D1560907

National Trade and Professional Associations Directory

MAIL LIST ORDER FORM

National Trade and Professional Associations (NTPA) lists over 7,500 national membership organizations representing business, labor and the professions. NTPA mailing lists can be selected as follows:

- by **State**, to target a specific geographic area.
- by **Budget**, to reach associations that fall within specific annual budget ranges.
- by **Year Established**, to contact groups on anniversaries.
- by **Subject**, to market to a specific industry or profession.
- by **Staff Size**, to contact organizations with a certain number of employees.
- or any or all combinations listed. Please contact us for details.

SELECTIONS:

Please call 301-986-1455 or visit www.bethesda-list.com/columbiabooks.html for a complete list of available selections.

☐ National (Total US)

☐ State(s): ______

☐ Budget: ______

☐ Staff Size: ______

☐ Year Established:

☐ Additional Selections: (*please inquire*) ______

PRICING:

$175 per thousand ($350 minimum) base rate plus applicable selection charges.
Multiple use license also available. Please inquire for pricing.

ADDITIONAL OPTIONS:

☐ **PHONE/FAX** • $300/thousand

☐ **EMAIL/WEB** • $300/thousand

Applicable selection charges and other fees may apply. For a complete list of selections and pricing, please visit us on the web at www.bethesda-list.com/columbiabooks.html or call 301-986-1455.

LIST FORMAT:

☐ **EMAIL** • (Add $35)

☐ **DISKETTE** • (Add $50)

NOTE: Check, money order or credit card information MUST accompany order, along with a clear copy of your mail piece.

SEND TO:

Bethesda List Center, Inc.
4833 Rugby Avenue, Suite 501
Bethesda, MD 20814-3910
PHONE: 301-986-1455 FAX 301-907-4870
EMAIL: info@bethesda-list.com
WEB: www.bethesda-list.com/columbiabooks.html

Order will not be processed without valid contact information

NAME: ______
TITLE: ______
COMPANY: ______
ADDRESS: ______
CITY/STATE/ZIP: ______
TELEPHONE: ______
FAX: ______
EMAIL: ______

☐ Check/Money Order enclosed

☐ Charge to credit card:

☐ VISA ☐ MASTERCARD

Complete Name on card: ______
Expiration Date: ______ CVN#: ______
Signature: ______
Date: ______

2007

National Trade and Professional Associations

of the United States

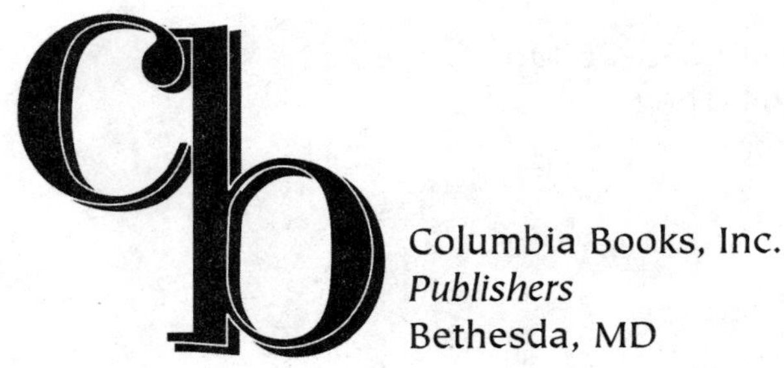

Columbia Books, Inc.
Publishers
Bethesda, MD

Managing Editor: Valerie S. Sheridan
Associate Editor: Megan E. Cimini
Associate Editor: Desiree V. Stephens
Associate Editor: Rachel A. Watson
Assistant Editor: Christy Talbot

Fourty-Second Edition – 2007

ISBN -10: 1-880873-52-4
ISBN-13: 978 1-880873-52-6
ISSN 0734-0734

Columbia Books, Inc.
Debra Mayberry, President

8120 Woodmont Ave., Suite110
Bethesda, MD 20814

Toll-free Customer Service: (888) 265-0600
Editorial Office: (202) 464-1662

2007 National Trade and Professional Associations

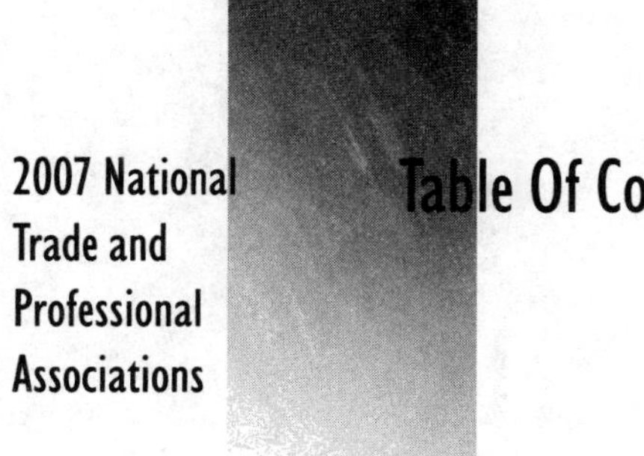

Table Of Contents

2007 National Trade and Professional Associations of the United States

Introduction

The *National Trade and Professional Associations (NTPA)* directory lists over 7,200 trade associations, professional societies, labor unions, and similar national groups. It is unique in providing a comprehensive listing focused on the trade associations segment of the U.S. non-profit community.

The associations listed in *NTPA* are an important segment of the American business community. Each has been formed to advance knowledge and provide support for a particular occupation, industry, or field of study. These voluntary, cooperative organizations provide learning opportunities and a central resource for technical information, mentoring and networking. In this sense, they reflect a long history, dating back to the craft and merchant guilds of medieval Europe.

The individual listings and indexes of *NTPA* provide an overview of association activity in the U.S. *NTPA* is intended as a resource for people and businesses interested in the organizations which serve a specific profession or operate in a particular area, or for those who have an interest in the U.S. trade associations community as a whole.

Associations vary widely in the types of benefits and services conferred by membership, as well as in organizational structure and types of members. The concepts of professionalism and advancement that are at the heart of any association's mission find different ways of expression in almost every case. What follows is a brief description of the kinds of information found in *NTPA*.

Executives and Staff

Every association requires a coordinator or administrator to handle its affairs. In many cases, particularly among smaller or more specialized societies, the administrator is an elected officer from the ranks of the association's membership. Such an elected volunteer will serve as President, Chair, or Secretary for a term of 1-3 years. Other small associations are managed by volunteers on a permanent basis. There are some 2,000-2,500 of these member-administered associations listed in NTPA. Typically, the description of such an organization will include a statement to the effect that the association has no paid officers or full-time staff.

Even within the associations that employ a professional staff, there are many groups that provide a range of services and are leaders in their industry but do so with a minimal staff. There are only a few hundred associations listed in NTPA whose employees number in the dozens or hundreds. The majority of the associations found in NTPA have a staff of 1-10 people, with an Exec. Director (the most common designation) and a small support staff.

For each listing in the main body of the book (the "Association Index") we list at least one contact person, whether it is an elected volunteer, a permanent volunteer or single administrator, or an executive who serves as chief of staff. They are the primary contacts for their associations, serving as liaison to the Board of Directors and C.E.O. for the organization.

In addition, where applicable, we have included names and titles of staff members who have been designated as contact in one of several administrative areas:

- Communications/Public Relations
- Government Relations

- Meetings & Conferences
- Education
- Administration/Finance
- Membership
- Publications
- Information Systems

Most of the organizations listed in NTPA do not have a specific contact for each of these administrative areas. But for those seeking more specific information about a larger organization's programs, the additional staff listings will serve to expedite an inquiry.

Association Size, History and Programs

As many as three statistical indicators of an association's size can be found in a typical NTPA listing. They are: number of members, number of full-time staff, and a budget size. Budget size is noted using one of fourteen budget categories in NTPA. A list of the organizations in each category can be found in the Budget Index.

Also included in each listing is a brief description of that association's history, purpose, membership, and programs. Again, these vary from association to association, depending on the age of the association and the type of membership it serves. Specific programs or subsidiaries are noted in the Historical Note, as well as any professional designations the association confers, political action committees and foundations, and alliances with other associations. Information on membership fees or dues is generally provided in this note.

Publications

Central to any association's role as a disseminator of information is the publication of newsletters, journals, and other periodicals for its membership. Any such serials published by the association and distributed to its members are included, along with a note on how frequently the publication appears (monthly, quarterly, etc.) and whether or not the publication regularly accepts advertising.

With the growth of digital communications, many associations now maintain an information presence on the World Wide Web in addition to or in place of traditional paper documents. The Web sites and e-mail addresses that provide access to these information resources are included in the contact information for each association, when available. As in many industries, the growth of association presence on the Web has been rapid. Since the 1996 edition, when we first began to include e-mail and Web addresses, the number of organizations with an Internet presence has grown, from a comparative handful to the majority of listed associations in this edition.

Meetings and Conventions

For many associations, the annual meeting or convention is the single most visible representation of the mission and goals of the association. Continuing education, professional networking, the exchange of ideas, and general fellowship combine to affirm an industry's continued vitality and the association's service to its members. NTPA lists recent conventions, meetings, trade shows, and similar functions sponsored by national associations, including the names and titles of the executive staff members with primary responsibilities coordinating such events.

Using NTPA

The main body of the book, called the *Association Index*, contains the full listing for each association, along with cross-references for recent name changes, etc., in alphabetical order by organization name. Following the Association Index are five separate indexes:

1. Subject Index

For users interested in particular industries or occupations, the Subject Index provides about 200 different categories. Associations may be listed in as many as four categories.

2. Geographic Index

Associations are cross-referenced based on the city and state in which they are headquartered.

3. Budget Index

An alphabetical list of associations in each of the fourteen budget categories.

4. Executive Index

Each executive listed in *NTPA* is listed here alphabetically, along with his or her association affiliation.

5. Acronym Index

Associations are often informally known by the abbreviations called Acronyms. The Acronym Index lists all such abbreviations, with the associations to which they refer.

6. Meeting Index

Organized by city within state, this index lists associations by the location of the coming year's annual meeting/s. Also included here are the facility, dates and projected attendance for each meeting, when available.

The last section of NTPA is a roster of U.S. Association Management Firms. These are companies who provide professional and administrative services to a number of client associations on a contract basis. There are over 350 such firms listed, with contact information and a list of association clients.

NTPA is now available online at AssociationExecs.com. Frequently updated with current information, AssociationExecs.com has customized search capabilities and allows for the exportation of data into desktop contact management programs. Please visit our website at columbiabooks.com for more information and subscription options.

DISTRIBUTION OF ASSOCIATION HEADQUARTERS BY STATE

Below is a breakdown of associations by state where they are headquartered.

State	Number of Associations	State	Number of Associations
District of Columbia	1,043	Oklahoma	56
Virginia	827	Iowa	55
Illinois	639	Oregon	49
New York	614	South Carolina	45
California	412	Alabama	42
Maryland	410	Nebraska	33
Texas	282	New Mexico	25
Pennsylvania	241	Nevada	21
Florida	236	Utah	21
Ohio	224	Louisiana	20
New Jersey	197	New Hampshire	19
Colorado	165	Mississippi	18
Georgia	156	Rhode Island	17
Missouri	141	Arkansas	15
Massachusetts	132	Delaware	15
Wisconsin	126	Montana	15
North Carolina	123	North Dakota	13
Indiana	114	Idaho	12
Minnesota	109	Vermont	11
Michigan	104	West Virginia	11
Tennessee	90	Maine	10
Kentucky	86	South Dakota	10
Arizona	77	Hawaii	6
Kansas	74	Wyoming	6
Washington	70	Alaska	0
Connecticut	59		

DISTRIBUTION BY BUDGET CATEGORY

Budgets included in each association's listing refer to the annual operating budget of the association. Listed below are the fourteen categories used in NTPA, along with the number of listees in each.

Budget Category	Number of Associations
under $10,000	540
$10-25,000	420
$25-50,000	430
$50-100,000	620
$100-250,000	953
$250-500,000	887
$500,000-1 Million	807
$1-2 Million	763
$2-5 Million	760
$5-10 Million	325
$10-25 Million	255
$25-50 Million	84
$50-100 Million	42
over $100 Million	32
No Budget Reported	1,282

DISTRIBUTION BY SELECTED SUBJECTS

Each association listed in NTPA may be cross-referenced in as many as four subject categories. Below are twenty-four common industry categories, with the number of associations in each.

Category	Number of Associations
Agriculture	167
Automotive Industry	145
Apparel and Textiles	135
Banking and Finance	145
Business	215
Chemicals and Chemical Industry	136
Communications and Telecommunications	127
Computers	185
Construction	206
Education	727
Electricity and Electronics	124
Food Industry	112
Government	428
Healthcare	326
Insurance Industry	162
Lawyers and the Law	203
Management	150
Manufacturing	667
Medicine	783
Nursing	105
Psychology and Psychiatry	166
Shipping and Trucking	146
Transportation	103
Wholesalers	120

2007 National Trade and Professional Associations

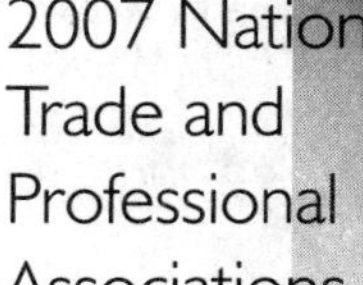

Association Index

The following listings include over 7,600 active national trade associations, professional societies, technical organizations, and labor unions. For each organization, the latest pertinent information has been compiled. Included among the current listings are references to organizations previously listed in NTPA that have since ceased operations, and cross-references to track association name changes.

AABB *(1947)*
8101 Glenbrook Road
Bethesda, MD 20814-2749
Tel: (301)907-6977 *Fax:* (301)907-6895
E-Mail: aabb@aabb.org
Web Site: www.aabb.org
Members: 8000 individuals
Staff: 70
Annual Budget: $10-25,000,000
Chief Executive Officer: Karen Shoos Lipton
Director, Public Relations: Jennifer Garfinkel

Historical Note
Scientists, physicians, nurses, medical technologists, donor recruitment professionals and administrators concerned with transfusion medicines and cellular therapies. Has an annual budget of approximately $17 million. Membership $98-198/year (individual); $350-6000/year (institutional).

Meetings/Conferences:
Annual Meetings: Fall/7,500
2007 - Anaheim, CA/Oct. 20-23
2008 - Montreal, QC, Canada/Oct. 4-7
2009 - New Orleans, LA/Oct. 24-27

Publications:
Transfusion Journal. m. adv.
AABB News. w. adv.
AABB Standards Source. q.
AABB PulsePoints. irreg.
AABB Regulatory Update. bi-w.
AABB Weekly Reports. w.

AABC Commissioning Group
1518 K St. NW
Suite 503
Washington, DC 20005
Tel: (202)737-7775 *Fax:* (202)638-4833
E-Mail: info@commissioning.org
Web Site: www.commissioning.org

AACC International *(1915)*
3340 Pilot Knob Road
St. Paul, MN 55121-2097
Tel: (651)454-7250 *Fax:* (651)454-0766
E-Mail: aacc@scisoc.org
Web Site: www.aaccnet.org
Members: 3000 individuals
Staff: 68
Annual Budget: $2-5,000,000
Executive Director: Steven C. Nelson, CMP
Chairman of the Board: Stuart Craig
E-Mail: aacc@scisoc.org
Director, Meetings and Conventions: Betty Ford
Vice President, Operations: Amy Hope

Historical Note
Founded in 1915 in Kansas City, MO, merged in 1923 with the American Society of Milling and Baking Technolog to form the American Association of Cereal Chemists; assumed current name in 2005. Incorporated in Minnesota in 1956. AACC International is an organization of cereal and food science professionals working in the grain-based foods field and/or studying cereal grains and their products. Encourages research in cereal grains, related materials, processing and utilization. Has offices in St. Paul, MN and Heverlee, Belgium. Membership: $120-1200/year (U.S. members).

Meetings/Conferences:
Annual Meetings: Fall/1,900
2007 - San Antonio, TX(San Antonio Convention Center)/Oct. 7-10

Publications:
Cereal Chemistry. bi-m.
Cereal Foods World. m. adv.
Food Science Catalog. semi-a.
Approved Methods of the AACC. a.

AACE International *(1956)*
209 Prairie Ave.
Suite 100
Morgantown, WV 26501
Tel: (304)296-8444 *Fax:* (304)291-5728
Toll Free: (800)858 - 2678
E-Mail: info@aacei.org
Web Site: www.aacei.org
Members: 5500 individuals
Staff: 12
Annual Budget: $1-2,000,000
Staff Director, Technical: Christian Heller
Staff Director, Education and Administration: Charla Miller
Manager, Finance: Carol S. Rogers

Historical Note
Founded as American Association of Cost Engineers; assumed its current name in 1991. A professional society of individuals interested in applying scientific principles to the solution of problems of cost management, engineering, estimating, cost control, planning and scheduling, project management and profitability. Membership: fees based on membership classification.

Meetings/Conferences:
Annual Meetings: July/1,000
2007 - Nashville, TN/July 15-18/700
2008 - Toronto, ON, Canada/June 29-July 2/800

Publications:
Cost Engineering. m. adv.
Cost Engineers Notebook. irreg.
Directory. a.
Transactions. a.

AACSB - the Association to Advance Collegiate Schools of Business *(1916)*
777 S. Harbour Island Blvd.
Suite 750
Tampa, FL 33602
Tel: (813)769-6500 *Fax:* (813)769-6559
Web Site: www.aacsb.edu
Members: 921 institutions
Staff: 38
Annual Budget: $2-5,000,000
President and Chief Executive Officer: John J. Fernandes
Vice President and Chief Financial Officer: Neil Bosland

Historical Note
Founded as American Association of Collegiate Schools of Business; Became American Association of Collegiate Schools of Business in 1973, and assumed its current name in 2001. Accrediting body for postsecondary business administration and accounting education programs.

Publications:
BizEd Magazine. bi-m. adv.

AAGL -- Advancing Minimally Invasive Gynecology Worldwide *(1972)*
6757 Katella Ave.
Cypress, CA 90630-5105
Tel: (714)503-6200 *Fax:* (714)503-6201
Toll Free: (800)554 - 2245
E-Mail: generalmall@aagl.com
Web Site: www.aagl.com
Members: 8000 individuals
Staff: 13
Annual Budget: $500-1,000,000
Executive Director: Linda Michels
Coordinator, Meetings: Jane Kalert
Executive Vice President and Medical Director: Franklin Loffer, M.D.

Historical Note
Founded as American Association of Gynecologic Laparoscopists; assumed its current name in 2005. Obstetricians and gynecologists interested in gynecological endoscopy, minimally invasive gynecology. Membership-$225 (physician); $95 (resident/fellows).

Meetings/Conferences:
Annual Meetings: Fall
2007 - Washington, DC(Marriott Wardman Park)/
2008 - Las Vegas, NV(Paris Hotel)/Oct. 29-Nov. 1/2000

Publications:
Journal of Minimally Invasive Gynecology (JMIG). bi-m. adv.

ABA Marketing Network *(1915)*
1120 Connecticut Ave. NW
Washington, DC 20036
Tel: (202)663-5268 *Fax:* (202)828-4540
Toll Free: (800)226 - 5377
E-Mail: marketingnetwork@aba.com

Web Site: www.aba.com/marketingnetwork
Members: 1679 individuals
Staff: 10
Annual Budget: $5-10,000,000
Executive Director: J. Douglas Adamson
Manager, Marketing and Communications: Mark DeBaugh
Publisher, Periodicals: Larry Price

Historical Note
An affiliate of American Bankers Association. Formerly (1947) Financial Advertisers Association, (1965) Financial Public Relations Association, (1970) Bank Public Relations and Marketing Association, and (2002) Bank Marketing Association. Membership: $950/year.

Meetings/Conferences:
Annual Meetings: *Fall*

Publications:
Bank Marketing Magazine. m. adv.
Marketing Edge Newsletter.

Abrasive Engineering Society *(1957)*
144 Moore Road
Butler, PA 16001
Tel: (724)282-6210 Fax: (724)234-2376
E-Mail: aes@abrasiveengineering.com
Web Site: www.abrasiveengineering.com
Members: 300 individuals
Staff: 1
Annual Budget: $25-50,000
Business Manager: Theodore L. Giese

Historical Note
Membership: $55/year (individual); $350/year (organization).

Meetings/Conferences:
Annual Meetings: *None Held*

Publications:
Proceedings, International Technical Conference.
Abrasive Users NewsFax. bi-w.

ACA International, The Association of Credit and Collection Professionals *(1939)*
4040 W. 70th St.
P.O. Box 39106
Minneapolis, MN 55439-0106
Tel: (952)926-6547 Fax: (952)926-1624
E-Mail: aca@acainternational.org
Web Site: www.acainternational.org
Members: 5300 credit, collection companies & professionals
Staff: 70
Annual Budget: $2-5,000,000
Chief Executive Officer: Gary D. Rippentrop, CAE
Vice President, Corporate Counsel: Rozanne Anderson
Director, Meetings and Conventions: Cathy Berg
Director, Communications: Tim Dressen
Vice President, Finance: Mike Henke
Director, Membership: Debra Kildahl
Chief Operating Officer: Toni Nuernberg
Director, Education: Carey Shandley
Vice President, Programs and Executive Director: Ted M. Smith, CAE

Historical Note
Founded as American Collectors Association; assumed its current name in 2001. ACA promotes the general welfare of the credit and collection profession. Activities include education, publishing, research, public affairs, group buying, public relations, conventions and trade shows. Sponsors and supports the American Collectors Political Action Committee (ACPAC).

Meetings/Conferences:
Annual Meetings: *Summer*
2007 - Chicago, IL(Hyatt Regency)/July 25-26/1200

Publications:
Collector. m. adv.

Academic Language Therapy Association
13140 Coit Rd.
Suite 320/LB-120
Dallas, TX 75240-5737
Tel: (972)233-9107 Ext: 224 Fax: (972)490-4219
E-Mail: helpline@altaread.org
Web Site: www.altaread.org
Members: 800 individuals
Annual Budget: $25-50,000
Executive Director: Pamela Silver

Historical Note
Membership: $60/year (individual); $30/year (student).

Meetings/Conferences:
Annual Meetings: *Spring*

Publications:
ALTA Bulletin. q. adv.

Academic Orthopaedic Society

Historical Note
Organization dissolved in 2003.

Academy for Eating Disorders
60 Revere Dr.
Suite 500
Northbrook, IL 60062
Tel: (847)498-4274 Fax: (847)480-9282
E-Mail: info@aedweb.org
Web Site: www.aedweb.org
Members: 1300 individuals
Executive Director: Sally Finney
E-Mail: info@aedweb.org

Meetings/Conferences:
2007 - Baltimore, MD(Baltimore Marriott Waterfront)/May 2-5/750

Publications:
International Journal of Eating Disorders. 8/yr. adv.

Academy of Accounting Historians *(1973)*
Case Western Reserve University, Weatherhead School of Management
10900 Euclid Ave.
Cleveland, OH 44106-7235
Tel: (216)368-2058 Fax: (216)368-4661
E-Mail: twelch001@gmail.com
Web Site: http://accounting.rutgers.edu/raw/aah
Members: 850 individuals
Administrative Coordinator: Tiffany Welch

Historical Note
AAH members are individuals and institutional affiliates with an interest in accounting/economic history. Membership: $45/year (individual); $95/year (organization/company); $95/year (institution); $10/year (student).

Meetings/Conferences:
Annual Meetings: *in conjunction with the American Accounting Ass'n*
2007 - Chicago, IL/Aug. 5-8

Publications:
Monograph Series. irreg.
Accounting Historians Notebook Newsletter. semi-a. adv.
Accounting Historians Journal. semi-a.

Academy of Ambulatory Foot and Ankle Surgery *(1972)*
1601 Walnut St.
Suite 1005
Philadelphia, PA 19102
Tel: (215)569-3303 Fax: (215)569-3310
Toll Free: (800)433 - 4892
E-Mail: aafas@aol.com
Web Site: www.academy-afs.org
Members: 1500 individuals
Staff: 3
Annual Budget: $250-500,000
Program Coordinator: Harriet Waloff

Historical Note
Members are podiatric surgeons who specialize in surgical procedures that do not require hospitalization. Incorporated in the State of Pennsylvania. Membership: $345/year.

Publications:
Journal of the Academy of Ambulatory Foot Surgery. a. adv.
Newsletter. bi-m. adv.

Academy of Aphasia *(1962)*
P.O. Box 26532
Minneapolis, MN 55426
Tel: (952)920-0484 Fax: (952)920-6098
E-Mail: contact@academyofaphasia.org
Web Site: www.academyofaphasia.org
Members: 200 individuals
Staff: 1
Annual Budget: $50-100,000
Director: Frances Laven

Historical Note
Members are researchers specializing in the study of total or partial loss of speech due to brain damage. Has no paid staff. Membership: $100/year.

Meetings/Conferences:
Annual Meetings: *October (location determined by availability of volunteer coordinator)*
2007 - Washington, DC

Publications:
Membership Directory. irreg.

Academy of Applied Science *(1963)*
24 Warren St.
Concord, NH 03301
Tel: (603)228-4530 Fax: (603)228-4730
E-Mail: admin@aas-world.org
Web Site: www.aas-world.org
Members: 300 individuals
Staff: 7
President: Robert Rines

Historical Note
Members are educators and professionals in applied science, engineering and similar disciplines. AAS sponsors programs that recognize and foster creativity and advancement in the applied sciences.

Academy of Behavioral Medicine Research *(1979)*
Department of Psychology, University of Miami
P.O. Box 248185
Coral Gables, FL 33124
Tel: (305)284-5507 Fax: (305)284-3402
E-Mail: pmccabe@miami.edu
Web Site: www.academyofbmr.org
Members: 300 individuals
Secretary: Philip McCabe, Ph.D.

Historical Note
ABMR members are individuals actively pursuing research in more than one aspect of behavioral science.

Meetings/Conferences:
Annual Meetings: *June*

Academy of Breastfeeding Medicine *(1993)*
140 Huguenot St., Third Floor
New Rochelle, NY 10801
Tel: (914)740-2115 Fax: (914)740-2101
Toll Free: (800)990 - 4ABM
E-Mail: abm@bfmed.org
Web Site: www.bfmed.org
Members: 500 individuals
Director, Membership: Alicia Dermer

Historical Note
Founded as Physicians Advocating Breastfeeding; became ABM in 1994. ABM provides education and technical information on breastfeeding and related medical issues for its members. Membership: $160/year.

Meetings/Conferences:
Annual Meetings: *Fall*

Publications:
Breastfeeding Medicine. q.
ABM Newsletter. q.

Academy of Certified Archivists *(1989)*
90 State St.
Suite 1009
Albany, NY 12207
Tel: (518)463-8644 Fax: (518)463-8656
E-Mail: aca@caphill.org
Web Site: www.certifiedarchivists.org
Members: 725 individuals
Executive Secretary: Steve Grandin

Historical Note
ACA promotes professional development for archivists, and administers the examination process culminating in the designation CA (Certified Archivist).

Academy of Clinical Laboratory Physicians and Scientists *(1966)*
ARUP Laboratories

500 Chipeta Way
Salt Lake City, UT 84108
Tel: (801)583-2787 Ext: 2087*Fax:* (801)584-5207
Web Site: www.aclps.org
*Members:*300 individuals
Annual Budget: $25-50,000
Secretary-Treasurer: Elizabeth L. Frank, Ph.D.

Historical Note

ACLPS members are physicians, scientists and educators primarily engaged in teaching, research and service in academic laboratory medicine, also known as clinical pathology. Membership: $100/year.

Meetings/Conferences:

Annual Meetings: June
2007 – San Diego, CA(UC San Diego)/June 7-9/150

Publications:

American Journal of Clinical Pathology. m. adv.

Academy of Country Music *(1964)*
4100 W. Alameda Ave.
Suite 208
Burbank, CA 91505
Tel: (818)842-8400 *Fax:* (818)842-8535
E-Mail: info@acmcountry.com
Web Site: www.acmcountry.com
*Members:*4000 individuals
Staff: 10
Executive Director: Bob Romeo
E-Mail: bobromeo@acmcountry.com

Historical Note

Formerly the Country and Western Music Academy. ACM is involved in numerous activities and events which promote country music, including an annual awards show. The Academy's members are individuals earning income from the country music industry. Membership: $75/year (individual).

Publications:

The Tempo. q. adv.

Academy of Criminal Justice Sciences *(1963)*
7339 Hanover Pkwy.
Suite A
Greenbelt, MD 20770
Tel: (301)446-6300 *Fax:* (301)446-2819
Toll Free: (800)757 - 2257
E-Mail: info@acjs.org
Web Site: www.acjs.org
*Members:*2,300 individuals
Staff: 2
Annual Budget: $500-1,000,000
Executive Director: Mittie D. Sutherland
E-Mail: execdir@acjs.org

Historical Note

ACJS is composed of professors, practitioners, researchers and institutions who deal with criminology, criminal justice, corrections and law. Membership: $75/year (individual); $250/year (institution).

Meetings/Conferences:

Annual Meetings: Annual
2007 – Seattle, WA(Sheraton)/March 13-17/1800

Publications:

ACJS Today. q. adv.
Justice Quarterly. q. adv.
ACJS Program Book. a. adv.
Journal of Criminal Justice Education. semi-a. adv.
Employment Bulletin. 2/week. adv.

Academy of Dental Materials *(1941)*
21 Grouse Terrace
Lake Oswego, OR 26506-9403
Tel: (503)636-0861 *Fax:* (503)675-2738
E-Mail: admtreas@comcast.net
Web Site: www.academydentalmaterials.org
*Members:*350 individuals
Staff: 2
Annual Budget: $50-100,000
Treasurer: Thomas Hilton
E-Mail: admtreas@comcast.net

Historical Note

Formerly (1983) American Academy for Plastics Research in Dentistry. Membership: $175/year.

Meetings/Conferences:

Semi-Annual Meetings: late Winter and Fall

Publications:

Dental Materials Journal. bi-m. adv.
ADM Newsletter. 2-3/year.
Transactions. irreg.

Academy of Dentistry for Persons with Disabilities *(1952)*
401 N. Michigan Ave.
Chicago, IL 60611
Tel: (312)527-6764 *Fax:* (312)673-6663
*Members:*350 individuals
Staff: 3
Annual Budget: $250-500,000
Executive Director: Kristen Smith

Historical Note

Established as the Academy for Oral Rehabilitation of Handicapped Persons by a group of dentists at a meeting of the American Dental Association in September 1952. Incorporated in Delaware in 1953. In February 1957 the name was changed to the Academy of Dentistry for the Handicapped, changed to current name in 1994. Affiliated with Special Care Dentistry. Membership: $170/year (individual).

Meetings/Conferences:

Annual Meetings: Spring

Publications:

Special Care in Dentistry. bi-m. adv.
Interface. bi-m. adv.

Academy of Dentistry International *(1974)*
P.O. Box 307
Hicksville, OH 43526
Tel: (419)542-0101 *Fax:* (419)542-6883
E-Mail: adintl@mindspring.com
Web Site: www.adint.org
*Members:*2400 individuals
Staff: 2
Annual Budget: $100-250,000
Executive Director: Dr. Robert L. Ramus
E-Mail: rramus@bright.net

Historical Note

An honorary international dental society established and incorporated in California, ADI promotes and fosters continuing education and service projects world-wide for the dental profession. Membership: $80/year.

Meetings/Conferences:

Annual Meetings: Fall with the American Dental Ass'n

Publications:

International Communicator. semi-a.

Academy of Dispensing Audiologists *(1977)*
401 N. Michigan Ave.
Suite 2200
Chicago, IL 60611
Toll Free: (866)493 - 5544
E-Mail: info@audiologist.org
Web Site: www.audiologist.org
*Members:*1000 individuals
Staff: 3
Annual Budget: $50-100,000

Historical Note

Professional organization of audiologists dispensing hearing aids in rehabilitative practice. Membership: $185/year (fellow/associate); $25/year (student).

Meetings/Conferences:

Annual Meetings: Summer

Publications:

ADA Feedback Newsletter. q. adv.
Membership Directory. a.

Academy of General Dentistry *(1952)*
211 E. Chicago Ave., Suite 900
Chicago, IL 60611-2670
Tel: (312)440-4300 *Fax:* (312)440-0559
Toll Free: (888)243 - 3368
E-Mail: msc@agd.org
Web Site: www.agd.org
*Members:*35000 individuals
Staff: 75
Annual Budget: $10-25,000,000
Executive Director: Christie Tarantino
Chief Financial Officer: Keith Bura
Associate Executive Director, Advocacy and Public Affairs: Daniel Buska
Director, Strategic Marketing and Product Development: Joe Dingee
Director, Membership Services: Tom Foley
Director, Meeting Services: Sarah McKinney
Director, Information Technology: Jason Paganessi

Historical Note

Serves the needs and represents the interests of general dentists. AGD fosters continued proficiency through quality continuing dental education in order to better serve the public. Has an annual budget of approximately $9.2 million. Membership: $209/year.

Meetings/Conferences:

Annual Meetings: Summer
2007 – San Diego, CA(San Diego Convention Center)/June 27-July 1/6000
2008 – Orlando, FL(Swan and Dolphin)/July 16-20/6000

Publications:

AGD Impact. 11/year. adv.
General Dentistry. bi-m. adv.

Academy of Homiletics *(1967)*
c/o San Francisco Theological Seminary
105 Kensington Road
San Anselmo, CA 94960
Tel: (415)451-2859 *Fax:* (415)451-2857
Web Site: www.homiletics.org
*Members:*400 individuals
Annual Budget: under $10,000
Treasurer: Jana Childers

Historical Note

Members are graduate schools of theology faculty teaching courses in homiletics.

Publications:

Homiletic Journal. semi-a.

Academy of International Business *(1959)*
7 Eppley Center Michigan State Univ.
East Lansing, MI 48824-1121
Tel: (517)432-1452 *Fax:* (517)432-1009
E-Mail: aib@aib.msu.edu
Web Site: http://aib.msu.edu
*Members:*3000 individuals
Staff: 4
Annual Budget: $500-1,000,000
Executive Director: G. Tomas M. Hult
Managing Director: Tunga Kiyak

Historical Note

Formerly (1959) Association for Education in International Business. Members are teachers and executives in the field of international business. Membership: $100/year (individual); $50/year (student); $50/year (low income).

Meetings/Conferences:

Annual Meetings: Fall
2007 – Indianapolis, IN/

Publications:

Journal of International Business Studies. 6/year. adv.
AIB Newsletter. 4/year. adv.
Membership Directory. bien. adv.
AIB Insights. q..

Academy of Laser Dentistry *(1993)*
P.O. Box 8667
Coral Springs, FL 33075
Tel: (954)346-3776 *Fax:* (954)757-2598
E-Mail: laserexec@laserdentistry.org
Web Site: www.laserdentistry.org
Members: 1100 individuals
Staff: 4
Executive Director: Gail Siminovsky
Member Services Coordinator: Heather Meiselman

Historical Note

ALD was formed by the merger of the American Academy of Laser Dentistry, the International Academy of Laser Dentistry and the North American Academy of Laser Dentistry in 1993. ALD promotes the advancement of research and education in laser applications in dentistry. Licensed dentists, auxiliaries, academic and research institutions, dental students, scientists and physicians are eligible for membership;

suppliers are eligible for corporate memberships. Membership: $350/year (dentists); $550/year (corporate); $105/year (auxiliaries); $30/year (student).

Meetings/Conferences:
Annual Meetings: Winter

Publications:
ALD Membership Directory. a.
Journal of the Academy of Laser Dentistry. q. adv.

Academy of Legal Studies in Business *(1924)*
Dept. of Finance, 120 Upham Hall
Miami University
Oxford, OH 45056
Tel: (513)529-2945 *Fax:* (513)523-8180
Toll Free: (800)831 - 2903
E-Mail: www.alsb.org
Members: 1000 individuals
Staff: 1
Annual Budget: $100-250,000
Executive Secretary: Dr. Daniel J. Herron

Historical Note
Formerly (1991) American Business Law Association. Members are teachers of business law, legal environment and other law-related courses in colleges and universities other than professional law schools. Membership: $60/year.

Meetings/Conferences:
Annual Meetings: August

Publications:
ALSB Newsletter. 3/year.
American Business Law Journal. q. adv.
Journal of Legal Studies Education. semi-a. adv.

Academy of Leisure Sciences *(1980)*
Univ. of Utah, Department of Parks, Recreation, and Tourism
College of Health, HPRN- 226
Salt Lake City, UT 84112
Tel: (801)581-4511 *Fax:* (801)581-4930
E-Mail: gary.ellis@health.utah.edu
Web Site: www.academyofleisuresciences.org
Members: 90 individuals
Secretary-Treasurer: Dr. Gary D. Ellis
E-Mail: gary.ellis@health.utah.edu

Historical Note
ALS members are academics specializing in the study of issues related to leisure, recreation, and management of businesses and agencies in the park, recreation, and tourism industries.

Academy of Managed Care Pharmacy *(1989)*
100 N. Pitt St.
Suite 400
Alexandria, VA 22314-3134
Tel: (703)683-8416 *Fax:* (703)683-8417
Toll Free: (800)827 - 2627
Web Site: www.amcp.org
Members: 4800 individuals
Staff: 28
Annual Budget: $2-5,000,000
Executive Director: Judith A. Cahill
Director, Communications: Carolyn Stables

Historical Note
AMCP's vision is improved of life through appropriate and accessible medication therapy. Its mission is to empower members to serve society by using sound medication management principles and strategies to achieve positive patient outcomes. Membership: $240/year (pharmacists and health care practicioners including physicians and nurses); $440/year (non-pharmacists); $85/year (students); $75/year (residents).

Meetings/Conferences:
Annual Meetings: April/October

Publications:
Journal of Manged Care Pharmacy. bi-m. adv.
AMCP News. m.

Academy of Managed Care Providers *(1993)*
1945 Palo Verde Ave.
Suite 202
Long Beach, CA 90815-3445
Tel: (562)682-3559 *Fax:* (562)799-3355
Toll Free: (800)297 - 2627
E-Mail: members@academymcp.org
Web Site: www.academymcp.org
Members: 2500 individuals
President: Dr. John Russell

Historical Note
Members are companies and individuals interested in the provision of quality managed care. Sponsors educational programs and other services. Membership: $175/year (individual); $125/year (internet members); $500/year (company).

Academy of Management *(1936)*
P.O. Box 3020
Briarcliff Manor, NY 10510-8020
Tel: (914)923-2607 *Fax:* (914)923-2615
E-Mail: aom@pace.edu
Web Site: www.aomonline.org
Members: 13000 individuals
Staff: 12
Annual Budget: $1-2,000,000
Executive Director: Nancy Urbanowicz

Historical Note
Members are professors who research and teach management, as well as doctoral students in management and business professionals interested in principles of management. Membership: $115/year (individual); $58/year (student).

Meetings/Conferences:
Annual Meetings: August/4,800

Publications:
Academy of Management Review. q. adv.
Academy of Management Journal. bi-m. adv.
Academy of Management Executive. q. adv.
Proceedings. a.
Academy of Management Leasing and Education. q. adv.
Annual Meeting Program. a. adv.

Academy of Marketing Science *(1971)*
P.O. Box 248012
Coral Gables, FL 33124
Tel: (305)284-6673 *Fax:* (305)284-3762
E-Mail: ams.sba@miami.edu
Web Site: www.ams-web.org
Members: 1500 individuals
Staff: 1
Executive Vice President and Director: Harold W. Berkman, Ph.D.
Coordinator: Sally Sultan

Historical Note
Professional (academicians and marketing executives) society concerned with fostering education in marketing, advancing the science of marketing and furthering professional standards in the discipline. Sponsors and supports the AMS Foundation which provides grants for both the advancement of the teaching of marketing and research in marketing. Membership: $75 (regular); $35 (students).

Meetings/Conferences:
Annual Meetings: May/300
2007 – Coral Gables, FL(Biltmore)/May 23-26/250

Publications:
Journal of the Academy of Marketing Science. q. adv.
Developments in Marketing Science and Proceedings. a. adv.
Newsletter. q. adv.

Academy of Medical-Surgical Nurses *(1991)*
E. Holly Ave., Box 56
Pitman, NJ 08071-0056
Tel: (856)256-2323 *Fax:* (856)589-7463
Toll Free: (866)877 - AMSN
E-Mail: amsn@ajj.com
Web Site: www.medsurgnurse.org
Members: 3000 individuals
Annual Budget: $100-250,000
Executive Director: Cynthia Hnatiuk, EdD, RN, CAE

Historical Note
AMSN seeks to represent members and promote the implementation of standards for the practice of adult/medical-surgical nursing. Also aims to support the use of guidelines for practice and enhance the image of the professional adult health/medical-surgical nurse. Membership: $75/year (individual).

Meetings/Conferences:
2007 – Las Vegas, NV

Publications:
AMSN News. q. adv.
MEDSURG Nursing Journal. bi-m. adv.

Academy of Motion Picture Arts and Sciences *(1927)*
8949 Wilshire Blvd.
Beverly Hills, CA 90211-1972
Tel: (310)247-3000 *Fax:* (310)859-9619
E-Mail: ampas@oscars.org
Web Site: www.oscars.org
Members: 6300 individuals
Staff: 136
Annual Budget: $25-50,000,000
Executive Director: Bruce Davis
Director, Communications: John M. Pavlik
Executive Administrator: Ric Robertson
Membership Administrator: Thomas Thanangaden

Historical Note
A professional honorary organization of motion picture craftsmen and craftswomen founded to advance the arts and sciences of motion pictures; foster cooperation among the creative leadership of the industry for cultural, educational and technological progress; recognize outstanding achievements through annual awards of merit (Oscars); conduct cooperative technical research and stimulate improvement of methods and equipment. Has an annual budget of approximately $33 million.

Meetings/Conferences:
Annual Meetings: Annual Academy Awards Ceremony in Spring

Publications:
Index to Motion Picture Credits. a.
Players Directory. 3/yr.
Academy Report. q.

Academy of Operative Dentistry *(1972)*
P.O. Box 14996
Gainesville, FL 32604
Tel: (352)371-0296 *Fax:* (352)371-4882
Web Site: http://operativedentistry.com
Members: 1200 individuals
Annual Budget: $100-250,000
Secretary: Gregory E. Smith, DDS

Historical Note
Membership: $165/year (individual).

Publications:
Journal of Operative Dentistry. 6/year.

Academy of Oral Dynamics *(1946)*
134 E. Church Road
Elkins Park, PA 19027-2208
Tel: (215)635-2336
Members: 85 individuals
Annual Budget: $10-25,000
Chairman of the Board: Bertram Kreger

Historical Note
Formerly (1950) International Academy of Oral Dynamics. Members are dentists interested in the application of biophysical principles to diagnose, restore and maintain the health of the mouth and its supporting structures. Has no paid officers or full-time staff. Membership: $25/year (active); $15/year (associate).

Meetings/Conferences:
Annual Meetings: Always Washington, DC(Sheraton/Hilton)/Spring/100

Publications:
Academy of Oral Dynamics Membership Letters. q.

Academy of Organizational and Occupational Psychiatry
P.O. Box 343
Ridgefield Park, NJ 07660
Tel: (877)789-6050 *Fax:* (877)789-2667
E-Mail: staff@aoop.org
Web Site: www.aoop.org
Members: 150 individuals
Staff: 2
President: Steve Pflanz

Historical Note
AOOP members are psychiatrists with an interest in the relationship of work to general well-being and

mental health. Organizational and occupational psychiatrists study the psychopathology brought to and resulting from work setting and utilize clinical, consultative, educational and preventive interventions and strategies to reduce symptoms and conflict, and facilitate health and well-being. Membership: $150/year (individual).

Meetings/Conferences:
Annual Meetings: January
2007 – Chicago, IL(University Club)/Apr. 14-15

Publications:
OOP News Bulletin. semi-a. adv.

Academy of Osseointegration *(1987)*
85 W. Algonquin Rd.
Suite 550
Arlington Heights, IL 60005
Tel: (847)439-1919 *Fax:* (847)439-1569
Toll Free: (800)656 - 7736
Web Site: www.osseo.org
Members: 5200 individuals
Staff: 14
Annual Budget: $2-5,000,000
Executive Director: Kevin Smith
E-Mail: kevinsmith@osseo.org
Director, Communications: Richard Bragaw
E-Mail: richardbragaw@osseo.org
Director, Finance: James Kmak
E-Mail: jameskmak@osseo.org
Director, Membership: Jean Lynch
Associate Director: Mike Scawney
Director, Meetings: Gina Seegers
Director, Information Systems: Charlene Taylor

Historical Note
AO was established to advance, promote and improve the art and science of rigid/living tissue interfaces (osseointegration). Members are dental specialists and general practitioners. Membership: $255/year (individual).

Meetings/Conferences:
Annual Meetings: Spring
2007 – San Antonio, TX(San Antonio Convention Center)/March 8-10/3200
2008 – Boston, MA(Hynes Convention Center)/Feb. 25-March 1/4000
2009 – San Diego, CA(Convention Center)/Feb. 26-March 1/3500

Publications:
Annual Meeting Program/Abstract Book. a. adv.
Membership Roster. a. adv.
Academy News newsletter. q. adv.
Internat'l Journal of Oral and Maxillofacial Implants. bi-m. adv.

Academy of Parish Clergy *(1968)*
2249 Florinda St.
Sarasota, FL 34231-4414
Tel: (941)922-8633
Web Site: www.apclergy.org
Members: 165 individuals
Staff: 2
Annual Budget: $10-25,000
Vice President, Administration: Paul J. Binder, APC
E-Mail: pjbinder2@juno.com

Historical Note
Formed in Indianapolis as a voluntary self-governing association of clergy who work together in an interfaith, ecumenical parish setting. Affiliated with the Association of Theological Schools and the Society for the Advancement of Continuing Education for Ministry. Membership: $60/year (individual); $30/year (retired); $25/year (subscription to journal only).

Meetings/Conferences:
Annual Meetings: Spring
2007 – Princeton Junction, NJ(Princeton University)/Apr. 24-26/90

Publications:
Sharing the Practice. q. adv.

Academy of Pharmaceutical Research and Science *(1965)*

Historical Note
An affiliate of American Pharmaceutical Association, which provides administrative support.

Academy of Political Science *(1994)*
475 Riverside Dr.
Suite 1274
New York, NY 10115-1274
Tel: (212)870-2500 *Fax:* (212)870-2202
Web Site: www.psqonline.org
Members: 140 institutions
Staff: 4
Annual Budget: $500-1,000,000
President: Demetrios Caraley

Historical Note
APS promotes objective, scholarly analyses of political, social, and economic issues.

Meetings/Conferences:
Annual Meetings: None held.

Publications:
Political Science Quarterly. q. adv.
Proceedings. irreg.

Academy of Prosthodontics *(1918)*
6177 Orchard Lake Rd.
Suite 120
West Bloomfield, MI 48322
Tel: (248)855-6655 *Fax:* (248)855-0803
Web Site: www.academyprosthodontics.org
Members: 130 individuals
Secretary-Treasurer: Dr. Jonathan Wiens

Historical Note
Founded as National Society of Denture Prosthetists; became Academy of Denture Prosthetics in 1940, and assumed its current name in 1991. Has no paid officers or full-time staff.

Meetings/Conferences:
Annual Meetings: Spring

Academy of Psychosomatic Medicine *(1953)*
5272 River Rd.
Suite 630
Bethesda, MD 20816
Tel: (301)718-6520 *Fax:* (301)656-0989
E-Mail: apm@apm.org
Web Site: www.apm.org
Members: 1000 individuals
Staff: 2
Annual Budget: $250-500,000
Executive Director: Norman E. Wallis, Ph.D.
E-Mail: apm@apm.org

Historical Note
Incorporated in Massachusetts in 1954. Works to advance medicine and allied health professions through interaction of mind, body and environment. Membership: $175/year (individual).

Meetings/Conferences:
Annual Meetings: October-November/400
2007 – Amelia Island, FL(Amelia Island Plantation)/Nov. 14-18

Publications:
Psychosomatics. bi-m. adv.
Directory of US Consultation-Liaison Training Programs. a.
APM Directory. a.

Academy of Radiology Research *(1994)*
1029 Vermont Ave. NW
Suite 505
Washington, DC 20005
Tel: (202)347-5872 *Fax:* (202)347-5876
E-Mail: rcruea@acadrad.org
Web Site: www.acadrad.org
Members: 25 organizational members
Staff: 2
Annual Budget: $250-500,000
Executive Director: Edward C. Nagy
E-Mail: info@acadrad.org
Director, Government Relations: Renee Cruea

Historical Note
The Academy is intended to focus attention on radiology as a discipline committed to basic and clinical research and dedicated to the translation of research advances into higher quality and more cost-effective patient care.

Publications:
Washington Update (online newsletter).

Academy of Rehabilitative Audiology *(1966)*
P.O. Box 952
DeSoto, TX 75123
Tel: (972)534-1281
E-Mail: ara@audrehab.org
Web Site: www.audrehab.org
Members: 385 individuals
Annual Budget: $10-25,000
Administrative Assistant: Karen Dannheim
E-Mail: ara@audrehab.org

Historical Note
Members hold graduate degrees in audiology, speech pathology, language or related fields and have had a minimum of two years post-degree experience. Membership: $50/year.

Meetings/Conferences:
Annual Meetings: Summer

Publications:
The Pinnacle Newsletter. 3/year.
The News Flash E-Mail Update.
Journal of the Academy of Rehabilitative Audiology. a.
Membership Directory. a.

Academy of Scientific Hypnotherapy *(1977)*

Historical Note
Address unknown in 2006.

Academy of Security Educators and Trainers *(1980)*
P.O. Box 802
Berryville, VA 22611-0802
Tel: (540)554-2540 *Fax:* (540)554-2558
Web Site: www.asetcse.org/
Members: 400 individuals
Staff: 2
Annual Budget: $10-25,000
Director: Dr. Richard W. Kobetz

Historical Note
Awards the CST ("Certified Security Trainer") designation. Membership: $50/year.

Meetings/Conferences:
Annual Meetings: Spring
2007 – Berryville, VA(Highlands Lodge)/Apr. 12-14
2008 – Berryville, VA(Highlands Lodge)/Apr. 3-5

Publications:
ASET Newsletter. semi-a.
World of Security Education. a.

Academy of Student Pharmacists *(1954)*
c/o American Pharmacists Ass'n
2215 Constitution Ave. NW
Washington, DC 20037
Tel: (202)429-7595 *Fax:* (202)628-0443
Toll Free: (800)237 - 2742
E-Mail: apha-asp@aphanet.org
Web Site: www.aphanet.org/students
Members: 24500 individuals
Staff: 4
Annual Budget: $500-1,000,000
Senior Manager, Student Development: Jessica Anciu
E-Mail: apha-asp@aphanet.org

Historical Note
A constitutent section of the American Pharmacists Association. Formerly (1987) the Student American Pharmaceutical Association and then American Pharmaceutical Association - Academy of Students of Pharmacy; assumed its current name in 2003. ASP provides students in pharmacy school with a resource for networking, education, and other professional benefits prior to actual APhA membership. Membership: $33/year, plus state and local dues.

Meetings/Conferences:
Semi-Annual Meetings: March in conjunction with APhA and October-November.

Publications:
Student Pharmacist. bi-m. adv.

Academy of Students of Pharmacy

Historical Note
Became American Pharmacists Ass'n - Academy of Students of Pharmacy in 2003.

Academy of Surgical Research *(1982)*

7500 Flying Cloud Dr.
Suite 900
Eden Prairie, MN 55344
Tel: (952)253-6240 *Fax:* (952)835-4774
E-Mail: manager@surgicalresearch.org
Web Site: www.surgicalresearch.org
Members: 400 individuals
Executive Director: Jim Manke, CAE

Historical Note
ASR promotes the advanced study of surgical practice.

Meetings/Conferences:
Annual Meetings: Fall

Publications:
Journal of Investigative Surgery. bi-m.

Academy of Veterinary Allergy and Clinical Immunology *(1960)*
330 Waukegan Road
Glenview, IL 60025
Tel: (847)729-5200 *Fax:* (847)729-5214
Web Site: www.avaci.org
Members: 300 individuals
Staff: 1
Annual Budget: $25-50,000
Treasurer: Richard Rossman, D.V.M.

Historical Note
Formerly (1993) Academy of Veterinary Allergy. AVACI members are veterinarians, physicians and other professionals with an interest in animal and comparative allergy research. Membership: $50/year (individual).

Meetings/Conferences:
Annual Meetings: in conjunction with American Animal Hospital Ass'n

Publications:
Journal of Veterinary Allergy & Clinical Immunology. q.
Membership List. q.

Academy of Veterinary Homeopathy *(1996)*
P.O. Box 9280
Wilmington, DE 19809
Toll Free: (866)652 - 1590
E-Mail: office@theAVH.org
Web Site: www.theavh.org
Members: 206
Executive Secretary: Stephanie Connell
E-Mail: office@theAVH.org

Historical Note
Sponsors research, accreditation, education, and other programs to advance the application of homeopathic methods in veterinary medicine.

Publications:
AVH Journal. q.

AcademyHealth *(1981)*
1801 K St. NW
Suite 701-L
Washington, DC 20006
Tel: (202)292-6700 *Fax:* (202)292-6800
E-Mail: info@academyhealth.org
Web Site: www.academyhealth.org
Members: 4000 individuals and organizations
Staff: 18
Annual Budget: $1-2,000,000
President and Chief Executive Officer: W. David Helms
Senior Manager, Meeting Operations: Gennice T. Carter
Chief Financial Officer: Deborah L. Edwards
Director, Communications: Christina E. Folz
Director, Information Technology: Stacy L. Halbert
Director, Government Relations: Jon Lawniczak
Director, Membership: Kristine Metter

Historical Note
Founded as Ass'n for Health Services Research; became Ass'n for Health Services Research and Health Policy in 2000 and assumed its current name in 2002. AcademyHealth members are individuals and organizations concerned with health services research. Membership: $200/year (individual); $2,000-$10,000/year (institution).

Publications:
Health Service Research. bi-m.

Access Technology Association *(1991)*
3612 Bent Branch Court
Falls Church, VA 22041
Tel: (703)942-4329
Members: 70 companies
Staff: 3
Annual Budget: $100-250,000
Executive Director: William J. Tobin, Ph.D.

Historical Note
Members are companies supplying products and services which expand workplace access for disabled individuals and professionals concerned with improving access to the workplace for disabled persons.

Publications:
Directory of Access Technology Products & Services. a. adv.
ATA Briefings Newsletter. m.

Accordion Federation of North America *(1955)*
1101 W. Orangethorpe Ave.
Fullerton, CA 92833
Tel: (818)994-1249
E-Mail: afna@musician.org
Members: 75 individuals
Annual Budget: $10-25,000
Treasurer: Sylvia Prior
E-Mail: afna@musician.org

Historical Note
AFNA members are primarily music teachers and music school owners. AFNA's primary purpose is to encourage young people to pursue their music study; a four-day series of contests is held annually.

Meetings/Conferences:
Annual Meetings: August

Accordionists and Teachers Guild International *(1940)*
334 S. Broadway
Pitman, NJ 08071
Tel: (856)854-6628
E-Mail: accordion3@comcast.net
Web Site: www.accordions.com/atg
Members: 175 individuals
Staff: 1
Annual Budget: $10-25,000
Executive Secretary: Joan Arnold Darrow
E-Mail: accordion3@comcast.net

Historical Note
Formerly the Accordion Teachers' Guild International (1998). ATGI members are accordion teachers, professional musicians, hobbyists, and students. Membership: $25/year (individual).

Meetings/Conferences:
Annual Meetings: Summer

Publications:
ATG Bulletin. 5/year. adv.

Accountants for the Public Interest *(1975)*
Univ. of Baltimore, Suite BC519
1420 N. Charles St.
Baltimore, MD 21201-0720
Tel: (410)837-6533 *Fax:* (410)837-6532
E-Mail: api36@juno.com
Web Site: www.geocities.com/api_woods/api/apihome.html
Members: 1650 individuals
Staff: 2
Annual Budget: $100-250,000
Executive Director: T.L. Woods
E-Mail: api36@juno.com

Historical Note
Through API affiliates, API volunteer accountants provide pro bono accounting assistance to non-profit organizations, small businesses, and individuals who need but cannot afford professional service. Membership: $45/year (individual); $275/year (company).

Publications:
What a Difference Knowledge Makes: A Guide to Intermediate Sanctions.
What a Difference Understanding Makes: A Guide to Nonprofit Management.
API's Complete Guide to Accounting Procedures for Non-Profit Organizations.
API's Complete Guide to the Nonprofit Audit.
Affiliate Newsbriefs.

ACCRA - Ass'n of Applied Community Researchers *(1962)*
P.O. Box 100127
Arlington, VA 22210
Tel: (703)522-4980 *Fax:* (703)522-4985
Web Site: www.accra.org
Members: 500 individuals
Staff: 9
Annual Budget: $250-500,000
Administrative Director: Sean A. McNamara

Historical Note
Formerly (1992) American Chamber of Commerce Researchers Ass'n. Promotes research in community development. Membership: fees based on membership type.

Meetings/Conferences:
Annual Meetings: Spring

Publications:
Membership Directory. a.
ACCRA Newsletter-Research in Review. q.
Applied Community Research Monographs Series.
Cost of Living Index. q.

Accreditation Association for Ambulatory Health Care *(1979)*
3201 Old Glenview Rd.
Suite 300
Wilmette, IL 60091
Tel: (847)853-6060 *Fax:* (847)853-9028
E-Mail: info@aaahc.org
Web Site: www.aaahc.org
Members: 1950 facilities and organizations
Staff: 30
Annual Budget: $2-5,000,000
Executive Director: John E. Burke, Ph.D.
Director, Marketing and Communications: Andrea Lee

Historical Note
AAAHC is the leading accrediting body in the United States for a variety of ambulatory health care providers, including free-standing ambulatory surgery centers (ASCs), medical group practices, college health centers, HMOs, and office-based surgical practices. Accreditation is conferred based upon in-depth initial and periodic site inspections of the practice to determine compliance with AAAHC quality standards.

Meetings/Conferences:
Annual Meetings: AAAHC schedules separate and specialized meetings throughout the year.

Publications:
Update. q.
Accreditation Handbook for Ambulatory Health Care. a.

Accreditation Council for Pharmacy Education *(1932)*
20 N. Clark St.
Suite 2500
Chicago, IL 60602-5109
Tel: (312)664-3575 *Fax:* (312)664-4652
E-Mail: techinfo@acpe-accredit.org
Web Site: www.acpe-accredit.org
Staff: 10
Executive Director: Peter H. Vlasses
E-Mail: techinfo@acpe-accredit.org

Historical Note
Established in 1932 as the American Council on Pharmaceutical Education and chartered in Maryland in 1939; assumed its current name in 2003. Sponsoring organizations are the American Ass'n of Colleges of Pharmacy, the American Pharmaceutical Ass'n, and the National Ass'n of Boards of Pharmacy. Accredits professional programs in pharmacy and providers of continuing pharmacy education.

Meetings/Conferences:
Annual Meetings: Semi-annual Meetings

Publications:
Accredited Professional Programs of Colleges & Schools of Pharmacy. a.
Accredited Providers of Continuing Pharmaceutical Education. a.

Accredited Gemologists Association *(1976)*
c/o G-Force Services
3315 Juanita St.

San Diego, CA 92105
Tel: (619)501-5444 *Fax:* (480)247-5958
Web Site: http://accreditedgemologists.org/
Members: 250 individuals
Annual Budget: $25-50,000
President: Joseph DuMouchelle, GG

Historical Note
Members must hold a "gemologist" diploma from the Gemological Institute of America or the Gemological Association of Great Britain and pass character, professional, and ethical investigation. Membership: $100/year.

Meetings/Conferences:
Annual Meetings: Tucson, AZ/February

Publications:
Update. bi-m.
Cornerstone. a.

Accredited Pet Cemetery Society *(1993)*
P.O. Box 12073
Kansas City, MO 64152
Tel: (816)891-8888 *Fax:* (816)891-8781
E-Mail: secretary@accreditedpetcemeterysociety.org
Web Site: www.accreditedpetcemeterysociety.org
Members: 15 individuals
Annual Budget: under $10,000
Secretary: Nancy Piper
E-Mail: secretary@accreditedpetcemeterysociety.org

Historical Note
APCS is composed of a group of pet cemeterians who operate quality properties and adhere to high standards of operation and professionalism. Members must endorse and support deed restriction of pet cemetery property and meaningful pet cemetery legislation. Members must serve actively on committees and attend yearly conferences with the emphasis on continuing education and incentive for achievement. Educational programs for the APCS focus on the newest trends in the pet death care profession such as community involvement, pet bereavement and support groups, and professional business management.

Publications:
APCS Bulletin. irreg.

Accredited Review Appraisers Council *(1987)*

Historical Note
An affiliate of National Ass'n of Master Appraisers, which provides administrative support.

Accrediting Bureau of Health Education Schools
7777 Leesburg Pike
Suite 314 North
Falls Church, VA 22043
Tel: (703)917-9503 *Fax:* (703)917-4109
E-Mail: info@abhes.org
Web Site: www.abhes.org
Members: 170 individuals
Staff: 5
Executive Director: Carol Moneymaker
E-Mail: info@abhes.org

Publications:
The Advantage. q.

Accrediting Commission for Career Schools and Colleges of Technology *(1993)*
2101 Wilson Blvd.
Suite 302
Arlington, VA 22201
Tel: (703)247-4212 *Fax:* (703)247-4533
E-Mail: info@accsct.org
Web Site: www.accsct.org
Members: 800 schools and institutions
Staff: 30
Executive Director: Elise Scanlon
E-Mail: escanlon@accsct.org

Historical Note
Founded as Accrediting Commission of the National Association of Trade and Technical Schools; became an independent organization in 1993. ACCSCT provides leadership and accreditation to a wide variety of schools and institutions.

Accrediting Council for Continuing Education and Training *(1974)*
1722 N St. NW
Washington, DC 20036
Tel: (202)955-1113 *Fax:* (202)955-1118
E-Mail: info@accet.org
Web Site: www.accet.org
Members: 246 institutions and 700 branches
Staff: 10
Annual Budget: $1-2,000,000
Executive Director: Roger J. Williams
E-Mail: rjwilliams@accet.org

Historical Note
Members are associations, private educational institutions, and companies who conduct continuing education and training programs. The Council's purpose is to provide accreditation to organizations that meet the quality standards established by ACCET. The Council has also attained registered status as an ISO 9001 quality system and is officially recognized by the U.S. Secretary of Education.

Meetings/Conferences:
Annual Meetings: Fall

Accrediting Council for Independent Colleges and Schools *(1912)*
750 First St. NE
Suite 980
Washington, DC 20002-4241
Tel: (202)336-6780 *Fax:* (202)842-2593
E-Mail: info@acics.org
Web Site: www.acics.org
Members: 600 individuals
Staff: 22
Annual Budget: $2-5,000,000

Historical Note
ACICS is an independent accrediting agency and its members include different national and international education institutions.

Publications:
Criterion. 3/year.

Accrediting Council on Education in Journalism and Mass Communications *(1947)*
Univ. of Kansas Sch. of Journalism, Stauffer-Flint Hall
1435 Jayhawk Blvd.
Lawrence, KS 66045-7575
Tel: (785)864-3973 *Fax:* (785)864-5225
Web Site: www.ukans.edu/~acejmc
Members: 23 associations
Staff: 3
Annual Budget: $100-250,000
Executive Director: Susanne Shaw
E-Mail: sshaw@ku.edu

Historical Note
ACEJMC members are journalism/media departments, education associations and professional organizations concerned with journalism education. Membership: $1,000/year (accredited school); $1,000-6,000/year (company).

Meetings/Conferences:
Three Meetings Annually:
2007 – Chicago, IL(Westin)/March 24- /75
2007 – St. Petersburg, FL(Westin)/March 24-24/75
2007 – Portland, WA(Westin)/May 4-5/100
2007 – Chicago, IL(Sheraton)/Aug. 31- /75

Publications:
Benefits of Accreditation. irreg.
Team Manual. bien.
Accredited Journalism and Mass Communications Education. a.

ACL - Association for Consortium Leadership *(1967)*
c/o Virginia Tidewater Consortium for Higher Education
1417 43rd St.
Norfolk, VA 23529
Tel: (757)683-3183 *Fax:* (757)683-4515
Web Site: www.acl.odu.edu
Members: 50 consortia of institutions
Staff: 3
Annual Budget: $25-50,000
Executive Director: Lawrence G. Dotolo, Ph.D.

Historical Note
Encourages voluntary cooperation between colleges and universities. ACL members are organizations whose chief purpose is to help colleges and universities cooperate with one another to improve education and strengthen management. Formerly known as the Cooperative Program of the American Association for Higher Education, and the Council for Interinstitutional Leadership (1994). Membership: $125/year (individual); $500/year (organization).

Meetings/Conferences:
Annual Meetings: Fall

Publications:
Consortium Staffs Salary Survey. semi-a.
Consortium Directory. a.
ACL Newsletter. 4-6/year.

ACME - World Association of Management Consulting Firms *(1929)*

Historical Note
See Association of Management Consulting Firms.

Acoustical Society of America *(1929)*
Two Huntington Quadrangle
Suite 1N01
Melville, NY 11747-4502
Tel: (516)576-2360 *Fax:* (516)576-2377
E-Mail: asa@aip.org
Web Site: http://asa.aip.org
Members: 7000 individuals
Staff: 7
Annual Budget: $2-5,000,000
Executive Director: Charles Schmid, Ph.D.

Historical Note
Incorporated in New York City in 1929, where its initial meeting was held May 10-11, 1929 with a charter membership of about 450. ASA is a member of the American Institute of Physics. Membership: $35/year (student); $100/year (associate); $120/year (member and fellows).

Meetings/Conferences:
Semi-Annual Meetings: Spring and Fall/1,000

Publications:
Journal of the Acoustical Soc. of America. m. adv.
Acoustics Research Letters online. q.

ACPA - College Student Educators Association *(1924)*
One Dupont Circle NW
Suite 300
Washington, DC 20036-1188
Tel: (202)835-2272 *Fax:* (202)296-3286
E-Mail: info@acpa.nche.edu
Web Site: www.myacpa.org
Members: 8000 individuals
Staff: 8
Annual Budget: $2-5,000,000
Executive Director: Gregory Roberts, Ed.S.
E-Mail: gr@acpa.nche.edu
Coordinator, Marketing and Public Relations: Rita Bowers
E-Mail: rb@acpa.nche.edu
Associate Executive Director, Information Technology and Convention Services: Peter D. Brown
E-Mail: pdb@acpa.nche.edu

Historical Note
American College Personnel Association, d/b/a ACPA - College Student Educators International, was established in 1924 to serve as a collective voice for the college student personnel profession, including faculty, graduate students, counselors, administrators, deans, department heads, and researchers. An independent association with 16 commissions, 6 standing committees, and 32 state and international divisions. Membership: $65-110/year (general); $150-1,100/year (institutional); $150-350/year (organization); $45/year (graduate student).

Meetings/Conferences:
Annual Meetings: Spring
2007 – Orlando, FL(Gaylord & Marriott)/March 31-4/6500
2008 – Atlanta, GA/March 29-Apr. 2
2009 – Washington, DC(Gaylord National on the Potomac)/March 28-Apr. 1

Publications:
ACPA Developments Newsletter (on-line). q. adv.

About Campus. bi-m. adv.
The Journal of College Student Development. bi-m. adv.

ACPA International *(1978)*

Historical Note
See Affiliated Conference of Practicing Accountants International.

Acrylamide Monomer Producers Association

Historical Note
Became North American Polyelectrolyte Producers Association in 2003.

Acrylonitrile Group *(1981)*
1250 Connecticut Ave. NW
Suite 700
Washington, DC 20036
Tel: (202)419-1500 *Fax:* (202)659-8037
E-Mail: angroup@regnet.com
Web Site: www.angroup.org
Members: 7 companies
Staff: 2
Annual Budget: $250-500,000
Executive Director: Robert J. Fensterheim

Historical Note
AN Group represents producers and users of the industrial chemical used to make plastics, fibers and synthetic rubber products. Membership fee: pro rata share of annual budget.

Actors' Equity Association *(1913)*
165 W. 46th St.
New York, NY 10036
Tel: (212)869-8530 *Fax:* (212)719-9815
E-Mail: info@actorsequity.org
Web Site: www.actorsequity.org
Members: 45000 individuals
Staff: 120
Annual Budget: $10-25,000,000
Eastern Regional Director, Supervisor of National Contracts: Carol Waaser
National Director, Finance and Administration: Steve DiPaola
National Director, Communications: David Lotz
E-Mail: info@actorsequity.org
National Director, Policy: Mary Lou Westerfield
President: Mark Zimmerman

Historical Note
Organized in New York City May 26, 1913 by a group of members of the former Actors' Society of America. It is an autonomous component of Associated Actors and Artists of America and represents actors and stage managers on the legitimate stage.

Meetings/Conferences:
Annual Meetings: *New York, NY*

Publications:
Equity News. 10/year.

Acute Long Term Hospital Association *(1996)*
625 Slater's Ln.
Suite 302
Alexandria, VA 22314
Tel: (703)518-9900 *Fax:* (703)518-9980
E-Mail: info@altha.org
Web Site: www.altha.org
Members: 175 Hospitals
Chief Executive Officer: William Walters
E-Mail: info@altha.org

Historical Note
Established in 1996 to promote the interests of long term acute care hospitals and their patients.

Publications:
ALTHA Insights. semi-a. adv.

ADARA *(1966)*
P.O. Box 480
Myersville, MD 21773
Tel: (301)293-8969 *Fax:* (301)293-9698
E-Mail: adaraorgan@aol.com
Web Site: www.adara.org
Members: 600 individuals
Staff: 1
Annual Budget: $50-100,000
Office Manager: Sherri Fleishell

Historical Note
Founded in St. Louis, Missouri in 1966 as Professional Rehabilitation Workers with the Adult Deaf and incorporated the following year. Became American Deafness and Rehabilitation Association in 1976, and ADARA: Professionals Networking for Excellence in Service Delivery with Individuals Who Are Deaf or Hard of Hearing in 1994. Membership: $55/year (domestic); $75/year (overseas).

Meetings/Conferences:
Biennial Meetings: Spring

Publications:
ADARA Journal. 3/year. adv.
ADARA UPDATE. q. adv.

ADED - the Association for Driver Rehabilitation Specialists *(1976)*
711 S. Vienna
Ruston, LA 71272
Tel: (318)257-5055 *Fax:* (318)255-4175
Toll Free: (800)290 - 2344
E-Mail: webmaster@driver-ed.org
Web Site: www.aded.net
Members: 570 individuals
Staff: 1
Annual Budget: $100-250,000
Co-Executive Director: Michael K. Shipp
E-Mail: webmaster@driver-ed.org

Historical Note
Members are driver rehabilitation specialists who provide driver evaluation and training for persons with disabilities and manufacturers/distributors of equipment used by persons with disabilities. Membership: $75/year (individual); $25/year (associate/student); $250/year (vendor); $500/year (corporate).

Meetings/Conferences:
Annual Meetings: *Summer*
2007 – Dallas, TX(Hyatt Regency)/July 27-31/300

Publications:
Newsbrake. q. adv.

Adhesion Society *(1977)*
Two Davidson Hall - 0201
Blacksburg, VA 24061
Tel: (540)231-7257 *Fax:* (540)231-3971
E-Mail: adhesoc@vt.edu
Web Site: www.adhesionsociety.org
Members: 514 individuals
Staff: 1
Office Manager: Esther Brann
E-Mail: adhesoc@vt.edu

Historical Note
Members are chemists, engineers, biologists, mathematicians, physicists, physicians, dentists and other professionals involved in adhesion science. Membership: $55/year (individual); $20/year (student/retiree).

Meetings/Conferences:
Annual Meetings: *February*

Publications:
Adhesion Society Newsletter Online.
Review of Adhesion Literature Online.
Proceedings of Adhesion Society. a.

Adhesive and Sealant Council *(1958)*
7979 Old Georgetown Rd.
Suite 500
Bethesda, MD 20814-2429
Tel: (301)986-9700 *Fax:* (301)986-9795
E-Mail: info@ascouncil.org
Web Site: www.ascouncil.org
Members: 120 companies
Staff: 8
Annual Budget: $1-2,000,000
President: Lawrence D. Sloan
E-Mail: larry.sloan@ascouncil.org
Director, Government Relations: Mark Collatz
E-Mail: mark.collatz@ascouncil.org
Director, Finance and Administration: Kate Zando
E-Mail: kate.zando@ascouncil.org

Historical Note
Formerly (1967) Rubber and Plastic Adhesive and Sealant Manufacturers Council. Members are makers of adhesives and sealants and their suppliers. Membership: $1,900-30,000/year, based on net sales (company).

Meetings/Conferences:
Semi-Annual Meetings: Spring and Fall
2007 – Savannah, GA(Hyatt Regency)/Apr. 15-18
2007 – Kansas City, MO(Hyatt Regency)/Oct. 7-10

Publications:
Catalyst Newsletter. 3/yr. adv.

Adjutants General Association of the United States *(1912)*
1300 Military Rd.
Lincoln, NE 68508-1090
Tel: (402)309-7107 *Fax:* (402)309-7128
E-Mail: terri.kattes@ne.ngb.army.mil
Web Site: www.agaus.org
Members: 54 state and territorial commands
Staff: 1
Annual Budget: under $10,000
President: Maj. Gen. Roger P. Lempke

Historical Note
Membership composed of the commander of the National Guard in each state, the District of Columbia, the Commonwealth of Puerto Rico, the Virgin Islands and Guam.

Meetings/Conferences:
Semi-Annual Meetings: early Feb./Washington, DC & Spring/various sites
2007 – Anchorage, AK/June 3-7

Administrators and Teachers in English as a Second Language *(1988)*

Historical Note
A section of NAFSA: Association of International Educators.

ADSC: The International Association of Foundation Drilling *(1972)*
14180 Dallas Pkwy.
Suite 510
Dallas, TX 75254
Tel: (214)343-2091 *Fax:* (214)343-2384
E-Mail: adsc@adsc-iafd.com
Web Site: www.adsc-iafd.com
Members: 900 companies and individuals
Staff: 9
Annual Budget: $1-2,000,000
Executive Director: S. Scot Litke
E-Mail: slitke@adsc-iafd.com
Director, Administration: Marilyn Ellis
Director, Meetings: Jan Hall
Memebership/Chapter Relations/Education Coordinator: Mike Moore

Historical Note
Founded in 1972 as the Association of Drilled Shaft Contractors; assumed its current name in 1995. ADSC seeks to advance technology in the drilled shaft, earth retention, micropile and other related industries. ADSC represents drilled shaft, anchored earth retention, micropile, and other related subcontractors, civil engineers, and equipment manufacturing firms world-wide. Provides scholarships and R&D support through its Industry Advancement Fund. Membership: $300-4,640/year (Contractors); varies by contract limit; $350-875/year (Associate); $95/year (Technical Affiliate).

Meetings/Conferences:
Semi-Annual Meetings: Winter/Summer
2007 – Orlando, FL(Buena Vista Palace Resort)/Jan. 31-Feb. 3/1500
2007 – Incline Village, NV(Hyatt Regency Lake Tahoe Resort)/July 25-28/200

Publications:
ADSC Membership Directory/Buyer's Guide. a. adv.
Foundation Drilling. 8/year. adv.
Technical Library Catalog. bien.

Adult Video Association *(1987)*

Historical Note
Superseded by Free Speech Coalition (see listing).

Advanced Medical Technology Association *(1903)*
701 Pennsylvania Ave. NW
Suite 800

Washington, DC 20004
Tel: (202)783-8700 *Fax:* (202)783-8750
E-Mail: info@advamed.org
Web Site: www.advamed.org
Members: 1,300 companies
Staff: 65
Annual Budget: $10-25,000,000
President and Chief Executive Officer: Stephen J. Ubl
Executive Vice President, Global Strategy/Analysis: Ralph Ives
Executive Vice President, Federal Government Relations: Megan Ivory
Senior Executive Vice President and Chief Administrative Officer: Kenneth Mendez
Senior Executive Vice President: David Nexon
Vice President, Membership: Frank S. Wilton

Historical Note

Established as the Wholesale Surgical Trade Association. Became Manufacturers Surgical Trade Association in 1944 and the Medical-Surgical Manufacturers Association in 1967. Merged in 1974 with the Health Industries Association to form the Health Industry Manufacturers Association, and assumed its current name in 2000. Represents manufacturers of health care technology, including medical devices, diagnostic products and health care information systems. Has an annual budget of approximately $12 million. Membership fee based on domestic sales volume.

Meetings/Conferences:

Annual Meetings: March
2007 – Chandler, AZ(Sheraton Wild Horse Pass)/March 7-9

Publications:

Medical Technology & Innovation.
In Brief. bi-w.

Advanced Transit Association *(1976)*
P.O. Box 220249
Boston, MA 02122-0013
E-Mail: membership@advancedtransit.org
Web Site: http://advancedtransit.org
Members: 120 individuals and 5 corporations
Annual Budget: $10-25,000
Treasurer: Lawrence Fabian
E-Mail: membership@advancedtransit.org

Historical Note

Members are transportation professionals and others interested in applying advanced technology and planning concepts to urban transportation. Promotes low-cost and service-effective urban transit modes, with the goal of including underserved urban areas. Has no paid officers or full-time staff. Membership: $35/year.

Meetings/Conferences:

Annual Meetings: Washington, DC/January

Publications:

Journal of Advanced Transportation. 3/year.
Newsletter. 6/yr.

Adventure Travel Trade Association *(1990)*
601 Union St., 42nd Floor
Seattle, WA 98101
Tel: (360)805-3131 *Fax:* (360)805-0649
E-Mail: info@adventuretravel.biz
Web Site: www.adventuretravelbusiness.com
Members: 300 corporations
Staff: 4
Annual Budget: $250-500,000
President: Shannon Stowell
E-Mail: info@adventuretravel.biz

Historical Note

Formerly (1997) Adventure Travel Society ATTA assists members in managing their businesses and marketing adventure travel and facilitates communication and business relationships within the adventure travel industry. Membership: $75/year (individual); $600/year (organization).

Meetings/Conferences:

Annual Meetings: Fall

Advertising and Marketing International Network *(1932)*
12323 Nantucket
Wichita, KS 67235
Tel: (316)531-2342 *Fax:* (316)722-8353
Web Site: www.aminworldwide.com
Members: 65 agencies
Staff: 2
Annual Budget: $250-500,000
Executive Director: Vaughn Sink

Historical Note

A world-wide network of cooperating, non-competitive advertising agencies in 60 cities which provide facilities and branch office services for its members. Formerly called the Continental Advertising Agency Network. Membership: $3,000/year (organization/company).

Publications:

AMIN News. m.

Advertising Council *(1942)*
261 Madison Ave., 11th Floor
New York, NY 10016-2303
Tel: (212)922-1500 *Fax:* (212)922-1676
Toll Free: (800)933 - 7727
E-Mail: info@adcouncil.org
Web Site: www.adcouncil.org
Members: 500 companies
Staff: 60
Annual Budget: $2-5,000,000
Chief Executive Officer and President: Peggy Conlon
E-Mail: info@adcouncil.org
Executive Vice President, Corporate Communications: Paula Veale
E-Mail: info@adcouncil.org

Historical Note

Founded in 1942 as the War Advertising Council. Reorganized after World War II and became the Advertising Council, Inc. Not a trade association in the accepted sense, the Ad Council is a private, non-profit organization of volunteers who conduct advertising campaigns in the public good.

Meetings/Conferences:

Biennial Meetings: Washington, DC/Spring

Publications:

Public Service Advertising That Changed A Nation.
Committment to Children.
Annual Report. a.
Public Service Advertising Bulletin. bi-m.
The Story of the Ad Council.

Advertising Media Credit Executives Association, International *(1953)*
8840 Columbia 100 Pkwy.
Columbia, MD 21045-2158
Tel: (410)992-7609 *Fax:* (410)740-5574
E-Mail: amcea@amcea.org
Web Site: www.amcea.org
Members: 300 individuals
Staff: 1
Annual Budget: $50-100,000
President: Mark Stepuszek

Historical Note

Members are credit executives of newspapers, magazines, radio and television stations. Membership: $200/year (new member).

Meetings/Conferences:

Annual Meetings: Fall

Publications:

News and Views Magazine. q. adv.

Advertising Photographers of America *(1985)*
5455 Wilshire Blvd.
Suite 1709
Los Angeles, CA 90036-4217
Tel: (323)933-1631 *Fax:* (323)933-9209
Toll Free: (800)272 - 6264
E-Mail: office@apa-la.org
Web Site: www.apa-la.org
Staff: 2
Executive Director: Constance Evans

Historical Note

APA members are established, independent advertising and commercial photographers. Associate members are photographers who have been in business less than three years. APA was started with four regional chapters in 1981; in 1985 the original chapters formed APA National with the desire to coordinate and communicate on a national level. Only individuals located over 100 miles from the nearest regional chapter may join APA National directly as a member-at-large. Membership: $250/year (general, at large); $125/year (associate); $50/year (assistant/student); $3,000-$25,000/year (sustaining supplier).

Publications:

News-in-Focus Newsletter. q. adv.

Advertising Research Foundation *(1936)*
641 Lexington Ave., 11th Floor
New York, NY 10022
Tel: (212)751-5656 *Fax:* (212)319-5265
E-Mail: info@thearf.org
Web Site: www.thearf.org
Members: 325 companies
Staff: 20
Annual Budget: $2-5,000,000
President and Chief Executive Officer: Robert Barocci
Vice President, Marketing and Membership: Cassandra Bates
Senior Vice President, Research and Standards: Bill Cook
Vice President and Director, Member Services: Diane Streckfuss
Vice President and Director, Operations: Felix Yang

Historical Note

Founded in 1936 by the Association of National Advertisers and the American Association of Advertising Agencies. The only industry-wide not-for-profit association with the mission to enhance profitable marketing through effective research.

Meetings/Conferences:

Annual Meetings: New York, NY(Hilton)

Publications:

Journal of Advertising Research. bi-m. adv.

AeA - Advancing the Business of Technology *(1943)*
5201 Great America Pkwy.
Suite 400
Santa Clara, CA 95054
Tel: (408)987-4200 *Fax:* (408)987-4298
Toll Free: (800)284 - 4232
E-Mail: csc@aeanet.org
Web Site: www.aeanet.org
Members: 2500 companies
Staff: 100
Annual Budget: $10-25,000,000
President and Chief Executive Officer: William T. Archey
E-Mail: csc@aeanet.org

Historical Note

Formerly (2000) American Electronics Association. Founded in California in 1943 by 25 electronics manufacturers, it is now the largest trade association serving the electronics, software, and information technology industries. Maintains a Washington office, one of its 18 offices in the U.S., and offices in Brussels, Tokyo, and Beijing. Formerly (1971) the Western Electronic Manufacturers Association (WEMA). Supports the American Electronics Association ElectroPAC. Has an annual budget of over $17.5 million. Membership: dues vary with size of company.

Meetings/Conferences:

Annual Meetings: September

AERA - Engine Rebuilders Association *(1922)*
330 Lexington Dr.
Buffalo Grove, IL 60089-6998
Tel: (847)541-6550 *Fax:* (847)541-5808
Toll Free: (888)326 - 2372
E-Mail: jan@aera.org
Web Site: www.aera.org
Members: 3200 companies
Staff: 10
Annual Budget: $1-2,000,000
President and Chief Executive Officer: John Goodman
Vice President, Operations: Jan Juhl

Historical Note

Founded in 1922 Midwest Grinders Association; assumed its current name in 1927. Active members include: automotive jobber machine shops, custom automotive machine shops, heavy-duty, diesel and industrial shops, production engine rebuilders, high performance, and marine shops. Associate membership is available for suppliers of automotive parts, tools, equipment, chemicals, and services. Membership: $295-550/year (company, based on number of shop personnel).

Meetings/Conferences:
Annual Meetings: April

Publications:
Specifications Manuals. a. adv.
Technical Bulletins. m.
ID Guides. a. adv.
Shop Talk Newsletter. m.
Directory. a. adv.

Aerobics and Fitness Association of America
(1983)
15250 Ventura Blvd.
Suite 200
Sherman Oaks, CA 91403
Tel: (818)905-0040 *Fax:* (818)990-5468
Toll Free: (877)968 - 7263
E-Mail: lpafaa@aol.com
Web Site: www.AFAA.com
Members: 150000 individuals
Staff: 50
President: Linda D. Pfeffer, RN
Vice President, Purchasing: Tony Eid
Vice President and Controller: Phillip Longsworth

Historical Note
AFAA is an international professional association for the education, training, and certification of fitness professionals. Publishes standards and guidelines in addition to providing educational materials, continuting education programs, and home study courses. Membership: $68/year (individual). Also has online courses.

Publications:
Injury Prevention and Exercise Progressions Workshop Manual.
Practical Yoga.
Practical Pilates.
Personal Fitness Training, Theory and Practice.
American Fitness Magazine. 6/year. adv.
Fitness: Theory and Practice Textbook.
MAT Science Workshop Manual.
Fitness Gets Personal.
Kickboxing: A Manual For Instructors.
Exercise Standards & Guidelines Reference Manual.
An Emerging Profession: The Fitness Practitioner Manual.
A Guide to Personal Training.
Indoor Cycling Workshop Manual.
The Metabolic Connection to Obesity Workshop Manual.

Aeronautical Repair Station Association *(1984)*
121 N. Henry St.
Alexandria, VA 22314-2903
Tel: (703)739-9543 *Fax:* (703)739-9488
E-Mail: arsa@arsa.org
Web Site: www.arsa.org
Members: 50
Staff: 7
Annual Budget: $500-1,000,000
Executive Director: Sarah MacLeod
E-Mail: sarahsays@arsa.org
Managing Director and General Counsel: Marshall Filler
Vice President, Quality: Paul Hawthorne

Historical Note
Established and incorporated in Washington, D.C. in June 1984, ARSA represents entities certified by national aviation authorities to perform maintenance and alterations on civil aviation products. Absorbed Airline Services Association in 1985. Membership: $250-7,500/year.

Meetings/Conferences:
Annual Meetings: Annual/250

Publications:
The Hotline. m. adv.

Aerospace and Electronic Systems Society

Historical Note
A technical society of the Institute of Electrical and Electronics Engineers (IEEE). Membership in the Society, open only to IEEE members, includes a subscription to a technical periodical in the field published by IEEE. All administrative support is provided by IEEE.

Aerospace Department Chairmen's Association
(1968)
School of Aeronautics and Astronautics
1280 Engineering Administration
West Lafayette, IN 47907-1280
Tel: (765)494-5345 *Fax:* (765)494-9321
Web Site: www.ecn.purdue.edu/ENGR
Members: 80 individuals
Annual Budget: under $10,000
Chairman: Dave Dolling

Historical Note
Promotes aerospace engineering education and research to stimulate the growth of the aerospace profession. Has no paid officers or full-time staff. Membership: $3/year.

Meetings/Conferences:
Annual Meetings: January

Publications:
Meeting Minutes. a. adv.

Aerospace Industries Association of America
(1919)
1000 Wilson Blvd.
Suite 1700
Arlington, VA 22209-3901
Tel: (703)358-1000 *Fax:* (703)358-1011
Web Site: www.aia-aerospace.org
Members: 105 regular members, 180 associate members
Staff: 40
President and Chief Executive Officer: John W. Douglass
E-Mail: burkholder@aia-aerospace.org
Communications Manager: Matt Grimison
E-Mail: burkholder@aia-aerospace.org
Director, Legislative Affairs: Patrick McCartan

Historical Note
Established in 1919 as the Aeronautical Chamber of Commerce of America, Inc. Name changed to Aircraft Industries Association of America, Inc. in 1945 and to Aerospace Industries Association of America in 1959. The National Center for Advanced Technologies is its non-profit affiliate. Membership fee based on percentage of sales.

Meetings/Conferences:
Semi-annual Meetings: Williamsburg, VA in May & Phoenix, AZ in November.

Publications:
Aerospace Facts and Figures. a.
AIA Update. 10/year.
Aerospace Statistical Mailing List. q.

Aerospace Medical Association *(1929)*
320 S. Henry St.
Alexandria, VA 22314-3579
Tel: (703)739-2240 *Fax:* (703)739-9652
Web Site: www.asma.org
Members: 3600 individuals
Staff: 6
Annual Budget: $500-1,000,000
Executive Director: Dr. Russell B. Rayman
Membership: Gloria Carter

Historical Note
Founded in Detroit, MI as The Aero Medical Society of the United States. Incorporated (1930) in Washington, DC. Name changed to the Aero Medical Association in 1947 and to the present name in 1959. Membership: $215/year (individual); $400/year (company).

Meetings/Conferences:
Annual Meetings: Spring
2007 – New Orleans, LA(Sheraton and Marriott)/May 13-17

Publications:
Aviation, Space, and Environmental Medicine. m. adv.

Aestheticians International Association *(1972)*
2611 N. Belt Line Rd.
Suite 101
Sunnyvale, TX 75182
Tel: (972)226-2309 *Fax:* (972)226-2339
Toll Free: (877)968 - 7539
E-Mail: aiathekey@aol.com
Web Site: www.dermascope.com
Members: 2000 individuals
Staff: 2
Annual Budget: $25-50,000
Director, Membership: Jennifer Fields
E-Mail: aiathekey@aol.com

Historical Note
Members are individuals owning or working in a skin care salon, together with manufacturers and distributors of skin care products. AIA produces trade shows for both the specialized industry and full cosmetology profession.

Meetings/Conferences:
Annual Meetings:

Publications:
Dermascope Magazine. m. adv.

AFCOM *(1981)*
742 E. Chapman Ave.
Orange, CA 92866
Tel: (714)997-7966 *Fax:* (714)997-9743
E-Mail: afcom@afcom.com
Web Site: www.afcom.com
Members: 2800 individuals
Staff: 11
Annual Budget: $2-5,000,000
President and Chief Executive Officer: Leonard Eckhaus

Historical Note
Founded as Association for Computer Operations Management; became Association for Data Center, Network, and Enterprise Systems Management in (1997), and assumed its current name in 2001. AFCOM members are managers of corporate, institutional and internet computer facilities. Membership: $184/year.

Publications:
DCM - Data Center Management Magazine. bi-m. adv.
Comminique Newsletter. bi-m.

Affiliated Conference of Practicing Accountants International *(1978)*

Historical Note
Address unknown in 2006.

Affiliated Warehouse Companies *(1953)*
P.O. Box 295
Hazlet, NJ 07730-0295
Tel: (732)739-2323 *Fax:* (732)739-4154
E-Mail: sales@awco.com
Web Site: www.awco.com
Members: 115 companies
Staff: 8
Annual Budget: $250-500,000
President: James McBride, III
E-Mail: sales@awco.com

Historical Note
Affiliated Warehouse Companies was organized in 1953 and remains the first third party warehouse marketing sales company owned and operated by its employees. Through its offices in Hazlet, NJ, La Grange, IL, and Fresno, CA, AWC performs the marketing and sales for third party warehouse companies in the United States, Canada, Mexico and Puerto Rico. Of equal importance, AWC assists the third party warehouse user by being a resource for rates, data, and information on warehousing and distribution at no charge or obligation.

Meetings/Conferences:
Semi-annual Meetings: Spring and Fall

Publications:
Directory. bien.
Newsletter. m.
Summary of Sales Work. w.
Public Warehouse Selection Process.
Database of Public Warehouse Users.

Affordable Housing Tax Credit Coalition *(1988)*
1900 K St. NW
Suite 1200
Washington, DC 20006
Tel: (202)419-2025 *Fax:* (202)828-3738
E-Mail: info@taxcreditcoalition.org
Web Site: www.taxcreditcoalition.org
Members: 75 companies
Staff: 1
Annual Budget: $100-250,000
Executive Director: Victoria E. Spielman

Historical Note
AHTCC members include syndicators, investors, lenders, developers, non-profit organizations and others with an interest in the low-income housing tax credit. Founded as the Coalition to Preserve the Low-Income Housing Tax Credit with the then-sole purpose of achieving a permanent extension, its goals were broadened after permanent extension was achieved in 1993. Membership: Annual dues vary by membership category.

Meetings/Conferences:
2007 - Key West, FL/Jan. 29-30

Publications:
AHTCC News. q.
Washington Alert. irreg.

AFIA-Alfalfa Processors Council *(1941)*
1501 Wilson Blvd.
Suite 1100
Arlington, VA 22209
Tel: (703)524-0810 *Fax:* (703)524-1921
E-Mail: afia@afia.org
Web Site: www.afia.org/industry_committee/AFIA_alfalfa_processors_council_members.htm
Members: 29 companies
Staff: 1
Annual Budget: $50-100,000
Contact: Joel Newman

Historical Note
Founded as the American Dehydrators Association; became American Alfalfa Processors Association in 1984. Merged with the American Feed Industry Association and assumed its current name in 2001. Members are suppliers to and operators of alfalfa processing firms. Provides market research and related services to members.

Meetings/Conferences:
Annual Meetings: February-March

Publications:
Bulletin. w. adv.

AFMA

Historical Note
Became Independent Film & Television Alliance in 2004.

Afram Films

Historical Note
A division of Motion Picture Association, which provides administrative support.

Africa Travel Association *(1975)*
347 Fifth Ave.
Suite 610
New York, NY 10016
Tel: (212)447-1926 *Fax:* (212)725-8253
E-Mail: africatravelasso@aol.com
Web Site: www.africa-ata.org
Members: 760 individuals
Staff: 5
Annual Budget: $50-100,000
Executive Director: Mira Berman
E-Mail: africatravelasso@aol.com

Historical Note
Mission of ATA is to promote the tourist attractions of the continent of Africa to the travel industry in North America and educate all interested travel agents, planners, and operators about the products and services offered by the travel and tourism industry in Africa. ATA works closely with individual African countries, tour and ground operators, incentive, meeting, convention planners, travel agents, airlines, hoteliers, and all other branches of the travel and leisure industry. ATA has broadened its programs to include business, economic and financial development in Africa.

Publications:
Africa Travel Magazine. q.
Membership Directory. a.

African American Contractors Association
3901 State St.
Chicago, IL 60609
Tel: (312)915-5960 Ext: 13 *Fax:* (312)567-9919
E-Mail: omaraaca@hotmail.com
Members: 2500 individuals
Staff: 6
President: Omar S. Shareef

Publications:
Mainstream.

African Studies Association *(1957)*
Rutgers University, Douglass Campus
132 George St.
New Brunswick, NJ 08901-1400
Tel: (732)932-8173 *Fax:* (732)932-3394
E-Mail: members@rci.rutgers.edu
Web Site: www.africanstudies.org
Members: 2200 individuals
Staff: 5
Annual Budget: $500-1,000,000
Executive Director: Carol L. Martin, Ph.D.

Historical Note
Membership: $45-150/year (individual); $220/year (institutions).

Meetings/Conferences:
Annual Meetings: Fall

Publications:
African Studies Review. 3/year. adv.
ASA NEWS. 3/year. adv.
History in Africa. a. adv.

African-American Library and Information Science Association *(1993)*
10920 Wilshire Blvd.
Suite 150-9132
Los Angeles, CA 90024-6502
Tel: (310)825-6060 *Fax:* (310)825-5019
Members: 100 individuals
Annual Budget: under $10,000
President: Itibari M. Zulu
E-Mail: imz@ucla.edu

Historical Note
Formed to address issues of under-representation within the library sciences profession and access to information resources for the African-American community at large. Has no paid officers or full-time staff. Membership: $20/year.

Meetings/Conferences:
Annual Meetings: March

African-American Natural Foods Association *(1990)*
P.O. Box 496177
Chicago, IL 60649-6177
Tel: (312)363-3939
Annual Budget: under $10,000
Chief Executive Officer: Cheryl Simms

Historical Note
Members are health food retailers, manufacturers and others with an interest in increasing the acceptance of natural foods in minority communities. Membership: $50-$75/year (individual); $100-$250/year (company).

Meetings/Conferences:
Quarterly Meetings:

African-American Women's Clergy Association *(1969)*
214 P St. NW
Washington, DC 20001
Tel: (202)518-8488 *Fax:* (202)518-1273
E-Mail: imageneshelter@aol.com
Web Site: www.houseofimagene.org
Members: 175 individuals
Chairperson: Bishop Imagene B. Stewart

Historical Note
Formerly (1990) American Women's Clergy Association. AAWCA members are lay and ordained women clergy.

AFSM International *(1976)*
1342 Colonial Blvd.
Suite 25
Ft. Myers, FL 33907
Tel: (239)275-7887 *Fax:* (239)275-0794
Toll Free: (800)333 - 9786
Web Site: www.afsmi.org
Members: 5000 individuals
Staff: 16
Annual Budget: $2-5,000,000
Chief Executive Officer: John Schoenwald
E-Mail: jschoenwald@afsmi.org
Vice President, Sales: Ron Churchill
Chief Financial Officer: Kevin Douglas
Vice President, Member Services: James Gaidry
Director, Events: Stephen Stidinger
E-Mail: sstidinger@afsmi.org

Historical Note
Members are executives and managers in the high technology services/support industry. Formerly (1985) Association of Field Service Managers and (1989) Association of Field Service Managers International. Membership: $200/year, first year; $175/year, renewal (individual).

Meetings/Conferences:
Annual Meetings: Fall

Publications:
AFSM Internat'l, S-Business. bi-m. adv.

AFT - Public Employees
555 New Jersey Ave. NW
Washington, DC 20001
Tel: (202)879-4549 *Fax:* (202)393-5672
E-Mail: pubemps@aft.org
Web Site: www.aft.org/pubemps
Members: 1300000 individuals
Staff: 9
President: Edward J. McElroy

Historical Note
Formerly (2002) Federation of Public Employees. AFT Public Employees is the division of the American Federation of Teachers representing state and local government employees who are members of the AFT. As the oldest public employee union in the AFL-CIO, the AFT has been a pioneer in the effort to bring meaningful collective bargaining rights to public employees at all levels of government. With more than 100,000 federal, state and local government employee members in 20 states, AFT Public Employees is the most diverse of the AFT's divisions, with more than 4,000 job titles represented.

Publications:
Public Employee Advocate. bi-m. adv.

AFT Healthcare *(1978)*
555 New Jersey Ave. NW
Washington, DC 20001
Tel: (202)879-4491
E-Mail: healthcare@aft.org
Web Site: www.afthealthcare.org
Members: 70000 individuals
Staff: 9
Annual Budget: $2-5,000,000
Director: Mary Lehman MacDonald
Deputy Director for Public Affairs: Janet Bass
Director, Federal Legislation: Tor Cowan
Assistant to President for Organizing: Phil Kugler
In-House Counsel: David J. Strom

Historical Note
Formerly (2002) Federation of Nurses and Health Professionals. The health care division of the American Federation of Teachers, AFT Healthcare is a union which organizes and represents a wide spectrum of health care professionals, including registered nurses, LPNs, medical technologists and technicians and school nurses.

Meetings/Conferences:
Annual Meetings: Summer

Publications:
Healthwire. bi-m.

AGN International - North America *(1978)*
2851 S. Parker Rd.
Suite 850
Aurora, CO 80014-2729
Tel: (303)743-7880 *Fax:* (303)743-7660
Web Site: www.agn-na.org
Members: 52 firms
Staff: 5
Annual Budget: $1-2,000,000
Executive Director: Rita J. Hood

Historical Note
Founded as Continental Association of CPA Firms; assumed its current name in 1997. Absorbed TAG International in 2002. Membership fee varies; company must have revenues in excess of $2m.

Meetings/Conferences:
Semi-annual Meetings: Fall and Spring

Publications:
Client Newsletter. q.
The Worldwide Linx. 3/yr.

Agribusiness Council *(1967)*
1312 18th St. NW
Suite 300
Washington, DC 20036
Tel: (202)296-4563 *Fax:* (202)887-9178
E-Mail: info@agribusinesscouncil.org
Web Site: www.agribusinesscouncil.org/
Members: 400 companies and organizations
Staff: 3
President and Chief Executive Officer: Nicholas E. Hollis
E-Mail: info@agribusinesscouncil.org
Historical Note
ABC is a consortium of companies, universities, foundations, and individuals. Its purpose is to stimulate and encourage agribusiness development both domestically and abroad. Identifies investment opportunities for agribusiness, supports research, and serves as an information and networking resource for its members. ABC manages an informal network of state agribusiness councils, providing start-up support and training. Agri-Energy Roundtable (AER) manages a series of overseas affiliates of ABC. AER is a UN accredited non-governmental organization.
Publications:
State Agribusiness Council Bulletin. semi-a.
Heritage Preservation Committee Reports. q.
Newsletter.

Agricultural and Food Transporters Conference *(1994)*
2200 Mill Rd.
Alexandria, VA 22314
Tel: (703)838-7999 *Fax:* (703)519-1866
E-Mail: fhall@trucking.org
Members: 500 companies
Staff: 2
Annual Budget: $250-500,000
Executive Director: Fletcher R. Hall
E-Mail: fhall@trucking.org
Historical Note
Formerly (2003) Agricultural Transportation Conference. Represents transporters of commercial agricultural and food products through lobbying, educational programs and communications. A conference of the American Trucking Associations.
Publications:
Horizons. m. adv.

Agricultural and Industrial Manufacturers' Representatives Association *(1961)*
7500 Flying Cloud Dr.
Suite 900
Eden Prairie, MN 55344
Tel: (952)253-6230 *Fax:* (952)853-4774
Web Site: www.aimrareps.org
Members: 110 companies, 23 associates
Staff: 3
Annual Budget: $100-250,000
Executive Director: Jim Manke, CAE
Historical Note
Formerly (1972) American Farm and Power Equipment Agents Association. Membership: $450/year.
Meetings/Conferences:
Annual Meetings: Fall
Publications:
AIMRA Newsline. m.
Directory. a.

Agricultural Communicators in Education
Historical Note
Became Association for Communication excellence in 2003.

Agricultural History Society *(1919)*
Department of History
University of Arkansas
Little Rock, AR 72204-1099
Tel: (501)569-8782 *Fax:* (501)569-3059
E-Mail: cfwilliams@ualr.edu
Members: 1000 individuals
Staff: 1
Annual Budget: $10-25,000
Executive Secretary: C. Fred Williams
Historical Note
Organized to stimulate interest in, promote the study of, and facilitate research and publication on the history of agriculture. Membership: $45/year.
Meetings/Conferences:
Annual Meetings: April, in conjunction with the Organization of American Historians.
Publications:
Agricultural History. q. adv.

Agricultural Publishers Association
Historical Note
Became APA: the Association of Leading Agricultural Media Companies in 2000.

Agricultural Relations Council *(1953)*
Historical Note
Merged with Agriculture Council of America in 1998.

Agricultural Retailers Association *(1955)*
1156 15th St. NW
Suite 302
Washington, DC 20005
Tel: (202)457-0825 *Fax:* (202)457-0864
Toll Free: (800)535 - 6272
E-Mail: ara@aradc.org
Web Site: www.aradc.org
Members: 1000 individuals
Staff: 5
Annual Budget: $1-2,000,000
President and Chief Executive Officer: Jack E. Eberspacher
Director, Communications: Stacy Mayuga
Vice President, Regulatory Policy and Corporate Relations: Jim Thrift
Historical Note
Formerly National Nitrogen Solutions Association and (1992) National Fertilizer Solutions Association. Absorbed the National AgriChemical Retailers Association in 1992. Members are dealers, manufacturers, and suppliers of related products and services, nutrient materials, pesticides and fertilizer organizations.

Agricultural Transportation Conference
Historical Note
Became Agricultural and Food Transporters Conference in 2003.

Agriculture Council of America *(1973)*
11020 King St.
Suite 205
Overland Park, KS 66210
Tel: (913)491-1895 *Fax:* (913)491-6502
E-Mail: info@agday.org
Web Site: www.agday.org
Members: 2500 individuals
Staff: 3
Annual Budget: $250-500,000
President and Chief Executive Officer: Eldon White
Historical Note
Members include producers, commodity groups/cooperatives, general farm organizations, railroads, port authorities, market development cooperators, private voluntary agencies, retailers and financial institutions, and food and agricultural companies. Works to promote and build public support on behalf of the industry. Serves as coordinator for National Agriculture Day. Absorbed Agricultural Relations Council in 1998. Membership fee varies according to type of membership.
Publications:
National Agday Educator Kit. a.
Newsletter (online).

AIM Global *(1972)*
125 Warrrendale Road, Suite 100
Warrendale, PA 15086
Tel: (724)934-4470 *Fax:* (724)934-4495
E-Mail: info@aimglobal.org
Web Site: www.aimglobal.org
Members: 800 companies
Staff: 8
President: Dan Mullen
E-Mail: info@aimglobal.org
Historical Note
AIM Global is a global association recognized as the worldwide authority on automatic identification, data collection, and networking in a mobile environment.
Meetings/Conferences:
Annual Meetings: Winter
2007 – Tampa, FL/Feb. 26-27
Publications:
Global Yearbook and Buyer's Guide. a.

Air & Surface Transport Nurses Association *(1980)*
7995 E. Prentice Ave., Suite 100
Greenwood Village, CO 80111
Tel: (720)498-0492 *Fax:* (303)770-1614
Toll Free: (800)897 - 6362
E-Mail: astna@gwami.com
Web Site: www.astna.org
Members: 1800 individuals
Staff: 2
Annual Budget: $100-250,000
Executive Director: Karen Wojdyla
Historical Note
Founded as National Flight Nurses Association; assumed its present name in 1999. Membership: $80/year (active); $75/year (inactive and affiliate).
Meetings/Conferences:
Annual Meetings: Fall
Publications:
Air Medical Journal. bi-m.
Wings, Wheels & Motors. q.

Air and Waste Management Association *(1907)*
One Gateway Center, Third Floor
420 Ft. Duquesne Blvd.
Pittsburgh, PA 15222-1435
Tel: (412)232-3444 *Fax:* (412)232-3450
E-Mail: info@awma.org
Web Site: www.awma.org
Members: 9000 organizations & individuals
Staff: 25
Annual Budget: $2-5,000,000
Finance Director: Bill Braun
Executive Director: Adrianne Carolla, CAE
Director, Publications: Andy Knopes
Director, Meetings and Education: Louise Wallach
Historical Note
Formerly (1989) Air Pollution Control Association. The Association provides a neutral forum where environmental professionals share technical and managerial information about air pollution control and waste management. Members are drawn from a wide range of disciplines and represent all viewpoints on environmental issues. Has an annual budget of over $5 million. Membership: $150/year (individual); $1,000/year (contributing); $350/year (organization); $100/year (new member).
Meetings/Conferences:
Annual Meetings: June
Publications:
EM. m. adv.
Journal of the A&WMA. m.
Resource Book & Membership Directory. a. adv.

Air Brake Association *(1894)*
Historical Note
Address unknown in 2006.

AIR Commercial Real Estate Association *(1960)*
800 W. Sixth St.
Suite 800
Los Angeles, CA 90017
Tel: (213)687-8777 *Fax:* (213)687-8616
Toll Free: (877)462 - 4732
Web Site: www.airea.com
Members: 1,600 individuals
Staff: 30
Annual Budget: $2-5,000,000
Executive Director: Tim Hayes
Historical Note
Founded as American Industrial Real Estate Association; assumed its current name in 2004. Members are real estate brokers specializing in industrial/commercial properties.
Publications:
Bulletin. m.

Industrial Multiple. w.
Newsletter. bi-w.

Air Conditioning Contractors of America *(1969)*
2800 Shirlington Road, Suite 300
Arlington, VA 22206
Tel: (703)575-4477 *Fax:* (703)575-4449
E-Mail: admin@acca.org
Web Site: www.acca.org
Members: 4030 companies
Staff: 20
Annual Budget: $5-10,000,000
President and Chief Executive Officer: Paul T. Stalknecht
E-Mail: paul.stalknecht@acca.org
Vice President, Administration and Finance/General Counsel: Hilary Atkins
Senior Vice President and Chief of Staff: Michael Honeycutt
Vice President, Research and Technology: Glenn Hourahan, P.E.

Historical Note
Formed by a consolidation of Air Conditioning and Refrigeration Contractors of America with the contractors of the National Warm Air Heating and Air Conditioning Association. From 1969 to 1978 known as the National Environmental Systems Contractors Association. Supports the Air Conditioning Contractors of America Political Action Committee. Membership: $325/year (company).

Meetings/Conferences:
Annual Meetings: February or March/600
2007 - Orlando, FL/March 5-8

Publications:
Insider. a. adv.
Contractor Excellence. q.
ACCA Alert. w.

Air Courier Conference of America

Historical Note
Became Express Delivery & Logistics Association in 2005.

Air Diffusion Council *(1960)*
1901 N. Roselle Rd.
Suite 800
Schaumburg, IL 60195
Tel: (847)706-6750 *Fax:* (847)706-6751
E-Mail: info@flexibleduct.org
Web Site: www.flexibleduct.org
Members: 50 companies
Staff: 2
Annual Budget: $50-100,000
Executive Director: Jack L. Lagershausen
E-Mail: info@flexibleduct.org

Historical Note
Members are makers and suppliers of flexible ducts for air distribution. Membership: $600-2,800/year (company).

Meetings/Conferences:
Semi-Annual Meetings:

Publications:
Flexible Duct Performance & Installation Standards Manual and Videotape.

Air Distributing Institute *(1947)*
4415 W. Harrison St., Suite 242-C
Hillside, IL 60162
Tel: (708)449-2933 *Fax:* (708)449-0837
Members: 27 companies
Staff: 2
Annual Budget: $25-50,000
General Manager: Patricia H. Keating

Historical Note
Members are manufacturers of prefabricated ducts, pipes and fittings used in residential housing.

Publications:
Bulletin. m.

Air Force Association *(1946)*
1501 Lee Hwy.
Arlington, VA 22209-1198
Tel: (703)247-5800 *Fax:* (703)247-5853
Web Site: www.afa.org
Members: 130,000 individuals
Staff: 65
Annual Budget: $10-25,000,000
President: Donald L. Peterson
Director, Communications: Chester Curtis
Director, Programs and Industry Relations: Mary Ellen Dobrowolski
Director, Government Relations: Kenneth A. Goss
Executive Director: John Shaud

Historical Note
Has military and civilian members. Promotes public understanding of aerospace power. Annual budget of approximately $11.5 million. Membership: $36/year.

Meetings/Conferences:
Annual Meetings: Washington, DC/September/7,000-8,000
2007 - Washington, DC(Marriott Wardman Park)/Sept. 24-26
2008 - Washington, DC(Marriott Wardman Park)/Sept. 15-17

Publications:
Air Force Magazine. m. adv.

Air Force Sergeants Association *(1961)*
5211 Auth Rd.
Suitland, MD 20746
Tel: (301)899-3500 *Fax:* (301)899-8136
Toll Free: (800)638 - 0594
E-Mail: staff@afsahq.org
Web Site: www.afsahq.org
Members: 132000 individuals
Staff: 32
Annual Budget: $2-5,000,000
Chief Executive Officer: Richard Dean
E-Mail: staff@afsahq.org

Historical Note
Formed May 3, 1961 by four noncommissioned Air Force officers, and incorporated in the District of Columbia. Members are enlisted personnel in the U.S. Air Force, Air National Guard and U.S. Air Force Reserve. Membership: $21/year (individual).

Publications:
Weekly Newsletter. w.
The Sergeants Magazine. 8/year. adv.

Air Line Pilots Association, International *(1931)*
1625 Massachusetts Ave. NW
Washington, DC 20036
Tel: (703)689-2270
Web Site: www.alpa.org
Members: 64000 individuals
Staff: 400
Annual Budget: $50-100,000,000
President: Capt. Duane E. Woerth
Director, Finance: Kevin Barnhurst
Director, Legal Department: Jonathan Cohen, CAE
Director, Government Affairs: Paul L. Hallisay
General Manager: Jalmer M. Johnson
Director, Communications: Don P. Skiados

Historical Note
Organized in Chicago in 1931 by pilot representatives of various air carriers under the leadership of David Behncke and chartered by the American Federation of Labor the same year. Once included the Air Line Employees Association and the Association of Flight Attendants which became independent chartered affiliates in 1963 and 1973, respectively. Absorbed Canadian Air Line Pilots Association in 1997, and now represents pilots at 49 airlines. Supports the Air Line Pilots Political Action Committee. Has an annual budget of approximately $99.0 million.

Meetings/Conferences:
Biennial meetings: Fall

Publications:
The Air Line Pilot. m. adv.

Air Medical Physician Association *(1992)*
951 E. Montana Vista Ln.
Salt Lake City, UT 84124
Tel: (801)263-2672 *Fax:* (801)534-0434
Web Site: www.ampa.org
Members: 400 individuals
Staff: 1
Annual Budget: $50-100,000
Executive Director: Pat Petersen

Historical Note
AMPA members are physicians with an interest in critical care air and ground transport.

Meetings/Conferences:
Annual Meetings: Spring

Publications:
Air Medical Physician Handbook.
Air Medical Journal.

Air Movement and Control Association International *(1955)*
30 W. University Dr.
Arlington Heights, IL 60004-1893
Tel: (847)394-0150 *Fax:* (847)253-0088
Web Site: www.amca.org
Members: 280 companies
Staff: 25
Annual Budget: $2-5,000,000
Executive Director: Barbara L. Morrison, Ph.D., CAE
E-Mail: bmorrison@amca.org
Director, Finance: Robert Harris
E-Mail: rharris@amca.org

Historical Note
Formerly (1977) Air Moving and Conditioning Association. Manufacturers of axial centrifugal fans, power roof ventilators, propeller fans, air curtains, ceiling fans, louvers, accoustic attenuators, dampers, shutters, and other air system components. Administers a Certified Ratings Program to insure that products bearing the AMCA seal meet criteria established by the AMCA Certified Rating Program. Member companies manufacture products for the commercial, industrial, and residential markets.

Meetings/Conferences:
Annual Meetings: Fall
2007 - Phoenix, AZ(J.W. Marriott)/Oct. 12-15

Publications:
Directory of Agricultural Products with Certified Ratings. a.
Techspecs. semi-a.
Publications Catalog.
Standards.
In Motion Magazine. adv.

Air Traffic Control Association *(1956)*
1010 King St., Suite 300
Alexandria, VA 22314-2944
Tel: (703)299-2430 *Fax:* (703)299-2437
E-Mail: info@atca.org
Web Site: www.atca.org
Members: 2300 individuals
Staff: 9
Annual Budget: $2-5,000,000
President: Paul P. Bollinger, Jr.
Director, Conference Services: Gail Hanline

Historical Note
An independent, non-profit professional organization founded by air traffic controllers seeking professional recognition. Includes all types of professionals working within the air traffic control system. Membership: $78/year (individual); $500-1,000/year (company).

Meetings/Conferences:
Semi-Annual Meetings: one international, one U.S.

Publications:
Quarterly of Air Traffic Control. q.
ATCA Bulletin. m. adv.
Conference Proceedings. a. adv.
Journal of Air Traffic Control. q. adv.

Air Transport Association of America *(1936)*
1301 Pennsylvania Ave. NW
Suite 1100
Washington, DC 20004-1707
Tel: (202)626-4000 *Fax:* (202)626-4181
E-Mail: ata@airlines.org
Web Site: www.airlines.org
Members: 19 U.S. airlines, 4 non-U.S. airlines
Staff: 75
Annual Budget: $10-25,000,000
President and Chief Executive Officer: James C. May
Vice President, Chief Financial Officer and Treasurer: Paul R. Archambeault
Vice President, Operations and Safety: Basil J. Barimo
Vice President, General Counsel and Secretary: David A. Berg
Senior Managing Director, Administration: Karen V. Evans
Vice President and Chief Economist: John P. Heimlich
Vice President, Policy: Patricia Higginbotham
Executive Vice President and Chief Operating Officer: John M. Meenan

Vice President, Government Affairs: Sharon L. Pinkerton

Historical Note

Organized January 5, 1936 at a meeting of airline representatives in Chicago, IL, ATA represents U.S. scheduled airlines in domestic and international passenger and cargo operations. Sponsors and supports the ATA Political Action Committee.

Meetings/Conferences:

Annual Meetings: Washington, DC/December

Publications:

Air Transport Ass'n of America: Annual Report of the U.S. Scheduled Airline Industry. a.

Airborne Law Enforcement Association *(1968)*

P.O. Box 3683
Tulsa, OK 74101-3683
Tel: (918)599-0705 *Fax:* (918)583-2353
E-Mail: homeoffice@alea.org
Web Site: www.alea.org
Members: 3500 individuals
Staff: 4
Annual Budget: $100-250,000
Executive Director: Sherry W. Hadley, C.A.E.
E-Mail: homeoffice@alea.org

Historical Note

Law enforcement officers who use both fixed and rotary wing aircraft, and who are engaged or interested in the use of aircraft in law enforcement, plus equipment suppliers. Officers elected every 2 years. Membership: $30/year (individual); $360/year (organization/company).

Meetings/Conferences:

Annual Meetings: Summer/800
2007 - Orlando, FL/July 18-21
2008 - Houston, TX/July 16-19

Publications:

Buyers Guide. a. adv.
Conference Issue. a. adv.
Air Beat Magazine. m. adv.

AirConditioning and Refrigeration Institute *(1953)*

4100 N. Fairfax Dr.
Suite 200
Arlington, VA 22203
Tel: (703)524-8800 *Fax:* (703)528-3816
E-Mail: ari@ari.org
Web Site: www.ari.org
Members: 236 companies
Staff: 43
Annual Budget: $5-10,000,000
President: William G. Sutton
Director, Communications: Joe Stevens

Historical Note

Formed in 1953 by a merger of the Refrigeration Equipment Manufacturers Association and the Air Conditioning and Refrigerating Machinery Association. Merged (1965) with the equipment manufacturers of the National Warm Air Heating and AirConditioning Association and (1967) with the Air Filter Institute. Represents manufacturers of air conditioning, refrigeration and heating equipment; membership is divided into sections according to product type. Co-sponsors the International Air Conditioning, Heating, Refrigerating and Ventilating Trade Exposition. Has an annual budget of approximately $7.2 million. Membership fee based on sales volume.

Meetings/Conferences:

Annual Meetings: November/500

Publications:

Minuteman Bulletin. m.
Statistical Profile. a.

AirConditioning and Refrigeration Wholesalers Association International *(1935)*

Historical Note

Formerly National Refrigeration Supply Jobbers Association and Refrigeration Equipment Wholesalers Association. Merged with North American Heating, Refrigeration and Airconditioning Wholesalers Ass'n in 2003 to form Heating, Airconditioning and Refrigeration Distributors Internat'l.

Aircraft Builders Council *(1955)*

4248 Park Glen Rd.
Minneapolis, MN 55416-4758
Tel: (952)928-4662 *Fax:* (952)929-1318
Web Site: www.aircraftbuilders.com
Administrator: Judy Harrington-Carlisle
E-Mail: jharrington@harringtoncompany.com

Historical Note

The Aircraft Builders Council is a comprehensive aerospace liability insurance program.

Meetings/Conferences:

Annual Meetings: September
2007 - Scottsdale, AZ(Fairmont Scottsdale Princess)/Sept. 23-25

Aircraft Electronics Association *(1958)*

4217 S. Hocker
Independence, MO 64055
Tel: (816)373-6565 *Fax:* (816)478-3100
E-Mail: info@aea.net
Web Site: www.aea.net
Members: 1200 companies
Staff: 9
Annual Budget: $2-5,000,000
President: Paula Derks
E-Mail: paulad@aea.net
Executive Assistant, Member Services: Linda Adams
E-Mail: lindaa@aea.net
Vice President, Administration and Meeting Management: Debra A. McFarland
E-Mail: debbiem@aea.net

Historical Note

Companies engaged in the manufacture, installation and servicing of aviation electronic equipment. Membership fee based on annual sales volume or size of personnel.

Meetings/Conferences:

Annual Meetings: Spring

Publications:

Avionics News. m. adv.

Aircraft Locknut Manufacturers Association

994 Old Eagle School Rd.
Suite 1019
Wayne, PA 19087-1866
Tel: (610)971-4850 *Fax:* (610)971-4859
E-Mail: info@almanet.org
Web Site: www.almanet.org
Members: 11 companies
Staff: 2
Annual Budget: $25-50,000
Executive Director: Robert H. Ecker

Historical Note

ALMA established a code of practice to ensure the highest standards of quality and reliability are met by threaded fasteners produced by its members.

Meetings/Conferences:

Semi-Annual Meetings: usually in California

Aircraft Owners and Pilots Association *(1939)*

421 Aviation Way
Frederick, MD 21701-4756
Tel: (301)695-2000 *Fax:* (301)695-2375
E-Mail: aopahq@aopa.org
Web Site: www.aopa.org
Members: 400000 individuals
Staff: 200
Annual Budget: $25-50,000,000
Executive Director: Bruce Landsberg
President: Phil Boyer
Senior Vice President, Publications: David Wright

Historical Note

AOPA is the world's largest aviation organization, representing more than 400,000 U.S. pilots. AOPA is a national advocate for operators of 94% of U.S. aircraft, the 206,000 general aviation aircraft for personal and business transportation. AOPA Air Safety Foundation (ASF) conducts continuing pilot education and safety training. ASF's 50,000-record general aviation accident database is the most comprehensive outside of government. Membership: $39/year (individual).

Meetings/Conferences:

Annual Meetings: Fall

Publications:

AOPA Pilot. m. adv.
ePilot Newsletter. m. adv.
AOPA's Airport Directory. bi-a. adv.
AOPA Flight Training. m. adv.

Airforwarders Association *(1990)*

1156 15th St. NW
Suite 900
Washington, DC 20005
Tel: (202)393-2818 *Fax:* (202)223-9741
E-Mail: bfried@airforwarders.org
Web Site: www.airforwarders.org
Members: 80 companies
Executive Director: Brandon Fried
E-Mail: bfried@airforwarders.org

Historical Note

Airforwarder Association members are air freight forwarding companies holding valid FAA Security Agreement Numbers. Associate members are airlines, truckers and other non-forwarders with an interest in the industry.

Publications:

Forward Newsletter. bi-m. adv.

Airline Industrial Relations Conference *(1971)*

1300 19th St. NW
Suite 750
Washington, DC 20036-1561
Tel: (202)861-7550 *Fax:* (202)861-7557
E-Mail: office@aircon.org
Web Site: www.aircon.org
Members: 32 companies
Staff: 4
Annual Budget: $250-500,000
Senior Vice President, Labor Relations: Robert A. Brodin
Vice President, General Counsel and Treasurer: Robert J. DeLucia

Historical Note

Also known as the AIR Conference. Used by its members as an information exchange for such matters as industrial and personnel relations, equal employment opportunity, and related issues.

Meetings/Conferences:

Quarterly Meetings:

Airline Suppliers Association

Historical Note

Became Aviation Suppliers Association in 2003.

Airlines Electronic Engineering Committee *(1949)*

2551 Riva Rd.
Annapolis, MD 21401
Tel: (410)266-2982 *Fax:* (410)266-2047
Web Site: www.arinc.com
Members: 27 companies
Staff: 14
Co-Chairman: Roy T. Oishi

Historical Note

Develops voluntary standards for electronic systems used in aircraft and serves as an advocate for the aircraft engineering community.

Publications:

AeroLine. m.

Airport Consultants Council *(1978)*

908 King St., Suite 100
Alexandria, VA 22314
Tel: (703)683-5900 *Fax:* (703)683-2564
E-Mail: info@acconline.org
Web Site: www.acconline.org
Members: 240 companies
Staff: 4
Annual Budget: $500-1,000,000
President: Paula Hochstetler
Membership and Marketing: Cari Hicks
Vice President: T. J. Schulz

Historical Note

ACC represents the majority of airport consulting firms in the United States. Member firms include architectural, engineering, planning, management, construction, marketing, economic consultants as well as firms that manufacture or supply airport equipment, products or other services. Membership fee: $1,750/year.

Publications:

ACC News Airport Consulting. q. adv.
ACC Outlook. w.
Guide to Selecting Airport Consultants & Membership Directory. a.

Airport Ground Transportation Association *(1946)*
154 University Center
8001 Natural Bridge Rd.
St. Louis, MO 63121-4499
Tel: (314)516-7271 *Fax:* (314)516-7272
E-Mail: admin@agtaweb.org
Web Site: www.agtaweb.org
Members: 350 individuals
Staff: 2
Annual Budget: $100-250,000
Executive Director: Ray Mundy

Historical Note
Members include airport authorities and operators and industry suppliers of ground transportation at airports and courtesy transportation providers. Membership: $330/year (organization/company).

Meetings/Conferences:
Semi-annual Meetings: February-March and September

Publications:
AGTA's Airport Ground Transportation Fees and Fares Summary. a.
AGTA Newsletter. bi-m. adv.

Airports Council International/North America *(1948)*
1775 K St. NW
Suite 500
Washington, DC 20006
Tel: (202)293-8500 *Fax:* (202)331-1362
E-Mail: postmaster@aci-na.org
Web Site: www.aci-na.org
Members: 168 operating organizations
Staff: 28
Annual Budget: $2-5,000,000
President: Gregory O. Principato
E-Mail: postmaster@aci-na.org
Executive Vice President, Operations and Legal Counsel: Patricia A. Hahn
E-Mail: postmaster@aci-na.org

Historical Note
Founded in 1948 as the Airport Operators Council, the organization became (1965) Airport Operators Council International, and (1991) Airports Association Council International following its merger with International Civil Airports Association; assumed its current name in 1993. Members are boards, commissions, and local governmental entities operating public airport facilities. Membership: $500-93,000/year, according to size of airport.

Meetings/Conferences:
Annual Meetings: Fall/1,800

Publications:
Airport Highlights. bi-w. adv.

Alexander Graham Bell Association for the Deaf and Hard of Hearing *(1890)*
3417 Volta Pl. NW
Washington, DC 20007
Tel: (202)337-5220 *Fax:* (202)337-8314
Toll Free: (866)337 - 5220
E-Mail: info@agbell.org
Web Site: www.agbell.org
Members: 5200 individuals
Staff: 22
Annual Budget: $2-5,000,000
Executive Director: K. Todd Houston, Ph.D.
Senior Director, Advocacy and Policy: Gerri Hanna
Senior Director, Marketing and Communications: Jessica Ripper
Senior Director, Membership and Chapters: Greg Zick

Historical Note
Founded by Alexander Graham Bell to promote the teaching of speech, speech-reading, and use of residual hearing to individuals who are deaf and hard of hearing. Has three sections: Parents Section; International Professional Section; and Deaf and Hard of Hearing Section. The Bell Association is a member of the Council on Education of the Deaf. Membership: $50/year.

Meetings/Conferences:
Biennial Meetings: usually June-July

Publications:
Volta Voices. bi-m. adv.
The Volta Review. q. adv.

Alfalfa Council

Historical Note
Organization dissolved in 2003; superseded by National Alfalfa Alliance.

Alkylphenols and Ethoxylates Research Council *(1998)*
1250 Connecticut Ave. NW
Suite 700
Washington, DC 20036
Tel: (202)419-1506 *Fax:* (202)659-8037
Toll Free: (866)273 - 7262
E-Mail: info@aperc.org
Web Site: www.aperc.org
Members: 6 companies
Staff: 2
Executive Director: Robert J. Fensterheim

Historical Note
Monitors regulatory developments affecting manufacturers in the chemical industry.

All-America Rose Selections *(1938)*
388 Market St., Suite 1400
San Francisco, CA 94111
Tel: (415)249-6776
E-Mail: rose@rose.org
Web Site: www.rose.org
Members: 15 commercial rose growers
Staff: 5
Annual Budget: $250-500,000
President: Steve Hutton

Historical Note
A non-profit corporation formed by rose producers and introducers to test new varieties of roses and determine which, if any, could be recommended to the public as exceptional.

Meetings/Conferences:
Annual Meetings: July, with the American Ass'n of Nurserymen, and November.

Publications:
Annual Winners brochure. a.
Quarterly newsletter (online). q.

Alliance for Children and Families *(1998)*
11700 W. Lake Park Dr.
Milwaukee, WI 53224-3099
Tel: (414)359-1040 *Fax:* (414)359-1074
Toll Free: (800)221 - 3726
E-Mail: pgoldberg@alliance1.org
Web Site: www.alliance1.org
Members: 330 agencies
Staff: 50
Annual Budget: $2-5,000,000
President and Chief Executive Officer: Peter Goldberg
E-Mail: pgoldberg@alliance1.org
Chief Operating Officer: Susan Dreyfus
Senior Vice President, Public Policy: Carmen Delgado Votaw

Historical Note
A nonprofit membership association representing child- and family- serving organizations in North America. Member organizations provide a variety of community-based programs and services to all generations, and serve nearly 8 million people each year in more than 6,700 communities. Motivated by a vision of a healthy society and strong communities, the Alliance's mission is to strengthen the capacities of North America's nonprofit child and family serving organizations to serve and to advocate for children, families, and communities.

Publications:
Directory of Member Agencies. a.
Families in Society. 10/year. adv.

Alliance for Community Media *(1976)*
666 11th St. NW
Suite 740
Washington, DC 20001-4542
Tel: (202)393-2650 *Fax:* (202)393-2653
E-Mail: acm@alliancecm.org
Web Site: www.alliancecm.org
Members: 900 individuals and organizations
Staff: 3
Annual Budget: $250-500,000
Executive Director: Anthony Riddle

Historical Note
Formerly (1992) National Federation of Local Cable Programmers. Organized to foster citizen participation in community television programming. Membership: $70/year, professional (individual); $225-575/year (organization).

Meetings/Conferences:
Annual Meetings: July
2007 – Minneapolis, MN

Publications:
Community Media Review. q. adv.
Community Media Resource Directory. a.

Alliance for Continuing Medical Education *(1975)*
1025 Montgomery Hwy.
Suite 105
Birmingham, AL 35216
Tel: (205)824-1355 *Fax:* (205)824-1357
E-Mail: acme@acme-assn.org
Web Site: www.acme-assn.org
Members: 2200 individuals
Staff: 10
Annual Budget: $1-2,000,000
Executive Director: Bruce Bellande, Ph.D.
Director, Professional Development: Bernie Halbun

Historical Note
A professional association concerned exclusively with continuing medical education. Membership: $285/year (individual).

Meetings/Conferences:
Annual Meetings: January
2007 – Phoenix, AZ(JW Marriott)/Jan. 17-20/1500
2008 – Miami, FL(Fountainbleau Resort)/Jan. 23-26/1500
2009 – San Fancisco, CA(JW Marriott)/Jan. 28-31/1500
2010 – New Orleans, LA(Hilton Riverpark)/Jan. 27-30/1000

Publications:
Alliance Connection. m. adv.
Best Practices in CME Accreditation. a.
CME Basics Course. a.
Journal for Continuing Education in Health Professions. q. adv.
CME Buyer's Guidebook. a. adv.
Membership Directory. a. adv.
Almanac. m. adv.
Best of Annual Conferences and Sessions. a.

Alliance for Nonprofit Management *(1998)*
1899 L St. NW, Sixth Floor
Washington, DC 20036
Tel: (202)955-8406 *Fax:* (202)721-0086
E-Mail: info@allianceonline.org
Web Site: www.allianceonline.org
Members: 1100 individuals
Staff: 6
Annual Budget: $1-2,000,000
Executive Director and Chief Executive Officer: Tangie Newborn
Deputy Director, Education: Heather Iliff
E-Mail: heather@allianceonline.org
Membership: Heidi Sorensen

Historical Note
Formerly (1998) Nonprofit Management Association. The Alliance for Nonprofit Management is a professional association of member organizations and individuals devoted primarily to helping nonprofit organizations increase their effectiveness and impact. The Alliance and its members work collectively and individually to develop, codify, and deliver practices in management and governance of nonprofit organizations.

Meetings/Conferences:
Annual Meetings: Summer
2007 – Atlanta, GA/July/500

Publications:
Gold Book Online.
PULSE!. bi-m.
Evaluation of Capacity Building and Lessons from the Field.
The Expanding Universe: New Directions in Non-profit Capacity Building.
Enhance. q.

Alliance for Responsible Atmospheric Policy *(1980)*
2111 Wilson Blvd., Suite 800
Arlington, VA 22201-3058
Tel: (703)243-0344 *Fax:* (703)243-2874
E-Mail: info@arap.org
Web Site: www.arap.org/
Members: 300 companies
Staff: 3
Annual Budget: $250-500,000
Executive Director: David Stirpe
E-Mail: info@arap.org

Historical Note
Formerly (1995) Alliance for Responsible CFC Policy. It is composed of companies who rely on alternatives to ozone depleting chlorofluorocarbons (CFCs). These alternatives are HCPCs and HFCs, used primarily as refrigerants, specialty solvents, agents for foamed plastics, etc.

Publications:
Newsletter. m.

Alliance for Telecommunications Industry Solutions *(1983)*
1200 G St. NW
Suite 500
Washington, DC 20005
Tel: (202)628-6380 *Fax:* (202)393-5453
E-Mail: atispr@atis.org
Web Site: www.atis.org
Members: 120 companies
Staff: 46
Annual Budget: $10-25,000,000
President and Chief Executive Officer: Susan Miller
Vice President, Marketing and Public Relations: John Bernhards
E-Mail: jbernhards@atis.org
Vice President, Finance and Operations: Bill Klein

Historical Note
ATIS, formerly (1993) known as Exchange Carriers Standards Association, is an organization of telecommunications carriers, manufacturers, service providers, and other companies that discuss technical planning and develop standards, guidelines, and procedures. ATIS sponsors more than 1,100 participants that are active in 23 industry committees and Incubator Solutions Program. They open forums that address network interconnection number portability, wireless, and improved data transmission, among other issues. Membership: Scaled by annual revenue.

Meetings/Conferences:
Annual Meetings: March

Publications:
ATIS Member Update.
ATIS Annual Report. a.
Tech Beat. bi-m.

Alliance for the Polyurethane Industry *(1985)*
1300 Wilson Blvd.
Arlington, VA 22209
Tel: (703)741-5656 *Fax:* (703)741-5655
E-Mail: api@plastics.org
Web Site: www.polyurethane.org
Members: 60 companies
Staff: 5
Annual Budget: $5-10,000,000
Executive Director: Richard E. Mericle, II
E-Mail: api@plastics.org

Historical Note
Founded as the Urethane Institute in 1959; became Society of the Plastics Industry - Polyurethane Division in 1985, and assumed its present name in 1999. Members are polyurethane chemical producers; systems formulators; machinery manufacturers; manufacturers of polyurethane flexible and rigid foams, coatings, adhesives, sealants, elastomers, and molded polyurethane products; and manufacturers of rigid polyisocyanurate foams.

Meetings/Conferences:
Annual Meetings: Fall

Publications:
Conference Proceedings.
Polyurethane News.
Technical, Marketing & Educational publications & audio visuals.

Alliance of Area Business Publications *(1979)*
4929 Wilshire Blvd., Suite 428
Los Angeles, CA 90010
Tel: (323)937-5514 *Fax:* (323)937-0959
Web Site: www.bizpubs.org
Members: 100 publications
Staff: 2
Annual Budget: $100-250,000
Executive Director: C. James Dowden

Historical Note
Members are local and regional business newspapers and magazines. AABP provides a forum for local business publications to cooperate, exchange information, and promote their publications in the national business community. Membership: $500-2,100/year.

Meetings/Conferences:
Semi-Annual Meetings: Winter(publishers), Summer(editors & publishers)
2007 – Denver, CO(Grand Hyatt Denver)/June 21-23

Publications:
AABP Directory. a.
Readership Survey. bien.
AABP Newsletter. q.

Alliance of Artists Communities *(1992)*
255 S. Main St.
Providence, RI 02903
Tel: (401)351-4320 *Fax:* (401)351-4507
E-Mail: aac@artistcommunities.org
Web Site: www.artistcommunities.org
Members: 160 organizations
Staff: 3
Annual Budget: $250-500,000
Executive Director: Deborah Obalil
Director, Programs and Communications: Caitlin Glass

Historical Note
AAC is a consortium of residency programs that provide artists with time, space and community to create new work.

Meetings/Conferences:
Annual: 100

Publications:
Artists' Communities, a Directory of Residencies. trien.

Alliance of Associations of Teachers of Japanese *(1963)*
Univ. of Colorado, East Asian Language & Literature Dept.
Box 279
Boulder, CO 80309-0279
Tel: (303)492-5487 *Fax:* (303)492-5856
E-Mail: ATJ@colorado.edu
Web Site: www.colorado.edu/ealld/atj
Members: 1000 individuals
Staff: 2
Annual Budget: $50-100,000
Executive Director: Susan Schmidt
President: Seiichi Makino

Historical Note
The Association of Teachers of Japanese merged with the National Council of Japanese Language Teachers to form the AATJ in 1999. Members have professional interests in the teaching of Japanese as a foreign language and in the allied fields of Japanese linguistics and literature.

Meetings/Conferences:
Annual: 300

Publications:
ATJ Newsletter. q. adv.
Journal of The Association of Teachers of Japanese. semi-a. adv.

Alliance of Automobile Manufacturers *(1999)*
1401 I St. NW
Suite 900
Washington, DC 20005
Tel: (202)326-5500 *Fax:* (202)326-5598
Web Site: www.autoalliance.org
Members: 13 companies
Staff: 36
Annual Budget: $10-25,000,000
President and Chief Executive Officer: Frederick L. Webber
Vice President, Communications and Public Affairs: Gloria Bergquist
Vice President, Government Affairs: Michael Stanton
General Counsel: John Whatley

Historical Note
Formerly (1972) Automobile Manufacturers Association, (1982) Motor Vehicle Manufacturers of the United States, (1992) American Automobile Manufacturers Association, and (1999) Alliance of American Automobile Manufacturers, AAAM is the trade association of U.S. automakers. Member companies produce 90% of North American light duty vehicles. Maintains additional offices in Sacramento, CA and Southfield, MI. Has an annual budget of approximately $30 million.

Meetings/Conferences:
Annual Meetings: June

Alliance of Black Telecommunications Employees *(1985)*
P.O. Box 6116
Somerset, NJ 08873-6119
E-Mail: webmaster@el200.abteinc.org
Web Site: www.abteinc.org
President and Chief Executive Officer: Merle Isler

Historical Note
Formed from the merger of Association of Black Laboratory Employees, Committee of Black AT&T Employees, and Employee Focus Group, a second group of AT&T Employees. ABTE works to promote positive dialogue on career advancement possibilities for African-Americans in the telecommunications industry.

Publications:
Newslink. q.

Alliance of Cardiovascular Professionals *(1957)*
P.O. Box 2007
Middleton, VA 23113
Tel: (804)632-0078 *Fax:* (804)639-9212
E-Mail: peggymcelgunn@comcast.net
Web Site: www.acp-online.org
Members: 3000 individuals
Staff: 5
Annual Budget: $250-500,000
Executive Director: Peggy McElgunn

Historical Note
The product of a merger of the National Society of Cardiopulmonary Technologists, the American Cardiology Technology Association, and the National Alliance of Cardiovascular Technologists. Formerly National Society for Cardiovascular and Pulmonary Technology, became National Society for Cardiovascular Technology/National Society for Pulmonary Technology in 1988. Absorbed American College of Cardiovascular Invasive Specialists in 1993, and Society for Cardiovascular Management in 1995. Assumed its current name in 1998. Membership: $67-95/year (individual); $1,000/year (silver); $2,000/year (gold); $3,000/year (platinum).

Meetings/Conferences:
Annual Meetings: Fall

Publications:
Strategies. q. adv.
The Beat Goes On. q. adv.
CP Digest. bi-m. adv.
Pulmonary News. q. adv.
Heart-to-Heart. q. adv.

Alliance of Claims Assistance Professionals *(1998)*
873 Brentwood Dr.
West Chicago, IL 60185-3743
Tel: (630)562-1000 *Fax:* (630)562-1448
E-Mail: askacap@charter.net
Web Site: www.claims.org
Members: 30 individuals
Annual Budget: under $10,000
President: Susan A. Dressler, CCAP

Historical Note
Members are claims assistance professionals who work for patients. Membership: $75/year.

Publications:
Membership List.

Alliance of Foam Packaging Recyclers *(1991)*
1298 Cronson Blvd., Suite 201

Crofton, MD 21114-2426
Tel: (410)451-8340 *Fax:* (410)451-8343
Toll Free: (800)944 - 8448
E-Mail: info@epspackaging.org
Web Site: www.epspackaging.org
Members: 50 companies
Staff: 3
Annual Budget: $100-250,000
Executive Director: Betsy Steiner
Managing Director, Advocacy: Diana Gentilcore

Historical Note
AFPR represents the expanded polystyrene packaging industry, including raw material suppliers, molders and equipment suppliers in the United States and Canada. Its mission is to support and provide leadership to the EPS foam packaging industry, to position the industry and its products advantageously and to address environmental concerns with packaging disposal issues.

Alliance of Information and Referral Systems *(1973)*
11240 Waples Mill Rd.
Suite 200
Fairfax, VA 22030
Tel: (703)218-2477 *Fax:* (703)359-7562
E-Mail: info@airs.org
Web Site: www.airs.org
Members: 557 individuals
Staff: 4
Annual Budget: $500-1,000,000
Director, Membership: Debra Hernandez

Historical Note
Members are organizations and individuals providing a contact point for those with various social problems so that they can be referred to others who can assist them. Membership: $85/year (individual/professional).

Meetings/Conferences:
Annual Meetings: *Spring*

Publications:
Journal of Information and Referral. a. adv.
AIRS Newsletter. bi-m. adv.
Directory of Information & Referral Services. a.

Alliance of Insurance Agents and Brokers
1768 Arrow Hwy., Suite 105
La Verne, CA 91750-5332
Tel: (909)392-0836 *Fax:* (909)392-0892
Toll Free: (866)280 - 3222
E-Mail: memberinfo@agentsalliance.com
Web Site: www.agentsalliance.com
Members: 700 individuals
Staff: 6
Executive Director: Ken Nigohosian

Historical Note
American Agents Alliance, dba Alliance of Insurance Agents and Brokers, represents independent agents and brokers.

Meetings/Conferences:
Annual Meetings: *Fall/1700*

Publications:
Alliance Alert. bi-w. adv.

Alliance of Motion Picture and Television Producers *(1924)*
15503 Ventura Blvd
Encino, CA 91436
Tel: (818)995-3600 *Fax:* (818)382-1793
Members: 25 companies
Staff: 15
Annual Budget: $500-1,000,000
President: Nicholas Counter, III
Senior Vice President, Legal and Business Affairs: Carol Lonbardini

Historical Note
Merger of Association of Motion Picture Producers (1924) and Alliance of Television Film Producers (1951) and Society of Independent Producers. In 1964, the Association of Motion Picture and Television Producers and the Alliance separated into two distinct organizations, but later merged in 1982 under the current title.

Alliance of National Staffing and Employment Resources
525 S.W. Fifth St.
Suite A
Des Moines, IA 50309-4501
Tel: (515)282-8192 *Fax:* (515)282-9117
Web Site: www.anserteam.com
Members: 62 firms
Staff: 1
Executive Director: Sheila Dietz

Historical Note
ANSER members are privately-owned staffing companies throughout the U.S.

Alliance of Nonprofit Mailers *(1980)*
1211 Connecticut Ave. NW
Suite 620
Washington, DC 20036-2701
Tel: (202)462-5132 *Fax:* (202)462-0423
E-Mail: alliance@nonprofitmailers.org
Web Site: www.nonprofitmailers.org
Members: 300 individuals
Staff: 3
Annual Budget: $500-1,000,000
Interim Executive Director: Ellenor A. Kirkconnell

Historical Note
A national association of nonprofit organizations and businesses interested in stabilizing nonprofit postal rates. Membership: sliding fee.

Meetings/Conferences:
Annual Meetings: *Spring/Early Summer*

Publications:
Alliance Report. w.

Alliance of Professional Tattooists *(1992)*
9210 E. Hwy. 1792
Maitland, FL 32751
Tel: (407)831-5549
E-Mail: info@safe-tattoos.com
Web Site: www.safe-tattoos.com
Staff: 1
Executive Assistant: Erin Stallings
E-Mail: info@safe-tattoos.com

Historical Note
APT promotes safe practices in the profession and provides public education about tattooing. Membership: $125/year.

Publications:
Skin Scribe Newsletter. m.

Alliance of Work/Life Professionals

Historical Note
Became Alliance for Work/Life Progress in 2003.

Allied Artists of America *(1914)*
15 Gramercy Park South
New York, NY 10003
Tel: (212)582-6411
E-Mail: garyerbe@alliedartistsofamerica.org
Web Site: www.alliedartistsofamerica.org
Members: 400 regular & 800 associates
Annual Budget: $10-25,000
President: Gary T. Erbe
E-Mail: garyerbe@alliedartistsofamerica.org

Historical Note
Membership consists of painters and sculptors. Initiated at a meeting at the Grand Union Hotel in New York, January 24, 1914. Purpose is to promote American art and furnish exhibition space for American artists. Membership: $40/year (individual); $25/year (associate).

Meetings/Conferences:
Annual Meetings: *Spring, third Wednesday in April in New York City*

Publications:
Annual Exhibition Catalogue. a. adv.
Newsletter. a.
International Artists Magazine. a.

Allied Finance Adjusters Conference *(1936)*
P.O. Box 20708
Chicago, IL 60620
Toll Free: (800)621 - 3016
E-Mail: fedauto@bellsouth.net
Web Site: www.alliedfinanceadjusters.com
Members: 200 companies
Staff: 1
Annual Budget: $250-500,000
Chairman: Bob Dube
E-Mail: fedauto@bellsouth.net

Historical Note
Membership is composed of professional liquidators, repossessors, and skip tracers. Membership fee varies with size of population of the city served.

Meetings/Conferences:
Annual Meetings: *Summer*

Publications:
Bulletin. m.
Allied News Newsletter. semi-a.
AFAC Directory. a.

Allied Stone Industries *(1958)*

Historical Note
Address unknown in 2005.

Allied Trades of the Baking Industry *(1920)*
c/o Cereal Food Processors
2001 Shawnee Mission Pkwy.
Mission Woods, KS 66205
Tel: (913)890-6300
E-Mail: atbi@atbi.org
Web Site: www.atbi.org
Members: 500 individuals
Annual Budget: $10-25,000
Secretary-Treasurer: Tim Miller

Historical Note
Members are salesmen working for companies servicing the baking industry. Has no paid officers or full-time staff. Membership: $25/year (individual); $250/year (corporate).

Meetings/Conferences:
Annual Meetings:

Publications:
The Allied Tradesman. 3/year. adv.

ALMA - the International Loudspeaker Association *(1965)*
191 Clarksville Rd.
Princeton Junction, NJ 08550
Tel: (609)799-8440 *Fax:* (609)799-7032
Web Site: www.alma.org
Members: 100 companies
Staff: 3
Annual Budget: $50-100,000
Director: Lynn McCullough

Historical Note
Founded as American Loudspeaker Manufacturers Association; assumed its current name in 2003. Membership: $500/year.

Meetings/Conferences:
Semi-Annual Meetings: *Winter and Spring*

Publications:
Statistical Program. q.
Manuals and Reports.
Buyers Guide. a. adv.

Alpha Chi Sigma *(1902)*
2141 N. Franklin Rd.
Indianapolis, IN 46219
Tel: (317)357-5944
E-Mail: national@alphachisigma.org
Web Site: www.alphachisigma.org
Members: 57000 individuals
Staff: 3
Annual Budget: $100-250,000
National Secretary: Patrick Johanns
E-Mail: national@alphachisigma.org

Historical Note
A professional fraternity of chemists and chemical engineers founded at the University of Wisconsin in December 1902 and incorporated in Wisconsin.

Meetings/Conferences:
Biennial Meetings: *Even years, always held on a university campus*

Publications:
The Hexagon. q.

Alpha Gamma Rho *(1904)*
10101 N. Ambassador Dr.
Kansas City, MO 64153
Tel: (816)891-9200 *Fax:* (816)891-9401
Web Site: www.agrs.org
Members: 55000 individuals
Staff: 9
Annual Budget: $1-2,000,000

Executive Director: Philip Josephson
E-Mail: phil@alphagammarho.org

Historical Note
Professional agricultural fraternity.

Meetings/Conferences:
Biennial Meetings: even years

Publications:
Sickle & Sheaf. q.

Alpha Kappa Psi *(1904)*
7801 E. 88th St.
Indianapolis, IN 46268-1233
Tel: (317)872-1553 *Fax:* (317)872-1567
Web Site: www.akpsi.com
Members: 160000 individuals
Staff: 8
Annual Budget: $500-1,000,000
Executive Director: Gary L. Epperson, CAE

Historical Note
Professional fraternity, business administration. Founded at New York University October 5, 1904 and incorporated in the State of New York the following year. Membership: $60/year (student); $25/year (alumnus), plus initiation and pledge fee.

Meetings/Conferences:
Biennial Meetings: uneven years in August

Publications:
Beacon Newsletter. q.
The Diary. q.

Alpha Omega International Dental Fraternity *(1907)*
191 Clarksville Rd.
Princeton Junction, NJ 08550
Tel: (609)799-6000 *Fax:* (609)799-7032
Toll Free: (877)677 - 8468
E-Mail: headquarters@ao.org
Web Site: www.ao.org
Members: 9000 individuals
Staff: 13
Annual Budget: $500-1,000,000

Historical Note
A professional, international dental fraternity formed through the merger of the Ramach Fraternity (formed at the Pennsylvania College of Dental Surgery in 1906) and the Alpha Omega Dental Fraternity (formed at the University of Maryland in 1907). The fraternity remains dedicated to the same mission as its founding fathers: serving as the voice of the Jew in dentistry, aiding dental education and encouraging professional excellence. Membership: $180/year (international), plus chapter dues.

Meetings/Conferences:
Annual Meetings: December

Publications:
The Alpha Omegan. q. adv.
Alpha Omega Scientific Journal.
Alpha Omega Newsletter.
AO Today. q. adv.
The Arouser. bi-a. adv.

Alpha Tau Delta *(1921)*
11252 Camarillo St.
Toluca Lake, CA 91602
Tel: (916)984-9150
E-Mail: info@atdnursing.org
Web Site: www.atdnursing.org
Members: 11000 individuals
Annual Budget: $25-50,000
National President: Susan Carson
E-Mail: info@atdnursing.org

Historical Note
ATD is a professional nursing fraternity affiliated with the Professional Fraternity Association. It supports chapters which offer workshops, seminars, scholarships, grants, and loans. Membership: $35/year (individual).

Meetings/Conferences:
Annual Meetings: Biennial Meetings: odd years.

Publications:
President's Letter. a.
Cap'tions.

Alpha Zeta Omega *(1919)*
4422 Porpoise Dr.
Tampa, FL 33617
Tel: (813)283-5040
E-Mail: drbruce@tampabay.rr.com
Web Site: www.azo.org
Members: 11000 individuals
Staff: 1
Annual Budget: $25-50,000
Director, Fraternal Affairs: Bruce Strell
E-Mail: drbruce@tampabay.rr.com

Historical Note
Professional pharmacy fraternity founded at the Philadelphia College of Pharmacy in December 1919.

Meetings/Conferences:
Annual Meetings: Second week in July/350

Publications:
The Azoan. a. adv.

Alpines International
7195 County Rd. 315
Silt, CO 81652
Tel: (970)876-2738
Web Site: www.alpinesinternationalclub.com
Members: 100 individuals
Secretary-Treasurer: Tina Antes

Historical Note
Members are owners and breeders of French Alpine and American Alpine dairy goats. Has no paid officers or full-time staff.

Meetings/Conferences:
Annual Meetings: Fall

Publications:
Alpines Internat'l Newsletter. bi-m.

Alternatives Fuel Vehicle Network
11621 San Antonio NE
Albuquerque, NM 87122
Tel: (505)856-8585 *Fax:* (505)856-5904
Members: 60 individuals
Staff: 2
Executive Director: Frank Burcham
E-Mail: frank.burcham@comcast.net
Director, Programs: David Burt
E-Mail: frank.burcham@comcast.net

Meetings/Conferences:
Annual Meetings: Annual
2007 – Albuquerque, NM(Marriott)/October/70

Aluminum Anodizers Council *(1988)*
1000 N. Rand Rd.
Suite 214
Wauconda, IL 60084
Tel: (847)526-2010 *Fax:* (847)526-3993
E-Mail: mail@anodizing.org
Web Site: www.anodizing.org
Members: 75 companies
Staff: 3
Annual Budget: $100-250,000
President: Gregory T. Rajsky
E-Mail: mail@anodizing.org

Historical Note
Formerly (1992) Architectural Anodizers Council. Members are manufacturers of anodized aluminum products. AAC advances, supports, and promotes the aluminum anodizing industry. AAC released the Anodized Aluminum Color Standards for Architectural Applications to assure color consistency when specifying anodized aluminum. Membership: $750-2,000/year (firm); $1,875-2,100/year (supplier); $550/year (associate); $75/year (professional).

Meetings/Conferences:
Annual Meetings: Fall
2007 – Chicago, IL(Marriott Lincolnshire)/Oct. 8-11/120

Publications:
Industry Guide Online. a.
Anodizing Newsline Newsletter. bi-m.
Regulatory Roundup. q.

Aluminum Association *(1933)*
1525 Wilson Blvd., Suite 600
Arlington, VA 22209
Tel: (703)358-2960 *Fax:* (703)358-2961
Web Site: www.aluminum.org
Members: 90 companies
Staff: 18
Annual Budget: $5-10,000,000
President: J. Stephen Larkin
Manager, Meetings and Corporate Secretary: Pamela Dorsey
Public Relations Director: Patrick Kelly
Vice President, Public Affairs: Robin R. King
Director, Administration and Treasurer: Carol A. Williams

Historical Note
Members are manufacturers of aluminum mill products and producers of aluminum. Associate members are suppliers to the industry.

Meetings/Conferences:
Semi-annual Meetings: Fall and early Spring/usually Washington, DC

Publications:
Aluminum Situation. m.
Aluminum Statistical Review. a.
Aluminum Now. m.
Aluminum Standards and Data. trien.
Aluminum Design Manual. trien.

Aluminum Extruders Council *(1951)*
1000 N. Rand Rd.
Suite 214
Wauconda, IL 60084
Tel: (847)526-2010 *Fax:* (847)526-3993
E-Mail: mail@aec.org
Web Site: www.aec.org
Members: 200 companies
Staff: 7
Annual Budget: $1-2,000,000
President: Rand A. Baldwin, CAE
Government Relations: Dick Penna
Director, Member Services: Gregory T. Rajsky
Special Events: Mary Jo Ritt

Meetings/Conferences:
Annual Meetings: March

Publications:
The Executive Report. m.

Aluminum Foil Container Manufacturers Association *(1955)*
10 Vecilla Ln.
Hot Springs Village, AR 71909
Tel: (501)922-7425 *Fax:* (501)922-0383
Web Site: www.afcma.org
Members: 12 companies
Staff: 2
Annual Budget: $50-100,000
Executive Director: Ed Doyle

Historical Note
Manufacturers of aluminum foil containers in the U.S. and Canada.

Meetings/Conferences:
Semi-Annual Meetings: late Winter-Spring and Fall/36

Amalgamated Printers' Association *(1958)*
6906 Colony Loop Dr.
Austin, TX 78724
Web Site: www.apa-letterpress.org
Members: 150 individuals
Annual Budget: under $10,000
Archivist: David L. Kent

Historical Note
Voluntary association of printers, typefounders, graphic artists, calligraphers, private presses, and type collectors interested in the preservation of letterpress printing. Has no permanent address or paid staff. Membership limited to 150. Officers change biennially. Membership: $25/year (individual).

Meetings/Conferences:
Annual Meetings: Typical Attendence:90
2007 – Oklahoma City, OK

Publications:
Membership List. a.
Cooperative Calendar. a.
Treasure Gems. a.

Amalgamated Transit Union *(1892)*
5025 Wisconsin Ave. NW, Third Floor
Washington, DC 20016-4139
Tel: (202)537-1645 *Fax:* (202)244-7824
E-Mail: dispatch@atu.org
Web Site: www.atu.org
Members: 180000 individuals
Staff: 25
Annual Budget: $5-10,000,000

International President: Warren S. George
International Executive Vice President: Michael J. Sing

Historical Note

Established in Indianapolis on September 15, 1892 as the Amalgamated Association of Street Railway Employees of America and affiliated with the American Federation of Labor in 1893. Became the Amalgamated Association of Street and Electric Railway Employees of America in 1903, the Amalgamated Association of Street, Electric Railway and Motor Coach Employees of America in 1934 and assumed its present name in 1964. The dominant union in the local transit and over the road bus industry with membership in the U.S. and Canada. Members are operating, maintenance and administrative employees. Sponsors and supports the Amalgamated Transit Union Political Contributions Committee.

Meetings/Conferences:
Triennial Meetings: 2007

Publications:
In Transit. bi-m.

Ambulance Manufacturers Division

Historical Note

An affiliate of the National Truck Equipment Association.

Ambulatory Pediatric Association *(1960)*

6728 Old McLean Village Dr.
Mclean, VA 22101
Tel: (703)556-9222 *Fax:* (703)556-8729
E-Mail: info@ambpeds.org
Web Site: www.ambpeds.org
Members: 2000 individuals
Staff: 3
Annual Budget: $1-2,000,000
Executive Director: Marge Degnon

Historical Note

Formerly (1969) Association for Ambulatory Pediatric Services. An organization for those working in child health care programs, either in teaching and patient care or pediatrics research. Membership: $200/year (physicians); $100/year (non-physicians); $50/year (physicians-in-training).

Meetings/Conferences:
Annual Meetings: Spring

Publications:
Ambulatory Pediatrics. 6/year. adv.
Newsletter. 3/year.

America Outdoors *(1991)*

P.O. Box 10847
Knoxville, TN 37939-0847
Tel: (865)558-3595 *Fax:* (865)558-3598
Toll Free: (800)524 - 4814
E-Mail: info@americaoutdoors.org
Web Site: www.adventurevacation.com
Members: 600 companies
Staff: 3
Annual Budget: $500-1,000,000
Executive Director: David L. Brown
Director, Communications: Robin Brown

Historical Note

AO members are professional outdoor recreation outfitters. Membership: $165-995/year, based on gross revenue from outfitting (corporate). Mission is the conservation and enhancement of quality outdoor experiences on America's land and waters.

Meetings/Conferences:
Annual Meetings: December

Publications:
America Outdoors Outfitter Directory & Vacation Guide. a. adv.
America Outdoors Newsletter. q. adv.

America's Blood Centers *(1962)*

725 15th St. NW
Suite 700
Washington, DC 20005
Tel: (202)393-5725 *Fax:* (202)393-1282
E-Mail: ABC@americasblood.org
Web Site: www.americasblood.org
Members: 77 centers
Staff: 19
Annual Budget: $2-5,000,000
Chief Executive Officer: Jim MacPherson
Manager, Conferences and Executive Services: Lon Beaston
E-Mail: lbeaston@americasblood.org
Executive Vice President: Celso Bianco
Director, Government and Public Relations: Robert Kepler

Historical Note

Formerly (1962-1971) Community Blood Bank Council and (1971-1996) Council of Community Blood Centers. Members are non-profit regional and community centers that collect blood only from volunteer donors. Membership fee based on annual blood collection.

Meetings/Conferences:
Semi-Annual Meetings: February and July/75-150

Publications:
ABC Newsletter. w. adv.

America's Community Bankers *(1992)*

900 19th St. NW
Suite 400
Washington, DC 20006-2105
Tel: (202)857-3100 *Fax:* (202)296-8716
Toll Free: (888)872 - 0275
E-Mail: info@acbankers.org
Web Site: www.americascommunitybankers.com
Members: 1250 savings institutions/banks
Staff: 100
Annual Budget: $10-25,000,000
President and Chief Executive Officer: Diane M. Casey-Landry
Executive Vice President and Managing Director, Government Relations: Robert Davis
Senior Meeting Planner: June Janny
President, ACB Business Partners: William Kroll
Senior Vice President, Regulatory Affairs: Patricia Milon
Director, Government Relations and COMPAC: Patrick O'Brien
Executive Vice President, Corporate Communications and Membership: Robert F. Schmermund

Historical Note

Established as the United States Savings and Loan League, it became the United States League of Savings Associations in 1975 and the United States League of Savings Institutions in 1983. In 1992, the United States League of Savings Institutions merged with the National Council of Community Bankers to form Savings and Community Bankers of America; assumed its current name in 1995. Supports the Savings Association Political Elections Committee. Has an annual budget of approximately 22.3 million.

Meetings/Conferences:
Annual Meetings: Fall

Publications:
Regulatory Report. m.
Community Bankers Magazine. m. adv.
Washington Perspective. w.
Operations Alert. bi-m.

America's Health Insurance Plans *(1995)*

601 Pennsylvania Ave. NW
South Bldg., Suite 500
Washington, DC 20004
Tel: (202)778-3200 *Fax:* (202)331-7487
Toll Free: (877)291 - 2247
E-Mail: ahip@ahip.org
Web Site: www.ahip.org
Members: 1300 organizations
Staff: 120
Annual Budget: $10-25,000,000
President and Chief Executive Officer: Karen M. Ignagni, CAE
Vice President, Finance, Facilities and Human Resources: Robert O. Borchardt
Executive Vice President, Regulatory Affairs: Diana Dennett
Special Counsel: Stephanie Kanwit
Chief Administrative Officer: Dan Leonard
Vice President, Communications: Susan Pisano
Executive Vice President: Charles Stellar
Senior Vice President, Federal Affairs: Scott Styles

Historical Note

Formerly American Association of Health Plans. Created by the merger of Group Health Association of America (GHAA) and the American Managed Care and Review Association (AMCRA); absorbed Health Insurance Association of America and became AHIP in 2003. AHIP's mission is to advance health care quality and affordability through leadership in the health care community, advocacy and services to member plans. Members are HMOs, PPOs and similar health plan providers.

Meetings/Conferences:
Annual Meetings: June/300

Publications:
Healthplan Magazine. 6/year. adv.

American Abstract Artists *(1936)*

194 Powers St.
Brooklyn, NY 11211
E-Mail: americanabart@aol.com
Web Site: www.americanabstractartists.org
Members: 95 individuals
Annual Budget: under $10,000
President: Don Voisine

Historical Note

Members are abstract painters and sculptors. Has no paid officers or full-time staff. Membership: $35/year.

Publications:
American Abstract Artists Journal. 2/year.

American Academy for Cerebral Palsy and Developmental Medicine *(1947)*

6300 N. River Rd.
Suite 727
Rosemont, IL 60018-4226
Tel: (847)698-1635 *Fax:* (847)823-0536
E-Mail: king@aaos.org
Web Site: www.aacpdm.org
Members: 1600 individuals
Staff: 3
Annual Budget: $250-500,000
Executive Director: Sheril King

Historical Note

The AACPDM is a multidisciplinary scientific society devoted to the study of cerebral palsy and other childhood onset disabilities, to promoting professional education for the treatment and management of these conditions, and to improving the quality of life for people with these disabilities. Membership: $175-$265/year.

Meetings/Conferences:
Annual Meetings: Fall
2007 – Vancouver, BC, Canada/Oct. 10-13/800

Publications:
Developmental Medicine & Child Neurology. m.
Newsletter. q.
Membership Roster. a.

American Academy of Actuaries *(1965)*

1100 17th St. NW
Siote 700
Washington, DC 20036-4601
Tel: (202)223-8196 *Fax:* (202)872-1948
Web Site: www.actuary.org
Members: 14500 individuals
Staff: 32
Annual Budget: $5-10,000,000
Executive Director: Kevin Cronin
Director, Finance and Administration: Joanne B. Anderson
E-Mail: anderson@actuary.org
Director, Professionalism/General Counsel: Lauren M. Bloom
E-Mail: bloom@actuary.org
Director, Communications: Noel Card
E-Mail: card@actuary.org
Director, Public Policy: Craig Hanna

Historical Note

The American Academy of Actuaries is the public policy organization for actuaries of all specialties within the United States. In addition to setting qualification standards and standards of actuarial practice, a major purpose of the Academy is to act as the public information organization for the profession. The Academy is nonpartisan and assists the public policy process through the presentation of clear, objective analysis. The Academy regularly prepares testimony for Congress, provides information to senior federal elected officials and congressional staff, comments on proposed federal regulations, and works closely with state officials on issues related to *insurance. Has an annual budget of approximately $6 million.*

Publications:
Enrolled Actuaries Report. q.
Actuarial Update. m.
Year Book. a.
Contingencies. bi-m. adv.
Academy Alert. irreg.

American Academy of Addiction Psychiatry *(1985)*
1010 Vermont Ave. NW
Suite 710
Washington, DC 20005-4959
Tel: (202)393-4484 *Fax:* (202)393-4419
E-Mail: kcw@aaap.org
Web Site: www.aaap.org
Members: 1000 individuals
Staff: 3
Annual Budget: $500-1,000,000
Executive Director: Kathryn Cates-Wessel
E-Mail: kcw@aaap.org

Historical Note
Founded as American Academy of Psychiatrists in Alcoholism and Addictions; assumed its current name in 1996. AAAP promotes education, research, prevention, and treatment of addictions, as well as improved training for psychiatrists and public information about the psychiatrist's role in addiction treatment. Membership: $215/year (general); $123/year (residents and retired); $90/year (medical students); $235/year (international); $215/year (affiliate).

Meetings/Conferences:
Annual Meetings: Winter

Publications:
AAAP Newsletter. q. adv.
American Journal on Addictions. 6/year. adv.
Membership Directory. a.

American Academy of Advertising *(1958)*
Coll. of Mass Communications, Texas Tech University Box 43082
Lubbock, TX 79409-3082
Tel: (806)742-3385 *Fax:* (806)742-1085
Web Site: www.americanacademyofadvertising.org
Members: 675 individuals
Staff: 1
Annual Budget: $500-1,000,000
Executive Director: Donald Jugenheimer

Historical Note
AAA members are primarily professors of advertising. Membership: $65/year, Student $35/year.

Meetings/Conferences:
Annual Meetings: Spring
2007 – Cincinnati, OH
2007 – Burlington, VT(Sheraton)/Apr. 12-15
2008 – San Mateo, CA(Marriott)/March 28-30

Publications:
AAA Newsletter. q.
Contact. q.
Journal of Advertising. q.
Proceedings. a.
Membership Directory. a.

American Academy of Allergy, Asthma, and Immunology *(1943)*
555 E. Wells St., Suite 1100
Milwaukee, WI 53202
Tel: (414)272-6071 *Fax:* (414)272-6070
E-Mail: info@aaaai.org
Web Site: www.aaaai.org
Members: 5300 individuals
Staff: 40
Annual Budget: $10-25,000,000
Executive Vice President: Kay A. Whalen, MBA, CAE
E-Mail: kwhalen@aaaai.org
Director, Research and Training: Rebecca Brandt
Associate Executive Vice President: Eric Lanke, CAE
Director, Communications and Membership: Michele Martinez

Historical Note
Formed by a merger of the American Association for the Study of Allergy and the Association for the Study of Asthma and Related Conditions as the American Academy of Allergy; became the American Academy of Allergy and Immunology in 1982 and assumed its present name in 1982. Has an annual budget of over $10 million. Membership: $300/year (fellows); $300/year (members).

Meetings/Conferences:
Annual Meetings: Spring
2007 – San Diego, CA/Feb. 23-27
2008 – Philadelphia, PA/March 14-18
2009 – Washington DC/March 13-17
2010 – New Orleans, LA/Feb. 26-March 2
2011 – San Francisco, CA/March 18-22
2012 – Orlando, FL/March 2-6

Publications:
Journal of Allergy and Clinical Immunology. m. adv.
AAAAI News. m. adv.

American Academy of Ambulatory Care Nursing *(1976)*
East Holly Ave.
P.O. Box 56
Pitman, NJ 08071-0056
Tel: (856)256-2350 *Fax:* (856)589-7463
Toll Free: (800)262 - 6877
E-Mail: aaacn@ajj.com
Web Site: www.aaacn.org
Members: 2100 individuals
Staff: 6
Annual Budget: $100-250,000
Executive Director: Cynthia Hnatiuk, EdD, RN, CAE

Historical Note
Formerly (1992) the American Academy of Ambulatory Nursing Administration, and (1995) American Academy of Ambulatory Care Nursing Administration. Members are registered nurses engaged in the care of ambulatory patients. Membership: $130/year (full membership).

Meetings/Conferences:
Annual Meetings: Spring/400
2007 – Las Vegas, NV(Sheraton)/March 29-Apr. 2

Publications:
Standards.
Viewpoint. bi-m. adv.
Telehealth Certification Prep. Materials.
Ambulatory Certification Prep. Materials.
Competency Assessment.
Ambulatory Nurse Staffing Bibliography.

American Academy of Anesthesiologist Assistants *(1973)*
P.O. Box 13978
Tallahassee, FL 32317
Tel: (850)656-8848 *Fax:* (850)656-3038
Toll Free: (866)828 - 5888
E-Mail: sandy@anesthetist.org
Web Site: www.anesthetist.org
Members: 400 individuals
Staff: 5
Annual Budget: under $10,000

Meetings/Conferences:
Annual Meetings: Spring

Publications:
The Anesthesia Record. 5/year. adv.

American Academy of Anti-Aging Medicine *(1993)*
1510 W. Montana St.
Chicago, IL 60614
Tel: (773)553-1000 *Fax:* (773)528-5390
E-Mail: A4M@worldhealth.net
Web Site: www.worldhealth.net
Members: 15000 individuals
President: Ronald Klatz, MD, DO

Historical Note
A4M promotes the development of technologies, pharmaceuticals, and processes that retard, reverse, or suspend the deterioration of the human body resulting from the physiology of aging, and provides continuing medical education for physicians.

Publications:
Anti-Aging Medical News. semi-a. adv.
World Heatlh Network. w. adv.

American Academy of Appellate Lawyers *(1990)*
15245 Shady Grove Rd.
Suite 130
Rockville, MD 20850
Tel: (301)258-9210 *Fax:* (301)990-9771
E-Mail: info@appellateacademy.org
Web Site: www.appellateacademy.org
Members: 250 individuals
Annual Budget: $50-100,000
Executive Director: Beth W. Palys, CAE

Historical Note
AAAL promotes the improvement of appellate advocacy through recognition of outstanding practitioners in the field. Membership, by invitation only, consists of lawyers who have focused substantially on appeals representation for at least 15 years.

Meetings/Conferences:
Biennial Meeting: 80-90 attendence
2007 – Boston, MA(Fairmont Copley Plaza)/Sept. 27-29

Publications:
Appellate Advocate newsletter. 3/year.

American Academy of Arts & Sciences *(1780)*
136 Irving St.
Cambridge, MA 02138-1205
Tel: (617)576-5000 *Fax:* (617)576-5050
E-Mail: membership@amacad.org
Web Site: www.amacad.org
Members: 3600 individuals
Staff: 34
Annual Budget: $2-5,000,000
Executive Officer: Leslie Cohen Berlowitz
E-Mail: membership@amacad.org

Historical Note
Founded during the American Revolution by John Adams and other individuals active in the nation's founding. Honors individual achievement in science, scholarship, the arts, business, and public affairs by election to membership, and conducts a wide-ranging program of study projects and conferences on emerging issues of intellectual inquiry and social concern. It maintains a Midwest and a Western Center and holds monthly meetings in Cambridge as well as occasional meetings in the Midwest, Far West, New York, and Washington, D.C.

Publications:
Bulletin of the American Academy of Arts and Sciences. m.
Daedalus. q.
Records. a.

American Academy of Audiology *(1988)*
11730 Plaza America Dr., Suite 300
Reston, VA 20190
Tel: (703)790-8466 *Fax:* (703)790-8631
Toll Free: (800)222 - 2336
E-Mail: info@audiology.org
Web Site: www.audiology.org
Members: 9700 individuals
Staff: 25
Annual Budget: $2-5,000,000
Executive Director: Laura Fleming Doyle, CAE
Director, Finance: Sandy Bishop
Director, Communications: Sydney Davis
Director, Education: Meggan Olek

Historical Note
AAA fellows hold graduate degrees in audiology and are licensed by a state to practice in the field. Students actively enrolled in graduate programs in audiology qualify as candidate members. Individuals holding Masters degrees and actively engaged in research, or in fields related to hearing care, are affiliate members. Membership is also available to international audiologists. Membership: $165/year.

Meetings/Conferences:
Annual Meetings: Spring
2007 – Denver, CO/Apr. 18-21/6000

Publications:
Journal of the American Academy of Audiology. 10/year. adv.
Audiology Today. bi-m. adv.

American Academy of Child and Adolescent Psychiatry *(1953)*
3615 Wisconsin Ave. NW
Washington, DC 20016-3007

Tel: (202)966-7300 *Fax:* (202)966-2891
Toll Free: (800)333 - 7636
Web Site: www.aacap.org
Members: 59000 individuals
Staff: 30
Annual Budget: $2-5,000,000
Executive Director: Virginia Q. Anthony
E-Mail: executive@aacap.org
Director, Meetings: Heidi Buttner Fiordi
E-Mail: hfiordi@aacap.org
Comptroller: Pat Clark
Membership Manager: Sha'Dana Cleaver
Director, Government Affairs and Deputy Executive Director: Kristin Krueger Ptakowski
E-Mail: kkrueger@aacap.org

Historical Note
Established in February 1953 as American Academy of Child Psychiatry and incorporated in Delaware in 1959; assumed its present name in 1986. Encourages medical contributions to the knowledge and treatment of psychiatric problems of children and their families. Membership: $60/year (trainee); $215/year (corresponding); $295/year (affiliate); $350/year (active/fellow).

Meetings/Conferences:
Annual Meetings: Fall
2007 – Boston, MA(Sheraton Boston Hotel)/Oct. 23-28
2008 – Chicago, IL(Sheraton)/Oct. 28-Nov. 2
2009 – Honolulu, HI(Hilton Hawaiian Village)/Oct. 27-Nov. 1

Publications:
AACAP Directory. bien.
AACAP Newsletter. bi-m.

American Academy of Clinical Neurophysiology *(1985)*
104 13th St.
Hudson, WI 54016
Tel: (715)381-3440 *Fax:* (715)381-3442
E-Mail: dtjorneh@pressenter.com
Web Site: www.aacnonline.com
Members: 800 individuals
Staff: 4
Executive Director: Dan Tjornechoj
E-Mail: dtjorneh@pressenter.com

Historical Note
Membership: $25-95/year (individual); $100/year (company).

Publications:
Neurology and Clinical Neurophysiology.
AACN Newsletter. semi-a.

American Academy of Clinical Psychiatrists *(1975)*
P.O. Box 458
Glastonbury, CT 06033-0458
Tel: (860)633-5045 *Fax:* (860)633-6023
E-Mail: aacpoth@aol.com
Web Site: www.aacp.com
Members: 500 individuals
Staff: 1
Annual Budget: $100-250,000
: Beverly Davidson

Historical Note
Members are mainly private clinicians and academicians. Disseminates scientific information relevant to clinical practice to its members. Membership: $50-175/year.

Meetings/Conferences:
2007 – Washington, DC(Wyndham Hotel)/March 30-Apr. 1

Publications:
The Clinical Psychiatry Quarterly. q.
Annals of Clinical Psychiatry.

American Academy of Clinical Sexologists *(1979)*

Historical Note
The education division of the American Board of Sexology (see separate listing).

American Academy of Clinical Toxicology *(1968)*
777 East Park Dr.
P.O. Box 8820
Harrisburg, PA 17105-8820
Tel: (717)558-7847 *Fax:* (717)558-7841
E-Mail: aact@pamedsoc.org
Web Site: www.clintox.org
Members: 630 individuals
Staff: 2
Annual Budget: $100-250,000
Interim Executive Director: Jan Reisinger

Historical Note
ACCT members are physicians, research scientists, and analytical chemists, veterinarians and pharmacists active in clinical toxicology. Membership: $165/year.

Meetings/Conferences:
Annual Meetings: Fall/650

Publications:
Journal Toxicology/Clinical Toxicology.
Current Awareness in Clinical Toxicology. m.

American Academy of Cosmetic Dentistry *(1984)*
5401 World Dairy Dr.
Madison, WI 53718
Tel: (608)222-8583 *Fax:* (608)222-9540
Toll Free: (800)543 - 9220
E-Mail: info@aacd.com
Web Site: www.aacd.com
Members: 7200 individuals
Staff: 22
Annual Budget: $5-10,000,000
Executive Director: Robert Hall, C.A.E.
E-Mail: bobh@aacd.org

Historical Note
AACD members are dental practitioners, educators and researchers with an interest in the field of cosmetic dentistry. Has Accreditation and Fellowship programs. Membership: $395/year (individual).

Meetings/Conferences:
Annual Meetings: April-May
2007 – Atlanta, GA/May 15-20
2008 – New Orleans, LA/May 6-10
2009 – Honolulu, HI/Apr. 28-May 2

Publications:
Academy Connection. bi-m.
Journal of Cosmetic Dentistry. 4/year. adv.

American Academy of Cosmetic Surgery *(1985)*
737 N. Michigan Ave., Suite 2100
Chicago, IL 60611-5405
Tel: (312)981-6760 *Fax:* (312)981-6787
Web Site: www.cosmeticsurgery.org
Members: 2000 individuals
Staff: 8
Annual Budget: $2-5,000,000
Executive Vice President: Jeffrey P. Knezovich, CAE
E-Mail: jknezovich@cosmeticsurgery.org
Manager, Communications: Charlie Baase
E-Mail: cbaace@cosmeticsurgery.org
Manager, Program and Operations: Lauraeyn Montgomery
E-Mail: lmontgomery@cosmeticsurgery.org
Director, Meetings and Curriculum: Moira Twitty

Historical Note
Formed by a merger of the American Association of Cosmetic Surgeons (1969) and the American Society of Cosmetic Surgeons (1982). Membership: $620/year (fellow); $475/year (associate); $345/year (corresponding); $100/year (resident).

Meetings/Conferences:
Annual Meetings: Winter
2007 – Phoenix, AZ(Biltmore Resort)/Jan. 25-28
2008 – Orlando, FL(Shingle Creek Resort)/Jan. 23-27/800

Publications:
Membership Directory. a. adv.
American Journal of Cosmetic Surgery. q. adv.
Cosmetic Surgery Newsline. q. adv.

American Academy of Craniofacial Pain *(1985)*
516 W. Pipeline Rd.
Hurst, TX 76053
Tel: (817)282-1501 *Fax:* (817)282-8012
Toll Free: (800)322 - 8651
E-Mail: central@aacfp.org
Web Site: www.aacfp.org
Members: 500 individuals
Staff: 2
Executive Director: Cordelia Mason
E-Mail: central@aacfp.org

Historical Note
Formerly (2001) American Academy of Head, Neck and Facial Pain. Members are dentists and other professionals concerned with disorders of the temporo-mandibular region. Membership: $250/year.

Publications:
Membership List. irreg.
TM Diary. semi-a. adv.

American Academy of Dental Group Practice *(1973)*
2525 E. Arizona Biltmore Circle, Suite 127
Phoenix, AZ 85016-2129
Tel: (602)381-1185 *Fax:* (602)381-1093
E-Mail: aadgp@aadgp.org
Web Site: www.aadgp.org
Members: 370 groups
Staff: 3
Annual Budget: $500-1,000,000
Executive Director: Robert A. Hankin, Ph.D.
Manager, Meetings: Nicole Almond

Historical Note
AADGP was formed to address the unique needs of dental groups. The Academy provides a national voice for the special interests of dental group practices and a liaison to other national dental organizations. Members also receive public recognition along with opportunities in professional improvement, peer contacts, and networking. Membership: $150/year per group and $10 per dentist within the group.

Meetings/Conferences:
Annual Meetings: Winter

Publications:
Contact. q. adv.

American Academy of Dental Practice Administration *(1956)*
1063 Whippoorwill Ln.
Palatine, IL 60067
Tel: (847)934-4404 *Fax:* (847)934-4410
E-Mail: aadpa@aol.com
Web Site: www.aadpa.org
Members: 250 individuals
Staff: 1
Annual Budget: $100-250,000
Executive Director: Kathleen Uebel

Historical Note
Membership: $450/year.

Meetings/Conferences:
Annual Meetings: March
2007 – Scottsdale, AZ(Hyatt Gainey Ranch)/Feb. 28-March 4/600

Publications:
The Communicator (newsletter). q.

American Academy of Dental Sleep Medicine *(1990)*
One Westbrook Corporate Ctr., Suite 920
Westchester, IL 60154
Tel: (708)273-9366 *Fax:* (708)492-0943
E-Mail: info@dentalsleepmed.org
Web Site: www.dentalsleepmed.org
Members: 800 individuals
Staff: 1
Annual Budget: $250-500,000
Coordinator: Lois Ligon

Historical Note
Founded as Sleep Disorders Dental Society; assumed its current name in 2006. ADSM works to facilitate a coordinated synergistic approach with the medical community for research, treatment, education and professional development in the utilization of dental appliances as an integral part of overall therapy in the treatment of sleep disorders. Membership: $295/year.

Meetings/Conferences:
Annual Meetings: Summer
2007 – Minneapolis, MN(Hilton)/June 8-10

Publications:
ADSM Dialogue. q. adv.
Sleep and Breathing. q. adv.

American Academy of Dermatology *(1938)*
930 E. Woodfield Rd.
Schaumburg, IL 60173
Tel: (847)330-0230 *Fax:* (847)330-8907

Toll Free: (888)462 - 3376
Web Site: www.aad.org
Members: 13700 individuals
Staff: 100
Annual Budget: $10-25,000,000
Executive Director: Ronald A. Henrichs, CAE
Director, Member Services: Kimberly Hoarle
Director, Meetings and Conventions: Timothy Moses
E-Mail: tmoses@aad.org
Director, Education: Gretchen Murphy
E-Mail: gmurphy@aad.org
Director, Communications: Allison Scherer
Deputy Executive Director: Carol Trumbold

Historical Note

Representing virtually all practicing dermatologists, AAD one of the largest dermatologic organization in the world. The Academy promotes and advances the science and art of medicine and surgery related to the skin; promotes the highest possible standards in clinical practice, education and research in dermatology and related disciplines; and supports and enhances patient care and promotes the public interest relating to dermatology. Has an annual budget of approximately $25 million. Membership: $750/year (individual, US & Canada).

Meetings/Conferences:

Annual Meetings:

Publications:

Dermatology Insights. 2/year. adv.
Dermatology World. m. adv.
Journal of the American Academy of Dermatology. m. adv.
Membership Directory. a. adv.

American Academy of Diplomacy *(1983)*
1800 K St. NW
Suite 1014
Washington, DC 20006
Tel: (202)331-3721 *Fax:* (202)833-4555
E-Mail: academy@academyofdiplomacy.org
Web Site: www.academyofdiplomacy.org
Members: 170 individuals
Staff: 2
Annual Budget: $50-100,000
President: Bruce Laingen
E-Mail: bplaingen@aol.com

Historical Note

AAD members are individuals who have served in high positions in the diplomatic corps or state department. Membership: $250/year.

Publications:

Newsletter. q.

American Academy of Disability Evaluating Physicians *(1987)*
150 N. Wacker Dr., Suite 1420
Chicago, IL 60606-1606
Tel: (312)658-1171 *Fax:* (312)658-1175
Toll Free: (800)456 - 6095
E-Mail: aadep@aadep.org
Web Site: www.aadep.org
Members: 1400 individuals
Staff: 5
Annual Budget: $1-2,000,000
Executive Director: Sandra L. Yost, MBA
E-Mail: aadep@aadep.org

Historical Note

AADEP members are physicians and osteopaths with an interest in impairment and disability evaluation. Membership: $450/year (individual).

Meetings/Conferences:

Annual Meetings: Winter

Publications:

Newsletter. q. adv.
Directory. a. adv.

American Academy of Emergency Medicine *(1994)*
555 E. Wells St., Suite 1100
Milwaukee, WI 53202-3816
Tel: (414)276-7390 *Fax:* (414)276-3349
Toll Free: (800)884 - 2236
E-Mail: info@aaem.org
Web Site: www.aaem.org
Members: 5000 individuals
Staff: 6
Annual Budget: $1-2,000,000
Executive Director: Kay A. Whalen, MBA, CAE
E-Mail: kwhalen@aaem.org
Associate Executive Director: Janet Wilson
E-Mail: jwilson@aaem.org

Historical Note

Membership: $345/year (individual).

Meetings/Conferences:

Annual Meetings: Winter
2007 – Las Vegas, NV(Caesar's Palace)/March 12-14
2008 – Amelia Island, FL(Amelia Island Plantation)/Feb. 6-9

Publications:

Journal of Emergency Medicine. 8/year.
Common Sense. bi-m.

American Academy of Environmental Engineers *(1955)*
130 Holiday Ct.
Suite 100
Annapolis, MD 21401
Tel: (410)266-3311 *Fax:* (410)266-7653
E-Mail: info@aaee.net
Web Site: www.aaee.net
Members: 2600 individuals
Staff: 4
Annual Budget: $50-100,000
President: Timothy J. Shea, Ph.D.

Historical Note

Originally (1955) the American Sanitary Engineering Intersociety Board; became the Environmental Engineering Intersociety Board in 1966 and assumed its present name in 1973. Members are board-certified environmental engineers. Membership: $150/year (individual).

Meetings/Conferences:

Annual Meetings: late October

Publications:

Environmental Engineer. q. adv.
Who's Who in Environmental Engineering. a.
Environmental Engineering Selection Guide. a.

American Academy of Environmental Medicine *(1965)*
7701 E. Kellogg Dr., Suite 625
Wichita, KS 67207-1705
Tel: (316)684-5500 *Fax:* (316)684-5709
E-Mail: centraloffice@aaem.com
Web Site: www.aaem.com
Members: 400 individuals
Staff: 3
Annual Budget: $250-500,000
Executive Director: De Rodgers

Historical Note

Originated as the Human Ecology Study Club. Formerly (1984) the Society for Clinical Ecology. Members are interested in studying the effects of the environment on human health. Membership: $420/year (M.D.); $250/year (organization).

Meetings/Conferences:

Annual Meetings: Fall

Publications:

Directory. a. adv.
Environmental Physician Newsletter. q. adv.

American Academy of Equine Art *(1980)*
c/o Kentucky Horse Park
4089 Iron Works Pkwy.
Lexington, KY 40511
Tel: (859)281-6031 *Fax:* (859)281-6043
Web Site: www.aaea.net
Members: 90 individuals
Staff: 1
Annual Budget: $50-100,000
Director: Shelley Hunter

Historical Note

Members are professional artists who are willing and qualified to exhibit works of equine art and to teach the subject. Membership: fees vary.

Meetings/Conferences:

Annual Meetings: Lexington, KY (Kentucky Horse Park), April, September

Publications:

Newsletter. 2/year.
Workshop Brochure. a.
Exhibition Perspectives. a.

American Academy of Estate Planning Attorneys *(1993)*
6050 Santo Rd.
Suite 240
San Diego, CA 92124
Tel: (619)453-2128 *Fax:* (858)874-5804
Toll Free: (800)846 - 1555
E-Mail: information@aaepa.com
Web Site: www.aaepa.com
Members: 130 law firms
Staff: 39
President: Robert G. Armstrong
E-Mail: robert@aaepa.com
Chief Executive Officer: Sanford M. Fisch
E-Mail: sandyf@aaepa.com
Director, Member Services: Jennifer Price
E-Mail: jenniferp@aaepa.com
Director, Continuing Legal Education: Dennis Sandoval
E-Mail: denniss@aaepa.com

Historical Note

AAEPA provides continuing education, individualized consulting services, and other products and services to member firms. Members are lawyers and law firms specializing in estate planning practice.

Meetings/Conferences:

Two Meetings Annually: Fall and Spring Summit

American Academy of Esthetic Dentistry *(1975)*
401 N. Michigan Ave.
Chicago, IL 60611
Tel: (312)321-5121 *Fax:* (312)673-6952
E-Mail: aaed@sba.com
Web Site: www.estheticacademy.org
Members: 138 individuals
Staff: 1
Annual Budget: $250-500,000
Executive Director: Julianne Bendel

Historical Note

Dentists and other health professionals concerned with esthetics in dentistry, medicine and psychology. Affiliated with the Federation of Prosthodontic Organizations. Membership: $500/year.

Meetings/Conferences:

Annual Meetings: August

Publications:

Journal of Esthetic Dentistry. q. adv.
Journal of Prosthetic Dentistry. q. adv.

American Academy of Facial Plastic and Reconstructive Surgery *(1964)*
310 S. Henry St.
Alexandria, VA 22314-3524
Tel: (703)299-9291 *Fax:* (703)299-8898
E-Mail: info@aafprs.org
Web Site: www.aafprs.org
Members: 2700 individuals
Staff: 14
Annual Budget: $1-2,000,000
Executive Vice President: Stephen Duffy
Director, Development, Research, and Humanitarian Programs: Ann Holton
Director, Publications and Marketing: Rita Chua Magness
Director, Education (CME) and Training: Carol Worthington

Historical Note

Formed by a merger (1964) of the American Society of Facial Plastic Surgery and the American Otorhinologic Society for Plastic Surgery. Membership: $25-495/year.

Meetings/Conferences:

Semi-annual Meetings: Spring and Fall

Publications:

Facial Plastic Times. m. adv.
Facial Plastic Surgery Today. q.
Membership Directory. a. adv.

American Academy of Family Physicians *(1947)*
11400 Tomahawk Creek Pkwy.
Leawood, KS 66211-2672
Tel: (913)906-6000 *Fax:* (913)906-6075
Toll Free: (800)274 - 2237
E-Mail: fp@aafp.org
Web Site: www.aafp.org

Members: 94300 individuals
Staff: 400
Annual Budget: $50-100,000,000
Executive Vice President: Douglas Henley, M.D.
Director, Meetings and Conventions: Sondra Biggs
Deputy Executive Vice President: Todd C. Dicus
Director, Membership Division: Colleen Lawler, CAE
Director, Strategic Planning and Marketing Division: Karen Mathes
Director, Publications Division and Publisher: Joetta Melton
Director, Research and Information Services: Gordon Schmittling
Vice President, Publishing and Communications: Michael Springer
Vice President, Marketing, Membership, and Meetings: Donna Valponi
Chief Financial Officer: Robert I. Watchinski

Historical Note

Founded in June 1947 in Atlantic City as the American Academy of General Practice. Name changed to the American Academy of Family Physicians in October 1971. Has an annual budget of approximately $75 million. Membership: $225/year (individual).

Publications:

American Family Physician. 2/m. adv.
AAFP News Now. m. adv.
Facts about Family Practice. irreg.
Family Practice Management. 10/year.
Annals of Family Medicine.

American Academy of Fertility Care Professionals *(1982)*

11700 Studt Ave., Suite C
St. Louis, MO 63141
Tel: (402)489-3733 *Fax:* (402)489-3733
E-Mail: aafcp@aol.com
Web Site: www.aafcp.org
Members: 91 individuals
Annual Budget: $25-50,000
President: Michele Chambers
E-Mail: aafcp@aol.com

Historical Note

Founded as American Academy of Natural Family Planning; assumed its current name in 2001. Purpose is to foster, advance, and promote quality natural family planning through service, education, leadership, and research. Has no paid officers or full-time staff.

Meetings/Conferences:

Annual Meetings: July

Publications:

Academy Activity. q.

American Academy of Fixed Prosthodontics *(1952)*

P.O. Box 1409
Bodega Bay, CA 94923-1409
Tel: (707)875-3040 *Fax:* (707)875-2927
Toll Free: (800)860 - 5633
E-Mail: secaafp@comcast.net
Web Site: www.fixedprosthodontics.org
Members: 600 individuals
Staff: 2
Annual Budget: $250-500,000
Secretary: Dr. Robert S. Staffanou, DDS, MS

Historical Note

Organized under the leadership of Dr. Stanley D. Tylman, Dr. Claude R. Baker and Dr. George H. Moulton at the Stevens Hotel, Chicago, February 5, 1951. Formerly (1991) American Academy of Crown and Bridge Prosthodontics. Has no paid staff. Membership: $449/year (United States); $500/year (Canada); $501/year (International).

Meetings/Conferences:

Annual Meetings: Chicago, IL/Winter/600-800
2007 - Chicago, IL(Marriott Downtown)/Feb. 23-24/800

Publications:

Journal of Prosthetic Dentistry. m. adv.
Newsletter. 2/year.

American Academy of Forensic Sciences *(1948)*

410 N. 21st St.
Colorado Springs, CO 80904
Tel: (719)636-1100 *Fax:* (719)636-1993
E-Mail: membship@aafs.org
Web Site: www.aafs.org
Members: 5500 individuals
Staff: 10
Annual Budget: $2-5,000,000
Executive Director: Anne Warren
E-Mail: awarren@aafs.org

Historical Note

Formed in St. Louis in 1948 and incorporated in Illinois in 1964. Cooperates with regional, national, and international organizations dedicated to the use of science in the administration of justice. The Forensic Sciences Foundation is the Academy's educational, research and testing arm. Membership: $145/year.

Meetings/Conferences:

Annual Meetings: February/2,200
2007 - San Antonio, TX(Convention Center)/Feb. 19-24
2008 - Atlanta, GA(Marriott)/Feb. 18-23

Publications:

Journal of Forensic Sciences. bi-m.
Newsletter. bi-m. adv.

American Academy of Gnathologic Orthopedics *(1969)*

2651 Oak Grove Rd.
Walnut Creek, CA 94598
Toll Free: (800)510 - 2246
Web Site: www.aago.com
Members: 160 individuals
Staff: 1
Annual Budget: $50-100,000
Executive Director: Jack L. Hockel

Historical Note

Established in Portland, Oregon to promote the Crozat-Wiebrecht philosophy; incorporated in Wisconsin. Members are dentists specializing in non-extraction orthodontic treatment of malformations of the face and jaw. Officers are elected annually. Membership: $350/year.

Meetings/Conferences:

Annual Meetings: Fall/125

Publications:

AAGO Journal. q. adv.

American Academy of Gold Foil Operators *(1952)*

One Woods End Rd.
Etna, NH 03750-4318
Web Site: www.goldfoil.org
Members: 300 individuals
Annual Budget: $25-50,000
Secretary-Treasurer: Robert C. Keene

Historical Note

Members are dentists performing restorative procedures utilizing gold foil and the rubber dam. Has no paid officers or full-time staff. Membership: $60/year.

Meetings/Conferences:

Annual Meetings: Fall/150

Publications:

Journal of Operative Dentistry. bi-m. adv.
Gold Leaf. semi-a.

American Academy of Head, Neck and Facial Pain

Historical Note

Became American Academy of Craniofacial Pain in 2001.

American Academy of Health Care Providers-Addictive Disorders *(1989)*

314 W. Superior St., Suite 702
Duluth, MN 55802
Tel: (858)693-7470
E-Mail: info@americanacademy.org
Web Site: www.americanacademy.org
Members: 2000 individuals
Staff: 6
Executive Director: Lorraine D. Grymala
E-Mail: lgrymala@americanacademy.org

Historical Note

The American Academy of Health Care Providers in the Addictive Disorders is a non-profit credentialing organization devoted to maintaining quality standards for the provision of treatment in the addictive disorders. The Academy was created to establish a core set of standards of competence for addition treatment professionals throughout the world.

Publications:

Academy E-News. bi-m.
Academy News. bi-a.
Internat'l Register of Health Care Providers in the Addictive Disorders. bi-a.
WAGER Report. w.

American Academy of Health Physics

1313 Dolley Madison Blvd., Suite 402
McLean, VA 22101
Tel: (703)790-1745 *Fax:* (703)790-2672
E-Mail: aahp@burkinc.com
Web Site: www.aahp-abhp.org
Members: 1600 individuals
Executive Director: Richard J. Burk, Jr.

Meetings/Conferences:

Annual Meetings:

Publications:

CHP News. m.

American Academy of Home Care Physicians *(1989)*

P.O. Box 1037
Edgewood, MD 21040-0337
Tel: (410)676-7966 *Fax:* (410)676-7980
E-Mail: aahcp@comcast.net
Web Site: www.aahcp.org
Members: 1300 individuals
Staff: 2
Annual Budget: $50-100,000
Executive Director: Constance F. Row, FACHE
E-Mail: aahcp@comcast.net
Director, Administrative and Member Services: Bernie Sciuto

Historical Note

AAHCP members are physicians and other home care professionals with an interest in the enhancement of quality home care. Membership: $150/year (individual); $150/year (agency); $2,000/year (corporate sponsor).

Meetings/Conferences:

Annual Meetings: Spring

Publications:

Frontiers newsletter. bi-m.

American Academy of Hospice and Palliative Medicine *(1988)*

4700 W. Lake Ave.
Glenview, IL 60025-1485
Tel: (847)375-4712 *Fax:* (877)734-8671
E-Mail: info@aahpm.org
Web Site: www.aahpm.org
Members: 2280 individuals
Staff: 12
Annual Budget: $500-1,000,000
Executive Director: Anne M. Cordes

Historical Note

Formerly the Academy of Hospice Physicians (1998). AAHPM members are physicians and other medical professionals dedicated to excellence in palliative medicine, through prevention and relief of suffering for patients and families of patients by providing education and clinical practice standards, fostering research, and facilitating personal and professional development. Membership: $285/year (physician); $145/year (affiliate); $50/year (student/resident).

Meetings/Conferences:

Annual Meetings: Summer

Publications:

AAHPM Bulletin. 4/yr. adv.
Journal of Palliative Medicine. 6/yr. adv.

American Academy of Implant Dentistry *(1952)*

211 E. Chicago Ave., Suite 750
Chicago, IL 60611
Tel: (312)335-1550 *Fax:* (312)335-9090
E-Mail: aaid@aaid-implant.org
Web Site: www.aaid-implant.org
Members: 2800 individuals
Staff: 9
Annual Budget: $1-2,000,000
Executive Director: J. Vincent Shuck
E-Mail: jvshuck@aaid-implant.org

Director, Administration: Joyce Sigmon, CAE
E-Mail: joyce@aaid-implant.org
Historical Note
Founded in Chicago in February 1952 as the American Academy of Implant Dentures and incorporated in Minnesota in October 1952. Name changed to American Academy of Implant Dentistry in 1966. Membership: $600/year (fellow/associety fellow); $275/year (general member).
Meetings/Conferences:
Annual Meetings: October
Publications:
AAID Newsletter. q. adv.
Journal of Oral Implantology. q. adv.

American Academy of Implant Prosthodontics
(1982)
Historical Note
Address unknown in 2006.

American Academy of Insurance Medicine *(1889)*
c/o Unconventional Planning
174 Colonnade Rd. Unit 25
Ottawa, ON K2E 7-J5
Tel: (613)226-9601 *Fax:* (613)721-3581
Toll Free: (888)211 - 3204
E-Mail: info@aaimedicine.org
Web Site: www.aaimedicine.org
Members: 500 individuals
Staff: 2
Annual Budget: $50-100,000
Executive Secretary: Ellyn Holzman, CMP
E-Mail: info@aaimedicine.org
Historical Note
Formerly (1991) Association of Life Insurance Medical Directors. Membership: $350/year (individual).
Publications:
Journal of Insurance Medicine. q. adv.

American Academy of Matrimonial Lawyers
(1962)
150 N. Michigan Ave., Suite 2040
Chicago, IL 60601
Tel: (312)263-6477 *Fax:* (312)263-7682
E-Mail: office@aaml.org
Web Site: www.aaml.org
Members: 1500 individuals
Staff: 2
Annual Budget: $250-500,000
Executive Director: Lorraine J. West
E-Mail: office@aaml.org
Historical Note
Members are attorneys specializing in the field of marriage and family law. Membership: $325/year.
Meetings/Conferences:
Semi-annual Meetings: November and March/300
Publications:
Proceedings. a.
Newsletter. q.
Journal of the AAML. 2/year.

American Academy of Maxillofacial Prosthetics
(1953)
Indiana University School of Dentistry
1121 W. Michigan St.
Indianapolis, IN 46202
E-Mail: sphaug@iupui.edu
Web Site: www.maxillofacialprosth.org
Members: 260 individuals
Staff: 1
Annual Budget: $50-100,000
Executive Secretary-Treasurer: Dr. Steven P. Haug
E-Mail: sphaug@iupui.edu
Historical Note
The Academy provides a forum for discussion and presentation of new materials, procedures and techniques in the field of facial prosthetic reconstruction. Membership: $260/year (individual); $250/year (organization/company).
Meetings/Conferences:
Annual Meetings: Fall
Publications:
Journal of Prosthetic Dentistry. m. adv.

American Academy of Mechanics *(1969)*
220 Norris Hall, MC-0219, Virginia Tech
Blacksburg, VA 24061
Tel: (540)231-6051 *Fax:* (540)231-2290
E-Mail: rbatra@vt.edu
Web Site: www.aamech.org
Members: 1200 individuals
Staff: 1
Annual Budget: $25-50,000
Secretary: Romesh Batra
E-Mail: rbatra@vt.edu
Historical Note
AAM members are individuals who have made significant contributions in the field of mechanics. Membership: $50/year (individual).
Publications:
Mechanics. m. adv.
Directory. irreg.

American Academy of Medical Acupuncture
(1987)
4929 Wilshire Blvd., Suite 428
Los Angeles, CA 90010
Tel: (323)937-5514 *Fax:* (323)937-0959
Web Site: www.medicalacupuncture.org
Members: 1900 individuals
Staff: 5
Annual Budget: $500-1,000,000
Executive Director: C. James Dowden
Historical Note
Membership: $285/year (individual).
Meetings/Conferences:
Annual Meetings: Spring/340
2007 – Baltimore, MD(Baltimore Marriott Waterfront)/Apr. 27-29
Publications:
AAMA Newsletter. bi-m.
AAMA Review Journal. semi-a. adv.

American Academy of Medical Administrators
(1957)
701 Lee St., Suite 600
Des Plaines, IL 60016
Tel: (847)759-8601 *Fax:* (847)759-8602
E-Mail: info@aameda.org
Web Site: www.aameda.org
Members: 3000 individuals
Staff: 7
Annual Budget: $1-2,000,000
President: Renee S. Schleicher, CAE
Vice President, Finance/Administration: Nancy L. Anderson, CPA
Director, Education: Holly Estal
Director, Membership and Communications: Von Yetzer
Historical Note
Founded in Boston in 1957. Healthcare administrators, including department heads, in both the federal and private sectors. The American College of Cardiovascular Administrators, American College of Healthcare Information Administrators, American College of Managed Care Administrators, the American College of Contingency Planners, the American College of Oncology Administrators, and the Federal Sector Healthcare Administrator are specialty groups of AAMA. Membership: $185/year (individual).
Meetings/Conferences:
Annual Meetings: Spring
Publications:
AAMA Executive. q. adv.
Academy in Motion e-newsletter. m. adv.
Journal of Cardiovascular Management. q. adv.
Journal of Oncology Management. q. adv.

American Academy of Medical Hypnoanalysts
(1974)
1022 Depot Hill Rd.
Broomfield, CO 80020
Tel: (303)465-2323 *Fax:* (303)465-1260
Toll Free: (888)454 - 9766
E-Mail: aamhmhj1@aamhm.com
Web Site: www.aamh.com
Members: 143 individuals
Annual Budget: $10-25,000
Executive Administrator: John A. Scott
Historical Note
Formerly the Society of Medical Hypnoanalysts. AAMH members include medical doctors, masters- and Ph.D.-level psychologists, social workers, counselors and nurses. Associate membership is open to any qualified mental health practitioner; clinical membership requires completion of a clinical training program. Membership: $185/year (clinical); $135/year (associate.
Meetings/Conferences:
Semi-annual Meetings: Spring and Fall
2007 – San Antonio, TX
Publications:
Journal of the AAMH (online). a. adv.

American Academy of Medical Management
(1987)
560 W. Crossville Rd.
Suite 103
Roswell, GA 30075
Tel: (770)649-7150 *Fax:* (770)649-7552
E-Mail: webmaster@ePracticeManagement.org
Web Site: www.epracticemanagement.org/
Members: 4500 individuals
Staff: 28
Annual Budget: $5-10,000,000
Executive Director: Roger G. Bonds
Historical Note
Founded as American College of Medical Staff Development; became American College of Medical Practice Management in 2000, and assumed its current name in 2001. Members are executives and managers in medical organizations.

American Academy of Microbiology *(1955)*
Historical Note
The professional services arm of the American Society for Microbiology.

American Academy of Ministry *(1992)*
P.O. Box 681868
Franklin, TN 37068-1868
Tel: (615)599-9889 *Fax:* (615)599-8985
E-Mail: mail@ministry.org
Web Site: www.ministry.org
Members: 1000 individuals
Staff: 2
Annual Budget: $25-50,000
Executive Director: Michael Duduit
Historical Note
An interdenominational professional and scholarly organization, AAM is organized to help ministers enhance their ministry gifts. Membership: $39/year.
Meetings/Conferences:
Annual Meetings: Summer
Publications:
Journal of the AAM. 2/year. adv.
Academy News. q.

American Academy of Natural Family Planning
Historical Note
Became American Academy of Fertility Care Professionals in 2001.

American Academy of Neurological and Orthopaedic Surgeons *(1977)*
Ten Cascade Creek Ln.
Las Vegas, NV 89113
Tel: (702)388-7390 *Fax:* (702)871-4728
E-Mail: aanos@aanos.org
Web Site: www.aanos.org
Members: 269 individuals
Staff: 3
Annual Budget: under $10,000
Chairman, Board of Directors and Academy: Kazem Fathie, Ph.D., M.D.
E-Mail: aanos@aanos.org
Executive Assistant: Nick Rebel
E-Mail: aanos@aanos.org
Historical Note
AANOS members are neurological and orthopaedic surgeons and other physicians. The Academy was formed to promote the combination of approaches from other disciplines (e.g., Neurosurgery, Orthopaedic Surgery, Spinal Surgery, Neurology) in the treatment of injury and disease in the neuromusculoskeletal system. The American Academy of Spinal Surgeons is a board under the auspices of AANOS; also known as the American Academy of

Neurological and Orthopaedic Surgery. Membership: $600/year.

Meetings/Conferences:
Annual Meetings: Las Vegas, NV
2007 – Las Vegas, NV

Publications:
Academy Newsletter. 6/year. adv.
Journal of Neurological and Orthopaedic Medicine and Surgery. 24/year. adv.
FAANOS Directory. 2/year. adv.
Journal (on line). 3/year. adv.

American Academy of Neurological Surgery *(1938)*

Historical Note
A research and certification program of American Ass'n of Neurological Surgeons, which provides administrative support

American Academy of Neurology *(1948)*

1080 Montreal Ave.
St. Paul, MN 55116-2311
Tel: (651)695-2717 *Fax:* (651)695-2791
Toll Free: (800)879 - 1960
E-Mail: memberservices@aan.com
Web Site: www.aan.com
Members: 19000 individuals
Staff: 105
Annual Budget: $10-25,000,000
Executive Director and Chief Executive Officer: Catherine Rydell

Historical Note
Founded and incorporated in Minnesota in 1948. Members are medical doctors who specialize in nerve and nervous system diseases. Has an annual budget of approximately $10 million.

Meetings/Conferences:
Annual Meetings: April
2007 – Boston, MA/Apr. 28-May 5
2008 – Chicago, IL/Apr. 12-19
2009 – Seattle, WA/Apr. 25-May 2

Publications:
Neurology Today. m. adv.
AANews. m. adv.
Neurology. bi-m. adv.

American Academy of Nurse Practitioners *(1985)*

P.O. Box 12846
Austin, TX 78711
Tel: (512)442-4262 *Fax:* (512)442-6469
Web Site: www.aanp.org
Members: 21000 individuals
Staff: 30
Annual Budget: $2-5,000,000
Executive Director: Dr. Judith S. Dempster
Director, Commnications: Nancy McMurrey
E-Mail: nmcmurrey@aanp.org

Historical Note
AANP promotes high standards of health care delivery by nurse practitioners and acts as a forum to enhance the identity and continuity of nurse practitioners. Maintains a Washington, DC office. Membership: $99/year (individual); supporting memberships available.

Meetings/Conferences:
Annual Meetings: June/1,700
2007 – Indianapolis, IN(Convention Center)/June 20-24

Publications:
AANP Smartbrief. d. adv.
Journal of the AANP. m. adv.
AANP Monitor. q.

American Academy of Nursing *(1973)*

555 E. Wells St., Suite 1100
Milwaukee, WI 53202-3823
Tel: (414)287-0289 *Fax:* (414)276-3349
E-Mail: info@aanet.org
Web Site: www.aannet.org/
Members: 1000 individuals
Staff: 3
Annual Budget: $100-250,000
Director, Administration: Annette Hess
E-Mail: info@aanet.org
Director, Meetings: Carina Tran
E-Mail: info@aanet.org

Historical Note
The American Academy of Nursing is a working body of nursing leaders and scholars in education, practice, administration. and research. Fellows are elected to membership based on their contributions to the profession. Following induction, members are designated Fellow of the American Academy of Nursing (FAAN). The Academy seeks to identify emerging nursing and health care issues, promote scholarly exploration, and propose solutions. Applicants must be sponsored by members and successfully complete the membership and selection process. Membership: $225/year (individual).

Meetings/Conferences:
Annual Meetings: October

Publications:
Nursing Outlook. bi-m. adv.

American Academy of Nutrition *(1985)*

1204-D Kenesaw
Knoxville, TN 37919-7736
Tel: (865)524-8079 *Fax:* (865)524-8339
Toll Free: (800)290 - 4226
E-Mail: aantn@aol.com
Web Site: www.nutritioneducation.com
Director, Education: Arthur Presser
E-Mail: aantn@aol.com

Historical Note
Founded in 1985, the American Academy of Nutrition was formed to meet the demand for an accredited independent study program in nutrition.

American Academy of Ophthalmology *(1896)*

P.O. Box 7424
San Francisco, CA 94120-7424
Tel: (415)561-8500 *Fax:* (415)561-8533
E-Mail: comm@aao.org
Web Site: www.aao.org
Members: 7000 individuals
Staff: 165
Annual Budget: $10-25,000,000
Executive Vice President: H. Dunbar Hoskins, Jr., M.D.
Director, Finance: Ben Bank
Director, Human Resources: Virginia Cunningham
Vice President, Member Services: Jill Hartle
Vice President, Meetings and Exhibits: Debra Rosencrance, CMP

Historical Note
Founded as the Western Ophthalmological, Otolaryngological and Rhinological Association. Name changed to Western Ophthalmologic and Otolaryngologic Association in 1899. Became the American Academy of Ophthalmology and Otolaryngology in 1903. In 1979 the Academy split into the American Academy of Ophthalmology and the American Academy of Otolaryngology. Absorbed the American Association of Ophthalmology, July 1, 1981. Maintains a Washington office. Sponsors and supports the American Academy of Ophthalmology Political Action Committee (OPHTH PAC). Has an annual budget of approximately $21.3 million. Memberships: $675/year.

Meetings/Conferences:
Annual Meetings: Fall/20,000

Publications:
Ophthalmology Journal. m.
Eyenet. m. adv.

American Academy of Optometry *(1922)*

6110 Executive Blvd., Suite 506
Rockville, MD 20852
Tel: (301)984-1441 *Fax:* (301)984-4737
E-Mail: loiss@aaoptom.org
Web Site: www.aaopt.org/
Members: 5000 individuals
Staff: 10
Annual Budget: $2-5,000,000
Executive Director: Lois Schoenbrun, CAE, FAAO
E-Mail: loiss@aaoptom.org
Director, Membership and Communications: Deborah Brandt
Director, Finance: Joni Hoskie
Manager, Meetings and Exhibits: Gloria Nehemiah

Historical Note
Supports research, education, and the dissemination of knowledge to foster and enhance excellence in basic and applied vision science. American Optometric Foundation and Ophthalmic Research Institute are affiliates of AAO. Membership: $215/year (full member); $25/year (student); $1,000/year (corporate sponsor).

Meetings/Conferences:
Annual Meetings: December/3,500

Publications:
Optometry and Vision Science. m. adv.
Newsletter. q. adv.
Directory. bien.

American Academy of Oral and Maxillofacial Pathology *(1946)*

214 N. Hale St.
Wheaton, IL 30187
Tel: (630)510-4552 *Fax:* (630)510-4501
Toll Free: (888)552 - 2667
E-Mail: aaomp@b-online.com
Web Site: http://aaomp.org
Members: 700 individuals
Annual Budget: $100-250,000
Co-Executive Secretary: Liz Lenard
E-Mail: aaomp@b-online.com
Co-Executive Secretary: Janet Svazas

Historical Note
Formerly (1994) American Academy of Oral Pathology.

Meetings/Conferences:
Annual Meetings: Spring
2007 – Kansas City, MO/May 4-9

Publications:
Newsletter. 3/year.
Membership Directory (online, for members only).

American Academy of Oral and Maxillofacial Radiology *(1949)*

P.O. Box 1010
Evans, GA 30809
Tel: (706)721-2607 *Fax:* (706)721-6276
E-Mail: mshrout@mail.mcg.edu
Web Site: www.aaomr.org
Members: 388 individuals
Staff: 1
Annual Budget: $50-100,000
Executive Director: Dr. Michael K. Shrout
E-Mail: mshrout@mail.mcg.edu

Historical Note
Formerly (1949) American Academy of Dental Roentgenologists, (1951) American Academy of Oral Roentgenology, and then (1967) American Academy of Dental Radiology. Membership: $90-$200/year (individual); $500-$1500/year (organization/company).

Meetings/Conferences:
Annual Meetings: Fall/125
2007 – Chicago, IL(Knickerbocker)/Nov. 28-Dec. 2/125
2008 – Pittsburgh, PA(Omni William Penn)/Oct. 29-Nov. 2/125
2009 – Louisville, KY(Seelbach Hilton)/Oct. 21-24/125

Publications:
AAOMR Newsletter. q.
Membership Roster. a.
Oral Surgery, Oral Medicine and Pathology, Oral Radiology and Endodontics. m.

American Academy of Oral Medicine *(1946)*

P.O. Box 2016
Edmonds, WA 98020
Tel: (425)778-6162 *Fax:* (425)771-9588
E-Mail: info@aaom.com
Web Site: www.aaom.com
Members: 800 individuals
Staff: 2
Annual Budget: $100-250,000
Executive Coordinator: Abraham Reiner, D.D.S.

Historical Note
Founded and incorporated in New York as the American Academy of Dental Medicine, AAOM assumed its present name in 1966. Purpose is to promote the study and dissemination of knowledge of the cause, prevention and control of diseases of the teeth and oral tissues; and to foster increased

scientific understanding and cooperation between the dental and medical professions. Membership: $185/year.

Meetings/Conferences:
Annual Meetings: April-May

Publications:
Clinician's Guides for Treatment of HIV Infected Patients.
Newsletter of the American Academy of Oral Medicine. 2/year. adv.
Clinician's Guides for Treatment of Oral Conditions in Geriatric Patients.
Clinician's Guides for Treatment of Oral Facial Pain.
Clinician's Guides for Treatment of Medically Compromised Patient.
Clinician's Guides for Treatment of Common Oral Conditions.

American Academy of Orofacial Pain *(1975)*
19 Mantua Rd.
Mt. Royal, NJ 08061
Tel: (856)423-7222 *Fax:* (856)423-3420
E-Mail: aaopco@talley.com
Web Site: www.aaop.org
Members: 315 individuals
Staff: 2
Annual Budget: $250-500,000
Executive Director: Ken Cleveland

Historical Note
AAOP is dedicated to alleviating pain and suffering through the promotion of excellence in education, research, and patient care in the field of orofacial pain and associated disorders.

Publications:
Journal of Orofacial Pain. q. adv.
AAOP News. q. adv.

American Academy of Orthopaedic Surgeons *(1933)*
6300 N. River Rd.
Rosemont, IL 60018-4262
Tel: (847)823-7186 *Fax:* (847)823-8125
Toll Free: (800)346 - 2267
Web Site: www.aaos.org
Members: 20000 individuals
Staff: 200
Annual Budget: $25-50,000,000
Chief Executive Officer: Karen L. Hackett, FACHE, CAE
Medical Director: Robert Haralson, III, M.D.
Chief Financial Officer: Richard J. Stewart
Chief Education Officer: Mark W. Wieting

Historical Note
Founded October 11, 1933 in Chicago. Incorporated in Illinois in 1948. AAOS fosters and assures the highest quality musculoskeletal health care through education of orthopaedists, other health care providers, and the public; promotion of research; communication with other professionals and the public; and leadership in the development of health care policy. Has an annual budget of approximately $40 million. Membership: $750/year (active fellows); $300/year (candidate members); $300/year (international).

Meetings/Conferences:
Annual Meetings: Winter
2007 - San Diego, CA/Feb. 14-18
2008 - San Francisco, CA/March 5-9
2009 - Las Vegas, NV/Feb. 25-March 1

Publications:
Journal of the AAOS. m. adv.
Bulletin. bi-m. adv.
OKO - Orthopaedic Knowledge Online.

American Academy of Orthotists and Prosthetists *(1970)*
526 King St., Suite 201
Alexandria, VA 22314
Tel: (703)836-0788 *Fax:* (703)836-0737
Web Site: www.oandp.org
Members: 3000 individuals
Staff: 9
Annual Budget: $1-2,000,000
Executive Director: Peter Rosenstein
E-Mail: prosentein@oandp.org
Deputy Executive Director: Chellie Blondes

Historical Note
Members are individuals who have been certified for practice by the American Board for Certification in Orthotics and Prosthetics. Membership: $330/year.

Meetings/Conferences:
2007 - San Francisco, CA(Marriott)/March 21-24/2000
2008 - Orlando, FL(Caribe Royal)

Publications:
Academician Newsletter. 10/year.
Journal of Prosthetics & Orthotics. q.

American Academy of Osteopathy *(1937)*
3500 DePauw Blvd., Suite 1080
Indianapolis, IN 46268
Tel: (317)879-1881 *Fax:* (317)879-0563
E-Mail: snoone@academyofosteopathy.org
Web Site: www.academyofosteopathy.org
Members: 2000 individuals
Staff: 6
Annual Budget: $500-1,000,000
Executive Director: Stephen J. Noone, CAE
E-Mail: snoone@academyofosteopathy.org

Historical Note
Founded July 6, 1937 in Chicago as The Section of Manipulative Therapeutics of the American Osteopathic Association. Name changed in 1938 to Osteopathic Manipulative Therapeutic and Clinical Research Association. Incorporated in 1944 as the Academy of Applied Osteopathy and became American Academy of Osteopathy in 1970. Affiliated with American Osteopathic Association. Membership: $205/year (individual).

Meetings/Conferences:
2007 - Colorado Springs, CO(Broadmoor)/March 21-25/1000
2008 - Dallas, TX(Intercontinental)/March 26-30/1000
2009 - Little Rock, AR(Peabody)/March 25-29/1000

Publications:
AAO Newsletter. 8/year. adv.
AAO Journal. q. adv.
AAO Yearbook. a.

American Academy of Otolaryngic Allergy *(1941)*
Executive Director: Jami Lucas

Historical Note
Formerly (1982) the American Society of Ophthalmologic and Otolaryngologic Allergy. Membership: $50-325/year.

Meetings/Conferences:
Annual Meetings: Fall/600

Publications:
Newsletter. q.

American Academy of Otolaryngology-Head and Neck Surgery *(1896)*
One Prince St.
Alexandria, VA 22314-3357
Tel: (703)836-4444 *Fax:* (703)683-5100
Web Site: www.entnet.org
Members: 11500 individuals
Staff: 80
Annual Budget: $10-25,000,000
Executive Vice President: David Nielsen, M.D.
Chief Technology Officer: Harry Biddle
Associate Director, Meetings: Erin LaFlair
Manager, Congressional Affairs: Jenny Lubold
Deputy Executive Vice President: Paul Markowski
Director, Communications and Publications: Jeanne McIntyre
E-Mail: jmcintyre@entnet.org

Historical Note
Founded as the Western Ophthalmological, Otolaryngological and Rhinological Association. Name changed to Western Ophthalmologic and Otolaryngologic Association in 1899. Became the American Academy of Ophthalmology and Otolaryngology in 1903, and assumed its present name in 1979 when the ophthalmologists left the Academy and established the American Academy of Ophthalmology. Merged with the American Council of Otolaryngology-Head and Neck Surgery on January 1, 1982. Functions as a national information, liaison, and promotional center of otolaryngological endeavors. Affiliated with the International Federation of Oto-Rhino-Laryngological Societies. Coordinates state and federal political action and organizes the Combined Otolaryngological Spring Meetings on behalf of ten otolaryngologic societies. Has an annual budget of approximately $17 million. Membership: $400/year (individual).

Meetings/Conferences:
Semi-Annual Meetings: Spring and Fall/8,500
2007 - Washington, DC/Sept. 16-19
2008 - Chicago, IL/Sept. 21-24
2009 - San Diego, CA/Sept. 13-16

Publications:
The Bulletin. m. adv.
Otolaryngology-Head and Neck Surgery. m. adv.

American Academy of Pain Management *(1988)*
13947 Mono Way, Suite A
Sonora, CA 95370-2807
Tel: (209)533-9744 *Fax:* (209)533-9750
E-Mail: aapm@aapainmanage.org
Web Site: www.aapainmanage.org
Members: 6000 individuals
Staff: 14
Annual Budget: $2-5,000,000
Executive Director: Kathryn A. Padgett, Ph.D.
Director, Communications and Advocacy: Lenore Duensing
Director, Education: Terry Finigian
Director, Print and Electronic Media: Carol Harper
Director, Sales: Jillian Manley

Historical Note
AAPM's primary function is to establish and monitor a national credentialling process in pain management, to identify individuals who have voluntarily sought and obtained credentialling in pain management, and to maintain a register of credentialed individuals. AAPM works to eliminate barriers to effective pain management through education, accredition, credentialling, and publication. Membership: $160/year (individual).

Meetings/Conferences:
2007 - Las Vegas, NV(Red Rock Resort)/Sept. 26-30/1200

Publications:
American Journal of Pain Management. q. adv.
Pain Practitioner. q. adv.
Currents (e-newsletter). m.

American Academy of Pain Medicine *(1983)*
4700 W. Lake Ave.
Glenview, IL 60025-1485
Tel: (847)375-4731 *Fax:* (877)734-8750
E-Mail: aapm@amctec.com
Web Site: www.Painmed.org
Members: 1200 individuals
Staff: 12
Annual Budget: $1-2,000,000
Executive Director: Jeffrey W. Engle, CMP, CAE
E-Mail: aapm@amctec.com

Historical Note
Formerly the American Academy of Algology. AAPM members are physicians and surgeons who spend a significant portion of their practice in treating and studying pain disorders. Membership: $325/year.

Meetings/Conferences:
Annual Meetings: always President's Day weekend

Publications:
AAPM Newsletter. q.
Pain Medicine. q. adv.
Membership Directory. a.

American Academy of Pediatric Dentistry *(1947)*
211 E. Chicago Ave., Suite 700
Chicago, IL 60611-2616
Tel: (312)337-2169 *Fax:* (312)337-6329
Web Site: www.aapd.org
Members: 6500 individuals
Staff: 18
Annual Budget: $5-10,000,000
Executive Director: John S. Rutkauskas, D.D.S.
Deputy Executive Director and General Counsel: Scott Litch
Manager, Membership and Marketing: Suzanne Wester

Historical Note
Formerly (1984) the American Academy of Pedodontics. Absorbed the American Academy of Pediatric Dentistry in 2002. Membership: $550/year.

Meetings/Conferences:
Annual Meetings: Spring/800

Publications:
Pediatric Dentistry Today (Newsletter). bi-m. adv.
Pediatric Dentistry. bi-m. adv.
Pediatric Dental Impressions. q.
Membership Directory. a. adv.

American Academy of Pediatrics *(1930)*
141 N.W. Point Blvd.
Elk Grove Village, IL 60007-1098
Tel: (847)434-4000 *Fax:* (847)434-8000
Toll Free: (800)433 - 9016
Web Site: www.aap.org
Members: 60000 individuals
Staff: 310
Annual Budget: $50-100,000,000
Executive Director: Errol Alden, M.D., FAAP
Director, Federal Affairs: Elizabeth J. Noyes
E-Mail: enoyes@aap.org

Historical Note
In 1922 the AMA's Section on Pediatrics dissented from the AMA in support of the Sheppard-Towner Act, a federal proposal to set up a small maternal and child health program. They were censured, causing the nation's pediatricians to realize that they needed a forum of their own. In 1930, 35 charter members founded the AAP in Detroit and chartered it in the State of Illinois. Maintains a Washington office.

Meetings/Conferences:
Annual Meetings: Fall/6,000

Publications:
Pediatrics. m. adv.
Pediatrics-in-Review. m.
AAP News. m. adv.

American Academy of Periodontology *(1914)*
737 N. Michigan Ave., Suite 800
Chicago, IL 60611
Tel: (312)787-5518 *Fax:* (312)787-3670
Toll Free: (800)282 - 4867
E-Mail: abperio@msn.com
Web Site: www.perio.org
Members: 7250 individuals
Staff: 40
Annual Budget: $5-10,000,000
Executive Director: Gerald M. Bowers, D.D.S.
Director, Scientific and Educational Affairs: Carol Dingeldey
Director, Publications and Marketing: Katie Goss
Director, Membership: Christi Lennox
Executive Secretary: Brenda J. Mayes
E-Mail: abperio@msn.com
Director, Business and Financial Affairs: Don Morin
Director, Information Technology: Margo Pecoulas
Director, Meetings and Continuing Education: Susan Schaus
Director, Public and Practice Affairs: Kimberly Suda-Blake

Historical Note
Originated in Cleveland February 21, 1914 as the Academy of Oral Prophylaxis and Periodontology. Became the American Academy of Periodontology in 1919. Incorporated in Michigan in 1934 and merged with the American Society of Periodontists in 1967. Reincorporated in Illinois in 1988. Membership open to qualified periodontists in the U.S. and Canada. Has an annual budget of approximately $6 million. Membership: $540/year (active).

Meetings/Conferences:
Annual Meetings: Winter/6,000
2007 – Washington, DC/Oct. 27-30
2008 – Seattle, WA/Sept. 6-9
2009 – Boston, MA/Sept. 12-15

Publications:
Annals of Periodontology.
Journal of Periodontology. m. adv.
AAP News. q.
Directory of Members. a.

American Academy of Physical Medicine and Rehabilitation *(1938)*
330 North Wabash Ave., Suite 2500
Chicago, IL 60611-7617
Tel: (312)464-9700 *Fax:* (312)464-0227
E-Mail: info@aapmr.org
Web Site: www.aapmr.org
Members: 6400 individuals
Staff: 32
Annual Budget: $2-5,000,000
Interim Executive Director: Lynda M. Leedy
Coordinator, Membership: Barbara A. Bogel
Director, Meetings and Conventions: Cathy Mason, CMP
Director, Education and Research: Cheryl Ritzi
E-Mail: info@aapmr.org
Director, Marketing, Communications and Membership: Steve Smith, MS, CAE
E-Mail: info@aapmr.org

Historical Note
Founded in 1938 as the Society of Physical Therapy Physicians, and icorporated September 1939 in Chicago. Name changed to American Society of Physical Medicine in 1944 and American Academy of Physical Medicine and Rehabilitation in 1955. AAPM&R is a society of Physiatrists, physicians who are Board-certified in physical medicine and rehabilitation. Aprox. 87% of all physiatrists practicing in the US are members of AAPM&R. The mission of the AAPM&R is to maximize the quality of life, while minimizing the incidence, severity, and prevalence of impairments, disabilities, and handicaps. Membership: $520/year (individual).

Meetings/Conferences:
Annual Meetings: October-November/2,000-2,300
2007 – Boston, MA(Hynes Convention Center)/Sept. 27-30
2008 – San Diego, CA(Marriott)/Nov. 20-23

Publications:
Membership Directory. January. adv.
The PM&R Resident. 3/year.
Archives of Physical Medicine and Rehabilitation. m. adv.
The Physiatrist (offical newsletter). 10/year. adv.

American Academy of Physician Assistants *(1968)*
950 N. Washington St.
Alexandria, VA 22314-1552
Tel: (703)836-2272 *Fax:* (703)684-1924
E-Mail: aapa@aapa.org
Web Site: www.aapa.org
Members: 39000 individuals
Staff: 83
Annual Budget: $10-25,000,000
Executive Vice President and Chief Executive Officer: Stephen C. Crane
Director, State Government Affairs: Ann Davis
Senior Vice President: Marilyn H. Fitzgerald
Vice President, Government and Professional Affairs: Nicole Gara
Vice President, Communications and Information Services: Nancy Hughes
Vice President, Finance/Administration: Robert A. Johnston
Vice President/Chief Operating Officer: Cheryl Kasunich
Vice President, Data Systems and Computer Operations: Kevin Marvelle
Director, Human Resources: Lynn Schoenfelder
Vice President, Professional Education and Industry Relations: Greg Thomas

Historical Note
Formed by a group of physician assistants at Duke University in April 1968. Sponsors the American Academy of Physician Assistants Political Action Committee and the Physician Assistant Foundation. Membership: $215/year.

Meetings/Conferences:
Annual Meetings: Semi-Annual Meetings
2007 – Philadelphia, PA/May 26-31

Publications:
AAPA News. twice m. adv.
AAPA Journal. m. adv.

American Academy of Physician Assistants in Occupational Medicine

Historical Note
An affiliate of American Academy of Physician Assistants, which provides administrative support.

American Academy of Podiatric Practice Management *(1961)*
10 Maple St., Suite 301
Middleton, MA 01949-2200
Tel: (978)646-9091 *Fax:* (978)646-9092
E-Mail: office@appm.org
Web Site: www.aappm.com
Members: 300 individuals
Annual Budget: $100-250,000
Executive Director: Gary W. Adams

Historical Note
Formerly (1993) the American Academy of Podiatric Administration, it was founded as American Academy of Practice Management in Podiatry and (1970) American Academy of Podiatric Management. AAPPM members are doctors of podiatric medicine interested in enhancing their professional efficiency and profits. Membership dues: sliding scale, starting at $195/year.

Publications:
AAPPM Newsletter. q.
Directory of Membership. a.

American Academy of Podiatric Sports Medicine *(1970)*
109 Greenwich Dr.
Walkersville, MD 21793
Tel: (301)845-9887 *Fax:* (301)845-9888
Toll Free: (888)854 - 3338
Web Site: www.aapsm.org
Members: 650 individuals
Staff: 3
Annual Budget: $100-250,000
Executive Director: Rita J. Yates
E-Mail: ritayates2@aol.com

Historical Note
Affiliated with the American Podiatric Medical Association. AAPSM members are medical professionals specializing in treatment of athletic injuries. Membership: $175/year.

Meetings/Conferences:
Annual Meetings: Summer
2007 – Philadelphia, PA

Publications:
Newsletter. q. adv.

American Academy of Political and Social Science *(1889)*
3814 Walnut Ave.
Philadelphia, PA 19104
Tel: (215)746-6500 *Fax:* (215)573-3003
E-Mail: phyllis.kaniss@sas.upenn.edu
Web Site: www.aapss.org
Members: 2000 individuals
Staff: 2
Executive Director: Phyllis Kaniss
E-Mail: phyllis.kaniss@sas.upenn.edu

Historical Note
AAPSS members are academics and others with an interest in the political and social sciences.

Meetings/Conferences:
Annual Meetings: April
2007 – Washington, DC(Reagan Hill Trade Center)/Apr. 29/50
2007 – Cambridge, MA(Harvard University)/

Publications:
Annals Journal. bi-m. adv.

American Academy of Procedural Coders

Historical Note
Became American Academy of Professional Coders in 2001.

American Academy of Professional Coders *(1988)*
2480 South 3850 West, Suite B
Salt Lake City, UT 84120
Tel: (801)236-2227 *Fax:* (801)236-2258
Toll Free: (800)626 - 2633 Ext:
E-Mail: aapc@aapc.com
Web Site: www.aapc.com
Members: 30000 individuals
Staff: 50

Executive Director: Terrill Curtis
Director, Marketing: Clare Bailey

Historical Note

Founded as American Academy of Procedural Coders; assumed its current name in 2001. AAPC members are medical coding professionals. Membership: $85/year.

Meetings/Conferences:

Annual Meetings: 3000

Publications:

AAPC Coding Edge. m. adv.

American Academy of Psychiatry and the Law *(1969)*

One Regency Dr., P.O. Box 30
Bloomfield, CT 06002-0030
Tel: (860)242-5450 *Fax:* (860)286-0787
Toll Free: (800)331 - 1389
E-Mail: office@aapl.org
Web Site: www.aapl.org
Members: 2000 individuals
Staff: 3
Annual Budget: $250-500,000
Executive Director: Jacquelyn T. Coleman, CAE

Historical Note

AAPL members are forensic psychiatrists and general psychiatrists who have a professional interest in psychiatry and the law and are members of the American Psychiatric Association, the American Academy of Child and Adolescent Psychiatry or a national organization equivalent to the APA. Membership: $250/year (individual); $55/year (trainee); $50/year (correspondent).

Meetings/Conferences:

Annual Meetings: October/650

Publications:

Journal of the AAPL. q.
Newsletter of the AAPL. 3/year.

American Academy of Psychoanalysis and Dynamic Psychiatry *(1956)*

One Regency Dr.
P.O. Box 30
Bloomfield, CT 06002-0030
Toll Free: (888)691 - 8281
E-Mail: info@aapsa.org
Web Site: www.aapsa.org
Members: 600 individuals
Staff: 3
Annual Budget: $250-500,000
Executive Director: Jacquelyn T. Coleman, CAE

Historical Note

Founded April 29, 1956 in Chicago as the Academy of Psychoanalysis. Incorporated in New York in 1956. Became the American Academy of Psychoanalysis in 1966, and assumed its current name in 2003. The Academy advocates an acceptance of all relevant and responsible psychoanalytic views of human behavior, rather than adherence to one particular doctrine. It holds that divergent views should be made available to psychoanalytic practitioners, candidates in training, and related behavioral scientists. Membership: $475/year.

Meetings/Conferences:

Semi-annual meetings: Spring and Winter

Publications:

Academy News. semi-a.
The Academy Forum. q.
Journal of American Academy of Psychoanalysis. q.

American Academy of Psychotherapists *(1955)*

5634 N.E. 29th Ave.
Portland, OR 97211
Tel: (503)282-2910 *Fax:* (503)282-2913
E-Mail: aapoffice@quest.net
Web Site: www.aapweb.com
Members: 600 individuals
Staff: 1
Office Director: Nancy R. Hunt

Historical Note

AAP is a professional society of practicing psychotherapists.

Publications:

AAP Newsletter. q.
Voices. q.
Directory. bien.

American Academy of Religion *(1909)*

Emory Univ., The Luce Center
825 Houston Mill Rd. NE, Suite 300
Atlanta, GA 30329-4246
Tel: (404)727-3049 *Fax:* (404)727-7959
E-Mail: aar@aarweb.org
Web Site: www.aarweb.org
Members: 9000 individuals
Staff: 14
Annual Budget: $1-2,000,000
Executive Director: Barbara DeConcini
Director, Membership and Technology Services: Joe DeRose
Director, Annual Meeting Program: Aislinn Jones
Director, Finance and Administration: Deborah Minor

Historical Note

Formerly (1964) National Association of Biblical Instructors. A member of the American Council of Learned Socs. and the National Humanities Alliance. Members include students, persons who study religion outside the field and members of the profession in colleges, universities and seminaries. Membership: $40-$145/year, based on income; $25/year (student).

Meetings/Conferences:

Annual Meetings: Winter
2007 – San Diego, CA/Nov. 17-20
2008 – Chicago, IL/Oct. 25-28
2009 – Montreal, QC, Canada/Nov. 7-10
2011 – San Francisco, CA/Nov. 18-21

Publications:

Openings: Employment Opportunities for Scholars of Religion. m. adv.
Spotlight on Teaching. semi-a. adv.
Journal of The AAR. q. adv.
Religious Studies News. q. adv.

American Academy of Research Historians of Medieval Spain *(1974)*

Department of History, University of California, Los Angeles
6265 Bunch Hall
Los Angeles, CA 90095-1473
E-Mail: tfruiz@history.ucla.edu
Web Site: www.uca.edu/aarhms
Members: 200 individuals
President: Teofilo F. Ruiz

Historical Note

An affiliated Society of the American Historical Association, the Academy serves to promote and facilitate the study of the history of the Iberian Peninsula during the Middle Ages.

Publications:

Newsletter. bi-a.

American Academy of Restorative Dentistry *(1928)*

2512 W. Kent St.
Broken Arrow, OK 74012
Tel: (918)455-2380 *Fax:* (918)455-8919
Web Site: www.restorativeacademy.com
Members: 400 individuals
Staff: 1
Annual Budget: $25-50,000
Executive Secretary: Cindy Metcalf

Historical Note

Members are dentists in general practice with an interest in advanced restorative procedures and materials. AARD produces a series of videotape lectures on topics relating to developments in the field.

Meetings/Conferences:

Annual Meetings:
2007 – Chicago, IL(Drake Hotel)/Feb. 24-25

Publications:

Journal of Prosthetic Dentistry. m. adv.

American Academy of Safety Education *(1962)*

Safety Science & Technology Dept.
Central Missouri State Univ.
Warrensburg, MO 64093
Tel: (660)543-4972
Members: 107 individuals
President: Chitaranjan Saran

Historical Note

An affiliate of National Safety Council, AASE members are instructors and educators in safety science. Has no paid officers or full-time staff.

Meetings/Conferences:

Nat'l Safety Conference.

Publications:

AASE Newsletter. semi-a.

American Academy of Sanitarians *(1966)*

1568 Le Grand Circle
Lawrenceville, GA 30043
Tel: (678)407-1051
E-Mail: gnoonan@charter.net
Web Site: www.sanitarians.org
Members: 300 individuals
Staff: 1
Annual Budget: under $10,000
Executive Secretary-Treasurer: Gary P. Noonan
E-Mail: gnoonan@charter.net

Historical Note

Members are licensed sanitarians with at least an M.A. in environmental health sciences, environmental management or public health. Membership: $50/year (individual).

Meetings/Conferences:

Annual Meetings: June, in conjunction with Nat'l Environmental Health Ass'n

Publications:

Newsletter. semi-a.
Roster of Diplomates. a.
Register of Professional Sanitarians. quinq.

American Academy of Sleep Medicine *(1975)*

One Westbrook Corporate Ctr., Suite 920
Westchester, IL 60154
Tel: (708)492-0930 *Fax:* (708)492-0943
E-Mail: aasm@aasmnet.org
Web Site: www.aasmnet.org
Members: 5000 individuals
Staff: 35
Annual Budget: $1-2,000,000
Executive Director: Jerome A. Barrett
Assistant Executive Director: Jennifer Markkanen

Historical Note

Founded as American Association of Sleep Disorder Centers in 1975. Became Association of Sleep Disorders Centers (1987) and American Sleep Disorders Association before assuming its current name in 1999. AASM members are institutions and individuals concerned with the clinical care of patients with sleep disorders. Membership: $200/year (individual); $1,000/year (center).

Meetings/Conferences:

Annual Meetings: In conjunction with the Sleep Research Soc.
2007 – Minneapolis, MN(Minneapolis Convention Center)/June 9-14/5000
2008 – Baltimore, MD(Baltimore Convention Center)/June 7-12/5000
2009 – Seattle, WA(Washington State Convention and Trade Center)/June 6-11/5000

Publications:

Membership Directory. a. adv.
Journal of Clinical Sleep Medicine. bi-m. adv.
Sleep. m.. adv.

American Academy of Somnology *(1986)*

P.O. Box 27077
Las Vegas, NV 89126-3124
Tel: (702)371-0947
Members: 75 individuals
Staff: 6
Annual Budget: under $10,000
President: David L. Hopper, Ph.D.

Historical Note

The Academy is an educational, scientific, and professional organization dedicated to advancing the understanding of sleep and sleep related processes. Certification of competence (diplomate status) is provided to qualified individuals by the American Board of Somnological Examiners. AAS bestows the title "fellow" and other recognition on individuals who have made outstanding contributions to the field of somnology. Membership: $35-95/year.

Meetings/Conferences:
Annual Meetings: July

Publications:
The Somnologist. q. adv.
Journal of Somnology. a. adv.

American Academy of Sports Physicians *(1979)*
17445 Oak Creek Ct.
Encino, CA 91316-2534
Tel: (818)501-4433 *Fax:* (818)501-8855
Members: 100 individuals
Staff: 1
Annual Budget: $10-25,000
Coordinator: Janie Zimmer

Meetings/Conferences:
Annual Meetings: last weekend in July

Publications:
AASP Newsletter. q.

American Academy of State Certified Appraisers
1438-F W. Main St.
Ephrata, PA 17522-1345
Tel: (717)721-3500 *Fax:* (717)721-3515
E-Mail: jjm@intercorpinc.net
Members: 4000 individuals
Staff: 2
Annual Budget: $100-250,000
Executive Director: John J. Matternas
E-Mail: jjm@intercorpinc.net

Publications:
Peer Review. q. adv.

American Academy of Teachers of Singing *(1922)*
600 W. 116th St., Suite 52A
New York, NY 10027-7042
Tel: (212)666-5951
E-Mail: rcwhitejr@earthlink.net
Web Site: www.americanacademyofteachersofsinging.org
Members: 35 individuals
Annual Budget: under $10,000
Chairman: Robert C. White, Jr.
E-Mail: rcwhitejr@earthlink.net

Historical Note
Membership: $100/year (individual).

Meetings/Conferences:
Annual Meetings: Five Meetings in the Academic Year.

American Academy of the History of Dentistry *(1951)*
284 Harvard St.
Brookline, MA 02446
Tel: (617)731-6767
E-Mail: info@histden.org
Web Site: www.histden.org
Members: 400 individuals
Staff: 1
Annual Budget: $10-25,000
President: David A. Chernin, D.M.D.

Historical Note
Seeks to stimulate interest, study, and research in the history of dentistry. Membership: $65/year (professional); $40/year (student).

Meetings/Conferences:
Annual Meetings: Fall, prior to American Dental Ass'n Annual Session/100
2007 – San Francisco, CA

Publications:
Journal of the History of Dentistry. 3/year. adv.

American Academy of Thermology *(1968)*
40 Medical Park, Suite 304
Wheeling, WV 26003
Tel: (304)242-2503 *Fax:* (304)242-2682
E-Mail: wpadmin@americanthermology.org
Web Site: www.americanthermology.org
Members: 250 individuals
Staff: 1
Annual Budget: $50-100,000
Executive Director: Srini Govindan M.D.

Historical Note
Membership composed of physicians (M.D. and D.O.) involved with the use of infrared and liquid cholesteric imaging in medical diagnosis. Formed as the American Thermographic Society, it assumed its present name in 1983. Membership: $200/year.

Meetings/Conferences:
Annual Meetings: Spring

Publications:
International Journal of Thermology. q.
Thermology Newsletter. q. adv.

American Academy of Veterinary and Comparative Toxicology *(1958)*
North Dakota State University, Veterinary Diagnostic Laboratory
P.O. Box 5406
Fargo, ND 58105-5406
Tel: (701)231-7529 *Fax:* (701)231-7514
Members: 220 individuals
Staff: 1
Annual Budget: $10-25,000
Secretary-Treasurer: Dr. Michelle S. Mostrom

Historical Note
Organized in 1957, and incorporated Jan. 15, 1958 in Salt Lake City. Formerly (1984) the American College of Veterinary Toxicologists. Concerned with education, research and exchange of proven methods and procedures in the field of veterinary toxicology. Encourages the use of uniform toxicologic nomenclature. Membership: $60/year.

Publications:
Veterinary and Human Toxicology. bi-m. adv.

American Academy of Veterinary Pharmacology and Therapeutics *(1977)*
Three Penny Lane Ct.
Wilmington, DE 19803-4023
Tel: (302)761-9690 *Fax:* (302)761-9680
E-Mail: aavptsec@aol.com
Web Site: www.aavpt.org
Members: 200 individuals
Annual Budget: $10-25,000
Secretary-Treasurer: Joe Gloyd, D.V.M
E-Mail: aavptsec@aol.com

Historical Note
Formerly (1981) American College of Veterinary Pharmacology and Therapeutics. Members are veterinary pharmacologists and veterinarians. Has no paid officers or full-time staff. Membership: $35/year (individual).

Meetings/Conferences:
Annual Meetings: with ACVIM forum/odd years & Biennial Symposium/even years
2007 – Monterey, CA(Asilomar Conference Center)/May 24-28

Publications:
Journal of Veterinary Pharmacology and Therapeutics. 6/year. adv.
Membership Directory (online).
Newsletter. 3/year. adv.

American Academy of Wound Management *(1995)*
1255 23rd St. NW
Suite 200
Washington, DC 20037-1125
Tel: (202)521-0368 *Fax:* (202)833-3636
E-Mail: woundnet@aawm.org
Web Site: www.aawm.org
Members: 1790 individuals
Staff: 2
Annual Budget: $250-500,000

Historical Note
AAWM provides board certification for physicians, nurses, therapists, and other healthcare professionals involved in wound care. Awards the trademarked designation Certified Wound Specialist (CWS). Membership: $400 (certification); $150 (certification renewal).

Publications:
AAWM News. q.
Nat'l Registry of Board Certified Wound Specialists. a.

American Academy on Communication in Healthcare *(1993)*
16020 Swingley Ridge Rd.
Suite 300
Chesterfield, MO 63017
Tel: (636)449-5080 *Fax:* (636)449-5051
Web Site: www.aachonline.org
Members: 425 individuals
Executive Director: Chris Pallozola

Historical Note
Membership: $195/year.

Meetings/Conferences:
Annual Meetings: Spring

Publications:
Medical Quarterly. q.

American Academy on Mental Retardation *(1960)*

Historical Note
The educational wing of the American Association on Mental Retardation.

American Accordionists Association *(1938)*
580 Kearny Ave.
Kearny, NJ 07032
Tel: (201)991-2233 *Fax:* (201)991-1944
E-Mail: AAA1938@aol.com
Web Site: www.ameracord.com
Members: 17000 individuals
Staff: 1
Annual Budget: $25-50,000
Executive Secretary: Maddalena Belfiore
E-Mail: AAA1938@aol.com

Historical Note
Members are teachers, manufacturers, importers, performers, amateurs and suppliers united to promote the use of the accordion and the development of accordion music. Membership: $50/year.

Publications:
AAA Journal. a. adv.
AAA Newsletter. q.

American Accounting Association *(1916)*
5717 Bessie Dr.
Sarasota, FL 34233-2399
Tel: (941)921-7747 *Fax:* (941)923-4093
Web Site: http://aaahq.org
Members: 9000 individuals
Staff: 15
Annual Budget: $2-5,000,000
Executive Director: Tracey E. Sutherland
E-Mail: tracey@aaahq.org

Historical Note
Founded as the American Association of University Instructors in Accounting; assumed its present name in 1935. The American Taxation Association is one of its sections.

Meetings/Conferences:
Annual Meetings: August
2007 – Chicago, IL/Aug. 5-8
2008 – Orange County, CA/Aug. 3-6
2009 – New York, NY/Aug. 2-5

Publications:
Accounting Horizons. q. adv.
Accounting Education News. 4/year. adv.
Issues in Accounting Education. q. adv.
Accounting Review. 5/year. adv.

American Acupuncture Association *(1972)*
4262 Kissena Blvd.
Flushing, NY 11355
Tel: (718)886-4431
Members: 400 individuals
Staff: 1
Chairman: Dr. David P.J. Hung

Historical Note
AAA members are physicians and other health professionals with an interest in acupuncture. Provides legislative support to the profession.

Meetings/Conferences:
Annual Meetings: always New York, NY/December

Publications:
Journal of Chinese Acupuncture. a.

American Advertising Federation *(1905)*
1101 Vermont Ave. NW
Suite 500
Washington, DC 20005-6306
Tel: (202)898-0089 *Fax:* (202)898-0159
Toll Free: (800)999 - 2231
E-Mail: aaf@aaf.org
Web Site: www.aaf.org

Members: 50000 individuals
Staff: 32
Annual Budget: $2-5,000,000
President and Chief Executive Officer: Wallace S. Snyder
Senior Vice President, Finance and Administration: Laurel Penhale
Executive Vice President, Government Affairs and Operations and General Counsel: Jeffry Perlman
Executive Vice President, Marketing and Communications: Peter W. Shih

Historical Note
Formed by a merger of the Advertising Federation of America and the Advertising Association of the West (formerly Pacific Advertising Association). Supports the Advertising Political Action Committee and the Advertising Hall of Fame. AAF represents all segments of the advertising industry and its views and concerns on public issues affecting advertising.

American Agents Alliance

Historical Note
See Alliance of Independent Agents and Brokers.

American Agents Association *(1980)*

P.O. Box 7079
Hilton Head, SC 29938
Tel: (843)785-2808 *Fax:* (843)785-9068
E-Mail: akaamerican@hargray.com
Members: 250 individuals
Staff: 2
Annual Budget: $10-25,000
President: James Fitzpatrick
E-Mail: akaamerican@hargray.com

Historical Note
AAA members are licensed insurance agents. Membership: $25/year.

Publications:
American Eagle Newsletter. bi-m.

American Aging Association *(1970)*

110 Chesley Dr.
Media, PA 19063-1755
Tel: (610)627-2626 *Fax:* (610)565-9747
E-Mail: ameraging@aol.com
Web Site: www.americanaging.org
Members: 200 individuals
Staff: 1
Annual Budget: $100-250,000
Executive Director: Arthur K. Balin, M.D., Ph.D., FACP

Historical Note
Formed to promote biomedical aging research with the long-term goal of increasing the span of healthy, productive life. Membership: $110/year (subscription); $50/year (lay); $50/year (student).

Meetings/Conferences:
Annual Meetings: Fall/200
2007 – San Antonio, TX

Publications:
AGE: The Journal of the American Aging Ass'n. q. adv.
AGE News. q. adv.

American Agricultural Economics Association *(1910)*

415 S. Duff, Suite C
Ames, IA 50010-6600
Tel: (515)233-3202 *Fax:* (515)233-3101
E-Mail: info@aaea.org
Web Site: www.aaea.org
Members: 2700 individuals
Staff: 8
Annual Budget: $1-2,000,000
Executive Director: Yvonne C. Bennett, CAE, SPHR
Association and Member Services Manager: Terri Haffner

Historical Note
Originated in 1910 as the American Farm Management Association. Became the American Farm Economic Association in 1918; assumed its current name in 1968. Incorporated in Iowa in 1968. Membership: $150/year (individual); $270/year (organization).

Meetings/Conferences:
Annual Meetings: Summer
2007 – Portland, OR/July 29-Aug. 1/1400

Publications:
American Journal of Agricultural Economics. 5/year. adv.
The Exchange. bi-m. adv.
Review of Agricultural Economics. q.. adv.
Choices magazine. q.. adv.

American Agricultural Editors Association *(1921)*

120 W. Main St.
P.O. Box 156
New Prague, MN 56071
Tel: (952)758-6502 *Fax:* (952)758-5813
E-Mail: ageditors@aol.com
Web Site: www.ageditors.com
Members: 400 individuals
Staff: 2
Annual Budget: $100-250,000
Executive Director: Den Gardner

Historical Note
Established and incorporated in Illinois. AAEA members are editors, writers, and photographers associated with agricultural publications. Membership: $150/year (individual).

Meetings/Conferences:
Annual Meetings: Fall

Publications:
Byline Newsletter. 10/year.
Membership Directory. a.

American Agricultural Law Association *(1980)*

P.O. Box 2025
Eugene, OR 97042
Tel: (541)485-1090 *Fax:* (541)302-1958
Web Site: www.aglaw-assn.org
Members: 650 individuals
Staff: 1
Annual Budget: $50-100,000
Interim Executive Director: Robert Achenbach
E-Mail: roberta@aglaw-assn.org

Historical Note
Attorneys, law professors, and others interested in agricultural law. Membership: $75/year (individual); $125/year (organization/company).

Meetings/Conferences:
Annual Meetings: Fall

Publications:
Agricultural Law Update. m.
Membership Directory. bi-a. adv.

American Agricultural Marketing Association *(1960)*

Historical Note
Affiliate of the American Farm Bureau Federation.

American Agriculture Movement *(1977)*

786 Cty. Rd. Q
Panhandle, TX 79068
Tel: (806)537-3750
Web Site: www.aaminc.org
Members: 42 state organizations
Staff: 2
Annual Budget: $250-500,000
National President: Buddy Vance

Historical Note
AAM is an umbrella organization composed of state organizations representing family farm producers for all sectors of agriculture. Membership: $100/year.

Meetings/Conferences:
Annual Meetings: Winter

Publications:
American Agriculture Movement Reporter. m. adv.

American Alliance for Health, Physical Education, Recreation and Dance *(1885)*

1900 Association Dr.
Reston, VA 20191
Tel: (703)476-3400 *Fax:* (703)476-9537
Toll Free: (800)213 - 7193
E-Mail: info@aahperd.org
Web Site: www.aahperd.org
Members: 26000 individuals
Staff: 71
Annual Budget: $2-5,000,000
Chief Executive Officer: Michael G. Davis
Membership: Eric Berkowitz
Vice President, Finance: Laura Myers
Director, Conventions: Sandra Sumner

Historical Note
The American Association for Advancement of Physical Education was founded at Adelphi Academy, Brooklyn, NY in 1885. In 1903 the name was changed to the American Physical Education Association and in 1938 to the American Association for Health, Physical Education and Recreation. Incorporated in the District of Columbia in 1969. Became the American Alliance for Health, Physical Education and Recreation in 1974, and assumed its present name in 1979. Composed of the American Association for Leisure and Recreation, American Association for Health Education, American Association for Active Lifestyles and Fitness, National Association for Girls and Women in Sports, National Association for Sport and Physical Education and the National Dance Association. Archival records available to researchers. Membership: $100/year (individual).

Meetings/Conferences:
Annual Meetings: Spring/8,000

Publications:
Journal of Physical Education, Recreation, and Dance. q. adv.
Research Quarterly for Exercise and Sport. q. adv.
Update. 9/year. adv.
Journal of Health Education. bi-m. adv.
Strategies. 8/year. adv.

American Alliance for Theatre and Education *(1987)*

7475 Wisconsin Ave., Suite 300A
Bethesda, MD 20814
Tel: (301)951-7977 *Fax:* (301)968-0144
E-Mail: aate.info@asu.edu
Web Site: www.aate.com
Members: 1000 individuals
Staff: 1
Annual Budget: $100-250,000
Administrative Director: Christy M. Taylor
E-Mail: aate.info@asu.edu

Historical Note
Created by the merger of American Association of Theatre for Youth with American Association of Theatre in Secondary Education in 1987. Both organizations were orginally divisions of the American Theatre Association (Children's Theatre Association and Secondary School Theatre Association) which were reorganized independently when ATA ceased operations in 1986. Incorporated in Arizona, AATE members are educators, artists, administrators and others serving young people in professional and community youth theatres and theatre educational programs. Membership: $98/year (individual); $131/year (organization); $60/year (students); $71/year (retired); add $20 outside U.S. and Canada.

Publications:
STAGE of the Art. q. adv.
Youth Theatre Journal. a. adv.

American Ambulance Association *(1979)*

8201 Greensboro Dr., Suite 300
McLean, VA 22102
Tel: (703)610-9018 *Fax:* (703)610-9005
Toll Free: (800)523 - 4447
E-Mail: aaa911@the-aaa.org
Web Site: www.the-aaa.org
Members: 950 companies
Staff: 5
Annual Budget: $1-2,000,000
Executive Vice President: Maria Bianchi
E-Mail: mbianchi@the-aaa.org

Historical Note
Product of a merger of the Ambulance Association of America formed in 1962 and the National Ambulance and Medical Services Association formed in 1963. Formerly (until 1979) known as the Ambulance and Medical Services Association of America. The majority of members are private ambulance services, but municipal and volunteer ambulance services can join as associate members. Membership: annual dues vary by number of ambulances operated.

Meetings/Conferences:
Annual Meetings: Winter/1,000

2007 – Las Vegas, NV(Hilton)/Nov. 28-Dec. 3
Publications:
Ambulance Industry Journal. q. adv.

American Amusement Machine Association *(1981)*
450 E. Higgins Rd., Suite 201
Elk Grove Village, IL 60007
Tel: (847)290-9088 *Fax:* (847)290-9121
E-Mail: information@coin-op.org
Web Site: www.coin-op.org
Members: 170 companies
Staff: 4
Annual Budget: $500-1,000,000
President: Michael Rudowicz
Manager, Marketing and Communications: Vanessa Cabrera
E-Mail: vcabrera@coin-op.org
Manager, Business: Tina Schwartz
E-Mail: tschwartz@coin-op.org
Historical Note
Founded in Des Plaines, Illinois as the Amusement Device Manufacturers Association; became the Amusement Game Manufacturers Association in 1982 and assumed its present name in 1985. Members are manufacturers, distributors and parts suppliers of coin-operated games and machines.
Meetings/Conferences:
Annual Meetings: Spring
Publications:
Membership Directory. a. adv.
Loose Change. m.

American Anaplastology Association *(1980)*
6060 Sunrise Vista Dr., Suite 1300
Citrus Heights, CA 95610-7098
Tel: (916)726-2910 *Fax:* (916)722-8149
E-Mail: aaa@anaplastology.org
Web Site: www.anaplastology.org
Staff: 1
Executive Director: Maryanne Bobrow, CAE, CMP
Historical Note
AAA is a noprofit educational organization dedicated to the art and science of rehabilitating patients with facial or somato disfigurements, thereby improving standards and advancing knowledge in prosthetic services and products. Founded to serve as an "information center" fostering communication among multidisciplined specialists involved in prosthetic rehabilitation. Membership is comprised of health care providers and researchers from the fields of medicine, dentistry, allied health, materials research and development, psychology, clinical cosmotology, and others. Membership: $185/yr (active); $95/yr (student); $95/yr (emeritus).
Meetings/Conferences:
Annual Meetings: Summer
Publications:
AAA Newsletter. semi-a.

American and Delaine-Merino Record Association *(1906)*
59419 Walters Rd.
Jacobsburg, OH 43933-9731
Tel: (740)686-2172 *Fax:* (740)686-2421
Web Site: www.admra.org
Members: 200 flocks
Staff: 1
Annual Budget: under $10,000
Secretary-Treasurer: Connie M. King
Historical Note
Registry office for owners and breeders of Merino sheep. Membership: $15 (lifetime); $20/year (annual dues).
Meetings/Conferences:
Annual Meetings: Harrisburg, PA(Keystone Int'l Livestock Expo)/October
Publications:
Consider Merinos. irreg.

American Angora Goat Breeder's Association *(1900)*
P.O. Box 195
Rocksprings, TX 78880
Tel: (830)683-4483
Members: 700 individuals
Staff: 1
Annual Budget: under $10,000
Secretary-Treasurer: Patty C. Shanklin
Historical Note
Breeders and fanciers of Angora goats.
Meetings/Conferences:
Annual Meetings: Rocksprings, TX/2nd Tuesday in October

American Angus Association *(1883)*
3201 Frederick Ave.
St. Joseph, MO 64506
Tel: (816)383-5100 *Fax:* (816)233-9703
E-Mail: angus@angus.org
Web Site: www.angus.org
Members: 35000 individuals
Staff: 30
Annual Budget: $2-5,000,000
Executive Vice President: John R. Crouch
Director, Industry and Member Communications: Sara Moyer
Historical Note
Formerly (1956) American Aberdeen-Angus Breeder's Association. The purpose of the association is: 1) to register purebred calves, 2) to inform and educate people about the breed, 3) to work to improve the breed. Member of the National Pedigree Livestock Council, National Cattlemen's Beef Association.
Publications:
Angus Journal. m. adv.
Angus Beef Bulletin. q. adv.

American Animal Hospital Association *(1933)*
12575 W. Bayaud Ave.
Lakewood, CO 80228
Tel: (303)986-2800 *Fax:* (303)986-1700
E-Mail: info@aahanet.org
Web Site: www.aahanet.org
Members: 34000 individuals
Staff: 61
Annual Budget: $5-10,000,000
Executive Director: John W. Albers, D.V.M.
E-Mail: info@aahanet.org
Manager, Communications: Constance Hardesty
E-Mail: info@aahanet.org
Historical Note
An association of animal hospitals and small animal practitioners. Founded in 1933 and incorporated in 1935 in Illinois. Has an annual budget of approximately $8.5 million.
Meetings/Conferences:
Annual Meetings: Spring
2007 – Denver, CO(Colorado Convention Center)/March 17-21
Publications:
Journal of the American Animal Hospital Association. bi-m.
AAHA Trends Magazine. bi-m. adv.

American Anthropological Association *(1902)*
2200 Wilson Blvd, Suite 600
Arlington, VA 22201
Tel: (703)528-1902 *Fax:* (703)528-3546
Web Site: www.aaanet.org
Members: 11000 individuals
Staff: 26
Annual Budget: $5-10,000,000
Executive Director: Bill Davis
Deputy Executive Director and Chief Financial Officer: Sandra Berlin
Director, Meetings: Lucille Dinon Horn
Director, Government Relations: Paul Nuti
Director, Publications: Susan Skomal
Director, Academic Relations: Kathleen Terry-Sharp
Manager, Membership Services: Richard Thomas
Historical Note
Established by members of the American Ethnological Society of New York, the Anthropological Society of Washington and Section H (Anthropology) of the American Association for the Advancement of Science. Incorporated in the District of Columbia in May, 1902. Specialty sections of AAA include: American Ethnological Society, Archeology Division, Association for Africanist Anthropology, Association for Feminist Anthropology, Association for Political and Legal Anthropology, Association of Black Anthropologists, Association of Latina and Latino Anthropologists, Anthropology of Religion Section, Association of Senior Anthropologists, Biological Anthropology Section, Central States Anthropological Society, Council on Anthropology and Education, Council for Museum Anthropology, Council on Nutritional Anthropology, Culture and Agriculture, General Anthropology Section, Middle East Section, National Association for the Practice of Anthropology, National Association of Student Anthropologists, Society for Anthropology in Community Colleges, Society for the Anthropology in Consciousness, Society for the Anthropology of Europe, Society for the Anthropology of North America, Society for the Anthropology of Work, Society for Cultural Anthropology, Society for Humanistic Anthropology, Society for Latin American Anthropology, Society for Psychological Anthropology, Society for Linguistic Anthropology, Society for Medical Anthropology, Society for Urban Anthropology, and Society for Visual Anthropology. Membership: several categories; for information contact AAA.
Meetings/Conferences:
Annual Meetings: November-December/4,500
Publications:
Visual Anthropology Review. semi-a. adv.
American Anthropologist. q. adv.
Guide to Departments of Anthropology. a.
Anthropology Newsletter. m. adv.
American Ethnologist. q. adv.
Ethos. q. adv.
Medical Anthropology Quarterly. q. adv.
Cultural Anthropology. q. adv.
Anthropology and Education Quarterly. q. adv.
Anthropology and Humanism. semi-a. adv.
Central Issues in Anthropology. semi-a. adv.
Journal of Linguistic Anthropology. semi-a. adv.
Museum Anthropology. 3/year. adv.

American Antiquarian Society *(1812)*
185 Salisbury St.
Worcester, MA 01609-1634
Tel: (508)755-5221 *Fax:* (508)753-3311
Web Site: www.americanantiquarian.org/
Members: 692 individuals
Staff: 50
Annual Budget: $2-5,000,000
President: Ellen S. Dunlap
Vice President, Administration: Edward J. Harris
Vice President, Development: John M. Keenum
Historical Note
A learned society founded in 1812 by Isaiah Thomas and others to collect and preserve materials related to American history before 1877; maintains an outstanding historical research library.
Publications:
Almanac: AAS Newsletter.
Proceedings of the AAS. semi-a.

American Apitherapy Society *(1978)*
5535 Balboa Rd.
Encino, CA 91316-1557
Tel: (818)501-0446 *Fax:* (818)995-9334
E-Mail: info@apitherapy.org
Web Site: www.apitherapy.org
Members: 350 individuals
Staff: 1
Annual Budget: $10-25,000
Office Manager: Rose Niwa
Historical Note
AAS members are beekeepers, health professionals and others with an interest in therapeutic applications of honey bee products, particularly honey bee venom. Has no paid officers or full-time staff. Membership: $45/year (individual).
Publications:
Journal of the American Apitherapy Society. q. adv.
Proceedings. irreg.
Directory. a.

American Apparel & Footwear Association *(1933)*
1601 N. Kent St., Suite 1200
Arlington, VA 22209
Tel: (703)524-1864
Toll Free: (800)520 - 2262

Web Site: www.apparelandfootwear.org
Members: 450 companies
Staff: 15
Annual Budget: $2-5,000,000
President and Chief Executive Officer: Kevin Burke
Director, Government Relations: Felicia Cheek
Director, International Trade: Nate Herman
Vice President, Industry Relations: Mary Howell
Senior Vice President Government Relations: Stephen Lamar
Director, Industry Programs: Susan Lapetina
Vice President, Membership: Joan McNeal
Chief Financial Officer: Ralph Reinecke
Executive Administrator: Marti Rust
Office Manager: Darrell Sumpter

Historical Note
Founded as Southern Garment Manufacturers Association; became American Apparel Manufacturers Association in 1960. Absorbed the National Association of Shirt, Pajama, and Sportswear Manufacturers in 1962, the Pacific Coast Garment Manufacturers Association in 1965, the Textile Merchants and Associated Industries of Chicago in 1965, the Corset and Brassiere Association in 1971, the Lingerie Industry Council in 1971, the New England Rainwear Manufacturers Association in 1974, the National Outerwear and Sportswear Association in 1983, the Headwear Institute of America in 1993, and the National Knitwear Manufacturers Association in 1993. Merged with The Fashion Association and Footwear Industries of America and assumed its current name in 2000. Intimate Apparel Council and Swimwear Industry Manufacturers Association are divisions of AAMA.

Meetings/Conferences:
Annual Meetings: Spring/350
2007 – Dana Point, CA(St. Regis)/Feb. 28-March 2/250

Publications:
Apparel Market Monitor.
Footwear Market Monitor.
International Trade Update. q..
AAFA Newsbreaker Email. w.
Membership Directory Online.
Trends Statistical Report. q.

American Apparel Manufacturers Association

Historical Note
Became American Apparel and Footwear Association in 2000.

American Apparel Producers Network *(1980)*

P.O. Box 720693
Atlanta, GA 30358
Tel: (404)843-3171 *Fax:* (413)702-3226
E-Mail: source@aapnetworks.net
Web Site: www.aapnetwork.net
Members: 210 companies
Staff: 2
Annual Budget: $100-250,000
Executive Director: Sue Strickland
E-Mail: source@aapnetworks.net

Historical Note
Formerly (1981) Southern Apparel Contractors and (1986) American Apparel Producers Association. AACA was established for "the purpose of domestic apparel sourcing in direct competition with imports." Membership: $1,450/year.

American Arbitration Association *(1926)*

335 Madison Ave., Tenth Floor
New York, NY 10017-4605
Tel: (212)716-5800 *Fax:* (212)716-5905
Toll Free: (800)778 - 7879
Web Site: www.adr.org
Staff: 800
Annual Budget: $50-100,000,000
President and Chief Executive Officer: William K. Slate, II
Senior Vice President, Marketing and Sales: Roy M. Arbeit
Vice President, U.S. and International Mediation Services: Neil Carmichael
Vice President, Elections: Kenneth Egger
Senior Vice President and Chief Operating Officer: John C. Emmert, Jr.
Vice President, Membership and Corporate Secretary: Jennifer Coffman Jester
Vice President, Neutrals Education: Harry Kaminsky
Senior Vice President, Program Development: Robert E. Meade
Senior Vice President, International, Legislative, and Research: Richard Naimark
Vice President, Corporate Communications: Kersten Norlin
Vice President, Publications: Ted E. Pons
Vice President, Human Resources: Morag Rollins
Senior Vice President and Chief Financial Officer: Frank Rossi
Vice President, Staff Education and Development: Gene Truncellito
General Counsel: Eric Tuchman
Vice President, Information Systems: Joseph Williams
Vice President, Management: Frank T. Zotto

Historical Note
Formed by a merger of the Arbitration Society of America and the Arbitration Foundation. Members are individuals and organizations united to promote the use of arbitration, mediation, democratic elections and other non-judicial processes for the settlement of all types of disputes. Has an annual budget of approximately $65 million.

Publications:
New York State No-Fault/SUM Arbitration Reporter. q.
Dispute Resolution Journal. q.
Arbitration in the Schools. m.
Dispute Resolution Times. q.
Labor Arbitration in Government. m.
Summary of Labor Arbitration Awards. m.
ADR and the Law. a.

American Architectural Manufacturers Association *(1936)*

1827 Walden Office Sq., Suite 550
Schaumburg, IL 60173-4268
Tel: (847)303-5664 *Fax:* (847)303-5774
Web Site: www.aamanet.org
Members: 270 companies
Staff: 12
Annual Budget: $1-2,000,000
President and Chief Executive Officer: Richard G. Walker
Marketing and Membership Manager: Janice Charletta
Technical Co-Director: John Lewis
Meetings Manager: Florence Nicolici
Technical Co-Director: Carl Wagus

Historical Note
Product of a merger (1962) of Sliding Glass Door and Window Institute (1954) and Aluminum Window Manufacturers Association (1936) to become the Architectural Aluminum Manufacturers Association. Absorbed (1971) Aluminum Siding Association, and assumed present name in 1984 after changing mission to include all framing materials. Members are manufacturers of storm windows, residential/commercial windows and doors, as well as sliding glass doors, siding, skylights, curtain walls and sun rooms. Membership: $1,500/year minimum (company).

Meetings/Conferences:
Annual Meetings: Fall/700
2007 – Marco Island, FL(Marriott)/Feb. 11-14
2007 – Huntington Beach, CA(Hyatt Regency)/June 10-13
2007 – Orlando, FL(Marriott Grand Lakes)/Oct. 14-17

American Art Therapy Association *(1969)*

1202 Allanson Rd.
Mundelein, IL 60060-3808
Tel: (847)949-6064 *Fax:* (847)566-4580
Toll Free: (888)290 - 0878
E-Mail: info@arttherapy.org
Web Site: www.arttherapy.org
Members: 4500 individuals
Staff: 5
Annual Budget: $250-500,000
Executive Director: Edward J. Stygar, Jr.
Assistant Executive Director and Convention Manger: Mary Buckley
E-Mail: info@arttherapy.org

Historical Note
AATA serves its members and the general public by providing standards of professional competence, and by disseminating knowledge relevant to the use of artistic processes and practices as tools for treatment, personal growth and the reconciliation of emotional conflict. Membership: $35/year (student); $85/year (professional); $120/year (organization).

Meetings/Conferences:
Annual Meetings: November

Publications:
Directory. bien.
Newsletter. q.
Proceedings. a.
Art Therapy Journal. q.

American Artists Professional League *(1928)*

c/o Salmagundi Club
47 Fifth Ave.
New York, NY 10003
Tel: (212)645-1345
E-Mail: aapl@verizon.net
Web Site: www.americanartisisprofessionalleague.org
Members: 750 individuals
Staff: 3
Annual Budget: $50-100,000
President: Konrad Hansalik

Historical Note
Members are professional painters, sculptors and graphic artists working in style of traditional realism. Has no paid officers or full-time staff. Membership: $40/year.

Meetings/Conferences:
Annual Meetings: New York, NY(Salmagundi Club)/November

Publications:
Catalog, Grand National Exhibition. a. adv.
Newsletter. a.

American Arts Alliance *(1977)*

1112 16th St. NW
Suite 400
Washington, DC 20036
Tel: (202)207-3850 *Fax:* (202)833-1543
E-Mail: info@americanartsalliance.org
Web Site: www.americanartsalliance.org
Members: 3000 Organizations
Staff: 1
Annual Budget: $250-500,000
Manager: Rachel Lyons

Historical Note
The American Arts Alliance is a national network of more than 3,000 members comprising the professional, nonprofit performing arts and presenting fields. For 27 years, the American Arts Alliance has been the premiere advocate for America's professional nonprofitart organizations, artists and their publics before the U.S. Congress and key policy makers. Through legislative and grassroots action, the American Arts Alliance advocates for national policies which recognize, enhance, and foster the contributions the arts make to America. Member art organizations include the Association of Performing Arts Presenters, Dance/USA, Opera America and Theatre Communications Group.

Publications:
Grassroots Kit for Arts Advocates. irreg.
Legislative Update. m.

American Ass'n of Ambulatory Surgery Centers *(1978)*

P.O. Box 5271
Jefferson City, TN 37602
Tel: (423)282-9712 *Fax:* (423)282-9712
E-Mail: info@aaasc.org
Web Site: www.aaasc.org
Members: 400 individuals
Staff: 2
Annual Budget: $100-250,000
Executive Director: Craig Jeffries
E-Mail: craigjeffries@aaasc.org

Historical Note
Founded as Soc. for Office Based Surgery; became American Soc. of Outpatient Surgeons in 1986, and assumed its current name in 1996). Promotes effective and reliable operation of the ambulatory surgery center as the best environment for outpatient surgery. Surgical specialists/board certified surgeons, nurses and administrators are admitted to membership. Membership: $350/year (individual); $250-1750/year (facility); and $500-$10,000 (corporate).

Publications:
Monitor. q.
Newsletter. q.

American Assembly for Men in Nursing *(1974)*
P.O. Box 130220
Birmingham, AL 35213
Tel: (205)802-7551 *Fax:* (205)802-7553
E-Mail: aamn@aamn.org
Web Site: www.aamn.org
Members: 250 individuals
Staff: 3
Annual Budget: $25-50,000
Contact: Byron McCain
E-Mail: aamn@aamn.org
Historical Note
Founded as National Male Nurses Association; assumed its current name in 1982. AAMN is a forum that enhances the nursing profession by supporting men in the profession. Membership: $80/year (R.N.s), $25-40/year (students).
Publications:
AAMN Interaction. q. adv.

American Association for Accreditation of Ambulatory Surgery Facilities *(1981)*
P.O. Box 9500
Gurnee, IL 60031
Toll Free: (888)545 - 5222
E-Mail: info@aaaasf.org
Web Site: www.aaaasf.org
Members: 900 individuals
Staff: 7
Annual Budget: $500-1,000,000
Executive Director: Jeff Pearcy
Historical Note
Formerly (1992) The American Association for Accreditation of Ambulatory Plastic Surgery Facilities. Members are ambulatory surgical facilities operated by American Board of Medical Specialties board certified surgeons.
Meetings/Conferences:
Biennial Symposium: (odd years)
Publications:
AAAASF News Newsletter. q. adv.

American Association for Active Lifestyles and Fitness *(1949)*
Historical Note
Merged (2005) with American Association for Leisure and Recreation to form the American Association for Physical Activity and Recreation.

American Association for Adult and Continuing Education *(1982)*
10111 Martin Luther King Jr. Hwy.
Suite 200C
Bowie, MD 20720
Tel: (301)459-6261 *Fax:* (301)459-6241
E-Mail: aaace10@aol.com
Web Site: www.aaace.org
Members: 1000 individuals
Staff: 1
Annual Budget: $500-1,000,000
Manager: Cle Anderson
E-Mail: aaace10@aol.com
Historical Note
The product of a merger between the Adult Education Association (founded in 1951) and the National Association for Public and Continuing Adult Education (founded in 1952). AAACE coordinates local, state, regional, and national adult education programs, publications, and legislation. Absorbed National Council of Administrators of Adult Education in 1992. Membership: $115/year (professional).
Meetings/Conferences:
Annual Meetings: Fall
Publications:
Adult Education Quarterly. q. adv.
Adult Learning. q. adv.

American Association for Aerosol Research *(1981)*
17000 Commerce Pkwy., Suite C
Mt. Laurel, NJ 08054
Tel: (856)439-9080 *Fax:* (856)439-0525
E-Mail: info@aaar.org
Web Site: www.aaar.org
Members: 1000 individuals
Staff: 3
Annual Budget: $250-500,000
Executive Director: Amy Williams
Historical Note
Promotes the research of small particles suspended in gases. Applications include air pollution research, production of fine powders, and the study of atmospheric chemistry and nuclear safety. Membership: $150/year (individual); $1400/year (organization).
Publications:
Membership Directory. a.
AAAR Newsletter. 3/year.
Aerosol Science and Technology. m. adv.

American Association for Affirmative Action *(1974)*
888 16th St. NW
Suite 800
Washington, DC 20006
Tel: (202)349-9855 Ext: 1857 *Fax:* (202)335-1399
Toll Free: (800)252 - 8952
E-Mail: execdir@affirmativeaction.org
Web Site: www.affirmativeaction.org
Staff: 2
Executive Director: ReNee S. Dunman
Historical Note
AAAA represents managers of affirmative action programs. Membership fee varies, based on number of employees.
Meetings/Conferences:
Annual Meetings: Spring

American Association for Agricultural Education *(1960)*
Texas A&M Univ., Campus Mail 2116
College Station, TX 77843-2116
Tel: (979)862-3419 *Fax:* (979)845-6296
Web Site: http://aaaeonline.org
Members: 300 individuals
Staff: 1
Annual Budget: $25-50,000
Treasurer: Dr. Timothy J. Murphy
Historical Note
Formerly Teacher Trainers Section of the Agricultural Division of the American Vocational Association, then American Association of Teacher Educators in Agriculture; name changed, yet still part of AVA. Officers elected annually; has no permanent headquarters. AAAE is dedicated to studying, applying, and promoting teaching and learning processes in agriculture. Membership: $60/year (individual).
Meetings/Conferences:
Annual Meetings: Annual Meeting with Ass'n for Career and Technical Education (ACTE).
Publications:
Journal of Agricultural Education. q.

American Association for Applied Linguistics *(1977)*
3416 Primm Ln.
Birmingham, AL 35216
Tel: (205)824-7700 *Fax:* (205)823-2760
Toll Free: (866)821 - 7700
E-Mail: aaal@primemanagement.net
Web Site: www.aaal.org
Members: 1300 individuals
Annual Budget: $100-250,000
Business Manager: Robert Ranieri
Historical Note
Individuals interested in multidisciplinary approaches to language issues and problems. Membership: $48/year (individual); $96/year (institution); $24/year (student).
Meetings/Conferences:
Annual Meetings: Spring
Publications:
AAA Letter.
AILA Review. a.
ARAL. a.

American Association for Artificial Intelligence *(1979)*
445 Burgess Dr.
Menlo Park, CA 94025-3442
Tel: (650)328-3123 *Fax:* (650)321-4457
Web Site: www.aaai.org
Members: 5000 individuals
Staff: 6
Annual Budget: $2-5,000,000
Executive Director: Carol M. Hamilton
Historical Note
Members are individuals interested in attempting to approximate the human thinking process with computers in such fields as visual data interpretation, expert systems, natural language processing, common sense reasoning, automated problem solving, and robotics. Membership: $95 (U.S./Canadian Institution); $135/year (foreign individual); $190/year (U.S./Canadian institution); $230/year (foreign company).
Meetings/Conferences:
Annual Meetings: July/August
Publications:
AI Magazine. q. adv.
Conference Proceedings. a.

American Association for Budget and Program Analysis *(1976)*
P.O. Box 1157
Falls Church, VA 22041
Tel: (703)941-4300 *Fax:* (703)941-1535
E-Mail: aabpa@aol.com
Web Site: www.aabpa.org
Members: 500 individuals
Staff: 1
Annual Budget: $25-50,000
National Executive Secretary: Christine Lawson
E-Mail: aabpa@aol.com
Historical Note
The result of a merger between the Budget Officers Conference and the American Public Policy Association, AABPA was chartered as a non-profit educational corporation in Washington, DC in 1976. Members, largely in the DC area, have an interest in program management and budget analysis. Membership: $45/year (individual); $150/year (corporate); $15/year (student).
Meetings/Conferences:
Semi-Annual Symposia: Spring and Fall
Publications:
Newsletter. bi-m.
Public Budgeting and Finance Journal. q. adv.

American Association for Cancer Education *(1947)*
256 WARF Bldg.
610 Walnut St.
Madison, WI 53726
Tel: (608)263-9515 *Fax:* (608)263-4497
E-Mail: hasahel@wisc.edu
Web Site: www.aaceonline.com
Members: 500 individuals
Annual Budget: $25-50,000
Executive Director: Heidi A. Sahel
Historical Note
Formerly (1966) Coordinators of Cancer Teaching. Membership includes scientists, surgeons, internists, radiation oncologists, pediatricians, gynecologists, osteopathic physicians, dentists, oncology nursing educators and professional educators. Concerned with cancer teaching in medical, dental and nursing schools, educational programs for the general public, for populations at special risk, and for cancer patients. Efforts involve developing and evaluating new educational strategies and methods, including the examination of objectives, courses, and evaluation instruments; expanding public education; fostering international cooperative efforts in cancer education; and furthering education in cancer prevention. Membership: $150/year.
Meetings/Conferences:
Annual Meetings: Fall/200
Publications:
Membership Directory.
President's Newsletter.
Journal of Cancer Education. q. adv.
American Ass'n for Cancer Education Newsletter. q.

American Association for Cancer Research
(1907)
615 Chestnut Ave., 17th Floor
Philadelphia, PA 19106
Tel: (215)440-9300 *Fax:* (215)440-9313
E-Mail: communications@aacr.org
Web Site: www.aacr.org
Members: 24000 individuals
Staff: 125
Annual Budget: $25-50,000,000
Chief Executive Officer: Margaret Foti, Ph.D., M.D.
E-Mail: foti@aacr.org
Publisher: Kathleen Case
E-Mail: publications@aacr.org
Director, Communications: Warren Froelich
E-Mail: communications@aacr.org
Managing Director, Programs: David Irvin
Chief Financial Officer: Mike Stewart

Historical Note
Founded 1907 in Washington, DC and incorporated in New York in 1940. An association of research workers for presentation and discussion of new or significant observations and problems in cancer, and to foster research on cancer. Membership: $175/year.

Meetings/Conferences:
Annual Meetings: *Spring/17,000*

Publications:
Clinical Cancer Research. semi-m. adv.
Cancer Research. semi-m. adv.
Cell Growth and Differentiation -
Molecular Cancer Research. m. adv.
Cancer Epidemiology, Biomarkers & Prevention. m. adv.
Molecular Cancer Therapeutics. m. adv.
CR. q. adv.

American Association for Career Education
(1980)
2900 Amby Pl.
Hermosa Beach, CA 90254-2216
Tel: (310)376-7378 *Fax:* (310)376-2926
Members: 500 individuals
Annual Budget: under $10,000
President: Pat Nellor Wickwire, Ph.D.

Historical Note
Incorporated in the District of Columbia in 1981. AACE connects education, work, and careers through Career Education for all ages. AACE members are professional educators, community leaders, parents, business leaders, government leaders and other interested individuals. Membership: $15/year (regular); $100/year (sustaining); $25/2 years (regular); $150/2 years (sustaining). Has no full-time staff.

Publications:
AACE Career Education Classics. irreg.
AACE Bonus Briefs. q.
AACE Careers Update. q. adv.
Career Education That Works. a.
AACE CareerGram. irreg.
AACE Distinguished Member Series. a.
AACE Forum. irreg.

American Association for Chinese Studies *(1958)*
CCNY North Academic Center, Room 4/116
Convent Ave. and 138th St.
New York, NY 10031
Tel: (212)650-8268 *Fax:* (212)650-8287
E-Mail: aacs@mail.com
Web Site: www.ccny.cuny.edu/aacs/
Members: 350 individuals
Staff: 2
Annual Budget: under $10,000
Executive Secretary: Peter Chow
E-Mail: aacs@mail.com

Historical Note
Formerly (1976) the American Association of Teachers of Chinese Language and Culture.

Meetings/Conferences:
Annual Meetings: *Fall*

Publications:
Newsletter. semi-a.
Journal of Chinese Studies. semi-a.

American Association for Clinical Chemistry
(1948)
2101 L St. NW
Suite 202
Washington, DC 20037-1558
Tel: (202)857-8739 *Fax:* (202)887-5093
Toll Free: (800)892 - 1400
Web Site: www.aacc.org
Members: 11000 individuals
Staff: 50
Annual Budget: $10-25,000,000
Executive Vice President: Richard G. Flaherty
Vice President, Marketing Programs: Jerry Goldsmith
E-Mail: jgoldsmith@aacc.org
Managing Editor, Publication: Joanna Grimes
Director, Meetings: Gail E. Mutnik
E-Mail: gmutnik@aacc.org
Vice President, Policy and Programming: Pamela Nash
E-Mail: pnash@aacc.org
Program Director, Government Affairs: Vince Stine

Historical Note
Incorporated in New York in 1949. Formerly (Jan. 1, 1976) American Association of Clinical Chemists. Members are chemists, physicians and other scientists specializing in clinical chemistry. Provides educational and professional development services to its members in order to improve the level at which chemistry is practiced in chemical laboratories. Membership: $185/year (full); $110/year (affiliate); $25/year (student.

Meetings/Conferences:
Annual Meetings: *Summer*
2007 - San Diego, CA/July 15-19
2008 - Washington, DC/July 27-31
2009 - Chicago, IL/July 19-23
2010 - Anaheim, CA/July 25-29

Publications:
Clinical Chemistry Journal. m. adv.
Clinical Laboratory News. m. adv.
Clinical and Forensic Toxicology News. q.
AACC News. bi-m.
Endocrinology & Metabolism. m.
Therapeutic Drug Monitoring & Toxicology. m.
Clinical Laboratory Strategies. m.
Market News. q.
Government Affairs Update. m.

American Association for Continuity of Care
(1982)
638 Prospect Ave.
Hartford, CT 06105
Tel: (860)586-7525 *Fax:* (860)586-7550
Members: 400 individuals
Staff: 1
Annual Budget: $100-250,000
Contact: Christine G. Leyden
E-Mail: cagleyden@aol.com

Historical Note
Incorporated in Washington, DC, AACC members are multi-disciplinary professionals involved in developing continuity of care, hospital discharge and home health care. Membership: $90/year (individual); $175-750/year (organization).

Publications:
Directory. a. adv.

American Association for Correctional and Forensic Psychology *(1953)*
c/o Central Coast Consultancy
897 Oak Park Blvd., Suite 124
Pismo Beach, CA 93449
Tel: (805)489-0665
E-Mail: pres@eaacp.org
Web Site: www.aa4cfp.org/cgi-bin/index.pl
Members: 250 individuals
Annual Budget: $25-50,000
President and Program Chairperson: John L. Gannon, Ph.D.

Historical Note
Affiliate of the American Correctional Association. Members of the AACFP are involved in criminal justice in a variety of ways - through administration, practice, teaching and research. The purpose of the association is to bring together behavorial scientists interested in the psychology of crime, to promote the development of psychological practice in criminal justice and law enforcement settings, and to stimulate research into the nature of criminal behavior. Membership: $45/year; $30/year (student).

Meetings/Conferences:
Annual Meetings: *Summer with American Correctional Ass'n*

Publications:
The Correctional Psychologist. q. adv.
Criminal Justice and Behavior Journal. q. adv.

American Association for Crystal Growth *(1968)*
25 Fourth St.
Somerville, NJ 08876
Tel: (908)575-0649 *Fax:* (908)575-0794
E-Mail: aacg@att.net
Web Site: www.crystalgrowth.org
Members: 600 individuals
Staff: 1
Annual Budget: $50-100,000
Executive Administrator: Laura A. Bonner
E-Mail: aacg@att.net

Historical Note
Formerly (1970) American Committee for Crystal Growth. Members include engineers, scientists, educators, technologists, marketing representatives and students, all with a strong interest in one or more facets of the crystal growth field. Affiliated with the International Organization for Crystal Growth. Membership: $50/year (individual); $20/year (student); $500/year (corporate affiliation).

Meetings/Conferences:
Annual Meetings: *Summer*
2007 - Salt Lake City, UT/Aug. 12-17

Publications:
AAGC Newsletter. 3/year. adv.

American Association for Dental Research *(1952)*
1619 Duke St.
Alexandria, VA 22314-3406
Tel: (703)548-0066 *Fax:* (703)548-1883
E-Mail: research@iadr.org
Web Site: www.dentalresearch.org
Members: 5000 individuals
Staff: 16
Annual Budget: $1-2,000,000
Executive Director: Christopher Fox, D.M.D., MP
Director, Meetings: Gwynn Breckenridge
Director, Publications: Linda Hemphill
Director, Marketing and Membership: Denise Setuff
Director, Finance: Darin Walsh

Historical Note
A division of International Association for Dental Research. Membership: $177/year (individual); $500-4,000/year (company).

Meetings/Conferences:
Annual Meetings: *Spring/6,000*

Publications:
Critical Reviews in Oral Biology and Medicine. m. adv.
Journal of Dental Reseach. m. adv.
Advances in Dental Research. q.

American Association for Employment in Education *(1934)*
3040 Riverside Dr., Suite 125
Columbus, OH 43221
Tel: (614)485-1111 *Fax:* (614)485-9609
E-Mail: aaee@osu.edu
Web Site: www.aaee.org
Members: 1000 institutions
Staff: 2
Annual Budget: $250-500,000
Executive Director: B.J. Bryant
E-Mail: aaee@osu.edu

Historical Note
Formerly (1934) National Institutional Teacher Placement Association and (1962) Association for School, College and University Staffing. Members are university career center directors and school system human resources administrators. Membership: $180/year (institution).

Meetings/Conferences:
Annual Meetings: *November*

Publications:
Teacher Supply and Demand Report in the U.S. a.
Directory of Public School Systems in the U.S.. a.
The Job Search Handbook for Educators. a.

Guide to Services & Activities for Teacher Employment. a.
National Directory for Employment in Education. a.
National Directory of Job and Career Fairs for Educators. a.

American Association for Fuel Cells *(1992)*

Historical Note
A project of the American Hydrogen Ass'n, which provides administrative support.

American Association for Functional Orthodontics *(1984)*
106 S. Kent St.
Winchester, VA 22601
Tel: (540)662-2200 *Fax:* (540)665-8910
Toll Free: (800)441 - 3850
E-Mail: aafo@adelphia.net
Web Site: www.aafo.org
Members: 2100 individuals
Staff: 4
Annual Budget: $250-500,000
Executive Director: Rachele M. Riley

Historical Note
An independent association of orthodontists, pedodontists, and general dentists from throughout the U.S., Canada, and over 20 foreign countries with interests in functional appliance treatment and TMJ therapy. Membership: $295/year.

Publications:
AAFO Members' Directory. bi-a.
The Functional Orthodontist. q. adv.

American Association for Geodetic Surveying *(1981)*

Historical Note
A member organization of the American Congress on Surveying and Mapping.

American Association for Geriatric Psychiatry *(1978)*
7910 Woodmont Ave., Suite 1050
Bethesda, MD 20814-3004
Tel: (301)654-7850 *Fax:* (301)654-4137
Web Site: www.aagponline.org
Members: 2000 individuals
Staff: 17
Annual Budget: $2-5,000,000
Executive Director: Christine M. DeVries
E-Mail: cdevries@aagponline.org
Director, Finance and Administration: Bellinda D'Agostino
Senior Director, Education and Research: Jeanine Rowe
E-Mail: jrowe@aagponline.org
Director, Governance: Carrie Stankiewicz
Director, Government Relations: Marjorie W. Vanderbilt

Historical Note
An organization of psychiatrists interested in aging. Purpose is to promote better understanding and care of the mental health of the elderly. Membership: $210/year (general member); $65/year (member-in-training).

Meetings/Conferences:
Annual Meetings:

Publications:
Membership Directory. a. adv.
AAGP Newsletter. bi-m. adv.
American Journal of Geriatric Psychiatry. bi-w. adv.

American Association for Hand Surgery *(1970)*
20 N. Michigan Ave., Suite 700
Chicago, IL 60602
Tel: (312)236-3307 *Fax:* (312)782-0553
E-Mail: contact@handsurgery.org
Web Site: www.handsurgery.org
Members: 1081 individuals
Staff: 4
Annual Budget: $500-1,000,000
Executive Director: Laura Downes Leeper, CAE
Meetings Manager: Rachel Elliott

Historical Note
AAHS members are hand surgeons in the disciplines of plastic, orthopaedic, and general surgery, and hand therapists. AAHS evolved from the Joseph L. Posch Hand Society which originally met in 1967, an alumnus group of hand surgeons who trained under Dr. Posch in Detroit, Michigan. Membership: $375/year (physician); $125/year (therapist).

Meetings/Conferences:
Annual Meetings: Winter

Publications:
Membership Roster. a.
Newsletter. q.

American Association for Health Education *(1937)*
1900 Association Dr.
Reston, VA 20191
Tel: (703)476-3437 *Fax:* (703)476-6638
Toll Free: (800)213 - 7193 Ext: 437
E-Mail: aahe@aahperd.org
Web Site: www.aahe.info.org
Members: 7500 individuals
Staff: 4
Annual Budget: $250-500,000
Executive Director: Becky J. Smith, Ph.D.
E-Mail: aahe@aahperd.org

Historical Note
Formerly (1996) the Association for the Advancement of Health Education. Until 1974 a division of the American Alliance for Health, Physical Education and Recreation, AAHE is now an independent member of the American Alliance for Health, Physical Education, Recreation and Dance. Membership: $125/year.

Meetings/Conferences:
Annual Meetings: With AAHPERD.
2007 – Baltimore, MD(Convention Center)/March 13-17/5000
2008 – Ft. Worth, TX(Convention Center)/Apr. 8-12/5000
2009 – Tampa, FL(Convention Center)/March 31-Apr. 4
2010 – Indianapolis, IN(Convention Center)/March 16-20/5000

Publications:
HE-XTRA. 4/year. adv.
American Journal of Health Education. bi-m. adv.
International Electronic Journal of Health Education (online). adv.

American Association for Health Freedom *(1992)*
4620 Lee Hwy.
Suite 210
Arlington, VA 22207
Tel: (703)294-6244 *Fax:* (703)624-6380
Toll Free: (800)230 - 2762
E-Mail: healthfreedom2000@yahoo.com
Web Site: www.healthfreedom.net
Members: 350 individuals
Staff: 4
Annual Budget: $250-500,000
Executive Director: Brenna Hill
E-Mail: healthfreedom2000@yahoo.com

Historical Note
Founded as American Preventive Medical Association; assumed its current name in 2001. Members are primarily health care practitioners who use complementary therapies, nutritional supplements or other alternatives to allopathic medicine; supplement manufacturers; and other individuals or businesses involved in the preventive health care industry. Membership: $350/year (professional); $165/year (associate); $100/year (consumer).

Publications:
Eye on Health Freedom Newsletter. m.

American Association for Homecare *(1982)*
625 Slaters Ln.
Suite 200
Alexandria, VA 22314-1171
Tel: (703)836-6263 *Fax:* (703)836-6730
E-Mail: info@aahomecare.org
Web Site: www.aahomecare.org
Members: 800 companies
Staff: 14
Annual Budget: $2-5,000,000
Chief Operating Officer: Sue Mairena
Vice President, Government Affairs: Walter Gorski
Director, Federal Policy: Ann Howard
Director, Education and Meetings: Kim Kianka
Senior Director, Membership and Database Operations: Melva E. Mazur
Director, Membership Sales: Tucker Ophof
E-Mail: tuckero@aahomecare.org
Vice President, Communications: Michael Reinemer

Historical Note
AAHomecare was formed in February 2000 by the merger of three nat'l associations - Home Health Services and Staffing Association (HHSSA), Health Industry Distributors Association (HIDA), and Nat'l Assn for Medical Equipment Services (NAMES). In December 2001, the American Homecare Association joined the new organization. AAHomecare represents companies and practitioners across the spectrum of healthcare practice. Membership fee varies, based on revenue.

Publications:
AA Homecare Update. w.
Financial Performance Survey. a.
Associate Member Directory. a.

American Association for Laboratory Accreditation *(1978)*
5301 Buckeystown Pike, Suite 350
Frederick, MD 21704
Tel: (301)644-3248 *Fax:* (301)662-2974
Web Site: www.a2la.org
Members: 1700 laboratories and individuals
Staff: 34
Annual Budget: $5-10,000,000
President: Peter S. Unger
Manager, Financial: Lisa C. Drake
Vice President: Roxanne M. Robinson
Manager, Business Development: Philip Smith

Historical Note
Members are interested in establishing and maintaining quality laboratory testing by accrediting laboratories. Accreditation is available to all laboratories meeting the requirements of ISO/IEC 17025 (2005) whether they are owned by private companies or government bodies. A2LA has over 1,700 accreditations in 46 states and 15 foreign countries. Membership does not imply accreditation. Membership: $50/year (individual); $100/year (institution); $200/year (organization).

Publications:
A2LA News. q.
A2LA Annual Report. a.
General Requirements for Accreditation. bien.

American Association for Laboratory Animal Science *(1950)*
9190 Crestwyn Hills Dr.
Memphis, TN 38125-8538
Tel: (901)754-8620 *Fax:* (901)753-0046
E-Mail: info@aalas.org
Web Site: www.aalas.org
Members: 11300 individuals
Staff: 30
Annual Budget: $2-5,000,000
Executive Director: Ann T. Turner, Ph.D., CAE
Director, Meetings and Financial Services: Betty Cartwright
Director, Education and Prof. Development: Nicole Duffee
Associate Executive Director and Director, Member Services: Judith S. Grisamore
Director, Communications and Marketing: Chris Lyons

Historical Note
Founded in 1950 and incorporated in Illinois in 1953 as the Animal Care Panel. Assumed its present name in 1966. Members are individuals professionally concerned with the production, care and study of laboratory animals.

Meetings/Conferences:
Annual Meetings: October-November
2007 – Charlotte, NC(Convention Center)/Oct. 14-18/4000
2008 – Indianapolis, IN/Nov. 9-13
2009 – Denver, CO/Nov. 8-12
2010 – Atlanta, GA/Oct. 10-14
2011 – San Diego, CA/Oct. 2-6

Publications:
AALAS Contemporary Topics. bi-m. adv.
Comparative Medicine. bi-m. adv.
Tech Talk. bi-m.
AALAS in Action. bi-m.

American Association for Leisure and Recreation *(1938)*

Historical Note

Merged (2005) with American Association for Active Lifestyle and Fitness to become American Association for Physical Activity and Recreation.

American Association for Marriage and Family Therapy *(1942)*

112 S. Alfred St.
Alexandria, VA 22314-3061
Tel: (703)838-9808 *Fax:* (703)838-9805
E-Mail: central@aamft.org
Web Site: www.aamft.org
Members: 23000 individuals
Staff: 30
Annual Budget: $2-5,000,000
Executive Director: Michael Bowers
E-Mail: central@aamft.org

Historical Note

Founded as American Association of Marriage Counselors; became American Association of Marriage and Family Counselors in 1970 and assumed its present name in 1978. Members are clinical therapists specially trained to conduct marriage and family therapy with individuals, couples and families. Includes 55 regional divisions in the U.S. and Canada, with members around the world. Membership: $168/year, plus state division dues.

Meetings/Conferences:

Annual Meetings: Fall

Publications:

Family Therapy magazine. bi-m. adv.
Journal of Marital and Family Therapy. q.

American Association for Medical Transcription *(1978)*

100 Sycamore Ave.
Modesto, CA 95354
Tel: (209)527-9620 *Fax:* (209)527-9633
Toll Free: (800)982 - 2182
E-Mail: aamt@aamt.org
Web Site: www.aamt.org
Members: 7500 individuals
Staff: 17
Annual Budget: $2-5,000,000
Executive Director: Peter Preziosi, Ph.D., CAE
Director, Communications: Lea Minkley-Sims

Historical Note

AAMT is a professional association for medical transcriptionists, supervisors, teachers, students, and other interested health personnel. Awards the "CMT" (Certified Medical Transcriptionist) designation by voluntary examination. Membership: $135/year (individual); $400/year (institution).

Meetings/Conferences:

Annual Meetings: August

Publications:

Plexus (Members Only). bi-m. adv.
AAMT Vitals (Members Only). w. adv.
Journal of the American Ass'n for Medical Transcription. bi-m. adv.

American Association for Paralegal Education *(1981)*

19 Mantua Rd.
Mt. Royal, NJ 08061-1006
Tel: (856)423-2829 *Fax:* (856)423-3420
E-Mail: info@aafpe.org
Web Site: www.aafpe.org
Members: 450institutionsandindividuals
Staff: 2
Annual Budget: $250-500,000
Executive Director: Meridyth M. Senes

Historical Note

Formerly (1981) American Association of Paralegal Educators. Members are institutions and individuals who provide training or continuing education to paralegals. Membership: $75/year (individual); $225/year (institution/sustaining/associate).

Meetings/Conferences:

Annual Meetings: Fall

Publications:

The Paralegal Educator. 3 times/yr. adv.
Newsletter. 3 times/yr.
Membership Directory. a. adv.

American Association for Pediatric Ophthalmology and Strabismus *(1974)*

P.O. Box 193832
San Francisco, CA 94119-3832
Tel: (415)561-8505 *Fax:* (415)561-8531
E-Mail: aapos@aao.org
Web Site: www.aapos.org
Members: 900 individuals
Staff: 3
Annual Budget: $100-250,000
Manager: Denise DeLosada Wilson

Historical Note

AAPOS supports eye surgeons and physicians concerned with amblyopia, strabismus, and other eye disorders affecting children ans adults. Membership: $300/year.

Publications:

Strabismus. bi-m. adv.
Journal of the American Ass'n for Pediatric Ophthalmology.

American Association for Public Opinion Research *(1946)*

P.O. Box 14263
Lenexa, KS 66285-4263
Tel: (913)310-0118 *Fax:* (913)599-5340
E-Mail: aapor-info@oamp.com
Web Site: www.aapor.org
Members: 1850 individuals
Staff: 5
Annual Budget: $100-250,000
Executive Coordinator: Michael Flanagan, CAE

Historical Note

Founded at a meeting at the Opera House in Central City, CO on July 29-31, 1946. AAPOR members are individuals engaged or interested in the methods and applications of public opinion and social research. Membership: $15-90/year.

Meetings/Conferences:

2007 - Anaheim, CA(Hyatt Regency Orange County)/May 16-20/900
2008 - New Orleans, LA(Sheraton New Orleans)/May 14-18/900

Publications:

Public Opinion Quarterly. q.
AAPOR News. 2/year.

American Association for Respiratory Care *(1947)*

9425 N. MacArthur Blvd., Suite 100
Irving, TX 75063-4706
Tel: (972)243-2272 *Fax:* (972)484-2720
Web Site: www.aarc.org
Members: 36000 individuals
Staff: 35
Annual Budget: $5-10,000,000
Executive Director: Sam P. Giordano
E-Mail: giordano@aarc.org

Historical Note

A professional organization of respiratory care personnel formed in Chicago and incorporated in the State of Illinois in 1947; assumed the name American Association for Inhalation Therapists in 1954; American Association for Inhalation Therapy in 1967; American Association for Respiratory Therapy in 1973; and its present name in 1986. Sponsored by the American College of Chest Physicians, the American Society of Anaesthesiologists and the American Thoracic Society In 1989, AARC conducted the nationwide survey of airplane passengers which led to a complete ban of smoking on commercial airline flights in the U.S. Sponsors and supports the AARC Political Action Committee. Has an annual budget of approximately $6 million. Membership: $60/year.

Meetings/Conferences:

Annual Meetings: Late Fall/6,000

Publications:

AARC Report. m.
AARC Times. m. adv.
Respiratory Care. m. adv.

American Association for State and Local History *(1940)*

1717 Church St.
Nashville, TN 37203-2991
Tel: (615)320-3203 *Fax:* (615)327-9013
E-Mail: membership@aaslh.org
Web Site: www.aaslh.org
Members: 6000 individuals & institutions
Staff: 8
Annual Budget: $1-2,000,000
President and Chief Executive Officer: Terry Davis
E-Mail: davis@asslh.org
Manager, Membership: Gina Sawyer
E-Mail: sawyer@aaslh.org
Director, Finance: Risa Woodward
E-Mail: woodward@aaslh.org

Historical Note

Formerly the Council of Historical Societies. Absorbed the Association of Historic Sites Officials in 1963. An organization of individuals and groups interested in promoting the study of state and local history in the U.S. and Canada. Membership: $60-250/year (individual); $30/year (student); $200/year, minimum (institution).

Meetings/Conferences:

Annual Meetings: Annual
2007 - Atlanta, GA(Omni Hotel)/Sept. 5-8

Publications:

History News. q. adv.
Dispatch Newsletter. m. adv.

American Association for the Advancement of Science *(1848)*

1200 New York Ave. NW
Washington, DC 20005
Tel: (202)326-6400 *Fax:* (202)789-0455
E-Mail: webmaster@aaas.org
Web Site: www.aaas.org
Members: 120000 individuals
Staff: 300
Annual Budget: $5-10,000,000
Chief Executive Officer: Alan I. Leshner
Chief Financial Officer: Phil Blair
Executive Director: Richard S. Nicholson
Senior Manager, Meetings, Marketing, Operations: Jill Perla

Historical Note

Founded in September, 1848 in Philadelphia with 461 charter members, AAAS was incorporated in Massachusetts in 1874. An umbrella association, the AAAS has nearly 300 affiliates-societies, academies and other organizations which effectively comprise the whole spectrum of U.S. science and engineering. Membership: $92/year (individual); $50/year (student).

Meetings/Conferences:

Annual Meetings: Winter/10000

2007 - San Francisco, CA/Feb. 15-19

Publications:

Science.

American Association for the Advancement of Slavic Studies *(1948)*

Harvard Univ., Third Floor
Eight Story St.
Cambridge, MA 02138-1205
Tel: (617)495-0677 *Fax:* (617)495-0680
E-Mail: aaass@fas.harvard.edu
Web Site: www.fas.harvard.edu/~aaass
Members: 4000 individuals
Staff: 5
Annual Budget: $500-1,000,000
Executive Director: Dmitry P. Gorenburg, PhD
Editor: Jolanta Davis
Comptroller: Galina Shaumyan
Convention Coordinator: Wendy Walker

Historical Note

Seeks to advance scholarly study, publication, and teaching relating to the former Soviet Union and Eastern Europe. Membership: $25-85/year, based on annual income (individual); $25/year (affiliate).

Meetings/Conferences:

Annual Meetings: Fall
2007 - New Orleans, LA(Marriott)/Nov. 15-18

Publications:

Newsnet Newsletter. 5/year. adv.
Slavic Review. q. adv.
Membership Directory.

American Association for the History of Medicine *(1925)*
c/o Department of Medical Humanities
East Carolina University, Brody School of Medicine
Greenville, NC 27858-4354
Tel: (252)744-2797 *Fax:* (252)744-2319
Web Site: www.histmed.org
Members: 1300 individuals
Annual Budget: $50-100,000
Secretary-Treasurer: Todd L. Savitt, Ph.D.
E-Mail: savittt@mail.ecu.edu

Historical Note
AAHM is a volunteer organization whose members include physicians and practitioners of other health sciences, professional historians, laboratory scientists, librarians, and individuals from other disciplines. Incorporated in New York in 1958. Membership: $70/year (individual); $80/year (organization/company).

Meetings/Conferences:
Annual Meetings: Spring

Publications:
Bulletin of the History of Medicine. q. adv.
Research in Progress. bien.
Membership Directory. bien.
AAHM Newsletter. 3/year.

American Association for the History of Nursing *(1980)*
P.O. Box 175
Lanoka Harbor, NJ 08734-0175
Tel: (609)693-7250 *Fax:* (609)693-1037
E-Mail: aahn@aahn.org
Web Site: www.aahn.org
Members: 500 individuals
Staff: 1
Annual Budget: $25-50,000
Executive Secretary: Janet L. Fickeissen
E-Mail: aahn@aahn.org

Historical Note
Members are individuals with an interest in the history of nursing. Membership: $100/year (regular); $150/year (agency); $50/year (student/retiree).

Meetings/Conferences:
Annual Meetings: Fall

Publications:
Nursing History Review. a.
Bulletin of AAHN. q. adv.

American Association for the Study of Hungarian History *(1970)*
Dept. of Admin. & Econ./Coll. of Professional Studies
St. Johns Univ., 8000 Utopia Pkwy.
Jamaica, NY 11439
Tel: (718)990-6161 Ext: 7438 *Fax:* (718)990-1882
Web Site: http://www2.h-net.msu.edu/~habsweb/aashh.htm
Members: 140 individuals
Annual Budget: under $10,000
Secretary-Treasurer: Susan Glanz
E-Mail: glanzs@stjohns.edu

Historical Note
AASHH members are academics specializing in the history of Hungary. Purpose is to further interest in Hungarian history and to encourage research in this field. The association also aims to cooperate with scholars and institutions with similar interests in Hungary. Organizes panels for participation at scholarly conferences. Has no paid officers or full-time staff. Membership: $10/year.

Meetings/Conferences:
Annual Meetings: in conjunction with the AHA & AAASS annual meetings

Publications:
AASHH Newsletter. q.

American Association for the Study of Liver Diseases *(1949)*
1729 King St., Suite 200
Alexandria, VA 22314
Tel: (703)299-9766 *Fax:* (703)299-9622
E-Mail: aasld@aasld.org
Web Site: www.aasld.org
Members: 2600 individuals
Staff: 22
Annual Budget: $5-10,000,000
Executive Director: Sherrie Cathcart
E-Mail: scathcart@aasld.org

Historical Note
Membership: $240/year.

Publications:
Directory. m.
Hepatology. m. adv.
Liver Transplantation. adv.
Newsletter. q.

American Association for the Surgery of Trauma *(1938)*
Department of Surgery, UMPC
P.O. Box 7533
Pittsburgh, PA 15213
Tel: (412)647-4848 *Fax:* (412)647-3247
E-Mail: peitzmanab@msx.umpc.edu
Web Site: www.aast.org
Members: 900
Staff: 1
Annual Budget: $500-1,000,000
Secretary-Treasurer: Andrew Peitzman, M.D.
E-Mail: peitzmanab@msx.umpc.edu

Historical Note
Organized June 14, 1938 in San Francisco. Promotes advancement of the surgical care of injured patients. Membership: $250/year.

Publications:
Journal of Trauma. m. adv.

American Association for Therapeutic Humor *(1987)*
247 East Front St.
Trenton, NJ 08540-6627
Tel: (609)392-0200 *Fax:* (609)392-0244
E-Mail: staff@aath.org
Web Site: www.aath.org
Members: 500 individuals
Staff: 1
Annual Budget: $10-25,000
President: Lenny David

Historical Note
Members are healthcare providers and others interested in the therapeutic aspects of humor. Membership: $50/year (individual).

Publications:
Laugh It Up Newsletter. bi-m.

American Association for Thoracic Surgery *(1917)*
900 Cummings Center, Suite 221-U
Beverly, MA 01915
Tel: (978)927-8330 *Fax:* (978)524-8890
Web Site: www.aats.org
Members: 1200 individuals
Executive Director: Robert P. Jones, Jr., Ed.D.

Historical Note
Organized in New York City in 1917.

Meetings/Conferences:
Annual Meetings: Spring/2,500

Publications:
Journal of Thoracic and Cardiovascular Surgery. m. adv.
Operative Techniques in Thoracic and Cardiovascular Surgery. q. adv.
Seminars in Thoracic and Cardiovascular Surgery. q. adv.
Pediatric Cardiac Surgery Annual. a. adv.

American Association for Vascular Surgery *(1952)*

Historical Note
Merged with Society for Vascular Surgery in 2003.

American Association for Vocational Instructional Materials *(1949)*
220 Smithonia Rd.
Winterville, GA 30683-9527
Tel: (706)742-5355 *Fax:* (706)742-7005
Toll Free: (800)228 - 4689
Web Site: www.aavim.com
Members: 6 U.S. states
Staff: 4
Annual Budget: $250-500,000
Director: Gary Farmer
E-Mail: gary@aavim.com

Historical Note
AAVIM is a consortium of states whose purpose is the development, publication and distribution of instructional materials (manuals, teacher keys, computer software, videos) in the areas of agriscience, technology education and consumer and life science education. Membership: $4,000/year.

Publications:
AAVIM Catalog. a.
PBTE Catalog. a.

American Association for Women in Community Colleges *(1973)*
P.O. Box 336603
Greeley, CO 80633-0611
Tel: (970)352-2079 *Fax:* (970)352-2080
E-Mail: aawcc@comcast.net
Web Site: www.aims.edu/aawcc
Members: 2000 individuals
Staff: 1
Annual Budget: $100-250,000
Vice President, Finances: Dr. Linda Myers
Vice President, Communications: Dr. Cheryl B. Crutcher
E-Mail: cheryl.crutcher@smcmail.maricopa.edu

Historical Note
Formerly (1993) American Association of Women in Community and Junior Colleges. AAWCC members are women faculty, administrators, staff members, trustees, students and others concerned with women's issues, programs and professional development in the community, junior or technical college setting. Membership: dues based on income (individual); $300/year (institution).

Meetings/Conferences:
Annual Meetings: Spring
2007 – Tampa, FL(Tampa Convention Center)/Apr. 14-17

Publications:
AAWCC Quarterly. q.

American Association for Women Podiatrists *(1965)*
1506 E. Franklin St., Suite 104
Chapel Hill, NC 27514
Tel: (919)960-8858 *Fax:* (919)960-2882
E-Mail: Jander1130@aol.com
Web Site: www.aawpinc.com/
Members: 800 individuals
Annual Budget: $25-50,000
President: Jane Anderson, DPM

Historical Note
Members must be members of the American Podiatric Medical Association. Maintains no paid staff. Membership: $75/year (individual).

Meetings/Conferences:
Annual Meetings: August, in conjunction with the American Podiatric Medical Association

Publications:
AAWP Newsletter. q. adv.

American Association for Women Radiologists *(1981)*
4550 Post Oak Place, Suite 342
Houston, TX 77027
Tel: (713)965-0566 *Fax:* (713)960-0488
E-Mail: admin@aawr.org
Web Site: www.aawr.org
Members: 2000 individuals
Staff: 2
Annual Budget: $25-50,000
Associate Account Executive: Angela Mason
E-Mail: admin@aawr.org

Historical Note
AAWR addresses concerns of women radiologists. AAWR promotes participation of women in other radiological organizations, encourages scientific advancement, and serves as a networking group. Formerly (1991) American Association of Women Radiologists. Membership: $125/year.

Publications:
Membership Directory. a.
AAWR Focus. q.

American Association of Advertising Agencies *(1917)*

405 Lexington Ave., 18th Floor
New York, NY 10174-1801
Tel: (212)682-2500 *Fax:* (212)682-8391
Toll Free: (800)536 - 7346
Web Site: www.aaaa.org
Members: 1200 companies
Staff: 80
Annual Budget: $10-25,000,000
President and Chief Executive Officer: O. Burtch Drake
Vice President and Director, Public Affairs: Kipp Cheng
Executive Vice President: Michael D. Donahue
Senior Vice President, Agency Relations and Membership: Harley M. Griffiths
Executive Vice President and Chief Financial Officer: James C. Martucci, Jr.
Senior Vice President, Conferences and Special Events: Karen A. Proctor, CMP

Historical Note
Maintains branch offices in San Francisco, CA, Charlotte, NC, and Washington, DC. Has an annual budget of approximately $15 million. Membership dues based on members' gross income.

Meetings/Conferences:
Annual Meetings: Spring

Publications:
Roster and Organization. adv.
The Reporter newsletter. bi-m.

American Association of Airport Executives *(1928)*
601 Madison St., Suite 400
Alexandria, VA 22314
Tel: (703)824-0500 *Fax:* (703)820-1395
Web Site: www.airportnet.org
Members: 4500 individuals
Staff: 70
Annual Budget: $2-5,000,000
President: Charles M. Barclay, AAE
E-Mail: charles.barclay@airportnet.org
Senior Vice President, Communications: Joan Lowden
E-Mail: joan.lowden@airportnet.org
Staff Vice President, Meetings: Jacky Sher Raker
E-Mail: jacky.sher@airportnet.org

Historical Note
A professional organization of individuals concerned with the management, operation and construction of civil airports. Awards the "A.A.E." (Accredited Airport Executive) designation. Sponsors and supports the AAAE Good Government Committee. Membership: $225/year (individual); $475/year (company/organization).

Publications:
Airport Report. bi-w.
Airport Magazine. bi-m.
Airport Report Express. 2/week.

American Association of Anatomists *(1888)*
9650 Rockville Pike, Suite 2408
Bethesda, MD 20814-3998
Tel: (301)634-7910 *Fax:* (301)634-7965
Web Site: http://anatomy.org
Members: 1800 individuals
Staff: 4
Annual Budget: $500-1,000,000
Executive Director: Andrea Pendleton
E-Mail: apendleton@anatomy.org

Historical Note
Established September 17, 1888 at Georgetown University, Washington, DC as the Association of American Anatomists. Name changed in 1908 to American Association of Anatomists. Incorporated in New York in 1947. Regular membership: $120/year; includes one journal.

Meetings/Conferences:
Annual Meetings: in conjunction with FASEB experimental biology meeting/Spring

Publications:
Anatomical Record. m. adv.
Developmental Dynamics. m. adv.
The New Anatomist. bi-m. adv.

American Association of Attorney-Certified Public Accountants *(1964)*
3921 Old Lee Hwy., Suite 71-A
Fairfax, VA 22030
Tel: (703)352-8064 *Fax:* (703)352-8073
E-Mail: info@attorney-cpa.com
Web Site: www.attorney-cpa.com
Members: 1400 individuals
Staff: 3
Annual Budget: $250-500,000
Executive Director: Clark Mulligan
E-Mail: info@attorney-cpa.com

Historical Note
Members are individuals "dually licensed" as both lawyer and CPA. Membership: $105/year, first two years; $210/year thereafter.

Meetings/Conferences:
Semi-annual meetings: Spring and Fall
2007 - Lake Tahoe, CA(Squaw Valley Resort)/June 23-29
2008 - Amelia Island, FL(Ritz-Carlton)/June 22-28

Publications:
Membership Directory. a. adv.
The Attorney-CPA. 4/year. adv.

American Association of Automatic Door Manufacturers *(1994)*
1300 Sumner Ave.
Cleveland, OH 44115-2851
Tel: (216)241-7333 *Fax:* (216)241-0105
E-Mail: aaadm@aaadm.com
Web Site: www.aaadm.com
Members: 13 companies
Staff: 3
Annual Budget: $50-100,000
Executive Director: John H. Addington

Historical Note
AAADM is a trade association of power operated automatic door manufacturers as defined and governed by ANSI/BHMA A156.10. The association promotes product safety by establishing uniform programs for training and certification of installers and service providers as well as inspection of installations. Membership: $10,250/year (company).

Meetings/Conferences:
Semi-Annual Meetings: Spring and Fall

American Association of Avian Pathologists *(1957)*
953 College Station Rd.
Athens, GA 30602-4875
Tel: (706)542-5645
E-Mail: aaap@uga.edu
Web Site: www.aaap.info
Members: 1000 individuals
Staff: 2
Annual Budget: $100-250,000
Secretary-Treasurer: Dr. Charles L. Hofacre

Historical Note
Affiliated with the American Veterinary Medical Association. Veterinarians specializing in poultry and their diseases. Membership: $110-130/year (individual).

Meetings/Conferences:
Annual Meetings: July, with the American Veterinary Medical Ass'n

Publications:
Avian Diseases. q. adv.
Directory. a.

American Association of Bank Directors *(1989)*
4701 Sangamore Rd.
Suite P15
Bethesda, MD 20816
Tel: (301)263-9841 *Fax:* (301)229-2443
E-Mail: info@aabd.org
Web Site: www.aabd.org
Executive Director: David Baris
E-Mail: dbaris@aabd.org

Historical Note
AABD represents bank and savings institution directors, providing educational programs, advocacy before the congress and federal banking agencies, and other services to its members. Membership: $695/year (directors); $795/year (associates).

Publications:
Course Guide-Institute for Bank Director Education. q.
Informational Booklet Series. q.
Newsletter. q.
Bank Director News. q.

American Association of Behavioral Therapists *(1987)*
c/o Bennett/Stellar University
2696 Mission Blvd.
San Diego, CA 92109-8272
Toll Free: (888)432 - 1122
Members: 1000 individuals
Annual Budget: $25-50,000
President: Dan J. Allen, Ph.D

Historical Note
Members are therapists and counselors who use behavioral science techniques, such as biofeedback, hypnosis, conditioned learning, and behavior modification to effect positive changes for improved mental health, habit control and personal improvement. Membership: $45/year.

Publications:
The Therapist Report. q.
Nat'l Directory of Behavioral Therapists. a.
Special Reports. irreg.

American Association of Bioanalysts *(1956)*
906 Olive St., Suite 1200
St. Louis, MO 63101-1434
Tel: (314)241-1445 *Fax:* (314)241-1449
E-Mail: aab@aab.org
Web Site: www.aab.org
Members: 4000 individuals
Annual Budget: $500-1,000,000
Administrator: Mark S. Birenbaum, Ph.D.

Historical Note
AAB was formed by a merger of the Council of American Bioanalysts (founded in 1953) and the National Association of Clinical Laboratories (founded in 1949). Merged with the International Society for Clinical Laboratory Technology in 1999. Members are directors, owners, managers, and supervisors of medical laboratories concerned with improving laboratory testing and procedures. Membership: $225/year (directors, owners); $75/year (managers, supervisors). AMS members include laboratory technologists and technicians.

Meetings/Conferences:
Annual Meetings: Summer
2007 - Orlando, FL(Rosen Centre Hotel)/May 17-19

Publications:
The AAB Bulletin. q. adv.
The AAB Update. irreg.

American Association of Birth Centers *(1983)*
3123 Gottschall Rd.
Perkiomenville, PA 18074-9546
Tel: (215)234-8068 *Fax:* (215)234-8829
E-Mail: aabc@birthcenters.org
Web Site: www.BirthCenters.org
Members: 300 individuals
Staff: 2
Annual Budget: $250-500,000
Executive Director: Kate Bauer
E-Mail: aabc@birthcenters.org

Historical Note
AABC (formerly NACC) is a not-for-profit membership organization which is a comprehensive resource on birth centers. Working on public and policy levels in government, industry and the health professions, AABC is dedicated to developing quality, holistic services for childbearing families that promote self-reliance and confidence in birth and parenting. AABC collects and disseminates information on birth centers. It sets national standards for birth center operations, promotes state regulations for licensure, and national accreditation by the Commission for the Accreditation of Birth Centers. Provides a Parent Information Service for consumers looking for birth centers. Membership: $25-135/year (individual); $400-1,200/year (organization/company).

Meetings/Conferences:
Annual Meetings: September-October
2007 - Anchorage, AK(Marriott)/Oct. 3-8/200

Publications:
NACC News. 3/year.
Membership Directory. a.

American Association of Blacks in Energy *(1977)*
927 15th St. NW

Suite 200
Washington, DC 20005-2304
Tel: (202)371-9530 *Fax:* (202)371-9218
Toll Free: (800)466 - 0204
E-Mail: aabe@aabe.org
Web Site: www.aabe.org
Members: 1200 individuals
Staff: 3
Annual Budget: $500-1,000,000
President: Robert L. Hill
E-Mail: bhill@aabe.org

Historical Note
AABE is a national association of energy professionals who are dedicated to include African American and other minorities into the discussion and development of energy policies, regulations, research and development technologies and environmental issues. Membership: $100/year (individual).

Publications:
Annual Report. bien.
AABE Energy News. q.

American Association of Botanical Gardens and Arboreta

Historical Note
Became American Public Gardens Association in 2005.

American Association of Bovine Practitioners *(1965)*
P.O. Box 3610
Auburn, AL 30162-1755
Tel: (334)821-0442 *Fax:* (334)821-9532
Toll Free: (800)269 - 2227
E-Mail: aapbhq@aabp.org
Web Site: www.aabp.org
Members: 6200 individuals
Staff: 3
Annual Budget: $500-1,000,000
Executive Vice President: M. Gatz Riddell

Historical Note
Membership is restricted to veterinarians. Membership: $95/year (individual); $15/year (student).

Meetings/Conferences:
Annual Meetings: Fall/1,400

Publications:
Bovine Practitioner. a. adv.
Membership Directory. a.

American Association of Business Valuation Specialists *(1995)*
P.O. Box 13089
Tallahassee, FL 32317
Tel: (850)878-3134 *Fax:* (850)878-1291
Toll Free: (800)878 - 3134
E-Mail: ems-rac@nettally.com
Web Site: www.aabvs.com
Members: 180 individuals
Staff: 4
Annual Budget: $10-25,000
President and Chief Executive Officer: Robert S. Rhinehart

Historical Note
Awards the designation BVS (Business Valuation Specialist). Membership: $60/year.

Meetings/Conferences:
Annual Meetings: Fall

Publications:
Business Update. q. adv.

American Association of Candy Technologists
175 Rock Rd.
Glen Rock, NJ 07452
Tel: (201)652-2655 *Fax:* (201)652-3419
E-Mail: aact@gomc.com
Web Site: www.aactcandy.org
Members: 650 individuals
Annual Budget: under $10,000
Executive Officer: Patrick Hurley

Historical Note
Has no paid officers or full-time staff. Membership: $30/year.

Meetings/Conferences:
Annual Meetings: September

American Association of Cardiovascular and Pulmonary Rehabilitation *(1985)*
401 N. Michigan Ave., Suite 2200
Chicago, IL 60611
Tel: (312)321-5146 *Fax:* (312)527-6635
E-Mail: aacvpr@smithbucklin.com
Web Site: www.aacvpr.org
Members: 3000 individuals
Staff: 9
Annual Budget: $1-2,000,000
Executive Director: Marie Bass, CAE

Historical Note
Established in New York and incorporated in Wisconsin, AACVPR is a multi-disciplinary professional society dedicated to the improvement of clinical practice, promotion of scientific inquiry and the advancement of education. Membership: $120/year.

Meetings/Conferences:
Annual Meetings: November
2007 – Salt Lake City, UT/Oct. 18-21

Publications:
Journal of Cardiopulmonary Rehabilitation. bi-m. adv.
Directory of Cardiopulmonary Rehabilitation Programs. a. adv.

American Association of Cereal Chemists

Historical Note
Became AACC International in 2005.

American Association of Certified Allergists *(1968)*
85 W. Algonquin Rd.
Suite 550
Arlington Heights, IL 60005-4425
Tel: (847)427-8111 *Fax:* (847)427-1294
Members: 550 individuals
Staff: 2
Annual Budget: $10-25,000
Executive Director: Rick Slawny

Historical Note
Membership: $75/year.

Publications:
President's Newsletter. semi-a.

American Association of Certified Appraisers *(1977)*

Historical Note
Merged with Nat'l Ass'n of Independent Fee Appraisers in 2002.

American Association of Certified Orthoptists *(1940)*
University of Iowa, Department of Opthamology
200 Hawkins Dr.
Iowa City, IA 52242
Tel: (319)356-3863 *Fax:* (319)384-9831
E-Mail: pamela-kutschke@iowa.edu
Web Site: www.orthoptics.org
Members: 300 individuals
Staff: 1
Annual Budget: $25-50,000
President: Pamela Kutschke
E-Mail: pamela-kutschke@iowa.edu

Historical Note
Founded in October 1940 in Cleveland as the American Association of Orthoptic Technicians; assumed its current name in 1966. AACO is a charter member of the International Orthoptic Association and a member of the American Orthoptic Council. Membership: $100/year.

Meetings/Conferences:
Annual Meetings: Fall, with American Academy of Ophthalmology

Publications:
Prism. q. adv.
AACO Directory. a.
American Orthoptic Journal. a. adv.

American Association of Chairmen of Departments of Psychiatry *(1967)*
c/o Lucille Meinsler, Suite 319
1594 Cumberland St.
Lebanon, PA 17042
Tel: (717)270-1673
E-Mail: aacdp@verizon.net
Web Site: www.aacdp.org
Members: 136 individuals
Staff: 1
Annual Budget: $10-25,000
Executive Secretary: Lucille F. Meinsler

Historical Note
AACDP is a forum for professional exchange among teaching psychaitrists. Has no paid officers or full-time staff.

Meetings/Conferences:
Semi-Annual Meetings:

American Association of Children's Residential Centers *(1957)*
11700 W. Lake Park Dr.
Milwaukee, WI 53224
Tel: (877)33A-ACRC *Fax:* (877)36A-ACRC
E-Mail: mskarich@alliance1.org
Web Site: www.aacrc-dc.org
Members: 160 individuals
Staff: 2
National. Coordinator: Maggie Skarich

Historical Note
Concerned with maintaining and enhancing sound clinical practice in residential treatment for children with emotional problems. Membership includes psychologists, psychiatrists, social workers, educators and child care specialists, as well as residential treatment agencies. A member of the National Consortium for Child Mental Health Services. Membership: $95/year (individual); $750/year (agency).

Meetings/Conferences:
Annual Meetings: October/150

Publications:
Residential Treatment for Children and Youth. q.
Contributions to Residential Treatment (CRT). a. adv.
AACRC Membership Directory. a.
Outcomes in Residential Treatment.

American Association of Christian Schools *(1972)*
2000 Vance Ave.
Chattanooga, TN 37404
Tel: (423)629-4280 *Fax:* (423)622-7461
E-Mail: national@aacs.org
Web Site: www.aacs.org
Members: 1200 schools
Staff: 5
Annual Budget: $1-2,000,000
Executive Director: Dr. Charles Walker

Historical Note
Maintains school accreditation and teacher/administrator certification programs.

Publications:
AACS Directory. a. adv.
Capital Comments. q. adv.
Journal for Christian Educators. q. adv.
Legal Report. semi-a.
Washington Flyer. w.

American Association of Classified School Employees *(1958)*
555 N.E. Berry St.
Sublimity, OR 97385
Tel: (503)769-2846 *Fax:* (503)769-3578
Toll Free: (800)252 - 6732
E-Mail: grychard@nsantium.k12.or.us
Web Site: www.aacse.org
Members: 260000 individuals
Annual Budget: $250-500,000
President: Gary Rychard

Historical Note
The oldest independent coalition of labor union representing teaching and non-teaching employees of the nation's school systems. Major emphasis is on national lobbying about educational issues. Has roughly 260,000 individual members in 42 states.

Publications:
Federal Update. m.

American Association of Clinical Endocrinologists *(1991)*

1000 Riverside Ave., Suite 205
Jacksonville, FL 32204-3339
Tel: (904)353-7878 *Fax:* (904)353-8185
Toll Free: (800)393 - 2223
E-Mail: info@aace.com
Web Site: www.aace.com
Members: 4800 individuals
Staff: 31
Annual Budget: $5-10,000,000
Chief Executive Officer: Donald C. Jones
Director, Communications: Sissy Crabtree
Director, Conventions: Sandra Goode
Chief Financial Officer: Doug Gregory
Director, Information Systems: Ashley Horn
Director, Legislation and Socioeconomists: Victoria Jeune
Director, CME: Lucille Killgore
Director, Administrative Services: Kim Neill
General Counsel: Chris L. Nuland
Director, Membership: Robert Thomas
Director, Chapters: Geoff Wynn

Historical Note
AACE is a professional medical organization devoted to the field of clinical endocrinology. The mission of the Association is to enhance the practice of clinical endocrinology. Members are physicians with special education, training and interest in the practice of clinical endocrinology.

Meetings/Conferences:
Annual Meetings: Spring
2007 – Seattle, WA(Sheraton)/Apr. 11-15

Publications:
AACE on Line (internet). m. adv.
First Messenger Newsletter. bi-m. adv.
Endocrine Practice Journal. bi-m. adv.

American Association of Clinical Urologists
(1969)
1111 N. Plaza Dr., Suite 550
Schaumburg, IL 60173
Tel: (847)517-1050 *Fax:* (847)517-7229
E-Mail: info@aacuweb.org
Web Site: www.aacuwb.org
Members: 4500 individuals
Staff: 6
Annual Budget: $250-500,000
Executive Director: Wendy J. Weiser

Historical Note
AACU members are licensed physicians whose practices are devoted primarily to urology. The purpose of the Association is to promote the science of urology in the best interests of the public and the medical profession, by the study and evaluation of socioeconomic factors which affect the practice of urology. Provides members with an opportunity to exert influence at a national level for the improvement of all aspects of the profession and to influence legislation and policies affecting the practice of medicine. Membership: $100/year (individual); $250/year (organization/company).

Meetings/Conferences:
Annual Meetings: Washington, D.C./July with the American Urological Ass'n.

Publications:
AACU News newsletter. irreg.
AACU Fax. irreg.

American Association of Code Enforcement
(1988)
5310 E. Main St., Suite 104
Columbus, OH 43213
Tel: (614)552-2633 *Fax:* (614)868-1177
Web Site: www.aace1.com
Members: 1400 individuals
Staff: 2
Annual Budget: $100-250,000
Management Executive: Sammi Soutar
E-Mail: aace@aace1.com

Historical Note
Membership: $60/year (active/associate).

Publications:
Perspective. bi-m. adv.
Nationwide Membership Directory.

American Association of Colleges for Teacher Education *(1917)*
1307 New York Ave. NW
Suite 300
Washington, DC 20005-4701
Tel: (202)293-2450 *Fax:* (202)457-8095
E-Mail: aacte@aacte.org
Web Site: www.aacte.org
Members: 780 institutions
Staff: 40
Annual Budget: $2-5,000,000
President and Chief Executive Officer: Sharon P. Robinson
Vice President, Professional Development and Membership: Judy Beck
Vice President, Research and Policy: M. Christopher Brown II
Director, Human Resources: Patricia B. Goldman
Vice President, Professional Issues: Carol E. Smith

Historical Note
Formed by a merger of the American Association of Teachers Colleges, the National Association of Colleges and Departments of Education and the National Association of Teacher Education Institutions of Metropolitan Districts. AACTE works to serve all learners by improving the education of educators. Dedicated to providing high-quality teachers, AACTE provides member services in advocacy, professional development, accountability, research, and information dissemination.

Meetings/Conferences:
Annual Meetings: February-March/2,000
2007 – New York, NY(Hilton)/Feb. 24-27
2008 – New Orleans, LA(Hilton Riverside)/Feb. 15-18
2009 – Chicago, IL(Hyatt Regency)/Feb. 6-9

Publications:
AACTE Directory of Members. a.
AACTE Briefs. 17/year. adv.
Journal of Teacher Education. bi-m. adv.

American Association of Colleges of Nursing
(1969)
One Dupont Circle NW
Suite 530
Washington, DC 20036
Tel: (202)463-6930 *Fax:* (202)785-8320
E-Mail: info@aacn.nche.edu
Web Site: www.aacn.nche.edu
Members: 600 schools of nursing
Staff: 35
Annual Budget: $1-2,000,000
Executive Director: Geraldine Bednash
Deputy Executive Director: Jennifer Ahearn
Director, Government Affairs: Debbie Campbell
Coordinator, Membership: Horacio Oliveira
Associate Executive Director: Robert Rosseter

Historical Note
Established to answer the need for a national organization devoted exclusively to furthering the goals of baccalaureate and graduate education in nursing. AACN members are schools of nursing at universities and four-year colleges. Member of the Federation of Associations of Schools of the Health Professions.

Meetings/Conferences:
Semi-Annual: Spring and Fall
2007 – Washington, DC(The Fairmont)/March 17-20/400
2007 – Washington, DC(The Fairmont)/Oct. 20-23/600

Publications:
Syllabus Newsletter (online). bi-m. adv.
Curriculum & Standards. a.
News Watch newsletter (online). m.
Journal of Professional Nursing. bi-m. adv.
AACN Issue Bulletin. a.

American Association of Colleges of Osteopathic Medicine *(1898)*
5550 Friendship Blvd., Suite 310
Chevy Chase, MD 20815-7231
Tel: (301)968-4100 *Fax:* (301)968-4101
Web Site: www.aacom.org
Members: 20 institutions
Staff: 25
Annual Budget: $2-5,000,000
President: Douglas L. Wood, D.O., Ph.D
Vice President, Finance and Administration: Nancy C. Cioffari
Vice President, Government Relations: Michael J. Dyer
Vice President, Medical Education: Linda Heun, Ph.D.
Vice President, Communications and Member Scvs.: Cathleen B. Kearns
Vice President, Research and Application Services: Thomas Levitan, Ph.D.

Historical Note
Established a national headquarters and permanent staff in 1972. Operates centralized application processing service. Represents the administration, faculty, and students of its member osteopathic medical schools in the U.S.

Publications:
AACOMAS Update.
Osteopathic Medical Education Report. a.
Debt, Career Plans and Opinions of Osteopathic Medical Students. a.

American Association of Colleges of Pharmacy
(1900)
1426 Prince St.
Alexandria, VA 22314-2815
Tel: (703)739-2330 *Fax:* (703)836-8982
E-Mail: mail@aacp.org
Web Site: www.aacp.org
Members: 2500 individuals
Staff: 15
Annual Budget: $2-5,000,000
Executive Vice President: Lucinda L. Maine
Communications Coordinator: Chandra T. Gilmore
Vice President, Policy and Advocacy: Will Lang
E-Mail: mail@aacp.org
Vice President Finance and Systems: Ronald G. Linder
E-Mail: mail@aacp.org
Senior Vice President: Kenneth W. Miller
E-Mail: mail@aacp.org

Historical Note
Founded in May 1900 as the American Conference of Pharmaceutical Faculties. Became the American Association of Colleges of Pharmacy in August 1925. Promotes pharmaceutical education and research. Includes a few foreign institutions. Member of the Coalition for Health Funding in Washington and the Federation of Associations of Schools of the Health Professions. Membership: $100/year (individual); $19,000 (institutions).

Meetings/Conferences:
2007 – Orlando, FL(Disney Yacht and Beach Club Resort)/July 14-18
2008 – Chicago, IL(Sheraton Chicago Hotel and Towers)/July 19-23

Publications:
AACP News. m. adv.
American Journal of Pharmaceutical Education. q. adv.

American Association of Colleges of Podiatric Medicine *(1932)*
15850 Crabbs Branch Way, Suite 320
Rockville, MD 20855
Tel: (301)948-9760 *Fax:* (301)948-1928
Toll Free: (800)922 - 9266
E-Mail: info@aacpm.org
Web Site: www.aacpm.org
Members: 200 hospitals, 8 colleges
Staff: 7
Annual Budget: $500-1,000,000
Executive Director: Moraith G. North

Historical Note
Established as the American Association of Colleges of Chiropody, it then became the American Association of Colleges of Podiatry and assumed its present name in 1968. Member of the National Association of Advisers in the Health Professions, and the Federation of Associations of Schools of the Health Professions. Membership: $500/year (organization).

Meetings/Conferences:
Semi-Annual Meetings:

American Association of Collegiate Registrars and Admissions Officers *(1910)*
One Dupont Circle NW
Suite 520
Washington, DC 20036

Tel: (202)293-9161 *Fax:* (202)872-8857
E-Mail: info@aacrao.org
Web Site: www.aacrao.org
Members: 9500 individuals
Staff: 16
Annual Budget: $2-5,000,000
Executive Director: Jerome Sullivan
E-Mail: info@aacrao.org
Director, Membership and Publications: Martha Henebry
E-Mail: info@aacrao.org

Historical Note
Founded in 1910 as the American Association of Collegiate Registrars. AACRAO is a voluntary, nonprofit professional education association of degree-granting postsecondary institutions, government agencies and higher education coordinating boards, private educational organizations, and education-oriented businesses. Its goal is to promote higher education and further the professional development of members working in admissions, enrollment management, financial aid, institutional research, records, and registration. Membership: $184/year (individual); institutional dues vary according to size of enrollment.

Meetings/Conferences:
Annual Meetings: Spring/3,500

Publications:
AACRAO Quarterly Journal, College & University. q. adv.

American Association of Community Colleges
(1920)
One Dupont Circle NW
Suite 410
Washington, DC 20036-1176
Tel: (202)728-0200 *Fax:* (202)833-2467
E-Mail: gboggs@aacc.nche.edu
Web Site: www.aacc.nche.edu
Members: 1132 two-year colleges
Staff: 46
Annual Budget: $5-10,000,000
President and Chief Executive Officer: George R. Boggs
Vice President, Government Relations: David Baime
E-Mail: dbaime@aacc.nche.edu
Director, Academic, Student and Community Development: Lynn Barnett
E-Mail: lbarnett@aacc.nche.edu
Vice President, Communications: Norma G. Kent
E-Mail: nkent@aacc.nche.edu
Vice President, Economic Development: James McKenney
E-Mail: jmckenney@aacc.nche.edu
Vice President, Membership and Information Services: Margaret Rivera
E-Mail: mrivera@aacc.nche.edu
Director, Meeting and Council Relations: Mary Ann Settlemire
E-Mail: msettlemire@aacc.nche.edu

Historical Note
The American Association of Community Colleges (AACC) is the national voice for two-year associate degree granting institutions in the U.S. Promoting the goals of community colleges and higher education, AACC works with higher education associations, the federal government, Congress, and other national associations that represent the public and private sectors. Membership: $95-50,000. Has an annual budget of approximately $8 million.

Meetings/Conferences:
Annual Meetings: April/2,500
2007 - Tampa, FL(Tampa Convention Center)/Apr. 14-17

Publications:
Community College Journal. bi-m. adv.
Community College Times. bi-w. adv.
AACC Membership Directory. a.

American Association of Community Psychiatrists *(1984)*
P.O. Box 570218
Dallas, TX 75228-0218
Tel: (972)613-0985 *Fax:* (972)613-5532
Web Site: www.communitypsychiatry.org
Members: 500 individuals
Staff: 1
Administrative Director: Frances Roton
E-Mail: frda1@airmail.net

Historical Note
AACP members are psychiatrists practicing in community mental health centers, or in similar programs which provide community care to populations of the mentally ill unrestricted by financial or other exclusionary policies. AACP promotes excellence in the care of patients through the organization of psychiatrists in community health centers, helps clarify and solve problems related to the practice of psychiatry in community health settings, provide public education, establishes liaisons with related professional organizations, and encourages training and research in psychiatry. Membership: $75/year (individual).

Meetings/Conferences:
Semi-Annual Meetings: in conjunction with American Psychiatric Ass'n/Spring and Institute of Hospital and Community Psychiatry/Fall

Publications:
Community Psychiatry Newsletter. q.

American Association of Community Theatre
(1986)
8402 Briar Wood Circle
Lago Vista, TX 78645
Tel: (512)267-0711 *Fax:* (512)267-0712
Toll Free: (866)687 - 2228
Web Site: www.aact.org
Members: 750 individuals
Staff: 4
Annual Budget: $100-250,000
Executive Director: Julie Angelo
E-Mail: angelo@aact.org

Historical Note
Members are community theater organizations, theater professionals and volunteers interested in community theater. Programs include community theatre festivals, insurance services, production and management resources, and other services. Membership: $30-55/year (individual); $55-450/year (organization).

Meetings/Conferences:
Annual Meetings: June/350

Publications:
Spotlight Magazine. bi-m. adv.
AACT Membership Directory. a. adv.
AACT Festival Handbook. bien.

American Association of Cosmetology Schools
(1924)
15825 N. 71st St., Suite 100
Scottsdale, AZ 85254
Tel: (480)281-0431 *Fax:* (480)905-0993
Toll Free: (800)831 - 1086
Web Site: www.beautyschools.org
Members: 650 schools
Staff: 4
Annual Budget: $1-2,000,000
Executive Director: Jim Cox
E-Mail: jim@beautyschools.org

Historical Note
Formerly (1991) National Association of Cosmetology Schools and (1993) Association of Accredited Cosmetology Schools. Membership: $850/year (single location); $550/year (additional locations).

Publications:
AACS Newsbreak. q. adv.
CEA Update. q. adv.

American Association of Credit Union Leagues
601 Pennsylvania Ave. NW
Suite 600 South
Washington, DC 20004-5777
Tel: (202)638-5777 *Fax:* (202)638-7729
Toll Free: (800)356 - 9655
Web Site: www.cuna.org/league
Members: 200 individuals
Staff: 1
Annual Budget: $250-500,000
Executive Director: Susan Newton

Historical Note
Founded as Association of Credit Union League Executives; assumed its current name in 1999. Administrative support provided by Credit Union National Association.

Meetings/Conferences:
Annual Meetings: January and July

Publications:
League Letter. q.

American Association of Critical-Care Nurses
(1969)
101 Columbia
Aliso Viejo, CA 92656-4109
Tel: (949)362-2000 *Fax:* (949)362-2020
Toll Free: (800)899 - 2226
E-Mail: info@aacn.org
Web Site: www.aacn.org
Members: 76900 individuals
Staff: 116
Annual Budget: $10-25,000,000
Chief Executive Officer: Wanda L. Johanson, RN, MN
E-Mail: info@aacn.org
Marketing Communications Manager: Chris Alvarez
Director, Marketing and Strategy Integration: Dana Woods

Historical Note
Founded September 22, 1969 at the Second Cardiac Nursing Symposium, as the American Association of Cardiovascular Nurses. Assumed its present name in 1972. Members are nurses in all areas of critical care, acute care, and progressive care such as cardiac intensive care, medical/surgical critical care, and trauma. Membership: $78/year (individual).

Meetings/Conferences:
Annual Meetings: May-June/10,000

Publications:
American Journal of Critical Care. bi-m. adv.
Critical Care Nurse. bi-m. adv.
AACN Clinical Issues in Critical Care Nursing. q.
AACN News. m. adv.

American Association of Crop Insurers *(1983)*
One Massachusetts Ave. NW
Suite 800
Washington, DC 20001-1401
Tel: (202)789-4100 *Fax:* (202)408-7763
E-Mail: aaci@mwmlaw.com
Web Site: www.cropinsurers.org
Members: 15 companies, 9,500 agents
Staff: 4
Annual Budget: $250-500,000
General Counsel and Executive Director: Michael R. McLeod

Historical Note
The American Association of Crop Insurers is a nonprofit industry service organization representing the interests of reinsured companies, private agents, and adjusters involved in the Federal crop insurance program. AACI's reinsured company members write more than 81% of the multiple peril crop insurance sold by private companies nationwide.

Meetings/Conferences:
Annual Meetings: Spring

Publications:
Crop Insurance Insider. m.

American Association of Dental Consultants
(1977)
10032 Wind Hill Dr.
Greenville, IN 47124
Tel: (812)923-2600 *Fax:* (812)923-2900
Toll Free: (800)896 - 0707
Web Site: www.aadc.org
Members: 450 individuals
Staff: 1
Annual Budget: $100-250,000
Executive Director: Judith K. Salisbury
E-Mail: JSALIS913@aol.com

Historical Note
Members are dentists, insurance consultants, benefits programs administrators, and other dental professionals. Membership: $100/year.

Meetings/Conferences:
Annual Meetings: Spring/350

Publications:
The Beacon. 3/year.

American Association of Dental Editors *(1931)*
750 North Lincoln Memorial Dr., Suite 422
Milwaukee, WI 53202
Tel: (414)272-2759 *Fax:* (414)272-2754
E-Mail: aade@dentaleditors.org
Web Site: www.dentaleditors.org

Members: 325 individuals
Staff: 2
Annual Budget: $25-50,000
Executive Director: Detlef B. Moore

Historical Note
The AADE was chartered in 1931 and is composed of active, interested people who are dedicated to improving communication within the dental profession and to elevating the standards of dental journalism. The organization exists to establish and encourage responsible editorial policy. Member publications represent state dental associations, component societies, dental specialty groups, dental schools, alumni, dental auxiliaries, students, and commercial publications. Membership: $40/year (individual); $130/year (organization).

Meetings/Conferences:
Annual Meetings: Fall, with the American Dental Ass'n

Publications:
Newsletter. q.
Membership Directory (online).

American Association of Dental Examiners *(1883)*
211 E. Chicago Ave., Suite 760
Chicago, IL 60611
Tel: (312)440-7464 *Fax:* (312)440-3525
E-Mail: info@aadexam.org
Web Site: www.aadexam.org
Members: 725 individuals
Staff: 3
Annual Budget: $100-250,000
Executive Director: Molly Nadler

Historical Note
Formerly the National Association of Dental Examiners, members are present and former members of state dental examining boards.

Publications:
The Composite. a.
The Bulletin. q.

American Association of Dental Schools

Historical Note
Became American Dental Education Association in 2000.

American Association of Diabetes Educators *(1974)*
100 W. Monroe, Suite 400
Chicago, IL 60603-1901
Tel: (312)424-2426 *Fax:* (312)424-2427
Toll Free: (800)338 - 3633
E-Mail: aade@aadenet.org
Web Site: www.diabeteseducator.org
Members: 11000 individuals
Staff: 24
Annual Budget: $5-10,000,000
Chief Executive Officer: Christopher E. Laxton
Chief Operating Officer: Thomas Corcoran
Director, Administration and Member Services: Nadine Cunix
Director, Communications: Diana Pihos
Director, Professional Development: Mary Sears
Director, Meeting Services: Marie Shaw
Chief Learning Officer: Lana Vukovljak
Director, Marketing: Michael Warner

Historical Note
Members are nurses, dietitians, physicians, pharmacists and other allied health professionals involved in teaching self-management to people with diabetes. Membership: $125/year.

Meetings/Conferences:
Annual Meetings: August

Publications:
AADE FYI. 4/year.
Today's Educator. 6/year. adv.

American Association of Directors of Psychiatric Residency Training *(1971)*
c/o Lucille Meinsler #319
1594 Cumberland St.
Lebanon, PA 17042
Tel: (717)270-1673
E-Mail: aadprt@verizon.net
Web Site: www.aadprt.org
Members: 428 individuals
Staff: 2
Administrative Manager: Lucille F. Meinsler

Historical Note
AADPRT was established to meet the needs of training directors, assistant/associate training directors, and residency training directors. Program directors generally hold institutional memberships. Programs with both general psychiatry and child/adolescent psychiatry training may hold combined memberships. Associate/Assistant directors hold individual memberships.

Meetings/Conferences:
Annual Meetings: January-March/500

Publications:
Newsletter. 3/year.
Academic Psychiatry. q.

American Association of Early Childhood Educators *(1990)*
3612 Bent Branch Ct.
Falls Church, VA 22041
Tel: (703)941-4329
Members: 5000 individuals
Staff: 3
Annual Budget: $10-25,000
Executive Director: William J. Tobin, Ph.D.

Historical Note
AAECE members are directors, teachers and teacher aides working in licensed childcare centers. Membership: $10/year (individual); $500/year (organization/company).

Meetings/Conferences:
Annual Meetings: Spring

Publications:
AAECE First Class Educator. q. adv.

American Association of Endodontists *(1943)*
211 E. Chicago Ave., Suite 1100
Chicago, IL 60611-2691
Toll Free: (800)872 - 3636
E-Mail: info@aae.org
Web Site: www.aae.org
Members: 5500 individuals
Staff: 22
Annual Budget: $2-5,000,000
Executive Director: James M. Drinan
E-Mail: jdrinan@aae.org
Assistant Executive Director, Education: Beverly Albert
Assistant Executive Director, Policy: Jill E. Cochran
E-Mail: jcochran@aae.org
Assistant Executive Director, Meeting Services: Lori B. Edmunds
E-Mail: ledmunds@aae.org
Manager, Membership: Carrie A. Gremer

Historical Note
Established February 25, 1943 in Chicago. Incorporated in Illinois in 1955. Promotes research on pulp conservation and endodontic treatment. Sponsors the American Board of Endodontics and the AAE Foundation. Membership: $495/year; $50/year (student).

Meetings/Conferences:
Annual Meetings: April/3,000
2007 – Philadelphia, PA(Philadelphia Convention Center)/Apr. 25-28
2008 – Vancouver, BC, Canada(Vancouver Convention and Exhibition Center)/Apr. 9-12
2009 – Orlando, FL(Gaylord Palms Resort and Convention Center)/Apr. 29-May 2
2010 – San Diego, CA(San Diego Convention Center)/Apr. 13-16
2011 – San Antonio, TX(San Antonio Convention Center)/Apr. 13-16

Publications:
Communique. q.
Endodontics: Colleagues for Excellence. semi.
Journal of Endodontics. m. adv.

American Association of Engineering Societies *(1979)*
1828 L St. NW
Suite 906
Washington, DC 20036
Tel: (202)296-2237 *Fax:* (202)296-1151
Toll Free: (888)400 - 2237
Web Site: www.aaes.org
Members: 26 societies
Staff: 3
Annual Budget: $1-2,000,000
Director, Engineering Workforce Commission (EWC): Dan Bateson
E-Mail: dbateson@aaes.org

Historical Note
Formerly the Engineers Joint Council, AAES is a multidisciplinary organization of engineering societies representing over 1,000,000 engineers in industry, government and education.

Meetings/Conferences:
Biannual Meetings: always Washington, DC/May and December

Publications:
Engineers' Salaries: Personal Salary Profile. a.
Engineering and Technology Degrees. a.
Engineering & Technology Enrollments. a.
Salaries of Engineers in Education. bien.

American Association of Equine Practitioners *(1954)*
4075 Iron Works Pkwy.
Lexington, KY 40511
Tel: (859)233-0147 *Fax:* (859)233-1968
E-Mail: aaepoffice@aaep.org
Web Site: www.aaep.org
Members: 8000 individuals
Staff: 16
Annual Budget: $2-5,000,000
Executive Director: David Foley
E-Mail: aaepoffice@aaep.org
Director, Public Relations: Sally Baker
Director, Finance and Operations: Brad Mitchell
E-Mail: aaepoffice@aaep.org

Historical Note
Members are veterinarians who specialize in treating horses. Membership: $255/year (individual); $25/year (veterinary students).

Meetings/Conferences:
Annual Meetings: December/3,500

Publications:
Equine Veterinary Education. m. adv.
AAEP Report. m.
Proceedings. a.
Member Directory. a.
Scientific Abstracts. a.

American Association of Exporters and Importers *(1921)*
1050 17th St. NW
Suite 810
Washington, DC 20036
Tel: (202)857-8009 *Fax:* (202)857-7843
E-Mail: hq@aaei.org
Web Site: www.aaei.org
Members: 425 individuals
Staff: 4
Annual Budget: $1-2,000,000
Chief Executive Officer: Hallock Northcott
Director, Meetings and Events: Kathy Corrigan
Director, Marketing and Membership: Terri Lankford

Historical Note
Primary mission of the AAEI is the promotion of fair and open trade among nations. AAEI is the only national association specifically representing both U.S. exporters and importers before the Executive Branch, Congress, the U.S. Trade Representative, U.S. Customs Service and the regulatory agencies. Became the American Importers Association in 1967 and assumed its present name in 1981. Membership fee: based on volume of business.

Meetings/Conferences:
Annual Meetings: Always New York, NY/May

Publications:
Customs Compliance Regulations Manual.
International Trade Alert. w.
Alertfax. d.
International Trade Quarterly. q.
Textile Quota Report. w.
Membership Directory. a.

American Association of Eye and Ear Hospitals *(1983)*
1100 Wilson Blvd., Suite 1200

Arlington, VA 22209
Tel: (703)243-8848 *Fax:* (703)243-8664
Web Site: www.aaeeh.org
Members: 13 facilities
Staff: 4
Executive Director: Robert B. Betz
E-Mail: rbetz@robertbetz.com

Historical Note
AAEEH represents specialty hospitals and related institutions emphasizing eye, ear, nose and throat patient care.

Meetings/Conferences:
Annual Meetings: Fall

American Association of Family and Consumer Sciences *(1909)*
400 N. Columbus St., Suite 202
Alexandria, VA 22314
Tel: (703)706-4600 *Fax:* (703)706-4663
Toll Free: (800)424 - 8080
E-Mail: staff@aafcs.org
Web Site: www.aafcs.org
Members: 11000 individuals
Staff: 13
Annual Budget: $2-5,000,000
Executive Director: Carolyn Jackson
Director, Finance and Administration: Dwight Theall
Director, Communications, Development, Member Services and Public Policy: Linda Wilson

Historical Note
Formerly (1994) American Home Economics Association. Founded at Lake Placid, NY on December 31, 1908 and incorporated in New York in 1909. Reincorporated in the District of Columbia in 1951. The purpose of AAFCS is to improve the quality and standards of individual and family life through programs that educate, influence public policy, disseminate information and publish research findings. The association's members include elementary, secondary and post-secondary educators and administrators, cooperative extension agents, other professionals in government, business and nonprofit sectors, and students preparing for the field. Membership: $82.50/year (active); $74.25/year (associate); $62/year (retired); $41.25/year (student).

Meetings/Conferences:
Annual Meetings: late June/2,000

Publications:
Family and Consumer Sciences Research Journal. q.
Journal of Family and Consumer Sciences Research Journal. q. adv.

American Association of Feline Practitioners *(1970)*
203 Towne Center Dr.
Hillsborough, NJ 08844-4693
Tel: (908)359-9351 *Fax:* (908)359-7619
Toll Free: (800)204 - 3514
E-Mail: info@aafponline.org
Web Site: www.aafponline.org
Members: 1800 individuals
Staff: 3
Annual Budget: $10-25,000
Managing Director: Joanne J. Cole, CAE, CMP

Historical Note
Members are veterinarians specializing in the treatment of cats. Membership: $145/year.

American Association of Food Stamp Directors *(1975)*

Historical Note
An affiliate of the American Public Welfare Association, which provides administrative support.

American Association of Franchisees and Dealers *(1992)*
P.O. Box 81887
San Diego, CA 92138-1887
Tel: (619)209-3775 *Fax:* (619)209-3777
Toll Free: (800)733 - 9858
E-Mail: benefits@aafd.org
Web Site: www.aafd.org
Members: 5000 individuals and companies
Staff: 6
Annual Budget: $500-1,000,000
Chairman and Chief Executive Officer: Robert L. Purvin, Jr.
Director, Member Services: Vickey Doescher
Director, Chapter Development: Stacie Power
Director, Supporting Member Services: Ron Soto

Historical Note
AAFD represents owners of franchised businesses. Membership: $69-290/year (individual); $1,000-5,000/year (corporate).

Meetings/Conferences:
Annual Meetings: Spring

Publications:
Franchisee Voice. q. adv.
Annual Members Guide. a. adv.
Chapter Alert Newsletter. irreg. adv.

American Association of Genitourinary Surgeons *(1886)*
c/o Lahey Clinic, Dept. of Urology
41 Mall Rd.
Burlington, MA 01805
Tel: (781)744-5796 *Fax:* (781)744-5767
Members: 200 individuals
Annual Budget: under $10,000
Secretary-Treasurer: David M. Barrett, M.D.
E-Mail: david.m.barrett@lahey.org

Historical Note
Organized October 16, 1886 in New York City. Has no paid officers or full-time staff.

Meetings/Conferences:
Annual Meetings: Spring/190-200

Publications:
AAGUS Newsletter. q.

American Association of Grain Inspection and Weighing Agencies *(1944)*
c/o Sioux City Inspection
840 Clark St.
Sioux City, IA 51101
Tel: (712)255-8073 *Fax:* (712)255-0959
Web Site: www.aagiwa.org
Members: 30 agencies and corporations
Annual Budget: $50-100,000
President: Tom Dahl

Historical Note
Established to provide a liaison between the Federal Grain Inspection Service and designated agencies. Has no paid officers or full-time staff.

Meetings/Conferences:
Annual Meetings: 70

Publications:
Chaff Newsletter. bi-m.
Grain-Gram. bi-w.

American Association of Gynecologic Laparoscopists

Historical Note
Became AAGL -- Advancing Minimally Invasive Gynecology Worldwide in 2005.

American Association of Handwriting Analysts *(1962)*

Historical Note
Address unknown in 2006.

American Association of Healthcare Administrative Management *(1968)*
11240 Waples Mill Rd.
Suite 200
Fairfax, VA 22030
Tel: (703)281-4043 Ext: 204 *Fax:* (703)359-7562
E-Mail: info@aaham.org
Web Site: www.aaham.org
Members: 2500 individuals
Staff: 6
Annual Budget: $500-1,000,000
Executive Director: Sharon Galler, CMP
E-Mail: info@aaham.org

Historical Note
AAHAM's goal is to promote patient account management as an integral part of financial management in the health care industry. Provides educational and professional development for its members. Membership: $150/year (individual).

Meetings/Conferences:
Annual Meetings: October

Publications:
Journal of Healthcare Administrative Management. 4/year. adv.
Legislative Currents. 6/year.

American Association of Healthcare Consultants *(1949)*
5938 N. Drake Ave.
Chicago, IL 60659
Tel: (773)866-2770 *Fax:* (773)463-3552
Toll Free: (888)350 - 2242
E-Mail: info@aahcmail.org
Web Site: www.aahc.net
Members: 100 individuals
Staff: 1
Annual Budget: $100-250,000
Executive Director: Linda Campbell, CMP, CAE

Historical Note
Formerly (1984) the American Association of Hospital Consultants. Membership: $325/year (individual); $1,795/year (company).

Publications:
Newsletter. q.
Directory. a.

American Association of Hip and Knee Surgeons *(1991)*
6300 N. River Rd.
Suite 615
Rosemont, IL 60018
Tel: (847)698-1200
E-Mail: helpdesk@aahks.org
Web Site: www.aahks.org
Members: 900 individuals
Staff: 2
Executive Officer: Priscilla Majewski

Meetings/Conferences:
2007 - Dallas, TX(Conference Center)/Nov. 2-4/700

Publications:
Journal of Arthoplasty. m.

American Association of Hispanic Certified Public Accountants

Historical Note
Became Association of Latino Professionals in Accounting and Finance in 2001.

American Association of Homes and Services for the Aging *(1961)*
2519 Connecticut Ave. NW
Washington, DC 20008-1520
Tel: (202)783-2242 *Fax:* (202)783-2255
E-Mail: info@aahsa.org
Web Site: www.aahsa.org
Members: 5600 facilities
Staff: 71
Annual Budget: $10-25,000,000
President and Chief Executive Officer: William L. Minnix, Jr., D. Min.
Chief Operating Officer and Senior Vice President, Member Services: Katrina Smith Sloan
Senior Vice President for Advocacy: Suzanne M. Weiss

Historical Note
Formerly (1994) American Association of Homes for the Aging. Primary nonprofit membership consists of community-based services for the aging, nursing homes, assisted independent housing, continuing care retirement communities, and senior housing. Provides administrative support to the International Association of Homes and Services for the Aging. Membership: annual dues vary.

Meetings/Conferences:
Annual Meetings: Fall

Publications:
Best Practices in Long Term Care. bi-m. adv.
Policy Update. a.

American Association of Hospital and Healthcare Podiatrists *(1950)*
8508 18th Ave.
Brooklyn, NY 11214
Tel: (718)259-1822 *Fax:* (718)259-4002
E-Mail: info@hospitalpodiatrists.org
Web Site: www.hospitalpodiatrists.org
Members: 800 individuals

Annual Budget: $25-50,000
Executive Director: Frank Rinaldi, DPM

Historical Note
Founded as American Association of Hospital Podiatrists. AAHHP members are podiatrists affiliated with hospitals. Grants fellowship status to members who document 3 years of in-hospital privileges and pass an appropriate examination. Membership: $75/year (individual).

Meetings/Conferences:
Annual Meetings: in conjunction with the American Podiatric Medical Ass'n/August

Publications:
Hospital Podiatrist. a. adv.
Newsletter. a. adv.

American Association of Hospital Dentists *(1937)*
401 N. Michigan Ave.
Chicago, IL 60611
Tel: (312)527-6764 *Fax:* (312)673-6663
E-Mail: scd@scdonline.org
Web Site: www.scdonline.org
Members: 800 individuals
Staff: 3
Annual Budget: $250-500,000
Executive Director: Kristen Smith

Historical Note
Formerly (1968) American Association of Hospital Dental Chiefs. Affiliated with Special Care Dentistry. Membership: $170/year (dentist).

Publications:
Interface Newsletter. bi-m. adv.
Special Care in Dentistry Journal. bi-m. adv.

American Association of Hospital Podiatrists

Historical Note
Became American Association of Hospital and Healthcare Podiatrists in 2002.

American Association of Housing Educators

Historical Note
Became Housing Education and Research Association in 2003.

American Association of Immunologists *(1913)*
9650 Rockville Pike
Bethesda, MD 20814-3994
Tel: (301)634-7178 *Fax:* (301)634-7887
E-Mail: infoaai@aai.faseb.org
Web Site: www.aai.org
Members: 5390 individuals
Staff: 8
Annual Budget: $500-1,000,000
Executive Director: M. Michelle Hogan, Ph.D.
Director, Public Policy and Government Affairs: Lauren Gross
Coordinator, Membership: Lisa McFadden

Historical Note
AAI was founded (1913) with 56 charter members, most of whom worked in the laboratories of Sir Almroth Wright, Mechnikov and Ehrlich. A member of the Federation of American Societies for Experimental Biology since 1942. Membership: $260/year (domestic individual); $300/year (international individual); $358.75/year (Canadian individual); $750-2000/year (organization/company).

Meetings/Conferences:
Annual Meetings: With Federation of American Socs. for Experimental Biology/15,000

Publications:
Journal of Immunology. semi-m.
AAI Newsletter. bi-m.

American Association of Independent News Distributors *(1971)*

Historical Note
AAIND members are independent newspaper dealers and distributors.

Publications:
Newsletter. q. adv.

American Association of Individual Investors *(1978)*
625 N. Michigan Ave., Suite 1900
Chicago, IL 60611-3110
Tel: (312)280-0170 *Fax:* (312)280-9883
Toll Free: (800)428 - 2244
Web Site: www.aaii.com
Members: 170,000 individuals
Staff: 39
Annual Budget: $10-25,000,000
President: John Markese

Historical Note
An independent non-profit corporation formed for the purpose of assisting individuals in becoming effective managers of their own assets through programs of education, information and research. Has an annual budget of approximately $12 million. Membership: $49/year.

Meetings/Conferences:
Annual Meetings: Fall
2007 – Orlando, FL(Hilton)/Nov. 8-10

Publications:
Computerized Investing. bi-m.
The Individual Investor. bi-m.
AAII Journal. m.

American Association of Industrial Veterinarians *(1954)*
6060 Sunrise Vistra Dr.
Suite 1300
Citrus Heights, CA 95610-7098
Tel: (916)722-8186 *Fax:* (916)722-8149
E-Mail: info@aaiv.org
Web Site: www.aaiv.org/
Members: 400 individuals
Staff: 1
Annual Budget: $25-50,000
Executive Director: Maryanne Bobrow, CAE, CMP

Historical Note
Formerly (1976) Industrial Veterinarian's Association. Membership: $50/year.

Meetings/Conferences:
Annual Meetings: July, with American Veterinary Medical Ass'n
2007 – Washington, DC/July 14-18

Publications:
AAIV Newsline. 3/year.
Directory. a.

American Association of Insurance Management Consultants *(1978)*
507 N. Kings Hwy.
Cherry Hill, NJ 08034
Tel: (856)779-2430 *Fax:* (856)667-6224
Toll Free: (888)280 - 0114
Web Site: www.aaimco.com
Members: 35 companies
Staff: 1
Annual Budget: under $10,000
Executive Director: Al Diamond

Historical Note
Founded to provide a platform for the exchange of information and the development of uniform standards and practices for firms and individuals providing professional consulting to the insurance industry. Has no paid officers or full-time staff.

Meetings/Conferences:
Semi-Annual Conferences:

Publications:
AAIMCO Connection. q. adv.

American Association of Integrated Healthcare Delivery Systems *(1993)*
4435 Waterfront Dr.
Suite 101
Glen Allen, VA 23060
Tel: (804)747-5823 *Fax:* (804)747-5316
E-Mail: info@aaihds.org
Web Site: www.aaihds.org
Members: 415 individuals
Staff: 16
Annual Budget: $500-1,000,000
President: William C. Williams, III, M.D.

Historical Note
Founded as American Association of Physician-Hospital Organizations; assumed its current name in 1997. AAIHDS members are physicians, hospital administrators, health plan executives and other individuals with an interest in physician-hospital organizations. An affiliate of National Association of Managed Care Physicians, which provides administrative support. Membership: $275/year (individual); $750/year (organization).

Meetings/Conferences:
Semi-Annual Meetings: Spring and Fall

Publications:
Integrated Healthcare Delivery System Newsletter. q.

American Association of Language Specialists *(1957)*
P.O. Box 39339
Washington, DC 20016-9339
Tel: (301)613-0310
Web Site: www.taals.net
Members: 150 individuals
Annual Budget: under $10,000
President: Teresa G. Willett

Historical Note
Professional association representing interpreters, translators, and precis writers working at the international level, either for conferences on a free-lance basis or for international organizations as permanent staff. Has no paid officers or full-time staff. Membership: $80/year.

Meetings/Conferences:
Annual Meetings: December in Washington, DC

Publications:
Yearbook. a.

American Association of Law Libraries *(1906)*
53 W. Jackson Blvd., Suite 940
Chicago, IL 60604
Tel: (312)939-4764 *Fax:* (312)431-1097
E-Mail: aallhq@aall.org
Web Site: www.aallnet.org
Members: 5000 individuals
Staff: 13
Annual Budget: $2-5,000,000
Executive Director: Susan E. Fox, CAE
Director, Finance and Administration: Lynn A. Cotteleer

Historical Note
Members are librarians of law libraries in schools, law firms, associations, the government, court systems and other institutions. Membership: $198/year.

Meetings/Conferences:
Annual Meetings: Summer/2,600
2008 – Portland, OR(Convention Center)/July 12-16

Publications:
AALL Spectrum. a. adv.
Directory & Handbook. a.
Law Library Journal. q. adv.
Index to Foreign Legal Periodicals. q.

American Association of Legal Nurse Consultants *(1989)*
401 N. Michigan Ave.
Chicago, IL 60611-4267
Toll Free: (877)462 - 2562
E-Mail: info@aalnc.org
Web Site: www.aalnc.org
Members: 3500 individuals
Staff: 12
Annual Budget: $250-500,000
Executive Director: Julianne Bendel

Historical Note
Promotes the professional advancement of Registered Nurses practicing in a consulting capacity in the legal profession and provides educational opportunities for legal nurse consultants. Membership: $145/year (individual); $225/year (company).

Meetings/Conferences:
Annual Meetings: April

Publications:
Network News. q.
Journal of Legal Nurse Consulting. q. adv.

American Association of Managed Care Nurses *(1994)*
4435 Waterfront Dr., Suite 101
Glen Allen, VA 23060
Tel: (804)747-9698 *Fax:* (804)747-5316
Web Site: www.aamcn.org
Members: 2000 individuals
Staff: 10
Annual Budget: $100-250,000

Senior Vice President: William C. Williams, III, M.D.

Historical Note

AAMCN members are nurses and other professionals with an interest in managed healthcare. Membership: $70/year (individual).

Publications:

Managed Care Weekly Update (e-news). w. adv.
Nurses' Notes Newsletter. q. adv.
Journal of Managed Care Medicine. q.

American Association of Managing General Agents *(1926)*

150 S. Warner Rd.
Suite 156
King of Prussia, PA 19406
Tel: (610)225-1999 *Fax:* (610)225-1996
Web Site: www.aamga.org
Members: 247 managing firms, 234 ass'ns.
Staff: 10
Annual Budget: $1-2,000,000
Executive Director: Bernd Heinze
E-Mail: bernie.heinze@aamga.org
Director, Education: Russ Rado

Historical Note

Members are independent insurance managers with contractual authority to perform managerial functions on behalf of insurance companies and syndicates. Membership: $850-2500/year (company).

Meetings/Conferences:

Annual Meetings: Spring/1,000

Publications:

AAMGA Newsletter. q.
AAMGA Yearbook and Directory. a. adv.
Annual Report. a.

American Association of Meat Processors *(1939)*

P.O. Box 269
One Meating Pl.
Elizabethtown, PA 17022
Tel: (717)367-1168 *Fax:* (717)367-9096
E-Mail: aamp@aamp.com
Web Site: www.aamp.com
Members: 1700 firms
Staff: 9
Annual Budget: $500-1,000,000
Executive Director: Stephen F. Krut
Director, Regulatory and Legislative Affairs: Andrea Brown
Exhibitor Coordinator: Jane Frey
Convention Registration: Nancy Matako
Convention Manager: Debbie Sirex
Assistant Executive Director: Jay B. Wenther

Historical Note

Founded as the National Frozen Food Locker Institute; became successively the National Frozen Food Locker Association, the Frozen Food Locker Institute, and the National Institute of Locker and Freezer Provisioners. Assumed its present name in 1973. AAMP is North America's largest meat trade association. Members are small to medium-sized meat, poultry, seafood and food businesses including packers, processors, wholesalers, home food service businesses, retailers, deli/catering operators, and industry suppliers. Membership: $150 (operator); $300/year (supplier); $75/year (Canadian); $100/year (international); $75/year (allied).

Meetings/Conferences:

Annual Meetings: Summer

Publications:

Membership Directory and Buyers' Guide. bi-a. adv.
AAMPlifier. semi-m. adv.
Capitol Line Up. semi-m. adv.

American Association of Medical Assistants *(1956)*

20 N. Wacker Dr., Suite 1575
Chicago, IL 60606-2903
Tel: (312)899-1500 *Fax:* (312)899-1259
E-Mail: info@aama-ntl.org
Web Site: www.aama-ntl.org
Members: 20000 individuals
Staff: 21
Annual Budget: $1-2,000,000
Executive Director: Donald A. Balasa, JD,CAE
Assistant Executive Director: Anna Johnson

Historical Note

AAMA was established to promote the medical assisting profession through continuing education and credentialing. Membership includes medical assistants, medical secretaries, bookkeepers, receptionists, technicians and office nurses. Administers CMA (Certified Medical Assistant) certification program. Assistant. Membership: $67/year (individual).

Meetings/Conferences:

Annual Meetings: Fall
2007 – Louisville, KY(Downtown Marriott)/Sept. 7-11
2008 – Chicago, IL(Hyatt O'Hare)/Oct. 17-21
2009 – Houston, TX(J.W. Marriott Galleria)/Sept. 11-15

Publications:

CMA Today. 6/year.
The Professional Medical Assistant. bi-m.

American Association of Medical Milk Commissions *(1907)*

1824 N. Hillhurst Ave.
Los Angeles, CA 90027
Tel: (323)664-1977 *Fax:* (323)664-0870
E-Mail: fleiss@usc.edu
Members: 6 individuals
Annual Budget: under $10,000
President: Paul M. Fleiss, M.D.
E-Mail: fleiss@usc.edu

Historical Note

Professional society of physicians on local Medical Milk Commissions supervising production of Certified Milk from dairies conforming to offical standards. Membership includes physicians, pathologists, pediatricians and veterinarians. Affiliated with the Certified Milk Producers Association of America.

Meetings/Conferences:

Semi-Annual Meetings: May, with Certified Milk Producers Ass'n of America, and September-October.

Publications:

Methods and Standards for the Production of Certified Milk. irreg.

American Association of Medical Society Executives *(1947)*

555 E. Wells St., 11th Floor
Milwaukee, WI 53202
Tel: (414)221-9275 *Fax:* (414)276-3349
E-Mail: aamse@aamse.org
Web Site: www.aamse.org
Members: 1200 individuals
Staff: 3
Annual Budget: $500-1,000,000

Historical Note

Professional organization of executives of medical societies. Formerly Medical Society Executives Association. Membership: $160-300/year (individual).

Meetings/Conferences:

Annual Meetings: Summer/325

Publications:

Hotline. m.
Who's Who in Medical Society Management - Directory. a. adv.

American Association of Mental Health Professionals in Corrections *(1940)*

P.O. Box 160208
Sacramento, CA 95816-0208
E-Mail: corrmentalhealth@aol.com
Members: 2000 individuals
Staff: 1
Annual Budget: $25-50,000
National President: J.S. Zil, M.D., J.D.
E-Mail: corrmentalhealth@aol.com

Historical Note

Founded in 1940 as the Medical Correctional Association. Membership: $55/year.

Meetings/Conferences:

Annual Meetings: With the American Psychiatric Association

Publications:

Corrective and Social Psychiatry Monograph Series. q. adv.

American Association of Minority Businesses *(1992)*

P.O. Box 35432
Charlotte, NC 28235
Tel: (704)596-1800 *Fax:* (704)599-6146
E-Mail: info@aambnet.com
Web Site: www.aambnet.com
Members: 17000 businesses/corporations
Staff: 3
Annual Budget: $250-500,000
President and Chief Executive Officer: Charles L. Kelly

Historical Note

AAMB is a network of minority business owners. Membership: $60/year (business owner); $100/year (associate); $1,000/year (corporate member); $250/year (alliance and association members).

Publications:

The Business Partner. q. adv.

American Association of Motor Vehicle Administrators *(1933)*

4301 Wilson Blvd., Suite 400
Arlington, VA 22203
Tel: (703)522-4200 *Fax:* (703)522-1553
Web Site: www.aamva.org
Members: 150 agencies
Staff: 80
Annual Budget: $25-50,000,000
President and Chief Executive Officer: Linda R. Lewis-Pickett
Chief Financial Officer: Sandy Afes
Deputy Chief Executive Officer: Mike Calvin
Vice President, Membership and Conference Services: Diane Graham
Vice President, Human Resources: Marvin Lynch
Chief Policy Officer: Tom Wolfsohn

Historical Note

Membership composed of state and provincial agencies responsible for the administration and enforcement of motor vehicle and traffic laws in the U.S. and Canada. AAMVA is composed of 67 jurisdictions representing 150 agencies and thousands of employees.

Meetings/Conferences:

Annual Meetings: Fall
2007 – Rapid City, SD(Best Western Ramkota Hotel)/Aug. 21-23/500

Publications:

MOVE Magazine. q. adv.

American Association of Museums *(1906)*

1575 I St. NW
Suite 400
Washington, DC 20005
Tel: (202)289-1818 *Fax:* (202)289-6578
Web Site: http://aam-us.org
Members: 14000 individuals
Staff: 90
Annual Budget: $5-10,000,000
Interim President and Chief Executive Officer: Kim Igoe
Vice President, Finance and Administration: Mary Bowie
Director, Government and Media Relations: Jason Y. Hall
Director, Meetings and Professional Education: Dean Phelus

Historical Note

AAM's institutional members include art museums, history museums, natural history museums, science museums, children's museums, historic buildings and sites, science/technology centers, aquariums, zoos, botanical gardens, arboreta, and military and maritime museums. Individual members include museum directors, curators, registrars, educators, exhibit designers, public relations officers, development officers, security managers, trustees, and volunteers. Corporate members include individual consultants as well as providers of commercial products and services. AAM's services include: accreditation, museum assessment programs, government affairs, technical information, continuing education, publications, international programs, and vendor-provided services. Affiliated with the International Council of Museums. Administers 12 standing professional committees. Has an annual budget of approximately $7 million. Membership fee: Individual based on salary; institution based on *operating budget; corporate individual based on salary; corporate company is flat fee.*

Meetings/Conferences:
Annual Meetings: Spring/5,000
2007 – Chicago, IL/May 13-17

Publications:
Museum News. bi-m. adv.
Aviso. m. adv.

American Association of Naturopathic Physicians *(1985)*
4435 Wisconsin Ave. NW
Suite 403
Washington, DC 20016
Tel: (202)237-8150 *Fax:* (202)237-8150
Toll Free: (866)538 - 2267
E-Mail: member.services@naturopathic.org
Web Site: www.naturopathic.org
Members: 1800 individuals
Staff: 3
Annual Budget: $500-1,000,000
Executive Director: Karen Howard
E-Mail: member.services@naturopathic.org

Historical Note
AANP represents licensable naturopathic physicians in the United States. Supports legislation to license and regulate naturopathic physicians in all states, in order to distinguish properly trained individuals. Provides referral service, accessible through the AANP web site and toll-free phone number. Membership: $400/year (individual); $2,500/year (organization).

Meetings/Conferences:
Annual Meetings: Autumn/500

Publications:
Referral Directory. a. adv.

American Association of Neurological Surgeons *(1931)*
5550 Meadowbrook Dr.
Rolling Meadows, IL 60008-3852
Tel: (847)378-0500 *Fax:* (847)378-0600
Toll Free: (888)566 - 2267
E-Mail: info@aans.org
Web Site: www.aans.org
Members: 6500 individuals
Staff: 41
Annual Budget: $10-25,000,000
Executive Director: Thomas A. Marshall
E-Mail: tam@aans.org
Director, Marketing: Kathleen T. Craig
E-Mail: ktc@aans.org
Associate Executive Director: Susan M. Eget
E-Mail: sme@aans.org
Dep. Executive Director: Ronald W. Engelbreit
E-Mail: rwe@aans.org
Director, Development: Michele Gregory
Director, AANS/CNS Washington Office: Katie Orrico, JD
E-Mail: korrico@neurosurgery.org
Director, Membership Services: Chris Ann Philips
E-Mail: cap@aans.org
Associate Executive Director, Education and Meetings: Joni Shulman

Historical Note
Founded October 10, 1931 as the Harvey Cushing Society. Incorporated in Illinois in 1956 and assumed its current name in 1967. Membership: $830/year (individual).

Meetings/Conferences:
Annual Meetings: Spring
2007 – Washington, DC(Convention Center)/Apr. 14-19
2008 – Chicago, IL(Convention Center)/March 29-Apr. 3

Publications:
Journal of Neurosurgery. m. adv.
AANS Bulletin. q. adv.

American Association of Neuromuscular & Electrodiagnostic Medicine *(1953)*
2621 Superior Dr. NW
Rochester, MN 55901
Tel: (507)288-0100 *Fax:* (507)288-1225
E-Mail: aanem@aanem.org
Web Site: www.aanem.org
Members: 5200 individuals
Staff: 15
Annual Budget: $1-2,000,000
Executive Director: Shirlyn A. Adkins, JD
Director, Health Policy and Advocacy: Megan Fogelson
Director, Member and Diplomate Services: Shelly D. Hansen
Director, Marketing and Communications: Brenda Riggott
Director, Meetings: Kathryn J. Smith
Director, Finance: Robin Splittstoesser
Director, Education: Stacie Stucky
Graphic Designer/Web Developer: Susan E. Yoder

Historical Note
Founded as the American Association of Electromyography and Electrodiagnosis; became the American Association of Electrodiagnostic Medicine in 1989; assumed its present name in 2004. The primary goal of AANEM is to increase the quality of patient care, specifically of those patients with disorders of skeletal muscle, neuromuscular function and the central and peripheral nervous systems, by contributing to the improvement in the methods of electrodiagnostic medicine through programs in education, research and quality assurance. Membership: $245/year (individual).

Meetings/Conferences:
Annual Meetings: Fall
2007 – Phoenix, AZ(J.W. Marriott/Desert Ridge)/Oct. 17-20/1000
2008 – Providence, RI(Rhode Island Convention Center)/Sept. 17-20/1000
2009 – San Diego, CA(Manchester Grand Hyatt)/Oct. 7-10/1000
2010 – Quebec City, QC, Canada(Quebec City Convention Centre)/Oct. 6-9
2011 – San Francisco, CA(San Francisco Hilton)/Sept. 14-17/1000

Publications:
Positive Waves Newsletter. 2/yr.
Practice Topics. q.
Minimonographs. irreg.
Muscle & Nerve Journal. m. adv.

American Association of Neuropathologists *(1924)*
Case Western Reserve Univ., Institute of Pathology
2085 Adelbert Rd.
Cleveland, OH 44106
Tel: (216)368-2488 *Fax:* (216)368-8964
E-Mail: aanp@cwru.edu
Web Site: www.neuropath.org
Members: 900 individuals
Annual Budget: $250-500,000
Secretary-Treasurer: George Perry

Historical Note
Founded as the Club of Neuropatholgists, this professional society of physicians assumed its present name in 1932. Provides a forum for the advancement of the study of diseases of the nervous system. Membership: $165/year.

Publications:
Neuropathology Newsletter. 3/year.
Membership Directory. a.
Journal of Neuropathology & Experimental Neurology. m.

American Association of Neuroscience Nurses *(1968)*
4700 W. Lake Ave.
Glenview, IL 60025-1485
Tel: (847)375-4733 *Fax:* (877)734-8677
Toll Free: (888)557 - 2266
E-Mail: info@aann.org
Web Site: www.aann.org
Members: 3700 individuals
Staff: 6
Annual Budget: $500-1,000,000
Executive Director: Diane Simmons, MPA
Manager: Laura Baerenklau
Director, Communications: Barbara Simmons

Historical Note
Membership is open to Registered Nurses who demonstrate an active or primary interest in neurosurgical or neurological nursing. Membership: $98/year (individual); $73.50/year (associate); $49/year (student).

Meetings/Conferences:
Annual Meetings: Spring/1,000
2007 – Orlando, FL(Gaylord Palms Resort)/Apr. 29-May 2/1000

Publications:
Journal of Neuroscience Nursing. bi-m. adv.
Synapse. bi-m. adv.

American Association of Nurse Anesthetists *(1931)*
222 S. Prospect Ave.
Park Ridge, IL 60068-4001
Tel: (847)692-7050 *Fax:* (847)692-6968
E-Mail: info@aana.com
Web Site: www.aana.com
Members: 30000 individuals
Staff: 70
Annual Budget: $5-10,000,000
Executive Director: Jeffery M. Beutler, CRNA, MS
Senior Director, Communications: Christopher Bettin, MA
E-Mail: cbettin@aana.org
Director, Accreditation and Education: Francis Gerbasi, CRNA, Ph.D.
E-Mail: fgerbasi@aana.com
Senior Director, Federal Affairs: Frank Purcell
Director, Programs and Meeting Services: Cindy Wood, CMD
Senior Director, Finance and Administrative Services: William E. Yeo, CPA, BBA
E-Mail: byeo@aana.com

Historical Note
Established in 1931 as the National Association of Nurse Anesthetists. Became the American Association of Nurse Anesthetists in 1939. Certifies nurse anesthetists and awards the CRNA (Certified Registered Nurse Anesthetist) designation. Has an annual budget of approximately $8 million. Sponsors and supports the CRNA Political Action Committee. Membership: $380/year.

Meetings/Conferences:
Annual Meetings: August

Publications:
AANA Journal. bi-m. adv.
AANA Newsbulletin. 11/year. adv.

American Association of Nurse Attorneys, The *(1982)*
P.O. Box 515
Columbus, OH 43216-2262
Toll Free: (877)538 - 2262
Web Site: www.taana.org
Members: 575 individuals
Staff: 2
Annual Budget: $50-100,000

Historical Note
Members are individuals holding degrees in both nursing and law and members of either profession who are pursuing a second degree in the other field. Sponsors the TAANA Foundation to provide educational opportunities and recognize achievement in the field. Membership: $165/year (nurse/attorney); $150/year (affiliate/associate); $90/year (student).

Publications:
Inside TAANA. q. adv.
Journal of Nursing Law. q. adv.
Membership Directory. a. adv.

American Association of Nutritional Consultants *(1980)*
714 E. Winona Ave.
Warsaw, IN 46580
Tel: (574)269-4060 *Fax:* (574)268-2120
Toll Free: (888)828 - 2262
E-Mail: registrar@aanc.net
Web Site: www.aanc.net
Members: 2000 individuals
Staff: 1
Executive Administrator: Tracy Perry
E-Mail: registrar@aanc.net

Historical Note
Members are professional consultants in the field of nutrition. Also serves as administrative offices for the American Naturopathic Medical Association. Membership: $60/year.

Meetings/Conferences:
2007 - Las Vegas, NV(Renaissance Las Vegas Hotel)/Nov. 15-18
2008 - Duck Key, FL(Hawk's Cay Resort)/Nov. 20-23
2009 - New Orleans, LA(Royal Sonesta Hotel)/Nov. 19-22

Publications:
Healthkeepers Magazine. q. adv.

American Association of Occupational Health Nurses *(1942)*
2920 Brandywine Rd.
Suite 100
Atlanta, GA 30341-5539
Tel: (770)455-7757 *Fax:* (770)455-7271
E-Mail: aaohn@aaohn.org
Web Site: www.aaohn.org
Members: 10000 individuals
Staff: 24
Annual Budget: $2-5,000,000
Executive Director: Ann R. Cox, CAE

Historical Note
Founded in Philadelphia in 1942 and incorporated in New York in 1952, AAOHN is the professional association of occupational health nurses. Formerly (1977) the American Association of Industrial Nurses, Inc. Incorporated in the state of Georgia in 1982. Membership: $185 plus chapter dues/year.

Meetings/Conferences:
Annual Meetings: April-May

Publications:
AAOHN News. m. adv.
AAOHN Journal. m. adv.

American Association of Oral and Maxillofacial Surgeons *(1918)*
9700 W. Bryn Mawr Ave.
Rosemont, IL 60018-5701
Tel: (847)678-6200 *Fax:* (847)678-6286
Toll Free: (800)822 - 6637
Web Site: www.aaoms.org
Members: 7000 individuals
Staff: 50
Annual Budget: $10-25,000,000
Executive Director: Dr. Bob Rinaldi
E-Mail: brinaldi@aaoms.org
Associate Executive Director and General Counsel: Mark Adams
Associate Executive Director, Advanced Education and Professional Affairs: Randi V. Andresen
E-Mail: randresen@aaoms.org
Chief Financial Officer: Scott Farrell
E-Mail: sfarrell@aaoms.org
Associate Executive Director, Continuing Education: Laura Jelinek
E-Mail: ljelinek@aaoms.org
Associate Executive Director, Communications and Publications: Janice Teplitz
E-Mail: jteplitz@aaoms.org
Associate Executive Director, Practice Management and Government Affairs: Karin Wittich

Historical Note
Formerly (1978) the American Society of Oral Surgeons. Members are surgeons specializing in surgery of the mouth, face and jaws. Operates the Oral and Maxillofacial Surgery Political Action Committee (OMSPAC) and the Oral and Maxillofacial Surgery Foundation (OMSF). Has annual budget of approximately $14 million. In addition to its annual meeting, AAOMS sponsors an annual Dental Implant Conference in December.

Meetings/Conferences:
Annual Meetings: Fall/3,500
2007 - Honolulu, HI(Hawaii Convention Center)/Oct. 10-13/5000

Publications:
AAOMS Today. bi-m. adv.
Journal of Oral and Maxillofacial Surgery. m. adv.

American Association of Oriental Medicine *(1981)*
P.O. Box 162340
Sacramento, CA 95816
Tel: (916)443-4770 *Fax:* (916)443-4766
Toll Free: (866)455 - 7999
E-Mail: info@aaom.org
Web Site: www.aaom.org
Members: 1200 individuals
Staff: 5
Annual Budget: $500-1,000,000
Executive Director: Bekah Christensen

Historical Note
Formerly (1996) American Association of Acupuncture and Oriental Medicine. Advocates the recognition of acupuncture and Oriental medicine with acupuncture as a reliable, cost effective and viable form of treatment. Membership: $240/year (individual); $400/year (organization); $35/year (student).

Meetings/Conferences:
Annual Meetings: Fall

Publications:
The American Acupuncturist. q. adv.
Membership Directory. a. adv.

American Association of Orthodontists *(1900)*
401 N. Lindbergh Blvd.
St. Louis, MO 63141-7816
Tel: (314)993-1700
Toll Free: (800)424 - 2841
E-Mail: info@aaortho.org
Web Site: www.braces.org
Members: 15000 individuals
Staff: 48
Annual Budget: $10-25,000,000
Executive Director: Chris P. Vranas, CAE
E-Mail: cvranas@aaortho.org
Director, Finance and Administration: Ronald T. Martin
E-Mail: rmartin@aaortho.org
Manager, Membership/Information: Sherry Nappier
E-Mail: snappier@aaortho.org

Historical Note
Formed in 1900 as The American Society of Orthodontists. Incorporated in Pennsylvania in 1917 as The American Association of Orthodontists and later, in 1965 after the headquarters was established in St. Louis, incorporated in Missouri. Sponsors the American Association of Orthodontists Foundation. Has an annual budget of approximately $10 million.

Meetings/Conferences:
Annual Meetings: Spring/16,000
2007 - Seattle, WA(Washington State Convention Center)/May 18-22

Publications:
American Ass'n of Orthodontists Bulletin. bi-m. adv.
American Journal of Orthodontics and Dentalfacial Orthopedics. m. adv.

American Association of Orthopaedic Medicine *(1982)*
600 Pembrook Park
Woodland Park, CO 80863
Tel: (719)475-0032 *Fax:* (719)687-5184
Toll Free: (800)992 - 2063
E-Mail: aaom@aaomed.org
Web Site: www.aaomed.org
Members: 600 individuals
Staff: 2
Annual Budget: $100-250,000
Executive Director: Maelu Fleck
E-Mail: aaom@aaomed.org

Historical Note
Professional association of physicians concerned with musculoskeletal system. Absorbed the Prolotherapy Association (founded in 1962). Membership: $300/year.

Meetings/Conferences:
Annual Meetings: February or March

Publications:
Journal of Orthopaedic Medicine. 3/year.
Newsletter. q.

American Association of Osteopathic Women Physicians
505 N. Lake Shore Dr.
Suite 6802
Chicago, IL 60611
Tel: (773)769-0880
President: Melicien A. Tettambel, D.O.

American Association of Owners and Breeders of Peruvian Paso Horses *(1962)*
3077 Wiljan Court, Suite A
Santa Rosa, CA 95407
Tel: (817)447-7574 *Fax:* (817)447-2450
E-Mail: mhwmd@aol.com
Web Site: www.aaobpph.org
Members: 500 individuals
Staff: 1
Annual Budget: $100-250,000
Executive Director: Donna Bearer

Historical Note
Absorbed into the North American Peruvian Horse Association in November 2005. Formed to establish a breed registry for the Peruvian Paso Horse (imported from Peru) and to encourage the breeding, training, and showing of the horse, as well as to inform the general public of the history and attributes of what has been called the "Cadillac of Pleasure Horses." Membership: $50/year.

Meetings/Conferences:
Annual Meetings: With National Championship Show

Publications:
Owner/Breeder Membership Directory. a.
AAOBPPH Newsletter. 3/year. adv.

American Association of Pastoral Counselors *(1963)*
9504A Lee Hwy.
Fairfax, VA 22031-2303
Tel: (703)385-6967 *Fax:* (703)352-7725
E-Mail: info@aapc.org
Web Site: www.aapc.org
Members: 3000 individuals
Staff: 6
Annual Budget: $500-1,000,000
Executive Director: Douglas M. Ronsheim
E-Mail: info@aapc.org

Historical Note
An international organization of clergy and other religious-oriented professionals whose ministry involves counseling and therapy. Membership: fees determined by membership type.

Meetings/Conferences:
Annual Meetings: April-May/600

Publications:
Newsletter. q. adv.
Magazine. bi-a. adv.
Directory. a. adv.

American Association of Pathologists' Assistants *(1972)*
1711 County Rd. B West
Suite 300N
Roseville, MN 55113-4036
Tel: (651)697-9264 *Fax:* (651)635-0307
Toll Free: (800)532 - 2272
E-Mail: oei@assocmgmt.org
Web Site: www.pathologistsassistants.org
Members: 950 individuals
Central Office Coordinator: Michelle Sok

Historical Note
Established and incorporated in Ohio. Members have received training in anatomical pathology and related topics and provide a variety of technical services under the direction of a pathologist. Membership: $100/year (fellow); $150/year (affiliate); $25 one-time fee (student).

Meetings/Conferences:
Annual Meetings: Fall
2007 - New Orleans, LA(Fairmont)/Sept. 8-14/350

Publications:
AAPA Newsletter. q. adv.

American Association of Petroleum Geologists *(1917)*
P.O. Box 979
Tulsa, OK 74101-0979
Tel: (918)584-2555 *Fax:* (918)560-2636
Toll Free: (800)364 - 2274
Web Site: www.aapg.org
Members: 30030 individuals
Staff: 60
Annual Budget: $10-25,000,000
Executive Director: Richard D. Fritz

E-Mail: rfritz@aapg.org
Director, Geosciences: Jim Blankenship
Director, Global Development: Brenda Cunningham
E-Mail: bcunning@aapg.org
Business Director: David Lange
Director, Communications: Larry M. Nation
E-Mail: lnation@aapg.org

Historical Note
Established in Tulsa, OK in 1917 to provide for the dissemination of scientific and technical ideas and data in the field of geology as it relates to exploration for and production of oil, natural gas and energy minerals and the environment. Originally the Southwestern Association of Petroleum Geologists; assumed its current name in 1918 and was incorporated in Colorado in 1924. A member society of the American Geological Institute. Has a budget of approximately $11 million. Membership: $62/year (full member); $10/year (student).

Meetings/Conferences:
Annual Meetings: Spring/7,600
2007 – Long Beach, CA/Apr. 1-4

Publications:
DEG Environment Geosciences. q. adv.
AAPG Bulletin. m. adv.
AAPG Explorer. m. adv.

American Association of Pharmaceutical Scientists *(1986)*
2107 Wilson Blvd., Suite 700
Arlington, VA 22201-3042
Tel: (703)243-2800 *Fax:* (703)243-9650
E-Mail: aaps@aaps.org
Web Site: www.aapspharmaceutica.com
Members: 13000 individuals
Staff: 47
Annual Budget: $10-25,000,000
Executive Director: John Lisack, Jr., CAE
Director, Finance and Administration: Maureen E. Downs
Director, Marketing: Peter Inchauteguiz
Director, Technology: Richard Lawson
Director, Public Outreach: Stacy May
Director, Meetings and Expositions: Sharon R. Pichon

Historical Note
Incorporated in Washington, DC. AAPS members are pharmaceutical scientists in academia, industry, government and other research institutions. Membership: $125/year.

Meetings/Conferences:
Annual Meetings: October-November/8,000
2007 – San Diego, CA(Convention Center)/Nov. 12-16

Publications:
AAPS NewsMagazine. adv.
Pharmaceutical Research. adv.
AAPS Journal.
AAPS Pharm Sci Tech.

American Association of Philosophy Teachers *(1978)*
Cal State Univ.
Dept. of Philosophy
Long Beach, CA 90840-2408
Tel: (562)985-4346
E-Mail: aapt@philosphers.net
Web Site: www.aapt-online.dhs.org
Members: 400 individuals
Annual Budget: $10-25,000
Executive Director: Betsy Newell Decyk
E-Mail: bdecyk@csulb.edu

Historical Note
Incorporated in 1976, the AAPT is an international organization with members in the US, Canada, Japan, South Africa and other countries. AAPT is dedicated to the development and improvement of philosophy teaching at all levels of schooling. Sponsors a biennial International Workshop/Conference on Teaching Philosophy. Has no paid officers or full-time staff. Membership: $25/year (individual).

Meetings/Conferences:
Annual Meetings: With the American Philosophical Ass'n.

Publications:
AAPT newsletter. 2/year. adv.

American Association of Phonetic Sciences *(1973)*
Box 14095, Univ. Station
Gainesville, FL 32604
Tel: (352)392-9221 *Fax:* (352)392-6170
Members: 100 individuals
Staff: 2
Annual Budget: under $10,000
Executive Secretary: William S. Brown, Jr., Ph.D.
E-Mail: wsbrown@csd.ufl.edu

Historical Note
Affiliated with International Society of Phonetic Sciences. Membership: $15/year.

Meetings/Conferences:
Annual Meetings: Fall

Publications:
AAPS Newsletter. semi-a. adv.

American Association of Physical Anthropologists *(1928)*
Dept. of Anthropology
SUNY College at Oneonta
Oneonta, NY 13820
Tel: (607)436-2017 *Fax:* (607)436-2653
Web Site: www.physanth.org/
Members: 1650 individuals
Annual Budget: $25-50,000
President: John H. Relethford

Historical Note
Founded in the District of Columbia in 1928. Affiliated with the International Association of Human Biologists, The American Association for The Advancement of Science (AAAS), and the Society for the Study of Human Biology. Membership: $115/year (individual).

Meetings/Conferences:
Annual Meetings: April/800
2007 – Philadelphia, PA/March 27-Apr. 3
2008 – Columbus, OH/Apr. 7-13

Publications:
AAPA Newsletter online. q.
Yearbook of Physical Anthropology. a.
American Journal of Physical Anthropology. m. adv.

American Association of Physician Specialists *(1952)*
2296 Henderson Mill Rd. NE
Suite 206
Atlanta, GA 30345-2739
Tel: (770)939-8555 *Fax:* (770)939-8559
Toll Free: (800)447 - 9397
Web Site: www.aapsga.org
Members: 2800 individuals
Staff: 12
Annual Budget: $2-5,000,000
Chief Executive Officer: William J. Carbone
E-Mail: wcarbone@aapsga.org

Historical Note
Membership is open to D.O.'s and M.D.'s from all specialty categories. Formerly the American Academy of Osteopathic Surgeons, became American Association of Osteopathic Specialists in 1984; assumed its current name in 1994. AAPS provides continuing medical education and board certification in numerous specialties. M.D.'s are accepted for associate membership. Membership: $545/year.

Meetings/Conferences:
Annual Meetings: June

Publications:
Member Notes. q. adv.
American Journal of Clinical Medicine. q. adv.

American Association of Physicians and Health Care Professionals
P.O. Box 13089
Tallahassee, FL 32317
Tel: (850)878-3134 *Fax:* (850)656-0510
Annual Budget: $50-100,000
Executive Director: Robert S. Rhinehart

Historical Note
Membership: $50/year.

Publications:
The Health Care Professional. 3/year. adv.

American Association of Physicists in Medicine *(1958)*
One Physics Ellipse
College Park, MD 20740-3846
Tel: (301)209-3350 *Fax:* (301)209-0862
E-Mail: aapm@aapm.org
Web Site: www.aapm.org
Members: 5531 individuals
Staff: 20
Annual Budget: $5-10,000,000
Executive Director: Angela R. Keyser
E-Mail: akeyser@aapm.org
Director, Finance and Administration: Cecilia Hunter
Director, Exhibits and Scientific Programs: Lisa R. Sullivan
Director, Information Services: Michael Woodward
E-Mail: woodward@aapm.org

Historical Note
Founded in Chicago in 1958 and incorporated in Washington in 1965. Promotes the application of physics to medicine and biology. A member society of the American Institute of Physics and the American Institute for Medical and Biological Engineering. Membership: $185/year.

Meetings/Conferences:
Annual Meetings: Summer
2007 – Minneapolis, MN/July 22-26
2008 – Houston, TX/July 27-31
2009 – Anaheim, CA/July 19-23

Publications:
Medical Physics. m. adv.

American Association of Physics Teachers *(1930)*
One Physics Ellipse
College Park, MD 20740-3845
Tel: (301)209-3300 *Fax:* (301)209-0845
E-Mail: aapt-exec@aapt.org
Web Site: www.aapt.org
Members: 10500 individuals
Staff: 26
Annual Budget: $2-5,000,000
Executive Officer: Dr. Bernard V. Khoury
E-Mail: bkhoury@aapt.org
Director, Membership and Subscriptions: Valerie Evans
E-Mail: vevans@aapt.org
Director, Meetings, Exhibits and Advertising: Carol Heimpel
E-Mail: cheimpel@aapt.org
Director, Finance: Frances Smith
E-Mail: fsmith@aapt.org

Historical Note
AAPT members are university, college, two-year college and high school physics teachers, students and friends. A member of the American Institute of Physics, AAPT is dedicated to advancing the teaching of physics and furthering the role of physics in our culture. Membership: $66-124/year (individual); $500/year (organization/company).

Meetings/Conferences:
Semi-Annual Meetings: *Winter & Summer*

Publications:
The Physics Teacher. 9/year. adv.
Physics Today.
American Journal of Physics. m. adv.
AAPT Announcer. q. adv.

American Association of Plastic Surgeons *(1921)*
900 Cummings Center, Suite 221-U
Beverly, MA 01915
Tel: (978)927-8330 *Fax:* (978)524-8890
Web Site: www.aaps1921.org
Members: 500 individuals
Staff: 1
Annual Budget: $100-250,000
Executive Director: Aurelie M. Alger
Director, Administration: Rebecca R. Bonsaint

Historical Note
Formerly (1942) American Association of Oral and Plastic Surgeons.

Meetings/Conferences:
Annual Meetings: Spring/700
2007 – , ID/May 20-23

Publications:
Plastic and Reconstructive Surgery. m. adv.

American Association of Poison Control Centers *(1958)*
3201 New Mexico Ave. NW
Suite 330
Washington, DC 20016
Tel: (202)362-7217

E-Mail: info@aapcc.org
Web Site: www.aapcc.org
Members: 20 individuals
Staff: 10
Executive Director: Anne Flanagan

Historical Note

AAPCC represents poison control centers and personnel in the field of clinical toxicology. Certifies regional poison centers and individual practitioners, and collects and publishes data on poison exposure in the U.S. Maintains, coordinates, and promotes a nationwide poison emergency phone number, 1-800-222-1222. AAPCC has a second web site, at www.1-800-222-1222.info, to help inform the public. Membership: varies.

Meetings/Conferences:
Annual Meetings: Fall/600

Publications:
Annual Report of the AAPCC's Toxic Exposure Surveillance System. a.

American Association of Police Polygraphists *(1977)*

P.O. Box 657
Waynesville, OH 45068
Tel: (541)598-7332 *Fax:* (937)488-1046
Toll Free: (888)743 - 5479
Web Site: www.policepolygraph.org
Members: 700 individuals
Staff: 1
Annual Budget: $25-50,000
Office Manager: Julie Gerspacher

Historical Note

Members are still polygraphists currently affiliated with a law enforcement agency, investigative agency or government service. Membership: $100/year.

Meetings/Conferences:
Annual Meetings: April/May

Publications:
The Police Polygraphist Journal. q. adv.

American Association of Political Consultants *(1969)*

600 Pennsylvania Ave. SE
Suite 330
Washington, DC 20003-6300
Tel: (202)544-9815 *Fax:* (202)544-9816
E-Mail: info@theaapc.org
Web Site: www.theaapc.org
Members: 1100 individuals
Staff: 1
Annual Budget: $100-250,000
Executive Director: Martha Lockwood

Historical Note

Organized in January 1969 in New York, AAPC is a bipartisan organization of political professionals. Members include strategy consultants, media specialists, pollsters, campaign managers, corporate public affairs officers, elected and appointed public officials, academics, fundraisers, lobbyists, Congressional staff members, and vendors of products and services in the field of politics. Membership: $60/year (student); $100/year (academic); $100/year (associate); $250/year (individual); $500/year (gold); $1,000/year (platinum).

Meetings/Conferences:
Annual Meetings: Fall
2007 - Miami, FL(Eden Roc Hotel)/Feb. 21-23

Publications:
AAPC Update. bi-w.

American Association of Port Authorities *(1912)*

1010 Duke St.
Alexandria, VA 22314-3589
Tel: (703)684-5700 *Fax:* (703)684-6321
E-Mail: info@aapa-ports.org
Web Site: www.aapa-ports.org
Members: 500 agencies and firms
Staff: 15
Annual Budget: $1-2,000,000
President and Chief Executive Officer: Kurt J. Nagle
Director, Communications: Aaron Ellis
Executive Vice President and General Counsel: Jean C. Godwin
Vice President, Government Relations: Susan Monteverde
Director, Membership Services: Edward L. O'Connell

Historical Note

Membership: $1195/year (sustaining); dues for Ports, based on revenues.

Meetings/Conferences:
Annual Meetings: Fall
2007 - Norfolk, VA

Publications:
AAPA Advisory. w. adv.
AAPA Alert. w.
AAPA Seaports of the Americas. a. adv.

American Association of Preferred Provider Organizations *(1984)*

222 S. First St., Suite 303
Louisville, KY 40202
Tel: (502)403-1122 *Fax:* (502)403-1129
Web Site: www.aappo.org
Members: 400 individuals
Staff: 3
Annual Budget: $1-2,000,000
President: Karen Greenrose
E-Mail: kgreenrose@aappo.org
Vice President: Julian Roberts

Historical Note

AAPPO was established in 1983 to advance awareness of the access, choice and flexibility that preferred provider organizations bring to American Healthcare. Representing over 400 individuals from nearly 110 PPO industry companies, AAPPO is dedicated to representing PPOs and their certified provider networks. Leads industry initiatives that improve health plan service for enrollees by listening and responding to needs voiced by enrollees, and works to keep employer and consumer healthcare costs to a minimum.

Meetings/Conferences:
Semi-Annual Meetings: Annual PPO Forum

Publications:
Market Report. a. adv.
State Federal Review. q. adv.
PPO Regulatory Guide. q. adv.
PPO Directory. a. adv.

American Association of Presidents of Independent Colleges and Universities *(1968)*

Box 7070
Provo, UT 84602-7070
Tel: (801)422-5624 *Fax:* (801)422-0617
E-Mail: john_stohlton@byu.edu
Web Site: www.aapicu.org
Members: 175 individuals
Annual Budget: $50-100,000
Executive Director: John B. Stohlton
E-Mail: john_stohlton@byu.edu

Historical Note

Formerly known as the American Association of Independent College and University Presidents; assumed its current name in 1969. Membership: $200/year.

Meetings/Conferences:
Annual Meetings: Third weekend in February, usually in Phoenix, AZ

Publications:
Private Higher Education. irreg.

American Association of Private Railroad Car Owners *(1977)*

630-B Constitution Ave. NE
Washington, DC 20002
Tel: (202)547-5696 *Fax:* (202)547-5623
Web Site: www.aaprco.com
Members: 512 individuals
Staff: 1
Annual Budget: $100-250,000
Executive Director: Diane Elliott

Historical Note

Membership: $500/year (Amtrak-qualified owner); $350/year (non-Amtrak owner); $90/year (associate/non-owner).

Meetings/Conferences:
Annual Meetings: Fall/250

Publications:
Private Varnish. bi-m. adv.
PV News Briefs. bi-m.

American Association of Professional Hypnotherapists *(1979)*

4149A El Camino Way
Palo Alto, CA 94306
Tel: (650)323-3224
Web Site: www.aaph.org
Members: 1500 individuals
Annual Budget: under $10,000
Director: Josie Hadley
E-Mail: aaph@earthlink.com

Historical Note

Members are hypnotherapists, clinical social workers, marriage and family therapists, psychologists, physicians, pastoral counselors, and others trained and experienced in the use of hypnosis in therapy. Membership: $55/year.

Publications:
Hypnotherapy Today. q. adv.
Nat'l Register of Professional Hypnotherapists. a.

American Association of Professional Landmen *(1955)*

4100 Fossil Creek Blvd.
Ft. Worth, TX 76137
Tel: (817)847-7700 *Fax:* (817)847-7704
Toll Free: (888)566 - 2275
Web Site: www.landman.org
Members: 7500 individuals
Staff: 9
Annual Budget: $2-5,000,000
Executive Vice President: Robin Forte
E-Mail: rforte@landman.org
Editor, Publications: Le'ann Pembroke Callihan
E-Mail: leannc@landman.org
Director, Education: Richard Rosprim

Historical Note

A professional society of oil, gas and mining landmen, independent lease brokers, oil operators and company exploration managers. Formerly (1992) the American Association of Petroleum Landmen. Membership: $100/year.

Meetings/Conferences:
Annual Meetings: June/1,000

Publications:
Landman. bi-m. adv.
Landmen's Directory & Guidebook. a. adv.
Landman 2. bi-m. adv.

American Association of Professional Sales Engineers *(1983)*

55969 Jayne Dr.
Elkhart, IN 46514-1325
Tel: (219)522-4837
Members: 600 individuals
Chairman and Chief Executive Officer: Thomas S. Hill

Historical Note

Membership: $125/year (individual); $10/year (student).

Publications:
Newsletter.

American Association of Psychiatric Administrators *(1961)*

P.O. Box 570218
Dallas, TX 75357-0218
Toll Free: (800)650 - 5888
E-Mail: frda1@airmail.net
Web Site: http://psychiatricadministrators.org
Members: 413 individuals
Staff: 1
Annual Budget: $10-25,000
Executive Director: Frances Roton

Historical Note

Affiliated with the American Psychiatric Association. Formerly (1975) Association of Medical Superintendents of Mental Hospitals. Has no headquarters or permanent staff. Officers change annually. Membership: $40/year.

Meetings/Conferences:
Semi-Annual Meetings: Spring/Fall. In conjunction with American Psychiatric Ass'n

Publications:
Psychiatrist Administrator. 3/year.
AAPANews Journal.

American Association of Psychiatric Technicians *(1991)*
2000 O St., Suite 250
Sacramento, CA 95814-5286
Tel: (916)443-1701 *Fax:* (916)329-9145
Toll Free: (800)391 - 7589
E-Mail: aapt@psych-health.com
Web Site: www.psychtechs.org
Members: 3500 individuals
Staff: 1
Executive Director: Keith Hearn
Historical Note
Administers an examination for mental health workers to receive the designation of Nationally Certified Psychiatric Technician.

American Association of Public Health Dentistry *(1937)*
P.O. Box 7536
Springfield, IL 62791
Tel: (217)391-0218 *Fax:* (217)793-0041
E-Mail: natoff@aaphd.org
Web Site: www.aaphd.org
Members: 800 individuals and organizations
Staff: 1
Annual Budget: $250-500,000
Executive Director: Pamela Tolson, CAE
E-Mail: natoff@aaphd.org
Historical Note
Formerly (1983) the American Association of Public Health Dentists. Membership: $100/year.
Meetings/Conferences:
Annual Meetings: usually in conjunction with American Dental Ass'n
2007 – Denver, CO(Marriott Tech Center)/Apr. 30-May 2
Publications:
Journal of Public Health Dentistry. q. adv.
Communique. q. adv.

American Association of Public Health Physicians *(1954)*
c/o American College of Preventive Medicine
1307 New York Ave. NW, Suite 200
Washington, DC 20005
Tel: (202)466-2044 *Fax:* (202)466-2662
E-Mail: rsr@acpm.org
Web Site: www.aaphp.org
Members: 200 individuals
Annual Budget: under $10,000
Director, Membership: Robert S. Rader
Historical Note
Incorporated in the state of Texas. AAPHP's mission is to promote the public health, represent public health physicians, educate the nation on the role and importance of the public health physician's knowledge and skills in practicing population medicine, and foster communication, education and scholarship in public health. Membership: $60/year; $30/year (AMA member).
Meetings/Conferences:
Annual Meetings: Spring
Publications:
AAPHP News. m. adv.
Bulletin. q. adv.

American Association of Public Welfare Attorneys *(1967)*
Historical Note
An affiliate of the American Public Welfare Association, which provides administrative support.

American Association of Radon Scientists and Technologists *(1986)*
2502 S. Fifth Ave.
Lebanon, PA 17042-9701
Tel: (717)949-3198 *Fax:* (717)949-3192
Toll Free: (866)772 - 2778 Ext:
E-Mail: office@aarst.org
Web Site: www.aarst.org
Members: 1100 individuals
Staff: 1
Annual Budget: $100-250,000
Executive Secretary: Caren Walmer
Historical Note
AARST members are manufacturers, scientists and others concerned with radon gas testing and remediation. Membership: $125/year (individual); $500/year (corporate); $75/year (associate and student).
Meetings/Conferences:
Annual Meetings: Fall/300
Publications:
Radon Reporter. q. adv.

American Association of Railroad Superintendents *(1896)*
P.O. Box 456
Tinley Park, IL 60477
Tel: (708)342-0210 *Fax:* (708)342-0257
E-Mail: aars@railroadsuperintendents.org
Web Site: www.railroadsuperintendents.org
Members: 500 individuals
Staff: 1
Annual Budget: $50-100,000
Administrative Manager: Pat Weissmann
E-Mail: aars@railroadsuperintendents.org
Historical Note
Promotes continuing education among its members. Membership: $50/year.
Meetings/Conferences:
Semi-annual Meetings: August and February
2007 – St. Augustine, FL(Renaissance Hotel World Golf Village)/Feb. 25-27/170
2007 – Chicago, IL(Indian Lakes)/July 29-30/200
Publications:
Proceedings. a.
AARS News. q.

American Association of Residential Mortgage Regulators *(1989)*
1255 23rd St. NW
Suite 200
Washington, DC 20037
Tel: (202)521-3999 *Fax:* (202)833-3636
Web Site: www.aarmr.org
Members: 100 individuals
Staff: 2
Exective Director: David A. Saunders
Historical Note
Members are state employees responsible for administration of residential mortgage oversight. Primary interests include model legislation and best practices.
Meetings/Conferences:
Annual Meetings: Fall
Publications:
Newsletter. q.

American Association of Retired Persons *(1958)*
601 E St. NW
Suite A-9
Washington, DC 20049
Tel: (202)434-2560
Toll Free: (888)687 - 2277
E-Mail: media@aarp.org
Web Site: www.aarp.org
Annual Budget: Over $100,000,000
Chief Executive Officer: William Novelli
Director, Federal Affairs: David Certner
Chief People Officer: Ellie Hollander
Chief Operating Officer: Thomas Nelson
Historical Note
AARP is the successor to National Association of Retired Teachers (founded 1947). AARP is a non-profit association providing services and representing members of the American workforce over the age of 50. Membership: $12.50/year.
Publications:
AARP Bulletin.
Modern Maturity.
My Generation.

American Association of Retirement Communities *(1974)*
c/o Jacksonville State Univ. Center for Econ. Development
700 Pelham Rd. North, 114 Merrill Hall
Jacksonville, AL 36265
Tel: (256)782-5700
E-Mail: aarc@jsu.edu
Web Site: www.the-aarc.org
Executive Director: Pat Shaddix
E-Mail: aarc@jsu.edu
Historical Note
AARC members are municipal development authorities, chambers of commerce, business and other organizations interested in retiree retention as an economic development strategy.
Meetings/Conferences:
Annual Meetings: usually Fall
Publications:
AARC Newsletter. q.

American Association of School Administrators *(1865)*
801 N. Quincy St., Suite 700
Arlington, VA 22203
Tel: (703)528-0700 *Fax:* (703)841-1543
Web Site: www.aasa.org
Members: 14000 individuals
Staff: 45
Annual Budget: $10-25,000,000
Executive Director: Paul D. Houston
E-Mail: phouston@aasa.org
Associate Executive Director, Children's Initiatives and Special Projects: Sharon Adams-Taylor
E-Mail: sadamstaylor@aasa.org
Associate Executive Director, Operations: Dyanne Hughes
E-Mail: dhughes@aasa.org
Associate Executive Director, Public Affairs: Bruce Hunter
E-Mail: bhunter@aasa.org
Associate Executive Director, Affiliate and Membership Services: C.J. Reid
E-Mail: creid@aasa.org
Associate Executive Director, Leadership Development and Communications: Claudia Mansfield Sutton
Historical Note
Founded as the National Association of School Superintendents, it became the Department of School Superintendents of the National Education Association in 1870, the Department of Superintendents of NEA in 1907 and assumed its present name in 1937. Absorbed the County and Intermediate Unit Superintendents of NEA in 1968. Has an annual budget of approximately $11 million. Membership: $304/year (individual).
Meetings/Conferences:
Annual Meetings: February-March/17,000
2007 – New Orleans, LA/March 1-4
2008 – Tampa, FL/Feb. 14-18
2009 – San Francisco, CA/Feb. 19-22
2010 – Phoenix, AZ/Feb. 11-14
Publications:
The Conference Daily. a. adv.
The Conference Program Book. a. adv.
The School Administrator. m. adv.

American Association of School Librarians *(1951)*
50 E. Huron
Chicago, IL 60611-2795
Tel: (312)280-4382 *Fax:* (312)280-5276
Toll Free: (800)545 - 2433 Ext: 4382
E-Mail: aasl@ala.org
Web Site: www.ala.org/aasl
Members: 9300 individuals
Staff: 11
Annual Budget: $500-1,000,000
Executive Director: Julie A. Walker
E-Mail: aasl@ala.org
Manager, Communications: Steven Hofman
E-Mail: aasl@ala.org
Historical Note
AASL's membership is composed of school library media specialists. A division of the American Library Association.
Meetings/Conferences:
Biennial meetings:
2007 – Reno, NV/Oct. 25-28
Publications:
AASL Hotlinks (online). m. adv.
Knowledge Quest. tri-m.
School Library Media. q. adv.

American Association of School Personnel Administrators *(1940)*
533B N. Mur-Len Rd.
Olathe, KS 66062
Tel: (913)829-2007 *Fax:* (913)829-2041
E-Mail: aaspa@aaspa.org
Web Site: www.aaspa.org
Members: 1800 individuals
Staff: 4
Annual Budget: $250-500,000
Executive Director: Jody Shelton, Ed.D
E-Mail: aaspa@aaspa.org

Historical Note
Founded as the American Association of Examiners and Administrators of Educational Personnel, it assumed its present name in 1959. AASPA provides leadership in promoting effective human resource practices within education through professional development activities and a resource-based network. Membership: $150/year (individual).

Meetings/Conferences:
Annual Meetings: October/800
2007 – Kansas City, MO/Oct. 17-20
2008 – Seattle, WA/Oct. 15-18
2009 – Hartford, CT/Oct. 13-16
2010 – Myrtle Beach, SC/Oct. 12-15

Publications:
Perspectives newsletter. 4/year.
Research Publications.

American Association of Sexuality Educators, Counselors and Therapists *(1967)*
P.O. Box 1960
Ashland, VA 23005-1960
Tel: (804)752-0026 *Fax:* (804)752-0056
E-Mail: aasect@aasect.org
Web Site: www.aasect.org
Members: 2000 individuals
Staff: 4
Annual Budget: $500-1,000,000
Executive Director: Stephen Conley, Ph.D.

Historical Note
Awards the designations Certified Sex Educator, Sex Counselor, Sex Therapist and Certified Supervisor to qualified members. Membership: $195/year (individual); $475/year (organizaton).

Meetings/Conferences:
Annual Meetings: Summer

Publications:
Contemporary Sexuality. m. adv.

American Association of Small Ruminant Practitioners *(1968)*
1910 Lyda Ave., Suite 200
Bowling Green, KY 42104
Tel: (270)793-0781 *Fax:* (270)782-0188
E-Mail: aasrp@aasrp.org
Web Site: www.aasrp.org
Members: 1100 individuals
Annual Budget: $25-50,000
Acting Executive Director: Peggy Logsdon
E-Mail: davidm7316@aol.com

Historical Note
Formerly (1988) American Association of Sheep and Goat Practitioners. Primarily an association of veterinarians, AASRP also includes veterinary student members, foreign libraries, and owners of sheep, goats, llamas, deer, and more exotic small ruminants. It is an educational association which encourages research and dissemination of new knowledge to practicing veterinarians. Membership: $50/year (U.S.A.); $55/year (foreign); and $15/year (student U.S.A.); $20/year (student foreign).

Meetings/Conferences:
Annual Meetings: With the AVMA

Publications:
The AASRP Newsletter, Wool & Wattles. q.

American Association of Spinal Cord Injury Nurses *(1983)*
75-20 Astoria Blvd.
Jackson Heights, NY 11370-1177
Tel: (718)803-3782 Ext: 324 *Fax:* (718)803-0414
Web Site: www.aascin.org
Members: 1100 individuals
Staff: 5
Annual Budget: $500-1,000,000
Associate Executive Director: Vivian Beyda, DPH
Program Manager: Stephen Sofer, Ph.D.

Historical Note
AASCIN members are nurses specializing in the care of spinal cord injuries. Limited to registered nurses (RN), licensed practical nurses (LPN), and licensed vocational nurses (LVN). Shares Administrative offices with American Paraplegia Society and the American Association of Spinal Cord Psychologists and Social Workers. Membership: $100/year (individual).

Meetings/Conferences:
Annual Meetings: September
2007 – Orlando, FL(Gaylord Palms)/Aug. 27-29
2008 – Orlando, FL(Gaylord Palms)/Aug. 11-13

Publications:
Membership Directory (on-line).
SCI Nursing Journal (e-journal). q.

American Association of Spinal Cord Injury Psychologists and Social Workers *(1986)*
75-20 Astoria Blvd.
Jackson Heights, NY 11370-1177
Tel: (718)803-3782 *Fax:* (718)803-0414
Web Site: www.aascipsw.org
Members: 530 individuals
Staff: 5
Annual Budget: $250-500,000
Associate Executive Director: Vivian Beyda, DPH
Program Manager: Stephen Sofer, Ph.D.

Historical Note
Members are psychologists and social workers who treat individuals with spinal cord injuries. Shares administrative offices with the American Paraplegia Society and the American Association of Spinal Cord Injury Nurses. Membership: $100/year (individual).

Meetings/Conferences:
2007 – Orlando, FL(Gaylord Palms)/Aug. 27-29
2008 – Orlando, FL(Gaylord Palms)/Aug. 11-13

Publications:
SCI Psychosocial Process (e-journal). q.
Membership Directory (on-line).

American Association of State Climatologists *(1976)*
Department of Geography, Rutgers University
54 Joyce Kilmer Ave.
Piscataway, NJ 08854-8054
Tel: (732)445-4741 *Fax:* (732)445-0006
Web Site: www.ncdc.noaa.gov/ol/climate/aasc.html
Members: 130 individuals
Staff: 1
Annual Budget: under $10,000
President: Dave Robinson

Historical Note
Established in Asheville, NC, by 16 state climatologists as a method of interaction on climatological matters. AASC now includes 49 states. Has no paid officers or full-time staff. Membership: $100/year.

Publications:
State Climatology. q.

American Association of State Colleges and Universities *(1961)*
1307 New York Ave. NW
Fifth Floor
Washington, DC 20005-4701
Tel: (202)293-7070 *Fax:* (202)296-5819
Web Site: www.aascu.org
Members: 425 institutions
Staff: 72
Annual Budget: $5-10,000,000
President: Constantine Curris, Ph.D.
Vice President, Membership Services: Christina Bitting
VicePresident, Communications: Susan Chilcott
Senior Vice President, Government Relations and Policy Analysis: Edward M. Elmendorf
Director, Meetings: Rosemary S. Lauth
Vice President, Academic Leadership and Change: George Mehaffy
Vice President, Administration and Finance: Wayne V. Sforza

Historical Note
Formerly the Association of State Colleges and Universities. Absorbed the Association of Upper Level Colleges and Universities and superseded the Association of Teachers of Education Institutions, founded in 1951. Has an annual budget of approximately $6.6 million. Membership fee based upon enrollment of institution.

Meetings/Conferences:
Annual Meetings: November/600

Publications:
Public Purpose Magazine. 5/yr.

American Association of State Highway and Transportation Officials *(1914)*
444 North Capitol St. NW
Suite 249
Washington, DC 20001
Tel: (202)624-5800 *Fax:* (202)624-5806
Members: 52 state governmental agencies
Staff: 50
Annual Budget: $5-10,000,000
Executive Director: John C. Horsley
E-Mail: jhorsley@aashto.org
Director, Management and Business Development: Jack Basso
E-Mail: jbasso@aashto.org
Director, Engineering and Technical Services: Anthony Kane
E-Mail: akane@aashto.org
Director, Policy and Government Relations: Janet Oakley
E-Mail: joakley@aashto.org
Director, Finance and Administration: Roger Roberts
E-Mail: rogerr@aashto.org
Director, Communications and Publications: Sunny Mays Schust
E-Mail: sunnys@aashto.org
Director, Meeting and Member Services: Hannah Whitney
E-Mail: hannahw@aashto.org

Historical Note
Founded as the American Association of State Highway Officials, it was reorganized and renamed in 1973 to represent transportation agencies. AASHTO members are the state highway and transportation departments of the 50 states, Puerto Rico, and the District of Columbia. Annual budget is approximately $8.1 million.

Publications:
AASHTO Quarterly. q.
AASHTO Journal Weekly Transportation Report. w.

American Association of State Social Work Boards

Historical Note
Became Association of Social Work Boards in 2000.

American Association of Stratigraphic Palynologists *(1967)*
c/o ConocoPhillips
P.O. Box 2197
Houston, TX 77252-2197
Tel: (281)293-3189 *Fax:* (281)293-3833
Web Site: www.palynology.org
Members: 617 individuals
Staff: 8
Annual Budget: $50-100,000
Secretary-Treasurer: Dr. Thomas D. Demchuk

Historical Note
Founded December 8, 1967 in Tulsa, Oklahoma with 31 charter members. Promotes the study of palynology, or the study of pollen and spores, especially as it relates to stratigraphic applications and biostratigraphy. Has no paid staff. Membership: $45/year (individual); $30/year (student); $15/year (retired); $70/year (institutional).

Publications:
Newsletter (online and print). q.
Palynology Journal. a.
Contribution Series. irreg.
Membership Directory. a.

American Association of Suicidology *(1968)*
5221 Wisconsin Ave. NW
Washington, DC 20015
Tel: (202)237-2280 *Fax:* (202)237-2282
E-Mail: info@suicidology.org
Web Site: www.suicidology.org
Members: 1000 individuals
Staff: 3
Annual Budget: $250-500,000
Executive Director: Dr. Alan L. Berman

Historical Note
Multi-disciplinary organization of professionals and concerned lay people. Makes available an up-to-date listing of suicide prevention centers and survivors' suicide support groups. Sponsors National Suicide Prevention Week. Membership: $140/year (individual); organization dues based on revenue.

Meetings/Conferences:
Annual Meetings: Spring
2007 – Boston, MA(Park Plaza)/Apr. 16-19/700

Publications:
Surviving Suicide. q. adv.
Suicide and Life Threatening Behavior. q. adv.
Newslink. q. adv.
Proceedings. a.

American Association of Sunday and Feature Editors *(1948)*
1117 Journalism Bldg., Room 4113
University of Maryland
College Park, MD 20742
Tel: (301)314-2631
E-Mail: aasfe@jmail.umd.edu
Web Site: www.aasfe.org
Members: 250 individuals
Staff: 1
Annual Budget: $50-100,000
Executive Director: Penny Bender Fuchs
E-Mail: aasfe@jmail.umd.edu

Historical Note
Concerned with the improvement of Sunday newspapers and newspaper features. Membership: $100/year (organization).

Meetings/Conferences:
Annual Meetings: Fall

Publications:
Style. semi-a.
Feedback. q.

American Association of Surgical Physician Assistants *(1973)*
4267 N.W. Federal Hwy, PMB 201
Jensen Beach, FL 34957
Toll Free: (888)882 - 2772 Ext:
E-Mail: aaspa@aaspa.com
Web Site: www.aaspa.com
Members: 540 individuals
Staff: 2
Annual Budget: $50-100,000
Executive Director: Linda Kotrba

Historical Note
Formerly the American Association of Surgeon Assistants. Membership: $125/year; $30/year (student).

Meetings/Conferences:
Annual Meetings: Fall, with the American College of Surgeons Clinical Congress

Publications:
Membership Directory. a.
Surgical Physician Assistant. m. adv.
Sutureline. q. adv.

American Association of Swine Practitioners

Historical Note
Became American Association of Swine Veterinarians in 2002.

American Association of Swine Veterinarians *(1969)*
902 First Ave.
Perry, IA 50220
Tel: (515)465-5255 *Fax:* (515)465-3832
E-Mail: aasv@aasv.org
Web Site: www.aasv.org
Members: 1400 individuals
Staff: 2
Annual Budget: $500-1,000,000
Executive Director: Thomas J. Burkgren, D.V.M., MBA
E-Mail: aasv@aasv.org

Historical Note
Formerly (2000) American Association of Swine Practitioners. Seeks to improve the quality of swine herd health programs and to enhance the scientific knowledge of veterinarians through continued education. Members are graduate veterinarians. Membership: $160/year.

Meetings/Conferences:
Annual Meetings: Spring/900
2007 – Orlando, FL/March 3-6/900
2009 – Dallas, TX/March 7-10/900
2010 – Omaha, NE/March 6-9/900

Publications:
Journal of Swine Health and Production. bi-m. adv.
Proceedings of the AASV Annual Meeting. a.

American Association of Teachers of Arabic *(1965)*
College of William & Mary, Modern Lang./Literature Dept.
P.O. Box 8795
Williamsburg, VA 23187
Tel: (757)221-3145 *Fax:* (757)221-3637
Web Site: www.wm.edu/aata
Members: 130 individuals
Staff: 5
Annual Budget: $10-25,000
Executive Director: John C. Eisele
E-Mail: jceise@facstaff.wm.edu

Historical Note
AATA's objective is to contribute to the enhancement of study, criticism and research in the field of Arabic language, literature, and linguistics. Affiliated in 1964 with the American Council on Teaching of Foreign Languages and in 1970 with the Middle East Studies Assn. Membership: $25/year (individual); $200/year (organization).

Meetings/Conferences:
Annual Meetings: With Middle East Studies Ass'n of North America

Publications:
Journal of the AATA and Notes for Contributors. a. adv.

American Association of Teachers of Esperanto *(1961)*
5140 San Lorenzo Dr.
Santa Barbara, CA 93111-2521
Tel: (805)967-5241
Members: 60 individuals
Annual Budget: under $10,000
Editor, AATE Bulletin: Dorothy Holland

Historical Note
AATE members are persons who are teaching or have taught Esperanto, and educators interested in Esperanto. Affiliated with the International League of Esperantist Teachers. AATE has no paid officers or staff. Membership: $30/year (individual).

Meetings/Conferences:
Annual Meetings: Annual meetings held in conjunction with the Esperanto League for North America.

Publications:
AATE Bulletin. q.

American Association of Teachers of French *(1927)*
MC-4510, Southern Illinois Univ.
Carbondale, IL 62901-4510
Tel: (618)453-5731 *Fax:* (618)453-5733
Web Site: www.frenchteachers.org
Members: 10000 individuals
Staff: 4
Annual Budget: $500-1,000,000
Executive Director: Jayne Abrate
E-Mail: abrate@siu.edu

Historical Note
Member of the Joint National Committee on Languages. Sponsors programs for students such as the French Honor Society at the high school level, a national french contest, summer scholarships, and a placement service. Membership: $45/year (U.S.); $50/year (foreign); $22/year (student).

Meetings/Conferences:
Annual Meetings: Summer

Publications:
AATF National Bulletin. q.
French Review. bi-m. adv.

American Association of Teachers of German *(1926)*
112 Haddontowne Ct.
Suite 104
Cherry Hill, NJ 08034
Tel: (856)795-5553 *Fax:* (856)795-9398
E-Mail: headquarters@aatg.org
Web Site: www.aatg.org
Members: 6000 individuals
Staff: 8
Annual Budget: $1-2,000,000
Executive Director: Helene Zimmer-Loew
E-Mail: helene@aatg.org

Historical Note
AATG sponsors a number of programs for students such as a national high school honor society, summer travel/study programs, and competitions. Also provides materials, awards, and job information for teachers. Membership: $30-60/year (based on salary).

Meetings/Conferences:
Annual Meetings: Fall

Publications:
AATG Newsletter. q.
Die Unterrichtspraxis. semi-a. adv.
German Quarterly. q. adv.

American Association of Teachers of Italian *(1924)*
Dept. of Modern Foreign Languages and Literatures
Nazareth Coll., 4245 East Ave.
Rochester, NY 14618
Tel: (585)389-2688 *Fax:* (585)586-2452
Members: 1200 individuals
Staff: 1
Annual Budget: $25-50,000
Treasurer: Maria Rosaria Vitti-Alexander
E-Mail: mrvittia@naz.edu

Historical Note
Allied with the Modern Language Association and the American Council on the Teaching of Foreign Languages. Secretary-Treasurer serves for 4 years; others officers change triennially. Membership: $45/year (individual); $60/year (institution).

Meetings/Conferences:
Annual Meetings: November, with the American Council on the Teaching of Foreign Languages/150

Publications:
Italica. q. adv.
AATI Newsletter. semi-a. adv.

American Association of Teachers of Slavic and East European Languages *(1941)*
P.O. Box 7039
Berkeley, CA 94707
Tel: (510)526-6614
E-Mail: aatseel@earthlink.net
Web Site: http://aatseel.org
Members: 1000 individuals
Staff: 1
Annual Budget: $50-100,000
Executive Director: Kathleen E. Dillon, Ph.D.
E-Mail: aatseel@earthlink.net

Historical Note
AATSEEL members are teachers of Slavic and East European languages. Membership: $25-60/year (varies by academic rank).

Publications:
Slavic and East European Journal. q. adv.
AATSEEL Newsletter. q. adv.

American Association of Teachers of Spanish and Portuguese *(1917)*
423 Exton Commons
Exton, PA 19341-2451
Tel: (610)363-7005 *Fax:* (610)363-7116
E-Mail: corporate@aatsp.org
Web Site: www.aatsp.org

Members: 15000 individuals
Staff: 4
Annual Budget: $250-500,000
Executive Director: Emily Spinelli
E-Mail: corporate@aatsp.org

Historical Note
Supports teachers of Spanish and Portugese at all levels through its publications, placement bureau, and other programs. Membership: $40/year.

Meetings/Conferences:
Annual Meetings: August/500

Publications:
Portuguese Newsletter. 2/year.
AATSP Professional Development Series Handbook for Teachers K-16.
Hispania. q. adv.
Enlace Newsletter. 2/year.

American Association of Teachers of Turkic Languages *(1985)*
Near Eastern Studies, 110 Jones Hall
Princeton University
Princeton, NJ 08544-1008
Tel: (609)258-1435 *Fax:* (609)258-1242
Web Site: www.princeton.edu/turkish/aatt.html
Members: 160 individuals
Annual Budget: under $10,000
Executive Secretary-Treasurer: Erika H. Gilson, Ph.D.
E-Mail: ehgilson@princeton.edu

Historical Note
AATT is a non-profit national association of professionals dedicated to the enhancement of study, criticism and research in the field of Turkic languages, literature and linguistics, and to improving and advancing the teaching and learning of Turkic. Membership: $15/year (individual); $25-500/year (institution); $7/year (student).

Meetings/Conferences:
Annual Meetings: Fall

Publications:
Bulletin. bi-a.

American Association of Textile Chemists and Colorists *(1921)*
P.O. Box 12215
Research Triangle Park, NC 27709
Tel: (919)549-8141 *Fax:* (919)549-8933
Web Site: www.aatcc.org
Members: 7000 individuals
Staff: 25
Annual Budget: $2-5,000,000
Executive Director: John Y. Daniels
E-Mail: danielsj@aatcc.org
Director, Membership Services: Birgit Patty
E-Mail: pattyb@aatcc.org
Director, Educational Programs: Peggy J. Pickett
E-Mail: pickettp@aatcc.org
Director, Publications: Sandy Thomas
E-Mail: thomass@aatcc.org

Historical Note
Founded in Boston in 1921 with 270 charter members and incorporated in Massachusetts. Promotes the increase of knowledge of the application of dyes and chemicals in the textile industry and the use of textile wet processing machinery. Membership: $80/year (individual); $500/year (minimum for companies, with sliding scale for size).

Meetings/Conferences:
Annual Meetings: Fall/3,000

Publications:
Membership Directory.
AATCC Review Magazine. m. adv.
Book of Papers from Internat'l Conference & Exhibition. a.
AATCC Technical Manual. a.

American Association of Tissue Banks *(1976)*
1320 Old Chain Bridge Rd.
Suite 450
McLean, VA 22101
Tel: (703)827-9582 *Fax:* (703)356-2198
E-Mail: aatb@aatb.org
Web Site: www.aatb.org
Members: 1350 individuals & institutions
Staff: 7
Chief Executive Officer: Robert Rigney
E-Mail: aatb@aatb.org

Historical Note
Incorporated in the State of Maryland. AATB members are individuals involved or interested in banking of tissues, cells or organs and institutions qualifying as accredited tissue banking facilities which participate in a tissue, cell or organ banking program including retrieval, processing, storage and distribution. AATB offers a program of Certification of Tissue Bank Personnel awarding the designation Tissue Bank Specialist (TBS). Membership: $150/year (individual); call for information on institutional membership.

Meetings/Conferences:
Semi-annual Meetings: Spring and late August-early September

Publications:
AATB Newsletter. q.
AATB Standards for Tissue Banking. irreg.
AATB Tissue & Cell Report. semi-a. adv.

American Association of University Administrators *(1970)*
c/o Rhode Island College, Roberts Hall 407
600 Mount Pleasant St.
Providence, RI 02908-1991
Tel: (401)456-2808 *Fax:* (401)456-8287
Web Site: www.aaua.org
Members: 900 individuals
Staff: 1
Annual Budget: $50-100,000
General Secretary: Dan King

Historical Note
A professional association of career educational administrators founded in Buffalo, New York. Develops and advances the standards for the profession of higher education administration. Membership: $100/year (individual); $250/year (sponsor); $500-1000/year (institutional members).

Meetings/Conferences:
Annual Meetings: Summer

Publications:
AAUA Communique Newsletter (online). q.

American Association of University Affiliated Programs for Persons with Developmental Disabilities

Historical Note
Became Association of University Centers on Disabilities in 2002.

American Association of University Professors *(1915)*
1012 14th St. NW
Suite 500
Washington, DC 20005-3465
Tel: (202)737-5900 *Fax:* (202)737-5526
E-Mail: aaup@aaup.org
Web Site: www.aaup.org
Members: 45000 individuals
Staff: 40
Annual Budget: $2-5,000,000
General Secretary: Roger A. Bowen
Director, Organizing and Services: Michael Mauer

Historical Note
AAUP provides economic and legisative information on higher education issues, and advocates in the interest of faculty in all types of universites and colleges. Promotes academic freedom and professional standards. Members are full and part-time teachers, scholars, graduate students, librarians and other academic professionals. Membership: $143/year (individual).

Meetings/Conferences:
Annual Meetings: June/400
2007 – Washington, DC(Omni Shoreham)/June 7-10/400
2008 – Washington, DC(Omni Shoreham)/June 12-15/400

Publications:
Academ. bi-m. adv.

American Association of Variable Star Observers *(1911)*
25 Birch St.
Cambridge, MA 02138
Tel: (617)354-0484 *Fax:* (617)354-0665
E-Mail: aavso@aavso.org
Web Site: www.aavso.org
Members: 3000 individuals
Staff: 12
Annual Budget: $250-500,000
Director: Arne Henden
E-Mail: aavso@aavso.org

Historical Note
Members are amateur and professional astronomers who gather and record data on stars which vary in brightness. Membership: $50/year.

Publications:
Women in the History of Variable Star Astronomy.
Manual for Visual Observing.
AAVSO Circular. m.
Bulletin. a.
Journal of AAVSO. semi-a.
Alert Notices. irreg.
Newsletter. semi-a.

American Association of Veterinary Clinicians *(1958)*
37 W. Broad St., Suite 480
Columbus, OH 43215-4132
Tel: (614)358-0417 *Fax:* (614)241-2215
E-Mail: tking@craiggroup.com
Web Site: www.craiggroup.com/aavc.htm/
Members: 476 individuals
Staff: 3
Annual Budget: $50-100,000
Executive Director: Tom King

Historical Note
AAVC's purpose is three-fold: to provide for the association of persons engaged in teaching clinical veterinary medicine, for the presentation and discussion of items of common interest and to further scientific progress by education and research in the field of clinical veterinary medicine. Membership: $8/year (individual).

American Association of Veterinary Immunologists *(1979)*
2118 Veterinary Medicine Bldg.
Iowa State University
Ames, IA 50011
Tel: (515)294-5097 *Fax:* (515)294-8500
Members: 260 individuals
Annual Budget: under $10,000
Secretary-Treasurer: Dr. Eileen Thacker

Historical Note
AAVI members are veterinarians and others with an interest in veterinary immunology. Membership: $15/year (individual); $5/year (student).

Publications:
AAVI Newsletter. 2/year.

American Association of Veterinary Laboratory Diagnosticians *(1958)*
P.O. Box 1770
Davis, CA 95617
Tel: (530)754-9719 *Fax:* (530)752-5680
Web Site: www.aavld.org
Members: 1200 individuals
Staff: 2
Annual Budget: $250-500,000
Secretary-Treasurer: Dr. Alex Ardans

Historical Note
AAVLD, formerly the Conference of Veterinary Laboratory Diagnosticians, was organized in 1956 with the express purpose of: dissemination of information relating to the diagnosis of animal disease, coordination of diagnostic activities of regulatory research in service laboratories, establishment of uniform diagnostic techniques and the improvement of existing ones, and the development of a body that could act in a consultant capacity to the United States Animal Health Association on uniform diagnostic criteria involved in regulatory animal disease programs. Membership: $75/year.

Meetings/Conferences:
Annual Meetings: October, with United States Animal Health Ass'n

Publications:
Membership Directory. a.

Journal of Veterinary Diagnostic Investigation. 6/year. adv.
Proceedings. a. adv.
Newsletter. q. adv.

American Association of Veterinary Parasitologists *(1956)*
c/o Phoenix Scientific, Inc.
3915 S. 48th St. Terrace
St. Joseph, MO 64503
Tel: (816)364-3777 Ext: 1375 *Fax:* (816)364-6021
Toll Free: (800)757 - 3664 Ext: 1375
Web Site: www.aavp.org
Members: 500 individuals
Staff: 1
Annual Budget: $25-50,000
Executive Secretary-Treasurer: Dr. Alan Marchiondo
E-Mail: alan.marchiondo@tevaUSA.com

Historical Note
Professional society for the promotion of veterinary parasitology and the dissemination of current scientific information. Affiliated with the American Veterinary Medical Association. Membership: $30/year (individual).

Meetings/Conferences:
Annual Meetings: With American Veterinary Medical Ass'n/200
2007 – Washington, DC/July 14-18
2008 – New Orleans, LA/July 19-22

Publications:
AAVP Newsletter. 3/year.
Proceedings. a.

American Association of Veterinary State Boards *(1957)*
4106 Central St.
Kansas City, MO 64111
Tel: (816)931-1504 *Fax:* (816)931-1604
Toll Free: (877)698 - 8482
E-Mail: info@aavsb.org
Web Site: www.aavsb.org
Members: 57 boards
Staff: 6
Annual Budget: $1-2,000,000
Executive Director: Charlotte P. Ronan
E-Mail: aavsb@aavsb.org

Historical Note
AAVSB members are members of state boards of veterinary examiners.

Meetings/Conferences:
Annual Meetings: in conjunction with the American Veterinary Medical Ass'n

Publications:
AAVSB Newsletter. q.
Membership Directory. a.

American Association of Wildlife Veterinarians *(1979)*
Wildlife Health Center, University of California - Davis
One Shields Ave.
Davis, CA 95616
Tel: (530)754-5701
E-Mail: djessup@ospr.dfg.ca.gov
Members: 250 individuals
Annual Budget: under $10,000
President: Dave Jessup

Historical Note
Members are veterinarians specializing in the health of wild animals in their natural habitat. Has no full-time staff.

Meetings/Conferences:
Annual Meetings: Summer with the Wildlife Disease Ass'n.

Publications:
Newsletter. q.
Membership Directory. irreg.

American Association of Women Dentists *(1921)*
216 W. Jackson Blvd., Suite 625
Chicago, IL 60606
Tel: (312)913-9327 *Fax:* (312)750-1203
Toll Free: (800)920 - 2293
E-Mail: info@aawd.org
Web Site: www.womendentists.org
Members: 1000 individuals
Staff: 3
Annual Budget: $100-250,000
Executive Director: Debbie Gidley

Historical Note
Founded as Association of American Women Dentists. Established to advance women in dentistry.

Meetings/Conferences:
Annual Meetings: Summer

Publications:
Chronicle. q. adv.
Woman Dental Journal. 10/year. adv.
Membership Directory. a. adv.

American Association of Women Emergency Physicians *(1983)*

Historical Note
Merged with American College of Emergency Physicians in 2000.

American Association of Zoo Keepers *(1967)*
3601 S.W. 29th St., Suite 133
Topeka, KS 66614
Tel: (785)273-9149 *Fax:* (785)273-1980
Toll Free: (800)242 - 4519
Web Site: www.aazk.org
Members: 2700 individuals
Staff: 3
Annual Budget: $100-250,000
Executive Director: Ed Hansen
E-Mail: zked9@cs.com
Managing Editor, AKF: Susan D. Chan
E-Mail: afkeditor@zk.kscoxmail.com
Administrative Secretary: Barbara Manspeaker
E-Mail: aazkoffice@zk.kscoxmail.com

Historical Note
Membership: $40/year (professional keepers); $35/year (other individuals); $125/year (organization/company).

Publications:
Animal Keepers' Forum. m. adv.
Conference Proceedings. a.

American Association of Zoo Veterinarians *(1945)*
581705 White Oak Rd.
Yulee, FL 32097
Tel: (904)225-3275 *Fax:* (904)225-3289
E-Mail: aazv@aol.com
Web Site: www.aazv.org
Members: 1200 individuals
Staff: 2
Annual Budget: $250-500,000

Historical Note
Organized to advance programs of preventive medicine, husbandry and scientific research in the field of veterinary medicine dealing with captive and free-ranging wild animals. Membership: $80/year (student); $95/year (domestic); $210/year (overseas).

Meetings/Conferences:
Annual Meetings: Fall

Publications:
The Journal of Zoo and Wildlife Medicine. q. adv.
Proceedings. a.
Directory (online, for members only).

American Association on Mental Retardation *(1876)*
444 North Capitol St. NW
Suite 846
Washington, DC 20001-1512
Tel: (202)387-1968 *Fax:* (202)387-2193
Toll Free: (800)424 - 3688
E-Mail: aanap@aamr.og
Web Site: www.aamr.org
Members: 8050 individuals
Staff: 10
Annual Budget: $2-5,000,000
Executive Director: M. Doreen Croser
E-Mail: dcroser@aamr.org
Director, Finance and Administration: Paul D. Aitken
E-Mail: pdaitken@aamr.org
Director, Publications: Bruce Appelgren

Historical Note
Organized June 6, 1876 in Elwyn, Pennsylvania as the Association of Medical Officers of American Institutions for Idiotic and Feeble-Minded Persons; changed name (1906) to American Association for the Study of the Feeble-Minded and became (1933) American Association on Mental Deficiency in 1933; assumed current name in 1987. Incorporated in Pennsylvania in 1938. AAMR is affiliated with the International Association for the Scientific Study of Mental Retardation. American Academy on Mental Retardation is the educational arm of AAMR. Membership: $80/year (individual).

Meetings/Conferences:
Annual Meetings: May/2,000

Publications:
AAMR Membership News. 4/year.
Innovations Series. irreg.
American Journal on Mental Retardation. bi-m. adv.
Mental Retardation. bi-m. adv.
FYI News & Notes. m. adv.
Monograph Series. irreg.

American Astronautical Society *(1954)*
6352 Rolling Mill Pl.
Suite 102
Springfield, VA 22152-2354
Tel: (703)866-0020 *Fax:* (703)866-3526
E-Mail: aas@astronautical.org
Web Site: www.astronautical.org
Members: 1500 individuals
Staff: 2
Annual Budget: $250-500,000
Executive Director: James R. Kirkpatrick

Historical Note
Founded by a small group of engineers, scientists and others who wished to initiate an American activity similar to the British Interplanetary Society to promote a substantive space program. Incorporated in the State of New York in 1954. Dedicated to the advancement of the astronautical sciences and spaceflight engineering and the encouragement of the astronautic arts. Regular memberships are for professionals involved in the field of astronautics and general space enthusiasts. Membership: $85/year (individual).

Meetings/Conferences:
2007 – Adelphi, MD(Marriott)/March 20-21/400

Publications:
Space Times/AAS Magazine. bi-m. adv.
Journal of the Astronautical Sciences. q.
Advances in the Astronautical Sciences.
Science and Technology Series.
AAS History Series.

American Astronomical Society *(1899)*
2000 Florida Ave. NW
Suite 400
Washington, DC 20009
Tel: (202)328-2010 *Fax:* (202)234-2560
E-Mail: aas@aas.org
Web Site: www.aas.org
Members: 6500 individuals
Staff: 11
Annual Budget: $5-10,000,000
Executive Officer: Dr. Robert W. Milkey
E-Mail: milkey@aas.org
Manager, Meetings and Conventions: Kelli Gilmore
Manager, Information Systems: Debbie Kovalsky
E-Mail: kovalsky@aas.org

Historical Note
Organized September 6, 1899, at the Yerkes Observatory, Green Bay, Wisconsin, as the Astronomical and Astrophysical Society of America. Name changed to American Astronomical Society in 1914. Incorporated in Illinois in 1928 and incorporated in DC in 1986. A member of the American Institute of Physics. Has an annual budget of $8.5 million. Membership: $105/year (individual); $35/first 2 years (junior); $800/year (corporate).

Meetings/Conferences:
Semi-annual meetings: Winter and Summer

Publications:
Bulletin of the American Astronomical Society. 4-5/year.

AAS Newsletter. 5/year.
Astrophysical Journal. 18/yr.
Astronomical Journal. m.
AAS Membership Directory. a. adv.
AAS Job Register. m.

American Auditory Society *(1973)*
352 Sundial Ridge Circle
Dammeron Valley, UT 84783
Tel: (435)574-0062 *Fax:* (435)574-0063
E-Mail: amaudsoc@aol.com
Web Site: www.amauditorysoc.org
Members: 2000 individuals
Annual Budget: $100-250,000
Executive Director: Wayne J. Staab, Ph.D.
E-Mail: amaudsoc@aol.com

Historical Note
Formerly (1982) American Audiology Society. Members are health professionals, audiologists, otolaryngologists, scientists, hearing aid manufacturers, educators of the hearing impaired and others with an interest in hearing. Membership: $55/year.

Meetings/Conferences:
Annual Meetings: in conjunction with American Academy of Audiology
2007 - Scottsdale, AZ(Embassy Suites)/Nov. 4-6/350

Publications:
Bulletin of the AAS. 3/year. adv.
Ear and Hearing. bi-m. adv.

American Auto Racing Writers and Broadcasters Association *(1955)*
922 North Pass Ave.
Burbank, CA 91505-2703
Tel: (818)842-7005 *Fax:* (818)842-7020
E-Mail: aarwba@compuserve.com
Web Site: www.aarwba.org
Members: 525 individuals
Annual Budget: under $10,000
President: Norma "Dusty" Brandel
E-Mail: aarwba@compuserve.com

Historical Note
Established in Indianapolis in 1955 with 17 charter members. Members are professional journalists who regularly cover auto racing and related sports events. Has no full-time staff. Membership: $45/year (individual); $65/year (affiliate); $300/year (association/corporation).

Meetings/Conferences:
Annual Meetings: May, usually in Indianapolis, IN

Publications:
All-America Team Program. a. adv.
Newsletter. m. adv.

American Automatic Control Council *(1957)*
311-RC Dept. of Elect. Engineering, Wright State Univ.
Dayton, OH 45435
Tel: (937)775-5062 *Fax:* (937)775-3936
Web Site: www.a2c2.org
Members: 8 societies
Staff: 8
Annual Budget: $250-500,000
Secretary: Pradeep Misra

Historical Note
Founded in Chicago, IL, in March, 1957, as North American Control Council, it assumed its present name in October of that year. AACC is a federation of sponsoring societies, including: American Institute of Aeronautics and Astronautics, American Institute of Chemical Engineers, American Society of Civil Engineers, American Society of Mechanical Engineers, Association of Iron and Steel Engineers, Institute of Electrical and Electronics Engineers, Instrumentation, Systems and Automation Society, International Society for Measurement and Control, and the Society for Computer Simulation. Serves as the U.S. representative in International Federation of Automatic Control. Membership: $800/year (organization).

Meetings/Conferences:
Annual Meetings: American Control Conference in June

Publications:
AACC Newsletter. semi-a.
Proceedings of the American Control Conference. a.

American Automotive Leasing Association *(1955)*
675 N. Washington St., Suite 410
Alexandria, VA 22314
Tel: (703)548-0777 *Fax:* (703)548-1925
E-Mail: aalafleet@aol.com
Web Site: www.aalafleet.com
Members: 12 companies
Staff: 2
Annual Budget: $250-500,000
Executive Director: Pamela Sederholm

Historical Note
Formed in late 1955 by 19 charter auto leasing companies in response to an effort by the IRS to deny leasing companies capital gains treatment on the sale of their used vehicles. Members are large and small commercial leasing and fleet management companies.

American Bail Coalition *(1992)*
1725 DeSales St. NW
Suite 800
Washington, DC 20036
Tel: (202)659-6547 *Fax:* (202)296-8702
Toll Free: (800)375 - 8390
Web Site: www.americanbailcoalition.com
Members: 5 companies
Staff: 1
Executive Director: Michael Carmichael

Historical Note
Supersedes National Association of Bail Insurance Companies (founded 1992). ABC's purpose is to protect and expand the commercial surety bail market. Members are companies who write contract and performance, appearance, surety, and other related bond instruments.

American Bakers Association *(1897)*
1350 I St. NW
Suite 1290
Washington, DC 20005-3300
Tel: (202)789-0300 *Fax:* (202)898-1164
E-Mail: info@americanbakers.org
Web Site: www.americanbakers.org
Members: 300 companies
Staff: 12
Annual Budget: $2-5,000,000
President: Robb S. MacKie, II
Manager, Conventions and Shows: Carol McDougall
Senior Vice President, Government Relations and Public Affairs: Lee Sanders
Vice President, Finance and Administration: Charles Wellard

Historical Note
Formed at a meeting in Walter Baker & Co.'s room in the Mechanics' Building, Boston, October 20, 1897 at which eleven states and two Canadian provinces were represented. Known originally as the National Association of Master Bakers and then the American Association of the Baking Industry, it has operated under its present name since 1921. Incorporated in Illinois in 1917, it is affiliated with the American Institute of Baking. Supports the BREAD Political Action Committee.

Meetings/Conferences:
Annual Meetings: Spring
2007 - Palm Springs, CA(La Quinta Resort)/March 18-21/200

Publications:
Bulletin. 2/m.

American Bandmasters Association *(1929)*
4250 Shorebrook Dr.
Columbia, SC 29206
Tel: (803)787-6540 *Fax:* (803)777-2151
E-Mail: wmoody@sc.rr.com
Web Site: www.americanbandmasters.org
Members: 372 individuals
Staff: 1
Annual Budget: $10-25,000
Secretary-Treasurer: Dr. William J. Moody

Historical Note
Formed at a meeting on July 5, 1929 at the Hotel Pennsylvania in New York City. Incorporated March 13, 1930 in the State of New York.

Meetings/Conferences:
Annual Meetings: March/300

Publications:
Journal of Band Research. 3/year.
Membership Directory. a.

American Bankers Association *(1875)*
1120 Connecticut Ave. NW
Washington, DC 20036
Tel: (202)663-5000
Toll Free: (800)226 - 5377
Web Site: www.aba.com
Members: 9000 individuals
Staff: 350
Annual Budget: $50-100,000,000
President and Chief Executive Officer: Edward L. Yingling
E-Mail: eyinglin@aba.com
Executive Director, Financial Institutions Policy and Regulatory Affairs: Wayne Abernathy
Executive Director, Communications: Virginia Dean
Executive Director, Congressional Relations and Public Policy: Floyd Stoner

Historical Note
Organized in Saratoga, NY, July 20-22, 1875. Absorbed the Charge Account Bankers Association and the Foundation for Full Service Banks in 1972. ABA represents over 90% of the nation's banks. The American Institute of Banking is a section of the ABA; BankPac is its political action committee, and the Bank Marketing Association is an affiliate of ABA. Has an annual budget of approximately $66 million.

Meetings/Conferences:
Annual Meetings: Fall

Publications:
ABA Trust and Investments. m.
Journal of Agricultural Lending. q.
ABA Bank Marketing. m. adv.
ABA Banking Journal. m. adv.
ABA Bankers News. w.
Trust Letter. m.

American Bankruptcy Institute *(1982)*
44 Canal Center Plaza, Suite 404
Alexandria, VA 22314-1592
Tel: (703)739-0800 *Fax:* (703)739-1060
E-Mail: info@abiworld.org
Web Site: www.abiworld.org
Members: 11500 individuals
Staff: 28
Annual Budget: $5-10,000,000
Executive Director: Samuel J. Gerdano
Director, Communications: Carolyn Kanon
Director, Membership: Chris Thackston

Historical Note
Incorporated in Virginia. The ABI provides a multi-disciplinary forum for the exchange of ideas and information on bankruptcy issues. American Board of Certification is certifying organization sponsored by ABI. Membership: $250/year (private sector individual); $95/year (government/academic individual).

Meetings/Conferences:
Annual and Semi-Annual Meetings: April and December
2007 - Washington, DC(JW Marriott)/Apr. 12-15

Publications:
ABI Law Review. 2/yr.
ABI Journal. 10/year. adv.
ABI Directory. a. adv.
ABI Update. 2/wk. adv.

American Baptist Homes and Hospitals Association *(1935)*
P.O. Box 851
Valley Forge, PA 19482-0851
Tel: (610)768-2411 *Fax:* (610)768-2453
Toll Free: (800)222 - 3872 Ext: 2411
Web Site: www.nationalministries.org/mission/abhha
Members: 128 institutions
Staff: 2
Director: Aundreia Alexander
E-Mail: aundreiaalexander@abc.usa

Historical Note
ABHHA members are retirement/nursing homes, hospitals, children's homes.
Publications:
Perspective Newsletter. q.

American Bar Association *(1878)*
321 N. Clark St.
Chicago, IL 60610
Tel: (312)988-5000 *Fax:* (312)988-6281
Toll Free: (800)285 - 2221
E-Mail: askaba@abanet.org
Web Site: www.abanet.org
*Members:*407741 individuals
Staff: 900
Annual Budget: Over $100,000,000
Executive Director: Henry F. White, Jr.
Associate Executive Director, Communications: Sarina Butler
Director, Membership Benefits: Paula Cleave
General Counsel: Darryl L. DePriest
Chief Financial Officer: John Hanle
Historical Note
Represents more than 50% of practicing lawyers in the U.S. Federally approved accrediting agency for law schools. The American Law Student Association is a division of the ABA. Maintains the nationally-honored Code of Professional Responsibility. Operates the Center for Professional Responsibility, and an information center for the bar admission and bar disciplinary agencies. Has an annual budget of $94 million. Membership: $95-$295/year (depending upon number of years admitted to the bar).
Meetings/Conferences:
Semi-Annual Meetings: February and August
2007 - Miami, FL/Feb. 7-13
2007 - San Francisco, CA/Aug. 9-15
2008 - Los Angeles, CA/Feb. 6-12
2008 - New York, NY/Aug. 7-12
2009 - Boston, MA/Feb. 11-17
2009 - Chicago, IL/July 30-Aug. 4
2010 - Orlando, FL/Feb. 3-9
2010 - San Franscisco, CA/Aug. 5-10
2011 - Atlanta, GA/Feb. 9-15
2011 - Toronto, ON, Canada/Aug. 5-10
Publications:
American Bar Association Journal. m. adv.

American Baseball Coaches Association *(1945)*
108 S. University Ave., Suite Three
Mt. Pleasant, MI 48858-2327
Tel: (989)775-3300 *Fax:* (989)775-3600
E-Mail: abca@abca.org
Web Site: www.abca.org
*Members:*6400 individuals
Staff: 4
Annual Budget: $500-1,000,000
Executive Director: Dave Keilitz
Historical Note
Formerly (1985) the American Association of College Baseball Coaches. Founded in New York, NY. ABCA includes members from every division of amateur baseball. Membership: $30/year (U.S.); $35/year (North America); $40/year (overseas).
Meetings/Conferences:
Annual Meetings: Winter
2007 - Orlando, FL(Orlando World Center)/Jan. 4-7
2008 - Philadelphia, PA(Marriott)/Jan. 3-6
2009 - San Diego, CA(J.W. Marriott)/Jan. 2-5
2010 - Dallas, TX(Hilton)/Jan. 7-10
2011 - Nashville, TN(Gaylord Opryland)/Jan. 6-9
Publications:
Coaching Digest. a. adv.
Directory. a. adv.
Covering All Bases. q.

American Bashkir Curly Registry *(1971)*
P.O. Box 151029
Ely, NV 89315
Tel: (775)289-4999
E-Mail: secretary@abcregistry.org
Web Site: www.abcregistry.org
*Members:*500 individuals
Staff: 2
Annual Budget: $50-100,000
Secretary: Sue Chilson
E-Mail: secretary@abcregistry.org
Historical Note
Members are owners and breeders of rare horses with curly coats. Membership: $35/year (individual).
Meetings/Conferences:
Annual Meetings: June in Ely, NV(Bristlecone Convention Ctr.)/100
Publications:
Curly Cues. q. adv.

American Bearing Manufacturing Association *(1933)*
2025 M St. NW
Suite 800
Washington, DC 20036
Tel: (202)367-1155 *Fax:* (202)367-2155
E-Mail: info.abma@smithbucklin.com
Web Site: www.abma-dc.org
*Members:*35 companies
Staff: 4
Annual Budget: $250-500,000
President: Richard E. Opatick, CAE
E-Mail: info.abma@smithbucklin.com
Historical Note
Formerly (1993) the Anti-Friction Bearing Manufacturers Association. Members are manufacturers of anti-friction bearings and of the major components used in their manufacture. Sponsors and supports the Bearing Technical Committee.

American Beefalo World Registry *(1983)*
10892 Yakima Valley Hwy.
Zillah, WA 98953
Toll Free: (866)374 - 2297
Web Site: www.abwr.org
*Members:*50 individuals
Staff: 1
Annual Budget: under $10,000
Office Manager: Ruby Ide
E-Mail: ideranch@earthlink.net
Historical Note
Formed in November, 1983 by a merger of the American Beefalo Association (1975), the World Beefalo Association and International Beefalo Breeders' Registry (1980). Absorbed the Bison Hybrid International Association. Maintains a registry of full-blood and percentage Beefalo stock (full-blood is an exact 3/8 bison and 5/8 bovine cross); also maintains a registry for bison cross animals not qualifying as Beefalo, and a Beefalo Meat Registry. Membership: $25/year.
Publications:
American Beefalo World Registry Newsletter. bi-m.

American Beekeeping Federation *(1943)*
P.O. Box 1337
Jesup, GA 31598
Tel: (912)427-4233 *Fax:* (912)427-8447
E-Mail: info@abfnet.org
Web Site: www.abfnet.org
Members: 1850 individuals
Staff: 3
Annual Budget: $250-500,000
Executive Director: Troy H. Fore, Jr.
E-Mail: info@abfnet.org
Historical Note
Formerly National Federation of Beekeepers Associations. Absorbed the Honey Industry Council of America in 1986. Members are honey producers, packers, shippers and suppliers. Membership: $250/year (commercial); $100/year (part-time); $35/year (hobbyist).
Meetings/Conferences:
Annual Meetings: January
Publications:
ABF Newsletter. bi-m. adv.
Membership Directory. a. adv.

American Benefits Council *(1967)*
1212 New York Ave. NW
Suite 1250
Washington, DC 20005-3987
Tel: (202)289-6700 *Fax:* (202)289-4582
E-Mail: info@abcstaff.org
Web Site: www.americanbenefitscouncil.org
*Members:*270 companies
Staff: 12
Annual Budget: $2-5,000,000
President: James A. Klein
E-Mail: jklein@abcstaff.org
Vice President, Health Policy: Paul W. Dennett
E-Mail: pdennett@abcstaff.org
Vice President, Retirement Policy: Lynn D. Dudley
E-Mail: ldudley@abcstaff.org
Director, Public Policy: Jon Jacobson
Director, Communications: Deanna Johnson, APR
Health Policy Legal Counsel: Kathryn Wilber
Historical Note
Founded as Association of Private Pension and Welfare Plans; assumed its current name in 2000. Focus is on government regulations and legislation concerning private, voluntary retirement savings and welfare benefit arrangements. Members are investment firms, attorneys, benefits administrators, banks, actuaries, associations, accounting firms and employer/plan sponsors. Sponsors and supports the American Benefits Council Political Action Committee.
Publications:
Membership Surveys.
Benefits Byte.
Policy Reports.
White Pages.

American Berkshire Association *(1875)*
P.O. Box 2436
West Lafayette, IN 47996-2436
Tel: (765)497-3618 *Fax:* (765)497-2959
E-Mail: berkshire@nationalswine.com
Web Site: www.americanberkshire.com
*Members:*500 individuals
Staff: 3
Annual Budget: $100-250,000
Breed Secretary: Lisa Kennedy
Historical Note
Breeders and promoters of Berkshire swine. Member of the National Pedigree Livestock Council. Membership: $20/year.
Meetings/Conferences:
Annual Meetings: July
Publications:
The Berkshire News. 10/year. adv.

American Beverage Association *(1919)*
1101 16th St. NW
Washington, DC 20036
Tel: (202)463-6732 *Fax:* (202)659-5349
E-Mail: info@ameribev.org
Web Site: www.ameribev.org
*Members:*300 firms
Staff: 40
Annual Budget: $5-10,000,000
President: Susan Neely
Executive Vice President: Jim B. Finkelstein
Senior Vice President, Communications: Kevin W. Keane
Vice President, State and Local Affairs: James A. McGreevey, III
Vice President, Scientific, Technical and Regulatory Affairs: Michael Redman
Historical Note
Established as the American Bottlers of Carbonated Beverages; became National Soft Drink Association in 1967 and assumed its current name in 2004. Absorbed the National Bottlers Association and the National Bottlers Protective Association. Members are soft drink makers and their suppliers. Has an annual budget of approximately $5 million.
Meetings/Conferences:
Annual Meetings: Fall/25,000
Publications:
Friday Facts. w.
Beverage eLinks. w.
Soft Drink Recycler. q.
Soft Drink Recyclers Newsletter.
Members and Buyers Guide. a.
Executive Briefs Newsletter. bi-m.

American Beverage Institute *(1991)*
1775 Pennsylvania Ave. NW
Suite 1200

Washington, DC 20006
Tel: (202)463-7110 *Fax:* (202)463-7107
Toll Free: (800)843 - 8877
E-Mail: abi@abionline.org
Web Site: www.abionline.org
Members: 4500 individuals
Staff: 5
Executive Director: John Doyle
General Counsel: Richard B. Berman

Historical Note
Founded to represent the retail beverage industry, ABI shares accurate information with legislators, retailers, their employees, and the public regarding the responsible service and consumption of wine, beer, and distilled spirits.

Publications:
ABI News Newsletter. q.

American Beverage Licensees *(1934)*
5101 River Rd.
Suite 108
Bethesda, MD 20816-1650
Tel: (301)656-1494 *Fax:* (301)656-7539
Web Site: www.ablusa.org
Members: 30000
Staff: 5
Annual Budget: $250-500,000
Executive Director: Harry Wiles

Historical Note
Founded as National Retail Liquor Package Stores Association; became National Liquor Stores Association in 1964, and National Association of Beverage Retailers in 1992 . Absorbed National Licensed Beverage Association and assumed its current name in 2001. Members are state associations representing private-sector liquor stores and on-premise retailers of alcoholic beverages.

Publications:
ABL Leader. m. adv.

American Biological Safety Association
1202 Allanson Rd.
Mundelein, IL 60060-3808
Tel: (847)949-1517 *Fax:* (847)566-4580
E-Mail: absa@absa.org
Web Site: www.absa.org
Members: 1000 individuals
Staff: 3
Executive Director: Edward J. Stygar, Jr.

Historical Note
ABSA provides members with information and research on best practices in laboratory safety and related topics. Membership $150/year.

Meetings/Conferences:
2007 – Nashville, TN

Publications:
Journal of the American Biological Safety Ass'n. q. adv.
ABSA Newsletter. q.

American Blind Lawyers Association *(1971)*

Historical Note
An affiliate of American Council of the Blind, which provides administrative support.

American Blonde D'Aquitaine Association *(1973)*
7407 VZ County Rd. 1507
Grand Saline, TX 75140
Tel: (903)570-0568 *Fax:* (903)569-1613
E-Mail: info@blondecattle.org
Web Site: www.blondecattle.org
Members: 70 individuals
Staff: 1
Annual Budget: $25-50,000
President: Pierre Livalldais
E-Mail: info@blondecattle.org

Historical Note
Members are breeders and fanciers of Blonde D'Aquitaine cattle. Merged with the National Blonde D'Aquitaine Foundation in 1985. Membership: $50/year.

Publications:
Blonde Bulletin. q. adv.
Membership Directory. a. adv.

American Board of Bioanalysis *(1968)*
906 Olive St., Suite 1200
St. Louis, MO 63101-1434
Tel: (314)241-1445 *Fax:* (314)241-1449
E-Mail: abb@abbcert.org
Web Site: www.abbcert.org
Administrator: Mark S. Birenbaum, Ph.D.

American Board of Forensic Psychology *(1980)*
300 Drayton St., Third Floor
Savannah, GA 31401
Tel: (912)234-5477
Toll Free: (800)255 - 7792
Web Site: www.abfp.com
Members: 200 individuals
Staff: 4
Annual Budget: $100-250,000
Executive Director: Thomas Grisso, PhD

Historical Note
Founded as the American Academy of Forensic Psychology; assumed its present name in 1999. Members are psychologists who have passed the Diplomate Examination in Forensic Psychology of the American Board of Professional Psychology. Membership: $165/year (individual).

Meetings/Conferences:
Annual Meetings: Spring

Publications:
Bulletin of the AAFP. a.
Directory of Diplomates. a.

American Board of Industrial Hygiene *(1960)*
6015 W. St. Joseph, Suite 102
Lansing, MI 48917
Tel: (517)321-2638 *Fax:* (517)321-4624
E-Mail: abih@abih.org
Web Site: www.abih.org
Members: 11 boardmembers
Staff: 5
Annual Budget: $500-1,000,000
Executive Director: Lynn O'Donnell, CIH

Historical Note
Certifies professionals who evaluate health and safety in the workplace employed by industry, labor unions, state, provincial and local governments, federal agencies, uniformed services and academia in the U.S., Canada, Australia and other countries. Membership: $100 (individual).

Publications:
Newsletter.

American Board of Medical Specialties *(1933)*
1007 Church St.
Suite 404
Evanston, IL 60201-5913
Tel: (847)491-9091 *Fax:* (847)328-3596
Web Site: www.abms.org
Members: 24 organizations
Staff: 17
Annual Budget: $2-5,000,000
President: Stephen H. Miller, MPH, M.D.
Director, Human Resources and Communications: Alexis L. Rodgers
Director, Information Services and Systems Development: Todd J. Tischendorf

Historical Note
Established as the Advisory Board for Medical Specialties, ABMS assumed its present name in 1970. As the parent organization for the 24 medical specialty Boards in the USA, it works closely with the American Hospital Association, the Association of American Medical Colleges, the American Medical Association and the Council of Medical Specialty Societies in the accreditation of programs in graduate and continuing medical education. The mission of ABMS is to maintain and improve the quality of medical care by assisting the Member Boards in their efforts to develop and utilize professional and educational standards for the evaluation and certification of physician specialists. The intent of the certification of physicians is to provide assurance to the public that a physician specialist certified by a Member Board of ABMS has successfully completed an approved educational program and an evaluation process which includes an examination designed to assess the knowledge, skills and experience required to provide quality patient care in that specialty. ABMS serves to coordinate the activities of its Member Boards and to provide information to the public, the government, the profession and its members concerning issues involving specialization and certification in medicine.

Meetings/Conferences:
Semi-Annual Meetings: March and September in Chicago at Chicago area hotels.

Publications:
ABMS Record (newsletter). q.
Annual Report & Reference Handbook. a.
The Official ABMS Directory of Board Certified Medical Specialists. a.

American Board of Nursing Specialties *(1991)*
610 Thornhill Ln.
Aurora, OH 44202
Tel: (330)995-9172 *Fax:* (330)995-9743
E-Mail: abnsceo@aol.com
Web Site: www.nursingcertification.org
Members: 23 organizations
Staff: 1
Chief Executive Officer: Bonnie Niebuhr
E-Mail: abnsceo@aol.com

Historical Note
ABNS works to increase public awareness of the value of quality nursing certification to healthcare. ABNS is an advocate for consumer protection by establishing and maintaining standards for professional specialty nursing certification. Member organizations of ABNS represent over a half million certified Registered Nurses around the world. The purposes of ABNS are to: provide a form for nursing certification collaboration, promote the value of nursing certification to various publics, provide a mechanism for accrediation and recognition of quality specialty nursing certification programs. Membership fee: varies.

American Board of Periodontology *(1939)*
4157 Mountain Rd., PBN 249
Pasadena, MD 21122
Tel: (410)437-3749 *Fax:* (410)437-4021
E-Mail: abperio@msn.com
Web Site: www.perio.org
Members: 1400 individuals
Staff: 2
Annual Budget: $250-500,000
Executive Director: Gerald M. Bowers, D.D.S.
E-Mail: abperio@msn.com

Historical Note
Membership: $125/year (individual).

Meetings/Conferences:
Annual Meetings: Fall/600-800

Publications:
Journal of Periodontology. a.
Annals of Periodontologya. a.

American Board of Podiatric Orthopedics and Primary Podiatric Medicine *(1978)*
3812 Sepulveda Blvd.
Suite 530
Torrance, CA 90505
Tel: (310)375-0700 *Fax:* (310)375-1589
Web Site: www.abpoppm.org
Members: 2850 individuals
Staff: 4
Annual Budget: $500-1,000,000
Executive Director: Marc A. Benard, D.P.M.
E-Mail: mbenard@abpoppm.org

Historical Note
An affiliate of American Podiatric Medical Association, ABPOPPM is the certifying board responsible for non-surgical aspects of foot care. It offers comprehensive examinations in two specialty areas: podiatric orthopedics and primary podiatric medicine. APBOPPM emphasizes excellence in podiatric care and strives to further the cause of podiatry in general. Membership: $200/year (diplomate); $150/year (board-qualified member).

Meetings/Conferences:
Annual Meetings: with the American Podiatric Medical Ass'n

Publications:
Newsletter. semi-a. adv.
Directory of Diplomates. a. adv.

American Board of Preventive Medicine *(1948)*
330 S. Wells St., Suite 1018
Chicago, IL 60606-7106

Tel: (312)939-2276 *Fax:* (312)939-2218
Web Site: www.abprevmed.org
Members: 11 individuals
Staff: 3
Executive Director: James Vanderploeg, MD, MPH
E-Mail: execdir@abprevmed.org

American Board of Professional Psychology *(1947)*
300 Drayton St., Third Floor
Savannah, GA 31401
Tel: (912)234-5477 *Fax:* (912)234-5120
Toll Free: (800)255 - 7792
E-Mail: office@abpp.org
Web Site: www.abpp.org
Members: 3500 individuals
Staff: 4
Annual Budget: $250-500,000
Executive Officer: David R. Cox
Assistant Executive Officer: Nancy McDonald
Historical Note
Formerly the American Board of Examiners in Professional Psychology, ABPP awards its diploma in the areas of clinical psychology, counseling psychology, school psychology, industrial/organizational psychology, clinical neuropsychology, forensic psychology, family psychology, clinical child and adolescent psychology, health psychology, behavioral psychology, group psychology, psychoanalysis in psychology, and rehabilitation psychology. Applicants must have a doctoral degree from a professional psychology program accredited by the APA or CPA and a licensure or certification at the independent level as a psychologist in the state, province, or territory in which the psychologist practices. Membership: $165/year (individual).
Meetings/Conferences:
Semi-annual Meetings:
2007 - San Francisco, CA(Moscone Center)/Aug. 17-20
Publications:
The Specialist. 2/yr.

American Board of Quality Assurance and Utilization Review Physicians *(1977)*
6640 Congress St.
New Port Richey, FL 34653
Tel: (727)569-0190 *Fax:* (727)569-0195
Toll Free: (800)998 - 6030
E-Mail: abqaurp@abqaurp.org
Web Site: www.abqaurp.org/
Members: 9000 certified members
Staff: 14
Accounting Specialist: Kim Gorman
E-Mail: abqaurp@abqaurp.org
Historical Note
ABQAURP provides education and certification programs in health care quality management and is accredited by the Accreditation Council for Continuing Medical Education (ACCME) for physicians. Membership: $245/year.
Meetings/Conferences:
Annual Meetings: Fall
Publications:
ABQAURP Diplomate Directory. online. adv.
Journal of Quality Health Care. q. adv.

American Board of Veterinary Practitioners *(1978)*
618 Church St., Suite 220
Nashville, TN 37219-2321
Tel: (615)250-7794 *Fax:* (615)254-7047
Toll Free: (800)697 - 3583
E-Mail: abvp@walkermgt.com
Web Site: www.abvp.com
Members: 700 individuals
Staff: 2
Annual Budget: $250-500,000
Executive Director: Dee Ann Walker, CAE
Historical Note
Certifying board for veterinarians who obtain advanced recognition through examination.
Meetings/Conferences:
Annual Meetings: Spring
Publications:
ABVP News. q.

American Boarding Kennels Association *(1977)*
1702 E. Pikes Peak Ave.
Colorado Springs, CO 80909
Tel: (719)667-1600 *Fax:* (719)667-0116
Toll Free: (877)570 - 7788
E-Mail: info@abka.com
Web Site: www.abka.com
Members: 3000
Staff: 8
Annual Budget: $1-2,000,000
Executive Director: James J. Krack, CKO, CAE
E-Mail: info@abka.com
Assistant Executive Director: Kathryn Eddy
E-Mail: info@abka.com
Historical Note
ABKA is your source for all pet care services. Members are boarding kennels, pet day care businesses, suppliers, individuals and others interested in the pet care industry. ABKA provides benefits, services and educational opportunities to pet care professionals and serves as a forum for the exchange of ideas among members. The association offers three levels of education and certification programs. Membership: $195/year.
Meetings/Conferences:
Annual Meetings: Fall
2007 - Sacramento, CA(Hyatt)/Oct. 17-20/400
Publications:
Pet Services Journal. bi-m. adv.
Boarderline E-Newsletter. bi-m. adv.

American Boat and Yacht Council *(1954)*
613 Third St.
Suite Ten
Annapolis, MD 21403
Tel: (410)990-4460 *Fax:* (410)990-4466
E-Mail: information@abycinc.org
Web Site: www.abycinc.org
Members: 700 individuals
Staff: 15
Annual Budget: $1-2,000,000
Director, Technical: John Adey
Manager: Judith Ramsey
Historical Note
Members are companies and individuals concerned with the design, construction, and maintenance of recreational boats and related equipment. Develops standards and technical information reports. Membership: $165/year minimum (company).
Meetings/Conferences:
Annual Meetings: February/Miami, FL
Publications:
Standards and Technical Information Reports for Small Craft. a.
American Boat and Yacht Council News. q.
Rules & Regulations for Recreational Boats. irreg.
Compliance Guidelines for Federal Boating Regulations. irreg.
Internat'l Navigation Rules (Inland). irreg.

American Boat Builders and Repairers Association *(1943)*
50 Water St.
Warren, RI 02885
Tel: (401)247-0318 *Fax:* (401)247-0074
E-Mail: info@abbra.org
Web Site: www.abbra.org
Members: 350 individuals and companies
Staff: 2
Annual Budget: $100-250,000
Managing Director: Mark Amaral
E-Mail: mamaral@abbra.org
Historical Note
Established as the Atlantic Coast Boat Builders and Repairers Association; assumed its present name in 1965. ABBRA was established to strengthen and encourage professionalism in the marine service industry. Membership: $100/year (individual); $375/year (company).
Publications:
ABBRACARD - Cruising and Repair Directory. a. adv.
Capstan. q. adv.

American Boiler Manufacturers Association *(1888)*
8221 Old Courthouse Rd.
Suite 207
Vienna, VA 22182-3839
Tel: (703)356-7172 *Fax:* (703)356-4543
Web Site: www.abma.com
Members: 115 companies
Staff: 4
Annual Budget: $500-1,000,000
President: W. Randall Rawson
E-Mail: randy@abma.com
Director, Meetings: Cheryl Jamall
E-Mail: cheryl@abma.com
Historical Note
Formerly (1960) American Boiler Manufacturers Association. Incorporated in New Jersey. Members are manufacturers and suppliers of steam and hot water generating systems. Membership: $4,000/year (minimum).
Meetings/Conferences:
Semi-Annual Meetings: January and June
Publications:
ABMA Buyers Guide. a. adv.
Boiler Systems Engineering Magazine. q. adv.

American Book Producers Association *(1980)*
160 Fifth Ave.
New York, NY 10010-7000
Tel: (212)645-2368 *Fax:* (212)242-6799
Toll Free: (800)209 - 4575
E-Mail: office@abpaonline.org
Web Site: www.abpaonline.org
Members: 55 companies
Annual Budget: $25-50,000
Administrator: David Katz
Historical Note
Members are companies or individuals that develop concepts for books, and, based on a contractual agreement with a publisher, a business or other source, may produce finished books or production-ready film, camera-ready mechanicals, finished manuscripts, art and layouts. Membership: $500/year (company).
Meetings/Conferences:
Monthly Meetings: Third Wednesday, except July and Aug.
Publications:
American Book Producers Directory. a.
Newsletter. m.

American Booksellers Association *(1900)*
200 White Plains Rd.
Tarrytown, NY 10591
Tel: (914)591-2665 *Fax:* (914)591-2720
Toll Free: (800)637 - 0037
E-Mail: info@bookweb.org
Web Site: www.bookweb.org
Members: 2100 companies
Staff: 50
Annual Budget: $5-10,000,000
Chief Executive Officer: Avin Mark Domnitz
Chief Financial Officer: Eleanor Chang
Chief Operating Officer: Oren Teicher
Historical Note
The trade association of U.S. retail bookstores. Started at the call of six booksellers in November, 1900, three from New York, and one each from Grand Rapids, Cleveland and St. Paul. Formally organized the following year with an initial membership of 748. ABA represents the interests of booksellers through education, research, and the dissemination of information. Membership: $175/year.
Meetings/Conferences:
Annual Meetings: June/38,000
Publications:
Bookselling This Week. w. adv.
Book Buyer's Handbook. a.

American Border Leicester Association *(1973)*
9838 S. Gribble Rd.
Canby, OR 97013-9364
Tel: (503)266-7156
Web Site: www.ablasheep.org
Members: 175 individuals
Staff: 10

Annual Budget: under $10,000
Secretary-Treasurer: Di Waibel

Historical Note
Members are breeders of sheep. Maintains a breed registry, promotes sheep shows and education. Membership: $15/year.

Meetings/Conferences:
Annual Meetings: during the Maryland Sheep and Wool Festival/1st Saturday in May

Publications:
Directory. a.
American Border Leicester Newsletter. q. adv.

American Brachytherapy Society *(1978)*
12100 Sunset Hills Rd.
Suite 130
Reston, VA 20190
Tel: (703)234-4078 *Fax:* (703)435-4390
E-Mail: rguggolz@drohanmgmt.com
Web Site: www.americanbrachytherapy.org
Members: 1100
Staff: 2
Annual Budget: $250-500,000
Executive Director: Richard A. Guggolz

Historical Note
Members are oncologists and physicists working in the field of brachytherapy. Memebership: $180/yr. Resident membership is free.

Meetings/Conferences:
2007 - Chicago, IL(Sheraton)/Apr. 29-May 1

Publications:
Newsletter. q. adv.

American Brahman Breeders Association *(1924)*
3003 South Loop West, Suite 140
Houston, TX 77054
Tel: (713)349-0854 *Fax:* (713)349-9795
E-Mail: abba@brahman.org
Web Site: www.brahman.org
Members: 1200 individuals
Staff: 8
Annual Budget: $500-1,000,000
Executive Vice President: Chris Shivers

Historical Note
Breeders and fanciers of Brahman beef cattle. Member of the National Pedigree Livestock Council. Membership: $100/year (active membership).

Meetings/Conferences:
Annual Meetings: February, in Houston

Publications:
The Brahman Journal. m. adv.

American Brahmousin Council
P.O. Box 88
Whitesboro, TX 76273
Tel: (903)564-3995
E-Mail: info@brahmousin.org
Web Site: www.brahmousin.org
Members: 95 ranches
Interim Director: Bob Cummins

Historical Note
Breeders of Brahmousin cattle.

Publications:
Brahmousin Connection. q. adv.

American Bralers Association *(1983)*
P.O.Box 75
Burton, TX 77835
Tel: (979)289-3021
Members: 200 individuals
Annual Budget: $25-50,000
President: Marcus Brosche

Historical Note
Maintains a registry of Bralers (a crossbreed of Brahman and Salers cattle). Has no paid officers or full-time staff. Membership: $25/year.

Meetings/Conferences:
Annual Meetings: February

Publications:
Bralers News. a. adv.

American Breed Association *(1977)*

Historical Note
Address unknown in 2001.

American Bridge Teachers' Association *(1957)*
14840 Crystal Cove Ct.
Suite 503
Ft. Myers, FL 33919-7417
Tel: (239)437-4106
E-Mail: abta@juno.com
Web Site: www.atbahome.com
Members: 500 individuals
Staff: 1
Annual Budget: $25-50,000
Business Secretary/Treasurer: Patricia A. Harrington
E-Mail: abta@juno.com

Historical Note
Membership: $35/year.

Meetings/Conferences:
Annual Meetings: Precedes Summer Nationals of the American Contract Bridge League

Publications:
ABTA Quarterly Magazine. q. adv.

American British White Park Association *(1975)*
P.O. Box 957
Harrison, AZ 72602
Toll Free: (877)900 - 2333
E-Mail: office@whitecattle.org
Web Site: www.whitecattle.org
Members: 527 individuals
Staff: 1
Annual Budget: $10-25,000
Executive Secretary: Sherry Parks

Historical Note
Founded as White Park Cattle Association of America; assumed its curent name in 1999. Breeders and fanciers of Park cattle. Membership fees vary.

Publications:
White Cattle Journal. q.

American Broncho-Esophagological Association *(1917)*
Division of Otolaryngology, Stanford University
801 Welch Rd.
Stanford, CA 94305-5739
Tel: (650)725-6500 *Fax:* (650)725-6685
Web Site: www.abea.net
Members: 400 individuals
Staff: 1
Annual Budget: under $10,000
Secretary: Peter Koltai

Historical Note
Established as the American Bronchoscopic Society; assumed its present name in 1928. Affiliated with the American Academy of Otolaryngology - Head and Neck Surgery.

Publications:
Annals of Otolaryngology. adv.

American Brush Manufacturers Association *(1917)*
2111 Plum St., Suite 274
Aurora, IL 60506-3268
Tel: (630)631-5217 *Fax:* (630)897-9140
E-Mail: info@abma.org
Web Site: www.abma.org
Members: 165 companies
Staff: 3
Annual Budget: $250-500,000
Executive Director: David Parr
E-Mail: info@abma.org

Historical Note
ABMA works to help American brush manufacturers by enhancing industry knowledge, by providng networking opportunities for, and promoting profitability for, its members. Absorbed the National Broom and Mop Council in 1982. Membership: $580-$2,300/year.

Meetings/Conferences:
Annual Meetings: March/300
2007 - St. Petersburg, FL(Renaissance)/March 14-17
2008 - Carlsbad, CA(La Costa)/March 12-15

Publications:
"Brush Up" - ABMA Newsletter. m.

American Bryological and Lichenological Society *(1898)*
Dept. of Biology, Stevens Halls
North Dakota State University
Fargo, ND 58105-5517
Web Site: www.unomaha.edu/~abls/
Members: 525 individuals
Annual Budget: $25-50,000
President-Elect: Theodore L. Esslinger
E-Mail: ted.esslinger@ndsu.edu
Secretary- Treasurer: Robert S. Egan

Historical Note
Originated in 1898 in Plymouth, New Hampshire, as the Sullivant Moss Chapter of the Agassiz Association. Became independent in 1900 under the name of Sullivant Moss Society Name changed to American Bryological Society in 1949 and to the American Bryological and Lichenological Society in 1969. Incorporated in Missouri in 1965. Affiliated with American Institute of Biological Sciences. Devoted to the study of all aspects of bryophytes and lichens. Membership: $45/year, with publications (individual); $70/year, with publications (organization).

Meetings/Conferences:
Annual Meetings: Summer
2007 - Xalapa, Mexico/Aug. 12-16
2008 - Monterey, CA/Aug. 10-15
2009 - Snowbird, UT

Publications:
Evansia. irreg.
The Bryologist. q.

American Buckskin Registry Association *(1938)*
1411 Hartnell Ave.
Redding, CA 96002-2113
Tel: (530)223-1420
Web Site: www.americanbuckskin.org
Members: 6000 individuals
Staff: 3
Annual Budget: $25-50,000
Office Manager: Georgi Jones
E-Mail: georgijones@aol.com

Historical Note
Established as the Buckskin Registry Association, it assumed its present name in 1965. Members are owners, breeders, and dealers of the Buckskin horse. Sponsors shows and other promotional events. Membership: $15/year (individual); $20/year (company).

Meetings/Conferences:
Annual Meetings: early November

Publications:
Newsletter. bi-m.

American Bureau of Metal Statistics *(1920)*
P.O. Box 805
Chatham, NJ 07928
Tel: (973)701-2299 *Fax:* (973)701-2152
E-Mail: info@abms.com
Web Site: www.abms.com
Members: 5 companies
Staff: 3
Annual Budget: $500-1,000,000
Executive Director: Patricia T. Foley
E-Mail: info@abms.com

Historical Note
Created on January 1, 1975 by a merger of the American Bureau of Metal Statistics (1920) with the Copper Institute (organized in 1927) and the United States Copper Association (established in 1934). Collects and disseminates statistical industry data on copper, lead, zinc and other non-ferrous metals. Collects and compiles statistical information for the Copper Development Association and other non-ferrous metal trade associations. Membership: dues assessed pro-rata.

Meetings/Conferences:
Semi-annual Meetings: June and December

Publications:
Non-Ferrous Metal Yearbook. a.
Industry Reports. m.

American Bureau of Shipping *(1862)*
16855 Northchase Dr.
Houston, TX 77060
Tel: (281)877-5800 *Fax:* (281)877-5803
E-Mail: abs-worldhq@eagle.org
Web Site: www.eagle.org
Members: 814 individuals

Staff: 1600
Annual Budget: Over $100,000,000
Chairman and Chief Executive Officer: Robert D. Somerville
E-Mail: abs-worldhq@eagle.org
President and Chief Operating Officer: Robert E. Kranek
E-Mail: abs-worldhq@eagle.org
Vice President, External Affairs: Stewart H. Wade

Historical Note
Certifies the mechanical and structural fitness of ships, mobile and fixed offshore drilling units, and other marine structures. Publishes over 50 Rules and Guides related to the design, construction and operational maintenance of ships, mobile offshore drilling units, containers, machinery and other marine equipment. Has an annual budget of approximately $140 million.

Meetings/Conferences:
Annual Meetings: usually Spring/New York, NY.

Publications:
Surveyor. 4/year.
Activities. 4/year.
Annual Report. a.

American Burn Association *(1967)*
625 N. Michigan Ave., Suite 2550
Chicago, IL 60611
Tel: (312)642-9260 *Fax:* (312)642-9130
Toll Free: (800)548 - 2876
E-Mail: info@ameriburn.org
Web Site: www.ameriburn.org
Members: 4000 individuals
Staff: 8
Annual Budget: $1-2,000,000
Executive Director: John Krichbaum, JD
E-Mail: krichbaum@ameriburn.org
Associate Executive Director: Susan M. Browning, MPH

Historical Note
Members are individuals concerned with the care, treatment and prevention of burns. Membership: $300/year (physicians); $125/year (non-physicians); plus initiation fee ($65).

Meetings/Conferences:
Annual Meetings: Spring
2007 - San Diego, CA(Manchester Grand Hyatt)/March 20-23
2008 - Chicago, IL(Hyatt Regency)/Apr. 29-May 2

Publications:
Journal of Burn Care and Rehabilitation. bi-m. adv.
Membership Directory (online). a.
Burn Care Resources in North America. bi-a.
Annual Meeting Abstract. a.
Education Resource Manual.

American Bus Association *(1926)*
700 13th St. NW
Suite 575
Washington, DC 20005-5923
Tel: (202)842-1645 *Fax:* (202)842-0850
Toll Free: (800)283 - 2877
E-Mail: abainfo@buses.org
Web Site: www.buses.org
Members: 3800 companies and other organizations
Staff: 23
Annual Budget: $5-10,000,000
President and Chief Executive Officer: Peter J. Pantuso
Chief Financial Officer: Eric Braendel
Senior Vice President, Meetings and Education: Lynn M. Brewer
Director, Marketing and Membership: Ginger D. Croce
Senior Vice President, Policy and External Affairs: Linda Bauer Darr
Senior Vice President, Government Affairs: Clyde Hart, Jr.
Vice President, Safety, Security and Regulatory Programs: Norm Littler

Historical Note
Formerly the Motor Bus Division and later the National Motor Bus Division of the American Automobile Association. Name changed to the National Association of Motor Bus Operators until 1960 when it became the National Association of Motor Bus Owners. Assumed its present name on Sept. 19, 1977. Members are privately owned bus companies, bus manufacturers, accessory manufacturers, travel-tourism businesses, and organizations and others concerned with bus service. Sponsors and supports the BusPac-Political Action Committee.

Meetings/Conferences:
Annual Meetings: Winter
2007 - Grapevine, TX/Jan. 27-31/3000
2008 - Virginia Beach, VA/Feb. 1-6/3000
2009 - Charlotte, VA/Jan. 7-12/3000

Publications:
Destinations. m. adv.
The Motorcoach Marketer. a. adv.

American Business Alliance for the Transition Economies of Eurasia

Historical Note
Became Europe and Eurasia Business Committee in 2000.

American Business Conference *(1981)*
1828 L St. NW
Suite 908
Washington, DC 20036
Tel: (202)822-9300 *Fax:* (202)467-4070
E-Mail: abc@americanbusinessconference.org
Web Site: www.americanbusinessconference.org
Members: 100 individuals
Staff: 4
Annual Budget: $1-2,000,000
President: John Endean
E-Mail: abc@americanbusinessconference.org

Historical Note
ABC is an association of 100 mid-size, high-growth companies, represented by their chief executive officers. Each member company generates from $25 million to $2 billion in revenue annually. Companies must maintain annual growth rates of approximately 15 percent a year to remain part of the ABC. Concerned with tax and regulatory reform, and preservation of the free enterprise system.

American Business Media *(1906)*
675 Third Ave., Seventh Floor
New York, NY 10017-5704
Tel: (212)661-6360 Ext: 3326 *Fax:* (212)370-0736
E-Mail: info@abmmail.com
Web Site: www.americanbusinessmedia.com
Members: 235 companies, 1700 publications
Staff: 16
Annual Budget: $2-5,000,000
President and Chief Executive Officer: Gordon T. Hughes, II
E-Mail: g.hughes@abmmail.com

Historical Note
Formed by a merger of Associated Business Publications (founded in 1906) and National Business Publications (founded in 1948). Absorbed Agricultural Publishers Association in 2002. Members are specialized business magazines with audited circulation.

Meetings/Conferences:
Annual Meetings: Spring/350

Publications:
Business Media Matters. bi-m. adv.
E News. w. adv.
Business Media News newsletter. bi-m. adv.
Inside the Beltway. w. adv.

American Business Women's Association *(1949)*
9100 Ward Pkwy.
P.O. Box 8728
Kansas City, MO 64114-0728
Tel: (816)361-6621 *Fax:* (816)361-4991
Toll Free: (800)228 - 0007
E-Mail: abwa@abwa.org
Web Site: www.abwa.org
Members: 50000 individuals
Staff: 25
Annual Budget: $2-5,000,000
Chief Executive Officer: Carolyn Bufton Elman
E-Mail: abwa@abwa.org
Chief Operating Officer: Rene Street
E-Mail: abwa@abwa.org

Historical Note
Dedicated to developing strong business skills in working women. Provides networking support. Membership: $50-100/year.

Meetings/Conferences:
Annual Meetings: Fall

Publications:
Prime Time Connection newsletter (online). q. adv.
Company Connection Business Owners (online). q. adv.
Express Network Newsletter (online). m. adv.
Leadership Edge Newsletter (online). q. adv.
Council Communications Newsletter (online). q. adv.
Women In Business Magazine. bi-m. adv.

American Butter Institute *(1908)*
2101 Wilson Blvd., Suite 400
Arlington, VA 22201
Tel: (703)243-5630 *Fax:* (703)841-9328
Web Site: www.butterinstitute.org
Members: 36 companies
Staff: 2
Annual Budget: $50-100,000
Executive Director: Jerome J. Kozak
Director, Membership Services: Anuja Miner
E-Mail: aminer@nmpf.org

Historical Note
Organized as the National Association of Creamery Butter Manufacturers in 1908, ABI represents manufacturers and packagers of the majority of creamery butter and butter products. ABI is one of the nation's oldest dairy product associations.

Publications:
Butter Market Situation and Outlook. q.

American Camp Association *(1910)*
5000 State Rd. 67 North
Martinsville, IN 46151-7902
Tel: (765)342-8456 *Fax:* (765)342-2065
E-Mail: aca@acacamps.org
Web Site: www.acacamps.org
Members: 6000 individuals
Staff: 30
Annual Budget: $2-5,000,000
Chief Executive Officer: Peg L. Smith
Standards: Wesley Bird
Director, Operations Research: Marge Scanlin

Historical Note
Established in 1910 as the Camp Directors Association. Became the Camp Directors' Association of America in 1924 and the American Camping Association in 1935; assumed its current name in 2004. Sponsors accreditation programs for camps and educational programs for camp director/owners. ACA offers over 250 products to camp and youth program directors through its direct-mail bookstore.

Meetings/Conferences:
Annual Meetings: Winter

Publications:
Camping Magazine. bi-m. adv.

American Cancer Society *(1913)*
1599 Clifton Rd. NE
Atlanta, GA 30329
Toll Free: (800)227 - 2345
Web Site: www.cancer.org
Members: 2000000 individuals
Staff: 6000
Annual Budget: Over $100,000,000
Chief Executive Officer: John R. Seffrin, Ph.D.

Historical Note
Formerly (1913) the American Society for the Control of Cancer. Incorporated in 1922. Name changed (1944) to American Cancer Society Inc. Has an annual budget of approximately $400 million.

Meetings/Conferences:
Annual Meetings: Atlanta, GA in November

Publications:
Cancer Cytopathology. bi-m.
Cancer.
Cancer Practice.
CA- a Cancer Journal for Clinicians. bi-m.
Cancer Facts and Figures. a.

American Canine Sports Medicine Association *(1991)*
P.O. Box 07412
Ft. Myers, FL 33919
E-Mail: postmaster@acsma.org
Web Site: www.acsma.org
Members: 400 individuals
Staff: 1
Executive Director: Gail Cook
E-Mail: postmaster@acsma.org

Historical Note
ACSMA promotes the application of sports medicine, e.g., exercise physiology and orthopedic health, in canine veterinary practice. Membership: $25/year (domestic); $35/year (foreign).

Publications:
ACSMA Newsletter. q.

American Car and Truck Rental Association *(1996)*

Historical Note
Address unknown in 2005.

American Cardiology Technologists Association *(1957)*

Historical Note
A division of American Society of Extra-Corporeal Technology.

American Cash Flow Association *(1990)*
P.O. Box 2668
Orlando, FL 32802-2668
Tel: (407)206-6523 *Fax:* (407)206-6515
Toll Free: (800)253 - 1294 Ext: 2166
Web Site: www.americancashflow.com
Members: 25000 individuals
Staff: 4
Managing Editor: Judy Arndt
President and Chief Executive Officer: Frederic Rewey
Manager, Client Relations: Cathy Simmons

Historical Note
Formerly (1997) the National Association of Entrepreneurs. ACFA members are professionals working in fields related to cash flow and debt instruments. ACFA provides certification programs leading to the Certified Cash Flow Consultant (CCFC) designation. Membership: $149/year.

Meetings/Conferences:
Annual Meetings: Spring

Publications:
Who's Who in the Private Mortgage Industry.
Who's Who in the Factoring Industry.
Who's Who in the Cash Flow Industry?.
Industry Resource Manual.
American Cash Flow Journal Newspaper. m. adv.

American Casual Furniture Fabric Association

Historical Note
A division of the Industrial Fabrics Association International.

American Catholic Correctional Chaplains Association *(1952)*
320 Cathedral St.
Baltimore, MD 21201
Tel: (410)547-5475 *Fax:* (410)625-8483
E-Mail: shull@archbalt.org
Web Site: www.catholiccorrectionalchaplains.org
Members: 150 individuals
Annual Budget: under $10,000
Executive Secretary: Sharon Hull

Historical Note
Formerly the American Catholic Prison Chaplains Association, ACCCA is affiliated with The American Correctional Chaplain Association. Membership: $40/year (individual); $20/year (retiree/volunteer).

Meetings/Conferences:
Annual Meetings: August, with the American Correctional Ass'n.

Publications:
ACCCA newsletter. 3/yr. adv.

American Catholic Historical Association *(1919)*
Catholic Univ. of America
Mullen Library, Room 318
Washington, DC 20064
Tel: (202)319-5079
E-Mail: cua-chracha@cua.edu
Web Site: http://research.cua.edu/acha
Members: 900 individuals
Staff: 2
Annual Budget: $25-50,000
Secretary-Treasurer: Rev. Robert Trisco
E-Mail: trisco@cua.edu

Historical Note
A professional society of those interested in the history of the Catholic church and the promotion of historical scholarship among Catholics. Sponsors the John Tarcy Ellis Dissertation Award, in support of graduate work on the history of the Catholic Church. Membership: $50/year (individual); $30/year (student).

Meetings/Conferences:
Annual Meetings: January, with the American Historical Ass'n, which plans all meetings
2007 – Atlanta, GA(Hilton, Marriott, Hyatt)/Jan. 4-7

Publications:
Catholic Historical Review. q. adv.

American Catholic Philosophical Association *(1926)*
Administration Bldg., Fordham Univ.
New York, NY 10458
Tel: (718)817-4081 *Fax:* (718)817-5709
E-Mail: secretary@acpa-main.org
Web Site: www.acpaweb.org
Members: 1500 individuals
Staff: 1
Annual Budget: $50-100,000
National Secretary: Michael Baur

Historical Note
Members are scholars and individuals interested in Catholic philosophy. Membership: $20-52/year (individual); $75/year (institution).

Meetings/Conferences:
Annual Meetings: Fall

Publications:
Proceedings of the ACPA. a.
The American Catholic Philosophical Quarterly. q. adv.

American Ceramic Society *(1898)*
735 Ceramic Pl.
Suite 100
Westerville, OH 43081
Tel: (866)721-3322 *Fax:* (614)889-6109
E-Mail: customerservice@ceramics.org
Web Site: www.ceramics.org
Members: 8000 individuals
Staff: 52
Annual Budget: $5-10,000,000
Director, Marketing and Meeting Services: Megan Mahan
Director, Publications and Meeting: Mark Mecklenborg

Historical Note
Founded February 6, 1898 by Edward Orton, Jr. with 15 charter members. Incorporated in Ohio in 1905. The National Institute of Ceramic Engineers, the Ceramic Manufacturing Council and the Ceramic Education Council are affiliated classes of ACerS. Members include scientists, engineers and industrialists who produce products related to ceramics and related materials. Membership fee varies.

Meetings/Conferences:
Annual Meetings: Spring/7,000

Publications:
Ceramics Monthly. m. adv.
Pottery Making Illustrated. 6/year. adv.
The American Ceramic Society Bulletin. m. adv.
Journal of the American Ceramic Society. m.
Ceramic Engineering and Science Proceedings. 9/yr.
Ceramic Source. a. adv.
International Journal of Applied Ceramic Technology. q. adv.

American Chain Association *(1971)*
6724 Lone Oak Blvd.
Naples, FL 34109-6834
Tel: (239)514-3441 *Fax:* (239)514-3470
E-Mail: bob@americanchainassn.org
Web Site: www.americanchainassn.org
Members: 5 companies
Staff: 3
Annual Budget: $50-100,000
Executive Director: Robert A. Reinfried

Historical Note
Formerly (1971) American Sprocket Chain Manufacturers; successor to Association of Roller and Silent Chain Manufacturers and Malleable Chain Manufacturers Institute. Membership: $2,500-15,000/year.

Meetings/Conferences:
Annual Meetings: June/10
2007 – Litchfield Park, AZ(Wigwam)/Apr. 1-4/6

American Chain of Warehouses *(1911)*
156 Flamingo Dr.
Beecher, IL 60401
Tel: (708)946-9792 *Fax:* (708)946-9793
Web Site: www.acwi.org
Members: 50 commercial warehouses
Staff: 2
Annual Budget: $100-250,000
Vice President: William L. Jurus
E-Mail: bjurus@acwi.org

Historical Note
Membership fees are set according to formula.

Meetings/Conferences:
Annual Meetings: May

Publications:
Report for Members. m.
Membership Directory. a.

American Chamber of Commerce Executives *(1914)*
4875 Eisenhower Ave., Suite 250
Alexandria, VA 22304
Tel: (703)998-0072 *Fax:* (703)212-9512
Toll Free: (800)394 - 2223
E-Mail: infol@acce.org
Web Site: www.acce.org
Members: 5900 individuals
Staff: 25
Annual Budget: $2-5,000,000
President: Mick Fleming
Vice President, Communication and Network Development: Cathy Lada
Vice President, Administration and Chief Financial Officer: Brenda Luper
Vice President, Member Relations: Chris Mead
Director, Administration: Maryann Niner
Vice President, Member Services and F.B.I.: Tamara Philbin
Vice President, Education: Kawania Wooten

Historical Note
Established 1914. Formerly National Association of Commercial Organization Secretaries and changed to American Chamber of Commerce Executives. Absorbed the National Association for Membership Development in 2003. Grants the professional CCE (Certified Chamber Executive) designation.

Meetings/Conferences:
2007 – Sacramento, CA/Aug. 1-4

Publications:
Chamber Executive. bi-m. adv.
Quorum Call. q.

American Cheese Society *(1982)*
304 W. Liberty St., Suite 201
Louisville, KY 40202
Tel: (502)583-3783 *Fax:* (502)589-3602
E-Mail: acs@hqtrs.com
Web Site: www.cheesesociety.org
Members: 700 individuals
Staff: 1
Annual Budget: $100-250,000
Executive Director: Marci Wilson

Historical Note
ACS encourages the understanding, appreciation, and promotion of America's farmstead and specialty cheeses. Members include producers, distributors, retailers, and others with an interest in the cheese industry. Membership: $75-750/year (individual); $1,875/year (company).

Meetings/Conferences:
Annual Meetings: August
Publications:
Annual Conference Report. a.
ACS Newsletter. q. adv.
Membership Directory.

American Chemical Society *(1876)*
1155 16th St. NW
Washington, DC 20036
Toll Free: (800)227 - 5558
E-Mail: help@acs.org
Web Site: www.chemistry.org
Members: 158000 individuals
Staff: 1750
Annual Budget: Over $100,000,000
Executive Director and Chief Executive Officer: Madeleine Jacobs
Treasurer and Director, Finance and Administration: Brian A. Bernstein
E-Mail: b_bernstein@acs.org
Director, Membership Division: Denise Creech
Acting Director, Education: Mary Kirchoff
Secretary and General Counsel: Flint H. Lewis
E-Mail: f_lewis@acs.org
Historical Note
Founded in New York City on April 6, 1876. Incorporated in 1877. Granted a national charter by the Congress in 1937. Encourages the advancement of all branches of chemistry in the broadest and most liberal manner. Has an annual budget of approximately $250 million. Membership: $127/year (regular/associate); $94/year (national); $64/year (student).
Publications:
Journal of Natural Products. m. adv.
Organic Process Research & Development. bi-m. adv.
Journal of Combinatorial Chemistry. bi-m. adv.
Organic Letters. bi-w. adv.
Accounts of Chemical Research. m.
Biochemistry. w. adv.
Chemical & Engineering News. w. adv.
Chemical Reviews. m. adv.
Industrial & Engineering Chemistry Research. bi-w. adv.
Inorganic Chemistry. bi-w. adv.
Journal of Agricultural and Food Chemistry. bi-w. adv.
Journal of the American Chemical Society. w. adv.
Journal of Chemical and Engineering Data. bi-m. adv.
Journal of Chemical Information and Modeling. bi-m. adv.
Journal of Medicinal Chemistry. bi-w. adv.
Macromolecules. bi-w. adv.
Organometallics. bi-w. adv.
Langmuir. bi-w. adv.
Chemical Research in Toxicology. m. adv.
Chemistry of Materials. bi-w. adv.
Bioconjugate Chemistry. bi-m. adv.
Chemcyclopedia. a. adv.
Biotechnology Progress. bi-m. adv.
Energy Fuels. bi-m. adv.
Crystal Growth & Design. m. adv.
Journal of Proteome Research. m. adv.
Nano Letters. m. adv.
Analytical Chemistry. bi-w. adv.
Environmental Science & Technology. bi-w. adv.
Biomacromolecules. m. adv.
Journal of Organic Chemistry. bi-w. adv.
Journal of Physical Chemistry, A. w. adv.
Journal of Physical Chemistry, B. w. adv.
ACS Chemical Biology. m. adv.
Molecular Pharmaceutics. bi-m. adv.
Journal of Chemical Theory and Computation. bi-m. adv.

American Chemical Society - Rubber Division
P.O. Box 499
Akron, OH 44309-0499
Tel: (330)972-7814 *Fax:* (330)972-5269
Members: 3000
Staff: 10
Annual Budget: $1-2,000,000
Executive Director: Edward L. Miller
Publications:
Rubber Chemistry and Technology. 5/year. adv.

American Chemistry Council *(1872)*
1300 Wilson Blvd.
Arlington, VA 22209-2307
Tel: (703)741-5000 *Fax:* (703)741-6000
Web Site: www.americanchemistry.com
Members: 133 companies
Staff: 175
Annual Budget: $25-50,000,000
President and Chief Executive Officer: Jack N. Gerard
Vice President, Communications: Lisa Harrison
Historical Note
Founded as Manufacturing Chemists' Association; absorbed Plastic Materials Manufacturers Association in 1950. Became Chemical Manufacturers Association in 1979, and assumed its current name in 2000. Began admitting Canadian companies to membership in 1953. Includes programs such as Ethylene Oxide Industry Council. Administers research on specific chemicals germane to industry activity. Has a core budget of approximately $28 million.
Meetings/Conferences:
Annual Meetings: Always White Sulphur Springs, WV/June
Publications:
Chemistry Business. 10/year.

American Cheviot Sheep Society *(1924)*
Route One
Box 120
New Richland, MN 56072
Tel: (765)465-8474
Web Site: www.cheviots.org
Members: 800 individuals
Staff: 1
Annual Budget: $10-25,000
Executive Secretary: Jo Bernard
Historical Note
Breeders and fanciers of Cheviot sheep. Member of the National Pedigree Livestock Council. Membership: $10 (lifetime).
Meetings/Conferences:
Annual Meetings: November, in Louisville, KY
Publications:
The Banner. m. adv.
Breeders Directory. a.
Cheviot Journal. a.

American Chianina Association *(1972)*
1708 N. Prarie View Rd.
P.O. Box 890
Platte City, MO 64079
Tel: (816)431-2808 *Fax:* (816)431-5381
E-Mail: amerchianina@earthlink.com
Web Site: www.chicattle.org
Members: 1044 individuals
Staff: 7
Annual Budget: $250-500,000
Chief Executive Officer: Glen Klippenstein
E-Mail: amerchianina@earthlink.com
Director, Marketing: Ed Miller
E-Mail: amerchianina@earthlink.com
Historical Note
Breeders and fanciers of Chianina beef cattle. Member of the National Pedigree Livestock Council. Membership: $50/year (individual and company).
Meetings/Conferences:
Annual Meetings: Always, Louisville, KY in November
Publications:
ACA Journal. 8/year. adv.

American Chiropractic Association *(1930)*
1701 Clarendon Blvd.
Arlington, VA 22209
Tel: (703)276-8800 *Fax:* (703)243-2593
E-Mail: memberinfo@acatoday.org
Web Site: www.acatoday.com
Members: 18000 individuals
Staff: 40
Annual Budget: $5-10,000,000
Executive Vice President: Kevin Corcoran, CAE
Vice President, Insurance Relations: Laurie Douglass
Vice President, Government Relations: John Falardeau
Vice President, Communications: Felicity Feather Clancy
Vice President, Meeting and Administration: Janet Ridgely
Vice President, Finance: Steve Stoupa
Vice President, Finance and Administration: John Wanda
Historical Note
Founded in 1930 as the National Chiropractic Association, it assumed its present name in 1963; chartered in Delaware. Sponsors the following specialty councils: Family Practice, Nutrition, Orthopedics, Neurology, Physiological Therapeutics, Sports Injuries and Physical Fitness, Diagnositc Imaging, Technique and Occupational Health. Promotes the philosophy, science and art of chiropractic, and the professional welfare of its members; promotes legislation defining chiropractic health care and public education of chiropractic. Conducts chiropractic surveys and statistical studies. Oversees the work of the ACA-PAC, its political action arm, and the American Chiropractic Foundation. Has an annual budget of approximately $6 million. Membership: $600/year.
Meetings/Conferences:
Annual Meetings: September
Publications:
Journal of the ACA (online). m. adv.
ACA Today. m. adv.
ACA Membership Directory. a. adv.

American Chiropractic Registry of Radiologic Technologists *(1982)*
52 W. Colfax St.
Palatine, IL 60067
Tel: (847)705-1178
Web Site: www.acrrt.com
Members: 2000 individuals
Staff: 2
Annual Budget: $50-100,000
Executive Vice President: Lawrence Pyzik, DC
Historical Note
Members are radiologic technologists working in chiropractic offices.
Meetings/Conferences:
Annual Meetings: annual
Publications:
Wavelengths Newsletter. q.

American Choral Directors Association *(1959)*
P.O. Box 2720
Oklahoma City, OK 73101
Tel: (405)232-8161 *Fax:* (405)232-8162
E-Mail: acda@acdaonline.org
Web Site: www.acdaonline.org
Members: 19000 individuals
Staff: 11
Annual Budget: $2-5,000,000
Executive Director: Gene Brooks, Ph.D.
Historical Note
A non-profit professional organization whose active membership is composed of choral musicians from schools, colleges and universities, community and industrial organizations, churches and professional groups. Active membership: $75/year.
Meetings/Conferences:
Biennial Meetings: Odd years
Publications:
The Choral Journal. 10/year. adv.

American Choral Foundation *(1954)*
Historical Note
A division of Chorus America, which provides administrative support.

American Cinema Editors *(1950)*
100 Universal City Plaza, Bldg 2352B
Room 202
Universal City, CA 91608
Tel: (818)777-2900 *Fax:* (818)733-5023
E-Mail: amercinema@earthlink.net
Web Site: www.ace-filmeditors.org
Members: 500 individuals
Staff: 3
Annual Budget: $100-250,000
Managing Director: Jennifer McCormick

E-Mail: amercinema@earthlink.net

Historical Note

An honorary professional society. Presents the annual "Ace Eddie" award for film editing. Membership, though international, is concentrated in the Los Angeles area. Membership: $250/year.

Publications:

Cinemeditor. bi-m. adv.

American Classical League *(1919)*

Miami University
Oxford, OH 45056
Tel: (513)529-7741 *Fax:* (513)529-7742
E-Mail: info@aclclassics.org
Web Site: www.aclclassics.org
Members: 4000 individuals
Staff: 5
Annual Budget: $25-50,000
Administrative Secretary: Geri Dutra

Historical Note

Members are high school and college teachers of Latin and Greek. Supports the Junior Classical League - high school Latin and Greek students. Membership: $35/year (individual); $15/year (student); $25/year (retired).

Meetings/Conferences:

Annual Meetings: Summer

Publications:

Classical Outlook. q. adv.

American Cleft Palate-Craniofacial Association *(1943)*

1504 E. Franklin St., Suite 102
Chapel Hill, NC 27514
Tel: (919)933-9044 *Fax:* (919)933-9604
E-Mail: info@aca-cpf.org
Web Site: http://ww.acpa-cpf.org
Members: 2600 individuals
Staff: 5
Annual Budget: $500-1,000,000
Executive Director: Nancy Smythe
E-Mail: info@aca-cpf.org

Historical Note

Founded in Harrisburg, PA, April 4, 1943 as the American Academy of Cleft Prosthesis. Became the American Association for Cleft Palate Rehabilitation in 1949 and later assumed its present name. Members consist of doctors, dentists and others concerned with facial birth defects. Membership: $150/year.

Meetings/Conferences:

Annual Meetings: Spring
2007 - Denver, CO(Omni Interlocken)/Apr. 23-28/550
2008 - Philadelphia, PA(Loews Hotel)/Apr. 14-19/550

Publications:

ACPA/CPF Newsletter. 4/year. adv.
Cleft Palate-Craniofacial Journal. bi-m. adv.
Directory. bi-a.

American Clinical and Climatological Association *(1884)*

Univ. of Cincinnati Dept. of Internal Medicine
231 Albert Sabin Way ML 0557
Cincinnati, OH 45267-0557
Tel: (513)558-0858 *Fax:* (513)558-0852
Web Site: www.accassoc.org
Members: 375 individuals
Annual Budget: $25-50,000
Secretary-Treasurer: Robert G. Luke, M.D.

Historical Note

Members are engaged in the clinical study of disease. Has no paid staff. Membership: (invitation only) $100/year.

Meetings/Conferences:

Annual Meetings: October/300-350

Publications:

Transactions of the American Clinical and Climatological Ass'n. a.

American Clinical Laboratory Association *(1971)*

1250 H St. NW
Suite 880
Washington, DC 20005
Tel: (202)637-9466 *Fax:* (202)637-2050
E-Mail: info@clinical-labs.org
Web Site: www.clinical-labs.org
Members: 24 organizations
Staff: 3
Annual Budget: $250-500,000
President: Alan Mertz
Senior Vice President: Jo Anne Glisson

Historical Note

Members are clinical laboratories licensed and regulated under Medicare and the Interstate Laboratory Program. Membership dues vary by organization size.

American Clinical Neurophysiology Society *(1946)*

One Regency Dr.
P.O. Box 30
Bloomfield, CT 06002-0030
Tel: (860)243-3977 *Fax:* (860)286-0787
E-Mail: acns@ssmgt.com
Web Site: www.acns.org
Members: 1450 individuals
Staff: 3
Annual Budget: $100-250,000
Executive Director: Jacquelyn T. Coleman, CAE

Historical Note

Formerly (1996) American Electroencephalographic Society, ACNS is a professional society of electroencephalographers and neurophysiologists.

Meetings/Conferences:

Annual Meetings: Fall

Publications:

Journal of Clinical Neurophysiology. 6/year.

American Cloak and Suit Manufacturers Association *(1919)*

P.O. Box 605039
Bayside, NY 11360-5039
Tel: (212)244-7300 *Fax:* (212)564-6166
Staff: 3
Annual Budget: $25-50,000
Executive Director: Peter Conticelli

Historical Note

Membership concentrated in the New York metropolitan area. Major function is to represent its members in bargaining with labor.

Meetings/Conferences:

Executive Board meetings: Every six weeks.

American Coal Ash Association *(1968)*

15200 E. Girard Ave., Suite 3050
Aurora, CO 80014-3955
Tel: (720)870-7897 *Fax:* (720)870-7889
E-Mail: info@acaa-usa.org
Web Site: www.acaa-usa.org
Members: 100 companies
Staff: 4
Annual Budget: $500-1,000,000
Executive Director: David C. Goss

Historical Note

Incorporated in 1968 as the National Ash Association in Washington, DC, ACAA moved to Alexandria, VA in 1994. ACAA has an international membership which includes both electric utility and non-utility producers of coal-combustion products (CCPs), marketers, consultants, and other organizations. ACAA's mission is to advance the management and use of CCPs in ways that are environmentall safe, technically sound, and commercially competitive.

Meetings/Conferences:

Quarterly Meetings:
2007 - Cincinnati, OH(N. Kentucky Convention Center)//600

Publications:

CCP Survey. a.

American Cocoa Research Institute *(1948)*

8320 Old Courthouse Rd.
Suite 300
Vienna, VA 22182
Tel: (703)790-5011 *Fax:* (703)790-5752
Members: 9 companies
Staff: 3
Annual Budget: $1-2,000,000
President: Lynn Munroe Bragg
Senior Vice President, Scientific Affairs: Leah C. Porter, Ph.D.

Historical Note

Affiliate of Chocolate Manufacturers Association, which provides administrative support. ACRI provides industry leadership in all scientific areas related to cocoa and promotes the chocolate industry's interests through legislative and regulatory programs and public relations.

Meetings/Conferences:

Annual Meetings: with the Chocolate Manufacturers Ass'n

American Coke and Coal Chemicals Institute *(1944)*

1255 23rd St. NW
Washington, DC 20037-1174
Tel: (202)452-1140 *Fax:* (202)833-3636
E-Mail: information@accci.org
Web Site: www.accci.org
Members: 60 companies
Staff: 3
Annual Budget: $500-1,000,000
President: David A. Saunders

Historical Note

Members are national and international firms representing companies which produce oven coke and metallurgical coal; producers and processors of chemicals derived from coal or tar; producers of integrated steel and builders of major components for the industry.

Meetings/Conferences:

Semi-Annual Meetings: Spring and Fall/150

Publications:

Foundry Facts. q.

American Collectors Association

Historical Note

Became ACA - the International Association of Credit and Collection Professionals in 2001.

American College Counseling Association *(1991)*

Historical Note

An affiliate of American Counseling Association, which provides administrative support.

American College for Advancement in Medicine *(1973)*

2411 Ridge Route
Suite 115
Laguna Hills, CA 92653-1339
Tel: (949)309-3521 *Fax:* (949)309-3538
Toll Free: (800)532 - 3688
E-Mail: info@acam.org
Web Site: www.acam.org
Members: 1000 individuals
Staff: 5
Annual Budget: $1-2,000,000
Executive Director: Sharon Urch

Historical Note

Members are physicians interested in preventive and nutritional medicine. Membership: $430/year.

Meetings/Conferences:

Semi-Annual Meetings: Spring and Winter
2007 - Chicago, IL/May 5-11

Publications:

Monthly Update. m. adv.
Clinical Practice of Alternative Medicine. q. adv.

American College Health Association *(1920)*

P.O. Box 28937
Baltimore, MD 21240
Tel: (410)859-1500 *Fax:* (410)859-1510
E-Mail: contact@acha.org
Web Site: www.acha.org
Members: 2500 individuals
Staff: 18
Annual Budget: $2-5,000,000
Executive Director: Col. Doyle Randol, USA (Ret.)
Director, Member Programs and Services: Susan Answorth
Communications Coordinator: Sharon Fisher
E-Mail: sharon@acha.org
Director, Development: Sukana Powers

Historical Note

Founded as the American Student Health Association. ACHA and its regional affiliates represent and serve physicians, nurses, health educators, administrative *and support staff who manage and staff college and university student health services. Membership: $130-160/year (professional); $35-80/year (student); $270-1840/year (institution).*

Meetings/Conferences:
Annual Meetings: Spring/1,800
2007 – San Antonio, TX(Marriott Rivercenter and Riverwalk)/May 29-June 2

Publications:
Action. q.
Journal of American College Health. bi-m. adv.

American College of Addictions Treatment Administrators *(1984)*

Historical Note
Merged with Nat'l Ass'n of Addiction Treatment Providers in 2003.

American College of Allergy, Asthma and Immunology *(1942)*

85 W. Algonquin Rd.
Suite 550
Arlington Heights, IL 60005-4460
Tel: (847)427-1200 *Fax:* (847)427-1294
E-Mail: diannekubis@acaai.org
Web Site: www.acaai.org
Members: 4200 individuals
Staff: 20
Annual Budget: $5-10,000,000
Executive Director: James R. Slawny
Director, Public Relations: JoAnn Faber
E-Mail: joannfaber@acaai.org
Director, Registration and Exhibits Manager: Dianne K. Kubis

Historical Note
Formerly (1987) American College of Allergists and (1995) American College of Allergy and Immunology. An organization of qualified allergists, physicians and scientists who have a special interest in allergy, asthma and/or immunology. Membership: $265/year.

Meetings/Conferences:
Annual Meetings: Winter/4,000
2007 – Dallas, TX(Gaylord Texan)/Nov. 9-14/4000
2008 – Seattle, WA(Washington State Convention Center)/Nov. 7-12/4000

Publications:
Allergy Watch. m.
ACAAI News. bi-m.
Annals of Allergy, Asthma and Immunology. m. adv.

American College of Angiology *(1954)*

2549 S.W. 23rd Cranbrook Pl.
Boynton Beach, FL 33436-5701
Members: 700 individuals
Staff: 5
Annual Budget: $100-250,000
Executive Director: Joan Shaffer
Meeting Coordinator: Carol Altruda

Historical Note
An interdisciplinary scientific organization composed of physicians and scientists interested in the study of blood circulation, lymph glands and the heart. Serves the growing need of medical, clinical and research scientists by providing the opportunity for the convenient interchange of technical research and clinical experiences associated with circulatory diseases. Maintains and sponsors the ACA Young Investigator Award Fund. Fellowship: $410/year (with journal), $185/year (without journal).

Meetings/Conferences:
Annual Meetings: Fall

Publications:
Journal of the American College of Cardiology. 6/yr. adv.

American College of Apothecaries *(1940)*

Research and Education Resource Center
2830 Summer Oaks Dr.
Bartlett, TN 38134-3811
Tel: (901)383-8119 *Fax:* (901)383-8882
E-Mail: aca@acainfo.org
Web Site: www.acainfo.org
Members: 1000 individuals
Staff: 5
Annual Budget: $500-1,000,000
Executive Vice President: Dr. D.C. Huffman, Jr.
E-Mail: aca@acainfo.org

Historical Note
Members are pharmacists owning ethical prescription pharmacies. Membership: $295/year.

Meetings/Conferences:
Annual Meetings: Fall

Publications:
Voice of The Pharmacist. q.
ACA Newsletter.
Patient's Newsletter. m.
Prescriber's Newletter. m.

American College of Bankruptcy *(1989)*

PMB 626A, 11350 Random Hills Rd.
Suite 800
Fairfax, VA 22030-6044
Tel: (703)934-6154 *Fax:* (703)802-0207
E-Mail: college@amercol.org
Web Site: www.amercol.org
Members: 650 individuals
Staff: 3
Annual Budget: $100-250,000
Executive Director: Suzanne A. Bingham
E-Mail: college@amercol.org

Historical Note
An honorary professional and educational association of bankruptcy and insolvency professionals. Its Fellows include commercial and consumer bankruptcy attorneys, insolvency accountants, corporate turnaround and renewal specialists, law professors, judges, government officials, and others involved in the bankruptcy and insolvency community. Nominees are extended an invitation to join based on a proven record of the highest standards of professionalism.

Publications:
College Columns. q.
ACB Directory. a.

American College of Cardiology *(1949)*

2400 N St. NW
Washington, DC 20037
Tel: (202)375-6000 *Fax:* (202)375-7000
Toll Free: (800)253 - 4636
Web Site: www.acc.org
Members: 26000 individuals
Staff: 200
Annual Budget: $25-50,000,000
Interim Chief Staff Officer: Tom Arend
Associate Executive Vice President, Advocacy: Karen J. Collishaw
Assistant Executive Vice President, Operations: Cathleen C. Gates
Senior Associate Executive Vice President, Education: Marcia Jackson, Ph.D.
Director, Communications: Sheila Strand

Historical Note
ACC is a professional society composed of 26,000 cardiovascular physicians and scientists around the world. ACC's mission is to foster optimal cardiovascular care and disease prevention through professional education, promotion of research, leadership in the development of standards and guidelines, and the formulation of health care policy. ACC operates a foundation that provides education and quality products and services. ACC's annual budget is approximately $41 million. Membership: $3500/year.

Meetings/Conferences:
Annual Meetings: Spring/23,000

Publications:
Affiliates in Training. bi-m. adv.
ACCEL (audiocassette). m.
ACC Current Journal Review. bi-m. adv.
Cardiology (newsletter). m. adv.
Journal of the American College of Cardiology. bi-m. adv.
Scientific Session News. a. adv.
CEO Briefing. m.

American College of Cardiovascular Administrators *(1986)*

701 Lee St., Suite 600
Des Plaines, IL 60016
Tel: (847)759-8601 *Fax:* (847)759-8602
E-Mail: info@aameda.org
Web Site: www.aameda.org
Members: 1000 individuals
Staff: 7
Annual Budget: $1-2,000,000
President and Chief Executive Officer: Renee S. Schleicher, CAE
Vice President, Finance and Administration: Nancy L. Anderson, CPA
Director, Education: Holly Estel
Director, Membership and Communications: Von Yetzer

Historical Note
ACCA is a specialty group of the American Academy of Medical Administrators. ACCA members are administrators in cardiovascular care.

Meetings/Conferences:
Management Conference: (also meets preceding the American College of Cardiology and American Heart Ass'n conventions)

Publications:
AIM (Academy in Action). m. adv.
ACCA Journal of Cardiovascular Management. q. adv.

American College of Chest Physicians *(1935)*

3300 Dundee Rd.
Northbrook, IL 60062-2348
Tel: (847)498-1400 *Fax:* (847)498-5460
Toll Free: (800)343 - 2227
E-Mail: accp@chestnet.org
Web Site: www.chestnet.org
Members: 16000 individuals
Staff: 60
Annual Budget: $10-25,000,000
Executive Vice President/Chief Executive Officer: Alvin Lever
Director, Leadership Activities: Darelene J. Buczak
Vice President, Finance: P. Stratton Davies, CPA
Vice President, Educational Resources: Ed Dellert
Vice President, Membership: Tracy Goode
Vice President, Operations: Donald R. Jones
Assistant Vice President, Meetings: David Larsen
Vice President, Health Affairs: Lynne G. Marcus
Vice President, Marketing: Richard Waters
Vice President and Executive Editor, CHEST: Stephen J. Welch

Historical Note
Founded in 1935 and incorporated in Illinois in 1942. Promotes the prevention of diseases of the chest. Membership: $324/year.

Meetings/Conferences:
Annual Meetings: Fall/3,600

Publications:
CHEST. m. adv.
Pulmonary Perspectives. q. adv.
Chest Soundings. q. adv.

American College of Chiropractic Orthopedists *(1954)*

1030 Broadway, Suite 101
El Centro, CA 92243
Tel: (760)370-9106 *Fax:* (760)352-3966
Web Site: www.accoweb.org
Members: 787 individuals
Annual Budget: $50-100,000
Contact: Bill Valusek

Historical Note
Members are chiropractic orthopedists and others with an interest in the field. Has no paid officers or full-time staff. Membership: $80/year.

Meetings/Conferences:
Annual Meetings: Spring.

Publications:
Membership Directory. a. adv.
Journal of the ACCO. q. adv.

American College of Clinical Pharmacology *(1969)*

3 Ellinwood Ct.
New Hartford, NY 13413-1105
Tel: (315)768-6117 *Fax:* (315)768-6119
Web Site: www.ACCP1.org
Members: 1000 individuals
Staff: 4
Annual Budget: $500-1,000,000
Executive Director: Susan Ulrich, R.Ph.
E-Mail: ACCP1ssu@AOL.com

Historical Note
Members of the College are health care professionals and biomedical/pharmaceutical scientists employed in academia, the pharmaceutical industry, contract clinical research organizations, private practice or government. There are four categories of membership offered by the college.

Meetings/Conferences:
Annual Meetings: Fall
2007 – San Francisco, CA(The Palace Hotel)/Sept. 9-11/300

Publications:
Newsletter. 3-4/year.
Journal of Clinical Pharmacology. m. adv.
Directory. a.

American College of Clinical Pharmacy *(1979)*
3101 Broadway, Suite 650
Kansas City, MO 64111
Tel: (816)531-2177 *Fax:* (816)531-4990
E-Mail: accp@accp.com
Web Site: www.accp.com
Members: 8700 individuals
Staff: 23
Annual Budget: $2-5,000,000
Executive Director: Michael S. Maddux
Manager, Operations: Richard Collins
Director, Research Institute: Robert Evenbaas
Director, Professional Development: Nancy Perrin
Director, Government and Professional Affairs: C. Edwin Webb

Historical Note
International society founded in October 1979 in Kansas City. Promotes the rational use of medications in health care, the advancement of knowledge regarding drug therapy and the development of clinical pharmacy. Membership: $30-200/year.

Meetings/Conferences:
Annual Meetings: Fall, Spring
2007 – Memphis, TN(Memphis Convention Center)/Apr. 22-25
2008 – Denver, CO(Colorado Convention Center)/Oct. 14-17

Publications:
Pharmacotherapy. m. adv.
PRN Report. bi-a.
ACCP Report. m. adv.
Residency & Fellowship Directory. a.

American College of Construction Lawyers *(1989)*
P.O. Box 4646
Austin, TX 78765
Tel: (512)343-1808 *Fax:* (512)451-2911
E-Mail: donna@clesolutions.com
Web Site: www.accl.org
Members: 150 individuals
Staff: 4
Annual Budget: $100-250,000
Executive Director: Donna Passons

Historical Note
ACCL is a national organization of lawyers who have demonstrated skill and experience in the practice or teaching of construction law, and are dedicated to the specialized practice of construction law. The group provides advanced professional workshops and educational programs. Membership: based upon nomination and election.

Meetings/Conferences:
2007 – Dana Point, CA(Ritz Carlton)/Feb. 22-25
2008 – San Antonio, TX(Hyatt Hill Country)/Feb. 21-24

American College of Contingency Planners *(1998)*
701 Lee St., Suite 600
Des Plaines, IL 60016
Tel: (847)759-8601 *Fax:* (847)759-8602
E-Mail: info@aameda.org
Members: 500 individuals
Staff: 7
Annual Budget: $1-2,000,000
President and Chief Executive Officer: Renee S. Schleicher, CAE

Historical Note
ACCP is a national specialty group of the American Academy of Medical Administrators. Members are disaster, emergency, and contingency planners in healthcare organizations.

Meetings/Conferences:
Annual Meetings: Fall/Typical Attendance: 450

Publications:
AIM (Academy in Motion). m. adv.
The AAMA Executive. q. adv.

American College of Counselors *(1984)*
12634 Gunnison Dr.
Indianapolis, IN 46236
Tel: (317)823-3427
Web Site: http://counselors.co.nr
Members: 150 individuals
Annual Budget: $25-50,000
Executive Director: Mary E. Oetjen

Historical Note
ACC members are professionals in counseling and related fields of human services. ACC promotes competent counseling by certifying people in the field who meet high standards of education, supervision and experience. ACC is an collegial, interdisciplinary organization. Benefits of membership include three newsletter issues a year, an annual journal, and educational opportunities. Membership: $150 (initial individual membership, plus application fees for certification as clinical member); $100/year thereafter.

Meetings/Conferences:
Annual Meetings: Fall

Publications:
ACC Courier. 3/year. adv.
CON-TEXT - Journal of the ACC. a. adv.
Membership Directory. a.

American College of Critical Care Medicine *(1988)*

Historical Note
A division of the Society of Critical Care Medicine.

American College of Dentists *(1920)*
839 Quince Orchard Blvd., Suite J
Gaithersburg, MD 20878-1614
Tel: (301)977-3223 *Fax:* (301)977-3330
E-Mail: info@facd.org
Web Site: www.facd.org
Members: 8000 individuals
Staff: 6
Annual Budget: $500-1,000,000
Executive Director: Stephen A. Ralls, D.D.S.

Historical Note
Founded in Cedar Rapids in 1920 and incorporated in Maryland in 1970. Membership: $150/year.

Meetings/Conferences:
Annual Meetings: Fall
2007 – San Francisco, CA/Sept. 26-27

Publications:
Journal of the American College of Dentists. q.
News and Views. q.

American College of Emergency Physicians *(1968)*
1125 Executive Circle
Irving, TX 75038-2522
Tel: (972)550-0911 *Fax:* (972)580-2816
Toll Free: (800)798 - 1822
E-Mail: info@acep.org
Web Site: www.acep.org
Members: 25000 individuals
Staff: 98
Annual Budget: $10-25,000,000
Executive Director: Dean Wilkerson
Director, Human Resources: Debbie Bridge
E-Mail: dbridge@acep.org
Associate Executive Director, Policy Division: W. Calvin Chaney
E-Mail: cchaney@acep.org
Associate Executive Director, Member Services Division: Robert Heard
E-Mail: rheard@acep.org
Associate Executive Director, Professional and Educational Publications Division: Tom Werlinich
E-Mail: twerlinich@acep.org

Historical Note
Provides courses in clinical practice and management to members in accordance with the continuing education requirements of the College. Sponsors and supports the National Emergency Medicine Political Action Committee and the Emergency Medicine Foundation. Has an annual budget of $17 million. Membership: $515/year.

Meetings/Conferences:
Annual Meetings: Fall
2007 – Seattle, WA(Convention Center)/Oct. 8-11/4000

Publications:
The Connection. m.
Em Today. bi-m.
24/7 Quarterly.
Annals of Emergency Medicine. m. adv.
ACEP News. m. adv.

American College of Epidemiology *(1979)*
1500 Sunday Dr., Suite 102
Raleigh, NC 27607
Tel: (919)861-5573 *Fax:* (919)787-4916
E-Mail: info@acepidemiology.org
Web Site: www.acepidemiology.org
Members: 850 individuals
Staff: 7
Executive Director: Peter Kralka
E-Mail: pkralka@olsonmgmt.com

Historical Note
Members are physicians and other health professionals with an interest in the study of human disease. Membership: $120-150/year (individual).

Meetings/Conferences:
Annual Meetings: Fall

Publications:
Annals of Epidemiology. bi-m.
Newsletter. q.

American College of Eye Surgeons *(1986)*
334 East Lake Rd.
Suite 135
Palm Harbor, FL 34685
Tel: (727)480-8542 *Fax:* (727)786-6622
E-Mail: quality@aces-abes.org
Web Site: www.aces-abes.org
Members: 800 individuals
Staff: 3
Executive Director: Carrol Roark
E-Mail: quality@aces-abes.org

Historical Note
ACES promotes quality ophthalmic surgical care; also suports the American Board of Eye Surgery (ABES). ABES establishes sub-specialty certification programs for ophthalmic surgeons. Certification currently available in cataract/implant, refractive surgery (incisional keratotomy and lasik), and penetrating keratoplasty. Membership: $275/year (individual); $300/year (corporate).

Meetings/Conferences:
Annual Meetings: February/225

Publications:
Newsletter. q.
Directory of Certified Physicians. a.
Clinical Guidelines. irreg.

American College of Foot and Ankle Orthopedics and Medicine *(1949)*
4350 East West Hwy., Suite 401
Bethesda, MD 20814-4410
Tel: (301)778-6539 *Fax:* (888)336-6832
Toll Free: (800)265 - 8263
E-Mail: info@acfaom.org
Web Site: www.acfaom.org
Members: 1100 individuals
Staff: 5
Annual Budget: $250-500,000
Executive Director: Norman E. Wallis, Ph.D.
E-Mail: info@acfaom.org

Historical Note
Formerly (1951) American College of Foot Orthopedists. An education and research association of podiatrists specializing in diseases and deformities of the foot and ankle. Affiliated with the American Podiatric Medical Association. Membership: $350/year.

Meetings/Conferences:
Annual Meetings: *August with the American Podiatric Medical Ass'n*
Publications:
ACFAOM Newsletter. q.
ACFAOM Defense Guide. a. adv.

American College of Foot and Ankle Surgeons *(1942)*
8725 W. Higgins Rd.
Suite 555
Chicago, IL 60631-2724
Tel: (773)693-9300 *Fax:* (773)693-9304
Toll Free: (800)421 - 2237
E-Mail: info@acfas.org
Web Site: www.acfas.org
Members: 6000 individuals
Staff: 15
Annual Budget: $2-5,000,000
Executive Director: J.C. (Chris) Mahaffey, CAE
Director, Finance: Steve King
Director, Health Policy: Julie K. Letwat, JD, MPH
Director, Education Curriculum and Alliances: Mary Meyers
Director, Marketing and Communications: Marsha Pedersen
Manager, Membership: Christine Rose
Historical Note
Formerly (1993) the American College of Foot Surgeons. ACFAS is a voluntary educational and scientific organization devoted to the ethical and competent practice of foot and ankle surgery and to the provision of high quality care for the foot and ankle surgery patient. ACFAS presents extensive scientific and educational programs, promotes methods to ensure a high standard of surgical practice, disseminates surgical knowledge, and provides information to the general public and to the health care community. Has a second web site at http://www.footphysicians.com. Membership: $495/year.
Meetings/Conferences:
Annual Meetings: *February-March/2,500*
Publications:
E-Updates. bi-w. adv.
The Bulletin. bi-m. adv.
Journal of Foot and Ankle Surgery. bi-m. adv.

American College of Forensic Examiners *(1992)*
2750 E. Sunshine
Springfield, MO 65804
Tel: (417)881-3818 *Fax:* (417)881-4702
Web Site: www.acfe.com
Members: 10000 individuals
Staff: 25
Annual Budget: $1-2,000,000
Founder and Chief Executive Officer: Robert L. O'Block, Ph.D.
Chief Association Officer: Megan Augustine
Historical Note
ACFE members are forensic examiners, mostly from the United States, that engage in the scientific aspects of forensic examination. Membership: $130/year (individual).
Publications:
The Forensic Examiner. q. adv.

American College of Forensic Psychiatry *(1981)*
P.O. Box 5870
Balboa Island, CA 92662
Tel: (949)673-7773 *Fax:* (949)673-7710
E-Mail: psychlaw@sover.net
Web Site: www.forensicpsychonline.com
Members: 350 individuals
Staff: 4
Executive Director: Ed Miller
E-Mail: psychlaw@sover.net
Publications:
American Journal of Forensic Psychiatry. q. adv.

American College of Gastroenterology *(1932)*
6400 Goldsboro Rd.
Suite 450
Bethesda, MD 20817-5848
Tel: (301)263-9000 *Fax:* (301)263-9025
E-Mail: acg.gi@acg.gi.org
Web Site: www.acg.gi.org
Members: 8,000 individuals
Staff: 8
Annual Budget: $1-2,000,000
Executive Director: Bradley C. Stillman
Historical Note
With members in over 30 countries worldwide, ACG promotes scholarly practice, teaching, and research in the digestive disease specialties.
Publications:
American Journal of Gastroenterology. m. adv.

American College of Health Care Administrators *(1962)*
300 N. Lee St., Suite 301
Alexandria, VA 22314
Tel: (703)739-7903 *Fax:* (703)739-7901
Toll Free: (888)882 - 2422
E-Mail: info@achac.org
Web Site: www.achca.org
Members: 3000 individuals
Staff: 10
Chief Executive Officer: Susan Burton, CAE
Historical Note
Formerly (1983) the American College of Nursing Home Administrators. ACHCA members manage and direct the daily operations of long-term care, subacute, and assisted living facilities. Membership: $230/year, active (individual).
Meetings/Conferences:
Annual Meetings: *Spring/800*

American College of Healthcare Architects
P.O. Box 14548
Lenexa, KS 66285-5340
Tel: (913)492-4307 *Fax:* (913)599-5340
E-Mail: acha-info@goamp.com
Web Site: www.healtharchitects.org
Executive Director: Francis M. Pitts

American College of Healthcare Executives *(1933)*
One N. Franklin St., Suite 1700
Chicago, IL 60606
Tel: (312)424-2800 *Fax:* (312)424-0023
E-Mail: ache@ache.org
Web Site: www.ache.org
Members: 30000 individuals
Staff: 100
Annual Budget: $10-25,000,000
Chief Executive Officer: Thomas C. Dolan, Ph.D., FACHE, CAE
Chief Operating Officer and Executive Vice President: Deborah Bowen
Vice President, Publications: Maureen Glass, CHE
Vice President, Membership: Cynthia Hahn, FACHE
Vice President, Marketing and Communications: Douglas Klegon, Ph.D.
Chief Information Officer and Vice President, Management Information Systems: Kimberly Mosley
Vice President, Research and Development: Peter Weil, Ph.D., FACHE
Historical Note
ACHE is an international professional society of nearly 30,000 healthcare executives. ACHE is known for its prestigious credentialing and educational programs. Its annual Congress on Healthcare management draws more than 4,000 participants each year. ACHE works toward its goal of improving the health status of society, by advancing healthcare management excellence. Also publishes an extensive catalog of publications in the area of healthcare administration. Has an annual budget of over $16,000,000. Membership: $325/year (Fellow/Diplomate); $285/year (Member).
Meetings/Conferences:
2007 – New Orleans, LA(Marriott-Sheraton)/March 19-22/4500
Publications:
Directory Online.
Journal of Healthcare Management. bi.
Healthcare Executive. bi-m. adv.
Frontiers of Health Services Management. q.

American College of Healthcare Information Administrators
701 Lee St., Suite 600
Des Plaines, IL 60016
Tel: (847)759-8601 *Fax:* (847)759-8602
President and Chief Executive Officer: Renee S. Schleicher, CAE
Historical Note
An affiliate of American Academy of Medical Administrators. ACHIA members are IT professionals in healthcare organizations.

American College of International Physicians *(1975)*
18700 Old Triangle Rd.
Triangle, VA 22172-0075
Tel: (703)221-1500 *Fax:* (703)360-6155
Toll Free: (877)422 - 4172
E-Mail: acip@acip.org
Web Site: www.acip.org
Members: 3000 individuals
Staff: 1
Annual Budget: $100-250,000
President: Alex P. Yadao, M.D.
E-Mail: acip@acip.org
Historical Note
Physicians educated in foreign countries and the U.S. who are licensed and practicing in the U.S. Main interests of the College are medical education, research, ethics and international activities. Absorbed the National Association of Foreign Medical Graduates in 1976. Membership: $175/year (individual).
Publications:
International Physician Newsletter. adv.

American College of Laboratory Animal Medicine *(1957)*
96 Chester St.
Chester, NH 03036
Tel: (603)887-2467 *Fax:* (603)887-0096
Web Site: www.aclam.org
Members: 700 individuals
Staff: 2
Annual Budget: $100-250,000
Executive Director: Dr. Melvin Balk
E-Mail: mwbaclam@gsi.net.net
Historical Note
Founded in 1957 as the American Board of Laboratory Animal Medicine. Incorporated in Illinois in 1957. Affiliated with the American Veterinary Medical Association and the American Association for Laboratory Animal Science. Established to encourage education, training, and research in laboratory animal medicine and to provide standards for veterinarians professionally concerned with the health of laboratory animals.
Meetings/Conferences:
Annual Meetings: *July, with American Veterinary Medical Ass'n*
Publications:
ACLAM Newsletter. 4/year.

American College of Legal Medicine *(1960)*
1111 N. Plaza Dr., Suite 550
Schaumburg, IL 60173
Tel: (847)969-0283 *Fax:* (847)517-7229
E-Mail: info@aclm.org
Web Site: www.aclm.org
Members: 1450 individuals
Staff: 3
Annual Budget: $250-500,000
Executive Director: Wendy J. Weiser
Administrative Director: Sue O'Sullivan
Historical Note
Founded and incorporated in Delaware in September, 1960. Members are doctors, lawyers, and other health care professionals interested in the interface between law and medicine. Fellows of the College must have both a medical and law degree or have performed significant service to the college over time. Membership: $270/year (fellow); $190/year (member/affiliate/corresponding); $35/year (student).
Meetings/Conferences:
Semi-Annual Meetings: *Spring/300 and Fall/150*
Publications:
Medical Legal Lessons. bi-m.
Legal Medicine Perspectives. bi-m. adv.
ACLM Newsletter. q. adv.

Journal of Legal Medicine. q.
Membership Directory. a.

American College of Managed Care Administrators *(1995)*
701 Lee St., Suite 600
Des Plaines, IL 60016
Tel: (847)759-8601 *Fax:* (847)759-8602
Web Site: www.aameda.org
Members: 475 individuals
Staff: 7
Annual Budget: $1-2,000,000
President and Chief Executive Officer: Renee S. Schleicher, CAE
E-Mail: Renee@aameda.org

Historical Note
ACMCA is a speciality group of the American Academy of Medical Administrators. ACMCA serves as a forum for exchanging information, and for credentialling and networking among managed care professionals. Funding is provided by AAMA.

Meetings/Conferences:
Annual Meetings: Fall

Publications:
The AAMA Executive. q. adv.
AIM (Academy in Motion). m. adv.

American College of Managed Care Medicine *(1995)*
4435 Waterfront Dr., Suite 101
P.O. Box 4913
Glen Allen, VA 23060
Tel: (804)527-1905 *Fax:* (804)747-5316
Toll Free: (800)722 - 0376
Web Site: www.acmcm.org
Members: 1000 individuals
Staff: 17
President: William C. Williams, III, M.D.
Vice President, Operations: Sloane Reed

Historical Note
ACMCM seeks to educate physicians about changes in health care environment and to prepare them to deliver cost-effective, appropriate managed care medicine to members of current and future health care delivery systems. An affiliate of National Association of Managed Care Physicians, which provides administrative support. Membership: $195/year (physicians); $250/year (other professionals); $1,500/year (organization).

Publications:
Journal of Managed Care Medicine. bi-a. adv.
Newsletter. m.
American Journal of Integrated Healthcare. bi-a. adv.

American College of Medical Genetics *(1991)*
9650 Rockville Pike
Bethesda, MD 20814-3998
Tel: (301)634-7127 *Fax:* (301)634-7275
E-Mail: acmg@acmg.net
Web Site: www.acmg.net
Members: 1450 individuals
Staff: 5
Annual Budget: $1-2,000,000
Executive Director: Michael S. Watson
Director, Administration: Melissa T. Forburger
E-Mail: acmg@acmg.net

Historical Note
ACMG members are physicians, laboratorians, and other health care professionals with an interest in genetics.

Meetings/Conferences:
Annual Meetings: March/1500
2007 – Nashville, TN(Renaissance Convention Center)/March 22-25/1500
2008 – Phoenix, AZ(Hyatt Regency)/March 13-16/1500
2009 – Tampa, FL(Marriott Waterside)/March 25-28/1500

Publications:
Genetics in Medicine. bi-m. adv.

American College of Medical Physics *(1982)*
12100 Sunset Hills Rd.
Suite 130
Reston, VA 20190-5202
Tel: (703)481-5001 *Fax:* (703)435-4390
Web Site: www.acmp.org
Members: 475 individuals
Staff: 2
Annual Budget: $100-250,000
Executive Director: Laureen Rowland
E-Mail: lrowland@drohanmgmt.com

American College of Medical Practice Executives *(1956)*
104 Inverness Terrace East
Englewood, CO 80112-5306
Tel: (303)799-1111 *Fax:* (303)643-4427
Toll Free: (877)275 - 6462
E-Mail: acmpe@mgma.com
Web Site: www.mgma.com/acmpe/index.cfm
Members: 5000 individuals
Staff: 9
Annual Budget: $1-2,000,000
President and Chief Executive Officer: William F. Jessee, M.D., FACMPE

Historical Note
Founded as the American College of Clinic Managers; became American College of Medical Group Administrators in 1976 and assumed its current name in 1993. A voluntary certification organization drawing its membership from the Medical Group Management Association. Membership: $265/year.

Meetings/Conferences:
Annual Meetings: With Medical Group Management Ass'n
2007 – Philadelphia, PA(Philadelphia Convention Center)/Oct. 28-31
2008 – San Diego, CA(San Diego Convention Center)/Oct. 19-22

Publications:
Executive View. bi-a..

American College of Medical Practice Management

Historical Note
Became American Academy of Practice Management in 2001.

American College of Medical Quality *(1973)*
4334 Montgomery Ave., Second Floor
Bethesda, MD 20814
Tel: (301)913-9149 *Fax:* (301)913-9142
Toll Free: (800)924 - 2149
E-Mail: acmq@acmq.org
Web Site: www.acmq.org
Members: 1000 individuals
Staff: 4
Annual Budget: $250-500,000
Executive Vice President: Bridget Brodie
E-Mail: acmq@acmq.org

Historical Note
Formerly (1991) the American College of Utilization Review Physicians. Organized and incorporated in the State of Pennsylvania, October 13, 1973 to set standards, provide continuing medical education and measure competence in the fields of quality assurance and utilization review. Members are doctors, related health personnel, hospitals, and health plans. Membership: $100/year (first year membership); $145/year (full member/M.D.); $285/year (first year affiliate); $125/year (affiliate member).

Meetings/Conferences:
2007 – Miami, FL(InterContinental Hotel)/Feb. 22-24

Publications:
American Journal of Medical Quality. bi-m. adv.
Focus. bi-m. adv.

American College of Medical Toxicology *(1993)*
11240 Waples Mill Rd.
Suite 200
Fairfax, VA 22030
Tel: (703)934-1223 *Fax:* (703)359-7562
E-Mail: info@acmt.net
Web Site: www.acmt.net
Members: 500 individuals
Staff: 2
Executive Director: Jerry Galler
E-Mail: info@acmt.net

Historical Note
ACMT is a professional, non-profit organization of physicians, certified in medical toxicology, dedicated to advancing the science and practice of medical toxicology.

Meetings/Conferences:
Annual Meetings: in conjunction with North American Congress of Clinical Toxicology

Publications:
Internet Journal of Medical Toxicology. q.

American College of Mental Health Administration *(1979)*
Five Waterside Place
Pittsburgh, PA 15222
Tel: (412)322-3969 *Fax:* (412)322-0655
Web Site: www.acmha.org
Members: 200 individuals
Staff: 1
Annual Budget: $50-100,000
Executive Director: Carolyn Maue
E-Mail: executive.director@acmha.org

Historical Note
ACMHA was established to further mental health administration as a practice and a profession, to foster research, and provide opportunites for professional education and communication. ACMHA members are clinician-administrators with knowledge and experience in both the administration of mental health programs and clinical care. Membership: $225/year (individual).

Meetings/Conferences:
Annual Meetings: Spring

American College of Mohs Micrographic Surgery and Cutaneous Oncology *(1967)*
511 E. Wells St., Suite 1100
Milwaukee, WI 53202
Tel: (414)347-1103 *Fax:* (414)276-2146
Toll Free: (800)500 - 7224
E-Mail: info@mohscollege.org
Web Site: www.mohscollege.org
Members: 810 individuals
Staff: 3
Annual Budget: $500-1,000,000
Executive Director: Georganne Dixon

Historical Note
Formerly (1987) American College of Chemosurgery. Members are physicians utilizing Mohs micrographic for the microscopically controlled excision of skin cancers. Membership open exclusively to physicians with fellowship training in Mohs surgery. Absorbed American College of Cryosurgery in 1997.

Meetings/Conferences:
2007 – Naples, FL(Registry Resort)/May 4-6

Publications:
Journal of Dermatologic Surgery. m.

American College of Mortgage Attorneys
15245 Shady Grove Rd.
Suite 130
Rockville, MD 20850-3222
Tel: (301)990-9075 *Fax:* (301)990-9771
Web Site: www.acmaatty.org
Members: 400 individuals
Staff: 4
Executive Director: Beverly I. Levy, CAE
E-Mail: blevy@mgmtsol.com

American College of Musicians *(1929)*
P.O. Box 1807
Austin, TX 78767
Tel: (512)478-5775 *Fax:* (512)478-5843
E-Mail: ngpt@aol.com
Web Site: www.pianoguild.com
Members: 115000 individuals
Staff: 12
Annual Budget: $1-2,000,000
President: Richard Allison

Historical Note
A standardizing agency granting degrees and diplomas to worthy musicians, ACM consists of two divisions: the National Guild of Piano Teachers and the National Fraternity of Student Musicians. Members are individuals whose qualifications make them eligible to judge.

Meetings/Conferences:
Annual Meetings: Not held
Publications:
Piano Guild Notes. bi-m.

American College of Neuropsychiatrists *(1939)*
28595 Orchard Lake Rd.
Suite 200
Farmington Hills, MI 48334
Tel: (248)553-0010 Ext: 295 *Fax:* (248)553-0818
E-Mail: acn-aconp@msn.com
Members: 800 Physicians
Staff: 2
Annual Budget: $100-250,000
Executive Director: Louis E. Rentz, DO, FACN
E-Mail: acn-aconp@msn.com
Historical Note
Affiliated with the American Osteopathic Association. Also known as American College of Osteopathic Neurologists and Psychiatrists. Membership: $300/year (individual).
Meetings/Conferences:
2007 - St. Pete Beach, FL(Tradewinds)/May 2-5
2007 - San Diego, CA/Sept. 30-Oct. 4
Publications:
ACN Newsletter. semi-a.
Journal Of The American College Of Neuropsychiatrists. semi-a. adv.

American College of Neuropsychopharmacology *(1961)*
545 Mainstream Dr., Suite 110
Nashville, TN 37228
Tel: (615)324-2360 *Fax:* (615)324-2361
E-Mail: acnp@acnp.org
Web Site: www.acnp.org
Members: 600 individuals
Staff: 6
Annual Budget: $250-500,000
Executive Director: Ronnie Wilkins
Historical Note
ACNP promotes the continuing study of diseases and conditions affecting the brain and subsequent behavior.
Meetings/Conferences:
Annual Meetings: December, by invitation only
2007 - Boca Raton, FL(Boca Raton Resort)/Dec. 9-13
Publications:
ACNP Bulletin.

American College of Nuclear Medicine *(1972)*
101 W. Broad St., Suite 614
Hazleton, PA 18201
Tel: (570)501-9661 *Fax:* (570)450-0863
Web Site: www.acnucmed.org
Members: 500 individuals
Staff: 2
Annual Budget: $50-100,000
Executive Director: Robert Powell
Historical Note
Members are scientists and physicians working in the field of nuclear medicine. Membership: $225/year.
Publications:
ACNM Report. q.

American College of Nuclear Physicians *(1974)*
c/o Society of Nuclear Medicine
1850 Samuel Morse Dr.
Reston, VA 20190-5316
Tel: (703)708-9000 *Fax:* (703)708-9015
E-Mail: vpappas@snm.org
Web Site: www.acnponline.org
Members: 500 individuals
Annual Budget: $250-500,000
Executive Director: Virginia M. Pappas, CAE
E-Mail: vpappas@snm.org
Historical Note
The Society of Nuclear Medicine manages ACNP. Members are physicians doing diagnostic work with radioactive pharmaceuticals. Members must pass a Specialty Board examination.
Meetings/Conferences:
Semi-Annual Meetings: Fall and Winter

American College of Nurse Practitioners *(1993)*
1111 19th St. NW
Suite 404
Washington, DC 20036
Tel: (202)659-2190 *Fax:* (202)659-2191
E-Mail: acnp@acnpweb.org
Web Site: www.acnpweb.org
Members: 3700 individuals
Staff: 4
Annual Budget: $250-500,000
Executive Director: Carolyn Hutcherson
E-Mail: carolyn@acnpweb.org
Director, Communications and Public Relations: Allison E. Beard
E-Mail: allison@acnpweb.org
Manager, Administration: Kimberly Williams
E-Mail: kim@acnpweb.org
Historical Note
ACNP provides advocacy on legislative, regulatory, and clinical practice areas that affect nurse practitioners. In addition to advocacy work, ACNP publishes a variety of information resources, sponsors educational events, and provides other membership benefits. Membership: $95/year (individual); $45/year (student).
Meetings/Conferences:
Annual Meetings:
Publications:
American Journal for Nurse Practitioners. 10/year. adv.
Nurse Practitioner World News. 10/year. adv.
ACNP Forum. q.
ACNP Washington Word. 6/yr.

American College of Nurse-Midwives *(1955)*
8403 Colesville Rd.
Suite 1550
Silver Spring, MD 20910
Tel: (240)485-1800 *Fax:* (240)485-1818
E-Mail: info@acnm.org
Web Site: www.midwife.org
Members: 7000 individuals
Staff: 30
Annual Budget: $2-5,000,000
Executive Director: Deanne Williams
Director, Global Outreach: Deborah Gordis
Editor-in-Chief: Tekoa King
Director, Professional Services: Marion McCartney
Director, Finance/Administration: Maria Nazareth
Historical Note
Formerly (1969) American College of Nurse-Midwifery. Membership: $125-315/year.
Publications:
Directory of Nurse-Midwifery Practices. adv.
Journal of Nurse-Midwifery and Women's Health. bi-m. adv.
Quickening. bi-m. adv.

American College of Nutrition *(1959)*
300 S. Duncan Ave., Suite 225
Clearwater, FL 33755
Tel: (727)446-6086 *Fax:* (727)446-6202
E-Mail: office@amcollnutr.org
Web Site: www.amcollnutr.org
Members: 1200 individuals
Staff: 4
Annual Budget: $250-500,000
Executive Director: Ece Yilmaz, CPA, MBA
Meeting Coordinator: Santa Henriquez
Historical Note
Merged with the American Nutritionists Association in 1992. Members are physicians, bachelor and advanced degree nutritionists, and registered dietitians. Officers change annually. Membership: $150/year.
Meetings/Conferences:
Annual Meetings: Fall
2007 - Orlando, FL(Hilton Resort)/Sept. 19-23/400
Publications:
Journal of ACN. bi-m. adv.
ACN Newsletter. q.

American College of Obstetricians and Gynecologists *(1951)*
P.O. Box 96920
Washington, DC 20090
Tel: (202)638-5577 *Fax:* (202)863-4980
E-Mail: communications@acog.org
Web Site: www.acog.org
Members: 49000 individuals
Staff: 218
Annual Budget: $25-50,000,000
Executive Vice President: Ralph W. Hale, M.D.
E-Mail: rhale@acog.org
Vice President, Finance: Richard Bailey
Vice President, Administration: Elsa P. Brown
E-Mail: ebrown@acog.org
Director, Membership: Bernice Rose
General Counsel: Penny Rutledge
E-Mail: prutledge@acog.org
Vice President, Fellowship: Albert Strunk
E-Mail: astrunk@acog.org
Vice President, Education: Sterling Williams, M.D.
E-Mail: swilliams@acog.org
Vice President, Practice: Stanley Zinberg
E-Mail: szinberg@acog.org
Historical Note
Doctors specializing in women's health care, including childbirth and female disorders. Formerly (1956) American Academy of Obstetrics and Gynecology. Promotes further education and standards of practice. Has an annual budget of approximately $42 million. Membership: $350/year.
Meetings/Conferences:
Annual Meetings: Spring/7,000
2007 - San Diego, CA/May 5-9
Publications:
ACOG Clinical Review. bi-m. adv.
Obstetrics and Gynecology. m. adv.

American College of Occupational and Environmental Medicine *(1916)*
25 Northwest Point Blvd.
Elk Grove Village, IL 60007
Tel: (847)818-1800 *Fax:* (847)818-9266
E-Mail: acoeminfo@acoem.org
Web Site: www.acoem.org
Members: 6000 individuals
Staff: 24
Annual Budget: $2-5,000,000
Executive Director: Barry S. Eisenberg
Director, Education: Barbara Choyke
Director, Communications: Marianne Dreger
Director, Information Services: Bud Romano
Historical Note
Established in Illinois in 1915 as the American Association of Industrial Physicians and Surgeons and chartered in Illinois in 1916. Became the Industrial Medical Association in 1951 and then the American Occupational Medical Association in 1974; assumed its present name in 1988 on merging with the American Academy of Occupational Medicine. Membership: $345/year, plus $25 application fee (individual).
Meetings/Conferences:
Semi-Annual Meetings: Spring and Fall/4,000
2007 - New Orleans, LA(New Orleans Marriott)/May 4-9
Publications:
MRO Update newsletter. 10/year.
CDME Review newsletter. q.
ACOEM Report. 10/year.
Journal of Occupational and Environmental Medicine. m. adv.
APAG Insights. 6/year.

American College of Oral and Maxillofacial Surgeons *(1975)*
1710 Route 29
Galway, NY 12074
Tel: (518)882-6729 *Fax:* (518)882-6730
Toll Free: (800)522 - 6676
E-Mail: info@acoms.org
Web Site: www.acoms.org
Members: 2300 individuals
Staff: 2
Annual Budget: $500-1,000,000
Executive Director: Daniel Lanka
Historical Note
ACOMS was formed for the purpose of enhancing patient care through the furthering of research and

education in oral and maxillofacial surgery. Membership: $295/year (individual).

Meetings/Conferences:
Annual Meetings: Spring

Publications:
Archives of Oral and Maxillofacial Surgery. a. adv.

American College of Osteopathic Emergency Physicians *(1975)*
142 E. Ontario St., Suite 1250
Chicago, IL 60611-2818
Tel: (312)587-3709 *Fax:* (312)587-9951
Toll Free: (800)521 - 3709
Web Site: www.acoep.org
Members: 1800 individuals
Staff: 4
Annual Budget: $1-2,000,000
Executive Director: Janice Wachtler

Historical Note
Represents osteopathic emergency physicians in U.S. Provides education, political representation, legal services, placement. Also represents students and residents. Membership: $450/year (individual).

Meetings/Conferences:
Annual Meetings: Spring
2007 - Phoenix, AZ(Wild Horse Pass Resort)/Apr. 10-14

Publications:
The Pulse - An Osteopathic OM Publication. a. adv.

American College of Osteopathic Family Physicians *(1950)*
330 E. Algonquin Rd.
Suite One
Arlington Heights, IL 60005
Tel: (847)952-5100 *Fax:* (847)228-9755
Toll Free: (800)323 - 0794
Web Site: www.acofp.org
Members: 20000 individuals
Staff: 15
Annual Budget: $2-5,000,000
Executive Director: Peter L. Schmelzer, CAE
Director, Meetings and Exhibits: Patt L. Moskal

Historical Note
Founded in California in 1950 and chartered in Illinois. Formerly the American College of General Practitioners in Osteopathic Medicine and Surgery (1993). An affiliate of the American Osteopathic Association. Membership: $250/year (individual).

Meetings/Conferences:
Annual Meetings: Spring

Publications:
Osteopathic Family Physician News. m. adv.

American College of Osteopathic Internists *(1941)*
Three Bethesda Metro Center, Suite 508
Bethesda, MD 20814
Tel: (301)656-8877 *Fax:* (301)656-7133
Toll Free: (800)327 - 5183
E-Mail: acoi@acoi.org
Web Site: www.acoi.org
Members: 3000 individuals
Staff: 6
Annual Budget: $1-2,000,000
Executive Director: Brian J. Donadio
E-Mail: bjd@acoi.org
Director, Administration: Susan B. Stacy

Historical Note
Educational association providing continuing medical education opportunities to a community of osteopathic internists and subspecialists. Membership: $150-400/year (individual).

Meetings/Conferences:
Annual Meetings: Fall
2007 - Boston, MA(Marriott Copley Place)/Oct. 10-14
2008 - Marco Island, FL(Marco Island Resort & Spa)/Oct. 8-13

Publications:
ACOI Online Site. m. adv.
ACOI Resident Newsletter. q. adv.
ACOInformation Newsletter. m. adv.
ACOI Annual Directory. a.

American College of Osteopathic Obstetricians and Gynecologists *(1934)*
2615 Merrick St.
Ft. Worth, TX 76107
Tel: (817)377-0421 *Fax:* (817)377-0439
Toll Free: (800)875 - 6360
Web Site: www.acoog.com
Members: 1000 individuals
Staff: 4
Annual Budget: $250-500,000
Executive Director: Steve P. Buchanan, D.O.
E-Mail: stbuchan@hsc.unt.edu
Associate Executive Director: Valerie Smith

Historical Note
Formed in Wichita, Kansas during the annual meeting of the American Osteopathic Association by ten charter practicing obstetricians and gynecologists in the profession of osteopathic medicine. Originally the American College of Osteopathic Obstetricians, the present name was assumed in 1949. Chartered in the State of Missouri. Membership: $375/year.

Meetings/Conferences:
Semi-annual Meetings: March and September-October

Publications:
Newsletter. q.
Membership Directory. a.

American College of Osteopathic Pain Management and Sclerotherapy *(1938)*
303 S. Ingram Ct.
Middletown, DE 19709
Tel: (302)376-8080 *Fax:* (302)376-8081
Toll Free: (800)471 - 6114
Web Site: http://acopms.com
Members: 190 individuals
Staff: 1
Annual Budget: $25-50,000
Executive Secretary: Linda J. Pavina
E-Mail: LindaPavina@aol.com

Historical Note
Formerly (1995) American Osteopathic Academy of Sclerotherapy. Founded in 1938 as the American Osteopathic Society of Herniologists. Members are physicians who treat by injecting certain medications (sclerosants) to stimulate the production of fibrous connective tissue to strengthen weakened areas. Affiliated with American Osteopathic Association.

Publications:
Get the Point. 2/year.

American College of Osteopathic Pediatricians *(1940)*
P.O. Box 11086
Richmond, VA 23230
Tel: (804)971-6333 *Fax:* (804)282-0090
E-Mail: acop@acopeds.org
Web Site: www.acopeds.org
Members: 1000 individuals
Staff: 11
Annual Budget: $100-250,000
Executive Director: Stewart A. Hinckley, CMP

Historical Note
Organized in 1940 in California and incorporated in 1967 in Illinois. Administrative management provided by America Osteopathic Healthcare Association. Membership: $300/year.

Publications:
Membership Directory (online).
The Pulse Newsletter. 4/year. adv.

American College of Osteopathic Surgeons *(1927)*
123 N. Henry St.
Alexandria, VA 22314-2903
Tel: (703)684-0416 *Fax:* (703)684-3280
E-Mail: info@facos.org
Web Site: www.facos.org
Members: 1978 individuals
Staff: 8
Annual Budget: $1-2,000,000
Executive Director: Guy D. Beaumont, Jr.
Director, Membership, Recruitment and Retention: Sonjya Johnson
Director, Post-Doctoral Training Standards and Evaluation: Don Kaveny
Director, Finance and Administration: Judy Mangum
Director, Education and Meetings: Cynthia Smith

Historical Note
Organized in June 1926 and incorporated in Missouri in 1927. Affiliated with the American Osteopathic Association. Membership: $540/year (individual).

Meetings/Conferences:
Annual Meetings: Fall/1,000
2007 - San Francisco, CA(Marriott)/Oct. 18-21/1000
2008 - Boca Raton, FL(Boca Raton Resort)/Sept. 11-14/1000

Publications:
ACOS News. m. adv.

American College of Physician Executives *(1975)*
4890 W. Kennedy Blvd., Suite 200
Tampa, FL 33609-2575
Tel: (813)287-2000 *Fax:* (813)287-8993
Toll Free: (800)562 - 8088
E-Mail: acpe@acpe.org
Web Site: www.acpe.org
Members: 10000 individuals
Staff: 22
Annual Budget: $2-5,000,000
Executive Vice President: Roger Schenke
Information Systems: Luke Barnes
Director, Membership: Judy Rochell

Historical Note
Formerly (1988) the American Academy of Medical Directors. ACPE is the national professional and educational association for physicians in management positions within all sectors of the health care field. Recognized by the AMA House of Delegates as the national specialty society representing physicians in management. Membership: $215/year (individual).

Meetings/Conferences:
Annual Meetings: Winter, Spring, Fall/400-700
2007 - Amelia Island, FL(Ritz Carlton)/Jan. 20-25
2007 - Orlando, FL(Hyatt Grand Cypress)/May 5-10
2007 - Tucson, AZ(Westin La Paloma)/Nov. 11-16

Publications:
Membership Directory (online). daily.
The Physician Executive. bi-m. adv.

American College of Physicians *(1915)*
190 N. Independence Mall West
Philadelphia, PA 19106
Tel: (215)351-2600 *Fax:* (215)351-2829
Toll Free: (800)523 - 1546
Web Site: www.acponline.org
Members: 115000 individuals
Staff: 360
Annual Budget: $25-50,000,000
Executive Vice President and Chief Executive Officer: John Tooker, M.D., MBA, FACP
Senior Vice President, Government Affairs and Public Policy: Robert Doherty
Senior Vice President, Operations: William Habingreither
Deputy Executive Vice President and Chief Operating Officer: John A. Mitas, M.D., FACP
Senior Vice President, Membership: Jim Ott
Senior Vice President, Finance: Charles Senior
Senior Vice President, Marketing and Communications: David Sgrignoli
Senior Vice President/Editor: Harold C. Sox, M.D., MACP
Director, Publishing: Robert Spanier
Director, Membership and International Activities: Eve C. Swiacki
Director, Convention and Meeting Services: Barbara Turner

Historical Note
Formerly American College of Physicians - American Society of Internal Medicine;
assumed its current name in 2003. Patterned after Great Britain's Royal College of Physicians, ACP was founded to foster communications among medical scientists, clinical researchers and practicing physicians. Merged with Congress of Internal Medicine in 1925 and American Society of Internal Medicine in 1999. Members are practicing internists. "Fellows" are certified internists recognized by their

colleagues for their scholarship and professional excellence. Has an annual budget of approximately $31 million.

Meetings/Conferences:
Annual Meetings: Spring/7,000
2007 – San Diego, CA/Apr. 19-21

Publications:
Annals of Internal Medicine. bi-m. adv.
ACP Observer. 11/year. adv.

American College of Physicians - American Society of Internal Medicine

Historical Note
Became American College of Physicians in 2003.

American College of Podiatric Radiologists *(1942)*
423 E. 23rd St., Suite 112
New York, NY 10010
Tel: (212)686-7500 Ext: 7144
Members: 65 individuals
Annual Budget: under $10,000
President: Steven Goldman, D.P.M

Historical Note
Established as the American College of Chiropodial Roentgenologists, it became the American College of Foot Roentgenologists in 1962 and assumed its present name in 1974. Affiliated with the American Podiatric Medical Association. Has no paid officers or full-time staff. Membership: $110/year (individual).

Meetings/Conferences:
Annual Meetings:

Publications:
Newsletter. m.
Journal. q.

American College of Preventive Medicine *(1954)*
1307 New York Ave. NW
Suite 200
Washington, DC 20005
Tel: (202)466-2044 *Fax:* (202)466-2662
E-Mail: info@acpm.org
Web Site: www.acpm.org
Members: 2000 individuals
Staff: 8
Annual Budget: $1-2,000,000
Executive Director: Michael Barry

Historical Note
Physicians specializing in preventive medicine, occupational medicine, public health and aerospace medicine. Membership: $290/year (associate); $145/year (affiliate); $55/year (resident).

Meetings/Conferences:
Annual Meetings: Spring

Publications:
ACPM Headlines (online). m.
American Journal of Preventive Medicine. bi-m.
ACPM News. q.

American College of Prosthodontists *(1970)*
211 E. Chicago Ave., Suite 1000
Chicago, IL 60611
Tel: (312)573-1260 *Fax:* (312)573-1257
Toll Free: (800)378 - 1260
E-Mail: acp@prosthodontics.org
Web Site: www.prosthodontics.org
Members: 2700 individuals
Staff: 9
Annual Budget: $2-5,000,000

Historical Note
Members are prosthodontists and dentists specializing in implant, esthetic, and reconstructive dentistry.

Meetings/Conferences:
Annual Meetings: Fall
2007 – Phoenix, AZ(Westin Kierland)/Oct. 31-Nov. 3/1000
2008 – Nashville, TX(Gaylord Opryland)/Oct. 29-Nov. 1/1000

Publications:
ACP Annual Session Program Guide. a. adv.
Journal of Prosthodontics. q. adv.
ACP Messenger. q. adv.
ACP Membership Directory. a. adv.

American College of Psychiatrists *(1963)*
122 S. Michigan Ave.
Chicago, IL 60603
Tel: (312)662-1020 *Fax:* (312)662-1025
Web Site: www.acpsych.org
Members: 600 individuals
Staff: 5
Annual Budget: $1-2,000,000
Executive Director: Maureen Shick
Administrative Assistant: Angel Waszak
E-Mail: angel@acapsych.org

Historical Note
An honorary society limited to 1,000 members. Membership: $370/year (individual).

Meetings/Conferences:
Annual Meetings: February/700

Publications:
Membership Directory. a.
Newsletter. q.
Proceedings. a.

American College of Psychoanalysts *(1969)*
434 Fox Run Ln.
Hampshire, IL 60140
Tel: (847)683-7517 *Fax:* (847)683-3130
Members: 240 individuals
Staff: 1
Annual Budget: $10-25,000
Executive Secretary: Deborah L. Quick

Historical Note
ACP members are medical doctors practicing psychoanalysis.

Meetings/Conferences:
Annual Meetings: May

Publications:
Newsletter. semi-a.

American College of Radiation Oncology *(1989)*
5272 River Rd.
Suite 630
Bethesda, MD 20816
Tel: (301)718-6575 *Fax:* (301)656-0989
E-Mail: info@acro.org
Web Site: www.acro.org
Members: 1200 individuals
Staff: 4
Annual Budget: $1-2,000,000
Executive Secretary: Norman E. Wallis, Ph.D.
E-Mail: info@acro.org

Historical Note
ACRO members are radiation oncologists, physicists and administrators. Membership: $300/year (individual); $180/year (associate).

Meetings/Conferences:
Annual Meetings: May
2007 – San Diego, CA(Hotel del Coronado)/Feb. 22-24

Publications:
ACRO Practice Management Guide. a.
ACRO Bulletin. q. adv.

American College of Radiology *(1924)*
1891 Preston White Dr.
Reston, VA 20191
Tel: (703)648-8900 *Fax:* (703)295-6773
Toll Free: (800)227 - 5463
E-Mail: info@acr.org
Web Site: www.acr.org
Members: 32000 individuals
Staff: 200
Annual Budget: $10-25,000,000
Director, Membership Services: Marcia Hendershot
Executive Director: Harvey L. Neiman
Chief Information Officer: Gary Pfaff
Chief Financial Officer: Peter Shavalay
Associate Executive Director and General Counsel: William Shields

Historical Note
Founded in June 1923 in San Francisco and incorporated in California in 1924. Purpose of the ACR is to improve the art and science of radiological practice through coordination of national radiological societies, promotion of research, standardization of procedures, safeguarding of patients and operators and continuing medical education. Has an annual budget of $18.2 million. Membership: $475/year.

Meetings/Conferences:
Annual Meetings: September/700
2007 – Washington, DC(Hilton Washington)/May 19-24
2008 – Washington, DC(Hilton Washington)/May 17-22
2009 – Washington, DC(Hilton Washington)/May 2-7

Publications:
American College of Radiology Bulletin. m. adv.

American College of Real Estate Lawyers *(1978)*
One Central Plaza
11300 Rockville Pike, Suite 903
Rockville, MD 20852-3034
Tel: (301)816-9811 *Fax:* (301)816-9786
Web Site: www.acrel.org
Members: 900 individuals
Staff: 2
Annual Budget: $500-1,000,000
Executive Director: Jill H. Pace

Historical Note
ACREL members are attorneys with at least ten years of specialization in real estate law. Membership is by invitation.

Publications:
ACREL News. q.

American College of Rheumatology *(1934)*
1800 Century Pl.
Suite 250
Atlanta, GA 30345-4300
Tel: (404)633-3777 *Fax:* (404)633-1870
E-Mail: acr@rheumatology.org
Web Site: www.rheumatology.org
Members: 6500 individuals
Staff: 40
Annual Budget: $5-10,000,000
Executive Vice President: Mark Andrejeski

Historical Note
The professional society for Rheumatologists and associated health professionals. Members are physicians, teachers, researchers, and individuals with an interest in diseases of the joints and connective tissues. Formerly (1989) American Rheumatism Association. Membership: $313/year.

Meetings/Conferences:
Annual Meetings: November

Publications:
Arthritis Care and Research. semi-m. adv.
Arthritis and Rheumatism. m. adv.
ACR News. m. adv.

American College of Sports Medicine *(1954)*
P.O. Box 1440
Indianapolis, IN 46206-1440
Tel: (317)637-9200 *Fax:* (317)634-7817
E-Mail: publicinfo@acsm.org
Web Site: www.acsm.org
Members: 20000 individuals
Staff: 36
Annual Budget: $5-10,000,000
Executive Vice President: James R. Whitehead
Deputy Executive Vice President and Chief Financial Officer: Paula Burkert
E-Mail: pburkert@acsm.org
Director, Communications: Christa Dickey
E-Mail: cdickey@acsm.org
Communications and Public Information: Adam Hoog
Assistant Executive Vice President, Publications and Certification: D. Mark Robertson
E-Mail: dmrobertson@acsm.org
Director, Membership: Chris Sawyer
E-Mail: csawyer@acsm.org
Director, Research, Administration and Programs: Jane Senior
E-Mail: jsenior@acsm.org
Senior Director, Human Resources and Operations: Lori Tobin
E-Mail: ltobin@acsm.org

Historical Note
ACSM promotes sports medicine and exercise science and their capacity to maintain and enhance physical fitness and general health. Membership includes team physicians, orthopedic surgeons, athletic trainers and

others. Affiliated with the Federation Internationale de Medicine Sportive. Membership: $195/year (professional); $135/year (associate); $80/year (student)

Meetings/Conferences:
Annual Meetings: Spring

Publications:
ACSM's Health and Fitness Journal. 6/year. adv.
Exercise and Sport Sciences Reviews. q. adv.
Medicine & Science in Sports & Exercise. m. adv.
Sports Medicine Bulletin. q.
Current Sports Medicine.

American College of Surgeons *(1913)*
633 N. St. Claire St.
Chicago, IL 60611-3211
Tel: (312)202-5000 *Fax:* (312)202-5001
E-Mail: postmaster@facs.org
Web Site: www.facs.org
Members: 66000 individuals
Staff: 210
Annual Budget: $25-50,000,000
Executive Director: Thomas R. Russell
Director, Advocacy and Health Policy: Cynthia Brown
Director, Member Services: Paul E. Collicott, MD, FACS
Director, Human Resources: Jean DeYoung
Director, Communications: Linn Meyer
Director, Conventions and Meetings: Felix Niespodziewanski
Director, Information Technology: Howard Tanzman

Historical Note
Founded in 1913 and incorporated in Illinois. A professional association of surgeons devoted to advancing the science of surgery and its competent practice. Has an annual budget of approximately $38 million. Membership: $440/year (individual).

Meetings/Conferences:
Semi-Annual Meetings: Spring and Fall
2007 - Las Vegas, NV/Apr. 22-25
2007 - New Orleans, LA/Oct. 7-11

Publications:
ACS NewsScope.
Bulletin of the ACS. m.
Journal of the American College of Surgeons. m. adv.

American College of Tax Counsel *(1980)*
1156 15th St., Suite 900
Washington, DC 20005-1704
Tel: (202)637-3243 *Fax:* (202)331-2714
E-Mail: info@actconline.org
Web Site: www.actconline.org
Members: 625 individuals
Staff: 4
Annual Budget: $100-250,000
Administrative Manager: Laura Harris
E-Mail: info@actconline.org

Historical Note
The College was established to foster and recognize excellence and to elevate standards in the practice of tax law. ACTC provides additional mechanisms for input by tax professionals in the development of tax laws and facilitates scholarly discussion and examination of tax policy issues. Membership: $200/year.

Publications:
American Journal of Tax Policy. semi-a.

American College of Theriogenologists *(1970)*

Historical Note
ACT is the examiniation and certifying body for veterinarians specializing in animal reproduction. Administrative support provided by Society for Theriogenology (same address).

American College of Toxicology *(1977)*
9650 Rockville Pike
Bethesda, MD 20814
Tel: (301)634-7840 *Fax:* (301)634-7852
Web Site: www.actox.org
Members: 850 individuals
Executive Director: Carol C. Lemire
E-Mail: clemire@actox.org
Director, Membership and Exhibits: Eve Gamzu Kagan
E-Mail: ekagan@actox.org

Historical Note
Incorporated in The State of Illinois. A multidisciplinary society composed of professionals having a common interest in toxicology. ACT educates and leads professionals in toxicology and related areas through exchange of information and an annual meeting.

Publications:
Internat'l Journal of Toxicology. bi-m.
Newsletter. q.

American College of Trial Lawyers *(1950)*
19900 MacArthur Blvd., Suite 610
Irvine, CA 92612
Tel: (949)752-1801 *Fax:* (949)752-1674
E-Mail: nationaloffice@actl.com
Web Site: www.actl.com
Members: 5400 individuals
Staff: 6
Annual Budget: $2-5,000,000
Executive Director: Dennis J. Maggi, CAE
E-Mail: nationaloffice@actl.com

Historical Note
An honorary society of lawyers, former lawyers and judges.

Meetings/Conferences:
Annual Meetings: Fall

Publications:
The Bulletin. q.

American College of Trust and Estate Counsel *(1949)*
3415 S. Sepulveda Blvd., Suite 330
Los Angeles, CA 90034
Tel: (310)398-1888 *Fax:* (310)572-7280
E-Mail: info@actec.org
Web Site: www.actec.org
Members: 2700 individuals
Staff: 10
Annual Budget: $500-1,000,000
Executive Director: Gerry Vogt
E-Mail: info@actec.org

Historical Note
Membership, by invitation only, consists of lawyers specializing in probate, estate, and trust law, and related procedures. Formerly (1990) American College of Probate Counsel. Membership: $500/year.

Meetings/Conferences:
Annual Meetings: February-March/1,200

Publications:
ACTEC Journal. q.
Studies. irreg.

American College of Veterinary Anesthesiologists *(1975)*
2511 CR 500E
Mahomet, IL 61853
E-Mail: info@acva.org
Web Site: www.acva.org
Executive Secretary: Dr. John Benson

Historical Note
Promotes best practices in the field by supporting educational institutions and research training at the undergraduate, graduate, and post-doctoral levels.

Publications:
Veterinary Anesthesia.

American College of Veterinary Dermatology *(1982)*
5610 Kearny Mesa Rd.
Suite B
San Diego, CA 92111
Tel: (858)560-9393
Web Site: www.acvd.org
Members: 144 individuals
Annual Budget: $10-25,000
Executive Secretary: Alexis Borich

Historical Note
ACVD members ar veterinarians certified in veterinary dermatology.

Meetings/Conferences:
Annual: Spring, held in conjunction with the American Academy of Veterinary Dermatology.

Publications:
Veterinary Dermatology Journal. q. adv.

American College of Veterinary Internal Medicine *(1972)*
1997 Wadsworth Blvd., Suite A
Lakewood, CO 80214-5293
Tel: (303)231-9933 *Fax:* (303)231-0880
Toll Free: (800)245 - 9081
E-Mail: acvim@acvim.org
Web Site: www.acvim.org
Members: 1600 individuals
Staff: 6
Annual Budget: $2-5,000,000
Executive Director: June Pooley
Manager, Exhibits and Sponsorship: Lucy Ackerman
Assistant Executive Director: Ruth Green

Historical Note
Governing organization for veterinary specialists who deal with the diagnosis and non-surgical treatment of diseases of the internal organs. Encompasses internal medicine, cardiology, oncology, and neurology. Members are board-certified veterinary specialists. Membership: $350year.

Meetings/Conferences:
Annual Meetings: Summer/4,000

Publications:
Specialists Newsletter. q.
Directory. a.
Proceedings. a. adv.
Journal of Veterinary Internal Medicine. bi-m. adv.

American College of Veterinary Nutrition *(1988)*
Six N. Pennell Rd.
Media, PA 19063-5520
Tel: (610)892-4812 *Fax:* (610)892-4813
E-Mail: wbamand@aol.com
Web Site: http://acvn.org
Members: 54 individuals
Staff: 1
Annual Budget: $10-25,000
Executive Director: Wilbur B. Amand, VMD

Historical Note
Formerly (1978) the American Association of Veterinary Nutritionists. AAVN advances and expands information and interest in nutrition for both well and diseased animals. Has no permanent address or paid staff; officers change biennially. Membership: $25/year.

Meetings/Conferences:
Annual Meetings: With American College of Internal Medicine

Publications:
Directory (online).

American College of Veterinary Ophthalmologists *(1971)*
P.O. Box 1311
Meridian, ID 83680
Tel: (208)466-7624 *Fax:* (208)466-7693
E-Mail: office06@acvo.org
Web Site: www.acvo.org
Members: 275 members
Staff: 2
Annual Budget: $250-500,000
Executive Director: Stacee Daniel

Historical Note
Affiliated with the American Veterinary Medical Association. ACVO's objectives are to advance ophthalmology in all phases of veterinary medicine, including training, continuing education, research, and practice. Prerequisites for membership include graduation from an accredited college of veterinary medicine, two years of training in an approved residency program, and successful completion of written, oral and practical examinations by the ACVO Examination Committee. Members must vest in the college. Membership: $250/year; there is no general membership fee required in order to join.

Meetings/Conferences:
2007 - Kona, HI/Oct. 21-27/700
2008 - Boston, MA/Oct. 15-18/700

Publications:
ACVO News. 2/year. adv.
Veterinary and Comparative Ophthalmology Journal. 6/year. adv.
Directory of Members. a. adv.

American College of Veterinary Pathologists *(1949)*
2810 Crossroads Dr., Suite 3800
Madison, WI 53718-7961
Tel: (608)433-2466 Ext: 149 *Fax:* (608)443-2474
E-Mail: info@acvp.org
Web Site: www.acvp.org
Members: 1540 individuals
Staff: 4
Annual Budget: $500-1,000,000
Executive Director: Wendy Coe

Historical Note
Membership: $200/year.

Meetings/Conferences:
Annual Meetings: Fall

Publications:
Veterinary Pathology Journal. 6/year. adv.
Proceedings. a.
Membership Directory. a.

American College of Veterinary Radiology *(1961)*
777 E. Park Dr.
P.O. Box 8820
Harrisburg, PA 17105-8820
Tel: (717)558-7865 *Fax:* (717)558-7841
E-Mail: administration@acvr.info
Web Site: www.acvr.org
Members: 230 individuals
Staff: 1
Annual Budget: $50-100,000
Executive Director: Robert D. Pechman, Jr.

Historical Note
Originally established as a specialty board in veterinary radiology under the jurisdiction of the American Veterinary Medical Association, by 1966 it had become the American Board of Veterinary Radiology with 11 charter members and was incorporated in Illinois. Assumed its present name in 1969. Membership: $125/year.

Publications:
Veterinary Radiology and Utrasound. bi-m. adv.

American College of Veterinary Surgeons *(1965)*
11 N. Washington St., Suite 720
Rockville, MD 20850
Tel: (301)610-2000 *Fax:* (301)610-0371
E-Mail: acvs@acvs.org
Web Site: www.acvs.org
Members: 1215 individuals
Staff: 5
Annual Budget: $1-2,000,000
Executive Director: Ann T. Loew, Ed.M.

Historical Note
Maintains rigid membership requirements including certification by examination.

Meetings/Conferences:
2007 – Chicago, IL(Sheraton Hotel & Towers)/Oct. 18-20
2008 – San Diego, CA(Manchester Grand Hyatt)/Oct. 18-20

Publications:
Symposium Proceedings. a. adv.
Newsletter. 3/year. adv.
Directory. bien. adv.

American Collegiate Retailing Association *(1949)*
208 Spindle Hall, Auburn Univ.
Auburn, AL 36849
Tel: (334)844-6458 *Fax:* (334)844-1340
E-Mail: forsysa@auburn.edu
Web Site: www.acraretail.org
Members: 300 individuals
Annual Budget: under $10,000
President: Sandra Forsythe
E-Mail: forsysa@auburn.edu

Historical Note
Established in 1948, ACRA is an organization of faculty from colleges with specialized curricula in retailing. Conducts annual Retail Management Conference with retail store executives, and attends the semi-annual meeting in New York each winter in conjunction with the National Retail Federation. Has no paid staff. Membership: $50/year.

Meetings/Conferences:
Semi-annual Meetings: January/April in New York, NY with Nat'l Retail Federation

Publications:
ACRA Newsletter. q.

American Community Cultural Center Association *(1978)*
149 Cannongate III
Nashua, NH 03063-1953
Tel: (603)886-2748 *Fax:* (603)886-7944
Executive Director: Milli Janz
E-Mail: millijanz@aol.com

Historical Note
ACCCA was founded to encourage the development of local cultural centers in the U.S. and abroad. Offers technical information and guidance on the development of cultural centers. Membership: $25/year.

American Comparative Literature Association *(1960)*
One University Station, B5003
Austin, TX 78712-0196
Tel: (512)471-1925 *Fax:* (512)471-8878
E-Mail: info@acla.org
Web Site: www.acla.org
Members: 800 individuals
Staff: 2
Annual Budget: $25-50,000
Secretary-Treasurer: E. Richmond-Garza

Historical Note
An allied organization of the Modern Language Association. Membership: $55/year (individual); $100/year (institution); $25/year (student).

Meetings/Conferences:
Annual Meetings: March

American Compensation Association

Historical Note
Merged with Canadian Compensation Association and became World at Work in 2000.

American Composers Alliance *(1937)*
648 Broadway, Room 803
New York, NY 10012
Tel: (212)362-8900 *Fax:* (212)925-6798
E-Mail: info@composers.com
Web Site: www.composers.com
Members: 320 individuals
Staff: 5
Annual Budget: $100-250,000
Executive Director: Jasna Radonjic
E-Mail: info@composers.com

Historical Note
Established in late 1937 by 48 musicians under the leadership of Aaron Copland, its first president, to protect the rights of its members and to promote the use and understanding of their music. Performing rights are assigned to Broadcast Music, Inc. Distributes members' music through its subsidiary, American Composers Edition. Membership: $75/year.

Meetings/Conferences:
Annual Meetings: New York, NY/Dec.

Publications:
Catalogues of New Music.

American Composites Manufacturers Association *(1979)*
1010 N. Glebe Rd.
Suite 450
Arlington, VA 22201
Tel: (703)525-0511 *Fax:* (703)525-0743
E-Mail: info@acmanet.org
Web Site: www.acmanet.org
Members: 1000 companies
Staff: 23
Annual Budget: $2-5,000,000
Executive Director: Melissa Henriksen, CAE
Director, Membership and Marketing: Shaine Anderson, CAE
Deputy Director: Sabeena Hickman, CAE
Director, Technical Services: Bob Lacovara
Director, Conferences and Meetings: Jeanne McCormack
Editor and Director, Communications: Andy Rusnak
Senior Director, Government Affairs: John Schweitzer
Director, Information Technology: Dan Sharma

Historical Note
Formerly (1992) Fiberglass Fabrication Association and then Composites Fabricators Association; assumed its current name in 2003. Incorporated in 1979 in Washington, DC. Absorbed Composites Institute in 2000. Membership is open to any person, firm or corporation performing the hand layup or sprayup method of fiberglass fabrication in open or closed molds or engaged in filament winding or resin transfer molding. Membership Fee: based on sales volume.

Meetings/Conferences:
Annual Meetings: Fall/2,000

Publications:
Composites Manufacturing Magazine. m. adv.

American Concrete Institute *(1904)*
38800 Country Club Dr.
Farmington Hills, MI 48331
Tel: (248)848-3700 *Fax:* (248)848-3701
Web Site: www.aci-int.org
Members: 16500 individuals
Staff: 84
Annual Budget: $5-10,000,000
Executive Vice President: William R. Tolley
E-Mail: bill.tolley@concrete.org
Director, Marketing and Membership: Diane L. Baloh
Editor-in-Chief: Rex C. Donahey, PE
E-Mail: rex.donahey@concrete.org
Director, Publishing and Event Services: Renee J. Lewis
E-Mail: renee.lewis@concrete.org

Historical Note
Founded in 1904 as the National Association of Cement Users; became the American Concrete Institute in 1913 and was incorporated in Michigan in 1964. ACI gathers and disseminates information for the improvement of the design, construction, manufacture and maintenance of concrete products and structures. Its members include designers, architects, civil engineers, educators, contractors, concrete craftsmen and technicians, materials suppliers, testing laboratories and manufacturers. Membership: $157/year (individual); $680/year (organization).

Meetings/Conferences:
Semi-Annual Meetings: Spring and Fall
2007 – Atlanta, GA(Hilton)/Apr. 22-26
2007 – Puerto Rico, PR(Wyndham El Conquistador)/Oct. 14-18
2008 – Los Angeles, CA(Century Plaza)/March 30-Apr. 3
2008 – St. Louis, MO(Renaissance Grand)/Nov. 2-6
2009 – San Antonio, TX(Marriott River Center)/March 15-19
2010 – Pittsburgh, PA
2010 – Chicago, IL(Sheraton)/March 21-25
2011 – Cincinnati, OH
2011 – Tampa, FL/Apr. 3-7
2012 – Dallas, TX(Hyatt Regency)/March 18-22
2012 – Toronto, ON, Canada(Sheraton Centre)/Oct. 21-25
2013 – Phoenix, AZ
2013 – Cleveland, OH
2014 – Washington, DC
2014 – San Francisco, CA

Publications:
Concrete International. m. adv.
ACI Structural Journal. bi-m.
ACI Materials Journal. bi-m.

American Concrete Pavement Association *(1964)*
500 New Jersey Ave. NW, Seventh Floor
Washington, DC 20001
Tel: (202)638-2272 *Fax:* (202)638-2688
E-Mail: info@pavement.com
Web Site: www.pavement.com
Members: 500
Staff: 14
Annual Budget: $250-500,000
President and Chief Executive Officer: Gerald F. Voight
E-Mail: jvoigt@pavement.com
Senior Vice President, Market Development and Communications: Robb Jolly

Historical Note
Formerly (1988) the American Concrete Paving Association. ACPA is dedicated to promoting concrete pavement for use in interstate highways, state and county highways, local roads and airports. Membership: Dues depend on the type of member company.

Meetings/Conferences:
Annual Meetings: late November or early December/400

Publications:
Concrete Pavement Progress. bi-m.
ACPA Action. m.
ACPA Today. q.

American Concrete Pipe Association *(1907)*
222 W. Las Colinas Blvd., Suite 641
Irving, TX 75039-5423
Tel: (972)506-7216 *Fax:* (972)506-7682
E-Mail: info@concrete-pipe.org
Web Site: www.concrete-pipe.org
Members: 125 companies
Staff: 8
Annual Budget: $1-2,000,000
President: Matt Childs
Director, Marketing: Karen Hunter
E-Mail: info@concrete-pipe.org
Comptroller: Wendy Lamber
E-Mail: info@concrete-pipe.org

Historical Note
The American Concrete Pipe Association is an international trade association whose U.S. and Canadian members account for approximately 75% of the precast concrete pipe, box culvert and manhole production in North America. The association sponsors research and engineering investigations and educational programs, and publishes technical and promotional literature. Provides administrative support to Concrete Pipe Associations, a joint venture with American Concrete Pressure Pipe Association (same address).

Meetings/Conferences:
Annual Meetings: March/April

Publications:
Newscast. m.
The Locator. a.
Resources. a.
Membership Directory. a.
Concrete Pipe News. q.

American Concrete Pressure Pipe Association *(1949)*
11800 Sunrise Valley Dr., Suite 309
Reston, VA 20191-5302
Tel: (703)391-9135 *Fax:* (703)391-9136
Web Site: www.acppa.org
Members: 6 companies
Staff: 2
Annual Budget: $250-500,000
President: David Prosser

Historical Note
Serves as the authoritative voice of the concrete pressure pipe industry, providing technical and educational information and activities.

Publications:
CPP Digest. q.

American Concrete Pumping Association *(1974)*
606 Enterprise Dr.
Lewis Center, OH 43035
Tel: (614)431-5618 *Fax:* (614)431-6944
Web Site: www.concretepumpers.com
Members: 450 companies
Staff: 4
Annual Budget: $250-500,000
Executive Director: Christie Collins

Historical Note
ACPA promotes concrete pumping and safety in concrete pumping. Membership: $100-600/year.

Meetings/Conferences:
Annual Meetings: Winter

Publications:
Concrete Pumping. q.
Update (newsletter). m.

American Conference for Irish Studies *(1960)*
Dept. of English
Stanford University
Stanford, CA 94305-2087
Web Site: www.acisweb.com
Members: 1400 individuals
Annual Budget: $10-25,000
Secretary: Matthew Jockers

Historical Note
Formerly (1988) American Committe for Irish Studies. Members include scholars interested in Irish history, language and culture. Affiliated with the American Historical Association and the Modern Language Association of America. Membership fee varies.

Meetings/Conferences:
Annual Meetings: Spring/200

Publications:
ACIS Newsletter. 3/year.
Irish Literary Supplement. 2/year. adv.

American Conference of Academic Deans *(1944)*
1818 R St. NW
Washington, DC 20009
Tel: (202)884-7419 *Fax:* (202)265-9532
Web Site: www.acad-edu.org
Members: 600 individuals
Staff: 1
Annual Budget: $100-250,000
Administrative Director: Laura Rzepka

Historical Note
Academic deans and chief academic officers of four-year colleges, community colleges and two-year institutions. Membership: $95/year.

Meetings/Conferences:
Annual Meetings: Winter
2007 – New Orleans, LA/Jan. 24-27

Publications:
Resource Handbook for Academic Deans.

American Conference of Cantors *(1953)*
213 N. Morgan St., Suite One-A
Chicago, IL 60607
Tel: (312)491-1034 *Fax:* (312)491-1087
E-Mail: info@accantors.org
Web Site: www.rj.org/acc
Members: 450 individuals
Staff: 3
Annual Budget: $250-500,000
Managing Director: Scott Colbert

Historical Note
Members serve in Jewish congregations in the United States and Canada. Affiliated with the Union of American Hebrew Congregations. Membership: 1.5% of annual salary.

Meetings/Conferences:
Annual Meetings: Summer
2007 – Kerhonkson, NY(Hudson Valley Resort and Spa)/June 24-28

Publications:
Koleinu. q.
Membership Directory. a.

American Conference of Governmental Industrial Hygienists *(1938)*
1330 Kemper Meadow Dr., Suite 600
Cincinnati, OH 45240-1634
Tel: (513)742-2020 *Fax:* (513)742-3355
E-Mail: mail@acgih.org
Web Site: www.acgih.org
Members: 4000 individuals
Staff: 18
Annual Budget: $2-5,000,000
Executive Director: A. Anthony Rizzuto
E-Mail: mail@acgih.org
Director, Operations: Amy Bloomhuff
E-Mail: mail@acgih.org

Historical Note
Formerly (1945) National Conference of Governmental Industrial Hygienists. A member-based organization, ACGIH is a community of professionals that works to advance worker health and safety through education and through development and dissemination of scientific and technical knowledge. Membership: $159/year (individual); $20/year (student); $30/year (retired); $600/year (organization).

Meetings/Conferences:
Annual Meetings: May, with American Industrial Hygiene Ass'n/10,000

Publications:
Industrial Ventilation Manual. trien..
TLVs and BEIs Book. a.
Guide to Occupational Exposure Values. a.
Journal of Occupational & Environmental Hygiene. m. adv.

American Congress of Community Supports and Employment Services
1875 I St. NW, 11th Floor
Washington, DC 20006
Tel: (202)466-3355 *Fax:* (202)466-7571
E-Mail: mkilmer@access.org
Web Site: www.accses.org
Executive Director: Marc Kilmer

Historical Note
ACCSES members are community organizations providing job training and related services.

Publications:
ACCESS Update newsletter.

American Congress of Rehabilitation Medicine *(1923)*
6801 Lake Plaza Dr., Suite B-205
Indianapolis, IN 46220
Tel: (317)915-2250 *Fax:* (317)915-2245
Web Site: www.acrm.org
Members: 800 individuals, 3 companies
Staff: 4
Annual Budget: $500-1,000,000
Executive Director: Richard D. Morgan, MBA
E-Mail: Rmorgan@acrm.org

Historical Note
Founded September 18, 1923 as the American College of Radiology and Physiotherapy. Name changed in 1926 to the American College of Physical Therapy and in 1930 to the American Congress of Physical Therapy. In 1945 it again changed its name to the American Congress of Physical Medicine, and in 1953 it became the American Congress of Physical Medicine and Rehabilitation. In 1967 it adopted its present name. Incorporated in Illinois in 1930. Provides education and networking opportunities to professionals throughout the field of medical rehabilitation. Membership: $75-240/year (individual); $1500-3,500/year (corporate partners).

Meetings/Conferences:
Annual Meetings: Fall

Publications:
Archives of Physical Medicine and Rehabilitation. m. adv.
Rehabilitation Outlook. q. adv.

American Congress on Surveying and Mapping *(1941)*
Six Montgomery Village Ave., Suite 403
Gaithersburg, MD 20879
Tel: (240)632-9716 *Fax:* (240)632-1321
E-Mail: curtis.sumner@acsm.net
Web Site: www.acsm.net
Members: 4500 individuals
Staff: 7
Annual Budget: $500-1,000,000
Executive Director: Curt W. Sumner

Historical Note
Founded in the District of Columbia in 1941 and incorporated there in 1951. Composed of four member organizations: the Cartographic and Geographic Information Society, the American Association of Geodetic Surveyors, the National Society of Professional Surveyors, and the Geographic Land Information Society. Affiliated with state land surveyor societies, also the Accreditation Board for Engineering and Technology, and the National Council of Examiners for Engineering and Surveying. Member of the International Federation of Surveyors, the International Cartographic Association, and the International Society of Mine Surveyors. Promotes the profession of surveying and mapping science. Sponsors and supports the ACSM/NSPS Political Action Committee. Membership: $133-215/year (individual); $1200/year (organization).

Meetings/Conferences:
Semi-annual Meetings: Spring and Fall

Publications:
ACSM Bulletin. bi-m. adv.

Cartography and Geographic Information Science. q. adv.
Surveying and Land Information Science. q. adv.

American Connemara Pony Society *(1956)*
P.O. Box 100
Middlebrook, VA 24459
Tel: (540)662-5953 *Fax:* (540)722-2277
Web Site: www.acps.org
Members: 900 individuals
Staff: 1
Annual Budget: $25-50,000
Secretary: Marynell Eyles

Historical Note
Members are breeders and trainers of the Connemara Pony. Sponsors shows and awards prizes for distinguished examples of the breed. Membership:$40/year.

Meetings/Conferences:
Annual Meetings: Fall

Publications:
The American Connemara. bi-m. adv.

American Construction Inspectors Association *(1959)*
12995 Sixth St., Suite 69
Yucaipa, CA 92399
Tel: (909)795-3039 *Fax:* (909)795-4039
Toll Free: (888)876 - 2242
E-Mail: office@acia.com
Web Site: www.acia-rci.org
Members: 1100 individuals
Staff: 2
Annual Budget: $250-500,000
Executive Director: Woneta Carnes
E-Mail: office@acia.com

Historical Note
Members are engineering, building, public works, and other specialized construction inspectors. Supports and sustains the Board of Registered Construction Inspectors. Membership: $125/year (individual); $250/year (company).

Meetings/Conferences:
Annual Meetings: November

Publications:
The Inspector Magazine. q. adv.

American Consultants League *(1984)*
c/o ETR
245 N.E. Fourth Ave., Suite 102
Delray Beach, FL 33483
Toll Free: (866)344 - 7200
E-Mail: support@earlyrise.com
Web Site: www.americanconsultantsleague.com
Members: 1025 individuals
Staff: 2
Annual Budget: $100-250,000
Executive Officer: Hubert Bermont
E-Mail: support@earlyrise.com

Historical Note
An association of part-time and full-time consultants in every field of expertise from all over the United States, Canada, and all foreign countries. Assists consultants in the setting up and managing of the business end of their consultancies by providing educational materials and continuing education through the Consultants Institute, a home study course which is the education arm of the League. Membership: $139/year.

Meetings/Conferences:
Annual Meetings: None held.

Publications:
Early To Rise newsletter. m.

American Copper Council *(1974)*
Two South End Ave., Suite 4C
New York, NY 10280
Tel: (212)945-4990 *Fax:* (212)945-4992
E-Mail: mcb@americancopper.org
Web Site: http://americancopper.org/
Members: 200 companies
Staff: 2
Annual Budget: $250-500,000
Executive Director: Mary Boland

Historical Note
Organized in 1974 as the successor to the Committee for the Release of Stockpile Copper, the Council represents all segments of the industry. The Council sponsors four quarterly seminars of interest to members of the copper industry.

Meetings/Conferences:
Biennial Meetings:

Publications:
Coppertalk Magazine. q.
Directory of Member Companies. a.

American Corn Growers Association *(1987)*
P.O. Box 18157
Washington, DC 20036
Tel: (202)835-0330 *Fax:* (202)463-0862
E-Mail: acga@acga.org
Web Site: www.acga.org
Staff: 3
Annual Budget: $500-1,000,000
Chief Executive Officer: Larry Mitchell
E-Mail: acga@acga.org
Director, Legislative Affairs: David L. Senter
E-Mail: acga@acga.org

Historical Note
ACGA is a progressive commodity association that works to protect farm interests and rural communities. ACGA represents the interests of corn producers in 28 states. Works to develop national legislation to protect the interests of corn producers and the rural communities that depend on them, and develops educational and promotional programs.

Meetings/Conferences:
Annual Meetings: Winter

Publications:
ACGA Newsletter. m.

American Corporate Counsel Association

Historical Note
Became Association of Corporate Counsel in 2003.

American Correctional Association *(1870)*
206 N. Washington St.
Suite 200
Alexandria, VA 22314
Tel: (703)224-0000 *Fax:* (703)224-0040
Toll Free: (800)222 - 5646
Web Site: www.aca.org
Members: 21000 individuals
Staff: 100
Annual Budget: $5-10,000,000
Executive Director: James A. Gondles, Jr., CAE
Director, Conventions, Advertising and Corporate Relations: Litsa Deck
Director, Membership and Financial Services: Cathy Gibney
Director, Publications and Communications: Gabriella Daley Klatt
Director, Government Affairs: Eric Schultz
Deputy Executive Director: Jeff Washington

Historical Note
Founded as the National Prison Association. Became the American Prison Association and assumed its present name in 1954. Membership is open to all individuals and organizations actively working in the correctional profession including wardens, psychologists, sociologists, probation officers, etc. Has an annual budget of over $10 million. Membership: $35/year (individual); $300/year (non-profit organization).

Meetings/Conferences:
Semi-annual Meetings: Winter/Summer

Publications:
Directory of Juvenile & Adult Corrections. a. adv.
Corrections Compendium. 6/yr. adv.
Corrections Today. 7/year. adv.
On the Line Newsletter. 5/year.
Proceedings. a.
Probation & Parole Directory. trien.
National Jail & Adult Detention Directory. trien.

American Correctional Chaplains Association *(1885)*
P.O. Box 661
Waupun, WI 53963-0661
Tel: (920)324-6298 *Fax:* (920)324-6254
Web Site: www.correctionalchaplains.org
Members: 450 individuals
Annual Budget: under $10,000
President: Paul Rogers
E-Mail: paul.rogers@doc.state.wi.us

Historical Note
An affiliate of American Correctional Association. Has no paid officers or full-time staff. Membership: $30/year (professional); $15/year (associate); $90/year (affiliate).

Meetings/Conferences:
Semi-annual Meetings: Jan. and Aug. in conjunction with American Correctional Ass'n

Publications:
Newsletter. q.

American Correctional Health Services Association *(1975)*
250 Gatsby Pl.
Alpharetta, GA 30022-6161
Toll Free: (877)918 - 1842
E-Mail: achsa@bellsouth.net
Web Site: http://achsa.org
Members: 900 individuals
Staff: 1
Annual Budget: $100-250,000
Executive Director: Willma Miles

Historical Note
Multidisciplinary society of health care professionals and representatives from diverse areas of the corrections field. An affiliate of the American Correctional Association. Its mission is to be the voice of the correctional healthcare profession, serving as an effective forum for communication addressing current issues and needs confronting correctional healthcare. ACHSA provides support, skill development, and education programs for healthcare personnel, organizations and decision makers involved in correctional healthcare, resulting in increased professionalism and a sense of community for correctional healthcare personnel and positive changes in health for detained and incarcerated individuals. Membership: $50/year (individual); $1,000/year (organization).

Meetings/Conferences:
Annual Meetings: Spring

Publications:
CorHealth. q. adv.

American Cotswold Record Association *(1878)*
18 Elm St.
P.O. Box 59
Plympton, MA 02367
Tel: (781)585-2026
E-Mail: acrasheep@aol.com
Members: 55 individuals
Staff: 1
Annual Budget: under $10,000
Secretary/Treasurer: Vicki Rigel
E-Mail: acrasheep@aol.com

Historical Note
Formerly (1904) American Cotswold Sheep Association. Members are breeders of purebred Cotswold sheep. Maintains a breed registry.

Meetings/Conferences:
Annual Meetings: Louisville, KY/November

Publications:
Cotswold News. 2/year.
Directory. a.

American Cotton Exporter's Association *(1975)*

Historical Note
The Webb-Pomerene Act registration of American Cotton Shippers Association.

American Cotton Shippers Association *(1924)*
88 Union Center, Suite 1204
P.O. Box 3366
Memphis, TN 38173
Tel: (202)296-7116 *Fax:* (901)527-8303
Toll Free: (800)238 - 7192
E-Mail: MAIL@acsa-cotton.org
Web Site: www.acsa-cotton.org
Members: 300 individuals
Staff: 7
Annual Budget: $10-25,000

Executive Vice President and General Counsel: Neal P. Gillen

Historical Note

Members are cotton merchants, cotton shippers, and exporters of raw cotton and firms allied with the industry. Its membership is composed of four Federated Associations: Atlantic Cotton Association; Southern Cotton Association; Texas Cotton Association; and the Western Cotton Shippers Association. Maintains the Cotton States Arbitration Board in conjunction with the NCTO. Maintains a Washington office. Known as American Cotton Exporters Association under Webb-Pomerene. Membership: $300/year.

Meetings/Conferences:

Annual Meetings: Spring

Publications:

Directory. a.
Washington Update Reports. irreg.
Export News. irreg.

American Council for Construction Education *(1974)*

1717 N. Loop 1604 East, Suite 320
San Antonio, TX 78232-1570
Tel: (210)495-6161 *Fax:* (210)495-6168
E-Mail: acce@acce-hq.org
Web Site: www.acce-hq.org
Members: 115 individuals
Staff: 3
Annual Budget: $100-250,000
Executive Vice President: Michael M. Holland

Historical Note

ACCE is the accrediting agency for postsecondary construction education programs. Recognized by the Council for Higher Education Accreditation. Membership: $120/year (individual); $700/year (company); $4,000/year (association voting).

Meetings/Conferences:

Semi-Annual Meetings: February and July

Publications:

Newsletter. q.
Annual Report. a.

American Council for Southern Asian Art *(1966)*

133 W. 17th St.
Suite Six-D
New York, NY 10011
Tel: (617)369-3227 *Fax:* (617)859-7031
Web Site: http://kaladarshan.arts.ohio-state.edu/acsaa/hp.html
Members: 280 individuals
Secretary: Joan Cummins

Historical Note

Formerly the American Committee for South Asian Art. ACSAA members are academics and others with an interest in the art of India, Pakistan, Nepal, Bangladesh, Sri Lanka, and South East Asia. Has no paid officers or full-time staff. Membership: $40/year.

Publications:

Bibliography of South Asian Art. bien.
Newsletter. semi-a.

American Council for Technology *(1979)*

11350 Williams Dr., Suite 610
Fairfax, VA 22031
Tel: (703)208-4800 *Fax:* (703)208-4805
E-Mail: act-iac@actgov.org
Web Site: www.actgov.org
Members: 50000 individuals
Staff: 6
Annual Budget: $500-1,000,000
Executive Director: Kenneth Allen

Historical Note

Formerly (2003) Federation of Government Information Processing Councils. ACT is the U.S. representative in the International Council for Information Technology in Government Administration (ICA). Members are information resources management councils as well as professionals at various government positions and levels. FGIPC is parent to the Industry Advisory Council which has 210 corporate members; dues $500-$5,000/year (company).

Meetings/Conferences:

Annual Meetings: Spring-Summer

Publications:

iAction newsletter. bi-m.

American Council for Trade in Services *(1994)*

Historical Note

ACTS represents the interests of U.S. service-industry companies involved in international trade. Membership: $6,000/year.

American Council of Engineering Companies *(1909)*

1015 15th St. NW, Eighth Floor
Washington, DC 20005-2605
Tel: (202)347-7474 *Fax:* (202)898-0068
E-Mail: acec@acec.org
Web Site: www.acec.org
Members: 5500 firms
Staff: 42
Annual Budget: $10-25,000,000
President/Chief Executive Officer: David A. Raymond
Vice President, Institute for Business Management: Jeff Beard
Director, Membership and Member Organization Services: Patrick Brookover
Vice President, Operations: Mary Ann Emely, CAE
Vice President, Government Affairs: Steven Hall
General Counsel: Charles Kim

Historical Note

Product of a merger of the American Institute of Consulting Engineers (1909) and the Consulting Engineers Council of the U.S.A. (1956). Members are independent, private practice engineering companies. Provides information on federal legislation, insurance, business practices, international markets and public relations to member firms. Sponsors and supports the ACEC Political Action Committee and the Environmental Business Action Council. Became American Council of Engineering Companies in 2001.

Publications:

Engineering, Inc.. bi-m. adv.
Last Word. w.

American Council of Hypnotist Examiners *(1980)*

700 S. Central Ave.
Glendale, CA 91204
Tel: (818)242-1159 *Fax:* (818)247-9379
E-Mail: hypnotismla@earthlink.net
Web Site: www.hypnotistexaminers.org
Members: 9200 individuals
Staff: 5
Annual Budget: $100-250,000
Executive Director: Gil Boyne
E-Mail: hypnotismla@earthlink.net

Historical Note

Membership: $50-100/year (individual).

Publications:

American Hypnotherapy Report. a.
Directory of Certified Members.
Internat'l Hypnotherapy Report Magazine. q.
Newsletter. irreg.

American Council of Independent Laboratories *(1937)*

1629 K St. NW
Suite 400
Washington, DC 20006-1633
Tel: (202)887-5872 Ext: 202 *Fax:* (202)887-0021
Web Site: www.acil.org
Members: 350 companies
Staff: 9
Annual Budget: $1-2,000,000
Executive Director: Joan Walsh Cassedy, CAE
E-Mail: jcassedy@acil.org
Meeting Planner: Beverly Adams
E-Mail: badams@acil.org
Coordinator, Membership: Tom Hutchcraft
Program Manager: Eddie Van Aken

Historical Note

Formerly (1954) American Council of Commercial Laboratories, (1994) American Council of Independent Laboratories, (1995) ACIL: the Association of Independent Scientific, Engineering and Testing Firms, and (1999) ACIL; resumed using the name American Council of Independent Laboratories in 2000. Members are third-party commercial engineering and scientific testing laboratories offering analytical, testing, R&D, and consulting services to industry, commerce, and government. Promotes code of ethics among members, works with standards and accrediting bodies on programs to improve laboratory performance, publishes manuals and guidelines for quality control, risk management, human resource management and safety. Sponsors and supports the Independent Laboratories Institute.

Meetings/Conferences:

Annual Meetings: Fall/250
2007 – Atlanta, GA(Inter-Continental Buckhead)/Oct. 13-16

Publications:

ACIL Newsletter. m.
Financial Management Survey. a.
Wage and Salary Survey. a.

American Council of Learned Societies *(1919)*

633 Third Ave.
New York, NY 10017-6795
Tel: (212)697-1505 *Fax:* (212)949-8058
Web Site: www.acls.org
Members: 68 societies, 21 affiliated ass'n
Staff: 20
Annual Budget: $2-5,000,000
President: Pauline Yu
Director, Publications and Information Technology: Candace Frede
Director, Finance: Lawrence R. Wirth

Historical Note

Organized in Washington DC September 19, 1919 by twelve scholarly organizations in the humanities and social sciences. Its immediate purpose was to provide U.S. representation in the International Academic Union. Its member organizations today are all national in scope and concerned with the advancement of fundamental research in the humanities and humanistic social sciences.

Meetings/Conferences:

Annual Meetings: Spring

Publications:

Annual Report. a.
Occasional Papers. irreg.

American Council of Life Insurers *(1976)*

101 Constitution Ave. NW
Washington, DC 20001-2133
Tel: (202)624-2000 *Fax:* (202)624-2319
E-Mail: media@acli.com
Web Site: www.acli.com
Members: 400 insurance companies
Staff: 160
Annual Budget: $25-50,000,000
President and Chief Executive Officer: Frank Keating
Vice President, Media Relations: Jack Dolan
Chief Operating Officer: Michael Hunter

Historical Note

Formerly (2000) American Council of Life Insurance. ACLI is a national trade association representing the interests of legal reserve life insurance companies in legislative, regulatory and judicial matters at the federal, state and municipal levels of government and at the NAIC. Its member companies hold more than 90 percent of the life insurance in force in the United States. Dues based in adjusted admitted assets and premiums.

Meetings/Conferences:

Annual Meetings: Fall/1,200
2007 – Washington, DC(Omni Shoreham Hotel)/Oct. 21-23

Publications:

Financial Security Insight. q. adv.
Consumer Brochure Series CD-ROM.
ACLI Digest (online). bi-m.

American Council of State Savings Supervisors *(1939)*

P.O. Box 1904
Leesburg, VA 20177
Tel: (703)669-5440 *Fax:* (703)669-5441
Web Site: www.acsss.org
Members: 130 individuals
Staff: 1
Annual Budget: $100-250,000
Executive Director: Andrea Falzarano, CAE
E-Mail: amfalz@acsss.org

Historical Note

Formerly (1987) National Association of State Savings and Loan Supervisors. Members are regulators of state-chartered thrift institutions. Educational arm is the Institute for Supervisory Education. Associate membership includes approximately 100 state-chartered thrift institutions.

Meetings/Conferences:
Annual Meetings: May/June

Publications:
The State Advisor. m. adv.

American Council of the Blind *(1961)*
1155 15th St. NW
Suite 1004
Washington, DC 20005
Tel: (202)467-5081 *Fax:* (202)467-5085
Toll Free: (800)424 - 8666
E-Mail: info@acb.org
Web Site: www.acb.org
Staff: 7
Annual Budget: $1-2,000,000
Executive Director: Melanie Brunson
E-Mail: info@acb.org

Historical Note
ACB is a national organization providing support and services to the visually impaired. Provides administrative support for a number of occupation-specific affiliates, including American Blind Lawyers Association, National Association of Blind Teachers, and Visually Impaired Data Processors International.

Publications:
Braille Forum. 10/yr.

American Council on Consumer Interests *(1953)*
415 S. Duff, Suite C
Ames, IA 50010-6600
Tel: (515)956-4666 *Fax:* (515)233-3101
Web Site: www.consumerinterests.org
Members: 350 individuals
Staff: 2
Annual Budget: $100-250,000
Executive Director: Terri Haffner

Historical Note
Founded at the University of Minnesota as the Council on Consumer Information with 21 charter members, for the purpose of stimulating the exchange of ideas among persons interested in the welfare of the consumer; adopted present name in 1969. ACCI is an affiliate member of the International Organization of Consumers Unions and the Consumer Federation of America. Membership: $110/year (individual); $295/year (subscribing organizations); $55/year (student/retired).

Meetings/Conferences:
Annual Meetings: March or April/250

Publications:
Consumer Interests Annual - online. a.
Journal of Consumer Affairs. semi-a.

American Council on Education *(1918)*
One Dupont Circle NW
Suite 800
Washington, DC 20036-1193
Tel: (202)939-9300 *Fax:* (202)833-4760
E-Mail: comments@ace.nche.edu
Web Site: www.acenet.edu
Members: 1800institutionsandassociations
Staff: 175
Annual Budget: $25-50,000,000
President: David Ward
Senior Vice President, Government and Public Affairs: Terry W. Hartle
Director, Finance: Yvonne Kankam-Boadu
Director, Meeting Services: Stephanie Marshall
Assistant Vice President, Public Affairs: Timothy McDonough
Chief Information Officer: Stephen Rose

Historical Note
Organized by eleven national educational associations to coordinate the work of educational institutions during World War I. It has always placed particular emphasis on higher education and today plays a leading role in the resolution of questions regarding higher education and the federal government. Has an annual budget of approximately $36 million.

Meetings/Conferences:
Annual Meetings: Winter/1,200

Publications:
Presidency. q. adv.
Higher Education and National Affairs. semi-m.

American Council on Exercise *(1985)*
4851 Paramount Dr.
San Diego, CA 92123
Tel: (858)279-8227 *Fax:* (858)279-8064
Toll Free: (800)825 - 3636
E-Mail: support@acefitness.org
Web Site: www.acefitness.org
Members: 55000
Staff: 50
Annual Budget: $5-10,000,000
President: Scott Goudeseune
Chief Science Officer: Dr. Cedric X. Bryant
Vice President, Operations: Graham Melstrand
Chief Financial Officer: Al Mirrnezam
Director, Corporate Communications: Kristie Spalding

Historical Note
The American Council on Exercise (ACE) is a not-for-profit, educational organization committed to enriching quality of life through safe and effective physical activity. It is the largest not-for-profit fitness certifying organization in the world, with over 65,000 instructors certified in 60 countries since 1986.

Meetings/Conferences:
2007 – Las Vegas, NV(Rio Hotel)/September/500

Publications:
ACE Certified News. bi-m. adv.
ACE Fitness Matters. bi-m. adv.

American Council on International Personnel *(1972)*
Executive Director: Lynn Frendt Shotwell
E-Mail: lynn_shotwell@acip.com

Historical Note
Membership is open to all companies and organizations that employ at least 1,000 persons worldwide, including overseas and U.S. affiliates and subsidiaries. ACIP's purpose is to serve the business community on immigration matters. Membership: $500/year.

Meetings/Conferences:
Annual Meetings: always Arlington, VA (Ritz-Carlton)/first week of June/220

Publications:
Bulletins. w.

American Council on Science and Health *(1978)*
1995 Broadway, Second Floor
New York, NY 10023-5860
Tel: (212)362-7044 *Fax:* (212)362-4919
E-Mail: acsh@acsh.org
Web Site: www.acsh.org
Members: 2500 individuals
Staff: 10
Annual Budget: $1-2,000,000
Executive and Medical Director: Gilbert Ross
E-Mail: ross@acsh.org
Associate Director: Jeff Stier
President: Dr. Elizabeth Whelan

Historical Note
A consumer education organization providing the public with scientifically accurate evaluations of food, chemicals, the environment and health. Membership: $25/year (general); $50/year (sustaining); $1,000 and greater/year (organization).

Publications:
Health Facts and Fears.com. w.
The ACSH Media Update. semi-a.

American Council on the Teaching of Foreign Languages *(1967)*
700 S. Washington St., Suite 210
Alexandria, VA 22321-4
Tel: (703)894-2900 *Fax:* (703)894-0798
E-Mail: headquarters@actfl.org
Web Site: www.actfl.org
Members: 8000 individuals
Staff: 16
Annual Budget: $2-5,000,000
Executive Director: Bret D. Lovejoy
Director, Education: Martha Abbott
Director, Communications: Steve Ackley
Director, Membership: Juliet Mason
E-Mail: headquarters@actfl.org

Historical Note
Founded in 1967 as part of the Modern Language Association of America and incorporated in 1974. Became a separate organization in 1977. Membership: $75/year.

Meetings/Conferences:
Annual Meetings: November/5,000

Publications:
Foreign Language Annals. bi-m. adv.

American Councils for International Education *(1974)*
1776 Massachusetts Ave. NW
Suite 700
Washington, DC 20036
Tel: (202)833-7522 *Fax:* (202)833-7523
E-Mail: general@americancouncils.org
Web Site: www.americancouncils.org
Members: 1500 individuals
Staff: 89
Annual Budget: $50-100,000,000
President and Co-Founder: Dan E. Davidson, Ph.D.
Vice President, Teaching, Learning and Citizen Exchange: Lisa Choate
Vice President, Higher Education: Jeanne-Marie Duval
Chief Financial Officer/Director, Finance and Administration: John Henderson
Vice President, Field Operations: David Patton
Director, Human Resources: Kitt Poole

Historical Note
Founded as American Council of Teachers of Russian; assumed its current name in 2000. AC advances research, training, and materials development in the fields of Russian and English language, literature, and area studies. Membership: $20/year (associate and full professors); $15/year (assistant professors, lecturers, and pre-college teachers); $10/year (students and retired persons); $200 (life membership); $100/year (institutions).

Meetings/Conferences:
Annual Meetings: Fall

Publications:
Russian Language Journal. a. adv.
ACTR Newsletter. 20/year. adv.

American Counseling Association *(1952)*
5999 Stevenson Ave.
Alexandria, VA 22304-3300
Toll Free: (800)347 - 6647
E-Mail: aca@counseling.org
Web Site: www.counseling.org
Members: 53000 individuals
Staff: 55
Annual Budget: $5-10,000,000
Executive Director: Richard Yep
Director, Government Relations: Scott Barstow
Convention and Meetings: Robin Hayes
Member Services: Jacki Walker

Historical Note
Formerly (1983) the American Personnel and Guidance Association and (1992) American Association for Counseling and Development. ACA is a private, non-profit organization dedicated to the growth and development of the counseling profession. ACA members, who must hold a master's degree or higher in counseling or a closely related field, work in education settings, mental health agencies, community organizations, correctional institutions, employment settings, rehabilitation programs, government, business, industry, research facilities, and private practice. Divisions include the following: American College Counseling Association; American Mental Health Counselors Association; American Rehabilitation Counseling Association; American School Counselor Association; Association for Adult Development and Aging; Association for Assessment in Counseling; Association for Counselor Education and Supervision; Association for Counselors and Educators in Government; Association of Gay, Lesbian and Bisexual Issues in Counseling; Counseling Association for Humanistic Education and Development; Association for Multicultural Counseling and Development; Association for Specialists in Group Work; Association for Spiritual, Ethical and Religious Values in Counseling; International Association of Addictions and Offender Counselors; International Association of Marriage and Family Counselors; National Career Development

Association; and National Employment Counseling Association. Has an annual budget of approximately $8 million. Membership: $113/year (professional); $85/year (retired/student).

Meetings/Conferences:
Annual Meetings: Spring/4,000
2007 - Detroit, MI/March 21-25

Publications:
Journal of Counseling and Development. q. adv.
Counseling Today Newspaper. m. adv.

American Countertrade Association

Historical Note
Became Global Offset and Countertrade Association in 2005.

American Court and Commercial Newspapers *(1930)*

P.O. Box 5337
Arlington, VA 22205
Tel: (703)812-0561 *Fax:* (703)812-4555
E-Mail: information@pnrc.org
Web Site: www.americanpressworks.com/
Members: 79 newspapers
Staff: 1
Annual Budget: $50-100,000
Executive Director: Rishi Hingoraney

Historical Note
Newspapers dealing primarily with court news, financial matters, real estate and business matters. Established as Associated Court and Commercial Newspapers, it assumed its present name in 1979. Membership: up to $2,100/year for 4 or more papers under common ownership.

Meetings/Conferences:
Semi-Annual Meetings:

American Craft Association

Historical Note
A program of the American Craft Council.

American Craft Council *(1943)*

72 Spring St., Sixth Floor
New York, NY 10012-4019
Tel: (212)274-0630 *Fax:* (212)274-0650
Toll Free: (800)724 - 0859
E-Mail: council@craftcouncil.org
Web Site: www.craftcouncil.org
Members: 30000 individuals
Staff: 26
Annual Budget: $2-5,000,000
Executive Director: Carmine Branagan
E-Mail: branagan@craftcouncil.org
Director, Finance and Administration: Michael W. McKay
E-Mail: mmckay@craftcouncil.org
Director, Shows: Reed McMillan

Historical Note
Founded in 1943, the American Craft Council is a national, nonprofit public educational organization. The mission of the Council is to promote understanding and appreciation of contemporary American craft. Programs include the award-winning bimonthly magazine, American Craft, annual juried craft shows presenting artists and their work, the Aileen Osborn Webb Awards honoring excellence in craft, a specialized library and archive on contemporary craft, workshops and seminars. Membership is open to all.

Meetings/Conferences:
Annual Meetings: Summer

Publications:
American Craft. bi-m. adv.

American Cream Draft Horse Association *(1944)*

193 Crossover Rd.
Bennington, VT 05201
Tel: (802)447-7612 *Fax:* (802)447-0711
E-Mail: info@americancreamdraft.org
Web Site: www.americancreamdraft.org
Members: 125 individuals
Annual Budget: under $10,000
Secretary-Treasurer: Nancy H. Lively

Historical Note
Members are owners and breeders of American Cream Draft Horses. Has no paid officers or full-time staff. Membership: $25/year (individual).

Publications:
Cream Newsletter. bi-a.
American Cream News. semi-a. adv.

American Criminal Justice Association/Lambda Alpha Epsilon *(1937)*

P.O. Box 601047
Sacramento, CA 95860-1047
Tel: (916)484-6553 *Fax:* (916)488-2227
E-Mail: acjalae@aol.com
Web Site: www.acjalae.org
Members: 4500 individuals
Staff: 1
Annual Budget: $100-250,000
Executive Secretary: Karen K. Campbell
E-Mail: acjalae@aol.com

Historical Note
Also known as Lambda Alpha Epsilon, its official title until 1970. Members include persons employed in areas concerned with the administration of criminal justice (e.g., law enforcement, corrections, courts, etc.) and persons enrolled in a program of study in the criminal justice field at a college or university. Membership: $36/year (initial); $30/year (renewal fee).

Meetings/Conferences:
Annual Meetings: Spring

Publications:
LAE Journal of the American Criminal Justice Ass'n. semi-a.
LAE Newsletter. semi-a.

American Crop Protection Association

Historical Note
Became CropLife America in 2002.

American Crossbred Pony Registry *(1957)*

22 Dove Island Rd.
Newton, NJ 07860
Tel: (973)383-3384
E-Mail: bvfarm@nac.net
Members: 150 individuals
Staff: 1
Annual Budget: under $10,000
Registrar: Dr. George Yeaton
E-Mail: bvfarm@nac.net

Historical Note
Registry certifies and registers bloodlines of crossbred hunter and driving ponies.

Meetings/Conferences:
Annual Meetings: Not held.

American Crystallographic Association *(1949)*

P.O. Box 96, Ellicott Station
Buffalo, NY 14205-0096
Tel: (716)898-8690 *Fax:* (716)898-8695
Web Site: www.hwi.buffalo.edu/ACA/
Members: 2200 individuals
Staff: 3
Annual Budget: $250-500,000
Director, Administrative Services: Marcia Colquhoun

Historical Note
Created in 1949 through a merger of the Crystallographic Society of America and the American Society of X-ray and Electron Diffraction. Incorporated in New York in 1971. Member of the American Institute of Physics. Membership: $75/year (individual); $600/year (company/organization); $15/year (student).

Publications:
Newsletter. q.
Transactions of the ACA. a.

American Culinary Federation *(1929)*

180 Center Place Way
St. Augustine, FL 32095
Tel: (904)824-4468 *Fax:* (904)825-4758
Toll Free: (800)624 - 9458
Web Site: www.acfchefs.org
Members: 19600 individuals
Staff: 30
Annual Budget: $2-5,000,000
Managing Director: Dawn Jantsch, CAE, APR
Education Development Director: Michael Baskette
E-Mail: mbaskette@acfchefs.net
Director, Event Management: Debra Bulak
E-Mail: dbulak@acfchefs.net

Historical Note
ACF is the premier professional organization for culinarians in America. With nearly 20,000 members and 240 chapters nationwide, ACF offers educational resources, training, professional certification, apprenticeship, and accreditation programs. In addition, the ACF is the presidium for the World Association of Cooks Societies (WACS), the international network of chefs associations, with more that eight million members globally.

Meetings/Conferences:
Annual Meetings: July
2007 - Orlando, FL(Orlando World Marriott Resort)/July 20-23

Publications:
Center of the Plate. m. adv.
Sizzle. q. adv.
Nat'l Culinary Review. m. adv.

American Cultural Resources Association *(1995)*

6150 E. Ponce de Leon Ave.
Stone Mountain, GA 30083
Tel: (770)498-5159 *Fax:* (770)498-3809
Web Site: www.acra-crm.org
Members: 120 firms, 30 associate members
Staff: 1
Annual Budget: $50-100,000
Contact: Scott Stull

Historical Note
ACRA provides professional support to firms in cultural resources consulting, historic preservation, architectural history, historical architecture, landscape architecture, and related disciplines. Membership: $150-1,000/year.

Meetings/Conferences:
Annual Meetings: Fall

Publications:
ACRA Newsletter. bi-m. adv.

American Custom Gunmakers Guild *(1983)*

22 Vista View Ln.
Cody, WY 82414-9606
Tel: (307)587-4297 *Fax:* (307)587-4297
E-Mail: acgg@acgg.org
Web Site: www.acgg.org
Members: 350 individuals
Staff: 1
Executive Director: Jan Billeb

Historical Note
ACGG was founded to be an association of individual craftsmen actively engaged in custom gunmaking, for the exchange of ideas, views, techniques, and the promotion of public interest and awareness of gun making as an art form. Membership (associate membership) is open to all interested in supporting the art of fine custom gunmaking. Associate membership: $95/year (individual associate); $180/year (commercial associate); $45/year (student).

Meetings/Conferences:
Annual Meetings: Winter
2007 - Reno, NV(Silver Legacy)/Jan. 26-28

Publications:
Informational Package/Membership Directory. a.
Directory of Custom Gunmaking Services. a.
Gunmaker. q. adv.

American Dairy Association *(1940)*

Historical Note
A wholly-owned subsidiary of Dairy Management Inc., which provides administrative support.

American Dairy Goat Association *(1904)*

209 W. Main St.
P.O. Box 865
Spindale, NC 28160
Tel: (828)286-3801 *Fax:* (828)287-0476
E-Mail: info@adga.org
Web Site: www.adga.org
Members: 12000 individuals
Staff: 12
Annual Budget: $1-2,000,000
Associate Manager: Shirley C. McKenzie

Historical Note
Members are breeders and fanciers of dairy goats. Formerly American Milch Goat Record Association and American Milk Goat Record Association. Member of the National Pedigree Livestock Council. Membership: $35/year (full member), $10/year (junior member).

Meetings/Conferences:
Annual Meetings: Fall

Publications:
ADGA Guidebook. a. adv.
ADGA News & Events Newsletter. q.
ADGA Directory. a.

American Dairy Products Institute *(1986)*
116 N. York St., Suite 200
Elmhurst, IL 60126
Tel: (630)530-8700 *Fax:* (630)530-8707
E-Mail: adpi@americandairyproducts.org
Web Site: www.adpi.org
Members: 225 companies
Staff: 10
Annual Budget: $500-1,000,000
Chief Executive Officer: Jim Page
Director, Membership Communications: Beth Sutton
E-Mail: bsutton@adpi.org

Historical Note
Product of a merger between the American Dry Milk Institute and the Whey Products Institute in 1986; the Evaporated Milk Association merged into Institute in 1987; a cheese division was formed in 1997. Seeks to promote the acceptance and utilization of processed dairy products, nationally and internationally, to maintain liaison and represent the industry in dealings with governmental agencies and regulatory bodies, to support technical and marketing research and to assemble and disseminate statistics and other information about processed dairy products.

Meetings/Conferences:
Annual Meetings: Chicago, IL/April

Publications:
Dry Milk Products Utilization and Production Trends. a.
Whey Products-Utilization and Production Trends. a.

American Dairy Science Association *(1906)*
1111 N. Dunlap Ave.
Savoy, IL 61874
Tel: (217)356-5146 *Fax:* (217)398-4119
E-Mail: adsa@assochq.org
Web Site: www.adsa.org
Members: 5200 individuals
Staff: 11
Annual Budget: $1-2,000,000
Executive Director: Brenda S. Carlson

Historical Note
Incorporated in the District of Columbia in 1906 as the National Association of Dairy Instructors and Investigators; assumed its current name in 1911. Members are equipment manufacturers and suppliers, farmers, educators, researchers, and breeders interested in strengthening all aspects of the dairy industry. Membership: $110/year (individual); $250/year (organization/company).

Meetings/Conferences:
Annual Meetings: June-July

Publications:
ADSA Today. m.
Mastitis Control and Milk Quality. irreg.
Dairy Management Practices, Housing and Cattle Health. irreg.
Abstracts & Annual Meeting Program. a. adv.
Journal of Dairy Science. m. adv.

American Dance Guild *(1956)*
P.O. Box 2006, Lenox Hill Station
New York, NY 10021
Tel: (212)932-2789
E-Mail: americandanceguild@hotmail.com
Web Site: www.americandanceguild.org
Members: 400 individuals
Staff: 1
Annual Budget: $100-250,000
President: Deborah Mauldin
E-Mail: americandanceguild@hotmail.com

Historical Note
Formerly known as (1956) Dance Teachers Guild, (1966) National Dance Teachers Guild, and (1968) National Dance Guild before assuming its current name, ADG serves the dance professional by providing a networking system for networking between dance artists and dance educators; an informed voice on behalf of the dance field to governmental, educational and corporate institutions and to the general public; international dance festivals, dance film festivals and conferences; educational publications and videos; and the ADG Fannie Weiss Scholarship. Membership: $50/year (individual); $25/year (senior, student); $100/year (company/institution).

Meetings/Conferences:
Annual Meetings: June

Publications:
American Dance magazine. 2/yr. adv.
Newsletter. 2/yr. adv.

American Dance Therapy Association *(1966)*
2000 Century Plaza, Suite 108
10632 Little Patuxent Pkwy.
Columbia, MD 21044
Tel: (410)997-4040 *Fax:* (410)997-4048
Web Site: www.adta.org
Members: 1200 individuals
Staff: 2
Annual Budget: $100-250,000
Spokesperson: Sally Totenbier
E-Mail: totenbier@houston.rr.com

Historical Note
Individuals and institutions concerned with the dance as a therapeutic agent. Awards the DTR and the ADTR designations to those meeting prescribed professional standards. Membership: $70-135/year.

Meetings/Conferences:
Annual Meetings: Fall

Publications:
American Journal of Dance Therapy. bi-a. adv.
Newsletter. q. adv.

American Dehydrated Onion and Garlic Association *(1956)*
980 Ninth St., Suite 230
Sacramento, CA 95814
Tel: (916)444-9260 *Fax:* (916)444-2746
Members: 2 companies
Staff: 1
Annual Budget: $100-250,000
Secretary-Treasurer: Bill Grigg

Historical Note
Members are U.S. companies that dehydrate onions and garlic serving industrial and food service customers. ADOGA members account for 90% of dried onions and garlic produced in the United States.

Publications:
ADOGA News Bulletin. irreg.

American Dental Assistants Association *(1924)*
35 E. Wacker Dr., Suite 1730
Chicago, IL 60601-2211
Tel: (312)541-1550 *Fax:* (312)541-1496
Web Site: www.dentalassistant.org
Members: 30500 individuals
Staff: 10
Annual Budget: $1-2,000,000
Executive Director: Lawrence Sepin
Director, Communications: Doug McDonough

Historical Note
Requires tripartite membership (local, state, and national). Membership: $100/year.

Meetings/Conferences:
Annual Meetings: Summer/1,000

Publications:
Newsletter. q. adv.
Dental Assistant Journal. 6/year. adv.

American Dental Association *(1859)*
211 E. Chicago Ave.
Chicago, IL 60611-2678
Tel: (312)440-2500 *Fax:* (312)440-2800
E-Mail: online@ada.org
Web Site: www.ada.org
Members: 140000 individuals
Staff: 400
Annual Budget: $50-100,000,000
Executive Director: James B. Bramson, DDS
E-Mail: online@ada.org
Associate Executive Director, Government Affairs: William Prentice
Associate Executive Director, Legal Affairs: Peter M. Sfikas
E-Mail: online@ada.org
Chief Financial Officer: Bill Zimmerman
E-Mail: online@ada.org

Historical Note
Founded August 3, 1859 in Niagara Falls. United with the Southern Dental Association in 1897 and changed its name to the National Dental Association; assumed its current name in 1922. Incorporated in Illinois. Supports the American Dental Political Action Committee, and maintains a Washington office. Has an annual budget of approximately $50 million.

Meetings/Conferences:
Annual Meetings: Fall/12,500
2007 – San Francisco, CA/Sept. 27-30
2008 – San Antonio, TX/Oct. 16-19
2009 – Honolulu, HI/Sept. 30-Oct. 3

Publications:
ADA News. bi-w. adv.
Journal of the ADA. m. adv.

American Dental Education Association *(1923)*
1400 K St. NW
Suite 1100
Washington, DC 20005
Tel: (202)289-7201 *Fax:* (202)289-7204
E-Mail: adea@adea.org
Web Site: www.adea.org
Members: 230 institutions
Staff: 40
Annual Budget: $5-10,000,000
Executive Director: Richard W. Valachovic, D.M.D., M.P.H
Associate Executive Director, Member Services: Jane Hamblin
E-Mail: adea@adea.org

Historical Note
Founded as American Association of Dental Schools in Omaha, NE on January 24, 1923 through a merger of the American Institute of Dental Teachers, Canadian Dental Faculties' Association, National Association of Dental Faculties and the Dental Faculties' Association of American Universities; incorporated in Illinois in 1960; assumed its current name in 2000. Membership includes all U.S. and Canadian dental schools and many other dental and allied institutions in Canada and the U.S. Provides an application service for people applying to dental school. Membership: free to staff and students of member institutions.

Meetings/Conferences:
Annual Meetings: March/2,000
2007 – Dallas, TX/March 29-Apr. 2
2008 – Phoenix, AZ/March 14-18

Publications:
Official Guide to Dental Schools. a.
Opportunities for Minority Students. bi-a.
Directory of Institutional Members. a. adv.
Bulletin of Dental Education. m. adv.
Journal of Dental Education Online. m. adv.

American Dental Hygienists' Association *(1923)*
111 Queen Anne Ave. North
Suite 501
Seattle, WA 98109-4955
Tel: (312)440-8900 *Fax:* (312)440-8929
E-Mail: mail@adha.net
Web Site: www.adha.org
Members: 35000 individuals
Staff: 40
Annual Budget: $5-10,000,000
Executive Director: Ann Battrell
Director, Member Services: Danielle Bright
E-Mail: member.services@adha.net
Director, Finance: Isaac Carpenter
E-Mail: finance@adha.net
Director, Administration and Special Projects: Karen Dunn Caspers
E-Mail: exec.office@adha.net

Historical Note
Membership: $155/year, plus constituent and component dues; $500/year (organization/company).

Meetings/Conferences:
Annual Meetings: June/1,000
2007 - New Orleans, LA(Sheraton)/June 20-27
2008 - Albuquerque, NM(Doubletree)/June 18-25
2009 - Washington, DC(Omni Shorehame Hotel)/June 16-24

Publications:
Access. 10/year. adv.
Journal of Dental Hygiene. q.. adv.
Education Update. semi-a.

American Dental Interfraternity Council *(1923)*
2800 College Ave., Suite 286
Alton, IL 62002-4742
Tel: (618)474-7201 *Fax:* (618)463-1882
E-Mail: kdickey@siue.edu
Web Site: www.ada.org
Members: 4 dental fraternities
Staff: 1
Annual Budget: under $10,000
Executive Director: Dr. Keith W. Dickey

Historical Note
A federation of professional Greek letter societies united to promote better public relations for the dental profession.

Meetings/Conferences:
Annual Meetings: Fall, in conjunction with the American Dental Ass'n annual meeting.

American Dental Society of Anesthesiology *(1953)*
211 E. Chicago, Suite 780
Chicago, IL 60611
Tel: (217)356-5146
Toll Free: (800)722 - 7788
E-Mail: adsahome@mac.com
Web Site: www.adsahome.org
Members: 3500 individuals
Staff: 2
Annual Budget: $250-500,000
Executive Director: R. Knight Charlton

Historical Note
Members are dentists with a special interest in pain control. Membership: $175/year (active member); $25/year (student).

Meetings/Conferences:
Annual Meetings: Spring/250

Publications:
Anesthesia Progress. q. adv.
Newsletter. bi-m.

American Dental Trade Association

Historical Note
Combined with Dental Trade Alliance in 2004.

American Design Drafting Association *(1959)*
105 East Main St.
Newburn, TN 38059
Tel: (731)627-0802 *Fax:* (731)627-9321
E-Mail: corporate@adda.org
Web Site: www.adda.org
Members: 2000 individuals
Staff: 2
Annual Budget: $100-250,000

Historical Note
Formerly (1960) Association of Professional Draftsmen and (1989) American Institute for Design and Drafting. Membership includes individuals, corporations and educational institutions and students. Seeks to promote improved quality and efficiency in the drafting/designing profession and industry. ADDA administers a curriculum certification program for schools with design/drafting programs and design/drafter certification programs. Membership: $75/year (individual); $215/year (educational institutions); $300/year (organization/company).

Meetings/Conferences:
Annual Meetings: Spring

Publications:
Design Drafting News. bi-m. adv.

American Dexter Cattle Association *(1912)*
4150 Merino Ave.
Watertown, MN 55388
Tel: (660)841-9502
E-Mail: info@dextercattle.org
Web Site: www.dextercattle.org
Members: 450 individuals
Staff: 1
Annual Budget: $50-100,000
Registrar: Chuck Daggett

Historical Note
Established as the American Kerry and Dexter Club; assumed its present name in 1957. Indigenous to Ireland, the Dexter is a breed used in both beef and dairy applications. Membership: $30/year (new and associate); $20/year (renewal).

Meetings/Conferences:
Annual Meetings: Summer

Publications:
Bulletin. bi-m.
Herd Book. a.

American Diabetes Association *(1940)*
1701 N. Beauregard St.
Alexandria, VA 22311
Tel: (703)549-1500 *Fax:* (703)836-7439
Toll Free: (800)342 - 2383
E-Mail: askada@diabetes.com
Web Site: www.diabetes.org
Members: 390000 individuals
Staff: 900
Annual Budget: Over $100,000,000
Chief Executive Officer: Lynn B. Nicholas
Executive Vice President, Development: Vaneeda Bennett
Executive Vice President, Marketing and Communications: Maura Connell
Executive Vice President/Chief Financial Officer: Debbie Johnson
Chief Scientific and Medical Officer: Richard Kahn, Ph.D.
Executive Vice President, Government Affairs and Advocacy: Jim Schlict

Historical Note
Founded in 1940 in Cincinnati as a professional society of medical doctors; converted in 1965 to a voluntary health agency. Operates as one nationwide organization. ADA is the nation's leading voluntary health organization concerned with the prevention and cure of diabetes. It provides support to millions who have the disease and educates health professionals and the general public.

Meetings/Conferences:
Annual Meetings: June

Publications:
Diabetes Spectrum. bi-m. adv.
Diabetes Forecast. m. adv.
Clinical Diabetes. bi-m. adv.
Diabetes. m. adv.
Diabetes Care. m. adv.

American Dialect Society *(1889)*
Dept. of English, MacMurray College
Jacksonville, IL 62650-2590
Tel: (217)479-7117 *Fax:* (217)245-0405
Web Site: www.americandialect.org
Members: 550 individuals
Staff: 1
Annual Budget: $10-25,000
Executive Secretary: Allan Metcalf
E-Mail: AAllan@aol.com

Historical Note
Members are educators and others interested in the English language in North America. Sponsors the Dictionary of American Regional English. Membership: $35/year (individual); $20/year (student).

Meetings/Conferences:
Annual Meetings: With the Linguistic Soc. of America in January.

Publications:
American Speech. q.
Newsletter of the American Dialect Society. 3/year. adv.
Publication of the American Dialect Society (PADS). a.

American Dietetic Association *(1917)*
120 S. Riverside Plaza
Suite 2000
Chicago, IL 60606
Tel: (312)899-0040 *Fax:* (312)899-4845
Toll Free: (800)877 - 1600
E-Mail: knowledge@eatright.org
Web Site: www.eatright.org
Members: 65000 individuals
Staff: 150
Annual Budget: $25-50,000,000
Chief Executive Officer: Ronald S. Moen
Senior Manager, Government and Political Affairs: Ronald Smith

Historical Note
The nation's largest professional society of dietetics professionals, ADA was established in Cleveland, OH in 1917 and incorporated in Illinois in 1923. Members are employed in health care organizations, schools, colleges, and universities as well as in business institutions and industry. Sponsors and supports the American Dietetic Association Political Action Committee. Has an annual budget of approximately $21.8 million. The American Dietetic Foundation, established in 1967, is ADA's educational and research arm. Membership: $200/year.

Meetings/Conferences:
Annual Meetings: October/10,000

Publications:
ADA Times. 6/yr. adv.
Journal of the American Dietetic Ass'n. m. adv.

American Disc Jockey Association *(1992)*
20118 N. 67th Ave.
Suite 300-605
Glendale, AZ 85308
Toll Free: (888)723 - 5776
E-Mail: office@adja.org
Web Site: www.adja.org
Members: 900 individuals
Staff: 8
President: Peter Merry, Jr.

Historical Note
ADJA represents the needs of professional mobile and night club DJ's and KJ's. The association promotes common standards, procedures, and benefits for its members. Membership: $60/year (associate); $120/year (individual/company).

Publications:
ADJA News Newsletter. q. adv.

American Donkey and Mule Society *(1967)*
P.O. Box 1210
Lewisville, TX 75067
Tel: (972)219-0781 *Fax:* (972)420-9980
E-Mail: adms@juno.com
Web Site: www.lovelongears.com
Members: 5000 individuals
Staff: 4
Annual Budget: $50-100,000
Secretary: Leah Patton
E-Mail: adms@juno.com

Historical Note
Breeders, owners, and organizations interested in donkeys and mules. Maintains five registries for donkeys, mules and zebra hybrids, stud books, and prepares and disseminates educational books and literature. Membership: $20/year; $27/year (Canada); $30/year (international).

Publications:
The Brayer Magazine. bi-m. adv.

American Down Association

Historical Note
Became American Down and Feather Section, HFPA in 2002.

American Driver and Traffic Safety Education Association *(1956)*
c/o Highway Safety Center
Indiana University of Pennsylvania
Indiana, PA 15705
Tel: (724)357-4051 *Fax:* (724)357-7595
Toll Free: (800)896 - 7703
Web Site: www.adtsea.iup.edu/adtsea
Members: 1000 individuals
Staff: 3
Annual Budget: $250-500,000
Chief Executive Officer: Allen Robinson, Ph.D.

Historical Note
A professional society of driving and safety educators; established as the American Driver and Safety Education Association, became the American Driver Education Association in 1957 and assumed its present name in 1963. Sponsors the National Student Safety Program. Membership: $25-100/year (individual); $400/year (organization/company).

Meetings/Conferences:
Annual Meetings: August/500

Publications:
ADTSEA New & Views. 4-7/year.
Chronicle of the ADTSEA. q. adv.

American Economic Association *(1885)*
2014 Broadway, Suite 305
Nashville, TN 37203-2418
Tel: (615)322-2595 *Fax:* (615)343-7590
E-Mail: aeainfo@vanderbilt.edu
Web Site: www.vanderbilt.edu/AEA
Members: 18000 individuals
Staff: 40
Annual Budget: $2-5,000,000
Secretary-Treasurer: John Siegfried
E-Mail: aeainfo@vanderbilt.edu

Historical Note
Founded in Saratoga, NY in 1885. Member of the American Council of Learned Societies and affiliated with the Social Science Research Council, the American Association for the Advancement of Science and the International Economic Association. Encourages economic research, particularly historical and statistical studies of industrial life. Serves as the umbrella organization for U.S. economists. Regular membership: $64-90/year (individual); $315/year (organization/company).

Meetings/Conferences:
Annual Meetings: Winter
2007 – Chicago, IL/Jan. 5-7
2008 – New Orleans, LA/Jan. 4-6
2009 – San Francisco, CA/Jan. 3-5

Publications:
American Economic Review. q. adv.
Journal of Economic Literature. q. adv.
Journal of Economic Perspectives. q. adv.

American Edged Products Manufacturers Association *(1947)*
21165 Whitfield Pl.
Suite 105
Potomac Falls, VA 20165
Tel: (703)433-9281 *Fax:* (703)433-0369
E-Mail: aepma@erols.com
Web Site: www.aepma.org
Members: 50 companies
Staff: 4
Annual Budget: $50-100,000
Executive Director: David W. Barrack

Historical Note
Formerly (2000) American Cutlery Manufacturers Association. Serves the domestic edged products industry by providing educational services, promoting communication and cooperation between members and governmental agencies and by sponsoring meetings and trade shows.

Meetings/Conferences:
Annual Meetings: Spring
2007 – Orlando, FL(Villas of Grand Cypress)/May 2-5

Publications:
AEPMA Newsletter. q. adv.
Membership Directory. a.

American Education Finance Association *(1975)*
8365 S. Armadillo Trail
Evergreen, CO 80439
Tel: (303)674-0857 *Fax:* (303)670-8986
Web Site: www.aefa.cc
Members: 650 individuals
Annual Budget: $250-500,000
Executive Director: Ed Steinbecher

Historical Note
AEFA encourages communications among groups and individuals in the education finance field, including academicians, researchers, policy makers and practitioners. Serving as a forum for a broad range of issues and concerns, AEFA concerns include traditional school finance concepts, issues of public policy, and teaching school finance. Membership: $95/year (individual); $45/year (student); $1,000/year (sustaining member).

Meetings/Conferences:
Annual Meetings: March-April
2007 – Baltimore, MD(Sheraton Inner Harbor)/March 22-24/325

Publications:
Conference Abstract. a. adv.
Membership Directory. a. adv.
Newsletter. q. adv.
Education, Finance and Policy Journal of AEFA. q. adv.

American Educational Research Association *(1915)*
1230 17th St. NW
Washington, DC 20036-3078
Tel: (202)223-9485 *Fax:* (202)775-1824
Web Site: www.aera.net
Members: 22000 individuals
Staff: 23
Annual Budget: $2-5,000,000
Executive Director: Felice J. Levine
Director, Communications and Outreach: Helaine Patterson
Director, Governmental Relations: Gerald E. Sroufe, Ph.D

Historical Note
Founded in 1915 in Cincinnati as the National Association of Directors of Educational Research, an affiliate of the National Education Association. In 1930 the name was changed to the American Educational Research Association. In 1968 the affiliation with NEA was dropped and the organization was incorporated in the District of Columbia. AERA is an international professional organization of educators; directors of research, testing, or evaluation in federal, state, and local agencies; counselors; evaluators; graduate students; and behavioral scientists concerned with educational research and its application to practice. Sponsors and supports the National Council on Measurement in Education. Membership: $45/year.

Meetings/Conferences:
Annual Meetings: Spring

Publications:
Journal of Educational and Behavioral Statistics. q. adv.
Review of Educational Research. q. adv.
Review of Research in Education. a. adv.
Educational Researcher. 9/year. adv.
American Educational Research Journal. q. adv.
Educational Evaluation and Policy Analysis. q. adv.

American Educational Studies Association *(1968)*
9785 Coleman Rd.
Roswell, GA 30075
Tel: (404)651-1192 *Fax:* (404)651-1009
Toll Free: (877)730 - 4865 Ext: 103
Web Site: www.uakron.edu/aesa
Members: 700 individuals
Annual Budget: $10-25,000
Treasurer: Deron Boyles

Historical Note
Concerned with the comprehensive view of education including the underlying philosophy, history, sociology and psychology of education and dedicated to research and the improvement of teaching in these areas. Has no paid officers or full-time staff. Membership: $45/year (individual); $105/year (institution).

Meetings/Conferences:
Semi-annual Meetings: Spring, conjunction with American Educational Research Ass'n

Publications:
AESA Newsletter. q.
Educational Studies. q. adv.

American Egg Board *(1976)*
1460 Renaissance Dr., Suite 301
Park Ridge, IL 60068
Tel: (847)296-7043 *Fax:* (847)296-7007
E-Mail: aeb@aeb.org
Web Site: www.aeb.org
Members: 250 producer companies
Staff: 20
Annual Budget: $10-25,000,000
President: Louis B. Raffel, CAE
Senior Vice President, Industry and Market Development: Joanne C. Ivy
Controller: Dennis Kane

Historical Note
AEG was originally established as the Poultry and Egg National Board, a federation of egg producers. Assumed its current name in 1973. An act of Congress in 1976 gave this official status, permitted dues check offs from egg producers, and authorized the appointment by the Secretary of Agriculture of the members of the Board. AEG is concerned with advertising, promotion and research activities for eggs and egg products. Has an annual budget of $18 million.

Publications:
Eggsaminer - Food Manufacturer Newsletter.
eggstra! - Retailer Newsletter. q.
Foodservice Newsletter. q.
News from AEB. m.

American Electrology Association *(1958)*
P.O. Box 687
Bodega Bay, CA 94923-0687
Tel: (707)875-9135 *Fax:* (707)875-3340
E-Mail: infoaea@electrology.com
Web Site: www.electrology.com
Members: 2000 individuals
Staff: 1
Annual Budget: $100-250,000
Executive Director: Patsy Kirby
E-Mail: infoaea@electrology.com

Historical Note
Founded in New Jersey in February 1958 as American Electrolysis Association; assumed its present name in 1986. Membership is composed of electrologists (permanent hair removers). Sponsors national certification program, national accreditation program and continuing education. Membership: $120/year (individual).

Meetings/Conferences:
Annual Meetings: Fall

Publications:
Electrology World. 3/year. adv.
Membership Directory. a.
Journal of Electrology. semi-a.

The American Electrophoresis Society *(1980)*
1201 Ann St.
Madison, WI 53713
Tel: (608)258-1565 *Fax:* (608)258-1569
E-Mail: matt-aes@tds.net
Web Site: www.aesociety.org
Members: 100 individuals
Staff: 1
Annual Budget: $10-25,000
Executive Director: Matt Hoelter
E-Mail: matt-aes@tds.net

Historical Note
Members are scientists striving to promote scientific advances in electrophoretic theory and applications. Membership: $75/year.

Publications:
AES Newsletter. 4/year.

American Electroplaters and Surface Finishers Society *(1909)*
1155 15th St. NW
Washington, DC 20005
Tel: (202)457-8401 *Fax:* (202)530-0659
E-Mail: aesf@aesf.org
Web Site: www.aesf.org
Members: 3500 individuals
Annual Budget: $1-2,000,000

Historical Note
Founded in New York City in 1909 as the National Electro-Platers Association; became American Electroplaters' Society in 1913 and assumed its present name in 1985. Incorporated in New Jersey in 1946. Promotes all aspects of electroplating and surface finishing. Membership: $125/year (U.S. members), $100/year (non-U.S. members).

Meetings/Conferences:
Annual Meetings: Summer/4,500

Publications:
Proceedings of Sur/Fin Conference. a. adv.
Plating and Surface Finishing Journal. m. adv.
AESF Shopguide. a. adv.

American Embryo Transfer Association *(1981)*
1111 N. Dunlap Ave.
Savoy, IL 61874
Tel: (217)398-2217 *Fax:* (217)398-4119
E-Mail: aeta@assochq.org
Web Site: www.aeta.org
Members: 363 companies and individuals
Staff: 3
Annual Budget: $25-50,000
Executive Director: Keely Roy
E-Mail: aeta@assochq.org

Historical Note
Seeks to promote the use of embryo transfer as a means to improve livestock and encourages cooperative relationships among companies and individuals engaged in embryo transfer. Has developed a certification program for embryo transfer companies in order to identify those who meet certain criteria in their commercial activities.

Meetings/Conferences:
Annual Meetings: Fall

Publications:
Closer Look. q. adv.
Convention Proceedings. a.

American Emu Association
P.O. Box 2502
San Angelo, TX 76902
Tel: (541)332-0675 *Fax:* (509)351-6236
E-Mail: info@aea-emu.org
Web Site: www.aea-emu.org
Members: 680 individuals
Annual Budget: under $10,000
Treasurer: Deitra McCleary
E-Mail: emulady76905@peoplepc.com

Historical Note
Members are emu (a flightless bird) raisers. Membership: $300/year (individual, first year); $100/year (renewal).

Meetings/Conferences:
Annual Meetings: Summer

Publications:
AEA EMUpdate. bi-m. adv.

American Endodontic Society *(1969)*
265 N. Main St.
Glen Ellyn, IL 60137
Tel: (773)519-4879 *Fax:* (630)858-0525
E-Mail: n2dontics@aol.com
Web Site: www.aesoc.com
Members: 7000 individuals
Staff: 2
Annual Budget: $100-250,000
Executive Director: Ramon Werts, D.D.S.
E-Mail: drdaddy@deltanet.com

Historical Note
Members are dentists specializing in root canal work. Membership: $150/year.

Meetings/Conferences:
Annual Meetings: Fall, usually in conjunction with the ADA Scientific Meeting

Publications:
AES Newsletter. q.

American Engineering Association *(1979)*
4116 S. Carrier Pkwy., Suite 280-809
Grand Prairie, TX 75052
Tel: (972)264-6428
E-Mail: info@aea.org
Web Site: www.aea.org
President: Billy E. Reed

Publications:
American Engineer. bi-m.

American Entomological Society *(1859)*
c/o Academy of Natural Sciences
1900 Ben Franklin Pkwy.
Philadelphia, PA 19103-1195
Tel: (215)561-3978 *Fax:* (215)299-1028
E-Mail: aes@acnatsci.org
Web Site: www.acnatsci.org/hosted/aes
Members: 400 individuals
Staff: 2
Annual Budget: $10-25,000
Office Manager: Suzanne Schecter
Coordinator: Tina R. LeMar

Historical Note
Founded as the Entomological Society of Phildelphia. In 1867 the name was changed to American Entomological Society The Society's library is housed and staffed by the Academy of Natural Sciences of Philadelphia. AES promotes the study of insects and publishes the results of pure research in the systematics and morphology of insects. Membership: $15/year (regular); $10/year (student).

Publications:
Entomological News. 5/year. adv.
Memoirs of the AES. irreg.
Transactions of the AES. q.

American Epilepsy Society *(1946)*
342 N. Main St.
West Hartford, CT 06117-2507
Tel: (860)586-7505 *Fax:* (860)586-7550
E-Mail: info@aesnet.org
Web Site: www.aesnet.org
Members: 2000 individuals
Staff: 3
Annual Budget: $1-2,000,000
Executive Director: M. Suzanne C. Berry, CAE, MBA

Historical Note
Founded as the American League Against Epilepsy; assumed its present name in 1959. Members are physicians, nurses, and scientists engaged in research and practice in epilepsy or closely related fields. Membership: $180/year (active member); $65 or $140/year (junior member); $135 or 210/year (outside North America).

Meetings/Conferences:
Annual Meetings: December
2007 – Philadelphia, PA/Nov. 30-Dec. 4
2008 – Seattle, WA/Dec. 5-9
2009 – Boston, MA/Dec. 4-8

Publications:
Journal of Epilepsy. 6/year.
Epilepsy Research. 9/year.
Epilepsia. m. adv.

American Equilibration Society *(1955)*
8726 N. Ferris Ave.
Morton Grove, IL 60053
Tel: (847)965-2888 *Fax:* (847)965-4888
E-Mail: aesdental@sprynet.com
Web Site: www.occlusion-tmj.org
Members: 1000 individuals
Staff: 5
Annual Budget: $500-1,000,000
Executive Director: Shel Marcus
E-Mail: aesdental@sprynet.com

Historical Note
Membership consists of dentists and physicians interested in the structure and functions of the temporomandibular region and related parts of the mouth. Membership: $340/year (individual).

Meetings/Conferences:
Annual Meetings: Winter/500

Publications:
Newsletter. 3/year.
Directory. a.

American Ethnological Society *(1842)*

Historical Note
Organized in 1842, "to make inquiries into the origin, progress and characteristics of the various races of man." Became inactive in the 1860s but was re-organized in 1871 as the Anthropological Institute, and shortly thereafter assumed its present name. A section of the American Anthropological Association.

American Evaluation Association *(1986)*
16 Sconticut Neck Rd.
Suite 290
Fairhaven, MA 02719
Tel: (508)748-3326 *Fax:* (508)748-3158
Toll Free: (888)232 - 2275
E-Mail: info@eval.org
Web Site: www.eval.org
Members: 4000 individuals
Annual Budget: $500-1,000,000
Executive Director: Susan Kistler

Historical Note
Formed in 1985 by the merger of the Evaluation Network and the Evaluation Research Society. AEA is an international organization of professionals involved in the practice or study of evaluation. Evaluation involves assessing the strengths and weaknesses of programs, policies, personnel, products and organizations to improve their effectiveness. AEA members represent many different disciplines including psychology, education, public administration and policy analysis, economics, public relations and marketing, auditing, health care, social work, sociology, and measurement and statistics. AEA's mission is to improve evaluation practice and methods, increase evaluation use and promote evaluation as a profession. Membership: $80/year (individual); $50/year (student).

Meetings/Conferences:
Annual Meetings: Typical Attendence: 1300
2007 – Baltimore, MD(Wyndham Inner Harbor)/Nov. 5-10
2008 – Denver, CO(Hyatt Convention Center)/Nov. 3-8
2009 – Orlando, FL(Rose Shingle Creek Resort)/Nov. 9-14

Publications:
New Directions for Program Evaluation. q.
American Journal of Evaluation. q.

American Family Therapy Academy *(1977)*
1608 20th St. NW, Fourth Floor
Washington, DC 20009
Tel: (202)483-0001 *Fax:* (202)483-0002
E-Mail: afta@afta.org
Web Site: www.afta.org
Members: 800 individuals
Staff: 5
Annual Budget: $250-500,000
Administrative Director: Barbro Miles
E-Mail: afta@afta.org

Historical Note
Formerly (1992) American Family Therapy Association. Members are teachers, researchers, and clinical therapists specially trained to work with couples and families. Its purpose is to advance therapies and theories that regard the family as a unit within a broader context; to promote research in family therapy; and to make information available to the public and practitioners in other fields. Membership: $232/year.

Meetings/Conferences:
Annual Meetings: June/300

Publications:
Membership Directory. a.
AFTA Monograph Series. 2/yr. adv.

American Farm Bureau Federation *(1919)*
600 Maryland Ave. SW
Suite 1000W
Washington, DC 20024
Tel: (202)406-3600 *Fax:* (202)406-3602
Web Site: www.fb.org
Members: 5.6 million individuals worldwide
Staff: 100
Annual Budget: $10-25,000,000
President: Robert Stallman
Director, Legislative Services: R. J. Karney
Director, Public Relations: Don Lipton
Executive Director, Public Policy: Mark Maslyn
Chief Administrative Officer and Secretary-Treasurer: Richard Newpher
General Counsel: Julie A. Potts

Historical Note
Members are the state Farm Bureaus in 50 states and Puerto Rico. These, in turn, represent nearly 3,000 county Farm Bureaus and over 5 million families. The American Agricultural Marketing Association, American Agricultural Insurance Company, and American Agricultural Communications System are affiliated companies. Has an annual budget of approximately $20 million.

Meetings/Conferences:
Annual Meetings: January/6,000

Publications:
Farm Bureau News. w.

American Farrier's Association *(1971)*
4059 Iron Works Pkwy.
Suite One
Lexington, KY 40511
Tel: (859)233-7411 *Fax:* (859)231-7862
Web Site: www.nofootnohorse.org
Members: 3400 individuals
Staff: 4
Annual Budget: $500-1,000,000
Executive Director: Bryan Quinsey

Historical Note
An association of professional horseshoers. Membership: $105/year.

Meetings/Conferences:
Annual Meetings: Spring
2007 – Albuquerque, NM(Convention Center)/Feb. 26-March 3
2008 – Lexington, KY(Convention Center)/Feb. 25-March 1/2000

Publications:
Professional Farrier. bi-m. adv.
AFA Newsletter. bi-m.

American Federation for Aging Research *(1981)*
70 W. 40th St., 11th Floor
New York, NY 10018
Tel: (212)703-9977 *Fax:* (212)997-0330
Toll Free: (888)582 - 2327
E-Mail: info@afar.org
Web Site: www.afar.org
Staff: 6
Annual Budget: $5-10,000,000
Executive Director: Stephanie Lederman
E-Mail: info@afar.org

Historical Note
AFAR members are physicians, scientists and others with an interest in research on aging.

Meetings/Conferences:
Annual Meetings: with the American Aging Ass'n (AGE)

Publications:
AFAR Newsletter. irreg.
Network Newsletter. bi-a.

American Federation for Medical Research *(1940)*
900 Cummings Center, Suite 221-U
Beverly, MA 01915
Tel: (978)927-8330 *Fax:* (978)524-8890
Web Site: www.afmr.org
Members: 2500 individuals
Staff: 6
Annual Budget: $2-5,000,000
Contact: Aurelie M. Alger

Historical Note
Promotes research in clinical and laboratory medicine. Membership: $180/year.

Meetings/Conferences:
Annual Meetings: Spring

Publications:
Journal of Investigative Medicine. bi-m. adv.
Journal of Investigative Medicine Supplement. semi-a. adv.
AFMR Newsletter. q.

American Federation of Astrologers, Inc. *(1938)*
6535 S. Rural Rd.
Tempe, AZ 85283
Tel: (480)838-1751 *Fax:* (480)838-8293
Toll Free: (888)301 - 7630
E-Mail: afa@msn.com
Web Site: www.astrologers.com
Members: 2500 individuals
Staff: 5
Annual Budget: $500-1,000,000
Executive Secretary: Robert W. Cooper
E-Mail: afa@msn.com

Historical Note
Organized to advance astrological education and research. Has members throughout the U.S. and in 54 foreign countries. Membership: $30/year (senior U.S. associate member); $45/year (foreign senior associate member); $45/year (U.S. associate member); $60/year (international associate member); $60/year (U.S. husband and wife membership); $75/year (international husband and wife membership); $50/year (U.S. group affiliate membership); $65/year (international group affiliate membership); $67/year (U.S. associate research member); $72/year (foreign associate research member); $600 (lifetime U.S. associate member); $1,000 (lifetime foreign associate member); $1,000 (lifetime U.S. research member); $1,400 (foreign lifetime research member).

Meetings/Conferences:
Biennial Meetings: even years, July/August

Publications:
AFA Bulletin. m.

American Federation of Government Employees *(1932)*
80 F St. NW
Washington, DC 20001-1528
Tel: (202)639-6419 *Fax:* (202)639-6441
E-Mail: communications@afge.org
Web Site: www.afge.org
Members: 200000 individuals
Staff: 200
Annual Budget: $2-5,000,000
President: John Gage
National Secretary/Treasurer: Jim Davis
Executive Assistant to National President: Brian DeWyngaert
Director, Communications: Enid Doggett
Director, Membership and Organization: Sharon Pinnock
General Counsel: Mark Roth

Historical Note
Established by dissidents from the National Federation of Federal Employees in 1932 who wished to extend the civil service classification system to skilled crafts in government. Chartered by the American Federation of Labor the same year. Sponsors and supports the American Federation of Government Employees Political Action Commitee. AFGE is the largest union representing Federal and District of Columbia workers.

Meetings/Conferences:
Triennial Meetings:

Publications:
Rep Wing. m.
The Government Standard. bi-m.

American Federation of Labor and Congress of Industrial Organizations *(1955)*
815 16th St. NW
Washington, DC 20006
Tel: (202)637-5000 *Fax:* (202)637-5058
Web Site: www.aflcio.org
Members: 53 Unions
Staff: 200
President: John J. Sweeney
Executive Vice President: Linda Chavez-Thompson
Secretary-Treasurer: Richard L. Trumka

Historical Note
The American Federation of Labor was founded in 1886 by 13 national unions on the principle of autonomy for its members. Samuel Gompers was the first president and served 38 years. In 1935 nine of its unions broke away under the leadership of John L. Lewis to form the Congress of Industrial Organizations to push industrial (as opposed to craft) unionism. After 20 years of independence, the AFL and CIO were merged in 1955. The AFL-CIO consists of 50 international unions, 50 state organizations and about 45,000 local unions. Has an annual budget of approximately $72.3 million.

American Federation of Musicians of the United States and Canada *(1896)*
1501 Broadway, Suite 600
New York, NY 10036
Tel: (212)869-1330 *Fax:* (212)764-6134
E-Mail: info@afm.org
Web Site: www.afm.org
Members: 100000 individuals
Staff: 75
Annual Budget: $5-10,000,000
President: Thomas F. Lee
Secretary-Treasurer: Sam Folio

Historical Note
Organized October 19, 1896 in Indianapolis as the American Federation of Musicians and chartered by the American Federation of Labor the same year. AFM represents the professional interests of musicians. Assumed its present name in 1965. Supports the AFM-Tempo Political Contributions Committee.

Meetings/Conferences:
Biennial meetings: odd years

Publications:
International Musician. m. adv.

American Federation of Police and Concerned Citizens *(1966)*
6350 Horizon Dr.
Titusville, FL 32780
Tel: (321)264-0911 *Fax:* (321)264-0033
E-Mail: policeinfo@aphf.org
Web Site: www.aphf.org
Members: 160000 individuals
Staff: 22
Annual Budget: $2-5,000,000
Executive Director: Donna M. Shepherd

Historical Note
Established as the United States Federation of Police, AFP & CC is is largely an educational organization, offering police survivor benefits, a placement service and various types of awards to its members. Conducts a nonprofit public charity. Merged with the American Law Enforcement Officers Association in 1977, and added "and Concerned Citizens" to its name in 1996. Membership: $36/year (active individual); $20/year (associate).

Publications:
Police Times Magazine. q. adv.

American Federation of School Administrators *(1971)*
1101 17th St. NW
Suite 408
Washington, DC 20036
Tel: (202)986-4209 *Fax:* (202)986-4211
E-Mail: afsa@admin.org
Web Site: www.admin.org
Members: 20000 individuals
Staff: 4
Annual Budget: $500-1,000,000
International President: Baxter Atkinson
Executive Vice President: Jill Levy

Historical Note
Established in 1971 as the School Administrators and Supervisors Organizing Committee. Assumed its present name on July 7, 1976. Affiliated with the AFL-CIO in 1976. Memberhip: $72/year.

Meetings/Conferences:
Annual Meetings: Summer

Publications:
AFSA News. 10/year.

American Federation of State, County and Municipal Employees *(1936)*
1625 L St. NW
Washington, DC 20036-5837
Tel: (202)429-1000 *Fax:* (202)429-1293
Web Site: www.afscme.org
Members: 1400000 individuals
Staff: 200
Annual Budget: $10-25,000,000
President: Gerald W. McEntee
Director, Public Affairs: Jean Boland
Director, Information Systems: Steven Gretsuk
Director, Finance: Charlie Jurgonis

Historical Note
Organized in Chicago on December 9, 1935 and chartered by the American Federation of Labor the following year. Merged (1978) with the Civil Service Employees Association of New York. Has an annual budget of approximately $88.2 million. Sponsors and supports the American Federation of State, County and Municipal Employees Political Action Committee.

Meetings/Conferences:
Annual Meetings:

Publications:
The Public Employee. bi-m.

American Federation of Teachers *(1916)*

555 New Jersey Ave. NW
Washington, DC 20001
Tel: (202)879-4440 *Fax:* (202)879-4576
E-Mail: online@aft.org
Web Site: www.aft.org
Members: 1050000 individuals
Staff: 250
Annual Budget: $50-100,000,000
President: Edward J. McElroy
Executive Vice President: Antonia Cortese

Historical Note

AFT was organized in Chicago, IL to represent the economic, social and professional interests of classroom teachers. Advocates public education policies including high academic and conduct standards for students and greater professionalism for teachers and school staff, high-quality public service through cooperative problem solving and workplace innovations, and high-quality health care provided by qualified professionals. AFT has an annual budget of approximately $71.2 million, and is an affiliated international union of the AFL-CIO. The Federation of Public Employees is a division of AFT. Sponsors and supports the AFT Cope Political Action Committee.

Meetings/Conferences:

Biennial Meetings: QuEST Conference in odd years, Convention in even years.

Publications:

Inside AFT.
American Educator. q. adv.
American Teacher. m. adv.
On Campus.
Public Service Reporter. bi-m.
PSRP Reporter.
Healthwire. bi-m.

American Federation of Television and Radio Artists *(1937)*
260 Madison Ave., Seventh Floor
New York, NY 10016
Tel: (212)532-0800 *Fax:* (212)532-2242
E-Mail: aftra@aftra.com
Web Site: www.aftra.com
Members: 74000 individuals
Staff: 200
Annual Budget: $25-50,000,000
National Executive Director: Kim Hedgpeth
E-Mail: aftra@aftra.com

Historical Note

Chartered August 16, 1937 by Associated Actors and Artistes of America as an autonomous branch union representing radio performers. Merged with the Television Authority in 1950. AFTRA negotiates on behalf of artists, performers, and journalists working in the entertainment and news media.

Meetings/Conferences:

Biennial Meetings: Summer/350

Publications:

AFTRA Magazine. q.

American Federation of Violin and Bow Makers *(1980)*
1201 South Main St.
Mt. Airy, MD 21771
Web Site: www.afvbm.com
Members: 120instrumentmakers,restorers
Staff: 9
Annual Budget: $50-100,000
President: Christopher Germain

Historical Note

Professional society of individuals who make and restore violins, violas, cellos and their bows. Address changes bienially in conjunction with the President. Membership: $300/year (individual).

Meetings/Conferences:

Annual Meetings: April

Publications:

Newsletter. q.
Membership Directory. a.

American Feed Industry Association *(1909)*
1501 Wilson Blvd., Suite 1100
Arlington, VA 22209-3199
Tel: (703)524-0810 *Fax:* (703)524-1921
Web Site: www.afia.org
Members: 600 companies
Staff: 20
President: Joel Newman
Public Information Specialist: Judy Pilgrim
Vice President, Public Relations: Rex A. Runyon
E-Mail: rrunyon@afia.org

Historical Note

Formerly (1985) American Feed Manufacturers Association. Absorbed Midwest Feed Manufacturers Association in 1975, National Feed Ingredients Association in 1992, and American Alfalfa Processors Association in 2001. Members are firms which manufacture formula feed and pet food to sell; firms which manufacture formula feed only for their own poultry or livestock; and firms which provide ingredients, services, equipment, and supplies to feed manufacturers.

Publications:

Newsletters (Feedgram, Feed Control Comment, Safety Gram).
AFIA Quarterly. 4/yr. adv.
Membership Directory & Buyers Guide. a. adv.

American Fence Association *(1962)*
800 Roosevelt Rd., Bldg. C
Suite 312
Glen Ellyn, IL 60137
Tel: (630)942-6598 *Fax:* (630)790-3095
Toll Free: (800)822 - 4342
E-Mail: afa@mindspring.com
Web Site: www.americanfenceassociation.com
Members: 2013 companies
Staff: 7
Annual Budget: $2-5,000,000
Executive Director: Lee Cumbragh

Historical Note

Formerly (1993) International Fence Industry Association. Membership: $365/year.

Meetings/Conferences:

Annual Meetings: Winter
2007 - Orlando, FL(Orange County Convention Center)/Jan. 31-Feb. 2
2008 - Las Vegas, NV(Mandalay Bay Convention Center)/Feb. 5-7

Publications:

Buyer's Guide. a.
ASTM Manual.
Across the Fence. q.
Fence Post. bi-m. adv.
Who's Who in Fencing. bi-a. adv.

American Fern Society *(1893)*
c/o Missouri Botanical Garden
P.O. Box 299
St. Louis, MO 63166-0299
Tel: (314)577-9522 *Fax:* (314)577-0830
Web Site: www.amerfernsoc.org
Members: 800 individuals
Annual Budget: $10-25,000
Membership: Dr. George Yatskievych

Historical Note

Founded in 1893 as the Linnaean Fern Chapter of the Aggasiz Association with 24 charter members. Became The American Fern Society in 1905 and was incorporated in the District of Columbia in 1936. Affiliated with the American Institute of Biological Sciences. Has an international membership of pteridologists, botanists and others interested in growing or studying ferns. Has no paid staff. Membership: $8-15/year (individual); $20/year (organization).

Meetings/Conferences:

Annual Meetings: August, with the American Institute of Biological Sciences

Publications:

American Fern Journal. q.
Fiddlehead Forum Newsletter. 5/year.

American Fiber Manufacturers Association *(1933)*
1530 Wilson Blvd., Suite 690
Arlington, VA 22209
Tel: (703)875-0432 *Fax:* (703)875-0907
E-Mail: feb@afma.org
Web Site: www.fibersource.com
Members: 27 manufacturers, 11 associate members
Staff: 8
Annual Budget: $1-2,000,000
President: Paul T. O'Day
E-Mail: feb@afma.org
Vice President: Dr. Robert H. Barker
E-Mail: feb@afma.org

Historical Note

Formerly (1988) the Man-Made Fiber Producers Association. Members are producers of chemically-based or cellulosic fibers such as polyester, nylon, rayon, etc.

Meetings/Conferences:

Annual Meetings: October

Publications:

World Directory of Manufactured Fiber Producers. a.
The Fiber Organon. m.
Manufactured Fiber Fact Book. a.
Guide to Manufactured Fibers. a.

American Fiberboard Association *(1991)*
853 N. Quentin Rd.
Suite 317
Palatine, IL 60067
Tel: (847)934-8394
E-Mail: afa@fiberboard.org
Web Site: www.fiberboard.org
Members: 4 companies
Staff: 1
Annual Budget: $50-100,000
Executive Director: Louis E. Wagner
E-Mail: lwagner@voyager.net

American Filtration and Separations Society *(1987)*
7608 Emerson Ave. South
Richfield, MN 55423
Tel: (612)861-1277 *Fax:* (612)861-7959
E-Mail: afs@afssociety.org
Web Site: www.afssociety.org
Members: 800 individuals
Staff: 1
Annual Budget: $250-500,000
Executive Manager: Suzanne Sower

Historical Note

Formed as a U.S. section of the Filtration Society (U.K.); reorganized as a separate organization in 1987. Members are engineers, scientists and others with an interest in fluid particle separation technology. Membership: $95/year (individual-U.S.); $105/year (individual-Canada and Mexico); $155/year (individual - non-North American); $2,000/year (company).

Meetings/Conferences:

Annual Meetings: Spring/1,000

Publications:

Filtration Journal. q.
AFS Newsletter. m. adv.

American Finance Association *(1940)*
University of California
Haas School of Business
Berkeley, CA 94720-1900
Tel: (510)642-2397 *Fax:* (510)525-6246
Web Site: www.afajof.org
Members: 5000 individuals
Staff: 2
Annual Budget: $250-500,000
Executive Secretary and Treasurer: David Pyle

Historical Note

Established in 1940 and incorporated in Illinois in 1952. Membership consists of both individuals and institutions interested in finance. Affiliated with Allied Social Sciences Association, which manages the annual convention. Membership: $80/year (individual), $776/year (organization).

Meetings/Conferences:

Annual Meetings: In conjunction with the Allied Social Sciences Ass'n

Publications:

Journal of Finance. bi-m. adv.

American Financial Services Association *(1916)*
919 18th St. NW
Washington, DC 20006
Tel: (202)296-5544 *Fax:* (202)223-0321
E-Mail: afsa@afsamail.org
Web Site: www.afsaonline.org
Members: 530 companies

Staff: 27
Annual Budget: $2-5,000,000
President and Chief Executive Officer: H. Randolph Lively, Jr.
E-Mail: rlively@afsamail.org
Vice President, Finance and Human Resources: Jeffrey Cohen
Vice President, Membership Services: Sheilah J. Harrison, CAE
E-Mail: sharrison@afsamail.org
Senior Vice President, Federal Government Affairs: William Himpler
President/Chief Executive Officer, AFSA Education Foundation: M. Susie Irvine
E-Mail: susie@afsamail.org
Senior Vice President and General Counsel: Robert E. McKew
E-Mail: remckew@afsamail.org
Vice President, Meetings and Conferences: Tom Morano
Vice President, Communications: Lynne Strang
E-Mail: lstrang@afsamail.org

Historical Note

The national trade association for providers of financial services to consumers and small businesses. Its member companies are consumer finance and sales finance companies, auto finance companies, and diversified financial services firms. Merged (1971) with the American Industrial Bankers Association which had, in 1965, absorbed the American Finance Conference. Established as the National Consumer Finance Association, it assumed its present name in 1983. Maintains the Consumer Credit Education Foundation and the Consumer Finance Political Action Committee.

Meetings/Conferences:
Annual Meetings: Fall/600

Publications:
Credit. 6/year. adv.
Auto Finance. q.
Consumer Finance Law Bulletin. m.
Independent Operations. q.

American Fire Safety Council *(1973)*
1909 K St. NW
Suite 400
Washington, DC 20006
Tel: (202)419-3269 *Fax:* (202)955-6215
E-Mail: info@fire-safety.net
Web Site: www.fire-safety.net
Members: 40 companies
Staff: 3
Annual Budget: $250-500,000
Program Manager: Mike Heimowitz

Historical Note

Fire Retardant Chemicals Association, d/b/a American Fire Safety Council, promotes fire safety while creating and maintaining the best possible industry climate for member companies to individually market their products and services. Membership fee varies, based on sales volume.

Meetings/Conferences:
Semi-annual Meetings: Spring and Fall

Publications:
Newsletter. m.

American Fire Sprinkler Association *(1981)*
9696 Skillman St.
Suite 300
Dallas, TX 75243
Tel: (214)349-5965 *Fax:* (214)343-8898
E-Mail: afsainfo@firesprinkler.org
Web Site: www.firesprinkler.com
Members: 700 companies
Staff: 16
Annual Budget: $1-2,000,000
President: Steve A. Muncy, CAE
Director, Education Services and Meetings: Marlene Garrett, CMP
Vice President, Engineering and Technical Services: Roland Huggins, P.E.
Director, Membership/Training: Lloyd M. Ivy
Vice President, Marketing and Communications: Janet K. Knowles

Historical Note

AFSA members are contractors, manufacturers, and suppliers of fire sprinkler systems, authorities having jurisdiction, and fire protection consultant firms. AFSA has a merit shop orientation. Membership fee based on sales volume.

Meetings/Conferences:
Annual Meetings: Fall
2007 - Phoenix, AZ(Marriott Desert Ridge)/Sept. 26-30
2008 - Washington, DC(Marriott Warden Park)/Oct. 15-19
2009 - San Diego, CA(Hyatt Manchester)/Oct. 14-18

Publications:
Contractor Network. 2/year.
Sprinkler Age. m. adv.

American Fisheries Society *(1870)*
5410 Grosvenor Ln.
Suite 110
Bethesda, MD 20814-2199
Tel: (301)897-8616 *Fax:* (301)897-8096
E-Mail: main@fisheries.org
Web Site: www.fisheries.org
Members: 8500 individuals
Staff: 23
Annual Budget: $2-5,000,000
Executive Director: Gus Rassam

Historical Note

Founded Dec. 20, 1870 in New York, NY as the American Culturists' Association, became (1878) the American Fish Cultural Association and assumed its current name in 1884. Incorporated in the District of Columbia in 1911. AFS promotes the conservation, development and wise use of commercial and recreational fisheries.

Meetings/Conferences:
Annual Meetings: August or September
2007 - San Francisco, CA(Marriott)/Sept. 2-6

Publications:
Fisheries - A Bulletin of the AFS. m. adv.
North American Journal of Fisheries Management. q.
North American Journal of Aquaculture. q.
Transactions of the American Fisheries Society. bi-m.
Journal of Aquatic Animal Health. q.

American Flint Glass Workers Union *(1878)*

Historical Note

Merged with United Steelworkers of America in 2003.

American Flock Association *(1985)*
Six Beacon St., Suite 1125
Boston, MA 02108
Tel: (617)303-6288 *Fax:* (617)542-2199
E-Mail: info@flocking.org
Web Site: www.flocking.org
Members: 66 companies
Staff: 2
Annual Budget: $100-250,000
Executive Director: Barrett F. Ripley

Historical Note

AFA represents all aspects of the flock industry, including flock suppliers, manufacturers and end users. Flock is very short fiber primarily used in coating paper, fabric, plastic, objects, etc. Membership: $925-2,750/year.

Meetings/Conferences:
Annual Meetings: Fall

Publications:
American Flock Ass'n Directory. bien.
Design with Flock in Mind.

American Floorcovering Alliance *(1979)*
210 W. Cuyler St.
Dalton, GA 30720-8209
Tel: (706)278-4101 *Fax:* (706)278-5323
Toll Free: (800)288 - 4101
E-Mail: afa@americanfloor.org
Web Site: www.americanfloor.org
Members: 190 companies
Staff: 2
Annual Budget: $50-100,000
Executive Director: Wanda Ellis

Historical Note

Founded as Carpet Manufacturers Marketing Association; became Dalton Floor Covering Market Association in 1991 and assumed its current name in 2001. AFA provides marketing services, employee benefits programs, and other services to members of the floor covering industry nationwide. Membership: $400/year.

Meetings/Conferences:
Biennial Meetings: usually in Dalton, GA

Publications:
Newsletter. m.
Directory. a.

American Floral Marketing Council *(1969)*

Historical Note

A council of the Society of American Florists.

American Folklore Society *(1888)*
Mershon Center, Ohio State Univ.
1501 Neil Ave.
Columbus, OH 43201-2602
Tel: (614)292-3375 *Fax:* (614)292-2407
Members: 1500 individuals
Staff: 3
Annual Budget: $250-500,000
Executive Director: Timothy Lloyd

Historical Note

Organized in Cambridge, MA on January 4, 1888 to collect, publish and preserve original folklore material. Membership: $85/year.

Meetings/Conferences:
Annual Meetings: October
2007 - Quebec City, QC, Canada(Hilton)/Oct. 17-21
2008 - Louisville, KY(Hyatt)/Oct. 22-26
2009 - Boise, ID(Grove Hotel)/Oct. 21-25

Publications:
Journal of American Folklore. q. adv.
American Folklore Society Newsletter. bi-m.

American Football Coaches Association *(1922)*
100 Legends Ln.
Waco, TX 76706
Tel: (254)754-9900
E-Mail: info@afca.com
Web Site: www.afca.com
Members: 10000 individuals
Staff: 12
Executive Director: Grant Teaff
Director, Membership and Events: Sandi Atkinson
Director, Marketing and Development: Mel Pulliam

Historical Note

Originally organized to promote college football and to discuss mutual problems. Later interests include a voice in the rule making process, the promotion of safe football playing techniques and the formulation and enforcement of a code of ethics. Membership: $40/year (coaches); $50/year (foreign members).

Meetings/Conferences:
Annual Meetings: January/7,000
2007 - San Antonio, TX(Convention Center)/Jan. 7-10/7300

Publications:
Summer Manual. a.
Proceedings Manual. a.
Directory. a.
The Extra Point. bi-m.

American Forage and Grassland Council *(1944)*
P.O. Box 94
Georgetown, TX 78627-0053
Toll Free: (800)944 - 2342
Web Site: www.afgc.org
Members: 4000 individuals
Staff: 1
Annual Budget: $50-100,000
Executive Secretary: Dana Tucker

Historical Note

Established July 17, 1944, at Rutgers University as the Joint Committee on Grassland Farming. Reorganized on December 19, 1957, as the American Grassland Council. The name was changed July 15, 1968, to the American Forage and Grassland Council. Membership: $30/year (individual); $50-1,000/year (organization/company) based on type and size.

Meetings/Conferences:
Annual Meetings: Spring

Publications:
The Forage Leader. q.
Membership Directory. a.
Proceedings. a.

American Foreign Law Association *(1925)*
c/o Bryan Cave LLP
1290 Ave. of the Americas
New York, NY 10104
Tel: (212)541-2258 *Fax:* (212)541-4630
E-Mail: alodell@bryancave.com
Members: 300 individuals
Staff: 2
Annual Budget: $10-25,000
Treasurer: Andrew L. Odell

Historical Note
AFLA promotes the advancement of learning through the study, understanding and practice of foreign, comparative and international law; cooperation with other professional societies interested in similar objectives; fostering legal research; and the publication and dissemination of legal materials. Membership: $90/year (individual); $40/year (foreign/non-resident); $35/year (student).

Meetings/Conferences:
Monthly Luncheon Meeting: September to May in New York City

Publications:
The American Journal of Comparative Law. q.
AFLA Newsletter. 3/year.

American Foreign Service Association *(1924)*
2101 E St. NW
Washington, DC 20037
Tel: (202)338-4045 *Fax:* (202)338-6820
E-Mail: afsa@afsa.org
Web Site: www.afsa.org
Members: 13000 individuals
Staff: 30
Annual Budget: $2-5,000,000
Executive Director: Susan Reardon
E-Mail: reardon@afsa.org
Director, Member Services: Janet Hedrick
E-Mail: hedrick@afsa.org
Editor: Steve Honley
E-Mail: honley@afsa.org
General Counsel: Sharon Papp
E-Mail: papps@state.gov

Historical Note
Professional association of Foreign Service employees. Acts as the elected representative of all Foreign Service personnel in the AID, FAS, FCS and USIA and State Department bargaining units. Membership fee varies, based on service grade.

Meetings/Conferences:
Annual Meetings: *Washington, DC/late Fall*

Publications:
Foreign Service Journal. m. adv.

American Foreign Service Protective Association *(1929)*
1716 N St. NW
Washington, DC 20036-2902
Tel: (202)833-4910 *Fax:* (202)833-4918
E-Mail: afspa@afspa.org
Web Site: www.afspa.org
Members: 25000 individuals
Chief Executive Officer: John P. Shumate
Office Manager: Vincent Myers

Historical Note
AFSPA members are Foreign Service personnel and other government employees assigned overseas. Primarily acts as a group insurance provider to its membership.

American Forensic Association *(1949)*
Box 256
River Falls, WI 54022
Tel: (715)425-3198 *Fax:* (715)425-9533
Toll Free: (800)228 - 5424
E-Mail: amforensicassoc@aol.com
Web Site: www.americanforensics.org
Members: 1200 individuals
Staff: 2
Annual Budget: $50-100,000
Executive Secretary: James W. Pratt

Historical Note
Established in 1949 to promote effective and responsible oral communication. Membership composed primarily of college and high school directors of debate and speech programs. Affiliated with the National Communication Association. Membership: $75/year (individual); $85/year (organization/company).

Meetings/Conferences:
Annual Meetings: *November, with Speech Communication Ass'n*

Publications:
Argumentation and Advocacy. q. adv.
Newsletter. 3/year. adv.

American Forest and Paper Association *(1993)*
1111 19th St. NW
Suite 800
Washington, DC 20036
Tel: (202)463-2700 *Fax:* (202)463-2785
E-Mail: info@afandpa.org
Web Site: www.afandpa.org
Members: 250 companies and trade ass'ns
Staff: 150
Annual Budget: $25-50,000,000
Vice President, Finance and Administraton and Chief Financial Officer: Ann W. Bittman
Senior Director, Marketing: Stephany East
Vice President, Congressional Affairs: Donna Harman
Senior Director, Human Resources and Development: Michael P. Hoagland
Vice President, Communications: Kristin Seeger
Senior Manager, Meetings: Susan Van Eaton

Historical Note
Formed by the merger of the American Forest Council (1932), American Paper Institute (1964) and the National Forest Products Association (1902) in 1993. AF&PA represents companies which grow, harvest and process wood and woodfiber; manufacture pulp, paper and paperboard products from both virgin and recovered fiber; and produce solid wood products. AF&PA divisions include: American Wood Council, Containerboard and Kraft Paper; Forest Resources, Paperboard, Paper and Pulp. Annual Budget: $38 million (2000). Membership: Dues are set and collected by each product group based on all member company primary paper sales, solid wood product sales and the cords of forest resources consumed in pulp production.

American Forest Resource Council *(2000)*
1500 S.W. First Ave., Suite 765
Portland, OR 97201
Tel: (503)222-9505 *Fax:* (503)222-3255
E-Mail: staff@afrc.ws
Web Site: www.afrc.ws
Members: 80 companies
Staff: 10
Annual Budget: $1-2,000,000
President: Tom Partin

Historical Note
AFRC was founded in October 2000 as a result of a merger between the Independent Forest Products Association (IFPA) and the Northwest Forestry Association (NFA). AFRC represents forest product manufacturers and forest landowners--from small, family-owned companies to large multi-national corporations--in 12 states, west of the Great Lakes.

Meetings/Conferences:
Annual Meetings: *March*

Publications:
AFRC Newsletter. bi-w.

American Forests *(1875)*
P.O. Box 2000
Washington, DC 20013-2000
Tel: (202)737-1944 *Fax:* (202)737-2457
E-Mail: info@amfor.org
Web Site: www.americanforests.org
Members: 148000 individuals
Staff: 25
Annual Budget: $250-500,000
Executive Director: Deborah Gangloff
E-Mail: gangloff@amfor.org
Vice President, Policy: Gerald Gray
E-Mail: ggray@amfor.org
Senior Vice President, Urban Ecosystems Center: Gary Moll
E-Mail: gmoll@amfor.org
Vice President, Development: Jeff Olson
E-Mail: gmoll@amfor.org

Historical Note
Formerly (1992) American Forestry Association. Founded September 10, 1875 in Chicago, IL for "the protection of the existing forests of the country from unnecessary waste, and the promotion of the propagation and planting of useful trees." Merged in 1882 with the American Forestry Congress. Membership: $25/year.

Meetings/Conferences:
Annual Meetings: *Fall*

Publications:
American Forests. q.

American Foundry Society *(1896)*
1695 N. Penny Ln.
Schaumburg, IL 60173-4555
Tel: (847)824-0181 *Fax:* (847)824-7848
Toll Free: (800)537 - 4237
Web Site: www.afsinc.org
Members: 9500 individuals
Staff: 37
Annual Budget: $5-10,000,000
Executive Vice President: Jerry Call
Director, Member Services: Rick Callavaro
Publisher, Modern Casting: Rolf Petersen
Senior Technical Director: Steve Robison

Historical Note
Founded as the American Foundrymen's Association; became American Foundrymen's Society in 1948 and assumed its present name in 2002. AFS is a technical and trade association of individuals and companies concerned with the castings industry. The Cast Metals Institute is the educational arm of the AFS.

Meetings/Conferences:
Annual Meetings: *April-May*
2007 – Houston, TX(Hilton Americas)

Publications:
Modern Casting. m. adv.
Transactions. a.
Labor Agreement Settlement Data. 9-12/year.
Nat'l Survey of Wages and Benefits in the Foundry Industry. a.
Engineered Casting Solutions. q. adv.

American Fracture Association *(1938)*

Historical Note
Address unknown in 2005.

American Frozen Food Institute *(1942)*
2000 Corporate Ridge, Suite 1000
McLean, VA 22102-7805
Tel: (703)821-0770 *Fax:* (703)821-1350
Web Site: www.affi.com
Members: 510 companies
Staff: 15
Annual Budget: $2-5,000,000
President and Chief Executive Officer: Leslie G. Sarasin, CAE
E-Mail: lsarasin@affi.com
Senior Director, Industrial Affairs: Lucas Darnell
E-Mail: ldarnell@AFFI.com
Senior Director, Conventions and Meetings: Jenny Mitchell
E-Mail: jmitchell@AFFI.com
Vice President, Legislative Affairs: Susan Siemietkowski

Historical Note
Formerly (1970) National Association of Frozen Food Packers. Absorbed the California Freezers Association in 1967. Supports the AFFI Political Action Committee. Affiliated with the International Frozen Food Association; Frozen Potato Products Institute; National Frozen Pizza Institute; National Yogurt Association; Texas-Mexico Frozen Food Council; and Food Industry Environmental Council.

Meetings/Conferences:
Annual Meetings: *Fall/1,800*

Publications:
Frozen Express. daily. adv.
Capitol Connection. w.
Membership Directory & Buyers Guide. a. adv.

American Fur Merchant's Association *(1898)*

Historical Note
A division of Fur Information Council of America, which provides administrative support.

American Furniture Manufacturers Association
Historical Note
Became American Home Furnishings Alliance in 2004.

American Galloway Breeders Association *(1888)*
310 W. Spruce St.
Missoula, MT 59802
Tel: (406)728-5719 *Fax:* (406)721-6300
E-Mail: info@americangalloway.com
Web Site: www.americangalloway.com
Members: 75 individuals
Annual Budget: under $10,000
President: Stephen Castner
Historical Note
Formed in Chicago, November 23, 1882 by U.S. and Canadian breeders of Galloway cattle. Incorporated in the State of Montana. Absorbed the Galloway Performance International in 1973. Membership: $75/year.
Meetings/Conferences:
Annual Meetings: October
Publications:
Midwest Galloway News. q. adv.
The Galloway Advantage. q. adv.

American Galvanizers Association *(1935)*
6881 S. Holly Circle, Suite 108
Centennial, CO 80012-1145
Tel: (720)554-0900 *Fax:* (720)554-0909
Toll Free: (800)468 - 7732
E-Mail: aga@galvanizeit.org
Web Site: www.galvanizeit.org
Members: 150 companies
Staff: 8
Annual Budget: $500-1,000,000
Executive Director: Philip G. Rahrig
Marketing Manager: John Krzywicki
Technical Director: Thomas J. Langill, Ph.D.
Historical Note
Organized in 1933 and incorporated in 1935 in the Commonwealth of Pennsylvania. Represents the after-fabrication hot dip galvinizing industry whose members provide anti-corrosion coatings to steel products. Formerly (1989) American Hot Dip Galvanizers Association.
Meetings/Conferences:
Annual Meetings: Spring/200
2007 – Cancun, Mexico(La Meridian)/March 26-30/150
Publications:
e-News. m.
Directory. a.
Newsletter. bi-m.

American Gaming Association *(1995)*
1299 Pennsylvania Ave. NW, Suite 1175
Washington, DC 20004
Tel: (202)552-2675 *Fax:* (202)552-2676
E-Mail: info@americangaming.org
Web Site: www.americangaming.org
Members: 50 companies
Staff: 10
President and Chief Executive Officer: Frank J. Fahrenkopf, Jr.
Vice President, Government Affairs: Walton Chambers
Vice President, Government Affairs: D. Brett Hale
Vice President, Government Affairs: Dorothy Jackson
Senior Vice President and Executive Director: Judy Patterson
Historical Note
Trade association representing the commercial casino industry.
Meetings/Conferences:
2007 – Las Vegas, NV(Convention Center)/Nov. 13-15
2008 – Las Vegas, NV(Convention Center)/Nov. 18-20
Publications:
Responsible Gaming Quarterly. q.
Inside the AGA. m.

American Gas Association *(1918)*
400 N. Capitol St., Suite 450
Washington, DC 20001
Tel: (202)824-7000 *Fax:* (202)824-7115
E-Mail: WEBMASTER@AGA.ORG
Web Site: www.aga.org
Members: 192 companies
Staff: 85
Annual Budget: $25-50,000,000
President and Chief Executive Officer: David N. Parker, CAE
General Counsel: Kevin B. Belford
Senior Vice President, Policy and Planning: Roger B. Cooper
Senior Vice President, Corporate Affairs and Corporate Secretary: Jay Copan
Chief Information Officer: Gary Gardner
Vice President, Communications: Greg Pruett
Executive Vice President, Public Affairs: Richard D. Shelby
Senior Vice President, Operations and Engineering Management: Lori S. Traweek
Historical Note
Formed by a merger of the Gas Institute and the Commercial Gas Association in 1918. Connected with the Gas Employees Political Action Committee (GASPAC). Has an annual budget of approximately $25 million. Supports the Natural Gas Vehicle Coalition.
Meetings/Conferences:
Annual Meetings: Fall
Publications:
American Gas Magazine. m. adv.

American Gastroenterological Association *(1897)*
4930 Del Ray Ave.
Bethesda, MD 20814
Tel: (301)654-2055 *Fax:* (301)654-5920
E-Mail: member@gastro.org
Web Site: www.gastro.org
Members: 13000 individuals
Staff: 65
Annual Budget: $10-25,000,000
Executive Vice President: Robert Greenberg
Vice President, Public Policy: Michael Roberts
Senior Vice President: Lynn P. Robinson
VIce President, Finance and Administration: Thomas J. Serena
Historical Note
Membership: $345-400/year, plus $40 application fee (individual); $95/year (first year fee for trainees).
Meetings/Conferences:
Annual Meetings: Spring
Publications:
Digestive Health and Nutrition. bi-m. adv.
Clinical Hepatology and Gastroenterology. m. adv.
AGA eDigest (online). w.
Gastroenterology. m. adv.
AGA Perspectives. m. adv.

American Gear Manufacturers Association *(1916)*
500 Montgomery St., Suite 350
Alexandria, VA 22314-1581
Tel: (703)684-0211 *Fax:* (703)684-0242
E-Mail: webmaster@agma.org
Web Site: www.agma.org
Members: 400 companies
Staff: 14
Annual Budget: $2-5,000,000
President: Joe T. Franklin, Jr., CAE
E-Mail: franklin@agma.org
Vice President, Technical Division: William Bradley
E-Mail: bradley@agma.org
Vice President, Administration Division: Kurt Medert
E-Mail: medert@agma.org
Vice President, Membership: Jan Potter
Historical Note
Members are gear manufacturers, makers of gear cutting and checking equipment, gearing teachers, suppliers to the industry and purchasers of gear products. Membership: $1,315-15,335/year, based on annual sales (company).
Meetings/Conferences:
Annual Meetings: Fall/Spring
2007 – Marco Island, FL(Marco Island Marriott)/March 15-17
2007 – Detroit, MI(Cobo Center)/Oct. 7-10/3000
Publications:
Gear Industry Journal. q. adv.

American Gelbvieh Association *(1971)*
10900 Dover St.
Westminster, CO 80021
Tel: (303)465-2333 *Fax:* (303)465-2339
E-Mail: info@gelbvieh.org
Web Site: www.gelbvieh.org
Members: 1700 individuals
Staff: 15
Annual Budget: $1-2,000,000
Executive Director: Wayne Vanderwert
Historical Note
Members are breeders and promoters of Gelbvieh cattle. Membership: $75/year (initial membership); $50/year (renewal).
Meetings/Conferences:
Annual Meetings: Denver, CO/Jan./300
Publications:
Gelbvieh World. 11/year. adv.

American Gem Society *(1934)*
8881 W. Sahara Ave.
Las Vegas, NV 89117-5865
Tel: (702)255-6500 *Fax:* (702)233-6122
Web Site: www.AGS.org
Members: 3600 individuals
Staff: 17
Annual Budget: $2-5,000,000
Executive Director and Chief Executive Officer: Ruth Batson
E-Mail: rbatson@ags.org
Deputy Executive Director: Cindy Ramsey
E-Mail: cramsey@ags.org
Historical Note
A professional association of U.S. and Canadian jewelers. Certifies members as Registered Jewelers, Certified Gemologists or Certified Gemologist Appraisers.
Meetings/Conferences:
Annual Meetings: Spring/800-1,000
Publications:
Spectra. bi-m.

American Gem Trade Association *(1981)*
3030 LBJ Freeway, Suite 840
Dallas, TX 75234
Tel: (214)742-4367 *Fax:* (214)742-7334
Toll Free: (800)972 - 1162
E-Mail: info@agta.org
Web Site: www.agta.org
Members: 750 firms
Staff: 16
Annual Budget: $2-5,000,000
Executive Director: Douglas K. Hucker
E-Mail: doug@agta.org
Manager, Marketing: Elizabeth Holt
E-Mail: elizabeth@agta.org
Manager, Trade Show: Mary Lou Keen
E-Mail: marylou@agta.org
Director, Laboratory: Kenneth Scarratt
Historical Note
Established in Tucson, AZ and incorporated in New York, AGTA is a trade association for the colored gemstone industry in the United States and Canada. Also operates a Geological Test Center in New York, NY. Membership: $250/year (affiliate); $500/year (firm).
Meetings/Conferences:
Annual Meetings: February, in Tucson, Arizona
Publications:
Prism Newsletter. q.
Directory. a.

American Genetic Association *(1903)*
P.O. Box 257
Buckeystown, MD 21717-0257
Tel: (301)695-9292
Web Site: www.theaga.org
Members: 850 individuals
Staff: 1
Executive Vice President: Dr. James E. Womack
E-Mail: jwomack@cvm.tamu.edu
Historical Note
Established as the American Breeders Association in December 1903 in St. Louis by a committee from the Association of Land Grant Colleges. Name changed in

1913 to the American Genetic Association when it was incorporated in the District of Columbia. Affiliated with the American Association for the Advancement of Science. A member society of the International Genetics Federation. Promotes the study of genetics and its application to plant and animal improvement and human welfare. Membership: $48/year (individual); $170/year (institution); $24/year (student); $45/year (joint); foreign membership rates are available.

Publications:
Journal of Heredity. bi-m. adv.

American Geographical Society *(1851)*
120 Wall St., Suite 100
New York, NY 10005-3904
Tel: (212)422-5456 *Fax:* (212)422-5480
E-Mail: ags@amcrgeog.org
Web Site: www.amergeog.org
Members: 3000 fellows and subscribers
Staff: 4
Annual Budget: $500-1,000,000
Executive Director: Mary Lynne Bird

Historical Note
Initiated in 1851 and incorporated on May 22, 1854, in New York as The American Geographical and Statistical Society; assumed current name in 1871. Over the years AGS has sponsored research projects, symposia and lectures and published books, periodicals and maps, awards and travel programs. Membership: $50/year (individual); $64/year (institutional); $1,000/year (organization).

Meetings/Conferences:
Annual Meetings: None held

Publications:
Focus on Geography. q. adv.
Ubique. 3/year.
Geographical Review. q. adv.

American Geological Institute *(1948)*
4220 King St.
Alexandria, VA 22302-1502
Tel: (703)379-2480 *Fax:* (703)379-7563
E-Mail: agi@agiweb.org
Web Site: www.agiweb.org
Members: 43 societies
Staff: 60
Annual Budget: $5-10,000,000
Executive Director: Christopher M. Keane
Director, Education and Development: Ann Benbow
Controller: Patrick Burks
Director, Information Systems: Sharon N. Tahirkheli

Historical Note
Founded in Washington in 1948, AGI was operated as part of the National Academy of Sciences, 1948-1962. Incorporated (1962) as a separate entity in the District of Columbia. A federation of societies, the Institute is a member of the American Association for the Advancement of Science, Commission on Professionals in Science and Technology, and the Board on Earth Sciences (NRC). Membership: $2/year (individual member societies).

Meetings/Conferences:
Semi-Annual Meetings: Spring and Fall

Publications:
Guide to Geoscience Departments. a. adv.
Geotimes. m. adv.
Directory of Geoscience Departments. a. adv.
Bibliography and Index of Geology. m.

American Geophysical Union *(1919)*
2000 Florida Ave. NW
Washington, DC 20009-1277
Tel: (202)462-6900 *Fax:* (202)328-0566
Toll Free: (800)966 - 2481
E-Mail: service@agu.org
Web Site: www.agu.org
Members: 45000 individuals
Staff: 150
Annual Budget: $10-25,000,000
Executive Director: Fred Spilhaus
Deputy Executive Director and Director, Publications: Judy Holoviak
Director, Development: Joanna Tahar
Director, Meetings: Brenda L. Weaver, CMP

Historical Note
Incorporated in 1972 in Washington, DC. Members are individual research scientists and others, including organizations, interested in supporting the objectives of AGU. AGU is dedicated to the study of Earth and its environment in space. Member society of the Renewable Natural Resources Foundation and the American Institute of Physics. Membership: $20/year (individual); $7/year (student).

Meetings/Conferences:
Semi-Annual Meetings: Spring and Fall
2007 - Acapulco, Mexico/May 22-25/3000
2007 - San Francisco, CA/Dec. 10-14/13000

Publications:
Virtual Choice. online daily.
Space Weather. online daily. adv.
Geophysical Research Letters. online daily.
Radio Science. online daily.
Tectonics. online daily.
Reviews of Geophysics. online daily.
Paleoceanography. online daily.
Internat'l Journal of Geomagnetism and Aeronomy. online daily.
Global Biogeochemical Cycles. online daily.
Nonlinear Processes in Geophysics. online daily.
Earth Interactions. online daily.
EOS, Transactions. online daily. adv.
Journal of Geophysical Research. online daily.
Water Resources Research. online daily.

American Geriatrics Society *(1942)*
350 Fifth Ave., Suite 801
New York, NY 10118-0801
Tel: (212)308-1414 *Fax:* (212)832-8646
Toll Free: (800)247 - 4779
Web Site: www.americangeriatrics.org
Members: 6100 individuals
Staff: 22
Annual Budget: $2-5,000,000
Executive Vice President: Linda Hiddemen Barondess
Associate Vice President, Professional Education and Special Projects: Nancy Lundebjerg
Manager, Governance and Public Policy: Julie Zaharatos

Historical Note
Founded in Atlantic City, NJ, in 1942. Incorporated in Rhode Island (1952) and later in New York (1963). Members are licensed physicians and allied health care professionals whose practice emphasis is in geriatric medicine and whose interests lie in geriatric medicine and gerontology. Membership: $195/year.

Meetings/Conferences:
Annual Meetings: Spring/2,000
2007 - Seattle, WA(Seattle Convention Center)/May 2-5/2500

Publications:
Journal of the American Geriatrics Society. m. adv.
Newsletter. bi-m. adv.
AGS Membership Directory. a.
Geriatrics Review Syllabus. trien.

American Glovebox Society *(1986)*
P.O. Box 9099
Santa Rosa, CA 95405
Tel: (707)527-0444 *Fax:* (707)578-4406
Toll Free: (800)530 - 1022
E-Mail: ags@gloveboxsociety.org
Web Site: http://gloveboxsociety.org
Members: 280 individuals
Staff: 5
Association Manager: Dorothy Calegari

Historical Note
Members are companies manufacturing equipment for remote or safe handling of toxic, radioactive, or infectious substances.

Meetings/Conferences:
Annual Meetings: August

Publications:
Enclosure Newsletter. q. adv.

American Goat Society *(1936)*
735 Oakridge Ln.
Pipe Creek, TX 78063-5658
Tel: (830)535-4247 *Fax:* (830)535-4561
E-Mail: office@americangoatsociety.com
Web Site: www.americangoatsociety.com
Members: 834 individuals
Staff: 1
Annual Budget: $10-25,000
Office Manager: Amy Kowalik

Historical Note
Breeders and fanciers of purebred dairy goats. Maintains herdbooks on eight breeds: French Alpine, Nubians, Saanens, Toggenburgs, LaMancha, Oberhasli, Pygmy and Nigerian Dwarf. Has an annual budget of approximately $20,000. Membership: $20/year (individual); $30/year (family); $10/year (junior); $15/year (senior - over 65).

Meetings/Conferences:
Annual Meetings: July

Publications:
The Voice of AGS. q. adv.
Yearbook. a. adv.
Buyers Guide. a. adv.
Roster of AGS Membership. a.

American Greyhound Track Operators Association *(1946)*
Melbourne Greyhound Park
1100 Wickham Rd.
Melbourne, FL 32935
Tel: (321)259-1143 *Fax:* (321)259-3437
Web Site: www.agtoa.com
Members: 48 tracks
Staff: 2
Annual Budget: $1-2,000,000
Managing Coordinator: Rob Christmas

Historical Note
Members are greyhound tracks. AGTOA represents the interests of its members, and is the American member organization of the World Greyhound Racing Federation.

Meetings/Conferences:
Annual Meetings: March

Publications:
Track Facts. a.

American Group Psychotherapy Association *(1942)*
25 E. 21st St., Sixth Floor
New York, NY 10010
Tel: (212)477-2677 *Fax:* (212)979-6627
Toll Free: (877)668 - 2472
E-Mail: info@agpa.org
Web Site: www.agpa.org
Members: 3000 individuals
Staff: 5
Annual Budget: $500-1,000,000
Chief Executive Officer: Marsha S. Block, CAE, CFRE
Director, Professional Development: Angela Moore Stephens, CAE

Historical Note
Includes psychiatrists, psychologists, social workers, psychiatric nurses and others in the mental health field interested in the theory, practice and research of group psychotherapy. Established on June 16, 1942 in New York City at the Jewish Board of Guidance as the American Group Therapy Association. Membership: $125/year, minimum based on annual professional income (individual); $60/year (student).

Meetings/Conferences:
Annual Meetings: February/1,200
2007 - Austin, TX(Hilton Austin)/March 5-10

Publications:
AGPA Newsletter. bi-m. adv.
International Journal of Group Psychotherapy. q. adv.
Group Connections. m..

American Guernsey Association *(1877)*
7614 Slate Ridge Blvd.
Reynoldsburg, OH 43068-0666
Tel: (614)864-2409 *Fax:* (614)864-5614
Web Site: www.usguernsey.com
Members: 1427 individuals
Staff: 9
Annual Budget: $500-1,000,000
Executive Secretary-Treasurer: Seth Johnson
E-Mail: sjohnson@usguernsey.com
Membership Records: Ida Albert

E-Mail: ialbert@usguernsey.com
Programs Coordinator: Brian Schewbly
E-Mail: bschewbly@usguernsey.com

Historical Note

Formerly (1987) American Guernsey Cattle Club. Members are breeders of Guernsey dairy cattle. Maintains herd registry. Member of the National Pedigree Livestock Council and the Purebred Dairy Cattle Association. Membership: $150/lifetime or $15/year.

Publications:

Guernsey Directory. every 18 months.
Guernsey Breeder's Journal. 10/year. adv.
Guernsey Sire Summary. semi-a.

American Guild of Hypnotherapists *(1975)*
2200 Veteran Blvd., Suite 108
Kenner, LA 70062-4005
Tel: (504)468-2900 *Fax:* (504)468-3213
Members: 685 individuals
Staff: 2
Annual Budget: under $10,000
President: Reg Sheldrick, Ph.D.
Executive Vice President, Communications: Dr. Grayce Lee

Historical Note

Membership: $50/year (initial registration); $35/year (renewal).

Publications:

Journal of Hypnotherapy. q.
Newsletter. irreg.

American Guild of Music *(1901)*
P.O. Box 599
Warren, MI 48090
Tel: (248)336-9388
E-Mail: agm@americanguild.org
Web Site: www.americanguild.org
Members: 5000 individuals
Staff: 1
Annual Budget: $50-100,000
Meetings and Conventions: Richard Chizmadia
E-Mail: richardchizmadia@americanguild.org

Historical Note

AGM members are music teachers, musicians, music retailers, and others interested in promoting music and music education. Sponsors regional and national competitions.

Meetings/Conferences:

Annual Meetings: July

Publications:

American Guild of Music NEWS. q. adv.

American Guild of Musical Artists *(1936)*
1430 Broadway, 14th Floor
New York, NY 10018
Tel: (212)265-3687 *Fax:* (212)262-9088
E-Mail: agma@musicalartists.org
Web Site: www.musicalartists.org
Members: 5700 individuals
Staff: 18
Annual Budget: $2-5,000,000
National Executive Director: Alan S. Gordon
E-Mail: agma@musicalartists.org

Historical Note

Founded March 11, 1936 in New York City by Lawrence Tibbett and Jascha Heifetz. Became an autonomous branch union of Associated Actors and Artistes of America August 30, 1937 and merged at the same time with the Grand Opera Artists Association. Absorbed the Grand Opera Choral Alliance in 1938. Acts as the exclusive bargaining agent for concert musical artists, opera singers, ballet dancers, modern dancers, and stage personnel in those fields. Membership: $78/year (individual).

Meetings/Conferences:

Semi-Annual Meetings:

Publications:

AGMAzine. q.

American Guild of Organists *(1896)*
475 Riverside Dr., Suite 1260
New York, NY 10115
Tel: (212)870-2310 *Fax:* (212)870-2163
Toll Free: (800)246 - 5115
Web Site: www.agohq.org
Members: 21000 individuals
Staff: 9
Annual Budget: $2-5,000,000
Executive Director: James E. Thomashower
E-Mail: jet@agohq.org
Editor: Anthony Baglivi
E-Mail: abaglivi@agohq.org
Director, Development and Communications: F. Anthony Thurman
E-Mail: fathurman@agohq.org

Historical Note

The AGO is the national professional association serving the organ and choral music fields. Chartered by the Board of Regents of the University of the State of New York in 1896, it now serves more than 20,000 members throughout the U.S. and abroad. The purpose of the AGO is to promote the organ in its historic and evolving roles, to encourage excellence in the performance of organ and choral music, and to provide a forum for mutual support, inspiration, education and certification of Guild members. Membership: $84/year.

Meetings/Conferences:

Biennial meetings: National Convention: Even years/1,500-2,000 attendees.
2008 – Minneapolis, MN(Hilton)/June 22-26/2000
2010 – Washington, DC/2000
2012 – Nashville, TN/2000

Publications:

The American Organist Magazine. m. adv.

American Guild of Variety Artists *(1939)*
363 Seventh Ave., 17th Floor
New York, NY 10001
Tel: (212)675-1003 *Fax:* (212)633-0097
E-Mail: agvany@aol.com
Members: 5000 individuals
Staff: 15
Annual Budget: $250-500,000
President: Rod McKuen
E-Mail: agvany@aol.com

Historical Note

An autonomous component of Associated Actors and Artistes of America (AFL-CIO).

American Hackney Horse Society *(1891)*
4059 Iron Works Pkwy.
Suite A-3
Lexington, KY 40511-8462
Tel: (859)255-8694 *Fax:* (859)255-0177
E-Mail: ahhscsl@qx.net
Web Site: www.hackneysociety.com
Members: 900 individuals
Staff: 2
Annual Budget: $100-250,000
Executive Secretary: Frances Bjalobok, M.S.

Historical Note

The registry for Hackney horses and ponies. Promotes the breeding, registering and showing of registered Hackney horses and Hackney ponies. Membership: $35/year (individual); $50/year (family); $15.00/year (junior); $500/year (life membership).

Meetings/Conferences:

Semi-annual Meetings:
2007 – Cincinnati, OH(Westin)/January

Publications:

Web Site - Marketplace. adv.
AHHS Stud Book. bien. adv.
AHHS Newsletter. q. adv.
Membership Directory. bien. adv.

American Hair Loss Council
125 Seventh Street, Suite 625
Pittsburgh, PA 15222
Tel: (412)765-3666
E-Mail: info@ahlc.org
Web Site: www.ahlc.org
Members: 130
Executive Secretary-Treasurer: Susan Kettering

Historical Note

AHLC members specialize in surgical and non-surgical treatments for progressive or illness-related hair loss. Has no paid officers or full-time staff. Membership: $275/year.

Publications:

AHLC News. q.

American Hampshire Sheep Association *(1889)*
15603 173rd Ave.
Milo, IA 50166
Tel: (641)942-6402 *Fax:* (641)942-6502
E-Mail: info@hampshires.com
Web Site: www.hampshires.com
Members: 900 individuals
Staff: 3
Annual Budget: $100-250,000
Contact: Tammy Bruce
Publications: Carrie Taylor

Historical Note

Members are breeders and fanciers of Hampshire sheep. AHSA is a member of the National Pedigree Livestock Council.

Meetings/Conferences:

Annual Meetings: Fall

Publications:

The Hampshire Heartbeat. q. adv.

American Handwriting Analysis Foundation *(1967)*
P.O. Box 6201
San Jose, CA 95150-6201
Tel: (408)377-6775
Toll Free: (800)826 - 7774
E-Mail: ahaf@iwhome.com
Web Site: www.handwritingfoundation.org
Members: 250 individuals
Staff: 5
Annual Budget: $10-25,000
President: Heidi H. Harralson

Historical Note

AHAF was established to educate the public and promote the growth of graphology. AHAF has established professional requirements for certification. Membership: $50/year (United States); $60/year (Canada/Mexico); $70/year (non-North American).

Meetings/Conferences:

Annual Meetings: summer

Publications:

In the Margin. q.
International Handwriting Analysis Journal. bi-m.

American Hanoverian Society *(1971)*
4067 Iron Works Pkwy.
Suite One
Lexington, KY 40511-8462
Tel: (859)255-4141 *Fax:* (859)255-8467
E-Mail: ahsoffice@aol.com
Web Site: www.hanoverian.org
Members: 2000 individuals
Staff: 4
Annual Budget: $250-500,000
Executive Director: Hugh Bellis-Jones
E-Mail: ahsoffice@aol.com

Historical Note

Members own and breed Hanoverian horses. Membership: $25-$80/year (individual).

Publications:

The Hanoverian. q. adv.
Yearbook. a. adv.
Stallion Directory and Yearbook. a. adv.

American Hardboard Association *(1952)*

Historical Note

Absorbed by Composite Panel Association in 2004.

American Hardware Manufacturers Association *(1901)*
801 N. Plaza Dr.
Schaumburg, IL 60173-4977
Tel: (847)605-1025 *Fax:* (847)605-1030
E-Mail: info@ahma.org
Web Site: www.ahma.org
Members: 800 companies
Staff: 25
President and Chief Executive Officer: Tim Farrell

Historical Note

AHMA is a premier trade association serving the home improvement industry. Member companies include approximately 800 manufacturers, as well as a smaller number of industry trade publications and agencies representing manufacturers.

Meetings/Conferences:
Annual Meetings: AHMA Hardware Show/Chicago, IL in April

Publications:
Washington Report. m.
Issue Briefing. m.
Eagle Newsletter. bi-m.
Employee Relations Report. m.

American Hardwood Export Council *(1989)*
1111 19th St. NW
Suite 800
Washington, DC 20036
Tel: (202)463-2720 *Fax:* (202)463-2787
E-Mail: michael_snow@afandpa.org
Web Site: www.ahec.org
Members: 135 companies
Staff: 20
Annual Budget: $2-5,000,000
Executive Director: Michael S. Snow

Historical Note
Founded by the merger of Hardwood Export Trade Council and National Lumber Exporters Association (1989). Exists to aid in the export of hardwoods and hardwood products overseas. A division of American Forest and Paper Association, which provides administrative support. Membership: $1,250-5,000/year (based on export value).

Meetings/Conferences:
Annual Meetings: In conjunction with the Nat'l Hardwood Lumber Ass'n

American Harp Society *(1962)*
P.O. Box 38334
Los Angeles, CA 90038-0334
Tel: (323)469-3050
Web Site: www.harpsociety.org
Members: 3300 individuals
Staff: 3
Annual Budget: $100-250,000
Executive Secretary: Kathleen Moon

Historical Note
Members are ndividuals interested in the lore and literature of the harp. Affiliated with the World Association of Harpists (Paris, France). Membership: $35/year.

Meetings/Conferences:
Annual Meetings: Summer
2007 - Chicago, IL(Roosevelt University)/June 18-21
2008 - Detroit, MI(St. John's Conference Center)/June 23-26

Publications:
American Harp Journal. bien. adv.

American Head and Neck Society *(1959)*
11300 W. Olympic Blvd., Suite 600
Los Angeles, CA 90064
Tel: (310)437-0559 *Fax:* (310)437-0585
E-Mail: admin@ahns.org
Web Site: www.headandneckcancer.org
Members: 1650 individuals
Staff: 1
Annual Budget: $50-100,000
Secretary: John Ridge, M.D.
E-Mail: admin@ahns.org

Historical Note
Members are fellows of the American College of Surgeons whose primary interest is head and neck surgery. Absorbed Society of Head and Neck Surgeons in 1998. Membership: $300/year.

Meetings/Conferences:
Annual Meetings: Spring

Publications:
E-newsletter. m. adv.

American Headache Society *(1959)*
19 Mantua Rd.
Mt. Royal, NJ 08061
Tel: (856)423-0043 *Fax:* (856)423-0082
E-Mail: ahshq@talley.com
Web Site: www.ahsnet.org
Members: 2400 individuals
Staff: 6
Annual Budget: $2-5,000,000
Executive Director: Linda K. McGillicuddy

Historical Note
Formerly (2000) American Association for the Study of Headache. Members are healthcare professionals with an interest in the illness of headache. Membership: $150/year (individual).

Meetings/Conferences:
Annual Meetings: June

Publications:
Headache: The Journal of Head & Face Pain. 10/year. adv.

American Health and Beauty Aids Institute *(1981)*
P.O. Box 19510
Chicago, IL 60619-0510
Tel: (708)333-8740 *Fax:* (708)333-8741
E-Mail: ahbai1@sbcglobal.net
Web Site: www.ahbai.org
Members: 11 companies
Staff: 3
Annual Budget: $250-500,000
Executive Director: Geri Duncan Jones

Historical Note
Members are makers of beauty products for ethnic consumers.

Meetings/Conferences:
Semi-Annual Meetings: Spring and Fall

Publications:
Associate Membership Directory. a. adv.
Salon Advantage News. q. adv.

American Health Care Association *(1949)*
1201 L St. NW
Washington, DC 20005
Tel: (202)842-4444 *Fax:* (202)842-3860
Web Site: www.ahca.org
Members: 10000 state licensed facilities
Staff: 75
Annual Budget: $10-25,000,000
President and Chief Executive Officer: Bruce Yarwood
Senior Vice President, Policy and Government Relations: David E. Hebert
Vice President, Administration and Human Resources: Penny L. Prue

Historical Note
A federation of state associations of health care facilities formed by a merger of the American Association of Nursing Homes and the National Association of Registered Nursing Homes (founded in 1949). Formerly (1974) the American Nursing Home Association. Absorbed (1984) National Council of Health Centers. Sponsors and supports the AHCA Political Action Committee. Membership: $7.55/bed/year.

Meetings/Conferences:
2007 - Boston, MA/Oct. 7-10
2008 - Nashville, TN/Oct. 5-8
2009 - Chicago, IL/Oct. 4-7

Publications:
Assisted Living Focus.
Provider Magazine. m. adv.
AHCA Notes. m.

American Health Information Management Association *(1928)*
233 N. Michigan Ave., Suite 2150
Chicago, IL 60601-5800
Tel: (312)233-1100 *Fax:* (312)233-1090
E-Mail: info@ahima.org
Web Site: www.ahima.org
Members: 40000 individuals
Staff: 85
Annual Budget: $10-25,000,000
Executive Vice President and Chief Executive Officer: Linda L. Kloss, RRA

Historical Note
Founded in Boston in 1928 as the Association of Record Librarians of North America. Became the American Association of Medical Record Librarians in 1935. Incorporated in Illinois in 1953, it became the American Medical Record Association in 1969 and assumed its present name in 1992. Has an annual budget of approximately $8 million. Membership: $145/year (active); $135/year (associate); $20/year (student).

Meetings/Conferences:
Annual Meetings: October/5,000
2007 - Philadelphia, PA/Oct. 6-11
2008 - Seattle, WA/Oct. 11-16
2009 - Dallas, TX/Oct. 3-8
2010 - Orlando, FL/Sept. 25-30

Publications:
Keeping Pace. a.
AHIMA Advantage. bi-m. adv.
In Confidence. bi-m.
Journal of AHIMA. 10/year. adv.

American Health Lawyers Association *(1971)*
1025 Connecticut Ave. NW
Suite 600
Washington, DC 20036-5405
Tel: (202)833-1100 *Fax:* (202)833-1105
E-Mail: info@healthlawyers.org
Web Site: www.healthlawyers.org
Members: 9500 individuals
Staff: 31
Annual Budget: $5-10,000,000
Executive Vice President and Chief Executive Officer: Peter Leibold
Director, Professional Resources: Cynthia Cohner
Director, Strategic Planning, Membership and Marketing: Kerry B. Hoggard, CAE, PAHM
Director, Programs: Anne H. Hoover
Deputy Executive Vice President and Chief Operating Officer: Wayne Miller

Historical Note
Founded as National Health Lawyers Association; merged with American Academy of Healthcare Attorneys, and assumed its current name in 1998. Members are private, corporate, government and institutional lawyers involved with or practicing law in the health care field. Membership is available to non-lawyers. Conducts non-partisan educational programs and publishes books and periodicals of interest to health attorneys and providers of health care. Membership: $150-315/year (full member); $20/year (student).

Publications:
Health Lawyers News. m. adv.
Journal of Health Law. q.
Health Law Digest. m.

American Health Planning Association *(1972)*
7245 Arlington Blvd., Suite 300
Falls Church, VA 22042
Tel: (703)573-3103 *Fax:* (703)573-1276
E-Mail: aphanet@aol.com
Web Site: www.ahpanet.org
Members: 150 organizations
Annual Budget: $50-100,000
President: Dean Montgomery

Historical Note
Members are state, regional and national health planning and other organizations. Formerly the Association of Areawide Health Planning Agencies and (1978) the American Association for Comprehensive Health Planning. Provides national voice for health care consumers, purchasers, providers and business and labor representatives who are interested in health planning to improve health care system. Has no paid staff. Membership: $50/year (individual); $500-1,000/year (organization); $250/year (affiliate); $25/year (student).

Publications:
Health Planning Bibliography. irreg.
Today in Health Planning. q.
Directory. a.

American Health Quality Association *(1973)*
1155 21st St. NW
Suite 202
Washington, DC 20036
Tel: (202)331-5790 *Fax:* (202)331-9334
E-Mail: info@ahqa.org
Web Site: www.ahqa.org
Members: 1200 individuals
Staff: 12
Annual Budget: $2-5,000,000
Executive Vice President: David Shulke
E-Mail: dshulke@ahqa.org
Public Affairs Associate: Jennifer Felsher
Vice President, Government Affairs: Todd Ketch

Senior Director, Finance: Jacqueline Oglesby Cook

Historical Note

Established as American Association of Professional Standards Review Organizations; became American Medical Peer Review Association in 1983, and assumed its present name in 1996. AHQA promotes health care quality through community-based, independent quality evaluation and improvement programs.

Meetings/Conferences:

Annual Meetings: Fall

2007 – New Orleans, LA(New Orleans Marriott)/Feb. 13-15

2008 – San Francisco, CA/Feb. 25-29

Publications:

AHQA Matters. bi-m.

American Healthcare Radiology Administrators *(1973)*

490-B Boston Post Rd.
Suite 101
Sudbury, MA 01776-3301
Tel: (978)443-7591 *Fax:* (978)443-8046
Toll Free: (800)334 - 2472
E-Mail: info@ahraonline.org
Web Site: www.ahraonline.org
Members: 3900 individuals
Staff: 10
Annual Budget: $2-5,000,000
Executive Director: Edward J. Cronin
Manager, Communications: Karen Guy-Dyer

Historical Note

Formerly (1986) American Hospital Radiology Administrators. Membership: $140/year.

Meetings/Conferences:

Annual Meetings: August/1,300

2007 – Orlando, FL(Gaylord Palms Hotel)/July 8-12

Publications:

Directory. a. adv.
Link. m. adv.
Radiology Management. q. adv.

American Heart Association *(1924)*

7272 Greenville Ave.
Dallas, TX 75231
Tel: (214)373-6300
Toll Free: (800)242 - 8721
Web Site: www.americanheart.org
Members: 29506 individuals
Annual Budget: Over $100,000,000
Chief Executive Officer: M. Cass Wheeler
Chief Operating Officer: Nancy A. Brown

Historical Note

Incorporated in New York in 1924. Reorganized in 1948 as a national voluntary health agency. Maintains 14 scientific councils which, through representatives to the AHA Research Committee, help determine the allocation of funds in research support, the nature and scope of professional education activities, and at which point knowledge is sufficiently advanced to be translated and applied to community-based education programs. Has an annual budget of approximately $560 million.

Meetings/Conferences:

Scientific Session: Fall/25,000

Publications:

Arteriosclerosis, Thrombosis and Vascular Biology. m. adv.
Cardiovascular Nursing. bi-m.
Circulation. bi-m. adv.
Circulation Research. m. adv.
Currents in Emergency Cardiac Care. q.
Hypertension. m. adv.
Stroke. m. adv.

American Heartworm Society *(1974)*

P.O. Box 667
Batavia, IL 60510-0667
Tel: (630)208-8398
E-Mail: heartwormsociety@earthlink.net
Web Site: www.heartwormsociety.org
Members: 1200 individuals
Vice President: Dr. John W. McCall
President: Dr. Charles Thomas Nelson

Historical Note

Members are practitioners and research scientists dedicated to research and dissemination of knowledge about canine heartworm disease. Membership: $25/year (member); $30/year (subscriber).

Meetings/Conferences:

Annual Meetings:

Publications:

American Heartworm Society Bulletin. q.
Proceedings of Heartworm Symposium. trien.

American Helicopter Society International *(1943)*

217 N. Washington St.
Alexandria, VA 22314-2538
Tel: (703)684-6777 *Fax:* (703)739-9279
E-Mail: staff@vtol.org
Web Site: www.vtol.org
Members: 6000 individuals
Staff: 6
Annual Budget: $1-2,000,000
Executive Director: M.E. "Rhett" Flater
Director, Meetings and Marketing: Dave Renzi

Historical Note

Founded and incorporated in 1943 in Connecticut.

Meetings/Conferences:

Annual Meetings: May

Publications:

Annual Forum Proceedings. a. adv.
Vertiflite. 4/year. adv.
AHS Internat'l Directory (online). a. adv.
Journal of the American Helicopter Society. q.

American Herbal Products Association *(1982)*

8484 Georgia Ave., Suite 370
Silver Spring, MD 20910-5604
Tel: (301)588-1171 *Fax:* (301)588-1174
E-Mail: info@ahpa.org
Web Site: www.apha.org
Members: 400 companies
Staff: 4
Annual Budget: $500-1,000,000
President: Michael McGuffin
E-Mail: mmcguffin@apha.org
Director, Administrator: Devon Powell
Director, Communications: Karen Robin
E-Mail: krobin@ahpa.org

Historical Note

A trade association representing manufacturers, distributors, raw material suppliers and service associates of herbal products. Membership: $1000-50,000/year (organization).

Meetings/Conferences:

Triennial:

Publications:

Newsletter. m. adv.
Membership Directory. a. adv.

American Herbalists Guild *(1989)*

141 Nob Hill Rd.
Cheshire, CT 06410
Tel: (203)272-6731 *Fax:* (203)272-8550
E-Mail: ahgoffice@earthlink.net
Web Site: www.americanherbalist.com
Members: 1100 individuals
Staff: 2
Annual Budget: $100-250,000
Executive Director: Tracy Romm

Historical Note

AHG is a professional, peer-review organization for herbalists specializing in the medicinal use of plants. Membership: $120/year (professional); $60/year (general); $50/year (student).

Meetings/Conferences:

Annual Meetings: Fall

Publications:

Journal of the American Herbalists Guild.
Mentorship Handbook.
Herbalist Newsletter Guild News & Views. q.
Directory of Herb Education. a.
Recommended Reading List. a.

American Hereford Association *(1881)*

P.O. Box 014059
Kansas City, MO 64101
Tel: (816)842-3757 *Fax:* (816)842-6931
E-Mail: aha@hereford.org
Web Site: www.hereford.org
Members: 11000 individuals
Staff: 35
Annual Budget: $5-10,000,000
Executive Vice President: Craig Huffhines
E-Mail: aha@hereford.org

Historical Note

Members are breeders of Hereford beef cattle. Absorbed the American Polled Hereford Association in 1995. A member of the National Pedigreed Livestock Council, AHA has an annual budget of approximately $6 million. Membership: $15/year.

Meetings/Conferences:

Annual Meetings: November in Kansas City, MO

Publications:

Hereford World. 11/year. adv.

American Hernia Society *(1997)*

P.O. Box 4834
Englewood, CO 80155
Tel: (303)567-7899 *Fax:* (303)771-2550
E-Mail: contact@americanherniasociety.org
Web Site: www.americanherniasociety.org
Members: 600 individuals
Staff: 2
Annual Budget: $100-250,000
Executive Director: Carol Goodard
E-Mail: contact@americanherniasociety.org

Historical Note

Membership: $100/year, plus $60 for journal subscription.

Meetings/Conferences:

2007 – Hollywood, FL(Diplomat Resort & Spa)/March 8-11/400

Publications:

Hernia Journal. q. adv.

American Highland Cattle Association *(1948)*

200 Livestock Exchange Bldg.
4701 Marion St.
Denver, CO 80216
Tel: (303)292-9102 *Fax:* (303)292-9171
E-Mail: info@highlandcattleusa.org
Web Site: www.highlandcattleusa.org
Members: 1500 individuals
Staff: 2
Annual Budget: $100-250,000
Manager, Operations: Ginnah Moses

Historical Note

Formerly (1994) American Scotch Highland Breeder's Association. Maintains a breed registry and promotes the Highland breed through research, education, and national events, including the Annual Show and Sale.

Meetings/Conferences:

Annual Meetings: Meetings: Semi-Annual; Conventions: Annual

Publications:

The Bagpipe. q. adv.

American Highway Users Alliance *(1932)*

1101 14th St. NW
Suite 750
Washington, DC 20005
Tel: (202)857-1200 *Fax:* (202)857-1220
Toll Free: (800)483 - 4544
Web Site: www.highways.org
Members: 300 companies and organizations
Annual Budget: $2-5,000,000
President and Chief Executive Officer: Gregory M. Cohen
Director, Membership: Cheryl J. Hollins

Historical Note

Founded as Highway Users Federation for Safety and Mobility; assumed current name in 1995. Product of a merger of the Automotive Safety Foundation (1937), Auto Industries Highway Safety Committee (1946) and National Highway Users Conference (1932). Absorbed the Auto Dealers Traffic Safety Council in 1970. Members are motorists, truckers and businesses who benefit from a safe national highway system and efficient movement of goods and people. Also includes manufacturers of vehicles, tires, and related accessories. membership: $250-$500,000/year (company/organization).

Publications:

Driving Ahead. m.

Rules of the Road. w.

American Historical Association *(1884)*
400 A St. SE
Washington, DC 20003
Tel: (202)544-2422 *Fax:* (202)544-8307
E-Mail: aha@historians.org
Web Site: www.historians.org
Members: 16231 individuals
Staff: 21
Annual Budget: $2-5,000,000
Executive Director: Arnita A. Jones
Controller: Randy Norrell
Membership Coordinator: Pamela Scott-Pinkney
Historical Note
An off-shoot of the American Social Science Association, the AHA came into being at the annual meeting of the ASSA in Saratoga, NY in 1884. AHA's founders were a group of historians who felt that the ASSA had over-specialized in such matters as prison reform, charity, etc. Incorporated by Congress in 1889 to promote historical studies, collect and preserve historical manuscripts and disseminate the fruits of historical research. A member of the American Council of Learned Societies. Membership: $34-165/year (individual); varies with income.
Meetings/Conferences:
Annual Meetings: Winter
2007 – Atlanta, GA(Hilton Marriot)/Jan. 4-7/6000
Publications:
Grants and Fellowships of Interest to Historians Online.
American Historical Review. 5/year. adv.
Perspectives (Newsletter). 9/year. adv.
Directory of Affiliated Societies.
Annual Report. a.
Directory of History Departments and Organizations. a.

American Hockey Coaches Association *(1947)*
Seven Concord St.
Gloucester, MA 01930
Tel: (781)245-4177 *Fax:* (781)245-2492
Web Site: www.ahcahockey.com
Members: 1300 individuals
Staff: 1
Annual Budget: $100-250,000
Executive Director: Joe Bertagna
Historical Note
Resolves local and intersectional differences on rules, officiating and recruiting in the sport of hockey. Membership: $25-315/year (individual/school).
Meetings/Conferences:
Annual Meetings: last week of April
Publications:
American Hockey Coaches Directory. a.
Newsletter. 8/year.

American Hockey League *(1936)*
One Monarch Pl.
Springfield, MA 01144
Tel: (413)781-2030 *Fax:* (413)733-4767
E-Mail: info@theahl.com
Web Site: www.theahl.com
Members: 27 clubs
Staff: 11
Annual Budget: $2-5,000,000
President and Chief Executive Officer: David A. Andrews
E-Mail: info@theahl.com
Vice President, Communications: Jason Chaimovich
E-Mail: info@theahl.com
Historical Note
AHL is a professional ice hockey league functioning as a development league for the National Hockey League. Each member club is affiliated, or has a working agreement, with an NHL team.
Meetings/Conferences:
Annual Meetings: as of 2004, AHL has four quarterly meetings of its Board of Governors
Publications:
AHL Official Rule Book. a. adv.
AHL Master Schedule. a. adv.
Annual Media Guide & Play Off Guide. a. adv.

American Holistic Medical Association *(1978)*
P.O. Box 2016
Edmonds, WA 98020
Tel: (425)967-0737 *Fax:* (425)771-9588
E-Mail: ahma@holisticmedicine.org
Web Site: www.holisticmedicine.org
Members: 900 individuals
Staff: 3
Annual Budget: $250-500,000
Executive Director: Jane Kantor
Historical Note
AHMA members are licensed physicians, medical and osteopathic students, and allied health care practitioners. Membership: $295/year.
Meetings/Conferences:
Annual Meetings: Spring
Publications:
Newsletter. q. adv.
Nat'l Referral Directory (online and print).
Directory of Members. a.

American Holistic Nurses Association *(1981)*
P.O. Box 2130
Flagstaff, AZ 86003-2130
Tel: (928)526-2196 Ext: 13 *Fax:* (928)526-2752
Toll Free: (800)278 - 2462 Ext: 13
E-Mail: info@ahna.org
Web Site: www.ahna.org
Members: 2700 individuals
Staff: 8
Annual Budget: $250-500,000
Communications and Marketing: Rebecca Lara
Historical Note
AHNA is a non-profit, educational association for nurses and allied health care professionals embracing the concept of holistic health, a harmony between mind, body and spirit. Provides a support system, communications network, recognition, research, and educational opportunities. Membership: $125/year.
Meetings/Conferences:
Annual Meetings: Summer
Publications:
Beginnings (newsletter). 5/year. adv.
Journal of Holistic Nursing. q. adv.

American Holistic Veterinary Medical Association *(1982)*
2218 Old Emmorton Road
Bel Air, MD 21015
Tel: (410)569-0795 *Fax:* (410)569-2346
E-Mail: office@ahvma.org
Web Site: www.ahvma.org
Members: 900 individuals
Staff: 4
Annual Budget: $100-250,000
Executive Director: Carvel G. Tiekert, D.V.M.
E-Mail: office@ahvma.org
Historical Note
Formerly (1985) the American Veterinary Holistic Medical Association. AHVMA members have an interest in unconventional systems of veterinary medicine as a complement to conventional approaches.
Meetings/Conferences:
Annual Meetings: Fall
Publications:
Journal of the AHVMA. 4/year. adv.

American Home Furnishings Alliance *(1905)*
P.O. Box HP-7
High Point, NC 27261
Tel: (336)884-5000 *Fax:* (336)884-5303
Web Site: www.ahfa.us
Members: 400 companies
Staff: 19
Annual Budget: $2-5,000,000
Chief Executive Officer: Andy S. Counts
Director, Communications: Pat Bowling
Historical Note
Founded as the Southern Furniture Manufacturers Association; became (1984) American Furniture Manufacturers Association when it merged with the National Association of Furniture Manufacturers and assumed its current name in 2004. Members are manufacturers of household and international furniture. Maintains a government affairs office in Washington, DC. Divisions include Summer and Casual Furniture Manufacturers Association, suppliers, transportation and logistics, marketing, finance, manufacturing, and human relations. Sponsors and supports the FurnPac political action committee.
Meetings/Conferences:
Annual Meetings: Fall
Publications:
AHFA Membership Directory. a.
The Furniture Executive. m.

American Homebrewers Association *(1978)*
736 Pearl St.
Boulder, CO 80302-5006
Tel: (303)447-0816 *Fax:* (303)447-2825
Toll Free: (888)822 - 6273
Web Site: www.beertown.org
Members: 9000 individuals
Staff: 23
Director: Paul Gatza
Publications:
Zymurgy for the Homebrewer and Beer Lover. 6/yr.

American Horse Council *(1969)*
1616 H St. NW, Seventh Floor
Washington, DC 20006
Tel: (202)296-4031 *Fax:* (202)296-1970
E-Mail: ahc@horsecouncil.org
Web Site: www.horsecouncil.org
Members: 2000 individuals
Staff: 6
Annual Budget: $500-1,000,000
President: James J. Hickey, Jr.
Director, Adminstration: Katherine A. Luedeke
Historical Note
The trade association of the equine industry. Members are organizations and individuals who need to be kept informed of tax and regulatory developments affecting such matters as breeding, racing, showing, pleasure riding, funding of livestock research, import-export restrictions and similar matters affecting those who live by horses. Membership: $25-5,000/year.
Meetings/Conferences:
Annual Meetings: April
2007 – Washington, DC(L'Enfant Plaza Hotel)/June 17-19
Publications:
AHC Newsletter. q.
Horse Industry Directory. a.
Tax Bulletin. bi-m.

American Horse Publications Association *(1970)*
49 Spinnaker Circle
South Daytona, FL 32119
Tel: (386)760-7743 *Fax:* (386)760-7728
E-Mail: ahorsepubs@aol.com
Web Site: www.americanhorsepubs.org
Members: 200 individuals
Staff: 200
Annual Budget: $50-100,000
Executive Director: Christine W. Brune
E-Mail: ahorsepubs@aol.com
Historical Note
An association of horse-oriented publications in the U.S. and Canada. Membership: $100-$200/year.
Meetings/Conferences:
Annual Meetings: Summer
2007 – Albuquerque, NM(Albuquerque Marriot Pyramid North)/June 21-23/150
Publications:
AHP For the Record. q.

American Horse Shows Association
Historical Note
Became Equestrian USA in 2002.

American Horticultural Society *(1922)*
7931 E. Boulevard Dr.
Alexandria, VA 22308
Tel: (703)768-5700 *Fax:* (703)768-8700
Toll Free: (800)777 - 7931
Web Site: www.ahs.org
Members: 36,000 individuals
Staff: 18
Annual Budget: $2-5,000,000
President and Chief Executive Officer: Katy Moss Warner

Membership and Business Operations Office Manager: Janet Daniels
E-Mail: jdaniels@ahs.org
Director, Communications: David J. Ellis
Director, Horticulture Programs: Tom Underwood
E-Mail: tunderwood@ahs.org

Historical Note

Merged in 1926 with the National Horticultural Society; incorporated in 1932 in the District of Columbia and consolidated in 1959 with the American Horticultural Council. AHS educates and inspires people of all ages to become successful and environmentally responsible gardeners by advancing the art and science of horticulture. Membership includes the widest range of horticultural concerns, with individuals, scientific organizations, institutions and commercial enterprises spanning interests from technical research to advanced amateur gardening. Membership: $35/year (individual); $5,000-10,000/year (corporate).

Publications:
The American Gardener. bi-m. adv.

American Horticultural Therapy Association *(1973)*
3570 E. 12th Ave.
Denver, CO 80206
Tel: (303)322-2482 *Fax:* (303)322-2485
Toll Free: (800)634 - 1603
E-Mail: info@ahta.org
Web Site: www.ahta.org
Members: 700 individuals
Staff: 2
Annual Budget: $100-250,000
Executive: Joy Harrison
Director, Special Projects: Stephanie Shulman

Historical Note

Formerly (1987) the National Council for Therapy and Rehabilitation Through Horticulture. Members are professional therapists, rehabilitation specialists and others using horticulture for rehabilitation. Membership: $95/year (individual with U.S. mailing address); $120/year (individual with Canadian address); $135/year (individual with mailing address outside the U.S. or Canada).

Meetings/Conferences:
Annual Meetings: Fall
2007 – Washington, DC/Oct. 26-27

Publications:
Newsletter. bi-m.
Journal of Therapeutic Horticulture. a.
AHTA Membership Directory. a. adv.

American Hospital Association *(1898)*
One N. Franklin
Chicago, IL 60606-3421
Tel: (312)422-3000 *Fax:* (312)422-4796
Web Site: www.aha.org
Members: 50000 individuals
Staff: 800
Annual Budget: $50-100,000,000
President: Richard J. Davidson
Executive Vice President, Advocacy and Public Policy: Richard Pollack
Senior Vice President, Strategic Communications: Richard H. Wade

Historical Note

Formerly (1906) Association of Hospital Superintendents of the United States and Canada. Has an annual budget of approximately $81 million. Sponsors the AHA Political Action Committee, established in 1978.

Meetings/Conferences:
Annual Meetings:

Publications:
Hospital Literature Index. q.
AHA News. w. adv.
Hospitals & Health Networks. semi-m. adv.
The Hospital Medical Staff. m.
Trustee. m. adv.
Hospital Statistics. a.
AHA Guide to the Health Care Field. a.
Health Facilities Management. m.
Medical Staff Leader. m.

American Hotel & Lodging Association *(1910)*
1201 New York Ave. NW
Suite 600
Washington, DC 20005-3931
Tel: (202)289-3100 *Fax:* (202)289-3106
E-Mail: joe@ahla.com
Web Site: www.ahma.com
Members: 10000 properties/1.4 million rooms
Staff: 60
Annual Budget: $10-25,000,000
President and Chief Executive Officer: Joseph A. McInerney
Vice President and Chief Information Officer: Laurence Barron
Executive Vice President, Public Policy: Marlene Colucci
Senior Vice President, Member and Industry Relations: Pam Hewlett Inman
Executive Vice President and Chief Financial Officer: Jorri Jeon
Vice President, Government Affairs: Kevin Maher
Vice President, Conventions and Events: Kimberly Miles, CMP

Historical Note

A federation of state hotel & motel associations. Formerly (1917) American Hotel Protective Association, (1962) American Hotel Association and (2000) American Hotel and Motel Association . Supports the American Hotel-Motel Political Action Committee. Has an annual budget of $18.4 million. Member of the Trade Show Bureau.

Publications:
Lodging Magazine. m. adv.
Directory of Hotel & Lodging Companies. a. adv.

American Humanist Association *(1941)*
1777 T St. NW
Washington, DC 20009-7125
Tel: (202)238-9088 *Fax:* (202)238-9003
Toll Free: (800)837 - 3792
E-Mail: aha@americanhumanists.org
Web Site: www.americanhumanist.org/hsfamily/huumanist.htm
Members: 7000 individuals
Staff: 12
Annual Budget: $500-1,000,000
Co-Executive Director: Tony Hileman
Co-Executive Director: Roy Speckhardt

Historical Note

AHA members are academics and other individuals interested in humanist philosophy. Membership: $50/year.

Meetings/Conferences:
Annual Meetings: Always in an academic or religous setting

Publications:
The Humanist. bi-m. adv.
Essays in Humanism. a.
The Communicator. q.
Religious Humanism. semi-a. adv.

American Humor Studies Association *(1974)*
3800 Lindell Blvd.
St. Louis, MO 63108-3414
Tel: (314)977-3068 *Fax:* (314)977-1514
Web Site: www.americanhumor.org
Members: 400 individuals
Staff: 1
Annual Budget: under $10,000
Executive Director: Janice McIntire-Strasburg
E-Mail: mcintire@slu.edu

Historical Note

Investigates American humor and popular culture topics to expand scholarship and understanding of American humor. An allied organization of the Modern Language Association of America and the American Literature Association. Membership: $20/year.

Meetings/Conferences:
Semi-Annual Meetings: May with ALA and December with MLA

Publications:
Studies in American Humor. a. adv.
To Wit (newsletter). semi-a. adv.

American Hungarian Educators Association *(1974)*
4515 Willard Ave., Apt. 2210
Chevy Chase, MD 20815-3685
Tel: (301)659-4759
Web Site: www.magyar.org/ahea
Members: 300 individuals
Staff: 1
Annual Budget: under $10,000
Executive Director: Eniko Molnar Basa

Historical Note

Chartered in the State of Maryland in 1976. Members are educators concerned with the teaching and dissemination of Hungarian history, language, literature, art and music. Works to further Hungarian studies in American and Canadian universities. Membership: $15/year.

Meetings/Conferences:
Annual Meetings: Spring
2007 – New York, NY(St. Johns College)/April/100
2008 – Pittsburgh, PA(Duquesne)/April/100

Publications:
American Hungarian Educator. a.
E-journal of the AHEA. a.

American Hydrogen Association *(1989)*
1739 W. Seventh Ave.
Mesa, AZ 85202-1906
Tel: (602)328-4238 Ext: 273 *Fax:* (480)967-6601
Toll Free: (888)493 - 7643
E-Mail: aha@clean-air.org
Web Site: www.clean-air.org
Members: 6200 individuals
Staff: 8
Annual Budget: $50-100,000
President: Roy E. McAlister
Editor: Byron Anderson
Director, Government Relations: Charles Terry

Historical Note

AHA is a non-profit association of individuals and institutions, technical and non-technical, with an interest in the promotion of renewable energy systems. Membership: $39/year (regular); $25/year (student); $2,500/year (corporate).

Publications:
Hydrogen Today. bi-m. adv.

American Hypnosis Association *(1972)*
18607 Ventura Blvd., Suite 310
Tarzana, CA 91356
Tel: (818)758-2730 *Fax:* (818)344-2262
Toll Free: (800)990 - 0426
Web Site: www.hypnosis.edu/aha/
Members: 1500 individuals
Staff: 6
Annual Budget: $25-50,000
President: George Kappas

Historical Note

AHA members are hypnotherapy professionals and other professionals with an interest in hypnosis and related fields. Membership: $25 initiation fee and $24/year (individual).

Meetings/Conferences:
Annual Meetings:

Publications:
American Hypnotherapist. q.

American Immigration Lawyers Association *(1946)*
918 F St. NW
Washington, DC 20004-1400
Tel: (202)216-2400 *Fax:* (202)783-7853
E-Mail: executive@aila.org
Web Site: www.aila.org
Members: 9000 individuals
Staff: 50
Annual Budget: $5-10,000,000
Executive Director: Jeanne A. Butterfield
Director, Membership: Jennifer English Lynch
Deputy Director, Finance and Administration: Susan D. Quarles

Historical Note

Formerly (1981) the Association of Immigration and Nationality Lawyers. Members are attorneys practicing in the field of immigration and nationality law. Membership: $225/year (less than three years of practice); $300/year (more than three years of practice).

Meetings/Conferences:
Annual Meetings: June/2,000
2007 - Orlando, FL(Orlando World Center Marriott Resort)/June 13-17
2008 - Vancouver, BC, Canada/June 25-28

Publications:
AILA Business Immigration News. q.
Directory. a. adv.
Immigration Law Today. bi-m. adv.

American Import Shippers Association *(1987)*
662 Main St.
New Rochelle, NY 10801
Tel: (914)633-3770 *Fax:* (914)633-4041
E-Mail: info@aisaship.com
Web Site: www.aisaship.com
Members: 250 companies
Staff: 5
Executive Director: Hubert Wiesenmaier
Vice President, Operations: Fred dela Pewa

Historical Note
Members are small to medium-sized U.S. firms importing textiles and apparel. Membership: $250/year plus service fee.

Publications:
ATTN - Apparel Trade & Transportation News. m.

American Importers and Exporters Meat Products Group *(1955)*
One Atlanta Plaza
Elizabeth, NJ 07206
Tel: (908)351-8000 *Fax:* (908)351-0761
Members: 30 companies
Staff: 3
President: George Gellert

Historical Note
Formerly (1983) Meat Products Group of the American Association of Exporters and Importers and (1992) American Importers Meat Products Group. Members are companies importing pork and pork products into the United States.

American Importers Association *(1999)*
214 7th St. North
Safety Harbor, FL 34695
Tel: (727)724-0900
Web Site: www.americanimporters.org
Members: 13,000
Director General: Phillip W. Byrd

Historical Note
AIA serves as a forum connecting exporters with importers and buyers in the U.S.

Publications:
AIA monthly e-newsletter. m.

American Incense Manufacturers Association *(1973)*
11745 S. Ironwood Dr.
Yuma, AZ 85367
Tel: (928)919-0346 *Fax:* (928)342-6202
Members: 4 companies
Annual Budget: under $10,000
President: Fred B. Block
E-Mail: fredbhb@msn.com

Historical Note
AIMA members are companies manufacturing incense in the United States. Industry suppliers may join as associated members. AIMA works to foster the growth of domestically manufactured incense, for export in the United States and abroad. Membership: $100/year.

Meetings/Conferences:
Annual Meetings: July
2007 - Addis Ababa, Ethiopia/July 2-4/20
2008 - Nome, AK/July 2-4/20
2009 - San Jose, Costa Rica/July 2-4
2010 - Hanoi, Vietnam/July 2-4

American Independent Business Alliance *(2000)*
222 S. Black Ave.
Bozeman, MT 59715-4716
Tel: (406)582-1255
E-Mail: info@amiba.net
Web Site: www.amiba.net
Members: 30 Independent Business Alliances
Staff: 2
Annual Budget: $100-250,000
Executive Director: Jennifer Rockne
E-Mail: jennifer@amiba.net
Director, Outreach: Jeff Milchen

Historical Note
Organized as an outgrowth of the Boulder Independent Business Alliance, AMIBA seeks to help communities establish Independent Business Alliances and to coordinate activities between IBAs nationwide. AMIBA provides resources to IBAs and works with them to help them succeed.

Meetings/Conferences:
Annual Meetings: Quarterly/10-20

American Indian Council of Architects and Engineers *(1976)*

Historical Note
Address unknown in 2006.

American Indian Science and Engineering Society
P.O. Box 9828
Albuquerque, NM 87119-9828
Tel: (505)765-1052 *Fax:* (505)765-5608
E-Mail: info@aises.org
Web Site: www.aises.org
Members: 3000 individuals
Staff: 10
Annual Budget: $2-5,000,000
Executive Director: Pamala Silas
Events Coordinator: Christy Davies

Historical Note
Membership: $25/year (student); $65/year (professional).

Meetings/Conferences:
Annual Meetings: Nov./2,000
2007 - Phoenix, AZ/Nov. 1-3/2200
2008 - Anaheim, CA/November

Publications:
Winds of Change Magazine. q. adv.
American Indian College Guide. a. adv.
Education Newsletter. q. adv.

American Indonesian Chamber of Commerce *(1949)*
317 Madison Ave., Suite 169
New York, NY 10017
Tel: (212)687-4505 *Fax:* (212)687-5844
E-Mail: aiccny@bigplanet.com
Web Site: www.aiccusa.org
Members: 50 individuals
Staff: 2
Annual Budget: $100-250,000
Executive Director: Wayne Forrest

Historical Note
The Chamber works to increase business and understanding between the United States and Indonesia and serves organizations and individuals involved commercially with Indonesia. Membership: $1000/year (corporate); $125/year (individual).

Meetings/Conferences:
Monthly Meetings:

Publications:
Outlook Indonesia. q.

American Industrial Hygiene Association *(1939)*
2700 Prosperity Ave., Suite 250
Fairfax, VA 22031
Tel: (703)849-8888 *Fax:* (703)207-3561
E-Mail: infonet@aiha.org
Web Site: www.aiha.org
Members: 12000 individuals
Staff: 57
Annual Budget: $10-25,000,000
Executive Director: Steven Davis, CAE
E-Mail: sdavis@aiha.org
Assistant Executive Director: Peter J. O'Neil, CAE
E-Mail: poneil@aiha.org

Historical Note
Absorbed American Academy of Industrial Hygiene in 1999. Promotes the study and control of environmental stresses arising in or from the work place or its products, in relation to the health or well-being of workers and the public. Has an annual budget of approximately $14 million. Membership: $166/year (individual); $300 and $990/year (organization).

Meetings/Conferences:
Annual Meetings: Summer
2007 - Philadelphia, PA/June 1-7

Publications:
Journal of Occupational and Environmental Hygiene. m. adv.
The Synergist. m. adv.

American Industrial Real Estate Association

Historical Note
Became AIR Commercial Real Estate Association in 2004.

American Innerspring Manufacturers *(1966)*
1918 N. Parkway
Memphis, TN 38112
Tel: (901)274-9030 *Fax:* (901)725-0510
Toll Free: (800)882 - 5634
E-Mail: aimy@aiminfo.org
Web Site: www.aiminfo.org
Members: 8 companies
Staff: 1
Annual Budget: $100-250,000
Executive Director: Marjory Walker

Historical Note
Formerly the Association of Innerspring Manufacturers. Members make innerspring units and box springs and sell them to mattress manufacturers.

Meetings/Conferences:
Annual Meetings: Spring

American Institute for Archaeological Research

Historical Note
See Archaeological Institute of America.

American Institute for Conservation of Historic and Artistic Works *(1973)*
1717 K St. NW
Suite 200
Washington, DC 20006
Tel: (202)459-9545 *Fax:* (202)452-9328
E-Mail: info@aic-faic.org
Web Site: http://aic.stanford.edu
Members: 3000 individuals
Staff: 6
Annual Budget: $500-1,000,000
Executive Director: Eryl Wentworth
E-Mail: info@aic-faic.org

Historical Note
Formerly (until 1973) an affiliate of the International Institute for Conservation of Historic and Artistic Works. The AIC is a professional organization of conservators, curators, educators, librarians and scientists. Purpose is to disseminate information on conservation, establish and encourage high standards of practice, and provide continuing education opportunities for conservators. Membership: $115/year (fellow or professional); $175/year (institution); $115/year (associate).

Meetings/Conferences:
Annual Meetings: June

Publications:
Journal. 3/year. adv.
Directory. a. adv.
Newsletter. bi-m. adv.
Abstracts of Annual Meeting. a.
Program of Annual Meeting. a. adv.

American Institute for CPCU - Insurance Institute of America *(1942)*
720 Providence Rd.
P.O. Box 3016
Malvern, PA 19355-0716
Tel: (610)644-2100 *Fax:* (610)640-9576
Toll Free: (800)644 - 2101
E-Mail: cserv@cpcuiia.org
Web Site: www.aicpcu.org
Members: 700 companies
Staff: 134
Annual Budget: $10-25,000,000
Senior Vice President, Marketing and Educational Services: Kenneth R. Dauscher, Ph.D., CPCU
Senior Vice President and Corporate Secretary: Christine L. Lewis, Ph.D., CPCU

President and Chief Executive Officer: Peter L. Miller
Senior Vice President, IRC/Publication: Elizabeth A. Sprinkel

Historical Note
Formerly (1992) the American Institute for Property and Liability Underwriters. The American Institute for CPCU (AICPCU) and the Insurance Institute of America (IIA) are independent organizations offering educational programs and professional certification to people in the property and liability insurance business. Chartered in 1942, AICPCU administers an education program that leads to the CPCU (Chartered Property Casualty Underwriter) designation. IIA programs offer both general education in insurance principles and specialist education in particular fields. The operations of IIA, founded in 1909, were merged with those of AICPCU of 1953; in 1996, a third arm, the Insurance Institute for Applied Ethics, was inaugurated. In 1998, the Insurance Research Council (IRC) was merged into and became a department of the AICPCU.

Meetings/Conferences:
Annual Meetings: Summer

Publications:
IRC Research Reports Periodical.
Report on Progress. a.
AICPCU/IIA Catalog. a.
AICPCU/IIA Key Information. a.
The Malvern Examiner. a.
Solutions. Semi-a.

American Institute for International Steel *(1950)*
1100 H St. NW
Suite 830
Washington, DC 20005
Tel: (202)628-3878 *Fax:* (202)737-3134
E-Mail: aiis@aiis.org
Web Site: www.aiis.org
Members: 200 companies
Staff: 3
President: David Phelps

Historical Note
An information-gathering organization that keeps its members informed concerning trade and tariff legislation and importing concerns. Founded during the Korean War at government urging to help alleviate the then-current steel shortage. Members are U.S. companies or U.S. affiliates of foreign producers engaged in the import and export of steel. Membership concentrated on the East, West, and Gulf coasts. Membership: $2,500/year plus tonnage assessment (regular); $900/year (associate); $5,000/year (non-mill sales rep).

Meetings/Conferences:
Annual Meetings: usually first Monday after Thanksgiving

Publications:
newsletter. bi-m.

American Institute for Maghrib Studies *(1984)*
c/o Center for Middle East Studies
845 N. Park Ave., Room 470
Tucson, AZ 85721
Tel: (520)626-6498 *Fax:* (520)621-9257
E-Mail: aimcmes@u.arizona.edu
Web Site: www.la.utexas.edu/research/mena/aims
Members: 250
Staff: 4
Annual Budget: $100-250,000
Executive Director: Kerry Adams
E-Mail: aimcmes@u.arizona.edu

Historical Note
AIMS members are individuals and institutions with an interest in the study of the Maghrib region of North Africa. Membership: $55/year (individual); $40/year (student); $500/year (institution).

Publications:
Journal of North African Studies.
Newsletter. semi-a.

American Institute for Medical and Biological Engineering *(1992)*
1901 Pennsylvania Ave. NW
Suite 401
Washington, DC 20006
Tel: (202)496-9660 *Fax:* (202)466-8489
E-Mail: info@aimbe.org
Web Site: www.aimbe.org
Members: 500 individuals, 500 organizations
Staff: 3
Annual Budget: $250-500,000

Publications:
Membership Directory. a.
The AIMBE News. q. adv.

American Institute for Patristic and Byzantine Studies *(1967)*
12 Minuet Ln.
Kingston, NY 12401
Tel: (845)336-8797 *Fax:* (845)331-1002
Members: 319 individuals
Staff: 3
Annual Budget: under $10,000
President: Dr. Constantine N. Tsirpanlis

Historical Note
Promotes research in eastern Patristic literature, history, theology, and culture. Founded as the American Society for Neo-Hellenic Studies; assumed its present name in 1981. Membership: $65/year (individual); $90/year (organization).

Publications:
Patristic and Byzantine Review. a. adv.

American Institute for Shippers Associations *(1961)*
P.O. Box 33457
Washington, DC 20033
Tel: (202)628-0933 *Fax:* (202)296-7374
E-Mail: info@shippers.org
Web Site: www.shippers.org
Members: 50 companies
Staff: 1
Annual Budget: $50-100,000
Executive Director: Bill Clark
E-Mail: info@shippers.org

Historical Note
Shippers associations are cooperatives formed for the purpose of consolidating freight to obtain volume transportation rates. Membership: $250-2,500/year, based on gross revenues.

Meetings/Conferences:
Annual Meetings: Spring-Early Summer/250

Publications:
AISA Guide to Shipping Cooperatives. a. adv.
AISA News. m.

American Institute of Aeronautics and Astronautics *(1963)*
1801 Alexander Bell Dr., Suite 500
Reston, VA 20191-4344
Tel: (703)264-7500 *Fax:* (703)264-7551
Toll Free: (800)639 - 2422
Web Site: www.aiaa.org
Members: 35000 individuals
Staff: 100
Annual Budget: $10-25,000,000
Executive Director: Robert S. Dickman
E-Mail: bobd@aiaa.org
Manager, Public Policy: Steve Howell
Director, Human Resources: Shirley Jacobson

Historical Note
Formed in 1963 by a merger of the American Rocket Society (1930) and the Institute of the Aeronautical Sciences (1932). Members are engineers, scientists, and students in the aerospace field. Maintains offices in Reston, Virginia and Los Angeles. Has an annual budget of over $15 million. Membership: $75/year (professional); $15/year (student).

Meetings/Conferences:
Annual Meetings: Winter

Publications:
AIAA Journal. m.
AIAA Student Journal. q.
Aerospace America. m. adv.
International Aerospace Abstracts. m.
Journal of Aircraft. bi-m.
Journal of Guidance, Control and Dynamics. bi-m.
Journal of Spacecraft and Rockets. bi-m.
Journal of Propulsion and Power. bi-m.
Journal of Thermophysics and Heat Transfer. q.

American Institute of Architects *(1857)*
1735 New York Ave. NW
Washington, DC 20006-5292
Tel: (202)626-7300 *Fax:* (202)626-7547
Toll Free: (800)242 - 3837
E-Mail: infocentral@aia.org
Web Site: www.aia.org
Members: 79000 individuals
Staff: 187
Annual Budget: $50-100,000,000
Executive Vice President and Chief Executive Officer: Christine W. McEntee
Chief Financial Officer: Richard J. James, CPA
General Counsel: Jay A. Stephens

Historical Note
Incorporated in New York on April 15, 1857; incorporated as The Western Association of Architects in 1889. As the umbrella organization of the U.S. architectural profession, AIA promotes the standards of architecture and interests of architects. Supports the American Architectural Foundation and the Architects Quality Government Fund Political Action Committee. Has an annual budget of approximately $35 million. Membership: $175/year (full member architect); associate and allied memberships available.

Meetings/Conferences:
Annual Meetings: Late Spring/23,000
2007 – San Antonio, TX/May 3-5
2008 – Boston, MA/May 15-17
2009 – San Francisco, CA/Apr. 30-May 2

Publications:
ARCHITECTURE. m. adv.
Memo. m.
AIA News Service. m.

American Institute of Architecture Students *(1956)*
1735 New York Ave. NW
Washington, DC 20006
Tel: (202)626-7472 *Fax:* (202)626-7414
E-Mail: mailbox@aias.org
Web Site: www.aias.org
Members: 6200 individuals
Staff: 5
Annual Budget: $500-1,000,000
Executive Director: Michael Geary, CAE

Historical Note
Formerly (1985) Association of Student Chapters, American Institute of Architects and (1958) National Association of Students of Architecture. Membership: $45/year (individual); $60/year (organization/company).

Meetings/Conferences:
Annual Meetings: Annual

Publications:
CRIT magazine. bien. adv.

American Institute of Baking *(1919)*

Historical Note
Research and educational center for the baking industry. Affiliated with the American Bakers Association.

American Institute of Bangladesh Studies *(1989)*
820 Williams Hall, University of Pennsylvania
36th & Spruce Sts.
Philadelphia, PA 19104-6305
Tel: (215)898-7475 *Fax:* (215)573-2138
Web Site: www.aibs.net
Members: 17 institutions
Annual Budget: $10-25,000
President: Guy Welbon, Ph.D
E-Mail: gwelbon@ccat.sas.upenn.edu

Historical Note
Members of the Institute are colleges and universities. Membership: $250/year (institution).

Meetings/Conferences:
Annual Meetings: Spring

American Institute of Banking *(1900)*

Historical Note
A section of the American Bankers Association.

American Institute of Biological Sciences *(1947)*

1444 I St. NW
Suite 200
Washington, DC 20005
Tel: (202)628-1500 *Fax:* (202)628-1509
Web Site: www.aibs.org
Members: 4500 individuals
Staff: 42
Annual Budget: $2-5,000,000
Executive Director: Richard T. O'Grady, Ph.D.
E-Mail: rogrady@aibs.org

Historical Note
Established within the National Academy of Sciences at a meeting of the Organizing Board in April, 1946. Incorporated as an independent, non-profit entity in the District of Columbia on January 12, 1955. Charter membership closed December 31, 1957. A federation of professional societies and research laboratories with an interest in the life sciences, AIBS also has individual members and promotes all aspects of the biological sciences, including agriculture, environment, and medicine. Absorbed the American Society of Professional Biologists in 1969. Membership: $70/year (individual); $125/year (library).

Meetings/Conferences:
Annual Meetings: Summer/3,000

Publications:
AIB U.S. Congress Handbook.
BioScience. 11/year. adv.
Membership Directory. irreg.
Annual Meeting Program. a. adv.

American Institute of Biomedical Climatology *(1958)*
1050 Eagle Rd.
Newtown, PA 18940-2818
Tel: (215)968-4483
Web Site: www.aibc.cc
Members: 58 individuals
Staff: 2
Annual Budget: under $10,000
Secretary-Treasurer: George W.K. King

Historical Note
Formerly (1987) the American Institute of Medical Climatology. Promotes the sciences of bioclimatology and biometerology, which address the relationship between climate, weather and the entire spectrum of life. Emphasizes human health and well-being. Membership: $45/year (individual); $250/year (corporate).

Meetings/Conferences:
Annual Meetings: usually Philadelphia PA(Drexel Univ.)/late October

Publications:
AIBC Journal. 3/year.
Med-Clime Currents. q.

American Institute of Building Design *(1950)*
2505 Main St., Suite 209B
Stratford, CT 06615
Toll Free: (800)366 - 2423
Web Site: www.aibd.org
Members: 1400 individuals
Staff: 2
Annual Budget: $250-500,000
Director, Operations: Bobbi Fasco
E-Mail: bobbi@aibd.org

Historical Note
Established in California as United Designers Association; assumed its present name in 1958. Seeks to unify the building design field, develop better design education standards, encourage inter-professional relations among designers and promote research into the aesthetic and technical aspects of the field. AIBD acts as a legislative watchdog for the building design profession, and provides professional support to residential design specialists. Membership: $165/year (individual); $1,500/year (company).

Meetings/Conferences:
Annual Meetings: Summer

Publications:
Home Design Journal. q. adv.
Design Lines Newsletter. q. adv.

American Institute of Certified Planners *(1978)*
1776 Massachusetts Ave. NW
Washington, DC 20036-1904
Tel: (202)872-0611 *Fax:* (202)872-0643
E-Mail: aicp@planning.org
Web Site: www.planning.org
Members: 10000 individuals
Staff: 5
Executive Director: Paul Farmer
Chief Operating Officer: Charlotte McCaskill
E-Mail: aicp@planning.org

Historical Note
The professional institute of the American Planning Association. Members are those members of APA who have met the required qualifications of education, experience and examination in the field of city and regional planning. Awards the designation "AICP". Membership: $70/year, plus membership in APA.

Meetings/Conferences:
Annual Meetings: Spring, with American Planning Ass'n

Publications:
Roster of Members. bi-a.
Planners Casebook. q.

American Institute of Certified Public Accountants *(1887)*
1211 Ave. of the Americas
New York, NY 10036-8775
Tel: (212)596-6200 *Fax:* (212)596-6213
E-Mail: service@aicpa.org
Web Site: www.aicpa.org
Members: 330000 individuals
Staff: 625
Annual Budget: Over $100,000,000
President and Chief Executive Officer: Barry C. Melancon
Vice President, Communications: Janice Maiman
Senior Vice President, Public Affairs: Jim O'Malley
Vice President, Congressional and Political Affairs: Mark G. Peterson

Historical Note
Founded as the American Association of Public Accountants. Became the Institute of Accountants in the U.S.A. in 1916 and the American Institute of Accountants in 1917. Merged in 1937 with the American Society of Certified Public Accountants. Became the American Institute of Certified Public Accountants in 1957. Administers the national uniform CPA exam. Supports the AICPA Effective Legislation Committee. Has an annual budget of over $100 million. Maintains offices in Jersey City, NJ and in Washington, DC.

Meetings/Conferences:
Annual Meetings: Fall

Publications:
CPA Letter. m.
Journal of Accountancy. m. adv.
Tax Adviser. m. adv.
Practicing CPA. m.

American Institute of Chemical Engineers *(1908)*
Three Park Ave.
New York, NY 10016-5991
Tel: (212)591-7338 *Fax:* (212)591-8888
Toll Free: (800)242 - 4363
E-Mail: xpress@aiche.org
Web Site: www.aiche.org
Members: 55000 individuals
Staff: 40
Annual Budget: $10-25,000,000
Executive Director: John A. Sofranko, Ph.D.
Director, Human Resources: Cathy Diana
Senior Director, Operations, Membership and Marketing: Bette Lawler

Historical Note
Organized June 22, 1908 in Philadelphia and incorporated in New York in 1910. A member of the Accreditation Board for Engineering and Technology, the American Association of Engineering Societies, the Chemical Heritage Foundation and related organizations. Sponsors research through its Center for Chemical Process Safety, Center for Waste Reduction Technologies, Process Data Exchange Institute, Design Institute for Physical Property Data, Research Institute on Food Engineering, and Design Institute for Emergency Relief Systems' Users' Group. A member society of the American Institute for Medical and Biological Engineering. Has an annual budget of approximately $21 million. Membership: $133/year.

Meetings/Conferences:
Semi-Annual Meetings: Spring and Fall

Publications:
Chemical Engineering Progress. m. adv.
Environmental Progress. q. adv.
Process Safety Progress. q. adv.
Symposium Series. bi-m.
Biotechnology Progess. bi-m.
Chemical Engineering Faculties. a.
AIChE Directory. a.
AIChExtra. m.
CHAPTER One. 8/year. adv.
AIChE Activities Directory. a.
Ammonia Plant Safety. a.
AIChE Journal. m. adv.

American Institute of Chemists *(1923)*
315 Chestnut St.
Philadelphia, PA 19106-2702
Tel: (215)873-8224 *Fax:* (215)925-1954
E-Mail: info@theaic.org
Web Site: www.TheAIC.org
Members: 5000 individuals
Staff: 3
Annual Budget: $100-250,000
Executive Director: Sharon Dobson

Historical Note
Founded in New York City in 1923 and incorporated in New York in 1926 and in Maryland in 1974. Engages in a broad range of programs for professional enhancement of the chemist and chemical engineer through its Fellow membership category, awards program, meetings, publications, and public relations activities. The AIC's National Certification Commission in Chemistry and Chemical Engineering (NCC) provides a professional credentialing system for members. Membership: $120/year (individual).

Meetings/Conferences:
Annual Meetings: Spring

Publications:
The Chemist. 6/year. adv.
Professional Directory. a. adv.

American Institute of Commemorative Art *(1951)*
P.O. Box 43602
Middletown, KY 40253-0602
Tel: (502)254-1375 *Fax:* (502)254-1375
Web Site: www.monuments-aica.com
Members: 54 firms
Staff: 2
Annual Budget: $50-100,000
Executive Director: Leland B. Longstreth
E-Mail: lelandb@monuments-aica.com

Historical Note
Members are devoted to high standards of design and ethics in the monument field. Membership: $400/year.

Publications:
Milestone. q.

American Institute of Constructors *(1971)*
P.O. Box 26334
Alexandria, VA 22314
Tel: (703)683-4999 *Fax:* (703)683-5480
E-Mail: admin@aicnet.org
Web Site: http://aicnet.org
Members: 1000 individuals
Staff: 4
Annual Budget: $250-500,000
Executive Director: Davin E. Hattaway
Executive Administrator: Kimberlee Weidenheimer

Historical Note
AIC serves as the qualifying body for individuals in the construction profession. Was the founding organization for the American Council for Construction Education, the recognized agency for accrediting colleges and universities that grant 4-year degrees in construction. Membership: $115-$250/year.

Publications:
Membership Directory. a. adv.
American Professional Constructor. bien.
Newsletter. q. adv.

American Institute of Engineers *(1990)*
4630 Appian Way, Suite 206

El Sobrante, CA 94803-1875
Tel: (510)758-6240
E-Mail: aie@members-aie.org
Web Site: www.members-aie.org
Members: 1,250 individuals
Staff: 2
Annual Budget: $50-100,000
Director: Joel Snyder, PE, CEng

Historical Note
AIE is a two level national and county professional association for engineers, scientists and mathematicians. Purpose is to represent, promote and advance the interests of American engineers, scientists, and mathematicians. Members hold a bachelor's degree or higher in engineering, science or mathematics, are members of another professional association, and are U.S. citizens. Membership: $100/year.

Meetings/Conferences:
Annual Meetings:

Publications:
AIE Alumni Directory, Statistical (US). bien. adv.
AIE Geographic Distribution Directory, Statistical (US). bien. adv.
AIE Members' Directory. a. adv.
AIE Perspectives. m. adv.

American Institute of Fishery Research Biologists *(1956)*
SUNY- Maritime College
6 Pennyfield Ave.
Bronx, NY 10648-4198
Tel: (718)409-7378 *Fax:* (718)409-7364
E-Mail: synodos@aol.com
Web Site: www.aifrb.org
Members: 1000 individuals
Staff: 1
Annual Budget: $10-25,000
President: Dr. Linda Jones
: Dr. Barbara Warkentine

Historical Note
Has no paid officers or full-time staff. Membership is subject to review and approval by Accrediation Committee based on professional accomplishment. Membership: $40/year, plus $10 initiation fee.

Meetings/Conferences:
Annual Meetings: Held in conjunction with American Fisheries Soc.
2007 – San Francisco, CA(Marriott Downtown)/Sept. 2-7/1500

Publications:
BRIEFS. bi-m.

American Institute of Floral Designers *(1962)*
720 Light St.
Baltimore, MD 21230
Tel: (410)752-3318 *Fax:* (410)752-8295
E-Mail: aifd@assnhqtrs.com
Web Site: www.aifd.org
Members: 550 individuals
Staff: 10
Annual Budget: $500-1,000,000
Executive Director: Thomas C. Shaner

Historical Note
Foundation provides financial support for educational purposes: scholarships, projects, and programs that facilitate the advancement and dissemination of knowledge in the field of floral design and related fields.

Meetings/Conferences:
Annual Meetings: July

Publications:
Newsletter. q. adv.

American Institute of Food Distribution *(1928)*
One Broadway
Elmwood Park, NJ 07407
Tel: (201)791-5570 *Fax:* (201)791-5222
E-Mail: info@foodinstitute.org
Web Site: www.foodinstitute.com
Members: 5500 individuals
Staff: 13
Annual Budget: $2-5,000,000
President: Brian L. Todd
E-Mail: btodd@foodinstitute.com

Historical Note
The Food Institute is an international food trade information and research organization serving, and maintained by, companies concerned with distribution of food products. Membership: $695/year (organization/company); E-Membership $395/year; $245/year (school/university).

Meetings/Conferences:
Annual Meetings: None Held

Publications:
Almanac of the Canning, Freezing, Preserving Industries. a.
HACCP & US Food Safety Guide.
Food Institute Report. w.
OSHA Manual. a.
Recall Manual.
Food Markets in Review (Series). a.
Food Industry Review. a.
Food Business Mergers & Acquisitions. a.
Daily Update. d. adv.

American Institute of Graphic Arts *(1914)*
164 Fifth Ave.
New York, NY 10010-5900
Tel: (212)807-1990 *Fax:* (212)807-1799
E-Mail: robyn-jordan@aiga.org
Web Site: www.aiga.org
Members: 17000 individuals
Staff: 14
Annual Budget: $2-5,000,000
Executive Director: Richard Grefe
E-Mail: grefe@aiga.org

Historical Note
AIGA advances excellence in graphic design as a discipline, profession and cultural force. Members are involved in design and production of books, magazines and periodicals as well as corporate, environmental, and promotional graphics. AIGA provides leadership in the exchange of ideas and information, the encouragement of critical analysis and research, and the advancement of education and ethical practice. Conducts interrelated programs of competitions, exhibitions, publications and educational activities to promote excellence in graphic design. Has 37 chapters nationwide which provide local programs. Membership: $235/year.

Meetings/Conferences:
Annual Meetings: Fall

Publications:
365: AIGA Year in Design. a.
Gain: AIGA Journal of Design for the Network Economy.
AIGA Journal of Design. 3/year.
Graphic Design USA. a.

American Institute of Homeopathy *(1844)*
801 N. Fairfax St., Suite 306
Alexandria, VA 22314-1757
Toll Free: (888)445 - 9988
E-Mail: aih@homeopathyusa.org
Web Site: www.homeopathyusa.org
Members: 150 individuals
Annual Budget: $50-100,000
President: Joyce Frye, D.O.

Historical Note
Members are doctors of medicine, dentistry and osteopathy in the U.S. and Canada. Has no paid officers or full-time staff. Membership: $250/year.

Meetings/Conferences:
Semi-annual Meetings: Spring and Fall

Publications:
AIH Handbook & Directory of Active Members. a.
American Journal of Homeopathic Medicine. q. adv.
Newsletter. q.

American Institute of Hydrology *(1981)*
300 Village Green Circle, Suite 201
Smyrna, GA 30080
Tel: (770)384-1634 *Fax:* (770)438-6172
E-Mail: aihydro@aol.com
Web Site: www.aihydro.org
Members: 1000organizationsandindividuals
Staff: 2
Annual Budget: $100-250,000
Manager: Cathryn Seaburn

Historical Note
Incorporated in March 1981 in the State of Minnesota. Registers and certifies hydrologists and hydrogeologists, provides a forum to discuss national and international issues, and provides educational courses. Membership: $120/year (individual); $200/year (organization/company); $15/year (student).

Publications:
Hydrological Science and Technology. q.
AIH Bulletin. q. adv.

American Institute of Indian Studies *(1961)*
1130 E. 59th St.
Chicago, IL 60637
Tel: (773)702-8638
E-Mail: aiis@uchicago.edu
Web Site: www.indiastudies.org
Members: 55 institutions
Staff: 2
President: Ralph W. Nicholas

Historical Note
Members include colleges and universities that support research in the art, archaeology and languages of India.

Meetings/Conferences:
Annual Meetings: With Asian Studies Conference

American Institute of Inspectors *(1989)*
65 Enterprise
Aliso Viejo, CA 92656
Tel: (541)273-6440 *Fax:* (949)715-6931
Toll Free: (800)877 - 4770
E-Mail: execdir@inspection.org
Web Site: www.inspection.org
Members: 280 individuals
Annual Budget: $25-50,000
Executive Director: Fred Droz

Historical Note
All members are home inspectors.

Meetings/Conferences:
Annual Meetings: October

Publications:
NADeFA News Roundup. bi-m. adv.
Roster. a.

American Institute of Marine Underwriters *(1898)*
14 Wall St.
New York, NY 10005
Tel: (212)233-0550 *Fax:* (212)227-5102
E-Mail: aimu@aimu.org
Web Site: www.aimu.org
Members: 100 companies
Staff: 4
Annual Budget: $500-1,000,000
President: James M. Craig
E-Mail: jcraig@aimu.org

Historical Note
AIMU traces its origins to 1820. Its member companies write ocean marine insurance in the United States. Membership: $1,200/year (associate); $1,500/year (subscriber); $2,500/year (corporate).

Meetings/Conferences:
Annual Meetings: New York, NY in November

Publications:
Weekly Bulletin. w.

American Institute of Mining, Metallurgical, and Petroleum Engineers *(1871)*
P.O. Box 270728
Littleton, CO 80127-0013
Tel: (303)948-4255 *Fax:* (303)948-4260
E-Mail: aime@aimehq.org
Web Site: www.aimehq.org
Members: 4 societies
Staff: 2
Annual Budget: $250-500,000
Executive Director: Rick Rolater
Executive Assistant: Michele Gottwald

Historical Note
Founded in Wilkes-Barre, Pennsylvania in 1871 as the American Institute of Mining Engineers to "further the arts and sciences employed to recover the earth's minerals and convert them to useful products." Incorporated in 1905, the name was changed in 1919 to American Institute of Mining and Metallurgical

Engineers after absorbing the American Institute of Metals. In 1957 the name American Institute of Mining, Metallurgical and Petroleum Engineers, Inc. was adopted and the Institute was reorganized into constituent societies: Minerals, Metals, & Materials Society; Society for Mining, Metallurgy, & Exploration; Society of Petroleum Engineers; and Iron and Steel Society In 1985, these societies became separately incorporated, autonomous organizations. Publications of these societies should be obtained directly from the society in question.

Meetings/Conferences:
Annual Meetings: Summer

American Institute of Oral Biology *(1943)*
P.O. Box 7184
Loma Linda, CA 92354-7184
Tel: (909)558-4671 *Fax:* (909)558-0285
E-Mail: jbarrientos@llu.edu
Web Site: www.aiob.org
Members: 4 individuals
Staff: 2
Annual Budget: $25-50,000
Executive Secretary: June Barrientos

Historical Note
Registration: $350/year; $400 for first year if registering onsite at annual meeting.

Meetings/Conferences:
Annual Meetings: Always in Palm Springs, CA/Late October/140
2007 – Palm Springs, CA(Hilton)/Oct. 19-22/125

Publications:
Proceedings Manual. a.

American Institute of Organbuilders *(1974)*
P.O. Box 130982
Houston, TX 77219-0982
Tel: (713)529-2212
E-Mail: execsec@pipeorgan.org
Web Site: www.pipeorgan.org
Members: 380 individuals
Staff: 1
Annual Budget: $25-50,000
Executive Secretary: Howard Maple

Historical Note
AIO was established to educate professional builders of pipe organs through lectures, discussion and publication of technical information. Members are individuals professionally engaged in some facet of the building, servicing and maintaining of pipe organs, including organ company executives, pipe and cabinet makers, and service and maintenance technicians. Membership: $80/year (individual).

Meetings/Conferences:
Annual Meetings: October

Publications:
Journal of American Organbuilding. q. adv.

American Institute of Parliamentarians *(1958)*
P.O. Box 2173
Wilmington, DE 19899-2173
Tel: (302)762-1811 *Fax:* (302)762-2170
Toll Free: (888)664 - 0428
E-Mail: aip@parliamentaryprocedure.org
Web Site: www.parliamentaryprocedure.org
Members: 1400 individuals
Staff: 2
Annual Budget: $50-100,000
Executive Director: Ann Iona Warner

Historical Note
Promotes the teaching of parliamentary procedure, training and certification of parliamentarians and the wider use of parliamentarians . Awards the designations CP (Certified Parliamentarian) and CPP (Certified Professional Parliamentarian). Membership: $45/year (regular); $50/year (associate); $20/year (full time student).

Publications:
The Communicator. q.
Parliamentary Journal. q.

American Institute of Physics *(1931)*
One Physics Ellipse
College Park, MD 20740-3843
Tel: (301)209-3100 *Fax:* (301)209-0843
E-Mail: aipinfo@aip.org
Web Site: www.aip.org
Members: 10 societies & 24 affiliates
Staff: 500
Annual Budget: $50-100,000,000
Executive Director and Chief Executive Officer: Marc H. Brodsky
E-Mail: brodsky@aip.org
Treasurer and Chief Financial Officer: Richard Baccante
E-Mail: rbaccant@aip.org
Vice President, Human Resources: Theresa C. Braun
E-Mail: tbraun@aip.org
Vice President, Physics Resources: James H. Stith
E-Mail: jstith@aip.org
Director, Media and Government Relations: Alicia Torres
E-Mail: atorres@aip.org
Senior Vice President, Publishing: Darlene A. Walters
E-Mail: dwalters@aip.org

Historical Note
Organized in New York under the leadership of Karl Compton and George Pegram as a means of preserving communication within the community of physicists whose energies were being dispersed into an increasing number of special fields. A federation of ten societies in physics: Acoustical Society of America, American Association of Physicists in Medicine, American Association of Physics Teachers, American Astronomical Society, American Crystallographic Association, American Geophysical Union, American Physical Society, American Vacuum Society, Optical Society of America, and Society of Rheology. Incorporated in New York in 1932. Has a budget of approximately $60 million.

Meetings/Conferences:
Annual Meetings: Not held.

Publications:
Applied Physics Letters. w. adv.
Graduate Program Book. a.
Journal of Applied Physics. semi-m.
Physics of Plasmas. m.
Directory of Organizations with Physics, Astronomy & Geophysics Staff. bien.
The Industrial Physicist. bi-m. adv.
Computing in Science and Engineering. bi-m. adv.
Physics of Fluids. m.
Review of Scientific Instruments. m. adv.
CHAOS: An Interdisciplinary Journal of Nonlinear Science. q.
Low Temperature Physics. m.
Current Physics Index. q.
Journal of Mathematical Physics. m.
Journal of Physical and Chemical Reference Data. q.
Physics Today. m. adv.
Journal of Chemical Physics. semi-m.

American Institute of Professional Bookkeepers *(1987)*
6001 Montrose Rd.
Suite 500
Rockville, MD 20852
Tel: (301)770-7300 *Fax:* (800)541-0066
Toll Free: (800)622 - 0121
E-Mail: info@aipb.org
Web Site: www.aipb.org
Members: 35000 individuals
Staff: 6
Co-President: Stanley I. Hartman
Co-President: Stephen Sahler

Historical Note
Offers examinations leading to the designation CB (Certified Bookkeeper), provides continuing education and other opportunities to is members.

Publications:
The General Ledger. m.

American Institute of Professional Geologists *(1963)*
1400 W. 122nd Ave.
Suite 250
Westminster, CO 80234
Tel: (303)412-6205 *Fax:* (303)253-9220
E-Mail: aipg@aipg.org
Web Site: www.aipg.org
Members: 5000 individuals
Staff: 4
Annual Budget: $500-1,000,000
Executive Director: William J. Siok
Publications Manager and Assistant Director: Wendy Davidson
Manager, Membership Services: Catherine Duran

Historical Note
Founded November 15, 1963 and incorporated in Colorado in 1964, AIPG is a member of the American Geological Institute. Awards the designation Certified Professional Geologist (CPG). Provides continuing education and advocacy programs in support of the profession. Membership: $120/year.

Meetings/Conferences:
Annual Meetings: late September-early October
2007 – Traverse City, MI(Park Place Hotel)/Oct. 7-11
2008 – Flagstaff, AZ/Sept. 20-25

Publications:
The Professional Geologist. bi-m. adv.
Membership Directory. a. adv.

American Institute of Service Body Manufacturers

Historical Note
An affiliate of the National Truck Equipment Association.

American Institute of Steel Construction *(1921)*
One E. Wacker Dr., Suite 700
Chicago, IL 60601-1802
Tel: (312)670-2400 *Fax:* (312)670-5403
E-Mail: membership@aisc.org
Web Site: www.aisc.org
Members: 10000 individuals
Staff: 60
Annual Budget: $2-5,000,000
President: H. Louis Gurthet
Director, Membership: Kelly M. Johnson

Historical Note
Fabricators of structural steel.

Publications:
Modern Steel Construction. m. adv.
AISC Engineering Journal. q.

American Institute of Stress *(1979)*
124 Park Ave.
Yonkers, NY 10703
Tel: (914)963-1200 *Fax:* (914)965-6267
E-Mail: stress125@optonline.net
Web Site: www.stress.org
Members: 5000 individuals
Staff: 4
Annual Budget: $50-100,000
President and Chairman: Paul J. Rosch, M.D.
E-Mail: stress125@optonline.net

Historical Note
AIS is a multidisciplinary professional society composed of health professionals, academics and others with an interest in the study of stress and its treatment. Membership: $90/year (fellow); $70/year (individual).

Publications:
Health and Stress: The Newsletter of the AIS. m.

American Institute of the History of Pharmacy *(1941)*
777 Highland Ave.
Madison, WI 53705-2222
Tel: (608)262-5378
E-Mail: aihp@aihp.org
Web Site: www.aihp.org
Members: 1000 individuals
Staff: 4
Annual Budget: $100-250,000
Executive Director: Dr. Gregory J. Higby

Historical Note
Founded in Madison, WI as a non-profit agency specializing in the history of pharmacy and drugs, with emphasis on the USA. Individual memberships are nationwide, governed by a nationally representative Council. The historical and publishing office has been at the University of Wisconsin School of Pharmacy since the founding. Fosters investigations, publications, teaching, and interest in the history of pharmacy; collects historical records and makes them available; sponsors awards and

educational grants. Membership: $50/year (individual); $100/year (organization/company).

Meetings/Conferences:
Annual Meetings: Spring, with American Pharmaceutical Ass'n
2007 – Atlanta, GA/March 16-19

Publications:
Apothecary's Cabinet.
AIHP Notes. irreg. adv.
Pharmacy in History. q.

American Institute of Timber Construction
(1952)
7012 S. Revere Pkwy., Suite 140
Centennial, CO 80112-3932
Tel: (303)792-9559 *Fax:* (303)792-0669
E-Mail: info@aitc-glulam.org
Web Site: www.aitc-glulam.org
Members: 510 companies and individuals
Staff: 7
Annual Budget: $500-1,000,000
Executive Vice President: R. Michael Caldwell
E-Mail: rmc@aitc-glulam.org
Director, Inspections Bureau: Ron Goff
E-Mail: rgoff@aitc-glulam.org
Manager, Technical Services: Jeff Linville
E-Mail: linville@aitc-glulam.org
Membership/Publications: Holly Mais
E-Mail: hcm@aitc-glulam.org
Accounting Manager/Meeting Planner: Shiel V. Sieli
E-Mail: svs@aitc-glulam.org

Historical Note
Members are manufacturers and erectors of laminated structural timber; and engineers, architects and other professionals involved in timber construction.

Meetings/Conferences:
Annual Meetings: Spring

Publications:
Lamlines. q.

American Institute of Ultrasound in Medicine
(1951)
14750 Sweitzer Ln.
Suite 100
Laurel, MD 20707-5906
Tel: (301)498-4100 *Fax:* (301)498-4450
Toll Free: (800)638 - 5352
Web Site: www.aium.org
Members: 10000 individuals
Staff: 30
Annual Budget: $2-5,000,000
Chief Executive Officer: Carmine M. Valente, Ph.D., CAE
Chief Financial Officer: Diane Eberle

Historical Note
Founded in Denver, CO, by 24 physicians attending the annual meeting of the American Congress of Physical Medicine and Rehabilitation who wished to expand the scope of physical medicine as a new specialty. Members are physicians, scientists, engineers and sonographers concerned with the use of diagnostic medical ultrasound. Membership: $250/year (physician); $140/year (non-physician).

Meetings/Conferences:
Annual Meetings: Spring/3,500

Publications:
Journal of Ultrasound in Medicine. m. adv.
Scientific Meeting Abstracts. a.
AIUM Reporter. m.

American Insurance Association *(1964)*
1130 Connecticut Ave. NW
Suite 1000
Washington, DC 20036
Tel: (202)828-7100 *Fax:* (202)293-1219
E-Mail: info@aiadc.org
Web Site: www.aiadc.org
Members: 270 companies
Staff: 150
Annual Budget: $10-25,000,000
President: Marc F. Racicot
Executive Vice President, Public Policy Management: Debra T. Ballen
E-Mail: dballen@aiadc.org
General Counsel and Senior Vice President: Craig A. Berrington
E-Mail: cberrington@aiadc.org
Senior Vice President, Government Affairs: Leigh Ann Pusey
Senior Vice President, Public Affairs: Julie Rochman

Historical Note
Formed by a merger of the National Board of Fire Underwriters (founded in 1866), the Association of Casualty and Surety Companies (founded in 1927) and the old American Insurance Association (founded in 1953). Supports the American Insurance Association Political Action Committee. Has an annual budget of approximately $21.6 million. Membership fee based on market share.

Publications:
AIA Advocate. 10/yr.

American Insurance Marketing and Sales Society *(1968)*
P.O. Box 35718
Richmond, VA 23235
Tel: (804)674-6466 *Fax:* (804)915-9435
Toll Free: (877)674 - 2742
E-Mail: info@aimssociety.com
Web Site: www.aimssociety.com
Members: 500 individuals
Staff: 2
Annual Budget: $100-250,000
Executive Director: Kitty Ambers, CPIA, CIC, CPSR
E-Mail: k.ambers@comcast.net

Historical Note
Formerly Certified Professional Insurance Agents Society; assumed its current name in 2004. Educates agents in the property casualty insurance profession about sales skills and provides a forum for agents to exchange sales and marketing ideas. Awards the CPIA (Certified Professional Insurance Agent) designation to members successfuly completing an educational program. Membership: $225/year (individual).

Meetings/Conferences:
Annual Meetings: Spring

Publications:
Quik Sales Tip Fax/Email. bi-w.
Bright Ideas Fax/Email. m.
Online Membership Directory.
Agency Ideas. q. adv.

American Insurers Highway Safety Alliance
(1920)

Historical Note
Absorbed by Property Casualty Insurance Association of America.

American Intellectual Property Law Association
(1897)
2001 Jefferson Davis Hwy., Suite 203
Arlington, VA 22202
Tel: (703)415-0780 *Fax:* (703)415-0786
E-Mail: aipla@aipla.org
Web Site: www.aipla.org
Members: 12000 individuals
Staff: 13
Annual Budget: $2-5,000,000
Executive Director: Michael K. Kirk
E-Mail: aipla@aipla.org
Director, Communications: James Crowne
E-Mail: aipla@aipla.org

Historical Note
Formerly (1914) Patent Law Association of Washington and (1984) the American Patent Law Association. Membership in this voluntary bar association consists of lawyers whose specialty is trademark, copyright and patent law. Fields of concern are patent, trademark, and copyright patent laws, and the federal rules and regulations that administer them. A member of National Council of Patent Law Associations. Membership: $225/year (active).

Publications:
AIPLA Quarterly Journal. q. adv.
Membership Directory. bien. adv.
Bulletin of AIPLA. 3/year. adv.
Economic Survey. bien.

American International Automobile Dealers Association *(1970)*
211 N. Union St., Suite 300
Alexandria, VA 22314
Tel: (703)519-7800 *Fax:* (703)519-7810
Toll Free: (800)462 - 4232
Web Site: www.aiada.org
Members: 10000 dealers
Staff: 20
Annual Budget: $2-5,000,000
President: Marianne McInerney
Communications Coordinator: Todd Kohlhepp
Director, Member Services: Kelly Martin

Historical Note
Formed in 1970 as the Volkswagen American Dealers Association. Assumed its present name in 1980. AIADA represents America's 10,000 international nameplate automobile dealers and their 330,000 employees who sell and service world-class automobiles. Only trade association exclusively dedicated to representing the nation's international nameplate automobile dealers before Congress, the administration, the industry, the media and the American public.

Meetings/Conferences:
Annual Meetings: Spring

Publications:
This Week in Washington. w.
Showroom Magazine. 8/year.
AIADA Newsletter. m.

American International Charolais Association
(1957)
11700 N.W. Plaza Circle
Kansas City, MO 64153
Tel: (816)464-5977 *Fax:* (816)464-5759
E-Mail: charolaisjournal@charolaisusa.com
Web Site: www.charolaisusa.com
Members: 4300 individuals
Staff: 20
Annual Budget: $1-2,000,000
Executive Vice President: J. Neil Orth
Director, Communications: Julie Olson

Historical Note
Formed (1957) by merger of American Charolais Breeders Association and International Charolais Association. Absorbed (1967) American Charbray Breeders Association. Members are breeders and fanciers of Charolais beef cattle. Member of the National Pedigree Livestock Council and the United States Beef Breeds Council. Membership: $50 initial fee, $35/year.

Meetings/Conferences:
Semi-Annual Meetings: 300

Publications:
Charolais Journal. m. adv.

American International Freight Association

Historical Note
Merged with Transportation Intermediaries Ass'n in 2002.

American International Marchigiana Society
(1973)
P.O. Box 198
Walton, KS 67151-0198
Tel: (620)837-3303
Web Site: www.marchigiana.org
Members: 50 individuals
Staff: 1
Annual Budget: under $10,000
Executive Secretary: Martie TenEyck

Historical Note
Founded in 1973, AIMS is an association that fosters raising of the marchigiana breed of cattle in the United States. Also known as the Marky Cattle Association. Membership: $100/year (initial fee per member); $25/year (per member, after first year).

Meetings/Conferences:
Annual Meetings: Kansas, Nebraska or Texas/month varies

Publications:
The Marky Newsletter. 6/year.

American Iron and Steel Institute *(1855)*
1140 Connecticut Ave. NW
Suite 705
Washington, DC 20036
Tel: (202)452-7100 *Fax:* (202)463-6573
Web Site: www.steel.org
Members: 200 companies and assoc. members

Staff: 60
Annual Budget: $25-50,000,000
Vice President, Finance and Administration: David E. Bell
Vice President, Government Relations: Walter "Chip" Foley
Vice President, Communications: Nancy Gravatt
Vice President, Manufacturing and Technology: Larry Kavanaugh
Vice President, Environment and Energy: James Schultz
Vice President, Public Policy, Tax and Trade: Barry Solarz

Historical Note
The American Iron Association was founded in 1855 and absorbed by the American Iron and Steel Association in 1864. This, in turn, was absorbed in 1912 by the American Iron and Steel Institute which had been incorporated March 31, 1908 in New York. Promotes the interests of the iron and steel industry.

Publications:
AISI Newsletter.
Annual Statistical Report. a.

American Iron Ore Association *(1882)*
614 SuperiorAve. West
Suite 915
Cleveland, OH 44113-8261
Tel: (218)722-7724 *Fax:* (218)720-6707
Web Site: www.aioa.org
*Members:*4 companies
Staff: 3
Annual Budget: $50-100,000
Contact Person: Frank Ongaro
E-Mail: ryan@lcaships.com

Historical Note
Established as the Western Iron Ore Association, it became the Lake Superior Iron Ore Association in 1895 and assumed its present name in 1957. Members are iron ore mining companies in the United States and Canada.

Publications:
Statistical Reports - Ore Consumed & Inventory (online).
Iron Ore - Statistical. a.

American Italian Historical Association *(1966)*
209 Flagg Pl.
Staten Island, NY 10304
Tel: (718)351-8800 *Fax:* (718)667-4598
Web Site: www.cmsny.org
*Members:*800 individuals
Annual Budget: under $10,000
Executive Director: Rev. Joseph Fugolo
E-Mail: offices@cmsny.org

Historical Note
AIHA members are academics and others with an interest in the study of the Italian experience in North America. Has no paid officers or full-time staff. Membership: $35/year (individual); $15/year (student); $50/year (institution).

Meetings/Conferences:
Annual Meetings: Fall

Publications:
Newsletter of AHIA. 3/year. adv.
Proceedings. a.

American Jail Association *(1981)*
1135 Professional Ct.
Hagerstown, MD 21740-5853
Tel: (301)790-3930 Ext: 13 *Fax:* (301)790-2941
E-Mail: jails@aja.org
Web Site: www.aja.org
*Members:*4200 individuals
Staff: 12
Annual Budget: $1-2,000,000
Executive Director: Gwyn Smith-Ingley
E-Mail: gwyns@aja.org
Assistant to the Executive Director: Sheryl Ebersole
E-Mail: sheryle@aja.org

Historical Note
Members are jail personnel and persons whose work is closely associated with jails. AJA was the result of a merger between the National Jail Association (1939) and the National Jail Managers Association (1973). Membership: $15/year (student); $36/year (individual, US); $42/year (Canada); $54/year (outside U.S. or Canada); $100/year (affiliate); $300/year (organization/company).

Meetings/Conferences:
Annual Meetings: Spring
2007 - Nashville, TN/May 20-24
2008 - Sacramento, CA/May 4-8
2009 - Louisville, KY/Apr. 26-30

Publications:
Legal Issues Manual.
Jail Directory. bien. adv.
Product Service Directory. a. adv.
Exploring Jail Operations.
Write It Right Bulletin. q.
American Jails Magazine. bi-m. adv.
Jail Operations Bulletin. m.
Jail Managers Bulletin. m.

American Jersey Cattle Association *(1868)*
6486 E. Main St.
Reynoldsburg, OH 43068-2362
Tel: (614)861-3636 *Fax:* (614)861-8040
E-Mail: info@usjersey.com
Web Site: www.usjersey.com
*Members:*2381 individuals
Staff: 34
Annual Budget: $2-5,000,000
Executive Secretary: Neal Smith

Historical Note
Breeders of Jersey dairy cattle. Member of the National Pedigree Livestock Council. Membership: $100/lifetime.

Meetings/Conferences:
Annual Meetings: June

Publications:
Jersey Directory. bien. adv.
Jersey Journal. m. adv.

American Jewish Correctional Chaplains Association *(1937)*
c/o Westchester Jewish Center
Rockland & Palmer Aves.
Mamaroneck, NY 10543
Tel: (914)698-2960 *Fax:* (914)698-3610
*Members:*50 individuals
Annual Budget: under $10,000
President: Rabbi Irving Koslowe

Historical Note
Affiliated with the American Correctional Association and the American Correctional Chaplains Association. Formerly National Council of Jewish Correctional Chaplains and National Council of Jewish Prison Chaplains. Membership: $10/year.

Meetings/Conferences:
Semi-annual Meetings: January and June

Publications:
Chaplaincy.

American Jewish Historical Society *(1892)*
15 W. 16th St.
New York, NY 10011
Tel: (212)294-6160 *Fax:* (212)294-6161
E-Mail: info@ajhs.org
Web Site: www.ajhs.org
*Members:*4000 individuals
Staff: 14
Annual Budget: $1-2,000,000
Interim Executive Director: David Solomon

Historical Note
The Society is a museum, library and archives and educational institution interested in public service. It is the repository for the archives of such organizations as the Council of Jewish Federations, the American Jewish Congress, and the Synagogue Council of America. Its collections provide information on current as well as past Jewish communal and institutional life, social welfare services, immigration, synagogue records, prominent Jewish individuals, the Colonial Period and the early 19th century, and the ties between American Jewry and events overseas. Members are historians, scholars, and lay people. Membership: $50/year.

Meetings/Conferences:
Annual Meetings: Spring/300

Publications:
Heritage (newsletter). q. adv.
American Jewish History. q. adv.

American Jewish Press Association *(1943)*
1225 New Hampshire Ave. NW
Suite 702
Washington, DC 20036
Tel: (202)250-6144 *Fax:* (202)250-6151
E-Mail: info@ajpa.org
Web Site: www.ajpa.org
*Members:*50 individuals
Annual Budget: $50-100,000
Executive Director: Toby Dershowitz

Historical Note
Members are Jewish community newspapers. Formerly the American Association of English Jewish Newspapers. Membership: $100/year (individual); $360/year (full newspaper).

Publications:
Membership Bulletin. 4/year.
Membership Directory. 1/year.

American Journalism Historians Association *(1981)*
OBU Box 61201, 500 W. University
Shawnee, OK 74804
Tel: (405)878-2221
E-Mail: carol.humphrey@okbu.edu
Web Site: www.berry.edu/ajha
*Members:*360 individuals
Annual Budget: $10-25,000
Secretary: Carol Sue Humphrey

Historical Note
AJHA members are academics and other individuals with an interest in the history of the media. Has no paid officers or full-time staff. Membership: $15/year (student/retiree); $35/year (individual); $45/year (organization/company)

Meetings/Conferences:
Annual Meetings: October

Publications:
AJHA Intelligencer Newsletter. q.
American Journalism Journal. q. adv.

American Judges Association *(1959)*
300 Newport Ave.
Williamsburg, VA 23185-4147
Tel: (757)259-1841 *Fax:* (757)259-1520
E-Mail: aja@ncsc.dni.us
Web Site: http://aja.ncsc.dni.us
*Members:*2000 individuals
Staff: 2
Annual Budget: $50-100,000
Association Manager: Shelley Rockwell

Historical Note
Formerly (1965) the National Association of Municipal Judges and (1972) the North American Judges Association. An independent organization of judges of all jurisdictions in the United States and Canada. Affiliated with the American Judges Foundation. Membership: $90/year.

Meetings/Conferences:
Annual Meetings: Fall/200-250
2007 - Vancouver, BC, Canada(Sheraton Wall Centre)
2008 - Maui, HI(Westin Maui)

Publications:
AJA Benchmark. q. adv.
Court Review. q. adv.

American Judicature Society *(1913)*
2700 University Ave.
Des Moines, IA 50311
Tel: (515)271-2281 *Fax:* (515)279-3090
Web Site: www.ajs.org
*Members:*6000 individuals
Staff: 12
Annual Budget: $1-2,000,000
President: Allan D. Sobel
E-Mail: asobel@ajs.org
Communications and Public Relations: Dawn Buzynski

Historical Note
AJS is a nonpartisan, nonprofit organization established in 1913 to promote the effective administration of justice. Membership consists of lawyers, judges and others interested in furthering this mission. Through reseach, educational programs and publications, AJS focuses primarily on judicial selection, judicial independence, judicial ethics, the jury, court administration and public understanding of the justice system. Membership: $75/year.

Meetings/Conferences:
Annual Meetings: in conjunction with American Bar Ass'n/Summer

Publications:
Judicature. bi-m. adv.
Judicial Conduct Reporter. q.

American Karakul Sheep Registry *(1965)*
11500 Hwy. Five
Boonville, MO 65233
Tel: (660)838-6340 *Fax:* (660)838-6322
E-Mail: aksr@i-land.net
Web Site: www.karakulsheep.com
Members: 80 individuals
Staff: 1
Annual Budget: under $10,000
Registrar: Rey Perera

Historical Note
Formerly Karakul Fur Sheep Registry, (1979) Empire Karakul Registry and (1985) American Karakul Fur Sheep Registry. AKSR promotes and perpetuates the Karakul purebred, originally imported from Russia. Membership: $15/year (individual).

Meetings/Conferences:
Biennial Show:

Publications:
Newsletter. 3-4/year.

American Kennel Club *(1884)*
260 Madison Ave., Fourth Floor
New York, NY 10016
Tel: (212)696-8200 *Fax:* (212)696-8299
E-Mail: info@akc.org
Web Site: www.akc.org
Members: 503 dog clubs
Staff: 410
Annual Budget: $10-25,000,000
President and Chief Executive Officer: Dennis B. Sprung
Chief Operating Officer: John Lyons
Chief Financial Officer: James T. Stevens

Historical Note
The principal registry of pure-bred dogs in the United States and the regulatory agency for dog shows, the AKC was established to advance the study, breeding, exhibiting, running and maintenance of the purity of thoroughbred dogs. Founded by show-giving clubs to bring order to the sport of dogs, the AKC has no individual members. Has an annual budget of approximately $20 million.

Publications:
Pure-Bred Dogs/American Kennel Gazette. m.

American Kinesiotherapy Association *(1946)*
P.O. Box 1390
Hines, IL 60141-1390
Toll Free: (800)296 - 2582
E-Mail: ccbkt@aol.com
Web Site: www.akta.org
Members: 500 individuals
Staff: 1
Executive Officer: Bridget Collins

Historical Note
Formerly (1987) American Corrective Therapy Association and (1967) Association for Physical and Mental Rehabilitation. Professional society of kinesiotherapists and exercise therapists. Kinesiotherapy is the application of scientifically based exercise principles adapted to enhance the strength, endurance and mobility of individuals with functional limitations, and of individuals requiring extended physical conditioning. Membership: $150/year (individual).

Meetings/Conferences:
Annual Meetings: Second week in July/150-200

Publications:
Mobility Newsletter. q. adv.
Journal of Clinical Kinesiology (online). q.

American Knife and Tool Institute *(1997)*
22 Vista View
Cody, WY 82414-9606
Tel: (307)587-8296 *Fax:* (307)587-8296
E-Mail: akti@akti.org
Web Site: www.akti.org
Members: 300 individuals
Executive Director: Jan Billeb

Historical Note
AKTI monitors legislative developments concerning the use, manufacture, and distribution of knives and tools in the U.S., and educates and informs the knife-using community on important issues.

Publications:
AKTI Update. 4/year.

American Ladder Institute *(1935)*
401 N. Michigan Ave.
Chicago, IL 60611-4267
Tel: (312)644-6610 *Fax:* (312)527-6705
E-Mail: rpietrzak@smithbucklin.com
Web Site: www.americanladderinstitute.org
Members: 34 companies
Staff: 2
Annual Budget: $100-250,000
Executive Director: Ron Pietrzak

Historical Note
Represents U.S. companies engaged in the research, development, manufacture, and safety of ladders. Works with government bodies, particularly ANSI, OSHA and CPSC, in addressing design and safety questions. Members include manufacturers of wood, metal, and fiberglass ladders. Suppliers to the industry are also eligible for membership as associates.

Meetings/Conferences:
Annual Meetings: Spring

Publications:
ALI Ladder Lines. q.

American Lamb Council

Historical Note
A division of the American Sheep Industry Association.

American Land Rights Association *(1978)*
P.O. Box 400
Battle Ground, WA 98604
Tel: (360)687-3087 *Fax:* (360)687-2973
E-Mail: administrator@landrights.org
Web Site: www.landrights.org
Members: 22000 individuals
Staff: 8
Annual Budget: $250-500,000
Executive Director: Charles S. Cushman

Historical Note
Formerly (1980) National Park Inholders Association, and then (1993) National Inholders Association. Members are individuals holding property, equity interest, grazing permits, leases or related claims to use on real estate in or adjacent to federally managed areas such as national parks, forests, refuges and other reserves in the public domain. Promotes the interests of these property owners and resource dependent communities through lobbying and activism. Maintains a Washington representative. Membership: $35/year.

Meetings/Conferences:
Annual Meetings: Irregular

Publications:
Land Rights Advocate. bi-m. adv.
Congressional Directory. bien.
Land Rights Action Guide. bien.
Land Rights Alert. m.
Private Property Congressional Vote Index. bien.

American Land Title Association *(1907)*
1828 L St. NW
Suite 705
Washington, DC 20036-5104
Tel: (202)296-3671 *Fax:* (888)329-2582
Toll Free: (800)787 - 2582
E-Mail: service@alta.org
Web Site: www.alta.org
Members: 2600 corporations
Staff: 17
Annual Budget: $2-5,000,000
Executive Vice President: James R. Maher
E-Mail: jim_maher@alta.org
Director, Education: Patricia L. Berman
E-Mail: pat_berman@alta.org
Director, Marketing: Cammy Davidge
Vice President, Operations: Mark Hernick
E-Mail: mark_hernick@alta.org
Director, Research: Richard McCarthy
E-Mail: rich_mccarthy@alta.org
Chief Counsel and Vice President, Public Policy: Edward Miller
Director, Communications: Lorri Lee Ragan
E-Mail: lorri_ragan@alta.org
Director, Technology: Kelly Romeo
E-Mail: kelly_romeo@alta.org
Director, Meetings/Conferences: Liza Trey
E-Mail: liza_trey@alta.org

Historical Note
Membership is composed of title insurers, agents, title abstracters, lawyers and other specialists in real estate settlement services. Supports the Title Industry Political Action Committee. Membership: Dues based on gross revenue for title service.

Meetings/Conferences:
Annual Meetings: Fall
2007 - Chicago, IL(Hilton)/Oct. 10-14
2008 - Koloa, HI(Hyatt Kauai)/Oct. 15-18

Publications:
ALTA e-News. w.
TITLE News. bi-m. adv.

American Landrace Association *(1950)*

Historical Note
Members are breeders and fanciers of landrace swine. Member of the National Pedigree Livestock Council. Membership: $50/year.

American Laryngological Association *(1878)*
Montefiore Medical Center, Third Floor
3400 Bainbridge Ave.
Bronx, NY 10467-2404
Tel: (718)920-2700 *Fax:* (718)405-9014
Web Site: www.alahns.org
Members: 250 individuals
Staff: 2
Annual Budget: $25-50,000
Secretary: Marvin P. Fried, M.D.
E-Mail: mfried@montefiore.org

Historical Note
Members are individuals concentrating on the advancement of medicine and surgery of the upper aerodigestive tract.

Meetings/Conferences:
Annual Meetings: Spring

Publications:
Transactions. a.

American Laryngological, Rhinological and Otological Society *(1895)*
555 N. 30th St.
Omaha, NE 68131
Tel: (402)346-5500 *Fax:* (402)346-5300
E-Mail: info@triological.org
Web Site: www.triological.org
Members: 1100 individuals
Staff: 3
Annual Budget: $1-2,000,000
Executive Secretary: Patrick Brookhouser, MD

Historical Note
Organized June 19, 1895 and incorporated December 5, 1917. Also known as the Triological Society. Membership: $110/year (individual).

Meetings/Conferences:
Annual Meetings: Spring

Publications:
Triologistics. 3/year.
Laryngoscope. m. adv.

American Law Institute *(1923)*
4025 Chestnut St.
Philadelphia, PA 19104-3099
Tel: (215)243-1600 *Fax:* (215)243-1636
Toll Free: (800)253 - 6397
Web Site: www.ali.org
Members: 3950 individuals
Staff: 85
Annual Budget: $5-10,000,000
Director: Lance Liebman
Deputy Director: Elena A. Cappella
Coordinator, Membership: Helene Cohen
Coordinator, Meetings: Sandrine Forgeron
Director, Office of Administrative Services: Joseph A. Mendicino, Jr.
E-Mail: jmendicino@ali-aba.org

Historical Note
Membership, by invitation only, consists of lawyers, judges, educators and government officials interested in simplifying, clarifying, and improving the law. ALI produces restatements of the law, model codes, and recommendations for reform. Its program of education is conducted in close cooperation with the American Bar Association through a joint committee known as American Law Institute/American Bar Association Continuing Professional Education (ALI-ABA). Membership: $250/year (practicing lawyers); $125/year (teachers and judges).

Meetings/Conferences:
Annual Meetings: Spring
2007 – San Francisco, CA/May 14-16
2008 – Washington, DC/May 12-14
2009 – Washington, DC(The Mayflower)/May 11-13
2010 – Washington, DC/May 17-19

Publications:
ALI-ABA Business Law Course Materials Journal. bi-m.
ALI Annual Meeting Proceedings. a.
CLE Journal. bien.
Practical Real Estate Lawyer. bi-m.
Practical Litigator. bi-m.
Practical Tax Lawyer. q.
ALI-ABA CLE Review. 11/year.
ALI-ABA Estate Planning Course Materials Journal. bi-m.
ALI Reporter. q.
Practical Lawyer. bi-m.

American Law Student Association *(1949)*

Historical Note
A Division of the American Bar Association.

American League of Financial Institutions *(1948)*

Historical Note
Absorbed by America's Community Bankers in 2002.

American League of Lobbyists *(1978)*
P.O. Box 30005
Alexandria, VA 22310
Tel: (703)960-3011
E-Mail: info@alldc.org
Web Site: www.alldc.org
Members: 800 individuals
Staff: 1
Annual Budget: $100-250,000
Executive Director: Patti Jo Baber
E-Mail: info@alldc.org

Historical Note
ALL is dedicated to enhancing the profession of lobbying throughout the United States. ALL helps its members to develop their professional skills, heighten their knowledge of the issues that affect them, and increase their exposure to the elected officials involved in public policy decisions. ALL also serves to inform the public about the substantive role of the lobbyist in the American governmental process. Membership: $195/year (regular); $85/year (government).

Publications:
ALL News. 4/year. adv.
ALL Directory. a. adv.

American League of Professional Baseball Clubs *(1900)*

Historical Note
Ceased independent operations in 2000; see Major League Baseball - Office of the Commissioner.

American Leather Chemists Association *(1903)*
1314 50th St., Suite 103
Lubbock, TX 79412
Tel: (806)744-1798 *Fax:* (806)744-1785
E-Mail: alca@leatherchemists.org
Web Site: www.leatherchemists.org
Members: 500 individuals
Staff: 3
Annual Budget: $100-250,000
Executive Secretary: Carol Adcock
E-Mail: carol.adcock@ttu.edu

Historical Note
Founded in 1903 and incorporated in New Jersey in 1937, ALCA is a member of the International Union of Leather Chemists Societies. ALCA advances the knowledge of science and engineering as it applies to leather and leather products industries. Membership: $112/year.

Meetings/Conferences:
Annual Meetings: June/400
2007 – Washington, DC(Marriott)/June 20-24

Publications:
Journal of the American Leather Chemists Association. m. adv.

American Legend Cooperative *(1985)*
P.O. Box 58308
Seattle, WA 98138
Tel: (425)251-3200 *Fax:* (425)251-3222
E-Mail: info@americanlegend.com
Web Site: www.americanlegend.com
Members: 800 individuals
Staff: 40
Annual Budget: $1-2,000,000
Chief Executive Officer: Edward Brenen

Historical Note
Formed in 1985 by a merger of the Great Lakes Mink Association and the Emba Mink Breeders Association (1942), ALC is a producer-owned cooperative organization that promotes ranch-raised mink and fox fur. Membership: 2% of gross sales/year.

Meetings/Conferences:
Semi-Annual Meetings: Winter and Spring

Publications:
American Legend Newsletter. m.

American Legislative Exchange Council *(1973)*
1129 20th St. NW, Fifth Floor
Washington, DC 20036
Tel: (202)466-3800 *Fax:* (202)466-3801
E-Mail: info@alec.org
Web Site: www.alec.org
Members: 2400 individuals
Staff: 30
Annual Budget: $5-10,000,000
Executive Director: Lori Roman

Meetings/Conferences:
Annual Meetings: Summer
2007 – Philadelphia, PA(Downtown Marriott)/July 25-29
2008 – Chicago, IL(Sheraton)/July 30-Aug. 2

Publications:
Inside ALEC. m. adv.
ALEC Policy Forum. q. adv.

American Library Association *(1876)*
50 E. Huron St.
Chicago, IL 60611-2795
Tel: (312)280-1392 *Fax:* (312)440-9374
Toll Free: (800)545 - 2433
E-Mail: ala@ala.org
Web Site: www.ala.org
Members: 64099
Staff: 259
Annual Budget: $25-50,000,000
Executive Director: Keith M. Fiels
Director, Public Information Office: Mark Gould
Director, Conference Services: Diedre Irwin Ross
Associate Executive Director, Washington Office: Emily Sheketoff
Director, Office for Information Technology Policy: Rick Weingarten

Historical Note
An educational association of U.S. libraries, librarians and library supporters, the ALA represents all types of libraries, including state, public, school, academic and special libraries serving persons in government, commerce, armed services, hospitals, prisons and other institutions. ALA has the following membership units (divisions), focusing on specific types of libraries or library services: American Association of School Librarians, Association for Library Trustees and Advocates, Reference and User Services Association, Association for Library Collections and Technical Services, Association for Library Service to Children, Association of College and Research Libraries, Association of Specialized and Cooperative Library Agencies, Library Administration and Management Association, Library and Information Technology Association, Public Library Association, Reference and User Services Association, and Young Adult Library Services Association (see separate listings). ALA also counts 57 independent library associations in states, regions and territories of the U.S. as chapters. 23 independent national and international organizations with purposes similar to the ALA are affiliates. Maintains a Washington, DC office. Has an annual budget of approximately $30 million. Membership: $25-100/year.

Meetings/Conferences:
Semi-Annual Meetings: Winter and Summer

Publications:
Young Adult Library Services. 4/year. adv.
Knowledge Quest. 5/year. adv.
Children and Libraries. 3/year. adv.
Documents to the People. q. adv.
Reference and User Services Quarterly. 4/year. adv.
Library Administration and Management. 4/year. adv.
American Libraries. 11/year. adv.
Choice. 11/year. adv.
College and Research Libraries News. 11/year. adv.
Booklist. semi-m. adv.
College and Research Libraries. bi-m. adv.
Information Technology and Libraries. 4/year. adv.
Library Resources and Technical Services. q. adv.
Library Technology Reports. 6/yr. adv.
Newsletter on Intellectual Freedom. bi-m.
Library Personnel News. q.

American Licensed Practical Nurses Association *(1984)*
1090 Vermont Ave. NW
Suite 800
Washington, DC 20005-4905
Tel: (202)682-9000 *Fax:* (202)682-0168
Members: 5000 individuals
Staff: 5
Annual Budget: $250-500,000
Executive Director and General Counsel: Paul M. Tendler

Historical Note
A professional association of licensed practical/vocational nurses. Membership: $50/year (individual).

Publications:
ALPNA Newsletter. q.

American Lighting Association *(1945)*
2050 Stemmons Freeway, Suite 10046
P.O. Box 420288
Dallas, TX 75342-0288
Tel: (214)698-9898 *Fax:* (214)698-9899
Toll Free: (800)605 - 4448
Web Site: www.americanlightingassoc.com
Members: 1200 firms
Staff: 8
Annual Budget: $1-2,000,000
President: Richard D. Upton
Director, Meetings and Conventions: Beth Bentley
Vice President, Membership: Eric Jacobson, CAE
Manager, Education: Nicole Juncan
Vice President, Public Relations and Communications: Larry Lauck
Director, Finance: Wendy Rollins

Historical Note
Members are manufacturers of lighting products, components, and accessories, manufacturers' representatives, showrooms and distributors. Formerly (1989) American Home Lighting Institute. Membership: $420-$20,400/year (organization/company).

Meetings/Conferences:
Annual Meetings: Fall/550-600

Publications:
Membership Directory. a. adv.
Lightrays. bi-m. adv.
Lighting Your Life.
Light Up Your Landscape.
Light Up Your Kitchen & Bath.

American Literary Translators Association *(1978)*
c/o UTD
Box 830688
Richardson, TX 75083-0688

Tel: (972)883-2093 *Fax:* (972)883-6303
E-Mail: jdickey@utdallas.edu
Web Site: www.literarytranslators.org
Members: 600 individuals
Staff: 3
Annual Budget: $25-50,000
Director: Rainer Schulte
Secretary: Jessie Dickey

Historical Note
Members are translators into English of books in literature and the humanities. Maintains the Translation Clearinghouse and Translation Library. Membership fee varies, based on type.

Meetings/Conferences:
Annual Meetings: December/150

Publications:
Translation Review. 2/year. adv.
ALTA Newsletter. 3/year.

American Lithotripsy Society *(1987)*
305 Second Ave., Suite 200
Waltham, MA 02451
Tel: (781)895-9098 *Fax:* (781)895-9088
E-Mail: als@lithotripsy.org
Web Site: www.lithotripsy.org
Members: 900 individuals
Staff: 5
Annual Budget: $500-1,000,000
Executive Director: Wesley E. Harrington, CAE

Historical Note
ALS was established to develop criteria for quality assurance and review, to validate and credential ESWL sites for training, establish training criteria, to provide support through data and experience to members for influencing third party reimbursers, to review and disseminate information on emerging ESWL technologies, to develop cost comparison data, establish liaison with related professional organizations, and to create a forum for the exchange of views regarding renal and billiary lithotripsy. Membership: $185/year (physician); $65/year (allied health care professional).

Meetings/Conferences:
Annual Meetings: Spring/300
2007 - Orlando, FL(Dolphin Hotels)/March 15-18/650

Publications:
Newsletter of the American Lithotripsy Soc. semi-a. adv.

American Littoral Society *(1961)*
Bldg. 18
Sandy Hook Highlands, NJ 07732
Tel: (732)291-0055 *Fax:* (732)872-8041
E-Mail: pat@littoralsociety.org
Web Site: www.littoralsociety.org
Members: 6000 individuals
Staff: 11
Annual Budget: $100-250,000
Executive Director: Tim Dillingham
Office Manager: Pat Coren

Historical Note
Founded in 1961 at the Sandy Hook Marine Laboratory and incorporated in 1962 in New Jersey. Promotes the study and conservation of the coastal zone habitat. Membership: $25/year (regular).

Meetings/Conferences:
Annual Meetings: Fall

Publications:
Coastal Reporter. semi-a.
Underwater Naturalist. q. adv.

American Logistics Association *(1920)*
1133 15th St. NW
Suite 640
Washington, DC 20005
Tel: (202)466-2520 *Fax:* (202)296-4419
E-Mail: membership@ala-national.org
Web Site: www.ala-national.org
Members: 2500 individuals
Staff: 12
Annual Budget: $2-5,000,000
President: John Molino
Vice President, Operations: L. Maurice Branch
Vice President, Exchange, MWR and Service Affairs: Frank Jepson
Vice President, Commissary Affairs: Alan Nissalke
Vice President, Government Affairs: Len Williams

Historical Note
A trade association of companies and individuals involved in marketing to the military - commissaries, exchanges, clubs, snack bars, ship's stores, mess halls, and service stations. Formerly the Quartermaster Association and (1972) Defense Supply Association. Membership: $50/year (individual); company dues based on annual gross military sales revenue.

Meetings/Conferences:
Annual Meetings: Fall

Publications:
Executive Briefing Newsletter (online). w.
Military Market Facts.
Worldwide Directory. a. adv.

American Loudspeaker Manufacturers Association

Historical Note
Became ALHA - The Internat'l Loudspeaker Ass'n, in 2003.

American Luggage Dealers Association *(1970)*
20 First Plaza NW
Suite 310
Albuquerque, NM 87102-3390
Tel: (505)246-0087 *Fax:* (505)246-0096
Web Site: www.luggagedealers.com
Members: 60 companies
Staff: 4
Annual Budget: $2-5,000,000
Executive Director: Frank Fine

Historical Note
Formed to develop a progressive merchandise program such as publication of catalogs and specific merchandise opportunities for independent luggage retailers.

Meetings/Conferences:
Semi-annual Meetings: Spring/Summer

Publications:
Fall Flyer. a.
Giftables Catalog. a.
Spring Flyer. a.
Newsletter. q.

American Lung Association *(1904)*
61 Broadway, Sixth Floor
New York, NY 10006
Tel: (212)315-8700 *Fax:* (212)315-8882
Toll Free: (800)586 - 4872
E-Mail: info@lungusa.org
Web Site: www.lungusa.org
Members: 10000 individuals
Staff: 150
Annual Budget: $25-50,000,000
President and Chief Executive Officer: John Kirkwood
Executive Vice President and Chief Operating Officer: Joseph Bergen
Senior Vice President, Program Services: Fran DuMelle

Historical Note
Established as the National Association for the Study and Prevention of Tuberculosis, it became the National Tuberculosis Association in 1918, the National Tuberculosis and Respiratory Disease Association in 1968 and assumed its present name in 1973. The American Thoracic Society is the ALA's medical section. A federation of state and local associations, ALA is dedicated to the control and prevention of all lung diseases and some of their related causes, including smoking, air pollution and occupational lung hazards.

Meetings/Conferences:
Annual Meetings: May

American Machine Tool Distributors Association *(1925)*
1445 Research Blvd., Suite 450
Rockville, MD 20850
Tel: (301)738-1200 *Fax:* (301)738-9499
Web Site: www.amtda.org
Members: 500 companies
Staff: 8
Annual Budget: $2-5,000,000
President: John J. Healy, CAE

Historical Note
Founded in 1925 in Cincinnati by 22 distributors of machine tools.

Meetings/Conferences:
Annual Meetings: Spring

Publications:
AMTDA Membership Directory. a. adv.
Tool Talk. m.

American Maine-Anjou Association *(1969)*
204 Marshall Rd.
P.O. Box 1100
Platte City, MO 64079-1100
Tel: (816)431-9950 *Fax:* (816)431-9951
E-Mail: maine@kc.rr.com
Web Site: www.maine-anjou.org
Members: 2500 individuals
Staff: 6
Annual Budget: $1-2,000,000
Executive Vice President: John A. Boddicker

Historical Note
Formerly (1971) the Maine-Anjou Society and (1975) the International Maine-Anjou Association. Members are breeders and fanciers of Maine-Anjou Beef Cattle. Member of the National Cattlemen's Association. Membership: $50/year.

Publications:
The Voice. bi-m. adv.
Commercial Connection.

American Malting Barley Association *(1945)*
740 N. Plankinton Ave., Suite 830
Milwaukee, WI 53203-2403
Tel: (414)272-4640
E-Mail: joann.amba@sbcglobal.net
Web Site: www.ambainc.org
Members: 10 companies
Staff: 3
Annual Budget: $500-1,000,000
President: Michael P. Davis

Historical Note
Founded as the Midwest Barley Improvement Association, it became the Malting Barley Improvement Association in 1954 and assumed its present name in 1982. Absorbed Malt Research Institute. Members are maltsters and brewers.

Meetings/Conferences:
Annual Meetings:

American Managed Behavioral Healthcare Association *(1994)*
1101 Pennsylvania Ave. NW, Sixth Floor
Washington, DC 20004
Tel: (202)756-7726 *Fax:* (202)756-7308
Web Site: www.ambha.org
Members: 9 organizations
Staff: 1
Annual Budget: $250-500,000
Executive Director: Pamela Greenberg, M.P.P.

Historical Note
AMBHA seeks to present and promote the industry's perspective in federal and state legislative and regulatory actions, and works to foster a broad understanding of managed behavioral healthcare's ability to deliver accessible, quality, cost-effective care. The association represents the industry to federal and state governments, mental health and substance abuse providers, associations and other key audiences. AMBHA supports and promotes the need for comprehensive managed behavioral care benefits in all private and public health care programs, including Medicare and Medicaid. AMBHA advocates open competition based on documented performance, positive clinical outcomes, consumer satisfaction and public accountability. Membership: $5,000-$70,000/year (company).

Meetings/Conferences:
Annual Meetings: Twice a year

American Management Association *(1923)*
1601 Broadway
New York, NY 10019-7420
Tel: (212)586-8100 *Fax:* (212)903-8168
Toll Free: (888)262 - 9699
E-Mail: rkelleher@amanet.org
Web Site: www.amanet.org
Members: 4464 corporate

Staff: 550
Annual Budget: $5-10,000,000
President and Chief Executive Officer: Edward T. Reilly
Executive Vice President, Chief Financial Officer, Treasurer: Vivianna Guzman

Historical Note
Merger (1973) of the American Management Association (1923), the American Foundation for Management Research (1960), the International Management Association (1956), the Presidents Association (1961) and the Society for Advancement of Management (1912) devoted to all types of management education. Maintains offices in Atlanta, GA; Watertown, MA; Chicago, IL; Hamilton, NY; Leawood, KS; New York, NY; San Francisco, CA; Saranac Lake, NY; and Washington, DC. Also maintains International offices and affiliated centers. AMA provides educational forums worldwide where members and their colleagues learn business skills and explore best practices of world-class organizations through interaction with each other and expert faculty practitioners.

Publications:
The Take-Charge Assistant. m.
Compensation & Benefits Review. bi-m.
Management Review. m. adv.
Organizational Dynamics. q.
H R Focus. m.

American Maritime Association *(1961)*
c/o American Maritime Safety, Inc.
445 Hamilton Ave., Suite 1204
White Plains, NY 10601-1833
Tel: (914)997-6959
Members: 28 companies
Staff: 1
Annual Budget: $100-250,000

Historical Note
An employer association created for the sole purpose of collective bargaining with the off-shore maritime unions.

Meetings/Conferences:
Annual Meetings: June, in New York City

American Maritime Congress *(1977)*
1300 I St. NW
Suite 250-W
Washington, DC 20005
Tel: (202)842-4900 *Fax:* (202)842-3492
E-Mail: info@us-flag.org
Web Site: www.us-flag.org
Members: 30 companies
Staff: 8
President: Gloria Cataneo Tosi

Historical Note
AMC members are U.S. ship operating companies having contracts with the Marine Engineers' Beneficial Association, a maritime union.

Publications:
AMC Washington Letter. w.

American Marketing Association *(1937)*
311 S. Wacker Dr., Suite 5800
Chicago, IL 60606
Tel: (312)542-9000 *Fax:* (312)542-9001
Toll Free: (800)262 - 1150
E-Mail: info@ama.org
Web Site: www.marketingpower.com
Members: 40000 individuals
Staff: 70
Annual Budget: $10-25,000,000
Chief Executive Officer: Dennis Dunlap
Senior Director, Publishing Group: Jack Hollfelder

Historical Note
Formerly (1915) National Association of Teachers of Advertising; (1926) National Association of Teachers of Marketing & Advertising; (1932) National Association of Teachers of Marketing; (1937) merged with American Marketing Society to form the American Marketing Association. The Academy of Health Service Marketing was absorbed by the AMA in 1994. Has an annual budget of over $7 million. AMBHA does not hold an annual convention or convocation, however holds a multiplicity of national conferences, seminars and forums throughout the year. Membership: $145/year (introductory); $25/year (student).

Publications:
Marketing News (Collegiate Edition). 8/yr. adv.
Marketing News (Professional Edition). 20/yr. adv.
Journal of International Marketing. q. adv.
Marketing Health Services. q. adv.
Journal of Marketing. q. adv.
Journal of Marketing Research. q. adv.
Marketing Research. q. adv.
Journal of Public Policy and Marketing. semi-a. adv.
Marketing Management. 6/yr. adv.

American Massage Therapy Association *(1943)*
500 Davis St., Suite 900
Evanston, IL 60201
Tel: (847)864-0123 *Fax:* (847)864-1178
Toll Free: (877)905 - 2700
E-Mail: info@amtamassage.org
Web Site: www.amtamassage.org
Members: 55000 individuals
Staff: 60
Annual Budget: $10-25,000,000
Executive Director: Elizabeth M. Lucas
E-Mail: info@amtamassage.org
Director, Professional Development: Andrea Haller
E-Mail: info@amtamassage.org
Director, Member Services: Lay Quek
E-Mail: info@amtamassage.org
Director, Finance: Sandor Szanjkovics
Director, Governance and Chapter Relations: Mark Tyle
E-Mail: info@amtamassage.org
Director, Communications and Marketing: Dean Vaeth
E-Mail: info@amtamassage.org

Historical Note
AMTA, founded in 1943, represents the massage therapy profession. Mission is to serve AMTA's members and advance the science and practice of massage therapy. AMTA also offers a free Find a Massage Therapist national locator service, www.findamassagetherapist.org, to help consumers find qualified massage therapists around the United States.

Meetings/Conferences:
2007 - Cincinnati, OH(Hilton)/Sept. 26-29/1000

Publications:
Hand's On. bi-m.
e-Touch Newsletter. m. adv.
Massage Therapy Journal. q. adv.

American Mathematical Association of Two Year Colleges *(1974)*
Southwest Tennessee CC
5983 Macon Cove
Memphis, TN 38134
Tel: (901)333-4643 *Fax:* (901)333-4651
E-Mail: amatyc@amatyc.org
Web Site: www.amatyc.org
Members: 3000 individuals
Staff: 4
Annual Budget: $250-500,000
President: Judy E. Ackerman
Director, Publications: Christine Shott
Office Director: Beverly Vance

Historical Note
A member of the Conference Board of the Mathematical Sciences and the Council of Scientific Society Presidents, AMATYC is the only national association exclusively devoted to improving mathematical education in the first two years of college. AMATYC members are teachers of mathematics and computer science in two-year colleges. Membership: $60/year (individual); $300/year (institution).

Meetings/Conferences:
Annual Meetings: October-November

Publications:
AMATYC News. 5/year.
AMATYC Review. semi-a.

American Mathematical Society *(1888)*
201 Charles St.
Providence, RI 02904-2294
Tel: (401)455-4000 *Fax:* (401)331-3842
Toll Free: (800)321 - 4267
E-Mail: ams@ams.org
Web Site: www.ams.org
Members: 30000 individuals
Staff: 250
Annual Budget: $10-25,000,000
Executive Director: John H. Ewing
Associate Executive Director, Special Projects: James Maxwell
Associate Executive Director, Meetings and Professional Services: Ellen Maycock
Chief Financial Officer: Constance W. Pass

Historical Note
Organized in New York City on November 24, 1888 by six members of the mathematics department of Columbia University as the New York Mathematical Soc; became the American Mathematical Society in 1894. Incorporated in the District of Columbia in 1923. Has an annual budget of approximately $21.5 million.

Meetings/Conferences:
Annual Meetings: With The Mathematical Ass'n of America/Winter/2,800
2007 - New Orleans, LA(Marriott/Sheraton)/Jan. 4-7
2008 - San Diego, CA(Convention Ctr.)/Jan. 6-9
2009 - Washington, DC(Marriott Wardman Park)/Jan. 7-10
2010 - San Francisco, CA(Moscone West Convention Center)/Jan. 6-9
2011 - New Orleans, LA(Marriott)/Jan. 5-8

Publications:
Abstracts of Papers Presented to the AMS. q.
Employment Information in the Mathematical Sciences. 5/year.
St. Petersburg Mathematical Journal. bi-m.
Sugaku Expositions. bien.
Mathematics of Computation. q.
Quarterly of Applied Mathematics. q.
Notices of the AMS. 10/year. adv.
Proceedings of the AMS. m.
Theory of Probability and Mathematical Statistics. 2/year.
Transactions of the AMS. m.
Transactions of the Moscow Mathematical Society. a.
Assistantships and Fellowships in the Mathematical Sciences. a.
Journal of the AMS. q.
Bulletin of the AMS. q.
Current Mathematical Publications. tri-w.
Mathematical Reviews. m. adv.
Memoirs of the American Mathematical Society. bi-m.

American Measuring Tool Manufacturers Association *(1973)*
1300 Sumner Ave.
Cleveland, OH 44115-2851
Tel: (216)241-7333 *Fax:* (216)241-0105
E-Mail: amtma@amtma.com
Web Site: www.amtma.com
Members: 75 companies
Staff: 3
Managing Director: Charles M. Stockinger

Historical Note
AMTMA members are companies that produce gauges and similar precison measuring tools for a wide variety of quality control applications.

American Meat Institute *(1906)*
1150 Connecticut Ave. NW, 12th Floor
Washington, DC 20036
Tel: (202)587-4200 *Fax:* (202)587-4300
E-Mail: memberservices@meatami.com
Web Site: www.meatami.com
Members: 1100 companies
Staff: 40
Annual Budget: $5-10,000,000
President and Chief Executive Officer: J. Patrick Boyle
Senior Vice President, Regulatory Affairs and General Counsel: Mark Dopp
Vice President, Convention and Member Services: Anne Halal, CAE
Vice President, Scientific Affairs: Randall Huffman, Ph.D.

Senior Vice President, Administration, Convention and Member Services: Ronald L. Nunnery
Senior Vice President, Public Affairs and Professional Development: Janet Riley
Vice President, Regulatory Affairs: Skip Seward

Historical Note
The national trade organization of the meat and poultry packing and processing industry. Founded in 1906 as the American Meat Packers Association, it became the Institute of American Meat Packers in 1919 and the American Meat Institute in 1940. Founded in 1944 as its research and education arm, the American Meat Institute Foundation was reestablished in 1992. AMI merged with the National Independent Meat Packers Association in 1982 and began managing the U.S. Hide Skin and Leather Association in 1990. The National Meat Canners Association became affiliated with AMI in 1992. Connected with the American Meat Institute Political Action Committee. Has an annual budget of approximately $8 million.

American Meat Science Association *(1948)*
1111 N. Dunlap Ave.
Savoy, IL 61874
Tel: (217)356-5368 *Fax:* (217)398-4119
E-Mail: information@meatscience.org
Web Site: www.meatscience.org
Members: 1066 individuals
Staff: 6
Executive Director: Thomas Powell
E-Mail: tpowell@meatscience.org

Historical Note
Established as the Reciprocal Meat Conference in 1948 and became the American Meat Science Association in 1964. Promotes education and research in meat and related subjects. Membership: $145/year (professional); $65/year (graduate student); $20/year (undergraduate).

Meetings/Conferences:
Annual Meetings: Summer

Publications:
Meat Science journal.
AMSA Newsletter. q.
Proceedings of the Reciprocal Meat Conference. a.

American Medallic Sculpture Association *(1982)*
P.O. Box 1201
Edmonds, WA 98020
Tel: (206)542-0608
E-Mail: amsanews@verizon.net
Web Site: www.amsamedals.org
Members: 130 individuals
Annual Budget: under $10,000
Secretary: Anne-Lise Deering

Historical Note
Organized in February, 1982 in New York City by a group of medallic artists to promote improvement in the art of the medal. Has no paid officers or full-time staff. Sponsors exhibitions, symposia, and other events. Membership: $35/year.

Publications:
Members Exchange. q.

American Medical Association *(1847)*
515 N. State St.
Chicago, IL 60610-4320
Tel: (312)464-5000 *Fax:* (312)464-4184
Toll Free: (800)621 - 8335
Web Site: www.ama-assn.org
Members: 260000 individuals
Staff: 1200
Annual Budget: Over $100,000,000
Executive Vice President/Chief Executive Officer: Michael D. Maves, MD, MBA
Chief Technology Officer: Michael J. Berkeley
Senior Vice President, Advocacy: Catherine D. DeAngelis, MD, MPH
Senior Vice President, Communications: Jon N. Ekdahl
Chief Marketing Officer: Gary C. Epstein
Chief Financial Officer and Vice President, Finance: Denise Hagerty
Chief Operating Officer: Bernard L. Hengesbaugh
Senior Vice President, Publishing and Business: Robert A. Musacchio
Senior Vice President, Governance and Operations: J. Todd Vande Hey
Senior Vice President, Professional Standards: Modena H. Wilson, MD, MHP

Historical Note
Established in Philadelphia in 1847 and incorporated in Illinois in 1897. Principal spokesman for the U.S. medical profession with about 2,000 local and regional medical societies. AMA and its affiliates support numerous political action committees throughout the country, including the American Medical PAC. In 1994, AMA absorbed the American Association of Senior Physicians. Has an annual budget of approximately $200 million. Membership: $420/year.

Meetings/Conferences:
Semi-Annual Meetings: June and December
2007 - Chicago, IL/June 23-27

Publications:
Archives of Pediatric and Adolescent Medicine. m. adv.
American Medical News. w. adv.
Journal of the American Medical Ass'n. w. adv.
Archives of Dermatology. m. adv.
Archives of General Psychiatry. m. adv.
Archives of Internal Medicine. m. adv.
Archives of Neurology. m. adv.
Archives of Ophthalmology. m. adv.
Archives of Otolaryngology. m. adv.
Archives of Surgery. m. adv.
Archives of Family Medicine.

American Medical Directors Association *(1976)*
10480 Little Patuxent Pkwy., Suite 760
Columbia, MD 21044-3506
Tel: (410)740-9743 *Fax:* (410)740-4572
Toll Free: (800)876 - 2632
E-Mail: info@amda.com
Web Site: www.amda.com
Members: 6900 individuals
Staff: 23
Annual Budget: $2-5,000,000
Executive Director: Lorraine Tarnove
E-Mail: ltarnove@amda.com
Director, Meetings: Megan Brey
E-Mail: mbrey@amda.com
Director, Membership: Cindy N. Hock, RN
Director, Clinical Affairs: Jacqueline Vance
E-Mail: jacquelinevance@amda.com

Historical Note
Members are physicians who provide care to patients in long term care facilities, either as medical director or attending physician. Awards the Certified Medical Director (CMD) designation. Membership: $180/year (individual).

Meetings/Conferences:
Semi-Annual Meetings: Spring and Summer
2007 - Hollywood, FL(Diplomat Hotel)/March 29-Apr. 1/2000

Publications:
AMDA Reports Newsletter. q.
Journal of the American Medical Directors. bi-m. adv.
Caring for the Ages. m. adv.

American Medical Group Association *(1949)*
1422 Duke St.
Alexandria, VA 22314-3403
Tel: (703)838-0033 *Fax:* (703)548-1890
E-Mail: dfisher@amga.org
Web Site: www.amga.org
Members: 295 medical groups
Staff: 27
Annual Budget: $2-5,000,000
Chief Executive Officer: Donald W. Fisher, Ph.D., CAE

Historical Note
Formerly (1974) American Association of Medical Clinics and (1996) American Group Practice Association. AGPA merged with the Unified Medical Group Association to form the American Medical Group Association in 1996. Members are group practice medical clinics. AMGA's mission is to shape the health care environment by advancing high quality, cost effective, patient-centered, and physician-directed health care. Serves as a strategic partner for medical groups, providing a package of services including political advocacy, educational and networking programs and publications, benchmarking data services, and financial and operations assistance. Sponsors and supports the Group Practice Association Political Action Committee (GROUPPAC).

Meetings/Conferences:
Annual Meetings: September/600
2007 - Scottsdale, AZ(Westin Kierland)/Feb. 28-March 3

Publications:
Group Practice Journal. 10/year. adv.
Medical Group Compensation and Productivity Survey. a. adv.
Medical Group Financial Operations Survey. a. adv.

American Medical Informatics Association *(1988)*
4915 St. Elmo Ave., Suite 401
Bethesda, MD 20814
Tel: (301)657-1291 *Fax:* (301)657-1296
E-Mail: mail@amia.org
Web Site: www.amia.org
Members: 3500 individuals
Staff: 12
Annual Budget: $2-5,000,000
President and Chief Executive Officer: Don E. Detmer, M.D.
Manager, Meetings: Dasha Cohen
Executive Vice President: Karen E. Greenwood
Vice President, Education: Jeffrey Williamson

Historical Note
Members are individuals interested in the application of information science and computer technology to all aspects of medical and health care, teaching and research. A member society of the American Institute for Medical and Biological Engineering. Membership: $250/year (individual); $1500-$10000/year (organization/company); $35/year (student).

Publications:
Symposium Procedures. a.
AMIA Alert. m.
Access AMIA. bi-w.
JAMIA Journal. bi-m. adv.
Proceedings of Symposium on Computer Applications in Medical Care. a.
Annual Membership Directory & Yearbook. a. adv.

American Medical Publishers' Association *(1961)*
71 Fifth Ave.
New York, NY 10003
Tel: (212)255-0200 *Fax:* (212)255-7007
E-Mail: info@ampaonline.org
Web Site: www.pspcentral.org/
Members: 60 companies
Staff: 1
Annual Budget: $50-100,000

Historical Note
Merged (Nov. 2005) with Association of American Publishers (AAP) into the Professional and Scholarly Publishing Division. Formerly (1974) Association of American Medical Book Publishers. Membership: $250-1,000/year, based on member's business.

Meetings/Conferences:
Annual Meetings: Spring

American Medical Rehabilitation Providers Association *(1969)*
1710 N St. NW
Washington, DC 20036
Tel: (202)223-1920 *Fax:* (202)223-1925
Toll Free: (888)346 - 4624
Web Site: www.amrpa.org
Members: 450 facilities
Staff: 4
Annual Budget: $1-2,000,000
Vice President, Government Relations and Policy Development: Carolyn C. Zollar
E-Mail: czollar@13x.com

Historical Note
Represents medical, residential and vocational Canadian and U.S. rehabilitation centers. Formed in 1969 by a merger of the Association of Rehabilitation Centers (founded in 1952 as the Conference of Rehabilitation Centers and Facilities) and the National Association of Sheltered Workshops and Homebound Programs (founded in 1954). Formerly (1975)

International Association of Rehabilitation Facilities, (1979) Association of Rehabilitation Facilities, and (1994) National Association of Rehabilitation Facilities.

Meetings/Conferences:
Annual Meetings: Spring and fall

Publications:
Off The Record. w.
The AMRPA Magazine. m.

American Medical Society for Sports Medicine *(1992)*
11639 Earnshaw St.
Overland Park, KS 66210-2763
Tel: (913)327-1415 *Fax:* (913)327-1491
E-Mail: office@amssm.org
Web Site: www.newamssm.org/
Members: 650 individuals
Staff: 2
Executive Director: Jody Gold
E-Mail: office@amssm.org

Historical Note
AMSSM provides support and continuing educations specific to primary care, non-surgical sports medicine physicians. Membership: $275/year (physicians); $225/year (fellows); $150/year (residents).

American Medical Student Association *(1950)*
1902 Association Dr.
Reston, VA 20191
Tel: (703)620-6600 *Fax:* (703)620-5873
Toll Free: (800)767 - 2266
E-Mail: amsa@www.amsa.org
Web Site: www.amsa.org
Members: 50000 individuals
Staff: 35
Annual Budget: $1-2,000,000
Executive Director: Paul R. Wright
Director, Public Relations: Kim Becker
E-Mail: prel@www.amsa.org
Associate Director, Program Development: Joan Hedgecock
E-Mail: joan_h@www.amsa.org
Director, Membership: Linda Killan

Historical Note
The AMSA is the oldest and largest independent association of physicians-in-training in the United States. Founded in 1950, AMSA is a student-governed, non-profit organization committed to representing the concerns of physicians-in-training.

Meetings/Conferences:
Annual Meetings: March
2007 - Washington, DC(Hyatt Regency Crystal City)/March 7-11
2008 - New Orleans, LA(Hyatt Regency)/March 12-16

Publications:
New Physician. 9/year. adv.

American Medical Technologists *(1939)*
710 Higgins Rd.
Park Ridge, IL 60068
Tel: (847)823-5169 *Fax:* (847)823-0458
Toll Free: (800)275 - 1268
E-Mail: mail@amt1.com
Web Site: www.amt1.com
Members: 32000 individuals
Staff: 19
Annual Budget: $2-5,000,000
Executive Director: Christopher A. Damon
Director, Marketing, Membership and Operations: Sharon Gautschy
Director, Publications and Meetings: Diane Powell, CMP
E-Mail: diane.powell@amt1.com

Historical Note
Founded in 1939 and incorporated in New Jersey. Grants the MT (Medical Technologist), MLT (Medical Laboratory Technician), RMA (Registered Medical Assistant), RDA (Registered Dental Assistant) and RPT (Registered Phlebotomy Technician), Certified Office Lab Technician, Certified Lab Consultant, Certified Medical Administrative Assistant, and Certified Allied Health Instructor designations. Membership: $90-125/year.

Meetings/Conferences:
Annual Meetings: June or July
2007 - Orlando, FL(Swan and Dolphin Resort)/July 9-14/300

Publications:
Journal of Continuing Education Topics And Issues. 3/year. adv.
AMT Events. 3/year. adv.

American Medical Women's Association *(1915)*
801 N. Fairfax St., Suite 400
Alexandria, VA 22314
Tel: (703)838-0500 *Fax:* (703)549-3864
E-Mail: info@amwa-doc.org
Web Site: www.amwa-doc.org
Members: 10000 individuals
Staff: 27
Annual Budget: $2-5,000,000
Executive Director: Linda D. Hallman
E-Mail: info@amwa-doc.org

Historical Note
Founded in November 1915 in Chicago and incorporated in Illinois in 1916 as the Medical Women's National Association. Reincorporated in New York in 1924 and name changed to American Medical Women's Association, Inc. in 1937. Membership restricted to women physicians, interns, residents and medical and osteopathic students. Friends of AMWA Category is open to both females and males. U.S. affiliate of the Medical Women's International Association. Membership: $225/year (physician); $80/year (resident); $50/year (associate); and $25/4 years (student).

Publications:
The Connection. bi-m.
Journal of the American Medical Women's Association. q. adv.

American Medical Writers Association *(1940)*
40 W. Gude Dr., Suite 101
Rockville, MD 20850-1192
Tel: (301)294-5303 *Fax:* (301)294-9006
E-Mail: amwa@amwa.org
Web Site: www.amwa.org
Members: 4700 individuals
Staff: 7
Annual Budget: $1-2,000,000
Executive Director: Donna Munari, CAE
E-Mail: dmunari@amwa.org

Historical Note
Originated September 25, 1940 at Rock Island, IL as the Mississippi Valley Medical Editors' Association; assumed its current name in 1948. Incorporated in Illinois in 1951. Concerned with the advancement and improvement of medical communications. Membership: $125/year (individual); $45/year (student).

Meetings/Conferences:
Annual Meetings: Fall

Publications:
AMWA Freelance Directory. on-line.
AMWA Membership Directory (online). a.
AMWA Journal. q. adv.

American Membrane Technology Association *(1985)*
2409 S.E. Dixie Hwy.
Stuart, FL 34994
Tel: (772)463-0820 *Fax:* (772)463-0860
Web Site: www.membranes-amta.org
Members: 300 individuals
Staff: 3
Annual Budget: $25-50,000
Administrative Director: Janet L. Jaworski

Historical Note
Founded as Natl Water Supply Improvement Association; became Water Supply Improvement Association in 1981, American Desalting Association in 1993, and assumed its current name in 2000. Members are individuals, government agencies and corporations with an interest in desalinization technology.

Publications:
Newsletter. m.
Conference Proceedings. bien.

American Men's Studies Association *(1991)*
22 East St.
Northampton, MA 01060
Tel: (413)586-0515
E-Mail: pat.sam@verizon.net
Web Site: www.mensstudies.org
Members: 150 individuals
Contact: Pat Samian

Historical Note
AMSA members are academics and others with an interest in the study of the male's social and historical context. Membership: $50/year (individual); $30/year (student).

Publications:
AMSA Newsletter. q.

American Mental Health Counselors Association *(1976)*
801 N. Fairfax St., Suite 304
Alexandria, VA 22314
Tel: (703)548-6002 *Fax:* (703)548-4775
Toll Free: (800)326 - 2642
Web Site: www.amhca.org
Members: 6000 individuals
Staff: 6
Annual Budget: $1-2,000,000
Executive Director/Chief Executive Officer: W. Mark Hamilton
Office Administration: Virginia Moore
Membership Information: Linda Morano
Director, Government Relations: Beth Powell

Historical Note
Members are professional mental health counselors working in a variety of community and non-school settings. Membership: $149/year (individual); $60/year (student).

Meetings/Conferences:
Annual Meetings: With the American Counseling Ass'n

Publications:
AMHCA Advocate. m. adv.
Journal of Mental Health Counseling. q. adv.

American Metal Detector Manufacturers Association *(1978)*
1881 W. State St.
Garland, TX 75042-6761
Tel: (972)494-6151 *Fax:* (972)494-1881
Members: 4 companies
Annual Budget: under $10,000
President: Charles Garrett

Historical Note
Has no paid officers or full-time staff.

American Metalcasting Consortium
5300 International Blvd.
North Charleston, SC 29418
Tel: (843)760-3537 *Fax:* (843)760-3349
E-Mail: amc@aticorp.org
Web Site: www.amc.aticorp.org
Members: 230 companies
Staff: 12
Annual Budget: $25-50,000,000
Director: Mike Gwyn

Historical Note
AMC is a coalition of four metalcasting organizations which aims to reestablish manufacting interests in specific areas. The coalition includes, The American Foundrymen's Society, Non-Ferrous Founders Society, North American Die Casting Association, and Steel Founders Society of America.

Publications:
AMC Annual Report. a.

American Meteorological Society *(1919)*
45 Beacon St.
Boston, MA 02108-3693
Tel: (617)227-2425 *Fax:* (617)742-8718
Web Site: www.ametsoc.org/AMS
Members: 11000 individuals
Staff: 45
Annual Budget: $5-10,000,000
Executive Director: Keith L. Seitter
Controller: Barry Mohan
E-Mail: bmohan@ametsoc.org

Historical Note
Founded December 29, 1919 in St. Louis and incorporated in the District of Columbia in 1920. Permanent headquarters were established in Boston in 1946 and the Society was reincorporated in Massachusetts in 1958. Certifies consulting

meteorologists, and grants Seal of Approval to television and radio meteorologists. Has an annual budget of approximately $15 million. Membership: $80/year (individual); $400-$1500/year (organization/company).

Meetings/Conferences:
Annual Meetings: Winter
2007 - San Antonio, TX/Jan. 14-18

Publications:
Journal of Atmospheric and Oceanic Technology. m.
Weather and Forecasting. semi-m.
Journal of Hydrometerology. semi-m.
Meteorological and Geoastrophysical Abstracts. a.
Bulletin of The AMS. m. adv.
Journal of Climate. bi-m.
Journal of Applied Meteorology. m.
Journal of the Atmospheric Sciences. m.
Journal of Physical Oceanography. m.
Monthly Weather Review. m.

American Microchemical Society *(1935)*
Two June Way
Middlesex, NJ 08846
Web Site: www.microchem.org
Members: 125 individuals
Annual Budget: under $10,000
Treasurer: Alvin Melveger
E-Mail: drajm@optonline.net

Historical Note
AMS members are analytic chemists with a special interest in the properties of chemicals when found in minute quantities. Has no paid officers or full-time staff.

Meetings/Conferences:
Annual Meetings:

Publications:
Microchemical Journal. bi-m.

American Microscopical Society *(1878)*
Bryn Mawr College
Dept. of Biology
Bryn Mawr, PA 19010
Tel: (610)526-5094 *Fax:* (610)526-5086
Web Site: www.amicros.org
Members: 510 individuals
Annual Budget: $10-25,000
Secretary: Stephen L. Gardiner
E-Mail: sgardine@brynmawr.edu

Historical Note
A professional society of microscopical biologists and microscopists established in 1878 to promote the use of the microscope in research and teaching. Membership: $19/year (student); $38/year (regular); $100/year (sustaining); $1,000 (life).

Meetings/Conferences:
Annual Meetings: January

Publications:
Invertebrate Biology.

American Mideast Business Associates *(1951)*
Four Kansas Rd.
Tuckerton, NJ 08087
Tel: (609)296-4783
Members: 175 corporations
Staff: 2
Annual Budget: $500-1,000,000
President: I.F. Yusif, CAE

Historical Note
Established in New York, NY as the Egyptian American Society Became (1960) American Arab Association for Commerce and Industry. Assumed its current name in 1987 to reflect growing membership interest in all Middle Eastern and North African countries. Members are both U.S and Arab transnationals. Provides consultation and translation services to non-members on a contract basis. Membership: $10,000/year (organization).

Meetings/Conferences:
Annual Meetings: Spring

Publications:
Bulletin. m.

American Milking Devon Association *(1978)*
135 Old Bay Rd.
New Durham, NH 03855
Tel: (603)859-6611
E-Mail: mdevons@worldpath.net
Web Site: www.milkingdevons.org
Members: 85 individuals
Annual Budget: under $10,000
Secretary/Registrar: Susan Randall

Historical Note
In 1623, two heifers and a bull from north Devonshire, England, were received by a member of the Plymouth Colony. Today the breed is a dual-purpose animal adapted to survive on a low-quality, high forage diet in severe climatic conditions and provide up to 12,000 pounds of milk. AMDA members are breeders and interested individuals. Has no paid officers or full-time staff. Membership: $5/year.

Meetings/Conferences:
Annual Meetings: May

American Milking Shorthorn Society *(1920)*
800 Pleasant St.
Beloit, WI 53511-5456
Tel: (608)365-3332 *Fax:* (608)365-6644
E-Mail: info@milkingshorthorn.com
Web Site: www.milkingshorthorn.com
Members: 350 individuals
Staff: 2
Annual Budget: $100-250,000
Executive Secretary: David J. Kendall

Historical Note
Breeders and fanciers of Milking Shorthorn dairy cattle. Formed in 1920 as the Milking Shorthorn Club within the framework of the American Shorthorn Breeders Association. Adopted its present name and became incorporated as a separate association in 1948. Member of the National Pedigreed Livestock Council and the Purebred Dairy Cattle Association. Membership: $45/year (full); $30/year (associate); $25/year (junior).

Meetings/Conferences:
Annual Meetings: Summer
2007 - West Lebanon, NH/June 27-30

Publications:
Milking Shorthorn Journal. bi-m. adv.

American Miniature Horse Association *(1978)*
5601 S. I-35 West
Alvarado, TX 76009
Tel: (817)783-5600 *Fax:* (817)783-6403
E-Mail: editor@amha.org
Web Site: www.amha.org
Members: 10000 individuals
Staff: 19
Annual Budget: $2-5,000,000
Editor: Melissa Powell

Historical Note
Absorbed the International Miniature Horse Registry in 1985. Members own and breed American Miniature horses. AMHA promotes the breed and maintains a permanent registry, the largest for miniature horses in the world with over 128,000 currently registered. AMHA is member-owned and governed. Membership: $50/year (individual); $70/year (new).

Meetings/Conferences:
Annual Meetings: Winter
2007 - Las Vegas, NV(Imperial Palace)/Feb. 22-25/350

Publications:
Miniature Horse World Magazine. bi-m. adv.

American Mobile Telecommunications Association *(1985)*

Historical Note
Merged with Industrial Telecommunications Association to form Enterprise Wireless Alliance in 2005.

American Mold Builders Association *(1973)*
701 E. Irving Park Rd.
Suite 207
Roselle, IL 60172
Tel: (630)980-7667 *Fax:* (630)980-9714
E-Mail: info@amba.org
Web Site: www.amba.org
Members: 350 organizations
Staff: 4
Annual Budget: $500-1,000,000
Executive Director: Jeanette Bradley
E-Mail: jbradley@amba.org

Historical Note
Members are manufacturers of molds. Membership: $150/quarter (organization).

Meetings/Conferences:
Annual Meetings: March

Publications:
AMBA Membership Directory. a. adv.
The American Mold Builder
. q. adv.

American Montessori Society *(1960)*
281 Park Ave. South, Sixth Floor
New York, NY 10010-6102
Tel: (212)358-1250 *Fax:* (212)358-1256
Web Site: www.amshq.org
Members: 8000 individuals
Staff: 13
Annual Budget: $2-5,000,000
Executive Director: Richard A. Ungerer

Historical Note
Members are teachers, schools and others interested in the approach to early learning through self-motivation developed by Dr. Maria Montessori in 1907. Membership rates available upon request.

Meetings/Conferences:
Annual Meetings: April
2007 - New York, NY(Marriott Marquis)/March 1-4/3500

Publications:
Teacher Membership Directory. a.
Montessori Life. q. adv.

American Monument Association *(1904)*

Historical Note
Address unknown in 2006.

American Morgan Horse Association *(1909)*
122 Bostwick Rd.
Shelburne, VT 05482
Tel: (802)985-4944 *Fax:* (802)985-8897
E-Mail: info@morganhorse.com
Web Site: www.morganhorse.com
Members: 10000 individuals
Staff: 17
Annual Budget: $2-5,000,000
Registrar: Tyler Atwood
Director, Membership and Programs: Erica Richard

Historical Note
Established as the Morgan Horse Club, Inc.; assumed its present name in 1971. Members are breeders, owners and trainers of the Morgan horse, a type of light horse which originated in Vermont around 1789. Membership: $50/year (individual); $15/year (junior).

Meetings/Conferences:
Annual Meetings: Winter/500
2007 - Atlanta, GA(Renaissance Waverly)/Feb. 15-17
2008 - Minneapolis, MN(Hyatt)/Feb. 14-16

Publications:
The Morgan Horse Magazine. m. adv.
AMHA Network and Morgan Sales Network. m. adv.
American Morgan Horse Register. a.

American Mosquito Control Association *(1935)*
15000 Commerce Pkwy.
Suite C
Mt. Laurel, NJ 08054
Tel: (856)439-9222 *Fax:* (856)439-0525
E-Mail: amca@mosquito.org
Web Site: www.mosquito.org
Members: 2000 individuals
Staff: 2
Annual Budget: $250-500,000
Contact: Sarah Gazi

Historical Note
Established in 1935 as the Eastern Association of Mosquito Control Workers and assumed its present name in 1944. Incorporated in New Jersey (1948), California (1974) and Louisiana (1986). Members are involved in the control of mosquitoes and other vectors. Has members throughout the world.

Membership: $65/year (individual); $85/year (company).

Meetings/Conferences:
Annual Meetings: Spring/700

Publications:
Wingbeats. q.
Journal of the AMCA. q. adv.
AMCA Newsletter. q.

American Motility Society *(1980)*
45685 Harmony Ln.
Belleville, MI 48111
Tel: (734)699-1130 *Fax:* (734)699-1136
E-Mail: admin@motilitysociety.org
Web Site: www.motilitysociety.org
Members: 250 individuals
Staff: 1
Managing Director: Lori Ennis

Historical Note
AMS members are physicians with an interest in gastrointestinal motility. Membership: $50/year (trainee); $100/year (non-trainee)..

American Motorcyclist Association *(1924)*
13515 Yarmouth Rd.
Pickerington, OH 43147-8214
Tel: (614)856-1900 *Fax:* (614)856-1920
Web Site: www.amadirectlink.com
Members: 270000 individuals
Staff: 100
President: Robert Rasor

Historical Note
Membership: $39/year (individual).

Publications:
American Motorcyclist. m. adv.

American Moving and Storage Association *(1936)*
1611 Duke St.
Alexandria, VA 22314-3482
Tel: (703)683-7410 *Fax:* (703)683-7527
E-Mail: info@moving.org
Web Site: www.promover.org
Members: 3400 companies
Staff: 28
Annual Budget: $2-5,000,000
President: Joseph M. Harrison
Vice President, Administration: John B. Brewer
Director, Advertising and Sales: Norma Gyouai
Vice President, Programs and Services: Patricia T. Jennings
Vice President, Int'l Programs: Sherry Koepke-Williams
Vice President, Membership and Government Traffic: Scott Michael
General Counsel: Bob Rothstein
Vice President, Business Development: Cindy Simpson
Vice President, Communications: David Sparkman

Historical Note
Formed by a merger of the Movers Conference of America (founded in 1943 as the Household Goods Carriers' Conference) and the American Movers Institute (founded in 1960). Founded in 1953 as the Household Goods Movers Group of ATA. Merged with National Moving and Storage Association and assumed its current name in 1998. Affiliated with American Trucking Associations. Membership: annual dues vary by size.

Meetings/Conferences:
Annual Meetings: Spring
2007 – Palm Springs, CA(La Quinta Resort)/Apr. 23-26

Publications:
AMSA Membership Directory. a. adv.
The Moving World. bi-w. adv.
Industry Calendar. a. adv.
AMSA E-mail Newsletter. w. adv.
Direction Magazine. m. adv.

American Murray Grey Association *(1970)*
P.O. Box 60748
Reno, NV 89506
Tel: (775)972-7526
E-Mail: amgaoffice@murraygreybeefcattle.com
Web Site: www.murraygreybeefcattle.com
Members: 200 individuals
Staff: 1
Annual Budget: $25-50,000
Executive Officer: John Gerow
E-Mail: amgaoffice@murraygreybeefcattle.com

Historical Note
Established as a national breed registry for Murray Grey Cattle. Members are breeders and fanciers of Murray Grey Beef Cattle. Member of the National Pedigree Livestock Council. Membership: $50/year.

Meetings/Conferences:
Annual Meetings: Fall

Publications:
Murray Grey News. q. adv.
AMGA Herd Book. bi-a. adv.

American Mushroom Institute *(1955)*
One Massachusetts Ave. NW
Suite 800
Washington, DC 20001
Tel: (202)842-4344 *Fax:* (202)408-7763
E-Mail: ami@mwmlaw.com
Web Site: www.americanmushroom.org
Members: 325 individuals
Staff: 3
Annual Budget: $250-500,000
President: Laura Phelps
E-Mail: ami@mwmlaw.com

Historical Note
AMI represents growers and marketers of cultivated mushrooms in the United States. Its major purposes are research and information dissemination, the development of better methods of growth and marketing of mushrooms, representation of the industry to governmental bodies and increasing the consumption of mushrooms. Membership: $350-$16,000/year, based on production; $300/year (non-growers).

Publications:
Mushroom News. m. adv.
Membership Directory. a. adv.
Mushroom News Flash. m. adv.

American Music Conference *(1947)*
5790 Armada Dr.
Carlsbad, CA 92008-4372
Tel: (760)431-9124 *Fax:* (760)438-7327
E-Mail: info@amc-music.org
Web Site: www.amc-music.org
Members: 211 organizations
Staff: 4
Annual Budget: $250-500,000
Executive Director: Robert Walker
Associate Executive Director: Laura Johnson
Project Manager: Sharon McLaughlin

Historical Note
AMC promotes the importance of music, music making and music education to the general public. Membership: $15/year (Collegiate); $25/year (Booster); $50/year (individual); $100/year (supporter); $250/year (sponsor); $500/year (sustainer); $1,000/year (visionary); $10,000/year (corporate).

Meetings/Conferences:
Annual Meetings: July

Publications:
AMC News. q.
AMC Year in Review. a.

American Music Therapy Association *(1950)*
8455 Colesville Rd.
Suite 1000
Silver Spring, MD 20910-3319
Tel: (301)589-3300 *Fax:* (301)589-5175
E-Mail: info@musictherapy.org
Web Site: www.musictherapy.org
Members: 5000 individuals
Staff: 10
Annual Budget: $500-1,000,000
Executive Director: Andrea H. Farbman, Ed.D.
E-Mail: farbman@musictherapy.org
Director, Communications and Conferences: Al Bumanis
E-Mail: bumanis@musictherapy.org
Director, Prof. Programs: Jane Creagan
E-Mail: info@musictherapy.org
Director, Membership Services: Angie Elkins
E-Mail: elkins@musictherapy.org
Director, Government Relations: Judy Simpson

Historical Note
Founded as National Association for Music Therapy; merged with American Association for Music Therapy and assumed its current name in 1998. Seeks to develop the therapeutic use of music in hospital and educational settings.

Meetings/Conferences:
Annual Meetings: Fall

Publications:
Music Therapy Matters. q. adv.
Music Therapy Perspectives. semi-a. adv.
Journal of Music Therapy. q.
Member Sourcebook. a. adv.

American Musicians Union *(1948)*
Eight Tobin Ct.
Dumont, NJ 07628
Tel: (201)384-5378
Members: 200 individuals
Annual Budget: under $10,000
President and Treasurer: Ben Intorre
Corresponding Secretary: Joe Garry

Historical Note
Formed by a small group of musicians who chose to remain independent of the AFL-CIO merger of labor unions; joined the National Federation of Independent Unions in 1961. Membership is open to all musicians and vocalists; contract books are provided at a modest cost, but members are not required to use the official contract form nor a binding wage scale. Has no paid officers or full-time staff. Membership: $27/year, plus $10 initiation fee.

Publications:
Quarternote. q. adv.

American Musicological Society *(1934)*
201 S. 34th St.
Philadelphia, PA 19104-6313
Tel: (215)898-8698 *Fax:* (215)573-3673
Toll Free: (888)611 - 4267
E-Mail: ams@sas.upenn.edu
Web Site: www.ams-net.org
Members: 3500 individuals
Staff: 2
Annual Budget: $100-250,000
Executive Director: Robert Judd

Historical Note
In 1929 the American Council of Learned Societies, feeling that "the history and science of music forms an important branch of learning," formed a standing committee on musicology. Out of this, the independent American Musicological Society was formed in 1934. It is a learned society of professional musicologists and educators. Membership: $45-100/year (individual); $85/year (organization).

Meetings/Conferences:
Annual Meetings: Fall

Publications:
Journal of The AMS. 3/year. adv.
Directory. a. adv.
Newsletter. semi-a.

American Mustang Association *(1962)*
P.O. Box 338
Yucaipa, CA 92399
E-Mail: mustang@netbox.com
Web Site: http://fp3.antelecom.net/fisherla/
Members: 150 individuals
Staff: 1
Annual Budget: under $10,000
Secretary: Mary Flory

Historical Note
Members are owners and breeders of the Mustang horse of the Western plains. Membership: $20/year.

Publications:
American Mustang World. q. adv.

American Name Society *(1951)*
Couper Admin. Bldg., AD 711
Binghamton Univ., SUNY
Binghamton, NY 13902-6000
Tel: (607)777-2143 *Fax:* (607)777-4830
Web Site: www.wtsn.binghamton.edu/ANS/
Members: 750individualsandinstitutions
Staff: 1
Annual Budget: $10-25,000
Treasurer: Dr. Michael F. McGoff

E-Mail: mmcgoff@binghamton.edu
Historical Note
A professional society of omnastic scholars and others interested in the study of the origin and meaning of names, geographic, personal, scientific, etc. Membership: $35/year (individual); $40/year (company/organization); $45/year (foreign).
Meetings/Conferences:
Annual Meetings: with the Linguistic Society of America
Publications:
ANS Newsletter. 3/year.
Names: A Journal of Omnastics. q.

American Naprapathic Association *(1909)*
164 Division St., Suite 202
Elgin, IL 60120-5533
Tel: (847)214-8642 *Fax:* (847)214-8645
E-Mail: anarfordns@aol.com
Web Site: www.naprapathy.org
Members: 140 individuals
Staff: 1
Annual Budget: $10-25,000
President: Dr. George Stretch
Historical Note
Members are practitioners of naprapathy, the science and system of manipulation (administered by the hands) designed to cure physical ailments. Membership: $180/year (individual); $150/year (organization/company).
Meetings/Conferences:
Semi-annual Meetings: 2nd Sunday in January and last weekend in June
Publications:
The Voice of Naprapathy. a.

American National CattleWomen *(1952)*
P.O. Box 3881
Englewood, CO 80155-2851
Tel: (303)694-0313 *Fax:* (303)694-2390
E-Mail: ancw@beef.org
Web Site: www.ancw.org
Members: 2800 individuals
Staff: 4
Executive Director: Marcie Hervey
Coordinator, Membership, Communications and Finance: Jackie Buehner
Historical Note
Members are women in the beef cattle industry. Promotes education and beef on behalf of the beef industry. Membership: $50/year (individual); $100/year, $500 or $1,000/year (company).
Meetings/Conferences:
2007 – Nashville, TN/Jan. 31-Feb. 3
2008 – Reno, NV/Feb. 6-9
2009 – Phoenix, AZ/Jan. 28-31
Publications:
The American CattleWoman. bi-m.

American National Metric Council *(1973)*
900 Mix Ave., Suite One
Hamden, CT 06514-5106
Tel: (203)287-9849
E-Mail: anmcmetric@pi-c.com
Members: 200 individuals
Staff: 2
Annual Budget: $50-100,000
President: Daniel L. Potts
Historical Note
Coordinates metric activities of commerce and industry. Membership: $50/year (individual); $50-2,500/year (organization).
Publications:
Metric Reporter. q.

American National Standards Institute *(1918)*
1819 L St. NW
Sixth Floor
Washington, DC 20036
Tel: (202)293-8020 *Fax:* (202)293-9287
E-Mail: info@ansi.org
Web Site: www.ansi.org
Members: 1000companies,organizations,etc.
Staff: 75
Annual Budget: $10-25,000,000
President and Chief Executive Officer: S. Joseph Bhatia
Vice President, International Policy: Gary Kushnier
E-Mail: gkushnie@ansi.org
Historical Note
ANSI is a private, non-profit organization that administers and coordinates the U.S. voluntary standardization and conformity assessment system. Its mission is to enhance U.S. competitiveness and quality of life by promoting, facilitating, and safeguarding the integrity of the voluntary standardization system. The Institute has an annual budget of approximately $16 million. Headquarters in Washington, D.C.; New York office at 25 W. 43nd St., 4th Floor, New York, NY 10036. Membership dues vary, based on membership category. Company member dues are based on global sales revenue.
Publications:
ANSI Reporter. q. adv.
What's New newsletter (online). bi-w.
Standards Action (Electronic). w.

American Natural Soda Ash Corporation *(1984)*
15 Riverside Ave.
Westport, CT 06880
Tel: (203)226-9056 *Fax:* (203)227-1484
Web Site: www.ansac.com
Members: 6 companies
Staff: 30
Annual Budget: $5-10,000,000
President and Chief Executive Officer: John Andrews
Executive Vice President and Chief Financial Officer: Thomas G. Dullinger
Historical Note
A Webb-Pomerene Act association. ANSAC is the sole authorized export organization for members' soda ash production.

American Nature Study Society *(1908)*
R.R. 2 Box 1010
Dingmans Ferry, PA 18328
Tel: (570)828-2319 *Fax:* (570)828-9695
E-Mail: peec@ptd.net
Web Site: www.peec.org
Members: 650 individuals
Staff: 1
Annual Budget: under $10,000
Executive Director: Jim Rienhardt
Historical Note
Founded in 1908, ANSS quickly became the leading organization serving and strengthening the Nature Study movement. Its main concern is nature and conservation education. The Society works to forge a bond between each generation of students and their natural environment. Members are science, nature study, and environmental education professionals. Membership: $25/year (individual); $18/year (organization)
Meetings/Conferences:
Annual Meetings: February, with American Ass'n for the Advancement of Science
Publications:
Eco Tones. a.
ANSS Newsletter. q.

American Nephrology Nurses Association *(1969)*
E. Holly Ave., Box 56
Pitman, NJ 08071-0056
Tel: (856)256-2320 *Fax:* (856)589-7463
Toll Free: (888)600 - 2662
E-Mail: anna@ajj.com
Web Site: www.annanurse.org
Members: 12000 individuals
Staff: 8
Annual Budget: $2-5,000,000
Executive Director: Mike Cunningham
E-Mail: cunninghamm@ajj.com
Director, Membership Services: Lou Ann Leary
E-Mail: learyl@ajj.com
Conference Manager: Mary O'Connor
E-Mail: oconnorm@ajj.com
Managing Editor: Gus Ostrum
E-Mail: ostrumg@ajj.com
Historical Note
Nurses specializing in the structure, function and diseases of the kidneys, as well as dieticians, physicians, social workers and technicians. Formerly the American Association of Nephrology Nurses and Technicians. Assumed its present name in 1984. Membership: $60/year (individual); $2,500/year (organization/company).
Meetings/Conferences:
Annual Meetings: Spring
2007 – Dallas, TX(Wyndham Anatole)/Apr. 22-25
Publications:
Nephrology Nursing Journal. bi-m.
Update. bi-m.
Publications List Available.

American Network of Community Options and Resources *(1970)*
1101 King St., Suite 380
Alexandria, VA 22314
Tel: (703)535-7850 *Fax:* (703)535-7860
Web Site: www.ancor.org
Members: 800 agencies
Staff: 9
Annual Budget: $1-2,000,000
Chief Executive Officer: Renee Pietrangelo
E-Mail: rpietrangelo@ancor.org
Director, Government Relations: Suellen Galbraith
E-Mail: sgalbraith@ancor.org
Director, Member Services: Jerri McCandless
E-Mail: jmccandless@ancor.org
Historical Note
Founded as National Association of Private Residential Facilities for the Mentally Retarded. In 1987 became National Association of Private Residential Resources. Adopted current name in 1993. Represents and assists agencies that provide private services and support for people with disabilities. Affiliated with the Consortium for Citizens With Disabilities; participates in the Commission on Accreditation of Rehabilitation Facilities, Accreditation Council on Services for People with Developmental Disabilities, and National Fire Protection Association. Membership fee based on agency budget.
Meetings/Conferences:
Three Meetings Annually: May/June, February/March, September.
Publications:
LINKS. m. adv.

American Neurological Association *(1875)*
5841 Cedar Lake Rd.
Suite 204
Minneapolis, MN 55416
Tel: (952)545-6284 *Fax:* (952)545-6073
E-Mail: ana@llmsi.com
Web Site: www.aneuroa.org
Members: 1400 individuals
Staff: 7
Annual Budget: $2-5,000,000
Executive Director: Linda Scher
Historical Note
Founded in 1875 and incorporated in Minnesota.
Meetings/Conferences:
Annual Meetings: Fall/700-900
2007 – Washington, DC(Marriott Wardman Park)/Oct. 7-10
Publications:
Annals of Neurology. m. adv.

American Neuromodulation Society
Historical Note
Became North American Neuromodulation Society in 2004.

American Neuropsychiatric Association *(1987)*
700 Ackerman Rd.
Suite 625
Columbus, OH 43202
Tel: (614)447-2077 *Fax:* (614)263-4366
E-Mail: anpa@osu.edu
Web Site: www.anpaonline.org/
Members: 700 individuals
Staff: 1
Annual Budget: $50-100,000
Executive Director: Sandra Bornstein
E-Mail: anpa@osu.edu
Meetings/Conferences:
Semi-annual Meetings:

Publications:
Journal of Neuropsychiatry & Clinical Neuroscineces. q.
Headlines Newsletter. q. adv.

American Neurotology Society *(1965)*
2720 Tartan Way
Springfield, IL 62711
Tel: (217)483-6966
Web Site: www.americanneurotologysociety.org
Members: 500 individuals
Annual Budget: under $10,000
Administrator: Shirley Gossard
Historical Note
ANS members are otologists/neurotologists and allied health professionals as affiliate members with an interest in hearing and balance disorders. Has no paid officers or full-time staff.
Publications:
Otology and Neurotology Journal.

American North Country Cheviot Sheep Association *(1962)*
10506 S. 875 East
Walkerton, IN 46574
Tel: (574)586-3778
E-Mail: anccsa@northcountrycheviot.com
Web Site: www.northcountrycheviot.com
Members: 300 individuals
Annual Budget: under $10,000
Secretary-Treasurer: Sandy Thomas
Historical Note
Members are breeders of purebred North Country Cheviot Sheep. Maintains registry. Has no paid officers or full-time staff. Membership: $10/year.
Meetings/Conferences:
Biennial Meetings: odd years
Publications:
Breeders Directory. bien.

American Nuclear Insurers *(1957)*
95 Glastonbury Blvd., Suite 300
Glastonbury, CT 06033-4412
Tel: (860)682-1301 *Fax:* (860)659-0002
Web Site: www.amnucins.com
Members: 100 companies
Staff: 79
President and Chief Executive Officer: George D. Turner
Historical Note
The product of a merger (1974) of the Nuclear Energy Property Insurance Association and the Nuclear Energy Liability Insurance Association, both established in 1957. From 1974 to 1978 known as the the Nuclear Energy Liability Property Insurance Association; assumed its current name in 1978.
Meetings/Conferences:
Annual Meetings: March

American Nuclear Society *(1954)*
555 N. Kensington Ave.
La Grange Park, IL 60526
Tel: (708)352-6611 *Fax:* (708)352-0499
Web Site: www.ans.org
Members: 11000 individuals
Staff: 49
Annual Budget: $5-10,000,000
Executive Director: Harry Bradley
E-Mail: execdir@ans.org
Director, Meetings and Exhibits: Mary Keenan
E-Mail: meetings@ans.org
Director, Public Communications: Sharon Kerrick
E-Mail: outreach@ans.org
Comptroller: Christian Krapp
Historical Note
Established December 11, 1954 in the National Academy of Sciences in Washington, DC to advance science and engineering relating to the atomic nucleus and allied sciences and arts. Has an annual budget of approximately $6.5 million. Membership: $112/year, based on age (individual).
Meetings/Conferences:
Semi-annual Meetings: Spring and Fall
Publications:
Re-actions. q.
ANS News. m.
Nuclear Technology. m.
Nuclear News. m. adv.
Nuclear Science and Engineering. m.
RSTD Proceedings. a.
Transactions. semi-a.
Nuclear Standards News. m.
Radwaste Magazine. q.

American Numismatic Society *(1858)*
96 Fulton St.
New York, NY 10038
Tel: (212)571-4470 *Fax:* (212)571-4479
E-Mail: info@amnumsoc.org
Web Site: www.numismatics.org
Members: 2000 individuals
Staff: 17
Annual Budget: $1-2,000,000
Executive Director: Ute Wartenberg Kagan, Ph.D.
Historical Note
Organized April 16, 1858 in New York City under the present name. Incorporated in 1865 as the American Numismatic and Archeological Society but reverted to original name in 1907. Its purpose is "the collection and preservation of coins and medals, with an investigation into the history, and other subjects connected therewith." Maintains a significant numismatic library and museum. Membership: $40/year (basic); $60/year (full); $30/year (student).
Meetings/Conferences:
Quarterly Meetings: Meetings held at ANS Headquarters, NY, NY.
Publications:
American Numismatic Society Magazine. 3/year. adv.
Numismatic Literature. a.
Colonial Newsletter. 3/year.
Museum Notes & Monographs (MNN).
Ancient Coins in North America (ACNAC). irreg.
American Journal of Numismatics. a.

American Nursery and Landscape Association *(1876)*
1000 Vermont Ave. NW
Suite 300
Washington, DC 20005-4914
Tel: (202)789-2900 *Fax:* (202)789-1893
Web Site: www.anla.org
Members: 3000 companies
Staff: 17
Annual Budget: $2-5,000,000
Executive Vice President: Robert J. Dolibois, CAE
Director, Member Resources: Kellee Magee
Director, Operations: Warren A. Quinn
Senior Director, Government Relations: Craig J. Regelbrugge
Historical Note
Formerly (1887) the American Association of Nurserymen, Florists and Seedmen and (1997) the American Association of Nurserymen. Garden Centers of America, Horticultural Research Institute, National Association of Plant Patent Owners, National Landscape Association, and Wholesale Nursery Growers of America are divisions of ANLA. Supports the Nursery Industry Political Action Committee. Membership Fee: based on volume of business.
Meetings/Conferences:
Annual Meetings: August/2,000
Publications:
ANLA Today. bi-m.
Update. tri-w.
Who's Who in the Nursery Industry. a. adv.

American Nurses Association *(1896)*
8515 Georgia Ave., Suite 400
Silver Spring, MD 20910-3492
Tel: (301)628-5000 *Fax:* (301)628-5001
Toll Free: (800)274 - 4262
Web Site: www.nursingworld.org
Members: 152,000 individuals
Staff: 170
Annual Budget: $10-25,000,000
Chief Executive Officer: Linda J. Stierle
General Counsel: Alice Bodley
Director, Finance: Larry Fisher
Director, Communications: Joan Meehan, APR
Chief Operating Officer: Bill Powers
Director, Marketing: Betty Whitaker
Historical Note
Founded in New York City in 1896. Incorporated 1901 as the Nurses Associated Alumnae of the United States and Canada. Became the American Nurses' Association in 1911 and was incorporated in the District of Columbia in 1917. The national professional organization of registered nurses, ANA is a federation composed of 54 constituent state and territorial associations. Sponsors and supports the ANA Political Action Committee. Has an annual budget of $22 million.
Meetings/Conferences:
Biennial meetings: even years in June
Publications:
The American Nurse. 6/year. adv.
American Journal of Nursing. m.
The Online Journal of Issues in Nursing (OJIN).

American Nurses in Business Association *(1992)*
Historical Note
Address unknown in 2004.

American Obesity Association *(1995)*
1250 24th St. NW
Suite 300
Washington, DC 20037-1124
Tel: (202)776-7711 *Fax:* (202)776-7712
E-Mail: executive@obesity.org
Web Site: www.obesity.org
Staff: 2
Annual Budget: under $10,000
Executive Director and Chief Executive Officer: Morgan Downey
E-Mail: executive@obesity.org
Historical Note
AOA is dedicated to promoting education, research, and community action that can improve the quality of life for people with obesity. Members include health professionals and others who are concerned with solving the problems of obesity. Membership: $25/year (individual); $50/year (health professional).
Publications:
AOA Newsletter. q. adv.

American Occupational Therapy Association *(1917)*
4720 Montgomery Ln.
P.O. Box 31220
Bethesda, MD 20824-1220
Tel: (301)652-2682 *Fax:* (301)652-7711
Toll Free: (800)377 - 8555
Web Site: www.aota.org
Members: 40000 individuals
Staff: 90
Annual Budget: $10-25,000,000
Executive Director: Fred Somers
Chief Operating Officer: Chris Bluhm
Chief Public Affairs Officer: Christina Metzler
Chief Financial Officer: Chuck Partridge
Chief Professional Affairs Officer: Maureen Peterson
Historical Note
AOTA is a national professional association established to represent the interests and concerns of occupational therapy practitioners and to improve the quality of occupational therapy services. Occupational therapy is a vital health care profession whose pracititioners help to restore and sustain the highest quality of productive life to persons recovering from illnesses or injuries, or coping with developmental disabilities, mental illness or changes resulting from the aging process. Current AOTA membership numbers more than 40,000 including registered occupational therapists, certified occupational therapy assistants and occupational therapy students. AOTA's major programs are directed toward assuring the quality of occupational therapy services, improving consumer access to health care and promoting the professional development of its members. Has an annual budget of $13.0 million. Membership: $187/year (individual).
Meetings/Conferences:
Annual Meetings: Spring/Summer/6-7,000

Publications:
American Journal of Occupational Therapy. 6/year. adv.
OT Practice. bi-m. adv.
AOTA Buyer's Guide. a. adv.
Special Interest Section Newsletters. q.

American Oil Chemists' Society *(1909)*
2710 S. Boulder Dr.
Urbana, IL 61802-6996
Tel: (217)359-2344 *Fax:* (217)351-8091
E-Mail: general@aocs.org
Web Site: www.aocs.org
Members: 4000 individuals
Staff: 9
Annual Budget: $5-10,000,000
Executive Vice President: Jean M. Wills
E-Mail: jeanw@aocs.org
Director, Finance and Operations: Gloria Cook
E-Mail: gloriac@aocs.org
Director, Meetings and Education: Jeffrey Newman
E-Mail: jeffn@aocs.org
Manager, Marketing and Sales: Lisa Spencer
E-Mail: lisas@aocs.org
Historical Note
Founded in 1909 in Memphis, TN as the Society of Cotton Products Analysts. Incorporated in Louisiana in 1922 as the American Oil Chemists' Society. Designed to be a forum for the exchange of ideas, information and experience for those with a professional interest in the sciences of fats, oils and related substances in ways that promote personal excellence and provide for a high standard of quality. Membership: $140/year (domestic); $145/year (foreign).
Meetings/Conferences:
Annual Meetings: Spring/2,500
2007 – Quebec City, QC, Canada(Quebec City Convention Center)/May 13-16
Publications:
Journal of Surfactants and Detergents. q. adv.
INFORM (Internat'l News on Fats, Oils, and Related Materials). m. adv.
Journal of the American Oil Chemists' Society. m. adv.
Lipids. m. adv.

American Oilseed Coalition *(1993)*
1300 L St. NW, Suite 1020
Washington, DC 20005-4168
Tel: (202)842-0463 *Fax:* (202)842-9126
Members: 6 associations
Staff: 3
Annual Budget: $100-250,000
Coordinator: Thomas A. Hammer
Historical Note
Successor to the Oilseed Council of America. A coalition of oilseed (canola, cottonseed, flaxseed, soybean, safflower and sunflower) growers, processors, handlers, exporters, and end users. The Council promotes long range government policies which ensure an adequate supply of oilseeds at economical prices.
Meetings/Conferences:
Annual Meetings: None held.

American Ophthalmological Society *(1864)*
P.O. Box 193940
San Francisco, CA 94119
Tel: (415)561-8578 *Fax:* (415)561-8531
E-Mail: aos@aao.org
Web Site: www.aosonline.org
Members: 319 individuals
Staff: 2
Annual Budget: $50-100,000
Secretary-Treasurer: Charles P. Wilkinson, M.D.
Historical Note
The oldest medical society in American medicine and the second oldest ophthalmology society in the world. Membership restricted to 225 active members. Awards the Howe Medal for distinguished service to ophthalmology. Membership: $300/year.
Meetings/Conferences:
Annual Meetings: May/250
Publications:
Transactions of the AOS. a.

American Optometric Association *(1898)*
243 N. Lindbergh Blvd.
St. Louis, MO 63141-7851
Tel: (314)991-4100 *Fax:* (314)991-4101
Toll Free: (800)365 - 2219
Web Site: www.aoanet.org
Members: 33000 individuals
Staff: 98
Annual Budget: $10-25,000,000
Executive Director: Michael Jones
Historical Note
Founded as the American Optical Association in 1898. Became the American Optometric Association in 1919. A federation of state optometric associations. Seeks to improve the quality, availability, and accessibility of eye/vision care, to represent the optometric profession to government, third parties and the public, and to assist members in conducting practices successfully in accordance with the highest standards of patient care and efficiency. Affiliated with the International Optometric and Optical League. Connected with the American Optometric Association Political Action Committee. Has an annual budget of approximately $19 million.
Meetings/Conferences:
Annual Meetings: Summer
Publications:
Optometry. m. adv.
AOA News. semi-m. adv.

American Optometric Student Association *(1968)*
243 N. Lindbergh Blvd.
St. Louis, MO 63141
Tel: (314)991-4100 *Fax:* (314)991-4101
Web Site: www.theaosa.org
Members: 5600 individuals
Staff: 2
Executive Director: Carol Freihaut
Historical Note
AOSA promotes the profession of optometry and enhances the education and welfare of optometry students. Membership: $25/year (individual); $100/year (group).
Meetings/Conferences:
Annual Meetings: Winter
Publications:
AOSA Foresight: Optometry Looking Forward. semi-a.

American Organization for Bodywork Therapies of Asia *(1990)*
1010 Haddonfield-Berlin Rd.
Suite 408
Voorhees, NJ 08043
Tel: (856)782-1616 *Fax:* (856)782-1653
E-Mail: office@aobta.org
Web Site: www.aobta.org
Members: 1400 individuals
Staff: 2
Annual Budget: $25-50,000
Office Manager: Angela Pflugfelder
Historical Note
Founded as American Shiatsu Association; became American Oriental Bodywork Therapy Association in 1990 and assumed its current name in 2001. Especially concerned with the establishment of appropriate standards for practice of all forms of oriental bodywork therapy. Membership: $30-150/year (individual, varies according to type); $500/year (school).
Meetings/Conferences:
Annual Meetings: Summer
Publications:
AOBTA Bulletin. q. adv.
Directory of Members. a.

American Organization of Nurse Executives *(1967)*
Liberty Place
325 Seventh St. NW
Washington, DC 20004
Tel: (202)626-2240 *Fax:* (202)638-5499
E-Mail: aone@aha.org
Web Site: www.aone.org
Members: 4000 individuals
Staff: 10
Annual Budget: $2-5,000,000
Chief Executive Officer: Pamela Thompson
Historical Note
Representing nurses in executive practice across the health care continuum, AONE is a corporate subsidiary of the American Hospital Association. Formerly (1978) American Society for Hospital Nursing Service Administrators and (1985) American Society for Nursing Service Administrators. In 1994 AONE absorbed the Council of Nurse Manager Affiliates. Membership: $200/year.
Meetings/Conferences:
Annual Meetings: Spring
Publications:
Nurse Leader.
Voice of Nursing Leadership.
AONE e-News Update. every 3 weeks. adv.

American Oriental Society *(1842)*
Hatcher Graduate Library
Univ. of Michigan
Ann Arbor, MI 48109-1205
Tel: (734)647-4760 *Fax:* (734)763-6743
Web Site: www.umich.edu/~aos/
Members: 1350 individuals
Staff: 4
Annual Budget: $50-100,000
Secretary-Treasurer: Jonathan Rodgers
E-Mail: jrodgers@umich.edu
Historical Note
Established in 1842 to encourage research in the languages and literatures of Asia and North Africa. Member of the American Council of Learned Societies. Membership: $50/year (regular); $1000 (life); $25/year (student).
Meetings/Conferences:
Annual Meetings: Spring
Publications:
Journal of The American Oriental Society. q.
American Oriental Series. irreg.
AOS Membership Directory.

American Ornithologists' Union *(1883)*
1313 Dolly Madison Blvd., Suite 402
McLean, VA 22101-3926
Tel: (703)790-1745 *Fax:* (703)790-2672
E-Mail: aou@aou.org
Web Site: www.aou.org
Members: 4000 individuals
Annual Budget: $100-250,000
Management Executive: Richard J. Burk, Jr.
Historical Note
Founded September 29, 1883 at the American Museum of Natural History in New York City with 21 charter members. Incorporated 1888 in the District of Columbia, reincorporated in 1987. Affiliated with the American Association for the Advancement of Science. Membership: $42/year.
Meetings/Conferences:
Annual Meetings: August
2007 – Laramie, WY(University of Wyoming)/Aug. 8-11
Publications:
The Auk. q. adv.
Ornithological Newsletter. bi-m.
Ornithological Monographs. irreg.
Membership List. trien.
Checklist of North American Birds. irreg.

American Orthopaedic Association *(1887)*
6300 N. River Rd.
Suite 505
Rosemont, IL 60018
Tel: (847)318-7330 *Fax:* (847)318-7339
E-Mail: info@aoassn.org
Web Site: www.aoassn.org
Members: 1200 individuals
Staff: 7
Annual Budget: $1-2,000,000
Executive Director: Kristin Glavin
Historical Note
Founded in 1887, AOA is the oldest orthopaedic association in the world. AOA's purpose is to identify, develop, recognize and engage leadership in orthopaedics. AOA's annual meeting is open to AOA members and invited guests only.

Meetings/Conferences:
Annual Meetings: Summer
Publications:
AOA News. q.

American Orthopaedic Foot and Ankle Society
(1969)
6300 North River Rd.
Suite 510
Rosemont, IL 60018-4264
Tel: (847)698-4654 *Fax:* (847)692-3315
Toll Free: (800)235 - 4855
E-Mail: aofasinfo@aofas.org
Web Site: www.aofas.org
Members: 1600 individuals
Staff: 7
Annual Budget: $1-2,000,000
Executive Director: Lousanne (Zan) Lofgren
E-Mail: zolfgren@aofas.org
Historical Note
Formerly (1983) American Orthopaedic Foot Society. AOFAS members are members of the American Academy of Orthopaedic Surgeons with an interest in the foot and ankle. Membership: $475/year (active); $75/year (resident/fellow); $250/year (international).
Meetings/Conferences:
2007 – Toronto, ON, Canada(Westin Harbor Castle)/July 12-15/450
Publications:
In-Stride Newsletter. q.
Foot and Ankle International. m.

American Orthopaedic Society for Sports Medicine *(1972)*
6300 N. River Rd.
Suite 500
Rosemont, IL 60018-4229
Tel: (847)292-4900 *Fax:* (847)292-4905
Toll Free: (877)321 - 3500
E-Mail: aossm@aossm.org
Web Site: www.sportsmed.org
Members: 2000 individuals
Staff: 11
Annual Budget: $1-2,000,000
Executive Director: Irvin Bomberger
Director, Communications: Eric Goodwin
Director, Research: Barton Mann
Managing Director: Camille Petrick
Director, Education: Janisse Selan
Historical Note
AOSSM members are orthopaedic surgeons and allied health professionals. AOSSM promotes the prevention, recognition and orthopedic treatment of sports injuries. Membership: $450/year.
Meetings/Conferences:
Annual Meetings: Summer
2007 – Calgary, AB, Canada(Telus Convention Centre)/July 12-15/1000
2008 – Orlando, FL(Marriott)/July 10-13/1000
Publications:
Prevention of Non-Contact ACL Injuries.
Sports Tips (Injury Prevention Guides).
Online Self Assessment.
Sports Medicine Update. 3/year.
American Journal of Sports Medicine. bi-m. adv.

American Orthopsychiatric Association *(1924)*
Department of Psychology, Box 871104
Arizona State University
Tempe, AZ 85287-1104
Tel: (480)727-7518 *Fax:* (480)965-8544
E-Mail: americanortho@gmail.com
Web Site: www.amerortho.org
Members: 650 individuals
Staff: 5
Annual Budget: $500-1,000,000
Director, Membership Services: Nicole Bruno
Historical Note
Founded in New York City in 1924 and incorporated in New York in 1937. Interdisciplinary association of mental health professionals concerned with the study of human behavior and development, and the promotion of mental health. Membership: $105/year (individual).
Meetings/Conferences:
Annual Meetings: Spring/1,500
Publications:
American Journal of Orthopsychiatry. q. adv.
ORTHO UPDATE Newsletter (Ortho Bulletin). q.

American Orthotic and Prosthetic Association
(1917)
330 John Carlyle St., Suite 200
Alexandria, VA 22314
Tel: (571)431-0876 *Fax:* (571)431-0899
E-Mail: info@aopanet.org
Web Site: www.aopanet.org
Members: 2000 companies
Staff: 25
Annual Budget: $2-5,000,000
Executive Director: Tyler J. Wilson
Director, Membership and Communications: Malissa R. Bennett
Senior Director, Government Affairs: Kathleen A. Dodson
Historical Note
AOPA is dedicated to quality patient care. The association represents companies that custom fit or manufacture componentry for patients with prostheses, artifical limbs, orthoses, and orthopedic braces. Membership: varies.
Meetings/Conferences:
Annual Meetings: Fall/1,500
Publications:
AOPA in Advance. bi.
O&P Almanac. m. adv.
The AOPA Yearbook. a. adv.

American Osteopathic Academy for Sports Medicine *(1977)*
2810 Crossroads Dr.
Suite 3800
Madison, WI 53718
Tel: (608)443-2477 *Fax:* (608)443-2474
E-Mail: info@aoasm.org
Web Site: http://aoasm.org
Members: 500 individuals
Staff: 2
Annual Budget: $50-100,000
Executive Director: Susan M. Rees
Historical Note
An affiliate of the American Osteopathic Association. Provides support and continuing education specific to primary care, nonsurgical sports medicine physicians. Membership: $325/year (physicians); $100/year (residents and interns).
Publications:
Sports Medicine Letter. bi-m.
Clinical Journal of Sport Medicine. bi-m. adv.

American Osteopathic Academy of Addiction Medicine *(1986)*
Historical Note
An affiliate of American Osteopathic Healthcare Association, which provides administrative support.

American Osteopathic Academy of Orthopedics
(1941)
P.O. Box 291690
Davie, FL 33329-1690
Tel: (954)262-1700 *Fax:* (954)262-1748
Toll Free: (800)741 - 2626
E-Mail: exec@aoao.org
Web Site: www.aoao.org
Members: 700 individuals
Staff: 2
Executive Director: Morton Morris, D.O.
Historical Note
Affiliated with the American Osteopathic Association. Membership: $350/year.
Meetings/Conferences:
Annual Meetings: Spring
Publications:
The Orthopod. semi-a.

American Osteopathic Association *(1897)*
142 E. Ontario St.
Chicago, IL 60611-2864
Tel: (312)202-8000 *Fax:* (312)202-8200
Toll Free: (800)621 - 1773
E-Mail: info@osteopathic.org
Web Site: www.osteopathic.org
Members: 33224 physicians
Staff: 164
Annual Budget: $10-25,000,000
Executive Director: John Crosby
Controller: Frank Bedford
Director, Education: Diane Burkhart, Ph.D.
Director, Publications: Michael Fitzgerald
Director, State, Specialty, and Socioeconomic Affaris: Michael Mallie
Director, Membership: Sherry McAuliffe
Director, Human Resources: Ollie McCarroll
Director, Quality and Research: Sharon McGill
Director, Government Relations: Sydney Olson
General Counsel: Josh Prober
Associate Executive Director: Jim Swartwout
Director, Communications: Karyn Szurgot
Associate Executive Director: Ann M. Wittner
Director, Information Technology: Mike Zarski
Historical Note
Organized in April 1897 as the American Association for the Advancement of Osteopathic Medicine. Became the American Osteopathic Association in 1901 and was incorporated in Illinois in 1923. A federation of divisional societies organized within state boundaries, the present association has numerous affiliations with other osteopathic organizations. It constitutes the official structure of the osteopathic profession. Has an annual budget of approximately $25 million. Membership: $590/year (individual).
Meetings/Conferences:
Annual Meetings: Fall
Publications:
The D.O. m. adv.
The Journal of the AOA. m. adv.

American Osteopathic Board of Physical Medicine and Rehabilitation *(1954)*
142 E. Ontario St., Fourth Floor, NW
Chicago, IL 60611-2818
Tel: (312)202-8103 *Fax:* (312)202-8224
E-Mail: pzenger@osteopathic.org
Web Site: www.aobpmr.org
Members: 323 individuals
Annual Budget: $10-25,000
Administrator: Pepper L. Zenger
E-Mail: pzenger@osteopathic.org
Historical Note
Affiliated with the American Osteopathic Association. Formerly (1995) the American Osteopathic Academy of Physical Medicine and Rehabilitation. Membership: $295/year.
Meetings/Conferences:
Annual Meetings: in conjunction with the American Osteopathic Ass'n
Publications:
Newsletter. irreg.
Directory. a.

American Osteopathic College of Allergy and Immunology *(1975)*
7025 E. Mc Dowell Rd.
Suite One-B
Scottsdale, AZ 85257
Tel: (480)585-1580
Members: 75 individuals
Annual Budget: under $10,000
Secretary-Treasurer: Dr. William Higgins
Historical Note
An affiliate of American Osteopathic Association, AOCAI provides opportunities for member osteopaths and students to continue studies as they relate to the field of immunology. Has no paid officers or full-time staff. Membership: $50/year.
Meetings/Conferences:
Annual Meetings: 2nd week in November in conjunction with the American Osteopathic Ass'n annual convention.
Publications:
Newsletter. irreg.

American Osteopathic College of Anesthesiologists *(1952)*
6500 N.W. Tower Dr., Suite 103
Kansas City, MO 64151-4414

Tel: (816)373-4700
E-Mail: osteoanest@aol.com
Members: 575 individuals
Staff: 3
Annual Budget: $100-250,000
Secretary-Treasurer: Bert M. Bez, D.O.

Historical Note
Advances the standards of practice and service in anesthesiology; aids in providing the opportunity for study and training in the specialty of anesthesiology. Membership: $300/year.

Meetings/Conferences:
Semi-annual Meetings: Spring and Fall

Publications:
Newsletter. 3/year.

American Osteopathic College of Dermatology *(1955)*
P.O. Box 7525
Kirksville, MO 63501-7525
Tel: (660)665-2184 *Fax:* (660)627-2623
Toll Free: (800)449 - 2623
Web Site: www.aocd.org
Members: 350 individuals
Staff: 3
Annual Budget: $100-250,000
Executive Director: Rebecca A. Mansfield

Historical Note
Membership: $300/year (individual); $5,000/year (organization).

Meetings/Conferences:
Annual Meetings: Semi-Annual With American Osteopathic Ass'n

Publications:
Directory. a. adv.
Newsletter. q. adv.

American Osteopathic College of Occupational and Preventive Medicine *(1984)*
307 Lake View Way NW
Leesburg, VA 20176
Tel: (800)443-8869 *Fax:* (703)443-0576
E-Mail: aocopm@adelphia.net
Web Site: www.aocopm.org/
Members: 350 individuals
Staff: 3
Annual Budget: $25-50,000
Executive Director: Thomas Loftus

Historical Note
Formerly (1995) American Osteopathic College of Preventive Medicine. Membership: $175/year (individual).

Meetings/Conferences:
Semi-annual meetings:

Publications:
Newsletter. q.
Directory. a.

American Osteopathic College of Pathologists *(1954)*
142 E. Ontario St.
Chicago, IL 60611-8224
Tel: (312)202-8197 *Fax:* (312)202-8224
Web Site: www.aocp-net.org
Members: 140 individuals
Staff: 1
Annual Budget: $25-50,000
Executive Director: Penny Evans

Historical Note
Provides continuing education opportunities and support to member pathologists.

Meetings/Conferences:
Semi-annual meetings:

Publications:
NOVA Newsletter. m.
Membership Directory. a. adv.

American Osteopathic College of Proctology
123 Henry St.
Alexandria, VA 22314
Tel: (703)684-0416 *Fax:* (703)684-3280
Web Site: www.aocpr.org
Members: 37 individuals
Staff: 1
Annual Budget: under $10,000
Executive Director: Paul Broderick, D.O.
E-Mail: proctodoc55@hotmail.com

Historical Note
Members specialize in disorders of the lower gastro-intestinal tract. Membership: $400/year.

Meetings/Conferences:
Annual Meetings: Fall
2007 – San Francisco, CA(San Francisco Marriott)/Oct. 18-21/40
2008 – Boca Raton, FL(Boca Raton Resort)/Sept. 11-14/40

American Osteopathic College of Radiology *(1941)*
119 E. Second St.
Milan, MO 63556-1331
Tel: (660)265-4011 *Fax:* (660)265-3494
Toll Free: (800)258 - 2627
E-Mail: aocrrb@nemr.net
Web Site: www.aocr.org
Members: 950 individuals
Staff: 5
Executive Director: Pamela A. Smith
E-Mail: aocrrb@nemr.net

Historical Note
Active members are accredited or certified radiologists who also hold the D.O. degree. Membership: $450/year.

Meetings/Conferences:
Annual Meetings: Fall/180

Publications:
Viewbox. q.

American Osteopathic College of Rheumatology
193 Monroe Ave.
Edison, NJ 08820-3755
Tel: (732)494-6688 *Fax:* (732)494-6689
E-Mail: bmaurer123@aol.com
Members: 300 individuals
Staff: 3
Annual Budget: $50-100,000
President: Sidney Malet, D.O.
Secretary-Treasurer: Robert S. Maurer, D.O.

Historical Note
Members are osteopathic doctors and trainees with an interest in the treatment of arthritis and related diseases.

Publications:
Newsletter. q.

American Osteopathic Colleges of Ophthalmology and Otolaryngology - Head and Neck Surgery *(1916)*
405 W. Grand Ave.
Dayton, OH 45405
Tel: (937)233-5653 *Fax:* (937)233-5673
Toll Free: (800)455 - 9404
E-Mail: info@aocoohns.org
Web Site: www.aocoohns.org
Members: 565 individuals
Staff: 2
Annual Budget: $100-250,000
Executive Vice President: Alvin Dubin
Administrative Director: Debra L. Bailey
E-Mail: aocoohns@aol.com

Historical Note
Formerly (1991) Osteopathic College of Ophthalmology and Otorhinolaryngology and (1993) Osteopathic Colleges of Ophthalmology and Otolaryngology and Head and Neck Surgery. Membership: $475/year.

Meetings/Conferences:
Annual Meetings: Spring/300

Publications:
Newsletter. q.
AOCOO-HNS Journal. a. adv.

American Ostrich Association *(1987)*
P.O. Box 166
Ranger, TX 76470
Tel: (254)647-1645 *Fax:* (254)647-1645
E-Mail: aoa@ostriches.org
Web Site: www.ostriches.org
Members: 100 individuals
Staff: 1
Annual Budget: $500-1,000,000
President: Carole A. Price
E-Mail: aoa@ostriches.org
Secretary/Treasurer: Glinda Cunningham

Historical Note
AOA supports the ostrich industry through government relations, promotions, referral services, and other programs. Membership: $150/year (domestic); $200/year (international).

Meetings/Conferences:
Annual Meetings: Winter

Publications:
American Ostrich Newsletter. q. adv.

American Otological Society *(1868)*
2720 Tartan Way
Springfield, IL 62711
Tel: (217)483-6966 *Fax:* (217)483-6966
Web Site: www.americanotologicalsociety.org
Members: 303 individuals
Annual Budget: $25-50,000
Secretary-Treasurer: Clough Shelton, M.D.
E-Mail: segossard@aol.com

Historical Note
AOS members are otologists and other health professionals with an interest in diseases of the ear.

Publications:
Otology and Neorology. adv.
Transactions of the AOS. a. adv.

American Pain Society *(1978)*
4700 W. Lake Ave.
Glenview, IL 60025-1485
Tel: (847)375-4715 *Fax:* (877)734-8758
E-Mail: info@ampainsoc.org
Web Site: www.ampainsoc.org
Members: 3400 individuals
Staff: 10
Annual Budget: $2-5,000,000
Executive Director: Cathy Underwood

Historical Note
APS is composed of physicians, dentists, psychologists, nurses, physical and occupational therapists and scientists interested in pain research and treatment. A national chapter of the International Association for the Study of Pain. Incorporated in the District of Columbia in 1978. Mission is to serve people in pain by advancing research, education, treatment and professional practice. Membership: $120-$275/year, depending on income (individual); $50/year (student); $150/year (affiliate).

Meetings/Conferences:
Annual Meetings: Spring

Publications:
Journal of Pain. 9/year. adv.
APS Bulletin. bi-m. adv.
APS Membership Directory. a. adv.

American Paint Horse Association *(1962)*
P.O. Box 961023
Ft. Worth, TX 76161-0023
Tel: (817)834-2742 *Fax:* (817)834-3152
E-Mail: askapha@apha.com
Web Site: www.apha.com
Members: 105000 individuals
Staff: 145
Annual Budget: $10-25,000,000
Director: Lex Smurthwaite
E-Mail: lex@apha.com

Historical Note
Merger of American Paint Stock Horse and American Paint Quarter Horse Associations. Collects, records, and preserves the pedigrees of Paint horses. Member of the National Pedigree Livestock Council and the American Horse Council. Membership: $25/year.

Meetings/Conferences:
2007 – June 24-July 7
2008 – June 22-July 5
2009 – June 21-July 4
2010 – June 20-July 3
2011 – June 26-July 9

Publications:
Paint Racing News. bi-m.
APHA Connection. q.
The Paint Horse Journal. m.
Breeders and Trainers Directory.

American Pancreatic Association *(1970)*
45 High Valley Dr.

Chesterfield, MO 63017
Tel: (314)392-3919 *Fax:* (314)754-9515
E-Mail: american-pancreatic-association@lettuceplanet.com
Web Site: www.american-pancreatic-association.org
Members: 375 individuals
Annual Budget: under $10,000
Secretary-Treasurer: Richard Bell
Meeting Manager: Marcia McIntyre

Historical Note

Formerly (1975) American Pancreatic Study Group. APA members are medical professionals with an interest in diseases of the pancreas. Has no paid officers or full-time staff.

Meetings/Conferences:

Annual Meetings: *always Chicago, IL/November*
2007 – Chicago, IL(Wyndham)/Nov. 1-3/200

American Paper Machinery Association

Historical Note

Became (2004) Association of Suppliers to the Paper Industry.

American Paraplegia Society *(1954)*

75-20 Astoria Blvd.
Jackson Heights, NY 11370-1177
Tel: (718)803-3782 Ext: 322 *Fax:* (718)803-0414
Web Site: www.apssci.org
Members: 525 individuals
Staff: 5
Annual Budget: $250-500,000
Associate Executive Director: Vivian Beyda, DPH
Program Manager: Stephen Sofer, Ph.D.

Historical Note

APS members are physicians and scientists with an interest in injuries and diseases of the spinal cord. Membership: $100/year (individual).

Meetings/Conferences:

2007 – Orlando, FL(Gaylord Palms)/Aug. 27-29
2008 – Orlando, FL(Gaylord Palms)/Aug. 11-13

Publications:

Membership Directory (on-line).
Journal of Spinal Cord Medicine. q. adv.

American Paso Fino Horse Association *(1964)*

P.O. Box 2363
Pittsburgh, PA 15230
Tel: (724)437-5170 *Fax:* (724)438-4471
Members: 500 individuals
President: Warren R. Hull

Historical Note

Members are breeders and owners of Paso Fino horses. Maintains stud book and breed registry.

Meetings/Conferences:

Annual Meetings: *Fall*

Publications:

American Paso Fino World. q.

American Pathology Foundation *(1959)*

1540 S. Coast Hwy.
Suite 203
Laguna Beach, CA 92651
Tel: (847)949-6055 *Fax:* (847)566-4580
Toll Free: (877)993 - 9935
Web Site: www.americanpathologyfoundation.org/
Members: 600 individuals
Staff: 3
Executive Director: Edward J. Stygar, Jr.
E-Mail: estygar3@covad.net

Historical Note

Formerly the Private Practitioners of Pathology Foundation. Members are board certified pathologists concerned with private practice. Membership: $175/year (individual).

Publications:

Newsletter. q.
Directory. a.

American Payroll Association *(1982)*

660 N. Main Ave., Suite 100
San Antonio, TX 78205-1217
Tel: (210)226-4600 *Fax:* (210)226-4027
E-Mail: info@americanpayroll.org
Web Site: www.americanpayroll.org
Members: 21000 individuals
Staff: 51
Annual Budget: $10-25,000,000
Executive Director: Daniel J. Maddux

Historical Note

APA was established to increase the payroll professional's skill level through education and mutual support and to obtain recognition for payroll work as a professional discipline. Awards the designation Certified Payroll Professional (CPP). Has an annual budget of $8.1 million. Membership: $165/year (individual).

Meetings/Conferences:

2007 – Las Vegas, NV/May 22-26
2008 – Austin, TX/
2009 – Long Beach, CA/

Publications:

Payroll Currently. bi-m.
Paytech. m. adv.
APA Directory. every eighteen months.
ePayXpress, e-journal. m.
The Payroll Source.

American Peanut Council *(1940)*

1500 King St., Suite 301
Alexandria, VA 22314
Tel: (703)838-9500 *Fax:* (703)838-9508
E-Mail: generalinfo@peanutsusa.com
Web Site: www.peanutsusa.com
Members: 225 producers and businesses
Staff: 8
Annual Budget: $2-5,000,000
President: Patrick Archer

Historical Note

Formerly National Peanut Council (1998). Founded in June 1940 and incorporated in Georgia in 1941, the Council counts among its members peanut farmers, shellers, brokers, special processors, the manufacturers of peanut products and peanut butter, and the allied support trades. As the umbrella organization for the entire peanut industry, the Council promotes increased peanut consumption, research and the dissemination of knowledge of new technology, as well as improved processing, storage, handling and packaging techniques. The Council also acts as a clearinghouse for information pertaining to actions by the federal government and is the industry forum for the exchange of ideas and information by the industry's leaders.

Meetings/Conferences:

Annual Meetings: *Summer/500*

Publications:

APC Newsletter. m.
USA Peanuts. a.
Peanut Industry Directory. a.

American Peanut Product Manufacturers *(1983)*

One Massachusetts Ave. NW
Suite 800
Washington, DC 20001
Tel: (202)842-2345 *Fax:* (202)408-7763
Members: 6 companies
Staff: 2
Annual Budget: $100-250,000
Counsel: Richard Pasco

Historical Note

APPMI members are food processors of products using peanuts.

Meetings/Conferences:

Annual Meetings: *None held.*

American Peanut Research and Education Society *(1968)*

376 Ag Hall
Oklahoma State University
Stillwater, OK 74078
Tel: (405)372-3052 *Fax:* (405)624-6718
Web Site: www.apres.okstate.edu
Members: 450 individuals
Staff: 2
Annual Budget: $50-100,000
Executive Officer: J. Ronald Sholar, Ph.D.

Historical Note

Organized in Norfolk, Virginia July 1968 as the American Peanut Research and Education Association as an outgrowth of the Peanut Improvement Working Group dating back to 1957. The present name was adopted in 1979. Membership, which is drawn from government, academia and private industry, now includes individuals from over 20 countries. Membership: $80/year (individual); $100/year (organizational); $80 (institutional); $20 (student).

Meetings/Conferences:

Annual Meetings: *July*
2007 – Birmingham, AL(Wynfrey Hotel)/July 10-14

Publications:

Peanut Science. semi-a.
APRES Proceedings. a.

American Peanut Shellers Association *(1919)*

P.O. Box 70157
Albany, GA 31708-0157
Tel: (229)888-2508 *Fax:* (229)888-5150
E-Mail: info@peanut-shellers.org
Web Site: www.peanut-shellers.org
Members: 200 companies
Staff: 4
Annual Budget: $2-5,000,000
Executive Director: John T. Powell
Director, Events and Publications: Miriam Crosby

Historical Note

Formerly (1994) Southeastern Peanut Association. Active members are companies engaged in peanut shelling and crushing; 198 associate members are firms serving the peanut industry in such areas as transportation, storage, insurance, implement manufacture, etc. Retains representation in Washington to promote the interests of the national peanut shellers. Membership: based on tonnage (active members); $400/year (associate member).

Publications:

Newsletter. m.
Membership Directory. a.

American Pediatric Society *(1888)*

3400 Research Forest Dr., Suite B-7
The Woodlands, TX 77381-4259
Tel: (281)419-0052 *Fax:* (281)419-0082
E-Mail: info@aps-spr.org
Web Site: www.aps-spr.org
Members: 1500 individuals
Staff: 3
Annual Budget: $100-250,000
Associate Executive Director: Kathy Cannon
E-Mail: kathyc@aps-spr.org

Historical Note

Organized September 18, 1888 and incorporated in New York in 1962. Membership: $255/year.

Meetings/Conferences:

Annual Meetings: *Spring/4,500*
2007 – Toronto, ON, Canada(Convention Center)/May 5-8/6000

Publications:

Pediatric Research. m. adv.

American Pediatric Surgical Association *(1970)*

60 Revere Dr., Suite 500
Northbrook, IL 60062
Tel: (847)480-9576 *Fax:* (847)480-9282
E-Mail: eapsa@eapsa.org
Web Site: www.eapsa.org
Members: 800 individuals
Annual Budget: $500-1,000,000
Executive Director: Melanie Stanton

Meetings/Conferences:

Annual Meetings: *May*
2007 – Orlando, FL(J.W. Marriott)/May 23-27/650

Publications:

Journal of Pediatric Surgery. m. adv.
APSA Membership Directory. a.
Newsletter. a.

American Peptide Society *(1990)*

Torrey Pines Institute, Room 2-136
3550 General Atomics Court
San Diego, CA 92121
Tel: (858)455-4752 *Fax:* (800)446-5596

E-Mail: aps_member@tpims.org
Web Site: www.ampepsoc.org
Members: 1000 individuals
General Manager: Donna Freher-Lyons

Historical Note

AmPepSoc is a scientific and educational organization. Members are involved in research in academia, industry and government covering all aspects of the chemistry and biology of peptides and small proteins. Membership: $125/year (individual); $50/year (student); $75/year (postdoctoral and retired).

Meetings/Conferences:

2007 - Montreal, QC, Canada

Publications:

Biopolymers (Peptide Science). bi-m. adv.

American Pet Boarding Association *(1989)*
22096 N. Pet Lane
Prairie View, IL 60069
Tel: (847)634-9444 *Fax:* (847)634-9460
Members: 189 individuals
Staff: 1
Annual Budget: $10-25,000
Executive Director: Robert X. Leeds

Historical Note

APBA's goal is to define valid criteria for the humane boarding care of companion animals and to recognize operating boarding facilities that meet this criteria by conferring Accredited Membership to them. Membership: $35/year.

Meetings/Conferences:

Annual Meetings: *Meetings are held during the first week in October.*

Publications:

Journal of Professional Pet Boarding. q. adv.

American Pet Products Manufacturers Association *(1958)*
255 Glenville Road
Greenwich, CT 06831-4148
Tel: (203)532-0000 *Fax:* (203)532-0551
Toll Free: (800)452 - 1225
Web Site: www.appma.org
Members: 750 companies
Staff: 15
Annual Budget: $2-5,000,000
Managing Director and Chief Operating Officer: Bob Vetere
E-Mail: bob@appma.org
Vice President and Deputy Managing Director: Andrew Darmohraj, CAE
E-Mail: andy@appma.org
Director, Member Services: Anne Ferrante
E-Mail: aferrante@appma.org
General Counsel and Director, Legislative Affairs: Gina Valeri
E-Mail: gina@appma.org

Historical Note

APPMA is a trade association for manufacturers and importers of pet products. Represents the pet products industry in the U.S., providing market research, legislative and regulatory monitoring, industry promotion, and other services to members.

Meetings/Conferences:

Annual Meetings: *June*

Publications:

APPMA E-Update. w.
APPMA Advisor Magazine. q.
Nat'l Pet Owners Survey. bien.

American Petroleum Institute *(1919)*
1220 L St. NW
Washington, DC 20005
Tel: (202)682-8000 *Fax:* (202)682-8115
Web Site: www.api.org
Members: 400 companies
Staff: 200
Annual Budget: $50-100,000,000
President and Chief Executive Officer: Red Cavaney, CAE
Policy and Communications: Jim Craig
Government Affairs: Jim Ford

Historical Note

Incorporated March 20, 1919 in New York, NY. API is the U.S. oil and natural gas industry's primary trade association. Membership consists of a broad cross section of oil, gas and allied companies in exploration, production, transportation, refining and marketing. API's mission is to influence public policy in support of a strong, viable U.S. oil and natural gas industry essential to meet the energy needs of consumers in an efficient, environmentally responsible manner. 2005 budget $100 + million, which includes special programs. Membership dues based on market share volumes.

American Pharmaceutical Association - Academy of Students of Pharmacy

Historical Note

Became Academy of Students of Pharmacy in 2003.

American Pharmacists Association *(1852)*
2215 Constitution Ave. NW
Washington, DC 20037-2985
Tel: (202)628-4410 *Fax:* (202)783-2351
Toll Free: (800)237 - 2742
E-Mail: infocenter@aphanet.org
Web Site: www.aphanet.org
Members: 53000 individuals
Staff: 100
Annual Budget: $25-50,000
Executive Vice President and Chief Executive Officer: John A. Gans, Pharm.D.
Senior Vice President, Business Development: James Appleby
Vice President, Finance and Administration: Roger K. Browning
Director, Meetings and Expositions: Windy K. Christner
Director, Executive Office Operations and Corporate Secretary: Linda K. Gainey
Vice President, Strategic Alliances and Business Development: Liz Keyes
Vice President, Professional Practice: Mitchel C. Rothholz
Vice President, Professional Education and Industry Relations: Karen K. Tracy
Vice President, Policy and Communications and Staff Counsel: Susan C. Winckler

Historical Note

Founded in Philadelphia in 1852 and incorporated in the District of Columbia in 1888, APhA is a national professional society of pharmacists. Its constituent sections include: Academy of Pharmacy Practice and Management, Academy of Pharmaceutical Research and Science, and Academy of Student Pharmacists. Sponsors and supports the APhA Political Action Committee. Membership: varies.

Meetings/Conferences:

Annual Meetings: *Spring/5,000*
2007 - Atlanta, GA/March 16-20

Publications:

Journal of the American Pharmacists Ass'n. bi-m. adv.
Student Pharmacist. q. adv.
Pharmacy Today. m. adv.
Journal of Pharmaceutical Sciences. m. adv.

American Philatelic Society - Writers Unit #30 *(1967)*
2501 Drexel St.
Vienna, VA 22180
Tel: (703)560-2413
E-Mail: ggrittenhagen@aphanet.org
Members: 250 individuals
Staff: 1
Annual Budget: under $10,000
Secretary-Treasurer: George Griffenhagen

Historical Note

APSWU members are journalists and editors specializing in philately. APSWU is Unit #30 of the American Philatelic Society. Membership: $10/year (U.S. member); $17.50/year (Canadian or Mexican member); $20/year (member in any other country).

Meetings/Conferences:

Annual Meetings: *in conjunction with the American Philatelic Soc.*

Publications:

Philatelic Communicator Journal. q.

American Philological Association *(1869)*
Univ. of Pennsylvania, 292 Logan Hall
249 S. 36th St.
Philadelphia, PA 19104-6304
Tel: (215)898-4975 *Fax:* (215)573-7874
E-Mail: apaclassics@sas.upenn.edu
Web Site: www.apaclassics.org
Members: 2900 individuals
Staff: 3
Annual Budget: $500-1,000,000
Executive Director: Adam D. Blistein
E-Mail: apaclassics@sas.upenn.edu

Historical Note

Organized in Poughkeepsie, New York in July, 1869 by classical scholars from the Classical Section of the American Oriental Society and the Greek Club of New York City. A member of the American Council of Learned Societies and National Humanities Alliance. APA membership primarily comprises university and college teachers of classical languages, literature and history. Membership: $20-196/year (individual, based on salary); $95/year (organization).

Meetings/Conferences:

Annual Meetings: *Winter*
2007 - San Diego, CA(Marriott)/Jan. 4-7
2008 - Chicago, IL(Hyatt)/Jan. 3-6

Publications:

APA Newsletter. bi-m. adv.
Transactions of the American Philological Ass'n (TAPA). semi-a. adv.
Classical Texts. irreg.
Meeting Abstracts. a.
Amphora (outreach publication). semi-a.
Meeting Program. a. adv.
Positions for Classicals and Archaeologists. m.
American Classical Studies. irreg.

American Philosophical Association *(1900)*
University of Delaware
31 Amstel Ave.
Newark, DE 19716-4797
Tel: (302)831-1112 *Fax:* (302)831-8690
E-Mail: apaonline@udel.edu
Web Site: www.apa.udel.edu/apa
Members: 10400 individuals
Staff: 7
Annual Budget: $500-1,000,000
Acting Executive Director: William Mann
Coordinator, Membership: Janet Sample
Coordinator, Meetings: Linda Smallbrook
E-Mail: apaonline@udel.edu

Historical Note

Formed in New York City in November, 1901 with 98 charter members. Merged in 1920 with the Western Philosophical Association, founded in 1900, and later with the Society of Philosophy, a Pacific Coast organization. Members are professors of philosophy at the college level, graduate students and others with a special interest in the field. A member of the American Council of Learned Societies and the Federation Internationale des Societes de Philosophie. Membership: $35-140/year (individual, by income).

Meetings/Conferences:

Three Meetings Annually: *March, April and December*

Publications:

Proceedings and Addresses. 5/year. adv.
Jobs for Philosophers. 5/year.
Philosophy & Law Newsletter. semi-a.
Philosophy & Medicine Newsletter. semi-a.
Feminism & Philosophy Newsletter. semi-a.
Teaching Philosophy Newsletter. semi-a.
Computer Use in Philosophy Newsletter. semi-a.
Philosophy and the Black Experience Newsletter. semi-a.

American Philosophical Society *(1743)*
104 S. Fifth St.
Philadelphia, PA 19106-3387
Tel: (215)440-3400 *Fax:* (215)440-3425
Web Site: www.amphilsoc.org
Members: 900 individuals
Staff: 32
Co-Executive Officer: Mary Maples Dunn, Ph.D.
Co-Executive Officer: Richard S. Dunn
Editor and Head of Publications: Mary McDonald
E-Mail: mmcdonald@amphilsoc.org
Director, Museum Exhibitions and Collections: Sue Ann Prince

Historical Note
Founded in 1743 in Philadelphia by Benjamin Franklin, APS evolved in 1769 through a merger of the American Philosophical Society and the American Society for Promoting Useful Knowledge; chartered in 1780 in Pennsylvania. The full name is the American Philosophical Society Held at Philadelphia for Promoting Useful Knowledge. A member of the American Council of Learned Societies. Promotes and advances all useful branches of knowledge through scholarly and scientific meetings (semi-annual); financial assistance to scholars; scholarly books, monographs, articles and newsletter; a library specializing in the history of science in America and its European background; and community service. The society, which includes about 100 Nobel laureates, recognizes excellence with awards and medals including the Magellanic Premium, the oldest scientific prize in America.

Meetings/Conferences:
Semi-Annual Meetings: Spring and Fall

Publications:
Memoirs. 3-4/year. adv.
Transactions. 5/year. adv.
APS News Newsletter. semi-a.
Proceedings. q.
Yearbook. a.

American Physical Society *(1899)*
One Physics Ellipse
College Park, MD 20740-3844
Tel: (301)209-3200 *Fax:* (301)209-0865
E-Mail: opa@aps.org
Web Site: www.aps.org
Members: 44000 individuals
Staff: 170
Annual Budget: $25-50,000,000
Executive Officer: Judy R. Franz, Ph.D.
E-Mail: franz@aps.org
Director, Meetings: Donna Baudrau
E-Mail: badreau@aps.org
Director, International Affairs: Amy Flatten
Director, Education and Outreach Programs: Ted Hodapp
Director, Membership: Trish Lettieri
E-Mail: lettieri@aps.org
Director, Public Affairs: Michael Lubell
E-Mail: lubell@aps.org

Historical Note
Founded in 1899, the Society's objective is the advancement and diffusion of the knowledge of physics. A constituent member of the American Institute of Physics. Has an annual budget of approximately $34 million. Membership: $25-100/year (individual).

Meetings/Conferences:
Annual Meetings: Spring

Publications:
Membership Directory. bien..
APS News. m.
Bulletin of the APS. m.
Physical Review Letters. w.
Reviews of Modern Physics. q.
The Physical Reviews A-E. m.
Physical Review Abstracts. bi-w.

American Physical Therapy Association *(1921)*
1111 N. Fairfax St.
Alexandria, VA 22314-1488
Tel: (703)684-2782 *Fax:* (703)684-7343
Toll Free: (800)999 - 2782
Web Site: www.apta.org
Members: 64000 individuals
Staff: 160
Annual Budget: $10-25,000,000
Chief Executive Officer: Francis J. Mallon
Senior Vice President, Education: Janet Bezner, PT
Senior Vice President, Practice, Analysis and Research Devel.: Andrew Guccione, Ph.D.
Chief Operating Officer: Charles "Chuck" Martin, CAE
Vice President, Government Affairs: Dave Mason
Senior Vice President, Governance, Components, and Meetings: Bonnie Polvinale, CMP

Historical Note
Founded as the American Women's Physical Therapeutic Association; became the American Physiotherapy Association in the 1930s and assumed its current name in 1948. APTA is a professional association of physical therapists, physical therapist assistants and physical therapy students. Sponsors and supports the Physical Therapy Political Action Committee (PTPAC). Membership: $245/year, plus chapter dues.

Meetings/Conferences:
Annual Meetings: Summer

Publications:
PT Bulletin Online. w. adv.
PT-e Clips.
PT, Magazine of Physical Therapy. m. adv.
Physical Therapy Journal. m. adv.

American Physical Therapy Association - Private Practice Section *(1956)*
1055 N. Fairfax St., Suite 100
Alexandria, VA 22314
Tel: (703)299-2410 *Fax:* (703)299-2411
Toll Free: (800)517 - 1167
E-Mail: privatepracticesection@apta.org
Web Site: www.ppsapta.org
Members: 4000 individuals
Staff: 2
Annual Budget: $1-2,000,000
Executive Director: Monica Baroody, CAE

Historical Note
Consists of members of the APTA who are in private practice.

Meetings/Conferences:
Annual Meetings: Fall

Publications:
IMPACT Newsletter. 11/year. adv.

American Physiological Society *(1887)*
9650 Rockville Pike
Bethesda, MD 20814-3991
Tel: (301)634-7164 *Fax:* (301)634-7241
E-Mail: info@the-aps.org
Web Site: www.the-aps.org
Members: 11000 individuals
Staff: 70
Annual Budget: $10-25,000,000
Executive Director: Martin Frank, Ph.D.
E-Mail: mfrank@the-aps.org
Manager, Membership Services: Linda Allen
E-Mail: lallen@the-aps.org
Education Officer: Marsha Lakes Matyas, PhD
E-Mail: mmatyas@the-aps.org
Director, Finance: Robert Price
E-Mail: rprice@the-aps.org
Public Affairs Officer: Alice Ra'anan
Publications Director and Executive Editor: Margaret Reich
E-Mail: mreich@the-aps.org

Historical Note
Founded December 30, 1887, at a meeting held in the physiology laboratory of the College of Physicians and Surgeons, New York City. Incorporated in Missouri in 1923. A member of the Federation of American Socs. for Experimental Biology (FASEB). Membership: $100/year (regular, corresponding); $65/year (affiliate); $15/year (students). Has an annual budget of over $10 million.

Meetings/Conferences:
Semi-Annual Meetings: Spring (with FASEB) and Fall

Publications:
Advances in Physiology Education. semi-a. adv.
American Journal of Physiology (Consolidated). m. adv.
American Journal of Physiology: Endocrinology and Metabolism. m. adv.
American Journal of Physiology: Gastrointestinal/Liver Physiology. m. adv.
American Journal of Physiology: Heart and Circulatory Physiology. m. adv.
American Journal of Physiology: Regulatory/Integrative/Comparative. m. adv.
American Journal of Physiology: Renal Physiology. m. adv.
Physiological Genomics. adv.
Journal of Applied Physiology. m. adv.
Journal of Neurophysiology. m. adv.
Physiological Reviews. q. adv.
The Physiologist. bi-m. adv.
News in Physiological Sciences. bi-m. adv.
American Journal of Physiology: Lung Cellular/Molecular Phys. m. adv.

American Phytopathological Society *(1908)*
3340 Pilot Knob Road
St. Paul, MN 55121-2097
Tel: (651)454-7250 *Fax:* (651)454-0766
E-Mail: aps@scisoc.org
Web Site: www.apsnet.org
Members: 5000 individuals
Staff: 60
Annual Budget: $2-5,000,000
Executive Vice President: Steven C. Nelson, CMP
Director, Membership and Communications: Michelle Bjerkness
E-Mail: mbjerkness@scisoc.org
Director, Meetings: Betty Ford

Historical Note
Founded December 30, 1908 in Baltimore with 130 charter members and incorporated in the District of Columbia in 1915. Promotes all aspects of knowledge of plant diseases, and promotes their control. Membership: $72/year (individual); $550-750/year (company).

Meetings/Conferences:
Annual Meetings: Summer/1,800-2,000
2007 – San Diego, CA/July 28-Aug. 1
2008 – Minneapolis, MN/July 26-30
2009 – Portland, OR/Aug. 1-5

Publications:
Molecular Plant-Microbe Interactions. m. adv.
Phytopathology. m.
Plant Disease. m. adv.
Phytopathology News. m. adv.

American Pilots' Association *(1884)*
499 South Capitol St. SW
Suite 409
Washington, DC 20003
Tel: (202)484-0700 *Fax:* (202)484-9320
E-Mail: contact@americanpilots.org
Web Site: www.americanpilots.org
Members: 59 state and other associations
Staff: 4
Annual Budget: $2-5,000,000
Executive Director and General Counsel: Paul G. Kirchner

Historical Note
APA members are groups or state licensed maritime pilots or federally licensed pilots in the Great Lakes region. Membership: $1,400/year (individual).

Meetings/Conferences:
Biennial Meetings: Even years

Publications:
On Station. q.

American Pinzgauer Association *(1973)*
P.O. Box 147
Bethany, MO 64424
Toll Free: (800)914 - 9883
E-Mail: info@pinzgauers.org
Web Site: www.pinzgauers.org
Members: 500 individuals
Staff: 1
Annual Budget: $25-50,000
Secretary: Jeff Cole

Historical Note
Owners and breeders of the Pinzgauer breed of cattle, which originated in the Pinzgau Valley region of Austria. Membership: $35/year (individual); lifetime membership: $200.

Meetings/Conferences:
Annual Meetings: Fall/100

Publications:
Pinzgauer Journal. q. adv.

American Pipe Fittings Association *(1938)*
201 Park Washington Court
Falls Church, VA 22046
Tel: (703)538-1786 *Fax:* (703)241-5603
E-Mail: info@apfa.com
Web Site: www.apfa.com
Members: 50 companies
Staff: 2

Annual Budget: $100-250,000
Executive Director: Clay D. Tyeryar, CAE

Historical Note
Formerly Pipe Fittings Manufacturers Association. Members are domestic producers of piping components and accessories and pipe hangers and supports. Seeks to promote use of American pipe fittings, contribute to development of standards, collect statistics, and cooperate with government agencies on matters affecting the industry.

Meetings/Conferences:
Semi-Annual Meetings: April and October/90

Publications:
The Pipeline. 4-5/year.

American Planning Association *(1909)*
122 S. Michigan Ave., Suite 1600
Chicago, IL 60603
Tel: (312)431-9100 *Fax:* (312)431-9985
Web Site: www.planning.org
Members: 37000 individuals
Staff: 80
Annual Budget: $10-25,000,000
Executive Director and Chief Executive Officer: Paul Farmer
Director, Conferences: Deene Alongi
Director, Marketing: Kenneth East
Director, Publications: Sylvia Lewis
Director, Policy: Jeff Soule
Director, Education: Carolyn Torma

Historical Note
Founded as the National Conference on City Planning, APA assumed its present name in 1978. Membership is open not only to practicing planners (city, local, state, regional, rural, privately or publicly employed), but to administrators, appointed commissioners, students and others. Includes the American Institute of Certified Planners, a professional institute which provides national certification of planners. Has an annual budget of approximately $15 million. Membership fee varies, based on annual salary: $80-156/year, plus chapter dues.

Meetings/Conferences:
Annual Meetings: Spring/3,000

Publications:
Journal of the American Planning Association. q.
The Commissioner newsletter. q.
Planning & Environmental Law. m.
Planning magazine. m.
Zoning Practice. m.
Practicing Planner (online). q.
Planning Advisory Service Reports. 6/yr.
PAS Memo. m.

American Plastics Council *(1991)*
1300 Wilson Blvd.
Arlington, VA 22209
Tel: (703)741-5000 *Fax:* (703)741-5695
Toll Free: (800)243 - 5790
Web Site: www.plastics.org
Members: 18 companies
Staff: 50
Annual Budget: $25-50,000,000
President: Rodney W. Lowman
Director, Communications: Rob Krebs

Historical Note
APC members include United States resin and monomer producers, representatives of the plastics industry, processors and suppliers. Focuses on plastics issues, industry statistics, and industry and public education programs.

American Podiatric Circulatory Society *(1979)*
5704 18th Ave.
Brooklyn, NY 11204
Tel: (718)236-7952 *Fax:* (718)236-7953
Members: 900 individuals
President: Dr. Stanley Goldstein

Historical Note
Membership: $35/year (individual).

Meetings/Conferences:
Annual Meetings: Winter

Publications:
APCS Bulletin. q. adv.

American Podiatric Medical Association *(1912)*
9312 Old Georgetown Road
Bethesda, MD 20814-1698
Tel: (301)571-9200 *Fax:* (301)530-2752
Toll Free: (800)275 - 2762
E-Mail: askapma@apma.org
Web Site: www.apma.org
Members: 11500 individuals
Staff: 57
Annual Budget: $10-25,000,000
Executive Director: Glenn B. Gastwirth, D.P.M.
Director, Scientific Affairs: James Christina, D.P.M.
Director, Legislative Advocacy: Faye Frankfort
Director, Public Relations: Amie Haer
Director, Publications: Maggie Kay
Deputy Executive Director: Jay Levrio, Ph.D.
Meetings Administrator: Anne R. Martinez
Director, Health, Policy and Practice: Nancy Parsley, DPM
Director, Finance: Denis Russell, CPA
Director, Membership Services: Beth Shaub
Director, Council on Podiatric Medical Education: Alan Tinkleman

Historical Note
Organized July 1, 1912 as the National Association of Chiropodists. Incorporated in New York in 1912; became the American Podiatry Association in 1958 and assumed its current name in 1984. Has over 50 component podiatry societies and numerous affiliates. Supports the Podiatry Political Action Committee, Fund for Podiatric Medical Education, and Foot Health Foundation of America. Has an annual budget of approximately $11 million. Membership: $725/year (individual members in practice five years minimum; dues reduced for individual members in practice less than five years, nearing retirement or fully retired).

Meetings/Conferences:
Annual Meetings: August/2,000

Publications:
APMA Alert. bi-m.
eNews. d.
APMA News. m. adv.
Journal of the American Podiatric Medical Association. m. adv.

American Podiatric Medical Students' Association *(1954)*
9312 Old Georgetown Rd.
Bethesda, MD 20814-1621
Toll Free: (800)295 - 2762 Ext: 263
E-Mail: apmsadcm@apma.org
Web Site: www.apmsa.org
Members: 1700 individuals
Staff: 1
Executive Director: Dorothy Cahill McDonald

Historical Note
APMSA represents students enrolled at the eight colleges of podiatric medicine in the U.S. Provides a forum to discuss and resolve issues in the profession of podiatry.

Meetings/Conferences:
Annual Meetings: Winter

Publications:
newsletter. q.
Graduation Handbook. a.

American Podiatric Medical Writers Association *(1985)*
P.O. Box 750129
Forest Hills, NY 11375
Tel: (718)897-9700
Members: 100 individuals
Staff: 3
Annual Budget: $10-25,000
Executive Director: Dr. Barry Block
E-Mail: bblock@prodigy.net

Historical Note
Established in New York City. Membership: $50/year (podiatrist); $25/year (non-podiatrist).

Meetings/Conferences:
Semi-Annual Meetings:
2007 - Philadelphia, PA(Marriott)/Aug. 16-19/100
2008 - Honolulu, HI(Hilton)/July 24-27/100

Publications:
APMWA Newsletter. q.

American Polarity Therapy Association *(1984)*
122 N. Elm St.
Suite 512
Greensboro, NC 27401
Tel: (336)574-1121 *Fax:* (336)574-1151
E-Mail: hq@polaritytherapy.org
Web Site: www.polaritytherapy.org
Members: 1400 individuals
Staff: 1
Annual Budget: $250-500,000
President: Damon Fazio

Historical Note
Membership: $66/year (individual); $44/year (student); $66/year (general).

Meetings/Conferences:
Annual Meetings: Bi-Annual

Publications:
magazine. a. adv.
Newsletter. q. adv.

American Police Academy

Historical Note
Educational arm of the National Association of Chiefs of Police.

American Political Science Association *(1903)*
1527 New Hampshire Ave. NW
Washington, DC 20036-1206
Tel: (202)483-2512 *Fax:* (202)483-2657
E-Mail: apsa@apsanet.org
Web Site: www.apsanet.org
Members: 15000 individuals
Staff: 25
Annual Budget: $2-5,000,000
Executive Director: Michael A. Brintnall
E-Mail: brintnall@apsanet.org
Director, Educational and Professional Programs: Linda Lopez
Director, Meetings and Conventions: Christina Marmon
Director, Member Services and Technology: Sean Twombly

Historical Note
Member of the American Council of Learned Societies. Membership: $74-179/year (full member), $35/year (student).

Meetings/Conferences:
Annual Meetings: Fall

Publications:
Directory of Political Science Faculty. trien.
Perspectives on Politics. q. adv.
American Political Science Review. q. adv.
PS: Political Science & Politics. q. adv.

American Polygraph Association *(1966)*
P.O. Box 8037
Chattanooga, TN 37414-0037
Tel: (423)892-3992 *Fax:* (423)894-5435
Toll Free: (800)272 - 8037
Web Site: www.polygraph.org
Members: 2500 individuals
Staff: 2
Annual Budget: $100-250,000
Manager: Robbie S. Bennett
E-Mail: apapolygraph@earthlink.net

Historical Note
The product of a merger of Academy of Scientific Interrogation, American Academy of Polygraph Examiners, and National Board of Polygraph Examiners. Membership: $125/year.

Meetings/Conferences:
2007 - New Orleans, LA(Hilton)/July 19-24

Publications:
APA Membership Directory. a. adv.
APA Newsletter. bi-m.
Polygraph. q.

American Polypay Sheep Association *(1980)*
15603 173rd Ave.
Milo, IA 50166
Tel: (641)942-6402 *Fax:* (641)942-6502
E-Mail: info@polppay.org
Web Site: www.polypay.org
Members: 225 individuals
Staff: 1
Annual Budget: $25-50,000
Secretary: Karey Claghorn

Historical Note
Breeders of polypay sheep, a breed developed to provide more pounds of lamb, more frequently. Membership: $50/year.

Meetings/Conferences:
Annual Meetings: Summer

Publications:
American Polypay Sheep News. q. adv.
Breeders Directory. irreg. adv.

American Pomological Society *(1848)*
103 Tyson Bldg.
University Park, PA 16802
Tel: (814)863-6163 *Fax:* (814)237-3407
E-Mail: aps@psu.edu
Web Site: http://americanpomological.org/
Members: 950 individuals
Staff: 1
Annual Budget: $10-25,000
Treasurer: Robert Crassweller

Historical Note
Formed in Buffalo, NY on September 1, 1848 at a conference called by the New York Agricultural Society. First called the North American Pomological Convention, the group became the American Pomological Congress in 1849 and the American Pomological Society in 1852. The first U.S. national association to promote fruit variety improvement. Membership: $40/year.

Meetings/Conferences:
Annual Meetings: With the American Soc. for Horticultural Science

Publications:
Journal American Pomological Society. q. adv.

American Postal Workers Union *(1971)*
1300 L St. NW
Washington, DC 20005
Tel: (202)842-4200 *Fax:* (202)842-4297
Web Site: www.apwu.org
Members: 332000 individuals
Staff: 90
Annual Budget: $10-25,000,000
President: William Burrus
Executive Vice President: C.J. "Cliff" Guffey
Secretary-Treasurer: Terry R. Stapleton

Historical Note
Product of a merger (1971) of National Association of Post Office and General Services Maintenance Employees (1937); National Association of Special Delivery Messengers (1932); National Federation of Post Office Motor Vehicle Employees (1925); National Postal Union; and United Federation of Postal Clerks (1966). Affiliated with AFL-CIO, APWU has an annual budget of about $18 million. Sponsors and supports the Committee on Political Action of the American Postal Workers Union.

Meetings/Conferences:
Biennial Meetings: Even years in Summer

Publications:
The American Postal Worker. m. adv.

American Poultry Association *(1873)*
P.O. Box 306
Burgettestown, PA 15021-0306
Tel: (513)598-4337
E-Mail: apasec@cinci.rr.com
Web Site: www.amerpoultryassn.com
Members: 3000 individuals
Staff: 1
Annual Budget: $25-50,000

Historical Note
The oldest livestock organization in North America, established in Buffalo, New York by a group of poultrymen interested in fostering purebred poultry. Membership: $10/year (individual); $20/year (organization/company); $25/year (international).

Meetings/Conferences:
Semi-Annual Meetings:

Publications:
APA News and Views. q.
APA Yearbook. a. adv.

American Poultry International *(1970)*
P.O. Box 16805
Jackson, MS 39236
Tel: (601)956-1715 *Fax:* (601)956-1755
E-Mail: apiltd@apipoultry.com
Web Site: www.apipoultry.com
Staff: 3
President and Chief Executive Officer: Gerald W. Holaday
Vice President and Chief Operating Officer: Leon Dye
Secretary-Treasurer: Karla A. Ford

Historical Note
Members are firms engaged in the poultry export industry.

Meetings/Conferences:
Triennial Meetings: Summer

American Prepaid Legal Services Institute *(1976)*
321 N. Clark, 19th Fl.
Chicago, IL 60610
Tel: (312)988-5751 *Fax:* (312)988-5710
E-Mail: info@apisi.org
Web Site: www.aplsi.org
Members: 650 individuals
Staff: 4
Annual Budget: $250-500,000
Executive Director: Alec M. Schwartz
Information Manager/Conference Planner: Catherine Denny
Legislative Counsel: Tori Jo Wible

Historical Note
Founded by the American Bar Association to serve as a national umbrella organization dedicated to the growth and development of prepaid legal services. Membership: $120/year (associate); $325/year (organization/company); $85/year (provider).

Meetings/Conferences:
Annual Meetings: Spring/150

Publications:
Regulation Reporter on Pre-Paid Legal Services. q.
API Newsbriefs. m.
Publications List Available.

American Printed Fabrics Council *(1966)*

Historical Note
Formed by members of the Textile Distributors Association to promote printed fabrics; administrative support provided by TDA.

American Printing History Association *(1974)*
P.O. Box 4519, Grand Central Station
New York, NY 10163
Tel: (212)930-9220 *Fax:* (212)930-0079
Web Site: www.printinghistory.org
Members: 800 individuals
Annual Budget: $25-50,000
Executive Secretary: Stephen Crook
E-Mail: scrook@printinghistory.org

Historical Note
APHA members are academics and others with an interest in the history of printing and its related skills and technologies. Membership: $45/year (individual); $55/year (institution).

Meetings/Conferences:
Annual Meetings: Winter

Publications:
APHA Newsletter. q.
Printing History. semi-a.

American Probation and Parole Association *(1975)*
P.O. Box 11910
Lexington, KY 40578-1910
Tel: (859)244-8000 *Fax:* (859)244-8001
E-Mail: appa@csg.org
Web Site: www.appa-net.org
Members: 3500 individuals
Staff: 15
Annual Budget: $2-5,000,000
Executive Director: Carl Wicklund
E-Mail: appa@csg.org

Historical Note
Members are probation/parole professionals and others. Membership: $50/year (individual); $150-$5,000/year (organization/company).

Meetings/Conferences:
Annual Meetings: Winter
2007 – Atlanta, GA(Sheraton Atlanta)/Feb. 11-14
2007 – Philadelphia, PA(Marriott Downtown)/July 8-11
2008 – Phoenix, AZ(Hyatt Regency)/Feb. 10-13/700

Publications:
Perspectives. q. adv.

American Professional Society on the Abuse of Children *(1987)*
P.O. Box 30669
Charleston, SC 29417
Tel: (843)764-2905 *Fax:* (803)753-9823
Toll Free: (877)402 - 7722
E-Mail: apsac@comcast.net
Web Site: www.apsac.org
Members: 2600 individuals
Staff: 4
Annual Budget: $500-1,000,000
Operations Manager: Daphne Wright

Historical Note
APSAC's aim is to ensure that everyone affected by child maltreatment receives the best possible professional care. Members include psychologists, social workers, physicians, attorneys, nurses, law enforcement officers, child protective service workers, administrators, researchers, and allied professionals who have dedicated a substantial portion of their professional lives to alleviating the problems caused by child maltreatment. Membership: $65-125/year.

Meetings/Conferences:
Annual Meetings: Summer

Publications:
APSAC Advisor. q. adv.
Child Maltreatment. q. adv.

American Property Tax Counsel
77 W. Washington St., Suite 900
Chicago, IL 60602
Toll Free: (877)829 - 2782
E-Mail: bulletin@aptcnet.com
Web Site: www.aptcnet.com
Members: 45 law firms
Annual Budget: $100-250,000
Contact: James P. Regan

American Prosthodontic Society *(1928)*
426 Hudson St.
Hackensack, NJ 07601
Tel: (201)440-7699 *Fax:* (201)440-7963
Toll Free: (877)499 - 3500
E-Mail: aps@prostho.org
Web Site: www.prostho.org
Members: 800 individuals
Staff: 2
Annual Budget: $100-250,000
Central Ofc. Secretary: Carol Bensky

Historical Note
Membership: $325/year (individual).

Meetings/Conferences:
Annual Meetings: Winter, in conjunction with the Chicago Dental Soc.
2007 – Chicago, IL(Westin River North)/Feb. 22-23/350

Publications:
Journal of Prosthetic Dentistry. m. adv.

American Psychiatric Association *(1844)*
1000 Wilson Blvd., Suite 1825
Arlington, VA 22209-3901
Tel: (703)907-7300 *Fax:* (703)907-7849
Toll Free: (888)357 - 7924
E-Mail: apa@psych.org
Web Site: www.psych.org
Members: 39000 individuals
Staff: 270
Annual Budget: $25-50,000,000
Chief Executive Officer and Medical Director: Jay Scully, Jr.

Historical Note
A professional society consisting solely of psychiatrists. The oldest national medical specialty society in the U.S., founded in Philadelphia in 1844 as the Association of Medical Superintendents of American Institutions for the Insane. In 1892 it became the American Medico-Psychological Association and in 1921 the American Psychiatric Association. Incorporated in the District of Columbia

in 1927. Has an annual budget of approximately $26.7 million. Membership: $540/year.

Meetings/Conferences:
Annual Meetings: Spring
2007 – San Diego, CA/May 19-24
2008 – Washington, DC/May 3-8
2009 – San Francisco, CA/May 16-21

Publications:
American Journal of Psychiatry. m. adv.
Psychiatric Services Journal. m. adv.
Psychiatric News. bi-m. adv.

American Psychiatric Nurses Association *(1987)*
1555 Wilson Blvd., Suite 602
Arlington, VA 22209
Tel: (703)243-2443 *Fax:* (703)243-3390
E-Mail: inform@apna.org
Web Site: www.apna.org
Members: 4900 individuals
Staff: 8
Annual Budget: $2-5,000,000
Executive Director: Nick Croce

Historical Note
APNA serves as a forum for dialogue among clinicians, teachers and researchers in the field of psychiatric nursing. Membership: $120/year (individual); $66/year (student).

Meetings/Conferences:
Annual Meetings: Fall

Publications:
Journal of the APNA. m. adv.
APNA News. q.

American Psychoanalytic Association *(1911)*
309 E. 49th St.
New York, NY 10017
Tel: (212)752-0450 *Fax:* (212)593-0571
E-Mail: centraloffice@apsa.org
Web Site: www.apsa.org
Members: 3500 individuals
Staff: 13
Annual Budget: $1-2,000,000
Executive Director: Dean K. Stein
Director, Scientific Programs and Meetings: Debra Eder
E-Mail: deder@apsa.org
Director, Public Affairs: Dottie Jeffries

Historical Note
Formed to study and advance psychoanalysis; to advocate and maintain standards for the training and practice of psychoanalysis; and to foster the integration of psychoanalysis with other branches of medicine.

Meetings/Conferences:
2007 – New York, NY/June 17-21
2007 – Denver, CO/June 20-24

Publications:
The American Psychoanalyst (newsletter). q.
Journal of the APsa.
Roster of the APsa.

American Psychological Association *(1892)*
750 First St. NE
Washington, DC 20002-4242
Tel: (202)336-5500 *Fax:* (202)336-5502
Toll Free: (800)374 - 2721
E-Mail: executiveoffice@apa.org
Web Site: www.apa.org/
Members: 151000 individuals
Staff: 500
Annual Budget: $50-100,000,000
Executive Vice President and Chief Executive Officer: Norman B. Anderson
Education Director: Cynthia Belar
Executive Director, Public Communications: Rhea K. Farberman
Deputy Chief Executive Officer and Chief Operating Officer: L. Michael Honaker
Vice President and Chief Financial Officer: Charles McKay
Executive Director, Publications: Gary R. VandenBos

Historical Note
Established on July 8, 1892 and incorporated in the District of Columbia in 1925. Has a number of semi-autonomous divisions which collectively advance psychology as a science, profession and means of promoting human welfare. Divisions include: Addictions; Adult Development and Aging; American Psychology-Law Society (see seperate listing); Applied Experimental and Engineering Psychology; Behavioral Neuroscience and Comparative Psychology; Child, Youth and Family Services; Clinical Neuropsychology; Clinical Psychology (see seperate listing); Consulting Psychology; Counseling Psychology; Developmental Psychology; Educational Psychology; Evaluation, Measurement and Statistics; Exercise and Sport Psychology; Experimental Analysis of Behavior; Experimental Psychology; Family Psychology (see seperate listing); General Psychology; Group Psychology and Group Psychotherapy; Health Psychology; History of Psychology; Humanistic Psychology; Media Psychology; Mental Retardation and Developmental Disabilities; Military Psychology; Peace Psychology; Population and Environmental Psychology; Psychoanalysis (see seperate listing); Psychological Hypnosis; Psychologists in Independent Practice (see seperate listing); Psychologists in Public Service; Psychology and the Arts; Psychology of Religion; Psychology of Women; Psychopharmacology and Substance Abuse; Psychotherapy; School Psychology; Rehabilitation Psychology; Society for Community Research and Action: Division of Community Psychology; Society for Consumer Psychology; Society for Industrial and Organizational Psychology (see seperate listing); Society for the Psychological Study of Lesbian and Gay Issues; Society for the Psychological Study of Ethnic Minority Issues; Society for the Study of Men and Masculinity; Society for the Psychological Study of Social Issues (see seperate listing); Society for the Teaching of Psychology; Society of Personality and Social Psychology; State Psychological Association Affairs; and Theoretical and Philosophical Psychology. Membership varies. Has an annual budget of approximately $80 million.

Meetings/Conferences:
Annual Meetings: August/18,000
2007 – San Francisco, CA/Aug. 16-19
2008 – Boston, MA/Aug. 14-17

Publications:
Journal of Counseling Psychology. q. adv.
Journal of Personality and Social Psychology. m. adv.
Behavioral Neuroscience. bi-m. adv.
Cultural Diversity and Ethnic Minority Psychology. q. adv.
Developmental Psychology. bi-m. adv.
Dreaming. adv.
Emotion. q. adv.
European Psychologist. q. adv.
Families, Systems and Health. q. adv.
GradPSYCH. q. adv.
History of Psychology. q. adv.
International Journal of Stress Management. q. adv.
Journal of Occupational Health Psychology. q. adv.
Journal of Experimental Psych: Human Perception & Performance. bi-m. adv.
Journal of Experimental Psychology: Learning, Memory, & Cognition. bi-m.
Rehabilitation Psychology News Newsletter. 3/year.
Journal of Educational Psychology. q. adv.
Experimental and Clinical Psychopharmacology. q. adv.
Health Psychology Journal. bi-m. adv.
Journal of Experimental Psychology: Applied. q. adv.
Journal of Family Psychology. q. adv.
Neuropsychology. bi-m. adv.
Psychological Assessment Journal. q. adv.
Psychology, Public Policy and Law. q. adv.
PsycSCAN: Behavior Analysis and Therapy. q.
APA Monitor. m. adv.
Journal of Psychotherapy Integration. q. adv.
Contemporary Psychology. m. adv.
Journal of Abnormal Psychology. q. adv.
Journal of Applied Psychology. q. adv.
Journal of Comparative Psychology. q. adv.
Journal of Consulting and Clinical Psychology. bi-m. adv.
Prevention and Treatment.
Psychological Methods. q. adv.
Journal of Experimental Psychology: Animal Behavior Processes. q. adv.
Journal of Experimental Psychology: General. q. adv.
Psychological Services. q. adv.
Psychological Abstracts. m.
Psychological Bulletin Journal. bi-m. adv.
Psychological Review. q. adv.
Psychology and Aging. q. adv.
PsycSCAN: Clinical Psychology. q.
PsycSCAN: Developmental Psychology. q.
PsycSCAN: LD/MR. q.
PsycSCAN: Applied Psychology. q.
Psychology of Aesthetics, Creativity and the Arts. q. adv.
Psychology of Men and Masculinity. q. adv.
School Psychology Quarterly. q. adv.
Training and Education in Professional Psychology. q. adv.
Review of General Psychology Journal. q. adv.
Consulting Psychology Journal: Practice and Research. q. adv.
Rehabilitation Psychology Journal. q. adv.
Psychotherapy: Theory Research & Practice Journal. q. adv.
Psychology of Women Quarterly Journal. q. adv.
Psychoanalytic Abstracts Journal. q. adv.
Group Dynamics: Theory, Practice & Research Journal. q. adv.
Psychology of Addictive Behaviors Journal. q. adv.
Clinician's Research Digest Newsletter. m. adv.

American Psychological Association - Division 43

Historical Note
A division of American Psychological Ass'n, which provides administrative support.

American Psychological Association - Division of Psychoanalysis
2615 Amesbury Road
Winston-Salem, NC 27103
Tel: (336)768-1113 *Fax:* (336)768-4445
E-Mail: div39@namgmt.com
Web Site: www.division39.org
Members: 4000 individuals
Staff: 1
Annual Budget: $250-500,000
Administrator: Ruth Helein

Historical Note
A semi-autonomous division of the American Psychological Association. Division members participate professionally in psychoanalytic theory, research and practice. Sections include: Childhood and Adolescence; Family Therapy; Psychoanalysis and Groups; Psychoanalytic Research Society; Psychologist-Psychoanalyst Clinicians; Psychologist-Psychoanalyst Practitioners; Women and Psychoanalysis; Local Chapters; and Social Responsibility; Membership: $75/year (individual); $45 (international affiliates); $15/year (students).

Meetings/Conferences:
Semi-annual Meetings: Spring and in conjunction with APA Meeting

Publications:
Journal of the American Psychoanalytic Ass'n.
Internat'l Journal of Psychoanalysis.
Psychoanalytic Abstracts. q.
Psychologist-Psychoanalyst Newsletter. q. adv.
Psychoanalytic Psychology Journal. q.

American Psychological Association - Division of Psychotherapy *(1968)*
6557 E. Riverdale St.
Mesa, AZ 85215
Tel: (602)363-9211 *Fax:* (480)854-8966
E-Mail: assnmgmt1@cox.net
Web Site: www.divisionofpsychotherapy.org
Members: 4500 individuals
Administrator: Tracey Martin

Historical Note
A semi-autonomous division of the American Psychological Association. This division is composed of individual members of the APA, who are interested in and/or active in psychotherapy theory research, practice and training. Membership: $40/annually.

Meetings/Conferences:
Semi-Annual Meetings: mid-Winter and Summer

Publications:
Psychotherapy Journal. q. adv.
Psychotherapy Bulletin. q. adv.

American Psychological Association - Society of Clinical Psychology *(1946)*
P.O. Box 1082
Niwot, CO 80544
Tel: (303)652-3126 *Fax:* (303)652-2723
Members: 6600 individuals
Staff: 2
Annual Budget: $250-500,000
Administrative Officer: Lynn Peterson

Historical Note
Division members are psychologists who are active in the practice, research, teaching, administration and/or study in the field of clinical psychology. Sections include: Clincial Geropsychology; Clinical Psychology of Women; Ethnic Minority Psychology; Society for a Science of Clinical Psychology; Associety of Medical School Psychologists; and Section on Emergency Crises. Membership: $60/year (individual); $30/year (student).

Publications:
Clinical Geropsychology Newsletter. 3/year.
Clinical Science Newsletter. 3/year.
Clinical Psychology of Women Newsletter. semi-a.
Clinical Psychology of Ethnic Minorities Newsletter. semi-a.
Clinical Psychology: Science and Practice Journal. q. adv.
Clinical Psychologist Newsletter. q. adv.
The Clinical Pyschologist.
Clinical Psychology: Science and Practice. 4/year.
Emergencies and Crises. semi-a.
Assessment Psychology. semi-a.

American Psychological Society *(1988)*
1010 Vermont Ave. NW, Suite 1100
Washington, DC 20005-4907
Tel: (202)783-2077 *Fax:* (202)783-2083
Web Site: www.psychologicalscience.org
Members: 15078 individuals
Staff: 12
Annual Budget: $1-2,000,000
Executive Director: Alan G. Kraut
Deputy Director: Sarah Brookhart
Director, Membership and Marketing: Louis E. Shomett
Director, Communications: Brian L. Weaver

Historical Note
APS addresses the needs and interests of scientific and academic psychologists as distinct from members of the professional community primarily engaged in clinical practice. APS members include psychologists engaged in scientific research or the application of scientifically grounded research findings without regard for specialties. The Society promotes, protects and advances the interests of scientifically oriented psychology in research, applications and the improvement of human welfare. Membership: $146/year (regular); $56/year (student); $86/year (retiree); $300/year (institution).

Meetings/Conferences:
Annual Meetings: Spring

Publications:
Observer. m. adv.
Current Directions in Psychological Science. bi-m. adv.
Psychological Science. m. adv.
Psychological Science in the Public Interest. 3/yr.

American Psychology-Law Society *(1968)*
238 Burnett Hall
University of Nebraska
Lincoln, NE 68588-0308
Tel: (402)472-3121 *Fax:* (402)472-4637
E-Mail: div41@comcast.com
Web Site: www.unl.edu/ap-ls
Members: 3000 individuals
Staff: 1
Annual Budget: under $10,000
Administrative Assistant: Lynn Peterson

Historical Note
AP-LS promotes the contributions of psychology to the understanding of law and legal institutions, the education of psychologists in legal matters and law personnel in psychological matters, and the application of psychology in the legal system. AP-LS became a division of the American Psychological Association in 1985.

Meetings/Conferences:
Biennial Conference: (even years)

Publications:
AP-LS Newsletter. 3/year. adv.
Law and Human Behavior. bi-m. adv.

American Psychopathological Association *(1910)*
c/o Dept. of Epidemiology, Columbia Univ.
722 W. 168th St., 7th Floor
New York, NY 10032
Tel: (212)304-5857
E-Mail: gah13@columbia.edu
Web Site: www.appassn.org
Members: 5000 individuals
Staff: 1
Annual Budget: under $10,000
Coordinator: Gary Heiman

Historical Note
Founded in New York City in 1910. Promotes research on problems of psychopathology. Membership: $100/year.

Meetings/Conferences:
Annual Meetings: New York, NY/March

Publications:
Comprehensive Psychiatry. bi-m. adv.

American Psychosomatic Society *(1943)*
6728 Old McLean Village Dr.
McLean, VA 22101
Tel: (703)556-9222 *Fax:* (703)556-8729
E-Mail: info@psychosomatic.org
Web Site: www.psychosomatic.org
Members: 915 individuals
Staff: 3
Executive Director: George K. Degnon, CAE

Historical Note
Organized in 1943 as the American Society for Research in Psychosomatic Problems and incorporated in 1944. Became The American Psychosomatic Society, Inc. in 1948. APS members are specialists from all medical and health-related disciplines, the behavioral sciences and the social sciences. Membership: $125/year (regular); $50/year (student).

Meetings/Conferences:
Annual Meetings: March

Publications:
Newsletter. semi-a.
Psychosomatic Medicine Journal. bi-m. adv.

American Psychotherapy Association *(1997)*
2750 E. Sunshine St.
Springfield, MO 65804
Tel: (417)823-0173 *Fax:* (417)823-9959
Toll Free: (800)205 - 9165
E-Mail: member@americanpsychotherapy.com
Web Site: www.americanpsychotherapy.com
Members: 5000 individuals
Staff: 7
Annual Budget: $100-250,000
Program Administrator: Jaime Wommack
Managing Editor: Heather Blades
Director, Certifications: Lisa Dill
Director, Continuing Education: Rachel Renfrow

Historical Note
APA promotes continuing education and training for psychotherapists, and serves as a voice for the profession. Awards Diplomate status to qualified members within the American Psychotherapy Association. Membership: $130/year.

Meetings/Conferences:
Annual Meetings: Fall

Publications:
Annals of the APA. q. adv.

American Public Communications Council *(1988)*
625 Slaters Lane, Suite 104
Alexandria, VA 22314
Tel: (703)739-1322 *Fax:* (703)739-1324
Toll Free: (800)868 - 2722
E-Mail: apcc@apcc.net
Web Site: www.apcc.net
Members: 1300 member companies
Staff: 11
Annual Budget: $2-5,000,000
President: Willard R. Nichols

Historical Note
Members are manufacturers, suppliers, distributors, owners and operators of public communications equipment.

Meetings/Conferences:
2007 – Miami Beach, FL(Loews)/June 27-29/600

Publications:
APCC Conference and Expo Showguide. a. adv.
Perspectives on Public Communication. m. adv.

American Public Gardens Association *(1940)*
100 West Tenth St., Suite 614
Wilmington, DE 19801
Tel: (302)655-7100 *Fax:* (302)655-8100
E-Mail: info@publicgardens.org
Web Site: www.publicgardens.org
Members: 1850 individuals and institutions
Staff: 6
Annual Budget: $250-500,000
Executive Director: Dan Stark
Manager: Tracy Matthews

Historical Note
Formerly American Association of Botanical Gardens and Arboreta; assumed current name in 2005. A non-profit, membership organization serving North American botanical gardens and arboreta, their professional staffs and their work on behalf of the public and the profession. Membership: $65-80/year (individual); $160-1,500/year (organization).

Meetings/Conferences:
Annual Meetings: Summer/350
2007 – Washington, DC(Hyatt Regency)/June 26-30
2008 – Pasadena, CA
2009 – St. Louis, MO

Publications:
The Public Garden: Journal of the AABGA. q. adv.
AABGA Newsletter. m. adv.

American Public Gas Association *(1961)*
201 Massachusetts Ave. NE, Suite C-4
Washington, DC 20002
Tel: (202)464-2742 *Fax:* (202)464-0246
Toll Free: (800)927 - 4204
Web Site: www.apga.org
Members: 590 systems
Staff: 8
Annual Budget: $2-5,000,000
President: Bert Kalisch
Executive Vice President: Dave Schryver

Historical Note
Members are municipal natural gas systems and their suppliers.

Meetings/Conferences:
Annual Meetings: July/August

Publications:
Directory of Municipal Natural Gas Systems. a. adv.
Newsletter. semi-m.

American Public Health Association *(1872)*
800 I St. NW
Washington, DC 20001
Tel: (202)777-2742 *Fax:* (202)777-2534
E-Mail: comments@apha.org
Web Site: www.apha.org
Members: 30000 individuals
Staff: 65

Annual Budget: $10-25,000,000
Executive Director: Georges Benjamin, M.D., FACP
Director, Communications: David Fouse
Director, Government Relations: Donald Hoppert

Historical Note
Established September 12, 1872 at Long Branch, NJ and incorporated in Massachusetts in 1918, APHA represents health professionals in over 40 disciplines in the development of health standards and policies. Membership: $160/year (individual).

Meetings/Conferences:
Annual Meetings: Fall/10,000-12,000
2007 – Washington, DC/Nov. 3-7
2008 – San Diego, CA/Oct. 25-29

Publications:
American Journal of Public Health. m. adv.
The Nation's Health. m. adv.

American Public Human Services Association
(1930)
810 First St. NE, Suite 500
Washington, DC 20002
Tel: (202)682-0100 *Fax:* (202)289-6555
Web Site: www.aphsa.org
Members: 4000 individuals
Staff: 60
Annual Budget: $2-5,000,000
Executive Director: Jerry W. Friedman
Deputy Executive Director, Leadership and Practice Development: Susan Christie
Communications and Member Services: Gary Cyphers
Deputy Executive Director, Policy and Government Affairs: Elaine Ryan

Historical Note
Formerly American Public Welfare Association (1998). APSHA represents the 50 cabinet-level, state human service departments, local public welfare agencies, and individuals concerned with social welfare policy and practice. APWA includes two councils, the National Council of State Human Service Administrators and the National Council of Local Public Human Service Administrators. It also includes eleven affiliates representing separate professional disciplines within public welfare: the American Association of Food Stamp Directors, the American Association of Public Welfare Attorneys, IT Solutions Management for Human Services, the National Association of State Child Care Administrators, the National Association of State TANF Administrators, the Association of Administrators of the Interstate Compact on the Placement of Children, the National Association of Hearing Officials, the National Association for Program Information and Performance Measurement, the National Association of Public Child Welfare Administrators, the National Staff Development and Training Association, and the National Association of State Medicaid Directors. Membership: $60/year. (individual); agency dues vary.

Publications:
Policy and Practice. q.
Public Human Services Directory. a.

American Public Power Association *(1940)*
2301 M St. NW, Suite 300
Washington, DC 20037-1484
Tel: (202)467-2900 *Fax:* (202)467-2910
Web Site: www.appanet.org
Members: 2000 utilities
Staff: 62
Annual Budget: $5-10,000,000
President and Chief Executive Officer: Alan H. Richardson
Director, Communications: Madalyn Cafruny
Vice President, Finance and Accounting: Bianca Donnally, CPA
Vice President, Publishing: Jeanne LaBella
E-Mail: jlabella@APPAnet.org
Senior Vice President, Government Relations: Joe Nipper
E-Mail: jnipper@APPAnet.org
Executive Vice President: David Penn
E-Mail: davepenn@APPAnet.org
Vice President, Information Services: Deborah Penn
E-Mail: debpenn@APPAnet.org
Senior Vice President, Member Services: Jeffrey Tarbert
E-Mail: jtarbert@APPAnet.org

Historical Note
Members are publicly-owned electric utility systems. Has an annual budget of approximately $8.0 million. Sponsors and supports the PowerPAC political action committee. Membership: based on kWh sales and revenues.

Meetings/Conferences:
Annual Meetings: June/2,000

Publications:
Public Power. bi-m. adv.
Public Power Weekly. w.

American Public Transportation Association
(1882)
1666 K St. NW, Suite 1100
Washington, DC 20006
Tel: (202)496-4800 *Fax:* (202)496-4324
E-Mail: info@apta.org
Web Site: www.apta.com
Members: 1600 organizations and individuals
Staff: 86
Annual Budget: $10-25,000,000
President: William W. Millar
Vice President, Program Management and Educ. Services: Pamela L. Boswell
Chief Counsel and Vice President, Government Affairs: Daniel Duff
Vice President, Finance and Administration: Samuel Kerns
Vice President, Member Services: Anthony M. Kouneski
Chief of Staff: Karol J. Popkin
Vice President, Communications/Marketing: Rosemary Sheridan

Historical Note
Founded in 1882 as the American Street Railway Association, it became the American Street and Inter-Urban Railway Association in 1905, and later the American Electric Railway Association. The name was changed in 1910 to American Transit Association, which merged in 1974 with the Institute of Rapid Transit (1961) to become American Public Transit Association, and assumed its current name in 2000. APTA members include transit systems, manufacturers, consultants, state departments of transportation and others with an interest in the industry. Has an annual budget of approximately $13 million.

Meetings/Conferences:
Annual Meetings: Fall

Publications:
Transit Fact Book. a.
Membership Directory. a.
Passenger Transport. w. adv.

American Public Works Association *(1894)*
2345 Grand Blvd., Suite 500
Kansas City, MO 64108-2641
Tel: (816)472-6100
Toll Free: (800)848 - 2792
Web Site: www.apwa.net
Members: 26800 individuals
Staff: 49
Annual Budget: $5-10,000,000
Deputy Executive Director/Chief Operating Officer: Kaye Sullivan
E-Mail: ksullivan@apwa.net
Director, Information Technology: Daniel Armstrong
E-Mail: darmstrong@apwa.net
Director, Marketing: David Dancy
E-Mail: ddancy@apwa.net
Director, Technical Services: Ann Daniels
E-Mail: adaniels@apwa.net
Director, Education: Patricia Kutt
E-Mail: pkutt@apwa.net
Director, Finance/Controller: Teri Newhouse
Director, Meetings: Dana Priddy
Coordinator, Member Services: Hend Shakntana
E-Mail: hshakntana@apwa.net

Historical Note
APWA is composed of government officials, engineers, administrators and others engaged in some aspect of public works. Merger (1937) of American Society of Municipal Engineers and International Association of Public Works Officials. Maintains a Washington, DC office. Has an annual budget of approximately $8 million.

Meetings/Conferences:
2007 – San Antonio, TX(Henry B. Gonzales Covention Center)/Sept. 9-12
2008 – New Orleans, LA(Morial Convention Center)/Sept. 17-20
2009 – Columbus, OH(Columbus Convention Center)/Sept. 13-16
2010 – Boston, MA(Boston Convention and Exhibit Center)/Aug. 15-Apr. 18
2011 – Denver, CO(Colorado Convention Center)/Sept. 18-21
2012 – Indianapolis, IN(Indianapolis Convention Center)/Aug. 26-29

Publications:
APWA Reporter. 11/year. adv.

American Purchasing Society *(1969)*
Eight E. Galena Blvd., Suite 203
Aurora, IL 60506-5035
Tel: (630)859-0250 *Fax:* (630)859-0270
E-Mail: propurch@mgci.com
Web Site: www.american-purchasing.com
Members: 4500 individuals
Staff: 7
Annual Budget: $500-1,000,000
President: Harry E. Hough

Historical Note
APS members include purchasing agents, buyers, procurement specialists, purchasing managers, purchasing executives and others who buy goods and services. APS was the first organization to certify buyers and purchasing managers. Concerned with improving purchasing performance in business through the education of its membership and the development of ethical standards of conduct in the marketplace. Conducts online training courses. Membership: $213/year (individual); $378/year (organization/company).

Meetings/Conferences:
2007 – Chicago, IL/Sept. 1- /25

Publications:
Purchasing Salaries and Employment Trends. a.
Annual Purchasing Benchmarking Report. a.
Professional Purchasing. m.
American Purchasing and Materials Management. a.

American Pyrotechnics Association *(1948)*
P.O. Box 30438
Bethesda, MD 20824-0438
Tel: (301)907-8181 *Fax:* (301)907-9148
E-Mail: info@americanpyro.com
Web Site: www.americanpyro.com
Members: 240 companies
Staff: 4
Annual Budget: $500-1,000,000
Executive Director: Julie Heckman
Technical Consultant: John A. Conkling, Ph.D.

Historical Note
Founded in 1948 and incorporated in Delaware, APA members are fireworks importers, distributors, suppliers and manufacturers. Absorbed the National Pyrotechnic Distributors Association in 1979.

Publications:
Bulletin. m.

American Quarter Horse Association *(1940)*
P.O. Box 200
Amarillo, TX 79168
Tel: (806)376-4811 *Fax:* (806)349-6409
E-Mail: aqhamall@aqha.org
Web Site: www.aqha.com
Members: 342,000 individuals
Staff: 330
Annual Budget: $25-50,000,000
Executive Vice President: Bill Brewer
E-Mail: aqhamall@aqha.org

Historical Note
Organized in 1940 to collect, register, and preserve the pedigree of American Quarter Horses. Member of the National Pedigree Livestock Council and the American Horse Council. Has an annual budget of $38 million. Membership: $30/year (individual).

Publications:
The American Quarter Horse Journal. m. adv.

The American Quarter Horse Racing Journal. m. adv.
America's Horse. bi-m.

American Quaternary Association *(1969)*
Illinois State Museum
1011 E. Ash St.
Springfield, IL 62703
Tel: (217)782-7475 *Fax:* (217)785-2857
Web Site: http://www4.nau.edu/amqua/
Members: 1000 individuals
Staff: 1
Annual Budget: $10-25,000
Secretary: Dr. Bonnie W. Styles
E-Mail: styles@museum.state.il.us

Historical Note
Established in 1969 and held its first meeting at Montana State University in Bozeman in 1970. Members are natural scientists studying the history of the environment during the last two million years. Affiliated with The International Quaternary Association. Membership: $8/year (individual); $4/year (student).

Meetings/Conferences:
Biennial meetings: even years

Publications:
Quaternary Times Newsletter. semi-a.
Program with Abstracts. bien.

American Rabbit Breeders Association *(1910)*
P.O. Box 426
Bloomington, IL 61702
Tel: (309)664-7500 *Fax:* (309)664-0941
E-Mail: arbapost@aol.com
Web Site: www.arba.net
Members: 30000 individuals
Staff: 8
Annual Budget: $500-1,000,000
Executive Director: Brad Boyce
E-Mail: arbapost@aol.com

Historical Note
Members are Commercial or Fancy breeders of rabbits and guinea pigs. Commercial breeders breed for profit and Fancy breeders breed for pleasure (about 90% of the membership). Founded as the National Breeders and Fanciers Association, it became the American Pet Stock Association in 1923, the American Rabbit and Cavy Association in 1928 and assumed its present name in 1954. ARBA has chartered about 1100 affiliated clubs, for fanciers of various types of rabbits. Membership: $15/year (adult); $8/year (youth).

Meetings/Conferences:
Annual Meetings: Fall/4,000-5,000
2007 – Grand Rapids, MI/Oct. 14-18

Publications:
ARBA Yearbook. a. adv.
Domestic Rabbits. bi-m. adv.

American Radio Relay League
225 Main St.
Newington, CT 06111-1494
Tel: (860)594-0200 *Fax:* (860)594-0303
Toll Free: (888)277 - 5289
E-Mail: hq@arrl.org
Web Site: www.arrl.org
Members: 151000 individuals
Staff: 110
Annual Budget: $5-10,000,000
Chief Executive Officer: David Sumner
Chief Development Officer: Mary Hobart
Chief Financial Officer: Barry J. Shelley

Historical Note
ARRL is a non-commercial membership association of amateur radio operators, organized for the promotion of interest in amateur radio communication and experimentation, for the establishment of radio networks to provide communications in the event of disasters or other emergencies, for the advancement of the radio art and related public welfare, for the representation of radio amateurs in legislative matters, and for the maintenance of fraternalism and a high standard of conduct among radio amateurs.

Publications:
The ARRL Letter. w.
QST. m. adv.
QEX. bi-m. adv.
NCJ. bi-m. adv.

American Radiological Nurses Association *(1981)*
7794 Grow Dr.
Pensacola, FL 32514
Tel: (850)474-7292 *Fax:* (850)484-8762
Toll Free: (866)486 - 2762
E-Mail: arna@puetzamc.com
Web Site: www.arna.net
Members: 1880 individuals
Staff: 2
Annual Budget: $100-250,000
Nurse Consultant: Belinda E. Puetz, Ph.D., RN
E-Mail: arna@puetzamc.com

Historical Note
ARNA members are professional nurses actively engaged in radiological nursing or with a radiological nursing background. Associate membership is available to licensed practical nurses actively employed in radiological nursing. Membership: $75/year (individual).

Meetings/Conferences:
Annual Meetings: Spring
2007 – Seattle, WA(Sheraton Seattle Hotel)/March 1-6

Publications:
Vision. q. adv.
ARNA Images. q. adv.

American Radium Society *(1916)*
53 W. Jackson Blvd., Suite 663
Chicago, IL 60604
Tel: (312)322-0730 *Fax:* (312)322-0732
E-Mail: info@americanradiumsociety.org
Web Site: www.americanradiumsociety.org
Members: 850 individuals
Staff: 2
Annual Budget: $100-250,000
Executive Director: Catherine Carey

Historical Note
Founded in 1916 by physicians interested in radiation therapy. Promotes the study of cancer in all its aspects.

Meetings/Conferences:
Annual Meetings: Spring/300

Publications:
The Cancer Journal.
Membership Directory. a.

American Railway Development Association *(1906)*
P.O. Box 44369
Eden Prairie, MN 55344-4369
Tel: (952)828-9750 *Fax:* (952)828-9751
Web Site: www.amraildevelop.org
Members: 200 individuals
Staff: 1
Annual Budget: $50-100,000
Executive Director: E. Gilbert Tyckoson, Jr.

Historical Note
Members are marketing, real estate and industrial development officers of railroads. ARDA's objective is to foster the industrial, real estate, natural resources and market development activities of North American railroads and through the advancement of ideas and education of its members further promote the effectiveness of railway development and related work. Membership: $75/year (individual).

Meetings/Conferences:
Annual Meetings: May/100

Publications:
ARDA Newsletter. 4-6/year.

American Railway Engineering and Maintenance of Way Association *(1883)*
8201 Corporate Dr., Suite 1125
Landover, MD 20785
Tel: (301)459-3200 *Fax:* (301)459-8077
Web Site: www.arema.org
Members: 5000 individuals
Staff: 9
Annual Budget: $1-2,000,000
Executive Director and Chief Executive Officer: Charles Emely, Ph.D.

Historical Note
Formerly American Railway Engineering Association. Absorbed Roadmaster and Maintenance of Way Association of America and American Railway Bridge and Building Association and assumed its current name in 1997. Founded to raise the standards and improve the methods of track and roadway maintenance of American railways. Membership: $120/year.

Meetings/Conferences:
Annual Meetings: Fall

Publications:
Proceedings. a. adv.
Membership Directory. a. adv.

American Rambouillet Sheep Breeders Association *(1889)*
1610 S. State Road 3261
Levelland, TX 79336-9230
Tel: (806)894-3081
E-Mail: arsba@hotmail.com
Web Site: www.rambouilletsheep.org
Members: 400 individuals
Staff: 1
Annual Budget: $50-100,000
Secretary: Burk Lattimore
E-Mail: arsba@hotmail.com

Historical Note
Members are breeders and fanciers of Rambouillet sheep. ARSBA's primary function is for registry of purebred Rambouillet sheep and secondarily to advertise and promote the breed. Membership: $15/year; $20 (after April 1).

Meetings/Conferences:
Annual Meetings: July

Publications:
Bouilletin. q. adv.

American Real Estate and Urban Economics Association *(1965)*
P.O. Box 9958
Richmond, VA 23228
Toll Free: (866)273 - 8321
E-Mail: areuea@areuea.org
Web Site: www.areuea.org
Members: 1254 individuals
Staff: 1
Annual Budget: $10-25,000
Secretary-Treasurer: John L. Glascock

Historical Note
Established and incorporated in 1965 as American Real Estate Association. Name changed in 1966 to American Real Estate and Urban Economics Association. Members are individuals both academically and commercially involved in real estate and urban economics. Membership: $65/year (individual); $350/year (inst. sponsor); $125/year (library); $1,000/year (inst. member); $30/year (student).

Meetings/Conferences:
Annual Meetings: January

Publications:
Real Estate Economics. q. adv.
News Bytes e-Mail Newsletter.

American Real Estate Society *(1985)*
c/o Donna Cooper, Florida Atlantic University
5353 Parkside Dr.
Jupiter, FL 33458
Web Site: www.aresnet.org
Members: 950 individuals
Staff: 1
Annual Budget: $250-500,000
Manager, Member Services: Donna Cooper

Historical Note
ARES is concerned with the creation and dissemination of knowledge concerning real estate finance, real estate investment analysis and decision making, real estate valuation, real estate market analysis and other closely-related areas. Has no paid staff. Membership: $105/year (academic); $450/year (organization/company); $1,500-6,000/year (major real estate companies and organizations).

Meetings/Conferences:
Annual Meetings: Spring

Publications:
ARES monographs. irreg.
ARES Newsletter. semi-a.
Journal of Real Estate Portfolio Management. 4/year. adv.

Journal of Real Estate Practice & Education. a. adv.
Journal of Real Estate Research. bi-m. adv.
ARES Annual Meeting Program. a.
ARES Membership Directory. on-line.
Journal of Real Estate Literature. semi-a. adv.
Journal of Housing Research.

American Recovery Association *(1965)*
5525 N. MacArthur Blvd.
Suite 135
Irving, TX 75038
Tel: (972)755-4755 *Fax:* (972)870-5755
Web Site: www.repo.org
Members: 275 repossession companies
Staff: 3
Annual Budget: $1-2,000,000
Membership Manager: Tricia Corkern

Historical Note
The world's largest organization of professional finance adjusters and repossession specialists. ARA members represent banks, credit unions, finance companies, leasing companies, savings and loan associations and other financial institutions involved in the recovery of collateral on defaulted installment contracts. Formerly (1972) American Repossessors Association, Inc. Membership: fees based on metropolitan statistical area of the city in which business is located.

Meetings/Conferences:
Annual Meetings: July/250

Publications:
ARA News and Views Newsletter. q.
National Membership Directory. a. adv.

American Recreation Coalition *(1979)*
1225 New York Ave. NW, Suite 450
Washington, DC 20005
Tel: (202)682-9530 *Fax:* (202)682-9529
E-Mail: arc@funoutdoors.com
Web Site: www.funoutdoors.com
Members: 100 associations & companies
Staff: 5
Annual Budget: $500-1,000,000
President: Derrick A. Crandall

Historical Note
Formed by the recreation industry and related organizations to present a united approach to such topics of legislative interest as land use and energy, and to educate the government and the public about the value of recreation.

American Red Brangus Association *(1956)*
3995 E. Hwy. 290
Dripping Springs, TX 78620-4205
Tel: (512)858-7285 *Fax:* (512)858-7084
E-Mail: arba@texas.net
Web Site: www.americanredbrangus.com
Members: 260 individuals
Staff: 1
Annual Budget: $250-500,000
Office Manager: Kim Reed
E-Mail: arba@texas.net

Historical Note
Founded in Austin, Texas. Members are breeders and fanciers of Red Brangus cattle, a crossbreed of Brahman and Angus cattle. Membership: $75/first year; dues thereafter based on stock size.

Meetings/Conferences:
Annual Meetings: November

Publications:
Bull Pen. m.
Membership Directory. a.

American Red Poll Association *(1883)*
P.O. Box 147
Bethany, MO 64424
Tel: (660)425-7318 *Fax:* (660)425-8374
E-Mail: info@redpollusa.org
Web Site: www.redpollusa.org
Staff: 3
Executive Vice President: Ken Harwell
E-Mail: kharwell@redpollusa.org

Historical Note
Members are breeders and fanciers of Red Poll beef cattle. Formerly (1976) Red Poll Cattle Club of America. Member of the National Pedigree Livestock Council. Absorbed The Red Poll Beef Breeders Internt'l in 1979.

Publications:
Red Poll Beef Journal. 3/year. adv.

American Registry of Certified Professionals in Agronomy, Crops and Soils

Historical Note
A membership activity of the American Society of Agronomy.

American Registry of Diagnostic Medical Sonographers *(1975)*
51 Monroe St.
Plaza East One
Rockville, MD 20850-2400
Tel: (301)738-8401 *Fax:* (301)738-0312
Toll Free: (800)541 - 9754
E-Mail: admin@ardms.org
Web Site: www.ardms.org
Members: 95000 individuals
Staff: 19
Annual Budget: $2-5,000,000
Executive Director: Dale R. Cyr

Historical Note
The ARDMS offers voluntary certification through examination to qualified sonographers and vascular technologists. Has certified over 35,000 individuals in these specialty areas: obstetrics & gynecology, abdomen, ophthamology, neurosonology, adult echocardiography, pediatric echocardiography and vascular technology. Membership: $45/year.

Meetings/Conferences:
Annual Meetings: None held.

Publications:
Registry Reports. q.
ARDMS Directory. a.
Examination and Information & Application Booklet. a.

American Registry of Medical Assistants *(1950)*
69 Southwick Road
Westfield, MA 01085-4729
Tel: (413)562-7336 *Fax:* (413)562-9021
Toll Free: (800)527 - 2762
E-Mail: arma@verizon.net
Members: 11500 individuals
Staff: 8
Annual Budget: $100-250,000
Director: Annette H. Heyman
Executive Secretary: Michelle P. Lesieur

Historical Note
ARMA provides updated information to its members, to advance the professional interests of medical assistants. Members include graduates of licensed medical assistant programs and other allied health professionals. Membership: $60 application fee; $30/year renewal.

Meetings/Conferences:
Annual Meetings: September

Publications:
Registry Connection. q.
Medical Assistant. a. adv.

American Registry of Radiologic Technologists *(1922)*
1255 Northland Drive
St. Paul, MN 55120
Tel: (651)687-0048 *Fax:* (651)687-0349
Web Site: www.arrt.org
Members: 235000 individuals
Staff: 43
Executive Director: Jerry B. Reid, Ph.D.

Historical Note
ARRT registrants are individuals qualilfied in the use of both ionizing and nonionizing radiation for the purposes of diagnostic medical imaging, interventional procedures, and therapeutic treatment. ARRT establishes standards of professional behavior and requirements for educational preparation and continuing education.

Publications:
Annual Report to Registered Technologists. a.

American Rehabilitation Counseling Association *(1957)*

Historical Note
A division of the American Counseling Association, which provides administrative support.

American Rental Association *(1955)*
1900 19th St.
Moline, IL 61265-4198
Toll Free: (800)334 - 2177
Web Site: www.ararental.org
Members: 6100 companies
Staff: 36
Annual Budget: $5-10,000,000
Executive Vice President: Christine Wehrman
E-Mail: chris.wehrman@ararental.org
Vice President, Association Services: Allison Box
E-Mail: allison.box@ararental.org
Senior Director, Corporate Communications/Publisher: Ken Hughes
Senior Director, Government Affairs: John McClelland
Director, Strategic and Volunteer Development: Kathy Nicoletto
Chief Financial Officer: Kathleen A. Schwartz
E-Mail: kathy.schwartz@ararental.org

Historical Note
Founded as the National Rental Owners Mutual Association, and formerly American Associated Rental Operators (1961). In 1986, the National Rental Service Association merged with ARA. ARA represents owners of privately owned or franchise rental businesses, and manufacturers and suppliers of rental products. The association covers most kinds of tangible personal properties found in the market today except apartments, cars, billboards or office space. Supports ARAPAC, its political action committee.

Meetings/Conferences:
Annual Meetings: Winter
2007 – New Orleans, LA/Feb. 12-15
2008 – Las Vegas, NV/Feb. 11-14
2009 – Atlanta, GA/Feb. 11-14
2010 – Orlando, FL/Feb. 8-11
2011 – Las Vegas, NV/Feb. 21-24

Publications:
Rental Pulse e-newsletter.
Daily Showtimes. a. adv.
ARA Advantage. m.
Rental Management. m. adv.
Marketing Messages. bi-m.

American Resort Development Association *(1969)*
1201 15th St. NW, Suite 400
Washington, DC 20005-2842
Tel: (202)371-6700 *Fax:* (202)289-8544
Web Site: www.arda.org
Members: 1000 companies & corporations
Staff: 30
Annual Budget: $5-10,000,000
President and Chief Executive Officer: Howard C. Nusbaum
E-Mail: hnusbaum@arda.org
Vice President, Marketing and Communications: LouAnn Burney
Vice President, Federal Relations: Sandra DePoy
Vice President, Finance and Administration: Rob Dunn
Vice President, Meetings and Conventions: Catherine Lacey

Historical Note
Formerly (1985) the American Land Development Association. Represents the recreational, resort and residential real estate development industry, including timesharing and vacation ownership resorts. Sponsors and supports the American Resort Development Association Political Action Committee. Membership: $1,200-12,500/year, based on annual gross income (company).

Publications:
Developments Magazine. 10/year. adv.
ARDA Advantage newsletter. q.

American Reusable Textile Association *(1982)*
P.O. Box 1053
Mulberry, FL 33860-1053
Tel: (863)660-5350
E-Mail: info@arta1.com
Web Site: www.arta1.com
Members: 70 companies and organizations
Staff: 1

Annual Budget: $25-50,000
Executive Director: William J. Carroll, Ph.D.
E-Mail: wcarroll@arta1.com

Historical Note
ARTA members are producers and distributors of apparel, diapers, and other reusable textiles, manufacturers of laundry equipment, and suppliers to the industry. Membership $600/year.

Meetings/Conferences:
Semi-Annual Meetings:

Publications:
The Reusable Textile. bi-m.

American Rhinologic Society *(1954)*
9 Sunset Terrace
Warwick, NY 10467
Tel: (845)988-1631 *Fax:* (845)986-1527
E-Mail: wendi.perez@gmail.com
Web Site: www.american-rhinologic.org
Members: 1100 individuals
Staff: 2
Annual Budget: $50-100,000
Secretary: Brent Senior, M.D.
Administrator: Wendi Perez

Historical Note
Formed in Chicago in 1954 by Dr. M.H. Cottle. Members are physicians who are diplomates of the American Board of Otolaryngology; promotes research and education on disorders and surgery of the nose. Membership: $270/year.

Meetings/Conferences:
Annual Meetings: Fall, with the American Academy of Otolaryngology
2007 - Washington, DC/Sept. 15-17/300
2008 - Chicago, IL/Sept. 20- /350

Publications:
American Journal of Rhinology. bi-m. adv.
Newsletter. q.

American Risk and Insurance Association *(1932)*
716 Providence Road
Malvern, PA 19355
Tel: (610)640-1997 *Fax:* (610)725-1007
E-Mail: aria@cpcuiia.org
Web Site: www.aria.org
Members: 500 individuals
Staff: 2
Annual Budget: $100-250,000
Executive Director: Tony Biacchi

Historical Note
A learned society devoted exclusively to furthering the science of risk management and insurance through education, research, literature and communications. Formerly (1961) American Association of University Teachers of Insurance. Membership: $120/year (individual); $221/year (organization); $500-$10,000/year (sponsoring institution).

Meetings/Conferences:
Annual Meetings: August/200
2007 - Quebec City, QC, Canada(Loews Le Concordia Hotel)/Aug. 5-8

Publications:
Risk Management and Insurance Review. semi-a.
Journal of Risk and Insurance. q. adv.

American Road and Transportation Builders Association *(1902)*
1219 28th St. NW
Washington, DC 20007-3712
Tel: (202)289-4434 *Fax:* (202)289-4435
Web Site: www.artba.org
Members: 5000 companies
Staff: 35
Annual Budget: $5-10,000,000
President and Chief Executive Officer: T. Peter Ruane, CAE
Senior Vice President, Government Relations: David Bauer
Senior Vice President and General Counsel: Randy Freedman
Vice President, Communications: Matt Jeanneret
Vice President, Chapter Relations and Grassroots Programs: Rich Juliano
Vice President, Congressional Relations: Jim Kolb
Vice President, Marketing and Membership Development: Eric Rothman
Vice President, Safety and Education: Brad Sant
Exec Vice President and Chief Operating Officer: Bill Toohey

Historical Note
Founded as American Road Makers, it became the American Road Builders Association in 1910, absorbed the Better Highway Information Foundation in 1969 and assumed its present name in 1977. Sponsors the ARTBA Political Action Committee. Membership fee: varies by division.

Meetings/Conferences:
Annual Meetings: Fall

Publications:
Washington Newsline. w.
Transportation Builder. m. adv.
ARTBA Newsletter. m. adv.

American Rock Mechanics Association *(1994)*
600 Woodland Terrace
Alexandria, VA 22302-3319
Tel: (703)683-1808 *Fax:* (703)683-1815
Web Site: www.armarocks.org
Members: 310 individuals
Staff: 1
Annual Budget: $25-50,000
Executive Director: Peter Smeallie
E-Mail: smeallie@armarocks.org

Historical Note
ARMA maintains U.S. membership in the International Society of Rock Mechanics, and represents professionals, firms, and students in rock mechanics and rock engineers. Membership: $65/year (individual); $500-5,000/year (corporation); $15/year (student).

Meetings/Conferences:
Annual Meetings: June

Publications:
ARMA Update (online). m. adv.

American Roentgen Ray Society *(1900)*
44211 Slatestone Court
Leesburg, VA 20176
Tel: (703)729-3353 *Fax:* (703)729-4839
Toll Free: (800)438 - 2777
Web Site: www.arrs.org
Members: 14500 individuals
Staff: 34
Annual Budget: $5-10,000,000
Executive Director: Susan B. Cappitell, MBA, CAE

Historical Note
Organized in 1900 in St. Louis as the Roentgen Society of the United States. Became the American Roentgen Ray Society in 1906. Incorporated in the District of Columbia in 1922. The purpose of the Society, as stated in its constitution, is the advancement of medicine through the science of radiology and its allied sciences. Membership: $235/year (individual).

Meetings/Conferences:
Annual Meetings: Spring/3,000

Publications:
American Journal of Roentgenology. m. adv.
ARRS Memo. q.

American Rolling Door Institute
P.O. Box 117
28 Lowry Dr.
West Milton, OH 45383-0117
Tel: (937)698-4188 *Fax:* (937)698-6153
Executive Director: Rosita S. Long

American Romagnola Association *(1974)*
3815 Touzalin, Suite 104
Lincoln, NE 68507
Tel: (402)466-3334 *Fax:* (402)466-3338
E-Mail: argbeef@aol.com
Web Site: www.americanromagnola.com
Members: 150 individuals
Staff: 1
Annual Budget: $50-100,000
Office Manager: Stephanie Nelson

Historical Note
Members are breeders of purebred Romagnola cattle, a beef breed originated in Italy. Maintains a breed registry. Membership: $45/year (lifetime).

Meetings/Conferences:
Annual Meetings: February

American Romney Breeders Association *(1912)*
744 Riverbanks Road
Grants Pass, OR 97527-9607
Tel: (541)476-6428
E-Mail: secretary@americanromney.org
Web Site: www.americanromney.org
Members: 450 individuals
Staff: 1
Annual Budget: $10-25,000
Secretary-Treasurer: Jean Kamenicky

Historical Note
Members are breeders and fanciers of Romney sheep. Maintains a registry of pedigrees. Has an annual budget of approximately $25,000. Membership: $15/year.

Meetings/Conferences:
Annual Meetings: November-December

Publications:
Romney Ramblings. q. adv.

American Saddlebred Horse Association *(1891)*
4083 Iron Works Pkwy.
Lexington, KY 40511
Tel: (859)259-2742 *Fax:* (859)259-1628
E-Mail: saddlebred@asha.net
Web Site: www.saddlebred.com
Members: 8000 individuals
Staff: 16
Annual Budget: $1-2,000,000
Executive Secretary: Alan F. Balch
E-Mail: a.balch@asha.net

Historical Note
Members are owners, breeders and others interested in American Saddlebred horses united to preserve a 5-generation pedigree of each horse of this breed in the world. Known as the American Saddle Horse Breeders Association before 1980. Membership: $60/year.

Meetings/Conferences:
Annual Meetings: Winter

Publications:
American Saddlebred Reference Directory. a. adv.
Membership Directory. a. adv.
American Saddlebred Magazine. bi-m. adv.

American Safe Deposit Association *(1924)*
P.O. Box 519
Franklin, IN 46131
Tel: (317)738-4432 *Fax:* (317)738-5267
E-Mail: tasda1@aol.com
Web Site: www.tasda.com
Members: 1800 banks
Staff: 2
Annual Budget: $100-250,000
Executive Director: Joyce A. McLin

Historical Note
TASDA is a federation of regional and local associations of banks, trust companies and others engaged in the safe deposit business. Formerly (1947) National Safe Deposit Advisory Council.

Meetings/Conferences:
Annual Meetings: Late Spring-Early Summer

Publications:
ACCESS Magazine. q. adv.
Educational Bulletin. q.

American Salers Association *(1974)*
19590 E. Main St., Suite 202
Parker, CO 80138
Tel: (303)770-9292 *Fax:* (303)770-9302
E-Mail: salersinfo@salerusa.org
Web Site: www.salersusa.org/
Members: 1000 individuals
Staff: 4
Annual Budget: $500-1,000,000
Executive Vice President: Sherry Doubet

Historical Note
Members are breeders of Salers cattle. Maintains registry of pedigreed Salers cattle. Membership: $50/year.

Meetings/Conferences:
Annual Meetings: January/conjunction with the Nat'l Western Stock Show/Denver, CO

Publications:
American Salers. q. adv.

American Salvage Pool Association *(1985)*
2100 Roswell Road
Suite 200C - PMB 709
Marietta, GA 30062
Tel: (678)560-6678 *Fax:* (678)560-9112
E-Mail: natalie@aspa.com
Web Site: www.aspa.com
Members: 180 companies
Staff: 1
Annual Budget: $250-500,000
Executive Director: Natalie Nardone
E-Mail: natalie@aspa.com

Historical Note
Incorporated in Florida. Members are firms specializing in the brokering of totally wrecked, water and hail damaged, and other recovered vehicles in conjunction with insurance companies and recovery personnel. Membership: $900-5,600/year (companies); $300/year (associates).

Meetings/Conferences:
Annual Meetings: Spring/200

Publications:
ASPA Report. q.
Directory. a. adv.
Convention Program. a. adv.

American School Band Directors' Association *(1953)*
P.O. Box 696
Guttenberg, IA 52052-0696
Tel: (563)252-2500
E-Mail: asbda@alpinenet.com
Web Site: www.asbda.com
Members: 1200 individuals
Staff: 1
Annual Budget: $25-50,000
Office Manager: Dennis L. Hanna
E-Mail: asbda@alpinenet.com

Historical Note
Organized in Cedar Rapids, Iowa, November 21-22, 1953. Members are professionally trained instrumental music teachers with at least seven years of experience. Officers change annually on September 1. Membership: $75/year (individual); $65/year (institution).

Meetings/Conferences:
2007 - Dearborn, MI(Hyatt Regency)/June 27-30

Publications:
School Band & Orchestra. q.
Bandworld Magazine. bi-m.

American School Counselor Association *(1952)*
1101 King St., Suite 625
Alexandria, VA 22314
Tel: (703)683-2722 *Fax:* (703)683-1619
Toll Free: (800)306 - 4722
E-Mail: asca@schoolcounselor.org
Web Site: www.schoolcounselor.org
Members: 17500 individuals
Staff: 7
Annual Budget: $2-5,000,000
Executive Director: Richard Wong
Director, Programs: Jill Cook
Coordinator, Meetings: Kelly Frey
Director, Administration: Stephanie J. Wicks

Historical Note
ASCA promotes professional school counseling activities that affect personal, academic and career development of students. ASCA is a division of the American Counseling Association. Membership: $115/year (professional); $115/year (affiliate); $60/year (student/retired).

Publications:
ASCA School Counselor. 6/yr. adv.
Professional School Counseling Journal. 5/year.

American School Food Service Association

Historical Note
Became School Nutrition Association in 2004.

American School Health Association *(1927)*
7263 State Route 43
Box 708
Kent, OH 44240
Tel: (330)678-1601 *Fax:* (330)678-4526
Toll Free: (800)445 - 2742
Web Site: www.ashaweb.org
Members: 2000 individuals
Staff: 10
Annual Budget: $1-2,000,000
Executive Director: Susan Wooley, Ph.D., CHES
E-Mail: swooley@ashaweb.org
Director, Meeting Planning: Mary Bamer Ramsier
E-Mail: mbramsi@ashaweb.org
Director, Editorial Services: Thomas M. Reed
E-Mail: treed@ashaweb.org
Director, Research and Sponsored Programs: Marcia Rubin, Ph.D, MHP
E-Mail: mrubin@ashaweb.org

Historical Note
Established in Cincinnati, OH in 1927, as the American Association of School Physicians. Became the American School Health Association in 1936. Incorporated in Ohio in 1971. ASHA supports and provides professional services to comprehensive school health programs and to protect and improve the health and well-being of children and youth. Membership: $95/year (individual); $195/year (institution).

Meetings/Conferences:
Annual Meetings: Fall/800

Publications:
Journal of School Health. 10/year. adv.
The PULSE. bi-y. adv.

American Schools Association *(1914)*
P.O. Box 577820
Chicago, IL 60657-7820
Tel: (773)732-0046 *Fax:* (773)782-0113
Toll Free: (800)230 - 2263
E-Mail: asaceu@hotmail.com
Web Site: www.asaceu.com
Staff: 2
Annual Budget: $100-250,000
President: Carl M. Dye
E-Mail: asaceu@hotmail.com

Historical Note
Main purpose is to coordinate educational counseling and consulting; home studies courses providing continuing education for professional certification maintenance, and training videos for the disabled.

Meetings/Conferences:
Annual Meetings: Chicago, IL/August

Publications:
Directory of College Transfer Information. bien.

American Schools of Oriental Research *(1900)*
656 Beacon St., 5th Fl.
Boston, MA 02215-2006
Tel: (617)353-6570 *Fax:* (617)353-6575
E-Mail: asor@bu.edu
Web Site: www.asor.org/
Members: 1300 individuals
Staff: 6
Annual Budget: $500-1,000,000
Executive Director: Douglas R. Clark

Historical Note
Members are universities and individuals involved in Middle Eastern research, especially Biblical archaeology, pre-history, ancient and medieval history. Membership: $50/year (minimum individual); $1,000/year (organization).

Meetings/Conferences:
Annual Meetings: November
2007 - San Diego, CA

Publications:
Bulletin. q.
Journal of Cuneiform Studies. a.
Newsletter. q. adv.
Near Eastern Archaeology. q. adv.

American Scientific Glassblowers Society *(1952)*
P.O. Box 778
Madison, NC 27025
Tel: (336)427-2406 *Fax:* (336)427-2496
E-Mail: natl-office@asgs-glass.org
Web Site: www.asgs-glass.org
Members: 950 individuals
Staff: 2
Annual Budget: $100-250,000
Executive Secretary: David Daenzer

Historical Note
Founded in Wilmington, DE in 1952 and incorporated in Delaware in 1954. Membership: $75/year.

Meetings/Conferences:
Annual Meetings: Summer

Publications:
Fusion. q. adv.
Symposium Proceedings. a.

American Seed Trade Association *(1883)*
225 Reinekers Lane, Suite 650
Alexandria, VA 22314-2875
Tel: (703)837-8140 *Fax:* (703)837-9365
Toll Free: (888)890 - 7333
Web Site: www.amseed.com
Members: 800 companies
Staff: 11
Annual Budget: $1-2,000,000
Chief Executive Officer: Richard T. Crowder
Vice President, Government Affairs: Leslie Cahill
E-Mail: lcahill@amseed.org
Vice President, Financial and Administration: Ann Jorss
E-Mail: ajorss@amseed.org
Vice President, Scientific and International Affairs: Bernice Slutsky
Director, Administrative Services: Barbara Surian
E-Mail: bsurian@amseed.org
Senior Director, International Marketing: Kent Swisher

Historical Note
Active members are producers of seeds for planting purposes. Affiliates are state seed associations while associates are suppliers to the industry and corresponding members are overseas seed companies. Sponsors the American Seed Research Foundation.

Meetings/Conferences:
Annual Meetings: June/1,000

Publications:
E-News Update. w.
ASTA Newsletter. m.
Corn and Sorghum Seed Conference Proceedings. a.
Soybean Seed Conference Proceedings. a.

American Seminar Leaders Association *(1988)*
2405 E. Washington Blvd.
Pasadena, CA 91104-2040
Tel: (626)791-1211 *Fax:* (626)798-0701
Toll Free: (800)735 - 0511
E-Mail: info@asla.com
Web Site: www.asla.com
Members: 3500 individuals
Staff: 7
Annual Budget: $500-1,000,000
President: June Davidson
Vice President: Alina Pogaceanu
Secretary-Treasurer: Geri Rouse

Historical Note
ASLA members are professional seminar and workshop leaders. Awards the CSL (Certified Seminar Leader) designation. Membership: $195/year.

Publications:
Directory of Seminar Leaders (online).
Newsletter. bi-m. adv.

American Seniors Housing Association *(1991)*
5100 Wisconsin Ave. NW, Suite 307
Washington, DC 20016
Tel: (202)237-0900 *Fax:* (202)237-1616
Web Site: www.seniorshousing.org
Members: 250 firms
Staff: 3
Annual Budget: $500-1,000,000
President: David S. Schless
E-Mail: dschless@seniorshousing.org
Director, Member Services: Doris Kerr
E-Mail: dkerr@seniorhousing.org
Vice President, Research and Policy: Ken Preede
E-Mail: kpreede@seniorhousing.org

Historical Note
The American Seniors Housing Association was formed in 1991 to address the unique challenges of housing the nation's growing population of older adults. ASHA provides leadership for the seniors

housing industry on legislative and regulatory matters, and promotes research and the exchange of information among the developers, operators, and financiers of all types of seniors housing.

Publications:
State of Seniors Housing. a.

American Sexually Transmitted Diseases Association *(1934)*
P.O. Box 13827
Research Triangle Park, NC 27709
Tel: (919)361-8400 *Fax:* (919)361-8425
E-Mail: info@ashastd.org
Members: 450 individuals
Annual Budget: $25-50,000
President and Chief Executive Officer: James R. Allen, MD, MPH

Historical Note
Member of the International Union Against Sexually Transmitted Infections. Founded as the American Neisserian Medical Association; became American Veneral Disease Association in 1967, and assumed its current name in 1996. Has no paid officers or full-time staff. Membership: $67/year (individual).

Publications:
Sexually Transmitted Diseases. 10/year. adv.

American Sheep Industry Association *(1955)*
9785 Marson Circle, Suite 360
Englewood, CO 80112-2692
Tel: (303)771-3500 *Fax:* (303)771-8200
E-Mail: prodgers2@earthlink.net
Web Site: www.sheepusa.org
Members: 80000 individuals
Staff: 9
Annual Budget: $2-5,000,000
Executive Director: Peter Orwick
E-Mail: porwick@sheepusa.org
Director, Prod. Education: Paul Rodgers
E-Mail: prodgers2@earthlink.net

Historical Note
ASI is a federation of state associations dedicated to the welfare and profitability of the sheep industry. Formerly (1989) the American Sheep Producers Council, ASI merged with the National Wool Growers Association in 1989. American Lamb Council and American Wool Council are divisions of ASI. Sponsors and supports RAMS-PAC. Has an annual budget of approximately $2 million.

Meetings/Conferences:
Annual Meetings: Winter

Publications:
Sheep Industry News. m. adv.

American Shetland Pony Club/American Miniature Horse Registry *(1888)*
81-B Queenwood Road
Morton, IL 61550-2923
Tel: (309)263-4044 *Fax:* (309)263-5113
E-Mail: info@shetlandminiature.com
Web Site: www.shetlandminiature.com
Members: 7500 individuals
Staff: 11
Annual Budget: $1-2,000,000
Director, Operations: Zona J. Schneider
Chief Financial Officer: Joe Schroeter

Historical Note
Members are owners and breeders of of Shetland ponies. A member of the National Pedigree Livestock Council. Founded by the American Shetland Pony Club, AMHR members are breeders and owners of American miniature horses. Membership: $45/year (individual).

Meetings/Conferences:
Annual Meetings: November

Publications:
The Journal Magazine. bi-m. adv.

American Shipbuilding Association
600 Pennsylvania Ave. SE, Suite 305
Washington, DC 20003
Tel: (202)544-8170 *Fax:* (202)544-8252
E-Mail: asa@usships.org
Web Site: www.americanshipbuilding.com
Members: 6 shipyards
Annual Budget: $500-1,000,000
President: Cynthia L. Brown
Director, Legislative Affairs: Amy E. Praeger

Historical Note
ASA is a trade association comprising American private sector shipyards. Membership: $100,000/year.

Publications:
American Shipbuilder News. m.

American Shire Horse Association *(1885)*
1211 Hill Harrell Road
Effingham, SC 29541-3178
Tel: (843)629-0072
E-Mail: secretary@shirehorse.org
Web Site: www.shirehorse.org
Members: 650 individuals
Staff: 1
Annual Budget: $25-50,000
Administrative Secretary: Pamela Correll

Historical Note
Members are owners and breeders of Shire horses. Records pedigrees of Shire draft horses and promotes their breeding. Membership: $25/years (domestic); $30/year (foreign); $200/5 years (company).

Meetings/Conferences:
Annual Meetings: February

Publications:
ASHA.
Directory of Shire Owners and Breeders. a.
Shire Newsletter. q.

American Short Line and Regional Railroad Association *(1913)*
50 F St. NW, Suite 7020
Washington, DC 20001-1536
Tel: (202)628-4500 *Fax:* (202)628-6430
E-Mail: aslrra@aslrra.org
Web Site: www.aslrra.org
Members: 400 railroads, 300 associated companies
Staff: 8
Annual Budget: $1-2,000,000
President: Richard F. Timmons
Executive Director, Membership Services: Kathleen M. Cassidy
Executive Director, Traffic and E-Commerce: K. Grant Ozburn, Jr.
Executive Director, Federal and Industry Programs: Matthew B. Reilly, Jr.
Executive Director, Administration: Stephen M. Sullivan

Historical Note
Absorbed (1998) Regional Railroads of America. ASLRRA represents short line and regional railroads in legislative/regulatory matters and industry relations. Membership: $925 - $5,000/year.

Meetings/Conferences:
Annual Meetings: Fall/1,100

Publications:
Views & News. w.

American Shorthorn Association *(1846)*
8288 Hascall St.
Omaha, NE 68124
Tel: (402)393-7200 *Fax:* (402)393-7203
E-Mail: bolze@shorthorn.org
Web Site: www.shorthorn.org
Members: 3000 individuals
Staff: 12
Annual Budget: $500-1,000,000
Executive Secretary/Treasurer: Ron Bolze

Historical Note
Absorbed the American Polled Shorthorn Society in 1991. Members are breeders and promoters of Shorthorn Beef Cattle. A member of the National Pedigree Livestock Council, the U.S. Beef Breeds Council and the National Cattlemen's Association. Membership: $35/year.

Meetings/Conferences:
Annual Meetings: Winter

Publications:
Shorthorn Country. m. adv.

American Shoulder and Elbow Surgeons *(1984)*
6300 N. River Road, Suite 727
Rosemont, IL 60018-4226
Tel: (847)698-1629 *Fax:* (847)823-0536
E-Mail: jones@aaos.org
Web Site: www.ases-assn.org
Members: 168 individuals
Staff: 2
Executive Officer: Emily Jones

Historical Note
Organized in 1982. Mission is to advance the science, encourage investigation, and disseminate knowledge of shoulder and elbow surgery in affiliation with the American Academy of Orthopaedic Surgeons. Members are orthopedic surgeons.

Publications:
Journal of Shoulder and Elbow Surgery.

American Shrimp Processors Association *(1962)*
P.O. Box 50774
New Orleans, LA 70150
Tel: (504)368-1571
Web Site: http://americanshrimpprocessorsassociation.org/
Members: 51 companies
Staff: 3
Annual Budget: $25-50,000
Managing Director: William Chauvin
E-Mail: kchauvin@shrimpcom.com

Historical Note
Formerly (1977) the American Shrimp Canners Association and the American Shrimp Canners and Processors Association. Assumed its present name in 1984. Membership: $500/year.

Meetings/Conferences:
Annual Meetings: Spring

Publications:
Currents newsletter.

American Shropshire Registry Association *(1884)*
P.O. Box 635
Harvard, IL 60033-0635
Tel: (815)943-2034
E-Mail: amshrops@stans.net
Web Site: www.shropshires.org
Members: 1000 individuals
Staff: 1
Annual Budget: $10-25,000
Secretary-Treasurer: Dale E. Blackburn, D.V.M.

Historical Note
ASRA is composed of breeders and fanciers of Shropshire sheep, which were introduced into the U.S. in 1855 from England and are bred both for their meat and wool production. ASRA registers and records the pedigrees of all purebred Shropshire sheep bred in America.

Meetings/Conferences:
Annual Meetings: Fall/100

Publications:
Shropshire Voice. 3/year. adv.

American Sightseeing International *(1947)*
2727 Steeles Ave. West, Suite 301
Toronto, ON M3J - 3G9
Tel: (416)736-4432 *Fax:* (416)663-4495
Toll Free: (866)349 - 0899
E-Mail: info@americansightseeing.org
Web Site: www.americansightseeing.org
Members: 150 Companies
Staff: 8
Annual Budget: $250-500,000
General Secretary: Christine Fournier

Historical Note
Established as the American Sightseeing Association (1971); assumed its present name in 1995.

Meetings/Conferences:
Annual Meetings: Fall

Publications:
World Wide Directory of Tours and Vacation Packages. adv.
ASI Worldwide Tour Planning Manual. a. adv.

American Simmental Association *(1969)*
One Simmental Way
Bozeman, MT 59718-8699
Tel: (406)587-4531 *Fax:* (406)587-9301
E-Mail: simmental@simmgene.com
Web Site: www.simmental.org
Members: 8702 individuals
Staff: 35

Annual Budget: $2-5,000,000
Executive Vice President: Jerry Lipsey, Ph.D.
Historical Note
Members are breeders of Simmental and Simbrah cattle. ASA provides research and data in breed and cross-breed genetics, production methods, and other issues.
Meetings/Conferences:
Annual Meetings: Winter
Publications:
The Register. m. adv.

American Skin Association *(1987)*
346 Park Ave. South, Fourth Floor
New York, NY 10010
Tel: (212)889-4858 *Fax:* (212)889-4959
Toll Free: (800)499 - 7546
Web Site: www.americanskin.org
Members: 300 individuals
Staff: 2
Annual Budget: $500-1,000,000
Managing Director: Joyce Weidler
E-Mail: joyce@americanskin.org
Historical Note
ASA is a not-for-profit association that raises support money for research and educates the public, particularly children, on the prevention and treatment of skin disorders. Membership: $25/year.
Meetings/Conferences:
Annual Meetings: usually Spring/New York, NY
Publications:
Skin Facts Newsletter. q.

American Sleep Apnea Association *(1990)*
1424 K St. NW, Suite 302
Washington, DC 20005-2410
Tel: (202)293-3650 *Fax:* (202)293-3656
E-Mail: asaa@sleepapnea.org
Web Site: www.sleepapnea.org
Members: 5000 individuals
Staff: 2
Annual Budget: $250-500,000
Executive Director: Edward Grandi
Historical Note
ASAA exists to promote understanding and awareness of sleep apnea and to support care-givers and patients. The Association is dedicated to reducing injury, disability, and death from sleep apnea and to enhancing the well-being of those affected by the disorder. Supports A.W.A.K.E., a network of mutual support groups. Membership: $25/year.
Meetings/Conferences:
Annual Meetings: none held.
Publications:
WAKE-UP CALL. q.

American Small Businesses Association
206 E. College St., Suite 201
Grapevine, TX 76051
Tel: (817)488-8770 *Fax:* (817)251-8578
Toll Free: (800)942 - 2722
E-Mail: info@asbaonline.org
Web Site: www.asbaonline.org
President: Bill Hill, Sr.
Historical Note
Membership: $48/year (associate); $60/year (full).

American Society for Adolescent Psychiatry *(1967)*
P.O. Box 570218
Dallas, TX 75357-0218
Tel: (972)686-6166 *Fax:* (972)613-5532
E-Mail: info@adolpsych.org
Web Site: www.adolpsych.org
Members: 800 individuals
Staff: 1
Annual Budget: $250-500,000
Executive Director: Frances Roton
Historical Note
In 1958 a group of New York psychiatrists formed the Society for Adolescent Psychiatry. Shortly thereafter similar groups were set up in Philadelphia, Los Angeles and Chicago. In 1967 these groups confederated into the present ASAP, which is now a confederation of psychiatric societies and members-at-large throughout the United States and Canada. Provides continuing education, clinical guidance, knowledge exchange, advocacy, and research support to professionals in adolescent psychiatry. Membership: $225/year.
Publications:
Annals of Adolescent Psychiatry. a.
Membership Directory. bi-a.
Newsletter. q. adv.

American Society for Aesthetic Plastic Surgery *(1967)*
11081 Winner's Circle
Los Alamitos, CA 90720
Tel: (212)921-0500 *Fax:* (212)921-0011
Toll Free: (800)364 - 2147
E-Mail: asaps@surgery.org
Web Site: www.surgery.org
Members: 2200 individuals
Staff: 32
Annual Budget: $2-5,000,000
Executive Director: Robert G. Stanton
E-Mail: bob@surgery.org
Manager, Media Relations: Adeena Colbert
E-Mail: asaps@surgery.org
Deputy Executive Director: Sue Dykema, CAE
E-Mail: sue@surgery.org
Historical Note
Members are specialists in the area of aesthetic plastic surgery certified by the American Board of Plastic Surgery. Membership: $750/year.
Meetings/Conferences:
Annual Meetings: Spring/2,600
2007 – New York, NY
Publications:
Aesthetic Surgery Journal.

American Society for Aesthetics *(1942)*
Marquette University, 707 N. 11th Room 322
P.O. Box 1881
Milwaukee, WI 53201-1881
Tel: (414)288-7831 *Fax:* (414)288-5415
E-Mail: asa@aesthetics-online.org
Web Site: www.aesthetics-online.org
Members: 500 individuals
Staff: 2
Annual Budget: $100-250,000
Secretary-Treasurer: Curtis L. Carter
Historical Note
Founded to advance the philosophical and scientific understanding of the arts and related fields, ASA promotes study, research, publication, and discussion of aesthetics. Member of the Council of Learned Societies. Membership: $70/year (individual); $136/year (organization).
Meetings/Conferences:
Annual Meetings: Fall
Publications:
Journal of Aesthetics and Arts Criticism. q. adv.
ASA Newsletter. 3/year.

American Society for Amusement Park Security and Safety *(1972)*
Riverside Park
P.O. Box 307
Agawam, MA 01001
Tel: (413)786-9390 *Fax:* (413)786-1332
Members: 115 individuals
Annual Budget: under $10,000
Secretary: Jason Freeman
Meetings/Conferences:
Annual Meetings: September
Publications:
Newsletter. semi-a.

American Society for Apheresis *(1981)*
3900 E. Timrod St.
Tucson, AZ 85711-4517
Tel: (520)327-8584 *Fax:* (520)322-6778
E-Mail: asfa@azstarnet.com
Web Site: www.apheresis.org
Members: 1000 individuals
Annual Budget: $50-100,000
Executive Director: Phillip A. Gutt, CAE
Historical Note
Members are health professionals with an interest in the removal and separation of blood components. Membership: $105/year (individual).
Meetings/Conferences:
Annual Meetings: Spring
Publications:
ASFA Newsletter. irreg.
Journal of Clinical Apheresis. q.

American Society for Artificial Internal Organs *(1955)*
P.O. Box C
Boca Raton, FL 33429-0468
Tel: (561)391-8589
E-Mail: info@asaio.com
Web Site: www.asaio.com
Members: 1000 individuals
Staff: 4
Annual Budget: $250-500,000
Administrative Assistant: Dina Manginelli
Historical Note
Established in June 1954. ASAIO members are physicians, scientists and engineers from academia, industry, research institutions and government agencies who have made significant contributions to the development and/or understanding of artificial organs. A member society of the American Institute for Medical and Biological Engineering. Membership: $250/year; $270/year (foreign); $50/year (students); $70 (foreign students).
Meetings/Conferences:
Annual Meetings: Spring
Publications:
ASAIO Abstracts. a.
ASAIO Journal. bi-m. adv.

American Society for Automation in Pharmacy *(1989)*
492 Norristown Road, Suite 160
Blue Bell, PA 19422
Tel: (610)825-7783 *Fax:* (610)825-7641
E-Mail: wal@computertalk.com
Web Site: www.asapnet.org
Members: 150 companies
Staff: 3
Annual Budget: $50-100,000
Executive Director: Bill Lockwood
Historical Note
Members are software solutions providers serving the pharmacy industry. Supports implementation of standards for electronic data interchange between pharmacies and suppliers.

American Society for Biochemistry and Molecular Biology *(1906)*
9650 Rockville Pike
Bethesda, MD 20814-3996
Tel: (301)634-7145 *Fax:* (301)634-7126
E-Mail: asbmb@asbmb.org
Web Site: www.asbmb.org
Members: 11000 individuals
Staff: 23
Annual Budget: $10-25,000,000
Executive Director: Barbara Gordon
Director, Publications: Nancy Rodnan
Historical Note
Formerly (1987) American Society of Biological Chemists. Founded December 26, 1906 in New York City under the leadership of Drs. John J. Abel and C.A. Herter; incorporated in New York in 1919. Purpose is the extension and dissemination of knowledge about biochemistry and molecular biology. A founder and constituent member of the Federation of American Socs. for Experimental Biology as well as the Pan American Association for Biochemistry and Molecular Biology. A member of the American Association for the Advancement of Science and the Council of Academic Socs. of the American Association of Medical Colleges. Has an annual budget of approximately $15 million. Membership: $140/year (regular); $70/year (associate); $20/year (undergraduate).
Meetings/Conferences:
Annual Meetings: Spring
2007 – Washington, DC(Convention Center)/Apr. 28-March 2

2008 - San Diego, CA(Convention Center)/Apr. 5-9

Publications:
Molecular and Cellular Proteomics. m. adv.
Journal of Lipid Research. m. adv.
Biochem and Molecular Biology Education. bi-m. adv.
Journal of Biological Chemistry. w. adv.

American Society for Bioethics and Humanities *(1998)*
4700 W. Lake Ave.
Glenview, IL 60025-1485
Tel: (847)375-4745 *Fax:* (877)734-9385
E-Mail: info@asbh.org
Web Site: www.asbh.org
Members: 1500 individuals
Staff: 4
Annual Budget: $250-500,000
Executive Director: Amy Claver

Historical Note
A professional society of more than 1,500 individuals, organizations and institutions interested in bioethics and humanities. Founded in January 1998 through the consolidation of three existing associations in the field: the Society for Health and Human Values (SHHV), the Society for Bioethics Consultation (SBC), and the American Association of Bioethics (AAB). ASBH promotes the exchange of ideas, scholarship, and research among people engaged in the fields of clinical and academic bioethics and the health-related humanities.

Meetings/Conferences:
Annual Meetings: Fall

Publications:
ASBH Exchange. 3/yr. adv.

American Society for Blood and Marrow Transplantation *(1993)*
85 W. Algonquin Road, Suite 550
Arlington Heights, IL 60005-4425
Tel: (847)427-0224 *Fax:* (847)427-9656
E-Mail: mail@asbmt.org
Web Site: www.asbmt.org
Members: 1300 individuals
Staff: 3
Annual Budget: $1-2,000,000
Executive Director: Alan K. Leahigh
E-Mail: alanleahigh@asbmt.org

Historical Note
ASBMT represents the interests of celluar therapy and blood and marrow transplantation clinicians and investigators. The society promotes rapid dissemination of basic and clinical research related to hematopoietic stem cell transplantation, and supports clinical guidelines and standards of care for marrow transplant patients.

Meetings/Conferences:
Annual Meetings: Winter
2007 - Keystone, CO(Keystone Resort)/Feb. 8-12/1750
2008 - San Diego, CA(Manchester Hyatt)/Feb. 13-17/1800

Publications:
Blood and Marrow Transplantation Reviews. q.
Biology of Blood and Marrow Tranplantation. m. adv.
ASBMT E-News. m.

American Society for Bone and Mineral Research *(1977)*
2025 M St. NW, Suite 800
Washington, DC 20036-3309
Tel: (202)367-1161 *Fax:* (202)367-2161
E-Mail: asbmr@smithbucklin.com
Web Site: www.asbmr.org
Members: 4000 individuals
Staff: 20
Annual Budget: $2-5,000,000
Executive Director: Ann Elderkin
Deputy Executive Director: Karen R. Hasson

Historical Note
ASBMR members are physicians and scientists who perform basic and clinical research in the fields of metabolic bone diseases and mineral metabolism. Membership: $210-215/year (individual); $80/year (trainee).

Meetings/Conferences:
Annual Meetings: Fall

Publications:
ASBMR News.
Primer on Metabolic Bone Diseases & Disorders of Mineral Metabolism.
Journal of Bone and Mineral Research. m. adv.
Membership Roster. bien. adv.

American Society for Cell Biology *(1960)*
8120 Woodmont Ave., Suite 750
Bethesda, MD 20814-2762
Tel: (301)347-9300 *Fax:* (301)347-9310
E-Mail: ascbinfo@ascb.org
Web Site: www.ascb.org
Members: 10000 individuals
Staff: 20
Annual Budget: $2-5,000,000
Executive Director: Joan R. Goldberg
Director, Marketing: Edward Newman
Director, Public Policy: Kevin Wilson

Historical Note
Formed in 1960 and incorporated in New York in 1961. Membership: $125/year.

Meetings/Conferences:
Annual Meetings: Fall/9,000
2007 - Washington, DC(Convention Center)/Dec. 1-5

Publications:
ASCB Directory. a.
ASCB Newsletter. m.
Molecular Biology of the Cell. m.

American Society for Clinical Investigation *(1909)*
35 Research Dr., Suite 300
Ann Arbor, MI 48103
Tel: (734)222-6050 *Fax:* (734)222-6058
E-Mail: asci@the-jci.org
Web Site: www.asci-jci.org
Members: 2700 individuals
Staff: 14
Annual Budget: $2-5,000,000
Executive Director: John Hawley

Historical Note
Founded (1909) as the American Society for the Advancement of Clinical Investigation; assumed current name in 1916. ASCI's objectives are to advance medical science, cultivate clinical research through the methods of natural science, correlate science with the art of medical practice and encourage scientific spirit among its members.

Meetings/Conferences:
Annual Meetings: Spring
2007 - Chicago, IL(Fairmont Hotel)/Apr. 13-15

Publications:
Journal of Clinical Investigation. m.

American Society for Clinical Laboratory Science *(1932)*
6701 Democracy Blvd., Suite 300
Bethesda, MD 20817
Tel: (301)657-2768 *Fax:* (301)657-2909
E-Mail: ascls@ascls.org
Web Site: www.ascls.org
Members: 13000 individuals
Staff: 4
Annual Budget: $1-2,000,000
Executive Vice President: Elissa Passiment, EdM
E-Mail: ascls@ascls.org
Director, Education: Joan Polancic
E-Mail: ascls@ascls.org

Historical Note
Formerly (1936) the American Society of Clinical Laboratory Technicians, the American Society of Medical Technologists (1972), and the American Society for Medical Technology (1993). Members have an associate, a B.S. degree, and/or clinical training or experience in a branch of medical technology, or the medical laboratory sciences. Supports the American Society for Clinical Laboratory Science Political Action Committee. Membership: $80/year, plus state dues.

Meetings/Conferences:
Annual Meetings: Summer
2007 - San Diego, CA/July 17-21

Publications:
Clinical Laboratory Science. q. adv.
ASCLS Today. m. adv.

American Society for Clinical Nutrition *(1959)*

Historical Note
Merged with American Society for Nutritional Sciences and Society for International Nutrition Research to become American Society for Nutrition in 2005.

American Society for Clinical Pathology *(1922)*
2100 W. Harrison St.
Chicago, IL 60612-3798
Tel: (202)541-4999 *Fax:* (312)738-1619
Toll Free: (800)621 - 2727
E-Mail: info@ascp.org
Web Site: www.ascp.org
Members: 140000 individuals
Staff: 145
Annual Budget: $10-25,000,000
Executive Vice President: John R. Ball, M.D., JD
Director, Communications: Nadine M. Filipiak
Vice President, Government Relations: Jeff P. Jacobs
Vice President, Educational Programs: Kathy Mauck
Director, Marketing: Elizabeth Parks
Director, Information Technology: Jennifer Schmidt
Director, Membership: Nanice Thompson

Historical Note
Formerly (1922) American Society of Clinical Pathologists; assumed its current name in 2002. ASCP's purpose is to promote public health and safety by appropriate application of pathology and laboratory medicine in the prevention, diagnosis and treatment of disease, to conduct educational programs and publish educational materials in the field of clinical and anatomic pathology and laboratory medicine, and to conduct a program for the examination and certification of medical laboratory personnel. Has an annual budget of approximately $20 million. Membership: $329/year (pathologist); $79/year (technologist).

Publications:
Pathology Today - The Physicians Newsletter. 6/yr.
Medical Technology Today. 12/yr.
Laboratory Medicine. 12/yr. adv.
ASCP e-Newsbriefs. 26/year. adv.
American Journal of Clinical Pathology. 12/yr. adv.

American Society for Clinical Pharmacology and Therapeutics *(1900)*
528 N. Washington St.
Alexandria, VA 22314
Tel: (703)836-6981
Web Site: www.ascpt.org
Members: 2000 individuals
Staff: 5
Annual Budget: $2-5,000,000
Executive Director: Sharon J. Swan
E-Mail: sharon@ascpt.org
Senior Director, Member Services: Melissa Llevellyn
Director, Meetings and Education: Bethany Oxer

Historical Note
Organized May 1, 1900, as the American Therapeutic Society merged in 1969 with the American College of Clinical Pharmacology and Chemotherapy (founded in 1963) and incorporated in the District of Columbia under its present name. Approximately 30% of ASCPT members are from academia and private practice, 60% from industry and 10% from government. Two-thirds of members are clinicians with hospital staff appointments and a subspecialty interest in clinical pharmacology and therapeutics. Membership: $330/year.

Meetings/Conferences:
Annual Meetings: Spring/1,400

Publications:
Clinical Pharmacology and Therapeutics. m.

American Society for Colposcopy and Cervical Pathology *(1964)*
20 W. Washington St., Suite One

Hagerstown, MD 21740
Tel: (301)733-3640 *Fax:* (301)733-5775
Toll Free: (800)787 - 7227
Web Site: www.asccp.org
Members: 3800 individuals
Staff: 4
Annual Budget: $1-2,000,000
Executive Director: Kathleen Graham Poole
E-Mail: kpoole@asccp.org
President: Daron Ferris, M.D.

Historical Note
Founded as American Society for Colposcopy and Colpomicroscopy to provide a forum for education in the diagnosis, etiology and treatment of pathologies of the cervix and lower genital tract. Members are gynecologists, pathologists, family phsysicians and others interested in promoting the study of female lower genital tract disease. Sponsors several continuing education programs throughout the year. Membership: $140/year (individual).

Meetings/Conferences:
Biennial Meeting: (even years)
2008 - Lake Buena Vista, FL/March 17-21

Publications:
The Home Study Program. q.
Journal of Lower Genital Tract Disease. q. adv.

American Society for Cytotechnology *(1979)*

1500 Sunday Dr., Suite 102
Raleigh, NC 27607
Tel: (919)861-5571 *Fax:* (919)787-4916
Toll Free: (800)948 - 3947
E-Mail: info@asct.com
Web Site: www.asct.com
Members: 1800 individuals
Staff: 3
Annual Budget: $50-100,000
Executive Director: Beth Denny

Historical Note
Members are individuals concerned with the evaluation of cells for early signs of malignancy. Full members must have passed a qualifying cytotechnology exam and have either graduated from a school of cytology or worked in the field for three years. Membership: $40/year.

Meetings/Conferences:
Annual Meetings: Spring; Held in conjunction with a regional Cytology Society.

Publications:
ACST Journal of Cytotechnology. q. adv.
ASCT News. m. adv.

American Society for Dental Aesthetics *(1976)*

635 Madison Ave., 13th Floor
New York, NY 10022
Tel: (212)751-3263 *Fax:* (212)755-3263
Toll Free: (800)454 - 2732
E-Mail: info@asdatoday.com
Web Site: www.asdatoday.com
Members: 160 individuals
Staff: 1
Annual Budget: $100-250,000
Executive Vice President: Marvin A. Fier, DDS

Historical Note
Members are dentists who have demonstrated excellence in an area of aesthetic dentistry. Applicants must be dentists for five years, then submit before-and-after photos of five cases for review. Fellowships to the Society are granted to members who have been active for five years and have advanced the Society's standards.

Meetings/Conferences:
Semi-annual Meetings: Spring and Fall

Publications:
Journal ASDA Today. q.

American Society for Dermatologic Surgery *(1970)*

5550 Meadowbrook Dr., #120
Rolling Meadows, IL 60008
Tel: (847)956-0900 *Fax:* (847)956-0999
E-Mail: ksvedman@asds.net
Web Site: www.asds.net
Members: 3500 individuals
Staff: 6
Annual Budget: $500-1,000,000
Executive Director: Katherine J. Svedman

Historical Note
ASDS was established to preserve and enhance the use of surgical modalities in the practice of dermatology. Membership: $400/year.

Meetings/Conferences:
Annual Meetings: Fall

Publications:
Dermatologic Surgery. m. adv.
Directory. a. adv.
Currents Newsletter. m. adv.
Annual Meeting Program Book. a. adv.

American Society for Eighteenth-Century Studies *(1969)*

Wake Forest U.
P.O. Box 7867
Winston-Salem, NC 27109
Tel: (336)727-4694 *Fax:* (336)727-4697
E-Mail: asecs@wfu.edu
Web Site: http://asecs.press.jhu.edu/
Members: 3000 individuals
Staff: 1
Annual Budget: $250-500,000
Executive Director: Byron R. Wells
Office Manager: Vickie Cutting

Historical Note
ASECS members are academics and others interested in the cultural history of the eighteenth century. Membership: $20-$65 (individual); $100-$130 (organization/company).

Meetings/Conferences:
Annual Meetings: Spring or Summer

Publications:
ASECS Directory. q. adv.
ASECS News Circular. q. adv.
ASECS Program of Annual Meeting. a. adv.
Eighteenth-Century Studies. q. adv.
Studies in Eighteenth Century Culture. a.

American Society for Engineering Education *(1893)*

1818 N St. NW, Suite 600
Washington, DC 20036
Tel: (202)331-3500 *Fax:* (202)265-8504
E-Mail: aseexec@asee.org
Web Site: www.asee.org
Members: 11000 individuals
Staff: 50
Annual Budget: $10-25,000,000
Executive Director: Dr. Frank L. Huband
Deputy Director: Robert Black
Manager, Meetings and Conferences: Patricia Greenwalt
Manager, Outreach: Eric Iversen
Manager, Global Action: Jennifer Johnson
Manager, Information Technology Department: Keith Mounts
Manager, Executive Office: Marian Tatu
Manager, Public Affairs: Kathy Tollerton
Manager, Member Services: Dwight Wardell
Chief Financial Officer: Charlotte Watson
Manager, Administrative Services and Awards: Sandra Wingate-Bey

Historical Note
Originated in 1893 as the Society for the Promotion of Engineering Education. Merged in 1946 with the Engineering College Research Association to form the American Society for Engineering Education. Incorporated in Pennsylvania in 1943. A member of the American Association of Engineering Societies, Accreditation Board for Engineering and Technology, the American Association for the Advancement of Science and the American Council on Education. A participating society of the World Federation of Engineering Organizations. Membership: $60/year (individual); $750-900/year (organization).

Meetings/Conferences:
Annual Meetings: Summer/3,000
2007 - Honolulu, HI/June 24-27
2008 - Pittsburgh, PA/June 22-25

Publications:
ASEE Action Newsletter. m.
PRISM Magazine. 9/year. adv.
COED (Computers in Education Division) Journal. q.
Engineering Design Graphics. 3/year. adv.
Engineering College Research and Graduate Directory. a. adv.
Mechanical Engineering News. q. adv.
Engineering Economist. q.
Journal of Engineering Education. q.
Journal of Engineering Technology. semi-a.
Directory of Undergraduate Engineering Statistics.
Directory of Engineering Technology Statistics.
Directory of Graduate Engineering Statistics.
Directory of Key Engineering Administrators.
ASEE Conference Proceedings. a.
College Industry Conference Proceedings.
Chemical Engineering Education. q. adv.
Civil Engineering Education. bi-a.

American Society for Engineering Management *(1979)*

P.O. Box 820
Rolla, MO 65402
Tel: (573)341-2101 *Fax:* (573)364-3500
Web Site: www.asem.org
Members: 800 individuals
Staff: 1
Annual Budget: $100-250,000
Executive Director: Jerry Westbrook
Manager, Member Services: Kellie Davis

Historical Note
Founded in 1979 by a group of engineering management professionals from academic, industrial, and governmental organizations to promote the development of engineering management as a professional discipline and academic specialty and to maintain a high professional standard among its members. Membership: $90/year (individual); $1,000-10,000/year (company).

Meetings/Conferences:
Annual Meetings: Fall

Publications:
Newsletter. q. adv.
Proceedings of Annual Meeting. a.
Engineering Management Journal. q. adv.

American Society for Enology and Viticulture *(1950)*

Box 1855
Davis, CA 95617-1855
Tel: (530)753-3142 *Fax:* (530)753-3318
E-Mail: society@asev.org
Web Site: www.asev.org
Members: 2600 individuals
Staff: 8
Annual Budget: $1-2,000,000
Executive Director: Lyndie McHenry Boulton

Historical Note
Formerly (1984) the American Society of Enologists. ASEV is an international, professional society dedicated to the interests of enologists, viticulturists and others in the fields of wine and grape production. Membership: $40/year (internatl student); $210/year (full); $225/year (internatl); $650/year (affiliate).

Meetings/Conferences:
Annual Meetings: June
2007 - Reno, NV(Grand Sierra Resort)/June 20-22/2000
2008 - Portland, OR(Oregon Convention Center)/June 18-20/2000

Publications:
American Journal of Enology and Viticulture. q. adv.

American Society for Environmental History *(1976)*

119 Pine St., Suite 301
Seattle, WA 98101
Tel: (206)343-0226 *Fax:* (206)343-0249
Web Site: www.aseh.net
Members: 1200 individuals
Annual Budget: under $10,000
Executive Director: Lisa Mighetto

Historical Note
ASEH members are teachers and researchers with an interest in human ecology and environmental history. Membership: $55/year (individual); $25/year (student); $100/year (institution).

Meetings/Conferences:
Annual Meetings: Spring
2007 - Baton Rouge, LA(Sheraton)/March 1-4/400
2008 - Boise, ID(Grove)/March 12-16/400

Publications:
ASEH News. q.
Environmental History. q.

American Society for Ethnohistory *(1953)*
Dept. of History, York University
Toronto, ON M3J 1-P3
E-Mail: ase@indiana.edu
Web Site: http://ethnohistory.org
Members: 700 individuals
Annual Budget: $50-100,000
Secretary-Treasurer: Carolyn Podruchny

Historical Note
Formerly (1966) American Indian Ethnohistoric Conference. Members are anthropologists, historians, art historians, geographers and other professionals interested in the research of the cultural history of non-industrial peoples. Has no paid officers or full-time staff. Membership: $30/year (individual); $50/year (institution); $20/year (student/retired).

Meetings/Conferences:
Annual Meetings: November

Publications:
Ethnohistory Journal. q. adv.

American Society for Experimental NeuroTherapeutics
555 E. Wells St., Suite 611
Milwaukee, WI 53202-3823
Tel: (414)273-8290 *Fax:* (414)276-3349
E-Mail: info@asent.org
Web Site: www.asent.org
Members: 275 individuals
Staff: 3
Annual Budget: $100-250,000
Executive Director: Anne Rushing

Historical Note
To provide a forum; to promote dialogue, understanding and cooperation; to develop information and seek consensus; to organize training and education for members of academia, industry and government.

Meetings/Conferences:
Annual Meetings: Spring

Publications:
NeuroRx. q.

American Society for Gastrointestinal Endoscopy *(1941)*
1520 Kensington Road, Suite 202
Oak Brook, IL 60523
Tel: (630)573-0600 *Fax:* (630)573-0691
Toll Free: (888)353 - 2743
E-Mail: info@asge.org
Web Site: www.asge.org and www.askasge.org
Members: 7500 individuals
Staff: 20
Annual Budget: $5-10,000,000
Executive Director: Patricia Blake
Chief Financial Officer: Sam Haroz
E-Mail: sharoz@asge.org
Director, Meetings and Education: Vanessa Kizart
E-Mail: vkizart@asge.org
Professional Education Officer: Gregory Paulos
Chief Development and Communications Officer: P. Joanne Ray

Historical Note
Formerly American Gastropic Club. Seeks to advance the use of endoscopy as a diagnostic technique.

Meetings/Conferences:
Annual Meetings: Spring

Publications:
ASGE News. bi-m. adv.
Gastrointestinal Endoscopy. m. adv.
Scope. bi-w.

American Society for Geriatric Dentistry *(1964)*
401 N. Michigan Ave.
Chicago, IL 60611
Tel: (312)537-6764 *Fax:* (312)673-6663
Members: 550 individuals
Staff: 3
Annual Budget: $250-500,000
Executive Director: Kristen Smith

Historical Note
Established and incorporated in Chicago, IL, ASGD is a component group of the Special Care Dentistry Association. Membership: $170/year.

Meetings/Conferences:
Semi-annual Meetings: Spring in Chicago. Fall with the American Dental Ass'n.

Publications:
SCD Interface Newsletter. m. adv.
Special Care in Dentistry. bi-m. adv.

American Society for Healthcare Central Service Professionals *(1967)*
One N. Franklin, Suite 2800
Chicago, IL 60606
Tel: (312)422-3700 *Fax:* (312)422-4577
E-Mail: ashcsp@aha.org
Web Site: www.ashcsp.org
Members: 1000 individuals
Staff: 5
Annual Budget: $250-500,000
Executive Director: Virginia Sylvestri

Historical Note
Formerly (1987) American Society for Hospital Central Service Personnel. An affiliate of the American Hospital Association. Membership: $85/year (individual).

Meetings/Conferences:
Annual Meetings: Fall/300

Publications:
Healthcare Central Service. q. adv.

American Society for Healthcare Engineering *(1962)*
One N. Franklin St., 28th Floor
Chicago, IL 60606
Tel: (312)422-3801 *Fax:* (312)422-4571
E-Mail: ashe@aha.org
Web Site: www.ashe.org
Members: 7200 individuals
Staff: 16
Annual Budget: $5-10,000,000
Executive Director: Dale Wooden, CHFM, SASHE
Director, Operations: Kate Wickham

Historical Note
Formerly (1995) American Society for Hospital Engineering. An affiliate of the American Hospital Association. Supports the American Hospital Association Political Action Committee (AHA-PAC). Membership: $125/year (active professional); $175/year (associate from non-member hospital); $25/year (retiree or student).

Meetings/Conferences:
Annual Meetings: June-July
2007 - New Orleans, LA(Convention Center)/July 8-11/3000

Publications:
Inside ASHE. bi-m. adv.
Management Monographs. as needed.
Directory of Planning Professionals for Health Facilities. a. adv.

American Society for Healthcare Environmental Services *(1986)*
One N. Franklin St.
Chicago, IL 60606
Tel: (312)422-3860 *Fax:* (312)422-4578
Web Site: www.ashes.org
Members: 2020 individuals
Staff: 4
Annual Budget: $500-1,000,000
Executive Director: Patti Costello
E-Mail: pcostello@aha.org

Historical Note
An affiliate of the American Hospital Association. ASHES members are directors, managers and supervisors of healthcare environmental services, housekeeping, textile, and land waste management departments. Membership: $105/$135 (individuals); $155 (suppliers).

Meetings/Conferences:
Annual Meetings: September
2007 - St. Louis, MO(America's Center)/Sept. 30-Oct. 4/1000

Publications:
ASHES Newsletter. bi-m. adv.
ASHES Members Directory (online). a. adv.
Annual Conference Proceedings Manual. a. adv.
E-Newsletter. m. adv.

American Society for Healthcare Food Service Administrators *(1967)*
340 W. Liberty St., Suite 201
Louisville, KY 40202
Toll Free: (800)620 - 6422 Ext: 268
Web Site: www.ashfsa.org
Members: 1300 individuals
Staff: 5
Annual Budget: $250-500,000
Executive Vice President: Keith Howard
E-Mail: khoward@hqtrs.com

Historical Note
An affiliate of the American Hospital Association, ASHFSA advances the effectiveness of food and nutrition services administration in the healthcare setting.

Meetings/Conferences:
Annual Meetings: Summer/600

Publications:
Healthcare Food Service Trends. q. adv.

American Society for Healthcare Human Resources Administration *(1964)*
One N. Franklin
Chicago, IL 60606
Tel: (312)422-3720 *Fax:* (312)422-4577
Web Site: www.ashhra.org
Members: 3000 individuals
Staff: 5
Annual Budget: $1-2,000,000

Historical Note
An affiliate of the American Hospital Association. Formerly (1975) American Society for Hospital Personnel Directors. Dedicated exclusively to the education and professional development of hospital personnel administrators. Membership: $100/year.

Meetings/Conferences:
Annual Meetings: Varies/500

Publications:
HR Pulse. q. adv.
JCAHO II. irreg.
ADA Job Description Manual.
Consultants Directory. a. adv.
Membership Roster. a. adv.

American Society for Healthcare Risk Management *(1980)*
One N. Franklin St.
Chicago, IL 60606
Tel: (312)422-3980 *Fax:* (312)422-4580
E-Mail: ashrm@aha.org
Web Site: www.ashrm.org
Members: 4600 individuals
Staff: 8
Annual Budget: $1-2,000,000
Executive Director: Elizabeth Summy
E-Mail: esummy@aha.org
Director, Professional and Technical Services: Pamela J. Para
E-Mail: ppara@aha.org
Manager, Communications and Publications: Joe Pixler

Historical Note
Formerly (1987) American Society for Hospital Risk Management. An affiliate of the American Hospital Association. Members are hospital employees involved in risk management, insurance personnel, hospital administrators, attorneys, physicians and healthcare management consultants. Membership: $110/year.

Meetings/Conferences:
Annual Meetings: Fall/2,000

Publications:
Directory (online, for members only). a.
e-news (online). w.
Conference Proceedings. a.
Journal of Healthcare Risk Management. q.
ASHRM Forum. bi-m.

American Society for Hispanic Art Historical Studies *(1975)*
Univ. of Illinois, 143 Art & Design Bldg.
408 E. Peabody Dr.
Champaign, IL 61820
Tel: (217)333-7139 *Fax:* (217)244-7688
Members: 150 individuals
General Secretary: Jordana Mendelson

Historical Note
ASHAHS members are academics and others with an interest in the art of Spain and Portugal. Membership: $20/year (individual); $30/year (institution); $10/year (student).

Publications:
Newsletter. bi-a.

American Society for Histocompatability and Immunogenetics *(1970)*
15000 Commerce Pkwy., Suite C
Mt. Laurel, NJ 08054
Tel: (856)638-0428 *Fax:* (856)439-0525
E-Mail: info@ashi-hla.org
Web Site: www.ashi-hla.org
Members: 1150 individuals
Staff: 6
Annual Budget: $1-2,000,000
Executive Director: Kimberly Glenn

Historical Note
Physicians, blood banks and others involved in the testing of blood to determine its compatability with organs to be used in transplants. Formerly (1984) the American Association for Clinical Histocompatibility Testing. Membership: $95/year (full member); $45/year (associate); $1,000/year (institution).

Meetings/Conferences:
Annual Meetings: Fall
2007 – Minneapolis, MN(Hyatt)/Oct. 8-12/900

Publications:
ASHI Quarterly. q. adv.
Human Immunology. m.

American Society for Horticultural Science *(1903)*
113 S. West St., Suite 200
Alexandria, VA 22314-2851
Tel: (703)836-4606 *Fax:* (703)836-2024
E-Mail: ashs@ashs.org
Web Site: www.ashs.org
Members: 4000 individuals
Staff: 14
Annual Budget: $2-5,000,000
Executive Director: Michael W. Neff

Historical Note
Founded in 1903 in Boston and incorporated in 1961 in the District of Columbia. Promotes and encourages national and international interest in scientific research and education in all branches of horticulture production, marketing, processing, and utilization of fruits, nuts, vegetables, flowers, ornamental and landscape plants). Membership: $105/year (individual); $300/year (corporate).

Meetings/Conferences:
2007 – Scottsdale, AZ(Westin)/July 16-19

Publications:
Journal of the ASHS. bi-m. adv.
HortScience. bi-m. adv.
ASHS Newsletter. m. adv.
HortTechnology. q. adv.

American Society for Information Science and Technology *(1937)*
1320 Fenwick Lane, Suite 510
Silver Spring, MD 20910
Tel: (301)495-0900 *Fax:* (301)495-0810
E-Mail: asis@asis.org
Web Site: www.asis.org
Members: 3800 individuals
Staff: 7
Annual Budget: $500-1,000,000
Executive Director: Richard B. Hill
E-Mail: rhill@asis.org
Manager, Membership Services and Meetings: Vanessa O. Foss

Historical Note
Founded in Washington, DC in 1937 as the American Documentation Institute and incorporated in Delaware the same year. Became the American Society for Information Science in 1968, and assumed its current name in 2000. Promotes the creation and application of knowledge concerning information and its transfer. Membership: $95/year (individual); $350-550/year (company).

Meetings/Conferences:
Semi-Annual Meetings: Fall and Spring

Publications:
Annual Review of Information Science and Technology. a.
Bulletin of ASIS. bi-m. adv.
Journal of ASIS. 14/year. adv.
Proceedings. a.
ASIS Handbook and Directory. a. adv.

American Society for Investigative Pathology *(1900)*
9650 Rockville Pike
Bethesda, MD 20814-3993
Tel: (301)634-7130 *Fax:* (301)634-7990
E-Mail: asip@asip.org
Web Site: www.asip.org
Members: 2000 individuals
Staff: 21
Annual Budget: $2-5,000,000
Executive Officer: Mark E. Sobel, MD, Ph.D
Director, Finance: James S. Douglas
Managing Editor: Maria Eiseman
Director, Meetings and Membership Services: Tara Snethen
Director, Marketing: Alta Wallington

Historical Note
Formed on July 1, 1976 by a merger of the American Society for Experimental Pathology (founded in 1913) and the American Association of Pathologists and Bacteriologists (founded in 1900). Formerly (1992) American Association of Pathologists. Membership: $180/year.

Meetings/Conferences:
Annual Meetings: Spring
2007 – Washington, DC(Convention Center)/Apr. 28-May 2/13000

Publications:
American Journal of Pathology. m. adv.
Journal of Molecular Diagnostics. q. adv.
ASIP Bulletin. bi-a.

American Society for Laser Medicine and Surgery *(1980)*
2404 Stewart Ave.
Wausau, WI 54401
Tel: (715)845-9283 *Fax:* (715)848-2493
E-Mail: information@aslms.org
Web Site: www.aslms.org
Members: 3557 individuals
Staff: 5
Annual Budget: $250-500,000
Secretary: Dr. Richard O. Gregory

Historical Note
Founded through an initial grant from the A. Ward Ford Memorial Institute in Wausau, and incorporated in the State of Wisconsin by 150 charter members.

Meetings/Conferences:
Annual Meetings: Spring
2007 – Grapevine, TX(Gaylord Texan Resort)/Apr. 11-15/2100

Publications:
Official ASLMS Newsletter. semi-a. adv.
Lasers in Surgery and Medicine. bi-m. adv.

American Society for Legal History *(1956)*
New York Law School
57 Worth St.
New York, NY 10013
Tel: (212)431-2883 *Fax:* (212)431-2830
E-Mail: wlapiana@nyls.edu
Web Site: www.h-net.msu.edu/~law/ASLH/aslh.htm
Members: 930 individuals
Staff: 1
Annual Budget: $25-50,000
Secretary/Treasurer: William P. LaPiana
E-Mail: wlapiana@nyls.edu

Historical Note
A member of the American Council of Learned Societies. Originated as a special interest section of the American Association of Law Schools. Membership fees vary.

Meetings/Conferences:
Annual Meetings: Third week in October/250
2007 – Tempe, AZ/Oct. 25-28

Publications:
Law & History Review. 3/year. adv.
Newsletter. semi-a.

American Society for Mass Spectrometry *(1969)*
2019 Galisteo St., Bldg. I
Santa Fe, NM 87505
Tel: (505)989-4517 *Fax:* (505)989-1073
E-Mail: office@asms.org
Web Site: www.asms.org
Members: 6000 individuals
Staff: 5
Annual Budget: $1-2,000,000
Executive Director: Judith Sjoberg

Historical Note
Members are academic and industrial chemists and scientists who use the mass spectrometer as an analytical and physical tool. Membership: $65/year; $40/year (full-time student).

Meetings/Conferences:
Annual Meetings: Spring
2007 – Indianapolis, IN/June 3-7
2008 – Denver, CO/June 1-5

Publications:
Journal of the ASMS. m.
Proceedings of the Annual Conference. a.

American Society for Microbiology *(1899)*
1752 N St. NW
Washington, DC 20036-2904
Tel: (202)737-3600 *Fax:* (202)942-9333
Web Site: www.asm.org/
Members: 43000 individuals
Staff: 110
Annual Budget: $25-50,000,000
Executive Director: Michael I. Goldberg, Ph.D.
Director, Education and Training: Amy L. Chang
Director, Meetings and Conferences: Nancy L. Elder
Director, Communications: Barbara Hyde
Director, Membership Services: Lorna D. Kent
Manager, Media Relations and Communications: James Sliwa

Historical Note
Founded in New Haven, CT in 1899 as the Society of American Bacteriologists. Became the American Society for Microbiology in 1960, and merged with the American Academy of Microbiology in 1969. Incorporated in the District of Columbia in 1947. A member of the International Union of Microbiological Societies. Promotes scientific knowledge of microbiology and related subjects through discussions, reports and publications. The American Academy of Microbiology is the professional services arm of the ASM.

Meetings/Conferences:
Annual Meetings: Spring

Publications:
Eukaryotic Cell.
Microbiology and Molecular Biology Reviews. q. adv.
Antimicrobial Agents and Chemotherapy. m. adv.
Applied and Environmental Microbiology. m. adv.
Infection and Immunity. m. adv.
Journal of Bacteriology. bi-m. adv.
Journal of Clinical Microbiology. m. adv.
Journal of Virology. m. adv.
Molecular and Cellular Biology. m. adv.
Clinical Microbiology Reviews.
Clinical Immunology.

American Society for Neurochemistry *(1969)*
9037 Ron Den Lane
Windermere, FL 34786
Tel: (407)876-0750
E-Mail: amazing@iag.net
Web Site: www.asneurochem.org

Members: 1000 individuals
Staff: 1
Annual Budget: $50-100,000
Executive Director: Sheilah Jewart

Historical Note
Organized in 1968-1969 by U.S., Canadian and Mexican members of the International Society for Neurochemistry and incorporated in the District of Columbia, August 6, 1969. Membership: $75/year.

Publications:
Membership Directory. a.
Transactions of the ASN. a. adv.

American Society for Nondestructive Testing *(1941)*
1711 Arlingate Lane
P.O. Box 28518
Columbus, OH 43228-0518
Tel: (614)274-6003 *Fax:* (614)274-6899
Toll Free: (800)222 - 2768
E-Mail: bblazar@asnt.org
Web Site: www.asnt.org
Members: 10000 individuals
Staff: 35
Annual Budget: $5-10,000,000
Executive Director: Wayne Holliday
Senior Manager, Marketing and Membership: Betsy Blazar
Senior Manager, Accounting and Finance: Mary Potter
E-Mail: mpotter@asnt.org

Historical Note
Founded in August 1941 with nine charter members as the American Industrial Radium and X-Ray Society; became Society for Nondestructive Testing in 1946 and assumed its current name in 1967. Incorporated in Ohio in 1988. Members are engineers, metallurgists and managers in the field of nondestructive testing for a variety of industries: chemicals, aerospace, construction, electronics, nuclear, metals, petroleum, food processing, transportation and automotive. Membership: $75/year (initial fee); $65/year (renewal).

Meetings/Conferences:
Semi-Annual Meetings: Spring and Fall

Publications:
Nondestructive Testing Handbook.
TNT - The NDT Technican. q. adv.
Materials Evaluation. m. adv.
Research in Nondestructive Evaluation. q.

American Society for Nutrition *(1928)*
9650 Rockville Pike
Bethesda, MD 20814
Tel: (301)634-7050 *Fax:* (301)634-7892
E-Mail: sec@nutrition.org
Web Site: www.nutrition.org
Members: 3500 individuals
Staff: 5
Annual Budget: $1-2,000,000
Director, Communications: Karen King
Interim Executive Officer: Frederick T. Spahr, CAE

Historical Note
Founded as American Institute of Nutrition by members of the American Society of Biological Chemists to provide for the publication of the Journal of Nutrition. Reorganized as a membership society in 1934; became American Society for Nutritional Sciences in 1996; Merged (2005) with American Soc. for Clinical Nutrition and Soc. for International Nutrition Research, and assumed its current name the same year. ASN represents practitioners and researchers in several disciplines concerned with nuitrition science, policy and practice. Membership: $150/year (regular members and associate members); $50/year (postdoctoral fellows); $30/year (students); $25/year (emeritus members).

Meetings/Conferences:
Annual Meetings: Spring, with Fed. of American Socs. for Experimental Biology/15,000
2007 - Washington, DC/Apr. 28-May 2

Publications:
American Journal of Clinical Nutrition. m. adv.
Journal of Nutrition. m. adv.
ASN Nutrition Notes. q. adv.

American Society for Parenteral and Enteral Nutrition *(1975)*
8630 Fenton St., Suite 412
Silver Spring, MD 20910-3803
Tel: (301)587-6315 *Fax:* (301)587-2365
Toll Free: (800)727 - 4567
E-Mail: aspen@nutr.org
Web Site: www.nutritioncare.org
Members: 5500 individuals
Staff: 17
Annual Budget: $2-5,000,000
Executive Director: Robin Kriegel, CAE
E-Mail: robink@aspen.nutr.org
Associate Executive Director: Patrick Mcgary
E-Mail: patrickm@aspen.nutr.org
Program Director for Marketing: Natalie Ortiz-Ramos
E-Mail: natalier@aspen.nutr.org

Historical Note
Physicians, dietitians, nurses, pharmacists, nutritionists, researchers, hospital administrators and others who work in specialized nutrition support. ASPEN is concerned with the care of patients who cannot digest food normally, and therefore have to be fed parenterally (intravenously) or enterally (by tube). Membership: $100-$165/year.

Meetings/Conferences:
Annual Meetings: Winter/3,000
2007 - Phoenix, AZ/Jan. 28-31

Publications:
Aspen eNews. q. adv.
Journal of Parenteral and Enteral Nutrition. bi-m. adv.
Nutrition in Clinical Practice. bi-m. adv.

American Society for Pediatric Neurosurgery *(1978)*
c/o Semmes-Murphy Clinic
1211 Union Ave., Suite 200
Memphis, TN 38104
Tel: (901)522-7700 *Fax:* (901)522-2600
Web Site: www.aspn.org
Members: 50 individuals
Staff: 1
Annual Budget: under $10,000
Secretary: Frederick A. Boop, M.D.

Historical Note
Membership: $100/year, new member initiation fee $100 additional.

Publications:
Journal of Neurosurgery - Pediatrics.
Newsletter. 4/year.

American Society for Pharmacology and Experimental Therapeutics *(1908)*
9650 Rockville Pike
Bethesda, MD 20814-3995
Tel: (301)634-7060 *Fax:* (301)634-7061
E-Mail: info@aspet.org
Web Site: www.aspet.org
Members: 4300 individuals
Staff: 15
Annual Budget: $5-10,000,000
Executive Officer: Christine K. Carrico, Ph.D.
E-Mail: ccarrico@aspet.org
Director, Public Affairs: James Bernstein
E-Mail: jbernstein@aspet.org

Historical Note
Organized at Johns Hopkins University on December 28, 1908 with 18 charter members. Incorporated in Maryland in 1933. A member of the Federation of American Societies for Experimental Biology, International Union of Pharmacology, and American Association for the Advancement of Science, and the U.S. Pharmacopeial Convention. Membership: $130/year.

Meetings/Conferences:
Annual Meetings: Spring
2007 - Washington, DC(Convention Center)/Apr. 28-May 2

Publications:
Drug Metabolism and Disposition. m. adv.
The Pharmacologist. q.
Molecular Interventions. bi-m. adv.
Clinical Pharmacology and Therapeutics. m. adv.
Journal of Pharmacology and Experimental Therapeutics. m. adv.
Molecular Pharmacology. m. adv.
Pharmacological Reviews. q. adv.

American Society for Photobiology *(1972)*
P.O. Box 1897
Lawrence, KS 66044
Tel: (785)843-1235 Ext: 210 *Fax:* (785)843-1287
Toll Free: (800)627 - 0629
E-Mail: phot@allenpress.com
Web Site: www.pol-us.net
Members: 1600 individuals
Staff: 6
Annual Budget: $250-500,000
Executive Secretary: Linda Hardwick

Historical Note
Founded in 1972 to further the scientific study of the effects of light on all living organisms. Membership: $110/year.

Publications:
ASP Newsletter. bi-m.
Photochemistry and Photobiology. bi-m. adv.

American Society for Photogrammetry and Remote Sensing *(1934)*
5410 Grosvenor Lane, Suite 210
Bethesda, MD 20814-2160
Tel: (301)493-0290 *Fax:* (301)493-0208
E-Mail: asprs@asprs.org.
Web Site: www.asprs.org
Members: 6500 individuals
Staff: 10
Annual Budget: $2-5,000,000
Executive Director: James R. Plasker
Program Manager: Jesse Winch
E-Mail: jwinch@asprs.org

Historical Note
Founded as the American Society of Photogrammetry in Washington, DC in 1934 with 12 charter members and incorporated the same year in DC. The mission of the ASPRS is to advance knowledge and improve understanding of mapping sciences and to promote the responsible applications of photogrammetry, remote sensing, geographic information systems (GIS), and supporting technologies. Membership: $105/year (active); $70/year (associate); $45/year (student).

Meetings/Conferences:
2007 - Tampa, FL(Marriott Tampa)/May 7-11
2008 - Portland, OR/Apr. 27-May 2

Publications:
Photogrammetric Engineering and Remote Sensing. m. adv.

American Society for Plasticulture *(1959)*
526 Brittany Dr.
State College, PA 16803-1420
Tel: (814)238-7045 *Fax:* (814)238-7051
E-Mail: info@plasticulture.org
Web Site: www.plasticulture.org
Members: 96 individuals
Annual Budget: $25-50,000
Executive Director: Patricia E. Heuser

Historical Note
Established in Lexington, KY as National Agricultural Plastics Association; assumed its current name in 1990. Provides a forum for the investigation and discussion of the applications of plastics used in agricultural production and marketing systems. Membership: $60/year (grower); $60/year (academic); $200/year (company); $600/year (sponsor).

Publications:
Conference Proceedings. every 18 mos..
Agri-Plastics Report. 4/year.

American Society for Political and Legal Philosophy *(1955)*
c/o Dept. Political Science, University of Chicago
5828 S. University Ave.
Chicago, IL 60637
Tel: (773)702-8052 *Fax:* (773)702-1689
Members: 500 individuals
Secretary-Treasurer: Prof. Jacob Levy

Historical Note
ASPLP members are academics and others with an active professional interest in the field of political/legal philosophy. Membership: $40/year.

Publications:
Nomos. a.

American Society for Precision Engineering
(1986)
P.O. Box 10826
Raleigh, NC 27605-0826
Tel: (919)839-8444 *Fax:* (919)839-8039
Web Site: www.aspe.net
Members: 800 individuals
Staff: 3
Annual Budget: $250-500,000
Manager, Meetings and Membership: Erika Deutsch-Layne

Historical Note
Represents all facets of precision engineering from research to application. Members are from academia, government, and industry. Membership: $65/year (individual); $1,000/year (corporate).

Publications:
Precision Engineering Journal. q. adv.
Proceedings of the ASPE Annual Meeting. a.
Proceedings of Topical Meetings. 2-3/yr.

American Society for Public Administration
(1939)
1301 Pennsylvania Ave. NW, Suite 840
Washington, DC 20004
Tel: (202)393-7878 *Fax:* (202)638-4952
E-Mail: info@aspanet.org
Web Site: www.aspanet.org
Members: 10000 individuals
Staff: 9
Annual Budget: $1-2,000,000
Executive Director: Antoinette Samuel
Senior Director: Matt Rankin
Senior Director, Membership and Database Management: Patricia Yearwood

Historical Note
A professional society dedicated to advancing excellence in public service and public management. Membership: $40-95/year (individual); group rates available for organizations.

Meetings/Conferences:
Annual Meetings: Spring
2007 - Washington, DC(Omni Shoreham)/March 23-27/1200

Publications:
Public Administration Review. bi-m. adv.
Public Administration Times. m. adv.

American Society for Quality *(1946)*
P.O. Box 3005
Milwaukee, WI 53201-3005
Tel: (414)272-8575 *Fax:* (414)272-1734
Toll Free: (800)248 - 1946
E-Mail: help@asq.org
Web Site: www.asq.org
Members: 100,000 individuals and organizations
Staff: 225
Annual Budget: $25-50,000,000
Executive Director and Chief Strategic Officer: Paul Borawski, CAE
Managing Director: Christopher Bauman
Senior Manager, Membership Growth and Development: Jeanine Becker
Managing Director: Debra Crawford
Managing Director: Brian LeHouillier
Managing Director: Laurel Nelson-Rowe
Managing Director: Steve R. Wnuk

Historical Note
Formerly (1997) American Society for Quality Control. Founded and incorporated in New York State in 1946. ASQ is concerned with the development, promotion and application of quality-related information and technology for the quality profession, private sector, government and academia. ASQ's mission is to facilitate continuous improvement and increase customer satisfaction by identifying, communicating and promoting the use of quality principles, concepts and technologies. Has an annual budget of approximately $45 million. Membership: $291/year (individual); $691/year (sustaining); $119/year (student).

Meetings/Conferences:
Annual Meetings: May

Publications:
Six Sigma Forum Magazine. q. adv.
Journal for Quality and Participation. q.
Software Quality Professional. q.
Quality Management Journal. q.
Journal of Quality Technology. q.
Quality Progress Magazine. m. adv.
Technometrics. q.
Quality Engineer. q.

American Society for Reconstructive Microsurgery *(1983)*
20 N. Michigan Ave., Suite 700
Chicago, IL 60602
Tel: (312)456-9579 *Fax:* (312)782-0553
Web Site: www.microsurg.org
Members: 500 individuals
Staff: 4
Executive Director: Krista A. Greco
E-Mail: greco@isms.org

Meetings/Conferences:
Annual Meetings: Typical Attendance: 300
2007 - Rio Grande, PR(Westin Rio Mar)/Jan. 13-16
2008 - Los Angeles, CA(Hyatt Century Plaza)/January/300

Publications:
Newsletter. 2/yr. adv.

American Society for Reproductive Medicine
(1944)
1209 Montgomery Hwy.
Birmingham, AL 35216-2809
Tel: (205)978-5000 *Fax:* (205)978-5005
E-Mail: asrm@asrm.org
Web Site: www.asrm.org
Members: 9000 individuals
Staff: 25
Annual Budget: $5-10,000,000
Executive Director: Robert W. Rebar, M.D.

Historical Note
Founded and incorporated in 1944 in California as the American Society for the Study of Sterility; became American Fertility Society in 1966 and assumed its present name in 1994. Promotes knowledge of all aspects of reproductive medicine including fertility. Provides administrative support to specialty divisions including Society for Assisted Reproductive Technology, Society of Reproductive Endocrinologists, and Society of Reproductive Surgeons. Membership: $195/year.

Meetings/Conferences:
Annual Meetings: Fall

Publications:
Sexuality, Reproduction and Menopause. q.
Menopausal Medicine.
Fertility & Sterility. m. adv.
ASRM News. q.

American Society for Stereotactic and Functional Neurosurgery *(1968)*
c/o Cleveland Clinic Foundation
9500 Euclid Ave S-31
Cleveland, OH 44195
Tel: (415)502-3744 *Fax:* (415)753-1772
Web Site: www.assfn.org
Members: 380 individuals
Annual Budget: under $10,000
Secretary-Treasurer: Ali R. Rezai

Historical Note
Formerly (1972) the American Branch of the World Society for Research in Stereoencephalotomy. Members are surgeons using advanced localization of targets in the brain to diagnose and treat disease and injury. Has no paid officers or full-time staff.

Meetings/Conferences:
Biennial Meetings: Odd years

Publications:
Stereotactic and Functional Neurosurgery. 8/year. adv.

American Society for Surgery of the Hand *(1946)*
6300 N. River Road, Suite 600
Rosemont, IL 60018-4256
Tel: (847)384-8300 *Fax:* (847)384-1435
E-Mail: info@assh.org
Web Site: www.assh.org
Members: 2200 individuals
Staff: 14
Annual Budget: $5-10,000,000
Executive Director: Mark Anderson, CAE
E-Mail: manderson@assh.org
Director, Meetings and Education: Angie Legaspi
E-Mail: alegaspi@assh.org

Historical Note
Established in 1946. Incorporated in Ohio in 1947. Membership: $530/year.

Meetings/Conferences:
Annual Meetings: Fall/2,500

Publications:
Journal of the American Society for Surgery of the Hand. q. adv.
Journal of Hand Surgery. bi-m. adv.

American Society for the Advancement of Sedation and Anesthesia in Dentistry *(1929)*
Six E. Union Ave.
Bound Brook, NJ 08805
Tel: (732)469-9050 *Fax:* (732)271-1985
E-Mail: info@sedation4dentists.com
Web Site: www.sedation4dentists.com
Members: 650 individuals
Annual Budget: under $10,000
Executive Secretary: David Crystal, D.D.S.

Historical Note
Founded in 1929 by Dr. M. Hillel Feldman for the training of dentists in the use of nitrous oxide and oxygen. Incorporated in New Jersey in 1929. As new drugs and techniques developed, the Society studied them and expanded its role to include all aspects of pain control. Formerly (1965) the American Society for the Advancement of General Anesthesia in Dentistry. Established the International Federation of Dental Anesthetic and Sedation at the 101st International Dental Congress on Modern Dental Anesthesia in December 1976 in Monaco. Membership: $85/year (individual); $35 initiation fee (organization).

Meetings/Conferences:
Annual Meetings: Winter/New York, NY(Jacob Javitz Center)

Publications:
Pain Control in Dentistry. semi-a. adv.

American Society for the Study of Orthodontics
(1945)
Five Diamond Ct.
Huntington, NY 11743
Tel: (631)271-9220
Members: 100 individuals
Staff: 1
Annual Budget: $10-25,000
President: Dr. Milton Bloch

Historical Note
Formerly (1962) New York Society for the Study of Orthodontics.

Meetings/Conferences:
Annual Meetings: November in conjunction with the greater New York Dental Meeting.

Publications:
International Journal of Orthodontics. irreg. adv.

American Society for Theatre Research *(1956)*
P.O. Box 1798
Boulder, CO 80306-1798
Toll Free: (888)530 - 1838
Web Site: www.astr.umd.edu
Members: 750 individuals
Staff: 1
Annual Budget: $25-50,000
Administrative Director: Nancy Erickson

Historical Note
Members are scholars of the theatre. Affiliated with the International Federation for Theatre Research. Membership: $60/year (regular).

Meetings/Conferences:
Annual Meetings: November

Publications:
Theatre Survey. semi-a. adv.
Directory of Doctoral Programs in Theatre Studies.
ASTR Newsletter. semi-a.

American Society for Therapeutic Radiology and Oncology *(1958)*
12500 Fair Lakes Circle, Suite 375
Fairfax, VA 22033-3882
Tel: (703)502-1550 *Fax:* (703)502-7852
Toll Free: (800)962 - 7876
E-Mail: meetings@astro.org
Web Site: www.astro.org
Members: 8500 individuals
Staff: 35
Annual Budget: $5-10,000,000
Executive Director: Laura Thevenot

Historical Note
Formerly (1984) the American Society of Therapeutic Radiologists. Members are physicians who limit their practice to radiation therapy. Membership: $235/year (active); $1,500/year (company/institution).

Meetings/Conferences:
Annual Meetings: Fall

Publications:
Astrogram.
ASTRONews. 3/year.

American Society for Training and Development *(1944)*
1640 King St.
P.O. Box 1443
Alexandria, VA 22313-2043
Tel: (703)683-8100 *Fax:* (703)683-8103
Toll Free: (800)628 - 2783
Web Site: www.astd.org
Members: 70000 individuals
Staff: 125
Annual Budget: $10-25,000,000
President and Chief Executive Officer: Anthony Bingham
E-Mail: mmarquardt@astd.org
Vice President, Finance and Administration: Steve Earnest
Vice President, Membership and Client Services: Lance Hall
Senior Director, Public Relations and Public Policy: Jennifer Homer
E-Mail: jhomer@astd.org

Historical Note
Formerly (1964) American Society of Training Directors. ASTD is a professional society of trainers and human resource development professionals. Has an annual budget of approximately $20 million. Membership: $150/year.

Meetings/Conferences:
Annual Meetings: Spring

Publications:
Learning Circuits. q.
T & D Magazine. m. adv.
Technical & Skills Training Magazine. 8/year. adv.
INFO-LINE. m.

American Society for Virology *(1981)*
Dept. of Medical Microbiology/Immunology at the University of Toledo Health Science Campus
3000 Arlington Ave., Mail Stop #1021
Toledo, OH 43614-2598
Tel: (419)383-5173 *Fax:* (419)383-2881
E-Mail: asv@asv.org
Web Site: www.asv.org
Members: 3100 individuals
Secretary-Treasurer: Dorothea L. Sawicki

Historical Note
ASV membership is open to any researcher interested or actively engaged in the study of viruses. Membership: $100year (full); $30/year (associate); $15/year (associate student).

Meetings/Conferences:
Annual Meetings: Summer
2007 – Corvallis, OR(Oregon State University)/July 14-18/1500

Publications:
Secretary-Treasurer's Newsletter. irreg.
President's Newsletter. irreg.

American Society of Abdominal Surgeons *(1959)*
One E. Emerson St.
Melrose, MA 02176-3195
Tel: (781)665-6102 *Fax:* (781)665-4127
E-Mail: office@abdominalsurg.org
Web Site: www.abdominalsurg.org
Members: 3000 individuals
Staff: 4
Annual Budget: $250-500,000
Executive Secretary: Louis F. Alfano, Sr., M.D.
E-Mail: office@abdominalsurg.org

Historical Note
Founded and incorporated in Delaware in 1959. Membership: $175/year (individual).

Publications:
The Surgeon. 2/year.
Journal of Abdominal Surgery. a. adv.

American Society of Access Professionals *(1980)*
1444 I St. NW, Suite 700
Washington, DC 20005-6542
Tel: (202)712-9054 *Fax:* (202)216-9646
E-Mail: asap@bostromdc.com
Web Site: www.accesspro.org
Members: 300 individuals
Staff: 1
Annual Budget: $250-500,000
Executive Director: Claire Shanley

Historical Note
Members are government employees, lawyers, journalists and others concerned with access to government data under current personal privacy and public information statutes. Membership: $25/year.

Meetings/Conferences:
Annual Meetings: Always Washington, DC/Fall

Publications:
ASAP Newsletter. irreg.

American Society of Addiction Medicine *(1954)*
4601 N. Park Ave., Suite 101 Arcade
Chevy Chase, MD 20815
Tel: (301)656-3920 *Fax:* (301)656-3815
E-Mail: email@asam.org
Web Site: www.asam.org
Members: 3000 Physicians
Staff: 11
Annual Budget: $2-5,000,000
Executive Vice President and Chief Executive Officer: Eileen McGrath, JD
E-Mail: emcgrath@asam.org
Director, Membership and Chapter Relations: Nancy Brighindi
Director, Finance: Lynda Jones
E-Mail: ljone@asam.org
Director, Meetings and Conferences: Sandy Metcalfe
E-Mail: smete@asam.org
Director, Credentialing Project and Administrator, Systems: Christopher Weirs
E-Mail: cweir@asam.org

Historical Note
ASAM serves as a medium for physicians and medical students who are interested in the diseases of alcoholism and drug dependency; to extend and disseminate knowledge and research in these fields; to encourage high quality care for individuals suffering from these problems; and to enlighten and inform medical opinion with regard to these issues. Maintains a certification program in addiction medicine. Membership: $250/year (individual physician member).

Meetings/Conferences:
Annual Meetings: Spring/1,500

Publications:
ASAM Patient Placement Criteria.
Principles of Addiction Medicine.
ASAM News. bi-m. adv.
Journal of Addictive Diseases. q. adv.

American Society of Agricultural Appraisers *(1980)*
1126 Eastland Dr. N. #100
P.O. Box 186
Twin Falls, ID 83303-0186
Tel: (208)733-2323 *Fax:* (208)733-2326
Toll Free: (800)488 - 7570
E-Mail: ag@amagappraisers.com
Web Site: www.amagappraisers.com
Members: 1200 individuals
Staff: 5
Annual Budget: $500-1,000,000
President: Jay Proost

Historical Note
The Society consists of three divisions: International Society of Livestock Appraisers, American Society of Farm Equipment Appraisers, and American Society of Equine Appraisers. Provides professional certification upon sucessful completion of a divisional examination and subscription to a code of ethics. Membership: $295 initial plus $55 semi-annual renewal (association).

Publications:
Appraiser Newsletter. q.

American Society of Agricultural Consultants *(1963)*
950 S. Cherry St., Suite 508
Denver, CO 80246-2664
Tel: (303)759-5091 *Fax:* (303)758-0190
E-Mail: asac@agri-associations.org
Web Site: www.agconsultants.org
Members: 200 individuals
Staff: 3
Annual Budget: $100-250,000
Account Manager: Nancy Hardiman

Historical Note
ASAC members are professional agricultural consultants with a minimum of two years consulting experience or have completed the required number of ASAC continuing courses. Associate and allied memberships are available for individuals and with a business tie to the industry. Operates a referral service for consultants. Membership: $300/year (consultant or associate); 500/year (allied).

Publications:
Newsletter. q.
Membership Directory. a.

American Society of Agronomy *(1907)*
677 S. Segoe Rd.
Madison, WI 53711-1086
Tel: (608)273-8080 *Fax:* (608)273-2021
E-Mail: headquarters@agronomy.org
Web Site: www.agronomy.org
Members: 6408 individuals
Staff: 33
Annual Budget: $5-10,000,000
Executive Vice President: Dr. Ellen Bergfeld

Historical Note
ASA is a scientific and educational organization, dedicated to fostering research, communications education, high standards, and professionalism among people working in, or otherwise interested in agronomy and related activities. Offers individual certification for professional agronomists and crop science specialists through the American Registry of Certified Professionals in Agronomy, Crops and Soils. Membership: $83/year; $510/year (sustaining member).

Meetings/Conferences:
Annual Meetings: Fall, held in conjunction with Crop Science Society of America and with Soil Science Society of America.
2007 – New Orleans, LA(Convention Center)/Nov. 4-8
2008 – Chicago, IL(Convention Center)/Oct. 26-26/4000

Publications:
Crop Science-Soil Science-Agronomy News. m. adv.
Journal of Environmental Quality. bi-m. adv.
Journal of Natural Resources & Life Sciences Education. semi-a. adv.
Agronomy Journal. bi-m. adv.

American Society of Andrology
1111 N. Plaza Drive, Suite 550
Schaumburg, IL 60173
Tel: (847)619-4909 *Fax:* (847)517-7229
E-Mail: debbie@wjweiser.com
Members: 750 individuals
Staff: 16
Annual Budget: $250-500,000
Administrative Director: Debbie Roller
E-Mail: debbie@wjweiser.com

Historical Note
ASA members are physicians and scientists specializing in the study of the male reproductive

system. Membership: $150/year (active); $160/year (active international); $40/year (trainee).

Meetings/Conferences:

Annual Meetings: Spring
2007 – New Orleans, LA(Hyatt Regency)/Apr. 18-24/300

Publications:

Journal of Andrology. bi-m. adv.

American Society of Anesthesia Technologists and Technicians *(1989)*
P.O. Box 624
Franklin Lakes, NJ 07417
Tel: (201)337-1555 *Fax:* (201)337-5073
E-Mail: asattinfo@aol.com
Web Site: www.asatt.org
Members: 1800 individuals
Staff: 1
Annual Budget: $100-250,000
Executive Director: Sheila Guston

Historical Note

ASATT was formed to address the needs of anesthesia support personnel and promote advances in anesthesia technology.

Meetings/Conferences:

Annual Meetings: Fall

Publications:

The Sensor. 4/year. adv.

American Society of Anesthesiologists *(1905)*
520 N. Northwest Hwy.
Park Ridge, IL 60068-2573
Tel: (847)825-5586 *Fax:* (847)825-1692
E-Mail: mail@asahq.org
Web Site: www.asahq.org
Members: 39000 individuals
Staff: 59
Annual Budget: $10-25,000,000
Executive Director: Ronald A. Bruns
Director, Finance: Rick Barwacz
Assistant Executive Director: Denise M. Jones
Director, Information Services: Janice L. Plack
Director, Communications: Gina Steiner
Director, Government and Legal Affairs: Ronald Szabat

Historical Note

Organized in 1905 in Brooklyn, NY, as the Long Island Society of Anesthetists. Became the New York Society of Anesthetists in 1912; incorporated in 1936 as the American Society of Anesthetists; assumed its current name in 1945. Membership: $450/year.

Meetings/Conferences:

Annual Meetings: Fall/15,000
2007 – San Francisco, CA(Convention Center)/Oct. 13-17
2008 – Orlando, FL(Convention Center)/Oct. 18-22

Publications:

Anesthesiology. m. adv.
Newsletter. m.

American Society of Animal Science *(1908)*
1111 N. Dunlap Ave.
Savoy, IL 61874-9510
Tel: (217)356-9050 *Fax:* (217)398-4119
E-Mail: asas@assochq.org
Web Site: www.asas.org
Members: 4450 individuals
Staff: 5
Annual Budget: $1-2,000,000
Executive Director: Meghan C. Wulster-Radcliffe

Historical Note

Founded in 1908 in Chicago as the American Society of Animal Nutrition. Became the American Society of Animal Production in 1912; assumed its current name in 1941. Membership: $110/year (individual); $450/year (organization/company).

Meetings/Conferences:

Annual Meetings: Summer
2007 – San Antonio, TX/July 8-12

Publications:

Newsletter. q.
Journal of Animal Science. m.

American Society of Appraisers *(1936)*
555 Herndon Pkwy., Suite 125
Herndon, VA 20170
Toll Free: (800)272 - 8258
E-Mail: frank@appraisers.org
Web Site: www.appraisers.org
Members: 6000 individuals
Staff: 25
Annual Budget: $2-5,000,000
Executive Vice President: Jerry F. Larkins
E-Mail: jerry@appraisers.org
Director, Meetings and Conferences: Janet Coe, CMP
E-Mail: janet@appraisers.org
Director, Finance and Administration: Harriet Cutshall
Managing Director, Education, Accreditation and Information Systems: Howard C. Ducat
E-Mail: howard@appraisers.org
Director, Membership and Development: Bonny F. Price
Director, Communications: Laurie M. Saunders

Historical Note

Formed by a merger of the Society of Technical Appraisers (founded in 1939) and the American Society of Technical Appraisers, ASA incorporated in 1952. Merged with the Association of Governmental Appraisers in 1985. ASA is an international organization of appraisal professionals and others interested in the appraisal professional. The oldest major appraisal organization representing all the disciplines of appraisal specialists, ASA's pffice in Herndon, VA also serves as its international headquarters.

Meetings/Conferences:

Annual Meetings: Summer
2007 – Hollywood, CA(Renaissance)/July 22-25

Publications:

The Machinery and Technical Specialties Journal. q.
Real Property Journal. q.
Directory of Professional Appraisers. a. adv.
Business Valuation Review. q.
Personal Property Journal. q.
ASA Professional. q. adv.

American Society of Architectural Illustrators
11756 W. Hopi St.
Avondale, AZ 85323
Tel: (623)433-8782 *Fax:* (623)444-7420
E-Mail: hq@asai.org
Web Site: www.asai.org
Members: 350 individuals
Contact: Tammy Horch

Historical Note

Members are firms and individuals involved in architecture, and specifically in the art of architectural rendering as a design and presentation tool. Sponsors an annual juried competition, exhibitions, and publications. Formerly known as American Society of Architectural Perspectivists.

American Society of Artists *(1972)*
P.O. Box 1326
Palatine, IL 60078
Tel: (312)751-2500
E-Mail: asoa@webtv.net
Web Site: www.americansocietyofartists.org
Members: 30000 individuals
Staff: 14
Annual Budget: $50-100,000
President: Nancy J. Fregin

Historical Note

An organization of professional artists, which sponsors art and crafts festivals and a lecture/demonstration service and other services for members.

Publications:

ASA Artisan. q. adv.
Art Lovers' Art and Craft Fair Bulletin. q. adv.

American Society of Association Executives & Center for Association Leadership *(1920)*
1575 I St. NW
Washington, DC 20005
Tel: (202)371-0940 *Fax:* (202)371-8315
Toll Free: (888)950 - 2723
E-Mail: asae@asaecenter.org
Web Site: www.asaecenter.org
Members: 24000 individuals
Staff: 106
Annual Budget: $10-25,000,000
President and Chief Executive Officer: John H. Graham, IV
Senior Vice President, Public Policy and Strategic Relations: James L. Clarke
Vice President and Publisher: Karl Ely, CAE
General Counsel: Jerald A. Jacobs
Chief Knowledge and Strategy Officer: Greta Kotler
Vice President, Meetings and Expositions: Amy Ledoux
Public Policy and APAC Manager: Carla Lochiatto
Senior Vice President and Managing Director, Membership and Business Development: Susan Robertson
Executive Vice President, President & Chief Executive Officer for Center for Association Leadership: Susan Sarfati
Vice President, Administration: Robert Skelton

Historical Note

Founded in Lenox, Massachusetts in 1920 as American Trade Association Executives, a successor organization to the National Trade Organization Secretaries. Became American Society of Association Executives in 1956. Absorbed Greater Washington Society of Association Executives in 2004. A professional society of paid employees of associations and societies, and suppliers of products and services to the association community. ASAE offers resources on association management, including education and training, publications, technology, research, career information, networking, and professional development. Certifies association executives and awards the CAE (Certified Association Executive) designation. Sponsors the ASAE Foundation and A-PAC. Membership: $275/year (associaton C.E.O.); $245/year (association staff); $375/year (associates/suppliers).

Meetings/Conferences:

SemiAnnual Meetings: August and December

Publications:

Journal of Association Leadership.
Associations Now. m. adv.
Meetings and Expositions. m.
Membership Developments. m.
Associate Member Update. q.
Communication News. m.
AMC Forum. q.
Technoscope. bi-m.
Executive IdeaLink. m.
Marketing Forum. bi-m.
Chapter Relations. bi-m.
Who's Who in Association Management. a. adv.
International News. bi-m.
Association Law & Policy. bi-w.
Government Relations. bi-m.
Dollars & Cents. m.
Association Educator. bi-m.

American Society of Baking *(1924)*
P.O. Box 1853
Sonoma, CA 95476
Tel: (707)935-0103 *Fax:* (707)935-0174
Toll Free: (866)920 - 9885
E-Mail: asbe@asbe.org
Web Site: www.asbe.org
Members: 2700 individuals
Staff: 2
Annual Budget: $250-500,000
President: Thomas J. Kuk
Membership Coordinator: Tammi Matthews

Historical Note

Formerly (1998) American Society of Bakery Engineers. Membership: $100/year.

Meetings/Conferences:

Annual Meetings: Always in Chicago(Chicago Marriott)/March/1,300

Publications:

Newsletter. q.
Proceedings. a.
Technical Bulletins. q.

American Society of Bariatric Physicians *(1950)*
2821 S. Parker Road, Suite 625
Aurora, CO 80014
Tel: (303)770-2526 Ext: 110 *Fax:* (303)779-4834
E-Mail: info@asbp.org
Web Site: www.asbp.org
Members: 1200 individuals
Staff: 4

Annual Budget: $500-1,000,000
Executive Director: Beth A. Little
Director, Continuing Medical Education: Harold C. Seim, M.D., M.P.H., FASBP

Historical Note

Members are physicians specializing in the treatment of obesity. Membership: $450/year.

Publications:

News from ASBP. bi-m. adv.
American Journal of Bariatric Medicine, The Bariatrician. q. adv.
Membership Directory. a. adv.

American Society of Body Engineers *(1945)*

2122 Fifteen Mile Road, Suite F
Sterling Heights, MI 48310
Tel: (586)268-8360 *Fax:* (586)268-2187
E-Mail: asbe@asbe.com
Web Site: www.asbe.com
Members: 1600 individuals
Staff: 3
Annual Budget: $25-50,000
President: Bill Bonner

Historical Note

Founded as American Society of Body Engineers; became American Society of Body and Design Engineers in 1991, and reverted to its original name in 2000. Members are automotive engineers and auto body designers. Membership: $75/year (individual).

Publications:

ASBE Newsletter. bi-m.
Body Engineering Technical Journal. semi-a. adv.

American Society of Breast Disease *(1976)*

P.O. Box 140186
Dallas, TX 75214
Tel: (214)368-6836 *Fax:* (214)368-5719
Web Site: www.asbd.org
Members: 600 individuals
Annual Budget: $25-50,000
Executive Director: Brooke Breslow
E-Mail: bbreslow@asbd.org

Historical Note

Formerly (1994) the Society for the Study of Breast Disease. Members are medical doctors, nurses, social workers, psychologists and others concerned with breast diseases. Has no paid officers or full-time staff. Membership: $150/year (doctors/psychologists); $100/year (auxiliary).

Meetings/Conferences:

Annual Meetings: Spring

Publications:

ASBD Advisor. q.
The Breast Journal. bi-m. adv.
Newsletter. q.

American Society of Brewing Chemists *(1934)*

3340 Pilot Knob Road
St. Paul, MN 55121
Tel: (651)454-7250 *Fax:* (651)454-0766
E-Mail: asbc@scisoc.org
Web Site: www.asbcnet.org
Members: 846 individuals
Staff: 17
Annual Budget: $100-250,000
Executive Assistant: Marci Smith

Historical Note

A professional society of brewing chemists. Formerly the Malt Analysis Standards Committee. Membership: $405/year (individual); $215/year (U.S. corporate); $29/year (U.S. student).

Meetings/Conferences:

Annual Meetings: Spring

Publications:

Journal. q.
Newsletter. q. adv.

American Society of Business Publication Editors *(1949)*

214 N. Hale St.
Wheaton, IL 60187
Tel: (630)510-4588 *Fax:* (630)510-4501
E-Mail: info@asbpe.org
Web Site: www.asbpe.org
Members: 800 individuals
Staff: 3
Annual Budget: $100-250,000
Executive Director: Janet Svazas

Historical Note

Formerly (1964) Society of Business Magazine Editors and (2000) American Society of Business Press Editors. Membership: $75/year.

Meetings/Conferences:

Annual Meetings: Summer
2007 – New York, NY(Roosevelt Hotel)/July 31-Aug. 2

Publications:

ASBPE Editor's Notes. bi-m. adv.

American Society of Cataract and Refractive Surgery *(1974)*

4000 Legato Road, Suite 850
Fairfax, VA 22033-4003
Tel: (703)591-2220 *Fax:* (703)591-0614
E-Mail: ascrs@ascrs.org
Web Site: www.ascrs.org
Members: 9200 individuals
Staff: 43
Annual Budget: $10-25,000,000
Executive Director: David A. Karcher
Director, Communications: John Ciccone
Director, Government Relations: Nancy Kaplan McCann
Director, Meetings and Conventions: Paula Schneider
Director, Operations: Pattye Whitmer

Historical Note

Incorporated in California as the American Intraocular Implant Soc; assumed its present name in 1986. ASCRS serves to disseminate and facilitate the flow of information concerning anterior segment, cataract and refractive surgery. Membership is offered to physicians interested in anterior segment surgery and committed to the advancement of ophthalmology. Membership: $315/year.

Meetings/Conferences:

Annual Meetings: Spring/5,200
2007 – San Diego, CA/Apr. 28-May 2/7000

Publications:

Journal of Cataract and Refractive Surgery. bi-m. adv.
EyeWorld. m. adv.

American Society of Certified Engineering Technicians *(1964)*

P.O. Box 239
Wesson, MS 39191
Tel: (601)643-9079
E-Mail: tim_latham@ascet.org
Web Site: www.ascet.org
Members: 2000 individuals
Staff: 2
Annual Budget: $50-100,000
General Manager: Tim Latham

Historical Note

ASCET's membership consists of certified and non-certified engineering technicians and technologists, and registered professional engineers and land surveyors. Membership is also available to students enrolled in engineering technology degree programs belonging to an ASCET Student Chapter. Certified members have received certification verification of their skills through testing programs conducted by a number of independent certification societies. Membership: $40/year (individual); $250-500/year (organization/company).

Meetings/Conferences:

Annual Meetings: last week in June

Publications:

Certified Engineering Technician. bi-m. adv.

American Society of Church History *(1888)*

409 Prospect St., Room S-127
New Haven, CT 06511
Tel: (203)432-3158 *Fax:* (203)432-5356
E-Mail: asch@yale.edu
Web Site: www.churchhistory.org
Members: 1566
Staff: 17
Annual Budget: $50-100,000
Executive Secretary: Kenneth P. Minkema

Historical Note

Affiliated with the American Historical Association. Membership: $50/year (individual); $75/year (organization/company).

Meetings/Conferences:

Semi-Annual Meetings: January, and (alternate years) early Spring, with AHA

Publications:

Church History. q. adv.

American Society of Cinematographers *(1919)*

P.O. Box 2230
Hollywood, CA 90078
Tel: (323)969-4333 *Fax:* (323)882-6391
Toll Free: (800)448 - 0145
E-Mail: office@theasc.com
Web Site: www.theasc.com
Members: 285 individuals
Staff: 20
Annual Budget: $1-2,000,000
President: Daryn Okada

Historical Note

Membership is by invitation.

Meetings/Conferences:

Monthly Meetings: October through June

Publications:

ASC eNewsletter.
American Cinematographer Video Manual. every 4 years. adv.
American Cinematographer Magazine. m. adv.

American Society of Civil Engineers *(1852)*

1801 Alexander Bell Dr.
Reston, VA 20191-4400
Tel: (703)295-6300 *Fax:* (703)295-6222
Toll Free: (800)548 - 2723
Web Site: www.asce.org
Members: 120000 individuals
Staff: 295
Annual Budget: $25-50,000,000
Executive Director: Patrick J. Natale, PE, FNSPE
E-Mail: pnatale@asce.org
Managing Director, Membership: Wendy B. Cowan
E-Mail: cdinges@asce.org
Managing Director, Professional and Technical: Jonathan Esslinger
E-Mail: jesslinger@asce.org
Director, International Relations: Meggan Farrell
E-Mail: mfarrell@asce.org
Managing Director, Publications: Bruce Gossett
E-Mail: bgossett@asce.org
Deputy Executive Director: Larry Roth
E-Mail: cdinges@asce.org

Historical Note

Founded November 5, 1852 in New York City as the American Society of Civil Engineers and Architects. Dormant 1855-1867. Revived in 1868 as the American Society of Civil Engineers and incorporated in New York in 1877. Membership: $135/year.

Meetings/Conferences:

Annual Meetings: Fall/1,750

Publications:

ASCE Publications Abstracts. bi-m.
Civil Engineering. m. adv.
Journals of 25 Technical Divisions. m.
Transactions. a.
ASCE News. m. adv.

American Society of Clinical Hypnosis *(1957)*

140 N. Bloomingdale Road
Bloomingdale, IL 60108-1017
Tel: (630)980-4740 *Fax:* (630)351-8490
E-Mail: info@asch.net
Web Site: www.asch.net
Members: 2500 individuals
Staff: 7
Annual Budget: $500-1,000,000
Executive Vice President: John E. Kasper, Ph.D., CAE

Historical Note

Established as the American Society of Clinical Hypnosis-Education and Research Foundation in 1962. Membership: $160/year.

Meetings/Conferences:

Annual Meetings: Spring/350

Publications:

American Journal of Clinical Hypnosis. q.

ASCH Newsletter. q.

American Society of Clinical Oncology *(1964)*
1900 Duke St., Suite 200
Alexandria, VA 22314
Tel: (703)299-0150 *Fax:* (703)299-1044
E-Mail: asco@asco.org
Web Site: www.asco.org
Members: 19 individuals
Staff: 118
Annual Budget: $10-25,000,000
Interim Executive Vice President and Chief Executive Officer: Joseph M. Bailes, M.D.
Vice President and Chief Operating Officer: Ron Beller, Ph.D.
Senior Director, Communications and Patient Information: Kristin Ludwig

Historical Note
Founded November 5, 1964 and incorporated in 1965 to promote the study of neoplastic diseases, clinical research and patient care. Members are academicians in universities, medical centers, teaching and research facilities affiliated with cancer centers, major hospitals, as well as physicians in community practice. Has an annual budget of $20 million dollars. Membership: $300/year (active U.S.); $315/year (active international); $50/year (affiliate).

Meetings/Conferences:
Annual Meetings: May

Publications:
Journal of Clinical Oncology. bi-m. adv.
Proceedings. a.
ASCO News. q.
Educational Book. a.
Policy Watch. m.

American Society of Clinical Psychopharmacology *(1992)*
P.O. Box 40395
Glen Oaks, NY 11004
Tel: (718)470-4007 *Fax:* (718)343-7739
Web Site: www.ascpp.org
Members: 1100 individuals
Staff: 3
Annual Budget: $250-500,000
Administrator: Jennifer Russo

Historical Note
ASCP's is devoted to improving clinical research; educating health providers in the importance of, the proper diagnosis of and the proper treatment of mental illness; to encourage interest in and assist in the educating of medical students, psychiatric residents and fellows; and educating the public and government as to the importance of destigmatizing, understanding and treating properly mental illnesses. Membership: $100/year.

Publications:
ASCP Update Newsletter. q.
Progress Notes Journal. q.

American Society of Colon and Rectal Surgeons *(1899)*
85 W. Algonquin Road, Suite 550
Arlington Heights, IL 60005-4460
Tel: (847)290-9184 *Fax:* (847)290-9203
Web Site: www.fascrs.org
Members: 2500 individuals
Staff: 8
Annual Budget: $1-2,000,000
Executive Director: James R. Slawny
Director, Registration/Exhibits Manager: Dianne K. Kubis

Historical Note
Founded in Columbus, Ohio in 1899 as the American Proctologic Society with 12 charter members. Incorporated in Delaware in 1947. Name changed in 1973 to the American Society of Colon and Rectal Surgeons. Sponsored the formation of the American Board of Colon and Rectal Surgery and in 1957 founded the American Society of Colon and Rectal Surgeons Research Foundation. Membership: $225/year (individual).

Meetings/Conferences:
Annual Meetings: Spring
2007 – St. Louis, MO
2008 – Boston, MA/June 7-11/1800
2009 – Hollywood, FL/May 2-6/1800

Publications:
Diseases of the Colon and Rectum. m. adv.

American Society of Comparative Law *(1951)*
Washington University School of Law
One Brookings Dr., Campus Box 1120
St. Louis, MO 63130
Tel: (314)935-6411 *Fax:* (314)935-5356
Web Site: www.comparativelaw.org
Members: 102 organizations
Annual Budget: $50-100,000
Secretary: Leila Sadat

Historical Note
Formerly (1992) American Association for the Comparative Study of Law. Has no paid officers or full time staff. Membership: $700/year (organization/company).

Publications:
American Journal of Comparative Law. q. adv.

American Society of Composers, Authors and Publishers *(1914)*
One Lincoln Plaza
New York, NY 10023
Tel: (212)621-6000 *Fax:* (212)724-9064
E-Mail: info@ascap.com
Web Site: www.ascap.com
Members: 260000 individuals
Staff: 550
Annual Budget: Over $100,000,000
Chief Executive Officer: John LoFrumento
President/Chairman of the Board: Marilyn Bergman
Executive Vice President and Director, Membership: Todd Brabec
Senior Vice President, Industry Affairs: Karen Sherry

Historical Note
America's first performing rights society, ASCAP was organized in 1914 by composer Victor Herbert and eight of his colleagues. The goal of ASCAP was to license all commercial users of copyrighted music so that the musical creative talent of this country and their publishers might receive just financial returns. Has an annual budget of approximately $500 million. Membership: $10/year (writers); $50/year (publishers).

Publications:
Inside Music. m.
Playback. bi-m. adv.

American Society of Concrete Contractors *(1964)*
2025 S. Brentwood Blvd.
St. Louis, MO 63144
Tel: (314)962-0210 *Fax:* (314)968-4367
Toll Free: (866)788 - 2722
E-Mail: ascc@ascconline.org
Web Site: www.ascconline.org
Members: 525 companies and individuals
Staff: 5
Annual Budget: $1-2,000,000
Executive Director: Bev Garnant

Historical Note
Formerly (1998) American Society for Concrete Construction. ASCC is a non-profit corporation founded in 1964 to enhance the capabilities of those who build in concrete. Members of ASCC are concrete contractors, decorative concrete contractors, material suppliers, equipment manufacturers, and others involved in concrete construction. ASCC provides an extensive Safety Program, concrete and safety hotlines, safety videos, safety bulletins, troubleshooting newsletters, and The Contractor's Guide to Quality Concrete Construction. Membership: dues based on annual sales volume $450-995/year (contractor companies); $250-2000/year (all other member categories).

Meetings/Conferences:
Semi-Annual Meetings: Winter and Summer

Publications:
Membership Bulletin. m.
Insurance Bulletin. 3-4/year.
Technical Bulletin.
Position Statements.
Membership Directory. a. adv.
Contractor's Guide to Quality Concrete Construction.
Employee Safety Handbook for Concrete Contractors.
Safety Manual for Concrete Construction.
Troubleshooting Newsletter. 2/year.
Safety Bulletin. 3-4/year.

American Society of Consultant Pharmacists *(1969)*
1321 Duke St.
Alexandria, VA 22314
Tel: (703)739-1300 *Fax:* (703)739-1321
Toll Free: (800)355 - 2727
E-Mail: info@ascp.org
Web Site: www.ascp.com
Members: 7000 individuals
Staff: 45
Annual Budget: $5-10,000,000
Executive Director: John Feather, Ph.D., CAE
E-Mail: jfeather@ascp.org
Director, Meetings and Conventions: Jackie Hajji
E-Mail: jfeather@ascp.org
Chief Financial Officer: Doug McAdoo
E-Mail: dmcadoo@ascp.com
Associate Executive Director and Chief Operating Officer: Phyllis Moret
Senior Director, Administration and Membership: Cheryl Rothbart
E-Mail: crothbarth@ascp.com
Director, Communications and Marketing: Linda Williams
E-Mail: jfeather@ascp.org

Historical Note
Pharmacists specializing in service to long-term care facilities and geriatric institutions. Sponsors and supports the ASCP Political Action Committee. Has an annual budget of approximately $7 million. Membership: $185/year (individual); $2,000/year (company).

Meetings/Conferences:
Annual Meetings: November

Publications:
Update Newsletter. bi-m.
Consultant Pharmacist Journal. m. adv.

American Society of Consulting Arborists *(1967)*
15245 Shady Grove Road, Suite 130
Rockville, MD 20850-3222
Tel: (301)947-0483 *Fax:* (301)990-9771
E-Mail: asca@mgmtsol.com
Web Site: www.asca-consultants.org
Members: 364 individuals
Staff: 4
Annual Budget: $250-500,000
Executive Director: Beth W. Palys, CAE

Historical Note
A professional society of individuals skilled in diagnosing problems and appraising the value of shade and ornamental trees. Membership: $225/year.

Meetings/Conferences:
Annual Meetings: Winter

Publications:
Arboricultural Consultant. q.

American Society of Consulting Planners *(1966)*

Historical Note
An affiliate of American Planning Association, which provides administrative support.

American Society of Contemporary Ophthalmology *(1977)*
7250 N. Cicero Ave., LL-6
Lincolnwood, IL 60712
Tel: (847)677-9093 *Fax:* (847)677-9094
Toll Free: (800)621 - 4002
E-Mail: iaos@aol.com
Members: 500 individuals
Staff: 3
Director: Randall T. Bellows, M.D.

Historical Note
Formerly (1989) the International Glaucoma Congress. Administrative support provided by the American Society of Contemporary Medicine and Surgery. Affiliated with the American College of Medicine. The International Glaucoma Congress is a division of ASCO. Membership: $275/year.

Meetings/Conferences:
Annual Meetings: In conjunction with the ASCMS and the ACM/Spring

Publications:
Annals of Ophthalmology. q. adv.

American Society of Crime Laboratory Directors *(1974)*
139-K Technology Dr.
Garner, NC 27529
Tel: (919)773-2044 *Fax:* (919)773-2602
Web Site: www.ascld.org
Members: 350 individuals
Annual Budget: under $10,000
President: Earl Wells
Meetings/Conferences:
Annual Meetings: usually Fall
Publications:
Membership Directory. a.
Newsletter. q.

American Society of Criminology *(1941)*
1314 Kinnear Road
Columbus, OH 43212-1156
Tel: (614)292-9207 *Fax:* (614)292-6767
E-Mail: asc41@infinet.com
Web Site: www.asc41.com
Members: 3200 individuals
Staff: 2
Annual Budget: $250-500,000
Administrator: Sarah M. Hall
Historical Note
Established in Berkeley, California as the Society for the Advancement of Criminology, it absorbed the Association of College Police Training Officials in 1947 and assumed its present name in 1956. Affiliated with the American Association for the Advancement of Science. Members are criminologists, psychologists, sociologists and students in institutions of higher learning. Membership: $30/year (student); $60/year (active); $125/year (institution).
Meetings/Conferences:
Annual Meetings: November/1,000+
Publications:
The Criminologist. bi-m. adv.
Criminology: An Interdisciplinary Journal. q. adv.

American Society of Cytopathology *(1951)*
400 W. Ninth St., Suite 201
Wilmington, DE 19801
Tel: (302)429-8802 *Fax:* (302)429-8807
E-Mail: asc@cytopathology.org
Web Site: www.cytopathology.org
Members: 3400 individuals
Staff: 6
Annual Budget: $500-1,000,000
Meeting Manager: Christy A. Myers
E-Mail: cmyers@cytopathology.org
Historical Note
Founded in 1951 as the Inter-Society Cytology Council. Incorporated in Delaware in 1966. Became American Society of Cytology in 1961; assumed current name in 1994. ASC members are physicians, cytotechnologists, and scientists employing the cytologic method of diagnostic pathology. Membership: $232/year (individual).
Meetings/Conferences:
Annual Meetings: November
2007 – Houston, TX(Hilton)/Nov. 2-7/900
2008 – Orlando, FL(Wyndham Palace Resort & Spa)/Nov. 7-9/900
2009 – Denver, CO(Hyatt Regency)/Nov. 13-18/900
Publications:
The ASC Bulletin. 8/year. adv.

American Society of Dermatological Retailers *(1989)*
320 Superior Ave., #395
Newport Beach, CA 92663-3501
Tel: (949)646-9098 *Fax:* (949)646-7298
Toll Free: (800)469 - 3739
E-Mail: dermdoc58@aol.com
Members: 10 individuals
Staff: 2
Annual Budget: $25-50,000
Medical Director: Jeffrey Lauber, M.D.
E-Mail: dermdoc58@aol.com
Historical Note
ASDR members are board-certified dermatologists concerned with marketing standards for skin care products.
Publications:
Skin Saver Newsletter. bi-m. adv.
Contemporary Products. bi-m. adv.

American Society of Dermatology *(1946)*
2721 Capital Ave.
Sacramento, CA 95816-6004
Tel: (916)446-5054 *Fax:* (916)446-0500
E-Mail: jeremy@aapsonline.org
Web Site: www.asd.org
Staff: 2
Executive Director: M. John Hanni, Jr., CAE
Historical Note
ASD is dedicated to preserving the practice of dermatology, freedom in medicine and economic freedom.

American Society of Dermatopathology *(1962)*
60 Revere Dr., Suite 500
Northbrook, IL 60062
Tel: (847)400-5820 *Fax:* (847)480-9282
E-Mail: info@asdp.org
Web Site: www.asdp.org
Members: 1100 individuals
Staff: 6
Annual Budget: $250-500,000
Executive Director: Leah McCrackin
E-Mail: info@asdp.org
Historical Note
Members are pathologists or dermatologists who have extra training or expertise in the study of skin biopsies. Membership: $250/year.
Meetings/Conferences:
Annual Meetings: Fall
Publications:
Journal of Cutaneous Pathology. m. adv.

American Society of Directors of Volunteer Services *(1968)*
One N. Franklin, 27th Floor
Chicago, IL 60606
Tel: (312)422-3939 *Fax:* (312)422-4575
E-Mail: asdvs@aha.org
Web Site: www.asdvs.org
Members: 1500 individuals
Staff: 4
Annual Budget: $250-500,000
Executive Director: Audrey Harris
Historical Note
Sponsored by the American Hospital Association. Members are directors of volunteer resources in hospitals and other health care institutions. Membership: $95/year.
Meetings/Conferences:
Annual Meetings: Fall
Publications:
Volunteer Services Administration. bi-m.
Newsletter for Society Members. q.

American Society of Echocardiography *(1975)*
1500 Sunday Dr., Suite 102
Raleigh, NC 27607-5163
Tel: (919)861-5574 *Fax:* (919)787-4916
E-Mail: ase@asecho.org
Web Site: www.asecho.org
Members: 9700 individuals
Staff: 14
Annual Budget: $2-5,000,000
Executive Director: Robin Wiegerink
Historical Note
Members are physicians, cardiac sonographers, and engineering scientists concerned with ultrasound diagnosis of heart disease. Incorporated in the state of Indiana. Membership: $75-120/year (individual).
Meetings/Conferences:
Annual Meetings: Summer
Publications:
Journal of the American Society of Echocardiography. m. adv.

American Society of Electroneurodiagnostic Technologists *(1959)*
6501 E. Commerce Ave., Suite 120
Kansas City, MO 64120
Tel: (816)931-1120 *Fax:* (816)931-1145
E-Mail: info@aset.org
Web Site: www.aset.org
Members: 2900 individuals
Staff: 5
Annual Budget: $500-1,000,000
Executive Director: Sheila R. Navis, CAE
Historical Note
Formerly (1987) the American Society of Electroencephalographic Technologists. ASET members include technologists, students, lab managers, physicians and institutions involved in EEG, evoked potentials, polysomnography, nerve conduction studies, intraoperative monitoring, and related electroneurodiagnostics. Membership: $80/year (individual); $350/year (organization/company).
Meetings/Conferences:
Annual Meetings: Summer
2007 – Orlando, FL/July 18-21/500
Publications:
ASET Newsletter. q.
Who's Who in Electroneurodiagnostics. a. adv.
American Journal of Electroneurodiagnostic Technology. q. adv.

American Society of Emergency Radiology *(1988)*
4550 Post Oak Place, Suite 342
Houston, TX 77027
Tel: (713)965-0566 *Fax:* (713)960-0488
E-Mail: aser@meetingmanagers.com
Web Site: www.erad.org
Members: 430 individuals
Acct. Executive: Sheryl Trotz
Historical Note
ASER members are health professionals with an interest in advancing and improving radiological aspects of emergency patient care.
Meetings/Conferences:
Annual Meetings: Fall
Publications:
Emergency Radiology Journal.

American Society of Equine Appraisers
Historical Note
A division of the American Society of Agricultural Appraisers.

American Society of Extra-Corporeal Technology *(1964)*
1512 Millikens Bend Road
Herndon, VA 20170-2829
Tel: (703)435-8556 *Fax:* (703)435-0056
Web Site: www.amsect.org
Members: 3000 individuals
Staff: 5
Annual Budget: $500-1,000,000
Executive Director: Stewart A. Hinckley, CMP
Director, Government Relations: Bob Reinshuttle
E-Mail: reinshuttle@comcast.net
Director, Membership Services: Joye Steward
E-Mail: joye@amsect.org
Historical Note
Perfusionists operate heart-lung machines. Formerly (until 1968) the American Society of Extracorporeal Circulation Technicians.
Meetings/Conferences:
Annual Meetings: Spring
Publications:
Journal of Extra-Corporeal Technology. q.
AmSect Today. 11/year. adv.

American Society of Farm Managers and Rural Appraisers *(1929)*
950 S. Cherry St., Suite 508
Denver, CO 80246-2664
Tel: (303)758-3513 *Fax:* (303)758-0190
E-Mail: asfmra@asfmra.org
Web Site: www.asfmra.org
Members: 2700 individuals
Staff: 10
Annual Budget: $1-2,000,000
Executive Vice President: Brian Stockman

Manager, Information Systems, Public Relations and Communications: Cheryl Cooley

Historical Note

ASFMRA members are agricultural professionals with an interest in understanding the interaction between the land and the forces that influence its markets and products. Awards the AAC (Accredited Agricultural Consultant), AFM (Accredited Farm Manager), ARA (Accredited Rural Appraiser), and RPRA (Real Property Review Appraiser) designations to members that meet field experience, educational, and ethical requirements. Membership: $200-500/year.

Meetings/Conferences:

2007 - Atlanta, GA(Hyatt)/Feb. 14-17

Publications:

Membership Directory. a.
Journal of the ASFMRA. a.
Newsletter. bi-m.

American Society of Forensic Odontology *(1975)*

P.O. Box 1989
Eureka, MT 59917
Tel: (250)426-2354 *Fax:* (250)426-7282
E-Mail: docben@cyberlink.bc.ca
Web Site: www.asfo.org
Members: 1200 individuals
Annual Budget: $10-25,000
Executive Director: Susan K. Rivera
E-Mail: docben@cyberlink.bc.ca

Historical Note

Founded to further the study of forensic dentistry. Members are dentists and others interested in the study of teeth for identification purposes, particularly in relation to malpractice, child abuse, and bite mark identification. Has no paid officers or full-time staff. Membership: $50/year.

Meetings/Conferences:

Annual Meetings: usually in conjunction with the American Academy of Forensic Sciences.

Publications:

Manual of Forensic Odontology. irreg.
Newsletter. 3/year.

American Society of Furniture Designers *(1981)*

144 Woodland Dr.
New London, NC 28127
Tel: (910)576-1273 *Fax:* (910)576-1573
E-Mail: info@asfd.com
Web Site: www.asfd.com
Members: 200 individuals and corporations
Staff: 1
Annual Budget: $25-50,000
Executive Director: Christine Evans

Historical Note

Founded in High Point, NC, ASFD is the only nationwide, non-profit membership organization for furniture designers. Membership: $225/year (individual); $600/year (organization/company).

Meetings/Conferences:

Semi-Annual Meetings: usually High Point, NC/April & October

Publications:

Pinnacle Awards Pressbook. a.
Bulletin. m.
Membership Directory. a.

American Society of Gas Engineers *(1954)*

2805 Barranca Parkway
Irvine, CA 92606
Tel: (949)733-4304 *Fax:* (949)733-4320
Web Site: www.asge-national.org
Members: 300 individuals
Staff: 1
Annual Budget: $10-25,000
Executive Director: Jerry Moore
E-Mail: jerry.moore@csa-international.org

Historical Note

Formerly (1973) Gas Appliance Engineers Society. Membership: $30-50/year (individual).

Meetings/Conferences:

2007 - Las Vegas, NV(Red Rock)/June 14-16/100

Publications:

ASGE News. q.

American Society of Gene Therapy *(1996)*

555 E. Wells St., Suite 1100
Milwaukee, WI 53202
Tel: (414)278-1341 *Fax:* (414)276-3349
E-Mail: info@asgt.org
Web Site: www.asgt.org
Members: 2800 individuals
Staff: 5
Executive Director: Elizabeth Dooley, CAE
E-Mail: edooley@asgt.org
Senior Meetings Manager: Nadine Kinnunen

Meetings/Conferences:

Annual Meetings: Summer
2007 - Seattle, WA(Convention Center)/May 30-June 3
2008 - Boston, MA(Hynes Convention Center)/May 28-June 1

American Society of General Surgeons *(1993)*

P.O. Box 4834
Englewood, CO 80155
Tel: (303)771-5948 *Fax:* (303)771-2550
E-Mail: asgs-info@theasgs.org
Web Site: www.theasgs.org
Members: 3600 individuals
Staff: 2
Annual Budget: $250-500,000
Executive Director: L. Jack Carow, III

Historical Note

ASGS members are board certified general surgeons and subspecialists who perform general surgery. Membership: $125/year (active); $50/year (candidate/corresponding); $25/year (resident); $100/year (senior).

Publications:

Surgfax. m.
Legislative Hotline.

American Society of Geolinguistics *(1965)*

CUNY, Baruch College, Dept. of Modern Languages
17 Lexington Ave., Box B6-280
New York, NY 10010-5585
Tel: (646)312-4220 *Fax:* (646)312-4211
Members: 110 individuals
Annual Budget: under $10,000
Secretary: Wayne H. Finke, Ph.D.
E-Mail: wayne_finke@baruch.cuny.edu

Historical Note

The Society was founded by Mario A. Pei of Columbia University in 1965. ASG gathers and disseminates up-to-date knowledge concerning the world's present-day languages; their distribution and population use; their relative practical importance, usefulness and availability from the economic, political and cultural standpoints; their genetic, historical and geographic affiliations and relationships; and their identification and use in spoken and written form. Has no paid staff. ASG is particularly interested in linguistic geography, languages in contact and conflict, language education and politics, language planning and macro-sociolinguistics. Membership fee: $35/year (regular); $25/year (retired/student); $40/year (organization/company).

Publications:

Geolinguistics. a.

American Society of Golf Course Architects *(1946)*

125 N. Executive Dr., Suite 106
Brookfield, WI 53005
Tel: (262)786-5960 *Fax:* (262)786-5919
E-Mail: info@asgca.org
Web Site: www.asgca.org
Members: 177 individuals
Staff: 3
Annual Budget: $25-50,000
Executive Secretary: Chad Ritterbusch

Meetings/Conferences:

Annual Meetings: Spring
2007 - Atlanta, GA(Westin Buckhead)/Apr. 28-May 2

Publications:

Suppliers Directory. a. adv.

American Society of Group Psychotherapy and Psychodrama *(1942)*

301 N. Harrison St., Suite 508
Princeton, NJ 08540
Tel: (609)452-1339 *Fax:* (732)605-7033
E-Mail: asgpp@asgpp.org
Web Site: www.asgpp.org
Members: 500 individuals
Staff: 1
Annual Budget: $100-250,000
Executive Director: Eduardo Garcia
E-Mail: asgpp@asgpp.org

Historical Note

Membership includes psychiatrists, psychologists, social workers, doctors, psychodramatists, sociologists and nurses. Membership: $50-100/year.

Meetings/Conferences:

Annual Meetings: Spring

Publications:

Journal of Action Methods, Psychodrama, Skill Training & Role Playing. q.
Psychodrama Network News. q. adv.
Membership Directory. a. adv.

American Society of Hair Restoration Surgery

737 N. Michigan Ave., Suite 2100
Chicago, IL 60611-5405
Tel: (312)981-6760 *Fax:* (312)981-6787
E-Mail: info@cosmeticsurgery.org
Web Site: www.cosmeticsurgery.org
Members: 300 individuals
Staff: 8
Executive Vice President: Jeffrey P. Knezovich, CAE

Historical Note

Affiliated with the Academy of Cosmetic Surgery.

Meetings/Conferences:

Annual Meetings: Winter
2007 - Phoenix, AZ(Biltmore Resort)/Jan. 25-28/800
2008 - Orlando, FL(Shinglecreek Resort)/Jan. 23-27/800

American Society of Hand Therapists *(1977)*

401 N. Michigan Ave., Suite 2200
Chicago, IL 60611-4267
Tel: (312)321-6866 *Fax:* (312)673-6670
E-Mail: asht@smithbucklin.com
Web Site: www.asht.org
Members: 2800 individuals
Staff: 7
Annual Budget: $500-1,000,000
Director, Operations and Member Services: Chelli Johnson

Historical Note

Members are registered or licensed occupational or physical therapists specializing in working with patients with hand problems. Membership: $225/year (individual).

Meetings/Conferences:

Annual Meetings: Fall
2007 - Phoenix, AZ/Oct. 4-7

Publications:

ASHT Times. bi-m.. adv.
Journal of Hand Therapy. q. adv.
Membership Directory. a. adv.

American Society of Head and Neck Radiology *(1976)*

2210 Midwest Rd., Suite 207
Oak Brook, IL 60523-8205
Tel: (630)574-0220 Ext: 226 *Fax:* (630)574-0661
Web Site: www.ashnr.org
Members: 410 individuals
Annual Budget: $250-500,000
Business Manager: Ken Cammarata
E-Mail: kcammarata@asnr.org

Historical Note

ASHNR members are physicians who are board certified in general radiology with an interest in the field of head and neck radiology. Membership: $175/year (individual).

Meetings/Conferences:

Annual Meetings: Fall
2007 - Seattle, WA(The Fairmont Olympic Hotel)/Sept. 26-30
2008 - Toronto, ON, Canada(Torono Hilton)/Sept. 10-14
2009 - New Orleans, LA(Sheraton)/Sept. 9-13

Publications:

ASHNR Newsletter. 3/yr.
American Journal of Neuroradiology. 10/yr.

American Society of Health-System Pharmacists *(1942)*
7272 Wisconsin Ave.
Bethesda, MD 20814-1439
Tel: (301)657-3000 *Fax:* (301)664-8877
E-Mail: evp@ashp.org
Web Site: www.ashp.org
Members: 30000 individuals
Staff: 200
Annual Budget: $25-50,000,000
Executive Vice President/Chief Executive Officer: Dr. Henri R. Manasse
E-Mail: evp@ashp.org
Vice President, Finance: Dave Edwards
E-Mail: evp@ashp.org
Senior Vice President, Operations: Stan Lowe
E-Mail: evp@ashp.org
Director, Government Affairs: Brian Meyer
E-Mail: evp@ashp.org
Director, Meeting Administration: Tana Stellato
E-Mail: evp@ashp.org
Director, Education Services: Judy Walter
E-Mail: evp@ashp.org
Corporate Counsel: Fern Zappala
E-Mail: evp@ashp.org
Deputy Executive Vice President: William Zellmer, M.P.H.
E-Mail: evp@ashp.org

Historical Note
Formerly (1994) American Society of Hospital Pharmacists. Founded in 1942 as an outgrowth of the Sub-Section of Hospital Pharmacy of the American Pharmaceutical Association. Incorporated in the District of Columbia in 1955, and reincorporated in Maryland in 1984. Sponsors and supports the American Society of Health-System Pharmacists Research and Education Foundation and the ASHP Political Action Committee. Has an annual budget of approximately $30 million.

Meetings/Conferences:
Semi-Annual Meetings: June and December

Publications:
ASHP News and Views. m.
AHFS Drug Information. a.
American Journal of Health-System Pharmacy. bi-w. adv.
International Pharmaceutical Abstracts. bi-m.

American Society of Heating, Refrigerating and Air-Conditioning Engineers *(1894)*
1791 Tullie Cir. NE
Atlanta, GA 30329
Tel: (404)636-8400 *Fax:* (404)321-5478
Toll Free: (800)527 - 4723
E-Mail: ashrae@ashrae.org
Web Site: www.ashrae.org
Members: 55000 individuals
Staff: 100
Annual Budget: $10-25,000,000
Executive Vice President and Secretary: Jeff Littleton
Director, Communications/Education: W. Stephen Comstock
Director, Technology: Bruce Hunn
Director, Member Services: Carolyn K. Kettering
Program Director, Government Affairs: Doug Read
Comptroller/Director, Administrative Services: Cindy Simmons

Historical Note
Organized in 1894 and incorporated in 1895 as the American Society of Heating and Ventilating Engineers. Became the American Society of Heating and Air-Conditioning Engineers in 1954. Merged in 1959 with the American Society of Refrigerating Engineers (established 1904) to form the American Society of Heating, Refrigerating and Air-Conditioning Engineers. Maintains a Washington office. Has an annual budget of approximately $18 million. Membership: $150/year (individual).

Meetings/Conferences:
2007 – Dallas, TX/Jan. 29-31

Publications:
HVAC&R Research Journal. q.
ASHRAE Journal. m. adv.
ASHRAE Transactions. semi-a.
ASHRAE Handbook. a.
ASHRAE Insights. m.

American Society of Hematology *(1958)*
1900 M St. NW, Suite 200
Washington, DC 20036
Tel: (202)776-0544 *Fax:* (202)776-0545
E-Mail: ash@hematology.org
Web Site: www.hematology.org
Members: 14800 individuals
Staff: 60
Annual Budget: $10-25,000,000
Executive Director: Martha L. Liggett
Director, Finance: Tiffany Ake
Director, Government Relations: Mila Becker
Director, Communications: Jenifer Hamilton
Director, Meetings: Ayuko Kimura-Fay
Acting Director, Education and Training: Michelle Klinke
Director, Membership: Michelle Moody
Director, Journal Publishing: Eleanor Tapscott

Historical Note
Membership: $195/year renewal (active membership); $225/year renewal (foreign).

Meetings/Conferences:
Annual Meetings: December
2007 – Atlanta, GA/Dec. 8-11

Publications:
Blood. bi-m. adv.
The Hematologist. 6/year.
Membership Directory. a.

American Society of Highway Engineers *(1958)*
113 Heritage Hills Road
Uniontown, PA 15401
Tel: (724)929-2760 *Fax:* (724)929-2234
E-Mail: info@highwayengineers.org
Web Site: www.highwayengineers.org
Members: 6000 individuals
Secretary: Terence D. Conner, P.E.
E-Mail: info@highwayengineers.org

Historical Note
ASHE was incorporated in Pennsylvania in 1958 with the conception and inception of the first chartered section credited to a small group of dedicated engineers from the Pennsylvania Department of Highways, in association with a group of outstanding contractors, material suppliers and consulting engineers in the Harrisburg area.

Meetings/Conferences:
Annual Meetings: Spring

Publications:
Scanner. q.

American Society of Home Inspectors *(1976)*
932 Lee St., Suite 101
Des Plaines, IL 60016-6546
Tel: (847)759-2820 *Fax:* (847)759-1620
Toll Free: (800)743 - 2744
E-Mail: hq@ashi.org
Web Site: www.ashi.org
Members: 6000 individuals
Staff: 14
Annual Budget: $2-5,000,000
Executive Director: Robert J. Paterkiewicz, CAE
Director, Communications: Sandy Bourseau
Director, Sales and Operations: Russell Daniels
Director, Chapter Relations and State Affairs: Bob Kociolek
Director, IT: Joe Kusiak
Director, Conferences and Meetings: Angela Orlando
Director, Membership and Marketing: Anthony Snyder

Historical Note
Sets standards for inspection professionals based on technical merit and experience. ASHI members are professional home inspectors; AHSI has 3,000 full members and 3,500 candidates. Membership: $300/year (candidate); $275/year (member).

Meetings/Conferences:
Annual Meetings: Mid-January

Publications:
ASHI Reporter. m. adv.
Annual Conference Proceedings. a.

American Society of Human Genetics *(1948)*
9650 Rockville Pike
Bethesda, MD 20814-3998
Tel: (301)634-7300 *Fax:* (301)530-7079
Toll Free: (866)486 - 4363
E-Mail: society@ashg.org
Web Site: www.faseb.org/genetics
Members: 6000 individuals
Staff: 10
Annual Budget: $1-2,000,000
Executive Director: Elaine Strass
Manager, Membership: Barbara Abbott
Executive Vice President: Dr. Joann A. Boughman
Exhibits Manager: Toney Vogel

Historical Note
Incorporated in North Carolina in 1952 and reincorporated in Maryland in 1985. ASHG provides leadership in research, education and service in human genetics. Membership: $120/year (regular); $60/year (student).

Meetings/Conferences:
Annual Meetings: Fall
2007 – San Diego, CA/Oct. 23-27
2008 – Philadelphia, PA/Nov. 12-15
2009 – Honolulu, HI/Oct. 20-24
2010 – San Antonio, TX/Oct. 5-9
2011 – Montreal, QC, Canada(ICHG)/Oct. 11-15
2012 – San Fransico, CA/Nov. 6-10
2013 – Boston, MA/Oct. 22-26

Publications:
Membership Directory. bien.
American Journal of Human Genetics. m. adv.

American Society of Hypertension *(1985)*
148 Madison Ave., Fifth Floor
New York, NY 10016
Tel: (212)696-9099 *Fax:* (212)696-0711
E-Mail: ash@ash-us.org
Web Site: www.ash-us.org
Members: 3200 individuals
Staff: 10
Annual Budget: $250-500,000
Executive Director: Torry Mark Sansone
E-Mail: tsansone@ash-us.org
Associate Executive Director: Melissa Levine

Historical Note
ASH members are individuals who have undertaken and accomplished meritorious original scientific investigation in the field of hypertension and/or related cardiovascular disease, and/or those involved in the diagnosis and treatment of hypertension and related cardiovascular disease. Professionals, paraprofessionals and students with a demonstrated interest in the field are eligible for associate membership. Membership: $150/year (full); $75/year (associate); $175/year (foreign); $15,000/year (corporate).

Meetings/Conferences:
Annual Meetings: Spring/2,600

American Society of Ichthyologists and Herpetologists *(1913)*
Biological Sciences Dept., Florida Internat'l Univ.
11200 S.W. Eighth St.
North Miami, FL 33199
Tel: (305)348-1235 *Fax:* (305)348-1986
E-Mail: asih@fiu.edu
Web Site: www.asih.org
Members: 2600 individuals
Annual Budget: $100-250,000
Secretary: Maureen A. Donnelly, PhD

Historical Note
Incorporated in the District of Columbia. Purpose is to advance the study of fishes, amphibians and reptiles. Has no paid officers or full-time staff; the Secretary stays in office 3-5 years. Membership: fees vary.

Meetings/Conferences:
Annual Meetings: Summer

Publications:
Copeia. q.

American Society of Indexers *(1968)*
10200 W. 44th Ave., Suite 304
Wheat Ridge, CO 80033
Tel: (303)463-2887 *Fax:* (303)422-8894
E-Mail: info@asindexing.org
Web Site: www.asindexing.org
Members: 900 individuals
Staff: 1
Annual Budget: $100-250,000
Executive Director: Jerry Bowman

Historical Note
Founded in 1968, ASI is a nonprofit organization that promotes excellence in indexing and provides information, guidance and aid to indexers. Members include freelance and salaried indexers, abstracters, librarians, editors, publishers and organizations employing indexers. Membership: $120/year (individual); $85/year (student); $250/year (organization).

Publications:
Key Words Newsletter. bi-m. adv.

American Society of Interior Designers *(1975)*
608 Massachusetts Ave. NE
Washington, DC 20002
Tel: (202)546-3480 *Fax:* (202)546-3240
E-Mail: asid@asid.org
Web Site: www.asid.org
Members: 38000 individuals and corporations
Staff: 41
Annual Budget: $10-25,000,000
Executive Director: Michael Alin
Deputy Executive Director: Thomas Banks
Director, Communications and Knowledge Resources: Michael Berens
Associate Executive Director: Kirstin Hellwig
Director, Finance and Administration: Rick Peluso
Director, Government and Public Affairs: Deanna Waldron
Director, Education: Jenifer Wilcox

Historical Note
Product of a consolidation of the American Institute of Interior Designers (1931) and the National Society of Interior Designers (1957). ASID is a leading professional association representing the interests of interior designers. Mission is to advise the interior design profession through knowledge generation and sharing advocacy of interior designers' right to practice professional and public education, and expansion of interior design markets.

Meetings/Conferences:
Annual Meetings: Winter-Spring
2007 - San Francisco, CA/March 15-18

Publications:
ASID Icon. 6/year. adv.
ASID Resources Guide and Industry Partner Directory. a. adv.

American Society of International Law *(1906)*
2223 Massachusetts Ave., N.W.
Washington, DC 20008-2864
Tel: (202)939-6000 *Fax:* (202)797-7133
E-Mail: services@asil.org
Web Site: www.ASIL.org
Members: 4000 individuals
Staff: 17
Annual Budget: $1-2,000,000
Executive Director: Charlotte Ku

Historical Note
Organized in 1906 and incorporated in 1950 by a special act of Congress. Promotes international relations on the basis of law and justice. Membership: $150/year (individual); $2,000/year (organization).

Meetings/Conferences:
Annual Meetings: Spring/700

Publications:
Newsletter. bi-m. adv.
International Legal Materials. 5/year. adv.
Proceedings of the ASIL. a. adv.
American Journal of International Law. q. adv.
Studies in Transnational Legal Policy. irreg.

American Society of Irrigation Consultants *(1970)*
P.O. Box 426
Rochester, MA 02770
Tel: (508)763-8140 *Fax:* (508)763-8102
E-Mail: info@asic.org
Web Site: www.asic.org
Members: 300 individuals
Staff: 3
Annual Budget: $25-50,000
Executive Director: Norman F. Bartlett

Historical Note
ASIC was established to advance education and skills and to exchange data, knowledge and experience related to landscape irrigation. Members are irrigation consultants, suppliers, and manufacturers involved in landscape irrigation. Membership: $300/year (associate); $300/year (professional).

Meetings/Conferences:
Annual Meetings: Spring

Publications:
ASIC Waterfront. q.
Newsletter. m.

American Society of Journalists and Authors *(1948)*
1501 Broadway, Suite 302
New York, NY 10036
Tel: (212)997-0947 *Fax:* (212)937-2315
E-Mail: execdir@asja.org
Web Site: www.asja.org
Members: 1100 individuals
Staff: 2
Annual Budget: $250-500,000
Executive Director: Brett Harvey

Historical Note
Established in 1948 as the Society of Magazine Writers, Inc. Became the American Society of Journalists and Authors, Inc. in 1975. Members are freelance nonfiction writers whose bylines appear on books and in leading periodicals. ASJA acts as an information center on freelance rights, and provides other services to members. Membership: $165/year.

Meetings/Conferences:
Annual Meetings: New York, NY/Summer

Publications:
Newsletter. m.
ASJA Directory of Members. a.

American Society of Laboratory Animal Practitioners *(1967)*
P.O. Box 125
Adamstown, MD 21710
Tel: (301)874-4826 *Fax:* (301)874-6195
E-Mail: aslap-info@aslap.org
Web Site: www.aslap.org
Members: 778 individuals
Annual Budget: $10-25,000
Secretary-Treasurer: Frederick M. Rock

Historical Note
ASLAP members are veterinarians engaged in laboratory animal practice. Affiliated with the American Veterinary Medical Association and the American Association for Laboratory Animal Science. Membership: $60/year; $22.50/year (student).

Meetings/Conferences:
Semi-annual Meetings: Summer and Fall, in conjunction with AVMA and AALAS

Publications:
Laboratory Animal Practitioner. q. adv.

American Society of Landscape Architects *(1899)*
636 I St. NW
Washington, DC 20001-3736
Tel: (202)898-2444 *Fax:* (202)898-1185
E-Mail: membership@asla.org
Web Site: www.asla.org
Members: 15000 individuals
Staff: 45
Annual Budget: $5-10,000,000
Chief Executive Officer and Executive Vice President: Nancy Somerville
E-Mail: nsomerville@asla.org
Director, Education and Academic Affairs: Ron Leighton
E-Mail: rleighton@asla.org
Managing Director, Member and Chapter Services: Mark Miles
E-Mail: mmiles@asla.org

Historical Note
Founded in New York City by eleven charter members and incorporated in Massachusetts in 1916. Absorbed the American Institute of Landscape Architects in 1982. Works closely with the Landscape Architecture Foundation. Has an annual budget of approximately $8.6 million. Membership: $280/year (individual) plus chapter dues.

Meetings/Conferences:
Annual Meetings: October
2007 - San Francisco, CA(Convention Center)/Oct. 5-9

Publications:
Landscape Architectural News Digest (LAND). 10/year. adv.
Landscape Architecture Magazine. m. adv.

American Society of Law Enforcement Trainers *(1987)*

Historical Note
Address unknown in 2006.

American Society of Law, Medicine and Ethics *(1972)*
765 Commonwealth Ave., Suite 1634
Boston, MA 02215
Tel: (617)262-4990 *Fax:* (617)437-7596
E-Mail: info@aslme.org
Web Site: www.aslme.org
Members: 4500 individuals
Staff: 8
Annual Budget: $500-1,000,000
Executive Director: Benjamin Moulton, JD, MPH
E-Mail: bmoulton@aslme.org
Director, Publications: Edward "Ted" Hutchinson
E-Mail: thutchinson@aslme.org
Director, Conference: Katie Kenney Johnson
E-Mail: kkenney@aslme.org

Historical Note
An outgrowth of two founding organizations: the Massachusetts Society of Examining Physicians (1911) and the Massachusetts Society of Law and Medicine (1971). Formerly (1992) American Society of Law and Medicine. Multi-disciplinary membership of professionals concerned with the interrelation of law, medicine, and health care. Membership: $200/year (individual); $320/year (institution).

Meetings/Conferences:
Annual Meetings: Summer

Publications:
American Journal of Law and Medicine. q. adv.
Journal of Law, Medicine & Ethics. q. adv.

American Society of Limnology and Oceanography *(1936)*
5400 Bosque Blvd., Suite 680
Waco, TX 76710
Tel: (254)399-9635 *Fax:* (254)776-3767
Toll Free: (800)929 - 2756
E-Mail: business@aslo.org
Web Site: http://aslo.org
Members: 1500 Libraries
Staff: 3
Annual Budget: $500-1,000,000
Business Manager: Helen Schneider Lemay

Historical Note
Founded January 1, 1936 in St. Louis as the Limnological Society of America. Assumed its present name in 1949 and was incorporated in Wisconsin in 1956. Membership: $75/year (individual).

Publications:
ASLO Bulletin. q. adv.
Limnology and Oceanography Journal. 6/year.

American Society of Lipo-Suction Surgery *(1982)*
737 N. Michigan Ave., Suite 2100
Chicago, IL 60611-5405
Tel: (312)981-6760 *Fax:* (312)981-6787
E-Mail: info@cosmeticsurgery.org
Web Site: www.cosmeticsurgery.org
Members: 2000 individuals
Staff: 8
Annual Budget: $2-5,000,000
Executive Director: Jeffrey P. Knezovich, CAE
E-Mail: jknezovich@cosmeticsurgery.org
Manager, Communications: Charlie Baase
E-Mail: cbaase@cosmeticsurgery.org
Manager, Programs and Operations: Lauraeyn Montgomery
E-Mail: lmontgomery@cosmeticsurgery.org
Director, Meetings and Curriculum: Moira Twitty

Historical Note
ASLSS members are surgeons with an interest in the removal of fatty tissue by suction.

Meetings/Conferences:
Annual Meetings: Winter
2007 - San Diego, CA(Manchester Grand Hyatt)/Jan. 25-28

Publications:
American Journal of Cosmetic Surgery. q. adv.
Membership Roster. a. adv.
Newsletter. q. adv.

American Society of Magazine Editors *(1963)*
810 Seventh Ave.
New York, NY 10019
Tel: (212)872-3700 *Fax:* (212)906-0128
E-Mail: asme@magazine.org
Web Site: www.asme.magazine.org
Members: 900 individuals
Staff: 3
Executive Director: Marlene Kahan
Assistant Director: Andrew Rhodes

Historical Note
A professional society of junior and senior magazine editors designed to allow magazine editors to discuss matters of mutual concern. ASME's varied program includes The National Magazine Awards, The Magazine Internship Program, Conferences, Members Lunches, Seminars, The Junior Editorial Seminar Series, The American Magazine Conference, and Special Advertising Sections guidelines. Affiliated with the Magazine Publishers of America. Membership: $250/year.

Meetings/Conferences:
Annual Meetings: Fall, with the Magazine Publishers of America.

Publications:
The Best American Magazine Writing. a.

American Society of Mammalogists *(1919)*
Oklahoma State University
Department of Zoology, 430 LSW
Stillwater, OK 74078
Tel: (405)744-9679 *Fax:* (405)744-7824
Web Site: www.mammalsociety.org
Members: 4500 individuals
Staff: 3
Annual Budget: $100-250,000
Secretary-Treasurer: Ronald A. Van Den Bussche
E-Mail: ravdb@okstate.edu

Historical Note
Founded and incorporated in the District of Columbia in April 1919. Affiliated with the International Union for the Conservation of Nature. Membership: $30/year (individual); $45/year (organization/company).

Meetings/Conferences:
Annual Meetings: June/800

Publications:
Journal of Mammalogy. 6/year. adv.
Mammalian Species. a.

American Society of Marine Artists *(1978)*
P.O. Box 369
Ambler, PA 19002
Tel: (215)283-0888
E-Mail: asma@icdc.com
Web Site: http://americansocietyofmarineartists.com
Members: 625 individuals
Staff: 1
Annual Budget: under $10,000
Executive Director: Nancy Stiles

Historical Note
Members are artists, collectors and historians. Membership: $45/year, plus $50 initiation fee.

Meetings/Conferences:
Annual Meetings: Fall/various coastal locations on the East Coast

Publications:
ASMA News. q.

American Society of Master Dental Technologists *(1976)*
146-21 13th Ave.
Whitestone, NY 11357-2420
Tel: (718)746-8355
E-Mail: asmdt1@aol.com
Web Site: www.asmdt.com
Members: 125 individuals
Staff: 1
Annual Budget: under $10,000
Executive Director: Susan Heppenheimer

Historical Note
A professional society formed to raise the educational standards of dental technicians. Awards the designation "MDT" (Master Dental Technologist). Membership: $100/year.

Meetings/Conferences:
Annual Meetings: Fall

American Society of Maxillofacial Surgeons *(1947)*
444 E. Algonquin Road
Arlington Heights, IL 60005
Tel: (847)228-3338 *Fax:* (847)228-0628
Toll Free: (800)849 - 4682
Web Site: www.maxface.org
Members: 350 individuals
Staff: 1
Annual Budget: $100-250,000
Administrative Manager: Peggy O'Carroll
E-Mail: po@plasticsurgery.org

Historical Note
ASMS is devoted to stimulating interest, advancing knowledge, and providing leadership and direction within the areas of maxillofacial and craniofacial surgery. Its members are dedicated to improving and promoting the highest levels of patient care. Membership: $300/year (individual).

Meetings/Conferences:
Annual Meetings: Fall, with the American Soc. of Plastic & Reconstructive Surgeons and the Plastic Surgery Educational Foundation

Publications:
Journal of Plastic & Reconstructive Surgery. 14/year. adv.
Maxillofacial News. 3/year. adv.

American Society of Mechanical Engineers *(1880)*
Three Park Ave.
New York, NY 10016-5990
Tel: (212)591-7000 *Fax:* (212)591-7674
Toll Free: (800)843 - 2763
E-Mail: infocentral@asme.org
Web Site: www.asme.org
Members: 125000 individuals
Staff: 405
Annual Budget: $50-100,000,000
Executive Director: Virgil R. Carter, FAIA
Managing Director, Public Affairs: Philip W. Hamilton
Director, Public Information: June Scangarello

Historical Note
Founded in 1880 and incorporated in New York in 1881, ASME is a technical society with 37 technical divisions and the International Gas Turbine Institute and extensive programs in the development of safety codes and equipment standards, educational guidance for student members, professional development, research and technology development and government relations. Conducts one of the largest technical publishing operations in the world. Has an annual budget of $60 million. Membership: $94/year.

Meetings/Conferences:
Semi-Annual Meetings: Summer and Winter

Publications:
Mechanical Engineering Magazine. m.
Journal of Medical Devices. q.
Journal of Computational and Nonlinear Dynamics. q.
Journal of Computing and Information Science in Engineering. q.
Applied Mechanics Reviews. m. adv.
ASME News. m. adv.
Journal of Applied Mechanics. q. adv.
Journal of Biomechanical Engineering. q. adv.
Journal of Dynamic Systems, Measurement and Control. q. adv.
Journal of Electronic Packaging. q. adv.
Journal of Energy Resources Technology. q. adv.
Journal of Engineering for Gas Turbines and Power. q. adv.
Journal of Engineering for Industry. q. adv.
Journal of Engineering Materials and Technology. q. adv.
Journal of Fluids Engineering. q. adv.
Journal of Heat Transfer. q. adv.
Journal of Mechanical Design. q. adv.
Journal of Microelectromechanical Systems. q. adv.
Journal of Offshore Mechanics and Arctic Engineering. q. adv.
Journal of Pressure Vessel Technology. q. adv.
Journal of Solar Energy Engineering. q. adv.
Journal of Tribology. q. adv.
Journal of Turbomachinery. q. adv.
Journal of Vibration and Acoustics. q. adv.
Mechanical Engineering. m. adv.
Heat Transfer - Recent Contents. bi-m.

American Society of Media Photographers *(1944)*
150 N. Second St.
Philadelphia, PA 19106
Tel: (215)451-2767 *Fax:* (215)451-0880
E-Mail: info@asmp.org
Web Site: www.asmp.org
Members: 5000 individuals
Staff: 8
Annual Budget: $1-2,000,000
Executive Director: Eugene Mopsik
Director, Communications: Peter Dyson
General Counsel: Victor Perlman

Historical Note
Known as Society of Photographers in Communications from 1971 to 1979. Became (1979) American Society of Magazine Photographers, and assumed its current name in 1992. Actively lobbies on behalf of photographers at the state and federal levels. Has 40 chapters nationwide. Membership: $125-300/year (individual).

Publications:
ASMP Professional Business Practices In Photography.
ASMP Bulletin. q. adv.
ASMP White Papers. irreg.

American Society of Military Comptrollers *(1949)*
415 N. Alfred St.
Alexandria, VA 22314-4650
Tel: (703)549-0360 *Fax:* (703)549-3181
Toll Free: (800)462 - 5637
Web Site: www.asmconline.org
Members: 18000 individuals
Staff: 9
Annual Budget: $2-5,000,000
Executive Director: Robert F. Hale

Historical Note
Founded in 1955, ASMC is the successor to the Society of Military Accountants and Statisticians. Membership: $26/year (individual); $250/year (company).

Meetings/Conferences:
Annual Meetings: May-June

Publications:
Armed Forces Comptroller. q.

American Society of Mining and Reclamation *(1973)*
3134 Montavesta Road
Lexington, KY 40502
Tel: (859)351-9032 *Fax:* (859)335-6529
E-Mail: asmr@insightbb.com
Web Site: http://ces.ca.uky.edu/assmr
Members: 450 individuals
Staff: 1
Annual Budget: $100-250,000
Executive Secretary: Richard I. Barnhisel

Historical Note
Formerly (1978) Council for Surface Mining and Reclamation Research in Appalachia and (1982) American Council for Reclamation Research; assumed its current name in 2001. ASMR members are mining companies, federal and state agencies, academics and others with an interest in reclamation of mined land. Membership: $50/year (individual); $120/year (organization/company); $10/year (student).

Publications:
ASMR Newsletter. 10/year.
Meeting Proceedings. a.
Membership Directory. a.
IALR Newsletter. a.

American Society of Missiology *(1972)*

100 E. 27th St.
Austin, TX 78705
Tel: (512)404-4855
E-Mail: asm@austinseminary.edu
Web Site: www.asmweb.org
Members: 625 individuals
Annual Budget: $50-100,000
Secretary-Treasurer: Arun W. Jones

Historical Note
Members are individuals interested in the scholarly study of theological, historical and social questions regarding the missionary dimension of the Christian church. Member of the Council of Socs. for the Study of Religion. Has no paid staff. Membership: $30/year.

Meetings/Conferences:
Annual Meetings: *Chicago, IL(Techny Towers)/third weekend in June*

Publications:
Missiology: an International Review. q. adv.

American Society of Music Arrangers and Composers *(1938)*
P.O. Box 17840
Encino, CA 91416
Tel: (818)994-4661 *Fax:* (818)994-6181
E-Mail: properimage2000@earthlink.net
Web Site: www.asmac.org
Members: 400 individuals
Staff: 1
Annual Budget: $10-25,000
President: John Clayton

Historical Note
Professional society for musicians and composers specializing in arrangement and orchestration, working in film, television and other theater arts industries.

Meetings/Conferences:
Annual Meetings: *Golden Score Awards Banquet.*

American Society of Naturalists *(1883)*
Florida State University
Dept. of Biological Sciences
Tallahassee, FL 32306
E-Mail: travis@neuro.fsu.edu
Web Site: www.amnat.org
Members: 1109 individuals
Staff: 1
Annual Budget: $25-50,000
President: Dr. Joseph Travis

Historical Note
ASN's purpose is to advance and diffuze knowledge of organic evolution and biological principles toward concept unification of the biological sciences. Membership: $75/year (U.S. individuals); $95/year (foreign individuals); $100.25/year (Canadian individuals); $49/year (U.S. students); $69/year (foreign students); $72.43/year (Canadian students).

Meetings/Conferences:
Annual Meetings: *in conjunction with the Soc. for the Study of Evolution, and the Soc. for Systematic Biology*

Publications:
The American Naturalist. m. adv.

American Society of Naval Engineers *(1888)*
1452 Duke St.
Alexandria, VA 22314-3458
Tel: (703)836-6727 *Fax:* (703)836-7491
E-Mail: asnehq@navalengineers.org
Web Site: www.navalengineers.org
Members: 5500 individuals
Staff: 10
Annual Budget: $1-2,000,000
Executive Director: Capt. Dennis K. Kruse, USN (Ret.)
E-Mail: dkruse@navalengineers.org
Manager, Membership: Danny Martin
E-Mail: dmartin@navalengineers.org
Manager, Meetings: Megan Sinesou
E-Mail: msinesiou@navalengineers.org
Director, Technical: David Stevenson
Director, Business and Operations: David Woodbury

Historical Note
Founded in the District of Columbia in 1888 and incorporated there in 1946. Naval Engineering includes all arts and sciences as applied in research, development, design, construction, operation, maintenance, and logistic support of: surface/sub-surface ships and marine craft; naval maritime auxiliaries; aviation and space systems; combat systems including command and control electronics, and ordinance systems; ocean structures; and associated shore facilities which are used by the naval and other military forces and civilian maritime organizations for the defense and well-being of the nation. Membership: $95/year (individual).

Meetings/Conferences:
Annual Meetings: *Spring*
2007 - Arlington, VA(Hyatt Regency Crystal City)/June 18-20

Publications:
Naval Engineers Journal. q. adv.

American Society of Nephrology *(1967)*
1725 I St. NW, Suite 510
Washington, DC 20006
Tel: (202)659-0599 *Fax:* (202)659-0709
E-Mail: email@asn-online.org
Web Site: www.asn-online.org
Members: 9400 individuals
Staff: 18
Annual Budget: $5-10,000,000
Executive Director: Karen L. Campbell, Ph.D.

Historical Note
Members are nephrologists. Membership: $250/year (domestic); $275/year (foreign).

Meetings/Conferences:
Annual Meetings: *Fall*
2007 - San Francisco, CA/Oct. 31-Nov. 5

Publications:
Journal of the American Society of Nephrology. m. adv.
NEPHCAP. q.

American Society of Neuroimaging *(1977)*
5841 Cedar Lake Road, Suite 204
Minneapolis, MN 55416
Tel: (952)545-6291 *Fax:* (952)545-6073
E-Mail: asn@llmsi.com
Web Site: www.asnweb.org
Members: 800 individuals
Staff: 2
Annual Budget: $250-500,000

Historical Note
Established as the Society for Computerized Tomography and Neuroimaging; assumed its present name in 1980. Members are specialists in CT scanning, MRI, neurosonology and other neurodiagnostic techniques. Membership: $285/year (active member); $100/year (junior member).

Meetings/Conferences:
Annual Meetings: *Spring*

Publications:
Journal of Neuroimaging. q. adv.

American Society of Neuroradiology *(1962)*
2210 Midwest Road, Suite 207
Oak Brook, IL 60523-8205
Tel: (630)574-0220 *Fax:* (630)574-0661
Web Site: www.asnr.org
Members: 3200 individuals
Staff: 19
Annual Budget: $5-10,000,000
Executive Director and Chief Executive Officer: James B. Gantenberg, CHE
E-Mail: jgantenberg@asnr.org
Director, Communciations and Media Management: Angelo Artemakis
Director, Scientific Meetings: Lora Tannehill, CMP
E-Mail: ltannehill@asnr.org

Historical Note
ASNR was founded in 1962 to develop and support standards for training in the practice of neuroradiology, to foster independent research in neuroradiology, and to promote a closer fellowship and exchange of ideas among neuroradiologists.

Meetings/Conferences:
Annual Meetings: *Spring/1,800*
2007 - Chicago, IL(Hyatt Regency Chicago)/June 9-15
2008 - New Orleans, LA(Morial Convention Center)/May 31-June 6

Publications:
American Journal of Neuroradiology. 10/year.

American Society of Neurorehabilitation *(1990)*
5841 Cedar Lake Road, Suite 204
Minneapolis, MN 55416
Tel: (952)545-6324 *Fax:* (952)545-6073
E-Mail: asnr@llmsi.com
Web Site: www.asnr.com
Members: 500 individuals
Staff: 2
Annual Budget: $100-250,000
Associate Executive Director: Renee Molstad

Historical Note
Members are physicians and other medical professionals with an interest in the rehabilitation of disorders of the nervous system. Membership: $125/year (nonphysician); $195/year (active); $150/year (certified).

Meetings/Conferences:
Annual Meetings: *Fall*

Publications:
Journal of Neurorehabilitation Newsletter. bien. adv.
Neurorehabilitation and Neural Repair. q. adv.

American Society of Newspaper Editors *(1922)*
11690-B Sunrise Valley Dr.
Reston, VA 20191
Tel: (703)453-1122 *Fax:* (703)453-1133
E-Mail: asne@asne.org
Web Site: www.asne.org
Members: 750 individuals
Staff: 11
Annual Budget: $1-2,000,000
Executive Director: Scott Bosley
Director, Diversity: Bobbi Bowman
Director, Online: Craig Branson
Senior Project Director: Diana Mitsu Klos
Systems Manager and Publications Assistant: Suzanne Martin
Office Manager: Chris Schmitt
Planner, Meetings: Alison Wilcox
Director, Communications: Kevin Wilcox

Historical Note
ASNE members are primarily directing editors with immediate responsibility for editorial or news policies at daily newspapers, wire services and other organizations in the U.S. and Canada. Membership: $195-$625/year; varies by circulation.

Meetings/Conferences:
Annual Meetings: *Spring*
2007 - Washington, DC(JW Marriott)/March 27-30
2008 - Washington, DC(Convention Center)/Apr. 13-16
2009 - Chicago, IL(Fairmont)/Apr. 28-May 1

Publications:
The American Editor. 6/yr.

American Society of Notaries *(1965)*
P.O. Box 5707
Tallahassee, FL 32314-5707
Tel: (850)671-5164 *Fax:* (850)671-5165
Toll Free: (800)522 - 3392
E-Mail: mail@notaries.org
Web Site: www.notaries.org
Members: 20000 individuals
Staff: 9
Annual Budget: $250-500,000
Executive Director: Kathleen M. Butler

Historical Note
ASN was organized to improve notarial practices and to uphold high standards for notaries public. Membership: $26/year.

Meetings/Conferences:
Annual Meetings: *August-September*

Publications:
American Notary. q.

American Society of Nuclear Cardiology *(1993)*
4550 Montgomery Ave.

Bethesda, MD 20814
Tel: (301)215-7575 *Fax:* (301)215-7113
E-Mail: admin@asnc.org
Web Site: www.asnc.org
Members: 4700 individuals
Staff: 10
Annual Budget: $2-5,000,000
Executive Director: Steve Carter

Historical Note

Members are professionals in cardiology, nuclear medicine, and radiology pursuing applications of nuclear science to cardiology.

Meetings/Conferences:

Annual Meetings: Fall

Publications:

Journal of Nuclear Cardiology. bi-m. adv.
Newsletter. bi-m.
Membership Directory. bien.

American Society of Ocularists *(1957)*

P.O. Box 608
Earlysville, VA 22936-0608
Tel: (434)973-4066
Toll Free: (866)973 - 4066
E-Mail: tzappone@ocularist.org
Web Site: www.ocularist.org
Executive Director: Toni Zappone

Historical Note

ASO members are technicians specializing in the fitting and fabrication of custom artifical eyes. Benefits of membership include research, education and standards.

Meetings/Conferences:

Annual Meetings: usually Fall

American Society of Ophthalmic Administrators *(1986)*

4000 Legato Road, Suite 700
Fairfax, VA 22033-4003
Tel: (703)591-2220 *Fax:* (703)591-0614
Toll Free: (800)451 - 1339
E-Mail: asoa@asoa.org
Web Site: www.asoa.org
Members: 2000 individuals
Staff: 3
Annual Budget: $500-1,000,000
Executive Director: Eileen Giaimo
Practice Administrator: Lynda Jones
Director, Finance: Suzanne Peeler
Director, Meetings and Covention: Paula Schneider

Historical Note

A division of the American Society of Cataract and Refractive Surgery. ASOA members are active administrators functioning in an ophthalmologists's practice. Membership: $250/year (individual); $550/year.

Meetings/Conferences:

Annual Meetings: Spring, with the American Soc. of Cataract and Refractive Surgery
2007 – San Diego, CA(Marriott San Diego Marina and Yacht Club)/Apr. 1- /2000

Publications:

Administrative Eyecare (AE). q. adv.

American Society of Ophthalmic Plastic and Reconstructive Surgery *(1969)*

222 S. Westmonte Dr., Suite 101
Altamonte Springs, FL 32714
Tel: (407)774-7880 *Fax:* (407)774-6440
E-Mail: asoprs@kmgnet.com
Web Site: www.asoprs.org
Members: 456 individuals
Executive Director: Barbara Fitzgerald Beatty

Historical Note

ASOPRS members are surgeons specializing in plastic and reconstructive surgery of the eyelids, orbits and lacrimal system.

Publications:

Ophthalmic Plastic and Reconstructive Surgery Journal. q.

American Society of Ophthalmic Registered Nurses *(1976)*

P.O. Box 193030
San Francisco, CA 94119
Tel: (415)561-8513 *Fax:* (415)561-8531
E-Mail: asorn@aao.org
Web Site: www.asorn.org
Members: 1000 individuals
Staff: 3
Annual Budget: $100-250,000
Executive Director: Lisa Brown

Historical Note

ASORN was established to assist the registered nurse involved in ophthalmic care to achieve a necessary and distinctive role in the health care system. Membership: $85/year.

Meetings/Conferences:

Annual Meetings: Fall, with the American Academy of Ophthalmology/400
2007 – New Orleans, LA/Nov. 9-12

Publications:

Insight. q. adv.

American Society of Orthopaedic Physician's Assistants

6300 N. River Road, Suite 727
Rosemont, IL 60018-4226
Tel: (847)823-7186 *Fax:* (847)823-0536
Toll Free: (800)998 - 6022
Web Site: www.asopa.org
Executive Director: Damaris Nunez

American Society of Pain Management Nurses *(1990)*

P.O. Box 15473
Lenexa, KS 66285-5473
Tel: (913)752-4975 *Fax:* (913)599-5340
Toll Free: (888)342 - 7766
E-Mail: aspmn@goamp.com
Web Site: www.aspmn.org
Members: 1700 individuals
Staff: 3
Annual Budget: $100-250,000
Executive Director: Janene Dawson

Historical Note

ASPMN represents professional nurses dedicated to promoting and providing optimal care of patients with pain, including the management of its sequelae. This is accomplished through education, standards, advocacy, and research. Membership: $60/year (individual); $1000/year (organization/company).

Meetings/Conferences:

Annual Meetings: Winter

Publications:

ASPMN Pathways. q. adv.
Pain Management Nursing. q. adv.

American Society of Papyrologists *(1961)*

Dept. of Classics ML 226, 410 Blegen Library
Univ. of Cincinnati
Cincinnati, OH 45221-0226
E-Mail: asp@papyrology.org
Web Site: www.papyrology.org
Members: 175 individuals
Annual Budget: $25-50,000
Treasurer: William A. Johnson

Historical Note

The ASP is an association of scholars and students concerned with classical and Egyptian antiquity, in particular with the editing and study of texts preserved on papyrus. Affiliated with the Association Internationale de Papyrologues, Brussels, Belgium. Has no paid officers or full-time staff. Membership: $40/year(regular); $30/year(associate).

Meetings/Conferences:

Annual Meetings: In conjunction with the American Philological Ass'n and the Archaeological Institute of America.

Publications:

American Studies in Papyrology. irreg.
Bulletin of the ASP. q. adv.

American Society of Parasitologists *(1924)*

Univ. of Nebraska
School of Biological Studies
Lincoln, NE 68588
Tel: (402)472-2754 *Fax:* (402)472-2083
Web Site: http://asp.unl.edu
Members: 1050 individuals
Staff: 1
Annual Budget: $250-500,000
Secretary - Treasurer: Dr. John Janovy

Historical Note

Society started by Henry Baldwin Ward. Formed in Washington under the leadership of a group of parasitologists from the Baltimore-Washington area, December 30, 1924 at a meeting of the American Association for the Advancement of Science. Incorporated in the District of Columbia in 1932. Membership: $35/year (student); $75 (individual); $215/year (organization/company in the U.S); $225/year (all other countries); $5 agent discount.

Meetings/Conferences:

Annual Meetings: Summer

Publications:

Journal of Parasitology. 6/year. adv.
Proceedings of the Annual Meeting of the ASP. a.
ASP Directory. a.
ASP Newsletter. q. adv.

American Society of Pediatric Hematology/Oncology *(1981)*

4700 W. Lake Ave.
Glenview, IL 60025-1485
Tel: (847)375-4716 *Fax:* (877)734-9557
E-Mail: info@aspho.org
Web Site: www.aspho.org
Members: 1000 individuals
Staff: 5
Annual Budget: $500-1,000,000
Executive Director: Cynthia S. Porter

Historical Note

Purpose is to advance the knowledge and understanding of pediatric hematology/oncology. Membership open to qualified professionals from all countries.

Publications:

Journal of Pediatric Blood and Cancer. 9/yr. adv.
President Letter. bi-m.
Membership Directory. a. adv.

American Society of Pediatric Nephrology *(1971)*

c/o Northwestern University, Feinberg School of Medicine. Pediatrics, W140
303 E. Chicago Ave.
Chicago, IL 60611-3008
Tel: (312)503-4000 *Fax:* (312)503-1181
E-Mail: aspn@northwestern.edu
Web Site: www.aspneph.com
Members: 525 individuals
Coordinator: Robyn Mann
E-Mail: aspn@northwestern.edu

Meetings/Conferences:

2007 – Toronto, ON, Canada/May 5-8
2008 – Honolulu, HI/May 3-6

American Society of Pension Professionals and Actuaries *(1966)*

4245 N. Fairfax Dr., Suite 750
Arlington, VA 22203
Tel: (703)516-9300 *Fax:* (703)516-9308
E-Mail: asppa@asppa.org
Members: 5000 individuals
Staff: 25
Annual Budget: $5-10,000,000
Executive Director: Brian H. Graff

Historical Note

Awards the designations MSPA and FSPA (Member and Fellow of the Society of Pension Actuaries), QPA (Qualified Pension Administrator), and CPC (Certified Pension Consultant).

Meetings/Conferences:

Annual Meetings: Washington, DC/Grand Hyatt/October

Publications:

ASPPA ASAP.
ASPPA Journal.
The Candidate Connection.

American Society of Perfumers *(1947)*

P.O. Box 1551
West Caldwell, NJ 07004
Tel: (201)991-0040 *Fax:* (201)991-0073
E-Mail: info@perfumers.org
Web Site: www.perfumers.org
Members: 300 individuals
Staff: 1

Annual Budget: $100-250,000
Business Manager: Jim Fassold

Historical Note

ASP's mission is to foster and encourage the art and science of perfumery in the United States while promoting professional exchange and a high standard of professional conduct within the fragrance industry. ASP is a sponsor of the the quadrennial World Perfumery Congress.

Publications:

Newsletter. semi-a.

American Society of PeriAnesthesia Nurses *(1980)*
10 Melrose Ave., Suite 110
Cherry Hill, NJ 08003-3696
Toll Free: (877)737 - 9696
E-Mail: aspan@aspan.org
Web Site: www.aspan.org
Members: 11000 individuals
Staff: 10
Annual Budget: $1-2,000,000
Executive Director: Kevin Dill
E-Mail: kdill@aspan.org
Director, Programs and Project Development: Jane Certo
E-Mail: jcerto@aspan.org

Historical Note

Formerly (1996) American Society of Post Anesthesia Nurses. ASPAN members are post-anesthesia, pre-anesthesia and ambulatory surgery nurses. Membership: $65/year (individual); $1,500/year (corporate).

Meetings/Conferences:

Annual Meetings: April/2,000

Publications:

PeriAnesthesia Journal of PeriAnesthesia Nursing. bi-m. adv.
Breathline. bi-m.

American Society of Pharmacognosy *(1959)*
3149 Dundee Road, Suite 260
Northbrook, IL 60062-2402
Tel: (623)202-3500 *Fax:* (847)656-2800
E-Mail: asphcog@aol.com
Web Site: www.phcog.org/
Members: 1200 individuals
Annual Budget: $250-500,000
Treasurer: David J. Slatkin, Ph.D.
E-Mail: asphcog@aol.com

Historical Note

Founded in 1959 and incorporated in the District of Columbia in 1965. Promotes the study of the composition, production, use and history of drugs of natural origin. Has no paid officers or full-time staff. Membership: $75/year.

Meetings/Conferences:

Annual Meetings: Summer/500
2007 – Portland, ME(Holiday Inn)/July 14-18/500

Publications:

Journal of Natural Products. m.
Newsletter. q.

American Society of Photographers *(1937)*
P.O. Box 1120
Caldwell, TX 77836
Toll Free: (800)638 - 9609
Web Site: www.asofp-online.com
Members: 800 individuals
Staff: 1
Annual Budget: $50-100,000
Executive Director: Doug Box

Historical Note

Membership in Professional Photographers of America is a pre-requisite for membership in ASP; members must be either a Master of Photography, a Photographic Craftsman, or a Photographic Specialist. Membership: $70/year (individual).

Meetings/Conferences:

Annual Meetings: July-August

Publications:

ASP Newsletter. q. adv.

American Society of Picture Professionals *(1966)*
117 S. Saint Asaph
Alexandria, VA 22314
Tel: (703)299-0219
E-Mail: cathy@aspp.com
Web Site: www.aspp.com
Members: 750 individuals
Staff: 1
Annual Budget: $500-1,000,000
Executive Director: Cathy D.P. Sachs

Historical Note

Members are image producers (e.g. photographers), stock photo agencies, and image users (publishers and independent photo editors and researchers). Provides networking and educational opportunities in the image transaction industry. Membership: $100/year.

Meetings/Conferences:

Regional Meetings: various locations within five regional chapters

Publications:

Membership Directory (online). a.
eNews Electronic Newsletter. m.
The Picture Professional. q. adv.

American Society of Plant Biologists *(1924)*
15501 Monona Dr.
Rockville, MD 20855-2765
Tel: (301)251-0560 *Fax:* (301)279-2996
E-Mail: info@aspb.org
Web Site: www.aspb.org
Members: 5000 individuals
Staff: 22
Annual Budget: $5-10,000,000
Executive Director: Crispin Taylor
Director, Public Affairs: Brian M. Hyps
E-Mail: bhyps@aspb.org
Director, Publications: Nancy Winchester
E-Mail: nancyw@aspb.org

Historical Note

Founded in 1924 as American Society of Plant Physiologists and incorporated in the District of Columbia the same year. Assumed its current name in 2001. Membership: $115/year (individual); $45/year (student); $65/year (postdoctoral).

Meetings/Conferences:

Annual Meetings: July-August
2007 – Chicago, IL/July 7-11

Publications:

Plant Physiology. m. adv.
ASPB Newsletter. bi-m. adv.
The Plant Cell. m. adv.

American Society of Plant Taxonomists *(1936)*
Dept. of Botany
Miami University
Oxford, OH 45056
Tel: (513)529-2755 *Fax:* (513)529-4243
Web Site: www.sysbot.org
Members: 1300 individuals
Staff: 1
Annual Budget: $100-250,000
Secretary: Michael A. Vincent, Ph.D.
E-Mail: vincema@muohio.edu

Historical Note

Founded in 1936 and incorporated in 1964. ASPT members are professional plant systematists and others interested in plant taxonomy and evolution. An affiliate of American Association for the Advancement of Science, American Institute of Biological Sciences, National Research Council, Botanical Society of America, and Association of Systematics Collections. Membership: $40/year (individual); $115/year (organization).

Meetings/Conferences:

Annual Meetings: Summer
2007 – Chicago, IL/July 7-11

Publications:

ASPT Newsletter. q.
Systematic Botany. q. adv.
Systematic Botany Monographs. irreg.
ASPT Membership Directory. a.

American Society of Plastic Surgeons *(1931)*
444 E. Algonquin Road
Arlington Heights, IL 60005-4654
Tel: (847)228-9900 *Fax:* (847)228-9131
Web Site: www.plasticsurgery.org
Members: 6000 individuals
Staff: 84
Annual Budget: $5-10,000,000
Executive Vice President: Paul Pomerantz, CAE
Comptroller: Michael Baldwin
Assistant Executive Director, Communications: Lynn Kahn, CAE
Assistant Executive Director, Member Services and Strategies: Carol L. Lazier, CAE, CMP
Assistant Executive Director, Government Relations: William Seward
Assistant Executive Director, Education, Meetings and Clinical Research: Bergitta Smith

Historical Note

Founded in New York City in 1931 and incorporated in New York in 1945 as American Society of Plastic and Reconstructive Surgeons; assumed its current name in 2001. Reincorporated in Illinois in 1975. Has an annual budget of approximately $8.6 million. Sponsors and supports the Plastic Surgery Educational Foundation and the ASPRS Political Action Committee.

Meetings/Conferences:

Annual Meetings: Fall/4,500

Publications:

Plastic and Reconstructive Surgery. m. adv.
Plastic Surgery News. m. adv.

American Society of Plastic Surgical Nurses *(1975)*
7794 Grow Dr.
Pensacola, FL 32514-7072
Tel: (850)473-2443 *Fax:* (850)484-8762
Toll Free: (800)272 - 0136
E-Mail: aspsn@puetzamc.com
Web Site: www.aspsn.org
Members: 1800 individuals
Staff: 2
Annual Budget: $250-500,000
Executive Director: Amy DeFaveri

Historical Note

Formerly American. Society of Plastic and Reconstructive Surgical Nurses; assumed its current name in 2001. Membership: $75/year (individual); $1,500/year (company).

Meetings/Conferences:

Annual Meetings: Fall

Publications:

Plastic Surgical Nursing. q. adv.
ASPRSNews. bi-m.

American Society of Plumbing Engineers *(1964)*
8614 W. Catalpa Ave., Suite 1007
Chicago, IL 60656-1116
Tel: (773)693-2773 *Fax:* (773)695-9007
E-Mail: aspehq@aspe.org
Web Site: www.aspe.org
Members: 6800 individuals
Staff: 11
Annual Budget: $1-2,000,000
Executive Director: Stanley M. Wolfson

Meetings/Conferences:

Biennial Meetings: Even years/4,500
2008 – Long Beach, CA(Convention Center)/Oct. 26-29

Publications:

Plumbing Systems and Design. bi-m.. adv.
ASPE Plumbing, Engineering Design Handbook. a. adv.
Model Plumbing Codes: A Comparison Study.
Domestic Water Heating Design Manual.
Engineered Plumbing Design II.
Advanced Plumbing Technology.

American Society of Podiatric Medical Assistants *(1964)*
2124 S. Austin Blvd.
Cicero, IL 60804
Tel: (708)863-6303 *Fax:* (708)863-5375
Toll Free: (888)882 - 7762
Web Site: www.aspma.org
Members: 1350 individuals
Annual Budget: $25-50,000
Executive Director: Sandra Lohrentz, PMAC
E-Mail: aspmaex@aol.com

Historical Note

Members must be employed by podiatrists who are members of APMA. Formerly (1985) American Society of Podiatric Assistants. An affiliate of the

American Podiatric Medical Association. Membership: $55/year.

Meetings/Conferences:
Annual Meetings: With the American Podiatric Medical Ass'n/Aug.

Publications:
The Journal of ASPMA. Quarterly.

American Society of Podiatric Medicine *(1944)*
1111 Lane Concourse Dr., Suite 111
Bay Harbor, FL 33154
Tel: (305)866-9608 *Fax:* (305)866-1750
Members: 110 individuals
Annual Budget: under $10,000
Secretary: Dr. Warren L. Simmonds

Historical Note
An affiliate of the American Podiatric Medical Association. Formerly (1972) American College of Podiatric Medicine.

Publications:
Newsletter. 3/year.

American Society of Podiatry Executives
410 N. Gadsden St.
Tallahassee, FL 32301
Tel: (850)224-4085 *Fax:* (850)681-0899
Members: 35 individuals
Annual Budget: under $10,000
President: Michael Schwartz

Historical Note
Founded as Conference of Podiatric Executives; assumed its current name in 1996. Members are directors of state podiatry associations. Has no paid officers or full-time staff. Membership: $125/year (individual).

Meetings/Conferences:
Semi-annual Meetings: February and August

American Society of Preventive Oncology *(1976)*
Room 330 WARF Bldg., 610 Walnut St.
Madison, WI 53726
Tel: (608)263-9515 *Fax:* (608)263-4497
Web Site: www.aspo.org
Members: 420 individuals
Staff: 1
Annual Budget: $100-250,000
Executive Director: Heidi A. Sahel

Historical Note
ASPO is a multi-disciplinary society committed to cancer prevention and control through scientific conferences and advocacy for cancer prevention and control research funding. Membership: $200/year (individual); $35/year (student).

Meetings/Conferences:
Annual Meetings: Spring
2007 – Houston, TX(Marriott)/March 15-18
2008 – Bethesda, MD(Hyatt Regency)/March 15-18

Publications:
Cancer Epidemiology, Biomarkers, and Prevention. m.

American Society of Primatologists *(1976)*
Loyola Univeristy, Dept. Of Psychology
6363 St. Charles Ave.
New Orleans, LA 70118
Tel: (504)865-3255
Web Site: www.asp.org
Members: 750 individuals
Staff: 1
Annual Budget: $50-100,000
Treasurer: Evan Zucker

Historical Note
Members are individuals specializing in the study of monkeys, apes, and other primates. Membership: $30/year.

Publications:
American Journal of Primatology. m.
ASP Bulletin. q.

American Society of Professional Estimators *(1956)*
2525 Perimeter Place Dr., Suite 103
Nashville, TN 37214
Tel: (615)316-9200 *Fax:* (615)316-9800
Toll Free: (888)378 - 6283
E-Mail: psmith@aspenational.org
Web Site: www.ASPEnational.org
Members: 3000 individuals
Staff: 4
Annual Budget: $250-500,000
Executive Director: Edward Walsh
Membership Coordinator: Tanya Laury
Certification Coordinator: Sue Parrish
Director, Administration: Patsy Smith

Historical Note
ASPE is composed of construction trade estimators. ASPE serves construction trade estimators by providing education, fellowship, and opportunity for professional development. Membership: $165/year, plus chapter dues.

Meetings/Conferences:
Annual Meetings: June-July

Publications:
Estimator Society Newsletter. bi-m. adv.
Standard Estimating Practice. a.
Estimating Today. m. adv.

American Society of Psychoanalytic Physicians *(1985)*
13528 Wisteria Dr.
Germantown, MD 20874
Tel: (301)540-3197 *Fax:* (301)540-3511
Web Site: www.aspp.net
Members: 280 individuals
Staff: 1
Annual Budget: under $10,000
Executive Director: Christine Cotter
E-Mail: cfcotter@yahoo.com

Historical Note
Formed by the merger of the American Society of Physician Analysts and the American Association of Psychoanalytic Physicians. Members are involved in private practice of psychoanalysis and analytically-oriented psychotherapy. Membership is by invitation.

Meetings/Conferences:
Annual Meetings: May, in conjunction with the American Psychiatric Ass'n

Publications:
Bulletin. semi-a. adv.

American Society of Psychopathology of Expression *(1964)*
74 Lawton St.
Brookline, MA 02446
Tel: (617)738-9821 *Fax:* (617)975-0411
Members: 100 individuals
Staff: 1
Annual Budget: under $10,000
President: Irene Jakab, M.D.

Historical Note
Members are psychiatrists, psychologists, art therapists, artists, and others interested in the problems of verbal and non-verbal expression. Membership: $25/year.

Publications:
Newsletter. semi-a. adv.
Proceedings. bien. adv.

American Society of Questioned Document Examiners *(1942)*
P.O. Box 18298
Long Beach, CA 90807
Tel: (562)901-3376 *Fax:* (562)901-3378
E-Mail: asqdeorders@aol.com
Web Site: www.asqde.org
Members: 132 individuals
Staff: 1
Annual Budget: $25-50,000
President: Howard C. Rile, Jr.
E-Mail: hcrqde@aol.com

Historical Note
Purpose is to foster education; sponsor scientific research; establish standards; and provide training in the field of questioned document examination and promote justice in matters that involve questions about documents. Membership: $100/year (individual).

Meetings/Conferences:
Annual Meetings: Summer/130
2007 – Boulder, CO(Harvest Millennium)/Aug. 11-16/130

Publications:
Journal of the ASQDE. semi-a. adv.
ASQDE News. semi-a.
Membership Directory. a.

American Society of Radiologic Technologists *(1920)*
15000 Central Ave. SE
Albuquerque, NM 87123-3917
Tel: (505)298-4500 Ext: 2 *Fax:* (505)298-5063
Toll Free: (800)444 - 2778 Ext: 2
E-Mail: customerinfo@asrt.org
Web Site: www.asrt.org
Members: 121000 individuals
Staff: 100
Annual Budget: $10-25,000,000
Chief Executive Officer: Lynn May
Director, Finance: diana bunnell
Vice President, Member Services: DuVonne Campbell
Director, Government Relations: Christine Lund
Chief Academic Officer: Salvatore Martino
Director, Human Resources: Gayla Mills
Director, Shipping and Receiving: John Padilla
Director, Education: Kevin Powers
Director, Information Services: Curt Schatz
Director, Marketing: Lisa Taute
Vice President, Communications: Nora Tuggle
Director, Continuing Education: Barbara Whitefield

Historical Note
Founded in Chicago as American Association of Radiologic Technicians; became American Society of Radiographers in 1930 and incorporated in Illinois in 1932. Became American Society of X-Ray Technicians in 1934 and American Society of Radiologic Technologists, Inc. in 1964. Promotes the science of radiation and imaging specialties. Membership: $115 (initial year); $105/year (renewal).

Meetings/Conferences:
Annual Meetings: Summer/600

Publications:
ASRT Scanner. m. adv.
Radiation Therapist. semi-a. adv.
Radiologic Technology. bi-m. adv.

American Society of Regional Anesthesia and Pain Medicine *(1976)*
520 Northwest Hwy.
Park Ridge, IL 60068-2573
Tel: (847)825-7246
E-Mail: g.hoormann@asahq.org
Web Site: www.asra.com
Members: 8,000 individuals
Staff: 5
Annual Budget: $1-2,000,000
Executive Secretary: Gary W. Hoorman
E-Mail: g.hoormann@asahq.org

Historical Note
Physicians and anesthetists interested in the induction of insensibility over a certain area by nerve blocking or field blocking, regional anesthesia for pain, surgery and obstetrics. Membership: $150/year (individual).

Publications:
Regional Anesthesia and Pain Medicine. bi-m. adv.
Newsletter. q.

American Society of Retina Specialists *(1982)*
PMB 2845 Notre Dame Blvd., Suite 370
Chico, CA 95928
Tel: (530)566-9181 *Fax:* (530)566-9192
E-Mail: cordie@retinaspecialists.org
Web Site: www.retinaspecialists.org
Members: 1783
Staff: 1
Managing Director: Cordie Miller

Historical Note
Founded as the Vitreous Society; assumed its current name in 2002.

Meetings/Conferences:
Annual Meetings: 1,000

American Society of Roommate Services *(1979)*
253 W. 72nd St., #1711
New York, NY 10023
Tel: (212)362-0162
Executive Officer: Michael Santomauro

Historical Note
ASRS members are roommate-finding agencies.
Publications:
Ins & Outs of the Roommate Biz. 3/year.

American Society of Safety Engineers *(1911)*
1800 E. Oakton St.
Des Plaines, IL 60018-2187
Tel: (847)699-2929 *Fax:* (847)768-3434
E-Mail: customerservice@asse.org
Web Site: www.asse.org
Members: 30000 individuals
Staff: 60
Annual Budget: $5-10,000,000
Executive Director and Secretary: Fred Fortman, Jr.
Director, Marketing and Communications: Kelly Fanella
Historical Note
Founded in 1911 as the United Association of Casualty Inspectors and merged with the National Safety Council in 1924, becoming its Engineering Section. It again became independent in 1947 as the American Society of Safety Engineers and incorporated in Illinois in 1962. Membership is open to individuals whose employment, education, and experience are safety-related. Membership: $135/year.
Meetings/Conferences:
Annual Meetings: June/1,900
Publications:
Journal of SH&E Research. q.
Professional Safety Journal. m. adv.
Society Update. m.

American Society of Sanitary Engineering *(1906)*
901 Canterbury Road, Suite A
Westlake, OH 44145
Tel: (440)835-3040 *Fax:* (440)835-3488
E-Mail: general.info@asse-plumbing.org
Web Site: www.asse-plumbing.org
Members: 2750 individuals
Staff: 9
Annual Budget: $500-1,000,000
Executive Director: Shannon Corcoran
E-Mail: shannon@asse-plumbing.org
Historical Note
Originated in January 1906 in the District of Columbia as the American Society of Inspectors of Plumbing and Sanitary Engineers. Became the American Society of Sanitary Engineering in 1914 and incorporated in the District of Columbia in 1937. Membership: $80-105/year (individual); $250/year (company).
Publications:
Plumbing Standards Magazine. q. adv.
ASSE Yearbook. a. adv.
Newsletter. m. adv.

American Society of Sephardic Studies *(1963)*
1225 Weaner St.
Wykagyl, NY 10804
Tel: (914)633-3728 *Fax:* (914)636-0608
Members: 120 individuals
Annual Budget: under $10,000
Director: M. Mitchell Serels, Ph.D.
Historical Note
ASOSS members are academics with an interest in Sephardic Jewish history, culture or language.
Meetings/Conferences:
Annual Meetings: always New York, NY/March
Publications:
Sephardic Scholar Journal. irreg.

American Society of Sugar Beet Technologists *(1935)*
800 Grant St., Suite 300
Denver, CO 80203
Tel: (303)832-4460 *Fax:* (303)832-4468
Web Site: www.bsdf-assbt.org
Members: 650 individuals
Staff: 2
Annual Budget: $10-25,000
Executive Vice President: Thomas K. Schwartz
Historical Note
Membership: $150/2 years (individual); $350 (company).
Meetings/Conferences:
Biennial Meetings: odd years in February-March
2007 - Salt Lake City, UT(Little America)/Feb. 28-March 3
2009 - Orlando, FL(Wyndham)/Feb. 25-28
Publications:
Journal of Sugar Beet Research. 2-3/year.

American Society of Tax Professionals *(1985)*
P.O. Box 1213
Lynnwood, WA 98046-1213
Tel: (425)774-1996 *Fax:* (425)672-0461
Toll Free: (877)674 - 1996
Web Site: taxbeacon.com/astp
Members: 150 individuals
Staff: 1
Annual Budget: $10-25,000
Executive Director: Carol Kraemer, CCCE
E-Mail: kraemerc@juno.com
Historical Note
Founded as National Association of Income Tax Preparers; assumed its current name in 1987. ASTP provides continuing education opportunities to its member tax preparers. Supports the Certified Tax Preparer (CTP) program. Institute of Tax Consultants is the certifying board for ASTP.
Meetings/Conferences:
Annual Meetings: September
Publications:
Tax Professionals Update. bi-m. adv.

American Society of Teachers for the Alexander Technique *(1987)*
P.O. Box 60008
Florence, MA 01062
Tel: (413)584-2359 *Fax:* (413)584-3097
Toll Free: (800)473 - 0620
E-Mail: info@amsat.ws
Web Site: www.amsat.ws
Members: 700 individuals
Executive Administrator: Indrani Kowlessar Gallagher
E-Mail: info@amsat.ws
Historical Note
Founded as North American Society of Teachers of the Alexander Technique; assumed its current name in 2000. Members are practitioners and trainees in the Alexander technique, an educational method that replaces harmful habitual movement patterns with balanced coordination of the individual, thus reducing body fatigue and strain. Qualified AmSAT teachers have completed an AmSAT-approved teacher training program of 1,600 hours over a minimum of three years. AmSAT is the largest professional association of certified teachers of the Alexander Technique in the country.
Publications:
Newsletter. 3/year. adv.
Teaching Members List. a.
List of Certified Training Courses. a.

American Society of Test Engineers *(1981)*
P.O. Box 389
Nutting Lake, MA 01865-0389
E-Mail: aste@earthlink.net
Web Site: www.astetest.org
Members: 500 individuals
Staff: 4
Executive Director: Michael E. Keller
E-Mail: mkeller@drc.com
Historical Note
Incorporated in the state of Illinois, ASTE members are engineers and companies involved in test engineering and related fields. Membership: $40/year (individual); $400/year (corporate).
Publications:
Newsletter. q.

American Society of Theatre Consultants *(1983)*
12226 Mentz Hill Road
St. Louis, MO 63128
Tel: (314)843-9218 *Fax:* (314)843-4955
Web Site: www.theatreconsultants.org
Members: 41 individuals
Annual Budget: $10-25,000
Secretary: Edgar L. Lustig
Historical Note
ASTC members are consultants specializing in the planning and design of theatres and other performing facilities. Has no paid officers or full-time staff.
Publications:
ASTC Newsletter. a.

American Society of Transplant Surgeons *(1974)*
1020 N. Fairfax St., Suite 200
Alexandria, VA 22314
Tel: (703)684-5990 *Fax:* (703)684-6303
Web Site: www.asts.org
Members: 900 individuals
Staff: 4
Annual Budget: $2-5,000,000
Executive Director: Katrina Crist
Historical Note
ASTS members are surgeons, scientists and physicians specializing in liver, heart, lung, pancreas, and kidney transplants. Membership: $350/year (individual).
Meetings/Conferences:
Annual Meetings: May-June
2007 - San Francisco, CA(Convention Center)/May 5-9/5000
Publications:
American Journal of Transportation. y. adv.
Chimera. q.

American Society of Transplantation *(1981)*
15000 Commerce Pkwy., Suite C
Mt. Laurel, NJ 08054
Tel: (856)439-9986 *Fax:* (856)439-9982
E-Mail: ast@ahint.com
Web Site: www.a-s-t.org
Members: 2600 individuals
Staff: 11
Annual Budget: $2-5,000,000
Executive Vice President: Susan J. Nelson
Historical Note
Formerly (1998) American Society of Transplant Physicians. AST promotes and encourages education and research in transplantation medicine and immunology, and provides a forum for the exchange of scientific information related to the field. Membership: $420/year.
Meetings/Conferences:
Annual Meetings: Spring
2007 - San Francisco, CA(Convention Center)/May 5-9
Publications:
American Journal of Transplantation. 12/year. adv.
AST Newsletter. bi-m.

American Society of Transportation and Logisitcs *(1946)*
1700 N. Moore St., Suite 1900
Arlington, VA 22209
Tel: (703)524-5011 *Fax:* (703)524-5017
E-Mail: info@astl.org
Web Site: www.astl.org
Members: 1000 individuals
Staff: 2
Annual Budget: $100-250,000
Executive Director: Laurie Denham
E-Mail: ldenham@astl.org
Historical Note
Organized in Chicago, IL on March 1, 1946 and incorporated later the same year in the state of Indiana as the American Society of Traffic and Transportation. Assumed its present name in 1984. A professional society of individuals involved in or concerned with the various management functions of transportation, physical distribution and logistics. Awards the CTL (Certified in Transportation and Logistics), PLS (Professional Designation in Logistics and Supply Chain Management) and DLS (Distinguished Logistics Professional) designations. Membership fee varies.
Meetings/Conferences:
Annual Meetings: Fall
2007 - Atlanta, GA(Convention Center)/Nov. 11-
2008 - Ft. Lauderdale, FL(Convention Center)/Nov. 16- /100
Publications:
Transportation Journal. q.

American Society of Travel Agents *(1931)*
1101 King St., Suite 200

Alexandria, VA 22314
Tel: (703)739-2782 *Fax:* (703)684-8319
E-Mail: askasta@astahq.com
Web Site: www.astanet.com
Members: 25000 individuals
Staff: 92
Annual Budget: $10-25,000,000
Executive Vice President and Chief Operating Officer: William A. Maloney
Senior Vice President, Sales and Marketing: Cheryl Ahearn
Vice President, Communications: Eileen E. Denne
Director, Member Services: Karen Roberts
Senior Vice President, General Counsel: Burton J. Rubin
Senior Vice President, Legal and Industry Affairs: Paul Ruden
Vice President, Communications: Kristina Rundquist

Historical Note
Established in 1931 in New York as the American Steamship and Tourist Agents' Association. The name was changed in 1944 to American Society of Travel Agents, Inc. Sponsors the American Society of Travel Agents Political Action Committee. Has an international membership of about 15%. Has an annual budget of approximately $12 million.

Meetings/Conferences:
Annual Meetings: Fall

Publications:
ASTA Network Magazine.
ASTA Agency Management. m.
Dateline ASTA. bi-w.

American Society of Trial Consultants *(1982)*

1941 Greenspring Dr.
Timonium, MD 21093
Tel: (410)560-7949 *Fax:* (410)560-2563
E-Mail: astcoffice@aol.com
Web Site: www.astcweb.org
Members: 440 individuals
Staff: 2
Annual Budget: $100-250,000
Executive Director: Ronald J. Matlon, Ph.D.

Historical Note
Organized in Phoenix, October, 1982. Formerly (1986) the Association of Trial Behavior Consultants, ASTC assumed its present name in January, 1987. Members are trial consultants from a variety of academic backgrounds who work within court systems on jury selection, community surveys, continuing legal education, courtroom visuals, witness preparation, language and law, legal interviewing and negotiation, post trial juror interviews, presentation strategy in the courtroom, trial simulations, voir dire strategy, etc. Membership: $185/year (individual member); $60/year (individual student member).

Meetings/Conferences:
Annual Meetings: Summer

Publications:
Court Call Newsletter. q. adv.
Jury Expert. m. adv.
Annual Directory of Members. a.

American Society of Tropical Medicine and Hygiene *(1951)*

60 Revere Dr., Suite 500
Northbrook, IL 60062-1577
Tel: (847)480-9592 *Fax:* (847)480-9282
E-Mail: info@astmh.org
Web Site: www.astmh.org
Members: 3000 individuals
Staff: 6
Annual Budget: $1-2,000,000
Executive Director: Sally Finney
Administrative Director: Judy DeAcetis
E-Mail: jdeacetis@astmh.org
Director, Conferences: Lyn Maddox
E-Mail: lmaddox@astmh.org

Historical Note
Organized November 17, 1951 in Chicago as an amalgamation of the American Society of Tropical Medicine, formed in 1903, and the National Malaria Society, founded in 1916. Incorporated in Delaware in 1952. Mission is to promote world health by increasing prevention and control of tropical diseases, through research and education. Membership: $160/year (individual); $80/year (post-doctoral student); $54/year (pre-doctoral student).

Meetings/Conferences:
Annual Meetings: Winter/1,500
2007 – Philadelphia, PA/Nov. 4-8/1500

Publications:
Health Hints for the Tropics. irreg.
American Journal of Tropical Medicine and Hygiene. m. adv.
Program and Abstracts of the Annual Meeting. a.
Clinical Consultants Directory. a.
Tropical Medicine and Hygiene News. bi-m.

American Society of Veterinary Ophthalmology *(1957)*

1416 W. Liberty Ave.
Stillwater, OK 74075
E-Mail: membership@asvo.org
Web Site: www.asvo.org
Members: 200 individuals
Staff: 1
Annual Budget: under $10,000
Secretary-Treasurer: Dr. V.A. Schultz

Historical Note
Founded in 1957 in Miami Beach during a meeting of the American Animal Hospital Association. Affiliated with American Veterinary Medical Association. Membership: $25/year.

Meetings/Conferences:
Annual Meetings: Spring, with American Animal Hospital Ass'n

Publications:
Directory. a.
Newsletter. q.

American Society of Wedding Professionals *(1992)*

c/o Make an Impression
792 Kinderkamack Rd.
River Edge, NJ 07661
Tel: (973)472-1800 Ext: 538 *Fax:* (973)574-7626
Toll Free: (800)526 - 0497 Ext: 538
E-Mail: lawrence@carroll.com
Web Site: www.sellthebride.com
Members: 100 individuals
Staff: 2
Annual Budget: $50-100,000
Executive Officer: Brian D. Lawrence
E-Mail: lawrence@carroll.com

Historical Note
ASWP members are wedding-related businesses. Membership: $149/year minimum (individual).

Publications:
The Wedding Expert's Guide to Sales and Marketing. irreg.
The Invitation Business Report. irreg.

American Society of Women Accountants *(1938)*

8405 Greensboro Dr., Suite 800
McLean, VA 22102
Tel: (703)506-3265 *Fax:* (703)506-3266
Toll Free: (800)326 - 2163
E-Mail: aswa@aswa.org
Web Site: www.aswa.org
Members: 5000 individuals
Staff: 10
Annual Budget: $250-500,000
Executive Director: Michelle Spencer

Historical Note
Composed of 100 chapters nationwide. ASWA seeks to enable women in all fields of accounting to achieve their full personal, professional, and economic potential as well as contributing to the future development of the profession. Membership: $96/year (regular).

Meetings/Conferences:
Annual Meetings: Fall

Publications:
Membership Directory On-Line. a. adv.
The Edge. 6/year. adv.

American Society of Writers on Legal Subjects

Historical Note
See Scribes.

American Society on Aging *(1954)*

833 Market St., Suite 511
San Francisco, CA 94103
Tel: (415)974-9600 *Fax:* (415)974-0300
Toll Free: (800)537 - 9728
E-Mail: info@asaging.org
Web Site: www.asaging.org
Members: 6000 individuals
Staff: 44
Annual Budget: $2-5,000,000
President and Chief Executive Officer: Gloria Cavanaugh

Historical Note
Founded as the Western Gerontological Society ASA's goal is the well-being of older Americans and their families. Membership includes educators, service providers, researchers, health and social service professionals, administrators, policy makers, business executives, advocates, students, and elders. Membership: $110/year (individual); $250/year (organization).

Meetings/Conferences:
Annual Meetings: March/3,500

Publications:
Healthcare and Aging. q.
Older Learner. q.
Maximizing Human Potential. q.
Dimensions. q.
Outword. q.
Generations. q. adv.
Aging Today. bi-m. adv.
Aging and Spirituality. q.
Networker. q.

American Sociological Association *(1905)*

1307 New York Ave. NW
Washington, DC 20005
Tel: (202)383-9005 *Fax:* (202)638-0882
E-Mail: executive.office@asanet.org
Web Site: www.asanet.org
Members: 13000 individuals
Staff: 25
Annual Budget: $2-5,000,000
Executive Officer: Sally T. Hillsman
Director, Meeting Services: Janet L. Astner
E-Mail: astner@asanet.org
Director, Information Technology: Kevin Brown
E-Mail: brown@asanet.org
Director, Publications: Karen Gray Edwards
E-Mail: edwards@asanet.org
Director, Public Affairs and Public Information: K. Lee Herring
E-Mail: herring@asanet.org

Historical Note
The American Sociological Association (ASA), founded in 1905, is a non-profit membership association dedicated to serving sociologists in their work, advancing sociology as a scientific discipline and profession, and promoting the contributions and use of sociology to society. As the national organization for over 13,000 sociologists, the Association is well positioned to provide a unique set of benefits to its members and to promote the vitality, visibility, and diversity of the discipline. Working at the national and international levels, the Association aims to articulate policy and implement programs likely to have the broadest possible impact for sociology now and in the future. Membership: $37-210/year (individual); $150-175/year (department).

Meetings/Conferences:
2007 – San Francisco, CA(Hilton)/Aug. 4-7

Publications:
Social Psychology Quarterly. adv.
Member Directory. bi-a. adv.
Guide to Graduate Departments.
ASA Employment Bulletin. m. adv.
ASA Footnotes. 9/year. adv.

American Software Association *(1991)*

Historical Note
A division of the Information Technology Association of America.

American Solar Energy Society *(1954)*

2400 Central Ave., Suite A
Boulder, CO 80301-2843
Tel: (303)443-3130 *Fax:* (303)443-3212
E-Mail: ases@ases.org
Web Site: www.ases.org
Members: 4500 individuals
Staff: 4

Annual Budget: $1-2,000,000
Executive Director: Brad Collins

Historical Note

Established in 1970 and incorporated in Florida. Formerly (1982) the International Solar Energy Society, American Section. Affiliated with the International Solar Energy Society. Membership: $60/year (individual).

Meetings/Conferences:

Annual Meetings: Spring

Publications:

Annual Proceedings. a.
Solar Today Magazine. bi-m. adv.
Passive Proceedings. a.

American Southdown Breeders Association *(1882)*
100 Cornerstone Road
Fredonia, TX 76842
Tel: (325)429-6226 *Fax:* (325)429-6225
Web Site: www.southdownsheep.org
Members: 1000 individuals
Staff: 1
Annual Budget: $10-25,000
Secretary-Treasurer: Gary Jennings
E-Mail: gary@southdownsheep.org

Historical Note

Breeders and fanciers of Southdown sheep. Membership: $10 (initial fee); $5/year thereafter.

Meetings/Conferences:

Annual Meetings: Fall

Publications:

The American Southdown Journal. 3/year. adv.
Southdown Handbook. trien. adv.

American Soybean Association *(1920)*
12125 Woodcrest Executive Dr., Suite 100
St. Louis, MO 63141-5009
Tel: (314)576-1770 *Fax:* (314)576-2786
Toll Free: (800)688 - 7692
E-Mail: scensky@soy.org
Web Site: www.soygrowers.com
Members: 26500 individuals
Staff: 20
Annual Budget: $25-50,000,000
Chief Executive Officer: Steve Censky
Director, Membership: Sue Dersheid
Executive Assistant and Meeting Planner: Julie Hawkins
Director, Finance: Brian Vausht

Historical Note

Develops and implements policies to increase the profitability of its members and the entire soybean industry, including export/market expansion, education, research and legislative action.

Meetings/Conferences:

Annual Meetings: Spring
2007 – Tampa, FL/March 1-3
2008 – Nashville, TN/Feb. 28-March 1/4000

Publications:

Leader Letter. m.
ASA Today. 10/year.

American Spa and Health Resort Association *(1982)*
Box 585
Lake Forest, IL 60045
Tel: (847)234-8851 *Fax:* (847)295-7790
Members: 30 companies
Annual Budget: under $10,000
Executive Director: Melanie Ruehle

Historical Note

Incorporated in Illinois, ASHRA promotes the public awareness of spas/health resorts and sets standards for membership.

American Specialty Toy Retailing Association *(1992)*
116 W. Illnois St., Suite 5E
Chicago, IL 60610
Tel: (312)222-0984 *Fax:* (312)222-0986
Toll Free: (800)591 - 0490
E-Mail: info@astratoy.org
Web Site: www.astratoy.org
Members: 870 individuals and companies
Annual Budget: $250-500,000
Executive Director: Kathleen McHugh

Historical Note

ASTRA represents the needs and interests of the specialty toy industry and promotes the sale and use of specialty toys through marketing, research and education. Membership: $200-$5,000/year, based on gross sales (retailers); $200/year (others).

Meetings/Conferences:

Annual Meetings: Spring

Publications:

Membership Directory. a.
Newsletter. q. adv.

American Speech-Language-Hearing Association *(1925)*
10801 Rockville Pike
Rockville, MD 20852-3279
Tel: (301)897-5700 *Fax:* (301)897-7355
Toll Free: (800)638 - 8255
E-Mail: actioncenter@asha.org
Web Site: www.asha.org
Members: 123000 individuals
Staff: 230
Annual Budget: $25-50,000,000
Executive Director: Arlene Pietranton, Ph.D.

Historical Note

ASHA is the professional, scientific, and credentialing association for more than 120,000 audiologists, speech-language pathologists, and speech, language, and hearing scientists. ASHA was founded in 1925 as the American Academy of Speech Correction. It became the American Society for the Study of Disorders of Speech in 1927 and the American Speech Correction Association in 1934. In 1947 the name was changed to the American Speech and Hearing Association and the organization incorporated in Kansas; assumed current name in 1979. ASHA is a member of the International Association of Logopedics and Phoniatrics; has an annual budget of $38 million; sponsors and supports the ASHA Political Action Committee; and has a membership of $200/year (individual).

Meetings/Conferences:

Annual Meetings: Fall/13,000
2007 – Boston, MA/Nov. 15-17

Publications:

American Journal of Audiology. 2/year. adv.
Contemporary Issues in Communication Sciences and Disorders. 2/yr.
American Journal of Speech-Language Pathology. q. adv.
Journal of Speech, Language, and Hearing Research. 6/year. adv.
Language, Speech and Hearing Services in Schools. q. adv.
ASHA Leader. bi-m. adv.

American Spice Trade Association *(1907)*
2025 M St. NW, Suite 800
Washington, DC 20036-3309
Tel: (202)367-1127 *Fax:* (202)367-2127
E-Mail: info@astaspice.org
Web Site: www.astaspice.org
Members: 220 spice companies
Staff: 3
Annual Budget: $500-1,000,000
Executive Director: Cheryl A. Deem

Historical Note

ASTA is a trade association with worldwide membership comprised of leading firms in the spice industry. It protects the interests and promotes the welfare of the industry and encourages activities and programs leading to the continued growth in spice consumption.

Meetings/Conferences:

Annual Meetings: Spring

American Spinal Injury Association *(1973)*
2020 Peachtree Rd. NW
Atlanta, GA 30309-1402
Tel: (404)355-9772 *Fax:* (404)355-1826
E-Mail: lesley_hudson@shepherd.org
Web Site: www.asia-spinalinjury.org
Members: 500 individuals
Staff: 3
Annual Budget: $250-500,000
Executive Secretary: Marianne G. Kaplan
Director, Meetings and Publications: Lesley M. Hudson
E-Mail: lesley_hudson@shepherd.org

Historical Note

ASIA members are Doctors of Medicine or Osteopathy and other allied health professionals. Membership: $250 - 350/year (individual).

Meetings/Conferences:

Annual Meetings: Spring

American Sportfishing Association *(1962)*
225 Reinekers Lane, Suite 420
Alexandria, VA 22314
Tel: (703)519-9691 *Fax:* (703)519-1872
Web Site: www.asafishing.org
Members: 767 companies
Staff: 15
Annual Budget: $2-5,000,000
President and Chief Executive Officer: Mike Nussman
E-Mail: mnussman@asafishing.org
Chief Financial Officer: Diane Carpenter
E-Mail: dcarpenter@asafishing.org
Vice President, Government Affairs: Gordon Robertson
E-Mail: grobertson@asafishing.org

Historical Note

Formed by the merger in 1995 of the Sport Fishing Institute and the American Fishing Tackle Manufacturers Association. ASA members are businesses that sell or manufacture any product used in serving and meeting the needs of recreational fishing and associated services including manufacturers, tackle and marine dealers, wholesalers, rep agencies, resource agencies, advocacy groups and publishers.

Publications:

American Sportfishing. q.

American Sports Builders Association *(1965)*
8480 Baltimore National Pike
#307
Ellicott City, MD 21043
Tel: (410)730-9595 *Fax:* (410)730-8833
Toll Free: (866)501 - ASB
Web Site: www.sportsbuilders.org
Members: 360 companies
Staff: 3
Annual Budget: $250-500,000
Executive Vice President: Carol T. Hogan, CAE

Historical Note

The only organization that represents builders, designers, and suppliers of materials for tennis courts, running tracks, synthetic and natural turf fields, and indoor and outdoor sport surfaces. Membership dues vary according to member category.

Meetings/Conferences:

Annual Meetings: November
2007 – Austin, TX(Hyatt Regency)/Dec. 1-5/275

Publications:

Newsletter. q.
Membership Directory. a. adv.

American Sports Medicine Association *(1978)*
660 W. Duarte Road
Arcadia, CA 91007
Tel: (626)445-1978
E-Mail: americansportsmedicine@hotmail.com
Members: 3550 individuals
Staff: 2
Annual Budget: $10-25,000
Chairman: Joe S. Borland, D.O.
E-Mail: americansportsmedicine@hotmail.com

Historical Note

Members are sports medicine trainers, skilled in the prevention and care of injuries as well as physical therapy under a physician's direction. Members must maintain their professional license annually. Provides continuing education and awards the designation CSMT (Certified Sports Medicine Trainer). Membership: $40/year.

Publications:

ASMA Newsletter. q. adv.

American Sportscasters Association *(1979)*
225 Broadway
New York, NY 10007
Tel: (212)227-8080 *Fax:* (212)571-0556
E-Mail: lschwa8918@aol.com

Web Site: http://americansportscasters.com
Members: 550 individuals
Staff: 3
Annual Budget: $100-250,000
President and Executive Director: Louis O. Schwartz
E-Mail: lschwa8918@aol.com

Historical Note
Members are radio and TV sportscasters; the ASA is the forerunner of the American Sportscasters Hall of Fame Trust. Founded the American Sportscasters' Hall of Fame in 1984. Membership: $50/year (individual); $250/year (company).

Meetings/Conferences:
Annual Meetings: Annual Hall of Fame Awards Dinner

Publications:
Insiders Sportsletter. q. adv.

American Staffing Association *(1966)*
277 S. Washington St., Suite 200
Alexandria, VA 22314
Tel: (703)253-2020 *Fax:* (703)253-2053
Toll Free: (800)315 - 3736
E-Mail: asa@americanstaffing.net
Web Site: www.americanstaffing.net
Members: 1700 companies
Staff: 30
Annual Budget: $5-10,000,000
President and Chief Executive Officer: Richard Wahlquist
E-Mail: rwahlquist@americanstaffing.net
Vice President, Communications and Research: Steve Berchem
E-Mail: sberchem@americanstaffing.net
Director, Finance and Administration: Melissa Cecchine
E-Mail: mcecchine@americanstaffing.net
Director, Publications: Luanne Crayton
E-Mail: lcrayton@americanstaffing.net
Senior Vice President, Public Affairs and General Counsel: Edward A. Lenz
E-Mail: elenz@americanstaffing.net
Assistant Vice President, Chapter Relations and Education: Tracy Rettie
E-Mail: trettie@americanstaffing.net
Manager, Information Systems: Ray Richards
E-Mail: rrichards@americanstaffing.net
Senior Meeting Planner: Lisa Simpson
E-Mail: lsimpson@americanstaffing.net
Director, Membership: Kelly Verberg
E-Mail: kverberg@americanstaffing.net

Historical Note
Formerly (1971) Institute of Temporary Services, (1994) National Association of Temporary Services, and (1999) National Association of Temporary and Staffing Services. Members are companies providing the full range of staffing services and human resource solutions, including temporary help, placement services, managed services and employee leasing to business and government. Sponsors and supports the American Staffing Association Staffing Political Action Committee. Membership: $450/year (associate); $240-60,000/year (company).

Meetings/Conferences:
Annual Meetings: Fall/850

Publications:
Staffing Law. q. adv.
Staffing Week. w. adv.
Staffing Success. bi-m. adv.
Directory. a. adv.

American Stamp Dealers' Association *(1914)*
3 School St., Suite 205
Glen Cove, NY 11542
Tel: (516)759-7000 *Fax:* (516)759-7014
E-Mail: asda@erols.com
Web Site: www.asdaonline.org
Members: 1000 individuals
Staff: 4
Annual Budget: $500-1,000,000
Executive Vice President: Joseph B. Savarese

Historical Note
Members are retailers and wholesalers of stamps, albums and other philatelic materials. Membership: $300/year.

Meetings/Conferences:
Semi-Annual Meetings: Spring and Fall

American Statistical Association *(1839)*
1429 Duke St.
Alexandria, VA 22314-3415
Tel: (703)684-1221 *Fax:* (703)684-2036
E-Mail: steve@amstat.org
Web Site: www.amstat.org
Members: 17000 individuals
Staff: 29
Annual Budget: $5-10,000,000
Executive Director and Secretary: William B. Smith, Ph.D.
Director, Operations: Stephen Porzio

Historical Note
Founded in Boston November 27, 1839 and incorporated in Massachusetts in 1841. ASA, a non-profit professional organization, fosters statistics and their application in the broadest manner, promotes unity and effective effort among all concerned with statistical problems and works to increase the contribution of statistics to human welfare. Membership: $85/year (regular); $25/year (student/senior member).

Meetings/Conferences:
Annual Meetings: Summer
2007 – Salt Lake City, UT(Convention Center)/July 29-Aug. 2
2008 – Denver, CO(Convention Center)/Aug. 3-7
2009 – Washington DC(Convention Center)/Aug. 2-6
2010 – Vancouver, BC, Canada(Convention Center)/Aug. 1-5

Publications:
Journal of Computational & Graphical Statistics. q. adv.
Proceedings. a. adv.
Stats-The Magazine for Students of Statistics. 3/year. adv.
Chance Magazine. q. adv.
LINK Newsletter.
Technometrics. q.
Journal of Agricultural, Biological and Environmental Statistics. q.
American Statistician. q. adv.
AMSTAT News. m. adv.
Current Index to Statistics. a.
Journal of the American Statistical Ass'n. q. adv.
Journal of Business and Economic Statistics. q. adv.
Journal of Educational & Behavioral Statistics. q.

American Stock Exchange *(1911)*
86 Trinity Place
New York, NY 10006-1881
Tel: (212)306-1000 *Fax:* (212)306-1152
Toll Free: (800)843 - 2639
E-Mail: amexfeedback@amex.com
Web Site: www.amex.com
Members: 864 individuals
Staff: 781
Annual Budget: $5-10,000,000
Chief Executive Officer: Neal L. Wolkoff
Contact: Daniel Charmas
Executive Vice President and Chief Information Officer: Antoine Shagoury
E-Mail: amexfeedback@amex.com

Historical Note
Founded as an outdoor market in New York before 1800, it became successively the New York Market Agency in 1908, the New York Curb Market Association in 1911, the New York Curb Market in 1921 with its move indoors, the New York Curb Exchange in 1929 and the American Stock Exchange in 1953. In 1998, AmEx merged with National Association of Securities, forming the NASDAQ-AmEx Market Group, under which the two stock exchanges operate; the two exchanges became independent again in 2003.

Meetings/Conferences:
Annual Meetings: New York City, 2nd Monday in April.

Publications:
Annual Report.
Fact Book.

American String Teachers Association *(1946)*
4153 Chain Bridge Road
Fairfax, VA 22030-4102
Tel: (703)279-2113 *Fax:* (703)279-2114
E-Mail: asta@astaweb.com
Web Site: www.astaweb.com
Members: 11500 individuals, schools, universities and corporate members
Staff: 10
Annual Budget: $500-1,000,000
Executive Director: Donna Sizemore Hale

Historical Note
Founded in 1946 and incorporated in Iowa in 1955. Absorbed National School Orchestra Association in 1998. Membership is open to teachers and performers of stringed instruments including guitar and harp, students, schools or libraries, and commercial institutions interested in supporting its programs. Sponsors a biannual National Solo Competition, summer workshops, conferences, and publications.

Meetings/Conferences:
2007 – Detroit, MI(Detroit Marriott Renaissance Hotel)/March 7-10

Publications:
ATSA e-News. m.
American String Teacher. q. adv.

American Student Dental Association *(1971)*
211 E. Chicago Ave., Suite 1160
Chicago, IL 60611
Tel: (312)440-2795 *Fax:* (312)440-2820
Toll Free: (800)621 - 8099 Ext: 2795
E-Mail: asda@asdanet.org
Web Site: www.asdanet.org
Members: 13000 individuals
Staff: 6
Annual Budget: $500-1,000,000
Executive Director: Nancy R. Honeycutt, CAE
Director, Communications: Lauren Wood

Historical Note
Founded in Chicago, Illinois in 1971 at a national conference for dental students. Seeks to involve its members in the interprofessional activities of the dental profession. Membership: $40/year.

Meetings/Conferences:
Annual Meetings: Summer

Publications:
ASDA News. m. adv.
Dentistry. q. adv.
ASDA Handbook. a. adv.
ASDA Guides to Post-Doctoral Dental Programs, Vols I,II,III. bi-a.
National Boards Examination Reprints.

American Studies Association *(1951)*
1120 19th St. NW, Suite 301
Washington, DC 20036
Tel: (202)467-4783 *Fax:* (202)467-4786
E-Mail: asastaff@theasa.net
Web Site: www.georgetown.edu/crossroads/asainfo.html
Members: 5000 individuals
Staff: 5
Annual Budget: $500-1,000,000
Executive Director: John F. Stephens, Ph.D.

Historical Note
Founded in 1951 and incorporated in 1951 to foster the study of American culture and civilization as an entity rather than from the viewpoint of a single discipline. Admitted to membership in the American Council of Learned Societies in 1958. Membership: individual fees vary according to income.

Meetings/Conferences:
Annual Meetings: Fall/1,500

Publications:
Directory of Graduate Programs in American Studies.
Encyclopedia of American Studies.
Guide to American Studies Resources. a. adv.
ASA Newsletter. q. adv.

American Subcontractors Association *(1966)*
1004 Duke St.
Alexandria, VA 22314-3588
Tel: (703)684-3450 *Fax:* (703)836-3482
E-Mail: asaoffice@asa-hq.com
Web Site: www.asaonline.com

Members: 6900 companies
Staff: 15
Annual Budget: $2-5,000,000
Executive Vice President: E. Colette Nelson
E-Mail: cnelson@asa-hq.com
Counsel, Construction Law and Contracts: Brian Cubbage
E-Mail: bcubbage@asa-hq.com
Director, Government Relations: Luke McFadden
Director, Communications: David Mendes
E-Mail: dmendes@asa-hq.com

Historical Note
ASA is a trade association representing subcontractors, specialty trade contractors, and material suppliers in the construction industry. Sponsors and supports the American Subcontractors Association Political Action Committee and the Subcontractors Legal Defense Fund.

Meetings/Conferences:
Semi-Annual Meetings: Spring and Fall

Publications:
The Contractor's Compass. q. adv.
ASA Today. w.

American Suffolk Horse Association
4240 Goehring Road
Ledbetter, TX 78946-5004
Tel: (979)249-5795
E-Mail: suffolks@cvtv.net
Web Site: www.suffolkpunch.com
Members: 200 individuals
Staff: 1
Annual Budget: under $10,000
Secretary: Mary Margaret Read

Historical Note
Members are owners and breeders of Suffolk horses. Membership: $20-25/year.

Publications:
Directory of Suffolk Owners and Breeders. irreg.

American Sugar Alliance *(1983)*
2111 Wilson Blvd., Suite 600
Arlington, VA 22201
Tel: (703)351-5055 *Fax:* (703)351-6698
E-Mail: info@sugaralliance.org
Web Site: www.sugaralliance.org
Members: 500 individuals
Staff: 4
Executive Director: Vickie R. Myers
Director, Media Relations: Phillip Hayes
Director, Economics and Policy Analysis: Jack Roney

Historical Note
A national coalition supporting America's cane, beet and corn farmers and dedicated to preserving a strong domestic sweetener industry.

Meetings/Conferences:
Annual Meetings: Summer
2007 - Napa Valley, CA(Silverado Resort and Spa)/Aug. 4-8
2008 - Big Island of Hawaii, HI(Fairmont Orchid)/Aug. 2-6

Publications:
The Sugar Beat. m.

American Sugar Cane League of the U.S.A. *(1922)*
P.O. Drawer 938
Thibodaux, LA 70302
Tel: (985)448-3707 *Fax:* (985)448-3722
E-Mail: jsimon@amsel.org
Web Site: www.amscl.org
Members: 675 producers, 13 manufacturers
Staff: 5
Annual Budget: $2-5,000,000
General Manager: Jim Simon

Historical Note
Formed by a merger of the Louisiana Sugar Planters Association (founded in 1887), the American Cane Growers Association (founded in 1919) and the Producers and Manufacturers Association (founded in 1921). Sponsors the American Sugar Cane League Political Action Committee.

Meetings/Conferences:
Annual Meetings: Thibodaux, LA/last Wednesday in February

Publications:
Sugar Bulletin. m. adv.

American Sugarbeet Growers Association *(1975)*
1156 15th St. NW, Suite 1101
Washington, DC 20005
Tel: (202)833-2398 *Fax:* (202)833-2962
E-Mail: info@americansugarbeet.org
Web Site: www.americansugarbeet.org
Members: 23 regional associations
Staff: 4
Annual Budget: $500-1,000,000
Executive Vice President: Luther A. Markwart
E-Mail: info@americansugarbeet.org
Vice President: Ruthann Geib
E-Mail: info@americansugarbeet.org

Historical Note
A federation of state and regional associations of sugarbeet growers. Formerly (1975) National Sugarbeet Growers Association.

Meetings/Conferences:
Annual Meetings: Winter

American Supply and Machinery Manufacturers Association

Historical Note
Became Industrial Supply Manufacturers Association in 2001.

American Supply Association *(1894)*
222 Merchandise Mart Plaza, Suite 1400
Chicago, IL 60654
Tel: (312)464-0090 *Fax:* (312)464-0091
E-Mail: info@asa.net
Web Site: www.asa.net
Members: 1000 companies
Staff: 11
Annual Budget: $5-10,000,000
Executive Vice President: Inge Calderon
Director, Meetings/Conventions: Ruth Mitchell

Historical Note
Merger (1970) of Central Supply Association of Chicago and the American Institute of Supply Associations. Members are plumbing, heating and cooling piping distributors and manufacturers. Sponsors and supports the ASA Political Action Committee.

Meetings/Conferences:
Annual Meetings: Fall/6,000

Publications:
Membership Directory. a. adv.
ASA Quarterly. q.
Operations Performance Report. a.

American Surgical Association *(1880)*
900 Cummings Center, Suite 221-U
Beverly, MA 01915
Tel: (978)927-8330 *Fax:* (978)524-8890
E-Mail: asa@prri.com
Web Site: www.americansurgical.info
Members: 1139 individuals
Staff: 1
Executive Director: Robert P. Jones, Jr., Ed.D.

Historical Note
Founded in 1880 in Philadelphia as the American Surgical Society, the name was subsequently changed to the American Surgical Association.

Meetings/Conferences:
Annual Meetings: Spring
2007 - Colorado Springs, CO(The Broadmoor)/Apr. 26-28

Publications:
Annals of Surgery. semi-a. adv.
Transactions. a.

American Swimming Coaches Association *(1958)*
5101 N.W. 21st Ave., Suite 200
Ft. Lauderdale, FL 33309
Tel: (954)563-4930 *Fax:* (954)563-9813
Toll Free: (800)356 - 2722
E-Mail: ASCA@LORNET.COM
Web Site: www.swimmingcoach.org
Members: 5174 individuals
Staff: 10
Annual Budget: $1-2,000,000
Executive Director: John Leonard

Historical Note
Membership: $65/year (U.S.); $80/year (foreign).

Meetings/Conferences:
Annual Meetings: September

Publications:
ASCA Newsletter. m.
Clinic Book. a.
Journal of Swimming Research. a.
ASCA Magazine. m.
Job Service. bi-w.
High School Recruiters Directory. a.

American Symphony Orchestra League *(1942)*
33 W. 60th St., Fifth Floor
New York, NY 10023-7905
Tel: (212)262-5161 *Fax:* (212)262-5198
E-Mail: league@symphony.org
Web Site: www.symphony.org
Members: 3490 individuals
Staff: 35
Annual Budget: $5-10,000,000
President and Chief Executive Officer: Henry Fogel
Manager, Advertising and Meetings: Steven Alter
Vice President and Chief Financial Officer: Charles Irmiter
Vice President and Chief Operating Officer: Jack McAuliffe
Vice President, Development: Stacey Weston

Historical Note
Founded in 1942 and chartered by Congress in 1962. ASOL's purpose is to ensure the artistic, organizational and financial strength of American orchestras. Services include: training programs, publications, research and analysis, technical assistance, and government relations for professional, avocational and youth orchestras, and for trustees, management staff, conductors, artistic staff and volunteers.

Meetings/Conferences:
Annual Meetings: June

Publications:
SYMPHONY Magazine. bi-m. adv.

American Tarentaise Association *(1973)*
P.O. Box 34705
North Kansas City, MO 64116-1105
Tel: (816)421-1993 *Fax:* (816)421-1991
E-Mail: info@usa-tarentaise.com
Web Site: http://usa-tarentaise.com
Members: 244 individuals
Annual Budget: $50-100,000
Executive Director: James A. Spawn

Historical Note
Tarentaise cattle originated in Southeastern France, and were recognized as a breed in 1866. The association is the official breed registry for Tarentaise cattle. Membership: $30/year.

Meetings/Conferences:
Annual Meetings: January

Publications:
Tarentaise Journal. m. adv.

American Taxation Association *(1975)*

Historical Note
A section of the American Accounting Association, which provides administrative support. Members are university professors teaching courses dealing with federal tax matters.

American Technical Education Association *(1928)*
North Dakota State College of Science
800 N. Sixth St.
Wahpeton, ND 58076-0002
Tel: (701)671-2240 *Fax:* (701)671-2260
Web Site: www.ateaonline.org
Members: 2000 organizations & individuals
Staff: 2
Annual Budget: $100-250,000
Executive Director: Betty Krump

Historical Note
Established in 1928 as the American Association of Technical High Schools and Institutes; assumed its present name in 1950 and was incorporated in New York in 1960. From 1944 to 1969, was affiliated with the American Vocational Association. Composed of post-secondary institutions, businesses and industrial organizations, ATEA is involved in expanding and improving the quality of technical education at the secondary level. Membership: $50/year (individual);

$300/year (industry/business); $200/year (institution/agency).

Meetings/Conferences:

Annual Meetings: Spring

Publications:

ATEA Journal. q. adv.

American Telemedicine Association *(1993)*
1100 Connecticut Ave. NW
Suite 540
Washington, DC 20036
Tel: (202)223-3333 *Fax:* (202)223-2787
Web Site: www.americantelemed.org/
Members: 1400 individuals
Annual Budget: $100-250,000
Executive Director: Jonathan D. Linkous
E-Mail: jlinkous@americantelemed.org
Deputy Executive Director: Alice J. Watland
E-Mail: awatland@americantelemed.org

Historical Note

Membership: $180/year (individual); $200/year (international); $75/year (student).

Publications:

Telemedicine Journal and e-Health. q. adv.
Membership Directory.
On-Line Member News Update.

American Teleservices Association *(1983)*
3815 River Crossing Pkwy., Suite 20
Indianapolis, IN 46240
Tel: (317)816-9336 *Fax:* (317)218-0323
E-Mail: contact@ataconnect.org
Web Site: www.ataconnect.org
Members: 2000companiesandindividuals
Staff: 2
Annual Budget: $1-2,000,000
Chief Executive Officer: Tim Searcy
E-Mail: contact@ataconnect.org
Director, Member Services: Karl Jacobs
E-Mail: contact@ataconnect.org

Historical Note

Founded as American Telemarketing Association; assumed its current name in 1998. ATA members are business executives who have significant management responsibilities for telephone-assisted marketing/sales/service activities, own or operate telemarketing service agencies, or are suppliers of goods/services to the telemarketing industry. Membership fee varies, based on company size.

Meetings/Conferences:

Semi-Annual Meetings: Spring and Fall

Publications:

Compendium of State Regulations. a.
Newsletter. m. adv.
On-Site Conference Program. semi-a. adv.
ATA Membership Services Referral Directory. a.

American Textile Machinery Association *(1907)*
201 Park Washington Court
Falls Church, VA 22046-4513
Tel: (703)538-1789 *Fax:* (703)241-5603
E-Mail: info@atmanet.org
Web Site: www.atmanet.org
Members: 100 companies
Staff: 5
Annual Budget: $500-1,000,000
President: Clay D. Tyeryar, CAE

Historical Note

Formerly (1933) National Association of Textile Machinery Manufacturers. Sponsors and supports the Textile Machinery Good Government Committee.

Meetings/Conferences:

Annual Meetings: Spring

Publications:

Product Directory Guide. every 4 years.
ATMA Executive Report. 6-8/year.

American Textile Manufacturers Institute *(1949)*

Historical Note

Superseded by National Council of Textile Organizations.

American Theatre and Drama Society

Historical Note

A focus group of the Association for Theatre in Higher Education.

American Theatre Critics Association *(1974)*
773 Nebraska Ave. West
St. Paul, MN 55117
Tel: (317)826-7894
E-Mail: atca_admin@msn.com
Web Site: www.americantheatrecritics.org
Members: 275 individuals
Annual Budget: $10-25,000
Administrator: Kathryn Burger
E-Mail: atca_admin@msn.com

Historical Note

Organized at the O'Neill Theater Center in Waterford, CT in 1974 to make possible greater communication among theater critics, to encourage freedom of expression in theater and theater criticism, to advance standards of criticism and to increase public awareness of the theater as a national resource. Membership is open only to professional writers who have been activelyemployed reviewing theatre on a regular and continuing basis. membership: $55/year.

Meetings/Conferences:

Semi-annual Meetings: Winter/Spring

Publications:

Critics Annual. a. adv.

American Theological Library Association *(1946)*
250 S. Wacker Dr., Suite 1600
Chicago, IL 60606-5889
Tel: (312)454-5100 *Fax:* (312)454-5505
Toll Free: (888)665 - 2852
E-Mail: atla@atla.com
Web Site: www.atla.com
Members: 496 individuals
Staff: 42
Annual Budget: $2-5,000,000
Executive Director: Dennis Norlin
E-Mail: dnorlin@atla.com
Director, Financial Services: Pradeep Gamadia
E-Mail: pgamadia@atla.com
Director, Member Services: Barbara Kemmis

Historical Note

An outgrowth of a Round Table on Libraries of the American Association of Theological Schools held in 1947. International membership includes persons from Christian, Jewish and non-Judeo-Christian traditions interested in the practice, support or promotion of theological librarianship, information systems or bibliography. Membership: $15-150/year (individual); $75-750/year (company); $75/year (affiliates).

Meetings/Conferences:

Annual Meetings: June
2007 – Philadelphia, PA/June 13-16
2008 – Ottawa, ON, Canada/June 25-28

Publications:

Newsletter. q. adv.
Proceedings. a.
Religion Index One: Periodicals. semi-a.

American Therapeutic Recreation Association *(1984)*
1414 Prince St., Suite 204
Alexandria, VA 22314
Tel: (703)683-9420 *Fax:* (703)683-9431
E-Mail: national@atra-tr.org
Web Site: www.atra-tr.org
Members: 4500 individuals
Staff: 5
Annual Budget: $500-1,000,000
Executive Director: Ann D. Huston, CTRS
E-Mail: national@atra-tr.org

Historical Note

Purpose is to advance the field of Therapeutic Recreation as an effective and efficient component of health care. Membership: $95/year (individual); $275/year (company).

Meetings/Conferences:

Semi-Annual Meetings: Spring and Fall

Publications:

Newsletter. bi-m. adv.
Employment Update. m. adv.
Annual in Therapeutic Recreation. a.

American Thoracic Society *(1905)*
61 Broadway, Fourth Floor
New York, NY 10006-2755
Tel: (212)315-8600 *Fax:* (212)315-6498
Web Site: www.thoracic.org
Members: 18000 individuals
Staff: 65
Annual Budget: $10-25,000,000
Executive Director: Carl Booberg
Director, Membership, Subscriptions and Database Services: Jeffrey Delgado
Director, Communications and Marketing: Brian Kell
Director, Info. Systems: Maribel Lim
Director, Educational Programs: Shane McDermott
Director, Meeting Services: Deborah Richardt, CMP
Director, Human Resources: Barbara Smith, GBA

Historical Note

Founded in 1905 as the American Sanatorium Association and became the American Trudeau Society in 1939; assumed its current name in 1960. Has an annual budget of approximately $22 million.

Meetings/Conferences:

Annual Meetings: Spring

Publications:

Proceedings of the American Thoracic Society. 4-6/yr. adv.
American Journal of Respiratory and Critical Care Medicine. m. adv.
ATS News. m.
American Journal of Respiratory Cell and Molecular Biology. m. adv.

American Thyroid Association *(1923)*
6066 Leesburg Pike, Suite 650
Falls Church, VA 22041
Tel: (703)998-8890 *Fax:* (703)998-8893
E-Mail: admin@thyroid.org
Web Site: www.thyroid.org
Members: 900 individuals
Staff: 3
Annual Budget: $1-2,000,000
Executive Director: Barbara R. Smith, CAE

Historical Note

Founded as the American Association for the Study of Goiter, it became the American Goiter Association in 1948 and assumed its present name in 1959. ATA is a professional organization of physicians and scientists dedicated to treatment and education regarding thyroid function and disease. Membership: $210/year (basic dues, plus journal).

Meetings/Conferences:

Annual Meetings: Fall
2007 – New York, NY(Sheraton New York)/Oct. 4-7
2008 – Chicago, IL(Chicago Sheraton Hotel and Towers)/Oct. 2-5
2009 – Palm Beach, FL(The Breakers Hotel)/Sept. 24-27

Publications:

Newsletter. 3/year.
Thyroid, A Journal. m. adv.
Annual Meeting Program Book. a.
Signal. 3/year.

American Tin Trade Association *(1928)*
P.O. Box 53
Richboro, PA 18954
Tel: (215)504-9725 *Fax:* (215)504-9726
Members: 60 companies
Annual Budget: $10-25,000
Secretary: Kay Salberg

Historical Note

Membership: $350/year.

Meetings/Conferences:

Semi-Annual Meetings: New York, NY/second Thursday in May and second Thursday in November/60

American Tinnitus Association *(1971)*
P.O. Box 5
Portland, OR 97207-0005
Tel: (503)248-9985 *Fax:* (503)248-0024
Toll Free: (800)634 - 8978
E-Mail: tinnitus@ata.org
Web Site: www.ata.org
Members: 18500 individuals
Staff: 10
Annual Budget: $1-2,000,000
Executive Director: Cheryl McGinnis

E-Mail: cheryl@ata.org
Director, Education: Barbara Sanders
E-Mail: barbara@ata.org

Historical Note
Physicians, audiologists, hearing aid dispensers and individuals who suffer from tinnitus, noises in the head or ears. ATA supports tinnitus research, provides information and referral to professionals and support groups, and conducts seminars for hearing professionals. Promotes public education regarding tinnitus. Membership: $35/year; $50/year (outside U.S.).

Publications:
Tinnitus Today. q. adv.

American Tort Reform Association *(1986)*
1101 Connecticut Ave. NW, Suite 400
Washington, DC 20036
Tel: (202)682-1163 *Fax:* (202)682-1022
Toll Free: (800)306 - 2872
Web Site: www.atra.org
Members: 300 individuals
Staff: 7
Annual Budget: $2-5,000,000
President: Sherman "Tiger" Joyce
E-Mail: sjoyce@atra.org
Director, Communications: Darren McKinney
Director, Public Affairs and Field Operations: Cari O'Malley

Historical Note
Members are individuals and organizations with a professional interest in reforming the civil justice system.

Publications:
Reform (newsletter). a.
Leaders Update. bi-w.
Legislative Watch. w.

American Traffic Safety Services Association *(1969)*
15 Riverside Pkwy., Suite 100
Fredericksburg, VA 22406
Tel: (540)368-1701 *Fax:* (540)368-1717
Toll Free: (800)272 - 8772
Web Site: www.atssa.com
Members: 1800 companies
Staff: 28
Annual Budget: $5-10,000,000
Executive Director: Roger Wentz
Director, Communications: Jim Baron
Director, Government Relations: Peter Bizzozero
Director, Training and Products: Donna Clark
Director, Finance and Administration: Mitu Lao
Director, Member Services: David McKee
Director, Meetings and Conventions: Melanie Myers
Associate Director, Volunteer Services: Elaine Ottley

Historical Note
Founded as the American Traffic Safety Control Devices Association. Became the American Traffic Services Association in 1971; assumed its present name in 1984. Members are companies providing traffic control and safety devices to government and industry. Membership: $75/year (individual); $775/year minimum (organization/company).

Meetings/Conferences:
2007 - San Antonio, TX(Convention Center)/Jan. 28-30
2008 - New Orleans, LA(Convention Center)/Feb. 10-12

Publications:
ATSSA Flash. bi-w.
ATSSA Signal. q.
ATSSA Membership Directory. a.

American Train Dispatchers Association *(1917)*
1370 Ontario St., Suite 1040
Cleveland, OH 44113-1701
Tel: (216)241-2630 *Fax:* (216)241-6286
Web Site: http://atdd.homestead.com/atddpg1.html
Members: 2600 individuals
Staff: 5
Annual Budget: $1-2,000,000
Secretary-Treasurer: Gary L. Melton

Historical Note
First organized as a local union in Spokane, Washington in 1917. Shortly developed into the Western Train Dispatchers' Association and, in 1918, organized as American Train Dispatchers Association. Chartered by AFL-CIO in 1957. In 1993, ATDA affiliated with the Brotherhood of Locomotive Engineers, and in 2004 re-established itself as an independent organization. Membership: $729/year (individual).

Meetings/Conferences:
Quadrennial Meetings: (2003)

Publications:
The Train Dispatcher. 6/year.

American Trakehner Association *(1974)*
1536 W. Church St.
Newark, OH 43055
Tel: (740)344-1111 *Fax:* (740)344-3225
E-Mail: atahorses@alltel.net
Web Site: www.americantrakehner.com
Members: 1400 individuals
Staff: 2
Annual Budget: $100-250,000
Executive Director: Kelly Gulick

Historical Note
Members are owners and breeders of Trakehner horses, a breed originating in Trakehnen, East Prussia. Unified with North American Trakhener Association in 2001. Membership: $75/year (individual); $750 (lifetime member).

Meetings/Conferences:
Annual Meetings: Fall

Publications:
Handbook. a. adv.
Newsletter. bi-m. adv.
American Trakehner. q. adv.

American Translators Association *(1959)*
225 Reinekers Lane, Suite 590
Alexandria, VA 22314
Tel: (703)683-6100
E-Mail: ata@atanet.org
Web Site: www.atanet.org
Members: 9700 individuals
Staff: 10
Annual Budget: $2-5,000,000
Executive Director: Walter W. Bacak, Jr.
E-Mail: walter@atanet.org

Historical Note
Members are translators and interpreters. Has a testing and accreditation program. Membership: $145/year (individual); $140/year (institution); $300/year (corporate); $65/year (student).

Meetings/Conferences:
Annual Meetings: Fall
2007 - San Francisco, CA(Hyatt Regency)/Oct. 31-Nov. 3/1500
2008 - Orlando, FL(Hilton)/Nov. 5-8/1500
2009 - New York, NY(Marriott)/Oct. 28-31/1800

Publications:
ATA Chronicle. m. adv.
Proceedings. a.

American Trauma Society *(1968)*
8903 Presidential Pkwy., Suite 512
Upper Marlboro, MD 20772-2656
Tel: (301)420-4189 *Fax:* (301)420-0617
Toll Free: (800)556 - 7890
E-Mail: info@amtrauma.org
Web Site: www.amtrauma.org/
Members: 3000 individuals
Staff: 8
Annual Budget: $1-2,000,000
Executive Director: Harry Teter

Historical Note
Dedicated to reducing needless death and disability through public awareness/education on trauma system development and trauma prevention. Membership includes both lay and professional individuals, institutions, and corporations. Membership: $50/year (general member); $145/year (physician); $250/year (sustaining); and $2500 for lifetime membership.

Meetings/Conferences:
Annual Meetings: Spring

Publications:
Promotional Media Resource Catalog. q. adv.
Traumagram. q.

American Truck Dealers *(1970)*
8400 Westpark Dr.
McLean, VA 22102
Tel: (703)821-7230 *Fax:* (703)749-4700
Toll Free: (800)352 - 6232
E-Mail: atd@nada.org
Web Site: http://atd.nada.org
Members: 2000 companies
Staff: 35
Executive Director: James H. Westlake
E-Mail: atd@nada.org

Historical Note
A division of National Automobile Dealers Association, ATD represents medium and heavy truck dealers. ATD members share in NADA's programs, services and benefits and can take advantage of ATD 20 Groups, a performance-based business forum for truck dealers.

Meetings/Conferences:
2007 - San Diego, CA(Convention Center)/Apr. 14-16/2500

Publications:
American Truck Dealer newsletter. m.

American Truck Stop Operators Association *(1981)*
P.O. Box 4949
Winston-Salem, NC 27115-4949
Tel: (336)774-5555 *Fax:* (336)744-1184
Members: 650 companies
Staff: 6
Annual Budget: $500-1,000,000
President and Chief Executive Officer: Lloyd L. Golding

Historical Note
Trade association of full facility truck stop operators. Membership: $500/year.

Publications:
Bulletin. m.

American Trucking Associations *(1933)*
2200 Mill Road
Alexandria, VA 22314-4677
Tel: (703)838-1700
E-Mail: atamembership@trucking.org
Web Site: www.truckline.com
Members: 3000 companies
Staff: 190
Annual Budget: $25-50,000,000
Senior Vice President and Chief of Staff: Dan Stanley
President and Chief Executive Officer: Bill Graves
E-Mail: atamembership@trucking.org
Senior Vice President and Chief of Staff: Dan Stanley
Director, Public Affairs and Deputy Press Secretary: Tiffany Wlazlowski
E-Mail: atamembership@trucking.org

Historical Note
A federation of state trucking associations, national truck conferences and individual motor carrier companies and suppliers. Formed by a merger of the American Highway Freight Association and the Federated Truck Associations of America. Sponsors and supports the political action committee TRUCK-PAC.

Meetings/Conferences:
Annual Meetings: Fall/4,000

Publications:
Transport Topics. w. adv.

American Tunaboat Association *(1921)*

Historical Note
Address unknown in 2006.

American Underground-Construction Association *(1976)*
3001 Hennepin Ave., South, Suite D202
Minneapolis, MN 55408
Tel: (212)465-5541 *Fax:* (212)631-3787
E-Mail: underground@auca.org
Web Site: www.auaonline.org
Members: 650 individuals and firms
Staff: 2
Annual Budget: $100-250,000
Executive Director: Susan R. Nelson

Historical Note
Formerly (1994) American Underground-Space Association. Membership consists of owners, engineers, architects, planners, developers, contractors, equipment/materials manufacturers and others interested in the development of underground infrastructure and commercial, industrial, residential, and transport structures. Membership: $70/year (individual); $500/year (company/institution).

Publications:
AUA News. q. adv.

American Urogynecologic Society *(1979)*
2025 M St. NW, Suite 800
Washington, DC 20036
Tel: (202)367-1167 *Fax:* (202)367-2167
E-Mail: info@augs.org
Web Site: www.augs.org
Members: 1200 individuals
Staff: 3
Annual Budget: $1-2,000,000
Executive Director: Steven C. Kemp, CAE
E-Mail: maryellen_watson@dc.sba.com
Convention Manager: Mary Ellen Watson
E-Mail: maryellen_watson@dc.sba.com

Historical Note
Membership: $250/year (individual).

Publications:
Quarterly Report. q.

American Urological Association *(1902)*
1000 Corporate Blvd.
Linthicum, MD 20190
Tel: (410)689-3700 *Fax:* (410)689-3800
Toll Free: (866)746 - 4282
E-Mail: aua@auanet.org
Web Site: www.auanet.org
Members: 15400 individuals
Staff: 80
Annual Budget: $10-25,000,000
Executive Director: Mike Sheppard
E-Mail: aua@auanet.org

Historical Note
Founded in 1902 and incorporated in Maryland. Has an annual budget of $12 million. Membership: $350/year.

Meetings/Conferences:
Annual Meetings: Spring/14,000
2007 – Anaheim, CA/May 19-24
2008 – Orlando, FL/May 17-22

Publications:
Health Policy Brief. m.
Journal of Urology. m. adv.
AUA News. m. adv.

American Venous Forum *(1989)*
PMB #311, 203 Washington St.
Salem, MA 01970
Tel: (978)744-5005 *Fax:* (978)744-5029
E-Mail: venous-info@administrare.com
Web Site: www.venous-info.com
Members: 260 individuals
Staff: 1
Executive Director: Robin Hoyle
President: Michael D. Dalsing
E-Mail: venous-info@administrare.com

American Veterinary Dental Society *(1976)*
618 Church St., Suite 220
Nashville, TN 37219
Toll Free: (800)332 - 2837
E-Mail: audf@walkermgt.com
Members: 1200 individuals
Annual Budget: $100-250,000
Management Executive: Dee Ann Walker, CAE

Historical Note
AVDS provides a common meeting ground and learning forum for those interested in veterinary dentistry, with the objectives of furthering the knowledge and recognition of the importance of veterinary dentistry among practicing veterinarians, students of veterinary medicine and the general public. Membership: $60/year (individual).

Meetings/Conferences:
Annual Meetings: October
2007 – Minneapolis, MN(Hyatt Regency)/Oct. 19-21

Publications:
Journal of Veterinary Dentistry. q. adv.

American Veterinary Distributors Association *(1976)*
2105 Laurel Bush Road, Suite 200
Bel Air, MD 21015
Tel: (443)640-1040 Ext: 105 *Fax:* (443)640-1031
E-Mail: jackie@ksgroup.org
Web Site: www.avda.net
Members: 75 companies
Annual Budget: $100-250,000
Executive Director: Jackwelyn Raley-King
Director, Meetings and Member Services: Kaymie T. Owen

Historical Note
AVDA members are distributors of animal healthcare products; associate members are manufacturers of animal healthcare products.

Meetings/Conferences:
Annual Meetings: Spring

Publications:
AVDA Distributor Newsletter. q.

American Veterinary Medical Association *(1863)*
1931 N. Meacham Road, Suite 100
Schaumburg, IL 60173-4360
Tel: (847)925-8070 *Fax:* (847)925-1329
Toll Free: (800)248 - 2862
E-Mail: avmainfo@avma.org
Web Site: www.avma.org
Members: 74000 individuals
Staff: 117
Annual Budget: $10-25,000,000
Executive Vice President: Dr. Bruce W. Little
Director, Marketing: Jim Flanigan

Historical Note
Founded in 1863 as the United States Veterinary Medical Association; assumed its current name in 1898. Incorporated in Illinois in 1917. AVMA's objective is to advance the art and science of veterinary medicine, including its relationship to public health, biological science, and agriculture. Sponsors the American Veterinary Medical Foundation and the American Veterinary Medical Association Political Action Committee. Membership: $250/year (individual).

Meetings/Conferences:
Annual Meetings: Summer

Publications:
American Journal of Veterinary Research. m. adv.
Journal of AVMA. semi-m. adv.

American Veterinary Society of Animal Behavior *(1975)*
Three Fox Valley Lane
Glen Mills, PA 19342
E-Mail: avsabe@yahoo.com
Web Site: www.avma.org/avsab
Members: 530 individuals
Annual Budget: $10-25,000
Treasurer: Lisa Radosta, DVM
E-Mail: avsabe@yahoo.com

Historical Note
Formerly the American Society of Veterinary Ethology. Membership restricted to veterinarians, veterinary students, and animal behavior consultants. Has no paid officers or full-time staff. Membership: $40/year (full member); $7.50/year (student).

Meetings/Conferences:
Annual Meetings: in conjunction with American Veterinary Medical Ass'n

Publications:
AVSAB Newsletter. 4/year.

American Viola Society *(1971)*
14070 Proton Road, Suite 1100
Dallas, TX 75244-5737
Tel: (972)233-9107 Ext: 204
E-Mail: info@avsnationaloffice.org
Web Site: www.americanviolasociety.org
Members: 1000 individuals
Annual Budget: $25-50,000
General Manager: Madeleine Crouch

Historical Note
AVS members are professional violists, teachers and amateur string players. Has no paid officers or full-time staff. Membership: 42/year (full member); $21/year (student).

Publications:
Journal of the American Viola Society. 2/year.
Membership Directory (online).

American Vocational Education Personnel Development Association *(1972)*
39 Bank St.
P.O. Box 232
Chatham, VA 24531
Tel: (434)432-2761 Ext: 3129 *Fax:* (434)432-9560
Members: 250 individuals
Annual Budget: under $10,000
President: Lillian H. Daughtry, Ph.D.

Meetings/Conferences:
Annual Meetings: in conjunction with the American Vocational Ass'n/December

Publications:
AVEPDA Review Newsletter. q.
Directory. a.

American Voice Input/Output Society *(1982)*
P.O. Box 20817
San Jose, CA 95160
Tel: (408)323-1783 *Fax:* (408)323-1782
E-Mail: info@avios.com
Web Site: www.avios.com
Members: 470 individuals
Staff: 2
Executive Director: William Meisel
E-Mail: wmeisel@tmaa.com

Historical Note
AVIOS members are academics, engineers, hardware manufacturers, and others with an interest in the development of voice interfaces with computers.

Publications:
Internat'l Journal of Speech Technology. a.

American Volleyball Coaches Association *(1981)*
2365 Harrodsburg Rd.
Suite A325
Lexington, KY 40504
Tel: (859)226-4205 *Fax:* (859)226-4338
Toll Free: (866)544 - 2822
E-Mail: info@avca.org
Web Site: www.avca.org
Members: 3200 individuals
Staff: 9
Annual Budget: $1-2,000,000
Executive Director: Kathy DeBoer
Assistant Executive Director: C. Todd Hamilton

Historical Note
AVCA is comprised of coaches from all levels who are committed to the development and advancement of volleyball throughout America. Membership: $50-310/year (individual).

Meetings/Conferences:
Annual Meetings: Winter

Publications:
AVC At the Net Electronic Newsletter. bi-w.
Coaching Volleyball. bi-m. adv.
AVCA Membership Directory. a.
Power Tips. m. adv.
Volleyball Records Book. a.

American Walnut Manufacturers Association *(1912)*
35 Village Court
Zionsville, IN 46077-5046
Tel: (317)873-8780 *Fax:* (317)873-8780
E-Mail: fryelarryr@aol.com
Web Site: www.walnutassociation.org
Members: 11 companies
Staff: 1
Annual Budget: $10-25,000
Executive Director: Larry R. Frye
E-Mail: fryelarryr@aol.com

Historical Note
First organized in 1912. AWMA is an international trade association representing manufacturers of walnut and other fine hardwood, lumber, dimension lumber, veneer, squares and gunstock blanks.

Meetings/Conferences:
Annual Meetings: Annual luncheon held in conjunction w/ the Nat'l Hardwood Lumber Ass'n
2007 - Washington, DC/Sept. 12-15/1200
2008 - San Francisco, CA(San Francisco Marriott)

American Warmblood Registry *(1981)*
P.O. Box 190
Larkspur, CO 80118
Tel: (303)681-3193 *Fax:* (775)667-0516
E-Mail: amerwarmblood@aol.com
Web Site: www.americanwarmblood.com
Members: 400 individuals
Staff: 4
Annual Budget: $250-500,000
President: Sonja K. Lowenfish
E-Mail: amerwarmblood@aol.com
Historical Note
Members are owners and breeders of Warmblood horses. Membership: $75/year.
Publications:
Internet-with monthly upgrades of news. adv.
Directory of Stallions at Stud. a. adv.
Warmblood News Magazine. m. adv.

American Watch Association *(1933)*
1201 Pennsylvania Ave. NW
Washington, DC 20044
Tel: (703)759-3377
Members: 45 companies
Staff: 2
Annual Budget: $250-500,000
Executive Director: Emilio G. Collado, III
Historical Note
Founded as the American Watch Assemblers Association; assumed its present name in 1951. Members are importers of watch and clock movements and cases, domestic manufacturers and assemblers.

American Watchmakers-Clockmakers Institute *(1960)*
701 Enterprise Dr.
Harrison, OH 45030
Tel: (513)367-9800 *Fax:* (513)367-1414
Toll Free: (866)367 - 2924
Web Site: www.awci.com
Members: 4000 individuals and institutions
Staff: 11
Annual Budget: $500-1,000,000
Executive Director: James E. Lubic
E-Mail: jlubic@awci.com
Assistant Executive Director: Lucy Fuleki
E-Mail: lfuleki@awci.com
Historical Note
Formed by the merger of the Horological Institute of America and United Horological Association of America, as the American Watchmakers Institute; adopted its present name in 1992. Offers correspondence courses and bench courses in clockmaking, watchmaking, and micro-electronics for watches, and an examination and certification program for master watchmakers and clockmakers. Membership: $83/year.
Publications:
Horological Times. m. adv.

American Water Resources Association *(1964)*
P.O. Box 1626
Middleburg, VA 20118-1626
Tel: (540)687-8390 *Fax:* (540)687-8395
E-Mail: info@awra.org
Web Site: www.awra.org
Members: 3100 individuals
Staff: 7
Annual Budget: $1-2,000,000
Executive Vice President: Kenneth D. Reid, CAE
E-Mail: info@awra.org
Director, Operations: Michael J. Kowalski, CAE
E-Mail: info@awra.org
Marketing Director: Terry Meyer
E-Mail: info@awra.org
Director, Publications: Charlene E. Young
E-Mail: info@awra.org
Historical Note
Incorporated in Illinois in March 1964, AWRA is a multidisciplinary non-profit scientific, educational association dedicated to the advancement of research, planning, management, development and education in water resources. Member society of the Renewable Natural Resources Foundation and World Water Council. Membership includes engineers, hydrologists, biologists, attorneys, chemists and social scientists. Membership: $150/year (individual); $325/year (institutional); $425/year (company).
Meetings/Conferences:
Annual Meetings: Fall/Winter
Publications:
Water Resources Impact. bi-m. adv.
Proceedings. a.
Journal of the AWRA. bi-m.
Membership Directory (online).

American Water Works Association *(1881)*
6666 W. Quincy Ave.
Denver, CO 80235-3098
Tel: (303)794-7711 *Fax:* (303)347-0804
Toll Free: (800)926 - 7337
E-Mail: custsvc@awwa.org
Web Site: www.awwa.org
Members: 49500 individuals
Staff: 170
Annual Budget: $10-25,000,000
Executive Director: Jack W. Hoffbuhr
E-Mail: custsvc@awwa.org
Director, Volunteer and Technical Support: Ed Baruth
E-Mail: custsvc@awwa.org
Director, Publishing: Monia Joda Baruth
E-Mail: custsvc@awwa.org
Technology Solutions: Robert Campoy
E-Mail: custsvc@awwa.org
Deputy Executive Director, Government Affairs: Tom Curtis
E-Mail: custsvc@awwa.org
Chief Financial Officer: Linda Laskey
E-Mail: custsvc@awwa.org
Deputy Executive Director: Paula MacIlwaine
E-Mail: custsvc@awwa.org
Director, Communications and Marketing: Jon Runge
E-Mail: custsvc@awwa.org
Historical Note
Organized at Washington University, St. Louis, MO on March 29, 1881 and incorporated in Illinois in 1912. Has an annual budget of approximately $20 million. Membership: $114/year (individual); organizational fee varies by size.
Meetings/Conferences:
Annual Meetings: June
Publications:
MainStream. q.
Opflow. m. adv.
AWWA Journal. m. adv.

American Waterways Operators *(1944)*
801 N. Quincy St., Suite 200
Arlington, VA 22203
Tel: (703)841-9300 *Fax:* (703)841-0389
Web Site: www.americanwaterways.com
Members: 375 companies
Staff: 22
Annual Budget: $2-5,000,000
President and Chief Executive Officer: Thomas A. Allegretti
E-Mail: tallegretti@vesselalliance.com
Chief Financial Officer and Senior Vice President: Lee H. Hill
E-Mail: lhill@vesselalliance.com
Senior Vice President, Government Affairs and Policy Analysis: Jennifer A. Kelly Carpenter
E-Mail: jcarpenter@vesselalliance.com
Historical Note
Members include domestic carriers transporting commodities by water, shipyards, terminals, and affiliated businesses. Works to preserve the coastal and inland commercial navigable waterways system and promote waterborne transportation. Supports the American Waterways Operators PAC.
Publications:
AWO Letter. bi-w.
Annual Report. a.

American Welara Pony Society *(1981)*
P.O. Box 401
Yucca Valley, CA 92286-0401
Tel: (760)364-2048 *Fax:* (760)364-2048
Web Site: www.WelaraRegistry.com
Members: 249 individuals, 231 businesses
Staff: 13
Annual Budget: $10-25,000
Registrar: John H. Collins
E-Mail: info@WelaraRegistry.com
Historical Note
AWPS was established to collect, record and preserve the pedigrees of Welara ponies (a cross of Arabian horse with Welsh pony), to publish a stud book, and to stimulate all other matters such as may pertain to the history, breeding, exhibiting, publicity, sale and improvement of the breed throughout the world. Membership: $16/year (individual); $28/year (organization).
Meetings/Conferences:
Annual Meetings: late Spring/150
Publications:
Introduction to the Welara CD-Rom.
Welara Journal. semi-a. adv.
Welara Journal CD-Rom. semi-a. adv.
Registry Stud Book. bien. adv.

American Welding Society *(1919)*
550 N.W. LeJeune Road
Miami, FL 33126
Tel: (305)443-9353 *Fax:* (305)443-7559
Toll Free: (800)443 - 9353
E-Mail: info@aws.org
Web Site: www.aws.org
Members: 49000 individuals
Staff: 90
Annual Budget: $10-25,000,000
Executive Director: Ray Shook
E-Mail: rshook@aws.org
Associate Executive Director: Cassie Burrell
Director, Member Services: Rhenda Mayo
Director, Convention and Expositions: John Ospina
Historical Note
Organized in March 1919 as an outgrowth of the Welding Committee of the Emergency Fleet Corporation, U.S. Shipping Board. Incorporated in New York in 1932. Annual budget is over $17 million. Membership: $75/year.
Meetings/Conferences:
Annual Meetings: Fall/20,000
2007 - Chicago, IL(McCormick Place)/Nov. 11-14/20000
Publications:
Inspection Trends. q. adv.
Welding Journal. m. adv.

American White/American Creme Horse Registry *(1936)*
90.000 Edwards Road
Naper, NE 68755-9707
Tel: (402)832-5560
Web Site: www.whitehorseranchnebraska.com/registry.htm
Members: 200 individuals
Staff: 2
Annual Budget: under $10,000
Secretary-Treasurer: Carley Daugherty
Historical Note
Founded as the American Albino Horse Club in 1936, became American Albino Association in 1964, and International American Albino Association in 1985. The Association does business as the American White/American Creme Horse Registry. Serves as a promotional agency for the registered breeds American White and American Creme. Membership: $15/year (domestic individual); $25/year (domestic family); $20/year (overseas individual); $30/year (overseas family).
Meetings/Conferences:
Annual Meetings: Naper, NE(White Horse Ranch)/Father's Day Weekend
Publications:
American White/American Creme Newsletter. q.

American Wholesale Booksellers Association *(1984)*
702 S. Michigan St.
South Bend, IN 46601
Tel: (219)232-8500 *Fax:* (303)265-9292
E-Mail: info@awba.com

Web Site: www.awba.com
Members: 20 wholesalers, 22 associates
Staff: 2
Annual Budget: $10-25,000
Executive Secretary: Patricia Walsh
Treasurer: Michael J. Raymond

Historical Note
Members are wholesale distributors for whom book sales constitute at least 75% of total sales. Membership: $350-700/year (depending on size).

Meetings/Conferences:
Tri-annual Meetings: Spring, Fall, Winter/20-100

Publications:
Directory of Members (online).
Handbook for Small Presses.

American Wholesale Marketers Association *(1945)*
2750 Prosperity Ave., Suite 530
Fairfax, VA 22031
Tel: (703)208-3358 *Fax:* (703)573-5738
Toll Free: (800)482 - 2962
E-Mail: pennyp@awmanet.org
Web Site: www.awmanet.org
Members: 1500 organizations
Staff: 8
Annual Budget: $2-5,000,000
President and Chief Executive Officer: Scott S. Ramminger
E-Mail: pennyp@awmanet.org
Corporate Secretary and Assistant to the President: Penny Paterson
E-Mail: pennyp@awmanet.org
Vice President, Marketing, Membership and Industry Affairs: Robert Pignato
E-Mail: robertp@awmanet.org

Historical Note
Formed (1992) by the merger of the National Candy Wholesalers Association and the National Association of Tobacco Distributors. AWMA promotes the interests of the wholesale distributors of convenience products and unites the members of the wholesale industry for its common good. In 1994 AWMA absorbed the National Association of Service Merchandising. Membership: $500-3,500/year (company).

Meetings/Conferences:
2007 – Las Vegas, NV(Hilton)/Feb. 21-23

Publications:
AWMA Members Only Newsletter. bi-m.
Buying Guide and AWMA Membership Directory. a. adv.
Distribution Channels. m. adv.
Legistatus. 8/year.

American Wind Energy Association *(1974)*
1101 14th St. NW, 12th Floor
Washington, DC 20005
Tel: (202)383-2500 *Fax:* (202)383-2505
Web Site: www.awea.org
Members: 650 individuals
Staff: 12
Annual Budget: $2-5,000,000
Executive Director: Randall S. Swisher
Director, Finance and Administration: Mary Childress
Deputy Executive Director and Director, Communications: Tom Gray
Director, Conferences and Education: Stephen Miner
Director, Legislative: Jaime Steve

Historical Note
AWEA is a national trade association that represents wind power plant developers, wind turbine manufacturers, utilities, consultants, insurers, financiers, researchers, wind power advocates, and others involved in the wind energy industry. Membership: $50/year (individual); $200/year (academic); $750/year (associate); $1,000-3,000/year (utility); $1,000-35,000/year (corporate).

Meetings/Conferences:
Annual Meetings: Spring

Publications:
AWEA Wind Energy Weekly. w.
Windletter. m.
Annual Conference Proceedings. a.
Membership Directory. a.

American Wine Society *(1967)*
3006 Latta Road
Rochester, NY 14612-3298
Tel: (585)225-7613
E-Mail: angel910@aol.com
Web Site: www.americanwinesociety.org
Members: 5000 individuals
Staff: 3
Annual Budget: $250-500,000
Executive Director: Angel E. Nardone
E-Mail: angel910@aol.com

Historical Note
AWS members include professional and amateur wine growers, winemakers, distributors, retailers and others with an interest in American or foreign wines. Membership: $75/year (professional); $52/year (individual).

Publications:
Home Wine Information. a.
AWS Journal. q. adv.
AWS News Newsletter. q. adv.

American Wire Cloth Institute *(1933)*
25 N. Broadway
Tarrytown, NY 10591
Tel: (914)332-0040 *Fax:* (914)332-1541
E-Mail: info@wireclothinstitute.org
Web Site: www.wireclothinstitute.org
Members: 16 companies
Staff: 2
Executive Director: Richard C. Byrne

Historical Note
Formerly (1978) the Industrial Wire Cloth Institute.

American Wire Producers Association *(1981)*
801 N. Fairfax St., Suite 211
Alexandria, VA 22314-1757
Tel: (703)299-4434 *Fax:* (703)299-9233
E-Mail: info@awpa.org
Web Site: www.awpa.org
Members: 85 companies
Staff: 5
Annual Budget: $250-500,000
Executive Director: Kimberly A. Korbel
Director, Meetings and Membership: Emily M. Bardach
Director, Government Affairs: Janet Kopenhaver
E-Mail: jkopenhaver@awpa.org

Historical Note
Founded as the Independent Wire Drawers Association; became the Independent Wire Producers Association in 1975 and assumed its present name in 1981 when it merged with the Specialty Wire Association. Members are companies producing wire by drawing metal through a die.

Meetings/Conferences:
Annual Meetings: Winter

Publications:
Imports Report. q.
Wireline. bi-m.

American Woman's Society of Certified Public Accountants *(1933)*
136 S. Keowee St.
Dayton, OH 45402
Tel: (937)222-1872 *Fax:* (937)222-5794
Toll Free: (800)297 - 2721
E-Mail: info@awscpa.org
Web Site: www.awscpa.org
Members: 1200 individuals
Staff: 6
Annual Budget: $250-500,000
Executive Director: Kim Fantaci
E-Mail: info@awscpa.org

Historical Note
AWSCPA provides its members with programs and opportunities for professional networking at meetings and seminars, and through publications and other services. The Society works to advance the professional interests and careers of women certified public accountants and to build a national presence for women CPA's throughout the country. Membership: $105/year.

Meetings/Conferences:
2007 – Orlando, FL(Coronado Springs)/Oct. 24-27

Publications:
AWSCPA Newsletter. q.
Network. semi-a.
Issues Paper. a.
Membership Directory. a.

American Women in Radio and Television *(1951)*
8405 Greensboro Dr., Suite 800
Vienna, VA 22102
Tel: (703)506-3290 *Fax:* (703)506-3266
E-Mail: info@awrt.org
Web Site: www.awrt.org
Members: 2800 individuals
Staff: 4
Annual Budget: $250-500,000
Executive Director: Maria E. Brennan

Historical Note
Prior to 1951 a group known as the Association of Women Broadcasters was an adjunct to the National Association of Radio and Television Broadcasters, the predecessor to the National Association of Broadcasters. AWB was discontinued in October 1950. The present organization was established at the Hotel Astor in New York on April 6-8, 1951 and consists of individuals in numerous job categories in the radio-TV industry and its affiliated or supporting organizations. The Foundation of American Women in Radio and Television is an educational subsidiary. Membership: $115/year.

Meetings/Conferences:
Annual Meetings: Spring

Publications:
CareerLine (online). m.
News & Views. bi-m.
Making Waves Magazine. q. adv.
Resource Directory.
Mentoring in Broadcasting.

American Wood Council *(1968)*

Historical Note
A product group of the American Forests and Paper Association.

American Wood Preservers Institute *(1921)*
2750 Prosperity Ave.
Suite 550
Fairfax, VA 22031-4312
Tel: (703)204-0500 *Fax:* (703)204-4610
Toll Free: (800)356 - 2974
Web Site: www.preservedwood.com
Members: 115 companies
Staff: 7
Annual Budget: $1-2,000,000
President: Parker Brugge
Membership/Meeting Coordinator: Elisabeth Heyedahl
Director, Environmental and Regulatory Affairs: George Parris, Ph.D.
Manager, Communications: Mel Pine
Technical Manager: Christopher Surak

Historical Note
The government relations and environmental affairs arm of the wood preserving industry. Members are wood treating companies, manufacturers and formulators of wood preserving chemicals, and related industry suppliers and manufacturers.

Meetings/Conferences:
Annual Meetings: October-November

Publications:
American Wood Preserver. bi-m.
AWPI letter. bi-m.

American Wood-Preservers' Association *(1904)*
P.O. Box 361784
Birmingham, AL 35236-1784
Tel: (205)733-4077 *Fax:* (205)733-4075
E-Mail: email@awpa.com
Web Site: www.awpa.com
Members: 1000 individuals
Staff: 2
Annual Budget: $100-250,000
Executive Vice President: Colin McCown

Historical Note
The American Wood-Preservers' Association is an international, nonprofit, technical society founded in 1904 to provide a common forum for exchange of information for all segments of the industry. The Association provides a link for technical interchange

between industry, research and users of treated wood. Membership: $150/year.

Meetings/Conferences:
Annual Meetings: Spring
2007 – St. Louis, MO(Hyatt Union Station)/May 6-8
2008 – Portland, OR(Marriott Downtown)/May 18-20

Publications:
AWPA Book of Standards. a.
AWPA Proceedings. a. adv.

American Wool Council *(1954)*

Historical Note
A division of the American Sheep Industry Association.

American Zinc Association *(1990)*
2025 M St. NW, Suite 800
Washington, DC 20036
Tel: (202)367-1151 *Fax:* (202)367-2232
Web Site: www.zinc.org
Members: 18 companies
Staff: 1
Annual Budget: $250-500,000
Executive Director: George F. Vary
E-Mail: gvary@zinc.org

Historical Note
AZA's mission is to promote the general welfare of the zinc industry; serve as a spokesgroup and information center for zinc; and monitor environmental and other issues pertinent to the zinc industry. Members are producers of zinc metal, oxide and dust selling in the United States, and consumers of zinc.

Meetings/Conferences:
Annual Meetings: 500

American Zoo and Aquarium Association *(1924)*
8403 Colesville Road, Suite 710
Silver Spring, MD 20910
Tel: (301)562-0777 *Fax:* (301)562-0888
Web Site: www.aza.org
Members: 5500 individuals
Staff: 26
Annual Budget: $2-5,000,000
Executive Director: Kristin L. Verhs
Director, Finance and Administration: Laura Benson

Historical Note
Formerly a branch of the American Institute of Park Executives and the National Recreation and Park Association, it became an independent organization in 1971 as American Association of Zoological Parks and Aquariums; assumed its current name in 1994.

Meetings/Conferences:
Annual Meetings: September/1,500

Publications:
AZA Membership Directory. a. adv.
Communique. m. adv.
Annual Conference Proceedings. a.

American-European Soda Ash Shipping Association *(1991)*
c/o Baker and McKenzie LLP
1114 Ave. of the Americas
New York, NY 10036-7703
Tel: (212)626-4496 *Fax:* (212)626-4120
Members: 6 companies
Acting Secretary: Charles H. Critchlow

Historical Note
AESSA members are producers of soda ash in the United States. A Webb-Pomerene Act association, AESSA promotes the export of U.S. natural soda ash to countries in the European community through the provision of joint storage, transportation and other related logistical and technical support.

American-Israel Chamber of Commerce and Industry *(1953)*
Three New York Plaza
Tenth Floor
New York, NY 10004
Tel: (212)232-8440 *Fax:* (212)365-3366
E-Mail: info@aicci.org
Web Site: www.aicci.org
Members: 300 individuals
Staff: 2
Annual Budget: $100-250,000
Executive Vice President: Ronny Bassan
E-Mail: info@aicci.org

Historical Note
A U.S. non-profit trade association whose purpose is to foster the growth and expansion of economic relations between the U.S. and Israel and to promote U.S. investment in Israel, Israeli exports to the U.S. and U.S. exports to Israel. Membership: $250/year (individual); $500/year (organization).

American-Uzbekistan Chamber of Commerce *(1993)*
1717 N St. NW
Washington, DC 20036
Tel: (202)828-4111
E-Mail: aucc@verizon.net
Web Site: www.aucconline.com
Members: 60 companies/individuals
Staff: 1
Annual Budget: $50-100,000
Executive Director: Robert S. Pace
E-Mail: aucc@verizon.net

Historical Note
AUCC promotes trade and investment between the U.S. and Uzbekistan. Membership: $3,000/year (corporate); $1,250/year (small business); $500/year (nonprofit); $100/year (professional).

Meetings/Conferences:
Annual Meetings: May

Americans for the Arts *(1960)*
1000 Vermont Ave. NW, Sixth Floor
Washington, DC 20005
Tel: (202)371-2830 *Fax:* (202)371-0424
E-Mail: info@artsusa.org
Web Site: www.americansforthearts.org
Members: 5000 organizations and individuals
Staff: 50
Annual Budget: $10-25,000,000
President and Chief Executive Officer: Robert L. Lynch
E-Mail: pwilliams@artsusa.org
Vice President, External Relations: T.C. Benson
E-Mail: pwilliams@artsusa.org

Historical Note
Americans for the Arts, formerly the National Assembly of Local Arts Agencies and American Council for the Arts, assumed its current name in 1996. With a 40-year record of service, it is dedicated to representing and serving local communities and creating opportunities for every American to participate in and appreciate the arts.

Meetings/Conferences:
Annual Meetings: Spring

Publications:
ArtsLink. q.
Monthly Wire. m. adv.
E-Clios. m. adv.
Monograph. bi-m.

Americas Association of Cooperative/Mutual Insurance Socs. *(1979)*
8201 Greensboro Dr., Suite 300
McLean, VA 22102
Tel: (703)245-8077 *Fax:* (703)610-9005
E-Mail: info@amg-inc.com
Members: 40 individuals
Staff: 1
Annual Budget: $250-500,000
Executive Director: Edward Potter
E-Mail: info@amg-inc.com

Historical Note
Formerly the North American Association of the International Cooperative Insurance Federation. AAC/MIS membership is open to cooperative and mutual insurance companies in the Western Hemisphere who are also members of the international organization, International Cooperative and Mutual Insurance Federation. Membership fee varies; $500/year minimum.

Meetings/Conferences:
Annual Meetings: Fall

Amerifax Cattle Association *(1977)*
P.O. Box 149
Hastings, NE 68902
Tel: (402)463-5289 *Fax:* (402)463-6652
Members: 150 individuals
Staff: 1
Annual Budget: $25-50,000
Executive Secretary: John Quirk
E-Mail: quirk@navix.net

Historical Note
Promotes the Amerifax breed of cattle. Maintains a herd book. Membership: $20/year; $50 initiation fee.

Meetings/Conferences:
Annual Meetings: January in Denver, CO

AMT - The Association For Manufacturing Technology *(1902)*
7901 Westpark Dr.
McLean, VA 22102
Tel: (703)893-2900 *Fax:* (703)893-1151
Toll Free: (800)524 - 0475
E-Mail: amt@amtonline.org
Web Site: www.amtonline.org
Members: 350 companies
Staff: 60
Annual Budget: $10-25,000,000
President: John Byrd
E-Mail: jgalloway@autonline.org
Vice President, Exhibitions: Peter Eelman
E-Mail: jgalloway@autonline.org
Vice President, Government Relations: Paul Freedenberg
Manager, Membership: Diyana Hrzic
Vice President, Finance and Human Resources: Linda Montfort
Vice President, Meetings: Christine Rasul

Historical Note
Formerly (1989) the National Machine Tool Builders Association; assumed its present name in 1992. Supports the Machine-Tool Political Action Committee.

Publications:
Directory of Member Products. a.
Economic Handbook of Machine Tool Industry. a.

Amusement and Music Operators Association *(1948)*
33 W. Higgins Road, Suite 830
South Barrington, IL 60010
Tel: (847)428-7699 *Fax:* (847)428-7719
Toll Free: (800)937 - 2662
E-Mail: jackamoa@aol.com
Web Site: www.amoa.com
Members: 1700 companies
Staff: 4
Annual Budget: $1-2,000,000
Executive Vice President: Jack Kelleher
E-Mail: jackamoa@aol.com

Historical Note
Established as the Music Operators of America; assumed its present name in 1977. Members are companies making, servicing or selling coin operated amusement, music, and vending equipment.

Meetings/Conferences:
Annual Meetings: Fall/8,000

Publications:
The Edge. bi-m.

Amusement Industry Manufacturers and Suppliers International *(1926)*
1250 S.E. Port St. Lucie Blvd., Suite C
Port St. Lucie, FL 34952
Tel: (772)398-6701 *Fax:* (772)398-6702
E-Mail: aimsinterl@aol.com
Web Site: www.aimsintl.org
Members: 61 companies
Staff: 2
Annual Budget: $50-100,000
Executive Director: John Hinde
E-Mail: aimsinterl@aol.com

Historical Note
Formerly (1934) Manufacturers Division, National Association of Amusement Parks and (1997) American Recreational Equipment Association. Members are makers of rides, walk-throughs and other equipment and devices purchased by carnivals, circuses and amusement parks. Membership: $360/year (individual): $100/year (associate).

Publications:
News Line. q.

Analytical and Life Science Systems Association *(1988)*
225 Reinekers Lane, Suite 625
Alexandria, VA 22314-2875
Tel: (703)836-1360 *Fax:* (703)836-6644
Web Site: www.alssa.org
Members: 100 companies
Staff: 3
Annual Budget: $500-1,000,000
President: Michael J. Duff

Historical Note
ALSSA is the trade association for suppliers of instruments, consumables, reagents, software and technology used in analysis and measurement in chemistry and the life sciences. The products supplied by ALSSA members are enabling equipment essential to scientific research and drug discovery. Membership: Annual dues are based on sales volume (company).

Meetings/Conferences:
Semi-Annual Meetings: Spring and Fall/55-70

Publications:
newsletter. m.
Annual report. a.

Analytical Laboratory Managers Association *(1980)*
2019 Galisteo St., Bldg. I-1
Santa Fe, NM 87505
Tel: (505)989-4683 *Fax:* (505)989-1073
E-Mail: alma@labmanagers.org
Web Site: http://labmanagers.org
Members: 450 individuals
Staff: 2
Annual Budget: under $10,000
Executive Secretary: Miquela Ortiz
E-Mail: alma@labmanagers.org

Historical Note
Founded as the University Laboratory Managers Association; assumed its present name in 1981. Created to promote the exchange of information about management and operation of analytical laboratories. Members include university, industrial and government laboratories. Membership: $80/year (individual); $250/year (corporate).

Meetings/Conferences:
Annual Meetings: Fall

Publications:
ALMA Bulletin. 3/year.

Aniline Association *(1982)*
11527 Bertram St.
Lake Ridge, VA 22192
Tel: (703)897-4444 *Fax:* (703)897-4646
Members: 5 companies
Staff: 4
Annual Budget: $50-100,000
General Counsel: Joseph E. Hadley, Jr.

Historical Note
Members are chemical companies producing and/or using aniline.

Animal Behavior Society *(1964)*
Indiana University
2611 E. Tenth St., Suite 170
Bloomington, IN 47408-2603
Tel: (812)856-5541 *Fax:* (812)856-5542
E-Mail: aboffice@indiana.edu
Web Site: www.animalbehavior.org
Members: 2200 individuals
Staff: 3
Annual Budget: $250-500,000
Society Manager: Steve Ramey
E-Mail: aboffice@indiana.edu

Historical Note
Professionals and students involved in animal behavior research. Membership: $57/year (individual); $40/year (student).

Publications:
Animal Behavior. m.
Newsletter. q.

Animal Health Institute *(1941)*
1325 G St. NW
Suite 700
Washington, DC 20005-3104
Tel: (202)637-2440 *Fax:* (202)393-1667
Web Site: www.ahi.org
Members: 23 companies
Staff: 10
Annual Budget: $2-5,000,000
President and Chief Executive Officer: Alexander S. Mathews
E-Mail: kmcclure@ahi.org
Vice President, Administration and Finance: Carolyn S. Ayers
E-Mail: cayers@ahi.org
Vice President, Regulatory, Scientific and International Affairs: Richard A. Carnevale, VMD
E-Mail: rcarnevale@ahi.org
General Counsel: Kent D. McClure
E-Mail: kmcclure@ahi.org
Vice President, Legislative and Public Affairs: Ronald B. Phillips
E-Mail: rphillips@ahi.org

Historical Note
AHI is the U.S. industry trade association representing companies that make medicines for pets and farm animals.

Publications:
Annual Report. a.
Congressional Directory. bien.

Animal Transportation Association *(1976)*
1111 East Loop North
Houston, TX 77029
Tel: (713)532-2177 *Fax:* (713)532-2166
E-Mail: info@aata-animaltransport.org
Web Site: www.aata-animaltransport.org
Members: 180 individuals
Staff: 3
Annual Budget: $50-100,000
Director, Administration: Alistair Macnab
E-Mail: info@aata-animaltransport.org
Administration Manager: James Haggarty
E-Mail: info@aata-animaltransport.org

Historical Note
Members include transport manufacturers, carriers, and shippers; animal welfare groups and breeders; zoos; and animal forwarders. Organized to improve conditions for safe transportation of animals by air, sea and ground travel. Formerly (1989) Animal Air Transportation Association. Membership: $180/year (individual); $375/year (company).

Meetings/Conferences:
Annual Meetings: Spring

Publications:
Conference Program. a. adv.
AATA Newsletter. q. adv.

Ankole Watusi International Registry *(1983)*
22484 W. 239th St.
Spring Hill, KS 66083-9306
Tel: (913)592-4050
E-Mail: watusi@aol.com
Web Site: http://members.aol.com/Watusi/index.html
Members: 86 individuals
Staff: 1
Annual Budget: $10-25,000
Executive Secretary: Dr. Elizabeth Lundgren
E-Mail: watusi@aol.com

Historical Note
Incorporated in Colorado. Breeders and fanciers of African Ankole Watusi cattle. Maintains pedigree registry and sponsors full blood and cross breeding programs. Membership: $25/year.

Meetings/Conferences:
Annual Meetings: Fall

Publications:
Watusi. q.

Antenna Measurement Techniques Association *(1979)*
22117 N.E. Tenth Place
Sammamish, WA 98074
Tel: (303)533-7225 *Fax:* (303)533-7379
E-Mail: secretary@amta.org
Web Site: www.amta.org
Members: 400 individuals
Annual Budget: $50-100,000
Coordinator, Meetings: Janet O'Neil
E-Mail: secretary@amta.org

Historical Note
Members are institutions and individuals concerned with the design and measurement of antennas. Membership: $30/year (individual).

Meetings/Conferences:
Annual Meetings: Fall

Publications:
Membership List. a.
Newsletter. semi-a.
Proceedings of Annual Meeting. a.

Antennas and Propagation Society

Historical Note
A technical society of the Institute of Electrical and Electronics Engineers (IEEE). Membership in the Society, open only to IEEE members, includes subscription to a technical periodical in the field published by IEEE. All administrative support is provided by IEEE.

Antiquarian Booksellers Association of America *(1949)*
20 W. 44th St.
Fourth Floor
New York, NY 10036-6604
Tel: (212)944-8291 *Fax:* (212)944-8293
E-Mail: hq@abaa.org
Web Site: www.abaa.org
Members: 475 companies
Staff: 1
Annual Budget: $250-500,000
Executive Director: Susan Benne
E-Mail: hq@abaa.org

Historical Note
Members are rare book dealers. Affiliated with the International League of Antiquarian Booksellers. Membership: $575/year (individual).

Publications:
Membership Directory. a.

Antique and Amusement Photographers International *(1993)*
P.O. Box 150
Eureka Springs, AR 72632
Tel: (479)253-8554 *Fax:* (479)253-8225
E-Mail: ted@oldtimephotos.org
Web Site: www.oldtimephotos.org
Members: 200 companies
Staff: 2
Annual Budget: $50-100,000
Executive Director: Gail Pierce Larimer
E-Mail: gail@oldtimephotos.org
Art Director: Ted Larimer
E-Mail: ted@oldtimephotos.org

Historical Note
Members are photography studios and photographers, primarily in the U.S. and Canada, specializing in costume photography and suppliers to the industry. Membership: $140-175/year.

Meetings/Conferences:
Annual Meetings: Winter
2007 – Las Vegas, NV(Gold Coast Hotel)/Feb. 6-8

Publications:
Flash Newsletter. q. adv.
AAPI Directory (online). q. adv.

Antique Appraisal Association of America *(1972)*

Historical Note
Address unknown in 2003; see also Appraisers Association of America.

Anxiety Disorders Association of America *(1980)*
8730 Georgia Ave.
Suite 600
Silver Spring, MD 20910
Tel: (240)485-1001 *Fax:* (240)485-1035
Web Site: www.adaa.org
Members: 1500 individuals
Staff: 10
Annual Budget: $1-2,000,000
President and Chief Executive Officer: Jerilyn Ross
Program Manager: Gina Mangiaracina
Business Manager: Heather Murray
Chief Operating Officer: Alies Muskin
Director, Conferences: Betsy Oliveto

Historical Note
Formerly (1990) Phobia Society of America. ADAA members include people who suffer from anxiety disorders and professionals who study and treat them. Its purpose is to provide information, education and support. Membership: $165/year (professional); $25/year (students). Individual supporters contribute online and by mail.
Publications:
Professional Membership Directory. a. adv.
ADAA Online Newsletter. q. adv.
Conference Program Book. a. adv.

AOAC International *(1884)*
481 N. Frederick Ave.
Suite 500
Gaithersburg, MD 20877-2417
Tel: (301)924-7077 *Fax:* (301)924-7089
Toll Free: (800)379 - 2662
E-Mail: aoac@aoac.org
Web Site: www.aoac.org
Members: 3700 individuals
Staff: 35
Annual Budget: $2-5,000,000
Executive Director: Dr. E. James Bradford, Ph.D.
E-Mail: jbradford@aoac.org
Senior Director, Publications, Marketing and Sales: Krystyna McIver
E-Mail: kmciver@aoac.org
Principal Scientific Liaison, Government and Industry: Anita Mishra
Senior Director, Membership and Professional Development: Brian Theil
E-Mail: btheil@aoac.org
Historical Note
Founded in 1884 as the Association of Official Agricultural Chemists, became the Association of Official Analytical Chemists in 1965 and assumed its present name in 1991. AOAC International is an independent international association whose primary focus is coordination of the development and validation of chemical and microbiological analytical methods by expert scientists working in industry, academic, and government laboratories worldwide. These scientists work within three validation programs operated by AOAC International: the AOAC Official Methods Program, the AOAC Peer-Verified Methods Program, and the AOAC Performance-Tested Methods Program. Membership: $85/year (individual); $750/year (organization/company).
Meetings/Conferences:
Annual Meetings: September/1,000
2007 - Anaheim, CA(Hyatt Regency Orange County)/Sept. 16-20
Publications:
Inside Laboratory Management. m. adv.
Official Methods of Analysis of AOAC INTERNAT'L. a.
Journal of AOAC INTERNAT'L. bi-m. adv.

AOC *(1964)*
1000 N. Payne St.
Alexandria, VA 22314-1652
Tel: (703)549-1600 *Fax:* (703)549-2589
Web Site: www.crows.org
Members: 14000 individuals
Staff: 11
Annual Budget: $2-5,000,000
Executive Director: Donald N. Richetti
Deputy Director: Andy Vittoria
Historical Note
Founded in 1964 as Association of Old Crows, AOC is a professional association comprised of individuals engaged in the science of electronic warfare, information operations and related disciplines. Members include scientists, engineers, managers, operators, educators, and military personnel in all grades. Grew from a similar World War II organization whose symbol was the raven. Membership: $35/year.
Meetings/Conferences:
Annual Meetings: Fall
Publications:
Journal of Electronic Defense. m. adv.

AORN *(1954)*
2170 S. Parker Road
Suite 300
Denver, CO 80231-5711
Tel: (303)755-6300 *Fax:* (303)750-2927
Toll Free: (800)755 - 2676
E-Mail: custserv@aorn.org
Web Site: www.aorn.org
Members: 40000 individuals
Staff: 110
Annual Budget: $10-25,000,000
President: William J. Duffy
E-Mail: custserv@aorn.org
Interim Executive Director: Ellen Murphy
Chief Financial Officer: James L. Cousin
E-Mail: custserv@aorn.org
President: William J. Duffy
E-Mail: custserv@aorn.org
Director, Meetings and Conventions: Julie McGrath
E-Mail: custserv@aorn.org
Historical Note
Professional organization that unites its members by providing education, representation, and standards for quality patient care. Membership: $65/year (individual).
Meetings/Conferences:
Annual Meetings: Late Winter-Early Spring
2007 - Orlando, FL/March 11-15
Publications:
ORPD. a. adv.
Surgical Services Management. q. adv.
AORN Standards and Recommended Practices. a.
AORN Journal. m. adv.

APA - The Engineered Wood Association *(1933)*
7011 S. 19th St.
Tacoma, WA 98466
Tel: (253)565-6600 *Fax:* (253)565-7265
E-Mail: help@apawood.org
Web Site: www.apawood.org
Members: 161 mills
Staff: 110
Annual Budget: $10-25,000,000
President: Dennis J. Hardman
E-Mail: help@apawood.org
Director, Communications: Jack Merry
E-Mail: help@apawood.org
Historical Note
Formerly (1964) Douglas Fir Plywood Association and (1994) American Plywood Association. Members are producers of plywood, oriented strandboard, and other engineered wood products. Members must meet the association's quality standards in order to use the APA Trademark on their products.
Meetings/Conferences:
Annual Meetings: Fall
Publications:
Engineered Wood Journal. semi-a.
Industry Newsletter. m.
Management Report. m.

APA: The Association of Leading Agricultural Media Companies *(1915)*
Historical Note
Merged with American Business Media in 2002.

APHSA - Information Systems Management
Historical Note
An affiliate of the American Public Welfare Association, which provides administrative support.

Apiary Inspectors of America *(1932)*
c/o Arkansas State Plant Board
One Natural Resources Dr.
Little Rock, AR 72205
Tel: (501)225-1598 *Fax:* (501)225-3590
E-Mail: elevi@mvtel.net
Members: 60 individuals
Staff: 1
Annual Budget: under $10,000
Secretary: Ed Levi
Historical Note
Formerly National Apiary Inspectors. Members are state apiarists of the U.S. and Canada. Has no paid officers or full-time staff. Membership: $35/year (individual); $100/year (state).
Meetings/Conferences:
Annual Meetings: January
Publications:
Proceedings of the Annual Conference. a.

APICS - The Association for Operations Management *(1957)*
5301 Shawnee Road
Alexandria, VA 22312-2317
Tel: (703)354-8851 *Fax:* (703)354-8106
Toll Free: (800)444 - 2742
E-Mail: webmaster@apicshq.org
Web Site: www.apics.org
Members: 65000 individuals
Staff: 100
Annual Budget: $25-50,000,000
Executive Director and Chief Operating Officer: Abe Eshkenazi, CPA, CHE, CAE
Director, Human Resources: Betsy Davis
Director, Information Systems: Sherry Martin, CNE, CCNA
E-Mail: s_martin@apicshq.org
Chief Financial Officer: Lynn Grossman Quinn, C.P.A., C.A.E.
Deputy Executive Director: Sarah C. Varner
Historical Note
Formerly (1997) the American Production and Inventory Control Society and then APICS - The Educational Society for Resource Management; assumed current name on January 1, 2005. APICS is a not-for-profit educational organization with headquarters in Alexandria, VA. Founded in 1957, APICS is a recognized global leader in professional certifications, education programs, and publications for manufacturing and service industry professionals across the entire supply chain. Administers the certification programs Certified in Production and Inventory Management (CPIM) and Certified in Integrated Resource Management (CIRM); is also the distributor of more than 800 business management publications and educational materials. Publishes a variety of publications, including the APICS Dictionary, and is a source for solutions, training and networking.
Meetings/Conferences:
Annual Meetings: Fall/5,000-8,000
Publications:
APICS Magazine. m. adv.
Production and Inventory Management Journal.
Journal of Operations Management. q.
APICS Conference Proceedings. a.

APICS - The Educational Society for Resource Management
Historical Note
Became APICS - The Association for Operations Management in 2005.

APMI International *(1958)*
105 College Road East
Princeton, NJ 08540-6692
Tel: (609)452-7700 *Fax:* (609)987-8523
E-Mail: info@mpif.org
Web Site: www.apmiinternational.org
Members: 2600 individuals
Staff: 3
Annual Budget: $500-1,000,000
Executive Director and Chief Executive Officer: C. James Trombino, CAE
Historical Note
Formerly (1994) American Powder Metallurgy Institute. APMI is a technical/professional society representing engineers, chemists, metallurgists, physicists, and other professionals involved in powder metal and advanced particulate materials technology. Membership: $95/year.
Meetings/Conferences:
Annual Meetings: Spring, in conjunction with the Metal Powder Industries Federation.
2007 - Denver, CO/May 13-6/1200
Publications:
Internat'l Journal of Powder Metallurgy. 6/year. adv.
Who's Who in P/M. a. adv.

Appalachian Hardwood Manufacturers *(1928)*

P.O. Box 427
High Point, NC 27261
Tel: (336)885-8315 *Fax:* (336)886-8865
E-Mail: ahmi@northstate.net
Web Site: www.appalachianwood.org
Members: 200 companies
Staff: 3
Annual Budget: $100-250,000
President: Mark A. Barford
E-Mail: ahmi@northstate.net

Meetings/Conferences:
Annual Meetings: Spring

Publications:
Newsletter. m.
Appalachian Hardwood Membership Directory. a.

Appaloosa Horse Club *(1938)*
2720 W. Pullman Road
Moscow, ID 83843
Tel: (208)882-5578 *Fax:* (208)882-8150
E-Mail: marketing@appaloosa.com
Web Site: www.appaloosa.com
Members: 28000 individuals
Staff: 42
Annual Budget: $5-10,000,000
Chief Executive Officer: Steve Taylor
Marketing Director: Krystina Burns
E-Mail: marketing@appaloosa.com

Historical Note
Owners and breeders of the Appaloosa horse. Member of the National Pedigree Livestock Council. Appaloosas are descendents of horses brought to America by Spanish explorers. Membership: $50/year (individual).

Meetings/Conferences:
Annual Meetings: Summer

Publications:
Appaloosa Journal. m. adv.

Apparel Graphics Institute *(1989)*
58 Boston Dr.
Suite 1000
Ocean Pines, MD 21811
Tel: (410)641-7300
E-Mail: mark@shopworx.com
Members: 600 individuals
Staff: 7
President: Mark L. Venit
E-Mail: mark@shopworx.com

Historical Note
Formerly (1995) Apparel Decorators Association International. AGI serves constituents in the apparel graphics industry, including textile screen printers, embroiderers and apparel retailers, as well as manufacturers and distributors of garments, apparel decorating equipment and supplies.

Apple Processors Association *(1987)*
1100 17th St. NW
Suite 1000
Washington, DC 20036
Tel: (202)785-6715 *Fax:* (202)331-4212
Web Site: www.appleprocessors.org
Members: 90 individuals
Staff: 3
Annual Budget: $100-250,000
President: Paul S. Weller, Jr.

Historical Note
APA is a national association dedicated to serving processors, marketers and suppliers to the apple industry.

Meetings/Conferences:
2007 – White Sulphur Springs, WV(Greenbrier)/June 20-22/100

Publications:
APAGram. bi-m.

Apple Products Research and Education Council *(1951)*
5775 Peachtree-Dunwoody Road
Suite 500-G
Atlanta, GA 30342-1558
Tel: (404)252-3663 *Fax:* (404)252-0774
E-Mail: info@appleproducts.org
Web Site: www.appleproducts.org
Members: 80 companies
Staff: 5
Annual Budget: $100-250,000
President: Andrew G. Ebert, Ph.D.

Historical Note
Members are producers of processed apple products; suppliers of equipment, packaging or ingredients to the apple processing industry; brokers and concentrate manufacturers.

Meetings/Conferences:
Annual Meetings: Spring

Publications:
Reference Manual for the Processed Apples Industry. irreg..

Appliance Parts Distributors Association *(1937)*
4700 W. Lake Ave.
Glenview, IL 60025-1468
Tel: (847)375-4713 *Fax:* (866)879-7505
Toll Free: (800)621 - 0298
E-Mail: rjacobshagen@narda.com
Web Site: www.apda.com
Members: 66 companies
Staff: 3
Annual Budget: $100-250,000
Executive Vice President: Rosemary Jacobshagen, CAE

Historical Note
Formerly Appliance Parts Jobbers Association. Administrative support provided by North American Retail Dealers Association (same address). Membership: based on the number of company branches.

Applied Research Ethics National Association *(1986)*
126 Brookline Ave.
Suite 202
Boston, MA 02115
Tel: (617)423-4112 *Fax:* (617)423-1185
Web Site: www.primr.org
Members: 875 individuals
Staff: 5
Annual Budget: under $10,000
Director: Amy L. Davis, JD, MPH
E-Mail: adavis@arena.org

Historical Note
ARENA is a professional association founded by the public interest group Public Responsibility in Medicine & Research to promote networking among professionals whose responsibilities include ethical issues. Members are administrators, health research professionals and others with an interest in the ethical aspects of biological research. Membership: $55/year (individual); $150/year (company).

Meetings/Conferences:
Semi-Annual Meetings: Spring and Fall

Publications:
ARENA Newsletter. q.

Appraisal Institute *(1991)*
550 W. Van Buren St.
Suite 1000
Chicago, IL 60607
Tel: (312)335-4100 *Fax:* (312)335-4400
E-Mail: info@appraisalinstitute.org
Web Site: www.appraisalinstitute.org
Members: 21000 individuals
Staff: 100
Annual Budget: $10-25,000,000
Chief Executive Officer: John Ross
Vice President, Human Resources: Sheila Barnes
E-Mail: sbarnes@appraisalinstitute.org
Director, Government Affairs: Bill Garber
E-Mail: info@appraisalinstitute.org
Vice President, Educational Programs and Publications: Larisa K. Phillips
E-Mail: lphillips@appraisalinstitute.org
Director, Membership Services: Anna Vogt

Historical Note
The result of the unification in 1991 of American Institute of Real Estate Appraisers and Society of Real Estate Appraisers, the Appraisal Institute is a professional association providing opportunities for professional education and enforcing a code of ethics and uniform standards of real estate appraisal practice. Sponsors and supports the political action committee APPAC and an education trust. Offers the designations MAI (Member, Appraisal Institute) and SRA (Senior Residential Appraiser). Has an annual budget of approximately $20 million.

Meetings/Conferences:
Annual Meetings: Summer

Publications:
Appraiser News in Brief. bi-w.
Appraisal Journal. q.
Valuation Insights and Perspectives. q.
MarketSource. q.
Annual Directory of Designated Members. a.
Education Course Catalogue. a.

Appraisers Association of America *(1949)*
386 Park Ave. South
Suite 2000
New York, NY 10016
Tel: (212)889-5404 *Fax:* (212)889-5503
E-Mail: aaa@appraisersassoc.org
Web Site: www.appraisersassoc.org
Members: 900 individuals
Staff: 3
Annual Budget: $250-500,000
Executive Director: Aleya Lehmann

Historical Note
A professional society composed primarily of personal property appraisers.

Meetings/Conferences:
Annual Meetings: Fall, in New York, NY

Publications:
The Appraiser. 2/year.

Aquacultural Engineering Society *(1993)*
c/o Freshwater Institute
P.O. Box 1889
Shepherdstown, WV 25443
Tel: (304)876-2815 *Fax:* (304)870-2208
E-Mail: info@aesweb.org
Web Site: www.aesweb.org
Members: 250 individuals
Annual Budget: under $10,000
Secretary-Treasurer: Brian J. Vinci
E-Mail: info@aesweb.org

Historical Note
AES members are aquacultural engineers and others with an interest in the field. Has no paid officers or full-time staff. Membership: $88/year (individual).

Meetings/Conferences:
Annual Meetings: usually Winter

Publications:
Aquacultural Engineering. bi-m.
AES Newsletter. bi-m. adv.

Aquatic Exercise Association *(1987)*
201 S. Tamiami Trail, #3
Nokomis, MI 34275
Tel: (941)486-8600 *Fax:* (941)486-8820
Toll Free: (888)232 - 9283
E-Mail: info@aeawave.com
Web Site: www.aeawave.com
Members: 6000 individuals
Staff: 20
Annual Budget: $1-2,000,000
Executive Director: Angie Proctor

Historical Note
AEA members are aquatic therapists or fitness professionals, facility operators, manufacturers of pool/fitness products and others with an interest in aquatic fitness and therapy programs. Membership: $52/year (individual); $225/year (small business); $400/year (company).

Publications:
AKWA Magazine. 6/yr. adv.

Aquatic Plant Management Society *(1961)*
P.O. Box 821265
Vicksburg, MS 39182-1265
Tel: (601)634-3722 *Fax:* (601)634-2430
Web Site: www.apms.org
Members: 600 individuals
Staff: 1
Annual Budget: $25-50,000
Treasurer: Robert Gunkel
E-Mail: Robert.C.Gunkel@erdc.usace.army.mil

Meetings/Conferences:
Annual Meetings: Mid-July

Publications:
Journal of Aquatic Plant Management. semi-a.
Newsletter of the APMS. 3/year.

Arabian Horse Association *(1950)*
10805 E. Bethany Dr.
Aurora, CO 80014
Tel: (303)696-4500 *Fax:* (303)696-4599
E-Mail: info@arabianhorses.org
Web Site: www.arabianhorses.org
Members: 41000 individuals
Staff: 60
Annual Budget: $10-25,000,000
Executive Vice President: Gary Zimmerman
Director, Communications: Susan Bavaria
E-Mail: info@arabianhorses.org
Historical Note
Promotes the Arabian breed of horses, and registers Arabians, Half-Arabians and Anglo-Arabians. Maintains show records of Arabian horse placings, produces films and videotapes, compiles statistics, and sponsors national competitions for adult and youth competitors. Membership: $25/year (base adult rate); $20/year (base youth rate); $55/year (business); $1,000 (lifetime membership).
Meetings/Conferences:
Annual Meetings: Fall
2007 – Tulsa, OK/November/600
2008 – Denver, CO(Marriott)/Nov. 19-23/600
Publications:
Arabian Horse. bi-m. adv.

Arabian Horse Registry of America *(1908)*
Historical Note
Organization dissolved in 2004. See Arabian Horse Association.

Archaeological Institute of America *(1879)*
656 Beacon St.
Boston, MA 02215-2006
Tel: (617)353-9361 *Fax:* (617)353-6550
E-Mail: aia@aia.bu.edu
Web Site: www.archaeological.org
Members: 11000 individuals
Staff: 30
Annual Budget: $5-10,000,000
Executive Director: Bonnie R. Clendenning
Historical Note
Founded in 1879 in Boston under the aegis of Charles Eliot Norton and chartered by the US Congress in 1906. Member of the American Council of Learned Societies and affiliate of the American Association for the Advancement of Science and numerous other societies and institutes. Membership: $32-$110/year.
Meetings/Conferences:
Annual Meetings: Winter/2,200
Publications:
Dig. bi-m. adv.
American Journal of Archaeology. q.
Archaeology. bi-m. adv.
Archaeological Fieldwork Opportunities Bulletin. a.
AIA Newsletter. q.

Archery Manufacturers and Merchants Organization
Historical Note
Became Archery Trade Association in 2002.

Archery Range and Retailers Organization *(1981)*
156 N. Main
Oregon, WI 53575
Tel: (608)835-9060 *Fax:* (608)835-9360
Toll Free: (800)234 - 7499
Web Site: www.archeryretailers.com
Members: 130 companies
Staff: 4
Annual Budget: $50-100,000
Executive Secretary: Lynn Stiklestad
Historical Note
Formerly (until 1980) known as the Archery Lane Operators Association, ARRO is primarily a cooperative buying association. Membership: $400/year (company).
Meetings/Conferences:
Annual Meetings: January

Archery Trade Association *(1946)*
860 East 4600 South
Suite 310
Salt Lake City, UT 84107
Tel: (801)261-2380 *Fax:* (801)261-2389
Toll Free: (866)266 - 2776 Ext: 1
E-Mail: info@archerytrade.org
Web Site: www.archerytrade.org
Members: 700 companies
Staff: 5
Annual Budget: $100-250,000
President and Chief Executive Officer: Jay McAninch
Historical Note
Founded as the Archery Manufacturers and Dealers Association, it became the Archery Manufacturers Association in 1952, Archery Manufacturers Organization in 1965, and Archery Manufacturers and Merchants Organization in 1994. Assumed present name in 2002. Members are producers and sellers to the archery consumer including manufacturers, distributors, sales representatives, dealers and the archery media. Membership: $150-15,000/year, based on archery sales (regular); $100/year (retail); $50-250/year (rep firm); $750/year (supporting).

Architectural Engineering Institute *(1998)*
1801 Alexander Bell Dr.
Reston, VA 20191-4400
Tel: (703)295-6300 *Fax:* (703)295-6222
E-Mail: aei@asce.org
Web Site: www.aeinstitute.org
Members: 4000 individuals
Staff: 2
Annual Budget: $100-250,000
Director: Patricia S. Brown
Historical Note
Formerly (1998) National Society of Architectural Engineers. An affiliate of American Society of Civil Engineers. Members are architectural engineers involved in engineering design and/or construction. membership: $140/year (individual); $500/year (industry).
Meetings/Conferences:
Annual Meetings: Fall
Publications:
The Team Newsletter. bi-a. adv.
Journal of Architectural Engineering. q.

Architectural Precast Association *(1966)*
6710 Winkler Road, Suite 8
Ft. Myers, FL 33919
Tel: (239)454-6989 *Fax:* (239)454-6787
E-Mail: info@archprecast.org
Web Site: www.archprecast.org
Members: 100 companies
Staff: 3
Annual Budget: $100-250,000
Executive Director: Fred L. McGee
E-Mail: info@archprecast.org
Historical Note
The APA is organized to serve the international, technical and business needs of architectural precast concrete manufacturers and their suppliers and to provide high standards of workmanship throughout the industry.
Meetings/Conferences:
Annual Meetings: Spring
Publications:
The Architectural Precaster. bi-m.

Architectural Woodwork Institute *(1953)*
1952 Isaac Newton Sq. West
Reston, VA 20190
Tel: (703)733-0600 *Fax:* (703)733-0584
Web Site: www.awinet.org
Members: 10 companies
Staff: 9
Annual Budget: $1-2,000,000
Executive Vice President: Judith B. Durham, CAE
E-Mail: jdurham@awinet.org
Director, Marketing and Communications: Philip Duvic
Director, QCP: Randy Estabrook
Director, Meetings and Conventions: Kimberly Haynes
Director, Member Services: Greg Heuer
Historical Note
Absorbed the Millwork Cost Bureau. Members are manufacturers and suppliers of paneling, fixtures, cases, laminates and doors. Membership: $600-3600/year (organization/company).
Meetings/Conferences:
Annual Meetings: Fall/over 700
Publications:
Quality Standards. a.
Design Solutions Journal. q. adv.
National Membership Directory. a. adv.

Archivists and Librarians in the History of the Health Sciences *(1975)*
1216 Fifth Ave.
New York, NY 10029
Tel: (212)822-7321
E-Mail: pgallagher@nyam.org
Web Site: www.library.ucla.edu/libraries/biomed/alhhs
Members: 220 individuals
Staff: 1
Annual Budget: under $10,000
Secretary-Treasurer: Patricia E. Gallagher
E-Mail: pgallagher@nyam.org
Historical Note
Formerly (1992) the Association of Librarians in the History of the Health Sciences. Members are librarians & archivists with responsibility for history of health science collections. Meets to discuss mutual concerns, view history of medicine collections, and to participate in continuing professional education. Membership $15/year (domestic); $21/year (overseas).
Meetings/Conferences:
Annual Meetings: With the American Ass'n for the History of Medicine
Publications:
The Watermark. q. adv.

Argentina-American Chamber of Commerce *(1919)*
630 Fifth Ave.
Suite 2518
New York, NY 10011
Tel: (212)698-2238
Members: 450 companies
Staff: 3
Annual Budget: $100-250,000
Executive Director: Soledad Matteozzi
Historical Note
Membership: $375/year (individual); $700/year (organization/company).
Meetings/Conferences:
Annual Meetings: Spring in New York, NY/4-500
Publications:
Argentine-American Business Review Directory. a. adv.
Argentine News-Letter. m.
Business Watch. m. adv.
Directory. a.

ARMA International *(1975)*
13725 W. 109th St.
Suite 101
Lenexa, KS 66215
Tel: (913)341-3808 *Fax:* (913)341-3742
Toll Free: (888)299 - 2372
E-Mail: hq@arma.org
Web Site: www.arma.org
Members: 10500 individuals
Staff: 28
Annual Budget: $5-10,000,000
Executive Director and Chief Executive Officer: Peter R. Hermann, CAE
E-Mail: phermann@arma.org
Director, Education: Marilyn Bier
E-Mail: mbier@arma.org
Corporate Secretary: Connie Hardy
E-Mail: connieh@arma.org
Director, Branding and Marketing: Cynthia Launchbaugh
E-Mail: claunch@arma.org
Director, Finance: Melanie Middlebrook
Director, Professional Resources: William Millican

E-Mail: wmillican@arma.org
Director, Public Relations/Advocacy: Bob Tillman
E-Mail: btillman@arma.org
Director, Membership Services: Anita Willis
E-Mail: awillis@arma.org

Historical Note

Founded as American Records Management Association. Absorbed Association of Records Executives and Administrators and became Association of Records Managers and Administrators in 1985; assumed its current name in 2000. Affiliated with the Institute of Certified Records Managers. Membership: $150/year.

Meetings/Conferences:

Annual Meetings: *Fall/5,000*

Publications:

Buyers Guide. a. adv.
ARMA Website. m. adv.
Enriched Emails. adv.
Information Management Journal. q. adv.

Armed Forces Broadcasters Association *(1982)*

P.O. Box 447
Sun City, CA 92586-0447
Tel: (951)672-7299 *Fax:* (951)679-5484
Members: 600 individuals
Staff: 1
Annual Budget: under $10,000
President: Mary Carnes

Historical Note

Enhances camaraderie among former, present, and future members of the military broadcasting community; provides employment search assistance. Membership: $20/year.

Meetings/Conferences:

Annual Meetings: *April, in LA, following the Nat'l Ass'n of Broadcasters Convention.*

Publications:

Transmitter. q.

Armed Forces Communications and Electronics Association *(1946)*

4400 Fair Lakes Court
Fairfax, VA 22033-3899
Tel: (703)631-6100 *Fax:* (703)631-6405
Toll Free: (800)336 - 4583
Web Site: www.afcea.org
Members: 33000 individuals
President and Chief Executive Officer: V.Adm. Herbert A. Browne, USN (Ret.)
E-Mail: promo@afcea.org

Historical Note

Originated in May 1946 as the Army Signal Association. Name changed to Armed Forces Communications Association in 1948; assumed its current name in 1954. Provides an ethical forum in which government and industry leaders and decision-makers can meet to exchange ideas and concepts, discuss current problems and solutions and identify future requirements in the technical disciplines of communications, electronics, intelligence and information systems. Fosters cooperation between free world industries, governments and C41 professionals. Membership: $35/year (individual).

Publications:

SIGNAL Magazine. m. adv.

Armed Forces Financial Network

Historical Note

A network of ATMs and POS terminals, located at or near U.S. military installations, that allow personnel at those bases access to their funds. AFFN is a joint venture of Association of Military Banks and Defense Credit Union Council.

Armed Forces Optometric Society *(1970)*

411 Sweetgrass Court
Great Falls, MT 59405
Tel: (406)452-5688
E-Mail: execdir@afos2020.org
Web Site: www.afos2020.org
Members: 800 individuals
Staff: 1
Executive Director: Steven R. Sem, O.D.
E-Mail: execdir@afos2020.org

Publications:

Newsletter. q.

Army Aviation Association of America *(1957)*

755 Main St.
Suite 4D
Monroe, CT 06468-2830
Tel: (203)268-2450 *Fax:* (203)268-5870
E-Mail: aaaa@quad-a.org
Web Site: www.quad-a.org
Members: 14500 individuals
Staff: 12
Annual Budget: $500-1,000,000
Executive Director: William R. Harris, Jr.
E-Mail: aaaa@quad-a.org

Historical Note

Quad-A represents active and retired U.S. Army aviators and defense contractors. Membership: $26/year.

Meetings/Conferences:

Annual Meetings: *Spring*

Publications:

Army Aviation. 10/year.

Art and Antique Dealers League of America *(1926)*

1040 Madison Ave.
New York, NY 10021-0111
Tel: (212)879-7558 *Fax:* (212)772-7197
Web Site: www.artantiquedealersleague.org
Members: 100 dealers
Staff: 1
Annual Budget: $10-25,000
Secretary and Executive Director: James Frankel

Historical Note

Oldest and principal antiques and fine arts organization in America. An outgrowth of the Antique Dealers Luncheon Club which on January 7, 1926 met at the Madison Hotel, New York City and formed the Antique and Decorative Arts League, which became the Art and Antique Dealers League of America, Inc., in 1942. Member of the International Art Dealers Confederation (CINOA - Confederation Internationale des Negociantes en Oeuvres d'Art), a worldwide organization encompassing 14 countries.

Meetings/Conferences:

Annual Meetings: *Annual Dinner & General Meeting - New York, NY/late January/75*

Publications:

Connoiseurs Quarterly. q. adv.

The Art and Creative Materials Institute *(1936)*

P.O. Box 479
Hanson, MA 02341-0479
Tel: (781)293-4100 *Fax:* (781)294-0808
Web Site: www.acminet.org
Members: 210 companies
Staff: 4
Annual Budget: $500-1,000,000
Executive Vice President: Deborah M. Fanning, CAE
E-Mail: debbief@acminet.org
Associate Director: Deborah S. Gustafson
E-Mail: debbieg@acminet.org

Historical Note

Formerly (1983) the Crayon, Water Color and Craft Institute and Art and Craft Materials Institute (1994). Members are makers of art and craft products. The Institute conducts a certification program to assure that these products are non-toxic or properly labelled if necessary. Membership fee varies, based on annual sales.

Meetings/Conferences:

Annual Meetings: *Spring*
2007 – Chicago, IL(Navy Pier)

Publications:

Institute Items. m.
List of Certified Products. q.

Art Dealers Association of America *(1962)*

575 Madison Ave.
New York, NY 10022
Tel: (212)940-8590 *Fax:* (212)940-6484
E-Mail: adaa@artdealers.org
Web Site: www.artdealers.org
Members: 166 dealers
Staff: 5
Administrative Vice President: Gilbert S. Edelson
E-Mail: adaa@artdealers.org

Historical Note

ADAA is a nonprofit membership organization composed of many of the nation's leading dealers in the fine arts.

Meetings/Conferences:

Annual Meetings: *Always held at ADAA's office in New York City.*

Publications:

Directory. a.

Art Directors Guild/Scenic, Title and Graphic Artists *(1960)*

11969 Ventura Blvd.
Suite 200
Studio City, CA 91604
Tel: (818)762-9995 *Fax:* (818)762-9997
Web Site: www.artdirectors.org
Members: 1500 individuals
Staff: 9
Executive Director: Scott Roth
Associate Executive Director: Missy Humphrey

Historical Note

Founded as the Society of Motion Picture Art Directors; became (1960 Society of Motion Picture and Television Art Directors and assumed its current name in 1999. ADG/STGA comprises the Art Directors Guild and the Scenic, Title and Graphic Artists, Local 800. ADG/STA is part of the International Alliance of Theatrical Stage Employees and Moving Picture Machine Operators of the U.S. and Canada. Members are creatives in the motion picture industry responsible for settings, props, backgrounds, and related areas.

Publications:

Perspective (newsletter). q.
Directory. a. adv.

Art Glass Association *(1986)*

P.O. Box 2537
Zanesville, OH 43702-2537
Tel: (740)450-6547 *Fax:* (740)454-1194
Toll Free: (866)301 - 2421
Web Site: www.artglassassociation.com
Members: 890manufacturersandretailers
Staff: 6
Annual Budget: $100-250,000
Executive Director: Bill Bird

Historical Note

Formerly (2003) Art Glass Suppliers Association International. AGA is the trade association of the art, decorative glass and ceramics industry. Members are retailers, wholesalers, studios of art glass and suppliers. Membership: $250/year (company); $100/year (individual/small business).

Publications:

Art Glass News Newsletter. q. adv.
AGSA Trade Show Directory. a. adv.

Art Glass Suppliers Association International

Historical Note

Became Art Glass Association in 2003.

Art Libraries Society of North America *(1972)*

232-329 March Road, Box 11
Ottawa, ON K2K -2E1
Tel: (613)599-3074 *Fax:* (613)599-7027
Toll Free: (800)817 - 0621
E-Mail: arlisna@igs.net
Web Site: www.arlisna.org
Members: 1300 individuals
Staff: 2
Annual Budget: $100-250,000
Executive Director: Elizabeth Clark

Historical Note

A professional organization of art information specialists. ARLIS/NA includes individual (librarians, historians, curators, and students) and institutional (colleges and universities, museums and galleries, historical societies and libraries) members. Membership: $85/year (individual member); $45/year (student or retired); $145/year (institutional).

Meetings/Conferences:

Annual Meetings: *February-March/600*
2007 – Atlanta, GA(Sheraton Midtown)/Apr. 26-May 1

Publications:
Art Documentation. bi-a. adv.
Handbook and List of Members. a. adv.

Art Therapy Credentials Board *(1993)*
Three Terrace Way, Suite B
Greensboro, NC 27403-3660
Toll Free: (877)213 - 2822
Web Site: www.atcb.org
Members: 4000 individuals
Staff: 1
Annual Budget: $250-500,000
Executive Director: Mickey Horner
Historical Note
ATCB is a certification board that offers two credentials to art therapists. ATCB's mission is to protect the public by promoting the competent and ethical practice of art therapy. The ATCB grants postgraduate registration after reviewing documentation of completion of graduate education and postgraduate supervised experience. The registered art therapist who successfully completes the written examination administered by the ATCB is qualified as board certified.
Publications:
ATCB Review. semi-a.

Arthroscopy Association of North America *(1982)*
6300 N. River Road
Suite 104
Rosemont, IL 60018-4228
Tel: (847)292-2262 *Fax:* (847)292-2268
Web Site: www.aana.org
Members: 1800 individuals
Staff: 8
Annual Budget: $2-5,000,000
Executive Director: Edward Goss
E-Mail: ed@aana.org
Director, Meetings and Office Manager: Holly Albert
E-Mail: holly@aana.org
Director, Information Systems: Tiffany Duensino
Historical Note
Incorporated in the State of Illinois in 1982. Membership: by invitation only; $525/year.
Meetings/Conferences:
Annual Meetings: Spring
2007 - San Francisco, CA/Apr. 26-29
2008 - Washington, DC/Apr. 24-27
2009 - San Diego, CA/Apr. 30-May 3
2010 - Hollywood, FL/May 20-23
Publications:
Arthroscopy, The Journal of Arthroscopic Related Surgery. bi-m. adv.
Newsletter-Inside AANA. bi-m.
Membership Directory. a.

Articulating Crane Council of North America
Historical Note
An affiliate of the National Truck Equipment Association.

Artist-Blacksmiths' Association of North America *(1973)*
P.O. Box 816
Farmington, GA 30638-0816
Tel: (706)310-1030 *Fax:* (706)769-7147
E-Mail: abana@abana.org
Web Site: www.abana.org
Members: 4800 individuals
Staff: 1
Annual Budget: $250-500,000
Central Office Executive Director: LeeAnn Mitchell
E-Mail: abana@abana.org
Historical Note
Members are professional blacksmiths, artists and others with an interest in blacksmithing techniques. Membership: $55/year (individual).
Publications:
Hammer's Blow. q. adv.
The Anvil's Ring. q. adv.

ASABE - the Society for Engineering in Agricultural, Food and Biological Systems *(1907)*
2950 Niles Road
St. Joseph, MI 49085
Tel: (269)429-0300 *Fax:* (269)429-3852
E-Mail: moore@asabe.org
Web Site: www.asae.org
Members: 9000 individuals
Staff: 31
Annual Budget: $2-5,000,000
Executive Vice President: M. Melissa Moore
Director, Standards and Technical Activities: Scott Cedarquist
Director, Meetings and Conferences: Michael Chesser
Director, Membership: Mark Crossley
Director, Publications: Donna M. Hull
Comptroller and Human Resources: Mark D. Zielke
Historical Note
Founded in Madison, WI in 1907 and incorporated in Michigan in 1935; assumed its current name in 2000. ASABE is a professional and technical society for engineering in agriculture, food, and biological systems. Membership: $90-118/year (individual).
Meetings/Conferences:
Annual Meetings: Summer/1,700
2007 - Minneapolis, MN/June 17-20
Publications:
Journal of Agricultural Safety & Health. q.
Resource. m. adv.
Transactions of the ASAE. bi-m.
ASAE Standards. a.
Applied Engineering in Agriculture. q.

Asbestos Cement Product Producers Association *(1972)*
PMB114-1235 Jefferson Davis Hwy.
Arlington, VA 22202
Tel: (703)560-2980 *Fax:* (703)560-2981
E-Mail: aia@chrysotile.com
Members: 10 companies
Staff: 1
Annual Budget: $25-50,000
President: Bob J. Pigg
Historical Note
Formerly (1989) the Association of Asbestos Cement Pipe Producers, and (1996) the Asbestos Cement Pipe Producers Association. An international association incorporated in Pennsylvania in 1972. Represents international manufacturers of asbestos-cement products.
Meetings/Conferences:
Annual Meetings: April
Publications:
Special Reports. irreg.

Asbestos Information Association/North America *(1970)*
PMB114-1235 Jefferson Davis Hwy.
Arlington, VA 22202-3283
Tel: (703)560-2980 *Fax:* (703)560-2981
Members: 5 companies
Staff: 1
Annual Budget: $50-100,000
President: Bob J. Pigg
E-Mail: aiabjpigg@aol.com
Historical Note
Incorporated in 1971. The science and education arm of U.S. and Canadian asbestos producers and asbestos products manufacturers. Provides information on asbestos and health.
Meetings/Conferences:
Annual Meetings: Washington, DC area, second or third week in September

Aseptic Packaging Council *(1989)*
2120 L St. NW
Suite 400
Washington, DC 20037
Tel: (202)478-6158 *Fax:* (202)223-9579
Toll Free: (800)277 - 8088
Web Site: www.aseptic.org
Members: 2 companies
Staff: 3
Executive Vice President: Erich Parker
Historical Note
Members are producers of drink-boxes and other aseptic (plastic-coated paper) products.

ASFE/The Best People on Earth *(1969)*
8811 Colesville Road
Suite G106
Silver Spring, MD 20910
Tel: (301)565-2733 *Fax:* (301)589-2017
E-Mail: info@asfe.org
Web Site: www.asfe.org
Members: 300companies, 1200branchoffices
Staff: 6
Annual Budget: $1-2,000,000
Executive Vice President: John P. Bachner
Director, Information Technology: Zach Fletcher
Historical Note
Formerly (1975) Associated Soil and Foundation Engineers, (1987) Association of Soil and Foundation Engineers, and (1993) ASFE/ The Association of Engineering Firms Practicing in the Geosciences. Seeks the enhancement of professionalism and the reduction of liability loss exposure. Membership: $525-9,850/year (company).
Publications:
Newslog. bi-m.
Membership Directory. a.

Asia America MultiTechnology Association *(1980)*
P.O. Box 7522
Menlo Park, CA 94026-7522
Tel: (650)738-1480
E-Mail: aama@aamasv.com
Web Site: www.aamasv.com
Members: 1100 individuals
Staff: 2
Annual Budget: $100-250,000
Executive Director: Leilynne Lau
E-Mail: aama@aamasv.com
Historical Note
Founded as Asian American Manufacturers Association; assumed its current name in 2002. Members manufacturer high technology computer-related products. Membership: $25/year (student); $50/year (individual manufacturer); $100/year (associate non-manufacturer); $450/year (business); $1,200/year (business associate); $500/year (life - one time fee).
Meetings/Conferences:
Annual Meetings: Fall
Publications:
AAMA Newsletter. m. adv.
Membership Directory. a. adv.

Asian American Certified Public Accountants *(1979)*
425 Washington St.
Third Floor
San Francisco, CA 94111
Tel: (415)981-9999
Members: 200 individuals
Contact: Arthur Louie
Historical Note
AACPA members are accountants of Asian ancestry.
Publications:
AACPA Newsletter. bi-m.
Directory of Accounting Firms. irreg.
Membership Directory. a.

Asian American Journalists Association *(1981)*
1182 Market St.
Suite 320
San Francisco, CA 94102
Tel: (415)346-2051 *Fax:* (415)346-6343
E-Mail: national@aaja.org
Web Site: www.aaja.org
Members: 2000 individuals
Staff: 9
Annual Budget: $1-2,000,000
Executive Director: Rene Astudillo
Historical Note
AAJA encourages Asian Americans and Pacific Islanders to enter the journalism profession and work towards fair coverage of Asian Americans. Members are journalists who receive the bulk of their economic support from employment as executives, reporters, editors, writers, photographers, producers, technicians and directors in news or news-oriented public affairs departments of print or broadcast companies. Members also include non-journalists who were at one time professional journalists and non-newsroom employers and students. Programs include scholarships, job listings, professional development, fellowships, and internship support. Membership:

$55/year, full (professional journalist); $55/year (associate non-journalist); $20/year (retired); $15/year (student).

Meetings/Conferences:
Annual Meetings: Annual

Publications:
AAJA Dateline. q.
AAJA Online. w.

Asian American Manufacturers Association

Historical Note
Became Asia American Multi-Technology Association in 2002.

Asian American Psychological Association *(1971)*
5025 N. Central Ave., PMB 527
Phoenix, AZ 85012
Tel: (602)230-4257
Web Site: www.aapaonline.org
Members: 400 individuals
Annual Budget: under $10,000
President: Alvin N. Alvarez, Ph.D.
E-Mail: aalvarez@sfsu.edu

Historical Note
AAPA provides a network and forum for member psychologists and psychology professionals. Has no paid officers or full-time staff. Membership: $35/year (professional); $12/year (student).

Meetings/Conferences:
Annual Meetings: August, just prior to American Psychological Ass'n convention

Publications:
The Asian American Psychological Newsletter. a.
AAPA Journal. a.

Asian/Pacific American Librarians Association *(1980)*
c/o Texas Womens Univ. Dept. of Library Science
P.O. Box 425439
Denton, TX 76204
Tel: (940)898-2607
E-Mail: linghwey@yahoo.com
Web Site: www.apalaweb.org
Members: 219 individuals
Annual Budget: under $10,000
Executive Director: Ling Hwey Jeng

Historical Note
APALA members are librarians and other information specialists of Asian/Pacific heritage. Has no paid officers or full-time staff. Membership: $20/year (individual); $50/year (institution); $10/year (student).

Meetings/Conferences:
Annual Meetings: in conjunction with the American Library Ass'n

Publications:
APALA Newsletter. q. adv.
Membership Directory. a. adv.

ASIS International *(1955)*
1625 Prince St.
Alexandria, VA 22314-2818
Tel: (703)519-6200 *Fax:* (703)519-6299
E-Mail: asis@asisonline.org
Web Site: www.asisonline.org
Members: 33000 individuals
Staff: 80
Executive Director: Michael J. Stack
E-Mail: asis@asisonline.org
Director, Government Affairs and Public Policy: Jack D.P. Lichtenstein
E-Mail: asis@asisonline.org
Director, Education: Susan A. Melnicove
E-Mail: asis@asisonline.org
Director, Marketing: Eileen Smith
E-Mail: asis@asisonline.org
Director, Publishing: Denny White
E-Mail: asis@asisonline.org

Historical Note
With more than 33,000 members worldwide, ASIS International is a preeminent organization for security management professionals that works to lead the way for advanced and improved security performance. Provides members, business, government and the public with access to a wide range of programs, information, professional certifications, and services. Administers three certifications: the PCI - Professional Certified Investigator, PSP - Physical Security Professional, PCI - Professional Certified Investigator, and CPP - Certified Protection Professional.

Meetings/Conferences:
Annual Meetings: Fall
2007 – Las Vegas, NV/Sept. 24-27

Publications:
Security Management Weekly (online). w.
Security Management Daily (online). d.
Security Industry Buyer's Guide. a.
Security Management Weekly (online). w. adv.
Dynamics. bi-m.

ASM International *(1913)*
9639 Kinsman Road
Materials Park, OH 44073-0002
Tel: (440)338-5151 *Fax:* (440)338-4634
Toll Free: (800)336 - 5152
E-Mail: customerservice@asminternational.org
Web Site: www.asminternational.org
Members: 43000 individuals
Staff: 120
Annual Budget: $10-25,000,000
Managing Director: Stanley C. Theobald

Historical Note
Originated in Detroit as the Steel Treaters Club in 1913; became the American Society for Steel Treating in 1920, the American Society for Metals in 1933 and assumed its present name in 1986. Incorporated in Ohio in 1920. ASM's mission is to gather, process and disseminate technical information on engineered materials through forums and meetings, education programs, publications and electronic media. Society of Carbide and Tool Engineers is a division of ASM. Has a budget of about $12 million.

Meetings/Conferences:
Annual Meetings: Fall

Publications:
Heat Treating Progress. m.
Alloy Digest. bi-m.
Electronic Device. q.
Metallurgical Transactions A. m.
Metallurgical Transactions B. q.
Journal of Thermal Spray Technology. q.
ASM News. m. adv.
Internat'l Materials Review. bi-m.
Journal of Phase Equilibria & Diffusion. q.
Journal of Material Engineering & Performance. q.
Advanced Materials and Processes. m. adv.

ASME International Gas Turbine Institute *(1946)*
5775 Glenridge Dr. NE
Suite C115
Atlanta, GA 30328-5380
Tel: (404)847-0072 *Fax:* (404)847-0151
E-Mail: igti@asme.org
Web Site: www.igti.asme.org
Members: 8000
Staff: 8
Annual Budget: $2-5,000,000
Manager, Conferences and Exhibitions: Judy Osborn
E-Mail: igti@asme.org

Historical Note
An eductional and technical institute of the American Society of Mechanical Engineers.

Meetings/Conferences:
Annual Meetings: Summer
2007 – Montreal, QC, Canada(Palais de Congres)/May 14-17/2500

Publications:
Source GT (on-line). adv.
Global Gas Turbine News newsletter. q.
Turbo Expo Conference Programs. a. adv.

Asphalt Emulsion Manufacturers Association *(1973)*
Three Church Circle
Suite 250
Annapolis, MD 21401
Tel: (410)267-0023 *Fax:* (410)267-7546
Web Site: www.aema.org
Members: 130 companies
Staff: 3
Annual Budget: $250-500,000
Executive Director: Michael R. Krissoff
E-Mail: krissoff@aema.org

Historical Note
Members are manufacturers of asphalt emulsion (active) and suppliers to the industry (associate). Membership: $1,500 plus $100/additional plant/year; $6,000 maximum (company)/year; $2,000/year (associate).

Meetings/Conferences:
Semi-Annual Meetings: Spring and Fall

Publications:
AEMA Directory. a. adv.
AEMA Newsletter. q. adv.

Asphalt Institute *(1919)*
2696 Research Park Dr.
Lexington, KY 40511
Tel: (859)288-4960 *Fax:* (859)288-4999
E-Mail: info@asphaltinstitute.org
Web Site: www.asphaltinstitute.org
Members: 85 companies
Staff: 26
Annual Budget: $2-5,000,000
President: Peter T. Grass

Historical Note
Founded as the Asphalt Association; assumed its present name in 1929. Members are companies that refine asphalt products, process finished asphalts, or are marketers with significant asphalt assets. AI affiliates include companies working with liquid asphalt through transporting, additive manufacturers, or equipment manufacturers. AI serves both users and producers of asphalt materials.

Meetings/Conferences:
Annual Meetings: December (by invitation only)

Publications:
ASPHALT Magazine. 3/yr. adv.
Catalog of Publications. a. adv.

Asphalt Recycling and Reclaiming Association *(1976)*
Three Church Circle
Suite 250
Annapolis, MD 21401-1902
Tel: (410)267-0023 *Fax:* (410)267-7546
Web Site: www.arra.org
Members: 200 companies
Staff: 2
Annual Budget: $100-250,000
Executive Director: Michael R. Krissoff
E-Mail: krissoff@arra.org

Historical Note
Promotes the collective interests of those individuals, firms or corporations engaged in the asphalt recycling industry as contractors, owners or manufacturers of equipment, engineers, suppliers and public highway officials. Membership: $1,350/year (organization/company).

Meetings/Conferences:
Semi-annual Meetings: Winter/Fall

Publications:
ARRA Newsletter. q. adv.
Membership Directory. a. adv.

Asphalt Roofing Manufacturers Association *(1915)*
1156 15th St. NW
Suite 900
Washington, DC 20005
Tel: (202)207-0917 *Fax:* (202)223-9741
E-Mail: rsnyder@kellencompany.com
Web Site: www.asphaltroofing.org
Members: 42 companies
Staff: 4
Annual Budget: $1-2,000,000
Executive Vice President: Russell K. Snyder
E-Mail: rsnyder@kellencompany.com
General Manager: Reed Hitchcock
Director, Communications: Joseph Hobson

Historical Note
Formerly (1969) Asphalt Roofing Industry Bureau. ARMA members are manufacturers of roll roofing, built-up roofing, residential roofing, asphalt shingles, and modifed bitumen roofing.

Meetings/Conferences:
Annual Meetings: Spring

Publications:
Industry Shipment Report. q.
Technical Bulletins. irreg.
ARMA Newsletter. q.

Aspirin Foundation of America *(1981)*
529 14th St. NW
Suite 807
Washington, DC 20045
Toll Free: (800)432 - 3247
E-Mail: info@aspirin.org
Web Site: www.aspirin.org
Members: 8 companies
Staff: 1
Annual Budget: $1-2,000,000
President: Thomas E. Bryant, M.D., J.D.

Ass'n of Learning Providers *(1978)*
12427 Hedges Run Dr.
Suite 120
Lake Ridge, VA 22192
Tel: (703)730-2838 *Fax:* (703)730-2857
Toll Free: (877)533 - 4914
Web Site: www.isaconnection.org
Members: 150 companies
Staff: 4
Annual Budget: $500-1,000,000
Executive Director: Pamela J. Schmidt
E-Mail: pschmidt@isaconnection.org
Membership Manager: Kristin Atkins
E-Mail: katkins@isaconnection.org
Manager, Finance and Administration: Lois Donovan
E-Mail: ldonovan@isaconnection.org
Historical Note
Members are training industry firms which produce generic and/or custom-designed training programs or consult for business and industry.
Meetings/Conferences:
Annual Meetings: March
Publications:
Newswire (online). 26/year.
Intercom. 3/year.

Ass'n of Procurement Technical Assistance Centers *(1986)*
P.O. Box 1607
Orange, TX 77631-1607
Tel: (409)886-0125 *Fax:* (409)886-2849
E-Mail: headquarters@aptac-us.org
Web Site: www.aptac-us.org
Members: 500 individuals
Staff: 2
Contact Person: Shelia Rhoads
E-Mail: headquarters@aptac-us.org
Historical Note
APTAC, d/b/a/ Association of Procurement Technical Assistance Centers, provides information and support for persons and organizations active in government procurement.
Meetings/Conferences:
Annual Meetings: Spring

Assembly of Episcopal Healthcare Chaplains *(1951)*
1326 N. Tenth St.
Beatrice, NE 68310
Tel: (402)223-7372
Web Site: www.episcopalchaplain.org
Members: 800 individuals
Annual Budget: $10-25,000
President: Jean Scribner
Historical Note
Founded as Assembly of Episcopal Hospitals and Chaplains; assumed its current name in 1999. Has no paid officers or full-time staff.
Meetings/Conferences:
Annual Meetings: usually in March, in conjunction with the Association of Professional Chaplains
Publications:
Chaplair. q.
Directory. irreg.

Assisted Living Federation of America *(1991)*
1650 King St.
Suite 602
Alexandria, VA 22314
Tel: (703)894-1805 *Fax:* (703)894-1831
Web Site: www.alfa.org
Members: 7000 organizations and companies
Staff: 26
Annual Budget: $5-10,000,000
President and Chief Executive Officer: Richard P. Grimes
Senior Vice President: Maribeth Bersahi
Chief Program Office: Marilen King
Finance: Nathan Nickens
Membership: Johnny White
Director, Public Policy: Paul Williams
Historical Note
Absorbed NARCF in 1997 and NASLIE in 1999. Formerly (1996) Assisted Living Facilities Association of America, ALFA members are providers of assisted living and other senior housing, state provider associations, and other businesses with an interest in the industry.
Meetings/Conferences:
2007 – Dallas, TX/May 14-17
Publications:
Assisted Living Executive. 9/yr. adv.

Assistive Technology Industry Association
401 N. Michigan Ave.
Chicago, IL 60611-4267
Tel: (312)321-5172 *Fax:* (312)673-6659
E-Mail: info@atia.org
Web Site: www.atia.org
Administrator: Kim Barnett

Associated Actors and Artistes of America *(1919)*
165 W. 46th St.
New York, NY 10036
Tel: (212)869-0358 *Fax:* (212)869-1746
E-Mail: actors1919@verizon.net
Members: 120000 individuals
Staff: 2
Annual Budget: $50-100,000
President: Theodore Bikel
Historical Note
Affiliated with AFL-CIO. Chartered by the American Federation of Labor on August 28, 1919, 4As is the successor organization to the White Rats Actors Union of America (established in 1910). An umbrella coordinating organization comprising autonomous branches: Actors' Equity Association, American Federation of Television and Radio Artists, American Guild of Musical Artists, American Guild of Variety Artists, Hebrew Actors Union, Italian Actors Union and screen Actors Guild.
Meetings/Conferences:
Biennial Meetings: Uneven years/Headquarters/Summer

Associated Air Balance Council *(1965)*
1518 K St. NW
Suite 503
Washington, DC 20005
Tel: (202)737-0202 *Fax:* (202)638-4833
E-Mail: info@aabc.com
Web Site: www.aabchq.com
Members: 140 companies
Staff: 5
Annual Budget: $500-1,000,000
Executive Director: Kenneth M. Sufka
E-Mail: info@aabc.com
Historical Note
Members are independent testers of air handling systems.
Meetings/Conferences:
Annual Meetings: Fall
2007 – Savannah, GA(Westin Savannah)/Oct. 18-21
Publications:
TAB Journal. q. adv.
Annual Membership Directory. a.

Associated Bodywork and Massage Professionals *(1987)*
1271 Sugarbush Dr.
Evergreen, CO 80439-9766
Tel: (303)674-8478 *Fax:* (303)674-0859
Toll Free: (800)458 - 2267
E-Mail: expectmore@abmp.com
Web Site: www.abmp.com
Members: 51,000 individuals
Staff: 33
Annual Budget: $5-10,000,000
Executive Director: Katie Armitage
President: Robert Benson
Executive Vice President: Les Sweeney
Historical Note
ABMP members are massage therapists, bodyworkers, somatic therapists and estheticians practicing a wide variety of massage bodywork and skin care therapies. Membership: $229/year (certified/esthetician); $199/year (professional/practitioner); $75/year (supporting); $49/year (student).
Publications:
ABMP Touch Resource Guide. a. adv.
Massage & Bodywork Magazine. bi-m. adv.
ABMP Successful Business Handbook. a.
Body Sense. semi-a. adv.
Different Strokes. bi-m.
Massage Marketplace. a. adv.
Skin Deep. bi-m. adv.
ABMP School Connector. q.
Knead To Know. q.

Associated Builders and Contractors *(1950)*
4250 N. Fairfax Dr.
Suite 900
Arlington, VA 22203
Tel: (703)812-2000 *Fax:* (703)812-8236
E-Mail: gotquestions@abc.org
Web Site: www.abc.org
Members: 23500 companies
Staff: 80
Annual Budget: $10-25,000,000
President and Chief Executive Officer: M. Kirk Pickerel, CAE
Vice President, Finance and Administration: Kathie Berry
Vice President, Special Projects: Michael Dunbar
Vice President, Workforce Development: Robert Piper
Vice President, Public Affairs: Gail A. Raiman
Director, Meetings: Tina Schneider
Vice President, Information Technology: Mary S. Schroer
Vice President, Government Affairs: William B. Spencer
Vice President, Member Services: Tim Welsh
Historical Note
Incorporated in Baltimore, MD in 1950. Members are merit shop construction companies. Sponsors and supports the Associated Builders and Contractors Political Action Committee. Has an annual budget of approximately $12 million. Membership fee varies by volume and is collected at chapter level.
Meetings/Conferences:
Annual Meetings: Winter
2007 – Nashville, TN(Gaylord Opryland)/March 21-25
Publications:
Construction Executive. m. adv.
National Membership Directory (online). w. adv.
Newsline.

Associated Business Writers of America *(1945)*
10940 S. Parker Road, #508
Parker, CO 80134
Tel: (303)841-0246 *Fax:* (303)841-2607
Members: 230 individuals
Staff: 1
Annual Budget: $10-25,000
Executive Director: Sandy Whelchel
Historical Note
An affiliate of the National Writers Association. The Associated Business Writers of America was established in 1946. The ABWA is composed of freelance writers whose aim is to better the image of the profession, to improve relations and communication with editors and other clients, and to strive for higher pay scales and more considerate handling of manuscripts. Membership: $98/year (individual); $250/year (group).
Meetings/Conferences:
Annual Meetings: with the Nat'l Writers Ass'n/June
Publications:
Authorship. q. adv.
Flash Market News (online). m.

Associated Church Press *(1916)*
1410 Vernon St.
Stoughton, WI 53589-2248

Tel: (608)877-0011 Fax: (608)877-0062
E-Mail: acpoffice@earthlink.net
Web Site: www.theacp.org
Members: 40 individuals
Staff: 1
Annual Budget: $50-100,000
Executive Director: Mary Lynn Hendrickson
E-Mail: acpoffice@earthlink.net

Historical Note
Formerly (1937) Editorial Council of the Religious Press. Protestant, Anglican, Catholic and Orthodox church-affiliated and independent periodicals in North America. Membership: $35/year (individual); $130-740/year, depending on circulation (company).

Meetings/Conferences:
Annual Meetings: *Spring*

Publications:
Newslog. q. adv.

Associated Collegiate Press, National Scholastic Press Association *(1921)*
2221 University Ave. SE
Suite 121
Minneapolis, MN 55414
Tel: (612)625-8335 Fax: (612)626-0720
E-Mail: rolni005@umn.edu
Web Site: www.studentpress.org
Members: 2000 individuals
Staff: 6
Annual Budget: $250-500,000
Executive Director: Tom E. Rolnicki
E-Mail: rolni005@umn.edu

Historical Note
Also known as the National Scholastic Press Association. Founded to promote the growth and quality of high school and college student publications.

Meetings/Conferences:
Annual Meetings: *Fall*

Publications:
Trends in High School Media. q. adv.
Trends in College Media. 3/year. adv.

Associated Construction Distributors International *(1974)*
1605 S.E. Delaware Ave.
Suite B
Ankeny, IA 50021
Tel: (515)964-1335 Fax: (515)964-7668
E-Mail: info@acdi.net
Web Site: www.acdi.net
Members: 37 construction distributors
Staff: 4
Annual Budget: $50-100,000
Executive Vice President: Tom Goetz

Historical Note
Members are distributors of construction supplies and equipment.

Meetings/Conferences:
Semi-annual Meetings: Spring and Fall

Publications:
ACDI Bulletin. m.
ACDI Directory. a.

Associated Construction Publications *(1938)*
30 Technology Pkwy. South
Norcross, GA 30092
Toll Free: (800)486 - 0014
Web Site: www.acppubs.com
Members: 14 regional publications
Staff: 48
Annual Budget: $2-5,000,000
Publisher and General Manager: John Weatherhead

Historical Note
A business unit of Reed Construction Data

Associated Cooperage Industries of America *(1915)*
2100 Gardiner Lane, Suite 100-E
Louisville, KY 40205-2947
Tel: (502)459-6113 Fax: (502)459-6114
E-Mail: aciainc@ncia.net
Web Site: www.acia.net
Members: 53 companies
Staff: 1
Annual Budget: $25-50,000
Secretary-Treasurer: Polly Wagner
E-Mail: aciainc@ncia.net

Historical Note
Promotes the interests of cooperage manufacturers and of those who use wooden barrels.

Meetings/Conferences:
Annual Meetings: *Fall*

Publications:
Newsletter. bi-m.

Associated Corset and Brassiere Manufacturers Association *(1933)*

Historical Note
An affiliate of United Infants' and Children's Wear Association, which provides administrative support.

Associated Equipment Distributors *(1919)*
615 W. 22nd St.
Oak Brook, IL 60523
Tel: (630)574-0650 Fax: (630)574-0132
E-Mail: info@aednet.org
Web Site: www.aednet.org
Members: 1200 companies
Staff: 20
Annual Budget: $2-5,000,000
President: Toby Mack
E-Mail: info@aednet.org
Director, Meetings and Conventions: Marcia Arger
E-Mail: info@aednet.org
Vice President, Operations: Matt Di Iorio
E-Mail: info@aednet.org
Director, Communications: Pam Gruebnau
E-Mail: info@aednet.org

Historical Note
Distributors and manufacturers of construction, mining, logging, and road maintenance equipment. Formerly National Distributors Association of Construction Equipment. Affiliated with the Canadian Association of Equipment Distributors. Affiliated with the AED Foundation.

Meetings/Conferences:
Annual Meetings: *Winter/3,000*
2007 – Las Vegas, NV(Convention Center)/Jan. 16-18
2008 – Chicago, IL(Convention Center)/Jan. 10-12

Publications:
Construction Equipment Distribution. m. adv.

Associated Funeral Directors International *(1939)*
P.O. Box 1347
Kingsport, TN 37662-1347
Tel: (423)392-1985 Fax: (423)392-1179
Toll Free: (800)346 - 7151
Members: 1700 funeral homes
Staff: 4
Annual Budget: $50-100,000
Executive Director: Richard A. Santore

Historical Note
Formerly (1992) the Associated Funeral Directors Service. Membership fee based on population of member's service area.

Meetings/Conferences:
Annual Meetings: *October*

Publications:
Today in Funeral Service. m. adv.
AFDI Membership Directory. a. adv.

Associated Fur Manufacturers *(1911)*

Historical Note
A division of Fur Information Council of America, which provides administrative support.

Associated General Contractors of America *(1918)*
2300 Wilson Blvd.
Suite 400
Arlington, VA 22201
Tel: (703)548-3118 Fax: (703)548-3119
E-Mail: info@agc.org
Web Site: www.agc.org
Members: 32000 companies
Staff: 75
Annual Budget: $10-25,000,000
Chief Executive Officer: Stephen E. Sandherr
E-Mail: sandhers@agc.org
Director, Congressional Relations, Tax and Fiscal Affairs: Heidi Blumenthal
Executive Director, Convention and Meeting Services: Rick Brown
Director, Communications: Carla Julian
Senior Director, Public Affairs: Kelley Keeler
E-Mail: keelerk@agc.org
General Counsel: Michael E. Kennedy
E-Mail: kennedym@agc.org
Chief Operating Officer: David R. Lukens
E-Mail: lukensd@agc.org
Executive Director, Publications: Donald A. Scott
E-Mail: scottd@agc.org
Senior Executive Director, Government and Public Affairs: Jeff Shoaf
E-Mail: shoafj@agc.org

Historical Note
Members are contracting firms responsible for the construction of commercial buildings, highways, industrial complexes and municipal-utilities and heavy-engineering facilities. Has an annual budget of approximately $17 million. Sponsors and supports the AGC Political Action Committee.

Meetings/Conferences:
Semi-Annual Meetings: March and Fall

Publications:
SmartBrief (online). bi-w.
News & Views. bi-w.
CONSTRUCTOR. m. adv.
National Newsletter. bi-w.
Directory and Buyers Guide. a. adv.

Associated Glass and Pottery Manufacturers *(1874)*
754 Cabin Hill Dr.
Greensburg, PA 15601-1660
Tel: (330)965-8728
Members: 18 companies
Staff: 1
Annual Budget: under $10,000
President: Robert Gonze

Historical Note
Manufacturers of semi-vitrified and vitrified ceramic and glass dinnerware and tableware. Membership: $75/year (organization/company).

Associated Locksmiths of America *(1956)*
3500 Easy St.
Dallas, TX 75247-6416
Tel: (214)819-9733 Fax: (214)819-9736
E-Mail: aloa@aloa.org
Web Site: www.aloa.org
Members: 10000 individuals
Staff: 20
Annual Budget: $1-2,000,000
Executive Director: Charles W. Gibson, Jr., CAE
Editor: Betty Henderson
E-Mail: aloa@aloa.org
Manager, Information Systems: Greg Jackson
Manager, Government Affairs: Paul Kanitra
Manager, PRP and Education: David Lowell, CML, CMS
Manager, Membership: Mary May
Manager, Meetings: JoAnne Mims
E-Mail: aloa@aloa.org
Comptroller: Kathy Romo

Historical Note
Membership: $125/year (individual); $500/year (company).

Meetings/Conferences:
Annual Meetings: *Summer/6,000*

Publications:
Keynotes. m. adv.

Associated Luxury Hotels *(1986)*
1000 Connecticut Ave. NW
#603
Washington, DC 20036
Tel: (202)887-7020 Fax: (202)887-0085
E-Mail: meetings@alhi.com
Web Site: www.alhi.com
Members: 70 hotels and resorts
Staff: 26
President and Chief Executive Officer: David Gabri, CAE

Associated Owners and Developers *(1994)*
P.O. Box 4163

McLean, VA 22103-4163
Tel: (703)734-2397 Ext: 411 *Fax:* (703)734-2908
E-Mail: aod@cbrmag.com
Members: 1832 individuals
Staff: 4
Annual Budget: $100-250,000
Founder and Chief Executive Officer: Harvey Kornbluh

Historical Note
AOD represents owner/developers from both the private and public sectors, enhancing their business opportunities through interaction with other owner/developers and assisting them in producing and maintaining projects which make economic sense. Membership: $250/year (individual); $500/year (company); $1,000/per region (affiliates).

Publications:
AOD News. q.

Associated Pipe Organ Builders of America *(1941)*
c/o Quimby Pipe Organs
P.O. Box 434
Warrensburg, MO 64093
Tel: (660)747-3066 *Fax:* (660)747-7920
Toll Free: (800)473 - 5270
E-Mail: qpo1@earthlink.net
Web Site: www.apoba.com
Members: 33 companies
Annual Budget: $25-50,000
President: Michael Quimby
E-Mail: qpo1@earthlink.net

Historical Note
Formerly Associated Organ Builders of America. Formed originally to set metal priorities during World War II. Has no permanent address or staff; officers rotate triennially.

Meetings/Conferences:
Annual Meetings: Spring

Associated Press Managing Editors *(1933)*
450 W. 33rd St.
New York, NY 10001
Tel: (212)621-1838 *Fax:* (212)506-6102
E-Mail: apme@ap.org
Web Site: www.apme.com
Members: 2000 individuals
Staff: 1
Annual Budget: $100-250,000
Administrator: Susan Clark

Historical Note
Members are editors of Associated Press newspapers.

Meetings/Conferences:
Annual Meetings: Fall

Publications:
APME Update. w.
APME News. q.

Associated Professional Sleep Socs. *(1986)*
One Westbrook Corporate Center
Suite 920
Westchester, IL 60154
Tel: (708)492-0930 *Fax:* (708)492-0943
Web Site: www.apss.org
Members: 2 societies
Staff: 40
Annual Budget: $1-2,000,000
Executive Director: Jerome A. Barrett
Staff: Jennifer Markkanen
E-Mail: jmarkkanen@aasmnet.org

Historical Note
A partnership comprising two sleep societies: Sleep Research Society, and the American Academy of Sleep Medicine. APSS provides a joint annual meeting and publications. Formerly (1993) Association of Professional Sleep Societies.

Meetings/Conferences:
Annual Meetings: May/June
2007 - Minneapolis, MN/June 9-14/5000

Publications:
Sleep. m. adv.

Associated Risk Managers *(1970)*
c/o ARM Partners, Gallagher Center
Two Pierce Place
Itasca, IL 60143
Tel: (630)285-4186 *Fax:* (630)285-4000
Web Site: www.armiweb.com
Members: 300 companies
Staff: 4
Annual Budget: $500-1,000,000
Executive Officer: Paul Ross

Historical Note
ARMI members are state/province affiliates representing independent agencies united to market insurance/risk management services to targeted industries, associations, professional societies and other organizations.

Meetings/Conferences:
Annual Meetings: May

Publications:
AN-ARM News. q.

Associated Schools of Construction *(1965)*
Colorado State University, Construction Management
102 Guggenheim
Ft. Collins, CO 80523
Tel: (970)491-7958 *Fax:* (970)491-2473
E-Mail: drfire107@mindspring.com
Web Site: www.ascweb.org
Members: 92 schools
Annual Budget: $50-100,000
Treasurer: Larry Grosse
E-Mail: drfire107@mindspring.com

Historical Note
ASC is a professional association for the development and advancement of construction education. Members are colleges and universities which have programs in the field of construction. Membership: $400/year.

Meetings/Conferences:
Annual Meetings: April
2007 - Flagstaff, AZ(Northern Arizona University)/Apr. 1- /150

Publications:
Journal of Construction Education. q.
ASC Annual Conference Proceedings. a.

Associated Specialty Contractors *(1950)*
Three Bethesda Metro Center
Suite 1100
Bethesda, MD 20814-5372
Tel: (301)657-3110 *Fax:* (301)215-4500
E-Mail: dgw@necanet.org
Web Site: www.assoc-spec-con.org
Members: 9 associations
Staff: 1
Annual Budget: $25-50,000
President: Daniel G. Walter
E-Mail: dgw@necanet.org

Historical Note
A federation of construction specialty associations: Finishing Contractors Assn; Mechanical Contractors Association of America; Plumbing-Heating-Cooling Contractors National Association; National Electrical Contractors Association; Sheet Metal and Air Conditioning Contractors' National Association; National Insulation Contractors Association; National Roofing Contractors Association; National Subcontractors Alliance; and Painting and Decorating Contractors of America. Formerly (1973) Council of Mechanical Specialty Contracting Industries, Inc. Membership: $2750/year.

Meetings/Conferences:
Semi-Annual Meetings: Spring/Fall

Associated Surplus Dealers *(1950)*

Historical Note
Ceased non-profit operations in 2001. ASD/AMD is now part of VNU Expositions, a subsidiary of VNU Business Media, Inc.

Associated Wire Rope Fabricators *(1976)*
P.O. Box 748
Walled Lake, MI 48390-0748
Tel: (248)994-7753 *Fax:* (248)994-7754
E-Mail: awrf@att.net
Web Site: www.awrf.org
Members: 300 companies
Staff: 1
Annual Budget: $100-250,000
Chief Executive: Jeffrey Gilbert
E-Mail: awrf@att.net

Meetings/Conferences:
Semi-Annual Meetings: Spring and Fall

Publications:
Slingmakers. q.

Associated Writing Programs

Historical Note
Became Association of Writers and writing Programs in 2004.

Association Chief Executive Council *(1988)*
P.O. Box 220
Annandale, VA 22003
Tel: (703)280-4622 *Fax:* (703)532-1798
E-Mail: kentonp1@aol.com
Members: 50 individuals
Staff: 1
Annual Budget: $10-25,000
Executive Director: Kenton Pattie

Historical Note
Council members are chief executive officers of trade & professional associations. Provides an exclusive, and confidential, trade and professional forum for C.E.O.'s to help each other solve leadership problems, work with boards and elected leaders, and give career development support. Membership: $500/year.

Meetings/Conferences:
Monthly Meetings: usually in Washington, DC area

Association Correctional Food Service Affiliates *(1969)*
4248 Park Glen Road
Minneapolis, MN 55416
Tel: (952)928-4658 *Fax:* (952)929-1318
Web Site: www.acfsa.org
Members: 1400 individuals
Staff: 3
Annual Budget: $500-1,000,000
Executive Director: Hope Cook

Historical Note
Membership: $59/year (foodservice); $384/year (vendor).

Meetings/Conferences:
Annual Meetings: August/1,000

Publications:
Insider Magazine. q. adv.
Directory. a. adv.

Association for Academic Surgery *(1966)*
11300 W. Olympic Blvd.
Suite 600
Los Angeles, CA 90064
Tel: (310)437-1606 *Fax:* (310)437-0585
Web Site: www.aasurg.org
Members: 3000 individuals
Staff: 6
Annual Budget: $250-500,000

Historical Note
Founded in 1966 as an organization serving the needs of academic surgeons, particularly those under 40 years of age. Dedicated to interchange of scientific, educational, social and political information relative to the surgical profession. Membership: $130/year (regular); $50/year (senior); $15/year (candidate).

Publications:
Journal of Surgical Research. m.

Association for Accounting Administration *(1983)*
136 South Keowee St.
Dayton, OH 45402
Tel: (937)222-0030 *Fax:* (937)222-5794
E-Mail: AAAinfo@cpadmin.org
Web Site: www.cpaadmin.org
Members: 650 individuals
Staff: 7
Annual Budget: $100-250,000
Executive Director: Kim Fantaci

Historical Note
Formerly (1994) Association of Accounting Administrators. Members are accounting administrators, high-level office managers and administrative partners in accounting firms and corporate accounting departments. Membership: $225/year (individual); $300/year (organization).

Meetings/Conferences:
Annual Meetings: June

Publications:
AAA Report. bi-m.

Membership Directory. a.

Association for Accounting Marketing *(1989)*
14 W. Third St.
Suite 200
Kansas City, MO 64105
Tel: (816)221-1296 *Fax:* (816)472-7765
E-Mail: info@accountingmarketing.org
Web Site: www.accountingmarketing.org
Members: 720 individuals
Staff: 3
Annual Budget: $100-250,000
Executive Director: Granville Loar
E-Mail: info@accountingmarketing.org
Historical Note
Formerly (1993) Association of Accounting Marketing Executives. AAM is a professional association serving individuals actively engaged in developing and implementing marketing programs for accounting firms. Executive membership is limited to full-time, in-house marketing executives; associate membership available to in-house accounting firm personnel whose reponsibilities include marketing and consultants to the accounting profession. Affiliate membership is also available. Membership: $300/year (first year); $250/year (renewal).
Meetings/Conferences:
Annual Meetings: Summer
Publications:
MarkeTrends. bi-m. adv.

Association for Adult Development and Aging *(1986)*
Historical Note
An affiliate of American Counseling Association, which provides administrative support.

Association for Advanced Life Underwriting *(1957)*
2901 Telestar Court
Falls Church, VA 22042
Tel: (703)641-9400 *Fax:* (703)641-9885
Toll Free: (888)275 - 0092
E-Mail: info@aalu.org
Web Site: www.aalu.org
Members: 1900 individuals
Staff: 14
Annual Budget: $5-10,000,000
Executive Vice President: David Stertzer
Vice President, Policy and Public Affairs: Thomas Korb
Director, Membership: Marilyn A. Maticic
Historical Note
Founded in 1957, AALU is the advocate for advance life insurance planning.
Meetings/Conferences:
Annual Meetings: Spring in Washington, DC/700
Publications:
Quarterly Update.
Washington Report. 125/year.
AALU Roster. a.

Association for Advancement of Behavior Therapy *(1966)*
305 Seventh Ave.
Suite 16A
New York, NY 10001-6008
Tel: (212)647-1890 *Fax:* (212)647-1865
E-Mail: membership@aabt.org
Web Site: www.aabt.org
Members: 4500 individuals
Staff: 10
Annual Budget: $1-2,000,000
Executive Director: Mary Jane Eimer, CAE
E-Mail: mjeimer@aabt.org
Director, Administration and Convention Manager: Mary Ellen Brown
E-Mail: mebrown@aabt.org
Director, Publications: David Teisler, CAE
E-Mail: teisler@aabt.org
Historical Note
Founded and incorporated in New York in 1966 as the Association for Advancement of the Behavioral Therapies. AABT is a professional, interdisciplinary organization concerned with the application of behavioral and cognitive sciences to understanding human behavior, developing interventions to enhance the human condition, and promoting the appropriate utilization of these interventions. Assumed its present name in 1968. Membership: $185/year (full member); $40/year (student).
Meetings/Conferences:
Annual Meetings: November
Publications:
Cognitive and Behavioral Practice. q. adv.
The Behavior Therapist. 8/year. adv.
Behavior Therapy. q. adv.

Association for Africanist Anthropology
Historical Note
A section of the American Anthropological Association.

Association for Ambulatory Behavorial Healthcare *(1965)*
11240 Waples Mill Road
#200
Fairfax, VA 22030
Tel: (703)934-0165 *Fax:* (703)359-7562
E-Mail: stephen@aabh.org
Web Site: www.aabh.org
Members: 384 individuals
Annual Budget: $100-250,000
President: Stephen Michael, MS
E-Mail: stephen@aabh.org
Historical Note
Formerly the American Association for Partial Hospitalization. Began in the 1960's as the Partial Hospitalization Study Group; it adopted its present name in 1979 to reflect the fact that the organization had grown into an extensive national network. AAPH is a multidisciplinary organization whose members share a common interest in the development, growth and improvement of partial hospitalization within the continuum of psychiatric treatment. Membership: $105/year (individual); $450/year (organization).
Meetings/Conferences:
Annual Meetings: August
Publications:
Milieu. bi-m.
Standards and Guidelines. 5/year.

Association for Applied and Clinical Sociology *(1978)*
Dept. of Soc., Anthropology & Criminology
712 Pray-Harold, EMU
Ypsilanti, MI 48197
Tel: (734)487-0012 *Fax:* (734)487-7010
E-Mail: sacs_aacs@emich.edu
Web Site: www.aacsnet.org
Members: 425 organizations
Staff: 1
Annual Budget: $25-50,000
Historical Note
Formerly (2005) Society for Applied Sociology. AACS provides a forum for sociologists to apply their knowledge, enhance understanding of knowledge and practice, and in increaseg the practical use of research and training. Membership: $80/year (individual); $195/year (organization/company).
Meetings/Conferences:
Annual Meetings: October
Publications:
The Useful Sociologist Newsletter. 3/year. adv.
Social Insight: Knowledge at Work. a.
Journal of Applied Sociology. a.

Association for Applied Interactive Multimedia *(1992)*
P.O. Box 892
Charleston, SC 29402-0892
E-Mail: seayj@ofc.edu
Web Site: www.aaim.org
Acting President: Jared A. Seay
E-Mail: seayj@ofc.edu
Historical Note
AAIM members are professionals who use and develop interactive multimedia. Membership: $40/year.
Publications:
Newsletter. q.

Association for Applied Psychophysiology and Biofeedback *(1969)*
10200 W. 44th Ave.
Suite 304
Wheat Ridge, CO 80033-2840
Tel: (303)422-8436 *Fax:* (303)422-8894
E-Mail: aapb@resourcenter.com
Web Site: www.aapb.org
Members: 1500 individuals
Staff: 4
Annual Budget: $250-500,000
Executive Director: Francine Butler, Ph.D.
Director, Membership: Ruth Gleason
Director, Finance: Chris Ruppert
E-Mail: aapb@resourcenter.com
Historical Note
Formerly (1988) the Biofeedback Society of America. Members are psychologists and other health care professionals who treat stress-related disorders with biofeedback or other applied psychophysiology techniques. Membership: $115/year.
Meetings/Conferences:
Annual Meetings: Spring
Publications:
Applied Psychophysiology and Biofeedback. q. adv.
Biofeedback: a Newsmagazine. q. adv.

Association for Arid Lands Studies *(1977)*
ICASALS, Box 41036
Texas Tech University
Lubbock, TX 79409-1036
Tel: (806)742-2218 *Fax:* (806)742-1954
E-Mail: ac.correa@ttu.edu
Web Site: www.iaff.ttu.edu/home/icasals/pages/aals.asp
Members: 250 individuals
Staff: 2
Executive Director: Dr. A.C. Correa
E-Mail: ac.correa@ttu.edu
Historical Note
Members are scientists, social scientists and other academics with an interest in the study of arid and semi-arid lands. Membership: $20/year.
Meetings/Conferences:
Annual Meetings: In conjunction with the Western Social Sciences Ass'n
2007 – Calgary, AB, Canada(Hyatt Regency)/Apr. 11-14
2008 – Denver, CO(Hyatt Regency Downtown)/Apr. 15-19
2009 – Albuquerque, NM(Hyatt Regency Downtown)/Apr. 15-18
2010 – Reno, NV(Hilton)/Apr. 14-17
Publications:
Forum of the AALS. a.

Association for Asian American Studies *(1970)*
Cornell University
420 Rockefeller Hall
Ithaca, NY 14850
Tel: (607)255-3320 *Fax:* (607)254-4996
E-Mail: ssh13@cornell.edu
Web Site: www.aaastudies.org/stat.tpl
Members: 810 individuals
Staff: 1
Administrative Manager: Stephanie Hsu
E-Mail: ssh13@cornell.edu
Historical Note
AAAS members are academics, students and others with an interest in the field. Membership: $30-80/year, varies by rank (faculty); $30/year (student).
Publications:
Journal. 3/year. adv.
Occasional Papers Newsletter. q.

Association for Asian Performance
Historical Note
A focus group of the Association for Theatre in Higher Education.

Association for Asian Studies *(1941)*
1021 E. Huron St.
Ann Arbor, MI 48104
Tel: (734)665-2490 *Fax:* (734)665-3801
Web Site: www.aasianst.org
Members: 8000 individuals
Staff: 10
Annual Budget: $1-2,000,000

Executive Director: Michael Paschal
Coordinator, Annual Meeting: Karen Fricke

Historical Note

Organized as the Far Eastern Association on June 9, 1941, the Association for Asian Studies assumed its present name in 1957 to reflect a growing interest in Asia east of the Middle East. A member of the American Council of Learned Socs. Membership: $35-90/year (individual).

Meetings/Conferences:

Annual Meetings: Spring
2007 – Boston, MA(Marriott)/March 22-25
2008 – Atlanta, GA
2009 – Chicago, IL

Publications:

Asian Studies Newsletter. q. adv.
Education About Asia. 3/yr. adv.
Meeting Abstract (Online). a.
Member Directory. bi-a.
Bibliography of Asian Studies (Online). a.
Journal of Asian Studies. q. adv.

Association for Assessment and Accreditation of Laboratory Animal Care International *(1965)*

5283 Corporate Dr.
Suite 203
Rockville, MD 21703
Tel: (301)696-9626 *Fax:* (301)696-9627
Toll Free: (800)926 - 0066
E-Mail: accredit@aaalac.org
Web Site: www.aaalac.org
Members: 630units,50sponsoringsocieties
Staff: 9
Annual Budget: $1-2,000,000
Executive Director: John G. Miller, DVM

Historical Note

Formerly (1996) American Association for Accreditation of Laboratory Animal Care. Established and incorporated in Illinois, AAALAC promotes high quality animal care and use in programs of research, breeding, teaching and testing through a voluntary accreditation program.

Publications:

AAALAC Connection Newsletter. 4/year.

Association for Assessment in Counseling *(1965)*

Historical Note

An affiliate of American Counseling Association, which provides administrative support.

Association for Behavior Analysis *(1974)*

1219 S. Park St.
Kalamazoo, MI 49001
Tel: (269)492-9310 *Fax:* (269)492-9316
E-Mail: mail@abainternational.org
Web Site: www.abainternational.org
Members: 4700 individuals
Staff: 5
Executive Director: Maria E. Malott, Ph.D.

Historical Note

Formerly (1979) Midwestern Association for Behavior Analysis. Members are individuals interested in the applied experimental and theoretical analysis of behavior and the enhancement of behavior analysis as a profession. Full members of ABA have at least a Master's degree in psychology or a related discipline and have demonstrated competence in either applied or experimental behavior analysis.

Meetings/Conferences:

Annual Meetings: Memorial Day Weekend
2007 – San Diego, CA(Hyatt)/May 25-29
2008 – Chicago, IL(Hilton)/May 23-27

Publications:

The Behavior Analyst. semi-a. adv.
The Analysis of Verbal Behavior. a. adv.
ABA Newsletter. 3/year. adv.

Association for Biblical Higher Education *(1947)*

5575 S. Semoran Blvd.
Suite 26
Orlando, FL 32822-1781
Tel: (407)207-0808 *Fax:* (407)207-0840
E-Mail: info@abhe.org
Web Site: www.abhe.org
Members: 144 colleges
Staff: 6
Annual Budget: $250-500,000
Executive Director: Larry McKinney

Historical Note

Established as Accrediting Association of Bible Institutes and Bible Colleges (1947), it became Accrediting Association of Bible Colleges (1957), American Association of Bible Colleges(1973), and changed back to Accrediting Assn of Bible Colleges (1994). In 2004, the name was changed again to the Assn for Biblical Higher Education in order to reflect its expansion of scope with graduate education accreditation and programmatic accrediation and in order to address its expansion of services to include affiliate institutions.

Meetings/Conferences:

Annual Meetings: Winter

Publications:

Newsletter. 4/year.

Association for Biology Laboratory Education *(1979)*

Dept. of Biology, Box 90338
Duke University
Durham, NC 27708-0338
Tel: (919)684-2301
Web Site: www.zoo.utoronto.ca/able
Members: 400 individuals
Annual Budget: $10-25,000
Tresurer: Alexander F. Motten

Historical Note

ABLE's primary purpose is to facilitate communication between college instructors who are actively involved with laboratory instruction in the various areas of biology, and to encourage the development and dissemination of reliable laboratory exercises. Has no paid officers or full-time staff. Membership: $35/year.

Meetings/Conferences:

Annual Meetings: June
2007 – Lexington, KY(University of Kentucky)/June 5-9

Publications:

Labstracts Newsletter. 3/year.
Proceedings. a.

Association for Birth Psychology *(1978)*

444 East 82nd St.
New York, NY 10028
Tel: (212)988-6617
E-Mail: birthpsychology@aol.com
Web Site: www.birthpsychology.org
Members: 360 individuals
Staff: 1
Annual Budget: under $10,000
Executive Director: Leslie Feher, Ph.D.
E-Mail: birthpsychology@aol.com

Publications:

Birth Psychology Bulletin. a.

Association for Borderlands Studies *(1976)*

Department of Geography
New Mexico State University
Las Cruces, NM 88003
Tel: (505)646-1892 *Fax:* (505)646-7430
Web Site: www.absborderlands.org
Members: 300 individuals
Staff: 1
Annual Budget: under $10,000
President: Christopher Brown
E-Mail: brownchr@nmsu.edu

Historical Note

Originally a scholarly organization studying the U.S.-Mexico border. ABS members now include academics and professionals concerned with other border regions worldwide. The executive officers change annually. Membership: $20/year (student); $35/year (professor).

Meetings/Conferences:

Annual Meetings: last full weekend in April
2007 – Calgary, AB, Canada(Hyatt Regency)/Apr. 10-16
2008 – Denver, CO(Hyatt Regency)/Apr. 15-19

Publications:

Journal of Borderlands Studies. semi-a.
La Frontera Newsletter. semi-a.

Association for Bridge Construction and Design *(1976)*

P.O. Box 23264
Pittsburgh, PA 15222
Tel: (412)392-8765 *Fax:* (412)392-8785
Web Site: www.abcdpittsburgh.org
Members: 250 individuals
Annual Budget: $10-25,000
President: Geoffrey Goldberg
Secretary: Jane-Ann Patton

Historical Note

Has no paid staff. Membership: $20/year (individual); $150/year (company).

Meetings/Conferences:

Annual Meetings: A monthly meeting held September through May

Publications:

Newsletter. m. adv.

Association for Business Communication *(1935)*

Baruch College/Communications Studies
One Bernard Baruch Way, Box B8-240
New York, NY 10010
Tel: (646)312-3726
E-Mail: myers@businesscommunication.org
Web Site: www.businesscommunication.org
Members: 1800 individuals
Staff: 2
Annual Budget: $100-250,000
Executive Director: Robert J. Myers

Historical Note

ABC is an international organization committed to fostering excellence in business communication scholarship, research, education and practice.

Meetings/Conferences:

Annual Meetings: Fall

Publications:

Business Communication Quarterly. q. adv.
Journal of Business Communication. q. adv.

Association for Business Simulation and Experiential Learning *(1974)*

Wayne State Univ.
Marketing Dept.
Detroit, MI 48202-3930
Tel: (313)577-4551 *Fax:* (313)577-5486
Web Site: www.absel.org
Members: 225 individuals
Staff: 1
Annual Budget: $25-50,000
Executive Director: Hugh M. Cannon, Ph.D.

Historical Note

ABSEL was created to encourage the association of business simulators and those interested in developing and using experiential learning techniques in the fields of business and administration. Membership: $60/year (individual).

Meetings/Conferences:

Annual Meetings: March

Publications:

Proceedings (Cumulative Archive on CD). a. adv.
Simulation & Gaming: An International Journal of Theory.
Design & Research.
Developments in Business Simulation & Experiential Exercises.
ABSEL News & Views. semi-a. adv.
Conference Program. a. adv.

Association for Canadian Studies in the United States *(1971)*

1220 19th St. NW
Suite 801
Washington, DC 20036
Tel: (202)233-9005 *Fax:* (202)775-0061
E-Mail: info@acsus.org
Web Site: www.acsus.org
Members: 1000 individuals
Staff: 2
Annual Budget: $100-250,000
Executive Director: David Archibald
E-Mail: info@acsus.org

Historical Note
Promotes the study of Canada at all educational levels. The core of its membership is comprised of university professors involved in teaching about Canada. Membership: $60/year (individual); $110/year (institution).
Meetings/Conferences:
Biennial Meetings: Odd years
Publications:
American Review of Canadian Studies. q. adv.
Canadian Studies Update. q.
Directory. bien.

Association for Career and Technical Education *(1926)*
1410 King St.
Alexandria, VA 22314
Tel: (703)683-3111 *Fax:* (703)683-7424
Toll Free: (800)826 - 9972
E-Mail: acte@acteonline.org
Web Site: www.acteonline.org
Members: 28000 individuals
Staff: 30
Annual Budget: $2-5,000,000
Executive Director: Janet B. Bray
E-Mail: acte@acteonline.org
Senior Director, Programs and Communications: Peter Magnuson
E-Mail: acte@acteonline.org
Senior Director, Public Policy: Seth Turner
Senior Director, Finance Operations: LeAnn Wilson
Historical Note
Founded as the National Society for the Promotion of Industrial Education; became (1918) the American Vocational Association before assuming its present name in 1999. Merged in 1925 with the Vocational Association of the Middle West to form the American Vocational Association and incorporated in Indiana in 1926. A federation of state vocational associations. The National Association of State Supervisors of Home Economics Education is a division of AVA. Membership: $60/year (individual).
Meetings/Conferences:
Annual Meetings: December/10,000
Publications:
Career Tech Update. bi-m.
Techniques. 8/year. adv.

Association for Career and Technical Education Research *(1966)*
320 Graham Hall
College of Education, Northern Illinois University
DeKalb, IL 60115-2867
Tel: (815)753-9056 *Fax:* (815)753-2100
E-Mail: djackman@niu.edu
Web Site: www.agri.wsu.edu/acter/
Members: 500 individuals
Annual Budget: under $10,000
President: Diane Jackman
E-Mail: djackman@niu.edu
Historical Note
Formerly American Vocational Education Research Association, AVERA (2005). Members are academics interested in methodology and other research issues in career education. Membership: $40/year (regular); $5/year (student).
Meetings/Conferences:
Annual Meetings: Winter
Publications:
The Beacon. q.
Career and Technical Education Research. q.

Association for Chemoreception Sciences *(1979)*
5841 Cedar Lake Road
Suite 204
Minneapolis, MN 55416
Tel: (952)646-2035 *Fax:* (952)545-6073
E-Mail: info@achems.org
Web Site: www.achems.org
Members: 725 individuals
Executive Director: Lori J. Anderson
Historical Note
Members are scientists interested in the physiological reception of chemical stimuli. Has no paid officers or full-time staff.
Meetings/Conferences:
Annual Meetings: April
Publications:
Newsletter. semi-a.

Association for Child Psychoanalysis *(1965)*
P.O. Box 253
Ramsey, NJ 07446
Tel: (201)825-3138 *Fax:* (201)825-3138
E-Mail: childanalysis@optonline.net
Web Site: www.childanalysis.org
Members: 600 individuals
Staff: 2
Annual Budget: $250-500,000
Administrator: Nancy Hall
E-Mail: childanalysis@optonline.net
Historical Note
Formerly (1971) American Association for Child Psychoanalysis. Membership: $150/year (individual); $75/year (candidates).
Meetings/Conferences:
Annual Meetings: Spring
Publications:
ACP Newsletter. q.
Abstracts. bien.

Association for Childhood Education International *(1892)*
17904 Georgia Ave.
Suite 215
Olney, MD 20832-2277
Tel: (301)570-2111 *Fax:* (301)570-2212
Toll Free: (800)423 - 3563
E-Mail: headquarters@acei.org
Web Site: www.acei.org
Members: 7000 individuals
Staff: 15
Annual Budget: $1-2,000,000
Executive Director: Gerald C. Odland
E-Mail: headquarters@acei.org
Editor and Director, Publications: Anne Watson Bauer
E-Mail: aceid@aol.com
Director, Membership and Marketing: Marilyn B. Gardner
E-Mail: aceimemb@aol.com
Director, Conferences Marketing: Lisa Wenger
E-Mail: aceimc@aol.com
Historical Note
Established in 1892 as the International Kindergarten Union. In 1931, merged with the National Council of Primary Education and became Association for Childhood Education International. ACEI is a professional organization for educators concerned with whole curriculum and whole child development from birth to age 15. It is the national accrediting body for university-level elementary education programs through the National Council for Accreditation of Teacher Education (NCATE). Membership: $45/year (individual); $65/year (institutional).
Meetings/Conferences:
Annual Meetings: Spring
2007 – Tampa, FL(Hyatt Regency)/May 2-5
Publications:
ACEI Exchange Newsletter. 6/year.
Childhood Education. bi-m. adv.
Journal of Research in Childhood Education. q. adv.

Association for Clinical Pastoral Education *(1967)*
1549 Clairmont Road
Suite 103
Decatur, GA 30033-4635
Tel: (404)320-1472 *Fax:* (404)320-0849
E-Mail: acpe@acpe.edu
Web Site: www.acpe.edu
Members: 3500 individuals
Staff: 9
Annual Budget: $500-1,000,000
Executive Director: Dr. Teresa Snorton
E-Mail: acpe@acpe.edu
Associate Director: Deryck Durston
E-Mail: acpe@acpe.edu
Historical Note
Formed (1967) by a combination of four CPE organizations: the Lutheran Council of the U. S. A., the Association of Clinical Pastoral Educators, the Council for Clinical Training and the Institute of Pastoral Care. Assumed present name in 1968.
Meetings/Conferences:
Annual Meetings: Spring/600
Publications:
ACPE News. bi-m. adv.

Association for College and University Religious Affairs *(1959)*
Northwestern University
1870 Sheridan Road
Evanston, IL 60208-1350
Tel: (847)491-7256
E-Mail: acuraonline@acuraonline.org
Web Site: www.acuraonline.org
Members: 95 individuals
Annual Budget: under $10,000
Secretary-Treasurer: Timothy S. Stevens, Ph.D.
Historical Note
Formerly (1991) Association for the Coordination of University Religious Affairs. An association of personnel involved in religious affairs at institutions of higher education. Membership: $35/year (individual); $60/year (institution).
Meetings/Conferences:
Annual Meetings: Fall
2007 – Philadelphia, PA(University of Pennsylvania)
Publications:
Dialogue on Campus. q.

Association for Commercial Real Estate
Historical Note
See NAIOP: The Association for Commercial Real Estate.

Association for Communication Administration *(1972)*
Historical Note
An affiliate of National Communication Association, which provides administrative support.

Association for Communication Excellence *(1913)*
Building 16, Mowry Road
P.O. Box 110811
Gainesville, FL 32611
Tel: (352)392-9588 *Fax:* (352)392-8583
E-Mail: ace@mail.ifas.ufl.edu
Web Site: www.aceweb.org
Members: 700 individuals
Staff: 1
Annual Budget: $50-100,000
Coordinator: Amanda Chambliss
E-Mail: ace@mail.ifas.ufl.edu
Historical Note
Founded as American Association of Agricultural College Editors; became Agricultural Communicators in Education in 1978, and assumed its current name in 2003. Members are writers, editors, broadcasters, graphic designers, teachers and researchers who are involved in the dissemination of agricultural, food science and natural resource information. Membership: $100/year.
Meetings/Conferences:
Annual Meetings: Summer/400
Publications:
SIGNALS Newsletter. bi-m.
Journal of Applied Communications. q.
Membership Directory. a.

Association for Commuter Transportation *(1976)*
1401 Peachtree St.
Suite 440
Atlanta, GA 30309
Tel: (678)916-4940 *Fax:* (678)244-4151
E-Mail: act@act-hq.com
Web Site: www.actweb.org
Members: 900 individuals & organizations
Staff: 5
Annual Budget: $250-500,000
Executive Director: Kevin Shannon

Historical Note
Formed in Savannah, Georgia in August 1976 by 31 charter van pool pioneers as the National Association of Van Pool Operators; assumed its present name in 1984. Absorbed the Association of Ridesharing Professionals in 1986. Members are corporations, employers, public agencies, transit authorities, van pool management companies, real estate developers and individuals involved in promoting alternatives to drive-alone commuting. Membership: $300/year (individual); $500/year (organization/company); $25/year (student).

Meetings/Conferences:
Semi-annual Meetings: Spring/Fall

Publications:
TMA Handbook.
TDM Review. q. adv.

Association for Comparative Economic Studies *(1972)*
Arizona State University
Box 873806
Tempe, AZ 85287-3806
Tel: (480)965-6524 *Fax:* (480)965-0748
Web Site: www.comparativeeconomics.org
Members: 700 individuals
Staff: 1
Annual Budget: $25-50,000
Executive Secretary: Josef C. Brada

Historical Note
A member of the Allied Social Science Associations. Formed by a merger of the Association for the Study of Soviet-Type Economics (1959) and the Association for Comparative Economics (1963). Membership: $40/year (individual); $65/year (organization/company).

Meetings/Conferences:
Annual Meetings: With the Allied Social Science Ass'n

Publications:
Journal of Comparative Economics. q. adv.
Comparative Economic Studies. q. adv.

Association for Comprehensive Energy Psychology *(1993)*
P.O. Box 910244
San Diego, CA 92191
Tel: (858)270-2103 *Fax:* (760)804-3704
E-Mail: acep@rutherfordassociates.com
Web Site: www.energypsych.org
Members: 600 individuals
Staff: 1
Annual Budget: $100-250,000
Administrator: Tamra Rutherford

Historical Note
ACEP members are psychotherapists and other care professionals interested in the integration of traditional mind/body therapies with current practice.

Publications:
Newsletter. q.

Association for Computational Linguistics *(1962)*
Three Landmark Center
East Stroudsburg, PA 18301
Tel: (570)476-8006 *Fax:* (570)476-0860
E-Mail: acl@aclweb.org
Web Site: www.aclweb.org
Members: 1600 individuals
Staff: 1
Annual Budget: $100-250,000
Business Manager: Priscilla Rasmussen
E-Mail: acl@aclweb.org

Historical Note
Formerly (1968) Association for Machine Translation and Computational Linguistics. Affiliated with the International Committee on Computational Linguistics. Computational linguistics deals with algorithms, models, and computer systems or components of systems for research on language and scholarly investigation.

Meetings/Conferences:
Annual Meetings: Summer

Publications:
Computational Linguistics. q.
Proceedings, Annual Meetings. a.
Proceedings, European Chapter Meetings. bien.
Proceedings, Conference on Applied Natural Language Processing. bien.

Association for Computers and the Humanities *(1978)*
McMaster Univ.
School of the Arts
Hamilton, ON L8S 4-M2
Tel: (905)525-9140 Ext: 23930 *Fax:* (905)527-6793
E-Mail: sgsinclair@gmail.com
Web Site: www.ach.org
Members: 380 individuals
Annual Budget: under $10,000
Executive Secretary: Stefan Sinclair

Historical Note
Formed to foster computer-aided scholarship and teaching in the humanities and arts fields. Membership: $75/year.

Publications:
Literary and Linguistic Computing. 4/year. adv.

Association for Computing Machinery *(1947)*
2 Penn Plaza
New York, NY 10121
Tel: (212)626-0500 *Fax:* (212)944-1318
Toll Free: (800)342 - 6626
E-Mail: webmaster@acm.org
Web Site: www.acm.org
Members: 75000 individuals
Staff: 94
Annual Budget: $25-50,000,000
Executive Director: John White
Director, Information Systems: Wayne S. Graves
Director, Financial Services: Russell Harris
Director, Membership: Lillian Israel
Director, Publications: Mark Mandelbaum

Historical Note
ACM was founded at Columbia University as the Eastern Association for Computing Machinery. Its constitution and by-laws were adopted in 1949 and it was incorporated in Delaware in 1954. It is the oldest and largest international professional association of computer professionals. ACM's purpose is to advance the skills of information technology professionals and students. Membership: $99/year (professional member); $198/year (professional membership plus access to ACM's online Portal); $42/year (student); $19/year (limited student membership).

Meetings/Conferences:
Annual Meetings: February-March

Publications:
Transactions on the Web. q.
Journal on Emerging Technologies in Computing Systems. q.
Transactions on Storage. q.
Transactions on Sensor Networks. q.
Ubiquity.
Transactions on Asian Language Information Processing. q.
Transactions on Database Systems. q.
Transactions on Internet Technology. q.
Journal of Experimental Algorithmics. q.
Transactions in Accesible Computing. q.
Journal on Computing and Cultural Heritage. q.
ACM Transactions on Mathematical Software. q.
Collected Algorithms from ACM. q.
Communications of the ACM. m. adv.
Computing Reviews. m. adv.
ACM Computing Surveys. q.
Journal of the ACM. bi-m.
Transactions on Programming Languages and Systems. bi-m.
Transactions on Information Systems. q.
Transactions on Graphics. q.
Transactions on Computer Systems. q.
Transactions on Modeling and Computer Simulation. q.
Transactions on Software Engineering & Methodology. q.
Transactions on Networking. bi-m.
Networker. q.
Transactions on Computer-Human Interaction. q.
Interactions. bi-m.
Wireless Networks. bi-m.
ACM Transactions on Database Systems. q.
Transactions on Multimedia Computing Communications and Applications. q.
Transactions on Speech and Language Processing. q.
Computers in Entertainment. q.
Crossroads: The International ACM Student Magazine.
Journal on Educational Resources in Computing. q.
TECHNews.
Transactions on Architecture and Code Optimization. q.
Transactions on Applied Perception. q.
Transactions on Computational Logic. q.
Transactions on Design Automation of Electronic Systems. q.
Transactions on Embedded Computing Systems. q.
Transactions on Information and System Security. q.
Transactions on Mathematical Software. q.
Transactions on Computational Biology and Bioinformatics. q.
Transactions on Knowledge Discovery in Data. q.
Transactions on Autonomous Adaptive Systems. q.

Association for Conflict Resolution *(1972)*
1015 18th St. NW
Suite 1150
Washington, DC 20036
Tel: (202)464-9700 *Fax:* (202)464-9720
E-Mail: acr@acrnet.org
Web Site: www.acrnet.org
Members: 7500 individuals
Staff: 11
Annual Budget: $1-2,000,000
Chief Executive Officer: David A. Hart

Historical Note
Founded as Society of Professionals in Dispute Resolution; merged with Academy of Family Mediators and Conflict Resolution Education Network to become ACR in 2001. Members are specialists in labor, environment, family, community and other types of dispute resolution. Incorporated in the State of New York. Membership fee varies.

Meetings/Conferences:
Annual Meetings: Fall

Publications:
ACResolution. q. adv.
Membership Directory. a. adv.
Conflict Resolution Quarterly. q.

Association for Conservation Information *(1938)*
c/o Fish, Game and Wildlife Division
P.O. Box 400
Trenton, NJ 08625-0400
Tel: (609)984-0837 *Fax:* (609)984-1414
Web Site: www.aci-net.org
Members: 65 individuals
Annual Budget: $10-25,000
Assistant Director: David Chanda

Historical Note
Organized originally as the American Association for Conservation Information, ACI works to upgrade the quality of all forms of communication in and among agencies devoted to the protection and management of natural resources and wildlife. Members are officials of state fish and game departments, parks, recreation, soil and forestry organizations, as well as affiliates of federal and regional natural resource agencies. Has no paid staff or permanent address. Officers change annually. Membership: $25/year (individual); $100/year (organization).

Meetings/Conferences:
Annual Meetings: Summer

Publications:
The Balance Wheel. q.
Membership Directory. a.

Association for Consumer Research *(1969)*
UMD LSBE, 11 Superior St.
Suite 210
Duluth, MN 55802
Tel: (218)726-7853 *Fax:* (218)726-6338
E-Mail: acr@acrwebsite.org
Web Site: www.acrwebsite.org
Members: 1700 individuals
Staff: 5
Annual Budget: $250-500,000
Executive Director: Rajiv Vaidyanathan

Historical Note
Members are business people, educators and government officials interested in consumer research. Membership: $30/year.

Meetings/Conferences:
Annual Meetings: *Even numbered years-Asia/Pacific; odd numbered years-Europe*

Publications:
Asia Pacific Advances in Consumer Research. bien.
Advances in Consumer Research. a.
European Advances in Consumer Research. bien.

Association for Continuing Higher Education *(1939)*
Trident Technical College
P.O. Box 118067, CE-M
Charleston, SC 29423-8067
Tel: (843)574-6658 *Fax:* (843)574-6470
Toll Free: (800)807 - 2243
E-Mail: michele.shinn@tridenttech.edu
Web Site: www.acheinc.org
Members: 1800 individuals
Staff: 1
Annual Budget: $100-250,000
Executive Vice President: Michele Shinn
E-Mail: michele.shinn@tridenttech.edu

Historical Note
Established as Association of University Evening Colleges by a group of evening college administrators attending the 1939 annual meeting of Association of Urban Universities; assumed its present name in 1973. Membership consists of individuals whose prime commitment is continuing education and regionally accredited institutions of higher learning which have programming or administrative units responsible for continuing education. Absorbed Committee for Continuing Education for School Personnel in 1990. Membership: $60/year (individual); $260/year (institution).

Meetings/Conferences:
Annual Meetings: *Fall/400*

Publications:
Journal of Continuing Higher Education. 3/year.
Five Minutes with ACHE. 10/year.
Proceedings. a.
Membership Directory. a.

Association for Continuing Legal Education *(1964)*
P.O. Box 4646
Austin, TX 78765
Tel: (512)453-4340 *Fax:* (512)451-2911
Web Site: www.aclea.org
Members: 566 individuals
Staff: 4
Annual Budget: $250-500,000
Executive Director: Donna Passons
E-Mail: donna@clesolutions.com

Historical Note
Formerly (1964) National Association of Continuing Legal Education Administrators and then (1995) Association for Continuing Legal Education. Members are organizations and individuals involved in providing continuing legal education. Holds two meetings each year. Membership: $195/year (individual); $180/year (additional members).

Meetings/Conferences:
Annual Meetings: *Summer and winter*
2007 – Nashville, TN(Loews Vanderbilt)/Jan. 27-30
2007 – Philadelphia, PA(Loews Philadelphia)/July 28-31

Publications:
Directory (online). a.
Newsletter. q.

Association for Convention Marketing Executives *(1990)*
204 E St. NE
Washington, DC 20002
Tel: (202)547-8030 *Fax:* (202)547-6348
E-Mail: smc@giuffrida.org
Web Site: www.acmenet.org
Members: 175 individuals
Staff: 4
Annual Budget: $50-100,000
Executive Director: Sheila Crowley

Historical Note
Active members are convention marketing executives affiliated with convention bureaus and centers whose chief objective is to establish and foster an effective marketing partnership. Membership: $325/year.

Meetings/Conferences:
Annual Meetings: *Winter*

Publications:
Newsletter. q. adv.
Membership Directory. a.

Association for Convention Operations Management *(1988)*
191 Clarksville Road
Princeton Junction, NJ 08550
Tel: (609)799-3712 *Fax:* (609)799-7032
E-Mail: info@acomonline.org
Web Site: www.acomonline.org
Members: 500 individuals
Staff: 4
Annual Budget: $250-500,000
Executive Director: Lynn McCullough

Historical Note
Members are convention service directors and managers, executives associated with convention facilities and bureaus, and industry suppliers. Membership: $225/year (active member); $225/year (affiliate).

Meetings/Conferences:
Annual Meetings: *Winter*
2007 – Toronto, ON, Canada(Westin Harbour Castle)/Jan. 5-7

Publications:
ACOMmodate. q.
Acom at a Glance.

Association for Corporate Growth *(1954)*
1926 Waukegan Road
Suite 1
Glenview, IL 60025-1770
Tel: (847)657-6730 *Fax:* (847)657-6819
Toll Free: (800)699 - 1331
E-Mail: acghq@tcag.com
Web Site: www.acg.org
Members: 9000 individuals
Staff: 10
Annual Budget: $2-5,000,000
Chief Executive Officer: Daniel Varroney
Manager, Member Services: Janice H. Wangman
E-Mail: janicew@tcag.com

Historical Note
Founded as the Association for Corporate Growth and Diversification by Peter Hilton and a group of businessmen. ACG was formed as a professional society and forum for ideas related to both external and internal growth - joint ventures, acquisitions and divestitures, and new or expanded products and services. Members are mergers and acquisitions specialists. Membership: $250/year (individual, plus variable chapter dues).

Meetings/Conferences:
Annual Meetings: *Spring*

Publications:
ACG Network Newsletter. m. adv.

Association for Counselor Education and Supervision *(1940)*

Historical Note
An affiliate of American Counseling Association, which provides administrative support.

Association for Counselors and Educators in Government *(1984)*

Historical Note
An organizational affiliate of the American Counseling Ass'n, which provides administrative support.

Association for Death Education and Counseling *(1976)*
60 Revere Dr.
Suite 500
Northbrook, IL 60062
Tel: (847)509-0403 *Fax:* (847)480-9282
E-Mail: info@adec.org
Web Site: www.adec.org
Members: 2000 individuals and institutions
Annual Budget: $250-500,000
Chief Staff Officer: Rick Koepke
Administrative Manager: Bret S. Beall, Ph.D.
Conference Administrator: Debbie Pederson
Communications Manager: Patricia Sullivan

Historical Note
ADEC members are individuals and institutions involved in counseling the dying and bereaved. Maintains a code of ethics and certification programs. Membership: $135/year (individual); $275/year (institution); $60/year (student); $70/year (65 or older).

Publications:
Forum Newsletter. q. adv.
Conference Proceedings. a.
Membership Directory. a.

Association for Direct Instruction *(1981)*
P.O. Box 10252
Eugene, OR 97440
Tel: (541)485-1293 *Fax:* (541)868-1397
Toll Free: (800)995 - 2464
Web Site: www.adihome.org
Members: 1200 individuals
Staff: 3
Director: Bryan Wickman
E-Mail: brywick@adihome.org
President: Gary Johnson
E-Mail: brywick@adihome.org

Historical Note
ADI members are public school teachers and university instructors with an interest in improving teaching methodology. Membership: $40/year (regular); $30/year (student); $75/year (sustaining membership); $150/year (institution). There is no longer a subscription category; please pay $40 (regular member price for same service).

Meetings/Conferences:
Annual Meetings: *always in Eugene, OR*

Publications:
Journal of Direct Instruction. 1/yr. adv.
Direct Instruction News. 3/yr. adv.

Association for Documentary Editing *(1978)*
128 Walnut St., Apt. 2
Everett, MA 02149
E-Mail: adcecere@hotmail.com
Web Site: etext.virginia.edu/ade
Members: 460 individuals

Historical Note
Members of the ADE work on editions in history, literature, philosophy, the arts, and the sciences. Many members are teachers or archivists as well as editors; others are full-time editors. All share the goal of promoting documentary editing through cooperation and exchange of ideas. Membership: $25/year.

Meetings/Conferences:
Annual Meetings: *Fall*

Publications:
Documentary Editing. q.
Membership Directory. a.

Association for Dressings and Sauces *(1926)*
5775 Peachtree-Dunwoody Road
Bldg. G, Suite 500
Atlanta, GA 30342-1558
Tel: (404)252-3663 *Fax:* (404)252-0774
E-Mail: ads@kellencompany.com
Web Site: www.dressings-sauces.org

Members: 180 companies
Staff: 5
President: Richard E. Cristol

Historical Note

Formerly (1973) Mayonnaise and Salad Dressings Institute. Members are manufacturers of mayonnaise, dressings, and prepared sauces; associate membership is available to suppliers.

Meetings/Conferences:

Annual Meetings: Spring and Fall

Publications:

ADS Directory. a.
ADS Information Heads Up. q.

Association for Education and Rehabilitation of the Blind and Visually Impaired *(1984)*
1703 N. Beauregard St.
Suite 440
Alexandria, VA 22311-1744
Tel: (703)671-4500 *Fax:* (703)671-6391
Toll Free: (877)492 - 2708
Web Site: www.aerbvi.org
Members: 4000 individuals
Staff: 5
Annual Budget: $500-1,000,000

Historical Note

The result of a consolidation of the American Association of Workers for the Blind (1895) and the Association for Education of the Visually Handicapped (1905) in 1984. Membership: $130/year (individual).

Meetings/Conferences:

Annual Meetings: Summer
2008 – Chicago, IL(Marriott Downtown)

Publications:

AER Report. bi-m. adv.
Re: view. q. adv.
Job Exchange online. m.

Association for Education in Journalism and Mass Communication *(1912)*
234 Outlet Pointe Blvd.
Suite A
Columbia, SC 29210-5667
Tel: (803)798-0271 *Fax:* (803)772-3509
E-Mail: aejmc@aejmc.org
Web Site: www.aejmc.org
Members: 3400 individuals
Staff: 8
Annual Budget: $500-1,000,000
Executive Director: Jennifer H. McGill
Convention Manager: Fred Williams

Historical Note

Formerly (1951) American Association for Teachers of Journalism. Membership: $100/year (individual); $125/year (organization); $600/year (council of affiliate member).

Meetings/Conferences:

Annual Meetings: Summer/over 1,500

Publications:

AEJMC News. bi-m. adv.
Journalism and Mass Communication Educator. q. adv.
Journalism and Mass Communication Monographs. q.
Journalism and Mass Communication Quarterly. q. adv.
Journalism and Mass Communication Directory. a. adv.
Journalism and Mass Communication Abstracts. a.

Association for Educational Communications and Technology *(1923)*
1800 N. Stonelake Dr.
Suite 2
Bloomington, IN 47404-1517
Tel: (812)335-7675 *Fax:* (812)335-7678
Toll Free: (800)677 - 2328
E-Mail: aect@aect.org
Web Site: www.aect.org
Members: 4500 individuals
Staff: 8
Annual Budget: $1-2,000,000
Executive Director: Dr. Phillip Harris
Director, Electronic Services: Larry Vernon

Historical Note

Founded in 1923 as the Department of Visual Instruction of the National Education Association. Incorporated in the District of Columbia in 1969. Reorganized in 1969 as a national affiliate of the National Education Association and became independent as the Association for Educational Communications and Technology in July 1974. Members are professionals such as microcomputer and audiovisual specialists, media services directors and television producers who require expertise in instructional technology. Membership: $95/year (individual).

Publications:

Educational Technology Research & Development. 4/year.
TechTrends. 6/year. adv.

Association for Electronic Health Care Transactions
3516 McKinley St. NW
Washington, DC 20015-2513
Tel: (202)244-6450
Web Site: www.afehct.org
Members: 70 individuals
Washington Representative: Tom Gilligan

Publications:

Washington Wire.

Association for Electronics Manufacturing of SME *(1985)*

Historical Note

Part of Engineering Materials Applications Community of SME, a program of Society of Manufacturing Engineers, which provides administrative support.

Association for Enterprise Opportunity *(1991)*
1601 N. Kent St.
Suite 1101
Arlington, VA 22209
Tel: (703)841-7760 *Fax:* (703)841-7748
E-Mail: aeo@assoceo.org
Web Site: www.microenterpriseworks.org
Members: 450 organizations
Staff: 17
Annual Budget: $2-5,000,000
Managing Director: Zulma Bianca
Chief Executive Officer: Amy McKenna Luz

Historical Note

AEO is the national association of organizations committed to microenterprise development. AEO provides its members with a forum, information and a voice to promote enterprise opportunity for people and communities with limited access to economic resources.

Meetings/Conferences:

Annual Meetings: May
2007 – Kansas City, MO(Hyatt Regency)/May 15-18
2008 – Anaheim, CA(Hyatt Regency)/May 19-22

Publications:

AEO Exchange. q.

Association for Equine Sports Medicine *(1982)*
CalPoly Pomona, College of Agriculture
3801 W. Temple Ave.
Pomona, CA 91768
Tel: (909)869-2156 *Fax:* (909)869-4454
Members: 350 individuals
Staff: 1
Annual Budget: $50-100,000
Executive Director: Holly M. Greene

Historical Note

AESM members are veterinarians, health professionals, horse owners, horse trainers and others interested in the medical treatment of horses involved in athletic competition. Membership: $60/year (U.S.).

Meetings/Conferences:

Annual Meetings: March

Publications:

AESM News. q. adv.
Newsletter. q. adv.
Conference Proceedings. a. adv.
Membership List. irreg.

Association for Evolutionary Economics *(1965)*
Bucknell Univ.
Dept. of Economics, Coleman Hall 154
Lewisburg, PA 17837
Tel: (570)577-3648 *Fax:* (570)577-2372
E-Mail: afee@bucknell.edu
Web Site: www.orgs.bucknell.edu/afee
Members: 550 individuals
Staff: 1
Annual Budget: $50-100,000
Association Coordinator: Helen M. Saver
E-Mail: afee@bucknell.edu

Historical Note

Includes institutional economists from the United States, Canada, Latin America, Western Europe, and Asia. Seeks to foster the development of economic study and of economics as a social science based on the complex interrelationships of man and society. A member of the Allied Social Science Associations. Membership: $35/year (individual); $40/year (library/institution); $15/year (student).

Meetings/Conferences:

Annual Meetings: With the Allied Social Science Ass'ns

Publications:

Journal of Economic Issues. q. adv.

Association for Experiential Education *(1972)*
3775 Iris Ave.
Suite Four
Boulder, CO 80301
Tel: (303)440-8844 *Fax:* (303)440-9581
Toll Free: (866)522 - 8337
Web Site: www.aee.org
Members: 2000 individuals
Staff: 6
Annual Budget: $500-1,000,000
Executive Director: Dr. Kristin Von Wald
Director, Membership: Christine Day
E-Mail: membership@aee.org
Manager, Finance: Ellen Jardine
E-Mail: finance@aee.org
Director, Publications: Natalie Kurylko
E-Mail: publications@aee.org
Director, Conference Services: Evan Narotsky
E-Mail: evan@aee.org
Director, Accreditation: Henry Wood
E-Mail: henry@aee.org

Historical Note

A not-for-profit international professional organization with roots in experiential education committed to the development, practice, and evaluation of experiential learning in all settings. Membership: $55-95/year (individual); $200-500/year (organization).

Meetings/Conferences:

Annual Meetings: Fall

Publications:

Jobs Clearinghouse. online. adv.
The AEE Horizon Newsletter (online). 3/year. adv.
Journal of Experiential Education. 3/year.

Association for Facilities Engineering *(1954)*
8160 Corporate Park Dr.
Suite 125
Cincinnati, OH 45242-3309
Tel: (513)489-2473 *Fax:* (513)247-7422
E-Mail: mail@afe.org
Web Site: www.afe.org
Members: 9000 individuals
Staff: 8
Annual Budget: $1-2,000,000
Executive Director: Michael Ireland
E-Mail: mireland@afe.org
Communications Manager: Gabriella Jacobs
E-Mail: gjacobs@afe.org

Historical Note

Formerly (1996) American Institute of Plant Engineers. Members are facility managers in charge of engineering, operations, and maintenance of industrial plants, office buildings, campuses, and other workplaces. AFE provides technical resources and support on enginnering issues affecting facilities management. Membership: $185/year.

Meetings/Conferences:

Annual Meetings: Fall

Publications:
Facilities Engineering Journal. bi-m. adv.

Association for Federal Information Resources Management *(1979)*
P.O. Box 2851
Washington, DC 20013
Web Site: www.affirm.org
Members: 565 individuals
Annual Budget: $25-50,000
Secretary: Kenneth Touloumes
E-Mail: kenneth.touloumes@titan.com

Historical Note
Membership, concentrated in the metropolitan Washington area, is composed of information & technology professionals employed by the U.S. government or government contractors. Has no paid officers or full-time staff.

Meetings/Conferences:
Monthly Luncheons: Washington, DC/September-June

Publications:
The Affirmation. m.
Membership Directory. a.

Association for Feminist Anthropology *(1988)*

Historical Note
A section of the American Anthropological Association.

Association for Financial Counseling and Planning Education *(1983)*
1500 W. Third Ave.
Suite 223
Columbus, OH 43212
Tel: (614)485-9650 *Fax:* (614)485-9621
E-Mail: sburns@afcpe.org
Web Site: www.afcpe.org
Members: 810 individuals
Staff: 2
Annual Budget: $500-1,000,000
Executive Director: Sharon Burns, Ph.D

Historical Note
AFCPE members are financial planners and counselors, educators, and other professionals involved in teaching budgetary and financial skills to consumers. Membership: $95/year.

Publications:
AFCPE Newsletter. q.
Financial Planning & Counseling Journal. semi-a.

Association for Financial Professionals *(1979)*
7315 Wisconsin Ave.
Suite 600 West
Bethesda, MD 20814-3211
Tel: (301)907-2862 *Fax:* (301)907-2864
E-Mail: afp@afponline.org
Web Site: www.afponline.org
Members: 14000 individuals
Staff: 60
Annual Budget: $10-25,000,000
President and Chief Executive Officer: James Kaitz
E-Mail: afp@afponline.org
Chief Operating Officer and Senior Vice President: Kevin Keller
E-Mail: afp@afponline.org
Chief Financial Officer: Erick Larsen, CPA
E-Mail: afp@afponline.org

Historical Note
Formerly Cash Management Practitioners Association and National Corporate Cash Managment Association; became Treasury Management Association in 1991 and assumed its present name in 1999. AFP supports its members throughout all stages of their careers with cutting edge research, continuing education, career development, professional certifications, publications, representations to key legislators and regulators, and the development of industry standards. Membership: $295/year (individual).

Meetings/Conferences:
Annual Meetings: Fall

Publications:
Membership Directory & Guide to Treasury Services. a.
AFP Exchange. q. adv.
Status Update of Current Issues. m.
Electronic Commerce Report. m.

Association for Financial Technology *(1972)*
34 North St.
New Albany, OH 43054
Tel: (614)895-1208 *Fax:* (614)895-3466
E-Mail: aft@aftweb.com
Web Site: www.aftweb.com
Members: 58 companies
Staff: 2
Annual Budget: $100-250,000
Executive Director: James R. Bannister
E-Mail: aft@aftweb.com

Historical Note
Established as the Multi-Bank Data Processing Organization; became National Association of Bank Servicers in 1975 and assumed its present name in 1994. AFT member companies provide systems applications and outsourcing services to banks, thrifts, credit unions and other financial institutions. Membership also includes suppliers of computer hardware and software, and other related products and services. Membership: $1,000/year.

Meetings/Conferences:
Semi-annual Meetings: Spring and Fall/75

Publications:
Newsletter. q. adv.

Association for Gay, Lesbian and Bisexual Issues in Counseling *(1974)*

Historical Note
An affiliate of American Counseling Association, which provides administrative support.

Association for General and Liberal Studies *(1961)*
English Dept. RB 297
Ball State University
Muncie, IN 47306
Tel: (765)285-8406 *Fax:* (765)285-2384
Web Site: www.bsu.edu/web/agls
Members: 300 individuals
Annual Budget: under $10,000
Executive Director: Paul Ranieri
E-Mail: pranieri@bsu.edu

Historical Note
AGLS members are individuals with an interest in higher education liberal arts and general education programs. Has no paid officers or full-time staff; the Director's position changes every three years. Membership: $30/year.

Meetings/Conferences:
Annual Meetings: October

Publications:
JGE: Journal of General Education. bi-a.
AGLS Newsletter. 3/year.

Association for Gerontology in Higher Education *(1974)*
1030 15th St. NW
Suite 420
Washington, DC 20005
Tel: (202)289-9806 *Fax:* (202)289-9824
E-Mail: aghetemp@aghe.org
Web Site: www.aghe.org
Members: 320 institutions
Staff: 4
Annual Budget: $500-1,000,000
Director: Derek D. Stepp

Historical Note
The association grew out of a committee of educators interested in the development and improvement of gerontological programs and resources in institutions of higher education. Its membership comprises colleges and universities in the U.S. and Canada concerned with gerontological education, training and research. Membership: $150-585/year (institution).

Meetings/Conferences:
Annual Meetings: February-March/500

Publications:
Nat'l Directory of Educational Programs in Gerontology and Geriatrics. bien.
Standards and Guidelines for gerontology programs.
AGHE Exchange. q. adv.

Association for Gnotobiotics *(1961)*
Nat'l Animal Disease Ctr., Animal Sup.
P.O. Box 70
Ames, IA 50010
Tel: (515)663-7458
Web Site: www.gnotobiotics.org
Members: 220 individuals
Annual Budget: under $10,000
Executive Secretary-Treasurer: Dr. LaWayne T. Nusz

Historical Note
Members are scientists interested in germ-free research and applications. Formerly (1968) Association for Applied Gnotobiotics. Has no paid officers or full-time staff. Membership: $20/year (individual); $250/year (organization).

Publications:
Newsletter. a.
Membership Directory. a.
Annual Meeting Abstract. a.

Association for Governmental Leasing and Finance *(1981)*
Executive Director: Ken Cleveland

Historical Note
Provides an exchange of information among tax-exempt issuers, investment banking firms, commercial banks and third party lease brokers primarily concerned with the tax-exempt lease purchase marketplace. Informs members of recent changes in federal, state and local laws and regulations as they affect tax-exempt project finance. Membership: $120/year (governmental member); $600/year (organization).

Meetings/Conferences:
Semi-annual Meetings: Spring and Fall

Publications:
Tax Exempt Leasing Letter. bi-m. adv.
Fifty State Survey. a.

Association for Graphic Arts Training *(1987)*
c/o Banta Publications
2600 E. Main St.
Spanish Fork, UT 94660
Tel: (801)798-5268 *Fax:* (801)798-1505
E-Mail: d.franks@enovationgraphics.com
Web Site: www.agatweb.org
Members: 100 individuals
President: Daryl Franks
E-Mail: d.franks@enovationgraphics.com

Historical Note
AGAT members are graphic arts trainers employed by printing companies, teachers and other individuals and companies with an interest in graphic arts instruction. Has no paid officers or full-time staff. Membership: $60/year (organization).

Meetings/Conferences:
Annual Meetings: Fall

Publications:
AGAT E Line Newsletter. q. adv.

Association for Health Services Research and Health Policy

Historical Note
Became AcademyHealth in 2002.

Association for Healthcare Philanthropy *(1967)*
313 Park Ave.
Suite 400
Falls Church, VA 22046
Tel: (703)532-6243 *Fax:* (703)532-7170
E-Mail: ahp@ahp.org
Web Site: www.ahp.org
Members: 3000 individuals
Staff: 12
Annual Budget: $2-5,000,000
President and Chief Executive Officer: William C. McGinly, Ph.D., CAE
E-Mail: ahp@ahp.org
Executive Vice President: Terence J. Rainey
E-Mail: ahp@ahp.org
Director, Membership and Communications: Kathy Renzetti
E-Mail: ahp@ahp.org
Director, Education and Meetings: Monika Schulz
E-Mail: ahp@ahp.org

Historical Note
Established as Developartners, became National Association for Hospital Development in 1968, and assumed its present name in 1991. A professional association of hospital and health care executives involved in hospital development and fund-raising programs. Membership: $395/year (individual); $600/year (organization). Institutional membership rate varies on number of dev. professionals.

Meetings/Conferences:
Annual Meetings: Fall
2007 – Philadelphia, PA/Oct. 3-7

Publications:
AHP Advanced Course Workbook.
AHP Foundation Self-Study Guide.
AHP Journal. semi-a. adv.
AHP Connect. 8/year. adv.
AHP Membership Directory & Buyers Guide. a. adv.
Annual Conference Tapes/CD.
AHP Report on Giving U.S./Canada CD.
AHP Development Primer Manual.

Association for Healthcare Resource and Materials Management *(1962)*
One N. Franklin
30th Floor
Chicago, IL 60606
Tel: (312)422-3840 *Fax:* (312)422-4573
E-Mail: ahrmm@aha.org
Web Site: www.ahrmm.org
Members: 4000 individuals
Staff: 7
Annual Budget: $1-2,000,000
Executive Director: Deborah Sprindzunas
E-Mail: dsprindzunas@aha.org
Director, Education: Cathy Futrell

Historical Note
Affiliated with the American Hospital Association. Formerly (1975) the American Society for Hospital Purchasing Agents, (1983) the American Society for Hospital Purchasing and Materials Management, (1994) American Society for Hospital Materials Management, and (1998) American Society for Healthcare Materials Management. Membership: $100/year (regular); $130/year (non-AHA).

Meetings/Conferences:
Annual Meetings: Summer
2007 – San Diego, CA(Marriott)/Aug. 12-15

Publications:
AHRMM Membership Roster. a.
Career Connection. adv.
Hospital Materials Management News. bi-m.
Conference Proceedings. a.
Technical Articles. q.
Healthcare Materials Management Newsletter. m.

Association for High Technology Distribution *(1985)*
100 N. 20th St.
Fourth Floor
Philadelphia, PA 19103-1443
Tel: (215)564-3484 *Fax:* (215)564-2175
E-Mail: ahtd@ahtd.org
Web Site: www.ahtd.org
Members: 250 companies
Staff: 3
Annual Budget: $250-500,000
Executive Director: Talbot M. Gee

Historical Note
Formerly (1995) Association of High Technology Distributors. AHTD members are distributors of industrial automation products; affiliate membership is available for manufacturers. Membership: $595/year (company).

Meetings/Conferences:
Semi-Annual Meetings: Spring and Fall

Publications:
AHTD Network Newsletter. 3/year.
Membership Directory. a.

Association for Hose and Accessories Distribution *(1985)*
105 Eastern Ave.
Suite 104
Annapolis, MD 21403-3300
Tel: (410)263-1014 *Fax:* (410)263-1659
Toll Free: (800)624 - 2227
E-Mail: info@nahad.org
Web Site: www.nahad.org
Members: 350 distributors, 250 manufacturers
Staff: 8
Annual Budget: $500-1,000,000
Executive Director: Joseph M. Thompson, Jr.
Director, Business Services: Diana J. Crompton, CPA
Manager, Program Development: Robb Fish
E-Mail: rfish@nahad.org
Membership Development Manager: Amy Luckado
E-Mail: aluckado@nahad.org
Conference and Communication Assistant: Lauren Miller
Conference Manager: Aimee Murphy
Office Manager: Janice Sunderland
Director, Communications and Conferences: Kristin B. Thompson

Historical Note
NAHAD is an international association of distributors and manufacturers of industrial hose and fittings. A member of the National Association of Wholesaler Distributors. Membership: $450-$735/year.

Meetings/Conferences:
Annual Meetings: Spring
2007 – Victoria, BC, Canada(Fairmont Hotel)/May 18-22

Publications:
Convention Guide. a. adv.
NAHAD News. bi-m.
Membership Directory. a. adv.

Association for Hospital Medical Education *(1956)*
109 Brush Creek Rd.
Irwin, PA 15642-9504
Tel: (724)864-7321
Web Site: www.ahme.org
Members: 700 individuals
Staff: 3
Annual Budget: $100-250,000
Executive Director: Margie Kleppick

Historical Note
Formerly (1968) Association of Hospital Directors of Medical Education. Members are hospital staff and administrators concerned with medical education, primarily at community hospitals. Membership: $495/year (individual); $1,500/year (institutional).

Meetings/Conferences:
Semi-Annual Meetings: Spring and Fall

Publications:
Transitional Year Program Directory (web). a.
AHME News. q. adv.
Guide to Graduate Medical Education.

Association for Humanist Sociology *(1976)*
213 Hillyer Place
Decatur, GA 30030
Tel: (404)373-2482
Web Site: www.humanistsoc.org
Members: 300 individuals
Annual Budget: $10-25,000
Treasurer: Brian S. Sherman, Ph.D.

Historical Note
AHS is an organization of sociologists disenchanted with conventional academic sociology and committed to making sociology relevant to human needs. AHS seeks to provide an active support network for sociologists committed to humanist values. Has no paid officers or full-time staff. Membership: $20-60/year, varies by annual income (individual); $110/year (library subscription).

Meetings/Conferences:
Annual Meetings: Fall

Publications:
Humanity and Society Jounal. q. adv.
Humanist Sociologist Newsletter. q. adv.

Association for Humanistic Psychology *(1962)*
1516 Oak St.
Suite 320A
Alameda, CA 94501-2947
Tel: (510)769-6495 *Fax:* (510)769-6433
E-Mail: ahpoffice@aol.com
Web Site: www.ahpweb.org
Members: 1840 individuals
Staff: 3
Annual Budget: $100-250,000
President: J. Bruce Francis
Director, Member Services: Bonnie Davenport

Historical Note
Founded in Palo Alto, CA in December 1962 as the American Association for Humanistic Psychology. Incorporated in California in 1965; assumed its present name in 1969. Purpose is to promote and protect the humanistic perspectives and practices worldwide. Membership: $49-69/year (individual); $149/year (organization).

Meetings/Conferences:
Annual Meetings: July/August

Publications:
AHP Perspective. bi-m. adv.
Journal of Humanistic Psychology. q.

Association for Informal Logic and Critical Thinking *(1983)*
P.O. Box 65
Philosophy and Religion Dept., Baker University
Baldwin City, KS 66006
Tel: (785)594-6451 *Fax:* (785)594-2522
Web Site: http://ailact.mcmaster.ca
Members: 200 individuals
Annual Budget: under $10,000
Secretary-Treasurer: Dr. Donald L. Hatcher
E-Mail: donaldhatcher@bakeru.edu

Historical Note
AILACT was established to promote the quality of research, teaching, and testing of informal logic and critical thinking at all levels and to facilitate discussion between its members. AILACT members are academics and teachers of courses in informal logic and critical thinking. Has no paid officers or full-time staff. Membership: $6/year (individual).

Publications:
IALACT Bulletin. 3/yr.

Association for Information and Image Management International *(1943)*
1100 Wayne Ave.
Suite 1100
Silver Spring, MD 20910-5603
Tel: (301)587-8202 *Fax:* (301)587-2711
Toll Free: (800)477 - 2446
E-Mail: aiim@aiim.org
Web Site: www.aiim.org
Members: 6000 individuals
Staff: 25
Annual Budget: $10-25,000,000
President: John F. Mancini
E-Mail: jmancini@aiim.org
Director, Standards and Content: Betsy Fanning
Vice President: Peggy Winton

Historical Note
Established and incorporated in Michigan as the National Microfilm Association, it became the National Micrographics Association in 1975 and assumed its present name in 1995. Merged with the International Information Management Congress in 1999. Members are users and manufacturers of equipment, supplies and services for the document management industry. Has an annual budget of approximately $12 million. Membership: $125/year (individual); $1,000/year (company, based on gross revenue.)

Meetings/Conferences:
Annual Meetings: Spring/40,000

Publications:
E-Doc. bi-m. adv.

Association for Information Media and Equipment *(1986)*
P.O. Box 9844
Cedar Rapids, IA 52409-9844
Tel: (319)654-0608 *Fax:* (319)654-0609
Web Site: www.aime.org
Members: 159
Staff: 1
Annual Budget: $25-50,000
Executive Director: Betty Gorsegner Ehlinger

Historical Note
AIME is an association of producers and distributors of educational films and video, companies who provide related equipment and services, and others who use information media materials and equipment. AIME is active in the areas of copyright, legislation to benefit school media centers and funds for materials, market research, new technology, and promotion of film and video as effective instructional tools. Membership fee varies by category of membership.

Publications:
AIME News Newsletter. 4/year.

Association for Information Systems *(1994)*
P.O. Box 2712
Atlanta, GA 30301-2712
Tel: (404)651-0348 *Fax:* (404)651-4938
Web Site: www.aisnet.org
Members: 4100 individuals
Staff: 3
Annual Budget: $1-2,000,000
Executive Director: Ephraim R. McLean

Historical Note
AIS members are academics with an interest in information systems and related fields.

Publications:
Communications of the Association for Information Systems. q.
Journal of the Association for Information Systems. q.

Association for Institutional Research *(1965)*
1435 E. Piedmont Dr.
Suite 211
Tallahassee, FL 32308
Tel: (850)385-4155 *Fax:* (850)385-5180
E-Mail: air@mailer.fsu.edu
Web Site: http://airweb.org
Members: 3100 individuals
Staff: 6
Annual Budget: $1-2,000,000
Executive Director: Terrence R. Russell, Ph.D.

Historical Note
Members are involved in research to improve institutions of postsecondary education. Membership: $115/year (individual); $410/year (organization/company); $30/year (graduate student).

Meetings/Conferences:
Annual Meetings: Spring/1,250

Publications:
Journal of Higher Education. bi-m.
Resources in Institutional Research. a.
Assessment Update. bi-m.
Resources in Institutional Research. a.
New Directions for Institutional Research. q.
Research in Higher Education. bi-m.

Association for Integrative Studies *(1979)*
Miami University
School of Interdisciplinary Studies
Oxford, OH 45056
Tel: (513)529-2213 *Fax:* (513)529-5849
Web Site: www.muohio.edu/ais
Members: 2500 individuals
Staff: 1
Annual Budget: $10-25,000
Executive Director: William H. Newell
E-Mail: aisorg@muohio.org

Historical Note
Established and incorporated in Ohio. AIS members are primarily faculty and administrators engaged in interdisciplinary teaching and research or who are interested in exploring interdisplinary topics and methodology. Membership: $40/year (individual); $100/year (institution); $15/year (student).

Meetings/Conferences:
Annual Meetings: Fall/125

Publications:
AIS Newsletter. q.
Issues in Integrative Studies. semi-a.

Association for International Agricultural and Extension Education *(1984)*
University of Florida - Institute of Food and Agricultural Sciences
219 Rolfs Hall, P.O. Box 110540
Gainesville, FL 32611-0540
Tel: (352)392-0502 Ext: 227 *Fax:* (352)392-9585
E-Mail: nplace@ufl.edu
Web Site: www.aiaee.org
Members: 300 individuals
Annual Budget: under $10,000
President-Elect: Nick T. Place, Ph.D.

Historical Note
AIAEE is a professional society composed of individuals working in international education or extension programs. Has no paid officers or full-time staff. Membership: $20/year (regular member); $10/year (member from a developing country).

Meetings/Conferences:
Annual Meetings: Spring

Publications:
The Informer. 3/year.

Association for International Agriculture and Rural Development *(1964)*
Dept. of Ag Economics, Mississippi State University
P.O. Box 5187
Mississippi State, MS 39762
Tel: (662)325-0549 *Fax:* (662)325-8777
Web Site: http://aiard.org
Members: 220 individuals
Annual Budget: under $10,000
Secretary-Treasurer: Joy Odom
E-Mail: odom@agecon.msstate.edu

Historical Note
Formerly (1989) Association of United States Directors of International Agriculture Programs. Members are international development professionals representing educational, research and extension interests in international agriculture. Affiliated with the National Association of State Universities and Land Grant Colleges. Has no paid officers or full-time staff. Membership: $35/year; $15/year (student).

Meetings/Conferences:
Annual Meetings: June/100

Association for Iron and Steel Technology *(1907)*
186 Thorn Hill Road
Warrendale, PA 15086
Tel: (724)776-6040 *Fax:* (724)776-1880
E-Mail: custserv@aist.org
Web Site: www.aist.org
Members: 10000 individuals
Staff: 25
Annual Budget: $2-5,000,000
Executive Director: Ronald E. Ashburn
Manager, Membership Programs: Bill Albaugh
Manager, Sales and Expositions: Gerry Kane
Manager, Membership Communications: Stacy Uarmecky

Historical Note
Originated in 1907 as the Association of Iron and Steel Electrical Engineers; became the Association of Iron and Steel Engineers in 1936. Merged with Iron and Steel Society and assumed its current name in 2004. AIST works to advance the technical development, production, processing and application of iron and steel. Membership: $115/year (regular American or foreign member); $57.50/year (young professional member); $25.00/year (international student).

Meetings/Conferences:
Annual Meetings: Spring (AISTECH)/Fall (MS&T)
2007 - Indianapolis, IN(Indiana Convention Center)/May 7-10
2007 - Detroit, MI/Sept. 17-20

Publications:
AIST Iron & Steel Technology. m. adv.
Convention Proceedings. a.
Directory of Iron & Steel Plants. a. adv.

Association for Jewish Studies *(1969)*
15 W. 16th St.
New York, NY 10011-6301
Tel: (917)606-8249 *Fax:* (917)606-8222
E-Mail: ajs@ajs.cjh.org
Web Site: www.brandeis.edu/ajs
Members: 1600 individuals
Staff: 1
Executive Director: Rona Sheramy, Ph.D.
E-Mail: ajs@ajs.cjh.org

Historical Note
Founded in 1969, AJS is a learned society and professional organization that seeks to promote, maintain and improve teaching, research and related endeavors in Jewish Studies in colleges, universities and other institutions of higher learning. AJS is a constituent society of the American Council of Learned Societies. Membership: $40/year (individual).

Publications:
AJS Perspectives. semi-a.
AJS Review. semi-a. adv.
Conference Program. a. adv.

Association for Library and Information Science Education *(1915)*
1055 Commerce Park Dr.
Suite 110
Oak Ridge, TN 37839
Tel: (865)425-0155 *Fax:* (865)481-0390
E-Mail: contact@alise.org
Web Site: www.alise.org
Members: 500
Staff: 3
Annual Budget: $100-250,000
Executive Director: Deborah York

Historical Note
Founded (1915) as the Association of American Library Schools; assumed its current name in 1983. Affiliate of American Library Association and International Federation of Library Associations, Medical Library Association, Special Libraries Association, and American Association of Law Libraries. Membership: $90/year (full-time faculty member, librarian, researcher, administrator); $75/year (part-time); $60/year (doctoral student).

Meetings/Conferences:
Annual Meetings: January, prior to the Winter American Library Ass'n meeting
2007 - Seattle, WA/Jan. 16-19

Publications:
KALIPER Report.
Journal of Education for Library & Information Science (JELIS). q.
Library and Information Science Education Statistical Report. a.
Membership Directory. a.

Association for Library Collections and Technical Services *(1957)*
50 E. Huron St.
Chicago, IL 60611-2795
Toll Free: (800)545 - 2433 Ext: 5038
E-Mail: alcts@ala.org
Web Site: www.ala.org/alcts
Members: 4200 individuals
Staff: 3
Annual Budget: $500-1,000,000
Executive Director: Charles Wilt
E-Mail: cwilt@ala.org

Historical Note
A division of the American Library Association formerly known as the Resources and Technical Services Division, ALCTS adopted its name in 1989. Membership: $55/year (individual); plus membership in ALA (individual).

Meetings/Conferences:
Annual Meetings: in conjunction with the American Library Ass'n
2007 - Washington, DC/June 21-27
2008 - Anaheim, CA/June 26-July 2
2009 - Chicago, IL/July 9-15
2010 - New York, NY/June 24-30

Publications:
ALCTS Newsletter Online. bi-m. adv.
Library Resources & Technical Services. q. adv.

Association for Library Service to Children *(1901)*
c/o American Library Ass'n
50 E. Huron St.
Chicago, IL 60611
Tel: (312)280-2163 *Fax:* (312)944-7671
Toll Free: (800)545 - 2433 Ext: 2163
E-Mail: alsc@ala.org
Web Site: www.ala.org/alsc
Members: 3600 individuals

Staff: 7
Annual Budget: $500-1,000,000
Interim Executive Director: Aimee Strittmatter
E-Mail: alsc@ala.org

Historical Note
ALSC is a division of American Library Association providing specialized resources for librarians in charge of libraries serving children.

Meetings/Conferences:
Biennial Meetings: Summer with the American Library Ass'n

Publications:
ALSConnect newsletter. q.
Children and Libraries Journal. 3/yr.

Association for Library Trustees and Advocates *(1961)*

50 E. Huron St.
Chicago, IL 60611
Tel: (312)280-2161 *Fax:* (312)280-3256
Toll Free: (800)545 - 2433
Web Site: www.ala.org/alta
Members: 1200 individuals
Staff: 2
Annual Budget: $100-250,000
Executive Director: Kerry Ward

Historical Note
Originally founded in 1890 as a section of the American Library Association, became a division of the ALA in 1961. Operated under the name American Library Trustee Association before (1999) assuming current name. Membership is restricted to ALA members. Annual meetings held in conjunction with the ALA. Membership: $50/year (individual).

Meetings/Conferences:
Annual Meetings: Summer/250

Publications:
The Voice. q.

Association for Living History, Farm and Agricultural Museums *(1970)*

8774 Route 45 NW
North Bloomfield, OH 44450-9701
Tel: (440)685-4410 *Fax:* (440)685-4410
Web Site: www.alhfam.org
Members: 800 individuals
Annual Budget: $50-100,000
Secretary-Treasurer: Judith Sheridan

Historical Note
Members include people working in living history, farms, house museums, agricultural museums and outdoor museums of history and folklife. ALHFAM has no paid officers or full-time staff. Membership: $20/year (individual); $50/year (organization).

Meetings/Conferences:
Annual Meetings: Summer
2007 – Santa Fe, NM(El Rancho de los Golordrinas)/June 2-6/125
2008 – Ottawa, ON, Canada(Canada Agmuseum)/125

Publications:
Living Historical Farms Bulletin. q. adv.
Proceedings. a.

Association for Local Telecommunications Services *(1987)*

Historical Note
Merged with COMPTEL/ASCENT in 2005.

Association for Management Information in Financial Services *(1980)*

3895 Fairfax Court
Atlanta, GA 30339
Tel: (770)444-3557 *Fax:* (770)444-9084
E-Mail: ami@amifs.org
Web Site: www.amifs.org
Members: 600 individuals
Staff: 1
Annual Budget: $250-500,000
Executive Director: Kevin Link

Historical Note
Formerly (1990) the National Association for Bank Cost Analysis and (1997) National Association for Bank Cost and Management Accounting. Membership open to individuals employed by any commercial bank, trust company, Federal Reserve bank, bank holding company, credit union or thrift institution. Membership: $295/year (individual); $995/year (organization/company)

Meetings/Conferences:
Annual Meetings: May-June/300-350

Publications:
Journal of Performance Management. 3/yr.
AMI Bulletin. q.

Association for Manufacturing Excellence *(1985)*

3115 N. Wilke Road
Suite G
Arlington Heights, IL 60004-1451
Tel: (224)232-5980 *Fax:* (224)232-5981
E-Mail: jaweitz@ame.org
Web Site: www.ame.org
Members: 4200 individuals
Staff: 5
Annual Budget: $2-5,000,000
Production Manager: JoAnn Weitzenfeld
E-Mail: jaweitz@ame.org

Historical Note
A not-for-profit organization founded to cultivate the understanding, analysis and exchange of world class productivity methods and their successful application in the pursuit of excellence. Membership: $150/year (individual), $190 (outside North America).

Meetings/Conferences:
Annual Meetings: Fall

Publications:
AME Newsletter. bi-m.
Target. q. adv.

Association for Maximum Service Television *(1956)*

P.O. Box 9897
Washington, DC 20016
Tel: (202)966-1956 *Fax:* (202)966-9617
E-Mail: mstv@mstv.org
Web Site: www.mstv.org
Members: 400 television stations
Staff: 5
Annual Budget: $1-2,000,000
President: David L. Donovan
Manager, Administration: April C.T. Lee

Historical Note
Formerly (1990) Association of Maximum Service Telecasters. Individuals, partnerships, firms and corporations who own and operate TV stations, UHF or VHF seeking to assure the highest technical quality for local and nationwide free over-the-air television service.

Meetings/Conferences:
Annual Meetings: Spring/350

Publications:
Newsletter. bi-m.

Association for Molecular Pathology *(1995)*

9650 Rockville Pike
Bethesda, MD 20814-3993
Tel: (301)634-7939 *Fax:* (301)634-7990
E-Mail: amp@asip.org
Web Site: www.amp.org
Members: 1300 individuals
Annual Budget: $500-1,000,000
Executive Officer: Mark E. Sobel, MD, Ph.D
Director, Meetings and Membership Services: Maricel M. Herrera, CMP
E-Mail: amp@asip.org
Director, Scientific Programs and Chief Operating Officer: Mary Williams, MT
E-Mail: amp@asip.org

Historical Note
AMP members are academics, scientists, researchers and others with an interest in molecular pathology. Membership: $175/year (M.D./Ph.D.); $100/year (BS or MS); $75/year (student/fellow/resident).

Meetings/Conferences:
Annual Meetings: Fall

Publications:
AMP Newsletter. 3/year.
The Journal of Molecular Diagnostics. 5/year. adv.

Association for Multicultural Counseling and Development *(1971)*

Historical Note
An affiliate of American Counseling Association, which provides administrative support.

Association for Philosophy of the Unconscious *(1971)*

Dept. of Philosophy, Georgetown Univ.
Washington, DC 20057
Tel: (202)687-7613 *Fax:* (202)687-4493
Members: 150 individuals
Annual Budget: under $10,000
President: Wilfried Ver Eecke
E-Mail: vereeckw@georgetown.edu

Historical Note
APU members are academics and others with an interest in psychoanalysis and philosophy. Membership: $5/year (individual); $2/year (student).

Meetings/Conferences:
Annual Meetings: with American Philosophical Ass'n, Eastern Division in December

Publications:
APU Newsletter. a.

Association for Play Therapy *(1982)*

2060 N. Winery Ave.
Suite 102
Fresno, CA 93703-2884
Tel: (559)252-2278 *Fax:* (559)252-2297
Web Site: www.a4pt.org
Members: 4600 individuals
Staff: 5
Annual Budget: $500-1,000,000
Executive Director: William M. Burns, CAE
General Manager: Kathryn Lebby, CMP
E-Mail: klebby@a4pt.org

Historical Note
Membership: $95/year (individual); $50/year (affiliate).

Meetings/Conferences:
Annual Meetings: October
2007 – Hollywood, CA

Publications:
APT Magazine. q. adv.
Internat'l Journal of Play Therapy. bi-a.

Association for Political and Legal Anthropology *(1976)*

Historical Note
A section of the American Anthropological Association. Established to foster communication and cooperation among scholars interested in the anthropological study of politics and the law.

Association for Politics and the Life Sciences *(1980)*

Political Science Department
Utah State University
Logan, UT 84322
Tel: (435)797-1316 *Fax:* (435)797-3751
E-Mail: david.goetze@usu.edu
Web Site: www.aplsnet.org
Members: 350 individuals
Annual Budget: $25-50,000
Executive Director: David Goetze
E-Mail: david.goetze@usu.edu

Historical Note
APLS is an international and interdisciplinary association of scholars, scientists and policymakers concerned with problems or issues that involve politics or public policy and one or more of the life sciences. Annual Membership: $55/year.

Publications:
Politics and the Life Sciences. semi-a. adv.

Association for Population/Family Planning Libraries and Information Centers, International *(1968)*

3718 Locust Walk
Philadelphia, PA 19104-6298
Tel: (212)898-5375
Web Site: www.aplici.org
Members: 120 individuals
Annual Budget: under $10,000
President: Nykia N. Perez

Historical Note
Members are librarians, information researchers, resource coordinators and the population and family-

planning related agencies that they serve. Incorporated in the District of Columbia in May 1972. Membership: $25/year (individual).

Publications:
APLICommunicator. q. adv.

Association for Postal Commerce *(1947)*
1901 N. Fort Myer Dr.
Suite 401
Arlington, VA 22209-1609
Tel: (703)524-0096 *Fax:* (703)524-1871
E-Mail: cmiller1@postcom.org
Web Site: http://postcom.org
Members: 1000 individuals
Staff: 4
Annual Budget: $1-2,000,000
President: Gene A. Del Polito, Ph.D.
E-Mail: genedp@postcom.org
Administrative Director: Caroline Miller
E-Mail: cmiller1@postcom.org
Vice President: Kate Muth

Historical Note
Established as Associated Third Class Mail Users; became the Third Class Mail Association in 1981, Advertising Mail Marketing Association in 1991, and assumed its present name in 1999. Members are firms who use or support the use of mail for advertising, marketing, or fund raising purposes. Membership: $1,000-19,000/year (organization).

Meetings/Conferences:
Annual Meetings: February, May and October

Publications:
PostCom Bulletin. w.
Postal Tech-Notes.
CEO Postal Update.
Membership Directory. a.
Postal Issues Summary. semi-a.
PostOps Update. m.
Postal Policy Report. m.

Association for Practical and Professional Ethics *(1990)*
618 E. Third St.
Bloomington, IN 47405-3602
Tel: (812)855-6450 *Fax:* (812)855-3315
E-Mail: appe@indiana.edu
Web Site: www.indiana.edu/~appe
Members: 650 individuals
Staff: 2
Annual Budget: $100-250,000
Executive Secretary: Brian Schrag
E-Mail: appe@indiana.edu

Historical Note
APPE members are academic and other professionals with an interest in the field of practical and professional ethics. Membership: $25-250/year (individual); $150/year (institution); $500/year (sustaining).

Meetings/Conferences:
Annual Meetings: Winter
2007 – Cincinnati, OH(Hilton Cincinnati Netherland Plaza)/Feb. 23-25

Publications:
Call for Papers. 1/yr.
Ethically Speaking Newsletter. 2/year.
Member Directory and Profiles. 1/yr.

Association for Preservation Technology International *(1968)*
4513 Lincoln Ave.
Suite 213
Lisle, IL 60532
Tel: (630)968-6400 *Fax:* (888)723-4242
E-Mail: information@apti.org
Web Site: www.apti.org
Members: 1500 individuals
Staff: 7
Annual Budget: $100-250,000
Administrative Director: Tim Seeden

Historical Note
Organized in Canada in 1968 and relocated to the United States in 1988. APT members are preservationists, architects, conservators, consultants, contractors, craftspersons, curators, developers, educators, engineers, historians, landscape architects, technicians and others involved in the systematic application of methods and materials to the maintenance, conservation and protection of historic buildings, sites and artifact resources for future use and appreciation. Membership: Graduated scale; phone calls for further information are welcome.

Meetings/Conferences:
Annual Meetings: Fall

Publications:
APT Bulletin. 3/yr.
Communique. q.

Association for Professionals in Infection Control and Epidemiology *(1972)*
1275 K St. NW
Suite 1000
Washington, DC 20005-4006
Tel: (202)789-1890 *Fax:* (202)789-1899
E-Mail: apic@apic.org
Web Site: www.apic.org
Members: 11500 individuals
Staff: 21
Annual Budget: $5-10,000,000
Chief Executive Officer: Kathy Warye
E-Mail: apic@apic.org
Senior Director, Education and Research: Shawn Boynes

Historical Note
Formerly (1992) Association for Practitioners in Infection Control. APIC members are physicians, nurses, medical technologists, sanitarians and others professionally concerned with the practice and management of infection control and epidemiology in all health settings. Membership: $155/year (domestic); $2,150/year (patron member).

Meetings/Conferences:
Annual Meetings: Summer
2007 – San Jose, CA/June 24-28
2008 – Denver, CO(Hyatt Regency Convention Center)/June 15-19
2009 – Fort Lauderdale, FL(Broward Convention Center)/June 7-9

Publications:
APIC Guidelines and Standards.
AJIC. bi-m. adv.
APIC News. bi-m. adv.

Association for Psychoanalytic Medicine *(1945)*
333 Central Park West
New York, NY 10025
Tel: (718)548-6088 *Fax:* (212)866-4817
Web Site: www.theapm.org
Members: 240 individuals
Staff: 2
Annual Budget: under $10,000
President: Dr. Lila J. Kalinich

Historical Note
Formerly Association for Psychoanalytic and Psychosomatic Medicine. Affiliated with American Psychoanalytic Association. Membership: $265/year.

Meetings/Conferences:
Annual Meetings: June, always in New York City

Publications:
Bulletin. a.

Association for Psychological Type *(1979)*

Historical Note
Address unknown in 2006.

Association for Public Policy Analysis and Management *(1979)*
P.O. Box 18766
Washington, DC 20036-8766
Tel: (202)496-0130 *Fax:* (202)496-0134
E-Mail: appam@appam.org
Web Site: www.appam.org
Members: 2000 individuals
Staff: 3
Annual Budget: $500-1,000,000
Executive Director: Erik Devereux
E-Mail: appam@appam.org
Membership and Business Affairs Coordinator: David Hartwell
E-Mail: appam@appam.org
Database and Information Systems Coordinator: Nadia Tyme

Historical Note
APPAM members are individuals and institutions with an interest in the teaching, research or practice of public policy analysis. Membership: $60-100/year (individual); $35/year (student); and $1,500/year (institution).

Meetings/Conferences:
Annual Meetings: Fall
2007 – Washington, DC(Washington Marriott)/Nov. 8-10/1400
2008 – Los Angeles, CA(Wilshire Grand Hotel)/Nov. 5-7/900

Publications:
Preliminary Conference Program. a. adv.
Final Conference Program. a. adv.
Journal of Policy Analysis and Mangement. q. adv.
APPAM News. q.

Association for Quality and Participation *(1977)*

Historical Note
Absorbed by American Society for Quality in 2002.

Association for Recorded Sound Collections *(1966)*
P.O. Box 543
Annapolis, MD 21404-0543
Tel: (410)956-5600 Ext: 248
Web Site: www.arsc-audio.org
Members: 1100 individuals
Staff: 1
Annual Budget: $25-50,000
Executive Director: Peter Shambarger
E-Mail: shambarger@sprynet.com

Historical Note
ARSC serves the scholarly interests and concerns of the private collector, discographer, librarian, sound archivist, historian, recording preservation engineer, and specialty dealer and appraiser. ARSC fosters the development of discographic information in all fields and periods of recording and encourages the preservation of historical recordings. Membership: $40/year (institutional); $80/year (sustaining member); and $36/year (individual).

Meetings/Conferences:
Annual Meetings: Spring

Publications:
Journal. semi-a. adv.
Newsletter. q. adv.
Membership Directory. bien. adv.

Association for Research in Nervous and Mental Disease *(1920)*
Dept. of Psychiatry, 1300 York Ave.
Room F-1231, Box 171
New York, NY 10021
Tel: (570)839-0296 *Fax:* (570)839-0297
E-Mail: arnmd@arnmd.org
Web Site: www.arnmd.org
Members: 500 individuals
Annual Budget: $500-1,000,000
Executive Director: Annlouise Goodermuth

Historical Note
Established as the Neuropsychiatric Research Society; assumed its present name in 1922. Membership: $150/year (individual).

Meetings/Conferences:
Annual Meetings: First Friday & Saturday in December in New York City

Publications:
Proceedings. a.

Association for Research in Otolaryngology *(1973)*
19 Mantua Road
Mt. Royal, NJ 08061
Tel: (856)423-0041 *Fax:* (856)423-3420
E-Mail: headquarters@aro.org
Web Site: www.aro.org
Members: 2000 individuals
Staff: 4
Annual Budget: $250-500,000
Executive Director: Darla Dobson
E-Mail: headquarters@aro.org

Historical Note
ARO is a scientific society of researchers who investigate basic science and clincal problems associated with hearing, speech, the sense of balance, smell, taste and diseases of the head and neck.

Membership: $110/year (regular); $50/year (associate).

Meetings/Conferences:
Annual Meetings: February

Publications:
Journal of the Association for Research in Otolaryngology. q. adv.
ARO Directory. a.

Association for Research in Vision and Ophthalmology *(1928)*
12300 Twinbrook Pkwy.
Suite 250
Rockville, MD 20852-1606
Tel: (240)221-2900 *Fax:* (240)221-0370
E-Mail: exec@arvo.org
Web Site: www.arvo.org
Members: 11370 individuals
Staff: 21
Annual Budget: $500-1,000,000
Executive Director: Joanne G. Angle
E-Mail: exec@arvo.org
Manager, Meetings: Nancy Copen
E-Mail: exec@arvo.org

Historical Note
Founded as the Association for Research in Ophthalmology and incorporated in New York in 1936; assumed its present name in 1970. Works to promote research opportunities in the vision sciences. Membership: $155/year (regular member); $70/year (student without journal); $75/year (student with IOVS).

Meetings/Conferences:
Annual Meetings: May

Publications:
ARVO Newsletter. semi-a.
Investigative Ophthalmology and Visual Science. m. adv.

Association for Retail Technology Standards *(1973)*
325 Seventh St. NW
Suite 1000
Washington, DC 20004
Tel: (202)626-8182 *Fax:* (202)626-8166
E-Mail: arts@arf.org
Web Site: www.nrf-arts.org
Members: 230 individuals
Staff: 3
Executive Director: Richard E. Mader

Historical Note
An affiliate of National Retail Federation, ARTS members are retailers and vendors of retail and business systems and software. ARTS promotes the adoption of standards for technology solutions in the retail sector. Membership: Based on annual sales.

Publications:
ARTS Member Monthly. m.

Association for Science Teacher Education *(1953)*
113 Radcliff Dr.
Pittsburgh, PA 15237
Tel: (412)624-2861
Web Site: http://theaste.org
Members: 850 individuals
Annual Budget: $50-100,000
Executive Secretary: Dr. Eugene Wagner

Historical Note
Founded as Association for the Education of Teachers of Science; assumed its current name in 2004. Affiliated with the National Science Teachers Association. Has no paid officers or full-time staff. Membership: $75/year.

Meetings/Conferences:
Annual Meetings: Spring, with the Nat'l Science Teachers Ass'n

Publications:
Journal of Elementary Science Education. semi-a.
Journal of Science Teacher Education. q.
AETS Newsletter. q.
Science Education. q. adv.

Association for Social Anthropology in Oceania *(1967)*
Melanesian Studies Resource Center, University of California
SSH Library 0175R
San Diego, CA 92093
Tel: (858)534-2029 *Fax:* (858)534-7548
Web Site: www.asao.org
Members: 375 individuals
Annual Budget: under $10,000
Treasurer: Kathy Creely

Historical Note
Formerly known as the Association for Social Anthropology in Eastern Oceania. Has no paid officers or full-time staff. Membership: $35/year (individual); $20/year (student).

Meetings/Conferences:
Annual Meetings: Alternates West & East Coasts & Hawaii/February
2007 - Charlottesville, VA(Omni Hotel)/Feb. 21-24

Publications:
ASAO Newsletter. 3/year.

Association for Social Economics *(1941)*
c/o Education Management Information Systems
7116 Wandering Oak Road
Austin, TX 78749
Tel: (512)288-5988 *Fax:* (512)288-5989
E-Mail: email@edmis.com
Web Site: www.socialeconomics.org
Members: 300 individuals
Annual Budget: $25-50,000
Secretary: Elba K. Brown-Collier

Historical Note
Formerly (1965) Catholic Economic Association. Has no paid officers or full-time staff. Membership: $35-45/year.

Meetings/Conferences:
Annual Meetings: In January, with the Allied Social Science Ass'n

Publications:
Forum for Social Economics. semi-a.
Review of Social Economy. q.

Association for Specialists in Group Work *(1973)*

Historical Note
A division of the American Counseling Association, which provides administrative support.

Association for Spiritual, Ethical and Religious Values in Counseling *(1955)*

Historical Note
A division of the American Counseling Association, which provides administrative support.

Association for Supervision and Curriculum Development *(1943)*
1703 N. Beauregard St.
Alexandria, VA 22311-1714
Tel: (703)578-9600 *Fax:* (703)575-5400
E-Mail: member@ascd.org
Web Site: www.ascd.org
Members: 175000 individuals
Staff: 200
Annual Budget: $25-50,000,000
Co-Executive Director and Chief Executive Officer: Gene R. Carter
Co-Executive Director and Chief Financial Officer: Eric Bellamy
E-Mail: member@ascd.org
Chief Human Resources and Administration Officer: Deborah Hall
E-Mail: member@ascd.org
Deputy Executive Director and Chief Constituent Partnerships Officer: Judy Seltz
E-Mail: member@ascd.org
Deputy Executive Director and Chief Program Development Officer: Michelle "Mikki" Lambert Terry
E-Mail: member@ascd.org

Historical Note
Formed in 1943 by a merger of the Society for Curriculum Study (1929) and the Department of Supervisors and Directors of Instruction of the National Education Association, to form the Department of Supervision and Curriculum Development of NEA. Changed to its present title in 1946. Became independent of NEA in 1975. Initiates and supports activities to provide educational equity for all students, and serves as a leader in education information services. ASCD has members in more than 135 countries; members include superintendents, principals, teachers, professors of education, school board members, students, and parents who share a commitment to quality education and a belief that all students can learn in a well-planned educational program. Membership: $29-189/year.

Meetings/Conferences:
Annual Meetings: Spring
2007 - Anaheim, CA(Anaheim Convention Center)/March 17-19

Publications:
Education Update. m.
Infobrief. q.
Research Brief. m.
Educational Leadership. m. adv.

Association for Surgical Education *(1980)*
Department of Surgery, SIU School of Medicine
P.O. Box 19655
Springfield, IL 62794-9655
Tel: (217)545-3835 *Fax:* (217)545-2431
Web Site: www.surgicaleducation.com
Members: 850 individuals and organizations
Staff: 2
Annual Budget: $100-250,000
Executive Director: Susan Kepner
E-Mail: skepner@siumed.edu

Historical Note
ASE works specifically to improve surgical education among medical students. Membership: $50/year (individual); $300/year (organization).

Meetings/Conferences:
Annual Meetings: April

Publications:
Focus on Surgical Education. q.

Association for Symbolic Logic *(1936)*
Vassar College
124 Raymond Ave., Box 742
Poughkeepsie, NY 12604
Tel: (845)437-7080 *Fax:* (845)437-7830
E-Mail: asl@vassar.edu
Web Site: www.aslonline.org
Members: 1450 individuals
Staff: 2
Annual Budget: $250-500,000
Administrator: Fran Whitney
E-Mail: asl@vassar.edu

Historical Note
Founded and incorporated in Rhode Island in 1936. Affiliated with the American Mathematical Society, the Conference Board of the Mathematical Sciences and the International Union for the History and Philosophy of Science. Promotes research and studies in mathematical logic and related fields. Membership: $76/year (individual); $625/year (institution); $1100/year (corporate associate); $3,000/year (corporate); $38/year (student).

Meetings/Conferences:
2007 - Gainesville, FL/March 10-13

Publications:
Bulletin of Symbolic Logic. q.
Journal of Symbolic Logic. q.
ASL Newsletter. q.

Association for Technology in Music Instruction *(1975)*
c/o College Music Society
312 E. Pine St.
Missoula, MT 59802
Tel: (406)728-1152 *Fax:* (406)721-9419
Web Site: www.music.org/atmi
Members: 300 individuals
Staff: 1
Annual Budget: under $10,000
President: Scott Lipscomb

Historical Note
Formerly (1986) National Consortium for Computer-Based Music Instruction. ATMI members are music teachers and others interested in the application of computers in music instruction. Membership: $40/year (individual); $40/year (foreign).

Meetings/Conferences:
Annual Meetings: In conjunction with the College Music Soc.
2007 - Salt Lake City, UT(Little America)/Nov. 15-18/400

Publications:
Technology Directory.
ATMI Newsletter. q.

Association for Textual Scholarship in Art History *(1991)*
112 Charles St.
Boston, MA 02114
Tel: (617)367-1679 *Fax:* (617)557-2962
Web Site: www.uml.edu/Dept/History/ArtHistory/ATSAH/
Members: 65 individuals
Annual Budget: under $10,000
President: Liana Cheney

Historical Note
ATSAH members are academics and others with an interest in the study and publication of primary sources for art history. Membership: $20/year.

Publications:
Newsletter. semi-a.

Association for the Advancement of Applied Sport Psychology *(1986)*
2810 Crossroads Dr.
Suite 3800
Madison, WI 53718
Tel: (608)443-2475 *Fax:* (608)443-2478
Members: 1000 individuals
Annual Budget: $100-250,000

Historical Note
AAASP promotes the development of psychological theory, research and intervention strategies in sport psychology; provides a forum for individuals who are interested in research and theory development and in the application of psychological principles in sport and exercise; and is also concerned with ethical and professional issues relating to the development of sport psychology and to the provision of psychological services in sport and exercise settings. Membership: $90/year (professional/affiliate); $50/year (student).

Meetings/Conferences:
Annual Meetings: September-October
2007 - Louisville, KY

Publications:
AAASP Newsletter. 3/year. adv.
Journal of Applied Sport Psychology. semi-a.

Association for the Advancement of Automotive Medicine *(1957)*
P.O. Box 4176
Barrington, IL 60011
Tel: (847)844-3880 *Fax:* (847)844-3884
E-Mail: info@aaam.org
Web Site: www.aaam.org
Members: 600 individuals
Staff: 3
Annual Budget: $250-500,000
Administrative Director: Irene Herzau
E-Mail: info@aaam.org

Historical Note
Formerly (1988) the American Association for Automotive Medicine. Organized in 1957 and incorporated in Florida. Encourages and promotes the growth and dissemination of new knowledge in the field of traffic and highway safety. Membership is composed of physicians, researchers, educators, engineers, administrators, and other highway and traffic medicine professionals. Membership: $260/year (individual); $2,600/year (company).

Meetings/Conferences:
Annual Meetings: Fall
2007 - Melbourne, Australia/Oct. 14-17/200

Publications:
Inroads. q.
Proceedings. a.

Association for the Advancement of Baltic Studies *(1968)*
14743 Braemar Crescent Way
Darnestown, MD 20878-3911
Tel: (301)977-8491 *Fax:* (301)977-8492
E-Mail: juberts.aabs@verizon.net
Web Site: http://depts.washington.edu/aabs/
Members: 700 individuals
Staff: 2
Annual Budget: $100-250,000
Administrative Executive Director: Anita Juberts
E-Mail: juberts.aabs@verizon.net

Historical Note
Formed to promote research and education in Baltic studies (history, literature, linquistics, social sciences). Membership is open to anyone wishing to support these aims. Membership: $60/year (individual); $25/student; $2,000 (life member).

Meetings/Conferences:
2008 - Bloomington, IN

Publications:
Journal of Baltic Studies. q. adv.

Association for the Advancement of Computing in Education *(1981)*
P.O. Box 1545
Chesapeake, VA 23327-1545
Tel: (757)366-5606 *Fax:* (757)997-8860
E-Mail: info@aace.org
Web Site: www.aace.org
Executive Director: Gary H. Marks
E-Mail: info@aace.org

Historical Note
AACE members are educators and academics interested in the application of information technology to teaching.

Meetings/Conferences:
Annual Meetings: Spring
2007 - San Antonio, TX/March 26-30

Publications:
EDUCTECH. 2/m.

Association for the Advancement of Cost Engineering

Historical Note
See AACE International.

Association for the Advancement of International Education *(1966)*
AAIE Office, Sheridan College
P.O. Box 1500
Sheridan, WY 82801-1500
Tel: (307)674-6446 Ext: 5201 *Fax:* (307)674-7205
E-Mail: aaie@sheridan.edu
Web Site: www.aaie.org
Members: 550 individuals
Staff: 2
Annual Budget: $250-500,000
Executive Director: Richard Krajczar
E-Mail: aaie@sheridan.edu
Executive Assistant: Annie Jenkins

Historical Note
AAIE is a support organization for American International schools abroad. Members include head administrators of American International schools located in major cities worldwide. U.S. membership includes superintendents of U.S. schools and college/university deans, presidents and others who have an interest in American international schools. Membership: $95-350/year; conference registration $220-360/year.

Meetings/Conferences:
Annual Meetings: Winter

Publications:
Conference Directory. a. adv.
Inter-Ed. 2/year. adv.

Association for the Advancement of Medical Instrumentation *(1967)*
1110 N. Glebe Road
Suite 220
Arlington, VA 22201
Tel: (703)525-4890 *Fax:* (703)276-0793
Toll Free: (800)332 - 2264
E-Mail: customerservice@aami.org
Web Site: www.aami.org
Members: 7000 individuals
Staff: 37
Annual Budget: $5-10,000,000
President: Michael J. Miller, JD
E-Mail: customerservice@aami.org
Executive Vice President: Elizabeth Bridgman
E-Mail: customerservice@aami.org
Vice President, Marketing and Communications: Steve Campbell
E-Mail: customerservice@aami.org
Vice President, Finance and Administration: Sylvia E. Chandler
E-Mail: customerservice@aami.org
Vice President, Education: Chris Dinegar
E-Mail: customerservice@aami.org
Vice President, Membership Development: Lori Freeman
E-Mail: customerservice@aami.org
Vice President, Standards Development: Joe Lewelling
E-Mail: customerservice@aami.org
Senior Vice President, Education and Government Programs: Leah Lough
E-Mail: customerservice@aami.org
Vice President, Standards, Policy and Procedures: Theresa Zuraski
E-Mail: customerservice@aami.org

Historical Note
A non-profit multi-disciplinary association of engineering, medicine and government professionals and organizations involved in the development, use and management of medical technology. Founded and incorporated in Massachusetts in 1967. Absorbed American College of Physician Inventors in 1997. Membership: $185/year (individual); varies (institutional/corporate).

Meetings/Conferences:
Annual Meetings: Spring and Fall
2007 - Boston, MA/June 16-18

Publications:
Biomedical Instrumentation & Technology Journal. bi-m. adv.
AAMI Membership Directory. a. adv.

Association for the Advancement of Psychoanalysis

Historical Note
Became Nat'l Ass'n for the Advancement of Psychoanalysis in 2003.

Association for the Advancement of Psychology *(1974)*
P.O. Box 38129
Colorado Springs, CO 80937-8129
Tel: (719)520-0688 *Fax:* (719)520-0375
Toll Free: (800)869 - 6595
Web Site: www.aapnet.org
Members: 6000 individuals
Staff: 2
Annual Budget: $250-500,000
Executive Director: Stephen M. Pfeiffer, Ph.D.
E-Mail: smpfeiffer@aapnet.org
Administrator: Karen Rivard
E-Mail: krivard@aapnet.org

Historical Note
Merged in 1975 with the Council for the Advancement of the Psychological Professions and Sciences (1971). Members are psychologists and educators. Works in close alliance with the American Psychological Association. Primarily a government liaison operation. Supports Psychologists for Legislative Action Now (PLAN). Membership: $95/year (individual); $150/year (organization/company).

Meetings/Conferences:
Annual Meetings: August, with the American Psychological Ass'n.

Publications:
AAP Advance Plan. q.

Association for the Advancement of Psychotherapy *(1939)*
Belfer Educational Center
1300 Morris Park Ave., Room 405
Bronx, NY 10461
Tel: (718)430-3503 *Fax:* (718)430-8907
Toll Free: (888)257 - 7924
E-Mail: info@ajp.org
Web Site: www.ajp.org
Members: 350 individuals
Staff: 2
Annual Budget: $100-250,000
President and Editor-in-Chief: T. Byram Karasu, M.D.

E-Mail: info@ajp.org
Historical Note
AAP serves as a forum for clinical and theoretical findings in the field of psychotherapy. Membership: $64/year (individual); $91/year (organization).
Meetings/Conferences:
Quarterly Meetings: always New York, NY
Publications:
American Journal of Psychotherapy. q.

Association for the Advancement of Wound Care *(1995)*
83 General Warren Blvd.
Suite 100
Malvern, PA 19355
Tel: (610)560-0500 Ext: 223 *Fax:* (610)560-0502
Toll Free: (866)229 - 2999 Ext:
E-Mail: tthomas@aawcone.org
Web Site: www.aawcone.org
Members: 1600 individuals
Staff: 1
Annual Budget: $100-250,000
Executive Director: Tina Thomas
E-Mail: tthomas@aawcone.org
Historical Note
AAWC is an interdisciplinary association serving medical professionals, patients and lay caregivers interested in wound care. Membership: $120/year (clinician); $50/year (student); $300/year (organization, industry or facility); $25/year (patient/lay caregiver).
Meetings/Conferences:
Annual Meetings: *Spring*
2007 - Tampa, FL(Convention Center)/Apr. 28-May 1
Publications:
Ostomy/Wound Management Journal. m. adv.
Wounds Official Journal. m. adv.
AAWC Newsletter. q.
AAWC Networking Directory. a. adv.

Association for the Behavioral Sciences and Medical Education *(1970)*
1460 N. Center Road
Burton, MI 48509
Tel: (810)715-4365 *Fax:* (810)715-4371
E-Mail: admin@absame.org
Web Site: www.absame.org
Members: 140 individuals
Staff: 2
Annual Budget: $25-50,000
Executive Director: Mark Vogel
E-Mail: vogel@absame.org
Coordinator, National Office: Cyndee Lehner
E-Mail: admin@absame.org
Meetings/Conferences:
Annual Meetings: *Fall*
2007 - Copper, CO(Copper Convention Center)/Oct. 17-21/150
Publications:
Annals of Behavioral Sciences & Medical Education. 2/year. adv.
Newsletter of ABSAME. q. adv.

Association for the Bibliography of History *(1978)*
Lockwood Library, Room 321
SUNY at Buffalo
Buffalo, NY 14260
Tel: (716)645-2817 *Fax:* (716)645-3859
Web Site: www.h-net.msu.edu/~histbibl/abh.html
Members: 100 individuals
Annual Budget: under $10,000
Secretary, Treasurer: Charles A. D'Aniello
E-Mail: lclcharl@acsu.buffalo.edu
Historical Note
Established in San Francisco at the 1978 annual meeting of the American Historical Association. Members are historians and librarians interested in developing better bibliographic tools and skills for historical research. Membership: $10/year.
Meetings/Conferences:
Annual Meetings:
Publications:
ABH Bulletin. 3/year. adv.

Association for the Calligraphic Arts *(1997)*
2774 Countryside Blvd., #2
Clearwater, FL 33761
E-Mail: aca@calligraphicarts.org
Web Site: www.calligraphicarts.org
Members: 800 individuals
Staff: 1
Annual Budget: $25-50,000
Executive Director: Joan Merrell
Publications:
Newsletter. q. adv.

Association for the Development of Religious Information Systems *(1971)*
P.O. Box 210735
Nashville, TN 37221-0735
Tel: (615)429-8744 *Fax:* (508)632-0370
E-Mail: editor@adris.org
Web Site: www.adris.org
Members: 500 individuals
Staff: 2
Annual Budget: under $10,000
Editor: Edward W. Dodds
Historical Note
ADRIS provides a forum for the exchange of information on religious-topic databases and information systems, bringing together academic, religious, and commercial users.
Publications:
ADRIS Newsletter. q.
Internat'l Directory of Religious Information Systems.

Association for the Education of Teachers of Science
Historical Note
Became Association for Science Teacher Education in 2004.

Association for the Environmental Health of Soils *(1989)*
150 Fearing St.
Amherst, MA 01002
Tel: (413)549-5170 *Fax:* (413)549-0579
Toll Free: (888)540 - 2347
E-Mail: info@aehs.com
Web Site: www.aehs.com
Members: 600 individuals
Staff: 6
Annual Budget: $250-500,000
Executive Director: Paul T. Kostecki, Ph.D.
Historical Note
AEHS is a multi-disciplinary association providing a forum for individual professionals concerned with soil protection and cleanup. Fields represented include chemistry, geology, hydrogeology, law, engineering, modeling, toxicology, regulatory science, public health and public policy. Membership: $125/year (individual) and $75/year (student).
Meetings/Conferences:
Annual Meetings: *March*
Publications:
Soil and Sediment Contamination. 6/year. adv.
Matrix Newsletter. bi-a. adv.
Soil & Groundwater Cleanup Magazine. 6/year.
International Journal of Phytoremediation. q.

Association for the Sociology of Religion *(1938)*
618 S.W. Second Ave.
Galva, IL 61434-1912
Tel: (309)932-2727 *Fax:* (309)932-2282
Web Site: www.sociologyofreligion.com
Members: 800 individuals
Staff: 1
Annual Budget: $100-250,000
Executive Officer: William H. Swatos, Jr., Ph.D
E-Mail: bill4329@hotmail.com
Historical Note
Formerly (1938) American Catholic Sociological Society; assumed present name in 1971. ASR is an international scholarly association that seeks to advance theory and research in the sociology of religion. Has no paid staff. Membership: $35/year (individual); $75/year (company).
Meetings/Conferences:
Annual Meetings: August, prior to the American Sociological Ass'n meeting/250
2007 - New York, NY(Marriott Marquis)/Aug. 13-15
2008 - Boston, MA(Park Plaza)/July 31-Aug. 2
2009 - San Francisco, CA(Sir Francis Drake)/Aug. 10-12
2010 - Atlanta, GA/Aug. 9-11
Publications:
News & Announcements. q.
Religion and the Social Order. a.
Sociology of Religion: A Quarterly Review. q. adv.

Association for the Study of African American Life and History *(1915)*
Howard University/ Powell Bldg.
525 Bryant St., Suite C142
Washington, DC 20059
Tel: (202)865-0053 *Fax:* (202)265-7920
E-Mail: executivedirector@asalh.net
Web Site: www.asalh.org
Members: 3300 individuals
Staff: 5
Annual Budget: $250-500,000
President: Sheila Y. Flemming-Hunter
E-Mail: executivedirector@asalh.net
Executive Director: Sylvia Y. Cyrus-Albritton
E-Mail: executivedirector@asalh.net
President: Sheila Y. Flemming-Hunter
E-Mail: executivedirector@asalh.net
Historical Note
Organized by Dr. Carter G. Woodson in Chicago September 9, 1915 as the Association for the Study of Negro Life and History and incorporated in the District of Columbia the same year. Assumed its present name in 1973. Promotes an appreciation of the life and history of Afro-Americans, creates an understanding of their present status and works to improve their promise for the future. Membership: fees vary.
Meetings/Conferences:
Annual Meetings: *October*
Publications:
Journal of African American History. 4/yr. adv.
Black History Bulletin. 2/yr. adv.
Annual Black History Theme Magazine and Products. a. adv.

Association for the Study of Classical African Civilizations *(1984)*
2274 W. 20th St.
Los Angeles, CA 90018
Tel: (323)730-1155 *Fax:* (323)731-0665
E-Mail: info@ascac.org
Web Site: www.ascac.org
Members: 1000 individuals
Staff: 2
International President: Nzinga Ratibisha Heru
E-Mail: info@ascac.org
Historical Note
ASCAC members are individuals with an interest in the study of African civilizations.
Publications:
Critical Commentaries. a.

Association for the Study of Dreams *(1983)*
1672 University Ave.
Berkeley, CA 94703
Tel: (209)724-0889 *Fax:* (209)724-9319
E-Mail: office@asdreams.org
Web Site: www.ASDreams.org
Members: 800 individuals
Staff: 1
Annual Budget: $25-50,000
Office Manager: Richard Wilkerson
E-Mail: office@asdreams.org
Historical Note
Incorporated in California, ASD was established as a multidisciplinary organization to promote the study of dreams. Members are individuals with serious interests in dreams. Among the disciplines represented are: anthropology, comparative literature, education, medicine, psychology, religion, and social work. Membership: $85/year (individual); $55/year

(student); $120/year (couple); and $150/year (patron).

Meetings/Conferences:

Annual Meetings: July

Publications:

Dream Time. q.
Dreaming Professional Journal. q.

Association for the Study of Food and Society *(1986)*

Dept. of Nutrition & Food Studies/NYU
35 W. Fourth St., Tenth Floor
New York, NY 10012-1172
Tel: (212)998-5580 *Fax:* (212)995-4194
Web Site: http://food-culture.org
Members: 200 individuals
Annual Budget: $10-25,000
Treasurer: Jennifer Berg

Historical Note

ASFS is an interdisciplinary international organization dedicated to the complex relationship between food and society. ASFS members are sociologists, anthropologists, nutritionists, dieticians and others with an interest in sociological aspects of food. Has no paid officers or full-time staff. Membership: $55/year; $30/year (student).

Meetings/Conferences:

Annual Meetings: Annual meetings in conjunction with the Food, Agriculture, and Human Values Society.

Publications:

Journal of Appetite. a.
Newsletter. semi-a.
Journal of the Ass'n for the Study of Food and Society. a.
Directory. a.
Abstracts of Annual Meeting. a.
ASFS Newsletter. semi-a.

Association for the Study of Higher Education *(1975)*

424 Erickson Hall
Michigan State University
East Lansing, MI 48824
Tel: (517)432-8805 *Fax:* (517)432-8806
E-Mail: ashemsu@msu.edu
Web Site: www.ashe.ws
Members: 1800 individuals
Staff: 2
Annual Budget: $100-250,000
Executive Director: Dennis Brown

Historical Note

ASHE is a professional society of scholars, researchers, practitioners and graduate students dedicated to the advancement of higher education as a field of study. Membership: $80/year (individual); $50/year (student); $50/year (emeritus).

Meetings/Conferences:

2007 – Louisville, KY(Marriott)/Nov. 7-10

Publications:

Review of Higher Education. q.
ASHE Newsletter. q.

Association for the Study of Nationalities *(1971)*

420 W. 118th St.
New York, NY 10027
Tel: (212)854-8487 *Fax:* (212)666-3481
E-Mail: gnb12@columbia.edu
Web Site: www.nationalities.org
Members: 825 individuals
Staff: 4
Annual Budget: $250-500,000
Treasurer: Gordon Bardos

Historical Note

ASN members are academics and others with an interest in the study of nationalities issues and ethnic problems in eastern Europe and the former USSR. Membership: $40/year (individual); $25/year (student); $194/year (institutional).

Meetings/Conferences:

Semi-annual Meetings: New York, NY/April & with AAASP/Fall

Publications:

Nationalities Papers. q.
Analysis of Current Events. m.
ASNet. q.
ASN Membership Directory. a.

Association for the Study of Play *(1974)*

East Tennessee State Univ.
P.O. Box 70548
Johnson City, TN 37614
Tel: (423)439-7903
Web Site: www.csuchico.edu/phed/tasp
Members: 180 individuals
Annual Budget: under $10,000
Treasurer: Laurelle Phillips

Historical Note

Formerly (1987) Association for the Anthropological Study of Play. TASP's broad focus includes many disciplines and scholarly interests involved with the study of play. Has no paid officers or full-time staff. Membership: $65/year (professional membership); $55/year (student/retiree); $25/year (institution).

Meetings/Conferences:

Annual Meetings:

Publications:

TASP Newsletter. 3/year.

Association for the Treatment of Sexual Abusers *(1984)*

4900 S.W. Griffith Dr.
Suite 274
Beaverton, OR 97005
Tel: (503)643-1023 *Fax:* (503)643-5084
Web Site: www.atsa.com
Members: 2300 individuals
Staff: 3
Annual Budget: $500-1,000,000
Executive Director: John Gruber

Historical Note

ATSA members are professionals treating sexual offenders and/or their victims. Among its activities are the development and dissemination of professional standards and practices in the field of sex offender research, evaluation and treatment. Membership: $140/year (individual); $35/year (student).

Meetings/Conferences:

Annual Meetings: Fall

Publications:

ATSA Standards and Guidelines.
ATSA Professional Code of Ethics.
Sexual Abuse: A Journal of Research and Treatment. q. adv.
The Forum: A Professional Newsletter. q.

Association for Theatre in Higher Education *(1986)*

P.O. Box 1290
Boulder, CO 80306-1290
Tel: (303)530-2167 *Fax:* (303)530-2168
Toll Free: (888)284 - 3737
E-Mail: info@athe.org
Web Site: www.athe.org
Members: 1,800 individuals
Annual Budget: $100-250,000
Administrative Director: Nancy Erickson

Publications:

ATHENEWS. 3/yr.
Membership Directory and Theatre Publications. a. adv.
Theatre Journal. q. adv.
Theatre Topics. semi-a.

Association for Transpersonal Psychology *(1971)*

P.O. Box 50187
Palo Alto, CA 94303
Tel: (650)424-8764 *Fax:* (650)618-1851
E-Mail: info@atpweb.org
Web Site: www.atpweb.org
Members: 1200 individuals
Staff: 1
Annual Budget: $100-250,000
Office Manager: David S. Molina
E-Mail: info@atpweb.org

Historical Note

ATP members are professionals and others with an interest in transpersonal psychology. Membership: $55/year (student); $50/year (international); $75/year (general); $95/year (professional); $150/year (organizational); $175/year (supporting).

Publications:

Directory of Professional Members. a.
Reflections E-Mail Newsletter. q.
Journal of Transpersonal Psychology. semi-a.
Listing of Schools and Programs. a.

Association for Tropical Biology and Conservation *(1963)*

Nat'l Museum of Natural History, Botany Dept., MRC-166
P.O. Box 37012
Washington, DC 20013-7012
Tel: (202)633-0920 *Fax:* (202)786-2563
E-Mail: kressj@si.edu
Web Site: www.atbio.org
Members: 1500 individuals
Staff: 3
Annual Budget: $50-100,000
Executive Director: W. John Kress

Historical Note

Membership: $25-65/year (individual); $120/year (institution).

Meetings/Conferences:

Annual: 400-1000

Publications:

Biotropica. q. adv.
Tropinet. q. adv.

Association for University and College Counseling Center Directors *(1951)*

University Counseling Center
Colorado State Univ.
Ft. Collins, CO 80523-8010
Tel: (970)491-1613 *Fax:* (970)491-2382
E-Mail: charles.davidshofer@colostate.edu
Web Site: www.auccd.org
Members: 600 individuals
Annual Budget: $25-50,000
Treasurer: Charles Davidshofer
E-Mail: charles.davidshofer@colostate.edu

Historical Note

Members are directors of counseling centers on college and university campuses. Has no paid officers or full-time staff. Membership: $130/year.

Meetings/Conferences:

Annual Meetings: October

Association for University Business and Economic Research *(1947)*

Univ. of Colorado
420 UCB
Boulder, CO 80309-0420
Tel: (303)492-8227 *Fax:* (303)492-3620
Web Site: www.auber.org
Members: 130 individuals
Staff: 1
Annual Budget: $10-25,000
Secretary-Treasurer: Richard Wobbekind
E-Mail: wobbekind@colorado.edu

Historical Note

AUBER is the professional association of business and economic research organizations in public and private universities.

Publications:

AUBER Newsletter. q.

Association for Unmanned Vehicle Systems International *(1972)*

2700 S. Quincy St.
Suite 400
Arlington, VA 22206
Tel: (703)845-9671 *Fax:* (703)845-9679
E-Mail: info@auvsi.org
Web Site: www.auvsi.org
Members: 5000 individuals
Staff: 9
Annual Budget: $500-1,000,000
Executive Director: Daryl Davidson
E-Mail: wherry@auvsi.org
Director, Conferences and Exposition Services: Staci Butler
Editor: Ramon Lopez
Manager, Chapter Relations and Membership: Karen McMullen
Director, Finance and Administration: Mary Alice Pickens
Manager, Marketing and Communications: Gretchen Wherry

Historical Note
Established in Dayton, Ohio as the National Association for Remotely Piloted Vehicles; assumed its present name in 1977. Members are companies and individuals concerned with the development and manufacture of unmanned vehicles. Membership: $50/year (individual); $750-5,000/year (corporate); $500/year (academic institution).

Publications:
Convention Proceedings. a. adv.
Membership Directory. a.
Unmanned Systems Magazine. bi-m. adv.

Association for Wedding Professionals International *(1995)*
6700 Freeport Blvd.
Sacramento, CA 95822
Tel: (916)392-5000 *Fax:* (916)392-5222
Toll Free: (800)242 - 4461
Web Site: www.afwpi.com
Members: 760 companies
Staff: 4
Executive Director: Richard Markel
E-Mail: richard@afwpi.com

Historical Note
AFWPI provides a referral and other promotional and professional services to wedding professionals.

Meetings/Conferences:
2007 – Ventura, CA(Crowne Plaza)/Apr. 22-25

Publications:
The Professional Connection. q. adv.
Membership Directory. semi-a. adv.

Association for Women Geoscientists *(1977)*
P.O. Box 30645
Lincoln, NE 68505-0645
Tel: (402)470-3110
E-Mail: office@awg.org
Web Site: www.awg.org
Members: 1200 individuals
Staff: 1
Annual Budget: $50-100,000
Business Manager: Janelle Gerry
E-Mail: office@awg.org

Historical Note
Established in 1977 in San Francisco as the Association of Women Geoscientists; assumed its present name in 1982 and was incorporated in California in 1983. A member society of the American Geological Institute. Membership includes men and women from petroleum and mineral industries, geotechnical and hydrogeologic consulting, academic faculty, regulatory agencies and research institutions. Membership: $50/year (professional); $100/year (institution); $500/year (corporate); $25/year (students or reduced income members).

Meetings/Conferences:
Semi-Annual Meetings: May and October

Publications:
AWG E-Mail News. m. adv.
Gaea Newsletter. bi-m. adv.

Association for Women in Communications *(1909)*
3337 Duke St.
Alexandria, VA 22314
Tel: (703)370-7436 *Fax:* (703)370-7437
E-Mail: info@womcom.org
Web Site: www.womcom.org
Members: 3500 individuals
Staff: 5
Annual Budget: $250-500,000
Administrator: Pamela Valenzuela, CAE

Historical Note
Founded as Theta Sigma Phi; absorbed Women in Communications, Inc., and assumed its current name in 1996. AWC seeks to improve opportunities for women in the communications industry. Membership: $90/year, plus local dues. Application fee: $50.

Publications:
The Matrix. q.
InterCom. m.

Association for Women in Computing *(1978)*
41 Sutter St., Suite 1006
San Francisco, CA 94104
Tel: (415)905-4663 *Fax:* (415)358-4667
E-Mail: info@awc-hq.org
Web Site: www.awc-hq.org
Members: 800 individuals
Annual Budget: $10-25,000
President: Mary DiFiore Crowe
E-Mail: president@awc-hq.org

Historical Note
AWC is a non-profit professional organization for women and men who have an interest in information and technology. AWC is dedicated to the advancement of women in technology fields. Membership: $25/year (independent/non-chapter); chapter membership fees vary.

Meetings/Conferences:
Annual Meetings: Spring

Publications:
The Source. a. adv.
National Directory. a. adv.

Association for Women in Management
927 15th St. NW
Suite 1000
Washington, DC 20005
Tel: (202)659-6364 *Fax:* (202)371-1467
E-Mail: awm@benefits.net
Web Site: www.womens.org
Staff: 1
President: Bonnie B. Whyte, CAE, CFCI

Historical Note
AWM was formed to support education and research to further development of women in the higher echelons of business. Membership: $199/year (introductory).

Association for Women in Mathematics *(1971)*
11240 Waples Mill Road
Suite 200
Fairfax, VA 22030
Tel: (703)934-0163 *Fax:* (703)359-7562
E-Mail: awm@awm-math.org
Web Site: www.awm-math.org
Members: 4500 individuals & institutions
Annual Budget: $250-500,000
Managing Director: Jennifer Lewis
E-Mail: awm@awm-math.org

Historical Note
Formerly (1973) Association of Women Mathematicians. Members represent education, industry, business and government. Membership: $40/year (individual); $80-120/year (organization).

Meetings/Conferences:
Annual Meetings: with American Mathematical Soc./Mathematical Ass'n of America/January
2007 – New Orleans, LA
2008 – San Diego, CA
2009 – Washington, DC

Publications:
AWM Newsletter. bi-m. adv.

Association for Women in Psychology *(1969)*
Psychology Dept., Mount St. Mary's College
12001 Chalon Road
Los Angeles, CA 90049
Tel: (310)954-4104
E-Mail: kdean@msmc.la.edu
Web Site: www.awpsych.org
Members: 2000 individuals
Annual Budget: $50-100,000
Membership Contact: Karol Dean

Historical Note
Formerly (1970) Association for Women Psychologists. Major objectives are to promote unbiased scientific research on gender in order to establish fact and eliminate myths and assumptions about the "natures" of women and men, to ensure equality of opportunity for women and men in the profession, and encourage research on issues of concern to women of color. Has no paid officers or full-time staff. Membership: $15-$85/year (individual).

Meetings/Conferences:
Annual Meetings: March

Publications:
AWP Member Directory. bien.
AWP Newsletter. 3/yr. adv.

Association for Women in Science *(1971)*
1200 New York Ave. NW
Suite 650
Washington, DC 20005-3920
Tel: (202)326-8940 *Fax:* (202)326-8960
Toll Free: (800)886 - 2947
E-Mail: awis@awis.org
Web Site: www.serve.com/awis
Members: 6000 individuals
Staff: 5
Annual Budget: $250-500,000
Executive Director: Nancy Bakowski

Historical Note
Founded in April, 1971 in Chicago, AWIS has 74 chapters in the U.S. and is dedicated to full participation for women in science, mathematics, engineering and technology. Affiliated with the Federation of Organizations for Professional Women, the American Association for the Advancement of Science, and the National Coalition for Women and Girls in Education. Sponsors the AWIS Predoctoral Awards. Membership: $20-60/year (based on income).

Meetings/Conferences:
Annual Meetings: held in conjunction with American Ass'n for Advancement of Science

Publications:
AWIS Magazine. q. adv.

Association for Women in Sports Media *(1987)*
P.O. Box F
Bayville, NJ 08721-0317
Tel: (732)581-0522
E-Mail: info@awsonline.org
Web Site: www.awsmonline.org
Members: 500 individuals
Annual Budget: $10-25,000
Secretary-Treasurer: Karen Wall Bush
E-Mail: info@awsonline.org

Historical Note
AWSM members are professional women in sports media and the women and men who support them in their work. Membership: $35/year (individual); $20/year (student).

Meetings/Conferences:
Annual Meetings: Summer/120
2007 – Dallas, TX

Publications:
AWSM Newsletter. q.
Membership Directory. a.

Association for Women Journalists
P.O. Box 2199
Ft. Worth, TX 76113
Tel: (817)685-3876
Web Site: www.awjdfw.org
Members: 150 individuals
Co-President: Jessamy Brown

Historical Note
The Association for Women Journalists is dedicated to supporting women in print and broadcast journalism and promoting the respectful treatment of women by the news media. Has no paid officers or full-time staff. Membership: $30/year.

Association for Women Veterinarians *(1947)*
310 N. Indian Hill Blvd.
Claremont, CA 91711-4611
Tel: (909)319-5552
Web Site: www.awv-women-veterinarians.org
Members: 300 individuals
Staff: 1
Annual Budget: under $10,000
President: Michelle LeBlanc

Historical Note
Founded as the Women's Veterinary Association, it became the Women's Veterinary Medical Association in 1950 and assumed its present name in 1980. Membership: $50/year (full with bulletin); $95/2 year (full); $5/year (student); $10/year (new graduate); $10/year (associate); $5/year (retiree).

Meetings/Conferences:
Annual Meetings: with the American Veterinary Medical Ass'n

Publications:
AWV Bulletin. q. adv.

Association for Women's Rights in Development *(1982)*
96 Spadina Ave.
Toronto, ON M5V2J-6
Tel: (416)594-3773 *Fax:* (416)594-0330
E-Mail: AWID@awid.org
Web Site: www.awid.org
Members: 1200 individuals
Staff: 5
Annual Budget: $250-500,000
Executive Director: Joanna Kerr
E-Mail: AWID@awid.org
Historical Note
AWID was founded in 1982 by a group of 26 North American scholars, practitioners and policy-makers at a Wingspread Conference in Racine, Wisconsin. Those who gathered at Wingspread created an organization dedicated to the full participation of women in the development process. Today AWID is an organization of over 1000 members providing a series of services and programs with the assistance of hundreds of dedicated volunteers. Membership: $15/year (income $25,000-$45,000); $65/year (income greater than $45,000); $150/year (organization).
Meetings/Conferences:
Triennial Meetings: (2008)
Publications:
AWID News. q.
Trialogue. a.
Membership Directory. bien.
Mailing List. a.

Association for Work Process Improvement *(1970)*
185 Devonshire St.
Suite M102
Boston, MA 02110-1407
Tel: (617)426-1167 *Fax:* (617)521-8675
Toll Free: (800)998 - 2974
E-Mail: info@tawpi.org
Web Site: www.tawpi.org
Members: 1300 individuals
Staff: 9
Annual Budget: $1-2,000,000
President and Chief Executive Officer: Frank Moran
Senior Vice President, Communications and Business Development: Melissa Comeau
Vice President, Administration and Chief Financial Officer: Alden Keyser
Historical Note
Formed by the merger of the Recognition Technologies Users Association , DEMA - The Association for Input Technology and Management, and the OCR/Scanner Fax Association in 1993. Users and marketers of electronic processing equipment focusing on document (data capture and desktop), remittance, data entry, character, mark read, optical bar code, magnetic ink character, image processing and voice recognition technologies. Membership: $195/year (domestic); $215/year (international).
Meetings/Conferences:
Annual Meetings: Summer/2,000
Publications:
TODAY-The Journal of Work Process Improvement. 5/year. adv.

Association of 1890 Research Directors *(1945)*
Historical Note
See Association of Research Directors.

Association of Academic Chairmen of Plastic Surgery
444 E. Algonquin Road
Arlington Heights, IL 60005
Toll Free: (800)526 - 9884
Web Site: www.aacplasticsurgery.org
Members: 290 individuals
Administrative Manager: Peggy O'Carroll

Association of Academic Health Centers *(1969)*
1400 16th St. NW
Suite 720
Washington, DC 20036
Tel: (202)265-9600 *Fax:* (202)265-7514
Web Site: www.ahcnet.org
Members: 104 institutions
Staff: 13
Annual Budget: $2-5,000,000
President and Chief Executive Officer: Steven A. Wartman, M.D., Ph.D
Vice President, Programs and Communications: Elaine R. Rubin, Ph.D.
Historical Note
Founded in 1969 and incorporated in Indiana as the Organization of University Health Center Administrators. Name changed in 1971 to Association for Academic Health Centers; assumed its current name in 1980. Represents academic health centers in the U.S. and Canada. AAHC is dedicated to improving the health of the people by advancing the leadership of academic health centers in health professions, education, biomedical and health services research, and health care delivery. Sponsors seminars and publications to address issues relevant to health, biomedical research and education, health care policy, and health care in the university setting.
Meetings/Conferences:
Annual Meetings: Fall
Publications:
Health Promotion Newsletter. q.
Membership Directory. a.

Association of Academic Health Sciences Library Directors *(1978)*
2150 N. 107th St.
Suite 205
Seattle, WA 98133
Tel: (206)367-8704 *Fax:* (206)367-8777
E-Mail: aahsl@sbims.com
Web Site: www.aahsl.org
Members: 125 institutions
Staff: 1
Annual Budget: $50-100,000
Executive Director: Shirley Bishop
Historical Note
Formed to provide a medium for communication among academic health sciences library directors for addressing common concerns on planning, program and policy developments; to extend contacts nationally to provide a forum for joint action. Compiles statistics on medical school libraries in the U.S. and Canada annually. Membership: $300/year.
Meetings/Conferences:
Annual Meetings: Fall
Publications:
AAHSLD News. q.
Annual Report. a.
Directory. a.
Annual Statistics of Medical School Libraries. a.

Association of Academic Physiatrists *(1967)*
1106 N. Charles St.
Suite 201
Baltimore, MD 21201
Tel: (410)637-8300 *Fax:* (410)637-8399
E-Mail: aap@physiatry.org
Web Site: www.physiatry.org
Members: 1200 individuals
Staff: 7
Annual Budget: $500-1,000,000
Executive Director: Carolyn L. Braddom, Ed.D.
E-Mail: aap@physiatry.org
Historical Note
Members are academic physicians specializing in physical medicine and rehabilitation. Affiliated with Association of American Medical Colleges. Membership: $150-450/year.
Meetings/Conferences:
Annual Meetings: February
Publications:
Directory. a.
Newsletter. q.
American Journal of Physical Medicine & Rehabilitation. bi-m. adv.

Association of Administrative Law Judges *(1970)*
601 S.W. Second Ave., 17th Floor
Portland, OR 97204
Tel: (503)326-3275 Ext: 3049
E-Mail: info@aalj.org
Web Site: www.aalj.org
Members: 830 individuals
Staff: 1
Annual Budget: $100-250,000
Secretary: Joel Elliott
Historical Note
Formed to protect the decisional independence of Federal Administrative Law Judges, to provide ongoing judical education, and defend the integrity of the hearing system. Incorporated in the State of Illinois in 1980, members are administrative law judges of the Social Security Agency of the U.S. Government. Officers are elected annually. Membership: $390/year.
Publications:
AALJ Newsletter/Report via e-mail/website. w.

Association of Administrators of the Interstate Compact on the Placement of Children *(1969)*
Historical Note
An affiliate of the American Public Welfare Association, which provides administrative support.

Association of Advanced Rabbinical and Talmudic Schools *(1973)*
11 Broadway, Suite 405
New York, NY 10004-1392
Tel: (212)363-1991 *Fax:* (212)533-5335
Members: 64 institutions
Staff: 4
Annual Budget: $250-500,000
Executive Vice President: Bernard Fryshman, Ph.D.
Historical Note
Formerly (1971) the Council of Roshei Yeshivas.
Meetings/Conferences:
Annual Meetings: Winter
Publications:
Handbook of the Accreditation Commission. a.

Association of African American Museums *(1978)*
P.O. Box 578
1350 Brush Row Road
Wilberforce, OH 45384
Tel: (937)376-4944 *Fax:* (937)376-2007
Web Site: www.blackmuseums.org
Members: 200 individuals
Staff: 5
Annual Budget: $25-50,000
Executive Director: William Billingsley
E-Mail: wbillingsley@ohiohistory.org
Historical Note
Founded and incorporated in 1978 as African-American Museums Association; assumed its current name in 1998. AAAM is the national voice of black museums in the U.S. AAAM helps its members in collecting, preserving, and interpreting the cultural objects and artifacts of black heritage worldwide. Membership is open to cultural organizations, historical societies and museums that collect, conserve, exhibit and interpret objects valuable to art, history, and science, as well as educational institutions and research centers. Membership: $15/year (student); $35/year (individual); $100-250/year (organization); $225-500/year (affiliates).
Meetings/Conferences:
Annual Meetings: late Summer
Publications:
AAAM Scrip. a. adv.
Heritage Directory. a.
AAAM Monthly Email Update. m.

Association of African Studies Programs *(1972)*
Dartmouth College, Dept. of History
6107 Reed Hall
Hanover, NH 03755-3506
Tel: (603)646-2365 *Fax:* (603)646-3353
Members: 40 programs
Annual Budget: under $10,000
Contact: Gail Vernazza

Association of Air Medical Services *(1980)*
526 King St.
Suite 415
Alexandria, VA 22314-3143
Tel: (703)836-8732 *Fax:* (703)836-8920
E-Mail: information@aams.org
Web Site: www.aams.org
Members: 500 companies
Staff: 7

Annual Budget: $2-5,000,000
Executive Director and Chief Executive Officer: Dawn M. Mancuso, CAE
Manager, Communications and Marketing: Blair Beggan
Manager, Membership: Melissa Porter, CME
Manager, Education and Meetings: Natasha Ross

Historical Note
Formerly (1988) ASHBEAMS (American Society of Hospital-Based Emergency Air Medical Services). Established in Houston, Texas and incorporated in Iowa, AAMS is an association of air and critical care ground medical transport services. The composition of medical and aviation people who belong to AAMS includes administrators, pilots, mechanics, paramedics, respiratory therapists, physicians, communication specialists, nurses, Part 135 operators and aircraft manufacturers. Membership: $94/year (individual); $4,800/year (organization/company).

Meetings/Conferences:
Annual Meetings: *Fall*

Publications:
Air Medical Journal. bi-m. adv.
AAMS News & Views Newsletter. m. adv.
Membership Directory. a. adv.
AAMS Capital Watch. m.
AAMS On the Fly. m.

Association of Alternate Postal Systems *(1975)*
1725 Oaks Way
Oklahoma City, OK 73131
Tel: (405)478-0161
E-Mail: aaps@cox.net
Web Site: www.aapsinc.org
Members: 110 companies
Staff: 1
Annual Budget: $100-250,000
Executive Director: John S. White
E-Mail: aaps@cox.net

Historical Note
Formerly (1990) the Association of Private Postal Systems. Members are companies delivering advertising mail to consumers. Membership: $340/year, minimum.

Meetings/Conferences:
Annual Meetings: *Spring*

Publications:
e-Newsletter. m.
Update. bi-m. adv.

Association of Alternative Newsweeklies *(1978)*
1250 I St. NW
Suite 804
Washington, DC 20005
Tel: (202)289-8484 *Fax:* (202)289-2004
E-Mail: rkarpel@aan.org
Web Site: http://aan.org
Members: 125 newspapers
Staff: 6
Annual Budget: $1-2,000,000
Executive Director: Richard Karpel
E-Mail: rkarpel@aan.org

Historical Note
AAN represents alternative newspapers like the Village Voice, Boston Phoenix, LA Weekly and Chicago Reader. Membership: $500-$2500/year (company).

Meetings/Conferences:
Annual Meetings: *June*

Association of American Chambers of Commerce in Latin America *(1967)*
1615 H St., N.W.
Washington, DC 20062-2000
Tel: (202)463-5485 *Fax:* (202)463-3126
Web Site: www.aaccla.org
Staff: 3
Executive Vice President: John Murphy
E-Mail: jmurphy@aaccla.org

Historical Note
Founded in 1967, AACCLA is the umbrella group for 23 American Chambers of Commerce in 21 Latin American/Caribbean nations. Representing over 20,000 companies and individuals managing the bulk of U.S. investments in the region, AACCLA advocates trade and investment between the U.S. and the countries of the region through free trade, free markets and free enterprise.

Association of American Colleges and Universities *(1915)*
1818 R St. NW
Washington, DC 20009
Tel: (202)387-3760 *Fax:* (202)265-9532
Toll Free: (800)297 - 3775
Web Site: www.aacu.org
Members: 1000 institutions
Staff: 45
Annual Budget: $5-10,000,000
President: Carol G. Schneider
Vice President, Communications: Debra Humphreys
Director, Membership: Dennis W. Renner

Historical Note
Founded in 1915, AAC&U is the leading national association devoted to advancing and strengthening liberal learning for all students.

Meetings/Conferences:
Annual Meetings: *Winter/1200*

Publications:
Peer Review. q.
Liberal Education. q.
Diversity Digest. q.

Association of American Editorial Cartoonists *(1957)*
3899 N. Front St.
Harrisburg, PA 17110
Tel: (717)703-3069 *Fax:* (717)703-3001
E-Mail: aaec@nc.rr.com
Web Site: www.editorialcartoonists.com
Members: 350 individuals
Staff: 1
Annual Budget: $50-100,000
Manager: Wanda R. Nicholson

Historical Note
Membership: $100/year (individual).

Meetings/Conferences:
2007 – Washington, DC(Mayflower Hotel)/July 4-7

Publications:
AAEC Notebook. q.
Membership Directory. bi-a.

Association of American Educators *(1994)*
27405 Puerta Real, Suite 230
Mission Viejo, CA 92691-6388
Tel: (949)595-7979 *Fax:* (949)595-7970
Toll Free: (800)704 - 7799
E-Mail: info@aaeteachers.org
Web Site: www.aaeteachers.org
Members: 5000 individuals
Staff: 12
Annual Budget: $2-5,000,000
Executive Director: Gary Beckner
E-Mail: info@aaeteachers.org

Historical Note
AAE represents the views of member teachers as advocates for professionalism, community involvement and local control of educational institutions. Absorbed National Association of Professional Educators in 2000.

Publications:
Education Matters newsletter. m.

Association of American Feed Control Officials *(1909)*
Office of IN State Chemist, Purdue Univ.
175 S. University St.
West Lafayette, IN 47907-2063
Tel: (765)494-1561
Web Site: www.AAFCO.org
Members: 325 individuals
Secretary-Treasurer: Dr. Rodney Noel

Historical Note
Officials of government agencies at the State, Provincial, Dominion and Federal levels engaged in the regulation of production, analysis, labeling, distribution and sale of animal feeds and livestock remedies.

Publications:
Official Publication. a.

Association of American Geographers *(1904)*
1710 16th St. NW
Washington, DC 20009-3198
Tel: (202)234-1450 *Fax:* (202)234-2744
E-Mail: gaia@aag.org
Web Site: www.aag.org
Members: 7500 individuals
Staff: 12
Annual Budget: $2-5,000,000
Executive Director: Douglas B. Richardson
Accounting Manager: Teri Martin
Director, Educational Affairs: Michael Solem

Historical Note
Founded in Philadelphia in 1904 at a meeting of the American Association for the Advancement of Science, and incorporated in the District of Columbia in 1937. Merged in 1948 with the American Society for Professional Geographers. A member of the American Council of Learned Societies. Membership: varies according to income.

Meetings/Conferences:
Annual Meetings: *Spring/3,500*

Publications:
AAG Newsletter. m. adv.
Annals. q. adv.
The Professional Geographer. q. adv.

Association of American Indian Physicians
1225 Sovereign Row, Suite 103
Oklahoma City, OK 73108
Tel: (405)946-7072 *Fax:* (405)946-7651
E-Mail: aaip@aaip.com
Web Site: www.aaip.com
Staff: 1
Executive Director: Margaret Knight
E-Mail: aaip@aaip.com

Historical Note
Sponsors continuing education and other programs that reflect the cultural heritage of Native Americans.

Association of American Law Schools *(1900)*
1201 Connecticut Ave. NW
Suite 800
Washington, DC 20036-2605
Tel: (202)296-8851 *Fax:* (202)296-8869
Web Site: www.aals.org
Members: 168 institutions
Staff: 23
Annual Budget: $2-5,000,000
Executive Vice President and Executive Director: Carl C. Monk
E-Mail: cmonk@aals.org

Historical Note
Organized in Saratoga Springs with 32 schools as charter members, AALS is an association of law schools and serves as the law teachers' learned society. AALS is legal education's principal representative to the federal government and to other national higher education organizations and learned societies. Incorporated in the District of Columbia in 1971. Membership: $4,813-19,242/year, varies by size of enrollment (school).

Meetings/Conferences:
Annual Meetings: *January/3,000*
2007 – Washington, DC/Jan. 2-6
2008 – New York, NY/Jan. 2-6

Publications:
AALS Newsletter. q.
Directory of Law Teachers. a.
Journal of Legal Education. q.
Placement Bulletin. bi-m.
Proceedings. a.

Association of American Medical Colleges *(1876)*
2450 N St. NW
Washington, DC 20037
Tel: (202)828-0400 *Fax:* (202)828-1125
Web Site: www.aamc.org
Members: 126 schools, 92 socs., 98 hospitals
Staff: 300
Annual Budget: $50-100,000,000
President and Chief Executive Officer: Darrell G. Kirch
Senior Vice President, Administrative Services: Barbara S. Friedman
Executive Vice President: Richard M. Knapp, Ph.D.
Vice President, Information Resources: Jeanne L. Mella
Senior Vice President, Communications: Elisa K. Siegel
Vice President, Membership/Constituent Service Office: Kathleen Turner

Historical Note
Seeks the advancement of medical education, biomedical research and the nation's health. Has an annual budget of approximately $60 million.
Publications:
Reporter. m.
Washington Highlights. w.
Academic Physician & Scientist. bi-m.
Academic Medicine. m. adv.

Association of American Pesticide Control Officials *(1947)*
P.O. Box 1249
Hardwick, VT 05843
Tel: (802)472-6956 *Fax:* (802)472-6957
E-Mail: aapco@vtlink.net
Web Site: http://aapco.ceris.purdue.edu/
Members: 55 individuals
Staff: 1
Annual Budget: $10-25,000
Secretary: Philip H. Gray
E-Mail: aapco@vtlink.net
Historical Note
An association composed of state pesticide regulatory officials dedicated to a uniform approach throughout the U.S. to the implementation of the Federal Insecticide, Fungicide, and Rodenticide Act, as amended. Membership: $125/year.
Meetings/Conferences:
Annual Meetings: August/150
2007 - Grand Rapids, MI/July 27-29
Publications:
Official Publication. a.

Association of American Physicians *(1886)*
45685 Harmony Ln.
Belleville, MI 48111
Tel: (734)699-1217
E-Mail: admin@aap-online.org
Web Site: www.aap-online.org
Members: 1500 individuals
Staff: 2
Annual Budget: $10-25,000
Executive Director: Lori Ennis
Historical Note
Members are medical school professors. Has no paid officers or full-time staff. Membership: $150/year.
Meetings/Conferences:
Annual Meetings: Spring/4,500
Publications:
Proceedings.

Association of American Physicians and Surgeons *(1943)*
1601 N. Tucson Blvd., Suite 9
Tucson, AZ 85716
Toll Free: (800)635 - 1196
E-Mail: aaps@aapsonline.org
Web Site: www.aapsonline.org
Members: 6000 individuals
Staff: 3
Annual Budget: $500-1,000,000
Executive Director: Jane M. Orient, M.D.
E-Mail: aaps@aapsonline.org
Historical Note
Represents physicians in the socio-economic aspects of medical practice. Supports the Association of American Physicians and Surgeons Political Action Committee. Membership: $225/year (individual).
Meetings/Conferences:
Annual Meetings: Fall
Publications:
Journal of American Physicians and Surgeons. q.
AAPS News Newsletter. m.

Association of American Plant Food Control Officials *(1946)*
Fertilizer/Ag Lime Control Service
University of Missouri - Columbia
Columbia, MO 65211-8080
Tel: (573)882-0007 *Fax:* (573)882-4543
E-Mail: slaterj@missouri.edu
Web Site: www.aapfco.org
Members: 185 individuals
Staff: 1
Annual Budget: $10-25,000
Secretary: Joseph Slater
E-Mail: slaterj@missouri.edu
Historical Note
Formerly (1967) Association of American Fertilizer Control Officials. Membership: $100/year.
Meetings/Conferences:
Annual Meetings: 1st week in August
2007 - Grand Rapids, MT(Amway Grand Hotel)/July 29-31
Publications:
Official Publication of AAPFCO. a.

Association of American Publishers *(1970)*
71 Fifth Ave.
New York, NY 10003
Tel: (212)255-0200 *Fax:* (212)255-7007
Web Site: www.publishers.org
Members: 320 companies
Staff: 25
Annual Budget: $5-10,000,000
President: Patricia Schroeder
Vice President: Kathryn Blough
Historical Note
Formed by a merger of the American Educational Publishers Institute (founded in 1942 and formerly known as the American Textbook Publishers Institute), and the American Book Publishers Council (founded in 1946 and which included the former Technical, Scientific and Medical Book Publishers). AAP is the voice of the American publishing industry. Maintains a Washington office.
Meetings/Conferences:
Annual Meetings: Spring
Publications:
Annual Report. a.
Industry Statistics Report. a.
AAP Monthly Report - Statistics. m.
Compensation & Personnel Policies Silver Report. a.

Association of American Railroads *(1934)*
50 F St. NW
Washington, DC 20001-1564
Tel: (202)639-2100 *Fax:* (202)639-2558
E-Mail: information@aar.org
Web Site: www.aar.org
Members: 65 railroads
Staff: 45
Annual Budget: $25-50,000,000
President and Chief Executive Officer: Edward R. Hamberger
E-Mail: information@aar.org
General Attorney: Janet L. Bartelmay
E-Mail: information@aar.org
Manager, Meeting Services: Stephanie Kilfeather
E-Mail: information@aar.org
Senior Vice President, Law and General Counsel: Louis P. Warchot
E-Mail: information@aar.org
Vice President, Communications: Peggy Wilhilde
E-Mail: information@aar.org
Historical Note
Founded in 1934 by a merger of the American Railway Association, the Association of Railway Executives and several other rail organizations. The oldest predecessor organization was Master Car Builders Association, founded in 1867. AAR presently serves as the joint agency of its individual railroad members to assure an efficient nationwide rail system. Activity areas include standards, operations, maintenance, safety, theoretical and applied research, economics, finance, accounting, communications, electronic data exchanges and public affairs. Maintains the Transportation Technology Center near Pueblo, Colorado, and Rail Inc. as a leading provider of information technology to North American railroads. Membership: determined by members' annual revenues.
Meetings/Conferences:
Annual Meetings: Not held; AAR divisions and departments meet separately.
Publications:
Railroad Facts. a.
Analysis of Class I Railroads. a.
Railroad Ten-year Trends. a.
Price List of Publications. a.

Association of American Seed Control Officials *(1949)*
MN Dept. of Agriculture
8831 Hillside Trail South
Cottage Grove, MN 55016
Tel: (651)201-6000
Web Site: www.seedcontrol.org
Members: 52 individuals
Annual Budget: under $10,000
Treasurer: Charles Dale
Historical Note
Members are U.S. and Canadian officials who administer state/provincial seed regulations. AASCO has one member from each state, one from Canada and one from the U.S. Dept. of Agriculture. Has no paid officers or full-time staff. Membership: $150/year (state organization).
Meetings/Conferences:
Annual Meetings: Summer
Publications:
Annual Meeting Proceedings.
Directory.
Administrative Practices Handbook.
Seed Inspectors Handbook.

Association of American State Geologists *(1906)*
Montana Bureau of Mines and Geology
1300 W. Park St.
Butte, MT 59701
Tel: (303)866-2611 *Fax:* (303)866-2461
E-Mail: vicki.cowart@state.co.us
Web Site: www.stategeologists.org
Members: 51 individuals
Annual Budget: under $10,000
Secretary: Edmond Deal
E-Mail: vicki.cowart@state.co.us
Historical Note
Founded in 1906 as the Association of State Geologists of the Mississippi Valley; assumed its present name May 12, 1908 in the District of Columbia. Members of the association are chief executives of State Geological Surveys in the 50 states and Puerto Rico.
Meetings/Conferences:
Annual Meetings: late Spring
2007 - , FL
2008 - Washington, DC
2009 - , MS
2010 - , IA
2012 - , TX
Publications:
The State Geologists Journal. a.
AASG Fact Book. a.

Association of American Universities *(1900)*
1200 New York Ave. NW
Suite 550
Washington, DC 20005
Tel: (202)408-7500 *Fax:* (202)408-8184
Web Site: www.aau.edu
Members: 63 universities
Staff: 20
Annual Budget: $2-5,000,000
President: Nils Hasselmo, Ph.D.
E-Mail: nils_hasselmo@aau.edu
Director, Human Resources and Meetings: Kim Moshlak
Director, Business and Finance: Susan Staton
Director, Communications and Public Affairs: Barry Toiv
Director, Federal Relations: Patrick White
Historical Note
Members are chief executives of major research universities. Affiliated with the Association of Graduate Schools.
Meetings/Conferences:
Semi-Annual Meetings: Spring and Fall
Publications:
University Research Funding in the News.
Report on Hearings and Markup.
Public Affairs Report.
Washington Report.

Association of American University Presses *(1937)*
71 W. 23rd St., Suite 901
New York, NY 10010-3506
Tel: (212)989-1010 *Fax:* (212)989-0275

E-Mail: info@aaupnet.org
Web Site: www.aaupnet.org
Members: 128 presses
Staff: 9
Annual Budget: $1-2,000,000
Executive Director: Peter J. Givler
Administrative Manager: Linda McCall
E-Mail: lmccall@aaupnet.org
Assistant Director/Controller: Timothy Muench
E-Mail: tmuench@aaupnet.org

Historical Note
AAUP is dedicated to the support of creative and effective scholarly communication. Its members are university presses and non-profit scholarly publishers who publish books and journals. AAUP's programs include cooperative marketing services, statistical analyses, and professional development opportunities. Membership: $2-13,000/year.

Meetings/Conferences:
Annual Meetings: May-June/800

Publications:
The Exchange Newsletter. q.
University Press Books for Public & Secondary School Libraries. a.
Directory. a.

Association of American Veterinary Medical Colleges *(1966)*
1101 Vermont Ave. NW
Suite 301
Washington, DC 20005
Tel: (202)371-9195 *Fax:* (202)842-0773
Toll Free: (877)862 - 2740
E-Mail: hbenedict@aavmc.org
Web Site: www.aavmc.org
Members: 55 institutions
Staff: 11
Annual Budget: $1-2,000,000
Executive Director: Lawrence E. Heider
E-Mail: leheider@aavmc.org

Historical Note
AAVMC coordinates the affairs of the 32 U.S. and Canadian veterinary medical colleges, and also 8 departments of comparative medicine, two animal medical centers and three international colleges of veterinary medicine. In addition, the association fosters the membership's teaching, research and service missions both nationally and internationally. Addressing the interests of producers and consumers of food and fiber, the interests of animal owners, and those of pet owners, AAVMC's principal goal is improving the quality of human and animal life.

Meetings/Conferences:
Annual Meetings: Spring
2007 – Washington, DC(Marriott Wardman Park)/March 3-5

Publications:
Journal of Veterinary Medical Education. 4/year.

Association of Analytical Chemists *(1941)*

Historical Note
See AOAC Internat'l

Association of Ancient Historians *(1974)*
Mercyhurst College, History Dept.
501 E. 38th St.
Erie, PA 16546-0001
Tel: (814)824-2345 *Fax:* (814)824-2182
Web Site: www.trentu.ca/aah/welcome.shtml
Members: 800 individuals
Annual Budget: under $10,000
Secretary-Treasurer: Randall S. Howarth

Historical Note
AAH was organized to provide ancient historians, as a group, an identity apart from classical philologists and to hold an annual meeting. Membership: $7.50/year (individual).

Meetings/Conferences:
Annual Meetings: Spring

Publications:
Newsletter. 3/year.
Publications of the AAH (monograph series). irreg.

Association of Applied IPM Ecologists *(1967)*
P.O. Box 526
Oxnard, CA 93030
Tel: (707)265-9349
E-Mail: director@aaie.net
Web Site: www.aaie.net
Members: 300 individuals
Staff: 1
Annual Budget: $25-50,000
Executive Director: Annika Forester

Historical Note
Founded as Association of Applied Insect Ecologists; assumed its current name in 2002. Members are specialists in agricultural pest control. AAIE serves as a forum for the exchange of ideas on IPM (Integrated Pest Management) practices. Membership: $100/year (professional); $50/year (general); $35/year (associate); $15/year (student).

Meetings/Conferences:
Annual Meetings: Winter/400

Publications:
AAIE Bulletin. q. adv.
AAIE Conference Program. a. adv.

Association of Art Editors *(1994)*
3912 Natchez Ave. South
St. Louis Park, MN 55416
Tel: (952)922-1374
E-Mail: pfreshman@mm.com
Web Site: www.artedit.org
Members: 80 individuals
Staff: 1
President: Phil Freshman
E-Mail: pfreshman@mm.com

Historical Note
AAE members are art editors and others involved in art-related publications. An affiliate of College Art Association. Has no paid officers or full-time staff. Membership: $20/year.

Meetings/Conferences:
Annual Meetings: in conjunction with College Art Ass'n

Publications:
Directory of Members (online).

Association of Art Museum Directors *(1916)*
41 E. 65th St.
New York, NY 10021
Tel: (212)754-8084 *Fax:* (212)754-8087
E-Mail: canagnos@aamd.org
Web Site: www.aamd.org
Members: 170 individuals
Staff: 4
Annual Budget: $100-250,000
Executive Director: Millicent Hall Gaudieri
Deputy Director: Christine Anagnos
Director, Government Affairs: Anita M. DiFanis

Historical Note
Works to establish and maintain high standards for members and the museums they represent. Membership: $1,400-5,400/year.

Meetings/Conferences:
Semi-annual Meetings:

Publications:
AAMD Salary Survey. a.
Professional Practices in Art Museums.

Association of Arts Administration Educators *(1975)*
Bolz Center for Arts Administration
975 University Ave.
Madison, WI 53706
Tel: (608)265-2735 *Fax:* (608)263-4161
E-Mail: ataylor@bus.wisc.edu
Web Site: www.artsadministration.org
Members: 250 students, affiliates, and univ. depts
Annual Budget: $10-25,000
Director: Andrew Taylor
E-Mail: ataylor@bus.wisc.edu

Historical Note
Members are directors of graduate level programs in arts administration. Affiliate membership is available to directors of undergraduate programs and other interested individuals. Has no paid officers or full-time staff. Membership: $25/year (individual); $50/year (affiliate); $125/year (associate); $275/year (organization).

Meetings/Conferences:
Annual Meetings: Spring

Publications:
Guide to Arts, Administration, Training and Research. bien.

Association of Asian-Pacific Community Health Organizations *(1987)*
300 Frank H. Ogawa Plaza
Oakland, CA 94612
Tel: (510)272-9536 *Fax:* (510)272-0817
E-Mail: webmaster@aapcho.org
Web Site: www.aapcho.org
Members: 14 organizations
Staff: 2
Executive Director: Jeffrey B. Caballero
E-Mail: webmaster@aapcho.org
Director, Programs: Nina Agbayani

Historical Note
AAPCHO represents community health organizations dedicated to promoting advocacy, collaboration and leadership that improves the health status and access of Asian Americans, Native Hawaiians and Pacific Islanders within the United States, its territories and freely associated states.

Association of Asphalt Paving Technologists *(1926)*
4711 Clark Ave.
Suite G
St. Paul, MN 55110
Tel: (651)293-9188 *Fax:* (651)293-9193
E-Mail: aapt@qwest.net
Web Site: www.asphalttechnology.org
Members: 850 individuals
Staff: 1
Annual Budget: $100-250,000
Administrative Secretary: Eileen Soler
E-Mail: aapt@qwest.net

Historical Note
Formed in Chicago in 1926 with 19 charter members and incorporated in Minnesota in 1969. Membership: $90/year.

Publications:
Asphalt Paving Technology. a.

Association of Attorney-Mediators *(1989)*
P.O. Box 741955
Dallas, TX 75374-1955
Tel: (972)669-8101 *Fax:* (972)669-8180
Toll Free: (800)280 - 1368
E-Mail: aam@airmail.net
Web Site: www.attorney-mediators.org
Members: 300 individuals
Staff: 11
Executive Director: Brenda Rachuig
E-Mail: aam@airmail.net

Historical Note
Members are mediators who are also attorneys.

Association of Authors' Representatives *(1991)*
676A Ninth Ave.
Suite 312
New York, NY 10036
Tel: (212)840-5777
E-Mail: aarinc@mindspring.org
Web Site: www.aar-online.org
Members: 350 individuals
Staff: 1
Annual Budget: $10-25,000
Administrative Secretary: Joanne Brownstein
E-Mail: aarinc@mindspring.org

Historical Note
Formerly the Society of Authors' Representatives, SAR merged with the Independent Literary Agents Association (est. 1977) to form the Association of Authors' Representatives. AAR membership is restricted to professional literary and dramatic agents.

Meetings/Conferences:
Annual Meetings: June

Publications:
AAR Newsletter. bi-a.
The Literary Agent. a.

Association of Automotive Aftermarket Distributors *(1977)*
5050 Poplar Ave., Suite 2020
Memphis, TN 38157-2001
Tel: (901)682-9090 *Fax:* (901)682-9098

Toll Free: (800)727 - 8112
E-Mail: info@partsplus.com
Web Site: www.partsplus.com
Members: 35 distributors
Staff: 18
Annual Budget: $5-10,000,000
President: Mike Lambert
E-Mail: info@partsplus.com
Director, Retail Marketing: Bob Barstow
E-Mail: info@partsplus.com
Account Manager: David Cowsert
E-Mail: info@partsplus.com
Director, Wholesale Marketing and Training: Gil Gunn
E-Mail: info@partsplus.com
Director, Sales: Dale Hobbs
E-Mail: info@partsplus.com

Historical Note
Provides purchasing and marketing services for members.

Meetings/Conferences:
Biennial Meetings:

Publications:
Parts Plus Magazine. 6/year.
Car Care Center Newsletter. 6/year.

Association of Average Adjusters of the U.S. *(1879)*
79 Palmer Dr.
Livingston, NJ 07039-1314
Tel: (973)597-0824
E-Mail: averageadjusters@aol.com
Web Site: www.usaverageadjusters.org
Members: 800 individuals
Annual Budget: $25-50,000
Secretary: Eileen M. Fellin, Jr.
E-Mail: averageadjusters@aol.com

Historical Note
Marine insurance and general average adjusters, ship and cargo surveyors and admiralty lawyers. Has no paid staff. Membership principally in New York area.

Meetings/Conferences:
Annual Meetings: October, in New York, NY

Publications:
Report of the Annual Meeting.
Bulletin. a.

Association of Avian Veterinarians *(1980)*
P.O. Box 811720
Boca Raton, FL 33481-1720
Tel: (561)393-8901 *Fax:* (561)393-8902
E-Mail: aavctrlofc@aol.com
Web Site: www.aav.org
Members: 3300 individuals
Staff: 8
Annual Budget: $250-500,000
Executive Director: Adina Rae Freedman, CAE

Historical Note
Members are veterinarians, technicians, and members of allied professions. Membership: $120/year.

Meetings/Conferences:
Annual Meetings: Summer

Publications:
Journal of Avian Medicine and Surgery. q. adv.
AAV News and Clinical Forum. q.

Association of Aviation Psychologists *(1964)*
P.O. Box 87150
College Park, GA 30337-0150
Tel: (770)471-6286
Web Site: www.avpsych.org
Members: 225 individuals
Annual Budget: under $10,000
President: Lori McDonnell

Historical Note
AAP is an informal group whose members are psychologists, behavioral scientists, and pilots concerned with aviation psychology including such topics as pilot/controller performance and flight safety and related fields. Has no paid officers or full-time staff. Membership: $35/year.

Meetings/Conferences:
Annual Meetings: With the Human Factors Society

Publications:
Newsletter. q.
Membership Directory. a.

Association of Battery Recyclers *(1976)*
P.O. Box 290286
Tampa, FL 33687
Tel: (813)626-6151 *Fax:* (813)622-8388
E-Mail: info@batteryrecyclers.com
Web Site: www.batteryrecyclers.com/
Members: 25 companies
Staff: 2
Annual Budget: $100-250,000
Secretary-Treasurer: Joyce Morales
E-Mail: joycemorales@aol.com

Historical Note
Formerly (1990) the Secondary Lead Smelters Association. Investigates means/methods to achieve compliance with OSHA and EPA regulations impacting the secondary lead smelting industry. Membership: $1,500/year (consultant); $4,500/year (associate); $2,500/month (secondary smelter).

Meetings/Conferences:
Semiannual Meetings:

Publications:
Monthly Regulatory Update. m.

Association of Biomedical Communications Directors *(1973)*
SUNY Stony Brook, L3 044 Health Science Ctr.
Stony Brook, NY 11794-8030
Tel: (631)444-3228 *Fax:* (631)444-3500
Web Site: www.abcdirectors.org/
Members: 95 individuals
Staff: 1
Annual Budget: $10-25,000
Executive Officer: Kathleen Gebhart

Historical Note
Members are directors of bio-medical communications units in a school or in an academic health science center, either of which must grant degrees in the field of health or life sciences. Membership: $110/year (active); $50/year (associate).

Meetings/Conferences:
Annual Meetings: Summer

Publications:
ABCD Exchange. q. adv.
The Journal of Biocommunication. q. adv.
Joint Membership Directory. a. adv.
Annual Survey of ABCD.

Association of Biomolecular Resource Facilities *(1988)*
2019 Galisteo Street, Bldg. I
Santa Fe, NM 87505
Tel: (505)983-8102 *Fax:* (505)989-1073
E-Mail: abrf@abrf.org
Web Site: www.abrf.org
Members: 800 individuals
Staff: 3

Historical Note
ABRF members are laboratories and other facilities with an interest in biomolecular research. Administrative support is provided by the Federation of American Socs. for Experimental Biology.

Publications:
Directory. irreg.

Association of Bituminous Contractors *(1968)*
815 Connecticut Ave. NW
Suite 620
Washington, DC 20006
Tel: (202)785-4440 *Fax:* (202)331-8049
Members: 100 companies
Staff: 1
Annual Budget: $100-250,000
Secretary and General Counsel: William H. Howe

Historical Note
Members are general and independent contractors constructing coal mines and coal mine facilities. Bargains with the United Mine Workers.

Meetings/Conferences:
Annual Meetings: March

Association of Black Anthropologists *(1970)*

Historical Note
A section of the American Anthropological Association.

Association of Black Cardiologists *(1974)*
6849-B2 Peachtree Dunwoody Rd. NE
Atlanta, GA 30328
Tel: (678)302-4222 *Fax:* (678)302-4223
E-Mail: abcardio@abcardio.org
Web Site: www.abcardio.org
Members: 620 individuals
Staff: 28
Annual Budget: $2-5,000,000
Chief Executive Officer: B. Waine Kong, Ph.D., J.D
E-Mail: bwainekong@abcardio.org

Historical Note
ABC members are primarily black cardiologists and other medical professionals with an interest in cardiovascular disease. Membership: $295/year (individual); $1,000/year (institution).

Meetings/Conferences:
Tri-annual Meetings: Spring/Summer/Fall/300

Publications:
ABC Newsletter. q.
ABC Directory. a.
Digest of Urban Cardiology. bi-m. adv.

Association of Black Foundation Executives *(1971)*
55 Exchange Pl.
New York, NY 10005
Tel: (212)982-6925 Ext: 510 *Fax:* (212)982-6886
E-Mail: information@abfe.org
Web Site: www.abfe.org/
Members: 200 individuals
President: Kenneth W. Austin
E-Mail: information@abfe.org

Historical Note
Membership is limited to the staff of grant-making foundations. Membership: $125/year (individual).

Association of Black Nursing Faculty in Higher Education *(1987)*
c/o ABNF Journal
5823 Queens Cove
Lisle, IL 60532
Tel: (630)969-3809 *Fax:* (630)969-3895
E-Mail: mfonza@msn.com
Web Site: www.abnf.net
Members: 175 individuals
Staff: 1
Annual Budget: $25-50,000
Preisdent: Marjorie A. Fonza, Ph.D.
E-Mail: mfonza@msn.com

Historical Note
Members are nursing faculty teaching at the college level. Membership: $75/year (individual).

Meetings/Conferences:
Annual Meetings: Summer
2007 – Chicago, IL(Marriott)/June 13-17/100

Publications:
ABNF Newsletter. q. adv.
ABNF Journal. q. adv.

Association of Black Psychologists *(1968)*
P.O. Box 55999
Washington, DC 20040-5999
Tel: (202)722-0808 *Fax:* (202)722-5941
E-Mail: abpsi_office@abpsi.org
Web Site: www.abpsi.org
Members: 1500 individuals
Staff: 2
Annual Budget: $250-500,000
President: Willie S. Williams

Historical Note
Organized at the 1968 San Francisco meeting of the American Psychological Association, ABPsi is an independent autonomous organization addressing the needs of black professionals and the mental health of the national black community by means of planning, programs, services, training and advocacy. Membership: Fees vary.

Meetings/Conferences:
Annual Meetings: August

Publications:
Journal of Black Psychology. quarterly. adv.
Psych Discourse. m. adv.

Association of Black Sociologists *(1970)*
4200 Wisconsin Ave. NW
PMB 106-257

Washington, DC 20016-2143
Tel: (202)365-1759 *Fax:* (781)723-6527
E-Mail: info@blacksociologists.org
Web Site: www.blacksociologists.org/
Members: 400 individuals
Annual Budget: $100-250,000
Executive Officer/Treasurer: Evita Bynum
E-Mail: evita.bynum@american.edu

Historical Note
Formerly (1977) Caucus of Black Sociologists. Membership: $55/year (individual).

Meetings/Conferences:
Annual Meetings: *Last week in August*

Publications:
Race and Society. semi-a.
The Griot newsletter. q.

Association of Boarding Schools, The *(1976)*
2141 Wisconsin Ave. NW
Suite H
Washington, DC 20007
Tel: (202)965-8982 *Fax:* (202)965-8988
Toll Free: (800)541 - 5908
E-Mail: ruzicka@schools.com
Web Site: www.schools.com
Members: 300 schools
Staff: 4
Annual Budget: $500-1,000,000
Director: Steven D. Ruzicka
E-Mail: tabs@schools.com

Historical Note
TABS is an independent, non-profit association that serves its member schools by improving public awareness of boarding schools, expanding the markets of students, and providing training for boarding school professionals. Membership: $1,080-$2,700/year.

Meetings/Conferences:
Annual Meetings: *In conjunction with NAIS*

Publications:
Boarding Schools Directory. a.

Association of Boards of Certification *(1972)*
208 Fifth St.
Ames, IA 50010-6259
Tel: (515)232-3623 *Fax:* (515)232-3778
E-Mail: abc@abccert.org
Web Site: www.abccert.org
Members: 94 agencies
Staff: 10
Executive Director: Stephen W. Ballou, Ph.D.
E-Mail: abc@abccert.org

Historical Note
Formerly (1982) Association of Boards of Certification for Operating Personnel in Water and Wastewater Utilities and (1986) Association of Boards of Certification for Operating Personnel. Members are government agencies certifying operating personnel and laboratory analysts concerned with water and pollution control. Membership: $50/year (individual member); $250/year (associate member); $300-1,800/year (certifying authority).

Meetings/Conferences:
Annual Meetings: *January*

Publications:
Certifier. bi-m.
Directory. a.

Association of Bone and Joint Surgeons *(1947)*
6300 N. River Road, Suite 727
Rosemont, IL 60018-4226
Tel: (847)698-1636 *Fax:* (847)823-4921
E-Mail: abjs@aaos.org
Web Site: www.abjs.org
Members: 270 individuals
Staff: 2
Annual Budget: $50-100,000
Executive Director: Colette Iocca Hohimer

Historical Note
Founded in Oklahoma City in April 1949 and incorporated the same year in Oklahoma.

Meetings/Conferences:
2007 – Lexington, KY(Radisson Plaza)/Apr. 11-15

Publications:
Clinical Orthopaedics and Related Research. m.

Association of Booksellers for Children *(1985)*
3900 Sumac Circle
Middleton, WI 53562
Tel: (608)836-6050 *Fax:* (608)836-1438
E-Mail: info@abfc.com
Web Site: www.abfc.com
Members: 600 individuals
Staff: 1
Annual Budget: $250-500,000
Executive Director: Anne Irish

Historical Note
ABC offers a support network for professional children's booksellers. Membership: $85/year (bookstores, associates); $50/year (authors, illustrators, literary agents).

Meetings/Conferences:
Annual Meetings: *Spring*

Publications:
Best Books for Children Catalog. a. adv.
ABC Newsletter. 3/year.

Association of Bridal Consultants *(1981)*
56 Danbury Road, Suite 11
New Milford, CT 06776
Tel: (860)355-0464 *Fax:* (860)354-1404
E-Mail: office@bridalassn.com
Web Site: www.bridalassn.com
Members: 3850 companies and individuals
Staff: 10
Annual Budget: $500-1,000,000
President: David M. Woods, III
Director, Education: Renee Grannis

Historical Note
Composed of independent consultants as well as owners and employees of wedding related businesses. Supersedes American Association of Professional Bridal Consultants (1955-1980). Awards the designations Professional Bridal Consultant, Accredited Bridal Consultant, and Master Bridal Consultant. Membership: $140-500/year.

Meetings/Conferences:
Annual Meetings: *Fall*

Publications:
Newsletter. bi-m. adv.
Retail Resource Directory. a.

Association of Business Support Services International *(1981)*

Historical Note
Ceased non-profit operations in 2002.

Association of Camp Nurses *(1990)*
8630 Thorsonveien NE
Bemidji, MN 56601
Tel: (218)586-2633 *Fax:* (218)586-8770
E-Mail: acn@campnurse.org
Web Site: www.campnurse.org
Members: 300 individuals
Annual Budget: $10-25,000
Executive Director: Linda Ebner Erceg
E-Mail: erceg@campnurse.org

Historical Note
ACN is a professional nursing organization established to work toward healthier camp communities through camp nursing practice. Membership: $50/year (individual).

Publications:
CompassPoint. q.

Association of Career Firms International *(1982)*
204 E St. NE
Washington, DC 20002
Tel: (202)547-6344 *Fax:* (202)547-6348
E-Mail: acf@acfinternational.org
Web Site: www.aocfi.org
Members: 1400 organizations
Staff: 6
Annual Budget: $50-100,000
Executive Director: Annette L. Summers

Historical Note
Formerly (1994) Association of Outplacement Consulting Firms, (1997) Association of Outplacement Consulting Firms International and then Association of Career Management Consulting Firms International before assuming its current name in 2004. Established at a dinner meeting at the Yale Club, New York City, on March 16, 1982 to promote standards of professional practice in the outplacement business, AOFCI works as a voice of career management consulting companies around the world, and has North American and European chapters. AOFCI's goal is to preserve, protect and enhance the career management consulting industry through its services, and to promote the maintenance by members of the highest standards of ethics and professional competence. Members make up 70% of the career management consulting industry around the world, and individual company members together employ thousands of professionals providing a wide range of career management services to clients. Some of these services are outplacement, executive coaching, and effective workforce deployment.

Publications:
Membership Directory.

Association of Career Management Consulting Firms International

Historical Note
Became Association of Career Firms International in 2004.

Association of Career Professionals International *(1989)*
204 E St. NE
Washington, DC 20002
Tel: (202)547-6377 *Fax:* (202)547-6348
E-Mail: info@acpinternational.org
Web Site: www.acpinternational.org
Members: 1250 individuals
Annual Budget: $25-50,000
Executive Director: Annette L. Summers

Historical Note
Founded as International Association of Outplacement Professionals; became International Association of Career Management Professionals in 1994 and assumed its current name in 2004. Established to build the professionalism and to meet the professional needs of outplacement practitioners; and to achieve recognition for that profession. Membership: $40/year (individual).

Publications:
IACMP Networks Newsletter. q.
IACMP Highlighter. m.

Association of Caribbean Studies *(1978)*
P.O. Box 22202
Lexington, KY 40522
Tel: (859)257-6966 *Fax:* (859)323-1072
Members: 1200 individuals
Staff: 3
Annual Budget: under $10,000
Executive Director: O.R. Dathorne, Ph.D.

Historical Note
Interdisciplinary scholarly society concerned with the Caribbean. Has no paid officers or full-time staff. Membership: $50/year (individual); $200/year (organization).

Meetings/Conferences:
Annual Meetings: *July/100*

Publications:
Journal of Caribbean Studies. 2-3/year. adv.
ACS Abstracts. a.

Association of Catholic Colleges and Universities *(1899)*
One Dupont Circle NW
Suite 650
Washington, DC 20036
Tel: (202)457-0650 *Fax:* (202)728-0977
E-Mail: accu@accunet.org
Web Site: www.accunet.org
Members: 217 institutions
Staff: 5
Annual Budget: $500-1,000,000
President and Chief Executive Officer: Richard Yanikoski
Vice President: Michael Galligan-Stierle
Director, Operations: Kathleen Laddbush

Historical Note
Founded in 1899, ACCU became (1904) the College and University Department of the National Catholic

Education Association. Later reassumed its status as an independent organization, but as an affiliate of the NCEA; reassumed the name ACCU in 1978. Incorporated in 2002.

Meetings/Conferences:
2007 - Washington, DC(Washington Court Hotel)/Feb. 3-5/250

Publications:
Current Issues in Catholic Higher Education. semi-a.
Update. q.

Association of Catholic Diocesan Archivists *(1979)*
Archdioces of Chicago Records Center
711 W. Monroe St.
Chicago, IL 60661
Tel: (312)831-0610 *Fax:* (312)831-0711
Members: 300 individuals
Annual Budget: $10-25,000
President: Joseph Coen
Permanent Secretariat: Peter O'Toole

Historical Note
Members are individuals responsible for the preservation of diocesan records and historical materials. They are committed to the active promotion of professionalism in the management of diocesan archives. Membership: $15/year (individual).

Meetings/Conferences:
Annual Meetings: Odd years with S.A.A., even years a summer meeting.

Publications:
ACDA Bulletin. q.

Association of Catholic TV and Radio Syndicators *(1975)*
75 Ryder Road
P.O. Box 308
Maryknoll, NY 10545-0308
Tel: (914)941-7636 Ext: 2384 *Fax:* (914)762-6567
Members: 70companiesandorganizations
Annual Budget: under $10,000
Membership Contact: Darlene R. Torres
E-Mail: dtorres@maryknoll.org

Historical Note
Affiliated with UNDA-USA, the U.S. arm of the international association of Catholic broadcasters. Members are producers and syndicators of Catholic radio and television programs. Has no paid officers or full-time staff. Membership: $50/year (individual), $100/year (organization).

Publications:
Directory. bi-a.
Proceedings. bi-a.

Association of Celebrity Personal Assistants *(1992)*
914 Westwood Blvd., PMB 507
Los Angeles, CA 90024
Tel: (310)281-7775
E-Mail: jobbank@celebrityassistants.org
Web Site: www.celebrityassistants.org
Members: 100 individuals
Staff: 11
Annual Budget: $25-50,000
President: Shelley Anderson

Historical Note
A non-profit, membership-based organization representing personal assistants to celebrities and other notables. Membership: $150/year.

Publications:
The Best Of The Best. bi-a. adv.
ACPA Membership Directory.

Association of Certified Fraud Examiners *(1988)*
World Headquarters - The Gregor Building
716 West Ave.
Austin, TX 78701-2727
Tel: (512)478-9000 *Fax:* (512)478-9297
Toll Free: (800)245 - 3321
E-Mail: info@cfenet.com
Web Site: www.acfe.com
Members: 34000 individuals
Staff: 50
President and Chief Executive Officer: Toby J.F. Bishop
E-Mail: jratley@cfenet.com
Vice President: Kathie S. Lawrence
E-Mail: klawrence@cfenet.com
Program Director: James D. Ratley
E-Mail: jratley@cfenet.com

Historical Note
ACFE is a global, 34,000-member professional association. Members are dedicated to fighting fraud. ACFE is one of the world's leading providers of anti-fraud training and education. Awards the designation Certified Fraud Examiner (CFE) to members who successfully complete a rigorous credential-granting curriculum.

Meetings/Conferences:
Annual Meetings: July

Publications:
Fraud Magazine. bi-m. adv.
CFE Exam Coach E-Newsletter. m. adv.
FraudInfo E-Newsletter. bi-w. adv.
Fraud Examiner E-Newsletter. m. adv.

Association of Certified Professional Secretaries *(1985)*
P.O. Box 89301
Tucson, AZ 85752-9301
Tel: (602)650-2659
Members: 300 individuals
Annual Budget: $10-25,000
Director, Membership: Roxanna D. Forbragd

Historical Note
Organized as a support network for individuals who have successfully completed the Certified Professional Secretaries examination administered by Professional Secretaries International. Membership: $50/year.

Publications:
ACPS Connection. 6/yr.

Association of Chairmen of Departments of Mechanics *(1970)*
Dept. of Engineering and Science Mechanics
223 Norris Hall ESM, MC0219
Blacksburg, VA 24061
Tel: (540)231-3243 *Fax:* (540)231-4574
E-Mail: esmhead@vt.edu
Members: 110 institutions
Staff: 1
Annual Budget: under $10,000
President: Ishwar K. Puri
E-Mail: esmhead@vt.edu

Historical Note
Has no paid officers staff or full-time staff.

Meetings/Conferences:
Semi-annual Meetings:

Association of Chartered Accountants in the United States *(1980)*
341 Lafayette St., Suite 4246
New York, NY 10012-2417
Tel: (212)334-2078 *Fax:* (212)431-5786
E-Mail: administration@acaus.org
Web Site: www.acaus.org
Members: 650 individuals
Staff: 1
Annual Budget: $50-100,000
Executive Director: Katerina Caterisano

Historical Note
ACAUS represents the interests of U.S.-based accountants chartered by institutes in England and Wales, Scotland, Ireland, Australia, Canada, New Zealand, and South Africa. Supports research on international accounting and provides programs and services linking its members to accounting practitioners worldwide. Membership: $95/year (individual).

Meetings/Conferences:
Three Annual Dinners: New York, NY; Chicago, IL; and Los Angeles, CA

Publications:
ACAUS Newsletter. a. adv.
Directory of Members. a. adv.

Association of Children's Museums *(1962)*
1300 L St. NW
Suite 975
Washington, DC 20005
Tel: (202)898-1080 *Fax:* (202)898-1086
E-Mail: acm@childrensmuseums.org
Web Site: www.childrensmuseums.org
Members: 495 museums and individuals
Staff: 9
Annual Budget: $1-2,000,000
Executive Director: Janet Rice Elman
Association Coordinator: Eliza Katz
Director, Finance and Administration: Nancy Silverman

Historical Note
Founded as Association of Youth Museum Directors; became American Association of Youth Museums in 1967 and Association of Youth Museums in 1988. Assumed its current name in 2001. Membership composed of museums with hands-on exhibits and programs targeted toward the educational needs of children. Membership: $250-1,600/year (museum, based on annual budget).

Meetings/Conferences:
Annual Meetings: Annual
2007 - Chicago, IL(Westin, Michigan Ave.)/May 10-11

Publications:
ACM Forum. q.
Hand to Hand. q.
ACM Membership Directory. a.
Capturing the Vision.
Collective Vision.
ACM Standards Document.
Salary Survey. trien.
The Case for Children's Museums.

Association of Children's Prosthetic-Orthotic Clinics
6300 N. River Road, Suite 727
Rosemont, IL 60018-4226
Tel: (847)698-1637 *Fax:* (847)823-0536
E-Mail: raymond@aaos.org
Web Site: www.acpoc.org
Members: 432 clinics
Staff: 3
Annual Budget: $25-50,000
Contact: Sheril King

Historical Note
ACPOC supports clinic teams through education, clinical research and annual meetings. Membership: $100/year (clinic chief); $50/year (associate).

Meetings/Conferences:
Annual Meetings:

Publications:
ACPOC Newsletter. q. adv.

Association of Chiropractic Colleges *(1977)*
4424 Montgomery, Suite 202
Bethesda, MD 20814
Tel: (301)652-5066 *Fax:* (301)913-9146
Toll Free: (800)284 - 1062
E-Mail: info@chirocolleges.org
Web Site: www.chirocolleges.org
Members: 19 institutions
Staff: 3
Annual Budget: $500-1,000,000
Executive Director: David S. O'Bryon, CAE

Historical Note
Formerly (1985) Association of Chiropractic College Presidents. ACC members are presidents of chiropractic colleges.

Meetings/Conferences:
Semi-annual Meetings: January and June

Publications:
Journal of Chiropractic Education. semi-a.

Association of Christian Librarians *(1957)*
P.O. Box 4
Cedarville, OH 45314
Tel: (937)766-2255 *Fax:* (937)766-2337
E-Mail: info@acl.org
Web Site: www.acl.org
Members: 500 individuals
Staff: 1
Annual Budget: $50-100,000
Executive Director: Nancy J. Olson
E-Mail: info@acl.org

Historical Note
Formerly (1981) Christian Librarians Fellowship. ACL members are primarily evangelical Christian academic librarians, as well as other interested librarians and individuals who subscribe to the purposes and position of the association. ACL is an organization

that promotes the professional and spiritual growth of its members and provides service to the academic library community worldwide. Membership fee varies, based on salary: $22-$65/year.

Meetings/Conferences:
Annual Meetings: June

Publications:
Christian Periodical Index. 2/year.
Christian Librarian. 3/yr. adv.

Association of Christian Schools International *(1978)*
731 Chapel Hills Dr.
Colorado Springs, CO 80920
Tel: (719)528-6906 *Fax:* (719)531-0631
E-Mail: info@acsi.org
Web Site: www.acsi.org
Members: 5000 schools
Staff: 150
Annual Budget: $10-25,000,000
President: Dr. Ken Smitherman
E-Mail: info@acsi.org
Vice President, Finance: Jere Elliott
E-Mail: info@acsi.org
Vice President, Academic Affairs: Derek Keenan, Ed.D.
E-Mail: info@acsi.org
Vice President, International Ministries: Philip M. Renicks
E-Mail: info@acsi.org
Vice President, Operations: Thomas A. Scott
E-Mail: info@acsi.org
Vice President, Executive Support: Taylor Smith, Jr.
E-Mail: info@acsi.org

Historical Note
ACSI is composed of privately funded schools with a religious orientation that work to effectively prepare students for life. The product of a merger on July 1, 1978 of the Western Association of Christian Schools, the Ohio Association of Christian Schools and the National Christian School Education Association.

Meetings/Conferences:
Annual Meetings: Summer

Publications:
Christian School Education. q. adv.
ACSI Directory. a. adv.
Christian Early Education. q. adv.
Christian School Comment. m.
Legal/Legislative Update. bi-m.

Association of Christian Teachers *(1990)*
P.O. Box 1193
Georgetown, TX 78627-1193
Tel: (512)819-0087
E-Mail: ppalmer549@aol.com
Chief Executive Officer: Paull Palmer
E-Mail: ppalmer549@aol.com

Association of Christian Therapists
6728 Old McLean Village Dr.
McLean, VA 22101
Tel: (703)556-9222 *Fax:* (703)556-8729
E-Mail: actheals@degnon.org
Web Site: www.actheals.org
Members: 1000 individuals
Staff: 3
Annual Budget: $100-250,000
Executive Director: George K. Degnon, CAE
Manager: Connie Mackay

Meetings/Conferences:
Annual Meetings: Fall

Publications:
InterAct. bi-m.
Journal of Christian Healing. q. adv.

Association of Cinema and Video Laboratories *(1953)*
1377 N. Serrano Ave.
Hollywood, CA 90027
Tel: (323)462-6171 *Fax:* (323)461-0608
Web Site: www.acvl.org
Members: 61 laboratories
Staff: 3
Annual Budget: $50-100,000
President: Beverly Wood

Historical Note
Formerly Association of Cinema Laboratories, ACVL provides an opportunity for the discussion and exchange of ideas in connection with the technical, administrative and managerial problems of the motion-picture and video laboratory industry. The Association is concerned with government relations, public and industry relations, product specifications, improvements of technical practices and procedures and other interest areas for film and video laboratories.

Meetings/Conferences:
Annual Meetings: June

Publications:
ACVL Handbook.

Association of Civilian Technicians *(1960)*
12620 Lake Ridge Dr.
Woodbridge, VA 22192
Tel: (703)494-4845 *Fax:* (703)494-0961
E-Mail: actnat@actnat.com
Web Site: www.actnat.com
Members: 23500 individuals
Staff: 10
Annual Budget: $1-2,000,000
President: Thomas G. Bastas
E-Mail: actnat@actnat.com

Historical Note
ACT is the largest union representing civilian National Guard Technicians. Membership: 0.007% of base pay/bi-weekly.

Meetings/Conferences:
Semi Annual Meetings: February/September/ Washington D.C.
2007 – Washington, DC/

Publications:
Technician Newsletter. m.

Association of Clinical Research Professionals *(1976)*
500 Montgomery St., Suite 800
Alexandria, VA 22314
Tel: (703)254-8100 *Fax:* (703)254-8101
E-Mail: office@acrpnet.org
Web Site: www.acrpnet.org
Members: 20000 individuals
Staff: 37
Annual Budget: $5-10,000,000
President and Chief Executive Officer: Thomas L. Adams, CAE
E-Mail: office@acrpnet.org
Chief Operating Officer: J. Alan Armstrong
E-Mail: office@acrpnet.org
Director, Certification and Accreditation: Carol McCullough
E-Mail: office@acrpnet.org
Director, Finance and Administration: Jim Thomasell
E-Mail: office@acrpnet.org
Manager, Membership Services and Customer Service: Debbie Timmons
E-Mail: office@acrpnet.org

Historical Note
Founded as Associates of Clinical Pharmacology; assumed its current name in 1997. ACRP members are clinical researchers and related health professionals. Membership: $120/year (individual).

Meetings/Conferences:
Annual Meeting: Spring
2007 – Seattle, WA(Washington State Convention Center)/Apr. 20-24

Publications:
Salary Survey. bien.
Monitor. bi-m. adv.

Association of Clinical Scientists *(1949)*
P.O. Drawer 1287
Middlebury, VT 05753
Tel: (802)462-2507 *Fax:* (802)462-2673
E-Mail: clinsci@sover.net
Web Site: www.clinicalscience.org
Members: 500 individuals
Staff: 1
Annual Budget: $100-250,000
Secretary-Treasurer: F. William Sunderman, Jr., M.D.

Historical Note
Organized as the Clinical Science Club in 1949. Became Association of Clinical Scientists in 1956. Chartered by the State of Pennsylvania as a nonprofit scientific organization in 1957. Affiliated with the American Association for the Advancement of Science and the Intersociety Pathology Council. Membership: $170/year (individual).

Meetings/Conferences:
Annual Meetings: Spring
2007 – Hershey, PA(Hershey Lodge)/May 16-20

Publications:
Annals of Clinical and Laboratory Science. q. adv.
Newsletter (Clinical Science Trumpet). q.

Association of College Administration Professionals *(1995)*
P.O. Box 1389
Staunton, VA 24402
Tel: (540)885-1873 *Fax:* (540)885-6133
E-Mail: acap@cfw.com
Web Site: www.acap.org
Members: 1500 individuals
Staff: 3
Annual Budget: $250-500,000
President: Stan Clark
E-Mail: acap@cfw.com

Historical Note
ACAP members are administrators in the business, student and academic services areas of colleges and universities. Membership: $75/year (individual); $195/year (institution).

Meetings/Conferences:
Annual Meetings: February
2007 – San Diego, CA/March 10-13

Publications:
Bulletin. m.

Association of College and Research Libraries *(1938)*
50 E. Huron St.
Chicago, IL 60611-2795
Tel: (312)280-2523 *Fax:* (312)280-2520
Toll Free: (800)545 - 2433 Ext: 2523
E-Mail: acrl@ala.org
Web Site: www.ala.org/acrl
Members: 13000 individuals
Staff: 14
Annual Budget: $2-5,000,000
Executive Director: Mary Ellen Davis
Associate Director: Mary Jane Petrowski
E-Mail: mpetrowski@ala.org

Historical Note
Represents academic and research librarians and libraries. This includes all types of academic libraries - community and junior college, college, and university - as well as comprehensive and specialized research libraries and their professional staffs. Formerly Association of College and Reference Libraries. A division of the American Library Association. Individuals must belong to ALA in order to join ACRL. Membership: $35/year.

Meetings/Conferences:
Semi-Annual Meetings: Mid-Winter, and Summer Annual Conference with American Library Ass'n
2007 – Baltimore, MD/March 29-Apr. 1

Publications:
C&RL News. 11/year. adv.
Choice. 11/year. adv.
College and Research Libraries. 6/year. adv.
Rare Books & Manuscripts Librarianship (RBM). semi-a. adv.

Association of College and University Auditors *(1958)*
342 N. Main St.
West Hartford, CT 06117-2507
Tel: (860)586-7561 Ext: 2 *Fax:* (860)586-7550
E-Mail: info@acua.org
Web Site: www.acua.org
Members: 500 institutions
Annual Budget: $250-500,000
Executive Director: Karen Hinen, CAE

Historical Note
Members are educational institutions with their own auditing staffs. Membership: $300/year (institution).

Meetings/Conferences:
Annual Meetings: September
2007 – Atlanta, GA(Omni)/Sept. 28-Oct. 3

Publications:
Newsletter. 4/year.
Directory (online). adv.
Journal. 3/year. adv.

Association of College and University Housing Officers-International *(1951)*
941 Chatham Ln., Suite 318
Columbus, OH 43221-2416
Tel: (614)292-0099 *Fax:* (614)292-3205
E-Mail: osuacuho@osu.edu
Web Site: www.acuho-i.org
Members: 5200 individuals
Staff: 11
Annual Budget: $2-5,000,000
Executive Director: Sallie Traxler
Director, Communications and Marketing: James Baumann
Corporate Relations Manager: Fred Comparato
Executive Assistant and Volunteer Coordinator: Judy Dallas
Director, Finance and Administration: Dan Griscom
Professional Development Coordinator: Jennie Long
Systems Manager: Gal Naor
Historical Note
Organized in 1952 at the Univ. of California, Berkeley, as a direct outgrowth of the first National Campus Housing Conference held in 1949 at the Univ. of Illinois. Added International to its name in 1981. Members are college and university staff members with responsibility for student residence, food service, developmental programming, administration and related operations and independent residence hall operators. Membership: $131/year (individual); $201-234/year (institution); $38/year (student or emeritus); $556/year (corporation).
Meetings/Conferences:
Annual Meetings: Summer
Publications:
Talking Stick. bi-m. adv.
International Directory. a. adv.
Journal of College and University Student Housing. semi-a. adv.

Association of College and University Museums and Galleries *(1980)*
Philip and Muriel Berman Museum of Art, Ursinus College
601 E. Main St.
Collegeville, PA 19426
Tel: (610)409-3500 *Fax:* (610)409-3664
E-Mail: lhanover@ursinus.edu
Web Site: www.acumg.org
Members: 400 individuals
Staff: 1
Annual Budget: $10-25,000
President: Lisa Tremper Hanover
E-Mail: lhanover@ursinus.edu
Historical Note
ACUMG promotes the welfare of college and university museums and galleries of all disciplines, as well as the welfare of the professional staffs of those museums and galleries. Membership: $25/year (individual); $50/year (institution); $75/year (corporate); $10/year (student).
Meetings/Conferences:
Annual Meetings: Spring
2007 – Chicago, IL(Northwestern University)/100
Publications:
News and Issues. q.

Association of College and University Printers *(1964)*
Arizona State University
Box 870401
Tempe, AZ 85287
Tel: (480)965-9833 *Fax:* (480)965-2234
E-Mail: iburxl@asu.edu
Members: 140 individuals
Annual Budget: $10-25,000
President: Bob Lane
E-Mail: iburxl@asu.edu
Historical Note
An informal group of managers of printing services in colleges and universities. ACUP membership is achieved principally by attending the annual conference. Officers change annually in May.
Meetings/Conferences:
Annual Meetings: usually at a university location

Association of College and University Telecommunications Administrators *(1971)*
152 W. Zandale Dr., Suite 200
Lexington, KY 40503
Tel: (859)278-3338 *Fax:* (859)278-3268
Web Site: www.acuta.org
Members: 2100 individuals
Staff: 10
Annual Budget: $1-2,000,000
Executive Director: Jeri A. Semer, CAE
Manager, Membership Development: Kellie Bowman
E-Mail: kbowman@acuta.org
Manager, Meetings: Lisa Cheshire
E-Mail: lcheshire@acuta.org
Business Manager: Margaret Riley
Manager, Communications: Pat Scott
E-Mail: pscott@acuta.org
Historical Note
Membership: $155-395/yr (college/university); $500-2,465/year (corporate affiliates); $175/year (associate).
Meetings/Conferences:
Annual Meetings: Summer
2007 – Hollywood, FL(Westin Diplomat Resort and Spa)/July 29-Aug. 2
2008 – Las Vegas, NV(Caesars Palace)/July 13-17
Publications:
Membership Directory. a. adv.
ACUTA News. m.
ACUTA Journal. q. adv.

Association of College Honor Societies *(1925)*
4990 Northwind Dr., Suite 140
East Lansing, MI 48823-5031
Tel: (517)351-8335 *Fax:* (517)351-8336
Web Site: http://achsnatl.org
Members: 67 societies
Staff: 1
Annual Budget: $10-25,000
Executive Director: Dorothy I. Mitstifer
E-Mail: dmitstifer@achsnatl.org
Historical Note
Organized in 1925 to consider problems of mutual interest, and recommend action leading toward appropriate classification and standards. Acts as the coordinating agency for college and university honor societies. Membership: fees vary, based on budget.
Meetings/Conferences:
Annual Meetings: February
Publications:
ACHS Member Directory. bien.

Association of College Unions International *(1914)*
120 W. 7th St., Suite 200
Bloomington, IN 47404-3925
Tel: (812)245-2284 *Fax:* (812)245-6710
E-Mail: acui@acui.org
Web Site: www.acui.org
Members: 950 colleges and universities
Staff: 12
Annual Budget: $1-2,000,000
Executive Director: Marsha Herman-Betzen
E-Mail: acui@acui.org
Director, Finance Administration: David Teske
E-Mail: acui@acui.org
Historical Note
Founded as the Association of College Unions; assumed its present name in 1961. ACUI is a professional association dedicated to enhancing campus life through programs, services, and facilities with the goal of unifying the union and activities field.
Meetings/Conferences:
Annual Meetings: Early Spring/1,000
Publications:
Bulletin. bi-m. adv.

Association of Collegiate Business Schools and Programs *(1988)*
7007 College Blvd., Suite 420
Overland Park, KS 66211-1524
Tel: (913)339-9356 *Fax:* (913)339-6226
E-Mail: info@acbsp.org
Web Site: www.acbsp.org
Members: 455 institutions
Staff: 5
Annual Budget: $1-2,000,000
Executive Director: Doug Viehland
E-Mail: info@acbsp.org
Historical Note
Accrediting organization for business schools and programs in colleges and universities. Membership: $1250/year (institution).
Meetings/Conferences:
Annual Meetings: June
2007 – Orlando, FL(Wyndham Plaza)/June 29-July 2
Publications:
Update. q. adv.
Business Education Week. w. adv.

Association of Collegiate Conference and Events Directors International *(1980)*
8037 Campus Delivery, Colorado State Univ.
Ft. Collins, CO 80523-8037
Tel: (970)491-5151 *Fax:* (970)491-0667
Toll Free: (877)502 - 2233
E-Mail: acced@lamar.colostate.edu
Web Site: www.acced-i.org
Members: 1200 individuals
Staff: 3
Annual Budget: $250-500,000
Executive Director: Deborah Blom
E-Mail: deborah.blom@colostate.edu
Director, Member Services and Education: Rebecca Dakin
E-Mail: diana.hakenholz@colostate.edu
Electronic Communication Coordinator: Lori Everhart
E-Mail: lori.everhart@colostate.edu
Historical Note
Formerly Association of Conference and Events Directors International (1998). ACCED-I members are collegiate conference and events directors, professionals who design, coordinate and market conferences and special events at their institutions. Membership: $225/year (individual); $450/year (organization/company/institution).
Meetings/Conferences:
Annual Meetings: March
2007 – Baltimore, MD(Renaissance)/March 25-28/450
Publications:
e-Communique. bi-m. adv.

Association of Collegiate Licensing Administrators
Historical Note
ACLA merged with Internat'l Collegiate Licensing Ass'n, a program division of Nat'l Ass'n of Collegiate Directors of Athletics, in 2003.

Association of Collegiate Schools of Architecture *(1912)*
1735 New York Ave. NW
Third Floor
Washington, DC 20006
Tel: (202)785-2324 *Fax:* (202)628-0448
E-Mail: info@acsa-arch.org
Web Site: www.acsa-arch.org
Members: 4000 individuals
Staff: 8
Annual Budget: $1-2,000,000
Executive Director: Michael Monti, Ph.D.
Historical Note
Members are U.S. and Canadian faculties of professional architectural degree programs. Membership includes over 200 colleges and universities worldwide.
Meetings/Conferences:
Annual Meetings: Spring
Publications:
Guide to Architecture Schools. quadren.
Journal of Architectural Education. q.
ACSA News. 9/year. adv.

Association of Collegiate Schools of Planning *(1959)*
6311 Mallard Trace
Tallahassee, FL 32312
Tel: (850)385-2054 *Fax:* (850)385-2084

E-Mail: ddodd@acsp.org
Web Site: www.acsp.org
Members: 125 schools
Staff: 1
Annual Budget: $100-250,000
Association Manager: Donna Dodd
E-Mail: ddodd@acsp.org

Historical Note

ACSP is a consortium of university-based programs offering degrees in urban and regional planning in the U.S. Supports research in planning curricula and instruction to promote the discipline. Membership: $350/year.

Meetings/Conferences:

Annual Meetings: Fall/800
2007 – Milwaukee, WI(Hilton Milwaukee City Center)/Oct. 18-21

Publications:

ACSP Update. q. adv.
Journal of Planning Education and Research. q. adv.

Association of Commercial Finance Attorneys *(1958)*

10451 Mill Run Circle, Suite 1000
Owings Mills, MD 21117-5519
Tel: (410)581-7400 *Fax:* (410)581-7410
Members: 350 individuals
Vice President: Jeremy Friedberg

Historical Note

ACF members are attorneys specializing in commercial finance and bankruptcy law. ACFA provides continuing education and publishes material relevant to the field for its members. Has no paid officers or full-time staff.

Publications:

Annual Update Proceedings.

Association of Communications Enterprises *(1992)*

Historical Note

Merged with COMPTEL in 2003 to form COMPTEL/ASCENT.

Association of Community Cancer Centers *(1974)*

11600 Nebel St., Suite 201
Rockville, MD 20852
Tel: (301)984-9496 *Fax:* (301)770-1949
Web Site: www.accc-cancer.org
Members: 675 institutions
Staff: 20
Annual Budget: $500-1,000,000
Deputy Executive Director: Christian Downs

Historical Note

Voting members are primarily community hospitals with cancer-care programs and onocology practices. Membership: $105/year (individual); $997.50/year (hospitals).

Publications:

Community Cancer Programs in the United States. adv.
Oncology Issues. bi-m. adv.

Association of Community College Trustees *(1972)*

1233 20th St. NW
Suite 301
Washington, DC 20036-2907
Tel: (202)775-4667 *Fax:* (202)223-1297
Web Site: www.acct.org
Members: 650 governing boards
Staff: 13
Annual Budget: $2-5,000,000
President and Chief Executive Officer: J. Noah Brown

Historical Note

Formerly (1972) the Council of Community College Boards, National School Boards Association. Membership: $545-2,185/year, based on enrollment (institution).

Meetings/Conferences:

Annual Meetings: Fall/1,500-2,000
2007 – San Diego, CA(Hyatt)

Publications:

Advisor. bi-m.
Trustee Quarterly. q. adv.

Association of Community Health Nursing Educators *(1978)*

10200 W. 44th Ave., Suite 304
Wheat Ridge, CO 80033
Tel: (303)422-0769 *Fax:* (303)422-8894
E-Mail: achne@resourcenter.com
Web Site: www.achne.org
Members: 400 individuals
Staff: 2
Annual Budget: $50-100,000
Management Executive: Francine Butler, Ph.D., CAE

Historical Note

Promotes the public's health by ensuring leadership and excellence in community and public health nursing education through excellence in practice and research. Has no paid officers or full-time staff; administrative support provided by New York State Nurses Association. Membership: $90/year (individual), $450/year (organization/company).

Publications:

ACHNE Newsletter. q. adv.
Proceedings of Spring Institute. a.

Association of Community Tribal Schools *(1982)*

616 Fourth Ave., West
Sisseton, SD 57262-1349
Tel: (605)698-3112
Web Site: www.wambdi.bia.edu/ACTS
Members: 30 schools
Annual Budget: $25-50,000
Executive Director: Dr. Roger Bordeaux

Historical Note

Founded as Association of Contract Tribal Schools. Has no paid officers or full-time staff.

Meetings/Conferences:

Annual Meetings: Spring

Publications:

Newsletter. q.

Association of Concert Bands *(1977)*

6613 Cheryl Ann Dr.
Independence, OH 44131-3718
Tel: (216)524-1897
Toll Free: (800)726 - 8720
E-Mail: acbsec@sbcglobal.net
Web Site: www.acbands.org
Members: 800bands,companiesandindividuals
Staff: 1
Annual Budget: $25-50,000
Secretary: Nada Vencl

Historical Note

Formerly (1983) Association of Concert Bands of America. Dedicated to the worldwide advancement of adult concert and community bands. Membership: $30/year (individual); $150/year (corporate); $50/year (organization).

Meetings/Conferences:

Annual Meetings: Spring
2007 – Pensacola, FL/Feb. 28-March 4

Publications:

Advance! ACB Magazine. 3/year. adv.

Association of Conservation Engineers *(1961)*

c/o Missouri Department of Conservation
P.O. Box 180
Jefferson City, MO 65102
Tel: (573)522-4115 Ext: 3739
E-Mail: greg.michalevich@mdc.mo.gov
Web Site: http://conservationengineers.org
Members: 300 individuals
Staff: 16
Annual Budget: $10-25,000
Secretary: Greg Michalevich

Historical Note

Members are engineers and allied personnel employed by state, federal and provincial conservation and recreation departments, who have a specialized interest in the areas of fish, wildlife, parks, forests and related conservation-recreation fields. Has no paid officers or full-time staff. Membership: $15/year (individual).

Meetings/Conferences:

Annual Meetings: Fall

Publications:

ACE Newsletter. semi-a. adv.
Membership Directory. a.

Association of Construction Inspectors

1224 N. Nokomis NE
Alexandria, MN 56308
Tel: (320)763-7525 *Fax:* (320)763-9290
E-Mail: aci@iami.org
Web Site: www.iami.org/aci.html
Members: 3000 individuals
Staff: 12
Annual Budget: $1-2,000,000
Executive Director: Robert G. Johnson
Managing Director: Dale Ekdahl
E-Mail: iami@iami.org

Historical Note

Membership: $165/year.

Meetings/Conferences:

Annual Meetings: Fall

Publications:

Conspect. q. adv.
Registry of Members. a.

Association of Consulting Chemists and Chemical Engineers *(1928)*

P.O. Box 297
Sparta, NJ 07871
Tel: (973)729-6671 *Fax:* (973)729-7088
E-Mail: info@chemconsult.org
Web Site: www.chemconsult.org
Members: 150 individuals
Staff: 1
Annual Budget: $25-50,000
Executive Secretary: Linda Townsend
E-Mail: info@chemconsult.org

Historical Note

Founded and chartered in 1928 in the state of New York, ACC&CE is a non-profit association of independent consulting chemists. ACC&CE serves the various scientific industries, using expertise based on a wide variety of technical and business knowledge. Membership directory accessible online through the association's URL address. Membership: $300/year.

Publications:

The Chemical Consultant. 3/yr. adv.
Consulting Services Directory. bien.

Association of Consulting Foresters of America *(1948)*

312 Montgomery St., Suite 208
Alexandria, VA 22314
Tel: (703)548-0990 *Fax:* (703)548-6395
Toll Free: (888)540 - 8733
E-Mail: director@acf-foresters.org
Web Site: www.acf-foresters.org
Members: 625 individuals
Staff: 3
Annual Budget: $100-250,000
Executive Director: Lynn C. Wilson
E-Mail: director@acf-foresters.org

Historical Note

Members are technically trained foresters who own their own businesses, demonstrate their professional competency and whose services are available to the general public on a fee or contract basis. Membership: $300/year.

Meetings/Conferences:

Annual Meetings: last week in June

Publications:

ACF Membership Specialization Directory. a. adv.
ACF Newsletter. bi-m.
The Consultant. a. adv.

Association of Cooperative Educators *(1965)*

P.O. Box 64047
St. Paul, MN 55164-0047
Tel: (651)355-5481 *Fax:* (651)355-5073
Web Site: www.uwcc.wisc.edu/ace/ace.html
Members: 200 individuals
Staff: 1
Annual Budget: $50-100,000
Executive Administrator: Leslie Mead

Historical Note

Founded in Banff as the Association for Cooperative Education, the name was changed in 1970 and reorganized in 1997 as a non-profit organization. Membership consists of individuals and organizations professionally engaged in educational, training or *personnel programs of cooperative organizations. Membership: $25-50/year (individual); $150/year (organization/company).*

Meetings/Conferences:
Annual Meetings: Annual institutes in August
2007 – Saskatoon, SK, Canada(Univ. of Saskatchewan)/May 29-June 2

Publications:
ACE News. q.
Newsletter. semi-a.
Membership List. a.

Association of Corporate Counsel *(1982)*
1025 Connecticut Ave. NW
Suite 200
Washington, DC 20036-5425
Tel: (202)293-4103 *Fax:* (202)293-4701
Web Site: www.acca.com
Members: 20000 individuals
Staff: 30
Annual Budget: $2-5,000,000
President and Chief Operating Officer: Frederick J. Krebs
Director, Communications: David Barre
Senior Vice President and Chief Financial Officer: Anne Bracken
E-Mail: bracken@acca.com
Vice President, Membership, Chapters and Communications: Robin Grossfeld
Senior Vice President and General Counsel: Susan Hackett
E-Mail: hackett@acca.com
Vice President, Law and Technology: Ron Peppe

Historical Note
ACC members are lawyers who practice law in a corporation or other private sector entity and who do not hold themselves out to the public for the practice of law. Organized in Dallas, Texas on March 11, 1982 by 52 corporate attorneys from 45 companies. Membership: $225/year.

Meetings/Conferences:
Annual Meetings: Fall

Publications:
The ACCA Docket Magazine. bi-m. adv.
ACCA News Newsletter. 2-4/year.

Association of Corporate Travel Executives *(1988)*
515 King St., Suite 340
Alexandria, VA 22314
Tel: (703)683-5322 *Fax:* (703)683-2720
E-Mail: info@acte.org
Web Site: www.acte.org
Members: 2500 individuals
Staff: 14
Annual Budget: $5-10,000,000
Executive Director: Susan Gurley
E-Mail: susan@acte.org
Deputy Executive Director: Megan Costello
E-Mail: megan@acte.org

Historical Note
ACTE members are senior level travel professionals from around the world. Membership: $300/year (individual).

Meetings/Conferences:
Annual Meetings: Spring

Publications:
ACTE Quarterly. bi-m. adv.
Update Newsletter. m. adv.
Membership Directory. a. adv.

Association of Cosmetologists and Hairdressers *(1985)*
1811 Monroe St.
Dearborn, MI 48124
Tel: (313)563-0360 *Fax:* (313)563-1448
Members: 3910 individuals
Staff: 4
Annual Budget: $2-5,000,000
President: Mary Ann Neuman

Historical Note
Membership includes hairdressers and cosmetologists, as well as wholesalers, manufacturers, buyers, distributors, and retailers. Membership: $150/year (individual).

Publications:
Newsletter. q.

Association of Coupon Professionals *(1988)*
200 E. Howard, Suite 280
Des Plaines, IL 60018
Tel: (847)297-7773 *Fax:* (847)297-8428
E-Mail: joanne.martori@acphq.org
Web Site: www.couponpros.org
Members: 60 companies
Annual Budget: $100-250,000
Executive Director: Joanne Martori, CAE
E-Mail: joanne.martori@acphq.org

Historical Note
Founded as Association of Coupon Processors; assumed its current name in 1996. ACP was established to improve industry business conditions, to assure continued use of coupons as a viable sales and marketing tool and to provide for the resolution of common industry concerns in the development, distribution and redemption of coupons. Membership fee varies, based on type: $500-3,000/year.

Publications:
Coupon Exchange. 10/yr.

Association of Crafts and Creative Industries *(1976)*

Historical Note
Formerly (1984) the Mid-America Craft Hobby Association. Membership is composed of professionals in the craft supply and creative industries. Object of ACCI is to offer a means of exchange to all those engaged in the buying, selling or manufacturing of craft, art, framing, miniature, notions, needlework and floral hobby merchandise. Membership: $75-150/year.

Association of Credit Union Internal Auditors *(1990)*
P.O. Box 1926
Columbus, OH 43216-1926
Tel: (866)254-8128 *Fax:* (614)221-2335
E-Mail: acuia@acuia.org
Web Site: www.acuia.org
Members: 660 Individuals
Annual Budget: $250-500,000
Executive Director: Brad L. Feldman, MPA

Historical Note
ACUIA provides continuing education and professional resources to its member auditors and the credit union community. Membership: $200-400/year (regular); $100/year (supervisory); $400/year (associate).

Meetings/Conferences:
2007 – Nashville, TN(Sheraton Downtown)/June 5-8

Publications:
The Audit Report. q. adv.

Association of Dark Leaf Tobacco Dealers and Exporters *(1947)*
310 N. Blythe Ave.
Gallatin, TN 37066
Tel: (615)452-3355
Members: 20 companies
Staff: 1
Annual Budget: under $10,000
President: Doug Bond

Historical Note
An affiliate of Burley and Dark Leaf Tobacco Export Association, ADLTDE was organized to promote the use of dark-fired and dark air-cured tobaccos, both domestically and abroad.

Meetings/Conferences:
Semi-annual Meetings: Spring/Fall - Springfield, TN, Golf and Country Club

Association of Defense Trial Attorneys *(1941)*
124 S.W. Adams St., Suite 600
Peoria, IL 61602
Tel: (309)676-0400 *Fax:* (309)676-3374
Web Site: www.adtalaw.com
Members: 700 individuals
Staff: 1
Annual Budget: $25-50,000
Assistant to the Secretary: Lynnette Baldovin
E-Mail: lbaldovin@hrva.com

Historical Note
Formerly (1988) the Association of Insurance Attorneys. ADTA members are attorneys who regularly represent insurance companies and self-insurers and are expert in the fields of law pertaining to dispute resolution for the insurance industry. A minimum of five years trial experience with insurance cases and insurance matters is required for admission. Membership is limited to one member selected from each city, town and municipality (with certain exceptions). A member's partners or associates may become associate members. Membership: $195/year (prime member); $125/year (associate).

Meetings/Conferences:
Annual Meetings: Spring/200

Publications:
Newsletter. semi-a.
Membership Roster. a.

Association of Defensive Spray Manufacturers *(1992)*
906 Olive St., Suite 1200
St. Louis, MO 63101-1434
Tel: (314)241-1445 *Fax:* (314)241-1449
E-Mail: adsm@pepperspray.org
Web Site: www.pepperspray.org
Members: 6 corporate members
Annual Budget: under $10,000
Executive Director: Mark S. Birenbaum, Ph.D.

Historical Note
ADSM's purpose is to permit manufacturers of non-lethal chemical weapons to join together to promote the industry as well as to address safety, quality control, marketing and other issues relevant to the industry. Membership: $1,000/year (corporate).

Association of Departments of English *(1962)*
26 Broadway, Third Floor
New York, NY 10004-1789
Tel: (646)576-5130
Web Site: www.ade.org
Members: 840 departments
Staff: 3
Director: David Laurence
E-Mail: dlaurence@mla.org

Historical Note
Formerly Association of Departments of English in American Colleges and Universities. ADE members are administrators of college and university-level departments of English. Sponsored by the Modern Language Association of America. Membership: $100 - $600/year (company).

Meetings/Conferences:
Annual Meetings: Summer

Publications:
Job Information List. q.
ADE Bulletin. 3/year.

Association of Departments of Foreign Languages *(1969)*
26 Broadway, Third Floor
New York, NY 10004-1789
Tel: (646)576-5140 *Fax:* (646)458-0033
E-Mail: adfl@mla.org
Web Site: www.adfl.org
Members: 1050 academic departments
Staff: 4
Annual Budget: $50-100,000
Director: Nelly Furman

Historical Note
Members are administrators of foreign language departments at the college/university level.

Publications:
ADFL Bulletin. 3/year.

Association of Destination Management Executives *(1995)*
11 Monument Ave., Suite 510
P.O. Box 2307
Dayton, OH 45401-2307
Tel: (937)586-3727 *Fax:* (937)586-3699
E-Mail: info@adme.org
Web Site: www.adme.org
Members: 200 companies
Staff: 2
Annual Budget: $250-500,000
Executive Vice President: Francine W. Rickenbach, C.A.E.
E-Mail: info@adme.org

Historical Note
ADME members are CEOs of destination management companies. Awards the designation DMCP (Destination Management Certified Professional). Membership: $425/year.

Meetings/Conferences:
2007 - Rancho Mirage, CA(Westin Mission Hills)/Feb. 7-11/160

Publications:
ADMExpressions. q. adv.

Association of Diesel Specialists *(1956)*
P.O. Box 13966
Research Triangle Park, NC 27709
Tel: (919)549-4800 *Fax:* (919)549-4824
E-Mail: info@diesel.org
Web Site: www.diesel.org
Members: 750 companies
Staff: 6
Annual Budget: $500-1,000,000
Membership Director: Paulette Becoat

Historical Note
Members are companies and individuals whose primary interest is the technology and service of diesel fuel injection, governor and turbocharger systems.

Meetings/Conferences:
Annual Meetings: August/September

Publications:
Nozzle Chatter. q. adv.

Association of Direct Response Fundraising Counsel *(1987)*
1612 K St. NW
Suite 510
Washington, DC 20006
Tel: (202)293-9640 *Fax:* (202)293-9641
E-Mail: adrfco@msn.com
Web Site: www.adrfco.com
Members: 40 companies
Staff: 2
Annual Budget: $100-250,000
General Counsel: Robert Tigner
E-Mail: adrfco@msn.com

Meetings/Conferences:
2007 - Washington, DC(Williard Intercontinental)/February/41

Publications:
FYI. 3-4/year.
In Brief. 3-4/year.

Association of Directory Marketing *(1990)*
1187 Thorn Run Road, Suite 630
Moon Township, PA 15108-3198
Tel: (412)269-0663 *Fax:* (412)269-0655
E-Mail: adm@admworks.org
Web Site: www.admworks.org
Members: 10 companies
Staff: 8
Annual Budget: $500-1,000,000
President and Chief Executive Officer: Herbert D. Gordon
E-Mail: adm@admworks.org
Senior Vice President: Nancy B. Augustine
E-Mail: adm@admworks.org

Historical Note
ADM members are certified marketing representatives/agencies, directory publishers and suppliers. Membership: varies based on annual billings.

Meetings/Conferences:
Annual Meetings: Fall

Publications:
ADM Flash. m.

Association of Directory Publishers *(1898)*
P.O. Box 1929
Traverse City, MI 49685-1929
Toll Free: (800)267 - 9002
Web Site: www.adp.org
Members: 277 companies
Staff: 1
Annual Budget: $500-1,000,000
President and Chief Executive Officer: R. Lawrence Angove
E-Mail: larry.angove@adp.org
Chief Operating Officer: Bonnie Pintozzi
E-Mail: bonnie.pintozzi@adp.org

Historical Note
Formerly (1992) the Association of North American Directory Publishers; assumed its current name in. ADP is the oldest and largest organization in the country representing the interests of telephone directory publishers.

Meetings/Conferences:
Semi-annual Meetings: Spring and Fall

Publications:
Membership Roster. a. adv.
Extra. a. adv.

Association of Diving Contractors International *(1968)*
5206 F.M. 1960 West, Suite 202
Houston, TX 77069
Tel: (281)893-8388 *Fax:* (281)893-5118
Toll Free: (888)232 - 4838
Web Site: www.adc-int.org
Members: 450 companies
Staff: 4
Annual Budget: $500-1,000,000
Executive Director: Ross Saxon, Ph.D.

Historical Note
Commercial diving and underwater contractors, manufacturers and suppliers of diving equipment, diving schools and ROV owners and operators. Membership: $25/year (individual); $250/year and up (organization/company) fee varies by volume.

Meetings/Conferences:
Annual Meetings: Winter

Publications:
Underwater Magazine. bi-m. adv.

Association of Earth Science Editors *(1967)*
101 Fire Academy Road
Socorro, NM 87801
Tel: (412)268-4708 *Fax:* (412)268-5677
E-Mail: maryanns@andres.cum.edu
Web Site: www.aese.org
Members: 275 individuals
Staff: 7
Annual Budget: $10-25,000
Central Office Manager: Mary Ann Schmidt
E-Mail: maryanns@andres.cum.edu

Historical Note
Founded to strengthen the profession of earth science editing, AESE promotes the exchange of ideas on problems of selection, editing and publication of research manuscripts, journals, serials, periodicals and maps pertaining to earth sciences. Affiliated with the American Geological Institute, Geological Society of America, Council of Science Editors, and American Association for the Advancement of Science. Membership: $30/year (individual).

Meetings/Conferences:
Annual Meetings: September or October/100

Publications:
Blueline. q.
Membership Directory. a.

Association of Ecosystem Research Centers *(1985)*
Univ. of Alabama
Biological Science Dept.
Tuscaloosa, AL 35487-0206
Tel: (205)348-1787 *Fax:* (205)348-1403
Members: 41 centers
Annual Budget: under $10,000
Treasurer: Amelia Ward
Program Administrator: Deborah Cook

Historical Note
AERC was established to improve coordination and communications among ecosystem research centers and to promote and expand their research programs. Membership: $40/year (individual); $400/year (center).

Publications:
AERC Newsletter. semi-a.
Directory of Member Centers. bien.

Association of Edison Illuminating Companies *(1885)*
P.O. Box 2641
Birmingham, AL 35291-0992
Tel: (205)257-2530 *Fax:* (205)257-2540
Web Site: www.aeic.org
Members: 111 investor-owned utilities
Staff: 4
Annual Budget: $250-500,000
Executive Director: Robert Huffman
E-Mail: diraeic@a6inter.net

Historical Note
Organized in 1885 by licensees of Thomas A. Edison for the advancement of electric service to the public for light, heat and power. Represents U.S. investor-owned utilities and international electric utilities providing technical expertise and information. Membership fee varies based on revenues; maximum $13,775/year.

Meetings/Conferences:
Annual Meetings: Fall

Publications:
AEIC Update. q.

Association of Educational Publishers *(1895)*
510 Heron Dr., Suite 201
Logan Township, NJ 08085
Tel: (856)241-7772 *Fax:* (856)241-0709
E-Mail: mail@edpress.org
Web Site: www.edpress.org
Members: 1500 companies & individuals
Staff: 8
Annual Budget: $500-1,000,000
Executive Director: Charlene F. Gaynor
E-Mail: cgaynor@edpress.org

Historical Note
Formerly (1998) Educational Press Association of America. Members are among the most respected names in school and teacher publications, children's magazines, software and supplemental publishers, educational foundations and associations, schools and school districts, and the education and trade press across the media. Services provided for CEOs, editorial, marketing and public relations professionals in education publishing. Membership: corporate fee varies; independents/freelancers $260/year.

Meetings/Conferences:
Annual Meetings: early Summer

Publications:
EP Online. semi-m.

Association of Educational Service Agencies *(1976)*
801 N. Quincy St., Suite 750
Arlington, VA 22203
Tel: (703)875-0739 *Fax:* (703)807-1849
E-Mail: info@aesa.us
Web Site: www.aesa.us
Members: 607 Individuals
Staff: 3
Annual Budget: $500-1,000,000
Executive Director: Brian Talbott

Historical Note
AESA members are public entities created by statute to provide educational support programs and services to local schools and school districts within a given geographic area.

Meetings/Conferences:
Annual Meetings: Winter

Publications:
AESA Perpectives - Journal. a.
AESA News. m.

Association of Educational Therapists *(1978)*
210 N. Glenoaks Blvd., Suite C
Burbank, CA 91502
Toll Free: (800)286 - 4267
E-Mail: aet@aetonline.org
Web Site: www.aetonline.org
Staff: 1
Management Executive: Janine Newell, CAE, CPC

Historical Note
AET defines and sets standards for the professional practice of educational therapy. Membership: $200/year.

Meetings/Conferences:
Annual Meetings: Fall

Association of Educators in Imaging and Radiologic Sciences *(1967)*
P.O. Box 90204
Albuquerque, NM 87199-0204
Tel: (505)823-4740 *Fax:* (505)823-4740
E-Mail: office@aeirs.org

Web Site: www.aeirs.org
Members: 500 individuals
Staff: 1
Executive Secretary: Valerie Christensen
E-Mail: office@aeirs.org

Historical Note
AERS members are professionals who have current registration with ARRT, NMTCB, ARDMS, or equivalent credentials and are employed in an educational position associated with an accredited radiological sciences program. Membership: $75/year (individual).

Meetings/Conferences:
Annual Meetings: Summer
2007 – Albuquerque, NM(Hyatt)/

Publications:
Radiologic Science and Education Journal. a.
AERS Spectrum Newsletter. q.

Association of Eminent Domain Professionals
P.O. Box 6721
West Palm Beach, FL 33405
Tel: (561)655-4144 *Fax:* (561)659-1824
E-Mail: aedp@aedp.org
Web Site: www.aedp.org
Staff: 2
Executive Secretary: Alison Pruitt
E-Mail: aedp@aedp.org

Association of Energy Engineers *(1977)*
4025 Pleasantdale Road, Suite 420
Atlanta, GA 30340
Tel: (770)447-5083 Ext: 210 *Fax:* (770)446-3969
E-Mail: info@aeecenter.org
Web Site: www.aeecenter.org
Members: 8500 individuals
Staff: 12
Annual Budget: $1-2,000,000
Executive Director: Albert Thumann

Historical Note
Licensed professional engineers, architects, utility managers and consultants with experience in energy management and environmental management, distributed generation, energy services, facilities management and security management. Membership: $155/year.

Meetings/Conferences:
Annual Meetings: Fall

Publications:
Retail Energy Newsletter. m.
Cogeneration & Distributed Generation. 3/year.
Merchant Power Newsletter. m.
Insight Newsletter. q.
Energy Engineering Journal. bi-m. adv.
Strategic Planning for Energy and the Environment Journal. q.
Wheeling and Transmission Newsletter. m.

Association of Energy Service Companies *(1956)*
10200 Richmond Ave., Suite 253
Houston, TX 77042
Tel: (713)781-0758 *Fax:* (713)781-7542
Toll Free: (800)692 - 0771
Web Site: www.aesc.net
Members: 687 companies
Staff: 5
Annual Budget: $1-2,000,000
Administrative Manager: Angela Fails

Historical Note
Formerly Association of Oilwell Servicing Contractors (1996).

Meetings/Conferences:
Semi-Annual Meetings: February and July

Publications:
Field Reports Newsletter. bi-m.
Well Servicing Magazine. bi-m. adv.
Directory. a.

Association of Energy Services Professionals, International *(1989)*
229 E. Ridgewood Road
Georgetown, TX 78628-9569
Tel: (512)864-7200
E-Mail: eboardman@aesp.org
Web Site: www.aesp.org
Members: 1200 individuals
Staff: 4
Annual Budget: $500-1,000,000
Executive Director: Elliot Boardman

Historical Note
Formerly (1994) Association of DSM Professionals. Members are professionals in the energy industry. Membership: $155/year.

Meetings/Conferences:
Annual: December

Publications:
Strategies Newsletter. q. adv.

Association of Environmental and Engineering Geologists *(1957)*
P.O. Box 460518
Denver, CO 80246
Tel: (303)757-2926 *Fax:* (303)757-2969
E-Mail: aeg@aegweb.org
Web Site: www.aegweb.org
Members: 3100 individuals
Staff: 3
Annual Budget: $500-1,000,000
Chief Staff Executive: Becky Roland

Historical Note
Founded by 12 charter members in Sacramento, CA as the California Association of Environmental and Engineering Geologists; assumed its present name and became an international organization in 1957. A member society of the American Geological Institute. Membership is open to anyone possessing a college degree in geology or engineering geology, or otherwise having a serious interest in the subject. Membership: $105/year (full member); $70/year (associate/affiliate); $25/year (student).

Meetings/Conferences:
Annual Meetings: Fall
2007 – Los Angeles, CA(Sheraton, Universal Studios)/Sept. 24-28/800

Publications:
Environmental and Engineering Geoscience. q.
AEG Directory. a. adv.
AEG News. q. adv.
AEG Program with Abstracts. a. adv.

Association of Environmental and Resource Economists *(1979)*
1616 P St. NW
Room 510
Washington, DC 20036
Tel: (202)328-5077 *Fax:* (202)939-3460
E-Mail: voigt@rff.org
Web Site: www.aere.org
Members: 800 individuals
Annual Budget: $25-50,000
Executive Secretary: Marilyn Voigt

Historical Note
AERE serves as an information resource for economists involved in natural resources policy planning and research. Membership: $30/year (individual); $15/year (student); $56-$125/year (student or personal membership for the U.S., Canada, and abroad, with subscription to the Journal of Environmental Economics and Management).

Meetings/Conferences:
Annual Meetings: January, in conjunction with Allied Social Science Ass'ns.

Publications:
AERE Newsletter. semi-a.
Journal of Environmental Economics and Management. bi-m.

Association of Environmental Engineering and Science Professors *(1963)*
2303 Naples Court
Champaign, IL 61822
Tel: (217)398-6969 *Fax:* (217)355-9232
Web Site: www.aeesp.org
Members: 700 individuals
Staff: 1
Annual Budget: $25-50,000
Business Secretary: Joanne Fetzner

Historical Note
Formerly (1972) American Association of Professors in Sanitary Engineering. Individuals working or teaching in the field of environmental engineering, including water quality and treatment, air quality, air pollution control and solid and hazardous waste management. Officers change annually. Membership: $40-70/year (individual); $500/year (company).

Meetings/Conferences:
Annual Meetings: Fall with the Water Environment Federation

Publications:
AEESP Newsletter. q. adv.

Association of Episcopal Colleges *(1962)*
The Episcopal Church Center
815 Second Ave., Suite 315
New York, NY 10017-4594
Tel: (212)716-6148 *Fax:* (212)986-5039
E-Mail: office@cuac.org
Web Site: www.cuac.org
Members: 11 colleges
Staff: 3
Annual Budget: $100-250,000
General Secretary: Rev. Dr. Don Thompson
E-Mail: office@cuac.org

Historical Note
Formerly (1965) Foundation for Episcopal Colleges, and (1966) Fund for Episcopal Colleges. The Association is a consortium of colleges with historic and current ties to the Episcopal Church. Its mission is the development of programs on and off campus which enhance the spiritual, intellectual and ethical growth of college students. Colleges and Universities in the Anglican Communion is its international equivalent, and shares administrative staff with AEC. Membership: $7,000/year (institution).

Meetings/Conferences:
Annual Meetings: Annual/15

Publications:
Views & News. a.

Association of Equipment Management Professionals *(1980)*
P.O. Box 1368
Glenwood Springs, CO 81602
Tel: (970)384-0510 *Fax:* (970)384-0512
E-Mail: info@aemp.org
Web Site: www.aemp.org/
Members: 1200 individuals
Staff: 2
Annual Budget: $250-500,000
Executive Director: Stan Orr, CAE

Historical Note
AEMP members are equipment managers from all equipment-intensive industries: construction, wood products, municipalities, utilities, gas and oil exploration, mining, solid waste, commercial farming, aviation ground equipment maintenance, and vocational technical schools. AEMP works to establish a positive relationship between users, manufacturers, government agencies and educators involved in the design and operation of equipment.

Meetings/Conferences:
Annual Meetings: Spring

Publications:
Membership Directory. a.
Up & Running. 6/year. adv.
Management Digest. bi-a.

Association of Equipment Manufacturers *(1894)*
6737 W. Washington St., #2400
Milwaukee, WI 53214-5647
Tel: (414)272-0943 *Fax:* (414)272-1170
Toll Free: (888)236 - 0442
E-Mail: aem@aem.org
Web Site: www.aem.org
Members: 700 companies
Staff: 50
Annual Budget: $5-10,000,000
President: Dennis J. Slater
E-Mail: aem@aem.org

Historical Note
Formerly (2001) Construction Industry Manufacturers Association (CIMA) and Equipment Manufacturers Institute (EMI). Subsidiaries include more than 60 bureaus, councils and committees of volunteer member executives covering areas including product safety and technical issues, market information, global public policy, and trade shows. Owns or co-

owns and operates four international trade shows: CONEXPO-CON/AGG (construction), CONEXPO Asia, ICUEE International Construction and Utility Equipment Exposition, IFPE international Exposition for Power Transmission and World of Asphalt Show and Conference. Maintains offices in Washington, DC; Ottawa, Canada; Beijing, China; and Brussels, Belgium.

Publications:
Activities Report. a.
Catalog Safety, Technical & Info Materials on Off-Road Constr Machines. a.
Directory. a.
Newsletter. m.

Association of Executive and Administrative Professionals *(1975)*
900 S. Washington St., Suite G13
Falls Church, VA 22046-4020
Tel: (703)237-8616 *Fax:* (703)533-1153
E-Mail: headquarters@naesaa.com
Web Site: www.naesaa.com
Members: 8000 individuals
Staff: 4
Annual Budget: $100-250,000
Director: Ruth Ludeman
Director, Membership: Susan Young
Historical Note
Formerly (1997) National Association of Executive Secretaries and (2006) National Association of Executive Secretaries and Administrative Assistants. Membership: $35/year.
Meetings/Conferences:
Annual Meetings: Fall
Publications:
Executive Secretary Salary Survey Report (online).
The Exec-U-Tary. 11/year.

Association of Executive Search Consultants *(1959)*
12 E. 41st St.
17th Floor
New York, NY 10017
Tel: (212)398-9556 *Fax:* (212)398-9560
E-Mail: aesc@aesc.org
Web Site: www.aesc.org
Members: 200 firms
Staff: 14
Annual Budget: $2-5,000,000
President: Peter Felix
E-Mail: aesc@aesc.org
Historical Note
Established as the Association of Executive Recruiting Consultants; assumed its present name in 1982. The Association consists of executive search firms that are committed to the high standards of professional practice outlined in the AESC Code of Ethics and Professional Practice Guidelines.
Publications:
AESC News: Retained Firms Newsletter (e-mail).
BlueSteps Senior Executives Newsletter.
AESC Researchers Networking Group Newsletter.
AESC News: Hiring Organizations Newsletter (e-mail).
Code of Ethics.
Professional Practice Guidelines.
Small Firm Forum Newsletter.

Association of Family and Conciliation Courts *(1963)*
6525 Grand Teton Plaza
Madison, WI 53719-1085
Tel: (608)664-3750 *Fax:* (608)664-3751
E-Mail: afcc@afccnet.org
Web Site: www.afccnet.org
Members: 1800 individuals
Staff: 5
Annual Budget: $250-500,000
Executive Director: Peter Salem, MA
E-Mail: afcc@afccnet.org
Historical Note
AFCC was established to develop and improve the practice and procedures of family counseling as a complement to the judicial process; to promote ethical standards in court-related marriage and divorce counseling; and to provide a forum for the exchange of ideas and assistance in establishing programs in this field. Members include lawyers, judges and marriage counselors. Membership: $125/year (individual); $300/year (institution); $40/year (student).
Meetings/Conferences:
Annual Meetings: May
Publications:
Family Courts Review. q. adv.
Newsletter. q. adv.

Association of Family Medicine Administration *(1983)*
11400 Tomahawk Creek Pkwy.
Leawood, KS 66211-2672
Tel: (800)274-2237 Ext: 6708 *Fax:* (913)906-6092
Toll Free: (800)274 - 2237 Ext: 6708
Web Site: www.afpa.net
Members: 376
Staff: 1
Executive Secretary: Dawn Sexton
E-Mail: dsexton@aafp.org
Historical Note
Formerly (1983) Association of Family Practice Administrators; assumed current name in 2005. AFMA members are administrators of residency programs in family medicine. Membership: $150/year (individual).
Publications:
Connection. q.

Association of Family Medicine Residency Directors *(1990)*
11400 Tomahawk Creek Pkwy., Suite 670
Leawood, KS 66211-2672
Tel: (913)906-6000 Ext: 6736 *Fax:* (913)906-6105
Toll Free: (800)274 - 2237 Ext: 6736
Web Site: www.afmrd.org
Members: 420 individuals
Staff: 4
Annual Budget: $50-100,000
Executive Director: Cynthia W. Weber, M.A.
E-Mail: cweber@aafp.org
Historical Note
Formerly (2004) Association of Family Practice Residency Directors. Members are directors of residency programs in family medicine. Membership: $350/year.
Meetings/Conferences:
Annual Meetings: always Kansas City, MO.
Publications:
Highlights. 3/year. adv.

Association of Family Practice Administrators
Historical Note
Became Association of Family Medicine Administration in 2005.

Association of Farmworker Opportunity Programs *(1971)*
1726 M St. NW, Suite 800
Washington, DC 20036-4525
Tel: (202)828-6006 *Fax:* (202)828-6005
E-Mail: wochinske@afop.org
Web Site: www.afop.org
Members: 53 organizations
Staff: 7
Annual Budget: $1-2,000,000
Executive Director: David Strauss
Finance Manager: Jaime Atienza
E-Mail: wochinske@afop.org
SAFE Manager: Hope Driscoll
DOL Project Manager: Reid Maki
Historical Note
AFOP is a federation of non-profit organizations and state agencies using federal grants to provide training leading to full-time employment for eligible migrant and seasonal farmworkers. Membership: $50/year (individual); $2000/year (organization/company).
Meetings/Conferences:
Quarterly Conferences:
Publications:
AFOP Washington Newsline. bi-m.

Association of Federal Communications Consulting Engineers *(1948)*
P.O. Box 19333, 20th St. Station
Washington, DC 20036-0333
Tel: (703)392-9090 *Fax:* (703)392-9559
Web Site: www.afcce.org
Members: 250 individuals
Annual Budget: $250-500,000
President: Michael D. Rhodes
Vice President: Ross J. Heide
Historical Note
An organization of professional engineering consultants serving the telecommunications industry. Associate membership composed of engineering executives of communications companies and radio equipment manufacturers. AFCCE maintains close relationship with the Federal Communications Commission. Officers change annually. Membership: $120-160/year.
Meetings/Conferences:
Annual Meetings: May-June
Publications:
Newsletter. q.
Membership Directory. a.

Association of Field Ornithologists *(1922)*
9672 N.E. Timberlane Place
Bainbridge Island, WA 98110-1358
Tel: (206)842-0772
Web Site: www.afonet.org
Members: 1200 individuals
Secretary: Lee H. Robison
Historical Note
AFO members are individuals with an interest in the study of birds and their habitats, particularly through the use of bird banding.
Publications:
AFO Afield.
Journal of Field Ornithology. q.
The Flock. bien.

Association of Film Commissioners International *(1979)*
314 N. Main, Suite 308
Helena, MT 59601
Tel: (406)495-8040 *Fax:* (406)495-8039
E-Mail: info@afci.org
Web Site: www.afci.org
Members: 307 individuals
Staff: 3
Annual Budget: $500-1,000,000
Chief Executive Officer: Bill Lindstrom
E-Mail: bill@afci.org
Director, Membership and Events: Sue Clark-Jones
Historical Note
Formerly (1990) Association of Film Commissioners. Members are officials serving as film commissioners. The purpose of the AFCI is to act as liaison between the visual communications industry and local governments or organizations in order to facilitate on-location production. Membership: $500/year.
Meetings/Conferences:
Annual Meetings: Spring
Publications:
Global Passport Directory. a.
Locations Magazine. a. adv.
AFCI Newsletter. q.

Association of Finance and Insurance Professionals *(1989)*
4100 Felps Drive, Suite C
Colleyville, TX 76034
Tel: (817)428-2434 *Fax:* (817)428-2534
E-Mail: info@afip.com
Web Site: www.afip.com
Members: 10000 individuals
Staff: 7
Annual Budget: $500-1,000,000
Executive Director: David N. Robertson
Historical Note
AFIP supports finance/insurance personnel and the finance/insurance industry for franchised automobile dealers in the U.S. and Europe. Membership: $670/year (individual for two years); $3500/year (company for two years).

Publications:
F & I Management Technology.
Management and Technology. bi.

Association of Financial Guaranty Insurors *(1986)*
Towers Group
15 West 39th St., 14th Floor
New York, NY 10018
Tel: (212)354-5020 *Fax:* (212)391-6920
E-Mail: margarettowers@towerspr.com
Web Site: www.afgi.org
Members: 11 corporations
Staff: 6
Annual Budget: $1-2,000,000
Executive Director: Robert E. Mackin
Contact: Margaret Towers
E-Mail: margarettowers@towerspr.com
Historical Note
AGFI members are firms that write financial guaranty insurance.

Association of Firearm and Toolmark Examiners *(1969)*
Prince George's County Police Department Lab
7600 Barlowe Road
Landover, MD 20785
Tel: (301)772-4613 *Fax:* (301)772-4631
E-Mail: teaton1050@aol.com
Web Site: www.afte.org
Members: 800 individuals
Staff: 9
Annual Budget: under $10,000
Secretary: Terry R. Eaton
E-Mail: teaton1050@aol.com
Historical Note
Represents firearm and toolmark examiners engaged in firearm and toolmark idenitification for legal system. Has no paid officers or full-time staff.
Meetings/Conferences:
Annual Meetings: Spring
Publications:
AFTE Journal. q.

Association of Fish and Wildlife Agencies *(1902)*
444 North Capitol St. NW
Suite 275
Washington, DC 20001
Tel: (202)624-7890 *Fax:* (202)624-7891
E-Mail: info@fishwildlife.org
Web Site: www.fishwildlife.org
Members: 300 individuals
Staff: 25
Annual Budget: $2-5,000,000
Executive Director: Matt Hogan
E-Mail: info@fishwildlife.org
Legislative Director: Gary J. Taylor
E-Mail: info@fishwildlife.org
Historical Note
Established as the National Association of Game Commissioners and Wardens, it became the International Association of Game, Fish and Conservation Commissioners in 1917 and assumed its previous name in 1976, and present name in 2006. Membership: $25/year (individual), $250/year (organization).
Meetings/Conferences:
Annual Meetings: September/250
Publications:
Newsletter. m.
Proceedings. a.

Association of Flight Attendants - CWA *(1945)*
501 Third St. NW
Washington, DC 20001
Tel: (202)434-1300 *Fax:* (202)434-1319
Toll Free: (800)424 - 2401
E-Mail: afatalk@afanet.org
Web Site: www.afanet.org
Members: 50000 individuals
Staff: 84
Annual Budget: $10-25,000,000
International President: Patricia A. Friend
General Counsel: David Borer
Communications: Corey Caldwell
International Vice President: George M. Donahue
Historical Note
Formerly (1973) the Steward and Stewardesses Division of the Air Line Pilots Association, International. An independent affiliate of AFL-CIO (Washington, DC), organized to negotiate pay, working conditions, benefits, and work rules on behalf of flight attendants on the nation's commercial air carriers. Sponsors and supports the Flight PAC Political Action Committee. Has an annual budget of approximately $19 million. Membership: $39/month.
Meetings/Conferences:
Annual Meetings: October
Publications:
Flight Log. q.

Association of Food and Drug Officials *(1896)*
2550 Kingston Rd., Suite 311
York, PA 17402
Tel: (717)757-2888 *Fax:* (717)755-8089
E-Mail: afdo@afdo.org
Web Site: www.afdo.org
Members: 600 individuals
Staff: 3
Annual Budget: $100-250,000
Executive Director: Denise C. Rooney
E-Mail: drooney@afdo.org
Historical Note
Founded in 1896 to promote the passage of federal regulations to prevent the misbranding and adulteration of foods, drugs, cosmetics and devices, and to promote uniformity among the states in regulating the above. Members are individuals concerned with the development and enforcement of uniform food, drug and other consumer protection laws. Membership: varies; $35-300/year.
Meetings/Conferences:
Annual Meetings: June, hosted in rotation by the six regional chapters of the ass'n
Publications:
Online Journal. 4/year.
Journal of the Ass'n of Food and Drug Officials. 5/year. adv.
AEDD eNews. m.

Association of Food Industries *(1906)*
3301 Route 66, Suite 205, Bldg. C
Neptune, NJ 07753
Tel: (732)922-3008 *Fax:* (732)922-3590
E-Mail: info@afius.org
Web Site: www.afius.org
Members: 850 companies
Staff: 5
Annual Budget: $500-1,000,000
President: Bob Bauer
Historical Note
Formed by a merger of the Bean Association, the Dried Fruit Association of New York and the Food Brokers Association. AFI also manages the National Association of Flavors and Food-Ingredient Systems, and Women in Flavor and Fragrance Commerce. Membership in AFI is now composed of the North American Olive Oil Association, National Honey Packers and Dealers Association, and Processed Foods and Nut and Agricultural Products. Formerly (1982) Association of Food Distributors. Membership: $1045-2685/year.
Meetings/Conferences:
Annual Meetings: April/May
Publications:
AFI Annual. a. adv.
AFI Newsletter. bi-m.
Meeting Minutes. m.
Bulletins. 2-3/wk.

Association of Food Journalists *(1974)*
38309 Genesee Lake Road
Oconomowoc, WI 53066
Tel: (262)965-3251
Web Site: www.afjonline.com
Members: 300 individuals
Staff: 1
Executive Director: Carol DeMasters
Historical Note
Formerly (1994) the Newspaper Food Editors and Writers Association. AFJ members are food journalists for newspapers, magazines, broadcast and cable media, cookbook authors, and internet food journalists. Membership: $75/year (individual).
Publications:
Newsletter. m.

Association of Foreign Investors in Real Estate *(1988)*
1300 Pennsylvania Ave. NW
Washington, DC 20004
Tel: (202)312-1400 *Fax:* (202)312-1401
E-Mail: afireinfo@afire.org
Web Site: www.afire.org
Members: 150 corporations
Staff: 3
Annual Budget: $1-2,000,000
Chief Executive: James A. Fetgatter, CPA
E-Mail: afireinfo@afire.org
Director, Meetings and Membership: Soo Aldrich
E-Mail: afireinfo@afire.org
Historical Note
Formerly (1998) Association of Foreign Investors in United States Real Estate. Members are foreign investors in U.S. real estate, and domestic firms providing services in the field. Membership: $6,500-8,000/year.
Meetings/Conferences:
Annual Meetings: Fall
Publications:
AFIRE News newsletter. bi-m.

Association of Foreign Trade Representatives *(1984)*
P.O. Box 300, Planetarium Stn.
New York, NY 10024-0300
Tel: (212)877-8900 *Fax:* (212)877-1905
E-Mail: mccabe@whoswho.com
Members: 200 individuals
Staff: 2
Annual Budget: under $10,000
Executive Director: John J. McCabe
E-Mail: mccabe@whoswho.com
Historical Note
Established in April, 1984 to provide a forum for the exchange of ideas and experiences relating to the advancement of trade. Members are consuls general, executive directors, trade commissioners, ministers and consuls, attaches, secretaries and officers from the commercial and information sections of sovereign states and provincial governments.

Association of Forensic Document Examiners *(1986)*
214 W. DesPlaines Lane
Hoffman Estates, IL 60194
Tel: (847)884-1871 *Fax:* (847)490-1104
E-Mail: expert@afde.org
Web Site: www.afde.org
Members: 40 individuals
Annual Budget: under $10,000
Membership Director: Darlene Hennessy
Historical Note
Established and incorporated in Illinois, AFDE provides continuing education in the field of forensic document examination and a forum for the exchange of information among colleagues. Admittance testing is required. AFDE provides a certification program involving the participation of non-members and members of the legal profession in the evaluation of candidates. Membership: $125/year (individual).
Meetings/Conferences:
Annual Meetings: October/75
Publications:
Journal of Forensic Document Examination. a.

Association of Former Agents of the U.S. Secret Service *(1970)*
525 S.W. Fifth St., Suite A
Des Moines, IA 50309-4501
Tel: (812)369-6291
E-Mail: afausss@assoc-mgmt.com
Web Site: www.oldstar.org
Members: 1400 individuals
Staff: 4
Annual Budget: $25-50,000
Executive Secretary: Stu Statham
E-Mail: afausss@assoc-mgmt.com

Historical Note
Dedicated to the welfare of former special agents of the U.S. Secret Service and of their families when in need; to the continuing improvement and effectiveness of law enforcement; and to awarding scholarships and honoring those law enforcement officers whose performance merits special recognition. Membership: $20/year.

Meetings/Conferences:
Annual Meetings: Fall

Publications:
Pipeline. q.
Directory. a.

Association of Former Intelligence Officers *(1975)*
6723 Whittier Ave., Suite 303A
McLean, VA 22101-4533
Tel: (703)790-0320 *Fax:* (703)991-1278
E-Mail: afio@afio.com
Web Site: www.afio.com
Members: 4500
Staff: 3
Annual Budget: $100-250,000
Executive Director: Elizabeth Bancroft

Historical Note
Founded in May 1975 by a group of intelligence professionals, who served with or retired from one of the U.S. intelligence organizations, civilian or military, concerned about the future of the U.S. intelligence system in consequence of prevalent media reporting. Chartered originally as the Association of Retired Intelligence Officers; present name was adopted in 1976. Incorporated as a non-profit organization in the State of Virginia. Membership: $40/year (individual); $1250/year (corporate).

Meetings/Conferences:
Annual Meetings: Fall

Publications:
Intelligencer. 2/year. adv.
Periscope newsletter. 2/year.
AFIO Weekly Intelligence Notes (e-mail). w.

Association of Former OSI Special Agents
P.O. Box 523135
Springfield, VA 22152-5135
Tel: (703)978-6198
E-Mail: lawd@afosisa.org
Web Site: www.afosisa-ncc.org
Executive Officer: Richard Law
E-Mail: lawd@afosisa.org

Historical Note
AFOSISA are former and current members of the Air Force Office of Special Investigations. Has no paid officers or full-time staff. Membership: $25/year (individual); $15/year (associate).

Publications:
Global Alliance. q.

Association of Fraternity Advisors *(1976)*
9640 N. Augusta Dr., Suite 433
Carmel, IN 46032
Tel: (317)876-1632 *Fax:* (317)876-3981
E-Mail: info@fraternityadvisors.org
Web Site: www.fraternityadvisors.org
Members: 1200 individuals
Staff: 2
Annual Budget: $500-1,000,000
Executive Director: Sue Kraft Fussell
Director, Membership Services: Amanda Bureau

Historical Note
AFA was established to serve professionals in higher education who advise fraternities and sororities. Membership: $80/year (individual).

Meetings/Conferences:
Annual Meetings: December/500

Publications:
Perspectives. q. adv.

Association of Free Community Papers *(1950)*
1630 Miner St., Box 1989
Idaho Springs, CO 80452
Tel: (303)567-0355 *Fax:* (781)459-7770
Toll Free: (877)203 - 2327
E-Mail: afcp@pobox.com
Web Site: www.afcp.org
Members: 350corporations,3,000papers
Staff: 3
Annual Budget: $2-5,000,000
Executive Director: Craig McMullin

Historical Note
Formerly (1987) National Association of Advertising Publishers. Members are publishers of free-circulation community newspapers Membership: $100/year.

Meetings/Conferences:
Annual Meetings: Spring

Publications:
Free Paper Ink. m. adv.

Association of Freestanding Radiation Oncology Centers *(1986)*
1875 Eye St. NW
12th Floor
Washington, DC 20006
Tel: (202)872-6767 *Fax:* (202)466-5938
Toll Free: (888)334 - 4542
E-Mail: sgell@ppsv.com
Web Site: www.afroc.org
Members: 350 individuals
Staff: 2
Annual Budget: $100-250,000
Executive Director: Sheila Gell
E-Mail: sgell@ppsv.com

Historical Note
AFROC's focus is on regulatory, legislative and socio-economic issues. AFROC has been highly successful in promoting independent, nonhospital-based cancer therapy centers, which are typically cost-effective for consumers and have high practice standards.

Meetings/Conferences:
Annual Meetings: June
2007 – Washington, DC(Grand Hyatt)/May 14-15

Publications:
Source. q.
Directory. a.

Association of Fund-Raising Distributors and Suppliers *(1992)*
1100 Johnson Ferry Rd., Suite 300
Atlanta, GA 30342
Tel: (404)252-3663 *Fax:* (404)252-0774
E-Mail: afrds@kellencompany.com
Web Site: www.afrds.org
Members: 650 companies
Staff: 5
Annual Budget: $250-500,000
Executive Director: Russell A. Lemieux
E-Mail: afrds@kellencompany.com

Historical Note
Formerly (2001) Association of Fund Raisers and Direct Sellers. Formed in 1992 by the merger of National Association of Product Fund Raisers and National Association of Direct Sellers. AFRDS members are distributors, manufacturers, suppliers, and brokers to the product fund raising industry. Membership: $295-1,500/year, based on company's sales and function (i.e., distributor, supplier/manufacturer, or affiliate).

Meetings/Conferences:
Annual Meetings: January/1,600
2007 – Las Vegas, NV(Paris Las Vegas)/Jan. 7-11
2008 – San Antonio, TX(San Antonio Convention Center)/Jan. 9-13
2009 – Las Vegas, NV(Paris Las Vegas)/Jan. 5-9

Publications:
AFRDS Advisor. q.
The Fundraising Edge. semi.

Association of Fundraising Professionals *(1960)*
1101 King St., Suite 700
Alexandria, VA 22314-2967
Tel: (703)684-0410 *Fax:* (703)684-0540
Toll Free: (800)666 - 3863
E-Mail: afp@afpnet.org
Web Site: www.afpnet.org
Members: 26,494 individuals
Staff: 60
Annual Budget: $5-10,000,000
President and Chief Executive Officer: Paulette V. Maehara, CFRE, CAE
E-Mail: afp@afpnet.org
Vice President, Membership/Chapter Services: Lori Gusdorf, CAE
E-Mail: afp@afpnet.org
Vice President, Communications and Marketing: Joyce O'Brien
E-Mail: afp@afpnet.org
Director, Management Information Systems: Wil Robinson
E-Mail: afp@afpnet.org
Vice President, Meetings: Lynn Smith
E-Mail: afp@afpnet.org
Vice President, Education and Research: Cathlene Williams, Ph.D., CAE
E-Mail: afp@afpnet.org

Historical Note
Formerly Association of Fund-Raising Directors and then (1978) the National Society of Fund Raisers, assumed its current name in 2000. AFP members are individual fund raisers with experience in directing, managing or counseling fund raising programs. Annual Budget: over $6 million. Membership: $200/year, plus local fees (individual).

Meetings/Conferences:
Annual Meetings: Spring

Publications:
Directory (Consultants and Resource Partners). a. adv.
Advancing Philanthropy. bi-m. adv.

Association of Gay and Lesbian Psychiatrists *(1985)*
4514 Chester Ave.
Philadelphia, PA 19143-3707
Tel: (215)222-2800
Web Site: www.aglp.org
Members: 650 individuals
Staff: 1
Annual Budget: $50-100,000
Executive Director: Roy Harker
E-Mail: rharker@aglp.org

Historical Note
Successor to the Caucus of Gay, Lesbian and Bisexual Members of the American Psychiatric Association, AGLP is an independent, professional organization of psychiatrists, psychiatric residents and medical students which serves as a voice for the concerns of lesbians and gay men within the psychiatric community. AGLP provides opportunities for affiliation and collaboration among psychiatrists who share these concerns.

Publications:
Journal of Gay and Lesbian Psychotherapy. q.
AGLP Newsletter. q.

Association of Genetic Technologists *(1975)*
P.O Box 15945-288
Lenexa, KS 66285-5945
Tel: (913)541-0497 *Fax:* (913)599-5340
Web Site: http://agt-info.org
Members: 1500 individuals
Staff: 4
Annual Budget: $250-500,000
Executive Director: Stephanie Newman

Historical Note
Founded as Association of Cytogenetic Technologists; assumed its current name in 1996. A non-profit professional organization established to promote cooperation and exchange of information among those engaged in classical cytogenetics, molecular and biochemical genetics, and to stimulate interest in genetics as a career.

Meetings/Conferences:
Annual Meetings: June
2007 – Denver, CO(Marriott Tech Center)/May 31-June 3

Publications:
Journal of the Association of Genetic Technologists. q. adv.

Association of Girl Scout Executive Staff *(1939)*
1801 N. Mill St., Suite R
Naperville, IL 60563
Tel: (630)369-7781 *Fax:* (630)369-3773
Web Site: www.agses.org
Members: 1200 individuals
Annual Budget: $100-250,000
Executive Director: Karen Renk, CAE

Administrative Assistant: Julie Neibch

Historical Note

Formerly (1955) National Association of Girl Scout Executives and (1975) Association of Girl Scout Professional Workers. AGSES members are executive staff employed by the national headquarters and local Girl Scout Councils.

Publications:

Inter/Com. q.

Association of Golf Merchandisers *(1989)*

P.O. Box 7247
Phoenix, AZ 85011-7247
Tel: (602)604-8250 *Fax:* (602)604-8251
E-Mail: info@agmgolf.org
Web Site: www.agmgolf.org
Members: 800 individuals and 140 companies
Staff: 2
Annual Budget: $250-500,000
Executive Director: Desane Blaney
E-Mail: info@agmgolf.org

Historical Note

Membership: $225/year (individual); $450/year (organization/company).

Meetings/Conferences:

Semi-annual Meetings: Winter

Publications:

AGM E-tailer. m.

Association of Gospel Rescue Missions *(1913)*

1045 Swift Ave.
Kansas City, MO 64116-4127
Tel: (816)471-8020 *Fax:* (816)471-3718
Toll Free: (800)624 - 5156
E-Mail: agrm@agrm.org
Web Site: www.rescuemissons.org
Members: 1200 individuals
Staff: 12
Annual Budget: $1-2,000,000
Executive Director: Rev. Stephen E. Burger
E-Mail: agrm@agrm.org
Business Administrator: Len Conner
Director, Development: Ken Fast
E-Mail: agrm@agrm.org
Director, Education: Rev. Michael Liimatta
E-Mail: agrm@agrm.org
Coordinator, District and Track: Gary Meek
E-Mail: agrm@agrm.org
Director, Communications: Phil Rydman
E-Mail: agrm@agrm.org

Historical Note

Members are rescue mission directors, staff and others affiliated with rescue missions. Membership: $50/year (individual); $250-3,700/year (organization/ company).

Meetings/Conferences:

Annual Meetings: Spring and Summer
2007 - Atlanta, GA(Hilton)/May 15-19/1000

Publications:

Rescue Magazine. bi-m. adv.
Happenings Newsletter. m. adv.
Executive Report. bi-m.
AGRM Directory. bien.

Association of Governing Boards of Universities and Colleges *(1921)*

One Dupont Circle NW
Suite 400
Washington, DC 20036
Tel: (202)296-8400 *Fax:* (202)223-7053
Web Site: www.agb.org
Members: 30000 individuals
Staff: 30
Annual Budget: $2-5,000,000
Vice President: Richard Novak
President: Richard D. Legon

Historical Note

Founded originally as an informal organization of public university trustees, AGB established an office in Washington with its first full-time staff in 1964. It now serves 30,000 trustees and regents on some 1,100 governing and coordinating boards of 1,700 public and private colleges and universities. Its purpose is to strengthen the performance of boards of higher education.

Meetings/Conferences:

Annual Meetings: Spring

Publications:

Trusteeship. bi-m.
Priorities.

Association of Government Accountants *(1950)*

2208 Mount Vernon Ave.
Alexandria, VA 22301
Tel: (703)684-6931
Toll Free: (800)242 - 7211
E-Mail: sfritzlen@agacgfm.org
Web Site: www.agacgfm.org
Members: 18000 individuals
Staff: 23
Annual Budget: $2-5,000,000
Executive Director: Relmond P. Van Daniker
Director, Communications: Marie S. Force
Deputy Executive Director, Member Services: Susan Fritzlen

Historical Note

Founded in 1950, AGA is an educational organization dedicated to the enhancement of public financial management. AGA serves the profesional interests of governmental financial managers and public accounting firms. Membership: $90/year (individual).

Meetings/Conferences:

Annual Meetings: Summer

Publications:

The Journal of Government Financial Management. q. adv.
AGA Today. bi-w. adv.
Certified Government Financial Management Topics. q. adv.

Association of Graduate Liberal Studies Programs *(1975)*

c/o Duke University
P.O. Box 90095
Durham, NC 27708
Tel: (919)684-1987 *Fax:* (919)681-8905
E-Mail: info@aglsp.org
Web Site: www.aglsp.org
Members: 125 institutions
Staff: 1
President: Donna Zapf
E-Mail: info@aglsp.org

Historical Note

AGLSP was founded in 1975 to promote the quality and growth of interdisciplinary graduate liberal studies programs at colleges and universities. Members are interested in maintaining the quality of interdisciplinary, graduate-level degree programs in liberal studies. Officers change bienially. Membership: $250/year (full or associate member); $40year (affiliate).

Meetings/Conferences:

Annual Meetings: Fall
2007 - Memphis, TN/

Publications:

Confluence, The Journal of Graduate Liberal Studies. bi-m.

Association of Graduate Schools in Association of American Universities *(1948)*

Historical Note

An affiliate of Ass'n of American Universities, which provides administrative support.

Association of Group Travel Executives *(1965)*

Historical Note

An affiliate of Travel Industry Association.

Association of Halfway House Alcoholism Programs of North America *(1966)*

860 N. Center St.
Mesa, AZ 85201
Tel: (480)610-8300 *Fax:* (480)834-5372
Toll Free: (800)861 - 0599
E-Mail: ahhap@aol.com
Web Site: www.ahhap.org/
Members: 300 individuals
President: Sterling Gildersleeve
E-Mail: ahhap@aol.com

Historical Note

AHHAP members are halfway house programs and individuals with an interest in the halfway house movement.

Publications:

AHHAP Membership Directory. a.
Communications and Services Newsletter. q.
Conference Proceedings. a.

Association of Health Insurance Advisors *(1990)*

2901 Telestar Court
Falls Church, VA 22042-1205
Tel: (703)770-8200 *Fax:* (703)770-8201
E-Mail: ahia@naifa.org
Web Site: www.ahia.net
Members: 4000 individuals
Staff: 5
Annual Budget: $1-2,000,000
Executive Vice President: Diane Boyle
Coordinator, Membership: Carey Karpick
E-Mail: ahia@naifa.org

Historical Note

Formerly (2002) Association of Health Insurance Agents. AHIA takes a lead role within the NAIFA federation with the National Association of Insurance Commissioners and on federal issues which impact members concerned with employee benefits, health, disability or long-term care health insurace, as well as Section 125 Plans and COBRA administration. AHIA plays a supportive role with state and local associations on state legislative issues. Membership: $115/year (individual).

Meetings/Conferences:

Annual Meetings: September
2007 - Washington, DC/Sept. 8-12

Publications:

Health Insurance Matters. 26/year.

Association of Health Insurance Agents

Historical Note

Became Association of Health Insurance Advisors in 2002.

Association of Healthcare Internal Auditors *(1981)*

2901 Telestar Ct.
Falls Church, VA 22042-1205
Tel: (703)770-8200 *Fax:* (703)770-8201
Toll Free: (888)275 - 2442
E-Mail: ahia@naifa.org
Web Site: www.ahia.org
Members: 1000 individuals
Staff: 2
Annual Budget: $250-500,000
Executive Vice President: Diane Boyle
E-Mail: dboyle@naifa.org

Historical Note

Formerly (1989) Healthcare Internal Audit Group. HIAG was established to promote cost containment and increased productivity in healthcare institutions through internal auditing. AHIA promotes excellence in its members, their institutions, and the healthcare internal audit profession. Provides educational opportunities and the sharing of ideas to foster its members' growth as healthcare professionals. Membership: $180/year (for first individual member of an organization who joins); $125 (for second, third or fourth individual member from that organization who joins); $75 (for fifth individual member from that organization who joins).

Meetings/Conferences:

Annual Meetings: Fall

Publications:

New Perspectives on Healthcare Auditing. 4/yr. adv.

Association of Higher Education Facilities Officers

1643 Prince St.
Alexandria, VA 22314
Tel: (703)684-1446 *Fax:* (703)549-2772
Web Site: www.appa.org
Members: 4500 individuals
Staff: 14
Annual Budget: $2-5,000,000
Executive Vice President: E. Lander Medlin, CAE
E-Mail: lander@appa.org

Senior Director, Finance and Administration: Chong-Hie Choi
E-Mail: choi@appa.org
Director, Knowledge Management: Steve Glazner
E-Mail: steve@appa.org
Director, Meetings, Conventions and Education: Suzanne Healy

Historical Note
Formerly (1991) the Association of Physical Plan Administrators of Universities and Colleges. Members are accredited non-profit institutions of higher education with an independent facilities department, and university or college systems offices which supervise the physical plants of two or more campuses. Membership: $240-1,060/year (based on enrollment and gross institutional expenditures).

Meetings/Conferences:
Annual Meetings: Summer

Publications:
Facilities Manager. q. adv.
Inside APPA. m. adv.
Membership Directory. a. adv.

Association of Hispanic Advertising Agencies
(1996)
8201 Greensboro Dr., Suite 300
McLean, VA 22102
Tel: (703)610-9014 *Fax:* (703)610-9005
Web Site: www.ahaa.org
Members: 250 companies
Staff: 5
Annual Budget: $1-2,000,000
Executive Director: Horacio Gavilan
E-Mail: hgavilan@ahaa.org
Administrator: Rick Garcia

Historical Note
AHAA's mission is to grow, strengthen and protect the Hispanic marketing and advertising industry by providing leadership in raising awareness of the value of the Hispanic market opportunities and enhancing the professionalism of the industry.

Meetings/Conferences:
Semi-Annual Meetings: Spring and Fall
2007 - Chicago, IL(Drake)/Apr. 25-27

Publications:
Standard Directory of Hispanic Advertising Agencies - AHAA Book. a. adv.

Association of Hispanic Arts *(1975)*
161 E. 106th St.
New York, NY 10029
Tel: (212)876-1242 *Fax:* (212)876-1285
E-Mail: ahanews@latinoarts.org
Web Site: www.latinoarts.org
Members: 5000 individuals
Staff: 4
Annual Budget: $500-1,000,000
Director: Nicholas Arture
E-Mail: nicolas@latinoarts.org

Historical Note
Founded in 1975 by a network of Hispanic Art Organization representatives for the purpose of addressing issues relevant to the growth and stability of the Hispanic Arts community. AHA services are open to all Hispanic arts organizations and individual artists.

Publications:
AHA Hispanic Arts News. q. adv.

Association of Home Appliance Manufacturers
(1967)
1111 19th St. NW
Suite 402
Washington, DC 20036
Tel: (202)872-5955 *Fax:* (202)872-9354
E-Mail: aham@aham.org
Web Site: www.aham.org
Members: 173 companies
Staff: 14
Annual Budget: $2-5,000,000
President: Joseph M. McGuire
E-Mail: jmcguire@aham.org
Vice President, Government Relations: David Calabrese
E-Mail: dcalabrese@aham.org
Director, Government Relations: Chris Hudgins
E-Mail: chudgins@aham.org
Director, Finance: Rita K. McClelland
E-Mail: rmcclelland@aham.org
Director, Communications and Marketing: Jill A. Notini
E-Mail: jnotini@aham.org

Historical Note
Formed in 1967 by a merger of the Consumer Products Division of the National Electrical Manufacturers Association and the American Home Laundry Manufacturers' Association. Composed of manufacturers and suppliers to the major appliance and portable appliance industry. Sponsors and supports the AHAM Political Action Committee, and periodically sponsors action groups to address issues facing the industry.

Meetings/Conferences:
Annual Meetings: Spring

Publications:
Major Home Appliance Industry Factbook. a.

Association of Home Office Life Underwriters
(1930)
2300 Windy Ridge Pkwy., Suite 600
Atlanta, GA 30339-8443
Tel: (770)984-3715 *Fax:* (770)984-6418
Web Site: www.ahou.org
Members: 1200 individuals
Annual Budget: $250-500,000
President: Roland Paradis

Historical Note
Formerly (2002) Home Office Life Underwriters Association. Membership: $100/year (domestic); $125/year (overseas).

Meetings/Conferences:
Annual Meetings: Spring

Publications:
On the Risk Magazine. 2/yr.
Proceedings. a.

Association of Image Consultants International
(1990)
431 E. Locust St., Suite 300
Des Moines, IA 50309
Tel: (515)282-5500 *Fax:* (515)243-2049
E-Mail: info@aici.org
Web Site: www.aici.org
Members: 600 individuals
Staff: 3
Annual Budget: $100-250,000
Membership Director: Kim Lau

Historical Note
Formed by the merger of the Association of Image Consultants (1982) and the Association of Fashion and Image Consultants (1983). AICI members include color and wardrobe analysts, personal shoppers, cosmetic and hair stylists, designers, manufacturers, retailers, product developers, etiquette and communications specialists, trainers, educators and students. Membership: $249/year (individual); $500/year (organization).

Meetings/Conferences:
Annual Meetings: July

Publications:
AICI Image Update. q. adv.

Association of Independent Commercial Producers *(1972)*
Three W. 18th St.
Fifth Floor
New York, NY 10011
Tel: (212)929-3000
E-Mail: info@aicp.com
Web Site: www.aicp.com
Members: 575 companies
Staff: 10
President and Chief Executive Officer: Matt Miller
E-Mail: info@aicp.com

Historical Note
Independent producers of television commercials and their suppliers.

Publications:
Membership Directory. a. adv.
AICP National News Newsletter. bi-m.

Association of Independent Corrugated Converters *(1974)*
P.O. Box 25708
Alexandria, VA 22313
Tel: (703)836-2422 *Fax:* (703)836-2795
Toll Free: (877)836 - 2422
E-Mail: info@aiccbox.org
Web Site: www.aiccbox.org
Members: 1100 companies
Staff: 9
Annual Budget: $1-2,000,000
President: Steven Young
E-Mail: syoung@aiccbox.org
Director, Education: David L. Core
Director, Operations: Zell Murphy
E-Mail: zmurphy@aiccbox.org
Director, Meetings and Member Services: Taryn Pyle
Webmaster/Systems Manager: Chris Richards
E-Mail: crichards@aiccbox.org

Historical Note
AICC is an international trade association representing a majority of the independent corrugated packaging manufacturers and their suppliers in North America.

Meetings/Conferences:
Semi-Annual Meetings: Spring and Fall

Publications:
Safety Check. q.
Quarterly Business Conditions. q.
The Business Owner. q.
Salary Wage and Benefits Survey. bien.
Comparative Cost Report. a.
Box Score. bi-m. adv.
Profile of the Independent Corrugated Converter. bien.
Sales Compensation Survey. bien.
AICC Membership Directory. a. adv.
Annual Report. a.

Association of Independent Information Professionals *(1987)*
8550 United Plaza Blvd., Suite 1001
Baton Rouge, LA 70809
Tel: (225)408-4400 *Fax:* (225)408-4422
Toll Free: (888)544 - 2447 Ext:
E-Mail: info@aiip.org
Web Site: www.aiip.org
Members: 700 individuals
Staff: 18
Annual Budget: $50-100,000
Association Coordinator: Jill Lamonte
E-Mail: info@aiip.org

Historical Note
AIIP members are owners of firms providing information-related services including online and manual research, document delivery, database design, library support, consulting, writing and publishing. Membership: $175/year (regular or associate); $50/year (student).

Meetings/Conferences:
Annual Meetings: Spring

Publications:
AIIP Connections. q. adv.
Membership Directory. a. adv.

Association of Independent Research Institutes
c/o Lewis Burke Assoc.
1000 Vermont Ave. NW, 11th Floor
Washington, DC 20005
Tel: (202)289-7475 *Fax:* (202)289-7454
E-Mail: airi@lewis-burke.org
Web Site: www.airi.org
Members: 89 research institutions
Contact: April Burke
E-Mail: airi@lewis-burke.org

Meetings/Conferences:
Annual Meetings: Fall

Association of Independent Trust Companies
(1989)
8 S. Michigan Ave., Suite 1000
Chicago, IL 60603
Tel: (312)223-1611 *Fax:* (312)580-0165
E-Mail: aitco@gss.net
Web Site: www.aitco.net
Members: 150 companies
Staff: 5
Annual Budget: $25-50,000
Executive Director: Kathleen Lukasik

Historical Note
Founded to create a source for education, information and networking opportunities in order to have better resources to operate, manage and compete. Membership: $350-750/year.

Meetings/Conferences:
Annual Meetings: Fall

Publications:
AITCO Advisor Newsletter. q. adv.

Association of Independent Video and Filmmakers *(1974)*

Historical Note
Address uknown in 2006.

Association of Industrial Metallizers, Coaters and Laminators *(1970)*

201 Springs St.
Ft. Mill, SC 29715
Tel: (803)802-7820 *Fax:* (803)802-7821
E-Mail: aimcal@aimcal.org
Web Site: www.aimcal.org
Members: 225 companies
Staff: 4
Annual Budget: $1-2,000,000
Executive Director: Craig Sheppard
E-Mail: aimcal@aimcal.org

Historical Note
AIMCAL represents companies who metallize, coat and laminate flexible substrates and their suppliers. Formerly (1973) Vacuum Metallizers Association. Membership: $1870/year (company).

Meetings/Conferences:
Semi-annual: Fall and Winter

Publications:
Glossary of Terms. bien.
Metallizing Technical Reference. bien.
Newsletter. 3/year.
Sourcebook. a.
Fall Conference Proceedings. a.

Association of Industrial Real Estate Brokers *(1956)*

Historical Note
no updated contact information as of 2006

Association of Industry Manufacturers' Representatives *(1972)*

1 Spectrum Pointe, Suite 150
Lake Forest, CA 92630
Tel: (949)859-2884 *Fax:* (949)855-2973
E-Mail: info@aimr.net
Web Site: www.aimr.net
Members: 350 firms
Staff: 13
Annual Budget: $100-250,000
Executive Director: Joe Miller

Historical Note
AIMR began as an auxiliary of the now defunct Association of Independent Manufacturers, first becoming independent in June 1976 in Minneapolis. Incorporated September 14, 1977. Formerly (1987) the Association of Independent Manufacturers Representatives. Members are independent manufacturers' representatives throughout the the United States; membership draws heavily in the plumbing, heating, and air conditioning fields. Membership: $295/year (organization).

Meetings/Conferences:
Annual Meetings: Spring

Publications:
AIM/R News. q.
Membership Directory. a.

Association of Information and Dissemination Centers *(1968)*

P.O. Box 3212
Maple Glen, PA 19002-8212
Tel: (215)654-9129 *Fax:* (215)654-9129
E-Mail: info@asidic.org
Web Site: www.asidic.org
Members: 64 organizations
Staff: 1
Annual Budget: $10-25,000
Secretariat: Donald T. Hawkins
E-Mail: info@asidic.org

Historical Note
Formerly (1976) the Association of Scientific Information Dissemination Centers. Members are industrial, educational and government information centers which build, maintain, search and/or distribute online databases, online or computer database vendors, producers and high volume searchers. Membership: $495/year (full member); $250/year (associate).

Meetings/Conferences:
Semi-Annual Meetings: Spring and Fall/65

Publications:
ASIDIC Newsletters. semi-a.

Association of Information Technology Professionals *(1951)*

401 N. Michigan Ave., Suite 2200
Chicago, IL 60611-4267
Tel: (312)673-5771 *Fax:* (312)527-6636
Toll Free: (800)224 - 9371
E-Mail: aitp_hq@aitp.org
Web Site: www.aitp.org
Members: 8000 individuals
Staff: 8
Annual Budget: $1-2,000,000

Historical Note
Formerly (1951) National Machine Accountants Association, (1962) Data Processing Management Association, and (1996) DPMA: the Association of Information Systems Professionals. AITP represents systems professionals across the United States and Canada. Members serve in technical positions in business, industry and governmental organizations throughout the world. AITP's mission is to promote the effective, responsible management of information technology to the benefit of its members, their employers and society. AITP offers education programs, peer networking opportunities, local chapter affiliations, and member entitlement programs.

Meetings/Conferences:
Annual Meetings: Fall/250

Publications:
Information Executive. m. adv.
Nanosecond. q. adv.

Association of Insolvency and Restructuring Advisors *(1981)*

221 Stewart Ave., Suite 207
Medford, OR 97501
Tel: (541)858-1665 *Fax:* (541)858-9187
E-Mail: aira@airacira.org
Web Site: www.airacira.org
Members: 2100 individuals
Staff: 7
Annual Budget: $100-250,000
Executive Director: Grant Newton
E-Mail: aira@airacira.org

Historical Note
Members are certified and licensed public accountants, lawyers, examiners, trustees and receivers concerned with the application of accounting procedures to insolvency proceedings. Offers courses and examinations leading to the designation Certified Insolvency and Restructuring Advisor (CIRA). Membership: $175/year (individual); $250/year (CIRA designee); $150/year (associate); $75/year (government/education member).

Meetings/Conferences:
Annual Meetings: Spring
2007 – Chicago, IL(Westin Chicago River North)/June 6-9

Publications:
AIRA Directory. a. adv.
AIRA Newsletter. bi-m. adv.
CIRA Courses: Parts 1-3. m.
CIRA Directory. a.
CDBV Courses: Parts 1-2. m.

Association of Insurance Compliance Professionals *(1985)*

12100 Sunset Hills Road, Suite 130
Reston, VA 20190
Tel: (703)234-4074 *Fax:* (703)435-4390
E-Mail: aicp@aicp.net
Web Site: www.aicp.net
Members: 1200 individuals
Staff: 2
Annual Budget: $250-500,000
Executive Director: Richard A. Guggolz

Historical Note
Formerly Society of State Filers (1998). AICP represents individuals involved or interested in statutes, state filing methods, and/or regulatory requirements. Associate members are consultants, attorneys, association managers, education/service organizations and other interested individuals. Membership: $175/year.

Meetings/Conferences:
Annual Meetings: Fall
2007 – Portland, OR(Hilton)/Oct. 28-31/650

Publications:
Newsletter. q.

Association of Internal Management Consultants *(1971)*

824 Caribbean Ct.
Marco Island, FL 34145
Tel: (239)642-0580 *Fax:* (239)642-1119
E-Mail: info@aimc.org
Web Site: www.aimc.org
Members: 250 individuals
Staff: 4
Annual Budget: $50-100,000
President: Dr. William Trotter

Historical Note
Established in Baltimore on February 19, 1971 by forty-two charter members under the leadership of Walter J. Sistek of the Maryland National Bank. Incorporated in the State of New York in 1975. Members are individuals engaged in the practice of internal management consulting, with five or more years experience and operating at a senior or project leader level. Membership: $195/year (individual); $575/year (corporate); $125/year (additional corporate members).

Meetings/Conferences:
Annual Meetings: Spring

Publications:
AIMC Forum. semi-a.
Membership Directory. a.

Association of International Automobile Manufacturers *(1964)*

2111 Wilson Blvd., Suite 1150
Arlington, VA 22201
Tel: (703)525-7788 *Fax:* (703)525-3289
Web Site: www.aiam.org
Members: 19 companies
Staff: 11
Annual Budget: $2-5,000,000
President and Chief Executive Officer: Timothy MacCarthy

Historical Note
Founded as the Imported Car Group; became Automobile Importers of America in 1965 and assumed its present name in 1990. AIAM is the trade association for U.S. subsidiaries of the international automobile companies. AIAM acts as the industry's voice and serves as a clearinghouse for industry-related information. Its purpose is to communicate the true makeup of today's automobile industry.

Association of International Education Administrators *(1981)*

c/o Dr. Darla Deardorff, AIEA Secretariat, Campus Box 90404, 2204 Erwin Road
Duke University
Durham, NC 27708-0404
Tel: (919)668-1928 *Fax:* (919)684-8749
E-Mail: aiea@duke.edu
Web Site: www.aieaworld.org
Members: 400 individuals
Staff: 1
Annual Budget: $100-250,000
Executive Director: Darla Deardorff

Historical Note
AIEA represents C.E.O.s at institutions of higher learning dedicated to the advancement of international education. Membership: $350/year (institutional); $30/year (associate).

Meetings/Conferences:
Annual Meetings: 250

Publications:
Journal of Studies in International Education. 2/year. adv.
AIEA Directory. a.

Association of International Photography Art Dealers *(1979)*
1609 Connecticut Ave. NW
Suite 200
Washington, DC 20009
Tel: (202)986-0105 *Fax:* (202)986-0448
E-Mail: info@aipad.com
Web Site: www.aipad.com
Members: 125 individuals
Staff: 4
Annual Budget: $500-1,000,000
Executive Director: Kathleen Ewing
Historical Note
Galleries and private dealers in fine art photography who have been in business for at least three years. Membership: $700/year, plus initiation fee (organization).
Meetings/Conferences:
Annual Meetings: Spring Trade Show in February or March
Publications:
Show Art Catalogue. a. adv.
Membership Directory. bien.
On Collecting Photographs. quinquen.

Association of Investment Management Sales Executives *(1977)*
1320 19th St. NW
Suite 300
Washington, DC 20036-1636
Tel: (202)296-3560 *Fax:* (202)371-8977
Toll Free: (800)343 - 5659
E-Mail: nkraich@tkgllc.org
Web Site: www.aimse.com
Members: 1400 individuals
Staff: 3
Annual Budget: $500-1,000,000
Executive Director: Norbert Kraich
Director, Meetings and Membership: Pam Svendsen
Historical Note
Incorporated in 1981, AIMSE provides marketing and sales educational programs for its members. Membership: $185/year (individual).
Meetings/Conferences:
Annual Meetings: April
Publications:
Advisor Newsletter. q.
Membership Directory. a.

Association of Iron and Steel Engineers
Historical Note
Became Association for Iron and Steel Technology in 2003.

Association of Jesuit Colleges and Universities *(1970)*
One Dupont Circle NW
Suite 405
Washington, DC 20036-1140
Tel: (202)862-9893 *Fax:* (202)862-8523
Web Site: www.ajcunet.edu
Members: 28 institutions
Staff: 9
Annual Budget: $500-1,000,000
President: Charles L. Currie, S.J.
E-Mail: ccurrie@ajcunet.edu
Director, Communications: Melissa Di Leonardo
E-Mail: mdleonardo@ajcunet.edu
Director, Federal Relations: Cyndy Littlefield
E-Mail: clittlefield@ajcunet.edu
Executive Director, JesuitNET: Richard Vigilante
E-Mail: vigilante@ajcunet.edu
Historical Note
Formed in 1970 when the Jesuit Educational Association split to form the Association of Jesuit Colleges and Universities and the Jesuit Secondary Education Association. Absorbed the Jesuit Research Council of America. A national voluntary service organization whose institutional members are the 28 Jesuit colleges and universities in the United States. The association respresents its members in shaping public policy for higher education, monitoring regulatory activities of government executive agencies and following the judicial decisions of the court.
Meetings/Conferences:
Annual Meetings:
Publications:
International Resource Book. a.
ACJU Connections. m.
AJCU Directory. a.

Association of Jewish Aging Services *(1960)*
316 Pennsylvania Ave. SE
Suite 402
Washington, DC 20003-1175
Tel: (202)543-7500 *Fax:* (202)543-4090
E-Mail: info@ajas.org
Web Site: www.ajas.org
Members: 125 facilities
Staff: 2
Annual Budget: $500-1,000,000
President and Chief Executive Officer: Harvey Tillipman
Historical Note
Formerly (1997) the North American Association of Jewish Homes and Housing for the Aging. AJAS members are non-profit organizations providing long term care and housing services for the aged.
Meetings/Conferences:
2007 – New Orleans, LA(Hilton New Orleans Riverside)/March 10-13/300
Publications:
The Scribe. q.
Directory. bien.
E-update (online). m.
Washington/CEO Update. q.

Association of Jewish Center Professionals *(1918)*
15 E. 26th St.
Ninth Floor
New York, NY 10010-1579
Tel: (212)786-5155 *Fax:* (212)481-4174
E-Mail: hrosenzweig@jcca.org
Web Site: www.ajcp.org
Members: 1100 individuals
Staff: 3
Annual Budget: $100-250,000
Executive Director: Harvey Rosenzweig
E-Mail: hrosenzweig@jcca.org
Historical Note
Formerly (1988) Association of Jewish Center Workers. A membership organization dedicated to enhancing the skills and growth of professionals and support staff employed in the Jewish Community Centers in order to provide quality service and programs to the community.
Meetings/Conferences:
Annual Meetings: Summer
Publications:
Th Connection. q.
Tasgal/Korobkin Lecture. bien.
Conference Papers. a.
Kesher. q.

Association of Jewish Family and Children's Agencies *(1972)*
620 Cranbury Road, Suite 102
East Brunswick, NJ 08816-5419
Tel: (732)432-7120 *Fax:* (732)432-7127
Toll Free: (800)634 - 7346
Web Site: www.ajfca.org
Members: 165 agencies
Staff: 7
Annual Budget: $500-1,000,000
President/Chief Executive Officer: Bert J. Goldberg
Historical Note
Members are local Jewish family and children's service agencies in the U.S. and Canada.
Meetings/Conferences:
Annual Meetings: April
2007 – New York, NY(Roosevelt)/500
Publications:
Executive Digest. m. adv.
Directory. a.

Association of Jewish Libraries *(1965)*
c/o NFJC, 330 Seventh Ave., 21st Floor
New York, NY 10010-1579
Tel: (212)725-5359 *Fax:* (212)678-8998
E-Mail: ajlibs@osu.edu
Web Site: www.jewishlibraries.org
Members: 1095 individuals
Staff: 1
Annual Budget: $25-50,000
Contact: Yossi Galron
Historical Note
Merger of the Jewish Library Association (founded in 1946) and the Jewish Librarians Association (founded in 1962). AJL is an international organization dedicated to the preservation and production of Judaic resources and culture. Membership: $50/year.
Meetings/Conferences:
Annual Meetings: June
Publications:
AJL Newsletter. q. adv.
Judaica Librarianship. irreg. adv.

Association of Junior Leagues International *(1921)*
90 William St., Suite 200
New York, NY 10038
Tel: (212)951-8300 *Fax:* (212)481-7196
E-Mail: info@ajli.org
Web Site: www.ajli.org
Members: 193000 individuals
Staff: 50
Annual Budget: $5-10,000,000
Executive Director: Susan Danish
Historical Note
The first Junior League was established in New York City in 1901 to promote volunteer service in the settlement houses of the city. This League was founded with the title of Junior League for the Promotion of Settlement Movements, later shortened to the Junior League. Subsequently, women in Boston, Brooklyn, Portland, Baltimore, Chicago and Cleveland began to organize Junior Leagues. From work in the settlement houses, early Junior Leagues rapidly expanded their programs to found well baby clinics, conduct classes in home nursing, establish orphanages and organize garment factories to employ needy women. The New York Junior League started the first residence for young working women. As Leagues multiplied, the need for an overall organization was recognized and, in 1921 the Association of the Junior Leagues of America was incorporated with 24 Leagues as charter members. Became the Association of Junior Leagues in 1971 and added International in 1989. AJLI helps each member League to fulfill its mission, of promoting voluntarism, developing the potential of women, and improving communities through programs and activities.
Meetings/Conferences:
Annual Meetings: Spring/850
Publications:
Association Update. 9/year.
What Works. 2/year.

Association of Labor Relations Agencies *(1951)*
c/o New Jersey PERC
Box 429
Trenton, NJ 08625-0429
Tel: (609)292-9830 *Fax:* (609)777-0089
Web Site: www.alra.org
Members: 75 agencies
Annual Budget: $50-100,000
Vice President: Robert Uackel
Historical Note
Formerly (1963) the Association of State Mediation Agencies, and (1978) the Association of Labor Mediation Agencies. Member agencies include those at the federal, state and local levels in the U.S. and federal and provincial levels in Canada. Has no paid officers or full-time staff. Membership: $250/year (organization/company).
Meetings/Conferences:
Annual Meetings: July/300
Publications:
ALRA Advisor. q.

Association of Latina and Latino Anthropologists

Historical Note
A section of the American Anthropological Association.

Association of Latino Professionals in Accounting and Finance *(1972)*
510 W. Sixth St., Suite 400
Los Angeles, CA 90014
Tel: (213)243-0004 *Fax:* (213)243-0006
E-Mail: info@nationalalpfa.org
Web Site: www.alpfa.org
Members: 2500 individuals
Staff: 3
Annual Budget: $500-1,000,000
Executive Director: Lisa Lopez
Vice President, Administration: Sharon Rivera
Historical Note
Formerly (2001) American Association of Hispanic Certified Public Accountants. ALPFA members are certified public accountants of Hispanic descent. Membership: $50/year (individual).
Meetings/Conferences:
Annual Meetings: Fall
Publications:
La Cuenta newsletter. q. adv.

Association of Leadership Educators *(1990)*
2120 Fyffe Road
Columbus, OH 43210
Tel: (614)247-5034 *Fax:* (614)292-9750
Web Site: http://leadershipeducators.org
Members: 180 individuals
Annual Budget: under $10,000
Executive Officer: Garee W. Earnest
E-Mail: earnest.1@osu.edu
Historical Note
ALE members are educators with an interest in leadership development curricula. Has no paid officers or full-time staff. Membership: $50/year (individual).
Meetings/Conferences:
Annual Meetings: Summer
Publications:
Journal of Leadership Education. semi-a.
Annual Conference Proceedings. a.
Newsletter. q.

Association of Legal Administrators *(1971)*
75 Tri-State International, #222
Lincolnshire, IL 60069-4435
Tel: (847)267-1252 *Fax:* (847)267-1329
E-Mail: ala@alanet.org
Web Site: www.alanet.org
Members: 9500 individuals
Staff: 36
Annual Budget: $5-10,000,000
Executive Director: John J. Michalik
E-Mail: jmichalik@alanet.org
Director, Conventions and Meetings: Kathleen M. Rossell
Director, Professional Development: Pamela A. Stong
E-Mail: pstong@alanet.org
Director, Member Services: Jan M. Waugh
E-Mail: jwaugh@alanet.org
Historical Note
Members are individuals responsible for the management and administration of private law firms, corporate legal departments and government agencies. Membership: $200-300/year (individual).
Meetings/Conferences:
Annual Meetings: Spring/1,700
2007 – Las Vegas, NV(Mandalay Bay Resort)/Apr. 30-May 3
Publications:
Directory. a. adv.
ALA News. 6/year. adv.
Legal Management: Journal of the Ass'n of Administrators. 6/year. adv.
Compensation Survey. a.

Association of Life Insurance Counsel *(1913)*
435 New Karner Road
Albany, NY 12205
Tel: (518)785-0721 *Fax:* (518)785-3579
E-Mail: alic@dgallc.net
Members: 850 individuals
Annual Budget: $50-100,000
Secretary/Treasurer: Phillip E. Stano
Historical Note
Members are legal counsels of life insurance companies. Membership: $150/year (individual).
Publications:
Membership Directory. a.
Proceedings of the ALIC. a.

Association of Literary Scholars and Critics *(1994)*
650 Beacon St., Suite 510
Boston, MA 02215
Tel: (617)358-1990 *Fax:* (617)358-1995
E-Mail: alsc@bu.edu
Web Site: www.bu.edu/literary
Members: 2000 individuals
Staff: 2
Annual Budget: $100-250,000
Executive Director: Michael Govin-Hart
E-Mail: alsc@bu.edu
Historical Note
A professional society for the study of literature, ALSC serves as a forum for anyone with serious critical or scholarly interests in literature. Membership: $25/year (individual).
Meetings/Conferences:
Annual Meetings: Fall
Publications:
Literary Imagination. semi-a.
ALSC Newsletter. q.

Association of Local Air Pollution Control Officials *(1971)*
444 North Capitol St. NW
Suite 307
Washington, DC 20001-1512
Tel: (202)624-7864 *Fax:* (202)624-7863
E-Mail: 4clnair@4clnair.org
Web Site: www.cleanairworld.org/
Members: 220 local air pollution agencies
Staff: 7
Annual Budget: $1-2,000,000
Executive Director: S. William Becker
Historical Note
ALAPCO represents air pollution control officials from over 150 major metropolitan areas across the United States. Shares headquarters and staff with the State and Territorial Air Pollution Program Administrators. In addition to its semi-annual meetings for members, the association sponsors an annual communications conference, the Air Toxics Control Conference.
Meetings/Conferences:
Semi-Annual Meetings: Spring and Fall
Publications:
Washington Update. w.

Association of Lutheran Secondary Schools *(1944)*
12800 N. Lake Shore Dr.
Mequon, WI 53097
Tel: (262)243-4210 *Fax:* (262)243-4428
Web Site: www.alss.org
Members: 90 schools
Staff: 1
Executive Director: Ross E. Stueber
Historical Note
Membership fees based on student enrollment of member schools.
Meetings/Conferences:
Annual Meetings: Spring
Publications:
The Leader's E-Compass. bi-w.

Association of Machinery and Equipment Appraisers *(1983)*
315 S. Patrick St.
Alexandria, VA 22314-3501
Tel: (703)836-7900 *Fax:* (703)836-9303
Toll Free: (800)537 - 8629
E-Mail: amea@amea.org
Web Site: www.amea.org
Members: 285 individuals
Staff: 2
Annual Budget: $50-100,000
Director, Member Services: Pamlea J. Reid
E-Mail: amea@amea.org
Historical Note
Members are appraisers of all different types of machinery and capital equipment. Conducts accreditation and certification programs for members; offer accredited and certified membership. Membership: $300/year; $600/year (associate).
Meetings/Conferences:
Annual Meetings: May
Publications:
Auction Summaries. bi-a.
Membership Directory. a.
AMEA Appraiser. q.

Association of Major City and County Building Officials *(1974)*
505 Huntmar Park Dr., Suite 210
Herndon, VA 20170
Tel: (703)437-0100 *Fax:* (703)481-3596
Web Site: www.ncsbcs.org
Members: 36 cities and counties
Staff: 1
Annual Budget: under $10,000
Contact: Carolyn Fitch
E-Mail: cfitch@ncsbcs.org
Historical Note
Provides a forum for the building officials of major cities and counties in the U.S. to discuss mutual interests and seek solutions to common problems in building code and public safety issues. Membership: $300/year.

Association of Managed Care Dentists
1223 Wilshire Blvd., Suite 483
Santa Monica, CA 90403
Tel: (310)453-3439 *Fax:* (310)453-7895
Toll Free: (800)864 - 6848
Web Site: www.amcd.org
President: John J. Maguire, D.D.S.
Historical Note
Formerly (1997) Association of Managed Care Providers. AMCD is a nonprofit organization that provides education, representation and a forum for dentists. Membership: $95/year (provider, $50 each add'l); $250/year (affiliated).

Association of Management Consulting Firms *(1929)*
380 Lexington Ave., Suite 1700
New York, NY 10168-0002
Tel: (212)551-7887 *Fax:* (212)551-7934
E-Mail: info@amcf.org
Web Site: www.amcf.org
Members: 50 firms
Staff: 6
Annual Budget: $1-2,000,000
President and Chief Executive Officer: Elizabeth A. Kovacs
E-Mail: info@amcf.org
Director, Programs: Kathleen Fish
E-Mail: info@amcf.org
Historical Note
Previously know as ACMFAssociation of Management Consulting Firms; ACMF merged with Institute of Management Consultants to form Council of Consulting Organizations in 1989; split in 1999. Oldest and largest organization representing management consulting firms in the world. Members are professional management consulting firms that must meet demanding membership requirements and pledge to uphold a strict and enforced code of professional conduct and standards of practice. ACMF member firms, 20% of which are foreign-based, employ over 55,000 management consultants in over 100 countries worldwide and have annual billings in excess of $5 billion.
Meetings/Conferences:
Annual Meetings: Fall
Publications:
Operating Benchmark Survey. a.

Association of Management/International Association of Management *(1975)*
P.O. Box 64841
Virginia Beach, VA 23467-4841
Tel: (757)482-2273 *Fax:* (757)482-0325
E-Mail: aomgt@inter-source.org
Web Site: www.aom-iaom.ubalt.edu
Members: 3800 individuals

Staff: 12
Annual Budget: $1-2,000,000
President and Chief Executive Officer: Dr. Willem A. Hamel, Ph.D.

Historical Note
Formerly the Association of Management (AoM). Assumed its present name in 1996. AoM/IAoM is a professional organization of academic professionals and practitioners of management who are taking scholarly pursuits toward bridging the management gap worldwide. Membership: $325/year.

Publications:
Journal of Leadership and Leaders. q. adv.
Journal of Management in Practice. q. adv.
Human Resources Management and organizational Behavior.
Business Functions and Applications.
Dissertation Research Journal.
Education: 21 Century World.
Computer Science and Information Management. q. adv.
Journal of Management Systems. q. adv.
Journal of Information Technology Management. q. adv.
Internat'l Association of Management Journal. q. adv.

Association of Marine Engine Manufacturers

Historical Note
An affiliate of Nat'l Marine Manufacturers Ass'n, which provides administrative support.

Association of Master of Business Administration Executives *(1970)*
388 E. Main St., Suite A
Branford, CT 06405
Tel: (203)315-5221 *Fax:* (203)483-6685
Members: 15000 individuals
Staff: 11
Contact: Joan Adamczyk

Historical Note
A membership organization providing career information and professional services.

Publications:
MBA Employment Guide. adv.
AMBA Network News. q.

Association of Maternal and Child Health Programs *(1944)*
1220 19th St. NW
Suite 801
Washington, DC 20036-2435
Tel: (202)775-0436 *Fax:* (202)775-0061
E-Mail: info@amchp.org
Web Site: www.amchp.org
Members: 600 individuals
Staff: 23
Annual Budget: $1-2,000,000
Chief Executive Officer: Peter Sybinsky
E-Mail: info@amchp.org
Director, Membership and Communications: Lisa Cain
E-Mail: info@amchp.org

Historical Note
Established as the Association of State and Territorial Maternal and Child Health and Crippled Children Directors; assumed its present name in 1987. Membership: $105/year (individual); $735/year (organization).

Meetings/Conferences:
Annual Meetings: Winter

Publications:
Pulse e-newsletter (online). 26/year.

Association of Medical Diagnostic Manufacturers *(1973)*
555 13th St. NW
Washington, DC 20004-1109
Tel: (202)637-6837 *Fax:* (202)637-5910
E-Mail: amdminfo@email.amdm.org
Web Site: www.amdm.org
Members: 75 companies
Staff: 2
Annual Budget: $50-100,000
Administrator: Daniel Dovi

Historical Note
Formerly (1995) Association of Microbiological Diagnostic Manufacturers. Membership open to any manufacturer, processor, repackager or distributor of medical diagnostic devices or device components. Membership: $275-1,400/year, based upon number of employees.

Meetings/Conferences:
Annual Meetings: October

Publications:
AMDM News. q.

Association of Medical Education and Research in Substance Abuse *(1976)*
125 Whipple St., Suite 300
Providence, RI 02908
Tel: (401)349-0000 *Fax:* (877)418-8769
E-Mail: isabel@amersa.org
Web Site: www.amersa.org
Members: 300 individuals
Staff: 2
Annual Budget: $50-100,000
Co-Director: Isabel Vieiera
E-Mail: isabel@amersa.org

Meetings/Conferences:
Annual Meetings: November

Publications:
Substance Abuse Journal. q.
Membership Directory. bien.

Association of Medical Illustrators *(1945)*
c/o Allen Press, Inc.
810 East Tenth St.
Lawrence, KS 66044
Tel: (866)393-4264
E-Mail: hq@ami.org
Web Site: www.ami.org
Members: 900 individuals
Staff: 4
Annual Budget: $250-500,000
Executive Director: Vanessa Reilly
E-Mail: hq@ami.org

Historical Note
Incorporated in the State of Illinois. AMI is dedicated to enhancing the professionalism and abilities of its members, and to advancing education and communication in medicine and health related fields. AMI has an international membership and operates an official placement service. Membership: $85/year (student), $230/year (professional and associate).

Meetings/Conferences:
Annual Meetings: Summer

Publications:
The Journal of Biocommunication. q.
Newsletter. q. adv.
Medical Illustration Sourcebook. a.
Membership Directory. a.

Association of Medical School Pediatric Department Chairs *(1961)*
c/o American Board of Pediatrics
111 Silver Cedar Court
Chapel Hill, NC 27514
Tel: (919)942-1993 *Fax:* (919)929-9255
Members: 146 Member Schools
Staff: 1
Annual Budget: $50-100,000
Coordinator: Jean M. Bartholomew

Historical Note
Members are chairs of pediatrics of U.S. and Canadian accredited medical schools. Membership: $510/year (institution).

Meetings/Conferences:
Annual Meetings: Spring
2007 – San Antonio, TX(Westin La Cantera)/March 7-12/300
2008 – Santa Fe, NM(Eldorado)/March 6-10/200
2009 – Savannah, GA(Westin Savannah Harbor)/March 5-9/200

Publications:
Directory. a.

Association of Meeting Professionals *(1982)*
2025 M St. NW
Washington, DC 20036
Tel: (202)973-8686 *Fax:* (202)973-8722
E-Mail: amps@courtesyassoc.com
Web Site: www.ampsweb.org
Members: 400 individuals
Staff: 3
Annual Budget: $100-250,000
Interim Executive Director: Leslie Thorton
Executive Director: Molly Bartkowski

Historical Note
AMP's mission is to provide local affordable opportunities for its members to gather and share information, and to promote excellence in and strengthen the value and crediblity of the meeting profession. Membership: $110/year (individual); $185-295/year (organization/company).

Publications:
AMPS Newsletter. m. adv.
AMPS Directory. a. adv.

Association of Membership and Marketing Executives *(1960)*
P.O. Box 1736
Sacramento, CA 95812-1736
Tel: (916)325-1284 *Fax:* (916)443-0469
E-Mail: drew.savage@calchamber.com
Web Site: www.ammeonline.org
Members: 85 individuals
Annual Budget: under $10,000
Vice President: Drew Savage

Historical Note
Has no paid officers or full-time staff.

Meetings/Conferences:
Annual Meetings: September, in conjunction with the Council of State Chambers of of Commerce

Publications:
Newsletter. q.

Association of Mental Health Librarians *(1964)*
Louis de la Parte Florida Mental Health Institute
13301 Bruce B. Downs Blvd.
Tampa, FL 33612
Tel: (813)974-4471 *Fax:* (813)974-7242
E-Mail: hanson@fmhi.usf.edu
Web Site: www.fmhi.usf.edu/amhl/
Members: 100 individuals
Annual Budget: under $10,000
President: Ardis Hanson
E-Mail: hanson@fmhi.usf.edu

Historical Note
Formed (1964) as the Society of Mental Health Librarians; assumed its present name in 1980. The Association provides an opportunity for the exchange of information and the continuing education of its members. Membership: $15/year.

Meetings/Conferences:
Annual Meetings: Fall

Association of Metropolitan Sewerage Agencies

Historical Note
Became National Association of Clean Water Agencies in 2005.

Association of Metropolitan Water Agencies *(1981)*
1620 I St. NW
#500
Washington, DC 20006
Tel: (202)331-2820 *Fax:* (202)785-1845
Web Site: www.amwa.net
Members: 200 agencies
Staff: 6
Annual Budget: $250-500,000
Executive Director: Diane VanDe Hei
Dep. Director: Michael Arceneaux
Director, Communications and Public Affairs: Carolyn Peterson

Historical Note
Established and incorporated in the District of Columbia, AMWA members are publicly-owned metropolitan, county and city water supply agencies serving populations of more than 100,000. Membership: based on population served.

Meetings/Conferences:
Annual Meetings: Fall

Publications:
Congressional Report. m.

Regulatory Report. m.
Federal Water Review. bi-m.

Association of Military Banks of America *(1959)*
P.O. Box 3335
Warrenton, VA 20188
Tel: (540)347-1044 *Fax:* (540)347-7964
E-Mail: ambahq@aol.com
Web Site: www.ambanq.org
Members: 120 banks
Annual Budget: $100-250,000
Administrative Assistant: Christine Jacobs

Historical Note
AMBA members are banks specializing in providing services to military personnel and banks operating on military bases.

Meetings/Conferences:
Annual Meetings: Fall

Publications:
AMBA Newsletter. q.
Membership Directory. a.

Association of Military Colleges and Schools of the U.S. *(1914)*
9429 Garden Court
Potomac, MD 20854-3964
Tel: (301)765-0695
Web Site: www.amcsus.org
Members: 45 institutions
Staff: 1
Annual Budget: $25-50,000
Executive Director: Dr. Lewis Sorley

Historical Note
Members are educational institutions with regionally accredited academic programs and Defense Department-approved military, naval, marine, or air programs. Absorbed the National Association of Military Schools in 1972.

Meetings/Conferences:
Annual Meetings: Spring

Association of Military Surgeons of the U.S. *(1891)*
9320 Old Georgetown Road
Bethesda, MD 20814-1653
Tel: (301)897-8800 *Fax:* (301)530-5446
Toll Free: (800)761 - 9320
E-Mail: amsus@amsus.org
Web Site: www.amsus.org
Members: 9000 individuals
Staff: 10
Annual Budget: $1-2,000,000
Executive Director: RAdm. Frederic G. Sanford, USN (Ret.)
E-Mail: amsus@amsus.org
Manager, Conventions: Linda L. Hines
E-Mail: amsus@amsus.org
Assistant Executive Director: Col. Steven C. Mirick, USAF, MSC (Ret.)
E-Mail: amsus@amsus.org

Historical Note
Established in 1891 and incorporated by an act of Congress in 1903. Membership consists of health care professionals or civilians employed by the armed services, the Public Health Service or Dept. of Veterans Affairs, or medical consultants. Membership: $45-525/year (individual).

Meetings/Conferences:
Annual Meetings: Fall/5,000

Publications:
Military Medicine. m. adv.

Association of Millwork Distributors *(1935)*
10047 Robert Trent Jones Pkwy.
New Port Richey, FL 34655-4649
Tel: (727)372-3665 *Fax:* (727)372-2879
Web Site: www.amdweb.com
Members: 1100 companies
Staff: 7
Annual Budget: $2-5,000,000
Executive Director and Chief Executive Officer: Rosalie Leone
E-Mail: rleone@amdweb.com

Historical Note
Formed by a merger of the Northern and Southern Sash and Door Jobbers Associations (both founded in 1935) as the National Sash and Door Jobbers Association; assumed its current name in 2006.

Meetings/Conferences:
Annual Meetings: October/3,000
2007 – Denver, CO/Nov. 1-6
2008 – Kissimmee, FL/Oct. 11-16
2009 – To Be Determined
2010 – Nashville, TN/Oct. 9-14

Publications:
Membership Directory and Products Guide. a. adv.
Millwork Sales Manual. a.
NSDJA News. m.
Millwork Product Guide. a.
Millwork Home Study. a.
Business Math Home Study. a.

Association of Moving Image Archivists *(1990)*
1313 North Vine St.
Hollywood, CA 90028
Tel: (323)463-1500 *Fax:* (323)463-1506
E-Mail: amia@amianet.org
Web Site: www.amianet.org
Members: 800 individuals
Staff: 2
Annual Budget: $50-100,000
Managing Director: Janice Simpson
E-Mail: amia@amianet.org

Historical Note
AMIA members are archivists, scholars, and institutions concerned with the preservation of film and video resources. Founded as Film and Television Archives Advisory Committee; assumed its current name in 1990. Membership: $75/year (individual); $250/year (non-profit); $500/year (company).

Meetings/Conferences:
Annual Meetings: Fall

Publications:
The Moving Image: Journal of AMIA. semi-a. adv.
AMIA Newsletter. q. adv.

Association of Muslim Scientists and Engineers *(1969)*
P.O. Box 38
Plainfield, IN 46168
Tel: (517)947-6338
E-Mail: office@amse.net
Web Site: www.amse.net
Members: 590 individuals
Staff: 1
Annual Budget: $10-25,000
Director: Iqbal Unus
E-Mail: office@amse.net

Historical Note
Established and incorporated in Indiana. Membership: $25/year (regular); $15/year (student).

Meetings/Conferences:
Annual Meetings: October

Publications:
AMSE Newsletter. irreg. adv.
Proceedings of AMSE Annual Conference. irreg. adv.
Directory of Members. irreg. adv.
Internat'l Journal of Science and Technology. semi-a. adv.

Association of Muslim Social Scientists *(1972)*
P.O. Box 669
Herndon, VA 20172
Tel: (703)471-1133 *Fax:* (703)471-3922
E-Mail: amss@amss.net
Web Site: www.amss.net
Members: 300 individuals
Annual Budget: under $10,000
President: Dr. Louay M. Safi
E-Mail: louay@amss.net

Historical Note
AMSS members are professors and graduate students in the social sciences, united to disseminate Islamic positions relevant to their various academic disciplines. Seeks to present an accurate portrayal and understanding of Islamic thought. Membership: $45/year (professional); $30/year (student).

Meetings/Conferences:
Annual Meetings: October

Publications:
American Journal of Islamic Social Sciences. q. adv.

Association of National Advertisers *(1910)*
708 Third Ave., 33rd Fl.
New York, NY 10017-4270
Tel: (212)697-5950 *Fax:* (212)661-8057
Web Site: www.ana.net
Members: 350 companies
Staff: 33
Annual Budget: $2-5,000,000
President and Chief Executive Officer: Robert D. Liodice

Historical Note
Founded in 1910 as the Association of National Advertising Managers; assumed its present name in 1914. ANA is dedicated exclusively to serving the interest of companies which advertise either regionally or nationally. Maintains a Washington office to lobby against restrictions of advertisers' rights. Membership: fees based on advertiser's expenditures.

Meetings/Conferences:
Annual Meetings: Fall

Publications:
The Advertiser. q.
Compendium of Legislative/Regulatory Issues. a.

Association of Natural Resource Enforcement Trainers *(1986)*
IGCS Room #W255D
Indianapolis, IN 46204
Tel: (317)232-4014 *Fax:* (317)232-8035
E-Mail: dlw800@yahoo.com
Web Site: www.anret.org
Members: 50 individuals
President: Dave Windsor
E-Mail: dlw800@yahoo.com

Association of Naval Aviation *(1975)*
2550 Huntington Ave., #202
Alexandria, VA 22303-1499
Tel: (703)960-6806 *Fax:* (703)960-6807
E-Mail: nafhgtr@aol.com
Web Site: www.anahq.org
Members: 10000 individuals
Staff: 4
Annual Budget: $250-500,000
Executive Director: Eric L. Wheeler

Historical Note
Seeks to support a strong U.S. maritime air posture. Membership: $40/year (individual); $2,500/year (organization/company).

Meetings/Conferences:
Annual Meetings: Spring

Publications:
Wings of Gold. q. adv.

Association of Neurosurgical Physician Assistants *(1991)*
4267 N.W. Federal Hwy, PMB 202
Jensen Beach, FL 34957
Toll Free: (888)942 - 6772
E-Mail: theanspa@aol.com
Web Site: www.anspa.org
Members: 250 individuals
Staff: 2
Annual Budget: under $10,000
Executive Director: Linda Kotrba

Historical Note
A specialty organization affiliated with the American Academy of Physician Assistants, ANSPA educates professionals and the lay public with respect to neurological surgery and the role of the physician assistant. Membership: $75/year (individual); $3000/year (company).

Meetings/Conferences:
Annual Meetings: Annual meeting at the American Association of Neurosurgical Surgeons (AANS)

Publications:
Newsletter. q. adv.
Surgical Physician Assistant. m. adv.

Association of North American Missions *(1942)*
P.O. Box 8667
Longview, TX 75607
Tel: (903)234-2075 *Fax:* (903)758-2799

E-Mail: bwiley@techteam.org
Web Site: www.anamissions.org
Members: 25 missions
Staff: 2
Annual Budget: $25-50,000
Chairman: Birne Wiley
E-Mail: bwiley@techteam.org

Meetings/Conferences:
Annual Meetings: May
2007 - Chicago, IL(Awana Hotel)/Apr. 18-20

Publications:
North American Missions. 3/year.
Update. bi-m.

Association of Nurses in AIDS Care *(1987)*

3538 Ridgewood Road
Akron, OH 44333
Tel: (330)670-0101 *Fax:* (330)670-0109
Toll Free: (800)260 - 6780
Web Site: www.anacnet.org
Members: 2500 individuals
Staff: 6
Annual Budget: $1-2,000,000
Executive Director: Dr. Adele Webb
E-Mail: adele@anacnet.org
Chief Financial Officer: Kathy Reihl
E-Mail: kathy@anacnet.org

Historical Note
ANAC members are nurses and other health professionals with an interest in the care of individuals with HIV. Membership: $70/year (individual); corporate dues vary.

Meetings/Conferences:
Annual Meetings: Fall
2007 - Orlando, FL(Swan)/Nov. 8-11/1000

Publications:
Journal of ANAC. bi-m. adv.
Newsletter. q. adv.

Association of Occupational and Environmental Clinics *(1987)*

1010 Vermont Ave. NW
Suite 513
Washington, DC 20005
Tel: (202)347-4976 *Fax:* (202)347-4950
Toll Free: (888)347 - 2632
E-Mail: aoec@aoec.org
Web Site: www.aoec.org
Members: 250 individuals
Staff: 4
Annual Budget: $2-5,000,000
Executive Director: Katherine H. Kirkland
Program Coordinator: Ingrid Denis

Historical Note
Established to enhance the practice of occupational/environmental medicine through information sharing and research. Membership criteria include commitment to teaching, research and public health response to occupational and environmental conditions. Individual membership is open to those who share the goals of AOEC. Membership: $40/year (individual); $250/year (clinic).

Meetings/Conferences:
Annual Meetings: Fall, in conjunction with American Public Health Ass'n
2007 - Washington, DC/Nov. 4-8

Publications:
Newsletter. q.

Association of Occupational Health Professionals in Healthcare *(1982)*

109 VIP Dr., Suite 220
Wexford, PA 15090
Tel: (724)935-6622 *Fax:* (724)935-1560
Toll Free: (800)362 - 4347
E-Mail: info@aohp.org
Web Site: www.aohp.org
Members: 985 individuals
Staff: 3
Annual Budget: $250-500,000
Executive Director: Judy Lyle
Account Manager: Annie West

Historical Note
Formerly (1994) Association of Hospital Employee Health Professionals. AOHP members are employee and occupational health professionals, safety officers, human resource administrators, risk managers, infection control practitioners and hospital administrators. Membership: $125/year (active); $50/year (student); $25/year (retired).

Meetings/Conferences:
2007 - Savannah, GA(Marriott Riverfront)/Sept. 26-29/300

Publications:
Journal of the AOHP. q. adv.
Make a Difference. a.

Association of Official Racing Chemists *(1947)*

P.O. Box 8400, Station T
Ottawa, ON K1G - 3H
Tel: (613)731-7137 *Fax:* (613)731-7984
Web Site: www.aorc-online.org
Members: 200 individuals
Staff: 1
Annual Budget: $25-50,000
Executive Director: Sharon K. McLellan

Historical Note
Formed in Chicago by a group of chemists from the United States and several other countries. The international membership consists of individuals concerned with detection of drugs in racing samples. Affiliated with the Association of Racing Commissioners International. There are currently 200 active members and 15 emeritus and honorary members.

Publications:
Proceedings. a.

Association of Official Seed Analysts *(1908)*

1763 E. University Blvd., Suite A
PMB #411
Las Cruces, NM 88001
Tel: (505)522-1437
E-Mail: aosaoffice@earthlink.net
Web Site: www.aosaseed.com
Members: 59 individuals
Staff: 1
Annual Budget: $100-250,000
Executive Assistant: Janice Osburn
E-Mail: aosaoffice@earthlink.net

Historical Note
Established in 1908 by 16 states, the U.S. Department of Agriculture and Canada. Cooperates with the International Seed Testing Association, the Society of Commercial Seed Technologists and the Commercial Seed Analysts Association of Canada. Membership: $150/year (individual); $500/year (organization).

Meetings/Conferences:
Annual Meetings: Summer/250-300
2007 - Cody, WY/June 8-11/300

Publications:
Seed Technologist News. 3/year.
Seed Technology. irreg.

Association of Official Seed Certifying Agencies *(1919)*

1601 52nd Ave., Suite One
Moline, IL 61265
Tel: (309)736-0120 *Fax:* (309)736-0115
Web Site: www.aosca.org
Members: 450 individuals
Staff: 2
Annual Budget: $100-250,000
Chief Executive Officer: Chet Boruff

Historical Note
Formerly (1968) The International Crop Improvement Association. Members are state seed certifying agencies and their employees.

Publications:
Genetic and Crop Standards.
Operating Procedures of the AOSCA.

Association of Oil Pipe Lines *(1947)*

1101 Vermont Ave. NW
Suite 604
Washington, DC 20005
Tel: (202)408-7970 *Fax:* (202)408-7983
E-Mail: aopl@aopl.org
Web Site: www.aopl.org
Members: 48 companies
Staff: 5
Annual Budget: $2-5,000,000
Executive Director: Benjamin Cooper
E-Mail: aopl@aopl.org
General Counsel: Michele Joy
E-Mail: aopl@aopl.org
Director, Public Affairs: Raymond Paul
E-Mail: aopl@aopl.org

Historical Note
Founded (1947) as the Committee for Pipe Line Companies, a voluntary, unincorporated association of common carrier pipeline companies. Later became the Committee for Oil Pipe Lines; assumed its current name in 1960.

Meetings/Conferences:
Semi-Annual Meetings: Winter in Washington, DC and June

Association of Old Crows

Historical Note
See AOC.

Association of Oncology Social Work *(1984)*

100 N. 20th St.
Fourth Floor
Philadelphia, PA 19103
Tel: (215)599-6093 *Fax:* (215)545-8107
E-Mail: info@aosw.org
Web Site: www.aosw.org
Members: 1100 individuals
Annual Budget: $50-100,000
Executive Director: Katherine Smolinski
E-Mail: info@aosw.org
Contact: Jessica Widing
E-Mail: info@aosw.org
Executive Director: Katherine Smolinski
E-Mail: info@aosw.org

Historical Note
Formerly the National Association of Oncology Social Workers. AOSW was established to enable professional social workers in oncology to better address the needs of clients, practitioners, managers, educators and researchers in the cancer field. Membership: $115/year (full member); $95/year (student/retired).

Meetings/Conferences:
Annual Meetings: Spring/400

Publications:
Journal of Psychosocial Oncology. q. adv.
AOSW News Newsletter. q.

Association of Operating Room Nurses

Historical Note
See listng under AORN.

Association of Operative Millers

Historical Note
Became International Association of Operative Millers in 2003.

Association of Organ Procurement Organizations *(1984)*

1364 Beverly Road, Suite 100
McLean, VA 22101
Tel: (703)556-4242 Ext: 204 *Fax:* (703)556-4852
E-Mail: organdonation@aopo.org
Web Site: www.aopo.org
Members: 58 organizations
Staff: 5
Annual Budget: $1-2,000,000
Executive Director: Paul M. Schwab
E-Mail: pschwab@aopo.org

Historical Note
AOPO members are organizations which obtain and transport vascular organs for transplantation. Membership: $7,100-11,600/year (organization).

Meetings/Conferences:
Annual Meetings: Summer

Publications:
Newsletter Update. q.

Association of Osteopathic State Executive Directors *(1918)*

2007 Apalachee Pkwy.
Tallahassee, FL 32301
Tel: (850)878-7364 *Fax:* (850)942-7538
E-Mail: admin@foma.org
Members: 58 individuals

Annual Budget: $10-25,000
Coordinator: Michelle Winn, CMP
E-Mail: admin@foma.org

Historical Note
Regular members are Osteopathic State executive directors; affiliate members include related medical associations. Has no paid officers or full-time staff.

Meetings/Conferences:
Annual Meetings: *Fall, with the American Osteopathic Ass'n*

Association of Otolaryngology Administrators *(1982)*
1805 Aromore Blvd.
Pittsburgh, PA 15221
Tel: (412)243-5156 *Fax:* (412)243-5160
E-Mail: aoa@oto-online.org
Web Site: www.oto-online.org
Members: 969 individuals
Staff: 1
Annual Budget: $100-250,000
Central Office Staff: Robin Wagner
E-Mail: aoa@oto-online.org

Historical Note
Active members are individuals responsible for the business aspects of an otolaryngology practice. Membership: $175/year.

Meetings/Conferences:
Annual Meetings: *Fall*

Publications:
Oto's Scope. q. adv.

Association of Paroling Authorities, International *(1961)*
Northwest Corner, Courthouse Square
P.O. Box 211
California, MO 65018
Tel: (573)796-2113 *Fax:* (573)796-2114
E-Mail: ghdh@aol.com
Web Site: www.apaintl.org
Members: 425 individuals
Staff: 2
Annual Budget: $50-100,000
Executive Secretary: Gail D. Hughes
E-Mail: ghdh@aol.com

Historical Note
Affiliate of the American Correctional Association. Membership is made up of paroling authorities, which includes both individuals and agencies. Membership: $50/year (individual); $300/year (agency).

Meetings/Conferences:
Annual Meetings: *Spring*

Publications:
APAI News. q. adv.
Paroling Authority Survey. a.

Association of Partners for Public Lands *(1977)*
2401 Blueridge Ave., Suite 303
Wheaton, MD 20902
Tel: (301)946-9475 *Fax:* (301)946-9478
E-Mail: appl@appl.org
Web Site: www.appl.org
Members: 80 organizations
Staff: 4
Annual Budget: $500-1,000,000
Executive Director: Donna L. Asbury
E-Mail: appl@appl.org

Historical Note
APPL supports its members in their missions of service and stewardship of America's public lands through education, information, and representation. APPL provides training courses, publications, an annual convention and trade show, and other programs to foster professional management practices and faciliate partnership among members and the federal agencies they serve.

Meetings/Conferences:
Annual Meetings: *Winter*

Publications:
Membership Directory. a.
Newswire. m.
Annual Report. a.

Association of Pathology Chairs *(1967)*
9650 Rockville Pike
Bethesda, MD 20814-3993
Tel: (301)634-7880 *Fax:* (301)634-7990
E-Mail: apc@asip.org
Web Site: www.apcprods.org
Members: 144 departments of pathology
Annual Budget: $250-500,000
Managing Officer: Mark E. Sobel, MD, Ph.D
Director, Finance: James S. Douglas
Director, Scientific Affairs, Communications, and Society Services: Priscilla Markwood

Historical Note
Formerly (1976) American Association of Chairmen of Medical School Departments of Pathology. Membership: $600/year (institution).

Meetings/Conferences:
2007 – Colorado Springs, CO(Cheyenne Mountain Springs)/July 18-21/250

Publications:
Newsletter. 2/yr.

Association of Pediatric Hematology/Oncology Nurses *(1976)*
4700 W. Lake Ave.
Glenview, IL 60025-1485
Tel: (847)375-4854 *Fax:* (877)734-8755
E-Mail: info@apon.org
Web Site: www.apon.org
Members: 2000 individuals
Staff: 3
Annual Budget: $250-500,000
Executive Director: Louise S. Miller
E-Mail: lmiller@amctec.com

Historical Note
Members are nurses specializing in care for children and adolescents with cancer and blood disorders and their families. Membership: $98/year (individual); $118/year (foreign individual); $2,500/year (company).

Meetings/Conferences:
Annual Meetings: *Fall/700*

Publications:
APON Counts. q. adv.
Journal of Pediatric Oncology Nursing. 6/year. adv.

Association of Pediatric Oncology Social Workers *(1977)*
c/o CBTF, 274 Madison St., Suite 1301
New York, NY 10016
Tel: (212)448-9494 *Fax:* (212)448-1022
Web Site: www.aposw.org
Members: 180 individuals
Annual Budget: $25-50,000
Executive Officer: Terry Moore

Historical Note
APOSW members are professional social workers employed in the field of pediatric oncology. Membership: $60/year (individual).

Meetings/Conferences:
Annual Meetings: *April*

Publications:
APOSW Update. q. adv.

Association of Pediatric Program Directors *(1980)*
6728 Old McLean Village Dr.
McLean, VA 22101
Tel: (703)556-9222 *Fax:* (703)556-8729
E-Mail: info@appd.org
Web Site: www.appd.org
Members: 1100 Individuals
Staff: 2
Executive Director: Laura E. Degnon

Meetings/Conferences:
Annual Meetings: *May*

Association of Performing Arts Presenters *(1957)*
1112 16th St. NW
Suite 400
Washington, DC 20036-4823
Tel: (202)833-2787 *Fax:* (202)833-1543
Toll Free: (888)820 - 2787
E-Mail: info@artspresenters.org
Web Site: www.artspresenters.org
Members: 1700 organizations
Staff: 20
Annual Budget: $2-5,000,000
President and Chief Executive Officer: Sandra Gibson
E-Mail: sgibson@artspresenters.org
Vice President, Programs: Kim Chan
Vice President, Finance and Operations: Mark Kimble
Vice President, External Affairs: Patrick Madden

Historical Note
Formerly (1974) Association of College and University Concert Managers, and (1989) Association of College, University and Community Arts Administrators. Members are arts organizations who present the professional, touring performing arts and managers of artists involved in the performing arts. Membership: $160-2,462/year (organization).

Meetings/Conferences:
Annual Meetings: *always New York, NY/2,000*

Publications:
Inside Arts. bi-m. adv.
Membership Directory. a.

Association of Personal Computer User Groups
3150 Payne Ave., Suite 12
Cleveland, OH 44114-4504
Tel: (301)423-1618
Toll Free: (800)558 - 6867
E-Mail: secretary@apcug.net
Web Site: www.apcug.net
Staff: 1
President: Ken Bundy

Association of Pet Dog Trainers *(1993)*
150 Executive Center Drive, Box 35
Greenville, SC 29615
Toll Free: (800)738 - 3647
E-Mail: information@apdt.com
Web Site: www.apdt.com
Members: 5227 individuals
Staff: 5
Annual Budget: Over $100,000,000
Executive Director: Richard Spencer

Historical Note
APDT provides continuing education and related services for member dog trainers.

Meetings/Conferences:
Annual Meetings: *Fall*

Publications:
APDT Newsletter. bi-m. adv.

Association of Philosophy Journal Editors *(1971)*
Journal of Philosophy, Columbia Univ.
1150 Amsterdam Ave., MC 4972
New York, NY 10027
Tel: (212)666-4419 *Fax:* (212)932-3721
Members: 95 journal members
Staff: 1
Annual Budget: under $10,000
Secretary-Treasurer: Michael Kelly

Historical Note
Membership: $10/year.

Meetings/Conferences:
Annual Meetings: *With the American Philosophical Ass'n, Eastern Division*

Association of Physician Assistant Programs *(1972)*

Historical Note
An affiliate of American Academy of Physician Assistants, which provides administrative support.

Association of Physician Assistants in Cardiovascular Surgery *(1981)*
P.O. Box 4834
Englewood, CO 80155
Tel: (303)221-5651 *Fax:* (303)771-2550
Toll Free: (877)221 - 5651
E-Mail: carol@goddardassociates.com
Web Site: www.apacvs.org
Members: 500 individuals
Staff: 2
Annual Budget: $50-100,000
Executive Director: Carol A. Goddard

Historical Note
APACVS members are surgical physician assistants specializing in cardiovascular surgery. Membership: $125/year (individual); $25/year (student).

Meetings/Conferences:
Annual Meetings: *Winter*

Publications:
Salary & Benefits Survey. a. adv.
Surgical Physician Assistant. adv.
APACVS Membership Directory. a. adv.
CardioVision. q. adv.

Association of Physician Assistants in Obstetrics and Gynecology *(1991)*
P.O. Box 1109
Madison, WI 53701-1109
Toll Free: (800)545 - 0636
Web Site: www.paobgyn.org
Members: 200 individuals
Staff: 1
Annual Budget: under $10,000
President: Judy Zaczek
Administrative Director: Kathy Mohelnitzky
Historical Note
APAOG is a specialty organization for physician assistants in OB-GYN affiliated with the American Academy of Physician Assistants.
Meetings/Conferences:
Annual Meetings: In conjunction with AAPA conference.
Publications:
The Monitor. 4/year.

Association of Plastic Surgery Assistants *(1974)*
3017 W. Charleston Blvd., Suite 80
Las Vegas, NV 89102
Tel: (702)870-0058 *Fax:* (702)870-0068
Toll Free: (800)753 - 7244
E-Mail: admin@plasticassistants.info
Web Site: www.plasticassistants.info
Members: 650 individuals
Staff: 1
Treasurer: Sandie Heitmann
Historical Note
Membership: $125/year.

Association of Polysomnographic Technologists *(1978)*
One Westbrook Corporate Ctr., Suite 920
Westchester, IL 60154
Tel: (708)492-0796 *Fax:* (708)273-9344
E-Mail: apt@aptweb.org
Web Site: www.aptweb.org
Members: 2500 individuals
Staff: 3
Annual Budget: $250-500,000
Coordinator: Christopher Waring
Historical Note
A constituent society of the Association of Professional Sleep Societies. Membership: $75/year (individual).
Meetings/Conferences:
Annual Meetings: June
Publications:
Annual Meeting Program. a. adv.
Membership Directory. a.
A2Z Newsletter. q. adv.

Association of Pool and Spa Professionals *(1956)*
2111 Eisenhower Ave.
Alexandria, VA 22314
Tel: (703)838-0083 Ext: 161 *Fax:* (703)549-0493
Web Site: www.theapsp.org
Members: 5500 companies
Staff: 50
Annual Budget: $5-10,000,000
President and Chief Executive Officer: Bill Weber
Senior Director, Communications and Marketing: Suzanne Barrows
Senior Director, Technical, Education and Government Relations: Carvin DiGiovanni
Chief Financial Officer: Leona Taylor
E-Mail: ltaylor@theapsp.org
Historical Note
Founded in Chicago, IL. Formerly (1956) known as the National Swimming Pool Institute. Absorbed the International Spa and Tub Institute in 1983. Represents all segments of the spa and pool industry. Has an annual budget of approximately $6 million.
Meetings/Conferences:
Annual Meetings: Fall

Association of Postgraduate Physician Assistant Programs *(1988)*
Dept. of Surgery, Norwalk Hospital
Norwalk, CT 06856
Tel: (203)852-2188
Web Site: www.appap.org
Historical Note
Affiliated with the American Academy of Physician Assistants and the Association of Physician Assistant Programs, APPAP member programs are postgraduate programs that offer structured curricula, including didactic and clinical components, to educate physician assistants for a defined period of time in a medical specialty. All programs must award a certificate, degree, or provide graduate academic credit.
Meetings/Conferences:
Annual Meetings: usually October

Association of Presbyterian Colleges and Universities *(1983)*
100 Witherspoon St.
Louisville, KY 40202-1396
Tel: (502)569-5364 *Fax:* (502)569-8766
Web Site: www.apcu.net
Members: 63 institutions
Staff: 2
Annual Budget: $100-250,000
Executive Director: Gary W. Luhr
E-Mail: gluhr@ctr.pcusa.org
Historical Note
Product of a merger of the Association of Presbyterian Colleges and the Presbyterian College Union.
Meetings/Conferences:
Annual Meetings: Summer
Publications:
Directory. a.

Association of Private Enterprise Education *(1974)*
313 Fletcher Hall
Univ. of Tennessee, 615 McCallie Ave.
Chattanooga, TN 37403-2598
Tel: (423)425-4118 *Fax:* (423)425-5218
Web Site: www.apee.org
Members: 362
Staff: 1
Secretary-Treasurer: J.R. Clark
E-Mail: j-clark@utc.edu
Historical Note
APEE members are scholars and entrepreneurs involved in research and/or teaching the basic economic principles of private enterprise. Membership: $70/year.
Meetings/Conferences:
Annual Meetings: Spring
2007 – Cancun, Mexico(Hilton)
2008 – Las Vegas, NV
Publications:
APEE Journal.

Association of Productivity Specialists *(1977)*
521 Fifth Ave., Suite 1700
New York, NY 10175
Tel: (212)286-0943
E-Mail: secretary@a-p-s.org
Web Site: www.a-p-s.org
Members: 1200 individuals
Staff: 2
Annual Budget: $10-25,000
Executive Secretary: Donna L. Matura
E-Mail: secretary@a-p-s.org
Historical Note
Membership: $50/year (individual); $1,500-4,000/year (organization/company).
Meetings/Conferences:
Annual Meetings: Typical Attendence: 100
Publications:
APS Review. q.

Association of Professional Ball Players of America *(1924)*
1820 W. Orangewood Ave., Suite 206
Orange, CA 92868
Tel: (714)935-9993 *Fax:* (714)935-0431
E-Mail: ballplayersassn@aol.com
Web Site: www.apbpa.org
Members: 9500 individuals
Staff: 2
Annual Budget: $250-500,000
Secretary-Treasurer: Richard Beverage
E-Mail: ballplayersassn@aol.com
Historical Note
APBPA members are professional baseball players, managers, coaches, scouts, and umpires.
Meetings/Conferences:
Annual Meetings: January

Association of Professional Chaplains *(1947)*
1701 E. Woodfield Road., Suite 760
Schaumburg, IL 60173
Tel: (847)240-1014 *Fax:* (847)240-1015
E-Mail: info@professionalchaplains.org
Web Site: www.professionalchaplains.org
Members: 3800 individuals
Staff: 4
Annual Budget: $1-2,000,000
Executive Director: Josephine N. Schrader, CAE
E-Mail: info@professionalchaplains.org
Historical Note
Unites the College of Chaplains and Association of Mental Health Clergy (1988). APC is an interfaith organization that provides certification, advocacy, and educational opportunities for pastoral care professionals serving in any specialized ministry setting.
Meetings/Conferences:
Annual Meetings: Spring, with the American Psychiatric Ass'n
Publications:
Chaplaincy Today. semi-a.
APC News. bi-m.
Journal of Pastoral Care. q. adv.

Association of Professional Color Imagers *(1968)*
Historical Note
A section of Photo Marketing Association-International, which provides administrative support.

Association of Professional Communication Consultants *(1983)*
211 E. 28th St.
Tulsa, OK 74114
Tel: (918)743-4793
Web Site: www.consultingsuccess.org
Members: 140 individuals
Annual Budget: under $10,000
President: Ken Davis
Historical Note
Formerly (1995) Association of Professional Writing Consultants. Members are full-time independent writing and communications consultants, part-time consultants who primarily teach in colleges and universities, in-company consultants, training professionals, and freelance writers and editors. Its purpose is to provide a network and group services for writing and communications consultants, to ensure the quality of seminars and other consulting practices, and to inform business and industry about the value of communicating effectively. Membership: $50/year.
Meetings/Conferences:
Annual Meetings: November
Publications:
Newsletter. q.
Membership Directory. q.
Bibliography. a.

Association of Professional Design Firms *(1985)*
601 108th Ave. NE
19th Floor
Bellevue, WA 98004
Tel: (425)943-3825 *Fax:* (425)943-3878
E-Mail: danae@apdf.org
Web Site: www.apdf.org
Members: 100 companies
Staff: 1
Annual Budget: $250-500,000
Executive Director and Chief Operating Officer: Danae Loran Willson
E-Mail: danae@apdf.org

Historical Note
Membership is open to firms engaged in graphic, industrial, and commercial interior design. APDF officers are elected annually. Membership: $1,500/yr.

Meetings/Conferences:
Annual Meetings: April

Publications:
Product Terms & Conditions. 8/yr.
Biz Brief. 8/year.
Financial Handbook For Design Firms. a.
Financial Survey. a.
Design Biz. 2/year.

Association of Professional Energy Managers *(1982)*
3916 W. Oak St., Suite D
Burbank, CA 91505
Tel: (818)972-2159 *Fax:* (818)972-2863
E-Mail: buschre@earthlink.net
Web Site: www.apem.org
Members: 500 individuals
President: Mark Martinez
E-Mail: buschre@earthlink.net

Historical Note
APEM members are individuals responsible for energy production, consumption or management decisions, including professional consultants, in all types of organizations. Promotes sustainable resource use through the exchange of information. Has no paid officers or full-time staff. Membership: $125/year (individual); $1,250/year (corporate).

Publications:
Professional Energy Manager. bi-m. adv.
Membership Directory. a.

Association of Professional Genealogists *(1979)*
P.O. Box 350998
Westminster, CO 80035
Tel: (303)465-6980 *Fax:* (303)456-8825
E-Mail: admin@apgen.org
Web Site: www.apgen.org
Members: 1700 individuals
Annual Budget: $100-250,000
Executive Director: Kathleen W. Hinckley
E-Mail: admin@apgen.org

Publications:
APG Quarterly. q. adv.
Directory of Professional Genealogists (online).

Association of Professional Investment Consultants *(1991)*
1726 M St. NW
Suite 403
Washington, DC 20036
Tel: (202)822-8600 *Fax:* (202)822-8686
E-Mail: apic@kelseymgmt.com
Web Site: www.apicsb.com
Members: 500
Staff: 2
Annual Budget: $500-1,000,000
Executive Director: Eric G. Scharf, CAE

Historical Note
Membership is composed exclusively of Smith Barney Financial consultants who work in the firm's Consulting Group. Provides a forum for members to exchange ideas, knowledge and information; to enhance their professional skills; to make their business needs known to each other and to the firm; and to interact with a peer group sharing common goals and interests.

Publications:
Oracle. q.

Association of Professional Landscape Designers *(1989)*
4305 N. Sixth St.
Suite A
Harrisburg, PA 17110
Tel: (717)238-9780 *Fax:* (717)238-9985
E-Mail: info@apld.org
Web Site: www.apld.org
Members: 1100 individuals
Staff: 4
Executive Director: Denise Calabrese
Director, Communications: Bethany Dennis

Historical Note
APLD members are professional landscape designers, allied vendors and students of landscape design. Awards Professional Landscape Designer Certification. Membership: $150/year (certified); $300/year (allied); $50/year (student); $150/year (associate).

Meetings/Conferences:
2007 – Pasadena, CA(Hilton)/March 4/200

Publications:
APLD Designer Newsletter. 4/yr. adv.

Association of Professional Material Handling Consultants *(1959)*

Historical Note
An affiliate of Material Handling Industry of America, which provides administrative support.

Association of Professional Model Makers *(1992)*
P.O. Box 165
Hamilton, NY 13346
Toll Free: (877)663 - 2766
E-Mail: info@modelmakers.org
Web Site: www.modelmakers.org
Members: 600 individuals
Staff: 3
Annual Budget: $50-100,000
Executive Director: Samanthi Martinez

Historical Note
APMM promotes the practice of model-making as an important component of design and manufacturing processes. Membership: $150/year (individual); $600/year (organization).

Meetings/Conferences:
Annual Meetings: Biennial

Publications:
Leading Edge Quarterly Newsletter (online). q.
APMM Directory. a. adv.
Vendor Directory. a. adv.

Association of Professional Researchers for Advancement *(1988)*
401 N. Michigan Ave.
Suite 2200
Chicago, IL 60611
Tel: (312)321-5196 *Fax:* (312)673-6966
E-Mail: info@aprahome.org
Web Site: www.aprahome.org
Members: 1900 individuals
Staff: 4
Annual Budget: $500-1,000,000
Executive Director: Julie Sutter

Historical Note
An outgrowth of the Minneapolis Prospect Research Association, formerly (1995) American Prospect Research Association. APRA members are professionals (including prospect researchers, directors of development, executive directors and consultants) who work in donor research at non-profit institutions throughout the world. Membership: $150/year.

Meetings/Conferences:
Annual Meetings: August
2007 – Chicago, IL/July 25-28

Publications:
Bulletin. m.
Connections. q.

Association of Professional Schools of International Affairs *(1989)*
2201 S. Gaylord St.
Denver, CO 80208
Tel: (303)871-4021
E-Mail: info@apsia.org
Web Site: www.apsia.org
Members: 30 institutions (full members); 19 affiliate members
Staff: 1
Annual Budget: $100-250,000
ExecutiveDirector: Daniel J. Whelan
E-Mail: info@apsia.org

Historical Note
Members are professional graduate schools of international affairs in the U.S., Europe and Asia. Membership: $1,000-5,000/year (institution).

Association of Professors and Researchers in Religious Education *(1970)*

Historical Note
Merged with Religious Education Association in 2004.

Association of Professors of Cardiology *(1990)*
9111 Old Georgetown Road
Bethesda, MD 20814-1699
Tel: (301)493-2330 *Fax:* (301)897-9745
E-Mail: sthayer@cardiologyprofessors.org
Web Site: www.cardiologyprofessors.org
Members: 116 institutions
Staff: 2
Annual Budget: $25-50,000
Administrative Coordinator: Susan C. Thayer
E-Mail: sthayer@cardiologyprofessors.org

Historical Note
APC states its purpose as to promote and engage in educational and scientific activities with respect to the science of cardiology. Members are Directors of Divisions of Cardiology of each accredited school in the United States and Puerto Rico. Membership: $350/year (institution).

Meetings/Conferences:
Semi-Annual Meetings: March and November

Association of Professors of Gynecology and Obstetrics *(1962)*
2130 Priest Bridge Dr., Suite 7
Crofton, MD 21114
Tel: (410)451-9560 *Fax:* (410)451-9568
Web Site: www.apgo.org
Members: 1500 individuals
Staff: 6
Annual Budget: $500-1,000,000
Executive Director: Donna Wachter
E-Mail: apgoadmin@apgo.org
Assistant, Publications: Kelly Collinson
E-Mail: apgoadmin@apgo.org
Specialist, Membership: Bonnie Fetsko
E-Mail: apgoadmin@apgo.org
Specialist, Meetings: Melissa Ganley
E-Mail: apgoadmin@apgo.org
Director, Communications: Pamela Johanssen
E-Mail: apgoadmin@apgo.org

Historical Note
Members are drawn from faculties of medical school departments of obstetrics and gynecology. Membership: $185/year (individual); $1,250/year (member departments); $1,000/year (institutional departments).

Meetings/Conferences:
Annual Meetings: February-March/600
2007 – Salt Lake City, UT(Grand American)/March 7-11/900
2008 – Orlando, FL(Disney Contemporary)/March 5-8/900
2009 – San Diego, CA(Manchester Grand Hyatt)/March 11-14/900

Publications:
APGO Educational Series On Women's Health. 3/year.
Instructional Objectives - Medical Students. trien.
Academic Positions Report. q.
APGO Newsletter. q. adv.

Association of Professors of Medicine *(1954)*
2501 M St. NW
Suite 550
Washington, DC 20037-1308
Tel: (202)861-7700 *Fax:* (202)861-9731
E-Mail: apm@im.org
Web Site: www.im.org/apm
Members: 150 individuals
Staff: 10
Annual Budget: $100-250,000
Contact: Tod Ibrahim

Historical Note
Chairpersons of medical school departments of medicine.

Publications:
APM E-Update. bi-w.
APM Update. q.
American Journal of Medicine. m. adv.

Association of Professors of Mission *(1952)*
100 E. 27th St.
Austin, TX 78705
Tel: (512)404-4855
E-Mail: asm@austinseminary.edu
Web Site: www.asmweb.org
Members: 190 individuals
Staff: 1
Annual Budget: under $10,000
Secretary-Treasurer: Aron W. James
E-Mail: asm@austinseminary.edu
Historical Note
APM members are professors teaching in the field of mission in colleges and seminaries. APM is a member of the Council on the Study of Religion. Membership: $15/year.
Meetings/Conferences:
Annual Meetings: June/usually in Chicago, IL/80-100

Association of Program Directors in Internal Medicine *(1978)*
2501 M St. NW
Suite 550
Washington, DC 20037
Tel: (202)887-9450 *Fax:* (202)887-9447
Toll Free: (800)622 - 4558
Web Site: www.apdim.med.edu
Members: 1100 individuals
Staff: 4
Annual Budget: $250-500,000
Vice President, Policy: Charles P. Clayton
E-Mail: aaim@im.org
Historical Note
Seeks to advance medical education through assisting accredited hospital internal medicine education programs. Membership: $675/year (institution); $100/year (individual).
Meetings/Conferences:
Semi-annual Meetings: Spring with American College of Physicians and Fall with Ass'n of American Medical Colleges
Publications:
Educational Clearinghouse Catalogue. bien. adv.
Program Directors Handbook. a. adv.
Chief Resident Handbook. a. adv.
APDIM. q. adv.

Association of Program Directors in Radiology *(1993)*
820 Jorie Blvd.
Oak Brook, IL 60523
Tel: (630)368-3737 *Fax:* (630)571-7837
E-Mail: apdr@rsna.org
Web Site: www.apdr.org
Members: 417 individuals
Staff: 3
Annual Budget: $25-50,000
Acct. Executive: Lise Thorsby
E-Mail: apdr@rsna.org
Historical Note
APDR members are directors of resident and fellowship training in radiology.
Meetings/Conferences:
Annual Meetings: Spring
2007 - Denver, CO(Hyatt Denver Convention Center)/Apr. 25-28
Publications:
Academic Radiology. m. adv.

Association of Program Directors in Surgery
6400 Goldsboro Road, Suite 450
Bethesda, MD 20817-5848
Tel: (301)320-1200 *Fax:* (301)263-9025
Web Site: www.apds.org
Members: 500 individuals
Executive Director: Bradley C. Stillman
Meetings/Conferences:
Annual Meetings: usually Spring
Publications:
Current Surgery. m.

Association of Progressive Rental Organizations *(1980)*
1504 Robin Hood Trail
Austin, TX 78703
Tel: (512)794-0095 *Fax:* (512)794-0097
Toll Free: (800)204 - 2776
Web Site: www.aprovision.org
Members: 4500 companies
Staff: 10
Annual Budget: $2-5,000,000
Executive Director: Bill Keese
Director, Communications: Shellie Faught
Director, Marketing: Cindy Ferguson
Director, Membership: Laurie Hill
Director, Government Affairs: Ron Waters
Historical Note
Members are television, appliance and furniture dealers who rent merchandise with an option to purchase. Membership: $375-550,000/year (dealers); $600/year (suppliers).
Meetings/Conferences:
Annual Meetings: Summer
Publications:
Rental Viewpoint (online). bi-w. adv.
Progressive Rentals. bi-m. adv.
APRO Show Guide. a. adv.
Who's Who in Rent to Own Directory. a. adv.

Association of Promotion Marketing Agencies Worldwide
Historical Note
Became Marketing Agencies Association Worldwide in 2003.

Association of Proposal Management Professionals
P.O. Box 668
Dana Point, CA 92629-0668
Tel: (949)493-9398 *Fax:* (949)240-4844
E-Mail: apmpinfo@aol.com
Web Site: www.apmp.org
Members: 1700 individuals
Staff: 1
Annual Budget: $250-500,000
Executive Director: David L. Winton
Historical Note
Members are executives and professionals who author or evaluate funding proposals. Thirteen chapters located throughout the United States and the United Kingdom. Membership: $75/year.
Meetings/Conferences:
Annual Meetings: Semi-Annual Meetings
Publications:
Perspective Newsletter (online). q.
Journal of the Association of Proposal Management Professionals. bi-a.
Conference Proceedings. a.

Association of Psychology Postdoctoral and Internship Centers *(1968)*
Ten G St. NE
Suite 440
Washington, DC 20002
Tel: (202)589-0600 *Fax:* (202)589-0603
E-Mail: appic@aol.com
Web Site: www.appic.org
Members: 600 internship sites
Staff: 2
Annual Budget: $250-500,000
Executive Director: Connie Hercey, M.P.A.
Historical Note
Formerly (1990) the Association of Psychology Intership Centers. Members are programs in psychology. APPIC was formed to foster the sharing of information about mutual concerns and interests with respect to internship training interests within the American Psychological Association. Membership: $450/year.
Meetings/Conferences:
Annual Meetings: August, with APA
Publications:
APPIC Newsletter. semi-a.
Internship & Postdoctoral Programs in Professional Psychology. a.

Association of Public Data Users *(1975)*
40 APB Associates
28300 Franklin Rd.
Southfield, MI 48034-1562
Tel: (248)354-6520 *Fax:* (248)354-6645
E-Mail: info@apdu.org
Web Site: www.apdu.org
Members: 350 individuals
Staff: 1
Annual Budget: $50-100,000
Administrator: Patricia Becker
E-Mail: info@apdu.org
Historical Note
Facilitates the utilization of public data through the sharing of knowledge about files and applicable software, and exchange of documentation. APDU is committed to increasing the knowledge base of its members about new sources of information and increasing the awareness of Federal agencies about the requirements of data users. Membership: $375/year (organization).
Meetings/Conferences:
Annual Meetings: Fall
Publications:
APDU e-Newsletter. q.
APDU Membership Directory. a.

Association of Public Health Laboratories *(1951)*
8515 Georgia Ave.
Suite 700
Silver Spring, MD 20036-3320
Tel: (240)485-2745 *Fax:* (240)485-2700
E-Mail: info@aphl.org
Web Site: www.aphl.org
Members: 275 individuals
Staff: 29
Annual Budget: $2-5,000,000
Executive Director: Scott J. Becker
E-Mail: sbecker@aphl.org
Chief Operating Officer: Carol Clark, CPA
E-Mail: cclark@aphl.org
Director, Communications and Membership: Jody DeVoll
E-Mail: info@aphl.org
Manager, Membership: Anna Dillingham
E-Mail: info@aphl.org
Senior Director, Professional Development: Eva Perlman
E-Mail: eperlman@aphl.org
Historical Note
Formerly Association of State and Territorial Public Health Laboratory Directors (1998). APHL works cooperatively with private and governmental groups to improve the quality of laboratory testing through training and national conferences, and extends such programs to the international community.
Meetings/Conferences:
Annual Meetings: Summer
Publications:
APHL Minute. bi-m.
E-Update (online). w.
NLTN Network News. q.

Association of Public Television Stations *(1980)*
666 11th St. NW
Suite 1100
Washington, DC 20001
Tel: (202)654-4200 *Fax:* (202)654-4236
Web Site: www.apts.org
Members: 146 stations and organizations
Staff: 18
Annual Budget: $2-5,000,000
President and Chief Executive Officer: John Lawson
E-Mail: john@apts.org
Vice President, Communications: Jeffrey Davis
E-Mail: jeffrey@apts.org
Senior Vice President and Chief Operating Officer: Mark Erstling
E-Mail: mark@apts.org
Vice President, Government Relations: Debra Sanchez
E-Mail: debra@apts.org
Vice President and General Counsel: Lonna Thompson
E-Mail: lonna@apts.org
Historical Note
Established in January, 1980 as the Association for Public Broadcasting. Became National Association of Public Television Stations in July, 1980; later readopted its original name and then assumed its present name in 1991. APTS represents public television before the federal government and provides research, planning, and communicaions support to the industry. Members are public television licensees.
Meetings/Conferences:
Annual Meetings: Spring.

2007 - Washington, DC(Ritz Carlton)/Feb. 12-14

Publications:
Transition.
Communique.
Washington Update.

Association of Public Treasurers of the United States and Canada *(1965)*
962 Wayne Ave., Suite 910
Silver Spring, MD 20910
Tel: (301)495-5560 *Fax:* (301)495-5561
E-Mail: info@aptusc.org
Web Site: www.aptusc.org
Members: 2000 individuals
Staff: 3
Annual Budget: $250-500,000
Executive Director: Kelley Noone

Historical Note
Founded as Municipal Treasurers Association of the United States and Canada; assumed its current name in 2001. Awards the Certified Municipal Finance Adminstrator credential (CMFA). Membership: $101-301/year (city/state); $356/year (firm/associate).

Meetings/Conferences:
Annual Meetings: August/450
2007 - San Diego, CA
2008 - Grand Rapids, MI

Publications:
Treasury Notes. m. adv.

Association of Public-Safety Communications Officers- International *(1935)*
351 N. Williamson Blvd.
Daytona Beach, FL 32114
Tel: (386)322-2500
Toll Free: (800)272 - 6911
E-Mail: apco@apco911.org
Web Site: www.apcointl.org
Members: 16000 individuals
Staff: 60
Annual Budget: $2-5,000,000
Executive Director: George S. Rice, Jr.
Director, IT Systems: Dennis Divine
E-Mail: divined@apco911.org
Director, Automated Frequency Coordination: Ron Haraseth
E-Mail: harasethr@apco911.org
Director, Marketing and Communications: Garry Mendez
E-Mail: mendezg@apco911.org
Director, Conference and Meeting Services: Barbra Myers
Chief Financial Officer: Tim Ryan
E-Mail: ryant@apco911.org
Director, APCO Institute: Candice Solie
Director, Member Services: Susan Stowell Corder

Historical Note
The oldest and largest public safety communications group, APCO is recognized by the Federal Communications Commission as the frequency coordination body for police, local government and 800 MHZ public safety radio services. Member of the Land Mobile Communications Council. Offers various training courses.

Meetings/Conferences:
Annual Meetings: Summer
2007 - Baltimore, MD(Baltimore Convention Center)/Aug. 5-9
2008 - Kansas City, MO(Kansas City Convention Center)/Aug. 3-8
2009 - Las Vegas, NV(Las Vegas Convention Center)/Aug. 9-14
2010 - Houston, TX(George R. Brown Convention Center)/Aug. 1-5
2011 - Philadelphia, PA(Pennsylvania Convention Center)/Aug. 7-12

Publications:
Public Safety Communications - APCO Bulletin. m. adv.

Association of Publication Production Managers *(1939)*

Historical Note
Merged with Women in Production in 2003 to form Partnership in Print Production.

Association of Racing Commissioners International *(1934)*
2343 Alexandria Dr., Suite 200
Lexington, KY 40504
Tel: (859)224-7070 *Fax:* (859)224-7071
Web Site: www.arci.com
Members: 500 individuals
Staff: 5
Annual Budget: $1-2,000,000
President and Chief Executive Officer: Edward J. Martin
Database and Information Technology Administrator: Kevin Crum
Office Manager: Eva M. Waters
E-Mail: ewaters@arci.com

Historical Note
Formerly National Association of State Racing Commissioners; assumed its current name in 29 Represents all forms of flat racing, as well as jai alai, and harness and greyhound racing. Member of the American Horse Council.

Meetings/Conferences:
Annual Meetings: Spring/400

Publications:
Weekly News Bulletins. bi-w.
Statistical Reports on Greyhound Racing. a.
Statistical Reports on Horse Racing. a.
Statistical Summary of Pari-Mutuel Wagering. a.

Association of Railway Museums *(1961)*
P.O. Box 370
Tujunga, CA 91043-0370
Tel: (818)951-9151 *Fax:* (818)951-9151
E-Mail: secretary@railwaymuseums.org
Web Site: www.railwaymuseums.org
Members: 130 museums
Staff: 2
Annual Budget: $10-25,000
Secretary: Ellen Fishburn
E-Mail: secretary@railwaymuseums.org

Historical Note
Members are museums displaying electric and steam railway equipment. Has no full-time staff. ARM is a Professional Affiliate Member of American Association of Museums. Membership: $100/year (museum); $60/year (non-profit affiliate); $175/year (commercial affiliate); $15/year (individual affiliate).

Meetings/Conferences:
Annual Meetings: Fall/200
2007 - Washington, PA(Pennsylvania Trolley Museum)

Publications:
Railway Museum Quarterly. q. adv.

Association of Real Estate License Law Officials *(1930)*
P.O. Box 230159
Montgomery, AL 36123-0159
Tel: (334)260-2902 *Fax:* (334)260-2903
Web Site: www.arello.org
Members: 73 jurisdictions
Staff: 2
Annual Budget: $50-100,000,000
Chief Executive Officer: Craig Cheatham
E-Mail: craig@arello.org

Historical Note
Formerly National Association of License Law Officials, as well as formerly the National Association of Real Estate License Law Officials. An association of all the Real Estate Commissions in the United States and territories. Purpose is to upgrade the states' regulation of the real estate industry. The organization is now international, with members from Australia, Africa, Asia, The Caribbean and Central America as well as the United States.

Meetings/Conferences:
Annual Meetings: Fall
2007 - New York, NY(Hyatt)/Sept. 14-17/350

Publications:
Boundaries. bi-m.
ARELLOgram. m.
Case Law Report. a.
Digest of Real Estate License Laws. a.
Directory. a.

Association of Real Estate Women *(1978)*
551 Fifth Ave., Suite 3025
New York, NY 10176-3099
Tel: (212)599-6181 *Fax:* (212)687-4016
E-Mail: info@arew.org
Web Site: www.arew.org
Members: 300 individuals
Staff: 2
Annual Budget: $100-250,000
Executive Director: Arlene Stock, CAE

Historical Note
Based in New York City, the Association of Real Estate Women (AREW) was founded in 1978 to provide opportunities for career development and networking with other real estate professionals.

Meetings/Conferences:
Annual Meetings: None held.

Association of Regulatory Boards of Optometry *(1919)*
1750 S. Brentwood Blvd., Suite 503
St. Louis, MO 63144
Tel: (314)785-6000 *Fax:* (314)785-6002
E-Mail: arbo@arbo.org
Web Site: www.arbo.org
Members: 56 boards
Staff: 4
Annual Budget: $500-1,000,000
Executive Director: Jennifer Parker

Historical Note
Founded as the International Association of Boards of Examiners in Optometry, assumed its present name in 1999. ARBO is the association of state, provincial, and territorial boards of optometry throughout North America. Its mission is to represent and assist Member Boards in regulating the practice of optometry for the public welfare.

Meetings/Conferences:
Annual Meetings: With the American Optometric Ass'n

Publications:
ARBO "Greensheet" Newsletter. q.

Association of Rehabilitation Nurses *(1974)*
4700 W. Lake Ave.
Glenview, IL 60025-1485
Tel: (847)375-4710 *Fax:* (877)734-9384
Toll Free: (800)229 - 7530
E-Mail: info@rehabnurse.org
Web Site: www.rehabnurse.org
Members: 5700 individuals
Staff: 10
Annual Budget: $1-2,000,000
Executive Director: Karen Nason
Director, Education: Mary Beth Brenner
E-Mail: info@rehabnurse.org
Director, Finance: Jim Gillmeister

Historical Note
ARN members are registered nurses concerned with or involved in the practice of rehabilitation nursing; non-voting membership is available for others interested in the field. Formed and supports the Rehabilitation Nursing Foundation as its research arm. Membership: $100/year (individual); $2,000/year (corporate).

Meetings/Conferences:
Annual Meetings: Fall
2007 - Washington, DC(Hilton Washington)/Oct. 3-6/1000

Publications:
Make a Difference Brochure.
ARN Network Newsletter. bi-m. adv.
Rehabilitation Nursing. bi-m. adv.

Association of Rehabilitation Programs in Computer Technology *(1978)*
c/o Western Michigan Univ., Educ. Studies Office
3421 Sangren Hall
Kalamazoo, MI 49008
Tel: (269)387-2053 *Fax:* (269)387-6184
Web Site: www.arpct.org
Members: 65 organizations
Annual Budget: $10-25,000
Membership: Robert Lenaway
E-Mail: bob.lenaway@wmich.edu

Historical Note
Formerly (1994) Association of Rehabilitation Programs in Data Processing. ARPCT membership includes rehabilitation programs as well as individuals interested in promoting computer technology as a career for persons with disabilities. Has no permanent

office or staff; officers elected annually. Membership: $75/year (individual); $325/year (organziation).

Publications:
Viewpoint. semi-a.

Association of Reporters of Judicial Decisions *(1982)*
c/o Truman S. Fuller, Reporter of Decisions, Supreme Court of Washington
Temple of Justice, P.O. Box 40929
Olympia, WA 98504-0929
Tel: (360)357-2090 *Fax:* (360)357-2099
Web Site: http://asjd.washlaw.edu
Members: 60 individuals
Treasurer: Truman S. Fuller

Historical Note
ARJD is composed of attorneys and their staff who edit and publish judicial opinions. Has no paid officers or full-time staff. Membership: $50/year (reporter); $30/year (staff).

Publications:
Catchline Newsletter. 3/year.
Directory. a.

Association of Reproductive Health Professionals *(1963)*
2401 Pennsylvania Ave. NW
Suite 350
Washington, DC 20037-1718
Tel: (202)466-3825 *Fax:* (202)466-3826
E-Mail: arhp@arhp.org
Web Site: www.arhp.org
Members: 11000 individuals
Staff: 12
Annual Budget: $2-5,000,000
President/Chief Executive Officer: Wayne C. Shields
E-Mail: wshields@arhp.org
Director, Development: Becca Ramati
Director, Communications: Janet Riessman
Director, Finance and Administration: Joseph M. Rodden
Director, Education: Amy M. Swann

Historical Note
Members are physicians, advanced practice clinicians and other professionals in reproductive health. Founded in 1963 as the Association of Planned Parenthood Physicians. Membership: $115/year (advanced practice clinicians); $175/year (physicians); $40/year (students, residents); includes subscription to Contraception Journal.

Meetings/Conferences:
Annual Meetings: Fall

Publications:
Newsletter. q.
Health & Sexualty. q. adv.
Contraception Journal. m. adv.
Clinical Proceedings. q.

Association of Research Directors *(1972)*
University of Maryland, Eastern Shore
Princess Anne, MD 21853
Tel: (410)651-6074 *Fax:* (410)651-7657
Web Site: www.umes.edu/ard
Members: 18 universities
Executive Director: Samuel L. Donald

Historical Note
Founded as Association of 1890 Research Directors. ARD coordinates food and agricultural research projects between member programs and the USDA, other federal and state agencies, and private industry. Has no paid officers or full-time staff.

Publications:
Proceedings.
Resource Guide and Directory. bien.

Association of Research Libraries *(1932)*
21 Dupont Circle NW
Suite 800
Washington, DC 20036
Tel: (202)296-2296 *Fax:* (202)872-0884
E-Mail: arlhq@arl.org
Web Site: www.arl.org
Members: 120 libraries
Staff: 25
Annual Budget: $2-5,000,000
Executive Director: Duane Webster
E-Mail: duane@arl.org
Deputy Executive Director: G. Jaia Barrett
E-Mail: jaia@arl.org
Assistant Executive Director, External Relations: Julia Blixrud
E-Mail: jblix@arl.org
Director, Organizational Learning Services: DeEtta Jones
E-Mail: deetta@arl.org

Historical Note
ARL's primary function is to identify and solve problems fundamental to large research libraries. Membership: $18,550/year.

Meetings/Conferences:
Semi-Annual Meetings: May and October
2007 – St. Louis, MO/May 22-25
2007 – Washington, DC/Oct. 16-19
2008 – Coral Gables, FL/
2008 – Washington, DC/
2009 – Houston, TX/
2009 – Washington, DC/

Publications:
ARL: A Bimonthly Report on Research Library Issues and Actions from ARL, CNI, SPARC. bi-m.
SPEC Kit. 6/yr.
ARL Statistics. a.
ARL Preservation Statistics. a.
ARL Salary Survey. a.

Association of Residents in Radiation Oncology *(1983)*
12500 Fair Lakes Circle, Suite 375
Fairfax, VA 22033
Tel: (703)502-1550 *Fax:* (703)502-7852
Toll Free: (800)962 - 7876
E-Mail: arro@arro.org
Web Site: www.arro.org
Members: 515 individuals
Staff: 1
Annual Budget: $50-100,000
Program Manager: Steven M. Smith

Historical Note
ARRO members are residents and clinical fellows in accredited radiation oncology programs. An affiliate of American Society for Therapeutic Radiology and Oncology

Meetings/Conferences:
Annual Meetings: With American Soc. for Therapeutic Radiology and Oncology

Association of Retail Marketing Services *(1957)*
10 Drs. James Parker Blvd., Suite 103
Red Bank, NJ 07701
Tel: (732)842-5070 *Fax:* (732)219-1938
E-Mail: info@goarms.com
Web Site: www.goarms.com
Members: 140 individuals
Staff: 6
Annual Budget: $250-500,000
Executive Director: Gerri Hopkins
Administrative Director: Lisa McCauley

Historical Note
Formerly (1982) Trading Stamp Institute of America and TSIA, Inc., The Association of Retail Marketing Services. Assumed its present name in 1983. ARMS is a market-information network for suppliers of premium and continuity plans, customer incentive programs, and motivation techniques for sales personnel. Membership: $350/year.

Meetings/Conferences:
Annual Meetings: Winter

Publications:
ARMS Supermarket Promotion Show Directory. a.

Association of Retail Travel Agents *(1963)*
4320 N. Miller Rd.
Scottsdale, AZ 85251
Toll Free: (800)969 - 6069
E-Mail: info@artaonline.com
Web Site: www.artaonline.com
Members: 1200 companies, 2200 individuals
Staff: 4
Annual Budget: $250-500,000
President: John K. Hawks, APR
E-Mail: info@artaonline.com
Vice President, Administration: Pat Funk
E-Mail: info@artaonline.com

Historical Note
ARTA represents small and independent professional travel agents. Its two primary activities are providing educational and training opportunities to agents and representing their point of view before industry, governmental and consumer organizations. Membership: $75/year (individual); $250/year (company).

Meetings/Conferences:
Semi-annual Meetings: Spring

Publications:
A Taste of ARTA.

Association of Rheumatology Health Professionals *(1965)*
1800 Century Place NE
Suite 250
Atlanta, GA 30345-4300
Tel: (404)633-3777 *Fax:* (404)633-1870
E-Mail: arhp@rheumatology.org
Web Site: www.rheumatology.org/arhp
Members: 750 individuals
Staff: 7
Annual Budget: $500-1,000,000
Executive Director: David Haag

Historical Note
Formerly (1994) Arthritis Health Professions Association. A professional membership society, the organization works to establish and disseminate scientific knowledge relevant to issues of access, quality and provision of appropriate arthritis care. Membership: $115/year (individual); $115/year (international); $75/year (associate).

Meetings/Conferences:
Annual Meetings: Fall, in conjunction with the American College of Rheumatology

Publications:
Arthritis Care & Research. q. adv.

Association of Rotational Molders, International *(1976)*
2000 Spring Road, Suite 511
Oak Brook, IL 60523-1850
Tel: (630)571-0611 *Fax:* (630)571-0616
Web Site: www.rotomolding.org
Members: 400 companies
Staff: 5
Annual Budget: $1-2,000,000
Executive Director and Chief Executive Officer: Jeffrey Arnold

Historical Note
Plastic fabricators employing Rotational Molding.

Meetings/Conferences:
Semi-Annual Meetings: April and October

Publications:
Rotation Magazine. bi-m. adv.

Association of Sales Administration Managers *(1981)*
P.O. Box 1356
Laurence Harbor, NJ 08879
Tel: (732)264-7722
E-Mail: ASAMNET@AOL.COM
Web Site: http://members.aol.com/ASAMNET
Members: 88 individuals
Annual Budget: under $10,000

Historical Note
ASAM's members are independent consultants and corporate employees providing sales and marketing services including: establishing broker/representative sales networks, field sales management, marketing and administrative services, meeting management, etc. Members provide a full range of services from product introduction to promotional programs to support the sales effort. Operating primarily in the Consumer Packaged Goods field, both Private Label and Branded, in all classes of trade. Members are open for selective consulting assignments.

Association of Sales and Marketing Companies *(1904)*

Historical Note
Merged with Grocery Manufacturers Ass'n in 2003.

Association of School Business Officials International *(1910)*

11401 N. Shore Dr.
Reston, VA 20190-4200
Tel: (703)478-0405 *Fax:* (703)478-7060
Toll Free: (866)682 - 2729
E-Mail: asboreq@asbointl.org
Web Site: www.asbointl.org
Members: 7000 individuals
Staff: 18
Annual Budget: $2-5,000,000
Executive Director: Anne W. Miller, Ph.D.
E-Mail: amiller@asbointl.org
Director, Finance and Administration: Thuan Huynh
E-Mail: thuynh@asbointl.org
Director, Government and Public Affairs: Ronald A. Skinner
E-Mail: rskinner@asbointl.org

Historical Note

ASBO members are school district-level business executives, professors of business and education, students, and businessmen of school-related firms. Members are dedicated to the professional stewardship of the investment in education, both public and private. Membership: $40-$495/year.

Meetings/Conferences:

Annual Meetings: Fall

Publications:

School Business Affairs Magazine. m. adv.
ASBO International Elevator Speeches. bi-m.

Association of Schools and Colleges of Optometry *(1941)*

6110 Executive Blvd., Suite 510
Rockville, MD 20852
Tel: (301)231-5944 *Fax:* (301)770-1828
E-Mail: nloewentritt@opted.org
Web Site: www.opted.org
Members: 19
Staff: 5
Annual Budget: $500-1,000,000
Executive Director: Martin A. Wall, CAE
E-Mail: mwall@opted.org
Manager, Professional and Board Services: Mary Eastman
Director, Career Promotion and Student Affairs: Enid-Mai Jones
Director, Communications and Corporate Affairs: Patricia O'Rourke
E-Mail: porourke@opted.org

Historical Note

ASCO represents professional programs of optometric education in the U.S. and abroad.

Meetings/Conferences:

Annual Meetings: June, with the American Optometric Ass'n

Publications:

Residency Directory online.
Faculty Survey Report. a.
Student Survey Report. a.
Journal of Optometric Education. q. adv.
Optometric Faculty Directory online.

Association of Schools of Allied Health Professions *(1967)*

1730 M St. NW
Suite 500
Washington, DC 20036
Tel: (202)293-4848 *Fax:* (202)293-4852
Toll Free: (800)497 - 8080
E-Mail: asahp1@asahp.org
Web Site: www.asahp.org
Members: 750schools,programs&individuals
Staff: 3
Annual Budget: $500-1,000,000
Executive Director: Thomas W. Elwood

Historical Note

Formerly (1974) Association of Schools of Allied Health Professions and (1992) American Society of Allied Health Professions. Membership includes allied health schools and programs, associations, and individual educators. Membership: $65-145/year (individual); $4,500/year (institution).

Publications:

Annual Report. a.
Strategic Plan.
Journal of Allied Health. q. adv.

Association of Schools of Journalism and Mass Communication *(1917)*

234 Outlet Pointe Blvd.
Columbia, SC 29210-5667
Tel: (803)798-0271 *Fax:* (803)772-3509
Web Site: www.asjmc.org
Members: 202 institutions
Staff: 8
Executive Director: Jennifer H. McGill

Historical Note

Founded as the Association of Accredited Schools and Departments of Journalism; became the American Association of Schools and Departments of Journalism in 1954 and assumed its present name in 1983. Absorbed the American Society of Journalism School Administrators in 1984. Shares administrative offices with Association for Education in Journalism and Mass Communication. Membership: $50/year (individual); $350/year (institution).

Meetings/Conferences:

Annual Meetings: Summer/2,000

Publications:

ASJMC/Administrator Demographic Survey. a.

Association of Schools of Public Health *(1941)*

1101 15th St. NW
Suite 910
Washington, DC 20005
Tel: (202)296-1099 *Fax:* (202)296-1252
E-Mail: info@asph.org
Web Site: www.asph.org
Members: 41 schools
Staff: 25
Annual Budget: $500-1,000,000
President and Chief Executive Officer: Dr. Harrison C. Spencer
E-Mail: rkelliher@asph.org
Deputy Executive Director: Allison J. Foster
E-Mail: afoster@asph.org
Director, Education and Research: Karen Helsing
Director, Grants and Contracts: Rita Kelleher
E-Mail: rkelliher@asph.org
Director, Practice and Workshop Development: Antigone Vickery
E-Mail: rkelliher@asph.org

Historical Note

The only national organization representing administration, faculty, and students of the country's accredited schools of public health. Established in 1941 to facilitate communication among leadership of the schools. Membership: $14,000/year (organization).

Meetings/Conferences:

Annual Meetings: Fall

Association of Science Museum Directors *(1960)*

c/o Illinois State Museum
502 S. Spring St.
Springfield, IL 62706
Tel: (217)782-7011 *Fax:* (217)782-1254
Members: 80 institutions
Annual Budget: under $10,000
Secretary-Treasurer: Dr. Bonnie W. Styles

Historical Note

Has no paid officers or full-time staff. Membership: $100 or $200/year, depending on museum operating budget.

Meetings/Conferences:

Annual Meetings: Mid-winter director's forum annual meeting.
2007 – Honolulu, HI(Bishop Museum)/Feb. 21-26

Association of Science-Technology Centers *(1973)*

1025 Vermont Ave. NW
Suite 500
Washington, DC 20005-6310
Tel: (202)783-7200 *Fax:* (202)783-7207
E-Mail: info@astc.org
Web Site: www.astc.org
Members: 543 institutions
Staff: 22
Annual Budget: $2-5,000,000
Executive Director: Bonnie VanDorn
E-Mail: bvandorn@astc.org
Director, Partnerships for Learning: Deanna Beane
E-Mail: dbbeane@astc.org
Membership Director: Diane K. Frendak
E-Mail: dfrendak@astc.org
Director, Meetings/Conferences: Cindy Kong
E-Mail: ckong@astc.org
Chief Financial Officer: Wendy Margolis
Administrative Director: Donna McMillan
E-Mail: dmcmillan@astc.org
Director, Research and Communications: Wendy Pollock

Historical Note

Members are science museums and related institutions united to increase public understanding of science and technology. Works to improve the operation and delivery of services of member institutions, with a special interest in informal education and programs targeted to traditionally underserved communities and constituencies. Membership: $500 to $3,000/year (based on budget and type of membership).

Meetings/Conferences:

Annual Meetings: Mid-October/1,400
2007 – Los Angeles, CA(California Science Center)/Nov. 3-6
2008 – Philadelphia, PA(Franklin Institute)/Oct. 18-21
2009 – Ft. Worth, TX(Ft. Worth Museum of Science & History)/Oct. 31-Nov. 3

Publications:

ASTC Journal: Dimensions. bi-m.
ASTC Conference Program. a. adv.
ASTC Directory. a.

Association of Senior Anthropologists

Historical Note

A section of the American Anthropological Association.

Association of Service and Computer Dealers International *(1981)*

131 N.W. First Ave.
Delray Beach, FL 33483
Tel: (561)266-9016 *Fax:* (561)266-9017
Web Site: www.ascdi.com
Members: 300 members
Staff: 4
Annual Budget: $250-500,000
President: Joseph Marion
E-Mail: jmarion@ascdi.com

Historical Note

Formerly (1994) American Society of Computer Dealers. Members are dealers, leasing companies, brokerage firms and refurbishment maintenance companies. Membership: $900/year (company).

Meetings/Conferences:

Annual Meetings: Semi-annual Meetings

Publications:

ASCDI NOW. bi-m.
Membership Directory. a.

Association of Seventh-Day Adventist Librarians *(1981)*

Weis Library, Columbia Union College
7600 Flower Ave.
Takoma Park, MD 20912-7796
Tel: (301)891-4222 *Fax:* (301)891-4204
E-Mail: lwisel@cuc.edu
Web Site: www.asdal.org
Members: 150 individuals
Annual Budget: under $10,000
Treasurer: Lee Marie Wisel
E-Mail: lwisel@cuc.edu

Historical Note

Promotes librarianship and library services to Seventh-Day Adventist institutions. Sponsors the D. Glenn Hilts Scholarship Program. Has no paid officers or full-time staff. Membership: $20/year.

Meetings/Conferences:

Annual Meetings: 50
2007 – Somerset West, South Africa(Helderberg College)
2008 – Loma Linda, CA(Loma Linda University)
2009 – Berrien Springs, MI(Andrews University)
2010 – Collegedale, TN(Southern Adventist University)

2011 – Angwin, CA(Pacific Union College)
Publications:
ASDAL Action Newsletter. semi-a. adv.
Seventh-Day Adventist Periodical Index. a.

Association of Shareware Professionals *(1987)*
P.O. Box 1522
Martinsville, IN 46151
Tel: (765)349-4740 *Fax:* (765)349-4744
E-Mail: execdir@asp-shareware.org
Web Site: www.asp-shareware.org
Executive Director: Richard Holler
Historical Note
ASP members are developers and distributors of shareware software for computers. Membership: $100/year.
Publications:
Aspects Newsletter. m. adv.

Association of Ship Brokers and Agents (U.S.A.) *(1934)*
510 Sylvan Ave., Suite 201
Englewood Cliffs, NJ 07632
Tel: (201)569-2882 *Fax:* (201)569-9082
E-Mail: asba@asba.org
Web Site: www.asba.org
Members: 130 companies
Staff: 2
Executive Director: Jeanne L. Cardona
E-Mail: asba@asba.org
Historical Note
Founded as the Association of Ship Brokers and Agents on January 9, 1934. Incorporated in 1954 and assumed its present name in 1970. Members are ship brokers and ship agents. Offers correspondence courses, distance learning courses and live seminars in maritime-related subjects that are available to the general public. Membership: $800/year (individual); $800/year (affiliate); $325/year (associate).
Meetings/Conferences:
Annual Meetings: always New York, NY/February
2007 – New York, NY/February/100
Publications:
American Tanker Rate Schedule. bi-a.
ASBA Newsletter. bi-m.
Yearbook. bi-a. adv.
ASBA Desk Book.

Association of SIDS and Infant Mortality Programs *(1987)*
c/o NY State center for SID
School of Social Welfare, Stony Brook University
Stony Brook, NY 11794-8232
Tel: (631)444-3690 *Fax:* (631)444-6475
Web Site: www.asip1.org/
Members: 75 individuals
President: Marie Chandick
E-Mail: marie.chandick@stonybrook.edu
Historical Note
Founded as Association of SIDS Program Professionals; assumed its current name in 1996. Members are health care and human service professionals providing services to those affected by Sudden Infant Death Syndrome and related conditions. Has no paid officers or full-time staff. Membership: $65/year (full); $40/year (associate).
Meetings/Conferences:
Annual Meetings: Spring
Publications:
Newletter. a.

Association of Small Business Development Centers *(1980)*
8990 Burke Lake Road
Burke, VA 22015
Tel: (703)764-9850 *Fax:* (703)764-1234
Web Site: www.asbdc-us.org
Members: 1100 centers
Staff: 5
Annual Budget: $1-2,000,000
President and Chief Executive Officer: Don Wilson
Historical Note
SBDCs are small business development centers which provide management and technical assistance to small business concerns and are jointly funded by federal and state governments. Previously the Small Business Development Center Directors Association.

Association of Small Foundations *(1995)*
4905 Del Ray Ave., Suite 308
Bethesda, MD 20814
Tel: (301)907-3337 *Fax:* (301)907-0980
E-Mail: asf@smallfoundations.org
Web Site: www.smallfoundations.org
Members: 2 million
Staff: 7
Chief Executive Officer: Tim Walter
E-Mail: asf@smallfoundations.org
Historical Note
Assists foundations that have few or no staff. Membership: $400/year.
Publications:
Annual Survey. a.
Professional Directory. a. adv.
Newsletter. q.

Association of Smoked Fish Processors *(1963)*
c/o Shuster Labs
85 John Rd.
Canton, MA 02120
Tel: (781)821-2200 *Fax:* (781)821-9266
Toll Free: (800)444 - 8705 Ext:
Members: 5 companies
Vice President: Michael Chubb
Historical Note
Members are food processors with an interest in smoked fish. Has no paid officers or full-time staff.

Association of Social Work Boards *(1979)*
400 S. Ridge Pkwy., Suite B
Culpeper, VA 22701
Tel: (540)829-6880 *Fax:* (540)829-0142
Toll Free: (800)225 - 6880
E-Mail: info@aswb.org
Web Site: www.aswb.org
Members: 49 states, two territories, seven Canadian provinces
Staff: 23
Annual Budget: $2-5,000,000
Executive Director: Donna DeAngelis
Manager, Accounting: Christine Breeden
Director, Communications: Troy Elliott
Meeting Planner: Jennifer Hoffman
Deputy Executive Director: Kathleen Hoffman
Historical Note
Founded as American Association of State Social Work Boards in 1979; assumed its current name in 2000. ASWB develops and administers the social work licensing examinations, and supports social work licensing boards in the protection of the public through legal regulation.
Meetings/Conferences:
Semi-Annual Meetings: Spring and Fall
Publications:
Association News. bi-m. adv.

Association of Specialists in Cleaning and Restoration International *(1946)*
9810 Patuxent Woods Dr.
Suite K
Columbia, MD 21046
Tel: (443)878-1000 *Fax:* (443)878-1010
Toll Free: (800)272 - 7012
E-Mail: info@ascr.org
Web Site: www.ascr.org
Members: 1350 companies
Staff: 13
Annual Budget: $1-2,000,000
Executive Directory and Assistant Secretary: Donald Manger
E-Mail: donaldm@ascr.org
Historical Note
Formerly (1984) the Association of Interior Decor Specialists. Divisions: Carpet & Upholstery Cleaning Institute (1971); Drapery Specialists Institute (1971); Mechanical Systems Hygiene Institute (1993); National Institute of Disaster Restoration (1968); National Institute of Rug and Drapery Cleaning (1946); and Water Loss Institute (1994). ASCRI is made up of owners, executives, and companies whose primary business purpose is to offer cleaning and restoration services and products. Membership: $650/year.
Meetings/Conferences:
Annual Meetings: Spring/400
Publications:
Cleaning & Restoration. m. adv.
Directory of Cleaning & Restoration Firms. a. adv.
Conference Directories. 2/year. adv.

Association of Specialized and Cooperative Library Agencies *(1944)*
50 E. Huron St.
Chicago, IL 60611
Tel: (312)280-4395 *Fax:* (312)944-8085
Toll Free: (800)545 - 2433 Ext: x4398
E-Mail: ascla@ala.org
Web Site: www.ala.org/ASCLA/
Members: 950 libraries
Staff: 1
Annual Budget: $50-100,000
Executive Director: Cathleen Bourdon
E-Mail: ascla@ala.org
Historical Note
A division of the American Library Association. Formerly known as the Association of State Library Agencies, Association of Hospital and Institution Libraries, and then (1974) Health and Rehabilitative Library Services before assuming its current name in 1978. Membership: $40/year (individual); $50/year (organization).
Meetings/Conferences:
Annual Meetings: With the American Library Ass'n
Publications:
Interface. q.

Association of Specialized and Professional Accreditors *(1993)*
1020 W. Byron St., Suite 8-G
Chicago, IL 60613-2987
Tel: (773)525-2160 *Fax:* (773)525-2162
E-Mail: aspa@aspa-usa.org
Web Site: www.aspa-usa.org
Members: 51 organizations
Staff: 1
Annual Budget: $250-500,000
Executive Director: Cynthia A. Davenport
E-Mail: aspa@aspa-usa.org
Historical Note
ASPA fosters good practice in accreditation of educational programs. ASPA also represents the interests of, and provides information about, specialty and professional accreditation organizations to higher education and to government. Membership fee varies based on size of organization; $6,500/year maximum. Members must meet definitions posted on web site.
Meetings/Conferences:
Semi-Annual Meetings: Spring and Fall
Publications:
Membership Directory. a.
Newsletter. semi-a.

Association of Specialty Cut Flower Growers *(1988)*
MPO Box 268
Oberlin, OH 44074-0268
Tel: (440)774-2887 *Fax:* (440)774-2435
E-Mail: ascfg@oberlin.net
Web Site: www.ascfg.org
Members: 600 individuals
Staff: 1
Executive Director: Judy M. Laushman
E-Mail: ascfg@oberlin.net
Historical Note
Mission of ASCFG is to unite and inform growers in the production and marketing of field and greenhouse specialty floral crops. Membership: $165/year.
Publications:
Cut Flower Quarterly. q. adv.

Association of State and Interstate Water Pollution Control Administrators *(1961)*
1221 Connecticut Ave. NW, Second Floor
Washington, DC 20036
Tel: (202)756-0600 *Fax:* (202)756-0605
E-Mail: admin1@asiwpca.org

Web Site: www.asiwpca.org
Members: 56 state government and interstate organizations
Staff: 6
Annual Budget: $500-1,000,000
Executive Director: Linda Eichmiller
Coordinator, Meetings: Jamie Kamin
Deputy Director: Sean Rolland

Historical Note

Members are the chief water pollution control administrators from 49 states, Guam, U.S. Virgin Islands, Puerto Rico, the District of Columbia, and 6 interstate agencies. Establishes objectives, policies, and standards for state water pollution control and groundwater protection.

Meetings/Conferences:

Annual Meetings: Summer

Publications:

Statements. m.

Association of State and Provincial Psychology Boards *(1961)*
P.O. Box 241245
7177 Halycon Summit Dr.
Montgomery, AL 36124-1245
Tel: (334)832-4580 *Fax:* (334)269-6379
Toll Free: (800)448 - 4069
Web Site: www.aspbb.org
Members: 63 jurisdictions
Staff: 10
Annual Budget: $2-5,000,000
Executive Officer and General Counsel: Stephen T. DeMers, Ed.d.
Associate Director Director: Amy C. Hilson

Historical Note

ASPPB represents psychology regulatory boards in the U.S. and Canada. It creates the Examination for Professional Practice in Psychology; provides a means for psychology boards to work together on common concerns; and serves as a clearinghouse for information on licensing requirements, professional discipline, and other topics. Formerly (1992) the American Association of State Psychology Boards. Membership: $350 (base) + $3 per licensee, maximum $2,750 (agency); $35/year (individual).

Meetings/Conferences:

Annual Meetings: October/125

Publications:

AASPB Newsletter. q.

Association of State and Territorial Chronic Disease Program Directors

Historical Note

Became Chronic Disease Directors in 2003.

Association of State and Territorial Dental Directors *(1947)*
105 Westerly Rd.
New Bern, NC 28560
Tel: (252)637-6333 *Fax:* (252)637-3343
E-Mail: dperkins@astdd.org
Web Site: www.astdd.org
Members: 59 individuals
Annual Budget: $250-500,000
Executive Director: M. Dean Perkins, DDS
E-Mail: dperkins@astdd.org

Historical Note

An affiliate of Association of State and Territorial Health Officials. Has no paid officers or full-time staff. Membership: $100/year (full member); $50/year (associate).

Meetings/Conferences:

Annual Meetings: Spring/200

Publications:

ASTDD News Briefs. q. adv.

Association of State and Territorial Directors of Nursing *(1935)*
1275 K St., NW, Suite 800
Washington, DC 20005-4006
E-Mail: askastdn@astdn.org
Web Site: www.astdn.org
Members: 40 voting, 50 associate and alumni
Annual Budget: $10-25,000
President: Joy Reed
E-Mail: askastdn@astdn.org

Historical Note

Established in 1935 as a council of the American Public Health Association, it later became Association of State and Territorial Directors of Public Health Nursing. In 1966 the name was changed to Association of State and Terrritorial Directors of Nursing. Affiliated with Association of State and Territorial Health Officials. Has no paid officers or full-time staff. Membership: $35/year (individual).

Meetings/Conferences:

Annual Meetings: May

Association of State and Territorial Health Officials *(1942)*
1275 K St. NW
Suite 800
Washington, DC 20005-4006
Tel: (202)371-9090 *Fax:* (202)371-9797
E-Mail: jcardin@astho.org
Web Site: www.astho.org
Members: 57 individuals
Staff: 40
Annual Budget: $2-5,000,000
Executive Director: George E. Hardy, Jr., M.D.
E-Mail: ghardy@astho.org
Associate Executive Director, Member Services: Rusty Boyce
Associate Executive Director, Policy and Programs: Jacalyn Carden

Historical Note

Formerly (1975) Association of State and Territorial Health Officers. Members are executive officers at public health agencies of the U.S. states and territories. Its purpose is to formulate and influence sound public health policy, and to promote policies that improve health and prevent disease, injury, and disability.

Meetings/Conferences:

Annual Meetings: Fall

Publications:

ASTHO Report. q.
Primary Care Network News. bi-w.

Association of State and Territorial Public Health Nutrition Directors *(1952)*
P.O. Box 1001
Johnstown, PA 15907-1001
Tel: (814)255-2829 *Fax:* (814)255-6514
E-Mail: cyndi@astphnd.org
Web Site: www.astphnd.org
Members: 175 individuals
Staff: 1
Annual Budget: $250-500,000
Executive Director: Susanne Gregory, MPH
Director, Operations: Cynthia Atterbury, M.P.A., R.D., L.A.N.

Historical Note

Members are directors of nutrition programs in the state and territorial public health agencies, coordinators and other Public Health Nutrition professionals. Affiliated with the Association of State and Territorial Health Officials. Membership: $400/year.

Meetings/Conferences:

Annual Meetings: Spring

Publications:

ASTPHND Newsletter. q.
Moving to the Future: Developing Community Based Nutrition Services.

Association of State and Territorial Solid Waste Management Officials *(1974)*
444 N. Capitol St. NW
Suite 315
Washington, DC 20001
Tel: (202)624-5828 *Fax:* (202)624-7875
Web Site: www.astswmo.org
Members: 56 states and territories
Staff: 9
Annual Budget: $1-2,000,000
Executive Director and Director, Government Affairs: Thomas J. Kennedy

Historical Note

Members are state employees who manage the regulatory solid waste and remedial action programs of state government.

Meetings/Conferences:

Semi-Annual Meetings: Spring and Fall

Publications:

Directory of State Waste Management Program Officials. a.

Association of State Correctional Administrators *(1960)*
213 Court St., Sixth Floor
Middletown, CT 06457-2906
Tel: (860)704-6410 *Fax:* (860)704-6420
Toll Free: (800)704 - 6420
E-Mail: exec@asca.net
Web Site: www.asca.net
Members: 60 individuals
Staff: 4
Annual Budget: $100-250,000
Executive Director: Camille G. Camp
E-Mail: exec@asca.net
Executive Director: George M. Camp
E-Mail: exec@asca.net

Historical Note

Formerly (1967) Correctional Administrators Association of America. ASCA's membership consists of the directors of all fifty state correctional agencies, the Federal Bureau of Prisons, and several large urban prison systems. Its purpose is to provide leadership and direction on national correctional policy and practice. Membership: $750/year.

Meetings/Conferences:

Semi-annual Meetings:

Publications:

Newsletter. m.

Association of State Dam Safety Officials *(1984)*
450 Old Vine St., Second Floor
Lexington, KY 40507
Tel: (859)257-5140 *Fax:* (859)323-1958
E-Mail: info@damsafety.org
Web Site: www.damsafety.org
Members: 2000 individuals
Staff: 4
Annual Budget: $500-1,000,000
Executive Director: Lori Spragens
E-Mail: lspragens@damsafety.org
Administrative Database Specialist: Maureen Hogle
Information Specialist: Sarah Mayfield
E-Mail: smayfield@damsafety.org
Director, Membership and Conference Coordinator: Susan Sorrell
E-Mail: sasorrell@damsafety.org

Historical Note

ASDSO was established to provide a forum for the exchange of ideas and experiences on dam safety issues; to foster interstate cooperation; provide information and assistance to state dam safety programs; provide representation of state interests before Congress and federal agencies; and improve the efficiency and effectiveness of state dam safety programs. Full voting membership is restricted to one state official from each of the 50 states and U.S. territories who is responsible for administering and managing dam safety programs. Associate membership is available for other state, local and federal officials concerned with dam safety. Affiliate membership is available for individuals representing the private sector. Membership: $400/year (state/voting member); $40/year (associate); $300/year (company/affiliate); $75/year (individual affiliate); $30/year (retired); $20/year (student member).

Meetings/Conferences:

Annual Meetings: Fall
2007 – Austin, TX(Hilton)/Sept. 9-13/850
2008 – Palm Springs, CA(Renaissance)/Sept. 7-11/850

Publications:

Summary of Laws on Dam Safety. irreg.
Annual Report. a.
Publication on State Requirements. irreg.
State Dam Safety Programs Update. bi-a.
ASDSO Newsletter (online). m.
Conference Proceedings. a.
Journal of Dam Safety. q. adv.

Association of State Drinking Water Administrators *(1984)*
1025 Connecticut Ave. NW
Suite 903

Washington, DC 20036
Tel: (202)293-7655 *Fax:* (202)293-7656
E-Mail: info@asdwa.org
Web Site: www.asdwa.org
Members: 50 states and 6 territories
Staff: 5
Annual Budget: $500-1,000,000
Executive Director: James Taft

Historical Note
Members include the 50 states and six territories. Individuals who work for state water regulatory agencies or local health departments are also eligible for associate membership.

Meetings/Conferences:
Annual Meetings: Fall

Publications:
Newsletter. bi-m.

Association of State Floodplain Managers *(1977)*
2809 Fish Hatchery Road, Suite 204
Madison, WI 53713-5020
Tel: (608)274-0123 *Fax:* (608)274-0696
E-Mail: asfpm@floods.org
Web Site: www.floods.org
Members: 1500 individuals
Staff: 7
Annual Budget: $500-1,000,000
Executive Director: Larry A. Larson
E-Mail: asfpm@floods.org
Administrator: Diane Alicia Brown
Coordinator, Certification Program: Anita Larson
E-Mail: asfpm@floods.org
Project Manager: Alan Lulloff

Historical Note
ASFPM is an organization of professionals involved in floodplain management, flood hazard mitigation, multi-objective watershed management, the National Flood Insurance Program and flood preparedness, warning and recovery. Membership: $80/year (individual); $250/year (agency); $150-600/year based on number of employees (corporate sponsorship).

Publications:
News & Views newsletter. 6/yr.
Insider. bi-m.
Nat'l Directory of Floodplain Managers. a.
Proceedings of Annual Conference. a.

Association of State Supervisors of Mathematics *(1960)*
P.O. Box 2120
Richmond, VA 23218
Tel: (804)786-5444
Toll Free: (800)786 - 5466
E-Mail: deborah.bliss@doe.virginia.gov
Web Site: http://smtc.uwyo.edu/assm/
Members: 173 Individuals
Annual Budget: under $10,000
Contact Person: Deborah Bliss

Historical Note
ASSM promotes interest in the study and teaching of mathematics. Has no paid officers or full-time staff. Membership: $50/year.

Meetings/Conferences:
2007 – Atlanta, GA/March 17-20
2008 – Salt Lake City, UT/Apr. 5-8
2009 – Washington, DC/Apr. 19-22

Association of State Wetland Managers *(1984)*
P.O. Box 269
Berne, NY 12023-9746
Tel: (518)872-1804 *Fax:* (518)872-2171
E-Mail: aswm@aswm.org
Web Site: www.aswm.org
Members: 950 individuals
Staff: 4
Annual Budget: $100-250,000
Executive Director: Jeanne Christie
E-Mail: aswm@aswm.org

Historical Note
Members are professionals involved in wetlands protection and management programs including members of the federal, state, local, private, not-for-profit and academic communities addressing wetland protection issues. Membership: $30/year (individual); $100/year (organization/company).

Publications:
Wetland News Newsletter. q. adv.

Association of Statisticians of American Religious Bodies *(1934)*
100 Witherspoon St., Room 2623
Louisville, KY 40202
Tel: (502)569-5161 *Fax:* (502)333-7161
E-Mail: jmarcum@ctr.pcusa.org
Members: 30 individuals
Annual Budget: under $10,000
Secretary-Treasurer: John P. Marcum, Jr.
E-Mail: jmarcum@ctr.pcusa.org

Historical Note
Members are persons at the denominational or national level with responsibility for gathering, compiling and publishing statistics of and for their religious bodies. The association provides a forum for the exchange of information and seeks to bring about such measure of standardization as may be necessary and possible for the correlation of religious statistical data. Has no paid staff. Membership: $15/year.

Meetings/Conferences:
Annual Meetings: Fall

Association of Steel Distributors *(1943)*
401 N. Michigan Ave.
Chicago, IL 60611-4267
Tel: (312)644-6610 *Fax:* (312)527-6705
E-Mail: rpietrzak@smithbucklin.com
Web Site: www.steeldistributors.org/
Members: 137 companies
Staff: 4
Annual Budget: $250-500,000
Executive Director: Ron Pietrzak

Historical Note
Members are service centers, warehouses, processors, traders and mills. Membership: $1,900/year.

Meetings/Conferences:
Semi-annual: Spring and Fall
2007 – Carlsbad, CA(La Costa Resort)/March 16-20/100

Publications:
ASD News & Views. 6/year. adv.

Association of Subspecialty Professors
2501 M St. NW
Suite 550
Washington, DC 20037-1308
Tel: (202)861-6900 *Fax:* (202)861-9731
E-Mail: asp@im.org
Web Site: www.im.org/asp
Staff: 10
Executive Vice President: Tod Ibrahim

Historical Note
ASP members are division chiefs and program directors of ACGME-accredited internal medicine subspecialty training programs in the U.S. and Canada. Membership: $250/year.

Meetings/Conferences:
Annual Meetings: Fall

Publications:
ASP E-Reports. m.
ASP Reports. 2/year.

Association of Supervisory and Administrative School Personnel *(1989)*
1300 Mercantile Lane, Suite 144
Largo, MD 20774
Tel: (301)925-7047 *Fax:* (301)925-2774
Members: 625 individuals
Staff: 2
Annual Budget: $250-500,000
Executive Director: Doris A. Reed

Historical Note
Formerly (1994) Association of School Based Administrators and Supervisors.

Publications:
AWARE newsletter. 6/year.

Association of Suppliers to the Paper Industry *(1933)*
201 Park Washington Court
Falls Church, VA 22046-4513
Tel: (703)538-1787 *Fax:* (703)241-5603
E-Mail: apmahq@aol.com
Web Site: www.papermachinery.org
Members: 32 companies
Staff: 5
Annual Budget: $100-250,000
Executive Director: Clay D. Tyeryar, CAE
Coordinator, Member Services: Sharon Kelly

Historical Note
Formerly (1971) Pulp and Paper Machinery Association, (1989) Pulp and Paper Machinery Manufacturers Association, and (2004) American Paper Machinery Association. ASPI members are companies provided goods and services to commercial paper producers. Membership: $2,205-$3,307/year.

Meetings/Conferences:
Semi-Annual Meetings: Spring and Fall

Publications:
Newsletter. m.

Association of Surfing Professionals - North America *(1983)*
P.O. Box 309
Huntington Beach, CA 92648
Tel: (714)536-3500 *Fax:* (714)536-4821
E-Mail: meg@aspworldtour.com
Web Site: www.aspnorthamerica.org
Members: 1200 individuals
Staff: 10
Annual Budget: $500-1,000,000
Administrative Director: Meg Bernaido
E-Mail: meg@aspworldtour.com

Historical Note
ASPNA is the North American arm of the international organization, headquartered in Queensland, Australia. Seeks to promote the sport of professional surfing for the benefit of its members, the sanctioned World Tour events, professional surfers and the public. Membership is open to professional and amateur surfers.

Publications:
Pro Surfing Guide. bi-a. adv.
ASP Media Guide. a.
ASP Newsletter. m.

Association of Surgical Technologists *(1969)*
6 West Dry Creek Circle
Littleton, CO 80120
Tel: (303)694-9130 *Fax:* (303)694-9169
Toll Free: (800)637 - 7433
Web Site: www.ast.org
Members: 19000 individuals
Staff: 23
Annual Budget: $2-5,000,000
Chief Executive Officer: William J. Teutsch
E-Mail: bteutsch@ast.org
Director, Continuing Education: Kevin Frey, CST, MS
Director, Publishing: Karen Ludwig
Director, Government Relations and Public Affairs: Ben Price, CST, BS

Historical Note
AST's primary concerns center on ensuring that surgical technologists are educationally qualified to administer surgical patient care through the support of accreditation, certification and continuing education. Membership $70/year.

Meetings/Conferences:
Annual Meetings: Annual

Publications:
ASFA Newsletter. q. adv.
Instructor's Newsletter. 2/year. adv.
Student Connection. q. adv.
Surgical Technology for the Surgical Technologist. adv.

Association of Talent Agents *(1937)*
9255 Sunset Blvd., Suite 930
Los Angeles, CA 90069
Tel: (310)274-0628 *Fax:* (310)274-5063
E-Mail: shellie@agentassociation.com
Web Site: www.agentassociation.com
Members: 120 companies
Staff: 2
Annual Budget: $250-500,000
Executive Director: Karen Stuart
E-Mail: atastuart@aol.com
Administrative Director: Shellie Jetton

Historical Note

Founded in 1937 as the Artists Managers Guild with the purpose of professionalizing the agency business. Assumed present name in 1979. Membership: $1,000/year (minimum).

Publications:

Newsletter. m.

Association of Teacher Educators *(1920)*

P.O. Box 793
Manassas, VA 20113
Tel: (703)331-0911 *Fax:* (703)331-3666
E-Mail: info@ate1.org
Web Site: www.ate1.org
Members: 4000 individuals
Staff: 2
Annual Budget: $250-500,000
Executive Director: David A. Ritchey, Ph.D., CAE

Historical Note

The ATE serves as a national voice for issues related to preservice, graduate and inservice teacher education and provides opportunities for professional development through its publications and national conferences, workshops and academies. Membership: $90/year (individual); $130/year (library).

Meetings/Conferences:

Annual Meetings: February/1,500
2007 - San Diego, CA(Manchester Grand Hyatt)/Feb. 17-21/2000

Publications:

Action in Teacher Education. q. adv.
Standards for Teacher Educators.
Creating a Culture of Quality and Credibility.
Character Education: The Foundation for Teacher Education.
ATE Newsletter. q. adv.

Association of Teachers of Latin American Studies *(1970)*

25258 63rd Ave.
Little Neck, NY 11362-2406
Tel: (718)428-1237
E-Mail: atlas0754@aol.com
Members: 727 individuals
Staff: 2
Annual Budget: $50-100,000
Executive Director: Daniel J. Mugan
E-Mail: atlas0754@aol.com

Historical Note

An organization of educators and other persons interested in the promotion of study about Latin America in U.S. educational institutions. Incorporated in 1973. Membership: $12/year.

Meetings/Conferences:

Annual Meetings: Semi-annual Meetings

Publications:

Perspective (newsletter). q. adv.
Curriculum Guides on Ecuador, Brazil, Argentina, Venezuela, and Chile.

Association of Teachers of Maternal and Child Health *(1968)*

1101 15th St. NW
Suite 910
Washington, DC 20005
Tel: (202)296-1099 *Fax:* (202)296-1252
E-Mail: kramiah@asph.org
Web Site: www.atmch.org
Members: 200 individuals
Annual Budget: $10-25,000
Manager, Educational Programs: Kalpana Ramiah
E-Mail: kramiah@asph.org

Historical Note

ATMCH members are academics in the field of maternal and child health. Administrative support provided by the Association of Schools of Public Health (same address). Membership: $75/year; $10/year (student).

Meetings/Conferences:

Semi-annual Meetings: Fall with APHA and Spring with AMCHP

Publications:

ATMCH News Newsletter. semi-a.

Association of Teachers of Preventive Medicine *(1942)*

1660 L St. NW
Suite 208
Washington, DC 20036-5603
Tel: (202)463-0550 *Fax:* (202)463-0555
Toll Free: (866)474 - 2876
E-Mail: info@atpm.org
Web Site: www.atpm.org
Members: 1000
Staff: 12
Annual Budget: $250-500,000
Director: Allison L. Lewis
E-Mail: info@atpm.org

Historical Note

Individual members include educators in preventive medicine and public health, physicians, nurses, health services researchers, and public health professionals; organizational members include academic departments and programs, health agencies, and graduate programs of public health. Membership: $175/year (individual); $700/year (institution).

Publications:

ATMP News Now. w. adv.
ATPM Quarterly Newsletter. q. adv.
American Journal of Preventive Medicine. q. adv.

Association of Teachers of Technical Writing *(1973)*

Department of English, University of North Texas
P.O. Box 911307
Denton, TX 76203
Tel: (940)565-2115
E-Mail: sims@unt.edu
Web Site: www.attw.org
Members: 1200 individuals
Executive Secretary: Brenda Sims
E-Mail: sims@unt.edu

Historical Note

ATTW provides communication among teachers of technical writing and develops technical communications as an academic discipline. Founded in 1973 with about a dozen members, ATTW is now an international organization. Membership includes teachers and students from all levels and all types of educational institutions, and technical writers from government and industry. Has no paid staff. Membership: $50/year (USA); $55/year (foreign); $75/year (library); $20/year (student).

Meetings/Conferences:

Annual Meetings: in conjunction with Conference on College Composition & Communication

Publications:

Technical Communication Quarterly journal. q. adv.
ATTW Bulletin Newsletter. semi-a.

Association of Technical and Supervisory Professionals *(1974)*

6307 Sonora Court
Plainfield, IL 60544
Tel: (815)439-0072
Web Site: www.atsp.net
Members: 420 individuals
Annual Budget: under $10,000
National Secretary: Pete Bridgeman

Historical Note

ATSP members are individuals involved in the Department of Agriculture's meat and poultry inspection programs. ATSP was formed to give members consultation rights with the Department of Agriculture, Meat and Poultry Inspection Managment Program and to promote the importance of a safe and sanitary supply of meat and poultry. Has no paid officers or full time staff. Membership: $62.50/year (individual).

Publications:

ATSP Newsletter. q.

Association of Technical Personnel in Ophthalmology *(1969)*

2025 Woodlane Dr.
St. Paul, MN 55125
Tel: (651)731-7225 *Fax:* (651)731-0410
Toll Free: (800)482 - 4858
E-Mail: atpomembership@jcahpo.org
Web Site: www.atpo.org
Members: 1300 individuals
Staff: 2
Annual Budget: $100-250,000
Coordinator: Mary Evans

Historical Note

ATPO members are certified and other technical personnel in ophthamology. ATPO's mission is to provide, expand, and support scientific and educational opportunities for allied health personnel in opthamology, and to act as an advocate for its members and the profession.

Meetings/Conferences:

Annual Meetings: Fall

Publications:

National Salary and Benefits Report. bien.
Viewpoints Newsletter. q. adv.

Association of Telehealth Service Providers *(1996)*

4702 S.W. Scholls Ferry Rd., Suite 400
Portland, OR 97225-2008
Tel: (503)922-0988 *Fax:* (503)222-2402
E-Mail: info@atsp.org
Web Site: www.atsp.org
Members: 1000 individuals
Staff: 3
Executive Director: William Engle

Historical Note

Founded as Association of Telemedecine Service Providers; assumed its current name in 2000. ATSP promotes and supports the use of telecommunications services and technology to expand health care options for patients and providers.

Publications:

ATSP Report on U.S. Telemedicine Acitivity. a.
The Dispatch. q.
ATSP TeleJournal. m.
ATSP Tele Updates. q.

Association of TeleServices International *(1942)*

12 Academy Ave.
Atkinson, NH 03811
Toll Free: (866)896 - 2874
E-Mail: admin@atsi.org
Web Site: www.atsi.org
Members: 400 companies
Staff: 3
Annual Budget: $500-1,000,000
Vice President/Secretary: Marcy Hewlett
E-Mail: admin@atsi.org

Historical Note

Formerly the Association of Telemessaging Services International (1998). Formed to represent the telephone answering service industry, ATSI has expanded with the industry and now represents the full range of messaging and communications service bureaus, including TAS, voice mail, voice store, forward, fax mailboxes, and interactive and broadcast fax. Formerly (1986) Associated Telephone Answering Exchanges. Membership: $600-1,800/yr. (company).

Meetings/Conferences:

Annual Meetings: May/June

Publications:

TeleCommunicator. bi-w. adv.

Association of Test Publishers *(1992)*

1201 Pennsylvania Ave. NW
Suite 300
Washington, DC 20004
Tel: (770)650-7592 *Fax:* (717)755-8962
Toll Free: (866)240 - 7909
Web Site: www.testpublishers.org
Members: 120 companies
Staff: 1
Annual Budget: $500-1,000,000
Executive Director: Dr. William G. Harris

Historical Note

Formerly (1993) Association of Personal Test Publishers. Members are publishers of standardized tests for use in educational, industrial, and clinical situations, as well as providers of assessment services and products. Membership: $4,750-20,000/year.

Meetings/Conferences:

2007 - Palm Springs, CA(Westin Mission Hills)/Feb. 5-7
2008 - Dallas, TX(Gaylord Texan)/March 3-5/700

Publications:
Test Publisher. q.
Journal of Applied Testing Technology (online).

Association of the Nonwoven Fabrics Industry

Historical Note
See INDA, Association of the Nonwoven Fabrics Industry.

Association of the United States Army *(1950)*
2425 Wilson Blvd.
Arlington, VA 22201-3385
Tel: (703)841-4300
Toll Free: (800)336 - 4570
E-Mail: ausa-info@ausa.org
Web Site: www.ausa.org
Members: 102000 individuals
Staff: 88
Annual Budget: $10-25,000,000
Director, Communications: John Grady
E-Mail: ausa-info@ausa.org
President and Chief Operating Officer: Gen. Gordon R. Sullivan, (Ret.)
E-Mail: ausa-info@ausa.org
Director, Communications: John Grady
E-Mail: ausa-info@ausa.org
Vice President, Finance and Administration: Lt.Gen. Thomas Rhame, USA(Ret.)
E-Mail: ausa-info@ausa.org
Vice President, Education: Lt.Gen. Theodore G. Stroup, Jr., USA(R
E-Mail: ausa-info@ausa.org
Vice President, Membership/Meetings: Roger Thompson
E-Mail: ausa-info@ausa.org

Historical Note
Formed by a merger of the U.S. Infantry Association and the U.S. Field Artillery Association in 1950. Absorbed (1955) the U.S. Antiaircraft Association. Active, retired and reserve military personnel. Has an annual budget of $12 million.

Meetings/Conferences:
Annual Meetings: always Washington, DC Convention Center.

Publications:
ARMY Magazine. m. adv.
AUSA News. m. adv.
Washington Update. m.

Association of the Wall and Ceiling Industries-International *(1918)*
803 W. Broad St., Suite 600
Falls Church, VA 22046-3108
Tel: (703)534-8300 *Fax:* (703)534-8307
E-Mail: info@awci.org
Web Site: www.awci.org
Members: 2000 companies, 17 chapters
Staff: 14
Annual Budget: $2-5,000,000
Executive Vice President: Steven A. Etkin, CAE
E-Mail: info@awci.org
Director, Communications: Laura M. Porinchak
E-Mail: info@awci.org

Historical Note
AWCI represents acoustics systems, ceiling systems, drywall systems, exterior insulation/finishing systems, fireproofing, flooring systems, insulation and stucco contractors, suppliers and manufacturers, and those in allied trades. Membership accounts for nearly 25% of related wall and ceiling construction volume in the United States. Membership: annual dues vary through chapters; $585/year (At-Large), $295/year (foreign contractors).

Meetings/Conferences:
Annual Meetings: Spring

Publications:
Mold: Cause, Effect, & Response.
Tech Notes. m.
Who's Who in the Wall and Ceiling Industry. a.
Members Only. m.
Construction Dimensions. m. adv.

Association of Theatre Movement Educators *(1972)*
130 W. Mill Station Dr.
Newark, DE 19711
Tel: (302)831-1084
Web Site: www.asu.edu/cfa/atme
Members: 170 individuals
Secretary: Joann Browning

Historical Note
Formerly the Society of Theatre Movement Specialists, a focus group of the Association for Theatre in Higher Education. ATME incorporated as an independent organization in 1993. Provides networking and professional support for faculty and instructors in movement education. Membership: $35/year (individual); $15/year (student).

Association of Theatrical Press Agents and Managers *(1928)*
1560 Broadway, Suite 700
New York, NY 10036-2501
Tel: (212)719-3666 *Fax:* (212)302-1585
E-Mail: info@atpam.com
Web Site: www.atpam.com
Members: 850 individuals
Staff: 9
Annual Budget: $1-2,000,000
Secretary-Treasurer: Gordon Forbes

Historical Note
Labor Union affiliated with the IATSE AFL-CIO. Membership: $180/year (individual).

Meetings/Conferences:
Annual Meetings: Annual meetings held locally.

Association of Theological Schools in the United States and Canada *(1918)*
10 Summit Park Dr.
Pittsburgh, PA 15275-1103
Tel: (412)788-6505 *Fax:* (412)788-6510
E-Mail: ats@ats.edu
Web Site: www.ats.edu
Members: 254 institutions
Staff: 20
Annual Budget: $2-5,000,000
Executive Director: Rev. Daniel O. Aleshire, Ph.D.
E-Mail: ats@ats.edu
Director, Communications: Nancy Merrill

Historical Note
ATS is a membership organization of graduate schools of theology in the U.S. and Canada. The primary purpose of ATS is the improvement of theological schools, which it seeks to attain by accrediting schools and by providing programs and services to its membership. Member institutions are Protestant, Roman Catholic, and Orthodox schools of theology, both university-related divinity schools and freestanding seminaries. The ATS Commission on Accrediting is recognized by the U.S. Department of Education and by the nongovernmental Council for Higher Education Accreditation. The Association began in 1918 as a small annual conference of predominantly Protestant theological schools. In 1936 it became an association and adopted standards for judging quality in theological education, and in 1938 it established its first list of accredited schools.

Meetings/Conferences:
2008 – Atlanta, GA(Renaissance)/June 21-23/350

Publications:
Bulletin. semi-a.
Colloquy Newsletter. 5/year.
Theological Education Journal. semi-a.
Membership List. a.
Fact Book on Theological Education. a.

Association of Third World Studies *(1983)*
P.O. Box 1232
Americus, GA 31709-1232
Tel: (229)931-2078 *Fax:* (229)931-2960
E-Mail: hisaacs@canes.gsw.edu
Web Site: http://itc.gsw.edu/atws
Members: 600 individuals
Staff: 1
Annual Budget: $25-50,000
Founder: Harold Isaacs, Ph.D.
E-Mail: hisaacs@canes.gsw.edu

Historical Note
ATWS members are academics, development specialists and others with an interest in 'third world' countries. Membership: $45/year.

Publications:
Journal of Third World Studies. bi-a. adv.
ATWS Conference Proceedings. a.
ATWS Newsletter. 3/year.

Association of Transportation Professionals *(1929)*
Three Church Circle, PMB 250
Annapolis, MD 21401
Tel: (410)267-0023 *Fax:* (410)267-7546
Web Site: www.atlp.org
Members: 700 individuals
Staff: 3
Annual Budget: $100-250,000
Executive Director: Lauren Michalski

Historical Note
Formerly (1929) Association of Practitioners before the Interstate Commerce Commission; (1984) Association of Interstate Commerce Commission Practitioners; (1994) Association of Transportation Practitioners; and then Association for Transportation Law, Logistics and Policy; assumed current name in 2005. Membership includes attorneys, transportation and logistics professionals as well as faculty and students of transportation. Membership: $95/year (individual); $65/year (gov't/academic).

Meetings/Conferences:
Annual Meetings: Summer

Publications:
Ass'n Highlights newsletter. bi-m. adv.
Journal of Transportation Law, Logistics and Policy. q. adv.
Annual Meeting Papers & Proceedings. a. adv.

Association of Traumatic Stress Specialists *(1989)*
P.O. Box 246
Phillips, ME 04966
Tel: (207)639-2433 *Fax:* (207)639-2434
E-Mail: admin@atss.info
Web Site: www.atss-hq.com
Members: 800 individuals
Staff: 2
Annual Budget: $100-250,000
Executive Director: Jo Halligan

Historical Note
Founded as International Association of Trauma Counseling; assumed its current name in 1997. ATSS members are actively engaged in the field of trauma counseling treatment. Offers certfication in three specializations: Certified Trauma Specialist, Certified Trauma Services Specialist, and Certified Trauma Responder. Membership: $75/year (individual).

Meetings/Conferences:
Semi-Annual Meetings:

Publications:
Trauma Lines. q. adv.

Association of Travel Marketing Executives *(1980)*
331 W. 57th St., Suite 482
New York, NY 10019
Tel: (212)765-0625 *Fax:* (212)765-0624
E-Mail: admin@atme.org
Web Site: www.atme.org
Members: 400 individuals
Staff: 2
Annual Budget: $50-100,000
Executive Director: Kristin Zern

Historical Note
Membership: $225/year, plus initiation fee.

Meetings/Conferences:
Annual Meetings: usually Spring

Publications:
Travel & Tourism Executive Report.
Directory. a.

Association of Trial Lawyers of America *(1946)*
1050 31st St. NW
Washington, DC 20007
Tel: (202)965-3500 *Fax:* (202)625-7312
Toll Free: (800)424 - 2725
E-Mail: info@atlahq.org
Web Site: www.atlanet.org
Members: 60000 individuals
Staff: 155
Annual Budget: $10-25,000,000

Chief Executive Officer: Jon Haber
Senior Vice President, State Affairs: Steve Bouchard
Vice President/Director, Media Relations: Carlton Carl
E-Mail: info@atlahq.org
Senior Vice President, Membership and Marketing: Jeanne Esti
Senior Vice President, Information Technology: Bob Jansto
Senior Vice President, Finance: Bob Michaels

Historical Note

Founded as the NACCA Bar Association (National Association of Claimant's Compensation Attorneys); became the American Trial Lawyers Association in 1964 and the Association of Trial Lawyers of America in 1972. Sponsors ATLA PAC, a political action committee; the National College of Advocacy; and publishes legal books and tapes through ATLA Press. Sponsors the Roscoe Pound Foundation (public policy research, seminars and publications) and the Civil Justice Foundation (grants in areas of injury prevention). Has an annual budget of approximately $19 million.

Meetings/Conferences:

Semi-annual Meetings: Summer/13,900/ Winter/1,500

Publications:

ATLA Law Reporter. 10/year. adv.
ATLA Advocate. 10/year.
Products Liability Law Reporter. 10/year.
Trial. m. adv.
Professional Negligence Law Reporter. 10/year.

Association of United States Night Vision Manufacturers *(1980)*

7040 Highfields Farm Dr.
Roanoke, VA 24018
Tel: (540)774-1783 *Fax:* (540)774-1802
Web Site: www.nightvisionassociation.com
Members: 10 companies
Staff: 1
Annual Budget: $10-25,000
Executive Director: Robert G. Williams

Historical Note

Members manufacture night vision devices, systems, or components.

Meetings/Conferences:

Annual Meetings: January, in Alexandria, VA

Association of Universities for Research in Astronomy *(1957)*

1200 New York Ave. NW
Suite 350
Washington, DC 20005
Tel: (202)483-2101 *Fax:* (202)483-2106
Web Site: www.aura-astronomy.org
Members: 39 institutions
Staff: 7
Annual Budget: $2-5,000,000
President: William S. Smith

Historical Note

A consortium of universities managing government-sponsored observatories in the U.S. and abroad. One-time membership fee: $10,000 per university.

Meetings/Conferences:

Annual Meetings: Spring

Association of University Anesthesiologists *(1953)*

520 N. Northwest Hwy.
Park Ridge, IL 60068-2573
Tel: (847)825-5586
E-Mail: aua@asahq.org
Web Site: www.auahq.org
Members: 700 individuals
Staff: 5
Annual Budget: under $10,000
Secretary: Steven J. Barker, Ph.D., M.D.

Historical Note

Formerly (1990) Association of University Anesthetists.

Meetings/Conferences:

Annual Meetings: Spring
2007 – Chicago, IL(Sheraton)/Apr. 26-28
2008 – Chapel Hill, NC(Washington Duke Inn and Golf Club)/May 16-18

Association of University Architects *(1955)*

Dept. of Campus Planning, Western Michigan Univ.
Kalamazoo, MI 49008
Tel: (269)387-4082
E-Mail: aua@auaweb.net
Web Site: www.auaweb.net
Members: 150 individuals
Annual Budget: $10-25,000
Membership Chair: Evie Asken

Historical Note

Licensed architects whose full-time job is the development of the university or system employing them. Has no paid officers or full-time staff. Membership: $50/year (individual).

Meetings/Conferences:

Annual Meetings: June, at various university locations

Publications:

Annual Report. a.
Newsletter/Roster. a.

Association of University Centers on Disabilities *(1968)*

Executive Director: George Jesien
E-Mail: gjesien@aauap.org
Director, Legislative Affairs: Donna Ledder Meltzer

Historical Note

Founded as American Association of University Affiliated Programs for Persons with Developmental Disabilities; assumed its current name in 2002. Members provide clinical settings in universities, teaching hospitals, and clinics operating exemplary services to teach graduate students and others studying developmental disorders such as mental retardation. Founded as the Association of University Affiliated Facilities, it assumed its present name in 2001. Membership: $3,000-7,000/year (based on size of institution).

Meetings/Conferences:

Annual Meetings: Fall/350

Publications:

AUC Digest. m.
Legislative in Brief. w.

Association of University Interior Designers *(1979)*

Purdue University
1665 FREH
West Lafayette, IN 47907-1665
Tel: (765)494-9762 *Fax:* (765)494-6609
Web Site: www.auid.org
Members: 85 individuals
Annual Budget: $10-25,000
Vice President: Terry Smith-Wright

Historical Note

Members are designers, architects, facility managers, etc., employed by universities to do in-house design work. Has no paid officers or full-time staff. Membership: $25/year (individual).

Meetings/Conferences:

Semi-Annual Meetings: June and October

Publications:

Clerestory. a.

Association of University Professors of Ophthalmology *(1966)*

P.O. Box 420369
San Francisco, CA 94142-0369
Tel: (415)561-8548 *Fax:* (415)561-8531
E-Mail: aupo@aao.org
Web Site: www.aupo.org
Members: 250 individuals
Staff: 2
Annual Budget: $50-100,000
Administrator: Lisa Brown

Meetings/Conferences:

Annual Meetings: Winter
2007 – Indian Wells, CA(Renaissance Esmeralda)/Feb. 1-3/300
2008 – Sarasota, FL(Ritz-Carlton)/Jan. 31-Feb. 2/300
2009 – Indian Wells, CA(Renaissance Esmeralda)/Jan. 29-31/300

Publications:

News & Views. q.
Membership Directory. a.

Association of University Programs in Health Administration *(1948)*

2000 N. 14th St., Suite 780
Arlington, VA 22201
Tel: (703)894-0940 *Fax:* (703)894-0941
E-Mail: aupha@aupha.org
Web Site: www.aupha.org
Members: 1200 individuals
Staff: 8
Annual Budget: $1-2,000,000
President and Chief Executive Officer: Lydia M. Reed
E-Mail: aupha@aupha.org

Historical Note

The Association of University Programs in Health Administration (AUPHA) is a not-for-profit association on university-based educational programs, faculty, practitioners, and provider organizations. Its members are dedicated to continuously improving the field of healthcare management and practice. It is the only non-profit entity of its kind that works to improve the delivery of health services throughout the world -- and thus the health of citizens -- by educating professional managers at the entry level.

Meetings/Conferences:

Annual Meetings: Spring
2007 – Orlando, FL/May 31-June 3
2008 – Washington, DC/June 5-8
2009 – Chicago, IL/June 25-28

Publications:

Journal of Health Administration Education. q.
AUPHA Exchange. q. adv.
Health Services Administration Education Directory. bien. adv.

Association of University Radiologists *(1953)*

820 Jorie Blvd.
Oak Brook, IL 60523
Tel: (630)368-3730 *Fax:* (630)571-7837
E-Mail: aur@rsna.org
Web Site: www.aur.org
Members: 3388 individuals
Staff: 5
Annual Budget: $500-1,000,000
Account Executive: Lise Swanson
E-Mail: aur@rsna.org

Historical Note

Members are full-time academic radiologists, involved in teaching and laboratory and clinical investigation. Membership: $150/year (individual); $60/year (individual associate or fellow).

Meetings/Conferences:

Annual Meetings: Spring/450
2007 – Denver, CO(Hyatt Denver Convention Center)/Apr. 25-28

Publications:

Academic Radiology. m.

Association of University Research Parks *(1986)*

12100 Sunset Hills Road, Suite 130
Reston, VA 20190
Tel: (703)234-4088 *Fax:* (703)435-4390
E-Mail: info@aurp.net
Web Site: www.aurp.net
Members: 320 companies and institutions
Staff: 3
Annual Budget: $250-500,000
Executive Director: Kathie St. Clair

Historical Note

Serves as a central clearing house for the exchange of information on the planning, construction, marketing, and management of university related research parks and technology incubators. Promotes university-industry relations and helps to facilitate the transfer of technology to the private sector. Works to promote technology-led economic development for communities. Membership: fees vary.

Meetings/Conferences:

Annual Meetings: Fall

Publications:

Reasearch Park Forum. m.

Association of University Technology Managers *(1974)*

60 Revere Dr., Suite 500
Northbrook, IL 60062

Tel: (847)559-0846 *Fax:* (847)480-9282
E-Mail: info@autm.net
Web Site: www.autm.net
Members: 3500 individuals
Staff: 12
Annual Budget: $2-5,000,000
Executive Director: Vicki Loise

Historical Note

Incorporated as a non-profit group in the state of Connecticut. Formerly (1989) Society of University Patent Administrators. AUTM helps protect faculty inventions, fosters a positive social and legislative climate for university technology transfer, and assists in licensing academic technologies. Members are individuals overseeing the marketing and sale of the results of research at educational institutions. Membership: $175/year.

Meetings/Conferences:

Annual Meetings: February-March
2007 – San Francisco, CA(San Francisco Marriott)/March 8-10/2000
2008 – San Diego, CA(San Diego Marriott)/Feb. 28-March 1/2000

Publications:

AUTM Licensing Survey. a.
AUTM Newsletter. bi-m.
AUTM Journal. bi-a.
AUTM Better World Report. a.

Association of Vacuum Equipment Manufacturers International *(1969)*

71 Pinon Hill Place
Albuquerque, NM 87122-1914
Tel: (505)856-6924 *Fax:* (505)856-6716
E-Mail: aveminfo@avem.org
Web Site: www.avem.org
Members: 86 companies
Staff: 2
Annual Budget: $250-500,000
Executive Secretary: Vivienne Harwood Mattox

Historical Note

Membership: $520-2500/year.

Meetings/Conferences:

Annual Meetings: Fall

Publications:

Directory/Index of Products and Services. a. adv.

Association of Vascular and Interventional Radiographers *(1988)*

12100 Sunset Hills Road, Suite 130
Reston, VA 20190-3221
Tel: (703)234-4055 *Fax:* (703)435-4390
E-Mail: info@avir.org
Web Site: www.avir.org
Members: 110 individuals
Staff: 2
Executive Director: Rebecca Page

Historical Note

AVIR members are cardiovascular and interventional radiographers and allied health care professionals. Membership: $60/year (active); $50/year (associate); $30/year (student); $85/year (international).

Meetings/Conferences:

Annual Meetings: Typical attendance at AVIR's annual meetings is about 300 people.
2007 – Seattle, WA/March 1-6/450

Publications:

AVIR International Informer. q. adv.

Association of Vision Science Librarians *(1968)*

c/o SUNY Coll. of Optometry, 33 W. 42nd St.
New York, NY 10036
Tel: (212)780-5094 *Fax:* (212)780-5904
Web Site: http://spectacle.berkeley.edu/~library
Members: 80 individuals
Annual Budget: under $10,000
Chairperson: Elaine Wells

Historical Note

Established in Beverly Hills, California, at the 1968 meeting of the American Academy of Optometry. Members are librarians whose collections or services collections provide information services in the field of vision science. Has no paid officers or staff.

Meetings/Conferences:

Annual Meetings: With the Medical Library Ass'n in May and the American Academy of Optometry in December

Association of Visual Merchandise Representatives *(1983)*

307 Cove Creek
Houston, TX 77042-1023
Tel: (713)782-5533 *Fax:* (713)785-1114
E-Mail: raguse@attglobal.net
Members: 30 individuals
Staff: 2
Annual Budget: under $10,000
President: Tom Raguse
E-Mail: raguse@attglobal.net

Historical Note

Members are sales representatives for manufacturers of mannequins and other products used in retail sales displays. Membership: $50/year (individual).

Publications:

Newsletter. irreg.

Association of Volleyball Professionals *(1983)*

6100 Center Dr.
Ninth Floor
Los Angeles, CA 90045
Tel: (310)426-8000 *Fax:* (310)426-8010
E-Mail: contact@avp.com
Web Site: www.avp.com
Members: 150 individuals
Staff: 15
Annual Budget: $5-10,000,000
Commissioner: Leonard Armato
E-Mail: contact@avp.com

Historical Note

Founded to organize sanctioned events for pro beach volleyball players, AVP now co-sponsors the AVP Tour, negotiates broadcast coverage of Tour events, and represents the Tour's players and sponsors. Membership fee varies, based on earnings.

Meetings/Conferences:

Annual Meetings:

Publications:

Newsletter. bi-m.

Association of Water Technologies *(1985)*

8201 Greensboro Dr., Suite 300
McLean, VA 22102
Tel: (703)610-9012 *Fax:* (703)610-9005
Toll Free: (800)858 - 6683
E-Mail: awt@awt.org
Web Site: www.awt.org
Members: 1500 individuals
Staff: 3
Annual Budget: $500-1,000,000
Executive Director: John H. Ganoe, CAE
Communications Manager: Lesley E. Hunter

Historical Note

The purpose of AWT is to provide small to medium-sized independent commercial water treatment companies with technical education, industry communication, access to information, group purchasing discounts, legislative affairs, and sound management techniques. It also provides certification of professional water technologists as well as regulatory monitoring. Membership: $625/year (associate member company); $375/year (full member company); $425/year (consultants/manufacturers representatives).

Meetings/Conferences:

Annual Meetings: Fall

Publications:

Annual Membership Directory and Buyer's Guide. a. adv.
Analyst. q. adv.

Association of Winery Suppliers *(1983)*

Two Basin Road
Windham, ME 04062
Tel: (207)892-3399
Members: 50 companies
Staff: 5
Executive Director: John Warner

Historical Note

Members are suppliers of materials and services to wineries with a minimum of 20 active accounts.

Meetings/Conferences:

Annual Meetings: Fall, always in Marin County, CA.

Publications:

Credit Report. m.

Association of Women in the Metal Industries *(1981)*

515 King St., Suite 420
Alexandria, VA 22314-3137
Tel: (703)739-8335 *Fax:* (703)684-6048
E-Mail: ehawkins@clarionmanagement.com
Web Site: www.awmi.org
Members: 1100 individuals, 25 corporations
Staff: 4
Annual Budget: $250-500,000
Executive Director: Carole M. Rogin
Director, Member Services: Elizabeth Hawkins
E-Mail: ehawkins@clarionmanagement.com

Historical Note

Founded in Oakland, CA, AWMI fosters the professional growth of women in the metal industries. Membership: $175/year.

Meetings/Conferences:

Annual Meetings: Fall
2007 – Palm Springs, CA(Esmerelda)/

Publications:

AWMI Metal Mail. q.

Association of Women Soil Scientists *(1981)*

1525 N. Elms Street
Flint, MI 48532-2034
Web Site: www.awss.org
Members: 200 individuals
Annual Budget: under $10,000
Membership Chair: Laura Merkel Craven

Historical Note

AWSS goals are to identify women employed as soil scientists and in the sciences in general, to share technical and career information, to enhance communication among members, and to assist and encourage women seeking employment in the field. Has no paid officers or full-time staff. Membership: $15/year (full member); $10/year (student).

Meetings/Conferences:

Annual Meetings: Held with Soil and Water Conservation Society and American Society of Agronomy
2007 – New Orleans, LA/Nov. 4-8

Publications:

Newsletter. q.
Membership Directory.

Association of Women Surgeons *(1981)*

5204 Fairmount Ave., Suite 208
Downers Grove, IL 60515-5056
Tel: (630)655-0392 *Fax:* (630)493-0392
E-Mail: info@womensurgeons.org
Web Site: www.womensurgeons.org
Members: 1700 individuals
Staff: 3
Annual Budget: $250-500,000
Executive Director: Judith K. Keel
E-Mail: info@womensurgeons.org

Historical Note

Membership: $200/year.

Meetings/Conferences:

Annual Meetings: Fall

Publications:

Membership Directory. bien.
AWS Newsletter. q.
AWScope. bi-m.

Association of Women's Health, Obstetric and Neonatal Nurses *(1969)*

2000 L St. NW
Suite 740
Washington, DC 20036
Tel: (202)261-2400
Toll Free: (800)673 - 8499
Web Site: www.awhonn.org
Members: 22000 individuals
Staff: 50
Annual Budget: $5-10,000,000
Executive Director: Karen Tucker Holmes
Contact: Gretchen Wright

Historical Note
Founded as Nurses Association of the American College of Obstetricians and Gynecologists; became an independent organization and assumed its current name in 1993. Members specialize in women's health, obstetric, or neonatal nursing.
Meetings/Conferences:
Annual Meetings: Summer
2007 – Orlando, FL/June 23-27/2200
Publications:
Every Woman. q.. adv.
JOGNN. bi-m. adv.
AWHONN Lifelines. bi-m. adv.

Association of Woodworking-Furnishings Suppliers *(1976)*
5733 Rickenbacker Road
Commerce, CA 90040
Tel: (323)838-9440 *Fax:* (323)838-9443
Toll Free: (800)946 - 2937
E-Mail: info@awfs.org
Web Site: www.awfs.org
Members: 450 companies
Staff: 10
Annual Budget: $2-5,000,000
Executive Director: Dale K. Silverman, CAE, SPHR
E-Mail: dale@awfs.org
Historical Note
Originally a chapter of the California Furniture Manufacturers Association, it became independent as the Association of Western Furniture Suppliers in 1978. Adopted its present name in 1990 to reflect the geographic broadening of its membership and the importance of woodworking machinery suppliers to the industry. AWFS represents companies that supply the home and commercial furnishings industry. Membership: $300/year (company).
Meetings/Conferences:
Annual Meetings: November-December and Biennial Trade Show/August (odd years)
2007 – Las Vegas, NV(Las Vegas Convention Center)/July 18-21
Publications:
The Suppliers Edge. m.

Association of Writers and Writing Programs *(1967)*
George Mason University
MS 1E3
Fairfax, VA 22030
Tel: (703)993-4301
E-Mail: awp@awpwriter.org
Web Site: www.awpwriter.org
Members: 25000 individuals
Staff: 12
Annual Budget: $500-1,000,000
Executive Director: D.W. Fenza
Historical Note
Formerly (2004) Associated Writing Programs. An organization of writers, teachers, students and educational institutions concerned with creative and professional writing. Founded at Brown University in 1967. Membership: $69/year (individual); $220-700/year (institution).
Meetings/Conferences:
Annual Meetings: Spring
Publications:
Guide to Writing Programs. bien.
The Writers Chronicle. 6/year. adv.
Job List. 7/year. adv.

Association of YMCA Professionals *(1871)*
12 Broad St., Suite 2-1
Westerly, RI 02891
Tel: (401)604-0034 *Fax:* (401)604-0036
E-Mail: john@aypymca.org
Web Site: www.aypymca.org
Members: 6500 individuals
Staff: 3
Annual Budget: $500-1,000,000
National Executive Director/Chief Executive Officer: John B. Coduri
E-Mail: john@aypymca.org
Historical Note
Formerly (1969) Association of Professional Directors of YMCAs in the United States; assumed current name in 2004. All YMCA employees who are committed to their professional development are elegible for membership. Membership: $125/year.
Meetings/Conferences:
Biennial Meetings:: (2004)
Publications:
Perspective. 8/year. adv.

Association on Higher Education and Disability *(1977)*
107 Commerce Dr.
Suite 204
Huntersville, NC 28078
Tel: (704)947-7779 *Fax:* (704)948-7779
E-Mail: ahead@ahead.org
Web Site: www.ahead.org
Members: 2200 individuals
Staff: 8
Annual Budget: $500-1,000,000
Executive Director: Stephan Smith
Historical Note
Members are committed to improving postsecondary educational opportunities for students with disabilities. Membership: $185/year (individual); $225-750/year (institution); $75/year (student). Formerly (1992) Association on Handicapped Student Service Programs in Postsecondary Education.
Meetings/Conferences:
Annual Meetings: Summer
2007 – Charlotte, NC/July 17-21
2008 – Reno, NV
2009 – Louisville, KY
Publications:
ALERT Newsletter. bi-m.
Journal of Postsecondary Education & Disability. q.
Proceedings of AHSSPPE Annual Conference. a.
Membership Directory. a.

Association on Programs for Female Offenders *(1960)*
3119 Hayward St.
Columbia, SC 29205-2632
Web Site: www.apfonews.org
Members: 150 individuals
Annual Budget: under $10,000
Historical Note
APFO members are corrections professionals and others with an interest in programs for female offenders. Has no paid officers or full-time staff. Membership: $25/year.
Meetings/Conferences:
Annual Meetings: in conjunction with the American Correctional Ass'n
Publications:
APFO Newsletter. irreg. adv.

ASTM International *(1898)*
100 Barr Harbor Dr.
P.O. Box C700
West Conshohocken, PA 19428-2959
Tel: (610)832-9500 *Fax:* (610)832-9555
Web Site: www.astm.org
Members: 30000 individuals
Staff: 160
Annual Budget: $25-50,000,000
President: James A. Thomas
Vice President, Global Cooperation: Kathleen Kono
Director, Educational Services: Scott Murphy
Vice President, Publications: John Pace
Director, Meetings: Betty Schultz
Historical Note
Originated in 1898 as the American Section of the International Association for Testing Materials; became the American Society for Testing and Materials in 1902 and incorporated in 1904. Assumed its current name in 2001. The world's largest source of voluntary consensus standards for materials, products, systems and services, ASTM also promotes related technical knowledge. Maintains a European office, as well as its headquarters in West Conshohocken, PA. Has an annual budget of $28 million. Membership: $75/year.
Publications:
Annual Book of ASTM Standards. a.
ASTM Standardization News. m. adv.
Cement and Concrete Aggregates Journal. semi-a.
Composites Technology & Research. q.
Geotechnical Testing Journal. q.
Journal of Forensic Science. q. adv.
Journal of Testing and Evaluation. bi-m.

At-sea Processors Association *(1985)*
4039 21st Ave. West, Suite 400
Seattle, WA 98199
Tel: (206)285-5139 *Fax:* (206)285-1841
E-Mail: apa@atsea.org
Web Site: www.atsea.org
Members: 7 companies
Staff: 6
Annual Budget: $1-2,000,000
Executive Director: Kevin C. Duffy
Director, Public Affairs: James L. Gilmore
Seattle Administrator: Michelle Savey
Historical Note
Represents firms operating at-sea processing fleets, providing regulatory and legislative advocacy.
Meetings/Conferences:
Annual Meetings: December

Athletic Equipment Managers Association *(1974)*
1200 S. State St.
Ann Arbor, MI 48109
Tel: (734)763-0249 *Fax:* (734)747-1189
Web Site: www.aema1.com
Members: 675 individuals
Staff: 2
Annual Budget: $10-25,000
Executive Director: Jon Falk
Historical Note
Membership: $60/year (individual).
Meetings/Conferences:
Annual Meetings: June/300
2007 – Reno, NV(John Ascuaga's Nugget)/June 6-9
Publications:
Newsletter. q.

Athletic Goods Team Distributors *(1970)*
Historical Note
A division of the National Sporting Goods Association.

Atlantic Independent Union *(1938)*
520 Cinnaminson Ave.
Palmyra, NJ 08065
Tel: (856)303-0776
Toll Free: (800)346 - 4731
Web Site: www.aiuunion.com
Members: 500 individuals
Staff: 2
President: John W. Kerr
Historical Note
Independent union representing workers in the petroleum and chemical industries.
Publications:
IU News Newspaper. a. adv.

ATP *(1972)*
201 ATP Tour Blvd.
Ponte Vedra Beach, FL 32082
Tel: (904)285-8000 *Fax:* (904)285-5966
Toll Free: (800)527 - 4811
Web Site: www.atptennis.com
Members: 800 individuals
Staff: 95
Annual Budget: $50-100,000,000
Chief Executive Officer Americas: Mark Young
Chief Marketing Officer: Phil Anderton
Chief Operating Officer: Philip Galloway
Historical Note
Founded in 1972 at Forest Hills, New York, as Association of Tennis Professionals; assumed its current name in 1990. Membership restricted to male touring professional tennis players and tournament members. Operates the official computerized player ranking system. Administers entry system for international tennis circuit and staffs tournaments. Also features approximately 77 tournaments in 34 countries. In 1990, ATP Tour began the ATP World Championship. Has an annual budget of

approximately $51 million. Membership: $300/year (Division II Player); $1000/year (Division I Player).

Meetings/Conferences:
Annual Meetings: November

Publications:
ATP Tennis Weekly. w.
Deuce. q.
Official Guide to Professional Tennis. a.

Attention Deficit Disorder Association
15000 Commerce Parkway
Suite C
Mt. Laurel, NJ 08054
Tel: (856)439-9099 *Fax:* (856)439-0525
President: Linda S. Anderson

Auction Marketing Institute *(1976)*

Historical Note
Absorbed by Nat'l Auctioneers Ass'n in 2003.

Audio Engineering Society *(1948)*
60 E. 42nd St.
Room 2520
New York, NY 10165-2520
Tel: (212)661-8528 *Fax:* (212)682-0477
Toll Free: (800)541 - 7299
E-Mail: hq@aes.org
Web Site: www.aes.org
Members: 11780 individuals
Staff: 19
Annual Budget: $2-5,000,000
Executive Director: Roger K. Furness
E-Mail: hq@aes.org

Historical Note
Members are professionals throughout the world active in audio engineering or acoustics. Membership: $75/year (individual); $750/year (organization/company).

Publications:
Journal of the Audio Engineering Society. 10/yr. adv.

Audio Publishers Association *(1986)*
8405 Greensboro Dr., Suite 800
McLean, VA 22102
Tel: (703)556-7172 *Fax:* (703)506-3266
Web Site: www.audiopub.org
Members: 300 companies
Staff: 4
Annual Budget: $250-500,000
Contact: Michelle Spencer
E-Mail: mspencer@audiopub.org

Historical Note
APA represents the concerns of audiobook publishers, collects data on the industry, and provides promotional opportunities to members.

Publications:
APA E-Newsletter. m.
Customer Attitude and Usage Study. b.
Resource Directory. a.

Audit Bureau of Circulations *(1914)*
900 N. Meacham Road
Schaumburg, IL 60173-4968
Tel: (847)605-0909 *Fax:* (847)605-0483
E-Mail: accounting@accessabc.com
Web Site: www.accessabc.com
Members: 4500 members
Staff: 320
Annual Budget: $10-25,000,000
President and Managing Director: Michael J. Lavery
Vice President, Finance and Administration: Paul J. Fajnor
Senior Vice President, Human Resources: Laura Ferraris
Executive Vice President, Marketing and Communications: Bruce Johnson
Vice President, Corporate Communications: Neal Lulofs
Vice President, Information Technology: Kaydene Stachelski
Vice President, Meetings: Susan Thomas

Historical Note
Members are newspapers and periodicals, advertisers and advertising agencies. Purpose is to audit claimed circulation figures and publish the results. Has an annual budget of approximately $22 million. Audits Web site activity, readership and subscriber demographics, and other alternative, advertiser-supported, census-based media.

Meetings/Conferences:
Annual Meetings: November/600

Publications:
Audit Reports. a.
Magazine Trends Report. a.
Canadian Newspaper Factbook. a.
Canadian Circulation of U. s.
Magazine Coverage Reports. a.
Rate Book. a.
County Penetration Report. semi-a.
FAS-FAX. semi-a.
News Bulletin. 3/year.
Publisher's Statements. semi-a.

Augustinian Educational Association *(1987)*
Cascia Hall, 2520 S. Yorktown
Tulsa, OK 74114
Tel: (918)746-2600
Members: 9 schools
Staff: 1
Annual Budget: under $10,000
Executive Secretary: Rev. Bernard Sciana

Historical Note
Members are schools administered by the Augustinian order.

Authors Guild *(1912)*
31 E. 28th St.
New York, NY 10016
Tel: (212)563-5904 *Fax:* (212)564-5363
E-Mail: staff@authorsguild.org
Web Site: www.authorsguild.org
Members: 8000 individuals
Staff: 12
Annual Budget: $500-1,000,000
Executive Director: Paul Aiken

Historical Note
A component organization of the Authors League of America. Membership is available to any individual who has had a book published by an established American publisher within seven years prior to application, or who has had three works of fiction or non-fiction published by magazines of general circulation within 18 months prior to application. Members receive free assistance with contract negotiations and publishing disputes, current information on the publishing industry, and access to group health insurance and other benefits. Membership: $90/year (first year).

Meetings/Conferences:
Annual Meetings: Winter/New York, NY

Publications:
Bulletin. q.

Authors League of America *(1912)*
31 E. 28th Street
New York, NY 10016
Tel: (212)564-8350
Members: 14500 individuals
Staff: 9
Executive Director: Paul Aiken

Historical Note
Promotes the professional interests of authors and dramatists in such areas as taxation, copyright and freedom of expression. Affiliated with the Authors Guild and the Dramatists Guild. Membership: $90/year.

Meetings/Conferences:
Annual Meetings: Late-February

Publications:
Authors Guild Bulletin. q.
Dramatists Guild Quarterly. q.

Auto Suppliers Benchmarking Association *(1997)*
4606 FM 1960 West, Suite 300
Houston, TX 77069
Tel: (281)440-5044 *Fax:* (281)440-6677
Toll Free: (888)739 - 8244
E-Mail: info@asbabenchmarking.com
Web Site: www.asbabenchmarking.com
Members: 1800 individuals
Staff: 14
Annual Budget: $1-2,000,000
Senior Vice President and Consultant: Paul Claymore

Historical Note
An autonomous division of The Benchmarking Network. Goal of ASBA is to provide useful benchmarking data to automotive suppliers in support of their quality program. Basic membership is available to employees of corporations whose main line of business is the manufacturing of parts, components or subassemblies for the automotive industry. No membership fee at this time, but participation in association activites is charged separately.

Meetings/Conferences:
Annual Meetings: Fall

Publications:
Newsletter. m.

Autoclaved Aerated Concrete Products Association
3701 County Road 544 East
Haines City, FL 33844
Tel: (863)419-2058 *Fax:* (863)419-2068
E-Mail: info@aerocontl.com
Web Site: www.aacpa.org
Members: 25 companies
Contact: Ronald Barnett
E-Mail: info@aerocontl.com

Historical Note
Members are companies that manufacture or use aerated concrete products for improved energy efficiency, fire resistance, and related applications.

Automated Builders Consortium *(1993)*

Historical Note
Address unknown in 2006.

Automated Electrified Monorails *(1990)*

Historical Note
A section of Material Handling Industry of America, which provides administrative support

Automated Imaging Association *(1984)*
900 Victors Way, Suite 140
Ann Arbor, MI 48108
Tel: (734)994-6088 *Fax:* (734)994-3338
Toll Free: (800)994 - 6099
E-Mail: info@machinevisiononline.org
Web Site: www.machinevisiononline.org
Members: 230 companies
Staff: 10
Annual Budget: $1-2,000,000
Executive Director: Jeffrey A. Burnstein

Historical Note
Established and managed by the Automation Technologies Council. Formerly (1989) the Automated Vision Association. Members are imaging manufacturers, users or suppliers of related equipment and services for the machine vision industry. Membership: $300-2,000/yr.

Publications:
Machine Vision Online. adv.
Machine Vision Systems Integrator Directory. a. adv.
Machine Vision Market Study. a.

Automated Mapping/Facilities Management International

Historical Note
See AM/FM International.

Automated Procedures for Engineering Consultants *(1966)*

Historical Note
APEC is an international non-profit association of professional design firms who have been developing computer software for use in building systems design through volunteer cooperative efforts. Membership: $600-1,800/year (based on firm size).

Automated Storage/Retrieval Systems *(1967)*

Historical Note
A section of Material Handling Industry of America which provides administrative support.

Automatic Fire Alarm Association *(1953)*
P.O. Box 951807
Lake Mary, FL 32795-1807
Tel: (407)833-9133 *Fax:* (407)833-9131
E-Mail: fire-alarm@afaa.org
Web Site: www.afaa.org
Members: 900 companies & individuals
Staff: 3

Annual Budget: $500-1,000,000
President and Executive Director: Tom Hammerberg
E-Mail: TomHammerberg@afaa.org

Historical Note
Members are manufacturers and installers of, and others interested in, fire alarm and detection equipment.

Meetings/Conferences:
Annual Meetings: *March San Diego, CA/March 12-13*
2007 - Colorado Springs, CO(Broadmoor)/Apr. 18-20
2008 - San Antonio, TX/

Publications:
Member e-Bulletin. m.

Automatic Guided Vehicle Systems *(1979)*

Historical Note
An affiliate of Material Handling Industry of America, which provides administrative support.

Automatic Indentification Manufacturers USA *(1972)*

Historical Note
See AIM USA.

Automatic Meter Reading Association *(1987)*
60 Revere Dr., Suite 500
Northbrook, IL 60062
Tel: (847)480-9628 *Fax:* (847)480-9282
E-Mail: amra@amra-intl.org
Web Site: www.amra-intl.org
Members: 1000 individuals
Staff: 4
Annual Budget: $1-2,000,000
Executive Director: Brian Pugliese
E-Mail: amra@amra-intl.org
Administrative Director: Janice Greenberg
E-Mail: amra@amra-intl.org
Communications Director: Marcie Valerio
E-Mail: amra@amra-intl.org

Historical Note
AMRA serves to advance the state of telemetry technology for meter reading, distribution, and control, and to provide a forum for research and development of standards, guidelines and practices. Membership: $225/year (full member); $175/year (associate).

Meetings/Conferences:
Annual Meetings: *Fall*

Publications:
AMRA News. m.

Automatic Transmission Rebuilders Association *(1954)*
2400 Latigo Ave.
Oxnard, CA 93030
Tel: (805)604-2000 *Fax:* (805)604-2003
E-Mail: dmadden@atra.com
Web Site: www.atra.com
Members: 3200 individuals
Staff: 30
Annual Budget: $1-2,000,000
Chief Executive Officer: Dennis Madden

Historical Note
Members are rebuilders and suppliers. Membership: $129/quarter.

Publications:
Directory. a. adv.
Gears Magazine. 9/yr. adv.
Good Guys Newsletter. m. adv.

Automotive Aftermarket Industry Association *(1999)*
7101 Wisconsin Ave., Suite 1300
Bethesda, MD 20814
Tel: (301)654-6664 *Fax:* (301)654-3299
E-Mail: aaia@aftermarket.org
Web Site: www.aftermarket.org
Members: 7566 companies
Staff: 40
Annual Budget: $10-25,000
President and Chief Executive Officer: Kathleen Schmatz
Vice President, Meetings: Michael E. Barratt, CMP
E-Mail: michael.barratt@aftermarket.org
Vice President, Government Affairs and International Trade: Lee Kadrich
Vice President, Market Research: Dan Kaplan
Vice President, Regulatory and Government Affairs: Aaron Lowe
Chief Finance/Operations Officer: Susan Medick, CPA, CAE
E-Mail: susan.medick@aftermarket.org
Director, Administration: Dedra Selby
Senior Vice President, Marketing and Member Relations: Richard White

Historical Note
Founded as the Automotive Parts and Accessories Association; assumed its current name in 1999. Absorbed Automotive Wholesale Distributors Association in 2004. Members are manufacturers, distributors, retailers and manufacturers' representatives who market automotive replacement parts and accessories and services. Membership: $200-3,500/year (organization).

Meetings/Conferences:
Annual Meetings: *Las Vegas, NV*

Publications:
Aftermarket Insider. bi-m.
AAIA Aftermarket Factbook. a.
AAIA Mini-Monitor. a.
AutoFacts. w.

Automotive Body Parts Association *(1980)*
P.O. Box 820689
Houston, TX 77282-0689
Tel: (281)531-0809 *Fax:* (281)531-9411
Toll Free: (800)323 - 5832
E-Mail: srodmani@sbcglobal.net
Web Site: www.autopba.com
Members: 180 companies
Staff: 2
Annual Budget: $250-500,000
Executive Director: Stanley A. Rodman
E-Mail: srodmani@sbcglobal.net

Historical Note
Founded and incorporated in California in 1980; re-incorporated in Texas in 1987. Formerly (1984) the Aftermarket Body Parts Distributors Association and (1990) the Aftermarket Body Parts Association. Absorbed (1997) Bumper Recycling Association of North America. Members are companies that distribute, supply and/or manufacture automotive bumpers and other auto body crash parts for auto dealers, body shops and garages. Membership: $500-1200/year (company); $200/year (associate).

Meetings/Conferences:
Annual: *Spring*

Publications:
Body Language Newsletter. m. adv.
Collision Parts Journal. semi-a. adv.
International Directory. a. adv.

Automotive Communication Council *(1941)*
7101 Wisconsin Ave., Suite 1300
Bethesda, MD 20814
Tel: (240)333-1089 *Fax:* (301)654-3299
E-Mail: acc@aftermarket.org
Web Site: www.acc-online.org/
Members: 65 companies
Annual Budget: $10-25,000
President: Dave Wheeler
E-Mail: acc@aftermarket.org

Historical Note
Formerly (1993) the Automotive Advertisers Council. Administrative services provided by the Automotive Service Industry Association. Promotes research to increase advertising effectiveness. Chief executive is the President, who is elected annually. Membership: $295/year (individual).

Meetings/Conferences:
Semi-annual: *Fall/Winter*

Publications:
ACC Newsletter. semi-a.

Automotive Fleet and Leasing Association *(1969)*
1000 Westgate Dr.
St. Paul, MN 55114
Tel: (651)290-6274 *Fax:* (651)290-2266
E-Mail: info@aflaonline.com
Web Site: www.aflaonline.org
Members: 300 individuals
Staff: 2
Annual Budget: $50-100,000
Executive Director: Dave Ewald

Historical Note
AFLA is designed to improve communications among buyers, sellers, fleet administrators, lending institutions, lessors, used vehicle marketers and allied automotive service companies. Membership: $200/year.

Meetings/Conferences:
Semi-annual Meetings: *Fall*

Publications:
The Forum Newsletter. q.
AFLA Conference Journal. a. adv.

Automotive Industry Action Group *(1982)*
26200 Lahser Road, Suite 200
Southfield, MI 48033-7100
Tel: (248)358-3570 *Fax:* (248)358-3253
E-Mail: webmaster@aiag.org
Web Site: www.aiag.org
Members: 1500 companies
Staff: 60
Annual Budget: $10-25,000,000

Historical Note
Composed largely of major North American vehicle manufacturers and their suppliers; also has some member companies that are vehicle manufacturers and suppliers in Europe, Asia and the Pacific area. AIAG's goal is to reduce costs and to improve productivity within the industry. Generally, activities focus on the automotive chain. The AIAG provides a forum for suppliers and manufacturers to indentify and solve common business problems. Membership: fees are based on annual corporate sales.

Meetings/Conferences:
Annual Meetings: late Summer

Publications:
Buyer's Guide. a. adv.
Actionline Magazine. m. adv.

Automotive Lift Institute, Inc. *(1945)*
P.O. Box 85
Cortland, NY 13045
Tel: (607)756-7775 *Fax:* (607)756-0888
E-Mail: info@autolift.org
Web Site: http://autolift.org
Members: 19 companies
Staff: 3
President: R.W. "Bob" O'Gorman

Historical Note
ALI is a trade association of U.S./Canadian manufacturers and exclusive distributors of automotive lifts that are used to completely raise motor vehicles for undercarriage service. Members sell more than 90% of the lifts marketed in the U.S. ALI promotes public awareness of safety in the use of lifts. Sponsors the ANSI Accredited ALI Automotive Lift Certification Program.

Meetings/Conferences:
Semi-annual:

Automotive Maintenance Repair Association *(1994)*
7910 Woodmont Ave., Suite 750
Bethesda, MD 20814-3073
Tel: (301)634-4954
E-Mail: amra@motorist.org
Web Site: www.4amra.com
Members: 108 companies
Staff: 4
Annual Budget: $500-1,000,000
President: Larry Hecker

Historical Note
AMRA represents automotive repair stores, manufacturers, trade groups, retailers and distributors. Activities includes developing standards of service, uniform inspection procedures, shop accreditation programs, and dispute resolution mechanisms. Membership: $100/year, minimum (organization/company).

Meetings/Conferences:
2007 - Chicago, IL/May 2- /75

Publications:
Directions Newsletter. q.
e-Directions Electronic Newsletter. semi-monthly.

Automotive Market Research Council *(1966)*
P.O. Box 13966

Research Triangle Park, NC 27709-3966
Tel: (919)549-4800 *Fax:* (919)549-4824
E-Mail: info@amrc.org
Web Site: www.amrc.org
Members: 375 individuals
Annual Budget: $50-100,000
Contact: Frank Hampshire
E-Mail: info@amrc.org

Historical Note

AMRC is a professional association for companies that manufacture autos and automotive parts, components, subassemblies, or accessories for sale as original or replacement equipment. Marketing research is a primary responsibility of the personnel who represent their companies in the council. Has no paid staff; administrative support is provided by the Motor and Equipment Manufacturers Association. All officers change annually. Membership: $450/year (individual); $75/year (additional members from the same organization/company).

Meetings/Conferences:

Semi-annual meetings: Spring and Fall

Publications:

Newsletter. 2/year.

Automotive Occupant Restraints Council *(1961)*

1081 Dove Run Road, Suite 403
Lexington, KY 40502-3500
Tel: (859)269-4240 *Fax:* (859)269-4241
E-Mail: info@aorc.org
Web Site: www.aorc.org
Members: 50 companies
Staff: 2
Annual Budget: $250-500,000
Administrator: Jill P. Mulholland

Historical Note

Formerly (1977) the American Safety Belt Council and (1989) American Seat Belt Council. Membership: $3,000-15,000/year.

Meetings/Conferences:

Annual Meetings: March

Automotive Oil Change Association *(1987)*

12810 Hillcrest, Suite 221
Dallas, TX 75230
Tel: (972)458-9468 *Fax:* (972)458-9539
Toll Free: (800)331 - 0329
Web Site: www.aoca.org
Members: 1200 companies
Staff: 5
Annual Budget: $1-2,000,000
Executive Director: Stephen M. Christie, CAE
Director, Meetings/Conventions: Joyce A. Laurie

Historical Note

Formerly (1993) National Association of Independent Lubes. AOCA members are owners of independent and franchise automobile oil and lubrication businesses. Membership: $300/year, minimum (corporate).

Meetings/Conferences:

Annual Meetings: Annual
2007 – Dallas, TX(Dallas Convention Center)/Apr. 28-May 2/3200
2008 – Las Vegas, NV(Mandalay Bay)/March 15-21
2009 – Atlanta, GA(Convention Center)/Apr. 19-21

Publications:

Oil Changing Times. bi-m.

Automotive Parts and Accessories Association

Historical Note

Became Automotive Aftermarket Industry Association.

Automotive Parts Remanufactuers Association *(1941)*

4215 Lafayette Center Dr.
Suite Three
Chantilly, VA 20151-1243
Tel: (703)968-2772 *Fax:* (703)968-2878
E-Mail: mail@apra.org
Web Site: www.bigrshow.com OR www.apra.org
Members: 1000 companies
Staff: 8
Annual Budget: $1-2,000,000
President: William C. Gager
Senior Vice President: Jeanie Magathan

Historical Note

Formerly Automotive Parts Rebuilders Association; assumed its current name in 2004. Membership: $200-3800/year (based on number of employees).

Meetings/Conferences:

Annual Meetings: Fall
2007 – Las Vegas, NV(Rivera Hotel)/Oct. 27-29

Publications:

The Global Connection. m. adv.
Global Sourcing Directory. a. adv.
APRA Membership Directory. a. adv.
E Connection (electronic newsletter). w. adv.

Automotive Presidents Council

Historical Note

A division of Motor and Equipment Manufacturers Association, which provides administrative support. Members are chief executive officers of MEMA-member companies.

Automotive Public Relations Council *(1974)*

P.O. Box 13966
Research Triangle Park, NC 27709-3966
Tel: (919)406-8811 *Fax:* (919)549-4824
Web Site: www.autopr.org
Members: 63 individuals
Staff: 1
Annual Budget: under $10,000
Director: Neal Zipser

Historical Note

An activity of the Motor and Equipment Manufacturers Association. APRC members are corporate and agency communicators. Membership: $295-425/year.

Meetings/Conferences:

Semi-annual Meetings: Spring and Fall

Automotive Recyclers Association *(1943)*

3975 Fair Ridge Dr.
Terrace Level North, Suite 20
Fairfax, VA 22033-2924
Tel: (703)385-1001 *Fax:* (703)385-1494
Web Site: www.a-r-a.org
Members: 1200 companies
Staff: 6
Annual Budget: $2-5,000,000
Executive Vice President: George K. Eliades, CAE
Director, Member Services: Kelly C. Badillo
Director, Meetings and Communications: Mark Mohay
Manager, Government Affairs: Ray Tarnowski

Historical Note

Incorporated in the State of New York. Formerly (1973) National Auto and Truck Wreckers Association, (1975) Association of Auto and Truck Recyclers, and (1989) Automotive Dismantlers and Recyclers; assumed its current name in 1993. Members are recyclers of domestic and foreign automobile, truck, and motorcycle parts. Supports its international membership through education programs, legislative representation, and professional certification. Membership: fees vary.

Publications:

Annual Convention Program Guide. a. adv.
Automotive Recycling Magazine. bi-m. adv.
Membership Directory/Buyers Guide. a. adv.

Automotive Service Association *(1986)*

1901 Airport Freeway
P.O. Box 929
Bedford, TX 76095-0929
Tel: (817)283-6205 *Fax:* (817)685-0225
Toll Free: (800)272 - 7467
E-Mail: asainfo@asashop.org
Web Site: www.asashop.org
Members: 12000 businesses
Staff: 34
Annual Budget: $5-10,000,000
President: Ron Pyle
E-Mail: ronp@asashop.org
Vice President, Service Repair Markets, Collision and Mechanical Division: Bill Haas
E-Mail: asainfo@asashop.org
Vice President, Finance: Mark Hale
E-Mail: markh@asashop.org
Executive Vice President: John Scully
E-Mail: johns@asashop.org
Manager, Meetings and Travel: Robbie Talley
E-Mail: robbiet@asashop.org
Vice President, Marketing and Communications: Angie Wilson

Historical Note

ASA was the result of a consolidation of Automotive Service Councils, Inc. (formed in 1955) and Independent Automotive Service Association (formed in 1951). Members are businesses providing automotive service in mechanical, auto body and other fields. Membership: $195/year.

Meetings/Conferences:

Annual Meetings: Spring and Trade Show/late Fall

Publications:

Division Bulletins. m.
AutoInc. m. adv.

Automotive Trade Association Executives *(1915)*

8400 Westpark Dr.
McLean, VA 22102
Tel: (703)821-7072 *Fax:* (703)556-8581
E-Mail: atae@nada.org
Web Site: www.atae.info
Members: 113 associations
Staff: 2
Annual Budget: $100-250,000
Executive Director: C. Alan Marlette
E-Mail: atae@nada.org

Historical Note

Members are executives of state and local automobile dealer associations.

Meetings/Conferences:

Semi-Annual Meetings: February and July

Automotive Training Managers Council *(1984)*

101 Blue Seal Dr. SE
Suite 101
Leesburg, VA 20175
Tel: (703)669-6670 *Fax:* (703)669-6126
E-Mail: info@atmc.org
Web Site: www.atmc.org
Members: 135 individuals
Staff: 3
Annual Budget: $50-100,000
President: Ernie Wagner
Director, Administrative: Bob Rodriguez

Historical Note

ATMC members are automotive aftermarket manufacturing and distributing concerns, each represented by a training department executive. ATMC provides a forum for the exchange of views and opinions regarding the training needs of the automotive trade; encourages study and research of training effectiveness; and promotes quality training. Membership: $125 (initiation fee), $300/year (full), $100 (advisory).

Meetings/Conferences:

Semi-Annual Meetings: Spring and Fall

Automotive Warehouse Distributors Association *(1947)*

Historical Note

Merged with Automotive Aftermarket Industry Association in 2004.

Aviation Distributors and Manufacturers Association International *(1943)*

100 N. 20th St., Fourth Floor
Philadelphia, PA 19103-1443
Tel: (215)564-3484 *Fax:* (215)963-9784
E-Mail: adma@fernley.com
Web Site: www.adma.org
Members: 90 companies
Staff: 3
Annual Budget: $100-250,000
Executive Director: Talbot M. Gee

Historical Note

Promotes friendly business relations and mutual confidence among its members and others in the industry; represents the distributors and manufacturers of aviation parts, supplies and equipment in all matters of national importance; and cooperates with various government agencies, including the Federal Aviation Administration. Membership fee varies, based on sales volume.

Meetings/Conferences:

Semi-Annual Meetings: Spring and Fall

Publications:
ADMA News. m.
Aviation Education News Bulletin. a.

Aviation Insurance Association *(1976)*
14 W. Third St., Suite 200
Kansas City, MO 64105
Tel: (816)221-8488 Ext: 136 *Fax:* (816)472-7765
Toll Free: (800)354 - 7918
Web Site: www.aiaweb.org
Members: 875 firms and individuals
Staff: 3
Annual Budget: $250-500,000
Executive Director: Gary Hicks
Historical Note
Membership: $150/year per firm.
Meetings/Conferences:
Annual Meetings: Spring
Publications:
Newsletter-The Binder. q.
Membership Directory. a.

Aviation Maintenance Foundation International *(1971)*
P.O. Box 456
Basin, WY 82410-0456
E-Mail: amfic@ix.netcom.com
Members: 6000 individuals
Staff: 8
Annual Budget: $500-1,000,000
President and Executive Director: Richard S. Kost
E-Mail: amfic@ix.netcom.com
Historical Note
Formerly (1988) the Aviation Maintenance Foundation. Incorporated in March, 1972. Members are aviation maintenance personnel, schools, companies and related organizations. Membership: $40/year.
Meetings/Conferences:
Annual Meetings: Fall/1,200
Publications:
AMFI Technical Bulletin. irreg.
Industry News. m.
Industry Statistical Surveys. a.
World of Aviation Maintenance. a.
SAMOLYOT (Russian Aviation/Aerospace). semi-a.
China Aerospace News Digest. m.

Aviation Safety Institute *(1973)*
Historical Note
Address unknown in 2006.

Aviation Suppliers Association *(1993)*
734 15th St. NW
Suite 620
Washington, DC 20005
Tel: (202)347-6899 *Fax:* (202)347-6894
E-Mail: info@aviationsuppliers.org
Web Site: www.aviationsuppliers.org
Members: 300 companies
Staff: 9
Annual Budget: $500-1,000,000
President: Michele Dickstein
Coordinator, Membership and Meetings: Jeanne Meade
E-Mail: jeanne@aviationsuppliers.org
Historical Note
Founded as Airline Suppliers Association; assumed its current name in 2003. Members are companies providing materials and services to commercial airlines. Membership: $1,000-$2,500/year.
Meetings/Conferences:
Annual Meetings: Annual

Publications:
The Update Report. m. adv.

Aviation Technician Education Council *(1961)*
2090 Wexford Court
Harrisburg, PA 17112-1579
Tel: (717)540-7121 *Fax:* (717)540-7121
E-Mail: info@atec-amt.org
Web Site: www.atec-amt.org
Members: 155 schools
Staff: 2
Annual Budget: $50-100,000
Executive Director: R. Dumaresq, Ph.D.
E-Mail: info@atec-amt.org
Historical Note
ATEC members are FAA-approved schools training aviation maintenance technicians.
Publications:
ATEC Newsletter. 3/yr.

AVS Science and Technology Society *(1953)*
120 Wall St., 32nd Floor
New York, NY 10005
Tel: (212)248-0200 *Fax:* (212)248-0245
Toll Free: (800)888 - 1021
Web Site: www.avs.org
Members: 6000 individuals
Staff: 7
Annual Budget: $2-5,000,000
Administrative Director: Yvonne Towse
E-Mail: yvonne@avs.org
Meeting Manager: Della Miller
E-Mail: della@avs.org
Historical Note
Established in 1953 as the Committee on Vacuum Techniques. Became American Vacuum Society in 1958, and assumed its current name in 2002. Incorporated in Massachusetts. A member of the American Institute of Physics, and affiliated with the International Union for Vacuum Science, Techniques and Applications. Membership: $75/year.
Meetings/Conferences:
Annual Meetings: Fall
Publications:
AVS Newsletter. bi-m.
Surface Science Spectra. q.
Journal of Vacuum Science & Technology A. bi-m. adv.
Journal of Vacuum Science & Technology B. bi-m. adv.

Awards and Recognition Association *(1980)*
4700 W. Lake Ave.
Glenview, IL 60025
Tel: (847)375-4800 *Fax:* (877)734-9380
Toll Free: (800)344 - 2148
E-Mail: info@ara.org
Web Site: www.ara.org
Members: 4000 companies
Staff: 12
Annual Budget: $2-5,000,000
Executive Director: David J. Bergeson, Ph.D.
E-Mail: dbergeson@amctec.com
Historical Note
Founded in San Francisco, CA in 1966 as Bay Area Trophy Dealers; incorporated in California in 1967 as Trophy Dealers of Northern California; eventually expanded its membership to become Trophy Dealers of America, Inc. Merged with American Awards Manufacturers Association in 1980 and became Trophy Dealers and Manufacturers Association before assuming current name in 1993. Membership: $185/year (retail dealer); $450/year (manufacturing supplier).
Meetings/Conferences:
Annual Meetings: Spring
2007 – Las Vegas, NV(Las Vegas Convention Center)/Feb. 20-25
Publications:
Recognition Review. m. adv.

Awards & Recognition Industry Educational Foundation
4700 W. Lake Ave.
Glenview, IL 60025-4185
Tel: (847)375-4800 *Fax:* (877)734-9380
Toll Free: (800)344 - 2148
E-Mail: info@ara.org
Web Site: www.ara.org/foundation/index.cfm

Ayrshire Breeders' Association *(1875)*
1224 Alton Creek Road, Suite B
Columbus, OH 43228
Tel: (614)335-0020 *Fax:* (614)335-0023
E-Mail: info@usayrshire.com
Web Site: www.usayrshire.com
Members: 1100 individuals
Staff: 2
Annual Budget: $100-250,000
Executive Secretary: Becky Payne
E-Mail: info@usayrshire.com
Historical Note
Breeders and fanciers of Ayrshire dairy cattle. Member of the National Society of Livestock Record Associations. Membership: $25/year.
Meetings/Conferences:
Annual Meetings:
Publications:
Ayrshire Digest. bi-m. adv.

Bakery, Confectionery, Tobacco Workers and Grain Millers International Union *(1886)*
10401 Connecticut Ave.
Kensington, MD 20895
Tel: (301)933-8600 *Fax:* (301)946-8452
Web Site: www.bctgm.org/
Members: 120000 individuals
Staff: 40
President: Frank Hurt
Historical Note
Founded as the Bakery, Confectionery, and Tobacco Workers' International Union. Organized on January 13, 1886 in Pittsburgh and chartered by the American Federation of Labor on February 23, 1887. Merged (1969) with American Bakery and Confectionery Workers' International Union. Affiliated with AFL-CIO, CLC. Formerly (until 1978) known as the Bakery and Confectionery Workers International Union of America. Merged with the Tobacco Workers International Union in August, 1978. Sponsors and supports the Bakery, Confectionery and Tobacco Workers International Union Political Action Committee.
Meetings/Conferences:
Quadrennial Convention: (2006)
Publications:
BCTGM News. bi-m.

Baking Industry Sanitation Standards Committee *(1949)*
P.O. Box 3999
Manhattan, KS 66505-3999
Tel: (785)537-4750 *Fax:* (785)565-6060
Toll Free: (866)342 - 4772
E-Mail: bissc@bissc.org
Web Site: www.bissc.org
Members: 100 companies and organizations
Staff: 2
Annual Budget: $100-250,000
Executive Director: Jon R. Anderson
E-Mail: bissc@bissc.org
Historical Note
Founded and supported by the American Bakers Association (ABA), the American Institute of Baking (AIB), the American Society of Baking (ASB), the Baking Industry Suppliers Association (BEMA), and the Biscuit and Cracker Manufacturers Association (B&CMA). Primary purpose is to develop, publish and promote the use of voluntary sanitation standards covering the design and construction of machinery and equipment used in the baking industry. Registration fee: $350/year (company).
Meetings/Conferences:
Annual Meetings: Winter/30
Publications:
BISSC Design Handbook, Spanish Version.
BISSC Design Handbook for Easily Cleanable Equipment.
ANSI / BISSC Standard Bakery Equipment-Sanitation Standard. quadren.
Directory of Registered Companies (online).

Balloon Manufacturers Association
Historical Note
A division of the Industrial Fabrics Association International.

Bank Administration Institute *(1924)*
One N. Franklin St.
Suite 1000
Chicago, IL 60606-3421
Tel: (312)683-2464 *Fax:* (312)683-2373
Toll Free: (800)284 - 4078
E-Mail: info@bai.org
Web Site: www.bai.org
Members: 1500 banks
Staff: 90

Annual Budget: $5-10,000,000
President and Chief Executive Officer: Deborah L. Bianucci
E-Mail: info@bai.org
Chief Administrative Officer: Ann R. Barcroft
E-Mail: info@bai.org
Chief Financial Officer: Thomas J. Dubnicka
Chief Operating Officer: James M. McNeil, C.O.O
E-Mail: info@bai.org

Historical Note

Provides information for member bankers in areas such as human resources, finance, strategic planning and marketing, accounting, corporate services, audit, taxes, retail, operations and technology, through its series of emerging issues studies, professional conferences and education programs.

Meetings/Conferences:
Annual Meetings:

Publications:
Banking Strategies Magazine. bi-m. adv.
Compliance Alert Newsletter. m.
Bank Fraud Newsletter. m.

Bank Insurance and Securities Association *(1981)*
303 W. Lancaster Ave.
Suite 2D
Wayne, PA 19087
Tel: (610)989-9047 *Fax:* (610)989-9102
E-Mail: bisa@bisanet.org
Web Site: www.bisanet.org
Members: 410 institutions
Staff: 10
Managing Director: Heywood Sloane

Historical Note

Founded as Bank Securities Association, BISA absorbed (2002) the Financial Institutions Insurance Association and assumed its current name at the same time. Works to foster the full integration of securities and insurance businesses with depository institutions' traditional banking businesses. BISA's goal is to advance profit wealth and risk management solutions through banks, thrifts and credit unions. BISA's member organizations, and executives in these organizations who thus work with BISA, include firms and executives in the securities, insurance, investment advisory, trust, private banking, retail, and capital market categories, and commerical divisions of depository institutions. Provides members with knowledge and support to help grow their businesses, and works to help create a legislative and regulatory environment healthy for members' future growth.

Meetings/Conferences:
Annual Meetings: Annual
2007 – Hollywood, FL/March 10-14/600

Publications:
Bank Insurance & Securities Marketing. q. adv.
BISM Online.

Bankers' Association for Finance and Trade *(1921)*
1120 Connecticut Ave. NW, Fifth Floor
Washington, DC 20036
Tel: (202)663-7575 *Fax:* (202)663-5538
Toll Free: (800)226 - 5377
E-Mail: baft@baft.com
Web Site: www.baft.org
Members: 162 banks
Staff: 9
Annual Budget: $1-2,000,000
Executive Director: Rebecca Morter
Communications Specialist: Emily Montfort
E-Mail: emily@baft.org
Director, Membership/Communications: Bruce Portillo
E-Mail: bruce@baft.org

Historical Note

Founded as Bankers' Association for Foreign Trade; assumed its curent name in 2000. BAFT is an association of financial institutions dedicated to fostering and promoting international trade, finance, and investment between the United States and its trading partners. BAFT has played a unique role in bringing together financial institutions worldwide which have an interest in business, commerce and finance in the United States. Membership fee varies, based on assets.

Meetings/Conferences:
Annual Meetings: April/May

Publications:
For Your Information. bi-m.

Baptist Communicators Association *(1954)*
1715-K S. Rutherford Blvd.
Suite 295
Murfreesboro, TN 37130-5957
Tel: (615)904-0152
E-Mail: bca.office@comcast.net
Web Site: http://baptistcommunicators.org
Members: 450 individuals
Staff: 1
Annual Budget: $10-25,000
Administrative Coordinator: Keith Beene
E-Mail: bca.office@comcast.net

Historical Note

Founded as Baptist Public Relations Association; assumed its current name in 1997. Main purpose is educational. Membership: $75/year.

Meetings/Conferences:
Annual Meetings: Spring

Publications:
BPRA Newsletter. bi-m.
BPRA Directory. a.

Barbecue Industry Association *(1958)*

Historical Note

Merged with Hearth Products Ass'n to form Hearth Patio and Barbecue Ass'n in 2001.

Barre Granite Association *(1889)*
P.O. Box 481
51 Church St.
Barre, VT 05641
Tel: (802)476-4131 *Fax:* (802)476-4765
E-Mail: castaldoj@barregranite.org
Web Site: www.barregranite.org
Members: 81 companies
Staff: 4
Annual Budget: $500-1,000,000
Executive Director: John Castaldo

Historical Note

Members are granite quarriers and manufacturers, dedicated to the production of granite monuments and other products. BGA provides a cemetery planning assistance program designed to expand cemetery areas or establish new cemetery sections.

Meetings/Conferences:
Annual Meetings: usually Barre, VT/May

Barzona Breeders Association of America *(1968)*
40323 E. CR-1315 Road
McCurtain, OK 74944-3291
Tel: (918)432-5433
Members: 80 individuals
Staff: 1
Annual Budget: $25-50,000
Contact: Nancy Duley

Historical Note

Breeders and fanciers of Barzona cattle. Officers elected annually. Membership: $75/year.

Baseball Writers Association of America *(1908)*
P.O. Box 610611
Bayside, NY 11361
Tel: (718)767-2582 *Fax:* (718)767-2583
E-Mail: bbwaa@aol.com
Web Site: www.baseballwriters.org/
Members: 800 individuals
Staff: 1
Annual Budget: under $10,000
Secretary-Treasurer: Jack O'Connell
E-Mail: bbwaa@aol.com

Historical Note

Members are sports writers on direct assignment to major league teams. Membership: $50/year (individual).

Basic Acrylic Monomer Manufacturers *(1986)*
17260 Vannes Court
Hamilton, VA 20158-3163
Tel: (540)751-2093 *Fax:* (540)751-2094
Web Site: www.bamm.net
Members: 5 manufacturers
Staff: 1
Annual Budget: $500-1,000,000
Executive Director: Elizabeth K. Hunt

Historical Note

Members are producers of the basic acrylic monomers. BAMM addresses health, environmental and regulatory issues concerning acrylic monomers.

Battery Council International *(1924)*
401 N. Michigan Ave.
Suite 2200
Chicago, IL 60611-4267
Tel: (312)644-6610 *Fax:* (312)527-6640
E-Mail: mdesmarais@smickbucklin.com
Web Site: www.batterycouncil.org
Members: 200 companies
Staff: 3
Annual Budget: $1-2,000,000
Executive Vice President: Maurice A. Desmarais, CAE

Historical Note

Established as the National Battery Manufacturers Association. Became the Association of American Battery Manufacturers in 1940; assumed its current name in 1969. BCI members are distributors, manufacturers and suppliers to the electrical storage battery industry. Maintains a Washington office. Membership dues based on sales volume.

Meetings/Conferences:
Annual Meetings: Spring/600

Publications:
Battery Replacement Data Book. a. adv.
Service Manual. irreg. adv.
Technical Manual. irreg. adv.

BCA *(1993)*
55 West 116th St.
Suite 234
New York, NY 10026
Toll Free: (800)308 - 8188
E-Mail: iaddison@thebca.net
Web Site: www.thebca.net
Members: 500 individuals
Staff: 3
Annual Budget: $100-250,000
President: Alex Askew
Director, Operations: Ieda Addison
E-Mail: iaddison@thebca.net

Historical Note

Formerly (1993) Black Culinarians Alliance; assumed current name in 2004. BCA is a national nonprofit organization that conducts networking in the foodservice, hospitality and related educational areas. Mission is to create awareness, exposure and educational opportunities for people of color in the foodservice (culinary arts) and hospitality fields and to provide a vehicle to support the professional development of young people of color who are considering culinary arts and/or hospitality as a career.

Publications:
Newsletter. q.
BCA Newsflash. q. adv.

Bearing Specialist Association *(1966)*
800 Roosevelt Rd.
Bldg. C, Suite 312
Glen Ellyn, IL 60137-5833
Tel: (630)858-3838 *Fax:* (630)790-3095
E-Mail: info@bsahome.org
Web Site: www.bsahome.org
Members: 58 companies
Staff: 3
Annual Budget: $500-1,000,000
Executive Secretary: Jerilyn Church, CAE

Historical Note

Formed by a merger of the Anti-Friction Bearing Distributors Association and the Association of Bearing Specialists. BSA serves as a forum for professionals in the bearing industry to exchange information, network and focus on problems relevant to the industry.

Meetings/Conferences:
Annual Meetings: Spring
2007 – Marco Island, FL(Marriott)/May 5-8
2008 – Tucson, AZ(Loews Ventana Canyon)/Apr. 26-30

Publications:
News and Views.

Bearing Technical Committee
Historical Note
A committee of the American Bearing Manufacturing Association.

Beauty and Barber Supply Institute
Historical Note
Became Professional Beauty Association in 2004.

Beef Improvement Federation *(1968)*
124 Weber Hall
Kansas State University
Manhattan, KS 66506
Tel: (785)532-5428 *Fax:* (785)532-7059
Web Site: www.beefimprovement.org/
Members: 80 organizations
Staff: 1
Annual Budget: $25-50,000
Executive Director: Twig Marston
Historical Note
Membership, by organization, consists of groups of beef cattle breeders and state improvement associations. Membership: $50-600/year.
Meetings/Conferences:
Annual Meetings: Spring/300
Publications:
Ideas into Action - BIF 25 Year History.
Proceedings - BIF Symposium and Annual Meeting. a.
Guidelines for Uniform Beef Improvement Programs. quinquen.
Genetic Prediction Proceedings. quinquen.

Beefmaster Breeders United *(1961)*
6800 Park Ten Blvd.
Suite 290 West
San Antonio, TX 78213
Tel: (210)732-3132 *Fax:* (210)732-7711
Web Site: www.beefmasters.org
Members: 6400 individuals
Staff: 14
Annual Budget: $1-2,000,000
Executive Vice President: Wendell E. Schronk
Historical Note
Formerly Beefmaster Breeders Universal; absorbed Foundation Beefmaster Association and assumed its current name in 1996. Owners and breeders of Beefmaster cattle. Member of the National Pedigree Livestock Council. Membership: $60/year.
Meetings/Conferences:
Annual Meetings: Fall
Publications:
The Beefmaster Cowman. m. adv.
Directory of BBU Members. a. adv.

Beer Institute *(1986)*
122 C St. NW
Suite 350
Washington, DC 20001
Tel: (202)737-2337 *Fax:* (202)737-7004
Toll Free: (800)379 - 2739
E-Mail: info@beerinstitute.org
Web Site: www.beerinstitute.org
Members: 95 brewers and suppliers
Staff: 11
Annual Budget: $2-5,000,000
Executive Vice President/General Counsel/Secretary: Arthur DeCelle
E-Mail: info@beerinstitute.org
President: Jeffrey G. Becker
E-Mail: info@beerinstitute.org
Executive Vice President/General Counsel/Secretary: Arthur DeCelle
E-Mail: info@beerinstitute.org
Director, Federal Government Affairs: Richard B. Goddard
E-Mail: info@beerinstitute.org
Director, Administration: Mary L. Kita
E-Mail: info@beerinstitute.org
Historical Note
Successor organization to the United States Brewers Association, formerly (1944) United Brewers Industrial Foundation and (1961) United States Brewers Foundation. Members are the major national breweries and suppliers to the brewing industry.
Publications:
Brewers Almanac. a.
Beer Industry News.

Beet Sugar Development Foundation *(1945)*
800 Grant St.
Suite 300
Denver, CO 80203
Tel: (303)832-4460 *Fax:* (303)832-4468
Web Site: www.bsdf-assbt.org
Members: 15 companies
Staff: 30
Annual Budget: $250-500,000
Executive Vice President: Thomas K. Schwartz
Historical Note
Members are U.S. and Canadian sugar beet companies and primary suppliers of sugar beet seed.

Behavior Genetics Association *(1972)*
447 UCB, Univ. of Colorado
Boulder, CO 80309-0447
Tel: (303)492-2826
Web Site: www.bga.org
Members: 500 individuals
Annual Budget: $10-25,000
Secretary: Mike Stallings
Historical Note
Organized May 9, 1972 in Illinois to promote scientific study of the interrelationships of genetic mechanisms and behavior of both animal and human, to aid and encourage education and training in the field, and to interpret and disseminate knowledge to the public. Affiliated with the International Genetics Association, American Association for the Advancement of Science (AAAS). Has no paid officers or full-time staff. Membership: $55/year (full member); $30/year (student).
Meetings/Conferences:
Annual Meetings: Summer/175
Publications:
Behavior Genetics. bi-m. adv.

Belgian American Chamber of Commerce in the United States *(1925)*
c/o Fortis Bank
153 E. 53rd St., 27th Floor
New York, NY 10022
Tel: (212)340-6271 *Fax:* (212)340-6270
E-Mail: info@belcham.org
Web Site: www.belcham.org
Members: 150 companies and organizations
Staff: 2
Annual Budget: $100-250,000
President: Jean Pierre Paulet
Executive Director: Tamara Zouboff
Historical Note
Membership: $350/year (individual); $800/year (business); $2000/year (corporate).
Meetings/Conferences:
Annual Meetings: usually June/New York, NY
Publications:
Listing of Belgian Companies in the United States. irreg.
Listing of Belgian Exporters/Importers. irreg.
BACC News. a. adv.

Belgian Draft Horse Corp. of America *(1887)*
P.O. Box 335
Wabash, IN 46992
Tel: (260)563-3205
E-Mail: belgian@belgiancorp.com
Web Site: www.belgiancorp.com
Members: 5500 individuals
Staff: 2
Annual Budget: $250-500,000
Secretary-Treasurer: Vicki Knott
E-Mail: belgian@belgiancorp.com
Historical Note
Originated as the American Association of Importers and Breeders of Belgian Draft Horses and assumed its present name in 1937. The pedigree association for owners and breeders of Belgian Draft Horses. Membership: $100/lifetime membership.
Meetings/Conferences:
Annual Meetings: December in Wabash, Indiana
Publications:
Belgian Newsletter. 3/year.
Belgian Review. a. adv.

Belt Association *(1934)*
225 W. 39th St.
New York, NY 10018
Tel: (212)398-5400 *Fax:* (212)398-7818
E-Mail: joey5400@aol.com
Members: 24 companies
Staff: 2
Annual Budget: $50-100,000
Executive Director: Sheldon M. Edelman
Historical Note
Membership originally consisted of manufacturers of ladies' belts. Absorbed the Association of Men's Belt Manufacturers in 1986.
Publications:
The Association. q.
Trade Directory. a.

Belted Galloway Society *(1951)*
P.O. Box 316
Bendersville, PA 17306-0316
Tel: (717)677-9655 *Fax:* (717)677-9755
E-Mail: beltiecows@aol.com
Web Site: www.beltie.org
Members: 900 individuals
Staff: 1
Annual Budget: $50-100,000
Secretary/Treasurer: Laura Glassmann
E-Mail: beltiecows@aol.com
Historical Note
A non-profit association of United States breeders of Belted Galloway cattle, known for the economical production of beef under range conditions. Maintains a pedigree registry and promotes the breed. Membership: $40/year, plus $50 initiation fee.
Meetings/Conferences:
Annual Meetings: Fall/50-100
Publications:
US Beltie News. m. adv.

BEMA - The Baking Industry Suppliers Association *(1918)*
7101 College Blvd.
Suite 1505
Overland Park, KS 66210
Tel: (913)338-1300 *Fax:* (913)338-1327
E-Mail: office@bema.org
Web Site: www.bema.org
Members: 200 companies
Staff: 2
Annual Budget: $500-1,000,000
President and Chief Executive Officer: Kerwin Brown
Historical Note
Founded as Bakery Equipment Manufacturers Association; later became BEMA - an International Association Serving the Baking and Food Industries before assuming its current name in 1999. BEMA represents bakery and food equipment manufacturers and suppliers. The association is committed to furthering the professionalism of its members with programs that enhance communications and promote technological advancement, education, safety, sanitation, marketing and good manufacturing practices. Membership: $1,250/year (corporate).
Meetings/Conferences:
Annual Meetings: Summer
2007 – San Diego, CA(Del Coronado)/June 24-26
Publications:
Bakery Equipment Product and Service Guide. tri-a.
BEMA Newsletter. q.

Benchmarking Network Association *(1992)*
4606 FM 1960 West
Suite 250
Houston, TX 77069
Tel: (281)440-5044 *Fax:* (281)440-6677
Toll Free: (800)856 - 5646
Web Site: www.benchmarkingnetwork.com
Members: 150000 individuals
Staff: 21
Annual Budget: $1-2,000,000
President: Mark T. Czarnecki
E-Mail: mczarnecki@benchmarkingnetwork.com

Historical Note
BNA assists in benchmarking activities and promotes communication between professionals in corporations involved in benchmarking. Members span industries and functional expertise. BNA sponsors a number of specialty groups, including Health Care Benchmarking, Human Resources Benchmarking, Accounting and Finance Benchmarking, and International Governmental Benchmarking. Membership: $149/year (individual).

Meetings/Conferences:
Annual Meetings: August

Publications:
Benchmarking. w. adv.

Beta Alpha Psi *(1919)*
1211 Ave. of the Americas, 19th Floor
New York, NY 10036-8775
Tel: (212)596-6090 *Fax:* (212)596-6288
E-Mail: bap@bap.org
Web Site: www.bap.org
Members: 210000 individuals
Staff: 3
Annual Budget: $1-2,000,000
Executive Director: Hadassah Baum

Historical Note
An honorary, professional accounting fraternity. Organized February 12, 1919 at the University of Illinois. Membership: $45/year.

Meetings/Conferences:
Annual Meetings: Summer

Publications:
Annual Report. a.

Beta Beta Beta *(1922)*
University of North Alabama
Box 5079
Florence, AL 35632
Tel: (256)765-6220 *Fax:* (256)765-6221
Web Site: www.tri-beta.org
Members: 11000 individuals
Staff: 1
Annual Budget: $50-100,000
Secretary/Treasurer: Kathy Roush
E-Mail: tribeta@una.edu

Historical Note
TriBeta is an honorary, professional society of biology professionals and students of the biological sciences. TriBeta alumni number over 200,000 since 1922.

Meetings/Conferences:
Biennial Meetings: even years

Publications:
Bios Journal. q.

Beta Phi Mu *(1948)*
School of Information Studies
Florida State University
Tallahassee, FL 32306-2100
Tel: (850)644-3907 *Fax:* (850)644-9763
E-Mail: beta_phi_mu@lis.fsu.edu
Web Site: www.beta-phi-mu.org
Members: 27000 individuals
Staff: 1
ExecutiveDirector: Wayne Wiegand
E-Mail: beta_phi_mu@lis.fsu.edu

Historical Note
Professional honor society for library and information studies.

Meetings/Conferences:
Annual Meetings: Winter and Summer, usually with American Library Ass'n

Publications:
Newsletter. semi-a.

Better Hearing Institute *(1973)*
515 King St.
Suite 420
Alexandria, VA 22314
Tel: (703)684-3391 *Fax:* (703)684-6048
Toll Free: (800)327 - 9355
E-Mail: mail@betterhearing.org
Web Site: www.betterhearing.org
Staff: 2
Annual Budget: $500-1,000,000
Executive Director: Sergei Kochkin, Ph.D.
E-Mail: mail@betterhearing.org

Historical Note
A non-profit educational organization dedicated to informing professionals and the public about hearing loss and hearing aids.

Better Lawn and Turf Institute

Historical Note
See Lawn Institute.

Bibliographical Society of America *(1904)*
P.O. Box 1537
Lenox Hill Station
New York, NY 10021
Tel: (212)452-2710
E-Mail: bsa@bibsocamer.org
Web Site: www.bibsocamer.org
Members: 500 individuals
Staff: 1
Annual Budget: $100-250,000
Executive Secretary: Michele E. Randall
E-Mail: bsa@bibsocamer.org

Historical Note
Organized in Washington, D.C. as an outgrowth of the Bibliographical Society of Chicago. Incorporated in 1927. A member of the American Council of Learned Societies. Membership is open to all interested in bibliographical problems and projects. Membership: $65/year plus $15 surcharge for non U.S. members.

Meetings/Conferences:
Annual Meetings: New York City/Winter

Publications:
Papers of the Bibliographical Society of America. q. adv.

BICSI *(1974)*
8610 Hidden River Pkwy.
Tampa, FL 33637-1000
Tel: (813)979-1991 *Fax:* (813)971-4311
Toll Free: (800)242 - 7405
E-Mail: bicsi@bicsi.org
Web Site: www.bicsi.org
Members: 20000 individuals
Staff: 56
Annual Budget: $10-25,000,000
Executive Director: David C. Cranmer, RCDD

Historical Note
BICSI provides training and knowledge assessment to designers and installers of information transport systems, including designers and installers of telecommunications wiring. Sponsors numerous meetings and educational opportunities, both domestically and abroad.

Meetings/Conferences:
Annual Meetings: Winter

Publications:
BICSI News. 6/year. adv.

Bicycle Product Suppliers Association *(1940)*
P.O. Box 187
Montgomeryville, PA 18936
Tel: (215)393-3144 *Fax:* (215)893-4872
E-Mail: bpsa@bpsa.org
Web Site: www.bpsa.org
Members: 100 companies
Staff: 2
Annual Budget: $50-100,000
Executive Director: Maureen Waddington
E-Mail: bpsa@bpsa.org

Historical Note
Formerly (1960) Cycle Jobbers Association and (1997) Bicycle Wholesale Distributors Association. An association of suppliers and distributors who serve the independent bicycle dealer channel of trade.

Meetings/Conferences:
Annual Meetings: Winter

Bicycle Shippers Association *(1993)*
9237 Dove Ct.
Gilroy, CA 95020
Tel: (408)846-9592 *Fax:* (408)846-9213
E-Mail: bsa@earthlink.net
Web Site: www.bikesa.com
Staff: 2
Executive Director: Angie Munson

Historical Note
Monitors regulations on overseas shipping as they apply to the bicycle industry. Fees range from $20-80/year based on volume commitment to BSA.

Billiard and Bowling Institute of America *(1940)*

Historical Note
A component of the Sporting Goods Manufacturers Association.

Billiard Congress of America *(1948)*
4345 Beverly St.
Suite D
Colorado Springs, CO 80918-5916
Tel: (719)264-8300 *Fax:* (719)264-0900
E-Mail: membership@bca-pool.com
Web Site: www.bca-pool.com
Members: 1300 companies
Staff: 9
Annual Budget: $2-5,000,000
Executive Director: Rob Johnson
E-Mail: rob@bca-pool.com
Director, Trade Shows: Carolyn Lewis

Historical Note
BCA is the billiard industry trade organization and promotes and sanctions events and helps increase awareness of and participation in the sport of billiards, while working with all members to increase the overall growth of billiards. Membership:$150-1,000/year (company).

Meetings/Conferences:
Annual Meetings: Held in conjunction with the Billiard Congress of America International Trade Expo.
2007 – Las Vegas, NV(Sands Convention Center)/Apr. 12-14/6000
2008 – Charlotte, NC(Convention Center)/Apr. 24-26/6000

Publications:
Membership Directory. a. adv.
Expo Directory. a. adv.
Billiards: Official Rule and Record Book. a.
BCA Break. q.

Billings Ovulation Method Association of the United States *(1990)*
P.O. Box 2135
St. Cloud, MN 56302
Tel: (651)699-8139 *Fax:* (651)654-6486
E-Mail: boma-usa@msn.com
Web Site: www.boma-usa.org
Members: 390 individuals
Staff: 1
Executive Director: Sue Ek
E-Mail: boma-usa@msn.com

Historical Note
BOMA members are teachers of the Billings Ovulation Method and others with an interest in natural family planning. Membership: $50/year (organization); $35/year (associate); $25-50/year (teacher).

Meetings/Conferences:
Biennial Meetings:

Publications:
Science Notes Newletter. bi-m.
Victoria Bulletin. q.
BOMA Teachers Directory. a.
BOMA News. q.

Binding Industries Association *(1955)*
100 Daingerfield Rd.
Alexandria, VA 22314
Toll Free: (800)910 - 4283
E-Mail: bparrott@piagatf.org
Web Site: www.bindingindustries.org
Members: 100 companies
Staff: 1
Annual Budget: $250-500,000

Historical Note
A special industry group of Printing Industries of America. Formerly (1971) Trade Binders and Loose Leaf Division of PIA and (2002) Binding Industries of America. Members are trade binders and loose leaf manufacturers or suppliers. Membership: $545-970/year.

Meetings/Conferences:
Annual Meetings: March

Publications:
The Binding Edge. q. adv.

Binders Bulletin. bi-m.

BioCommunications Association *(1931)*
220 Southwind Lane
Hillsborough, NC 27278
Tel: (919)245-0906
E-Mail: bca@bca.org
Web Site: www.bca.org
Members: 300 individuals
Staff: 1
Annual Budget: $250-500,000
Manager, Central Office: Nancy Hurtgen

Historical Note
Formerly (1997) Biological Photographic Association. Membership: $100/year (individual).

Meetings/Conferences:
Annual Meetings: Summer/300

Publications:
Journal of Biocommunication. q.

Bioelectromagnetics Society *(1978)*
2412 Cobblestone Way
Frederick, MD 21702-2626
Tel: (301)663-4252 *Fax:* (301)694-4948
E-Mail: bemsoffice@aol.com
Web Site: www.bioelectromagnetics.com
Members: 850 individuals
Staff: 1
Annual Budget: $250-500,000
Executive Director: Gloria Parsley

Historical Note
A scientific society promoting research concerned with the interaction of electromagnetic energy with biological systems. Membership: $50/year (individual); $500/year (organization).

Meetings/Conferences:
Annual Meetings: June

Publications:
Bioelectromagnetics Journal. bi-m.
Bioelectromagnetics Newsletter. bi-m. adv.
Annual Meeting Abstract Book. a.

Biological Stain Commission *(1922)*
Univ. of Rochester Medical Center, Pathology Dept.
601 Elmwood Ave., Box 626
Rochester, NY 14642-0001
Tel: (585)275-2751 *Fax:* (585)442-8993
Web Site: www.biostains.org/
Members: 80 individuals
Staff: 4
Annual Budget: $100-250,000
Contact: Matthew Frank
E-Mail: mfrank@biostains.org

Historical Note
BSC seeks to standardize biological stains and promote their perfection and use. Originated as a special committee of the National Research Council and later became the Commission on Biological Stains. Incorporated in New York in 1943 as the Biological Stain Commission, Inc. Tests samples submitted by manufacturers and those approved are awarded the Certified Biological Stain distinction. Membership: $40/year (individual).

Meetings/Conferences:
Annual Meetings:

Publications:
Biotechnic & Histochemistry. bi-m. adv.

Biomedical Engineering Society *(1968)*
8401 Corporate Dr.
Suite 140
Landover, MD 20785-2224
Tel: (301)459-1999 *Fax:* (301)459-2444
E-Mail: info@bmes.org
Web Site: www.bmes.org
Members: 3700 individuals
Staff: 5
Annual Budget: $500-1,000,000
Executive Director: Barbara Dunlavey
E-Mail: barbara.dunlavey@bmes.org
Director, Marketing and Communications: Stephanie O. Darby

Historical Note
Incorporated February 1, 1968 in order to give equal representation to those interested in biomedical and engineering issues. Promotes biomedical engineering knowledge and its practical application. A member society of the American Institute for Medical and Biological Engineering. Membership: $175/year.

Meetings/Conferences:
Annual Meetings: Fall/1,300
2007 – Los Angeles, CA(Wilshire Grand)/2500

Publications:
Annals of Biomedical Engineering. m. adv.
BMES Bulletin. q. adv.
BMES Membership Directory. a. adv.

Biomedical Marketing Association
10293 N. Meridian St.
Suite 175
Indianapolis, IN 46290-1073
Tel: (317)816-1640 *Fax:* (317)816-1633
Toll Free: (800)278 - 7886
E-Mail: info@bmaonline.org
Web Site: www.bmaonline.org
Members: 300 individuals
Staff: 5
Annual Budget: $250-500,000
Executive Director: Michael F. Ward
E-Mail: info@bmaonline.org

Historical Note
Members are dignostic marketers in the biomedical field. Membership: $245/year (domestic); $295/year (international).

Meetings/Conferences:
Annual Meetings: Spring

Publications:
Membership Directory. a. adv.
Diagnostic Insight (online). q. adv.

Biophysical Society *(1957)*
9650 Rockville Pike
Bethesda, MD 20814-3998
Tel: (301)634-7114 *Fax:* (301)634-7133
E-Mail: society@biophysics.org
Web Site: www.biophysics.org
Members: 7400 individuals
Staff: 12
Annual Budget: $2-5,000,000
Executive Director: Rosalba Kampman
Convention and Exhibits Manager: Lauren Chelf
Publications Manager: Dianne McGavin
E-Mail: dmcgavin@biophysics.org
Membership Manager: Maxine McIntosh
Information Systems Administrator: Drita Tibbs

Historical Note
Founded in Columbus, Ohio in 1957. Members are individuals interested in applying physical laws and techniques to the investigation of biological phenomena. Membership: $150/year (individual).

Meetings/Conferences:
2007 – Baltimore, MD(Convention Center)/March 3-7
2008 – Long Beach, CA(Convention Center)/Feb. 2-6
2009 – Fort Lauderdale, FL(Convention Center)/March 7-11

Publications:
Newsletter. 6/year. adv.
Directory. a. adv.
Call for Papers. a. adv.
Biophysical Journal. m. adv.

Biotech Medical Management Association *(1993)*
10592 Perry Hwy., #300
Wexford, PA 15090
Tel: (724)934-8440 *Fax:* (866)706-8622
Toll Free: (888)990 - 2662
E-Mail: general@bmma.org
Web Site: www.bmma.org
Members: 1,500 individuals
Executive Director: Mark G. Fuller

Historical Note
Formerly U.S. Biotech Medical Management Association (1998). BMMA creates a forum for the open exchange of ideas and information between biotechnology-oncology manufacturers and the insurance payer community. Members include managed care professionals and other concerns that deal with biotechnology and oncology.

Publications:
BMMA Journal. 4/year. adv.
BMMA Newsletter.

Biotechnology Industry Organization *(1993)*
1225 Eye St. NW
Suite 400
Washington, DC 20005
Tel: (202)962-9200 *Fax:* (202)962-9201
E-Mail: info@bio.org
Web Site: www.bio.org
Members: 1150 companies
Staff: 80
Annual Budget: $25-50,000,000
President and Chief Executive Officer: James C. Greenwood
E-Mail: info@bio.org

Historical Note
Product of the merger of the Industrial Biotechnology Association and the Association of Biotechnology Companies in 1993. BIO represents biotechnology companies, academic institutions and state biotechnology centers in all 50 states and more than 33 countries. BIO members are involved in the research and development of health care, agricultural and environmental biotechnology products.

Meetings/Conferences:
Annual Meetings: April-May

Publications:
BIO News. bi-m.
BIO Milestone Report.
BIO Membership Directory.
BIO Bulletin. m.
Editors' and Reporters' Guide to BioTechnology. a.

Biscuit and Cracker Manufacturers' Association *(1901)*
8484 Georgia Ave.
Suite 700
Silver Spring, MD 20910-5604
Tel: (443)545-1645 *Fax:* (410)290-8585
Web Site: www.thebcma.org
Members: 350 companies
Staff: 5
Annual Budget: $500-1,000,000
President: Francis P. Rooney
Contact: Kathy Kinter

Historical Note
Established in Cincinnati in 1901, B&CMA promotes the cookie and cracker baking indutry. Absorbed the Biscuit Bakers Institute in 1965. Membership: annual dues vary, based on gross sales (bakers); $750/year (suppliers to bakers).

Meetings/Conferences:
Semi-Annual Meetings:: April Convention and October Technical Conference

Publications:
BCMA Bulletin. semi-m.
BCMA Membership Directory. a.

Bituminous and Aggregate Equipment Bureau *(1960)*

Historical Note
An affiliate of Association of Equipment Manufacturers, which provides administrative support.

Bituminous Coal Operators Association *(1950)*
1776 Eye St. NW
Washington, DC 20006
Tel: (202)783-3195 *Fax:* (202)783-4862
Members: 6 company groups
Staff: 4
Annual Budget: $2-5,000,000
President: David Young

Historical Note
BCOA was formed in 1950 to represent mine operators in negotiation of the National Bituminous Coal Wage Agreement, in order to avoid the chaotic situation resulting from separate company negotiations with the United Mine Workers of America. Dues are established by the Board of Directors, using tonnage produced as the basis.

BKR International *(1972)*
19 Fullton St.

Suite 306
New York, NY 10038
Tel: (212)964-2115 *Fax:* (212)964-2133
E-Mail: bkr@bkr.com
Web Site: www.bkr.com
Members: 107 companies
Staff: 5
Annual Budget: $500-1,000,000
Executive Director: Maureen M. Schwartz

Historical Note

Formerly known as the National Group of CPA Firms and (1989) The National CPA Group. BKR is an international affiliation of accounting firms in 140 cities in 66 countries around the world, formed to provide services to its member firms: professional development programs, exchange of management information, development of technical and promotional materials, interfirm peer reviews, availability of specialized knowledge, marketing brochures, comprehensive marketing programs for specialized services, newsletters on personal finance planning, year-end tax planners, office technology and benefits surveys. Membership: 0.8% of collections, minimum $1.2 million-maximum $2.2 million (company).

Meetings/Conferences:

Semi-annual Meetings: Spring and Fall/150

Publications:

Directory of Members. a.
Marketing Materials. q.
Newsletter. bi-m.
Directory of Specialists. bien.

Black Americans in Publishing *(1979)*
P.O. Box 6275
FDR Station
New York, NY 10150
Tel: (212)772-5951 *Fax:* (212)857-1145
E-Mail: baip@baip.org
Web Site: www.baip.org
Members: 250 individuals
Annual Budget: under $10,000
President: Lynette Velasco

Historical Note

Founded as Black Women in Publishing; assumed its current name in 2003. BAIP is a professional association of women and men of color who work in the print media including editors, writers, designers, photographers, publicists, financial analysts, production managers, personnel directors and freelancers.

Meetings/Conferences:

Annual Meetings: January

Publications:

BWIP Newsletter. m.
Interface. q.

Black Broadcasters Alliance *(1997)*
711 W. 40th St.
Suite 330
Baltimore, MD 21211
E-Mail: e-mail@thebba.org
Web Site: www.thebba.org
Staff: 2
Chairman: Eddie Edwards Sr.
E-Mail: e-mail@thebba.org

Historical Note

The BBA promotes equality and opportunities for African Americans and others employed in the broadcasting industry. Membership: $50/year (individual); $1,000/year (company); $25/year (student).

Publications:

The Communique. bi-a.

Black Caucus of the American Library Association *(1970)*
c/o Langston Hughes Community Library
100-01 Northern Blvd.
Corona, NY 11368
Tel: (718)651-1100 *Fax:* (718)651-6258
Web Site: www.bcala.org
Members: 1100 individuals
Staff: 1
Annual Budget: $50-100,000
President: Andrew P. Jackson

Historical Note

Organized in 1970 at the midwinter meeting of the American Library Association in Chicago, IL. Has no paid officers or full-time staff. Membership: $20/year.

Publications:

BCACA Newsletter. bi-m. adv.
Membership Directory. bien.

Black Coaches Association *(1987)*
201 S. Capitol
Suite 495
Indianapolis, IN 46225
Tel: (317)829-5600 *Fax:* (317)829-5601
Toll Free: (877)789 - 1222 Ext:
E-Mail: info@bcasports.org
Web Site: www.bcasports.org
Members: 3344 individuals
Staff: 4
Annual Budget: $1-2,000,000
Executive Director: Floyd Keith
Information Technology Consultant: Christopher L. Bradley
Director, Operations and Administration: Lauren I. Peterson
Director, Membership Services: Kennedy Wells
Director of Marketing and Events: Glenda K. Wilson

Historical Note

BCA members are African-American and other minority athletic coaches at the professional, high school, college, junior college, and secondary school levels. Membership fees vary.

Meetings/Conferences:

Annual Meetings: May
2007 – Indianapolis, IN(Hyatt Regency)/400
2007 – Miami, FL(Doral Golf Resort)/May 30-June 2/300
2008 – Atlanta, GA

Publications:

Newsletter. m.
BCA Journal. q. adv.

Black Culinarians Alliance

Historical Note

Became BCA in 2004.

Black Data Processing Associates *(1975)*
6301 Ivy Ln.
Suite 700
Greenbelt, MD 20770
Tel: (301)220-2180 *Fax:* (301)220-2185
Toll Free: (800)727 - 2372
E-Mail: info@bdpa.org
Web Site: www.bdpa.org
Members: 4000 individuals
Staff: 4
Annual Budget: $1-2,000,000
Executive Director: Vercilla A. Brown
E-Mail: info@bdpa.org
President: Wayne Hicks
E-Mail: info@bdpa.org

Historical Note

Dedicated to being the premier provider of Information Technology resources to the African American community. BDPA is a professional organization open to all persons without regard to race or sex in accordance with existing national and local chapter bylaws. Membership: $75/year (individual); $15/year (student).

Meetings/Conferences:

Annual Meetings: Summer

Publications:

Black IT Professional Magazines. semi-a. adv.
Quarterly Chapter Publications. q. adv.
Nat'l Journal. q. adv.

Black Entertainment and Sports Lawyers Association *(1979)*
P.O. Box 441485
Ft. Washington, MD 20749-1485
Tel: (301)248-1818 *Fax:* (301)248-0700
Toll Free: (866)273 - 4935
E-Mail: beslamailbox@aol.com
Web Site: www.besla.org
Members: 600 individuals
Staff: 1
Annual Budget: $50-100,000
Executive Administrator: Rev. Phyllicia M. Hatton
E-Mail: beslamailbox@aol.com

Historical Note

Founded by a group of prestigious black lawyers to encourage attorneys to develop an expertise in the fields of entertainment and sports law and related areas of specialization and to nurture and enhance individuals' aptitudes in these fields. BESLA members represent leading celebrities and professionals in entertainment and sports industries. Membership: $130/year (general); $105/year (associate); $40/year (law students).

Meetings/Conferences:

Annual Meetings: October

Publications:

BESLA Bulletin (e-news). q.

Black Filmmaker Foundation *(1978)*
11 W. 42nd St., Ninth Floor
New York, NY 10036
Tel: (212)253-1690 *Fax:* (212)253-1689
Web Site: www.dvrepublic.org
Members: 2000 individuals
Staff: 4
Annual Budget: $250-500,000
President: Warrington Hudlin
E-Mail: hudlin@dvrepublic.org

Historical Note

Established in 1978, The Black Filmaker Foundation develops and administers programs that assist emerging filmakers and builds audiences for their work. Hosts the BFF DUCAB, and an online discussion forum accessible through its web site dedicated to public discussion of contemporary media.

Publications:

DV Republic newsletter (online). w.

Black Psychiatrists of America *(1969)*
866 Carlston Ave.
Oakland, CA 94610
Tel: (510)834-7103 *Fax:* (415)695-9830
E-Mail: wlawsonpsy@aol.com
Members: 650 individuals
Annual Budget: $25-50,000
President: Ramona Davis, M.D.
E-Mail: wlawsonpsy@aol.com

Historical Note

Organized in Miami, Florida and incorporated in New York, BPA membership includes black psychiatrists in the United States, Canada, and the Caribbean. BPA is a non-profit, professional organization promoting excellence within the field with particular emphasis on the concerns of ethnic minority groups and the economically depressed. Has no paid staff. Membership: $150/year (individual).

Meetings/Conferences:

Semi-annual Meetings: Odd years with APA/May, even years with NMA/Aug.

Publications:

BPA Annals. a. adv.
BPA Newsletter. q. adv.

Black Retail Action Group *(1970)*
P.O. Box 1192
Rockefeller Center Station
New York, NY 10085
Tel: (212)319-7751 *Fax:* (212)997-5102
E-Mail: info@bragusa.org
Web Site: www.bragusa.org
Members: 300 individuals
Annual Budget: $50-100,000
Vice President, Operations: J.J. Thomas
E-Mail: info@bragusa.org

Historical Note

Founded by members of the former National Negro Retail Advisory Group, BRAG promotes the participation of Blacks and other minorities in retailing, especially in managerial and executive positions, and provides professional development, networking, and educational opportunities. Membership: $50/year (individual); $25/year (student).

Meetings/Conferences:

Annual Meetings: Fall, always New York City.

Publications:

BRAG About Progress. semi-a.
BRAG Journal. a. adv.

Black Theatre Association

Historical Note

A focus group of the Association for Theatre in Higher Education.

Black Theatre Network *(1986)*
4748A Michigan Ave.
St. Louis, MO 63111
Tel: (314)352-1123
E-Mail: btnoffice@sbcglobal.net
Web Site: www.blacktheatrenetwork.org
Members: 500theatercompanies/subscribers
Annual Budget: $10-25,000
Office Manager: Eddie Webb

Historical Note

BTN is dedicated to increasing awareness, appreciation, and production of Black Theatre in the African Diaspora. Network members are theatre professionals and academics. Membership: $75/year (individual); $35/year (retired/student); $110/year (institution).

Publications:
Black Theatre Network News/BTNews. q. adv.

Black Tie Bureau

Historical Note

A division of Internat'l Formalwear Ass'n which proivides administrative support.

Blue Cross and Blue Shield Association *(1946)*
225 N. Michigan Ave.
Chicago, IL 60601
Tel: (312)297-6000 *Fax:* (312)297-6609
Web Site: www.bluecares.com
Members: 55 companies
Staff: 700
Annual Budget: Over $100,000,000
President and Chief Executive Officer: Scott P. Serota
Senior Vice President, Human Resources and Administrative Services: William J. Colbourne
Vice President, Federal Relations: Jack Ericksen
Senior Vice President, Office of Policy and Representation: Mary Nell Lenhard
Senior Vice President, General Counsel and Corporate Secretary: Roger G. Wilson

Historical Note

Formerly Blue Cross Association and National Association of Blue Shield Plans; merged in 1978 to become the Blue Cross and Blue Shield Association. Members must be medical and/or hospital plans and operate according to established standards. Offers information, consulting, representation and operation services to members. Member plans represent over 68.1 million health care consumers. Has an annual budget of approximately $131 million.

Meetings/Conferences:
Annual Meetings: November

Publications:
Inquiry. q.

BMC - A Foodservice Sales and Marketing Council *(1980)*
P.O. Box 150229
Arlington, TX 76015
Tel: (682)518-6008 *Fax:* (682)518-6476
E-Mail: assnhqtrs@aol.com
Web Site: www.bmcsales.com
Members: 22 food marketing companies
Staff: 2
Annual Budget: $50-100,000
Executive Director: Pamela L. Bess

Historical Note

Founded as Broker Management Council; assumed its current name in 2003. BMC members are independent institutional food service brokers who specialize in institutional deli, bakery, school, hotel and restaurant food service products.

Board of Certified Safety Professionals *(1969)*
208 Burwash Ave.
Savoy, IL 61874-9510
Tel: (217)359-9263 *Fax:* (217)359-0055
E-Mail: bcsp@bcsp.org
Web Site: www.bcsp.org
Members: 11,000 individuals
Staff: 15
Annual Budget: $1-2,000,000
Executive Director: Roger L. Brauer, Ph.D., CSP, CPE
E-Mail: roger@bcsp.org
Director, Finance and Human Resources: Dennis Archer
Manager, Communications and Marketing: Heather Murphy
E-Mail: heather@bcsp.org
Manager, Business Systems: Bharat Philiph-Patel
Examination Director: Steven Schoolcraft

Historical Note

Members are all certificate holders; all these certificate holders are safety professionals. BCSP provides standards for the industry and conducts certification examinations.

Publications:
BCSP Newsletter. semi-a.

Board of Trade of the Wholesale Seafood Merchants *(1933)*
Seven Dey St.
Suite 805
New York, NY 10007
Tel: (212)732-4340 *Fax:* (212)732-6644
Members: 400 individuals
Staff: 2
Annual Budget: $25-50,000
Executive Secretary: Albert Altesman

Historical Note

The credit exchange for U.S. and Canadian wholesale seafood merchants.

Meetings/Conferences:
Annual Meetings: New York, NY

Boating Writers International *(1970)*
108 Ninth St.
Wilmette, IL 60091
Tel: (847)736-4142
E-Mail: info@bwi.org
Web Site: www.bwi.org
Members: 350 individuals, 100 supporting corporations
Staff: 1
Annual Budget: $25-50,000
Executive Director: Gregory Proteau

Historical Note

Individuals who write about boating and allied outdoor sports for magazines, newspapers, television and radio. Reports on legislation affecting boating and seeks to encourage boating as a recreational and competitive sport. Membership: $30/year (active); $40/year (associate); $150/year (supporting).

Meetings/Conferences:
Two Meetings Annually: Usually February in Miami, FL and
October in Fort Lauderdale, FL

Publications:
Boating Writers Journal. m.

Body and Hoist Manufacturers Committee

Historical Note

An affiliate of the National Truck Equipment Council.

Bond Market Association *(1977)*

Historical Note

Merged with the Securities Industry Association in 2006 to form the Securities Industry and Financial Markets Association (SIFMA).

Book Industry Study Group, Inc. *(1976)*
19 W. 21st St.
Suite 905
New York, NY 10010
Tel: (646)336-7141 *Fax:* (646)336-6214
E-Mail: info@bisg.org
Web Site: www.bisg.org/
Members: 200individualsandorganizations
Staff: 3
Annual Budget: $100-250,000
Executive Director: Michael Healy

Historical Note

Members are publishers, manufacturers, suppliers, wholesalers, retailers, librarians and others engaged professionally in the development, production and dissemination of books and journals. Purpose is to sponsor and encourage research within and about the publishing industry, to increase readership, improve distribution of books of all kinds, and expand the market for books.

Meetings/Conferences:
Annual Meetings: September, in New York, NY

Publications:
Used-Book Sales. irreg.
BISG Bulletin. m.
Book Industry Trends. a.
Under the Radar. irreg.

Book Manufacturers' Institute *(1920)*
Two Armand Beach Dr.
Suite 1-B
Palm Coast, FL 32137-2612
Tel: (386)986-4552 *Fax:* (386)986-4553
Web Site: www.bmibook.org
Members: 100 companies
Staff: 3
Annual Budget: $250-500,000
Executive Vice President: Bruce W. Smith

Historical Note

Established as the Employing Bookbinders of America; assumed its present name in 1933. Membership fee varies, based on sales volume.

Meetings/Conferences:
Annual Meetings: Fall/250

Publications:
Directory. a.

Botanical Society of America *(1906)*
4474 Castleman Ave.
P.O. Box 299
St. Louis, MO 63166
Tel: (314)577-9566 *Fax:* (314)577-9515
E-Mail: bsa-manager@botany.org
Web Site: www.botany.org
Members: 2800 individuals
Staff: 2
Annual Budget: $250-500,000
Executive Director: William Dahl
Administrative Assistant: Wanda Lovan

Historical Note

The American Botanical Club was organized in 1883 as a segment of the American Association for the Advancement of Science. In 1894, 25 members of this group constituted themselves the Botanical Society of America. This merged in 1906 with the Society for Plant Morphology and Physiology (formed in 1896) and the American Mycological Society (formed in 1903). The present Society was formed in a meeting in New York City, and later incorporated in Connecticut (1939). An affiliate of the American Association for the Advancement of Science and an adherent society of the American Institute of Biological Sciences. Goals are to promote research and teaching, cooperation among scientists and to disseminate knowledge of plants for application to practical problems. Membership: $80/year.

Meetings/Conferences:
Annual Meetings: August

Publications:
Botany For The Next Millennium. a.
Careers In Botany. a.
American Journal of Botany. m. adv.
Plant Science Bulletin. q.
Directory and Handbook. a.
Abstracts. a.

Bowling Inc.

Historical Note

Became United States Bowling Congress in 2005.

Bowling Proprietors Association of America *(1932)*
P.O. Box 5802
Arlington, TX 76005-5802
Tel: (817)649-5105 *Fax:* (817)633-2940
Toll Free: (800)343 - 1329
Web Site: www.bpaa.com
Members: 3300 individuals
Staff: 20
Annual Budget: $2-5,000,000
Director, Meetings: Leanne Norton
E-Mail: bpaainc@aol.com

Historical Note

Supports the Bowling Proprietors' Association of America Political Action Committee. Mission is to enhance the profitability of its members in a growing, prosperous and united bowling industry.

Meetings/Conferences:
Annual Meetings: Summer
Publications:
Marketing Trends. m.
BPAA Access. q.
Bowling Center Management. m. adv.
Capital Comment. q.

Bowling Writers Association of America *(1934)*
8501 Manor Lane
Fox Point, WI 53217
Tel: (414)351-6085
E-Mail: sjames2652@wi.rr.com
Web Site: www.bowlingwriters.com
Members: 280 individuals
Staff: 1
Annual Budget: $10-25,000
Executive Director: Steve James
Historical Note
Formerly (1931) National Bowling Writers' Association. Membership: $20/year (full member); $30/year (associate).
Meetings/Conferences:
Annual Meetings: With American Bowling Congress tournament
2007 – Las Vegas, NV/June 24-29/100
Publications:
BWAA Update. semi-a.

BPA Worldwide *(1931)*
Two Corporate Dr., Ninth Floor
Shelton, CT 06484
Tel: (203)447-2800 *Fax:* (203)447-2900
E-Mail: info@bpaww.com
Web Site: www.bpaww.com
Members: 5500publicationsandcompanies
Staff: 130
Annual Budget: $10-25,000,000
President and Chief Executive Officer: Glenn Hansen
E-Mail: info@bpaww.com
Senior Vice President, Communications: Peter D. Black
Senior Vice President, Finance and Administration: Doreen Castignoli
Manager, Information Technology: Jim McGuire
Historical Note
Formerly Controlled Circulations Audit and then (1931) Business Publications Audit of Circulation, before assuming its current name. BPAA Worldwide is a provider of circulation marketing intelligence for business publications, consumer magazines, e-newsletters, e-products and e-events, other events, newspapers, and web sites. Through annual audits, BPA Worldwide verifies circulation claims for roughly 2,500 publications and provides the information to advertiser companies and advertising agencies. Serves members in more than 25 countries. Has an annual budget of approximately $16 million.
Publications:
Consumer TRAC.
Business TRAC.

Brake Manufacturers Council *(1973)*
P.O. Box 13966
Research Triangle Park, NC 27709-3966
Tel: (919)406-8841 *Fax:* (919)406-1306
E-Mail: bmc@mema.org
Web Site: www.brakecouncil.org
Members: 29 companies
Staff: 2
Annual Budget: $50-100,000
Executive Director: Brent Hazelett
Historical Note
Formerly (1994) Brake System Parts Manufacturers Council. Formed by a group of companies making brake systems parts to expand the market for their products and to conduct friction material testing. A product line group of Motor and Equipment Manufacturers Association, which provides administrative support
Meetings/Conferences:
Annual Meetings: Spring, Fall and Winter

Brass and Bronze Ingot Industry *(2000)*
200 S. Michigan Ave.
Suite 1100
Chicago, IL 60604-2480
Tel: (312)372-4000 *Fax:* (312)939-5617
Members: 11 companies
Staff: 1
Annual Budget: $10-25,000
Attorney: P. Bowman
Historical Note
Formerly the Brass and Bronze Ingot Manufacturers.
Publications:
Resource Directory. adv.
Annual Survey. a.

Braunvieh Association of America *(1984)*
3815 Touzalin Ave.
Suite 103
Lincoln, NE 68507
Tel: (402)466-3292 *Fax:* (402)466-3293
E-Mail: braunaa@attglobal.net
Web Site: www.braunvieh.org
Members: 350 individuals
Staff: 2
Annual Budget: $250-500,000
Office Manager: Stephanie Nelson
Meetings/Conferences:
Annual Meetings: Winter/150
Publications:
Braunvieh World. q. adv.

Brazilian American Chamber of Commerce *(1968)*
509 Madison Ave.
Suite 304
New York, NY 10022-5501
Tel: (212)751-4691 *Fax:* (212)751-7692
Web Site: www.brazilcham.com
Members: 400 organizations
Staff: 5
Annual Budget: $500-1,000,000
Executive Director: Sueli Bonaparte
E-Mail: sueli@brazilcham.com
Historical Note
Founded as the Brazilian-American Association, it incorporated and assumed its present name in 1968. Members are Brazilian and U.S. business persons concerned with promoting trade and investment between the business communities of both nations. Membership: $400/year (individual); $850/year (corporate); $1,650/year (contributing); $5,000/year (sponsor); $10,000/year (patron).
Meetings/Conferences:
Annual Meetings: Semi-annual/250
Publications:
Brazilian American Business Review/Directory. a. adv.
News Bulletin. m. adv.

Brazilian Studies Association *(1994)*
V U Station B 350031
Vanderbilt University
Nashville, TN 37235-0031
Tel: (615)342-1764 *Fax:* (615)343-6002
E-Mail: brasa@vanderbilt.edu
Web Site: www.brasa.org
Members: 700 individuals
Staff: 3
Annual Budget: $10-25,000
Executive Director: Marshall C. Eakin, Ph.D.
E-Mail: brasa@vanderbilt.edu
Historical Note
BRASA members are academics and others with an interest in the study of Brazil. Membership: $70/year (institution); $40/year (faculty); $20/year (academic); $15/year (student).
Publications:
Proceedings. semi-a. adv.
BRASAnotes. semi-a. adv.

Brewers Association *(1983)*
736 Pearl St.
Boulder, CO 80302
Tel: (303)447-0816 *Fax:* (303)447-2825
Toll Free: (888)822 - 6273
E-Mail: ibs@aob.org
Web Site: www.beertown.org
Members: 1350 individuals
Staff: 4
Director: Paul Gatza
Historical Note
Formerly (1988) Institute for Fermentation and Brewing Studies and (2004) Institute for Brewing Studies. Members are professional brewers at micro, regional, large and pub breweries, suppliers to the industry, and other interested individuals. Publishes information on brewing techniques and brewery operations. Membership: $145/year (minimum, based on affiliation to industry), $225/year (company/organization, minimum).
Meetings/Conferences:
Annual Meetings: Spring
Publications:
Brewers Resource Directory. bien. adv.
New Brewer. bi-m. adv.
Brewery Planner.

Brewers' Association of America *(1941)*
736 Pearl St.
Boulder, CO 80302
Tel: (303)447-0816 *Fax:* (303)447-2825
Web Site: www.brewersadvocate.org
Members: 270 Breweries
Staff: 2
Annual Budget: $100-250,000
President: Charles Papazian
Historical Note
Founded as the Small Brewers Association, it assumed its present name on September 11, 1952. Members are breweries and suppliers to the industry. Focus is on sales marketing and issues affecting the industry.
Meetings/Conferences:
Annual Meetings: Spring and Fall
Publications:
Special Studies.
Bulletin. q.
Legal Newsletter. m.

Brick Industry Association *(1934)*
1850 Centennial Park Dr.
Suite 301
Reston, VA 20191-1542
Tel: (703)620-0010 *Fax:* (703)620-3928
E-Mail: brickinfo@bia.org
Web Site: www.gobrick.com
Members: 200 companies
Staff: 16
Annual Budget: $2-5,000,000
President and Chief Executive Officer: Richard Jennison
Historical Note
Founded as Structural Clay Products Institute and became Brick Institute of America in 1972; merged with National Association of Brick Distributors and assumed its current name in 1998.
Meetings/Conferences:
Annual Meetings: Spring
2007 – Orlando, FL(Gaylord Palms)/March 29-31/700
Publications:
Brick News (online). bi-m. adv.
Brick in Architecture. q.
Technical Notes (online).

Bridge Grid Flooring Manufacturers Association *(1985)*
201 Castle Dr.
West Mifflin, PA 15122
Tel: (412)469-3985
E-Mail: bgfma@aol.com
Members: 3 companies
Staff: 1
Annual Budget: $100-250,000
Executive Director: Ed Flanagan
E-Mail: bgfma@aol.com
Historical Note
BGFMA serves to educate and inform bridge owners and engineers regarding the use of bridge grid flooring systems, including open steel grid, grid reinforced concrete, and exodermic bridge decks.
Meetings/Conferences:
Semi-annual Meetings.
Publications:
Gridline. q.
Bridge Grid Flooring Systems.

Bright Belt Warehouse Association *(1945)*
P.O. Box 12004

Raleigh, NC 27605
Tel: (919)828-8988
E-Mail: fctcc-bbwa@mindspring.com
Members: 180 warehouses
Staff: 2
Annual Budget: $50-100,000
Managing Director: Terry Campbell

Historical Note
Represents the flue-cured tobacco warehouse industry.

Meetings/Conferences:
Annual Meetings: June

BritishAmerican Business Inc. *(1920)*
52 Vanderbilt Ave., 20th Floor
New York, NY 10017-3808
Tel: (212)661-4060 *Fax:* (212)661-4074
Web Site: www.babinc.org
Members: 4500 individuals
Staff: 9
Annual Budget: $500-1,000,000
Chief Executive Officer: Richard Fursland
Director, Membership and Communications: Maria Allen
Director, Special Events: Wendy Mendenhall

Historical Note
Founded as British-American Chamber of Commerce, BABi is a business organization that encourages trade and investments, and cultivates reciprocal interest in, and comity between the United States and the United Kingdom. Provides promotional opportunities, business contacts and information services to its member companies. Membership: $995/year (corporate); $495/year (associate).

Meetings/Conferences:
Annual Meetings: September

Publications:
BABi Handbook. a.
Network New York London. q. adv.
UK&USA Magazine. q. adv.
Membership Directory. a.

Broadcast Cable Credit Association *(1972)*
550 W. Frontage Rd.
Suite 3600
Northfield, IL 60093
Tel: (847)881-8757 *Fax:* (847)784-8059
E-Mail: info@bccacredit.com
Web Site: www.bccacredit.com
Members: 450 stations
Staff: 8
Annual Budget: $1-2,000,000
President/Chief Executive Officer: Mary Collins

Historical Note
A subsidiary of the Broadcast Cable Financial Management Association, Inc. Formerly known as BCA-Credit Information from 1976 to 1985. Became the Broadcast Credit Association in 1985 and assumed its present name in 1990.

Meetings/Conferences:
Annual Meetings:
2007 – Las Vegas, NV(Rio Suites)/May 22-24

Publications:
The Financial Manager/Credit Topics. bi-m. adv.
Credit and Collection Survey. bien.

Broadcast Cable Financial Management Association *(1961)*
550 W. Frontage Rd.
Suite 3600
Northfield, IL 60093
Tel: (847)716-7000 *Fax:* (847)716-7004
E-Mail: info@bcfm.com
Web Site: www.bcfm.com
Members: 1280 individuals
Staff: 5
Annual Budget: $1-2,000,000
President and Chief Executive Officer: Mary Collins

Historical Note
Formerly the Institute of Broadcasting Financial Management. Became the Broadcast Financial Management Association in 1977; assumed its present name in 1990. Membership fee varies, base $365/year (individual).

Meetings/Conferences:
Annual Meetings: May/800-1,200
2007 – Las Vegas, NV(Rio Suites Hotel)/May 22-24

Publications:
Monthly Update. m.
Membership Directory. a. adv.
The Financial Manager. bi-m. adv.

Broadcast Designers' Association *(1978)*
9000 W. Sunset Blvd.
Suite 900
Los Angeles, CA 90069
Tel: (310)789-1505 *Fax:* (310)788-7616
Web Site: www.bda.tv
Members: 3800 companies and individuals
Staff: 26
Annual Budget: $5-10,000,000
President and Chief Executive Officer: Jim Chabin
E-Mail: jim@promax.tv

Historical Note
BDA members are designers, artists, illustrators and others involved in design for electronic media and screen design. BDA fosters the exchange of ideas, information and experience, while serving as a resource for young talent interested in the televison communications arts/design field. Membership: $255/year (professional); $405/year (company); $575/year (corporate); $2,600/year (corporate patron).

Meetings/Conferences:
Annual Meetings: June
2007 – New York, NY(Hilton)/June 12-14

Publications:
BDA Awards Annual. a.
BDA online. bi-w. adv.
DNA Magazine. a. adv.
BDA Directory. a. adv.

Broadcast Education Association *(1955)*
1771 N St. NW
Washington, DC 20036
Tel: (202)429-3935 *Fax:* (202)775-2981
E-Mail: beainfo@beaweb.org
Web Site: www.beaweb.org
Members: 1520 individuals
Staff: 3
Annual Budget: $250-500,000
Executive Director: Heather Birks
Office Manager: Traci Bailey

Historical Note
Formerly (1973) Association for Professional Broadcasting Education. Institutional members are colleges and universities with degree-granting programs in radio and television, film, multi-media telecommunications, and communications. Individual members are professors and college students.

Meetings/Conferences:
Annual Meetings: Spring, with Nat'l Ass'n of Broadcasters
2007 – Las Vegas, NV(Convention Center)/Apr. 18-21/1800

Publications:
Journal of Radio Studies. semi-a. adv.
Feedback. 6/year. adv.
Journal of Broadcasting & Electronic Media. q. adv.

Broadcast Technology Society

Historical Note
A technical society of the Institute of Electrical and Electronics Engineers (IEEE).

Broker Management Council

Historical Note
Became BMC - A Foodservice Sales and Marketing Council in 2003.

Brominated Solvents Committee *(1999)*

Historical Note
Organization defunct in 2006.

Brotherhood of Locomotive Engineers and Trainmen *(1863)*
1370 Ontario St.
Cleveland, OH 44113-1702
Tel: (216)241-2630 *Fax:* (216)241-6516
E-Mail: execstaff@ble-t.org
Web Site: www.ble-t.org
Members: 56000 individuals
Staff: 40
Annual Budget: $10-25,000,000
President: Don M. Hahs
First Vice President: Edward Rodzwicz
National Secretary-Treasurer: William C. Walpert

Historical Note
Established in Detroit May 8, 1863 as Division Number One, Brotherhood of the Footboard, the nation's senior labor union. After 1864 became the Grand International Division of the Brotherhood of Locomotive Engineers. Later the BLE was affiliated with the AFL-CIO and Canadian Labor Congress. Absorbed by the International Brotherhood of Teamsters in 2004, becoming a division of the Rail Conference of the IBT and assuming its current name at the same time. Sponsors and supports the Brotherhood of Locomotive Engineers Political Action Committee.

Meetings/Conferences:
Quinquennial Meetings: (2006)

Publications:
Locomotive Engineer and Trainman Newsletter. m.
Locomotive Engineers and Trainmen Journal. q.

Brotherhood of Maintenance of Way Employees *(1887)*
20300 Civic Center Dr.
Suite 320
Southfield, MI 48076-4169
Tel: (248)948-1010 *Fax:* (248)948-7150
Web Site: www.bmwe.org/
Members: 55000 individuals
Staff: 50
Annual Budget: $5-10,000,000
President: Freddie N. Simpson
Secretary-Treasurer: Perry Geller

Historical Note
Now a Division of the Rail Conference of the International Brotherhood of Teamsters, this organization was originally established in July 1887 in Alabama as the Order of Railroad Trackmen. On October 13, 1891 the Brotherhood of Railway Section Foremen of North America, founded in La Porte City, Iowa, merged with the Order of Railroad Trackmen to become the International Brotherhood of Railway Track Foremen of America. Became the Brotherhood of Railway Trackmen in 1896 and absorbed the United Brotherhood of Railroad Trackmen (Canadian) in 1900, affiliating with the American Federation of Labor the same year. Became the United Brotherhood of Maintenance of Way Employees and Railway Shop Laborers in 1918 and then the Brotherhood of Maintenance of Way Employees 1925. Merged with the Brotherhood of Teamsters in 2005. Has a budget of about $8 million.

Meetings/Conferences:
Quadriennial Meetings: July 2006

Publications:
BMWE Journal. m.

Brotherhood of Railroad Signalmen *(1901)*
917 Shenandoah Shores Road
Front Royal, VA 22630-6418
Tel: (540)622-6522 *Fax:* (540)622-6532
E-Mail: signalman@brs.org
Web Site: www.brs.org
Members: 11000 individuals
Staff: 20
Annual Budget: $1-2,000,000
President: W.D. Pickett
E-Mail: signalman@brs.org

Historical Note
Organized in the signal tower of the Altoona, Pennsylvania railroad yard in 1901 and chartered by the American Federation of Labor in 1914. Sponsors and supports the Brotherhood of Railroad Signalmen Political Action Committee.

Meetings/Conferences:
Triennial Meetings: Summer 2004

Publications:
The Signalmen's Journal. q. adv.

Brotherhood Railway Carmen/TCU *(1890)*
Three Research Place

Rockville, MD 20850-3279
Tel: (301)948-4910 *Fax:* (301)948-1369
Web Site: http://members.aol.com/tcucarmen
Members: 20000 individuals
Staff: 6
President: Richard A. Johnson

Historical Note
The result of a merger on September 9, 1890 of the Brotherhood of Car Repairers of North America (founded in Cedar Rapids October 27, 1888) and the Carmen's Mutual Aid Association (founded in Minneapolis on November 23, 1888). Merged with the Car Inspectors, Repairers and Oilers Mutual Benefit Association in 1891 and with the Brotherhood of Railway Carmen of Canada the next year. Affiliated with the American Federation of Labor in 1910. Merged with Transportation Communications International Union in 1986. Membership: $318/year (individual).

Meetings/Conferences:
Quniquennial Meetings: (2009)

Publications:
TCU Interchange. m.

Brown Swiss Cattle Breeders Association of the U.S.A. *(1880)*

800 Pleasant St.
Beloit, WI 53511-5496
Tel: (608)365-4474 *Fax:* (608)365-5577
E-Mail: info@brownswissusa.com
Web Site: www.brownswissusa.com
Members: 907 individuals
Staff: 10
Annual Budget: $500-1,000,000
Executive Secretary: David J. Kendall

Historical Note
Members are breeders and fanciers of Brown Swiss dairy cattle. Member of the National Society of Livestock Record Associations. Membership: $20/one year, $80/five years (individual).

Meetings/Conferences:
Annual Meetings: Summer

Publications:
Sire Summary. 4/year.
Brown Swiss Bulletin. m. adv.

Budget Furniture Forum

Historical Note
A forum of the National Office Products Association.

Builders Hardware Manufacturers Association *(1925)*

355 Lexington Ave., 17th Floor
New York, NY 10017-6603
Tel: (212)297-2122 *Fax:* (212)370-9047
Web Site: www.buildershardware.com
Members: 80 companies
Staff: 5
Annual Budget: $250-500,000
Executive Director: Peter S. Rush

Historical Note
Formerly (1961) Hardware Manufacturers Statistical Association.

Meetings/Conferences:
Semi-Annual Meetings: Spring/Fall

Publications:
Directory of Certified Locks & Latches. a.
Directory of Certified Door Closers. a.
Directory of Certified Exit Devices. a.
Directory of Certified Electromagnetic & Delayed Egress Locks. a.
ANSI/BHMA Standards.
Membership Directory. a.

Building Commissioning Association

1400 S.W. Fifth Ave., #700
Portland, OR 97201
Tel: (503)595-4446 *Fax:* (503)295-0820
Toll Free: (877)666 - 2292
E-Mail: info@bcxa.org
Web Site: www.bcxa.org
Members: 570
Staff: 2
Contact: Amy Pallari

Historical Note
BCA members are architects, planners, engineers, advocates, and other professionals involved in commissioned building. BCA provides standards of practice, peer review, and other services to enhance the building commissioning process. Membership fee varies according to type.

Building Environment and Thermal Envelope Council

Historical Note
An affiliated council of National Institute of Building Sciences, which provides administrative support.

Building Material Dealers Association *(1915)*

12550 S.W. Main St.
Suite 200
Tigard, OR 97223-6112
Tel: (503)624-0561 *Fax:* (503)620-1016
Toll Free: (800)666 - 2632
E-Mail: bmda@bmda.com
Web Site: www.bmda.com
Members: 1200 individuals
Staff: 20
Executive Director: Marie Escamilla
E-Mail: bmda@bmda.com

Historical Note
Members are companies that retail building materials. Membership fee varies.

Publications:
Oregon & Washington Law Manuals. bien.

Building Owners and Managers Association International *(1907)*

1201 New York Ave. NW
Suite 300
Washington, DC 20005
Tel: (202)408-2662 *Fax:* (202)326-6377
E-Mail: webmaster@boma.org
Web Site: www.boma.org
Members: 19000 individuals and companies
Staff: 34
Annual Budget: $5-10,000,000
President and Chief Operating Officer: Henry Chamberlain, CAE
Senior Vice President: Patricia M. Areno, CAE
Communications, Marketing, and Meetings: Lisa M. Prats, CAE

Historical Note
Formerly (1968) National Association of Building Owners and Managers. International membership, including building owners, developers, managers, service companies, investors, brokers, and third-party management firms. Members include over 100 federated associations in North America and around the world. The Building Owners and Managers Institute International, an associated educational institute, provides educational programming (see separate listing). Has an annual budget of approximately $7 million. Membership fee varies.

Meetings/Conferences:
Annual Meetings: June/July
2007 - New York, NY(Javitz Center)/July 21-24/5000

Publications:
BOMA e-News. m. adv.
Convention Directory. a. adv.
Experience Exchange Report. a.
Currents. m. adv.
The BOMA magazine. m. adv.

Building Owners and Managers Institute International *(1970)*

1521 Ritchie Hwy.
Arnold, MD 21012
Tel: (410)974-1410 *Fax:* (410)974-1935
E-Mail: service@bomi-edu.org
Web Site: www.bomi-edu.org
Members: 30000 individuals
Staff: 55
Annual Budget: $2-5,000,000
President: Dan Baum
E-Mail: dbaum@bomi-edu.org
Interim Chief Operating Officer/Chief Financial Officer/Vice President, Finance and Administration: Sherry Hewitt

Historical Note
BOMI provides course materials and professional certification for building managers (RPA - Real Property Administrator), building engineers (SMA - Systems Maintenance Administrator), and corporate facilities managers (FMA - Facilities Management Administrator). BOMI serves developers, fee managers, multinational corporations and governments in 8 countries.

Meetings/Conferences:
Annual Meetings: June, with Building Owners and Managers Ass'n Internat'l

Publications:
BOMI Institute Update. semi-a.
Institute Educator. bi-m.
SPP Journal. semi-a.

Building Seismic Safety Council

Historical Note
An affiliated council of National Institute of Building Sciences, which provides administrative support.

Building Service Contractors Association International *(1965)*

10201 Lee Hwy.
Suite 225
Fairfax, VA 22030
Tel: (703)359-7090 *Fax:* (703)352-0493
Toll Free: (800)368 - 3414
Web Site: www.bscai.org
Members: 2000 companies
Staff: 13
Annual Budget: $2-5,000,000
Executive Vice President: Carol A. Dean
Director, Communications: Denise Anderson
Director, Meetings: Karen Bilak, CMP
Vice President, Administration/Finance: Gail R. McCauley
E-Mail: gmccauley@bscai.org
Director, Exhibitions/Sales/Marketing: Elizabeth Price
E-Mail: kbilak@bscai.org
Director, Advertising: Barbara Woodward
E-Mail: bwoodward@bscai.org

Historical Note
Formerly (1974) National Association of Building Service Contractors. Members are companies offering cleaning, maintenance, security and janitorial services, and their suppliers. Awards the designations CBSE (Certified Building Service Executive), RBSM (Registered Building Service Manager), and CSSP (Certified Sanitary Supply Professional). Membership: $145-5500/year (based on annual gross service sales of prior business year.)

Meetings/Conferences:
Annual Meetings: Spring
2007 - Chicago, IL(McCormick Place Hyatt)/Apr. 13-17/1000

Publications:
Member Resource Book. a.
Compensation & Benefits Survey. bi-a.
Financial & Operating Ratios Survey. bi-a.
SERVICES magazine. m. adv.
Member Resource Department Catalog. a.

Building Service Managers Institute *(1957)*

Historical Note
A component of the Environmental Management Association.

Building Stone Institute *(1919)*

Executive Vice President: Jeff Buczkiewicz

Historical Note
Formerly (1955) International Cut Stone Quarrymen's Association. Members are stone dealers, contractors, quarry owners and importers/exporters.

Meetings/Conferences:
Annual Meetings: February

Publications:
Building Stone Magazine. q. adv.
Who's Who in the Stone Business. a. adv.
Industry News Update. m. adv.
Buyer's Guide. a. adv.
Stone Information Manual. a.

Building Systems Councils of the National Association of Home Builders *(1943)*

Historical Note
An affiliate of National Association of Home Builders, which provides administrative support.

Bulgarian-U.S. Business Council *(1974)*
Historical Note
A program of U.S. Chamber of Commerce, which provides administrative support.

Bulk Carrier Conference *(1956)*
7437 Timothy's Way
Easton, MD 21061
Tel: (410)820-7884 *Fax:* (410)820-4210
Members: 20 companies
Staff: 1
Annual Budget: $100-250,000
General Manager: Reginald Mutter

Burlap and Jute Association *(1923)*
Historical Note
Members are importers of burlap and jute. An affiliate of Textile Bag and Packaging Association, which provides administrative support. Membership: $250/year (corporate).

Burley Auction Warehouse Association *(1946)*
620 South Broadway
Suite 201
Lexington, KY 40508-3150
Tel: (859)255-4504 *Fax:* (859)255-4534
E-Mail: bawa@gte.net
Members: 225 companies
Staff: 2
Annual Budget: $50-100,000
Executive Director: Donna C. Graves
E-Mail: bawa@gte.net
Historical Note
Members are warehouse companies selling burley tobacco at auction in the eight burley-producing states. Membership: $200/per million pounds burley tobacco sold.
Meetings/Conferences:
Annual Meetings: June

Burley Tobacco Growers Cooperative Association *(1922)*
620 South Broadway
Lexington, KY 40508
Tel: (859)252-3561 *Fax:* (859)231-9804
Web Site: www.burleytobacco.com
Members: 180000 individuals
Staff: 9
Annual Budget: $1-2,000,000
Chief Executive Officer: Danny McKinney

Buses International Association *(1981)*
P.O. Box 9337
Spokane, WA 99209-9337
Tel: (509)328-2494 *Fax:* (509)325-5396
E-Mail: billluke@ztc.net
Web Site: www.busesintl.com
Members: 100 individuals
Staff: 1
Annual Budget: under $10,000
Executive Director: William A. Luke
E-Mail: billluke@ztc.net
Historical Note
Members are management-level personnel in the bus industry or its suppliers. Membership: $30/year.
Meetings/Conferences:
Annual Meetings: Not held.
Publications:
Buses International. q.

Business and Institutional Furniture Manufacturers Association International *(1973)*
2680 Horizon Dr. SE
Suite A-1
Grand Rapids, MI 49546-7500
Tel: (616)285-3963 *Fax:* (616)285-3765
E-Mail: email@bifma.org
Web Site: www.bifma.org
Members: 260 companies
Staff: 5
Annual Budget: $500-1,000,000
Executive Director: Thomas Reardon
E-Mail: treardon@bifma.org
Historical Note
The voice of the office furnishings industry, BIFMA members are manufacturers and suppliers of goods and services to the industry.
Publications:
Membership Directory. a. adv.
Newsletter. q. adv.

Business and Professional Women/USA *(1919)*
1900 M St. NW
Suite 310
Washington, DC 20036
Tel: (202)293-1100 *Fax:* (202)861-0298
Web Site: www.bpwusa.org
Members: 30000 individuals
Staff: 12
Annual Budget: $1-2,000,000
Chief Executive Officer: Deborah L. Frett
Director, Public Policy: Elisabeth Gehl
Director, Member Services: Beth Robbins
Director, Communications: Sherry Saunders
Historical Note
Business and Professional Women/USA, founded in 1919, promotes equity for all women in the workplace through advocacy, education and information. With 1,500 local organizations across the country and members in every congressional district, BPW/USA is the leading advocate for millions of workingwomen on work-life balance and workplace equity issues. The BPW/PAC assists women and pro-women - candidates who support BPW's legislative platform by providing campaign contributions and endorsements. The BPW Foundation, established in 1956 by BPW/USA, empowers working women to acheive their full potential and partners with employers to build successful workplaces.
Meetings/Conferences:
Annual Meetings: Summer
Publications:
BusinessWoman. 3/year. adv.

Business Council *(1933)*
P.O. Box 20147
Washington, DC 20041
Tel: (202)298-7650 *Fax:* (202)785-0296
Web Site: www.businesscouncil.com
Members: 200 individuals
Staff: 3
Annual Budget: $500-1,000,000
Executive Director: Philip E. Cassidy
Historical Note
Established originally as the Business Advisory Council to the Department of Commerce, it assumed its present name in 1961 and broke away from the Department of Commerce. The Business Council is a forum for the exchange of ideas between top corporate executives and government officials.
Meetings/Conferences:
Tri-annual Meetings: (1)Washington, DC/(2)Williamsburg, VA

Business Forms Management Association *(1958)*
319 S.W. Washington
Suite 710
Portland, OR 97204-2618
Tel: (503)227-3393 *Fax:* (503)274-7667
E-Mail: bfma@bfma.org
Web Site: www.bfma.org
Members: 600 individuals
Staff: 2
Annual Budget: $250-500,000
Executive Director: Andrew Palatka, CAE
Manager, Office Services: Tonya Macalino
Historical Note
An international, non-profit association of individuals interested in the effective management of forms and related information resources management. Members are form designers, analysts, systems managers and IS managers. Membership: $175/year (member-at-large or chapter member).
Meetings/Conferences:
Annual Meetings: May/500
2007 – St. Louis, MO(Hilton)/May 6-10/350
Publications:
Infocus. bi-m. adv.

Business Higher Education Forum *(1979)*
2025 M St. NW
Suite 800
Washington, DC 20036
Tel: (202)367-1189 *Fax:* (202)367-2189
E-Mail: info@bhef.com
Web Site: www.bhef.com
Members: 75 individuals
Staff: 4
Annual Budget: $500-1,000,000
Executive Director: Brian Fitzgerald
E-Mail: info@bhef.com
Historical Note
An alliance of corporate CEO's and university presidents dedicated to cooperative links between higher education and corporate America. Studies education's relation to workplace competitiveness and other issues of mutual interest to business and education.
Meetings/Conferences:
Annual Meetings:
Publications:
Meeting Highlights. semi-a.

Business History Conference *(1954)*
P.O. Box 3630
Wilmington, DE 19807
Tel: (302)658-2400 Ext: 243 *Fax:* (302)655-3188
Web Site: www.h-net.org/~business/bhcweb/
Members: 315 individuals
Staff: 1
Annual Budget: under $10,000
Secretary-Treasurer: Roger Horowitz
Historical Note
Membership: $55/year.
Meetings/Conferences:
Annual Meetings: spring, in a university environment
Publications:
Enterprise & Society. q. adv.

Business Marketing Association *(1922)*
400 N. Michigan Ave.
Suite 1510
Chicago, IL 60611-1607
Tel: (312)822-0005 *Fax:* (312)822-0054
Toll Free: (800)664 - 4262
E-Mail: bma@marketing.org
Web Site: www.marketing.org
Members: 3500 individuals
Staff: 3
Annual Budget: $1-2,000,000
Executive Director: Richard I. Kean
E-Mail: rkean@marketing.org
Manager, Information Services: Rodney Branch
E-Mail: bma@marketing.org
Manager, Member Services: Michele Coughlin
Historical Note
Formerly the Business/Professional Advertising Association. Membership: $185/year.
Meetings/Conferences:
Annual Meetings: Annual
Publications:
Market Smart. q.

Business Products Credit Association *(1875)*
607 Westridge Dr.
O'Fallon, MO 63366
Tel: (636)272-3005 *Fax:* (636)272-2973
Web Site: www.bpca.org
Members: 341 companies
Staff: 6
Annual Budget: $500-1,000,000
President and Chief Executive Officer: C. David Schmucker
Manager, Member Services: Debbie Schmucker
Historical Note
Founded in 1875 as Stationers and Publishers Board of Trade and Incorporated in 1879; became Stationery & Office Equipment Board of Trade, Inc., and amended its certificate of incorporation in 1994 to become Business Products Credit Association, Inc., its current title. BPCA is a credit and financial reporting bureau servicing its membership of manufacturers, factors, and wholesalers in the office products, filing supplies, office furniture, graphic arts, writing supplies, advertising specialty, janitorial and sanitary supply and forms industries. Also involved in

consulting with members' debtors, including out of court reorganizations and liquidations.

Meetings/Conferences:
Annual Meetings: 70

Publications:
Ledger. semi-a. adv.

Business Professionals of America *(1966)*
5454 Cleveland Ave.
Columbus, OH 43231-4021
Tel: (614)895-7277 Ext: 106 *Fax:* (614)895-1165
Web Site: www.bpa.org
Members: 55000 individuals
Staff: 8
Annual Budget: $1-2,000,000
President and Chief Executive Officer: Marty Richards, III
Director, Communications: Stephen Dziura
E-Mail: sdziura@bpa.org
Director, Education: Becky Hannah

Historical Note
Formerly (1988) Office Education Association. A non-profit vocational student organization for students enrolled in high school and post secondary business and/or office education programs. Membership: $10/year (individual).

Meetings/Conferences:
Annual Meetings: Spring/4,000

Publications:
Communique. q. adv.
Advisors Bulletins. bi-m. adv.

Business Software Alliance *(1988)*
1150 18th St. NW
Suite 700
Washington, DC 20036
Tel: (202)872-5500 *Fax:* (202)872-5501
E-Mail: info@bsa.org
Web Site: www.bsa.org
Staff: 62
President: Robert W. Holleyman, II
E-Mail: info@bsa.org
Vice President, Enforcement: Robert M. Kruger
E-Mail: info@bsa.org
Vice President, Legal Affairs: Neil McBride

Historical Note
BSA members are producers of business software for personal computers. BSA promotes the continued growth of the software industry through its intenational programs. Its public policy, education, and enforcement programs are designed to eradicate software piracy, advance strong intellectual property protection, and remove other barriers to international markets.

Business Technology Association *(1926)*
12411 Wornall Road
Kansas City, MO 64145
Tel: (816)941-3100 *Fax:* (816)941-4838
Toll Free: (800)505 - 2821
E-Mail: info@bta.org
Web Site: www.bta.org
Members: 2000 companies
Staff: 15
Annual Budget: $2-5,000,000
Executive Director: Albert Darling, Jr.
E-Mail: bert@bta.org
General Counsel: Robert C. Goldberg
Director, Membership and Marketing: Robin Keller

Historical Note
Founded in 1926 as the National Association of Typewriter Dealers. Became the National Typewriter and Office Machine Dealers Association and later National Office Machine Dealers Association. Assumed its present name in 1994 after a merger with LANDA (Local Area Network Dealers Association). International association of independent office equipment and systems resellers. Sponsors and supports the Business Technology Political Action Committee (BTA-PAC). Has an annual budget of approximately $2 million. Membership: $395/year (organization).

Meetings/Conferences:
Annual Meetings: Spring/22,000

Publications:
Office Technology. m. adv.
The Membership Directory. a. adv.
Hotline. bi-w. adv.

Cab Manufacturers Council

Historical Note
A council of the Equipment Manufacturers Institute.

Cable & Telecommunications Association for Marketing *(1976)*
201 N. Union St.
Suite 440
Alexandria, VA 22314-2642
Tel: (703)549-4200 *Fax:* (703)684-1167
E-Mail: info@ctam.com
Web Site: www.ctam.com
Members: 5500 individuals
Staff: 30
Annual Budget: $5-10,000,000
President and Chief Executive Officer: Char Beales
E-Mail: char@ctam.com
Senior Vice President, Finance and Administration: Daniel J. Cassidy
Senior Vice President, Communications: Ann E. Cowan
E-Mail: anne@ctam.com
Senior Vice President and General Manager, Corporate Initiatives: Seth Morrison
E-Mail: seth@ctam.com

Historical Note
Founded as Cable and Television Administration and Marketing Society; became (1995) Cable and Telecommunications: A Marketing Society and assumed its current name in 1996. Supports marketing executives and management in the cable and telecommunications industry through numerous educational programs, publications, conferences, and other activities. Membership: $295/year.

Meetings/Conferences:
Annual Meetings: March-August/3,000

Publications:
CTAM Pulse. 6/year. adv.
CTAM Magazine. m. adv.

Cable and Telecommunications Human Resources Association *(1993)*
1755 Park St.
Suite 260
Naperville, IL 60563
Tel: (630)416-1166 *Fax:* (630)416-9798
E-Mail: cthra@cthra.com
Web Site: www.cthra.com
Members: 100 companies
Staff: 1
Executive Director: Pamela Williams, CAE

Historical Note
CTHRA represents human resource professionals in the telecommunications industry. Membership: $175/year.

Publications:
Membership Directory (online). a.
Compensation Survey. a.

Cable and Telecommunications: A Marketing Society

Historical Note
See Cable and Telecommunications Association for Marketing.

Cabletelevision Advertising Bureau *(1980)*
830 Third Ave., Second Floor
New York, NY 10022-7522
Tel: (212)508-1200 *Fax:* (212)832-3268
Web Site: www.onetvworld.org
Members: 200 companies
Staff: 24
Annual Budget: $2-5,000,000
President/Chief Executive Officer: Sean Cunningham
Vice President, Sales and Marketing: Danielle DeLauro
Vice President and Chief Financial Officer: Jimmie Spears
Vice President, Research and Insights: Ira Sussman
Senior Vice President, Director Sales and Marketing: Chuck Thompson

Historical Note
CAB's purpose is to assist members in maximizing advertising revenues and to promote the use of cable as an advertising medium. Members include systems operators representing more than 85% of the nation's cable subscribers and virtually all ad-supported cable programming services.

Meetings/Conferences:
Annual Meetings: Spring

Publications:
Cable Network Profiles. a.
Cable TV Facts. a.
Cable TV Facts User's Guide.

CADD Council

Historical Note
An affiliated council of National Institute of Building Sciences, which provides administrative support.

Cajal Club

Historical Note
A social organization, sponsored by American Ass'n of Anatomists, for members with an interest in neuroanatomy.

Calendar Marketing Association *(1989)*
214 N. Hale St.
Wheaton, IL 60187
Tel: (630)510-4564 *Fax:* (630)510-4501
E-Mail: info@CalendarAssociation.org
Web Site: www.calendarassociation.org/
Members: 150 companies
Staff: 5
Executive Director: Mike Hansen
E-Mail: info@CalendarAssociation.org

Historical Note
Members are calendar designers, printers, publishers, marketers and distributors. Membership: $159/year (individual); $350/year (organization/company).

Publications:
State of the Calendar. a.
Calendar News. q. adv.

California Dried Fruit Export Association *(1925)*
710 Striker Ave.
Sacramento, CA 95834-1112
Tel: (916)561-5900 *Fax:* (916)561-5906
E-Mail: richn@dfaofca.com
Web Site: www.cdfea.org
Members: 33 companies
Staff: 3
Annual Budget: $25-50,000
President and Chief Executive Officer: Richard W. Novy

Historical Note
A Webb-Pomerene Act Association of dried fruit and tree nut exporters.

California Redwood Association *(1916)*
405 Enfrente Dr.
Suite 200
Novato, CA 94949
Tel: (888)225-7339 *Fax:* (415)382-8531
E-Mail: info@calredwood.org
Web Site: www.calredwood.org
Members: 6 companies
Staff: 6
Annual Budget: $1-2,000,000
President: Christopher Grover
E-Mail: chris@calredwood.org
Vice President: Charles Jourdain

Historical Note
CRA promotes the use of redwood, providing technical services to manufacturers, specifiers and builders and maintaining high product quality through its Redwood Inspection Service division.

Meetings/Conferences:
Annual Meetings: September

Callerlab-International Association of Square Dance Callers *(1971)*
467 Forrest Ave.
Suite 118
Cocoa, FL 32922
Tel: (321)639-0039 *Fax:* (321)639-0851
E-Mail: info@callerlab.org
Web Site: www.callerlab.org
Members: 3000 individuals
Staff: 6
Annual Budget: $250-500,000
Executive Director: Jerry Reed
E-Mail: info@callerlab.org

Historical Note
An organization of currently active square dance callers. Incorporated in the State of California. Membership: $75/year.

Meetings/Conferences:
Annual Meetings: Mon.-Wed. before Easter
2007 - Colorado Springs, CO(Sheraton)/Apr. 2-4

Publications:
Direction. bi-m.

Calorie Control Council *(1966)*
5775 Peachtree-Dunwoody Road, Suite 500, Bldg. G
Atlanta, GA 30342-1558
Tel: (404)252-3663 *Fax:* (404)252-0774
E-Mail: ccc@kellencompany.com
Web Site: www.caloriecontrol.org
Members: 60 companies
Staff: 3
Annual Budget: $500-1,000,000
Executive Vice President: Lyn O'Brien Nabors

Historical Note
An international association of manufacturers of low-calorie and reduced fat foods and beverages. Objectives include maintaining and enhancing communication between the low-calorie food and beverage industry, government and regulatory bodies, scientific and medical professionals and consumers.

Meetings/Conferences:
Annual Meetings: November

Publications:
Calorie Control Commentary.
Calorie Control Focus. m.

Calorimetry Conference *(1947)*
Merck Research Labs, WP-78-302
P.O. Box 4
West Point, PA 19486
Tel: (215)652-3531 *Fax:* (215)652-5299
Web Site: www.calcon.org
Members: 250 individuals
Annual Budget: $10-25,000
Secretary-Treasurer: Karen C. Thompson, Ph.D.
E-Mail: karen_thompson@merck.com

Historical Note
Scientists interested in the measurement of heat. Formerly (1950) the Low Temperature Calorimetry Conference. Membership: $20/year.

Campus Computer Resellers Alliance

Historical Note
A division of National Association of College Stores, which provides administrative support.

Campus Safety, Health and Environmental Management Association *(1954)*
1121 Spring Lake Dr.
Itasca, IL 60143
Tel: (630)775-2227 *Fax:* (630)285-1139
Web Site: www.cshema.org
Members: 950 individuals
Staff: 1
Annual Budget: $100-250,000
Division Manager: Sloane Grubb

Historical Note
Founded as Campus Safety Association; assumed its cutrrent name in 1996. A division of National Safety Council, CSHEMA represents college and university safety professionals. Promotes the image and importance of the field, defines responsibilities, provides opportunities to learn and to mentor, develops skills and sets up ideal situations for networking. Membership fee varies: $250/year minimum.

Meetings/Conferences:
Annual Meetings: June-July
2007 - Boston, MA(Seaport Boston)/July 21-25

Can Manufacturers Institute *(1938)*
1730 Rhode Island Ave. NW
Suite 1000
Washington, DC 20036
Tel: (202)232-4677 *Fax:* (202)232-5756
E-Mail: webmaster@cancentral.com
Web Site: www.cancentral.com
Members: 28 companies
Staff: 7
Annual Budget: $10-25,000,000
President: Robert B. Budway
E-Mail: webmaster@cancentral.com
Vice President, Finance: Christa Matte
E-Mail: webmaster@cancentral.com

Historical Note
Absorbed the Carbonated Beverage Container Manufacturers Association in 1974. Has an annual budget of approximately $11 million.

Meetings/Conferences:
Annual Meetings: Washington, DC/Spring

Publications:
Can Shipments Report. q.
Executive Focus. q.
Federal/State Review. q.

Canadian-American Business Council *(1987)*
1900 K St. NW
Suite 100
Washington, DC 20006
Tel: (202)496-7340 *Fax:* (202)496-7756
E-Mail: canambusco@mckennalong.com
Web Site: www.canambusco.org
Members: 130 individuals
Staff: 3
Executive Director: Scotty Greenwood
E-Mail: canambusco@mckennalong.com

Historical Note
Founded to represent businesses and individuals with business interests in U.S. and Canada.

Publications:
Newsletter. bi-m.
Membership Directory. a.

Canon Law Society of America *(1939)*
108 N. Payne St.
Suite C
Alexandria, VA 22314-2906
Tel: (703)739-2560 *Fax:* (703)739-2562
E-Mail: coordinator@clsa.org
Web Site: www.clsa.org
Members: 1600 individuals
Staff: 2
Annual Budget: $250-500,000
Executive Coordinator: Arthur J. Espelage
E-Mail: coordinator@clsa.org

Historical Note
Individuals interested in the study of church law and ecclesiastical jurisprudence. Membership: $100/year.

Meetings/Conferences:
Annual Meetings: Fall/450

Publications:
Roman Replies and CLSA Advisory Opinions. a.
Proceedings. a.
CLSA Newsletter. q.

Cantors Assembly *(1947)*
c/o Jewish Theological Seminary
3080 Broadway, Suite 603
New York, NY 10027
Tel: (212)678-8834 *Fax:* (212)662-8989
E-Mail: caoffice@aol.com
Web Site: www.cantors.org
Members: 195 individuals
Staff: 3
Annual Budget: $250-500,000
Contact: Jay Neufeld

Historical Note
Promotes and advances the traditions of Conservative Judaism. Membership: $700/year.

Meetings/Conferences:
Annual Meetings: Spring
2007 - Los Angeles, CA/May 6-10

Publications:
Proceedings. a.
Journal of Synagogue Music. semi-a.

Capital Markets Credit Analysts Society *(1989)*
25 North Broadway
Tarrytown, NY 10591
Tel: (914)332-0040 *Fax:* (914)332-1541
E-Mail: cmcas@cmcas.com
Web Site: www.cmcas.org
Members: 500 individuals
Staff: 3

Historical Note
CMCAS is a professional society whose membership consists primarily of managers and analysts in credit risk departments that directly support their employers' capital market activities. CMCAS provides its members with opportunities to broaden their understanding of events that affect capital market activities; assists members who are seeking continuing education to keep abreast of issues affecting their profession; and provides ethical standards for the guidance of its members in their professional relations with each other and the public. Membership: $350/year.

Publications:
Directory. a.

Captive Insurance Companies Association *(1971)*
4248 Park Glen Road
Minneapolis, MN 55416-4758
Tel: (952)928-4655 *Fax:* (952)929-1318
E-Mail: cica@harringtoncompany.com
Web Site: www.captiveassociation.com
Members: 200 individuals
Staff: 2
Annual Budget: $250-500,000
President: Dennis P. Harwick
E-Mail: cica@harringtoncompany.com
Staff Liaison: Anthony LeClerc

Historical Note
Single insurance companies completely owned by a parent organization or industry. Membership: $700/year (company).

Meetings/Conferences:
Annual Meetings: Spring

Car Care Council *(1968)*
7101 Wisconsin Ave., Suite 1300
Bethesda, MD 20814
Tel: (240)333-1088
E-Mail: info@carcarecouncil.org
Web Site: www.carcare.org
Annual Budget: $500-1,000,000
Executive Director: Richard White
Communications Coordinator: Marcella Tilli

Historical Note
CCC members are automotive aftermarket manufacturers, distributors, jobbers, service providers, associations and communications organizations. CCC provides public service messages on auto maintenance to radio, television, newspapers and magazines. Coordinates National Care Care Month each April.

Meetings/Conferences:
Annual Meetings: November, with the Automotive Aftermarket Industry Week

Publications:
Aftermarket Insider magazine. bi-m.

Carbonated Beverage Institute *(1945)*
Three Border Ln.
Woodstock, VT 05091-1251
Tel: (802)457-1504 *Fax:* (802)457-4810
E-Mail: vermonthoyt@netscape.net
Members: 12 bottlers
Secretary: Donald Hoyt
E-Mail: vermonthoyt@netscape.net

Meetings/Conferences:
Annual Meetings: January

Cardiovascular Credentialing International
1500 Sunday Dr.
Suite 102
Raleigh, NC 27607
Tel: (919)861-4539 *Fax:* (919)787-4916
Toll Free: (800)326 - 0268
Web Site: www.cci-online.org

Career College Association *(1991)*
Ten G St. NE
Suite 750
Washington, DC 20002-4213
Tel: (202)336-6700 *Fax:* (202)336-6828
E-Mail: cca@career.org
Web Site: www.career.org/career.html
Members: 1350 colleges and allied member organizations

Staff: 24
Annual Budget: $2-5,000,000
President: Nick Glakas
E-Mail: nickg@career.org
General Counsel: Nancy Broff
E-Mail: nancyb@career.org
Director, Events: Katie Calabrese
E-Mail: katiec@career.org
Communications Manager: Lisa Kelley
E-Mail: cca@career.org
Vice President, Government Affairs: Bruce Leftwich
E-Mail: brucel@career.org
Executive Director, Career College Foundation: Bob Martin
E-Mail: bobm@career.org
Vice President, Membership: Mark Robbins
E-Mail: cca@career.org

Historical Note
In 1950, the National Association and Council of Accredited Commercial Schools and the National Council of Business Schools merged to form the National Association and Council of Business Schools. This, in turn, merged with the American Association of Business Schools (formerly the American Association of Commercial Colleges) to form the United Business Schools Association in 1962. Became the Association of Independent Colleges and Schools in 1973. Assumed its present name after the Association of Independent Colleges and Schools consolidated with the National Association of Trade and Technical Schools in 1991. Sponsors and supports the CCA Political Action Committee.

Publications:
CCA Link. q.. adv.
Connector. m.

Career Planning and Adult Development Network *(1979)*
543 Vista Mar Ave.
Pacifica, CA 94044
Tel: (408)272-3085 *Fax:* (408)272-8851
E-Mail: dick@careertrainer.com
Web Site: www.careernetwork.org
Members: 1000 individuals
Staff: 1
Annual Budget: $100-250,000
Executive Director and Editor: Richard L. Knowdell
E-Mail: dick@careertrainer.com

Historical Note
CPADN members are career counselors, educators and human resource specialists. Membership: $49/year (individual); $64/year (foreign).

Meetings/Conferences:
Annual Meetings: late October-early November
2007 - Sacramento, CA(Hyatt Regency)/Nov. 7-11/800

Publications:
Career Planning & Adult Development Newsletter. b.
Career Planning & Adult Development Journal. q. adv.

Cargo Airline Association *(1947)*
1220 19th St. NW
Suite 400
Washington, DC 20036
Tel: (202)293-1030 *Fax:* (202)293-4377
E-Mail: info@cargoair.org
Web Site: www.cargoair.org
Members: 24 companies
Annual Budget: $100-250,000
President: Stephen A. Alterman
Senior Vice President: Yvette Roso
Director, Government Affairs: Julia Krauss Torrey

Historical Note
Founded as Air Freight Forwarders Association; became Air Freight Association of America in 1977 and assumed its current name in 1997.

Meetings/Conferences:
Annual Meetings: June or August in Washington, DC

Carpet and Rug Institute *(1969)*
310 Holiday Ave.
P.O. Box 2048
Dalton, GA 30722-2048
Tel: (706)278-3176 *Fax:* (706)278-8835
Toll Free: (800)882 - 8846
E-Mail: wbraun@carpet-rug.org
Web Site: www.carpet-rug.com
Members: 122 companies
Staff: 15
Annual Budget: $2-5,000,000
President: Werner Braun
Director, Government Affairs: Frank Hard
E-Mail: wbraun@carpet-rug.org

Historical Note
Formed by a merger of the American Carpet Institute (1928) and the Tufted Textile Manufacturers Association (1945). CRI sponsors technical conferences and other programs for floorcovering manufacturers and installers.

Publications:
Appearance Change Reference Scales CRI 2003 Industry Statistics.

Carpet and Upholstery Cleaning Association *(1971)*

Historical Note
A division of the Association of Specialists in Cleaning and Restoration.

Carpet Cushion Council *(1976)*
23 Courtney Circle
Bryn Mawr, PA 19010
Tel: (610)527-3880
E-Mail: carpetcushion@msn.com
Web Site: www.carpetcushion.org
Members: 35 individuals
Staff: 1
Annual Budget: $100-250,000
Contact: G. William Haines

Historical Note
Involved in public relations to encourage distribution and use of separate carpet cushions. Works with regulatory agencies at the national, state, and local levels. Formerly a division of the Carpet and Rug Institute, the Council is now independent and incorporated in the District of Columbia. Membership: based on sales volume.

Meetings/Conferences:
Annual Meetings: Fall/50

Publications:
Fact Sheets. bi-m.

Carwash Owner's and Supplier's Association *(1983)*
1822 South St.
Racine, WI 53404
Tel: (262)639-2320 *Fax:* (262)639-4393
E-Mail: cosa@wi.net
Staff: 3
Annual Budget: $10-25,000
Director: Ed Holbus
E-Mail: cosa@wi.net

Historical Note
COSA's primary objective is to raise the public image of the industry. Membership: $300/year.

Publications:
COSA's Questions & Answers. m. adv.

Case Management Society of America *(1990)*
8201 Cantrell Road., Suite 230
Little Rock, AR 72227-2448
Tel: (501)225-2229 *Fax:* (501)221-9068
E-Mail: cmsa@cmsa.org
Web Site: www.cmsa.org
Members: 9800 individuals
Staff: 25
Annual Budget: $2-5,000,000
Associate Executive Director: Jeanne Boling
E-Mail: jboling@acminet.com
Director, Information Systems: Fred Howard
Executive Director: Cheri Lattimer
Senior Director, Operations and Business Strategy: Danielle Marshall
E-Mail: dmarshall@acminet.com
Senior Director, Human Resources: Randall Van Den Berghe

Historical Note
CMSA is an international professional society of health care professionals engaged in case management on all levels. Absorbed (1996) Individual Case Management Association. Membership: fees based on membership type.

Meetings/Conferences:
Annual Meetings: Spring
2007 - Denver, CO(Hyatt Regency)/June 19-23

Publications:
Case in Point. bi-m.
CMSA @ Work. q.
Lippincott Professional Case Management. bi-m.

Cashmere and Camel Hair Manufacturers Institute *(1984)*
Six Beacon St., Suite 1125
Boston, MA 02108
Tel: (617)542-7481 *Fax:* (617)542-2199
E-Mail: info@cashmere.org
Web Site: www.cashmere.org
Members: 17 companies
Staff: 4
President: Karl H. Spilhaus

Historical Note
Trade association of manufacturers of cashmere and camel hair products.

Casket and Funeral Supply Association of America *(1913)*
49 Sherwood Terrace, Suite Y
Lake Bluff, IL 60044
Tel: (847)295-6630 *Fax:* (847)295-6647
Web Site: www.cfsaa.org
Members: 175 companies
Staff: 3
Annual Budget: $250-500,000
Executive Director: George W. Lemke
E-Mail: lemke@cfsaa.org

Historical Note
Formerly (1993) Casket Manufacturers Association of America. Membership fee based on sales volume.

Meetings/Conferences:
Annual Meetings: Fall/190-200

Publications:
CFSA Newsletter. m.

Cast Iron Soil Pipe Institute *(1949)*
5959 Shallowford Rd.
Suite 419
Chattanooga, TN 37421
Tel: (423)892-0137 *Fax:* (423)892-0817
Web Site: www.cispi.org
Members: 4 foundries
Staff: 9
Annual Budget: $500-1,000,000
Executive Vice President: William H. LeVan
E-Mail: blevan@mindspring.com

Historical Note
Manufacturers of cast iron soil pipe and fittings.

Meetings/Conferences:
Annual Meetings: November/December

Cast Metals Institute

Historical Note
Not a trade association. The educational branch of the American Foundrymen's Society.

Cast Stone Institute *(1927)*
813 Chestnut St.
P.O. box 68
Lebanon, PA 17042
Tel: (717)272-3744 *Fax:* (717)272-5147
E-Mail: staff@caststone.org
Web Site: www.caststone.org
Members: 70 individuals
Staff: 3
Annual Budget: $50-100,000,000
Executive Director: Mimi Harlan
E-Mail: staff@caststone.org

Historical Note
CSI represents manufacturers of cast stone and the architects, engineers, concrete technologists, and contractors who specify, design, and use cast stone. Membership fees: $3,500/year (Producer); $300/year (Associate).

Meetings/Conferences:
Annual Meetings:

Publications:
Cast in Stone. q.

Casting Industry Suppliers Association *(1919)*
14175 W. Indian School Rd.
Suite B4-505
Goodyear, AZ 85338-8405
Tel: (623)547-0920 *Fax:* (623)536-1486
E-Mail: cisa@cox.net
Web Site: www.cisa.org
Members: 70 companies
Staff: 3
Annual Budget: $250-500,000
Executive Director: Roger A. Hayes
E-Mail: cisa@cox.net

Historical Note
Founded in 1919, it became the Casting Industry Supplier Association in 1986. Members are makers of supplies to the metal coating industry.

Publications:
Bulletin. m.
Directory. a.

Casual Furniture Retailers *(1980)*
214 N. Hale St.
Wheaton, IL 60187
Tel: (630)510-4562 *Fax:* (630)510-4501
Toll Free: (800)956 - 2237
Web Site: www.casualfurniture.org
Members: 200 retailers
Staff: 2
Annual Budget: $100-250,000
Executive Director: Janet Svazas

Historical Note
Formerly (1998) National Association of Casual Furniture Retailers. Incorporated in Illinois. Members are retailers; manufacturers and sales representatives qualify as associate members.

Meetings/Conferences:
Annual Meetings: Fall

Publications:
Membership Directory. a.

Casualty Actuarial Society *(1914)*
4350 N. Fairfax Dr.
Suite 250
Arlington, VA 22203
Tel: (703)276-3100 *Fax:* (703)276-3108
E-Mail: office@casact.org
Web Site: www.casact.org
Members: 3900 individuals
Staff: 25
Annual Budget: $2-5,000,000
Executive Director: Cynthia Ziegler, CPCU, AAI, AAE
Director, Communications and Research: J. Michael Boa
Director, Meeting Planner Services: Kathleen Dean
Director, Admissions: J. Thomas Downey
E-Mail: office@casact.org
Directorm Finance and Operations: Todd P. Rogers

Historical Note
Formerly (1921) Casualty Actuarial and Statistical Society of America. Membership contigent upon examination. Actuaries dealing in property, casualty, and similar risk exposures. Affiliated with the American Academy of Actuaries. Membership: $375/year.

Meetings/Conferences:
Semi-annual Meetings: May and Nov./700

Publications:
Forum. 3-4/year.
Syllabus of Examination. a.
Future Fellows. q.
Proceedings. a.
Yearbook. a.
Actuarial Review. q.
Discussion Paper Program. a.

Catalogue Raisonne Scholars Association *(1993)*
15 Lawrence Hall Dr.
Suite Two
Williamstown, MA 01267
Tel: (413)597-2335
Web Site: www.catalogueraisonne.org
Members: 10 individuals
President: Nancy Mowll Mathews
E-Mail: nmathews@williams.edu

Historical Note
Affiliated with College Art Association, CRSA members research descriptive annotation of works of art. Has no paid officers or full-time staff. Membership: $20/year (individual).

Meetings/Conferences:
Annual Meetings: In conjunction with College Art Ass'n

Publications:
Newsletter. semi-a.

Catecholamine Club *(1969)*
Dept. of Veterinary Medicine and Molecular Bioscience
University of California-Davis
Davis, CA 95616-5224
Tel: (530)752-7409 *Fax:* (530)752-4698
Members: 350 individuals
Annual Budget: $10-25,000
Secretary-Treasurer: Richard Vulliet, Ph.D.

Historical Note
Members are researchers in neuroscience interested in the properties of the ammonia-based chemical compounds known as catecholamines. Has no paid officers or full-time staff.

Meetings/Conferences:
Annual Meetings: in conjunction with Society for Neuroscience

Catfish Farmers of America *(1968)*
1100 Hwy. 82 East
Suite 202
Indianola, MS 38751
Tel: (662)887-2699 *Fax:* (662)887-6857
Web Site: www.catfishfarmersamerica.org
Members: 1400 farms
Staff: 3
Annual Budget: $250-500,000
Executive Vice President: Hugh Warren, III

Historical Note
CFA represents the national farm-raised catfish industry. Membership: $40/year.

Meetings/Conferences:
Annual Meetings: Winter in the Southeastern United States

Publications:
The Catfish Journal. m. adv.

Catfish Institute *(1986)*
1100 Hwy. 82 East
P.O. Box 924
Indianola, MS 38751
Tel: (662)887-2988 *Fax:* (662)887-6857
E-Mail: info@catfishinstitute.com
Web Site: www.catfishinstitute.com
Members: 11 feed mills
President: Henry Gantz
E-Mail: info@catfishinstitute.com

Historical Note
Members are catfish farmers and processors.

Catholic Academy for Communication Arts Professionals *(1972)*
1645 Brook Lynn Dr.
Dayton, OH 45432-1933
Tel: (937)458-0265 *Fax:* (937)458-0263
E-Mail: admin@catholicacademy.org
Web Site: www.catholicacademy.org
Members: 250 individuals
Staff: 2
Annual Budget: $100-250,000
Office Administrator: Sue West

Historical Note
Formerly (1972) UNDA-USA, National Catholic Association for Broadcasters/Communications; assumed its current name in 2002. An afflilate of SIGNIS, the Catholic World Association for Communication. Absorbed the Catholic Broadcasters Association in 1948. Membership: $210/year (individual); $575/year (organization).

Meetings/Conferences:
Annual Meetings: Fall

Publications:
Newsletter (online).

Catholic Biblical Association of America *(1936)*
314 Caldwell Hall
The Catholic University of America
Washington, DC 20064
Tel: (202)319-5519 *Fax:* (202)319-4799
E-Mail: cua-cathbib@cua.edu
Web Site: http://cba.cua.edu
Members: 1450 individuals
Staff: 2
Annual Budget: $250-500,000
Executive Secretary: Joseph Jensen, O.S.B.
E-Mail: cua-cathbib@cua.edu

Historical Note
Members are Catholic and non-Catholic Biblical scholars. Member of the Council of Societies for the Study of Religion. Membership: $35/year (individual).

Meetings/Conferences:
Annual Meetings: August in a university setting

Publications:
Old Testament Abstracts. 3/year. adv.
Catholic Biblical Quarterly. q. adv.
Catholic Biblical Quarterly monograph series. iireg.

Catholic Book Publishers Association *(1987)*
8404 Jamesport Dr.
Rockford, IL 61108
Tel: (815)332-3245 *Fax:* (815)332-3476
E-Mail: cbpa3@aol.com
Web Site: www.cbpa.org
Members: 100publishers,svcs,ind.members
Annual Budget: $50-100,000
Executive Director: Terry Wessels
E-Mail: cbpa3@aol.com

Historical Note
Members are publishers specializing in books of interest to the Catholic community. CBPA faciliates the exchange of professional information and cooperation concerning Catholic book publishing in the United States and abroad. Membership: $250-750/year (publisher); $200/year (service company); $100/year (individual).

Publications:
CPBA Directory. a. adv.
The Spirit of Books Catalog. semi-a. adv.

Catholic Campus Ministry Association *(1969)*
1118 Pendleton St.
Suite 300
Cincinnati, OH 45202-8805
Tel: (513)842-0167 *Fax:* (513)842-0171
Toll Free: (888)714 - 6631
E-Mail: info@ccmanet.org
Web Site: www.ccmanet.org
Members: 1200 individuals
Staff: 6
Annual Budget: $500-1,000,000
Director, Member Services: Chrysta Bolinger

Historical Note
Formerly (1968) National Newman Chaplains Association. CCMA is a national organization of individuals and groups of campus ministers who associate to foster their theological and professional growth and to promote the ministry of the Catholic Church in higher education. Membership: $110/year (individual); $125/year (organization).

Meetings/Conferences:
2007 – San Diego, CA(Town and Country)/Jan. 4-7/350

Publications:
CCMA Directory. a. adv.
Crossroads. bi-m. adv.

Catholic Charities USA *(1910)*
1731 King St.
Alexandria, VA 22314
Tel: (703)549-1390 *Fax:* (703)549-1656
Web Site: www.catholiccharitiesusa.org
Members: 3000 individuals
Staff: 50
Annual Budget: $1-2,000,000
President: Rev. Larry Snyder
Manager, Media and Relations: Shelly Borgsiewicz
Director, Mission Integration and Catholic Identity: Robert Colbert
Vice President, Social Policy: Candy Hill
Chief Operating Officer: Pat Huidston

Senior Vice President, Planning and External Relations: John Keightly
Senior Vice President, Programs and Services: Stuart Pope

Historical Note
Catholic Charities USA is one of the nation's largest private network of social service agencies, institutions, and individuals who seek to support families, reduce poverty and empower communities. Membership: $25/year (individual); Agency/institutional dues vary.

Meetings/Conferences:
Annual Meetings: Fall

Publications:
Charities USA. q.

Catholic Health Association of the United States *(1915)*
4455 Woodson Road
St. Louis, MO 63134-3797
Tel: (314)427-2500 *Fax:* (314)427-0029
Web Site: www.chausa.org
Members: 2000 organizations
Staff: 85
Annual Budget: $10-25,000,000
President and Chief Executive Officer: Sr. Carol Keehan, DC
Special Assistant to the President for Communications: Fred Caesar
Vice President, Communications: Ed Giganti
Vice President, General Counsel: Lisa Gilden
Senior Vice President, Finance and Operations: Rhonda Mueller
Vice President, Mission Services: Patricia A. Talone, Ph.D.

Historical Note
Formerly (1979) Catholic Hospital Association. Has an annual budget of approximately $19 million.

Meetings/Conferences:
Annual Meetings: June
2007 – Chicago, IL(Marriott Downtown)/June 17-19
2008 – San Diego, CA(Manchester Grand Hyatt)/June 22-24

Publications:
Catholic Health World. 22/year. adv.
Health Progress. bi-m. adv.

Catholic Library Association *(1921)*
100 North St.
Suite 224
Pittsfield, MA 01201-5109
Tel: (413)443-2252 *Fax:* (413)442-2252
E-Mail: cla@cathla.org
Web Site: www.cathla.org
Members: 1000 individuals and institutions
Staff: 9
Annual Budget: $100-250,000
Executive Director: Jean R. Bostley, SSJ
E-Mail: cla@cathla.org

Historical Note
CLA membership is open to all librarians for the purpose of initiating, fostering and encouraging any activity or library program which will promote literature and libraries, not only of a Catholic nature but also an ecumenical spirit. Membership: $45-150/year (individual); $100-300/year (institution/company).

Meetings/Conferences:
Annual Meetings: With Nat'l Catholic Educational Ass'n
2007 – Baltimore, MD/Apr. 10-13
2008 – Indianapolis, IN/March 25-28
2009 – Anaheim, CA/Apr. 14-17

Publications:
Catholic Periodical and Literature Index. q.
Membership Directory/Handbook. biennial. adv.
Convention Program. a. adv.
Catholic Library World. q. adv.

Catholic Medical Association *(1932)*
P.O. Box 920480
Needham, MA 02492-0006
Tel: (781)455-0259 *Fax:* (781)455-0357
E-Mail: info@cathmed.org
Web Site: www.cathmed.org
Members: 3500 individuals
Staff: 4
Annual Budget: $50-100,000
Executive Director: Anne H. DeLong

Historical Note
Formed in 1932 and incorporated in Washington, DC in 1964, CMA (formerly the National Federation of Catholic Physicians' Guilds) coordinates the activities of local guilds, upholds the principles of the Catholic faith and morality as related to the science and practice of medicine, communicates Catholic medical ethics to the medical profession and the community at large, supports Catholic hospitals in the application of Catholic moral principles, and enables Catholic physicians to work together with deeper mutual support and understanding. Membership: $50 for first year, $200/year for every subsequent year; $50 (retired); $50 (associate); $50/year (student or resident).

Meetings/Conferences:
Annual Meetings: Fall

Publications:
Linacre Quarterly. q. adv.

Catholic Press Association *(1911)*
3555 Veterans Memorial Hwy., Suite O
Ronkonkoma, NY 11779-7636
Tel: (631)471-4730 *Fax:* (631)471-4804
Web Site: www.catholicpress.org
Members: 258 individuals
Staff: 6
Annual Budget: $500-1,000,000

Historical Note
Founded in Columbus, Ohio, August 24-25, 1911 by forty-seven charter member publications. Incorporated the following year in New York. Membership: based on size and frequency of publications.

Meetings/Conferences:
Annual Meetings: Spring

Publications:
Catholic Journalist. m. adv.
Catholic Press Directory. a. adv.

Catholic Theological Society of America *(1946)*
John Carroll University
20700 North Park Blvd.
University Heights, OH 44118
Tel: (216)397-1631 *Fax:* (216)397-1804
Web Site: www.jcu.edu/ctsa
Members: 1400 individuals
Staff: 1
Annual Budget: $10-25,000
Executive Director: Dolores Christie

Historical Note
Members are individuals engaged in scholarly research, writing, and teaching of theology in seminaries and universities. Membership: salary-based.

Meetings/Conferences:
Annual Meetings: June/500

Publications:
CTSA Proceedings. a.

Caucus for Television Producers, Writers & Directors *(1974)*
P.O. Box 11236
Burbank, CA 91510-1236
Tel: (818)843-7572 *Fax:* (818)846-2159
E-Mail: caucuspwd@aol.com
Web Site: www.caucus.org
Members: 160 individuals
Staff: 1
Annual Budget: $50-100,000
Administrator: Penny S. Rieger
E-Mail: caucuspwd@aol.com

Historical Note
The Caucus provides support to content creators in the broadcast and cable television industries.

Meetings/Conferences:
Quarterly Meetings: Los Angeles, CA

Publications:
Caucus Journal. semi-a.

Caucus for Women in Statistics *(1970)*
7732 Rydal Terrace
Rockville, MD 20855
Tel: (301)827-0218 *Fax:* (301)594-2297
E-Mail: anevius@cvm.fda.gov
Web Site: www.statwomen.org
Members: 300 individuals
Annual Budget: under $10,000
Treasurer: Anna Nevius

Historical Note
CWS is a networking and professional forum supporting women in statistics-oriented professions. Has no paid officers or full-time staff.

Meetings/Conferences:
Annual Meetings: August

Publications:
Newsletter. q.
Membership Directory. a.

CBA *(1950)*
P.O. Box 62000
Colorado Springs, CO 80962
Tel: (719)265-9895 Ext: 1345 *Fax:* (719)272-3510
Toll Free: (800)252 - 1950 Ext: 1345
E-Mail: info@cbaonline.org
Web Site: www.cbaonline.org
Members: 3300 stores and companies
Staff: 40
Annual Budget: $5-10,000,000
President: William R. Anderson
E-Mail: banderson@cbaonline.org
Chief Operating Officer: Dorothy Gore
E-Mail: dgore@cbaonline.org
Meetings Director: Scott Graham
E-Mail: sgraham@cbaonline.org
Director, Marketing and Communications: Leon C. Wirth
E-Mail: lwirth@cbaonline.org

Historical Note
Founded as Christian Booksellers Association; assumed its current name in 1997. CBA is worldwide network of 2500 Christian stores. CBA supplies its member store owners with training, publications, trade shows and market research.

Meetings/Conferences:
Annual Meetings: July/13,000 and January/7000
2007 – Indianapolis, IN(Indiana Convention Center)/Jan. 29-Feb. 2
2007 – Atlanta, GA(Georgia World Congress Center)/July 8-12

Publications:
Aspiring Retail. m. adv.

CCIM Institute *(1950)*
430 N. Michigan Ave.
Suite 800
Chicago, IL 60611-4092
Tel: (312)321-4460 *Fax:* (312)321-4530
Toll Free: (800)621 - 7027
E-Mail: pr@ccim.com
Web Site: www.ccim.com
Members: 16000 individuals
Staff: 55
Annual Budget: $10-25,000,000
Executive Vice President: Susan J. Groeneveld, CCIM, CAE

Historical Note
Incorporated (1967) in Chicago, the CCIM Institute is an affiliate of the National Association of Realtors. CCIM Institute functions as a professional association of real estate practitioners who have successfully completed its certification program or are working toward it. Awards Certified Commercial Investment Member (CCIM) designation upon completion of its curriculum. Membership: $495/year (designee); $495/year (candidate).

Meetings/Conferences:
Annual Meetings: Fall

Publications:
Commercial Investment Real Estate. bi-m. adv.

CDLA: the Computer Leasing and Remarketing Association *(1981)*

Historical Note
See Computer Leasing and Remarketing Association.

Cedar Shake and Shingle Bureau *(1915)*
P.O. Box 1178
Sumas, WA 98295-1178
Tel: (604)820-7700 *Fax:* (604)820-0266
E-Mail: info@cedarbureau.com
Web Site: www.cedarbureau.org

Members: 450 companies
Staff: 10
Annual Budget: $1-2,000,000
Director, Operations: Lynne Christensen
E-Mail: info@cedarbureau.com

Historical Note

The Cedar Shake and Shingle Bureau is a non-profit trade association founded in 1915 that promotes the use of Certi-label (tm) cedar roofing and sidewall products. The Cedar Bureau offers the marketplace an attractive combination: quality Certi-label (tm) products manufactured, sold and applied by quality people. The organization provides installation instructions, educational seminars and technical advice. Founded in 1915 as Shingle Branch of West Coast Lumber Manufacturers Association. Incorporated as the Red Cedar Shingle Bureau in 1926. Absorbed (1963) the Red Cedar Shingle & Handsplit Shake Bureau. Adopted its present name in 1988.

Publications:

Certi-Scene. 26/year. adv.
Membership Directory and Buyers Guide. a. adv.

Ceilings and Interior Systems Construction Association *(1950)*

1500 Lincoln Hwy.
Suite 202
St. Charles, IL 60174-2386
Tel: (630)584-1919 *Fax:* (630)584-2003
E-Mail: cisca@cisca.org
Web Site: www.cisca.org
Members: 600 firms
Staff: 3
Executive Director: Bonny Luck
E-Mail: cisca@cisca.org

Historical Note

Formerly (1970) National Acoustical Contractors Association. Membership: $565/year and up.

Meetings/Conferences:

2007 – Orlando, FL(Walt Disney World)/Apr. 4-8/1000

Publications:

Interior Construction. bi-m. adv.

Cellular Telecommunications and Internet Association

Historical Note

Became CTIA - The Wireless Association in 2005.

Cellulose Insulation Manufacturers Association *(1982)*

136 S. Keowee St.
Dayton, OH 45402
Tel: (937)222-2462 *Fax:* (937)222-5794
Toll Free: (888)881 - 2462
E-Mail: cima@cellulose.org
Web Site: www.cellulose.org
Members: 20 insulation manufacturers
Staff: 3
Annual Budget: $250-500,000
Executive Director: Daniel Lea
E-Mail: cima@cellulose.org

Historical Note

Formerly (1992) Cellulose Industry Standards Enforcement Program. Founded in 1982 as the Cellulose Industry Standards Enforcement Program to enforce and document compliance with government and industry standards for cellulose insulation by member companies. Originally devoted exclusively to standards development through ASTM and ISO.

Cement Employers Association *(1936)*

122 E. Broad St., Second Floor
Bethlehem, PA 18018
Tel: (610)868-8060
E-Mail: emcgehee@cementemployers.com
Members: 27 companies
Staff: 2
Annual Budget: $250-500,000
Executive Director: Elton McGehee
E-Mail: emcgehee@cementemployers.com

Historical Note

A grouping of cement companies united to promote personnel and industrial relations.

Meetings/Conferences:

Annual Meetings: Fall/50-60
2007 – San Antonio, TX(The Hotel Contessa)/February/40

Cement Kiln Recycling Coalition

1001 Connecticut Ave. NW
Suite 615
Washington, DC 20036
Tel: (202)466-6802 *Fax:* (202)466-5009
E-Mail: info@ckrc.org
Web Site: www.ckrc.org
Members: 19 organizations
Staff: 5
Annual Budget: $1-2,000,000
Executive Director: Mike Benoit
Director, Government Affairs: Michelle Lusk

Historical Note

CKRC has adopted a comprehensive Environmental Policy Statement which mandates that its members be responsible stewards of the environment and conduct their businesses in a manner protective of human health and the environment. Members include most of the major cement companies engaged in the use of hazardous waste-derived fuel as well as companies involved in the collection, processing, management and marketing of such fuel for use in cement kilns.

Publications:

CKRC Newsletter. q..

Cemented Carbide Producers Association *(1955)*

30200 Detroit Road
Cleveland, OH 44145-1967
Tel: (440)899-0010 *Fax:* (440)892-1404
Web Site: www.ccpa.org
Members: 23 companies
Staff: 5
Annual Budget: $50-100,000
Comissioner: J. Jeffery Wherry

Historical Note

Members are makers of sintered carbide containing tungsten.

Center for Exhibition Industry Research *(1978)*

401 N. Michigan Ave.
Suite 2200
Chicago, IL 60611
Tel: (312)527-6735 *Fax:* (312)673-6722
E-Mail: info@ceir.org
Web Site: www.ceir.org
Members: 350 companies
Staff: 5
Annual Budget: $1-2,000,000
President and Chief Executive Officer: Douglas Ducate, CEM, CMP
Manager, Communications, Research and Operations: Tracy L. Nickless
Executive Director: Julie Sutter

Historical Note

Formed in 1978, CEIR promotes the growth of the exhibitions industry through research, information, and communications.

Publications:

Membership Directory (online). a. adv.
Newsletters. bi-m. adv.
Research Reports. bi-m.

Center for Livable Communities *(1977)*

Historical Note

Formerly Ass'n for Community Design. CLC is a division of American Institute of Architects, which provides administrative support.

Center for Waste Reduction Technologies *(1991)*

Three Park Ave.
New York, NY 10016-5991
Tel: (212)591-7462 *Fax:* (212)591-8895
E-Mail: cwrt@aiche.org
Web Site: www.aiche.org/cwrt
Members: 20 companies
Staff: 3
Annual Budget: $500-1,000,000
Director: Joseph E.L. Rogers
E-Mail: cwrt@aiche.org

Historical Note

CWRT is an international non-profit professional organization, affiliated with the American Institute of Chemical Engineers. The Center promotes the chemical, petroleum and pharmaceutical manufacturing industries.

Meetings/Conferences:

Annual Meetings: with AIChE meetings

Publications:

CWRT News. bi-m.

Central Conference of American Rabbis *(1889)*

355 Lexington Ave., 18th Floor
New York, NY 10017-6603
Tel: (212)972-3636 *Fax:* (212)692-0819
E-Mail: info@ccarnet.org
Web Site: www.ccarnet.org
Members: 1800 individuals
Staff: 15
Annual Budget: $1-2,000,000
Executive Vice President: Rabbi Paul J. Menitoff
E-Mail: info@ccarnet.org

Historical Note

Professional rabbinic organization of Reform Judaism.

Meetings/Conferences:

Annual Meetings: Spring

Publications:

CCAR Yearbook. a.
Journal of Reform Judaism. q. adv.

Central Office Executives Association of the National Panhellenic Conference *(1943)*

Historical Note

A division of National Panhellic Council, which provides administrative support.

Central Station Alarm Association *(1950)*

440 Maple Ave.
Suite 201
Vienna, VA 22180
Tel: (703)242-4670 *Fax:* (703)242-4675
E-Mail: admin@csaaul.org
Web Site: www.csaaul.org
Members: 150 companies
Staff: 4
Annual Budget: $1-2,000,000
Executive Vice President: Stephen P. Doyle
E-Mail: director@csaaul.org
Director, Marketing and Communications: Celia Besore
E-Mail: communications@csaaul.org
Vice President, Finance: Madeline Fullerton
E-Mail: finance@csaaul.org
Director, Member Services: Claudia Harper
Director, Meetings and Conventions: John McDonald

Historical Note

Underwriters Laboratories-listed and FM-approved central stations and suppliers to the burglar/fire alarm industry. Formerly (1950-1989) Central Station Electrical Protection Association.

Meetings/Conferences:

2008 – Grand Cayman Islands

Publications:

CSAA Signals. as needed. adv.
CSAA Dispatch Newsetter. q. adv.
Directory. a. adv.

Ceramic Manufacturers Association *(1925)*

1100-H Brandywine Blvd.
P.O. Box 3388
Zanesville, OH 43702-3388
Tel: (740)452-4541 *Fax:* (740)452-2552
Members: 215 companies
Annual Budget: $25-50,000
Manager, Association and Events: Gayla Fleming
E-Mail: gfleming@offinger.com

Historical Note

Formerly (1991) American Association of Ceramic Industries. CerMA is a trade association representing manufacturers of ceramic products. Members are corporations and individuals in the ceramic industry. Membership: $95/year (individual); $300/year (corporate); $25/year (associate).

Meetings/Conferences:

Semi-annual Meetings: Spring and Fall

Publications:

CerMA Member Directory. a. adv.

Ceramic Tile Distributors Association *(1978)*

800 Roosevelt Road, Bldg. C

Suite 312
Glen Ellyn, IL 60137
Tel: (630)545-9415 *Fax:* (630)790-3095
Toll Free: (800)938 - 2832
E-Mail: questions@ctdahome.org
Web Site: www.CTDAhome.org
Members: 600 companies
Staff: 3
Annual Budget: $500-1,000,000
Executive Director: Richard Church

Historical Note

A national trade association of wholesale distributors of ceramic tile. Incorporated in Illinois. CTDA's goals are to increase members' professionalism through information, education and product knowledge and to promote use of ceramic tile in the U.S. Membership: $550/year.

Meetings/Conferences:

2007 - Dana Point, CA(Laguna Cliffs Marriott)/Nov. 7-11

Publications:

News & Views. q.

Ceramic Tile Institute of America *(1957)*
12061 Jefferson Blvd.
Culver City, CA 90230
Tel: (310)574-7800 *Fax:* (310)821-4655
E-Mail: ctioa@earthlink.net
Web Site: www.ctioa.org
Members: 150 companies
Annual Budget: $250-500,000
Executive Director: Gray LaFortune
E-Mail: ctioa@earthlink.net

Historical Note

Formerly Ceramic Tile Institute. Members are installers and makers of ceramic tiles. Membership: varies.

Meetings/Conferences:

Annual Meetings: October

Certification Board for Urologic Nurses and Associates *(1972)*
E. Holly Ave.
Box 56
Pitman, NJ 08071-0056
Tel: (856)256-2351 *Fax:* (856)589-7463
E-Mail: cbuna@ajj.com
Web Site: www.cbuna.org
Members: 500 individuals
Staff: 3
Executive Director: Michael Brennan

Historical Note

Founded as American Board of Urologic Allied Health Professionals; assumed its current name in 1996.

Certified Claims Professional Accreditation Council *(1980)*
P.O. Box 441110-1110
Ft. Washington, MD 20749-1110
Tel: (301)292-1988 *Fax:* (301)292-1787
Web Site: www.lattmag.com
Members: 300 individuals
Staff: 2
Annual Budget: $10-25,000
Administrator: Dale L. Anderson

Historical Note

CCPAC was established to certify individuals in all levels of the domestic and international transportation industry. Membership: $50/year (individuals); $200/year (company).

Meetings/Conferences:

Annual Meetings: in conjunction with the Transportation Claims and Prevention Council

Publications:

Proclaim. q. adv.
Passport to Claims Professionalism. bien.
Pocket CCPAC Directory. bien.

Certified Contractors NetWork *(1995)*
134 Sibley Ave.
Ardmore, PA 19003
Tel: (610)642-9505 *Fax:* (610)642-5842
Toll Free: (866)868 - 7895
E-Mail: info@contractors.net
Web Site: www.contractors.net
Members: 100 companies
Staff: 5
Annual Budget: $500-1,000,000
Chief Executive Officer: Richard Kaller
E-Mail: info@contractors.net

Historical Note

CCN provides training and consulting services to independent contractors.

Certified Milk Producers Association of America *(1908)*
8300 Pine Ave.
China, CA 91710
Tel: (909)393-0960 *Fax:* (415)583-7328
Members: 6 farms
Staff: 2
Annual Budget: under $10,000
President: Boyd Clarke

Historical Note

Members are farms producing raw "certified" (pure, but unpasteurized) milk. CMPAA is affiliated with the American Association of Medical Milk Commissions. Membership fee based on production.

Meetings/Conferences:

Annual Meetings: May, with American Ass'n of Medical Milk Commissions.

Publications:

Newsletter. q.

Certified Professional Insurance Agents Society

Historical Note

Became American Insurance Marketing and Sales Society in 2004.

Cervical Spine Research Society *(1973)*
6300 N. River Rd.
Suite 727
Rosemont, IL 60018-4226
Tel: (847)698-1628 *Fax:* (847)823-0536
Web Site: www.csrs.org
Staff: 3
Executive Director: Peggy Wlezien

Meetings/Conferences:

2007 - San Francisco, CA(Palace Hotel)/Nov. 29-Dec. 1

CFA Institute *(1990)*
560 Ray C. Hunt Dr.
Charlottesville, VA 22903-2981
Tel: (434)951-5499 *Fax:* (434)951-5262
Toll Free: (800)247 - 8132
E-Mail: info@cfainstitute.org
Web Site: www.cfainstitute.org
Members: 71887 individuals
Staff: 210
Annual Budget: $50-100,000,000
President and Chief Executive Officer: Jeffrey J. Diermeir, CFA
E-Mail: info@cfainstitute.org

Historical Note

Formed (1990) as the Association for Investment Management and Research, the CFA Institute was formed by a merger of the Financial Analysts Federation and the Institute of Chartered Financial Analysts. The CFA Institute is a professional organizations for financial analysts and portfolio managers. Awards the CFA (Chartered Financial Analyst) designation to members upon completion of three levels of testing and the satisfaction of professional work experience and ethical practice requirements. Membership: $225/year (non-CFA charterholders); $225/year (CFA charterholders).

Publications:

AIMR Exchange. bi-m.
CFA Digest. q.
Financial Analysts Journal. bi-m. adv.

CHA - Certified Horsemanship Association *(1967)*
5318 Old Bullard Road
Tyler, TX 75703-3612
Tel: (903)509-2473 *Fax:* (903)509-2474
Toll Free: (800)399 - 0138
E-Mail: HORSESAFTY@aol.com
Web Site: www.cha-ahse.org
Members: 2500 individuals
Staff: 5
Annual Budget: $250-500,000
Director, Membership: Carol Parker
E-Mail: clandwehr@cha-ahse.org
Director, Programs: Julie Goodnight
E-Mail: clandwehr@cha-ahse.org
Director, Development: Christy Landwehr
E-Mail: clandwehr@cha-ahse.org

Historical Note

Formerly (1990) the Camp Horsemanship Association and The Association for Horsemanship Safety and Education (1998). Founded in Texas in 1967 and incorporated in Michigan in 1972. Members are camp owners, camp directors, colleges, stables, riding instructors and others interested in riding instruction and safety. CHA provides manuals and safety equipment for riding programs and also conducts certification clinics for riding instructors. Membership: $125/year (organization); $35/year (individual).

Meetings/Conferences:

Annual Meetings: Fall

Publications:

The instructor Magazine. q. adv.
Membership Directory. a. adv.

Chain Drug Marketing Association *(1926)*
43157 W. Nine Mile Rd.
P.O. Box 995
Novi, MI 48376-0995
Tel: (248)449-9300 *Fax:* (248)449-4634
E-Mail: cdma@chaindrug.com
Web Site: www.chaindrug.com
Members: 101 organizations
Staff: 16
Annual Budget: $2-5,000,000
President: James R. Devine
E-Mail: cdma@chaindrug.com
Vice President, Marketing: Judy Aspinall
E-Mail: cdma@chaindrug.com
Director, Information Technology: Brandon Curtis
E-Mail: cdma@chaindrug.com

Historical Note

CDMA members are regional drug chains from across North America. Association markets over 800 products under the name Quality Choice to its members. Membership: $200/month (individual); corporate dues vary by size.

Meetings/Conferences:

Semi-Annual Meetings:

Publications:

Making the Connection. q.

Chain Link Fence Manufacturers Institute *(1960)*
10015 Columbia Rd.
Suite B-215
Columbia, MD 21046
Tel: (301)596-2583 *Fax:* (301)596-2594
E-Mail: clfmihq@aol.com
Web Site: www.chainlinkinfo.org
Members: 54 companies
Staff: 2
Annual Budget: $100-250,000
Executive Vice President: Mark Levin
E-Mail: clfmihq@aol.com

Meetings/Conferences:

Annual Meetings: Summer

Publications:

Linkletter. m.

Chamber Music America *(1977)*
305 Seventh Ave.
New York, NY 10001-6008
Tel: (212)242-2022 Ext: 28 *Fax:* (212)242-7955
E-Mail: gevans@chamber-music.org
Web Site: www.chamber-music.org
Members: 8000 individuals
Staff: 12
Annual Budget: $2-5,000,000
Chief Executive Officer: Margaret M. Lioi
E-Mail: mlioi@chamber-music.org
Membership: Gregory Evans
E-Mail: mlioi@chamber-music.org
Meetings/Conventions: David Ezer
E-Mail: dezer@chamber-music.org

Historical Note

Incorporated in New York in September, 1977. Members are conductorless ensembles, one musician to a part (instrumental or vocal), performing concerts for professional fees, presenters of chamber music concerts, training institutions and individuals and

businesses interested in the development and growth of the chamber music field. Membership: $35-85/year (individual), $115-365/year (organization).

Meetings/Conferences:
Annual Meetings: January

Publications:
Chamber Music Magazine. bi-m.
Membership Directory. a.
CMA Matters. q.

Chamber of Commerce of the Apparel Industry *(1936)*
29 Bloomingburg Road
Middletown, NY 10940-8426
Tel: (845)781-7337
Members: 1300 individuals
Staff: 6
President: Howard Birne

Historical Note
Membership concentrated in the New York City area. Primary purpose is the administration of workers' compensation for the industry, as authorized by the New York State Insurance Fund.

Chamber of Shipping of America *(1917)*
1730 M St. NW
Suite 407
Washington, DC 20036-4517
Tel: (202)775-4399 *Fax:* (202)659-3795
Web Site: www.knowships.org
Members: 26 companies
Staff: 3
Annual Budget: $500-1,000,000
President/Chief Executive Officer: Joseph J. Cox
Director, Maritime Affairs: Kathy J. Metcalf

Historical Note
Founded as American Institute of Merchant Shipping as the result of the merger of Committee of American Steamship Lines (1952), Pacific American Steamship Association (1919) and American Merchant Marine Institute (1938). Became U.S. Chamber of Shipping in 1996, and assumed its current name in 1998. CSA members are U.S.-based companies which own, operate, or charter oceangoing tankers, container ships, and other merchant vessels engaged in domestic or international trade. Represents members' interests in dealings with international and domestic agencies concerned with merchant shipping.

Meetings/Conferences:
Annual Meetings: usually Washington, DC

Publications:
Environmental Criminal Liability in U.S. - A Handbook For The Marine Industry.

Charles Homer Haskins Society *(1982)*
Department of History
Ball State University
Muncie, IN 47306
Tel: (765)285-8783 *Fax:* (765)285-5612
Web Site: www.haskins.cornell.edu
Members: 180 individuals
Treasurer: Frederick Suppe
E-Mail: fsuppe@bsu.edu

Historical Note
Members are academic specializing in the study of Viking, Anglo-Saxon, Anglo-Norman, and early Angevin medieval history. Membership: $50/year (individual); $30/year (student).

Publications:
Haskins Soc Journal. a.
Anglo-Norman Anonymous Newsletter. q.

Check Payment Systems Association *(1952)*
2025 M St. NW
Suite 800
Washington, DC 20036-2422
Tel: (202)367-1144 *Fax:* (202)367-2144
E-Mail: info@cpsa-check.org
Web Site: www.cpsa-checks.org
Members: 60 companies
Staff: 2
Annual Budget: $250-500,000
Executive Director: Wade Delk

Historical Note
Formerly Bank Stationers Section of Lithographers and Printers National Association and the Bank Stationers Association, then became Financial Stationers Association and assumed its present name in 1999. Absorbed the Payment Systems Education Association in 1990.

Meetings/Conferences:
Annual Meetings: Summer

Publications:
The Indelible Check.
Guideline to Enhanced Check Security.

Cheiron: The International Society for the History of Behavioral and Social Sciences *(1968)*
Dept. of Psychology, Univ. of Guelph
Guelph, ON N16 2-WI
Tel: (262)595-2112 *Fax:* (262)595-2602
Web Site: www.psych.yorku.ca/orgs/cheiron
Members: 350 individuals
Staff: 2
Annual Budget: under $10,000
Executive Officer: Andrew Winston

Historical Note
Scholars in the United States and other countries interested in the history of the behavioral and social sciences. Membership: $20/year.

Meetings/Conferences:
Annual Meetings: Third Week in June/80-120

Publications:
Cheiron Newsletter. semi-a. adv.

Chemical Coaters Association International *(1970)*
P.O. Box 54316
Cincinnati, OH 45254
Tel: (513)624-6767 *Fax:* (513)624-0601
Toll Free: (800)926 - 2848
Web Site: www.ccaiweb.com
Members: 1000individualsandcompanies
Staff: 4
Annual Budget: $100-250,000
Executive Director: Anne Goyer

Historical Note
Users and suppliers of industrial cleaners, paints, coatings and equipment. Membership: $65/year (domestic individual), $1,000/year (domestic corporation); $135/year (individual, overseas), $1,500/year (corporation, overseas); $15 one-time membership processing fee.

Meetings/Conferences:
Annual Meetings: Spring

Publications:
Finishing Touch Newsletter. q.

Chemical Fabrics and Film Association *(1927)*
1300 Sumner Ave.
Cleveland, OH 44115-2851
Tel: (216)241-7333 *Fax:* (216)241-0105
E-Mail: cffa@chemicalfabricsandfilm.com
Web Site: www.chemicalfabricsandfilm.com
Members: 35 companies
Staff: 3
Executive Secretary: Charles M. Stockinger

Historical Note
Established as the Pyroxylin Coated Fabric Manufacturers, CFFA became the Vinyl Fabrics Institute and assumed its present name in 1971. Members are manufacturers of vinyl and urethane products.

Chemical Heritage Foundation *(1982)*
315 Chestnut St.
Philadelphia, PA 19106-2702
Tel: (215)925-2222 *Fax:* (215)925-1954
Toll Free: (888)224 - 6006
E-Mail: info@chemheritage.org
Web Site: www.chemheritage.org
Members: 29 organizations
Staff: 55
Annual Budget: $10-25,000,000
President: Arnold Thackray
Director, Communications and Marketing: Shelley Wilks Geehr
Vice President, Finance and Administration: Miriam Fisher Schaefer

Historical Note
Founded under of the auspices of the American Chemical Society and the American Institute of Chemical Engineers, CHF is recognized as the central agency for preserving, studying and communicating the history of the chemical industry. CHF's mission is to advance the heritage of the chemical and molecular sciences by collecting and disseminating information about historical resources, promoting public understanding, encouraging research, scholarship, and popular writing, publishing resource guides and historical materials, conducting oral histories, creating traveling exhibits, and taking other appropriate steps to make known the achievements of chemical scientists and the chemical process industries.

Publications:
Chemical Heritage. q. adv.

Chemical Industry Data Exchange
401 N. Michigan Ave.
Chicago, IL 60611-4267
Tel: (312)321-5145 *Fax:* (312)321-5158
E-Mail: memberservices@cidx.org
Web Site: www.cidx.org
Executive Director: JoAnne Norton

Historical Note
CIDX promotes standards to improve the efficiency of transactions across the chemical industry supply chain. Members are chemical producers and companies active in the chemicals industry.

Chemical Producers and Distributors Association *(1975)*
1430 Duke St.
Alexandria, VA 22314
Tel: (703)548-7700 *Fax:* (703)548-3149
Web Site: www.cpda.com
Members: 90 companies
Staff: 5
Annual Budget: $500-1,000,000
President: Warren E. Stickle, Ph.D.
Director, Legislative Affairs: Diane Schute

Historical Note
Until 1979, Pesticide Formulators Association, and formerly the Pesticide Producers Association, CPDA assumed its present name in 1987. Incorporated in the District of Columbia in 1975. Member are small to medium sized pesticide formulators, manufacturers and distributors.

Meetings/Conferences:
Annual Meetings: Summer

Publications:
Executive News. m.
Legislative and Regulatory Journal. m.
FAX-Flashed. bi-w.

Chemical Sources Association *(1972)*
1100 Valley Brook Ave.
P.O. Box 790
Lyndhurst, NJ 07071-0790
Tel: (201)896-4100 *Fax:* (201)896-8660
E-Mail: diane@afius.org
Web Site: www.chemsources.org
Members: 200 individuals
Staff: 3
Annual Budget: $25-50,000
Counsel: Patrick J. McNamara

Historical Note
Created to seek sources of supply and encourage production of various chemicals either not commonly found in the marketplace or newly created products used as flavoring ingredients. Membership: $325/year (company).

Publications:
Patent Compendiums (online). a.

Chemical Waste Transporation Institute *(1982)*

Historical Note
A division of the Hazardous Waste Management Association.

Cherry Marketing Institute *(1988)*
P.O. Box 30285
Lansing, MI 48909-7785
Tel: (517)669-4264 *Fax:* (517)669-3354
Web Site: www.usacherries.com
Members: 1200 cherry growers
Staff: 8
Annual Budget: $500-1,000,000
President/ Executive Director: Philip J. Korson, II

Historical Note
Serves as the national promotional organization for cherry growers in Michigan, Utah, Wisconsin and New York. Provides marketing information, research, product development, and product promotion.
Meetings/Conferences:
Annual Meetings: January

Chester White Swine Record Association *(1930)*
P.O. Box 9758
Peoria, IL 61612-9758
Tel: (309)691-0151 *Fax:* (309)691-0168
E-Mail: cpspeoria@mindspring.com
Web Site: www.cpsswine.com/chester/chesterwhites.htm
Members: 1050 individuals
Staff: 3
Annual Budget: $250-500,000
Director, Promotions: Jack Wall
Historical Note
Breeders of Chester White swine. The Chester White Breed originated in Chester County, PA, in the early 19th century. Member of the National Pedigree Livestock Council.
Publications:
Chester White Journal. bi-m. adv.

Chi Eta Phi Sorority *(1932)*
3029 13th St. NW
Washington, DC 20009
Tel: (202)232-3858 *Fax:* (202)232-3460
E-Mail: chietaphi@erols.com
Web Site: www.chietaphi.com
Members: 8000 individuals
Staff: 1
Annual Budget: $100-250,000
17th Supreme Basileus: Carolyn Mosley
E-Mail: chietaphi@erols.com
Contact: Lillian Stokes
Historical Note
A professional sorority of registered and student nurses, Chi Eta Phi was established to develop a corps of nursing leaders, encourage continuing education, recruit for the nursing and health professions, develop working relationships with other professional groups, and stimulate a close and friendly relationship among members. Membership: $75/year.
Meetings/Conferences:
Annual Meetings: July/500
Publications:
Chi Line Newsletter. semi-a.
Glowing Lamp. a.
Directory. a.

Chief Administrators of Catholic Education
Historical Note
An affiliate of the National Catholic Educational Association which provides administrative support.

Chief Executives Organization *(1958)*
7920 Norfolk Ave.
Suite 400
Bethesda, MD 20814
Tel: (301)656-9220 *Fax:* (301)656-9221
Toll Free: (800)634 - 2655
Members: 1400 individuals
Staff: 15
Annual Budget: $2-5,000,000
Executive Director: Brien Biondi
Historical Note
Members are individuals formerly in the Young Presidents' Organization who have become 49, the mandatory retirement age. Formerly (1983) Chief Executives Forum. Membership: $1150/year.
Meetings/Conferences:
Semi-Annual Meetings: Spring and Fall
Publications:
Compass. q.

Chief Officers of State Library Agencies *(1973)*
201 E. Main St.
Suite 1405
Lexington, KY 40507
Tel: (859)514-9166 *Fax:* (859)514-9166
Web Site: www.cosla.org
Members: 52 individuals
Staff: 1
Annual Budget: $50-100,000
Association Director: Tracy Tucker
Historical Note
An independent organization of the chief officers of state and territorial agencies designated as the state library administrative agency and responsible for statewide library development. COSLA provides a continuing mechanism for dealing with the problems and challenges faced by the heads of the state agencies which are responsible for statewide library development.
Meetings/Conferences:
Annual Meetings: Winter
Publications:
COSLA Directory. a.

Chief Petty Officers Association *(1969)*
5520-G Hempstead Way
Springfield, VA 22151-4009
Tel: (703)941-0395 *Fax:* (703)941-0397
E-Mail: cgcpoa@aol.com
Web Site: www.uscgcpoa.org
Members: 12000 individuals
Staff: 2
Annual Budget: $100-250,000
Executive Director: Thomas R. Scaramastro
Historical Note
Chief Petty Officers of the U.S. Coast Guard, active, retired and reserve. Constituent member of the Combined Organization of Military Associations. Membership: $24/year.
Meetings/Conferences:
Annual Meetings: August
Publications:
The Chief. q. adv.

Chief Warrant and Warrant Officers Association, United States Coast Guard *(1929)*
James Creek Marina
200 V. St. SW
Washington, DC 20024
Tel: (202)554-7753 *Fax:* (202)484-0641
E-Mail: cwoauscg@verizon.net
Web Site: www.cwoauscg.org
Members: 3600 individuals
Staff: 1
Annual Budget: $50-100,000
Executive Director: Ed Swift
E-Mail: cwoauscg@verizon.net
Historical Note
CWOA members are active, reserve and retired warrant officers and chief warrant officers.
Meetings/Conferences:
Annual Meetings: April
2007 - Bowie, MD(Comfort Inn)/Apr. 11-14/50
Publications:
CWO News. bi-m.

Child Neurology Society *(1971)*
1000 W. County Road E
Suite 290
St. Paul, MN 55126
Tel: (651)486-9447 *Fax:* (651)486-9436
E-Mail: nationaloffice@childneurologysociety.org
Web Site: www.childneurologysociety.org
Members: 1300 individuals
Staff: 2
Annual Budget: $100-250,000
Executive Director: Mary E. Currey, CMP
E-Mail: nationaloffice@childneurologysociety.org
Historical Note
Established in Minneapolis, MN, the Society advances child neurology by providing a scientific forum for professionals in the field. Membership: $225/year (active).
Meetings/Conferences:
Annual Meetings: Fall
Publications:
Annals of Neurology. m. adv.
CNS Newsletter. q. adv.

Child Welfare League of America *(1920)*
440 First St. NW, Third Floor
Washington, DC 20001-2085
Tel: (202)638-2952 *Fax:* (202)638-4004
Web Site: www.cwla.org
Members: 1153 individuals
Staff: 150
Annual Budget: $10-25,000,000
President/Chief Executive Officer: Shay Bilchik
Senior Vice President, Operations: Kathy Barbell
Co-Director, Government Affairs: Tim Briceland-Betts
Vice President, Finance/Chief Financial Officer: Nancy Moll
Co-Director, Government Affairs: John Sciamanna
Vice President, Corporate Communications and Development: Linda Spears
Vice President, Membership and Program Services: Dana Wilson
Historical Note
Has an annual budget of approximately $18 million.
Meetings/Conferences:
Annual Meetings: Washington, DC/March
Publications:
Children's Voice Magazine. bi-m. adv.
Child Welfare: Journal of Policy, Practice & Program. bi-m. adv.
CWLA Children's Monitor Newsletter. m.
CWLA Directory of Member Agencies. a.

Children's Book Council *(1945)*
12 W. 37th St., Second Floor
New York, NY 10018
Tel: (212)966-1990 *Fax:* (212)966-2073
E-Mail: info@cbcbooks.org
Web Site: www.cbcbooks.org
Members: 80 publishers
Staff: 8
Annual Budget: $1-2,000,000
Executive Director: Robin Adelson
Historical Note
CBC is a trade association of producers of children's books and related materials promoting reading and literature for children. Sponsors Children's Book Week each November and Young People's Poetry Week each April.
Meetings/Conferences:
Annual Meetings: September
2007 - New York, NY
Publications:
CBC Features. semi-a.

Children's Literature Association *(1972)*
P.O. Box 138
Battle Creek, MI 49016-0138
Tel: (269)965-8180 *Fax:* (269)965-3568
Members: 700 individuals
Staff: 1
Annual Budget: $100-250,000
Administrator: Kathryn Kiessling
Historical Note
The ChLA promotes serious scholarship and criticism in children's literature. Members are teachers, academics, critics, scholars, students, librarians, and institutions. Presents annual awards for excellence in children's literature. Membership: $75/year (individual); $145/year (institution).
Meetings/Conferences:
Annual Meetings: Summer
2007 - Newport News, VA(Christopher Newport University)/June 14-16/250
Publications:
Children's Literature: An International Journal. a.
ChLA Quarterly. q.

China Clay Producers Association *(1978)*
4885 Riverside Dr.
Suite 108
Macon, GA 31210
Tel: (478)757-1211 *Fax:* (478)757-1949
E-Mail: info@georgiamining.org
Web Site: www.kaolin.com
Members: 4 companies
Staff: 1
Annual Budget: $250-500,000
Executive Vice President: Lee R. Lemke

Historical Note
A trade group of kaolin producers. Supports the China Clay Producers Group Political Action Committee.

Chinese American Food Society *(1975)*
P.O. Box 194
Ashton, MD 20861
E-Mail: manager@cafsnet.org
Web Site: www.cafsnet.org
Members: 300 individuals
Annual Budget: under $10,000
President-Elect: Martin Lo

Historical Note
CAFS is an academic and professional organization which brings together professionals residing in North America with interests in food science and technology, as well as in Chinese culture, to provide technical consultation to industry and organizations. Has no paid officers or full-time staff. Membership: $20/year (individual).

Meetings/Conferences:
Annual Meetings: *usually in conjunction with Institute of Food Technologists*

Publications:
CAFS Newsletter. q. adv.
Science & Technology Monograph Series.

Chinese American Medical Society *(1964)*
41 Elizabeth St.
Suite 403
New York, NY 10013
Tel: (212)965-0723 *Fax:* (212)965-1876
Web Site: www.camsociety.org
Members: 860 individuals
Annual Budget: $10-25,000
Executive Director: H.H. Wang, M.D.
E-Mail: hw5@columbia.edu

Historical Note
Formerly (1985) American Chinese Medical Society. CAMS members are physicians of Chinese ancestry residing in the United States or Canada. Has no paid officers or full-time staff. Membership: $100/year (individual); $25/year (residency).

Meetings/Conferences:
Semi-Annual Meetings: Spring and Fall, usually in New York, NY/200

Publications:
CAMS Newsletter. 3-4/year.
Membership Directory. a.

Chinese Language Teachers Association *(1962)*
Univ. of Hawaii, Center for Chinese Studies
Moore Hall 416
Honolulu, HI 96822
Tel: (808)956-2692 *Fax:* (808)956-2682
Web Site: http://clta.osu.edu
Members: 800individualsandorganizations
Staff: 1
Annual Budget: $50-100,000
Executive Director: Cynthia Ning

Historical Note
Affiliated with the Association for Asian Studies, the Modern Language Association, and the American Council for the Teaching of Foreign Languages. Membership: $30-90/year (individual, varies by income); $120/year (organization).

Meetings/Conferences:
Annual Meetings: *November, with the American Council for the Teaching of Foreign Languages.*
2007 – San Antonio, TX/Nov. 16-18

Publications:
Journal of the CLTA. 3/year. adv.
Monograph. irreg.
Newsletter. 3/year. adv.

Chinese-American Librarians Association *(1983)*
P.O. Box 4992
Irvine, CA 92616
Tel: (949)552-5615 *Fax:* (949)857-1988
Web Site: www.cala-web.org
Members: 1000 individuals
Annual Budget: $10-25,000
Executive Director: Sally C. Tseng
E-Mail: sctseng888@yahoo.com

Historical Note
Formerly the Mid-West Chinese American Librarians Association. Affiliated with the American Library Association. Has no paid staff. Membership: $30/year (individual).

Meetings/Conferences:
Annual Meetings:
2007 – Washington, DC/June 21-27

Publications:
CALA Newsletter. 2/year.
Journal of Library and Information Science. semi-a.
Membership Directory. a. adv.

Chiropractic Council on Physiological Therapeutics and Rehabilitation *(1920)*
Seven Mystic Ln.
Malvern, PA 19355
Web Site: www.ccptr.org
Members: 250 individuals
Annual Budget: under $10,000
Contact: Jan Sharp, DC, DACRB

Historical Note
Members are chiropractors with an interest in the application of physiotherapy and rehabilitation to the practice of chiropractic. Has no paid officers or full-time staff.

Meetings/Conferences:
Annual Meetings: *June*

Publications:
Physiotherapy Briefs. irreg.

Chlorinated Paraffins Industry Association *(1984)*
1250 Connecticut Ave. NW
Suite 700
Washington, DC 20036
Tel: (202)419-1500 *Fax:* (202)659-8037
E-Mail: rfensterheim@regnet.com
Web Site: www.regnet.com/cpia
Staff: 2
Executive Director: Robert J. Fensterheim

Historical Note
CPIA is composed of manufacturers, distributors, and users of chlorinated paraffins, used in lubricants, plastics, and flame retardants.

Publications:
Status Report. irreg.

Chlorine Chemistry Council *(1992)*
1300 Wilson Blvd.
Arlington, VA 22209
Tel: (703)741-5000 *Fax:* (703)741-6084
Web Site: www.c3.org
Annual Budget: $5-10,000,000
Executive Director: Clifford T. Howlett, Jr.

Historical Note
A council of the Chemical Manufacturers Association. Membership: based on production/use of chlorine.

Publications:
Newsline. w.

Chlorine Institute *(1924)*
1300 Wilson Blvd.
Rosslyn, VA 22209
Tel: (703)741-5760 *Fax:* (703)741-6068
Web Site: www.chlorineinstitute.org
Members: 220 companies
Staff: 12
Annual Budget: $2-5,000,000
President: Arthur Dungan

Historical Note
Members are companies engaged in the production, packaging, distribution or use of chlorine, caustic soda, caustic potash, sodium hypochlorite; the distribution and use of hydrogen chloride; or any company interested in the development and improvement of the cholo-alkali industry. The Halogenated Solvents Industry Alliance became affiliated with the Institute in 1992. Membership: $2,900/year.

Meetings/Conferences:
2007 – Houston, TX(JW Marriott)/March 18-21
2007 – Nashville, TN(Loew's Vanderbilt)/Sept. 30-Oct. 3/200

Publications:
Annual Report. a.
Insider. m.

Chlorobenzene Producers Association *(1979)*

Historical Note
An affiliate of the Synthetic Organic Chemical Manufacturers Association, which provides administrative support.

Chocolate Manufacturers Association *(1923)*
8320 Old Courthouse Rd.
Suite 300
Vienna, VA 22182
Tel: (703)790-5011 *Fax:* (703)790-5752
E-Mail: info@chocolateusa.org
Web Site: www.chocolateusa.org
Members: 8 companies
Staff: 10
Annual Budget: $100-250,000
President: Lynn Munroe Bragg

Historical Note
Founded as the Association of Cocoa and Chocolate Manufacturers of the United States; assumed its present name in 1958. An affiliate of National Confectioners Association (same Address).

Choreographers Guild *(1971)*

Historical Note
An affiliate of Society of Stage Directors and Choreographers. Members are professional choreographers working in television, film, video and theater.

Choristers Guild *(1949)*
2834 W. Kingsley Road
Garland, TX 75041-2498
Tel: (972)271-1521 *Fax:* (972)840-3113
E-Mail: choristers@choristerguild.org
Web Site: www.choristersguild.org
Members: 5000 individuals
Staff: 9
Annual Budget: $1-2,000,000
Executive Director: Jim Rindelaub

Historical Note
Members are directors of children's and youth choirs in churches and schools seeking to enhance the religious and musical training of their students. Incorporated in the states of Tennessee and Texas. Membership: $65/year (American members); $90/year (Canadian members); $105/year (foreign members outside Canada); $25/year (student); $55/year (library rate).

Meetings/Conferences:
Annual Meetings: *6 per year/70*

Publications:
The Chorister. 6/year.

Chorus America *(1977)*
1156 15th St. NW
Suite 310
Washington, DC 20005-1704
Tel: (202)331-7577 *Fax:* (202)331-7599
E-Mail: service@chorusamerica.org
Web Site: www.chorusamerica.org
Members: 1100 organizations and individuals
Staff: 9
Annual Budget: $500-1,000,000
President and Chief Executive Officer: Ann Meier Baker
E-Mail: service@chorusamerica.org
Office Manager: Adam Hall
E-Mail: adam@chorusamerica.org

Historical Note
Formerly (1987) the Association of Professional Vocal Ensembles. Professional members are choral organizations which employ a minimum of 25% of the total ensemble membership or twelve professional singers. Chorus America promotes the professional growth and quality of the choral art, and occupational respectability and opportunity for its performers. Administers the American Choral Foundation (see separate listing). Membership: $50/year (individual); .01% of operating budget or $100 minimum (organization), with $500 maximaum.

Meetings/Conferences:
Annual Meetings: *Annual*

Publications:
The Voice of CHORUS AMERICA. q. adv.

Christian College Consortium *(1971)*

50 Stark Hwy. South
Dunbarton, NH 03046-4406
Tel: (603)774-6623 *Fax:* (603)774-6628
E-Mail: tenglund@earthlink.net
Web Site: www.ccconsortium.org
Members: 13 colleges
Staff: 1
Annual Budget: $100-250,000
President: Thomas H. Englund
E-Mail: tenglund@earthlink.net

Historical Note
Organized in 1971, the Consortium consists of thirteen colleges united by regional accreditation, concentration upon liberal arts studies, educational strengths that can be shared, nationwide distribution and a common affirmation of faith.

Meetings/Conferences:
Annual Meetings: March
2007 - Indian Wells, CA(The Miramonte Resort)/March 21-24

Christian Educators Association International *(1953)*
P.O. Box 41300
Pasadena, CA 91114
Tel: (626)798-1124 *Fax:* (626)798-2346
E-Mail: info@ceai.org
Web Site: www.ceai.org
Members: 7500 individuals
Staff: 20
Executive Director: Finn Laursen

Historical Note
CEAI members are professional educators (teachers, administrators and support personnel) serving in public and private schools.

Publications:
CEAI Newsletter. 4/year.
Teachers of Vision. 6/year. adv.

Christian Labor Association of the United States of America *(1931)*
405 Centerstone Court
P.O. Box 65
Zeeland, MI 49464
Tel: (616)772-9164 *Fax:* (616)772-9830
E-Mail: christianlabor@yahoo.com
Members: 3000 individuals
Staff: 11
Annual Budget: $250-500,000
Contact: Clarence Merrill
E-Mail: christianlabor@yahoo.com

Historical Note
Independent labor union. Works to support Christian principles in the workplace and promote cooperation between management and labor through union representation.

Publications:
Christian Labor Herald. q.

Christian Legal Society *(1961)*
8001 Braddock Road, Suite 300
Springfield, VA 22151
Tel: (703)642-1070 *Fax:* (703)642-1075
E-Mail: clshq@clsnet.org
Web Site: www.clsnet.org
Members: 4000 individuals
Staff: 25
Annual Budget: $2-5,000,000
Chief Executive Officer and Executive Director: Samuel B. Casey

Historical Note
A Christian organization of lawyers, judges, law professors and students, and interested laypeople, advocating justice and religious freedom. Membership: $175/year (attorneys); $25/year (law students); $50/year (associates).

Publications:
Christian Lawyer Digest. q.
Christian Lawyer. bi-a. adv.

Christian Management Association *(1976)*
P.O. Box 4090
San Clemente, CA 92674
Tel: (949)487-0900 *Fax:* (949)487-0927
Toll Free: (800)727 - 4262
E-Mail: cma@cmaonline.org
Web Site: www.cmaonline.org
Members: 3000 individuals
Staff: 8
Annual Budget: $1-2,000,000
Chief Executive Officer: John Pearson
Manager, Member Services: Sandy Huston
Director, Conferences and Meetings: Marsha Lyons

Historical Note
Formerly Christian Ministries Management Association; assumed its present name in 1990. Non-profit organization assisting C.E.O.'s and managers of churches and Christian organizations. Membership: $199/year (individual); $349/year (organization).

Meetings/Conferences:
Annual Meetings: February

Publications:
Christian Ministries Salary Survey. bien.
Christian Management Report. bi-m. adv.
Membership Directory. a. adv.
Publications List Available.

Christian Medical & Dental Associations *(1931)*
P.O. Box 7500
Bristol, TN 37621-7500
Tel: (423)844-1000 *Fax:* (423)844-1005
Toll Free: (888)230 - 2637
E-Mail: main@cmda.org
Web Site: www.cmda.org
Members: 17000 individuals
Staff: 70
Annual Budget: $5-10,000,000
Executive Director: David Stevens, M.D.
Associate Executive Director: Gene Rudd, M.D.

Historical Note
Founded as Christian Medical & Dental Society; assumed current name in 2000. Members are Christian medical and dental personnel, some of whom serve as medical missionaries. Membership: $250/year (individual practicing member); $75/year (missionary); $25/year (student); $150/year (new member).

Meetings/Conferences:
Annual Meetings: Summer
2007 - Orlando, FL(The Buena Vista Palace)/June 20-24/600

Publications:
Today's Christian Doctor. 4/year. adv.
Christian Doctors Digest Audio Journal. 7/year.

Christian Schools International *(1920)*
3350 E. Paris Ave.
Grand Rapids, MI 49512
Tel: (616)957-1070 *Fax:* (616)957-5022
Toll Free: (800)635 - 8288
E-Mail: info@csionline.org
Web Site: www.csionline.org
Members: 500 Protestant private schools
Staff: 35
Annual Budget: $2-5,000,000
President and Chief Executive Officer: David Koetje
Director, Consulting: James De Korne
E-Mail: info@csionline.org
Business Manager: John Wolters

Historical Note
Established as the National Union of Christian Schools, it assumed its present name in 1978. Serves Christian schools which seek to integrate Christian faith and culture. Provides employee benefit programs, curriculum and periodical publications, and services to school boards and administrators.

Meetings/Conferences:
Annual Meetings: July/August
2007 - Harbor Springs, MI(Boyne Highlands Resort)/July 25-28/500

Publications:
Board Agenda. q.
The Christian School Teacher. 3/year.
Administrator. q.
Christian Home and School. q. adv.
Christian School Directory. a.

Christian Stewardship Association
4700 W. Lake Ave.
Glenview, IL 60025
Tel: (847)375-4741 *Fax:* (866)597-1806
E-Mail: csa@stewardship.org
Web Site: www.stewardship.org

Chronic Disease Directors *(1988)*
2872 Woodcock Blvd., Suite 220
Atlanta, GA 30341
Tel: (770)458-7400 *Fax:* (770)458-7401
E-Mail: info@chronicdisease.org
Web Site: www.chronicdisease.org
Members: 59 program directors
Staff: 6
Annual Budget: $2-5,000,000

Historical Note
Founded as Association of State and Territorial Chronic Disease Program Directors, CDD members work to mobilize resources for treatment of chronic disease.

Meetings/Conferences:
Annual Meetings: Winter

Publications:
Chronic Disease Chronicles. semi-a.
Chronic Disease Directors eBulletin. m.

Church and Synagogue Library Association *(1967)*
2920 S.W. Dolph Ct.
Suite 3A
Portland, OR 97219
Tel: (503)244-6919 *Fax:* (503)977-3734
Toll Free: (800)542 - 2752
E-Mail: csla@worldaccessnet.com
Web Site: www.cslainfo.org
Members: 1600 libraries
Staff: 2
Annual Budget: $50-100,000
Administrator: Judith M. Janzen
E-Mail: csla@worldaccessnet.com

Historical Note
An outgrowth of library workshops held for several years by the library school of Drexel University in Philadelphia, CSLA provides educational guidance for library services in religious institutions. A member of the Council of National Library Associations. Membership: $35-$40/year (individual); $55-$65/year (church); $200/year (institution).

Meetings/Conferences:
Annual Meetings: June/July
2007 - Valley Forge, PA(Hilton)/July 15-17/200
2008 - Greensville, SC(Hilton)/July 19-22/200

Publications:
Congregational Libraries Today. bi-m. adv.

Church Music Publishers Association *(1926)*
P.O. Box 158992
Nashville, TN 37215
Tel: (615)791-0273 *Fax:* (615)790-8847
Web Site: www.cmpamusic.org
Members: 30 companies
Staff: 1
Annual Budget: $10-25,000
Secretary-Treasurer: Jerry Weimer

Historical Note
Formerly Church and Sunday School Music Publishers Association. Members publish music for Christian churches and schools. Membership: $450/year (organization).

Meetings/Conferences:
Annual Meetings: Spring

CIES, The Food Business Forum *(1953)*
8455 Colesville Road
Silver Spring, MD 20910
Tel: (301)563-3383 *Fax:* (301)563-3386
E-Mail: us.office@ciesnet.com
Web Site: www.ciesnet.com
Members: 500 companies
Staff: 30
Annual Budget: $1-2,000,000
Chief Executive Officer: Allen McClay
E-Mail: us.office@ciesnet.com

Historical Note
Formerly the International Association of Chain Stores - North American Headquarters, International Center for Companies of the Food Trade and Industry-North America Headquarters (1989) and Food Business Forum (1996). Provides management research on

problems related to food distribution and serves as an international forum where food chain store executives can meet to exchange ideas and information. Membership: $900-$16,000/year based on sales volume (organization).

Meetings/Conferences:
2007 - Shanghai, China/June 20-22
2008 - Berlin, Germany/June

Publications:
Food Business News. 10/year.

Cigar Association of America *(1937)*
1707 H St., NW, Suite 800
Washington, DC 20006
Tel: (202)223-8204 *Fax:* (202)833-0379
Members: 68 companies
Staff: 5
Annual Budget: $2-5,000,000
President: Norman F. Sharp

Historical Note
Established in 1937 as the Cigar Manufacturers Association of America, Inc. Became the Cigar Association of America, Inc. in 1974 through a merger of the Cigar Research Council, the Cigar Manufacturers Association of America, the Cigar Institute of America and the State and Local Tax Council. Represents the producers of about 95% of the cigars sold in the U.S. Sponsors the Cigar Political Action Committee.

Meetings/Conferences:
Annual Meetings: Fall
2007 - Charleston, SC(Charleston Place)/Oct. 11-14/180

Publications:
Import Export Report. m.
Trademark Bulletin. bi-m.

CIIT Centers for Health Research *(1974)*
Six Davis Dr.
P.O. Box 12137
Research Triangle Park, NC 27709-2137
Tel: (919)558-1204 *Fax:* (919)558-1400
E-Mail: emangum@ciit.org
Web Site: www.ciit.org
Staff: 130
Annual Budget: $10-25,000,000
President and Chief Executive Officer: William F. Greenlee, Ph.D.
E-Mail: wgreenlee@ciit.org
Director, Computational Biology: Melvin E. Andersen, Ph.D.
Director, Human Resources and Administrative Services: Rusty Bramlage, MBA, MPH, SPHR, CCP
Director, Biological Sciences/Director, Center for Development Dosimetry: David Dorman, DVM., Ph.D.
Chief Financial Officer and Vice President, Finance and Operations: Helen N. Schinkel, MBA, CPA

Historical Note
Founded as Chemical Industry Institute of Toxicology; assumed its current name in 2000. CIIT's mission is to promote the use of the best possible science for human health risk assessments, and to enhance public health through the conduct of leading edge, interdisciplinary research that elucidates the mechanisms of action of chemicals on biological systems. Funding provided by member companies of the American Chemistry Council, through Long-Range Funding Initiative. CIIT also receives funding from federal grants and industry contracts and has an annual budget of roughly $21 million.

Meetings/Conferences:
Annual Meetings: October

Publications:
CIIT Activities Newsletter. q.

Circuits and Systems Society

Historical Note
See IEEE Circuits and Systems Society

CISA Export Trade Group *(1988)*

Historical Note
A division of Casting Industry Suppliers Association (CISA).

City and Regional Magazine Association *(1978)*
4929 Wilshire Blvd., Suite 428
Los Angeles, CA 90010
Tel: (323)937-5514 *Fax:* (323)937-0959
Toll Free: (866)799 - 2762
Web Site: www.citymag.org
Members: 100 companies
Staff: 4
Annual Budget: $500-1,000,000
Executive Director: C. James Dowden

Historical Note
Membership composed of ABC or BPA-audited, general news, paid subscription city and regional magazines. CRMA represents member magazines on major national and regional policy issues, encourages high editorial and journalistic standards, provides professional development and training opportunities, compiles industry research and data, and promotes city and regional magazines as a major media market. Associate memberships are available to any person, firm, or corporation engaged in a business allied to the publishing of city or regional consumer magazines. Membership: $400-3,500/year (magazine).

Meetings/Conferences:
Annual Meetings: Typical Attendance: 600
2007 - Denver, CO(Grand Hyatt Denver)/May 5-7/500

Publications:
Communicator. m.

Civil Aviation Medical Association *(1948)*
P.O. Box 23864
Oklahoma City, OK 73123-2864
Tel: (405)840-0199 *Fax:* (405)848-1053
Web Site: www.civilavmed.com
Members: 800 individuals
Staff: 1
Annual Budget: $50-100,000
Executive Vice President: James L. Harris, M.Ed.
E-Mail: jimlharris@aol.com

Historical Note
Established in 1948 as the Airline Medical Examiners Association, it assumed its present name in 1955. CAMA is composed of physicians concerned with the welfare and growth of civil aviation, including aviation medical examiners and physicans who are pilots, aviation medical educators, flight instructors, and fixed-base operators. Membership: $100/year (individual); $250/year (organization/company).

Meetings/Conferences:
Annual Meetings: Fall
2007 - San Diego, CA(Marriott Mission Valley)/Oct. 10-14/150

Publications:
Flight Physician. q. adv.

Classification Society of North America *(1969)*
Univ. of Illinois, IDS Dept.
601 S. Morgan St., M/C 294
Chicago, IL 60607-7124
Tel: (312)996-2676 *Fax:* (312)413-0385
Web Site: www.cs-na.org
Members: 200 individuals
Annual Budget: $10-25,000
Secretary/Treasurer: Stanley L. Sclove, Ph.D.

Historical Note
A non-profit, interdisciplinary organization whose purposes are to promote the scientific study of classification and clustering, including systematic methods of creating classifications from data, and to disseminate scientific and educational information related to its fields of interest. Members are researchers in the fields of psychology, statistics, computer science, biology, business applications, education, engineering, mathematics and sociology. Membership: $60/year (individual).

Meetings/Conferences:
2007 - Champaign, IL(University of Illinois)/June 7-10/150

Publications:
Classification Literature Automated Search Service. a. adv.
Journal of Classification. 2/year. adv.

Classroom Publishers Association *(1948)*
P.O. Box 269
Columbus, OH 43218
Tel: (614)486-0831
Members: 6 companies
Annual Budget: $50-100,000
Contact: Kent Johnson

Historical Note
Founded as the Classroom Periodical Publishers Association; assumed its present name in 1978. Has no paid officers or full-time staff.

Clay Minerals Society *(1962)*
3635 Concorde Pkwy.
Suite 500
Chantilly, VA 20151
Tel: (703)652-9960 *Fax:* (703)652-9951
E-Mail: cms@clays.org
Web Site: www.clays.org
Members: 800
Staff: 1
Annual Budget: $250-500,000
Office Advisor: J.M. Elzea Kogel

Historical Note
Incorporated in the District of Columbia, July 18, 1962. Supersedes the Committee on Clay Minerals of the National Academy of Sciences/National Research Council. Members are clay mineralogists and others interested in the scientific study and applications of clays and related silicate minerals. Membership: $70/year (subscribing member); $35/year (non-subscribing member); $15/year (students).

Meetings/Conferences:
Annual Meetings: Summer
2007 - Santa Fe, NM/June 2-7

Publications:
Clays and Clay Minerals. bi-m.
Workshop Lecture Series. irreg.
Elements.
Meeting Abstracts. a.

Cleaning Equipment Trade Association *(1980)*
968 Lake St., South
Suite 202
Forest Lake, MN 55025
Tel: (651)982-0010 *Fax:* (651)982-0030
Toll Free: (800)441 - 0111
Web Site: www.ceta.org
Members: 325 companies
Staff: 3
Annual Budget: $500-1,000,000
Managing Director: Carol Wasieleski
E-Mail: carol@ceta.org

Historical Note
Formerly the Cleaning Equipment Manufacturers Association, CETA assumed its present name in 1990. Members are manufacturers, distributors and component suppliers of powered cleaning systems. Membership: $325-1,000/year (company).

Meetings/Conferences:
Annual Meetings:

Publications:
Clean-Up Newsletter. q.

Cleaning Management Institute *(1964)*
c/o Nat'l Trade Publications
13 Century Hill Dr.
Latham, NY 12110-2197
Tel: (518)783-1281 *Fax:* (518)783-1386
Web Site: www.cminstitute.net
Members: 850 individuals
Staff: 3
Annual Budget: $250-500,000
Executive Director: Katrine Gauigan
Assistant Director: Nicole Older
E-Mail: nolder@ntpinc.com
Publisher: Humphrey S. Tyler
E-Mail: hstyler@ntpmedia.com

Historical Note
Successor organization to the American Institute of Maintenance (1958) in 1985. Members are individuals and companies involved in building cleaning and maintenance management. Membership: $129/year.

Meetings/Conferences:
Annual Meetings: 7-10 yearly, across the U.S.

Publications:
Training Publications and Testing.
CM/Cleaning & Maintenance Management Magazine. m. adv.
NETWORKING Newsletter. m.

Networking Directory. a.

Clerkship Directors in Internal Medicine *(1989)*
2501 M St. NW, Suite 550
Washington, DC 20037-1308
Tel: (202)861--935 *Fax:* (202)861-9731
E-Mail: cdim@im.org
Web Site: www.im.org/cdim
Staff: 10
Executive Director: Tod Ibrahim
Historical Note
A member organization of Alliance for Academic Internal Medicine, CDIM fosters excellence in the education of students in the core clerkship in internal medicine at accredited medical schools in the U.S. and Canada.
Meetings/Conferences:
Annual Meetings: Fall
Publications:
CDIM News. 2/year.

Cleveland Bay Horse Society of North America *(1885)*
P.O. Box 483
Goshen, NH 03752
Tel: (603)863-5193 *Fax:* (603)863-5193
E-Mail: cbhsna@aol.com
Web Site: www.clevelandbay.org
Members: 150 individuals
Annual Budget: under $10,000
Secretary: Faye Mulvey
Historical Note
Formerly (1992) Cleveland Bay Horse Society of America. Members are breeders or fanciers of purebred Cleveland Bay horses. Has no paid officers or full time staff; acts as a contact for registry maintained by Cleveland Bay Horse Society, United Kingdom. Membership: $45/year (individual); $60/year (family).
Publications:
Baywatch Newsletter. 6/year. adv.

Clinical and Laboratory Standards Institute *(1968)*
940 W. Valley Road, Suite 1400
Wayne, PA 19087-1898
Tel: (610)688-0100 *Fax:* (610)688-0700
Toll Free: (800)447 - 1888
E-Mail: customerservice@clsi.org
Web Site: www.clsi.org
Members: 2100 organizations
Staff: 26
Annual Budget: $2-5,000,000
Executive Vice President: Glen Fine, MS, MBA
E-Mail: gfine@clsi.org
Vice President, Membership and Marketing: Louise Games, MBA
E-Mail: louisec@clsi.org
Director, Standards and Quality: Jennifer K. McGeary, MT (ASCP), MSHA
Vice President, Finance and Administration: Lola R. Pugliese, MBA, MS
E-Mail: lpugliese@clsi.org
Director, Communications: Timothy Roscoe
Director, Standards and Development: Lois Schmidt, DA
Vice President, Standads: John J. Zlockie, MBA
E-Mail: jzlockie@clsi.org
Historical Note
Formerly NCCLS (2005). Develops voluntary consensus standards for health care testing. Affiliated with the American National Standards Institute.
Meetings/Conferences:
Annual Meetings: Spring/250
Publications:
CLSI eNews (online).
Standards. irreg.

Clinical Immunology Society *(1986)*
555 E. Wells St., Suite 1100
Milwaukee, WI 53202-3823
Tel: (414)224-8095 *Fax:* (414)272-6070
E-Mail: info@clinimmsoc.org
Web Site: www.clinimmsoc.org
Members: 750 individuals
Staff: 1
Annual Budget: $250-500,000
Executive Director: Denise Lemke
E-Mail: info@clinimmsoc.org
Historical Note
The mission of the Clinical Immunology Society is to facilitate education, translational research and novel approaches to therapy in clinical immunology to promote excellence in the care of patients with immunologic/inflammatory disorders. CIS is an international professional organization which includes more than 750 clinicians, investigators and trainees. The CIS is governed by a Council consisting of an elected Executive Committee and appointed Councilors.
Publications:
Clinical Immunology. m.

Clinical Laboratory Management Association *(1971)*
989 Old Eagle School Road, Suite 815
Wayne, PA 19087
Tel: (610)995-9580 *Fax:* (610)995-9568
Web Site: www.clma.org
Members: 6400 individuals
Staff: 23
Annual Budget: $2-5,000,000
Chief Executive Officer: Dana Proscal
Director, Business Development: Charles Fenstermaker
Director, Administration: Joe Wisniewski
Historical Note
Established as the American Association of Clinical Laboratory Supervisors and Administrators; became Clinical Laboratory Management Association in 1976. Changed names, becoming CLMA - Leadership in Clinical Systems Management in 2000, and reverted to its previous name in 2002. Members are laboratory supervisors, managers and executives and their suppliers. Membership: $120/year.
Meetings/Conferences:
Annual Meetings: Fall
Publications:
Clinical Leadership and Management Review. bi-m. adv.
Vantage Point. m. adv.
CLMA Email Alert (online). 2/m. adv.

Clinical Ligand Assay Society *(1974)*
3139 S. Wayne Road
Wayne, MI 48184-1220
Tel: (734)722-6290 *Fax:* (734)722-7006
E-Mail: clas@clas.org
Web Site: www.clas.org
Members: 400 individuals
Staff: 2
Annual Budget: $250-500,000
Executive Director: Daisy S. McCann
E-Mail: clas@clas.org
Liaison, Membership: Alicia Scott
E-Mail: clas@clas.org
Liaison, Exhibition: Diane Shaw
E-Mail: clas@clas.org
Historical Note
Founded as the Clinical Radioassay Society, CLAS assumed its present name in 1981. Ligand Assay is a specialty of clinical laboratory medicine by which substances (drugs, hormones, etc.) are measured in minute quantities. Membership: $140/year (regular); $50/year (associate).
Meetings/Conferences:
Annual Meetings: Spring
Publications:
Proceedings (Syllabus). a.
Newsletter. bi-m. adv.
Journal of Clinical Ligand Assay. q. adv.

Clinical Orthopaedic Society *(1912)*
P.O. Box 11086
Richmond, VA 23230-1086
Tel: (804)565-6366 *Fax:* (804)282-0090
E-Mail: cos@societyhq.com
Web Site: www.cosociety.org
Members: 750 individuals
Staff: 3
Annual Budget: $100-250,000
Executive Director: Stewart A. Hinckley, CMP
Historical Note
Members are orthopaedic surgeons. Membership: $165/year (individual).
Meetings/Conferences:
Annual Meetings: Fall/250
Publications:
Journal of the Southern Orthopaedic Ass'n. q.

Clinical Social Work Federation *(1971)*
P.O. Box 3740
Arlington, VA 22203
Tel: (703)522-3866 *Fax:* (703)522-9441
E-Mail: nfscwlo@aol.com
Web Site: www.cswf.org
Members: 11000 individuals
Staff: 2
Annual Budget: $100-250,000
Executive Director: Richard P. Yanes
President: Abigail Grant
Historical Note
Formerly (1997) the National Federation of Socs. for Clinical Social Work, CSWF is an advocacy organization for state societies of social workers.
Meetings/Conferences:
Annual Meetings: Spring and Fall
Publications:
Access. 2-3/year. adv.

Closed Circuit Television Manufacturers Association *(1986)*
Historical Note
An affiliate of Electronic Industries Association, which provides administrative support.

Closure Manufacturers Association *(1981)*
P.O. Box 1358
Kilmarnock, VA 22482
Tel: (804)435-9580 *Fax:* (804)435-2203
E-Mail: djwilliamson@closuremanfucaturers.org
Web Site: www.closuremanufacturers.org
Members: 43 companies
Staff: 1
Annual Budget: $250-500,000
President: Darla Williamson
Historical Note
Founded as the Closure Committee of the Glass Packaging Institute, CMA later became (1984) an independent affiliate of the Institute and then became independently incorporated in 2006. Members are companies that make metal and plastic and composite closures for all types of containers and make plastic containers. Associate members are allied suppliers.
Meetings/Conferences:
Semi-annual Meetings: Spring and Fall
2007 – Phoenix, AZ(Pointe South Mountain)/Feb. 3-March 5
2008 – Long Boat Key, FL(Long Boat Key Club)/Feb. 9-11
Publications:
The Closure Report. 3/year.

Clothing Manufacturers Association of the U.S.A. *(1933)*
730 Broadway, Tenth Floor
New York, NY 10003
Tel: (212)529-0823 *Fax:* (212)529-1739
Members: 100 companies
Staff: 2
Annual Budget: $100-250,000
Executive Director: Robert A. Kaplan
Historical Note
Recognized by the Federal Government as the official liaison and spokesperson for the U.S. men's and boy's tailored clothing manufacturing industry. Represents employer members in national collective bargaining negotiations with the Union. Conducts annual problem-solving seminar. Membership: annual dues based on sales volume or fee determined each year in December.
Publications:
Clothing Industry.
Statistical Report on Sales, Production, and Profit in Men's and Boy's. a.
Publications List Available.

Clowns of America, International *(1960)*
P.O. Box C
Richeyville, PA 15358-0532
Tel: (724)938-8765

Toll Free: (888)522 - 5696
E-Mail: askus@coai.org
Web Site: www.coai.org
Members: 7000 individuals
Annual Budget: $50-100,000
Business Manager: Shirley Long
E-Mail: coaibusinessmgr@aol.com

Historical Note
Formerly (1968) Clown Club of America and Circus Clown Club. Members are amateur, semi-professional and professional clowns. Membership: $30/year (new members); $25/year (individual); $12/year (family).

Meetings/Conferences:
Annual Meetings: April

Publications:
New Calliope. bi-m. adv.

Club Managers Association of America *(1927)*
1733 King St.
Alexandria, VA 22314-2720
Tel: (703)739-9500 *Fax:* (703)739-0124
E-Mail: cmaa@cmaa.org
Web Site: www.cmaa.org
Members: 6500 individuals
Staff: 37
Annual Budget: $2-5,000,000
Chief Executive Officer: James B. Singerling, CCM,CEC
Senior Vice President, Professional Development: Cyd Bougae
Senior Director, Conferences and Meetings: Guy Doria
Chief Operating Officer: Kathi Driggs
Vice President and Chief Development Officer, The Club Foundation: Seth Gregg
Senior Vice President, Membership Operations: Kim Pasquale
Senior Vice President, Marketing and Communications: Ron Rosenbaum

Historical Note
Established and incorporated in Michigan in 1927, CMAA is the professional association for managers of the leading private membership clubs in the US and abroad. Membership: $625/year.

Meetings/Conferences:
Annual Meetings: Winter
2007 – Anaheim, CA(Anaheim Marriott)/Feb. 23-27

Publications:
Club Management Magazine. m. adv.
At Your Service. bi-m.
Outlook. m.

Clydesdale Breeders of the United States *(1879)*
17346 Kelly Road
Pecatonica, IL 61063
Tel: (815)247-8780 *Fax:* (815)247-8337
E-Mail: secretary@clydesusa.com
Web Site: www.clydesusa.com
Members: 900 individuals
Staff: 2
Annual Budget: $100-250,000
Secretary: Betty J. Groves
E-Mail: secretary@clydesusa.com

Historical Note
Members own and breed Clydesdale horses. Formerly the American Clydesdale Association and Clydesdale Breeders Association of the U.S. CBUS is responsible for all registration of eligible horses and the transfer of ownership.

Meetings/Conferences:
Annual Meetings: always in Springfield, IL

Publications:
The Stud Book.
The Clydesdale News. adv. adv.
The Lead Horse.
Clydesdale. a. adv.

Coal Exporters Association of the United States *(1945)*

Historical Note
An affiliate of Nat'l Mining Ass'n, which provides administrative support.

Coal Technology Association *(1975)*
601 Suffield Dr.
Gaithersburg, MD 20878
Tel: (301)294-6080
E-Mail: barbarasak@aol.com
Web Site: www.coaltechnologies.com
Members: 11 companies
Staff: 2
Annual Budget: $100-250,000
Vice President: Barbara A. Sakkestad
E-Mail: barbarasak@aol.com

Historical Note
Organized in Houston, August, 1975. Pipeline and energy companies and manufacturers interested in pipeline delivery of coal and coal technologies with special interests in transportation. Formerly the Slurry Transport Association and Slurry Technology Association. Assumed present name in 1988. Membership: $2,000-15,000/year.

Meetings/Conferences:
Annual Meetings: Clearwater, FL (Sheraton Sand Key)/March, April or May

Publications:
Proceedings, International Technical Conference on Coal Utilization. a.
Inside Pipeline. m.

Coalition for Government Procurement *(1979)*
1990 M St. NW, Suite 400
Washington, DC 20036
Tel: (202)331-0975 *Fax:* (202)822-9788
E-Mail: info@thecap.org
Web Site: www.coalgovpro.org
Members: 220 companies, 10 associations
Staff: 3
Annual Budget: $100-250,000
Executive Vice President: Larry Allen
Director, Policy: Kathryn Coulter

Historical Note
Founded as Coalition for Common Sense in Government Procurement; assumed its current name in 1988. Members are firms who provide commercial goods to the federal government, and related associations.

Publications:
Off the Shelf. m.

Coalition for Juvenile Justice *(1974)*
1710 Rhode Island Ave. NW, Tenth Floor
Washington, DC 20036
Tel: (202)467-0864 *Fax:* (202)887-0738
E-Mail: info@juvjustice.org
Web Site: www.juvjustice.org
Members: 1500 individuals
Staff: 3
Annual Budget: $500-1,000,000
Executive Director: David Doi
E-Mail: davedoi@juvjustice.org
Deputy Director: Nancy Gannon
E-Mail: gannon@juvjustice.org

Historical Note
Formerly (1994) National Coalition of State Juvenile Justice Advisory Groups.

Meetings/Conferences:
Annual Meetings: Spring

Publications:
Annual Report. a.

Coalition of Automotive Associations

Historical Note
Non-profit organization formed to provide administrative support for the Specialty Equipment Market Association and Auto International Association.

Coalition of Black Trade Unionists *(1972)*
1828 L St. NW
Washington, DC 20036
Tel: (202)429-1203 *Fax:* (202)429-1102
Web Site: www.cbtu.org
Members: 50 chapters, 26 internat'l unions
Staff: 3
Executive Director: Michael Williams

Historical Note
Organized to bring more blacks into the labor movement.

Coalition of Essential Schools *(1984)*
1814 Franklin St., Suite 700
Oakland, CA 94612
Tel: (510)433-1451 *Fax:* (510)433-1455
Web Site: www.essentialschools.org
Members: 1000 schools
Staff: 10
Executive Director: Lewis Cohen
Director, Strategic Communications: Brett Bradshaw

Meetings/Conferences:
Annual Meetings: November

Publications:
Horace Newsletter. 5/year.
Membership List. irreg.

Coalition of Higher Education Assistance Organizations *(1980)*
1101 Vermont Ave. NW, Suite 400
Washington, DC 20005-3586
Tel: (202)289-3910 *Fax:* (202)371-0197
E-Mail: jcriseuolo@wpllc.net
Web Site: www.coheao.com
Members: 365 organizations
Staff: 3
Annual Budget: $100-250,000
Executive Director: Harrison Wadsworth
E-Mail: hwadsworth@wpllc.het

Historical Note
COHEAO members are colleges/universities, billers and collectors of student loans. Specialty conferences are held as necessary.

Meetings/Conferences:
Semi-Annual Meetings: Annual/January and Mid-Year/August

Publications:
Torch Newsletter. bi-m.

Coalition of Labor Union Women *(1974)*
815 16th St. NW, Second Floor South
Washington, DC 20006
Tel: (202)508-6969 *Fax:* (202)508-6968
E-Mail: getinfo@cluw.org
Web Site: www.cluw.org
Members: 210000 individuals
Staff: 2
Annual Budget: $100-250,000
Executive Director: Carol Rosenblatt
E-Mail: csrosenblatt@cluw.org

Historical Note
Founded in 1974 to work towards full equality of opportunities and rights for employed women. Members are women in the labor movement, and others interested in advancing the participation of women within unions. Concerned with such issues as labor law reform, passage of ERA, child care, safety in the workplace and pay equity. Membership: $50/year.

Publications:
CLUW News. bi-m.

Coalition of Publicly Traded Partnerships *(1983)*
1801 K St. NW, Suite 500
Washington, DC 20006
Tel: (202)973-3150 *Fax:* (202)973-3101
Web Site: www.ptpcoalition.org
Members: 20 companies
Staff: 2
Annual Budget: $100-250,000
Director: Mary Lyman

Historical Note
CPTP is a trade association representing publicly traded partnerships, corporations which are general partners of PTP's and attorneys, accountants and investment bankers who work with them. Sponsors and supports the Coalition of Publicly Traded Partnerships Political Action Committee. Membership: $15,000/year (large PTP's); $11,000 (small PTP's); $6,000/year (all others).

Coalition of Service Industries *(1982)*
1090 Vermont Ave. NW, Suite 420
Washington, DC 20005
Tel: (202)289-7460 *Fax:* (202)775-1726
E-Mail: csi@uscsi.org
Web Site: www.uscsi.org
Members: 65 companies
Staff: 5
Annual Budget: $500-1,000,000
President: J. Robert Vastine, Jr.
E-Mail: vastine@uscsi.org

Historical Note
Promotes public awareness of the service industry in the U.S. Service industries including: health fields, accounting, banking, financial services, insurance, engineering, construction, communications, advertising, professional services and transportation. Membership: $5,000-$25,000/year.

Coalition of Visionary Resources *(1999)*
194 Main St.
Butler, NJ 07405-1025
Tel: (973)838-2280 *Fax:* (973)838-2270
E-Mail: info@covr.net
Web Site: www.covr.net
Members: 200 organizations and individuals
Staff: 1
Administrator: Patricia Bush
Historical Note
Formerly (2002) Coalition of Visionary Retailers. Represents retailers, manufacturers, importers, publishers, and other organizations and individuals that specialize in new age, metaphysical and spirituality products. Provides mentoring, purchasing discounts, an awards program and other opportunities to members. Membership: $80/year.
Publications:
Inside COVR. q.. adv.

Coblentz Society *(1954)*
c/o Smiths Detection
14 Commerce Dr.
Danbury, CT 06810
Tel: (203)207-9724 *Fax:* (203)207-9780
Web Site: www.coblentz.org
Members: 600 individuals
Annual Budget: under $10,000
Secretary: Dr. David Schiering
Historical Note
The Coblentz Society exists to foster understanding and application of vibrational spectroscopy. It presents several awards in recognition of scientific achievement in the field. Has no paid officers or full-time staff.
Publications:
Coblentz Society Mailings. q.

Cocoa Merchants' Association of America *(1924)*
One North End Ave., 13th Floor
New York, NY 10282-1101
Tel: (212)201-8819 *Fax:* (212)785-5475
E-Mail: cmaa@cocoamerchants.com
Web Site: www.cocoamerchants.com
Members: 75 corporations
Annual Budget: $250-500,000
Secretary-Treasurer: Frank Schiumo
E-Mail: cmaa@cocoamerchants.com
Historical Note
CMAA regular members are importing dealers of cocoa beans and cocoa products. Associate membership is available for chocolate manufacturers, merchants domiciled in foreign countries, domestic commission houses, service companies and government agencies. Has no paid staff. Membership: $750-$5,000/year (organization/company).
Meetings/Conferences:
Semi-annual Meetings:
Publications:
Annual Report.

Coffee Sugar and Cocoa Exchange *(1882)*
Historical Note
A subsidiary of New York Board of Trade (see separate listing).

Coin Laundry Association *(1960)*
1315 Butterfield Rd., Suite 212
Downers Grove, IL 60515
Tel: (630)963-5547 *Fax:* (630)963-5864
Toll Free: (800)570 - 5629
E-Mail: info@coinlaundery.org
Web Site: www.coinlaundry.org
Members: 3000 individuals
Staff: 8
Annual Budget: $1-2,000,000
Executive Director: Brian Wallace
E-Mail: brian@coinlaundry.org
Director, Membership and Meeting Planning: Sue Lally
E-Mail: sue@coinlaundry.org
Director, Administration: Kathy Sherman
Historical Note
Established as the National Automatic Laundry and Cleaning Council, it assumed its present name in 1983. Members are self-service laundry and dry cleaning establishments together with manufacturers and distributors of the equipment, services and supplies they use. Membership: $295 for first year (individual); $195 for second year (individual); $550-6,500/year (company).
Meetings/Conferences:
Annual Meetings: Spring Trade Show/22,000
Publications:
CLA Management Guidelines. m.
CLA Journal. m. adv.
Manufacturer & Supply Directory. a. adv.

COLA
9881 Broken Land Pkwy., Suite 200
Columbia, MD 21046
Tel: (410)381-6581 *Fax:* (410)381-8611
Toll Free: (800)981 - 9883
E-Mail: info@cola.org
Web Site: www.cola.org
Members: 7500 individuals
Staff: 70
Chief Executive Officer: Douglas A. Biegel
E-Mail: info@cola.org
Director, Research, Development, Sales and Marketing: Conigsby Burdon
E-Mail: info@cola.org
Public Relations Associate: Caroline Chetelat
E-Mail: info@cola.org
Superviser, Information Resource Center: Symone Hurt
E-Mail: info@cola.org
Director, Education and Communications: Catherine Johnson
E-Mail: info@cola.org
Chief Operating Officer: Gerard Weiss
E-Mail: info@cola.org
Historical Note
Formerly (1997) Commission on Office Laboratory Accreditation. Sponsors programs and services, including online education and national symposia, to support excellence in medicine and patient care.
Publications:
Insights. bi-m.

Cold Finished Steel Bar Institute *(1971)*
201 Park Washington Court
Falls Church, VA 22046
Tel: (703)538-3543 *Fax:* (703)241-5603
E-Mail: info@cfsbi.com
Web Site: www.cfsbi.com
Members: 20 companies
Staff: 1
Annual Budget: $100-250,000
Executive Director: Clay D. Tyeryar, CAE
Meetings/Conferences:
Semi-annual Meetings: Washington, DC(Watergate)/June and November/50

Cold Formed Parts and Machine Institute *(1937)*
25 N. Broadway
Tarrytown, NY 10591-3201
Tel: (914)332-0040 *Fax:* (914)332-1541
E-Mail: info@cfpmi.org
Web Site: www.cfpmi.org
Members: 8 companies
Staff: 2
Annual Budget: $25-50,000
Executive Director: Richard C. Byrne
Historical Note
Founded as Tubular and Split Rivet Council; later became Tubular Rivet and Machine Institute, and assumed its current name in 2002. Develops and publishes metric and inch engineering standards as well as safety standards for the use of rivet setting machines.
Meetings/Conferences:
Triennial Meetings::
Publications:
Directory. irreg.

Coleopterists Society
Dept. of Entomology, 413 Bio. Sciences
University of Georgia
Athens, GA 30602-2603
Tel: (706)542-2094 *Fax:* (706)542-2279
E-Mail: treasurer@coleopsoc.org
Web Site: www.coleopsoc.org/
Members: 570 individuals
Annual Budget: $25-50,000
Treasurer: Floyd Shockley
E-Mail: treasurer@coleopsoc.org
Historical Note
A professional society organized exclusively for scientific and educational purposes. Members are concerned with the study of living and fossil beetles. Membership: $40/year (individual); $80/year institutional subscription to Coleopterists Bulletin.
Meetings/Conferences:
Annual Meetings: December/with the Entomological Soc. of America
Publications:
Coleopterists Bulletin. q.

Collaborative Family Healthcare Association *(1993)*
P.O. Box 20838
Rochester, NY 14602-0838
Tel: (585)482-8210 *Fax:* (585)482-2901
E-Mail: info@cfha.net
Web Site: www.cfhcc.org
Business Manager: Bill Steger
E-Mail: info@cfha.net
Historical Note
CFHA is a diverse group of physicians, nurses, psychologists, social workers, and other professionals interested in multidisciplinary approaches to family health care.
Publications:
Families, Systems, and Health. irreg.

Collectibles and Platemakers Guild
Historical Note
Became Gift and Collectibles Guild in 2003.

Collector Car Appraisers International *(1980)*
24 Myrtle Ave.
Buffalo, NY 14204
Tel: (716)855-1931
Members: 25 individuals
Staff: 3
Annual Budget: $25-50,000
President: James T. Sandoro
Historical Note
Members are licensed and bonded individuals with at least ten years experience handling antique, classic, special interest collector cars, trucks, motorcycles, etc. Certifies members to act as expert witnesses in law suits and arbitration. Maintains a 3,740 volume library. Membership: $1,000/year.
Publications:
Actual Cash Value, Car Guide. a.

College and University Computer Users Conference *(1956)*
Historical Note
See CUMREC.

College and University Professional Association for Human Resources *(1946)*
2607 Kingston Pike, Suite 250
Knoxville, TN 37919
Tel: (865)637-7673 *Fax:* (865)637-7674
Toll Free: (877)287 - 2474
E-Mail: abrantley@cupahr.org
Web Site: www.cupahr.org
Members: 1800 colleges and universities
Staff: 25
Annual Budget: $2-5,000,000
Chief Executive Officer: Andy Brantley
E-Mail: abrantley@cupahr.org
Director, Conferences and Meetings: Susan Reichbart, CMP
E-Mail: sreichbart@cupahr.org
Director, Research and Information Systems: Ray Sizemore
E-Mail: rsizemore@cupahr.org
Historical Note
Formerly (2000) College and University Personnel Association. Members are colleges and universities united to improve the effectiveness of their human

resource management. Membership: $270-2155/year (organization, depending on budget).

Meetings/Conferences:
Annual Meetings: Late Summer or early Fall/1,000
2007 - Baltimore, MD(Baltimore Marriott Waterfront)/Nov. 8-11

Publications:
Benefits Survey. a. adv.
CUPAHR News. bi-w. adv.
CUPAHR Journal. semi-a. adv.
Salary Surveys. a. adv.

College Art Association *(1911)*
275 Seventh Ave., 18th Floor
New York, NY 10001-6708
Tel: (212)691-1051 *Fax:* (212)627-2381
E-Mail: nyoffice@collegeart.org
Web Site: www.collegeart.org
Members: 14000 individuals
Staff: 30
Annual Budget: $2-5,000,000
Executive Director: Susan Ball
Manager, Member Services: Doreen Davis
E-Mail: ddavis@collegeart.org
Director, Media and Communications: John Menick

Historical Note
Founded at the Cincinnati Art Museum in May, 1911 at a meeting of the Western Drawing and Manual Training Association. A professional organization of art historians, studio artists and museum professionals united to improve the standards of art scholarship, art teaching and art history. Member of the American Council of Learned Socs., National Humanities Alliance, American Arts Alliance and the American Council on the Arts. Membership: $50-275/year (individual); $275/year (institution).

Meetings/Conferences:
Annual Meetings: Winter
2007 - New York, NY/Feb. 14-17
2008 - Dallas, TX/Feb. 20-23

Publications:
CAA Newsletter. bi-m. adv.
CAA Reviews. on-line.
The Art Bulletin. q. adv.
Careers. bi-m. adv.
Art Journal. q. adv.

College Athletic Business Management Association *(1951)*
P.O. Box 16428
Cleveland, OH 44116
Tel: (440)892-4000 *Fax:* (440)892-4007
Web Site: www.cabma.com
Members: 474 individuals
Annual Budget: $10-25,000
Membership Coordinator: Brian Horning

Historical Note
Affiliated with National Collegiate Athletic Association. Members are business and ticket managers, directors of athletics and their assistants, fundraisers, facilities managers, systems managers, and individuals performing similar duties under different titles. Has no paid officers or full-time staff. Membership: $100/year (individual); $300/year (institution).

Meetings/Conferences:
Annual Meetings: January, with Nat'l Collegiate Athletic Ass'n

Publications:
Convention Notes. a.

College Band Directors National Association *(1941)*
University of Texas
P.O. Box 8028
Austin, TX 78713
Tel: (512)471-5883 *Fax:* (512)471-6589
Web Site: www.cbdna.org
Members: 1000 individuals
Annual Budget: $25-50,000
Secretary: Richard Floyd

Historical Note
Membership: $60/year.

Meetings/Conferences:
Annual Meetings:

Publications:
Newsletter. q.

College English Association *(1939)*
Arts & Sciences Hilbert Coll.
5200 S. Park Ave.
Hamburg, NY 14075
Tel: (716)649-7900 *Fax:* (716)649-0702
Web Site: http://www2.widener.edu/~cea/
Members: 1200 individuals
Annual Budget: $25-50,000
Executive Director: Charles Ernst

Historical Note
Concerned with practical applications of scholarship to teaching English literature and language at the college level. Membership: $30/year (individual); $30/year (institution).

Meetings/Conferences:
Annual Meetings: April

Publications:
The CEA Forum. semi-a. adv.
The CEA Critic. 3/year.

College Fraternity Editors Association *(1923)*
330 S. Campus Ave.
Oxford, OH 45056
Tel: (513)523-1907 Ext: 237 *Fax:* (513)523-7292
Web Site: www.cfea.org
Members: 80 fraternities and sororities
Annual Budget: $10-25,000

Historical Note
Organized December 1, 1923 in New York City. Membership consists of full-time editors of fraternity magazines. Has no paid officers or full-time staff.

Meetings/Conferences:
Annual Meetings: Summer

Publications:
Public Relations Manual. a. adv.
Speakers Bureau. a. adv.
The Fraternity Editor. q. adv.

College Gymnastics Association *(1950)*
52 Evelyn Road
Needham, MA 02494
Tel: (617)444-3893
Web Site: www.collegegymnastics.com
Members: 60 individuals
Annual Budget: under $10,000
Executive Director: Richard Aronson

College Media Advisers *(1954)*
University of Memphis
Department of Journalism
Memphis, TN 38152
Tel: (901)678-2403 *Fax:* (901)678-4798
Web Site: www.collegemedia.org
Members: 750 individuals
Staff: 2
Annual Budget: $50-100,000
Executive Director: Ronald Spielberger
E-Mail: rsplbrgr@memphis.edu

Historical Note
Established as the National Council of College Publication Advisors; assumed its present name in 1983 to reflect the growing importance of electronic media. Members are advisers to college student newspapers, yearbooks, magazines, radio and TV stations. Membership: $60/year.

Meetings/Conferences:
Semi-annual Meetings: Mid-March in New York City and Fall
2007 - New York, NY(Roosevelt Hotel)/March 15-17
2007 - Washington, DC(Hilton)/Oct. 25-28
2008 - New York, NY/
2008 - Kansas City, MO(Marriott)/Oct. 30-Nov. 2

Publications:
College Media Review. q. adv.
CMA Newsletter. m.

College Music Society *(1958)*
312 E. Pine St.
Missoula, MT 59802
Tel: (406)721-9616 *Fax:* (406)721-9419
E-Mail: cms@music.org
Web Site: www.music.org
Members: 9500 individuals
Staff: 8
Annual Budget: $1-2,000,000
Executive Director: Robby D. Gunstream
Director, Professional Development: Peter S. Park

Historical Note
CMS members are college teachers of music. CMS is a professional consortium of college, conservatory and university faculty dedicated to gathering, considering and disseminating ideas on the philosophy and practice of music as an integral part of higher education, and to developing and increasing communication among the various disciplines of music. Membership: $65/year (individual).

Meetings/Conferences:
Annual Meetings: Fall
2007 - Salt Lake City, UT(Little America)/Nov. 15-18/400

Publications:
Source Books in American Music. a.
Music Vacancy List. w. adv.
CMS Reports. irreg.
Directory of Music Faculties. a.
Monographs and Bibliographies in American Music. irreg.
College Music Symposium. a. adv.
CMS Newsletter. bi-m. adv.

College of American Pathologists *(1947)*
325 Waukegan Road
Northfield, IL 60093-2750
Tel: (847)832-7000 *Fax:* (847)832-8000
Toll Free: (800)323 - 4040
Web Site: www.cap.org
Members: 16000 individuals
Staff: 400
Annual Budget: Over $100,000,000
Executive Vice President: Nicki Norris
E-Mail: sgrear@cap.org
Vice President, Education Division: Constance Filling
E-Mail: sgrear@cap.org
Vice President, Communication Services Division: Sandra B. Grear
E-Mail: sgrear@cap.org
Vice President, Information Services Division: Matthew Hartzman
Senior Vice President, Operations: Michael J. Miller
E-Mail: sgrear@cap.org
Vice President, Finance Division: Stephen Myers
Vice President, Advocacy Division: John H. Scott

Historical Note
Founded and incorporated on May 14, 1947. Fellowship in the CAP is restricted to pathologists certified by the American Board of Pathology. Has an annual budget of over $100 million. Membership: $300/year.

Meetings/Conferences:
Semi-Annual Meetings: Spring with USCAP; Fall with American Soc. of Clinical Pathologists

Publications:
CAP Today. m. adv.

College of Diplomates of the American Board of Orthodontics *(1979)*
3260 Upper Bottom Road
St. Charles, MO 63303
Tel: (636)922-5551 *Fax:* (636)244-1650
E-Mail: cdabo@charter.net
Web Site: www.cdabo.org
Members: 1800 individuals
Staff: 1
Annual Budget: $50-100,000
Executive Director: Karen Seiler

Historical Note
Limited to diplomates of the American Board of Orthodontics. Promotes continuing education and certification among orthodontists. Membership: $100/yr.

Meetings/Conferences:
Annual Meetings: Summer
2007 - Half Moon Bay, CA(Ritz Carlton)/July 15-19

College of Healthcare Information Management Executives *(1992)*
3300 Washtenaw Ave., Suite 225

Ann Arbor, MI 48104-4250
Tel: (734)665-0000 *Fax:* (734)665-4922
E-Mail: staff@cio-chime.org
Web Site: www.cio-chime.org
Members: 750 individuals
Staff: 8
President and Chief Executive Officer: Rich A. Correll
E-Mail: staff@cio-chime.org

Historical Note

The mission of the College of Healthcare Information Management Executives (CHIME) is to serve the professional needs of healthcare Chief Information Officers, and to advance strategic application of information technology in innovative ways aimed at improving the effectiveness of healthcare delivery.

Meetings/Conferences:

Annual Meetings: Fall/300

College of Optometrists in Vision Development *(1970)*

215 W. Garfield St., Suite 210
Aurora, OH 44202
Tel: (330)995-0718 *Fax:* (330)995-0719
Toll Free: (888)268 - 3770
E-Mail: info@covd.org
Web Site: www.covd.org
Members: 1700 individuals
Staff: 2
Annual Budget: $250-500,000
Executive Director: Stephen C. Miller, O.D.

Historical Note

Members are optometrists, vision therapists, optometry students and faculty, vision science researchers and others concerned with vision development and vision therapy, particularly in the area of learning-related vision problems and visual information processing problems. Formed by a merger of the National Optometric Society for Developmental Vision Care, the National Society for Vision and Perception Training and the Southwest Developmental Vision Society Provides Board certification in the area of vision development and therapy.

Meetings/Conferences:

Annual Meetings: Fall

Publications:

Visions newsletter. bi-m.
Membership Directory and Desk Reference. a. adv.
Journal of Optometric Vision Development. q. adv.

College Reading and Learning Association *(1967)*

Central Community College
Hastings, NE 68902-1024
Tel: (402)461-2519 *Fax:* (402)460-2135
Web Site: www.crla.net
Members: 1000 individuals
Staff: 1
Annual Budget: $50-100,000
Member Coordinator: Vicki Papineau

Historical Note

Formerly Western College Reading Association and Western College Reading and Learning Association. CRLA members are educators involved in college and adult literacy and learning programs.

Meetings/Conferences:

Annual Meetings: Fall

Publications:

CRLA Newsletter. q.
Journal of College Reading & Learning. semi-a.

College Savings Foundation

1050 17th St. NW, Suite 1000
Washington, DC 20036
Tel: (202)223-2631 *Fax:* (202)223-2634
E-Mail: khamor@mindspring.com
Web Site: www.college-savings-foundation.org
Members: 14 firms
Executive Director: Kathy Hamor
E-Mail: khamor@mindspring.com

Historical Note

CSF members are firms that offer 529 college savings plans, investment managers who include 529s in their portfolio management plans, and other interested firms and professionals.

Meetings/Conferences:

2007 - Miami, FL(Miami Beach Resort and Spa)/Feb. 7-9

College Savings Plans Network *(1992)*

c/o Nat'l Ass'n of State Treasurers
P.O. Box 11910
Lexington, KY 40578-1910
Tel: (859)244-8175 *Fax:* (859)244-8053
E-Mail: cspn@csg.org
Web Site: www.collegesavings.org
Members: 50 States
Staff: 1
Program Manager: Chris Hunter
E-Mail: cspn@csg.org

Historical Note

CSPN members are state government officials who manage higher education tuition savings programs. Membership: $500-$1,500/year.

Meetings/Conferences:

Annual Meetings: Spring

College Sports Information Directors of America *(1957)*

Univ. of North Alabama, P.O. Box 5038
Florence, AL 35632
Tel: (256)765-4595 *Fax:* (256)765-4659
E-Mail: sportsinformation@una.edu
Web Site: www.cosida.com
Members: 1800 individuals
Annual Budget: $25-50,000
Secretary: Jeff Hodges

Historical Note

Originally a section of the American College Public Relations Association. Became independent in 1957. Selects Academic All-American teams in football, basketball, baseball, volleyball, and softball and a post-graduate scholarship. Has no paid officers or full-time staff.

Meetings/Conferences:

Annual Meetings: Summer

Publications:

CoSIDA Digest. m. adv.
CoSIDA Directory. a. adv.

College Swimming Coaches Association of America *(1922)*

PMB 503
10115 E. Bell Rd., Suite 107
Scottsdale, AZ 85260
Tel: (480)628-5488 *Fax:* (480)699-4852
Web Site: www.cscaa.org
Members: 850 individuals
Staff: 3
Annual Budget: $100-250,000
Executive Director: Phil Whitten
E-Mail: swimphil@aol.com

Historical Note

Chartered in the State of Florida on September 14, 1967. Officers rotate trienially. Membership: $50-100/year.

Meetings/Conferences:

Annual Meetings:

Publications:

Poolside Magazine. q.
Top Teams Poll. 8/year. adv.
Top Times Listing. 8/year. adv.

College Theology Society *(1954)*

Iona College
715 North Ave.
New Rochelle, NY 10801
Tel: (914)637-2744 *Fax:* (914)633-2248
Members: 850 individuals
Annual Budget: $25-50,000
Secretary: Elena Prolario-Foley

Historical Note

Formerly (1967) Society of Catholic College Teachers of Sacred Doctrine. Member of the Council on the Study of Religion. Members are devoted to the study and the teaching of religion. Membership: $50/year (regular member); $25/year (student member).

Publications:

Horizons: The Journal of the College Theology Society. semi-a. adv.
Annual Publication of the College Theology Soc.. a.

Collegiate Commissioners Association *(1939)*

2201 Richard Arrington Blvd.
Birmingham, AL 35203
Tel: (205)458-3000 *Fax:* (205)458-3031
Members: 32 individuals
Annual Budget: $50-100,000
Secretary-Treasurer: Greg Sankey

Historical Note

Founded as National Association of Football Commissioners; became the National Association of Collegiate Commissioners in 1948 and assumed its present name in 1965. Members are commissioners and staffs of the major collegiate athletic conferences of the U.S. Publishes a number of annual handbooks for officials. Has no paid staff or permanent headquarters. Membership fee: $500/year.

Publications:

Football Rules Illustrated for Coaches, Players and Fans. a.
Collegiate Commissioners Ass'n Directory. a.
Manual of Football Officiating. a.
Basketball Officials' Manual. a.

Colombian American Association *(1927)*

30 Vesey St., Suite 506
New York, NY 10007
Tel: (212)233-7776 *Fax:* (212)233-7779
E-Mail: andean@nyet.net
Members: 100 individuals
Staff: 3
Annual Budget: $25-50,000
Executive Secretary: Linda Calvet

Historical Note

Seeks to facilitate commerce and trade between the Republic of Colombia and the United States, to foster and advance cultural relations and good will between the two nations, and to encourage safe and sound investments. Membership: $250/year (individual); $500/year (corporate); $2,000/year (supporting).

Publications:

Colombian Newsletter. m.

Color Association of the United States *(1915)*

315 W. 39th St., Studio 507
New York, NY 10018
Tel: (212)947-7774 *Fax:* (212)594-6987
E-Mail: caus@colorassociation.com
Web Site: www.colorassociation.com
Members: 1000 companies
Staff: 3
Annual Budget: $250-500,000
Director: Margaret Walch
E-Mail: caus@colorassociation.com
Director, Membership: Christine Chow
E-Mail: caus@colorassociation.com

Historical Note

Formerly (1954) Textile Color Card Association of America., CAUS is a New York-based organization that represents leaders in every branch of fashion, textiles, design industries and general trade in which color is a factor. The association serves as the authority and arbiter of commercial colors in the US. Membership: $550/year (individual); $1050/year (company).

Meetings/Conferences:

Annual Meetings: New York,NY

Publications:

CAUS Color Design/Newsletter. m.
Seasonal Color Forecasts. bi-a.
Standard Color Reference of America. Every 10 yrs.
Trend Reports.

Color Marketing Group *(1962)*

5845 Richmond Hwy, #410
Alexandria, VA 22303-1865
Tel: (703)329-8500 *Fax:* (703)329-0155
E-Mail: cmg@colormarketing.org
Web Site: www.colormarketing.org
Members: 1300 individuals
Staff: 8
Annual Budget: $1-2,000,000
Executive Director: Jaime Stephens
Manager, Conferences: Jenny Gibson

Historical Note

Membership: $715/year.

Meetings/Conferences:
Semi-Annual Meetings: Spring and Fall
Publications:
Color Chips. bien.

Color Pigments Manufacturers Association *(1925)*
300 N. Washington St., Suite 102
Alexandria, VA 22314
Tel: (703)684-4044 *Fax:* (703)684-1795
E-Mail: cpma@cpma.com
Web Site: www.pigments.org
Members: 50 companies
Staff: 4
Annual Budget: $500-1,000,000
President: J. Lawrence Robinson, CAE
E-Mail: cpma@cpma.com
Historical Note
Formerly (1993) Dry Color Manufacturers Association. Members are manufacturers of organic and inorganic color pigments.
Meetings/Conferences:
Annual Meetings: White Sulphur Springs, WV/June
2007 – Philadelphia, PA/June 13-14/50
Publications:
Newsletter. m.

Colorado Ranger Horse Association *(1938)*
1510 Greenhouse Road
Wampum, PA 16157
Tel: (724)535-4841
E-Mail: crha@adelphia.net
Web Site: www.coloradoranger.com
Members: 3100 individuals
Staff: 1
Annual Budget: under $10,000
Executive Secretary: Laurel Kosior
E-Mail: crha@adelphia.net
Historical Note
Members are owners, breeders and enthusiasts of Colorado Ranger horses. Records and registers horses that can trace unbroken and direct descent from one of two foundation sires, Patches 1 and Max 2. Membership: $20/year (new member); $15/year (renewal).
Meetings/Conferences:
Annual Meetings: September
Publications:
CRHA Bloodhorse. irreg.
Rangerbred News. bi-m. adv.
CRHA Brochure. irreg.

Columbia Sheep Breeders Association of America *(1942)*
2821 State Hwy. 182
Nevada, OH 44849
Tel: (740)482-2608
Web Site: www.columbiasheep.org
Members: 600 individuals
Staff: 1
Annual Budget: $50-100,000
Office Manager: Phyllis Gerber
E-Mail: csbagerber@udata.com
Historical Note
Members are breeders and fanciers of Columbia sheep.
Meetings/Conferences:
Annual Meetings: Summer
Publications:
Speaking of Columbias. q. adv.

Combustion Institute *(1954)*
5001 Baum Blvd., Suite 635
Pittsburgh, PA 15213-1851
Tel: (412)687-1366 *Fax:* (412)687-0340
E-Mail: office@combustioninstitute.org
Web Site: www.combustioninstitute.org
Members: 4000 individuals
Staff: 3
Executive Administrator: Sue Steiner Terpack
E-Mail: office@combustioninstitute.org
Historical Note
An international organization with sections in several foreign countries, including Canada. Absorbed the Standing Committee on Combustion Symposia in 1954. The Institute is a non-profit, educational organization with the purpose of promoting and disseminating knowledge in the field of combustion science. Membership: $40/year.
Meetings/Conferences:
Biennial Meetings: even years
Publications:
Combustion and Flame. m.
Proceedings. bien.

Comics Magazine Association of America *(1954)*
355 Lexington Ave., 17th Floor
New York, NY 10017-6603
Tel: (212)297-2122 *Fax:* (212)370-9047
Members: 5 companies
Annual Budget: $50-100,000
Executive Director: Holly J. Munter-Koenig
Historical Note
Sponsors the Comics Code Authority, an agency for pre-publication evaluation of all editorial and advertising matter appearing in comic books.
Meetings/Conferences:
Annual Meetings: Winter in New York, NY

Commercial Finance Association *(1943)*
225 W. 34th St., Suite 1815
New York, NY 10122
Tel: (212)594-3490 *Fax:* (212)564-6053
E-Mail: info@cfa.com
Web Site: www.cfa.com
Members: 312banks&commercialinstitutions
Staff: 15
Annual Budget: $2-5,000,000
Executive Director and Secretary: Bruce H. Jones
E-Mail: info@cfa.com
Director, Government Relations: Brian Cove
Director, Education: Michael Keller
Historical Note
Founded as the National Conference of Commercial Receivable Companies, it became the National Commercial Finance Conference in 1953, the National Commercial Finance Association in 1983, and assumed its present name in 1991. Members are banks and commercial finance and factoring companies. Membership: $2,000-9,000/year (organization).
Meetings/Conferences:
Annual Meetings: Fall/1,400
2007 – Phoenix, AZ(J.W. Marriott Desert Ridge Resort and Spa)/Nov. 7-9
Publications:
Secured Lender. bi-m. adv.
Compendium of Commercial Finance Law. a.

Commercial Food Equipment Service Association *(1963)*
2211 W. Meadowview Road, Suite 20
Greensboro, NC 27407
Tel: (336)346-4700 *Fax:* (336)346-4745
E-Mail: hprice@cfesa.com
Web Site: www.cfesa.com
Members: 450 companies
Staff: 5
Annual Budget: $250-500,000
Executive Director: Carla Strickland
Director, Membership Services: Heather Price
E-Mail: hprice@cfesa.com
Historical Note
Members are companies with a minimum of three years experience in servicing or repairing food preparation equipment for hotels, restaurants or institutions.
Meetings/Conferences:
Semi-annual Meetings: May and September
Publications:
Newsletter. bi-m.
Directory. a.

Commercial Internet Exchange Association
Historical Note
Became United States Internet Service Providers Association in 2003.

Commercial Law League of America *(1895)*
70 E. Lake St., Suite 630
Chicago, IL 60601
Tel: (312)781-2000 *Fax:* (312)781-2010
Toll Free: (800)978 - 2552
E-Mail: info@clla.org
Web Site: www.clla.org
Members: 3000 individuals
Staff: 10
Annual Budget: $1-2,000,000
Executive Vice President: David R. Watson
Director, Administrative: Leslie Campbell
Director, Education: Paula Lucas
Historical Note
Members are commercial and bankruptcy law professionals. CCLA's mission is to act as a source of professional services in the field, to promote standards of professionalism, and to foster economic opportunities for its members in service to the credit industry. Participates with the American Board of Certification (Alexandria, VA), which certifies attorneys specializing in bankruptcy and creditors' rights law. Membership: $195/year.
Meetings/Conferences:
Annual Meetings: July/600-800
2007 – Chicago, IL(Westin - Michigan Ave.)/Apr. 19-22
Publications:
DePaul Business & Commercial Law Journal. q. adv.
Bankruptcy & Insolvency Section Newsletter. m.
Debt3. bi-m. adv.

Commercial Mortgage Securities Association *(1994)*
30 Broad St., 28th Floor
New York, NY 10004-2304
Tel: (212)509-1844 *Fax:* (212)509-1895
E-Mail: infoi@cmbs.org
Web Site: www.cmbs.org
Members: 309 corporations
Staff: 14
Chief Executive Officer: Dottie Cunningham
E-Mail: dottie@cmbs.org
Managing Director, Finance/Administration: Jane Gelfand
Historical Note
Founded as Commercial Real Estate Secondary Market and Securitization Association; assumed its present name in 1999. CMSA represents and promotes an orderly and ethical global institutional secondary market for the sale of commerical mortage loans and equity investments.
Meetings/Conferences:
Annual Meetings: Winter
Publications:
CMBS World. q. adv.

Commercial Real Estate Women
Historical Note
See National Network of Commercial Real Estate Women.

Commercial Real Estate Women Network *(1989)*
1201 Wakarusa Dr., Suite C3
Lawrence, KS 66049-3803
Tel: (785)832-1808 *Fax:* (785)832-1551
E-Mail: gaila@crewnetwork.org
Web Site: www.crewnetwork.org
Members: 6500 individuals
Staff: 15
Annual Budget: $2-5,000,000
Chief Executive Officer: Gail S. Ayers
Historical Note
CREW Network is the product of a merger (1989) of Women in Commercial Real Estate National Network and Commercial Real Estate Women. Starting in 1989, known as National Network of Commercial Real Estate Women until (2001) assumed current name. CREW Network provides a national communication network for women involved in all fields of commercial real estate and assists in the formation of new local groups in cities not currently represented in the National Network. Member organizations are existing, independent, local groups with goals similar to those of the National Network. Membership: $70/year (individual).
Meetings/Conferences:
Annual Meetings: Fall
2007 – Denver, CO(Hyatt Regency)/Oct. 3-6
Publications:
CREW Network Newsletter. q. adv.
Directory. a. adv.

Commercial Refrigerator Manufacturers Division - ARI *(1933)*
Historical Note
An affiliate of Air-Conditioning and Refrigeration Institute, which provides administrative support.

Commercial Vehicle Safety Alliance *(1982)*
1101 17th St. NW, Suite 803
Washington, DC 20036-4713
Tel: (202)775-1623 *Fax:* (202)775-1624
Web Site: www.cvsa.org
Members: 67 agencies
Staff: 12
Annual Budget: $1-2,000,000
Executive Director: Stephen F. Campbell
E-Mail: stephenc@cvsa.org
Director, Administration: Paul M. Bomgardner
E-Mail: paulb@cvsa.org
Historical Note
Members are state, territorial and provincial agencies responsible for commercial motor vehicle safety enforcement in the U.S., Canada and Mexico. Membership: $500/year (trucking and bus companies and safety suppliers); $700/year (organization); $3,750/year (state/province).
Meetings/Conferences:
Semi-annual Meetings: Spring and Fall
Publications:
The Guardian. bi-m.

Commission on Accreditation for Law Enforcement Agencies *(1979)*
10302 Eaton Place, Suite 100
Fairfax, VA 22030-2215
Tel: (703)352-4225
Toll Free: (800)368 - 3757
E-Mail: calea@calea.org
Web Site: www.calea.org
Members: 800 law enforcement agencies
Staff: 16
Annual Budget: $2-5,000,000
Executive Director: Sylvester Daughtry, Jr.
E-Mail: sdaughtry@calea.org
Historical Note
Established though union of International Chiefs of Police and Black Law Enforcement Executives. Membership fee varies, based on size of agency.
Meetings/Conferences:
Three Meetings Annually: Spring/Summer/Fall
2007 - Greensboro, NC
2007 - Montreal, QC, Canada
2007 - Colorado Springs, CO
Publications:
Commission Update. irreg.

Commission on Accreditation of Allied Health Education Programs *(1994)*
1361 Park St.
Clearwater, FL 33756
Tel: (727)210-2350 *Fax:* (727)210-2354
Web Site: www.caahep.org
Members: 70 sponsoring organizations
Staff: 4
Annual Budget: $500-1,000,000
Executive Director: Kathleen Megivern
E-Mail: megivern@caahep.org
Director, Accreditation Services: Lori Schroeder
Historical Note
CAAHEP is the national accrediting agency for health programs in 20 occupations. Formerly (1994) the Committee on Allied Health Education and Accreditation. Membership: $3000/year (sponsoring organization); $450/year (accredited institution).
Meetings/Conferences:
Annual Meetings: Spring
2007 - Orlando, FL(Rosen Center)/Apr. 13-14/90
Publications:
Communique. 3/year.

Commission on Certification of Work Adjustment and Vocational Evaluation Specialists *(1981)*
1835 Rohlwing Road, Suite E
Rolling Meadows, IL 60008
Tel: (847)342-1796 *Fax:* (847)394-2108
E-Mail: info@ccwaves.org
Web Site: www.ccwaves.org
Members: 2000 individuals
Staff: 1
Annual Budget: $50-100,000
Administrator: Cindy Chapman
Historical Note
CCWAVES offers qualified candidates the opportunity to obtain certification in vocational evaluation. The primary purpose of this certification is to provide assurances that those professionals engaged in vocational evaluation can meet acceptable standards of quality to service the best interests of clients, other practitioners, individuals in allied professions and the public.
Publications:
Wavelengths. q.

Commission on Professionals in Science and Technology *(1953)*
1200 New York Ave. NW, Suite 390
Washington, DC 20005
Tel: (202)326-7080 *Fax:* (202)842-1603
E-Mail: info@cpst.org
Web Site: www.cpst.org
Members: 700 individuals
Staff: 3
Annual Budget: $250-500,000
Executive Director: Lisa M. Frehill
Historical Note
Formerly (1986) Scientific Manpower Commission. A private non-profit corporation formed by 14 scientific societies to provide data on the education and employment of scientists and engineers. Concerned with the recruitment, training and utilization of scientific personnel. Membership: $120/year (individual); $700/year (society); $800/year (corporate).
Meetings/Conferences:
Commissioners' Meetings: May and November/Washington, DC
Publications:
Professional Women & Minorities: A Total Human Resources Data Compendium. bien.
Salaries of Scientists, Engineers & Technicians. bien.
CPST Comments. 8/year.

Commissioned Officers Association of the United States Public Health Service *(1947)*
8201 Corporate Dr., Suite 200
Landover, MD 20785
Tel: (301)731-9080 *Fax:* (301)731-9084
Web Site: www.coausphs.org
Members: 7000 individuals
Staff: 5
Annual Budget: $500-1,000,000
Executive Director: Gerard M. Farrell
Historical Note
Membership: $60 - 105/year.
Meetings/Conferences:
Annual Meetings: Summer
Publications:
Proceedings Program. a. adv.
Frontline. 10/year. adv.

Committee for Private Offshore Rescue and Towing (C-PORT) *(1987)*
619 Severn Ave., Suite 201
P.O. Box 4070
Annapolis, MD 21403
Toll Free: (866)847 - 3609
E-Mail: c-port@wpa.org
Web Site: www.c-port.org
Members: 188 companies
Staff: 3
Annual Budget: $50-100,000
Interim Executive Director: Melissa Moskal
Historical Note
Established in Washington, DC, C-PORT is the trade association for the small boat towing and salvage industry. C-PORT administers the ACAPT Industry Certification Program. Membership: $300/year minimum.
Meetings/Conferences:
Annual Meetings: Winter
Publications:
C-PORT News.

Committee of 200 *(1982)*
980 N. Michigan Ave., Suite 1575
Chicago, IL 60611-7540
Tel: (312)255-0296 *Fax:* (312)255-0789
E-Mail: sgilpin@c200.org
Web Site: www.c200.org
Members: 494 individuals
Staff: 9
Annual Budget: $2-5,000,000
President: Susan Gilpin
Chief Financial Officer and Chief Operating Officer: Debra Gold
Manager, Administration: Cindy Kudart
Director, Member Programs: Sioban Lombardi
Director, Outreach/Education and Mentoring Programs: Meghan G. O'Brien
Director, Membership: Amy E. O'Keefe
Historical Note
C200 is an international organization of leading business women. Three-quarters of its members are entrepreneurs; most others are senior executives of major corporations. Membership is by invitation only. Encourages entrepreneurship and seeks to promote women in executive positions. Membership: $1,800/year (individual).
Meetings/Conferences:
Semi-Annual Meetings: Spring and Fall/125
Publications:
C200 Network. q.

Committee of American Axle Producers
Historical Note
Address unknown in 2006.

Committee of Annuity Insurers *(1982)*
c/o Davis & Harman, LLP
1455 Pennsylvania Ave. NW, Suite 1200
Washington, DC 20004
Tel: (202)347-2230 *Fax:* (202)393-3310
E-Mail: cai@davis-harman.com
Web Site: www.annuity-insurers.org
Members: 29 companies
Counsel: Joseph F. McKeever, III
E-Mail: cai@davis-harman.com
Historical Note
CAI monitors federal tax policy regarding annuities and related financial instruments. Members are life insurance companies that sell insurance.

Committee on History in the Classroom *(1971)*
Deptartment of History
Purdue University
West Lafayette, IN 47907-1365
Tel: (765)494-4122 *Fax:* (765)496-1755
Web Site: www.theaha.org/affiliates/comt_his_classroom.htm
Members: 200 individuals
Secretary-Tresurer: Grodon R. Mork
Historical Note
CHC members are history teachers from both the secondary and post-secondary levels and others with an interest in the scholarship of teaching. Has no paid officers or full-time staff. Annual meetings held in conjunction with American Historical Association. Membership: $10/year (individual).
Meetings/Conferences:
Annual Meetings: in conjunction with AHA annual meeting
Publications:
Newsletter.

Committee on Lesbian and Gay History *(1979)*
Brown University
Box 1939, UH 201
Providence, RI 09219
Tel: (401)863-3488 *Fax:* (401)863-2075
Web Site: www.usc.edu/clgh
Members: 350 individuals and organizations
Staff: 6
Annual Budget: under $10,000

Historical Note
CLGH members are scholars from a variety of disciplines and others with an interest in the study of homosexuality in the past and present. CLGH also seeks to prevent discrimination against gay, lesbian and transgendered historians. Membership: $10/year (individual); $25/year (organization).
Meetings/Conferences:
Annual Meetings: in conjunction with AHA annual meeting
Publications:
CLGH Newsletter. 2/year. adv.

Committee on State Taxation
Historical Note
See Council on State Taxation.

Commodity Exchange *(1933)*
Historical Note
See New York Mercantile Exchange.

Communications Fraud Control Association *(1985)*
3030 N. Central Ave., Suite 707
Phoenix, AZ 85012-2715
Tel: (602)265-2322 *Fax:* (602)265-1015
E-Mail: fraud@cfca.org
Web Site: www.cfca.org
Members: 150 individuals
Staff: 3
Annual Budget: $250-500,000
Executive Director: Frances Feld, CAE
E-Mail: fraud@cfca.org
Historical Note
Representing companies and individuals in the communications industry, and agencies and professionals involved in the investigation of communications fraud, CCFA is a leading international association for communications fraud control education and information. It was created to foster and promote cooperation inside and outside the communications industry regarding communications fraud control. Membership consists of more than 250 carriers, private network owners, end-users and government and law enforcement agencies worldwide. CCFA offers educational programs around the world that create valuable learning and networking opportunities, and offers a limited number of opportunities to vendors to exhibit at conferences. Membership: $50-275/year (individual); $880-2,200/year (corporate).
Meetings/Conferences:
Annual Meetings: Winter
Publications:
CFCA Communicator. q.
Fraud Alert. w.

Communications Marketing Association *(1974)*
P.O. Box 36275
Denver, CO 80227
Tel: (303)988-3515 *Fax:* (303)988-3517
Web Site: www.commktga.com
Members: 400 individuals
Staff: 1
Annual Budget: $50-100,000
Executive Director: Mercy Contreras
E-Mail: mercycontreras@comcast.net
Historical Note
CMA members are independent manufacturers, independent sales representative firms and distributors of cellular and two-way radio equipment.
Meetings/Conferences:
Annual Meetings: Fall
Publications:
CMA Update Newsletter. q.

Communications Media Management Association *(1946)*
20423 State Rd. Seven
Suite F6-491
Boca Raton, FL 33498
Tel: (561)988-2681 *Fax:* (973)543-0166
E-Mail: cmma@cmma.net
Web Site: www.cmma.net
Members: 160 individuals
Staff: 1
Annual Budget: $100-250,000
Executive Director: Jody B. Rosen, APR
E-Mail: executive.director@cmma.net
Historical Note
Formerly (1980) Industrial Audio-Visual Association and (1994) Audio Visual Management Association. CMMA is a professional society of individuals managing comunications media departments in business, government and education. Membership: $350/year.
Meetings/Conferences:
Semi-Annual: Spring/Fall
Publications:
CMMA Visions. q.

Communications Society *(1952)*
Historical Note
See IEEE Communications Society

Communications Supply Service Association *(1976)*
5700 Murray St.
Little Rock, AR 72209
Tel: (501)252-2772 *Fax:* (501)562-7616
Toll Free: (800)252 - 2772
Web Site: www.cssa.net
Members: 258 companies
Staff: 27
Annual Budget: $5-10,000,000
President: Larry Hoaglan
E-Mail: larryh@cssa.net
Historical Note
CSSA members are small independent telephone companies. Membership: $100/year (individual).
Meetings/Conferences:
Annual Meetings: in conjunction with the Nat'l Telephone Cooperative Ass'n
Publications:
The Member Link. m.

Communications Workers of America *(1938)*
501 Third St. NW
Washington, DC 20001-2797
Tel: (202)434-1100 *Fax:* (202)434-1279
Web Site: http://cwa-union.org
Members: 630000 individuals
Staff: 600
Annual Budget: $50-100,000,000
President: Larry Cohen
Historical Note
Established in Chicago June 5, 1938 as the National Federation of Telephone Workers, it was named the Communications Workers of America in 1947; joined the Congress of Industrial Organizations in 1949 and merged with Telephone Workers Organizing Committee. Absorbed International Union of Electronic, Electrical, Salaried Machine and Furniture Workers in 2001. Has a budget of approximately $65 million. Sponsors and supports the CWA-COPE Political Action Committee. Absorbed (1987) the International Typographical Union, (1990) United Telegraph Workers.
Meetings/Conferences:
Annual Meetings: Spring/4,000
Publications:
CWA News. m.
CWA Newsletter. bi-w.
The Sector News. m. adv.

Community Action Partnership *(1968)*
1100 17th St. NW, Suite 500
Washington, DC 20036
Tel: (202)265-7546 *Fax:* (202)265-8850
E-Mail: info@communityactionpartnership.com
Web Site: www.communityactionpartnership.com
Members: 1400 individuals
Staff: 10
Annual Budget: $1-2,000,000
National President: Derrick Len Span
Director, Strategic Communications: Lisa Holland
National Vice President: Avril Weisman
Historical Note
Founded as National Community Action Agency Executive Directors Association; became National Association of Community Action Agencies in 1982, and assumed its current name in 2002. CAP members are community action and limited purpose agencies. Membership: $175-925/year.
Meetings/Conferences:
Annual Meetings: Fall, National Convention
2007 – San Diego, CA(Manchester Grand Hyatt)/Aug. 28-31
2008 – Chicago, IL(Chicago Marriott Magnificent Mile)/Aug. 25-30
2009 – Philadelphia, PA(Philadelphia Downtown Marriott)/Sept. 2-5
Publications:
The Promise. q.
CAA Executive's Handbook.
Community Action Directory. a.

Community Associations Institute *(1973)*
225 Reinekers Lane, Suite 300
Alexandria, VA 22314
Tel: (703)548-8600 *Fax:* (703)684-1581
Web Site: www.caionline.org
Members: 17000 firms and associations
Staff: 45
Annual Budget: $2-5,000,000
Chief Executive Officer: Tom Skiba
Acting Vice President, Finance/Controller: Stephen C. Albert
E-Mail: SAlbert@caionline.org
Vice President, Chapter Relations: Dawn Bauman
E-Mail: caidirect@caionline.org
Vice President, Education/Executive Director, Research Foundation: Michele Jerome
E-Mail: MJerome@caionline.org
Historical Note
Sponsored by the National Association of Home Builders and the Urban Land Institute. Composed of community and condominium owners, builders and managers. Absorbed (1975) National Federation of Condominium Associations and the Condominium Research and Education Society Membership: $50-265/year (home owner/associations); $315-550/year (professionals/firms).
Meetings/Conferences:
Annual Meetings:
Publications:
Journal of Community Ass'n Law. 2/year.
Community Manager. bi-m.
Community Association Law Reporter. m.
Common Ground Magazine. bi-m. adv.
Ledger Quarterly. q.

Community Banking Advisors Network *(1995)*
10831 Old Mill Road, Suite 400
Omaha, NE 68154
Tel: (402)778-7922 *Fax:* (402)778-7931
Toll Free: (888)475 - 4476
E-Mail: info@bankingcpas.com
Web Site: www.bankingcpas.com
Members: 30 firms
Staff: 6
Executive Director: Nancy Drennen
Historical Note
CBAN is an association of CPA firms that concentrate a substantial portion of their business on providing financial and consulting services to community banks and financial institutions. Member firms are accepted on a territorial protected basis.
Meetings/Conferences:
Annual Meetings:
Publications:
Members' Bulletin (online). m.

Community Broadcasters Association *(1954)*
3605 Sandy Plains Road, Suite 240462
Marietta, GA 30066
Toll Free: (800)215 - 7655
Web Site: www.communitybroadcasters.com
Members: 2,800 broadcasters
Contact: Amy Brown
Historical Note
CBA members are Class-A and other low-power television stations in the U.S.

Community College Association for Instruction and Technology *(1971)*
Historical Note
Address unknown in 2006.

Community College Business Officers
P.O. Box 5565

Charlottesville, VA 22905
Tel: (434)293-2825 *Fax:* (434)245-8453
E-Mail: info@ccbo.org
Web Site: www.ccbo.org
Members: 335
Staff: 30
Annual Budget: $100-250,000
Executive Director: Dr. Bob Hassmiller
E-Mail: bob@ccbo.org

Historical Note
Membership: $200/year.

Meetings/Conferences:
Annual Meetings: Fall

Publications:
Bottom Line. 4/year.

Community College Journalism Association *(1968)*
3376 Hill Canyon Ave.
Thousand Oaks, CA 91360-1119
Tel: (805)492-4440 *Fax:* (805)492-9800
Web Site: www.ccjaonline.org/
Members: 300 individuals
Staff: 1
Annual Budget: under $10,000
Executive Secretary-Treasurer: Steven Ames
E-Mail: docames@adelphia.net

Historical Note
Formerly the Junior College Journalism Association. Members are journalism instructors in community and junior colleges. Affiliated with the Association for Education in Journalism. Membership: $40/year.

Meetings/Conferences:
Semi-annual Meetings: Aug. with AEJMC and Fall with ACP/CMA
2007 – Washington, DC/Aug. 9-12
2007 – Washington, DC/Oct. 25-28
2008 – Chicago, IL/Aug. 6-9
2008 – Kansas City, MO/Oct. 30-Nov. 2
2009 – Boston, MA/Aug. 5-8

Publications:
Community College Journalist. q. adv.
Newsletter. q.

Community Colleges Humanities Association *(1979)*
Essex County College
303 University Ave.
Newark, NJ 07102
Tel: (973)877-3577 *Fax:* (973)877-3578
Web Site: www.ccha-assoc.org
Members: 850 individuals
Staff: 1
Annual Budget: $50-100,000
Executive Director: David A. Berry
E-Mail: berry@essex.edu

Historical Note
Members are administrators and humanities faculty from two-year colleges. Membership: $40/year (individual); $250-$850/year (institution).

Meetings/Conferences:
2007 – San Antonio, TX(St. Anthony Hotel)/Oct. 25-27/400

Publications:
Community College Humanities Review. a.
Community College Humanist. 3/year.

Community Development Society *(1969)*
17 S. High St., Suite 200
Columbus, OH 43215
Tel: (614)221-1900 Ext: 217 *Fax:* (614)221-1989
E-Mail: CDS@assnoffice.com
Web Site: www.comm-dev.org
Members: 1000 individuals
Staff: 2
Annual Budget: $50-100,000
Executive Director: Peggy Blankenship
Executive Assistant: Lori Landry

Historical Note
CDS members are academics and pratitioners in community development. Membership: $25/year (student); $55/year (individual); $200/year (organization/company).

Publications:
Practice Series. q.
Journal of the CDS. semi-a.
Vanguard Newsletter. q.
CDS Membership Directory. a.

Community Development Venture Capital Alliance *(1995)*
330 Seventh Ave., 19th Floor
New York, NY 10001
Tel: (212)594-6747 *Fax:* (212)594-6717
E-Mail: cdvca@cdvca.org
Web Site: www.cdvca.org
Members: 100corporationsandorganizations
Staff: 13
Annual Budget: $1-2,000,000
President: Kerwin Tesdell
E-Mail: ktesdell@cdvca.org
Director, Program Development and Membership: Kelly Williams

Historical Note
CDVCA is an alliance of venture capital funds and other organizations dedicated to entrepreneurial solutions to community development and long-term investment in economically disadvantaged areas. Acts as a source of information and technical assistance to members. Membership: $500/year.

Meetings/Conferences:
Annual: Winter

Publications:
CDVCA Ventures (online). 3/yr.

Community Financial Services Association of America *(1999)*
515 King St., Suite 300
Alexandria, VA 22314
Tel: (703)684-1029 *Fax:* (703)684-1219
E-Mail: cfsa@multistate.com
Web Site: www.cfsa.net
Members: 160 companies
Staff: 10
Annual Budget: $2-5,000,000
Executive Director: John McIntyre

Historical Note
CFSA members provide paycheck advances and related financial services for consumers.

Meetings/Conferences:
Annual: 800
2007 – Paradise Island, Bahamas/Feb. 28-March 4

Community Leadership Association *(1979)*
1240 S. Lumpkin St.
Athens, GA 30602
Tel: (706)542-0301 *Fax:* (706)542-7007
E-Mail: info@communityleadership.org
Web Site: www.communityleadership.org
Members: 2200 individuals
Staff: 4
Annual Budget: $500-1,000,000
Executive Director: James D. Maloney Jr., CAE
E-Mail: info@communityleadership.org

Historical Note
Founded in 1979 by 40 community leadership organizations as the National Association of Community Leadership Organizations; became National Association for Community Leadership in 1989, and assumed its present name in 2000. Members are community leadership organizations at the state and local levels and their graduate groups. CLA is dedicated to nurturing leadership in communities throughout the world serves as an information clearinghouse, develops and provides training and education in leadership, and helps members enhance their graduate capacity in serving their respective communities. Membership: $150/year minimum to $500/year.

Meetings/Conferences:
Annual Meetings: Spring
2007 – Grand Rapids, MI(Amway Grand Rapids)/May 3-6/700

Community Transportation Association of America *(1989)*
1341 G St. NW, Tenth Floor
Washington, DC 20005
Tel: (202)628-1480 *Fax:* (202)737-9197
Toll Free: (800)891 - 0590
Web Site: www.ctaa.org
Members: 500 individuals
Staff: 25
Annual Budget: $5-10,000,000
Executive Director: Dale J. Marsico
Director, Communications: Scott Bogren
Director, Membership: Caryn Souza

Historical Note
CTAA is a professional association focusing on serving transit agencies in rural areas, small cities and wherever elderly, disabled or poor persons do not have access to conventional public transit. CTAA members include transit operators, human service agencies, consultants, industry suppliers and state officials. Membership: $125/year (individual); $225/year (organization); $125/year, plus $10/vehicle/year (transit system); $500/year (supplier).

Meetings/Conferences:
Annual Meetings: Spring

Publications:
Rail Magazine. 4/year. adv.
Community Transportation Magazine. 9/year. adv.

Comparative and International Education Society *(1956)*
339 ZEB Bldg.
Florida International University
Miami, FL 33199
Tel: (305)348-2450 *Fax:* (305)348-1515
Web Site: www.cies.ws/
Members: 1500 individuals
Staff: 1
Annual Budget: $25-50,000
Secretary: Lynn Ilon

Historical Note
Formerly (1974) Comparative Education Society CIES members are comparative educators and others who work in the more applied areas of international education. Membership: $35/year (individual); $67/year (organization); $20/year (students).

Meetings/Conferences:
Annual Meetings: March

Publications:
CIES Newsletter. 3/year.
Comparative Education Review. q. adv.

Competitive Telecommunications Association *(1981)*

Historical Note
See COMPTEL

Components, Packaging, and Manufacturing Technology Society *(1950)*

Historical Note
An affiliate of Institute of Electrical and Electronics Engineers, which provides administrative support.

Composite Can and Tube Institute *(1933)*
50 S. Pickett St., Suite 110
Alexandria, VA 22304-7206
Tel: (703)823-7234 *Fax:* (703)823-7237
E-Mail: ccti@cctiwdc.org
Web Site: www.cctiwdc.org
Members: 80 companies
Staff: 4
Annual Budget: $250-500,000
Executive Vice President: Kristine J. Garland
E-Mail: ccti@cctiwdc.org

Historical Note
Formed in New York, NY as the National Fibre Can and Tube Institute; assumed its present name in 1970. Members are manufacturers of composite (paperboard) cans, tubes, spools, cores, fibre drums, ribbon blocks, mailing packages, cones and bobbins, and suppliers to those manufacturers. Membership: $1,800/year (supplier); manufacturers' dues based on sales volume.

Meetings/Conferences:
Annual Meetings: Spring/100

Publications:
Wages, Benefits, and Workers' Compensation Survey. Bien. adv.
Industry Marketing Report. trien.. adv.
Tube and Core Statistical Report. m.
Cantube Bulletin. bi-m. adv.
Machine Guarding Album. trien. adv.
Industry Directory. a. adv.

Technical Notebook (also available on CD). a. adv.

Composite Panel Association *(1960)*
18922 Premiere Court
Gaithersburg, MD 20879-1574
Tel: (301)670-0604 *Fax:* (301)840-1252
E-Mail: info@pbmdf.com
Web Site: www.pbmdf.com
Members: 38 companies
Staff: 17
Annual Budget: $2-5,000,000
President: Thomas A. Julia
E-Mail: tjulia@cpamail.org
Vice President, Membership and Administration: Jeannie Ervin
Senior Vice President: Chris Leffel
E-Mail: cleffel@cpamail.org

Historical Note
Formed in 1997 by the consolidation of the National Particleboard Association and Canadian Particleboard Association, CPA represents North American particleboard and medium density fiberboard manufacturers.

Meetings/Conferences:
Semi-Annual Meetings:

Publications:
Second Wave. semi-a. adv.
North America Particleboard/MDF Industry Shipments and Downstream Market Survey. a.
Buyers & Specifiers Guide to Particleboard & MDF. a.
North American Particleboard/MDF Plant Capacity. a.

Composites Manufacturing Association of SME

Historical Note
CMA is part of Engineering Materials Applications Community of SME, a program of Society of Manufacturing Engineers, which provides administrative support.

Compressed Air and Gas Institute *(1915)*
1300 Sumner Ave.
Cleveland, OH 44115-2851
Tel: (216)241-7333 *Fax:* (216)241-0105
E-Mail: cagi@cagi.org
Web Site: www.cagi.org
Members: 35 companies
Staff: 3
Annual Budget: $250-500,000
Secretary-Treasurer: John H. Addington

Historical Note
The Compressed Air and Gas Institute is a non-profit organization of companies which manufacture air and gas compressors, air or gas dryers, or pneumatic tools and machinery; products which have many applications in construction, manufacturing, mining, and the process and natural gas industries. The forerunner of the present Institute, the Compressed Air Society, was formed in 1915 to provide an instrument for solving the problems common to all member companies and to promote the industry. In 1933 the group became the Compressed Air Institute. The name Compressed Air and Gas Institute was adopted in 1945.

Meetings/Conferences:
Annual Meetings: Semi-Annual
2007 - Marco Island, FL(Marco Island Marriott)/May 4-7

Compressed Gas Association *(1913)*
4221 Walney Rd., Fifth Floor
Chantilly, VA 20151
Tel: (703)788-2700
E-Mail: cga@cganet.com
Web Site: www.cganet.com
Members: 160 companies
Staff: 14
Annual Budget: $2-5,000,000
Chief Executive Officer: Marc J. Meteyer
Manager, Meetings and Membership: Nancy Flower
C.A.O.: Michael Tiller
E-Mail: cga@cganet.com

Historical Note
Established as the Compressed Gas Manufacturers Association, it assumed its present name in 1949; absorbed the International Acetylene Association. CGA member companies include manufacturers, distributors and transporters of compressed, liquefied and cryogenic gases, as well as manufacturers of valves, cylinders, transportation equipment and other products related to the compressed gas industry. The mission of the CGA is to promote the safe manufacture, transportation, storage, transfilling, and disposal of industrial and medical gases and their containers. Membership: based on annual sales/revenues.

Meetings/Conferences:
Annual Meetings: February-March
2007 - St. Petersburg, FL(Renaissance Vinoy)/March 18-21
2007 - Ft. Lauderdale, FL(Harbor Beach Marriott)/March 16-18/250

Publications:
Compressions. m.

COMPTEL *(1981)*
1900 M St. NW, Suite 800
Washington, DC 20036
Tel: (202)296-6650 *Fax:* (202)296-7585
Web Site: www.comptel.org
Members: 300 companies
Staff: 17
Annual Budget: $2-5,000,000
President and Chief Executive Officer: Earl Comstock
Vice President, Communications: Margaret Boles
President and Chief Executive Officer: Earl Comstock
Executive Vice President, Business Development and Member Relations: Terry Monroe

Historical Note
Founded as Association of Long Distance Telephone Companies. Absorbed American Council of Competitive Communications in 1984, becoming Competitive Telecommunications Association. Absorbed America's Carriers Telecommunications Association and assumed the name COMPTEL in 1999. Merged with Association of Communications Enterprises and assumed the name COMPTEL/ASCENT in 2003; COMPTEL/ASCENT merged with the Association for Local Telecommunications Services (ALTS) in 2005 and assumed current name at the same time.
Members are long distance carriers, resellers, vendors and others with an interest in the telecommunications industry.

Meetings/Conferences:
Semi-annual Conferences: April and September

Publications:
Membership Memo Newsletter. m.

Computer and Automated Systems Association of SME *(1975)*

Historical Note
Part of Engineering Materials Applications Community of SME, a program of Society of Manufacturing Engineers, which provides administrative support.

Computer and Communications Industry Association *(1972)*
666 11th St. NW, Suite 600
Washington, DC 20001-4542
Tel: (202)783-0070 *Fax:* (202)783-0534
E-Mail: ccia@ccianet.org
Web Site: www.ccianet.org
Members: 35 companies
Staff: 9
Annual Budget: $1-2,000,000
President and Chief Executive Officer: Edward J. Black
Director, Government Affairs: Ken Kurokawa

Historical Note
Formerly (1976) Computer Industry Association. Members are manufacturers and providers of computer information processing and telecommunications-related products and services. Companies are represented by senior executives. It represents the interests of its members in domestic and foreign trade, federal procurement policy, telecommunication and technology policy, and intellectual property issues. Membership: $3,500-55,000/year (company).

Publications:
Executive Briefing Book. q.
CEO Report. bi-w.
International Trade Report. irreg.
Federal Procurement Policy Update. irreg.
Telecommunications Report. irreg.
Technology Report. irreg.
Intellectual Property Report. irreg.

Computer Assisted Language Instruction Consortium *(1983)*
214 Centennial Hall
San Marcos, TX 78666
Tel: (512)245-1417 *Fax:* (512)245-9089
E-Mail: info@calico.org
Web Site: www.calico.org
Members: 780 individuals
Staff: 1
Annual Budget: $50-100,000
Coordinator: Esther Horn
E-Mail: info@calico.org

Historical Note
Formerly (1991) Computer Assisted Language Learning and Instruction. Established at Brigham Young University, CALICO is a consortium of academic, business, research, manufacturing and government members involved in the field of computer-assisted language instruction. Membership: $50/year (individual); $90/year (institution); $140/year (corporation).

Meetings/Conferences:
Annual Meetings: Spring/450
2007 - San Marcos, TX(Texas State University)/May 22-26/400

Publications:
The CALICO Journal. 3/ year. adv.
CALICO Monograph Series. a.
Resource Guide. a. adv.

Computer Ethics Institute *(1985)*
c/o Brookings Institution
1775 Massachusetts Ave. NW
Washington, DC 20036
Tel: (202)797-6000 *Fax:* (202)797-6004
Web Site: www.brook.edu/its/cei/cei_hp.htm
Members: 250 individuals
Secretary: Cynthia Darling

Historical Note
Founded as Coalition for Computer Ethics; incorporated under its current name in 1992. CEI serves as a forum that focuses on the ethical issues raised by computer and information technology. Members are firms and individuals active in the computer industry.

Publications:
Working Papers/Monograph Series. irreg.

Computer Event Marketing Association *(1990)*
1512 Weiskopf Loop
Round Rock, TX 78664
Tel: (512)310-8330 *Fax:* (512)682-0555
E-Mail: cema@cemaonline.com
Web Site: www.cemaonline.com
Members: 500 individuals
Staff: 2
Annual Budget: $100-250,000
Executive Director: Erika Brunke
Membership Services Director: Olga Rosenbrook
E-Mail: olga@cemaonline.com

Historical Note
CEMA is dedicated to the unique needs of event professionals in the information technology industry. Its purpose is to bring together exhibit and event marketing managers, marketing communication professionals, show management, and industry associates to partner in ways that will increase their company's event quality and success. Membership: $275/year (individual); $675/year (company).

Meetings/Conferences:
Annual Meetings: July

Publications:
CEMA Communicator. m.

Computer Game Developers Association

Historical Note
See International Game Developers Association

Computer Law Association *(1971)*
401 Edgewater Place, Suite 600
Wakefield, MA 01880-6200
Tel: (781)876-8877 *Fax:* (781)224-1239
E-Mail: askcla@cla.org
Web Site: www.cla.org
Members: 2200 individuals
Staff: 2
Annual Budget: $50-100,000
Executive Director: Susan Donegan

Historical Note
Members are concerned with legal problems arising from the invention, evolution, production, marketing, acquisition and use of computer communications technology. Membership: $100/year.

Publications:
Computer Law Ass'n Newsletter. q.
Membership Directory. a.

Computer Measurement Group *(1975)*
151 Fries Mill Road, Suite 104
P.O. Box 1124
Turnersville, NJ 08012-2016
Tel: (856)401-1700 *Fax:* (856)401-1708
Toll Free: (800)436 - 7264
E-Mail: cmahq@cmg.org
Web Site: www.cmg.org
Members: 3000 individuals
Staff: 10
Annual Budget: $2-5,000,000
Senior Conference Coordinator/Office Manager: Barbara Hazard

Historical Note
Membership: $175/year (U.S).

Meetings/Conferences:
Annual Meetings: December/2,000

Publications:
CMG Journals. q.
CMG Proceedings. a.
CMG Bulletin. q.

Computer Oriented Geological Society *(1982)*
P.O. Box 37024
Denver, CO 80237-0246
Tel: (303)816-5453 *Fax:* (303)279-0909
Web Site: www.cogsnet.org
Members: 1000 individuals
Executive Officer: Tom Bresnahan

Historical Note
COGS is a professional society composed of geologists who are using computers in their research. Has no paid officers or full-time staff. Membership: $25/year (individual); $15/year (student).

Publications:
COGSletter. irreg.

Computer Security Institute *(1974)*
600 Harrison St.
San Francisco, CA 94107
Tel: (415)947-6320 *Fax:* (415)947-6023
E-Mail: csi@cmp.com
Web Site: www.gocsi.com
Members: 5000 individuals
Staff: 16
Annual Budget: $1-2,000,000

Historical Note
Membership services designed for data processing managers, security officers, auditors and others with an interest in computer security. Membership: $224/year (domestic and Canada); $264/year (international).

Meetings/Conferences:
Semi-Annual Meetings: June and November

Publications:
Computer Security Journal. q.
Computer Security Alert Newsletter. m.
Computer Security Buyers Guide. a.

Computer Society *(1946)*

Historical Note
See IEEE Computer Society

Computer Society of the Institute of Electrical and Electronics Engineers *(1951)*

Historical Note
See IEEE Computer Society

Computer Use in Social Services Network *(1981)*

Historical Note
Absorbed by the organization Computer Use in Social Services Network in 2001.

Computer-based Patient Record Institute

Historical Note
Became CPRI-HOST in 2000.

Computerized Medical Imaging Society *(1977)*
Georgetown University Medical Center
Box 571414
Washington, DC 20057-1414
Tel: (202)687-2121 *Fax:* (202)687-1662
Members: 125 individuals
Staff: 1
Annual Budget: under $10,000
Administrator: Sylvia Brown

Historical Note
Formerly (1988) Computerized Radiology Society. Members are radiologists interested in using the computer to scan X-rays of selected planes of the body. Membership: $60/year.

Meetings/Conferences:
Annual Meetings: With American Ass'n for the Advancement of Science

Publications:
Computerized Medical Imaging & Graphics. bi-m. adv.

Computing Research Association *(1972)*
1100 17th St. NW, Suite 507
Washington, DC 20036-4632
Tel: (202)234-2111 *Fax:* (202)667-1066
E-Mail: info@cra.org
Web Site: www.cra.org
Members: 250 institutions
Staff: 9
Annual Budget: $2-5,000,000
Executive Director: Andrew Bernat
E-Mail: info@cra.org
Director, Government Affairs: Peter Harsha
E-Mail: info@cra.org

Historical Note
Formerly (1986) Computing Science Board and (1990) Computing Research Board. CRA members are U.S. and Canadian academic departments of computer science and computer engineering and industrial and government laboratories engaging in basic computer research. Membership: $650-10,000/year (organization).

Meetings/Conferences:
Biennial Meetings:

Publications:
Computing Research News. 5/year. adv.

Computing Technology Industry Association *(1982)*
1815 S. Meyers Road, Suite 300
Oakbrook Terrace, IL 60181-5228
Tel: (630)678-8300 *Fax:* (630)678-8384
E-Mail: info@comptia.org
Web Site: www.comptia.org
Members: 15000 companies
Staff: 115
Annual Budget: $50-100,000,000
President and Chief Executive Officer: John A. Venator
E-Mail: info@comptia.org
Vice President, Marketing and Communications: Laurel Chivari
Chief Operating Officer: Brian A. McCarthy
E-Mail: info@comptia.org
Director, Global Communications: Brian Pelletier
E-Mail: info@comptia.org
Vice President, Membership Development: David Raab
Vice President, Education and Training: William Vanderbilt

Historical Note
Formerly (1986) Association of Better Computer Dealers and ABCD: The Microcomputer Industry Association (1993). Members are microcomputer resellers who provide technical assistance, training and full maintenance to customers and leading microcomputer software and hardware manufacturers and distributors. Membership: $150-20,000/year (corporation).

Meetings/Conferences:
Annual Meetings: Fall

Concord Grape Association *(1969)*
5775 Peachtree-Dunwoody Road, Suite 500-G
Atlanta, GA 30342-1558
Tel: (404)252-3663 *Fax:* (404)252-0774
E-Mail: info@concordgrape.org
Web Site: www.concordgrape.org
Members: 10 companies
Staff: 4
Annual Budget: $25-50,000
President: Pamela A. Chumley

Historical Note
Founded as the Concord Grape Council, it became the American Concord Grape Association in 1974 and assumed its present name in 1980. Members are firms engaged in the processing of a substantial quantity of Concord grapes in North America.

Publications:
Membership Directory. a.

Concrete Anchor Manufacturers Association *(1995)*
1603 Boone's Lick Road
St. Charles, MO 63301
Tel: (636)925-2212 *Fax:* (636)946-3336
E-Mail: info@concreteanchors.org
Web Site: www.concreteanchors.org
Members: 23 companies and organizations
Staff: 2
Annual Budget: $50-100,000
Executive Director: James A. Borchers
E-Mail: jborchers@concreteanchors.org

Historical Note
CAMA was established in 1996 to serve as an organized voice for the post-installed anchor industry. CAMA monitors issues and decisions affecting the industry and is often called upon by regulatory bodies for industry input and comment; also serves as an industry liaison and resource to state departments of transportation.

Concrete Foundations Association *(1975)*
P.O. Box 204
Mt. Vernon, IA 52314-1602
Tel: (319)895-6940 *Fax:* (319)895-8830
Web Site: www.cfawalls.org
Members: 385
Staff: 4
Annual Budget: $500-1,000,000
Executive Director: J. Edward Sauter
E-Mail: esauter@cfawalls.org
Tech Manager: Jim Baty
E-Mail: jbaty@cfawalls.org

Historical Note
Formerly (1990) the Poured Concrete Wall Contractors Association of America. Membership: $150-600/year.

Meetings/Conferences:
Annual Meetings: Summer

Publications:
Newsletter. 6/yr. adv.

Concrete Pipe Associations

Historical Note
Formed to handle matters of common concern to American Concrete Pipe Association and American Concrete Pressure Pipe Association. Administrative support provided by ACPA.

Concrete Plant Manufacturers Bureau *(1958)*
900 Spring St.
Silver Spring, MD 20910
Tel: (301)587-1400 *Fax:* (301)587-1605
E-Mail: nmaher@cpmb.org
Web Site: www.cpmb.org
Members: 11 companies
Staff: 2
Annual Budget: $50-100,000
Executive Secretary: Robert A. Garbini

Historical Note
An affiliate of the National Ready Mixed Concrete Association. Primary purpose is developing engineering standards.

Publications:
Concrete Plant Standards of the CPMB. irreg.

Concrete Reinforcing Steel Institute *(1924)*
933 N. Plum Grove Rd.
Schaumburg, IL 60173-4758
Tel: (847)517-1200 *Fax:* (847)517-1206
E-Mail: info@crsi.org
Web Site: www.crsi.org
Members: 270 firms
Staff: 20
Annual Budget: $2-5,000,000
Financial Administrator: Susan O'Sullivan

Historical Note
Members are firms engaged in the production and fabrication of reinforcing bars and accessories. Absorbed the Associated Reinforcing Bar Producers in 1982 and the Fusion Bonded Coaters Association in 1985.

Meetings/Conferences:
Annual Meetings: Spring

Publications:
Shop Talk. q.

Concrete Sawing and Drilling Association *(1972)*
11001 Danka Way North, Suite One
St. Petersburg, FL 33716
Tel: (727)577-5004 *Fax:* (727)577-5012
E-Mail: info@csda.org
Web Site: www.csda.org
Members: 500 companies
Staff: 3
Annual Budget: $500-1,000,000
Executive Director: Patrick A. O'Brien

Historical Note
CSDA's members are contractors of concrete sawing and drilling and producers of diamond sawblades, drills, and equipment. CSDA's mission is to promote the use of professional sawing and drilling contractors and their methods. Sponsors operator certification and other continuing education programs. Membership: fees vary based on manufacturing volume.

Meetings/Conferences:
Annual Meetings: always 1st quarter.
2007 - Maui, HI(Westin)/Feb. 23-27

Publications:
Concrete Openings Magazine. q. adv.

Conductors Guild *(1975)*
5300 Glenside Dr., Suite 2207
Richmond, VA 23228-3983
Tel: (804)553-1378 *Fax:* (804)553-1876
E-Mail: guild@conductorsguild.net
Web Site: www.conductorsguild.org
Members: 1700 individuals
Staff: 4
Annual Budget: $100-250,000
Executive Director: R. Kevin Paul
E-Mail: guild@conductorsguild.net

Historical Note
Formerly a sub-group of the American Symphony Orchestra League, the Guild became an independent entity in 1985. Guild members are conductors, students and institutions with an interest in the field. Membership: $70/year (regular/associate); $40/year (student); $80/year (institution).

Meetings/Conferences:
Annual Meetings: Winter

Publications:
Conductors Guild Membership Directory. a.
Conductor Opportunities Bulletin. m.
Podium Notes Newsletter. q.
Journal of the Conductors' Guild. semi-a.

Conference Board of the Mathematical Sciences *(1960)*
1529 18th St. NW
Washington, DC 20036
Tel: (202)293-1170 *Fax:* (202)293-3412
E-Mail: lkolbe@maa.org
Web Site: www.cbmsweb.org
Members: 16 professional societies
Staff: 2
Annual Budget: $25-50,000
Administrative Officer: Ronald C. Rosier
Administrative Coordinator: Linda Kolbe

Historical Note
A group of professional societies formed to present their point of view to the Government, CBMS consists of: American Mathematical Society, Association for Symbolic Logic, Institute of Mathematical Statistics, Mathematical Association of America, National Council of Teachers of Mathematics, Society for Industrial and Applied Mathematics, American Mathematical Association of Two-Year Colleges, American Statistical Association, Association for Women in Mathematics, National Council of Supervisors of Mathematics, Society of Actuaries, Institute for Operations Research and the Management Sciences, Association of State Supervisors of Mathematics, National Association of Mathematicians and Benjamin Banneker Association.

Meetings/Conferences:
Annual Meetings:

Conference for the Study of Political Thought *(1969)*
Department of Politics
Pitzer College
Claremont, CA 91711
Tel: (909)607-3178 *Fax:* (909)621-8481
Members: 500 individuals
Annual Budget: under $10,000
Secretary-Treasurer: Sharon Nickel-Snowiss
E-Mail: ssnowiss@pitzer.edu

Historical Note
CSPT members are academics and others with an interest in the study of political theory. Membership: $18-30/year (individual); $12/year (student).

Publications:
CSPT Newsletter. semi-a.
Proceedings. a.

Conference of Business Economists
28790 Chagrin Blvd., Suite 350
Cleveland, OH 44122
Tel: (216)464-2137 *Fax:* (216)464-0397
Members: 100 individuals
Staff: 5
Executive Director: David L. Williams
E-Mail: dwilliams@Admgt.com

Publications:
Directory. a.

Conference of Chief Justices *(1949)*
Nat'l Center for State Courts
300 Newport Ave.
Williamsburg, VA 23185
Tel: (757)259-1841 *Fax:* (757)259-1520
E-Mail: ccj@ncsc.dni.us
Web Site: http://ccj.ncsc.dni.us
Members: 58 individuals
Staff: 1
Association Manager: Brenda A. Williams
E-Mail: ccj@ncsc.dni.us

Meetings/Conferences:
Semi-annual Meetings:

Conference of Consulting Actuaries *(1950)*
3880 Salem Lake Dr.
Suite H
Long Grove, IL 60047-6400
Tel: (847)719-6500 *Fax:* (847)719-6506
E-Mail: conference@ccactuaries.org
Web Site: www.ccactuaries.org
Members: 1200 individuals
Staff: 5
Annual Budget: $1-2,000,000
Executive Director: Rita K. DeGraaf
E-Mail: conference@ccactuaries.org

Historical Note
Formerly (1991) Conference of Actuaries in Public Practice. A professional membership organization for actuaries working as consultants in life, health, property and casualty insurance and in the pension planning and employee benefits fields. Affiliated with the American Academy of Actuaries and Society of Actuaries. Awards the designations "FCA", "MCA", and "ACA" (Fellow, Member, and Associate of the Conference of Consulting Actuaries).

Meetings/Conferences:
Annual Meetings: Fall
2007 - San Antonio, TX(Westin La Cantera)/Oct. 21-24

Publications:
The Consulting Actuary. 2-3/year.
Annual Meeting Outlines. a.
Meeting Outline and Transcript.
The Proceedings. a.

Conference of Educational Administrators of Schools and Programs for the Deaf *(1868)*
P.O. Box 1778
St. Augustine, FL 32085-1778
Tel: (904)810-5200 *Fax:* (904)810-5525
E-Mail: nationaloffice@ceasd.org
Web Site: www.ceasd.org
Members: 800 individuals
Staff: 2
Annual Budget: $50-100,000
Executive Director: Joseph P. Finnegan, Jr.

Historical Note
CEASD's purpose is to promote effective management of educational programs for the deaf. Orginially known as the Association of Superintendents and Principals, a splinter group from the Convention of American Instructors of the Deaf (established 1850). Formerly (until 1980) known as the Conference of Executives of American Schools for the Deaf, Inc. CEASD is a member of the Council on Education of the Deaf.

Meetings/Conferences:
Biennial Meetings: with Convention of American Instructors of the Deaf

Publications:
American Annals of the Deaf. 5/year. adv.

Conference of Historical Journals *(1982)*
Dept. of History, Old Main 416
University of Arkansas
Fayetteville, AR 72701
Tel: (501)575-5884
Web Site: www.uark.edu/depts/histinfo/history/CHJ/
Members: 160 individuals
Secretary-Treasurer: Jeannie M. Whayne

Historical Note
CHJ members are editors of serial publications focusing on history and others with an interest in the field. Membership: $25/year (individual).

Meetings/Conferences:
Annual Meetings: in conjunction with AHA annual meeting

Publications:
Editing History.

Conference of Major Superiors of Men, U.S.A. *(1956)*
8808 Cameron St.
Silver Spring, MD 20910
Tel: (301)588-4030 *Fax:* (301)587-4575
E-Mail: postmaster@cmsm.org
Web Site: www.cmsm.org
Members: 275 individuals
Staff: 6
Annual Budget: $250-500,000
Executive Director: Rev. Ted Keating
E-Mail: postmaster@cmsm.org

Historical Note
Formerly the Conference of Major Superiors of Men's Institutes. Members are major superiors of the various Roman Catholic religious orders of men in the U.S.

Meetings/Conferences:
Annual Meetings: August

Publications:
CMSM Bulletin. m.
CMSM Forum. q.
Directory. a.
Justice and Peace Alert. m.

Conference of Minority Public Administrators *(1971)*

Historical Note
An affiliate of American Society for Public Administration, whioch provides administrative support.

Conference of Minority Transportation Officials *(1971)*
818 18th St. NW, Suite 850
Washington, DC 20006
Tel: (202)530-0551 *Fax:* (202)530-0617
Toll Free: (877)782 - 6686

E-Mail: comto@comto.org
Web Site: www.comto.org
Members: 2000 individuals
Staff: 4
Annual Budget: $500-1,000,000
Executive Director/Chief Executive Officer: Julie A. Cunningham

Historical Note

The Conference of Minority Transportation Officials (COMTO) is a nationwide association of professionals from a wide spectrum of transportation related industries and backgrounds. COMTO was formed in 1971 to provide a forum for minority professionals in the transportation industry. Membership, as the name suggests, is predominantly made up of minority professionals and organizations who have joined the association to continue the development of professional growth and influence through interaction with COMTO's programs and its people. Provides scholarships and the opportunity for networking, training and continued education. Has over 2,200 members in 27 chapters in cities throughout the United States. Membership: $60/year (individual); $1,000-5,000/year (organization/company).

Meetings/Conferences:
Annual Meetings: Summer

Publications:
Cable Express. m. adv.

Conference of Philosophical Socs. *(1976)*
Div. of Liberal Arts, D'Youville Coll.
Buffalo, NY 14201-2486
Tel: (716)881-7786
Members: 90 societies
Annual Budget: under $10,000
President: G. John M. Abbarno

Historical Note

COPS members are philosophical societies. Has no paid officers or full-time staff.

Publications:
COPS Newsletter. semi-a.
Directory of Philosophical Socs. irreg.
Philosophical Calendar. bi-m.

Conference of Radiation Control Program Directors *(1968)*
205 Capital Ave.
Frankfort, KY 40601-2832
Tel: (502)227-4543 *Fax:* (502)227-7862
Web Site: www.crcpd.org
Members: 884 individuals
Staff: 10
Annual Budget: $500-1,000,000
Interim Executive Director: Charles M. Hardin

Historical Note

Members are or have been employed by state, local or foreign radiation control programs. The CRCPD provides a forum for the exchange of information between radiation control programs of states, and between the states and federal government. Membership: $50-125/year.

Meetings/Conferences:
Annual Meetings: Spring
2007 - Spokane, WA(Red Lion)/May 21-24/400
2008 - Greensboro, NC(Marriott)/May 19-22/400

Publications:
Newsbrief. bi-m. adv.
Radon Bulletin. bi-m.
Directory of Radiological Health Program Directors. a. adv.
Annual Proceedings. a.

Conference of Research Workers in Animal Diseases *(1920)*
Colorado State University
Dept. of MIP
Ft. Collins, CO 80523-1682
Tel: (970)491-5740 *Fax:* (970)491-1815
Web Site: www.cvmbs.colostate.edu/microbiology/crwad/index.htm
Members: 400 individuals
Staff: 1
Annual Budget: $25-50,000
Executive Director: Dr. Robert P. Ellis
E-Mail: robertellis@colostate.edu

Historical Note

Approximately 325 presentations of unpublished research results of studies in animal health and disease are presented annually. Membership: $130/year.

Meetings/Conferences:
Annual Meetings: Fall/Winter

Publications:
Newsletter (online). a.
Proceedings of the CRWAD Annual Meeting. a.

Conference of State Bank Supervisors *(1902)*
1155 Connecticut Ave. NW, Suite 500
Washington, DC 20036-4306
Tel: (202)296-2840 *Fax:* (202)296-1928
Toll Free: (800)886 - 2727 Ext:
Web Site: www.csbs.org
Members: 54 state regulatory organizations
Staff: 27
Annual Budget: $2-5,000,000
President and Chief Executive Officer: Neil Milner, CAE
General Counsel: John Gorman
E-Mail: jgorman@csbs.org
Senior Vice President, Mortgage: Bill Matthews
Vice President, Regulatory: Mary Beth Puccinelli
E-Mail: mbpuccinell@csbs.org
Executive Vice President, Policy: John Ryan
E-Mail: jryan@csbs.org
Vice President, Membership and Banker Relations: Ed Smith
E-Mail: esmith@csbs.org
Vice President, Regulatory: Michael Stevens
Senior Vice President, Education: Roger Stromberg
Vice President, Communications: Mary White
E-Mail: mwhite@csbs.org
Senior Vice President, International: Leslie Woolley
E-Mail: leslie.woolley@csbs.org

Historical Note

Founded in 1902 as the National Association of Supervisors of State Banks; assumed current name in 1970. CSBS is the professional organization of the state bank regulators of the 50 States, Guam, Puerto Rico, the Virgin Islands, and Washington, DC. Associate membership offered to state-chartered commercial and mutual savings banks.

Meetings/Conferences:
Annual Meetings: Spring
2007 - Coeur d'Alene, ID(Coeur d'Alene Resort)/May 30-Jan. 1/350

Publications:
A Profile of State Chartered Banking. bien.
CSBS Examiner. w.

Conference of State Court Adminstrators *(1955)*
Nat'l Center for State Courts
300 Newport Ave.
Williamsburg, VA 23185-4147
Tel: (757)259-1841 *Fax:* (757)259-1520
Toll Free: (800)877 - 1233
Web Site: http://cosca.ncsc.dni.us
Members: 56 individuals
Staff: 1
Association Manager: Shelley Rockwell

Historical Note

Established as National Conference of Court Administrative Officers; became (1972) National Conference of State Court Administrators and assumed its present name in 1975. Administration provided by National Center for State Courts.

Meetings/Conferences:
Annual Meetings: Late Summer/100
2007 - Mackinac Island, MI(Grand Hotel)
2008 - Anchorage, AK(Hotel Captain Cook)

Conference on Asian History *(1953)*
East Asian Studies Center
Indiana University
Bloomington, IN 47405
Tel: (812)855-3765 *Fax:* (812)855-7762
Members: 400 individuals
Chairman: George M. Wilson

Historical Note

An affiliate of the American Historical Association, Conference members are historians specializing in the history of Asia. Membership: $10/year.

Meetings/Conferences:
Annual Meetings: in conjunction with American Historical Ass'n

---

Conference on College Composition and Communication *(1949)*
1111 W. Kenyon Road
Urbana, IL 61801
Tel: (217)328-3870 *Fax:* (217)328-9645
Toll Free: (800)369 - 6283
Web Site: www.ncte.org/groups/cccc
Members: 6000 individuals
Staff: 1
Annual Budget: $250-500,000
Executive Secretary-Treasurer: Kent D. Williamson

Historical Note

A subsidiary of the National Council of Teachers of English, to which members of the Conference must first belong and which provides administrative support. Members are teachers of freshman English at the college level. Membership: $75/year (individual).

Meetings/Conferences:
Semi-annual Meetings: Spring/3,000
2007 - New York, NY(Hilton)/March 21-24

Publications:
College Composition and Communication. q. adv.

Conference on Consumer Finance Law *(1926)*
Oklahoma City University School of Law
2501 N. Blackwelder
Oklahoma City, OK 73106
Tel: (405)521-5363 *Fax:* (405)521-5089
E-Mail: ccflqr@ccfl.com
Web Site: www.theccfl.com
Members: 1,400 lawyers and financial institutions
Staff: 1
Annual Budget: $25-50,000
Executive Director: Alvin C. Harrell
E-Mail: ccflqr@ccfl.com

Historical Note

Formerly (1984) Conference on Personal Finance Law. The objects of the Conference are to encourage research in the commercial law, banking, and consumer finance fields, to promote by discussion and publication the improvement of legal procedures affecting credit law and installment finance, and to afford a forum at which lawyers may meet and exchange opinions. Membership: $95/year.

Meetings/Conferences:
Semi-Annual: Spring/Summer w/American Bar Ass'n

Publications:
Consumer Finance Law Quarterly Report. q. adv.

Conference on English Education *(1963)*
1111 W. Kenyon Road
Urbana, IL 61801-1096
Tel: (217)328-3870 *Fax:* (217)328-9645
Web Site: www.ncte.org/groups/cee
Members: 2000 individuals
Staff: 1
Annual Budget: under $10,000
Executive Director: Kent D. Williamson

Historical Note

A subsidiary of the National Council of Teachers of English, to which all members of the Conference must first belong and which provides administrative support. Members are state and local supervisors of English instruction and college English education teachers. Membership: $45/year.

Meetings/Conferences:
Annual Meetings: Fall

Publications:
English Education. q. adv.

Conference on English Leadership *(1970)*
1111 W. Kenyon Road
Urbana, IL 61801-1096
Tel: (217)278-3607 *Fax:* (217)328-0977
Toll Free: (800)369 - 6283 Ext: 3607
Web Site: www.ncte.org/groups/cel
Members: 1700 individuals
Staff: 2
Annual Budget: $50-100,000

Executive Director: Kent D. Williamson
Liaison: Felisa Love
E-Mail: flove@ncte.org

Historical Note
Formerly (1992) the Conference for Secondary School English Department Chairpersons. A subsidiary of the National Council of Teachers of English, to which all members of the Conference must first belong, and which provides administrative support. Membership: $65/year (individual).

Meetings/Conferences:
Annual Meetings: In conjunction with the Nat'l Council of Teachers of English
2007 - New York, NY/Nov. 21-23/150
2008 - San Antonio, TX/Nov. 23-25/200

Publications:
English Leadership Quarterly. q.

Conference on Faith and History *(1967)*
Huntington University
Dept. of History
Huntington, IN 47650
Tel: (260)359-4242
E-Mail: cfh@huntington.edu
Web Site: www.huntington.edu/cfh
Members: 600 individuals
Annual Budget: $10-25,000
Secretary: Paul Michelson

Historical Note
Incorporated in 1969. CFH represents academic historians and others with an interest in the relationship of faith and history. Membership: $20/year (individual); $15/year (student/retired).

Meetings/Conferences:
Annual Meetings: in conjunction with American Historical Ass'n meeting

Publications:
Fides et Historia. semi-a. adv.
Newsletter. semi-a.

Conference on Jewish Social Studies *(1933)*
Stanford University, Bldg. 200, Room 11
Stanford, CA 94305-2024
Tel: (650)723-7589
E-Mail: jss@leland.stanford.edu
Members: 1400 individuals
Staff: 2
President: Steven J. Zipperstein

Historical Note
Academics and others with an interest in Jewish social studies.

Publications:
Jewish Social Studies. 3/year.

Conference on Latin American History *(1926)*
University of California at Davis
One Shields Ave.
Davis, CA 95616
Tel: (530)752-3046 *Fax:* (530)752-5655
E-Mail: clah@ucdavis.edu
Web Site: www.h-net.msu.edu/~clah/
Members: 850 individuals
Annual Budget: under $10,000
Executive Secretary: Tom Holloway
E-Mail: clah@ucdavis.edu

Historical Note
CLAH sponsors several prizes and awards in recognition of achievement in historiography of Latin America. Has no paid officers or full-time staff. Membership: $40/year (professional); $25/year (emeritus); $15/year (student).

Meetings/Conferences:
Annual Meetings: In conjunction with the American Historical Ass'n.

Publications:
Newsletter. semi-a. adv.
Membership List. a.

Congress of Chiropractic State Associations *(1968)*
P.O. Box 2054
Lexington, SC 29071
Tel: (803)356-6809 *Fax:* (803)356-6826
E-Mail: cocsa@sc.rr.com
Web Site: www.cocsa.org
Members: 60 organizations
Staff: 2
Annual Budget: $100-250,000
Executive Director: Janet Jordan, CAE

Historical Note
CCSA represents the state organizations which support the profession and science of chiropractic medicine in the U.S. Membership: $300/year.

Meetings/Conferences:
Annual Meetings: November

Congress of Independent Unions *(1958)*
303 Ridge St.
Alton, IL 62002
Tel: (618)462-2447 *Fax:* (618)462-5579
Members: 10 independent labor unions
Staff: 7
Annual Budget: $250-500,000
President: R. Richard Davis

Meetings/Conferences:
Annual Meetings: October/November

Publications:
CIU News. a.

Congress of Lung Association Staffs *(1912)*
1150 18th St., Suite 900
Washington, DC 20036
Tel: (202)785-3355 *Fax:* (202)452-1805
Web Site: www.lungus.org
Members: 1000 individuals
Staff: 3
Annual Budget: $100-250,000
Executive Director: Janet M. Widmer
Manager, Membership Services: Christopher Dyer

Historical Note
Formerly National Conference of Tuberculosis Workers, and (1973) National Respiratory Disease Conference. Members are professional staff of American Lung Association offices throughout the country. Membership: $25/year (individual).

Meetings/Conferences:
Annual Meetings: May

Publications:
CLAS Action Report. q.

Congress of National Black Churches *(1978)*

Historical Note
Address unknown in 2005.

Congress of Neurological Surgeons *(1951)*
10 North Martingale Road, Suite 190
Schaumburg, IL 60173
Tel: (847)240-2500 *Fax:* (847)240-0804
Toll Free: (877)517 - 1267
E-Mail: info@1cns.org
Web Site: www.neurosurgeon.org/index.asp
Members: 5500 individuals
Staff: 2
Annual Budget: $500-1,000,000
President: Richard E. Ellenbogen, MD, FACS
E-Mail: info@1cns.org

Historical Note
A professional society with members both from the United States and a number of foreign countries. Membership: $285/year.

Meetings/Conferences:
Annual Meetings: Fall
2007 - San Diego, CA/Sept. 15-20
2008 - Orlando, FL/Sept. 20-25
2010 - San Francisco, CA/Oct. 16-21
2011 - Washington, DC/Oct. 1-6
2012 - Chicago, IL/Sept. 29-Oct. 4
2013 - San Fracisco, CA/Oct. 19-24

Publications:
Video Perspectives in Neurological Surgery. 4/y.
Clinical Neurosurgery. a.
Newsletter. q.
Concepts. adv. adv.
Neurosurgery. m. adv.

Congress on Research in Dance *(1965)*
SUNY-Brockport Dance Department
350 New Campus Dr.
Brockport, NY 14420-2939
Tel: (716)395-2590 *Fax:* (716)345-5413
Web Site: http://cordance.org
Members: 822 individuals
Staff: 1
Annual Budget: $25-50,000
Director, Administration: Ginger Macchi Carlson
E-Mail: gcarlson@brockport.edu

Historical Note
Initally known as the Committee on Research in Dance; assumed its current name in 1979. Members are dance scholars who conduct research in dance and dance-related fields such as anthropology, body sciences, education, film, history, music, philosophy, psychology, sociology, theatre and the visual arts. CORD also has an international membership. Membership: $75/year (regular); $115/year (institution); $35/year (student/retired); $90-127/year (international); $50/year (student/retired international).

Publications:
Annual Conference Proceedings. a.
Dance Research Journal. bi-a. adv.
Newsletter. bi-a. adv.

Connected International Meeting Professionals Association *(1980)*
9200 Bayard Place
Fairfax, VA 22032
Tel: (512)684-0889 *Fax:* (267)390-5193
E-Mail: susan2@cimpa.org
Web Site: www.cimpa.org
Members: 2940 individuals
Staff: 6
Annual Budget: $2-5,000,000
President: Andrea Sigler, Ph.D.
E-Mail: asigler@cimpa.org

Historical Note
An online association of meetings and incentive professionals. Awards the CIMP (Certified Internet Meeting Professional) designation. Membership: Free

Meetings/Conferences:
Annual Meetings: Fall

Publications:
Tech-Savvy: Journal of Technology, Meetings and Incentives. q. adv.
MICE Magazine.
Meetings & Incentives. q. adv.
Internat'l Meetings Newsletter. bi-w. adv.
Course Catalogue. q.

Conservation and Preservation Charities of America
c/o Maguire/Maguire Assn. Mgmt.
21 Tamal Vista Blvd., Suite 209
Corte Madera, CA 94925
Toll Free: (800)626 - 6685
Web Site: www.conservenow.org
Members: 61 organizations
Secretary: Vance G. Martin

Historical Note
CPCA is a consortium of environmental stewardship organizations. CPCA acts as a central focus for charitable giving dedicated to the protection of the natural habitat and historic treasures. Sponsors workplace giving campaigns in support of its member organizations.

Conservative Orthopaedics International Association *(1982)*
6872 Arlington
Suite 201
West Bloomfield, MI 48322
Tel: (313)563-0360
E-Mail: drcastor.coia@gmail.com
Members: 4201 individuals
Staff: 4
Annual Budget: $2-5,000,000
President: Dr. Stephen R. Castor
E-Mail: drcastor.coia@gmail.com

Historical Note
Members are doctors of medicine, chiropractic, osteopathy, and other individuals interested in non-surgical treatment for the prevention and rehabilitation of musculoskeletal related disorders. Membership: $175/year.

Meetings/Conferences:
Annual Meetings: Winter
2008 - Sydney, Australia(Regent)

Publications:
Bulletin. bi-m.

Newsletter. m.

Consolidated Tape Association *(1974)*
c/o New York Stock Exchange
11 Wall St., 21st Floor
New York, NY 10005
Tel: (212)656-2052 *Fax:* (212)656-5848
Members: 9 organizations
Annual Budget: under $10,000
Administrator: Patricia Hussey
E-Mail: phussey@nyse.com
Historical Note
CTA members are stock exchanges and the National Association of Securities Dealers. CTA melds the reporting of transactions from the various stock exchanges.
Publications:
Activity Report. m.
Statistical Releases. w.

Consortium for Advanced Manufacturing International *(1972)*
119 N.E. Wilshire Blvd., Suite E
Burleson, TX 76028
Tel: (817)426-5744 *Fax:* (817)426-5799
E-Mail: admin@cam-i.org
Web Site: www.cam-i.org
Members: 100companiesandorganizations
Staff: 7
Annual Budget: $1-2,000,000
Member Services: Nancy Thomas
Historical Note
Founded as Computer Aided Manufacturing International; assumed its current name in 1997. Members are companies throughout the world interested in computer-assisted manufacturing and the general field of robotics. About two-thirds of the membership is from the United States. Membership: $25,000/year.
Publications:
Library Catalogue. q.

Consortium for Graduate Study and Management *(1966)*
5585 Pershing, Suite 240
St. Louis, MO 63112-4621
Tel: (314)877-5500 *Fax:* (314)877-5505
Toll Free: (888)865 - 6814
E-Mail: arandop@cgsm.org
Web Site: www.cgsm.org
Members: 13 schools, 140 supply companies
Staff: 17
Executive Director: Peter Aranda
E-Mail: arandop@cgsm.org
Historical Note
CGSM is an alliance of 13 universities working to faciliate the entry of minorities into managerial positions in business.
Meetings/Conferences:
Annual Meetings: Typical attendance at CGSM conferences is about 1,000 people.

Consortium for School Networking
1710 Rhode Island Ave. NW, Suite 900
Washington, DC 20036-3007
Tel: (202)861-2676 *Fax:* (202)861-0888
Toll Free: (866)267 - 8747
Web Site: www.cosn.org
Members: 450 organizations
Staff: 6
Annual Budget: $1-2,000,000
Chief Executive Officer: Keith Krueger
E-Mail: keith@cosn.org
Historical Note
CoSN promotes the development and use of internet and information technologies for K-12 learning. Members are school districts, states, nonprofits and commercial organizations, all of whom share the goal of promoting the state of the art in computer networking technologies in schools.
Publications:
Member News. 24/year.
Washington Update (e-newsletter). 12/year.

Consortium of Behavioral Health Nurses and Associates *(1987)*
1733 H St., Suite 330
PMB 1214
Blaine, WA 98230
Toll Free: (800)876 - 2236
E-Mail: cbhna@aol.com
Web Site: www.cbhna.org
Members: 1000 individuals
Staff: 4
Annual Budget: $100-250,000
Executive Director: Randy Bryson
Historical Note
Founded as National Consortium of Chemical Dependency Nurses; assumed its current name in 2002. CBHNA members are registered and licensed practical nurses specializing in the treatment of chemical dependency. Provides certification for members. Membership: $75/year.
Meetings/Conferences:
Annual Meetings: Fall
Publications:
CD Nurse Briefing Newsletter. q. adv.

Consortium of College and University Media Centers *(1971)*
1200 Comm. Bldg.
Iowa State University
Ames, IA 50011-3243
Tel: (515)294-1811 *Fax:* (515)294-8089
E-Mail: ccumc@ccumc.org
Web Site: www.ccumc.org
Members: 750 individuals
Staff: 2
Annual Budget: $100-250,000
President: Aileen Scales
Historical Note
Members are college and university media center managers, film/video rental librarians, film/video producers, distributors and other interested individuals and organizations. Membership: $325/year (company/institution).
Meetings/Conferences:
Annual Meetings: Fall
2007 – Gainesville, FL/Oct. 18-22/200
Publications:
CCUMC Leader Newsletter. q.
College and University Media Review. semi-a.
Directory. a.

Consortium of Social Science Associations *(1981)*
1522 K St. NW, Suite 836
Washington, DC 20005
Tel: (202)842-3525 *Fax:* (202)842-2788
E-Mail: cossa@cossa.org
Web Site: www.cossa.org
Members: 110 orgnizations
Staff: 4
Annual Budget: $250-500,000
Executive Director: Howard J. Silver
E-Mail: cossa@cossa.org
Historical Note
Established and incorporated in the District of Columbia, COSSA represents the full range of social and behavioral science disciplines with 17 member and 24 affiliate scholarly associations and 69 contributing universities/independent research institutions. Orginally created to lobby for the restoration of funds for social and behavioral science research cut from the National Science Foundation budget, COSSA now monitors research and research funding in most federal agencies which award significant external grants. COSSA provides information and guidance to social science groups unfamiliar with government processes and represents the social sciences in legislative relations.
Publications:
COSSA Washington Update -. bi-w.

Construction Equipment Council
Historical Note
A council of the Equipment Manufacturers Institute.

Construction Equipment Electronics Bureau
Historical Note
A bureau of the Construction Industry Manufacturers Association.

Construction Financial Management Association *(1981)*
29 Emmons Dr., Suite F-50
Princeton, NJ 08540
Tel: (609)452-8000 *Fax:* (609)452-0474
E-Mail: info@cfma.org
Web Site: www.cfma.org
Members: 6000 individuals
Staff: 20
Annual Budget: $2-5,000,000
President and Chief Executive Officer: William M. Schwab
E-Mail: info@cfma.org
Historical Note
Members are accountants, controllers, financial managers and CPAs in the construction industry concerned with financial management tax, techonology and risk management issues. Officers are elected annually. Membership: $195/year
Meetings/Conferences:
Annual Meetings: Spring
2007 – Phoenix, AZ(Marriott's Desert Ridge)/May 19-23
Publications:
State of CFMA Report. a.
Computerization Survey for the Construction Industry. bi-a.
Annual Financial Survey Report. a. adv.
CFMA Building Profits. bi-m. adv.
Financial Management Accounting for the Construction Industry. a.

Construction Innovation Forum
1625 S. Woodward Ave., P.O. Box 3402
Bloomfield Hills, MI 48302
Tel: (248)409-1500 *Fax:* (248)409-1503
E-Mail: info@cif.org
Web Site: www.cif.org
President: Brenda Romano
Historical Note
CIF is a professional association organized to recognize and foster technical advances in the construction industry.

Construction Management Association of America *(1982)*
7918 Jones Branch Dr., Suite 540
McLean, VA 22102
Tel: (703)356-2622 *Fax:* (703)356-6388
E-Mail: info@cmaanet.org
Web Site: www.cmaanet.org
Members: 2200 firms and individuals
Staff: 8
Annual Budget: $1-2,000,000
Executive Director: Bruce D'Agostino
E-Mail: bdagostino@cmaanet.org
Historical Note
CMAA is comprised of firms and individuals that provide total management of construction projects, from conception through completion as a professional service.
Meetings/Conferences:
Annual Meetings: Fall
Publications:
e-Advisor. bi-m.
CM Advisor. bi-m.

Construction Marketing Research Council *(1992)*
c/o CPMA, 4625 S. Wendler Dr., Suite 111
Tempe, AZ 85282
Tel: (602)431-1441 *Fax:* (602)431-0637
Web Site: http://cmrc.net
Members: 25 companies
Annual Budget: $10-25,000
Treasurer: Jim McMahon
Historical Note
CMRC members are professionals in the construction products industry with responsibilites for their firms' corporate strategic planning and the conduct of marketing research activities. Membership is restricted to the highest level marketing research or planning professional within a company. Associate non-voting membership is available for other individuals in different groups within the same company. Has no paid officers or full-time staff. Membership: $300/year.
Meetings/Conferences:
Semi-annual Meetings: April and October

Construction Metrication Council

Historical Note
An affiliated council of National Institute of Building Sciences, which provides administrative support.

Construction Owners Association of America *(1994)*
Two Paces West, Suite 1710
Atlanta, GA 30339
Tel: (770)433-0820 *Fax:* (404)577-3551
Toll Free: (800)994 - 2622
E-Mail: coaa@coaa.org
Web Site: www.coaa.org
Members: 400 individuals
Staff: 3
Annual Budget: $250-500,000
Managing Executive: Kim Fisher

Historical Note
Membership: $350/year (regular); $1000/year (associate).

Publications:
The Owner's Perspective magazine. q. adv.

Construction Specifications Institute *(1948)*
99 Canal Center Plaza, Suite 300
Alexandria, VA 22314-1791
Toll Free: (800)689 - 2900
E-Mail: csi@csinet.org
Web Site: www.csinet.org
Members: 16000 individuals
Staff: 38
Annual Budget: $5-10,000,000
Executive Director: Karl F. Borgstrom, Ph.D.

Historical Note
A not-for-profit technical organization dedicated to the advancement of construction technology through communication, research, education, and service. CSI serves the interests of architects, specifiers, engineers, contractors, product manufacturers, and others in the construction industry. Has an annual budget of approximately $7 million. Membership: $155/year.

Meetings/Conferences:
Annual Meetings: Spring
2007 – Baltimore, MD

Publications:
Construction Specifier. m. adv.
CSI Newsdigest. m.

Construction Writers Association *(1957)*
P.O. Box 5586
Buffalo Grove, IL 60089-5586
Tel: (847)398-7756 *Fax:* (847)590-5241
E-Mail: office@constructionwriters.org
Web Site: www.constructionwriters.org
Members: 275 individuals
Staff: 2
Annual Budget: $50-100,000
Executive Director: Sheila Wertz
E-Mail: office@constructionwriters.org

Historical Note
Membership: $100/year (individual); $200/year (corporate).

Meetings/Conferences:
2007 – Washington, DC/May
2007 – Chicago, IL/October

Publications:
CWA News Newsletter. q.

Consultant Dietitians in Health Care Facilities *(1975)*
2219 Cardinal Dr.
Waterloo, IA 50701
Tel: (319)235-0991 *Fax:* (319)235-7224
E-Mail: cdhcf@cdhcf.org
Web Site: www.cdhcf.org
Members: 5100 individuals
Annual Budget: $100-250,000
Executive Coordinator: Marla Carlson

Historical Note
A dietetic practice group of the American Dietetic Association. Membership: $20/year (individual), plus ADA membership.

Meetings/Conferences:
Annual Meetings: in conjunction with the American Dietetic Ass'n

Publications:
The Consultant Dietitian Newsletter. q.

Consumer Bankers Association *(1919)*
1000 Wilson Blvd., Suite 2500
Arlington, VA 22209-3912
Tel: (703)276-1750 *Fax:* (703)528-1290
Web Site: www.cbanet.org
Members: 200 corporate; 270 associate
Staff: 23
Annual Budget: $5-10,000,000
President: Joe Belew
Vice President, Membership: Jerry R. Baugh
Vice President, Communications: Fritz Elmendorf
Vice President, Administration and Conferences: Jayne Ellen Hunt
VicePresident and Director, Government Relations: Marcia Z. Sullivan

Historical Note
Formerly (1919) Morris Plan Bankers Association. Sponsors and supports the Consumer Bankers Association Political Action Committee (CONPAC). Members are federally-insured financial institutions with a primary interest in retail banking.

Meetings/Conferences:
Annual Meetings: Fall
2007 – San Diego, CA(Manchester Grand Hyatt)/Sept. 23-26

Publications:
CBA Reports. bi-w.

Consumer Credit Insurance Association *(1951)*
542 S. Dearborn, Suite 400
Chicago, IL 60605
Tel: (312)939-2242 *Fax:* (312)939-8287
Web Site: www.cciaonline.com
Members: 140 companies
Staff: 5
Annual Budget: $1-2,000,000
Executive Vice President: William F. Burfeind, III

Historical Note
Members are companies that sell or service insurance and related debt protection products provided in connection with credit transactions.

Meetings/Conferences:
Annual Meetings: Spring
2007 – Destin, FL(Hilton Sandestin)/Apr. 28-March 1/180

Consumer Data Industry Association *(1906)*
1090 Vermont Ave. NW, Suite 200
Washington, DC 20005-4905
Tel: (202)371-0910 *Fax:* (202)371-0134
E-Mail: info@cdiaonline.org
Web Site: www.cdiaonline.org
Members: 600 bureaus and collection agencies
Staff: 17
Annual Budget: $5-10,000,000
President and Chief Executive Officer: Stuart K. Pratt
Vice President, Public Relations: Norman Magnuson

Historical Note
Founded as National Association of Retail Credit Agencies, it became the National Association of Mercantile Agencies in 1908 and the Associated Credit Bureaus of America in 1937; assumed its present name in 2000. Membership is divided into three classes: Credit Reporting Offices, Collection Service Offices, and Specialized Reporting Services. Supports the ACB Political Action Committee.

Meetings/Conferences:
Annual Meetings: June

Publications:
Communicator. m.

Consumer Electronics Association *(1996)*
2500 Wilson Blvd.
Arlington, VA 22201-3834
Tel: (703)907-7600 *Fax:* (703)907-7690
E-Mail: cea@CE.org
Web Site: www.ce.org
Members: 2000
Staff: 130
Chief Executive Officer: Gary Shapiro
Vice President, Sales and Business Development: Dan Cole
Vice President, Communications: Jeff Joseph
Vice President, Technology and Standards: Ralph Justis

Historical Note
Formerly the Consumer Electronics Group of the Electronic Industries Association, became Consumer Electronics Manufacturers Association in 1996, and assumed its current name in 2000. Absorbed Professional Audio/Video Retailers Association in 2004.

Publications:
Consumer Magazine.
Visions Magazine. bi-m.

Consumer Electronics Society

Historical Note
See IEEE Consumer Electronics Society

Consumer Federation of America *(1968)*
1620 I St. NW, Suite 200
Washington, DC 20006
Tel: (202)387-6121 *Fax:* (202)265-7989
E-Mail: cfa@consumerfed.org
Web Site: www.consumerfed.org
Members: 280 organizations
Staff: 25
Annual Budget: $2-5,000,000
Executive Director: Stephen Brobeck
Membership: Mel H. Crawford

Historical Note
A broad coalition of consumer groups united to advance consumer interests. Membership consists of consumer organizations, labor unions, rural-electric cooperatives and state and local consumer protection officials. Supports the C.F.A. Political Action Fund.

Meetings/Conferences:
Annual Meetings: Consumer Assembly, Washington, DC

Publications:
CFA News. m.

Consumer Healthcare Products Association *(1881)*
900 19th St. NW, Suite 700
Washington, DC 20006
Tel: (202)429-9260 *Fax:* (202)223-6835
Web Site: www.chpa-info.org
Members: 180 companies
Staff: 32
Annual Budget: $5-10,000,000
President: Linda A. Suydam
Director, Communications and Media Relations: Elizabeth Assey
Vice President, Finance and Operations and Treasurer: Roman G. Blazauskas
Vice President, Communications and Strategic Initiatives: Virginia Cox
Director, Information and Technology: Kenneth W. Hoffman
Director, Meetings: Kass Kassouf
Vice President, Government Relations: Kevin J. Kraushaar
Vice President, Corporate Development: Theodore L. Peterson
Senior Vice President, Policy and International Affairs: David C. Spangler
Membership and Corporate Development Manager: Phyllis M. Taylor

Historical Note
Organized in New York City on November 26, 1881, as the Proprietary Medicine Manufacturers and Dealers Association; became Nonprescription Drug Manufacturers Association in 1989, and assumed its present name in 1999. Members are producers of medicines and dietary supplements for self-care sold without a prescription. Has an annual budget of approximately $6.7 million. Membership fee based on sales volume.

Meetings/Conferences:
Annual Meetings: Spring/600
2007 – Naples, FL(Ritz-Carlton Golf Resort)/March 15-17

Publications:
Legislative News. irreg.
Executive Newsletter. semi-m.
Membership Directory. a.

Consumer Specialty Products Association *(1914)*
900 17th St. NW, Suite 300
Washington, DC 20006-2111
Tel: (202)872-8110 *Fax:* (202)872-8114
Web Site: www.cspa.org

Members: 260 companies
Staff: 30
Annual Budget: $2-5,000,000
President: D. Christopher Cathcart
Senior Vice President, Legal Affairs/General Counsel: Stephen S. Kellner
E-Mail: skellner@csma.org

Historical Note
Established as the National Association of Insecticide and Disinfectant Manufacturers, became Chemical Specialities Manufacturers Association in 1948, and assumed its current name in 2001. Sponsors the CSPA Political Action Committee (CSPA-PAC).

Meetings/Conferences:
Semi-Annual Meetings: Mid-year meeting in April-May, annual meeting in December

Publications:
Formulators Forum. bien.
Executive Newswatch. bi-w.
Legislative Report. q.

Contact Lens Association of Ophthalmologists *(1963)*

2025 Woodlane Dr.
St. Paul, MN 55125-2998
Tel: (800)284-3937 Ext: 247 *Fax:* (651)357-1384
E-Mail: jmassare@clao.org
Web Site: www.clao.org
Members: 1000 individuals
Staff: 3
Annual Budget: $250-500,000
Executive Director: John S. Massare, Ph.D.
E-Mail: jmassare@clao.org

Historical Note
Founded in New York, NY, by a group of members of the American Academy of Ophthamology. CLAO provides comprehensive ophthalmologists and other eyecare professionals with education and training in contact lenses and related eyecare science. Membership: $295/year.

Meetings/Conferences:
Annual Meetings:
2007 – Las Vegas, NV(Caesars Palace)/Oct. 5-6

Publications:
CLAO Journal. bi-m. adv.
CLAOGram. m.

Contact Lens Council *(1982)*

8201 Corporate Drive, Suite 850
Landover, MD 20785
Tel: (301)459-2618 *Fax:* (301)459-1802
Toll Free: (800)884 - 4252
E-Mail: clc@thecli.com
Web Site: www.contactlenscouncil.org
Members: 6 organizations
Staff: 2
Annual Budget: $500-1,000,000
Executive Director: Edward L. Schilling, III

Historical Note
CLI members are contact lens manufacturers, producers and professional associations with an interest in the safe use of contact lenses and public education on vision correction. CLI is affiliated with and supported by the Contact Lens Institute. Membership: $20,000-$80,000/year (organization).

Contact Lens Manufacturers Association *(1961)*

5335 Wisconsin Ave
Suite 440
Washington, DC 20015
Tel: (402)465-4122 *Fax:* (402)465-4187
E-Mail: clmassociation@aol.com
Web Site: www.clma.net
Members: 110 companies
Staff: 2
Annual Budget: $500-1,000,000
Administrative Director: Pamela B. Witham
E-Mail: clmassociation@aol.com

Historical Note
CLMA members are contact lens laboratories, as well as material, solution and equipment manufacturers.

Meetings/Conferences:
Annual Meetings: Fall

Publications:
Contact Report Newsletter. 6/year.

Contact Lens Society of America *(1955)*

441 Carlisle Dr.
Herndon, VA 20170
Tel: (703)437-5100 *Fax:* (703)437-0727
Toll Free: (800)296 - 9776
E-Mail: clsa@clsa.info
Web Site: www.clsa.info
Members: 1200individualsandcompanies
Staff: 6
Annual Budget: $500-1,000,000
Executive Director: Tina M. Schott

Historical Note
Members are fitters, as well as manufacturers, of contact lenses. Membership: $130/year (individual); $600/year (company).

Meetings/Conferences:
Annual Meetings: Spring

Publications:
CLSA Eyewitness Magazine. q.

Containerization and Intermodal Institute *(1960)*

960 Holmdell Rd.
Suite Two
Holmdel, NJ 07733-2100
Tel: (732)817-9131 *Fax:* (732)817-9133
E-Mail: cii@bsya.com
Members: 300 companies
Annual Budget: under $10,000
Executive Director: Barbara Spector Yeninas
E-Mail: cii@bsya.com

Historical Note
Formerly (1960) Bulk Packaging and Containerization Institute, and (1967) The Containerization Institute. Membership includes transportation carriers; domestic and import-export lessors of containers and unit-load devices; terminal and port managers; and importers and exporters.

Meetings/Conferences:
Annual Meetings: September

Continental Basketball Association *(1946)*

195 Washington Ave.
Albany, NY 12210
Tel: (518)694-0100 *Fax:* (518)694-0101
E-Mail: info@cbahoopsonline.com
Web Site: www.cbahoopsonline.com
Members: 8 clubs
Staff: 6
Annual Budget: $1-2,000,000
Vice President, Basketball Operations: Eric Chapman
Director, Public/Media Relations: Kris Kamann

Historical Note
Established April 23, 1946 as the Eastern Basketball League, it later became the Eastern Basketball Association and assumed its present name on Jan. 1, 1978.

Meetings/Conferences:
Semi-annual Meetings: June and October

Publications:
CBA Media Guide. a.

Continental Dorset Club *(1898)*

P.O. Box 506
North Scituate, RI 02857-0506
Tel: (401)647-4676 *Fax:* (401)647-4679
E-Mail: cdcdorset@aol.com
Web Site: www.dorsets.homestead.com
Members: 1893 individuals
Staff: 1
Annual Budget: $50-100,000
Executive Secretary/Treasurer: Debra Hopkins
E-Mail: cdcdorset@aol.com

Historical Note
Breeders and fanciers of Dorset sheep. Member of the National Pedigree Livestock Council.

Publications:
Dorset Connection. a.

Contract Furnishings Forum

Historical Note
A forum of the Business Products Industry Association.

Contract Packaging Association *(1992)*

1601 N. Bond St.
Naperville, IL 60563
Tel: (630)544-5053 Ext: 108 *Fax:* (630)544-5055
E-Mail: info@contractpackaging.org
Web Site: www.contractpackaging.org
Members: 100 companies
Staff: 6
Annual Budget: $250-500,000
Executive Director: Stan Zelesnick

Historical Note
Founded as Contract Packagers Association; absorbed Contract Manufacturers Association and became Contract Manufacturing and Packaging Association in 1999 before assuming its current name in 2004. CPA helps its member companies lower their operating costs and improve their performance. Membership: $1,500/year (active membership).

Meetings/Conferences:
Semi-annual Meetings: April and October

Publications:
Newsletter. bi-m.

Contract Services Association of America *(1965)*

1000 Wilson Blvd., Suite 1800
Arlington, VA 22209
Tel: (703)243-2020 *Fax:* (703)243-3601
E-Mail: info@csa-dc.org
Web Site: www.csa-dc.org
Members: 235 companies
Staff: 9
Annual Budget: $1-2,000,000
President: Christopher L. Jahn
Vice President, Public Policy: Cathy Garman
Vice President, Business Management/Deputy Secretary: Kurt C. McMillan
Director, Professional Development: Malcolm Munro
Director, Legislative and Regulatory Affairs: Kent Sholars
Director, Membership: Cara Wedemeyer

Historical Note
CSA members are companies performing technical and support services for federal, state, and local governments. CSA supports commitment of Contracting-Out, and greater reliance on the private sector to perform services for the government. Sponsors and supports the CSA Political Action Committee. Membership: $300-16,000/year (company, based on gross revenue).

Publications:
Linkage Magazine. q.
Service Scope. m.

Contract Stationers Forum

Historical Note
A forum of the Business Products Industry Association.

Contractors Pump Bureau *(1938)*

6737 W. Washington St., Suite 2400
Milwaukee, WI 53214
Tel: (414)272-0943 *Fax:* (414)272-1170
Web Site: aem.org
Members: 15 companies
Staff: 1
Annual Budget: under $10,000
Director, Technical and Safety Services: Russell E. Hutchison
E-Mail: rhutchison@aem.org

Historical Note
Members are manufacturers of contractor type pumps and manufacturers of pump engines involved in the construction industry. A bureau of the Association of Equipment Manufacturers.

Control Systems Society *(1954)*

Historical Note
See IEEE Control Systems Society

Controlled Environment Testing Association

1500 Sunday Dr., Suite 102
Raleigh, NC 27607
Tel: (919)861-5576 *Fax:* (919)787-4916
E-Mail: info@cetainternational.org
Web Site: www.cetainternational.org
Members: 250 individuals
Executive Director: Peter Kralka

Historical Note
CETA promotes quality assurance within the controlled environment testing industry

Meetings/Conferences:
Annual Meetings: Spring
Publications:
Performance Review. q.

Controlled Release Society *(1973)*
3650 Annapolis Lane North, Suite 107
Minneapolis, MN 55447-5434
Tel: (763)512-0909 *Fax:* (763)765-2329
E-Mail: info@controlledrelease.org
Web Site: www.controlledrelease.org
Members: 2800 individuals
Staff: 4
Executive Director: Ronda Thompson
Historical Note
Members are firms and individuals concerned with basic and applied research on controlled release delivery systems. Maintains an office in Geneva, Switzerland and Tokyo, Japan. Membership: $80/year (individual); $300/year (company).
Meetings/Conferences:
Annual Meetings: Summer
2007 – Long Beach, CA/July 7-11
2008 – New York, NY/July 12-16
Publications:
Newsletter. 3/year.
Proceedings. a.
Journal of Controlled Release. q.

Controllers Council *(1985)*
Historical Note
An affiliate of the Institute of Management Accountants, which provides administrative supoort.

Convention Industry Council *(1949)*
8201 Greensboro Dr., Suite 300
McLean, VA 22102
Tel: (703)610-9030 *Fax:* (703)610-9005
Toll Free: (800)752 - 8982
E-Mail: cmp@cmponline.org
Web Site: www.conventionindustry.org
Members: 29 associations
Staff: 5
Annual Budget: $1-2,000,000
President and Chief Executive Officer: Mary Power, CAE
Historical Note
Formerly (1999) Convention Liaison Council. Members are associations directly involved in the convention, exposition, trade show, and meeting industry, and travel and tourism generally. Provides a focal point for the industry to exchange information, recommend solutions to industry problems, develop programs to serve the industry and to create a public awareness of the size of the industry. Sponsors Certified Meeting Professional (CMP) Program and Hall of Leaders Recognition. Membership: $1,600/year.
Publications:
CIC Manual.

Converting Equipment Manufacturers Association *(1984)*
2166 Gold Hill Road
Ft. Mill, SC 29708
Tel: (803)802-7820 *Fax:* (803)802-7821
E-Mail: cema@cema-converting.org
Web Site: www.cema-converting.org
Members: 75 companies
Staff: 3
Annual Budget: $50-100,000
Executive Director: Craig Sheppard
Historical Note
Membership open to any company or corporation engaged on a commercial scale in the manufacture of coaters, laminators, slitters/rewinders, printing presses, metalizers, sheeters, extruders, calenders, forming, bag or envelope machinery used to perform a complete web converting function. Membership: $1,150/year (full); $765/year (associate).
Meetings/Conferences:
Annual Meetings: May or June
Publications:
CEMA Scope. q.

Conveyor Equipment Manufacturers Association *(1933)*
6724 Lone Oak Blvd.
Naples, FL 34109-6834
Tel: (239)514-3441 *Fax:* (239)514-3470
Web Site: www.cemanet.org
Members: 88 companies
Staff: 4
Annual Budget: $250-500,000
Executive Vice President: Robert A. Reinfried
Historical Note
Founded as the Association of Conveyor and Material Preparation Equipment Manufacturers; became the Conveyor Association in 1935 and assumed its present name in 1945. A member of the Machinery and Allied Products Institute.
Meetings/Conferences:
Semi-Annual Meetings: March and September/150
2007 – Palm Desert, CA(Marriott)/March 9-13
2007 – Chicago, IL(Hilton)/Sept. 20-21/60
Publications:
Bulletin. 2/year.
Directory. a.

Cookie and Snack Bakers Association *(1962)*
1128 Maple Dr. NW
Cleveland, TN 37312
Tel: (423)472-5856
Web Site: www.casba.us
Members: 25 processors; 55 allied
Staff: 1
Annual Budget: $50-100,000,000
Executive Director: Craig Parrish
E-Mail: csparrish@worldnet.att.net
Historical Note
Members are bakery and snack food processors.
Meetings/Conferences:
Annual Meetings: Fall

Cookware Manufacturers Association *(1922)*
P.O. Box 531335
Mountain Brook, AL 35253
Tel: (205)823-3448 *Fax:* (205)823-3449
Web Site: www.cookware.org
Members: 25 companies
Staff: 1
Annual Budget: $100-250,000
Executive Vice President: Hugh J. Rushing
E-Mail: hrushing@cookware.org
Historical Note
Formerly (until 1963) the Aluminum Wares Association and (until 1981) the Metal Cookware Manufacturers Association.
Meetings/Conferences:
Annual Meetings: Spring/60
Publications:
Consumer Guide to Cookware. a.
Enginnering Standards Manual for Cookware/Bakeware. a.

Cooling Technology Institute *(1950)*
Box 73383
Houston, TX 77273
Tel: (281)583-4087 *Fax:* (281)537-1721
E-Mail: vmanser@cti.org
Web Site: www.cti.org
Members: 400 corporations
Staff: 3
Annual Budget: $500-1,000,000
Administrator: Virginia A. Manser
E-Mail: vmanser@cti.org
Historical Note
Promotes improvement in technology, design, performance and maintenance of cooling towers. Also concerned with water and air pollution and conservation of water as a natural resource. Membership: $495/year.
Meetings/Conferences:
Annual Meetings: Winter
Publications:
CTI Journal. semi-a. adv.
CTI News. q.

Cooperative Education and Internship Association *(1963)*
16 Santa Ana Place
Walnut Creek, CA 94598
Tel: (925)947-5581 *Fax:* (925)906-0922
Toll Free: (800)824 - 0449
E-Mail: info@ceiainc.org
Web Site: www.ceiainc.org
Members: 1200 individuals
Staff: 3
Annual Budget: $250-500,000
Association Executive: Deborah Dodds
E-Mail: info@ceiainc.org
Historical Note
Formerly (2003) Cooperative Education Association. Represents all aspects of cooperative education, the integration of classroom work and practical experience in an organized college program. CEA's primary goal is to promote opportunities for students to integrate periods of academic study with curriculum-related, paid, productive work experiences that maximize benefits to all students, employers and educators involved. Membership: $110/year (individual); $290/year (organization).
Meetings/Conferences:
Annual Meetings:
Publications:
CEA Membership Directory. a.
Journal of Cooperative Education. 3/year.
President's Newsbrief. q.
Experience Magazine. 2-3/year.

Cooperative Education Association
Historical Note
Became (2003) Cooperative Education and Internship Association.

Cooperative Work Experience Education Association *(1978)*
2910 E. Moore, Suite 122
Searcy, AR 72143
Tel: (501)278-2245 *Fax:* (501)278-2249
E-Mail: haroldv@ssmail.k12.ar.us
Members: 1300 individuals
Annual Budget: under $10,000
Treasurer: Harold A. Valentine
E-Mail: haroldv@ssmail.k12.ar.us
Historical Note
CWEEA members are coordinators of cooperative education and other education professionals with an interest in cooperative work experience programs. Has no paid officers or full-time staff.
Publications:
Newsletter. q. adv.
Membership Directory. a.

Coordinating Council for Women in History *(1969)*
211 Marginal Way, #733
P.O. Box 9715
Portland, ME 04104-5015
Tel: (207)780-5239
Web Site: www.theccwh.org
Members: 800 individuals
Annual Budget: $10-25,000
Executive Director: Jennifer Scanlon
Treasurer: Maureen Elgersman Lee
Historical Note
Formerly (1995) Coordinating Committee on Women in the Historical Profession/Conference Group on Women's History. CCWH is concerned with the advancement of women at all levels in the profession and with the study of women's history. Membership: $20-$75/year, based on salary (individual); $20/year (graduate student).
Meetings/Conferences:
Annual Meetings: in conjunction with AHA annual meeting/January
2007 – Atlanta, GA/Jan. 4-7
Publications:
CCWH Newsletter. q. adv.

Coordinating Research Council *(1942)*
3650 Mansell Road, Suite 140
Alpharetta, GA 30022
Tel: (678)795-0506 *Fax:* (678)795-0509
Web Site: www.crcao.org
Members: 800 individuals
Staff: 6
Annual Budget: Over $100,000,000
Executive Director: Brent K. Bailey
E-Mail: bkbailey@crcao.org
Deputy Director: Christopher J. Tennant

Historical Note
Coordinates research between the petroleum, automotive equipment, transportation industries, and government.
Meetings/Conferences:
Annual Meetings: None held.
Publications:
Annual Report. a.

Copier Dealers Association *(1977)*
6500 N.W. 21st Ave., Suite One
Ft. Lauderdale, FL 33309
Web Site: www.cdainfo.org
Members: 70 companies
Staff: 2
Annual Budget: $25-50,000
Membership Secretary: Britt Sikes
Historical Note
CDA members are independent companies in document imaging and copying. Has no paid officers or full-time staff.
Meetings/Conferences:
Three Meetings Annually: Spring, Summer, and Fall

Copper and Brass Fabricators Council *(1964)*
1050 17th St. NW, Suite 440
Washington, DC 20036-5561
Tel: (202)833-8575 *Fax:* (202)331-8267
E-Mail: copbrass@aol.com
Members: 20 companies
Staff: 4
Annual Budget: $500-1,000,000
President: Joseph L. Mayer
Government Affairs Counsel: John E. Arnett
E-Mail: arnettje@aol.com
Historical Note
Formerly (1966) Copper & Brass Fabricators Foreign Trade Association, Inc. The CBFC was organized to stem the flood of unlawful imports of brass mill products, minimize the compliance costs of federal regulations, and deal with brass mill industry problems. Membership: dues vary according to company size.
Meetings/Conferences:
Annual Meetings: February

Copper and Brass Servicenter Association *(1951)*
994 Old Eagle School Road, Suite 1019
Wayne, PA 19087-1802
Tel: (610)971-4850 Ext: 19 *Fax:* (610)971-4859
Web Site: www.cbsa.copper-brass.org
Members: 82 companies
Staff: 2
Annual Budget: $250-500,000
Executive Vice President: R. Franklin Brown, Jr.
E-Mail: fbrown@cbsa.copper-brass.org
Executive Assistant: Diana M. Lubragge
Historical Note
Formerly (1976) Copper and Brass Warehouse Association. CBSA is composed of wholesale distributors (Servicenters) of fabricated copper and brass mill products; the associate members are mills (fabricators who manufacture such products) and metal strip platers.
Meetings/Conferences:
Annual Meetings: Spring
2007 – Phoenix, AZ(Sheraton Wild Horse)/230
2008 – Aventura, FL(Turnberry Isle Fairmont)/Apr. 9-12/230
Publications:
Sources Handbook. 5/year.
Guide to Brass Mills & Strip Platers. 3/year.
Membership Directory. a.
Report - Statistical Survey. m.
CBSA Capsules Newsletter. m.
Guide for Marketing Copper, Brass, and Bronze. 5/year.

Copper Development Association *(1963)*
260 Madison Ave.
New York, NY 10016-2401
Tel: (212)251-7200 *Fax:* (212)251-7234
Toll Free: (800)232 - 3282
Web Site: www.copper.org
Members: 71 companies
Staff: 31
Annual Budget: $10-25,000,000
President and Chief Executive Officer: Andrew G. Kireta, Sr.
Vice President, Environmental Science and Government Relations: W. Ray Arnold
E-Mail: akiretasr@cda.copper.org
Vice President, Finance and Administration: Lorraine Herzing Mills
E-Mail: akiretasr@cda.copper.org
Historical Note
Supersedes the Copper and Brass Research Association as the market and technical development arm of the copper and brass industry. Membership is open to copper producers and brass mill, wire mill and foundry fabricators of copper and copper alloys with production facilities in the USA. Has an annual budget of approximately $10 million.
Meetings/Conferences:
Semi-Annual: Summer/Winter
Publications:
Copper Topics. semi-a.
Annual Data. a.

Copyright Society of the U.S.A. *(1953)*
352 Seventh Ave., Room 739
New York, NY 10036
Tel: (212)354-6401 *Fax:* (212)354-2847
Web Site: www.csusa.org
Members: 1000 individuals
Staff: 2
Annual Budget: $100-250,000
Administrator: Amy Nickerson
Historical Note
Established to foster interest in and advance the study of copyright law and of rights in literature, music, art, the theatre, motion pictures and other forms of intellectual property. Established the Walter J. Derenberg Copyright Library in 1976. Membership: $175/year (individual); $700-1,200/year (company).
Meetings/Conferences:
Semi-Annual Meetings: January-March and June
Publications:
Journal of the CSUSA. q.

Copywriter's Council of America *(1964)*
Historical Note
Address unknown in 2006.

Cordage Exporters Association
Historical Note
A Webb-Pomerene association, organized to promote commodity export, CEA is operated by the Cordage Institute.

Cordage Institute *(1920)*
994 Old Eagle School Road, Suite 1019
Wayne, PA 19087-1866
Tel: (610)971-4854 *Fax:* (610)971-4859
E-Mail: info@ropecord.com
Web Site: www.ropecord.com
Members: 83 companies
Staff: 3
Annual Budget: $250-500,000
Executive Director: Robert H. Ecker
Historical Note
Membership consists of manufacturers of natural and synthetic cordage (rope, twine and netting) and fiber and machinery suppliers. Merged with the American Cordage and Netting Manufacturers in 1990. Membership: annual dues vary based on class.
Meetings/Conferences:
Annual Meetings: Spring
Publications:
Ropecord News. bi-m. adv.
Rope Cord Directory. m.
Standards, Technical Information Manual.
Newsletter. bi-m.

CoreNet Global *(1961)*
260 Peachtree Street, NW, Suite 1500
Atlanta, GA 30303
Tel: (404)589-3200 *Fax:* (404)589-3201
Toll Free: (800)726 - 8111
Web Site: www.corenetglobal.org
Members: 7000 individuals
Staff: 51
Annual Budget: $5-10,000,000
Chief Executive Officer: Prentice Knight, Ph.D.
Chief Operating Officer/Chief Financial Officer: Peter Holland
Chief Membership Officer: Sherri Parman, CPA
Historical Note
Founded as Industrial Development Research Council; became International Development Research Council in 1994, before merging with NACORE International and assuming its current name in 2002. CoreNet Global members are executives of industrial corporations engaged in corporate real estate site selection and facility planning. Membership: $600/year (service providers); $495/year (corporate real estate executives).
Meetings/Conferences:
Semi-annual Meetings: Spring and Fall
Publications:
CRE Leader. q. adv.

Corn Refiners Association *(1913)*
1701 Pennsylvania Ave. NW
Suite 950
Washington, DC 20006-5805
Tel: (202)331-1634 *Fax:* (202)331-2054
E-Mail: info@corn.org
Web Site: www.corn.org/
Members: 9 companies
Staff: 7
Annual Budget: $1-2,000,000
President: Audrea Erickson
Senior Director, Regulatory Affairs: Tony Walker
E-Mail: info@corn.org
Historical Note
Formerly (1923) American Manufacturers' Association of Products from Corn; (1932) Associated Corn Products Manufacturers; (1966) Corn Industries Research Foundation. Represents the corn wet milling industry in the U.S. Members operate plants which produce corn syrup, corn starch, dextrose, corn oil and various animal feed ingredients.
Meetings/Conferences:
Biennial Meetings: June/600
Publications:
Corn Annual. a.

Corporate Facility Advisors
2000 N. 15th St., Suite 101
Arlington, VA 22201
Tel: (703)528-3500 *Fax:* (703)528-0113
E-Mail: tom@corfac.com
Web Site: www.corfac.com
Members: 805 individuals
Annual Budget: $100-250,000
Executive Director: Thomas P. Bennett
E-Mail: tom@corfac.com
Historical Note
CORFAC International member firms, located in 46 major North American cities, 35 European cities and Hong Kong, provide a full spectrum of coordinated commercial real estate services, including brokerage, counseling valuation, finance, project management and asset management. Membership: $3500/year (organization).
Meetings/Conferences:
Semi-annual Meetings: February and September/150-170

Corporate Housing Providers Association
7150 Winton Dr., Suite 300
Indianapolis, IN 46268
Tel: (317)328-4631 *Fax:* (317)280-8527
E-Mail: info@chpaonline.org
Web Site: www.chpaonline.org
Staff: 2
Executive Director: Mary Ann Passi, CAE
Historical Note
Founded as Association of Interim Housing Providers; assumed its current name in 2002.

Correctional Education Association *(1945)*
8182 Lark Brown Road, Suite 202
Elkridge, MD 21075
Tel: (443)459-3080 *Fax:* (443)459-3088
Toll Free: (800)783 - 1232
E-Mail: ceaoffice@aol.com
Web Site: www.ceanational.org

Members: 3000 individuals
Staff: 3
Annual Budget: $250-500,000
Executive Director: Stephen J. Steurer
Assistant Director: Heather Comstock

Historical Note
One of the largest affiliates of the American Correctional Association and one of two with a national headquarters and paid staff, CEA is a nonprofit professional association serving educators and administrators who provide services to students in correctional settings. Its members include adult and juvenile educational administrators, academic and vocational educators, correctional officers, counselors, clinicians, researchers and institution librarians. Membership: $50/year (individual); $85/year (library); $85/year (institution); $275/year (corporate); $1,000 (life).

Meetings/Conferences:
2007 – Atlanta, GA(Marriott Marquis)/July 8-11

Publications:
Directory. a. adv.
Journal of Correctional Education. q. adv.
CEA Newsletter. q. adv.
CEA Yearbook. a.

Correctional Vendors Association
3000 K St. NW, Suite 500
Washington, DC 20007-5101
Tel: (202)672-5579 *Fax:* (202)672-5399
Members: 50 individuals
President: Kate Leonard

Historical Note
CVA supports the goals of the State & Federal Correctional Industries Inmate Work Programs, their employees, inmates and vendors who supply products and services to them. Has no paid officers or full-time staff.

Meetings/Conferences:
Annual Meetings: No meetings held.

Corrugated Polyethylene Pipe Association

Historical Note
An affiliate of Plastics Pipe Institute, which provides administrative support.

Cosmetic Executive Women *(1954)*
21 E. 40th St., Suite 1700
New York, NY 10016
Tel: (212)685-5955 *Fax:* (212)685-3334
E-Mail: cew@cew.org
Web Site: www.cew.org
Members: 1300 individuals
Staff: 7
President: Carlotta Jackobson
E-Mail: cjacobson@cew.org
Chief Business Officer: Margie French
Director, Development: Lisa Klein
Director, Publishing: Kate Sweeney

Historical Note
Formerly (1981) Cosmetic Career Women; assumed its current name in 2003. Organized in 1954 and incorporated in New York in 1959. Membership is limited to women who have served at least 3 years in an executive capacity in business, and who are presently in the cosmetic industry. The CEW Foundation, established in 1993, develops and manages cancersandcareers, an online and offline resource for women undergoing cancer treatment.

Meetings/Conferences:
Annual Meetings: always New York, NY

Publications:
CEW News. q.

Cosmetic Industry Buyers and Suppliers *(1948)*
36 Lakeville Road
New Hyde Park, NY 11040
Tel: (516)775-0220 *Fax:* (516)328-9789
Web Site: www.cibsonline.com
Members: 800 individuals
Annual Budget: $25-50,000
Executive Director: Joseph A. Palazzolo

Historical Note
Members are individuals providing and obtaining essential oils, chemicals, packaging and other goods for the cosmetic industry. Membership concentrated in the New York City area. Has no paid staff. Officers change annually.

Cosmetic, Toiletry and Fragrance Association *(1894)*
1101 17th St. NW, Suite 300
Washington, DC 20036-4702
Tel: (202)331-1770 *Fax:* (202)331-1969
Web Site: www.ctfa.org
Members: 600 companies
Staff: 50
Annual Budget: $10-25,000,000
President and Chief Executive Officer: Pamela G. Bailey
Vice President and General Counsel: Thomas J. Donegan, Jr.
Vice President, Government Affairs: John Hurson
Vice President, Public Affairs: Irene L. Malbin
Vice President, Administration: Cheryl Schiappa
E-Mail: schiappac@ctfa.org
Vice President, Legislative Relations: Michael Thompson
Vice President, Meetings: Jean Tulipane, CMP

Historical Note
Founded as the Manufacturing Perfumers Association of the United States, it became the American Manufacturers of Toilet Articles in 1921, the Associated Manufacturers of Toilet Articles in 1932, the Toilet Goods Association in 1935 and assumed its present name in 1971. Sponsors the Cosmetic, Toiletry and Fragrance Association Political Action Committee. Founded the CTFA Foundation in 1986. Has an annual budget of approximately $10.5 million.

Meetings/Conferences:
Annual Meetings:

Publications:
Tech/Reg Notes. irreg.
CTFA Newsletter. bi-w.
Annual Report. a.
Who's Who Membership Directory. a. adv.
CIR Development. q.

Cost Management Group *(1991)*

Historical Note
A special interest group of Institute of Management Accountants, which provides administrative support.

Costume Society of America *(1973)*
P.O. Box 73
Earleville, MD 21919-0073
Tel: (410)275-1619 *Fax:* (410)275-8936
Toll Free: (800)272 - 9447
E-Mail: national.office@costumesocietyamerica.com
Web Site: www.costumesocietyamerica.com
Members: 1800 individuals
Staff: 3
Annual Budget: $100-250,000
President: Rosalyn Lester
E-Mail: national.office@costumesocietyamerica.com
Manager: Kaye Kittle Boyer, CAE
E-Mail: national.office@costumesocietyamerica.com

Historical Note
CSA works to advance the global understanding of all aspects of dress and appearance. CSA members are costume professionals and enthusiasts interested in the study, collection, preservation, presentation and interpretation of dress and appearance in societies of the past, present and future. Dues vary from individual to business categories. Visit website for more information.

Meetings/Conferences:
Annual Meetings: May-June

Publications:
CSA News. 3/year. adv.
Dress Journal. a.
CSA Membership Directory. a. adv.
Symposium Abstract. a.

Cottage Industry Miniaturists Trade Association *(1980)*
4244 Spring Creek Ln.
Bellingham, WA 98226
Tel: (866)326-9386 *Fax:* (360)733-5169
E-Mail: 2006@cimta.org
Web Site: www.cimta.org
Members: 600 individuals
Annual Budget: $50-100,000

Historical Note
Members are handcrafters of dollhouse miniatures. Sponsors trade shows and seminars for members. Membership: $100/year.

Publications:
CIMTA Newsletter, Inc. q.

Cotton Council International *(1956)*
1521 New Hampshire Ave. NW
Washington, DC 20036-1205
Tel: (202)745-7805 *Fax:* (202)483-4040
E-Mail: cottonusa@cotton.org
Web Site: www.cottonusa.org
Members: 21 companies
Staff: 20
Annual Budget: $10-25,000,000
Executive Director: Allen Terhaar
E-Mail: aterhaar@cotton.org
Fiscal Director: Delorise A. Winter
E-Mail: dwinter@cotton.org

Historical Note
The overseas operations arm of the National Cotton Council of America. CCI's primary goal is to increase exports of American-grown cotton.

Publications:
CCI FAX. w.

Cotton Warehouse Association of America *(1969)*
1156 15th St. NW
Suite 315
Washington, DC 20005-1714
Tel: (202)331-2121 *Fax:* (202)331-2112
E-Mail: cwaa@cottonwarehouse.org
Web Site: www.cottonwarehouse.org
Members: 125 companies
Staff: 3
Annual Budget: $100-250,000
Executive Vice President: Donald L. Wallace, Jr.
E-Mail: cwaa@cottonwarehouse.org

Historical Note
Formed in 1969 by a merger of the American and the National Cotton Compress and Cotton Warehouse Associations. Supports the Cotton Warehouse Government Relations Committee.

Meetings/Conferences:
Annual Meetings: June

Publications:
Cotton Comments. m.

Council for Adult and Experiential Learning *(1974)*
55 E. Monroe St., #1930
Chicago, IL 60603-5720
Tel: (312)499-2600 *Fax:* (312)499-2601
E-Mail: cael@cael.org
Web Site: www.cael.org
Members: 2300institutionsandindividuals
Staff: 130
Annual Budget: $10-25,000,000
President: Pamela Tate
Director, Public Policy: Amy Sherman

Historical Note
Established in 1974 as Council for the Advancement of Experiential Learning (CAEL), it assumed its present name in 1985 to reflect changing program priorities. A non-profit, higher education association whose basic mission is the advancement of experiential learning and the improvement of services to adult learners. Membership: $75/year (individual); $275-475/year (institution); $275/year (organization).

Meetings/Conferences:
Annual Meetings: November

Publications:
CAEL Forum & News. q. adv.

Council for Advancement and Support of Education *(1974)*
1307 New York Ave. NW, Suite 1000
Washington, DC 20005-4701
Tel: (202)328-2273 *Fax:* (202)387-4973
E-Mail: info@case.org
Web Site: www.case.org
Members: 3236
Staff: 90
Annual Budget: $10-25,000,000

Vice President, Business and Finance: Donald Falkenstein
Vice President, Communications and Marketing: Rae Goldsmith
Vice President, Member and Volunteer Relations: Donna Hasslinger
President: John Lippincott
Vice President, International Operations: Joanna Motion
Vice President, Research and Information Services: Chris Thompson
Vice President, Professional Development: Norma Walker

Historical Note
Product of a merger (1974) of American College Public Relations Association and American Alumni Council. Formerly (1975) AAC/ACPRA. Of CASE's individual and organizational members, roughly 21,000 and 2,700 respectively are in the United States. Has an annual budget of approximately $16 million.

Meetings/Conferences:
Annual Meetings: Summer
2007 – Chicago, IL(Chicago Marriott Downtown)/July 8-10

Publications:
CASE CURRENTS. 9/year. adv.

Council for Affordable and Rural Housing *(1980)*
1112 King St.
Alexandria, VA 22314-3022
Tel: (703)837-9001 *Fax:* (703)837-8467
E-Mail: carh@carh.org
Web Site: www.carh.org
Members: 231 individuals
Staff: 4
Executive Director: Colleen M. Fisher

Historical Note
CARH represents managers and developers of subsidized or federally-assisted housing.

Publications:
Newsletter. bi-m.

Council for Agricultural Science and Technology *(1972)*
4420 W. Lincoln Way
Ames, IA 50014-3447
Tel: (515)292-2125 *Fax:* (515)292-4512
Web Site: www.cast-science.org
Members: 1200 individuals
Staff: 7
Annual Budget: $500-1,000,000
Executive Vice President: John Bonner
E-Mail: jbonner@cast-science.org
Director, Development: Amanda Wall
E-Mail: amwall@cast-science.org

Historical Note
Chartered in the State of Iowa as a non-profit corporation to provide accurate information to the government, the news media and the public about national or regional agricultural subjects of broad concern. Membership: $25-2500/year (individual); dues vary (organization/company).

Publications:
Issue Papers. irreg.
Special Publications. irreg.
NewsCAST. q.
Task Force Reports. irreg.

Council for American Private Education *(1971)*
13017 Wisteria Dr.
PMB 457
Germantown, MD 20874-2112
Tel: (301)916-8460 *Fax:* (301)916-8485
E-Mail: cape@capenet.org
Web Site: www.capenet.org
Members: 18 organizations
Staff: 2
Annual Budget: $100-250,000
Executive Director: Joseph W. McTighe
E-Mail: cape@capenet.org

Historical Note
Represents national organizations for private elementary and secondary schools. Actively voices private school positions on public policy issues affecting private education.

Meetings/Conferences:
Semi-annual Meetings: Washington, DC/March and October

Publications:
Outlook. m.

Council for Art Education *(1983)*
P.O. Box 479
Hanson, MA 02341-0479
Tel: (781)293-4100 *Fax:* (781)294-0808
E-Mail: debbief@acminet.org
Web Site: www.acminet.org/cfae.htm
Members: 4 organizations
Staff: 2
Annual Budget: $25-50,000
Executive Vice President/Clerk: Deborah M. Fanning, CAE

Historical Note
CFAE promotes art education and school art programs, primarily through the National Youth Art Month program.

Meetings/Conferences:
Annual Meetings: Summer

Publications:
YAM News. q.

Council for Chemical Research *(1979)*
1730 Rhode Island Ave. NW, Suite 302
Washington, DC 20036
Tel: (202)429-3971 *Fax:* (202)429-3976
Web Site: www.ccrhq.org
Members: 200 organizations
Staff: 3
Annual Budget: $500-1,000,000
Executive Director: Donald B. Anthony, Sc.D.

Historical Note
CCR members are university, government, and private industry laboratories engaged in research.

Meetings/Conferences:
Annual Meetings: Annual

Publications:
CCR News. m.

Council for Children with Behavioral Disorders

Historical Note
CCBD is a division of the Council for Exceptional Children.

Council for Christian Colleges and Universities *(1976)*
321 Eighth St. NE
Washington, DC 20002
Tel: (202)546-8713 *Fax:* (202)546-8913
E-Mail: council@cccu.org
Web Site: www.cccu.org
Members: 169 institutions
Staff: 59
Annual Budget: $5-10,000,000
President: Dr. Paul R. Corts
Executive Vice President: Dr. Richard L. Gathro
Vice President, Professional Development and Research: Dr. Ronald P. Mahurin
Director, Communications: Nate Mouttet
Vice President, Finance/Administration: Kyle H. Royer

Historical Note
Incorporated in the District of Columbia as Christian College Coalition in 1982; became the Coalition for Chrisitan Colleges and Universities in 1995 and assumed its current title in 1999. CCCU members are accredited four-year colleges and universities that apply a Christ-centered philosophy to higher education. Membership fee varies, $1,800-8,600/year, based on full-time enrollment.

Meetings/Conferences:
Annual Meetings: Winter

Publications:
The News. m.
Resource Guide to Christian Higher Education. a.

Council for Educational Diagnostic Services

Historical Note
CEDS is a division of the Council for Exceptional Children.

Council for Electronic Revenue Communication Advancement
600 Cameron St., Suite 309
Alexandria, VA 22314
Tel: (703)340-1655 *Fax:* (703)340-1658
E-Mail: cerca@cerca.org
Web Site: www.cerca.org
Members: 75 companies
Staff: 4
Annual Budget: $250-500,000
Executive Director: Michael Cavanagh
E-Mail: cerca@cerca.org

Historical Note
CERCA members are companies with an interest in advancing electronic commerce with government revenue agencies. Membership: $25-$75/year (individual); $600-$4,800/year, based on sales (corporate); $2,400/year (government agency).

Publications:
CERCA News. q.

Council for Elementary Science International *(1920)*
College of Education Mail Stop 282
University of Nevada, Reno
Reno, NV 89557
Tel: (775)784-4961 Ext: 2004 *Fax:* (775)327-5345
Web Site: www.cesiscience.org/
Members: 1000 individuals
Annual Budget: $10-25,000
President and Editor, CESI Science: David T. Crowther
E-Mail: crowther@unr.edu

Historical Note
CESI members are teachers, administrators and others with an interest in the teaching of science at the preschool, elementary and middle school levels. Annual meetings are held in conjunction with the NSTA. Membership: $20/year.

Meetings/Conferences:
Annual Meetings: in conjunction with the Nat'l Science Teachers Ass'n

Publications:
CESI SCience. q. adv.

Council for Ethics in Economics *(1982)*
191 W. Nationwide Blvd., Suite 300B
Columbus, OH 43215-3605
Tel: (614)221-8661 *Fax:* (614)221-8707
E-Mail: cee@businessethics.org
Web Site: www.businessethics.org
Members: 140 individuals
Staff: 3
Annual Budget: $250-500,000
President: Michael Distelhorst
E-Mail: cee@businessethics.org

Historical Note
The Council is an association of leaders in business, education and other professions, working together to strengthen the ethical fabric of business and economic life. Membership: $100 (individual); moving scale prices for organizations.

Publications:
Ethics in Economics. q. adv.

Council for European Studies *(1970)*
Columbia University
420 W. 118th St., MC 3310
New York, NY 10027
Tel: (212)854-4172 *Fax:* (212)854-8808
E-Mail: ces@columbia.edu
Web Site: www.councilforeuropeanstudies.org
Members: 1000 individuals
Staff: 10
Annual Budget: $250-500,000

Historical Note
Founded in 1970, the Council for European Studies (CES) is the leading academic organization for the study of Europe. The Council produces and recognizes outstanding multidisciplinary research in European studies through a range of programs, including conferences, publications, special events, and awards.

Meetings/Conferences:
Biennial Meetings: (even years)
2008 – Chicago, IL(Drake Hotel)

Publications:
European Studies Forum. bi-a. adv.

Council for Exceptional Children *(1922)*
1110 N. Glebe Road, Suite 300
Arlington, VA 22201
Toll Free: (800)224 - 6830

E-Mail: cec@cec.sped.org
Web Site: www.cec.sped.org
Members: 44000 individuals
Staff: 45
Annual Budget: $5-10,000,000
Executive Director: Bruce Ramirez
E-Mail: cec@cec.sped.org
Associate Executive Director, Public Policy: Deborah Ziegler
E-Mail: cec@cec.sped.org

Historical Note

Formerly (1958) International Council for Exceptional Children. CEC is a professional organization whose members include teachers, administrators, teacher educators, students, support services, professionals and parents. Its goals include the promotion of professional standards of practice for persons involved in the education of exceptional persons; the extension of special education services to exceptional children not presently being served; and the support of the development and advancement of new knowledge, technology, methodology, curriculum and materials. Special divisions within CEC (which publish their own periodicals, see below) include: Council for Children with Behavioral Disorders; Career Development; Council for Educational Diagnostic Services; Mental Retardation; Children with Communication Disorders; Early Childhood; Administrators of Special Education; Association for the Gifted; Technology and Media; Research; and Council of Administrators of Special Education. Hosts symposia and other professional development events. Sponsors and supports the CEC Children's Action Network (CEC-CAN).

Meetings/Conferences:

Annual Meetings: Spring
2007 – Louisville, KY/Apr. 18-21
2008 – Boston, MA/Apr. 2-5

Publications:

Assessment for Effective Intervention. q.
Communication Disorders. q.
Early Intervention. q.
Exceptional Children. q. adv.
Teaching Exceptional Children. bi-m. adv.
Behavioral Disorders. q.
Career Development for Exceptional Individuals. 2/yr.
Education and Training in Developmental Disabilities. q.
Learning Disabilities Research and Practice. q.
Teacher Education and Special Education. q.
Journal for the Education of the Gifted. q.
Journal of Special Education Technology. q.

Council for Higher Education Accreditation *(1996)*

One Dupont Circle NW
Suite 510
Washington, DC 20036-1135
Tel: (202)955-6126 *Fax:* (202)955-6129
E-Mail: chea@chea.org
Web Site: www.chea.org
Members: 3000 degree granting colleges and universities
Staff: 8
Annual Budget: $1-2,000,000
President: Judith Eaton
E-Mail: chea@chea.org

Historical Note

CHEA is an organization of colleges and universities serving as the national advocate for voluntary self-regulation through accreditation. It is supported by member institutions.

Meetings/Conferences:

2007 – Washington, DC(Omni Shoreham)/Jan. 29-31

Publications:

CHEA Almanac of External Quality Review. bi-a..

Council for International Tax Education *(1982)*

P.O. Box 1012
White Plains, NY 10602
Tel: (914)328-5656 *Fax:* (914)328-5757
E-Mail: info@citeusa.org
Web Site: www.citeusa.org
Members: 400 individuals
Staff: 4
Annual Budget: $1-2,000,000
Executive Director: William H. Green

Historical Note

Founded as FSC/DISC Tax Association; assumed its current name in 2002. Members are companies and individuals engaged in international business on the tax, legal and accounting aspects of doing business overseas. Membership: $295/year (individual); $595/year (company).

Publications:

International Tax Newsletter. q.

Council for Jewish Education *(1926)*

11 Olympia Lane
Monsey, NY 10952-2829
Tel: (914)368-8657
Members: 350 individuals
Annual Budget: $25-50,000
Contact: Morton Summer

Historical Note

Formerly (until 1981) the National Council for Jewish Education. Members are college and university teachers of Hebrew and faculty of Jewish teacher training schools. Has no paid officers or full-time staff.

Meetings/Conferences:

Annual Meetings: Joint meetings with CJCS.

Publications:

Journal of Jewish Education. 3/year.

Council for Learning Disabilities *(1968)*

11184 Antioch Rd.
Box 405
Overland Park, KS 66210
Tel: (913)491-1011 *Fax:* (913)491-1012
Web Site: www.cldinternational.org
Members: 2000 individuals
Annual Budget: $100-250,000
Executive Director: Andrea Falzarano, CAE

Historical Note

CLD members are educators, diagnosticians, psychologists, physicians, optometrists, and speech, occupational and physical therapists working with individuals having specific disorders involving reading, writing, speaking, listening, thinking and mathematics. A member of the National Joint Committee on Learning Disabilities, CLD promotes and encourages high standards for serving the learning disabled and for conducting research including taking positions on legislation and professional practices. Membership: $45/year (individual)

Publications:

Learning Disability Quarterly. q. adv.

Council for Marketing and Opinion Research *(1992)*

110 National Dr., Second Floor
Glastonbury, CT 06033
Tel: (860)657-1881 *Fax:* (860)682-1010
E-Mail: info@cmor.org
Web Site: www.cmor.org
Members: 160 individuals
Staff: 4
Annual Budget: $500-1,000,000
Director, Operations: Donna Gillin
E-Mail: info@cmor.org

Historical Note

CMOR was established by four major survey research industry associations to address the critical issues of restricting prohibitive legislation and respondent cooperation.

Council for Museum Anthropology *(1975)*

Historical Note

CMA is a section of American Anthropological Ass'n, which provides administrative support.

Council for Near-Infrared Spectroscopy *(1986)*

9036 Green Valley Ct.
Douglasville, GA 30134
Tel: (770)947-1344
E-Mail: campclan@prodigy.net
Web Site: www.irdc-chambersburg.org
Members: 256 individuals
President: B. H. Campbell
E-Mail: campclan@prodigy.net

Historical Note

Affiliated with the Society for Applied Spectroscopy, purpose of CNIRS is to advance the art and science of near infrared spectroscopy.

Meetings/Conferences:

Annual Meetings: Semi-annual in even-numbered years

Publications:

NIR Spectrum. q.

Council for Opportunity in Education *(1981)*

1025 Vermont Ave. NW, Suite 900
Washington, DC 20005-3516
Tel: (202)347-7430 *Fax:* (202)347-0786
Web Site: www.trioprograms.org
Members: 930institutions, 10regionalorgs.
Staff: 25
Annual Budget: $2-5,000,000
President: Arnold L. Mitchem, Ph.D.
Vice President, Communications: Susan Trebach
Vice President, Government Relations: Heather Valentine

Historical Note

Founded as National Council of Equal Opportunity Associations; assumed its current name in 2000. COE members are regional organizations, institutions of higher education and agencies concerned with equality of educational opportunity and access. Membership: $1,000/year (organization).

Meetings/Conferences:

Annual Meetings: September

Publications:

Journal. semi-a.
Nat'l Trio Directory of Funded Programs. bien.
Equality Newsletter. bi-m. adv.

Council for Professional Recognition *(1985)*

2460 16th St. NW
Washington, DC 20009-3575
Tel: (202)265-9090 *Fax:* (202)265-9161
Toll Free: (800)424 - 4310
E-Mail: cda@cdacouncil.org
Web Site: www.cdacouncil.org
Members: 100000 individuals
Staff: 35
Annual Budget: $2-5,000,000
Chief Executive Officer: Carol Brunson Day, Ph.D.

Historical Note

Formerly (1987) Child Development Associate National Credentialing Program and (2000) Council for Early Childhood Professional Recognition. Concerned with improving the standards of child care through establishing standards and credentialing staff of child care facilities.

Meetings/Conferences:

Annual Meetings: None held.

Publications:

Nat'l Directory of Early Childhood Teacher Preparation Institutions.
Council News & Views. 3/year.
Council Newsletter.

Council for Resource Development *(1972)*

One Dupont Circle NW
Suite 365
Washington, DC 20036-1176
Tel: (202)822-0750 *Fax:* (202)822-5014
E-Mail: crd@crdnet.org
Web Site: www.crdnet.org
Members: 1500 individuals
Staff: 2
Annual Budget: $250-500,000
Executive Director: Polly Binns
E-Mail: crd@crdnet.org

Historical Note

An affiliate of the American Association of Community Colleges. CRD members are presidents and development administrators of two-year colleges. Membership: $175/year.

Meetings/Conferences:

Annual Meetings: always Washington, DC in November or December/550-700

Publications:

Resource Papers.
Dispatch Express (fax broadcast newsletter).
Dispatch Newsletter. q. adv.
Membership Directory. a.
Federal Funding to Two-Year Colleges. a.

Council for Responsible Nutrition *(1973)*
1828 L St. NW, Suite 900
Washington, DC 20036-5104
Tel: (202)776-7929 *Fax:* (202)204-7980
Web Site: www.crnusa.org
Members: 73 companies
Staff: 10
Annual Budget: $2-5,000,000
President and Chief Executive Officer: Steven M. Mister, CAE
Vice President, Communications: Judy Blatman
Historical Note
Members are manufacturers and distributors of dietary supplements, ingredients, and other nutritional products. Membership: based on annual supplement sales.
Meetings/Conferences:
Annual Meetings: Fall

Council for Spiritual and Ethical Education *(1898)*
220 College Ave., Suite 312
Athens, GA 30601
Tel: (678)354-4043 *Fax:* (678)623-5634
Toll Free: (800)298 - 4599
E-Mail: info@csee.org
Web Site: www.csee.org
Members: 300 schools
Staff: 3
Annual Budget: $500-1,000,000
Executive Director: David Streight
Associate Director: Matthew Hicks
Historical Note
CSEE provides independent school leaders, chaplains, community service coordinators, and teachers with publications, programs and information to encourage the moral, ethical, and spiritual development of young people. Membership: $250-1,850/year.
Meetings/Conferences:
Annual Meetings: Spring
Publications:
Connections Newsletter. 9/year.

Council for the Advancement of Standards in Higher Education *(1979)*
One Dupont Circle NW
Suite 300
Washington, DC 20036-1188
Tel: (202)862-1400 *Fax:* (202)296-3286
Web Site: www.cas.edu
Members: 36 organizations
Staff: 1
Executive Director: Phyllis Mable
Historical Note
CAS members are professional organizations whose members are involved in providing higher education services.
Meetings/Conferences:
Semi-Annual Meetings: April and November
Publications:
Self Assessment Guides (on compact disk). bien. adv.
CAS Book of Professional Standards in Higher Education (6th edition). bien. adv.
Book of Frameworks for Assessing Learning and Development Outcomes.

Council for Urban Economic Development *(1967)*
Historical Note
See International Economic Development Council (IEDC).

Council of 1890 College Presidents and Chancellors *(1913)*
Historical Note
Address unknown in 2004.

Council of Administrators of Special Education *(1952)*
1005 State University Dr.
Ft. Valley, GA 31030-4313
Tel: (478)825-7667 *Fax:* (478)825-7811
Web Site: www.casecec.org
Members: 5300 individuals
Staff: 2
Annual Budget: $250-500,000
Executive Director: Luann Purcell
E-Mail: lpurcell@bellsouth.net
Historical Note
A division of the Council for Exceptional Children. Dues are $60/year plus membership in CEC.
Publications:
Journal of Special Education Leadership. 2/year. adv.
In Case Newsletter. 6/year. adv.

Council of Advisers to Foreign Students and Scholars
Historical Note
A section of NAFSA: Association of International Educators.

Council of American Instructors of the Deaf *(1850)*
P.O. Box 377
Bedford, TX 76095-0377
Tel: (817)354-8414
E-Mail: caid@swbell.net
Web Site: www.caid.org
Members: 1250 individuals
Staff: 1
Annual Budget: $50-100,000
Office Manager: Helen Lovato
E-Mail: caid@swbell.net
Historical Note
Incorporated in 1897 by act of Congress. Members are teachers, administrators, educational interpreters, residential personnel and other concerned professionals involved in the education of the deaf. CAID is a member of the Council on Education of the Deaf and the Deaf and Hard of Hearing Alliance. Membership: $55/year (individual).
Meetings/Conferences:
Biennial Meetings: Uneven years/June
Publications:
American Annals of the Deaf. q. adv.
American Annals of the Deaf (Reference issue). a. adv.
News'n Notes Newsletter. q. adv.
Conference Proceedings. bien. adv.

Council of American Jewish Museums *(1978)*
2000 E. Asbury Ave., Suite 157
Denver, CO 80208
Tel: (303)871-3015 *Fax:* (303)871-3037
E-Mail: cajm@jewishculture.org
Web Site: www.jewishculture.org/cajm
Members: 75 institutions
Staff: 1
Annual Budget: $100-250,000
Executive Director: Joanne Kauvar
E-Mail: cajm@jewishculture.org
Historical Note
CAJM represents a broad spectrum of Jewish community museums and galleries which recognize professional standards of operation and programming. CAJM works to strengthen the Jewish museum field in North America through training of museum staff and volunteers, information exchang and advocacy. Membership: $250-1000/year (institution).
Meetings/Conferences:
Semi-annual Meetings: January and June
2007 – Toronto, ON, Canada/Jan. 21-24
Publications:
CAJM Newsletter. semi-a.

Council of American Maritime Museums *(1974)*
c/o Columbia River Maritime Museum
1792 Marine Dr.
Astoria, OR 97103
E-Mail: president@councilofamericanmaritimemuseums.org
Web Site: www.americanmaritimemuseums.org
Members: 75 museums
Annual Budget: under $10,000
President: Jerry Ostermiller
Historical Note
Affiliated with the International Congress of Maritime Museums and the American Association of Museums. Has no paid officers or full-time staff. Membership: $75/year.
Publications:
Gamming Newsletter. semi-a.

Council of American Master Mariners *(1936)*
2700 Broening Hwy., Suite 115
Dunbar Bldg.
Baltimore, MD 21222-4190
Tel: (410)285-7800 *Fax:* (410)285-7803
E-Mail: counciAMM@aol.com
Web Site: www.mastermariner.org
Members: 1300 individuals
Staff: 2
Annual Budget: $25-50,000
President: Tom Bradley
Secretary and Treasurer: Captain David R. Smith
Historical Note
CAMM is a professional non-profit organization of shipmasters who now command or have commanded American Flag ocean-going vessels. The stated objective of the Council is to render a public service by voicing, as the need arises, the opinion of Master Mariners concerning professional subjects of common interest to them and of concern to the Maritime Industry. Membership: $60/year.
Meetings/Conferences:
Annual Meetings: Spring
Publications:
Sidelights. q.

Council of American Overseas Research Centers *(1980)*
NHB Room CE-123, MRC 178
P.O. Box 37012
Washington, DC 20013-7012
Tel: (202)633-1599 *Fax:* (202)786-2430
E-Mail: caorc@caorg.org
Web Site: www.caorc.org
Members: 19 centers
Staff: 6
Annual Budget: $500-1,000,000
Executive Director: Mary Ellen Lane
Historical Note
Established to "advance higher learning and scholarly research by providing a forum for communication and cooperation among American overseas advanced research centers."

Council of American Survey Research Organizations *(1975)*
170 N. Country Road, Suite Four
Port Jefferson, NY 11777
Tel: (631)928-6954 *Fax:* (631)928-6041
E-Mail: casro@casro.org
Web Site: www.casro.org
Members: 250 companies
Staff: 5
Annual Budget: $1-2,000,000
President: Diane K. Bowers
Historical Note
CASRO is the national trade association for full-service, for profit survey research companies and their affiliated services. Membership: $865-19,000/year.
Meetings/Conferences:
Annual Meetings: Fall
Publications:
CASRO Comments. bi-m.

Council of Archives and Research Libraries in Jewish Studies *(1974)*
330 Seventh Ave., 21st Floor
New York, NY 10001
Tel: (212)629-0500 Ext: 215 *Fax:* (212)629-0508
E-Mail: nfjc@jewishculture.org
Web Site: www.jewishculture.org
Members: 34 institutions
Staff: 1
Annual Budget: under $10,000
Executive Director: Richard A. Siegel
Historical Note
Founded by the National Foundation for Jewish Culture in conjunction with the National Endowment for the Humanities, CARLJS members include the Jewish divisions of major North American municipal, university and Jewish community libraries and archives. CARLJS fosters cooperative efforts to enhance preservation of and access to collections. Membership: $100/year (full).

Meetings/Conferences:
Annual Meetings: June

Council of Better Business Bureaus *(1971)*
4200 Wilson Blvd., Suite 800
Arlington, VA 22203-1838
Tel: (703)247-9347 *Fax:* (703)525-8277
E-Mail: cbbb@bbb.org
Web Site: www.bbb.org
Members: 300 Companies; 150 Bureaus
Staff: 125
Annual Budget: $10-25,000,000
Chief Executive Officer: Steven J. Cole

Historical Note
CBB was formed by a merger (1971) of the Association of Better Business Bureaus (founded in 1921) and the National Better Business Bureau (founded in 1912). CBB membership consists of national companies and local Better Business Bureaus. Promotes sound business-consumer relations and a self-regulating environment for ethical business practice.

Meetings/Conferences:
Annual Meetings: Fall

Publications:
BBB Wise Giving Guide. q..
National Advertising Division Case Reports. m.
Council of Better Business Bureaus Annual Report. a.
Give But Give Wisely. bi-m.

Council of Chief State School Officers *(1927)*
One Massachusetts Ave. NW, Suite 700
Washington, DC 20001-1431
Tel: (202)336-7000 *Fax:* (202)408-8072
Web Site: www.ccsso.org
Members: 56 individuals
Staff: 70
Annual Budget: $10-25,000,000
Executive Director: Gene Wilhout
Director, Communications: Kara Schlosser
Director, Meeting Services: Marie Terova

Historical Note
CCSSO members head departments of elementary and secondary education in the states, the District of Columbia, the Department of Defense Education Activity, and five U.S. extra-state jurisdictions. CCSSO provides leadership, advocacy, and technical assistance on major educational issues. The Council seeks member consensus on major educational issues and expresses their views to civic and professional organizations, federal agencies, Congress, and the public.

Meetings/Conferences:
Annual Meetings: November

Publications:
The Council Brochure. a.
Council Quarterly. q.
Chief Line. w.
Hill Notes. w.
State Education Agency Directory. a.

Council of Colleges of Acupuncture and Oriental Medicine *(1982)*
3909 National Dr., Suite 125
Burtonsville, MD 20866
Tel: (301)476-7791 *Fax:* (301)476-7792
E-Mail: executivedirector@ccaom.org
Web Site: www.ccaom.org
Members: 50 schools
Staff: 2
Annual Budget: $250-500,000
Executive Director: David M. Sale
E-Mail: executivedirector@ccaom.org
CNT Program Manager/Finance Administrator: Paula Diamond

Historical Note
CCAOM is a membership organization for accredited and candidate acupuncture and Oriental medicine colleges. Incorporated in the District of Columbia in 1982. Mission is to advance acupuncture and Oriental medicine by promoting educational excellence within the field. Membership: $1,100/year (accredited schools); $550/year (candidate schools).

Meetings/Conferences:
Semi-Annual Meetings: May and October

Publications:
CCAOM News. a.

Council of Colleges of Arts and Sciences *(1965)*
P.O. Box 8795
Williamsburg, VA 23187-8795
Tel: (757)221-1784 *Fax:* (757)221-2184
E-Mail: info@ccas.net
Web Site: www.ccas.net
Members: 1600 individuals
Staff: 2
Annual Budget: $250-500,000
Executive Director: Ernie Peck

Historical Note
Organized in 1965 by the arts and sciences deans from the National Association of State Universities and Land-Grant Colleges (NASULGC). Until 1988, CCAS members were deans of arts and sciences at state-supported colleges and universities. Membership eligibility was changed in 1988 to include arts and science deans at all accredited, bachelor degree granting-institutions. Membership: $150-450/year (based on the number of BA/BS degrees awarded).

Meetings/Conferences:
Annual Meetings: November/500-600

Publications:
CCAS Member Directory. a.
CCAS Annual Meeting Program. a.
CCAS Newsletter. bi-m. adv.

Council of Communication Management *(1955)*
65 Enterprise
Aliso Viejo, CA 92656
Toll Free: (866)463 - 6226
E-Mail: membership@ccmconnection.com
Web Site: www.ccmconnection.com
Members: 270 individuals
Staff: 2
Annual Budget: $100-250,000
Contact: Fred Droz

Historical Note
Formerly (1955) the Industrial Communication Council. CCM provides a network through which managers, consultants and educators, who work at the policy level in organizational communication can help one another advance the practice of communication in business. Membership: $300/year.

Meetings/Conferences:
Annual Meetings: Spring

Publications:
CCM Communicator. m.

Council of Consulting Organizations *(1989)*

Historical Note
Formed as an umbrella organization with two divisions: ACME, the Association of Management Consulting Firms and the Institute of Management Consultants (listed separately). An affiliate organization is the Foundation for Excellence in Consulting and Management. ACME-The Association of Management Consulting Firms became a division of CCO in 1989.

Council of Dance Administrators *(1967)*
1315 Floyd Ave., P.O. Box 843007
Richmond, VA 23284-3007
Tel: (215)204-4347 *Fax:* (215)204-4347
Members: 25 individuals
President: Martha Curtis, Ed.D
E-Mail: lkahlich@temple.edu

Historical Note
Members are administrators of dance departments in educational institutions.

Meetings/Conferences:
Annual Meetings: November

Council of Defense and Space Industry Associations *(1964)*
1000 Wilson Blvd., Suite 1800
Arlington, VA 22201
Tel: (703)243-2020 *Fax:* (703)243-8539
E-Mail: codsia@ndia.org
Web Site: www.codsia.org
Members: 7 associations
Staff: 1
Annual Budget: $50-100,000
Administrative Officer: Timothy M. Nunnally-Olsen
E-Mail: codsia@ndia.org

Historical Note
Established June 30, 1964, by industry associations having common interests in the defense and space fields, CODSIA functions as a voluntary, coordinating, non-profit, consultative body. It addresses policies, regulations, directives and procedures relating to the supplier-purchaser relationship between government and industry. Members are Aerospace Industries Association, American Electronics Association, American Shipbuilding Association, Contract Services Association, Electronic Industries Alliance, Manufacturers' Alliance for Productivity and Innovation, Professional Services Council, and National Defense Industrial Association.

Meetings/Conferences:
Triannual Meetings:

Council of Development Finance Agencies *(1982)*
815 Superior Ave., Suite 1301
Cleveland, OH 44114
Tel: (216)920-3073 *Fax:* (216)771-4938
E-Mail: info@cdfa.net
Web Site: www.cdfa.net
Members: 165 agencies
Staff: 1
Annual Budget: $250-500,000
Executive Director: Toby Rittner

Historical Note
Formerly (1992) Council of Industrial Development Bond Issuers. Established and incorporated in the District of Columbia. CDFA members are state, city, and county public agencies and special authorities whose primary purpose is the provision of economic development financing. Membership fee varies based on type and volume of business: $275-4,200/year.

Meetings/Conferences:
Annual Meetings: Fall
2007 – Miami, FL/May 22-24

Publications:
Newsletter (online). m.

Council of Educational Facility Planners, International *(1921)*
9180 E. Desert Cove Dr., Suite 104
Scottsdale, AZ 85260
Tel: (480)391-0840 *Fax:* (480)391-0940
E-Mail: contact@cefpi.org
Web Site: www.cefpi.org
Members: 3000 companies and individuals
Staff: 10
Annual Budget: $1-2,000,000
Executive Director: Thomas Kube
Director, Public/Government/Regulatory Affairs: Janell Wells

Historical Note
Formerly (1967) National Council on Schoolhouse Construction. Members are companies and persons who plan, design, build, equip and maintain educational facilities. Membership: $230 new, $180/year renewal (individual);$600 new, $500/year renewal (company).

Meetings/Conferences:
Annual Meetings: Fall

Publications:
Consultants Directory. a.
The Communicator. q. adv.
Educational Facility Planner. q. adv.

Council of Engineering and Scientific Society Executives *(1949)*
P.O. Box 130656
St. Paul, MN 55113
Tel: (952)838-3268 *Fax:* (651)765-2890
E-Mail: info@cesse.org
Web Site: www.cesse.org
Members: 1100 individuals
Annual Budget: $100-250,000
Secretariat: Corie Dacus
E-Mail: info@cesse.org

Historical Note
Formerly (1972) Council of Engineering and Scientific Society Secretaries. Has no paid officers or full-time staff.

Meetings/Conferences:
Annual Meetings: Summer/800

Publications:
CESSE Quill. 3/year.

Council of Fashion Designers of America *(1962)*
1412 Broadway, Suite 2006
New York, NY 10018
Tel: (212)302-1821 *Fax:* (212)768-0515
E-Mail: info@cfda.com
Web Site: www.cfda.com
Members: 275 individuals
Staff: 7
Executive Director: Peter D. Arnold
E-Mail: info@cfda.com
Historical Note
The CFDA is a not-for-profit trade association whose membership consists of more than 275 of America's foremost fashion and accessory designers. CFDA Foundation, Inc. is a seperate, not-for-profit company which was organized to raise funds for charity and industry activities. CFDA membership is by invitation, and new candidates recommended by two current members, are voted in by the Board of Directors annually.
Meetings/Conferences:
Annual Meetings: Always in New York, NY
Publications:
Annual Report. a.

Council of Fleet Specialists *(1967)*
160 Symphony Way
Elgin, IL 60120
Tel: (816)801-7964 *Fax:* (630)672-7418
E-Mail: info@cfshq.com
Web Site: www.cfshq.com
Members: 210 individuals
Staff: 6
Annual Budget: $250-500,000
Executive Vice President: Margaret Walker
E-Mail: info@cfshq.com
Historical Note
Members are distributors of parts and servicers for heavy-duty trucks. Membership: $800/year.
Meetings/Conferences:
Annual Meetings: Spring/1,100
Publications:
Parts/Equipment Buyers' Guide & Services Directory. a. adv.

Council of Graduate Schools *(1961)*
One Dupont Circle NW
Suite 430
Washington, DC 20036-1173
Tel: (202)223-3791 *Fax:* (202)331-7157
Web Site: www.cgsnet.org
Members: 450 institutional members
Staff: 13
Annual Budget: $2-5,000,000
President: Debra Stewart
Director, Government Relations and Public Affairs: Patricia McAllister
Director, Meetings and Member Services: Heidi Miller
Director, Finance and Operations: Deborah Narcisso
E-Mail: dnarcisso@cgs.nche.edu
Historical Note
CGS is an organization of over 450 institutions of higher education in the United States, Canada and other countries that are engaged in graduate education, research, scholarship and the preparation of candidates for advanced degrees. Mission of CGS is to improve and advance graduate education. To this end, CGS conducts advocacy in the federal policy arena, research, and the development and dissemination of best practices.
Meetings/Conferences:
Annual Meetings: Winter
Publications:
Membership Directory. a.
Directory. a.
Newsletter. m.

Council of Graphological Socs. *(1974)*
P.O. Box 20175
Columbus, OH 46356
Tel: (614)538-9145
Toll Free: (800)255 - 0739
E-Mail: ellenbowers@netscape.net
Staff: 2
Annual Budget: under $10,000
President: Ellen Bowers
E-Mail: ellenbowers@netscape.net
Historical Note
COGS serves as a coordinating council for independent graphological organizations to promote and advance the profession of graphology.
Meetings/Conferences:
Annual Meetings: August
Publications:
The Journal of Graphological Sciences. adv.
Graphology and the Courts.

Council of Hotel and Restaurant Trainers *(1971)*
P.O. Box 2835
Westfield, NJ 07091
Toll Free: (800)463 - 5918
E-Mail: chart@chart.org
Web Site: www.chart.org
Members: 350 organizations
Staff: 3
Annual Budget: $25-50,000
Executive Director: Tara Davey
Director, Marketing: Lisa L. Marovec, FMP
Historical Note
CHART members are training or human resource professionals employed by multi-unit food service and lodging organizations with the authority and responsibility for the design and implementation of training and development programs. Membership: $195/year, plus initiation fee.
Meetings/Conferences:
Semi-Annual Meetings: March and August
2007 – Charleston, SC/
2007 – Tucson, AZ/
Publications:
Training Flash e-newsletter. m.
FlipCHART Newsletter. bien.

Council of Independent Colleges *(1956)*
One Dupont Circle NW
Suite 320
Washington, DC 20036
Tel: (202)466-7230 *Fax:* (202)466-7238
Web Site: www.cic.edu
Members: 500 colleges
Staff: 20
Annual Budget: $2-5,000,000
President: Richard Ekman
Executive Vice President: Russell Y. Garth
Vice President, Communications: Laura McCoy
Historical Note
Formerly (1981) Council for the Advancement of Small Colleges. Members are independent four-year colleges of liberal arts and sciences and state, regional, and national organizations with an interest in those colleges. Sponsoring memberships are available for corporations and foundations. CIC provides leadership and faculty development programs and sponsors projects on curricular reform and other educational topics. Acquired the Consortium for the Advancement of Private Higher Education in 1993. Membership: $1,965-6,375/year, based on enrollment (institution); $225/year (affiliate).
Meetings/Conferences:
Annual Meetings: January
Publications:
CIC Independent Newsletter. q.

Council of Independent Restaurants of America *(1999)*
3500 E. Sunrise Dr.
Tucson, AZ 85718
Tel: (520)577-8181 *Fax:* (520)577-9015
Web Site: www.dineoriginals.com
Members: 700 individuals
Staff: 4
Annual Budget: $500-1,000,000
President: Don Luria
E-Mail: CIRApresident@aol.com
Publications:
Chapter Leader Reports. q.
CIRA Perspective. q.

Council of Industrial Boiler Owners *(1978)*
6035 Burke Centre Pkwy., Suite 360
Burke, VA 22015-3717
Tel: (703)250-9042 *Fax:* (703)239-9042
Web Site: www.cibo.org
Members: 80 companies
Staff: 4
Annual Budget: $500-1,000,000
President: Robert D. Bessette
Manager, Meetings/Administration: B.J. Ogden
Historical Note
CIBO was founded to address technical and public policy issues affecting industrial boilers. Members are owners and operators of non-utility boilers as well as manufacturers, consultants and suppliers. In addition to its annual meeting, CIBO sponsors several technical conferences each year. Membership: $11,000/year (active); $5,500/year (associate); $1,000/year (university/educational affiliate).
Meetings/Conferences:
Annual Meetings: October/85-100
2007 – Phoenix, AZ(South Points Mountain Resort)/Oct. 17-19
Publications:
Seminar/Conference Proceedings. 2-4/year.

Council of Infrastructure Financing Authorities *(1988)*
1808 K St. NW, Suite 500
Washington, DC 20006
Tel: (202)973-3100 *Fax:* (202)973-3101
E-Mail: cifa@navigantconsulting.com
Web Site: www.cifanet.org
Executive Director: Richard T. Farrell
E-Mail: cifa@navigantconsulting.com
Historical Note
CIFA is an organization of state and local agencies that have authority to assist and facilitate the issuance of debt financing for public infrastructure purposes. It is the only national organization dedicated exclusively to the service and representation of public environmental financing authorities, many of which issue debt, manage state loan funds, and provide various mechanisms to enhance credit arrangement and generally facilitate public financing. Membership: $1,000-5,000/year (full member); $1,000/year (associate member); $250-5,000/year (affiliate member).
Meetings/Conferences:
Semi-Annual Meetings: Legislative Conference/Spring & Workshop/Fall

Council of Institutional Investors *(1985)*
1730 Rhode Island. NW, Suite 512
Washington, DC 20036
Tel: (202)822-0800 *Fax:* (202)822-0801
E-Mail: info@cii.org
Web Site: www.cii.org
Members: 305 individuals and companies
Staff: 7
Annual Budget: $2-5,000,000
Executive Director: Ann Yerger
E-Mail: info@cii.org
Historical Note
Members include employee benefit plans, non-profit foundations and non-profit endowment funds. The Council studies and discusses issues, policies and practices affecting its membership.
Meetings/Conferences:
Semi-Annual Meetings: Spring and Fall
Publications:
Alerts. w.
CII Central. m.

Council of Insurance Agents and Brokers *(1913)*
701 Pennsylvania Ave. NW
Suite 750
Washington, DC 20004-2608
Tel: (202)783-4400 *Fax:* (202)783-4410
E-Mail: ciab@ciab.com
Web Site: www.ciab.com
Members: 300 corporate members
Staff: 25
Annual Budget: $10-25,000,000
President: Ken A. Crerar
Vice President, Member Services: Alison Bowman, ARM
Senior Vice President: Barbara Haugen
Vice President, Industry Affairs: Coletta I. Kemper
Vice President, Marketing and Communications: Maura Nelson

Chief Financial Officer: Gerry Van DeVelde
Senior Vice President, Government Affairs: Joel Wood

Historical Note

Formerly (1993) the National Association of Casualty and Surety Agents. The Council represents 300 of the nation's largest commercial property and casualty insurance agencies and brokerage firms. Council members annually place some 80% of the commercial property/casualty insurance premiums in the United States. Council members, who operate both nationally and internationally, specialize in a wide range of insurance products and risk management services for business, industry, government and the public.

Meetings/Conferences:

Annual Meetings: Always at White Sulphur Springs, WV(Greenbrier)/Oct./1,500

Publications:

Leaders Edge. m.

Council of Insurance Company Executives *(1911)*

Historical Note

A standing committee of the Council of Insurance Agents and Brokers, which provides administrative support.

Council of International Investigators *(1955)*

2150 N. 107th St., Suite 205
Seattle, WA 98133-9009
Tel: (206)361-8889 *Fax:* (206)367-8777
Toll Free: (888)759 - 8884
E-Mail: information@cii2.org
Web Site: www.cii2.org
Members: 350 individuals
Staff: 2
Annual Budget: $25-50,000
Executive Director: Shirley Bishop

Historical Note

Membership is open to any individual within a firm, partnership, or corporation engaged in private investigation, private patrol operation or related security positions. Membership: $150/year.

Meetings/Conferences:

Semi-Annual Meetings:

Publications:

Councillor. bi-m. adv.
Internat'l Focus. q. adv.
Roster. a.

Council of Landscape Architectural Registration Boards *(1961)*

144 Church St. NW, Suite 201
Vienna, VA 22180
Tel: (703)319-8380 *Fax:* (703)319-8290
E-Mail: info@clarb.org
Web Site: www.clarb.org
Members: 48 state & provincial boards
Staff: 8
Annual Budget: $500-1,000,000
Executive Director: Clarence L. Chaffee
E-Mail: CChaffee@clarb.org
Director, Member Services: Elizabeth A. Isbell
Director, Examinations: James T. Penrod
E-Mail: JPenrod@clarb.org

Historical Note

An independent service organization whose only members are the legally constituted state regulatory agencies. CLARB's main objectives are to promote high standards for landscape architecture registration; foster the enactment of uniform laws for landscape architecture; compile, maintain and transmit certified records of qualified practitioners for registration; and equalize and improve examination of applicants through a uniform national licensing examination. Membership: $1,800/year (state board).

Meetings/Conferences:

Annual Meetings: September/75

Council of Large Public Housing Authorities *(1981)*

1250 I St. NW
Suite 901-A
Washington, DC 20005
Tel: (202)638-1300 *Fax:* (202)638-2364
E-Mail: info@clpha.org
Web Site: www.clpha.org
Members: 56 individuals
Staff: 6
Annual Budget: $500-1,000,000
Executive Director: Sunia Zaterman
Deputy Director: Debbie Gross
E-Mail: dgross@clpha.org
Communications Director: Pat Lewis
Office Manager/Meeting Planner: Patricia Redmon
E-Mail: predmon@clpha.org
Legislative Director: Blenda Riddick

Historical Note

Established in response to the perceived threat to funding of the nation's low-income housing programs, CLPHA members are large public housing authorities. CLPHA works to improve public, low-income housing stock through legislation in Congress and administrative actions by federal agencies. Membership: dues vary by number of units managed.

Meetings/Conferences:

Annual Meetings: Fall

Publications:

Newsletter.

Council of Literary Magazines and Presses *(1967)*

154 Christopher St., Suite 3C
New York, NY 10014-9110
Tel: (212)741-9110 *Fax:* (212)741-9112
E-Mail: info@clmp.org
Web Site: www.clmp.org
Members: 347 literary publishers
Staff: 4
Annual Budget: $500-1,000,000
Executive Director: Jeffrey Lependorf

Historical Note

Formerly (1990) Coordinating Council of Literary Magazines. Membership open to any noncommercial literary magazine or press that publishes at least one issue or one book per year. Sponsors granting programs, regional meetings, publications, technical assistance and an advertising program. Membership fee varies, $55-600/year, based on annual budget.

Publications:

CLMP Newswire. bi-m.
CLMPages Newsletter. q.
Directory of Literary Magazines. a.

Council of Logistics Management

Historical Note

Became Council of Supply Chain Management Professionals in 2005.

Council of Manufacturing Associations *(1907)*

1331 Pennsylvania Ave. NW, Suite 600
Washington, DC 20004-1790
Tel: (202)637-3000 *Fax:* (202)637-3182
E-Mail: council@nam.org
Members: 230 associations
Staff: 3
Annual Budget: $250-500,000

Historical Note

A division of National Association of Manufacturers, CMA is composed of associations representing manufacturers in specific industries. Membership: $600-2,300/year, based on annual budget.

Meetings/Conferences:

Semi-annual Meetings: Aug. and Dec.

Publications:

Council Update. 2/m.
Association Revenue Forecast.
Ass'ns Council Membership Directory. a.
Manufacturing Trade Ass'ns. bien.

Council of Medical Specialty Socs. *(1965)*

51 Sherwood Terrace, Suite M
Lake Bluff, IL 60044-2232
Tel: (847)295-3456 *Fax:* (847)295-3759
E-Mail: mailbox@cmss.org
Web Site: www.cmss.org
Members: 20 medical societies
Staff: 2
Annual Budget: $250-500,000
Executive Vice President: Walter J. McDonald, M.D., F.A.

Historical Note

Founded as the Tri-College Council by the American College of Obstetricians and Gynecologists, the American College of Physicians and the American College of Surgeons. As other specialty societies joined, the present name was adopted in 1967. Incorporated in the state of Illinois in 1976. Today, eighteen societies with an aggregate membership of over 350,000 physicians are represented. Each member society represents one of the 25 specialties with a certifying board sanctioned by the American Board of Medical Specialties. Provides a forum for discussion, action and policy formulation on national issues affecting medical practice. Membership: $1/year.

Meetings/Conferences:

Semi-Annual Meetings: Spring in Chicago, IL and Fall
2007 – March 16-17
2007 – Nov. 17-18
2008 – March 21-22
2008 – Nov. 14-15

Publications:

CMSS Report. q.

Council of Multiple Listing Service

P.O. Box 3159
Durham, NC 27715-3159
Tel: (919)383-0044 *Fax:* (919)383-0035

Meetings/Conferences:

2007 – Seattle, WA
2008 – Chicago, IL
2009 – , MN
2010 – Lake Tahoe, CA

Council of Musculoskeletal Specialty Socs.

6300 N. River Road, Suite 727
Rosemont, IL 60018-4226
Tel: (847)698-1629 *Fax:* (847)823-0536
Web Site: www.comss.org
Members: 22 organizations
Executive Officer: Penelope Johnson

Historical Note

COMSS is a coordinating body for professional societies in orthopaedics and related sciences.

Council of Nephrology Nurses and Technicians

Historical Note

A professional council of the National Kidney Foundation.

Council of Nephrology Social Workers

Historical Note

A professional council of the National Kidney Foundation.

Council of Petroleum Accountants Socs. *(1961)*

3900 E. Mexico Ave., Suite 602
Denver, CO 80210-3945
Tel: (303)300-1131 *Fax:* (303)300-3733
Web Site: www.copas.org
Members: 3200 individuals
Staff: 3
Executive Director: Jon H. Gear
E-Mail: jgear@copas.org

Historical Note

Members are accountants involved in, or closely related to, the oil and gas industry. Sponsors the National Oil and Gas Accounting School with the Professional Development Institute at University of North Texas.

Publications:

COPAS Accounts. q. adv.
Bulletins. irreg.
Interpretations. irreg.
Research Papers. irreg.

Council of Professional Associations on Federal Statistics *(1980)*

1429 Duke St., Suite 402
Alexandria, VA 22314-3402
Tel: (703)836-0404
E-Mail: copafs@aol.com
Web Site: http://members.aol.com/copafs
Members: 17 organizations, 50 affiliates
Staff: 2
Annual Budget: $100-250,000
Executive Director: Edward J. Spar
E-Mail: copafs@aol.com

Historical Note

Established to monitor the priorities, scope and compatibility of the federal statistical effort. Has a multidisciplinary membership of associations and also *has 60 affiliate organizations. Membership: $2,000-15,000/year (associations), $1,000-3,000/year (other organizations).*

Meetings/Conferences:
Quarterly Meetings: Washington, DC

Council of Protocol Executives *(1988)*
101 W. 12th St., Suite PHH
New York, NY 10011
Tel: (212)633-6934 *Fax:* (212)633-6934
E-Mail: copeorg@aol.com
Web Site: www.councilofprotocolexecs.org
Members: 300 individuals
Staff: 1
Executive Director: Edna Fine Greenbaum
E-Mail: copeorg@aol.com
President: Felice Axelrod
E-Mail: copeorg@aol.com

Historical Note
COPE members coordinate executive meetings in the public and private sectors. Has no paid officers or full-time staff. Membership: $200/year.

Meetings/Conferences:
Annual Meetings: Winter

Publications:
Newsletter. q.
Protocol Directory. a.

Council of Real Estate Brokerage Managers *(1968)*
430 N. Michigan Ave., Suite 300
Chicago, IL 60611-4092
Tel: (312)321-4432 *Fax:* (312)329-8882
Toll Free: (800)621 - 8738
E-Mail: info@crb.com
Web Site: www.crb.com
Members: 7000 individuals
Staff: 8
Annual Budget: $2-5,000,000
Chief Executive Officer: Ginny Shipe
E-Mail: gshipe@crb.com
Vice President, Membership and Education: Tara Maric

Historical Note
Formerly (2002) Real Estate Brokerage Managers Council. Awards the designation Certified Real Estate Brokerage Manager (CRB). An affiliate of National Association of Realtors. Membership: $185/year (individual).

Meetings/Conferences:
Annual Meetings: November, in conjunction with the Nat'l Ass'n of Realtors

Publications:
Real Estate Business Magazine. bi-m. adv.
Issue and Trends Newsletter. q.

Council of Residential Specialists *(1976)*
430 N. Michigan Ave., Third Floor
Chicago, IL 60611-4092
Tel: (312)321-4400 *Fax:* (312)329-8882
Toll Free: (800)462 - 8841
Web Site: www.crs.com
Members: 47000 individuals
Staff: 40
Annual Budget: $5-10,000,000
Chief Executive Officer: Nina Cottrell
E-Mail: ncottrell@crs.com
Director, Marketing: Eric Berkland
E-Mail: eberkland@crs.com
Director, Education: Mary Beth Ciukaj
E-Mail: mbciukaj@crs.com
Director, Communications: Mike Fenner
Director, Products: Richard Lawson
E-Mail: rlawson@crs.com
Director, Member Benefits: Colleen McMahon
E-Mail: cmcmahon@crs.com
Vice President, Operations: Carol Raabe
E-Mail: craabe@crs.com
Director, Meetings and Special Events: Octavia Toso
E-Mail: ttoso@crs.com

Historical Note
An affiliate of the National Association of Realtors and Council of Residential Specialists, awards the Certified Residential Spectialist (CRS) designation. Membership: $120/year.

Meetings/Conferences:
Annual Meetings: in conjunction with the Nat'l Ass'n of Realtors.

Publications:
The Residential Specialist. bi-m. adv.
CRS Directory of Members. a. adv.

Council of Science Editors *(1957)*
12100 Sunset Hills Road, Suite 130
Reston, VA 20190-5202
Tel: (703)437-4377 *Fax:* (703)435-4390
E-Mail: cse@councilscienceeditors.org
Web Site: www.councilscienceeditors.org
Members: 1200 individuals
Staff: 5
Annual Budget: $250-500,000
Executive Director: Kathy Hoskins

Historical Note
Founded in 1957 and incorporated in 1965 in the District of Columbia as Council of Biology Editors; assumed its current name in 1999. Membership consists of individuals concerned with writing, editing and publishing in the life sciences and related fields. Membership: $125/year (individual).

Meetings/Conferences:
Annual Meetings: Spring/250
2007 – Austin, TX(Hilton Austin)/May 18-22

Publications:
Membership Directory. a.
Science Editor/CBE Views. bi-m. adv.

Council of Scientific Society Presidents *(1973)*
1155 16th St. NW, Room 1015
Washington, DC 20036-4800
Tel: (202)872-4452 *Fax:* (202)872-4079
E-Mail: cssp@acs.org
Web Site: www.cssp.us
Members: 100 societies and 3 federations
Staff: 3
Annual Budget: $250-500,000
President: Martin A. Apple, Ph.D.
E-Mail: cssp@acs.org

Historical Note
Formerly (1977) Committee of Scientific Society Presidents. Members are past and current presidents and presidents-elect of scientific societies. CSSP is a leadership-development organization that exists to promote science, improve national science policy, and focus on related issues.

Meetings/Conferences:
Semi-Annual Meetings: Washington, DC/May and December

Publications:
CSSP News OnLine. 3/year.
CSSP News. q.
CSSP Congressional Sourcebook. a.
Email Directory of Members and Alumni. bi.

Council of Societies for the Study of Religion *(1969)*
c/o Elius Bonginba
Rice University, P.O. Box 1842, MS-156
Houston, TX 77251-1842
Tel: (713)348-5721 *Fax:* (713)348-5725
E-Mail: cssr@rice.edu
Web Site: www.cssr.org
Members: 12 societies
Staff: 4
Annual Budget: $100-250,000
Coordinator: Mary Ann Clark

Historical Note
Formerly (1985) Council on the Study of Religion. An umbrella group for learned societies concerned with the study of religion. Membership fee varies, based on number of constituents.

Meetings/Conferences:
Annual Meetings: Fall

Publications:
CSSR Bulletin. q. adv.
Directory of Departments and Programs of Religion. a. adv.
Religious Studies Review. q. adv.

Council of State Administrators of Vocational Rehabilitation *(1940)*
4733 Bethesda Ave., Suite 330
Bethesda, MD 20814
Tel: (301)654-8414 *Fax:* (301)654-5542
Web Site: www.rehabnetwork.org
Members: 80 Agencies
Staff: 4
Annual Budget: $500-1,000,000
Director, Business Relations: Kathy West-Evans

Historical Note
Composed of the chief administrators of the public vocational rehabilitation agencies for physically and mentally handicapped persons in the states, District of Columbia, and the territories.

Council of State and Territorial Epidemiologists *(1951)*
2872 Woodcock Blvd., Suite 303
Atlanta, GA 30341
Tel: (770)458-3811 *Fax:* (770)458-8516
Web Site: www.cste.org
Members: 874 individuals
Staff: 10
Annual Budget: $2-5,000,000
Executive Director: Pat McConnon
E-Mail: pmcconnon@cste.org
Director, Operations: Beverly McLeod

Historical Note
Formerly (1986) Conference of State and Territorial Epidemiologists. Affiliated with Association of State and Territorial Health Officials. Members are public health epidemiologists employed by the various states and territories. Membership: $450-650/year (state/territory); $30/year (individual).

Meetings/Conferences:
Annual Meetings: Spring

Publications:
Washington Report.
Newsletter. q.

Council of State Association Presidents *(1975)*
800 Perry Hwy., Suite Three
Pittsburgh, PA 15229
Tel: (412)366-1177 *Fax:* (412)366-8804
E-Mail: csap@robertcraven.com
Web Site: www.csap.org
Members: 52 states and territories
Staff: 2
Annual Budget: $25-50,000
Business Manager: Robert Craven

Historical Note
Membership: $295/year (organiztion).

Meetings/Conferences:
Semi-Annual Meetings:

Council of State Chambers of Commerce *(1947)*
c/o NCCBI, P.O. Box 2508
Raleigh, NC 27602
Tel: (919)836-1400 *Fax:* (919)836-1425
Members: 43 chambers
Annual Budget: $50-100,000
Treasurer: Phillip J. Kirk, Jr.

Historical Note
Founded in 1947 as the National Association of State Chambers of Commerce, COSC is a federation of state and regional chambers of commerce. Assumed its present name in 1948. Has no paid officers or full-time staff.

Meetings/Conferences:
Annual Meetings: October and January

Council of State Community Development Agencies *(1974)*
1825 K St. NW, Suite 515
Washington, DC 20006
Tel: (202)293-5820 *Fax:* (202)293-2820
Web Site: www.coscda.org
Members: 48 state agencies
Staff: 5
Annual Budget: $250-500,000
Executive Director: Dianne E. Taylor
E-Mail: dtaylor@coscda.org

Historical Note
Members are employees of state community affairs agencies representing all 50 states. Formerly (1992) Council of State Community Affairs Agencies.

Meetings/Conferences:
Annual Meetings: September

Publications:
National Line. bi-w.

Council of State Governments *(1933)*
P.O. Box 11910
Lexington, KY 40578-1910
Tel: (859)244-8103 *Fax:* (859)244-8067
Web Site: www.csg.org
Members: 50 states, 5 territories
Staff: 190
Annual Budget: $10-25,000,000
Executive Director: Daniel M. Sprague
General Counsel/Director, Washington Office: James Brown
Director, Operations: Sarah Pitt
Director, Membership Services: Mike Robinson
Deputy Director: Laura Williams

Historical Note
Founded as the American Legislators Association; assumed its present name in 1933. The Council seeks to preserve and strengthen the role of the state in the federal system. Serves as a research and service agency for the 50 state governments and for associations of state officials. Has an annual budget of approximately $12 million.

Meetings/Conferences:
Annual Meetings: December

Publications:
State Leadership Directories. a.
The Book of the States. a.
State Government News. m.

Council of Supply Chain Management Professionals *(1963)*
2805 Butterfield Road, Suite 200
Oak Brook, IL 60523
Tel: (630)574-0985 *Fax:* (630)574-0989
E-Mail: cscmpadmin@cscmp.org
Web Site: www.cscmp.org
Members: 7000 individuals
Staff: 30
Annual Budget: $5-10,000,000
Executive Vice President: Maria A. McIntyre
E-Mail: cscmpadmin@cscmp.org
Director, Marketing/Communications: Paul Accardo
Manager, Finance: Paul Blair
Director, Education/Roundable Services: Kathleen L. Hedland
Director, Meeting Services: Louise A. Pochelski
Director, Operations: James Schulze
Manager, Information Services: Janine M. Stuck

Historical Note
Formerly (1985) National Council of Physical Distribution Management and then Council of Logistics Management; assumed its current name on January 1, 2005. CSCMP is a professional organization of individuals concerned with transportation, warehousing, inventory, materials, logistics and/or physical distribution management. Has an annual budget of approximately $8 million. Membership: $250/year (individual).

Meetings/Conferences:
Annual Meetings: Fall/3,500

Publications:
Logistics Comment. 5/yr.
Journal of Business Logistics. 2/yr.

Council of Teaching Hospitals

Historical Note
A council of the Association of American Medical Colleges.

Council of the Americas *(1958)*
680 Park Ave.
New York, NY 10021
Tel: (212)628-3200 *Fax:* (212)249-1880
E-Mail: inforequest@as-coa.org
Web Site: www.counciloftheamericas.org
Members: 235 corporations
Staff: 11
Annual Budget: $1-2,000,000
President and Chief Executive Officer: Susan Segal
E-Mail: ssegal@as-coa.org
Director, Communications: Mara Lemos
Senior Director, Public Policy: Michele Levy
Chief Financial Officer: Peter Reilly

Historical Note
Founded in New York City in 1958 as the United States Inter-American Council, Inc. The name was changed in 1965 to Council for Latin America, Inc. and in 1970 to Council of the Americas, Inc. Members are corporations doing business in Latin America. Maintains a Washington office. Affiliate of The Americas Society Membership: $7,500-45,000/year.

Meetings/Conferences:
Annual Meetings: May/Washington, DC

Publications:
Review Magazine.
Americas Society Update.
Washington Report. q.
Mexico Bulletin.

Council of the Great City Schools *(1956)*
1301 Pennsylvania Ave. NW, Suite 702
Washington, DC 20004-1701
Tel: (202)393-2427 *Fax:* (202)393-2400
Web Site: www.cgcs.org
Members: 66 school districts
Staff: 16
Annual Budget: $2-5,000,000
Executive Director: Michael Casserly
Director, Management Services: Robert Carlson
Director, Communications: Henry Duvall
E-Mail: hduvall@cgcs.org
Director, Academic Achievment: Ricki Price-Baugh
E-Mail: mcasserly@cgcr.org
Director, Special Projects: Shirley Schwartz
Director, Legislative Services: Jeff Simering
Director, Research: Jason Snipes
Director, Finance/Administration and Conferences: Teresita T. ValeCruz

Historical Note
Members are large city school districts. Formerly known as the Research Council for the Great Schools Improvement. Advocates on behalf of inner-city students through legislation, research, and media relations. Membership: $22,500-42,000/year.

Meetings/Conferences:
2007 – Washington, DC(Marriott)/March 16-20/300

Publications:
The Urban Educator. m.
Urban Indicator and Urban Legislator. irreg.
Annual Report. a.

Council of Theatre Chairs and Deans

Historical Note
A focus group of the Association for Theatre in Higher Education.

Council of Vehicle Associations *(1992)*

Historical Note
Address unknown in 2005.

Council of Writers Organizations *(1979)*

Historical Note
Organization reported defunct in 2004.

Council of Writing Program Administrators *(1978)*

Historical Note
See National Council of Writing Program Administrators.

Council on Anthropology and Education

Historical Note
A section of the American Anthropology Association.

Council on Botanical and Horticultural Libraries *(1970)*
c/o Hunt Inst. for Botanical Documentation, C.M.U.
5000 Forbes Ave.
Pittsburgh, PA 15213-3890
Tel: (412)268-7301 *Fax:* (412)268-5677
Web Site: www.cbhl.net
Members: 240 individuals
Annual Budget: under $10,000
Secretary: Charlotte Tancin
E-Mail: ctancin@cmu.edu

Historical Note
Members are libraries and individuals with an interest in botanical and horticultural subjects. Has no paid officers or full-time staff. Membership: $55/year (individual); $105/year (organization); $35/year (student/retiree).

Meetings/Conferences:
Annual Meetings: Spring

Publications:
Newsletter. 3-4/year.
Directory of Member Libraries. a.

Council on Certification of Health, Environmental and Safety Technologists
208 Burwash Ave.
Savoy, IL 61874-9510
Tel: (217)359-2686 *Fax:* (217)359-0055
E-Mail: cchest@cchest.org
Web Site: www.cchest.org
Members: 3,700 individuals
Staff: 3
Annual Budget: $250-500,000
Executive Director: Roger L. Brauer, Ph.D., CSP, CPE

Historical Note
Founded as a joint venture between American Board of Industrial Hygiene and Board of Certified Safety Professionals, CCHEST examines and certifies safety practitioners and establishes standards for certification, including the OHST, CHST and STS. CCHEST is administered by the Board of Certified Safety Professionals.

Publications:
CCHEST Newsletter. a.

Council on Chiropractic Education *(1971)*
8049 N. 85th Way
Scottsdale, AZ 85258-4321
Tel: (480)443-8877 *Fax:* (480)483-7333
Web Site: www.cce-usa.org
Members: 16 programs and institutions
Staff: 5
Annual Budget: $500-1,000,000
Executive Director: Martha S. O'Connor
E-Mail: cce@cce-usa.org

Historical Note
Members are programs offering the doctor of chiropractic degree. Provides accreditation. Accreditation fee varies, based on enrollment; $80 per FTE/year.

Meetings/Conferences:
Semi-Annual: January and July

Council on Chiropractic Orthopedics *(1967)*
1202 County Road
Onalaska, WI 54650
Tel: (608)781-2225 *Fax:* (608)781-2495
E-Mail: wellness2U@aol.com
Web Site: www.ccodc.org/
Members: 400 individuals
Annual Budget: $10-25,000
President: Leo Bronston, D.C.
E-Mail: wellness2U@aol.com

Historical Note
A division of the American Chiropractic Association. Members are chiropractors with an interest in orthopedics. Membership: $100/year (individual).

Meetings/Conferences:
Annual Meetings: March/April

Publications:
Orthopedic Briefs. bi-m.
Directory. a.

Council on Diagnostic Imaging to the A.C.A. *(1936)*
P.O. Box 567
Wake Forest, NC 27588
Tel: (919)562-6570
E-Mail: cdisec@nc.rr.com
Web Site: www.dacbr.com/cdi_homepage.htm
Members: 1000 individuals
Staff: 1
Annual Budget: $100-250,000
Secretary-Treasurer: Kathy Thom
E-Mail: cdisec@nc.rr.com

Historical Note
A part of the American Chiropractic Association. Founded as the National Council of Chiropractic Roentgenologists, it later became the Council on Roentgenography, (1964) the American Council on Chiropractic Roentgenology, (1968) the Council on

Roentgenology to the A.C.A. and assumed its present name in 1986. Membership: $60/year.

Publications:
TDI. semi-a.
Topics in Diagnostic Radiology and Advanced Imaging. sem-a.

Council on Education of the Deaf *(1960)*
Gallaudet University, FH 207
800 Florida Ave. NE
Washington, DC 20002
Tel: (202)651-5525 *Fax:* (202)651-5749
E-Mail: ced@gallaudet.edu
Web Site: www.deafed.net
Members: 7 organizations
Staff: 2
Annual Budget: $25-50,000
Executive Director: Roslyn Rosen
E-Mail: ced@gallaudet.edu

Historical Note
An umbrella organization of associations concerned with education of the deaf, including the Alexander Graham Bell Association for the Deaf, the Convention of American Instructors of the Deaf, the Conference of Educational Administrators Serving the Deaf, the Association of College Educators: Deaf and Hard of Hearing, the National Association of the Deaf, and the American Society for Deaf Children. Maintains certification programs for teacher education programs and individual professionals and accredation reviews for university teacher preparation programs.

Meetings/Conferences:
Annual Meetings: 2 Board meetings per/year

Council on Employee Benefits *(1946)*
4910 Moorland Lane
Bethesda, MD 20814
Tel: (301)664-5940 *Fax:* (301)664-5944
Web Site: www.ceb.org
Members: 225 companies
Staff: 3
Annual Budget: $500-1,000,000
Executive Director: Vicki A. Schieber
E-Mail: vschieber@ceb.org

Historical Note
An organization for employers for the exchange of information on all aspects of employee benefit plans. Founded as the Federation of Employee Benefit Associations; became the Council on Employee Benefit Plans in 1950 and assumed its present name in 1961. Membership: $1,500/year (company).

Meetings/Conferences:
Semi-Annual Meetings: Spring

Council on Fine Art Photography *(1982)*
5613 Johnson Ave.
West Bethesda, MD 20817-3503
Tel: (301)897-0083
Members: 50 individuals
Staff: 14
Executive Director: Lowell Anson Kenyon

Historical Note
Members are fine art photographers employing silver processes. The International Museum Photographers Association is a division of CFAP.

Meetings/Conferences:
Annual Meetings: always Washington, DC/June

Publications:
Perspective on Photography.
Contemporary Photographer. m.
Daguerre Report. m.

Council on Forest Engineering *(1978)*
620 S.W. Fourth St.
Corvallis, OR 97333
Tel: (541)754-7558 *Fax:* (541)754-7559
E-Mail: office@cofe.org
Web Site: www.cofe.org
Members: 360 individuals
Staff: 1
Administrative Secretary: Sylvia Aulerich
E-Mail: office@cofe.org

Historical Note
COFE members are individuals with an interest in forest engineering. Membership: $10/year (individual).

Publications:
Newsletter. semi-a.
Proceedings. a.

Council on Foundations *(1949)*
1828 L St. NW
Washington, DC 20036
Tel: (202)466-6512 *Fax:* (202)785-3926
E-Mail: info@cof.org
Web Site: www.cof.org
Members: 2000 foundations
Staff: 100
Annual Budget: $10-25,000,000
President and Chief Executive Officer: Steven Gunderson
Editor: Allan Clyde
Vice President and General Counsel: Janne Gallagher
Vice President, Finance and Administration: Ellen Hobby
Vice President, Constituency Services: Char Mollison
Senior Vice President, Philathropic Leadership: Joanne Scanlan

Historical Note
Founded in 1949 as a non-profit membership association for grantmaking foundations and corporations. Membership includes independent foundations, community foundations, corporate grantmakers, public foundations, operating foundations and foreign foundations. COF promotes responsible and effective philanthropy, secures public policy supportive of philanthropy and provides advisory services to its members.

Meetings/Conferences:
Annual Meetings: Spring

Publications:
Corporate Update. q.
Council Columns Newsletter. bi-m.
Family Foundation Update. q.
Foundation News Magazine. bi-m. adv.
Annual Report. a.
Community Foundation Quarterly. q.
Foundation Management Report. bien.
Washington Update. irreg.
Communications Update. q.
International Dateline. q.
Foundation Salary Update. a.

Council on Governmental Ethics Laws *(1978)*
P.O. Box 60996
Jacksonville, FL 32236-0996
Tel: (904)693-0094 *Fax:* (904)434-8831
E-Mail: director@cogel.org
Web Site: www.cogel.org
Members: 40 individuals
Staff: 1
Annual Budget: $100-250,000
Executive Director: Tony Kramer
E-Mail: director@cogel.org

Historical Note
COGEL is the international professional association for agencies and individuals with responsibilities in governmental ethics, elections, campaign finance, freedom of information, and lobby law regulation. Membership: $150/year (individual); $395/year (agency).

Meetings/Conferences:
Annual Meetings: fall-WInter

Publications:
Campaign Finance Update. a.
Ethics Update. a.
Lobbying Update. a.
Freedom of Information Update. a.
COGEL Guardian. q.

Council on Governmental Relations *(1948)*
1200 New York Ave. NW, Suite 320
Washington, DC 20005
Tel: (202)289-6655 *Fax:* (202)289-6698
Web Site: www.cogr.edu
Members: 138 individuals
Staff: 3
President: Anthony DeCrappeo

Historical Note
Formerly (1995) a division of the National Association of College and University Business Officers, COGR is now an independent entity. Members are research university administrators with an interest in government regulations, policies and practices as they effect institutional conduct.

Council on Library-Media Technicians *(1967)*
c/o Lemont Public Library District
50 E. Wend St.
Lemont, IL 60439-6439
Tel: (630)257-6541 *Fax:* (630)257-7737
Web Site: http://colt.ucr.edu/
Members: 150 individuals and institutions
Annual Budget: under $10,000
President: Jackie Lakatos
E-Mail: jlakatos@lemontlibrary.org
Executive Director: Margaret R. Barron

Historical Note
Formerly (1973) Council on Library Technology, (1977) Council on Library Technical-Assistants, and (1989) Council on Library-Media Technical-Assistants. Affiliated with the American Library Association. Members are library employees responsible for multiple tasks in circulation, technical services and public service. Membership: $45/year (individual); $70/year (organization).

Meetings/Conferences:
Annual Meetings: Summer

Publications:
Library Mosaics. bi-m. adv.
Membership Directory and Data Book. a.
Conference Proceedings. a.

Council on Licensure, Enforcement and Regulation *(1980)*
403 Marquis Ave., Suite 200
Lexington, KY 40502-2140
Tel: (859)269-1289 *Fax:* (859)231-1943
E-Mail: clear@mis.net
Web Site: www.clearhq.org
Members: 409 individuals and agencies
Staff: 5
Annual Budget: $500-1,000,000
Executive Director: Pamela Brinegar

Historical Note
Formerly (1991) National Clearinghouse on Licensure, Enforcement and Regulation. Members include licensing boards and agencies in the 50 states, territories and Canada. Its mission is to improve the quality and understanding of professional and occupational regulation. Membership: $195/year (individual), $195-2,600/year (board/agency).

Meetings/Conferences:
Annual Meetings: Fall
2007 – Atlanta, GA(Westin Peachtree Plaza)/Sept. 6-8

Publications:
Clear Exam Review. semi-a. adv.
CLEAR News. q. adv.
Resource Briefs. a.

Council on Occupational Education *(1971)*
41 Perimeter Center East NE, Suite 640
Atlanta, GA 30346
Toll Free: (800)917 - 2081 Ext: 21
Web Site: www.council.org
Members: 432 institutions
Staff: 10
Annual Budget: $1-2,000,000
Executive Director and President: Dr. Gary Puckett

Historical Note
Formerly Commission on Occupational Education Institutions (1971). Members are post-secondary schools and institutions that are committed to career and workforce development.

Meetings/Conferences:
Annual Meetings: Fall

Publications:
Handbook of Accreditation.
Councilor. irreg.
Guidelines for Visiting Teams.
Self Study Manual.
Policies and Rules.

Council on Oceanic Engineering Society

Historical Note
A subsidiary of the Institute of Electrical and Electronics Engineers. Membership in the Society, open only to IEEE members, includes subscription to a technical periodical in the field published by IEEE. All administrative support is provided by IEEE.

Council on Renal Nutrition
Historical Note
A professional council of the National Kidney Foundation.

Council on Resident Education in Obstetrics and Gynecology *(1967)*
P.O. Box 96920
Washington, DC 20090-6920
Tel: (202)863-2554 *Fax:* (202)863-4994
Toll Free: (800)673 - 8444
Web Site: www.acog.org
Members: 7 societies
Annual Budget: $500-1,000,000
Associate Director: DeAnne Nehra
E-Mail: dnehra@acog.org
Historical Note
Founded by the American College of Obstetricians and Gynecologists, CREOG members are specialty professional societies with an interest in residency training in obstetrics and gynecology.
Meetings/Conferences:
2007 - Salt Lake City, UT(Grand America Hotel)/March 7-10
Publications:
CREOG Council News Newsletter. 3/year.
Basic Science Monographs in Obstetrics & Gynecology. irreg.

Council on Social Work Education *(1952)*
1725 Duke St., Suite 500
Alexandria, VA 22314-3457
Tel: (703)683-8080 *Fax:* (703)683-8099
Web Site: www.cswe.org
Members: 3500 individuals
Staff: 35
Annual Budget: $2-5,000,000
Executive Director: Julia M. Watkins
E-Mail: jwatkins@cswe.org
Director, Member and Information Services: Jennifer J. Johnson
E-Mail: info@cswe.org
Manager, Information Services: Eddie Wong
E-Mail: info@cswe.org
Historical Note
Accredits Baccalaureate and Masters degree programs of social work at colleges and universities. Formed by a merger of the National Association of Schools of Social Administration and the American Association of Schools of Social Work.
Meetings/Conferences:
Annual Meetings: Winter
2007 - San Francisco, CA/Nov. 27-30
Publications:
Directory. a.
Journal of Social Work Education. 3/year. adv.
Social Work Education Reporter. 3/year. adv.
Summary Information on Master of Social Work Programs. a.
Statistics on Social Work Education. a.

Council On State Taxation *(1969)*
122 C St. NW, Suite 330
Washington, DC 20001-2109
Tel: (202)484-5222 *Fax:* (202)484-5229
E-Mail: dsmith@statetax.org
Web Site: www.statetax.org
Members: 580 multi state corporate taxpayers
Staff: 10
Annual Budget: $2-5,000,000
President and Executive Director: Douglas L. Lindholm
E-Mail: dsmith@statetax.org
Legislative Director: Joseph Crosby
Tax Counsel: Steve Kranz
E-Mail: dsmith@statetax.org
Contact: Diann Smith
E-Mail: dsmith@statetax.org
Historical Note
Organized as an advisory committee to the Council of State Chambers of Commerce in 1969, COST became separately incorporated in in 1992. COST members are state and local tax professionals of multistate and multinational corporate taxpayers. COST provides educational programs and government affairs representation for its members. Membership: $3,000/year.
Meetings/Conferences:
Annual Meetings: Fall
Publications:
COST Practitioner Connection. bi-w.
COST Conscious. bi-w.
COST Membership Directory. a. adv.
COST Linchpin. q.

Council on Technology Teacher Education *(1950)*
Illinois State University
Department of Technology
Normal, IL 61790
Tel: (309)438-3661 *Fax:* (309)438-8626
Web Site: http://teched.vt.edu/ctte/t
Members: 900 individuals
Annual Budget: $10-25,000
Executive Officer: Prof. Klaus M. Schmidt
Historical Note
Formerly (1986) American Council on Industrial Arts Teacher Education. Has no paid staff. An affiliate of the International Technology Education Association (ITEA). Membership: $25/year, plus ITEA membership.
Meetings/Conferences:
Annual Meetings: March, with Internat'l Technology Education Ass'n
Publications:
CTTE Newsletter. semi-a.
CTTE Yearbook. a.
Journal of Technology Education. semi-a.

Council on the Safe Transportation of Hazardous Articles *(1972)*
7803 Hill House Court
Fairfax Station, VA 22039
Tel: (703)451-4031 *Fax:* (703)451-4207
E-Mail: mail@costha.com
Web Site: www.costha.com
Members: 150 individuals
Staff: 5
Administrator: Lara Mehr Currie
Historical Note
COSTHA represents shippers, carriers, manufacturers and others in the transportation industry. COSTHA is dedicated to promoting regulatory compliance and safety in the hazardous materials transportation industry.
Meetings/Conferences:
2007 - Scottsdale, AZ/Apr. 22-25
Publications:
What to Do When the DOT Hazardous Materials Inspector Calls.
Newsletter. q.

Counseling Association for Humanistic Education and Development *(1952)*
Historical Note
A division of the American Counseling Ass'n, which provides administrative support.

Counselors of Real Estate *(1953)*
430 N. Michigan Ave.
Chicago, IL 60611-4089
Tel: (312)329-8427 *Fax:* (312)329-8881
E-Mail: info@cre.org
Web Site: www.cre.org/
Members: 1100 individuals
Staff: 8
Annual Budget: $1-2,000,000
President: Mary Walker Fleischmann
Director, Communications: Gloria Bowman
Historical Note
The Counselors of Real Estate (CRE) is the professional consulting affiliate of the National Association of Realtors. Members are awarded the CRE (Counselor of Real Estate) designation. CREs are a respected source for professional advice on all types of property and land-related matters. Membership is by invitation only.
Meetings/Conferences:
Annual Meetings: With Nat'l Ass'n of Realtors
Publications:
Real Estate Issues. q.
The Counselor. bi-m.
CRE Member Directory. a.

Country Music Association *(1958)*
One Music Circle South
Nashville, TN 37203
Tel: (615)244-2840 *Fax:* (615)726-0314
Toll Free: (800)788 - 3045
Web Site: www.cmaworld.com
Members: 5000 individuals
Staff: 30
Annual Budget: $1-2,000,000
Executive Director: Edwin W. Benson, Jr.
Vice President, Events and Program Development: Bobette Dudley
Associate Executive Director: Tammy Genovese
Director, Membership and Online Marketing: Daphne Larkin
Vice President, Strategic Marketing: Rick Murray
Senior Director, Communications: Wendy Pearl
Senior Director, Finance and Administration: Amy Smart
Director, Board Administration: Peggy Whitaker
Historical Note
Membership is open to any individual or organization deriving income from country music. Membership: $50-$100/year (individual), $125-$5,000/year (organization).
Meetings/Conferences:
Annual Meetings: always Nashville, TN/Fall
Publications:
Close-Up. bi-m.

Country Radio Broadcasters, Inc. *(1970)*
819 18th Ave. South
Nashville, TN 37203-3218
Tel: (615)327-4487 *Fax:* (615)329-4492
E-Mail: info@crb.org
Web Site: www.crb.org
Members: 2500 individuals
Staff: 5
Annual Budget: $1-2,000,000
Executive Director: Ed Salamon
Historical Note
Members are country radio broadcasters, music industry personnel, record label officials, publishers, songwriters and performers. Sponsors panels, workshops, speakers, and presentations to expose members to all facets of the broadcasting and music industries.
Meetings/Conferences:
Annual Meetings: always Spring in Nashville, TN(Nashville convention center)/2800
2007 - Nashville, TN(Nashville Convention Center)/Feb. 28-March 2
Publications:
CRB Executive Memo. w. adv.
CRB Agenda Guide. a. adv.

County Executives of America *(1970)*
1100 H St. NW, Suite 910
Washington, DC 20005
Tel: (202)628-3585 *Fax:* (202)737-0556
Toll Free: (800)296 - 8438
Web Site: www.countyexecutives.org
Members: 709 individuals
Staff: 8
Annual Budget: $250-500,000
Executive Director: Michael G. Griffin
E-Mail: mgriffin@countyexecutives.org
Historical Note
Founded as National Council of Elected County Executives; assumed current name in 1997. Represents the chief elected officers of over 700 counties throughout the U.S.
Meetings/Conferences:
Quarterly Meetings:
Publications:
County Executive Summary. m. adv.

CPA Associates International *(1957)*
301 Rte. 17 North
Rutherford, NJ 07070
Tel: (201)804-8686 *Fax:* (201)804-9222
E-Mail: homeoffice@cpaai.com
Web Site: www.cpaai.com
Members: 146 firms
Staff: 3
Annual Budget: $500-1,000,000
President: James F. Flynn

Historical Note
Members are accounting firms.
Publications:
Not For Profit Client Newsletter.
Outlook. q.
Business Advisory Client Newsletter. q.
CPA Associates Directory. a.
Medical Client Newsletter. q.
Year-End Tax Planning Guide. a.
Tax Outlook. q.
Construction Newsletter. q.
Law Firm Client Newsletter.

CPA Auto Dealer Consultants Association *(1996)*
Che Valmont Plaza
Fourth Floor
Omaha, NE 68154
Tel: (402)778-7922 *Fax:* (402)778-7931
Toll Free: (888)475 - 4476
E-Mail: info@autodealercpas.net
Web Site: www.autodealercpas.net
Members: 22 firms
Staff: 6
Executive Director: Nancy Drennen
Historical Note
Formerly Construction Industry CPA/Consultants Association. CADCA is an association of CPA firms that concentrate a substantial portion of their business on providing financial and consulting services to auto dealers, beyond traditonal tax and audit work. Members are accepted on a territorially exclusive basis.
Meetings/Conferences:
Semi-annual Meetings:
Publications:
Members' Bulletin. m.

CPA Construction Industry Association *(1991)*
10831 Old Mill Road, Suite 400
Omaha, NE 68154
Tel: (402)778-7922 *Fax:* (402)778-7931
Toll Free: (888)475 - 4476
Web Site: www.the-apa.com
Staff: 4
Executive Director: Nancy Drennen
Historical Note
CICPAC is an association of CPA firms that provide services to construction contractors beyond traditional compliance work. Members are accepted on a territorially excluse basis with a limit of one member in each Metropolitan Statistical Area.
Publications:
Members Bulletin. q.
Construction Industry Advisor (Client Newsletter). q.

CPA Manufacturing Services Association *(1995)*
One Valmont Plaza
Fourth Floor
Omaha, NE 68154
Tel: (402)778-7922 *Fax:* (402)778-7931
Toll Free: (888)475 - 4476
E-Mail: info@manufacturingcpas.com
Web Site: www.manufacturingcpas.com
Members: 13 firms
Staff: 6
Executive Director: Nancy Drennen
Historical Note
MSA is a national association of CPA firms that provide industry specific services to manufacturers, especially CPA firms that specialize in providing accounting services beyond traditional tax and audit. Membership is on a territorially protected basis.
Meetings/Conferences:
Semi-Annual Meetings:
Publications:
Members' Bulletin. m.

CPAmerica International *(1978)*
11801 Research Dr.
Alachua, FL 32615
Tel: (386)418-4001 *Fax:* (386)418-4002
Toll Free: (800)992 - 2324
E-Mail: info@cpamerica.org
Web Site: www.cpamerica.org
Members: 70 firms, 10,000 professionals
Staff: 12
Annual Budget: $1-2,000,000
President: Douglas H. Thompson, Jr.
E-Mail: info@cpamerica.org
Historical Note
Founded as Accounting Firms Associated, assumed its present name in 1999. CPAmerica International is an international network of independent public accounting firms founded to pursue and ensure excellence in accounting, financial and business consulting services.
Meetings/Conferences:
Annual Meetings: August

CPCU Society *(1944)*
Kahler Hall
720 Providence Rd.
Malvern, PA 19355
Tel: (610)251-2728 *Fax:* (610)251-2780
Toll Free: (800)932 - 2728
E-Mail: membercenter@cpcusociety.org
Web Site: www.cpcusociety.org
Members: 26000 individuals
Staff: 35
Annual Budget: $5-10,000,000
Executive Vice President: James R. Marks, CAE
Vice President, Communications and Marketing: Pi-Lan Hsu
Vice President, Finance and Administration: Cathy Karch
Vice President, Member Services and Continuing Education: Barry Midwood
E-Mail: bmidwood@cpcusociety.org
Historical Note
Founded as Society of Chartered Property and Casualty Underwriters; became (1995) Chartered Property Casualty Underwriters Society before assuming its current name in 2001. Membership is composed of insurance professionals who have been awarded the designation Chartered Property Casualty Underwriter (CPCU) by the American Institute for Chartered Property Casualty Underwriters. Membership: $160/year.
Meetings/Conferences:
Annual Meetings: Fall/3,500
2007 - Honolulu, HI(Hawaiian Convention Center)/Sept. 8-11/5000
Publications:
CPCU News. 6/year.
CPCU Yearbook. a.

Craft & Hobby Association *(1940)*
319 E. 54th St.
P.O. Box 348
Elmwood Park, NJ 07407
Tel: (201)794-1133 *Fax:* (201)797-0657
E-Mail: hia@hobby.org
Web Site: www.hobby.org
Members: 6000 corporations
Staff: 20
Annual Budget: $5-10,000,000
Chief Executive Officer: Steve Berger
Vice President, Finance and Administration: Dale Atherton
Vice President, Marketing, Member Services, and Education: Sandy Ghezzi
Vice President, Meetings and Expositions: Tony Lee
Historical Note
Founded in Chicago as the Model Industry Association with 87 charter members; became (1956) the Hobby Industry Ass'n before (2004) absorbing the Association of Crafts & Creative Industries to form the present organziation. CHA represents manufacturers, wholesalers, retailers, publishers and others affiliated with the craft and hobby industry. Has an annual budget of approximately $5.5 million.
Meetings/Conferences:
Annual Meetings: *Held during trade show in Winter*
Publications:
CHA Show Directory. a.
Membership Directory. a.
Size of Industry Survey.
Horizons. m.
Nationwide Consumer Survey. a.

Craft Retailers Association for Tomorrow *(2001)*
100 N. 20th St.
Fourth Floor
Philadelphia, PA 19103-1443
Tel: (215)963-9785 *Fax:* (215)564-2175
E-Mail: info@craftonline.org
Web Site: www.craftonline.org
Members: 152 members
Staff: 2
Historical Note
CRAFT members are galleries and shops that feature handmade craftwork of U.S. origin, and artists, partnerships, and corporations who supply a product and/or service to retailer members.
Meetings/Conferences:
2007 - Philadelphia, PA

Cranberry Institute *(1952)*
3203-B Cranberry Highway
East Wareham, MA 02538
Tel: (508)295-4132 *Fax:* (508)759-6294
Toll Free: (800)295 - 4132
E-Mail: cinews@earthlink.net
Web Site: www.cranberryinstitute.org
Members: 1200 growers and handlers
Staff: 2
Annual Budget: $100-250,000
Executive Director: Jere Downing
E-Mail: jdd@capecod.net
Historical Note
Members are cranberry growers and handlers in the United States and Canada. Membership: $50-100/year (individual); by assessment (organization/company).
Publications:
Cranberry Institute Newsletter. bi-m.

Crane Certification Association of America *(1984)*
P.O. Box 89707
Vancouver, WA 98687-7907
Tel: (360)834-3805 *Fax:* (360)834-3507
Toll Free: (800)447 - 3402
E-Mail: admin@ccaaweb.net
Web Site: www.ccaaweb.net/
Staff: 1
Executive Officer: Maureen Craig
Historical Note
Promotes crane safety through improvements to the certification process and participation in government forums. Membership: $250/year.
Publications:
CCAA Newsletter. q. adv.

Crane Manufacturers Association of America *(1955)*
Historical Note
A section of Material Handling Industry of America which provides administrative support.

Cranial Academy *(1947)*
8202 Clearvista Pkwy., Suite 9D
Indianapolis, IN 46256-1457
Tel: (317)594-0411 *Fax:* (317)594-9299
E-Mail: info@cranialacademy.org
Web Site: www.cranialacademy.org
Members: 1200 individuals
Staff: 2
Annual Budget: $250-500,000
Executive Director: Sidney N. Dunn
E-Mail: info@cranialacademy.org
Historical Note
Affiliated with the American Academy of Osteopathy. Formerly (1960) Osteopathic Cranial Association. Members are osteopaths, physicians, dentists, and students who have studied osteopathy in the cranial field.
Meetings/Conferences:
Annual Meetings: June/150
2007 - Tucson, AZ(Marriott University Park)/June 21-24/150
Publications:
Cranial Letter. q.
Directory. a.

Creative Education Foundation *(1954)*
289 Bay Road
Hadley, MA 01035
Tel: (413)559-6614 *Fax:* (413)559-6615
Toll Free: (800)447 - 2774
Web Site: www.creativeeducationfoundation.org

Historical Note
CEF is the center for Applied Imagination - helping individuals, organizations, and communities transform themselves as they confront real-world challenges. Members share an interest in applying imagination, creative problem solving, and creative thinking. Membership: $175/year (Guild Member, includes one-year subscription to the Journal of Creative Behavior); $75/year (Associate Member). Members also receive discounted tele- and web-conferencing services.

Meetings/Conferences:
Annual Meetings: June

Publications:
The Journal of Creative Behavior. q.

Credit Professionals International *(1930)*
525B N. Laclede Station Road
St. Louis, MO 63119
Tel: (314)961-0031 *Fax:* (314)961-0040
E-Mail: creditpro@creditprofessionals.org
Web Site: www.creditprofessionals.org
Members: 500 individuals
Staff: 1
Annual Budget: $50-100,000
Contact Person: Charlotte Rancilio
E-Mail: creditpro@creditprofessionals.org

Historical Note
Formerly (1987) Credit Women - International and (1990) CWI: Credit Professionals. Members are persons employed in credit or collections departments of business firms, professional offices or companies. Membership: $55/year.

Meetings/Conferences:
Annual Meetings: Summer/600
2007 - Norfolk, VA(Renaissance Hotel)/June 21-24
2008 - Albuquerque, NM/June/75

Publications:
CPI Credit Connection. q. adv.
CPI Education Manual. a. adv.
Credit Professional Magazine. a. adv.

Credit Research Foundation *(1949)*
8840 Columbia 100 Pkwy.
Columbia, MD 21045
Tel: (410)740-5499 *Fax:* (410)740-4620
E-Mail: crf_info@crfonline.org
Web Site: www.crfonline.org
Members: 600 corporations
Staff: 4
Annual Budget: $500-1,000,000
President: William Terrence "Terry" Callahan, CCE, CRF
E-Mail: crf_info@crfonline.org

Historical Note
CRF is a membership organization dedicated to developing and enhancing the skills, talents and knowledge of credit professionals. Members are cash managers, credit executives, treasurers, and others responsible for any portion of the credit function in an organization. Sponsors research and education programs to advance the industry. Affiliated with the National Association of Credit Management. Membership: $795/year (corporate).

Meetings/Conferences:
Annual Meetings: Spring

Publications:
Credit Scoring.
Credit Decisioning Study.

Credit Union Executives Society *(1962)*
5510 Research Park Dr.
Madison, WI 53711-5377
Tel: (608)271-2664 *Fax:* (608)271-2303
Toll Free: (800)252 - 2664
E-Mail: cues@cues.org
Web Site: www.cues.org
Members: 4000 individuals
Staff: 53
Annual Budget: $10-25,000,000
President and Chief Executive Officer: Fred Johnson
Vice President, Publications: Mary Arnold
Senior Vice President and Chief Information Officer: Barbara Kachelski, CAE
Vice President, Institutes, Conferences, and Meetings: Krista Korfmacher, CMP
Vice President, Membership: Kristina Mattson
Senior Vice President and Chief Financial Officer: Dennis Porter
Chief Operating Officer and Senior Vice President: Linda Stemper-Johnson, CAE, CMP

Historical Note
Formerly (1970) CUES Managers Society. Members are credit union CEOs and other senior management personnel. CUES divisions include Directors Educational Forum and Financial Suppliers Forum. Membership: $595/year.

Meetings/Conferences:
Annual Meetings: June

Publications:
FYI Management Memo. w (email). adv.
Credit Union Management Magazine. m. adv.
Credit Union Directory. online.

Credit Union National Association *(1934)*
P.O. Box 431
Madison, WI 53701-0431
Tel: (608)231-4000 *Fax:* (608)231-4263
Toll Free: (800)356 - 9655
E-Mail: webmaster@cuna.org
Web Site: www.cuna.org
Members: 51 state credit union leagues
Staff: 310
Annual Budget: $25-50,000,000
President and Chief Executive Officer: Daniel A. Mica

Historical Note
Formerly (1970) CUNA International Inc. CUNA is the principal national trade association serving the nation's 12,300 credit unions through leagues in 50 states and the District of Columbia. Its affiliate organizations, including CUNA Service Group, provide financial products and services for credit unions. Certifies qualified credit union employees and awards the CCUE (Certified Credit Union Executive) designation. Sponsors and supports the Credit Union Legislative Action Council (CULAC). Street address is 5710 Mineral Point Road, Madison, WI 53701. Has an annual budget over $30 million.

Publications:
The Point.
Executive Newsletter. m.
The Credit Union Magazine. m. adv.
Strategic Planning.

Cremation Association of North America *(1913)*
401 N. Michigan Ave.
Chicago, IL 60611-4267
Tel: (312)245-1077 *Fax:* (312)321-4098
E-Mail: cana@smithbucklin.com
Web Site: www.cremationassociation.org
Members: 1300 companies
Staff: 3
Annual Budget: $500-1,000,000
Executive Director: Kevin Hacke

Historical Note
Formerly (1976) Cremation Association of America. Members are crematories, cemeteries, funeral directors and suppliers. Membership: $350/year (regular, consultant, association, supplier); $175/year (affiliate).

Meetings/Conferences:
Annual Meetings: August
2007 - San Francisco, CA(Fairmont Hotel)/Aug. 15-18/500
2008 - Montreal, QC, Canada(Le Centre Sheraton Montreal)/Aug. 6-9/500

Publications:
Cremationist Magazine. q. adv.
CANA Update Newsletter. bi-m. adv.

Crop Insurance Research Bureau *(1964)*
10800 Farley St., Suite 330
Overland Park, KS 66210-1412
Tel: (913)338-0470 *Fax:* (913)339-9336
Toll Free: (888)274 - 2472
E-Mail: cirb@cropinsurance.org
Web Site: www.cropinsurance.org
Members: 32 companies
Staff: 2
Annual Budget: $250-500,000
President: Paul L. Horel
E-Mail: cirb@cropinsurance.org

Historical Note
Members are crop insurance and other related companies. Sponsors CIRB-PAC and crop insurance industry research. Provides industry liaison to the U.S. Department of Agriculture.

Meetings/Conferences:
Annual Meetings: February

Publications:
CIRB Notes. bi-m. adv.

Crop Science Society of America *(1955)*
677 South Segoe Road
Madison, WI 53711
Tel: (608)273-8080 *Fax:* (608)273-2021
E-Mail: headquarters@agronomy.org
Web Site: www.crops.org
Members: 2868 individuals
Staff: 33
Annual Budget: $1-2,000,000
Executive Vice President: Dr. Ellen Bergfeld

Historical Note
Founded in 1955 and incorporated in Wisconsin in 1963, the Crop Science Society of America is an educational and scientific organization. CSSA's members work to advance the discipline of crop science by acquiring and disseminating information about crops in relations to seed genetics and plant breeding; crop physiology; crop production, quality and ecology; crop germplasm resources; and environmental quality. Membership: $83/year (individual member); $510/year (sustaining member).

Meetings/Conferences:
Annual Meetings: Fall, with American Soc. of Agronomy and Soil Science Soc. of America
2007 - New Orleans, LA(Convention Center)/Nov. 4-8/4000
2008 - Chicago, IL(Convention Center)/Oct. 26-30/4000

Publications:
Crop Science. bi-m. adv.
Journal of Environmental Quality. q. adv.
Journal of Natural Resources & Life Sciences Education. semi-a. adv.
Crop Science-Soil Science-Agronomy News. m. adv.

CropLife America *(1933)*
1156 15th St. NW, Suite 400
Washington, DC 20005
Tel: (202)296-1585 *Fax:* (202)463-0474
E-Mail: info@croplifeamerica.org
Web Site: www.croplifeamerica.org
Members: 86 companies
Staff: 35
Annual Budget: $5-10,000,000
President and Chief Executive Officer: Jay J. Vroom
Executive Vice President and Chief Operating Officer: Patrick Donnelly
Executive Vice President, General Counsel, and Secretary: Douglas T. Nelson
Director, Communications: A. Allen Noe
Senior Vice President, Government Affairs: George Rolofson

Historical Note
Formerly (1933) Agricultural Insecticides and Fungicides Manufacturers' Association, (1949) Agricultural Insecticide and Fungicide Association, (1994) National Agricultural Chemicals Association, and (2002) American Crop Protection Association. CropLife America is a trade association of the manufacturers, formulators, and distributors of agricultural crop protection, pest control, and biotechnology products. Membership is composed of companies that produce, sell and distribute virtually all the active ingredients used in crop protection chemicals. Has an annual budget of approximately $7.3 million.

Meetings/Conferences:
Annual Meetings: White Sulphur Springs, WV(Greenbrier Hotel)/Fall/650

Publications:
Annual Report. a.
Growing Possibilities. q.

Cross Country Ski Areas Association *(1976)*
259 Bolton Road

Winchester, NH 03470
Tel: (603)239-4341 *Fax:* (603)239-6387
Toll Free: (877)779 - 2754
E-Mail: ccsaa@xcski.org
Web Site: www.xcski.org
Members: 350 ski areas, suppliers and retailers
Staff: 2
Annual Budget: $100-250,000
President and Executive Director: Chris Frado
E-Mail: ccsaa@xcski.org

Historical Note

Formerly (1983) National Ski Touring Operators Association and (1988) Cross Country Ski Areas of America. CCSAA is the industry representative of cross country ski area operators. It was formed to promote cross country skiing in North America, protect the interests of ski area operators and establish safety guidelines for skiers. Membership: $350-500/year.

Meetings/Conferences:
Annual Meetings: always at member ski areas/April

Publications:
Nordic Network newsletter. q. adv.
Best of Cross Country Skiing Directory. a.

CrossSphere *(1951)*

Historical Note

National Tour Association became CrossSphere in 2004, but reverted to its original name in 2005.

Cruise Lines International Association *(1975)*
80 Broad St., Suite 1800
New York, NY 10004
Tel: (212)921-0066 *Fax:* (212)921-0549
E-Mail: clia@cruising.org
Web Site: www.cruising.org
Members: 19 cruise lines; 17,000 agencies
Staff: 21
Annual Budget: $5-10,000,000
President and Chief Executive Officer: Terry L. Dale
Executive Vice President and Chief Marketing Officer: Robert L. Sharak

Historical Note

Founded as International Passenger Ship Association; assumed its current name in 1984. CLIA promotes cruise and passenger vessel vacationing to selling agents and the buying public.

Meetings/Conferences:
Three Meetings Annually:

Cryogenic Engineering Conference *(1954)*
Fermilab, MS347
P.O. Box 500
Batavia, IL 60510-0500
Tel: (630)840-3238 *Fax:* (630)840-4989
Web Site: www.cec-icmc.org
Members: 1000 individuals
Annual Budget: $100-250,000
Secretary: Jay Theilacker

Historical Note

CEC members are scientists and engineers involved in research on extreme cold. Has no paid officers or full-time staff.

Meetings/Conferences:
Biennial Meetings: Odd Years
2007 – Chattanooga, TN(Convention Center)/July 17-20
2009 – Tucson, AZ(J.W. Marriott Starr Pass)/June 28-July 2

Publications:
Advances in Cryogenic Engineering. bien.

Cryogenic Society of America *(1964)*
c/o Huget Advertising
218 Lake St.
Oak Park, IL 60302
Tel: (708)383-6220 *Fax:* (708)383-9337
E-Mail: csa@cryogenicsociety.org
Web Site: www.cryogenicsociety.org
Members: 500 individuals
Staff: 2
Annual Budget: $50-100,000
Executive Director: Laurie Huget

Historical Note

Founded in Los Angeles in September 1964 and incorporated in California the same year. Reincorporated in Illinois in 1984. Absorbed the Helium Society in 1971. Promotes the engineering and science of low temperatures. Membership: $63/year (individual), $420/year minimum (corporate).

Meetings/Conferences:
Biennial Meetings:

Publications:
Cold Facts. q. adv.

CTIA - The Wireless Association *(1984)*
1400 16th St. NW, Suite 600
Washington, DC 20036
Tel: (202)785-0081 *Fax:* (202)785-0721
Web Site: www.ctia.org
Members: 396 companies
Staff: 100
Annual Budget: $10-25,000,000
President and Chief Executive Officer: Steve Largent
Senior Vice President and General Counsel: Michael F. Altschul
Vice President, Policy: Carolyn Brandon
Vice President, Finance and Administration: Rocco Carlitti
Vice President, Government Affairs: Jot Carpenter
Executive Vice President: Bobby Franklin
Vice President, Operations: Robert Mesirow
Vice President, External and State Affairs: K. Dane Snowden
Vice President, Public Affairs: John Walls

Historical Note

Founded as Cellular Communications Industry Association; later became Cellular Telecommunications Industry Association, and then Cellular Telecommunications and Internet Association before assuming its current name in 2004. Members are companies holding licenses, permits or having a reasonable expectation of receiving a cellular authorization from the FCC. Absorbed the Cellular Radio Communications Association in 1985. The CTIA represents more than 90% of licensed cellular operators, as well as manufacturers of cellular equipment and other interests providing services and products to the cellular industry. Membership: $1,000-135,000/year (based on size of market). Annual Budget approx. $10,000,000.

CUMREC International *(1956)*

Historical Note

Founded in 1956 and known as CUMREC (College University Machine Records Conference), the organization later became the College and University Computer Users Association (CUCUA). However, the organization maintains the acronymn CUMREC as its trade name. Members are adminstrators of records management and data processing in colleges and universities. Membership: $280/year.

CUNA International *(1934)*

Historical Note

See the Credit Union National Association.

Custom Electronic Design and Installation Association *(1989)*
7150 Winton Dr., Suite 300
Indianapolis, IN 46268
Toll Free: (800)669 - 5329
E-Mail: info@cedia.org
Web Site: www.cedia.org
Members: 3000 companies
Staff: 26
Annual Budget: $5-10,000,000
Executive Director: Billilynne Keller

Historical Note

Members are electronic systems professionals of custom designed electronic systems. Membership: $500/year (designers and installers, affiliates); $1,000/year (manufacturers, nat'l distributors); $300/year (sales representatives, consultants); $500-2,000/year (regional distributors).

Meetings/Conferences:
Annual Meetings: Fall

Publications:
Online Newsletter. w.
Membership Directory. y. adv.
Newsletter. q.

Custom Tailors and Designers Association of America *(1881)*
19 Mantua Road
Mt. Royal, NJ 08061
Tel: (856)423-1621 *Fax:* (856)423-3420
E-Mail: ctdahq@talley.com
Web Site: www.ctda.com
Members: 350 individuals
Annual Budget: $100-250,000
Executive Director: Meridyth M. Senes
E-Mail: ctdahq@talley.com

Historical Note

Trade association for men's custom tailoring industry. Formerly the Merchant Tailors and Designers Association of America. Membership: $325/year for tailors; %575/year for vendors.

Meetings/Conferences:
Annual Meetings: late Winter/200
2007 – Las Vegas, NV/Feb. 12-14

Customer Relations Institute *(1986)*
P.O. Box 880774
San Diego, CA 92168-0774
Tel: (858)486-8300 *Fax:* (858)486-8595
Toll Free: (800)544 - 0414
Web Site: www.tomhinton.com
Members: 500 individuals
Staff: 12
Annual Budget: $500-1,000,000

Historical Note

An international training and consulting consortium specializing in customer service, team building, leadership and performance excellence in the workplace. CRI also conducts customer satisfaction surveys.

Publications:
Heart and Soul: A Strategy for Business Renaissance. q.
Customer Focused Quality: What To Do On Monday Morning. q.
Leadership Lessons I Learned on the Links. q.
The Spirit of Service. q.

Customs and International Trade Bar Association *(1917)*
1875 Connecticut Ave. NW
Washington, DC 20009
Tel: (202)986-8011 *Fax:* (202)986-8102
E-Mail: myschwec@llgm.com
Web Site: www.citba.org
Members: 350 individuals
Annual Budget: $25-50,000
President: Melvin S. Schwechter

Historical Note

Formerly (1982) Association of the Customs Bar. Attorneys admitted to practice before the United States Court of International Trade (previously the United States Customs Court) and specializing in customs and international trade law in the United States. Membership: $75/year (individual).

Meetings/Conferences:
Annual Meetings: Annual and semi-annual; 75

Publications:
Newsletter. a.

CWLA - Child Mental Health Division *(1948)*
440 First St. NW, Third Floor
Washington, DC 20001-2085
Tel: (202)638-2952 *Fax:* (202)634-4004
E-Mail: lspears@cwla.org
Web Site: www.cwla.org/programs/bhd/mentalhealth.htm
Members: 100 individuals
President and Chief Executive Officer: Shay Bilchik
Vice President, Corporate Communications and Development: Linda Spears
E-Mail: lspears@cwla.org

Historical Note

Founded as American Association of Psychiatric Services for Children; became an affiliate of Child Welfare Leage of America in 1997 before assuming its current name.

Meetings/Conferences:
Annual Meetings: February-March
2007 – Washington, DC/Feb. 26-28
2008 – Washington, DC/Feb. 25-27

Publications:
Child Welfare Journal. 6/yr. adv.
Children's Voice. 6/yr. adv.

Cystic Fibrosis Foundation *(1955)*
6931 Arlington Road
Bethesda, MD 20814
Tel: (301)951-4422 *Fax:* (301)951-6378
Toll Free: (800)344 - 4823
E-Mail: info@cff.org
Web Site: www.cff.org
Members: 80 chapters
Staff: 550
President and Chief Executive Officer: Robert J. Beall, Ph.D.

Historical Note
The Cystic Fibrosis Foundation was established in 1955 to assure the development of the means to cure and control cystic fibrosis and to improve the quality of life for those with the disease.

Meetings/Conferences:
Annual Meetings: North American C.F. Conference

Publications:
Annual Report. a.
Commitment. bien.

Czech and Slovak-U.S. Business Council *(1974)*

Historical Note
A program of U.S. Chamber of Commerce, which provides administrative support.

Czechoslovak History Conference *(1975)*
Salisbury Univ.
Dept. of History
Salisbury, MD 21801
Tel: (410)543-6129 *Fax:* (410)677-5038
Members: 140 individuals
Staff: 1
Annual Budget: under $10,000
Secretary-Treasurer: Gregory C. Ference

Historical Note
CHC members are academics and others with an interest in the history of Czechoslovakia, its predecessor and successor states, and its historic peoples. Membership: $15/year (individual); $20/year (organization/company); $5/year (student).

Meetings/Conferences:
Annual Meetings: Held in conjunction with the American Ass'n for the Advacement of Slavic Studies (AAASS).
2007 – New Orleans, LA(Marriott)/Nov. 15-16
2008 – Philadelphia, PA(Marriott)/Nov. 20-23

Publications:
Newsletter. 2 times/year. adv.

Dairy Management *(1994)*
10255 W. Higgins Road, Suite 900
Rosemont, IL 60018-5616
Tel: (847)803-2000 *Fax:* (847)803-2077
Toll Free: (800)853 - 2479
Web Site: www.dairyinfo.com
Members: 20 member organization units
Staff: 86
Annual Budget: $1-2,000,000
Chief Executive Officer: Thomas P. Gallagher

Historical Note
Formed by the merger of the United Dairy Industry Association and the National Dairy Promotuion and Research Board, Dairy Management Inc. works to increase the demand for dairy products through the development and execution of an industry-wide, market-driven business plan that invests resources in a strategic manner and provides the best possible economic advantage to dairy farmers.

Meetings/Conferences:
Annual Meetings: September

Publications:
Catalogue of Nutrition Education Materials. a.
Dairy Council Digest. bi-m.
Nutrition News. q.

Dalton Floor Covering Market Association

Historical Note
Became American Floorcovering Alliance in 2001.

Dance Critics Association *(1974)*
Old Chelsea Station
P.O. Box 1882
New York, NY 10011
E-Mail: contactus@dancecritics.org
Web Site: www.dancecritics.org
Members: 266 individuals
Annual Budget: $25-50,000
Treasurer: Mary Cargill
E-Mail: contactus@dancecritics.org

Historical Note
Professionals who review dance either on a regular basis or freelance; teachers, historians, publicists and others interested in dance writing. Conducts workshops on subjects of practical interest to dance critics, also holds symposiums and mini-conferences. Membership: $40/year (individual); $20/year (student); $65/year (organization).

Meetings/Conferences:
Annual Meetings: usually New York, NY/June-July

Publications:
DCA News. q.
Membership Directory. bien.

Dance Educators of America *(1932)*
P.O. Box 607
Pelham, NY 10803-0607
Tel: (914)636-3200 *Fax:* (914)636-5895
Toll Free: (800)229 - 3868
E-Mail: dea@deadance.com
Web Site: www.deadance.com
Members: 2000 individuals
Staff: 4
Annual Budget: $100-250,000
Executive Director: Vickie Sheer
E-Mail: dea@deadance.com
Administrator, Training School: Charles M. Kelley
E-Mail: dea@deadance.com

Historical Note
Promotes the education of teachers in the performing arts, including dance and stage arts. Conducts seminars and workshops to advance the theory and practice of dance education. Membership: $150/year (individual); $250/year (couple).

Meetings/Conferences:
Three Meetings Annually: Summer, various locations
2007 – Knoxville, TN/June 24-29/400
2007 – Atlantic City, NJ/June 25-29
2007 – Las Vegas, NV/June 16-21

Publications:
DEA Tap Dancing Dictionary. a. adv.
DEA Workshops and Competitions. a. adv.

Dance Masters of America *(1884)*
P.O. Box 610533
Bayside, NY 11631
Tel: (718)225-4013 *Fax:* (718)225-4293
E-Mail: dmamann@aol.com
Web Site: www.dma-national.org
Members: 2500 individuals
Staff: 2
Annual Budget: $250-500,000
Executive Secretary: Robert Mann
E-Mail: dmamann@aol.com

Historical Note
An organization of dance teachers. Formerly (1926) known as the American National Association, Masters of Dancing. Membership: $62/year, plus local chapter dues.

Meetings/Conferences:
Annual Meetings: July/500

Publications:
DMA Bulletin. q.
DMA Bulletin. bi-m. adv.
DMA Magazine. q. adv.

Dance/USA *(1982)*
1111 16th St. NW
Suite 300
Washington, DC 20036
Tel: (202)833-1717 *Fax:* (202)833-2686
E-Mail: danceusa@danceusa.org
Web Site: www.danceusa.org
Members: 358 organizations and individuals
Staff: 9
Annual Budget: $1-2,000,000
Executive Director: Andrea Snyder
Deputy Director: Bob Fogelgren
Director, Member Services: Ann Norris

Historical Note
Dance/USA, the national service organization for not-for-profit, professional dance, seeks to advance the artform of dance by addressing the needs, concerns and interests of professional dance. Dance/USA members include ballet, modern, ethnic, jazz, culturally specific, traditional and tap companies as well as dance service organizations and other organizations concerned with non-profit professional dance. Membership: $50-250/year (individual); $150-$8,700/year (organization/company).

Meetings/Conferences:
2007 – Chicago, IL/June 14-16/400

Publications:
Dance/USA Journal. 2/year.
Member Bulletin (online). m.
Spin (online). w.

Dangerous Goods Advisory Council *(1978)*
1100 H St. NW, Suite 740
Washington, DC 20005
Tel: (202)289-4550 *Fax:* (202)289-4074
E-Mail: info@dgac.org
Web Site: www.hmac.org
Members: 210 companies
Staff: 10
Annual Budget: $1-2,000,000
President: Alan I. Roberts
Director, Education and Training/Course Instructor: E. Vaughn Arthur
Vice President and Director, Technical Scvs.: Michael Morrissette

Historical Note
Founded as Hazardous Materials Advisory Council, a committee of the Transportation Association of America; became an autonomous organization in 1978, and assumed its current name in 2003. DGAC represents shippers, carriers of all modes, container manufacturers and reconditioners, emergency response and waste clean-up companies, and other firms and associations involved in hazardous materials transportation. Membership: dues based on gross annual sales or revenues.

Meetings/Conferences:
Semi-Annual Meetings: May and November

Publications:
Dangerous Goods Dispatch. m.
Federal Register Extract. bi-m.

Danish-American Chamber of Commerce (USA) *(1931)*
885 Second Ave., 18th Fl.
New York, NY 10017
Tel: (212)705-4945 *Fax:* (212)754-1904
E-Mail: daccny@daccny.com
Web Site: www.daccny.com
Members: 160 companies
Staff: 1
Annual Budget: $50-100,000
Executive Director: Nargis McGuinness
E-Mail: daccny@daccny.com

Historical Note
Formed through a merger of the Danish-American Trade Council (1964) and the Danish Luncheon Club (1931). Members are concentrated in the New York City area. Membership: $80/year (individual); $350/year (corporate), sustaining members $1,000/year.

Meetings/Conferences:
Monthly Meetings: in New York City

Publications:
Newsletter. 5/year. adv.

Data Interchange Standards Association *(1987)*
7600 Leesburg Pike, Suite 430
Falls Church, VA 22043
Tel: (703)970-4480 *Fax:* (703)970-4488
E-Mail: info@disa.org
Web Site: www.disa.org
Members: 800 companies
Staff: 12
Annual Budget: $5-10,000,000
President and Chief Executive Officer: Jerry C. Connors

Historical Note
DISA is a not-for-profit corporation that serves the electronic commerce community by providing education about EDI and related technologies, and

managing the development of industry standards for electronic data interchange.

Data Management Association International *(1988)*
P.O. Box 5786
Bellevue, WA 98006-5786
Tel: (425)562-2636 *Fax:* (425)562-0376
E-Mail: damai@dama.org
Web Site: www.dama.org
Members: 3000 individuals
Annual Budget: $25-50,000
Vice President, Communications: Peter Aiken

Historical Note
Founded as Data Administration Management Association International; assumed its current name in 2002. Promotes understanding, development, and practice of managing information and data as a key enterprise asset.

Meetings/Conferences:
Annual Meetings: Spring

Publications:
DAMA News. bi-m.
DM Review Magazine.

Decision Sciences Institute *(1969)*
Georgia State Univ., College of Business
35 Broad St.
Atlanta, GA 30303
Tel: (404)651-4073 *Fax:* (404)651-4008
Web Site: www.decisionsciences.org
Members: 3500 individuals
Staff: 5
Annual Budget: $500-1,000,000
Executive Director: Carol J. Latta
E-Mail: clatta@gsu.edu

Historical Note
Formerly (1985) American Institute for Decision Sciences. Membership consists mainly of business school faculties and management specialists who use quantitative and behavioral techniques to apply theories of administrative decision-making. Membership: $70/year (U.S.); $70/year (U.S. and international).

Meetings/Conferences:
Annual Meetings: Fall/1,500

Publications:
Decision Sciences Journal of Innovative Education. bien.
Decision Line. bi-m. adv.
Decision Sciences Journal. q. adv.

Deep Foundations Institute *(1976)*
326 Lafayette Ave.
Hawthorne, NJ 07506
Tel: (973)423-4030 *Fax:* (973)423-4031
E-Mail: dfihq@dfi.org
Web Site: www.dfi.org
Members: 1700 individuals and organizations
Staff: 4
Annual Budget: $1-2,000,000
Executive Director: Theresa Rappaport

Historical Note
Incorporated in New Jersey in January, 1976. Concerned with the design, installation and stability of deep foundations of all types. Members are project owners, consulting engineers, contractors, educators and suppliers. Membership: $95/year (individual); corporate membership scaled by sales volume and/or number of employees.

Meetings/Conferences:
Annual Meetings: Fall/150-250
2007 – Colorado Springs, CO(The Broadmoor)/Oct. 11-13/350

Publications:
Deep Foundations Magazine. q. adv.
Membership Roster. bi-a.
Foundations Industry Desk Directory. bi-a. adv.

Defense Credit Union Council *(1963)*
601 Pennsylvania Ave. NW, Suite 600
Washington, DC 20004-2601
Tel: (202)638-3950 *Fax:* (202)638-3410
E-Mail: dcuc1@cuna.com
Web Site: www.dcuc.org
Members: 300 credit unions
Staff: 4
Annual Budget: $250-500,000
President and Chief Executive Officer: Roland Arteaga
E-Mail: dcuc1@cuna.com

Historical Note
Members are credit unions serving military and civilian employees of the Department of Defense.

Meetings/Conferences:
Annual Meetings:

Publications:
Alert. m. adv.
Director of Defense Credit Unions. bien.
Statistical Report of Defense Credit Unions. a.

Defense Fire Protection Association *(1984)*
P.O. Box 1310
Falls Church, VA 22041-0310
Tel: (703)521-3926 *Fax:* (703)521-0849
E-Mail: dfpa@aol.com
Web Site: www.dfpa.org
Staff: 3
Executive Director: Ron Fisher
E-Mail: dfpa@aol.com

Defense Research Institute *(1960)*
150 N. Michigan Ave., Suite 300
Chicago, IL 60601
Tel: (312)795-1101 *Fax:* (312)795-0747
Toll Free: (800)667 - 8108
E-Mail: dri@dri.org
Web Site: www.dri.org
Members: 22000 individuals
Staff: 28
Annual Budget: $5-10,000,000
Executive Director: John R. Kouris
Meetings and Customer Svc.: Tonya Almond
Director, Education: Jennifer Cout

Historical Note
Members are defense lawyers, insurance and manufacturing executives, and defendants. The Institute's primary purpose is to increase the professional skill and enlarge the knowledge of defense lawyers. Products and professional liability, insurance, environmental and equal opportunity law are some of the subjects with which members are concerned. Operates an arbitration service and provides a Brief Bank Index and Expert Witness Index. Membership: $125/year.

Meetings/Conferences:
Annual Meetings: With Internat'l Ass'n of Defense Counsel

Publications:
For the Defense. m.

Delta Dental Plans Association *(1965)*
1515 W. 22nd St., Suite 1200
Oak Brook, IL 60523
Tel: (630)574-6001 *Fax:* (630)574-6999
E-Mail: cs@ddpa.org
Web Site: www.deltadental.com
Members: 37 dental plans
Staff: 19
Annual Budget: $5-10,000,000
President and Chief Executive Officer: Kim E. Volk
Vice President and Chief Financial Officer: Stephen White
E-Mail: swhite@ddpa.org

Historical Note
The professional association of Delta Dental. Delta Dental is one of the country's largest dental benefits carriers, and is composed of a nationalwide system of dental health service organizations.

Meetings/Conferences:
Annual Meetings: June

Publications:
Newsletters. 6/yr.
Membership Directory. a.

Delta Nu Alpha Transportation Fraternity *(1940)*
1451 Elm Hill Pike, Suite 255
Nashville, TN 37210
Tel: (615)360-6863 *Fax:* (615)360-1891
E-Mail: carolh24@msn.com
Web Site: www.deltanualpha.org
Members: 500 individuals
Staff: 4
Administrator: Carol Hackett

Historical Note
Professional fraternity. Membership: $35-$125/year (individual).

Meetings/Conferences:
Annual Meetings: Fall

Publications:
Journal of Transportation. semi-a. adv.
Proceedings. a.
The Alphian. m.. adv.

Delta Omicron *(1909)*
910 Church St.
Jefferson City, TN 37760
Tel: (865)471-6155
E-Mail: doexecsec@aol.com
Web Site: www.delta-omicron.org
Members: 26000 individuals
Staff: 1
Annual Budget: $25-50,000
Executive Secretary: Julie Hensley
E-Mail: doexecsec@aol.com

Historical Note
An international music fraternity founded on September 6, 1909 at the Cincinnati Conservatory of Music and incorporated in the State of Ohio the same year.

Meetings/Conferences:
Triennial Meetings: Summer

Publications:
The Wheel of Delta Omicron. q.
The Whistle. a.

Delta Phi Epsilon *(1920)*
3401 Prospect St. NW
Washington, DC 20007
Tel: (202)337-9702
Web Site: www.deltaphiepsilon.net
Members: 7000 individuals
General Secretary: Terence Boyle

Historical Note
Professional foreign service fraternity.

Publications:
The Sun. q.
The Tramp. a.
The Galley. a.
Membership Directory. bien.

Delta Pi Epsilon *(1936)*
P.O. Box 4340
Little Rock, AR 72214
Tel: (501)219-1866 *Fax:* (501)219-1876
Web Site: www.dpe.org
Members: 11000 individuals
Staff: 2
Annual Budget: $100-250,000
Executive Director: Dr. Robert B. Mitchell
E-Mail: rbmitchell@ualr.edu

Historical Note
Professional society in graduate business education. Founded at New York University in 1936 and incorporated in the State of New York, December 3, 1937. Reincorporated in Minnesota in 1983 and in Arkansas in 1988. Members are teachers of business subjects. National Membership: $30/year.

Meetings/Conferences:
Annual Meetings: November

Publications:
DPE Journal. 3/year.

Delta Sigma Delta *(1882)*
296 15th Ave.
Nekoosa, WI 54457
Tel: (715)325-6320 *Fax:* (715)325-3057
Toll Free: (800)335 - 8744
Web Site: www.deltsig.com
Members: 28000 individuals
Staff: 2
Annual Budget: $250-500,000
Scribe: John H. Prey, D.D.S.
E-Mail: supremescribe@delstig.com

Historical Note
A professional dental fraternity founded at the University of Michigan on November 15, 1882. Membership: By invitation only.

Meetings/Conferences:
Annual Meetings: Fall/150-200
2007 – San Francisco, CA/Sept. 27-30

Publications:
Desmos of Delta Sigma Delta. q.

Delta Sigma Pi *(1907)*
330 S. Campus Ave., Box 230
Oxford, OH 45056-0230
Tel: (513)523-1907 *Fax:* (513)523-7292
E-Mail: centraloffice@dspnet.org
Web Site: www.dspnet.org
Members: 161000 individuals
Staff: 16
Annual Budget: $1-2,000,000
Executive Director: William C. Schilling
Associate Executive Director: Shandra R. Gray

Historical Note
Professional fraternity, commerce and business administration, founded at New York University November 7, 1907.

Meetings/Conferences:
Biennial Meetings: Odd years/750

Publications:
The Deltasig. q.

Delta Society *(1977)*
875 124th Ave. NE, Suite 101
Bellevue, WA 98005
Tel: (425)679-5500 *Fax:* (425)679-5539
E-Mail: info@deltasociety.org
Web Site: www.deltasociety.org
Members: 10000 individuals
Staff: 11
Annual Budget: $1-2,000,000
President and Chief Executive Officer: Lawrence J. Norvell
Vice President, Finance: Jon Eastlake

Historical Note
The Society is an international, educational, research and service resource on the relationships between people, animals and nature. Members include veterinarians, psychiatrists, health workers, volunteers, administrators, teachers, and pet owners. Membership: $50/year, with subscription.

Meetings/Conferences:
Annual Meetings: May

Publications:
Pet Partners Newsletter (part of InterActions). 2/yr.
InterActions. 2/yr.

Delta Theta Phi *(1900)*
38640 Butternut Ridge Road
Elyria, OH 44035
Tel: (440)458-4381 *Fax:* (440)458-4380
Toll Free: (800)783 - 2600
E-Mail: dtpoffice@alltel.net
Web Site: www.deltathetaphi.org
Members: 100000 individuals
Staff: 3
Annual Budget: $100-250,000
Executive Director: Catherine K. Smith

Historical Note
Professional legal fraternity formed at the Cleveland Law School of Baldwin Wallace College in 1900 as Delta Phi Delta. On September 27, 1913 created Delta Theta Phi by a merger of Alpha Kappa Phi, Delta Phi Delta and Theta Lambda Phi. Merged with Sigma Nu Phi legal fraternity in 1989. Membership: $60 (one-time student initation fee); $60 (alumni one-time fee). Alumni dues may also apply.

Meetings/Conferences:
Biennial Meetings: Odd years in Summer

Publications:
Adelphia Law Journal. a.
The Paper Book. q.

Delta Waterfowl Foundation *(1911)*
P.O. Box 3128
Bismarck, ND 58502
Tel: (701)222-8857
E-Mail: delta@deltawaterfowl.org
Web Site: www.deltawaterfowl.org
Members: 40000 companies and individuals
Staff: 20
Annual Budget: $2-5,000,000
President: Rob Olson
E-Mail: delta@deltawaterfowl.org

Historical Note
Formerly North American Wildlife Foundation (1993). Aims to help maintain, restore and advance sound natural resource and wildlife management programs. Supported by both individual and corporate members interested in its aims.

Publications:
Delta Waterfowl Report. q. adv.

Dental Dealers of America *(1944)*
123 S. Broad St., Suite 1960
Philadelphia, PA 19109-1020
Tel: (215)731-9975 *Fax:* (215)731-9984
Members: 45 wholesale distributors
Staff: 2
Annual Budget: $25-50,000
Executive Director: Edward B. Shils, Ph.D.
President: Fred Salzman

Historical Note
Founded to help educate the dental industry suppliers about industry problems and marketing and distribution trends. Membership: $275-$10,000/year (organization).

Meetings/Conferences:
Annual Meetings: February in Chicago at the Fairmont, held in conjunction with the Dental Manufacturers of America. Meeting in the Fall held with the American Dental Association.

Publications:
DDA Membership Directory. bi-a.

Dental Group Management Association *(1951)*
2525 E. Arizona Biltmore Circle, Suite 127
Phoenix, AZ 85016
Tel: (602)381-8980 *Fax:* (602)381-1093
E-Mail: dgma@aadgp.org
Web Site: www.dgma.org
Members: 200 individuals
Staff: 1
Annual Budget: $10-25,000
Executive Director: Robert A. Hankin, Ph.D.

Historical Note
Dental group business managers and others concerned with group practice management. Membership: $150/year.

Meetings/Conferences:
Annual Meetings: With American Academy of Dental Group

Publications:
Directory. a.
DGMA Communicator Newsletter. q. adv.

Dental Manufacturers of America *(1932)*

Historical Note
Merged with American Dental Trade Association to form Dental Trade Alliance in 2004.

Dental Trade Alliance *(1882)*
4222 King St. West
Alexandria, VA 22302-1597
Tel: (703)379-7755 *Fax:* (703)931-9429
E-Mail: info@dentaltradealliance.org
Web Site: www.dmanews.org
Members: 200 companies
Staff: 5
Annual Budget: $1-2,000,000
Chief Executive Officer: Gary W. Price
E-Mail: info@dentaltradealliance.org

Historical Note
Founded as American Dental Trade Association; combined with the Dental Manufacturers Association and assumed its current name in 2004. Membership: $1,250-49,000/year.

Meetings/Conferences:
Annual Meetings: Fall/450

Publications:
Update. bi-m.

Dermatology Nurses' Association *(1982)*
E. Holly Ave., Box 56
Pitman, NJ 08071-0056
Tel: (856)256-2330 *Fax:* (856)589-7463
Toll Free: (800)454 - 4362
E-Mail: dna@ajj.com
Web Site: www.dna.inurse.com
Members: 2200 individuals
Staff: 2
Annual Budget: $500-1,000,000
Executive Director: Cynthia Hnatiuk, EdD, RN, CAE

Historical Note
Established as a non-profit organization in 1981, the DNA serves its members through a national structure, regionally and locally in the U.S. and internationally. Licensed registered nurses, licensed practice nurses, licensed vocational nurses and individuals involved or interested in the care of the dermatology patient are eligible for membership in the association. Membership: $60/year (Active); $50/year (Associate).

Meetings/Conferences:
Annual Meetings: Spring

Publications:
Dermatology Nursing. bi-m.
DNA Focus. bi-m. adv.
Product Guide. a.
Membership Directory. a.

Design Management Institute *(1976)*
29 Temple Pl., Second Floor
Boston, MA 02111-1350
Tel: (617)338-6380 *Fax:* (617)338-6570
Web Site: www.dmi.org
Members: 1200 design teams and firms
Staff: 10
Annual Budget: $1-2,000,000
President: Earl N. Powell
E-Mail: epowell@dmi.org
Systems Manager: Christopher Hancock
E-Mail: cthancock@dmi.org
Vice President, Operations: John Tobin
E-Mail: jtobin@dmi.org

Historical Note
Members are in-house design teams and consulting design firms. Sponsors the Centers for Research, Education & Information, and other operations focusing on current issues in design management. Membership: $400/year (individual); $300/year (academic); $1,600-6,400/year (company).

Publications:
DMI News. bi-m. adv.
Design Management Journal. q. adv.
Directory of Members. a.

Design Professionals Association *(1986)*

Historical Note
Address unknown in 2006.

Design-Build Institute of America *(1993)*
1100 H St. NW, Suite 500
Washington, DC 20005-5476
Tel: (202)682-0110 *Fax:* (202)682-5877
Toll Free: (866)692 - 0110
E-Mail: dbia@dbia.org
Web Site: www.dbia.org
Members: 900 companies/organizations
Staff: 15
Annual Budget: $2-5,000,000
President: Walker Lee Evey
Chief Financial Officer: Timothy J. Fargo
E-Mail: TFargo@dbia.org
Vice President, Education and Professional Development: Lisa Washington
Director, Information and Edtior, DATELINE: Jennifer Whedener

Historical Note
DBIA is a professional association founded to promote Design-Build project delivery and to develop practices for users and practitioners. Design-Build includes professional design and construction (and frequently additional services such as finance, real estate and operation) under a single source responsiblity contract. Members include companies and individuals concerned with integrated architecture, engineering and construction services. Membership: $100-$7,500/year; dues vary based on annual volume.

Meetings/Conferences:
Annual Meetings: Fall

Publications:
Design Build Magazine. q. adv.
DATELINE. m. adv.
PerSpective.

Destination Marketing Association International *(1914)*

2025 M St. NW, Suite 500
Washington, DC 20036-3309
Tel: (202)296-7888 *Fax:* (202)296-7889
E-Mail: mnelson@destinationmarketing.org
Web Site: www.destinationmarketing.org
Members: 550 convention & visitor bureaus
Staff: 16
Annual Budget: $2-5,000,000
President and Chief Executive Officer: Michael D. Gehrisch
Vice President, Information Technology: Tom Chao
Executive Vice President: Elaine Rosquist
Vice President, Membership and Business Development: Sandi Talley

Historical Note

Formerly (1975) International Association of Convention Bureaus and then International Association of Convention and Visitors Bureaus; assumed current name in 2005. Represents 600 member bureaus in over 20 countries. Founded in 1914 to promote sound professional practices in the solicitation and servicing of meetings and conventions. Runs the on-line Meetings Industry Network (MINT(R)) with a broad spectrum of data on client meetings, sponsors two "Destinations Showcase (TM)" tradeshow events where IACVB members exhibit their destinations to meeting professionals, offers educational programs for members, provides public relations for the industry, and represents CVBs on legislative and regulatory issues. Member bureaus represent all significant travel/tourism-related businesses at the local and regional level, and also serve as the primary contact points in their destinations for a large number of convention and meeting professionals and tour operators. Is also involved with a variety of travel and tourism organizations such as the Travel Industry Association of America and many meetings- and convention-oriented associations such as Meeting Professionals International, American Society of Association Executives, and the Professional Convention Management Association.

Meetings/Conferences:

Annual Meetings: Summer
2007 – Pittsburgh, PA/July 18-21/900

Developmental Disabilities Nurses Association *(1992)*

1733 H St, Suite 330
PMB 1214
Blaine, WA 98230
Toll Free: (800)888 - 6733
E-Mail: ddnahq@aol.com
Web Site: www.ddna.org
Members: 1200 individuals
Staff: 1
Annual Budget: $250-500,000
Executive Director: Randy Bryson

Historical Note

DDNA members are registered, licensed practical and licensed vocational nurses with an interest in developmental disabilities nursing. Administers a professional certification program for achievement of the Certified Developmental Disabilities Nurse (CDDN) credential. Membership: $55/year (individual).

Publications:

DDNA News Network. q. adv.

Devon Cattle Association *(1918)*

11035 Waverly
Olathe, KS 66061
Tel: (913)583-1723
E-Mail: reddevons@netzero.com
Web Site: http://devoncattle.com
Members: 96 individuals
Staff: 2
Annual Budget: $10-25,000
Secretary: Sandy Brashears
E-Mail: reddevons@netzero.com

Historical Note

Breeders of Devon beef cattle. Formerly (1971) American Devon Cattle Club.

Meetings/Conferences:

Annual Meetings: Fall

Publications:

DCA Newsletter. q.

Diamond Council of America *(1944)*

3212 W. End Ave., Suite 202
Nashville, TN 37203
Tel: (615)385-5301 *Fax:* (615)385-4955
Toll Free: (877)283 - 5669
Web Site: www.diamondcouncil.org/
Members: 64 exec members, 1875 locations
Annual Budget: $250-500,000
President and Chief Executive Officer: Terry Chandler

Historical Note

Conducts correspondence course and certifies employees in diamonds and colored stones. Supplies members with merchandising tools, advertising copy, displays, etc. to feature diamonds and other gems as a professional specialty.

Publications:

The DCA Jeweler. bi-m.

Diamond Manufacturers and Importers Association of America *(1932)*

630 Fifth Ave., Suite 2406
New York, NY 10111
Tel: (212)245-3160
Toll Free: (800)223 - 2244
Web Site: www.dmia.net
Members: 150 companies
Staff: 2
Annual Budget: $10-25,000
President: Ronald J. Friedman

Historical Note

Formerly the Diamond Manufacturers Association. Members are importers, cutters and polishers of rough diamonds.

Dibasic Esters Group *(1995)*

1850 M St. NW
Suite 700
Washington, DC 20036-5810
Tel: (202)721-4145 *Fax:* (202)296-8120
E-Mail: rossj@socma.com
Members: 3 companies
Staff: 2
Annual Budget: $250-500,000
Executive Director: Jessica Ross

Historical Note

An affiliate of the Synthetic Organic Chemical Manufacturers Association, DBE was formed to address the EPA's and Consumer Product Safety Commission's testing consent order under TSCA Section 4 for three Dibasic Esters: Dimethyl Succinate (DMS);
Dimethyl Glutarate (DMG) and Dimethyl Adipate (DMA).

Diecasting Development Council *(1987)*

Historical Note

An affiliate of North American Die Casting Association, which provides administrative support.

Dielectrics and Electrical Insulation Society

Historical Note

A technical society of the Institute of Electrical and Electronics Engineers (IEEE). Membership in the Society, open only to IEEE members, includes subscription to a technical periodical in the field published by IEEE. All administrative support is provided by IEEE.

Dietary Managers Association *(1960)*

406 Surrey Woods Dr.
St. Charles, IL 60174-2386
Tel: (630)587-6336 *Fax:* (630)587-6308
Toll Free: (800)323 - 1908
E-Mail: info@dmaonline.org
Web Site: www.dmaonline.org
Members: 16000 individuals
Staff: 23
Annual Budget: $1-2,000,000
Executive Director: William S. St. John, CAE
E-Mail: info@dmaonline.org
Financial Administrator: Jennifer Karson
E-Mail: info@dmaonline.org

Historical Note

Formerly (1984) the Hospital, Institution and Educational Food Service Society DMA is an organization of professionals dedicated to excellence in the food service industry. Sponsors and supports the DMA Political Action Committee. Membership: $70/year (active); $75/year (associate); $90/year (certified).

Meetings/Conferences:

Annual Meetings: August
2007 – San Diego, CA(Hyatt Regency)/July 1-5
2008 – Philadelphia, PA(Wyndham Philadelphia)/July 27-31
2009 – Atlanta, GA(Hyatt Regency)/Aug. 9-13

Publications:

Dietary Manager Magazine. 10/yr. adv.

Digital Imaging Marketing Association

Historical Note

A section of the Photo Marketing Ass'n-Internat'l.

Digital Media Association *(1998)*

1029 Vermont Ave. NW, Suite 850
Washington, DC 20005-6320
Tel: (202)775-2660
E-Mail: info@digmedia.org
Web Site: www.digmedia.org
Staff: 2
Executive Director: Jonathan Potter

Historical Note

DiMA serves the digital media industry through its representation and advocacy of Internet related issues. Membership fees start at $20,000 for Board members to $10,000 for voting members.

Digital Printing and Imaging Association *(1992)*

10015 Main St.
Fairfax, VA 22031-3489
Tel: (703)385-1339 *Fax:* (703)359-1336
Toll Free: (888)385 - 3588
E-Mail: assist@sgia.org
Web Site: www.dpia.org
Members: 900 companies
Staff: 4
Annual Budget: $1-2,000,000
President: Mike Robertson
Vice President, Conventions and Conferences: Sylvia Hall
Vice President, Government Affairs: Marci Kinter
Director, Communications and Service Development: Daniel Marx

Historical Note

Formerly an independent association, DPI affiliated with the Screenprinting and Graphic Imaging Association International in 1995. DPI's membership represents large format digital output firms, reprographic companies, photo labs, screen printers, service bureaus, quick printers and other commercial printers/suppliers. Its mission is to serve as a forum to advance the electronic imaging field by: helping all graphic industry segments that provide or use digital printing devices to become more productive; responding to industry needs and concerns; promoting progress and excellence in digital pre-press, printing, and imaging, as well as related processes and techniques; and improving the industry's ability to serve its markets and customers. Membership: $250-$1,000/year (organization/company).

Meetings/Conferences:

Annual Meetings: Meetings held in conjunction with SGIA.
2007 – Orlando, FL(Orange County Convention Center)/Oct. 24-27
2008 – Atlanta, GA(Georgia World Congress Center)/Oct. 15-18
2009 – New Orleans, LA(Morial Convention Center)/Nov. 18-21
2010 – Las Vegas, NV(Las Vegas Convention Center)/Oct. 12-15

Publications:

KwikScan. 8/year.
Membership Directory. a.
Industry Update Weekly. w.
RIP Newsletter. q.

Diplomatic and Consular Officers, Retired *(1952)*

1801 F St. NW
Washington, DC 20006-4497
Tel: (202)682-0500 *Fax:* (202)842-3295
Toll Free: (800)344 - 9127
E-Mail: dacor@dacorbacon.org
Members: 3000 individuals

Staff: 4
Annual Budget: $250-500,000
Executive Director: Richard McKee

Historical Note
Members are principally active and retired Foreign Service officers. Now accepts members with overseas experience from other government agencies.

Meetings/Conferences:
Annual Meetings: Washington, DC in Spring.

Publications:
Dacor Bulletin. m.
Dacor Directory of Members. bien.

Direct Marketing Agency Council *(1917)*

Historical Note
An affiliate of Direct Marketing Association, which provides administrative support.

Direct Marketing Association *(1917)*

1120 Ave. of the Americas
New York, NY 10036-6700
Tel: (212)768-7277 *Fax:* (212)302-6714
E-Mail: dma@the-dma.org
Web Site: www.the-dma.org
Members: 6517 individuals
Staff: 150
Annual Budget: $25-50,000,000
President and Chief Executive Officer: John A. Greco, Jr.
Senior Vice President and Chief Financial Officer: Marcel Schloss

Historical Note
Formerly (1983) Direct Mail/Marketing Association and Direct Mail Advetising Association. Absorbed the Business Mail Foundation and the Mailing List Users and Suppliers Association. Sponsors and supports the DMA Political Action Committee and the DMA Nonprofit Federation. Has an annual budget of approximately $35 million.

Meetings/Conferences:
Annual Meetings: Fall

Publications:
DMA Insider.
Fact Book. a.
Washington Report (Members Only). m.
Direct Line (Members Only). 10/year. adv.
Journal of Direct Marketing. q.
Dateline: DMA (Members Only). q.
Washington Update. m.
The DMA Publications Catalog. bien.

Direct Marketing Insurance and Financial Services Council

1120 Avenue of the Americas
New York, NY 10036-8096
Tel: (212)768-7277 *Fax:* (212)768-4546
Members: 3600 member companies
Annual Budget: $100-250,000
Staff Contact: Kevin Thurman

Historical Note
DMIFSC is a council of Direct Marketing Association, which provides administrative support. DMIFSC members are DMA members who market insurance and financial services.

Meetings/Conferences:
Annual Meetings: April

Publications:
DMIC Councilgram. q.
DMIC Roster. a.

Direct Selling Association *(1910)*

1667 K St. NW
Suite 1100
Washington, DC 20006-1660
Tel: (202)452-8866 *Fax:* (202)452-9010
E-Mail: info@dsa.org
Web Site: www.dsa.org
Members: 500 companies
Staff: 35
Annual Budget: $5-10,000,000
President and Chief Executive Officer: Neil H. Offen, CAE
Vice President, Education and Meeting Services: Melissa K. Brunton
Director, International Department: Kimberly Harris Blinton
Vice President, Finance: Kathy Lindner
Executive Vice President and Chief Operating Officer: Joseph N. Mariano
Director, Communications and Media Relations: Amy Robinson

Historical Note
Formerly (1969) National Association of Direct Selling Companies. Manufacturers and distributors retailing products via door-to-door, party plan and other direct-to-consumer methods. Supports the Direct Selling Association Political Action Committee and the Direct Selling Education Foundation. Serves as the Secretariat for the World Federation of Direct Selling Associations. Membership: $1,500-135,000/year (corporate).

Meetings/Conferences:
Annual Meetings: Spring/550

Publications:
Action Needed Bulletin. irreg.
Advisory Memorandum. irreg.
News from Neil. m.
Legigram. q.
State Status Sheet. w.

Directional Crossing Contractors Association *(1991)*

13355 Noel Road, Suite 1940
Dallas, TX 75240
Tel: (972)386-9544 *Fax:* (972)386-9547
Members: 95 organizations
Staff: 2
Executive Secretary: Richard A. Gump, Jr.

Historical Note
DCCA is a trade association promoting the interests of the directional crossing contracting industry. Membership: $1,500/year (regular); $1,000/year (associate); $150/year (technical affiliate); $1,000/year (industry affiliate).

Meetings/Conferences:
Semi-annual Meetings: Spring and Fall

Directors Educational Forum

Historical Note
A division of the Credit Union Executives Society

Directors Guild of America *(1936)*

7920 Sunset Blvd.
Los Angeles, CA 90046
Tel: (310)289-2000 *Fax:* (310)289-2029
Toll Free: (800)421 - 4173
Web Site: www.dga.org
Members: 13400 individuals
Staff: 85
National Executive Director: Jay D. Roth
President: Michael Apted
Chief Financial Officer: Reginald D. Barnes
Director, Communications and Media Relations: Morgan Rumpf

Historical Note
Independent labor union.

Meetings/Conferences:
Biennial meetings: Odd years

Publications:
DGA Directory of Members. a. adv.
DGA Quarterly. q. adv.
Commercial Agreement.
Basic Agreement.

Directors of Health Promotion and Public Health Education *(1946)*

1101 15th St. NW, Suite 601
Washington, DC 20005
Tel: (202)659-2230 *Fax:* (202)659-2339
E-Mail: director@dhpe.org
Web Site: www.dhpe.org
Members: 55 individuals
Staff: 2
Annual Budget: $500-1,000,000
Executive Director: Rose Marie Matulionis, MSPH

Historical Note
Founded as Conference of State and Territorial Directors of Public Health Education; became Association of State and Territorial Directors of Public Health Education in 1996; assumed its current name in 1998. Membership: $25/year (individual); $200/year (organization).

Publications:
ASTDHPPHE Tech'l Assistance Guide and Application.

Disaster Preparedness and Emergency Response Association *(1962)*

P.O. Box 797
Longmont, CA 80502
Tel: (970)532-3362 *Fax:* (970)532-2979
E-Mail: dera@disasters.org
Web Site: www.disasters.org
Members: 1100 individuals
Staff: 3
Annual Budget: $25-50,000
Executive Director: Bascombe J. Wilson
Director, Education and Training: Robert Dockery
Director, Government Liasion: Steve Keene
Coordinator, Membership: James K. Lucas

Historical Note
DERA is an international network of individuals and organizations active in disaster preparedness and response. Sponsors research projects, technical publications, and other programs to inform members. Membership: $45/year (individual); $250/year (company).

Publications:
Disaster Resource Center Update. s.
DisasterCom Newsletter. q.

Disaster Recovery Institute International

Historical Note
Became DRI International in 2003.

Disease Management Association of America *(1997)*

701 Pennsylvania Ave. NW, Suite 700
Washington, DC 20004
Tel: (202)357-5980 *Fax:* (202)478-5113
Web Site: www.dmaa.org
Members: 160 corporations
Staff: 8
Annual Budget: $2-5,000,000
President and Chief Executive Officer: Tracey Moorhead

Meetings/Conferences:
Annual Meetings: Fall

Publications:
Disease Management. q. adv.
DMAA E-News. w. adv.

Display Distributors Association *(1968)*

c/o Daniels Display
1267 Mission St.
San Francisco, CA 94103-2766
Tel: (415)861-4400 *Fax:* (415)861-4496
Toll Free: (800)862 - 4400
Members: 16 companies
Staff: 2
Annual Budget: $50-100,000
President: Daniel Benjamin

Historical Note
Members are companies manufacturing or distributing display products and store fixtures. Incorporated in the State of Illinois. Membership: $1,200/year (organization).

Meetings/Conferences:
Semi-annual Meetings: New York, NY/June & Chicago, IL/December

Distance Education and Training Council *(1926)*

1601 18th St. NW
Washington, DC 20009-2529
Tel: (202)234-5100 *Fax:* (202)332-1386
Web Site: www.detc.org
Members: 100 distance educational institutions
Staff: 6
Annual Budget: $1-2,000,000
Executive Director: Michael P. Lambert
E-Mail: mike@detc.org

Historical Note
Founded as National Home Study Council; assumed its current name in 1994. A federally-recognized accrediting agency and trade association whose members serve 80-90% of all correspondence students.

Meetings/Conferences:
Annual Meetings: Spring/200
2007 – Tucson, AZ(Omni Tucson)/Apr. 15-17

Publications:
Directory of Accredited Institutions (online). a.
DETC News. 2/year.

Distilled Spirits Council of the U.S. *(1933)*
1250 I St. NW, Suite 400
Washington, DC 20005
Tel: (202)628-3544 *Fax:* (202)682-8876
Web Site: www.discus.org
Members: 12 companies
Staff: 48
Annual Budget: $10-25,000,000
President and Chief Executive Officer: Peter H. Cressy
Senior Vice President, Public Affairs and Communications Office: Frank Coleman
Senior Vice President, Government Relations: Mark Gorman
Senior Vice President, General Counsel and Corporate Secretary: Lynne J. Omlie
Historical Note
DISCUS represents producers and marketers of distilled spirits. Merger of the Distilled Spirits Institute (1933), the Bourbon Institute (1958), and Licensed Beverage Industries (1946). Absorbed the Tax Council-Alcoholic Beverage Industries. Connected with the Distilled Spirits Council Political Action Committee (DISPAC). Has an annual budget of approximately $14 million.
Publications:
Summary of State Laws and Regulations.

Distillers Grains Technology Council *(1945)*
c/o Lutz Hall, Room 435
Univ. of Louisville
Louisville, KY 40292
Tel: (502)852-1575 *Fax:* (502)852-1577
Toll Free: (800)759 - 3448
E-Mail: distillergrains@louisville.edu
Members: 8 companies (full members); 20 companies (associate members)
Staff: 2
Annual Budget: $50-100,000
Executive Vice President: Charlie Staff
E-Mail: distillergrains@louisville.edu
Historical Note
Formerly (1997) Distillers Feed Research Council. Members are beverage and ethanol distillers who process by-products of the distilling process for other uses (e.g., livestock feed, fuel additives, pharmaceutical products).
Meetings/Conferences:
Annual Meetings: Spring/70

Distribution and LTL Carriers Association *(1939)*
4218 Roanoke Road, Suite 200
Kansas City, MO 64111-4735
Tel: (816)753-0411
E-Mail: dltlca@dltl.org
Web Site: http:/www.dltl.org
Members: 200 companies
Staff: 3
Treasurer: Gary Dahl
E-Mail: dltlca@dltl.org
Historical Note
Founded as Regular Common Carriers Conference; merged with Regional and Distribution Carriers Conference and assumed its current name in 1997. Members are highway common carriers and less-than-truckload haulers of general commodity freight.
Meetings/Conferences:
Semi-Annual Meetings: *Fall and Winter/100*
Publications:
Highway Motor Carrier Newsletter. bi-w. adv.

Distribution Business Management Association *(1986)*
2938 Columbia Ave., Suite 1102
Lancaster, PA 17603
Tel: (717)295-0033 *Fax:* (717)299-2154
E-Mail: dbminfo@dbm-assoc.com
Web Site: www.dcenter.com
Members: 13500 individuals
Staff: 7
Annual Budget: $1-2,000,000
Executive Director: Amy Z. Thorn
Manager, Administration: Sue Munford
Historical Note
DBM members are companies and professional involved in warehousing and distribution, including warehouses, manufacturers of equipment, construction companies and material handling professionals and consultants. DBM conducts a certificate program sponsored by several universities.
Publications:
Distribution Business Management Journal. 2/yr. adv.

Distribution Contractors Association *(1961)*
Woodcreek Plaza, Suite 460
101 W. Renner Road
Richardson, TX 75082-2024
Tel: (972)680-0261 *Fax:* (972)680-0461
E-Mail: dca@dca-online.org
Web Site: www.dca-online.org
Members: 180 companies
Staff: 4
Annual Budget: $500-1,000,000
Executive Vice President: Dennis J. Kennedy
Manager, Administrative Services: Teri Korson
Member Services and Manager, Meeting: Melissa Leslie
Manager, Publications: Cason Pilliod
Historical Note
Membership consists of firms engaged in underground pipeline construction and manufacturers and suppliers of construction equipment to the gas distribution industry. Membership: $2,000/year (full member); $750/year (associate).
Meetings/Conferences:
Annual Meetings: Winter
2007 – Paradise Island, Bahamas(Atlantis)/Jan. 20-25/300
2008 – Indian Wells, CA(Esmeralda Resort)/Feb. 12-17/300
Publications:
DCA Update. m.
DCA Directory. a. adv.
DCA Benchmark. a.
DCA News Newsletter. m.

Distributive Education Clubs of America *(1947)*
1908 Association Dr.
Reston, VA 20191-1594
Tel: (703)860-5000 *Fax:* (703)860-4013
Web Site: www.deca.org
Members: 190000 individuals; 5000 chapters
Staff: 20
Annual Budget: $2-5,000,000
Executive Director: Edward L. Davis, Ph.D.
E-Mail: ed_davis@deca.org
Meeting Specialist: Larry Lorenzi
E-Mail: trvelclass@aol.com
Historical Note
Members are students and educators concerned with distribution, marketing, merchandising and management.
Meetings/Conferences:
2007 – Orlando, FL/Apr. 28-May 1
2008 – Atlanta, GA/Apr. 26-29
2009 – Anaheim, CA/Apr. 29-May 2
2010 – Louisville, KY/Apr. 24-27
2011 – Orlando, FL/Apr. 30-May 3
2012 – Salt Lake City, UT/Apr. 21-24
2013 – Anaheim, CA/Apr. 24-27
Publications:
DECA Dimensions. q. adv.
DECA Advisor. m. adv.

Diving Equipment and Marketing Association *(1972)*
3750 Convoy St., Suite 310
San Diego, CA 92111
Tel: (858)616-6408 *Fax:* (858)616-6495
Toll Free: (800)862 - 3483
Web Site: www.dema.org
Members: 1575 companies
Staff: 6
Annual Budget: $1-2,000,000
Executive Director: Tom Ingram
Historical Note
Formerly (1994) Diving Equipment Manufacturers Association. Membership: $300-12,000/year.
Meetings/Conferences:
Annual Meetings: January/10,000
Publications:
Trade Show Directory. a.

Document Management Industries Association *(1946)*
433 E. Monroe Ave.
Alexandria, VA 22301
Tel: (703)836-6232 *Fax:* (703)836-2241
E-Mail: dmia@dmia.org
Web Site: www.dmia.org
Members: 2400 companies
Staff: 48
Annual Budget: $5-10,000,000
Executive Vice President: Peter L. Colaianni, CAE
Vice President; Membership, Marketing and Education: Debbie Ayres
Vice President, Operations: Marj Green, CFC, CPSS
Vice President, New Media: Brad Holt
Vice President, Information Services and Technical Programming: Dennis McGarry
Vice President, Meetings and Expositions: Michael E. Pramstaller, CFC,CAE
Historical Note
Formerly (1996) National Business Forms Association. Has an annual budget of approximately $5.2 million.
Meetings/Conferences:
Annual Meetings: October/700
2007 – Las Vegas, NV
Publications:
Print Solutions Weekly e-newsletter. w.
Print Solutions Magazine.
FORM. m. adv.
Independent Management Report. m.
Business Printing Technologies Report. bi-m.
Who's Who in Business Printing and Information Management Services. a.

Dog Writers' Association of America *(1935)*
173 Union Road
Coatesville, PA 19320
Tel: (610)384-2436 *Fax:* (610)384-2471
E-Mail: rhydowen@aol.com
Web Site: www.dwaa.org
Members: 530 individuals
Annual Budget: under $10,000
Secretary: Pat Santi
E-Mail: rhydowen@aol.com
Historical Note
DWAA members write professionally on the subject of dogs. Membership: $40/year (individual).
Meetings/Conferences:
Annual Meetings: New York, NY/2nd weekend in Feb./200
Publications:
Members Bulletin. m.
Newsletter. m.
Membership Roster. a.

Domestic Petroleum Council *(1975)*
101 Constitution Ave. NW, Suite 800
Washington, DC 20001-2133
Tel: (202)742-4300 *Fax:* (202)742-4505
E-Mail: info@dcpusa.org
Web Site: www.dcpusa.org
Members: 24 companies
Annual Budget: $250-500,000
President: William F. Whitsitt
E-Mail: info@dcpusa.org
Historical Note
DPC members are the largest U.S. independent companies involved in exploration and/or production of natural gas and petroleum.
Meetings/Conferences:
Semi-Annual: Spring, Washington, DC/Winter. Houston, TX

Door and Access Systems Manufacturers' Association, International *(1968)*
1300 Sumner Ave.
Cleveland, OH 44115-2851
Tel: (216)241-7333 *Fax:* (216)241-0105
E-Mail: dasma@dasma.com
Web Site: www.dasma.com

Members: 90 companies
Staff: 4
Annual Budget: $100-250,000
Executive Director: John H. Addington
E-Mail: dasma@dasma.com

Historical Note
Formerly (1972) Midwest Garage Door Manufacturers Association and National Association of Garage Door Manufacturers, merged with Door and Operator Remote Controls Manufacturers Association and assumed its current name in 1996. DASMA is organized into three product specific divisions: Commercial and Residential Garage Door Division, Operator and Electronics Division, and Rolling Door Division. Membership: $5,750/year (minimum).

Meetings/Conferences:
Annual Meetings: Winter/200

Publications:
Door & Access Systems Magazine. q. adv.

Door and Hardware Institute *(1934)*
14150 Newbrook Dr.
Chantilly, VA 20151-2223
Tel: (703)222-2010 *Fax:* (703)222-2410
E-Mail: jheppes@dhi.org
Web Site: www.dhi.org
Members: 5200 individuals
Staff: 30
Annual Budget: $5-10,000,000
Chief Executive Officer: Jerry Heppes, CAE
E-Mail: jheppes@dhi.org
Director, Finance: Suzanne Shomers
E-Mail: sshomers@dhi.org
Director, Meetings and Conventions: Marcia Slakie

Historical Note
Founded as National Contract Hardware Association; became National Builders Hardware Association in 1954. Merged with American Society of Architectural Hardware Consultants and assumed its current name in 1975. Members are distributors and manufacturers of doors and builders' hardware, and architectural hardware and certified door consultants. Membership: $225/year.

Meetings/Conferences:
Annual Meetings: Fall/3,500-4,000
2007 – Nashville, TN(Opryland)/Oct. 15-20

Publications:
The Plan Room. q.
DHI Membership Directory. a. adv.
Doors and Hardware. m. adv.

Dramatists Guild of America *(1921)*
1501 Broadway, Suite 701
New York, NY 10036
Tel: (212)398-9366 *Fax:* (212)944-0420
Web Site: www.dramaguild.com
Members: 6500 individuals
Staff: 8
Annual Budget: $500-1,000,000
Associate Director: Ralph Sevush

Historical Note
An affiliate of the Authors League of America. The Guild is the professional association of playwrights, composers and lyricists. Members are entitled to use the Guild's "Approved Production Contract". Membership: $75-125/year.

Publications:
Newsletter. bi-m. adv.
The Dramatists Guild Resource Directory. a.
The Dramatist Magazine. bi-m. adv.

Drapery Specialists Institute *(1971)*

Historical Note
A division of the Association of Specialists in Cleaning and Restoration International.

Dredging Contractors of America *(1935)*
503 D St. NW, Suite 150
Washington, DC 20001
Tel: (202)737-2674 *Fax:* (202)737-2677
Web Site: www.dredgingcontractors.org
Members: 25 companies
Staff: 2
Annual Budget: $500-1,000,000
Executive Director: Jim Rausch

Historical Note
Formerly the National Association of Dredging Contractors.

Meetings/Conferences:
Annual Meetings: March

DRI International *(1988)*
1400 Eye St. NW
Suite 1050
Washington, DC 20005
Tel: (202)962-3979 *Fax:* (202)962-3939
E-Mail: driinfo@drii.org
Web Site: www.drii.org
Members: 3000 individuals
Staff: 9
Annual Budget: $2-5,000,000
Executive Director: Becca Dietrich
Meeting Planner: Paula Boyles
IT and Web Support: Brian Gorg
Manager, Finance: Cyndi Peterson
Manager, Education: Howie Southworth

Historical Note
Founded as Disaster Recovery Institute International, DRI represents professionals working in business continuity management. Awards the designations CBCP (Certified Business Continuity Professional), ABCP (Associate Business Continuity Planner), CFCP (Certified Functional Continuity Professional), and MBCP (Master Business Continuity Professional). Membership: $75-100/year.

Meetings/Conferences:
Semi-Annual Meetings: March

Publications:
DRI Newsletter. q.

Drilling Engineering Association
c/o IADC, 10370 Richmond Ave., Suite 760
Houston, TX 77042
Tel: (713)292-1945 Ext: 222 *Fax:* (713)292-1946
Web Site: www.dea.main.com
Members: 50 companies
Secretary-Treasurer: Mike Killalea

Historical Note
DEA was established to advance the technology related to drilling wells. Has no paid officers or full-time staff. Membership: One time fee, $500(full); $200 (associate).

Meetings/Conferences:
Annual Meetings: Quarterly Meetings

Driver Employer Council of America *(1967)*
1225 I St. NW, Suite 1000
Washington, DC 20005
Tel: (202)371-0100 *Fax:* (202)842-0011
Members: 25 companies
Staff: 2
Annual Budget: $50-100,000
General Counsel: Peter A. Susser

Historical Note
Formerly (1992) the Driver Leasing Council of America. Members are companies leasing truck drivers to motor carriers.

Driving School Association of America *(1973)*
111 W. Pomona Blvd.
Monterey Park, CA 91754
Tel: (323)728-2100 *Fax:* (323)722-0485
Members: 275 firms
Annual Budget: $10-25,000
Co-Founder and Editor: George R. Hensel

Historical Note
DSAA is a trade association composed of professional, state-licensed driving schools in the U.S. and Canada, and spokesmen of state associations. Affiliated with the IVV, an international organization of driving schools headquartered in Europe. Membership: $250/year.

Meetings/Conferences:
Annual Meetings: November

Publications:
Dual News. q. adv.
Dual News Bulletin. bi-m.

Drug and Alcohol Testing Industry Association *(1995)*
1325 G St. NW, Suite 500, #5001
Washington, DC 20005
Tel: (202)903-2420 *Fax:* (202)315-3579
Toll Free: (800)355 - 1257
E-Mail: datia@wpa.org
Web Site: www.datia.org
Members: 1100 companies
Staff: 3
Annual Budget: $500-1,000,000
Executive Director: Melissa Moskal

Historical Note
Founded as National Association of Collection Sites, DATIA represents drug and alcohol service providers, including collection sites, laboratories and testing manufactures. Membership: $159-$1,500/year.

Meetings/Conferences:
Annual Meetings: Spring

Publications:
eNewsweekly. w.
Drug-Alcohol Testing Industry News. bi-m.

Drug Information Association *(1965)*
800 Enterprise Road, Suite 200
Horsham, PA 19044
Tel: (215)442-6100 *Fax:* (215)442-6199
E-Mail: dia@diahome.org
Web Site: www.diahome.org
Members: 3 individuals
Staff: 37
Annual Budget: $1-2,000,000
Executive Director: David Maola
E-Mail: dia@diahome.org
Manager, Worldwide Marketing: Liza Zoks
E-Mail: dia@diahome.org

Historical Note
Members are individuals from the pharmaceutical industry, government, and academia responsible for processing and disseminating information on medicine and drugs in medicine, biology, pharmacy, and allied human/animal fields. Maintains a computer-access information line: (215) 628-9999. Membership: $100/year (individual).

Meetings/Conferences:
Annual Meetings:

Publications:
Drug Information Journal. 4/yr. adv.
DIA Today. 8/yr. adv.

Drug, Chemical and Allied Trades Association

Historical Note
Became Drug, Chemical and Associated Technologies Ass'n in 2003.

Drug, Chemical and Associated Technologies Association *(1890)*
One Washington Blvd., Suite Seven
Robbinsville, NJ 08691
Tel: (609)448-1000 *Fax:* (609)448-1944
Toll Free: (800)640 - 3228
E-Mail: info@dcat.org
Web Site: www.dcat.org
Members: 350 companies
Staff: 4
Annual Budget: $1-2,000,000
Executive Director: Margaret M. Timony

Historical Note
Formerly (1890) Drug, Chemcial and Allied Trades Association; assumed its current name in 2003. One of the oldest trade associations representing pharmaceutical, chemical, nutritional and related industries.

Publications:
Digest. q.
Membership Directory. a.

Ductile Iron Pipe Research Association *(1915)*
245 Riverchase Pwky. East, Suite 0
Birmingham, AL 35244
Tel: (205)402-8700 *Fax:* (205)402-8730
E-Mail: info@dipra.org
Web Site: www.dipra.org
Members: 7 companies
Staff: 22
President: Troy F. Stroud
E-Mail: info@dipra.org

Historical Note
Established as the Cast Iron Pipe Publicity Bureau, it later became the Cast Iron Pipe Institute, and the Cast

Iron Pipe Research Association in 1928. Assumed its present name in 1979.

Meetings/Conferences:
Semi-Annual Meetings: April and October.

Publications:
Ductile Iron Pipe News. semi-a.
Ductile Iron Pipe Installation Guide.

Ductile Iron Society *(1958)*
28938 Lorain Road, Suite 202
North Olmstead, OH 44070-4014
Tel: (440)734-8040 *Fax:* (440)734-8182
Web Site: www.ductile.org
Members: 90 companies
Staff: 2
Annual Budget: $100-250,000
Executive Director: John V. Hall

Historical Note
Ductile Iron is a casting material having properties similar to cast steel and processing characteristics similar to cast iron. Membership: $1,800 - $8,000/year (foundaries); $1760/year associate.

Publications:
Ductile Iron News. 3/year.

Dude Ranchers' Association *(1926)*
P.O. Box 2307
Cody, WY 82414
Tel: (307)587-2339
E-Mail: info@duderanch.org
Web Site: www.duderanch.org
Members: 100 guest ranches
Staff: 2
Annual Budget: $100-250,000
Executive Director: Colleen Hodson
E-Mail: info@duderanch.org

Historical Note
Organized in Bozeman, Montana in November 1926 to protect the image of the dude ranch industry, promote ranch properties as a tourist vacation, work with public lands, game and fish departments and preserve the western way of life. Membership: $750-2,200/year.

Meetings/Conferences:
Annual Meetings: Winter

Publications:
The Dude Rancher Directory. a.

Early Childhood Education Institute
1800 K St. NW, Suite 718
Washington, DC 20006
Tel: (202)466-4214 *Fax:* (202)466-7414
Executive Director: Randy Dyer, CAE

Early Sites Research Society *(1973)*
P.O. Box 4175
Independence, MO 64050
Tel: (816)254-4658
E-Mail: sidiggit@aol.com
Web Site: www.diggit.org
Members: 400 individuals
Annual Budget: $25-50,000
Director: Neil Steede
E-Mail: sidiggit@aol.com

Historical Note
Membership, concentrated in the Northeast, is composed of archaeologists involved in exploring unidentified antiquities.

Meetings/Conferences:
Semi-annual Meetings: Spring and Fall

Publications:
Newsletter. q. adv.
Early Sites Journal. a. adv.
Monographs. irreg. adv.

Earthmoving Equipment Manufacturers Council

Historical Note
A council of the Equipment Manufacturers Institute.

Earthquake Engineering Research Institute *(1948)*
499 14th St., Suite 320
Oakland, CA 94612-1934
Tel: (510)451-0905 *Fax:* (510)451-5411
E-Mail: eeri@eeri.org
Web Site: www.eeri.org
Members: 2300 individuals
Staff: 8
Annual Budget: $1-2,000,000
Executive Director: Susan K. Tubbesing
Manager, Editorial and Publications: Eloise Gilland
Controller and Member Relations: Sonya Hollenbeck

Historical Note
EERI advances the science and practice of earthquake engineering to protect people and property from the effects of damaging earthquakes. EERI's programs draw on its unique interdisciplinary membership, fostering communication among those disciplines to bridge the gap between new knowledge, design, practice, and policy. Membership: $150/year (individual); $275/year (organization).

Meetings/Conferences:
Annual Meetings: Winter

Publications:
Workshop Proceedings. quadren.
Spectra Journal. q.
Membership Roster. a.
EERI Newsletter. m.

Ecological Society of America *(1915)*
1707 H St. NW, Suite 400
Washington, DC 20006
Tel: (202)833-8773 *Fax:* (202)833-8775
E-Mail: esahq@esa.org
Web Site: www.esa.org
Members: 9000 individuals
Staff: 30
Annual Budget: $2-5,000,000
Executive Director: Katherine McCarter
E-Mail: esahq@esa.org
Director, Public Affairs: Nadine Lymn

Historical Note
Organized December 1915 in Columbus, Ohio at the annual meeting of the American Association for the Advancement of Science. A professional society of individuals interested in the study of living things in relation to their environment. Member society of the American Institute of Biological Sciences. Represented on the Council of the American Association for the Advancement of Science and the National Research Council. Membership: $20-80/year, varies by income (individual); special rates for students and for individuals in developing countries.

Publications:
Frontiers in Ecology and the Environment. m. adv.
Bulletin of the Ecological Soc of America. q. adv.
Ecological Applications. 6/year. adv.
Ecological Monographs. q. adv.
Ecology. m. adv.

Econometric Society *(1930)*
New York University
269 Mercer St., Seventh Floor
New York, NY 10003
Tel: (972)640-7951 *Fax:* (972)640-6698
E-Mail: econometrica@econometricsociety.org
Web Site: www.econometricsociety.org
Members: 4000 individuals
Staff: 2
Annual Budget: $100-250,000
Executive Director: Julie P. Gordon, Ph.D.

Historical Note
An international society for the advancement of economic theory in its relation to mathematics and statistics. Organized in Cleveland, Ohio, December 29, 1930 with Professor Irving Fisher of Yale University as the first president.

Meetings/Conferences:
Semi-annual: Winter/Summer

Publications:
Econometrica. bi-m. adv.

Economic History Association *(1940)*
500 Camino Real
Santa Clara University
Santa Clara, CA 95053-0385
Tel: (408)554-4348 *Fax:* (408)554-2331
E-Mail: afield@scu.edu
Web Site: www.eh.net
Members: 900 individuals
Annual Budget: $100-250,000
Executive Director: Alexander J. Field
E-Mail: afield@scu.edu

Historical Note
A member of the American Council of Learned Societies. Membership: $20-60/year (individual); $160-170/year (organization/company).

Meetings/Conferences:
Annual Meetings: September

Publications:
Journal of Economic History. q. adv.

Ecotourism Society

Historical Note
See International Ecotourism Society

ECRI *(1955)*
5200 Butler Pike
Plymouth Meeting, PA 19462-1298
Tel: (610)825-6000 *Fax:* (610)834-1275
E-Mail: info@ecri.org
Web Site: www.ecri.org
Members: 3800 hospitals
Staff: 250
Annual Budget: $25-50,000,000
President and Chief Executive Officer: Jeffrey C. Lerner, Ph.D.
E-Mail: info@ecri.org
Vice President, Information Services and Technology Assessment: Vivian H. Coates
E-Mail: info@ecri.org
Vice President, Finance: G. Dan Downing
E-Mail: info@ecri.org
Manager, Communications: Laurie Menyo
Executive Vice President and Chief Operating Officer: Anthony J. Montagnolo
Executive Vice President and General Counsel: Ronni P. Solomon
E-Mail: info@ecri.org

Historical Note
Offers evaluation, testing, and technical assistance services related to health care technology, clinical engineering and healthcare environmental management. Founded as the Graduate Pain Research Institute in 1968 and assumed its present name in 1980. Has an annual budget of approximately $29 million.

Meetings/Conferences:
Annual Meetings: Annual; October; 200

Publications:
Health Devices Sourcebook. a.
Healthcare Product Comparison System. m.
Health Devices Inspection and Environmental Maintenence System.
Health Devices Alerts. w.
Health Risk Control. m.
Health Care Environmental Management. m.
Operating Room Risk Management System. m.
Healthcare Hazard Monitor. m.
Health Standards Directory. a.

Ecuadorean American Association *(1932)*
30 Vesey St., Suite 506
New York, NY 10007
Tel: (212)233-7776 *Fax:* (212)233-7779
E-Mail: andean@nyet.net
Web Site: www.ecuadoreanamerican.org
Members: 27 individuals
Staff: 3
Annual Budget: $25-50,000
Program Director: Montserrat Hernandez
E-Mail: andean@nyet.net

Historical Note
Promotes greater knowledge and understanding of modern Ecuador; seeks to disseminate information on current events and on economic and financial matters of concern to investors in Ecuador; and promotes commercial and cultural relations and good will among the people of the two countries. Membership: $150/year (individual); $350/year (corporate); $1,000/year (sustaining).

Meetings/Conferences:
Annual Meetings:

EDA Consortium *(1989)*
111 W. St. John St., Suite 220
San Jose, CA 95113-1104
Tel: (408)287-3322 *Fax:* (408)283-5283

E-Mail: karla@edac.org
Web Site: www.edac.org
Members: 110 companies
Staff: 3
Annual Budget: $500-1,000,000
Executive Director: Pamela Parrish

Historical Note

Founded as Electronic Design Automation Consortium. EDA Consortium members are companies engaged in the development, manufacture and sale of design tools to the electronic engineering community. The Consortium's mission is to foster communication and cooperation between EDA companies, customers and stakleholders, driving industry-wide solutions to industry-wide problems. Membership: based on company revenues.

Meetings/Conferences:

Annual Meetings: January

Publications:

Market Statistics Service. q.

Edison Electric Institute *(1933)*
701 Pennsylvania Ave. NW
Washington, DC 20004-2696
Tel: (202)508-5000 *Fax:* (202)508-5360
Toll Free: (800)334 - 4688
Web Site: www.eei.org
Members: 200 companies
Staff: 200
Annual Budget: $50-100,000,000
President: Thomas R. Kuhn, CAE
Vice President, Corporate Affairs/Corporate Secretary: Edwin R. Anthony
Vice President, Policy and Public Affairs: M. William Brier
Vice President, General Counsel: Edward H. Comer
Vice President, International Programs: John J. Easton, Jr.
Senior Vice President, Policy Issues Management and Internal Operations: Lynn H. LeMaster
Executive Vice President, Business Operations: David K. Owens

Historical Note

EEI's members are the nation's shareholder-owned electric utility companies, which generate and distribute about 70% of the country's electricity. Membership also includes international affiliates, made up of power companies in every part of the world, and associates, who are electric power industry suppliers. EEI provides national leadership in legislative and regulatory arenas on public policy issues affecting its members and in promoting the development and use of efficient electrotechnologies. The association's other activities include administering the Power Political Action Committee (POWERPAC), providing forums for its members to exchange information and ideas, and serving as the authoritative information source on the shareholder-owned electric utility industry.

Meetings/Conferences:

Annual Meetings: Convention and Expo
2007 - Denver, CO(Hyatt Regency Convention Center)/June 17-20/100

Publications:

Electric Perspectives Magazine. bi-m. adv.

Edison Welding Institute *(1984)*
1250 Arthur E. Adams Dr.
Columbus, OH 43221-3585
Tel: (614)688-5000 *Fax:* (614)688-5001
E-Mail: info@ewi.org
Web Site: www.ewi.org
Members: 300 companies
Staff: 160
Annual Budget: $10-25,000,000
President and Chief Executive Officer: Dr. Henry J. Cialone
Vice President, Government Programs Office: Harvey Castner
Director, Technology and Innovation: Chris Conrardy
Chief Financial Officer: Robert Myers
Vice President and Chief Operating Officer: Phil Weisenbach

Historical Note

EWI provides practical welding and joining solutions through technical assistance, contract research, consultative services and training to more than 250 member companies, including the Office of Naval Research, for which it operates the Navy Joining Center. EWI's more than 150 engineers and staff can quickly isolate and solve urgent manufacturing problems or investigate failed components in the field, at members' sites, or in the EWI laboratories. The EWI staff works hand-in-hand with members to assess critical problems, develop solutions, optimize designs, and achieve positive results.

Meetings/Conferences:

Annual Meetings: Fall

Publications:

Insights Newsletter. q.
Research Reports. m.

Editorial Freelancers Association *(1974)*
71 W. 23rd St., Suite 1910
New York, NY 10010
Tel: (212)929-5400 *Fax:* (212)929-5439
E-Mail: info@the-efa.org
Web Site: www.the-efa.org
Members: 1200 individuals
Staff: 1
Annual Budget: $100-250,000
Co-Executive Director: J.P. Partland
Office Administrator: Judi Greenstein
Co-Executive Director: Martha Schueneman

Historical Note

EFA is a professional organization comprising editors, writers, indexers, proofreaders, researchers, translators and other self-employed workers in the publishing and communications industries. Absorbed Freelance Editors Association in 2000. Membership: $75-105/year.

Meetings/Conferences:

Annual Meetings: always New York, NY(EFA Offices)/June/60-100

Publications:

EFA Newsletter ("The Freelancer"). bi-m. adv.

Education Credit Union Council *(1972)*
P.O. Box 7558
Spanish Fort, AL 36577
Tel: (251)626-3399 *Fax:* (251)626-3565
E-Mail: ecuclbw@aol.com
Web Site: www.ecuc.org
Members: 350 credit unions
Staff: 1
Annual Budget: $250-500,000
Executive Director: Lorraine B. Zerfas
E-Mail: ecuclbw@aol.com

Historical Note

Members are credit unions serving educational institutions. Membership: $350/year (organization).

Meetings/Conferences:

Annual Meetings: February
2007 - Pointe Vedra Beach, FL(Marriott)/Feb. 17-20

Publications:

Chalktalk. bi-m.

Education Industry Association *(1990)*
One Stoney Creek Way
Potomac, MD 20854
Toll Free: (800)252 - 3280
Web Site: www.educationindustry.org
Members: 800 individuals
Staff: 2
Annual Budget: $100-250,000
Executive Director: Steve Pines
E-Mail: spines@educationindustry.org

Historical Note

Founded as Association of Educators in Private Practice; became Association of Education Practitioners and Providers in 2002, and assumed its current name in 2004. Members are educators working in private, corporate or other alternative settings. Membership:$150/year (governing); $500-5,000/year (corporate).

Meetings/Conferences:

Annual Meetings: Summer

Publications:

EIA Directory. a.
Enterprising Educators Newsletter. q.

Education Law Association *(1954)*
300 College Park
Dayton, OH 45469-0528
Tel: (937)229-3589 *Fax:* (937)229-3845
E-Mail: ela@educationlaw.org
Web Site: www.educationlaw.org
Members: 1750 individuals
Staff: 4
Annual Budget: $250-500,000
Executive Director: Mandy Bingaman Schrank
E-Mail: ela@educationlaw.org

Historical Note

Formerly (1996) National Organization on Legal Problems of Education; assumed its current name in 1997. Membership consists of law and education professors, school administrators, school attorneys, etc. Purpose is to promote research and publication in the field of school law. Membership: $145/year; $50/year (student).

Meetings/Conferences:

Annual Meetings: Fall
2007 - San Diego, CA(Catamaran)/Nov. 14-17/500

Publications:

School Law Reporter. m.
ELA Notes. q. adv.
NOLPE Case Citation Series. a.
Yearbook of Education Law. a.

Education Society

Historical Note

See IEEE Education Society

Education Writers Association *(1947)*
2122 P St. NW, Suite 201
Washington, DC 20037
Tel: (202)452-9830 *Fax:* (202)452-9837
E-Mail: ewa@ewa.org
Web Site: www.ewa.org
Members: 900 individuals
Staff: 6
Annual Budget: $500-1,000,000
Executive Director: Lisa J. Walker
E-Mail: lwalker@ewa.org
Assistant Director: Lori Crouch
E-Mail: lcrouch@ewa.org
Coordinator, Administrative: Tracee Eason
E-Mail: teason@ewa.org
Coordinator, Marketing and Membership: Michelle Everett
E-Mail: meverett@ewa.org

Historical Note

Members are staff members of newspapers, magazines and broadcasting stations or are freelancers. Absorbed the National Council for the Advancement of Education Writing in 1975. Membership: $65/year.

Meetings/Conferences:

Annual Meetings: Spring

Publications:

Nat'l Award for Education Reporting. a.
Education Reform. irreg.
Annual Meeting brochure. a. adv.
The Education Reporter. bi-m. adv.
Covering the Education Beat. irreg.

Educational Paperback Association *(1975)*
P.O. Box 1399
East Hampton, NY 11937
Tel: (631)329-3315
E-Mail: edupaperback@aol.com
Web Site: www.edupaperback.org
Members: 100 companies
Staff: 1
Executive Secretary: Marilyn Abel
E-Mail: edupaperback@aol.com

Historical Note

Membership: $500/year (wholesaler); $700/year (publisher).

Meetings/Conferences:

Annual Meetings: January
2007 - Savannah, GA(Hyatt Regency)/Jan. 31-Feb. 3

Educational Theatre Association *(1929)*
2343 Auburn Ave.
Cincinnati, OH 45219
Tel: (513)421-3900 *Fax:* (513)421-7033
E-Mail: info@edta.org
Web Site: www.edta.org
Members: 1000 individuals
Staff: 28

Annual Budget: $2-5,000,000
Executive Director: Michael Peitz
E-Mail: mpeitz@edta.org

Historical Note

Founded as Theatre Education Association; assumed current name in 1999. The Educational Theatre Association is an association of theatre educators and artists. Goal of EdTA is to advance quality theatre on the high school level. Membership: $75/year (adults); $21/year (students) plus school fee of $50.00.

Publications:

Dramatics Magazine. 9/year. adv.
Teaching Theatre Journal. q. adv.
STLA Bulletin. 2/year.

EDUCAUSE *(1962)*

1150 18th St. NW, Suite 1010
Washington, DC 20036
Tel: (202)872-4200 *Fax:* (202)872-4318
E-Mail: info@educause.edu
Web Site: www.educause.edu
Members: 130 individuals
Staff: 43
Annual Budget: $10-25,000,000
President: Brian L. Hawkins
Vice President: Mark A. Luker

Historical Note

Formerly (1984) Interuniversity Communications Council. A non-profit consortium of colleges, universities and other nonprofit institutions and companies in the education field, EDUCUASE works to facilitate the introduction, use and management of information technology. Also has an office in Boulder, CO. EDUCAUSE has an annual budget of approximately $6 million; membership fee varies, based on full-time enrollment.

Meetings/Conferences:

Annual Meetings: Fall
2007 - Seattle, WA/Oct. 23-26
2008 - Orlando, FL/Oct. 28-31
2009 - Denver, CO/Oct. 27-30
2010 - Anaheim, CA/Oct. 12-15

Publications:

Cause/Effect. q.
EDUCOM Review. bi-m.

EEG and Clinical Neuroscience Society *(1964)*

805 W. Liberty Dr.
Wheaton, IL 60187
Tel: (630)653-2244 *Fax:* (630)653-6233
E-Mail: clinicaleeg@aol.com
Web Site: www.ecnsweb.org
Members: 1000individuals&organizations
Staff: 4
Annual Budget: $100-250,000
Production Manager: Kevin Kjellberg
E-Mail: clinicaleeg@aol.com

Historical Note

Founded as American Medical Electroencephalographic Association; merged with American Psychiatric Electrophysiology Association and assumed its current name in 1998. Membership: $185/year. Subscriptions $96/year (US); $116/year (foreign).

Meetings/Conferences:

Annual Meetings: Fall

Publications:

Clinical EEG. 4/year. adv.
Neuroscience.

EIFS Industry Members Association *(1981)*

3000 Corporate Center Dr., Suite 270
Morrow, GA 30260-4116
Tel: (770)968-7945 *Fax:* (770)968-5818
Toll Free: (800)294 - 3462
E-Mail: sklamke@eima.com
Web Site: www.eima.com
Members: 230 companies
Staff: 2
Annual Budget: $1-2,000,000
Executive Director: Stephan E. Klamke
E-Mail: sklamke@eima.com

Historical Note

Formerly (1993) the Exterior Insulation Manufacturers Association. Established for EIFS (exterior insulation finish systems) manufacturers only, EIMA includes manufacturers, suppliers, distributors, applicator/contractors, and affiliated building professionals. EIMA is a trade association representing member firms involved in the exterior insulation and finish systems (EIFS) industry. Membership: dues vary by type of member on a sliding scale.

Meetings/Conferences:

Annual Meetings: Winter

Eight Sheet Outdoor Advertising Association *(1953)*

P.O. Box 2680
Bremerton, WA 98310
Tel: (360)377-9867 *Fax:* (360)377-9870
Toll Free: (800)874 - 3387
E-Mail: davidjacobs@esoaa.org
Web Site: www.esoaa.com
Members: 130 companies
Staff: 2
Annual Budget: $100-250,000
Executive Director: David Jacobs

Historical Note

Members are owners of eight-sheet outdoor poster panels (Jr 8 Poster Panels) which are small 6' x 12' panels used in outdoor advertising. Formerly (until 1979) known as the Junior Panel Outdoor Advertising Association.

Publications:

Rate and Allotments Book. a.
Eight-Sheet Report. m.
Sources. a.

Elastic Fabric Maunfacturers Council *(1915)*

Historical Note

A council of the Northern Textile Association.

Electric Drive Transportation Association *(1990)*

1350 I St. NW, Suite 1050
Washington, DC 20005
Tel: (202)408-0774 *Fax:* (202)408-7610
E-Mail: info@electricdrive.org
Web Site: www.electricdrive.org
Members: 82 companies and agencies
Staff: 6
President: Brian Wynne
E-Mail: info@electricdrive.org
Vice President, Government Policy and Legislation: Genevieve Cullen
E-Mail: info@electricdrive.org

Historical Note

Formerly (1990) Electric Vehicle Association of the Americas; assumed its current name in 2003. Advances commercialization of electric vehicles in the United States, Canada and Latin America through comprehensive public information and market development programs.

Meetings/Conferences:

Biennial Meetings: even years

Publications:

EV Update. bi-m.

Electric Power Research Institute *(1973)*

3412 Hillview Ave.
Palo Alto, CA 94304-1395
Tel: (650)855-2000 *Fax:* (650)855-2800
Toll Free: (800)313 - 3774
E-Mail: askepri@epri.com
Web Site: www.epri.com
Members: 660 utilities
Staff: 750
Annual Budget: $250-500,000
President and Chief Executive Officer: Steven R. Specker
E-Mail: askepri@epri.com
Director, Washington Relations: Barbara Tyron
E-Mail: askepri@epri.com

Historical Note

EPRI is an organization concerned with research relating to the production, transmission, distribution and utilization of electric power. Membership includes both publicly and privately held electric utility organizations. Maintains a Washington, DC office.

Publications:

EPRI Journal (online).

Electric Power Supply Association *(1997)*

1401 New York Ave. NW, 11th Floor
Washington, DC 20005-2110
Tel: (202)628-8200 *Fax:* (202)628-8260
E-Mail: epsainfo@epsa.org
Web Site: www.epsa.org
Members: 95 companies
Staff: 20
Annual Budget: $2-5,000,000
President and Chief Executive Officer: John E. Shelk
Vice President, Regulatory Policy: Nancy Bagot
Director, Finance and Administration: Shannon Gordon
Vice President, Legislative Affairs: Eugene F. Peters

Historical Note

Formerly (1987) Congeneration Coalition of America; became (1991) Cogeneration and Independent Power Coalition of America; merged with Independent Power Producers Working Group and became Electric Generation Association in 1992; merged with National Independent Energy Producers and assumed its current name in 1997. EPSA is primarily concerned with encouraging federal and state legislation and regulation favorable to the development of full wholesale and retail competition. Members are competitive electric generators, power marketers and suppliers to the industry. Membership: $12,000-150,000/year (organization/company).

Meetings/Conferences:

2007 - Palm Beach Gardens, FL(PGA Resort)/Jan. 25-28/120

Publications:

EPSA Report. q.
Restructing Matters. m.

Electric Vehicle Association of the Americas

Historical Note

Became Electric Drive Transportation Association in 2003.

Electrical and Computer Engineering Department Heads Association *(1985)*

300 W. Adams, Suite 1210
Chicago, IL 60606-5114
Tel: (312)559-3724 *Fax:* (312)559-3329
E-Mail: information@ecedha.org
Web Site: www.ecedha.org
Members: 280 individuals
Staff: 3
Executive Director: Robert M. Janowiak

Historical Note

Founded as National Electrical Engineering Department Heads Association; assumed its current name in 2001. Members are educators chairing collegiate electrical engineering programs.

Meetings/Conferences:

Annual Meetings: March

Publications:

Directory of Electrical & Computer Engineering Departments. a.

Electrical Apparatus Service Association *(1933)*

1331 Baur Blvd.
St. Louis, MO 63132
Tel: (314)993-2220 *Fax:* (314)993-1269
E-Mail: easainfo@easu.com
Web Site: www.easa.com
Members: 2200 firms
Staff: 16
Annual Budget: $2-5,000,000
President and Chief Executive Officer: Linda J. Raynes, CAE
E-Mail: lraynes@easa.com
Product Development Manager: Carl M. Fields
E-Mail: cfields@easa.com
Communications Manager: Randy Joslin
E-Mail: rjoslin@easa.com
Manager, Meetings and Exhibitions: Dale Shuter
Finance and Customer Svc. Manager: Richard Tutka
E-Mail: rtutka@easa.com

Historical Note

Established as the National Industrial Service Association; assumed its present name in 1961. Members are firms selling, servicing and rebuilding electric motors, generators, transformers and related equipment. Membership: $359-950/year (active); $899/year (associate).

Meetings/Conferences:

Annual Meetings: Summer
2007 - Minneapolis, MN(Convention Center)/June 24-27/3000

Publications:
Yearbook - Directory. a.
Currents - Newsletter. m.

Electrical Equipment Representatives Association *(1948)*

P.O. Box 419264
Kansas City, MO 64141-6264
Tel: (816)561-5323 *Fax:* (816)561-1991
E-Mail: eera@eera.org
Web Site: www.eera.org
Members: 100 companies
Annual Budget: $100-250,000
Executive Director: Jane Male, CAE
E-Mail: eera@eera.org

Historical Note
Founded to advance the quality and increase the effectiveness of Manufacturers Representatives in the Electrical Equipment Industry. Membership: $1100/year.

Meetings/Conferences:
Annual Meetings: May/235
2007 – Phoenix, AZ(Marriott Desert Ridge)/

Publications:
EERA Directory. a.

Electrical Generating Systems Association *(1965)*

1650 S. Dixie Hwy., Suite 500
Boca Raton, FL 33432-7462
Tel: (561)750-5575 *Fax:* (561)395-8557
E-Mail: e-mail@egsa.org
Web Site: www.egsa.org
Members: 330 companies
Staff: 5
Executive Director: Jalane Kellough

Historical Note
Founded as the Engine Generator Set Manufacturers Association, it became the Electrical Generating Systems Marketing Association in 1973 and assumed its present name in 1985. Formed in 1965 by 14 companies manufacturing engine generator sets, who were interested in standardizing specifications for products to be purchased by the U.S. government, primarily the military. In 1972, dealers and distributors of electrical generating equipment were invited to become full members, and the focus of the association was changed to developing programs which would be of benefit to them. Membership is international. Membership: $180-725/year (company)

Publications:
Powerline Magazine. bi-m.
Buyers Guide. a.

Electrical Insulation Conference *(1956)*

215 Burrage St.
Lunenburg, MA 01462
Tel: (978)582-9346
E-Mail: swalker@electricalinsulation.org
Web Site: www.electricalinsulation.org
Members: 200 individuals
Staff: 1
Executive Director: Sharon Walker
E-Mail: swalker@electricalinsulation.org

Historical Note
EIC is a technical organization founded to support research and exchange in the field of electrical insulation technology.

Meetings/Conferences:
Biennial Meeting: Fall, with the Electrical Manufacturing and Coil Winding Ass'n

Publications:
IEEE Electrical Insulation. 6/year. adv.

Electrical Manufacturing and Coil Winding Association *(1977)*

P.O. Box 278
Imperial Beach, CA 91933
Tel: (619)435-3629 *Fax:* (619)435-3639
E-Mail: info@emcwa.org
Web Site: www.emcwa.org
Members: 300 individuals
Staff: 2
Annual Budget: $1-2,000,000
Executive Director: Charles E. Thurman

Historical Note
Formerly the North American Council of the International Coil Winding Association and (1993) International Coil Winding Association. Membership: $50/year (individual); $300/year (organization/company).

Meetings/Conferences:
Annual Meetings: September-October
2007 – Nashville, TN(Opryland Convention Center)/Sept. 24-26

Publications:
Electrical Manufacturing & Coil Winding. a. adv.
Conference Proceedings. a.
EMCWA News Letter. bi-m.
Membership Directory. a. adv.
Conference Proceedings. a.

Electrical Overstress/Electrostatic Discharge Association *(1982)*

7900 Turin Rd., Bldg. Three
Rome, NY 13440-2069
Tel: (315)339-6937 *Fax:* (315)339-6793
E-Mail: info@esda.org
Web Site: www.esda.org
Members: 1400 individuals
Staff: 4
Annual Budget: $1-2,000,000
Operations Manager: Lisa Pimpinella

Historical Note
EOS/ESD is concerned with the advancement of the theory and practice of electrical overstress avoidance, with emphasis on electrostatic discharge phenomena. Members are government, industry and academic organizations involved in research and development; electronic equipment manufacturers and users; and manufacturers and users of EOS/ESD effects reduction products and methods. Also known as the ESD Association and Electrostatic Discharge Association. Membership: $60/year (U.S.); $70/year (foreign).

Meetings/Conferences:
Annual Meetings: September/550
2007 – Anaheim, CA(Disneyland Hotel)/Sept. 16-21

Publications:
Tutorial Note. a.
Threshold. bi-m.
Membership Roster. a.
EOS/ESD Symposium Proceedings. a.
EOS/ESD Standards. irreg.

Electricity Consumers Resource Council *(1976)*

1333 H St. NW
Eighth Floor, West Tower
Washington, DC 20005-4707
Tel: (202)682-1390 *Fax:* (202)289-6370
E-Mail: elcon@elcon.org
Web Site: www.elcon.org
Members: 38 member companies & 7 affiliates
Staff: 5
Annual Budget: $1-2,000,000
Executive Director: John A. Anderson
E-Mail: janderson@elcon.org
Vice President, Technical Affairs: John P. Hughes
Vice President, Government and Public Affairs: Marc Yacker

Historical Note
Members are industrial consumers of electricity who support regulatory practices that assure adequate supplies of electricity at prices based on cost of service.

Meetings/Conferences:
Annual Meetings: Washington, DC/October

Publications:
Profiles on Electricity Issues.
ELCON Report. q.

Electrochemical Society *(1902)*

65 S. Main St., Bldg. D
Pennington, NJ 08534-2839
Tel: (609)737-1902 *Fax:* (609)737-2743
E-Mail: ellen.tiano@electrochem.org
Web Site: www.electrochem.org
Members: 8000 individuals
Staff: 20
Annual Budget: $2-5,000,000
Executive Director and Chief Executive Officer: Roque J. Calvo, CAE
E-Mail: roque.calvo@electrochem.org
Director, Meetings: Stephanie Plassa
Director, Finance: Carolyn R. Wroblewski
Dep. Executive Director: Mary E. Yess
E-Mail: mary.yess@electrochem.org

Historical Note
Formed in Philadelphia April 3, 1902 as the American Electrochemical Society, it became the Electrochemical Society, Inc. in 1930 and incorporated in New York. Membership: $98/year (active); $18/year (student).

Meetings/Conferences:
Semi-Annual Meetings:

Publications:
Electrochemical and Solid State Letters. m.
Journal of The Electrochemical Society. m.
Interface Magazine. q. adv.

Electrocoat Association *(1997)*

P.O. Box 541083
Cincinnati, OH 45254-1083
Toll Free: (800)579 - 8806
E-Mail: kmglothin@electrocoat.org
Web Site: www.electrocoat.org
Members: 150 companies
Staff: 2

Historical Note
Members represent associations, corporations and individuals who have an economic or educational interest in electrocoating.

Meetings/Conferences:
Biennial: 500
2008 – Indianapolis, IN(Marriott Indianapolis Downtown)/May 14-16/500

Publications:
Electrocoating: A Guidebook For Finishers. a.

Electromagnetic Compatibility Society *(1957)*

Historical Note
See IEEE Electromagnetic Compatibility Society

Electron Devices Society *(1951)*

Historical Note
A technical society of the Institute of Electrical and Electronics Engineers (IEEE). Membership in the Society, open only to IEEE members, includes subscriptions to technical periodicals in the field published by IEEE. All administrative support is provided by IEEE.

Electronic Commerce Code Management Association *(1999)*

2980 Linden St., Suite E-2
Bethlehem, PA 18017
Tel: (610)861-5990 *Fax:* (610)861-5992
Web Site: www.eccma.org
Members: 300 corporations and organizations
Staff: 14
Annual Budget: $500-1,000,000
Executive Director: Peter R. Benson

Historical Note
Members are companies and executives involved in formulating or implementing electronic procurement and marketing strategies.

Publications:
newsletter. m.

Electronic Data Processing Auditors Association *(1969)*

Historical Note
See Information Systems Audit and Control Association.

Electronic Design Automation Consortium

Historical Note
Became EDA Consortium in 2003.

Electronic Distribution Show Corporation *(1935)*

222 S. Riverside Plaza, Suite 2160
Chicago, IL 60606
Tel: (312)648-1140 *Fax:* (312)648-4282
Web Site: www.edsc.org
Members: 500 companies
Staff: 5
Annual Budget: $500-1,000,000

Show Manager: Gretchen A. Oie
E-Mail: gretchen@edsc.org

Historical Note

Formerly (1996) Electronic Industry Show Corporation. Members are manufacturers who sell their products through electronics distributors. EDSC's main purpose is to conduct an annual trade show for these manufacturers. Affiliated with Electronic Industries Association, Electronic Representatives Association, and National Electronic Distributors Association.

Meetings/Conferences:

Annual Meetings: April/7,500-8,000

Publications:

Bulletin. m.

Electronic Forum on Sound Technology *(1994)*

Historical Note

An affiliate of Ass'n for Computing Machinery, which provides administrative support.

Electronic Funds Transfer Association *(1977)*

11350 Random Hills Rd., Suite 800
Fairfax, VA 22030
Tel: (703)934-6052 *Fax:* (703)934-6058
E-Mail: eftassoc@efta.org
Web Site: www.efta.org
Members: 400 companies
Staff: 4
Annual Budget: $500-1,000,000
President and Chief Executive Officer: H. Kurt Helwig

Historical Note

Dedicated to the advancement of electronic payment systems and commerce. Members include financial institutions, EFT networks, bank card associations, retailers, information processors, equipment, card and software manufacturers and vendors, Internet providers, telecommunications companies, state governments, and federal agencies. Membership: varies with the type of participation; $1,250/year (Government); $7,000/year (corporate); $18,000/year (sustaining); $4,000/year (Associate).

Meetings/Conferences:

semi-annual meetings: Spring/1,200

Publications:

E-News (online). m.

Electronic Industries Alliance *(1924)*

2500 Wilson Blvd.
Arlington, VA 22201
Tel: (703)907-7500 *Fax:* (703)907-7501
Web Site: www.eia.org
Members: 2300 companies
Annual Budget: $25-50,000,000
President: David McCurdy
Chief Operating Officer: Charles L. Robinson

Historical Note

Formerly Radio Manufacturers Association (1924-50); Radio-Television Manufacturers Association (1950-53); Radio-Electronics-Television Manufacturers Association (1953-57). Became Electronic Industries Association on August 5, 1957. Includes former Magnetic Recording Industry Association. Absorbed Association of Electronic Manufacturers in 1975, Institute of High Fidelity in 1980, and Mobile Electronics Association in 1992. Consumer Electronics Manufacturers Association and Electronic Components, Assemblies, Equipment and Supplies Association are sections of EIA. Sponsors the Joint Electron Device Engineering Council, the Electronics Political Action Committee, the Electronic Industries Foundation, and Consumer Electronics Shows. Members are companies involved in the manufacture of electronic components, parts, systems and equipment for communications, industrial, government and consumer uses. Has an annual budget of approximately $42 million.

Meetings/Conferences:

Semi-annual meetings: Spring in Washington, DC and Fall on the West Coast

Publications:

Annual Report.
Publication Index.
Executive Report. q.
Market Trends. m.
Market Data Book. a.
EIA Trade Directory. a.

Electronic Messaging Association

Historical Note

Became EMA - The E-Business Forum in 1999.

Electronic Retailing Association *(1990)*

2000 N. 14th St., Suite 300
Arlington, VA 22201
Tel: (703)841-1751 *Fax:* (703)841-1860
Toll Free: (800)987 - 6462
E-Mail: comtact@retailing.org
Web Site: www.retailing.org
Members: 400 companies
Staff: 12
Annual Budget: $2-5,000,000
President and Chief Executive Officer: Barbara Tulipane
Vice President, Meetings: Kara Kelley
Director, Communications: Molly Alton Mullins

Historical Note

Formerly (1994) National Infomercial Marketing Association and (1998) NIMA International. ERA promotes the growth, development and acceptance of the electronic retailing industry. Members (direct response companies and their suppliers) are involved in infomercial and short-form commercials, television shopping channels, and internet and multimedia marketing. Membership: $1,000-$23,000/year (corporate).

Meetings/Conferences:

Annual Meetings: Fall

Publications:

e-news. w. adv.
Electronic Retailer Magazine.

Electronic Transactions Association *(1990)*

1101 16th St. NW, Suite 402
Washington, DC 20036
Tel: (202)828-2635 *Fax:* (202)828-2639
Toll Free: (800)695 - 5509
E-Mail: info@electron.org
Web Site: www.electron.org
Members: 500 companies
Staff: 8
Annual Budget: $2-5,000,000
Executive Director: Carla Balakgie, CAE

Historical Note

Founded as Bankcard Services Association; assumed its current name in 1996. ETA members are bankcard service providers who are actively engaged in providing a full range of services to qualified merchants, who act as intermediaries between merchants and settlement banks. Other classes of membership include: credit card issuers and suppliers to the industry (associate); and financial institutions.

Meetings/Conferences:

Semi-annual: Spring/Fall

Publications:

Transaction Trends. m. adv.

Electronics Representatives Association *(1935)*

444 N. Michigan Ave., Suite 1960
Chicago, IL 60611
Tel: (312)527-3050 *Fax:* (312)527-3783
Toll Free: (800)776 - 7377
E-Mail: info@era.org
Web Site: www.era.org
Members: 10000 individuals
Staff: 5
Annual Budget: $1-2,000,000
Vice Chairman and Chief Executive Officer: Raymond J. Hall

Historical Note

Founded as the Representatives of Radio Parts Manufacturers, it became the Representatives of Electronic Parts Manufacturers in 1942 and assumed its present name in 1959.

Publications:

Locator of Manufacturer's Representatives. a.
The Representor. q.

Electronics Technicians Association International *(1978)*

Five Depot St.
Greencastle, IN 46135
Tel: (765)653-8262 *Fax:* (765)653-4287
Toll Free: (800)288 - 3824
E-Mail: eta@tds.net
Web Site: www.eta-sda.org
Members: 4000 individuals
Staff: 16
Annual Budget: $500-1,000,000
President: Dick Glass

Historical Note

Incorporated November 14, 1978 in the State of Indiana. Members are involved in such fields as medical, fiber optics, industrial, computer, and military electronics, as well as satellite and wireless communications and telecommunications, sound equipment and other electronic service. Operates a Certified Electronics Technician Program. One of seven organizations appointed by the FCC to administer FCC commercial license exams. Absorbed the Satellite Dealers Association (SDA), and the Indiana Electronic Service Association (IESA) in 1996. Membership: $25/year (individual), $250/year (company).

Meetings/Conferences:

Annual Meetings: Summer
2007 – Las Vegas, NV(Flamingo Hotel)/Feb. 25-27/250

Publications:

High Tech News. m. adv.

Elevator Industries Association *(1947)*

Seven Woodpath Dr.
Northport, NY 11768
Tel: (631)757-0887 *Fax:* (631)757-1129
Members: 27 companies
Staff: 1
Executive Consultant: Richard M. Wheeler

Embroidery Council of America *(1973)*

20 Industrial Ave., #26
Fairview, NJ 07002-1614
Tel: (201)943-7730
E-Mail: info@embroiderycouncil.org
Web Site: www.schiffli.org
Members: 30 companies
Staff: 2
Executive Director: J. Jeager
President: Vincent Mesiano

Historical Note

Formerly Schiffli Lace and Embroidery Institute. Members are manufacturers of machine-made embroidery and laces under union contract.

Meetings/Conferences:

Annual Meetings: None held.

Embroidery Trade Association *(1990)*

12300 Ford Road, Suite 135
Dallas, TX 75234
Toll Free: (888)628 - 2545
E-Mail: info@embroiderytrade.org
Web Site: www.embroiderytrade.org
Members: 2000 companies
Staff: 6
Annual Budget: $250-500,000
Executive Director: John S. Swinburn, CAE
E-Mail: john@embroiderytrade.org

Historical Note

ETA members are companies and individuals involved in the embroidery industry. Sponsorship: $175/year (individual); $1,000/year (company).

Publications:

Member Minute. w.

Emergency Department Practice Management Association *(1997)*

8405 Greensboro Dr., Suite 800
McLean, VA 22102
Tel: (703)506-3292 *Fax:* (703)506-3266
E-Mail: info@edpma.org
Web Site: www.edpma.org
Annual Budget: $500-1,000,000
Managing Director: Cherilyn Cepriano

Meetings/Conferences:

Annual Meetings: Spring

Emergency Medicine Residents' Association *(1974)*

1125 Executive Circle
Irving, TX 75038-2522
Tel: (972)550-0920 *Fax:* (972)580-2829
Toll Free: (800)798 - 1822

Web Site: www.emra.org
Members: 5000 individuals
Staff: 3
Annual Budget: $250-500,000
Executive Director: Michele Byers, CAE
E-Mail: mbyers@emra.org

Historical Note

Members are physicians training in the specialty of emergency medicine, and medical students interested in emergency medicine. Membership: $50/year.

Meetings/Conferences:

Semi-Annual Meetings: Spring and Fall

Publications:

Career Opportunity Guide. a. adv.
Antibiotic Guide. a.
EM Resident. bi-m.

Emergency Nurses Association *(1970)*

915 Lee St.
Des Plaines, IL 60016-6569
Tel: (847)460-4095 *Fax:* (847)460-4006
Toll Free: (800)900 - 9659 Ext: 4095
E-Mail: execinfo@ena.org
Web Site: www.ena.org
Members: 31000 individuals
Staff: 67
Annual Budget: $5-10,000,000
Executive Director: David Westman
E-Mail: execinfo@ena.org

Historical Note

Formerly (1974) National Emergency Department Nurses Association and the Emergency Department Nurses Association. Assumed its present name in 1984. Members are registered nurses committed to emergency nursing. Membership: $80/year.

Meetings/Conferences:

Annual Meetings: Fall/4,000
2007 – Salt Lake City, UT/Sept. 26-29
2008 – Minneapolis, MN/Sept. 24-27
2009 – Baltimore, MD/Oct. 7-9
2010 – Portland, OR/Sept. 22-25

Publications:

ENA Connection. bi-m. adv.
Management Update. q.
Journal of Emergency Nursing. bi-m. adv.

Emissions Markets Association

1400 I St., N.W., Suite 1050
Washington, DC 20006
Tel: (202)962-0405 *Fax:* (202)962-3930
E-Mail: info@environmentalmarkets.org
Web Site: www.environmentalmarkets.org
Members: 270 individuals
Staff: 3
Annual Budget: $250-500,000
Executive Director: Laura LeMunyan

Historical Note

EMA promotes market-based trading solutions for environmental management. Membership: $695/year (individual). Corporate memberships available.

Meetings/Conferences:

Annual Meetings: Semi-annual (Spring Meeting, Fall Internat'l Conf.)

Publications:

The Emissions Trader. q. adv.

Employee Assistance Professionals Association *(1971)*

4350 N. Fairfax Dr., Suite 410
Arlington, VA 22203
Tel: (703)387-1000 *Fax:* (703)522-4585
E-Mail: info@eap-association.org
Web Site: www.eapassn.org
Members: 7000 individuals
Staff: 10
Annual Budget: $2-5,000,000
Chief Executive Officer: John Maynard, Ph.D.
E-Mail: info@eap-association.org
Director, Finance and Operations: Chris Drake
Manager, Conference and Events: Shannon Welch
E-Mail: info@eap-association.org

Historical Note

Members are individuals involved in employee assistance programs. Formerly (1989) Association of Labor-Management Administrators and Consultants on Alcoholism. Sponsors continuing education and awards the designation CEAP (Certified Employee Assistance Professional). Membership: fees vary according to membership type.

Meetings/Conferences:

Annual Meetings: Fall

Publications:

Journal of Employee Assistance. q. adv.

Employee Assistance Society of North America *(1984)*

3650 Annapolis Lane North, Suite 107
Minneapolis, MN 55447
Tel: (763)765-2385 *Fax:* (763)765-2329
E-Mail: easna@bostrom.com
Web Site: www.easna.org
Members: 300 individuals
Annual Budget: $100-250,000
Contact: Judy Bourdeau

Historical Note

EASNA members are professionals involved in employee assistance. Membership: $90/year (U.S.), $120/year (Canada), $50/year (student), $55/year (student/Canada).

Meetings/Conferences:

Annual Meetings: Spring

Publications:

The Source. q. adv.
Employee Assistance Quarterly.
EASNA Membership Directory. bien. adv.

Employee Benefit Research Institute *(1978)*

2121 K St. NW, Suite 600
Washington, DC 20037-1896
Tel: (202)659-0670 *Fax:* (202)775-6312
E-Mail: info@ebri.org
Web Site: www.ebri.org
Members: 300 companies
Staff: 30
Annual Budget: $2-5,000,000
President and Chief Executive Officer: Dallas L. Salisbury

Historical Note

Members are businesses, plan sponsors, consultants and others interested in employee benefit plans. The Institute's main purpose is to conduct public policy research, particularly in the area of retirement, health, and welfare plans. Established September, 1978 in Washington, DC. Membership: $4,000-28,500/year.

Publications:

EBRI's Washington Bulletin. w.
Issue Briefs. m.
EBRI Notes.

Employee Involvement Association *(1942)*

P.O. Box 2307
Dayton, OH 45401-2307
Tel: (937)586-3724 *Fax:* (937)586-3699
E-Mail: eia@meinet.com
Web Site: www.eianet.org
Members: 400 companies
Staff: 1
Annual Budget: $250-500,000
Executive Director: Francine W. Rickenbach, C.A.E.
E-Mail: eia@meinet.com

Historical Note

Formerly (1992) National Association of Suggestion Systems. EIA represents manager and administrators of programs and/or systems which are designed to encourage employee involvement through the recognition of employee ideas and suggestions for company improvement. Membership: $250/year.

Meetings/Conferences:

Annual Meetings: Fall
2007 – Nashville, TN(Hilton)/Sept. 19-21/200

Publications:

Statistical Report. a. adv.
New Horizons. q. adv.
Membership Directory. a. adv.

Employee Relocation Council/Worldwide ERC *(1964)*

1717 Pennsylvania Ave. NW, Suite 800
Washington, DC 20006
Tel: (202)857-0857 *Fax:* (202)659-8631
E-Mail: cthompson@erc.org
Web Site: www.erc.org/index.shtml
Members: 13000 individuals
Staff: 45
Annual Budget: $10-25,000,000
Executive Vice President: H. Cris Collie, III,CAE
Chief Financial Officer: Laura Macary Fitch
Vice President, Research and Education: Jan Hatfield-Goldman
Senior Vice President, Operations: Tina Lung
Senior Vice President: Karen A. Reid
Vice President, Meetings and Membership: Cici Thompson
Vice President, Web Strategy and Services: Christine Wilson

Historical Note

Organized by a handful of large companies that wished to reduce the impact of relocation on their employees' productivity, efficiency and morale. Mission is to provide leadership, advocacy, education and networking to professionals and stakeholders in the mobile global workforce through specialized training, credentialing, meetings and exchange of information. Formerly (1973) Employee Relocation Real Estate Advisory Council.

Publications:

Globility newsletter (online). m.
ERC Directory. a. adv.
Mobility magazine. m. adv.
Roster of Members and Resource Guide. a. adv.
Worldwide ERC Advantage (online). m.

Employee Services Management Association *(1941)*

568 Spring Road, Suite Nine
Elmhurst, IL 60126-3896
Tel: (630)559-0020 *Fax:* (630)559-0025
E-Mail: esmahq@esmassn.org
Web Site: www.esmassn.org
Members: 2000 companies; 20 local chapters
Staff: 6
Annual Budget: $500-1,000,000
Executive Director: Patrick B. Stinson
E-Mail: pbstinson@esmassn.org

Historical Note

Founded as the National Industrial Recreation Association; became National Employee Services and Recreation Association in 1982, and assumed its present name in 2000. Members include managers of such programs as employee assistance, pre-retirement planning, fitness, child care, sports, travel and educational and cultural programs in business, the government and military. Membership: $185/year (company).

Meetings/Conferences:

Annual Meetings: Spring

Publications:

Employee Services Management. 6/year. adv.

Employee Stock Ownership Association *(1979)*

Historical Note

See ESOP Association.

Employers Council on Flexible Compensation *(1981)*

927 15th St. NW, Suite 1000
Washington, DC 20005
Tel: (202)659-4300 *Fax:* (202)371-1467
E-Mail: info@ecfc.org
Web Site: www.ecfc.org
Members: 650companiesandorganizations
Staff: 9
Annual Budget: $1-2,000,000
President: Bonnie B. Whyte, CAE, CFCI

Historical Note

A national, non-profit association committed to the promotion and improvement of flexible compensation plans. Professional membership is open to public and private employers, including non-profit organizations, companies, accounting firms, consulting actuaries, and others that design or administer flexible benefit plans. Membership fee based upon size and type of organization.

Meetings/Conferences:

Annual Meetings: March, in Washington, DC area

Publications:

Flex Reporter. q.
Legislative Alerts.
ECFC Bulletins. bi-w.
CapitoLetter. m.

Employment Management Association *(1969)*

Historical Note

A division of Society for Human Resource Management, which provides administrative support.

EMTA - Trade Association for the Emerging Markets *(1990)*

360 Madison Ave., 18th Floor
New York, NY 10017
Tel: (646)637-9100 *Fax:* (646)637-9128
E-Mail: sortiz@emta.org
Web Site: www.emta.org
Members: 100 institutions
Staff: 7
Annual Budget: $2-5,000,000
Executive Director: Michael M. Chamberlin
E-Mail: mchamb@emta.org
General Counsel: Aviva Werner
E-Mail: awerner@emta.org

Historical Note

EMTA is the principal trade group for the Emerging Markets trading and investment community and is dedicated to promoting the orderly development of fair, efficient, and transparent trading markets for Emerging Markets into the global capital markets. Full members are market participants that actively trade or invest in Emerging Markets instruments. Associate Members are market participants that trade or invest in Emerging Markets instruments, but which are smaller and less active than Full Members. Affiliate Members are firms that have a strong interest in the Emerging Markets trading and investment industry (such as advisors, law firms, accounting firms, vendors, rating agencies, data providers and consulting firms) but which do not themselves trade or invest in Emerging Markets instruments. Membership: $25,000/year (Sell-Side Full Member); $15,000/year (Buy-Side 1st Tier Member); $15,000/year (Sell-Side Associate Member); $10,000/year (Buy-Side 2nd Tier Member); $5,000/year (Sell-Side Affiliate Member); and $5,000/year (Buy-Side 3rd Tier Member).

Meetings/Conferences:

Annual Meetings: December

Publications:

Trading Volume Survey. q.
Bulletin Newsletter. q. adv.

Emulsion Polymers Council *(1995)*

1250 Connecticut Ave. NW, Suite 700
Washington, DC 20036
Tel: (202)419-1500 *Fax:* (202)659-8037
E-Mail: epc@regnet.com
Web Site: www.regnet.com/epc
Members: 9 companies
Staff: 2
Executive Director: Robert J. Fensterheim

Historical Note

EPC represents regulatory professionals at companies which produce emulsion polymers, chemical compounds used in a variety of coating and other industrial applications. Membership fee varies, based on production.

Endocrine Fellows Foundation *(1990)*

5959 W. Century Blvd., Suite 575
Los Angeles, CA 90045
Toll Free: (877)877 - 6515
E-Mail: endocrinefellows@sbcglobal.net
Web Site: www.endocrinefellows.org
Members: 600 individuals
Staff: 2
Annual Budget: $500-1,000,000
Executive Director: Marilyn Fishman
E-Mail: endocrinefellows@sbcglobal.net

Historical Note

EFF provides support to endocrine fellows in education, research grant funding and career guidance. The foundation also provides fellows and endocrinology professionals with research results on developments in endocrinology, metabolism and diabetology.

Meetings/Conferences:

Annual Meetings: Summer

Publications:

EndoTrends. q.

Endocrine Society *(1916)*

8401 Connecticut Ave., Suite 900
Chevy Chase, MD 20815-5817
Tel: (301)941-0200 *Fax:* (301)941-0259
Toll Free: (888)363 - 6274
E-Mail: societyservices@endo-society.org
Web Site: www.endo-society.org
Members: 13000 individuals
Staff: 65
Annual Budget: $10-25,000,000
Chief Executive Officer: Scott Hunt
E-Mail: shunt@endo-society.org
Director, Development and Client Services: Nancy Chill
E-Mail: nchill@endo-society.org
Director, Meeting and CME Services: Ken Fox
Director, Membership and Professional Affairs: Terry Jacobson
E-Mail: tjacobson@endo-society.org
Senior Director, Business Operations: Joseph Janela
Senior Director, Meetings and Education: Wanda Johnson
E-Mail: wjohnson@endo-society.org
Director, Government and Professional Affairs: Janet B. Kreizman
Senior Director, Journal Publications: Lenne Miller
E-Mail: lmiller@endo-society.org
Director, Portal: Wendy Raulin
Senior Director, Governance and Policy: Joan Zaro, PhD
E-Mail: jzaro@endo-society.org

Historical Note

Founded as the Association for Study of Internal Secretions, the Endocrine Society is a professional society of scientists, educators, clinicians, practicing physicians, nurses and students with an interest in research, study and clinical practice of endocrinology.

Meetings/Conferences:

Annual Meetings: June/5,000

Publications:

Endocrine News. bi-m.
Endocrine Reviews. bi-m. adv.
Endocrinology. m. adv.
Journal of Clinical Endocrinology and Metabolism. m. adv.
Molecular Endocrinology. m. adv.

Energy and Environmental Building Association *(1982)*

10740 Lyndale Ave., South, Suite 10W
Bloomington, MN 55420
Tel: (952)881-1098 *Fax:* (952)881-3048
E-Mail: information@eeba.org
Web Site: www.eeba.org
Members: 4000 individuals
Staff: 4
Annual Budget: $1-2,000,000
Executive Director: Kathleen Guidera

Historical Note

Formerly (2001) Energy Efficient Building Association. EEBA members are architects, builders, building material suppliers, and others with an interest in energy-efficient, environmentally responsible construction. Membership: $195/year (individual); $275/year (small business); $495/year (corporate).

Meetings/Conferences:

Annual Meetings: Fall

Publications:

EEBA News. q.

Energy Bar Association *(1946)*

1020 19th St. NW, Suite 525
Washington, DC 20036
Tel: (202)223-5625 *Fax:* (202)833-5596
E-Mail: admin@eba-net.org
Web Site: www.eba-net.org
Members: 2200 individuals
Staff: 3
Annual Budget: $500-1,000,000
Administrator: Lorna Johnston Wilson

Historical Note

Members are lawyers and non-attorney professionals engaged in promoting proper administration of federal laws relating to the production, development, conservation, transmission, and economic regulation of energy. Formerly (1977) Federal Power Bar Association and (1999) Federal Energy Bar Association. Membership: $110/year (private practitioner and non-attorney members); $60/'year (graduates from law school who have graduated within three years of the current calendar year); $30/year (government or academic); $20/year (student).

Meetings/Conferences:

Annual Meetings: Semi-Annual, held in May and November

Publications:

Court-Related Opinions. q.
Energy Law Journal. semi-a. adv.
Directory. a.

Energy Frontiers International *(1980)*

1110 N. Glebe Road, Suite 610
Arlington, VA 22201-4714
Tel: (703)276-6655 *Fax:* (703)276-7662
Web Site: www.energyfrontiers.org
Members: 56 companies
Staff: 3
Annual Budget: $250-500,000
President: Michael Koleda

Historical Note

Formerly (1996) the Council on Alternate Fuels. Energy Frontiers International is a joint effort by companies in the energy industry to augment their internal efforts to keep abreast of advances in a broad range of emerging energy technologies worldwide.

Publications:

Proceedings for Annual Spring Meeting. a.

Energy Security Council *(1981)*

5555 San Felipe St., Suite 100
Houston, TX 77056-3634
Tel: (713)296-1893 *Fax:* (713)296-1895
E-Mail: info@energysecuritycouncil.org
Web Site: www.energysecuritycouncil.org
Members: 350 individuals
Staff: 2
Annual Budget: $100-250,000
Executive Director: Gary Bourdreaux
E-Mail: info@energysecuritycouncil.org

Historical Note

Founded as Petroleum Industry Security Council; assumed its current name in 1999. ESC provides support to security professionals and business developers in the energy industry. Membership: $150/year (individual); $300/year (company); $1,000/year (corporate).

Publications:

ES Annual Report. a.
Intelligence Report. w.

Energy Telecommunications and Electrical Association *(1928)*

5005 Royal Lane, Suite 190
Irving, TX 75063
Tel: (972)929-3169 Ext: 203 *Fax:* (922)915-6040
Toll Free: (888)503 - 8700 Ext: 203
E-Mail: entelec@entelec.org
Web Site: www.entelec.org
Members: 140 companies
Staff: 6
Annual Budget: $500-1,000,000
Executive Manager: Blaine Siske

Historical Note

Formerly (until 1978) the Petroleum Industry Electrical Association. Members are companies and corporations in the energy industries employing personnel having managerial, engineering or technical responsibility in the electrical, electronics, communications and allied fields. Membership: $495/year.

Meetings/Conferences:

Annual Meetings: April
2007 – Houston, TX(Hilton Americas)/Apr. 11-13/1750

Energy Traffic Association *(1941)*

3303 Main St., Suite 207
Houston, TX 77002-9321
Tel: (713)528-2868
Web Site: www.energytraffic.org
Members: 100 companies
Annual Budget: $25-50,000
Executive Director: Russell Powell

Historical Note
Formerly (1997) Shippers Oil Field Traffic Association. ETA members work in logistics or related company functions for shippers in the energy industry.
Meetings/Conferences:
Annual Meetings: Spring
Publications:
Membership Directory. a.
SOFTA Newsletter. m.

Engine Manufacturers Association *(1968)*
Two N. Lasalle St., Suite 2200
Chicago, IL 60602
Tel: (312)827-8700 *Fax:* (312)827-8737
E-Mail: ema@enginemanufacturers.org
Web Site: www.enginemanufacturers.org
Members: 27 companies
Staff: 6
Annual Budget: $5-10,000,000
President: Jed R. Mandel
E-Mail: jmandel@emamail.org
Tech. Director: Roger T. Gault
E-Mail: rgault@emamail.org
Executive Vice President: Kevin Kokrda
E-Mail: kkokrda@emamail.org
Director, Finance: Todd Sharafinski
E-Mail: tsharafinski@emamail.org
Director, Public Affairs: Joseph L. Suchecki
E-Mail: jsuchecki@emamail.org
Manager, Meetings and Member Services: Muriel J. Walter
E-Mail: mwalter@emamail.org
Historical Note
Formerly (1968) Internal Combustion Engine Institute. Members are manufacturers of internal combustion engines used for any purpose except aircraft or passenger car use.
Meetings/Conferences:
Annual Meetings:
Publications:
Engine Fluids Data Book. adv.

Engine Service Association *(1970)*
Historical Note
Merged with Outdoor Power Equipment Ass'n in 2002.

Engineered Wood Association
Historical Note
See APA - The Engineered Wood Association.

Engineering College Magazines Associated *(1920)*
Historical Note
Members are staff of student-produced magazines in colleges of engineering across the U.S. ECMA promotes communication skills, good journalism and publishing practices, and camaraderie among students. Membership: $150/year.

Engineering in Medicine and Biology Society *(1950)*
445 Hoes Lane
Piscataway, NJ 08854
Tel: (732)981-3433 *Fax:* (732)465-6435
E-Mail: emb-exec@ieee.org
Members: 7800 individuals
Staff: 2
Executive Director: Laura J. Wolf
E-Mail: emb-exec@ieee.org
Historical Note
A technical society of the Institute of Electrical and Electronics Engineers (IEEE). Membership in the Society open only to IEEE members. Benefits of membership in the Society include subscription to a technical periodical in the field published by IEEE. All administrative support provided by IEEE.
Meetings/Conferences:
Annual Meetings: Fall
2007 – Lyon, France(Convention Center)/Aug. 22-27
2008 – Vancouver, BC, Canada(Vancouver Convention & Exhibition Center)/Aug. 20-25
2009 – Minneapolis, MN(Hilton)/Sept. 3-6
Publications:
IEEE/Transaction on Medical Imaging. m.
IEEE/Transactions on Biomedical Engineering. m.
IEEE/Transactions on Information Technology in Biomedicine. q.
IEEE/Transactions on Neural Systems and Rehabilitation Engineering. q.
IEEE/Transactions on Nano Bioscience. q.
IEEE/Engineering in Medicine and Biology Magazine. bi-m.
IEEE/ACM Transactions on Computational Biology and Bioinformatics.

Engineering Management Society *(1950)*
Historical Note
A technical society of the Institute of Electrical and Electronics Engineers (IEEE). Membership in the Society, open only to IEEE members, includes subscription to a technical periodical in the field published by IEEE. All administrative support is provided by IEEE.

Engraved Stationery Manufacturers Association
Historical Note
Became International Engraved Graphics Association in 2000.

Enlisted Association of the National Guard of the United States *(1972)*
3133 Mount Vernon Ave.
Alexandria, VA 22305
Tel: (703)519-3846 *Fax:* (703)519-3849
Toll Free: (800)234 - 3264
E-Mail: eangus@eangus.org
Web Site: www.eangus.org
Members: 84000 individuals
Staff: 9
Annual Budget: $1-2,000,000
Executive Director: MSG Michael P. Cline
E-Mail: eangus@eangus.org
Historical Note
EANGUS represents enlisted men and women of the Army and Air National Guard. Membership: varies by state (individual); $100-1000/year (organization/company).
Meetings/Conferences:
Annual Meetings: Summer
2007 – Oklahoma City, OK(Westin Hotel)/Aug. 12-15/2000
Publications:
New Patriot Magazine. q. adv.
New Patriot Newsletter. m. adv.
Legislative Updates. w. adv.
Congressional Report. d.
Army Times. w. adv.
Air Force Times. w. adv.

Enteral Nutrition Council *(1983)*
Historical Note
Members are manufacturers and marketers of enteral formulas, foods for special dietary use, and medical foods.

Enterprise Computer Telephony Forum *(1995)*
Historical Note
ECTF members are suppliers, developers, systems integrators and users of computer telephony integration technology. Promotes international standards for computer telephony technology and implementation of such standards throughout the industry. Membership: $12,000/year (principal); $6,000/year (small company principal); $2,500/year (auditing/user).

Enterprise Wireless Alliance *(1953)*
8484 Westpark Dr., Suite 630
McLean, VA 22102
Tel: (703)528-5115 *Fax:* (703)524-1074
E-Mail: info@ita-relay.com
Web Site: www.ita-relay.com
Members: 3100 licensed dealers
Staff: 30
Annual Budget: $2-5,000,000
President and Chief Executive Officer: Mark F. Crosby
Senior Vice President: Andre Cote
E-Mail: andre@ita-relay.com
Chief Information Officer: Howard Levitas
E-Mail: hlevitas@ita-relay.com
Vice President, Administration: Karin L. Norton
E-Mail: karin@ita-relay.com
Executive Director: Donald J. Vasek
E-Mail: dvasek@ita-relay.com
Historical Note
Formerly Industrial Telecommunications Association; absorbed American Mobile Telecommunications association and assumed its current name in 2005. EWA is an FCC-certified frequency advisory committee and national trade association that represents the interests of the private wireless (private land mobile radio) industry. In addition to regulatory and legislative representations before the FCC and US Congress, EWA provides system engineering, licensing, FCC research and refarming transition strategies. EWA is supported by more than 3,600 members and 12 trade associations. EWA also has the support of a number of independent market councils: the Council of Independent Communications Suppliers, Telephone Maintenance Frequency Advisory Committee, USMSS and the Texicab and Livery Communications Council. Membership rates: $95-2,500/year; varies by number of radio units in operation.
Meetings/Conferences:
Annual Meetings: Fall
Publications:
Private Wireless Magazine. m. adv.

Entertainment Services and Technology Association *(1987)*
875 Sixth Ave., Suite 1005
New York, NY 10005
Tel: (212)244-1505 *Fax:* (212)244-1502
Web Site: www.esta.org
Members: 460 companies
Staff: 7
Annual Budget: $1-2,000,000
Executive Director: Lori Rubinstein
E-Mail: lrubinstein@esta.org
Historical Note
Formerly (1994) Theatrical Dealers Association. ESTA's members are manufacturers, dealers, distributors, production companies, service companies, consultants, designers and others providing goods and services to the live entertainment industry in North America and around the world. These companies work in the areas of lighting, sound, rigging, soft goods, scenery, props, electrical distribution, costumes, special effects, computer software and show control.
Publications:
Protocol. q. adv.
Membership Directory. a. adv.

Entertainment Software Association *(1994)*
575 Seventh St. NW, #300
Washington, DC 20004
Tel: (202)223-2400
E-Mail: esa@theesa.com
Web Site: www.theesa.com
Members: 35 companies
Staff: 30
President: Douglas S. Lowenstein
Vice President, Congressional Relations: Ed Desmond
Senior Vice President, Intellectual Property Enforcement: Ric Hirsch
Senior Vice President and General Counsel: Gail Markels
Vice President, Intellectual Property Policy: Stevan Mitchell
Senior Vice President: Carolyn Rauch
Historical Note
Founded as Interactive Digital Software Association; assumed its current name in 2003. ESA represents interactive entertainment software publishers. Services include an annual industry trade show, an anti-piracy program, industry research, and government relations. Entertainment Software Rating Board is a division of IDSA
Meetings/Conferences:
Annual Meetings: Spring

Entomological Society of America *(1889)*
10001 Derekwood Lane, Ste 100
Lanham, MD 20706-4876
Tel: (301)731-4535 *Fax:* (301)731-4538
E-Mail: esa@entsoc.org
Web Site: www.entsoc.org
Members: 5700 individuals

Staff: 7
Annual Budget: $2-5,000,000
Executive Director: Paula G. Lettice
Director, Communications: Alan Kahan
E-Mail: akahan@entsoc.org
Director, Meetings: Judy Miller
E-Mail: jmiller@entsoc.org
Society Relations Officer: Lisa Spurlock
E-Mail: lspurlock@entsoc.org
Director, Membership and Marketing: Chris Stelzig
E-Mail: cstelzig@entsoc.org

Historical Note

Formed in 1953 by the consolidation of the American Association of Economic Entomologists (1889) and the Entomological Society of America (1906). Incorporated in the District of Columbia in 1954. In 1992 the American Registry of Professional Entomologists became the certification program for the ESA. Provides Board Certification for interested individuals. Membership: $137/year.

Meetings/Conferences:

Annual Meetings: December
2007 - San Diego, CA(Town and Country Hotel)/Dec. 10-13

Publications:

ESA Newsletter. m. adv.
Arthropod Management Tests. a.
Annals of ESA. bi-m. adv.
American Entomologist. q. adv.
Environmental Entomology. bi-m. adv.
Journal of Economic Entomology. bi-m. adv.
Journal of Medical Entomology. bi-m. adv.

Envelope Manufacturers Association *(1933)*

500 Montgomery St., #550
Alexandria, VA 22314-1565
Tel: (703)739-2200
Web Site: www.envelope.org
Members: 250 companies
Staff: 7
Annual Budget: $1-2,000,000
President and Chief Executive Officer: Maynard H. Benjamin, CAE
E-Mail: mhbenjamin@envelope.org
Manager, Educational Services and Systems Administration: Kim Moses
E-Mail: kmoses@envelope.org
Senior Vice President: Tonya Muse, CAE

Historical Note

EMA was formed by a merger of the American Envelope Manufacturers Association (founded in 1909) and the Bureau of Envelope Manufacturers (founded in 1916). Formerly (1995) Envelope Manufacturers Association of America.

Meetings/Conferences:

Semi-annual Meetings: Spring and Fall/250

Publications:

Newsletter. q.

Environmental and Engineering Geophysical Society *(1992)*

1720 S. Bellaire St., Suite 110
Denver, CO 80222
Tel: (303)531-7517 *Fax:* (303)820-3844
E-Mail: staff@eegs.org
Web Site: www.eegs.org
Members: 700 individuals
Staff: 5
Administrative Assistant: Jayma File
E-Mail: staff@eegs.org

Historical Note

Members are individuals and corporations with an interest in geophysics and applied environmental engineering. Membership fees vary.

Meetings/Conferences:

Annual Meetings: Spring

Publications:

Fast TIMES: The EEGS Newsletter. q. adv.
Journal of Environmental and Engineering Geophysics. q. adv.

Environmental Assessment Association

1224 N. Nokomis NE
Alexandria, MN 56308
Tel: (320)763-4320 *Fax:* (320)763-9290
E-Mail: eaa@iami.org
Web Site: www.iami.org/eaa.cfm
Members: 5000 individuals
Annual Budget: $1-2,000,000
Executive Director: Robert G. Johnson
Associate Executive Director: Dale Ekdahl

Historical Note

Members are environmental inspectors and other professionals, primarily in the real estate industry, involved in environmental hazard detection and mitigation. Membership: $195/year.

Meetings/Conferences:

Annual Meetings: usually Las Vegas, NV/Fall

Publications:

Environmental Times. m. adv.

Environmental Bankers Association *(1994)*

510 King St., Suite 410
Alexandria, VA 22314
Tel: (703)549-0977 *Fax:* (703)548-5945
Toll Free: (800)966 - 7475
E-Mail: eba@envirobank.org
Web Site: http://envirobank.org
Members: 76 banks and affiliates
Staff: 2
Annual Budget: $100-250,000
Executive Co-Director: D.J. Telego
Executive Co-Director: T.C. Telego

Historical Note

EBA voting members are banks, trust companies, credit unions, savings and loan associations, and other financial services organizations with an interest in environmental risk management and related issues. Active participants are bankers from Trust or Credit offices with responsibility for environmental liability, and financial services officers with environmental interests. Affiliate members are from law firms, consulting and insurance organizations. Membership: $500-$1,250/year.

Meetings/Conferences:

Semi-annual Meeting: January and June

Publications:

Your Financial Institution & the Environment. a.
Bank Notes. bi-m. adv.

Environmental Business Association, The *(1989)*

1150 Connecticut Ave. NW
Ninth Floor
Washington, DC 20036-4129
Tel: (202)828-4100 *Fax:* (202)828-4130
E-Mail: teba@bode.com
Members: 55 companies
Annual Budget: $50-100,000
President: William H. Bode

Historical Note

TEBA members represent all segments of the environmental industry -- consultants, laboratories, remediation companies, disposal firms, recyclers and technology innovators. TEBA facilitates arrangements and information exchange among members to develop business opportunities. Services include sponsoring seminars, monthly meetings, industry trends, changes in technology and legislation. Membership: $500/year (individual); corporate dues vary based on revenue.

Meetings/Conferences:

Annual Meetings: June

Environmental Design Research Association *(1968)*

P.O. Box 7146
Edmond, OK 73083-7146
Tel: (405)330-4863 *Fax:* (405)330-4150
E-Mail: edra@edra.org
Web Site: www.edra.org
Members: 700 individuals
Staff: 3
Annual Budget: $100-250,000
Executive Director: Janet Singer
E-Mail: edra@edra.org

Historical Note

Mission is to advance the art and science of environmental design research, to improve understanding of the interrelationships between people and their built and natural surroundings, and to help create environments responsive to human needs. EDRA members are designers and other professionals with an interest in environmental design research. Membership: $100/year (individual); $65/year (student); $300/year (organization/company).

Meetings/Conferences:

Annual Meetings: Spring-Summer
2007 - Sacramento, CA(Sheraton Grand Hotel)/May 30-June 3

Publications:

Design Research News. q.
Proceedings of Annual Meeting. a.

Environmental Industry Associations *(1968)*

4301 Connecticut Ave. NW, Suite 300
Washington, DC 20008-2304
Tel: (202)244-4700 *Fax:* (202)966-4824
Toll Free: (800)424 - 2869
E-Mail: membership@envasns.org
Web Site: www.envasns.org
Members: 2000 companies
Staff: 35
Annual Budget: $5-10,000,000
President and Chief Executive Officer: Bruce J. Parker
General Counsel: David Biderman
Director, Public Affairs and Industry Research: Alice Jacobsohn
Comptroller: Patricia Lyndane
Director, Federal Relations: William H. Sells

Historical Note

Formerly (1994) National Solid Wastes Management Association. Restructured in 1994. EIA now includes the National Solid Waste Management Association and the Waste Equipment Technology Association.

Meetings/Conferences:

Annual Meetings: Spring/14,000

Environmental Information Association *(1983)*

6935 Wisconsin Ave., Suite 306
Chevy Chase, MD 20815-6112
Tel: (301)961-4999 *Fax:* (301)961-3094
Toll Free: (888)343 - 4342
E-Mail: info@eia-usa.org
Web Site: www.eia-usa.org
Members: 500 individuals
Staff: 5
Annual Budget: $250-500,000
Coordinator, Membership and Meetings: Lisa Mihalik
Manager, Development and Communication: Kelly Rutt

Historical Note

Formerly (1991) National Asbestos Council and (1993) NAC/The Environmental Information Association. Serves as an information clearinghouse for building owners, environmental professionals, and the public concerning asbestos and other environmental health hazards to building occupants, industrial sites and other facilities. Membership: $105/year (individual); $400/year (corporate); $35/year (student); $1,000/year (executive).

Meetings/Conferences:

Annual: Typical Attendence: 200-250

2007 - Charlotte, NC(Charlotte Marriott City Center)/March 17-21/300

Publications:

NetNews. w.
Indoor Environment Connection. m. adv.
Inside EIA. m. adv.

Environmental Mutagen Society *(1969)*

1821 Michael Faraday Dr., Suite 300
Reston, VA 20190
Tel: (703)438-8220 *Fax:* (703)438-3113
E-Mail: emshq@ems-us.org
Web Site: www.ems-us.org
Members: 800 individuals
Annual Budget: $250-500,000
Executive Director: Tonia Masson

Historical Note

Members are scientists of diverse backgrounds and varied interests working in the field of molecular genetics and mutagenesis, whether in academia, industry or government. Focus is to encourage the study of mutagens in the human environment, particularly as they affect public health.

Meetings/Conferences:

Annual Meetings: Fall
2007 - Atlanta, GA(Hyatt Regency)/Oct. 21-24/500

2008 – Rio Grande, PR(Westin Rio Mar)/Oct. 18-22/500

Publications:

Environmental and Molecular Mutagenesis. 8/year.
EMS Newsletter. bi-a.
Membership Roster. irreg.

Environmental Technology Council *(1982)*
734 15th St. NW, Suite 720
Washington, DC 20005
Tel: (202)783-0870 *Fax:* (202)737-2038
E-Mail: mail@etc.org
Web Site: www.etc.org
Members: 15 companies
Staff: 3
Annual Budget: $1-2,000,000
Executive Director: David R. Case
ViceP., Government Relations: Scott L. Slesinger

Historical Note

Established in Washington, DC and incorporated in Delaware. Formerly (1994) Hazardous Waste Treatment Council. Trade association of environmental management firms engaged in waste treatment, recycling and disposal as well as engineering and consulting firms engaged in the cleanup of contaminated sites. Membership: $8,000-96,000/year, based on revenues (company); $2,500/year for firms outside the industry.

Meetings/Conferences:

Quarterly Meetings: Washington, DC/January, April, July, and October

Publications:

Environmental Technology Council Reports. bi-w.
Conference Proceedings. a.

EPDM Roofing Association *(2003)*
515 King St., Suite 420
Alexandria, VA 22314-3137
Tel: (703)684-5020 *Fax:* (703)684-6048
E-Mail: info@epdmroofs.org
Web Site: www.epdmroofs.org
Director, Member Services: Tonya S. Rideout

Historical Note

Members are manufacturers of single-ply roofing products and their suppliers.

EPS Molders Association *(1994)*
1298 Cronson Blvd., Suite 201
Crofton, MD 21114
Tel: (410)451-8341 *Fax:* (410)451-8343
Toll Free: (800)607 - 3772
E-Mail: info@epsmolders.org
Web Site: www.epsmolders.org
Members: 50 individuals
Staff: 4
Annual Budget: $250-500,000
Executive Director: Betsy Steiner

Historical Note

EPSMA represents the views of the manufacturers of expanded polystyrene and insulation products and associated industry groups. Membership fee varies.

Meetings/Conferences:

Annual Meetings: Annual

Publications:

EPS Newsline. q.

Epsilon Sigma Phi *(1927)*
P.O. Box 357340
Gainesville, FL 32635-7340
Tel: (352)378-6665 *Fax:* (352)375-0722
E-Mail: espoffice@espnational.org
Web Site: www.espnational.org
Members: 9000 individuals
Staff: 1
Annual Budget: $100-250,000
Executive Director: Linda D. Cook
E-Mail: espoffice@espnational.org

Historical Note

ESP is an organization of professional staff in U.S. land grant universities and U.S. Department of Agriculture Extension programs. Established in Montana January 10, 1927. Membership: $30/year (active); $150/lifetime membership.

Meetings/Conferences:

2007 – Charleston, SC(Francis Marion Hotel)/Sept. 8-14
2008 – Indianapolis, IN(Galaxy III)/Sept. 14-18

Publications:

The ESP Connection. q.

Equipment and Tool Institute *(1947)*
126 North Salem St., Suite 206
Apex, NC 27502
Tel: (919)629-8122 *Fax:* (603)971-2375
E-Mail: info@etools.org
Web Site: www.etools.org
Members: 60 companies
Staff: 3
Annual Budget: $500-1,000,000

Historical Note

Members are manufacturers of automotive service equipment and tools.

Meetings/Conferences:

Annual Meetings: Spring

Publications:

News and Views Newsletter. 2/year.

Equipment Leasing Association of America *(1961)*
4301 N. Fairfax Dr., Suite 550
Arlington, VA 22203-1608
Tel: (703)527-8655 *Fax:* (703)527-2649
Web Site: www.elaonline.com
Members: 800 companies
Staff: 26
Annual Budget: $5-10,000,000
President: Kenneth E. Bentsen
Vice President, State Government Relations: Dennis Brown, CAE
Vice President, Marketing and Communication: Donald Ethier, CAE
Vice President, Meetings and Conventions: Sally A. Maloney
Vice President, Professional Development: Lesley Sterling

Historical Note

Founded as Association of Equipment Lessors; became American Association of Equipment Lessors in 1974 and assumed its present name in 1992. Members are companies whose principal business is leasing equipment to business users. Sponsors the Equipment Leasing Association Capital Investment-Lease Political Action Committee.

Meetings/Conferences:

Annual Meetings: Fall

Publications:

Equipment Leasing Today (ELT). m. adv.
Journal of Equipment Lease Finance. semi-a.

Equipment Service Association *(1959)*
1605 Industrial Dr.
Carlisle, PA 17013
Tel: (717)243-1264 *Fax:* (717)243-8865
Toll Free: (866)372 - 3155
E-Mail: equipservassn@yahoo.com
Web Site: www.2esa.org
Members: 142 companies
Annual Budget: $50-100,000
Executive Director: Janet E. Brown
E-Mail: equipservassn@yahoo.com

Historical Note

Organized as the International Hydraulic Equipment Rebuilders Association at a meeting of hydraulic jack rebuilders convoked by the Hydraulic Jack Manufacturers Association. Members are companies who rebuild pneumatic, electric and hydraulic equipment. Has no paid officers or full time staff. Membership: $260/year.

Meetings/Conferences:

Annual Meetings: Spring/200

Publications:

The Leader in Service Newsletter. m. adv.
Membership Directory. a. adv.

ERISA Industry Committee *(1977)*
1400 L St. NW, Suite 350
Washington, DC 20005
Tel: (202)789-1400 *Fax:* (202)789-1120
E-Mail: eric@eric.org
Web Site: www.eric.org
Members: 114 companies
Staff: 9
President: Mark J. Ugoretz
Senior Vice President: Janice Gregory
Director, Communications: Brendan I. Lacivita

Historical Note

ERIC represents the employment benefit and retirement security interests of America's major enterprises. Members administer private sector retirement, health plans and other benefits for some 25 million active and retired workers and their beneficiaries.

Meetings/Conferences:

Annual Meetings: usually Washington, DC

Publications:

ERIC Executive Report. w.

ESOP Association *(1979)*
1726 M St. NW, Suite 501
Washington, DC 20036
Tel: (202)293-2971 *Fax:* (202)293-7568
Toll Free: (866)366 - 3832
E-Mail: amy@esopassociation.org
Web Site: www.esopassociation.org
Members: 2200 companies and professionals
Staff: 10
Annual Budget: $2-5,000,000
President: J. Michael Keeling, CAE
E-Mail: michael@esopassociation.org
Vice President, Membership Development: Lisa R. Betts
E-Mail: lisa@esopassociation.org
Vice President, Meetings and Conferences: Rosemary A. Clements
E-Mail: rose@esopassociation.org
Controller: Joel S. Goza
E-Mail: joel@esopassociation.org
Director, Communications: Amy Gwiazdowski
E-Mail: esop@esopassociation.org
Vice President, Administration: Gwenn E. Rosenthal
E-Mail: gwenn@esopassociation.org

Historical Note

Formed in May 1979 as the ESOP Association of America through a merger of the National Association of ESOP Companies and the Employee Stock Ownership Council of America, both formed in 1977; assumed its present name in July, 1982. Incorporated in California. Members are companies with employee stock ownership plans and professionals who specialize in these plans. Sponsors and supports ESOP PAC. Membership: $550-3600/year.

Meetings/Conferences:

Annual Meetings: May-June/1,000
2007 – Washington, DC/May 15-16

Publications:

ESOP Report. m.

Espionage Research Institute *(2001)*
10903 Indian Head Hwy., Suite 304
Ft. Washington, MD 20744
Tel: (240)273-8823 *Fax:* (301)292-4635
E-Mail: k3do@earthlink.net
Web Site: www.espionbusiness.com
Members: 97 individuals
Staff: 3
President: Glenn H. Whidden
E-Mail: k3do@earthlink.net

Historical Note

Supersedes the former Business Espionage Controls and Countermeasures Association (1990-2001). ERI members are counterespionge practitioners, developers of espionage-protection technologies, and companies actively deploying counterespionage solutions. Membership: $125/year.

Meetings/Conferences:

Annual Meetings: usually Washington, DC area

Publications:

The Business Espinoage Report. m.

Estuarine Research Federation *(1969)*
P.O. Box 510
Port Republic, MD 20676-0510
Tel: (410)586-0997 *Fax:* (410)586-9226
E-Mail: barnes@erf.org
Web Site: www.erf.org
Members: 2000 individuals
Staff: 3

Annual Budget: $100-250,000
Executive Director: Joy A. Bartholomew
Chief Operations Officer: Janet Barnes
E-Mail: barnes@erf.org

Historical Note

ERF is a multidisciplinary organization of individuals who study the structure and function of estuaries, and the effect of human activities on these environments. Promotes research in estuarine and coastal waters, and is available as a source of advice in matters concerning estuaries and the coastal zone. Membership: $95/year (individual); $245-600/year (institutional, domestic).

Meetings/Conferences:

Biennial Meetings: Odd years
2007 - Providence, RI(Convention Center)/Nov. 4-8

Publications:

Estuaries and Coasts. 6/year.
Newsletter. q.

ETAD North America *(1982)*
1850 M St. NW, Suite 700
Washington, DC 20036
Tel: (202)721-4154 *Fax:* (202)296-8120
E-Mail: helmest@socma.com
Web Site: www.etad.com
Members: 9 companies
Staff: 3
Annual Budget: $250-500,000
Executive Director: Dr. C. Tucker Helmes

Historical Note

Founded as United States Operating Committee of ETAD; became United States Dye Manufacturers Operating Committee of ETAD in 1993 and assumed its current name in 2001. The international association, ETAD (Ecological and Toxicological Association of Dyes and Organic Pigment Manufacturers) was formed in 1974 to combine scientific and technical resources within companies in the dyestuffs industry to address ecotoxicological problems. In 1977 American companies formed the Dyes Environmental and Toxicology Organization (DETO); in 1982 most DETO members decided to join ETAD, and the two organizations were merged. ETAD North America represents the interests of manufacturers and formulators of dyes in the region with regard to environmental and health hazards in the manufacture, processing, shipment, use and disposal of their products. Affiliated with the Synthetic Organic Chemical Manufacturers Association, which provides administrative support.

Meetings/Conferences:

Annual Meetings: Spring

Publications:

Questions and Answers About the Use and Handling of Dyes.
Handling Dyes Safely- A Guide for the Protection of Workers Handling Dyes.
Annual Report. a.

Ethics Officer Association *(1992)*
411 Waverly Oaks Road, Suite 324
Waltham, MA 02452
Tel: (781)647-9333 *Fax:* (781)647-9399
Web Site: www.theecoa.org
Members: 1100 individuals
Staff: 8
Executive Director: Keith T. Darcy

Historical Note

Membership: $950/year (basic); $3,500/year (organization/company).

Meetings/Conferences:

Semi-Annual Meetings: April and November

Ethylene Oxide Industry Council

Historical Note

A program of the Chemical Manufacturers Association.

Ethylene Oxide Sterilization Association *(1995)*
11527 Bertram St.
Lake Ridge, VA 22192-7453
Tel: (703)897-4444 *Fax:* (703)897-4646
E-Mail: hadmck@aol.com
Web Site: www.eosa.org
Members: 25 companies
Staff: 4
Annual Budget: $100-250,000

Historical Note

EOSA proactively addresses the merits of ethylene oxide steriliztion. Members are persons and companies with an interest in the sterilization of medical devices, scientific instruments, and spice fumigation. Membership fee varies, based on sales: $500-7500/year.

Meetings/Conferences:

Three Meetings Annually: usually in conjunction with AAMI

EUCG *(1973)*
20165 N. 67th Ave., Suite 122A
Glendale, AZ 85308
Tel: (623)572-4140 *Fax:* (623)572-4141
E-Mail: eucgexec@cox.net
Web Site: www.eucg.org
Members: 115 companies
Staff: 1
Annual Budget: $250-500,000
Executive Director: Pat Kovalesky
E-Mail: eucgexec@cox.net

Historical Note

Founded as Electric Utility Cost Group. Assumed its current name in 1996. EUCG is an association of utility professionals that meets semi-annually to discuss electric utility issues and problems. Enabling members to draw on the electric energy community; EUCG provides members with feedback on utility and plant specific problems, to increase competitiveness and value. Membership: $900-5,300/year.

Meetings/Conferences:

Semi-Annual Meetings:
2007 - Savannah, GA(Hyatt Riverfront)/March 25-25
2007 - Denver, CO(City Center Marriot)/Sept. 30-30

Europe and Eurasia Business Committee

Historical Note

An affiliate of United States Chamber of Commerce, which provides administrative support.

European-American Business Council *(1989)*
1325 G St. NW
Suite 500
Washington, DC 20005
Tel: (202)449-7705 *Fax:* (202)449-7704
Web Site: www.eabc.org
Members: 50 companies
Staff: 3
Annual Budget: $500-1,000,000
President and Chief Executive Officer: Michael Maibach

Historical Note

Formerly (1992) the European Community Chamber of Commerce in the United States and (1997) the European-American Chamber of Commerce. EABC members are European and American companies concerned with U.S. and European political activity affecting transatlantic trade. Membership: $12,000/year (company).

Publications:

Policy Review. m.
Jobs, Trade & Investment. a.

Evangelical Christian Publishers Association *(1974)*
4816 S. Ash Ave., Suite 101
Tempe, AZ 85282
Tel: (480)966-3998 *Fax:* (480)966-1944
E-Mail: info@ecpa.org
Web Site: www.ecpa.org
Members: 272 companies
Staff: 10
Annual Budget: $500-1,000,000
President and Chief Executive Officer: Mark Kuyper
Vice President, Business Development: Kelly Gallagher
Vice President, Operations: Chestine Gosnell
Manager, Membership Services: Jo Meegan
E-Mail: jmeegan@ecpa.org

Historical Note

ECPA is an international, non-profit trade organization serving the Christian publishing industry by promoting excellence and professionalism, sharing relevant data, stimulating Christian fellowship, raising the effectiveness of member publishing houses, and equipping them to meet the need of the changing marketplace.

Meetings/Conferences:

Semi-Annual Meetings: April-May and October-November

Evangelical Church Library Association *(1970)*
P.O. Box 353
Glen Ellyn, IL 60138-0353
Tel: (630)375-7865 *Fax:* (847)296-0754
E-Mail: judi@eclalibraries.org
Web Site: www.eclalibraries.org
Members: 350 individuals
Staff: 1
Annual Budget: $10-25,000
Treasurer: Judi Turek

Historical Note

Established to assist churches in setting up and maintaining library resource centers. Membership: $30/year (individual); $100/year (publishers).

Publications:

Church Libraries. q. adv.

Evangelical Council for Financial Accountability *(1979)*
440 W. Jubal Early Dr., Suite 130
Winchester, VA 22601
Tel: (540)535-0103 *Fax:* (540)535-0533
Toll Free: (800)323 - 9473
E-Mail: info@ecfa.org
Web Site: www.ecfa.org
Members: 1200 organizations
Staff: 11
Annual Budget: $1-2,000,000
President: Ken Behr
Vice President: Dan Busby
E-Mail: info@ecfa.org

Historical Note

Accreditation agency for religious charities. Seal granted to members who meet ECFA's "Seven Standards of Responsible Stewardship."

Publications:

Focus on Accountability. q.
Member List. a.

Evangelical Press Association *(1948)*
P.O. Box 28129
Minneapolis, MN 55428
Tel: (763)535-4793 *Fax:* (763)535-4794
E-Mail: director@epassoc.org
Web Site: www.epassoc.org
Members: 325 organizations
Staff: 3
Annual Budget: $100-250,000
Executive Director: Doug Trouten
E-Mail: director@epassoc.org

Historical Note

EPA is a fellowship of more than 300 Christian magazines, newspapers, and newsletters, including editors and publishers. Membership fees vary.

Meetings/Conferences:

Annual Meetings: May
2007 - Colorado Springs, CO(Doubletree)//400

Publications:

Liaison. q.
Membership Directory. a. adv.
Guide to Freelancers. a. adv.

Evangelical Training Association *(1930)*
P.O. Box 327
Wheaton, IL 60187
Tel: (630)540-7800
Toll Free: (800)369 - 8291
E-Mail: moreinfo@etaworld.org
Web Site: www.etaworld.org
Members: 200 colleges and seminaries
Staff: 8
Annual Budget: $500-1,000,000
President: Yvonne E. Thigpen

Historical Note

Active member seminaries and colleges present courses using ETA materials to prepare students for professional church leadership and to train church volunteers. These courses lead to the Associate Teacher Diploma, the Standard Teacher Diploma or *the Graduate Teacher Diploma. Formerly (1990) Evangelical Teacher Training Association. Membership: $100/year (organization).*

Meetings/Conferences:
Biennial Meetings: Odd years in February

Evaporative Cooling Institute *(1989)*
MSC Box 3ECI-NMSU
P.O. Box 30001
Las Cruces, NM 88003-8001
Tel: (505)646-4104 *Fax:* (505)646-2960
E-Mail: moreinfo@evapcooling.org
Web Site: www.evapcooling.org/index.htm
Members: 15 companies
Annual Budget: under $10,000
Executive Director: Robert Foster

Historical Note
Promotes research in and applications of evaporative air conditioning. Membership: $60/year (individual); $300/year (organization).

Meetings/Conferences:
Semi-annual Meetings:

Publications:
Cool Air News. a. adv.
Membership Services Directory. a. adv.

Evidence Photographers International Council *(1968)*
600 Main St.
Honesdale, PA 18431
Tel: (570)253-5450 *Fax:* (570)253-5011
Toll Free: (800)356 - 3742
E-Mail: epicheadquarters@verizon.net
Web Site: www.epicheadquarters@verizon.net
Members: 2000 individuals
Staff: 5
Annual Budget: $50-100,000
Executive Director: Robert Jennings

Historical Note
EPIC is a non-profit educational and scientific organization dedicated to the advancement of forensic photography in civil evidence and law enforcement. Membership: $75/year.

Meetings/Conferences:
Annual Meetings: Fall

Publications:
Journal of Evidence Photography. semi-a. adv.
Newsletter. q.

Executive Women in Government
P.O. Box 1046
Laurel, MD 20725-1046
Tel: (301)725-3500 *Fax:* (301)725-5323
E-Mail: info@execwomeningov.org
Web Site: www.execwomeningov.org
President: Marylouise Uhlig
E-Mail: info@execwomeningov.org

Historical Note
EWG members are women employed by the federal government at the Senior Executive Service, GS-15 or equivalent military rank; political apointees requiring confirmation and elected officials.

Executive Women International *(1938)*
515 S. 700 East, Suite 2A
Salt Lake City, UT 84102-2801
Tel: (801)355-2800 *Fax:* (801)355-2852
Toll Free: (800)394 - 1229
E-Mail: ewi@executivewomen.org
Web Site: www.executivewomen.org
Members: 6000 individuals
Staff: 5
Annual Budget: $500-1,000,000
Executive Director: Tara Ross
E-Mail: tara@executivewomen.org
Coordinator, Member Services and Marketing: Heather Hans
E-Mail: heather@executivewomen.org

Historical Note
Formerly (1978) Executives' Secretaries, Inc. Members are firms, each of which is represented by individuals engaged in executive and administrative positions. EWI provides an environment for the promotion of member firms, the enhancement of personal and professional development, and the encouragement of community involvement. Membership is by invitation only and through company representation.

Meetings/Conferences:
Annual Meetings: September

Publications:
Pulse. bi-m. adv.

Exercise-Safety Association *(1978)*
P.O. Box 547916
Orlando, FL 32854-7916
Tel: (407)246-5090
E-Mail: askesa@exercisesafety.com
Web Site: www.exercisesafety.com
Members: 20000 individuals
Staff: 5
Executive Director: Kim Foy
E-Mail: askesa@exercisesafety.com

Historical Note
ESA is a professional training organization, providing safety training and certification for fitness instructors and health facilities. Membership: $25/year.

Publications:
ESA News Newsletter. q. adv.
ESA Catalogue Directory. a. adv.

Exhibit Designers and Producers Association *(1954)*
1100 Johnson Ferry Rd.
Suite 300
Atlanta, GA 30342
Tel: (404)303-7310 *Fax:* (404)252-0774
E-Mail: edpa@edpa.com
Web Site: www.edpa.com
Members: 375 companies
Staff: 5
Annual Budget: $250-500,000
Executive Director: Pete Dicks

Historical Note
Members are designers, builders, and suppliers of displays for exhibits, trade shows, and events. Sets standards for creators of exhibits and promotes education in the use of three-dimensional media. Member of the Center for Exposition Industry Research and the International Federation of Exhibition Services (IFES).

Meetings/Conferences:
Annual Meetings: December/150
2007 – Marco Island, FL(Marco Island Marriott Resort)/Nov. 28-30

Publications:
EDPA Communications newsletter (online). m. adv.
EDPA Today newsletter. q. adv.
Membership Directory. a. adv.

Exhibition Services and Contractors Association *(1970)*
2260 Corporate Cir., Suite 400
Henderson, NV 89014-7701
Tel: (702)319-9561 *Fax:* (702)450-7732
Toll Free: (877)792 - 3722
E-Mail: info@esca.org
Web Site: www.esca.org
Members: 160 firms
Annual Budget: $100-250,000
Executive Director: Susan L. Schwartz, CEM
E-Mail: sschwartz@esca.org
Member Relations Coordinator: Tricia Prestwood-Hanisko

Historical Note
Formerly (2001) Exposition Service Contractors Association. Members are full-service general exposition contractors, and specialty firms related to the exposition service industry such as security, audio-visual, electrical and floral companies. Member of the Trade Show Bureau. Has no paid officers or full-time staff. Membership: $500-700/year.

Meetings/Conferences:
Semi-Annual Meeting: December, with Internat'l Ass'n for Exposition Management, and Summer Educational Conference

Publications:
ESCA Extra. m. adv.
ESCA Voice Newsletter. q. adv.

Exhibition Validation Council *(1981)*

Historical Note
Established by the Center for Exhibition Industry Research to develop a standardized form for reporting attendance and other data from trade shows, and to act as a clearinghouse where information on trade shows can be registered. A subsidiary of the Center for Exhibition Industry Research.

Exotic Wildlife Association *(1967)*
105 Henderson Branch Road West
Ingram, TX 78025
Tel: (830)367-7761 *Fax:* (830)367-7762
E-Mail: info@exoticwildlifeassociation.com
Web Site: www.exoticwildlifeassociation.com
Members: 2500 individuals
Staff: 4
Annual Budget: $250-500,000
Executive Director: Charly Seale

Historical Note
Membership: $150/year (individual).

Meetings/Conferences:
Annual Meetings: Spring

Publications:
Game Ranch Directory. a. adv.
Exotic Wildlife. bi-m. adv.
Fair Safari. bi-a. adv.

Expanded Shale, Clay and Slate Institute *(1952)*
2225 E. Murray Holladay Road, Suite 102
Salt Lake City, UT 84117
Tel: (801)272-7070 *Fax:* (801)272-3377
E-Mail: info@escsi.org
Web Site: www.escsi.org
Members: 10 companies
Staff: 3
Annual Budget: $250-500,000
President: John P. Ries, P.E.
E-Mail: jries@escsi.org
Office Manager: Robyn Rytting
E-Mail: rrytting@escsi.org

Historical Note
Founded as the Expanded Shale Institute; assumed its present name in 1955. Members are manufacturers of rotary kiln produced expanded shale, clay and slate lightweight aggregate. ESCSI promotes the extensive use of rotary kiln produced lightweight aggregate in the concrete masonry, ready-mix and precast markets. Based on research and development, educational material is disseminated to all phases of the building industry. The association works closely with other technical organizations to maintain product quality, life-safety and professional integrity throughout the construction industry and related building code bodies.

Meetings/Conferences:
Annual Meetings: May/September
2007 – Grapevine, TX(Gaylord Texan)/May 8-10/50
2007 – New York, NY/September/30

Publications:
Information Sheets. irreg.

Expansion Joint Manufacturers Association *(1955)*
25 N. Broadway
Tarrytown, NY 10591-3201
Tel: (914)332-0040 *Fax:* (914)332-1541
E-Mail: ejma@ejma.org
Web Site: www.ejma.org
Members: 9 companies
Staff: 2
Annual Budget: $10-25,000
Secretary: Richard C. Byrne

Historical Note
EJMA's Technical Committee prepares industry standards. Cooperates with ASME in the development of engineering standards for metallic expansion joints for use in piping systems.

Meetings/Conferences:
Semi-annual Meetings:

Expediting Management Association *(1978)*
534 Bridlecreek Green SW
Calgary, AB T2Y 3-P2
Tel: (403)201-6401 *Fax:* (403)201-6402
Web Site: www.expedite.org
Members: 100 companies

Staff: 10
Annual Budget: $10-25,000
Executive Administrator: Patricia Murphy
E-Mail: murphydp@telusplanet.net

Historical Note

Established in Greenwich, Connecticut and incorporated in Texas; EMA members are individuals actively engaged in managerial or supervisory positions in the profession of expediting. Membership: $100/year (individual).

Meetings/Conferences:

Annual Meetings: September

Publications:

EMAnator. bi-m. adv.
Expediting Checklist.
Expediting Handbook.

Export Institute

Historical Note

Became Export Institute of the United States in 2001

Export Institute of the United States *(1964)*

6901 W. 84th St., Suite 317
Minneapolis, MN 55438
Tel: (952)943-1505
Toll Free: (800)943 - 3171
E-Mail: jrj@exportinstitute.org
Web Site: www.exportinstitute.com
Members: 440 individuals
Staff: 8
Annual Budget: $500-1,000,000
Director: John R. Jagoe

Historical Note

Formerly (1964) Export Institute; assumed current name in 2001. Institute members are international traders that provide consulting services, market research, online export classes and export-related publications. Membership: $95/year.

Meetings/Conferences:

Annual: 600

Publications:

Foreign Customer Lists. a.
Export Sales and Marketing Manual. a.

Express Carriers Association *(1991)*

P.O. Box 4376
Allentown, PA 18105
Toll Free: (866)322 - 7447
E-Mail: eca@expresscarriers.com
Web Site: www.expresscarriers.com
Members: 185 companies
Staff: 1
Annual Budget: $100-250,000
Executive Director: Cheryle Williamson

Historical Note

A national association of shippers, carriers and vendors of products and services of the transportation industry. Membership: $520/year (organization).

Meetings/Conferences:

Annual Meetings: Spring

2007 - Orlando, FL(Portofino)/May 14-17/400

Publications:

Service Directory. a. adv.
Quarterly Newsletter Expressions. q.

Express Delivery & Logistics Association *(1976)*

6309 Beachway Dr.
Falls Church, VA 22044
Tel: (703)998-7121 *Fax:* (703)998-7123
E-Mail: info@expressassociation.org
Members: 100 companies
Staff: 3
Annual Budget: $250-500,000
Executive Director: Sue Presti

Historical Note

Formerly (1976) Air Courier Conference of America; assumed current name in 2005. Members are express delivery and logistics companies.

Meetings/Conferences:

Annual Meetings: March/400

Publications:

XLA Express. bi-m.
XLA Alerts. irreg.
XLA Policy Bulletins. irreg.

Extra Touch Florists Association *(1994)*

197 Woodlawn Pkwy., Suite 104-280
San Marcos, CA 92069
Toll Free: (888)419 - 1515
Web Site: www.etfassociation.org
Members: 13000 individuals
Staff: 50
Annual Budget: $2-5,000,000
Contact: Marilee Just

Historical Note

Founded as Florists Telegraph Delivery Association; became FTD Association in 1998, and assumed its current name in 2001. A partner of InterFlora, Inc., the international florists' delivery organization. Provides collaborative marketing, educational programs, and networking opportunities to member florists. Membership: $800/year.

Meetings/Conferences:

Annual Meetings: August

Publications:

Fax Flash.
The Extratouch Online.

Eye Bank Association of America *(1961)*

1015 18th St. NW, Suite 1010
Washington, DC 20036-5504
Tel: (202)775-4999 *Fax:* (202)429-6036
E-Mail: info@restoresight.org
Web Site: www.restoresight.org
Members: 112 eye banks
Staff: 5
Annual Budget: $1-2,000,000
President: Patricia Aiken-O'Neill
Director, Finance: Dorothy Robinson
Manager, Meetings and Education: Malene Ward

Historical Note

Established in 1961 by the Committee on Eye Banks of the American Academy of Ophthalmology to obtain, medically screen and deliver donor eyes to surgeons for corneal transplantation, and to research centers to aid in the discovery of the causes and cures of many types of blindness. EBAA represents eye banks nationwide and internationally.

Publications:

Insight. 8/year.
Membership Directory. a.

Fabricators and Manufacturers Association, International *(1970)*

833 Featherstone Road
Rockford, IL 61107
Tel: (815)399-8770 *Fax:* (815)484-7770
E-Mail: info@fmanet.org
Web Site: www.fmanet.org
Members: 1,800 individuals
Staff: 83
Annual Budget: $5-10,000,000
President and Chief Executive Officer: Gerald M. Shankel
Director, Expositions: Mark Hoper
Director, Communications: Pat Lee
Director, Membership Services and Research: Nancy Olson
Director, Education: Jim Warren

Historical Note

The primary educational organization serving the metal-forming and fabricating industry. Services focus on providing technical information through publications, conferences and seminars, expositions, newsletters and the Metal Authority to companies and individuals involved in sheet metal fabricating, pressworking, roll forming, coil processing, plate and structural fabricating. Originally known as the Fabricating Machinery Association; became the Fabricating Manufacturers Association in 1975 and assumed its present name in 1985. Membership: $25-1850/year.

Meetings/Conferences:

Annual Meetings: Exposition: Odd Years - Chicago, IL/Even Years - Varies

Publications:

FMA Connections Newsletter. bi-m.
Stamping Journal. m. adv.
The Fabricator. 12/year. adv.
TPJ, The Tube & Pipe Journal. 8/year. adv.
Practical Welding Today. 6/year. adv.

Family and Consumer Sciences Education Association *(1927)*

Family/Consumer Sciences, Central Washington Univ.
400 E. Eighth University Way
Ellensburg, WA 98926-7565
Tel: (509)963-2766 *Fax:* (509)963-2787
E-Mail: hubbards@cwu.edu
Web Site: www.cwu.edu/~fandcs/fcsea
Members: 900 individuals
Staff: 2
Annual Budget: $50-100,000
Executive Director: Dr. Jan Bowers, Ph.D.

Historical Note

Established as Dept. of Supervisors and Teachers of Home Economics of the National Education Association; became the Dept. of Home Economics in 1938, Home Economics Education Association in 1969, and assumed its current name in 1995. A nongovernance affiliate of the NEA. Membership: $25/year.

Meetings/Conferences:

Semi-annual Meetings: June with American Ass'n of Family and Consumer Sciences; December with Ass'n for Career and Technical Education.

Publications:

The Educator newsletter. semi-a.
Bulletin. semi-a.

Family Firm Institute *(1986)*

200 Lincoln St., Suite 201
Boston, MA 02111
Tel: (617)482-3045 *Fax:* (617)482-3049
Web Site: www.ffi.org
Members: 1400 individuals
Staff: 4
Annual Budget: $1-2,000,000
Executive Director: Judy L. Green
E-Mail: judy@ffi.org

Historical Note

FFI members include practitioners, academics, and other individuals who advise, study, research and consult with family-owned businesses. Provides educational and networking opportunities for individuals and organizations interested in issues pertinent to family-owned business. Membership: $580/year (consultant/advisor); $300/year (educator), $2,000/year (organizational), $80/year (student).

Meetings/Conferences:

Annual Meetings: Fall

2007 - Miami, FL(Fairmont Turnderry Isle Resort)/Oct. 17-20

Publications:

FFI Newsletter. m.
Family Business Review. q. adv.
Membership Directory. a.
Family Business Bibliography. a.
Directory of Consultants & Speakers. a.
Conference Proceedings. a.
FFI Practitioner. semi-a.

Family, Career, and Community Leaders of America *(1945)*

1910 Association Dr.
Reston, VA 20191-1584
Tel: (703)476-4900
E-Mail: natlhdqtrs@fcclainc.org
Web Site: www.fcclainc.org
Members: 220000 individuals
Staff: 25
Annual Budget: $2-5,000,000
Executive Director: Alan T. Rains, Jr.
E-Mail: arains@fcclainc.org
Associate Executive Director, Government Programs and Communications: Carolyn W. Brown
E-Mail: cbrown@fcclainc.org
Chief Financial Officer: David Hunt
E-Mail: dhunt@fcclainc.org

Historical Note

Founded as the Future Homemakers of America, assumed its present name in 1999. Sponsored by the Department of Education and the American Association of Family and Consumer Sciences. Members are family and consumer sciences students *through grade 12. Absorbed the New Homemakers of America in 1965. Membership: $8/year.*

Meetings/Conferences:
Annual Meetings: July
2007 – Anaheim, CA/July 7-13

Publications:
Teen Times. q.
The Adviser. 3/year.

Farm Credit Council *(1982)*
50 F St. NW, Suite 900
Washington, DC 20001
Tel: (202)626-8710 *Fax:* (202)626-8718
Toll Free: (800)525 - 2345
Web Site: www.fccouncil.com
Members: 5 district councils and farm credit banks
Staff: 10
Annual Budget: $2-5,000,000
President and Chief Executive Officer: Ken Auer
Senior Vice President, General Counsel and Secretary: Charles Dana
Director, Meetings: Michele Lucas
Director, Communications: Mike Mason
Executive Vice President, Government Affairs: W. Jeffrey Shipp

Historical Note
Represents the Farm Credit System and its 100 local credit association members, who make loans available to agricultural producers, rural homebuyers, farmer cooperatives, and rural utilities.

Meetings/Conferences:
Annual Meetings: Winter
2007 – Palm Springs, CA(Marriott)/Jan. 14-16

Publications:
The Insider. bi-w.

Farm Equipment Council

Historical Note
A council of the Equipment Manufacturers Institute.

Farm Equipment Manufacturers Association *(1950)*
1000 Executive Pkwy., Suite 100
St. Louis, MO 63141-6369
Tel: (314)878-2304 *Fax:* (314)878-1742
E-Mail: fema@farmequip.org
Web Site: www.farmequip.org
Members: 700 companies
Staff: 5
Annual Budget: $500-1,000,000
Executive Vice President: Robert K. Schnell
Director, Membership Services: Hannah Hammontree
E-Mail: hannah@farmequip.org
Vice President: Vernon F. Schmidt
E-Mail: vschmidt@farmequip.org
Convention Manager: Sarah Stevener
E-Mail: sarah@farmequip.org

Historical Note
Founded as the Allied Farm Equipment Manufacturers Association; assumed its present name in 1956. Membership: $235-920/year (company).

Meetings/Conferences:
Semi-Annual Meetings: Spring and Fall

Publications:
Shortliner. bi-m.

Farm Equipment Wholesalers Association *(1945)*
P.O. Box 1347
Iowa City, IA 52244
Tel: (319)354-5156 *Fax:* (319)354-5157
E-Mail: info@fewa.org
Web Site: www.fewa.org
Members: 190 companies
Staff: 2
Annual Budget: $100-250,000
Executive Vice President: Patricia Collins
Office Manager: Jane L. Hotz

Historical Note
FEWA is the international trade association of independent wholesale distributors engaged in marketing farm and related power equipment products including light industrial, commercial, irrigation, lawn and garden products. Membership: dues based on a sliding scale.

Meetings/Conferences:
Annual Meetings: November
2007 – New Orleans, LA(Sheraton)/Oct. 24-27

Publications:
FEWA Membership Directory. a.
FEWA Cross Index. a.
TIPS Newsletter. m.

Farmers Educational and Co-operative Union of America *(1902)*
5619 DTC Pkwy., Suite 300
Greenwood Village, CO 80111-3136
Tel: (303)337-5500 *Fax:* (303)771-1770
Toll Free: (800)347 - 1961
E-Mail: info@nfu.org
Web Site: www.nfu.org
Members: 250000 individuals
Staff: 20
Annual Budget: $2-5,000,000
President: David J. Frederickson
Director, Education: Jennifer Luitjens Bahr
E-Mail: jennifer.luitjens@nfu.org
Vice President, Government Relations: Tom Buis
Director, Communications: Emily Eisenberg
Director, Economic and Cooperative Development: Jeff Moser
E-Mail: jeff.moser@nfu.org
Vice President, Administration: Clay Pederson
E-Mail: clay.pederson@nfu.org

Historical Note
Also known as National Farmers Union, Farmers Union. Maintains offices in Aurora, CO and Washington, D.C. Members are farm families throughout the nation united for legislative, cooperative and educational purposes.

Meetings/Conferences:
Annual Meetings: 500-800

Publications:
National Farmers Union News. m.

Farmstead Equipment Association Council *(1945)*

Historical Note
Merger (1967) of Barn Cleaner, Cattle Feeder, Silo Unloader Association and Barn Equipment Association. A council of the Equipment Manufacturers Institute.

Fashion Accessories Shippers Association *(1986)*
350 Fifth Ave., Suite 2030
New York, NY 10118
Tel: (212)947-3424 *Fax:* (212)629-0361
Web Site: www.geminishippers.com
Members: 225 companies
Staff: 5
Executive Director: Harold Sachs
President: Sara Mayes

Fashion Association Division, AAFA *(1955)*

Historical Note
A division of American Apparel Ass'n, which provides administrative support.

Fashion Group International *(1931)*
8 W. 40th St., Seventh Floor
New York, NY 10018
Tel: (212)302-5511 *Fax:* (212)302-5533
E-Mail: info@fgi.org
Web Site: www.fgi.org
Members: 5000 individuals
Staff: 8
Annual Budget: $1-2,000,000
President: Margaret Hayes
E-Mail: MHayes@fgi.org
Director, Regional Services: Cheryl Ingersoll
E-Mail: Cheryl@fgi.org
Director, Membership Services: Trish Maffei

Historical Note
Members are men and women executives with a minimum of three years experience representing all facets of the fashion industry including manufacturing, marketing, designing, retailing, communications and education. Includes 26 U.S. chapters and 7 overseas chapters overseas. Membership: $145-$210/year.

Meetings/Conferences:
Annual Meetings: New York, NY/December

Publications:
FGI Bulletin newsletter. 3/year.
Fashion Trend Report. semi-a.
Membership Directory. a. adv.

Fastener Industry Coalition

Historical Note
A affiliate of National Fastener Distributors Association, which provides administrative support.

FCIB-NACM Corp. *(1919)*
8840 Columbia 100 Pkwy.
Columbia, MD 21045-2158
Tel: (410)423-1840 *Fax:* (410)423-1845
Toll Free: (888)256 - 3242
E-Mail: fcib_info@fcibglobal.com
Web Site: www.fcibglobal.com
Members: 850 companies & institutions
Staff: 6
Annual Budget: $1-2,000,000
President and Chief Operating Officer: Kenneth Garrison
Director, North American Operations: Aneta Spilman

Historical Note
A subsidiary of the National Association of Credit Management. Formerly (1967) the Foreign Credit Interchange Bureau. Membership: $840/year (corporate).

Meetings/Conferences:
Annual Meetings: European Meetings - 3/year in various cities; North American Meetings - 5/year in various cities and 2/year in New York, NY

Publications:
FCIB Minutes of Round Table Conference. 3/year.
Newsletter. q.
FCIB Bulletin. q. adv.
Credit and Collection Survey. q.
Country Credit Reports. on demand.

Federal Administrative Law Judges Conference *(1947)*
2000 Pennsylvania Ave. NW, Suite 200
Washington, DC 20006
Tel: (202)675-3065
E-Mail: judges@faljc.com
Web Site: www.faljc.org
Members: 360 individuals
Annual Budget: $10-25,000
Executive Administrator: Joel M. Paul
E-Mail: judges@faljc.com

Historical Note
Formerly (1973) Federal Trial Examiners Conference. Members are judges who preside at administrative hearings within federal agencies. Has no permanent staff. Officers are elected annually. Membership: $65/year.

Meetings/Conferences:
Annual Meetings: September

Publications:
Directory. a.
Newsletter. q.

Federal and Armed Forces Librarians Roundtable *(1972)*
c/o American Library Ass'n
1615 New Hampshire Ave. NW
Washington, DC 20009
Tel: (202)628-8410 *Fax:* (202)628-8419
E-Mail: rscott@alawash.org
Members: 550 individuals
Staff: 1
Annual Budget: under $10,000
Staff Liason: Reginald Scott

Historical Note
Founded as Federal Librarians Roundtable; assumed its current name in 2002. An affiliate of the American Library Association. FAFLRT is a membership unit established to promote a field of librarianship not within the scope of any single division of the ALA. Individuals may join the FAFLRT after first joining the ALA. Membership: $15/year (individual); $20/year (institution).

Meetings/Conferences:
Annual Meetings: in conjunction with the American Library Ass'n

Publications:
Federal and Armed Forces Libraries. q. adv.

Federal Bar Association *(1920)*
2215 M St. NW
Washington, DC 20037
Tel: (202)785-1614 *Fax:* (202)785-1568
E-Mail: fba@fedbar.org
Web Site: www.fedbar.org
Members: 15500 individuals
Staff: 18
Annual Budget: $1-2,000,000
Executive Director: Jack D. Lockridge
E-Mail: fba@fedbar.org

Historical Note
Members are attorneys currently or formerly employed by the Federal Government or who have a substantial interest in federal law as evidenced by admission to practice before a federal court or agency. Membership: $95/year (attorneys admitted to first bar five or more years); $50/year (retired attorneys or those admitted to first bar less than five years); $10/year (law student), plus section/committee dues where applicable.

Meetings/Conferences:
Annual Meetings: Summer

Publications:
The Federal Lawyer. 10/year. adv.

Federal Bureau of Investigation Agents Association *(1981)*
P.O. Box 250
New Rochelle, NY 10801
Tel: (914)235-7580 *Fax:* (914)235-8235
E-Mail: fbiaa@fbiaa.org
Web Site: www.fbiaa.org
Members: 12000 individuals
Staff: 3
Executive Director: Glenn Kelly
National Administrator: Gabriele Scibelli

Historical Note
Membership: $78/year; $26/year (retired or associate).

Meetings/Conferences:
Biennial Meetings: (2003)

Publications:
FBI Agent. 4/year.

Federal Communications Bar Association *(1936)*
1020 19th St., N.W., Suite 325
Washington, DC 20036-6101
Tel: (202)293-4000 *Fax:* (202)293-4317
E-Mail: fcba@fcba.org
Web Site: www.fcba.org
Members: 2800 individuals
Staff: 3
Annual Budget: $500-1,000,000
Executive Director: Stanley D. Zenor

Historical Note
FCBA members are involved in the development, interpretation, implementation and practice of communications law and policy. Voting members are members in good standing of the Bar of any state and who are (a) eligible to practice before an agency of government or (b) employees of an agency of the government. Non-voting membership is available to professionals in allied fields, including engineers, consultants, economists, government relations officials, foreign lawyers and law students at accredited law schools. Membership: dues vary.

Meetings/Conferences:
Annual Meetings: May, usually in mid-Atlantic region

Publications:
FCBA Directory. a.
Federal Communications Law Journal. q.
FCBA News. m.

Federal Education Association *(1956)*
1201 16th St. NW, Suite 117
Washington, DC 20036
Tel: (202)822-7850 *Fax:* (202)822-7867
E-Mail: fea@feaonline.org
Web Site: www.feaonline.org
Members: 5500 individuals
Staff: 10
Annual Budget: $500-1,000,000
Executive Director: H.T. Nguyen

Historical Note
Formerly Overseas Education Association (1996). A Federal labor union affiliated with the National Education Association, FEA represents teachers on overseas and stateside military bases. Membership: $300/year.

Meetings/Conferences:
Annual Meetings: July

Publications:
Journal. q.

Federal Facilities Council *(1953)*
500 Fifth St. NW
Washington, DC 20001
Tel: (202)334-3374 *Fax:* (202)334-3370
Web Site: http://www7.nationalacademies.org/ffc
Members: 130 individuals
Staff: 2
Annual Budget: $500-1,000,000
Executive Director: Lynda Stanley

Historical Note
Formerly (1994) Federal Construction Council. Members are professional employees of federal agencies and members of the Board on Infrastructure and the Constructed Environment of the National Research Council. Encourages cooperation among the sponsoring federal agencies. Sponsors six standing committees composed of federal agency employees and private-sector liaisons.

Federal Judges Association *(1982)*
111 W. Washington St., Suite 1100
Chicago, IL 60602
Tel: (312)641-1441 *Fax:* (312)641-1288
Web Site: http://federaljudgesassoc.org
Staff: 1
Registered Agent: Kevin M. Forde

Historical Note
Formed "to seek the highest quality of justice for the people of the United States," the Association seeks to preserve the ability of the federal judiciary to attract and retain the best qualified people for judicial service and to preserve the independence of the judiciary from intrusion, intimidation, coercion or domination from any source. Membership: $200/year (individual).

Meetings/Conferences:
Quadrennial Meetings:

Publications:
In Camera. q.

Federal Law Enforcement Officers Association *(1977)*
P.O. Box 326
Lewisberry, PA 17339
Tel: (717)938-2300 *Fax:* (717)932-2262
E-Mail: fleoa@fleoa.org
Web Site: www.fleoa.org
Members: 24000 individuals
Staff: 4
Annual Budget: $2-5,000,000
President: Art Gordon

Historical Note
FLEOA represents law enforcement officers and special agents from over sixty agencies of the federal government. Membership: $105/year (regular); $40/year (retiree, resignee); $45/year (associate).

Publications:
Newsletter. bi-m. adv.

Federal Managers Association *(1913)*
1641 Prince St.
Alexandria, VA 22314-2818
Tel: (703)683-8700 *Fax:* (703)683-8707
E-Mail: info@fedmanagers.org
Web Site: www.fedmanagers.org
Staff: 5
Annual Budget: $1-2,000,000
Executive Director: Didier-Kim Q. Trinh

Historical Note
Organized in 1913 in Washington, DC as the National Association of Supervisors, with members solely from the U.S. Navy. Disbanded in 1922, but was reactivated in 1933. In 1950, the association became the National Association of Supervisors, Department of Defense; in 1968 became the National Association of Supervisors, Federal Government; and in 1979 assumed its present name. Membership includes managers and supervisors in all federal agencies. Membership: $72/year.

Meetings/Conferences:
Annual Meetings: Spring

Publications:
The Federal Manager. q. adv.
The Washington Report. bi-w.

Federal Network for Sustainability *(2000)*
1112 16th St. NW, Suite 240
Washington, DC 20036
Tel: (202)628-6100 *Fax:* (202)393-5043
E-Mail: fns@federalsustainability.org
Web Site: www.federalsustainability.org
Members: 12 agencies
Management Executive: Christian May

Historical Note
FNS is a consortium of government agencies organized to disseminate information about responsible energy use throughout the federal government.

Federal Physicians Association *(1979)*
3003 Van Ness NW, W-112
Washington, DC 20008-4116
Web Site: www.fedphy.org
Members: 500 individuals
Staff: 1
Annual Budget: $25-50,000

Historical Note
Founded by a group of physicians concerned with the worsening situation of the physician in federal government employment, FPA has focused its efforts on ensuring that highly qualifed doctors will continue to consider federal employment both rewarding and desirable. A key component of FPA's program has been promotion of the Physician's Comparability Allowance, an annual bonus granted to physicians in various capacities among the various U.S. government agencies. Membership: $100/year (individual).

Meetings/Conferences:
Annual Meetings: Fall

Publications:
Federal Physician. q. adv.

Federal Probation and Pre-trial Officers Association *(1955)*
110 E. Court Ave., Room 127
Des Moines, IA 50309
Tel: (515)284-6207
E-Mail: info@fppoa.org
Web Site: www.fppoa.org
Members: 1000 individuals
Staff: 80
Annual Budget: $10-25,000
Secretary: Jerry L. Evans

Publications:
The Connection. q.

Federal Water Quality Association *(1941)*
P.O. Box 14303
Washington, DC 20044-4303
Tel: (202)566-2582 *Fax:* (202)566-2825
E-Mail: fwqa5@earthlink.net
Web Site: www.fwqa.org
Members: 175 individuals
Annual Budget: under $10,000
President: Mary Belefski

Historical Note
Formerly the Federal Sewage Research Association; now affiliated with the Water Environment Federation. Membership consists of federal employees, consultants, industry and association representatives concerned with sewage/industrial waste treatment and disposal, non-point source pollution, water quality, and other environmental concerns. 80% of members are in the Washington area. Membership: $12/year (WEF members); $15/year (non-WEF members). Has no paid officers or full-time staff.

Publications:
FWQA Newsletter. 6-8/year.

Federally Employed Women *(1968)*
1666 K St. NW, Suite 440
Washington, DC 20036

Tel: (202)898-0994 *Fax:* (240)266-3232
E-Mail: few@few.org
Web Site: www.few.org
Members: 5000 chapters
Staff: 5
Annual Budget: $500-1,000,000
President: Patricia Wolfe

Historical Note

Most members are employees of the Federal government. The association's goal is to end sex discrimination and increase job opportunities for women in government service. Membership: $25/year (national dues, plus regional and chapter dues); $35/year (member-at-large), $250/year (lifetime).

Meetings/Conferences:
Annual Meetings: July

Publications:
FEW News and Views. bi-m. adv.

Federated Ambulatory Surgery Association *(1974)*

700 N. Fairfax St., Suite 306
Alexandria, VA 22314-2040
Tel: (703)836-8808 *Fax:* (703)549-0976
E-Mail: fasa@fasa.org
Web Site: www.fasa.org
Members: 5708 individuals
Staff: 12
Annual Budget: $2-5,000,000
Executive Vice President: Kathy Bryant

Historical Note

First incorporated in Arizona in 1974 as the Society for the Advancement of Freestanding Ambulatory Surgical Care; became the Freestanding Ambulatory Surgery Association in 1984 and assumed its present name in 1986. Membership: $500/year (individual); $500-2,000/year (facility); $500/year (auxiliary).

Meetings/Conferences:
Annual Meetings: Spring/600

Publications:
FASA Update. bi-m. adv.

Federation of American Hospitals *(1966)*

801 Pennsylvania Ave. NW, Suite 245
Washington, DC 20004-2604
Tel: (202)624-1500 *Fax:* (202)737-6462
E-Mail: info@fah.org
Web Site: www.fah.org
Members: 1700hospital&healthcaresystems
Staff: 20
Annual Budget: $5-10,000,000
President: Charles N. Kahn, III

Historical Note

FAH changed its name to the Federation of American Health Systems (1986), then (2001) went back to its current name. Originally an association of investor-owned hospitals, FAH members now include a broad range of health-care delivery systems. Sponsors the Federation of American Hospitals Political Action Committee (FedPAC).

Meetings/Conferences:
Annual Meetings: Winter/1800
2007 – Washington, DC(Marriott Wardman Park)/March 4-7

Publications:
Hospital Outlook. q.
Annual Report. a.
Directory. a. adv.

Federation of American Scientists *(1945)*

1717 K St. NW, Suite 209
Washington, DC 20036
Tel: (202)546-3300 *Fax:* (202)675-1010
E-Mail: fas@fas.org
Web Site: www.fas.org
Members: 3500 individuals
Staff: 20
Annual Budget: $2-5,000,000
President: Henry Kelly
E-Mail: fas@fas.org
Director, Corporate, Foundation and Public Outreach: Jeff M. Aron

Historical Note

Engages in research and advocacy on science-and-society issues, especially global security. Membership: $15/year (student); $25/year (individual); $50/year (supporting member).

Meetings/Conferences:
Annual Meetings: Winter

Publications:
FAS Public Interest Report. q.
Secrecy News. w.

Federation of American Socs. for Experimental Biology *(1912)*

9650 Rockville Pike
Bethesda, MD 20814-3998
Tel: (301)634-7000 *Fax:* (301)634-7651
Web Site: www.faseb.org
Members: 22 member societies
Staff: 110
Annual Budget: $10-25,000,000
Executive Director: Frederick R. Rickles, M.D.
Manager, Financial Services: David Craven
Director, Public Affairs: Dr. Howard H. Garrison
Director, Human Resources: Maureen Murphy, Ph.D.
Director, Information Technology: Guy Riso
Director, Scientific Meetings and Conferences: Geri Swindle

Historical Note

In 1912 the American Physiological Society, the American Society of Biological Chemists and the American Society of Pharmacology and Expermental Therapeutics formed the Federation of American Societies for Experimental Biology (FASEB). The Federation was joined by the American Society of Experimental Pathology (now known as American Association for Investigative Pathology) in 1913, the American Institute of Nutrition in 1940, the American Association of Immunologists in 1942, the American Society for Cell Biology and the Biophysical Society in 1991, the American Association of Anatomists in 1993, and The Protein Society in 1995. Incorporated in the District of Columbia in 1954. Has an annual budget of approximately $16 million.

Meetings/Conferences:
2007 – Washington, DC(Washington Convention Center)/Apr. 28-May 2

Publications:
FASEB Newsletter. m. adv.
FASEB Journal. m. adv.
FASEB Directory. a. adv.

Federation of Analytical Chemistry and Spectroscopy Societies *(1972)*

2019 Galisteo, Bldg. One
Santa Fe, NM 87505
Tel: (505)820-1648 *Fax:* (505)989-1073
E-Mail: facssc@facssc.org
Web Site: www.facss.org/facss/index.php
Members: 7 organizations
Staff: 2
Annual Budget: $100-250,000
Executive Assistant: Cindi Lily

Historical Note

Members are the analytical division of the American Chemical Society, the Chromatography Forum of the Delaware Valley, the Coblentz Society, the Instrument Society of America, the Society for Applied Spectroscopy, the Association of Analytical Chemists, and the analytical division of the Royal Society of Chemistry. Purpose is to provide a national forum for analytical chemistry through an exhibition and technical papers.

Meetings/Conferences:
Annual Meetings: Fall
2007 – Memphis, TN(Cook Convention Center)/Oct. 12-18

Federation of Associations of Regulatory Boards *(1973)*

1603 Orrington Ave., Suite 2080-F
Evanston, IL 60201
Tel: (847)328-7909 *Fax:* (847)864-0588
E-Mail: farb@farb.org
Web Site: www.farb.org
Members: 100 individuals
Annual Budget: $50-100,000
Executive Director: Dale Atkinson
E-Mail: farb@farb.org

Historical Note

Formerly (1985) Federation of Associations of Health Regulatory Boards, this association is now open to any regulated profession. Membership: $75/year (individual); $750/year (association).

Meetings/Conferences:
Annual Meetings: January-February

Publications:
FARB Facts Newsletter. 3/year.

Federation of Behavioral, Psychological and Cognitive Sciences *(1980)*

750 First St. NE, Suite 909
Washington, DC 20002
Tel: (202)336-5920 *Fax:* (202)336-5953
E-Mail: federation@fbpcs.org
Web Site: www.thefederationonline.org
Members: 19societies&118academicdepts.
Staff: 3
Annual Budget: $100-250,000
Executive Director: Barbara Wanchisen, Ph.D.

Historical Note

A coalition of scientific societies and academic departments. Members are research scientists who study behavioral, psychological and cognitive processes and the physiological bases of these processes with an aim to apply their research to health, education and human development. Membership: $11/year per member (societies); $200-$500/year (academic departments).

Meetings/Conferences:
Annual Meetings: always Washington, DC/December: (FBPCS Office)

Publications:
Annual Report. a. adv.
Science Seminar Public Policy Transcripts. 6/yr. adv.
Federation News Newsletter. m. adv.

Federation of Defense and Corporate Counsel *(1936)*

11812-A N. 56th St.
Tampa, FL 33617
Tel: (813)983-0022 *Fax:* (813)988-5837
Web Site: www.thefederation.org
Members: 1283 individuals
Staff: 2
Annual Budget: $500-1,000,000
Executive Director: Martha J. Streeper

Historical Note

Founded in 1936 as the Federation of Insurance Counsel; incorporated in Illinois in 1973. Became Federation of Insurance and Corporate Counsel in 1985 and assumed its present name in 2001. Members are lawyers who are actively engaged in the legal aspects of the insurance business, officials and executives of insurance companies, and corporate counsel engaged in defense of claims. Membership: $250/yr.

Meetings/Conferences:
Semi-Annual Meetings: Winter and Summer
2007 – Scottsdale, AZ(Fairmont Scottsdale Princess)/Feb. 25-March 4
2007 – Sun Valley, ID(Sun Valley Resort)/July 22-29

Publications:
FDCC Quarterly. q.

Federation of Diocesan Liturgical Commissions

415 Michigan Ave. NE, Suite 70
Washington, DC 20017-0039
Tel: (202)635-6990 *Fax:* (202)529-2452
E-Mail: nationaloffice@fdlc.org
Web Site: www.fdlc.org
Members: 400 individuals
Staff: 4
Executive Director: Lisa A. Tarker

Historical Note

FDLC is an association of diocesan liturgical commissions in the United States.

Meetings/Conferences:
2007 – Hartford, CT(Bradley Airport Sheraton)/Oct. 9-13
2008 – Milwaukee, WI

Publications:
FDLC Newsletter. 6/year. adv.

Federation of Environmental Technologists *(1981)*

9451 N. 107th St.
Milwaukee, WI 53224-1105
Tel: (414)354-0070 *Fax:* (414)354-0073
E-Mail: info@fetinc.org
Web Site: www.fetinc.org
Members: 700 individuals
Staff: 2
Annual Budget: $100-250,000
Executive Director: Barbara Hurula
E-Mail: info@fetinc.org

Historical Note

FET assists members in interpretation of and compliance with environmental regulations.

Meetings/Conferences:

Annual Meetings: March
2007 – Milwaukee, WI(Four Points Sheraton)/March 12-14

Publications:

Environotes Newsletter. m.

Federation of Government Information Processing Councils

Historical Note

Became American Council for Technology in 2003.

Federation of International Trade Associations *(1984)*

1900 Campus Commons Dr.
Reston, VA 20191
Tel: (703)620-1588 *Fax:* (703)620-4922
Toll Free: (800)969 - 3482
E-Mail: info@fita.org
Web Site: www.fita.org
Members: 460 clubs and associations
Staff: 10
Annual Budget: $250-500,000
Chairman: Nelson T. Joyner
Director, Member Services: Kimberly Park

Historical Note

FITA's members are 460 world trade clubs and international trade associations located throughout North America. Aggregate membership exceeds 400,000.

Meetings/Conferences:

Annual Meetings: None held

Publications:

E-mail newsletter. bi-w. adv.
Membership Directory. a. adv.

Federation of Materials Socs. *(1972)*

910 17th St. NW, Suite 800
Washington, DC 20006
Tel: (202)296-9282
E-Mail: betsyhou@ix.netcom.com
Web Site: www.materialsocieties.org
Members: 14 societies
Staff: 1
Annual Budget: $50-100,000
Executive Director: Betsy Houston

Historical Note

Promotes cooperation among societies concerned with the understanding, development and application of materials and processes.

Meetings/Conferences:

Biennial Meetings:

Publications:

FMS Update. w..

Federation of Modern Painters and Sculptors *(1940)*

113 Greene St.
New York, NY 10012
Tel: (212)966-4864
E-Mail: info@fedart.org
Web Site: http://fedart.org
Members: 51 individuals
Staff: 4
Annual Budget: under $10,000
Acting Co-President: Lynda Caspe
E-Mail: info@fedart.org
Acting Co-President: Anneli Arms
E-Mail: info@fedart.org

Historical Note

Professional painters and sculptors. Purpose is to improve the economic and working conditions of professional artists and facilitate the exhibition of their work. Has no permanent headquarters or paid staff. Membership concentrated in the New York area. Membership: $30/year.

Federation of Podiatric Medical Boards *(1936)*

6551 Malta Dr.
Boynton Beach, FL 33437-7037
Tel: (561)477-3060
Members: 50 states
Staff: 1
Executive Director: Larry I. Shane

Historical Note

FPMB represents the collective interests of the state licensing boards for podiatric medicine. It is responsible for the administrative aspects of the Podiatric Medical Licensing Examination for STATES (PMLExis), and maintains a file of state board, public record disciplinary findings. Membership fee varies, based on number of state licensees.

Meetings/Conferences:

Annual Meetings: Spring

Publications:

Federation News. q. adv.
Directory of State Licensing Examination Information and Directory. a.

Federation of Socs. for Coatings Technology *(1922)*

492 Norristown Road
Blue Bell, PA 19422-2350
Tel: (610)940-0777 *Fax:* (610)940-0292
E-Mail: fsct@coatingstech.org
Web Site: www.coatingstech.org
Members: 7000 individuals
Staff: 13
Annual Budget: $2-5,000,000
Executive Vice President: Robert F. Ziegler

Historical Note

Established June 15, 1922 as the Federation of Paint and Varnish Production Clubs. Became the Federation of Societies for Paint Technology in 1959. The name was later changed to Federation of Societies for Coatings Technology. Membership: $60/year.

Meetings/Conferences:

Annual Meetings: Fall/8,000

Publications:

JTC Research. q.
JTC CoatingsTech. m. adv.
Membership Directory. a. adv.
Convention Program Book. a. adv.

Federation of Spine Associations

Historical Note

An affiliate of American Association of Orthopaedic Surgeons, which provides administrative support.

Federation of State Boards of Physical Therapy

509 Wythe St.
Alexandria, VA 22314-1917
Tel: (703)299-3100 *Fax:* (703)299-3110
Toll Free: (800)881 - 1430
Web Site: www.fsbpt.org
Members: 400 individuals
Staff: 30
Annual Budget: $5-10,000,000
Chief Executive Officer: William Hatherill

Publications:

Federation Forum. q.

Federation of State Humanities Councils *(1977)*

1600 Wilson Blvd., Suite 902
Arlington, VA 22209-2505
Tel: (703)908-9700 *Fax:* (703)908-9706
E-Mail: info@statehumanities.org
Web Site: http://ww.statehumanities.org
Members: 65 councils
Staff: 5
Annual Budget: $500-1,000,000
President: Esther Mackintosh
Manager, Information Services: Matthew Even
Vice President: John Matthews
Director, Conferences and Finance: Elizabeth Paine

Historical Note

FSHC assists state councils in achieving their common mission: the integration of the humanities into American life. FSHC monitors Congressional legislation and plans legislative forums. The Federation also forms partnerships with other national organizations on behalf of the state councils and coordinates an annual national conference of state humanitites councils.

Meetings/Conferences:

Annual Meetings: Fall/350-400

Federation of State Medical Boards of the United States *(1912)*

P.O. Box 619850
Dallas, TX 75261-9850
Tel: (817)868-4000 *Fax:* (817)868-4099
E-Mail: alpp@fsmb.org
Web Site: www.fsmb.org
Members: 70 boards
Staff: 110
Annual Budget: $10-25,000,000
President and Chief Executive Officer: James N. Thompson, M.D.
Senior Vice President and Chief Operating Officer: Dale L. Austin
Vice President, Examination and Post Licensure Assessment Services: Carol A. Clothier
Vice President, Membership Centers and Services: Tim R. Knettler
Vice President, Government Relations, Policy and Education: Lisa A. Robin

Historical Note

Voluntary national organization of state medical boards, the Federation was organized at the Congress Hotel, Chicago on February 29, 1912 with a charter membership of ten boards and eighteen fellows. It was incorporated in 1966. Maintains disciplinary information submitted by state boards on physicians. In collaboration with the National Board of Medical Examiners offers United States Medical Licensing Examination, and is the only medical licensing examination in the U.S. for allopathic physicians. Keeps statistics regarding requirements for licensure for ready reference to inquiries. Has an annual budget of $10 million. Membership: $2,000/year (state board).

Meetings/Conferences:

Annual Meetings: Spring

Publications:

InMedEd Newsletter. q.
Guide to the Essentials of a Modern Medical Practice Act. bi-a.
The EXCHANGE.
The Journal of Medical Licensure & Discipline. q.
FSMB Newsline. m.
Directory. a.
Guidebook on Medical Discipline. a.
Elements of a Modern State Medical Board.

Federation of Straight Chiropractors and Organizations *(1978)*

2276 Wassergass Road
Hellertown, PA 18055
Toll Free: (800)521 - 9856
E-Mail: fsco@juno.com
Web Site: www.straightchiropractic.com
Members: 1200 individuals
Staff: 1
Annual Budget: $100-250,000
Administrative Assistant: Renee Hillman

Historical Note

FSCO members are chiropractors and others with an interest in the practice of traditional chiropractic. Traditional chiropractic is defined as the correction of vertebral sudluxations to improve function and potential for health. Membership: $400/year.

Publications:

President's Update. bi-m.
FSCO Insider. bi-m.

Federation of Tax Administrators *(1937)*

444 N. Capitol St. NW, Suite 348
Washington, DC 20001
Tel: (202)624-5890 *Fax:* (202)624-7888
E-Mail: harley.duncan@taxadmin.org
Web Site: www.taxadmin.org
Members: 52 agencies
Staff: 10
Annual Budget: $500-1,000,000
Executive Director: Harley Duncan

Historical Note
Established by the National Association of Tax Administrators, the North American Gasoline Tax Conference and the National Tobacco Tax Association. FTA subsequently absorbed all three founding organizations. Members are the tax agencies of the 50 state governments, the District of Columbia and New York City. Its mission is to foster good tax administration.

Meetings/Conferences:
Annual Meetings: June

Publications:
Tax Administrators News. m.
Directory of State Tax Administrators. a.

Fellowship of United Methodists in Music and Worship Arts *(1956)*
P.O. Box 24787
Nashville, TN 37202
Tel: (615)749-6875 *Fax:* (615)749-6874
E-Mail: fummwa@aol.com
Web Site: www.fummwa.org
Members: 2200 individuals
Staff: 1
Annual Budget: $100-250,000
Executive Director: David L. Bone
E-Mail: fummwa@aol.com

Historical Note
Formerly (1974) National Fellowship of United Methodist Musicians, (1979) Fellowship of United Methodist Musicians, and (1995) Fellowship of United Methodists in Worship, Music and Other Arts. Membership: $55/year.

Meetings/Conferences:
Biennial meetings: Uneven years

Publications:
Worship Arts. bi-m. adv.

Felt Manufacturers Council *(1961)*

Historical Note
A council of the Northern Textile Association.

Ferroalloys Association *(1971)*

Historical Note
An affiliate of Non-Ferrous Founders Society, which provides administrative support.

Fertilizer Institute *(1970)*
820 First St. NE, Suite 430
Washington, DC 20002
Tel: (202)962-0490 *Fax:* (202)962-0577
E-Mail: informationfi@tfi.org
Web Site: www.tfi.org
Members: 175 individuals and organizations
Staff: 17
Annual Budget: $2-5,000,000
President: Ford B. West
Vice President, Public Affairs: Kathy O. Mathers
Vice President, Economic Services: Dr. Harry Vroomen
Director, Communications: Harriet Wegmeyer

Historical Note
Product of a merger of the National Plant Food Institute (1955) and Agricultural Nitrogen Institute (1951). Formerly (1970) National Plant Food Institute. Members are brokers, producers, importers, retailers and manufacturers of fertilizer and fertilizer-related equipment. Supports the FERT Political Action Committee.

Meetings/Conferences:
Annual Meetings: February

Publications:
TFI Advocate. m.

Fiber Society *(1941)*
North Carolina State University
College of Textiles, P.O. Box 8301
Raleigh, NC 27695-8301
Tel: (919)515-6555 *Fax:* (919)515-3733
Web Site: http://fs.tx.ncsu.edu/
Members: 400 individuals
Staff: 1
Annual Budget: $25-50,000
Secretary: Subhash K. Batra

Historical Note
A professional group of researchers on fibers, fiber based products and fibrous materials. Membership: $30/year.

Fiberglass Tank and Pipe Institute *(1987)*
11150 S. Wilcrest Dr., Suite 101
Houston, TX 77099-4343
Tel: (281)568-4100 *Fax:* (281)568-9998
Web Site: www.fiberglasstankandpipe.com
Members: 10 companies
Staff: 2
Annual Budget: $250-500,000
Executive Director: Sullivan D. Curran

Historical Note
Formerly (1995) Fiberglass Petroleum Tank and Pipe Institute, FTPI promotes and protects the interests and image of the fiberglass-reinforced thermosetting plastic tank and pipe manufacturing industry. In addition, the Institute develops, exchanges and disseminates information of benefit to its members. Members are domestic manufacturers. Membership: $4,400 minimum.

Meetings/Conferences:
Semi-Annual Meetings: Spring and Fall

Fibre Box Association *(1940)*
25 Northwest Point Blvd., Suite 510
Elk Grove Village, IL 60007
Tel: (847)364-9600 *Fax:* (847)364-9639
E-Mail: fba@fibrebox.org
Web Site: www.fibrebox.org
Members: 154 companies
Staff: 7
Annual Budget: $2-5,000,000
President: Bruce Benson

Historical Note
Members are makers of corrugated boxes. FBA represents 95% of the U.S. corrugated paper board packing industry.

Meetings/Conferences:
Annual Meetings: Spring

Publications:
Fibre Box Handbook. 3/year.
Labor Bulletin. m.
Statistical Summary. m.
Statistical Report. m.

Fibre Channel Industry Association *(1993)*
P.O. Box 29920
San Francisco, CA 94129
Tel: (415)561-6270 *Fax:* (415)561-6120
Toll Free: (800)272 - 4618
Web Site: www.fibrechannel.org
Executive Director: Chris Lyon
E-Mail: Clyon@fibrechannel.org

Historical Note
FCIA was formed to encourage the utilization of Fibre Channel and to complement the activities of the American National Standards Institute T11 committee by providing a support structure for system integrators, peripheral manufacturers, software developers, component manufacturers, communications companies and computer service providers. Membership: $20,000 (sponsor); $12,000/year (principal); $8,000/year (associate); $2,500/year (observer); $475 (individual observer).

Publications:
FCA Storage Area Networks.
FCA Newsletter. q.

Fiduciary and Risk Management Association *(1989)*
P.O. Box 48297
Athens, GA 30604
Tel: (706)354-0083 *Fax:* (706)353-3994
Web Site: www.thefirma.org
Members: 820 individuals
Staff: 1
Executive Director: Hale Mast
E-Mail: hale4@ix.netcom.com

Historical Note
Founded as National Association of Trust Audit and Compliance Professionals; assumed its current name in 2000. Members are audit and compliance professionals. Membership: $100/year (regular member); $125/year (sustaining member).

Meetings/Conferences:
Annual Meetings: Spring

Film and Bag Federation *(1986)*
1667 K St. NW, Suite 1000
Washington, DC 20006
Tel: (202)974-5200 *Fax:* (202)296-7675
E-Mail: ywade@socplas.org
Web Site: www.plasticsindustry.org
Members: 60 companies
Staff: 2
Annual Budget: $100-250,000
Executive Director: Donna Dempsey
Assistant Manager: Yvonne Wade

Historical Note
Formerly Plastic Bag Association (1998). Members are U.S. and Canadian manufacturers and suppliers of plastic retail bags. Membership: $2,000/year.

Meetings/Conferences:
Semi-Annual Meetings:

Publications:
Newsletter - FBF Info Fax. q.

Filter Manufacturers Council *(1971)*
P.O. Box 13966
Research Triangle Park, NC 27709-3966
Tel: (919)406-8817 *Fax:* (919)406-1306
Web Site: www.filtercouncil.org
Members: 25 companies
Staff: 2
Annual Budget: $100-250,000
Contact: Robin Bumpass

Historical Note
Formerly (1989) Automotive Filter Manufacturers Council. A product line council of Motor and Equipment Manufacturers Association, which provides administrative support.

Meetings/Conferences:
Semi-annual Meetings: Spring and Fall

Publications:
Technical Service Bulletins. q.

Financial and Insurance Conference Planners *(1958)*
401 N. Michigan Ave.
Chicago, IL 60611
Tel: (312)245-1023 *Fax:* (312)321-5150
E-Mail: info@icpanet.com
Web Site: www.ficpnet.com
Members: 500 individuals
Staff: 5
Annual Budget: $2-5,000,000
Executive Director: Steve Bova, CAE
E-Mail: info@icpanet.com

Historical Note
Founded as Insurance Convention Planners Association; became Insurance Conference Planners Association in 1976, ICPA-An Association of Insurance and Financial Service Conference Planners in 2004, and assumed its current name in 2005. Membership: $250/year.

Meetings/Conferences:
2007 - Scottsdale, AZ(Scottsdale Princess Fairmont)/Nov. 11-15/650

Publications:
Directory. a. adv.

Financial and Security Products Association *(1973)*
5300 Sequoia Rd. NW, Suite 205
Albuquerque, NM 87120
Tel: (505)839-7958 *Fax:* (505)839-0017
Toll Free: (800)843 - 6082
E-Mail: info@fspa1.com
Web Site: http://fspa1.com
Members: 265 dealers and manufacturers
Staff: 2
Annual Budget: $100-250,000
Executive Director: John M. Vrabec

Historical Note
Established as the National Independent Bank Equipment and Suppliers Association; later became the Nat'l Independent Bank Equipment and Systems Association before assuming its present name in 2005. Membership: $395/year.

Meetings/Conferences:
Annual Meetings: Spring/300

Publications:
NIBESA News. m. adv.

Financial Executives International *(1931)*

200 Campus Dr.
Florham Park, NJ 07932-0674
Tel: (973)765-1000 *Fax:* (973)765-1018
Web Site: www.fei.org
Members: 15000 individuals
Staff: 40
Annual Budget: $5-10,000,000
President and Chief Executive Officer: Colleen S. Cunningham
Vice President and Chief Financial Officer: Paul Chase

Historical Note
Formed by eight corporate controllers in New York City as the Controllers Institute of America, December 29, 1931 and incorporated December 31 of that year in the District of Columbia. Became Financial Executives Institute in 1962, and assumed its present name in 2001. A professional organization of individuals performing the duties of C.F.O., Controller, Treasurer or Vice President of Finance. Has an annual budget of $8.5 million. Membership: $450/year.

Meetings/Conferences:
Annual Meetings: October/1,000

Publications:
Financial Executive. bi-m. adv.
FEI Members Directory. bien.

Financial Management Association International *(1970)*
Univ. of South Florida, College of Bus. Admin.
4202 E. Fowler Ave., BSN 3331
Tampa, FL 33620-5500
Tel: (813)974-2084 *Fax:* (813)974-3318
E-Mail: fma@coba.usf.edu
Web Site: www.fma.org
Members: 12000individualsandinstitutions
Staff: 9
Annual Budget: $500-1,000,000
Special Events Coordinator: Karen Wright
E-Mail: kwright@fma.org

Historical Note
Members are college professors of financial management and corporate and organizational financial officers. Membership: $100/year (individual); $190/year (organization).

Meetings/Conferences:
Annual Meetings: October/1,200
2007 – Orlando, FL(Caribe Royale Resort)/Oct. 17-20
2008 – Dallas, TX(Gaylord Opryland Texas)/Oct. 8-11
2009 – Reno, NV(Nugget Hotel)/Oct. 21-24
2011 – Denver, CO(Adam's Mark Hotel)/Oct. 19-22

Publications:
Journal of Applied Finance. bi-a.
Financial Management. q. adv.

Financial Managers Society *(1949)*
100 W. Monroe St., Suite 810
Chicago, IL 60603-1959
Tel: (312)578-1300 *Fax:* (312)578-1308
Toll Free: (800)275 - 4367
E-Mail: info@fmsinc.org
Web Site: www.fmsinc.org
Members: 1600 individuals
Staff: 8
Annual Budget: $2-5,000,000
President and Chief Executive Officer: Richard A. Yingst
Director, Marketing: Jennifer Doak
Vice President and Director, Professional Development: Diane Walter
E-Mail: dianew@fmsinc.org

Historical Note
The Financial Managers Society, Inc., is the only individual membership society exclusively for finance & accounting professionals from financial institutions. FMS members are CFOs, controllers, CEOs, COOs, treasurers, investment officers and internal auditors from banks, thrifts and credit unions. Membership: $425/year (individual); $495/year (affiliate).

Meetings/Conferences:
Annual Meetings: May
2007 – Grapevine, TX(Gaylord Opryland Texas)/June 24-26
2008 – Orlando, FL(Royal Pacific Resort)/June 19-26
2009 – Keystone, CO(Keystone Resort)/June 21-23
2010 – Scottsdale, AZ(Sheraton Wild Horse Pass)/June 20-22

Publications:
FMS Update. bi-weekly. adv.

Financial Marketing Association
Historical Note
A division of the Credit Union Executives Society

Financial Markets Association *(1990)*
7799 Leesburg Pike, Suite 800-N
Falls Church, VA 22043-2413
Tel: (703)749-1579 *Fax:* (703)749-1688
Web Site: www.securagroup.com/affiliates/fma/index.htm
Members: 300 individuals
Staff: 1
Annual Budget: $100-250,000
Managing Director: Dorcas Pearce

Historical Note
FMA focuses on the educational and training needs of professionals working with financial institution treasury and capital markets, securities investing and fiduciary activities. Unlike other organizations, FMA works for individual bankers, not member banks. Membership: $150/year (new); $99/year (renewal).

Publications:
Market Solutions. q.

Financial Markets Association - USA *(1958)*
P.O. Box 156
Parlin, NJ 08859
Tel: (732)316-0384
E-Mail: info@fma-usa.org
Web Site: www.fma-usa.org
Members: 300 individuals
Administrator: Robert J. Tum-Suden

Historical Note
Formerly (1988) Forex Association of North America, and (1997) Forex U.S.A. Members are foreign exchange and money market traders and brokers. Membership: $200/year.

Meetings/Conferences:
Annual Meetings: June

Financial Operation Association
Historical Note
A division of the Credit Union Executives Society.

Financial Planning Association
4100 E. MIssissippi Ave., Suite 400
Denver, CO 80246-3053
Tel: (303)759-4900 *Fax:* (303)759-0749
Toll Free: (800)322 - 4237
E-Mail: fpa@fpanet.org
Web Site: www.fpanet.org
Members: 27500 individuals
Staff: 70
Annual Budget: $10-25,000,000
Executive Director/Chief Executive Officer: Marvin W. Tuttle, Jr, CAE
President: Daniel B. Moisand, CFP

Historical Note
Formed by a merger of the Institute of Certified Financial Planners and the International Association for Financial Planning; the resulting organization assumed its present name in 1999. Established in Denver, CO, FPA has roughly 27,500 members in 100 local chapters. Membership: $285/year (individual).

Meetings/Conferences:
Annual Meetings: Fall
2007 – Seattle, WA/Sept. 8-11/3000

Publications:
Solutions. 6/yr.
Journal of Financial Planning. m. adv.

Financial Services Roundtable *(1993)*
1001 Pennsylvania Ave. NW, Suite 500 South
Washington, DC 20004
Tel: (202)289-4322 *Fax:* (202)628-2507
E-Mail: info@fsround.org
Web Site: www.fsround.org
Members: 100 companies
Staff: 35
Annual Budget: $5-10,000,000
Executive Director and General Counsel: Richard M. Whiting
President and Chief Executive Officer: Steve Bartlett
Executive Vice President, External Affairs/President, Government Affairs Council: Lisa McGreevy
Senior Vice President, Government Affairs: Scott Talbott

Historical Note
Founded as the Bankers Roundtable; the result of a merger in 1993 of the Association of Bank Holding Companies and the Association of Reserve City Bankers. Assumed its current name in 1999.

Meetings/Conferences:
Semi-Annual Meetings: Spring and Fall

Publications:
Newsletter. m.
Government Affairs Bulletin. m.

Financial Services Technology Consortium *(1993)*
44 Wall St., 12th Floor
New York, NY 10005
Tel: (212)461-7116 *Fax:* (646)349-3629
Web Site: www.fstc.org
Members: 56companiesandorganizations
Staff: 3
Executive Director: Zachary Tumin
E-Mail: zachary.tumin@fstc.org

Historical Note
FSTC sponsors product testing, development programs, and other projects to ensure the continued viability of new technologies in the financial sector.

Meetings/Conferences:
Annual Meetings: Spring

Financial Services Technology Network
Eight S. Michigan Ave., Suite 1000
Chicago, IL 60603
Tel: (312)782-4951 *Fax:* (312)580-0165
Members: 45 corporations
Staff: 10
Annual Budget: $250-500,000
Executive Director: Kathleen Lukasik

Historical Note
Previously known as National Trust Aids Systems Association. Members are companies involved in technology services.

Meetings/Conferences:
Semi-Annual Meetings:

Financial Suppliers Forum
Historical Note
A division of the the Credit Union Executives Society

Financial Women International *(1921)*
1027 W. Roselawn Ave.
Roseville, MN 55113
Tel: (651)487-7632 *Fax:* (866)807-6081
E-Mail: info@fwi.org
Web Site: www.fwi.org
Members: 900 individuals
Annual Budget: $500-1,000,000
Contact Person: Ann Kvaal

Historical Note
Formerly (1989) the National Association of Bank Women. Members are managers, directors and officers from all sectors of the financial services industry. FWI's mission is to serve women in the financial services industry who seek to expand their personal and professional capabilities through self-directed growth in a supportive environment. Membership: $79-199/year (individual).

Meetings/Conferences:
Annual Meetings: Fall/500
2007 – San Juan, PR/Sept. 30-Oct. 2

Finishing Contractors Association *(1997)*
8150 Leesburg Pike, Suite 1210
Vienna, VA 22182
Tel: (703)448-9001 *Fax:* (703)448-9002
Toll Free: (866)322 - 3477
E-Mail: fca@finishingcontractors.org
Web Site: www.finishingcontractors.org
Members: 1150 companies
Staff: 4
Annual Budget: $1-2,000,000
Chief Executive Officer: Vincent R. Sandusky

Historical Note
FCA members are union contractors. FCA represents companies which are signatory to agreements with the International Brotherhood of Painters and Allied Trades. Areas covered include painting, drywall, glass, flooring, and signs.
Publications:
Finishing News Newsletter. q.

Finnish American Chamber of Commerce *(1948)*
866 United Nations Plaza
New York, NY 10017
Tel: (212)821-0225 *Fax:* (212)750-4418
E-Mail: faccnyc@verizon.net
Web Site: www.facc-ny.com
Members: 200 companies
Staff: 1
Annual Budget: $50-100,000
Executive Director: Maarit Bystedt
E-Mail: faccnyc@verizon.net
Historical Note
Membership: $80/year (individual); $550/year (company); $1,600/year (sustaining).
Meetings/Conferences:
Annual Meetings: always New York, NY/May-June/50
Publications:
Headlines. q. adv.

Finnsheep Breeders Association *(1971)*
HC 65, Box 517
Hominy, OK 74035
Tel: (918)885-1284
Web Site: www.finnsheep.org
Members: 601 individuals
Annual Budget: $10-25,000
Secretary: Cynthia Smith
Historical Note
FSBA members are owners and breeders of Finnsheep. Maintains a breed registry. Has no paid officers or full-time staff. Membership: $20/year (individual), $35/lifetime.
Publications:
Finnsheep Short Tales Newsletter. semi-a.
Breeders' Directory. a.

Fire and Emergency Manufacturers and Services Association *(1966)*
P.O. Box 147
Lynnfield, MA 01940-0147
Tel: (781)334-2771 *Fax:* (781)334-2771
E-Mail: info@femsa.org
Web Site: www.femsa.org
Members: 150 companies
Staff: 1
Annual Budget: $50-100,000
Executive to the Board: Karen H. Burnham
Historical Note
Formerly (1990) the Fire Equipment Manufacturers and Services Association. Established and incorporated in Delaware, FEMSA members are companies that manufacture vehicles, protective clothing, hoses and nozzles, breathing apparatus, rescue tools and other products and services used by fire fighters. FEMSA's primary public policy concern is federal product liability.
Meetings/Conferences:
Annual Meetings: Fall
2007 – Monterey, CA/Oct. 3-7
2008 – Tucson, AZ(El Conquistador)/Oct. 8-12
Publications:
FEMSA News. q.

Fire Apparatus Manufacturers' Association *(1946)*
P.O. Box 397
Lynnfield, MA 01940-0397
Tel: (781)334-2911 *Fax:* (781)934-2911
E-Mail: info@fama.org
Web Site: www.fama.org
Members: 104 companies
Staff: 1
Annual Budget: $50-100,000
Executive Assistant to the Board: Karen H. Burnham
Historical Note
Formerly a division of the National Truck Equipment Association, FAMA became an independent organization in 1997. Members are manufacturers of fire suppression material and equipment and other firefighting components. Membership: $1,500/year (company).
Meetings/Conferences:
Semi-Annual Meetings: Spring/Fall
2007 – Key West, FL/March 23-27
2007 – Monterey, CA/Oct. 3-6
Publications:
FAMA Flyer. q.

Fire Equipment Manufacturers' Association *(1925)*
1300 Sumner Ave.
Cleveland, OH 44115-2851
Tel: (216)241-7333 *Fax:* (216)241-0105
E-Mail: fema@taol.com
Web Site: www.femalifesafety.org
Members: 24 companies
Staff: 3
Annual Budget: $100-250,000
Executive Director: John H. Addington
Historical Note
Established as the Fire Extinguisher Manufacturers' Association, Inc., it assumed its present name in 1936. Members are companies making devices that control or extinguish fires in residential or commercial buildings. Membership: sliding scale.
Meetings/Conferences:
Annual Meetings: Fall/50

Fire Suppression Systems Association *(1982)*
5024-R Campbell Blvd.
Baltimore, MD 21236-5974
Tel: (410)933-3454 *Fax:* (410)931-8111
Web Site: www.fssa.net
Members: 94 installers, 14 manufacturers
Staff: 3
Annual Budget: $100-250,000
Executive Director: Crista LeGrand, CMP
Historical Note
Founded in Chicago and incorporated in the State of Illinois. Members are designers, suppliers and installers of special hazard fire suppression equipment, gases and dectectors.
Meetings/Conferences:
Annual Meetings: Winter
Publications:
FYI (Electronic). m.
Membership Directory.

Fixed Income Analysts Society *(1975)*
360 Madison Ave., 15th Floor
New York, NY 10017
Tel: (646)637-9243 *Fax:* (646)637-9118
E-Mail: fiasi@fiasi.org
Web Site: www.fiasi.org
Members: 300 individuals
Staff: 5
Annual Budget: $50-100,000
President: John Finnerty
E-Mail: fiasi@fiasi.org
Historical Note
FIASI members are individuals regularly engaged as fixed income professionals, including persons who specialize in credit research as well as those specializing in quantitative research. Membership: $160/year, plus $50 initiation (individual).
Meetings/Conferences:
Annual Meetings: June

Flavor and Extract Manufacturers Association of the United States *(1909)*
1620 I St. NW, Suite 925
Washington, DC 20006
Tel: (202)293-5800 *Fax:* (202)463-8998
Web Site: www.femaflavor.org
Members: 850 individuals
Staff: 18
Annual Budget: $2-5,000,000
Executive Director: Brian Bursjek
Historical Note
Formerly the Flavoring Extract Manufacturers Association of the U.S. Merged with the National Manufacturers of Beverage Flavors in 1965.
Meetings/Conferences:
Annual Meetings: Annual
Publications:
Regulatory and Legislative Update. q.

Fleet Reserve Association *(1924)*
125 N. West St.
Alexandria, VA 22314-2754
Tel: (703)683-1400
E-Mail: news-fra@fra.org
Web Site: www.fra.org
Members: 1500000 individuals
Staff: 30
Annual Budget: $2-5,000,000
National Executive Secretary: Joseph L. Barnes
Historical Note
One of the oldest and largest associations representing the interests of sea services enlisted personnel with regard to pay and benefits. Chartered by Congress in 1997. Annual membership: $20/individual.
Publications:
On Watch Newsletter. bi-m.
Naval Affairs Magazine. m. adv.

Fleischner Society *(1969)*
4550 Post Oak Place, Suite 342
Houston, TX 77027
Tel: (713)965-0566 *Fax:* (713)960-0488
Web Site: www.fleischner.org
Members: 65 individuals
Annual Budget: $50-100,000
Contact, Meetings: Pam Waslawski
Historical Note
Named for Dr. Felix Fleischner, an eminent chest radiologist, the society is dedicated to advancing the knowledge of chest diagnosis, with an emphasis on radiology. Membership is international and interdisciplinary, although the majority of members are Americans and radiologists.
Meetings/Conferences:
Annual Meetings: Spring
Publications:
Syllabus of Course Material. a.

Flexible Intermediate Bulk Container Association *(1984)*
P.O. Box 24792
Minneapolis, MN 55424
Tel: (952)412-8867 *Fax:* (661)339-0023
Toll Free: (866)600 - 8880
E-Mail: info@fibca.com
Web Site: http://fibca.com
Members: 50 companies
Staff: 1
Annual Budget: $50-100,000
Executive Vice President: Bruce Cuthbertson
Historical Note
Members are companies manufacturing flexible intermediate bulk containers, and their suppliers. Membership: $1,500/year.

Flexible Packaging Association *(1950)*
971 Corporate Blvd., Suite 403
Linthicum, MD 21090
Tel: (410)694-0800 *Fax:* (410)694-0900
E-Mail: fpa@flexpack.org
Web Site: www.flexpack.org
Members: 130 companies
Staff: 6
Annual Budget: $2-5,000,000
President: Marla Donahue
Director, Technology and Regulatory Affairs: Ram Singhal
Director, Business and Economic Research: Robert Zaborowski
Historical Note
Includes former Industrial Bag and Cover Association and Waxed Paper Institute. Formerly (1979) National Flexible Packaging Association. FPA is a trade association of manufacturers, converters and suppliers of paper, metal foil, and plastic or cellulose film. Membership: dues vary by sales (company).
Meetings/Conferences:
Annual Meetings: March/200
2007 – Aventura, FL(Fairmont Turnberry)/Feb. 28-March 2
2008 – Orlando, FL(Marriott JW)
Publications:
Flexible Packaging Magazine. m.

Membership Directory. a.
State of the Industry Report. a.
FPA Networks. a.
Association e-News.

Flexographic Prepress Platemakers Association *(1997)*
2105 Laurel Bush Road, Suite 200
Bel Air, MD 21015
Tel: (443)640-1045 *Fax:* (443)640-1031
E-Mail: fppa@ksgroup.org
Web Site: www.fppa.net
Members: 50 individuals
Staff: 3
Annual Budget: $100-250,000
Executive Director: Fred C. Stringfellow
E-Mail: fppa@ksgroup.org

Historical Note
FPPA's purpose is to create, promote and enhance high standards within the flexographic pre-press platemaking industry, to provide leadership through vision and direction, to strengthen education at all levels and to further the best interests of the industry. Membership is open to businesses who are involved in or supply to the flexographic industry.

Meetings/Conferences:
Annual Meetings: Spring
2007 - Scottsdale, AZ(Doubletree Paradise Valley Resort)/Feb. 18-20/100

Publications:
On Target Newsletter.

Flexographic Technical Association *(1958)*
900 Marconi Ave.
Ronkonkoma, NY 11779-7212
Tel: (631)737-6020 *Fax:* (631)737-6813
E-Mail: memberinfo@flexography.org
Web Site: www.flexography.org
Members: 1700 businesses
Staff: 21
Annual Budget: $2-5,000,000
President: Mark Cisternino
E-Mail: markc@flexography.org
Director, Marketing: Sharon Cox

Historical Note
Founded in 1958, the Flexographic Technical Association has led the way as a key resource for those in the flexographic industry. Members include printers, suppliers, consumer product companies, prepress and design houses and education institutions. FTA provides its members with technical information, support, products, seminars, conferences, networking opportunities, awards competitions and more.

Meetings/Conferences:
Annual Meetings: Spring/2,000
2007 - Montreal, QC, Canada(Palais des Congres)/May 6-9
2008 - Dallas, TX(Wyndham Anatole)/Apr. 27-30
2009 - Orlando, FL(Disney Coronado Springs Resort)/May 3-6

Publications:
FLEXO Magazine. m. adv.

Flight Safety Foundation *(1947)*
601 Madison St., Suite 300
Alexandria, VA 22314
Tel: (703)739-6700 *Fax:* (703)739-6708
Web Site: www.flightsafety.org
Members: 800 airlines, orgs. & individuals
Staff: 20
Annual Budget: $2-5,000,000
President and Chief Executive Officer: Stuart Matthews
Director, Technical Programs: James M. Burin
Director, Finance and Administration: Juan G. Gonzalez, CPA
Director, Membership and Development: Ann Hill
Senior Editor: Mark Lacagnina
Executive Vice President: Robert H. Vandel

Historical Note
An international, independent non profit association supported by airlines, aerospace manufacturers, aviation professionals, corporate flight departments and others interested in flight safety. Membership: $100/year (indiv.); $1,000-25,000/year (company)

Meetings/Conferences:
Annual Meetings: Winter

Publications:
European Seminar Proceedings. a. adv.
Accident Prevention Bulletin. m.
Airport Operations Safety Bulletin. bi-m.
Aviation Mechanics Bulletin. bi-m.
Cabin Crew Safety Bulletin. bi-m.
FSF Flight Safety Digest. m.
Helicopter Safety Bulletin. bi-m.
Human Factors Bulletin. bi-m.
Newsletter. bi-m.
Corporate Seminar Proceedings. a. adv.
Internat'l Seminar Proceedings. a. adv.

Floor Covering Installation Contractors Association *(1982)*
7439 Millwood Dr.
West Bloomfield, MI 48322-1234
Tel: (248)661-5015 *Fax:* (248)661-5018
E-Mail: info@fcica.com
Web Site: www.fcica.com
Members: 200 companies
Staff: 3
Annual Budget: $100-250,000
Executive Vice President: Kimberly Oderkirk

Historical Note
Established in 1982 and incorporated in Georgia. FCICA represents the floor covering contractor industry. Membership: $350-950/year (full member), $700-2,500/year (associate).

Meetings/Conferences:
Annual Meetings: Spring
2007 - San Francisco, CA(Argonaut)/March 14-17/150

Publications:
Floor Contractor. q. adv.
Bottom Line E-News. bi-m. adv.

Flue-Cured Tobacco Cooperative Stabilization Corporation *(1946)*
1304 Annapolis Dr.
Raleigh, NC 27608
Tel: (919)821-4560 *Fax:* (919)821-4564
E-Mail: fcmembers@ipass.net
Web Site: www.ustobaccofarmer.com
Members: 50000 individuals
Staff: 37
Annual Budget: $1-2,000,000
General Manager: L. Arnold Hamm

Historical Note
Flue-cured tobacco producers' marketing cooperative for six southern states and adminstrator of federal price support program for flue-cured tobacco. Membership: $5/year (individual).

Meetings/Conferences:
Annual Meetings: Always in Raleigh, NC(Scott Pavilion, NC State Fairgrounds)/last Friday in May/800-1,000

Publications:
Newsletter. m.

Fluid Controls Institute *(1921)*
1300 Sumner Ave.
Cleveland, OH 44115-2851
Tel: (216)241-7333 *Fax:* (216)241-0105
E-Mail: fci@fluidcontrolsinstitute.org
Web Site: www.fluidcontrolsinstitute.org
Members: 32 companies
Staff: 4
Annual Budget: $25-50,000
Executive Secretary: John H. Addington

Historical Note
Manufacturers of devices for fluid control, such as temperature and pressure regulators, strainers, gauges, control valves, solenoid valves, steam traps, etc. Established as the National Association of Steam and Fluid Specialty Manufacturers, it became the National Steam Specialty Club in 1941 and assumed its present name in 1955.

Meetings/Conferences:
Semi-annual Meetings: Spring and Fall
2007 - Amelia Island, FL(Amelia Island Plantation)/March 30-Apr. 3

Fluid Fertilizer Foundation *(1982)*

Historical Note
The research and educational arm of the Agricultural Retailers Association.

Fluid Power Distributors Association *(1974)*
P.O. Box 1420
Cherry Hill, NJ 08034-0054
Tel: (856)424-8998 *Fax:* (856)424-9248
E-Mail: info@fpda.org
Web Site: www.fpda.org
Members: 475 companies
Staff: 8
Annual Budget: $500-1,000,000
Executive Director: Kathleen A. DeMarco
E-Mail: KathyDeMarco@fpda.org

Historical Note
Membership is composed of distributors and manufacturers of hydraulic and pneumatic equipment and motion control technology. Services provided to members include management training, technical information updates, and statistical and financial information. Membership: $400-2,500/year (corporate).

Meetings/Conferences:
Semi-Annual Meetings: Spring and Fall

Publications:
FPDA Express. m. adv.
FPDA News. 6/year. adv.
Directory. a.

Fluid Power Society *(1957)*
P.O. Box 1420
Cherry Hill, NJ 08004
Toll Free: (800)303 - 8520
E-Mail: info@ifps.org
Web Site: www.ifps.org
Members: 3500 individuals
Staff: 7
Annual Budget: $500-1,000,000
Managing Director: Paul Prass

Historical Note
FPS is the international organization for fluid power (hydraulics, pneumatics, vacuum and electronics technologies) and motion control professionals. The Society provides education, certification and professional services. Membership: $60/year

Meetings/Conferences:
Annual Meetings:

Publications:
Fluid Power Journal.. bi-m. adv.
Certification Directory.. a. adv.
Membership Directory.. a. adv.

Fluid Sealing Association *(1933)*
994 Old Eagle School Road, Suite 1019
Wayne, PA 19087-1866
Tel: (610)971-4850 *Fax:* (610)971-4859
E-Mail: INFO@fluidsealing.com
Web Site: www.fluidsealing.com
Members: 60 companies
Staff: 5
Annual Budget: $250-500,000
Executive Director: Robert H. Ecker

Historical Note
Formerly (1970) Mechanical Packing Association. FSA is an international association of manufacturers of mechanical packings, sealing devices, gaskets, rubber expansion joints, and allied products.

Meetings/Conferences:
Annual Meetings: Spring and Fall
2007 - Marco Island, FL(Marriott Resort)/Apr. 25-27/120

Publications:
Newsletter. semi-a.
Technical Manuals & Standards.

Foil Stamping and Embossing Association *(1992)*
2150 S.W. Westport Dr., Suite 101
Topeka, KS 66614
Tel: (785)271-5816 *Fax:* (785)271-6404
Web Site: www.fsea.com
Members: 350 companies
Staff: 11
Annual Budget: $500-1,000,000
Executive Director: Jeff Peterson
E-Mail: jeff@petersonpublications.com

Historical Note
FSEA is a non-profit international trade association of foil stampers, embossers, die cutters and industry suppliers working together for the advancement of the industry. Membership: $175-500/year (active); $250-750/year (associate). Membership: rates are dependent upon the number of employees.

Meetings/Conferences:
Annual Meetings: October-November

Publications:
Inside Finishing Magazine. q. adv.
FSEA Annual Directory. a. adv.

Food and Drug Law Institute *(1949)*
1000 Vermont Ave. NW, Suite 200
Washington, DC 20005-4903
Tel: (202)371-1420 *Fax:* (202)371-0649
Toll Free: (800)956 - 6293
E-Mail: comments@fdli.org
Web Site: www.fdli.org
Members: 538 companies
Staff: 16
Annual Budget: $2-5,000,000
President and Chief Executive Officer: Jerome Halperin
Vice President, Membership and Marketing: Albert Auer
Vice President, Publications and Programs: Rita Fullem
Director, Operations: Carol D. Gavin

Historical Note
Formerly (1965) Food Law Institute. FDLI is a non-profit, educational organization working to promote an understanding of the laws, regulations, and policies affecting the public health aspects of foods, drugs, cosmetics, medical devices, biological products, and veterinary medical products. Members are manufacturers, suppliers, law firms, consultants, associations, research groups, public relations firms and others associated with the food, drug, medical devices, cosmetics and biologics industries. Membership: $25-10,000/year.

Meetings/Conferences:
Annual Meetings: Spring

Publications:
Food and Drug Law Journal. q.
Directory of the Food and Drug Administration. bien.
Update magazine. bi-m. adv.

Food Distribution Research Society *(1960)*
Univ. of Florida
1161 McCarty Hall A
Gainesville, FL 32611
Tel: (352)392-1826 Ext: 403 *Fax:* (352)846-0988
Web Site: http://fdrs.ag.utk.edu/
Members: 200 individuals
Annual Budget: $25-50,000
Contact: Allen Wysocki
E-Mail: wysocki@ufl.edu

Historical Note
Informally established in 1960 as the Food Distribution Research Conference, the organization became formally recognized and assumed its present name in 1967. The Society encourages and implements food distribution research and serves as an information clearinghouse for past, current, and future food industry issues. Has no paid staff. Membership fee: $10/year (student); $40/year (professional/academic/government); $50/year (library); $135/year (company).

Meetings/Conferences:
Annual Meetings: Fall

Publications:
Journal of Food Distribution Research. 3/year.
Newsletter. 3/year.

Food Industry Association Executives *(1927)*
P.O. Box 2510
Flemington, NJ 08822
Tel: (908)782-7833 *Fax:* (908)782-6907
E-Mail: fiae@earthlink.net
Web Site: www.fiae.net
Members: 170 individuals
Staff: 2
Annual Budget: $100-250,000
President/Chief Executive Officer: Barbara McConnell
Vice President, Administration: Kathy Shiarappa

Historical Note
Formerly (1959) the National Grocery Secretaries Association. Members are executives of retail grocer associations on the national, state and local levels. Membership: $150-650/year (active); $500/year (affiliate).

Publications:
ExecuNews. q.
FIAE. m.
Membership Directory. a.

Food Industry Suppliers Association *(1968)*
1207 Sunset Dr.
Greensboro, NC 27408
Tel: (336)274-6311 *Fax:* (336)691-1839
Web Site: www.fisanet.org
Members: 120 companies
Staff: 2
Annual Budget: $50-100,000
Executive Director: Stella Jones

Historical Note
Affiliated with National Association of Wholesaler-Distributors. Members are distributors who sell equipment and supplies to the food processing industry. Membership: $685/year (distributor/manufacturer); $425/year (associate).

Meetings/Conferences:
Annual Meetings: Fall/150

Publications:
FISA Distributor News. q.

Food Machinery Service Institute *(1932)*

Historical Note
Established as the United Saw Service Association, it assumed its present name in 1983. An autonomous division of the Meat Industry Supplier Association.

Food Marketing Institute *(1977)*
655 15th St. NW, Suite 700
Washington, DC 20005
Tel: (202)452-8444
E-Mail: fmi@fmi.org
Web Site: www.fmi.org
Members: 1500 companies
Staff: 140
Annual Budget: $25-50,000,000
President and Chief Executive Officer: Timothy Hammonds
Senior Vice President: Karen H. Brown
Senior Vice President: John Motley
Senior Vice President: Michael Sansolo
Senior Vice President: Brian Tully

Historical Note
Formed Jan. 3, 1977 by a merger of the Super Market Institute, Inc. and the National Association of Food Chains. Absorbed Food Distributors International in 2002. Members are food retailers and wholesalers. Supports the Food Marketing Institute Political Action Committee. Has an annual budget of approximately $32 million.

Meetings/Conferences:
2007 - Chicago, IL/May 5-8

Food Processing Machinery and Supplies Association *(1885)*
200 Daingerfield Road
Alexandria, VA 22314
Tel: (703)684-1080 *Fax:* (703)548-6563
Toll Free: (800)331 - 8816
E-Mail: info@fpmamail.com
Web Site: www.processfood.com
Members: 500 companies
Staff: 10
Annual Budget: $250-500,000
Executive Director: Nancy Janssen

Historical Note
Formerly (1968) Canning Machinery and Supplies Association, and then Food Processing Machinery and Suppliers Association; assumed its current name in 2002. Absorbed the Beverage Machinery Manufacturers Association in 1987. Membership: dues based on annual sales.

Meetings/Conferences:
Annual Meetings: Fall

Publications:
Blue Book Buyer's Guide. a. adv.

Food Processors Institute *(1973)*

Historical Note
A division of the National Food Processors Association, the FPI meets the educational and training needs of the food processing industry. Also known as the National Food Processors Institute.

Food Products Association *(1907)*
1350 I St. NW Suite 300
Washington, DC 20005
Tel: (202)639-5900 *Fax:* (202)639-5932
Members: 400 companies
Staff: 1
Annual Budget: $10-25,000,000
President and Chief Executive Officer: Cal Dooley

Historical Note
Formerly the National Food Processors Association, the Food Products Association is the largest trade association serving the food and beverage industry.

Food Sanitation Institute *(1957)*

Historical Note
A component of the Environmental Management Association.

Food Shippers of America *(1954)*
6166 Borror Road
Grove City, OH 43123
Tel: (614)875-3955
Web Site: www.foodshippersofamerica.org
Members: 66
Staff: 1
Executive Director: John Murphy

Historical Note
FSA promotes improvement in supply chain efficiency, emphasizing transportation service. Members are carriers, distributors, and related companies serving the food industry. Membership: $150/year.

Meetings/Conferences:
Annual Meetings: Winter

Foodservice and Packaging Institute *(1933)*
150 S. Washington St., Suite 204
Falls Church, VA 22046
Tel: (703)538-2800 *Fax:* (703)538-2187
E-Mail: fpi@fpi.org
Web Site: www.fpi.org
Members: 25 companies
Staff: 3
Annual Budget: $500-1,000,000
President: John R. Burke
E-Mail: jburke@fpi.org
Director, Member Services and Administration: Elizabeth T. Phillips

Historical Note
Formerly (1987) the Single Service Institute. Manufacturers of one-time use cups, plates, bowls, wraps, straws and other similar products used for food service; nestable containers, placemats, prepackaging trays, egg cartons, etc made from paper, plastic aluminum and other materials. Formed by the merger in 1966 of the Paper Cup and Container Institute (1933), the Paper Plate Association (1948) and the Linen and Lace Paper Institute (1954). Absorbed the Food Tray and Board Association in 1971 (formerly Pulp and Paper Prepackaging Association.) Absorbed the Egg Packaging Association in 1975. Membership: varies by sales volume.

Meetings/Conferences:
Semi-Annual Meetings:

Publications:
State of the Food Service Packaging Industry. a.
Member Product Directory. a.
Single Service News. q.
Indispensable Info. q.
Executive Briefs. bi-m.

Foodservice Consultants Society International *(1979)*
304 W. Liberty St., Suite 201
Louisville, KY 40202-3068
Tel: (502)583-3783 *Fax:* (502)589-3602
E-Mail: fcsi@fcsi.org
Web Site: www.fcsi.org
Members: 1200 individuals
Staff: 5

Annual Budget: $1-2,000,000
Executive Vice President: David L. Drain
Director, Public Relations: Travis Doster

Historical Note
The result of a merger in 1979 between the Food Facilities Consultants Society (founded in 1955) and the International Society of Food Service Consultants (founded in 1958). A professional society for consultants in design, equipment, engineering and management to the foodservice industry and furthers research, development and education in the foodservice field. Membership: $385/year (individual), $450-1,900/year (company).

Publications:
The Forum Newsletter.
The Consultant. q. adv.
The Spec Sheet Newsletter.
Membership Directory. a. adv.

Foodservice Equipment Distributors Association *(1933)*
2250 Point Blvd.
Suite 200
Elgin, IL 60606
Tel: (224)293-6500 *Fax:* (224)293-6505
E-Mail: feda@feda.com
Web Site: www.feda.com
Members: 290 companies
Staff: 6
Annual Budget: $100-250,000
Executive Vice President: Raymond W. Herrick, II, CAE

Historical Note
Formerly (1972) Food Service Equipment Industry, Inc. Dealers in and distributors of foodservice equipment and supplies.

Meetings/Conferences:
Annual Meetings: March

Publications:
FEDA News & Views. bi-m. adv.

The Foodservice Group, Inc. *(1978)*
630 Village Trace, Bldg. 15
Suite A
Marietta, GA 30067
Tel: (770)989-0049 *Fax:* (770)956-7498
E-Mail: kreynolds@fsgroup.com
Web Site: www.fsgroup.com
Members: 42 companies
Staff: 1
Annual Budget: $50-100,000
Executive Director: Kenneth W. Reynolds

Historical Note
Formerly (1978) National Foodservice Marketing Associates. Members are independent food service brokers.

Football Writers Association of America *(1941)*
18652 Vista Del Sol
Dallas, TX 75287
Tel: (972)713-6198
Web Site: www.sportswriters.net/fwaa/
Members: 900 individuals
Staff: 1
Executive Director: Steve Richardson

Historical Note
Established to improve working conditions in college press boxes. Now picks All-America Football team, national championship football team, college coach of the year, winner of the Outland Award, and college football defensive player of the year. Membership: $40/year.

Meetings/Conferences:
Annual Meetings: Winter
2007 – Glendale, AZ/Jan. 5-9

Publications:
The 5th Down. 5/year. adv.

Footwear Distributors and Retailers of America *(1944)*
1319 F St. NW, Suite 700
Washington, DC 20004
Tel: (202)737-5660 *Fax:* (202)638-2615
E-Mail: ptmangione@fdra.org
Web Site: www.fdra.org
Members: 81 companies
Staff: 4
Annual Budget: $500-1,000,000
President: Peter T. Mangione
Director, Communications: Margaret A. Lew
Director, Financial Services: Faith Lewis

Historical Note
Founded as the Popular Price Shoe Retailers Association, it became the National Association of Shoe Chain Stores in 1965, the Volume Footwear Retailers Association in 1969, the Volume Footwear Retailers of America in 1972, Footwear Retailers of America in 1985 and assumed its present name in 1985. Absorbed International Footwear Association in 1990. Sponsors and supports the FDRA Political Action Committee.

Meetings/Conferences:
Annual Meetings: Spring

Publications:
Customs Report. m.
Employee Relations. m.
Labor Digest. m.
Executive Bulletin. m.

Foreign Press Association *(1918)*
333 E. 46th St., Suite 1K
New York, NY 10017
Tel: (212)370-1054 *Fax:* (212)370-1058
E-Mail: fpanewyork@aol.com
Web Site: www.foreignpressnewyork.com
Members: 400 individuals
Staff: 1
Annual Budget: $25-50,000
Director: Suzanne Adams

Historical Note
FPA members are foreign newspaper and broadcast correspondents stationed in the United States. Membership: $75/year (individual).

Publications:
FPA News Newsletter. bi-m.
FPA Directory of Members. a. adv.

Forest History Society *(1946)*
701 William Vickers Ave.
Durham, NC 27701
Tel: (919)682-9319 *Fax:* (919)682-2349
E-Mail: recluce2@duke.edu
Web Site: www.lib.duke.edu/forest
Members: 2000 individuals
Staff: 8
Annual Budget: $500-1,000,000
President and Secretary: Steve Anderson
E-Mail: recluce2@duke.edu

Historical Note
Preceded by two unincorporated organizations, the Forest Products History Foundation (1946-52) and the American Forest History Foundation (1951-55), the Forest History Society was incorporated in Minnesota in 1955. In 1984 it affiliated with Duke University and moved to Durham, NC. A non-profit educational institution advancing the historical understanding of humankind's interaction with the physical environment. Membership: $55/year (individual); $250/year (corporate); $130/year (institution).

Publications:
Environmental History. q. adv.
Forest Timeline. a.
Forest History Today. a. adv.

Forest Industries Telecommunications *(1947)*
1565 Oak St.
Eugene, OR 97401
Tel: (541)485-8441 *Fax:* (541)485-7556
E-Mail: license@landmobile.com
Web Site: www.landmobile.com
Members: 1800 companies
Staff: 6
Annual Budget: $500-1,000,000
Executive Vice President: Kenton E. Sturdevant

Historical Note
Organized in 1947 to assist the forest industry in radio matters before the FCC. Recognized by the FCC as the official representative of the Forest Products Radio Service. Assists all industry and business categories with FCC licensing and frequency coordination services.

Meetings/Conferences:
Annual Meetings: Fall

Publications:
Two Way Transmissions. q.

Forest Products Society *(1947)*
2801 Marshall Court
Madison, WI 53705-2295
Tel: (608)231-1361 *Fax:* (608)231-2152
Web Site: www.forestprod.org
Members: 2500 individuals
Staff: 11
Annual Budget: $1-2,000,000
Executive Vice President: Carol Lewis

Historical Note
Formerly (1995) Forest Products Research Society. Focus is on wood industry development, research, production, distribution and use, including all phases from logging to finished product and use of by-products.

Meetings/Conferences:
Annual Meetings: Summer/400-500

Publications:
Wood Design Focus. q. adv.
Forest Products Journal. m. adv.

Forest Resources Association *(1934)*
600 Jefferson Plaza, Suite 350
Rockville, MD 20852
Tel: (301)838-9385 *Fax:* (301)838-9481
E-Mail: fra@forestresources.org
Web Site: www.forestresources.org
Members: 1000 companies
Staff: 13
Annual Budget: $1-2,000,000
President: Richard Lewis, CAE

Historical Note
Founded as American Pulpwood Association; assumed its current name in 2000. Members are consumers, producers and distributors of wood fiber and companies who offer products on services to the forest products industry. Membership fee varies, based on volume of wood handled.

Meetings/Conferences:
Annual Meetings: Spring/500

Publications:
Forest Operations Review. adv.
FRA Bulletin. m. adv.

Forestry Conservation Communications Association *(1944)*
P.O. Box 3217
Gettysburg, PA 17325
Tel: (717)338-1505 *Fax:* (717)334-5656
E-Mail: fcca@SSO.org
Web Site: www.fcca-usa.org
Members: 200 organizations
Staff: 1
Annual Budget: $100-250,000
Executive Manager: Ralph Haller

Historical Note
Certified by the FCC as the radio frequency coordinator for the Forestry Conservation Radio Service. Has no paid officers.

Meetings/Conferences:
Annual Meetings: July

Publications:
FCAA Newsletter. q.

Forestry Equipment Council

Historical Note
A council of the Equipment Manufacturers Institute.

Forging Industry Association *(1913)*
25 West Prospect Ave., Suite 300
Cleveland, OH 44115
Tel: (216)781-6260 *Fax:* (216)781-0102
E-Mail: info@forging.org
Web Site: www.forging.org
Members: 210 companies
Staff: 12
Annual Budget: $1-2,000,000
Executive Vice President: Charles H. Hageman
E-Mail: charlie@forging.org
Director, Marketing and Industry Meetings: Donald Farley
E-Mail: don@forging.org
Director, Training Services: George Layne
E-Mail: glayne@forging.org

Executive Director, Forging Industry Educational and Research Foundation: Karen Lewis
E-Mail: karen@forging.org
Director, Research and Education: George Mochnal
E-Mail: george@forging.org
Treasurer: Diane Rothaermel
E-Mail: diane@forging.org

Historical Note
Formerly Drop Forging Association. Members are producers of forgings and raw materials, major equipment and supplies used in the forging industry. In addition to its annual meeting, FIA sponsors Forge Fair, a triennial international symposium. Absorbed members of Open Die Forging Institute in 1981. Affiliated with Forging Industry Education and Research Foundation (FIERF).

Meetings/Conferences:
Annual Meetings: Biennial
2007 - Huntington Beach, CA(Hyatt Regency)/May 4-8/200

Publications:
Forging Capability Guide. bi-a.
FIA QuickRead. m.
Safety and Health Newsletter. bi-m.

Forming and Fabricating Community of SME

Historical Note
A professional group sponsored by the Society of Manufacturing Engineers.

Forum for Investor Advice

P.O. Box 3216
Merceville, NJ 08619
E-Mail: investoradvice@optonline.net
Web Site: www.investoradvice.org
Members: 65 organizations
Staff: 5
Annual Budget: $1-2,000,000
Executive Director: Barbara Levin

Historical Note
Formerly Mutual Fund Forum, FIA is an association of financial services organizations that distribute mutual funds or other investment products. The organization's primary role is to provide information and research to its constituencies, which include its member firms, the investing public, financial advisors, and the financial press.

Meetings/Conferences:
Semi-annual Meetings:

Publications:
Media Guide.. a.
Mutual Fund Forum.

Foster Family-Based Treatment Association *(1987)*

294 Union St.
Hackensack, NJ 07601
Tel: (201)343-2246 Ext: 113 *Fax:* (201)489-4593
Toll Free: (800)414 - 3382 Ext: 113
E-Mail: ffta@ffta.org
Web Site: www.ffta.org
Members: 400 agencies
Staff: 3
Annual Budget: $250-500,000
Executive Administrator: David Schild
Administrator: Melissa Cole

Historical Note
FFTA supports administrators, researchers, educators, treatment foster parents, and others interested in strengthening family-based treatment foster care. Membership: $450-$2000/year, based on budget.

Meetings/Conferences:
2007 - Orlando, FL(Disney's Coronado Springs Resort)/July 29-Aug. 1/700

Publications:
FOCUS. q. adv.
TFC e-news (online). m.

Foundation for Advances in Medicine and Science *(1983)*

P.O. Box 485
Mahwah, NJ 07430-0485
Tel: (201)818-1010 *Fax:* (201)818-0086
Toll Free: (800)443 - 0263
E-Mail: scanning@fams.org
Web Site: www.fams.org
Members: 350 individuals
Staff: 4
Executive Director: Tony Bourgholtzer

Historical Note
The Foundation for Advances in Medicine and Science Inc. (FAMS) is a nonprofit educational foundation established in 1983. Mission is to advance medicine and science worldwide via the exchange of knowledge and information. FAMS accomplishes this mission by sponsoring conferences, holding educational seminars and publishing scientific journals. Membership: $1,000/year (corporate); $200/year (participating sponsor); $50/year (individual member); $30/year (student).

Meetings/Conferences:
Annual Meetings: Spring
2007 - Monterey, CA(Portola Plaza)/Apr. 10-12/400

Foundation for Independent Higher Education *(1958)*

1920 N St. NW, Suite 210
Washington, DC 20036
Tel: (202)367-0333 *Fax:* (202)367-0334
E-Mail: fihe@fihe.org
Web Site: www.fihe.org
Members: 650 colleges/universities, 36 ass'ns
Staff: 4
Annual Budget: $1-2,000,000
President: Dr. William E. Hamm
Vice President, Advancement: Charles H. Beady
E-Mail: cbeady@fihe.org
Vice President, Programs: Michelle D. Guilliard
E-Mail: mgilliard@fihe.org

Historical Note
Formerly (1987) Independent College Funds of America. The Foundation is the national headquarters for a federation of 34 state and regional associations representing independent colleges and universities. One of the nation's largest fund-raising organizations for independent higher education, it is dedicated to broadening financial support and understanding of independent higher education and its contributions to the nation.

Meetings/Conferences:
Annual Meetings: Spring
2007 - Atlanta, GA(Ritz-Carlton)/50

Publications:
Directory of State Associations and Colleges Represented. a.
Annual Report. a.

Foundation for International Meetings *(1983)*

1110 N. Glebe Road, Suite 580
Arlington, VA 22201
Tel: (703)908-0707 *Fax:* (703)908-0709
Web Site: www.imminetwork.com
Members: 800 individuals
Staff: 8
Annual Budget: $50-100,000
Director, Member Services: Stefanie Gramm

Historical Note
Founded in Washington, DC in 1983. Members are C.E.O.'s of associations and corporations which have ongoing international meeting or trade programs. Membership: $475/year, (by invitation).

Meetings/Conferences:
Annual Meetings: Washington, DC

Publications:
Internat'l Meetings. q.

Foundation for Pavement Preservation *(1992)*

8613 Cross Park Dr.
Austin, TX 78754-4565
Toll Free: (866)862 - 4587
E-Mail: info@fp2.org
Web Site: www.fp2.org
Staff: 1
Executive Director: Gerry Eller

Historical Note
Founded as the Foundation for Pavement Rehabilitation and Maintenance Research; assumed present name in 1999.

Foundation for Russian-American Economic Cooperation *(1989)*

2601 Fourth Ave., Suite 310
Seattle, WA 98121
Tel: (206)443-1935 *Fax:* (206)443-0954
Web Site: www.fraec.org
Members: 90 companies
Staff: 20
Annual Budget: $2-5,000,000
President: Carol Vipperman
E-Mail: carolv@fraec.org
Director, Finance and Administration: Shelly Sutherland

Historical Note
Membership, concentrated in the Pacific Northwest, consists of businesses seeking to enter the Russian market or improve their market share in Russia. Supports initiatives and programs to enhance the business environment in the former Soviet Union, and to improve communications between members and business contacts abroad. Membership fee varies; $250-10,000/year.

Fragrance Foundation *(1949)*

145 E. 32nd St.
New York, NY 10016-6002
Tel: (212)725-2755 *Fax:* (212)779-9058
E-Mail: info@fragrance.org
Web Site: www.fragrance.org
Members: 175 companies
Staff: 7
Annual Budget: $1-2,000,000
Executive Director: Mary Ellen Lapsansky
President: Rochelle R. Bloom

Historical Note
The Fragrance Foundation is the educational arm of the fragrance industry. Mission is to enhance the image of the fragrance industry and expand the appreciation and use of fragrances in all their forms across all distribution channels in the Americas. Full membership: fee based on annual sales volume; $5,000/year (voting member).

Publications:
Recognition Awards Journal. a. adv.
Directory. a.

Fragrance Materials Association of the United States *(1979)*

1620 I St. NW
Suite 925
Washington, DC 20006
Tel: (202)293-5800 *Fax:* (202)463-8998
E-Mail: info@fmafragrance.org
Web Site: www.fmafragrance.org
Members: 65 companies
Staff: 12
Annual Budget: $500-1,000,000
Executive Director: Brian Bursjek
Communications Director: Chris McCarthy

Historical Note
FMA promotes the U.S. fragrance industry through legislative and regulatory work. Its activities are closely coordinated with those of the Research Institute for Fragrance Materials, which undertakes scientific research to support product safety for the industry.

Publications:
Regulatory and Legislative Update. q.
FMA Bulletin. m.

Fraternal Field Managers Association *(1935)*

c/o SBOT, P.O. Box 100
Temple, TX 76503
Tel: (254)773-1575
Web Site: www.ffma.info
Members: 75 organizations
Annual Budget: $10-25,000
Secretary-Treasurer: Gene McBride

Historical Note
Members are sales managers of fraternal life insurance societies. Awards the designation FIC (Fraternal Insurance Counselor). A section of the National Fraternal Congress of America. Has no paid officers or full-time staff. Membership: $50-1,000/year, based on assets.

Fraternity Executives Association *(1930)*

3205 Players Lane
Memphis, TN 38125
Tel: (317)872-8000
Web Site: www.fea-inc.org
Members: 72 fraternities

Annual Budget: $100-250,000
Treasurer: Melanie Schild

Historical Note
Formerly (1970) College Fraternity Secretaries Association. Serves chief executive officers of fraternal organizations. Has no paid officers or full-time staff.

Publications:
News and Notes. m.

Free Speech Coalition *(1990)*
P.O. Box 10480
Canoga Park, CA 91309
Tel: (818)348-9373 *Fax:* (818)886-5914
Toll Free: (866)372 - 9373
E-Mail: publications@freespeechcoalition.com
Web Site: www.freespeechcoalition.com
Staff: 11
Executive Director: Michelle L. Freridge

Historical Note
FSC is the trade association representing the adult entertainment industry. FSC was founded in 1992 by the consolidation of predecessors trade associations, including Adult Video Association and Adult Film Association of America. FSC monitors legislative and regulatory actions affecting the industry, educates members on their legal responsibilities, and provides litigation support on key issues.

Publications:
PresSpeaker. q. adv.
X-Press. w.

Freestanding Insert Council of North America *(1997)*
4700 W. Lake Ave.
Glenview, IL 60025-1485
Tel: (847)375-4737 *Fax:* (877)734-9892
Toll Free: (888)374 - 0081
E-Mail: swalsh@connect2amc.com
Web Site: www.fsicouncil.org/
Annual Budget: $1-2,000,000
Executive Officer: Mark Engle

Freight Transportation Consultants Association *(1959)*
8683 W. Sahara Ave., Suite 240
Las Vegas, NV 89117
Tel: (703)967-2347 *Fax:* (702)967-2348
Toll Free: (800)691 - 7161
E-Mail: info@transportpros.org
Web Site: www.transportpros.org
Members: 37 companies
Staff: 1
Annual Budget: $10-25,000
Manager: Steve Fernlund

Historical Note
FTCA members are individuals and companies providing services in freight logistics and related disciplines. Goals of TFCA include maintaining a high level of professionalism in the Freight Tranportation Consultant profession. Membership: fees vary, $150-350/year.

Meetings/Conferences:
Annual Meetings: usually Spring

French-American Chamber of Commerce *(1896)*
122 E. 42nd St., Suite 2015
New York, NY 10168
Tel: (212)867-0123 *Fax:* (212)867-9050
E-Mail: info@faccnyc.org
Web Site: www.faccnyc.org
Members: 4100 members nationwide; 500 local
Staff: 38
Annual Budget: $2-5,000,000
Manager, Sponsorship/Advertising: Martin Bischoff
E-Mail: mbischoff@faccnyc.org
Event Planner: Veronique De Bock
E-Mail: vdebock@faccnyc.org
Director, Membership: Alexandre Frenette
E-Mail: afrenette@faccnyc.org

Historical Note
Formerly (1977) French Chamber of Commerce in the United States. Furthers trade and fosters economic, commercial and financial relations between the U.S. and France. Also provides a forum for French and American business and professional people with international interests. Operates eighteen chapters in the U.S. and an office in Paris. Membership: $200-$650/year.

Publications:
French-American News. q. adv.
Directory. a. adv.

Fresh Produce and Floral Council *(1965)*
16700 Valley View Ave.
Suite 130
La Mirada, CA 90638
Tel: (714)739-0177 *Fax:* (714)739-0226
E-Mail: fpfc@aol.com
Web Site: www.fpfc.org
Members: 725 individuals
Staff: 3
Annual Budget: $500-1,000,000
President: Linda Stine
Coordinator, Event: Pauleen Yoshikane

Historical Note
Formerly (1994) Fresh Produce Council. Incorporated in California, FPFC's primary purpose is promoting, through communication and education, fresh fruit, vegetable and floral products. It also acts as a trade organization providing an environment for better communication within the industry. Membership: $450/year.

Publications:
Fresh Digest. 6/year. adv.

Fresh Produce Association of the Americas *(1944)*
P.O. Box 848
Nogales, AZ 85628
Tel: (520)287-2707 *Fax:* (520)287-2948
E-Mail: info@fpaota.org
Web Site: www.fpaota.org
Members: 125 companies
Staff: 7
Annual Budget: $500-1,000,000
President: Lee Frankel
Coordinator, Events: Marlene Miles
Director, Communications: Allison Moore
Director, Public Affairs: Martha Rascon
Accounting/Member Relations: Conchita Singh

Historical Note
Formerly known as West Mexico Vegetable Distributors Association, FPAA represents U.S. firms engaged in the marketing of Mexican-grown fruits and vegetables to international markets. Membership: $1,500/year.

Publications:
Newsletter. m.
Newsletter. w.

Friction Materials Standards Institute *(1948)*
23 Woodland Road, Suite B-3
Madison, CT 06443
Tel: (203)245-8425 *Fax:* (203)245-8537
E-Mail: fmsiinc@aol.com
Web Site: www.fmsi.org
Members: 90 companies
Staff: 2
Annual Budget: $100-250,000
Executive Director: Patrick T. Healey

Historical Note
Formerly Brake Lining Manufacturers Association. Manufacturers of brake linings and clutch facings.

Meetings/Conferences:
Annual Meetings: June

Publications:
Automotive Data Book. a.
Brake Block Identification Catalog. a.

Frozen Potato Products Institute *(1958)*
2000 Corporate Ridge, Suite 1000
McLean, VA 22102
Tel: (703)821-0770 *Fax:* (703)821-1350
Members: 6 companies
Staff: 2
Annual Budget: $50-100,000
Executive Director: Michael Gill

Historical Note
A product division of American Frozen Food Instiitute, which provides administrative support.

Fuel Cell Power Association
P.O. Box 1408
Great Falls, VA 22066
Tel: (202)669-7575
E-Mail: fcpa@advocatesinc.com
Web Site: www.advocatesinc.com/fcpa
Members: 4 companies
Staff: 2
Executive Director: Jeffrey S. Abboud

Fulfillment Management Association *(1948)*
60 E. 42nd St., Suite 1166
New York, NY 10165
Tel: (303)604-7362 *Fax:* (303)604-7840
E-Mail: fma@neodata.com
Web Site: www.fmanational.org
Members: 425 individuals
Annual Budget: $50-100,000
Director, Membership Services: Deb Jackson

Historical Note
Established as the Subscription Fulfillment Managers Association, it assumed its present name in 1972. Members are direct mail fulfillment, marketing and circulation executives. Membership is concentrated in New York, Chicago, and Washington, DC. Has no paid staff. Membership: $140/year

Meetings/Conferences:
Monthly Meetings: New York, NY(The Princeton Club)/3rd Wednesday
2007 – New York, NY(The Princeton Club)/200

Publications:
Job Listings Bulletin. m.
Membership Directory. a. adv.

Fulfillment Services Association of America *(1986)*
3030 Malmo Dr.
Arlington Heights, IL 60005-4728
Tel: (847)364-1222 *Fax:* (847)364-1268
Members: 1450 individuals
Staff: 4
Annual Budget: $100-250,000
Executive Vice President: Frederick J. Herzog

Historical Note
Formerly (2002) Association of Publishing and Fulfillment Services.

Meetings/Conferences:
Annual Meetings: Held in Illinois

Funeral Consumers Alliance *(1963)*
33 Patchen Road
South Burlington, VT 05403
Tel: (802)865-8300 *Fax:* (802)865-2626
Toll Free: (800)765 - 0107
E-Mail: info@funerals.org
Web Site: www.funerals.org
Members: 120 societies
Staff: 3
Annual Budget: $50-100,000
Executive Director: Joshua Slocum

Historical Note
Formerly (1995) Continental Association of Funeral and Memorial Socs. and Funeral and Memorial Socs. of America (1999). Members are non-profit consumer groups dedicated to protecting a consumer's right to choose a meaningful, affordable funeral. Membership fee varies, based on group membership dues collected.

Meetings/Conferences:
Biennial Meetings: Even years/100

Publications:
FAMSA Directory of Member Societies. irreg.
Newsletter. q.

Fur Commission USA *(1944)*
PMB 506, 826 Orange Ave.
Coronado, CA 92118-2698
Tel: (619)575-0139 *Fax:* (619)575-5578
E-Mail: furfarmers@aol.com
Web Site: www.furcommission.com
Members: 650minkandfoxfarmingfamilies
Staff: 4
Annual Budget: $250-500,000
Executive Director: Teresa Platt

Historical Note
Formerly (1995) National Board of Fur Farm Organizations, Fur Farm Animal Welfare Coalition, Mink Farmers Research Foundation. Members are

U.S. mink and fox farmers; these members represent 420 mink farming families, on 330 farms in 28 states.

Meetings/Conferences:

Annual Meetings: Fall

Publications:

Fur Animal Research Newsletter. 4/year.
Fur Farm Letter. 6/year. adv.

Fur Conservation Institute of America *(1970)*

Historical Note

A subsidiary of the Fur Information Council of America.

Fur Industry Marketing Institute *(1962)*

Historical Note

A subsidiary of the Fur Information Council of America.

Fur Information Council of America *(1985)*

8424-A Santa Monica Blvd., Suite 860
West Hollywood, CA 90069
Tel: (323)848-7940 *Fax:* (323)848-2931
E-Mail: info@fur.org
Web Site: www.fur.org
Members: 300 individuals
Staff: 5
Annual Budget: $500-1,000,000
Executive Director and Membership Services Director: Keith Kaplan

Historical Note

Absorbed (1962) Fur Industry Marketing Institute, (1971) Fur Conservation Institute of America, and (1972) American Fur Industry. Formerly known as Fur Information and Fashion Council; assumed its current name in 1985. FICA is the largest organization representing the fur trade. Member retailers and manufacturers account for over 80% of U.S. fur sales.

Meetings/Conferences:

Annual Meetings: usually New York, NY/February

Publications:

Newsletter. m.
Consumer Buying Guide. a.
Fur Fashion Trends Media Kit. a.

Fur Merchants Employers Council

Historical Note

An informal committee representing management in labor negotiations; otherwise inactive. Nominal support provided by Fur Information Council of America.

Furniture Manufacturers Alliance

Historical Note

An alliance of the Business Products Industry Association.

Fusion Power Associates *(1979)*

Two Professional Dr., Suite 249
Gaithersburg, MD 20879
Tel: (301)258-0545 *Fax:* (301)975-9869
E-Mail: fpa@compuserve.com
Web Site: http://fusionpower.org
Members: 400 individuals
Staff: 3
Annual Budget: $250-500,000
President: Stephen O. Dean, Ph.D.
Vice President, Administration and Finance: Ruth Watkins

Historical Note

Incorporated in California in 1979, the association is concerned with the development of practical applications of fusion science and technology. Membership: $60/year (individual); $500/year (small business); $1,000/year (non-voting institution); $1,800/year (voting institution).

Publications:

Executive Newsletter. bi-m.
Fusion Power Report. bi-w.

Futon Association International *(1975)*

46639 Jones Ranch Road
Friant, CA 93626
Tel: (559)868-4187 *Fax:* (559)868-4185
Web Site: www.specialtysleepnet.com
Members: 85 manufacturers and distributors
Staff: 1
Annual Budget: $100-250,000
Executive Director: Tambra Jones
E-Mail: tambra@netptc.net

Historical Note

Formerly (1990) the Waterbed Assoc. Members are manufacturers, distributors, and retailers or specialty matresses and bedding. Membership: sliding scale based on sales.

Meetings/Conferences:

Annual Meetings: Spring

Publications:

Newsletter. q.
Membership Directory. a.

Future Business Leaders of America-Phi Beta Lambda *(1942)*

1912 Association Dr.
Reston, VA 20191-1591
Tel: (703)860-3334 *Fax:* (703)758-0749
Toll Free: (866)500 - 5610
E-Mail: general@fbla.org
Web Site: www.fbla-pbl.org
Members: 250000 individuals
Staff: 13
Annual Budget: $2-5,000,000
President and Chief Executive Officer: Jean M. Buckley
Director, Education: Barbara Small

Historical Note

Future Business Leaders of America-Phi Beta Lambda is a nonprofit 501(c)(3) educational association of student members preparing for careers in business and business-related fields. The association has four divisions: FBLA for high school students; FBLA-Middle Level for middle-level students; PBL for postsecondary students;and a Professional Division for Business people, educators, and parents who support the goals of the association. Membership: $4/year (middle level); $6/year (high school); $10/year (college); $23/year (professional).

Meetings/Conferences:

Annual Meetings: July
2007 – Chicago, IL/June 23-July 1/7000

Publications:

Middle Level Advisers Hotline. 3/year. adv.
PBL Business Leader. 3/year. adv.
Advisers' Hotline. 3/year. adv.
Professional Edge. 3/year. adv.
NLC Guide. a. adv.
NFLC Guide. a. adv.
Tomorrow's Business Leader. q. adv.
PBL Business Leader. 3/yr. adv.

Futures Industry Association *(1955)*

2001 Pennsylvania Ave. NW
Suite 600
Washington, DC 20006-1823
Tel: (202)466-5460 *Fax:* (202)296-3184
E-Mail: info@futuresindustry.org
Web Site: www.futuresindustry.org
Members: 190 firms
Staff: 18
Annual Budget: $2-5,000,000
President: John M. Damgard
E-Mail: jdamgard@futuresindustry.org
Senior Vice President, Communications: Mary Ann Burns
E-Mail: maburns@futuresindustry.org
Senior Vice President, Administration/Conference Director: Julia Greenway, CMP
E-Mail: jgreenway@futuresindustry.org
Chief Operating Officer: Jeff Morgan
E-Mail: jmorgan@futuresindustry.org
Director, Communications: Tracy Wahler
Executive Vice President and General Counsel: Barbara Wierzynski

Historical Note

Formerly (1975) Association of Commodity Exchange Firms. Founded to represent the brokerage community, FIA now acts as a principal spokesman for the futures and options industry in general.

Meetings/Conferences:

Semi-Annual Meetings: Spring and Fall

Publications:

Weekly Bulletin. w.
E-Marketbeat Newsletter. freq.
Futures Industry Magazine. bi-m. adv.
Futures Trading Volume Report. m.

Galiceno Horse Breeders Association *(1959)*

Box 219
Godley, TX 76044
Tel: (817)389-3547
Members: 600 individuals
Annual Budget: under $10,000
Secretary: Chris Giles

Historical Note

Members are owners and breeders of Galiceno horses. Membership: $20/year.

Publications:

Newsletter. q.

GAMA International *(1952)*

2901 Telestar Court, Suite 140
Falls Church, VA 22042-1205
Tel: (703)770-8184 *Fax:* (703)770-8182
Toll Free: (800)345 - 2687
E-Mail: gamamail@gama.naifa.org
Web Site: www.gamaweb.com
Members: 5000 individuals
Staff: 15
Annual Budget: $2-5,000,000
Chief Executive Officer: Jeff Hughes

Historical Note

Founded as General Agents and Managers Conference of NALU; became General Agents and Managers Association in 1991, and assumed its current name in 1997. Provides educational and training opportunities for those engaged in field management within the life insurance and financial services industry. Membership: $10-300/year(individual member, depending on member individual's company's partners in management growth status).

Meetings/Conferences:

Annual Meetings: March/2,500
2007 – Toronto, ON, Canada/March 18-21
2008 – San Francisco, CA/March 16-19
2009 – Atlanta, GA/March 22-25

Publications:

GAMA International Journal. bi-m. adv.

Game Manufacturers Association *(1975)*

280 N. High St., Suite 230
Columbus, OH 43215
Tel: (614)255-4500 *Fax:* (614)255-4499
E-Mail: custserv@gama.org
Web Site: www.gama.org
Members: 730 organizations
Staff: 9
Annual Budget: $1-2,000,000
Executive Director: Anthony Gallela
E-Mail: president@gama.org

Historical Note

Formerly (1986) GAMA. Members are companies that manufacture historical, fantasy, science fiction, and adult games which are played on tables, computers, boards, or plain paper for the adventure game, hobby, and game markets. Membership: $400/year (full member); $100/year (associate); $75/year (retailer); $300/year (distributor); $50/year (communicating); $90/year (club and convention).

Meetings/Conferences:

Semi-Annual Meetings: Spring and Summer

Publications:

Newsletter. q. adv.
GAMA Source Directory. a.
Retail Handbook. a. adv.
Manufacturers Handbook. a. adv.
Show Books. q. adv.

Gamma Iota Sigma *(1965)*

17 S. High St.
Suite 200
Columbus, OH 43215
Tel: (614)221-1900 *Fax:* (614)221-1989
E-Mail: grand@gammaiotasigma.org
Web Site: www.gammaiotasigma.org
Members: 1000 individuals
Staff: 1
Annual Budget: $50-100,000
Executive Director: Melinda Vance
E-Mail: grand@gammaiotasigma.org

Historical Note

Student professional insurance fraternity. Member of Professional Fraternity Association.

Meetings/Conferences:
Annual Meetings: Spring
Publications:
The Sextant. semi-a.

Garden Writers Association *(1948)*
10210 Leatherleaf Court
Manassas, VA 20111-4245
Tel: (703)257-1032 *Fax:* (703)257-0213
E-Mail: info@gardenwriters.org
Web Site: www.gwaa.org
Members: 1700 individuals
Staff: 5
Annual Budget: $250-500,000
Executive Director: Robert C. LaGasse, CAE
Historical Note
Membership: $85/year, (individual); $275/year, (organization).
Meetings/Conferences:
Annual Meetings: Fall
Publications:
Quill & Trowel Newsletter. bi-m. adv.

Gas Appliance Manufacturers Association *(1935)*
2107 Wilson Blvd., Suite 600
Arlington, VA 22201
Tel: (703)525-7060 *Fax:* (703)525-6790
E-Mail: information@gamanet.org
Web Site: www.gamanet.org
Members: 210 companies
Staff: 25
Annual Budget: $5-10,000,000
Vice President and Chief of Staff: Thomas Warren Parker
President: Jack W. Klimp
Vice President, Secretary and General Counsel: Joseph M. Mattingly
Historical Note
Founded as the Association of Gas Appliance and Equipment Manufacturers; assumed its present name in 1946. Absorbed the Institute of Appliance Manufacturers (founded in 1872) in 1967. GAMA represents manufacturers of appliances, components and products used in connection with space heating, water heating and commercial food service. In addition to gas-fired appliances, GAMA's scope includes certain oil-fired and electrical appliances.
Meetings/Conferences:
Annual Meetings: Spring/500
2007 – St. Petersburg, FL(Renaissance Vinoy Resort)/May 5-8
2008 – Colorado Springs, CO(The Broadmoor)/May 17-20
2009 – Santa Ana Pueblo, NM(Hyatt Regency Tamaya Resort)
Publications:
GAMA Reports. m.
Statistical Highlights. m.
GAMAzine. bi-a. adv.

Gas Machinery Research Council *(1952)*
3030 LBJ Fwy., Suite 1300, LB-60
Dallas, TX 75234
Tel: (972)620-4024 *Fax:* (972)620-1613
Web Site: www.gmrc.org
Members: 80 companies
Staff: 1
Annual Budget: $1-2,000,000
Vice President: Marsha Short
Historical Note
A subsidiary of Southern Gas Association. Founded as Pipeline and Compressor Research Council; assumed its current name in 2001. Members are companies in the natural gas, oil and petrochemical industries interested in mechanical and fluid systems design. Membership: Fees vary.
Meetings/Conferences:
Annual Meetings: Fall
2007 – Dallas, TX(Hyatt Reunion)/Oct. 1-3/700
2008 – Albuquerque, NM(Hyatt/ABQ Convention Center)/Oct. 6-8
Publications:
Gas Machinery Journal. a. adv.
GMC Today.

Gas Processors Association *(1921)*
6526 E. 60th St.
Tulsa, OK 74145-9202
Tel: (918)493-3872 *Fax:* (918)493-3875
E-Mail: gpa@gasprocessors.com
Web Site: www.gasprocessors.com
Members: 100 companies
Staff: 7
Annual Budget: $500-1,000,000
Executive Director: Mark Sutton
E-Mail: msutton@swbell.net
Director, Technical Services: Ronald G. Bruner
Director, Industry Affairs: Johnny Dreyer
Historical Note
Established in 1921 as Association of Natural Gasoline Manufacturers and became Natural Gasoline Association of America in 1922. The name was changed to Natural Gas Processors Association in 1961 and Gas Processors Association in 1974. Membership consists of firms handling natural gasoline and other hydrocarbon products at gas-processing plants.
Meetings/Conferences:
Annual Meetings: March/1,800
2007 – San Antonio, TX/March 12-14
2008 – Dallas, TX/March 3-5
2009 – San Antonio, TX/March 9-11
Publications:
Proceedings. a.

Gas Processors Suppliers Association *(1927)*
6526 E. 60th St.
Tulsa, OK 74145-9202
Tel: (918)493-3872 *Fax:* (918)493-3875
E-Mail: gpsa@gasprocessors.com
Web Site: http://gpsa.gasprocessors.com
Members: 325 companies
Staff: 6
Annual Budget: $100-250,000
Secretary: Mark Sutton
E-Mail: msutton@gasprocessors.com
Historical Note
Formerly (1974) Natural Gas Processors Suppliers Association. GPSA is comprised of companies that provide supplies, equipment, or services to the gas processing industry. Membership: $300/year.
Meetings/Conferences:
Annual Meetings: with Gas Processors Ass'n/1,800
Publications:
Engineering Data Book.

Gas Technology Institute *(1941)*
1700 S. Mount Prospect Road
Des Plaines, IL 60018-1804
Tel: (847)768-0500 *Fax:* (847)768-0501
E-Mail: publicrelations@gastechnology.org
Web Site: www.gastechnology.org
Members: 325 companies and organizations
Staff: 340
Annual Budget: Over $100,000,000
President and Chief Executive Officer: David Carroll
Executive Director, Educational Group: Michael Dugan
Vice President, Washington Operations: Melanie Kenderdine
Director, Information Technology: Thomas Sheridan
Historical Note
Founded as Gas Research Institute; combined with Institute of Gas Technology and assumed its current name in 2000. Members are companies involved in the production, transmission and distribution of natural gas. Has an annual budget of approximately $130 million.
Publications:
Annual Report. a.
GTI Journal. semi-a.
Proceedings of the Internat'l Gas Research Conference. trien.
FERC R&C Plan and Program. a.

Gas Turbine Association *(1995)*
P.O. Box 1408
Great Falls, VA 22066
Tel: (202)669-7575 *Fax:* (703)757-8274
Web Site: www.gasturbine.org
Members: 15 companies
Staff: 2
Annual Budget: $100-250,000
Executive Director: Jeffrey S. Abboud
Historical Note
GTA's mission is to represent the gas turbine industry before public, governmental and quasi-governmental bodies; to collect and publish industry, economic and other statistical data; to encourage the use of gas turbines in specific markets through promotional and/or market development programs; to help member companies solve common environmental, health and safety problems; to develop recommended industry standards; and to increase public knowledge and understanding of gas turbines and the industry through educational and information programs. Membership: $1,000-22,500/year (organization/company).

Gases and Welding Distributors Association *(1947)*
100 N. 20th St., Fourth Floor
Philadelphia, PA 19103-1443
Tel: (215)564-3484 *Fax:* (215)564-2175
E-Mail: gawda@gawda.org
Web Site: www.gawda.org
Members: 1000 companies
Staff: 3
Annual Budget: $2-5,000,000
Executive Director: Kent Van Amborg
Historical Note
Founded as National Welding Supply Association; assumed its current name in 2002. GAWDA promotes the safe operation and economic vitality of distributors of industrial gases and related welding equipment and supplies.
Meetings/Conferences:
Annual Meetings: Fall
Publications:
Welding & Gases Today. q. adv.
GAWDA Connection. bi-w. adv.
Safety Organizer. m.

Gasification Technologies Council *(1995)*
1110 N. Glebe Road, Suite 610
Arlington, VA 22201
Tel: (703)276-0110 *Fax:* (703)276-0141
E-Mail: jchildress@gasification.org
Web Site: www.gasification.org
Members: 40 companies
Executive Director: James M. Childress
Historical Note
GTC members are companies involved in the gasification of coal, coke and heavy oils. Membership: $15,000/year (regular); $10,000/year (associate); $5,000/year (affililate).
Meetings/Conferences:
Annual: Fall

Gasket Fabricators Association *(1979)*
994 Old Eagle School Road, Suite 1019
Wayne, PA 19087-1866
Tel: (610)971-4850 *Fax:* (610)971-4859
E-Mail: info@gasketfab.com
Web Site: www.gasketfab.com
Members: 113 companies
Staff: 5
Annual Budget: $100-250,000
Executive Director: Robert H. Ecker
Historical Note
National trade association of gasket fabricators whose products include metallic and non-metallic sealing devices and allied products. Membership: $950/year.
Meetings/Conferences:
Semi-Annual Meetings: Spring and Fall
Publications:
Directory.
Newsletter.
Technical Handbook.

Gasoline and Automotive Service Dealers Association *(1931)*
372 Doughty Blvd., Suite Four
Inwood, NY 11096-1366
Tel: (516)371-6201 *Fax:* (516)371-1579
Members: 1000 companies, 120 associates
Staff: 7
Annual Budget: $250-500,000
Executive Director: Ralph Bombardiere

Historical Note

Formerly (1977) Gasoline Merchants. Members are owners and/or operators of service stations or auto repair facilities. GASDA seeks to strengthen professionalism in the industry. Membership: $175/year (individual); $420/year (company).

Publications:

Newsletter. irreg.
Directory and Buyers Guide. a.
Bulletin. m.

Gastroenterology Research Group *(1955)*

4930 Del Ray Ave.
Bethesda, MD 20814-2513
Tel: (301)272-0032 *Fax:* (301)272-1774
E-Mail: grg@gastro.org
Web Site: www.gastroresearch.org
Members: 1200 individuals
Annual Budget: $10-25,000
President: John Del Valle, M.D.

Historical Note

Affiliated with American Gastroenterological Association and American Association for the Study of Liver Disease. Membership: $40/year (full membership); $10/year (trainee membership).

Meetings/Conferences:

Semi-Annual Meetings: Spring and Fall

Publications:

GRG Newsletter. semi-a.

Gelbray International *(1981)*

P.O. Box 2177
Ardmore, OK 73402
Tel: (580)223-5771 *Fax:* (580)226-5773
Members: 150 ranches
Staff: 1
Annual Budget: under $10,000
Secretary: Don M. Yeager

Historical Note

Gelbray International was established for the registration and promotion of Gelbray cattle. Membership: $25/year (individual).

Publications:

American Beef Cattleman. a. adv.
Gelbray Newsletter. irreg. adv.

Gemological Institute of America *(1931)*

5345 Armada Dr.
Carlsbad, CA 92008
Tel: (760)603-4000 *Fax:* (760)603-4003
Toll Free: (800)421 - 7250
Web Site: www.gia.edu
Staff: 1100
Annual Budget: $10-25,000,000
Acting President: Donna M. Baker
E-Mail: president@gia.edu
Vice President, Education: Brook Ellis
Vice President, Marketing and Public Relations: Kathryn Kimmel

Historical Note

GIA is a notprofit organization that sets standards and conducts continuing education in support of all facets of the gemstone industry.

Meetings/Conferences:

Annual Meetings: Tucson, AZ/February/250

Publications:

Gems & Gemology. q. adv.
The Loupe. q. adv.

General Aviation Manufacturers Association *(1970)*

1400 K St. NW, Suite 801
Washington, DC 20005
Tel: (202)393-1500 *Fax:* (202)842-4063
Web Site: www.gama.aero
Members: 51 companies
Staff: 13
Annual Budget: $2-5,000,000
President and Chief Executive Officer: Peter J. Bunce
Director, Communications: Katie Pribyl
Vice President, Government Affairs: Brian Riley
Senior Vice President, Operations: Ron Swanda

Historical Note

An outgrowth of the former Utility Aircraft Council of the Aerospace Industries Association. Members of GAMA are manufacturers of general aviation aircraft equipment and components. Works on airport/airway technical matters, product liability, and safety issues to develop a better climate for growth of general aviation. Supports the General Aviation Political Action Committee (GAMAPAC).

Publications:

GAMA Statistical Databook. a.
GAMA Airplane Shipment Reports. q.

General Federation of Women's Clubs *(1890)*

1734 N St., N.W.
Washington, DC 20036-2990
Tel: (202)347-3168 *Fax:* (202)835-0246
E-Mail: gfwc@gfwc.org
Web Site: www.gfwc.org
Members: 150000 individuals
Staff: 20
Annual Budget: $1-2,000,000
Executive Director: Natasha Kalteis
Director, Public Policy: Katie Kikta
Director, Public Relations: Mima Kriem-Miller
Director, Meetings and Conventions: Marisa Krisfalusi
Director, Finance: Beverly Manlove
Director, Programs: Pat Nolan
President: Jacquelyn Pierce

Historical Note

GFWC is a non-denominational, non-partisan, international service organization of volunteer women's clubs dedicated to community service. Membership: $10/year.

Meetings/Conferences:

Annual Meetings: Summer/1,000
2007 – Philadelphia, PA(Marriott)/

Publications:

GFWC Clubwoman Magazine. q. adv.

General Merchandise Distributors Council *(1970)*

1275 Lake Plaza Dr.
Colorado Springs, CO 80906-3583
Tel: (719)576-4260 *Fax:* (719)576-2661
E-Mail: info@gmdc.org
Web Site: www.gmdc.org
Members: 870 companies
Staff: 18
Annual Budget: $5-10,000,000
President and Chief Executive Officer: David T. McConnell
E-Mail: dmcconnell@gmdc.org
Vice President, Membership Services: Jerry G. Barnes
E-Mail: jbarnes@gmdc.org
Senior Director, Finance and Administration: Ann McConnell
E-Mail: amcconnell@gmdc.org
Senior Vice President, Marketing and Development/Chief Operating Officer: Dan Nelson
E-Mail: dnelson@gmdc.org
Vice President, Information Technology: Michael Winterbottom
E-Mail: mwinterbottom@gmdc.org

Historical Note

Founded as a national trade association for the general merchandise and health and beauty care operations of wholesale grocers, supermarket retailers, dry cleaners, merchandisers, wholesale druggists and suppliers of these products to the retail trade. Membership: $2,000/year (wholesaler); $2,500/year (supplier).

Meetings/Conferences:

2007 – Scottsdale, AZ(J.W. Marriott Desert Ridge Resort and Spa)/June 1-5
2007 – Palm Desert, CA(J.W. Marriott Desert Springs Resort and Spa)/Sept. 7-10

Publications:

Off the Shelf. q.
Membership Directory. a.

Generic Pharmaceutical Association *(1981)*

2300 Clarendon Blvd., Suite 400
Arlington, VA 22201
Tel: (703)647-2480 *Fax:* (703)647-2481
E-Mail: info@gphaonline.org
Web Site: www.gphaonline.org
Members: 40 individuals
Staff: 9
Annual Budget: $2-5,000,000
President and Chief Executive Officer: Kathleen D. Jaeger
Vice President, Public Affairs and Development: Christine Simmon

Historical Note

Founded as Generic Pharmaceutical Industry Association; absorbed National Pharmaceutical Alliance and National Association of Pharmaceutical Manufacturers and assumed its current name in 2000. GPHA members are manufacturers and distributors of generic medicines, as well as the providers of technical services and goods to these firms. Membership: dues based on sales volume.

Genetics Society of America *(1931)*

9650 Rockville Pike
Bethesda, MD 20814-3998
Tel: (301)634-7300 *Fax:* (301)634-7079
Web Site: www.genetics-gsa.org
Members: 4000 individuals
Staff: 12
Annual Budget: $1-2,000,000
Executive Director: Elaine Strass

Historical Note

Organized in 1931 in New Orleans as an outgrowth of the Genetics Section of the American Society of Zoologists and the Botanical Society of America. Incorporated in Maryland in 1984. Membership: $120/year (full member), $50/year (student).

Publications:

Genetics. m.
Membership Directory. bien.
GSA Newsletter. 3/yr.

Geochemical Society *(1955)*

Dept. of Earth and Planetary Sciences
Washington Univ., One Brookings Dr.
St. Louis, MO 63130-4899
Tel: (314)935-4131 *Fax:* (314)935-4121
E-Mail: office@gs.wastl.edu
Web Site: http://gs.wustl.edu
Members: 2800 individuals
Staff: 1
Annual Budget: $100-250,000
Business Manager: Seth Davis

Historical Note

Founded November 7, 1955 and incorporated in the District of Columbia in 1956. Encourages the application of chemistry to the solution of geological and cosmological problems.

Meetings/Conferences:

Annual Meetings: Summer or Fall/1,600

Publications:

G3 - Geochemistry, Geophysics, Geosystems.
Reviews in Mineralogy & Geochemistry. q.
Geochemical News. q. adv.
Geochimica et Cosmochimica Acta. semi-m.
Elements magazine. bi-m. adv.

Geological Society of America *(1888)*

3300 Penrose Pl.
Box 9140
Boulder, CO 80301
Tel: (303)357-1000 *Fax:* (303)357-1074
Toll Free: (800)472 - 1988
E-Mail: mcummiskey@geosociety.org
Web Site: www.geosociety.org
Members: 18000 individuals
Staff: 50
Annual Budget: $5-10,000,000
Executive Director: John W. Hess
E-Mail: jhess@geosociety.org
Senior Director, IT: Todd Berggren
E-Mail: tberggren@geosociety.org
Director, Communications and Marketing: Ann Cairns
Director, Meetings: Melissa Cummiskey
Controller: Kay Dragon
E-Mail: kdragon@geosociety.org
Director, Membership: Pat Kilmer
Director, Education and Outreach: Gary Lewis
E-Mail: glewis@geosociety.org
Director, Strategic Initiatives: Deborah Nelson
Director, Publications: Jon Olsen
E-Mail: jolsen@geosociety.org

Historical Note

Founded in 1888 and incorporated in New York in 1929. GSA includes topical divisions, specializing in Archaeological Geology, Coal Geology, Engineering

Geology, Geobiology/Geomicrobiology, Geology and Society, Geophysics, Geoscience Education, History of Geology, Hydrogeology, International Division, Limneology, Planetary Geology, Quaternary Geology and Geomorphology, Sedimentary Geology, and Structural Geology and Tectonics. GSA has six regional sections, each of which holds its own annual meeting in the spring. Also has 35 member, associated and allied societies. GSA is a member society of the American Geological Institute. Membership: $65/year (members/fellows).

Meetings/Conferences:
Annual Meetings: Fall
2007 - Denver, CO/Oct. 28-31
2008 - Chicago, IL/Oct. 26-30
2009 - Portland, OR/Oct. 18-21

Publications:
Geological Society of America Bulletin. bi-m.
Environmental & Engineering Geoscience. q.
GSA Today. m. adv.
Geology. m. adv.

Geoscience and Remote Sensing Society *(1962)*
c/o Office of Naval Research
800 N. Quincy St.
Arlington, VA 22217
Tel: (703)696-4123 *Fax:* (703)696-2710
E-Mail: jay.pearlman@boeing.com
Web Site: www.grss-ieee.org/
Members: 2100 individuals
Executive Vice President: Dr. Charles A. Luther

Historical Note
A technical society of the Institute of Electrical and Electronics Engineeers (IEEE). Membership in the Society, open only to IEEE members, includes a subscription to a technical periodical in the field published by IEEE. Has no paid officers or full-time staff.

Meetings/Conferences:
2007 - Barcelona, Spain

Publications:
GRSS Newsletter.
Transactions on Geoscience and Remote Sensing Journal. bi-m.

Geoscience Information Society *(1965)*
University of Cincinnati Geology, Mathematics, and Physics Library
ML 0153, 240 Braunstein Hall
Cincinnati, OH 45221
Tel: (513)556-1582 *Fax:* (513)556-1930
E-Mail: goodenam@mail.uc.edu
Web Site: www.geoinfo.org
Members: 200 individuals
Annual Budget: $10-25,000
Secretary: Angela Gooden

Historical Note
Founded in Kansas City, GIS was incorporated in the District of Columbia in 1966. Affiliated with the Geological Society of America and the American Geological Institute. GIS membership includes national and international representation from colleges and universities, business and industry, publishing, geological surveys, geological societies and other aspects of the field. Membership: $40/year (individual); $75/year (institution); $15/year (student or retired); $100/year (sustaining).

Meetings/Conferences:
Annual Meetings: Fall

Publications:
GIS Newsletter. bi-m.
Proceedings. a.
Membership Directory. a.

Geospatial Information Technology Association *(1982)*
14456 E. Evans Ave.
Aurora, CO 80014
Tel: (303)337-0513 *Fax:* (303)337-1001
E-Mail: info@gita.org
Web Site: www.gita.org
Members: 2200 individuals
Staff: 11
Annual Budget: $2-5,000,000
Executive Director: Robert Samborski
E-Mail: bsamborski@gita.org
Director, Communications and Membership: Elizabeth Roberts
E-Mail: eroberts@gita.org
Director, Operations: Henry Rosales
E-Mail: hrosales@gita.org

Historical Note
GITA is a non-profit, educational association which fosters information exchange and educational opportunities and scientific research and development in the field of geospatial information technology. Membership: $95/year (individual).

Meetings/Conferences:
Annual Meetings: Spring/3,200
2007 - San Antonio, TX(Convention Center)/March 4-7/3000

Publications:
Geospatial Technology Report. a.
GIS for Oil & Gas Conference Proceedings. a.
GITA Networks. bi-m. adv.
Conference Proceedings. a.

Geothermal Energy Association *(1987)*
209 Pennsylvania Ave. SE
Washington, DC 20003
Tel: (202)454-5261 *Fax:* (202)454-5265
E-Mail: research@geo-energy.org
Web Site: www.geo-energy.org/
Members: 50 corporations
Staff: 4
Annual Budget: $250-500,000
Executive Director: Karl Gawell
Manager, Business and Special Projects: Mihaela-Daniela Stratulat

Historical Note
Founded as National Geothermal Association; assumed its current name in 1994. Shares administrative offices with Geothermal Resources Council. GEA is composed of U.S. companies who support the expanded use of geothermal energy and are developing geothermal resources worldwide for electrical power generation and direct heat uses. Membership: $500/year (individual); $1000/year corporate); $5000/year (board); $75/year (associate).

Meetings/Conferences:
Annual Meetings: October

Publications:
GEA Newsletter. m.
First Alert Newsletter. m.

Geothermal Resources Council *(1972)*
P.O. Box 1350
Davis, CA 95617-1350
Tel: (530)758-2360 *Fax:* (530)758-2839
E-Mail: grc@geothermal.org
Web Site: www.geothermal.org
Members: 800 individuals
Staff: 3
Annual Budget: $500-1,000,000
Executive Director: Ted J. Clutter

Historical Note
Members are individuals interested in the development and production of geothermal energy. Street address is 2001 Second St., Davis, CA. Membership: $100/year (individual); $480/year (basic company/institution).

Meetings/Conferences:
Annual Meetings: Summer

Publications:
GRC Bulletin. 6/year. adv.
Annual Meeting Transactions. a.
Special Reports. irreg.
Membership Directory. a. adv.

German American Business Association *(1990)*
727 Industrial Road, Suite 107
San Carlos, CA 94070
Tel: (415)276-2375
E-Mail: info@gaba-network.org
Web Site: www.gaba-network.org/
Members: 30 individuals
Staff: 4
Annual Budget: $100-250,000
President: Caroline Raynaud
Vice President, Public and Media Relations: Thomas Neubert

Historical Note
GABA is a business league promoting business between local German-American businesses. Membership: $50/year (individual).

Meetings/Conferences:
Annual Meetings: Bi-monthly meetings, held second Tuesday of the month

Publications:
GABA eNews. m.

German American Chamber of Commerce *(1947)*
75 Broad St.
21st Floor
New York, NY 10004
Tel: (212)974-8830 *Fax:* (212)974-8867
E-Mail: info@gaccny.com
Web Site: www.gaccny.com
Members: 2000 corporations
Staff: 32
Annual Budget: $2-5,000,000
President and Chief Executive Officer: Dr. Ben W. Bunse
Director, Marketing and Business Development: Ingo Bentz
Director, Communications: Nicola Michels
Director, Membership Services: Inge Orth

Historical Note
Established as a guide and liaison for U.S. and German businesses who want to practice in both the United States and Germany. Now acts as a service organization for members and non-members. Membership: $500/year.

Meetings/Conferences:
Semi-Annual Meetings: March, New York, NY/June, Bonn, Germany

Publications:
United States-German Economic Yearbook. a. adv.
American Subsidiaries of German Firms. a. adv.
Membership Directory. a. adv.
German American Trade. a. adv.

Gerontological Society of America *(1945)*
1030 15th St. NW, Suite 250
Washington, DC 20005-1503
Tel: (202)842-1275 *Fax:* (202)842-1150
E-Mail: geron@geron.org
Web Site: www.geron.org
Members: 5000 individuals
Staff: 23
Annual Budget: $2-5,000,000
Executive Director: Carol A. Schutz

Historical Note
An outgrowth of the Club for Research in Aging, organized in 1939. Incorporated in New York in 1945 to promote scientific study of aging; reincorporated in Washington, D.C. in 1980. A member of the American Association for the Advancement of Science, and the International Association of Gerontology Leadership Council of Aging Organizations. Members are researchers, educators and professionals in the field of aging. Membership: $135/year; $65/year (students).

Meetings/Conferences:
Annual Meetings: Fall/3,500
2007 - San Francisco, CA(San Francisco Hilton)/Nov. 16-20/3500

Publications:
Public Policy and Aging Report. q.
Gerontology News. m. adv.
Journal of Gerontology: Series A: Biological & Medical Sciences. m. adv.
Journal of Gerontology: Series B: Psychological & Social Sciences. bi. adv.
The Gerontologist. bi-m. adv.

Gift and Collectibles Guild *(1977)*
77 W. Washington St., Suite 1716
Chicago, IL 60602
Tel: (312)236-3930 *Fax:* (312)236-3927
E-Mail: giftguild@sbcglobal.net
Web Site: www.collectiblesguild.org
Members: 100 companies
Staff: 1
Annual Budget: $25-50,000
Managing Director: Karen Feil

Historical Note
Formerly (1988) the Collector Platemakers Guild and then Collectibles and Giftmakers Guild; became Collectibles and Platemakers Guild in 2001, and assumed its current name in 2003. GCG is a trade association of makers or importers of commemorative or limited edition plates who wish to encourage plate collecting as a hobby.

Meetings/Conferences:
Annual Meetings: July

Publications:
Member News. 6/year. adv.

Gift Associates Interchange Network *(1974)*
1100 Main St.
Buffalo, NY 14209
Tel: (716)887-9508 *Fax:* (716)887-9599
E-Mail: info@gaingroup.com
Web Site: www.gaingroup.com
Members: 254 companies
Staff: 4
Director, Membership Services: Donna Mostellar

Historical Note
Formerly (1995) Giftware Associates Interchange. Members are manufacturers and importers of giftware and china. Membership: $620-650/year.

Meetings/Conferences:
Semi-Annual Meetings: Spring and Fall

Publications:
Directory. irreg.

Gift Association of America *(1952)*
115 Rolling Hills Road
Johnstown, PA 15905
Tel: (814)288-1460 *Fax:* (814)288-1483
E-Mail: info@giftassn.com
Web Site: www.giftassn.com
Members: 900 businesses
Staff: 3
Annual Budget: $50-100,000
President and Chairman: Michael L. Russo

Historical Note
Offers programs and continuing education to professionals in the gift industry. Membership: $65/year (retail), $115/year (wholesale).

Meetings/Conferences:
Semi-annual Meetings:

Publications:
GAA Newsletter. q. adv.
Membership Directory. bien. adv.

Girls Incorporated *(1945)*
120 Wall St., Third Floor
New York, NY 10005-3904
Tel: (212)509-2000 *Fax:* (212)509-8708
Toll Free: (800)374 - 4475
E-Mail: communications@girls-inc.org
Web Site: www.girlsinc.org
Members: 840000 individuals
Staff: 65
Annual Budget: $5-10,000,000
President and Chief Executive Officer: Joyce M. Roche
Media Contact: Taiia Smart Young

Meetings/Conferences:
Annual Meetings: Holds fundraisers every year.

Publications:
Girls Ink. q.

Giving Institute *(1935)*
4700 W. Lake Ave.
Glenview, IL 60025
Tel: (847)375-4709 *Fax:* (866)263-2492
Toll Free: (800)462 - 2372
E-Mail: info@aafrc.org
Web Site: www.aafrc.org
Members: 38 companies
Annual Budget: $500-1,000,000
Executive Director: James M. Weir

Historical Note
Members are consulting firms specializing in services to nonprofit organizations. Founded to promote ethical practice and professional standards in the fund-raising consultant field. Has no full-time employees. Formerly the American Association of Fundraising Counsel.

Giving USA Foundation
4700 W. Lake Ave
Glenview, IL 60025-1485
Tel: (847)375-4709 *Fax:* (866)607-0913
Toll Free: (800)462 - 2372
E-Mail: info@givinginstitute.org
Web Site: www.aafrc.org/gusa/

Glass Art Society *(1971)*
3131 Western Ave., Suite 414
Seattle, WA 98121
Tel: (206)382-1305 *Fax:* (206)382-2630
E-Mail: info@glassart.org
Web Site: www.glassart.org
Members: 3800 individuals
Staff: 5
Annual Budget: $500-1,000,000
Executive Director: Pamela Koss

Historical Note
The Glass Art Society is a professional organization whose purpose is to encourage excellence in, to advance education in, and to promote the appreciation and development of glass arts, and to support the worldwide community of artists who work with glass. Membership: $50/year minimum (individual); $25/year (student); $250/year (organization/company).

Meetings/Conferences:
Annual Meetings: Summer

Publications:
Newsletter. bi-m. adv.
Membership Roster. a.
Glass Art Society Journal. a. adv.
Conference Program. a. adv.

Glass Association of North America *(1994)*
2945 S.W. Wanamaker Dr., Suite A
Topeka, KS 66614-5321
Tel: (785)271-0208 *Fax:* (785)271-0166
Web Site: www.glasswebsite.com
Members: 250 companies
Staff: 8
Annual Budget: $500-1,000,000
Executive Vice President: Stanley L. Smith

Historical Note
Formed by the merger of the Flat Glass Marketing Association (1949), the Glass Tempering Association (1958), and the Laminators Safety Glass Association (1971) in 1994. Absorbed the North American Association of Mirror Manufacturers in 1999. Membership: $600-$7,000/year (corporate).

Meetings/Conferences:
Semi-Annual Meetings: March and Fall

Publications:
Glass Reflections. m.
Safety Bulletins. m.

Glass Packaging Institute *(1945)*
515 King St., Suite 420
Alexandria, VA 22314
Tel: (703)684-6359 *Fax:* (703)684-6048
E-Mail: info@gpi.org
Web Site: www.gpi.org
Members: 45 companies and associate members
Staff: 7
Annual Budget: $1-2,000,000
President: Joseph J. Cattaneo
Director, Public Affairs: Andrew Bopp

Historical Note
Formerly (1976) Glass Container Manufacturers Institute, Inc.

Glass, Molders, Pottery, Plastics and Allied Workers International Union *(1988)*
608 E. Baltimore Pike
P.O. Box 607
Media, PA 19063-0607
Tel: (610)565-5051 *Fax:* (610)565-0983
E-Mail: gmpiu@gmpiu.org
Web Site: www.gmpiu.org
Members: 51000 individuals
Staff: 75
Annual Budget: $5-10,000,000
International President: John P. Ryan
Director, Communications: Richard Kline

Historical Note
Product of a merger between the Glass, Pottery, Plastics and Allied Workers and the International Molders and Allied Workers Union in 1988. Supports the Glass, Molders, Pottery, Plastics and Allied Workers Political Education League. Membership: $14/month (individual).

Meetings/Conferences:
Quadrennial Convention: (2004)
2008 – Las Vegas, NV(Rio Hotel and Casino)/800

Publications:
GMP Horizons. m.

Glazing Industry Code Committee *(1983)*
2945 S.W. Wanamaker Dr., Suite A
Topeka, KS 66614-5321
Tel: (785)271-0208 *Fax:* (785)271-0166
E-Mail: gicc@galzingcodes.org
Web Site: www.glazingcodes.org
Members: 17 companies
Staff: 8
Administrator: Stanley L. Smith

Historical Note
GICC represents the glass and glazing industry before the model building codes. Members are industry companies and associations.

Meetings/Conferences:
Triennial Meetings:

Global Association of Risk Professionals *(2000)*
100 Pavonia Ave., Suite 405
Jersey City, NJ 07310
Tel: (201)222-0054 *Fax:* (201)222-5022
E-Mail: rich.apostolik@garp.com
Web Site: www.garp.com
Members: 49000 individuals
Staff: 16
President and Chief Executive Officer: Richard Apostolik
Associate Director, Marketing and Relationship Management: Lara Daghlian

Historical Note
GARP's international membership includes a variety of professionals from the finance industry who share a common interest in financial risk management practice and research.

Publications:
Newsletter (online). m.

Global Health Council *(1971)*
1701 K St. NW, Suite 600
Washington, DC 20006-1503
Tel: (202)833-5900 *Fax:* (202)833-0075
E-Mail: ghc@globalhealth.org
Web Site: www.globalhealth.org
Members: 3023 individuals
Staff: 42
Annual Budget: $5-10,000,000
President and Chief Executive Officer: Nils Daulaire
Vice President, Membership Resources: Kathryn Guare

Historical Note
Formerly National Council for International Health (1998). GHC seeks to promote and improve people's health worldwide through advocacy and leadership in identifying and sharing best practices to serve the needs of those who have yet adequately benefited from the globalized world economy. Membership: $120/year (individual, regular); $20/year (supporting e-member); $60/year (student); $250-25,000/year (organization).

Meetings/Conferences:
Annual Meetings: June

Publications:
Global Healthlink. bi-m. adv.
Global Health Directory. a.
Global AIDSLink newsletter. bi-m. adv.

Global Offset and Countertrade Association *(1986)*
818 Connecticut Ave. NW, 12th Floor
Washington, DC 20006
Tel: (202)887-9011 *Fax:* (202)872-8324
E-Mail: goca@globaloffset.org
Web Site: www.globaloffset.org
Members: 500 individuals
Staff: 1
Annual Budget: $50-100,000

Deputy Director: Katherine Houston

Historical Note

Formed (1986) as American Countertrade Association; assumed current name in 2005.

Meetings/Conferences:

Semi-Annual Meetings: Spring and Fall

Glove Shippers Association *(1989)*
P.O. Box 1908
San Juan Capistrano, CA 92693
Tel: (949)425-0888 *Fax:* (949)425-9232
Toll Free: (877)877 - 8780
Members: 1100 companies
Staff: 5
Annual Budget: $100-250,000
Managing Director: James A. Murphy

Historical Note

Absorbed the Latex Advisors Association in 1998. GSA members are manufacturers and distributors of gloves and related medical products. Membership: $500-1500/year.

Meetings/Conferences:

Annual Meetings: Spring

Publications:

Medical and Latex Newsletter.
Latex Advisor. q. adv.

Glutamate Association (United States) *(1977)*
P.O. Box 14266
Washington, DC 20044-4266
Tel: (202)783-6135 *Fax:* (202)637-5910
Web Site: www.msgfacts.com
Members: 9 companies
Staff: 4
Executive Director: Martin J. Hahn

Historical Note

Provides information on glutamic acid and its salts, including monosodium glutamate (MSG). Serves as a regulatory and scientific liaison for industry concerning glutamates.

Meetings/Conferences:

Annual Meetings: November, in Teaneck, NJ

Glycerine and Oleochemicals Association *(1983)*

Historical Note

A division of the Soap and Detergent Association.

Gold Institute *(1976)*

Historical Note

Merged with Nat'l Mining Ass'n in 2003.

Golf Coaches Association of America *(1958)*
1225 W. Main St., Suite 110
Norman, OK 73069
Tel: (405)329-4222 *Fax:* (405)573-7888
Toll Free: (866)422 - 2669
E-Mail: gcaa@collegiategolf.org
Web Site: www.collegiategolf.com
Members: 650 individuals
Staff: 5
Annual Budget: $500-1,000,000
Executive Director: Gregg Grost
Director, Member Services: Sharon Beery
Director, Communications: Dustin Roberts

Historical Note

Formerly (1969) NCAA Golf Coaches Association. Members are golf coaches at all levels throughout the U.S. and Canada. Membership: for Head Coaches, $195/year (Division I); $175/year (Division II); $165/year (Division III); $155/year (NAIA); $100/year (NJCAA); Membership for Assistant Coaches, $75/year (PGA/LPGA Member); $75/year (Retired Members, Associate Members and High School.

Meetings/Conferences:

Annual Meetings: Held in Orlando, FL late January of each year in conjunction with the PGA Merchandise Show/225

Golf Course Builders Association of America *(1972)*
727 O St.
Lincoln, NE 68508
Tel: (402)476-4444 *Fax:* (402)476-4489
Web Site: www.gcbaa.org
Members: 360 companies
Staff: 3
Executive Director: Paul Foley

Historical Note

GCBAA is a trade association representing all segments of the golf course construction industry. Members are golf course builders and suppliers to the golf course construction industry. GCBAA was founded in 1972, and its members represent all segments of the golf course construction industry.

Meetings/Conferences:

Semi-annual Meetings: Summer/ Winter
2007 - Monterey, CA(Hyatt)/Aug. 1-4

Publications:

Earth Shaping News Newsletter. q. adv.
Directory. a. adv.

Golf Course Superintendents Association of America *(1926)*
1421 Research Park Dr.
Lawrence, KS 66049-3859
Tel: (785)841-2240 *Fax:* (785)832-3665
Toll Free: (800)472 - 7878 Ext:
E-Mail: infobox@gcsaa.org
Web Site: www.gcsaa.org
Members: 22000 individuals
Staff: 125
Annual Budget: $10-25,000,000
Chief Executive Officer: Stephen F. Mona, CAE
E-Mail: smona@gcsaa.org
Director, Communications: Jeff Bollig
E-Mail: jbollig@gcsaa.org
Senior Manager, Executive Administration: Ray Buckingham
Director, Finance and Member Solutions: Kathleen Burden
Director, Membership: Dave Fearis
Senior Manager, Government Relations: Chava McKeel
Senior Manager, Information Technology: Leslie Renzelman

Historical Note

GCSAA strives to provide education programs either in formal educational settings or at home or office through the use of videotapes, educational cassettes, and computers as well as conventional printed matter. Has a U.S. and international membership. Membership: $250/year (individual or organization); $55/year (student).

Meetings/Conferences:

Annual Meetings: Winter/22,000

Publications:

News Weekly. w. adv.
Golf Course Management Magazine. m. adv.
News On Line. m.
Leader Board. semi-m.
Greens and Grassroots e-newsletter.

Golf Range Association of America *(1991)*
P.O. Box 1265
New Canaan, CT 06840-1265
Tel: (203)972-6201 *Fax:* (203)972-1667
E-Mail: rangeassoc@aol.com
Web Site: www.golfrange.org
Members: 850 individuals
Annual Budget: $250-500,000
President: Steven J. DiCostanzo
E-Mail: steve@golfrange.org
Executive Vice President: Mark Silverman
E-Mail: mark@golfrange.org

Historical Note

Formerly (2001) Golf Range and Recreation Association of America. Membership: $149/year.

Publications:

Golf Range Magazine. bi-m. adv.
The Golf Range Encyclopedia. a.

Golf Writers Association of America *(1946)*
10210 Greentree Road
Houston, TX 77042-1232
Tel: (713)782-6664 *Fax:* (713)781-2575
E-Mail: golfwritersinc@aol.com
Web Site: www.gwaa.com
Members: 860 individuals
Staff: 1
Annual Budget: $25-50,000
Secretary-Treasurer: Melanie Hauser

Historical Note

Membership: $50/year.

Meetings/Conferences:

Semi-annual Meetings: Augusta, GA/April (Masters Tournament) and June in conjunction with the U.S. Open Golf Tournament

Publications:

Newsletter. 11/year.

Gospel Music Association *(1964)*
1205 Division St.
Nashville, TN 37203
Tel: (615)242-0303 Ext: 235 *Fax:* (615)254-9755
Web Site: www.gospelmusic.org
Members: 5000 individuals
Staff: 16
Annual Budget: $1-2,000,000
President: John Styll

Historical Note

The Gospel Music Association was founded in 1964 to support, encourage and promote the development of all kinds of gospel music. Over the years, the dynamics of those efforts have grown as the diversity and visibility of gospel music has increased. GMA's annual events include the Dove Awards, Gospel Music Week, Seminar in the Rockies, and others. As an umbrella organization, GMA members include recording and publishing executives, artists, church musicians, broadcasters, retailers, concert promoters, and others involved with gospel music. Membership: $85/year (professional); $60/year (associate).

Meetings/Conferences:

Annual Meetings: Spring

Publications:

GMA Today. q. adv.
GMail. w. adv.
The Christian Music Networking Guide. a. adv.

Government Finance Officers Association of the United States and Canada *(1906)*
203 N. LaSalle St., Suite 2700
Chicago, IL 60601-1210
Tel: (312)977-9700 *Fax:* (312)977-4806
E-Mail: inquiry@gfoa.org
Web Site: www.gfoa.org
Members: 14500 individuals
Staff: 65
Annual Budget: $5-10,000,000
Executive Director: Jeffrey L. Esser
E-Mail: jesser@gfoa.org
Chief Financial Officer: John Jurkash
E-Mail: jjurkash@gfoa.org
Information Technology Manager: Dennis Podgorski
Membership Coordinator: Jennifer Roberts
E-Mail: jroberts@gfoa.org

Historical Note

Formerly (1984) Municipal Finance Officers Association of the United States and Canada. Members are finance officers from city, county, and state governments, school, and other special districts; retirement systems and others in the U.S. and Canada interested in government finance.

Meetings/Conferences:

Annual Meetings: Spring
2007 - Anaheim, CA/June 10-13
2008 - Ft. Lauderdale, FL/June 15-20
2009 - Seattle, WA/June 28-1

Publications:

Newsletter. semi-m.
GAAFR Review. m.
Public Investor. m.
Government Finance Review. bi-m. adv.
Pension & Benefits Update. bi-m.

Government Management Information Sciences *(1971)*
P.O. Box 365
Bayville, NJ 08721-0365
Toll Free: (800)460 - 7454
E-Mail: gmishdqrs@mindspring.com
Web Site: www.gmis.org
Members: 600 government agencies
Staff: 2
Annual Budget: $250-500,000
Executive Secretary: John P. Moody

Historical Note

GMIS is an organization of local governments involved in information technology and educational institutions dealing in the affairs of state, county, or municipal governments. GMIS is affiliated with five foreign countrys. GMIS has 20 state chapters. Agency membership: $75-400/year, based on agency's EDP budget.

Meetings/Conferences:

Annual Meetings: Summer/400

2007 - Reno, NV(John Ascuaga's Nugget Casino Resort)/June 24-27/580

Publications:

General Education Material Newsletter. bi-m. adv.

Governmental Research Association *(1914)*

Samford University
402 Samford Hall
Birmingham, AL 35229-7017
Tel: (205)726-2482 *Fax:* (205)726-2900
Web Site: www.graonline.org
Members: 165 individuals
Annual Budget: under $10,000
Secretary: James W. Williams, Jr.

Historical Note

Members work in privately sponsored government research organizations, universities, chambers of commerce and governmental agencies. Membership: $75/year.

Publications:

GRA Reporter. q.
GRA Directory. a.

Governors Highway Safety Association *(1969)*

750 First St. NE, Suite 720
Washington, DC 20002-4241
Tel: (202)789-0942 *Fax:* (202)789-0946
E-Mail: headquarters@ghsa.org
Web Site: www.ghsa.org
Members: 54 states and territories
Staff: 4
Annual Budget: $500-1,000,000
Executive Director: Barbara L. Harsha
Director, Communications: Jonathan Adkins
Director, Administration: Denise Alston

Historical Note

Founded as National Association of Governors' Highway Safety Representatives; assumed its current name in 2002. Members are state officials who administer the Highway Safety Act.

Meetings/Conferences:

Annual Meetings: September

2007 - Portland, OR(Portland Hilton Hotel)/Sept. 23-26
2008 - Scottsdale, AZ(Fairmont Scottsdale Princess)/Sept. 5-9
2009 - Savannah, GA

Publications:

Newsletter. q.
e-Newsletter. 6-8/year.

Graduate Management Admission Council *(1970)*

1600 Tysons Blvd., Suite 1400
McLean, VA 22102
Tel: (703)749-0131 *Fax:* (703)749-0169
E-Mail: gmacmail@gmac.com
Web Site: www.gmac.com
Members: 136 institutions
Staff: 90
Annual Budget: $50-100,000,000
President and Chief Executive Officer: David A. Wilson
Chief Operating Officer: Nicole M. Chestang
Vice President, Communications: Linda Phair
General Counsel/Secretary: Sherri Sampson

Historical Note

Members are graduate schools of management or business administration.

Meetings/Conferences:

Annual Meetings:

2007 - Philadelphia, PA(Marriott)/June 14-16/600
2008 - Chicago, IL(Marriott)/June 19-21/600

Publications:

Graduate Management News. bi-m.
Dean's Digest. bi-m.

Grain Elevator and Processing Society *(1930)*

301 Fourth Ave. South, Suite 365
P.O. Box 15026
Minneapolis, MN 55415-0026
Tel: (612)339-4625 *Fax:* (612)339-4644
E-Mail: info@geaps.com
Web Site: www.geaps.com
Members: 3000 individuals
Staff: 7
Annual Budget: $1-2,000,000
Executive Vice President and Secretary: David Kresci
Communications Manager: Chuck House

Historical Note

GEAPS is an international professional society that provides news, information, continuing education and other services to grain handling and processing operations. Regular members are individuals who are associated directly with the grain, feed, milling and processing industries in an operations management or supervisory capacity. Affiliate membership is available for academics and government officials. Associate membership is available to suppliers of products, equipment or services to the industry. Membership: $145/year.

Meetings/Conferences:

Annual Meetings: late Winter/1,800

2007 - Grapevine, TX(Opryland Convention Center)/March 3-6/1800

Publications:

In-Grain (newsletter). m.
Proceedings of the International Technical Conference. a.
DirectaSource Buyers Guide and Member Directory. a. adv.

Grain Equipment Manufacturers Council

Historical Note

A council of the Equipment Manufacturers Institute.

Graphic Artists Guild *(1967)*

90 John St., Suite 403
New York, NY 10038-3202
Tel: (212)791-3400 *Fax:* (212)791-0333
Toll Free: (800)500 - 2672
E-Mail: admin@gag.org
Web Site: www.gag.org/
Members: 3500 individuals
Staff: 7
Annual Budget: $500-1,000,000
President: John Schmelzer
Administrative Director: Patricia McKiernan
Membership: Barbara Pannone

Historical Note

The Guild is a labor organization working to improve industry conditions and standards, and to protect the economic interests of member artists. The long-range goals of the Guild are: financial and professional respect, education and research, valued benefits, and organizational development. Full membership is open to any creators of original work intended for graphic presentation, either in original form or in reproduction. Members are illustrators, graphic designers, surface designers, production artists, cartoonists, computer artists and designers of accesories and wearable art. Associate members are professional in allied fields. Has absorbed the Illustrators Guild, Cartoonist Guild, and Textile Designers Guild. Membership: $55-$270/year.

Publications:

Guild News. bi-m.
Directory of Illustration. a. adv.
Graphic Artists Guild Handbook: Pricing and Ethical Guidelines. bien.

Graphic Arts Employers of America *(1887)*

Historical Note

A division of Printing Industries of America, of which it was the originating organization. Represents graphic arts firms whose production departments are partially or wholly organized. Formerly (1981) the Graphic Arts Union Employers of America (UEA).

Graphic Arts Marketing Information Service *(1966)*

100 Daingerfield Road
Alexandria, VA 22314-2888
Tel: (703)519-8179 *Fax:* (703)548-3227
Members: 75 companies
Staff: 2
Annual Budget: $500-1,000,000
Executive Director: Jacqueline M. Bland

Historical Note

GAMIS is a section of market researchers of Printing Industries of America, dedicated to providing its members with current, relevant market data and information on print media through member-directed research studies. Membership: $3100-8250/year (organization/company).

Publications:

Statistical Handbook for the Graphic Arts. bi-a.

Graphic Arts Sales Foundation *(1983)*

113 E. Evans St.
West Chester, PA 19380-3336
Tel: (610)431-9780 *Fax:* (610)436-5238
E-Mail: info@gasf.org
Members: 1200 individuals
Staff: 5
Annual Budget: $250-500,000
Chief Executive Officer: Richard Gorelick
E-Mail: info@gorelickandassociates.com
Administrator: Judy M. Miller

Historical Note

GASF is the largest training organization in the graphic arts industry offering one-day, five-day and custom in-house industry-specific education programs for C.E.O.'s, marketing executives, sales managers, salespeople, print buyers, customer service representatives, estimators, and production supervisors. GASF offers a professional certification program for graphic arts sales representatives in the graphic arts industry (CGASR).

Meetings/Conferences:

Annual Meetings: Programs are distributed by regional trade assn's throughout the year.

Publications:

Monographs. bi-m.

Graphic Arts Technical Foundation *(1924)*

200 Deer Run Road
Sewickley, PA 15143-2600
Tel: (412)741-6860 *Fax:* (412)741-2311
Toll Free: (800)910 - 4283
E-Mail: gain@gain.net
Web Site: www.gain.net
Members: 13000individualsandcompanies
Staff: 56
Annual Budget: $5-10,000,000
President and Chief Executive Officer: Michael Makin
Conference Coordinator: Ned Herrick
Executive Vice President and Chief Operating Officer: George H. Ryan
E-Mail: GRYAN@GATF.ORG
Senior Sales Coordinator: Chuck Sweeney
Vice President, Training: James Workman

Historical Note

Formerly (1924) Lithographic Technical Foundation; assumed current name in 1964 to reflect the Foundation's commitment to all aspects of printing. GATF is a member supported, nonprofit, scientific, technical, and educational organization dedicated to the advancement of graphic communications industries worldwide. A research and education foundation, it produces publications, training programs, research studies and quality control devices. Its Print and Graphics Scholarship Foundation, established in 1956, is a nonprofit corporation that awards scholarships to two and four year programs leading to a career in graphic communications. In 1999, GATF consolidated with Printing Industries of America (PIA). Membership: corporate fee based on sales volume.

Meetings/Conferences:

Annual Meetings: Fall

Publications:

GATFWORLD Magazine. bi-m. adv.
Process Controls Catalog. a.
Publications Catalogue. semi-a.
Training Programs Catalogue. semi-a.

Graphic Communications Conference, IBT *(1889)*

1900 L St. NW, Ninth Floor
Washington, DC 20036

Tel: (202)462-1400 *Fax:* (202)721-0600
Web Site: www.gciu.org
Members: 150000 individuals
Staff: 60
Annual Budget: $2-5,000,000
President: George Tedeschi

Historical Note

The Amalgamated Lithographers of America and the International Photoengravers Union of North America merged on September 7, 1964 to form the Lithographers and Photoengravers International Union. This, in turn, merged September 4, 1972 with the International Brotherhood of Bookbinders (founded 1892) to form the Graphic Arts International Union which merged July 1, 1983 with the International Printing and Graphic Communications Union to form the present organization. GCIU merged with the International Brotherhood of Teamsters and assumed its curent name in 2005.

Publications:

GraphiCommunicator. 8/year.

Graphic Communications International Union

Historical Note

Became Graphic Communications Conference/IBT in 2005.

Gravure Association of America *(1947)*
1200-A Scottsville Road
Rochester, NY 14624
Tel: (585)436-2150 *Fax:* (585)436-7689
E-Mail: gaa@gaa.org
Web Site: www.gaa.org
Members: 212 companies
Staff: 9
Annual Budget: $1-2,000,000
President and Chief Executive Officer: Bill Martin
E-Mail: bmartin@gaa.org
Executive Director, GEF: Laura Wayland-Smith Hatch
E-Mail: lwshatch@gaa.org

Historical Note

Formed (1988) through the merger of the Gravure Technical Association and the Gravure Research Insitute. Members are gravure printers, converters, suppliers, and users. Supports the Gravure Education Foundation, established in 1979.

Publications:

Gravure Magazine. bi-m. adv.

Greater Blouse, Skirt and Undergarment Association *(1933)*
1359 Broadway, Suite 1814
New York, NY 10018
Tel: (212)563-5052 *Fax:* (212)563-5373
Web Site: www.greaterblouse.org
Members: 150 garment factories
Staff: 6
Annual Budget: $500-1,000,000
Executive Director: Teddy Lai

Historical Note

Formerly (1967) Greater Blouse and Skirt Contractors Association. Membership: $1020/year (company).

Meetings/Conferences:

Annual Meetings: Early Fall

Publications:

Greater Voice Newsletter. q. adv.
Anniversary Journal. a. adv.

Greater Washington Board of Trade *(1889)*
1725 I St. NW, Suite 200
Washington, DC 20006
Tel: (202)857-5900 *Fax:* (202)223-2648
E-Mail: info@bot.org
Web Site: www.bot.org
Members: 1200 firms
Staff: 37
Annual Budget: $5-10,000,000
President: James Dinegar
E-Mail: info@bot.org
Vice President, Government Relations: Scott Sterling
E-Mail: info@bot.org
Vice President, Communications: Marie Tibor
E-Mail: info@bot.org

Historical Note

Serves as a regional chamber of commerce for the Washington metro area. Represents firms that employ more than 60% of the area's private work force. Membership: $450/year, minimum.

Meetings/Conferences:

Annual Meetings: November

Publications:

Across the Board. bi-m. adv.

Greek Food and Wine Institute *(1992)*
34-80 48th St.
Long Island City, NY 11101
Tel: (718)729-5277 *Fax:* (718)361-9725
Members: 18 companies
Staff: 4
Annual Budget: $100-250,000
Executive Vice President: Kathy Spiliotopolous
E-Mail: kspilio@aol.com

Historical Note

GFWI is a non-profit educational and promotional organization dedicated to increasing awareness of the quality, variety and uses of Greek foods, wines and spirits. Members include food, wine and spirts producers, importers and distributors in Greece and the US. The Institute directs its efforts towards promotional activities such as symposia, tastings and special events. Membership: $5,000/year (member); $25,000/year (board member); $1,000/year (restaurant member).

Publications:

Gastronomia Newsletter. semi-a.

Green Hotels Association
P.O. Box 420212
Houston, TX 77242-0212
Tel: (713)789-8889 *Fax:* (713)789-9786
E-Mail: green@greenhotels.com
Web Site: www.greenhotels.com
Members: 325 hotels
Staff: 3
President: Patricia Griffin

Historical Note

Committed to help hotels save water, save energy, and reduce solid waste, in order to help protect beautiful destinations valued by the public.

Publications:

Greening Newsletter. bi-m. adv.
Membership Conservation Guidelines & Ideas. 4-5/yr.

Greeting Card Association *(1941)*
1156 15th St. NW, Suite 900
Washington, DC 20005
Tel: (202)393-1778 *Fax:* (202)223-9741
E-Mail: info@greetingcard.org
Web Site: www.greetingcard.org
Members: 300 companies
Staff: 6
Annual Budget: $500-1,000,000
Executive Vice President: Valerie Cooper, CAE
Director, Membership Services: Mila Albertson
Executive Director: Kathy Prunty

Historical Note

Originally founded as the Greeting Card Association to confront the paper shortage during World War II; became the National Association of Greeting Card Publishers in 1967 and assumed its original name in 1983. Membership fee based on annual sales volume.

Meetings/Conferences:

Annual Meetings: Fall

Publications:

Greetings Etc. (includes GCA newsletter). bi-m. adv.
Industry Directory of Publishers and Suppliers. bi-a. adv.
Directory of Greeting Card Sales Representatives. bi-a.

Grocery Manufacturers Association *(1908)*
2401 Pennsylvania Ave. NW
Second Floor
Washington, DC 20037
Tel: (202)337-9400 *Fax:* (202)337-4508
E-Mail: info@gmabrands.com
Web Site: www.gmabrands.com
Members: 131 companies
Staff: 40
Annual Budget: $5-10,000,000
President and Chief Executive Officer: C. Manly Molpus
Vice President, Government Affairs: Steve Arthur
Vice President, Administration and Meetings: Hilarie Hoting
Vice President, Industry Affairs and Membership: Steve Sibert

Historical Note

Formerly Grocery Manufacturers of America; assumed current name in 2005. Members are manufacturers of branded products sold in grocery stores and retail outlets. Absorbed Association of Sales and Marketing in 2003. Sponsors and supports the GMA Political Action Committee (GMA-PAC). Has an annual budget of approximately $8.0 million.

Meetings/Conferences:

Annual Meetings: White Sulphur Springs, WV in June

Publications:

GMA Executive Update newsletter. w.
Washington Report. m.
State Legislative Reporting and Analysis Service. w.

Ground Water Protection Council *(1983)*
13308 N. MacArthur Blvd.
Oklahoma City, OK 73142
Tel: (405)516-4972 *Fax:* (405)516-4973
Web Site: www.gwpc.org
Members: 1500 individuals
Staff: 7
Annual Budget: $1-2,000,000
Executive Director: Mike Paque, CAE
Coordinator, Member Services: Dan Yates

Historical Note

GWPC provides a forum for discussion of ground water protection, source water and wellhead protection, and underground injection practices. Forums and projects bring together state and federal regulatory agencies and the industries subject to regulation to work on issue resolution. Membership: $75/year (individual); corporate fee varies.

Meetings/Conferences:

Annual Meetings: Winter

Groundwater Management Districts Association *(1975)*
P.O. Box 905
Colby, KS 67701-0905
Tel: (785)462-3915 *Fax:* (785)462-2693
Web Site: www.gmdausa.org
Members: 140 individuals
Staff: 1
Annual Budget: under $10,000
Secretary-Treasurer: Wayne Bossert

Historical Note

Membership includes districts, consulting organizations and individuals concerned with the management and conservation of water resources. Seeks effective information transfer between member districts, associations, and organizations responsible for water resource management. Affiliated with the National Water Resources Association. Membership: $20/year (individual); $90/year (affiliate); $150/year (organization); $200/year (district).

Meetings/Conferences:

Annual Meetings: In conjunction with the Nat'l Water Resources Ass'n

Publications:

Proceeding of Annual Conference. a.

Group for the Use of Psychology in History *(1971)*
John Jay College - CUNY
555 W. 57th St., Suite 601
New York, NY 10019
Tel: (212)237-8432
E-Mail: strozier2@aol.com
Web Site: https://www.historians.org/affiliates/group_use_psychology_his.htm
Members: 400 individuals
Executive Officer: Charles B. Strozier
E-Mail: strozier2@aol.com

Historical Note

Members are academics and others with an interest in the integration of disciplines of psychology and

history. Has no paid officers or full-time staff. Membership: $22/year.

Meetings/Conferences:
Annual Meetings: in conjunction with AHA annual meeting

Publications:
Psychohistory Review. q.

Guild of American Luthiers *(1972)*
8222 South Park Ave.
Tacoma, WA 98408
Tel: (253)472-7853
E-Mail: orders@luth.org
Web Site: www.luth.org
Members: 3400 individuals
Staff: 6
Annual Budget: $100-250,000
President and Editor: Timothy L. Olsen

Historical Note
Non-profit educational organization. Members are professional and amateur builders and repairers of string musical instruments and other interested individuals. Membership: $45/year (domestic); $49/year (Canada); $55/year (overseas).

Meetings/Conferences:
Triennial Meetings: usually Summer

Publications:
American Lutherie. q. adv.

Guild of Book Workers *(1906)*
521 Fifth Ave., Suite 1740
New York, NY 10175
Tel: (212)292-4444
Members: 900 individuals
Annual Budget: $10-25,000
Secretary: C. Burkhard

Historical Note
Established to continue and foster the growth of the handbook crafts, including binding, calligraphy, illumination, papermaking and printing. An affiliate of the American Institute of Graphic Arts from 1948 to 1978. Has no paid staff; all contact handled through mail. Membership: $75/year (U.S. members); $85/year (Canadian members); $90/year (all members outside U.S. and Canada).

Meetings/Conferences:
Annual Meetings: Fall

Publications:
Guild of Book Workers Journal. semi-a.
Newsletter. bi-m. adv.

Guild of Italian American Actors *(1937)*
Canal Street Station
P.O. Box 123
New York, NY 10013-0123
Tel: (212)420-6590
E-Mail: info@giaa.us
Web Site: www.giaa.us
Members: 270 individuals
Annual Budget: $10-25,000
President: Guy Palumbo
E-Mail: info@giaa.us

Historical Note
An autonomous component of the Associated Actors and Artistes of America, which chartered it in 1938. Founded in 1937 and also known as Italian Actors Union; assumed its current name in 1998. Membership: $400/year initiation fee, plus $60/year.

Meetings/Conferences:
Annual Meetings: April

Guild of Natural Science Illustrators *(1968)*
Box 652, Ben Franklin Station
Washington, DC 20044-0652
Tel: (301)309-1514
E-Mail: gnsihome@his.com
Members: 1000 individuals
Staff: 3
Annual Budget: $25-50,000
Administrative Assistant: Leslie Becker

Historical Note
Originally formed by illustrators at the Smithsonian Institution, the GNSI now includes foreign members. The Guild's purpose is to promote the techniques and understanding of scientific illustration and to encourage professionalism among its members. Membership: $85/year (domestic); $105/year (overseas).

Meetings/Conferences:
Annual Meetings: Summer

Publications:
Newsletter. 10/year. adv.
Membership Directory. a.
Journal of Natural Science Illustration. a.

Guitar and Accessories Marketing Association *(1924)*
P.O. Box 757
New York, NY 11105
Tel: (212)795-3630 *Fax:* (212)795-3630
E-Mail: assnhdqs@earthlink.net
Web Site: http://discoverguitar.com
Members: 46 companies
Staff: 2
Annual Budget: $25-50,000
Executive Vice President: Jerome Hershman

Historical Note
Established as the National Association of Musical Merchandise Manufacturers, it became the Guitar and Accessory Manufacturers of America in 1963, became the Guitar and Accessories Music Marketing Association in 1982 and assumed its present name in 1992. Members are distributors of domestic fretted instruments and allied accessories.

Meetings/Conferences:
Annual Meetings: With Nat'l Ass'n of Music Merchants in Anaheim, CA(Marriott)/Jan./50

Publications:
Newsletter. q.

Gynecologic Oncology Group *(1970)*
1600 JFK Blvd., Suite 1020
Philadelphia, PA 19103-2800
Tel: (215)854-0770 *Fax:* (215)854-0716
Web Site: www.gog.org
Members: 54 institutions
Staff: 25
Annual Budget: $500-1,000,000
Executive Director: John R. Kellner

Historical Note
Members are teaching hospitals and research institutions.

Meetings/Conferences:
Semi-Annual Meetings: January and July

Gynecologic Surgery Society *(1979)*
2440 M St. NW, Suite 801
Washington, DC 20037
Tel: (202)293-2046 *Fax:* (202)778-6195
E-Mail: information@gynecologicsurgerysociety.org
Web Site: www.gynecologicsurgerysociety.org
Members: 1000 individuals
Staff: 1
Annual Budget: $100-250,000
Chairman: John Marlow, M.D.

Historical Note
Formerly (1993) Gynecologic Laser Society and (1995) Gynecologic Laser and Advanced Technology Society Membership: $95/year (individual).

Meetings/Conferences:
Biennial Meetings: Spring

Publications:
Journal of Gynecologic Surgery. q. adv.
GLS Newlsetter. q. adv.

Gypsum Association *(1930)*
810 First St. NE, Suite 510
Washington, DC 20002
Tel: (202)289-5440 *Fax:* (202)289-3707
E-Mail: info@gypsum.org
Web Site: www.gypsum.org
Members: 10 companies
Staff: 8
Annual Budget: $1-2,000,000
Executive Director: Michael Gardner
Director, Government and Regulatory Affairs: Amy Foscue
Assistant Executive Director: Robert A. Wessel

Historical Note
Members are U.S. and Canadian manufacturers of gypsum board products. GA provides technical information and assistance to the construction industry and code enforcement community regarding gypsum board.

Meetings/Conferences:
Annual Meetings: Fall

Halogenated Solvents Industry Alliance *(1980)*
1300 Wilson Blvd., 12th Fl.
Arlington, VA 22209
Tel: (703)741-5780 *Fax:* (703)741-6077
E-Mail: contact@hsia.org
Web Site: www.hsia.org
Members: 50 companies
Staff: 2
Annual Budget: $500-1,000,000
Executive Director: Stephen P. Risotto
Director, Scientific Programs: Dr. Paul Dugard

Historical Note
HSIA members are producers, users, distributors and equipment manufacturers for chlorinated solvents.

Publications:
HSIA Solvents Update. bi-m.

Halon Alternatives Research Corp. *(1989)*
2111 Wilson Blvd., Eighth Floor
Arlington, VA 22201-3001
Tel: (703)524-6636 *Fax:* (703)243-2874
E-Mail: harc@harc.org
Web Site: www.harc.org
Members: 50 companies
Staff: 1
Annual Budget: $100-250,000
Executive Director: Tom Cortina

Historical Note
A trade association representing producers, distributors, users of halons, and others with an interest in finding replacement agents. Membership: $6,000/year (voting member); $1,000/year (general member).

Publications:
HARC News. 2-4/year.

Hand Knitting Association

Historical Note
A committee of the National Needlework Association.

Hand Tools Institute *(1935)*
25 N. Broadway
Tarrytown, NY 10591-3201
Tel: (914)332-0040 *Fax:* (914)332-1541
E-Mail: HTI@HTI.org
Web Site: www.HTI.org
Members: 60 companies
Staff: 3
Annual Budget: $250-500,000
Executive Director: Richard C. Byrne

Historical Note
Absorbed the Vise Manufacturers Association in 1969. Formerly (1973) Service Tools Institute.

Meetings/Conferences:
Semi-annual Meetings: Winter/Fall

Publications:
Directory. a.

Handweavers Guild of America *(1969)*
1255 Buford Hwy., Suite 211
Suwanee, GA 30024
Tel: (678)730-0010 *Fax:* (678)730-0836
E-Mail: weavespindye@weavespindye
Web Site: www.weavespindye.org
Members: 9000 individuals
Staff: 8
Annual Budget: $250-500,000
Executive Director: Sandra Bowles
E-Mail: executivedirector@weavespindye.org

Historical Note
Individuals, companies, and organizations promoting interest in and creation of fiber arts. Membership: $35/year (domestic), $40/year (foreign).

Meetings/Conferences:
Biennial Meetings: Even years

Publications:
Shuttle Spindle & Dyepot. q. adv.

HARDI - Heating, Airconditioning, and Refrigeration Distributors International *(1947)*
1389 Dublin Road

Columbus, OH 43215
Tel: (614)488-1835 *Fax:* (614)488-0482
E-Mail: hardimail@hardinet.org
Web Site: www.hardinet.org
Members: 450 wholesalers
Staff: 10
Annual Budget: $1-2,000,000
Executive Vice President and Chief Operating Officer: Donald Frendberg
E-Mail: hardimail@hardinet.org
Director, Education: James Healy
E-Mail: hardimail@hardinet.org

Historical Note
Affiliated with the National Association of Wholesaler-Distributors. Absorbed (1969) North American Association of Sheet Metal Distributors. Formerly National Heat Wholesalers Association; National Heating and Air Conditioning Wholesalers; and North American Heating and Airconditioning Wholesalers Association (1994); absorbed Airconditioning and Refrigeration Wholesalers International and assumed its current name in 2003.

Meetings/Conferences:
2007 – Orlando, FL(Orlando World Center Marriott Resort)/Oct. 6-9
2008 – Phoenix, AZ(J.W. Marriott Desert Ridge Resort and Spa)/Oct. 25-28
2009 – Orlando, FL(J.W. Marriott Orlando Grand Lakes)/Oct. 31-Nov. 3

Publications:
Distribution Today. bi-m. adv.

Hardwood Manufacturers Association *(1935)*
400 Penn Center Blvd., Suite 530
Pittsburgh, PA 15235
Tel: (412)829-0770 *Fax:* (412)829-0844
E-Mail: info@hardwood.org
Web Site: www.hardwood.org
Members: 156 individuals
Staff: 4
Annual Budget: $500-1,000,000
Executive Vice President: Susan Regan

Historical Note
Formerly Southern Hardwood Producers Inc. and Southern Hardwood Lumber Manufacturers Association. Assumed present name in 1984. Southern Cypress Manufacturers Association is a division of HMA.

Meetings/Conferences:
Annual Meetings: March

Publications:
Link Newsletter. m.

Hardwood Plywood and Veneer Association *(1921)*
P.O. Box 2789
Reston, VA 20195
Tel: (703)435-2900 *Fax:* (703)435-2537
E-Mail: hpva@hpva.org
Web Site: www.hpva.org
Members: 196 companies
Staff: 9
Annual Budget: $1-2,000,000
President: E.T. "Bill" Altman, CAE
Manager, Marketing, Publications and Government Affairs: Curt Alt
Financial Manager: Myrna Downey
Manager, Convention Planner and Membership Services: Ketti Tyree

Historical Note
Absorbed (1998) Fine Hardwood Veneer Association. Established in Chicago in 1921 as the Plywood Manufacturers Association. Formerly Plywood Manufacturing Institute, (1964) Hardwood Plywood Institute, and (1992) Hardwood Plywood Manufacturers Association. Absorbed the Southern Plywood Manufacturers Association in 1953. HPVA members include plywood manufacturers, veneer facilities, industry suppliers, and wholesale stocking distributors. Affiliated with American Forest and Paper Association, International Conference of Building Officials, Southern Building Code Congress, Building Officials and Code Administrators International, and the U.S. Dept. of Commerce National Voluntary Laboratory Accreditation Program. Membership: dues based on sales volume.

Meetings/Conferences:
Semi-Annual Meetings: Spring and Fall
2007 – Hilton Head, SC(Westin Resort Hilton Head Island)/March 24-26
2007 – Salt Lake City, UT(Salt Lake City Marriott Downtown)/Sept. 9-11

Publications:
Where to Buy Hardwood Plywood and Veneer. a. adv.
Hardwood Plywood & Veneer News (online). bi-w.. adv.

Hardwood Research Council *(1953)*

Historical Note
A program of the National Hardwood Lumber Association.

Harness Horsemen International *(1964)*
64 State Route 33
Manalapan, NJ 07726-8301
Tel: (732)683-1580 *Fax:* (732)683-1578
Members: 40000 individuals
Staff: 2
Annual Budget: $250-500,000
President: Dominic H. Frinzi

Historical Note
HHI represents owners, trainers, and drivers of standardbred racehorses working in the U.S. and Canada.

Meetings/Conferences:
Semi-annual Meetings: Winter and Summer

Publications:
Directory of Associations. irreg.
Careers in Harness Racing. irreg.
News from Harness Horsemen Internat'l. irreg.

Harness Tracks of America *(1954)*
4640 E. Sunrise Dr., Suite 200
Tucson, AZ 85718-4576
Tel: (520)529-2525 *Fax:* (520)529-3235
E-Mail: info@harnesstracks.com
Web Site: www.harnesstracks.com
Members: 34 pari-mutuel harness tracks
Staff: 4
Annual Budget: $500-1,000,000
Executive Vice President: Stanley F. Bergstein
E-Mail: info@harnesstracks.com

Historical Note
A trade association for North American harness race tracks. Issues monthly economic studies, reports, position papers, daily newsletters, and special surveys on legal and legislative matters affecting the sport and industry.

Meetings/Conferences:
Annual Meetings: Winter

Publications:
Executive Newsletter. d.
Promotions Newsletter. m.
Track Topics. w.
Surveys. m.
Directory. a. adv.

Harvey Society *(1905)*
Golding Bldg., Room 601
13000 Morris Park Ave.
Bronx, NY 10641
Tel: (718)430-8646 *Fax:* (718)430-8697
Web Site: www.harveysociety.org
Members: 1700 individuals
Staff: 1
Annual Budget: $25-50,000
Secretary: Dr. Robert H. Singer

Historical Note
Named after William Harvey, British physician who discovered the circulation of the blood in the 17th century, the Society consists of individuals interested in or capable of making a contribution to the literature of medicine. Membership: $50/year.

Meetings/Conferences:
Annual Meetings: Always in New York, NY

Publications:
The Harvey Lectures. a.

Hazardous Materials Advisory Council

Historical Note
Became Dangerous Goods Advisory Council in 2003.

Headwear Information Bureau *(1989)*
302 W. 12th St., PH-C
New York, NY 10014
Tel: (212)627-8333
Web Site: www.hatsworldwide.com
Members: 80 individuals and companies
Staff: 2
Annual Budget: $10-25,000
Executive Director: Casey Bush
E-Mail: MILICASE@aol.com

Historical Note
Formerly (1989) Millinery Institute of America and then Headwear Information Bureau, HIB members are designers and manufacturers/importers of men's and women's hats and suppliers to the industry. HIB promotes men's and women's fashion headwear to press, retailers and consumers. Membership: $25-$125/month.

Publications:
Milligram Newsletter. m.

Health & Sciences Communications Association *(1959)*
39 Wedgewood Dr., Suite A
Jewett City, CT 06351-2428
Tel: (860)376-5915 *Fax:* (860)376-6621
E-Mail: HeSCAOne@sbcglobal.net
Web Site: www.hesca.org
Members: 250 individuals
Staff: 2
Annual Budget: $100-250,000
Executive Director: Ron Sokolowski
E-Mail: HeSCAOne@sbcglobal.net

Historical Note
Organized in 1959 as the Council on Medical Television as part of the Institute for Advancement of Medical Communication. Incorporated in North Carolina in 1964 under its own charter. Became the Health Sciences Communications Association in 1972. A professional association of individuals interested in application of educational technology to the health sciences field. Membership: $150/year (individual); $195/year (organization); $75/year (student).

Meetings/Conferences:
Annual Meetings: Spring
2007 – Toronto, ON, Canada(Sheraton Centre Toronto)/June 14-17

Publications:
HeSCA Feedback. q. adv.
Journal of Biocommunication. q.
Membership Catalog. a.

Health Care Compliance Association *(1996)*
5780 Lincoln Dr., Suite 120
Minneapolis, MN 55436
Tel: (952)988-0141 *Fax:* (952)988-0146
Toll Free: (888)580 - 8373
E-Mail: info@hcca-info.org
Web Site: www.hcca-info.org
Members: 3800 individuals
Staff: 16
Annual Budget: $2-5,000,000
Chief Executive Officer: Roy Snell
E-Mail: rsnell@hcca-info.org
Director, Communications: Margaret Dragon
Deputy Chief Executive Officer: Claudia Hoffacker

Publications:
Compliance Today. m. adv.
This Week in Corporate Compliance (online). w. adv.

Health Care Education Association
P.O. Box 50603
Amarillo, TX 79159-0603
Toll Free: (888)298 - 3861
E-Mail: hcea03@cox.net
Web Site: www.hcea-info.org
Members: 400 individuals
Staff: 4
President: Kim Crosby
E-Mail: hcea03@cox.net

Historical Note
HCEA supports and mentors health care educators. Membership: $95/year.

Publications:
HCEA Newsletter. q. adv.

Health Care Institute
Historical Note
A component of the Environmental Management Association.

Health Forum *(1927)*
One N. Franklin St.
Chicago, IL 60606
Tel: (312)422-2806 *Fax:* (312)422-4506
Toll Free: (800)821 - 2039
Web Site: www.healthforum.com
Members: 1300organizationsandindividuals
Staff: 10
Annual Budget: $5-10,000,000
President and Chief Executive Officer: Neil J. Jesuele
E-Mail: njesuel1@aha.org
Chief Operating Officer: John Sukenik
E-Mail: jsukenik@healthforum.com
Historical Note
Founded as Association of Western Hospitals;later became the Healthcare Forum. Absorbed the publishing and data/information services divisions of American Hospital Association and asusmed its current name in 1998. HF is a provider of executive education and applied research for healthcare leaders. Forum members, individuals and organizations, are drawn from all 50 states and countries around the world. Also maintains offices in San Francisco and Washington. Has an annual budget of over $9 million. Membership: $500/year (individual); $1,600/year (organization).
Publications:
Health Forum Journal. bi-m. adv.

Health Industry Business Communications Council *(1984)*
2525 E. Arizona Biltmore Circle
Suite 127
Phoenix, AZ 85016
Tel: (602)381-1091 *Fax:* (602)381-1093
E-Mail: info@hibcc.org
Web Site: www.hibcc.org
Members: 900 individuals
Staff: 20
Annual Budget: $500-1,000,000
President: Robert A. Hankin, Ph.D.
Director, Communications: Sara Polansky
Historical Note
Membership: $150/year (individual); $2,500/year (organization).
Publications:
Health Industry Lines. q. adv.

Health Industry Distributors Association *(1902)*
310 Montgomery St.
Alexandria, VA 22314-1516
Tel: (703)549-4432 *Fax:* (703)549-6495
Web Site: www.hida.org
Members: 185 companies
Staff: 20
Annual Budget: $5-10,000,000
President and Chief Executive Officer: Matthew J. Rowan
Director, Government Affairs: Jennifer Bogenrief
Vice President, Trade Show: Ian Fardy
Vice President and Executive Director, HIDA Educational Foundation: Elizabeth B. Hilla
Vice President, Member Relations: Yvonne Noel
Chief Financial Officer: Lyn Rawdon
Vice President, Industry Relations/Program Development: Andrew Van Ostrand
Historical Note
Founded as the American Surgical Trade Association; assumed its present name in 1983. Trade association for all sectors of the medical products distribution industries. Sponsors the HIDA Educational Foundation, the Health Industry Distributors Association Political Action Committee (HIDA-PAC), and the HIDA Service Corporation. Membership fee varies, based on annual sales.
Meetings/Conferences:
2007 - Austin, TX(Hyatt Regency Lost Pines Resort and Spa)/Feb. 27-March 2
Publications:
HIDA 411. m. adv.
Selling. m. adv.

Health Industry Group Purchasing Association
(1990)
1100 Wilson Blvd., Suite 1200
Arlington, VA 22209
Tel: (703)243-9262 *Fax:* (703)243-8664
E-Mail: info@higpa.org
Web Site: www.higpa.org
Staff: 8
President and Chief Executive Officer: Robert B. Betz
Director, Communications: Carolyn Hickey
Historical Note
Members are organizations providing economies of scale to health care providers through group purchasing.
Publications:
CapitolLine Newsletter.

Health Industry Representatives Association
(1978)
138 Garfield St.
Denver, CO 80206
Tel: (303)756-8115 *Fax:* (303)756-5699
E-Mail: info@hira.org
Web Site: www.hira.org
Members: 185 companies, 65 associates
Staff: 2
Annual Budget: $100-250,000
Executive Director: Karen A. Hone
Historical Note
Independent manufacturers representatives who sell medical equipment and other products in the health care field. Formerly (1985) Health Associated Representatives.
Meetings/Conferences:
Annual Meetings: Summer
Publications:
Communicator. m.

Health Ministries Association
295 W. Crossville Road, Suite 130
Roswell, GA 30075
Tel: (770)640-9555 *Fax:* (770)640-1095
Toll Free: (800)280 - 9919
E-Mail: info@hmassoc.org
Web Site: www.hmassoc.org
Members: 1,300 individuals
Staff: 4
Annual Budget: $250-500,000
Executive Director: Charles B. Dillehay
Historical Note
HMA members are health care professionals working in faith-based organizations. Membership: $100/year.
Meetings/Conferences:
2007 - San Antonio, TX(Hyatt Riverwalk)/June 21-24/500

Health Physics Society *(1956)*
1313 Dolley Madison Blvd., Suite 402
McLean, VA 22101-3926
Tel: (703)790-1745 *Fax:* (703)790-2672
E-Mail: hps@burkinc.com
Web Site: www.hps.org
Members: 7000 individuals
Staff: 12
Annual Budget: $1-2,000,000
Executive Secretary: Richard J. Burk, Jr.
Historical Note
Founded and incorporated in the District of Columbia in 1956. Reincorporated in Tennessee in 1969. Fosters the protection of humankind and the environment from radiation. Affiliated with the International Radiation Protection Association. Membership: $105/year.
Meetings/Conferences:
Annual Meetings: Summer.
Publications:
Health Physics Journal. m. adv.
Newsletter. m. adv.
Membership Handbook. a.

Healthcare Billing and Management Association
(1992)
1540 South Coast Hwy., Suite 203
Laguna Beach, CA 92651
Toll Free: (877)640 - 4262 Ext: 203
E-Mail: info@hbma.org
Web Site: www.hbma.org
Members: 500 individuals
Staff: 5
Annual Budget: $500-1,000,000
Executive Director: Brad Lund
Historical Note
Founded as International Billing Association; assumed its current name in 1998. Members are companies providing third-party medical billing services. Membership: dues based on number of employees.
Meetings/Conferences:
2007 - Scottsdale, AZ(Hilton)/March 8-10
Publications:
Newsletter. m.

Healthcare Compliance Packaging Council *(1990)*
131 E. Broad St., Suite 206
Falls Church, VA 22046
Tel: (703)538-4030 *Fax:* (703)538-6305
Web Site: www.unitdose.org
Members: 80corporationsandindividuals
Staff: 3
Annual Budget: $250-500,000
Executive Director: Peter G. Mayberry
Historical Note
Members are companies and individuals in the pharmaceutical packaging industry with an interest in promoting unit-dose blister packaging. Membership: $5,000/year (corporate); $2,500/year (associate); $500/year (educational institution); $1,000/year (trade association); $195/year (individual).
Meetings/Conferences:
Semi-Annual Meetings: Washington, DC/Fall and Philadelphia, PA/Spring
Publications:
Unit-Dose Alert. q.

Healthcare Convention and Exhibitors Association *(1930)*
1100 Johnson Ferry Road
Suite 300
Atlanta, GA 30342
Tel: (404)252-3663 *Fax:* (404)252-0774
E-Mail: hcea@kellencompany.com
Web Site: www.hcea.org
Members: 680 companies
Staff: 7
Executive Vice President: Eric Allen
Associate Director: Jackie Beaulieu
Director, Communications: Jennifer Palcher
Historical Note
Formerly (1973) Medical Exhibitors Association and (1990) Health Care Exhibitors Association. Trade association of nearly 700 organizations united by their common desire to increase the effectiveness and efficiency of healthcare conventions and exhibits. Membership: $595/year (domestic); $695/year (overseas).
Meetings/Conferences:
Annual Meetings: June
2007 - Philadelphia, PA(Pennsylvania Convention Center)/June 9-12/700
Publications:
Directory of Healthcare Meetings/Conventions. a. adv.
Insight Magazine. semi-a. adv.
Association Alert Newsletter. semi-a. adv.
Inbox Informer E-Newsletter. m. adv.

Healthcare Distribution Management Association *(1876)*
901 N. Glebe Road, #1000
Arlington, VA 22203
Tel: (703)787-0000 *Fax:* (703)935-3200
Web Site: www.healthcaredistribution.org
Members: 400 companies
Staff: 42
Annual Budget: $5-10,000,000
President and Chief Executive Officer: John M. Gray
Senior Vice President, Industry Relations: Lisa Clowers
Director, Public Relations and Communications: Amanda Forster

Executive Vice President and Chief Operating Officer: Nancy E. Hanagan
Vice President, Finance and Administration: Cheryl Jordan
Senior Vice President, Government Relations: Scott Melville
Director, Member Services: Pamela C. Moore

Historical Note
Established as Western Wholesale Druggists; became National Wholesale Druggists' Association in 1881 assumed its present name in 2002. Sponsors and supports the NWDA Political Action Committee. Absorbed the Druggists Service Council in 1971. Merged (1984) with Drug Wholesalers Association. Has an annual budget of approximately $8 million. Membership fee varies, based on sales volume.

Meetings/Conferences:
Annual Meetings: Fall

Healthcare Financial Management Association *(1946)*
Two Westbrook Corporate Center, Suite 700
Westchester, IL 60154-5700
Tel: (708)531-9600 *Fax:* (708)531-0032
Toll Free: (800)252 - 4362
Web Site: www.hfma.org
Members: 32000 individuals
Staff: 80
Annual Budget: $10-25,000,000
President and Chief Executive Officer: Richard L. Clarke, FHFMA
E-Mail: dclarke@hfma.org
Director, Professional Development: Joseph Abel
E-Mail: Jabel@hfma.org
Director, Chapter Relations: Eileen M. Crow
E-Mail: Ecrow@hfma.org
Senior Vice President: Edwin C. Czopek
E-Mail: Eczopek@hfma.org
Assistant to the President: Heather Etheridge
Editor in Chief: Rob Fromberg
Vice President, Product Development: Richard Gundling
E-Mail: rgunding@hfma.org
Vice President, Marketing and Business Development: Lee Guthrie
Controller: Daniel Johansson
E-Mail: Djohansson@hfma.org
Director, Information Technology: Daniel E. Keck
E-Mail: Dkeck@hfma.org
Director, Research and Development: Janice Wiitala
E-Mail: jwiitala@hfma.org

Historical Note
Formerly (1946) the American Association of Hospital Accountants and (1982) the Hospital Financial Management Association. Offers designation of Fellow and Certified Healthcare Financial Professional. Members are directly or indirectly associated with financial management in healthcare organizations in the U.S., Canada, and several other countries, and belong to one of 70 local chapters. Membership: $215/year.

Meetings/Conferences:
Annual Meetings: June/1,500

Publications:
Healthcare Financial Management. m. adv.
Patient Accounts. m.

Healthcare Information and Management Systems Society *(1961)*
230 E. Ohio St., Suite 500
Chicago, IL 60611-3269
Tel: (312)664-4467 *Fax:* (312)664-6143
E-Mail: himss@himss.org
Web Site: www.himss.org
Members: 13000 individuals
Staff: 70
Annual Budget: $10-25,000,000
President and Chief Executive Officer: H. Stephen Lieber
Director, Information Technology: Jeremy Landfare
Director, Federal Affairs: Thomas A. Leary, MALA
Vice President, Meeting Services: Karen Malone
Executive Vice President and Chief Operating Officer: R. Norris Orms, CAE
Director, Member Relations: Erica Pantuso
Vice President, Communications: Fran Peveiler
Vice President, Government Relations: David Roberts
Vice President, Education: Margaret F. Schulte, DBA, FACHE
Senior Vice President and Chief Financial Officer: Marcia Zitowski

Historical Note
Formerly (1987) Hospital Management Systems Society HIMSS provides leadership in health care for the management of systems, information and change. Members include CIO's, Information Systems, Management Engineering, Clinical Systems, and Telecommunications. Absorbed CPRI-HOST, a health care information technology advocacy organization, in 2002. Membership: $110/year; (individual members); $195/year (foreign membership).

Meetings/Conferences:
Annual Meetings: February-March
2007 – New Orleans, LA/Feb. 25-March 1
2008 – Orlando, FL/Feb. 24-28

Publications:
The Journal of Healthcare Information Management. q.
Compensation Survey. a.
Leadership Survey: Trends in Health Care Information Systems. a.
HIMSS Insider.
Advocacy Dispatch and Standards Insight.
Proceedings of Annual Conference. a.
HIMSS eNews. w.

Healthcare Leadership Council *(1990)*
1001 Pennsylvania Ave. NW, Suite 550 South
Washington, DC 20004
Tel: (202)452-8700 *Fax:* (202)296-9561
Web Site: www.hlc.org
Members: 50 individuals
Staff: 16
President: Mary Grealey
Vice President, Communications: Michael V. Freeman
Vice President, Finance and Administration: David Wiermanski

Historical Note
A coalition of health care providers including physicians, health insurers, hospitals, pharmceutical companies, and medical technology firms. Affiliated with the National Committee for Quality Healthcare.

Healthcare Marketing and Communications Council *(1934)*
1525 Valley Center Pkwy., Suite 150
Bethlehem, PA 18017-2279
Tel: (610)868-8299 *Fax:* (610)868-8387
E-Mail: mary@hmc-council.org
Web Site: www.hmc-council.org
Members: 1500 individuals
Staff: 5
Annual Budget: $500-1,000,000
Executive Director: Mary Lacquaniti
E-Mail: mary@hmc-council.org

Historical Note
Founded as Pharmaceutical Advertising Club; later became Pharmaceutical Advertising Council, and assumed its current name in 1995. Membership, concentrated in the mid-Atlantic region, consists of marketing and communications professionals serving the health care industry. Membership: $150/year.

Meetings/Conferences:
Monthly Meetings: various mid-Atlantic locations (8/year)

Publications:
HMC News. 9/year.
Membership Directory. a. adv.

Hearing Industries Association *(1955)*
515 King St., Suite 420
Alexandria, VA 22314-3103
Tel: (703)684-5744 *Fax:* (703)684-6048
Web Site: www.hearing.org
Members: 34 companies
Staff: 4
Annual Budget: $1-2,000,000
President: Carole M. Rogin
Director, Government Relations: Andrew Bopp
Director, Member Services: Elizabeth Hawkins

Historical Note
Formerly (1977) the Hearing Aid Industry Conference.

Meetings/Conferences:
Annual Meetings: February/100
2007 – Key Largo, FL(Ocean Reef Club)/Feb. 14-17

Publications:
HIA Update. m.

Heart Rhythm Society *(1979)*
1400 K St. NW, Suite 500
Washington, DC 20005
Tel: (202)464-3400 *Fax:* (202)464-3401
Web Site: www.hrsonline.org
Members: 3500 individuals
Staff: 25
Annual Budget: $5-10,000,000
Chief Executive Officer: James H. Youngblood
First Vice President and Secretary: Bruce D. Lindsay

Historical Note
Founded (1979) as the North American Society of Pacing and Electrophysiology; became Heart Rhythm Society in 2003. An organization of physicians, scientists and allied professionals thoughout the world dedicated to the study and management of cardiac arrhythmias, NASPE is an international leader in science, education and advocacy for cardiac arrhyhmia professionals and patients, and a primary source of information on heart rhythm disorders. NASPE's mission is to improve the care of patients by promoting research, education and optimal healthcare policies and standards.

Meetings/Conferences:
Annual Meetings: Spring/5,000

Publications:
Heart Rhythm Journal.

Hearth Patio & Barbecue Association *(1980)*
1901 N. Moore St., Suite 600
Arlington, VA 22209-2105
Tel: (703)522-0086 *Fax:* (703)522-0548
E-Mail: hpba@hpba.org
Web Site: www.hpba.org
Members: 2600 companies
Staff: 24
Annual Budget: $2-5,000,000
Director, Communications: Leslie G. Wheeler
Comptroller/Executive Administrator: Cathy Centra
E-Mail: centra@hpba.org
Director, Government Affairs and General Counsel: Jack Goldman
E-Mail: goldman@hpba.org
Director, Market Research: Donald Johnson
E-Mail: johnson@hpba.org
Director, Hearth Education: Susan Kalish
E-Mail: hpba@hpba.org
Director, Advertising and Sales: Betteanne Leahy
E-Mail: leahy@hpba.org
Director, Meetings and Expositions: Kelly Van Denmark
Director, Communications: Leslie G. Wheeler

Historical Note
Founded as Hearth Products Association; merged (2001) with Barbecue Industry Association and assumed its current name at the same time. Represents and promotes the interests of the hearth, barbecue and patio products industries in North America. HPBA's members include manufacturers, retailers, distributors, manufacturers' representatives, and other firms and individuals involved in these industries.

Meetings/Conferences:
Annual Meetings: Spring/9,000

Publications:
HPA Membership Directory. a. adv.

Heat Exchange Institute *(1933)*
1300 Sumner Ave.
Cleveland, OH 44115-2851
Tel: (216)241-7333 *Fax:* (216)241-0105
E-Mail: hei@heatexchange.org
Web Site: www.heatexchange.org
Members: 20 companies
Staff: 3
Annual Budget: $50-100,000
Secretary-Treasurer: John H. Addington

Historical Note
Members are manufacturers of heat exchange and/or vacuum apparatus such as steam jet ejectors, steam surface condensers, closed feedwater heaters, power plant heat exchangers, and deaerators.

Meetings/Conferences:
Annual Meetings:

Heavy Duty Brake Manufacturers Council
P.O. Box 13966
Research Triangle Park, NC 27709-3966
Tel: (919)549-4800 *Fax:* (919)549-4824
Members: 10 companies
Staff: 2
Executive Director: Timothy R. Kraus

Historical Note
A product line group of Motor and Equipment Manufacturers Association. Coordinates research in heavy duty brake standards and testing procedures.

Heavy Duty Business Forum *(1977)*
P.O. Box 13966
Research Triangle Park, NC 27709-3966
Tel: (919)549-4800 *Fax:* (919)549-4824
E-Mail: hdma@mema.org
Members: 50 individuals
Staff: 2
Annual Budget: $50-100,000
Executive Director: Timothy R. Kraus

Historical Note
A discussion group affiliated with the Heavy Duty Manufacturers Association, concerned with issues affecting makers of manufacturers of products for Class 6, 7, and 8 trucks. Membership, by invitation only, is composed of top-level management and marketing executives and is limited to fifty members. Membership: $450/year.

Heavy Duty Manufacturers Association *(1982)*
P.O. Box 13966
Research Triangle Park, NC 27709-3966
Tel: (919)406-8808 *Fax:* (919)549-4824
E-Mail: info@hdma.org
Web Site: www.hdma.org
Members: 120 companies
Staff: 3
Annual Budget: $2-5,000,000
Managing Director: Timothy R. Kraus

Historical Note
HDMA is the one of the market segment associations of the Motor and Equipment Manufacturers Association. HDMA was formed in 1982 to provide a focus on issues involving manufacturers of components and equipment for class 6, 7 and 8 trucks, buses and off-road equipment. Membership: $900-17,000/year, based on annual sales volume.

Meetings/Conferences:
Annual Meetings: March, and Biennial Heavy Duty Dialogue Conference in February.

Publications:
Heavy Duty Newsletter. 6/year.
Heavy Truck Maintenance in the USA. a. adv.
Diesel Download (electronic). bi-w.

Heavy Duty Representatives Association *(1974)*
4015 Marks Road, Suite 2B
Medina, OH 44256
Tel: (330)725-7160 *Fax:* (330)722-5638
Toll Free: (800)763 - 5717
E-Mail: TruckSvc@aol.com
Web Site: www.hdra.org
Members: 70 companies
Staff: 1
Annual Budget: $25-50,000
Executive Director: Cara R. Giebner

Historical Note
Independent sales agents, representing manufacturers of parts, equipment and accessories for the heavy-duty vehicle, and equipment market. Associate membership open to manufacturers in the heavy-duty trucking industry.

Publications:
Between the Lines. m.

Hebrew Actors Union *(1887)*
31 E. Seventh St.
New York, NY 10003
Tel: (212)674-1923
Members: 225 individuals
Staff: 3
Annual Budget: $10-25,000
President: Bernard Sauer

Historical Note
An autonomous branch union of Associated Actors and Artists of America. An affiliate of the AFL-CIO. Membership: $20/year.

Meetings/Conferences:
Semi-annual Meetings: New York, NY in March and September/60-100

Helicopter Association International *(1948)*
1635 Prince St.
Alexandria, VA 22314-2818
Tel: (703)683-4646 *Fax:* (703)683-4745
Toll Free: (800)435 - 4976
Web Site: www.rotor.com
Members: 1400 individuals
Staff: 33
Annual Budget: $5-10,000,000
President: Matthew Zuccaro
Chief Financial Officer: Henry J. D'Souza
E-Mail: henry.d'souza@rotor.com
Vice President, Information Systems: Edward DiCampli
E-Mail: ed.dicampli@rotor.com
Director, Marketing and Expositions: Marilyn F. McKinnis
E-Mail: marilyn.mckinnis@rotor.com
Executive Vice President and Corporation Secretary: Elizabeth W. Meade
E-Mail: elizabeth.meade@rotor.com
Director, Communications/Editor: Martin Pociask
E-Mail: marty.pociask@rotor.com

Historical Note
Began as the California Helicopter Association with seven charter members. Became the Helicopter Association of America in 1951 and assumed its present name in 1981. Now has an international membership from over 70 countries. Membership consists of companies that own and operate helicopters for hire, use helicopters for private and corporate transport and helicopters in public service. Associate members are manufacturers and servicers to the industry. Membership: annual dues vary, based on helicopter fleet size (regular); annual dues vary, based on company's gross revenue (associate); $60/year (individual sustaining); $60/year (pilot/mechanic/technician); $35/year (student).

Meetings/Conferences:
Annual Meetings: Winter/14,000-15,000

Publications:
Maintenance Update. q.
Preliminary Accident Reports. q.
Helicopter Annual. a. adv.
Operations Update. m.
Rotor Magazine. q. adv.

Hellenic-American Chamber of Commerce *(1947)*
960 Avenue of the Americas
New York, NY 10001
Tel: (212)629-6380 *Fax:* (212)564-9281
E-Mail: hellenicchamber-nyc@att.net
Web Site: www.hellenicamerican.cc
Members: 250 companies
Executive Secretary: Stamatis Gikas
E-Mail: hellenicchamber-nyc@att.net

Meetings/Conferences:
Annual Meetings: Annual Meeting in October held in New York City.

Help Desk Institute *(1989)*
6385 S. Tejon, Suite 1200
Colorado Springs, CO 80903
Tel: (719)268-0174 *Fax:* (719)268-0184
Toll Free: (800)248 - 5667
E-Mail: support@thinkhdi.com
Web Site: www.thinkhdi.com/
Members: 5300 individuals
Founder and Chief Executive Officer: Ron Muns
E-Mail: support@thinkhdi.com

Historical Note
Institute members are software support sites and professionals involved in the provision of telephonic software support services. Membership: $275/year (individual); $495/year (organization/company).

Publications:
Practice Report. a.
Salary Survey. a.
Support World. bi-m. adv.
Focus Book Series. q.

Herb Growing & Marketing Network *(1990)*
P.O. Box 245
Silver Spring, PA 17575-0245
Tel: (717)393-3295 *Fax:* (717)393-9261
E-Mail: herbworld@aol.com
Web Site: www.herbworld.com
Members: 2000 companies/individuals
Staff: 3
Annual Budget: $100-250,000
Director: Maureen Rogers
E-Mail: herbworld@aol.com

Historical Note
HGMN was designed to provide practical information on all segments of the industry with an emphasis on marketing and locating wholesale sources. Members are growers, distributors, retailers and suppliers of materials to the industry. Membership: $95/year; $110/year (outside North America).

Publications:
Busine$s Herbal Connection Newsletter. m.
Herbal Green Pages. a. adv.

Herpetologists' League *(1936)*
c/o Dr. Lora Smith
P.O. Box 519
Bainbridge, GA 39818
Tel: (229)246-7374 *Fax:* (229)734-6650
E-Mail: hleague@bellsouth.net
Web Site: www.inhs.uiuc.edu/cbd/HL/HL.html
Members: 1400 individuals and institutions
Staff: 1
Annual Budget: $100-250,000
Treasurer: Dr. Lora Smith
E-Mail: lsmith@jonesctr.org

Historical Note
International membership organization. Fosters the study of the biology of amphibians and reptiles. Regular membership: $50/year (individual), $300/year (organization).

Meetings/Conferences:
Annual Meetings: Summer

Publications:
Herpetologica. q.
Herpetological Monographs. a.

High Speed Ground Transportation Association *(1983)*

Historical Note
Address unknown in 2006.

High Technology Crime Investigation Association
4021 Woodcreek Oaks Blvd., Suite 156, #209
Roseville, CA 95747
Tel: (916)408-1751 *Fax:* (916)408-7543
Web Site: www.htcia.org
Members: 3000 individuals
Staff: 2
Annual Budget: $50-100,000
Executive Secretary: Carol Hutchings
E-Mail: exec_secty@htcia.org

Historical Note
HTCIA members are law enforcment professionals and corporate security with an interest in the application of technology to criminal and civil investigations. Membership: $50/year.

Meetings/Conferences:
Annual Meetings: Fall

Hispanic Association of Colleges and Universities *(1986)*
8415 Data Point Dr., Suite 400
San Antonio, TX 78229
Tel: (210)692-3805 *Fax:* (210)692-0823
E-Mail: hacu@hacu.net
Web Site: www.hacu.net
Members: 200 colleges and universities
Staff: 31
Annual Budget: $2-5,000,000
President and Chief Executive Officer: Antonio R. Flores, Ph.D.
Director, Membership: Donna Fiedler Arrendondo
Director, Conferences and Special Events: Lilly A. Cardenas
Director, Information Technology: Harold Giese
Chief Financial Officer: Magda Gonzales

Director, Education Collaborative: Rene Gonzalez

Historical Note

Institutions of higher education in the U.S., Puerto Rico, Latin America, and Spain may be eligible to become HACU-member institutions. Membership fee varies based on enrollment: $825-2,200/year.

Meetings/Conferences:

Annual Meetings: October/800

Publications:

The Voice. m. adv.
Annual Report. q.

Hispanic Dental Association *(1990)*
1224 Centre West, Suite 400B
Springfield, IL 62704
Toll Free: (800)852 - 7921
E-Mail: hispanicdental@hdassoc.org
Web Site: www.hdassoc.org
Members: 2500 students and professionals
Staff: 3
Annual Budget: $250-500,000
Executive Director: Rebecca Jeppesen
E-Mail: hispanicdental@hdassoc.org

Historical Note

Membership: $125/year (individual, first-year introductory membership); Student - no fee, sponsored for 2006.

Meetings/Conferences:

Annual Meetings: Typical Attendence: 200

Publications:

HDA News & Reports. q. adv.

Hispanic Elected Local Officials *(1976)*
1301 Pennsylvania Ave. NW, Suite 550
Washington, DC 20004-1763
Tel: (202)626-3169 *Fax:* (202)626-3043
Members: 100 individuals
Annual Budget: under $10,000
Constituency Services: Mary Gordon Gerente

Historical Note

HELO serves as a forum for communication and exchange among Hispanic local government officials within the framework of the National League of Cities. HELO objectives include encouraging participation of Hispanic officials in NLC, identifying qualified Hispanic officials for service in NLC as well as for other national positions, promoting issues of interest to Hispanics, and establishing liaisons with other state and national organizations concerned with municipal government or issues of particular concern to the Hispanic community. Membership: $35-55/year (individual).

Meetings/Conferences:

Annual Meetings: March and December, during Nat'l League of Cities meetings

Publications:

Constituency and Member Group Report. q.
HELO Membership Directory. a.

Hispanic National Bar Association *(1972)*
815 Connecticut Ave. NW, Suite 500
Washington, DC 20006
Tel: (202)223-4777 *Fax:* (202)223-2324
E-Mail: info@hnba.com
Web Site: www.hnba.com
Members: 25000 individuals
Staff: 2
Annual Budget: $100-250,000
Executive Director: Antonio Arocho

Historical Note

Founded in California as La Raza National Bar Association; assumed present name in 1980, and was re-incorporated in Washington, DC in 1983. Members are Hispanic attorneys, judges, law professors and law students. Membership: $20-10,000/year.

Meetings/Conferences:

Annual Meetings: Fall

Publications:

Noticias. q. adv.

Hispanic Organization of Latin Actors *(1977)*
107 Suffolk St., Suite 302
New York, NY 10002
Tel: (212)253-1015 *Fax:* (212)253-9651
E-Mail: holagram@hellohola.org
Web Site: www.hellohola.org
Members: 400 individuals
Staff: 2
Annual Budget: $50-100,000
Executive Director: Manuel Alfaro
E-Mail: holagram@hellohola.org
Special Projects Director: Manuel Herrera
E-Mail: holagram@hellohola.org

Historical Note

HOLA is an arts service organization committed to exploring and expanding available opportunities for projecting Hispanic artists and their culture into the mainstream of Anglo-American industry and culture. Membership: $50/year (individual).

Meetings/Conferences:

Biennial Meetings: January (odd years)

Publications:

For Our Members Only. as needed.
La Nueva Ola Newsletter. q.
Directory of Hispanic Talent. bi-a. adv.

Histochemical Society *(1950)*
P.O. Box 85630, University Station
Seattle, WA 98145-1630
Tel: (206)616-5895 *Fax:* (206)616-5842
E-Mail: mail@histochemcialsociety.org
Web Site: www.histochemicalsociety.org/
Members: 550 individuals
Annual Budget: $50-100,000
Executive Director: William Stahl, Ph.D.

Historical Note

Founded in 1950 and incorporated in 1963 in New York. Affiliated with the International Federation of Socs. for Histochemistry and Cytochemistry. Society members are qualified scientists who employ histochemical and cytochemical techniques in their research. Organization encourages scientific research to advance and promulgate knowledge concerning the interrelationship of chemical constitution and detailed morphologic structure of organisms in normal and pathologic states. Membership: $50/year (individual); $20/year (student).

Meetings/Conferences:

Annual Meetings: Spring

Publications:

Knowledge Base.
Proceedings. a.
The Journal of Histochemistry and Cytochemistry. m. adv.
Newsletter. semi-a.

Historians Film Committee/Film & History *(1970)*
Center for the Study of Film and History
Route Three, Box 80
Cleveland, OK 74020
Tel: (918)243-7637 *Fax:* (918)243-5995
Web Site: www.filmandhistory.org.
Members: 3000 individuals and libraries
Chair: Peter C. Rollins
E-Mail: RollinsPC@aol.com

Historical Note

The Historians Film Committee exists to further the use of film sources in teaching and research, to disseminate information about film and film use to historians and other social scientists, to work for an effective system of film preservation so that scholars may have ready access to film archives, and to organize periodic conferences and seminars dealing with film. HFC is affiliated with the American Historical Society. Membership: $50/year (individual); $80/year (institution).

Meetings/Conferences:

Annual Meetings: in conjunction with AHA, PCA/ACA, and OAH annual meetings

Publications:

Film & History: Interdisciplinary Journal of Film & Television Studies. semi-a.
Research Materials. a.

Historians of American Communism *(1982)*
P.O. Box 1216
Washington, CT 06793
Tel: (860)868-7408 *Fax:* (860)868-0080
Members: 165 individuals
Annual Budget: under $10,000
General Secretary: Daniel Leab

Historical Note

HAC members are academics and others with an interest in the study of American communism. Membership: $32/year (individual/organization/company).

Meetings/Conferences:

Annual Meetings: In conjunction with AHA and OAH

Publications:

HOAC Newsletter. 2/year. adv.
American Communist History journal. 2/year. adv.

Historians of Islamic Art *(1983)*
Asian Art Dept., Brooklyn Museum of Art
200 Eastern Parkway
Brooklyn, NY 11238
Web Site: www.historiansofislamicart.org/
Members: 250 individuals
Secretary/Treasurer: Aimee Froom
E-Mail: Aimee.Froom@brooklynmuseum.org

Historical Note

Formerly North American Historians of Art. HIA members are academics and others with an interest in the study of the art of the Islamic world. Membership: $25/year (regular); $15/year (student); $40/year (couple); $50/year (institution).

Meetings/Conferences:

Annual Meetings: generally in conjunction with CAA or MESA

Publications:

Directory. a.
HIA Newsletter. 2/year.

Historians of Netherlandish Art *(1983)*
23 S. Adelaide Ave.
Highland Park, NJ 08904
Tel: (732)937-8394
E-Mail: rbelkin@aol.com
Web Site: www.hnanews.org
Members: 660 individuals
Staff: 1
Annual Budget: $10-25,000
Administrator: Kristin Lohse Belkin
E-Mail: rbelkin@aol.com

Historical Note

HNA comprises academics, art professionals, publishers and book dealers. Fosters communication and collaboration on the study of northern European Art in the period 1350-1750. Members: $45/year (individual); $100/year institutional); $25/year (student).

Publications:

Directory of Members. quadrenn.
The HNA Newsletter and Review of Books. semi-a.

History of Earth Sciences Society *(1982)*
P.O. Box 455
Poncha Springs, CO 81242
Tel: (719)539-4113 *Fax:* (719)539-4542
Web Site: http://historyearthscience.org
Members: 500 individuals
Annual Budget: $10-25,000
Treasurer: Ed Rogers
E-Mail: erogers@geology-books.com

Historical Note

Seeks to foster the study of all phases of history of the earth sciences. Has no paid officers or full-time staff. Membership: $42/year (individual); $72/year (institution), $47/year (foreign individual); $77/year (foreign institution).

Meetings/Conferences:

Annual Meetings: Summer

Publications:

Earth Sciences History. semi-a.

History of Economics Society *(1972)*
Univ. of New Hampshire, Dept. of Economics
Durham, NH 03824
Tel: (603)862-3336 *Fax:* (603)862-3383
E-Mail: hes@orbit.unh.edu
Web Site: www.eh.net/HE/HisEcSoc
Members: 400 individuals
Annual Budget: $10-25,000
Secretary-Treasurer: Neil Niman
E-Mail: hes@orbit.unh.edu

Historical Note
Membership: $30/year (individual).
Meetings/Conferences:
Annual Meetings: Summer
Publications:
Journal of the History of Economic Thought. semi-a. adv.

History of Education Society *(1960)*
220 McKay Educational Building
Slippery Rock Univ.
Slippery Rock, PA 16057-1326
Tel: (724)738-4557 *Fax:* (724)738-4548
Web Site: www.sru.edu/depts/scc/hes/heshome.htm
Members: 600 individuals
Staff: 2
Annual Budget: $50-100,000
Journal Editor: Richard J. Altenbaugh
Historical Note
For the advancement of interest, study, and research in the history of education. Membership: $40/year (individual), $57/year (institution).
Meetings/Conferences:
Annual Meetings: Fall
Publications:
History of Education Quarterly. q. adv.
The Network. m.

History of Science Society *(1924)*
P.O. Box 117360
3310 Turlington Hall, University of Florida
Gainesville, FL 32611-7360
Tel: (352)392-1677 *Fax:* (352)392-2795
E-Mail: info@hssonline.org
Web Site: www.hssonline.org
Members: 3000 individuals and institutions
Staff: 3
Annual Budget: $250-500,000
Executive Director: Robert J. Malone
Historical Note
Founded in 1924 to foster interest in the history of science and its social and cultural relations. Member society of the American Council of Learned Societies. Membership: $91/year (individual); $30/year (student and retired); $429/year (institution).
Meetings/Conferences:
Annual Meetings: Fall
Publications:
Guide to the History of Science. trien. adv.
Isis. q. adv.
HSS Newsletter. q. adv.
Osiris. a. adv.
Current Bibliography. a.

Hobby Manufacturers Association *(2005)*
P.O. Box 315
Butler, NJ 07405-0315
Tel: (973)283-9088 *Fax:* (973)838-7124
E-Mail: info@hmahobby.org
Web Site: www.hmahobby.org
Members: 260 companies
Staff: 3
Annual Budget: $100-250,000
Executive Director: Patricia S. Koziol
Historical Note
Serves the model hobby industries. HMA members include manufacturers, distributors and publishers involved in the industry. Membership: $200-1500/year.
Meetings/Conferences:
Annual Meetings: Fall/20,000
Publications:
Newsletter. q.

Hoist Manufacturers Institute *(1968)*
Historical Note
An affiliate of Material Handling Industry of America, which provides administrative support.

Holistic Dental Association *(1980)*
P.O. Box 151444
San Diego, CA 92175
E-Mail: info@holisticdental.org
Web Site: www.holisticdental.org
Members: 200 individuals
Staff: 1
Annual Budget: $25-50,000
Executive Director: Dr. R.S. Shepard
E-Mail: info@holisticdental.org
Historical Note
Members are dentists and other health professionals with an interest in a holistic approach to the practice of dentistry. Membership: $250/year (dental practitioner); $50/year (dental student); $125/year (others).
Meetings/Conferences:
Annual Meetings: Spring
Publications:
Communicator Newsletter. q. adv.

Holstein Association USA *(1885)*
One Holstein Place
Brattleboro, VT 05302-0808
Tel: (802)254-4551 *Fax:* (802)254-8251
Toll Free: (800)952 - 5200
E-Mail: info@holstein.com
Web Site: www.holsteinusa.com
Members: 30000 individuals
Staff: 140
Annual Budget: $10-25,000,000
Chief Executive Officer and Executive Secretary: John M. Myer
E-Mail: info@holstein.com
Historical Note
Formerly (1988) Holstein-Friesian Association of America, (1994) Holstein Association U.S.A. Members are breeders of Holstein dairy cattle. Member of the National Pedigreed Livestock Council. Has an annual budget of approximately $15 million. Membership: $25/year.
Meetings/Conferences:
2007 - Knoxville, TN/June 23-26
Publications:
The Holstein Pulse. q.

Home Baking Association *(1943)*
2931 S.W. Gainsboro Road
Topeka, KS 66614-4413
Tel: (785)478-3283 *Fax:* (785)478-3024
Web Site: www.homebaking.org
Members: 38 companies
Staff: 4
Annual Budget: $100-250,000
President: Barbara Heldorf
Historical Note
An association of the millers of wheat flour and corn meal, manufacturers of branded food ingredients used in home baking, and their allied trades formed for the purpose of conducting an educational program on behalf of those products. Formerly Self Rising Flour Institute and (1989) Self-Rising Flour and Corn Meal Program.
Meetings/Conferences:
Annual Meetings: Fall

Home Builders Institute
Historical Note
A subsidiary of the National Association of Home Builders of the U.S.

Home Fashion Products Association *(1968)*
355 Lexington Ave., 17th Fl.
New York, NY 10017-6603
Tel: (212)297-2122 *Fax:* (212)370-9047
Members: 100 companies
Annual Budget: $50-100,000
Executive Director: Carolynn Jennings
Historical Note
Formerly (1981) National Curtain, Drapery, and Allied Products Association. Members are producers of all window and bed decor products and related accessories as included in a curtain or drapery retail assortment. Membership: $200-3,000/year.
Meetings/Conferences:
Semi-annual Meetings: New York, NY (members' showrooms)/Spring and Fall

Home Furnishings International Association *(1923)*
P.O. Box 420807
Dallas, TX 75342-0807
Tel: (214)741-7632 *Fax:* (214)742-9103
Toll Free: (800)942 - 4663
E-Mail: info@hfia.com
Web Site: www.hfia.com
Members: 1800 individuals
Staff: 7
Annual Budget: $2-5,000,000
President: Mary Frye
Director, Membership: Christy Hodges
E-Mail: info@hfia.com
Historical Note
HFIA members are officers, managers, and employees of stores which stock home furnishings for retail sales. Associate members are consulting, design, manufacturing and supplier firms; affiliate members are individuals with an interest in the industry. Membership: $180/year, minimum; $320/year (associate); $180/year (affiliate).
Meetings/Conferences:
Annual Meetings: January and July Markets
Publications:
Home Furnishings Review. m. adv.

Home Healthcare Nurses Association *(1999)*
228 Seventh St. SE
Washington, DC 20003
Tel: (202)546-7424 *Fax:* (202)547-3540
E-Mail: hhna_info@nahc.org
Web Site: www.hhna.org
Members: 800 individuals
Staff: 1
Annual Budget: $100-250,000
Executive Director: Marcia Barnett
E-Mail: hhna_info@nahc.org
Historical Note
HHNA promotes the specialty of home healthcare nursing. Administrative support provided by National Association for Home Care. Membership: $100/year.
Meetings/Conferences:
Annual Meetings: Spring
Publications:
HHNA Forum. q. adv.
Home Healthcare Nurse. m. adv.

Home Improvement Research Institute *(1981)*
3922 Coconut Palm Dr.
Tampa, FL 33619
Tel: (813)627-6750 *Fax:* (813)627-7063
Web Site: www.hiri.org
Members: 80 companies
Staff: 3
Annual Budget: $500-1,000,000
Managing Director: Fred Miller
Senior Research Analyst: Richard Johnston
Historical Note
Formerly (1990) the Do-It-Yourself Research Institute. Members are manufacturers, wholesalers and retailers, trade associations and trade publications involved in the home improvement market (e.g. home repair and renovation, landscaping/gardening, etc.). Membership: $10,000/year.
Meetings/Conferences:
Annual Meetings: Spring/Fall
2007 - Adelphi, MD(Marriott)/Apr. 25- /125
Publications:
News Update. m.
Size of Industry Study. 2/year.
Home Improvement Market: A Reference Guide. a.
Remodeler Study. bien.
E-Business Tracking Study. a.
Product Purchase Tracking Study. bien.

Home Sewing Association *(1928)*
P.O. Box 1312
Monroeville, PA 15146-5712
Tel: (412)372-5950 *Fax:* (412)372-5953
E-Mail: info@sewing.org
Web Site: www.sewing.org
Members: 900 companies
Staff: 4
Annual Budget: $1-2,000,000
Executive Director: Joyce Perhac
E-Mail: info@sewing.org

Historical Note
Formerly (1976) the National Notion Association; a new National Notion Association was incorporated at this time with different objectives, and a separate organization called the National Home Sewing Association (NHSA) was formed. In 1978 NHSA merged with the American Home Sewing Council to create American Home Sewing Association; became American Home Sewing and Craft Association in 1990. Absorbed the International Sewing Machine Association in 1996; assumed its current name in 1997. Members are manufacturers of all types of home sewing items, as well as fabric stores, wholesalers and chains. Affiliate members include manufacturers' representatives, educators, and buying offices. Associate members include manufacturers of display equipment and supplies. Membership: varies according to sales volume or number of stores.

Meetings/Conferences:
Semi-Annual Meetings: Spring and Fall(Trade Show)/4,000
2007 - Las Vegas, NV(Rio Hotel)/Sept. 18-20/1500

Publications:
Trade and Show Journal semi-a.. adv. adv.
HSA Connections. bi-m.

Home Wine and Beer Trade Association *(1979)*
P.O. Box 1373
Valrico, FL 33595
Tel: (813)685-4261 *Fax:* (813)681-5625
E-Mail: hwbta@aol.com
Web Site: www.hwbta.org
Members: 300 individuals
Staff: 1
Annual Budget: $50-100,000
Executive Director: Dee Roberson
E-Mail: hwbta@aol.com

Historical Note
HWBTA members are manufacturers, distributors, retailers, and others with an interest in the home brewing/home winemaking trade. Membership: $100/year (retailer); $500/year (wholesaler/manufacturer).

Meetings/Conferences:
Annual Meetings: Summer

Publications:
HWBTA Advocate Newsletter. q. adv.

Homeland Security Industries Association *(2003)*
666 11th St. NW, Suite 315
Washington, DC 20001
Tel: (202)331-3096 *Fax:* (202)331-8191
E-Mail: info@hsianet.org
Web Site: www.hsianet.org
Members: 400 companies
Staff: 7
Executive Officer: Steve Ellis
E-Mail: info@hsianet.org

Hoo-Hoo International

Historical Note
See International Concatenated Order of Hoo-Hoo.

Hop Growers of America *(1956)*
P.O. Box 9218
Yakima, WA 98909
Tel: (509)248-7043 *Fax:* (509)248-7044
E-Mail: doug@usahops.org
Web Site: www.usahops.org
Members: 240 growers, state associations
Staff: 2
Annual Budget: $100-250,000
Executive Director: Douglas MacKinnon
E-Mail: doug@usahops.org

Historical Note
HGA provides marketing statistics, promotion, and research to U.S. hop growers, and serves as liaison between its membership and the world brewing industry. Membership is concentrated in Washington, Oregon, and Idaho. Membership: $100/year (full member); associate memberships available.

Meetings/Conferences:
Annual Meetings: Winter

Publications:
Newsletter. m. adv.

Horizontal Earth Boring Equipment Manufacturers Council

Historical Note
A council of the Equipment Manufacturers Institute.

Horticultural Research Institute *(1962)*
1000 Vermont Ave., NW, Suite 300
Washington, DC 20005
Tel: (202)789-5980 Ext: 3014 *Fax:* (202)741-4852
Web Site: www.anla.org/research
Members: 255 companies 25 associations
Staff: 2
Annual Budget: $250-500,000
Program Administrator: Teresa Jodon
E-Mail: tjodon@anla.org

Historical Note
The research arm of the American Nursery and Landscape Association, HRI promotes, directs, publishes and funds environmental horticultural research to benefit the nursery and landscape industry. Membership: $200/year (individual); $300/year (association).

Meetings/Conferences:
Annual Meetings: July, with American Nursery and Landscape Ass'n

Publications:
New Horizons Newsletter. bi-a.
Journal of Environmental Horticulture. q.

Hosiery Association, The *(1905)*
3623 Latrobe Dr., Suite 130
Charlotte, NC 28211
Tel: (704)365-0913 *Fax:* (704)362-2056
E-Mail: hosieryTHA@aol.com
Web Site: www.hosieryassociation.com
Members: 420 manufacturers
Staff: 8
Annual Budget: $1-2,000,000
President: Sally Kay
Director, Sales: Mike Austell
Executive Assistant: Jeanna Sheldon
Vice President: Sheila Simpson

Historical Note
Founded as the National Association of Hosiery Manufacturers, assumed its present name in 1999. Manufacturers of hosiery as well as suppliers of raw materials, machinery and packaging. Members make and distribute more than 85% of U.S. hosiery, including socks and pantyhose.

Publications:
Directory of Hosiery Manufacturers, Distributors and Suppliers. a. adv.
Hosiery News. m. adv.
Hosiery Insider.
Hosiery: The Opportunity Industry.

Hospice and Palliative Nurses Association *(1986)*
One Penn Center West Suite 229
Pittsburgh, PA 15276
Tel: (412)787-9301 *Fax:* (412)787-9305
E-Mail: hpna@hpna.org
Web Site: www.hpna.org
Members: 8000 individuals
Staff: 15
Annual Budget: $500-1,000,000
Chief Executive Officer: Judy Lentz
Director, Membership: Deena Butcher
Office Manager: Amy Kellmeyer
Director, Education/Research: Dena Jean Sutermaster

Historical Note
Formerly (1997) the Hospice Nurses Association, HPNA members are members of the nursing team specializing in hospice and palliative care. Associate members are professionals, para-professionals, and/or volunteers engaged in or interested in palliative and hospice care. Membership: $85/year RN (voting); $45/year (Senior RN); $85/year (associate); $70/year (LPN/LVN); $35/year (nursing ass't.); $45/year (student nurse).

Meetings/Conferences:
2007 - Salt Lake City, UT(Salt Palace Convention Center)/Feb. 14-17/2000

Publications:
Hospice and Palliative Core Curriculum.
Statement of the Scope and Standards of Hospice and Palliative Nursing.
Competencies of Non-Cancer Diagnosis.
Competencies for All Levels of Nursing.
Journal of Hospice & Palliative Nursing. bi-m. adv.

Hospice Association of America *(1985)*
228 Seventh St. SE
Washington, DC 20003
Tel: (202)546-4759 *Fax:* (202)547-9559
Web Site: www.hospice-america.org
Members: 2800 hospices
Executive Director: Janet E. Neigh

Historical Note
HAA members are hospices, related healthcare organizations, and medical professionals.

Meetings/Conferences:
Annual Meetings: in conjunction with NAHC/Fall and Educational Conference/Feb.

Publications:
Hospice Forum Newsletter. bi-w. adv.

Hospital Presidents Association *(1983)*
801 Main St., Suite Nine
Concord, MA 01742
Tel: (978)369-1290 *Fax:* (978)369-5101
Members: 55 individuals
Annual Budget: $25-50,000
President: Joel P. Davidson

Historical Note
HPA is an educational association dedicated to the design and presentation of programs for the most advanced practitioners of health care management among the Chief Executive Officers of hospitals in the U.S. and abroad. Has no paid officers or full-time staff. Membership: $500/year.

Hospitality Financial and Technology Professionals *(1952)*
11709 Boulder Lane, Suite 110
Austin, TX 78726
Tel: (512)249-5333 *Fax:* (512)249-1533
Toll Free: (800)646 - 4387
E-Mail: hftp@hftp.org
Web Site: www.hftp.org
Members: 4000 individuals
Staff: 20
Annual Budget: $1-2,000,000
Chief Executive Officer and Executive Vice President: Frank I. Wolfe, CAE
E-Mail: frank.wolfe@hftp.org
Director, Communications: Eliza Selig

Historical Note
HFTP is a professional society for finanical and technology personnel working in hotels, resorts, clubs, casinos, restaurants, and other hospitality-related businesses. Founded (1952) as the National Association of Hotel Accountants, it later became the National Association of Hotel-Motel Accountants and then (1975) the International Association of Hospitality Accountants; assumed its current name in 1997. Provides continuing education and networking opportunities to more than 4,000 members around the world, and produces the hospitality shows HITEC and OHNTEC. Also administers the examination, and awards the certification, for the Certified Hospitality Account Executive (CHAE) and Certified Hospitality Technology Professional (CHTP) designations. Membership: $295/year (individual; includes affiliation with one chapter).

Meetings/Conferences:
Annual Meetings: Fall

Publications:
Bottomline. bi-m. adv.

Hospitality Institute of Technology and Management *(1980)*
670 Transfer Road, Suite 21-A
St. Paul, MN 55114
Tel: (651)646-7077 *Fax:* (651)646-5984
Web Site: www.hi-tm.com
Members: 25 individuals
Staff: 3
President: Oscar P. Snyder, Jr., Ph.D.
E-Mail: osnyder@hi-tm.com

Historical Note
Members are professionals involved in all aspects of commercial and non-commercial foodservice systems. Membership: $60/year (individual); $525/year (corporation).

Meetings/Conferences:
Annual Meetings: Spring

Publications:
Journal of Foodservice Systems. q. adv.

Hospitality Sales and Marketing Association International *(1927)*
8201 Greensboro Dr., Suite 300
McLean, VA 22102
Tel: (703)610-9024 *Fax:* (703)610-9005
E-Mail: info@hsmai.org
Web Site: www.hsmai.org
Members: 7000 individuals
Staff: 12
Annual Budget: $2-5,000,000
President and Chief Executive Officer: Robert Gilbert, CHME, CHA
Director, Development: Melanie Penoyar
E-Mail: fbrasseux@hsmai.org
Vice President, Communications: Jason Smith
Associate Executive Director: Ilsa Whittemore

Historical Note
Formerly (1983) Hotel Sales Management Association International and (1992) Hotel Sales and Marketing Association International. Awards the CHME (Certified Hospitality Marketing Executive) designation. Membership: $295/year (individual).

Publications:
HSMAI Update. m.
HSMAI Marketing Review. q.

Hotel Brokers International *(1959)*
1420 N.W. Vivion Road, Suite 111
Kansas City, MO 64118-4511
Tel: (816)505-4315 *Fax:* (816)505-4319
E-Mail: info@hotelbrokersintl.org
Web Site: www.hbihotels.com
Members: 145 individuals
Staff: 2
Annual Budget: $500-1,000,000
Managing Director: Glenda Webb

Historical Note
Founded as the Motel Brokers of America; became the American Hotel and Motel Brokers in 1984, Hotel-Motel Brokers of America in 1985, and assumed its present name in 2001. Members are real estate agents specializing in the sale of motel and hotel properties. Membership: $550/year (individual); $5,160/year (company).

Meetings/Conferences:
Semi-Annual Meetings: Winter/Summer
2007 – Las Vegas, NV(Harrah's)/Jan. 30-Feb. 1/75

Publications:
TransActions by HBI. a.
Innside Issues. q.

Hotel Electronic Distribution Network Association *(1991)*
7600 Leesburg Pike, Suite 430
Falls Church, VA 22043
Tel: (703)970-2070 *Fax:* (703)970-4488
E-Mail: info@hedna.org
Web Site: www.hedna.org
Members: 200 corporations
Staff: 4
Executive Director: Heidi S. Gallacher
E-Mail: info@hedna.org

Historical Note
HEDNA sponsors educational seminars and other events to promote the use of electronic booking systems in the hospitality industry.

Meetings/Conferences:
Annual Meetings: Spring

Hotel Employees and Restaurant Employees International Union *(1891)*

Historical Note
Merged with UNITE in 2004 to form UNITE HERE

Household Goods Forwarders Association of America *(1962)*
5904 Richmond Highway, Suite 404
Alexandria, VA 22303
Tel: (703)317-9950 *Fax:* (703)317-9960
E-Mail: info@hhgfaa.org
Web Site: www.hhgfaa.org/
Members: 1600 companies
Staff: 5
Annual Budget: $2-5,000,000
President: Terry Head
General Manager: Bel Carrington
E-Mail: terryhead@look.net

Historical Note
Active members (86) are companies transporting household goods by the door-to-door container method for the Department of Defense, national accounts and individuals. Associate members (1500) are suppliers and related organization, here and abroad. Membership: $250/month (active); $500/year (associate).

Meetings/Conferences:
Annual Meetings: Fall/1,000

Publications:
e-Portal Electronic News.
The Portal Magazine. bi-m.

Housing Education and Research Association *(1965)*
Montana State Univ. Extension
P.O. Box 173580
Bozeman, MT 59717-3580
Tel: (406)994-3451 *Fax:* (406)994-5417
Web Site: www.housingeducators.org
Members: 70 libraries
Staff: 1
Annual Budget: $10-25,000
Executive Director: Michael Vogel

Historical Note
Founded as American Association of Housing Educators; assumed its current name in 2003. Members are educators, researchers, and policy makers.

Meetings/Conferences:
Annual Meetings: Oct./100

Publications:
Housing and Society Journal. 2/year.
In House Newsletter. q. adv.

Human Behavior and Evolution Society *(1988)*
836 Oldfather Hall, Univ. of Nebraska
Lincoln, NE 68588-0368
Tel: (402)472-6240 *Fax:* (402)472-9642
Web Site: www.hbes.com
Treasurer: Raymond Haymes

Historical Note
HBES is an interdisciplinary organization founded to promote the exchange of ideas and research findings using evolutionary theory to better understand human nature. Has no paid officers or full-time staff. Membership: $60/year (individual); $35/year (student).

Publications:
Evolution and Human Behavior.
Newsletter. q.

Human Biology Association *(1974)*
Ohio Univ., Dept. of Social Medicine
309 Grosvenor Hall
Athens, OH 45701
Tel: (740)593-2128 *Fax:* (740)593-1730
E-Mail: iceg@ohio.edu
Web Site: www.humbio.org
Members: 300 individuals
Staff: 1
Annual Budget: $25-50,000
Secretary/Treasurer: Gillian H. Ice
E-Mail: iceg@ohio.edu

Historical Note
Formerly (1995) Human Biology Council. HBA promotes research and teaching in human biology and related fields, encourages communication and utilization of results obtained from such research, stimulates discussion among human biologists, and aids in the training of persons engaged in scholarly research in the human biological disciplines. Council members are physical anthropologists, medical doctors, dentists, public health officers, geneticists, nutritionists and related professions. Membership: $80/year (fellow); $40/year (student).

Meetings/Conferences:
Annual Meetings: Spring

Publications:
American Journal of Human Biology. bi-m. adv.

Human Factors and Ergonomics Society *(1957)*
P.O. Box 1369
Santa Monica, CA 90406-1369
Tel: (310)394-1811 *Fax:* (310)394-2410
E-Mail: info@hfes.org
Web Site: www.hfes.org
Members: 4800 individuals
Staff: 6
Annual Budget: $1-2,000,000
Executive Director: Lynn Strother

Historical Note
Established (1957) in Tulsa, OK, HFES is a multidisciplinary society whose members are engaged in research on problems of the safety, comfort and convenience of people in the environment. Formerly known as the Human Factors Society of America and then the Human Factors Society (1992). Membership: $180/year (individual); $35/year (student).

Meetings/Conferences:
Annual Meetings:
2007 – Baltimore, MD(Baltimore Waterfront Marriott)/Oct. 1-5
2008 – New York, NY/Sept. 22-26

Publications:
Cumulative Index (online).
Human Factors. q.
Proceedings of Annual Meeting. a.
Bulletin. m. adv.
Ergonomics in Design. q. adv.
Journal of Cognitive Engineering and Decision Making. a.

Human Resource Planning Society *(1977)*
317 Madison Ave., Suite 1509
New York, NY 10017
Tel: (212)490-6387 *Fax:* (212)682-6851
E-Mail: info@hrps.org
Web Site: www.hrps.org
Members: 3500 individuals
Staff: 7
Annual Budget: $1-2,000,000
President and Chief Executive Officer: Walter J. Cleaver
Manager, Communications: Lisa Boyd
Director, Marketing and Programs: Dillian Waldron

Historical Note
Manpower planning and development specialists, staffing analysts, business planners and others concerned with planning for employee recruitment, development and utilization. Membership: $200/year (individual); $1,500/year (organization); $1,000/year (research sponsor).

Meetings/Conferences:
Annual Meetings: Spring

Publications:
Human Resource Planning. q.
Membership Directory. a.
Research Symposium Proceedings. bi-a.
Case Studies of HR Planning Practice. irreg.

Hungarian-U.S. Business Council *(1974)*

Historical Note
A program of U.S. Chamber of Commerce, which provides administrative support.

Hybrids and Manufacturing Technology Components Society

Historical Note
A subsidiary of the Institute of Electrical and Electronics Engineers. Membership in the Society, open only to IEEE members, includes subscription to a technical periodical in the field published by IEEE. All administrative support is provided by IEEE.

Hydraulic Institute *(1917)*
Nine Sylvan Way
Parsippany, NJ 07054-3802
Tel: (973)267-9700 *Fax:* (973)267-9055
Web Site: www.pumps.org
Members: 98 manufacturers of pumps

Staff: 8
Annual Budget: $1-2,000,000
Executive Director: Robert K. Asdal
Controller: Laura DiPrimo
Events and Education: Valerie Reid
E-Mail: vreid@pumps.org
Member Services and Communications: Mary Silver

Historical Note
Members of the Hydraulic Institute are major United States pump manufacturers. HI develops and disseminates standards for the industry, encourages continued technical development, and pursues appropriate activities in support of the industry. Membership: dues based on company revenue.

Meetings/Conferences:
Annual Meetings: February

Publications:
Pump Forum Newsletter. 3/year.
Pump Standards.
Engineering Data Book.
Membership Directory. a.

Hydronics Institute Division of GAMA *(1915)*
2107 Wilson Blvd., Suite 600
Arlington, VA 22201
Tel: (908)464-8200 *Fax:* (908)464-7818
Web Site: www.gamanet.org
Members: 63 companies
Staff: 4
Annual Budget: $500-1,000,000
Office Manager: Janine Brady
E-Mail: information@gamanet.org

Historical Note
Merger (1970) of Better Heating-Cooling Council (1950) and Institute of Boiler and Radiator Manufacturers (1915). Became a division of the Gas Appliance Manufacturers Association in 1995. The Institute is a trade association of manufacturers of hydronic heating and cooling equipment including boilers, various types of heating units, their accessories and controls.

Meetings/Conferences:
Semi-Annual Meeting: Absecon, NJ(Seaview Country Club)/October

---

Hydroponic Merchants Association *(1997)*
10210 Leatherleaf Court
Manassas, VA 20111-4245
Tel: (703)392-5890 *Fax:* (703)257-0213
E-Mail: info@hydromerchants.org
Web Site: www.hydromerchants.org
Members: 191 companies
Staff: 5
Annual Budget: $50-100,000
Executive Officer: Robert C. LaGasse, CAE

Historical Note
HMA addresses the needs of retail, manufacturing, wholesale and other interests in the hydroponic industry. Membership: $250/year (company).

Meetings/Conferences:
Annual Meetings: June

Publications:
HMA Newsletter. q. adv.
Membership Directory. a.
Industry and Market Surveys. irreg.

Hydroponic Society of America *(1978)*
P.O. Box 1183
El Cerrito, CA 94530-1183
Tel: (650)968-4070 *Fax:* (650)968-4051
Web Site: www.hsa.hydroponics.org
Members: 700companiesandindividuals
Staff: 1
Annual Budget: $50-100,000
Operations Manager: Dan Lubkeman
E-Mail: justdan@slip.net

Historical Note
Organized to promote the development of hydroponics, i.e., the growing of plants in nutrient solutions, without soil. Membership: $40/year (North America); $60/year (outside North America); $250/year (corporation); $20/year (student).

Meetings/Conferences:
Annual Meetings: Spring

Publications:
Newsletter. bi-m. adv.
Conference Proceedings. a.
Directory.

IBFI, The International Association for Document and Information Management Solutions *(1953)*

Historical Note
Absorbed by Document Management Industries Ass'n in 2003.

ICAAAA Coaches Association *(1919)*
3927 Benton St. NW
Washington, DC 20007
Tel: (202)965-1907 *Fax:* (202)466-8987
Members: 115 schools
Staff: 1
Annual Budget: under $10,000
Secretary-Treasurer: Walter Krolman
E-Mail: wjjk3927@juno.com

Historical Note
Track and field coaches from eastern colleges and universities affiliated with the Intercollegiate Association of Amateur Athletes of America (ICAAAA). Has no paid staff. Membership: $15/year (individual).

Meetings/Conferences:
Three Meetings Annually: March, May and September

Ice Skating Institute *(1959)*
17120 Dallas Pkwy., Suite 140
Dallas, TX 75248-1187
Tel: (972)735-8800 *Fax:* (972)735-8815
Web Site: www.skateisi.com
Members: 60000 individuals
Staff: 13
Annual Budget: $2-5,000,000
Executive Director: Peter Martell
Managing Director, Member Services/Programs: Patti Feeney

Historical Note
Membership comprised of ice rink owners, operators, instructors, builders/suppliers, skaters and retail shops. Sponsors educational seminars and judge's certification, as well as the annual World Recreational Team Championships in August, an annual Winter Classic in January, ISI Synchronized Skating Championships in April, ISI Adult Championships in September, the trade show/conference (listed below), and consumer shows in conjunction with the national skating events. Membership: $7/year (individual); $55/year (associate); $275/year (ice rink); $425/year (builder/supplier).

Meetings/Conferences:
Annual Meetings: May

Publications:
Directory. a. adv.
Resreational Ice Skating. q. adv.
ISI EDGE. bi-m. adv.

Icelandic American Chamber of Commerce *(1986)*
c/o Consul General of Iceland
800 Third Ave., 36th Fl.
New York, NY 10022-7604
Tel: (212)593-2700 *Fax:* (212)593-6269
E-Mail: info@icelandtrade.com
Web Site: www.icelandtrade.com
Members: 110 companies
Staff: 1
Annual Budget: $25-50,000
Executive Director: Petur Oskarsson

Historical Note
Facilitates businesses relationships between Iceland and U.S. firms. Membership: $60/year (individual), $200/year (company).

Publications:
Newsletter. q.

ICOM, International Communications Agency Network *(1950)*
P.O. Box 490
Rollinsville, CO 80474
Tel: (303)258-9511 *Fax:* (303)484-4087
E-Mail: burandt@icomagencies.com
Web Site: www.icomagencies.com
Members: 80 agencies
Staff: 2
Annual Budget: $250-500,000
Executive Director: Gary Burandt

Historical Note
Chartered in California as the National Federation of Advertising Agencies. Changed its name to International Federation of Advertising Agencies in 1979, to the International Communications Agency Network in 1998, and assumed its present name in 1999. Members are non-competing local advertising agencies, about 32% of which are American. Membership: $1,500-5,000/year (.0009% of annual revenue).

Meetings/Conferences:
Annual Meetings: Spring

Publications:
Newsletter. m.
Membership Directory. a.
Client Directory. a.

IDEA, The Health and Fitness Association *(1982)*
10455 Pacific Center Ct.
San Diego, CA 92121-4339
Tel: (858)535-8979 *Fax:* (858)535-8234
Toll Free: (800)999 - 4332 Ext: 7
E-Mail: contact@ideafit.com
Web Site: www.ideafit.com
Members: 20000 individuals
Staff: 40
Chief Executive Officer: Peter Davis
E-Mail: davisp@ideafit.com
Vice President, Marketing: Bernie Schroder
Chief Operating Officer: Rick Schwartz
E-Mail: schwartzr@ideafit.com

Historical Note
Formerly (1990) International Dance-Exercise Association, (1993) IDEA: The Association for Fitness Professionals, (1997) IDEA,The International Association of Fitness Professionals and then IDEA, The Health and Fitness Association before assuming its current name. Since 1982, this organization has provided health and fitness professionals with unbiased data, pertinent information, education resources, career development resources, and industry leadership. IDEA's membership includes personal trainers, program and fitness directors, business owners and managers, and group fitness instructors.

Meetings/Conferences:
Three Meetings Annually: Winter, Spring, and Summer

Publications:
IDEA Fitness Manager. 5/year.
IDEA Trainer Success. 5/year. adv.
IDEA Fitness Journal. 10/year. adv.

IEEE - Nuclear and Plasma Sciences Society *(1963)*

Historical Note
A technical society of the Institute of Electrical and Electronics Engineers (IEEE). Membership in the Society, open only to IEEE members, includes subscription to technical periodicals in the field published by IEEE. All administrative support provided by IEEE.

IEEE Circuits and Systems Society

Historical Note
A technical society of the Institute of Electrical and Electronics Engineers (IEEE). Membership in the Society, open only to IEEE members, includes a subscription to a technical periodical in the field published by IEEE. All administrative support is provided by IEEE.

IEEE Communications Society *(1952)*
Three Park Ave.
New York, NY 10017
Tel: (212)705-8900 *Fax:* (212)702-8999
E-Mail: webmaster@comsoc.org
Web Site: www.comsoc.org
Members: 50000 individuals
Staff: 20
Annual Budget: $10-25,000,000
Executive Director: Jack Howell
E-Mail: j.howell@comsoc.org

Historical Note
A subsidiary of the Institute of Electrical and Electronics Engineers, ComSoc members are industry professionals with a common interest in

communications technologies. Membership in the Society is open only to IEEE members. Administrative support is provided by IEEE.

Publications:
IEEE/ACM Transactions on Networking Journal. bi-m.
IEEE Communications Magazine. m. adv.
IEEE Network, The Magazine of Computer Communications. q.
IEEE Personal Communications: Nomadic Communications & Computing. bi-.
Journal on Selected Areas in Communications. 9/year.
Transactions on Communications Journal. m.

IEEE Computer Society *(1946)*
1730 Massachusetts Ave. NW
Washington, DC 20036-1992
Tel: (202)371-0101 *Fax:* (202)728-9614
Web Site: www.computer.org
Members: 95000 individuals
Staff: 127
Annual Budget: $25-50,000,000
Executive Director: David W. Hennage, Ph.D.
Director, Administration: Violet S. Doan

Historical Note
IEEE membership represents nearly 100,000 of the world's computer professionals. Two out of five members live and work outside the United States in 150 countries. The Computer Society generates a diverse array of 20 application and research oriented periodicals, publishes a variety of books, and holds as many as 150 conference proceedings per year. Programs in education, accreditation, standards, and technical activities are also services provided to members and the profession. Offices include: Washington, DC; Los Alamitos, CA; Tokyo, Japan. Other service centers include: Beijing, China; Moscow, Russia. Membership: $76/year (Society only); $124-146/year (IEEE and Society membership).

Meetings/Conferences:
Annual Meetings: The Computer Society organizes more than 125 conferences, symposia, and technical workshops each year throughout the world.

Publications:
IEEE Transactions on Computational Biology and Bioinformatics. q.
IEEE Security and Privacy. bi-m.
IT Professional. bi-m. adv.
IEEE Intelligent Systems. bi-m. adv.
IEEE Internet Computing. bi-m. adv.
IEEE Transactions on Multimedia. q.
IEEE Transactions on Visualization and Computer Graphics. q.
Computer Magazine. m. adv.
IEEE Design & Test. q. adv.
IEEE Computer Graphics & Applications. bi-m. adv.
IEEE MICRO. bi-m. adv.
IEEE SOFTWARE. bi-m. adv.
IEEE Transactions on Computers. m.
IEEE Transactions on Knowledge and Data Engineering. bi-m.
IEEE Transactions on Networking KS. bi-m.
IEEE Transactions on Parallel and Distributed Systems. m.
IEEE Transactions on Pattern Analysis and Machine Intelligence. m.
IEEE Transactions on Software Engineering. q.
IEEE Transactions on VLSI. q.
IEEE Annals of the History of Computing. q.
IEEE Computing in Science & Engineering. q. adv.
IEEE Multimedia. q. adv.

IEEE Consumer Electronics Society *(1965)*
Historical Note
A technical society of the Institute of Electrical and Electronics Engineers (IEEE). Membership in the Society, open only to IEEE members, includes a subscription to a technical periodical in the field published by IEEE. All administrative support is provided by IEEE.

IEEE Control Systems Society *(1954)*
Historical Note
A technical society of the Institute of Electrical and Electronics Engineers (IEEE). Membership in the Society, open only to IEEE members, includes a subscription to a technical periodical in the field published by IEEE. All administrative support is provided by IEEE.

IEEE Council on Superconductivity *(1987)*
Historical Note
A technical society of the Institute of Electrical and Electronics Engineers (IEEE). Membership in the Society, open only to IEEE members, includes subscription to a technical periodical in the field published by IEEE. All administrative support is provided by IEEE.

IEEE Education Society *(1963)*
Historical Note
A technical society of the Institute of Electrical and Electronics Engineers (IEEE). Membership in the Society, open only to IEEE members, includes a subscription to a technical periodical in the field published by IEEE. Administrative support provided by IEEE.

IEEE Electromagnetic Compatibility Society *(1957)*
Historical Note
A technical society of the Institute of Electrical and Electronics Engineers (IEEE). Membership in the Society, open only to IEEE members, includes a subscription to a technical periodical in the field published by IEEE. All administrative support is provided by IEEE.

IEEE Industry Applications Society
799 N. Beverly Glen
Los Angeles, CA 90077
Tel: (310)446-8370 *Fax:* (310)446-8390
Web Site: www.ewh.ieee.org/soc/ias
Members: 11500 individuals
Staff: 2
Annual Budget: $500-1,000,000
Administrator: Robert Myers

Historical Note
IAS members are individuals interested in the global development, design, manufacture and application of electrical systems, apparatus, devices and controls to the processes and equipment of industry and commerce; the promotion of safe, reliable and economic installations; industry leadership in energy conservation and environmental, health and safey issues; the creation of voluntary engineering standards and recommended practices; and professional development. IAS is a technical society of the Institute of Electrical and Electronics Engineers (IEEE). Membership in IAS is open only to IEEE members.

Meetings/Conferences:
Annual Meetings: Fall

Publications:
Industry Applications Magazine. bi-m. adv.
Transactions on Industry Applications Journal. m.

IEEE Instrumentation and Measurement Society *(1950)*
799 N. Beverly Glen
Los Angeles, CA 90077
Tel: (310)446-8280 *Fax:* (310)446-8390
Web Site: www.ewh.ieee.org/soc/im
Members: 6500 individuals
Staff: 2
Annual Budget: $500-1,000,000
Executive Director: Robert Myers

Historical Note
The I&M Society is a technical society of the Institute of Electrical and Electronics Engineers (IEEE). Provides support to scientists and technicians working in the design and development of electrical and electronic instruments and equipment to measure, monitor, and/or record physical phenomena of all types. Membership: $18/year (IEEE members).

Meetings/Conferences:
Annual Meetings: Spring

Publications:
IEEE Instrumentation & Measurement Magazine. bi-m. adv.
Transactions on Instrumentation and Measurement. bi-m.

IEEE Magnetics Society *(1964)*
2025 M St. NW, Suite 800
Washington, DC 20036
Tel: (202)973-8676 *Fax:* (202)973-8722
E-Mail: Magsoc@courtesyassoc.com
Web Site: www.ieeemagnetics.org/
Members: 3500 individuals
Annual Budget: $500-1,000,000
Executive Director: Diane Melton
E-Mail: Magsoc@courtesyassoc.com

Historical Note
Members are interested in theory, design and applications of magnetic materials and devices. A technical society of the Institute of Electrical and Electronics Engineers (IEEE). Membership in the Society is open only to IEEE members. Administrative support is provided by IEEE.

Publications:
IEEE Transactions on Magnetics. bi-m. adv.

IEEE Microwave Theory and Techniques Society
Eight Richard Rd.
Bedford, MA 01730
Tel: (781)258-5494 *Fax:* (781)275-8179
Web Site: www.mtt.org
Members: 9000 individuals
Administrator: Richard A. Sparks

Historical Note
A technical society of the Institute of Electrical and Electronics Engineers (IEEE). Membership in the Society, open only to IEEE members, includes a subscription to a technical periodical in the field published by IEEE. All administrative support provided by IEEE.

Publications:
MTT-S Newsletter. q.
IEEE Microwave & Guided Wave Letters. m.
Journal of Solid-State Circuits. m.
Journal of Lightwave Technology. m.
Transaction on Applied Superconductivity. q.
Transactions on Very Large Scale Integration Systems.
IEEE Transactions on Microwave Theory and Techniques Journal. m.

IEEE Power Electronics Society *(1987)*
799 N. Beverly Glen
Los Angeles, CA 90077
Tel: (310)466-8280 *Fax:* (310)466-8390
Web Site: www.pels.org/
Members: 5000 individuals
Staff: 3
Annual Budget: $250-500,000
Administrator: Robert Myers

Historical Note
A technical society of the Institute of Electrical and Electronics Engineers. Supports professionals working in the field of power electronics technology, including electronic components, circuit theory and design techniques, and the development of analytical tools for electronic power conversion. Membership: $18/year.

Meetings/Conferences:
Semi-Annual Meetings:
2007 - Orlando, FL
2008 - Rhodes, Greece

Publications:
Transactions on Power Electronics. q.
PELS Newsletter. q.
IEEE Power Electronics Letters (online).

IEEE Power Engineering Society
Historical Note
An affiliate of Institute of Electrical and Electronics Engineers, which provides administrative support.

IEEE Signal Processing Society *(1948)*
P.O. Box 1331
Piscataway, NJ 08855-1331
Tel: (732)562-3888 *Fax:* (732)235-1627
E-Mail: sp.info@ieee.org
Web Site: www.ieee.org/sp/index.html

Members: 20000 individuals
Staff: 12
Annual Budget: $5-10,000,000
Executive Director: Mercy Kowalczyk

Historical Note
Formerly the Acoustics, Speech and Signal Processing Society. Concerned with the theory and application of filtering, coding, transmitting, estimating, detecting, analyzing, recognizing, sythesizing, recording and reproducting signals by digital or analog devices or techniques. SPS is a technical society of the Institute of Electrical and Electronic Engineers (IEEE). Membership: $27/year.

Meetings/Conferences:
Annual Meetings: *Spring*
2007 - Oahu, HI/May 15-19
2008 - Las Vegas, NV/April
2009 - Taipei, Taiwan/April
2010 - Dallas, TX/March

Publications:
Transactions on Audio, Speech and Language Processing. 8/year.
Transactions on Signal Processing Journal. m.
Signal Processing Letters. m.
Transactions on Multimedia. 8/year.
Signal Processing Magazine. bi-m. adv.
Transactions on Image Processing. m.
Journal of Selected Topics in Signal Processing. bi-m.
Transactions on Information Forensics and Security. q.

IEEE Society on Social Implications of Technology
Purdue University
South Bend, IN 46614
E-Mail: kperusich@sbcglobal.net
Web Site: www.ieee.org/ssit/
Members: 2000 individuals
President: Karl Perusich
E-Mail: kperusich@sbcglobal.net

Historical Note
A technical society of the Institute of Electrical and Electronics Engineers (IEEE). Membership includes a subscription to a technical periodical in the field published by IEEE. Has no paid officers or full-time staff.

Publications:
IEEE Technology and Society Magazine. q.

IGAF Worldwide *(1977)*
3235 Satellite Blvd., Bldg. 400 Suite 300
Duluth, GA 30096
Tel: (678)417-7730 *Fax:* (678)999-3959
Toll Free: (800)CPA - IGAF
E-Mail: info@igafworldwide.org
Web Site: www.igafworldwide.org
Members: 150 accounting firms
Staff: 4
Annual Budget: $1-2,000,000
President: Kevin Mead
Marketing and Communications Manager: Debra Helwig

Historical Note
Founded as International Group of Accounting Firms; assumed its current name in 2005. IGAF members are full-service public accountants and chartered accountants.

Publications:
The Exchange. bi-m.

Illuminating Engineering Society of North America *(1906)*
120 Wall St., 17th Fl.
New York, NY 10005-4001
Tel: (212)248-5000 *Fax:* (212)248-5017
Web Site: www.iesna.org
Members: 10000 individuals
Staff: 20
Annual Budget: $2-5,000,000
Executive Vice President: William H. Hanley, CAE
E-Mail: whanley@iesna.org
Marketing: Sue Foley
E-Mail: sfoley@iesna.org
Director, Educational and Tech Development: Rita Harrold
E-Mail: rharrold@iesna.org
IT: Brigitte Houngbedji
E-Mail: bhoungbedji@iesna.org
Director, Member Services: Valerie Landers
E-Mail: vlanders@iesna.org

Historical Note
Organized February 13, 1906, with 178 charter members and incoporated in New York in 1907. Membership: $150/year (individual); $500 1st year (company).

Meetings/Conferences:
Annual Meetings: *Summer/700*

Publications:
Lighting Design and Application. m. adv.
Leukos. q.

Illustrators' Guild

Historical Note
A division of the Graphic Artists Guild Association for free-lance illustrators.

IMAGE Society *(1987)*
P.O. Box 6221
Chandler, AZ 85246-6221
E-Mail: image@asu.edu
Web Site: www.public.asu.edu/~image
Members: 500 individuals
Staff: 1
President: Eric G. Monroe, Ph.D
E-Mail: image@asu.edu

Historical Note
Members are individuals concerned with visual and related simulation technologies and applications.

Meetings/Conferences:
Annual Meetings: *Summer*

Publications:
Resource Guide. a. adv.
Proceedings. a. adv.
Images Newsletter. semi-a. adv.

Imaging Supplies Coalition for International Intellectual Property Protection *(1994)*
P.O. Box 35
Avalon, NJ 08202-0035
Tel: (609)967-3222 *Fax:* (609)967-7011
E-Mail: info@isc-inc.org
Web Site: www.isc-inc.org
Members: 9 companies
Staff: 1
Annual Budget: $100-250,000
President and Chief Executive Officer: William R. Duffy

Historical Note
ISC represents manufacturers, distributors, licensees, and other companies in the imaging industry. Works to eliminate counterfeiting and telemarketing fraud in the imaging supplies industry.

Publications:
ISC Newsletter. q.

Immigration and Ethnic History Society *(1965)*
Univ. of Wisconsin
Dept. of History
River Falls, WI 54022
Tel: (715)425-3164 *Fax:* (715)425-0657
Web Site: www.iehs.org
Members: 800 individuals
Staff: 1
Annual Budget: under $10,000
Secretary: Betty A. Bergland

Historical Note
Historians, sociologists, economists and others interested in immigration to the U.S. and Canada. Affiliated with the American Historical Association and the Organization of American Historians. Membership: $30/year (individual), $15/year (student), $100/year (organization/company).

Meetings/Conferences:
Annual Meetings: *April, with the Organization of American Historians*

Publications:
Immigration and Ethnic History Newsletter. semi-a.
Journal of American Ethnic History. q.

In-Plant Printing and Mailing Association *(1964)*
710 Regency Dr., Suite Six
Kearney, MO 64060
Tel: (816)902-4762 *Fax:* (816)902-4766
E-Mail: ipmainfo@ipma.org
Web Site: www.ipma.org
Members: 1700 individuals
Staff: 5
Annual Budget: $500-1,000,000

Historical Note
Founded as the In-Plant Printing Management Association, it became IPMA-A Graphic Communications Management Association in 1982 and In-Plant Management Association in 1986; assumed its current name in 1994. IPMA is the professional association for corporate publishing (creation, production, distribution) professionals who work for educational institutions, government, and private industry. IMPA exists to provide corporate publishing and distribution professionals the resources to attain greater productivity and cost effectiveness through education, certification and information exchange and to promote the value of in-house publishing and distribution while advocating high ethical standards and environmental and safety awareness. Membership: $160/year (individual); $320/year (vendor/associate).

Meetings/Conferences:
Annual Meetings: *Spring*

Publications:
Perspectives. m. adv.
Inside Edge Magazine. m.

In-Tix

Historical Note
See International Ticketing Association.

Incentive Federation *(1984)*
5008 Castle Rock Way
Naples, FL 34112
Tel: (239)775-7527 *Fax:* (239)775-7537
E-Mail: incentiveFed@aol.com
Web Site: www.incentivecentral.org
Members: 150 companies
Staff: 2
Annual Budget: $100-250,000
Executive Director: Howard C. Henry, CAE
E-Mail: incentiveFed@aol.com

Historical Note
Membership: $100-3,000/year (corporate).

Meetings/Conferences:
Annual Meetings: *usually Spring/New York, NY(Javits Convention Center)*

Publications:
Research Studies. semi-a.
Newsletter. q.

Incentive Manufacturers and Representatives Association *(1963)*
1801 N. Mill St., Suite R
Naperville, IL 60563
Tel: (630)369-7786 *Fax:* (630)369-3773
Toll Free: (888)285 - 4672
Web Site: www.imra1.org
Members: 325 companies
Staff: 4
Annual Budget: $250-500,000
Executive Director: Thomas F. Renk, CAE, CMP
E-Mail: tom@imraorg.net

Historical Note
Formerly (1977) National Premium Manufacturers Representatives, Inc. Members are incentive marketing specialists. Membership: $495/year.

Meetings/Conferences:
Annual Meetings: *Spring*

Publications:
Incentive Manager's Handbook. a.
News and Views. q. adv.
Inside IMRA. m. adv.

Incentive Marketing Association *(1956)*
1801 N. Mill St., Suite R
Naperville, IL 60563
Tel: (630)369-7780 *Fax:* (630)369-3773
Web Site: www.incentivemarketing.org
Members: 400 companies
Annual Budget: $250-500,000
Executive Director: Karen Renk, CAE
E-Mail: karen@incentivemarketing.org
Director, Communications: Patricia Childers

Historical Note
Formerly (1990) the National Premium Sales Executives and (2000) Association of Incentive Marketing. Members are professional premium/incentive marketing executives. Membership: $595/year.

Meetings/Conferences:
Annual Meetings:

Publications:
IMA Newsletter. m.
Directory. a. adv.

INDA, Association of the Nonwoven Fabrics Industry *(1968)*
P.O. Box 1288
Cary, NC 27512
Tel: (919)233-1210 *Fax:* (919)233-1282
E-Mail: rholmes@inda.org
Web Site: www.inda.org
Members: 300 Companies
Staff: 20
Annual Budget: $2-5,000,000
President: Rory Holmes
Director, Finance: Annette Balint
Director, Marketing: Peggy Blake
Coordinator, Education: Deanna Lovell
Director, Government Affairs: Peter C. Mayberry

Historical Note
Formerly (1972) the Disposables Association and (1977) the International Nonwovens and Disposables Association. Suppliers of fibers, adhesives, chemicals, fluff pulp, plastic film and related materials; roll goods producers; machinery and equipment suppliers; finishers and converters; and marketers of finished products. Membership: based upon revenues.

Independent Affiliation of Independent Accounting Firms *(1978)*
9200 S. Dadeland Blvd., Suite 510
Miami, FL 33156-2703
Tel: (305)670-0580 *Fax:* (305)670-3818
Members: 135 companies
Staff: 4
Annual Budget: $1-2,000,000
Executive Director: Arthur D. Goessel, CAE
E-Mail: art@accountants.org

Historical Note
Provides services to a global network of independent accounting firms. Maintains an educational foundation. Membership: $3,750/yr (average); $7,000/yr (maximum).

Meetings/Conferences:
Annual Meetings: May

Publications:
Talent Bank and Resource Guide Internet Site (online). a. adv.
Internat'l Tax Summary (online). a.
Newsletter (online). m.
Membership Directory (online). a.

Independent Armored Car Operators Association *(1971)*
102 E. Ave. J
Lancaster, CA 93535
Tel: (661)726-9864 *Fax:* (661)949-7877
Web Site: www.iacoa.com
Members: 127 companies
Staff: 1
Annual Budget: $100-250,000
Executive Secretary: John Margaritis

Historical Note
IACOA's purpose is to promote the high standards within the entire armored transportation/services industry. Membership: $450/year.

Publications:
IACOA Newsletter. q.

Independent Association of Accredited Registrars
3942 N. Upland St.
Arlington, VA 22207
Tel: (703)533-9539 *Fax:* (703)533-1612
E-Mail: info@iaar.org
Web Site: www.iaar.org
Annual Budget: $50-100,000
Executive Director: Milton M. Bush, J.D., CAE

Independent Association of Questioned Document Examiners *(1969)*
403 W. Washington Ave.
Red Oak, IA 51566-2146
Tel: (712)623-9130
Members: 150 individuals
Public Relations: Robert Larson
E-Mail: robertl@heartland.net

Historical Note
Members are professional examiners of questionned documents.

Meetings/Conferences:
Annual Meetings: Always in September or October.

Publications:
IAQDE Newsletter. m.
IAQDE Journal. q.
IAQDE Membership Directory & Bylaws. a.

Independent Automotive Damage Appraisers Association *(1947)*
P.O. Box 12291
Columbus, GA 31917-2291
Tel: (706)649-9907 *Fax:* (706)569-5173
Toll Free: (800)369 - 4232
E-Mail: admin@iada.org
Web Site: www.iada.org
Members: 108 companies
Staff: 2
Annual Budget: $1-2,000,000
Executive Vice President: John Williams
E-Mail: admin@iada.org

Historical Note
Founded by a group of independent appraisers sponsored and screened in selected areas after World War II by the Association of Casualty and Surety Companies and the Association of Mutual Companies.

Meetings/Conferences:
Annual Meetings: June/200
2007 - Orlando, FL(Omni Resort)/June 14-15/120

Publications:
IADA News. irreg.
IADA Service Directory. a. adv.
Watchline. q.

Independent Bakers Association *(1967)*
P.O. Box 3731
Washington, DC 20007-3212
Tel: (202)333-8190 *Fax:* (202)337-3809
E-Mail: napyle@yahoo.com
Web Site: www.independentbaker.com
Members: 350 companies
Staff: 2
Annual Budget: $250-500,000
President: Nicholas A. Pyle

Historical Note
Members are baking companies not part of any national chain. Sponsors BakePAC, a political action committee.

Meetings/Conferences:
Three Meetings Annually: February, usually in Florida, June in Washington, DC and November, usually in California.

Publications:
The Independent. a.
Regulatory Update. m.

Independent Cash Register Dealers Association

Independent Community Bankers of America *(1930)*
1615 L St. NW
Suite 900
Washington, DC 20036
Tel: (202)659-8111 *Fax:* (202)861-5503
Toll Free: (800)422 - 8439
E-Mail: info@icba.org
Web Site: www.icba.org
Members: 5400 financial institutions
Staff: 180
Annual Budget: $10-25,000,000
President and Chief Executive Officer: Camden R. Fine
Director, Communications: Timothy Cook
Chief Financial Officer: Harold L. DeVries
Director, Legislative Affairs: Ronald K. Ence
Director, IBPAC: Abbey Fox
Bank Operations: Ann Grochala
Director, Education: Gregory Martinson
Senior Vice President, State/Regional Operations: Paul McGuire
Executive Director, Sauk Centre Office: Mark Raitor
Regulatory Counsel: Robert Rowe
Agriculture/Rural America Representative: Mark Scanlan
Director, Marketing: Anthony Sidiropoulos
Executive Vice President and Chief Operating Officer: Karen Thomas
Director, Payments Policy: Viveca Ware

Historical Note
Founded as Independent Bankers Association of America and assumed its present name in 1999. Membership consists of community financial institutions. Supports the Independent Bankers Political Action Committee. Has an annual budget of approximately $13 million. Membership fee based upon the size of the institution.

Meetings/Conferences:
Annual Meetings: Spring

Publications:
The Independent Banker. m. adv.
Washington Weekly Report. w.
Community Bank Director. q.

Independent Computer Consultants Association *(1976)*
11131 S. Towne Square, Suite F
St. Louis, MO 63123-7817
Tel: (314)892-1675 *Fax:* (314)487-1345
Toll Free: (800)774 - 4222
E-Mail: execdirector@icca.org
Web Site: www.icca.org
Members: 1000 companies
Staff: 2
Annual Budget: $250-500,000
Executive Director: Joyce Burkard
E-Mail: execdirector@icca.org

Historical Note
ICCA is a national network of independent computer consultants representing a wide variety of resources serving computer-related needs. ICCA's goal is to support the success of independent computer consultants in providing professional services to their clients. Through chapters, educational conferences and programs, government and vendor relations activities, publications and electronic forums, ICCA encourages high standards of performance, increases understanding of computer resources, and enhances recognition of the computer consulting profession. Membership: $175/year (for 1 member firm), $225/year (for 2-9 member firm), $275/year (for 10 member firm).

Meetings/Conferences:
Annual Meetings: Spring

Publications:
The Independent. bi-m. adv.

Independent Cosmetic Manufacturers and Distributors *(1974)*
1220 W. Northwest Hwy.
Palatine, IL 60067-1803
Tel: (847)991-4499 *Fax:* (847)991-8161
Toll Free: (800)334 - 2623
Web Site: www.icmad.org
Members: 750 individuals and companies
Staff: 6
Annual Budget: $500-1,000,000
Executive Director: Penni Jones
E-Mail: pjones@icmad.org

Historical Note
Membership fee based upon annual sales volume.

Meetings/Conferences:
Annual Meetings: June

Publications:
Labeling Guide.
Digest. m.

Independent Distributors Association *(1958)*
13370 Branch View Lane, Suite 175
Dallas, TX 75234-5771
Tel: (972)241-1124 *Fax:* (972)484-3599
E-Mail: info@idaparts.org
Web Site: www.idaparts.org
Members: 450 companies
Staff: 2
Annual Budget: $100-250,000
Executive Director: Nancy Estes

E-Mail: info@idaparts.org

Historical Note

Formerly (1987) Associated Independent Distributors. Manufacturers and distributors of replacement parts for construction equipment.

Meetings/Conferences:

Annual Meetings: Fall/450

Publications:

Universal. bi-m.

Independent Distributors of Electronics Association

6312 Darlington Ave.
Buena Park, CA 90621
Tel: (714)670-0200 *Fax:* (714)670-0201
E-Mail: info@IDofEA.org
Web Site: www.idofea.org

Historical Note

IDEA members are companies that sell electronic components.

Independent Educational Consultants Association *(1976)*

3251 Old Lee Hwy., Suite 510
Fairfax, VA 22030
Tel: (703)591-4850 *Fax:* (703)591-4860
Toll Free: (800)808 - 4322
E-Mail: info@iecaonline.com
Web Site: www.iecaonline.com
Members: 600 individuals
Staff: 6
Annual Budget: $1-2,000,000
Executive Director: Mark H. Sklarow
E-Mail: msklarow@iecaonline.com
Manager, Member Services: Janice Berger
E-Mail: janice@iecaonline.com
Manager, Communications: Sarah Brachman
E-Mail: sarah@iecaonline.com
Director, Conference and Information Services: Susan Studnicki

Historical Note

IECA was founded as a non-profit professional association of established educational consultants. To be eligible for membership, individuals must have a master's degree or comparable training, a minimum of three years experience in the profession, extensive campus visits, and professional references, and meet IECA's professional standards and subscribe to its Principles of Good Conduct. Membership: $600/year (professional member); $300/year (associate member); $60/year (student).

Meetings/Conferences:

Semi-Annual Meetings: Spring and Fall.
2007 – Boston, MA(Westin Copley Place)/Apr. 25-28/1300
2007 – Los Angeles, CA(Hollywood Renaissance)/Nov. 6-10/1200

Publications:

Conference Directory. semi-a. adv.
Information Bulletin. q.
IECA Directory. a.
Newsletter. m. adv.

Independent Electrical Contractors *(1957)*

4401 Ford Ave., Suite 1100
Alexandria, VA 22302
Tel: (703)549-7351 *Fax:* (703)549-7448
Toll Free: (800)456 - 4324
E-Mail: info@ieci.org
Web Site: www.ieci.org
Members: 3200 companies/75 chapters
Staff: 11
Annual Budget: $2-5,000,000
Chief Executive Officer and Executive Vice President: Lawrence W. Mullins
Vice President, Apprenticeship and Training: Robert W. Baird
E-Mail: bbaird@icci.org
Vice President, Member and Chapter Development: Mark Crowley
Director, Finance: Marilyn Myers
Vice President, Government Affairs: Brian Worth

Historical Note

Formerly (1981) Associated Independent Electrical Contractors of America. A federation of state and local groups promoting the common business interests of the electrical construction industry, particularly the independent electrical contractor. Membership: $195/year (individual); $100/year (company).

Publications:

IEC Magazine. bi-m. adv.
Executive Exchange. m.

Independent Feature Project *(1979)*

104 W. 29th St., 12th Fl.
New York, NY 10001-5310
Tel: (212)465-8200 *Fax:* (212)465-8525
Web Site: www.ifp.org
Members: 3800 individuals
Staff: 5
Annual Budget: $1-2,000,000
Executive Director: Michelle Byrd
E-Mail: mbyrd@ifp.org
Senior Director Finance and Operations: Mitchell Micich
E-Mail: mmicich@ifp.org

Historical Note

IFP members are independent feature film directors and producers. Membership: $65/year (student); $100/year (individual).

Meetings/Conferences:

Annual Meetings: September-October

Publications:

Filmmaker. q. adv.

Independent Film and Television Alliance *(1980)*

10850 Wilshire Blvd., Ninth Floor
Los Angeles, CA 90024-4321
Tel: (310)446-1000 *Fax:* (310)446-1600
E-Mail: info@ifta-online.org
Web Site: www.ifta-online.org
Members: 170 companies
Staff: 30
Annual Budget: $5-10,000,000
President and Chief Executive Officer: Jean M. Prewitt
Vice President, Research and Publications: William Anderson
Vice President and General Counsel: Susan Cleary
Vice President, Finance: Robert Newman
Executive Vice President: Jonathan Wolf

Historical Note

Founded as American Film Marketing Association; became AFMA in 1997 and assumed its current name in 2004. Member companies are engaged in the international distribution, marketing, production or financing of independently-produced motion pictures and television programming. IFTA fosters the interests of its members in areas of copyright protection and trade barrier problems, and operates the American Film Market in November of each year in Santa Monica, CA. Membership: $6,000/year.

Meetings/Conferences:

Semi-annual meetings: Meeting in September, and Film Market in November

Publications:

IFTA Bulletin. w.
Fact Book. a.

Independent Forest Products Association

Historical Note

Merged with Northwest Forestry Association and became American Forest Resource Council in 2000.

Independent Free Papers of America *(1980)*

107 Hemlock Dr.
Rio Grande, NJ 08242
Tel: (609)886-0141 *Fax:* (609)889-8359
Toll Free: (800)441 - 4372
Web Site: www.ifpa.com
Members: 347 free newspapers
Staff: 1
Annual Budget: $250-500,000
Executive Director: Gary Rudy
E-Mail: gary@ifpa.com

Historical Note

Publishers of locally distributed and independently owned free circulation shopping guides and community newspapers. Membership: $75/year.

Meetings/Conferences:

Semi-Annual Meetings:

Publications:

The Independent Publisher. m. adv.

Independent Insurance Agents and Brokers of America *(1896)*

127 S. Peyton St.
Alexandria, VA 22314-2803
Toll Free: (800)221 - 7917
E-Mail: info@iiaba.org
Web Site: www.independentagent.com
Members: 25000 agencies
Staff: 75
Annual Budget: $10-25,000,000
Chief Executive Officer: Robert Rusboldt
E-Mail: info@iiaba.org
Assistant Vice President, Federal Government Affairs: John Prible

Historical Note

Formerly (1976) National Association of Insurance Agents, Inc. Supports the National Agents Political Action Committee (Insur-PAC). Membership: dues based on a state-by-state basis.

Meetings/Conferences:

Annual Meetings: Fall/4,000
2007 – Washington, DC(Marriott Wardman Park)/Apr. 25-29

Publications:

Independent Agent Magazine. m. adv.

Independent Investors Protective League *(1970)*

P.O. Box 5031
Ft. Lauderdale, FL 33310
Tel: (954)749-1551 *Fax:* (954)749-1553
Members: 3000 individuals
Staff: 2
Annual Budget: $25-50,000
Executive Vice President: Merrill Sands

Historical Note

Membership: $5/year (individual).

Meetings/Conferences:

Annual Meetings: December

Independent Laboratory Distributors Association

P.O. Box 1464
Fairplay, CO 80440
Tel: (719)836-9091 *Fax:* (719)836-9112
Toll Free: (888)878 - 4532
E-Mail: kbretcko@ilda.org
Web Site: www.ilda.org
Members: 60 companies
Staff: 3
Annual Budget: $50-100,000
Manager: Kathi Bretcko

Historical Note

ILDA is a trade association representing small businessmen (revenues between $500,000 and $40 million) whose primary endeavor is stocking and reselling products used by research, industrial, life science, education and/or government laboratories. Membership: $750/year, varies by annual sales volume (distributor member); $2,000-$3,000/year, varies by annual sales volume (associate member).

Publications:

ILDA Distributor Newsletter. q.
ILDA Update News. m.

Independent Liquid Terminals Association *(1974)*

1444 I St. NW, Suite 400
Washington, DC 20005
Tel: (202)842-9200 *Fax:* (202)326-8660
E-Mail: info@ilta.org
Web Site: www.ilta.org
Members: 75 terminal owners and operators, 300 suppliers
Staff: 7
Annual Budget: $1-2,000,000
President: E. David Doane
E-Mail: ddoane@ilta.org
Director, Meetings and Information Services: Renita Gross
Director, Government Relations and Education Services: Melinda Whitney

Historical Note

Members are firms that are owners and operators of bulk liquid terminals and/or aboveground storage tank facilities; and pipeline companies.

Meetings/Conferences:
Annual Meetings: Conference and trade show in June; membership meeting in November

Publications:
Supplier Member Directory. a.
Terminal Member Directory. a.
Conference & Trade Show brochure. a.
Newsletter. m.
Annual Operating Conference Proceedings. a.

Independent Lubricant Manufacturers Association *(1948)*
651 S. Washington St.
Alexandria, VA 22314
Tel: (703)684-5574 *Fax:* (703)836-8503
E-Mail: ilma@ilma.org
Web Site: www.ilma.org
Members: 295 companies
Staff: 6
Annual Budget: $1-2,000,000
Executive Director: Celeste M. Powers, CAE
Director, Meetings and Communications: Carla Magone

Historical Note
Independent blenders and compounders of lubricants, metalworking fluids, and greases. Originally called the Independent Oil Compounders Association; assumed its current name in 1980. Membership: $1,675/year (regular member); $1,675/year (associate); $1,675/year (international).

Meetings/Conferences:
Semi-annual Meetings: Spring and Fall

Publications:
ILMA FlashPoint. w. adv.
ILMA Compoundings. m. adv.
ILMA Membership Directory. a. adv.

Independent Manufacturers Representative Forum

Historical Note
A forum of the Business Products Industry Association.

Independent Medical Distributors Association *(1978)*
5204 Fairmount Ave.
Downers Grove, IL 60515
Toll Free: (866)463 - 2937
Web Site: www.imda.org
Members: 70 companies
Staff: 4
Annual Budget: $250-500,000
Executive Director: Judith K. Keel

Historical Note
Members are specialty sales and marketing companies that distribute innovative medical technologies. Membership is also open to manufacturers of such medical devices.

Meetings/Conferences:
Annual Meetings: Annual
2007 – Coeur d'Alene, ID(Coeur d'Alene Resort)/June 2-May 5

Publications:
Update. m.

Independent Office Products and Furniture Dealers Association *(1904)*
301 N. Fairfax St., Suite 200
Alexandria, VA 22314-2696
Tel: (703)549-9040 *Fax:* (703)683-7552
Toll Free: (800)542 - 6672
E-Mail: info@iopfda.org
Web Site: www.iopfda.org/
Members: 2000 companies
Staff: 10
Annual Budget: $2-5,000,000
President: Chris Bates
Director, Marketing and Member Services: Melinda Myers
Director, Government Affairs: Michael Ochs

Historical Note
The Independent Office Products and Furniture Dealers Association, formerly the Business Products Industry Association, is the trade association for independent dealers of office products and office furniture. IOPFDA is comprised of two membership divisions: NOPA, the National Office Products Alliance, representing office products dealers and their trading partners, and the OFDA, the Office Furniture Dealers Alliance, representing office furniture dealers and their trading partners.

Meetings/Conferences:
Annual Meetings: Fall

Publications:
Office World News. bi-m. adv.
Office Furniture and Design. bi-m. adv.

Independent Pet and Animal Transportation Association International *(1978)*
745 Winding Trail
Holly Lake Ranch, TX 75765
Tel: (903)769-2267 *Fax:* (903)769-2867
E-Mail: info@ipata.com
Web Site: www.ipata.com
Members: 200 companies
Staff: 1
Annual Budget: $100-250,000
Administrative Coordinator: Cherie Derouin
E-Mail: info@ipata.com

Historical Note
Members are companies providing animal transportation services. Membership: $150/year (organization/company).

Meetings/Conferences:
Annual: Fall
2007 – San Francisco, CA

Publications:
Membership Directory. a.
Paw Prints Newsletter. bi-m.

Independent Petroleum Association of America *(1929)*
1201 15th St. NW, Suite 300
Washington, DC 20005
Tel: (202)857-4722 *Fax:* (202)857-4799
Web Site: www.ipaa.org
Members: 5500 companies
Staff: 25
Annual Budget: $2-5,000,000
President: Barry Russell
Vice President, Government Relations: Lee Fuller
Vice President, Meetings: Tina Hamlin
Vice President, Economics and International Affairs: Fred Lawrence
Vice President, Administration and Chief of Staff: Teresa McCafferty
Vice President, Capital Markets: William Moyer

Historical Note
Members are small producers of oil and natural gas and their suppliers. Sponsors and supports the Independent Petroleum Political Action Committee. Has an annual budget of approximately $3 million.

Meetings/Conferences:
Semi-Annual Meetings::

Publications:
Petroleum Independent. m. adv.

Independent Photo Imagers *(1982)*
405 Capitol St., Suite 910
Charleston, WV 25301
Tel: (304)720-6482 *Fax:* (304)720-6484
E-Mail: info@ipiphoto.com
Web Site: www.ipiphoto.com
Members: 400
Staff: 3
President: Brent Bowyer
E-Mail: info@ipiphoto.com

Historical Note
IPI members are individuals who own independent photofinishing laboratories and imaging businesses at a total of over 520 locations nationwide.

Meetings/Conferences:
Annual Meetings: Annual

Publications:
PMA. a.

Independent Professional Painting Contractors Association of America *(1982)*
P.O. Box 1759
Huntington, NY 11743-0630
Tel: (631)423-3654
Members: 45 companies
Staff: 1
Annual Budget: under $10,000
Executive Director: Heinz K. Hoffmann

Historical Note
Founded to fill the need for an independent painting contractors association, IPPA represents open-shop painting contractors only. Has no paid officers or full-time staff. Membership concentrated in the New York/Long Island metropolitan area. Membership: $125/year (full member); $85/year (associate); $45/year (outside New York metro area).

Meetings/Conferences:
Annual Meetings: Meetings every second Wedneday of the month, except July and August; seminars held quarterly.

Publications:
Independent Brush Stroke. m.

Independent Professional Representatives Organization *(1988)*
34157 W. 9 Mile Road
Farmington Hills, MI 48335
Toll Free: (800)420 - 4268
E-Mail: ray@avreps.org
Web Site: www.avreps.org
Members: 70 individuals
Staff: 2
Annual Budget: $25-50,000
Executive Director: Raymond Wright
E-Mail: ray@avreps.org

Historical Note
Established and incorporated in Missouri, I-PRO members are independent manufacturers' representatives of audio-visual specialty products. Membership: $550/year, average (corporate).

Independent Research Libraries Association *(1972)*
c/o Virginia Historical Society
P.O. Box 7311
Richmond, VA 23221-0311
Tel: (804)342-9656 *Fax:* (804)355-2399
E-Mail: cbryan@vahistorical.org
Web Site: http://irla.lindahall.org
Members: 20 institutions
Annual Budget: under $10,000
President: Charles F. Bryan, Jr.
E-Mail: cbryan@vahistorical.org

Historical Note
Members are independently-supported research libraries that are not part of a larger institution (e.g., a university). Has no paid officers or full-time staff.

Meetings/Conferences:
Annual Meetings:

Independent Scholars of Asia *(1981)*
2321 Russell St., Suite 3-C
Berkeley, CA 94705-1959
Tel: (510)849-3791
Web Site: www.hypersphere.com/isa
Members: 132 organizationsandindividuals
Staff: 4
Annual Budget: under $10,000
National Director: Ruth-Inge Heinze, Ph.D.
E-Mail: riheinze@global.net

Historical Note
A non-profit, non-partisan professional organization affiliated with the Association for Asian Studies. Represents specialists in Asian affairs who prefer to stay independent, are looking for a tenured position in academia, are considering an alternative career, or are planning a career in the field of Asian studies. ISA disseminates information on upcoming events, vacancies, available grants and fellowships, inquiries, reports on research in progress, and book reviews. ISA also maintains a referral file. Has no paid staff. Membership fees: $18/year (general); $12/year (supportive or student); $18/year (organization/company).

Meetings/Conferences:
Annual Meetings: Spring

Publications:
Proceedings of International Conference. a.
Independent Scholars of Asia Newsletter. 3/year.

Independent Sealing Distributors *(1992)*
105 Eastern Ave., Suite 104
Annapolis, MD 21403-3300
Tel: (410)263-1014 *Fax:* (410)263-1659
E-Mail: info@isd.org

Web Site: www.isd.org
Members: 170 companies
Staff: 6
Annual Budget: $250-500,000
Executive Director: Joseph M. Thompson, Jr.
Accounting Manager: Diana J. Crompton, CPA
Membership Development Manager: Amy Luckado
Communications and Conferences Assistant: Lauren Miller
Conference Manager: Aimee Murphy
Director, Conferences and Communications: Kristin B. Thompson
E-Mail: kthompson@isd.org

Historical Note
ISD is an international trade association representing distributors and manufacturers of mechanical and hydraulic seals and gaskets. ISD is a member of the National Association of Wholesaler Distribution (NAW). Membership: $250-1,750/year (corporate).

Meetings/Conferences:
Semi-Annual Meetings: Fall and Spring
2007 – Colorado Springs, CO/Oct. 31-Nov. 2

Publications:
ISD Insider Newsletter. q. adv.
ISD Annual Membership Directory. a. adv.

Independent Sector *(1980)*
1200 18th St. NW, Suite 200
Washington, DC 20036
Tel: (202)467-6100 Fax: (202)467-6101
E-Mail: info@independentsector.org
Web Site: www.independentsector.org
Members: 500 institutions
Staff: 44
Annual Budget: $5-10,000,000
President and Chief Executive Officer: Diana Aviv
Vice President, Finance and Administration: Malvina Kay
Senior Vice President, Public Policy and Government Affairs: Patricia Read
Vice President, Resource Development: Sherry Rockey
Senior Vice President, Nonprofit Sector Programs and Practice: Peter Shirras

Historical Note
Formed by a merger of the Coalition of National Voluntary Organizations and the National Council on Philanthropy. Purpose is to encourage giving, volunteering and not-for-profit initiative.

Meetings/Conferences:
Annual Meetings: Fall/600-800

Publications:
Annual Meetings. a.

Independent Terminal Operators Association *(1970)*
1150 Connecticut Ave. NW, Ninth Floor
Washington, DC 20036-4129
Tel: (202)828-4100 Fax: (202)828-4130
E-Mail: itoa@bode.com
Members: 15 companies
Annual Budget: $10-25,000
Secretary and General Counsel: William H. Bode

Historical Note
Represents independent petroleum distributors. Has no paid officers or full-time staff.

Independent Turf and Ornamental Distributors Association *(1990)*
526 Brittany Dr.
State College, PA 16803
Tel: (814)238-1573 Fax: (814)238-7051
E-Mail: info@itoda.org
Web Site: www.itoda.org
Members: 70 companies
Annual Budget: $50-100,000
Executive Director: Patricia E. Heuser

Historical Note
Members are distributors and manufacturers of turf and lawn equipment and supplies. ITODA provides management training, product line information, and other programs to strengthen the independent distributors position in the marketplace.

Indian Arts and Crafts Association *(1974)*
4010 Carlisle NE, Suite C
Albuquerque, NM 87107
Tel: (505)265-9149 Fax: (505)265-8251
E-Mail: info@iaca.com
Web Site: www.iaca.com
Members: 750 companies and craftpersons
Staff: 4
Annual Budget: $250-500,000

Historical Note
IACA promotes, protects, and preserves Native American Indian arts and crafts. Membership: fees vary.

Meetings/Conferences:
2007 – Albuquerque, NM/March 30-31

Publications:
Newsletter. m. adv.
Directory. a. adv.

Indian Dental Association (USA) *(1983)*
146-02 89th Ave.
Jamaica, NY 11435
Tel: (718)523-8438
Members: 275 individuals
Annual Budget: under $10,000
President: Nilesh Patel

Historical Note
IDA(USA) members are dentists of Asian-Indian heritage.

Publications:
IDA Newsletter Sampark. m. adv.

Indian Educators Federation *(1967)*
2301 Yale Blvd. SE, Suite E-1
Albuquerque, NM 87106
Tel: (505)243-4088 Fax: (505)243-4098
Toll Free: (888)433 - 2382
Web Site: www.ief-aft.org
Members: 800 individuals
Staff: 1
Annual Budget: $100-250,000
President: Patrick Carr

Historical Note
Formerly the National Council of BIA Educators. IEFW members are teachers in schools operated by the Bureau of Indian Affairs. Affiliated with the American Federation of Teachers.

Publications:
Union Educator. m. adv.

Indiana Limestone Institute of America *(1928)*
Stone City Bank Bldg., Suite 400
Bedford, IN 47421
Tel: (812)275-4426 Fax: (812)279-8682
Web Site: www.iliai.com
Members: 85 companies
Staff: 2
Annual Budget: $100-250,000
Executive Director: Jim Owens
E-Mail: jim@iliai.com

Historical Note
Incorporated in 1928, ILI is the successor to the Quarryman's Club, an outgrowth of the Bedford Stone Club, which had been formed for promotional and political reasons. Absorbed the National Association for Indiana Limestone. As now constituted, ILI is the promotional arm of the Indiana Limestone Industry for limestone used as a building product and sets standards of quality and workmanship.

Meetings/Conferences:
Semi-annual Meetings: Spring/Fall

Publications:
Indiana Limestone Handbook. bien.

Indoor Tanning Association
2025 M St. NW, Suite 800
Washington, DC 20036
Toll Free: (888)377 - 0477
Web Site: www.theita.com
Executive Director: John Overstreet

Industrial Asset Management Council *(2002)*
6625 Corners Pkwy., Suite 200
Norcross, GA 30092
Tel: (770)325-3461 Fax: (770)263-8825
E-Mail: iamc@conway.com
Web Site: www.iamc.org
Members: 367 individuals
Staff: 10
Annual Budget: $500-1,000,000
Executive Director: Ronald Starner

Industrial Association of Juvenile Apparel Manufacturers *(1933)*

Historical Note
An affiliate fo United Infants' and Children's Wear Association, which provides administrative support.

Industrial Chemical Research Association *(1985)*
6872 Arlington Dr.
Suite 201
West Bloomfield, MI 48322-2719
Tel: (313)563-0360
Members: 5109 individuals
Staff: 5
Annual Budget: $2-5,000,000
President: Harold Castor

Historical Note
Members are manufacturers, marketers, researchers, formulators, salesmen, executive officers, and suppliers of industrial chemicals united to promote research, safe practices, and increased selling efficiency in the industrial chemical industry. Membership: $175/yr.

Publications:
Newsletter. bi-m.
Bulletin Update. irreg.

Industrial Designers Society of America *(1965)*
45195 Business Court, #250
Dulles, VA 20166
Tel: (703)707-6000 Fax: (703)787-8501
E-Mail: idsa@idsa.org
Web Site: www.idsa.org
Members: 3400 individuals
Staff: 13
Annual Budget: $1-2,000,000
Executive Director: Kristina Goodrich
E-Mail: kristinag@idsa.org
Director, Marketing and Communications: Gigi Jarvis

Historical Note
The product of a merger of American Society of Industrial Designers (1944), Industrial Designers Institute (1938) and Industrial Design Education Association. Membership: $148-238/year, plus chapter dues ($22-55/year).

Meetings/Conferences:
Annual Meetings: Early Fall

Publications:
Innovation: the Journal of IDSA. q. adv.
Design Perspectives. m. adv.

Industrial Diamond Association of America *(1946)*
P.O. Box 29460
Columbus, OH 43229
Tel: (614)797-2265 Fax: (614)797-2264
Web Site: www.superabrasives.org
Members: 190 individuals
Staff: 2
Annual Budget: $100-250,000
Executive Director: Terry M. Kane
E-Mail: Tkane-IDA@insight.rr.com

Historical Note
Members are concerned with industrial diamonds, either as material suppliers, importers, dealers or manufacturers of diamond tools.

Publications:
Finer Points. q. adv.

Industrial Electronics Society *(1974)*

Historical Note
A technical society of the Institute of Electrical and Electronics Engineers (IEEE). Membership in the Society, open only to IEEE members, includes a subscription to a technical periodical in the field published by IEEE. All administrative support is provied by IEEE.

Industrial EMS Society

Historical Note
A division of the National Association of Emergency Medical Technicians.

Industrial Fabrics Association International *(1912)*
1801 County Road B West
Roseville, MN 55113-4061
Tel: (651)222-2508 Fax: (651)631-9334

Toll Free: (800)225 - 4324
E-Mail: generalinfo@ifai.com
Web Site: www.ifai.com
*Members:*2000 companies
Staff: 70
Annual Budget: $5-10,000,000
President: Stephen M. Warner, CAE
E-Mail: smwarner@ifai.com
Vice President, Communications and Publisher: Mary Hennessy
Vice President, Conference Management: Todd V. Lindemann

Historical Note
Founded as the National Canvas Goods Manufacturers Association, it became the Canvas Products Association International in 1956 and assumed its present name in 1980. IFAI is a trade association comprised of fiber producers, weavers, coaters, laminators, finishers, dyers, non-woven producers, and producers of goods made from industrial fabrics. Divisions include The Casual Furniture Fabric Association, Professional Awning Manufacturers Association, Banner, Flag and Graphics Association, Geosynthetic Materials Association, Marine Fabricators Association, Narrow Fabrics Institute, Safety and Protective Products Division, Tent Rental Division, Transportation Division, Truck Cover & Tarp Association, Inflatable Recreational Products Division, Lightweight Structures Association, and United States Industrial Fabrics Institute.

Meetings/Conferences:
Annual Meetings: Fall/6,500

Publications:
Fabric Architecture. bi-m. adv.
IFAI Membership Directory. a. adv.
In Tents. bi-m. adv.
Marine Fabricator. q. adv.
Upholstry Journal. bi-m. adv.
Buyers' Guide. a. adv.
Industrial Fabric Products Review. m. adv.
GFR. m. adv.

Industrial Fasteners Institute *(1931)*
1717 E. Ninth St.
Suite 1105
Cleveland, OH 44114
Tel: (216)241-1482 *Fax:* (216)241-5901
Web Site: www.industrial-fasteners.org
*Members:*125 individuals
Staff: 5
Annual Budget: $1-2,000,000
Managing Director: Robert J. Harris
E-Mail: rharris@indfast.org
Secretary and Treasurer: Jewetta Haselbusch
E-Mail: jhaselbusch@indfast.org
Director, Engineering: Charles J. Wilson
E-Mail: cwilson@indfast.org

Historical Note
An association of leading North American manufacturers of bolts, nuts, screws, rivets and all types of special formed parts. Also, suppliers of equipment, materials and services used in fastener manufacturing.

Meetings/Conferences:
Annual Meetings: Fall and Spring

Publications:
Inch Fastener Standards, 7th Ed.. trien.
Metric Fastener Standards, 3rd Ed.. trien.
Fastener/Fastening Text Book Catalog. a.
Compliance Guide to U.S. Fastener Quality Act of 1999. a.

Industrial Foundation of America *(1960)*
402 E. San Antonio Ave.
Boerne, TX 78006
Tel: (830)249-7899 *Fax:* (800)628-2397
Toll Free: (800)592 - 1433
E-Mail: IFA@ifa-america.com
Web Site: www.ifa-america.com
*Members:*800 organizations
Staff: 6
Annual Budget: $500-1,000,000
Executive Director: William C. Smith, Jr
E-Mail: IFA@ifa-america.com

Historical Note
IFA represents different construction, trucking, oil drilling, retail interests, and medically related services throughout the United States. Services include performing employment screenings and serving as a consumer reporting agency. Membership: $125/year.

Industrial Heating Equipment Association *(1929)*
P.O. Box 54172
Cincinnati, OH 45254
Tel: (513)231-5613 *Fax:* (513)624-0601
E-Mail: ihea@ihea.org
Web Site: www.ihea.org
*Members:*57 companies
Staff: 6
Annual Budget: $100-250,000
Executive Vice President: Anne Goyer

Historical Note
Formerly (1954) Industrial Furnace Manufacturers Association. Members are manufacturers of industrial furnaces, ovens, combustion equipment, induction and dielectric heaters. Membership: $2,500-7,900/year (organization).

Meetings/Conferences:
Annual Meetings: Spring

Publications:
IHEA Newsletter. q.
Legislative and General News Reports. irreg.
Membership and Information Directory. a.
News Compendium. irreg.
Combustion Technology Manual.

Industrial Metal Containers and Wire Decking Product Section

Historical Note
A section of Material Handling Industry of America which provides administrative support.

Industrial Minerals Association - North America *(2002)*
2011 Pennsylvania Ave. NW
Suite 301
Washington, DC 20006
Tel: (202)457-0200 *Fax:* (202)457-0287
E-Mail: info@ima-na.org
Web Site: www.ima-na.org
*Members:*80 companies and organizations
President: Mark G. Ellis

Historical Note
IMA-NA members are companies producing or using ball clay, mica, talc, and related mineral resources in a wide variety of applications.

Industrial Perforators Association *(1961)*
5157 Deerhurst Crescent Cir.
Boca Raton, FL 33486
Tel: (561)447-7511
E-Mail: iperf@iperf.org
Web Site: www.iperf.org
Members: 18 companies
Staff: 2
Annual Budget: $50-100,000
Executive Secretary: Delores Morris
E-Mail: iperf@iperf.org

Historical Note
Members are companies making perforated metal products.

Meetings/Conferences:
Triannual Meetings:

Publications:
Designers Handbook. irreg.

Industrial Research Institute *(1938)*
2200 Clarendon Blvd.
Suite 1102
Arlington, VA 22201
Tel: (703)647-2580 *Fax:* (703)647-2581
Web Site: www.iriinc.org
*Members:*231 companies
Staff: 11
Annual Budget: $2-5,000,000
President: Edward Bernstein

Historical Note
Founded in 1938 under the auspices of the National Research Council and incorporated in New York in 1945. A company-membership association that works to improve the management of technological innovation in industry and to promote interaction among industry, government and academe in science and technology. Membership: $5,600/year (company).

Meetings/Conferences:
Annual Meetings: Spring/500-600
2007 – Rancho Mirage, CA(Rancho Las Palmas Resort)/May 6-9

Publications:
Research Technology Management. bi-m. adv.

Industrial Telecommunications Association

Historical Note
Became Enterprise Wireless Alliance in 2005.

Industrial Truck Association *(1951)*
1750 K St. NW
Suite 460
Washington, DC 20006
Tel: (202)296-9880 *Fax:* (202)296-9884
E-Mail: indtrk@earthlink.net
Web Site: www.indtrk.org
*Members:*22 manufacturers, 60 associated firms
Staff: 5
Annual Budget: $1-2,000,000
Executive Director: William J. Montwieler

Historical Note
Founded as the Electric Industrial Truck Association, it assumed its present name in 1951. Members are manufacturers of powered and non-powered lift trucks as well as their major component suppliers. Membership: $6000-$100,000/year (organization/company).

Meetings/Conferences:
Annual Meetings: Fall/300
2007 – Banff, AB, Canada/Sept. 8-10/300

Publications:
Membership Directory. a.

Industrial/Ag Mower Manufacturers Council

Historical Note
A council of the Equipment Manufacturers Institute.

Industry Coalition on Technology Transfer *(1984)*
1700 K St. NW
Suite 1250
Washington, DC 20006
Tel: (202)282-5994 *Fax:* (202)282-5100
*Members:*3 organizations
Staff: 3
Annual Budget: $25-50,000
Executive Secretary: Eric L. Hirschhorn

Historical Note
ICOTT is composed of trade associations whose members' products and technical data are subject to United States export controls. ICOTT advises U.S. Government officials of industry concerns about export controls.

Industry Council for Tangible Assets *(1983)*
P.O. Box 1365
Severna Park, MD 21146-8365
Tel: (410)626-7005 *Fax:* (410)626-7007
Web Site: www.ictaonline.org
*Members:*450 firms
Staff: 2
Annual Budget: $100-250,000
Executive Director: Eloise Ullman

Historical Note
Promotes the interests of those individuals, partnerships, firms, associations and corporations who are engaged in the business of manufacturing, importing, distributing or selling at retail any tangible asset, including any precious metal, coin, antique or art object. Membership: $300/year minimum (based on sales volume).

Meetings/Conferences:
Annual Meetings: No conventions held - Board of Directors meets three times a year.

Publications:
Washington Wire. q.

Infant and Juvenile Manufacturers Association *(1912)*

Historical Note
Address unknown in 2006.

Infectious Diseases Society of America *(1963)*
66 Canal Center Plaza
Suite 600
Alexandria, VA 22314
Tel: (703)299-0200 *Fax:* (703)299-0204
E-Mail: info@idsociety.org
Web Site: www.idsociety.org
Members: 7600 individuals
Staff: 25
Annual Budget: $5-10,000,000
Executive Director: Mark Leasure
Historical Note
IDSA represents physicians, scientists, and other health care professionals primarily involved with infectious disease treament and related disciplines. Membership: $225/year (domestic); $270/year (overseas); $115/year (member in training).
Meetings/Conferences:
Annual Meetings: Fall/3,500
Publications:
IDSA News. q.
Clinical Infectious Diseases. bi-m. adv.
Journal of Infectious Disease. bi-m. adv.

Inflatable Advertising Dealers Association
136 S. Keowee St.
Dayton, OH 45402
Tel: (937)222-1024 *Fax:* (937)222-5794
E-Mail: info@inflatableads.com
Web Site: www.inflatableads.com
Members: 125 individuals
Staff: 7
Executive Director: Kim Fantaci
E-Mail: info@inflatableads.com
Meetings/Conferences:
Annual Meetings: Winter
Publications:
Air News. bi-m. adv.

Inflatable Boat Association
Historical Note
A division of Industrial Fabrics Association International.

InfoCom International *(1939)*
11242 Waples Mill Road
Suite 200
Fairfax, VA 22030
Tel: (703)273-7200 *Fax:* (703)278-8082
Toll Free: (800)659 - 7469
E-Mail: icia@infocomm.org
Web Site: www.infocomm.org
Members: 2500 companies; 600 associates
Staff: 50
Annual Budget: $10-25,000,000
Executive Director: Randal Lemke
E-Mail: icia@infocomm.org
Historical Note
InfoCom International is a leading international trade association for the professional audiovisual communications industry. The Association produces InfoComm, a leading AV industry trade show. Also manages InfoComm expositions in China, elsewhere in Asia, and Europe. Provides education, certification, information, business tools and networking opportunities for the AV industry worldwide.
Publications:
Compensation and Benefits Survey. a.
Membership Newsletter. 4/year.
InfoComm News and Information Network. online.
Membership Director. a.

Information Processing Administratrators of Large School Systems
Historical Note
IPALSS is a functional affiliate of the International Society for Technology in Education.

Information Storage Industry Consortium *(1991)*
3655 Ruffin Road
Suite 335
San Diego, CA 92123-1833
Tel: (858)279-7230 *Fax:* (858)279-8591
E-Mail: insic@insic.org
Web Site: www.insic.org
Members: 70 companies and organizations
Staff: 6
Executive Director: Paul D. Frank
E-Mail: paul@insic.org
Historical Note
Founded as National Storage Industry Consortium; assumed current name in 2002. INSIC members are computer data storage manufacturers and other companies, universities and government laboratories with an interest in research in the field.
Meetings/Conferences:
Annual Meetings: Summer
2007 – Monterey, CA(Portola Plaza Hotel)/July 15-18

Information Systems Audit and Control Association *(1969)*
3701 Algonquin Road
Suite 1010
Rolling Meadows, IL 60008
Tel: (847)253-1545 *Fax:* (847)253-1443
E-Mail: exec@isaca.org
Web Site: www.isaca.org
Members: 47000 individuals
Staff: 38
Annual Budget: $10-25,000,000
Chief Executive Officer: Susan M. Caldwell
Marketing Manager: Bob Abramson
Chief Financial Officer: Scott Artman
Education Manager: Elia Fernandez
Director, Research and Academic Relations (Foundation): Thomas Lamm
Director, Membership Services: Diane Nelson
Chief Operating Officer: Ronald Riba
Chief Professional Development Officer: Terence Trsar
Historical Note
Formerly (1994) EDP Auditors Association, ISACA was formed to provide continuing professional education and development in information systems audit techniques and standards to its membership of auditors, managers and systems specialists. Maintains a research and education subsidiary, the IT Governance Institute. Membership: $120/year, plus $30 new member processing fee.
Meetings/Conferences:
Annual Meetings: Summer
Publications:
CISM Review Manual. a.
Information Systems Control Journal. bi-m. adv.
Global Communique. bi-m. adv.
CISA Review Manual. a.

Information Systems Security Association *(1984)*
7044 S. 13th St.
Oak Creek, WI 53154
Tel: (414)908-4949 *Fax:* (414)768-8001
Toll Free: (800)370 - 4772
Web Site: www.issa.org
Members: 13500 individuals
Annual Budget: $500-1,000,000
Historical Note
Members are professionals responsible for the protection of information databases. Membership: $95/year (individual).
Meetings/Conferences:
Annual Meetings: March
Publications:
The ISSA Journal. m. adv.

Information Technologies Credit Union Association *(1959)*
P.O. Box 160
Del Mar, CA 92014-0160
Tel: (858)792-3883 *Fax:* (858)792-3884
E-Mail: itcua@itcua.org
Web Site: www.itcua.org
Members: 300 credit unions
Annual Budget: $100-250,000
Executive Director: Katherine E. Clark
E-Mail: kathy@itcua.org
Historical Note
Formerly (1993) the International Telephone Credit Union Association. Members were credit unions serving telephone companies. Now open to all credit unions.
Meetings/Conferences:
Annual Meetings: Spring

Information Technology Association of America *(1961)*
1401 Wilson Blvd.
Suite 1100
Arlington, VA 22209
Tel: (703)522-5055 *Fax:* (703)525-2279
Web Site: www.itaa.org
Members: 500 corporations
Staff: 38
Annual Budget: $5-10,000,000
Senior Vice President, Communications: Bob Cohen
Senior Vice President, Global Affairs: Allen Miller
Senior Vice President and Counsel, Internet Division: Mark Uncapher
Historical Note
Formerly (1985) the Association of Data Processing Service Organizations and (1991) ADAPSO, the Computer Software and Services Industry Association. Consists of four divisions: American Software Association, Information Technology Services, Processing and Network Services, and Systems Integration. Absorbed the Association of Independent Software Companies in 1972. Membership fee based on size of company.
Publications:
Agenda. m.

Information Technology Industry Council *(1916)*
1250 I St. NW
Suite 200
Washington, DC 20005-3922
Tel: (202)737-8888 *Fax:* (202)638-4922
Web Site: www.itic.org
Members: 32 companies
Staff: 30
Annual Budget: $2-5,000,000
President: Rhett B. Dawson
Senior Vice President, Government Relations: Ralph Hellman
Vice President, Industry Statistics: Helga Sayadian
Historical Note
Formerly (1962) Office Equipment Manufacturers Institute, (1973) Business Equipment Manufacturers Association, and (1994) Computer and Business Equipment Manufacturers Association. ITI represents providers of computers, business and telecommunications equipment, software and services. Acts on domestic and international issues that affect the high-technology industry. ITI serves as the Secretariat for the American National Standards Institute Committee, Information Technology (X3).
Meetings/Conferences:
Semi-annual Meetings: Spring and Fall
Publications:
Annual Report. a.
ITI Washington Letter. bi-w.

Information Theory Society
Historical Note
A technical society of the Institute of Electrical and Electronics Engineers (IEEE). Membership in the Society, open only to IEEE members, includes a subscription to a technical periodical in the field published by IEEE. All admninistrative support is provided by IEEE.

Infrared Data Association *(1993)*
P.O. Box 3883
Walnut Creek, CA 94598
Tel: (925)943-6546 *Fax:* (925)943-5600
Web Site: www.irda.org
Members: 80 companies
Staff: 3
Annual Budget: $250-500,000
Executive Director: Ronald Brown
E-Mail: ron@irda.org
Historical Note
IRDA is a consortium of companies united to develop and promote interoperable, low-cost infrered data connection standards that support a broad range of appliances, computers, and communication devices.

Infusion Nurses Society *(1973)*
220 Norwood Park South
Norwood, MA 02062

Tel: (781)440-9408 *Fax:* (781)440-9409
Toll Free: (800)694 - 0298
Web Site: http://ins1.org
Members: 5,700 individuals
Staff: 18
Annual Budget: $2-5,000,000
Chief Executive Officer: Mary Alexander, CRNI
E-Mail: mary.alexander@ins1.org
Executive Vice President: Chris Hunt
E-Mail: chris.hunt@ins1.org

Historical Note
Formerly the National Intravenous Therapy Association; assumed its current name in 2001. Membership consists primarily of Registered Nurses involved in the clinical practice of infusion therapies. Membership: $90/year.

Meetings/Conferences:
Annual Meetings: Spring
2007 – Orlando, FL/June 2-7/1500
2008 – Phoenix, AZ/May 3-8/1500

Publications:
Journal of Infusion Nursing. bi-m. adv.
INS Newsline. bi-m. adv.
Convention Program. a. adv.

Inland Marine Underwriters Association *(1930)*
14 Wall St.
Suite 820
New York, NY 10005
Tel: (212)233-0550 *Fax:* (212)227-5102
Web Site: www.imua.org
Members: 400 companies
Staff: 2
Annual Budget: $500-1,000,000
President and Chief Executive Officer: Ronald G. Thornton, CPCU

Historical Note
IMUA is a non-profit insurance trade association that addresses problems of common concern to companies underwriting Inland Marine and transportation insurance.

Meetings/Conferences:
2007 – Charleston, SC(Wild Dunes)/Apr. 15-18/150

Publications:
Newsroom Articles newsletter. q.
Reports and Bulletin. irreg.
Inland Marine Insurance Fact Book. a.
Advantage newsletter. q.

InSight
401 N. Michigan Ave.
Suite 2400
Chicago, IL 60611
Tel: (312)673-4979 *Fax:* (312)673-6721
E-Mail: info@insight-net.org
Web Site: www.insight-net.org/
Staff: 2
Executive Director: David Schmahl

Historical Note
Founded as the Technology and Information Management Education Society. Assumed its present name in 1999.

Institute for Alternative Agriculture

Historical Note
See Henry A. Wallace Institute for Alternative Agriculture.

Institute for Briquetting and Agglomeration *(1949)*
P.O. Box 297
Manitowish Waters, WI 54545
Tel: (715)543-2750 *Fax:* (715)543-2751
Web Site: www.agglomeration.org
Members: 225 individuals
Staff: 1
Annual Budget: $50-100,000
Executive Director: Thomas Feldkamp
E-Mail: tnfeldkamp@centurytel.net

Historical Note
Organized in 1949 as International Briquetting Association; adopted present name in 1967. Members shape and form materials such as charcoal, lime, ores, chemicals, metal swarf and powders, coal fines, coke breeze, wood waste, etc. which require size enlargement for efficient use. Membership: $50/year (individual); $100/year (organization/company).

Meetings/Conferences:
Biennial Meetings: odd years

Publications:
Proceedings. bien. adv.
Newsletter. q.

Institute for Business & Home Safety *(1971)*
4775 E. Fowler Ave.
Tampa, FL 33617
Tel: (813)286-3400 *Fax:* (813)286-9960
Toll Free: (866)657 - 4247
Web Site: www.ibhs.org
Members: 130 members, 100 associate members
Staff: 22
Annual Budget: $2-5,000,000
President and Chief Executive Officer: Harvey G. Ryland
E-Mail: hryland@ibhs.org

Historical Note
IBHS is an initiative of the insurance industry to assist in the industry's effort to reduce deaths, injuries, property damage, economic losses, and human suffering caused by natural disasters.

Publications:
Disaster Safety Review. q.

Institute for Certification of Computing Professionals *(1973)*
2350 E. Devon Ave.
Suite 115
Des Plaines, IL 60018
Tel: (847)299-4227 *Fax:* (847)299-4280
Toll Free: (800)843 - 8227
E-Mail: office@iccp.org
Web Site: www.iccp.org
Members: 27 associations
Staff: 3
Annual Budget: $500-1,000,000
Executive Director: Kewal Dhariwal
E-Mail: office@iccp.org

Historical Note
ICCP is supported by 27 major international computer societies. It certifies professionals within the computer information processing industry, operating certification programs which lead to the designations: Certified Computing Professional (CCP) and Associate Computing Professional (ACP). Membership: $50/year (individual).

Meetings/Conferences:
Annual Meetings: Third Week in January

Publications:
ICCP Certification News. 3/year. adv.

Institute for Hospital Clinical Nursing Education *(1967)*

Historical Note
An affiliate of American Hospital Association, which provides administrative support.

Institute for Operations Research and the Management Sciences *(1952)*
7240 Parkway Dr.
Suite 310
Hanover, MD 21076
Tel: (443)757-3500 *Fax:* (443)757-3515
Toll Free: (800)446 - 3676
E-Mail: informs@informs.org
Web Site: www.informs.org
Members: 10000 individuals
Staff: 35
Annual Budget: $5-10,000,000
Executive Director: Mark G. Doherty, CAE
E-Mail: mark.doherty@informs.org
Director, Meetings: Teresa V. Cryan
Director, Accounting and Member Services: Jacqueline Johns
E-Mail: jacquie.johns@informs.org
Director, Information Technology: Randy Kiefer
E-Mail: randy.kiefer@informs.org
Director, Public Relations: Barry List
E-Mail: barry.list@informs.org
Director, Marketing, Research and Product Development: Mary Magrogan
E-Mail: mary.magrogan@informs.org
Director, Publication Services: Patricia Shaffer
E-Mail: pat.shaffer@informs.org

Historical Note
Formerly Operations Research Society of America; merged with The Institute of Management Sciences and assumed its current name in 1995. Founded in 1952 and incorporated in the District of Columbia. A member society of the International Federation of Operational Research Societies. Members are investigators, students, teachers and managers that deal with the application of scientific methods to decision making, especially to optimize the allocation of resources. Membership: $125/year; $31/year (retired); $31/year (student).

Meetings/Conferences:
2007 – Seattle, WA/Nov. 4-7

Publications:
INFORMS Transactions on Education (online).
PubsOnLine Suite (online only). 54/year.
Decision Analysis. q. adv.
Interfaces Journal. bi-m.
Mathematics of Operations Research Journal. q. adv.
Manufacturing & Service Operations Management Journal. q. adv.
Organization Science Journal. bi-m. adv.
INFORMS Journal on Computing. q. adv.
Management Science Journal. m. adv.
Information Systems Research Journal. q. adv.
OR/MS Today Magazine. bi-m. adv.
Marketing Science Journal. q. adv.
Operations Research Journal. bi-m. adv.
Transportation Science Journal. q. adv.

Institute for Polyacrylate Absorbents *(1985)*
1850 M St. NW
Suite 700
Washington, DC 20036-5810
Tel: (301)651-5051 *Fax:* (202)296-8120
Members: 13 companies
Staff: 2
Annual Budget: $250-500,000
Executive Director: John F. "Jack" Murray

Historical Note
An affiliate of the Synthetic Organic Chemical Manufacturers Association, IPA represents manufacturers and users of absorbent polymers made of cross-linked polyacrylates and manufacturers and users of acrylic acid or its salts. It addresses the scientific, regulatory and related issues which are likely to impact the manufacture, use and disposal of fluid-absorbing polyacrylates.

Institute for Professionals in Taxation *(1976)*
1200 Abernathy Road NE
Suite L-2
Atlanta, GA 30328-5662
Tel: (404)240-2300 *Fax:* (404)240-2315
E-Mail: ipt@ipt.org
Web Site: www.IPT.org
Members: 4300 individuals
Staff: 12
Annual Budget: $2-5,000,000
Executive Director: Billy D. Cook

Historical Note
Members are corporate sales/property income tax representatives and attorneys, accountants and other professionals representing corporate clients in these fields. Membership: $225-350/year.

Meetings/Conferences:
Annual Meetings: June

Publications:
Property Taxation.
Drop Shipment Survey. a.
Property Tax Report. m.
Sales Tax Report. m.
IPT Membership Directory. a.
Sales Taxation. a.

Institute for Responsible Housing Preservation *(1989)*
401 Ninth St. NW
Suite 900
Washington, DC 20004
Tel: (202)585-8739 *Fax:* (202)585-8080
E-Mail: info@housingpreservation.org
Web Site: www.housingpreservation.org
Members: 70 companies
Staff: 1

Annual Budget: $100-250,000
Executive Director: Linda D. Kirk

Historical Note
IRHP members are owners and managers of Low Income Housing Preservation and Resident Housing Act (1990) housing and ELIHPA housing and concerned professionals. Membership: $5/unit/year.

Publications:
Responsible Owner. m.
Washington Alert. irreg.

Institute for Supply Management *(1915)*
2055 E. Centennial Circle
P.O. Box 22160
Tempe, AZ 85285-2160
Tel: (480)752-6276 *Fax:* (480)752-7890
Toll Free: (800)888 - 6276
Web Site: www.ism.ws
Members: 43000 individuals
Staff: 80
Annual Budget: $10-25,000,000
Chief Executive Officer: Paul Novak, CPM
Senior Vice President and Secretary: Holly LaCroix Johnson
Vice President, Marketing and Sales: Cindy Urbaytis
Senior Vice President and Treasurer: Deborah Webber

Historical Note
Founded as National Association of Purchasing Agents; became National Association of Purchasing Management in 1968, and assumed its current name in 2001. Sponsors the Certified Purchasing Manager (C.P.M.) program of professional competency. Has an annual budget of approximately $17 million. Membership: $100/year, plus affiliate dues.

Meetings/Conferences:
Annual Meetings: May/3,000
2007 – Las Vegas, NV(Bally's Convention Center)/May 6-9/3000
2008 – St. Louis, MO(Convention Center)/May 4-7/3000

Publications:
Journal of Supply Chain Management. q.
Inside Supply Management. m.
Report on Business. m.

Institute of Behavioral and Applied Management
Eastern Illinois University
3004 Lumpkin Hall
Charleston, IL 61920
Tel: (217)581-6034
Web Site: www.ibam.com/
Members: 150 individuals
Annual Budget: $10-25,000
President: Melody Wollan, PhD, PHR

Historical Note
IBAM members are educators and other professionals interested in organizational behavior and management theory. Has no paid officers or full-time staff. Membership: $50/year.

Meetings/Conferences:
Annual Meetings: Fall

Publications:
Proceedings. a. adv.
Journal of Behavioral and Applied Management online. 3/year.

Institute of Business Appraisers *(1978)*
P.O. Box 17410
Plantation, FL 33318
Tel: (954)584-1144 *Fax:* (954)584-1184
Toll Free: (800)299 - 4130
E-Mail: ibahq@go-iba.org
Web Site: www.go-iba.org
Members: 3500 individuals
Staff: 12
Annual Budget: $1-2,000,000
Executive Director: Michele G. Miles
Technical Director: Raymond C. Miles

Historical Note
Members are actively involved in the valuation and appraisal of midsize and smaller businesses. Membership: $495/year.

Publications:
IBA Business Appraisal Practice. q.
IBA Newsletter. m.
IBA Directory. a.

Institute of Career Certification International *(1994)*
204 E St. NE
Washington, DC 20002
Tel: (202)547-8001 *Fax:* (202)547-6348
E-Mail: info@careercertification.org
Web Site: www.careercertification.org
Members: 325 individuals
Annual Budget: $10-25,000
Management Executive: Michael Giuffrida

Historical Note
Founded as Outplacement Institute; became International Board for Career Management Certification in 1999, assumed its present name in 2003. Members are professional counselors and coaches specializing in career consulting and related fields. Has no paid officers or full-time staff.

Institute of Caster Manufacturers *(1933)*
Historical Note
An affiliate of Material Handling Industry of America, which provides administrative support.

Institute of Certified Business Counselors *(1975)*
18615 Willamette Dr.
West Linn, OR 97068
Tel: (503)675-1856 *Fax:* (503)292-8237
Toll Free: (877)422 - 2674
E-Mail: inquiry@i-cbc.org
Web Site: www.i-cbc.org
Members: 160 individuals
Annual Budget: $25-50,000
Administrator: Mary Ann Gray

Historical Note
ICBC members are primarily professional intermediaries specializing in assisting clients in the successful operation of the sale or purchase of businesses. Membership: $350/year.

Meetings/Conferences:
Annual Meetings: Fall

Publications:
CBC Counselor - The Certified Business Counselor. bi-m. adv.

Institute of Certified Healthcare Business Consultants *(1975)*
307 N. Michigan Ave.
Suite 800
Chicago, IL 60601-5309
Tel: (312)360-0384 *Fax:* (312)360-0388
Toll Free: (800)447 - 1684
E-Mail: info@ichbc.org
Web Site: www.ichbc.org
Members: 275 individuals
Staff: 3
Executive Director: Barbara Boden

Historical Note
Formerly Institute of Certified Professional Business Consultants (1998). Members provide business and financial management or consulting services to physicians, dentists, and other healthcare professionals. Awards the CHBC (Certified Healthcare Business Consultant) designation through classroom and online certification program.

Meetings/Conferences:
Annual Meetings: With National Association of Health Care Consultants and Society of Medical-Dental Consultants

Publications:
ICHBC Directory (online).

Institute of Certified Management Accountants *(1972)*
Historical Note
An affiliate of Institute of Management Accountants, which provides administrative support.

Institute of Certified Professional Managers *(1974)*
James Madison University
MSC5504
Harrisonburg, VA 22807
Tel: (540)568-3247 *Fax:* (540)801-8650
Toll Free: (800)568 - 4120
E-Mail: icpmcm@jmu.edu
Web Site: www.icpm.biz
Members: 10000 individuals
Staff: 5
Annual Budget: $250-500,000
Executive Director: Robert Reid, CM
Director, Operations: Lynn S. Powell, CM

Historical Note
Members are professional managers. Offers management training and certification. Applicants that meet eligibility requirements and successfully complete the three assessment exams earn the certified manager designation or CM.

Meetings/Conferences:
Annual Meetings:

Publications:
Management World. 6/year.
Newsletter. 2/year.

Institute of Certified Records Managers *(1975)*
5818 Molloy Rd.
Syracuse, NY 13211
Tel: (315)234-1904 *Fax:* (315)474-1784
Toll Free: (877)244 - 3128
E-Mail: admin@icrm.org
Web Site: www.icrm.org
Members: 1040 applicants and candidates
Annual Budget: $100-250,000
Regent for Public Relations: Steve Golden

Historical Note
Developed by the American Records Management Association in 1966, the ICRM was incorporated in 1975. It is a separate and independent organization from its sponsoring associations, which include: Association of Records Managers and Administrators, National Association of Government Archivists and Records Administrators, the Society of American Archivists, and the Association for Information and Image Management. ICRM is a certifying organization of professional records managers and administrative officers who specialize in the field of Records and Information Management Programs. All members have received the Certified Records Manager (CRM) designation. ARMA provides administrative support for the ICRM secretariat. Membership: $150/year (regular); $10/year (retired).

Meetings/Conferences:
Annual Meetings: Fall

Publications:
ICRM Newsletters. q.
CRM Examination Handbook. irreg.
Membership Directory. a.

Institute of Certified Travel Agents *(1964)*
148 Linden St.
Suite 305
Wellesley, MA 02482-0012
Tel: (781)237-0280 *Fax:* (781)237-3860
Toll Free: (800)542 - 4282
E-Mail: info@thetravelinstitute.com
Web Site: www.icta.com
Members: 7000 individuals
Staff: 21
Annual Budget: $2-5,000,000
Executive Vice President and General Manager: Maureen Kennedy

Historical Note
A non-profit, educational institution chartered in Washington in 1964 to promote professionalism in the travel industry. Now based in Wellesley, Massachusetts, it conducts a training program leading to certification and the CTC ("Certified Travel Counselor") designation, various geography courses and entry-level training. Membership: $95/year(individual).

Publications:
Travel Counselor Magazine. bi-m. adv.

Institute of Chemical Waste Management
Historical Note
A division of the Hazardous Waste Management Association.

Institute of Clean Air Companies *(1960)*
1730 M St. NW
Suite 206
Washington, DC 20036-4535
Tel: (202)457-0911 *Fax:* (202)331-1388

Web Site: www.icac.com
Members: 61 corporations
Staff: 7
Annual Budget: $250-500,000
Executive Director: Dave Foerter
E-Mail: dfoerter@icac.com

Historical Note
Formerly (1992) the Industrial Gas Cleaning Institute. Members are manufacturers of industrial air pollution control and monitoring equipment for stationary sources. Membership: $4,500/year.

Meetings/Conferences:
Annual Meetings: Spring

Publications:
Clean Air Technology News. bien.
Executive Update. w.
Organization Directory. a.
Market Forecast. a.
Statistical Reports. q.

Institute of Diving *(1977)*
17314 Panama City Beach Pkwy.
Panama City Beach, FL 32413
Tel: (850)235-4101
E-Mail: momits@bellsouth.net
Web Site: www.instituteofdiving.com
Members: 600 individuals and companies
Staff: 2
Annual Budget: $100-250,000
Director: Douglas R. Hough
E-Mail: momits@bellsouth.net

Historical Note
Members are sports, commercial and military divers, individuals, organizations and corporations interested in diving and diving-related activities. Supports the Museum of Man in the Sea, which is dedicated to the preservation of artifacts, equipment, and archives of subjects ranging from diving history to aquaculture, marine biology, life support systems, remotely operated vehicles, oceanography, photography, and the ecology of the sea. Membership: $25/year.

Meetings/Conferences:
Annual Meetings: Panama City, FL/Spring

Publications:
IOD Newsletter. q. adv.

Institute of Electrical and Electronics Engineers *(1884)*
3 Park Ave., 17th Floor
New York, NY 10016-5997
Tel: (212)419-7900 *Fax:* (212)752-4929
E-Mail: corporate.communications@ieee.org
Web Site: www.ieee.org
Members: 360000 individuals worldwide
Staff: 700
Annual Budget: Over $100,000,000
Executive Director: Jeffry W. Raynes, CAE
E-Mail: corporate.communications@ieee.org

Historical Note
Merger (1963) of the American Institute of Electrical Engineers (1884) and Institute of Radio Engineers (1912). Includes sections in Canada and throughout the world, with members in over 150 countries. Maintains and provides administrative support for the following subsidiary groups: Aerospace and Electronic Systems Society; Antennas and Propagation Society; Broadcast Technology Society; Circuits and Systems Society; Communications Society; Components, Packaging and Manufacturing Technology Society; Computer Society; Consumer Electronics Society; Control Systems Society; Dielectrics and Electrical Insulation Society; Education Society; Electromagnetic Compatibility Society; Electron Devices Society; Engineering Management Society; Engineering in Medicine and Biology Society; Geoscience and Remote Sensing Society; Industrial Electronics Society; Industry Applications Society; Information Theory Society; Instrumentation and Measurement Society; Lasers and Electro-Optics Society; Magnetics Society; Microwave Theory and Techniques Society; Neural Networks Council; Nuclear and Plasma Sciences Society; Oceanic Engineering Society; Power Electronics Society; Power Engineering Society; Professional Communications Society; Reliability Society; Robotics and Automation Council; Signal Processing Society; Society on Social Implications of Technology; Solid-State Circuits Council; Systems, Man and Cybernetics Society; Ultrasonics, Ferroelectrics and Frequency Control Society; and Vehicular Technology Society. Has an annual budget of over $110 million. In addition to its New York City headquarters, the IEEE maintains a library, the Center for the History of Electrical Engineering at Rutgers University in New Brunswick, New Jersey; a multi-department complex called the IEEE Operations Center in Piscataway, NJ; and an office in Washington, DC. The DC office also serves as headquarters for IEEE-USA, the Institute's professional development and political advocacy division.

Meetings/Conferences:
Annual Meetings: Winter

Publications:
The Institute. bi-m. adv.
Proceedings of the IEEE. m.
IEEE Spectrum. m. adv.
IEEE Potentials. q.

Institute of Electrical and Electronics Engineers Computer Society

Historical Note
See IEEE Computer Society

Institute of Environmental Sciences and Technology *(1953)*
5005 Newport Dr.
Suite 506
Rolling Meadows, IL 60008-3841
Tel: (847)255-1561 *Fax:* (847)255-1699
E-Mail: iest@iest.org
Web Site: www.iest.org
Members: 1600 individuals
Staff: 9
Annual Budget: $500-1,000,000
Executive Director: Julie Kendrick
Director, Communications Services: Robert Burrows
Director, Programs and Administrative Services: Corrie Roesslein

Historical Note
Formed by a merger of the Institute of Environmental Engineers (founded in 1955) and the Society of Environmental Engineers. Absorbed the American Association for Contamination Control in 1973. IEST is an international professional society that serves members and the industries they represent through education and the development of recommended practices and standards. Membership: $125/year (individual).

Meetings/Conferences:
Annual Meetings: Spring

Publications:
Journal of the Institute of Environmental Sciences and Technology. a. adv.
Proceedings. a.

Institute of Food Technologists *(1939)*
525 W. Van Buren
Suite 1000
Chicago, IL 60607-3814
Tel: (312)782-8424 *Fax:* (312)782-8348
Toll Free: (800)IFT - FOOD
E-Mail: info@ift.org
Web Site: www.ift.org
Members: 27000 individuals
Staff: 60
Annual Budget: $10-25,000,000
Executive Vice President: Barbara Byrd Keenan, CAE
E-Mail: bbkeenan@ift.org
Chief Human Resources Officer: Kelley Ahuja
Director, Finance: Mark Barenie
E-Mail: mbarenie@ift.org
Director, Information Technology: Marc Bernstein
Director, Meetings and Exposition Services.: Stan Butler
E-Mail: svbutler@ift.org
Director, Government Relations: Ted Cartwright
Internet Editor: James H. Giese
Vice President, Communications: Roy Hlavacek
E-Mail: rghlavacek@ift.org
Media Relations Manager: James Klapthor
E-Mail: jnklaptor@ift.org
Executive Director, Communications: Heather Monroe Lang
Director, Knowledge and Learning Experiences: Bob Moore
E-Mail: bmoore@ift.org
Director, Science Communications: Rosetta Newsome
E-Mail: rlnewsome@ift.org
Vice President, Science, Communications and Government Relations: Fred Shank
E-Mail: frshank@ift.org
Editor-In-Chief, Food Technology: Bob Swientek
E-Mail: bswientek@ift.org
Vice President, Foundation Development: Tekla Syers
Vice President, Strategic Intiatives: Heidi Voorhees
Director, Membership Relations: Gail Wiseman
E-Mail: gawiseman@ift.org

Historical Note
Founded in 1939 and incorporated in Illinois. IFT is a non-profit society with 27,000 members, who work in food science, technology and related professions in industry, academia and government. As the society for food science and technology, IFT's mission is to advance the science and technology of food through the exchange of knowledge, and by doing so, to bring sound science to the public discussion of food issues.

Meetings/Conferences:
Annual Meetings: Summer/19,000
2007 – Chicago, IL(McCormick Place)/July 28-Aug. 1

Publications:
Journal of Food Science. m.
Food Technology. m. adv.

Institute of Hazardous Materials Management *(1984)*
11900 Parklawn Dr.
Suite 450
Rockville, MD 20852
Tel: (301)984-8969 *Fax:* (301)984-1516
E-Mail: ihmminfo@ihmm.org
Web Site: www.ihmm.org
Members: 12000 individuals
Staff: 7
Annual Budget: $500-1,000,000
Executive Director: John H. Frick, Ph.D., CHMM

Historical Note
Professional Certification Board certifies for Certified Hazardous Materials Manager upon successful completion of qualifications and test. Annual maintenance fee: $70.

Meetings/Conferences:
Annual: 500-700

Publications:
Newsletter. q.
Directory of Hazardous Materials Management. a.

Institute of Industrial Engineers *(1948)*
3577 Parkway Lane
Suite 200
Norcross, GA 30092
Tel: (770)449-0460 *Fax:* (770)441-3295
Toll Free: (800)494 - 0460
Web Site: www.iienet.org
Members: 17000 individuals
Staff: 35
Annual Budget: $5-10,000,000
Executive Director: John Powers
E-Mail: jpowers@iienet.org

Historical Note
Founded and chartered in Columbus, Ohio as the American Institute of Industrial Engineers; assumed its present name in 1981. Member of the Accreditation Board for Engineering and Technology and the Council of Engineering Examiners. Absorbed the Industrial Management Society in 1982. IIE's mission is to serve the professional needs of industrial engineers and all individuals involved in improving quality and productivity related to industrial engineering. Has an annual budget of approximately $5 million. Membership: $125/year, $20/year (student).

Meetings/Conferences:
Annual Meetings: May/2,000

Publications:
Industrial Engineer.
IIE Transactions. q.
The Engineering Economist. q.
Industrial Management. bi-m. adv.

Institute of Inspection Cleaning and Restoration Certification *(1972)*
2715 E. Mill Plain Blvd.

Vancouver, WA 98661
Tel: (360)693-5675 *Fax:* (360)693-4858
E-Mail: info@iicrc.org
Web Site: www.iicrc.org
Members: 16000 individuals
Staff: 10
Annual Budget: $1-2,000,000
Executive Administrator: Tom Hill
E-Mail: tom@iicrc.org

Historical Note

Formerly (1993) the International Institute of Carpet and Upholstery Certification. Members are firms and individuals concerned with fabric restoration. IICR establishes standards, codifies ethics and certifies companies and individuals.

Publications:

International Directory of Certified Professionals. a.
Newsletter. 2/year.

Institute of Internal Auditors *(1941)*

247 Maitland Ave.
Altamonte Springs, FL 32701-4201
Tel: (407)937-1100 *Fax:* (407)937-1101
Web Site: www.theiia.org
Members: 105000 individuals
Staff: 100
Annual Budget: $10-25,000,000
President: Dave A. Richards
Chief Advocacy Officer: Dominique Vincerti
Director, International and Regional Conferences: Augusto Baeta
Chief Operating Officer: Albert Holzinger
President: Dave A. Richards

Historical Note

IIA provides professional development and educational services, certification, standards and research to the internal auditing profession. Membership is composed of internal auditors, comptrollers and accountants in companies, government and organizations. Grants the CIA (Certified Internal Auditor), CCSA (Certification in Control Self-Assessment), CGAP (Certified Government Auditing Professional) and CFSA (Certified Financial Services Auditor) designations. Has an annual budget of approximately $24 million. Membership: $70-125/year. Has a second URL address at http://www.itaudit.org.

Meetings/Conferences:

Annual Meetings: Summer
2007 – Amsterdam, Netherlands/

Publications:

FSA Times. q. adv.
Audit Wire. bi-m. adv.
CSA Sentinel. 3/year. adv.
CAE Bulletin. bi-m.. adv.
The Gaming Auditorium. q. adv.
Internal Auditor. bi-m. adv.
Tone At The Top. 4/year.
IIA Educator. q..

Institute of International Bankers *(1966)*

299 Park Ave., 17th Floor
New York, NY 10171
Tel: (212)421-1611 *Fax:* (212)421-1119
E-Mail: iib@iib.org
Web Site: www.iib.org
Members: 230 banks
Staff: 10
Annual Budget: $2-5,000,000
Executive Director/General Counsel: Lawrence R. Uhlick
E-Mail: iib@iib.org

Historical Note

The Institute is a trade association engaged in lobbying on behalf of foreign banks doing business in the United States.

Meetings/Conferences:

Annual Meetings: always Washington, DC/March

Publications:

International Banking Focus. 11/year.
Institute News.

Institute of International Container Lessors *(1971)*

555 Pleasantville Road
Suite 140 South
Briarcliff Manor, NY 10510-1955
Tel: (914)747-9100 *Fax:* (914)747-4600
E-Mail: info@iicl.org
Web Site: www.iicl.org
Members: 12 companies
Staff: 7
Annual Budget: $500-1,000,000
President: Steven Blust
Director, Technical Services: Gary Danback

Historical Note

Members lease marine cargo containers and container chassis to ship operators and others on a broad international basis. Sponsors an inspectors' certification and examination testing program; distributes technical manuals; and is active in regulatory, tax, communications and customs fields.

Publications:

IICL Inspection Directory. a. adv.
News from IICL Newsletter. semi-a.

Institute of International Finance *(1983)*

1333 H St. NW
Suite 800E
Washington, DC 20005-4770
Tel: (202)857-3600 *Fax:* (202)775-1430
E-Mail: info@iif.com
Web Site: www.iif.com
Members: 350 financial institutions
Staff: 65
Annual Budget: $10-25,000,000
Managing Director: Charles H. Dallara
First Deputy Managing Director and Chief Economist: Yusuke Horiguchi
Director, Membership Administration: Eric Lescar
Director, Global Events: Sue Newman

Historical Note

Created as a center for the dissemination of information to member organizations and a forum in which lending institutions can communicate with borrowing countries, multilateral organizations and regulators, in order to improve the processs of international lending. Members include commercial banks from developed and developing countries. Associate members include development banks, trading companies, export credit agencies and multinational corporations.

Meetings/Conferences:

Semi-Annual Meetings: Usually at Washington, DC headquarters

Publications:

Economic Review. m.
Comparative Country Statistics. a.
Capital Flows to Emerging Market Economies. 2/year.
Survey of Debt Restructuring. 2/year.

Institute of Judicial Administration *(1952)*

40 Washington Square Park, Room 314
New York, NY 10012
Tel: (212)998-6149 *Fax:* (212)995-4036
E-Mail: alison.kinney@nyu.edu
Web Site: www.law.nyu.edu/institutes/judicial
Members: 1600 individuals
Staff: 3
Annual Budget: $500-1,000,000
Executive Co-Director: Samuel Estreicher
E-Mail: estreicher@juris.law.nyu.edu
Executive Co-Director: Oscar Chase
Program Coordinator: Alison Kinney

Historical Note

Founded by Arthur T. Vanderbilt in 1952 at the New York University School of Law. Members are judges, lawyers and others concerned with improving the operation of the court system. Membership is by invitation. Membership: $100-500/year.

Institute of Makers of Explosives *(1913)*

1120 19th St. NW
Suite 310
Washington, DC 20036-3605
Tel: (202)429-9280 *Fax:* (202)293-2420
E-Mail: info@ime.org
Web Site: www.ime.org
Members: 32 companies
Staff: 8
Annual Budget: $1-2,000,000
President: J. Christopher Ronay

Historical Note

Members are U.S. and Canadian producers of commercial explosives. Sponsors the I.M.E. Political Action Committee. Membership: based on sales.

Meetings/Conferences:

Annual Meetings: Fall and Spring

Publications:

Publications List Available.

Institute of Management Accountants *(1919)*

10 Paragon Dr.
Montvale, NJ 07645
Tel: (201)573-9000 *Fax:* (201)474-1600
Toll Free: (800)638 - 4427
E-Mail: ima@imanet.org
Web Site: www.imanet.org
Members: 67000 individuals
Staff: 94
Annual Budget: $10-25,000,000
President and Chief Executive Officer: Paul Sharman

Historical Note

IMA is an association of accounting, financial, and information management professionals established as the National Association of Cost Accountants. Became the National Association of Accountants in 1957 and assumed its current name in 1991. Has an annual budget of approximately $16.1 million. Awards the designations CFM (Certified in Financial Management) or CMA (Certified Management Accountant) to management accountants or financial managers who pass the examinations, have at least two years experience, and agree to comply with the IMA's standards of ethical conduct. Controllers Council, Cost Management Group, and Small-Business Council are special interest groups supported by IMA. Membership: $185/year (regular individual member); $185/year (foreign individual member); $95/year (academic or retired); $37/year (student).

Meetings/Conferences:

Annual Meetings: June

Publications:

Strategic TechNotes. bi-w.
Management Accounting Quarterly. q.
Strategic Finance. m. adv.
Small Business Update. m.
Controller's Quarterly. m.
Cost Management Update. m.
IMA Focus. bi-m.

Institute of Management Consultants USA *(1968)*

2025 M St. NW
Suite 800
Washington, DC 20036
Tel: (202)367-1134 *Fax:* (202)367-2134
Toll Free: (800)221 - 2557
E-Mail: office@imcusa.org
Web Site: www.imcusa.org
Members: 2000 individuals
Staff: 3
Annual Budget: $500-1,000,000
Acting Executive Director: Megan Renner

Historical Note

IMC USA members are individual management consultants. IMC USA awards the CMC (Certified Management Consultant) designation. Offers free CMC Referral Service. Presents consulting skills workshop in major U.S. cities. A member of the International Council of Management Consulting Institutes. Membership: $345/year (certified member); $295/year (member); $25/year (student); $174/year (affiliate).

Meetings/Conferences:

Annual Meetings: April-May/150

Institute of Mathematical Statistics *(1935)*

P.O. Box 22718
Beachwood, OH 44122
Tel: (216)295-2340 *Fax:* (216)295-5661
Web Site: www.imstat.org
Members: 4000 individuals
Staff: 4
Annual Budget: $500-1,000,000
Executive Director: Elyse R. Gustafson
E-Mail: erg@imstat.org

Historical Note

Established September 12, 1935 during the joint meeting of the American Mathematical Society and

the Mathematical Association of America in Ann Arbor. IMS seeks to foster the development and dissemination of the theory and applications of statistics and probability. Member of the Conference Board of the Mathematical Sciences. Membership: $60/year (individual); $450/year (institution); $750/year (corporate).

Meetings/Conferences:
Annual Meetings: Summer

Publications:
Annals of Probability. q.
Annals of Statistics. bi-m.
Institute of Mathematical Statistics Bulletin. bi-m. adv.
Statistical Science. q.
Annals of Applied Probability. q.

Institute of Medicine *(1970)*
500 Fifth St. NW
Washington, DC 20001
Tel: (202)334-2352 *Fax:* (202)334-1412
E-Mail: iomwww@nas.edu
Web Site: www.iom.edu
Members: 1550 individuals
Staff: 150
Annual Budget: $10-25,000,000
Executive Officer: Susanne Stoiber
E-Mail: sstoiber@nas.edu
Director, Communications: Bethany Hardy

Historical Note
Private membership organization established in 1970 under the charter of the National Academy of Sciences to address issues associated with public policies for the advancement of human health.

Meetings/Conferences:
Annual Meetings: October in Washington, D.C.

Publications:
IOM News. bi-m.

Institute of Nautical Archaeology *(1973)*
P.O. Drawer HG
College Station, TX 77841-5137
Tel: (979)845-6694 *Fax:* (979)847-9260
E-Mail: ina@tamu.edu
Web Site: http://ina.tamu.edu/
Members: 1000 individuals
Staff: 26
Annual Budget: $500-1,000,000
President: Donny L. Hamilton, Ph.D.
E-Mail: ina@tamu.edu

Historical Note
Originally called the American Institute of Nautical Archaeology. Members are interested in underwater archaeological excavation. Membership: $30/year (individual); $100/year (organization).

Publications:
INA Quarterly. q.

Institute of Navigation *(1945)*
3975 University Dr.
Suite 390
Fairfax, VA 22030
Tel: (703)383-9688 *Fax:* (703)383-9689
E-Mail: membership@ion.org
Web Site: www.ion.org
Members: 4000 individuals
Staff: 6
Annual Budget: $1-2,000,000
Director, Operations: Lisa Beaty
E-Mail: membership@ion.org

Historical Note
Members are individuals interested in advancing the science of space, land, air, and marine navigation. Membership: $45/year (individual), $350-750/year (organization).

Publications:
ION Newsletter. q.
Navigation Journal. q.
Newsbulletin. 4-6/year.
Proceedings. 3/year.

Institute of Noise Control Engineering *(1971)*
Iowa State University
210 Marston
Ames, IA 50011
Tel: (515)294-6142 *Fax:* (515)294-3528
E-Mail: ibo@inceusa.org
Web Site: www.inceusa.org
Members: 1100 individuals
Staff: 5
Annual Budget: $100-250,000
Executive Director: P.D. Schomer
E-Mail: ed@inceusa.org

Historical Note
Incorporated in Washington, DC, INCE is a non-profit professional organization concerned with the advancement of noise control technology with particular emphasis on engineering solutions to environmental noise problems. Membership: $70/yr.

Meetings/Conferences:
Triennial Convention: Winter

Publications:
Noise Control Engineering Journal. bi-m.
Noise/News International. q. adv.

Institute of Nuclear Materials Management *(1958)*
60 Revere Dr.
Suite 500
Northbrook, IL 60062
Tel: (847)480-9573 *Fax:* (847)480-9282
E-Mail: inmm@inmm.org
Web Site: www.inmm.org
Members: 800 individuals
Staff: 2
Annual Budget: $250-500,000
Executive Director: Leah McCrackin

Historical Note
Members are individuals and companies concerned with the managing and safeguarding of nuclear materials. Membership: $50/year.

Meetings/Conferences:
Annual Meetings: Summer
2007 – Tucson, AZ(Marriott)/July 15-19

Publications:
Journal of Nuclear Materials Management. q. adv.
Proceedings. a.

Institute of Nuclear Power Operations *(1979)*
700 Galleria Pkwy. SE
Suite 100
Atlanta, GA 30339-5957
Tel: (770)644-8000 *Fax:* (770)644-8549
Members: 28 members, 54 participants
Staff: 347
Annual Budget: $50-100,000,000
President and Chief Executive Officer: Alfred C. Tollison, Jr.
Treasurer: David W. Weeks

Historical Note
Established in late 1979, incorporated in Delaware, to promote the highest levels of safe and reliable nuclear power plant operation. Members are electric utilities owning a share in a nuclear power plant, operating one, or holding a license to construct one. Has an annual budget of over $60 million.

Meetings/Conferences:
Annual Meetings: March

Publications:
The Nuclear Professional. q.

Institute of Outdoor Advertising

Historical Note
The marketing/promotion arm of the Outdoor Advertising Association of America.

Institute of Packaging Professionals *(1989)*
1601 N. Bond St.
Naperville, IL 60563
Tel: (630)544-5050 *Fax:* (630)544-5055
Toll Free: (800)432 - 4085
E-Mail: info@iopp.org
Web Site: www.iopp.org
Members: 7000 individuals
Staff: 6
Annual Budget: $1-2,000,000
Executive Director: Edwin O. Landon
Manager, Awards, Events and Certification: Carole Schiller
Manager, Member Services: Kelly Staley

Historical Note
Formed in 1989 by a merger of the Packaging Institute International (1939) and the Society of Packaging Professionals (1946), the Institute is a society of individuals whose objectives include educating the packaging professional, advancing packaging technology, and increasing the value of packaging in the marketplace. Membership: $150/year (individual).

Publications:
Who's Who in Packaging. a. adv.

Institute of Paper Science and Technology *(1929)*
500 10th St. NW
Atlanta, GA 30332-0620
Tel: (404)894-5700 *Fax:* (404)894-4778
Toll Free: (800)558 - 6611
Web Site: www.ipst.gatech.edu
Members: 50 manufacturers
Staff: 200
Annual Budget: $10-25,000,000
Director: Jim Frederick

Historical Note
Formerly (1989) the Institute of Paper Chemistry (Appleton, WI). Name affiliated with Georgia Tech, IPST is an educational research center for manufacturers of pulp paper. Has an annual budget of approximately $20 million.

Meetings/Conferences:
Annual Meetings: Atlanta, GA/Spring

Publications:
Abstract Bulletin.

Institute of Public Utilities *(1965)*
Michigan State University
240 Nisbet Bldg.
East Lansing, MI 48823
Tel: (517)355-1876 *Fax:* (517)355-1854
E-Mail: ipu@msu.edu
Web Site: www.ipu.msu.edu/
Members: 28 companies
Staff: 5
Annual Budget: $250-500,000
Coordinator, Operations: Katherine "Sue" Carpenter
E-Mail: ipu@msu.edu

Historical Note
IPU members are regulated and competitive utility companies. An independent research organization, IPU promotes study, research, teaching, and training in the field of public uilities. $12,000/year (company).

Publications:
MSU Public Utilities Papers. a.

Institute of Real Estate Management *(1933)*
430 N. Michigan Ave.
Chicago, IL 60611-4090
Tel: (312)329-6000 *Fax:* (800)338-4736
Toll Free: (800)837 - 0706
E-Mail: custserv@irem.org
Web Site: www.irem.org
Members: 16000 individuals
Staff: 65
Annual Budget: $10-25,000,000
Executive Vice President and Chief Executive Officer: Russell C. Salzman
Manager, Planning and Governance: Diane Miller

Historical Note
An affiliate of National Association of REALTORS, IREM is a professional association dedicated to serving the needs of real estate management professionals worldwide. Awards three professional designations: Certified Property Manager (CPM); Accredited Residential Manager (ARM); and Accredited Management Organization (AMO). Membership: $495/year (CPM); $75/year (ARM); $440/year (AMO); $175/year (Associate Member).

Meetings/Conferences:
Annual Meetings: Fall with the National Association of Realtors

Publications:
Journal of Property Management. bi-m. adv.
Income/Expense Analyses. a.

Institute of Scrap Recycling Industries *(1987)*
1325 G St. NW
Suite 1000
Washington, DC 20005-3104
Tel: (202)737-1770 *Fax:* (202)626-0900
E-Mail: isri@isri.org

Web Site: www.isri.org
Members: 1200 companies
Staff: 30
Annual Budget: $5-10,000,000
President: Robin K. Wiener
E-Mail: RobinWiener@isri.org
Vice President, Member Services, Meetings, Marketing, and Communications: Chuck Carr
E-Mail: ChuckCarr@isri.org
Vice President, Government Relations and General Counsel: Scott Horne
E-Mail: ScottHorne@isri.org
Vice President, Finance: Ed Szrom
E-Mail: isri@isri.org

Historical Note
ISRI was formed by the merger (1987) of the Institute of Scrap Iron and Steel (founded 1928) and the National Association of Recycling Industries (founded 1913). ISRI members are companies that process, broker, and consume scrap commodities, including metals, paper, plastics, glass, rubber, electronics, and textiles. The Institute provides education, advocacy, and compliance training, and promotes public awareness of the value and importance of recycling to the production of the world's good and services.

Meetings/Conferences:
Annual Meetings: April

Publications:
ISRI Digest. m.
Scrap Magazine. bi-m. adv.
Membership Directory. a. adv.

Institute of Shortening and Edible Oils *(1936)*
1750 New York Ave. NW
Suite 120
Washington, DC 20006
Tel: (202)783-7960 *Fax:* (202)393-1367
E-Mail: info@iseo.org
Web Site: www.iseo.org
Members: 18 companies
Staff: 2
Annual Budget: $250-500,000
President: Robert M. Reeves
E-Mail: info@iseo.org

Historical Note
ISEO is a trade association representing the refiners of edible fats and oils in the United States. Its members represent approximately 90-95% of the edible fats and oils produced domestically, which are used in numerous foods including margarine, shortening, cooking and salad oils, confections and toppings and used as ingredients in a wide variety of foods. Formerly the Institute of Shortening Manufacturers.

Meetings/Conferences:
Annual Meetings: Late Winter/Early Spring

Publications:
Food Fats and Oils. quinquenn.
Directory of Edible Oil Industry in the US. a.

Institute of Store Planners *(1961)*
25 N. Broadway
Tarrytown, NY 10591
Tel: (914)332-1806 *Fax:* (914)332-1541
Toll Free: (800)379 - 9912
E-Mail: adminisp@ispo.org
Web Site: www.ispo.org
Members: 1100 individuals
Staff: 2
Annual Budget: $100-250,000
Administrator: Edie Tella
E-Mail: adminisp@ispo.org

Historical Note
Members are store planners and designers, visual merchandisers, educators, as well as contractors and suppliers to the industry. Membership: $175/year (professional), $500/year (trade).

Meetings/Conferences:
Annual Meetings:

Publications:
ISP Newsletter. q.

Institute of Tax Consultants *(1980)*

Historical Note
The Institute is the certifying board for the American Society of Tax Professionals.

Institute of Transportation Engineers *(1930)*
1099 14th St. NW
Suite 300 West
Washington, DC 20005-3438
Tel: (202)289-0222 *Fax:* (202)289-7722
E-Mail: ite_staff@ite.org
Web Site: www.ite.org
Members: 16000 individuals
Staff: 28
Annual Budget: $5-10,000,000
Executive Director and Chief Executive Officer: Thomas W. Brahms
Associate Executive Director, Administration and Finance: Peter W. Frentz

Historical Note
Founded in Pittsburgh in 1930 and incorporated in 1954 in Connecticut as the Institute of Traffic Engineers; assumed its present name in 1976. Members are individual professionals responsible for planning, designing, and operating surface transportation facilities.

Meetings/Conferences:
Annual Meetings: August-September
2007 – Pittsburgh, PA(David L. Lawrence Convention Center)/Aug. 5-8
2008 – Anaheim, CA(Anaheim Convention Center)/Aug. 17-20
2009 – San Antonio, TX(Homer B. Gonzales Convention Center)/Aug. 9-12
2010 – Vancouver, B.C., Canada(Vancouver Convention and Exhibition Center)/Aug. 8-11

Publications:
ITE Journal. m. adv.

Institute on Religion in an Age of Science *(1954)*
310 Windham Dr.
Booneville, MS 38829
Tel: (662)720-1241
E-Mail: webmaster@iras.org
Web Site: www.iras.org
Members: 400 individuals
Annual Budget: $25-50,000
Secretary: Bill Stone

Historical Note
IRAS aims to understand, interpret, and advance, in the light of the sciences and critical scholarship, the continuing functions of evolving religion that guide humanity's relation to the ultimate conditions of its destiny. Has no paid officers or full-time staff. Member of the Council on the Study of Religion. Affiliate Society of the American Association for the Advancement of Science. Membership: $60/year (individual); $65/year (joint); $100/year (organization); $40/year (student).

Meetings/Conferences:
Annual Meetings: Always Star Island, NH in July or August/50

Publications:
IRAS Newsletter. 3/year.
Zygon, Journal of Religion and Science. q. adv.
Science and Spirit.

Institutional and Service Textile Distributors Association *(1944)*
1609 Connecticut Ave. NW
Suite 200
Washington, DC 20009
Tel: (202)986-0105 *Fax:* (202)986-0448
E-Mail: istdatextiles@aol.com
Web Site: www.istda.org
Members: 18 companies
Staff: 4
Annual Budget: $50-100,000
Executive Secretary: Kathleen Ewing

Historical Note
Members are wholesale distributors of U.S. textiles to hospitality and health care industries such as hospitals, hotels, nursing homes and restaurants. Member sales total approximately $750 million annually. Membership: $1,000-3,000/year minimum, based on sales.

Meetings/Conferences:
Semi-Annual Meetings: Winter and Spring

Institutional Carpet Maintenance Council *(1971)*

Historical Note
A division of the Association of Specialists in Cleaning and Restoration.

Instructional Telecommunications Council *(1977)*
One Dupont Circle
Suite 360
Washington, DC 20036-1176
Tel: (202)293-3110 *Fax:* (202)822-5014
Web Site: www.itcnetwork.org
Members: 500 institutions
Staff: 2
Annual Budget: $100-250,000
Executive Director: Loren Brumm

Historical Note
Founded as Instructional Telecommunications Consortium; assumed its current name in 1993. Members are educators and organizations involved in higher education instructional telecommunications and distance learning. Membership: $450/year (institution).

Meetings/Conferences:
Annual Meetings: April/50-100

Publications:
ITC News. 10/yr.

Instrumentation Testing Association *(1984)*
631 N. Stephanie St.
Suite 279
Henderson, NV 89014
Tel: (702)568-1445 *Fax:* (702)568-1446
E-Mail: ita@instrument.org
Web Site: www.instrument.org
Members: 97 agencies
Staff: 2
Annual Budget: $100-250,000
Executive Director: Tony M. Palmer

Historical Note
Formerly (1988) Instrumentation Testing Service. Established and incorporated in the state of Illinois. ITA members are public and private agencies utilizing instrumentation for the conduct or enhancement of water, wastewater and industrial waste. Associate membership is available for instrument manufacturers, consultants, and regulatory agencies responsible for the supervision of facilities which utilize instrumentation. Membership: $250-3,000/year.

Meetings/Conferences:
Annual Meetings: Fall

Publications:
ITA Analyzer News. q. adv.
Test Evaluation Reports.

Insulated Cable Engineers Association *(1925)*
P.O. Box 1568
Carrollton, GA 30117
Tel: (770)830-0369 *Fax:* (770)830-8501
E-Mail: info@icea.net
Web Site: www.icea.net
Members: 90 individuals
Staff: 3
Annual Budget: $50-100,000
Secretary-Treasurer: Thomas P. Arnold

Historical Note
Formerly (1979) known as the Insulated Power Cable Engineers Association, Inc. ICEA is a professional society of engineers who develop standards to promote the reliability and safety of insulated wire and cable. Membership: $1,800/year.

Meetings/Conferences:
Annual Meetings: usually September

Publications:
ICEA Activities.
Publications List Available.

Insulating Concrete Form Association *(1995)*
1730 Dewes St.
Suite Two
Glenview, IL 60025
Tel: (847)657-9730 *Fax:* (847)657-9728
Toll Free: (888)864 - 4232
E-Mail: icfa@forms.org
Web Site: www.forms.org
Executive Director: Joseph E. Lyman
E-Mail: icfa@forms.org

Historical Note
ICFA represents manufacturers and marketers of concrete form systems for building construction. Membership: $4,000/year (manufacturer); $2,500/year (supplier/associate); $100/year (individual).
Publications:
ICFA Dialog magazine. q. adv.

Insulation Contractors Association of America *(1977)*
1321 Duke St.
Suite 303
Alexandria, VA 22314
Tel: (703)739-0356 *Fax:* (703)739-0412
E-Mail: icaa2005@insulate.org
Web Site: www.insulate.org
Members: 300 companies
Staff: 2
Annual Budget: $250-500,000
Executive Director: Michael Kwart
E-Mail: icaa2005@insulate.org
Historical Note
Incorporated in the District of Columbia in December 1977, with 32 charter members. Members are residential and commercial insulation contractors and suppliers. Membership: $600-5,000/year (organization, based on gross sales).
Meetings/Conferences:
Annual Meetings: September-October
Publications:
Member Bulletin. irreg.
Insulation Contractors Report. bi-m.
Membership Directory. a.

Insurance Accounting and Systems Association *(1928)*
P.O. Box 51340
Durham, NC 27717-3409
Tel: (919)489-0991 *Fax:* (919)489-1994
E-Mail: info@iasa.org
Web Site: www.iasa.org
Members: 1700 companies
Staff: 6
Annual Budget: $500-1,000,000
Executive Director: Joseph Pomilia
E-Mail: info@iasa.org
Historical Note
Formed as the Insurance Accounting and Statistical Association at a meeting of representatives of 8 Illinois and Indiana life insurance companies at Peoria, IL on April 14, 1928. Adopted the name Insurance Accounting and Systems Association in 1983 and incorporated in 1986. The IASA serves life, property and liability, reinsurance and health care companies through the study, research, and development of modern insurance theory, practice, and procedures. Membership: $300/year (company).
Meetings/Conferences:
Annual Meetings: May or June
Publications:
Interpreter. q.

Insurance Conference Planners Association
Historical Note
Became Financial and Insurance Conference Planners in 2006.

Insurance Consumer Affairs Exchange *(1976)*
P.O. Box 746
Lake Zurich, IL 60047
Tel: (847)991-8454
E-Mail: info@icae.com
Web Site: www.icae.com
Members: 110 individuals
Executive Director: Nancy Brebner
Historical Note
Forum for dialogue with professionals interested in consumer-related matters in the insurance industry and issues of consumer affairs in general. Has no paid officers or full-time staff. Membership: $150/year (individual); $300/year (organization/company).
Publications:
ICAE Catalyst. a.

Insurance Information Institute *(1959)*
110 William St.
New York, NY 10038
Tel: (212)346-5500 *Fax:* (212)732-1916
Toll Free: (800)942 - 4242
E-Mail: iiilibrary@aol.com
Web Site: www.iii.org
Members: 275 companies
Staff: 38
Annual Budget: $5-10,000,000
President: Gordon Stewart
Director, News Media: John Spagnudo
Historical Note
An association of property and casualty insurance companies whose activities include public education, information dissemination, and media relations. Maintains library database, as well as a toll-free consumer hotline. Has an annual budget of approximately $5 million.
Publications:
Insurance Facts. a.
III Insurance Daily. d.
Insurance Issues Update. m.

Insurance Institute for Highway Safety *(1959)*
1005 N. Glebe Rd.
Suite 800
Arlington, VA 22201-4751
Tel: (703)247-1500 *Fax:* (703)247-1588
E-Mail: rrader@iihs.org
Web Site: www.iihs.org
Staff: 70
Annual Budget: $10-25,000,000
President: Brian O'Neill
Director, Media Relations: Russ Rader
Historical Note
An independent non-profit research and communications organization working to reduce property losses, deaths and injuries on the nation's highways. Supported by automobile insurers.
Meetings/Conferences:
Annual Meetings: None held.
Publications:
Status Report. m.
The Year's Work. a.

Insurance Loss Control Association *(1931)*
P.O. Box 2075
Columbus, OH 43216-2075
Tel: (614)221-9950 *Fax:* (614)221-2335
E-Mail: ilca.director@insurancelosscontrol.org
Web Site: www.insurancelosscontrol.org
Members: 350 individuals
Staff: 6
Annual Budget: under $10,000
Historical Note
Established as the Association of Mutual Fire Insurance Engineers, it became the Association of Mutual Insurance Engineers in 1968, and assumed its present name in 1980. ILCA enables loss control professionals to increase their knowledge about fire prevention and protection. Membership: $20/year (individual).
Meetings/Conferences:
Annual Meetings: Fall
Publications:
ILCA Help Newsletter. q. adv.

Insurance Marketing Communications Association *(1923)*
P.O. Box 473054
Charlotte, NC 28247
Tel: (704)543-1776 *Fax:* (866)210-2481
Web Site: www.imcanet.com
Members: 180 companies
Staff: 1
Annual Budget: $100-250,000
Executive Director: September Seibert
E-Mail: tseibert@imcanet.com
Historical Note
Formerly the Insurance Advertising Conference; assumed its present name in 1984. Members represent mutual, stock and direct writer, property and casualty insurance companies. Membership: $500/year (company).
Meetings/Conferences:
Annual Meetings: June
Publications:
Update (online). bi-m.
Membership Roster. a.

Integrated Waste Services Association *(1991)*
1331 H St. NW
Suite 801
Washington, DC 20005
Tel: (202)467-6240 *Fax:* (202)467-6225
E-Mail: iwsa@wte.org
Web Site: www.wte.org
Members: 50 companies
Staff: 3
Annual Budget: $1-2,000,000
President: Ted Michaels
Office Manager: Ira McNeil
Historical Note
IWSA, representing the waste-to-energy industry, promotes integrated solutions to municipal solid waste management problems.

Intellectual Property Owners Association *(1972)*
1255 23rd St. NW
Suite 200
Washington, DC 20037
Tel: (202)466-2396 *Fax:* (202)466-2893
E-Mail: info@ipo.org
Web Site: www.ipo.org
Members: 500 institutions and individuals
Staff: 8
Annual Budget: $1-2,000,000
Executive Director: Herbert C. Wamsley
Government Relations and Legislative Counsel: Dana R. Colarulli
Information Technology Coordinator: Nicholas Evans
Director, Meetings and Events: Megan Griggs
Chief Operating Executive: Jessica K. Landacre
Historical Note
Founded as Intellectual Property Owners; assumed its current name in 1997. Members are holders of patents, trademarks and copyrights. Primary concern is to promote effective and affordable patent, trademark and copyright laws as an increased incentive for innovation and creativity. Membership: $115-250/year (individual); $425-22,500/year (institution).
Publications:
IPO Daily News. d.

Intelligent Transportation Society of America *(1991)*
1100 17th St. NW
Suite 1200
Washington, DC 20036
Tel: (202)285-9057 *Fax:* (202)484-3483
E-Mail: editor@itsa.org
Web Site: www.itsa.org
Members: 500 organizations
Staff: 24
Annual Budget: $5-10,000,000
President and Chief Executive Officer: Neil D. Schuster
Historical Note
Formerly (1994) Intelligent Vehicle Highway Society of America, ITS America fosters the acceleration of the development and deployment of intelligent transporation systems. ITS refers to the application of advanced computer, information and communication technologies to surface transportation. Members include transportation systems manufacturers, academic research centers and public transportation agencies. Composed of 24 state chapters in 33 states. Membership: $500-15,000/year (organization/company).
Meetings/Conferences:
Annual Meetings: Spring
Publications:
Weekly Briefing. w. adv.
Annual Report. a.
ITS America News. m.
Proceedings of Annual Meeting. a.

Inter American Press Association *(1942)*
1801 S.W. Third Ave.
Miami, FL 33129
Tel: (305)634-2465 *Fax:* (305)635-2272
E-Mail: info@sipiapa.org
Web Site: www.sipiapa.org
Members: 1300 newspapers and magazines
Staff: 11

Annual Budget: $1-2,000,000
Executive Director: Julio E. Munoz, Ph.D
E-Mail: jmunoz@sipiapa.org

Historical Note
The Inter American Press Association is a non-profit organization dedicated to defending freedom of expression and of the press throughout America. Membership: fees based on circulation.

Publications:
NotiSip/IAPA News. bi-m. adv.
Hora de Cierre. q. adv.

Inter-America Travel Agents Society *(1954)*
248 S. Alden St.
Philadelphia, PA 19139
Tel: (215)471-5321
*Members:*392 individuals
Annual Budget: $10-25,000
Executive Director: Joanne Ussery

Historical Note
ITAS members are African-American owned and operated travel agencies and agents. Has no paid officers or full-time staff. Membership: $100-150/year (individual); $300/year (organization/company).

Publications:
ITAS Newsletter. q. adv.

Inter-American Bar Association *(1940)*
1211 Connecticut Ave. NW
Suite 202
Washington, DC 20036
Tel: (202)466-5944 *Fax:* (202)466-5946
E-Mail: iaba@iaba.org
Web Site: www.iaba.org
*Members:*2500 individuals
Staff: 5
Annual Budget: $100-250,000
Secretary-General: Harry A. Inman
E-Mail: iaba@iaba.org
Office Manager: Patricia De La Riva
E-Mail: iaba@iaba.org

Historical Note
Founded in 1940 by a group of jurists and lawyers representing 44 professional organizations throughout 17 nations of the Western Hemisphere to fill the need for an unbiased and professional forum for the discussion of comparative law. Membership: $170/year (junior); $150/year (senior); $50/year (student).

Meetings/Conferences:
Annual Meetings: Spring

Publications:
Newsletter. q.
Proceedings. a.

Inter-Industry Conference on Auto Collision Repair *(1979)*
5125 Trillium Blvd.
Hoffman Estates, IL 60192
Tel: (847)590-1198 *Fax:* (800)590-1215
Toll Free: (800)422 - 7872
Web Site: www.i-car.com
Members: 100 individuals
Staff: 55
Annual Budget: $5-10,000,000
Executive Vice President and Chief Executive Officer: Thomas C. McGee, Jr.
E-Mail: tom.mcgee@i-car.com
Controller: Mike Brey
Director, Corporate Administration: Margaret Knell
Manager, Meetings: Pat Perren
Director, Human Resources: Shirley Pincus
Executive Director, Educational Foundation: Ron Ray
E-Mail: ron.ray@i-car.com
Director, Business Development and Field Operations: Rick Tuuri

Historical Note
I-CAR's mission is to research, develop and deliver technical education programs on collision repair, in order to raise the level of available knowledge and improve communication within the collision repair, insurance and related industries. Members are major auto manufacturers, insurance companies, auto collision repair shops, tool, equipment, and supply manufacturers and related industry and trade associations. Membership: $500/year (individual); $2,500/year (corporate); $5,000/year (sustaining); $500/year (educational partner).

Meetings/Conferences:
Annual Meetings: Summer

Inter-Society Color Council *(1931)*
11491 Sunset Hills Rd.
Suite 301
Reston, VA 20190
Tel: (703)318-0263 *Fax:* (703)318-0514
E-Mail: iscc@iscc.org
Web Site: www.iscc.org
*Members:*860 individuals
Staff: 2
Annual Budget: $50-100,000
Office Manager: Cynthia Sturke
E-Mail: iscc@iscc.org

Historical Note
Members are concerned with descriptions and specifications of color and their application to color problems. Established December 29, 1931 at the Museum of Science and Industry in New York City. Membership: $75/year (individual); $10/year (student).

Meetings/Conferences:
Annual Meetings: Spring

Publications:
ISCC Newsletter. 6/year.

Interactive Advertising Bureau *(1996)*
116 E. 27th St., Seventh Floor
New York, NY 10016
Tel: (212)380-4700 *Fax:* (212)380-4702
E-Mail: greg@iab.net
Web Site: www.iab.net
*Members:*250 companies
Staff: 15
Chief Executive Officer: Greg Stuart
E-Mail: greg@iab.net
Vice President, Membership Services: Andrew Kraft

Historical Note
Formerly (2003) Internet Advertising Bureau. IAB evaluates and recommends standards and practices for online advertising and sponsors research on behalf of its members. Merged with Internet Local Advertising and Commerce Association in 1998.

Publications:
IAB Informer. m.

Interactive Audio Special Interest Group *(1994)*
c/o MIDI Manufacturers Association
P.O. Box 3173
La Habra, CA 90632-3171
Tel: (714)736-9774 *Fax:* (714)736-9775
Web Site: www.iasig.org
*Members:*150 individuals
Managing Director: Tom White

Historical Note
Formerly the Association of Interactive Audio and Music Professionals, IA-SIG is an autonomous organization sponsored by the MIDI Manufacturers Association. IA-SIG members are companies and individuals involved in interactive audio development. Membership: $150/year (non-MMA corporate members); $75/year (MMA corporate members; $25/year (individual).

Meetings/Conferences:
Semi-annual Meetings:

Interactive Digital Software Association

Historical Note
Became Entertainment Software Association in 2003.

Interactive Multimedia and Collaborative Communications Association *(1982)*
P.O. Box 756
Syosset, NY 11791-0756
Tel: (516)818-8184 *Fax:* (516)922-2170
Web Site: www.imcca.org
Members: 1000 individuals
Staff: 1
Annual Budget: $100-250,000
Executive Director: Carol Zelkin

Historical Note
Founded as International Teleconferencing Association; absorbed National Telecommuting and Telework Association in 1994, and assumed its current name in 2000. IMCCA provides a clearinghouse for the exchange of information between users, researchers, and providers in the field of teleconferencing. Membership: $100/year (individual), $500/year (organizational); $250/year (small business), $30/year (student).

Intercoiffure America/Canada *(1933)*
5151 Reed Road
Columbus, OH 43220
Tel: (614)457-7712 *Fax:* (614)457-7794
Web Site: www.intercoiffure.us
*Members:*350 companies
Annual Budget: $100-250,000
President: Kenneth E. Anders

Historical Note
Formerly (1966) International des Coiffures de Dames and (2003) Intercoiffure America. The North American section of Intercoiffure Mondiale, headquartered in Paris. Members are beauty salon owners. Membership: $695/year.

Meetings/Conferences:
Annual Meetings: in conjunction with Intercoiffure World Congress

Intercollegiate Broadcasting System *(1940)*
367 Windsor Hwy
New Windsor, NY 12553-7900
Tel: (845)565-0003 *Fax:* (845)565-7446
E-Mail: ibs@ibsradio.org
Web Site: www.ibsradio.org
*Members:*800 stations
Staff: 8
Annual Budget: $100-250,000
Director, Operations: Fritz Kass

Historical Note
IBS is a nationwide, non-profit association of college and university broadcasting stations. Membership: $95/year.

Meetings/Conferences:
Annual Meetings: March

Publications:
IBS Station Manager's Newsletter. m. adv.
Journal of College Radio. q. adv.

Intercollegiate Men's Choruses, an International Association of Male Choruses *(1915)*
109 McCain Auditorium
Kansas State University
Manhattan, KS 66506-4706
Tel: (785)532-5740 *Fax:* (785)532-5709
E-Mail: polich@ksu.edu
Web Site: www.cco.caltech.edu/~dgc/imc.html
*Members:*70 choruses
Staff: 1
Annual Budget: under $10,000
Executive Director: Gerald Polich

Historical Note
Formerly (1988) the Intercollegiate Musical Council, The National Association of Male Choruses. Promotes research, publication and production of quality music for male choruses. Inactive during and after World War II, the Council was revived in 1952; annual seminars have been held since 1954. Membership: $40/year (minimum).

Publications:
Quodlibet (Newsletter). semi-a.

Intercollegiate Tennis Association *(1956)*
174 Tamarack Circle
Skillman, NJ 08558-2021
Tel: (609)497-6920 *Fax:* (609)497-9766
E-Mail: itatennis2@aol.com
Web Site: www.itatennis.com
*Members:*2300 individuals
Staff: 6
Annual Budget: $500-1,000,000
Executive Director: David A Benjamin
E-Mail: dab1945@aol.com
Director, Communications: Casey Angle

Historical Note
Formerly (1958) National Collegiate Tennis Coaches Association and (1992) the Intercollegiate Tennis Coaches Association. ITA is the governing body of collegiate tennis; administers a number of national

championships, as well as a comprehensive ranking system for teams, singles and doubles, and awards honors to players and coaches. Membership: $125-305/year (coach); $595/year (corporation); $70/year (associates); $60/year (alumni); $60/year (collegiate parent); $40/year (junior); $250/year (federation); $95/year (association).

Meetings/Conferences:
Annual Meetings: December/300

Publications:
ITA Coaches Directory (online). a.
ITA Scorebook. a. adv.
Ass'n News included in Tennis Week. m.

Interferry *(1976)*
1619 Warren Gardens
Victoria, BC V8S 1-S9
Tel: (250)592-9612 *Fax:* (250)592-9613
E-Mail: info@interferry.com
Web Site: www.interferry.com
Members: 200 companies
Staff: 2
Annual Budget: $100-250,000
Chief Executive Officer: Len Roueche
E-Mail: len.roueche@interferry.com

Historical Note
Founded (1976) as the Internationql Marine Transit Association; assumed its current name in 2001. Membership includes ferry operators, naval architects, manufacturers, suppliers, shipyards, government agencies, support services, marine engineering and planning consultants, and specialists in marine transit. Membership: $250/year (individual); $800/year (company).

Meetings/Conferences:
Annual Meetings: Fall
2007 - Stockholm, Sweden(The Grand Hotel)/Sept. 28-30

Publications:
Interferry News. w.
Conference Proceedings. a. adv.

Interior Design Educators Council *(1962)*
7150 Winston Dr.
Suite 300
Indianapolis, IN 46268
Tel: (317)328-4437 *Fax:* (317)280-8527
E-Mail: info@idec.org
Web Site: www.idec.org
Members: 600 individuals
Staff: 2
Annual Budget: $250-500,000
Executive Director: Jeff Beachum

Historical Note
IDEC members are teachers of interior design in colleges and universities in the U.S. and Canada, concerned with the advancement of education and research in interior design. IDEC concentrates on the establishment and strengthening of lines of communication among educators, practitioners, educational institutions and other organizations concerned with interior design education. Membership: $250/year (individual).

Meetings/Conferences:
Annual Meetings: Spring/300
2007 - Austin, TX/March 4-11

Publications:
IDEC Record. semi-a.
The Journal of Interior Design. semi-a.

Interior Design Society *(1973)*
3910 Tinsley Dr.
Suite 101
High Point, NC 27265-3610
Tel: (336)886-6100 Ext: 6122 *Fax:* (336)801-6110
Toll Free: (800)888 - 9590 Ext: 6122
E-Mail: idsinfo@nhfa.org
Members: 3500 individuals
Staff: 3
Annual Budget: $500-1,000,000
Executive Director: Faye Laverty
E-Mail: idsinfo@nhfa.org

Historical Note
A division of National Home Furnishings Association, which provides administrative support.

Publications:
Portfolio. q.

Interlocking Concrete Pavement Institute *(1993)*
1444 I St. NW
Suite 700
Washington, DC 20005-6542
Tel: (202)712-9036 *Fax:* (202)408-0285
Toll Free: (800)241 - 3652
E-Mail: icpi@icpi.org
Web Site: www.icpi.org
Members: 80 companies
Staff: 8
Annual Budget: $2-5,000,000
Executive Director: Charles A. McGrath, CAE
Director, Engineering: Rob Burak
Director, Meetings: Julie Elfand
Technical Director: David R. Smith

Historical Note
The mission of ICPI is to increase the use of segmental concrete pavement systems in North America. Membership: $500-20,000/year.

Meetings/Conferences:
Semi-Annual Meetings: Winter and Summer
2007 - Orlando, FL/Feb. 22-24/200

Publications:
ICPI Tech Specs. 1-2/year.
Activities Update. q. adv.
Industry Survey. a.
Interlocking Concrete Pavement Magazine. q. adv.
Membership Directory. a.

Intermarket Agency Network *(1967)*
5307 S. 92nd St.
Hales Corners, WI 53130
Tel: (414)425-8800 *Fax:* (414)425-0021
Web Site: www.intermarketnetwork.com
Members: 22 companies
Staff: 1
Annual Budget: $25-50,000
Executive Director: Bill Eisner

Historical Note
Founded as Intermarket Association of Advertising Agencies; assumed its current name in 2001. IAN members are small and mid-size advertising agencies, averaging $2-30 million in billings annually. Membership: $1,750/year.

Meetings/Conferences:
Semi-Annual Meetings: Winter and Summer/25

Publications:
Newsletter. m.

Intermediaries and Reinsurance Underwriters Association *(1967)*
971 Rte. 202 North
Branchburg, NJ 08876
Tel: (908)203-0211 *Fax:* (908)203-0213
Web Site: www.irua.com
Members: 60 companies
Staff: 2
Executive Director: Mary K. Clancy
E-Mail: mkclancy@irua.com
Office Administrator: Amy Metaxas

Historical Note
Formerly Independent Reinsurance Underwriters Association (1998). Membership: $4,000/year (company).

Meetings/Conferences:
Semi-Annual Meetings: Spring and Fall

Publications:
Journal of Reinsurance. q.

Intermodal Association of North America *(1991)*
11785 Beltsville Drive
Suite 1100
Calverton, MD 20705
Tel: (301)982-3400 *Fax:* (301)982-4815
E-Mail: IANA@intermodal.org
Web Site: www.intermodal.org
Members: 600 companies
Staff: 22
Annual Budget: $2-5,000,000
President: Joanne F. "Joni" Casey
Vice President, Member Services and Business Development: Thomas J. Malloy
Manager, Marketing: Maggie Miller
E-Mail: maggie.miller@intermodal.org
Vice President, Administration and Programs: Constance M. Sheffield

Historical Note
Formed by the merger of the Intermodal Transportation Association with the Intermodal Marketing Association and the National Railroad Intermodal Association in 1991. Members are motor, rail and water transportation companies and allied services. IANA promotes the benefits of intermodal freight transportation and encourages its growth through innovation and dialogue. Membership: dues vary according to intermodal revenues.

Publications:
Intermodal Market Trends and Statistics. q.
Intermodal Freight Transportation Book (4th Edition).
Intermodal Product and Supplier Directory. a. adv.
Intermodal Insights Newsletter. m. adv.
Best Practices for Inspecting Intermodal Equipment.

Intermodal Conference

Historical Note
A conference of the Transporation Intermediaries Association.

International Academy for Child Brain Development *(1958)*
8801 Stenton Ave.
Wyndmoor, PA 19038
Tel: (215)233-2050 *Fax:* (215)233-9312
E-Mail: institutes@iahp.org
Web Site: www.IAHP.ORG
Members: 300 individuals
Staff: 115
Annual Budget: under $10,000
Director: Janet Doman
E-Mail: institutes@iahp.org

Historical Note
IACBD members are physicians, psychologists and other professionals with an interest in child brain development.

Meetings/Conferences:
Annual Meetings: Fall

International Academy of Behavioral Medicine, Counseling and Psychotherapy *(1979)*
3208 N. Academy Blvd.
Suite 160
Colorado Springs, CO 80917
Tel: (719)594-9304 *Fax:* (719)597-0166
Toll Free: (800)411 - 7359
E-Mail: addicteduc@aol.com
Members: 1000 individuals
Annual Budget: $50-100,000
Vice President, International Affairs: William Simon
E-Mail: addicteduc@aol.com

Historical Note
Formerly (1988) the American Academy of Behavioral Medicine. Incorporated in the State of Texas as an outgrowth of a regional group of southwestern therapists, the Academy has a membership of psychologists, psychiatrists and others interested in the general field of behavioral medicine and health care. Membership: $75/year.

Publications:
Membership Roster. a.
Journal of the AABM. irreg.
Newsletter. q.

International Academy of Compounding Pharmacists
P.O. Box 1365
Sugar Land, TX 77487
Toll Free: (800)927 - 4227
E-Mail: iacpinfo@iacprx.org
Web Site: www.iacprx.org
Members: 1460 individuals
Executive Director: L.D. King
E-Mail: iacpinfo@iacprx.org

Historical Note
IACP members are state-licensed pharmacists who provide and promote compounding services utilitizing their knowledge and skill in the art of preparing, mixing, assembling, packaging, or labeling drugs/devices.

Publications:
The Link. m.

International Academy of Gnathology - American Section *(1964)*
3868 Riviera Dr.
Suite 3B
San Diego, CA 92109-6351
Tel: (858)273-9263 *Fax:* (858)274-9587
E-Mail: jimbenson_99@yahoo.com
Web Site: www.gnathologyusa.org/
Members: 500 individuals
Secretary-Treasurer: James M. Benson, DDS
Historical Note
Members are dentists.
Meetings/Conferences:
Biennial Meetings: usually Fall
Publications:
Journal of Gnathology. a.

International Academy of Health Care Professionals *(1984)*
333 Glen Read Rd.
Suite 180
Old Brookville, NY 11545-1945
Tel: (516)759-4630
Members: 38 individuals
Staff: 2
Annual Budget: under $10,000
Executive Director: Henry H. Reiter, Ph.D
Historical Note
IAHCP members are physicians, psychologists, nurses and social workers.
Publications:
Newsletter. irreg.

International Academy of Oral Medicine and Toxicology *(1984)*
8297 Champions Gate Blvd.
Suite 193
Champions Gate, FL 33896
Tel: (863)420-6373 *Fax:* (863)419-8136
E-Mail: info@iaomt.org
Web Site: www.iaomt.org
Members: 444 individuals
Staff: 1
Annual Budget: $100-250,000
Executive Director: Kim Smith
E-Mail: info@iaomt.org
Historical Note
IAOMT members are dentists and other medical professionals with an interest in the biocompatibility of materials. Membership: $425 (initial); $350/year (renewal).
Meetings/Conferences:
2007 - Tucson, AZ(Marriott)/March 15-17/200
Publications:
Membership Directory. 2/year.
Bio-Probe Newsletter. bi-m.
In Vivo Newsletter. q.

International Academy of Trial Lawyers *(1954)*
5841 Cedar Lake Rd.
Suite 204
Minneapolis, MN 55416
Tel: (952)546-2364 *Fax:* (952)545-6073
E-Mail: lindascher@llmis.com
Web Site: www.iatl.net
Members: 800 individuals
Staff: 3
Annual Budget: $1-2,000,000
Executive Director: Linda Wilkerson
Historical Note
Members are defense and plaintiff attorneys who have had a minimum of 12 years of trial or appellate practice. The Academy works for the enhancement and protection of the jury system and the enhancement of integrity within the profession. Membership: $600/year (individual).
Meetings/Conferences:
Annual Meetings: Spring/200
2007 - Chicago, IL(Four Seasons)/Apr. 10-15/300
Publications:
IATL Bulletin. 3/year.
Student Advocacy Report. a.
Dean's Address. a.

International Accounts Payable Professionals
P.O. Box 590373
Orlando, FL 32859-0373
Tel: (407)351-3322 *Fax:* (407)345-8351
E-Mail: inquire@iappnet.org
Web Site: www.iappnet.org
Members: 4000 individuals
Executive Director: Nelda Barkley
Historical Note
Awards the designation CAPP (Certified Accounts Payable Professional). Membership: $225/year
Meetings/Conferences:
Annual Meetings: Spring

International Advertising Association *(1938)*
521 Fifth Ave.
Suite 1807
New York, NY 10175
Tel: (212)557-1133 *Fax:* (212)983-0455
Web Site: www.iaaglobal.org
Members: 5100 individuals
Staff: 5
Annual Budget: $1-2,000,000
IAA World President: Joseph Ghossoub
Manager, Information Systems: Karl Kam
Executive Administrator: Arlene Kerins
Coordinator, Education: Nubia Martinez
E-Mail: marie@iaaglobal.org
Director, Membership Services: Marie J. Scotti
E-Mail: marie@iaaglobal.org
Historical Note
Formerly (1954) Export Advertising Association. IAA is the only global partnership of advertisers, agencies, the media, and related service providers. Its principal objectives are to protect freedom of commercial speech and consumer choice, to promote the value of advertising and to encourage self-regulation. Membership: $200/year (individual), $9,000/year (corporate); $405/year (organization).
Meetings/Conferences:
Annual Meetings: even years
Publications:
IAA Annual Report and Membership Directory. a. adv.

The International Air Cargo Association *(1994)*
P.O. Box 661510
Miami, FL 33266-1510
Tel: (786)265-7011 *Fax:* (786)265-7012
E-Mail: secgen@tiaca.org
Web Site: www.tiaca.org
Members: 335 individuals
Staff: 4
Secretary General: Daniel C. Fernandez
E-Mail: secgen@tiaca.org
Director, Operations: Leslie Herren
Historical Note
TIACA members include all major components of the industry - air and surface carriers, forwarders, shippers, vendors, manufacturers, airports, countries, financial institutions and consultants. TIACA also represents regional, national and city air cargo associations, service providers to the industry and educational institutions and their students involved in air cargo training. TIACA acts as a catalyst to improve industry cooperation, promote innovation, share knowledge, enhance quality and efficiency, develop educational and trade vehicles, and act as the voice of the industry whenever and wherever possible.
Meetings/Conferences:
Annual Meetings: Fall
2008 - Kuala Lumpur, Malaysia(Kuala Lmpur Convention Center)
Publications:
TIACA Times. q.

International Alliance for Women *(1980)*
8405 Greensboro Dr., Suite 800
McLean, VA 22102
Tel: (703)506-3284 *Fax:* (905)305-1548
Toll Free: (866)533 - 8429
E-Mail: info@tiaw.org
Web Site: www.tiaw.org
Members: 30000 individuals
Staff: 2
Annual Budget: $100-250,000
Executive Director: Maxine Westaway
Historical Note
Alliance members are executive and professional women. Membership: $150/year, plus $25 initiation fee (individual); $5 per member, $400 minimum (group).
Publications:
eConnections.
Alliance Newsletter. bi-m. adv.
Membership Directory. a.
eBulletins.

International Alliance for Women in Music *(1976)*
Box 2731, Rollins College
1000 Holt Ave.
Winter Park, FL 32789-4499
E-Mail: slackman@rollins.edu
Web Site: www.iawm.org
Members: 300 individuals
Staff: 1
Annual Budget: under $10,000
Contact: Susan Cohn Lackman
E-Mail: slackman@rollins.edu
Historical Note
Formerly (1995) American Women Composers. Members are women composers, performers, musicologists, and their supporters. Maintains a music library and holds various symposia and concerts throughout the year. The organization was formed to establish a network of support and encouragement for female musicians; to gain status and recognition for female musicians; to offer financial assistance for female efforts in the compositional arena; and to provide a forum for the interchange of ideas through workshops, meetings, and performances. Membership: $20/year (senior/student); $40/year (individual); $50/year (organization/company); $75/year (board affiliate).
Publications:
Women and Music: A Journal of Gender and Culture.
IAWM Journal. q.
News/Updates. bi-a.

International Alliance of Technology Integrators
1100 College St.
Northfield, MN 55057-2835
Tel: (507)664-9548 *Fax:* (786)551-2952
Web Site: www.iati.org
Staff: 2
Annual Budget: $10-25,000,000
Executive Director: Scott Davis
Historical Note
Member companies, restricted to one per market, are proven leaders in information technology integration in their respective markets.

International Alliance of Theatrical Stage Employees and Moving Picture Technicians of the U.S., Its Territories and Canada *(1893)*
1430 Broadway, 20th Floor
New York, NY 10018
Tel: (212)730-1770 *Fax:* (212)921-7699
Web Site: www.iatse-intl.org
Members: 105000 individuals
Staff: 30
Annual Budget: $2-5,000,000
President: Thomas Short
General Secretary-Treasurer: James Wood
Historical Note
Established in New York City on July 20, 1893 as the National Alliance of Theatrical Stage Employees of the United States and chartered by the American Federation of Labor in 1894. In 1899, with the acceptance of two Canadian locals, the words "and Canada" were added, and in 1902 "International" was subsituted for "National." When the union was granted jurisdiction over motion picture projectionists in 1914, the present name was adopted.
Meetings/Conferences:
Biennial Meetings: Odd Years
Publications:
The Organizer.
The Official Bulletin. q.

International Allied Printing Trades Association *(1896)*
1900 L St. NW, Eighth Floor
Washington, DC 20036
Tel: (202)462-1400 *Fax:* (202)721-0641
Members: 2 labor unions
Secretary-Treasurer: Robert Lacey

Historical Note
Exercises jurisdiction throughout the United States and Canada in regard to the Allied Printing Trades Label. Member unions are the Graphic Communications Conference/IBT and the Printing, Publishing & Media Workers Sector of the C.W.A. Adopted and owned by the Association, the label designates the products of the labor of its members.

International Aloe Science Council *(1981)*
415 E. Airport Fwy
Suite 150
Irving, TX 75062-6332
Tel: (972)258-8772 *Fax:* (972)258-8777
E-Mail: iasc1@msn.com
Web Site: www.iasc.org
Members: 275 Companies
Staff: 3
Annual Budget: $250-500,000
Executive Director: Gene Hale
E-Mail: iasc1@msn.com

Historical Note
Formerly known as the National Aloe Science Council (1990). The International Aloe Science Council is a non-profit trade organization for the Aloe Vera industry world-wide. Membership includes aloe growers, processors, finished goods manufacturers, marketing companies, insurance companies, equipment suppliers, printers, sales organizations, physicians, scientists and researchers. Membership: $1,100-2,000/year (organization/company).

Publications:
Inside Aloe. 8/year. adv.

International American Albino Association *(1936)*

Historical Note
The International American Albino Association does business and is listed as the American White/American Creme Horse Registry (AWACHR).

International Analgesia Society
3100 Wellington Pkwy.
Birmingham, AL 35243-9846
Tel: (205)967-5009
Staff: 1
Executive Director: Robert E. Hamric, DMD

Historical Note
Members are dentists and medical professionals in the science of pain reduction.

International and American Associations of Clinical Nutritionists *(1983)*
15280 Addison Rd.
Suite 130
Addison, TX 75001
Tel: (972)407-9089 *Fax:* (972)250-0233
E-Mail: khenry@clinicalnutrition.com
Web Site: www.iaacn.org
Staff: 5
Annual Budget: $250-500,000
Executive Secretary: Winna C. Henry
E-Mail: khenry@clinicalnutrition.com

Historical Note
IAACN represents clinical nutritionists in all of the licensed health care fields. Merged with International Academy of Nutrition and Preventive Medicine in 1997. Sponsors the Certified Clinical Nutritionist (CCN) designation through the Clinical Nutrition Certification Board and Columbia Assessment Services, Inc. Five levels of membership. Professional: $295/year (individual).

Publications:
IAACN Insight. q. adv.
Journal of Applied Nutrition. q. adv.

International Andalusian and Lusitano Horse Association
101 Carnoustie North
Suite 200
Birmingham, AL 35242
Tel: (205)995-8900 *Fax:* (205)995-8966
Web Site: www.ialha.org
Members: 1900 individuals
Staff: 6
Executive Director: Martina Philpott

Historical Note
IALHA is the largest membership organization in the country devoted to Iberian horses and related interests.

Publications:
The Andalusian. 4/year. adv.

International Anesthesia Research Society *(1922)*
Two Summit Park Dr.
Suite 140
Cleveland, OH 44131-2571
Tel: (216)642-1124 *Fax:* (216)642-1127
E-Mail: iarshq@iars.org
Web Site: www.iars.org
Members: 15000 individuals
Staff: 7
Executive Director: Anne F. Maggiore
E-Mail: iarshq@iars.org

Meetings/Conferences:
Annual Meetings: Spring
2007 – Orlando, FL(Wyndham Palace)/March 23-27/1000

Publications:
Anesthesia & Analgesia. m. adv.

International Animated Film Society, ASIFA-Hollywood *(1972)*
2114 Burbank Blvd.
Burbank, CA 91506
Tel: (818)842-8330 *Fax:* (818)842-5645
E-Mail: asifaalert-subscribe@yahoogroups.com
Web Site: www.asifa-hollywood.org
Members: 1200 individuals
Staff: 2
Annual Budget: $250-500,000
President: Antran Manoogian
E-Mail: asifaalert-subscribe@yahoogroups.com

Historical Note
U.S. chapter of the international organization. ASIFA members are professional animators and others with an interest in film animation. Sponsors programs for film preservation and exhibition. Membership: $45/year (individual); $20/year (student).

Publications:
2Q (Zoetrope Quarterly). q.
Annie Awards Annual Program Book. a. adv.

International Association Colon Hydro Therapy *(1989)*
P.O. Box 461285
San Antonio, TX 78246-1285
Tel: (210)366-2888 *Fax:* (210)366-2999
E-Mail: iact@healthy.net
Web Site: www.i-act.org
Members: 1000 individuals
Staff: 5
Annual Budget: $100-250,000
Executive Director: A.R. Hoenninger, Ph.D.
E-Mail: iact@healthy.net

Historical Note
Formerly (1995) the American Colon Therapy Association. IACT members are colon hygiene therapists and other health care professionals. Educational certification is provided by the group. Membership: $150/year.

Publications:
IACT Newsletter. q. adv.
IACT Membership Directory. a.

International Association for Business and Society *(1990)*
Duquesne University
600 Forbes Ave.
Pittsburgh, PA 15282
Tel: (412)396-4005 *Fax:* (412)396-1359
E-Mail: iabs@iabs.net
Web Site: www.iabs.net
Members: 300 individuals
Executive Director: Jenn Griffin

Historical Note
IABS is a learned society devoted to research and teaching about the relationships between business, government and society.

Meetings/Conferences:
Annual Meetings: Summer

Publications:
Business & Society Journal. q.
IABS Newsletter. 3/year.

International Association for Cold Storage Construction *(1981)*
1500 King St., Suite 201
Alexandria, VA 22314-2730
Tel: (703)373-4300 *Fax:* (703)373-4301
E-Mail: email@iacsc.org
Web Site: www.iacsc.org
Members: 165 companies
Staff: 3
Annual Budget: $100-250,000
President and Chief Executive Officer: J. William Hudson

Historical Note
Trade association for the low-temperature facility construction industry. Formerly (1989) National Association of Cold Storage Contractors. Membership: $700/year.

Meetings/Conferences:
Annual Meetings: Fall

Publications:
Newsletter. 2/yr. adv.
Directory. a. adv.

International Association for Computer Information Systems *(1960)*
220 College of Business Administration
Oklahoma State University
Stillwater, OK 74078
Tel: (405)744-8632 *Fax:* (405)744-5180
Web Site: www.iacis.org
Members: 500 individuals
Annual Budget: $50-100,000
Managing Director: Dr. G. Daryl Nord
E-Mail: dnord@okstate.edu

Historical Note
Formerly (1987) Society for Data Educators and (1990) Association for Computer Educators. IACIS members are individuals with a particular interest in all levels of computers. Membership: $50/year (individuals); $175/year (institutions).

Meetings/Conferences:
Annual Meetings: September-October

Publications:
Journal of Computer Information Systems. q.

International Association for Computer Systems Security *(1981)*
Six Swarthmore Lane
Dix Hills, NY 11746
Tel: (631)499-1616 *Fax:* (631)462-9178
E-Mail: iacssjalex@aol.com
Web Site: www.iacss.com
Members: 800 individuals
Staff: 16
Annual Budget: $100-250,000
President and Founder: Robert J. Wilk, P.Eng, CSSP
E-Mail: iacssjalex@aol.com

Historical Note
Members are organizations and individuals with an interest in the security of computer information systems. Certifies individuals as Computer Systems Security Professionals (CSSP) since 1983.

Publications:
Security and Control of your PC/Micro Network.

International Association for Continuing Education and Training *(1968)*
1620 I St. NW
Suite 615
Washington, DC 20006
Tel: (202)463-2905 *Fax:* (202)463-8498
E-Mail: iacet@iacet.org
Web Site: www.iacet.org
Members: 720 organizations
Staff: 3
Annual Budget: $1-2,000,000

Executive Director: Scott Farrow

Historical Note

Formerly (1990) the Council on the Continuing Education Unit. Members are educational institutions, hospitals, professional societies and others providing continuing education. Seeks to standardize and improve the quality of continuing education and training.

Publications:

IACET Reporter Newsletter. m.
Membership Directory (online).

International Association for Dental Research *(1920)*

Historical Note

See American Association for Dental Research.

International Association for Exhibition Management *(1928)*

8111 LBJ Fwy., Suite 750
Dallas, TX 75251-1313
Tel: (972)458-8002 *Fax:* (972)458-8119
E-Mail: iaem@iaem.org
Web Site: www.iaem.org
Members: 3500 individuals
Staff: 23
Annual Budget: $1-2,000,000
President: Steven G. Hacker, CAE
E-Mail: shacker@iaem.org
Chief Operating Officer: Cathy Breden, CAE, CMP
Marketing and Communications Manager: Michelle Mackey

Historical Note

Formed in Cleveland in 1928 as the National Association of Exhibit Managers; adopted its present name in 2000. Members are managers of shows, exhibits and expositions; associate members are industry suppliers. Awards the designation CEM (Certified in Exposition Management). Member of the Center for Exhibition Industry Research. IAEM Services, Inc. is a for-profit subsidiary, offering publications and other services. Operates a fax-on-demand service: (214) 353-6140. Dues are based on Annual Exhibition Revenues derived from the exhibition industry.

Meetings/Conferences:

Semi-Annual Meetings: June and December

Publications:

E2: Exhibitons and Events. m. adv.

International Association for Food Protection *(1911)*

6200 Aurora Ave., Suite 200W
Des Moines, IA 50322-2864
Tel: (515)276-3344 *Fax:* (515)276-8655
Toll Free: (800)369 - 6337
E-Mail: info@foodprotection.org
Web Site: www.foodprotection.org
Members: 3000 individuals
Staff: 12
Annual Budget: $2-5,000,000
Executive Director: David W. Tharp
Director, Membership: Julie Cattanach
Assistant Director: Lisa K. Hovey

Historical Note

Founded as the International Association of Dairy and Milk Inspectors; became the International Association of Milk Sanitarians in 1938, the International Association of Milk and Food Sanitarians in 1949, and then the International Association of Milk, Food and Environmental Sanitarians in 1966 before assuming its present name in 2000. Members are professionals from the industry, government, and academia with an interest in sanitary food product handling practices. Membership: $100-185/year (individual); $750-5,000/year (sustaining); $115-220/year (Canada and Mexico); $130-265/year (international).

Meetings/Conferences:

Annual Meetings: Summer
2007 - Lake Buena Vista, FL(Disney Contemporary Resort)/July 8-11/1600
2008 - Columbus, OH(Hyatt Regency)/Aug. 3-6/1800

Publications:

Food Protection Trends. m. adv.
Journal of Food Protection. m. adv.

International Association for Healthcare Security and Safety *(1968)*

P.O. Box 538
Glendale Heights, IL 60139
Tel: (630)871-9936 *Fax:* (630)871-9938
Toll Free: (888)353 - 0990
E-Mail: iahss@iahss.org
Web Site: www.iahss.org
Members: 1700 individuals
Staff: 5
Annual Budget: $250-500,000
Executive Director: James J. Balija, CAE
E-Mail: iahss@iahss.org

Historical Note

Formerly (1991) International Association for Hospital Security. An affiliate of the American Hospital Association. IAHSS is a non-profit organization of healthcare security and safety executives around the world. Membership: $175/year (general member); $100/year (senior member); $50/year (associate member).

Meetings/Conferences:

Annual Meetings: Summer
2007 - Boston, MA/July 24-27

Publications:

IAHSS Newsletter. q. adv.
Journal of Healthcare Protection Management. bi-a.

International Association for Human Resource Information Management *(1980)*

P.O. Box 1086
Burlington, MA 01803
Toll Free: (800)946 - 6363
E-Mail: moreinfo@ihrim.org
Web Site: www.ihrim.org
Members: 3000 individuals
Staff: 5
Annual Budget: $2-5,000,000
President and Chief Executive Officer: Lynne Mealy

Historical Note

Formerly the Association of Human Resource System Professionals (HRSP), HRSP unified with its Canadian counterpart (CHRSP) in 1996 and assumed its current name. IHRIM members are human resource or information systems professionals concerned with the development, maintenance and operation of human resource information and management systems. Membership: $195/year (individual).

Meetings/Conferences:

Annual Meetings: Spring

Publications:

IHRIM Journal. q. adv.
IHRIM Link. bi-m. adv.

International Association for Hydrogen Energy *(1975)*

5783 S.W. 40th St.
#303
Miami, FL 33155
Tel: (305)284-4666 *Fax:* (305)284-4792
E-Mail: ayfer@iahe.org
Web Site: www.iahe.org
Members: 2600 individuals
Staff: 4
Annual Budget: $100-250,000
President: T. Nejat Veziroglu, Ph.D.
E-Mail: ayfer@iahe.org

Historical Note

Established at the Hydrogen Economy Miami Energy Conference in Miami in March 1974 and incorporated in Florida in 1975. Members, hailing from 86 countries, are scientists and engineers professionally involved in the development of hydrogen energy. Membership: $140/year (individual); $80/year (associate); $950/year (institution).

Meetings/Conferences:

Annual Meetings: Summer

Publications:

International Journal of Hydrogen Energy. 15/year. adv.
Conference Proceedings. a.

International Association for Identification *(1915)*

2535 Pilot Knob Road, Suite 117
Mendota Heights, MN 55120-1120
Tel: (651)681-8566 *Fax:* (651)681-8443
E-Mail: iaisecty@theiai.org
Web Site: www.theiai.org
Members: 6000 individuals
Staff: 8
Annual Budget: $500-1,000,000
Chief Operating Officer: Joseph P. Polski
Planner, Education Program: James Gettemy
Planner, Conference: Candance Murray

Historical Note

Organized in 1915 in Oakland, CA as the International Association for Criminal Identification; assumed its present name in 1920. Absorbed the International Association for Voice Identification in 1981. Membership consists of persons engaged in forensic identification, investigation and scientific examination of physical evidence. IAI promotes research in forensic sciences and is responsible for six international certification programs for Latent Print Examiners, Voice Print Examiners, Crime Scene Technicians, Bloodstain Pattern Analysis, Footwear and Tiretrack Examination and Forensic Art. Membership: $60/year (U.S. members); $50/year (foreign members); $30/year (U.S. student members); $25/year (foreign student members).

Meetings/Conferences:

Annual Meetings: Summer
2007 - San Diego, CA(Town and Country Convention Center)/July 22-27

Publications:

IAI Membership Directory. a. adv.
Journal of Forensic Identification. bi-m.

International Association for Impact Assessment *(1980)*

1330 23rd St. South, Suite C
Fargo, ND 58103
Tel: (701)297-7908 *Fax:* (701)297-7917
E-Mail: info@iaia.org
Web Site: www.iaia.org
Members: 2500 individuals
Staff: 4
Annual Budget: $500-1,000,000
Chief Executive Officer: Rita Hamm
E-Mail: info@iaia.org

Historical Note

Founded and chartered in Atlanta, GA, IAIA is a professional society. Members are professionals from around the world who assess environmental, social and technological impact for both the private and public sectors. Members are corporate planners and managers, public interest advocates, government planners and administrators, private consultants and policy analysts, and university teachers and their students. Membership: $80/year (individual); $110/year (joint); $50/year (student/retired); corporate rate varies.

Meetings/Conferences:

Annual Meetings: June/500

Publications:

Impact Assessment & Project Appraisal. q. adv.
IAIA Newsletter. q. adv.

International Association for Insurance Law - United States Chapter *(1963)*

P.O. Box 9001
Mt. Vernon, NY 10552
Tel: (914)966-3180 Ext: 110 *Fax:* (914)966-3264
Web Site: www.aidaus.org
Members: 700 individuals
Annual Budget: $50-100,000
Executive Director: Stephen C. Acunto
E-Mail: sa@cinn.com
Conference Director: Bill Yankus
E-Mail: byankus@cinn.com

Historical Note

The national affiliate of the Association Internationale de Droit des Assurances (AIDA), U.S. Chapter members are attorneys, professors, regulators and others who are interested in international or comparative aspects of insurance law and regulation. In addition to supporting the work of AIDA on an international basis, the U.S. Chapter sponsors *seminars on regulation, publishes a regular bulletin of the international working group on pollution, publishes a newsletter, and serves as a vehicle through which its members can become involved with international projects or make contact with fellow professionals overseas. Membership: $100/year (individual).*

Publications:
AIDA-US Newsletter. q.

International Association for Jazz Education
(1968)
P.O. Box 724
Manhattan, KS 66505
Tel: (785)776-8744 *Fax:* (785)776-6190
Web Site: www.iaje.org
Members: 9000 individuals
Staff: 11
Annual Budget: $1-2,000,000
Executive Director: Bill McFarlin
E-Mail: bill@iaje.org

Historical Note
Formerly the National Association of Jazz Educators, it became international in 1989. Members are music teachers at all educational levels, librarians, musicians, and representatives from the music industry. IAJE is a member of the Music Educators National Conference. Membership: $70/year (individual); $250-8,000/year (company).

Meetings/Conferences:
Annual Meetings: January/3,500
2007 – New York, NY(Hilton and Sheraton)
2008 – Toronto, ON, Canada(Royal York and Crowne Plaza)/Jan. 9-12
2009 – Seattle, WA

Publications:
Jazz Educators Journal. bi-m. adv.

International Association for Language Learning Technology *(1965)*
c/o Instructional Media Services, Concordia College
Moorhead, MN 56562
Tel: (218)299-3464 *Fax:* (218)299-3246
E-Mail: business@iallt.org
Web Site: http://iallt.org
Members: 500 individuals
Staff: 1
Annual Budget: $10-25,000
Treasurer: Ron Balko
E-Mail: business@iallt.org

Historical Note
Members are involved in the administration or operation of language learning facilities and foreign language programs. Founded as the National Association of Language Lab Directors, it became the National Association Learning Laboratories and later became the International Association for Learning Laboratories before assuming its present name in 1982. Affiliated with the American Council on the Teaching of Foreign Languages and the Computer Assisted Language Learning Consortium. Membership: $50/year or $90/2 years (educational member); $75/year or $140/2 years (commercial member).

Meetings/Conferences:
Biennial meetings: Summer

Publications:
IALLT Journal of Language Learning Technologies. bi-a. adv.

International Association for Mathematical Geology *(1968)*
4 Cataraqui St., Suite 310
Kingston, ON K7K 1-Z7
Tel: (613)544-6878 *Fax:* (613)531-0626
E-Mail: office@iamg.org
Web Site: www.iamg.org
Members: 500 individuals
Annual Budget: $50-100,000
Administrative Coordinator: Pamela Lyons
E-Mail: office@iamg.org

Historical Note
Founded at the XXIII International Geological Congress, Prague, Czechoslovakia in 1968. Professional geologists, mathematicians and others interested in the application and use of mathematics in geological research and technology. Affiliated with the International Statistical Institute and the International Union of Geological Sciences. Has no paid officers or full-time staff.

Meetings/Conferences:
Annual Meetings: Fall

Publications:
Natural Resources Research. q.
Computers & Geosciences. 10/year.
Mathematical Geology. 8/year.
Studies in Mathematical Geology Series.

International Association for Modular Exhibitry
(1987)
155 West St., Unit Three
Wilmington, MA 01887-3064
Tel: (978)988-1100 *Fax:* (978)988-1128
Members: 47 companies
Staff: 7
Annual Budget: $100-250,000
Executive Director: Irving Sacks
E-Mail: isacks6421@aol.com

Historical Note
IAME members are companies with an interest in promoting the use of modular exhibits for trade shows and museums.

Meetings/Conferences:
Annual Meetings:

Publications:
Newsletter. q.

International Association for Near Death Studies *(1981)*
P.O. Box 502
East Windsor Hill, CT 06028
Tel: (860)882-1211 *Fax:* (860)882-1212
E-Mail: services@iand.org
Web Site: www.iands.org
Members: 1200 individuals
Staff: 1
Administrative Assistant: Janet Scollo
E-Mail: services@iand.org

Historical Note
IANDS works to build understanding of near-death and near-death like experiences through research, education and support.

Publications:
Vital Signs. q. adv.
Journal of Near-Death Studies. q.

International Association for Orthodontics
(1961)
750 N. Lincoln Memorial Dr., Suite 442
Milwaukee, WI 53202
Tel: (414)272-2757 *Fax:* (414)272-2754
E-Mail: worldheadquarters@iaortho.org
Web Site: www.iaortho.org
Members: 3600 individuals
Staff: 4
Annual Budget: $500-1,000,000
Executive Director: Detlef B. Moore

Historical Note
Formerly International Academy of Orthodontics. IAO trains general and pediatric dentists in the practice of orthodontics. Membership: $198/year.

Meetings/Conferences:
Annual Meetings: Fall/500-600

Publications:
International Journal of Orthodontics. q. adv.
Orthodontic Suppliers Directory. a.
Membership Directory. a.

International Association for Philosophy and Literature *(1976)*
Department of Philosophy
Stony Brook University
Stony Brook, NY 11794-3750
Tel: (631)632-7592 *Fax:* (631)632-7522
E-Mail: hsilverman@ms.cc.sunysb.edu
Web Site: www.iapl.info
Members: 3000 individuals
Staff: 2
Annual Budget: $10-25,000
Executive Director: Prof. Hugh J. Silverman
E-Mail: hsilverman@ms.cc.sunysb.edu

Historical Note
IAPL members are scholars and educators interested in interdisciplinary approaches to philosophy and literature. Membership: $45/year.

Meetings/Conferences:
Annual Meetings: April-May

Publications:
Continuum Books.
Textures-Philosophy/Literature/Culture Book Series.
Contemporary Studies in Philosophy and Literature. a.

International Association for Philosophy of Law and Social Philosophy - American Section *(1963)*
Univ. of Hawaii Coll. of Philosophy, 2530 Dole St.
Honolulu, HI 96822-2383
Tel: (808)956-8954 *Fax:* (808)956-9228
Members: 325 individuals
Staff: 1
Annual Budget: under $10,000
Executive Director: Ken Kipnis
E-Mail: kkipnis@hawaii.edu

Historical Note
AMINTAPHIL members are professors of philosophy, law and the social sciences in the United States and Canada. Membership: $15/year (individual).

Meetings/Conferences:
Biennial Meeting:

Publications:
Newsletter. q.
Conference Proceedings. bien.

International Association for the Leisure and Entertainment Industry *(1993)*
10 Briarcrest Sq.
Hershey, PA 17033
Tel: (717)533-0534 *Fax:* (717)533-0535
Toll Free: (888)464 - 6498
E-Mail: info@ialei.org
Web Site: www.ialei.org
Members: 860 companies
Staff: 5
Annual Budget: $500-1,000,000
Executive Director: Tracy Sarris
Director, Finance and Tradeshows: Ray Sjolander
E-Mail: ray@ialei.com

Historical Note
Founded as International Association of Family Entertainment Centers; assumed its current name in 1999. Members are owners and operators of location-based family entertainment centers, as well as developers and suppliers who serve the family entertainment center industry. Provides research, education, publications and discounts on products to promote successful center operations. Owns and sponsors Fun Expo. Membership: $275-350/year.

Meetings/Conferences:
Annual Meetings: Fall/8,500

Publications:
Membership Directory and Buyers' Guide. a. adv.
Fun Extra. m. adv.

International Association for the Study of Cooperation in Education *(1979)*
P.O. Box 390
Readfield, ME 04355
Tel: (207)685-3171 *Fax:* (207)685-4455
Web Site: www.iasce.net
Members: 1000 individuals
Annual Budget: under $10,000
Publications Chair: Kathryn Markovchick
E-Mail: kathrynm@maine.edu

Historical Note
Members are educators and other professionals with an interest in the use of cooperative activities in education. Has no paid officers or full-time staff. Membership: $20/year (individual); $35/year (company).

Publications:
Cooperative Learning. 3/year.

International Association for the Study of Organized Crime *(1984)*
P.O. Box 50484

Washington, DC 20091
E-Mail: iasoc_office@yahoo.com
Web Site: www.iasoc.net
Members: 350 individuals
Annual Budget: under $10,000
Executive Director: Jay Albanese
E-Mail: iasoc_office@yahoo.com

Historical Note
Researchers, investigators, and educators interested in the study of organized crime. Has no paid staff. Membership: $25/year (individual member living in U.S. or Canada); $55/year (individual member outside North America).

Meetings/Conferences:
Annual Meetings: *held in conjunction with American Society of Criminology in November*

Publications:
Trends in Organized Crime. q. adv.

International Association for the Study of Pain *(1973)*
909 N.E. 43rd St., Suite 306
Seattle, WA 98105-6020
Tel: (206)547-6409 *Fax:* (206)547-1703
E-Mail: iaspdesk@iasp-pain.org
Web Site: www.iasp-pain.org
Members: 6300 individuals
Staff: 12
Annual Budget: $1-2,000,000
Executive Officer: Louisa E. Jones
E-Mail: iaspdesk@iasp-pain.org

Historical Note
Founded in Seattle, Washington, IASP was incorporated in Washington, DC in 1974. Members are scientists, physicians and other health professionals actively engaged in pain research and those who have a special interest in diagnosis and treatment of pain syndromes. Membership: $110-175/year (individual).

Meetings/Conferences:
Triennial Meetings: *Summer*
2008 – Glasgow, United Kingdom(Scottish Convention Center)/Apr. 17-22/4000

Publications:
IASP Newsletter. q.
Pain: Clinical Updates. q.
Pain. m. adv.
Directory of Members. a.

International Association for Truancy and Dropout Prevention *(1911)*
P.O. Box 2188
Knoxville, TN 37901
Tel: (865)594-1506 *Fax:* (865)594-1504
Web Site: www.iatdp.org/
Members: 400 individuals
Annual Budget: $10-25,000
Executive Director: Jimmie Thacker

Historical Note
Founded as National League to Promote School Attendance; became International Association of Pupil Personnel Workers in 1957, and assumed its current name in 2004. IATDP members are pupil personnel workers, social workers and others concerned with school attendance. Membership: $35/year.

Meetings/Conferences:
Annual Meetings: *October*

Publications:
IAPPW Directory. a.
IAPPW Journal for Truancy and Dropout Prevention. semi-a.

International Association of Accident Reconstruction Specialists *(1980)*
P.O. Box 534
Grand Ledge, MI 48837-0534
Tel: (517)622-3135
Web Site: www.iaars.org
Members: 130 individuals
Secretary-Treasurer: Bill Brandt

Historical Note
Composed of members and associates from 38 states, as well as abroad. Membership comprised of law enforcement officers and civilian personnel.

Publications:
Centerline. irreg.

International Association of Addictions and Offender Counselors *(1974)*
c/o American Counseling Ass'n
5999 Stevenson Ave.
Alexandria, VA 22304
Tel: (703)823-9800 Ext: 222 *Fax:* (703)823-4786
Toll Free: (800)347 - 6647 Ext: 222
Web Site: www.counseling.org
Members: 958 individuals
Director, Publications: Carolyn Baker

Historical Note
Formerly (1990) Public Offenders Counselors Association. IAAOC advocates the development of effective counseling and rehabilitation programs for people with substance abuse problems, other addictions and adult and/or juvenile public offenders. A division of the American Counseling Association. Membership: $45/year (professional); $30/year (student/retired).

Meetings/Conferences:
Annual Meetings: *Spring, with the American Counseling Ass'n*
2007 – Detroit, MI(Convention Center)/March 21-25/300

Publications:
IAAOC News newsletter. 3/year. adv.
Journal of Addictions & Offender Counseling. semi-a. adv.

International Association of Administrative Professionals *(1942)*
10502 N.W. Ambassador Dr.
Kansas City, MO 64153
Tel: (816)891-6600 *Fax:* (816)891-9118
E-Mail: service@iaap-hq.org
Web Site: www.iaap-hq.org
Members: 40000 individuals
Staff: 30
Annual Budget: $2-5,000,000
Executive Director: Donald Bretthauer, CAE
E-Mail: executivedirector@iaap-hq.org
Manager, Education and Professional DeVice: Susan Fenner, Ph.D.
Manager, Conventions and Meetings: Inge Hafkemeyer
Manager, Membership Services: Robin Parrish
Manager, Certification: Kathy Schoneboom
Manager, Communications: Rick Stroud
Controller: Suzanne Tuff

Historical Note
Formerly (1998) Professional Secretaries International. Formerly (1981) National Secretaries Association (International). Incorporated in the State of Missouri, IAAP is a non-profit professional association sponsoring the Institute for Certifying Secretaries which awards the designation "Certified Administrative Professional" (CAP). IAAP services include the IAAP Research and Educational Foundation, a nonprofit trust which coordinates and authorizes research, distributes findings and provides public instruction related to the administrative profession. Membership: $15 initial fee; $48/year renewal.

Meetings/Conferences:
Annual Meetings: *Summer/1,700*
2007 – Tampa, FL(Convention Center)/July 29-Apr. 1
2008 – Reno, NV(Hilton)/July 20-23
2009 – Minneapolis, MN(Convention Center)/July 26-29
2010 – Boston, MA(Hynes Convention Center)/July 18-21
2011 – Montreal, QC, Canada(Montreal Convention Center)/July 24-27

Publications:
Office PRO. 9/year. adv.
IAAP Bits and Bytes Newsletter.

International Association of Airport Duty Free Stores *(1970)*
2025 M St. NW, Suite 800
Washington, DC 20036-3309
Tel: (202)367-1184 *Fax:* (202)429-5154
E-Mail: iaadfs@iaafds.org
Web Site: www.IAADFS.ORG
Members: 475 companies
Staff: 3
Annual Budget: $1-2,000,000
Associate Executive Director: Michael L. Payne
Associate Executive Director: Steven G. Antolick

Historical Note
Provides market research and professional development to member stores and suppliers. Membership: $450/year.

Meetings/Conferences:
Annual Meetings: *Spring*
2007 – Ft. Lauderdale, FL(Broward County Convention Center)/Apr. 22-26

Publications:
Show Guide. a. adv.
Membership Directory. a. adv.

International Association of Amusement Parks and Attractions *(1918)*
1448 Duke St.
Alexandria, VA 22314-3403
Tel: (703)836-4800 *Fax:* (703)836-4801
E-Mail: iaapa@iaapa.org
Web Site: www.iaapa.org
Members: 5000 companies
Staff: 36
Annual Budget: $10-25,000,000
President and Chief Executive Officer: Charlie Bray
Vice President, Membership and Marketing Services: Ana Elisa Benavent
Vice President, Government Relations: Randall P. Davis
Vice President, Finance and Support Services: Tom Fischetti
Vice President, Exhibitions/Conventions and Meeting Services: David Lee
Executive Vice President: Susan Mosedale

Historical Note
Formed as National Association of Amusement Parks, Pools and Beaches; formed in a merger of the National Association of Amusement Parks and the American Association of Pools and Beaches. Became (1964) the International Association of Amusement Parks; assumed its present name in 1972. Absorbed the National Water Slide Association in 1982. Sponsors and supports the International Association of Amusement Parks and Attractions Political Action Committee. Organizes the IAAPA Attractions Expo Trade Show.

Meetings/Conferences:
Annual Meetings: *Fall*

Publications:
On Site Convention Guide. a. adv.
Sponsorship Program. a. adv.
Funworld. m. adv.

International Association of Approved Basketball Officials *(1921)*
P.O. Box 1300
Germantown, MD 20875-1300
Tel: (301)540-5180 *Fax:* (301)540-5182
E-Mail: iaabo@erols.com
Web Site: www.iaabo.org
Members: 16000 individuals
Staff: 4
Annual Budget: $250-500,000
Executive Director: Paul J. Loube

Historical Note
A recruiting and training association for basketball officials. Membership: $40/year (individual).

Meetings/Conferences:
Semi-Annual Meetings: *Spring and Fall*

Publications:
Sportorials. 7/year.
Basketball Handbook. a.

International Association of Aquatic and Marine Science Libraries and Information Centers *(1975)*
Harbor Branch Oceanographic Institution, 5600 U.S. 1 North
Ft. Pierce, FL 34946
Tel: (772)465-2400 Ext: 201 *Fax:* (772)465-2446
E-Mail: iamslic@ucdavis.edu
Web Site: www.iamslic.org
Members: 350librariesandinformationctrs.
Annual Budget: under $10,000
Librarian: Kristen L. Metzger
E-Mail: iamslic@ucdavis.edu

Historical Note
Formerly (1975) the Marine Science Library Association; became the International Association of Marine Science Libraries and Information Centers, and assumed its present name in 1991. Membership: $35/year.

Meetings/Conferences:
Annual Meetings: Fall

Publications:
Newsletter. q.
Proceedings. a.
Directory of Marine Science Libraries and Information Centers. irreg.

International Association of Arson Investigators *(1949)*
12770 Boenker Road
Bridgeton, MO 63044
Tel: (314)739-4224 *Fax:* (314)739-4219
E-Mail: marsha@firearson.com
Web Site: www.firearson.com
Members: 7500 individuals
Staff: 3
Annual Budget: $500-1,000,000
Office Manager: Marsha Sipes

Historical Note
Formed at Purdue University by U.S. and Canadian representatives of the insurance industry, fire services, law enforcement agencies and law firms. Membership: $65/year (individual or company) and $15 initiation fee.

Meetings/Conferences:
Annual Meetings: Spring

Publications:
The Fire and Arson Investigator. q. adv.

International Association of Art Critics *(1948)*
340 E. 80th St., Suite 14K
New York, NY 10021
Tel: (212)249-2763
E-Mail: board@aicausa.org
Web Site: www.aicausa.org
Members: 300 individuals
Vice President, Membership: Phyllis Tuchman
E-Mail: board@aicausa.org

Historical Note
The U.S. branch of the international organization, headquartered in Paris, France. Has no paid officers or full-time staff. Membership: $60/year, (initial); $45/year (renewal).

Publications:
Newsletter. q.

International Association of Asian Studies

Historical Note
An affiliate of National Association of African American Studies, which provides administrative support.

International Association of Assembly Managers *(1923)*
635 Fritz Dr., Suite 100
Coppell, TX 75019
Tel: (972)906-7441 *Fax:* (972)906-7418
Toll Free: (800)935 - 4226
E-Mail: webmaster@iaam.org
Web Site: www.iaam.org
Members: 3200 individuals
Staff: 21
Annual Budget: $2-5,000,000
Executive Director: Dexter G. King, CFE
Director, Research and Development: Don Hancock, Ph.D.
Education Coordinator: Rodney Williams

Historical Note
Formerly (1996) International Association of Auditorium Managers. IAAM members are managers of auditoriums, arenas, convention centers, stadiums and performing arts centers representing the most prominent sports, entertainment and convention facilities. Sponsors executive development courses in public assembly facility management. Member of the Center for Exhibition Industry Research and the Convention Industry Council. Membership: $290/year (active); $415/year (allied).

Meetings/Conferences:
Annual Meetings: Summer/2,500

Publications:
Facility Manager. bi-m. adv.
IAAM News. bi-w. adv.
IAAM Guide to Members and Services. a. adv.

International Association of Assessing Officers *(1934)*
314 W. 10th St.
Kansas City, MO 64105
Tel: (816)701-8100 *Fax:* (816)701-8149
Toll Free: (800)616 - 4226
E-Mail: daniels@iaao.org
Web Site: www.iaao.org
Members: 8000 individuals
Staff: 19
Annual Budget: $2-5,000,000
Executive Director: Lisa Daniels
Director, Administration: Angela Blazevic

Historical Note
Formerly (1959) the National Association of Assessing Officers. Members are professionals involved in the administration of property assessments. Awards the CAE (Certified Evaluater), RES (Residential Evaluation Specialist), Cadastal Mapping Specialist (CMS), Personal Property Specialist (PPS) and Assessment Administration Specialist (AAS) designations. Sponsors numerous educational programs. Membership: $175/year.

Meetings/Conferences:
Annual Meetings: Fall/1,500

Publications:
Fair & Equitable Magazine. m.
Assessment Journal. q. adv.

International Association of Association Management Companies *(1964)*
100 N. 20th St., Fourth Floor
Philadelphia, PA 19103-1443
Tel: (215)564-3484 *Fax:* (215)963-9784
E-Mail: info@iaamc.org
Web Site: www.iaamc.org
Members: 200 companies
Staff: 4
Annual Budget: $250-500,000
Executive Vice President: Sue Pine
Administrative Director: Daniele Casterta

Historical Note
Founded as the Multiple Association Management Institute in 1964; changed its name to IAMC in 1977 and assumed its present name, IAAMC, in August, 1996 to better fit the organization's mission. Membership consists of companies engaged in the management of two or more organizations on a professional client basis; member companies are located in the United States, Canada and Europe. Membership: $400-4,000/year (ranges according to total AMC annual income).

Meetings/Conferences:
Semi-Annual Meetings: Summer and Winter

Publications:
Management Information Survey. a.
Associate Directory. a.
Membership Directory (online). a.
IAAMC News Update. q.
Legal Update. q.

International Association of Attorneys and Executives in Corporate Real Estate *(1990)*
20106 S. Sycamore Dr.
Frankfort, IL 60423
Tel: (815)464-6019 *Fax:* (815)464-8334
E-Mail: lcarreras@aecre.org
Web Site: www.aecre.org
Members: 225 individuals
Staff: 3
Annual Budget: $100-250,000
Executive Vice President and Director: Lisa Carreras
E-Mail: lcarreras@aecre.org

Historical Note
AECRE provides a collegial forum for real estate executives and attorneys to explore corporate real estate issues of common interest. The organization sponsors different educational programs, including workshops. Membership: $300/year (individual).

Meetings/Conferences:
Annual Meetings: Spring/100; Fall/50

Publications:
Corporate Real Estate and The Law. 3/yr. adv.

International Association of Audio Information Services *(1978)*
c/o 1090 Don Mills Rd.
Suite 303
Toronto, ON M3C 3-R6
Tel: (416)422-4222 Ext: 224 *Fax:* (416)422-1633
Toll Free: (800)567 - 6755
E-Mail: hlusignan@nbrscanada.com
Web Site: www.iaais.org
Members: 140 reading services
Annual Budget: $10-25,000
President: Heather Lusignan
E-Mail: hlusignan@nbrscanada.com

Historical Note
Founded as the National Association of Radio Reading Services, assumed its present name in 1999. In the late 1970's, the 15 reading services on the air formed the Association of Radio Reading Services; numbers grew rapidly afterwards, and today 157 transmittal sites exist in all states. Membership open to audio information services for blind and other print-handicapped persons. Has no paid officers or full-time staff. Membership: $200/year.

Meetings/Conferences:
Annual Meetings: Spring

Publications:
IAAIS Newsletter. q. adv.
Directory of Radio Reading Services. a.

International Association of Audio Visual Communicators *(1957)*
57 W. Palo Verde Ave.
P.O. Box 250
Ocotillo, CA 92259-0250
Tel: (760)358-7000 *Fax:* (760)358-7569
Web Site: www.cindys.org
Members: 5200 individuals
Staff: 4
Annual Budget: $500-1,000,000
Contact: Sheemon Wolfe

Historical Note
Founded as Industry Film Producer Association; later became Information Film Producers of America. Became (1985) Association of Visual Communicators, and assumed its current name in 1997. Members are audio-visual professionals using the media of film, video, slides, filmstrips, multi-image and interactive media to communicate information. Membership: $100/year (individual), $20/year (full-time student); $275 - $1,000 (3 - 20 members).

Meetings/Conferences:
Semi-annual Meetings: Fall/Spring

International Association of Auto Theft Investigators *(1952)*
P.O. Box 223
Clinton, NY 13323
Tel: (315)853-1913 *Fax:* (315)793-0048
Web Site: www.IAATI.org
Members: 4000 individuals
Staff: 2
Annual Budget: $50-100,000
Executive Director: John Abounader
E-Mail: jvabounader@iaati.org

Historical Note
Established and incorporated at the University of Oklahoma in Norman, OK. Active members include local and state police officers and national government agents. Affiliate members are from the insurance industry, car rental firms, and various automobile associations. Membership: $35 (first year); $30/year (renewal).

Meetings/Conferences:
Annual Meetings: Summer

Publications:
APB. q. adv.
E-News. q. adv.

International Association of Baptist Colleges and Universities *(1915)*
8120 Sawyer Brown Rd., Suite 108
Nashville, TN 37221-1410
Tel: (615)673-1896 *Fax:* (615)662-1396
Web Site: www.baptistcolleges.org

Members: 51 institutions
Staff: 3
Annual Budget: $100-250,000
Executive Director: Bob R. Agee
E-Mail: bob_agee@baptistschools.org
Director, Communications: Tim Fields
E-Mail: tim_fields@baptistschools.org

Historical Note
Incorporated as the Southern Association of Baptist Colleges and Schools in 1915; changed its name to the Association of Southern Baptist Colleges and Schools; assumed its current name in 2006. Consists of the presidents and chief academic officials of Baptist colleges, universities, Bible schools and academies.

Meetings/Conferences:
2007 - Williamsburg, VA(Marriott Williamsburg)/June 3-5

Publications:
Baptist Educator. q.

International Association of Bedding and Furniture Law Officials *(1936)*
c/o Dept of Labor & Industry/Bedding and Upholstery Section
7th & Forster Sts., Room 1623
Harrisburg, PA 17120-0019
Tel: (717)787-6848 *Fax:* (717)787-6925
E-Mail: scree@state.pa.us
Web Site: www.dli.state.pa.us
Members: 30 individuals
Annual Budget: under $10,000
Contact: Sandra Cree
E-Mail: scree@state.pa.us

Historical Note
Organized to secure the adoption of uniform bedding and upholstery laws; members supervise the inspection of bedding materials and upholstered furniture at the state and local levels. Has no permanent staff or address. Membership: $50/year.

Meetings/Conferences:
Annual Meetings: Spring

International Association of Black Professional Fire Fighters *(1970)*
P.O. Box 693835
Miami, FL 33269-3835
Tel: (305)651-2066 *Fax:* (305)249-5230
Web Site: www.iabpff.org
Members: 8000 individuals
Staff: 3
Annual Budget: $100-250,000
Executive Director: Teresa Everett

Historical Note
Members are black firefighters and related professionals. Membership: $30/year (individual); $60/year (organization); $350/year (corporation).

Meetings/Conferences:
Biennial Meetings: even years

International Association of Bomb Technicians and Investigators *(1973)*
P.O. Box 160
Goldvein, VA 22720-0160
Tel: (540)752-4533 *Fax:* (540)752-2796
E-Mail: admin@iabti.org
Web Site: www.iabti.org
Members: 4000 individuals
Staff: 2
Annual Budget: $250-500,000
Executive Director: Ralph Way
E-Mail: admin@iabti.org

Historical Note
Membership: $50/year.

Meetings/Conferences:
Annual Meetings: Spring

Publications:
Directory. annual. adv.
Newsletter. bi-m.

International Association of Bridge, Structural, Ornamental and Reinforcing Iron Workers *(1896)*
1750 New York Ave. NW, Suite 400
Washington, DC 20006
Tel: (202)383-4800 *Fax:* (202)638-4856
E-Mail: iwmagazine@iwintl.org
Web Site: www.ironworkers.org
Members: 135000 individuals
Staff: 70
Annual Budget: $10-25,000,000
President: Joseph Hunt
General Secretary: Michael Fitzpatrick

Historical Note
Organized in Pittsburgh, PA on February 4, 1896 as the International Association of Bridge and Structural Iron Workers. Chartered by the American Federation of Labor in 1903. Formerly (1917) the International Association of Bridge, Structural and Ornamental Iron Workers and Pile Drivers and (1997) International Association of Bridge, Structural and Ornamental Iron Workers.

Meetings/Conferences:
Quinquennial Meetings:

Publications:
The Ironworker. m.

International Association of Broadcast Monitors *(1981)*
64 Bean Road
Plainfield, NH 03781
Tel: (603)469-3054 *Fax:* (603)469-3155
Toll Free: (800)236 - 1741
E-Mail: info@iabm.com
Web Site: www.iabm.com
Members: 110 companies
Staff: 1
Executive Director: Audra Bucklin
E-Mail: info@iabm.com

Historical Note
Members are companies that monitor radio and/or television programming, print media and advertising. Membership: $250/year (domestic); $350/year depending on membership category

Publications:
Membership Directory. a.

International Association of Business Communicators *(1970)*
One Hallidie Plaza, Suite 600
San Francisco, CA 94102
Tel: (415)544-4700 *Fax:* (415)544-4747
Toll Free: (800)776 - 4222
Web Site: www.iabc.com
Members: 13000 individuals
Staff: 28
Annual Budget: $2-5,000,000
President: Julie A. Freeman, ABC, APR
Education and Development Group Leader: Chris Grossgart

Historical Note
IABC is the product of a merger (1970) of the International Council of Industrial Editors (1941) and the American Association of Industrial Editors (1938). Absorbed Corporate Communicators Canada (1942) in 1974. Members are communication and public relations professionals. Membership: $234/year, plus chapter and regional dues.

Meetings/Conferences:
Annual Meetings: Spring/1,500

Publications:
Communications World. bi-m. adv.
CW Bulletin. m. adv.

International Association of Campus Law Enforcement Administrators *(1958)*
342 N. Main St.
West Hartford, CT 06117-2507
Tel: (860)586-7517 *Fax:* (860)586-7550
E-Mail: info@iaclea.org
Web Site: www.iaclea.org
Members: 1700 individuals, 1100 institutions
Staff: 8
Chief Staff Officer: Peter J. Berry, CAE
E-Mail: pberry@iaclea.org

Historical Note
Formerly National Association of College and University Security Directors, and (until 1980) International Association of College and University Security Directors.

Meetings/Conferences:
Annual Meetings: Summer

Publications:
Membership Directory. a. adv.
Campus Law Enforcement Journal. bi-m. adv.

International Association of Career Consulting Firms *(1987)*
1910 Cochran Road
Manor Oak Two, Suite 740
Pittsburgh, PA 15220
Tel: (303)623-1770 *Fax:* (303)623-1775
Toll Free: (800)565 - 2182
E-Mail: inquiries@iaccf.com
Web Site: www.iaccf.com
Members: 14 firms
Annual Budget: $25-50,000
President: Christine Webb

Historical Note
Founded as National Association of Career Development Consultants; assumed its current name in 1992. An association of career consulting firms committed to client service and satisfaction; professional and ethical standards; and advancement of the industry. Has no paid officers or full-time staff. Membership: $300/year.

Meetings/Conferences:
Semi-Annual Meetings:

Publications:
IACCF Newsletter. q.

International Association of Career Management Professionals

Historical Note
Became Association of Career Professionals International in 2004.

International Association of Chiefs of Police *(1893)*
515 N. Washington St., Suite 400
Alexandria, VA 22314-2340
Tel: (703)836-6767 *Fax:* (703)836-4543
Toll Free: (800)843 - 4227
E-Mail: information@theiacp.org
Web Site: www.theiacp.org
Members: 18000 individuals
Staff: 85
Annual Budget: $5-10,000,000
Executive Director: Daniel N. Rosenblatt
E-Mail: rosenblatt@theiacp.org

Historical Note
Formerly (1895) National Chiefs of Police Union; (1898) National Association of Chiefs of Police; (1902) Chiefs of Police of the United States and Canada. Has an annual budget of approximately $7 million. Membership: $100/year (individual).

Meetings/Conferences:
Annual Meetings: Fall/6,000
2007 - New Orleans, LA/Oct. 13-17
2008 - San Diego, CA/Nov. 8-12
2009 - Denver, CO/Oct. 3-7

Publications:
Police Chief Magazine. m. adv.

International Association of Clerks, Recorders, Election Officials and Treasurers *(1971)*
2400 Augusta Dr., Suite 250
Houston, TX 77057-0296
Toll Free: (800)890 - 7368
Web Site: www.iacreot.com
Members: 2000 individuals and companies
Staff: 5
Annual Budget: $500-1,000,000
Executive Director: Tony Sirvello, III
E-Mail: tjsthree@msn.com

Historical Note
IACREOT was established to provide a forum for the exchange of information among government officials, to improve the standards of operation that will best serve the public, to encourage the passage of uniform laws governing the operation of state and local offices, and to provide a unified voice on matters of importance to governmental officials. Membership: $135/year (elected and appointed officials), $85/year (deputies).

Meetings/Conferences:
Annual Meetings: Summer

Publications:
IACREOT News. q. adv.

International Association of Clothing Designers and Executives *(1911)*
124 W. 93rd St., Suite 3E
New York, NY 10025
E-Mail: newyorkiacde@nyc.rr.com
Web Site: www.iacde.com
Members: 400 individuals
Staff: 2
Annual Budget: $250-500,000
Executive Director: Mina Henry
E-Mail: newyorkiacde@nyc.rr.com

Historical Note
Founded as the National Association of Clothing Designers, changed its name in 1919 to International Association of Clothing Designers, and assumed present name in 1994. Membership figure includes both designers and industrial members. Membership: $400/year (full member); $700/year (supplier).

Meetings/Conferences:
Semi-annual Meetings: May and September

Publications:
IACDE Annual Directory. a. adv.
International Designer. a.
Bulletin. q.
Style Forecast. semi-a.

International Association of Color Manufacturers *(1972)*
1620 I St. NW, Suite 925
Washington, DC 20006
Tel: (202)293-5800 *Fax:* (202)463-8998
E-Mail: info@iacmcolor.org
Web Site: www.iacmcolor.org
Members: 15 companies
Staff: 5
Annual Budget: $250-500,000
Executive Director: Brian Bursjek

Historical Note
Manufacturers of certified colors for food, drugs, and cosmetics. Formerly (1993) the Certified Color Manufacturers Association.

International Association of Conference Center Administrators *(1976)*
1270 N. Wickham Road, Suite 16-111
Melbourne, FL 32935
Tel: (772)562-4017 *Fax:* (772)562-4017
E-Mail: info@iacca.org
Web Site: www.iacca.org
Members: 285 individuals
Staff: 1
Annual Budget: $50-100,000
Executive Director: Janet Begley

Historical Note
IACCA's mission is to stimulate high professional standards of conference center leadership; to provide for an exchange of experienced-gained knowledge, including knowledge of successful practices; to provide for the development of materials, standards, and other aids for the progress of conference center administration; and to interpret the role and contribution of conference centers to related groups and the public. Membership: $245/year (executive); $195/year (associate); $245/year (business associate); $70/year (student/affiliate).

Meetings/Conferences:
2007 – Little Rock, AR(C.A. Vines Arkansas 4-H Center)/Nov. 5-9
2008 – Green Lake, WI(Green Lake Conference Center)/Nov. 3-7

Publications:
Association News. m.
IACCA Journal. irreg.
Take Ten. q.

International Association of Conference Centers *(1981)*
243 N. Lindbergh Blvd.
St. Louis, MO 63141
Tel: (314)993-8575 *Fax:* (314)993-8919
E-Mail: info@iacconline.org
Web Site: www.iacconline.org
Members: 128 individuals
Staff: 5
Annual Budget: $1-2,000,000
Executive Vice President: Thomas E. Bolman, CAE
Director, Member Services: Jerry L. White

Historical Note
Membership: $1,210-4,660 (organization); $550 (individual).

Meetings/Conferences:
Annual Meetings: Spring
2007 – New Brunswick, NJ(The Heldrich)/Apr. 19-22

Publications:
Center Lines. q.
Membership Directory. a.

International Association of Convention and Visitors Bureaus

Historical Note
Became Destination Marketing Association International in 2005.

International Association of Corporate and Professional Recruitment *(1976)*
327 N. Palm Dr., Suite 201
Beverly Hills, CA 90210
Tel: (310)550-0304 *Fax:* (213)413-1914
E-Mail: office@iacpr.org
Web Site: www.iacpr.org
Members: 250 individuals
Staff: 3
Annual Budget: $250-500,000
Executive Director: Kay Kennedy, IACPR
E-Mail: office@iacpr.org

Historical Note
Formerly (1991) the National Association of Corporate and Professional Recruiters and (1995) International Association of Corporate and Professional Recruiters. Founded in New York and incorporated in Illinois, IACPR was established to address the common concerns of corporate staffing executives and executive search consultants. Members are professionals with at least ten years experience in the recruiting of executives. Membership: $400/year (individual).

Meetings/Conferences:
Annual Meetings: Fall

Publications:
Impact. semi-a.
Quick Takes. q.

International Association of Correctional Officers *(1977)*
P.O. Box 81826
Lincoln, NE 68501-1826
Tel: (402)464-0602
Toll Free: (800)255 - 2382 Ext:
Members: 13000 individuals
Staff: 3
Annual Budget: $25-50,000
Administrator: Cece Hill

Historical Note
Officers in federal, state and local correctional facilities. Formerly (1978) the American Association of Correctional Facility Officers and (until 1986), the American Association of Correctional Officers. Membership: $35/year (individual), $20/year (supporting), $10/year (student).

Publications:
The Keeper's Voice. semi-a. adv.

International Association of Correctional Training Personnel *(1974)*
P.O. Box 6604
Jefferson City, MO 65102
Tel: (573)896-4560
E-Mail: iactp@earthlink.net
Web Site: www.iactp.org
Members: 450 individuals
Annual Budget: under $10,000
President: Linda Rubin

Historical Note
Formerly (1992) the American Association of Correctional Training Personnel. Formed in Carbondale, IL to improve the quality of correctional training. An affiliate of the American Correctional Association and The American Jail Association. Membership: $35/yr. in the U.S. (individual); $50/yr. (foreign); $20/yr. (full-time student); $50/yr. (agency/library); $350/yr (agency).

Meetings/Conferences:
Annual Meetings: with the Internat'l Trainers Conference in October and in April at the site of upcoming conference.

Publications:
The Correctional Trainer. q. adv.

International Association of Counseling Services *(1972)*
101 S. Whiting St., Suite 211
Alexandria, VA 22304-3416
Tel: (703)823-9840 *Fax:* (703)823-9843
E-Mail: iacsinc@earthlink.net
Web Site: http://iacsinc.org
Members: 170 centers and agencies
Staff: 2
Annual Budget: $100-250,000
Executive Officer: Nancy E. Roncketti
E-Mail: iacsinc@earthlink.net

Historical Note
Formerly the American Board on Professional Standards in Vocational Counseling and then the American Board on Counseling Services before assuming its current name. Established to evaluate counseling services. Accredits university/college counseling centers. Accreditation fee: $800/year (company).

Meetings/Conferences:
Annual Meetings: Held in conjunction with Association of University and College Counseling Center Directors
2007 – Indianapolis, IN

Publications:
IACS Newsletter. q.
Directory of Counseling Services (online; accessible through web site).
Professional Series. irreg.

International Association of Counselors and Therapists *(1990)*
RR #2
Box 22468
Laceyville, PA 18623
E-Mail: info@iact.org
Web Site: www.iact.org
Members: 5000 individuals
Staff: 2
Annual Budget: $50-100,000
Chief Executive Officer: Robert Otto
E-Mail: info@iact.org

Historical Note
IACT provides a forum in which helping and healing professionals may exchange information, techniques, and methodologies. Membership: $50/year (individual).

Publications:
Unlimited Human! Magazine. q. adv.

International Association of Culinary Professionals *(1978)*
304 West Liberty St., Suite 201
Louisville, KY 40202
Tel: (502)581-9786 *Fax:* (502)589-3602
Toll Free: (800)928 - 4227
E-Mail: iacp@hqtrs.com
Web Site: www.iacp.com
Members: 2700 individuals
Staff: 11
Annual Budget: $500-1,000,000
Executive Director: Lieann O'Brien

Historical Note
Founded in 1978 as the Association of Cooking Schools; became (1985) International Association of Cooking Schools; (1988) International Association of Cooking Professionals and assumed its current name in 1990. The IACP is a not-for-profit professional society of individuals employed in, or providing services to the culinary industry (cooking schools, cooking educators, cooking students, culinary specialists, caterers, and food writers). IACP's mission is to be a resource and support system for food professionals, and to help its members achieve and sustain success at all levels of their careers through education, information and peer contacts in an ethical, responsible and professional climate. Membership: $950/year (corporate); $385/year (small business); $360/year (cooking school).

Meetings/Conferences:
Annual Meetings: Spring/600
2007 - Chicago, IL(Chicago Hilton Hotel)/Apr. 11-14
2008 - New Orleans, LA(Hilton New Orleans Riverside)/Apr. 16-19

Publications:
Food Forum. q. adv.

International Association of Defense Counsel *(1920)*
One N. Franklin St., Suite 1205
Chicago, IL 60606
Tel: (312)368-1494 *Fax:* (312)368-1854
E-Mail: info@iadclaw.org
Web Site: www.iadclaw.org
Members: 2500 individuals
Staff: 10
Annual Budget: $2-5,000,000
Executive Director: Oliver Yandle
E-Mail: oyandle@iadclaw.org
Director, Marketing and Communications: Mary Beth Kurzak
E-Mail: mkurzak@iadclaw.org

Historical Note
Formerly (1986) International Association of Insurance Counsel. Members are defense attorneys and insurance and corporate counsel; membership is by invitation only. Membership: $580/year.

Meetings/Conferences:
Semi-Annual Meetings:: Winter and Summer

Publications:
Defense Counsel Journal. q.
IADC News. q.

International Association of Diecutting and Diemaking *(1972)*
651 Terra Cotta Ave., Suite 132
Crystal Lake, IL 60014
Tel: (815)455-7519 *Fax:* (815)455-7510
Toll Free: (800)828 - 4233
E-Mail: pmolitor@iadd.org
Web Site: www.iadd.org
Members: 700 individuals
Staff: 3
Annual Budget: $500-1,000,000
Chief Executive Officer: Cynthia C. Crouse
E-Mail: cccrouse@iadd.org
Member Relations Coordinator: Jill May
Administrative and Meetings Assistant: Peggy Molitar

Historical Note
Founded as the Diemakers and Diecutters Association; became (1980) the National Association of Diemakers and Diecutters in 1980 and assumed its present name in 1991. Members are firms involved in diemaking, diecutting and related equipment and supply areas. Membership: $395/year (company); $95/year (associate); $725/year (patron).

Meetings/Conferences:
Semi-Annual Meetings: March and September

Publications:
Directory of Members. a. adv.
Cutting Edge Newsletter. m. adv.

International Association of Dive Rescue Specialists *(1978)*
201 N. Link Lane
Ft. Collins, CO 80524
Tel: (970)482-1562 *Fax:* (970)482-0893
Toll Free: (800)423 - 7791
Web Site: www.iadrs.org
Members: 1000 individuals
Staff: 1
Annual Budget: $10-25,000
Executive Director: Blades Robinson
E-Mail: brobinson@iadrs.org
Director, Operations: Susan Watson
E-Mail: swatson@iadrs.com

Historical Note
IADRS is an information network for dive rescue authorities including state and federal agencies, military, coast guard, police and fire departments, equipment manufacturers and volunteer teams. Membership: $25/year (individual).

Meetings/Conferences:
Annual Meetings: Fall
2007 - Colorado Springs, CO(Sheraton)/Sept. 26-29

Publications:
Association News. bi-m.. adv.

International Association of Drilling Contractors *(1940)*
Box 4287
Houston, TX 77210-4287
Tel: (713)292-1945 *Fax:* (713)292-1946
E-Mail: info@iadc.org
Web Site: www.iadc.org
Members: 1000 companies
Staff: 25
Annual Budget: $2-5,000,000
President: A. Lee Hunt, Jr.
E-Mail: info@iadc.org

Historical Note
Formerly (1972) American Association of Oilwell Drilling Contractors. Sponsors and supports the IADC Political Action Committee.

Meetings/Conferences:
2007 - Galveston, TX(Moody Gardens Hotel)/Oct. 31-Nov. 2

Publications:
Drill Bits Newsletter. m.
Drilling Contractor. bi-m. adv.

International Association of Eating Disorders Professionals *(1985)*
P.O. Box 1295
Pekin, IL 61555-1295
Toll Free: (800)800 - 8126
E-Mail: info@iaedp.com
Web Site: www.iaedp.com
Members: 800 individuals
Staff: 3
Annual Budget: $250-500,000
Managing Director: Bonnie Harkin
E-Mail: info@iaedp.com

Historical Note
IAEDP members are professionals working in the field of eating disorders. Awards the designation Certifed Eating Disorders Specialist or Certified Eating Disorders Associate upon completion requirements. Membership: $150/year (individual); $500/year (organization).

Publications:
Certification Manual. irreg.
Connections Newsletter. q. adv.
Guidelines for Eating Disorders in Higher Education.

International Association of Electrical Inspectors *(1928)*
901 Waterfall Way, Suite 602
Richardson, TX 75080-7702
Tel: (972)235-1455 *Fax:* (972)235-3855
E-Mail: customerservice@iaei.org
Web Site: www.iaei.org
Members: 26000 individuals
Staff: 15
Annual Budget: $2-5,000,000
Chief Executive Officer and Executive Director: James W. Carpenter
Director, Publishing and Marketing: Kathryn P. Ingley

Historical Note
Members consist of inspectors, utilities, insurance groups, dealers, contractors, electricians, manufacturers and testing laboratories. IAEI cooperates in the formulation of standards for the safe installation and use of electrical materials, devices, and appliances. Membership: $90/year (individual); $200-5,000/year (organization/company).

Meetings/Conferences:
Annual Meetings: September and October

Publications:
1&2 Family Electrical Systems. trien. adv.
Analysis of National Electrical Code. trien. adv.
Analysis of National Electrical Code (video). trien. adv.
Ferm's Fast Finder Index. trie. adv.
Soares Grounding. trien. adv.
IAEI News. bi-m. adv.
Membership Directory. a. adv.

International Association of Electronic Keyboard Manufacturers *(1963)*
c/o Korg USA
316 S. Service Road
Melville, NY 11747-3201
Tel: (631)390-6500 *Fax:* (631)390-6501
Members: 20 companies
Staff: 1
Annual Budget: under $10,000
President: Mike Kovins

Historical Note
Founded as the National Association of Electronic Organ Manufacturers; became the National Association of Electronic Keyboard Manufacturers in 1983 and assumed its present name in 1990. Affiliated with the American Music Conference. Membership: $100/year.

Meetings/Conferences:
Annual Meetings: Trade Shows with the Nat'l Ass'n of Music Merchants/Jan. and June

International Association of Electronics Recyclers
P.O. Box 16222
Albany, NY 12212-1622
Toll Free: (888)989 - 4237
E-Mail: info@iaer.org
Web Site: www.iaer.org
Members: 107
Staff: 2
Founder and President: Peter R. Muscanelli
E-Mail: info@iaer.org

Historical Note
Members are electronics manufacturers, recyclers and affiliated distributor organizations seeking alternatives to landfill dumping of electronics components and material.

Publications:
IAER Industry Report. bien.
IAER Newsletter. m.

International Association of Emergency Managers *(1952)*
201 Park Washington Court
Falls Church, VA 22046-4527
Tel: (703)538-1795 *Fax:* (703)241-5603
E-Mail: info@iaem.com
Web Site: www.iaem.com
Members: 2800 individuals
Staff: 6
Annual Budget: $500-1,000,000
Executive Director: Elizabeth B. Armstrong, CAE
Editor: Karen Thompson

Historical Note
Founded as United States Civil Defense Council; became National Coordinating Council on Emergency Management in 1983, and assumed its current name in 1998. Members are representatives of city and county government departments responsible for civil defense and emergency management. Membership: $170-500/year.

Meetings/Conferences:
Annual Meetings: Fall
2007 - Reno, NV(Silver Legacy Resort)/Nov. 11-15

Publications:
Bulletin. m.

International Association of Equine Dentistry
2436 South, I-East
Suite 376, PMB 203
Denton, TX 76205
Tel: (804)492-5318
Toll Free: (877)642 - 1931
E-Mail: salaminder@aol.com
Web Site: www.iaeqd.org
Staff: 1
Secretary: Ken Fletcher
E-Mail: salaminder@aol.com

Historical Note
IAED awards examination and certification of veterinary dentists.

International Association of Fairs and Expositions *(1920)*
Box 985

Springfield, MO 65801
Tel: (417)862-5771 *Fax:* (417)862-0156
Web Site: www.fairsandexpos.com
Members: 2300 fairs and organizations
Staff: 15
Annual Budget: $1-2,000,000
President: Jim Tucker
Chief Operating Officer and Chief Financial Officer: Max Willis

Historical Note
Membership consists of individual agricultural fairs and regional associations of agricultural fairs. IAFE is a member of the Trade Show Bureau.

Meetings/Conferences:
Annual Meetings: Las Vegas, NV/Fall

Publications:
Fairs and Expositions. 10/year. adv.
Directory. a.

International Association of Financial Crimes Investigators *(1968)*
873 Embarcadero Dr., Suite Five
El Dorado Hills, CA 95762
Tel: (916)939-5000 *Fax:* (916)939-0395
E-Mail: admin@iafci.org
Web Site: www.iafci.org
Members: 3900 individuals
Staff: 4
Annual Budget: $250-500,000
Executive Director: Janis Moffett, CMP
E-Mail: admin@iafci.org

Historical Note
Founded as International Association of Credit Card Investigators; assumed its current name in 1996. IAFCI promotes the establishment of effective international card and cheque security programs, the suppression of fraudulent use of cards and travelers cheques, and the detection and apprehension of those responsible. Membership: $115/year (regular); $65/year (law enforcement members).

Publications:
IAFCI News. q. adv.

International Association of Fire Chiefs *(1873)*
4025 Fair Ridge Dr., Suite 300
Fairfax, VA 22033-2868
Tel: (703)273-0911 *Fax:* (703)273-9363
Web Site: www.iafc.org
Members: 12000 individuals
Staff: 30
Annual Budget: $2-5,000,000
Executive Director: Garry Briese, CAE
Director, Communications: Jennifer Ashley
Director, Finance: Rob Bataria
Director, Government Relations: Alan Caldwell
Director, Membership Services: Gillian Goodman
Director, Human Resources and Administration: Vicki Lee

Historical Note
Formerly (1926) National Association of Fire Engineers. Members are chief fire officers and others concerned with fire prevention, protection and emergency services management. Membership: $160-240/year (individual); $750/year (company).

Meetings/Conferences:
Annual Meetings: Fall

Publications:
On-Scene Newsletter. bi-w. adv.

International Association of Fire Fighters *(1918)*
1750 New York Ave. NW
Washington, DC 20006-5395
Tel: (202)737-8484 *Fax:* (202)737-8418
E-Mail: pr@iaff.org
Web Site: www.iaff.org
Members: 267,000 individuals
Staff: 110
Annual Budget: $10-25,000,000
President: Harold A. Schaitberger
Communications, Media, and Web Management: Jeff Zack

Historical Note
IAFF is the 12th largest union among the 54 unions that make up the AFL-CIO. Sponsors the John P. Redmond Education Foundation and the IAFF Burn Foundation. FIREPAC is the IAFF's Political Action Committee.

Meetings/Conferences:
Biennial Meetings: Even years/Summer
2008 – San Diego, CA

Publications:
The International Fire Fighter. bi-m.

International Association of Fitness Professionals *(1982)*

Historical Note
See IDEA, the Health and Fitness Source.

International Association of Food Industry Suppliers *(1911)*
1451 Dolley Madison Blvd.
McLean, VA 22101-3850
Tel: (703)761-2600 *Fax:* (703)761-4334
E-Mail: info@iafis.org
Web Site: www.iafis.org
Members: 500 companies
Staff: 9
Annual Budget: $2-5,000,000
President and Chief Executive Officer: Stephen C. Schlegel
Director, Client Services: Annette Damey
Director, Business Development: Andrew Drennan
Senior Vice President: Steven M. Perry
Vice President, Finance and Administration: Robyn Roche
Manager, Membership: Jan Rogers

Historical Note
Formerly the Dairy and Ice Cream Machinery and Supplies Association, the Dairy Industries Supply Association, and (1963) Dairy and Food Industries Supply Association. Absorbed the National Association of Food and Dairy Equipment Manufacturers in 1976. Members are manufacturers and distributors of dairy and food industry machinery, equipment, ingredients, and supplies. Membership: $400-3,350/year (company).

Meetings/Conferences:
Annual Meetings: Spring/400

Publications:
Membership Directory. a. adv.
IAFIS Reporter. m.

International Association of Forensic Nurses *(1992)*
E. Holly Ave.
P.O. Box 56
Pitman, NJ 08071-0056
Tel: (856)256-2425 *Fax:* (856)589-7463
E-Mail: iafn@ajj.com
Web Site: www.iafn.org
Members: 2800 individuals
Staff: 8
Annual Budget: $250-500,000
Executive Secretary: Kimberly Marrero
Public Relations Director and Managing Editor: Janet D'Alesandro

Historical Note
IAFN members are registered nurses participating in the application of nursing science to public or legal proceedings, including assault nurse examiners, clinical trauma nurses, correctional nurse specialists, crisis intervenors, death investigators, forensic clinical nurse specialists, forensic geriatric nurses, forensic gynecology specialists, forensic psychiatric nurses, grief counselors, legal nurse consultants, nurse attorneys, and other nursing roles defined as forensic practice. Membership: $115/year (individual).

Meetings/Conferences:
Annual Meetings: Fall

Publications:
On the Edge. q. adv.
Journal of Forensic Nursing. q. adv.

International Association of Forensic Toxicologists *(1965)*
5500 Nathan Shock Dr.
Baltimore, MD 21224
Tel: (410)550-2711 *Fax:* (410)550-2468
E-Mail: info@tiaft.org
Web Site: www.tiaft.org
Members: 1400 individuals
Past President: Marilyn A. Huestis

Historical Note
Members are medical examiners, coroners and other professionals with an interest in forensic toxicology. Has no paid officers or full-time staff. Membership: $35/year.

Meetings/Conferences:
Annual Meetings: Fall

Publications:
TIAFT Bulletin. q.

International Association of Geophysical Contractors *(1971)*
2550 N. Loop West, Suite 104
Houston, TX 77092
Tel: (713)957-8080 *Fax:* (713)957-0008
E-Mail: iagc@iagc.org
Web Site: www.iagc.org
Members: 235 companies
Staff: 5
Annual Budget: $100-250,000
President: Gordon C. Gill

Historical Note
IAGC represents companies that provide geophysical services (geophysical data acquistion, seismic data ownership and licensing, geophysical data processing and interpretation, and associated services and product providers) to the oil and gas industry.

Meetings/Conferences:
Annual Meetings: May

Publications:
IAGC Newsletter. q.

International Association of Golf Administrators *(1968)*
3740 Cahuenga Blvd.
North Hollywood, CA 91604
Tel: (818)980-3630 *Fax:* (818)508-6729
E-Mail: iaga@aol.com
Web Site: www.iaga.org
Members: 180 individuals
Staff: 1
Annual Budget: $50-100,000
Managing Director: Frances Nee
E-Mail: iaga@aol.com

Historical Note
Members are executives of state, regional, or national amateur golf associations. Membership: $125-150/year.

Meetings/Conferences:
Annual Meetings: Fall

Publications:
IAGA Roster. a.

International Association of Healthcare Central Service Materiel Management *(1958)*
213 W. Institute Pl., Suite 307
Chicago, IL 60610
Tel: (312)440-0078 *Fax:* (312)440-9474
Toll Free: (800)962 - 8274
E-Mail: mailbox@iahcsmm.org
Web Site: www.iahcsmm.com
Members: 9000 individuals
Staff: 7
Annual Budget: $500-1,000,000
Executive Director: Betty Hanna

Historical Note
Established in 1958 as the National Association of Hospital Central Service Personnel. Became the International Association of Hospital Central Service Management in 1969 and adopted its present name in 1989. Membership consists of persons serving in a technical, supervisory or management capacity in hospital departments responsible for the management and distribution of supplies. Active members are managers, supervisors, and technicians of Central Service departments in the U.S. and worldwide. Membership: $40.00/year.

Meetings/Conferences:
Annual Meetings: May
2007 – Atlanta, GA(Omni)/Apr. 29-May 2

Publications:
Communique. bi-m.

International Association of Heat and Frost Insulators and Asbestos Workers *(1904)*
9602 M. L. King Jr. Hwy
Lanham, MD 20706
Tel: (301)731-9101 *Fax:* (301)731-5058
Web Site: www.insulators.org/index.htm

Members: 21000 individuals
Staff: 15
Annual Budget: $2-5,000,000
General President: James A. Grogan
General Secretary-Treasurer: James P. "Bud" McCourt

Historical Note
Chartered on September 22, 1904 by the American Federation of Labor as the National Association of Heat, Frost, General Insulators and Asbestos Workers of America. The word "International" came into the title after the acceptance of Canadian locals in 1910. Sponsors and supports the International Association of Heat and Frost Insulators and Asbestos Workers Political Action Committee.

Publications:
The Asbestos Worker. q.

International Association of Home Safety and Security Professionals *(1992)*
P.O. Box 2044
Erie, PA 16512-2044
Tel: (814)504-3291
E-Mail: iahssp@aol.com
Executive Director: Bill Phillips
E-Mail: iahssp@aol.com

Historical Note
Membership is open to security consultants, alarm-systems installers, locksmiths, security officers, home automation systems installers, safe technicians, law enforcement officers, authors, researchers, educators, manufacturers, distributors, retailers, and others who provide safety and security related services or products to, for, or about the residential market. Membership: $150 (professional); $250 (allied); $125 (associate).

Meetings/Conferences:
Annual Meetings: Spring

Publications:
The Home Protector. 10/year.
Home Safety & Security Experts Directory. a.

International Association of Homes and Services for the Aging

Historical Note
A division of the American Association of Homes and Services for the Aging, which provides administrative support.

International Association of Hydrogeologists *(1956)*
c/o The University of Texas at Austin
Geological Science Dept., One University Station C1100
Austin, TX 78712-0254
Tel: (512)471-3317 *Fax:* (512)471-9425
E-Mail: iah@iah.org
Web Site: www.iah.org
Members: 400 individuals
Annual Budget: under $10,000
President: Jack Sharp

Historical Note
Membership: $70/year (individual); $30/year (student); $300/year (corporate). Has no full time staff.

Meetings/Conferences:
Annual Meetings: Fall

Publications:
Hydrogeology. bi-m.

International Association of Hygienic Physicians *(1978)*
4620 Euclid Blvd.
Youngstown, OH 44512-1633
Tel: (330)788-0526 *Fax:* (330)788-0093
Web Site: www.iahp.net
Members: 50 individuals
Staff: 1
Annual Budget: $10-25,000
Secretary-Treasurer: Mark A. Huberman
E-Mail: mhuberman@zoominternet.net

Historical Note
Founded as International Association of Professional Natural Hygienists; assumed its current name in 1995. IAHP promotes the clinical advancement of its profession, ethical responsibility, certification of other professionals and the accreditation of schools or training programs, and the health freedom of its membership. Members are limited to Primary Care Doctors specializing in the supervision of fasting as an integral part of Natural Hygienic care. Members must be graduates of a university and have a medical practice. Membership: $50/year.

Meetings/Conferences:
Annual Meetings: Summer

Publications:
IAPNH Newsletter. q.

International Association of Ice Cream Vendors *(1969)*
100 N. 20th St., 4th Floor
Philadelphia, PA 19103-1443
Tel: (215)564-3484 *Fax:* (215)564-2175
E-Mail: iaicv@fernley.com
Web Site: www.iaicv.org
Members: 130 companies
Staff: 3
Annual Budget: $100-250,000

Historical Note
IAICV is dedicated to the education and communication of responsible and ethical practice in the ice cream vending industry. The association promotes and enhances a quality image for safe ice cream vending and the success of the industry. Membership: $300/year (individual); $550-750/year (company).

Meetings/Conferences:
Annual Meetings: November/300

Publications:
Directory. a. adv.
Chimes. 3/year. adv.

International Association of Industrial Accident Boards and Commissions *(1914)*
5610 Medical Circle, Suite 24
Madison, WI 53711
Tel: (608)663-6355 *Fax:* (608)663-1546
E-Mail: workcomp@iaiabc.org
Web Site: www.iaiabc.org
Members: 350 individuals
Staff: 6
Annual Budget: $1-2,000,000
Executive Director: Greg Krohm

Historical Note
Members are governmental units, companies and others interested in improving workers compensation laws and their administration. Membership: $1000-10,000/year (active), $1000/year (associate).

Meetings/Conferences:
Annual Meetings: Fall

Publications:
IAIABC Journal. semi-a. adv.
IAIABC Newsletter. bi-m. adv.

International Association of Infant Massage *(1986)*
P.O. Box 6370
Ventura, CA 93006
Tel: (805)644-8524 *Fax:* (805)830-1729
Toll Free: (800)248 - 5432
E-Mail: iaim4us@aol.com
Web Site: www.iaim-us.com
Members: 3000 individuals
Staff: 3
Annual Budget: $250-500,000
Executive Director: Susan Campbell
E-Mail: iaim4us@aol.com
Business Administrator: Jennifer Campbell
Communications: Andrea Kelly

Historical Note
IAIM trains and certifies individuals as instructors in infant massage. Membership: $85/year (certified instructor); $85/year (student-pending instructor); $65/year (supporting).

Meetings/Conferences:
Annual Meetings: Autumn

Publications:
Tender Loving Care newsletter. bi-a. adv.
Tender Loving Care e-newsletter. m.

International Association of Insurance Receivers
174 Grace Blvd.
Altamonte Springs, FL 32714
Tel: (407)682-4513 *Fax:* (407)682-3175
Web Site: www.iair.org
Members: 400 individuals
Staff: 4
Annual Budget: $50-100,000
Executive Director: Paula Keyes

Historical Note
Membership: $225/year.

Meetings/Conferences:
Annual Meetings: December

Publications:
The Insurance Receiver. q.

International Association of Jewish Vocational Services *(1939)*
1845 Walnut St., Suite 640
Philadelphia, PA 19103-4701
Tel: (215)854-0233 *Fax:* (215)854-0212
Web Site: www.iajvs.org
Members: 29 affiliate agencies
Staff: 3
Annual Budget: $500-1,000,000
Executive Director: Genie Cohen
E-Mail: coheng@iajvs.org

Historical Note
Formerly (1976) the Jewish Occupational Council and (1990) National Association of Jewish Vocational Services. Voluntary Jewish vocational guidance, employment, training and rehabilitation organizations in the U.S., Canada and Israel.

Publications:
Newsletter. q.
Conference Proceedings. a.
Administrators' Newsletter. irreg.

International Association of Law Enforcement Firearms Instructors *(1981)*
25 Country Club Road, Suite 707
Gilford, NH 03249-6909
Tel: (603)524-8787 *Fax:* (603)524-8856
E-Mail: info@ialefi.com
Web Site: www.ialefi.com
Members: 8000 individuals
Staff: 3
Annual Budget: $500-1,000,000
Executive Director: Robert D. Bossey

Historical Note
IALEFI members are certified fierarms instructors from police departments, security agencies, etc. Membership: $55/year (individual); $550/year (sponsor).

Meetings/Conferences:
Annual Meetings: Spring

Publications:
Firearms Instructor Magazine. q.
IALEFI Directory. a.

International Association of Law Enforcement Intelligence Analysts *(1980)*
P.O. Box 13857
Richmond, VA 23225
Web Site: www.ialeia.org
Members: 1650 individuals
Staff: 1
Annual Budget: $50-100,000
President: Lisa Palmieri

Historical Note
IALEIA members are presently or formerly employed in a specialized law enforcement intelligence capacity, sworn or civilian, by a government entity. Membership: $50/year (individual); $250/year (corporate).

Meetings/Conferences:
Annual Meetings: in conjunction with the Internat'l Ass'n of Chiefs of Police

Publications:
Intelscope Magazine. trien. adv.
IALEIA Journal. semi-a.
Member Directory. a. adv.

International Association of Lighting Designers *(1969)*
200 World Trade Center, Suite 9-104
222 Merchandise Mart
Chicago, IL 60654
Tel: (312)527-3677 *Fax:* (312)527-3680

Web Site: www.iald.org
Members: 700 individuals
Staff: 4
Annual Budget: $500-1,000,000
Executive Vice President: Marsha L. Turner, CAE
Manager, Member Services: Renee Campbell
Office Manager: Rebecca Rock
Manager, Marketing and Communications: Heather Ryndak

Historical Note

The International Association of Lighting Designers (IALD) is an internationally recognized organization dedicated solely to the concerns of independent, professional lighting designers. Founded in 1969, the IALD now has 600 members worldwide. As the only global organization that focuses on independent lighting design, the IALD provides a worldwide forum for the accomplished lighting designer as well as those just entering the profession.

Meetings/Conferences:

Annual Meetings: Spring

Publications:

Newsletter. m. adv.

International Association of Lighting Management Companies *(1952)*

431 E. Locust St., Suite 300
Des Moines, IA 50309-1999
Tel: (515)243-2360 *Fax:* (515)243-2049
E-Mail: director@nalmco.org
Web Site: www.nalmco.org
Members: 120 individuals
Staff: 2
Annual Budget: $250-500,000
Executive Director: Julie Garrison
E-Mail: director@nalmco.org
Associate Director: Molly Lopez, CAE

Historical Note

Formerly (until 1978) the National Association of Lighting Maintenance Contractors and (1987) International Association of Lighting Maintenance Contractors. Companies that clean, repair, maintain and manage commercial and industrial lighting fixtures. Offers members a tradeshow and convention, various educational products, videos, certification programs and seminars. Membership: $750-4,100/year (based on sales which must be more that $10,000).

Meetings/Conferences:

Annual Meetings: April or May

Publications:

LM&M. q. adv.
Directory. a. adv.

International Association of Machinists and Aerospace Workers *(1888)*

9000 Machinists Place
Upper Marlboro, MD 20772-2687
Tel: (301)967-4500 *Fax:* (301)967-4587
E-Mail: websteward@goiam.org
Web Site: www.iamaw.org
Members: 650000 individuals
Staff: 225
Annual Budget: Over $100,000,000
President: R. Thomas Buffenbarger
General Counsel: Allison Beck
Director, IAM Education Center: James Leslie
General Secretary-Treasurer: Warren Mart
Director, Legislative and Political Action: Richard P. Michalski
Director, Strategic Resources: Stephen R. Sleigh
Director, Communications: Richard S. Sloan

Historical Note

Founded May 5, 1888 in Atlanta, Georgia as the Order of United Machinists and Mechanical Engineers. Became the National Association of Machinists in 1889 and the International Association of Machinists in 1891. Absorbed the Industrial Union of Marine and Shipbuilding Workers of America in 1988. Assumed its present name in 1964. Sponsors and supports the International Association of Machinists and Aerospace Workers Political Action Committee. On October 1, 1991 the Pattern Makers' League of North America was merged with IAMAW. In 1994 IAMAW merged with the International Woodworkers of America - U.S. Has an annual budget of approximately $101.3 million. Membership: $326/year minimum (individual).

Meetings/Conferences:

Quadrennial Meetings: (2008)

Publications:

IAM Journal. q.

International Association of Marriage and Family Counselors *(1989)*

Texas A&M Univ. at Corpus Christi
6300 Ocean Drive
Corpus Christi, TX 78412
Tel: (361)825-2307 *Fax:* (361)825-2732
Toll Free: (800)347 - 6647 Ext: 222
E-Mail: director@iamfc.com
Web Site: www.iamfc.com
Members: 4728 individuals
Staff: 3
Annual Budget: $50-100,000
Executive Director: Robert L. Smith, Ph.D.
E-Mail: director@iamfc.com

Historical Note

A division of the American Counseling Association, IAMFC was formed to meet the need to focus on the problems connected with marital and family issues. IAMFC members are ACA members whose primary work-related responsibilities or interests are in the area of marriage and family, specifically marriage counseling, marital therapy, divorce counseling, mediation, and family counseling or therapy. Membership: $24/year (student, retired); $39/year (professional).

Meetings/Conferences:

Annual Meetings: Spring, with the ACA

Publications:

Family Digest Newsletter. q.
The Family Journal: Counseling and Therapy for Couples & Families. q.

International Association of Milk Control Agencies *(1935)*

Dept. of Agriculture
Div. of Dairy Industry Services
Albany, NY 12235-1715
Tel: (518)457-5731 *Fax:* (518)485-5816
Web Site: www.state.me.us/agriculture/ahi/mmc/iamca/
Members: 26 agencies
Annual Budget: $25-50,000
Secretary-Treasurer: Charlie Huff

Historical Note

Membership: $150/year.

Meetings/Conferences:

Annual Meetings: Summer
2007 - Portland, ME(Sheraton)/Aug. 4-8

Publications:

Proceedings. a.
Membership Directory. a.

International Association of Music Libraries, United States Branch *(1955)*

201 Virginia Road
Concord, MA 01742
E-Mail: iaml-us@musiclibraries.org
Web Site: www.iamlus.org
Members: 200 individuals and libraries
Annual Budget: under $10,000
President: Mary W. Davidson

Historical Note

One of 22 affiliated national organizations worldwide, IAML-US promotes the preservation of musical materials and documentation at libraries and similar institutions. Has no paid officers or full-time staff. Membership: $45/year (individual); $63/year (organization).

Meetings/Conferences:

Annual Meetings: in conjunction with the Music Library Ass'n
2007 - Pittsburgh, PA(Hilton Pittsburgh)/Feb. 26-March 3
2008 - Newport, RI/Feb. 17-24

Publications:

Fontes Artis Musicae. q. adv.

International Association of Natural Resource Pilots *(1972)*

27102 Cty. Road A
Spooner, WI 54801
Tel: (715)635-7788
Web Site: www.ianrp.org
Members: 225 individuals
Treasurer: Fred Kruger

Historical Note

IANRP members are pilots and aircrew members employed by federal, state and provincial natural resource/conservation agencies in the United States and Canada. Has no paid officers or full-time staff. Membership: $15/year.

Meetings/Conferences:

Annual Meetings: August

Publications:

Conservation Aeronautics. q. adv.

International Association of Ocular Surgeons *(1981)*

4711 God Rd.
Suite 408
Skokie, IL 60076
Tel: (312)440-0699 *Fax:* (312)440-0580
Toll Free: (847)568 - 1527
Members: 1000 individuals
Staff: 3
Annual Budget: $50-100,000
Director: Randall T. Bellows, M.D.

Historical Note

A division of American Soc. of Contemporary Ophthalmology, which provides administrative support.

Publications:

Annals of Opthamology. q. adv.

International Association of Official Human Rights Agencies *(1949)*

444 N. Capitol St. NW, Suite 536
Washington, DC 20001
Tel: (202)624-5410 *Fax:* (202)624-8185
E-Mail: iaohra@sso.org
Web Site: www.sso.org/iaohra
Members: 200 agencies
Staff: 1
Annual Budget: $100-250,000
President: James L. Stowe
E-Mail: jlstowe@columbus.gov

Historical Note

Members are state and local government human rights and human relations agencies responsible for human rights law enforcement. Provides support services and training for human rights professionals.

Publications:

IAOHRA Newsletter. q.
Membership Directory. a.

International Association of Operative Millers *(1896)*

5001 College Blvd., Suite 104
Leawood, KS 66211
Tel: (913)338-3377 *Fax:* (913)338-3553
E-Mail: info@iaom.info
Web Site: www.iaom.info
Members: 1500 individuals
Staff: 3
Annual Budget: $250-500,000
Executive Vice President: Gary A. Anderson
E-Mail: gary.anderson@iaom.info
Director, Communications: Melinda Farris

Historical Note

Founded in 1896 as the Association of Operative Millers; assumed its current name in 2003. Members are millers, superintendents, engineers, plant managers, and others in the flour milling, cereal milling, and grain and seed industry. Membership: $195/year.

Meetings/Conferences:

2007 - Overland Park, KS(Sheraton and Overland Park Convetion Center)/May 5-9/1000
2008 - Orlando, FL(Rosen Plaza Hotel/Orange County Convention Center)/May 12-16/1000

Publications:
Membership Directory. a. adv.
International Miller. q. adv.

International Association of Personal Protection Agents *(1989)*
12110 Grandview Road
Grandview, MO 64030
Toll Free: (888)567 - 6621
E-Mail: IAPPAinfo@tiu.org
Web Site: www.iappa.org
Members: 600 individuals
Staff: 3
Annual Budget: $10-25,000
Executive Director: Dr. Stephen R. Barnhart
Historical Note
Founded as International Bodyguard Association; assumed its current name in 1996. IAPPA represents members in 50 countries worldwide. Members are professional bodyguards with at least one year of experience working for a public or private organization. Membership: $40/year (individual); $250/year (company).
Meetings/Conferences:
Annual Meetings: Ontario, CA March; Washington, D.C. August
Publications:
The IAPPA Advisor. q. adv.
Membership Directory. a.

International Association of Pet Cemeteries *(1971)*
5055 Rte. 11
P.O. Box 163
Ellenburg Depot, NY 12935
Tel: (518)594-3000 *Fax:* (518)594-8801
Toll Free: (800)952 - 5541
E-Mail: iaopc@aol.com
Web Site: www.iaopc.com
Members: 165 cemeteries
Staff: 2
Annual Budget: $50-100,000
Contact: Stephen Drown
E-Mail: iaopc@aol.com
Historical Note
Founded in Chicago as the National Association of Pet Cemeteries, it assumed its present name in 1978. Membership: $110/year (individual); $150/year (organization/company).
Publications:
Membership Directory. a.
News and Views. bi-m. adv.

International Association of Physicians in AIDS Care *(1995)*
33 N. LaSalle St., Suite 1700
Chicago, IL 60602-2601
Tel: (312)795-4930 *Fax:* (312)795-4938
E-Mail: iapac@iapac.org
Web Site: www.iapac.org
Members: 12800 individuals
Staff: 12
Annual Budget: $2-5,000,000
President and Chief Executive Officer: Jose M. Zuniga
Director, Membership: Cathy Cordova
Director, Operations: Perry Smrz
Historical Note
IAPAC is a nonprofit professional association representing 10,800 physicians and other healthcare professionals in 83 countries. IAPAC develops and implements global educational and advocacy strategies to better the quality of care for all people living with HIV/AIDS and other coinfectious diseases. Membership: $140/year (individual); $5,000/year (corporate).
Publications:
Journal of IAPAC. q. adv.
IAPAC Monthly. m. adv.
HIV and Hepatitis Monthly Brief. m.

International Association of Plastics Distributors *(1956)*
4707 College Blvd., Suite 105
Leawood, KS 66211-1667
Tel: (913)345-1005 *Fax:* (913)345-1006
E-Mail: iapd@iapd.org
Web Site: www.iapd.org
Members: 450 companies
Staff: 6
Annual Budget: $1-2,000,000
Executive Director: Susan E. Avery
Editor, IAPD Magazine: Janet Thill
Historical Note
Formerly United Plastics Distributors Association and then (1970) National Association of Plastics Distributors. Membership: fees based on sales, $600-5,000/year (company).
Meetings/Conferences:
Annual Meetings: Fall
2007 – Dallas, TX(Hyatt Regency Dallas at Reunion)/Oct. 4-7
Publications:
The IAPD Magazine. bi-m. adv.

International Association of Plumbing and Mechanical Officials *(1926)*
5001 E. Philadelphia
Ontario, CA 91761
Tel: (909)472-4100 *Fax:* (909)472-4150
E-Mail: iapmo@iapmo.org
Web Site: www.iapmo.org
Members: 3700 individuals
Staff: 70
Annual Budget: $10-25,000,000
Executive Director: G.P. Russ Chaney
Historical Note
Formerly (1966) Western Plumbing Officials Association. IAPMO members are government officials, agencies, industries and others interested in the promotion of the Uniform Plumbing and Mechanical Codes, which IAPMO sponsors and publishes. Membership: $50/year (individual); $350/year (organization/company).
Meetings/Conferences:
Annual Meetings: Spring and Fall
2007 – San Diego, CA(Doubletree San Diego)/Sept. 23-27
Publications:
Uniform Mechanical Code. trien.
Official Magazine. bi-m. adv.
Newsletter. irreg.
Minutes of Annual Meeting. a.
Directory of Listed Plumbing Products. m.
Directory of Water Conserving Products. m.
Directory of Listed Plumbing Products for Manufactured Housing & RVs. irreg.
Uniform Plumbing Codes. trien.
Uniform Swimming Pool, Spa & Hot Tub Code. trien.
Uniform Solar Energy Code. trien.

International Association of Printing House Craftsmen *(1919)*
7042 Brooklyn Blvd.
Minneapolis, MN 55429-1370
Tel: (763)560-1620 *Fax:* (763)560-1350
Toll Free: (800)466 - 4274
E-Mail: director@iaphc.org
Web Site: www.iaphc.org
Members: 6500 individuals
Staff: 2
Annual Budget: $250-500,000
President and Chief Executive Officer: Kevin P. Keane
E-Mail: kkeane1069@aol.com
Vice President, International Events and Director, Member Services: Leslie Addy
Vice President, Communications: Cindy Johnson
Historical Note
IAPHC is open to persons employed in or retired from the graphic arts industry. Membership: $100/year.
Meetings/Conferences:
Annual Meetings: August/1,000
Publications:
Know More Notes. irreg.
Craftsmen Communicator. irreg.

International Association of Privacy Professionals
266 York St.
York, ME 03909
Tel: (207)351-1500 *Fax:* (207)351-1501
Toll Free: (800)266 - 6501
E-Mail: information@privacyassociation.org
Web Site: www.privacyassociation.org
Staff: 2
Annual Budget: $250-500,000
Executive Director: J. Trevor Hughes
Meetings/Conferences:
Annual Meetings: Winter

International Association of Professional Security Consultants *(1984)*
525 S.W. Fifth St., Suite A
Des Moines, IA 50309-4501
Tel: (515)282-8192 *Fax:* (515)282-9117
E-Mail: iapsc@iapsc.org
Web Site: www.iapsc.org
Members: 120 individuals
Staff: 1
Annual Budget: $50-100,000
Executive Director: Kathy Rinkenberger
Historical Note
Members are independent, non-product affiliated, security management technical and forensic consultants. Membership: $450/year.
Meetings/Conferences:
Annual Meetings: Spring
Publications:
Newsletter.
Membership Directory.

International Association of Pupil Personnel Workers
Historical Note
Became International Association for Turancy and Dropout Prevention in 2004.

International Association of Railway Operating Officers *(1892)*
17 Elizabeth Lane
Cabot, AZ 72023
Tel: (501)605-0158 *Fax:* (501)605-8209
Web Site: www.iaroo.org
Members: 500 individuals
Staff: 1
Annual Budget: $10-25,000
Secretary-Treasurer: W.N. Hull
E-Mail: whull33051@aol.com
Historical Note
Membership: $25/year.
Meetings/Conferences:
Annual Meetings: Chicago, IL(Hilton), September
Publications:
The Modern Locomotive Handbook.

International Association of Refrigerated Warehouses *(1891)*
1500 King Street, Suite 201
Alexandria, VA 22314-2730
Tel: (703)373-4300 *Fax:* (703)373-4301
E-Mail: email@iarw.org
Web Site: www.iarw.org
Members: 700 companies
Staff: 8
Annual Budget: $2-5,000,000
President and Chief Executive Officer: J. William Hudson
Historical Note
Formerly (1972) National Association of Refrigerated Warehouses. Members are operators of public refrigerated warehouses. Membership: varies by size of operation.
Meetings/Conferences:
Annual Meetings: Spring/650
2007 – Phoenix, AZ(Sheraton Wild Horse Pass)/Apr. 21-26
2008 – Marco Island, FL(Marriott)/Apr. 19-24
2009 – San Antonio, TX(Westin La Cantera)/Apr. 18-23
2010 – San Antonio, TX(Westin La Cantera)/Apr. 24-29
Publications:
Cold Connection (online). w.
Cold Facts. bi-m. adv.
Annual Directory of Public Refrigerated Warehouses. a. adv.

International Association of Rehabilitation Professionals *(1977)*
3540 Soquel Ave., Suite A

Santa Cruz, CA 95062
Tel: (831)464-4802 *Fax:* (831)576-1417
Toll Free: (800)240 - 9095
Web Site: www.rehabpro.org
Members: 2800 individuals
Staff: 4
Annual Budget: $500-1,000,000
Executive Director: Glenn Zimmermann
E-Mail: glenn@btfenterprises.com

Historical Note
Formerly (2000) National Association of Rehabilitation Professionals in the Private Sector. Incorporated in Pennsylvania. Members are individuals in private sector companies or non-profit organizations that provide rehabilitation services. Membership: $155/year (individual).

Publications:
Rehabilitation Professional. bi-m. adv.
NARPPS National Directory. a. adv.

International Association of Round Dance Teachers *(1976)*
355 N. Orchard, Suite 200
Boise, ID 83706
Tel: (208)377-1232 *Fax:* (208)377-1236
Toll Free: (800)346 - 7522
E-Mail: roundalab@roundalab.org
Web Site: www.roundalab.org
Members: 1400 individuals
Staff: 1
Annual Budget: $100-250,000
Executive Administrator: Al Shaw
E-Mail: roundalab@roundalab.org

Historical Note
A professional international society of individuals who teach round dancing at any phase. Membership: $70/Renewal Teaching Unit (international); $60 (U.S.); $65 (Canada).

Meetings/Conferences:
Annual Meetings: June/200-250

Publications:
Cueing Guidelines. irreg.
Convention Proceedings and Directory. a.
Journal. q.
Roundalab Manual. a.
Six Phase Standards of Round Dancing. a.

International Association of School Librarianship *(1971)*
PMB 292, 1903 W. Eighth St.
Erie, PA 16505
E-Mail: iaslpres@gmail.com
Web Site: www.iasl-slo.org
Members: 700 individuals
Staff: 1
Annual Budget: $25-50,000
President: Peter Genco
E-Mail: iaslpres@gmail.com

Historical Note
IASL is concerned with the establishment and development of school librarianship around the world. Currently has members in over 70 countries. IASL members are librarians, administrators, and others concerned with school library media programs and services. Membership fees vary, based on location.

Meetings/Conferences:
Annual Meetings: July
2007 – Taipei, Taiwan(Gis Convention Center)/July 16-20

Publications:
IASL Newsletter. 3/yr. adv.
IASL Conference Proceedings. a.
School Libraries Worldwide. semi-a. adv.

International Association of Skateboard Companies *(1995)*
22431 Antonio Pkwy., Suite B160-412
Rancho Santa Margarita, CA 92688
Tel: (949)589-8863 *Fax:* (949)589-3604
Web Site: www.skateboardiasc.org
Members: 50 companies
Staff: 2
Annual Budget: $100-250,000
Executive Director: John Bernarads

Historical Note
Pushing skateboarding forward.

Meetings/Conferences:
Annual Meetings: Winter/Fall

Publications:
Grapevine Newsletter. m. adv.
Concrete Wave.
TWB. m. adv.
Skate Boarder. m. adv.

International Association of Speakers Bureaus *(1986)*
7150 Winston Dr., Suite 300
Indianapolis, IN 46268
Tel: (317)328-7790 *Fax:* (317)280-8527
E-Mail: info@iasbweb.org
Web Site: www.iasbweb.org
Members: 115speakersbureausandagencies
Staff: 2
Annual Budget: $100-250,000
Executive Vice President: James D. Montoya, CAE

Historical Note
Founded as International Group of Agents and Bureaus; became International Group of Speakers Bureaus in 1991, and assumed its current name in 2001. Members are bureaus, agencies or management companies who actively book professional speakers. Membership: $500/year.

Meetings/Conferences:
Annual Meetings: April/75
2007 – Ft. Worth, TX/Apr. 26-28

Publications:
Bureau Talk. q.

International Association of Special Investigation Units *(1984)*
8015 Corporate Dr., Suite A
Baltimore, MD 21236
Tel: (410)931-3332 *Fax:* (410)931-2060
E-Mail: iasiu@managementalliance.com
Web Site: www.iasiu.org
Members: 4600 individuals
Staff: 10
Executive Director: Dawn Lipsey
E-Mail: iasiu@managementalliance.com

Meetings/Conferences:
2007 – Las Vegas, NV(Caesar's Palace)/Sept. 9-12
2008 – Atlanta, GA(Marriott Marquis)/Sept. 7-10

Publications:
Seminar Journal. a. adv.
Online Membership Directory and Search. d. adv.
SIU Today. q. adv.

International Association of Structural Movers *(1983)*
P.O. Box 2637
Lexington, SC 29071-2637
Tel: (803)951-9304 *Fax:* (803)951-9314
Web Site: www.iasm.org
Members: 370 companies
Staff: 2
Annual Budget: $250-500,000
Staff Executive: N. Eugene Brymer, APR, CAE

Historical Note
Members are movers of heavy structural products, trusses, barns, houses and machinery. Has a small international membership. Membership: $260-735.

Meetings/Conferences:
Annual Meetings: February
2007 – Tucson, AZ/Feb. 14-18
2008 – Minneapolis, MN/Feb. 20-24

Publications:
The Structural Mover. 4/year. adv.

International Association of Tool Craftsmen *(1953)*
3710 Kasper St.
Racine, WI 53402-3542
Tel: (309)782-5776
Members: 200 individuals
Staff: 1
Annual Budget: $10-25,000
Secretary: Michael Kubarth

Historical Note
Independent labor union.

Meetings/Conferences:
Biennial meetings: Uneven years in Fall

Publications:
Tool and Die Journal. a.

International Association of Tour Managers - North American Region *(1961)*
9500 Rainier Ave., South, Suite 603
Seattle, WA 98118
Tel: (206)725-7108 *Fax:* (206)725-4020
E-Mail: chairman@tourmanager.org
Web Site: www.tourmanager.org
Members: 1000 individuals
Staff: 3
Annual Budget: $500-1,000,000
Chair: Scott McGraw

Historical Note
Affiliated with American Society of Travel Agents, European Tour Operators Association, National Federation of Tourist Guide Associations, Professional Association of Tour Managers; membership: $125/year ($65/year for students); associate membership available to tour operators.

Meetings/Conferences:
Annual Meetings: Winter

Publications:
IATM International Newsletter London Headquarters. q. adv.
IATM Newsletter North American Region. 4/year. adv.

International Association of Used Equipment Dealers *(2001)*
214 Edgewood Dr., Suite 100
Wilmington, DE 19809-3255
Tel: (302)765-3571 *Fax:* (302)765-3571
Web Site: www.iaued.org
Members: 50
Staff: 1
Annual Budget: $100-250,000
President: Darryl D. McEwen
E-Mail: darryl@iaued.org

International Association of Wildland Fire *(1983)*
P.O. Box 261
Hot Springs, SD 57747-0261
Tel: (206)600-5113 *Fax:* (605)890-2348
Toll Free: (800)440 - 4293
E-Mail: iawf@iawfonline.org
Web Site: www.iawfonline.org
Members: 700 individuals
Staff: 1
Annual Budget: $50-100,000
Executive Director: Bill Gabbert

Historical Note
IWAF members are academics and professionals with an interest in wildland fires.

Meetings/Conferences:
Annual Meetings: Three year rotation: United States, Canada, Australia

Publications:
Internat'l Journal of Wildland Fire. q.
Wildfire Magazine. m.

International Association of Women Ministers *(1919)*
579 Main St.
Stroudsburg, PA 18360
Tel: (570)421-7751 *Fax:* (570)421-7718
E-Mail: iawmpage@aol.com
Web Site: www.geocities.com/womenministers
Members: 350 individuals
Annual Budget: $10-25,000
Treasurer: Carol Brown

Historical Note
IAWM active members are ordained, licensed and recorded women clergy and women who meet the requirements for ordination, but whose denominations do not authorize women to serve as ministers. Other membership categories are retired, student, fraternal and sustaining. Membership: sliding scale (based on income).

Meetings/Conferences:
Annual Meetings: July

Publications:
Woman's Pulpit. q.

International Association of Women Police
(1915)
1417 Derby Cty. Crescent
Oakville, ON L6M --4N8
Tel: (905)847-1065
Web Site: www.iawp.org
Members: 3000 individuals
Annual Budget: $100-250,000
Business Manager: Wendy Wilson

Historical Note
Originally founded as the International Policewoman's Association in 1915 and disbanded in 1932; reorganized under its present name in 1956. Members are full-time law enforcement officers with powers of arrest. Men have been eligible for full membership since 1976. Membership: $40/year (American members); $20/year (international members).

Meetings/Conferences:
Annual Meetings: Fall

Publications:
Women Police. q. adv.

International Association of Workforce Professionals *(1913)*
1801 Louisville Road
Frankfort, KY 40601-3922
Tel: (502)223-4459 *Fax:* (502)223-4127
Toll Free: (888)898 - 9960
E-Mail: iapes@iapes.org
Web Site: www.iawponline.org
Members: 11000 individuals
Staff: 3
Annual Budget: $500-1,000,000
Coordinator, Membership Services: Paige Stodhill
Office Manager: Mary Riddell
E-Mail: iapes@iapes.org

Historical Note
Formerly (1952) International Association of Public Employment Services and then International Association of Personnel in Employment Security; assumed current name in 2003. Members are involved in unemployment compensation and job placement in local, state and federal agencies. Membership: $42/year (individual).

Meetings/Conferences:
Annual Meetings: June-July/1,500

Publications:
Workforce System Report.
Workforce Professional. 6/year. adv.

International Atherosclerosis Society *(1979)*
6535 Fannin, M.S. A-601
Houston, TX 77030
Tel: (713)797-9620 *Fax:* (713)797-9507
E-Mail: ias@bcm.tmc.edu
Web Site: www.athero.org
Members: 13329 individuals
Staff: 3
Annual Budget: $100-250,000
Executive Director: Ann Stephens Jackson

Historical Note
IAS promotes, at an international level, the advancement of science, research and teaching in the field of atherosclerosis. Members are physicians, scientists and other health professionals. Membership: $10/year (individual); $3/member/year (organization/company).

Meetings/Conferences:
Triennial Meetings: (2006)

Publications:
IAS Newsletter. semi-a.
Proceedings of Symposia. trien.

International Aviation Ground Support Association *(2002)*
201 Park Washington Court
Falls Church, VA 22046-4527
Tel: (703)538-1786 *Fax:* (703)241-5603
Staff: 2
Executive Director: Clay D. Tyeryar, CAE

International Aviation Womens Association
(1989)
P.O. Box 1088
Edgewater, MD 21037
Tel: (410)571-1990
E-Mail: info@iawa.org
Web Site: www.iawa.org
Members: 150 individuals
Annual Budget: $10-25,000
President: Joanne W. Young
E-Mail: info@iawa.org

Historical Note
IAWA members are women who are senior aviation defense attorneys, executives and managers in the aviation insurance industry, the aviation/aerospace manufacturing industry, airlines and related government agencies. Has no paid officers or full-time staff. Membership: $65/year (individual).

Meetings/Conferences:
Annual Meetings: September-October

Publications:
IAWA Newsletter. q.
Membership Directory. a.

International Banana Association *(1983)*
1901 Pennsylvania Ave. NW, Suite 1100
Washington, DC 20006
Tel: (202)303-3400
E-Mail: info@eatmorebananas.com
Web Site: www.eatmorebananas.com
Members: 7 companies
Staff: 2
Annual Budget: $500-1,000,000
Executive Director: Tim Debus

Historical Note
Trade association of the banana industry.

International Beverage Dispensing Equipment Association *(1971)*
4145 Amos Ave.
Baltimore, MD 21215
Tel: (410)764-0616 *Fax:* (410)764-6799
E-Mail: ibdea@cornerstoneassoc.com
Web Site: www.ibdea.org
Members: 200 individuals
Staff: 2
Annual Budget: $250-500,000
Executive Director: Marvin Howard
E-Mail: ibdea@cornerstoneassoc.com

Historical Note
Established as the National Soda Dispensing Equipment Association; became National Beverage Dispensing Equipment Association in 1982 and assumed its current name in 1996. Members are companies which sell, rent or service beverage dispensing equipment. Membership: $325-925/year (regular); $625/year (associate).

Meetings/Conferences:
Annual Meetings: March

Publications:
IBDEA News, Periodical. m.
IBDEA Report. q. adv.
IBDEA Annual Membership Directory. a. adv.

International Beverage Packaging Association
(1947)
631 N. Stephanie St., Suite 564
Henderson, NV 89014
Tel: (702)210-7638 *Fax:* (702)566-7166
E-Mail: info@ibpa.org
Web Site: www.ibpa.org
Members: 800 individuals
Annual Budget: $50-100,000
President: Paul V. Altimier
E-Mail: info@ibpa.org

Historical Note
IBPA members represent all facets of the beverage packaging industry including soft drink, beer, bottled water and juice. Has no paid officers or full-time staff.

Meetings/Conferences:
Biennial Meeting: concurrent with FPM&SA's Internat'l Exposition

Publications:
Membership Directory. a.
NBPA's Voice. q.

International Biometric Society *(1947)*
1444 I St. NW, Suite 700
Washington, DC 20005-6542
Tel: (202)712-9049 *Fax:* (202)216-9646
E-Mail: ibs@bostrom.com
Web Site: www.tibs.org
Members: 6500 individuals
Staff: 3
Annual Budget: $500-1,000,000
Executive Director: Claire Shanley

Historical Note
The Biometric Society was founded at Woods Hole, MA in September 1947 as a result of a report at the First International Biometric Conference. Became the International Biometric Society in 1994. Promotes the application of mathematical and statistical methods and applications in pure and applied biological sciences. Membership: $50/year (individual); $300/year (organization/company).

Meetings/Conferences:
Annual Meetings: March and June, and International Meetings biennially, even years

Publications:
Journal of Agricultural, Biological and Environmental Statistics. q.
Biometrics. q. adv.
Biometric Bulletin. q. adv.

International Bluegrass Music Association
(1985)
Two Music Circle South, Suite 100
Nashville, TN 37203
Tel: (615)256-3222 *Fax:* (615)256-0450
Toll Free: (888)438 - 4262
E-Mail: info@ibma.org
Web Site: www.ibma.org
Members: 2400 individuals
Staff: 4
Annual Budget: $250-500,000
Executive Director: Dan Hays
E-Mail: danh@ibma.org
Director, Special Projects: Nancy Cardwell
E-Mail: nancyc@ibma.org
Director, Marketing and Public Relations: Shari Lacy
Director, Member and Convention Services: Jill Snider
E-Mail: jill@ibma.org

Historical Note
Bluegrass music trade association representing musicians, broadcasters, record manufacturers and distributors, writers and event promoters. Membership: $40-65/year (individual); $150/year (organization/company); $15/year (youth, 16 and under).

Meetings/Conferences:
Annual Meetings: September
2007 - Nashville, TN/Oct. 1-7

Publications:
Internat'l Bluegrass. bi-m.
Blue Hot Bluegrass E-Newsletter. bi-m.

International Board for Career Management Certification

Historical Note
Became Institute of Career Certification International in 2003.

International Bottled Water Association *(1958)*
1700 Diagonal Road, Suite 650
Alexandria, VA 22314
Tel: (703)683-5213 *Fax:* (703)683-4074
Toll Free: (800)928 - 3711
E-Mail: ibwainfo@bottledwater.org
Web Site: www.bottledwater.org
Members: 1200 companies
Staff: 13
Annual Budget: $2-5,000,000
President: Joseph K. Doss
E-Mail: Jdoss@bottledwater.org
Vice President, Government Relations: Patrick Donoho
E-Mail: Pdonoho@bottledwater.org
Vice President, Communications: Stephen R. Kay
E-Mail: Skay@bottledwater.org

Historical Note
Membership consists of owners and operators of bottled water plants, dealers, distributors and industry suppliers. Established as American Bottled Water Association, it assumed its present name in 1982. Membership: fees based on sales.

Meetings/Conferences:
Annual Meetings: November/3,000

Publications:
Technical Newsletter.
Newsletter. w.
Bottled Water Reporter. bi-m. adv.
Membership Roster. a. adv.

International Bowling Pro Shop and Instructors Association *(1990)*

Executive Director: John F. Berglund, CAE

Historical Note
Formerly the International Bowling Pro Shop Association (1994). IBPSIA members are retailers, manufacturers and interested individuals. Membership: $200/year (U.S, Mexican and Canadian retailers); $400/year (U.S., Mexican and Canadian wholesalers); $275/year (foreign); $475/year (foreign associates).

Meetings/Conferences:
Annual Meetings: November

Publications:
The Industry Standard. bi-m. adv.

International Brangus Breeders Association *(1949)*

P.O. Box 696020
San Antonio, TX 78269-6020
Tel: (210)696-4343 *Fax:* (210)696-8718
Web Site: www.int-brangus.org
Members: 2500 individuals
Staff: 10
Annual Budget: $500-1,000,000
Executive Vice President: Dr. Joseph M. Massey
Advisor and Director, Administration: Suzanne N. Johnson

Historical Note
Breeders and merchandisers of Brangus beef cattle. Member of the National Society of Livestock Record Associations. Membership: $70/year.

Meetings/Conferences:
Annual Meetings: Always in February/March and October

Publications:
Brangus Journal. m. adv.

International Bridge, Tunnel and Turnpike Association *(1932)*

1146 19th St. NW, Suite 800
Washington, DC 20036-3725
Tel: (202)659-4620 *Fax:* (202)659-0500
E-Mail: info@ibtta.org
Web Site: www.ibtta.org
Members: 250companiesandorganizations
Staff: 9
Annual Budget: $1-2,000,000
Executive Director: Patrick Jones
Director, Government Affairs: Neil Gray
E-Mail: neilgray@ibtta.org
Director, Public Affairs: Wanda Klayman
E-Mail: wklayman@ibtta.org
Director, Technology Program: Tim McGuckin
E-Mail: mcguckin@ibtta.org
Director, Meetings: Nicole Neuman
E-Mail: nneuman@ibtta.org
Director, Administration and Finance: Barbara O'Connor
E-Mail: oconnor@ibtta.org

Historical Note
Founded as the American Toll Bridge Association, it became the American Bridge, Tunnel and Turnpike Association in 1948 and assumed its present name in 1964. Membership consists of public agencies, private companies, and support organizations operating toll facilities. Membership: sliding scale.

Meetings/Conferences:
Annual Meetings: Fall/700

Publications:
Toll Industry Statistics. a.

International Brotherhood of Boilermakers, Iron Ship Builders, Blacksmiths, Forgers and Helpers *(1880)*

753 State Ave., Suite 570
Kansas City, KS 66101
Tel: (913)371-2640
Web Site: www.boilermakers.org
Members: 80000 individuals
Staff: 150
Annual Budget: $25-50,000,000
International President: Newton B. Jones
Director, Research and Collective Bargaining: L.G. Beauchamp
Director, Construction Division: Dale Branscum
Director, Educations and Training Services: Don Caswell
Director, Organizing: W.M. Creeden
Administrative Assistant to International President: Byran King
Legislative Director: Bridget D. Martin
General Counsel: Joe Morland
International Secretary-Treasurer: Jerry Willburn

Historical Note
Organized in Chicago August 6, 1881 as the National Boilermaker and Helpers Protective and Benevolent Union. Renamed the International Brotherhood of Boilermakers and Iron Ship Builders Protective and Benevolent Union of the United States and Canada in 1883. Merged with the National Brotherhood of Boilermakers in 1893 to form the International Brotherhood of Boilermakers and Iron Ship Builders of America. Chartered by the American Federation of Labor in 1897, it became the International Brotherhood of Boilermakers, Iron Ship Builders and Helpers of America in 1912 and merged in 1951 with the International Brotherhood of Blacksmiths, Forgers and Helpers and adopted its present name. Merged with United Cement, Lime, Gypsum and Allied Workers International Union in 1984; Stove, Furnace and Allied Appliance Workers and Western Energy Workers in 1994; and the Metal Polishers, Buffers, Platers and Allied Workers International Union in 1997. Has a budget of about $27 million. The union represents 85,000 members in 420 lodges across the United States and Canada. Members perform work in construction, shipbuilding, railroad, manufacturing, and service industries.

Meetings/Conferences:
Annual Meetings: Every 5 years (2006)

Publications:
Boilermaker Reporter. bi-m.

International Brotherhood of Correctional Officers

Historical Note
A unit of the National Association of Government Employees.

International Brotherhood of Electrical Workers *(1891)*

900 Seventh St. NW
Washington, DC 20001
Tel: (202)833-7000 *Fax:* (202)728-7676
E-Mail: journal@ibew.org
Web Site: www.ibew.org
Members: 750000 individuals
Staff: 250
Annual Budget: $5-10,000,000
International President: Edwin D. Hill
International Secretary-Treasurer: Jon F. Walters

Historical Note
Established in St. Louis November 21, 1891 as the National Brotherhood of Electrical Workers and chartered by the American Federation of Labor the same year. Assumed its present name in 1899 after the acceptance of the first Canadian local. Sponsors and supports the International Brotherhood of Electrical Workers Committee on Political Education.

Meetings/Conferences:
Quadrennial Meetings:

Publications:
IBEW Journal. m.

International Brotherhood of Magicians *(1922)*

11155-C Southtowne Square
St. Louis, MO 63123-7823
Tel: (314)845-9200 *Fax:* (314)845-9220
E-Mail: office@magician.org
Web Site: www.magician.org
Members: 15000 individuals
Staff: 7
Annual Budget: $100-250,000
Executive Secretary: Sindie Richison
E-Mail: office@magician.org

Historical Note
Includes an international membership of professional and amateur magicians and their suppliers. Membership: $40/year.

Meetings/Conferences:
Annual Meetings: late June-July
2007 – Reno, NV
2008 – Louisville, KY

Publications:
Linking Ring. m. adv.

International Brotherhood of Police Officers

Historical Note
A division of the National Association of Government Employees.

International Brotherhood of Teamsters, AFL-CIO *(1903)*

25 Louisiana Ave. NW
Washington, DC 20001
Tel: (202)624-6800 *Fax:* (202)624-6918
Web Site: www.teamster.org
Members: 1400000 individuals
Staff: 300
Annual Budget: $50-100,000,000
General President: James P. Hoffa
Director, Communications: Brett Caldwell
General Secretary-Treasurer: C. Thomas Keegel
Director, Government Affairs: Michael Mathis
General Counsel: Pat Szymanski

Historical Note
Established in Niagara Falls, New York in 1903 as the International Brotherhood of Teamsters through the merger of the Teamsters National Union (founded in 1902) and the Team Drivers International Union (founded in 1899). Became the International Brotherhood of Teamsters, Chauffeurs, Warehousemen and Helpers of America in 1940 and assumed its present name in 1991. Formerly affiliated with the American Federation of Labor, it was expelled for corruption in 1957. After 30 years as an independent union, it reaffiliated with the AFl-CIO in 1987. Has an annual budget of approximately $87.8 million.

Meetings/Conferences:
Quinquennial Meetings:

Publications:
Teamster. 6/year.

International Buckskin Horse Association *(1971)*

P.O. Box 268
Shelby, IN 46377
Tel: (219)552-1013
E-Mail: ibha@netnitco.net
Web Site: www.ibha.net
Members: 3500 individuals
Staff: 4
Annual Budget: $100-250,000
Executive Secretary: Richard E. Kurzeja
E-Mail: ibha@netnitco.net

Historical Note
IBHA was incorporated in 1971 to register, preserve the pedigree, and promote activity of buckskin, dun, red dun and grulla horses. IBHA has proven to be the largest and most progressive registry for these types of horses, creating interest and demand through national, state, family and individual activities plus increased marketability of IBHA registered horses. Maintains a registry of Buckskin, Dun, Red Dun and Grulla horses. Membership: $25/year.

Meetings/Conferences:
Annual Meetings: Spring

Publications:
Horse Circuit News. m. adv.

International Builders Exchange Executives *(1948)*

4047 Naco Perrin, Suite 201A
San Antonio, TX 78217
Tel: (210)653-3900 *Fax:* (210)653-3912
Toll Free: (877)692 - 9638
E-Mail: info@bxnetwork.org
Web Site: www.bxnetwork.com
Members: 103 organizations
Staff: 2
Annual Budget: $100-250,000
Executive Vice President: Brenda L. Romano

E-Mail: info@bxnetwork.org

Historical Note

Members are executive heads of local building trade associations in the United States and Canada.

Meetings/Conferences:

Annual Meetings: June

Publications:

Construction Executive Report. bi-m.

International Business Brokers Association *(1984)*

401 N. Michigan Ave., Suite 2200
Chicago, IL 60611-4267
Toll Free: (888)686 - 4222
E-Mail: admin@ibba.org
Web Site: www.ibba.org
Members: 1450 individuals
Staff: 5
Annual Budget: $1-2,000,000
President: Maurice A. Desmarais, CAE

Historical Note

Members are individuals specializing in the sales of businesses of all sizes.

Meetings/Conferences:

Semi-annual Meetings: Spring/Fall

Publications:

Newsletter. q. adv.
Membership Directory. a. adv.
Weekly Communication E-Mail. w.

International Business Music Association *(1971)*

151 Broadmoor Lane
Iowa City, IA 52245-9313
Tel: (319)339-9851
E-Mail: info@ibma.net
Web Site: www.ibma.net
Members: 94 businesses
Staff: 8
Annual Budget: $10-25,000
President: Dan Hart
E-Mail: info@ibma.net

Historical Note

IBMA is an organization dedicated to serving business music and sound contracting companies by providing a vehicle for the exchange of ideas on matters of common interest and by promoting the interest and general welfare of the business music industry. Membership: $175/year (organization/company).

Meetings/Conferences:

Annual Meetings: September or October

Publications:

IBMA Newsletter. q. adv.

International Cadmium Association *(1980)*

9222 Jeffery Rd.
Great Falls, VA 22066
Tel: (703)759-7400 *Fax:* (703)759-7003
Web Site: www.cadmium.org
Members: 30 companies
Staff: 2
Annual Budget: $250-500,000
Senior Consultant: Hugh Morrow
E-Mail: icdamorrow@aol.com

Historical Note

Formerly a committee of the Zinc Institute, the association is the marketing, research and promotional arm of the cadmium industry. The International Cadmium Association (ICdA) was formed by the merger of the Cadmium Council (North America) and the Cadmium Association (Europe). Annual meetings are held alternately in North America and Europe. Members are producers and consumers of cadmium. Membership fee based on annual cadmium production or consumption.

Meetings/Conferences:

Annual Meetings: June

International Card Manufacturers Association *(1990)*

P.O. Box 727
Princeton Junction, NJ 08550-1028
Tel: (609)799-4900 *Fax:* (609)799-7032
E-Mail: info@icma.com
Web Site: www.icma.com
Members: 220 companies
Staff: 7
Annual Budget: $500-1,000,000
Executive Director: Jeffrey E. Barnhart

Historical Note

ICMA is a non-profit trade association of plastic card manufacturers and personalizers, supported by suppliers and other industry participants. Membership: $1,000-2,500/year.

Meetings/Conferences:

Annual Meetings: Fall
2007 – San Diego, CA

Publications:

Buyers Guide. a.
Card Flash (Fax). m.
Directory. a. adv.
Card Manufacturing. 8/year. adv.

International Cargo Gear Bureau *(1966)*

321 W. 44th St.
New York, NY 10036
Tel: (212)757-2011 *Fax:* (212)757-2650
E-Mail: incargear@aol.com
Web Site: www.icgb.com
Members: 35 companies
Staff: 9
Annual Budget: $1-2,000,000
President: Charles G. Visconti

Historical Note

Members are makers and users of material handling equipment ashore and afloat.

Publications:

Directory. bien.

International Cargo Security Council *(1969)*

1400 I St. NW, Suite 1080
Washington, DC 20005
Tel: (202)962-0190 *Fax:* (202)962-3939
Toll Free: (800)976 - 0403
E-Mail: admin@cargosecurity.com
Web Site: www.cargosecurity.com
Members: 1200 companies and individuals
Staff: 4
Annual Budget: $250-500,000
Executive Director: Joe Baker, Jr.

Historical Note

Formerly National Cargo Security Council; assumed its current name on January 1, 2005. ICSC members are drawn from the full spectrum of the air, truck/rail, and maritime cargo security industry.

Meetings/Conferences:

Annual Meetings: May/June, 500

Publications:

Cargo Security Report Newsletter. q. adv.

International Carwash Association *(1953)*

401 N. Michigan Ave.
Chicago, IL 60611
Tel: (312)321-5199 *Fax:* (312)245-1085
Toll Free: (888)422 - 8422
E-Mail: ica@sba.com
Web Site: www.carcarecentral.com
Members: 3000 companies
Staff: 18
Annual Budget: $2-5,000,000
Executive Director: Mark O. Thorsby
E-Mail: ica@sba.com

Historical Note

Formerly American Auto Laundry Association (1958) and Automatic Car Wash Association International (1975); absorbed the National Car Wash Council in 1982 and Professional Detail Association in 1996. Membership: $225/year (operator); $645/year (manufacturer).

Meetings/Conferences:

Annual Meetings: Spring

Publications:

ICA Update. m.
ICA Cost of Doing Business Benchmark Study. bi-a.
ICA Study of Consumer Carwashing Attitudes and Habits. bi-a.
Membership Directory/Buyers Guide. a. adv.

International Cast Polymer Association *(1974)*

1010 N. Glebe Road, Suite 450
Arlington, VA 22201
Tel: (703)525-0511 *Fax:* (703)525-0743
E-Mail: icpa@icpa-hq.org
Web Site: www.icpa-hq.com
Members: 385 companies
Staff: 21
Annual Budget: $500-1,000,000
Executive Director: Sabeena Hickman, CAE
Director, Communications: Andy Rusnak
Director, Legislative and Regulatory Affairs: H. Patrick Toner

Historical Note

Formerly (1993) Cultured Marble Institute. Manufacturers and suppliers of polyester resin-based synthetic marble, onyx and granite-densified products. ICPA promotes quality in the cast polymer products industry. Membership: $650-1,850/year (based on annual volume).

Meetings/Conferences:

Annual Meetings: February

Publications:

Cast Polymer Connection. bi-m. adv.
Membership Directory "The Resource". a.

International Castor Oil Association *(1957)*

521 Pomona Road
Cinnaminson, NJ 08077
Tel: (856)786-2983 *Fax:* (215)717-1220
E-Mail: ICOA@ICOA.org
Web Site: www.ICOA.org
Members: 52 individuals
Annual Budget: $25-50,000
Secretary-Treasurer: David P. Dingley
E-Mail: ICOA@ICOA.org
Administrative Assistant: Donna McGeehan
E-Mail: ICOA@ICOA.org

Historical Note

Formed in New York City on May 1, 1957 by members of the former Linseed-Castorseed Association of New York and incorporated in the State of New Jersey in 1963. Includes foreign members. Crushers of castor seed and exporters, importers, processors, consumers and distributors of castor oil. Membership: $700/year (members).

Meetings/Conferences:

Annual Meetings: Spring

Publications:

Annual.
The Processing of Castor Meal for Detoxicification and Deallergeration.
The Chemistry of Castor Oil and Its Derivatives and Their Applications.

International Cemetery and Funeral Association *(1887)*

107 Carpenter Dr., Suite 100
Sterling, VA 20164-4468
Tel: (703)391-8400 *Fax:* (703)391-8416
Toll Free: (800)645 - 7700
E-Mail: gen4@icfa.org
Web Site: www.icfa.org
Members: 7000 individuals
Staff: 14
Annual Budget: $2-5,000,000
Chief Operating Officer, Internal Affairs: Joseph W. Budzinski
Director, Communications and Membership Services: Linda Budzinski
General Counsel, External Chief Operating Officer: Robert M. Fells

Historical Note

Formerly (1944) the Association of American Cemetery Superintendents, (1945) and (1996) the American Cemetery Association. Merged with the National Association of Cemeteries in 1980. Absorbed the Pre-Arrangement Association of American in 1996. Members are cemetery and funeral home owners and managers.

Meetings/Conferences:

Annual Meetings: Spring
2007 – Las Vegas, NV(Mandalay Bay)/March 20-23

Publications:

ICFA WIRELESS Newsletter. bi-w. adv.
Internat'l Cemetery Management Magazine. m. adv.

International Ceramic Association *(1958)*

17098 Pheasant Meadow Lane SW

Prior Lake, MN 55372
Tel: (952)447-6421
E-Mail: admin@ceramic-ica.com
Web Site: www.ceramic-ica.com
Members: 3000 companies
Annual Budget: $10-25,000
Treasurer: Helen Daum

Historical Note

Members are suppliers of raw materials, manufacturers, distributors and teachers of ceramics. Maintains the International Ceramics Association Educational Foundation. Incorporated in the State of Illinois in August, 1958 as the National Ceramics Association, it assumed its present name in 1982. Membership fee varies, $15-200/year.

Meetings/Conferences:
Annual Meetings: Summer

Publications:
Trade Journal. q. adv.
Blue Book. a.

International Chain Salon Association *(1972)*

2323 Georgetown Circle
Aurora, IL 60504-6712
Toll Free: (866)444 - 4272
E-Mail: mmelaniphy@icsa.cc
Web Site: www.icsa.cc
Members: 70 chains
Staff: 1
Annual Budget: $50-100,000
Director: Margie Melaniphy
E-Mail: mmelaniphy@icsa.cc

Historical Note

Formerly (1985) the National Beauty Salon Chain Association. Membership: $900-1500/year.

Meetings/Conferences:
Annual Meetings:

Publications:
Annual Financial & Employee Operating Performance Survey. a.
Link. q. adv.

International Chemical Workers Union Council/UFCW *(1944)*

1799 Akron Peninsula Road, Suite 300
Akron, OH 44313-4847
Tel: (330)926-1444 *Fax:* (330)926-0816
E-Mail: icwucreg3@aol.com
Web Site: www.icwuc.org
Members: 35000 individuals
Staff: 35
Annual Budget: $2-5,000,000
President: Larry V. Gregoire
Secretary Treasurer: Frank Cyphers
E-Mail: icwucreg3@aol.com

Historical Note

Founded as International Council of Chemical and Allied Industries Union in Akron, Ohio September 7, 1940. Renamed International Chemical Workers Union, this organization received a charter from the American Federation of Labor in September, 1944. Merged with United Food and Commercial Workers International Union and assumed its current name in 1996. Maintains a Washington office. Sponsors and supports the Labor Investment of Voter Education Political Action Committee. Membership fee varies.

Meetings/Conferences:
Triennial meetings: (2008)

International Childbirth Education Association *(1960)*

P.O. Box 20048
Minneapolis, MN 55420-0048
Tel: (952)854-8660
E-Mail: info@icea.org
Web Site: www.icea.org
Members: 8000 individuals
Staff: 7
Annual Budget: $250-500,000
President: Connie Kishbaugh

Historical Note

Association concerned with family-centered maternity care with minimal medical intervention. An international group functioning in 32 countries, ICEA membership is predominantly concentrated in the U.S. Membership: $30/year (individual).

Meetings/Conferences:
Annual Meetings: Summer

Publications:
Internat'l Journal of Childbirth Education. q. adv.
ICEA Bookmarks. q.

International Chiropractors Association *(1926)*

1110 N. Glebe Road, Suite 650
Arlington, VA 22201
Tel: (703)528-5000 *Fax:* (703)528-5023
Toll Free: (800)423 - 4690
E-Mail: icachome@msn.com
Web Site: www.chiropractic.org
Members: 8000 individuals
Staff: 15
Annual Budget: $2-5,000,000
Executive Director: Ronald M. Hendrickson

Historical Note

Established in 1926 as the Chiropractic Health Bureau, it assumed its present name in 1941. A professional society of Doctors of Chiropractic which supports the International Chiropractors Political Action Committee (ICPAC). Membership: $560/year (doctor).

Meetings/Conferences:
Annual Meetings: Spring

Publications:
Internat'l Review of Chiropractic. bi-m. adv.
ICA Today. q. adv.
ICA Membership Directory. a. adv.
FACTS Bulletin. irreg.

International City/County Management Association *(1914)*

777 N. Capitol St. NE, Suite 500
Washington, DC 20002
Tel: (202)289-4262 *Fax:* (202)962-3500
Web Site: www.icma.org
Members: 8300 individuals
Staff: 120
Annual Budget: $10-25,000,000
Executive Director: Bob O'Neill

Historical Note

Founded as the International City Managers Association, it became the International City Management Association in 1969 and assumed its present name in 1991. Also known as ICMA - The Professional Local Government Management Association. A professional society of local government administrators. Has an annual budget of approximately $15 million.

Meetings/Conferences:
Annual Meetings: Fall

Publications:
Management Information Service. m.
Municipal Year Book. a.
Public Management. m. adv.
Urban Data Service. m.
ICMA Newsletter. bi-w. adv.

International Claim Association *(1909)*

One Thomas Circle NW, Tenth Floor
Washington, DC 20005
Tel: (202)452-0143 *Fax:* (202)833-3636
E-Mail: ica@claim.org
Web Site: www.claim.org
Members: 21 individuals
Staff: 2
Annual Budget: $250-500,000
Executive Director: Christopher M. Murphy
E-Mail: cmurphy@claim.org

Historical Note

Members are life and health insurance companies represented by claims employees and officers. Membership: $600/year (corporate); $100/year (individual).

Meetings/Conferences:
Annual Meetings: Fall
2007 – Kissimmee, FL(Gaylord Palms)/Sept. 30-Oct. 2

Publications:
ICA News. q.
Proceedings. a.

International Clarinet Association *(1990)*

P.O. Box 1310
Lyons, CO 80540
Tel: (801)867-4336 *Fax:* (212)457-6124
E-Mail: execdirector@clarinet.org
Web Site: www.clarinet.org/
Members: 3700 individuals
Annual Budget: $25-50,000
Executive Director: So Rhee
E-Mail: execdirector@clarinet.org

Historical Note

ICA members include teachers, manufacturers, amateur musicians and others with an interest in the clarinet. Membership: $50/year (general); $95/2 years (general); $45/2 year (student).

Meetings/Conferences:
Annual Meetings: early July
2007 – Vancouver, BC, Canada(University of British Columbia)/July 4-8

Publications:
Clarinet Journal. q. adv.

International Coach Federation

2365 Harrodsburg Road, Suite A-4325
Lexington, KY 40504
Tel: (859)219-3580 *Fax:* (859)226-4411
E-Mail: icfoffice@coachfederation.org
Web Site: www.coachfederation.org
Members: 11000 individuals
Staff: 13
Executive Director: Lisa Simon

Meetings/Conferences:
Annual Meetings: Fall

Publications:
Coaching World E-newsletter. m. adv.

International Code Council *(1994)*

5203 Leesburg Pike, Suite 600
Falls Church, VA 22041
Tel: (703)931-4533 *Fax:* (703)379-1546
Toll Free: (888)422 - 7253
E-Mail: webmaster@iccsafe.org
Web Site: www.iccsafe.org
Members: 3 associations
Staff: 4
Annual Budget: $500-1,000,000
Chief Executive Officer: James Lee Witt

Historical Note

Successor to Council of American Building Officials, which it formally absorbed in 1997, ICC was organized by its member associations to serve as the coordinating body for building and construction code formulation. Absorbed Southern Building Code Congress International, Building Officials and Code Administrators International, and International Conference of Building Officials in 2003.

International College of Applied Kinesiology *(1975)*

6405 Metcalf Ave., Suite 103
Shawnee Mission, KS 66202-3929
Tel: (913)384-5336 *Fax:* (913)384-5112
E-Mail: info@icakusa.com
Web Site: www.icakusa.com
Members: 600 individuals
Staff: 8
Annual Budget: $250-500,000
Executive Director: Terry Kay Underwood

Historical Note

Membership: $400/year.

Publications:
Membership Directory. a. adv.

International College of Cranio-Mandibular Orthopedics *(1979)*

619 N. 35th St., Suite 307
Seattle, WA 98103
Tel: (206)633-4355 *Fax:* (206)633-4352
Toll Free: (800)446 - 1763
Web Site: www.tmj-iccmo.org
Staff: 1
Executive Secretary: Hallie Truswell

Historical Note

ICCMO members are doctors and other health professionals interested in the physiology of the head and neck and especially the health effects of improper jaw alignment.

Publications:
ICCMO Newsletter. 3/year. adv.
Journal of Craniomandibular Orthopedics. 3/year. adv.

International College of Dentists, U.S.A. Section *(1928)*
51 Monroe St., Suite 1400
Rockville, MD 20850-2408
Tel: (301)251-8861 *Fax:* (301)738-9143
E-Mail: reg-sg@icd.org
Web Site: www.icd.org
Members: 10000 individuals
Staff: 3
Annual Budget: $500-1,000,000
Secretary General and Registrar: Robert E. Brady, DMD
E-Mail: reg-sg@icd.org
Historical Note
Members are dentists who have made an outstanding contribution to the profession of dentistry.
Meetings/Conferences:
Annual Meetings: Fall
Publications:
Key. a.
Keynotes. semi-a.
Globe. a.

International College of Surgeons *(1935)*
1516 N. Lake Shore Dr.
Chicago, IL 60610-1607
Tel: (312)642-3555 *Fax:* (312)787-1624
Toll Free: (800)766 - 3427
E-Mail: info@icsglobal.org
Web Site: www.icsglobal.org
Members: 7000 individuals
Staff: 5
Annual Budget: $500-1,000,000
Executive Director: Max C. Downham
Director, ICS Membership: Patricia Binfa
Controller: Jennifer Tran
Historical Note
Founded in Geneva, Switzerland in 1935 and incorporated in the District of Columbia in 1940, ICS is a federation of general surgeons and surgical specialists. Has an annual budget of approximately $1 million.
Meetings/Conferences:
Annual Meetings: Spring (U.S. Section) and Biennial International Meetings
Publications:
Journal of International Surgery. q. adv.

International Commercial Flooring Specifiers
Historical Note
See COMSPEC - International Commercial Flooring Specifiers.

International Communication Association *(1950)*
1500 21st St.
Washington, DC 20036
Tel: (202)955-1444 *Fax:* (202)955-1448
E-Mail: icahdq@icahdq.org
Web Site: www.icahdq.org
Members: 3238 individuals
Staff: 6
Annual Budget: $500-1,000,000
Executive Director: Michael L. Haley
Historical Note
Founded in December 1950 in Chicago as the National Society for the Study of Communication; assumed present name in 1969 when it was incorporated in Ohio. A founding member of the Council of Communication Societies and Council of Communications Associations and an affiliate of the American Association for the Advancement of Science. Encourages the systematic study of communication theories, processes and skills. Not to be confused with the International Communications Association.
Meetings/Conferences:
Annual Meetings: Spring
2007 – San Francisco, CA(Hilton)/May 24-28/2000
Publications:
Communication Theory. q. adv.
Human Communication Research. q. adv.
ICA Newsletter. 10/year. adv.
Journal of Communication. q. adv.

International Communications Agency Network
Historical Note
Became ICOM, International Communications Agency Network in 1999.

International Community Corrections Association *(1964)*
1730 Rhode Island Ave. NW
Suite 403
Washington, DC 20006
Tel: (202)828-5605 *Fax:* (202)828-5609
E-Mail: icca@iccaweb.org
Web Site: www.iccaweb.org
Members: 1100 individuals
Staff: 1
Annual Budget: $250-500,000
President: Terry Marshall
Historical Note
An affiliate of the American Correctional Association. Formerly (1989) International Halfway House Association; and (1995) International Association of Residential and Community Alternatives. Members are public and private agencies involved in providing community-based correctional programming and services. Membership: $50/year (individual); $150-950/year (organization).
Meetings/Conferences:
Annual Meetings: Fall
Publications:
Research Conference Proceedings. a.
ICCA Journal on Community Corrections. q. adv.

International Compressor Remanufacturers Association *(1965)*
6501 Robertson Dr.
Corpus Christi, TX 78415
Tel: (361)851-9900 *Fax:* (361)851-9908
E-Mail: mreeves@bradleyhermetics.com
Web Site: www.icracomp.com
Members: 60 individuals
Staff: 2
Annual Budget: $10-25,000
Executive Director: Maria Reeves
E-Mail: mreeves@bradleyhermetics.com
Historical Note
ICRA was established to foster the trade, commerce and interest of those engaged in the business of remanufacturing compressors and repairing similar equipment. Membership: $500/year (organization/company).
Meetings/Conferences:
Annual Meetings: Winter
Publications:
Newsletter. q.

International Computer Music Association *(1974)*
2040 Polk St., Suite 330
San Francisco, CA 94109
Tel: (734)878-3310 *Fax:* (734)878-3031
E-Mail: icma@umich.edu
Web Site: www.computermusic.org
Members: 700 individuals
Staff: 2
President: Perry Cook
Historical Note
ICMA are computer hardware/software companies, composers, musicians and others with an interest in computer music. Membership: $50/year (individual); $15/year (student); $150/year (corporation).
Publications:
ARRAY Newsletter. 3/year. adv.
ICMC Proceedings. a.
ICMA Membership Directory.

International Concatenated Order of Hoo-Hoo *(1892)*
Box 118
Gurdon, AR 71743-0118
Tel: (870)353-4997 *Fax:* (870)353-4151
Toll Free: (800)979 - 9950
E-Mail: info@hoo-hoo.org
Web Site: www.hoo-hoo.org
Members: 6000 individuals
Staff: 1
Annual Budget: $100-250,000
Executive Secretary: Beth A. Thomas
E-Mail: info@hoo-hoo.org
Historical Note
Does business under "Hoo-Hoo International" and "International Order of Hoo-Hoo". Members are represenatives of the forest products and lumber industry, lumber associations and lumber press. Originated in Gurdon, Arkansas when several lumber executives were stranded by a railroad washout. International in scope with chapters in Canada, Australia, and New Zealand. Membership: $21.99/year (membership is based on recommendation by a current member).
Meetings/Conferences:
Annual Meetings: September
Publications:
Log & Talley. q. adv.

International Concrete Repair Institute *(1988)*
3166 S. River Road, Suite 132
Des Plaines, IL 60018
Tel: (847)827-0830 *Fax:* (847)827-0832
Web Site: www.icri.org
Members: 1400companiesandindividuals
Staff: 6
Annual Budget: $500-1,000,000
Executive and Technical Director: Kelly Page
Historical Note
ICRI members are contractors, manufacturers, engineers and others concerned with improving the quality of concrete repairs through communication and education. Formerly (1993) International Association of Concrete Repair Specialists. Membership: $100-2,000/year.
Meetings/Conferences:
Semi-Annual Conventions:
Publications:
Concrete Repair Bulletin. bi-m. adv.
Who's Who in Concrete Repair Membership Directory. a. adv.

International Conference of Building Officials *(1922)*
Historical Note
Merged with International Code Council in 2003.

International Conference of Funeral Service Examining Boards *(1900)*
1885 Shelby Lane
Fayetteville, AR 72704
Tel: (479)442-7076 *Fax:* (479)442-7090
E-Mail: cfseb@cfseb.org
Web Site: www.cfseb.org
Members: 130 individuals
Staff: 4
Annual Budget: $250-500,000
Executive Director: Dalene Paull
Historical Note
Formerly (1998) Conference of Funeral Service Examining Boards of the United States. Members are executive secretaries and board members of state and provinical agencies, licensing embalmers and funeral directors in the U.S. and Canada. Associate members are mortuary science schools accredited by the American Board of Funeral Service. Membership: $250/year (organization/company).

International Conference of Police Chaplains *(1973)*
P.O. Box 5590
Destin, FL 32540
Tel: (850)654-9736 *Fax:* (850)654-9742
E-Mail: icpc@icpc.gccoxmail.com
Web Site: www.icpc4cops.org
Members: 2800 individuals
Staff: 6
Annual Budget: $250-500,000
Executive Director: Dr. Charles R. Lorrain
Director, Marketing and Fundraising: Stuart Nelson
E-Mail: icpc@icpc.gccoxmail.com
Historical Note
ICPC members are volunteer and paid law enforcement chaplains. ICPC assists law enforcement agencies seeking to start chaplaincy programs. Membership: $125/year.

Meetings/Conferences:
Annual Meetings: July/600
2007 – Grand Rapids, MI/June 25-29
Publications:
Chaplains Handbook. irreg.
Directory of Police Chaplains. m.
Newsletter. q.

International Conference of Symphony and Opera Musicians *(1962)*
1609 Tammany Dr.
Nashville, TN 37206
Tel: (615)227-2379 *Fax:* (615)259-9140
Web Site: www.icsom.org
Members: 4500 individuals
Staff: 9
Annual Budget: $250-500,000
Secretary: Laura Ross
Historical Note
Members are professional symphony, opera and ballet musicians united to promote the welfare of and make more rewarding the livelihood of the orchestral performer and to disseminate inter-orchestra information through correspondence and a newsletter. Affiliated with the American Federation of Musicians. Membership: fees vary.
Meetings/Conferences:
Annual Meetings: August
2007 – Minneapolis, MN
Publications:
Senza Sordino. bi-m.

International Congress of Oral Implantologists *(1975)*
248 Lorraine Ave., Third Floor
Upper Montclair, NJ 07043-1454
Tel: (973)783-6300 *Fax:* (973)783-1175
Toll Free: (800)442 - 0525
E-Mail: icoi@dentalimplants.com
Web Site: www.dentalimplants.com
Members: 7000 individuals
Staff: 7
Annual Budget: $1-2,000,000
Executive Director: R. Craig Johnson
E-Mail: icoi@dentalimplants.com
Historical Note
ICOI is a dental implant education and research organization. Members are dentists, oral surgeons, research personnel and others involved in oral implant procedures. Sponsors several seminars and meetings annually. Membership: $350/year (U.S.); $275/year (overseas); $150/year (Affiliate Society).
Publications:
Implant Dentistry Journal. q. adv.
ICCI World News. q. adv.

International Contract Center Benchmarking Consortium *(1998)*
4606 FM 1960 West, Suite 250
Houston, TX 77069
Tel: (281)440-5044 *Fax:* (281)440-6677
Toll Free: (888)739 - 8244
E-Mail: info@iccbc.org
Web Site: www.iccbc.org
Members: 3700 individuals
Staff: 14
Annual Budget: $1-2,000,000
Executive Director: Paul Claymore
Historical Note
An autonomous division of The Benchmarking Network, ICCBC members are individuals and companies operating customer service or information call centers. Provides information on industry best practices to members.
Publications:
Newsletter. w.

International Coordinating Committee on Solid State Sensors and Actuators Research *(1981)*
c/o Berkeley Sensor & Actuator Center, Suite 1770
Berkeley, CA 94720-1770
Tel: (510)643-6690 *Fax:* (510)525-9037
E-Mail: sensor@eecs.berkeley.edu
Members: 35 organizations
Staff: 1
Annual Budget: $250-500,000
Chairman: Richard S. Muller
Historical Note
Promotes the international exchange of scholarly information on developments in the field.
Meetings/Conferences:
Biennial Meetings: Typically held in June of odd-numbered years.
Publications:
Digest of International Conference on Sensors & Actuators. bien.

International Copper Association *(1960)*
260 Madison Ave., 16th Floor
New York, NY 10016
Tel: (212)251-7240 *Fax:* (212)251-7245
E-Mail: info@copperinfo.org
Web Site: www.copperinfo.com
Members: 33 companies, 9 associate members
Staff: 12
Annual Budget: $10-25,000,000
President: Francis J. Kane
E-Mail: fkane@copper.org
Director, Communications and Member Relations: Steve Kukoda
Vice President, Administration and Finance: Gerald J. McGee
E-Mail: gmcgee@copper.org
Historical Note
International Copper Association, Ltd. (ICA) was organized in 1989 when the copper industry's worldwide research arm, the International Copper Research Association, Inc. (INCRA), was restructured to include market development activities. ICA, formed by primary copper producing and fabricating companies throughout the world, assists the copper industry in maintaining the use of copper where traditionally utilized, in meeting competition from other materials, in expanding and extending markets in established and new areas, and in developing new applications for the metal. Has an annual budget of approximately $15 million. Membership fee: $2.50/ton/year (producer); $50,000/year (associate).
Meetings/Conferences:
Annual Meetings: New York City/June

International Corrugated Packaging Foundation *(1985)*
113 S. West St.
P.O. Box 25708
Alexandria, VA 22313
Tel: (703)549-8580 *Fax:* (703)549-8670
E-Mail: info@aiccbox.org
Web Site: www.icpfbox.org
Staff: 2
Annual Budget: $100-250,000
President: Robin Jackson
E-Mail: robin.icp@aiccbox.org
Historical Note
Established in Virginia and incorporated in Illinois, ICPF is a not-for-profit foundation formed for the purposes of research, education and scholarship for the corrugated packaging industry.
Publications:
ICPF Direct. q.

International Council for Small Business *(1956)*
School of Business and Public Management
2115 G. St. NW, Suite 403
Washington, DC 20052
Tel: (202)994-0704 *Fax:* (202)994-4930
E-Mail: icsb@gwu.edu
Web Site: www.icsb.org
Members: 1800 individuals
Staff: 2
Annual Budget: $50-100,000
Executive Administrator: Susan Duffy
E-Mail: icsb@gwu.edu
Historical Note
Formerly (1977) National Council for Small Business Management Development. Questions concerning the Journal should be directed to: Editor, Tom Witt at the Bureau of Business Research, West Virginia University, P.O. Box 6025, Morgantown, WV 26506-6025. Membership: $65/year (individual); $500/year (organization/company).
Meetings/Conferences:
Annual Meetings: June
Publications:
ICSB Bulletin. q. adv.
Journal of Small Business Management. q. adv.

International Council of Air Shows *(1968)*
751 Miller Dr. SE, Suite F-4
Leesburg, VA 20175
Tel: (703)779-8510 *Fax:* (703)779-8511
E-Mail: icas@airshows.org
Web Site: www.airshows.org
Members: 900 companies and organizations
Staff: 5
Annual Budget: $1-2,000,000
Historical Note
Members consist of event organizers, producers and air show performers and event service organizations. Membership: $175/year.
Meetings/Conferences:
Annual Meetings: Las Vegas, NV/December/1,500
Publications:
Newsletter. 24/year.
Directory. a.
Airshows Magazine. q. adv.

International Council of Cruise Lines *(1965)*
2111 Wilson Blvd., Eighth Floor
Arlington, VA 22201-3001
Tel: (703)522-8463 *Fax:* (703)522-3811
Toll Free: (800)545 - 9338
E-Mail: info@iccl.org
Web Site: www.iccl.org
Members: 16 cruise lines; 70 associates
Staff: 11
Annual Budget: $1-2,000,000
President: J. Michael Crye
Director, Communications: Christine Fischer
Director, Membership Programs: Katherine Harrison Shore
Executive Vice President: Thomas E. Thompson
Historical Note
The mission of the ICCL is to participate in the regulatory and policy development process and ensure that all measures adopted provide for a safe, secure and healthy cruise ship environment. Membership: $35,000/year (company).
Publications:
Even Keel. q.

International Council of Employers of Bricklayers and Allied Craftworkers *(1987)*
P.O. Box 21462
Washington, DC 20009
Tel: (202)457-9040 *Fax:* (202)457-9051
E-Mail: maquiline@icebac.org
Web Site: www.icebac.org
Members: 5000 companies
Staff: 2
Annual Budget: $250-500,000
Executive Director: Fred Kinateder
Historical Note
Formerly (1996) International Council of Employers of Bricklayers and Allied Craftsmen. Members are contractors who are signatory to collectively-bargained labor agreements with the International Union of Bricklayers and Allied Craftworkers.
Meetings/Conferences:
Annual Meetings: Fall
Publications:
ICE Voice. a.

International Council of Fine Arts Deans *(1964)*
Penn State University
111 Arts Bldg.
University Park, PA 16802-2900
Tel: (814)865-2593 *Fax:* (814)865-2018
Web Site: www.icfad.org
Members: 300 individuals
Staff: 1
Annual Budget: $50-100,000
Executive Director: Richard Durst
E-Mail: rdurst1@psu.edu

Historical Note
Members are deans of university schools of the arts. Membership: $350/year (institutional).
Meetings/Conferences:
Annual Meetings: November/October
Publications:
Membership Directory. a.
Update Newsletter. 3/year.

International Council of Library Association Executives *(1975)*
Historical Note
A program of American Library Association, which provides administrative support.

International Council of Psychologists *(1941)*
8302 York Rd. (B-45)
Elkins Park, PA 19027
Tel: (215)884-5964
E-Mail: mattikg@comcast.net
Web Site: http://icpsych.tripod.com
Members: 1200 individuals
Staff: 2
Annual Budget: $50-100,000
Secretary-General: Dr. Matti Gershenfeld
E-Mail: mattikg@comcast.net
Historical Note
Established as National Council of Women Psychologists in the U.S.A. Became (1947) International Council of Women Psychologists, and (1959) International Council of Psychologists. Purpose is to advance psychology and the applicaton of its scientific findings throughout the world. ICP seeks to strengthen international bonds between psychologists and to widen, deepen, and clarify channels of communication between individual psychologists. Membership: $85/year (individual).
Meetings/Conferences:
Annual Meetings: July-August/250
Publications:
Convention Proceedings. a.
Directory of Members. trien-quadren.
International Psychologist. bi-m.

International Council of Shopping Centers *(1957)*
1221 Avenue of the Americas, 41st Floor
New York, NY 10020-1099
Tel: (646)728-3800 *Fax:* (732)694-1755
E-Mail: icsc@icsc.org
Web Site: www.icsc.org
Staff: 132
Annual Budget: $25-50,000,000
President and Chief Executive Officer: Michael P. Kerchval
Staff Vice President, Finance and Controller: Glen Hale
E-Mail: ghale@icsc.org
Chief Operating Officer: Robert A. Mallia
E-Mail: rmallia@icsc.org
Staff Vice President, Conventions and Conferences: Lorraine Mazza
E-Mail: lmazza@icsc.org
Senior Vice President, Programs and Services: Marvin Morrison
E-Mail: mmorrison@icsc.org
Senior Staff Vice President and Chief Global Marketing Officer: Jay Starr
E-Mail: jstarr@icsc.org
Historical Note
Owners, developers, managers, retailers and suppliers of shopping centers. Sponsors professional accreditation programs for Certified Shopping Center Manager (CSM), Certified Marketing Director (CMD) and Certified Leasing Specialist (CLS). Sponsors and supports the ICSC Political Action Committee. Research analysts produce updates on the economic impact of U.S. and Canadian shopping centers, tenant sales in malls and center revenues and expenses. The ICSC Library contains information from surveys, periodicals, reference texts and computer data bases on most areas of shopping center retailing activities. ICSC holds 200 seminars and conferences annually. Also has offices in London and Singapore. Membership: $100/year (individual), $500/year (company).
Meetings/Conferences:
Semi-annual Meetings: Spring and Fall
2007 – Las Vegas, NV(Convention Center)/May 20-23
Publications:
SCTXra. w.
Monthly Mall Merchandise Index. m.
Journal of Shopping Center Research. semi-a.
Government Relations Report.
Shopping Centers Today. m. adv.
Research Quarterly. q.
Retail Challenge. q.
Legal Update. tri-a.
National Issues Update. m.
Directory of Products & Services. a. adv.
Membership Directory. a.
Value Retail News.

International Council on Education for Teaching *(1953)*
1000 Capitol Dr.
Wheeling, IL 60090-5863
Tel: (847)465-0191 *Fax:* (847)465-5617
E-Mail: icet@nl.edu
Web Site: www.nl.edu/icet
Members: 500 individuals
Staff: 4
Annual Budget: $250-500,000
Executive Director: Dr. Darrell Bloom
E-Mail: icet@nl.edu
Historical Note
ICET is an international, non-governmental association of educational organizations, institutions, and individuals dedicated to the improvement of teacher education and all forms of education and training related to national development. ICET works to foster international cooperation in improving the quality of the preparation of teachers and education specialists, to promote cooperation between higher education, government, and the private sector to develop a world-wide network of resources, and to provide an international forum for the exchange of information. Membership: $40/year (individual); $400/year (organization/company).
Publications:
Newsletter. irreg.
Proceedings. a.
International Yearbook on Teacher Education. a.

International Council on Hotel, Restaurant and Institutional Education *(1946)*
2810 N. Parham Rd., Suite 230
Richmond, VA 23294
Tel: (804)346-4800 *Fax:* (804)346-5009
Web Site: www.chrie.org
Members: 2500 individuals
Staff: 6
Annual Budget: $500-1,000,000
Executive Vice President: Kathy McCarty
E-Mail: kmccarty@chrie.org
Historical Note
I-CHRIE members are schools, colleges, and universities offering programs of study in hotel and restaurant management, foodservice management and culinary arts. Also includes the enhancement of professionalism at all levels of the hospitality and tourism industry, or businesses that provide food, lodging and travel services. Founded as the National Council on Hotel and Restaurant Education, it assumed its present name in 1959. Membership: $155/year (individual); $555/year (organization).
Meetings/Conferences:
Annual Meetings: Summer/1,000
Publications:
HOSTEUR Magazine. semi-a. adv.
Journal of Hospitality and Tourism Education. q. adv.
Journal of Hospitality and Tourism Research. q. adv.
Conference Proceedings. a. adv.
Guide to College Programs in Hospitality & Tourism. a. adv.
CHRIE Communique. m. adv.

International Council on Systems Engineering *(1990)*
2150 N. 107th St., Suite 205
Seattle, WA 98133-9009
Tel: (206)361-6607 *Fax:* (206)367-8777
Toll Free: (800)366 - 1164
E-Mail: info@incose.org
Web Site: www.incose.org
Members: 2000 individuals
Administrative Executive: Shirley Bishop
Meetings/Conferences:
Annual Meetings: Summer
Publications:
Insight Newsletter. q. adv.
Journal.

International Crystal Federation
c/o Collier, Shannon, Rill & Scott
3050 K St. NW, Suite 400
Washington, DC 20007
Tel: (202)342-8580 *Fax:* (202)342-8451
Members: 80 individuals
Staff: 1
Counsel: Michael R. Kershow
Historical Note
The ICF is a not-for-profit international organization of manufacturers, distributors and suppliers of crystal. Function of ICF is to monitor and respond to U.S. federal and state laws regulations, and international laws and regulations, pertaining to the crystal glass industry. Holds an annual technical conference.

International Customer Service Association *(1981)*
401 N. Michigan Ave., Suite 2200
Chicago, IL 60611-4267
Tel: (312)321-6800 *Fax:* (312)321-6869
Toll Free: (800)360 - 4272
E-Mail: icsa@smithbucklin.com
Web Site: www.icsa.com
Members: 3200 individuals
Staff: 10
Annual Budget: $2-5,000,000
Executive Director: Julie Sutter
Historical Note
Members are customer service management professionals. Incorporated in Illinois May 13, 1981. Membership: $195/year.
Meetings/Conferences:
Annual Meetings: Fall/1,000
Publications:
Compensation Study. bien.
ICSA News. bi-m.
Benchmarking Study. bien.
Membership Directory. a.
ICSA Journal. semi-a. adv.

International Cut Flower Growers Association *(1936)*
P.O. Box 99
Haslett, MI 48840
Tel: (517)655-3726 *Fax:* (517)655-3727
E-Mail: icfg@voyager.net
Web Site: www.rosesinc.org
Members: 300 individuals
Staff: 4
Executive Secretary: Jay Stawarz
E-Mail: icfg@voyager.net
Historical Note
Founded as Roses Incorporated; assumed its current name in 2000. Members produce greenhouse roses in the United States and Canada.
Meetings/Conferences:
Annual Meetings: Spring
Publications:
Bulletin. m.

International Dairy Foods Association *(1990)*
1250 H St. NW, Suite 900
Washington, DC 20005-3952
Tel: (202)737-4332 *Fax:* (202)331-7820
E-Mail: membership@idfa.org
Web Site: www.idfa.org
Members: 525 companies
Staff: 55
Annual Budget: $2-5,000,000
President and Chief Executive Officer: Constance E. Tipton
Vice President, Regulatory Affairs and Counsel: Clay Detlefsen

Vice President, Finance and Administration: Sam J. DiCarlo
Vice President, Regulatory Affairs: Cary Frye
Vice President, Marketing: Tom Nagle
Vice President, Communications and Meetings: Susan E. Ruland

Historical Note
IDFA is the umbrella organization for three separate constituent associations: Milk Industry Foundation, National Cheese Institute, International Ice Cream Association. IDFA is the dairy foods trade association working with industry, legislators, regulators and the public on issues affecting the dairy processing industry. Sponsors and supports the Ice Cream, Milk, and Cheese Political Action Committee.

Meetings/Conferences:
Annual Meetings: Fall
2007 – Oct. 24-27

Publications:
Alert!. irreg.
IDFA Membership Directory. a.
News Update. m.
Hotline. irreg.

International Dairy-Deli-Bakery Association *(1964)*
P.O. Box 5528
Madison, WI 53705-0528
Tel: (608)310-5000 *Fax:* (608)238-6330
E-Mail: iddba@iddba.org
Web Site: www.iddba.org
Members: 1450 companies
Staff: 20
Executive Director: Carol L. Christison
E-Mail: cchristison@iddba.org
Director, Membership, Registration and Exhibits: Lucie Arendt
E-Mail: larendt@iddba.org
Director, Education: Mary Kay O'Connor
E-Mail: mcconnor@iddba.org

Historical Note
Formerly (1985) the International Cheese and Deli Association, (1991) International Dairy-Deli Association. Members are companies involved in the production, processing or selling of deli, dairy and bakery products. Membership: $450/year (company).

Meetings/Conferences:
Annual Meetings: June

Publications:
Legisletter Newsletter. m.
What's In Store Trend Report. a.
Dairy-Deli-Bakery Wrap Up. q.
Dairy-Deli-Bakery Digest. m.
Research Publication. a.

International Desalination Association *(1973)*
P.O. Box 387
Topsfield, MA 01983
Tel: (978)887-0410 *Fax:* (978)887-0411
E-Mail: info@idadesal.org
Web Site: www.idadesal.org/
Members: 1000firms,individuals&agencies
Staff: 4
Annual Budget: $250-500,000
Secretary General: Patricia A. Burke
E-Mail: pab@idadesal.org

Historical Note
Established as the National Water Supply Improvement Association, became the Water Supply Improvement Association in 1982, and assumed its present name in 1985 upon merging with the International Desalination and Environmental Association. Members are producers and users of water desalinization equipment. In addition to the biennial meetings, the associaton holds regional affiliate meetings in even years and several seminars/workshops. Membership: $85/year (individual), $750/year (corporation), $500/year (small firms), $25/year (student/library).

Meetings/Conferences:
Biennial Meetings: Fall

Publications:
Desalination Directory. bi-a.
Newsletter. bi-m.
International Desalination and Reuse Quarterly. q.
Inventory Report. bi-a.
Proceedings of Biennial Conference. bien.
Membership Directory. a.

International Development Research Council
Historical Note
Merged with NACORE International to form Global Corporate Real Estate Network in 2002.

International Digital Enterprise Alliance *(1966)*
1421 Prince St., Suite 230
Alexandria, VA 22314-2805
Tel: (703)837-1070 *Fax:* (703)837-1072
E-Mail: info@idealliance.org
Web Site: www.idealliance.org
Members: 200 companies and organizations
Staff: 9
Annual Budget: $2-5,000,000
President and Chief Executive Officer: David Steinhardt

Historical Note
Organized as Graphic Communications Computer Association, became Graphic Communications Association in 1966, and assumed its present name in 2002. Has a broad-based membership to advance user driven, cross industry solutions for publishing and content related process by developing standards, fostering business alliances and identifying best practices.

International Disk Drive Equipment and Materials Association *(1986)*
470 Lakeside Dr.
Sunnyvale, CA 94085
Tel: (408)991-9430 *Fax:* (408)991-9434
Web Site: www.idema.org
Members: 100 individuals
Staff: 4
Annual Budget: $2-5,000,000
President: Mark Geenen

Historical Note
IDEMA was founded to promote the disk drive industry by holding trade shows, conferences and meetings and by setting industry standards. Membership: $300/year (individual); $995-25000/year (organization/company).

Meetings/Conferences:
Semi-Annual Meetings: Spring and Fall

Publications:
Insight (online).

International District Energy Association *(1909)*
125 Turnpike Rd., Suite 4
Westborough, MA 01581-2841
Tel: (508)366-9339 *Fax:* (508)366-0019
E-Mail: idea@districtenergy.org
Web Site: www.districtenergy.org
Members: 850 individuals
Staff: 3
Annual Budget: $1-2,000,000
President: Rob Thornton

Historical Note
Formerly (1969) National District Heating Association, (1985) International District Heating Association, and (1994) International District Heating and Cooling Association. Absorbed (1988) North American District Heating and Cooling Institute. Members are owners/operators of District (central) heating and cooling systems, suppliers of centralized piping systems and appurtenances that produce hot water, and architects/engineers associated with the design of such systems.

Meetings/Conferences:
Annual Meetings: June

Publications:
District Energy Now. m.
District Energy. q. adv.
Proceedings. a.

International Documentary Association *(1982)*
1201 W. Fifth St.
Suite M320
Los Angeles, CA 90017-1461
Tel: (213)534-3600 *Fax:* (213)534-3610
E-Mail: administration@documentary.org
Web Site: www.documentary.org
Members: 2800 individuals
Staff: 5
Annual Budget: $500-1,000,000
Executive Director: Sandra J. Ruch

Historical Note
The International Documentary Association is a non-profit association founded in 1982 to promote non-fiction film and video, to support the efforts of documentary film and video makers around the world and to increase public appreciation and demand for documentary film and television programs. Membership consists of foreign as well as American members and includes producers, directors, writers, editors, camera operators, musicians, researchers, technicians, journalists, broadcast and cable programmers, academics, distributors and members of the general public. Membership: $85/year (individual); $150/year (organization/company).

Meetings/Conferences:
Annual Meetings: Board of Trustees Meeting
2007 – New York, NY/Sept. 1- /20
2008 – Los Angeles, CA/Dec. 1- /20

Publications:
IDA Membership Directory & Survival Guide. bien.
Documentary Magazine. 8/year. adv.

International Door Association *(1973)*
P.O. Box 246
28 Lowry Dr.
West Milton, OH 45383-0246
Tel: (937)698-8042 *Fax:* (937)698-6153
Toll Free: (800)355 - 4432
Web Site: www.doors.org
Members: 1600 individuals
Staff: 10
Annual Budget: $1-2,000,000
Managing Director: Christopher S. Long

Historical Note
Formerly (1986) Door and Operator Dealers of America and (1997) Door and Operator Dealers Association and Far Western Garage Door Association. Members are producers and installers of garage door systems.

Meetings/Conferences:
Annual Meetings: Summer

Publications:
International Door and Operator Industry. bi-m.

International Double Reed Society *(1972)*
2423 Lawndale Rd.
Finksburg, MD 21048-1401
Tel: (410)871-0658 *Fax:* (410)871-0659
Web Site: www.idrs.org
Members: 4600 individuals
Staff: 1
Annual Budget: $50-100,000
Executive Secretary-Treasurer: Norma Hooks
E-Mail: norma4IDRS@verizon.net

Historical Note
Members are performers, teachers, students and manufacturers of double reed instruments (e.g., bassoon, oboe). Membership: $35-400/year.

Meetings/Conferences:
Annual Meetings: Summer
2007 – Ithaca, NY(Ithaca College)/June 12-16
2008 – Provo, UT(Brigham Young University)/

Publications:
Double Reed. q. adv.

International Downtown Association *(1954)*
1250 H St. NW, 10th Floor
Washington, DC 20005
Tel: (202)393-6801 *Fax:* (202)393-6869
Web Site: www.ida-downtown.org
Members: 700 individuals
Staff: 6
Annual Budget: $500-1,000,000
President: David M. Feehan
Director, Information and Policy: Chandrim Basak
Business and Office Manager: Lori Pizzo
Director, Events: Trina Soto-Clarke
Director, Membership and Marketing: Elizabeth C. Wells

Historical Note
Formerly (1986) International Downtown Executives Association. Members are downtown development organizations represented by a chief executive officer; city, county or state agencies involved with downtown economic development; and individuals and corporations with an interest in downtown

development. Operates a subsidiary for program development, the Downtown Development Foundation. Membership: $300/year (individual); $225-2,550/year, based on budget (company).

Meetings/Conferences:
Annual: Fall
2007 - New York, NY(Marriott Marquis)/Sept. 15-18

Publications:
Membership Roster. q.
Downtown News Briefs. q.

International Dyslexia Association *(1949)*
Chester Bldg., Suite 382
8600 La Salle Rd.
Baltimore, MD 21286-2044
Tel: (410)296-0232 *Fax:* (410)321-5069
Toll Free: (800)222 - 3123
Web Site: www.interdys.org
Members: 12000 individuals
Staff: 15
Annual Budget: $2-5,000,000
Executive Director: Megan Cohen

Historical Note
Formerly (1997) The Orton Dyslexia Society, IDA is an international organization disseminating information on specific language disabilities-dyslexia. Membership: $60/year (individual); $100/year (family); $395/year (institution).

Meetings/Conferences:
Annual Meetings: Fall
2007 - Dallas, TX(Adam's Mark Hotel)/Nov. 14-17/3500

Publications:
Membership Newsletter. bi-a.
Perspectives on Dyslexia. q. adv.
Journal - Annals of Dyslexia. a.
Annual Conference Program. a. adv.

International Economic Development Council *(2001)*
734 15th St. NW
Suite 900
Washington, DC 20005
Tel: (202)223-7800 *Fax:* (202)223-4745
E-Mail: jfinkle@iedconline.org
Web Site: www.iedconline.org
Members: 4300 individuals
Staff: 30
Annual Budget: $2-5,000,000
President and Chief Executive Officer: Jeffrey A. Finkle
Vice President, Training, Certification and Communications: Jill Frick
Vice President, Conferences: Richard Heffernan
Senior Legislative Associate: Laura Powars

Historical Note
Established in 2001 through the merger of the Council for Urban Economic Development (CUED) and the American Economic Development Council (AEDC), the IEDC is the largest membership association serving economic and community development professionals and those in allied fields.

Meetings/Conferences:
Semi-Annual Meetings: Summer and Fall
2007 - Phoenix, AZ(West Kierland Resort)/Sept. 16-19

Publications:
Economic Development Journal. q. adv.
Economic Development Now. bi-m.
Federal Directory. a.
Budget Overview. a.

International Ecotourism Society *(1990)*
733 15th St. NW, Sutie 1000
Washington, DC 20005
Tel: (202)347-9203 *Fax:* (202)387-7915
E-Mail: ecomail@ecotourism.org
Web Site: www.ecotourism.org
Members: 900 individuals
Staff: 8
Annual Budget: $250-500,000
Executive Director: Martha Honey
Director, Finance and Administration: Najah Abdullah
Director, International Programs: Amos Bien

Historical Note
Society members include park managers, tour operators, conservation professionals and others with an interest in the development of ecology-centered tourism. Membership: $35-1000/year.

Publications:
Digital Traveler. m.
TIES Quarterly Newsletter. q. adv.
International Membership Directory (online).

International Electrical Testing Association *(1972)*
106 Stone St.
P.O. Box 687
Morrison, CO 80465
Tel: (303)697-8441 *Fax:* (303)697-8431
Toll Free: (888)300 - 6382
E-Mail: neta@netaworld.org
Web Site: www.netaworld.org
Members: 1000 individuals
Staff: 5
Annual Budget: $250-500,000
Executive Director: Jayne Tanz
E-Mail: neta@netaworld.org
Member Services Coordinator: Dennice McMonigal

Historical Note
Formerly (2005) the National Electrical Testing Association. Members are independent firms in testing, analysis and maintenance of electrical power systems; associate members are firms supplying services for the power systems industry. Membership: based on employees (company); $75/year (individual).

Meetings/Conferences:
Annual Meetings: March

Publications:
NETA Conference Program. a. adv.
NETA World. q. adv.

International Electrology Educators *(1979)*

Historical Note
A committee affiliate of the Society of Clinical and Medical Electrologists, which provides administrative support.

International Electronic Article Surveillance Manufacturers Association
1800 K St. NW, Suite 718
Washington, DC 20006
Tel: (202)466-4214 *Fax:* (202)466-7414
E-Mail: ieasma@fsmail.net
Web Site: www.ieasma.org
Members: 12 companies
Staff: 7
Annual Budget: $250-500,000
Executive Vice President: Randy Dyer, CAE
Meeting Coordinator: Elvie Lou

Historical Note
IEASMA members are manufacturers of equipment which provides inventory security for retail and industrial stores or outlets. Membership: varies, based on gross sales.

Publications:
IEASMA Newsletter. bi-m.

International Embryo Transfer Society *(1974)*
1111 N. Dunlap Ave.
Savoy, IL 61874-9510
Tel: (217)356-3182 *Fax:* (217)398-4119
E-Mail: iets@assochg.org
Web Site: www.iets.org
Members: 1100 individuals
Staff: 2
Annual Budget: $100-250,000
Executive Secretary: Jennifer Gavel
E-Mail: iets@assochg.org
Business Manager: Charles L. Sapp
E-Mail: iets@assochg.org

Historical Note
Active members are persons interested in the technology of embryo transfer with a veterinary, master's or doctorate degree in a field related to embryo transfer. Membership: $110/year (individual); $55/year (student).

Meetings/Conferences:
Annual Meetings: January

Publications:
Embryo Transfer Newsletter. q. adv.

International Energy Credit Association *(1923)*
8325 Lantern View Lane
St. John, IN 46373
Tel: (219)365-7313 *Fax:* (219)365-0327
Web Site: www.ieca.net
Members: 900 individuals
Staff: 2
Annual Budget: $250-500,000
Executive Vice President: Robert Raichle, CCE
E-Mail: rprco@aol.com

Historical Note
Founded as American Petroleum Credit Association; became International Petroleum Credit Association in 1992, and assumed its current name in 2000. Members are credit and financial executives with companies whose product is a petroleum derivative. Allied members are vendors to the industry. Membership: $300/year (individual).

Meetings/Conferences:
Annual Meetings: October

Publications:
IECA Journal. 3/year.

International Engineering Consortium *(1944)*
300 W. Adams St., Suite 1210
Chicago, IL 60606-1154
Tel: (312)559-4100 *Fax:* (312)559-4111
E-Mail: info@iec.org
Web Site: www.iec.org
Members: 73 universities
Staff: 50
Executive Director: Roger Plummer
Manager, Publications: Elizabeth Santana

Historical Note
Formerly (1974) National Electronics Conference and (1993) National Engineering Consortium. An engineering education organization sponsored by major technological universities.

Publications:
Annual Review of Communications. a.

International Engraved Graphics Association *(1911)*
P.O. Box 290249
Nashville, TN 37229-0249
Tel: (615)366-1094 Ext: 209 *Fax:* (615)366-4192
E-Mail: engraved1@earthlink.net
Members: 80 companies
Staff: 1
Annual Budget: $50-100,000
Manager: Harris B. Griggs

Historical Note
Founded in 1911 as the National Association of Steel and Copper Plate Engravers; became Engraved Stationery Manufacturers Association in 1938 and assumed its present name in 2000. Administrative support provided by Printing Industry Association of the South (same address).

Meetings/Conferences:
Semi-annual Meetings: Winter and Summer

Publications:
ESMA Newsletter. q.

International Entertainment Buyers Association *(1970)*
P.O. Box 128376
Nashville, TN 37212
Tel: (615)463-0161 *Fax:* (615)463-0163
Toll Free: (888)999 - 4322
E-Mail: info@ieba.org
Web Site: www.ieba.org
Members: 500 individuals
Staff: 1
Annual Budget: $100-250,000
Executive Director: Patti Burgart
E-Mail: info@ieba.org

Historical Note
IEBA is dedicated to entertainment buyers, artists, managers and publicity persons. Membership: $150/year.

Publications:
Membership Directory. a. adv.
Newsletter. m. adv.

International Erosion Control Association *(1972)*
3001 S. Lincoln Ave., Suite 8
Steamboat Springs, CO 80487
Tel: (970)879-3010 *Fax:* (970)879-8563
Toll Free: (800)455 - 4322
E-Mail: ecinfo@ieca.org
Web Site: www.ieca.org
Members: 1900 individuals
Staff: 9
Annual Budget: $1-2,000,000
Executive Director: Ben Northcutt
E-Mail: ecinfo@ieca.org
Historical Note
Landscape contractors, architects, engineers, and suppliers, as well as government officials concerned about soil erosion. Membership: $95/year (individual), $295/year (corporate).
Publications:
Products/Services Directory. bi-a. adv.
Erosion Control Journal. bi-m. adv.
IECA Compilations.
Membership Directory. a.
Newsletter. q.
Proceedings. a.

International Executive Housekeepers Association *(1930)*
1001 Eastwind Dr., Suite 301
Westerville, OH 43081-3361
Tel: (614)895-7166 *Fax:* (614)895-1248
Toll Free: (800)200 - 6342
E-Mail: excel@ieha.org
Web Site: www.ieha.org
Members: 5000 individuals
Staff: 6
Annual Budget: $1-2,000,000
Chief Executive Officer: Beth B. Risinger
E-Mail: brisinger@ieha.org
Director, Communications: Audi Vance
Historical Note
Formerly (1996) National Executive Housekeepers Association. A professional organization for administrators of housekeeping programs in commercial, institutional and industrial facilities. Membership: $150/year (individual).
Meetings/Conferences:
Annual Meetings: Fall
Publications:
Executive Housekeeping Today. m. adv.

International Fabricare Institute *(1972)*
14700 Switzer Lane
Laurel, MD 20707
Tel: (301)622-1900 *Fax:* (240)295-0685
Toll Free: (800)638 - 2627
E-Mail: communications@ifi.org
Web Site: www.ifi.org
Members: 5000 companies
Staff: 32
Annual Budget: $2-5,000,000
Chief Executive Officer: William E. Fisher
Historical Note
The product of a merger (1972) of the American Institute of Laundering (1883) and the National Institute of Drycleaning (1907), IFI is a leading national and international association for drycleaners and launderers. Members also include manufacturers and suppliers of cleaning equipment, retailers, garment manufacturers, and others concerned with professional garment cleaning and serviceability. Membership: $385-1,450/year.
Meetings/Conferences:
Biennial Meetings: April-July, odd years/25,000.
2007 - New Orleans, LA/May 17-20
Publications:
Fabricare Magazine. m. adv.
Resources (a seven bulletin series). bi-m.
Clothes Care Gazette. m.

International Facility Management Association *(1980)*
One E. Greenway Plaza, Suite 1100
Houston, TX 77046-0194
Tel: (713)623-4362 *Fax:* (713)623-6124
E-Mail: ifma@ifma.org
Web Site: www.ifma.org
Members: 18000 individuals
Staff: 54
Annual Budget: $5-10,000,000
President and Chief Executive Officer: David J. Brady
E-Mail: david.brady@ifma.org
Vice President, Communications: Donald A. Young
E-Mail: donald.young@ifma.org
Historical Note
Founded as the National Facility Management Association; assumed its present name in 1982. Regular membership is open to any individual who is an in-house member or manager of a department responsible for facility planning, design, or management; and to those providing products or services. Electronic membership: $245/year; mail option membership: $275/year.
Meetings/Conferences:
Annual Meetings: Fall
2007 - New Orleans, LA/Oct. 24-26/6000
Publications:
IFMA News. m. adv.
Conference Proceedings. a.
Facility Management Journal. bi-m. adv.
FM Guide & Directory. a. adv.

International Family Recreation Association *(1982)*
P.O. Box 520
Gonzales, FL 32560-0520
Tel: (850)937-8354
Web Site: www.funoutdoors.com/node/view/785
Members: 9500 individuals
Staff: 5
Annual Budget: $100-250,000
Executive Officer: K.W. Stephens
Historical Note
Commercial and individual advocates of family recreation and the management of an organized customer base. Supports recommendations and legislation advantageous to recreation, leisure and travel. Promotes recreation, leisure, and travel safety policies and public participation in family recreational, leisure and travel activities. Membership: $49/year (family/individual); $100 (commercial).
Meetings/Conferences:
Annual Meetings: November
Publications:
The Recreation Advisor. 5/year. adv.
The Recreation Digest. q. adv.

International Federation for Artificial Organs *(1977)*
10 W. Erie St., Suite 200
Painesville, OH 44077-3270
Tel: (440)358-1102 *Fax:* (440)358-1104
Web Site: www.isao-society.org
Members: 1000 individuals
Staff: 3
Annual Budget: $100-250,000
Editor-in-Chief: Paul S. Malchesky, D.Eng.
E-Mail: PaulSMalchesky@aol.com
Historical Note
Formerly (1977) International Society for Artificial Organs; assumed current name in 2004. Members are involved in the research, development or application of artificial organs. Membership: $180/year.
Meetings/Conferences:
Biennial Meetings: Odd years
Publications:
Artificial Organs. m. adv.

International Federation for Choral Music *(1982)*
Univ. of Illinois Performing Arts Dept.
1040 W. Harrison St., Room L-042
Chicago, IL 60607-7130
Tel: (312)996-8744 *Fax:* (312)996-0954
Web Site: http://ifcm.net/index.php
Members: 2000 individuals
Staff: 3
Annual Budget: $1-2,000,000
Vice President: Dr. Michael J. Anderson
Historical Note
The Federation was formed to strengthen cooperation between national and international organizations interested in choral music, encourage formation of new choral organizations, promote international exchange programs and the inclusion of choral music in general education, and to inform the public of occurrences in the choral field. Membership: $40/year (individual); $125-2,500 (organization/company).
Meetings/Conferences:
Triennial Meetings:
Publications:
International Choral Bulletin. q. adv.
World Census of Choral Music. a.

International Federation of Inspection Agencies - Americas Committee
3942 N. Upland St.
Arlington, VA 22207
Tel: (703)533-9539 *Fax:* (703)533-1612
E-Mail: ifianac@aol.com
Annual Budget: $50-100,000
Executive Director: Milton M. Bush, J.D., CAE
Historical Note
IFIA-NAC monitors standards, safety procedures, and rules and regulations to determine their impact on member companies and suggest potential improvements.

International Federation of Nurse Anesthetists *(1985)*
183 Heatherton Way
Winston-Salem, NC 27104
Tel: (336)768-5107
E-Mail: souellette@triad.rr.com
Web Site: www.ifna.info
Members: 45000 individuals
Staff: 1
President: Sandra M. Ouellette, CRNA, MEd, FAAN
E-Mail: souellette@triad.rr.com
Historical Note
IFNA represents and promotes nurse anesthetists internationally through the education activities and continuing education programs.

International Federation of Pharmaceutical Wholesalers *(1984)*
10569 Crestwood Dr.
Manassas, VA 20109
Tel: (703)331-3714 *Fax:* (703)331-3715
E-Mail: info@ifpw.org
Web Site: www.ifpw.com
Members: 50 companies
Staff: 4
Annual Budget: $250-500,000
President: William Goetz
Director, Finance and Technology: Christopher Goetz
Historical Note
Membership: $250-$5,000/year (corporate).
Publications:
Focus. bi-w.

International Federation of Professional and Technical Engineers *(1918)*
8630 Fenton St., Suite 400
Silver Spring, MD 20910
Tel: (301)565-9016 *Fax:* (301)565-0018
E-Mail: ifpte@ifpte.org
Web Site: www.ifpte.org
Members: 80000 individuals
Staff: 18
Annual Budget: $1-2,000,000
President: Gregory J. Juneman
General Counsel: Julia A. Clark
Communications: Candace R. Rhett
Historical Note
Founded in Washington, DC, July 1, 1918 as the International Federation of Draftsmen's Unions and affiliated with the American Federation of Labor. Became the International Federation of Technical Engineers' Architects' and Draftsmen's Unions in 1919, the American Federation of Technical Engineers in 1953 and assumed its present name in 1973.
Meetings/Conferences:
Triennial Meetings: July
Publications:
Outlook. bi-m.

International Festivals and Events Association *(1956)*
2603 Eastover Terrace

Boise, ID 83706
Tel: (208)433-0950 *Fax:* (208)433-9812
Web Site: www.ifea.com
Members: 2000 individuals
Staff: 12
Annual Budget: $1-2,000,000
President/Chief Executive Officer: Steve Wood Schmader, CFEE
E-Mail: schmader@ifea.com
Senior Vice President: Kaye Campbell, CFEE
E-Mail: kaye@ifea.com

Historical Note

Members are primarily individuals employed by the administrations of community and civic festivals and events, along with event suppliers, chambers of commerce, municipalities, corporations and more. Membership: $150-746/year.

Meetings/Conferences:

Annual Meetings: Fall
2007 - Atlanta, GA(Omni Hotel)/Sept. 17-21

Publications:

Affiliate Connection (online newsletter). m.
IE - The Business of International Events magazine. q. adv.
IFEA Weekly Update (e-mail broadcast). w.

International Financial Services Association *(1924)*

Nine Sylvan Way, First Floor
Parsippany, NJ 07054-3802
Tel: (973)656-1900 *Fax:* (973)656-1915
E-Mail: info@intlbanking.org
Web Site: www.ifsaonline.org
Members: 250 businesses
Staff: 5
Annual Budget: $1-2,000,000
President: Dan Taylor
Vice President: Patricia Barry

Historical Note

Formerly (1998) United States Council on International Banking. USCIB members are banks involved in international operations.

Publications:

IFSA Newsletter. q.
Network. q.

International Fire Marshals Association *(1906)*

One Batterymarch Park
Quincy, MA 02169
Tel: (617)984-7423 *Fax:* (617)984-7056
E-Mail: ifma@nfpa.org
Web Site: www.nfpa.org/ifma
Members: 1800 individuals
Staff: 2
Executive Secretary: Steven F. Sawyer
E-Mail: ssawyer@nfpa.org

Historical Note

Founded in 1906 as Fire Marshals Association of North America, it reorganized as a section of the National Fire Protection Association in 1927. Assumed its current name in 2000. Members are fire marshals, fire prevention officers or similar government officials charged with investigating or preventing fires.

Meetings/Conferences:

Annual Meetings: with the National Fire Protection Association
2007 - Boston, MA/June 3-7
2008 - Las Vegas, NV

Publications:

Fire Marshals Directory. a.
Fire Marshals. q.

International Fire Photographers Association *(1964)*

143 40th St.
New Orleans, LA 70124
Tel: (504)482-9616 *Fax:* (504)486-4946
Members: 200 individuals
Staff: 6
Annual Budget: under $10,000
President: Chris E. Mickal

Historical Note

Fire photographers affiliated with fire departments, law enforcement, insurance, and related services dedicated to promoting the use of photography in fire investigations and in fire prevention education. Also works to establish harmonious relationships with news media and related agencies. Certification program awards designations of Journeyman, Craftsman and Master Fire Photographer. Non-voting corporate membership is available to manufacturers, dealers and distributors of photographic equipment. Membership: $35/year; $37.50/year (Canadian); $40/year (overseas); $100/year (company).

Meetings/Conferences:

Annual Meetings: Summer

Publications:

Membership Manual. a.
Fire Photography Journal. q. adv.

International Firestop Council

P. O. Box 1562
Westford, MA 01886
Toll Free: (877)241 - 3769
E-Mail: info@firestop.org
Web Site: www.firestop.org
Members: 32 comapnies
Staff: 3
Annual Budget: $50-100,000
Executive Director: Hubert T. Dudley

International Food Additives Council *(1980)*

5775 Peachtree-Dunwoody Rd., Suite 500-G
Atlanta, GA 30342-1558
Tel: (404)252-3663 *Fax:* (404)252-0774
E-Mail: ifac@assnhq.com
Web Site: www.ifacmem.org
Members: 11 companies
Staff: 3
Annual Budget: $100-250,000
President: Andrew G. Ebert, Ph.D.

Historical Note

Information clearing house concerning the use in food and safety of food additives. Members are companies engaged in the manufacture, sale, reformulation and commercial use of food additives. Serves as a regulatory and scientific liaison for industry concerning food additives.

Publications:

Food Additives.

International Food Information Council *(1985)*

1100 Connecticut Ave. NW, Suite 430
Washington, DC 20036
Tel: (202)296-6540 *Fax:* (202)296-6547
E-Mail: foodinfo@ific.org
Web Site: www.ific.org
Members: 34 companies
Staff: 25
Annual Budget: $5-10,000,000
Chief Executive Officer: David B. Schmidt
Director, Media Relations: Nick Alexander

Historical Note

IFIC serves as an information and educational resource on food safety and nutrition.

Publications:

Food Insight. bi-m.

International Food Service Executives' Association *(1901)*

2609 Surfwood Dr.
Las Vegas, NV 89128
Tel: (702)430-9217 *Fax:* (702)430-9223
E-Mail: hq@ifsea.com
Web Site: www.ifsea.com
Members: 2000 individuals
Staff: 2
Annual Budget: $250-500,000
President: Edward Manley

Historical Note

The oldest food service trade association. Formerly (1957) International Stewards' and Caterers' Association and (1977) Food Service Executives' Association, Inc. Administers the Certified Food Executive (CFE) program. Membership: $125/year.

Meetings/Conferences:

Annual Meetings: Summer
2007 - Kansas City, MO(Marriott Hotel)/Apr. 6-9/1000

Publications:

Hotline. q. adv.

International Food, Wine and Travel Writers Association *(1956)*

1142 S. Diamond Bar Blvd., #177
Diamond Bar, CA 91765
Tel: (877)439-8729 *Fax:* (877)439-8929
E-Mail: admin@ifwtwa.org
Web Site: www.ifwtwa.org
Members: 465 individuals
Staff: 2
Annual Budget: $100-250,000
Administrative Director: Patricia A. Anis
E-Mail: admin@ifwtwa.org

Historical Note

Established in Paris, France in 1956. Headquarters moved to California in 1981. Members are freelance and/or staff writers, editors, and photographers specializing in food, wine and/or travel writing. Associate memberships are available for individuals or companies in the travel and hospitality industries. Membership: $125/year (regular member); $235/year (associate); plus $50 initiation fee.

Publications:

Directory. a. adv.
Press Pass. m.

International Foodservice Distributors Association *(1956)*

201 Park Washington Ct.
Falls Church, VA 22046-4621
Tel: (703)532-9400 *Fax:* (703)538-4673
Web Site: www.ifdaonline.org
Members: 131 corporations
Staff: 13
Annual Budget: $2-5,000,000
President and Chief Executive Officer: Mark S. Allen
Senior Vice President, Industry Relations: Steve Potter

Historical Note

Formerly a division of Food Distributors International, IFDA reformed as an independent organization in 2002. IFDA provides education services, government representation, and industry research in support of its member distributors.

International Foodservice Editorial Council *(1956)*

P.O. Box 491
Hyde Park, NY 12538-0491
Tel: (845)229-6973 *Fax:* (845)229-6993
E-Mail: ifec@aol.com
Web Site: www.ifeconline.com
Members: 250 individuals
Staff: 2
Annual Budget: $100-250,000
Executive Director: Carol Lally
E-Mail: ifec@aol.com

Historical Note

IFEC is a non-profit international organization of communicators working in the foodservice industry. Its purpose is to facilitate the exchange of ideas between editors and other communicators and help advance the foodservice industry through media communications. Members include editors, publicists, marketers, educators, representatives of multi-unit operations, foodservice home economists, consultants and others active in foodservice communications. Membership: $225/year (individual).

Meetings/Conferences:

Annual Meetings: Fall
2007 - Austin, TX(Omni)/Oct. 23-26/185

Publications:

IFEC Newsletter. m.
Directory. a.

International Foodservice Manufacturers Association *(1952)*

Two Prudential Plaza
180 N. Stetson Ave., Suite 4400
Chicago, IL 60601
Tel: (312)540-4400 *Fax:* (312)540-4401
E-Mail: ifma@ifmaworld.com
Web Site: www.ifmaworld.com
Members: 600 companies
Staff: 18
Annual Budget: $5-10,000,000
President and Chief Executive Officer: Michael J Licata
Vice President, Member Services: Lea D. Eisenburg

E-Mail: lea_eisenberg@ifmaworld.com
Senior Vice President and Chief Financial Officer: Anthony J. Marchese
E-Mail: tmarchese@ifmaworld.com
Vice President, Communications: Janet E. Rustigan
E-Mail: janet_rustigan@ifmaworld.com
Vice President, Marketing: Doug Smith
E-Mail: dsmith@ifmaworld.com

Historical Note
Founded as the Institutional Food Manufacturers of America; became the Institutional Food-Service Manufacturers Association in 1964 and assumed its present name in 1970. Members are manufacturers of food, equipment and supplies for the away-from-home feeding market. Has an annual budget of $6 million.

Meetings/Conferences:
Annual Meetings: late February
2007 - Orlando, FL(J.W. Marriott Orlando, Grande Lakes)/March 4-7

Publications:
IFMA World. 5/year.
Membership Directory (online).

International Formalwear Association *(1973)*
401 N. Michigan Ave.
Chicago, IL 60611
Tel: (312)321-5139 *Fax:* (312)321-5150
E-Mail: ifa@sba.com
Web Site: www.formalwear.org
Members: 325 companies
Staff: 2
Annual Budget: $250-500,000
Executive Director: Karin S. Hurley

Historical Note
Formerly a division of the Menswear Retailers of America, became autonomous in 1981 as the American Formalwear Association. Assumed its present name in 1987. Membership: $195-695/year.

Publications:
Formalwords Newsletter Online. bi-m. adv.
Membership Roster Online. a. adv.

International Formula Council *(1988)*
5775 Peachtree-Dunwoody Rd.
Bldg. G, Suite 500
Atlanta, GA 30342-1558
Tel: (404)252-3663 *Fax:* (404)252-0774
E-Mail: info@infantformula.org
Web Site: www.infantformula.org
Members: 5 companies
Staff: 4
Executive Director: Mardi K. Mountford

Historical Note
Formed through the merger of Infant Formula Council (1970) and Enteral Nutrition Council (1983). IFC is an international association of formulated nutrition products, infant formula and adult nutritionals.

Meetings/Conferences:
Annual Meetings: February-March

International Foundation for Telemetering *(1964)*
5959 Topanga Canyon Blvd., Suite 150
Woodland Hills, CA 91367
Tel: (818)884-9568 *Fax:* (818)884-9671
Web Site: www.telemetry.org
Treasurer: Lawrence P. James

Historical Note
IFT is a technical organization concerned with the theory and practice of telemetry. Has no paid officers or full-time staff.

Publications:
ITC Proceedings. a.

International Foundation of Employee Benefit Plans *(1954)*
18700 W. Bluemound Rd.
Brookfield, WI 53045
Tel: (262)786-6700 *Fax:* (262)786-8670
E-Mail: pr@ifebp.org
Web Site: www.ifebp.org
Members: 35000 individuals
Staff: 140
Annual Budget: $10-25,000,000
Chief Executive Officer: Michael Wilson
Senior Director, Information Services and Publications: Dee Birschel
Senior Director, CIBS: Daniel W. Graham
Senior Director, Accounting and Finance: W. Albert Hamwright, Jr.
Senior Director, Education: Mary Jost
E-Mail: maryj@ifebp.org
Senior Director, Administration: John W. Steinbach
Director, Public Relations and Advertising: Stacy Van Alstyne
E-Mail: stacyv@ifebp.org
Senior Director, MIS: David Van Zeeland
E-Mail: dvz@ifebp.org

Historical Note
Formerly (1973) National Foundation of Health, Welfare and Pension Plans. Membership consists of individuals working in the field of employee benefits and compensation. Has an annual budget of approximately $20 million. Membership: $575/year (organizations); $295/year (individuals).

Meetings/Conferences:
Annual Meetings: Fall/6,000
2007 - Anaheim, CA/Nov. 4-7/6000

Publications:
Benefits and Compensation Digest. q. adv.
In-Focus. q.
Employee Benefits Digest. m.
Legal-Legislative Reporter News Bulletin. m.

International Franchise Association *(1960)*
1501 K St. NW, Suite 350
Washington, DC 20005
Tel: (202)628-8000 *Fax:* (202)628-0812
E-Mail: ifra@frachise.org
Web Site: www.franchise.org
Members: 32000
Staff: 28
Annual Budget: $5-10,000,000
President: Matt Shay
Director, Political Affairs: Victoria J. Adams
Vice President, Government Relations: David French
Vice President, Communications and Media Relations: Terry Hill
Vice President, Marketing and Development: Scott Lehr
Vice President, Operations: Debra A. Moss

Historical Note
Membership consists of companies franchising the distribution of their goods or services, unit owners (franchisees) and companies supplying products and services to franchise businesses. Sponsors and supports the Franchising Political Action Committee and the IFA Educational Foundation.

Meetings/Conferences:
Annual Meetings: Fall/1,200-1,500

Publications:
IFA Insider Newsletter. bi-w.
Franchising World Magazine. bi-m.
Franchise Opportunities Guide. semi-a.
IFA Smart Brief Email. bi-w.

International Frozen Food Association *(1974)*
2000 Corporate Ridge, Suite 1000
McLean, VA 22102
Tel: (703)821-0770 *Fax:* (703)821-1350
Members: 40 companies and associations
Staff: 2
Annual Budget: $10-25,000
Director General: Leslie G. Sarasin, CAE

Historical Note
Federation of associations and companies involved in distribution, production or marketing of frozen food for international markets. Affiliated with the American Frozen Food Institute.

International Fruit Tree Association *(1958)*
P.O. Box 5006
Wenatchee, WA 98807-5006
Tel: (509)884-5651 *Fax:* (509)884-1858
E-Mail: business@ifruittree.org
Web Site: www.ifruittree.org
Staff: 2
Annual Budget: $100-250,000
Executive Director: Susan Pheasant
E-Mail: business@ifruittree.org

Historical Note
Founded in Hartford, Michigan in 1958. Membership: $85/year (domestic or foreign).

Meetings/Conferences:
Annual Meetings: February-March

Publications:
Compact Fruit Tree. 3/year.

International Function Point Users Group *(1984)*
191 Clarksville Rd.
Princeton Junction, NJ 08550
Tel: (609)799-4900 *Fax:* (609)799-7032
E-Mail: ifpug@ifpug.org
Web Site: www.ifpug.org
Members: 650 companies
Staff: 5
Annual Budget: $500-1,000,000
Executive Director: Cheryl Oribabor

Historical Note
Members are companies and individuals employing the function point measurement process for business management. Membership: $250/year.

Meetings/Conferences:
Semi-Annual Meetings: Spring and Fall

Publications:
IFPUG Newsletter. semi-a. adv.

International Furnishings and Design Association *(1947)*
191 Clarksville Rd.
Princeton Junction, NJ 08550
Tel: (609)799-3423 *Fax:* (609)799-7032
E-Mail: info@ifda.com
Web Site: www.ifda.com
Members: 2000 individuals
Staff: 2
Annual Budget: $250-500,000
Executive Director: Lynn McCullough

Historical Note
Formerly (1987) National Home Fashions League. IFDA members are executives from diverse industries related to residential and commercial furnishings including interior and product design, communications, manufacturing, retailing, education, architecture and finance. Membership: $225/year (individual).

Meetings/Conferences:
Annual Meetings: Fall

Publications:
IFDA Directory. a. adv.
IFDA Network. q. adv.

International Furniture Rental Association *(1967)*

Historical Note
Address unknown in 2006.

International Furniture Suppliers Association *(1929)*
3910 Tinsley Dr.
Suite 101
High Point, NC 27265-3610
Tel: (336)801-6130 *Fax:* (336)801-6102
Toll Free: (800)888 - 9590 Ext: 6130
E-Mail: mpierce@mhfa.org
Web Site: www.ifsa-info.com/
Members: 50 companies
Staff: 1
Annual Budget: $100-250,000
Executive Director: Mike Pierce

Historical Note
Organized under the auspices of the National Association of Furniture Manufacturers, members are wholesale furniture distributors. Formerly (1992) National Wholesale Furniture Association.

Meetings/Conferences:
Annual Meetings: Annual/January/100

Publications:
Home Furnishings Industry Supplier. q. adv.

International Furniture Transportation and Logistics Council *(1926)*
P.O. Box 889
Gardner, MA 01440
Tel: (978)632-1913 *Fax:* (978)630-2917
Web Site: www.iftlc.org

Members: 150 individuals
Staff: 2
Annual Budget: $50-100,000
Managing Director: Raynard F. Bohman, Jr.

Historical Note

Founded as National Furniture Traffic Conference; assumed its current name in 2000. Members are logistics and shipping professionals employed in the various segments of the furniture industry.

Meetings/Conferences:

Annual Meetings: Spring

Publications:

Ocean Shipping News Summary. m.
The Furniture Transporter. m.
Traffic Newsletter. m.

International Game Developers Association

870 Market St., Suite 1181
San Francisco, CA 94102-3002
Tel: (415)738-2104 *Fax:* (415)738-2178
E-Mail: info@igda.org
Web Site: www.igda.org
Members: 2500 individuals
Staff: 2
Annual Budget: $250-500,000
Executive Director: Jason Della Rocca

Historical Note

IGDA members are developers of entertainment software. Membership: $100/year (individual); $25/year (student).

Publications:

IGDA Newletter. m. adv.

International Glaucoma Congress *(1977)*

Historical Note

A division of the American Society of Contemporary Ophthalmology.

International Glove Association *(1902)*

P.O. Box 146
Brookville, PA 15825
Tel: (814)328-5208 *Fax:* (814)328-2308
E-Mail: gloves@alltel.net
Web Site: www.iga-online.com
Members: 75 companies
Staff: 3
Annual Budget: $100-250,000
Executive Director: Carol Burdge
E-Mail: gloves@alltel.net

Historical Note

Founded as Work Glove Institute, became (1967) Work Glove Manufacturers Association and then (1991) International Hand Protection Association, before absorbing National Industrial Glove Distributors Association and assuming its current name in 2003. Members are manufacturers of work gloves and related workplace safety material.

Meetings/Conferences:

Annual Meetings: June

Publications:

InTouch Newsletter. bi-m.

International Graphic Arts Education Association *(1923)*

1899 Preston White Dr.
Reston, VA 20191
Tel: (703)264-7200 *Fax:* (703)620-0994
Web Site: www.igaea.org
Members: 800 individuals
Staff: 1
Annual Budget: $25-50,000
Contact: Darcy Harris

Historical Note

Founded in 1936 as the National Graphic Arts Education Association. Adopted the present name in 1950 and was incorporated in 1969. Members are teachers of printing, photography and the graphic arts. Membership: $40/year (individual).

Meetings/Conferences:

Annual Meetings: Summer, always in a university setting
2007 – Rochester, NY(Rochester Institute of Technology)

Publications:

The Communicator. bi-m. adv.
Visual Communications Journal. a.

International Graphoanalysis Society *(1929)*

842 Fifth Ave.
New Kensington, PA 15068
Tel: (724)472-9701 *Fax:* (276)501-1931
E-Mail: greg@igas.com
Web Site: www.igas.com
Members: 15000 individuals
Staff: 6
Annual Budget: $250-500,000
President: Greg Greco
E-Mail: greg@igas.com

Historical Note

Graphoanalysis is the analysis of handwriting for personality assessment. Used in such areas as testing for employment and education counseling. Absorbed the American Institute of Grapho Analysis in 1949. Membership: $90/year.

Meetings/Conferences:

Semi-annual meetings: Attendance 1,000

Publications:

IGAS Journal. m.

International Grooving and Grinding Association *(1972)*

12573 State Rte. 9-W
West Coxsackie, NY 12192-1709
Tel: (518)731-7450 *Fax:* (518)731-7490
Web Site: www.igga.net
Members: 37 companies
Staff: 2
Annual Budget: $100-250,000
Executive Director: John H. Roberts

Historical Note

IGGA is a professional association that promotes the use of grooving and diamond-grinding of highways, airports, municipal streets, rural roads, parking areas, sidewalks, industrial floors, and other surfaces constructed with portland cement concrete or asphalt concrete. IGGA works with the public and private sectors to develop and communicate specifications and standards, promote and transfer technology, provide legislative and regulatory support, and communicate the best possible practices in the texturing of pavement and pavement systems.

Meetings/Conferences:

Annual Meetings:

International Ground Source Heat Pump Association *(1987)*

Oklahoma State University
374 Cordell South
Stillwater, OK 74078
Tel: (405)744-5175 *Fax:* (405)744-5283
Toll Free: (800)626 - 4747
E-Mail: mcarthl@okstate.edu
Web Site: www.igshpa.okstate.edu/
Members: 2800 individuals
Staff: 10
Annual Budget: $500-1,000,000
Executive Director: James Bose
Assistant Director: Lisa McArthur
E-Mail: mcarthl@okstate.edu

Historical Note

Members are manufacturers, distributors and installers of ground service heat pumps, which utilize the earth as the heat exchanges. Membership: $105/year (individual); $400-1,325/year (company).

Publications:

IGSHPA Membership Directory. a. adv.
Geo Outlook. q. adv.

International Group of Accounting Firms

Historical Note

Became IGAF Worldwide in 2005.

International Guards Union of America *(1947)*

Route 8, Box 32-14
Amarillo, TX 79118-9427
Tel: (806)622-2424 *Fax:* (806)622-3500
Web Site: www.amaonline.com/igua
Members: 1,800 individuals
Annual Budget: $10-25,000
General President: Joseph A. Roybal

Historical Note

Originally affiliated with the Building Services Employees International Union, IGUA became an independent union in 1948. Independent labor union. Guards, watchmen and others hired to protect personnel and property. Has no paid officers or full-time staff. Membership: $5/month.

Meetings/Conferences:

Triennial Meetings: (2007)

Publications:

IGUA Newsletter. q.

International Guild of Candle Artisans *(1965)*

1640 Garfield
Fremont, NE 68025
Web Site: www.igca.net
Members: 700 companies and individuals
Staff: 1
Annual Budget: $25-50,000
Contact: Andy Hastings

Historical Note

Incorporated in 1969, IGCA members are individuals and companies with an interest in candle making. Membership: $50 first year, $30/year renewal.

Publications:

Candlelighter Yearbook and Buyers Guide. a.
Candlelighter Newsletter. m. adv.

International Guild of Professional Electrologists *(1979)*

Historical Note

Address unknown in 2006.

International Guild of Symphony, Opera and Ballet Musicians *(1985)*

12724 19th Ave. NE
Seattle, WA 98125
Tel: (206)365-8925
E-Mail: mkocmieroski@hotmail.com
Web Site: www.igsobm.org
Members: 400 individuals
President: Matthew Kocmieroski
E-Mail: mkocmieroski@hotmail.com

Historical Note

Independent labor union. IGSOBM members are musicians, music librarians, and others who work in not-for-profit music organizations, including regional symphonies and orchestras. Has no paid officers or full-time staff.

International Hand Protection Association

Historical Note

Became International Glove Association in 2003.

International Hard Anondizing Association *(1989)*

P.O. Box 579
Moorestown, NJ 08057-0579
Tel: (856)234-0330 *Fax:* (856)727-9504
Web Site: www.ihanodizing.com
Members: 40 companies
Staff: 3
Annual Budget: $10-25,000
Executive Director: Denise Downing

Historical Note

IHAA was formed by companies in the hard anodizing business to provide a forum for the exchange of technical information and to act as a clearing house for information about the industry. Membership: $400/year (corporate).

Meetings/Conferences:

Biennial Meetings: Fall

International Health Evaluation Association *(1972)*

Historical Note

Address unknown in 2006.

International Health, Racquet and Sportsclub Association *(1981)*

263 Summer St., Eighth Floor
Boston, MA 02210
Tel: (617)951-0055 *Fax:* (617)951-0056
Toll Free: (800)228 - 4772
E-Mail: info@ihrsa.org
Web Site: http://cms.ihrsa.org/IHRSA/viewPage.cfm?pageId=2
Members: 350 companies, 5200 clubs
Staff: 60
Annual Budget: $5-10,000,000

President and Chief Executive Officer: Joe Moore
Vice President, Publishing: Jay Ablondi
E-Mail: jma@ihrsa.org
Executive Vice President, Public Policy: Helen A. Durkin
E-Mail: gr@ihrsa.org
Vice President, Information Technology: Tom Durkin
Vice President, Meetings and Trade Shows: William Dussor
E-Mail: wdd@ihrsa.org
Chief Operating Officer: Anita Horne Lawlor
E-Mail: ahl@ihrsa.org
Vice President, Sales: Meredith Poppler
E-Mail: mm@ihrsa.org
Director, Human Resources: Regina Satagaj Orrock
E-Mail: rso@ihrsa.org

Historical Note

Formed as International Racquet Sports Association as the result of a merger between the National Court Clubs Association and the National Tennis Association; became IRSA-the Association of Quality Clubs in 1991, and assumed its current name in 1995. Members are commercial, for-profit health and sport clubs, as well as manufacturers and suppliers. Has an annual budget of approximately $8 million. Membership fee varies, based on annual revenues.

Meetings/Conferences:

Annual Meetings: Spring

Publications:

Club Business International. m. adv.
Club Business Latin America. bi-m. adv.
Club Business Europa. q. adv.

International Hearing Society *(1951)*

16880 Middlebelt Rd.
Livonia, MI 48154
Tel: (734)522-7200
E-Mail: chelms@ihsinfo.org
Web Site: www.ihsinfo.org
Members: 3000 individuals
Staff: 10
Annual Budget: $1-2,000,000
Executive Director: Cindy Helms
E-Mail: chelms@ihsinfo.org

Historical Note

Founded as Society of Hearing Aid Audiologists, became National Hearing Aid Society in 1966 and assumed its current name in 1992. Professional association of hearing instrument specialists. Membership: $275/year.

Meetings/Conferences:

Annual Meetings: Fall

Publications:

The Hearing Professional. bi-m.

International Herb Association

P.O. Box 5667
Jacksonville, FL 32247-5664
Tel: (904)399-3241 *Fax:* (904)396-9467
E-Mail: info@iherb.org
Web Site: www.iherb.org/
Members: 200 individuals
Annual Budget: $10-25,000
Treasurer: Marge Powell

Historical Note

Formerly (1994) International Herb Growers and Marketers Association. Has no full-time staff. Membership: $100/year.

Publications:

IHA Newsletter. q. adv.

International Home Furnishings Market Authority

P.O. Box 5244
High Point, NC 27262
Tel: (336)869-1000 *Fax:* (336)889-6999
Toll Free: (800)874 - 6492
E-Mail: tcovington@northstate.net
Web Site: www.highpointmarket.org
Members: 2300 exhibitors
Staff: 4
President: Brian Casey
Vice President, Operations: Tammy Covington

Historical Note

Formerly (1989) the Furniture Factories' Marketing Association of the South and then International Home Furnishings Marketing Association; assumed its current name in 2001. IHFMA acts as the introductory wholesale market for a range of finished products, including home furnishings, gift and decorative accessories, lighting, and area floor covering.

Meetings/Conferences:

Annual Meetings: High Point, NC
2007 - Apr. 19-26/80000
2008 - Apr. 10-17/80000
2009 - Apr. 23-30/80000
2010 - Apr. 15-22/80000

International Home Furnishings Representatives Association *(1934)*

P.O. Box 670
High Point, NC 27261-0670
Tel: (336)499-6489 *Fax:* (866)528-8634
E-Mail: ihfra@northstate.net
Web Site: www.IHFRA.org
Members: 1500
Staff: 2
Annual Budget: $250-500,000
Executive Director: Kathy Parks
E-Mail: ihfra@northstate.net
Membership Coordinator: Elaine M. Burns, CHR
E-Mail: ihfra@northstate.net

Historical Note

Formerly (1967) National Wholesale Furniture Salesmens' Association and (1972) National Home Furnishings Representatives Association. A federation of local home furnishings representatives associations. Membership: $105-$225/year, national + chapter dues, (individual); $105/year (at-large).

Meetings/Conferences:

Annual Meetings: Spring

Publications:

Opportunity Center News (Broadcast Fax). m. adv.
Opportunity Center. m. adv.

International Horn Society *(1970)*

P.O. Box 630 158
Lanai City, HI 96763-0158
Tel: (808)565-7273 *Fax:* (808)565-7273
E-Mail: exec-secretary@hornsociety.org
Web Site: www.hornsociety.org
Members: 3500 individuals
Staff: 4
Annual Budget: $100-250,000
Executive Secretary: Heidi Vogel
E-Mail: exec-secretary@hornsociety.org

Historical Note

IHS members are professional players, instructors and students of the French horn. Membership: $35/year (individual); $50/year (library).

Meetings/Conferences:

Annual Meetings: Annual Membership Meetings-Spring/Summer
2007 - La-Chaux-de-Fonds, Switzerland(Music Conservatory)/July 8-14/450
2008 - Denver, CO(Denver Univ. - Lamond School of Music)/July/450

Publications:

Horn Call Journal. 3/yr. adv.

International Hot Rod Association *(1970)*

9 1/2 E. Main St.
Norwalk, OH 44857
Tel: (419)663-6666 *Fax:* (419)663-4472
E-Mail: comments@ihra.com
Web Site: www.ihra.com
Members: 17500 individuals
Staff: 18
Annual Budget: $2-5,000,000
President: Aaron Polburn
Director, Marketing: Jim Marchyshyn
Director, Operations: Sharon Ramlow

Historical Note

Sanctioning body for professional drag racing strips, providing rules, regulations, and guidelines. Members are drivers and their sponsors, tracks, and spectators.

Publications:

Drag Review Newspaper. bi-w. adv.
Official Drag Racing Rule Book. a. adv.

International Housewares Association *(1938)*

6400 Shafer Ct., Suite 650
Rosemont, IL 60018-4929
Tel: (847)292-4200 *Fax:* (847)292-4211
Web Site: www.housewares.org
Members: 1700 companies
Staff: 28
Annual Budget: $5-10,000,000
President: Philip J. Brandl
Manager, Membership and Executive Services: Judy Colitz
E-Mail: jcolitz@housewares.org
Vice President, Finance and Information Technology: Dean Kurtis
E-Mail: dkurtis@housewares.org
Vice President, International: Derek Miller
E-Mail: dmiller@housewares.org
Vice President, Trade Show: Mia Rampersad
E-Mail: mrampersad@housewares.org
Vice President, Marketing and Trade Development: Perry Reynolds
E-Mail: preynolds@housewares.org

Historical Note

Formerly (2002) National Housewares Manufacturers Association. Serves manufacturers of kitchen tools and gadgets, cookware and bakeware items, serving and buffet products, glassware and china, bath and closet accessories, small electrical appliances, outdoor products and accessories, gourmet and specialty foods, decorative accessories, pet supplies, hardware, cleaning products and tabletop products. Membership: $300/year (regular); $400/year (associate).

Publications:

International Housewares Membership Directory. a.
IHA Reports (online). bi-m.
IHA State of the Industry Report. a.
Housewares Around the World Directory. a.
Show Directory. a.

International Housewares Representatives Association

175 N. Harbor Dr., Suite 3807
Chicago, IL 60601
Tel: (312)240-0774 *Fax:* (312)240-1005
E-Mail: info@ihra.org
Web Site: www.ihra.org
Members: 250 companies
Staff: 3
Executive Director: William Weiner
E-Mail: info@ihra.org

Historical Note

IHRA members are manufacturer representatives. Membership: $195/year.

International Hydrofoil Society *(1970)*

P.O. Box 51
Cabin John, MD 20818
Web Site: www.foils.org
Members: 240 individuals
Staff: 1
Annual Budget: under $10,000
Secretary: Kenneth Spaulding
E-Mail: secretary@foils.org

Historical Note

Represents organizations and individuals interested in the design, construction, and operation of hydrofoil craft. Membership: $20/year (regular); $2.50/year (student).

Meetings/Conferences:

Annual Meetings: Spring

Publications:

Newsletter. q.

International Hydrolized Protein Council *(1976)*

P.O. Box 14266
Washington, DC 20044-4266
Tel: (202)783-6135 *Fax:* (202)637-5910
Members: 14 companies
Staff: 2
General Counsel: Martin J. Hahn

Historical Note

Members are companies producing or using hydrolized proteins.

International Ice Cream Association *(1900)*

1250 H St. NW, Suite 900
Washington, DC 20005-3952
Tel: (202)737-4332 *Fax:* (202)331-7820
E-Mail: membership@idfa.org
Web Site: www.idfa.org

Members: 80 companies
Staff: 55
Annual Budget: $1-2,000,000
President and Chief Executive Officer: Constance E. Tipton

Historical Note

IICA represents manufacturers, distributors, and marketers of ice cream, frozen yogurt and other frozen desserts. IICA's activities range from legislative and regulatory advocacy to market research, industry training and education. Administrative support provided by International Dairy Foods Association. Membership fee based on volume.

Meetings/Conferences:

Annual Meetings: in conjunction with the International Dairy Foods Association/Fall

Publications:

Ice Cream Labeling Manual. irreg.
Frozen Dessert Plant Code Listing. irreg.
Dairy Facts. a.

International Imaging Industry Association *(1946)*

701 Westchester Ave., Suite 317-W
White Plains, NY 10604-3002
Tel: (914)285-4933 *Fax:* (914)285-4937
E-Mail: i3ainfo@i3a.org
Web Site: www.i3a.org
Members: 40 companies
Staff: 4
Annual Budget: $500-1,000,000
President: Lisa A. Walker
E-Mail: i3ainfo@i3a.org

Historical Note

Formerly (1997) National Association of Photographic Manufacturers and (2001) Photographic and Imaging Manufacturers Association. Membership fee varies, based on annual sales.

Meetings/Conferences:

Annual Meetings: November

Publications:

Membership Directory (online).
Eye on Imaging newsletter. 6/yr.
Eye on Standards newsletter. 6/yr.
Proceedings (online).

International Inflight Food Service Association *(1965)*

5775 Peachtree-Dunwoody Road, Bldg. G, Suite 500
Atlanta, GA 30342
Tel: (404)252-3663 *Fax:* (404)252-0774
E-Mail: ifsa@kellencompany.com
Web Site: www.ifsanet.com
Members: 400 businesses
Staff: 5
Annual Budget: $500-1,000,000
Executive Administrator: Pamela A. Chumley
Director, Meetings: Sharon Collins
E-Mail: ifsa@kellencompany.com
Manager, Communciatons: Scott Piper
E-Mail: ifsa@kellencompany.com

Historical Note

Members are domestic and international airlines, caterers and their suppliers. Membership: $100-1,000/year.

Meetings/Conferences:

Annual Meetings: Spring

Publications:

Membership Directory. a.
IECA/IFSA Review. q. adv.

International Institute for Lath and Plaster *(1976)*

P.O. Box 1663
Lafayette, CA 94549
Tel: (925)283-5160 *Fax:* (925)283-5161
Web Site: www.iilp.org
Members: 52 individuals
Staff: 2
Annual Budget: $25-50,000
Secretary: Frank Nunes

Historical Note

Formed by the merger of the Associated Institute for Lath and Plaster and the International Council for Lathing and Plastering (founded 1952 and formerly the National Bureau for Lathing and Plastering). A federation of organizations representing contractors, unions and makers of lathing and plastering supplies.

International Institute of Ammonia Refrigeration *(1971)*

1110 N. Glebe Road, Suite 250
Arlington, VA 22201
Tel: (703)312-4200 *Fax:* (703)312-0065
E-Mail: information@iiar.org
Web Site: www.iiar.org
Members: 1400 members
Staff: 6
Annual Budget: $1-2,000,000
President: M. Kent Anderson
E-Mail: information@iiar.org

Historical Note

Established in 1971 to promote the safe use of ammonia as a refrigerant. IIAR's purposes include public education, promotional and standards development programs, and legislative/regulatory concerns. Membership includes manufacturers, contractors, consulting engineers, wholesalers, and end users of ammonia refrigeration products.

Meetings/Conferences:

Annual Meetings: March/900

Publications:

Annual Meeting Proceedings. a.
IIAR Newsletter. bi-m.
Membership Directory. a.
Standards & Safety Bulletins. irreg.

International Institute of Connector and Interconnection Technology *(1958)*

3406 46th Terrace East
Bradenton, FL 34203
Toll Free: (800)854 - 4248
E-Mail: info@iicit.org
Web Site: www.iicit.org
Members: 2500 individuals
Staff: 4
Annual Budget: $250-500,000
Managing Director: Cindy Barnes
E-Mail: cbarnes114@iicit.org

Historical Note

Formerly (1988) the Electronic Connector Study Group. IICIT membership is open to engineers, manufacturers, sales representatives and any other people involved with any type of connector or interconnection application. IICIT has members from 90% of the major connector manufacturers and various interconnection related companies, such as wire manufacturers, platers, testing and evaluation labs, etc. Membership: $35/year (individual); $225-$1,200 (corporate).

Meetings/Conferences:

Annual Meetings: Fall/1,000

Publications:

Proceedings. a (also on CD-Rom).
IICIT News. q.

International Institute of Fisheries Economics and Trade *(1982)*

Dept of Agricultural & Resource Economic
Oregon State University
Corvallis, OR 97331-3601
Tel: (541)737-1416 *Fax:* (541)737-2563
E-Mail: iifet@oregonstate.edu
Web Site: www.oregonstate.edu/dept/IIFET
Members: 400 individuals
Executive Director: Ann L. Shriver
E-Mail: iifet@oregonstate.edu

Historical Note

IIFET is organized to promote the discussion of factors which affect international trade in seafoods, and fisheries policy questions. Designed to be attractive to individuals from governments, industries, and universities from all over the world, a major goal of the organization is to facilitate cooperative research and data exchange. Membership: $50/year (individual); $250/year (organization).

Meetings/Conferences:

Biennial: 400-500

Publications:

Membership Directory. bien.
IIFET Newsletter. semi-a. adv.

International Institute of Forecasters *(1981)*

53 Tesla Ave.
Medford, MA 02155
Tel: (781)234-4077 *Fax:* (509)357-5530
Web Site: http://forecasters.org
Members: 500 individuals
Annual Budget: $100-250,000
President: Geoff Allen
Business Manager: Pamela Stroud

Historical Note

Members are decision makers, forecasters and researchers involved with forecasting in the management, social, engineering and behavioral sciences. IIF is interested in research on forecasting methods and processes. Has no paid officers or full-time staff. Membership: $120/year (individual).

Meetings/Conferences:

Annual Meetings: Summer/650
2007 – New York, NY(Marriott Marquis)/June 24-27
2008 – Nice, France/June 22-27/300

Publications:

International Journal of Forecasting. q. adv.
Newsletter. q.
Foresight, the International Journal of Applied Forecasting. 3/yr. adv.

International Institute of Municipal Clerks *(1947)*

8331 Utica Ave., Suite 200
Rancho Cucamonga, CA 91730
Tel: (909)944-4162 *Fax:* (909)944-8545
E-Mail: hq@iimc.com
Web Site: www.iimc.com
Members: 10000 individuals
Staff: 11
Annual Budget: $1-2,000,000
Interim Executive Director: Chris Shalby
E-Mail: chriss@iimc.com

Historical Note

Founded in 1947 at French Lick, Indiana as the National Institute of City and Town Clerks. Became the National Institute of Municipal Clerks in 1949 and the International Institute of Municipal Clerks in 1960. Membership consists of persons serving as Clerks, Secretaries or Recorders at the state, provincial, county or local level of government. Awards the CMC (Certified Municipal Clerk) designation. Membership: $60-450/yr. (varies by population).

Meetings/Conferences:

Annual Meetings: Spring

Publications:

Sample Proclamations.
IIMC Meeting Administration Handbook.
City Council Rules of Procedure.

International Institute of Synthetic Rubber Producers *(1960)*

2077 S. Gessner, Suite 133
Houston, TX 77063-1123
Tel: (713)783-7511 *Fax:* (713)783-7253
E-Mail: info@iisrp.com
Web Site: www.iisrp.com
Members: 49 companies
Staff: 6
Annual Budget: $1-2,000,000
Managing Director and Chief Executive Officer: James L. McGraw
Director, Programs: Leon Loh

Historical Note

Has an international membership. Membership: $19,000/year (organization/company).

Meetings/Conferences:

Annual Meetings: April or May/250-300
2007 – New Delhi, India(Hyatt)/Apr. 16-19/150

Publications:

Worldwide Rubber Statistics. a.
Synthetic Rubber Manual. trien.
Proceedings. a.

International Insurance Society *(1965)*

101 Murray St.
New York, NY 10007-2165
Tel: (212)815-9291 *Fax:* (212)815-9297

E-Mail: ej@iisonline.org
Web Site: www.iisonline.org
Members: 1200 individuals
Staff: 4
Annual Budget: $1-2,000,000
Executive Director: Colleen McKenna Tucker
President and Chief Executive Officer: Patrick W. Kenny

Historical Note
IIS facilitates international understanding, the transfer of ideas and innovations, and the development of personal networks across insurance markets through a joint effort of leading executives and academics on a worldwide basis. Membership: $100/year (individual); $1,500/year (corporate).

Meetings/Conferences:
Annual Meetings: Summer

Publications:
Annual Report. a.
Seminar and Proceedings Manual. a.
Governors' Journal Newsletter. q.

International Intellectual Property Alliance *(1984)*
1747 Pennsylvania Ave. NW, Suite 825
Washington, DC 20006
Tel: (202)833-4198 *Fax:* (202)872-0546
E-Mail: info@iipa.com
Web Site: www.iipa.com
Members: 6 trade associations
Staff: 5
President: Eric H. Smith
Senior Vice President: Steven Metalitz
Vice President and General Counsel: Maria Strong

Historical Note
IIPA is an umbrella organization concerned with protection of U.S. intellectual property in international markets.

International Interactive Communication Society *(1983)*

Historical Note
Merged with Association of Internet Professionals in 2000.

International Interior Design Association *(1994)*
222 Merchandise Mart Plaza
Suite 1540
Chicago, IL 60654-1104
Tel: (312)467-1950 *Fax:* (312)467-0779
Toll Free: (888)799 - 4432
E-Mail: iidahq@iida.org
Web Site: www.iida.org
Members: 12000 individuals
Staff: 15
Annual Budget: $2-5,000,000
Executive Vice President: Cheryl Durst
Director, Government and Regulatory Affairs: Mike Hanlon
Senior Director, Education and Professional Development: Susan Heath
Senior Director, Membership: Heather Jakusz
Senior Vice President, Development, Corporate and Foundation Relations: Dennis Krause
E-Mail: dkrause@adelphia.net
Senior Director, Communications and Marketing: Jocelyn Pysarchuk
E-Mail: jpysarchuk@iida.org

Historical Note
Formed (1994) by the merger of Council of Federal Interior Designers, Institute of Business Designers, and International Society of Interior Designers, IIDA is a professional networking and educational association, committed to excellence in interior design, with members in eight specialty forums, nine regions, and more than 30 chapters around the world. Members are professionals from various facets of the interior design industry.

Meetings/Conferences:
Annual Meetings: June/Chicago, IL

Publications:
Design Matters. w. adv.
Custom. q.
Perspective. q. adv.

International Iridology Practitioners Association *(1982)*
P.O. Box 339
Pinehurst, TX 77362-0339
Toll Free: (888)682 - 2208
E-Mail: iipacentraloffice@iridologyassn.org
Web Site: www.iridologyassn.org
Members: 500 individuals
Staff: 1
Annual Budget: $10-25,000
President: Dave Carpenter

Historical Note
Promotes the art and science of iridology, providing for the exchange of research and information leading to the development of a national standard for the industry.

Meetings/Conferences:
Semi-Annual Meetings: February and August

Publications:
IIPA Newsletter. 4/year. adv.
Iridology Review. 3/year.

International Isotope Society *(1986)*
26 Dewey Rd.
Lexington, MA 02420-1018
Tel: (781)862-3457 *Fax:* (781)863-8856
E-Mail: iis@intl-isotope-soc.org
Web Site: www.intl-isotope-soc.org
Members: 650 individuals
Treasurer: Jennie G. Ahern

Historical Note
IIS members are academics and researchers involved in the study and application of chemical isotopes. Has no paid officers or full-time staff. Membership: $50/year (regular member); $350/year (associate).

Meetings/Conferences:
Triennial Meetings: Summer (2006)

Publications:
IIS Newsletter. semi-a. adv.
Journal of Labelled Compounds & Radiopharmaceuticals. m. adv.
Proceedings of International Symposium. trien.

International Jelly and Preserve Association *(1918)*
5775 Peachtree-Dunwoody Rd., Suite 500-G
Atlanta, GA 30342-1558
Tel: (404)252-3663 *Fax:* (404)252-0774
E-Mail: ijpa@kellencompany.com
Web Site: www.jelly.org
Members: 78 companies
Staff: 4
Annual Budget: $100-250,000
President: Pamela A. Chumley

Historical Note
Formerly (1978) the National Preservers Association. Members are producers of fruit jams, preserves, jellies, marmalades, pie fillings, fruit butters and manufacturers of bakers supplies or processed fruit products used as industrial ingredients; brokers; and suppliers of packaging materials or equipment to the preserving industry.

Meetings/Conferences:
Annual Meetings: Spring

Publications:
Direct Line. q.

International Kitchen Exhaust Cleaning Association *(1988)*
12339 Carroll Ave.
Rockville, MD 20852
Tel: (301)230-0099 *Fax:* (301)231-4871
E-Mail: info@ikeca.org
Web Site: www.ikeca.org
Members: 150 companies
Staff: 4
Annual Budget: $100-250,000
Executive Director: Glenn Fellman

Historical Note
Promotes fire safety in restaurants and professionalism in the kitchen exhaust cleaning industry. Membership: $375/year (company).

Publications:
IKECA Journal. q. adv.

International Labor Communications Association *(1955)*
815 16th St. NW
Washington, DC 20006
Tel: (202)974-8037 *Fax:* (202)974-8038
E-Mail: ilca@aflcio.org
Web Site: www.ilcaonline.org
Members: 600
Staff: 2
Annual Budget: $100-250,000
Media Coordinator: Alec Dubro

Historical Note
Formerly (1984) International Labor Press Association. Formed by a merger of the International Labor Press of America (1911) and the CIO Editors and Public Relations Conference (1940). Members are editors of union papers. Membership: varies, depending on circulation and type of membership.

Meetings/Conferences:
Biennial Conventions: Odd years
2007 –

Publications:
ILCA Reporter. bi-m. adv.

International Lactation Consultant Association *(1985)*
1500 Sunday Dr., Suite 102
Raleigh, NC 27607
Tel: (919)861-5577 *Fax:* (919)787-4916
E-Mail: info@ilca.org
Web Site: www.ilca.org
Members: 4600 individuals
Staff: 5
Annual Budget: $250-500,000
Executive Director: Jim Smith

Historical Note
Goals of ILCA are to facilitate networking among lactation consultants and other professionals interested in promoting, protecting and supporting breast feeding; to establish guidelines for competent, ethical lactation consultant practice; to foster the development of professional standards and ethical practice for International Board Certified Lactation Consultants; to inform all health care professionals of the importance of human milk and breastfeeding and the consequences of artificial feeding; to serve as an authoritative professional advisory body for women's and children's health; to cooperate with organizations with similar aims; to stimulate and support research in the field; and to support implementation of the International Code of Marketing of Breast-Milk Substitutes and all subsequent WHA resolutions. ILCA Members are professionals working to prevent and solve breastfeeding problems and to encourage a social environment that effectively supports breastfeeding families. Members include lactation consultants, midwives, nurses, maternal child health workers, physicians, childbirth educators, medical and nursing educators, maternal and infant health advocates, dieticians and nutrition specialists, speech therapists, occupational therapists, anthropologists, researchers, social workers, and volunteer counselors. Membership: dues vary.

Meetings/Conferences:
Annual Meetings: July-August/1,000

Publications:
Journal of Human Lactation. q. adv.
eGlobe (online). m.

International Laser Display Association *(1986)*
3721 S.E. Henry St.
Portland, OR 97202
Tel: (503)407-0289
Web Site: www.laserist.org
Members: 28 individuals
Staff: 1
Annual Budget: $25-50,000
Executive Director: David Lytle

Historical Note
ILDA members are individuals involved in the laser entertainment and display industry. Membership: $125/year (individual); $50/year (student); corporate and affiliate membership varies, maximum $1,000/year.

Publications:
Laserist. q. adv.

International Lead Zinc Research Organization *(1958)*
2525 Meridian Pkwy., Suite 100
P.O. Box 12036

Research Triangle Park, NC 27709-2036
Tel: (919)361-4647 *Fax:* (919)361-1957
E-Mail: rputnam@ilzro.org
Web Site: www.ilzro.org
Members: 43 companies
Staff: 16
Annual Budget: $5-10,000,000
President: Stephen Wilkinson
Vice President, Materials Sciences: Frank Goodwin
E-Mail: fgoodwin@ilzro.org
Treasurer: Scott Mooneyham
Director, Communications: Rob Putnam
E-Mail: rputnam@ilzro.org

Historical Note
Established in New York and incorporated in North Carolina, ILZRO members are miners and refiners of lead and zinc. Trade association of the lead and zinc industry worldwide. Focus on research and development to detect new uses for the metals and refine existing uses. Has an annual budget of approximately $5.3 million.

Meetings/Conferences:
Annual Meetings: November

Publications:
Annual Review. a.
R&D Focus. q.
Environmental Health Newsletter. q.

International League of Electrical Associations *(1936)*
12165 W. Center Rd., Suite 59
Omaha, NE 68144
Tel: (402)330-7227 *Fax:* (402)330-7283
E-Mail: info@electricalcouncil.com
Web Site: www.ileaweb.org
Members: 35 organizations
Staff: 1
Annual Budget: $10-25,000
Executive Manager: R. E. "Skip" Morris

Historical Note
Formerly known as International Association of Electrical Leagues; assumed current name in 1979. A federation of state, provincial and local organizations in the electrical industry. Membership: $250/year.

Meetings/Conferences:
2007 – Toronto, ON, Canada(Novotel)/July 18-21

Publications:
Membership Directory. a.
Bulletins. irreg.

International League of Professional Baseball Clubs *(1884)*
55 S. High St., Suite 202
Dublin, OH 43017
Tel: (614)791-9300 *Fax:* (614)791-9009
E-Mail: office@ilbaseball.com
Web Site: www.ilbaseball.com
Members: 14 clubs
Staff: 3
Annual Budget: $250-500,000
President: Randy Mobley
E-Mail: office@ilbaseball.com

Historical Note
The oldest minor league in baseball.

Publications:
Record Book. a.

International Legal Fraternity of Phi Delta Phi *(1869)*
1426 21st St. NW
Washington, DC 20036
Tel: (202)223-6801 *Fax:* (202)223-6808
Toll Free: (800)368 - 5606
E-Mail: info@phideltaphi.org
Web Site: www.phideltaphi.org
Members: 200000 individuals
Staff: 4
Annual Budget: $500-1,000,000
Executive Director: Tim Wheat

Historical Note
Professional international legal fraternity. Membership: $75 initiation fee; voluntary alumni dues.

Meetings/Conferences:
Biennial Meetings: odd years in August

Publications:
The Headnoter. q.

International Licensing Industry Merchandisers' Association *(1985)*
350 Fifth Ave., Suite 1408
New York, NY 10118
Tel: (212)244-1944 *Fax:* (212)563-6552
E-Mail: info@licensing.org
Web Site: www.licensing.org
Members: 1000 companies
Staff: 6
Annual Budget: $1-2,000,000
President: Charles Riotto
E-Mail: criotto@licensing.org
Vice President, Member Relations: Louise Q. Caron
E-Mail: louise@licensing.org
Director, Marketing and Communications: Jennifer Coleman
Director, Operations: Mary Verdegaal

Historical Note
LIMA is a leading trade association for the licensing industry. Headquartered in New York, with offices in the UK, Germany, Japan and China, and members around the world.

Meetings/Conferences:
Annual Meetings: 200-300 attendees

Publications:
Licensing Industry Survey. a.
LIMA Bottomline Newsletter. q.
Licensing Resource Directory. a. adv.

International Listening Association *(1979)*
Box 744
River Falls, WI 54022
Tel: (715)425-3377 *Fax:* (715)425-9533
Toll Free: (800)452 - 4505
E-Mail: ilistening@aol.com
Web Site: www.listen.org
Members: 400 individuals
Staff: 1
Annual Budget: $50-100,000
Executive Director: James W. Pratt

Historical Note
ILA members are academics and others with an interest in expanding our understanding of effective listening. Membership: $75/year (individual); $425/year (organization).

Meetings/Conferences:
Annual Meetings: Spring
2007 – Frankfurt, Germany/July 18-21

Publications:
Listening Professional. a.
Listening Post. q. adv.
International Journal of Listening. a.

International Liver Transplantation Society *(1992)*
17000 Commerce Pkwy., Suite C
Mt. Laurel, NJ 08054
Tel: (856)439-0500 *Fax:* (856)439-0525
E-Mail: ilts@ahint.com
Web Site: www.ilts.org
Members: 700 individuals
Staff: 1
Annual Budget: $500-1,000,000

Historical Note
Membership: $190/year (physician); $95/year (non-physician).

Meetings/Conferences:
Annual Meetings: Summer

Publications:
Liver Transplantation Journal. bi-m. adv.
ILTS Newsletter. q. adv.

International Longshore and Warehouse Union *(1937)*
1188 Franklin St., Fourth Floor
San Francisco, CA 94109
Tel: (415)775-0533 *Fax:* (415)775-1302
E-Mail: info@ilwu.org
Web Site: www.ilwu.org
Members: 58000 individuals
Staff: 25
Annual Budget: $2-5,000,000
President: James Spinosa
Office Manager and Executive Secretary: Linda Kuhn
Editor and Communications Director: Steve Stallone

Historical Note
ILWU was founded by Harry R. Bridges and NLRB certified as the International Longshoremen's and Warehousemen's Union. Members are longshoremen, warehousemen, bargemen, cannery workers, chemical/chemical processing workers, shipscalers, fishermen, and tourism employees; there are members in both the United States and Canada. Inlandboatmen's Union of the Pacific is its Marine Division. Affiliated with the AFL-CIO in 1988.

Meetings/Conferences:
Triennial Meetings: Spring

Publications:
The Dispatcher. 11/year.

International Longshoremen's Association, AFL-CIO *(1892)*
17 Battery Pl., Suite 930
New York, NY 10004
Tel: (212)425-1200 *Fax:* (212)425-2928
Web Site: www.ila2000.org
Members: 116000 individuals
Staff: 30
Annual Budget: $5-10,000,000
President: John Bowers, CAE

Historical Note
Established in Detroit in 1892 as the National Longshoremen's Association of the United States. Became the International Longshoremen's Association in 1895 and was chartered by the American Federation of Labor in 1896. Expelled for corruption and racketeering by the AFL in 1953, the ILA was an independent union until 1959, when it re-affiliated with AFL-CIO.

Meetings/Conferences:
Triennial Meetings:

Publications:
Directory. bien.
ILA Newsletter. 4-5/year.

International Magnesium Association *(1943)*
1000 N. Rand Rd., Suite 214
Wauconda, IL 60084
Tel: (847)526-2010 *Fax:* (847)526-3993
E-Mail: gpatzer@tso.net
Web Site: www.intlmag.org/
Members: 120 companies
Staff: 2
Annual Budget: $500-1,000,000
Executive Vice President: Greg Patzer
E-Mail: gpatzer@tso.net
Administrative Coordinator: Eileen Hobut

Historical Note
IMA's purpose is to develop and increase the international use and acceptance of magnesium metal and its alloys in all product forms. Regular membership is open to organizations or individuals directly engaged in the production, manufacture or marketing of metallic magnesium in some product form; and those supplying materials, equipment or services to the industry.

Meetings/Conferences:
Annual Meetings: May-June

Publications:
Magnesium Update. w.
Annual Conference Proceedings. a.

International Magnetics Association *(1959)*
Eight S. Michigan Ave., Suite 1000
Chicago, IL 60603
Tel: (312)456-5590 *Fax:* (312)580-0165
E-Mail: ima@gss.net
Web Site: www.intl-magnetics.org
Members: 35 companies
Staff: 2
Annual Budget: $50-100,000
President: Lowell Bosley

Historical Note
Established as the Permanent Magnet Producers Association; became Magnetic Materials Producers Association in 1967 and assumed its current names in 2002. Absorbed Magnetics Distributors and Fabricators Association in 2003. MMPA members are manufacturers of permanent and soft ferrite magnetic

materials. Membership: $1,200-4,800/year (corporate).

Meetings/Conferences:
Annual Meetings: Spring, always Florida

Publications:
Technical Standards.

International Maintenance Institute *(1961)*
P.O. Box 751896
Houston, TX 77275-1896
Tel: (281)481-0869 *Fax:* (281)481-8337
Toll Free: (800)207 - 1773
E-Mail: iminst@swbell.net
Web Site: www.imionline.org
Members: 2500 individuals
Staff: 1
Annual Budget: $100-250,000
Executive Secretary: Joyce Rhoden
E-Mail: iminst@swbell.net

Historical Note
Membership: $50/year, plus chapter dues.

Publications:
IMI News. bi-m.
The Maintenance Journal. bi-m. adv.

International Management Council *(1935)*

Historical Note
Merged with National Management Association in 2004.

International Manufacturers Representatives Association *(1958)*

Historical Note
Address unknown in 2006.

International Map Trade Association *(1981)*
2629 Hermosa Ave.
PMB 281
Hermosa Beach, CA 90254
Tel: (310)376-7731 *Fax:* (310)376-7287
E-Mail: imta@maptrade.org
Web Site: www.maptrade.org
Members: 800 companies
Staff: 4
Executive Director: Sandy Hill
E-Mail: imta@maptrade.org
Conference Coordinator: Linda Hill
E-Mail: imta@maptrade.org

Historical Note
Formerly (1993) the International Map Dealers Association. Membership comprised of retail stores featuring maps; distributors; manufacturers; wholesalers; and publishers. The purposes of the association are to stimulate the sale and use of maps and related material, to promote high standards of professional competence, conduct, and ethics, and to foster communication and cooperation among publishers, wholesalers, retailers, and others in the map industry. Incorporated in Florida. Membership: $150/year.

Meetings/Conferences:
Annual Meetings: Fall

Publications:
Membership Directory. a. adv.
Newsletter. m. adv.

International Maple Syrup Institute *(1975)*
5014 Rte. Seven
Ferrisburg, VT 05456
Tel: (802)877-2250 *Fax:* (802)610-1020
E-Mail:
info@internationalmaplesyrupinstitute.com
Web Site:
www.internationalmaplesyrupinstitute.com
Members: 15000 individuals
Staff: 1
Executive Secretary: Larry Myott

Meetings/Conferences:
Annual Meetings: Fall/350

International Marina Institute *(1986)*
444 North Capitol St. NW, Suite 645
Washington, DC 20001-1559
Toll Free: (866)367 - 6622
E-Mail: info@marinaassociation.org
Web Site: www.imimarina.org
Members: 600 individuals
Staff: 3
Annual Budget: $500-1,000,000
Executive Director: Jim Frye, CMM
E-Mail: info@marinaassociation.org

Historical Note
Membership: $150-185/year (individual); $375/year (organization/company)

Meetings/Conferences:
Annual Meetings: December.

Publications:
Dock Lines. bi-w.
IMI Catalog. a.

International Marking and Identification Association *(1910)*
655 Rockland Rd.
Suite 5
Lake Forest, IL 60044
Tel: (847)283-9810 *Fax:* (847)283-9808
E-Mail: info@marking-id.org
Web Site: www.marking-id.org
Members: 300 companies
Staff: 1
Annual Budget: $100-250,000
Executive Director: Gene Griffiths

Historical Note
Founded as International Stamp Manufacturers Association; later became Marking Device Association International before assuming its current name in 2002. IMIA members are manufacturers of embossing seals, notary seals, rubber and metal stamps, plates, signs, and other hand-held marking devices. Membership: $375-2,995/year.

Meetings/Conferences:
Annual Meetings: Fall, with trade show/700
2007 – Baltimore, MD/July 12-14/500

Publications:
MDAI Seal Manual. a. adv.
MDAI Membership Directory. a.
MDAI Newsletter Update. bi. adv.

International Masonry Institute *(1970)*
42 East St.
Annapolis, MD 21401
Tel: (410)280-1305 *Fax:* (301)261-2855
Web Site: www.imiweb.org
Staff: 170
Annual Budget: $25-50,000,000
President: Joan B. Calambokidis
Director, Communications: Hazel Bradford
National Director, Market Development and Technical Services: David Sovinski

Historical Note
A Labor/Management Trust established between the International Union of Bricklayers and Allied Craftsmen and contractors who employ BAC members. IMI conducts market development, and research and development craft training.

Publications:
IMI Today. bi-m.

International Memorialization Supply Association *(1955)*
P.O. Box 663
Export, PA 15632
Toll Free: (800)864 - 4174
E-Mail: info@imsa-online.com
Web Site: www.imsa-online.com
Members: 102 companies
Staff: 8
Annual Budget: $10-25,000
Contact: David Yearsley
E-Mail: info@imsa-online.com

Historical Note
Formerly (until 1980) known as the Cemetery and Funeral Supply Association and (until 1994) the International Cemetery Supply Association. Suppliers of equipment, materials and services to the cemetery and funeral industry united to improve the quality of materials made available to and by cemetery suppliers; to improve communication with the public; and to meet needs of access to information. Membership: $100/year (company).

Meetings/Conferences:
Semi-annual: with American Cemetery Association

International Metal Decorators Association
(1934)
9616 Deereco Rd.
Timonium, MD 21093
Tel: (410)252-5205 *Fax:* (410)628-8079
E-Mail: info@metaldecorators.org
Web Site: www.nmda.org
Members: 850 individuals
Staff: 2
Annual Budget: $250-500,000
President: Rick Clendenning
E-Mail: info@metaldecorators.org

Historical Note
Members are individuals in firms that apply decoration and supplies and services to metal surfaces through lithography or rollercoating. Membership: $65/year.

Publications:
International Metal Decorator. q. adv.

International Microelectronics and Packaging Society *(1967)*
611 Second St. NE
Washington, DC 20002-4909
Tel: (202)548-4001 *Fax:* (202)548-6115
E-Mail: imaps@imaps.org
Web Site: www.imaps.org
Members: 5400 individuals
Staff: 13
Annual Budget: $2-5,000,000
Executive Director: Michael O'Donoghue

Historical Note
Formed in 1996 by the merger of the International Society for Hybrid Microelectronics and the International Electronic Packaging Society IMAPS promotes close interaction between the complementary technologies of ceramics, thin and thick films, semiconductor packaging, surface mount technology, multichip modules, semiconductor devices, and monolithic circuits. Formed in the fall of 1967 by a small group of engineers in the San Francisco Bay area. Membership: $60/year (individual); $500/year (organization); $150/year (associate organization); $100/year (affiliate organization).

Meetings/Conferences:
Annual Meetings: Fall

Publications:
Directory of IMAPS Members. a.
Advancing Microelectronics. bi-m. adv.
IMAPS Journal. q.
Technical Proceedings. a.
Industry Guide. a. adv.

International Microwave Power Institute *(1966)*
7076 Drinkard Way
Mechanicsville, VA 23111
E-Mail: impi@impi.org
Web Site: www.impi.org
Members: 300 individuals
Staff: 2
Annual Budget: $100-250,000
Executive Director: Kimberly D. Thies
E-Mail: execdir@impi.org

Historical Note
Members are engineers, educators, home economists and scientists interested in non-communication aspects of microwave power. Membership: $160/year (individual); $1,500/year (organization).

Meetings/Conferences:
Annual Meetings: July

Publications:
Microwave World. tri. adv.
Journal of Microwave Power. q.

International Military Community Executives Association *(1971)*
1530 Dunwoody Village
Parkway Suite 203
Atlanta, GA 30338
Tel: (770)396-2101 *Fax:* (770)396-2198
E-Mail: imcea@imcea.com
Web Site: www.imcea.com
Members: 1070 individuals

Staff: 5
Annual Budget: $250-500,000
Executive Director: Sari Jill Schneider
E-Mail: sarischneider@imcea.com

Historical Note

Formerly (1989) the International Military Club Executives Association. Founded in 1972 for management personnel including all branches of the armed services. Some benefits of joining include training programs and certification. IMCEA is open to all personnel involved in morale, welfare and recreation, (MWR) activities, including clubs, bowling and golf managers. Membership: $225/year (regular; for first person or installation; $25 for each individual after that), $495/year (associate).

Meetings/Conferences:

Regional Meetings: throughout U.S., Europe, and the Far East

Publications:

MWR Today. m. adv.
Annual Directory and Buyers Guide. a. adv.

International Miniature Cattle Breeders Society *(1984)*
25204 156th Ave. SE
Covington, WA 98042
Tel: (253)631-1911 *Fax:* (253)631-5774
E-Mail: info@minicattle.com
Web Site: www.minicattle.com
Members: 4534 individuals
Staff: 4
Founding Director: Dick Gradwohl
E-Mail: info@minicattle.com

Historical Note

IMCBS represents breeders and ranchers of 24 breeds of mini- and mid-size miniature cattle. Membership: $100/year.

Meetings/Conferences:

Annual Meetings: Annual/Typical Attendance 3-4,000

Publications:

Newsletter. q.

International Mobile Air Conditioning Association *(1958)*

Historical Note

Absorbed by Mobile Air Conditioning Society in 2005.

International Mobile Telecommunications Association *(1994)*

Historical Note

Founded in 1994 as International Mobile Telecommunications Association. An international counterpart to American Mobile Telecommunications Association (same address); incorporated as a separate organization in 1996. Assumed its current name in 2000. IWTA provides industry input on government regulations for the commercial trunked radio industry in the 60+ countries where specialized mobile radio systems operate. Sponsors several international meetings and seminars throughout the year. Membership: $500/year (individual); $1,000/year (organization).

International Motion Picture and Lecturers Association

Historical Note

Became Travel Adventure Cinema Society in 2000.

International Motor Press Association *(1962)*
Four Park St.
Harrington Park, NJ 07640
Tel: (201)750-3533 *Fax:* (201)750-2010
E-Mail: info@impa.org
Web Site: www.impa.org
Members: 500 individuals
Staff: 1
Annual Budget: $50-100,000
Treasurer: Mike Geylin
E-Mail: info@impa.org

Historical Note

IMPA is a professional group of writers and editors producing auto articles for the press, radio or TV. Concentrated in the New York area, IMPA is the U.S. Chapter of the International Federation of Automotive Journalists. Membership: $50/year.

Meetings/Conferences:

Monthly Meetings: Third Thursdays

Publications:

IMPACT. m.

International Multimedia Telecommunications Consortium *(1994)*
Bishop Ranch 6, 2400 Camino Ramon, Suite 375
San Ramon, CA 94583
Tel: (925)275-6600 *Fax:* (925)275-6691
Web Site: www.imtc.org
Members: 61 corporations
Secretary: Jim Polizotto
E-Mail: secretary@imtc.org

Historical Note

IMTC fosters and facilitates the development of interoperable multimedia teleconferencing solutions based on open international standards. Membership: $5,000/year (voting).

International Municipal Lawyers Association *(1935)*
1110 Vermont Ave. NW, Suite 200
Washington, DC 20005-3522
Tel: (202)466-5424 *Fax:* (202)785-0152
Web Site: www.imla.org
Members: 1500 cities and counties
Staff: 9
Annual Budget: $1-2,000,000
Executive Director and General Counsel: Henry W. Underhill, Jr.
E-Mail: hunderhill@imla.org

Historical Note

Formerly (1995) the National Institute of Municipal Law Officers. IMLA was founded by municipal attorneys attending an annual conference of the United States Conference of Mayors in 1935 as an organization of municipalities acting through their chief legal officer. Participates in federal and state cases of nation-wide importance and serves as a source of local government legal information. Membership fee based on population.

Meetings/Conferences:

Annual Meetings: Fall/700
2007 – Nashville, TN/Oct. 28-31

Publications:

The Municipal Lawyer. bi-m.

International Municipal Signal Association *(1896)*
165 E. Union St.
P.O. Box 539
Newark, NY 14513
Tel: (315)331-2182 *Fax:* (315)331-8205
Toll Free: (800)723 - 4672
Web Site: www.imsasafety.org
Members: 10000 individuals
Staff: 6
Annual Budget: $1-2,000,000
Executive Director: Marilyn E. Lawrence
E-Mail: mel@imsasafety.org
Executive Assistant: Sharon Earl

Historical Note

Members are government employees and municipal contractors involved in public safety operations: traffic signal installation and maintenance, fire alarm systems, street lights, radio communications, etc. Sustaining membership is available to persons in private corporations responsible for promoting public safety. Membership: $60/year (individual); $50/year (3 or more individuals from the same agency); $350/year (sustaining).

Meetings/Conferences:

Annual Meetings: July-August
2007 – Louisville, KY(Louisville Marriott Downtown)/Aug. 15-22

Publications:

IMSA Journal. bi-m. adv.

International Museum Theater Alliance *(1990)*
Wildlife Theater, Central Park Zoo
830 Fifth Ave.
New York, NY 10021
Tel: (212)439-6542
Web Site: www.imtal.org
Members: 150 individuals
Annual Budget: under $10,000
Secretary: Jillian Finkle

Historical Note

The International Museum Theatre Alliance, formed in 1990, is a professional resource and networking organization for museum and theatre professionals using theatre as an interpretive technique. Membership: $15/year (student); $25/year (artist); $35/year (museum professional); $50-75/year (institution).

Publications:

Insights. q. adv.

International Nanny Association *(1985)*
2020 Southwest Fwy., Suite 208
Houston, TX 77098
Tel: (713)526-2670 *Fax:* (713)526-2667
Toll Free: (888)878 - 1477
E-Mail: INA@nanny.org
Web Site: www.nanny.org
Members: 700 individuals
Staff: 2
Annual Budget: $100-250,000
President: Pat Cascio
E-Mail: director@nanny.org

Historical Note

INA is a non-profit association whose members are nannies, nanny placement agencies and others with an interest in the field. Membership: $85-275/year, based on membership level.

Meetings/Conferences:

Annual Meetings: June

Publications:

INA Vision Newsletter. q. adv.
Directory of Agencies, Programs, and Services. a. adv.

International Narcotic Enforcement Officers Association *(1958)*
112 State St., Suite 1200
Albany, NY 12207-2079
Tel: (518)463-6232 *Fax:* (518)432-3378
E-Mail: ineoa@iopener.net
Web Site: www.ineoa.org
Members: 10000 individuals
Staff: 6
Annual Budget: $250-500,000
Executive Director: John J. Bellizzi

Historical Note

Established in Albany, NY in October, 1960, and incorporated in the state of New York in the same year. In recognition of its growing international membership, the present name was adopted in 1963. Membership: $40/year.

Meetings/Conferences:

Annual Meetings: October

Publications:

International Drug Report. q. adv.
Narc Officer. bi-m. adv.

International Natural Sausage Casing Association *(1964)*
12339 Carroll Ave.
Rockville, MD 20852-1867
Tel: (301)231-8383 *Fax:* (301)231-4871
E-Mail: insca@aol.com
Web Site: www.insca.org
Members: 250 companies
Staff: 2
Annual Budget: $250-500,000
Executive Administrator: Paul Tranvankha
E-Mail: insca@aol.com

Historical Note

Formerly (1965) Natural Casing Institute. Membership: $1,250/year (organization/company).

Meetings/Conferences:

Semi-annual: Spring/Europe; Fall/North America

Publications:

Newsletter. q.
Yearbook. a. adv.

International Network of Merger and Acquisition Partners *(1973)*
525 S.W. Fifth St., Suite A
Des Moines, IA 50309
Tel: (515)282-8192 *Fax:* (515)282-9117
E-Mail: info@imap.com
Web Site: www.imap.com
Members: 50 companies

Staff: 1
Annual Budget: $50-100,000
Executive Director: Mary Mycka

Historical Note

Formerly (1982) National Association of Merger and Acquisition Consultants, (1995) International Association of Merger and Acquisition Professionals, and (2005) International Merger and Acquisition Professionals. Members are specialists in selling, buying, and merging medium-sized public and private businesses.

Meetings/Conferences:
Semi-annual Meetings: Spring and Fall/50

Publications:
IMAP Briefs. q.

International Neural Network Society *(1987)*
2810 Crossroads Dr., Suite 3800
Madison, WI 53718
Tel: (608)443-2461 *Fax:* (608)443-2474
E-Mail: inns@reesgroupinc.com
Web Site: www.inns.org
Members: 1000 individuals
Staff: 4
Annual Budget: $100-250,000
Executive Director: Susan M. Rees

Historical Note

INNS promotes research into models of brain and behavioral processes, and the development of computing applications which utilize concepts obtained from neural modelling. Members are neural network scientists and other professionals interested in neurocomputing and theoretical neuroscience. Membership: $80/year (individual); $20/year (student).

Meetings/Conferences:
Annual Meetings: Summer

Publications:
Journal of Neural Networks. m. adv.
INNS Newsletter. m.

International Neuropsychological Society *(1967)*
700 Ackerman Road, Suite 625
Columbus, OH 43202-1559
Tel: (614)263-4200 *Fax:* (614)263-4366
E-Mail: ins@osu.edu
Web Site: www.the-ins.org
Members: 4500 individuals
Staff: 2
Executive Secretary: Robert Bornstein, Ph.D.

Publications:
Journal of the International Neuropsychological Society. 7/year. adv.

International Newspaper Financial Executives *(1947)*
21525 Ridgetop Circle, Suite 200
Sterling, VA 20166
Tel: (703)421-4060 *Fax:* (703)421-4068
E-Mail: infehq@infe.org
Web Site: www.infe.org
Members: 1000 individuals
Staff: 4
Annual Budget: $500-1,000,000
Executive Director and Vice President: Robert J. Kasabian
E-Mail: infehq@infe.org

Historical Note

Formerly (1984) Institute of Newspaper Controllers and Finance Officers. The international newspaper association for financial accounting and business management. Membership: $300-700/year (individual).

Meetings/Conferences:
Annual Meetings: June

Publications:
INFE E-Mail Newsletter. w.

International Newspaper Group *(1974)*
4335 N.W. 36th Terrace
Gainesville, FL 32605
Tel: (352)371-9475
Web Site: www.azcentral.org
Members: 250 individuals
Staff: 1
Annual Budget: $50-100,000
Secretary-Treasurer: Martin Donner
E-Mail: mdonner2@cox.net

Historical Note

ING members are executives responsible for newspaper production and operations, and suppliers to the industry.

Meetings/Conferences:
Annual Meetings: Fall

Publications:
Information Flyer. semi-a.

International Newspaper Marketing Association *(1930)*
10300 N. Central Expy., Suite 467
Dallas, TX 75231
Tel: (214)373-9111 *Fax:* (214)373-9112
E-Mail: inma@inma.org
Web Site: www.inma.org
Members: 1100 individuals
Staff: 5
Annual Budget: $500-1,000,000
Executive Director: Earl Wilkinson
Manager, Membership and Marketing: Brooke Bode
Associate Director: Maria E. Terrell

Historical Note

Founded in 1930 as the National Newspaper Promotion Association. The name was changed in 1967 to the International Newspaper Promotion Association to reflect the makeup of the membership, which is composed of members from more than 40 countries including the United States and Canada. In 1987, INMA assumed its present name. INMA's mission is to provide newspapers with professional leadership and assistance in creating effective marketing of the total newspaper. Membership fee based on newspaper circulation size.

Meetings/Conferences:
Annual Meetings: May/500-600

Publications:
IDEAS Magazine. m. adv.
Best in Print. a.

International Nubian Breeders Association *(1956)*
P.O. Box 927
Irrigon, OR 98744
Tel: (541)922-4893
E-Mail: secretary@i-n-b-a.org
Web Site: www.i-n-b-a.org
Members: 400 individuals
Annual Budget: under $10,000
Secretary-Treasurer: Michelle Osborne
E-Mail: secretary@i-n-b-a.org

Historical Note

Monitors and proposes revisions to the breed standard, awards outstanding animals and breeders, and provides a forum for breeders to learn about, advertise, and promote their breed. Has no paid officers or full-time staff. Membership: $10/year (domestic); $14/year (foreign).

Meetings/Conferences:
Annual Meetings: October/November

Publications:
Nubian Newsletter. q.

International Nurses Society on Addictions *(1974)*
P.O. Box 10752
Raleigh, NC 27605
Tel: (919)821-1292 *Fax:* (919)833-5743
E-Mail: jim@recanc.com
Web Site: www.intnsa.org
Members: 700 individuals
Staff: 4
Annual Budget: $100-250,000
Executive Director: Jim Scarborough
E-Mail: jim@recanc.com

Historical Note

Formerly (1983) National Nurses Society on Alcoholism; assumed its current name in 2000. A national specialty nursing organization for nurses whose field of practice is substance abuse/addictions nursing, including clinicians, educators, managers and researchers. Incorporated the Drug and Alcohol Nursing Association. Membership: $120/year (individual).

Meetings/Conferences:
Annual Meetings: Fall

Publications:
Journal of Addictions Nursing. q. adv.
Int NSA Today Newsletter. q. adv.

International Oceanic Society *(1978)*
1018 Harmon Cove Towers
Secaucus, NJ 07094
Tel: (201)392-3438
E-Mail: PGuibor@aol.com
Members: 250 individuals
Staff: 3
Annual Budget: $100-250,000
Executive Director: Pierre Guibor, M.D.

Historical Note

Formerly (1978) International Oculoplastic Society; assumed current name in 2004. IOS is an interspecialty diving surgical society with an international constituency. Members are doctors interested in diving. Membership: $1,000/year (individual).

Meetings/Conferences:
Annual Meetings: Spring

Publications:
IOS Journal. q.
Newsletter. m. adv.

International Oil Mill Superintendents Association *(1894)*
940 Mesa Vista Dr.
Crowley, TX 76036
Tel: (334)491-1754 *Fax:* (334)491-3109
E-Mail: general@iomsa.org
Web Site: www.iomsa.org
Members: 500 individuals
Staff: 1
Annual Budget: $25-50,000
Secretary-Treasurer: Linda Paukert
E-Mail: lmpaukert@aol.com

Historical Note

Founded in Waco, Texas on May 2, 1894 as the Oil Mill Superintendents Association of Texas. Several years later the name was changed to the National Oil Mill Superintendents Association to reflect the fact that the membership included individuals from other cotton-growing states. In the 1950s the present name was assumed because the membership had come to include individuals from other countries growing edible oil seeds. Absorbed the International Oil Seed Superintendents Association and the Tri-States Oil Mill Superintendents Association in 1996. Membership: $100/year (domestic); $100/year (foreign).

Meetings/Conferences:
Annual Meetings: June

Publications:
Oil Mill Gazetteer. m. adv.

International Oil Scouts Association *(1924)*
P.O. Box 940310
Houston, TX 77094
Web Site: www.oilscouts.org
Members: 100 individuals
Annual Budget: under $10,000
Treasurer: John Reedy

Historical Note

Formerly (1960) National Oil Scouts and Landmen's Association. Federation of regional associations of oil scouts and landmen. Records production in oil and gas fields and compiles exploratory well listings, in the U.S., Canada, and abroad. has no paid officers or full-time staff. Membership: $75/year.

Meetings/Conferences:
Annual Meetings: June

Publications:
IOSA Newsletter. q.
Directory. a. adv.
Magazine. a. adv.
Yearbook. semi-a.

International Order of the Golden Rule *(1928)*
P.O. Box 28689
St. Louis, MO 43146-1189
Toll Free: (800)637 - 8030
Web Site: www.ogr.org
Staff: 18
Executive Director: William A. Edmunds
Director, Education: Mark B. Allen

Director, Communications: Janet J. Protzel
E-Mail: jprotzel@ogr.org
Director, Meetings and Travel: Kathryn J. Thomas

Historical Note
Incorporated as a 501 (c)(3) not-for-profit organization. OGR members are locally- and family-owned funeral homes. OGR promotes the image of the independent funeral home owner/operator, and provides membership services through its for-profit subsidiary, Golden Services Group. Membership: varies, average $1,500/year.

Publications:
The Independent. bi-m. adv.

International Organization for the Education of the Hearing Impaired *(1967)*

Historical Note
A section of the Alexander Graham Bell Association for the Deaf.

International Organization of Citrus Virologists *(1959)*

Historical Note
Address unknown in 2006.

International Organization of Masters, Mates and Pilots *(1887)*

700 Maritime Blvd.
Linthicum Heights, MD 21090
Tel: (410)850-8700 *Fax:* (410)850-0973
E-Mail: iommp@bridgedeck.org
Web Site: www.bridgedeck.org
Members: 6800 individuals
Staff: 50
Annual Budget: $2-5,000,000
President: Capt. Timothy A. Brown
E-Mail: president@bridgedeck.org
International Secretary-Treasurer: Glen P. Banks
E-Mail: sec-treas@bridgedeck.org
International Comptroller: John A. Gorman
E-Mail: jgorman@bridgedeck.org
Executive Director, MITAGS: Glen Paine
E-Mail: gpaine@mitags.org
Director, Communications: Lisa Rosenthal
International Counsel: John Singleton
E-Mail: jsingleton@bridgedeck.org

Historical Note
Affiliated with the AFL-CIO. Supports the Maritime Institute for Research and Industrial Development.

Publications:
Master, Mate & Pilot. 6/year.
Wheelhouse Weekly email. w.

International Oxygen Manufacturers Association *(1943)*

1255 23rd St. NW
Suite 200
Washington, DC 20037-1174
Tel: (202)521-9300 *Fax:* (202)833-3636
E-Mail: ioma@iomaweb.org
Web Site: www.iomaweb.org
Members: 140 companies
Staff: 2
Annual Budget: $250-500,000
Executive Director: David A. Saunders

Historical Note
IOMA members are the manufacturers of all of the industrial and medical gases (oxygen, nitrogen, argon, acetylene, carbon dioxide, hydrogen, etc.) or of equipment and supplies (plants, cylinders, valves, tanks, etc.) used by the industrial gas companies.

Meetings/Conferences:
Annual Meetings: Fall/300

International Ozone Association-Pan American Group Branch *(1976)*

P.O. Box 876
Scottsdale, AZ 85252
Tel: (480)529-3787 *Fax:* (480)361-7725
Web Site: www.int-ozone-assoc.org
Members: 900 individuals
Staff: 2
Annual Budget: $50-100,000
Contact: Ron Caron

Historical Note
Formerly (1978) the International Ozone Institute, Inc., IOA-PAGB represents the interests of environmental and other scientific communities, application engineers, users, manufacturers of ozone generation and contacting equipment, ozone analyzers, monitors and control equipment, as well as the interests of various supporting industries and professions. International Coordinating office located in Lille, France. Membership: $80/year (individual), $180-600/year (organization).

Meetings/Conferences:
Biennial World Congress: Odd years

Publications:
Ozone Science and Engineering: The Journal of IOA. bi-m. adv.
OZONews. bi-m. adv.

International Packaged Ice Association *(1917)*

P.O. Box 1199
Tampa, FL 33601-1199
Tel: (813)258-1690 *Fax:* (813)251-2783
Toll Free: (800)742 - 0627
Web Site: www.packagedice.com
Members: 225 companies
Staff: 5
Annual Budget: $250-500,000
Executive Director: Jane W. McEwen
E-Mail: jane@packagedice.com

Historical Note
Manufacturers and distributors of ice and their suppliers. Founded as the National Association of Ice Industries, it became the National Ice Association in 1958, Packaged Ice Association in 1980, and assumed its present name in 1998.

Meetings/Conferences:
Annual Meetings: Fall

Publications:
Ice World Journal. a. adv.
Membership Directory. a. adv.

International Paralegal Management Association *(1984)*

P.O. Box 659
Avondale Estates, GA 30002-0659
Tel: (404)292-4762 *Fax:* (404)292-2931
E-Mail: mike@paralegalmanagement.org
Web Site: www.paralegalmanagement.org
Members: 600 individuals
Staff: 3
Annual Budget: $250-500,000
Executive Director: Michael J. Mazur, Jr.

Historical Note
Organized as an outgrowth of a Steering Committee of the Paralegal Manager's Conference, the IPMA is an association of professionals responsible for managerial and administrative duties related to paralegal personnel. Membership: $175/year (regular); $150/year (associate); $1,100/year (sustaining corporate member); $275/year (sustaining individual member).

Meetings/Conferences:
Annual Meetings: Fall
2007 – Phoenix, AZ(Westin Kirkland)/Oct. 10-13
2008 – Boston, MA

Publications:
Paralegal Management. bi-m. adv.
Conference Proceedings. a. adv.
Conference Brochure. a.
Directory of Legal Assistant Managers. a.
Compensation and Benefit Survey. a. adv.

International Parking Institute *(1962)*

P.O. Box 7167
Fredericksburg, VA 22404-7167
Tel: (540)371-7535 *Fax:* (540)371-8022
Web Site: www.parking.org
Members: 1300 organizations
Staff: 7
Annual Budget: $1-2,000,000
Executive Director: Kim E. Jackson

Historical Note
Formerly known as the International Municipal Parking Congress and (1995) Institutional and Municipal Parking Congress; until 1962 IPI was a branch of the National League of Cities. Members are cities, colleges, hospitals, airports, port authorities, civic centers, state/federal government agencies, commercial parking operators and others concerned with parking, as well as suppliers and consultants. Membership: $375-545/year.

Meetings/Conferences:
Annual Meetings: Spring/2000

2007 – Tampa, FL(Tampa Convention Center)/May 20-23

Publications:
The Parking Professional. m. adv.
Who's Who in Parking Member Directory. a.
Parking Buyers Guide. a. adv.
Guide to Parking Consultants. bi-a. adv.
Parking 101.
Parking Management: The Next Level.

International Pediatric Nephrology Association *(1971)*

David Geffen School of Medicine at UCLA
10833 Le Conte Ave.
Los Angeles, CA 90095
Tel: (310)206-9295
Web Site: www.ipna-online.org
Members: 1600 individuals
Annual Budget: $500-1,000,000
Treasurer: Isidro B. Salusky

Historical Note
IPNA members are physicians specializing in pediatric kidney disease. Has no paid officers or full-time staff. Membership: $125/year.

Meetings/Conferences:
Triennial Meetings:

Publications:
Pediatric Nephrology Journal. m. adv.
Proceedings. trien.

International Pediatric Transplant Association

17000 Commerce Pkwy., Suite C
Mt. Laurel, NJ 08054
Tel: (856)439-0500 *Fax:* (856)439-0525
E-Mail: ipta@ahint.com
Web Site: www.iptaonline.org
Members: 925
Staff: 3
Annual Budget: $100-250,000
Executive Director: Amy Williams

Meetings/Conferences:
Annual Meetings: Spring
2007 – Cancun, Mexico

Publications:
Pediatric Transplantation. m. adv.

International Perimetric Society *(1974)*

University of Iowa
Dept. of Neurology
Iowa City, IA 52242
Tel: (319)356-8758 *Fax:* (319)356-4505
Web Site: www.perimetry.org
Members: 200 individuals
Annual Budget: $25-50,000
President: Michael Wall, M.D.

Historical Note
Members are ophthamologists and other professionals working in the area of visual field testing.

Meetings/Conferences:
Biennial Meetings: even years

Publications:
Proceedings. bien.

International Pharmaceutical Excipients Council of the Americas *(1991)*

1655 N. Ft. Myer Dr., Suite 700
Arlington, VA 22209
Tel: (703)875-2127 *Fax:* (703)525-5157
E-Mail: info@ipecamericas.org
Web Site: www.ipecamericas.org
Members: 55 companies
Staff: 3
Annual Budget: $500-1,000,000
Secretary-Treasurer: Alan Mercill
E-Mail: ipecamer@aol.com
Director, Membership Services: Kimberly Beals, CAE
E-Mail: ipecamer@aol.com

Historical Note
Members are companies with an interest in the otherwise inert chemicals used as vehicles for

medicines. Membership: $8-20,000/year (full corporate); $1,000/year (associate).

Meetings/Conferences:
Annual Meetings: Fall

Publications:
GMP Auditing Guidance.
Compendial Horomonization Reports. irreg.
Excipient Supplier GMP Assessment Guidance. a.
IPEC - Americas' News. m.
New Equipment Safety Evaluation Guidelines. irreg.
Excipient Master File Guidance.
Signature Change Guidance.

International Phototherapy Association *(1981)*
PhotoTherapy Centre
1300 Richards St., #205
Vancouver, BC V6B 3-G6
Tel: (604)689-9709 *Fax:* (604)633-1505
Web Site: www.phototherapy-centre.com
Members: 225 individuals
Chairperson and Director: Judy Weiser
E-Mail: jweiser@phototherapy-centre.com

Historical Note
IPA members are psychologists, psychiatric nurses, social workers, therapists and other professionals with an interest in the use of still and moving pictures as tools for treatment, personal growth and reconciliation of emotional conflict.

International Physical Fitness Association *(1960)*
415 W. Court St.
Flint, MI 48503
Tel: (810)239-2166 *Fax:* (810)239-9390
Toll Free: (877)520 - 4732
E-Mail: contact@ipfa.us
Web Site: www.ipfa.us/index.html
Members: 2000 fitness centers
Staff: 1
Annual Budget: $10-25,000
President: Jerry Kahn

Historical Note
Formerly (1975) Universal Gym Affiliates. IPFA coordinates reciprocity for its member gyms and clubs, allowing member facilities to offer access to sister fitness clubs worldwide. Membership: $100/year (center).

Meetings/Conferences:
Annual Meetings: Fall

Publications:
Membership Roster. a.

International Piano Guild *(1929)*

Historical Note
A division of the American College of Musicians, which provides administrative support.

International Planetarium Society *(1970)*
P.O. Box 1812
Greenville, NC 27835
Tel: (252)328-9365 *Fax:* (252)328-9371
E-Mail: 102424.1032@compuserve.com
Web Site: www.ips-planetarium.org
Members: 700 individuals
Annual Budget: $50-100,000
Treasurer: Shawn Laatsch

Historical Note
Members are planetarium personnel and suppliers. Until 1976 known as the International Society of Planetarium Educators. Has no paid officers or full-time staff. Membership: $50/year (individual), $200/year (institution).

Meetings/Conferences:
Biennial Meetings: Even years

Publications:
Directory of Worlds Planetariums. bien. adv.
Planetarian. q. adv.

International Plant Propagators Society *(1950)*
2616 25th Ave. NE
PMB 582
Seattle, WA 98105
Tel: (206)543-8602 *Fax:* (206)685-2692
Web Site: www.ipps.org
Members: 2400 individuals
Staff: 1
Annual Budget: $100-250,000
Secretary: John A. Wott
E-Mail: jwott@IPPS.org

Historical Note
IPPS is an educational organization representing members in 40 countries worldwide. Members are professionals in the science of plant propagation. Membership fee varies.

Meetings/Conferences:
Annual Meetings: Regional Meetings Held in 10 Regions. See Web Site.

Publications:
Combined Proceedings. a.

International Plate Printers', Die Stampers' and Engravers' Union of North America *(1893)*
3957 Smoke Rd.
Doylestown, PA 18901-1556
Tel: (215)340-2843
Members: 200 individuals
Staff: 2
Annual Budget: $10-25,000
Secretary-Treasurer: James Kopernick

Historical Note
Organized in Boston in 1892 as the National Steel and Cooper Plate Printers of the United States of America and affiliated with the American Federation of Labor in 1898. Accepted Canadian members in 1901 and became the International Plate Printers and Die Stampers Union of North American in 1921. A merger with the International Steel and Copper Plate Engravers League in 1925 resulted in adoption of the present title. Members are employed in the printing of U.S. and Canadian currency as well as stocks, bonds and foreign currency.

International Platform Association *(1831)*

Historical Note
Address uknown in 2006.

International Precious Metals Institute *(1976)*
5101 N. Twelfth St.
Suite C
Pensacola, FL 32504
Tel: (850)476-1156 *Fax:* (850)476-1548
E-Mail: mail@impi.org
Web Site: www.ipmi.org
Members: 1000 individuals
Staff: 3
Annual Budget: $500-1,000,000
Executive Director: Dr. Larry Manziek
E-Mail: mail@impi.org

Historical Note
Members are miners, refiners, producers and users of precious metals, as well as research scientists and mercantilists. The Institute was formed Nov. 18, 1976, to encourage the exchange of information and technology in the precious metals industry. Cooperates with the American Society for Metals, the American Electroplaters' Society, the American Institute of Mining Engineers, the American Society for Testing and Materials and the Manufacturing Jewelers and Silversmith Association. Membership: $90/year (individual), $750-2,000/year (corporate).

Meetings/Conferences:
Annual Meetings: June/400-450
2007 - Miami, FL(Doral)/June 9-12

Publications:
IPMI Membership Directory. a. adv.
IPMI News and Reviews. q.
Buyers Guide. a. adv.

International Prepress Association

Historical Note
Became IPA - the Association of Graphic Solutions Providers.

International Private Infrastructure Association
5530 Wisconsin Ave., Suite 920
Chevy Chase, MD 20815
Tel: (301)656-9011 *Fax:* (301)657-1051
E-Mail: assocmail@aol.com
Executive Director: Jay McCrensky

Historical Note
Founded as International Private Energy Association; assumed its current name in 2002.

International Professional Groomers *(1988)*
120 Turner
Elk Grove Village, IL 60007
Tel: (847)758-1938 *Fax:* (847)758-8031
Web Site: www.ipgchg.org
Members: 800 individuals
Staff: 5
Annual Budget: under $10,000
President: Judy Kurpiel
E-Mail: jkurpiel@aol.com

Historical Note
IPG represents the professional pet grooming industry, providing continuing education to members and information to the public on the proper care and humane treatment of pets. Awards the designation Certified Master Groomer (CMG) to individuals successfully completing a certification program. Membership: $50/year (individual); $25/year (company); $25/year (concurrent).

Publications:
Newsletter. q. adv.

International Professional Rodeo Association *(1957)*
P.O. Box 83377
Oklahoma City, OK 73148
Web Site: www.iprarodeo.com
Members: 3500 individuals
Staff: 9
Annual Budget: $1-2,000,000
Membership: Pam Queen
E-Mail: pam@iprarodeo.com
Executive Director: Butch Stewart
Editor, Pro Rodeo World: Tom Strickland

Historical Note
Formerly Interstate Rodeo Association (1963) and the International Rodeo Association (1983). Governing body for professional rodeo. Membership: $230/year.

Meetings/Conferences:
Annual Meetings: In conjunction with International Finals Rodeo January

Publications:
Pro Rodeo World. m. adv.
IFR Program. a. adv.

International Psychogeriatric Association *(1981)*
550 Frontage Rd., Suite 3759
Northfield, IL 60093
Tel: (847)501-3310 *Fax:* (847)501-3317
E-Mail: ipa@ipa-online.org
Web Site: www.ipa-online.org
Members: 1400 individuals
Staff: 4
Annual Budget: $250-500,000
Executive Director: Susan M. Oster, CAE

Historical Note
Members are health care professionals and academics with an interest in developments in mental health care related to the elderly. Membership: $110 for 1 year, $200 for 2 years (individual); $225/year (organization/company).

Meetings/Conferences:
Annual Meetings: Summer
2007 - Osaka, Japan/Oct. 14-18/1500
2009 - Montreal, Canada/Oct. 1-5/1500

Publications:
IPA Bulletin. q.
International Psychogeriatrics. q.

International Psychohistorical Association *(1976)*
266 Monroe Ave.
Wyckhoff, NJ 07481-1951
Web Site: www.psychohistory.us/
Members: 250 individuals
Staff: 1
Annual Budget: $10-25,000
Secretary: Henry W. Lawton
E-Mail: hwlipa@aol.com

Historical Note
Membership is open to scholars from all disciplines who are interested in advancing the study and practice of psychohistory. Membership: $25/year; $1,000/lifetime.

Publications:
Psychohistorical Bibliography.
Psychohistory News. q. adv.

Membership Directory. a.
Convention Directory. a.

International Public Management Association for Human Resources *(1906)*
1617 Duke St.
Alexandria, VA 22314
Tel: (703)549-7100 *Fax:* (703)684-0948
Toll Free: (800)220 - 4762
E-Mail: ipma@ipma-hr.org
Web Site: www.ipma-hr.org
Members: 7000 individuals, 1300 agencies
Staff: 20
Annual Budget: $2-5,000,000
Executive Director: Neil E. Reichenberg, CAE
Director, Membership and Communication: Joe Grimes
Chief Operating Officer: Sima Hassassian
Director, Professional Development: Carrie Hoover
Director, Government Affairs: Tina Ott-Chiappetta

Historical Note
Formerly (1906) Civil Service Assembly of the United States and Canada; (1957) Public Personnel Association; then (1973) consolidated with Society for Personnel Administration to form International Personnel Management Association. Assumed its current name in 2003. Membership: $145/year (individual); corporate membership fee varies.

Meetings/Conferences:
Annual Meetings: Fall/700
2007 – Chicago, IL(Marriott Downtown)/Sept. 29-Oct. 3

Publications:
IPMA News. m. adv.
Public Personnel Management. q. adv.
Agency Issues. bi-w.

International Public Relations Association - U.S. Section *(1955)*
University of South Alabama, UCOM 1127
Mobile, AL 36688-0002
Tel: (251)380-2813 *Fax:* (251)380-2850
E-Mail: secretariat@ipra.org
Web Site: www.ipra.org
Members: 700 individuals
Staff: 3
Annual Budget: $500-1,000,000
President: Don K. Wright

Historical Note
IPRA members are senior public relations professionals. International headquarters is in London, England. Membership: GBP 150/year (individual).

Publications:
IPRA Gold Papers. trien. adv.
IPRA Members Register. a. adv.
IPRA News. q. adv.
Front Line 21 Review. q. adv.

International Radio and Television Society *(1939)*
420 Lexington Ave., Suite 1601
New York, NY 10170
Tel: (212)867-6650 *Fax:* (212)867-6653
Web Site: www.irts.org
Members: 1000 individuals
Staff: 6
Annual Budget: $1-2,000,000
President: Joyce M. Tudryn
Director, Member Programs and Development: Jim Cronin
Academic Programs: Amy Peloso

Historical Note
Formerly (1962) Radio and Television Executives Society. Originally formed by a merger in 1952 of the Radio Executives Club (1939) and the American Television Society (1940). Members are professionals in radio, television, cable, advertising, and related areas, as well as interested members of the general public. IRTS sponsors conventions and educational programs for college broadcasters. Membership: $50/year.

Publications:
Gold Medal Annual. a. adv.
Yearbook and Directory. a. adv.

International Reading Association *(1956)*
800 Barksdale Rd., P.O. Box 8139
Newark, DE 19714-8139
Tel: (302)731-1600 *Fax:* (302)731-1057
Toll Free: (800)336 - 7323
E-Mail: pubinfo@reading.org
Web Site: www.reading.org
Members: 80000 individuals
Staff: 100
Annual Budget: $10-25,000,000
Executive Director: Alan E. Farstrup

Historical Note
Founded January 1, 1956 through a merger of the International Council for the Improvement of Reading Instruction and the National Association for Remedial Teaching. Members are classroom teachers, reading specialists, consultants, administrators, supervisors, college teachers, researchers, psychologists, and librarians. Promotes the study of reading techniques, teaching methods, and literacy worldwide. Has an annual budget of approximately $15 million. Membership: $36/year, minimum (individual member; special rates available for students).

Meetings/Conferences:
Annual Meetings: April/May
2007 – Toronto, ON, Canada/May 13-17
2008 – Atlanta, GA/May 4-8
2009 – Phoenix, AZ/Feb. 21-25
2009 – Minneapolis, MN/May 2-7
2010 – New Orleans, LA/Apr. 18-22
2011 – Orlando, FL/May 8-12
2012 – Minneapolis, MN/May 4-8

Publications:
Reading Teacher. 8/year. adv.
Reading Online.
Journal of Adolescent & Adult Literacy. 8/year. adv.
Lectura y Vida. 4/year.
Reading Research Quarterly. 4/year.

International Real Estate Federation - American Chapter *(1951)*
2000 N. 15th St., Suite 101
Arlington, VA 22201
Tel: (703)524-4279 *Fax:* (703)991-6256
E-Mail: info@fiabci-usa.com
Web Site: www.fiabci-usa.com
Members: 500 individuals
Staff: 1
Annual Budget: $100-250,000
Secretary General: Susan S. Newman
E-Mail: info@fiabci-usa.com

Historical Note
Members are real estate professionals and those in related fields. U.S. chapter of FIABCI, headquartered in Paris, with 6,000 members in 56 countries worldwide. Membership: $435-485/year (individual); $2,000/year (national associations); $3,500/year (company).

Meetings/Conferences:
Semi-Annual:

Publications:
FIABCI Directory. a. adv.
Newsletter. bi-a.

International Real Estate Institute *(1975)*
1224 N. Nokomis Ave. NE
Alexandria, MN 56308
Tel: (320)763-4648 *Fax:* (320)763-9290
E-Mail: irei@iami.org
Web Site: www.iami.org/irei
Members: 5000 individuals
Staff: 16
Annual Budget: $1-2,000,000
Executive Director: Robert G. Johnson

Historical Note
Formerly (1984) the International Institute of Valuers. The primary objective of IREI is to provide professional recognition and a method to easily network with real estate professionals both internationally as well as within the United States. The Institute is also committed to providing the most current international real estate information possible through various publications and conferences. Members represent the area of real estate valuation, finance investment and development and management on an international level. Membership: $195/year (individual); $1,200/year (corporate); $150/year (associate).

Meetings/Conferences:
Annual Meetings: May

Publications:
The International Property Report.
Registry of Members. a.
International Real Estate Journal. semi-a. adv.
The International Real Estate Newsletter. q. adv.

International Reciprocal Trade Association *(1979)*
140 Metro Park Dr.
Rochester, NY 14623
Tel: (585)424-2940 *Fax:* (585)424-2964
Web Site: www.irta.com
Members: 180 organizations
Staff: 2
Annual Budget: $100-250,000
Executive Director: Krista Vardabash

Historical Note
Formerly (1994) International Association of Trade Exchanges. Members are organizations serving as clearinghouses for the barter exchange of goods and services among business firms, or who act as principals or intermediaries in the barter exchange of goods and services nationally and internationally. Formed to foster the common interests of the commercial barter industry worldwide. Supports the Barter Political Action Committee (BARTERPAC). Membership: $450-3,500/year.

Meetings/Conferences:
Semi-Annual Meetings: *Spring and Fall*

Publications:
IRTA Update. m.
The Trader. irreg.

International Recording Media Association *(1970)*
182 Nassau St., Suite 204
Princeton, NJ 08542-7005
Tel: (609)279-1700 *Fax:* (609)279-1999
E-Mail: info@recordingmedia.org
Web Site: www.recordingmedia.org
Members: 450 companies
Staff: 5
Annual Budget: $1-2,000,000
Executive Director: Guy Finley
President: Charles Van Horn
Director, Communications: Michael Bevel
Executive Director: Guy Finley
Director, Finance and Administration: Gail Muller

Historical Note
Founded as the International Tape Association, it became (1981) the International Tape/Disc Association and then (1995) ITA - International Association of Magnetic and Optical Recording Manufacturers before assuming current name. Members are manufacturers of optical/laser, blank computer, audio and video, and recording media and equipment. Membership: Based on volume, $480-6,000/year (company).

Meetings/Conferences:
Annual Meetings: March

International Refrigerated Transportation Association *(1994)*
1500 King St.
Alexandria, VA 22314
Tel: (703)373-4300 *Fax:* (703)373-4301
E-Mail: email@irta.org
Web Site: www.irta.org
Members: 200 individuals and companies
Staff: 4
Annual Budget: $50-100,000
President and Chief Executive Officer: J. William Hudson

Historical Note
Membership consists of executives in the refrigerated transportation industry. Includes importers, exporters, manufacturers, suppliers, attorneys, transportation providers, claims agents, ports, warehouses, receivers and consignees.

Meetings/Conferences:
Annual Meetings: Spring
2007 – Phoenix, AZ(Sheraton Wild Horse Pass)/Apr. 21-26
2008 – Marco Island, FL(Marco Island Marriott)/Apr. 19-24

2009 - San Antonio, TX(Westin La Cantera)/Apr. 18-23

Publications:
The IRTA Report. q. adv.

International Regional Magazine Association *(1960)*
P.O. Box 53
Georgetown, TX 78627-0053
Tel: (512)819-9500
Web Site: www.regionalmagazines.org
Members: 41 publications
Staff: 1
Annual Budget: $50-100,000
Executive Director: Herman Kelly

Historical Note
Formerly (1994) Regional Publishers Association. Founded to foster the interchange of publishing knowledge among regional magazines. IRMA provides a means by which members can assist one another in solving problems unique to regional publishing. In most cases, members are not competing for the same markets, so they discuss matters frankly and trade information freely. IRMA members are publishers of state and regional, as opposed to municipal, magazines. Membership: $450/year.

Publications:
E -Signature. 6/year.
Directory. a.

International Reprographic Association *(1927)*
401 N. Michigan Ave.
Chicago, IL 60611
Tel: (312)245-1026 *Fax:* (312)527-6705
Toll Free: (800)833 - 4742
E-Mail: info@irga.com
Web Site: www.irga.com
Members: 500 companies
Staff: 7
Annual Budget: $1-2,000,000
Executive Director: Steve Bova, CAE
E-Mail: info@irga.com

Historical Note
Membership consists of digital printing companies and reprographics equipment manufacturers and suppliers. Formerly (until 1973) known as the International Association of Blue Print and Allied Industries and (1973-1980) as the International Reprographic Blueprint Association. Membership: $425-1495/year (based on category and employee count).

Meetings/Conferences:
Annual Meetings: Spring
2007 - Dallas, TX(Gaylord Texan)/May 9-11

Publications:
Repro Report. bi-m. adv.
IRgA News Digest. m. adv.

International Research Council of Neuromuscular Disorders *(1982)*
1600 Sheridan Dr.
Lancaster, OH 43130
Tel: (740)687-5002 *Fax:* (740)687-5003
Members: 362 individuals
Staff: 2
Annual Budget: $100-250,000
Executive Director: James R. Grilliot, D.C.

Historical Note
IRCND members are health professionals with an interest in diseases of the neuromuscular system.

Publications:
Newsletter. a.

International Right of Way Association *(1934)*
19750 S. Vermont Ave.
Torrance, CA 90502-1144
Tel: (310)538-0233 *Fax:* (310)538-1471
E-Mail: info@irwaonline.org
Web Site: www.irwaonline.org
Members: 10000 individuals
Staff: 21
Annual Budget: $1-2,000,000
Executive Vice President: Dennis Stork
E-Mail: stork@irwaonline.org
Manager, Human Resources and Executive Assistant: Linda Alexander
Vice President, Member Services and Administration: Armando Apodaca, CAE
E-Mail: apodaca@irwaonline.org
Chief Financial Officer: Fred Nasri

Historical Note
Members are individuals responsible for acquiring land over which to run power and telephone lines, pipelines, and roads. Founded as the Southern California Right of Way Association. Formerly (1980) known as the American Right of Way Association. Membership: $130/year (individual).

Meetings/Conferences:
Annual Meetings: June/1,000
2007 - Sacramento, CA/June 17-20
2008 - Austin, TX/June 22-25
2009 - Indianapolis, IN/June 28-July 1
2010 - Calgary, AB, Canada/June 27-30

Publications:
Right of Way. bi-m. adv.

International Road Federation *(1948)*
500 Montgomery St.
Madison Place, Fifth Floor
Alexandria, VA 22314
Tel: (703)535-1001 *Fax:* (703)535-1007
E-Mail: info@internationalrailroadfederation.org
Members: 750companies&governmentagencies
Staff: 8
Annual Budget: $2-5,000,000
Director General and Chief Executive Officer Washington, D.C. Office: C. Patrick Sankey

Historical Note
An international organization representing road associations in over 120 countries. Provides consulting and administrative services in highways and transportation. Membership: $500-15,000/year (organization).

Publications:
Annual Report. a.
Fellowship Directory. a.
World Highways. bi-m. adv.
Who's Who. a.
Proceedings of World and Regional Meetings.

International Rural Sociology Association *(1976)*
International Program in Agriculture
2120 Fyffe Rd.
Columbus, OH 43210
Tel: (614)292-7252 *Fax:* (614)292-1757
E-Mail: hansen.4@osu.edu
Web Site: www.irsa-world.org/index.html
Members: 6 regional associations
Annual Budget: $25-50,000
Secretary/Treasurer: David O. Hanson
E-Mail: hansen.4@osu.edu

Historical Note
IRSA's member organizations are regional associations representing a total of 1,600 academics and professionals in the sociology of rural populations.

Meetings/Conferences:
Quadrennial Meetings: Summer

Publications:
IRSA Items. a.
Congress Program. quad.
Membership Directory. a.

International Safe Transit Association *(1948)*
1400 Abbott Rd., Suite 160
East Lansing, MI 48823-1900
Tel: (517)333-3437 *Fax:* (517)333-3813
E-Mail: ista@ista.org
Web Site: www.ista.org
Members: 800 companies
Staff: 6
Annual Budget: $250-500,000
Executive Director: Edward Church
E-Mail: echurch@ista.org
Director, Member Services: Meredith Dougherty

Historical Note
Formerly (1974) National Safe Transit Committee, Inc. Members are shippers, carriers, manufacturers, packagers, package designers, and testing laboratories interested in reducing damage to goods in transit. Formerly (1992) the National Safe Transit Association. Formerly (1994) National/International Safe Transit Association. Membership: $525/yr. (company).

Meetings/Conferences:
Annual Meetings: April-May
2007 - Orlando, FL(Coronado Springs)/March 27-30/350

Publications:
Preshipment Testing Newsletter. q. adv.
Proceedings/Projects. a.
Directory. a. adv.

International Safety Equipment Association *(1933)*
1901 N. Moore St., Suite 808
Arlington, VA 22209
Tel: (703)525-1695 *Fax:* (703)528-2148
E-Mail: isea@safetyequipment.org
Web Site: www.safetyequipment.org
Members: 80 companies
Staff: 6
Annual Budget: $1-2,000,000
President: Daniel K. Shipp
Technical Director: Janice Comer Bradley, CSP
Public Affairs Director: Daniel I. Glucksman
Marketing Communications Advisor: Joseph L. Walker

Historical Note
Members manufacture and market all types of apparel, supplies and equipment used for the protection of workers.

Publications:
ISEA Washington Report. m.
Safety Signals Newsletter.
Membership Directory. a.
ISEA Buyers Guide. a.
Protection Update. 4/year.

International Sanitary Supply Association

Historical Note
Became ISSA in 2005.

International Saw and Knife Association *(1965)*
12880 Bel-Red Rd.
Bellevue, WA 98005
Tel: (425)454-7627 *Fax:* (425)454-4274
Toll Free: (800)395 - 1650
E-Mail: mikel@eastsidesaw.com
Web Site: www.iska.org/
Members: 200 companies
Annual Budget: $10-25,000
Secretary: Mike Lindsay
E-Mail: mikel@eastsidesaw.com

Historical Note
Members are companies repairing, selling, manufacturing, or servicing large band and circular saws, paper knives, shear blades, circular slitters, and metal cutting bands. Formerly the National Association of Saw Shops, assumed its present name in 1983. Has no paid officers or full-time staff. Membership: $150-200/year (individual).

Publications:
Newsletter.
Membership List. a.

International Security Management Association *(1982)*
P.O. Box 623
Buffalo, IA 52728
Tel: (563)381-4008 *Fax:* (563)381-4283
E-Mail: isma3@aol.com
Web Site: www.isma.com
Members: 400 individuals
Staff: 2
Annual Budget: $500-1,000,000
Business Manager: Susan Pohlmann
E-Mail: isma3@aol.com

Historical Note
ISMA members are corporate security directors and executives of full service security service firms.

Meetings/Conferences:
Semi-annual Meetings: January and June

Publications:
Newsletters. q.
News Postings. m.
Membership Directory. a.

International Security Officers, Police, and Guards Union *(1937)*
411 Hempstead Ave., Suite 101
West Hempstead, NY 11552-2333
Tel: (718)836-3508
Members: 7000 individuals
Staff: 2
Annual Budget: $50-100,000
President: Frank W. Mancini, Jr.

Historical Note
An independent labor union founded as Independent Watchmen's Association. The present name was assumed around 1981-82. Represents guards and security personnel in all phases of private industry and those employed on the city, state, or federal levels.

Meetings/Conferences:
Annual Meetings: Quinquennial Meetings

International Shooting Coaches Association *(1984)*
17446 S.W. Granada Dr.
Beaverton, OR 97007
Tel: (503)642-5873 *Fax:* (503)649-5182
E-Mail: bawilli@attglobal.net
Members: 200 individuals
Editor, ISCA Newsletter: Don Williams
E-Mail: bawilli@attglobal.net

Historical Note
Founded as American Shooting Coaches Association; assumed its current name in 1985. Members are archery, pistol, rifle and shotgun coaches. Has no paid officers or full-time staff. Membership fee varies, based on certification and national standing.

Publications:
On Target Newsletter. q.

International Sign Association *(1944)*
707 N. Saint Asaph St.
Alexandria, VA 22314
Tel: (703)836-4012 *Fax:* (703)836-8353
Toll Free: (888)672 - 7446
Web Site: www.signs.org
Members: 2200 manufacturers
Staff: 21
Annual Budget: $2-5,000,000
President and Chief Executive Officer: Lori M. Anderson
Director, Technical and Regulatory Affairs: Bill Dundas
Director, Government Relations: David Hickey
Senior Vice President, Tradeshows: K. Brian McNamara
E-Mail: brian.mcnamara@signs.org
Director, Communications and Marketing: Janay Rickwalder
Vice President, Finance and Administration: Bill Winslow

Historical Note
Formerly (1995) National Electric Sign Association, ISA members are manufacturers of all types of on-premise signs and the materials for them. They are also suppliers to the industry. Membership fee varies, based on company size.

Meetings/Conferences:
Annual Meetings: Spring/15-17,000

Publications:
ISA Directory. a. adv.

International Silk Association *(1950)*
c/o Soritex
One Madison St.
East Rutherford, NJ 07073
Tel: (973)472-4200 *Fax:* (973)472-0222
Members: 25 silk converters and importers
Staff: 1
Annual Budget: $10-25,000
President: William Katterman

Historical Note
North American arm of the international organization headquartered in Lyon, France.

Meetings/Conferences:
Annual Meetings: Fall

International Silo Association *(1907)*
332 Brookview Dr.
Luxemburg, WI 54217
Tel: (920)265-6235
E-Mail: info@silo.org
Web Site: www.silo.org
Members: 14 companies
Staff: 1
Annual Budget: $25-50,000
Executive Officer: Joe Shefchik
E-Mail: info@silo.org

Historical Note
Formerly (1956) the National Association of Silo Manufacturers and (1990) the Feed Automation Association. Members manufacture crop storage facilities.

Meetings/Conferences:
Annual Meetings: January/100

Publications:
Newsletter. q.

International Sleep Products Association *(1915)*
501 Wythe St.
Alexandria, VA 22314-1917
Tel: (703)683-8371 *Fax:* (703)683-4503
E-Mail: info@sleepproducts.org
Web Site: www.sleepproducts.org
Members: 600 companies
Staff: 21
Annual Budget: $5-10,000,000
President: Richard M. Doyle
Vice President and Chief Financial Officer: Robert Bobowski, CPA
Associate, Government Relations: David Bright
Director, Marketing and Member Services: Deb Chapman
Director, Meetings and Trade Show Management: Catherine Lyons
Vice President, Research and Statistics: Patricia Martin
Vice President, Communications: Nancy Shark
Vice President, Marketing and Member Services: Debi Sutton
Executive Vice President and General Counsel: Ryan Trainer

Historical Note
Formerly (1986) National Association of Bedding Manufacturers. Affiliate organizations include the Better Sleep Council and the Sleep Products Safety Council.

Meetings/Conferences:
Biennial Meetings: Spring
2008 – Baltimore, MD/March 12-15

Publications:
Sleep Savvy. 6/year. adv.
BEDtimes. m. adv.

International Slurry Surfacing Association *(1962)*
Three Church Circle, PMB 250
Annapolis, MD 21401
Tel: (410)267-0023 *Fax:* (410)267-7546
Web Site: www.slurry.org
Members: 200 companies
Staff: 3
Annual Budget: $250-500,000
Executive Director: Michael R. Krissoff

Historical Note
Formerly known as the International Slurry Seal Association (1990). Members are contractors and suppliers of asphalt slurry seal. Provides information, technical assistance, and networking opportunities. Membership: $350/year (associate), $1,700/year (active); $75/year (government); $1,100/year (international).

Publications:
ISSA Report. bi-m.
Membership Directory. a.
Convention Proceedings. a.

International Snowmobile Manufacturers Association *(1995)*
1640 Haslett Rd., Suite 170
Haslett, MI 48840
Tel: (517)339-7788 *Fax:* (517)339-7798
Web Site: www.snowmobile.org/
Members: 4 manufacturers
Staff: 2
Annual Budget: $500-1,000,000
President: Edward J. Klim

Historical Note
Formerly (1995) the International Snowmobile Industry Association. Organized and incorporated in Michigan. ISMA serves the interests of the snowmobile manufacturing industry as well as recreational snowmobiling.

International Society for Adolescent Psychiatry & Pyschology *(1985)*
223 Sunset Blvd.
Bronx, NY 10473
Web Site: www.isap-web.org
Members: 500 individuals
Staff: 1
Annual Budget: $10-25,000
Administrative Director: Rosalie Landy
E-Mail: rlandy7257@aol.com

Historical Note
ISAP members are psychiatrists, pyschologists, and allied professionals specializing in adolescence. Membership: $120/year (individual).

Meetings/Conferences:
Quadrennial Meetings:: usually Summer (2007)
2007 – Montreal, QC, Canada(Fairmont Queen Elizabeth Hotel)/July 4-7

Publications:
ISAPP Newsletter (online). semi-a.

International Society for Analytical Cytology
60 Revere Dr., Suite 500
Northbrook, IL 60062
Tel: (847)205-4722 *Fax:* (847)480-9282
E-Mail: isac@isac-net.org
Web Site: www.isac-net.org
Members: 1900 individuals
Staff: 2
Annual Budget: $500-1,000,000
Executive Director: Richard Koepke

Historical Note
Members are scientists interested in the study of the cell. Membership: $110/year (individual).

Publications:
Communications in Clinical Cytometry. bi-m. adv.
Cytometry. m. adv.

International Society for Antiviral Research *(1987)*
2025 M St. NW, Suite 800
Washington, DC 20036
Tel: (202)973-8790 *Fax:* (202)331-0111
E-Mail: isar@courtesyassoc.com
Web Site: www.isar-icar.com
Members: 981
Manager, Meetings and Events: Amy Kirson

Historical Note
ISAR is an interdisciplinary organization supporting investigators involved in basic, applied, and clinical research in the field of antiviral chemotherapy.

Meetings/Conferences:
Annual: 350
2007 – Palm Springs, CA(Westin Mission Hills)/Apr. 29-May 3

International Society for Chronobiology *(1937)*
University of Texas, Medical Branch
Dept. of Anatomy and Neurosciences
Galveston, TX 77555-1069
Tel: (409)772-1294 *Fax:* (409)762-9382
Members: 300 individuals
Annual Budget: $10-25,000
Secretary-Treasurer: Norma H. Rubin, Ph.D.

Historical Note
Founded at Ronneby, Sweden as Societas pro Studio Rhythmi Biologici, it assumed its present name in 1971. Seeks to further the development of studies on temporal parameters of biological variables (chronobiologic variation) and to pursue related scientific and educational purposes; to encourage the development of centers of chronobiological research; and to work toward the establishment of chronobiology as an academic discipline in its own right. Its principal activity is sponsorship of international conferences. Has no paid officers or full-time staff. Membership: $82/year.

Publications:
Chronobiology International. q. adv.

International Society for Clinical Densitometry *(1993)*
342 N. Main St.
West Hartford, CT 06117
Tel: (860)586-7563 *Fax:* (860)586-7550

E-Mail: iscd@iscd.org
Web Site: www.iscd.org
Members: 5600 individuals
Staff: 8
Annual Budget: $2-5,000,000
Executive Director: M. Suzanne C. Berry, CAE, MBA
Associate Director: Martin Rotblatt, CAE

Meetings/Conferences:
2007 – Tampa, FL(Marriott Waterside)/March 14-17

Publications:
Journal of Clinical Densitometry. q. adv.
SCAN Newsletter. q.

International Society for Developmental Psychobiology *(1967)*
College of William and Mary, Psychology Dept.
229 Millington Hall
Williamsburg, VA 23187
Tel: (757)221-3894
E-Mail: phunt@wm.edu
Web Site: www.isdp.org
Members: 300 individuals
Annual Budget: $10-25,000
Secretary: Pamela S. Hunt
E-Mail: phunt@wm.edu

Historical Note
Formed to promote research into the relationship between behavioral and biological aspects of the developing organism at all levels of organization; membership open to any person engaged in the scientific study of human or animal development and holding a doctorate degree. Has no paid officers or full-time staff. Membership: fees vary.

Publications:
Developmental Psychobiology Journal. bi-m. adv.
Newsletter. 3/year. adv.
Membership Directory. a. adv.

International Society for Ecological Economics *(1989)*
P.O. Box 44194
West Allis, WI 53214
Tel: (414)453-0030 *Fax:* (877)230-5110
E-Mail: secretariat@ecoeco.org
Web Site: www.ecoeco.org/
Members: 1000 individuals
Staff: 1
Annual Budget: $100-250,000

Historical Note
Members are researchers, academics, and other professionals who study the impact of economic models and policies on the environment. Membership: $15-130/year.

Meetings/Conferences:
Annual Meetings: Summer or Fall

Publications:
Ecological Economics Journal. m.

International Society for Ecological Modelling-North American Chapter *(1983)*
PMB 255, 550 M Ritchie Highway
Severna Park, MD 21146
E-Mail: dmauriello@isemna.org
Web Site: www.isemna.org
Members: 150 individuals
Annual Budget: under $10,000
Treasurer: David Mauriello

Historical Note
The International Society for Ecological Modelling promotes the international exchange of general knowledge, ideas and scientific results in the area of the application of systems analysis and simulation to ecology, environmental science and natural resource management using mathematical and computer modelling of ecological systems. Has no paid officers or full-time staff. Membership: $10/year (student); $20/year (regular); $186/year (student and ecological modelling); $206/year (regular and ecological modelling).

Meetings/Conferences:
Annual Meetings: August

Publications:
ECOMOD Newsletter. q.

International Society for Educational Planning *(1970)*
Bacon Hall, Suite 312-J
SUNY-Buffalo, 1300 Elmwood Ave.
Buffalo, NY 14222-1095
Tel: (716)878-5028 *Fax:* (716)878-5833
Web Site: www.isep.info/
Members: 350 individuals
Annual Budget: under $10,000
Journal Editor: P. Rudy Mattai

Historical Note
Members are school administrators and school district executives. Has no paid officers or full-time staff.

Publications:
Educational Planning. q.

International Society for Experimental Hematology *(1972)*
2025 M St. NW, Suite 800
Washington, DC 20036-3309
Tel: (202)367-1183 *Fax:* (202)367-2183
E-Mail: iseh@dc.sba.com
Web Site: www.iseh.org
Members: 1400 individuals
Staff: 1
Annual Budget: $500-1,000,000
Executive Director: Patrice McKenney

Historical Note
ISEH promotes the scientific knowledge and clinical application of basic hematology and immunology through research, publications, and other activities. Incorporated in Texas in 1972. Membership: $130/year (full member); $26/year (associate); $5,000/year (corporate).

Meetings/Conferences:
Annual Meetings: Summer

Publications:
Experimental Hematolgy. 13/year. adv.

International Society for General Semantics *(1943)*
2260 College Ave.
Ft. Worth, TX 76110
Tel: (817)922-9950 *Fax:* (817)922-9903
E-Mail: igs@time-binding.org
Web Site: www.time-binding.org
Members: 2000 individuals
Staff: 2
Annual Budget: $100-250,000
Executive Director: Steve Stockdale

Historical Note
Members are educators, trainers, writers and scientists interested in how language shapes thought, behavior and communication with others. The Society stimulates and sponsors research in colleges and universities and other institutions through the publication of papers, articles, and books. Membership: $40/year.

Meetings/Conferences:
Annual Meetings: One every 2-3 years

Publications:
ETC: A Review of General Semantics. q. adv.
Time-Bindings.
The General Semantics Bulletin. a.

International Society for Heart and Lung Transplantation *(1981)*
14673 Midway Road, Suite 200
Addison, TX 75001
Tel: (972)490-9495 *Fax:* (972)490-9499
E-Mail: ishlt@ishlt.org
Web Site: www.ishlt.org
Members: 2250 individuals
Staff: 4
Annual Budget: $1-2,000,000
Executive Director: Amanda W. Rowe
E-Mail: amanda.rowe@ishlt.org
Director, Meetings: Lisa Edwards
Director, Membership: Phyllis Glenn

Historical Note
Formerly (1991) International Society for Heart Transplantation. Encourages and stimulates discussion of problems of interest and concern in the field of heart and lung transplantation, and promotes educational opportunities for professionals in the field. Membership: $250/year (individual).

Meetings/Conferences:
Annual Meetings: Spring

Publications:
Journal of Heart and Lung Transplantation. m. adv.

International Society for Infectious Diseases *(1986)*
181 Longwood Ave.
Boston, MA 02115
Tel: (617)277-0551 *Fax:* (617)731-1541
E-Mail: info@isid.org
Web Site: www.isid.org
Members: 30000 individuals
Staff: 5
Executive Director: Norman R. Stein
E-Mail: info@isid.org

Publications:
International Journal of Infectious Diseases. q.

International Society for Magnetic Resonance in Medicine *(1994)*
2118 Milvia, Suite 201
Berkeley, CA 94704
Tel: (510)841-1899 *Fax:* (510)841-2340
E-Mail: info@ismrm.org
Web Site: www.ismrm.org
Members: 6,200 individuals
Staff: 13
Annual Budget: $2-5,000,000
Executive Director: Roberta Kravitz
Accounting: Mariam Barzin
Education Coordinator: Tamara Bell
E-Mail: tamara@ismrm.org
Director, Membership: Anne DeLemos
Director, Education: Robert Goldstein
E-Mail: bob@ismrm.org
Membership and Study Group Coordinator: Kristina King
Director, Electronic Communications: Saly Moran
Associate Executive Director: Jennifer Olson
E-Mail: jennifer@ismrm.org
Director, Meetings: Katie Simmons
Publications Coordinator: Sara Vasquez
E-Mail: sara@ismrm.org

Historical Note
Formed as a merger of the Society for Magnetic Resonance Imaging and the Society of Magnetic Resonance in Medicine in 1994. Name changed from Society of Magnetic Resonance to International Society for Magnetic Resonance in Medicine in 1996. Membership consists of physicians and scientists promoting the applications of magnetic resonance techniques to medicine and biology. Membership: $245/yr (full member), $80/yr (technologist member) and $30/yr (student member, associate member and student technologist).

Meetings/Conferences:
Annual Meetings: April-May
2007 – Berlin, Germany(ICC Berlin)/May 19-25/5500

Publications:
Journal of Magnetic Resonance Imaging. m. adv.
MR Pulse Newletter. 3/year.
Proceedings of the Scientific Meeting. y.
Magnetic Resonance in Medicine. m. adv.

International Society for Minimally-Invasive Cardiac Surgery *(1997)*
900 Cummings Ctr., Suite 221-U
Beverly, MA 01915
Tel: (978)927-8330 *Fax:* (978)524-8890
E-Mail: ismics@prri.com
Web Site: www.ismics.org
Staff: 4
Executive Director: Aurelie M. Alger
E-Mail: aalger@prri.com
Administrator: Lindsay Rappa
Manager, Meeting: Pamela Wilson

Meetings/Conferences:
Annual Meetings: Summer

Publications:
Heart Surgery Forum. 4/yr. adv.

International Society for Molecular Plant Microbe Interactions *(1990)*

3340 Pilot Knob Rd.
St. Paul, MN 55121
Tel: (651)454-7250 *Fax:* (651)454-0766
E-Mail: ismpmi@scisoc.org
Web Site: www.ismpinet.org
Members: 400 individuals
Staff Contact: Amy Hope

Historical Note
Membership: $45/year (individual); $30/year (post-doc); $15/year (student).

Publications:
Molecular Plant-Microbe Interactions Journal. m. adv.

International Society for Performance Improvement *(1962)*
1400 Spring St., Suite 260
Silver Spring, MD 20910
Tel: (301)587-8570 *Fax:* (301)587-8573
E-Mail: info@ispi.org
Web Site: www.ispi.org
Members: 10000 individuals
Staff: 12
Annual Budget: $2-5,000,000
Executive Director: Richard D. Battaglia, CAE

Historical Note
Formerly (1973) National Society for Programmed Instruction and (1995) National Society for Performance and Instruction. ISPI is dedicated to increasing performance in the workplace through the application of performance technologies. ISPI members include performance technologists, training directors, human resource managers, instructional technologists, human factors practitioners and organizational development consultants working in a variety of settings including business, industry, universities, government agencies, health services, banks and the armed forces. ISPI has 60 chapters located throughout the world. Membership: $145/year (active member); $60/yr (student); $60/yr (retired).

Meetings/Conferences:
Annual Meetings: Spring

Publications:
Performance Improvement Journal. 10/year. adv.
Performance Improvement Quarterly. q.

International Society for Pharmaceutical Engineering *(1980)*
3109 W. Dr. Martin Luther King Jr. Blvd., Suite 250
Tampa, FL 33607
Tel: (813)960-2105 *Fax:* (813)264-2816
E-Mail: customerservice@ispe.org
Web Site: www.ispe.org
Members: 23000 individuals
Staff: 50
Annual Budget: $2-5,000,000
President and Chief Executive Officer: Robert Best
Director, Event Operations: Kindra Bess
Director, Continuing Education: Donna Clark
Director, Customer Services: Christian De Sousa
Director, Int'l Sales: Dave Hall
Editor and Director, Publications: Gloria Hall
Executive Vice President and Chief Financial Officer: Susan Humphreys Klein
Director, Training: Alicia Montes
Director, Professional Certification: Jerry Roth, PE

Historical Note
ISPE is the Society of choice for more than 23,000 pharmaceutical manufacturing professionals from 81 countries. ISPE aims to be the catalyst for "Engineering Pharmaceutical Innovation" by providing Members with opportunities to develop technical knowledge, exchange practical experience, and collaborate with global regulatory agencies. Founded in 1980, ISPE has worldwide headquarters in Tampa, Florida, USA; Brussels, Belgium, and an office in Singapore to serve Asia-Pacific. Visit www.ispe.org for additional Society news and information.

Meetings/Conferences:
Annual Meetings: November
2007 – Las Vegas, NV(Caesar's Palace)/Nov. 4-7

Publications:
Pharmaceutical Engineering. bi-m. adv.

International Society for Pharmacoeconomics and Outcomes Research *(1995)*
3100 Princeton Pike, Bldg. 3, Suite E
Lawrenceville, NJ 08648
Tel: (609)279-0773 *Fax:* (609)219-0774
Web Site: www.ispor.org
Members: 3000 individuals
Staff: 8
Annual Budget: $2-5,000,000
Executive Director: Marilyn Dix Smith, Ph.D.

Historical Note
Founded as Association for Pharmacoeconomics and Outcomes Research; absorbed International Society for Economic Evaluation of Medicines and assumed its current name in 1998. Members are researchers who study the relative effectiveness of treatments and procedures, their cost effectiveness and quality of life. Membership: $75/year (individual); $30/year (student).

Meetings/Conferences:
Annual Meetings: Spring
2007 – Crystal City, VA(Marriott)/May 19-23/1500

Publications:
Value In Health. bi-m. adv.
ISPOR Connections. bi-m. adv.

International Society for Pharmacoepidemiology
5272 River Rd., Suite 630
Bethesda, MD 20816
Tel: (301)718-6500 *Fax:* (301)656-0989
E-Mail: ispe@paimgmt.com
Web Site: www.pharmacoepi.org
Members: 500
Annual Budget: $500-1,000,000
Executive Secretary: Mark Epstein, Sc.D.

Historical Note
ISPE members are scientists and researchers using epidemiologic approaches to study the use, effectiveness, value and safety of pharmaceuticals.

Meetings/Conferences:
Annual Meetings: Summer

International Society for Plastination *(1984)*
University of Tennessee
2407 River Dr.
Knoxsville, TN 37996-4500
Tel: (865)974-5822 *Fax:* (423)974-2215
Web Site: www.kfunigraz.ac.at/anawww/plast/index.htm
Members: 200 individuals
Treasurer: Roger Henry, DVM

Historical Note
Members are professionals with an interest in the use of curable polymers in the preparation of biological specimens. Membership: $75/2-years.

Meetings/Conferences:
Biennial Meetings:

Publications:
Journal of the International Society of Plastination. semi-a. adv.

International Society for Preventive Oncology *(1980)*
55 Lake Avenue North, Box 20
Worcester, MA 01655
Tel: (508)856-1822 *Fax:* (508)856-1824
E-Mail: editor@cancerprev.org
Web Site: www.cancerprev.org
Members: 600 individuals
Staff: 6
Annual Budget: $100-250,000
Secretary General: Herbert E. Neiburgs, M.D.
E-Mail: editor@cancerprev.org

Historical Note
ISPO members are medical doctors, scientists and other professionals who are actively involved in preventive oncology.

Meetings/Conferences:
Annual Meetings: Summer

Publications:
Cancer Detection & Prevention. bi-m.
Proceed of International Symposium on Prevention & Detection of Cancer. bien.

International Society for Prosthetics and Orthotics - United States *(1970)*
P.O. Box 3188
Dublin, OH 43016
Tel: (614)659-0197 *Fax:* (614)336-8596
Web Site: www.usispo.org
Members: 310 individuals
Staff: 1
Annual Budget: $10-25,000
U.S. Coordinator: Dianne Farabi

Historical Note
Established in Copenhagen, Denmark. Incorporated in Dover, Delaware. Membership: $110/year.

Meetings/Conferences:
Annual Meetings:

Publications:
Prosthetics and Orthotics International. 3/year. adv.
Membership Directory. irreg.

International Society for Quality of Life Research
6728 Old McLean Village Dr.
McLean, VA 22101
Tel: (703)556-9222 *Fax:* (703)556-8729
E-Mail: info@isoqol.org
Web Site: www.isoqol.org/

International Society for Quality-of-Life Studies *(1995)*
1800 Kraft Dr., Suite 111
Blacksburg, VA 24061-0236
Tel: (540)231-5110 *Fax:* (540)961-4162
E-Mail: sirgy@vt.edu
Web Site: www.isgols.org
Members: 300 individuals
Staff: 2
Annual Budget: $25-50,000
Executive Director and Secretary: M. Joseph Sirgy
E-Mail: sirgy@vt.edu

Historical Note
ISQOLS was founded to stimulate interdisciplinary research in quality-of-life studies and closer cooperation among scholars. Members are academic and government social/behavioral science researchers drawn from such fields as marketing, management, applied psychology, applied sociology, political science, economics, public administration, educational administration, family/child development, leisure/recreation studies, and technology management. Membership: $50/year (individual); $100/year (corporate/institutional); $25/year (student/retired researchers).

Meetings/Conferences:
Annual Meetings: Fall
2007 – San Diego, CA(San Diego Marriott)/Dec. 6-9

Publications:
Journal of Happiness Studies. q. adv.
Social Indicators Research. 10/year. adv.
Journal of Macromarketing. semi-a. adv.
Social Indicators Network News. q. adv.
Applied Research in Quality of Life. q. adv.

International Society for Research on Aggression *(1972)*
Dept. of Psychology, Augusta State University
2500 Walton Way
Augusta, GA 30904
Tel: (706)667-4615 *Fax:* (706)737-1538
E-Mail: drichardson@aug.edu
Web Site: www.israsociety.com
Members: 250 individuals
Annual Budget: under $10,000
Executive Secretary: Deborah S. Richardson
E-Mail: drichardson@aug.edu

Historical Note
ISRA members are academics, scientists and other professionals with an interest in the field of aggression. Has no paid officers or full-time staff. Membership: $60/year.

Meetings/Conferences:
Biennial Meetings: in even-numbered years.
Publications:
Aggressive Behavior. 6/year.
Bulletin. 3/year.

International Society for Respiratory Protection
2577 N. Lightwood Ave.
Bethel Park, PA 15102
Tel: (412)386-4055
E-Mail: jisrp-editor@att.net
Web Site: www.isrp.com.au
Members: 12 corporations
Editor: Ziqing Zhuang
E-Mail: jisrp-editor@att.net
Historical Note
ISRP promotes the health and safety of users of respiratory protection devices and all aspects of respiratory care. Membership: $45/year (individual); $400/year (corporation).
Publications:
ISRP Quarterly. q.
Journal of ISRP.

International Society for Technology in Education *(1979)*
175 W. Broadway
Suite 300
Eugene, OR 97401-3003
Tel: (541)302-3777 *Fax:* (541)302-3778
Toll Free: (800)336 - 5191
E-Mail: iste@iste.org
Web Site: www.iste.org
Members: 13000 individuals, corporate and organizational affiliate members
Staff: 70
Annual Budget: $5-10,000,000
Deputy Chief Executive Officer: Leslie Conery, Ph.D.
Senior Director, Marketing and Communications: Steve Abbott
Historical Note
Product of a merger in 1989 of the International Council for Computers in Education and the International Association for Computing in Education. With its parent organizations ICCE and IACE, ISTE has been serving technology-using educators since 1979. In 2002, ISTE merged with the National Educational Computing Association, the supporting non-profit behind the National Educational Computing Conference (NECC), held annually since 1979. ISTE maintains seven special interest groups: Special Interest Group for Logo Educators (SIGLogo), Special Interest Group for Teacher Educators (SIGTE), Hyper/Multi-Media Special Interest Group (HyperSIG), Special Interest Group for Computer Science (SIGCS), Special Interest Group for Telecommunications (SIG/Tel), Special Interest Group for Technology Coordinators (SIGTC), and Special Interest Group for Special Education Technology (SIGSET). The Information Processing Administrators of Large School Systems is a functional affiliate of ISTE. Membership: $58/year (domestic); $78/year (overseas), plus SIG dues.
Meetings/Conferences:
Semi-annual Meetings: November-December and June
2007 - Atlanta, GA/June 24-27
Publications:
Learning & Leading with Technology. 8/year. adv.
Journal of Research on Computing in Education. q.
Computer Assisted English Language Learning Journal. q.
ISTE Update. 12/yr.
Logo Exchange (publication of SIGLogo). q.
Journal of Computing in Teacher Education (publication of SIGTE). q. adv.
HyperNEXUS (publication of HyperSIG). q.
Journal of Computer Science Education (publication of SIGCS). q.
Telecommunications in Education News (publication of SIG/Tel). q.
SIGTC Connections (publication of SIGTC). q.

International Society for the Comparative Studies of Civilizations *(1961)*
Department of History
New College of Florida
Sarasota, FL 34243
Tel: (941)355-4513 *Fax:* (941)359-4475
Web Site: www.iscsc.net
Members: 250 institutions
Staff: 2
Annual Budget: $10-25,000
President: Lee D. Snyder
E-Mail: lsnyder@ncf.edu
Historical Note
Founded in 1961 in Salzburg, Austria, ISCSC moved its headquarters to the U.S. in 1970 and was reconstituted over a two-year period. Members are scholars and other individuals interested in the study of the history and evolution of world cultures. Membership fee: $50/year (individual); $60/year (institution).
Publications:
ISCSC newsletter (online). adv.
Comparative Civilizations Review. semi-a. adv.

International Society for the Performing Arts
(1949)
P.O. Box 909
Rye, NY 10580-0909
Tel: (914)921-1550 *Fax:* (914)921-1593
Web Site: http://ispa.org
Members: 500 individuals and organizations
Staff: 4
Annual Budget: $250-500,000
Chief Executive Officer: Johann Zietsman
E-Mail: jzietsman@ispa.org
Historical Note
ISPA represents executives and directors of concert and performance halls, festivals, performing companies,and artist competitions; government cultural officials; artists' managers; and other interested parties with a professional involvement in the performing arts, internationally. Membership: $550/year (individual).
Meetings/Conferences:
Semi-Annual Meetings: June, international; December, New York, NY
2007 - New York, NY/Jan. 16-18
2007 - Brussels, Belgium/June 7-10
Publications:
Membership Directory. a. adv.

International Society for the Study of Dissociation *(1984)*
8201 Greensboro Dr., Suite 300
McLean, VA 22102
Tel: (703)610-9000 *Fax:* (703)610-9005
E-Mail: issd@issd.org
Web Site: www.issd.org
Members: 1500 individuals
Staff: 2
Annual Budget: $250-500,000
Contact: Spencer Boulter
Historical Note
Formerly (1994) International Society for the Study of Multiple Personality and Dissociation. Incorporated in Georgia, ISSD members are professionals in psychology, psychiatry, medicine, nursing, sociology, social work, anthropology, philosophy, theology and other disciplines seriously involved in the study and treatment of multiple psychological processes. Membership: $125/year (regular); $50/year (affiliate); $60/year (student/retiree).
Meetings/Conferences:
Annual Meetings: November
Publications:
Journal of Trauma and Dissociation. q. adv.
Guidelines for Treatment.
Newsletter. bi-m.
Membership Directory. a.

International Society for the Study of Subtle Energies and Energy Medicine *(1989)*
11005 Ralston Rd.
Suite 210
Arvada, CO 80004
Tel: (303)425-4625 *Fax:* (303)425-4685
E-Mail: issseem2@comcast.com
Web Site: www.issseem.org
Members: 1500 individuals
Staff: 5
Annual Budget: $250-500,000
Chief Executive Officer: C. Penny Hiernu
E-Mail: issseem2@comcast.com
Historical Note
ISSSEEM members are interested in integrating traditional knowledge about subtle energies and the healing process with modern scientific method and theory. Membership: $75/year (individual); $150/year (organization).
Meetings/Conferences:
Annual Meetings: June
2007 - Boulder, CO(Millenium)/June 21-27
Publications:
Bridges Magazine. q.
Subtle Energies & Energy Medicine Journal. 3/year.

International Society for Third-Sector Research
(1992)
Wyman Park Bldg., Room 559
3400 N. Charles St.
Baltimore, MD 21218-2688
Tel: (410)516-4678 *Fax:* (410)516-4870
E-Mail: istr@jhu.edu
Web Site: www.istr.org
Members: 700 individuals & institutions
Staff: 2
Annual Budget: $250-500,000
Executive Director: Margery Berg Daniels
E-Mail: istr@jhu.edu
Historical Note
ISTR is an international association that promotes research and education in the fields of civil society, philanthropy, and the nonprofit sector. ISTR is an organization committed to building a global community of scholars and interested others, dedicated to the creation, discussion and advancement of knowledge pertaining to the Third Sector and its impact on human and planetary well-being and international development. Holds biennial conferences. Membership: $100/year (individual); $80/year (student); $200/year (institution).
Meetings/Conferences:
Biennial Meetings:
2008 - Barcelona, Spain
Publications:
ISTR Reports. irreg.
Membership Directory (online). a.
Inside ISTR Newsletter (online). q.
Voluntas Journal. q. adv.

International Society for Traumatic Stress Studies *(1985)*
60 Revere Dr., Suite 500
Northbrook, IL 60062
Tel: (847)480-9028 *Fax:* (847)480-9282
E-Mail: istss@istss.org
Web Site: www.istss.org
Members: 2500 individuals
Staff: 8
Annual Budget: $500-1,000,000
Executive Director: Richard Koepke
Historical Note
Formerly (1991) Society for Traumatic Stress Studies. Established in Washington and incorporated in Ohio. Society members include mental health, social service, clergy and legal professionals who work with combat veterans, victims of crime and other forms of violence, survivors of natural and technological disasters, persons suffering from duty-related stress, and individuals who have suffered physical trauma. Membership: $100/year.
Meetings/Conferences:
Annual Meetings: November
Publications:
Traumatic StressPoints Newsletter. q. adv.
Journal of Traumatic Stress. q. adv.

International Society of Air Safety Investigators
(1964)
107 E. Holly Ave., Suite 11
Sterling, VA 20164-5405
Tel: (703)430-9668 *Fax:* (703)430-4970
E-Mail: isasi@erols.com
Web Site: www.isasi.org

Members: 1354 individuals
Staff: 1
Annual Budget: $100-250,000
International Office Manager: Ann Schull
E-Mail: isasi@erols.com
Executive Assistant: Richard Stone
E-Mail: isasi@erols.com

Historical Note

Established August 31, 1964 in Washington, DC to promote development of improved aircraft accident investigation procedures. Has an international membership from 41 countries. Formerly (1977) the Society of Air Safety Investigators. Membership: $60/year (individual); $500/year (company).

Meetings/Conferences:

Annual Meetings: Fall

Publications:

Proceedings. a. adv.
The Forum. q.

International Society of Applied Intelligence *(1993)*
TX State Univ.-San Marcos, Dept. of Computer Science
601 University Dr.
San Marcos, TX 78666-4616
Tel: (512)245-3409 *Fax:* (512)245-8750
Web Site: http://isai.cs.txstate.edu
Members: 50 individuals
Staff: 2
Annual Budget: $50-100,000
President: Moonis Ali, Ph.D.

Historical Note

ISAI members are academics, computer scientists and others with an interest in the applications of artificial intelligence. Membership: $125/year (individual); $50/year (student); $545/year (institution).

Meetings/Conferences:

Annual Meetings: Summer
2007 – Kyoto, Japan/June 6-29/250
2008 – Wyoclaw, Poland/June 1-1/250

Publications:

Internat'l Journal of Applied Intelligence. bi-m.
ISAI Newsletter. q. adv.
IEA/AIE Conference Proceedings. a.

International Society of Appraisers *(1979)*
1131 S.W. Seventh St., Suite 105
Renton, WA 98055
Tel: (206)241-0359 *Fax:* (206)241-0436
Toll Free: (888)472 - 4732
E-Mail: isa@isa-appraisers.org
Web Site: www.isa-appraisers.org
Members: 1400 individuals
Staff: 8
Annual Budget: $500-1,000,000
Executive Director: Jorge Sever
Controller: Leslie Wall-Becker

Historical Note

Founded and chartered in Illinois. Members are appraisers, specializing in Fine Arts, gems, and jewelry, antiques and collectibles, household items, and machinery and equipment. ISA offers courses in appraisal principles, theory, practice, and various speciality courses, and provides referrals to professional appraisers. Became a non-profit organization in 1993 and tax exempt in 1995. Membership: $380/year (initiation); $380/year (after first year).

Meetings/Conferences:

Annual Meetings: Spring

Publications:

Professional Appraisers Information Exchange. q. adv.
ISA Membership Directory. a. adv.

International Society of Arboriculture *(1924)*
P.O. Box 3129
Champaign, IL 61826-3129
Tel: (217)355-9411 *Fax:* (217)355-9516
Toll Free: (888)472 - 8733
E-Mail: isa@isa-arbor.com
Web Site: www.isa-arbor.com
Members: 20000 individuals
Staff: 20
Annual Budget: $2-5,000,000
Executive Director: Jim Skiera

Historical Note

Formerly (1976) International Shade Tree Conference. Membership: $105/year (individual); $500/year (company).

Meetings/Conferences:

Annual Meetings: August/800-900
2007 – Honolulu, HI/July 28-Aug. 1
2008 – St. Louis, MO/July 26-30
2009 – Providence, RI/July 25-29
2010 – Chicago, IL/July 24-28

Publications:

Arborist News. bi-m. adv.
Journal of Arboriculture. bi-m.
Member Directory. a. adv.

International Society of Arthroscopy, Knee Surgery and Orthopaedic Sports Medicine *(1977)*
2678 Bishop Dr., Suite 250
San Ramon, CA 94583-2338
Tel: (925)807-1197 *Fax:* (925)807-1199
E-Mail: isakos@isakos.com
Web Site: www.isakos.com
Members: 1600 individuals
Staff: 3
Annual Budget: $100-250,000
Executive Director: Michele Johnson
E-Mail: isakos@isakos.com

Historical Note

Formerly International Society of the Knee; merged with International Arthroscopy Association and assumed its current name in 1995. Membership: $125/year (domestic); $200/year (overseas).

Meetings/Conferences:

Biennial Meetings: Spring
2007 – Florence, Italy/May 27-31

Publications:

Arthroscopy Journal. 9/year.
Newsletter. 2/year.

International Society of Barristers *(1965)*
806 Legal Research Bldg.
625 S. State St.
Ann Arbor, MI 48109-1215
Tel: (734)763-0165 *Fax:* (734)764-8309
Web Site: www.internationalsocietyofbarristers.com
Members: 800 individuals
Staff: 1
Annual Budget: $100-250,000
Administrative Secretary: John W. Reed

Historical Note

Members are trial lawyers interested in encouraging advocacy under the adversary system and preserving the right to a jury trial. Membership: $650/year.

Meetings/Conferences:

Annual Meetings: Late Winter

Publications:

Newsletter. irreg.
ISOB Quarterly. q.

International Society of Bassists *(1967)*
14070 Proton Rd., Suite 100
Dallas, TX 75244
Tel: (972)233-9107 Ext: 204 *Fax:* (972)490-4219
E-Mail: info@isbworldoffice.com
Web Site: www.isbworldoffice.com
Members: 2700 individuals
Annual Budget: $50-100,000
General Manager: Madeleine Crouch

Historical Note

Members are teachers, students, reseachers and manufacturers of the double bass. ISB also serves to stimulate public interest in the double bass and improve performance standards. Membership: $40/year (domestic), $45/year (overseas).

Meetings/Conferences:

Biennial Meetings: Spring/Summer

Publications:

Bass World. 3/year. adv.

International Society of Beverage Technologists *(1953)*
8110 S. Suncoast Blvd.
Homosassa, FL 34446
Tel: (352)382-2008 *Fax:* (352)382-2018
E-Mail: isbt@bevtech.org
Web Site: www.bevtech.org
Members: 1000 individuals
Staff: 2
Annual Budget: $250-500,000
Executive Director: Elizabeth McLeod
E-Mail: isbt@bevtech.org

Historical Note

Formerly (1995) Society of Soft Drink Technologists. ISBT is a professional society of individuals engaged in the beverage industry. Membership: $150/year.

Meetings/Conferences:

Annual Meetings: April-May

Publications:

Seminar Proceedings. a.
Technical Manuals. a.
Annual Meeting Proceedings. a.
Newsletter. q.

International Society of Certified Electronics Technicians *(1970)*
3608 Pershing Ave.
Ft. Worth, TX 76107
Tel: (817)921-9101 *Fax:* (817)921-3741
Toll Free: (800)946 - 0201
E-Mail: info@iscet.org
Web Site: www.iscet.org
Members: 2000 individuals
Staff: 5
Annual Budget: $100-250,000
Executive Director: Mack Blakely

Historical Note

An affiliate of the National Electronic Service Dealers Association. Tests for and awards the CET (Certified Electronics Technician) designation. Publishes technical information, conducts technical training and product serviceability inspections. Only CETs are eligible for membership. Membership: $35/year.

Meetings/Conferences:

Annual Meetings: With the National Electronic Service Dealers Association in August.

Publications:

ISCET Update. q.
ProService (online). bi-m.
ProService Directory. a. adv.

International Society of Certified Employee Benefit Specialists *(1981)*
18700 W. Bluemound Rd., P.O. Box 209
Brookfield, WI 53008-0209
Tel: (262)786-8771 *Fax:* (262)786-8650
E-Mail: iscebs@iscebs.org
Web Site: www.iscebs.org
Members: 4000 individuals
Staff: 4
Annual Budget: $1-2,000,000
Executive Director: Daniel W. Graham
Director, Operations: Sandra L. Becker
Director, Chapter Services and Development: Pamela White Wu

Historical Note

An affiliate of the International Foundation of Employee Benefit Plans, ISCEBS members are graduates of a professional certification program co-sponsored by the Foundation and the Wharton School, Univ. of Pennsylvania. Membership: $155/year (individual).

Meetings/Conferences:

Annual Meetings: Typical Attendance: 600
2007 – Seattle, WA(The Westin Seattle)/Sept. 16-19
2008 – Orlando, FL(Disney's Yacht and Beach Club Resort)/Sept. 21-24
2009 – San Diego, CA(Manchester Grand Hyatt)/Oct. 4-7

Publications:

Benefits Quarterly. q.
Newsbriefs. bi-m.
ISCEBS Membership Directory. a.

International Society of Chemical Ecology *(1983)*
Dept. of Entomology, North Dakota State University
Fargo, ND 58105

Tel: (701)231-6444 *Fax:* (701)231-8557
Web Site: www.chemecol.org
Members: 650 individuals
Annual Budget: $50-100,000
Secretary: Stephen P. Foster

Historical Note

Formed to promote the understanding of the origin, function, and significance of natural chemicals that mediate interactions with and among organisms. Has no paid staff. Membership: $35/year.

Meetings/Conferences:

Annual Meetings: Summer
2007 – Jena, Germany
2008 – University Park, PA(Penn State Univ.)
2009 – Neuchatel, Switzerland

Publications:

Journal of Chemical Ecology. m. adv.
ISCE Newsletter. 3/year. adv.

International Society of Cleaning Technicians

Historical Note

Became Society of Cleaning and Restoration Technicians in 2004.

International Society of Communication Specialists *(1984)*

201 Blue Sky Dr.
Marietta, GA 30068-3511
Tel: (770)973-0662 *Fax:* (770)973-1410
E-Mail: ecs91@aol.com
Web Site: www.iscs.cc
Members: 70 companies
Staff: 1
Annual Budget: $100-250,000
Executive Director: Ed Sanner

Historical Note

ISCS members are companies that represent on-location audio and video recording services for the association community. Membership: $275/year (company).

Meetings/Conferences:

Annual Meetings: January

International Society of Copier Artists *(1982)*

759 President St., Suite 2H
Brooklyn, NY 11215
Tel: (718)638-3264
E-Mail: isca4art2b@aol.com
Web Site: http://members.aol.com/ISCA4ART2B/I.S.C.A./homepage.html
Members: 125 individuals
Annual Budget: under $10,000
Director: Louise Neaderland
E-Mail: isca4art2b@aol.com

Historical Note

Founded to promote the use of the copier as a creative tool. Membership: $30/year (contributing artist); $90-110/year (supporting member).

Meetings/Conferences:

Annual Meetings: Not held.

International Society of Crime Prevention Practitioners *(1978)*

P.O. Box 476
Simpsonville, SC 29681
Tel: (864)884-8466
Web Site: www.iscpp.org
Members: 1300 individuals
Staff: 2
Annual Budget: $100-250,000
Executive Director: Donna Weglewski, ICPS

Historical Note

Membership includes practitioners from civic organizations, law enforcement, private security, business, government, education, mass media, and other groups and agencies. ISCPP's mission is to establish and support a permanent network of crime prevention practitioners who can provide leadership, foster cooperation, encourage information exchange, and extend and improve crime prevention education and programs internationally. Absorbed National Crime Prevention Institute in 1997. Membership: $35/year (individual).

Meetings/Conferences:

Annual Meetings: October

International Society of Explosives Engineers *(1974)*

30325 Bainbridge Rd.
Cleveland, OH 44139-2295
Tel: (440)349-4400 *Fax:* (440)349-3788
E-Mail: isee@isee.org
Web Site: www.isee.org
Members: 4500 individuals
Staff: 12
Annual Budget: $1-2,000,000
Executive Director and General Counsel: Jeffrey L. Dean, CAE
E-Mail: isee@isee.org

Historical Note

ISEE is a professional society dedicated to promoting the safe and controlled use of explosives in mining, quarrying, construction, manufacturing, forestry, and many other commercial pursuits. Membership: $75/year (individual); $375/year (company).

Meetings/Conferences:

Annual Meetings: Winter

Publications:

Journal of Explosives Engineering. bi-m. adv.

International Society of Exposure Analysis *(1989)*

c/o JSI Research & Training Institute
44 Farnsworth St.
Boston, MA 02210-1211
Tel: (617)482-9485 *Fax:* (617)482-0617
E-Mail: iseamail@jsi.com
Web Site: www.iseaweb.org
Members: 390 individuals
Secretariat Contact: Carol Rougvie

Historical Note

ISEA represents a variety of professionals with an interest in the statistical analysis of risk factors, environmental exposure, and related issues. Has no paid officers or full-time staff.

Meetings/Conferences:

2007 – Research Triangle Park, NC/Oct. 14-18
2008 – Los Angeles, CA

Publications:

Journal of Exposure Analysis and Environmental Epidemiology. bi-m.

International Society of Facilities Executives *(1989)*

200 Corporate Place, Suite 2B
Peabody, MA 01960
Tel: (978)536-0108 *Fax:* (978)536-0199
E-Mail: isfe@isfe.org
Web Site: www.isfe.org
Members: 250 individuals
Annual Budget: $100-250,000

Historical Note

ISFE, founded by the Massachusetts Institute of Technology, is a professional organization for senior facilities executives with ultimate responsibilities for their corporate and institutional assets. ISFE provides a forum to exchange knowledge and experience in asset management. Membership: $290/year (professional), $175/year (associate), $2,500 (corporate).

Meetings/Conferences:

Annual Meetings: always Cambridge, MA(Royal Sonesta)/200

Publications:

Health / FM. semi-a.
Executive Briefs. q.
Executive Updates. m.

International Society of Fire Service Instructors *(1960)*

2425 Hwy. 49 East
Pleasant View, TN 37146
Toll Free: (800)435 - 0005
E-Mail: info@isfsi.org
Web Site: www.isfsi.org
Members: 7000 individuals
Staff: 16
Resource Consultant: May Caldwell
E-Mail: info@isfsi.org

Historical Note

Founded as International Society of Fire Service Instructors; became Alliance for Fire and Emergency Management in 1995; resumed its original name in 1997. Members are individuals responsible for the training of fire, police, ambulance and rescue personnel, and the public. Membership: $75/year (individual).

Meetings/Conferences:

Annual Meetings: July

Publications:

The Instructor. m. adv.

International Society of Hair Restoration Surgery *(1992)*

13 S. Second St.
Geneva, IL 60134
Tel: (630)262-5399 *Fax:* (630)262-1520
Toll Free: (800)444 - 2737
E-Mail: info@ishrs.org
Web Site: www.ishrs.org
Members: 700 individuals
Executive Director: Victoria Ceh

International Society of Hospitality Consultants *(1988)*

515 King St., Suite 420
Alexandria, VA 22314
Tel: (703)684-6681 *Fax:* (703)684-6048
Web Site: www.ishc.com
Members: 180 individuals
Staff: 3
Annual Budget: $500-1,000,000
Director, Administration: Carole M. Rogin
Director, Membership Services: Elizabeth Hawkins

Historical Note

ISHC provides networking and professional support to principals and management at consulting firms in the hospitality industry. Membership is by invitation only.

Meetings/Conferences:

Annual Meetings: Fall
2007 – Hong Kong, China(Intercontinental)/Oct. 5-11/150

Publications:

Cap Ex. quinquen. adv.

International Society of Hotel Association Executives *(1946)*

9589 S.E. Wyndham Way
Portland, OR 97086
Tel: (503)777-8407 *Fax:* (503)788-2151
E-Mail: admin@ishae.org
Web Site: www.ishae.org
Members: 75 individuals
Staff: 1
Annual Budget: $50-100,000
Executive Director: Philip Peach
E-Mail: admin@ishae.org

Historical Note

Formerly (1974) American Hotel Trade Association Executives. Affiliated with the American Hotel and Lodging Association. Members include CEOs of hotel and lodging associations in the U.S. and Canada. Officers change annually. Membership: $200/year.

Publications:

Newsletter. q.

International Society of Livestock Appraisers

Historical Note

A division of the American Society of Agricultural Appraisers.

International Society of Meeting Planners *(1981)*

1224 N. Nokomis Ave.
Alexandria, MN 56308
Tel: (320)763-4919 *Fax:* (320)763-9290
E-Mail: ismp@iami.org
Web Site: www.iami.org/ismp.cfm
Members: 2800 individuals
Staff: 6
Executive Director: Robert G. Johnson

Historical Note

ISMP provides certification and networking opportunities to meeting industry professionals in the U.S. and abroad.

Publications:

Global Connections. q. adv.

International Society of Orthopaedic Surgery - U.S. Chapter

Historical Note
U.S. Chapter of the international research organization, headquarterd in Brussels. Administrative support provided by American Academy of Orthopaedic Surgeons.

International Society of Parametric Analysts
(1979)
P.O. Box 3185
Chandler, AZ 85244
Tel: (480)917-4747 *Fax:* (480)792-6930
E-Mail: ispaoffice@earthlink.net
Web Site: www.ispa-cost.org
*Members:*400 individuals
Staff: 1
Annual Budget: $100-250,000
Service Coordinator: Allison Brown

Historical Note
Members are estimators, project managers, cost analysts, and other professionals working principally in the field of defense and weapons systems. Membership: $55/year.

Meetings/Conferences:
Annual Meetings: Summer

Publications:
Parametric World Newsletter. 3-4/year. adv.
Journal of Parametrics. 1/year. adv.
Annual Conference Tutorials. a. adv.
ISPA Directory. a. adv.
Annual Conference Proceedings. a. adv.

International Society of Political Psychology
(1978)
Moynihan Institute of Global Affairs
346 Eggers Hall
Syracuse, NY 13244
Tel: (315)443-4470 *Fax:* (315)443-9085
E-Mail: ispp@maxwell.syr.edu
Web Site: http://ispp.org
*Members:*900 individuals
Staff: 2
Annual Budget: $100-250,000
Central Office Administrator: Radell Roberts
E-Mail: ispp@maxwell.syr.edu

Historical Note
ISPP members include psychologists, political scientists, psychiatrists, historians, sociologists, economists, anthropologists, as well as journalists, government officials and others. Membership: $70/year.

Meetings/Conferences:
Scientific Conference: usually July/400
2007 – Portland, OR
2008 – Paris, France

Publications:
Political Psychology Journal. bi-m. adv.
ISPP News Newsletter. semi-a.
Advances in Political Philosophy. a.

International Society of Psychiatric Consultation Liaison Nurses *(1986)*
2810 Crossroads Dr., Suite 3800
Madison, WI 53718
Tel: (608)443-2463 *Fax:* (608)443-2474
Toll Free: (866)330 - 7227
E-Mail: info@ispn-psych.org
Web Site: www.ispn-psych.org/html/ispcln.html
*Members:*250 individuals
Annual Budget: $25-50,000
Division Director: Karen Ragaisis

Historical Note
ISPCLN provides a forum for the discussion of psychiatric issues within the nursing community. Membership: $75/year.

Publications:
Connections. q. adv.

International Society of Psychiatric-Mental Health Nurses *(1971)*
2810 Crossroads Dr., Suite 3800
Madison, WI 53718
Tel: (608)443-2463 *Fax:* (608)443-2474
Toll Free: (866)330 - 7227
E-Mail: info@ispn-psych.org
Web Site: www.ispn-psych.org
*Members:*850 individuals
Staff: 2
Annual Budget: $100-250,000
Executive Director: Bruce Wheeler
Coordinator, Membership: Theresa Vollstadt

Historical Note
Founded as Alliance of Psychaitric and Mental Nurses; assumed its current name in 1999. Membership: $115/year.

Meetings/Conferences:
Annual Meetings: Spring

Publications:
ISPN Newsletter. semi-a. adv.
Perspectives in Psychiatric Care. q. adv.
Journal of Child and Adolescent Psychiatric Nursing. q. adv.
Archives in Psych Nursing. adv.

International Society of Refractive Surgery of the American Academy of Ophthalmology *(2003)*
655 Beach St.
San Francisco, CA 94109-1336
Tel: (415)561-8581 *Fax:* (415)561-8575
E-Mail: member-services@aao.org
Web Site: www.isrs.org
*Members:*3500 individuals
Staff: 7
Director, Membership: Jill Hartle

Historical Note
Founded as International Society of Refractive Keratoplasty; became ISRS in 1995. ISRS/AAO promotes research, education, and exchange to advance the ethical practice of refractive surgery. Membership: $175/year.

Meetings/Conferences:
Annual Meetings: Fall

Publications:
Journal of Refractive Surgery. bi-m. adv.

International Society of Restaurant Association Executives *(1935)*
5024-R Campbell Blvd.
Baltimore, MD 21236
Tel: (410)931-8100 Ext: 120 *Fax:* (410)931-8111
Web Site: www.israe.org
*Members:*200 individuals
Staff: 2
Annual Budget: $100-250,000
Executive Director: Crista LeGrand, CMP

Historical Note
Membership composed of executive staff of state and national restaurant associations.

Publications:
ISRAE Newsletter (electronic). m.

International Society of Statistical Science
(1982)

Historical Note
Address unknown in 2006.

International Society of Transport Aircraft Trading *(1983)*
5517 Talon Ct.
Fairfax, VA 22032-1737
Tel: (703)978-8156 *Fax:* (703)503-5964
E-Mail: istat@istat.org
Web Site: www.istat.org
Members: 1400 individuals
Staff: 1
Annual Budget: $500-1,000,000
Executive Director: Dawn O'Day Foster
E-Mail: istat@istat.org

Historical Note
ISTAT provides a communications medium for those engaged in the purchase, sale, financing, appraisal or insuring of transport category aircraft. Membership: $400/year (individual).

Meetings/Conferences:
Annual Meetings: March

Publications:
Member Directory. a.
Conference Proceedings. 2/yr.
JeTrader. bi-m.

International Society of Travel and Tourism Educators *(1980)*
23220 Edgewater
St. Clair Shores, MI 48082
Tel: (586)294-0208
E-Mail: joannb@istte.org
Web Site: www.istte.org
Members: 150 individuals
Staff: 3
Annual Budget: $100-250,000
Executive Director: Joanne Bruss
E-Mail: joannb@istte.org

Historical Note
Founded as Society of Travel and Tourism Educators; assumed its current name in 1997. ISTTE members are teachers and administrators of programs that offer degrees in the areas of travel and tourism. Membership: $75/year (individual); $125/year (organization/company).

Publications:
ISTTE Membership Directory. a.
Journal of Teaching in Travel & Tourism.
Travel and Tourism Books in Print. a. adv.
News and Views. q. adv.

International Society of Weekly Newspaper Editors *(1954)*
c/o Inst. of Internat'l Studies, Missouri Southern State University
3950 E. Newman Road
Joplin, MO 64801-1595
Tel: (417)625-9736 *Fax:* (417)659-4445
E-Mail: stebbins-c@mssu.edu
Web Site: www.iswne.org
*Members:*300 individuals
Staff: 1
Annual Budget: $10-25,000
Executive Director: Dr. Chad D. Stebbins

Historical Note
Sponsors the Golden Quill Award for excellence in writing of editorials in weekly newspapers and the Eugene Cervi Award for that weekly newspaper person who has served as the conscience of the community. Membership: $50/year.

Meetings/Conferences:
Annual Meetings: July

Publications:
Grassroots Editor. q.
Newsletter. m.

International Society of Weighing and Measurement *(1916)*
15245 Shady Grove Rd., #130
Rockville, MD 20850
Tel: (301)258-1115 *Fax:* (301)990-9771
E-Mail: staff@iswm.org
Web Site: www.iswm.org
*Members:*900 individuals
Staff: 3
Annual Budget: $250-500,000
Executive Director: Karen Hutchison

Historical Note
Formerly (1985) National Men's Scale Association. Members are engaged in the weighing and measurement industry. Membership: $130/year (individual); $285/year (dealers); $3465/year (manufacturer).

Meetings/Conferences:
Biennial Meetings: 300

Publications:
ISWM News. q. adv.
Membership Directory and Product Guide. a.

International Spa Association *(1991)*
2365 Harrodsburg Rd., Suite A325
Lexington, KY 40504-4326
Tel: (859)226-4326 *Fax:* (859)226-4445
Toll Free: (888)651 - 4772
E-Mail: ispa@ispastaff.com
Web Site: www.experienceispa.com
*Members:*2500 companies
Staff: 14
President: Lynne Walker McNees
E-Mail: ispa@ispastaff.com
Director, Research and Development: Stefanie Ashley
Director, Membership: Laura Bertke
Vice President: Becky Brooks
Director, Communications: Debra Locker
Editor: Julie Wilson

Historical Note
Seeks to increase awareness of the spa industry and educate the public and industry professionals about the lifelong benefits of the spa experience. Members include club spas, cruise ship spas, day spas, destination spas, resort/hotel spas, medical spas and mineral spring spas, as well as suppliers to the industry.

Meetings/Conferences:
Annual Meetings: Fall
2007 – Kissimmee, FL(Gaylord Palms Resort and Convention Center)/Nov. 12-15
2008 – Las Vegas, NV(The Venetian)/Nov. 10-13

Publications:
Pulse. bi-m. adv.
Directory. a. adv.
Conference Magazine. a. adv.

International Special Events Society *(1986)*
401 N. Michigan Ave.
Chicago, IL 60611-4267
Tel: (312)321-6853 *Fax:* (312)673-6953
Toll Free: (800)688 - 4737
E-Mail: info@ises.com
Web Site: www.ises.com
Members: 4100 individuals
Staff: 4
Annual Budget: $1-2,000,000
Executive Director: Kevin Hacke
E-Mail: khacke@smithbucklin.com

Historical Note
ISES is an umbrella organization for the many different disciplines comprising the special event industry. ISES members include caterers, decorators, special event producers, meeting planners, destination management companies, rental companies, hotel sales managers, convention center managers, and other professionals. ISES has 40 chapters, providing professional and networking services to members worldwide. Membership: approximately $399/year (individual).

Meetings/Conferences:
Annual Meetings: Summer

Publications:
International Fax.
Eventworld. m.
Membership Directory. a. adv.

International Sport Show Producers Association *(1970)*
P.O. Box 480084
Denver, CO 80248-0084
Tel: (303)892-6800 Ext: 25 *Fax:* (303)892-6322
Web Site: www.sportshow.org
Members: 15 companies
Staff: 7
Annual Budget: under $10,000
Executive Secretary: Dianne Seymour

Historical Note
ISSPA members are producers of sports and vacation shows serving major North American markets.

Meetings/Conferences:
Annual Meetings: Summer

Publications:
Sports & Vacation Show Directory & Calendar. a.

International Sports Heritage Association *(1971)*
P.O. Box 3093
Ponte Vedra Beach, FL 32004-3093
Tel: (904)955-0126 *Fax:* (904)683-2189
E-Mail: info@sportsheritage.org
Web Site: www.sportshalls.com
Members: 125 organizations
Staff: 1
Annual Budget: $25-50,000
Executive Director: Karen Bednarski

Historical Note
Formerly the Association of Sports Museums and Halls of Fame, the association adopted its present name in 1989. Membership: $115-$175/year.

Meetings/Conferences:
Annual Meetings: Fall, usually at a Hall of Fame

Publications:
Honoring our Heroes.
Newsletter (electronic). bi-m. adv.
Organizing a Sports Museum/Hall of Fame.
Membership Directory. adv. adv.

International Sports Massage Federation *(1983)*

Historical Note
An international program administered by the United States Sports Massage Federation (same address).

International Staple, Nail and Tool Association *(1966)*
512 W. Burlington Ave., Suite 203
La Grange, IL 60525-2245
Tel: (708)482-8138 *Fax:* (708)482-8186
E-Mail: isanta@ameritech.net
Web Site: www.isanta.org/
Members: 19 companies
Staff: 2
Executive Vice President: John Kurtz

Historical Note
Founded as the Industrial Stapling Manufacturer's Institute, it became the Industrial Stapling and Nailing Technical Association in 1972 and assumed its present name in 1982. Financed and directed by manufacturers of machine-driven staples, nails and similar fasteners and their power tools.

Publications:
Safety Standards. quinquen.
Evaluation Reports. bien.

International Stress Management Association - U.S. Branch *(1973)*
111 Lake Harbor Dr.
Johnson City, TN 37615-2973
E-Mail: info@isma-usa.org
Web Site: www.isma-usa.org
Members: 100 individuals
Annual Budget: under $10,000
Secretary: Carolyn S. Massello, DBA

Historical Note
Formerly (1980) American Association for the Advancement of Tension Control and (1992) International Stress and Tension Control Association. ISMA members are individuals with an interest in the dissemination and acquisition of scientific knowledge for stress management, related disorders and tension control strategies. Has no paid officers or full-time staff. Membership: $65/year.

Meetings/Conferences:
Annual Meetings: Spring
2007 – Chicago, IL/

Publications:
International Journal of Stress Management. q.
Newsletter. 2/year.

International Studies Association *(1959)*
324 Social Sciences, Univ. of Arizona
Tucson, AZ 85721
Tel: (520)621-7715 *Fax:* (520)621-5780
E-Mail: isa@arizona.edu
Web Site: www.isanet.org
Members: 3500 individuals
Staff: 9
Annual Budget: $500-1,000,000
Executive Director: Thomas J. Volgy
Director, Administration: Dana B. Larsen

Historical Note
A professional society with multinational and multidisciplinary membership concerned with the communication of national, international, and transnational issues, concerns, and ideas. Special areas of interest are directed within sectional subunits. Membership: based upon annual income.

Meetings/Conferences:
Annual Meetings: Spring

Publications:
International Studies Perspectives. 3/yr.
International Studies Review. 3/yr.
International Studies Quarterly. q.

International Swaps and Derivatives Association *(1985)*
360 Madison Ave., 16th Floor
New York, NY 10017
Tel: (212)901-6000 *Fax:* (212)901-6001
E-Mail: isda@isda.org
Web Site: www.isda.org
Members: 370 firms and institutions
Staff: 27
Chief Executive Officer: Robert Pickel
E-Mail: isda@isda.org
Director, Administration: Corrinne Greasley
E-Mail: isda@isda.org
Director, Communications: Louise Marshall
E-Mail: isda@isda.org

Historical Note
Founded as International Swap Dealers Association; assumed its current name in 1993. Represents firms, primarily financial institutions, corporations and government entities who deal in privately-negotiated derivatives, as well as firms who provide services to such institutions. ISDA's mission is to encourage the productive development of interest rate, currency, commodity, and equity swaps as financial products. Has an annual budget of approximately $10 million. Membership fee varies, based on type of firm and degree of activity.

Publications:
Market Survey/Margin Survey/Ops Survey. semi-a.
Newsletter. 5/year.

International Tax Institute *(1961)*
c/o Shearman & Sterling LLP
599 Lexington Ave.
New York, NY 10022
Tel: (212)848-4106 *Fax:* (646)848-4106
E-Mail: pblessing@shearman.com
Members: 75 individuals
Staff: 1
Annual Budget: $50-100,000
President: Peter H. Blessing

Historical Note
Formerly (1971) Institute on U.S. Taxation of Foreign Income. A professional organization of tax executives, lawyers and accountants concerned with taxation of international business income.

Meetings/Conferences:
Annual Meetings: Meetings and seminars held throughout the year

International Technical Caramel Association *(1975)*
1900 K St. NW, Suite 100
Washington, DC 20006
Tel: (202)496-7111 *Fax:* (202)496-7281
Members: 6 companies
Staff: 1
Annual Budget: $50-100,000
Administrator: Francine Higgenbotham

Historical Note
Members are corporations in the food coloring industry.

Meetings/Conferences:
Semi-Annual Meetings:

International Technology Education Association *(1939)*
1914 Association Dr.
Reston, VA 20191-1539
Tel: (703)860-2100 *Fax:* (703)860-0353
E-Mail: itea@iteaconnect.org
Web Site: www.iteaconnect.org
Members: 7000 individuals
Staff: 16
Annual Budget: $1-2,000,000
Executive Director and Chief Executive Officer: Kendall N. Starkweather
Editor-in-Chief: Katie De La Paz
Meeting Planner: Susan Perry
Coordinator, Membership: Lari Price

Historical Note
ITEA has an international membership, composed primarily of members in North America. Membership consists of teachers, supervisors and university faculty interested in advancing technology and science education. Affiliates of the ITEA are: Technology Education for Children Council, Council on Technology Teacher Education, and Council for Supervisors. Membership: $60/year (individual); $180/year (institution).

Meetings/Conferences:
Annual Meetings: Spring

2007 – San Antonio, TX(Convention Center)/March 15-17/2000

Publications:
Technology & Children. q. adv.
The Technology Teacher. 8/year. adv.

International Test and Evaluation Association *(1980)*
4400 Fair Lakes Ct., Suite 104
Fairfax, VA 22033-3899
Tel: (703)631-6220 *Fax:* (703)631-6221
E-Mail: itea@itea.org
Web Site: www.itea.org
Members: 2000 individuals
Staff: 5
Annual Budget: $500-1,000,000
Executive Director: Lori Freeman
Assistant Director: Eileen Redd

Historical Note
A professional society of engineers and testers concerned with the technology, process and management of test and evaluation. Members are concerned primarily with industrial and defense products (autos, tanks, aircraft, spacecraft, command and control, simulation, weapon systems, etc). Membership: $45/year (individual); $675/year (corporate).

Meetings/Conferences:
Annual Meetings: Fall

Publications:
Journal of Test and Evaluation. q. adv.

International Textile and Apparel Association *(1944)*
P.O. Box 1360
Monument, CO 80132-1360
Tel: (719)488-3716
E-Mail: itaaoffice@itaaonline.org
Web Site: www.itaaonline.org
Members: 1000 individuals
Staff: 2
Annual Budget: $100-250,000
Executive Director: Sandra Hutton

Historical Note
An outgrowth of regional conferences of textile and clothing professors held under the auspices of the Home Economics Section of the Association of Land-Grant Colleges, ITAA was established in 1970. As a part of this change, the Association was incorporated in Oklahoma. Active members are persons engaged in college or university instruction, research, and/or administration in textiles, clothing or a related area. Formerly (1991) Association of College Professors of Textiles and Clothing. Membership $95/year (individual).

Meetings/Conferences:
Annual Meetings: November/500
2007 – Los Angeles, CA(Omni)/Nov. 5-10

Publications:
ITAA Newsletter. bi-m.
The Clothing & Textiles Research Journal. q.
ITAA Proceedings. a.
ITAA Monographs. irreg.

International Theatre Equipment Association *(1971)*
770 Broadway, Fifth Floor
New York, NY 10003-9595
Tel: (646)654-7680 *Fax:* (646)654-7694
Web Site: www.itea.com
Members: 150 companies
Staff: 2
Annual Budget: $250-500,000
Executive Director: Robert Sunshine

Historical Note
Merger of Theatre Equipment Dealers Association and the Supply Manufacturers Association founded in 1933. Added International to its name in 1996. Membership: $300/year.

Publications:
ITEA Newsletter (online). q.

International Thermographers Association *(1973)*

Historical Note
A section of the Printing Industries of America, which provides administrative support.

International Ticketing Association *(1980)*
330 W. 38th St., #605
New York, NY 10018
Tel: (212)629-4036 *Fax:* (212)629-8532
E-Mail: info@intix.org
Web Site: www.intix.org
Members: 1300 organizations
Staff: 5
Annual Budget: $1-2,000,000
President: Jeffrey Larris
Director, Special Projects: Ann Gennardo
E-Mail: amgenn@intix.org
Deputy Director: Kathleen O'Donnell
E-Mail: kathyo@intix.org
Attorney: Daniel Wasser
Comptroller: Cindy Wong
E-Mail: cindyw@intix.org

Historical Note
Incorporated as Box Office Management International, INTIX members are box office managers, treasurers, marketing and systems directors and other administrators from the performing arts and sports fields; performing arts centers; entertainment facilities; and industry vendors and suppliers. Membership: $50-500/year.

Publications:
INTIX Dictionary. a.
INTIX E-Bulletin. 8/year. adv.
INTIX Directory. a.

International Tire and Rubber Association

Historical Note
Merged with Tire Association of North America in 2002 to form Tire Industry Association.

International Titanium Association *(1984)*
2655 W. Midway Blvd., Suite 300
Broomfield, CO 80020
Tel: (303)404-2221 *Fax:* (303)404-9111
E-Mail: info@titanium.org
Web Site: www.titanium.org
Members: 400 individuals
Staff: 2
Annual Budget: $250-500,000
Executive Director: Jennifer Simpson
E-Mail: info@titanium.org
Member Services: Stacey Blicker
E-Mail: info@titanium.org

Historical Note
Founded as Titanium Development Association; assumed its current name in 1995. Formed to promote titanium metal; seeks to expand existing markets and develop new markets for titanium.

Meetings/Conferences:
Annual Meetings: Fall
2007 – Orlando, FL(Rosen Shingle Creek)/Oct. 7-9

Publications:
Buyers Guide. a. adv.
Titanium Newsletter. m. adv.
Conference Proceedings. a.
Products and Services Guide. a.
Statistics. a.

International Trade Commission Trial Lawyers Association *(1984)*
P. O. Box 6186, Ben Franklin Station
Washington, DC 20004
E-Mail: admin@itctla.org
Web Site: www.itctla.org
Members: 350 individuals
Staff: 1
Annual Budget: under $10,000
President: Kent R. Stevens

Historical Note
Composed of attorneys who practice or are otherwise interested in Section 337, of the U.S. Tarriff Act, which regulates international protection of U.S. intellectual property. Membership: $80/year (government attorneys); $50/year (non-government attorneys and students).

Meetings/Conferences:
Annual Meetings: Washington, DC/Nov.

Publications:
337 Reporter. m.

International Trademark Association *(1878)*
1133 Ave. of the Americas
New York, NY 10036
Tel: (212)768-9887 *Fax:* (212)768-7796
E-Mail: info@inta.org
Web Site: www.inta.org
Members: 4550 firms and organizations
Staff: 35
Annual Budget: $5-10,000,000
Executive Director: Alan C. Drewsen
E-Mail: executivedirector@inta.org
Manager, Conferences: Lois Blankstein
Director, Education: Ann Eng
Manager, Publications: Mary McGrane
E-Mail: publications@inta.org

Historical Note
Established in New York City as The United States Trademark Association in 1878 by twelve manufacturers responding to the need to protect their trademarks. Incorporated in the state of New York January 8, 1887. INTA is the largest international membership organization that supports and advances trademarks as essential to commerce throughout the world. Changed to the International Trademark Association in 1993. INTA is located in 120 countries. Membership: $850/year (regular), $700/year (associate).

Meetings/Conferences:
Annual Meetings: April-May/5,000
2007 – Chicago, IL/Apr. 28-May 2
2008 – Berlin, Germany/May 17-21
2009 – Seattle, WA/May 16-20
2010 – Boston, MA/May 22-26
2011 – San Francisco, CA/May 14-18
2012 – Washington, DC/May 5-9

Publications:
Trademark Reporter. bi-m.
Bulletin. tri-m.
Trademark Checklist. a.

International Transactional Analysis Association *(1958)*
2186 Rheem Dr., B-1
Pleasanton, CA 94588
Tel: (925)600-8110 *Fax:* (925)600-8112
E-Mail: itaa@itaa-net.org
Web Site: www.itaa-net.org
Members: 1600 individuals
Staff: 2
Annual Budget: $500-1,000,000
Office Manager: Ken Fogleman
E-Mail: itaa@itaa-net.org

Historical Note
Founded in 1950-1951 by Dr. Eric Berne as the San Francisco Social Psychiatry Seminars, Inc. Became International Transactional Analysis Association, Inc. in 1958. ITAA is a scientific organization established to investigate and promote the use of transactional analysis (TA) in psychotherapy, education, business and other fields of human interaction. Professional membership includes individuals from the fields of psychotherapy, business, education, religion, medicine and industry. Associate membership is available for those whose interest is not related to their profession. Membership: $86/year, regular (individual); $62/year, associate (individual).

Meetings/Conferences:
Semi-annual Meetings: Annual Conference and Spring Meeting.

Publications:
Membership Directory. a. adv.
Transactional Analysis Journal. q. adv.
Script Newsletter. 9/year. adv.

International Transplant Nurses Society *(1992)*
1739 E. Carson St., Box 351
Pittsburgh, PA 15203
Tel: (412)343-4867 *Fax:* (412)343-3959
E-Mail: itns@msn.com
Web Site: www.itns.org
Members: 1365 individuals
Staff: 3
Annual Budget: $250-500,000
Executive Director: Beth A. Kassalen
E-Mail: itns@msn.com

Historical Note
ITNS active members are registered nurses, associate members and LVN's and LPN's licensed to practice in the United States with an interest in the specialty of transplantation nursing. Membership: $50/year (active); $30/year (associate).

Meetings/Conferences:
Annual Meetings: Fall

Publications:
ITNS Newsletter. q. adv.

International Trauma Anesthesia and Critical Care Society

Historical Note
Became Trauma Care International; kept the acronym ITACCS.

International Travel Writers and Editors Association *(1972)*

1224 N. Nokomis Ave. NE
Alexandria, MN 56308
Tel: (320)763-4919 *Fax:* (320)763-9290
E-Mail: ismp@iami.org
Web Site: www.iami.org/ismp
Members: 3000 individuals
Staff: 3
Annual Budget: $500-1,000,000
Executive Director: Robert G. Johnson

Historical Note
Membership: $85/year (individual).

Meetings/Conferences:
Annual Meetings: Spring

Publications:
Complete Book of International Meeting Planning. irreg.
Global Connection - Newsletter. q.

International Truck Parts Association *(1974)*

7127 Braeburn Place
Bethesda, MD 20817-4909
Tel: (202)544-3090 *Fax:* (301)229-7331
Web Site: www.itpa.com
Members: 120 companies
Staff: 1
Annual Budget: $10-25,000
Executive Director: Venlo J. Wolfsohn

Historical Note
Members are dealers in used and rebuilt parts for heavy duty trucks. Membership: $450/year.

Meetings/Conferences:
2007 - Branson, MD(Chateau on the Lake)/Apr. 6-8/75

Publications:
Membership Directory. a.
Newsletter. m.

International Trumpet Guild *(1975)*

241 E. Main St., Suite 247
Westfield, MA 01086-1633
Tel: (413)568-1913
E-Mail: treasurer@trumpetguild.org
Web Site: www.trumpetguild.org
Members: 7000 individuals
Annual Budget: $250-500,000
Treasurer: David C. Jones
E-Mail: treasurer@trumpetguild.org

Historical Note
ITG members are professional and amateur trumpet players and teachers of the trumpet. Has no paid officers or full-time staff. Membership: $40/year.

Meetings/Conferences:
Annual Meetings: Summer

Publications:
ITG Journal. q. adv.

International Tuba-Euphonium Association *(1972)*

2253 Downing St.
Denver, CO 80205
Tel: (303)832-4676 *Fax:* (303)832-0839
E-Mail: itea@denverbrass.org
Web Site: www.iteaonline.org
Members: 2700 individuals
Annual Budget: $50-100,000
Treasurer: Kathleen Aylsworth Brantigan
E-Mail: itea@denverbrass.org

Historical Note
Founded as Tubists Universal Brotherhood Association; assumed its current name in 2001. ITEA members are professional musicians, music teachers and amateur players of the tuba, euphonium and related instruments. Membership: $45/year.

Meetings/Conferences:
Annual Meetings: Summer

Publications:
Membership Roster. a.
ITEA Journal. q. adv.

International Turfgrass Society *(1969)*

c/o Everglades Research & Education Ctr.
P.O. Box 8003
Belle Glade, FL 33430-8003
Tel: (561)993-1574
Web Site: www.uoguelph.ca/GTI/itsweb/index.html
Members: 325 individuals
Director: T. Karl Donneberger

Historical Note
ITS members are academics and others with an interest in turfgrass science. Has no paid officers or full-time staff. Membership: $220/year (regular); $1,000 (sustaining).

Meetings/Conferences:
Quadrennial: 2009
2009 - Santiago, Chile(Crowne Plaza Hotel)/July 12-17

Publications:
Proceedings of Conference. quadren.

International Union of Bricklayers and Allied Craftsworkers *(1865)*

1776 I St. NW
Washington, DC 20006
Tel: (202)783-3788 *Fax:* (202)393-0219
Toll Free: (888)880 - 8222
E-Mail: askbac@bacweb.org
Web Site: www.bacweb.org
Members: 100000 individuals
Staff: 65
Annual Budget: $5-10,000,000
President: John J. Flynn
Co-Director, Communications: Eileen Betit

Historical Note
Organized October 16, 1865 in Painters Hall, Philadelphia as the Bricklayers International Union of the United States of North America. Around 1870 it was renamed the National Union of Bricklayers of the United States of America. About 1880 it became the Bricklayers and Masons International Union of America and, after plasterers were included in 1910, the Bricklayers, Masons and Plasterers' International Union of America. It affiliated with the American Federation of Labor in 1916 and assumed its present name in 1975. Sponsors and supports the International Union of Bricklayers and Allied Craftsworkers Political Action Committee.

Publications:
Chalkline. bi-m.
Journal. bi-m.

International Union of Electronic, Electrical, Salaried, Machine, and Furniture Workers-CWA *(1949)*

501 Third St. NW
Washington, DC 20001
Tel: (202)434-1228 *Fax:* (202)434-1250
Web Site: www.iue-cwa.org
Members: 75000 individuals
Staff: 75
Annual Budget: $10-25,000,000
President: James D. Clark
Director, Communications: Laure Asplen
General Counsel: Peter Mitchell

Historical Note
Chartered November 2, 1949 by the Congress of Industrial Organizations after the expulsion on grounds of being a Communist front, of the United Electrical, Radio and Machine Workers of America. In 1987, United Furniture Workers of America merged with IUE to form the Furniture Division of IUEETSMW. Has a budget of about $17 million. Founded as the International Union of Electrical, Radio and Machine Workers (AFL-CIO), it became the International Union of Electronic, Electrical, Technical, Salaried and Machine Workers (AFL-CIO) in 1983, and assumed its present name in 1987. Merged with Communication Workers of America (CWA) in 2001.

Meetings/Conferences:
Quadrennial meetings: Annual Conference.

Publications:
CWA News. bi-m.
Conference Proceedings. a.

International Union of Elevator Constructors *(1901)*

7154 Columbia Gateway Dr.
Columbia, MD 21046
Tel: (410)953-6150 *Fax:* (410)953-6169
E-Mail: contact@iuec.org
Web Site: www.iuec.org
Members: 25000 individuals
Staff: 11
Annual Budget: $2-5,000,000
General President: Dana A. Brigham
Assistant to the President: James H. Chapman, Jr.

Historical Note
Established in Pittsburgh July 18, 1901 as the National Union of Elevator Constructors. Became the International Union of Elevator Constructors in 1903 and received a charter from the American Federation of Labor.

Publications:
The Elevator Constructor. m.

International Union of Industrial Service Transport Health Employees *(1970)*

18 E. 31st St.
New York, NY 10016
Tel: (212)696-5545 *Fax:* (212)696-5556
Members: 10600 individuals
Staff: 22
Annual Budget: $2-5,000,000
President: William Perry

Historical Note
Labor union formerly known as the International Federation of Health Professionals. Assumed its present name in 1990. Members are medical personnel, blue and white collar workers and transport workers united to oppose the influence of "third party" health insurance organizations destructive of the classical doctor- patient relationship.

Meetings/Conferences:
Quadrennial Meetings: Summer (2004)

Publications:
District 6 Voice. m.

International Union of Journeymen Horseshoers and Allied Trades *(1874)*

93 Lake Ave.
Suite 103
Danbury, CT 06810
Tel: (203)205-0101 *Fax:* (203)205-0006
E-Mail: info@iujat.org
Web Site: www.iujat.org
Members: 50000 individuals
Staff: 2
Annual Budget: $10-25,000
International President: S. Richard Elliott

Historical Note
Formerly (2000) International Union of Journeymen Horseshoers of the United States and Canada. Provides training and information on efficient, proper and humane horseshoes to the professional and amateur horseman as well as working to obtain equitable wages for horseshoers. Membership is $720/year (individual).

Meetings/Conferences:
Triennial Meetings: (2004)

International Union of Operating Engineers *(1896)*

1125 17th St. NW
Washington, DC 20036
Tel: (202)429-9100 *Fax:* (202)778-2616
Web Site: www.iuoe.org
Members: 400000 individuals
Staff: 160

Annual Budget: $10-25,000,000
General President: Vincent Giblin
General Secretary and Treasurer: Christopher Hanley

Historical Note
Established in Chicago, IL on December 7, 1896 as the National Union of Steam Engineers and received a charter from the American Federation of Labor the following year. Became the International Union of Steam Engineers in 1898 following the acceptance of Canadian locals. Responding to changes in technology, it was renamed the International Union of Steam and Operating Engineers, which in 1927 merged with the International Brotherhood of Steam Shovel and Dredgemen, assuming its present name in 1928. Absorbed the United Welders International Union in 1969. Has an annual budget of approximately $15 million. Sponsors and supports the Engineers Political Education Committee.

Meetings/Conferences:
Quinquennial Meetings: Spring 2007

Publications:
International Operating Engineer. bi-m.

International Union of Painters and Allied Trades *(1887)*
1750 New York Ave. NW
Washington, DC 20006
Tel: (202)637-0700 *Fax:* (202)637-0771
E-Mail: mail@iupat.org
Web Site: www.iupat.org
Members: 140000 individuals
Annual Budget: $10-25,000,000
President: James A. Williams
Communications: Kelly Luzier

Historical Note
Organized in Baltimore March 15, 1887 as the Brotherhood of Painters and Decorators. Became the Brotherhood of Painters, Decorators and Paperhangers of America in 1890, and International Brotherhood of Painters and Allied Trades in 1969. Absorbed the United Scenic Artists, the National Paperhangers Association and the National Union of Sign Painters. Merged with the Amalgamated Glass Workers International Association in 1915. Assumed its present name in 1999.

Meetings/Conferences:
Quinquennial Meetings: (2004)

Publications:
The Painters and Allied Trades Journal. 6/year.

International Union of Petroleum and Industrial Workers *(1945)*
8131 E. Rosecrans Ave.
Paramount, CA 90723
Tel: (562)630-6232 *Fax:* (562)408-1073
Toll Free: (800)624 - 5842
E-Mail: petroleumworkers@aol.com
Members: 5000 individuals
Staff: 6
Annual Budget: $1-2,000,000
International President: George R. Beltz
International Secretary-Treasurer: Pamela Parlow

Historical Note
Founded and incorporated in 1945 as the Independent Petroleum Workers Union; affiliated with the Seafarer's International Union of North America (AFL-CIO) in 1962; adopted its present name in 1971.

Meetings/Conferences:
Quinquennial Meetings: (2005)

Publications:
IUPIW Views. q.

International Union of Police Associations, AFL-CIO *(1978)*
1421 Prince St., Suite 400
Alexandria, VA 22314
Tel: (703)549-7473 *Fax:* (703)683-9048
E-Mail: iupa@iupa.com
Web Site: www.iupa.org
Members: 80000 individuals
Staff: 15
Annual Budget: $1-2,000,000
President: Sam A. Cabral
E-Mail: iupa@iupa.com
Executive Vice President: Dennis J. Slocumb
E-Mail: iupa@iupa.com

Historical Note
Established in December, 1978 in Washington, DC, when those members who wanted to affiliate with the AFL-CIO split away from the International Conference of Police Associations. IUPA is the only labor union charted by the AFL-CIO that exclusively represents law enforcement officers. IUPA's over 110,000 members are full-time employees of law enforcement agencies, ranging from officers on field level assignments to first rank supervisors. Mission of IUPA is to protect and advance officers' wages, benefits and work conditions; members are from over 500 agencies thoroughout the United States, Caribbean area and Canada, in municipal, county, state, federal, corrections, university, and hospital law enforcement agencies.

Meetings/Conferences:
Biennial meetings: even years

Publications:
Police Union News. bi-m.

International Union Security, Police and Fire Professionals of America *(1948)*
25510 Kelly Rd.
Roseville, MI 48066
Tel: (586)772-7250 *Fax:* (586)772-9644
Toll Free: (800)228 - 7492
E-Mail: spfpapres@aol.com
Web Site: www.spfpa.org
Members: 30000 individuals
Staff: 20
Annual Budget: $2-5,000,000
President: David L. Hickey
E-Mail: spfpapres@aol.com

Historical Note
Founded as International Union, United Plant Guard Workers of America; assumed its current name in 2000. SPFPA is an independent labor union representing security professionals.

Meetings/Conferences:
Quinquennial Meetings: (2005)

Publications:
The Security Link. semi-a.

International Union, United Automobile, Aerospace and Agricultural Implement Workers of America *(1935)*
8000 E. Jefferson Ave.
Detroit, MI 48214
Tel: (313)926-5000 *Fax:* (313)823-6016
Web Site: www.uaw.org
Members: 710000 individuals
Staff: 800
Annual Budget: Over $100,000,000
President: Ron Gettelfinger

Historical Note
Chartered by the American Federation of Labor August 26, 1935 in Detroit under the name, United Automobile Workers of America. Joined the Congress of Industrial Organizations in 1938, then became independent (after the formation of AFL-CIO) in 1968. Affiliated with the AFL-CIO in 1981. Has an annual budget of approximately $389.7 million.

Meetings/Conferences:
Triennial Meeting:

Publications:
Skill Magazine. q.
Research Bulletin. q.
Solidarity Magazine. m.

International Vessel Operators Hazardous Materials Association *(1972)*
10 Hunter Brook Lane
Queensbury, NY 12804
Tel: (518)761-0263 *Fax:* (518)792-7781
Web Site: www.vohma.com
Members: 53
Staff: 3
Administrator: Lara Mehr Currie
E-Mail: lara@vohma.com

Historical Note
VOHMA is an international organization composed of representatives of many ocean common carriers of the world, operating under the flags of a number of nations, dedicated to improving the understanding and uniform application of rules and regulations governing maritime transportation of dangerous goods. VOHMA's primary focus is to foster the safe handling of hazardous materials in shipment by sea, and to offer the expertise of the ocean carriers in forging regulatory development. Actively comments on proposed regulations and is in frequent contact with the U.S. Department of Transportation's PHMSR and the U.S. Coast Guard. VOHMA provides a variety of services and benefits to its members, ranging from discounts on technical and educational publications and programs, to opportunities to network and share information.

International Visual Literacy Association *(1968)*
c/o Waubonsee Community College
Route 47, Waubonsee Dr.
Sugar Grove, IL 60554
Tel: (630)466-7900 *Fax:* (630)466-2882
E-Mail: kstewart@waubonsee.edu
Web Site: www.ivla.org
Members: 320 individuals
Staff: 1
Annual Budget: under $10,000
Executive Treasurer: Karen J. Stewart

Historical Note
Professionals involved in visual communication and visual literacy in relation to education. Affiliated with the Association for Educational Communications and Technology. Incorporated in New York in 1968, IVLA's purpose is to provide a multidisciplinary forum for exploration, presentation, and discussion of visual communication; to serve as an organizational base for professionals interested in visual literacy projects, programs, and research; to promote and evaluate projects intended to increase the use of visuals in education and communications. Membership: $40/year (individual in U.S. or Canada), $45/year (individual foreign), $20/year (student), $500 (life).

Publications:
Review newsletter. q.
Journal of Visual Literacy. semi-a.

International Warehouse Logistics Association *(1891)*
2800 S. River Rd., Suite 260
Des Plaines, IL 60018
Tel: (847)813-4699 *Fax:* (847)813-0115
Toll Free: (800)525 - 0165
E-Mail: email@iwla.com
Web Site: www.iwla.com
Members: 625 companies
Staff: 10
Annual Budget: $2-5,000,000
President and Chief Executive Officer: Joel Hoiland
Director, Member Services: Scott Brewster
Director, Operations: Karen Cioni
Vice President and Chief Operating Officer: Alex Glann
E-Mail: email@iwla.com

Historical Note
The product of a merger of the American Warehouse Association and the Canadian Association of Warehousing and Distribution Sevices. IWLA represents the warehouse logistics industry.

Meetings/Conferences:
Annual Meetings: Spring/550

Publications:
IWLA Newsgram. m. adv.
Resource Guide to Logistic Professionals. a. adv.

International Water Resources Association *(1972)*
Southern Illinois University
4535 Faner Hall
Carbondale, IL 62901-4516
Tel: (618)453-5138 *Fax:* (618)453-6465
E-Mail: iwra@siu.edu
Web Site: www.iwra.siu.edu
Members: 2000 individuals
Staff: 4
Annual Budget: $50-100,000
Executive Director: Ben Dziegielewski

Historical Note
IWRA members are individuals and organizations with an interest in water resource management. Membership: $75/year (individual); $30/year (student/retiree); $270/year (institution); $430/year (corporation).

Meetings/Conferences:
Annual Meetings: Fall

Publications:
IWRA Update Newsletter. q.
Water Internat'l. q.

International Waterlily and Water Gardening Society *(1984)*

6828 26th St. West
Bradenton, FL 34207
Tel: (941)756-0880
E-Mail: info@iwgs.org
Web Site: www.iwgs.org
Members: 500 individuals
Staff: 1
Annual Budget: $100-250,000
Executive Director: Paula Biles
E-Mail: info@iwgs.org

Historical Note
Formerly (1985) the Water Lily Society and (1998) International Water Lily Society. Established and incorporated at Lilypons, MD, IWGS is concerned with all aspects of water gardening. Membership: $30/year (individual); $75/year (organization); $75-500/year (company).

Meetings/Conferences:
Annual Meetings: August

Publications:
Water Garden Journal. q.

International Webmasters Association *(1996)*

119 E. Union St., Suite F
Pasadena, CA 91103
Tel: (626)449-3709 *Fax:* (626)449-8308
Web Site: www.iwanet.org
Members: 22000 individuals
Staff: 4
Annual Budget: $100-250,000
Executive Director: Richard S. Brinegar
Membership: Claudia Garcia

Historical Note
IWA is a membership association organized to benefit its members. Membership includes: webmasters, web site developers, graphic designers, multimedia specialists and others who participate in the development, monitoring and management of Web sites. Membership: $49/year.

International Weed Science Society *(1972)*

University of California, Davis - Plant Sciences Dept.
One Shields Ave., MS 4
Davis, CA 95616-8780
Tel: (530)752-7386 *Fax:* (530)752-4604
Members: 550 individuals
President: Remal E. Valverde
Secretary-Treasurer: Albert J. Fischer

Historical Note
Members are institutions and individuals concerned with the study of weeds and their control. IWSS is a sponsor of the International Weed Control Congress, held quadrennially. Has no full-time staff. Membership fees: $15/year (individual); $50/year (associate); $200/year (lifetime).

Meetings/Conferences:
Quadrenniel: Held in conjunction with the Weed Science Society of America
2008 - Vancouver, BC, Canada

Publications:
Newsletter. semi-a.
Symposia Proceedings. irreg.

International Wild Rice Association *(1969)*

5213 Lake Washburn Rd. NE
Outing, MN 56662
E-Mail: iwra@brainerd.net
Web Site: www.wildrice.org/
Members: 100 individuals
Staff: 1
Annual Budget: $10-25,000
President: Doug McInturff
E-Mail: iwra@brainerd.net

Historical Note
Membership: $100/year.

Meetings/Conferences:
Annual Meetings: January

Publications:
Manomin News. q.

International Window Cleaning Association *(1989)*

14 West Third St.
Suite 200
Kansas City, MO 64105
Tel: (816)471-4922 *Fax:* (816)472-7765
Toll Free: (800)875 - 4922
E-Mail: debn@robstan.com
Web Site: www.iwca.org
Members: 700 companies
Staff: 7
Annual Budget: $250-500,000
Executive Director: Debra Nemec
Associate Director: Mandie Bannwarth

Historical Note
Trade association of the window cleaning industry with members in the United States and foreign countries. IWCA provides opportunities for networking, seminars and a trade show at its annual convention. Lobbies on issues that affect the industry and works to upgrade the image of the industry. Membership: $225-750/year, based on gross sales (corporate).

Meetings/Conferences:
2007 - Nashville, TN(Opryland Hotel)/Jan. 30-Feb. 3

Publications:
Professional Window Cleaner Magazine. q. adv.

International Window Film Association *(1991)*

P.O. Box 3871
Martinsville, VA 24115
Tel: (276)666-4932 *Fax:* (276)666-4933
E-Mail: information@iwfa.com
Web Site: www.iwfa.com
Members: 800 individuals
Staff: 3
Annual Budget: $250-500,000
Executive Director: Darrell Smith
E-Mail: admin@iwfa.com

Historical Note
IWFA members are manufacturers, distributors, and installers of window film. Membership: $175/year (installer); $10000/year, plus assessment (manufacturer); $2500/year (distributor).

Meetings/Conferences:
Annual: IWFA's annual meeting is held every year as part of the SEMA show, in the first week of November.

Publications:
Newsletter. 4/year.
Legislative Chart. m.
Legislative Bulletin. m.

International Women's Writing Guild *(1976)*

P.O. Box 810, Gracie Station
New York, NY 10028-0082
Tel: (212)737-7536 *Fax:* (212)737-9469
E-Mail: iwwg@iwwg.org
Web Site: www.iwwg.org
Members: 3200 individuals
Staff: 3
Annual Budget: $100-250,000
Executive Director: Hannelore Hahn
E-Mail: iwwg@iwwg.org

Historical Note
A broad-based, grass roots alliance open to all women connected with the written word, regardless of previous professional accomplishments. A network for the personal and professional empowerment of women through writing. Membership: $35/year (domestic); $45/year (foreign).

Meetings/Conferences:
Annual Summer Conference: Saratoga Springs, NY(Skidmore College), 2nd week in August/450

Publications:
Network. 6/year. adv.

International Wood Products Association *(1956)*

4214 King St., West
Alexandria, VA 22302
Tel: (703)820-6696 *Fax:* (703)820-8550
E-Mail: info@iwpawood.org
Web Site: www.iwpawood.org
Members: 220 companies
Staff: 3
Annual Budget: $1-2,000,000
Executive Vice President: Brent McClendon, CAE
Member Services and Programs: Annette Ferri
Manager, Government and Member Outreach: Suzanne Morgan

Historical Note
Formerly (1982) Imported Hardwood Plywood Association, Imported Hardwood Products Association, (1993) International Hardwood Products Association, and IHPA - The International Wood Products Association. Assumed its present name in 1999. IWPA is committed to the promotion and enhancement of trade in all imported wood and wood products. Membership consists of U.S. importers, overseas suppliers, manufacturers, ports, steamship companies, wholesalers, custom brokers, consultants, retailers, sales representatives, agents and other organizations and government agencies related to the forest products industry. Sponsors and supports the International Wood Products Association Political Action Committee.

Meetings/Conferences:
Annual Meetings: Spring
2007 - San Diego, CA(Loews Coronado Bay)/March 28-30/350
2008 - Orlando, FL(Royal Pacific)/March 5-7/350

Publications:
Imported Wood Magazine. a. adv.
Imported Wood: The Guide to Applications, Sources, and Trends. adv.
IWPA eNews. w.
IHPA Industry Standards. irreg.
Import Wood Statistics. q.
World Trade Outlook Newsletter. a.

International Writing Centers Association *(1983)*

Penn State University
206 Boucke Bldg.
University Park, PA 16802-5900
Tel: (814)865-9243 *Fax:* (814)863-9627
Web Site: www.writingcenters.org
Members: 400 individuals
Annual Budget: under $10,000
President: Jon Olson

Historical Note
An affiliate of National Council of Teachers of English, IWCA was founded to foster communication among writing centers and to provide a forum for concerns. Members are writing center directors and staff members. Has no paid officers or full-time staff. Membership: $10/year, plus subscriptions.

Meetings/Conferences:
Semi-Annual Meetings:

Publications:
Writing Center Journal. bi-a. adv.
Writing Lab Newsletter. m. adv.

Internet Advertising Bureau

Historical Note
Became Interactive Advertising Bureau in 2003.

Internet Alliance *(1982)*

1111 19th St. NW, Suite 1180
Washington, DC 20036
Tel: (202)861-2476
Web Site: www.internetalliance.org
Members: 10 companies
Staff: 1
Annual Budget: $500-1,000,000
Executive Director: Emily Hackett

Historical Note
The Alliance is the successor to Videotex Industry Association (founded 1981). Founded as Interactive Services Association; merged with the National Association for Interactive Services in 1994, and assumed its current name in 1998. Promotes the personal use of network-based interactive electronic services in homes, offices, and public locations. It is the premier organization of Internet policy professionals representing the Internet online industry at the state, federal and international levels. Membership consists of companies developing mass market electronic information and transaction services

and all other components of the industry. Membership: $20,000/year (company).

Meetings/Conferences:
Annual Meetings: Summer

Publications:
Daily Cyber Brief. d.
Annual Conference Proceeding. a.
Membership Directory & Handbook. a. adv.

Internet Society *(1992)*
1775 Wiehle Ave., Suite 102
Reston, VA 20190-5108
Tel: (703)326-9880 *Fax:* (703)326-9881
E-Mail: info@isoc.org
Web Site: www.isoc.org
Members: 20000 individuals
Staff: 14
Annual Budget: $2-5,000,000
President and Chief Executive Officer: Lynn St. Amour

Historical Note
ISOC members are technologists, developers, educators, researchers, government representatives, business people and others with an interest in internet technologies and applications. Membership: $1,250-100,000/year (corporate); free (individuals and students).

Meetings/Conferences:
Annual Meetings: Summer

Publications:
ISOC Member Briefings. m.

Intersocietal Accreditation Commission *(1990)*
8830 Stanford Blvd., Suite 306
Columbia, MD 21045
Tel: (410)872-0100 *Fax:* (410)872-0030
Toll Free: (800)838 - 2110
Web Site: www.icavl.org
Members: 5000 laboratories
Staff: 13
Annual Budget: $1-2,000,000
Executive Director: Sandra Katanick, CAE

Historical Note
Founded as the Intersocietal Commission for the Accreditation of Vascular Laboratories, assumed its present name in 1999. Establishes standards for the accreditation of laboratories performing noninvasive vascular testing, echocardiography, nuclear cardiology, nuclear medicine, and magnetic resonance imaging. Publishes study material for laboratories interested in the accreditation process.

Intersociety Council For Pathology Information *(1957)*
9650 Rockville Pike
Bethesda, MD 20814-3993
Tel: (301)634-7200 *Fax:* (301)634-7990
E-Mail: icpi@asip.org
Web Site: www.pathologytraining.org
Members: 5 societies
Staff: 2
Annual Budget: $100-250,000
Executive Officer: Mark E. Sobel, MD, Ph.D
Administrator: Donna Stivers

Historical Note
Incorporated in 1968, the Committee serves as a central source of information about pathology and careers in pathology.

Publications:
Directory of Pathology Training Programs. a.

Interstate Council on Water Policy *(1959)*
51 Monroe St.
Suite PE-08A
Rockville, MD 20850
Tel: (301)984-1908 *Fax:* (301)984-5841
E-Mail: icwp2005@yahoo.com
Web Site: www.icwp.org
Members: 70 agencies, businesses and associations
Staff: 4
Annual Budget: $50-100,000

Historical Note
Established in 1959 and incorporated in Washington, DC in 1977. Formerly (1990) the Interstate Conference on Water Policy. Members are state and regional agencies concerned with conservation, development and administration of water and land-related resources. Multi-state, interstate and intrastate agencies, as well as non-profit organizations and educational institutions, are eligible for associate membership; business and trade associations may apply for affiliate membership. Membership: $500/year (affiliate); $1,250/year (associate), $1,875-$3,750/year (state).

Publications:
ICWP Bulletin.
ICWP Policy Statement & Bylaws. a.
Membership Directory. a.
Proceedings. a.

Interstate Natural Gas Association of America *(1944)*
10 G St. NE, Suite 700
Washington, DC 20002
Tel: (202)216-5900 *Fax:* (202)216-0870
Web Site: www.ingaa.org
Members: 39 companies
Staff: 26
Annual Budget: $5-10,000,000
President: Donald F. Santa, Jr.
Senior Vice President, Regulatory Affairs: Terry D. Boss
Vice President, General Counsel and Secretary: Joan Dreskin
Vice President, Legislative Affairs: Martin E. Edwards, III

Historical Note
Established in Kansas City, Missouri on January 11, 1944 as the Independent Natural Gas Association of America by representatives of fourteen natural gas companies. In 1974 it assumed its present name and limited its voting membership to gas transmission companies, producers and distributors becoming associate members. Sponsors the Interstate Natural Gas Association of America Political Action Committee (INGAA-PAC). Has an annual budget of approximately $5.3 million.

Meetings/Conferences:
Annual Meetings: Fall/400

Publications:
Regulatory Update. q.

Interstate Oil and Gas Commission *(1935)*
P.O. Box 53127
Oklahoma City, OK 73152-3127
Tel: (405)525-3556 *Fax:* (405)525-3592
E-Mail: iogcc@iogcc.state.ok.us
Web Site: www.iogcc.state.ok.us
Members: 700 individuals
Staff: 15
Annual Budget: $1-2,000,000
Executive Director: Christine Hansen
Manager, Communications: Alesha Leemaster

Historical Note
Formerly (1991) the Interstate Oil and Gas Compact Commission. The Interstate Oil and Gas Commission represents the governors of 37 states to champion our nation's oil and natural gas resources while protecting health, safety, and the environment.

Meetings/Conferences:
2007 - New Orleans, LA(Omni Royal)/Sept. 23-25

Publications:
Summary of State Statutes and Regulations for Oil and Gas Production. a.
Compact Comments, IOGCC Newsletter. m.
Marginal Oil and Gas: Fuel for Economic Growth. a.
Directory of Interstate Oil Commission and State Gas Agencies. a.

Intersure, Ltd. *(1966)*
Three Hotel St.
Warrenton, VA 20186
Tel: (540)349-0969 *Fax:* (540)349-0971
E-Mail: intersur@staffnet.com
Web Site: www.intersurepartners.com
Members: 45 insurance agencies
Staff: 2
Annual Budget: $50-100,000
Executive Officer: Millie Curtis
E-Mail: intersur@staffnet.com

Historical Note
Formerly (1980) the Association of International Insurance Agents; became Intersure: The International Insurance Agents Association; assumed its present title in 1985.

Meetings/Conferences:
Quarterly Meetings:

Investigative Reporters and Editors *(1975)*
138 Neff Annex
University of Missouri
Columbia, MO 65211
Tel: (573)882-2042 *Fax:* (573)882-5431
E-Mail: info@ire.org
Web Site: www.ire.org
Members: 5200 individuals
Staff: 18
Annual Budget: $1-2,000,000
Executive Director: Brant Houston
E-Mail: brant@ire.org

Historical Note
A non-profit educational organization of individuals involved or concerned with investigative journalism. Membership fees vary.

Meetings/Conferences:
Annual Meetings: June/1,000
2007 - Phoenix, AZ(Arizona Biltmore Resort and Spa)/June 7-10

Publications:
IRE Journal. bi-m. adv.
Uplink. bi-m. adv.
IRE Books. bien.

Investment Adviser Association *(1937)*
1050 17th St. NW, Suite 725
Washington, DC 20036-5503
Tel: (202)293-4222 *Fax:* (202)293-4223
E-Mail: iaa@investmentadviser.org
Web Site: www.investmentadviser.org
Members: 400 firms
Executive Director: David G. Tittsworth
General Counsel: Karen Barr
Director, Member Services: Glenda L. Henning

Historical Note
Formerly Investment Counsel Association of America; assumed present name in 2005. IAA is a not-for-profit association that exclusively represents the interests of federally registered investment adviser firms. Membership: $2,300-$7,400/year (based on assets under management).

Publications:
IAA Compliance Guide.
IAA Newsletter. m.
IAA Investment Adviser.
Blue Sky Survey.
Directory of Member Firms.

Investment Casting Institute *(1950)*
136 Summit Ave.
Montvale, NJ 07645-1720
Tel: (201)573-9770 *Fax:* (201)573-9771
Web Site: www.investmentcasting.org
Members: 200 companies
Staff: 5
Annual Budget: $500-1,000,000
Executive Director: Michael Perry
E-Mail: mperry@investmentcasting.org

Historical Note
Formed in 1950 and holding its first annual meeting in 1953, ICI members are companies employing the precision, investment casting process and suppliers to the industry.

Meetings/Conferences:
Semi-annual Meetings: Spring and Fall

Publications:
Incast Magazine. m. adv.

Investment Company Institute *(1940)*
1401 H St. NW, Suite 1200
Washington, DC 20005-2148
Tel: (202)326-5800
Web Site: www.ici.org
Members: 9,300 companies
Staff: 167
Annual Budget: $25-50,000,000
President: Paul Schott Stevens

Historical Note
Members are open-end and closed-end investment companies registered under the Investment Company Act of 1940, and their advisers and principal

underwriters, as well as unit investment trust sponsors. Formerly (1961) National Association of Investment Companies. Absorbed the Association of Mutual Fund Plan Sponsors in 1973, the Unit Investment Trust Association in 1985, and the Association of Publicly Traded Investment Funds in 1987. Has an annual budget of approximately $40 million. Sponsors the Investment Company Institute Political Action Committee (ICIPAC).

Meetings/Conferences:
Annual Meetings: Spring in Washington, DC

Publications:
(Mutual Fund) Trends. m.
Perspective. s.
Service Directory. a. adv.
Investment Company Fact Book. a.

Investment Counsel Association of America

Historical Note
Became Investment Adviser Association in 2005.

Investment Management Consultants Association *(1985)*
5619 DTC Parkway, Suite 500
Greenwood Village, CO 80111
Tel: (303)770-3377 *Fax:* (303)770-1812
E-Mail: imca@imca.org
Web Site: www.imca.org
Members: 5500 individuals
Staff: 18
Annual Budget: $5-10,000,000
Executive Director: Lee Zimmerman
E-Mail: imca@imca.org
Director, Conferences: Marcy Donaldson

Historical Note
Incorporated in Colorado, IMCA was established to provide opportunities for the exchange of information and education about management consulting; encourage the practice of high standards of professional conduct in the profession; broaden public understanding of it; and protect the interests of the profession. Absorbed Institute for Certified Investment Management Consultants in 2002. Membership: $395/year (individual).

Meetings/Conferences:
Semi-Annual Meetings: Spring and Fall

Publications:
The Journal of Investment Consulting. 2/year.
The Monitor. bi-m.

Investment Program Association *(1985)*
1140 Connecticut Ave. NW, Suite 1040
Washington, DC 20036
Tel: (202)775-9750 *Fax:* (202)331-8446
E-Mail: contact@ipa-dc.org
Web Site: www.ipa-dc.org
Members: 150 companies
Staff: 4
Annual Budget: $500-1,000,000
Vice President: Emily BonGiorni
E-Mail: contact@ipa-dc.org

Historical Note
Formerly (1991) Investment Partnership Association. A national trade association for direct investment program sponsors, broker/dealers and partnership services firms. Serves as the industry advocate before Congress, regulatory agencies, and the media. Sponsors and supports the Invest America Political Action Committee. Membership: $2,500/year (minimum).

Publications:
Technical Bulletin. irreg.

Investment Recovery Association *(1981)*
638 W. 39th St.
Kansas City, MO 64111
Tel: (816)561-5323 *Fax:* (816)561-1991
E-Mail: info@invrecovery.org
Web Site: www.invrecovery.org
Members: 300 companies
Annual Budget: $100-250,000
Executive Director: Jane Male, CAE
E-Mail: info@invrecovery.org

Historical Note
Members are firms that have an established investment recovery program providing for the disposition of recyclable products, capital assets, or surplus materials. Membership: $300/year; $450/year (associate).

Meetings/Conferences:
Semi-annual Meetings: Spring/Fall
2007 - Scottsdale, AZ(Doubletree)/May 7-9
2007 - Orlando, FL(Rosen)/Sept. 14-17

Publications:
Newsletter. 6/year. adv.

Iota Tau Tau *(1925)*
641 Benfield Rd.
Severna Park, MD 21146
Tel: (410)647-6781
Members: 500 individuals
Staff: 1
Annual Budget: $10-25,000
Executive Officer: Catherine M. Osborne

Historical Note
Founded November 11, 1925 at Southwestern University, Los Angeles. Originally an honorary legal sorority, now also open to men. Has no permanent address or paid staff. The officers change every two years. Membership: $20/year.

Publications:
The Double Tau. bien.

IPA - The Association of Graphic Solutions Providers *(1896)*
7200 France Ave. South, Suite 223
Edina, MN 55435
Tel: (952)896-1908 *Fax:* (952)896-0181
Toll Free: (800)255 - 8141
E-Mail: info@ipa.org
Web Site: www.ipa.org
Members: 500 companies
Staff: 6
Annual Budget: $1-2,000,000
President: Steve Bonoff
E-Mail: info@ipa.org

Historical Note
Members produce pre-press material for the graphics industry. Formerly (1968) the American Photoengravers Association and (1980) the American Photoplatemakers Association and (until 1984) International Association of Photoplatemakers; became (1984) International Prepress Association before later assuming its current name. Merged with PERI, Inc. (1980) and Graphic Preparatory Association (1988).

Meetings/Conferences:
Annual Meetings: Fall

Publications:
The Prepress Bulletin. bi-m. adv.
IPA News. m. adv.

IPC - Association Connecting Electronics Industries *(1957)*
3000 Lakeside Dr., Suite 309 South
Bannockburn, IL 60015
Tel: (847)615-7100 *Fax:* (847)615-5637
E-Mail: info@ipc.org
Web Site: www.ipc.org
Members: 2,300 companies
Staff: 65
Annual Budget: $10-25,000,000
President: Dennis P. McGuirk
Director, Environmental Policy: Fran Abrams
Director, Membership: Neal Bender
Vice President, Standards Technology and International Relations: David W. Bergman, CAE
Vice President, Industry Programs: Anthony Hilvers
Director, Government Relations: John Kania
Director, Production and Fulfillment: Lynn Rahman
Director, Market Research: Sharon Starr
Vice President, Marketing and Communications: Kim Sterling

Historical Note
Established as the Institute of Printed Circuits, it became the Institute for Interconnecting and Packaging Electronic Circuits in 1978, more commonly known as IPC. Assumed its current name in 1999. Members are designers, manufacturers, and users of printed circuit boards and electronic assemblies. Has an annual budget of approximately $15 million. Membership: $1,000/year (company).

Meetings/Conferences:
2007 - Los Angeles, CA/Feb. 20-22

Publications:
IPC Review. m.

IPC - Surface Mount Equipment Manufacturers Association *(1987)*
1333 H St. NW, 11th Floor - West
Washington, DC 20005
Tel: (202)962-0460 *Fax:* (202)962-0464
Web Site: www.smema.org
Members: 80 companies
Staff: 1
Annual Budget: $50-100,000
Chief Executive Officer and Vice President, Administration: Bernie Klos
Executive Director: John Kania

Historical Note
Founded as Surface Mount Equipment Manufacturers Association; became part of IPC and assumed its current name in 1999. IPC-SMEMA members are companies manufacturing equipment or producing software for surface mount board production (a process of placing and securing electrical components on printed circuit boards). IPC-SMEMA's objectives are to develop and promote standards for the interface and operation of equipment; to assure users that each machine in their production line will interface effectively and smoothly with others; to advance the technology; and to investigate areas where the association may act to the benefit of all its members. Membership: $1,000/year (company).

Meetings/Conferences:
Annual Meetings: Winter-Spring
2007 - Los Angeles, CA(Convention Center)/Feb. 20-27

Publications:
Electronics newsletter. irreg.

Ireland Chamber of Commerce in the U.S. *(1988)*
556 Central Ave.
New Providence, NJ 07974
Tel: (908)286-1300 *Fax:* (908)286-1200
E-Mail: info@iccusa.org
Web Site: www.iccusa.org
Members: 750 individuals
Staff: 3
Annual Budget: $500-1,000,000
President and Chief Executive Officer: Maurice A. Buckley

Historical Note
ICCUSA is a corporate and professional membership organization promoting the interests of Ireland and expanding trade opportunities between the U.S. and Ireland. Membership: $250/year (individual); $500/year (professional); $1000/year (corporate, and renewing founder); $10,000/year (founder; first year).

Publications:
Newsletter. q. adv.

Irish Blacks Cattle Society *(1971)*
25377 Weld County Road 17
Johnstown, CO 80534
Tel: (970)587-2252
E-Mail: mmboney@webtv.net
Web Site: www.irishblacks.com
Members: 50 individuals
Annual Budget: under $10,000
President: Maurice W. Boney

Historical Note
Members are breeders of Irish Black cattle. Has no paid officers or full-time staff.

Publications:
BFS Newsletter. irreg.

Iron and Steel Society

Historical Note
Merged with Association of Iron and Steel Engineers to form Association for Iron and Steel in 2003.

Iron Casting Research Institute *(1939)*
2802 Fisher Rd.
Columbus, OH 43204
Tel: (614)275-4201 *Fax:* (614)275-4203
E-Mail: icri@ironcasting.org
Web Site: www.ironcasting.org

Members: 17 companies
Staff: 4
Annual Budget: $250-500,000
Executive Director: Bruce T. Blatzer
E-Mail: icri@ironcasting.org
Manager, Member Services: Susan J. Lambert
E-Mail: icri@ironcasting.org

Historical Note
Founded as Gray Iron Research Group; assumed its current name in 1982. Members are iron casting companies.

Publications:
Newsletter. bi-m.

Irrigation Association *(1949)*
6540 Arlington Blvd.
Falls Church, VA 22042-6638
Tel: (703)536-7080 *Fax:* (703)536-7019
E-Mail: membership@irrigation.org
Web Site: www.irrigation.org
Members: 1600 companies
Staff: 11
Annual Budget: $2-5,000,000
Executive Director: Deborah M. Hamlin, CAE
Manager, Membership: Mike Hemsley
E-Mail: membership@irrigation.org
Director, Education: Dennis McKernan
Director, Meetings: Denise Stone

Historical Note
Formerly the Sprinkler Irrigation Association, it adopted its present name in 1976 and absorbed the Drip Irrigation Association in 1979. Members are manufacturers, designers, suppliers, consultants, and contractors of all irrigation systems. Membership: $100/year (individual), $350-$14,000/year (company).

Meetings/Conferences:
Annual Meetings: Fall
2007 – San Diego, CA(Convention Center)/Dec. 9-11/7000

Publications:
Preliminary and Final Show Directory. a. adv.
Conference Proceedings. a.
Membership Directory and Buyers Guide. a. adv.

ISA *(1945)*
67 Alexander Dr., Box 12277
Research Triangle Park, NC 27709
Tel: (919)549-9411 *Fax:* (919)549-8288
E-Mail: info@isa.org
Web Site: www.isa.org
Members: 30000 individuals
Staff: 70
Annual Budget: $10-25,000,000
Executive Director: Robert Renner
Director, Finance and Administration: Ken Hilgers
E-Mail: khilgers@isa.org
Director, Education and Member Services: Dale Lee
E-Mail: dlee@isa.org
Associate Director, Publishing Services: T.S. (Chip) Lee
E-Mail: tlee@isa.org

Historical Note
Founded in Pittsburgh on April 28, 1945 by representatives of 18 local instrument societies from the U.S. and Canada as Instrument Society of America; assumed its current name in 2000. Incorporated initially in Pennsylvania, now a North Carolina corporation. A charter member of the American Automatic Control Council, an affiliate of the American Institute of Physics, member of American National Standard Institute, American Association for the Advancement of Science and U.S. representative to the International Measurement Confederation. Formed a subsidiary, ISA Services, Inc. in 1986. Has a budget of approximately $16 million. Membership: $85/year.

Meetings/Conferences:
Annual Meetings: Fall/18000

Publications:
ISA Proceedings. q.
ISA Directory of Automation. a. adv.
InTech. m. adv.
ISA Transactions. q.

ISDA - The Office Systems Cooperative *(1973)*
19 Valley View Dr.
Suffield, CT 06078
Tel: (860)463-6262 *Fax:* (860)668-9912
Web Site: www.isdanet.net
Members: 125 companies
Staff: 4
Annual Budget: $500-1,000,000
Executive Director: Herb Lyon
Administrative Coordinator: Erin Decker

Historical Note
Formerly (1981) International Systems Dealers Association. Members are dealers of office filing systems and microfilm equipment. Membership: $300-960/year (organization/company).

Publications:
News & Views. q. adv.
Office Systems Management. q. adv.

Islamic Medical Association of North America *(1967)*
101 W. 22nd St., Suite 106
Lombard, IL 60148
Tel: (630)932-0000
E-Mail: hq@imana.org
Web Site: www.imana.org
Members: 3000 individuals
Staff: 3
Annual Budget: $100-250,000
President: Rehana Kausar, M.D.
Manager: Usman R. Durrani

Historical Note
IMA members are Muslim physicians and health professionals. Membership: $200/year (individual); $2,500 (life membership).

Meetings/Conferences:
Annual Meetings: Summer

Publications:
JIMA - Journal of the Islamic Medical Association. q. adv.
IMANA News newsletter. q. adv.

ISSA *(1923)*
7373 N. Lincoln Ave.
Lincolnwood, IL 60712-1799
Tel: (847)982-0800 *Fax:* (847)982-1012
Toll Free: (800)225 - 4772
E-Mail: info@issa.com
Web Site: www.issa.com
Members: 5000 companies
Staff: 25
Annual Budget: $5-10,000,000
Executive Director: John P. Garfinkel
Director, Legislative Affairs: William C. Balek
Director, Membership Services and Operations: Joan F. Cooke
Director, Conventions and Meetings: LeeAnn Nowling
Director, Communications and Publications: Lisa Veeck

Historical Note
Formerly National Sanitary Supply Association and then International Sanitary Supply Association; assumed current name in 2005. Members are manufacturers, distributors, wholesalers, manufacturer representatives, publishers and associate members engaged in the manufacture and/or distribution of cleaning and maintenance products. Sponsors and supports the Sanitary Supply Political Action Committee (Clean-PAC) and the ISSA Foundation, its educational arm. Membership: $390-2,800/year.

Meetings/Conferences:
Annual Meetings: Fall/15,000

Publications:
ISSA Today. 10/year. adv.
Education Catalog. a.
ISSAlert. irreg.
Membership Directory. a.
ISSA Legislative and Regulatory Update. m.

IT Financial Management Association *(1988)*
P.O. Box 30188
Santa Barbara, CA 93130
Tel: (805)687-7390 *Fax:* (805)687-7382
E-Mail: info@itfma.com
Web Site: www.itfma.com
Members: 950 individuals
Staff: 1
Annual Budget: $100-250,000
President and Director: Terence A. Quinlan
E-Mail: info@itfma.com

Historical Note
Formerly (1996) Finanacial Managment for Data Processing and then (2001) IS Financial Management Association; assumed its current name in 2002. ITFMA provides educational programs and services for the financial management of information technology organizations. Services include seminars, education certificates, conferences and job clearinghouse service. Membership: $75/year (individual); $400-1,200/year (facility).

Meetings/Conferences:
Annual Meetings: Spring
2007 – Nashville, TN(Gaylord Opryland Hotel)/March 26-30/125
2007 – Las Vegas, NV(Mirage Resort)/June 25-29/250

Publications:
Journal of IT Financial Management. q.
Membership Directory. a.

Italy-America Chamber of Commerce *(1887)*
730 Fifth Ave., Suite 600
New York, NY 10019
Tel: (212)459-0044 *Fax:* (212)459-0090
E-Mail: info@italchamber.org
Web Site: www.italchamber.org
Members: 1200 individuals
Staff: 9
Annual Budget: $1-2,000,000
Secretary General: Franco De Angelis
Director, Communications: Carlo Santoro
Director, Marketing: Federico Tozzi

Historical Note
Formerly American Chamber of Commerce for Trade with Italy, it is the oldest foreign trade chamber in the U.S. An independent, private, not-for-profit corporation devoted to fostering trade between Italy and the U.S. through information, education, and travel services. Affiliated with the U. S. Chamber of Commerce and is a founding member of the European-American Chamber of Commerce. Membership: $500/year.

Meetings/Conferences:
Annual Meetings: June

Publications:
Target Italy. q. adv.
IACC Inform. m. adv.
Trade with Italy. bi-m. adv.
US-Italy Trade Directory. a. adv.
Guide for Exporting to the United States.

Japan Automobile Manufacturers Association *(1967)*
1050 17th St. NW, Suite 410
Washington, DC 20036-5503
Tel: (202)296-8537 *Fax:* (202)872-1212
E-Mail: jama@jama.org
Web Site: www.jama.org
Members: 14 companies
Staff: 6
Contact: Charley Powers

Historical Note
JAMA supports the production of Japanese-made automobilies and vehicles.

Publications:
Japan Auto Trends. q.

Jean Piaget Society *(1970)*
Dept. of Human Development, Larsen Hall, Harvard Univ.
Cambridge, MA 02138-1205
Tel: (617)495-3446 *Fax:* (617)495-3626
Web Site: www.piaget.org
Members: 600 individuals
Staff: 1
Annual Budget: $10-25,000
Manager, General Office: Kurt W. Fischer

Historical Note
The Piaget Society, a.k.a. Society for the Study of Knowledge and Development, includes researchers and practitioners in the fields of psychology, education, philosophy and psychiatry who are interested in the nature of human knowledge. Has no paid officers or full-time staff. Membership: $30/year (student); $70/year (regular).

Meetings/Conferences:
Annual Meetings: late May-June

Publications:
Newsletter. semi-a.
Symposium Proceedings. a.
Cognitive Development (journal). q. adv.

Jesuit Association of Student Personnel Administrators *(1954)*
St. Joseph's Univ.
5600 City Ave.
Philadelphia, PA 19131
Tel: (610)660-1045 *Fax:* (610)660-1069
Web Site: http://jaspa.creighton.edu
Members: 28 institutions
Annual Budget: under $10,000
President: Susan Donovan

Historical Note
Members are administrators of student personnel programs in Jesuit universities/colleges. Has no paid officers or full-time staff. Membership: based on a sliding scale.

Meetings/Conferences:
Annual Meetings: Spring

Publications:
JASPA Newsletter. 6/year.
Directory. a.

Jesuit Secondary Education Association *(1970)*
1616 P St. NW, Suite 400
Washington, DC 20036
Tel: (202)667-3888 *Fax:* (202)387-6305
E-Mail: jsea@jsea.org
Web Site: www.jsea.org
Members: 48 schools
Staff: 6
Annual Budget: $100-250,000
President: Ralph Metts, SJ
Executive Secretary: Kathreja Mills

Historical Note
Formerly, with the Association of Jesuit Colleges and Universities, a part of the Jesuit Education Association.

Publications:
AJCU/JSEA Directory. a.
JSEA News Bulletin. 8/year.

Jewelers Board of Trade *(1884)*
95 Jefferson Blvd.
Warwick, RI 02888-1046
Tel: (401)467-0055 *Fax:* (401)467-1199
E-Mail: jbtinfo@jewelersboard.com
Web Site: www.jewelersboard.com
Members: 3200 businesses
Staff: 58
Annual Budget: $2-5,000,000
President: Dione D. Kenyon

Historical Note
A credit reporting agency, JBT also provides collection services and mailing lists specific to the jewelry industry. Membership: $740/year (company).

Publications:
Confidential Reference Book. B.
New Claims/Bankruptcy Report. w.
Service Bulletin. w.
New Name Bulletin. w.

Jewelers of America *(1957)*
52 Vanderbilt Ave., 19th Floor
New York, NY 10017-3827
Tel: (646)658-0246 *Fax:* (646)658-0256
Toll Free: (800)223 - 0673
E-Mail: info@jewelofam.org
Web Site: www.jewelers.org
Members: 12500 stores
Staff: 16
Annual Budget: $2-5,000,000
President: Matthew A. Runci
E-Mail: matt@jewelofam.org

Historical Note
Formed as Retail Jewelers of America; the result of a merger between American National Retail Jewelers Association (founded 1906) and National Jewelers Association (founded 1942); assumed its current name in 1980. Membership: based on annual sales, number of employees or number of stores.

Meetings/Conferences:
Semi-Annual Meetings: February and July in New York, NY

Publications:
J Report. 6/year.

Jewelers Shipping Association *(1956)*
125 Carlsbad St.
Cranston, RI 02920
Tel: (401)943-6020 *Fax:* (401)943-1490
Toll Free: (800)688 - 4572
Web Site: www.jewelersshipping.com
Members: 1500 companies
Staff: 50
Annual Budget: $1-2,000,000
Managing Director: David Roche
General Manager: Mark Green
Contact: Mike Silva

Historical Note
Membership: $10/year.

Meetings/Conferences:
Annual Meetings: Providence, RI/Fall

Publications:
Journal of Commerce. d.

Jewelers Vigilance Committee *(1912)*
25 W. 45th St., Suite 400
New York, NY 10036
Tel: (212)997-2002 *Fax:* (212)997-9148
Toll Free: (800)564 - 6582
Web Site: www.jvclegal.org
Members: 3000 companies
Staff: 6
Annual Budget: $500-1,000,000
Executive Director and General Counsel: Cecilia L. Gardner
E-Mail: clgjvc@aol.com
Marketing and Development: Amy Greenbaum
E-Mail: agjvc@aol.com

Historical Note
JVC is the "legal arm and guardian of the jewelry industry, advocating legal compliance and ethical practices." JVC monitors legislation, provides government agency liaison, trade liaison, and consumer dispute resolution services.

Meetings/Conferences:
Annual Meetings: July/New York, NY(Javits Center)

Publications:
JVC Membership Directory. a.
Legal Reference for the Industry.
News and Views. 3/year.
Retailer's Legal Handbook.
Legal Compliance In Plain English.
Manufacturer's Legal Handbook.

Jewelers' Security Alliance of the U.S. *(1883)*
Six E. 45th St.
New York, NY 10017
Tel: (212)687-0328 *Fax:* (212)808-9168
Toll Free: (800)537 - 0067
E-Mail: jsa2@jewelerssecurity.org
Web Site: www.jewelerssecurity.org
Members: 19500 jewelry businesses
Staff: 6
Annual Budget: $1-2,000,000
President: John J. Kennedy
E-Mail: jsa2@jewelerssecurity.org
Manager, Membership Services: Helen M. Buck
E-Mail: jsa2@jewelerssecurity.org

Historical Note
Founded by 17 manufacturing jewelers in New York, NY to offer crime prevention assistance to traveling salespersons. Membership: $85-3000/year.

Meetings/Conferences:
Annual Meetings: January, New York City

Publications:
JSA Manual of Jewelry Security. bien. adv.
Newsletter. 2/year. adv.
Crime Bulletin. 10-15/year.

Jewelry Industry Distributors Association *(1946)*
701 Enterprise Dr.
Harrison, OH 45030
Tel: (513)367-2357 *Fax:* (513)367-1414
Web Site: www.jida.info
Members: 135 companies
Staff: 4
Annual Budget: $250-500,000
Executive Director: Jim Lubic

Historical Note
Formerly (1984) the Watch Material and Jewelry Distributors Association of America.

Meetings/Conferences:
Annual Meetings: Spring, with American Jewelry Marketing Association

Publications:
News and Views. q.

Jewelry Information Center *(1946)*
52 Vanderbilt Ave., 19th Floor
New York, NY 10017
Tel: (646)658-0240 *Fax:* (646)658-0245
Toll Free: (800)459 - 0130
E-Mail: info@jic.org
Web Site: www.jic.org
Members: 850 companies
Staff: 2
Annual Budget: $500-1,000,000
Media Liason: Helena Krodell
Public Relations Coordinator: Amanda Berg

Historical Note
The promotional and educational arm of the fine jewelry industry, JIC provides news, trends, and statistics about the fine jewelry industry to the media and otherwise promotes fine jewelry. JIC members are manufacturers, importers, refiners, equipment and tool and watch suppliers, stone dealers, precious metal fabricators and retailers with a 50/50 split between suppliers and retailers. Membership: $95-10,000/year (based on number of employees).

Publications:
LINK. 4/year.

Jewish Book Council
15 E. 26th St., 10th Floor
New York, NY 10010-1579
Tel: (212)532-4297 *Fax:* (212)481-4174
E-Mail: jbc@jewishbooks.org
Web Site: www.jewishbookcouncil.org
Staff: 1
Director: Carolyn Hessel

Historical Note
An affiliate of Jewish Community Centers Association of North America.

Publications:
Jewish Book Annual. a.

Jewish Community Centers Association of North America *(1917)*
15 E. 26th St.
New York, NY 10010-1579
Tel: (212)532-4949 *Fax:* (212)481-4174
E-Mail: info@jcca.org
Web Site: www.jcca.org
Members: 275 agencies
Staff: 40
Annual Budget: $2-5,000,000
President: Allan Finkelstein
E-Mail: info@jcca.org

Historical Note
An association of Jewish Community Centers, YM-YWHAs and Camps. Founded as the National Jewish Welfare Board, it absorbed the Council of Young Men's Hebrew and Kindred Associations in 1921. Assumed the name JWB in 1977 and its present name in 1990.

Meetings/Conferences:
Biennial Meetings: Even years/1,200

Publications:
Circle. q.
Briefing for JCC Presidents. 5/year.

Jewish Education Service of North America *(1939)*
111 Eighth Ave., 11th Floor
New York, NY 10011
Tel: (212)284-6950 *Fax:* (212)284-6951
Web Site: www.jesna.org
Members: 2000 individuals
Staff: 36
Annual Budget: $2-5,000,000
President: Dr. Donald A. Sylvan

Director, Marketing and Communication: Rika Levin-Reisman
E-Mail: rlevin@jesna.org

Historical Note

Formerly (1981) the American Association for Jewish Education. The Jewish education, advocacy, planning, coordinating and service agency for the federated Jewish community in North America. Helps local federations and central agencies for Jewish education undertake activities in research, program and human service development, information and resource dissemination, and consultations. Membership: $100/year (individual); for institutions, fee varies by size.

Publications:
JESNA eNewsletter.
Agenda: Jewish Education. q.
Directory of Central Agencies for Jewish Education. q.

Jewish Educators Assembly *(1951)*
P.O. Box 413
Cedarhurst, NY 11516
Tel: (516)569-2537 *Fax:* (516)295-9039
E-Mail: jewisheducators@jewisheducators.org
Web Site: www.jewisheducators.org
Members: 500 individuals
Staff: 3
Annual Budget: $100-250,000
Executive Director: Edward Edelstein

Historical Note

The Jewish Educators Assembly is an organization of Jewish education professionals, including educational directors of congregational schools, day school headmasters, youth directors, educational consultants, bureau directors, college professors, camp directors, family educators, academicians, and nursery directors functioning within the Conservative movement. Membership: $150/year (basic), $25/year (retired, student).

Meetings/Conferences:
Annual Meetings: Winter
2007 – , NJ

Publications:
Beineinu. m.
V'Aleh Hachadashot. 3/year.

Jewish Funeral Directors of America *(1927)*
Seaport Landing, 150 Lynnway, Suite 506
Lynn, MA 01902
Tel: (781)477-9300 *Fax:* (781)477-9393
E-Mail: info@jfda.com
Web Site: www.jfda.org
Members: 125 firms
Staff: 1
Annual Budget: $250-500,000
Executive Director: Florence Pressman, CAE
E-Mail: jfdamer@aol.com

Historical Note

JFDA's purpose is to preserve the traditions and customs of the Jewish funeral service as recognized and practiced by those of the Jewish faith; to enrich and strengthen its association as an exemplar of Jewish values; to fomulate and advocate the highest principles, ideals and ethics of the funeral profession; to conduct a Jewish funeral association for the mutual benefit of its members and the performance of its religious functions though professional cooperation to foster other activities for the perpetuation and advancement of the funeral profession and its relationship to Judaism.

Meetings/Conferences:
Annual Meetings: November

Publications:
The Jewish Funeral Director. a. adv.
JFDA Newsletter. 3/year.

Jewish Social Service Professionals Association *(1965)*
620 E. Cranbury Rd.
Suite 102
East Brunswick, NJ 08816
Tel: (732)432-7346 *Fax:* (732)432-7127
Toll Free: (800)634 - 7346
E-Mail: ajfca@ajfca.org
Web Site: www.ajfca.org
Members: 300 individuals
Staff: 1
Annual Budget: $500-1,000,000
President and Chief Executive Officer: Bert J. Goldberg

Historical Note

Established in 1964 as the National Association of Jewish Family, Children's and Health Services. Known as National Association of Jewish Family, Children's and Health Professionals until 1987. Membership: $25-100/year (individual).

Meetings/Conferences:
Annual Meetings: May

Publications:
Executive Digest. m.
Tachlis Newsletter. q.

Jockey Club *(1894)*
40 E. 52nd St.
New York, NY 10022
Tel: (212)371-5970 *Fax:* (212)371-6123
Toll Free: (800)444 - 8521
E-Mail: contactus@jockeyclub.com
Web Site: www.jockeyclub.com
Members: 100 individuals
Staff: 14
President: Alan G. Marzelli

Historical Note

A service organization to the racing industry which encourages the development of thoroughbred horses, establishes regulations governing them and sets the foundation for rules adopted by all racing states. Members are individual owners/breeders and others connected with the racing industry.

Publications:
The Fact Book. m.

Jockeys' Guild *(1940)*
P.O. Box 150
Monrovia, CA 91017-0150
Tel: (626)305-5605 *Fax:* (626)305-5615
E-Mail: info@jockeysguild.com
Web Site: www.jockeysguild.com
Members: 800 individuals
Staff: 13
Annual Budget: $1-2,000,000
Director: Wayne Gertmenian
E-Mail: info@jockeysguild.com

Historical Note

Established as the Jockey's Community Fund and Guild, it assumed its present name in 1946. Members are licensed flat riding jockeys. Major thrust is to offer financial aid to needy members.

Meetings/Conferences:
Annual Meetings: First week in December

Publications:
Jockey News. bi-m.

Joint Council of Allergy, Asthma, and Immunology *(1975)*
50 N. Brockway St., Suite 3-3
Palatine, IL 60067
Tel: (847)934-1918 *Fax:* (847)934-1820
E-Mail: info@jcaai.org
Web Site: www.jcaai.org
Members: 2 organizations
Staff: 3
Annual Budget: $250-500,000
Executive Director: Donald W. Aaronson, M.D.
E-Mail: info@jcaai.org

Historical Note

The political affairs liaison for the two major national allergy organizations: the American Academy of Allergy, Asthma & Immunology and the American College of Allergy, Asthma & Immunology. Membership: $175/year.

Meetings/Conferences:
Annual Meetings: Spring
2007 – Washington, DC

Publications:
New News You Can Use. w.

Joint Electron Device Engineering Council *(1941)*
2500 Wilson Blvd.
Arlington, VA 22201
Tel: (703)907-7558 *Fax:* (703)907-7583
Web Site: www.jedec.org
Members: 300 companies
Staff: 10
Annual Budget: $1-2,000,000
Senior Coordinator: Arlene Collier

Historical Note

Affiliated with the Electronic Industries Association. Members are manufacturers of solid state products. Membership: $4,000-8,000/year.

Meetings/Conferences:
Semi-annual Meetings: Spring and Fall

Publications:
JEDEC Engineering Publications.

Journalism Education Association *(1924)*
103 Kedzie Hall, Kansas State University
Manhattan, KS 66506-1501
Tel: (785)532-5532 *Fax:* (785)532-5484
Toll Free: (866)523 - 5523
E-Mail: jea@spub.edu
Web Site: www.jea.org
Members: 2200 individuals
Staff: 2
Annual Budget: $250-500,000
Executive Director: Linda S. Puntney

Historical Note

Established as National Association of Journalism Directors in 1924, it became a division of National Education Association in 1937; it has since severed this tie, and in 1963 assumed its present name. Members are principally secondary school journalism teachers and advisers. Membership: $35/year (individual); $40/year (institution).

Meetings/Conferences:
Semi-annual Meetings: April and November/3,000-3,500

Publications:
Communication: Journalism Education Today. q. adv.
Newswire. 3/year. adv.

Judge Advocates Association *(1943)*
720 Seventh St. NW, 3rd Floor
Washington, DC 20001-3716
Tel: (202)448-1712 *Fax:* (202)628-0080
E-Mail: jaa@jaa.org
Web Site: www.jaa.org
Members: 400 individuals
Annual Budget: $25-50,000
President: Karl F. Schneiders

Historical Note

Members are lawyers who serve or have served in the Armed Forces or who practice before the U.S. Court of Appeals for the Armed Forces and U.S. Courts of Appeals for Veterans Cause. Promotes improvement of military legal and judicial system. Membership: $50/year.

Meetings/Conferences:
Annual Meetings: In conjunction with the American Bar Association

Publications:
The Military Advocate. q. adv.

Juice Products Association *(1957)*
1156 15th St. NW, Suite 900
Washington, DC 20005
Tel: (202)785-3232 *Fax:* (202)223-9741
E-Mail: jpa@kellencompany.com
Web Site: www.juiceproducts.org
Members: 66 regular, 60 associates
Staff: 1
Annual Budget: $250-500,000
Executive Director: Carol Freysinger

Historical Note

Established by a group of citrus juice processors in Dallas, TX in Jan., 1957 as the National Association of Citrus Juice Processors and incorporated in Florida in June of that year; became the National Orange Juice Association in 1960, and National Juice Products Association in 1966; absorbed Processed Apples Institute and assumed its present name in 2003. Absorbed the International Jelly and Preserves Association in 2004. JPA's objectives are the promulgation of uniform standards and uniform advertising and labeling practices for juice and fruit products; the promotion of high standards of quality for juice and fruit products; liaison between Federal and state regulatory agencies; and promotion of research. Membership: $4,000/year.

Meetings/Conferences:
Annual Meetings: Spring/400
2007 - Monarch Beach, CA(St. Regis Resort)/Apr. 15-18/350

Publications:
Newsletter. m.
Membership Directory. q.

Justice Research and Statistics Association *(1974)*
777 N. Capitol St. NE, Suite 801
Washington, DC 20002
Tel: (202)842-9330 *Fax:* (202)842-9329
E-Mail: cjinfo@jrsa.org
Web Site: www.jrsa.org
Members: 300 individuals and institutions
Staff: 21
Annual Budget: $2-5,000,000
Executive Director: Joan C. Weiss
Director, Finance and Administration: Sandy Dayton
Director, Information and Member Services: Karen F. Maline
Director, Research: Stan Orchowsky, Ph.D.
Director, Training and Technical Assistance: James Zepp

Historical Note
JRSA is funded primarily by Justice Department grants. JRSA members include directors of state criminal justice statistics analysis centers and individuals engaged in applied statistical analysis in criminal and juvenile justice agencies and academia. The Association's purpose is to promote the exchange of criminal justice statistics in the states, and to provide training. Membership: $75/year (individual); $300/year (organization); $49/year (student).

Meetings/Conferences:
Annual Meetings: October/250

Publications:
Directory of Justice Issues in the States. a.
Justice Research and Policy Journal. semi-a.
JRSA Forum. q.

Juvenile Products Manufacturers Association *(1962)*
15000 Commerce Pkwy., Suite C
Mt. Laurel, NJ 08054-2255
Tel: (856)638-0420 *Fax:* (856)439-0525
E-Mail: achezem@ahint.com
Web Site: www.jpma.org
Members: 325 companies
Staff: 16
Annual Budget: $1-2,000,000
President: Robert Waller, Jr., CAE
Trade Show Director: Chris Brown
Director, Communications: Amy Chezem
Director, Member Services: Kandi Mell
E-Mail: jpma@ahint.com

Historical Note
Members are engaged in the manufacture, importation or exclusive distribution of juvenile products for general sale to retail distribution channels.

Meetings/Conferences:
Annual Meetings: Early Spring
2007 - Orlando, FL/Apr. 23-5

Publications:
Retail Rattle. q.
Connections. q.

JWB Jewish Chaplains Council *(1946)*
15 E. 26th St., 10th Floor
New York, NY 10010-1579
Tel: (212)532-4949 *Fax:* (212)481-4174
E-Mail: info@jcca.org
Web Site: www.jcca.org/JWB/index.html
Members: 400 individuals
Annual Budget: under $10,000
Executive Director: Rabbi David Lapp
Communications Manager: Miriam Rinn

Historical Note
Members are Jewish chaplains in the Army, Air Force, and Department of Veterans Affairs. Formerly Association of Jewish Chaplains of the Armed Forces. Has no paid officers or full-time staff. Membership: $10/year.

Meetings/Conferences:
Biennial Meetings: Winter-Spring

Publications:
CHAPLINES Newsletter. q.

Kamut Association of North America *(1990)*
P.O. Box 6447
Great Falls, MT 59406
Tel: (406)452-7227 *Fax:* (406)452-7175
Toll Free: (800)644 - 6450
Web Site: www.kamut.com/index2.html
Members: 90 individuals
Staff: 2
Annual Budget: $25-50,000
Executive Assistant: Debby Blyth
E-Mail: debby@kamut.com

Historical Note
KANA members are growers, processors and distributors of kamut grain.

Kappa Delta Epsilon *(1933)*
5115 Ashmont Ct.
Dunwoody, CA 30338
Tel: (770)393-1766 *Fax:* (770)395-7130
Web Site: www.kappadeltaepsilon.org
Members: 40000 individuals
Staff: 1
Annual Budget: $50-100,000
Secretary: Lynda Goodwin

Historical Note
An honorary professional educational fraternity founded in Washington, DC, March 25, 1933. KDE recognizes through its membership outstanding students preparing to enter the teaching profession and those actively engaged in teaching or related professions. Membership: $10/year, plus $25 initiation fee.

Meetings/Conferences:
Biennial National Meeting: even-numbered years

Publications:
The Current. 3/year.

Kappa Delta Pi *(1911)*
3707 Woodview Trace
Indianapolis, IN 46268-1158
Tel: (317)871-4900 *Fax:* (317)704-2323
Toll Free: (800)284 - 3167
E-Mail: admin@kdp.org
Web Site: www.kdp.org
Members: 55000 individuals
Staff: 25
Annual Budget: $2-5,000,000
Executive Director: Pamela K. Buckley
E-Mail: buckleyp@kdp.org
Director, Development: Cara Lathrop
E-Mail: cara@kdp.org
Director, Marketing and Membership: Faye Snodgress

Historical Note
Educational honor society. Includes honor students, faculty, and teacher practitioners in education. Membership: $35/year.

Meetings/Conferences:
Biennial Meetings:
2007 - Louisville, KY(Marriott)/Nov. 1-3/1500

Publications:
Educational Forum. q. adv.
Kappa Delta Pi Record. q. adv.
New Teacher Advocate. q. adv.

Kappa Kappa Iota *(1921)*
1875 E. 15th St.
Tulsa, OK 74104-4610
Tel: (918)744-0389 *Fax:* (918)744-0578
Toll Free: (800)678 - 0389
E-Mail: kappa@galstar.com
Web Site: www.kappakappaiota.org
Members: 7000 individuals
Staff: 2
Annual Budget: $100-250,000
Executive Director: Pat Fluegel
E-Mail: kappa@galstar.com

Historical Note
Established in Stillwater, OK, Kappa Kappa Iota is an organization formed to promote the advancement of education by providing an effective network for the exchange of education and teaching practices by educators. Membership: $20 plus state and local dues/year (individual).

Meetings/Conferences:
Annual Meetings: June/400
2007 - Savannah, GA(Hilton DeSoto)/June 30-July 3/350

Publications:
Kappa Profile. q.

Kappa Psi Pharmaceutical Fraternity *(1879)*
S.W. Oklahoma State University School of Pharmacy
100 Campus Dr.
Weatherford, OK 73096
Tel: (580)774-7171 *Fax:* (580)774-7125
E-Mail: kappapsi@swosu.edu
Web Site: www.kappa-psi.org
Members: 56000 individuals
Staff: 2
Annual Budget: $100-250,000
Executive Director: Dr. Scott Long
E-Mail: executivedirector@kappa-psi.org

Historical Note
Founded at Russell Military Academy, New Haven, CT. Kappa Psi is a professional fraternity in pharmacy. Membership: $35/year (individual).

Meetings/Conferences:
Biennial Meetings: August (odd years)

Publications:
The Mask. q. adv.

Keramos Fraternity *(1902)*
P.O. Box 999, K6-24
Richland, WA 99352
Tel: (509)372-3108 *Fax:* (509)376-3108
Web Site: www.ceramics.org/keramos
Members: 8000 individuals
Annual Budget: under $10,000
General Secretary: Dr. Bradley R. Johnson

Historical Note
A professional fraternity of ceramic engineers. Has no paid officers or full-time staff. Meets concurrently with the Annual Meeting of the American Ceramic Society. Membership: $10/year (individual).

Meetings/Conferences:
Annual Meetings: Spring

Publications:
Keragram. q.

Keyboard Teachers Association International *(1963)*

Historical Note
A division of Music Teachers Association International, which provides administrative support.

Kitchen Cabinet Manufacturers Association *(1955)*
1899 Preston White Dr.
Reston, VA 20191-5435
Tel: (703)264-1690 *Fax:* (703)620-6530
E-Mail: info@kcma.org
Web Site: www.kcma.org
Members: 360 manufacturers
Staff: 5
Annual Budget: $500-1,000,000
Executive Vice President: C. Richard Titus
E-Mail: dtitus@kcma.org
Director, Member Services and Marketing: Janet Titus
E-Mail: jtitus@kcma.org

Historical Note
Formerly National Institute of Wood Kitchen Cabinets. Became the National Kitchen Cabinet Association in 1962 and assumed its present name in 1990. Members are manufacturers of assembled prefinished kitchen cabinets. Absorbed the Decorative Laminate Products Association in 1995. Membership: $535/year (minimum, based on member company's sales volume).

Meetings/Conferences:
Annual Meetings: May

Publications:
Directory of Certified Cabinet Manufacturers. a.

Kite Trade Association International *(1983)*
P.O. Box 443
Otis, OR 97368
Tel: (541)994-9647 *Fax:* (541)994-4552
Toll Free: (800)243 - 8548

E-Mail: exdir@kitetrade.org
Web Site: www.kitetrade.org
Members: 300 companies
Staff: 2
Annual Budget: $100-250,000
Executive Director: Maggie Vohs, CAE
E-Mail: exdir@kitetrade.org

Historical Note
Membership: $75-450/year (organization/company).

Meetings/Conferences:
Annual Meetings: January

Publications:
Tradewinds. q. adv.
Directory. a.

The Knitting Guild Association *(1984)*
1100-H Brandywine Blvd.
Zanesville, OH 43701-7303
Tel: (740)452-4541 *Fax:* (740)452-2552
E-Mail: tkga@tkga.com
Web Site: www.tkga.com
Members: 12000 individuals
Staff: 2
Annual Budget: $500-1,000,000
Executive Director: Penny Sitler
E-Mail: psitler@tkga.com

Historical Note
Founded as Knitting Guild of America; assumed its current name in 2003. Provides an opportunity for communication and education to those persons wishing to advance the quality of workmanship and creativity in their knitting. Membership: $27/year.

Meetings/Conferences:
Annual Meetings: Spring

Publications:
Cast On Magazine. q. adv.

KWPN of North America *(1983)*
P.O. Box O
Sutherlin, OR 97479
Tel: (541)459-3232 *Fax:* (541)459-2967
E-Mail: office@kwpn-na.org
Web Site: www.kwpn-na.org
Members: 1350 individuals
Staff: 4
Office Manager: Silvia Monas
E-Mail: office@kwpn-na.org

Historical Note
KWPN is the North American branch of the international breed registry headquartered in the Netherlands. Keeps pedigree records and provides other services to member owners and breeders of purebred Dutch Warmblood horses. Formerly the Dutch Warmblood Studbook/North America.

Meetings/Conferences:
Annual Meetings: March
2007 – Austin, TX/March 1-4

Publications:
Breeder's Directory. a.
NA/WPN Newsletter. q.
Stallion Directory. a.

Label Packaging Suppliers Council *(1990)*
7406 Spring Village Dr., HP 106
Springfield, VA 22150
Tel: (703)569-9896 *Fax:* (703)569-9848
Web Site: www.lpsc.net
Members: 85 individuals
Staff: 1
Annual Budget: $25-50,000
Executive Administrator and Secretary-Treasurer: Betty B. Horn

Publications:
LPSC Bulletin. bi-m.

Label Printing Industries of America *(1976)*

Historical Note
An affiliate of Printing Industries of America, which provides administrative support.

Labor and Employment Relations Association *(1947)*
University of Illinois, 121 Labor and Industrial Relations
504 E. Armory
Champaign, IL 61820
Tel: (217)333-0072 *Fax:* (217)265-5130
E-Mail: lera@uicu.edu
Web Site: www.irra.uiuc.edu
Members: 3,500 individuals
Staff: 3
Annual Budget: $250-500,000
Executive Director: Paula D. Wells
E-Mail: lera@uicu.edu

Historical Note
LERA is a member of Allied Social Science Associations, and is affiliated with International Industrial Relations Association. Membership: $75/year (United States); $87/year (foreign).

Meetings/Conferences:
Semi-Annual: Meets with Allied Social Science Associations

Publications:
Proceedings. a.
Perspectives on Work. bi-a.
IRRA Newsletter. q.
Volume of Research. a.
Membership Directory. quadrennial.

Laboratory Animal Management Association *(1984)*
7500 Flying Cloud Dr., Suite 900
Eden Prairie, MN 55344
Tel: (952)253-6235 Ext: 114 *Fax:* (952)835-4774
Web Site: www.lama-online.org
Members: 550 individuals
Staff: 5
Annual Budget: under $10,000
Executive Director: Jim Manke, CAE

Historical Note
Formerly the Laboratory Animal Manager Association. LAMA members are managers of laboratory animal facilities.

Publications:
LAMA Lines. bi-m.
The LAMA Review. q. adv.
Membership Directory. a.

Laboratory Products Association *(1988)*
225 Reinekers Lane, Suite 625
Alexandria, VA 22314
Tel: (703)836-1360 *Fax:* (703)836-6644
Web Site: www.lpanet.org
Members: 125 companies
Staff: 3
Annual Budget: $500-1,000,000
President: William C. Strackbein
E-Mail: wstrackbein@lpanet.org
Manager, Meeting and Member Services: Katherine French Carter
E-Mail: membershipservice@lpanet.org

Historical Note
Originally part of the Scientific Apparatus Makers Association (SAMA) which was founded in 1914 and reorganized in 1988.

Meetings/Conferences:
Semi-annual Meetings: Spring/125 and Fall/125

Laborers' International Union of North America *(1903)*
905 16th St. NW
Washington, DC 20006-1765
Tel: (202)737-8320 *Fax:* (202)737-2754
E-Mail: rgreer@liuna.org
Web Site: www.liuna.org
Members: 840000 individuals
Staff: 150
Annual Budget: $50-100,000,000
General President: Terence M. O'Sullivan
Director, Public Affairs: Linda Fisher
Director, Legislative and Political: Donald J. Kaniewski

Historical Note
Organized in Washington, DC, April 13, 1903, as the International Hod Carriers and Building Laborers' Union of America and chartered by the AFL-CIO. Reflecting the expanding scope of its organization, it changed its name twice in 1912, first to the International Hod Carriers' and Common Laborers' Union of America, and next to the International Hod Carriers', Building and Common Laborers' Union of America. Merged in 1918 with the Compressed Air and Foundation Workers' International Union (founded in 1904) and in 1929 with the Tunnel and Subway Constructors' International Union (founded in 1910). Adopted its present name September 20, 1965. Has an annual budget of approximately $57.4 million. Sponsors and supports the Laborers' Political League, Laborers' Health & Safety Fund on North America, Laborers-Employers Cooperation and Education Trust, Laborers-ACG-Education and Training Fund.

Meetings/Conferences:
Quinquennial Conventions: Fall

Publications:
The Laborer. q.

Lacrosse USA

Historical Note
See U.S. Lacrosse.

Ladies Professional Golf Association *(1950)*
100 International Golf Dr.
Daytona Beach, FL 32124
Tel: (386)274-6200 *Fax:* (386)274-1099
E-Mail: feedback@lpga.com
Web Site: www.lpga.com
Members: 1600 professional golfers
Staff: 65
Annual Budget: $25-50,000,000
Senior Director, National Accounts: Eric Albrecht
Vice President, Professional Development: Betsy Clark, Ph.D.
Executive Vice President and Chief Legal Officer: Libba Galloway
Senior Vice President and Chief Operating Officer: Christopher Higgs
Senior Vice President, Project Development and Member Services: Mindy Moore
Senior Director, National Partnerships: Kathie Vu
Vice President, Communications: Connie Wilson
Vice President, Finance and Administration: Ken Wooten

Historical Note
The LPGA is the governing body for women's professional golf in the United States. Members are golf teachers, coaches, golf professionals and facility managers.

Meetings/Conferences:
Annual Meetings: Winter

Publications:
LPGA Media Guide. a.

Lake Carriers' Association *(1892)*
614 W. Superior Ave. West, Suite 915
Cleveland, OH 44113-1383
Tel: (216)621-1107 *Fax:* (216)241-8262
E-Mail: info@lcaships.com
Web Site: www.lcaships.com
Members: 12 companies
Staff: 4
Annual Budget: $500-1,000,000
President: James H. I. Weakley
Vice President, Operations: Richard W. Harkins
E-Mail: harkins@lcaships.com
Secretary-Treasurer: Carol Ann Lane
Vice President, Corporate Communications: Glen Nekvasil

Historical Note
Established in 1892 as the successor organization to Cleveland Vessel Owners Association (1880) and Lake Carriers' Association of Buffalo (1885). Members are U.S.-Flag Great Lakes vessel operators engaged in transportation of iron ore, coal, grain, limestone, cement and petroleum products.

Meetings/Conferences:
Annual Meetings: With Canadian Shipowners Ass'n

Publications:
Annual Report. a.

Lamaze International *(1960)*
2025 M St. NW, Suite 800
Washington, DC 20036
Tel: (202)367-1128 *Fax:* (202)367-2128
Toll Free: (800)368 - 4404
E-Mail: lamaze@dc.sba.com
Web Site: www.lamaze.org
Members: 3000
Staff: 15
Annual Budget: $500-1,000,000
Executive Director: Linda L. Harmon, MPH
Education Program Coordinator: Amy Pettit

Historical Note
Formerly (1998) the American Society for Psychoprophylaxis in Obstetrics. Founded and incorporated in New York in 1960. Begun as a medical society, the membership now includes childbirth educators, parents and physicians. Promotes prepared childbirth by the Lamaze method. Membership: $40/year (parent), $95/year (professional), $95/year (phycisian/nurse midwife).

Meetings/Conferences:
Annual Meetings: Fall
2007 – Phoenix, AZ(Sheraton Wild Horse Pass)/Sept. 8-10

Publications:
Journal of Perinatal Education. q. adv.
GENESIS. q.

Lambda Alpha Epsilon *(1937)*

Historical Note
See American Criminal Justice Association.

Lambda Kappa Sigma *(1913)*
W179S6769 Muskego Dr.
Muskego, WI 53150-9607
Toll Free: (888)LKS - 1913
E-Mail: lks@lks.org
Web Site: www.lks.org
Members: 18000 individuals
Staff: 3
Annual Budget: $100-250,000
Executive Director: Joan Rogala, CAE

Historical Note
Lambda Kappa Sigma promotes the profession of pharmacy among women, promoting the advancement of women in the profession and contributing to philanthropic endeavors of interest to its members. Membership: $40/year (students); $70/year (alumni).

Meetings/Conferences:
Biennial Meetings: Summer

Publications:
Blue & Gold Triangle. 3/year. adv.
Alumni News.

Land Improvement Contractors of America *(1951)*
3080 Ogden Ave., Suite 300
Lisle, IL 60532
Tel: (630)548-1984 *Fax:* (630)548-9189
E-Mail: nlica@aol.com
Web Site: www.licanational.com
Members: 2200 companies
Staff: 3
Annual Budget: $500-1,000,000
Executive Vice President: Wayne Maresch
Office Manager: Eileen Levy

Historical Note
Dedicated to the professional conservation of soil and clean water. Membership fee varies by state. Has 30 state chapters.

Meetings/Conferences:
Annual Meetings: Winter

Publications:
Membership Directory. a.
LICA News. 10/year.

Land Mobile Communications Council *(1967)*
8484 Westpark Dr.
Suite 630
McLean, VA 22102
Tel: (703)528-5115 *Fax:* (703)524-1074
E-Mail: donald.vasek@enterprisewireless.org
Web Site: www.lmcc.org
Members: 21 organizations
Annual Budget: $10-25,000
President: Ralph Haller

Historical Note
Members are organizations representing users of mobile radio communication apparatus such as railroads, business, trucking companies and public safety services. Works to insure the allocation of a sufficient part of the radio spectrum to meet their requirements. Has no paid officers or full-time staff.

Meetings/Conferences:
Annual Meetings: Spring in Washington, DC

Land Trust Alliance *(1982)*
1331 H St. NW, Suite 400
Washington, DC 20005-4734
Tel: (202)638-4725 *Fax:* (202)638-4730
E-Mail: lta@lta.org
Web Site: www.lta.org
Members: 2057 organizations and individuals
Staff: 34
Annual Budget: $2-5,000,000
President: Randolph N. Wentworth
Director, Information Services: Rob Aldrich
Director, Public Policy: Russell Shay
E-Mail: rshay@lta.org

Historical Note
Formerly (1991) Land Trust Exchange. Members are local and regional non-profit land conservation groups and other concerned organizations and individuals. Membership: $35-1,000/year (individual); $225-2,500/year (organization).

Publications:
Conservation Easement Handbook.
Landscape. 3/year. adv.
Exchange. q.
National Directory of Conservation Land Trusts.

Laser and Electro-Optics Manufacturers' Association *(1985)*
123 Kent Rd.
Pacifica, CA 94044
Tel: (650)738-1492
Web Site: www.leoma.com
Members: 40 companies
Staff: 1
Annual Budget: $100-250,000
Executive Director: C. Breck Hitz

Historical Note
Formerly (1991) Laser Association of America. Members are companies with an interest in laser technology. Membership: Dues range from $200/year - $22,000/year, based on revenue.

Publications:
Newsletter. irreg.

Laser Institute of America *(1968)*
13501 Ingenuity Dr., Suite 128
Orlando, FL 32826
Tel: (407)380-1553 *Fax:* (407)380-5588
Toll Free: (800)345 - 2737
E-Mail: lia@laserinstitute.org
Web Site: www.laserinstitute.org
Members: 1657 individuals
Staff: 18
Annual Budget: $2-5,000,000
Executive Director: Peter M. Baker
E-Mail: lia@laserinstitute.org
Director, Conferences: Beth Cohen
E-Mail: bcohen@laserinstitute.org
Chief Financial Officer: Jeannette Gabay
E-Mail: cfo@laserinstitute.org
Director, Education: Richard Greene

Historical Note
Established in February 1968 in California as the Laser Industry Association by a group of laser pioneers, inventors, and industry leaders. The name was changed to Laser Institute of America in 1972. The Institute is dedicated to fostering lasers, laser applications and laser safety worldwide as well as sponsoring educational and training courses, conferences and symposia on laser-related information. Membership: $100/year (individual); $650/year or $850/year (corporation); $350/year (institution).

Meetings/Conferences:
Annual Meetings: Fall
2007 – San Francisco, CA(Marriott)/March 19-22
2008 – Lake Buena Vista, FL(Hilton Walt Disney)/Oct. 29-Nov. 1

Publications:
ICALEO Proceedings. a.
Journal of Laser Applications. 4/year. adv.
ANSI Z136 Series of Laser Safety Standards. irreg.
Membership Directory. a. adv.
Members' Newsletter. bi-m. adv.

Lasers and Electro-Optics Society *(1964)*

Historical Note
A technical society of Institute of Electrcal and Electronics Engineers, which provides administrative support.

Latin American Management Association *(1973)*

Historical Note
Address unknown in 2006.

Latin American Studies Association *(1966)*
946 William Pitt Union, University of Pittsburgh
Pittsburgh, PA 15260
Tel: (412)648-7929 *Fax:* (412)624-7145
E-Mail: lasa@pitt.edu
Web Site: http://lasa.international.pitt.edu
Members: 5000 individuals
Staff: 4
Annual Budget: $100-250,000
Executive Director: Reid Reading

Historical Note
Members are both teachers and scholars concerned with the promotion of Latin American Studies. Membership: $30-78/year, based on income (individual), $150/year (non-profit organizazation); $250/year (for-profit organization).

Publications:
LASA Member Directory. a.
Latin American Research Review. 3/yr. adv.
LASA Forum. q. adv.
LASA North America: A Select Listing of Institutions, Courses and Programs. a.

Latin Business Association *(1976)*
120 S. San Pedro St., Suite 530
Los Angeles, CA 90012
Tel: (213)628-8510
E-Mail: info@lbausa.com
Web Site: www.lbausa.com
Members: 2000 individuals
Staff: 5
Annual Budget: $250-500,000
Director, Marketing and Operations: Jimmy Dichirico
E-Mail: info@lbausa.com

Meetings/Conferences:
Monthly Meetings:

Publications:
LBA Business Journal. m.

Latin Chamber of Commerce of U.S.A. *(1965)*
1401 W. Flagler St.
P.O. Box 350824
Miami, FL 33135
Tel: (305)642-3870 *Fax:* (305)642-0653
E-Mail: info@camacol.org
Web Site: www.camacol.org
Members: 2500 businesses
Staff: 35
Annual Budget: $500-1,000,000
President: William Alexander
Director, Government Relations: Wilfredo (Willy) Gort
Contact: Betty Gradera

Historical Note
Formerly (1990) Latin Chamber of Commerce. CAMA-COL promotes trade between the U.S. and Latin America.

Meetings/Conferences:
Annual Meetings: always last week in April

Publications:
Revista Camacol. m.
Members Directory. bien.

Laundry and Dry Cleaning International Union *(1959)*
307 Fourth Ave., Suite 405
Pittsburgh, PA 15222
Tel: (412)471-4829 *Fax:* (412)471-1840
Members: 11000 individuals
Staff: 15
Annual Budget: $250-500,000
President: Mary O'Brien

Historical Note
Organized in Washington May 12, 1959 by locals formerly members of the Laundry, Dry Cleaning and Dye House Workers' International Union (which had

been expelled from the AFL-CIO in December, 1957). Chartered by the AFL-CIO. Sponsors and supports the League of Voter Education Political Action Committee.

Law and Society Association *(1964)*
Hampshire House, Box 33615
University of Massachusetts
Amherst, MA 01003-3615
Tel: (413)545-4617 *Fax:* (413)577-3194
E-Mail: lsa@lawandsociety.org
Web Site: www.lawandsociety.org
Members: 1500 individuals
Staff: 4
Annual Budget: $250-500,000
Executive Officer: Ronald M. Pipkin
E-Mail: pipkin@lawandsociety.org
Coordinator, Administrative: Lissa Ganter
E-Mail: ganter@lawandsociety.org
Coordinator, Membership: Judy Rose
E-Mail: rose@lawandsociety.org

Historical Note
Members are social science and legal professionals and others interested in exploring the relationships between law and society. Membership: $25-170/year (individual); $134/year (organization/company).

Meetings/Conferences:
Annual Meetings: Spring
2007 – Berlin, Germany/July 25-28/1500

Publications:
Law and Society Review. q. adv.
Law and Society Newsletter. q.

Lawn and Garden Dealers' Association *(1985)*
2411 E. Skelly Dr., Suite 105
Tulsa, OK 74105
Toll Free: (800)752 - 5296
E-Mail: info@lgda.com
Web Site: www.lgda.com
Members: 2000 companies
Staff: 5
Annual Budget: $500-1,000,000
Contact Person: Dr. Paul Martin

Historical Note
Members are in the professional lawn and garden industry and include lawn equipment dealers, nurseries, small engine repair, and landscape and irrigation companies. Membership fee: $45/year. Street address is 2411 East Skelly Dr., Suite 105, Tulsa, OK, 74105.

Meetings/Conferences:
Annual Meetings: Fall

Publications:
Lawn & Garden Newsletter. q. adv.

Lawn and Garden Marketing and Distribution Association *(1969)*
2105 Laurel Bush Rd., Suite 200
Bel Air, MD 21015
Tel: (443)640-1080 *Fax:* (443)640-1031
E-Mail: lgmda@ksgroup.org
Web Site: www.lgmda.org
Members: 300 companies
Staff: 3
Annual Budget: $250-500,000
Contact: Steven T. King, CAE
E-Mail: lgmda@ksgroup.org

Historical Note
Founded as Lawn and Garden Distributors Association; became National Lawn and Garden Distributors Association in 1979 and assumed its current name in 1997. Members are wholesale distributors and manufacturers of lawn and garden supplies. There is also an affiliate classification. Promotes the growth and profitability of the lawn and garden industry through effective and efficient marketing and distribution of products and services. Membership: $1000/year (depending on classification).

Meetings/Conferences:
Annual Meetings: June/July
2007 – Dallas, TX(Westin Centre Park)/Jan. 17-19/125

Publications:
Grassroots. q.
Membership Directory. a. adv.

Lawn Institute *(1957)*
Two E. Main St.
East Dundee, IL 60008
Tel: (847)649-5555 *Fax:* (847)649-5678
Toll Free: (800)405 - 8873
E-Mail: info@turfgrasssod.org
Web Site: www.lawninstitute.com
Staff: 6
Executive Director: T. Kirk Hunter
E-Mail: info@turfgrasssod.org

Historical Note
Organized by midwestern bluegrass harvesters as Better Lawn and Turf Institute; membership now includes growers of improved turfgrasses as well as distributor groups, associations and suppliers such as fertilizer, chemical and equipment companies. Adminstered by Turfgrass Producers International (same address).

Leading Jewelers Guild *(1958)*
P.O. Box 69604
Los Angeles, CA 90069
Tel: (310)820-3386 *Fax:* (310)820-3530
Web Site: www.love-story.com
Members: 27 companies and 150 stores
Staff: 10
Executive Director: James West

Historical Note
LJC is a coalition of independent jewelers and jewelry retailers. Provides cooperative purchasing and marketing programs to its members and administers a number of registered trademarks on their behalf, including Love Story Diamonds.

Leaf Tobacco Exporters Association *(1939)*
3716 National Dr., Suite 114
Raleigh, NC 27612
Tel: (919)782-5151
Members: 45 companies
Staff: 2
Annual Budget: $100-250,000
Executive Vice President: J.T. Bunn

Historical Note
Affiliated with the Tobacco Association of the U.S., which provides administrative support.

Meetings/Conferences:
Annual Meetings: May, at the Greenbrier in White Sulphur Springs, WV

Leafy Greens Council *(1976)*
33 Pheasant Lane
St. Paul, MN 55127
Tel: (651)484-3321 *Fax:* (651)484-1098
Web Site: www.leafy-greens.org
Members: 100 individuals
Staff: 1
Annual Budget: $25-50,000
Executive Director: Ray L. Clark, Jr.

Historical Note
Growers, shippers, packers and sellers of spinach, cabbage, lettuce and other fresh leafy green vegetables. Founded in 1976 as the National Spinach Association. Became the Leafy Greens Council in 1977.

Meetings/Conferences:
Annual Meetings: usually coincides with United Fresh Fruit and Vegetable Association/May
2007 – Chicago, IL

League for Innovation in the Community College *(1968)*
4505 E. Chandler Blvd., Ste. 250
Phoenix, AZ 85048
Tel: (480)705-8200 *Fax:* (480)705-8201
Web Site: www.league.org
Members: 700 community colleges
Staff: 12
Annual Budget: $500-1,000,000
Interim President and Chief Executive Officer: Gerardo E. de los Santos

Historical Note
A national consortium of 20 districts established to stimulate innovation in community college education. Assists its members in experimenting in teaching, learning, student services and other aspects of community college operation, and in sharing the results of these experiments. Membership: $55/year (per education institution).

Publications:
League Connections. m.
League Reports. 10/year.

League of American Theatres and Producers *(1930)*
226 W. 47th St.
Sixth Floor
New York, NY 10036-1487
Tel: (212)764-1122 *Fax:* (212)944-8229
E-Mail: league@broadway.org
Web Site: www.livebroadway.com
Members: 500 individuals
Staff: 30
Annual Budget: $1-2,000,000
Contact: Charlotte St. Martin

Historical Note
The League is a professional trade association of the tax-paying legitimate theatre. Members include producers, theatre owners and operators, and local presenters. Programs include labor relations and negotiations; marketing, economic and media research; urban environment improvement programs; government relations; institutional public relations and promotion; tourism promotion; and presentation with the American Theatre Wing of the Antoinette Perry "Tony" Awards. Membership: $650/year (individual).

Publications:
League Line. bi-m.
Stage Specs. a.

League of Federal Recreation Associations *(1960)*

Historical Note
Membership, concentrated in the Washington, D.C. area, is composed of state, county and federal government employee associations which sponsor recreational and employee benefit activities. Membership: $19/year (associate), $50-150/year (agency).

League of Historic American Theatres *(1976)*
334 N. Charles St., Second Floor
Baltimore, MD 21201
Tel: (410)659-9533 *Fax:* (410)837-9664
Toll Free: (877)627 - 0833
E-Mail: info@lhat.org
Web Site: www.lhat.org
Members: 500 individuals
Staff: 3
Annual Budget: $250-500,000
Executive Director: Fran Holden
E-Mail: info@lhat.org

Historical Note
Members are historic and restored theatres, firms which specialize in theatre rehabilitation, operation, or other professional services, and individuals interested in historic theatre preservation. Membership: $290-$840/year (theatre); $475-$975/year (firm/supplier); $210/year (institution); $105/year (individual); $60/year (student).

Meetings/Conferences:
Annual Meetings: Summer
2007 – Boston, MA(Boston Park Plaza)/July 25-28/250

Publications:
Membership Directory. a. adv.
Newsletter. q. adv.
Conference Program. a. adv.

League of Resident Theatres *(1965)*
1501 Broadway, Suite 2401
New York, NY 10036
Tel: (212)944-1501 *Fax:* (212)768-0785
Web Site: www.lort.org
Members: 76 theatres
Staff: 2
Management Associate: Adam Knight

Historical Note
Members are professional resident theatres.

Meetings/Conferences:
Annual Meetings:

Leather Apparel Association *(1990)*
19 W. 21st St., Suite 403
New York, NY 10010
Tel: (212)727-1210 *Fax:* (212)727-1218

E-Mail: info@leatherassociation.com
Web Site: www.leatherassociation.com
Members: 100 companies
Staff: 1
Annual Budget: $250-500,000
Executive Director: Richard Harrow
Contact: Fran Harrow

Historical Note
Promotes the sale of leather garments through publicity, education, and business support services. Membership fee based on annual gross domestic sales.

Meetings/Conferences:
Annual Meetings: October

Publications:
Member Communique. m.

Leather Industries of America *(1917)*
3050 K St., NW, Suite 400
Washington, DC 20007
Tel: (202)342-8497 *Fax:* (202)342-8583
E-Mail: info@leatherusa.com
Web Site: www.leatherusa.com
Members: 70 companies
Staff: 2
Annual Budget: $1-2,000,000
President: John Wittenborn
Coordinator, Meeting, Membership and Statistical Communications: Christine Burt
E-Mail: chris@leatherusa.com
Controller: Mary Agnes Gustavson
E-Mail: maggie@leatherusa.com

Historical Note
Formed by a merger of the National Association of Tanners, the Morocco Manufacturers National Association and the Patent and Enameled Leather Manufacturers Association as the Tanners' Council of America; it absorbed the Leather Industries of America in 1975 and assumed this name in 1986. LIA members are U.S. businesses involved in the tanning, finishing, manufacturing or selling of leather. General membership is available for companies with an interest in the industry. Membership: $1,000-50,000/year.

Meetings/Conferences:
Annual Meetings: Summer

Publications:
Buyer's Guide.
U.S. Leather Industry Statistics. a.
Membership Directory. a.

Legal Marketing Association *(1986)*
1926 Waukegan Rd., Suite 1
Glenview, IL 60025-1770
Tel: (847)657-6717 *Fax:* (847)657-6819
E-Mail: carlw@tcag.com
Web Site: www.legalmarketing.org
Members: 2500 individuals
Staff: 8
Annual Budget: $1-2,000,000
Executive Director: Carl A. Wangman, CAE
Communications/Website Manager: Dan Lobring

Historical Note
Formed (1986) as the National Association of Law Firm Marketing Administrators; became (1990) National Law Firm Marketing Association and assumed its present name in 1999. LMA serves the needs of and maintains professional standards for those involved in marketing for the legal profession. Membership: $375/year, plus initiation fee and chapter dues.

Meetings/Conferences:
Annual Meetings: Spring

Publications:
Strategies Journal. m. adv.

Lepidoptera Research Foundation *(1962)*
9620 Heather Rd.
Beverly Hills, CA 90210
Tel: (310)399-6016 *Fax:* (310)399-2805
Members: 700 individuals
President and Editor: Rudolf H.T. Mattoni

Historical Note
Membership, concentrated in the western U.S., consists of professional and amateur lepidopterists. Publishes and disseminates information on the biology of butterflies and moths, as well as conservation issues relevant to lepidoptera.

Publications:
Journal of Research on the Lepidoptera. irreg.
Newsletter. irreg.

Liability Insurance Research Bureau *(1990)*
3025 Highland Pkwy., Suite 800
Downers Grove, IL 60515-1291
Tel: (630)724-2252 *Fax:* (630)724-2260
Toll Free: (888)711 - 7572
E-Mail: lirb@lirb.org
Web Site: www.lirb.org
Members: 252 insurance companies
Staff: 6
Annual Budget: $500-1,000,000
Vice President and General Counsel: Paul C. Dispensa
E-Mail: pdispensa@lirb.org

Historical Note
Spun off from Property Loss Research Bureau. Provides legal research, consulting, and educational services in auto liability and CGL lines. Members are stock and mutual insurance companies.

Publications:
Homeowners Liability, Auto, Commercial and Environmental Law Reviews. m.

Liaison Committee of Cooperating Oil and Gas Associations *(1957)*
1718 Columbus Rd. SW
P.O. Box 535
Granville, OH 13023-0535
Tel: (740)587-0444 *Fax:* (740)587-0446
Members: 25 associations
Annual Budget: under $10,000
Secretary-Treasurer: Thomas E. Stewart

Historical Note
The committee was established to facilitate communication among state and regional oil and gas associations. Has no paid or full-time staff.

Meetings/Conferences:
Annual Meetings: Summer

Library Administration and Management Association *(1957)*
50 E. Huron St.
Chicago, IL 60611-2795
Tel: (312)280-5036 *Fax:* (312)280-5033
Toll Free: (800)545 - 2433 Ext: 5036
Web Site: www.ala.org/lama
Members: 5000 individuals
Staff: 2
Annual Budget: $250-500,000
Executive Director: Lorraine Olley
E-Mail: lolley@ala.org
Marketing Specialist: Fred Reuland
E-Mail: freuland@ala.org

Historical Note
Founded as Library Administration Division of the American Library Association; it remains a division of the ALA. Membership (restricted to ALA members): $50/year (individual); $15/year (student).

Meetings/Conferences:
Annual Meetings: in conjunction with the American Library Association/Summer

Publications:
Library Administration & Management. q. adv.

Library and Information Technology Association *(1966)*
50 E. Huron St.
Chicago, IL 60611-2795
Tel: (312)280-4270 *Fax:* (312)280-3257
Toll Free: (800)545 - 2433 Ext: 4270
E-Mail: lita@ala.org
Web Site: www.lita.org
Members: 3500 individuals
Staff: 3
Annual Budget: $250-500,000
Executive Director: Mary C. Taylor
E-Mail: mtaylor@ala.org

Historical Note
LITA provides its members with a forum to discuss and learn about the development and implementation of information technology in libraries. A division of the American Library Association formerly known as the Information Science and Automation Division, LITA adopted its current name in 1978. Membership: $45/year (individual); $75/year (organization).

Meetings/Conferences:
Annual Meetings:
2007 - Denver, CO(Marriott)/Oct. 4-7

Publications:
Information Technology and Libraries. q. adv.

Library Binding Institute *(1935)*
4300 S. US Hwy. One
#203-296
Jupiter, FL 33417
Tel: (561)745-6821 *Fax:* (561)775-0089
Web Site: www.lbibinders.org
Members: 76 companies
Annual Budget: $100-250,000
Executive Director: Debra Nolan

Historical Note
Members are firms binding books for libraries, their suppliers and certain libraries with an in-house binding capacity.

Meetings/Conferences:
Semi-Annual Meetings: Spring and Fall

Publications:
endpaper. m.
The New Library Scene. q. adv.

Licensing Executives Society *(1965)*
1800 Diagonal Rd., Suite 280
Alexandria, VA 22314
Tel: (703)836-3106 *Fax:* (703)836-3107
Web Site: www.usa-canada.les.org
Members: 4500 individuals
Staff: 5
Annual Budget: $2-5,000,000
Director: Kenneth Schoppmann
E-Mail: schoppk@les.org
Director, Meetings: Eleanor de Leon
Manager, Membership: Christine Mercado
E-Mail: mercadoc@les.org

Historical Note
Membership consists of individuals concerned with licensing patents, trademarks, trade secrets, processes and other intellectual property. Membership in the United States and Canada is 3,600. Membership: $135/year (individual).

Meetings/Conferences:
Annual Meetings: Fall

Publications:
Viewpoints.
Les Nouvelles (Int'l Journal). q.
Membership Directory. a.

Life Insurers Council *(1910)*
2300 Windy Ridge Pkwy., Suite 600
Atlanta, GA 30339-8443
Tel: (770)951-1770 *Fax:* (770)984-0441
Web Site: www.loma.org
Members: 62 companies and 38 associates
Staff: 2
Annual Budget: $100-250,000
Contact: Christine Yeh

Historical Note
Established as Southern Casualty and Surety Conference, it became Southern Industrial Insurers' Conference in 1917, the Industrial Insurers Conference in 1925, Life Insurers Conference in 1948, and assumed its present name in 1997. Members are home service life insurance companies writing accident, life, and health insurance; Pre-Need funeral insurance companies; and non-life insurance company affiliate members which provide a service in the life insurance industry. Encourages the exchange of ideas between members, strives to maintain high standards of business conduct, and represents its members in connection with legislative, regulatory, and consumer matters.

Meetings/Conferences:
Annual Meetings: May

Publications:
Newsletter Compliance Report. m.

Life Office Management Association *(1924)*

Historical Note
Known by its acronym LOMA.

Lift Manufacturers Product Section - Material Handling Institute *(1990)*
Historical Note
A section of Material Handling Institute, which provides administrative support.

Light Aircraft Manufacturers Association *(1984)*
22 Deer Oaks Ct.
Pleasanton, CA 94588
Tel: (925)426-0771
E-Mail: info@lama.bz
Web Site: www.lama.bz
Members: 400 individuals
Staff: 5
Annual Budget: $10-25,000
President: Lawrence P. Burke
Historical Note
LAMA members are manufacturers of light and ultralight aircraft and suppliers of parts. Has no paid officers or full-time staff. Membership: $50/year (individual); $125/year (company).
Publications:
LAMA Newsletter. irreg. adv.
LAMA Membership Directory. irreg.

Lighter Association *(1986)*
1700 Pennsylvania Ave.
Suite 400
Washington, DC 20006
Tel: (202)349-4190 *Fax:* (202)349-4199
E-Mail: info@lighterassociation.org
Web Site: www.lighterassociation.org
Members: 10 companies
Staff: 1
Annual Budget: $100-250,000
General Counsel: David H. Baker
Historical Note
Members are manufacturers, suppliers and distributors of lighters. Membership: $4,000-48,000 (company).

Lightning Protection Institute *(1955)*
P.O. Box 99
Maryville, MO 64468
Toll Free: (800)488 - 6864
E-Mail: lpi@lightning.org
Web Site: www.lightning.org
Members: 100 companies
Staff: 4
Annual Budget: $25-50,000
Executive Director: Bud Van Sickle
Historical Note
Members are manufacturers and installers of lightning protection equipment. The LPI Professional Division has a membership of about 100 engineers and others.
Meetings/Conferences:
Annual Meetings: Fall
Publications:
Newsletter. q.
Technical Letter. q.
Golf Course Protection. a.

Lignin Institute *(1990)*
5775 Peachtree-Dunwoody Rd., Suite 500-G
Atlanta, GA 30342
Tel: (404)252-3663 *Fax:* (404)252-0774
E-Mail: LI@kellencompany.com
Web Site: www.lignin.org
Members: 40 individuals
Staff: 3
Annual Budget: $100-250,000
President: Pete Dicks
Contact: Pat Cohen
Technical Director: Andrew G. Ebert, Ph.D.
Historical Note
The Institute is a trade association for manufacturers and distributors of lignin products. Lignin is a co-product of the wood pulping process with applications in construction and other heavy industries.
Meetings/Conferences:
Semi-Annual meetings: Midyear meeting held in May; annual meeting held in November
Publications:
Dialogue Newsletter. a.

Lignite Energy Council *(1974)*
P.O. Box 2277
Bismarck, ND 58502-2277
Tel: (701)258-7117 *Fax:* (701)258-2755
E-Mail: lec@lignite.com
Web Site: www.lignite.com
Members: 304 companies
Staff: 10
Annual Budget: $2-5,000,000
President: John W. Dwyer
E-Mail: jdwyer@lignite.com
Director, Technology: Dave Allard
E-Mail: dallard@lignite.com
Director, Research and Development: Harvey Ness
E-Mail: hness@lignite.com
Director, Member Services and Education: Renee Walz
E-Mail: rwalz@lignite.com
Historical Note
LEC's members include the major producers of lignite, major reserve holders, investor-owned utilities, rural electric cooperatives, and businesses providing goods or services to the lignite industry. LEC promotes policies and directs activities that maintain a viable lignite industry and enhance the development of the Upper Midwest's lignite resources for the benefit of consumers, producers, utilities, and other users and businesses providing goods or services to the lignite industry.
Meetings/Conferences:
2007 – Bismarck, ND(Civic Center)/Oct. 24-25/400
Publications:
Lignite Update. bi-m.
Member Update. bi-m.
Inside Scoop. m.
Buyer's Directory. a.

LIMRA International *(1916)*
300 Day Hill Rd.
Windsor, CT 06095
Tel: (860)688-3358 *Fax:* (860)298-9555
Toll Free: (800)235 - 4672
Web Site: www.limra.com
Members: 800 companies
Staff: 250
Annual Budget: $25-50,000,000
President and Chief Executive Officer: Robert A. Kerzner
Director, Public Relations: Howard S. Drescher
E-Mail: hdrescher@limra.com
Historical Note
Founded as the Life Insurance Sales Research Bureau in 1916; merged with the Life Officers Association in 1945 to form the Life Insurance Agency Management Association; became Life Insurance Marketing and Research Association in 1974; and assumed its present name in 1994. Members are life insurance and financial services companies around the world. Has an annual budget of approximately $24.4 million.
Meetings/Conferences:
Annual Meetings: October/1,500
Publications:
Marketfacts. q.

Linguistic Association of Canada and the United States *(1974)*
Center for the Study of Languages, MS-36, Rice University
Houston, TX 77251-1892
Tel: (713)348-2820 *Fax:* (713)348-5846
E-Mail: lchen@rice.edu
Web Site: www.lacus.org
Members: 500 individuals
Annual Budget: under $10,000
Secretary-Treasurer: Lilly Lee Chen
Historical Note
Established and incorporated in Illinois, LACUS is an educational and scientific organization that promotes the objective study of language. Has no paid officers or full-time staff. Membership: $50 (USD)/year; $58 (CND)/year.
Meetings/Conferences:
Annual Meetings: July, August/100
Publications:
LACUS Forum. a. adv.

Linguistic Society of America *(1924)*
1325 18th St. NW, Suite 211
Washington, DC 20036-6501
Tel: (202)835-1714 *Fax:* (202)835-1717
E-Mail: lsa@lsadc.org
Web Site: www.lsadc.org
Members: 7000 individuals
Staff: 3
Annual Budget: $250-500,000
Executive Director: Margaret Reynolds
E-Mail: lsa@lsadc.org
Associate Executive Director: Mary Niebuhr
E-Mail: lsa@lsadc.org
Historical Note
Founded December 28, 1924 at the American Museum of Natural History in New York City and incorporated in 1940 in the District of Columbia. A constituent member of the American Council of Learned Societies; affiliate of Permanent International Committee of Linguistics (CIPL); founding member of the Consortium of Social Science Associations (COSSA). Domestic Membership: $30/year (student); $75/year (individual); $120/year (organization). Foreign Membership: $40/year (student); $85/year (individual).
Meetings/Conferences:
Annual Meetings: January/1,000
Publications:
Language. q. adv.
LSA Bulletin. q. adv.
Annual Meeting Handbook. a. adv.

Lipizzan Association of North America *(1968)*
P.O. Box 1133
Anderson, IN 46015-1133
Tel: (765)644-3904 *Fax:* (765)641-1208
E-Mail: lana@lipizzan.org
Web Site: www.lipizzan.org
Members: 175 individuals
Staff: 9
Annual Budget: $25-50,000
Director: Sandra Heaberlin
Historical Note
Members own and breed Lipizzan horses. Formerly (1980) the Royal International Lipizzan Club. Formerly (1992) the Lippizan Association of America; assumed this name following a merger with the Lippizan Society of North America. LANA's prime objective is to provide members with accessible, verifiable pedigree information, from America and oversees breeders. Membership: $45/year.
Publications:
Haute Ecole. q.
Directory. a.

Literary Managers and Dramaturgs of the Americas *(1985)*
Village Station
P.O. Box 728
New York, NY 10014
Tel: (212)561-0315
E-Mail: lmdanyc@hotmail.com
Web Site: www.lmda.org
Members: 600 individuals
Staff: 1
Annual Budget: $25-50,000
President: Liz Engelman
E-Mail: lmdanyc@hotmail.com
Historical Note
Formerly (1990) Literary Managers and Dramaturgs of America. LMDA is the national network of literary managers and dramaturgs founded in 1985 to affirm, examine and encourage these emerging professions. Provides a job bank, script exchange, and other programs to members. Membership: $25-60/year (individual); $130/year (institution).
Publications:
LMDA Guide to Programs in Dramaturgy.
LMDA Internships Guide.
The LMDA Review. q.
The Script Exchange. 5/year.
The LMDA Sourcebook.
Production Notebooks: Theatre in Process.
Dramaturgy in American Theatre: A Source Book.

Lithuanian-U.S. Business Council *(2000)*

Historical Note
A program of U.S. Chamber of Commerce, which provides administrative support.

Livestock Industry Institute *(1970)*
Historical Note
A division within the Livestock Marketing Association.

Livestock Marketing Association *(1976)*
10510 N.W. Ambassador Dr.
Kansas City, MO 64153-1278
Tel: (816)891-0502 *Fax:* (816)891-7926
Toll Free: (800)821 - 2048
E-Mail: lmainfo@lmaweb.com
Web Site: www.lmaweb.com
Members: 778 businesses
Staff: 35
Annual Budget: $10-25,000,000
Chief Executive Officer: Mark Mackey
Director, Information: John J. McBride
E-Mail: jmcbride@lmaweb.com
Chief Financial Officer: Vincent Nowak
Vice President, Government and Industry Affairs: Nancy J. Robinson
E-Mail: nrobinson@lmaweb.com
Historical Note
Formed by a merger (July 1, 1976) of the Competitive Livestock Marketing Association and the National Livestock Dealers Association. Sponsors the LMA Political Action Committee.
Meetings/Conferences:
Annual Meetings: June
2007 – Springfield, MO/June 14-17
Publications:
Membership Directory. a.
LMA InfoLink. bi-m.
The Risk Manager. bi-m.

Livestock Publications Council *(1974)*
910 Currie St.
Ft. Worth, TX 76107
Tel: (817)336-1130 *Fax:* (817)232-4820
Web Site: www.livestockpublications.com
Members: 175 publications
Staff: 1
Annual Budget: $100-250,000
Executive Director: Diane E. Johnson
Historical Note
Organized in a Texas meeting and incorporated in Colorado. Members are magazines, newspapers and other periodicals devoting at least 50% of their average content to the livestock industry. Membership: $150/year.
Meetings/Conferences:
Annual Meetings: July/August
Publications:
Actiongram (newsletter). m.
LPC Directory of Members. a.

Loading Dock Equipment Manufacturers
Historical Note
An affiliate of Material Handling Industry of America, which provides administrative support.

Locomotive Maintenance Officers' Association *(1905)*
Historical Note
A program of the Railway Supply Institute, which provides administrative support.

Log Home Builders Association of North America *(1967)*
22203 State Rte. 203
Monroe, WA 98272
Tel: (360)794-4464
Web Site: www.loghomebuilders.org
Members: 16900 companies
Staff: 4
Annual Budget: $500-1,000,000
President: DeWelle F. "Skip" Ellsworth
Vice President: Robert Johnson
Executive Vice President: Mike Simmons
Historical Note
Formerly (1976) Log House Association of North America.
Publications:
Log House Builders Journal. irreg. adv.
Log House Builders Association Newsletter. irreg. adv.

Log Homes Council *(1985)*
Historical Note
A division of Building Systems Councils of NAHB.

Logistics Conference
Historical Note
A conference of the Transporation Intermediaries Association.

LOMA *(1924)*
2300 Windy Ridge Pkwy., Suite 600
Atlanta, GA 30339-8443
Tel: (770)951-1770 *Fax:* (770)984-0441
Toll Free: (800)275 - 5662
E-Mail: askloma@loma.org
Web Site: www.loma.org
Members: 1250 companies
Staff: 175
Annual Budget: $10-25,000,000
President and Chief Executive Officer: Thomas P. Donaldson, FLMI, CLU
E-Mail: askloma@loma.org
Historical Note
Formerly (1996) Life Office Management Association. LOMA sponsors education, training, employee development programs, networking, and research to promote effective management in life & health insurance companies and other related organizations. Has an annual budget of approximately $18 million. Membership fee varies, based on premium income.
Meetings/Conferences:
Annual Meetings: Fall
2007 – Quebec City, QC, Canada(Quebec City Hilton Hotel)/Sept. 16-18
2008 – San Diego, CA(Manchester Hyatt)/Sept. 21-23
Publications:
The Changing Reinsurance Industry.
LOMA Membership Directory. q.
RESOURCE Magazine. m. adv.

Lutheran Education Association *(1942)*
7400 Augusta St.
River Forest, IL 60305
Tel: (708)209-3343 *Fax:* (708)209-3458
E-Mail: lea@lea.org
Web Site: www.lea.org
Members: 3500 individuals
Staff: 6
Annual Budget: $250-500,000
Executive Director: Jonathan Laabs
E-Mail: lea@lea.org
Director, Publications and Communications: Ed Grube
E-Mail: lea@lea.org
Historical Note
LEA is a professional organization that links, equips, and affirms educators in Lutheran ministries. Membership: $85/year.
Meetings/Conferences:
Triennial Meetings: Spring
2007 – Nashville, TN(Gaylord Opryland)/March 15-17/400
Publications:
Lutheran Education. 4/year. adv.
Monograph Series. 3/year.
Shaping the Future. 4/year. adv.

Lutheran Educational Conference of North America *(1910)*
First Financial Center
110 S. Phillips Ave., Suite 306
Sioux Falls, SD 57104
Tel: (605)782-4003 *Fax:* (605)782-4008
Web Site: www.lutherancolleges.org
Members: 43 colleges, 2 church bodies
Staff: 3
Annual Budget: $250-500,000
President: Ralph Wagoner
Director, Lutheran College Fairs: Laurie Brill
Historical Note
Members are Lutheran colleges, and church body boards of higher education. Formerly (until 1967) known as the National Lutheran Educational Conference, it is the oldest inter-Lutheran organization in North America. Membership: $500-3,000/year, based on type of institution.
Meetings/Conferences:
Annual Meetings: January-February

Machine Knife Association *(1933)*
30200 Detroit Rd.
Cleveland, OH 44145-1967
Tel: (440)899-0010 *Fax:* (440)892-1404
E-Mail: jjw@wherryassoc.com
Web Site: www.mka.org
Members: 8 companies
Staff: 2
Executive Secretary: J. Jeffery Wherry
Historical Note
Formerly (1991) Machine Knife Manufacturers Association.
Meetings/Conferences:
Semi-annual Meetings: Spring/Fall

Machine Printers and Engravers Association of the United States *(1960)*
Two Regency Plaza, Suite Seven
Providence, RI 02903
Tel: (401)831-3309
E-Mail: mpea74@aol.com
Members: 30 individuals
Staff: 1
Annual Budget: $25-50,000
President: Albert A. Poitras
E-Mail: mpea74@aol.com
Historical Note
Independent labor union formed by a merger of the Friendly Society of Engravers and Sketchmakers (founded in 1878) and the Machine Printers Beneficial Association (founded in 1874).
Meetings/Conferences:
Annual Meetings: Fall

Machine Vision Association of SME *(1984)*
Historical Note
Part of Engineering Materials Applications Community of SME, a program of Society of Manufacturing Engineers, which provides administrative support.

Machinery Dealers National Association *(1941)*
315 S. Patrick St.
Alexandria, VA 22314-3501
Tel: (703)836-9300 *Fax:* (703)836-9303
Toll Free: (800)872 - 7807
E-Mail: office@mdna.org
Web Site: www.mdna.org
Members: 400 individuals
Staff: 5
Annual Budget: $250-500,000
Executive Vice President: Mark Robinson
E-Mail: office@mdna.org
Historical Note
Represents used industrial machinery dealers. Membership: $900/year.
Meetings/Conferences:
Annual Meetings: Spring/400
Publications:
Used Machinery Buyers Guide. a.
MDNA News. m.

Machining Technology Association of SME *(1991)*
Historical Note
Part of Engineering Materials Applications Community of SME, a program of Society of Manufacturing Engineers, which provides administrative support.

Magazine Publishers of America *(1919)*
810 Seventh Ave., 24th Floor
New York, NY 10019
Tel: (212)872-3700 *Fax:* (212)888-4217
Toll Free: (888)567 - 3228
E-Mail: mpa@magazine.org
Web Site: www.magazine.org
Members: 220 companies, 800 magazines
Staff: 40
Annual Budget: $5-10,000,000
President and Chief Executive Officer: Nina B. Link
Executive Vice President, Government Affairs: James Cregan

Manager, Membership: Leecia Manning
Chief Financial Officer: Richard J. O'Rourke
Executive Vice President and Chief Marketing Officer: Ellen Oppenheim
Executive Vice President and General Manager: Michael Pashby
Vice President, Communications: Howard Polskin

Historical Note
Members are publishers of consumer and other magazines issued not less than four times a year. Founded as the National Association of Periodical Publishers; became National Publishers Association in 1920, National Association of Magazine Publishers in 1947, Magazine Publishers Association in 1952 and assumed its present name in 1987. Affiliated with American Society of Magazine Editors and Media Credit Association. Has an annual budget of approximately $7.9 million.

Meetings/Conferences:
Annual Meetings: Fall/600-650

Publications:
Sales Edge. w.
Behind the Numbers. m.
Magazine. bi-m.
MPA Newsletter of International Publishing. 8/year.
MPA Washington Newsletter. m.

Magic Dealers Association *(1946)*
15528 Illinois Ave.
Paramount, CA 90723
Tel: (562)531-1991
E-Mail: mda@sterlingmaic.com
Web Site: www.magicdealers.com
Members: 110 companies
Annual Budget: under $10,000
President: Gerald Kirchner
E-Mail: mda@sterlingmaic.com

Historical Note
Incorporated in the state of Maryland in 1947. The organization exists to assist with networking magic-related businesses and provide a common bond of integrity. The members consist of retailers, wholesalers, jobbers, publishers, and inventors who develop, manufacture and sell magic-related products. Membership: $150/year.

Meetings/Conferences:
Annual Meetings: With International Brotherhood of Magicians or Society of American Magicians

Magnet Distributors and Fabricators Association *(1991)*

Historical Note
Was absorbed by International Magentics Association in 2003.

Mail Systems Management Association *(1981)*
P.O. Box 1145
Riverside, IL 60546
Tel: (708)442-8589 *Fax:* (708)853-0471
Toll Free: (800)955 - 6762
Web Site: www.msmanational.org
Members: 2000 individuals
Staff: 1
Annual Budget: $50-100,000
Executive Assistant and Treasurer: Barbara Fahy

Historical Note
MSMA members are responsible for oversight and management of mail delivery at companies, government offices, and organizations. Provides continuing education and support for mail systems industry professionals, including the certification CMDSM (Certified Mail and Distribution Systems Manager). Membership: $75/year (individual); $175/year (company).

Publications:
Postscripts. m.

Mailing & Fulfillment Service Association *(1920)*
1421 Prince St., Suite 410
Alexandria, VA 22314-2806
Tel: (703)836-9200 *Fax:* (703)548-8204
Toll Free: (800)333 - 6272
E-Mail: mfsa@mfsanet.org
Web Site: www.mfsanet.org
Members: 700 companies
Staff: 11
Annual Budget: $1-2,000,000
President and Chief Executive Officer: David A. Weaver
E-Mail: DAWeaver@MFSAnet.org
Director, Finance and Accounting: Ruth M. Clark
Director, Membership: Tyler T. Keeney
Manager, Communications: Kimberly Kight
Director, Postal Affairs: Leo Raymond

Historical Note
Founded as Mail Advertising Service Association International; assumed its current name in 2001. Members are producers of direct commercial mail, letter shops, list brokers, fulfillment operations and data processing service bureaus.

Meetings/Conferences:
Annual Meetings: Spring or Summer

Publications:
Pricing Study. bien.
Performance Profiles. a.
Postal Points. 18/yr.
Employment Points. 6/yr.
Membership Directory. a. adv.
Postscripts Newsletter. m. adv.
Cost Ratio Survey. a.
Wage, Salary and Fringe Benefits Survey. bien.

Major Indoor Soccer League *(1984)*
1175 Post Rd. East
Westport, CT 06880
Tel: (203)222-4900 *Fax:* (203)221-7300
Toll Free: (866)647 - 5638
E-Mail: info@misl.net
Web Site: www.misl.net
Members: 10 clubs
Staff: 9
Commissioner: Stephen M. Ryan
E-Mail: sryan@misl.net
Vice President, Marketing and Communications: Jaye Cavallo

Historical Note
Founded as National Professional Soccer League; assumed its current name in 2001. MISL is the oldest running indoor soccer league in North America. MISL actively pursues corporate sponsorships and provides a variety of promotional opportunities at the local, regional, and national levels.

Publications:
MISL Guide and Record Book. a. adv.

Major League Baseball - Office of the Commissioner *(1921)*
245 Park Ave.
New York, NY 10167
Tel: (212)931-7800 *Fax:* (212)949-5654
Web Site: www.majorleaguebaseball.com
Members: 30 clubs
Staff: 70
Annual Budget: $2-5,000,000
Commissioner: Bud Selig
Executive Vice President, Baseball Operations: Sandy Alderson
President and Chief Operating Officer: Bob DuPuy

Historical Note
Founded to provide oversight and assure the integrity of the sport, the Office of the Commissioner works to promote baseball and protect the interests of its member franchises. Formerly a coordinating body for the separate activities for the National and American Leagues, in 2000 the Office of the Commissioner became the sole adminstrating body for major league baseball.

Meetings/Conferences:
Annual Meetings: Winter

Major League Baseball Players Association *(1966)*
12 E. 49th St., 24th Floor
New York, NY 10017
Tel: (212)826-0808 *Fax:* (212)752-4378
E-Mail: feedback@mlbpa.org
Web Site: www.bigleaguers.com
Members: 1200 individuals
Staff: 30
Executive Director and General Counsel: Donald Fehr
Director, Communications: Greg Bouris
Director, Business Affairs and Licensing: Judy Heeter

Historical Note
Independent labor union, representing approximately 1200 major league baseball players.

Meetings/Conferences:
Annual Meetings: First week in December

Major League Soccer *(1995)*
110 E. 42nd St., 10th Floor
New York, NY 10017
Tel: (212)450-1200 *Fax:* (212)450-1300
E-Mail: feedback@mlsnet.com
Web Site: www.mlsnet.com
Members: 10 teams
Commissioner: Don Garber
E-Mail: mlsgarber@mlsnet.com
President, MLS and Soccer United Marketing: Mark Abbott

Historical Note
Promotes the sport of soccer in general and serves as the central administrative office for its member franchises.

Man and Cybernetics Systems Society

Historical Note
A subsidiary of the Institute of Electrical and Electronics Engineers. Membership in the Society, open only to IEEE members, includes subscription to a technical periodical in the field published by IEEE. All administrative support is provided by IEEE.

Managed Funds Association *(1991)*
2025 M St. NW, Suite 800
Washington, DC 20036-3309
Tel: (202)367-1140 *Fax:* (202)367-2140
Toll Free: (800)425 - 4632
E-Mail: hq@mfainfo.org
Web Site: www.mfainfo.org
Members: 1200 individuals
Staff: 12
Annual Budget: $2-5,000,000
President: John G. Gaine

Historical Note
Founded as the Managed Futures Association; assumed its present name in 1999. Members are individuals involved in hedge funds, commodity funds, and funds of funds. Dedicated to protecting and advancing the broad interests of its members by representing the industry to regulatory and legislative governing bodies and to the investing public. Member/industry services include production of investment brochures, monthly newsletters and other publications. MFA also provides industry conferences, both in the U.S. and worldwide. Membership: $250-40,000/year.

Meetings/Conferences:
Semi-Annual: 700
2007 – Key Biscayne, FL(Ritz Carlton)/Feb. 11-13
2007 – Chicago, IL(Fairmont)/June 11-13

Publications:
The MFA Reporter. m.

Management Association for Private Photogrammetric Surveyors *(1982)*
1760 Reston Pkwy., Suite 515
Reston, VA 20190
Tel: (703)787-6996 *Fax:* (703)787-7550
E-Mail: info@mapps.org
Web Site: www.mapps.org
Members: 170 companies
Staff: 4
Annual Budget: $250-500,000
Executive Director: John M. Palatiello
E-Mail: info@mapps.org

Historical Note
MAPPS members are companies providing photogrammetry and computer based geographic information services. Membership: $1250/year.

Meetings/Conferences:
Semi-Annual Meetings: January and July

Publications:
Capitol Coverage. bi-m.
Flightline Newsletter. bi-m.

Manufactured Housing Association for Regulatory Reform *(1985)*
1331 Pennsylvania Ave. NW, Suite 508
Washington, DC 20004

Tel: (202)783-4087 *Fax:* (202)783-4075
Members: 40 companies
Staff: 2
Annual Budget: $250-500,000
President: Danny D. Ghorbani

Historical Note

Formerly the Association for Regulatory Reform. MHARR represents the interests and views of producers of manufactured housing. Dedicated to the reform of unnecessary regulation of American housing industry.

Meetings/Conferences:

Annual Meetings: Varies

Publications:

MHARR Review. m.
MHARR News. irreg.
MHARR Washington Update. bi-m.
Regulatory, Legislative and Legal Position Papers. irreg.

Manufactured Housing Institute *(1936)*

2101 Wilson Blvd., Suite 610
Arlington, VA 22201-3062
Tel: (703)558-0400 *Fax:* (703)558-0401
E-Mail: info@mfghome.org
Web Site: www.manufacturedhousing.org
Members: 300 companies
Staff: 18
Annual Budget: $2-5,000,000
President: Chris S. Stinebert
E-Mail: chris@mfghome.org
Director, Meetings and Education: Suzanne Thulin Clegg
E-Mail: sclegg@mfghome.org
Vice President, Government Affairs: Brian Cooney
E-Mail: brian@mfghome.org
Vice President, Technical Activities: Mark Nunn
E-Mail: mark@mfghome.org
Executive Vice President: Michael O'Brien, CAE
E-Mail: mobrien@mfghome.org
Vice President, Public Affairs: Bruce A. Savage, CAE
E-Mail: bruce@mfghome.org

Historical Note

Established as Trailer Coach Manufacturers Association. Became Mobile Homes Manufacturers Association in 1956 and the Manufactured Housing Institute in 1975. Absorbed the National Manufactured Housing Federation in 1991 and the National Manufactured Housing Finance Association in 1992. MHI members are corporations involved in the manufactured housing industry. Primary functions are governmetal relations, monitoring of construction standards, public relations, community operations, site development and statistical services. Supports the MHI Political Action Committee. Membership: dues vary, based on production.

Meetings/Conferences:

Annual Meetings: October

Publications:

Modern Homes. 6/year. adv.
Modern Homes Development. 6/year. adv.
Quarterly Economic Report. q.
Manufacturing Report. m.
Quick Facts. a.

Manufacturers Alliance/MAPI *(1933)*

1600 Wilson Blvd., Suite 1100
Arlington, VA 22209
Tel: (703)841-9000 *Fax:* (703)841-9514
E-Mail: info@mapi.net
Web Site: www.mapi.net
Members: 450 manufacturing companies
Staff: 37
Annual Budget: $5-10,000,000
President and Chief Executive Officer: Dr. Thomas J. Duesterberg
Director, Communications: James F. Engelhardt
E-Mail: jengelhardt@mapi.net
Vice President, Finance: Tracy Hollingsworth
Vice President and General Counsel: Frederick T. Stocker
E-Mail: fstocker@mapi.net

Historical Note

Formerly (1989) Machinery and Allied Products Institute; became (1996) Manufacturers Alliance for Productivity and Innovation/MAPI before assuming its curent name. The Alliance is a policy research organization whose members are companies drawn from the producers and users of capital goods and allied products. Includes leading companies in heavy industry, automotive, electronics, precision instruments, telecommunications, computers, office systems, aerospace, oil/gas, chemicals and similar high technology industries. Conducts original research in economics, law, and management and provides professional analysis of issues critical to the economic performance of the private sector. Operates 25 councils in various management disciplines, and acts as national spokesperson for policies which stimulate technological advancement and economic growth.

Meetings/Conferences:

Annual Meetings: June in Washington, DC/50 (Exec. Committee & Board of Trustees).
2007 – Washington, DC/June 14-15

Publications:

Economic Reports. irreg.
Legal Analysis & Regulations. irreg.
Policy Reviews. irreg.

Manufacturers Council of Small School Buses

Historical Note

An affiliate of the National Truck Equipment Association.

Manufacturers Elevating and Work Platform Council

Historical Note

A council of the Equipment Manufacturers Institute.

Manufacturers of Aerial Devices and Digger-Derricks Council

Historical Note

A council of the Equipment Manufacturers Institute.

Manufacturers of Emission Controls Association *(1976)*

1730 M St. NW, Suite 206
Washington, DC 20036
Tel: (202)296-4797 *Fax:* (202)331-1388
E-Mail: info@meca.org
Web Site: www.meca.org
Members: 46 companies
Staff: 4
Contact: Antonio Santos

Historical Note

MECA provides technical information on emission control technology for motor vehicles.

Meetings/Conferences:

Annual Meetings: March, in Washington, DC

Manufacturers of Telescoping and Articulating Cranes Council

Historical Note

A council of the Equipment Manufacturers Institute.

Manufacturers Representatives of America *(1978)*

P.O. Box 150229
Arlington, TX 76015
Tel: (682)518-6008 *Fax:* (682)518-6476
E-Mail: assnhqtrs@aol.com
Web Site: www.mra-reps.com
Members: 250salesandmarketingcompanies
Staff: 2
Annual Budget: $100-250,000
Executive Director: Pamela L. Bess

Historical Note

Members are manufacturers' representatives in the paper, plastic, packaging, and sanitary supply fields.

Manufacturers Standardization Society of the Valve and Fittings Industry *(1924)*

127 Park St. NE
Vienna, VA 22180-4602
Tel: (703)281-6613 *Fax:* (703)281-6671
E-Mail: info@mss-hq.com
Web Site: www.mss-hq.com
Members: 86 companies
Staff: 3
Annual Budget: $250-500,000
Executive Director: Robert O'Neill

Historical Note

An engineering society devoted to development and publication of standards and specifications for the valve and fittings industry. Membership: $1,800/year (company).

Meetings/Conferences:

Annual Meetings: April-May/115
2007 – Marco Island, FL(Marco Island beach Resort)/May 7-10/160
2008 – Orange Beach, CA(Perdido Beach Resort)/Apr. 28-March 1/160

Publications:

Standards for Valves, et. a.

Manufacturers' Agents Association for the Foodservice Industry *(1949)*

2814 Spring Rd., Suite 211
Atlanta, GA 30339
Tel: (770)433-9844 *Fax:* (770)433-2450
E-Mail: info@mafsi.org
Web Site: www.mafsi.org
Members: 700 companies
Staff: 3
Annual Budget: $500-1,000,000
Executive Director: Alison Cody
E-Mail: acody@mafsi.org

Historical Note

Formerly (1993) Marketing Agents for Food Service Industry. Members are independent manufacturers' representatives.

Meetings/Conferences:

Annual Meetings: February, in a resort area/450

Publications:

Outfront. q. adv.
Annual Report. a.

Manufacturers' Agents National Association *(1947)*

One Spectrum Pointe, Suite 150
Lake Forest, CA 92630
Tel: (949)859-4040 *Fax:* (949)855-2973
Toll Free: (877)626 - 2776
E-Mail: mana@manaonline.org
Web Site: www.manaonline.org
Members: 6600 companies
Staff: 15
Annual Budget: $2-5,000,000
President: Bryan Shirley
E-Mail: bshirley@manaonline.org
Executive Vice President: Helen Degli-Angeli
E-Mail: helen@manaonline.org

Historical Note

MANA promotes sucessful and profitable relationships among multi-line sales agencies, the principals/manufacturers they represent, and their joint customers. Membership: $199/year (sales agencies); $229/year (manufacturers).

Publications:

E-Mail Newsletter. m.
Directory of Manufacturers' Sales Agencies (online). w. adv.
Research Bulletins and Special Reports.
Agency Sales Magazine. m. adv.

Manufacturing Jewelers and Suppliers of America *(1903)*

45 Royal Little Dr.
Providence, RI 02904
Tel: (401)274-3840 *Fax:* (401)274-0265
Toll Free: (800)444 - 6572
E-Mail: mjsa@mjsainc.com
Web Site: www.mjsainc.com
Members: 1650 companies
Staff: 23
Annual Budget: $2-5,000,000
President and Chief Executive Officer: Frank Dallahan
Chief Financial Officer: James K. McCarty
Editor: Tina Wojtkiclo

Historical Note

Established as the New England Manufacturing Jewelers' and Silversmiths' Association, MJSA is the trade association for all segments of the American jewelry manufacturing and supply industry. Membership includes American, foreign and retail companies.

Meetings/Conferences:

Annual Meetings: Annual

Publications:

AJM Magazine. m. adv.

Manuscript Society *(1948)*
1960 E. Fairmont Dr.
Tempe, AZ 85282-2884
E-Mail: manuscrip@cox.net
Web Site: www.manuscript.org
Members: 1400 individuals
Staff: 3
Annual Budget: $50-100,000
Executive Director: Edward C. Oettinger
E-Mail: manuscrip@cox.net
Historical Note
Formerly (1953) National Society of Autograph Collectors. Members are dealers, curators, collectors and others interested in original manuscripts, autographs, letters and documents. Membership: $35/year (individual); $35/year (institution).
Meetings/Conferences:
Annual Meetings: Spring/100
Publications:
Manuscripts. q.
News. q.

Maple Flooring Manufacturers Association *(1897)*
60 Revere Dr., Suite 500
Northbrook, IL 60062
Tel: (847)480-9138 *Fax:* (847)480-9282
E-Mail: mfma@maplefloor.org
Web Site: www.maplefloor.org
Members: 195 companies
Staff: 4
Annual Budget: $250-500,000
Executive Director: John R. Waxman
Director, Technical: Daniel Heney
Historical Note
MFMA maintains technical and general information on maple flooring and represents manufacturing mills and allied product manufacturers, distributors, and flooring contractors who use maple flooring. Membership: $450/year (associate company), $800/year (allied manufacturer).
Meetings/Conferences:
Annual Meetings: Spring
2008 – San Diego, CA(Rancho Bernardo Inn)/March 6-8/250

Maraschino Cherry and Glace Fruit Processors *(1906)*
Historical Note
A section of the Association of Food Industries.

Marble Institute of America *(1944)*
28901 Clemens Rd., Suite 100
Cleveland, OH 44145-1166
Tel: (440)250-9222 *Fax:* (440)250-9223
E-Mail: miainfo@marble-institute.com
Web Site: www.marble-institute.com
Members: 1700 companies
Staff: 9
Annual Budget: $2-5,000,000
Executive Vice President: Garis F. Distelhorst, CAE
E-Mail: gdistelhorst@marble-institute.com
Director, Meeting and Events: Helen Distelhorst
E-Mail: hdistelhorst@marble-institute.com
Director, Education: James Hieb
Director, Membership: Cathy Mayer
Director, Technical: Charles Muehlbauer
Historical Note
Absorbed the National Association of Marble Dealers in 1962. Members include producers, exporters/importers, distributors, fabricators, finishers, installers and industry suppliers. Membership: $750/year (domestic company), $825/year (foreign company).
Meetings/Conferences:
Annual Meetings: Fall/600
2007 – Las Vegas, NV
Publications:
Cutting Edge. m. adv.
Various Technical and Consumer Advisories.
Dimension Stone Design Manual. quadren.
Dimension Stones of the World-Vols. I and II.

Marine Corps Reserve Association *(1926)*
2020 General Booth Blvd., Suite 200
Virginia Beach, VA 23454
Tel: (757)301-2032 *Fax:* (757)301-6884
Toll Free: (800)927 - 6270
E-Mail: mcra@mcrassn.org
Web Site: www.mcrassn.org/
Members: 5000 individuals
Staff: 2
Annual Budget: $250-500,000
Executive Director: Richard H. Esau, Jr.
E-Mail: resau@mcrassn.org
Historical Note
Founded as Marine Corps Reserve Officers Association; assumed its current name in 2003. MCRA serves to support the Marine Corps, its Reserve Component, and Marine Reservists. Members are active, former and retired Marine Corps Reservists. Membership: $15-50/year (individual), $250-1,000/year (small business), $1,000-10,000/year (corporate).
Meetings/Conferences:
Annual Meetings: Spring/500
Publications:
The Word. bi-m. adv.
Nat'l Network Directory. a. adv.

Marine Engineers Beneficial Association *(1875)*
444 N. Capitol St., Suite 800
Washington, DC 20001
Tel: (202)638-5355 *Fax:* (202)638-5369
E-Mail: mebahq@d1meba.org
Web Site: www.meba.us
Members: 35000 full and affiliate members
Staff: 69
Annual Budget: $5-10,000,000
President: Ron Davis
Secretary-Treasurer: Bill Van Loo
Historical Note
Founded in 1875, MEBA is the oldest labor union in America and represents licensed engine, radio and deck officers on U.S.-flag ocean-going ships.
Meetings/Conferences:
Annual Meetings: Third Monday of March/40
Publications:
Marine Officer. bi-m.
Telex Times. w.

Marine Fabricators Association
1801 County Rd. B West
St. Paul, MN 55113-4061
Tel: (651)222-2508 *Fax:* (651)631-9334
Toll Free: (800)209 - 1810
E-Mail: bhungiville@ifai.com
Web Site: www.marinecanvas.com
Members: 300 companies
Staff: 1
Annual Budget: $50-100,000
Managing Director: Beth L. Hungiville
E-Mail: bhungiville@ifai.com
Historical Note
MFA represents firms and individuals engaged in the design, construction, and installation of marine fabric products, providing certification and product standards. Membership: based on company's annual sales, begins at $290/year.
Meetings/Conferences:
Annual Meetings: Winter
Publications:
MFA Newsletter.
Fabric Specifier Guide.
Membership Directory. a.
Time Standards Manual.
Marine Fabricator. q. adv.
Upholstery Journal. q. adv.

Marine Retailers Association of America *(1971)*
P.O. Box 1127
Oak Park, IL 60304
Tel: (708)763-9210 *Fax:* (708)763-9236
E-Mail: mraa@mraa.com
Web Site: http://mraa.com
Members: 3000 companies
Staff: 2
Annual Budget: $500-1,000,000
President: Phil Keeter
E-Mail: mraa@mraa.com
Historical Note
Members are manufacturers, distributors and dealers in marine equipment. Membership: $150-5,000/year.
Meetings/Conferences:
Annual Meetings: Fall
Publications:
MRAA Newsletter. m.

Marine Technology Society *(1963)*
5565 Sterrett Place, Suite 108
Columbia, MD 21044
Tel: (410)884-5330 *Fax:* (410)884-9060
E-Mail: mtsmbrship@erols.com
Web Site: www.mtsociety.org
Members: 3000 individuals
Staff: 4
Annual Budget: $500-1,000,000
Executive Director: Judith Krauthamer
E-Mail: mtsdir@erols.com
Manager, Membership: Emily Speight
E-Mail: mtsmbrship@erols.com
Historical Note
Founded and incorporated in New York in 1963. Membership: rates vary.
Meetings/Conferences:
Annual Meetings: Fall/2,500
Publications:
Underwater Intervention Conference Proceedings. a.
Education & Training Programs in Oceanography & Related Fields. irreg.
Marine Technology Society Journal. q. adv.
MTS Currents Newsletter. bi-m.
MTS Conference Proceedings. a.

Maritime Law Association of the U.S. *(1899)*
Curtis, Mallet-Prevost, Colt & Mosle
101 Park Ave.
New York, NY 10178
Tel: (212)696-6000 *Fax:* (212)696-1559
Web Site: www.mlaus.org
Members: 3450 individuals
President: Lizabeth L. Burrell
Historical Note
Founded to represent the U.S. in the Comite Maritime Internationale. Works to unify and improve maritime law, and to educate members in the field. Affiliated with the American Bar Association. Has no paid officers or full-time staff. Membership: $135/year (individual).
Meetings/Conferences:
Semi-Annual: Spring/1st Friday in May/New York, NY. Fall/ alternates between port cities (even years) and other locations.
Publications:
MLA Proceedings. semi-a.
MLA Reports. semi-a.

Marketing Agencies Association Worldwide *(1969)*
460 Summer St.
Stamford, CT 06901
Tel: (203)978-1590 *Fax:* (203)969-1499
Web Site: www.maaw.org
Members: 85 agencies
Staff: 1
Annual Budget: $250-500,000
Contact: Keith McCracken
Historical Note
Founded as Council of Sales Promotion Agencies; became Association of Promotion Marketing Agencies Worldwide in 1995, and assumed its current name in 2003. A trade association of sales promotion agencies with at least two years experience. 50% of MAAW membership is foreign. Membership: $3,700/year (full member); $1,000/year (associate).
Meetings/Conferences:
Semi-annual Meetings: Spring and Fall
2007 – Berlin, Germany/May
Publications:
MAA Newsletters. q.
Membership Roster. bi-a.

Marketing and Advertising Global Network *(1946)*
1017 Perry Hwy., Suite 5
Pittsburgh, PA 15237

Tel: (412)366-6850 Fax: (412)366-6840
E-Mail: mxdirector@verizon.net
Web Site: www.magnetglobal.org
Members: 36 companies
Staff: 1
Annual Budget: $250-500,000
Executive Director: Cheri D. Gmiter
E-Mail: mxdirector@verizon.net

Historical Note
Founded as the Midwestern Advertising Agency Network; later became Mutual Advertising Agency Network and assumed its present name in 1999. Membership: $6,500/year (corporate).

Publications:
MAGNET Matters. 3/year.

Marketing Education Association *(1982)*
P.O. Box 27473
Tempe, AZ 85285-7473
Tel: (602)750-6735
E-Mail: mea@nationalmea.org
Web Site: www.nationalmea.org
Members: 600 individuals
Staff: 2
Annual Budget: $50-100,000
Executive Director: Rod Davis
E-Mail: mea@nationalmea.org

Historical Note
Formerly (1985) Marketing and Distributive Education Association and then (1989) National Marketing and Distributive Education Services Center. Formed by a merger of the Council of Distributive Teacher Educators (founded in 1960), National Association of Distributive Education Local Supervisors, National Association of Distributive Education Teachers (founded in 1957) and National Association of State Supervisors of Distributive Education (founded in 1947). MEA fosters the development and expansion of education for and about marketing as a discrete, clearly defined profession. Members are high school and postsecondary marketing educators as well as university-level teacher educators and collegiate marketing teacher education students. Membership: $30/first year; $56/year (renewal); $15/year (student member); $111/year (executive member); $200/year (institution).

Meetings/Conferences:
Annual Meetings: *June with MarkEd Resource Center*

Publications:
Meadvocate. a. adv.

Marketing Research Association *(1954)*
110 National Dr., Second Floor
Glastonbury, CT 06033
Tel: (860)682-1000 Fax: (860)682-1010
E-Mail: email@mra-net.org
Web Site: www.mra-net.org
Members: 2650 individuals
Staff: 19
Annual Budget: $1-2,000,000
Executive Director: Larry Brownell
E-Mail: email@mra-net.org

Historical Note
Formerly (1971) Marketing Research Trade Association. Members are companies and individuals involved in the design, administration, or analysis of market research studies. Membership: $223/year (individual), $446-$1,187/year (company).

Meetings/Conferences:
Semi-Annual Meetings: Spring and Fall

Publications:
E-Mail Newsletter. m. adv.
E-Mail Newsletter Student Focus. m.
Alert! Newsleter. m. adv.
Blue Book, Research Service Directory. a. adv.

Marky Cattle Association

Historical Note
See American International Marchigiana Society.

Mason Contractors Association of America *(1950)*
33 S. Roselle Rd.
Schaumburg, IL 60193
Tel: (847)301-0001 Fax: (847)301-1110
Toll Free: (800)536 - 2225
E-Mail: info@masoncontractors.com
Web Site: www.masoncontractors.com
Members: 1000 individuals
Staff: 8
Annual Budget: $1-2,000,000
Executive Director: Michael Adelizzi
Director, Professional Development: Colin Faul
E-Mail: info@masoncontractors.com
Controller: Liz Fidoruk
Director, Engineering: Rashod Johnson
Director, Government Affairs: Marian Marshall
Director, Information Technology: Timothy O'Toole
Director, Workforce Development: Melissa Polivka

Historical Note
Membership: $400-2000/year.

Meetings/Conferences:
Annual Meetings: *late Winter/6,000*

Publications:
Masonry Magazine. m. adv.

Masonry Heater Association of North America *(1986)*
1252 Stock Farm Rd.
Randolph, VT 05060
Tel: (802)728-5896 Fax: (802)728-6004
Web Site: http://mha-net.org
Members: 80 individuals
Staff: 1
Annual Budget: $25-50,000
Administrator: Beverly J. Marois

Historical Note
MHA was founded to promote the use of masonry heaters, increase public awareness of its advantages, and encourage reasonable governmental regulation of this unique wood burning appliance. Trade association representing the United States and Canada. Membership: $100/year (affiliate); $200/year (voting).

Publications:
MHA News Newsletter. q.

Masonry Society, The *(1977)*
3970 Broadway St., Suite 201-D
Boulder, CO 80304-1135
Tel: (303)939-9700 Fax: (303)541-9215
E-Mail: info@masonrysociety.org
Web Site: www.masonrysociety.org
Members: 660 individuals
Staff: 4
Annual Budget: $250-500,000
Executive Director: Phillip Samblanet
E-Mail: info@masonrysociety.org

Historical Note
TMS is a professional/technical association dedicated to the advancement of scientific, engineering, architectural and construction knowledge of masonry. The Society stimulates research and education and disseminates information on masonry materials, design and construction. Members are architects, engineers, manufacturers of masonry products, contractors, craftsmen, building officials, educators, researchers, suppliers, students and others having an interest in masonry. Membership: $125/year (regular); $35/year (student); $295/year (company/organization).

Meetings/Conferences:
2007 – St. Louis, MO/June 1-3
2007 – Pittsburgh, PA/Nov. 8-13/100

Publications:
Proceedings of the North American Masonry Conference. every 4 years.
TMS Journal. 1/year.
Membership Directory. bien.
TMS News. 4/year.

Mass Finishing Job Shops Association *(1981)*
808 13th St.
East Moline, IL 61244-1628
Tel: (309)755-1101 Fax: (309)755-1121
E-Mail: kvfquad@netexpress.net
Web Site: www.mfjsa.com
Members: 33 companies
Annual Budget: under $10,000
Executive Director: Terry Larson
E-Mail: kvfquad@netexpress.net

Historical Note
Members are companies providing advanced metal finishing services.

Meetings/Conferences:
Semi-annual Meetings: Fall & Spring

Mass Marketing Insurance Institute *(1969)*
14 W. Third, Suite 200
Kansas City, MO 64105
Tel: (816)221-7575 Fax: (816)472-7765
E-Mail: gary@robstan.com
Web Site: www.mi2.org
Members: 300 companies
Staff: 2
Annual Budget: $250-500,000
Executive Director: Gary Hicks

Historical Note
MI2 provides a forum for professionals engaged in marketing, sales and administration of employee benefits such as worksite marketing, payroll deduction and other mass marketed services. Membership: $395/year (manufacturers/administrators/vendors); $495/year (producers/brokers).

Meetings/Conferences:
Annual Meetings: *Spring*

Publications:
Membership Services Catalogue. a.
Worksite Insights. m.
Membership Directory. a.

Master Brewers Association of the Americas *(1887)*
3340 Pilot Knob Rd.
St. Paul, MN 55121
Tel: (651)454-7250 Fax: (651)454-0766
E-Mail: mbaa@scisoc.org
Web Site: www.mbaa.com
Members: 2300 individuals
Staff: 10
Annual Budget: $1-2,000,000
Executive Vice President: Steven C. Nelson, CMP
Manager, Publications: Karen Cummings
E-Mail: mbaa@mbaa.com
Director, Operations: Jody Grider
E-Mail: jgrider@scisoc.org
Vice President, Operations: Amy Hope
E-Mail: ahope@scisoc.org

Historical Note
Founded as the Master Brewers Association of America in 1887, it assumed its present name in 1979. It was formed with the purpose of promoting, advancing, improving and protecting the professional interest of brew and malt house production personnel . The MBAA disseminates technical and practical information, promotes training, and encourages the furthering of knowledge through the cooperation and interaction of its members.

Meetings/Conferences:
Annual Meetings: *Fall*
2007 – Nashville, TN(Gaylord Opryland Hotel)/Oct. 26-28
2008 – Honolulu, HI(Hawaii Convention Center)/Aug. 3-6

Publications:
MBAA Communicator. q. adv.
MBAA Technical Quarterly. q. adv.

Master Printers of America *(1945)*
5097 Coral Reef Dr.
Johns Island, SC 29455-8169
Tel: (843)768-0127
Members: 9000 individuals
Staff: 3
Annual Budget: $500-1,000,000
Advisor: Brian Gill

Historical Note
A division of Printing Industries of America, which provides administrative support. Members are open shop printers.

Meetings/Conferences:
Annual Meetings: *Spring*

MasterCard International *(1966)*
2000 Purchase St.
Purchase, NY 10577
Tel: (914)249-2000 Fax: (914)249-4206
Web Site: www.mastercardinternational.com

Members: 25000 financial institutions
Staff: 4000
Annual Budget: Over $100,000,000
Vice President, Global Communications and Corporate Public Relations: Sharon Gasmin

Historical Note
Administers the MasterCard credit card and other MasterCard products for 25,000 member financial institutions around the world. Formerly (1979) Interbank Card Association.

Publications:
Member News. q.

Material Handling Equipment Distributors Association *(1954)*
201 U.S. Hwy. 45
Vernon Hills, IL 60061-2398
Tel: (847)680-3500 *Fax:* (847)362-6989
E-Mail: connect@mheda.org
Web Site: www.mheda.org
Members: 650 companies
Staff: 7
Annual Budget: $1-2,000,000
Executive Vice President: Liz Richards
E-Mail: lrichards@mheda.org
Manager, Meetings and Events: AnnaMaria Kendall
Manager, Communications: Evelyn McWilliams
E-Mail: emcwilliams@mheda.org

Historical Note
Membership: $415-1,550/year (company).

Meetings/Conferences:
Annual Meetings: Spring/750-1,000

Publications:
Membership Directory. a.
The MHEDA Journal. q.

Material Handling Industry of America *(1945)*
8720 Red Oak Blvd., Suite 201
Charlotte, NC 28217-3992
Tel: (704)676-1190 *Fax:* (704)676-1199
Web Site: www.mhia.org
Members: 700 companies
Staff: 30
Annual Budget: $10-25,000,000
Chief Executive Officer: John B. Nofsinger
Director, Membership: Victoria Wheeler
E-Mail: vwheeler@mhia.org

Historical Note
Founded as Material Handling Institute; became Material Handling Industry Association in 1995 assumed its current name in 2002. A member of the Manufacturers Alliance for Productivity and Innovation. Makers of industrial material handling and logistics equipment and systems such as conveyors, racks, hoists and cranes, lift trucks, and information technologies. Membership: $2,000/year, (company).

Meetings/Conferences:
Annual Meetings: Spring

Publications:
On the MHove. q.
e-MHove. m.
The Exhibitor. m.
Membership Roster. a.

Materials and Methods Standards Association *(1962)*
4000 Pinemont
Houston, TX 77292
Tel: (713)682-8411 Ext: 116 *Fax:* (713)688-2448
Toll Free: (800)669 - 0115
E-Mail: leigh@texrite.com
Web Site: www.mmsa.ws
Members: 40 companies
Staff: 1
Annual Budget: $10-25,000
President: Leigh Hightower
E-Mail: leigh@texrite.com
Secretary/Treasurer: Steven Fine
E-Mail: sbfine@laticrete.com

Historical Note
Incorporated in 1962 in Texas as the Mortar Manufacturers Standards Association; became Methods and Materials Standards Association in 1977 and assumed its present name in 1984. Membership is composed of manufacturers of ceramic tile and ceramic tile installation products. MMSA is represented on the Tile Council of America and the ANSI A108/118/136 committees. MMSA member committees develop information and ANSI standards for the industry as technology dictates. Membership: $300/year (company).

Meetings/Conferences:
Biennial: Held in conjunction with the Services Convention and Total Solutions Convention.

Materials Handling and Management Society *(1947)*

Historical Note
An affiliate of Material Handling Industry of America, which provides administrative support.

Materials Marketing Associates *(1963)*
136 S. Keowee St.
Dayton, OH 45402
Tel: (937)222-1024 *Fax:* (937)222-5794
E-Mail: email@mma4u.com
Web Site: www.mma4u.com
Members: 15 companies
Staff: 3
Annual Budget: $50-100,000
Executive Director: Kim Fantaci

Historical Note
MMA's members are chemical distributors representing manufacturers marketing chemical raw material specialties to makers of coatings, inks, pharmaceuticals, adhesives, cosmetics, plastics, soaps, detergents, etc. Membership: $2,000/year (organization/company).

Meetings/Conferences:
Annual Meetings: February
2007 - Phoenix, AZ/February/40

Publications:
Newsletter. m.

Materials Properties Council *(1966)*
P.O. Box 1942
New York, NY 10156
Tel: (216)658-3847 *Fax:* (216)658-3854
E-Mail: mpc@forengineers.org
Web Site: www.forengineers.org/mpc/
Members: 600 individuals
Staff: 3
Annual Budget: $500-1,000,000
Executive Director: Martin Prager, Ph.D.

Historical Note
Formerly (1986) The Metal Properties Council. MPC is an outgrowth of the ASTM-ASME Joint Committee on the Effect of Temperature on the Properties of Metals which was founded in 1925 to meet the apparent need for information on the subject in the construction of central power stations. After 40 years it was apparent that a permanently staffed organization was needed to ensure the availability of valid data on materials to meet advancing technology. MPC was founded in 1966 to meet this need. Sponsored by American Society of Mechanical Engineers, American Society for Testing and Materials, American Society for Metals, Engineering Foundation and American Welding Society

Meetings/Conferences:
Annual Meetings: Second Thursday in October/25

Publications:
Yearbook. a.

Materials Research Society *(1973)*
506 Keystone Dr.
Warrendale, PA 15086-7573
Tel: (724)779-3003 *Fax:* (724)779-8313
E-Mail: info@mrs.org
Web Site: www.mrs.org
Members: 13000 individuals
Staff: 40
Annual Budget: $2-5,000,000
Executive Director: John B. Ballance, CAE
Director, Information Services: Michael C. Driver
Director, Meeting Activities: Patricia A. Hastings
Director, Membership Affairs: Gail A. Oare
Director, Finance and Administration: Robert H. Pachavis
Director, Planning: Sandra DeVincent Wolf

Historical Note
Members are individuals adopting a multi-disciplinary approach towards the problems of research on materials. Membership: $25/year (student); $105/year (individual).

Meetings/Conferences:
2007 - San Francisco, CA(Moscone West)/Apr. 9-13
2007 - Boston, MA(Hynes Convention Center)/Nov. 26-30

Publications:
MRS Bulletin. m.
Journal of Materials Research. m.

Materials Technology Institute *(1977)*
1215 Fern Ridge Pkwy., Suite 206
St. Louis, MO 63141-4401
Tel: (314)576-7712 *Fax:* (314)576-6078
E-Mail: mtiadmin@mti-global.org
Web Site: www.mti-global.org
Members: 56 companies
Staff: 8
Annual Budget: $500-1,000,000
Director, Operations: Debby Ehret

Historical Note
Established and incorporated in New York in 1977 as Materials Technology Institute of the Chemical Process Industries. MTI was formed to avoid duplication in investigations pertaining to materials of construction and equipment used in the process industries and to provide opportunites for the exchange of information. Membership: $8,700-51,400/year, based on total sales.

Meetings/Conferences:
Annual Meetings: October

Publications:
Newsletter. semi-a.

Mathematical Association of America *(1915)*
1529 18th St. NW, Suite 600
Washington, DC 20036
Tel: (202)387-5200 *Fax:* (202)265-2384
Toll Free: (800)741 - 9415
E-Mail: maahq@maa.org
Web Site: www.maa.org
Members: 33000 individuals
Staff: 30
Annual Budget: $2-5,000,000
Executive Director: Tina H. Straley
Associate Executive Director and Director, Publications: Donald J. Albers
Associate Executive Director, Membership, Marketing and Meetings: James D. Gandorf, CAE
Director, Finance: Sharon L. Tryon

Historical Note
Founded in Columbus, Ohio in 1915 to promote the teaching of mathematics, especially on the collegiate level. A constituent member of the Conference Board of the Mathematical Sciences. Membership: $89-122/year, varies by number of journals subscribed (individual); $150/year (institution).

Meetings/Conferences:
Semi-annual Meetings: Winter, with the American Mathematical Society, and Summer

Publications:
American Mathematical Monthly. 10/year. adv.
Mathematics Magazine. 5/year. adv.
College Mathematics Journal. 5/year. adv.
Focus Newsletter. bi-m. adv.

Meals On Wheels Association of America *(1973)*
203 S. Union St.
Alexandria, VA 22314-3355
Tel: (703)548-5558 *Fax:* (703)548-8024
E-Mail: mowaa@mowaa.org
Web Site: www.mowaa.org
Members: 900 programs and corporate members
Staff: 6
Annual Budget: $500-1,000,000
Chief Executive Officer: Enid A. Borden
Fiscal Officer: Elizabeth Doyle
Director, Policy and Legislation: Peggy Ingraham

Historical Note
Members are organizations providing meals, particularly to the elderly, disabled and homebound. MOWAA represents these organizations by providing training/technical assistance and legislative support. MOWAA consists of organizations throughout the

United States and Canada. Membership: $95/year (general member); $175/year (organizational member); $200 or $300/year (corporate member).

Meetings/Conferences:
Annual Meetings: Fall

Publications:
Membership Directory (online, for members only).
MOWAA News. m. adv.

Measurement, Control and Automation Association *(1918)*
P.O. Box 3698
Williamsburg, VA 23187-3698
Tel: (757)258-3100 *Fax:* (757)258-3100
Web Site: www.measure.org
Members: 150 companies
Staff: 2
Annual Budget: $250-500,000
President: Cynthia A. Esher
E-Mail: esher@measure.org

Historical Note
MCAA is a trade association representing manufacturers and distributors of instrumentation and systems used in industrial process measurement and control. MCAA disassociated from the SAMA Group of Associations in 1994. Membership: annual dues vary by sales volume (company).

Meetings/Conferences:
Annual Meetings: Spring
2007 - Dallas, TX(Hilton)/May 20-22/130

Publications:
Industrial Business Circles Report. 2/yr.
Membership Directory (online). m.
Measuring Markets - Economic Newsletter. q.

Meat Importers' Council of America *(1962)*
1901 N. Ft. Myer Dr.
Arlington, VA 22209
Tel: (703)522-1910 *Fax:* (703)524-6039
Toll Free: (800)522 - 1910
Members: 160 companies
Staff: 1
Annual Budget: $250-500,000
Executive Director: Laurie Bryant

Meetings/Conferences:
Annual Meetings: Fall

Meat Industry Suppliers Alliance *(1948)*
200 Daingerfield Rd.
Alexandria, VA 22314
Tel: (703)684-1080 *Fax:* (703)548-6563
E-Mail: misahq@aol.com
Members: 30 companies
Staff: 2
Annual Budget: $100-250,000
President: George O. Melnykovich, Ph.D.
Director, Member Services: Cheryl Clark

Historical Note
Founded as Meat Industry Supply and Equipment Association; became Meat Industry Suppliers Association in 1981. Absorbed the Meat Machinery Manufacturers Institute and the Food Machinery Service Institute in 1984. Merged with the Meat, Poultry and Seafood Council of the Food Processing Machinery Association and assumed its current name in 2003. Members are suppliers to the meat, poultry and seafood packing and processing industries.

Publications:
Buyer's Guide on CD. a. adv.
e-Newsletters. m.

Meat Machinery Manufacturers Institute *(1938)*

Historical Note
An autonomous division of the Meat Industry Supplier Association.

Mechanical Association Railcar Technical Services *(1901)*
2146 Windsor Ave. SW
Roanoke, VA 24015
Tel: (540)343-8991 *Fax:* (540)343-2410
E-Mail: admin@marts-rail.org
Web Site: www.marts-rail.org
Members: 500companiesandindividuals
Annual Budget: $10-25,000
Secretary-Treasurer: John Robertson

Historical Note
Founded as Interchange Car Inspectors, it became the Railway Car Department Officers Association the same year, the Master Car Builders Association in 1926, Car Department Officers Association in 1928, and assumed its present name in 1999. Companies and individuals involved in the construction, maintenance and repair of freight and passenger railway cars. Membership: $20/year (individual); $100/year (company)

Meetings/Conferences:
Annual Meetings: September

Publications:
Proceedings. a.

Mechanical Contractors Association of America *(1889)*
1385 Piccard Dr.
Rockville, MD 20850-4340
Tel: (301)869-5800 *Fax:* (301)990-9690
Toll Free: (800)556 - 3693
E-Mail: info@mcaa.org
Web Site: www.mcaa.org
Members: 2300 companies
Staff: 30
Annual Budget: $5-10,000,000
Executive Vice President and Chief Executive Officer: John R. Gentille
E-Mail: jgentille@mcaa.org
Director, Publications: Adrienne Breedlove
Executive Director, Strategic Events Management: Cynthia Buffington
Chief Financial Officer: Gail Gannon
Director, Membership: Jan Letow
Executive Director, Government and Labor Relations: John McNerney
Director, Information Technology: Lu Ann Steele

Historical Note
Founded as the Master Steam and Hot Water Fitters Association; assumed its present name in 1956. MCAA represents mechanical contractors (i.e. heating, piping, air conditioning and plumbing contractors) who employ primarily union labor. The National Certified Pipe Welding Bureau, Mechanical Service Contractors of America, and the Plumbing Contractors of America are departments of MCAA.

Meetings/Conferences:
Annual Meetings: February

Publications:
MCAA National Update. w.
The Reporter. m.
Membership Directory. a. adv.

Mechanical Power Transmission Association *(1933)*
6724 Lone Oak Blvd.
Naples, FL 34109-6834
Tel: (239)514-3441 *Fax:* (239)514-3470
E-Mail: bob@mpta.org
Web Site: http:/www.mpta.org
Members: 20 companies
Staff: 2
Annual Budget: $25-50,000
Executive Director: Robert A. Reinfried

Historical Note
Formerly Multiple V-Belt Drive and Mechanical Power Transmission Association. Membership: $500-3,850/year.

Meetings/Conferences:
Annual Meetings: April
2007 - Litchfield Park, AZ(Wigwam)/Apr. 1-4/45
2008 - Litchfield Park, AZ(Wigwam)/Apr. 6-9/45

Mechanical Service Contractors of America *(1971)*
1385 Piccard Dr.
Rockville, MD 20850
Tel: (301)869-5800 *Fax:* (301)990-9690
Toll Free: (800)556 - 3653
Web Site: www.mcaa.org/msca
Members: 750 companies
Staff: 2
Annual Budget: $500-1,000,000
Executive Director: Barbara A. Dolim
Associate Director: Sobeida Orantes

Historical Note
Formerly (1990) National Mechanical Equipment Services and Maintenance Burecau (SMB). A department of the Mechanical Contractors Association of America, MSCA members are employers of United Association of Journeymen and Apprentices of the Plumbing and Pipe Fitting Industry of the United States and Canada labor who are involved in service and maintenance work in the heating, ventilating, air conditioning and process piping industries. MSCA promotes the interests of service contractors by acting as a clearinghouse for information and by providing liaison between the contractor and the UA.

Publications:
Dateline MSCA. m.
MCAA Reporter. m.

Media Communications Association International *(1968)*
2810 Crossroads Dr., Suite 3800
Madison, WI 53718
Tel: (608)443-2464 *Fax:* (608)443-2474
E-Mail: info@mca-i.org
Web Site: www.mca-i.org
Members: 3000 individuals
Staff: 2
Annual Budget: $1-2,000,000
Executive Director: Susan Rees
Manager, Membership: Amy Bayer

Historical Note
Founded in 1968 as the National Industrial Television Association. Merged in 1973 with the Industrial Television Society to become the International Industrial Television Association. Became International Television Association in 1978 and assumed its current name in 2000. National organization of professional video communicators: individuals in non-broadcast video who use videotape and equipment in organizational settings producing, writing and editing video programs. Membership: $150/year (individual), $425/year (organization).

Publications:
MCA-I News. bi-m. adv.
Membership Directory. a.

Media Credit Association *(1903)*
919 Third Ave., 22nd Floor
New York, NY 10022
Tel: (212)872-3700 *Fax:* (212)888-4623
Web Site: www.magazine.org/mca
Members: 850 magazines
Staff: 3
Annual Budget: $100-250,000
Coordinator, Records: Janice Mitchell
E-Mail: jmitchell@magazine.org

Historical Note
Since 1903 the MCA has been the primary source of credit information to the magazine industry. The MCA provides a Credit Guideline Service to all members of the Magazine Publishers of America (MPA).

Meetings/Conferences:
Annual Meetings:

Publications:
Handbook of Media Credit Executives. a.

Media Human Resources Association *(1949)*

Historical Note
Organization defunct in 2006.

Media Rating Council *(1964)*
370 Lexington Ave., Room 902
New York, NY 10017-6588
Tel: (212)972-0300 *Fax:* (212)972-2786
E-Mail: abruncaj@mindspring.com
Web Site: www.mrc.htsp.com
Members: 80 companies
Staff: 2
Annual Budget: $250-500,000
Executive Director: George Ivie

Historical Note
Formerly (1983) Broadcast Rating Council and (1997) Electronic Media Rating Council. MRC was established by broadcast industry, trade groups and major networks to maintain industry confidence in the integrity of broadcast rating services. Conducts an accreditation system involving regular audits by professional CPA firms of all aspects of the operation

of the independent companies which produce radio, TV, cable and print ratings.

Meetings/Conferences:
Annual Meetings: usually New York, NY/Summer and Fall

Media Research Directors Association *(1947)*
c/o Brody & Associates
900 Palisade Avenue, Suite 20C
Ft. Lee, NJ 07024
Tel: (646)654-5909 *Fax:* (646)654-5901
Web Site: www.mrda.org
Members: 80 individuals
Annual Budget: $25-50,000

Historical Note
The MRDA is organized to build awareness, advance standards, promote new technology, and educate media and marketing professionals in all areas of media research. Has no paid officers or full-time staff.

Publications:
MRDA News & Views Newsletter. bi-m.
MRDA Membership Directory. a.

Medical Device Manufacturers Association *(1992)*
1919 Pennsylvania Ave. NW, Suite 660
Washington, DC 20006
Tel: (202)349-7171 *Fax:* (202)349-7176
E-Mail: mdmainfo@medicaldevices.org
Web Site: www.medicaldevices.org/public/
Annual Budget: $250-500,000
Executive Director: Mark B. Leahy

Historical Note
Supersedes Smaller Manufacturers Medical Device Association. MDMA represents manufacturers of medical devices, diagnostic products, and health care information systems. Membership fee varies, based on revenues.

Meetings/Conferences:
Annual Meetings: May

Publications:
MDMA. bi-weekly. adv.

Medical Group Management Association *(1926)*
104 Inverness Terrace East
Englewood, CO 80112-5306
Tel: (303)799-1111 *Fax:* (303)643-4439
Toll Free: (877)275 - 6462
E-Mail: marketing@mgma.com
Web Site: www.mgma.com
Members: 19000 individuals
Staff: 150
Annual Budget: $10-25,000,000
President and Chief Executive Officer: William F. Jessee, M.D., FACMPE
Vice President and Chief Financial Officer: Eric Cauble, CPA
Vice President and Chief Information Officer: Gary C. Fox
E-Mail: marketing@mgma.com

Historical Note
MGMA is a leading national voice for medical group practice. MGMA members represent over 200,000 practicing physicians. Leads the profession and assists members through information, education, networking and advocacy.

Meetings/Conferences:
Annual Meetings: Fall
2007 – Philadelphia, PA/Oct. 7-10
2008 – San Diego, CA/Oct. 19-22
2009 – Denver, CO/Oct. 11-14

Publications:
MGMA APA Matrix. 9/year.
MGMA e-Connexion. bi-w.
MGMA Connexion. 10/year. adv.

Medical Library Association *(1898)*
65 E. Wacker Place, Suite 1900
Chicago, IL 60601-7298
Tel: (312)419-9094 *Fax:* (312)419-8950
E-Mail: info@mlahq.org
Web Site: www.mlanet.org
Members: 4700 individuals and institutions
Staff: 19
Annual Budget: $1-2,000,000
Executive Director: Carla J. Funk
E-Mail: funk@mlahq.org
Director, Membership Services: Beverly Bradley
Director, Research and Information Systems: Kate E. Corcoran
Government Relations: Mary Langman
Director, Financial and Administrative Services: Ray Naegele
E-Mail: naegele@mlahq.org
Public Relations: Evelyn Shaevel
E-Mail: mlaedo1@mlahq.org

Historical Note
Founded as the Association of Medical Librarians; assumed its current name in 1907 and incorporated in Maryland in 1934. Membership: $150/year (individual); $235-545/year (institution).

Meetings/Conferences:
2007 – Philadelphia, PA/May 18-23
2008 – Chicago, IL/May 16-21

Publications:
Journal of the MLA. q. adv.
MLA News. 10/year. adv.

Medical Marketing Association *(1965)*
575 Market St., Suite 2125
San Francisco, CA 94105
Tel: (415)927-5732 *Fax:* (415)927-5734
Toll Free: (800)551 - 2173
E-Mail: mma@mmanet.org
Web Site: www.mmanet.org
Members: 1100 individuals
Annual Budget: $250-500,000
Executive Director: Sheri Thomas

Historical Note
MMA is a professional association comprised of over 1,000 medical marketers from the pharmaceutical, device, diagnostic, and marketing/advertising industries. Membership: $199/year (individual).

Meetings/Conferences:
Annual Meetings: Summer
2007 – San Francisco, CA/300

Publications:
Roadmap. a. adv.
MMA Directory. a. adv.
e-news (online). m. adv.

Medical Mycological Society of the Americas *(1966)*
c/o Annette Fothergill
430 CR 2720
Mico, TX 78056
Tel: (210)567-6074
E-Mail: fothergill@uthscsa.edu
Members: 350 individuals
Secretary-Treasurer: Annette Fothergill
E-Mail: fothergill@uthscsa.edu

Historical Note
Membership: $20/year.

Meetings/Conferences:
Annual Meetings: May, in conjunction with the American Soc. for Microbiology.

Publications:
Newsletter. 2/year.

Medical Records Institute *(1979)*
425 Boylston St., Fourth Floor
Boston, MA 02116
Tel: (617)964-3923 *Fax:* (617)964-3926
E-Mail: info@medrecinst.com
Web Site: www.medrecinst.com
Members: 4000 affiliates
Staff: 7
Annual Budget: $1-2,000,000
Executive Director: C. Peter Waegemann
Director, Educational Programming: Linda McLaughlin

Historical Note
Formerly (1988) the Institute for Medical Record Economics. Members are medical record, computer professionals and others concerned with research and education in medical documentation.

Meetings/Conferences:
Annual Meetings: Spring

Publications:
Toward an Electronic Patient Record. 10/year.

Medical-Dental-Hospital Business Associates *(1939)*
8201 Greensboro Dr., Third Floor
McLean, VA 22102
Tel: (703)610-9016 *Fax:* (703)610-9005
Web Site: www.mdhba.org
Members: 60 companies
Staff: 2
Annual Budget: $50-100,000
Executive Director: Jennifer English Lynch
E-Mail: jlynch@mdhba.org

Historical Note
Founded as Medical-Dental-Hospital Bureaus of America; assumed its current name in 1996. MDHBA members are owners/general managers of collection bureaus, credit bureaus and accounts receivable management agencies. Membership: varies by company size.

Meetings/Conferences:
Annual Meetings: Fall

Publications:
Newscope. m.

Medieval Academy of America *(1925)*
104 Mt. Auburn St., Fifth Floor
Cambridge, MA 02138
Tel: (617)491-1622 *Fax:* (617)492-3303
E-Mail: speculum@medievalacademy.org
Web Site: www.medievalacademy.org
Members: 3900 individuals
Staff: 5
Annual Budget: $500-1,000,000
Executive Director: Richard K. Emmerson
E-Mail: speculum@medievalacademy.org

Historical Note
Member American Council of Learned Societies. Members are scholars with an interest in the period 500-1500 AD. Membership: $55-70/year (individual); $25/year (sudent/retired); $70-80/year (organization).

Meetings/Conferences:
Annual Meetings: Spring

Publications:
Medieval Academy News. 3/year.
Speculum: A Journal of Medieval Studies. q. adv.

Meeting Professionals International *(1972)*
3030 LBJ Fwy., Suite 1700
Dallas, TX 75234
Tel: (972)702-3000 *Fax:* (972)702-3070
E-Mail: feedback@mpiweb.org
Web Site: www.mpiweb.org
Members: 19000 individuals
Staff: 72
Annual Budget: $10-25,000,000
Chief Executive Officer: Bruce MacMillan
Vice President, Marketing and Brand Management: Edjuan Bailey
Vice President, Membership and Chapter Relations: Elaine Jaspram
Chief Financial Officer: Greg Lohrentz

Historical Note
Formerly (1994) Meeting Planners International. MPI members manage meetings and related activities for associations, corporations, and educational institutions, or provide goods and services to the meetings industry. Membership: $325/year.

Meetings/Conferences:
Semi-Annual Meetings: Summer and Winter

Publications:
Newsbytes. w. adv.
Membership Directory. a. adv.
The Meeting Professional. m. adv.

MEMA Information Services Council *(1972)*
P.O. Box 13966
Research Triangle Park, NC 27709-3966
Tel: (919)406-8830 *Fax:* (919)549-8733
E-Mail: info@miscouncil.org
Web Site: www.miscouncil.org
Members: 50 companies
Staff: 3
Annual Budget: $10-25,000
Council Director: Chris Gardner

Historical Note
A peer group within the Motor and Equipment Manufacturers Association, the MISC serves as a forum for industry interaction, education and idea exchange regarding matters of common interest to

data processing managers and related executives in automotive manufacturing companies. Membership: $600/year (company), which includes the conference fee for the annual fall conference for one member.

Meetings/Conferences:
Semi-annual Meetings: Spring and Fall

Publications:
MISC E-news. m.
Member Company Profiles. a.
Membership Roster. a.

MENC: The National Association for Music Education *(1907)*
1806 Robert Fulton Dr.
Reston, VA 20191
Tel: (703)860-4000 *Fax:* (703)860-1531
Toll Free: (800)336 - 3768
Web Site: www.menc.org
Members: 80000 individuals
Staff: 68
Annual Budget: $2-5,000,000
Executive Director: John J. Mahlmann
Dep. Executive Director: Michael Blakeslee

Historical Note
Established as the Music Supervisors National Conference, it assumed its present name in 1934. A professional organization of music teachers, administrators and students. The Society for Research in Music Education, the Society for Music Teacher Education and the Society for General Music are councils of MENC. Affiliated with numerous other musical organizations.

Meetings/Conferences:
Biennial Meetings: Even years/6-8,000

Publications:
Teaching Music Magazine. 5/year. adv.
Music Educators Journal. 5/year. adv.
Journal of Research in Music Education. q.

Messenger Courier Association of the Americas *(1987)*
1156 15th St. NW, Suite 900
Washington, DC 20005
Tel: (202)785-3298 *Fax:* (202)223-9741
Web Site: www.mcaa.com
Members: 400 companies
Staff: 3
Annual Budget: $250-500,000
Executive Director: Robert L. DeCaprio
E-Mail: bdecaprio@kellencompany.com

Historical Note
The MCAA was formed in 1987 to promote, encourage, broaden and advance the interests of those engaged in the messenger courier industry and its related services. Membership: more than $475/year (organization).

Meetings/Conferences:
Annual Meetings: Spring
2007 – Orlando, FL(Portofino Bay)/May 14-20

Publications:
On Time Newsletter. m. adv.
Messenger Courier Magazine. q. adv.
MCAA Membership Directory and Network Guide. semi-a. adv.

Metal Building Contractors and Erectors Association *(1968)*
P.O. Box 499
Shawnee Mission, KS 66201
Tel: (913)432-3800 *Fax:* (913)432-3803
Toll Free: (800)866 - 6722
E-Mail: mbcea@kc.rr.com
Web Site: www.mbcea.org
Members: 325 companies
Staff: 12
Annual Budget: $250-500,000
Executive Director: Angela M. Cruse

Historical Note
Founded as Metal Building Dealers; became Systems Builders Association in 1984, and assumed its current name in 2002. Membership: $500/year (contractor); $750/year (industry); $500/year (chapter).

Meetings/Conferences:
Annual Meetings: Winter

Publications:
MBCEA Network Newsletter. q.

Metal Building Manufacturers Association *(1956)*
1300 Sumner Ave.
Cleveland, OH 44115-2851
Tel: (216)241-7333 *Fax:* (216)241-0105
E-Mail: mbma@mbma.com
Web Site: www.mbma.com
Members: 68 companies
Staff: 6
General Manager: Charles M. Stockinger

Historical Note
A trade association representing building systems manufacturers, roofing systems manufacturers and suppliers to the industry. Merged with Metal Roofing Systems Association in 1998.

Metal Construction Association *(1983)*
4700 W. Lake St.
Glenview, IL 60025
Tel: (847)347-4718 *Fax:* (877)665-2234
E-Mail: mca@metalconstruction.org
Web Site: www.metalconstruction.org
Members: 100 companies
Staff: 8
Annual Budget: $500-1,000,000
Executive Vice President: Mark Engle
Senior Manager: Julie Weldon

Historical Note
The MCA is dedicated to promoting the use of metal in construction. Initiatives include market development, educational programs, issue and product awareness campaigns, and publication of technical guidelines and specifications manuals. The Metal Construction Association also monitors and confronts challenges affecting the industry, such as code restrictions, fire testing, and wind load regulations.

Meetings/Conferences:
2007 – Scottsdale, AZ(Marriott)/Jan. 12-15

Publications:
Membership Directory. a.
MCA News. q.

Metal Findings Manufacturers Association *(1930)*
30-R Houghton St.
Providence, RI 02904
Tel: (401)861-4667 *Fax:* (401)861-0429
E-Mail: info@mfma.net
Web Site: www.mfma.net
Members: 60 companies
Annual Budget: under $10,000
Executive Officer: John Augustyn
E-Mail: info@mfma.net

Historical Note
Makers of metal parts and fittings used in the assembly of jewelry. Has no paid staff or permanent address. Officers change every two years. Membership: $200/year (organization/company).

Meetings/Conferences:
Annual Meetings: May in the Providence region.

Metal Finishing Suppliers Association *(1925)*
1155 15th St. NW, Suite 500
Washington, DC 20005
Tel: (202)457-8402 *Fax:* (202)530-0659
Web Site: www.mfsa.org
Members: 165 companies
Staff: 1
Annual Budget: $250-500,000

Historical Note
Membership: $1,100-10,100/year (corporate).

Meetings/Conferences:
Semi-Annual Meetings: Spring and Fall

Publications:
Newsletter. 2/yr.

Metal Framing Manufacturers Association *(1981)*
401 N. Michigan Ave.
Chicago, IL 60611
Tel: (312)644-6610 Ext: 6806 *Fax:* (312)321-4098
E-Mail: mfma@smithbucklin.com
Web Site: www.metalframingmfg.org
Members: 7 companies
Staff: 2
Annual Budget: $10-25,000
Executive Director: Jack M. Springer

Historical Note
Membership: $1,600/year.

Meetings/Conferences:
Annual Meetings: None held

Publications:
MFMA Standards Publication 2004. a.
Guidelines for the Use of Metal Framing. a.

Metal Injection Molding Association

Historical Note
A constituent association of the Metal Powder Industries Federation.

Metal Powder Industries Federation *(1944)*
105 College Rd., East
Princeton, NJ 08540-6692
Tel: (609)452-7700 *Fax:* (609)987-8523
E-Mail: info@mpif.org
Web Site: www.mpif.org
Members: 275 companies
Staff: 15
Annual Budget: $2-5,000,000
Executive Director and Chief Executive Officer: C. James Trombino, CAE
E-Mail: jtrombino@mpif.org
Vice President, Membership and Industry Relations: James R. Dale
Director, Communications: Donni Magid
E-Mail: dmagid@mpif.org

Historical Note
Represents the international trade, commercial and technological interests of the metal powder producing and consuming industries. The Federation consists of the following constituent associations: the Powder Metallurgy Parts Association, Metal Powder Producers Association, Powder Metallurgy Equipment Association, Refractory Metals Association, Advanced Particulate Materials Association and Metal Injection Molding Association.

Meetings/Conferences:
2007 – Denver, CO(Denver Covention Center)/May 13-16/1500

Publications:
Advances in P/M and Particulate Materials. a.

Metal Powder Producers Association

Historical Note
A constituent member of the Metal Powder Industries Federation.

Metal Powder Technology Association *(1985)*

Historical Note
A constituent unit of the Metal Powder Industries Federation.

Metal Service Center Institute *(1907)*
4201 Euclid
Rolling Meadows, IL 60008
Tel: (847)485-3000 *Fax:* (847)485-3001
E-Mail: info@msci.org
Web Site: www.msci.org
Members: 400 companies
Staff: 12
Annual Budget: $5-10,000,000
President: M. Robert Weidner, III
Vice President, Finance and Administration: Jonathan Kalkwarf

Historical Note
Formerly (1907) American Iron and Steel and Heavy Hardware Association; (1932) American Steel and Heavy Hardware Association; (1959) American Steel Warehouse Association, Inc. and then Steel Service Center Institute; assumed its current name in 2002. Annual Budget: $6.2 million.

Meetings/Conferences:
Annual Meetings: May/1,000

Publications:
Forward Magazine. bi-m. adv.
Metals Activity Report. m.

Metal Treating Institute *(1933)*
1550 Roberts Dr.
Jacksonville Beach, FL 32250-3222
Tel: (904)249-0448 *Fax:* (904)249-0459
Web Site: heattreatonline.com
Members: 310 companies
Staff: 3

Annual Budget: $500-1,000,000
Chief Executive Officer: M. Lance Miller, JD, CAE
Executive Vice President: Tom Morrison

Historical Note
Membership fee varies; approximately $1,000-$3,000/year (company).

Meetings/Conferences:
Semi-Annual Meetings: Spring and Fall
2007 – Keystone, CO(Keystone Resort)/July 10-15/150
2007 – Bahamas, Bahamas(The Atlantis)/Aug. 24-29/150

Publications:
MTInsight. m.

Metaphysical Society of America *(1950)*
University of Alabama, Dept. of Philosophy
Huntsville, AL 35899
Tel: (205)895-6555 *Fax:* (205)895-6949
Web Site: www.acls.org/metaphys.htm
*Members:*600 individuals
Staff: 1
Annual Budget: under $10,000
President: Lenn Goodman
Secretary-Treasurer: Brian Martine

Historical Note
Promotes the consideration of fundamental philosophical issues from a wide range of historical and contemporary perspectives. A member of the American Council of Learned Societies. Membership: $15/year.

Meetings/Conferences:
Annual Meetings: March
2007 – Nashville, TN(Vanderbilt University)/March 11-12

Methacrylate Producers Association *(1988)*
17260 Vannes Ct.
Hamilton, VA 20158-3163
Tel: (540)751-2093 *Fax:* (540)751-2094
Web Site: www.mpausa.org
*Members:*4 manufacturers
Staff: 2
Annual Budget: $250-500,000
Executive Director: Elizabeth K. Hunt

Historical Note
Members are manufacturers of basic methacrylate monomers. MPA serves to pool health, safety and environmental information; to sponsor testing when appropriate; and to communicate the industry's views on regulatory matters.

Methanol Institute *(1989)*
4100 N. Fairfax Dr., Suite 740
Arlington, VA 22203
Tel: (703)248-3636 *Fax:* (703)248-3997
Toll Free: (888)275 - 0768
E-Mail: mi@methanol.org
Web Site: www.methanol.org
*Members:*15 corporations
Staff: 3
Annual Budget: $1-2,000,000
President and Chief Executive Officer: John E. Lynn
Vice President, Communications and Policy: Gregory A. Dolan

Historical Note
Works to support the use of clean reformulated and oxygenated gasoline, and to encourage the development of emerging methanol-powered fuel cells. Membership: $75,000/year (company).

Publications:
Insider Report. w.

Methods Time Measurement Association for Standards and Research *(1951)*

Historical Note
See MTM Association for Standards and Research.

Metropolitan Symphony Managers Association

Historical Note
A sub-group of the American Symphony Orchestra League without dues structure or separate headquarters.

Mexican Restaurant and Cantina Association *(2002)*
908 Eighth St., Suite 200
Louisville, KY 40203
Tel: (502)736-9530 *Fax:* (502)736-9531
Toll Free: (800)489 - 8324
E-Mail: jstraughan@mexrca.com
Web Site: www.mexrca.com
*Members:*500 companies
Staff: 3
Executive Director: Joe Straughan

Historical Note
MR&CA members are kitchen equipment manufacturers, industry suppliers, independent and franchised operators of Mexican-themed restaurants, and producers of frozen Mexican entrees. Provides liaison between Mexican foodservice and government agencies. Researches industry data and statistics. Membership: $99/year.

Meetings/Conferences:
Annual Meetings: usually San Antonio, TX/May and Chicago, IL/July

Publications:
MR&CA News. q. adv.
La Cocina Mexicana. bi-m. adv.

Mexican-American Grocers Association *(1977)*
405 N. San Fernando Rd.
Los Angeles, CA 90031
Tel: (323)227-1565 *Fax:* (323)227-6935
*Members:*14000 individuals
Staff: 10
Annual Budget: $1-2,000,000
President and Chief Executive Officer: Steven A. Soto

Historical Note
MAGA members are food store owners, manufacturers, processors, brokers, distributors, and service providers who cater to the Hispanic market in the United States. Membership: varies according to membership classification.

Meetings/Conferences:
Annual Meetings: Winter

Publications:
MAGAzine. 8/year. adv.

Microbeam Analysis Society *(1968)*
307 East Ash
P.O. Box 30
Columbia, MO 65201
Toll Free: (800)462 - 7636
E-Mail: RossLM@missouri.edu
Web Site: www.microbeamanalysis.org
*Members:*1600 individuals
Staff: 2
Annual Budget: $10-25,000
Membership Services Chair: Lou Ross

Historical Note
Formerly (1973) Electron Probe Analysis Society of America. Society's purpose is to advance and diffuse knowledge concerning the principles and applications of microbeam instruments or related instrumentation, and to provide continuity, advanced planning, and a financing mechanism for annual meetings.

Meetings/Conferences:
Annual Meetings: Summer

Publications:
Microscopy Microanalysis Journal. bi-m. adv.
MicroNews. 3/year.

Microscopy Society of America *(1942)*
230 E. Ohio St., Suite 400
Chicago, IL 60611-3265
Tel: (312)644-1527 *Fax:* (312)644-8557
Toll Free: (800)538 - 3672
E-Mail: businessoffice@microscopy.org
Web Site: www.microscopy.org
*Members:*4000 individuals
Staff: 2
Annual Budget: $500-1,000,000
Deputy Director: Cynthia L. Keillor

Historical Note
Formerly (1992) the Electron Microscopy Society of America. Established November 27, 1942 as the Electron Microscope Society of America at the Second National Chemical Exposition in Chicago and incorporated in Delaware. An affiliate of the American Institute of Physics and the American Association for the Advancement of Science. Membership: $45/year (individual); $15/year (student), $375/year (organization).

Meetings/Conferences:
Annual Meetings: August/2,000-2,500

Publications:
Journal. bi-m. adv.
Proceedings. a.
Directory. bi-a.

Microwave Theory and Techniques Society

Historical Note
See IEEE Microwave Theory and Techniques Society.

Middle East Librarians' Association *(1972)*
University of Pennsylvania Libraries
3420 Walnut St.
Philadelphia, PA 19104-6206
Tel: (215)898-2196 *Fax:* (215)898-0559
*Members:*200 individuals
Annual Budget: under $10,000
Secretary-Treasurer: William J. Kopycki

Historical Note
Members are librarians and others who support the study or dissemination of information about the Middle East. Has no paid officers or full-time staff. Membership: $30/year.

Meetings/Conferences:
Annual Meetings: November, with the Middle East Studies Ass'n

Publications:
MELA Notes: Journal of Middle East Librarianship. bi-a. adv.

Middle East Studies Association of North America *(1966)*
University of Arizona
1219 N. Santa Rita Ave.
Tucson, AZ 85721
Tel: (520)621-5850 *Fax:* (520)626-9095
E-Mail: mesana@u.arizona.edu
Web Site: www.mesa.arizona.edu
*Members:*2700 individuals
Staff: 5
Annual Budget: $250-500,000
Executive Director: Amy W. Newhall
Editor, Newsletter: Nadia Hlibka
Assistant Director and Meeting Planner: Mark J. Lowder
Executive Assistant and Exhibit Coordinator: Shirley Nelson
Manager, Membership: Sara Palmer

Historical Note
Organized by a group of U.S. and Canadian scholars concerned with the study of the Middle East, from Morocco to Pakistan, Turkey to the Sudan. Membership: $90/year (regular), $40/year (student), $500/year (organization).

Meetings/Conferences:
Annual Meetings: late October-December

Publications:
Newsletter. q. adv.
International Journal of Middle East Studies. q. adv.
MESA Bulletin. semi-a. adv.

MIDI Manufacturers Association *(1984)*
P.O. Box 3173
La Habra, CA 90632-3173
Tel: (714)736-9774 *Fax:* (714)736-9775
E-Mail: info@midi.org
Web Site: www.midi.org
*Members:*80 companies
President: Tom White

Historical Note
MMA members are companies involved in the design and manufacture of MIDI (Musical Instrument Digital Interface) hardware or software and the application of audio technology to a wide variety of fields including stage and theater, performance, recording, multimedia computing, film and broadcast. Establishes MIDI specifications as an open standard. Sponsors the Interactive Audio Special Interest Group, an autonomous group for developers of PC and set top games and other multimedia applications. Membership: $400-$1,600/year, based on sales (company).

Meetings/Conferences:
Annual Meetings: January

Publications:
Complete MIDI 1. 0 Specifications.

Midwives Alliance of North America *(1982)*
375 Rockbridge Rd.
Suite 172-313
Lilburn, GA 30047
Toll Free: (888)923 - 6262
E-Mail: info@mana.org
Web Site: www.mana.org
Members: 1200 individuals
Annual Budget: $10-25,000
Secretary: Trinlie Wood
E-Mail: secretary@mana.org

Historical Note
Founded to build cooperation among midwives and to promote midwifery as a standard of health care for women and childbirth. A member of the International Confederation of Midwives, MANA participates in the North American Registry of Midwives. Absorbed the National Midwives Association in 1985. Membership: $25/year (associate); $50-75/year (voting); $50/year (supporting groups).

Meetings/Conferences:
Annual Meetings: November

Publications:
MANA News. q. adv.

Military Chaplains Association of the U.S. *(1925)*
P.O. Box 7056
Arlington, VA 22207
Tel: (703)533-5890
E-Mail: chaplains@mca-usa.org
Web Site: www.mca-usa.org
Members: 1875 individuals
Staff: 1
Annual Budget: $50-100,000
Executive Director: Gary R. Pollitt
E-Mail: chaplains@mca-usa.org

Historical Note
A professional association of military chaplains, including active, reserve, former and retired chaplains of all religious faiths. Members include chaplains of the Veterans Administration and Civil Air Patrol as well as the Armed Forces. Membership: $35/year.

Meetings/Conferences:
Annual Meetings: Spring

Publications:
Military Chaplain. bi-m. adv.

Military Impacted Schools Association *(1986)*
1600 Hwy. 370
Bellevue, NE 68005
Tel: (402)293-4005 *Fax:* (402)291-7982
Toll Free: (800)291 - 6472
E-Mail: carolmisa@aol.com
Web Site: www.militaryimpactedschoolsassociation.org
Members: 55 school districts
Annual Budget: $100-250,000
Chief Executive Officer: John Deegan

Historical Note
MISA is composed of school districts that serve children from military installations. Members are school districts with military personnel.

Meetings/Conferences:
Semi-annual Meetings:

Publications:
Military Impacted Schools Legislative Newsletter. m.

Military Officers Association of America *(1929)*
201 N. Washington St.
Alexandria, VA 22314-2539
Tel: (703)549-2311 *Fax:* (703)838-8173
Toll Free: (800)234 - 6622
E-Mail: msc@moaa.org
Web Site: www.moaa.org
Members: 370000 individuals
Staff: 95
Annual Budget: $10-25,000,000
President: VADM Norbert R. Ryan, USN(Ret.)
Director, Public Relations: Col. Marvin J. Harris, USAF(Ret.)
Director, Contract Services and Marketing: Col. Michael Jordan, USAF(Ret.)
Director, Print and Electronic Publications: Col. Warren Lacy, USA(Ret.)
Director, Government Relations: Col. Steven P. Stobridge, USAF (Ret.)
Secretary and General Counsel: Capt. Peter C. Wylie, USN(Ret.)
Chief Financial Officer: Col. Glenn R. Zauber, USAF(Ret.)

Historical Note
Formerly (2003) Retired Officers Association. Composed of retired and active members of the Army, Navy, Air Force, Marine Corps, Coast Guard, National Oceanic and Atmospheric Administration, and the U.S. Public Health Service, and widow(er)s of the above as auxiliary members. Represents about two-thirds of the total retired officer community. Established in Los Angeles February 23, 1929 with 63 members to counsel and render assistance to its members in connection with their retired status. Moved to Washington in 1944 and expanded its purpose to include representing its members' rights and interests when service matters are considered by the federal government. Now takes positions on a variety of personnel and healthcare issues. Has an annual budget of approximately $12 million. Membership: $22/year.

Meetings/Conferences:
Annual Meetings: Fall

Publications:
Military Officer. m. adv.
Today's Officer Online. q. adv.

Military Operations Research Society *(1966)*
1703 N. Beauregard St., Suite 450
Alexandria, VA 22311
Tel: (703)933-9070 *Fax:* (703)933-9066
E-Mail: morsoffice@mors.org
Web Site: www.mors.org
Members: 3000 individuals
Staff: 5
Annual Budget: $500-1,000,000
Executive Vice President: Brian Engler
Vice President, Administration: Natalie Strawn Kelly
Manager, Communications: Corrina Ross Witkowski

Historical Note
A professional society incorporated in the Commonwealth of Virginia for the purpose of enhancing the quality and effectiveness of military operations research. Conducts a classified symposium annually and workshops as needed.

Publications:
Phalanx. q.
Military Operations Research. q.

Milk Industry Foundation *(1908)*
1250 H St. NW, Suite 900
Washington, DC 20005-3952
Tel: (202)737-4332 *Fax:* (202)331-7820
E-Mail: membership@idfa.org
Web Site: www.idfa.org
Members: 110 companies
Staff: 55
Annual Budget: $1-2,000,000
President and Chief Executive Officer: Constance E. Tipton

Historical Note
MIF represents processors, manufacturers, distributors and marketers of fluid milk, cultured products, cream products, and other dairy products. MIF's activities range from legislative and regulatory advocacy to market research, industry training and education. Administrative support provided by International Dairy Foods Association. Membership fee based on volume.

Meetings/Conferences:
Three Meetings Annually: in conjunction with the International Dairy Foods Association

Publications:
Milk Labeling Manual. irreg.
Dairy Plant Manuals Library. irreg.
Dairy Facts. a.

Milking Machine Manufacturers Council

Historical Note
A council of the Equipment Manufacturers Institute.

Million Dollar Round Table *(1927)*
325 W. Touhy Ave.
Park Ridge, IL 60068-4265
Tel: (847)993-4925 *Fax:* (847)518-8921
E-Mail: jbutera@mdrt.org
Web Site: www.mdrt.org
Members: 35000 individuals
Staff: 83
Executive Vice President: John J. Prast, CAE, LLIF
E-Mail: prast@mdrt.org
Public Relations Coordinator: Jessica Butera
Director, Membership Services: Thomas Ensign
Director, Information Services: William Jesse
E-Mail: jesse@mdrt.org
Director, Meetings and Services: Ray Kopcinski
E-Mail: rayk@mdrt.org
Director, Finance and Administration: Patrick Koziol
E-Mail: pkoziol@mdrt.org

Historical Note
Members are life insurance financial service advisors who rank in the top 1% in the world. Members must qualify annually. Membership: $450/year (individual).

Meetings/Conferences:
Annual Meetings: June-7,000
2007 - Denver, CO/June 10-13
2008 - Toronto, ON, Canada/June 22-25/7000

Publications:
MDRT Minute. m.
Proceedings. a.
Round The Table. bi-m.

Mine Safety Institute of America *(1912)*
319 Paintersville Rd.
Hunker, PA 15139
Tel: (724)925-5150 Ext: 146
E-Mail: sikora.lisa@dol.gov
Web Site: www.miningorganizations.org/msia.htm
Members: 400 individuals
Annual Budget: under $10,000
Assistant Secretary-Treasurer: Lisa Sikora
E-Mail: sikora.lisa@dol.gov

Historical Note
Founded as Mine Inspectors' Institute of America; assumed its current name in 1998. Members are state, provincial and federal mine inspectors in the United States and Canada. Has no paid officers or full-time staff.

Meetings/Conferences:
Annual Meetings: Summer

Mineral Economics and Management Society *(1990)*
P.O. Box 1248
Kennett Square, PA 19348
Tel: (610)925-1860 *Fax:* (610)925-1861
Web Site: www.minecon.com/index.html
Members: 200 individuals
Annual Budget: $10-25,000
Treasurer: Mark C. Roberts

Historical Note
MEMS is a professional society for mineral, energy and natural resource economists, managers, consultants, financiers, policy analysts, geologists, engineers and others with an interest in the economics of the minerals, energy and materials industries. Membership: $45/year (individual); $20/year (student).

Meetings/Conferences:
Annual Meetings: Spring

Publications:
MEMS Newsletter. 3/year.
Resources Policy Journal.
MEMS Conference Proceedings. a.
Membership Directory. a.

Mineralogical Society of America *(1919)*
3635 Concorde Pkwy., Suite 500
Chantilly, VA 20151-1125
Tel: (703)652-9950 *Fax:* (703)652-9951
E-Mail: business@minsocam.org
Web Site: www.MINSOCAM.org
Members: 2200 individuals
Staff: 5
Annual Budget: $500-1,000,000
Executive Director: J. Alexander Speer, Ph.D.
E-Mail: j_a_speer@minsocam.org

Historical Note
Established at Harvard University on December 30, 1919; incorporated in the District of Columbia in 1937. A professional society of mineralogists, petrologists, geochemists, crystallographers and others interested in the study of minerals. A member society of the American Geological Institute. Membership: $55/year.

Meetings/Conferences:
Annual Meetings: Fall, with Geological Soc. of America
2007 – Denver, CO
2008 – Houston, TX

Publications:
American Mineralogist. 8/year.
Reviews in Mineralogy and Geochemistry. a.
Monographs and Textbooks. a.
Elements. 6/year. adv.

Minerals, Metals and Materials Society, The *(1871)*
184 Thorn Hill Rd.
Warrendale, PA 15086
Tel: (724)776-9000 *Fax:* (724)776-3770
E-Mail: TMSgeneral@tms.org
Web Site: www.tms.org
Members: 13000 individuals
Staff: 35
Annual Budget: $2-5,000,000
Executive Director: Alexander R. Scott
E-Mail: scott@tms.org
Manager, Finance and Administration: Peter DeLuca
Director, Communications: Robert Makowski
Director, Meeting, Marketing and Membership: Dan Steighner
E-Mail: steighner@tms.org

Historical Note
The Metals Branch of the American Institute of Mining, Metallurgical and Petroleum Engineers (AIME, founded in 1871) was established in 1947. From 1957-1988, it was known as The Metallurgical Society. The Society was separately incorporated in 1985. Membership: $80/year.

Meetings/Conferences:
Annual Meetings: Winter

Publications:
TMS Letters Online.
Journal of Electronic Materials. m.
JOM. m. adv.
Metallurgical and Materials Transactions A and B. m. adv.

Mini-Compact Excavators Manufacturers Council

Historical Note
A council of Equipment Manufacturers Institute.

Miniature Book Society *(1983)*
402 York Ave.
Delaware, OH 43015
Tel: (740)369-5517
E-Mail: kking@midohio.net
Web Site: www.mbs.org
Members: 320
Treasurer: Kathy King
E-Mail: kking@midohio.net

Historical Note
Members are artisans, publishers of miniature-format books, curators and collectors. Has no paid officers of full-time staff. Membership: $40/year (individual); $50/year (company).

Meetings/Conferences:
2007 – Seattle, WA/Oct. 12-15

Publications:
Membership Directory. a.
MBS Newsletter. q.

Miniature Cattle Breeds Registry

Historical Note
The registration arm of International Miniature Cattle Breeders Society

---

Mining and Metallurgical Society of America *(1908)*
476 Wilson Ave.
Novato, CA 94947-4236
Tel: (415)897-1380
E-Mail: info@mmsa.net
Web Site: www.mmsa.net
Members: 350 individuals
Staff: 1
Annual Budget: $25-50,000
Executive Director: Alan K. Burton

Historical Note
Members are individuals concerned with the conservation of the nation's mineral resources and the well-being of the mining and metallurgical industries. Membership: $100/year.

Meetings/Conferences:
Annual Meetings: In conjuction with the American Institute of Mining, Metallurgical and Petroleum Engineers

Publications:
MMSA News. q.

Missouri Fox Trotting Horse Breed Association *(1948)*
P.O. Box 1027
Ava, MO 65608
Tel: (417)683-2468 *Fax:* (417)683-6144
E-Mail: foxtrot@getgoin.net
Web Site: http://mfthba.com
Members: 8500 individuals
Staff: 6
Administrator: Donna Watson

Historical Note
Members are owners and breeders of Missouri Fox Trotting horses. Membership: $15/year.

Meetings/Conferences:
Annual Meetings: Fourth Saturday in October on show grounds in Ava, MO.

Publications:
MFTHBA Journal. m. adv.
Show & Celebration Book. a. adv.

Mobile Air Conditioning Society Worldwide *(1981)*
P.O. Box 88
Lansdale, PA 19446
Tel: (215)631-7020 *Fax:* (215)631-7017
E-Mail: info@macsw.org
Web Site: www.macsw.org
Members: 1600 companies
Staff: 10
Annual Budget: $1-2,000,000
President and Chief Operating Officer: Elvis L. Hoffpauir
E-Mail: elvis@macsw.org
Events Manager: Bob Hensel
Vice President, Sales and Marketing: Marion J. Posen
E-Mail: marion@macsw.org
Director, Operations: Maria Whitworth
E-Mail: maria@macsw.org

Historical Note
Provides technical training, information, and communications for professionals in the automotive aftermarket specializing in car air conditioning systems. Incorporated in the Commonwealth of Pennsylvania. Membership: $400/year (service/installation/distribution); $700/year (manufacturer/supplier); $200/year (service installer).

Meetings/Conferences:
Annual Meetings: Winter
2007 – Phoenix, AZ(Phoenix Hyatt)/Feb. 1-3/2500

Publications:
Action Magazine. bi-m.
MACS Service Reports. m.

Mobile Industrial Caterers' Association International *(1965)*
304 W. Liberty St., Suite 201
Louisville, KY 40202
Tel: (502)583-3783 *Fax:* (502)589-3602
Toll Free: (800)620 - 6422
Web Site: www.mobilecaterers.com
Members: 130 companies
Staff: 4
Annual Budget: $100-250,000
Executive Administrrator: Joe Broom
Director, Conferences: Nick Hall

Historical Note
Members are companies providing food service at job sites and similar remote locations.

Meetings/Conferences:
Semi-annual Meetings: Spring and Fall

Publications:
MICA Newsletter. m.
MICA Handbook and Roster. a.

Modern Greek Studies Association *(1968)*
Box 622
Kent, OH 44240
Tel: (330)672-0910 *Fax:* (330)672-4025
E-Mail: mgsa@kent.edu
Web Site: www.hnet.uci.edu/classics/mgsa/
Members: 400 individuals
Staff: 1
Annual Budget: $25-50,000
Executive Director: S. Victor Papacosma

Historical Note
MSGA defines its scope broadly to include not only post-Independence Greece but also the period of Ottoman rule and later Byzantine Empire, as well as those of early Byzantine, Hellenistic and classical times that have bearing on the modern period. Membership: $50/year; $25/year (student); $75/year (organization).

Meetings/Conferences:
Biennial Meetings: Fall

Publications:
MGSA Bulletin. semi-a. adv.
Journal of Modern Greek Studies. bi-a. adv.

Modern Language Association of America *(1883)*
26 Broadway
Third Floor
New York, NY 10004-1789
Tel: (646)576-5000 *Fax:* (646)458-0030
Web Site: www.mla.org
Members: 30000 individuals
Staff: 88
Annual Budget: $5-10,000,000
Executive Director: Rosemary G. Feal
Director, Convention Programs: Maribeth T. Kraus
E-Mail: mkraus@mla.org

Historical Note
Founded at Columbia University, December 27-28, 1883 and incorporated in 1900 to elevate the study and teaching of modern languages to the status then held by the classics; members are college-level teachers of modern languages. A member of the American Council of Learned Societies. Has an annual budget of approximately $8 million. Membership: $35/year (new member, first year); $25-$125/year (reinstating member, based on income); $20/year (student member, maximum of seven years).

Meetings/Conferences:
Annual Meetings: Always December 27-30

Publications:
MLA Newsletter. q.
Publications of the Modern Language Association (PMLA). bi-m. adv.
ADE Bulletin. 3/year.
ADFL Bulletin. 3/year.
MLA International Bibliography. a.

Modular Building Institute *(1983)*
413 Park St.
Charlottesville, VA 22902-4737
Tel: (434)296-3288 *Fax:* (434)296-3361
Toll Free: (888)811 - 3288
E-Mail: info@mbinet.org
Web Site: www.mbinet.org
Members: 210 individuals
Staff: 6
Annual Budget: $250-500,000
Executive Director: Tom Hardiman, CAE
E-Mail: info@mbinet.org

Historical Note
Formerly Mobile Modular Office Association, assumed its current name in 1993. Members are companies involved in the manufacturing and marketing of factory-built commercial structures. MBI promotes modular commercial construction as an alternative to conventional building. Membership: $250-$9,500/year (company).

Publications:
Commercial Modular Construction Magazine. q. adv.
MMI News For Members. q.

Industry Survey. a.

Modular Building Systems Council *(1942)*

Historical Note

A division of the Building Systems Councils of the National Association of Home Builders.

Mohair Council of America *(1966)*

P.O. Box 5337
San Angelo, TX 76902-5337
Tel: (325)655-3161 *Fax:* (325)655-4761
Toll Free: (800)583 - 3161
E-Mail: mohair@mohairusa.com
Web Site: www.mohairusa.com
Members: 10500 individuals
Staff: 3
Executive Director: Zane Willard
E-Mail: mohair@mohairusa.com

Historical Note

Members are Angora goat breeders. Street Address is: 233 W. Twohig, San Angelo, TX.

Meetings/Conferences:

Semi-annual meetings:

Molluscan Shellfish Institute *(1908)*

Historical Note

An affiliate of National Fisheries Institute, which provides administrative support.

Monorail Manufacturers Association *(1933)*

Historical Note

A section of Material Handling Industry of America, which provides administrative support.

Montadale Sheep Breeders Association *(1945)*

2514 Willow Rd. NE
Fargo, ND 58102
Tel: (701)297-9199
E-Mail: info@montadale.com
Web Site: www.montadale.com
Members: 300 individuals
Staff: 1
Annual Budget: under $10,000
Secretary-Treasurer: Mildred E. Moore
E-Mail: info@montadale.com

Historical Note

Members are breeders and fanciers of Montadale sheep. Membership: $20/year (senior member); $10/year (junior member).

Meetings/Conferences:

Semi-annual Meetings: June and November

Publications:

Montadale Mover Express. 3/year. adv.

Monument Builders of North America *(1906)*

401 N. Michigan Ave., Suite 2400
Chicago, IL 60611
Toll Free: (800)233 - 4472
E-Mail: info@monumentbuilders.org
Web Site: www.monumentbuilders.org
Members: 840 companies
Staff: 7
Annual Budget: $500-1,000,000
Executive Director: Ernest Stewart

Historical Note

Formed by a merger of the Monument Builders of America (formerly Memorial Craftsmen of America, founded in 1906) and the Canadian Granite and Marble Dealers. Members are manufacturers, retailers, wholesalers and suppliers of cemetery markers and monuments. Membership: $390/year (company).

Meetings/Conferences:

Annual Meetings: Winter
2007 – Cincinnati, OH(Hyatt)/Jan. 19-22

Publications:

MB News. m. adv.

Mortgage Bankers Association *(1914)*

1919 Pennsylvania Ave. NW
Washington, DC 20006-3438
Tel: (202)557-2700 *Fax:* (202)833-1305
E-Mail: info@mortgagebankers.org
Web Site: www.mortgagebankers.org
Members: 2900 institutions
Staff: 135
Annual Budget: $25-50,000,000
President and Chief Executive Officer: Jonathan L. Kempner
Senior Vice President, Commercial/Multifamily: Gail Davis Cardwell
Senior Vice President, Communications and Marketing: Cheryl Crispin
Senior Vice President, Research and Business Development/Chief Economist: Douglas G. Duncan, Ph.D.
Senior Vice President, Corporate Relations: Paul Green
Senior Vice President Multiple Family/Governance: Cheryl Patton Malloy
Senior Vice President, Government Affairs: Kurt P. Pfotenhauer
Vice President and General Counsel: Phyllis K. Slesinger
Senior Vice President, Operations: Jayne Somes-Schloesser

Historical Note

Formed to promote growth and excellence in the real estate finance industry. Encourages sound business practices that serve the needs of investors and borrowers. Informs members of changes in law, regulations, and pending legislation that affect the real estate and mortgage business. Members include mortgage companies, commercial banks, thrifts, life insurance companies, and other instituions. Supports the Mortgage Bankers Political Action Committee (MORPAC). Has an annual budget of approximately $30.7 million.

Meetings/Conferences:

Annual Meetings: October

Publications:

MBA NewsLink. adv.
MBA Commercial NewsLink. w. adv.
MBA Tech NewsLink. w. adv.
Mortgage Banking magazine. m. adv.
National Delinquency Survey. q.

Mortgage Insurance Companies of America *(1973)*

1425 K St. NW, Suite 210
Washington, DC 20005
Tel: (202)682-2683 *Fax:* (202)842-9252
Web Site: www.privatemi.com
Members: 6 companies
Staff: 6
Annual Budget: $10-25,000,000
Executive Vice President: Suzanne C. Hutchinson

Historical Note

MICA represents the private mortgage insurance industry.

Publications:

Private MI Perspective. q.
Fact Book & Membership Directory. a.

Motion Picture and Television Credit Association *(1956)*

4102 W. Magnolia Blvd., Suite A
Burbank, CA 91505-2747
Tel: (818)729-0220 *Fax:* (818)729-0225
Members: 75 companies
Staff: 3
Annual Budget: $50-100,000
President: Donna Cottone
Executive Director: Seta Kasperian
Administrator: Norma Myara
Administrator: Nanci Ann Tommone

Historical Note

Established as the Motion Picture and Television Credit Managers Association, it assumed its present name in 1966. Membership: $1,200/year (organization).

Meetings/Conferences:

Monthly Luncheon: (Beverly Garland Holiday Inn)/50

Publications:

Industry Credit Interchange.

Motion Picture Association *(1945)*

1600 I St. NW
Washington, DC 20006
Tel: (202)393-1966 *Fax:* (202)393-7674
E-Mail: duckworth@mpaa.org
Web Site: www.mpaa.org
Members: 7 companies
Annual Budget: $5-10,000,000
Chairman and Chief Executive Officer: Dan R. Glickman
Director, Internal and External Affairs: Tara Duckworth
Executive Vice President, Government Affairs: John Feehery

Historical Note

Fomerly (1994) American Motion Picture Export Company. A Webb-Pomerene Act association affiliated with the Motion Picture Association of America, MPA is dedicated to improving the freedom of movement of films and television in international distribution. MPA's national headquarters is in Encino, CA.

Motion Picture Association of America *(1922)*

1600 I St. NW
Washington, DC 20006
Tel: (202)293-1966 *Fax:* (202)296-7410
E-Mail: duckworth@mpaa.org
Web Site: www.mpaa.org
Members: 8 companies
Staff: 142
Annual Budget: $5-10,000,000
Chairman and Chief Executive Officer: Dan R. Glickman
Senior Vice President: Fritz E. Attaway
Director, Internal and External Affairs: Tara Duckworth
Vice President, Trade and Federal Affairs: Bonnie Richardson
Executive Vice President, Industry Affairs/Association Development: Vans Stevenson
Vice President, Educational Affairs: Richard Taylor

Historical Note

Formerly (1945) Motion Picture Producers and Distributors of America. Membership includes the principal producers and distributors of films in the United States. Affiliated with the Motion Picture Association, MPAA's headquarters is in Encino, CA.

Motor and Equipment Manufacturers Association *(1904)*

P.O. Box 13966
Research Triangle Park, NC 27709-3966
Tel: (919)549-4800 *Fax:* (919)549-4824
E-Mail: info@mema.org
Web Site: www.mema.org
Members: 700 companies
Staff: 70
Annual Budget: $10-25,000,000
President and Chief Executive Officer: Robert McKenna
Director, Communications: Margaret Beck
Vice President, Finance and Human Resources: Wendy Earp
Vice President, Automotive Aftermarket Suppliers Association: Chris Gardner

Historical Note

Serves manufacturers of automotive aftermarket and original equipment used on, in or for the servicing of cars, trucks and buses; conducts market research. MEMA's TRANSNET and ANSINET Divisions provide computerized electronic data interchange services. Divisionalized by product lines, market segments and executive peer groups. Also serves as an association management service for other associations in related fields. Maintains offices in Washington, DC, Japan, and Mexico City. Has an annual budget of approximately $14 million. Membership: $900-17,000/year, based on sales volume.

Publications:

Customer Credit & Sales Directory. 3/year.
Latin America Automotive Insight. m.
MEMA Newsletter. bi-m.
Focus Magazine. q. adv.
OE Suppliers Newsletter. bi-m.
Heavy Duty Newsletter. bi-m.
Japan Automotive Insight. m.
Market Analysis. bi-m.
International Buyers Guide. bien.
Market Research Studies. irreg.

Motorcycle Industry Council *(1914)*

Two Jenner St., Suite 150
Irvine, CA 92618-3806
Tel: (949)727-4211 *Fax:* (949)727-4217
Web Site: www.mic.org
Members: 310 manufacturers
Staff: 100
Annual Budget: $2-5,000,000
President: Tim Buche

Historical Note
Formerly (1970) Motorcycle, Scooter and Allied Trades Association. Represents motorcycle manufacturers and members of allied trades.
Meetings/Conferences:
Annual Meetings: *Established by Board of Directors annually during Feb.-April period.*
Publications:
Motorcycle Statistical Annual. a.

Motorcycle Safety Foundation *(1973)*
Two Jenner St., Suite 150
Irvine, CA 92618-3806
Tel: (949)727-3227 *Fax:* (949)727-4217
Web Site: www.msf-usa.org
Members: 10 companies
Staff: 18
Annual Budget: $5-10,000,000
President: Tim Buche
Historical Note
Founded by the five leading manufacturers and distributors of motorcycles for the purpose of public motorcycle safety education, licensing improvement, public information and research. Membership: dues based on marketshare.
Meetings/Conferences:
Annual Meetings: *March*
Publications:
Safe Cycling. q.

Motorist Information and Services Association *(1988)*
229 Madrona Ave. SE
Salem, OR 97302
Tel: (503)373-0864
E-Mail: info@misaonline.org
Web Site: www.misaonline.org
Members: 125 individuals
Annual Budget: $10-25,000
Executive Director: Cheryl Gribskov
E-Mail: info@misaonline.org
Historical Note
MISA represents firms and organizations involved in highway information signage and other technologies developed to deliver pertinent information to motorists on the highway. Membership: $50/year (government employee); $100/year (individual); $200/year (organization/company); $250/year (multi-state operator).
Publications:
MISA Messenger. q. adv.
Membership Directory. a. adv.

Mountain Rescue Association *(1959)*
P.O. Box 880868
San Diego, CA 92168-0868
Tel: (858)229-4295 *Fax:* (619)374-7072
E-Mail: mra@kayley.com
Web Site: www.mra.org
Members: 91 units
Annual Budget: $50-100,000
Executive Secretary: Kayley Trujillo
Historical Note
Since 1958, accredits mountain rescue units. MRA members are mountain rescue units in the United States and Canada and other countries. Promotes high standards, mutual aid response, research and education programs.
Meetings/Conferences:
Annual Meetings: *Semi-annual Conference.*
2007 – Weber County, UT
Publications:
Blue Book. a.
Rescue Forum Magazine. q. adv.
Conference Minutes. semi-a.

Mounted Breakers Manufacturers Bureau
Historical Note
A bureau of the Construction Industry Manufacturers Association.

Movement Disorder Society *(1985)*
555 E. Wells St., Suite 1100
Milwaukee, WI 53202
Tel: (414)276-2145 *Fax:* (414)276-3349
E-Mail: info@movementdisorders.org
Web Site: www.movementdisorders.org
Members: 2300 individuals
Staff: 5
Annual Budget: $2-5,000,000
Executive Director: Caley A. Kleczka
Historical Note
MDS is a scholarly scientific society devoted to research in the field of movement disorders. Membership: $200/year.
Publications:
Movement Disorders Journal. m. adv.
Directory of Members. a.
Newsletter. q. adv.

MTM Association for Standards and Research *(1951)*
1111 E. Touhy Ave., Suite 280
Des Plaines, IL 60018
Tel: (847)299-1111 *Fax:* (847)299-3509
Web Site: www.mtm.org
Members: 1000 individuals
Staff: 8
Annual Budget: $1-2,000,000
Executive Director: Dirk Rauglas
Contact: Lillian Burns
Historical Note
Membership consists of industrial psychologists, industrial engineers, academicians and corporate members. Conducts research and training on the efficiency of human motion. Also known as Methods Time Measurement Association for Standards and Research. Membership: $40/year (individual); $750/year (company).
Meetings/Conferences:
Annual Meetings: *Chicago, IL/October*
Publications:
Journal. q.
Research Reports. irreg.

Mu Phi Epsilon *(1903)*
4705 N. Sonora Ave., Suite 114
Fresno, CA 93722-3947
Tel: (559)277-1898 *Fax:* (559)277-2825
Toll Free: (888)259 - 1471
E-Mail: mpeieo@aol.com
Web Site: http://homumuphiepsilon.org
Members: 70000 individuals
Staff: 2
Annual Budget: $100-250,000
Executive Secretary Treasurer: Gloria Debatin
Historical Note
An international professional music fraternity founded November 13, 1903 at the Metropolitan College of Music, Cincinnati, Ohio. Membership is open to music majors or minors enrolled in schools where chapters exist. Concert artists, teachers, composers and other music leaders are also included. Membership: $18-$25/year.
Publications:
The Triangle. q.

Mulch and Soil Council *(1971)*
10210 Leatherleaf Ct.
Manassas, VA 20111-4245
Tel: (703)257-0111 *Fax:* (703)257-0213
E-Mail: info@mulchandsoilcouncil.org
Web Site: www.mulchandsoilcouncil.org
Members: 104 companies
Staff: 5
Annual Budget: $100-250,000
Executive Director: Robert C. LaGasse, CAE
Historical Note
Founded as National Bark Producers Association; became National Bark and Soil Producers Association in 1988 and assumed its current name in 2001. Members are manufacturers of bark and soil products and industry suppliers.
Meetings/Conferences:
Annual Meetings: *Fall*
Publications:
Capitol Hill Report. q.
Bark Producers Report. q.
Special Regional Releases. irreg.

Multi-Housing Laundry Association *(1959)*
1500 Sunday Dr., Suite 102
Raleigh, NC 27607
Tel: (919)861-5579 *Fax:* (919)787-4916
Toll Free: (800)380 - 3652
Web Site: www.mhla.com
Members: 40 companies
Staff: 3
Annual Budget: $500-1,000,000
Executive Director: David Feild
Historical Note
Formerly National Association of Coin Laundry Equipment Operators; assumed its current name in 1982.
Meetings/Conferences:
Annual Meetings: *June*
Publications:
MLA News. bi-m. adv.

Multi-Level Marketing International Association *(1985)*
11956 Bernardo Plaza St.
Suite 313
San Diego, CA 92128
Tel: (949)854-0484 *Fax:* (949)854-7687
E-Mail: info@mlmia.com
Web Site: www.mlmia.com
Members: 5000 individuals
Staff: 2
Annual Budget: $250-500,000
Chief Executive Officer/President Emeritus: Doris Wood
Executive Director: Del Hickman
Historical Note
Established and incorporated in California as a not-for-profit organization, MLMIA members are companies which market their products and services directly to consumers through distributors, suppliers to the industry, and distributors who interface with consumers. Maintains branch offices in England, Canada, and Malaysia. Membership: $1,200-12,000/year (company); $600/year (support); $60/year (distributor).
Meetings/Conferences:
Semi-Annual Meetings: Winter and Summer
Publications:
Connecting Point. q.
Support Directory. q.
Corporate Directory. q.

Municipal Arborists and Urban Foresters Society
Historical Note
A special interest group within the International Society of Aboriculture.

Municipal Waste Management Association *(1982)*
1620 I St. NW, Suite 300
Washington, DC 20006
Tel: (202)293-7330 *Fax:* (202)293-2352
Web Site: www.usmayors.org/uscm/mwma
Members: 200localgovernmentorganizations
Staff: 4
Annual Budget: $50-100,000
Senior Program Manager: Susan Jarvis
Historical Note
Formerly (1991) the National Resource Recovery Association. Affiliated with U. S. Conference of Mayors; members are concerned with the processing of municipal solid waste for the production of recyclable materials, heat, energy, and other purposes. Active members are local government organizations; associate members are from the private sector. Membership: $300-5,000/year, varies by population (active member); $250-750/year, varies by number of employees (associate).
Meetings/Conferences:
Annual Meetings: *Always in Washington, DC/March-April/300 1992(Vista International)*

Musculoskeletal Tumor Society *(1977)*
Medical Center East, South Tower, Suite 4200
Nashville, TN 37232-8774
Tel: (615)343-4400 *Fax:* (615)343-1028
E-Mail: msts@vanderbilt.edu
Web Site: www.msts.org
Members: 180 individuals
Staff: 1
Annual Budget: $100-250,000
Executive Director: Marla Holderby
E-Mail: msts@vanderbilt.edu

Historical Note
MSTS advances the science of orthopaedic oncology and promotes high standards of patient care. Has one full-time staff member.

Meetings/Conferences:
Annual Meetings: Spring/200
2007 – St. Louis, MO(Ritz Carlton)/May 10-12/250
2008 – Phoenix, AZ(The Biltmore)/Nov. 6-8
2009 – Boston, MA(Westin Copley Place)/Sept. 22-24/250

Publications:
Clinical Orthopaedics and Related Research. m. adv.

Museum Computer Network *(1967)*
232-329 March Road, Box 11
Ottawa, ON K2K -2E1
Tel: (613)254-9772 *Fax:* (613)599-7027
Toll Free: (888)211 - 1477
E-Mail: mcn@igs.net
Web Site: www.mcn.edu
Members: 800 individuals
Annual Budget: $100-250,000
Contact: Helene Mcdonald

Historical Note
Membership: $75/year (individual); $250/year (institution/vendor); $300/year (industry/corporate).

Publications:
Spectra Newsletter. q. adv.
Membership Directory. a.

Museum Education Roundtable *(1969)*
P.O. Box 15727
Washington, DC 20003-4303
Tel: (202)547-8378 *Fax:* (202)547-8344
E-Mail: info@mer-online.org
Web Site: www.mer-online.org/
Members: 1000 individuals
Staff: 1
Annual Budget: $50-100,000
President: Mychalene Giampaoli

Historical Note
Members are museum educators, teachers, museums and schools. Membership: $40/year (individual); $120/year (institution); $25/year (student); $60/year (library).

Publications:
Journal of Museum Education. 3/year.
Network Newsletter. semi-a.

Museum Store Association *(1955)*
4100 E. Mississippi Ave., Suite 800
Denver, CO 80246-3055
Tel: (303)504-9223 *Fax:* (303)504-9585
Web Site: www.museumdistrict.com/about/about msa.cfm
Members: 3000 museums and companies
Staff: 10
Annual Budget: $1-2,000,000
Executive Director: Beverly Barsook

Historical Note
A professional organization affiliated with the American Association of Museums.

Meetings/Conferences:
Annual Meetings: May/1,500

Publications:
Product News. q.
Management Insights. bi-m.
Museum Store. q. adv.
Directory. a. adv.

Museum Trustee Association *(1986)*
2025 M St. NW, Suite 800
Washington, DC 20036-3309
Tel: (202)367-1180 *Fax:* (202)367-2180
E-Mail: office@mta-hq.org
Web Site: www.mta-hq.org
Members: 200 individuals
Staff: 2
Annual Budget: $250-500,000
Administrative Manager: Megan Renner

Historical Note
Founded as the Trustee Committee of the American Association of Museums, MTA was separately incorporated in 1986 as the Museum Trustee Committee for Research and Development and subsequently assumed its current name. MTA is the American Association of Museum's affiliate for trustee affairs. Membership: fee varies; $100/year minimum (individual); $200/year minimum (organization).

Meetings/Conferences:
Annual: Fall

Publications:
MTA Briefings. q. adv.

Music and Entertainment Industry Educators Association *(1978)*
1900 Belmont Blvd.
Nashville, TN 37212-3757
Tel: (615)460-6946
E-Mail: office@meiea.org
Web Site: www.meiea.org
Members: 650 individuals
Staff: 2
Annual Budget: $10-25,000
President: Dr. Rebecca Chappell

Historical Note
Established in Nashville, TN in 1978 as the Music Industry Educators Association, it assumed its present name in April 1986. Members are individuals, educational institutions and companies concerned with establishing educational standards for the creative production and management aspects of the music and recording industry. Membership: $50/year (individual); $150/year (company); $100/year (educational institution); $15/year (student).

Meetings/Conferences:
Annual Meetings: Spring
2007 – Pomona, CA(California State Polytechnic University)

Publications:
MEIEA Notes. q.

Music Critics Association of North America *(1957)*
722 Dulaney Valley Rd., Suite 259
Baltimore, MD 21204
Tel: (410)435-3881 *Fax:* (410)435-3881
E-Mail: musiccritics@aol.com
Web Site: www.mcana.org
Members: 230 individuals
Staff: 1
Annual Budget: $10-25,000
Managing Director: Robert Leininger
E-Mail: musiccritics@aol.com

Historical Note
Added "of North America" to its name in 1994. Members are classical music critics from the various communications media. Seeks to improve the caliber of music criticism and to promote an interest in music in the U.S. and Canada. Membership: $100/year (individual); $35/year (students).

Meetings/Conferences:
Annual Meetings: usually late summer

Publications:
Critical Issues. 3/year.

Music Distributors Association *(1939)*
13610 92nd St.
Alto, MI 49302
Tel: (616)765-9912 *Fax:* (616)765-3479
Web Site: www.musicdistributors.org
Members: 125 companies
Staff: 2
Annual Budget: $50-100,000
Executive Officer: Glenda Plummer

Historical Note
Formerly (1977) the National Association of Musical Merchandise Wholesalers. Two-thirds of member companies are domestic, one-third overseas. Membership: $650/year (active); $325/year (international).

Meetings/Conferences:
Semi-annual Meetings: following National Association of Music Merchants

Publications:
Newsletter. 6-10/year.

Music Industry Conference *(1923)*

Historical Note
An affiliate of MENC (same address), which provides administrative support.

Music Library Association *(1931)*
A-R Editions
8551 Research Way, Suite 180
Middleton, WI 53562
Tel: (608)836-5825 *Fax:* (608)831-8200
E-Mail: mla@areditions.com
Web Site: www.musiclibraryassoc.org
Members: 3 individuals and institutions
Staff: 1
Annual Budget: $250-500,000
President: Bonna Boettcher

Historical Note
MLA promotes the active study of the material history and culture of music, as well as best practices in music conservation in the library community.

Meetings/Conferences:
2007 – Pittsburgh, PA/Feb. 28-March 4

Publications:
Music Cataloging Bulletin. m.
Notes. q. adv.
Music Library Association Newsletter. q.

Music Publishers' Association of the United States *(1895)*
243 Fifth Ave., Suite 236
New York, NY 10016
Tel: (212)327-4044
Web Site: www.mpa.org
Members: 75 music publishers
Staff: 1
President: Lauren Keiser
E-Mail: laurenk@carlfischer.com

Historical Note
Serves as a forum for publishers to deal with the music industry's vital issues, including copyright laws, copyright infringements, and the need for further reform. Keeps its members informed of the latest technology and production sophistication in graphics, engraving, computerization, and printing. Informs its constituents of new laws, decisions, and regulations affecting the industry. Fosters relations among the publishing industry, schools, dealers, performers, and composers.

Meetings/Conferences:
Annual Meetings: Summer

Publications:
Directory of Music Publishers. a.

Music Teachers National Association *(1876)*
441 Vine St., Suite 505
Cincinnati, OH 45202-2811
Tel: (513)421-1420 *Fax:* (513)421-2503
Toll Free: (888)512 - 5278
E-Mail: mtnanet@mtna.org
Web Site: www.mtna.org
Members: 24000 individuals
Staff: 17
Annual Budget: $1-2,000,000
Executive Director: Gary Ingle

Historical Note
Founded by Theodore Presser in Delaware, Ohio on December 26, 1876 with 62 charter members, MTNA is a non-profit organization of independent and collegiate music teachers. Membership: $59/year, plus state and local dues.

Meetings/Conferences:
Annual Meetings: Spring
2007 – Toronto, ON, Canada(Sheraton Centre Toronto)/March 23-27
2008 – Denver, CO(Hyatt/Colorado Convention Center)/March 29-Apr. 2/2000

Publications:
American Music Teacher. bi-m. adv.

Mutual Fund Education Alliance *(1971)*
100 N.W. Englewood Rd., Suite 130
Kansas City, MO 64118
Tel: (816)454-9422 *Fax:* (816)454-9322
E-Mail: webservices@mfea.com
Web Site: www.mfea.com

Members: 37 fund companies.; 1500 mutual funds
Staff: 5
Managing Director: Michelle Smith
E-Mail: webservices@mfea.com

Historical Note
Formerly No-Load Mutual Fund Association; assumed its present name in 1989. MFEA is an association for investment companies who market their shares directly to the public. Provides investor education and data, including on its web site.

Meetings/Conferences:
Semi-Annual Meetings: Winter and Fall

Mycological Society of America *(1932)*
c/o Allen Mktg., 810 E. 10th St.
Lawrence, KS 66044
Tel: (785)843-1235 Ext: 296 *Fax:* (785)843-1274
Web Site: www.msafungi.org
Members: 1400 individuals
Staff: 2
Annual Budget: $500-1,000,000
Association Manager: Kay Rose

Historical Note
Founded in New Orleans in 1932 as an outgrowth of the Microbiological Section of the Botanical Society of America, and incorporated in 1966 in the District of Columbia. Members are individuals interested in the study of fungi. Affiliated with the American Association for the Advancement of Science, International Union of Microbiological Societies, Latin American Mycological Society and the American Institute of Biological Sciences. Membership: $98/year (individual), $190/year US/ $205 Canada (organization); $50/year (student).

Meetings/Conferences:
Annual Meetings: Summer/350

Publications:
Inoculum. bi-m. adv.
Mycologia Online.
Mycologia. bi-m. adv.
Mycologia Memoirs. irreg.

Mystery Shopping Providers Association
12300 Ford Rd., Suite 135
Dallas, TX 75234
Tel: (972)406-1104 *Fax:* (972)755-2561
E-Mail: info@mysteryshop.org
Web Site: www.mysteryshop.org/
Members: 150 companies
Staff: 6
Annual Budget: $250-500,000
Executive Director: John S. Swinburn, CAE

Meetings/Conferences:
Annual Meetings: Fall

Mystery Writers of America *(1945)*
17 E. 47th St., Sixth Floor
New York, NY 10017
Tel: (212)888-8171 *Fax:* (212)888-8107
E-Mail: mwa@mysterywriters.org
Web Site: www.mysterywriters.org
Members: 2800 individuals
Staff: 2
Annual Budget: $100-250,000
Office Manager: Margery L. Flax

Historical Note
Members are professional writers of crime and mystery stories and novels. Unpublished writers are affiliate members; publishers and agents are associate members. Membership: $80/year.

Meetings/Conferences:
Annual Meetings: Spring/New York, NY/700-800

Publications:
Third Degree. 10/yr. adv.
MWA Annual. a. adv.

NAADAC -- the Association for Addiction Professionals *(1972)*
901 N. Washington St., Suite 600
Alexandria, VA 22314-1535
Tel: (703)741-7686 *Fax:* (800)377-1136
Toll Free: (800)548 - 0497
E-Mail: naadc@naadc.org
Web Site: www.naadac.org
Members: 18000 individuals
Staff: 11
Annual Budget: $1-2,000,000
Executive Director: Cynthia Moreno Tuohy, NCAC II, CCDC III
Director, Finance and Operations: Jeff Crouse
E-Mail: jcrouse@naadc.org

Historical Note
Founded as National Association of Alcoholism and Drug Abuse Counselors; assumed its current name in 2001. NAADAC represents addiction counselors working in hospitals, treatment centers, private practice, councils and agencies on alcoholism and drug abuse, and employee assistance programs. Incorporated in Arlington, VA. Administers certifying examinations leading to the National Certified Addiction Counselor (NCAC) and Master Addiction Counselor designations. Membership: $100/year (individual); $350/year (company).

Meetings/Conferences:
Annual Meetings: Summer

Publications:
Addiction Professional. bi-m.
The Counselor Magazine. bi-m. adv.
NAADAC Newsletter. bi-m.

NABIM - the International Band and Orchestral Products Association *(1920)*
P.O. Box 757
New York, NY 10033
Tel: (212)795-3630 *Fax:* (212)795-3630
Toll Free: (866)496 - 8742
E-Mail: assnhdqs@earthlink.net
Web Site: www.nabim.org
Members: 34 companies
Staff: 2
Annual Budget: $25-50,000
Executive Vice President: Rob Sulkow

Historical Note
Formerly (2003) National Association of Band Instrument Manufacturers. Membership fee varies by sales.

Meetings/Conferences:
Annual Meetings: Fall

Publications:
Newsletter. bi-m.

NACE International *(1943)*
1440 S. Creek Dr.
Houston, TX 77084-4906
Tel: (281)228-6200 *Fax:* (281)228-6300
Toll Free: (800)797 - 6223
E-Mail: firstservice@nace.org
Web Site: www.nace.org
Members: 16000 individuals
Staff: 70
Annual Budget: $10-25,000,000
Executive Director: Tony Keane, CAE
Director, Conferences and Exhibitions: Cassie Davie
Director, Membership and Program Services: Teri Elliott
Director, Technical Activities: Linda Goldberg
Director, Publications: Gretchen Jacobson
Director, Public Affairs: Cliff Johnson
Director, Information Systems: John Perry
Senior Director, New Business and Program Development: Helena Seelinger
Controller: Rhonda Wagner

Historical Note
Formerly (1993) the National Association of Corrosion Engineers. NACE advances the knowledge of corrosion engineering and science in all major industries through education, certification, standards, publications, and public awareness. Membership: $90/year (individual); $500-$5,000/year (corporate).

Meetings/Conferences:
Annual Meetings: Spring
2007 – Nashville, TN(Convention Center)/Apr. 22-26

Publications:
Corrosion - The Journal of Science and Engineering. m. adv.
Materials Performance. m. adv.

NACHA - The Electronic Payments Association *(1974)*
13665 Dulles Technology Dr., Suite 300
Herndon, VA 20171
Tel: (703)561-1100 *Fax:* (703)787-0996
E-Mail: info@nacha.org
Web Site: www.nacha.org
Members: 12000 financial institutions
Staff: 48
Annual Budget: $5-10,000,000
President and Chief Executive Officer: Elliott C. McEntee
Senior Director, Conference Marketing and Publications: Deb Evans-Doyle
Senior Director, Electronic Commerce Solutions: Julie Hedlund
Director, Public Relations: Michael Herd
Senior Director, International and Corporate Payments: Priscilla Holland, AAP
Senior Director, Education Services: Scott Lang, AAP
General Counsel: Jane Larimer
Senior Director, Membership Communications and Affiliate Services: Ian Macoy
Senior Director, Finance and Administration: Pam Moore
Executive Vice President: William B. Nelson
Senior Director, National Marketing: Robin Reeder
Senior Director, Network Services: Deborah Shaw, AAP
Senior Director, Private/Public Partnerships: Helena Sims

Historical Note
Founded as National Automated Clearing House Association; assumed its current name in 2000. NACHA is a trade association that forms the cooperative foundation for the automated clearing house (ACH) payments system through a network of 21 ACH associations nationwide. NACHA is responsible for establishing the rules for the exchange of ACH transactions between financial institutions. It also provides marketing and educational support to the banking industry. NACHA has 12,000 members, through direct memberships and a network of regional payment associations.

Meetings/Conferences:
Annual Meetings: Spring/1,000

Publications:
Electronics Payment Journal. 6/year.
Affiliate Forum. 3/year.
NACHA Operating Rules & Guidelines. a.

NADD: Association for Persons with Developmental Disabilities and Mental Health Needs *(1983)*
132 Fair St.
Kingston, NY 12401-4802
Tel: (845)331-4336 *Fax:* (845)331-4569
Toll Free: (800)331 - 5362
Web Site: www.thenadd.org
Members: 1500 individuals
Staff: 4
Annual Budget: $500-1,000,000
Chief Executive Officer: Robert Fletcher, D.S.W.

Historical Note
Founded as National Association for the Dually Diagnosed Mental Illness/Mental Retardation. Mission is to advance mental wellness for persons with mental health needs who have development disabilities, through the promotion of excellence in mental health care. Membership: $98/year (individual); $450-600/year (organization/company).

Meetings/Conferences:
Annual Meetings: Fall

Publications:
NADD Bulletin. 6/yr. adv.

NAFSA: Association of International Educators *(1948)*
1307 New York Ave. NW, Eighth Floor
Washington, DC 20005-4701
Tel: (202)737-3699 *Fax:* (202)737-3657
Toll Free: (800)836 - 4994
E-Mail: inbox@nafsa.org
Web Site: www.nafsa.org
Members: 9000 individuals
Staff: 55
Annual Budget: $5-10,000,000
Executive Director and Chief Executive Officer: Marlene M. Johnson
E-Mail: inbox@nafsa.org
Senior Director, Member Relations and Leadership Services: Frank Doyle
E-Mail: inbox@nafsa.org

Associate Executive Director, Public Policy: Vic Johnson
E-Mail: inbox@nafsa.org
Chief Financial Officer: Bill Newman
E-Mail: inbox@nafsa.org
Associate Executive Director, Organizational Advancement: Will Philipp
E-Mail: inbox@nafsa.org
Senior Director, Conferences and Meetings: Valerie Royal
E-Mail: inbox@nafsa.org
Deputy Executive Director, Member Relations: Betty Soppelsa
E-Mail: inbox@nafsa.org
Deputy Executive Director, Development Services: Bob Stableski
E-Mail: inbox@nafsa.org

Historical Note
Founded in 1948 as National Association of Foreign Student Advisors. NAFSA has nearly 9,000 members worldwide including in 80 foreign countries, making it the largest professional membership association in the world concerned with the advancement of effective international educational exchange. NAFSA members are foreign student advisors, international admissions officers, ESL teachers and administrators, study-abroad administrators, overseas educational advisors, community support groups, and sponsored program administrators; other members are from sister associations and foundations, international and within-nation corporations, research centers, community organizations and cultural groups.

Meetings/Conferences:
Annual Meetings: May
2007 – Minneapolis, MN/May 27-June 1/7000

Publications:
International Educator. bi-m. adv.
NAFSA News. w. adv.
NAFSA Directory (online).

NAGMR Consumer Product Brokers *(1949)*
1503 Near Thicket Lane
Stevenson, MD 21153
Tel: (410)653-6560 *Fax:* (410)484-4261
Web Site: www.nagmr.com
Members: 40 firms
Staff: 2
Annual Budget: $25-50,000
Executive Director: Steve Dimond

Historical Note
Founded as National Association of Drug Manufacturer's Representatives; became (1976) National Association of Diversified Manufacturers' Representatives, (1978) National Association General Merchandise Representatives, and assumed its current name in 1998. Membership: $590-2,000/year.

Meetings/Conferences:
Annual Meetings: Fall

Publications:
The Representative (online). m.
Membership Roster. a.

Nail Manufacturers Council *(1989)*

Historical Note
A division of the American Beauty Association.

NAIR -- the International Association of Bowling Lane Specialists *(1973)*
5806 W. 127th St.
Alsip, IL 60803
Tel: (708)371-8237 *Fax:* (708)371-8283
E-Mail: nairbowllanecare@email.msn.com
Web Site: www.nairbowl.org
Members: 55 companies
Staff: 1
Executive Secretary: Nancy Surprenant
E-Mail: nairbowllanecare@email.msn.com

Historical Note
Founded as National Association of Independent Resurfacers; assumed its current name in 2001. Members are companies engaged in the installation and refinishing, injecting and repairing of bowling lanes.

Meetings/Conferences:
Annual Meetings: Fall

Publications:
NAIR News. q.

NALS *(1929)*
314 E. Third St., Suite 210
Tulsa, OK 74120-2409
Tel: (918)582-5188 *Fax:* (918)582-5907
E-Mail: info@nals.org
Web Site: www.nals.org
Members: 6000 individuals
Staff: 7
Annual Budget: $500-1,000,000
Executive Director: Tammy Hailey, CAE

Historical Note
Established as the California Association of Legal Secretaries, it became Legal Secretaries, Inc. in 1940, National Association of Legal Secretaries in 1950, and assumed its present name in 2003. Has certification programs leading to designations as Certified Paralegal Professional (CPP), Professional Legal Secretary (PLS), and Accredited Legal Secretary (ALS). Membership: $90/year (national).

Meetings/Conferences:
Annual Meetings: Summer/600
2007 – Tulsa, OK(Doubletree Warren Place)/March 6-10
2007 – St. Louis, MO(Sheraton Westport)/Oct. 9-14

Publications:
@LAW. q. adv.

NAMM - the International Music Products Association *(1901)*
5790 Armada Dr.
Carlsbad, CA 92008-4391
Tel: (760)438-8001 *Fax:* (760)438-7327
E-Mail: info@namm.org
Web Site: www.namm.org
Members: 9600 companies
Staff: 62
President and Chief Executive Officer: Joe Lamond
E-Mail: joel@namm.org
Director, Administration: Cathy Hughes
E-Mail: cathyh@namm.org
Director, Public Affairs and Government Relations: Mary Luehrsen
E-Mail: maryl@namm.org
Chief Financial Officer: Larry Manley
E-Mail: larrym@namm.org
Marketing and Communications Director: Scott Robertson
E-Mail: scottr@namm.org
Director, Professional Development: Ken Wilson

Historical Note
Founded as National Association of Music Merchants; became NAMM - the International Music Products Association in 1997. Members are musical instrument retailers and manufacturers and their suppliers.

Meetings/Conferences:
Semi-Annual Trade Shows: The NAMM Show/Anaheim, CA/81,000, and Summer Session/Austin, TX/20,000
2007 – Austin, TX/July 27-31

Publications:
Compensation and Benefits. a.
Music USA. a.
Playback. bi-m.
Cost of Doing Business Report. a.

NANDA International *(1972)*
100 N. 20th St., Suite 400
Philadelphia, PA 19103
Tel: (215)545-8105 *Fax:* (215)545-8107
Toll Free: (800)647 - 9002
E-Mail: info@nanda.org
Web Site: www.nanda.org
Members: 500 individuals
Staff: 10
Executive Director: Joseph Braden

Historical Note
Formerly North American Nursing Diagnosis Association; assumed its current name in 1992. NANDA members are registered nurses and other health professionals with an interest in nursing diagnosis. Membership: $85/year.

Publications:
NANDA Nursing Diagnosis Journal. q.
NANDA Book. bien.

NARTE *(1982)*
167 Village St.
Medway, MA 02053
Tel: (508)533-8333 *Fax:* (508)533-3815
Toll Free: (800)896 - 2783
E-Mail: narte@narte.org
Web Site: www.narte.org
Members: 5200 individuals
Staff: 4
Annual Budget: $250-500,000
Executive Director: Russell V. Carstensen
E-Mail: narte@narte.org
Director, Operations: Laura Holmberg
E-Mail: narte@narte.org

Historical Note
Founded (1982) as National Association of Radio and Telecommunications Engineers; assumed its current name in 2002. NARTE is a non-profit certification agency, formed by telecommunication industry leaders concerned about potential proliferation of pseudo-qualified engineers and technicians that could result as a by-product of Federal deregulation. Expanded in 1988 to include the field of electromagnetic compatibility at the request of the NAVAIR of the US Navy. Certifies qualified engineers and technicians in the fields of telecommunications, electromagnetic compatibilty/interference (EMC/EMI), electro static discharge control (ESD), and wireless systems installation, and was certified as a Commercial Operators license examination manager by the Federal Communications Commission in August, 1993. Also established the Association of Access Engineering Specialists. Membership: $25-75/year.

Publications:
NARTE News. q. adv.

NASFM *(1956)*
4651 Sheridan St., Suite 470
Hollywood, FL 33021
Tel: (954)893-7300 *Fax:* (954)893-7500
E-Mail: nasfm@nasfm.org
Web Site: www.nasfm.org
Members: 400 manufacturers, 30 designer members, 100 visual merchandising members, 250 suppliers
Staff: 11
Annual Budget: $1-2,000,000
Executive Director: Klein S. Merriman
E-Mail: kleinmerriman@nasfm.org
Director, Communications: Tracy Dillon
Director, Sales and Marketing: Karen Doodeman
E-Mail: karendoodeman@nasfm.org
Director, Education and Administration: Pamela Presley

Historical Note
Members are providers of store fixtures. Membership: $1,100-2,200/year.

Meetings/Conferences:
Annual Meetings: October/November: 250
2007 – Laguna Beach, CA(St. Regis)/Nov. 5-7/250

Publications:
NASFM News newsletter. m.
Buyers' Guide/Membership Directory. a. adv.
NASFM Magazine. bi-m. adv.

NaSPA: the Network and System Professionals Association *(1986)*
7044 S. 13th St.
Oak Creek, WI 53154
Tel: (414)908-4945
E-Mail: sherer@naspa.com
Web Site: www.naspa.com
Members: 29000 individuals
Staff: 22
Annual Budget: $2-5,000,000
President: Scott P. Sherer
E-Mail: sherer@naspa.com
Director, Finance: Margaret Zizis
E-Mail: m.ziziz@naspa.com

Historical Note
Founded as National Systems Programmers Association; became (1994) NaSPA: the Association for Corporate Computing Professionals, and assumed its current name in 1997. Established and incorporated in Wisconsin. NaSPA members are technical professionals in corporate computing

environments. Membership: $49.95/year (individual).

Publications:
Network Support Magazine. bi-m. adv.
Technical Support Magazine. m. adv.

NASTD - Technology Professionals Serving State Government *(1978)*
P.O. Box 11910
Lexington, KY 40578-1910
Tel: (859)244-8187 *Fax:* (859)244-8001
Web Site: www.nastd.org
Members: 1000 individuals
Staff: 4
Annual Budget: $500-1,000,000
Executive Director: Karen Britton

Historical Note
Founded as National Association of State Telecommunications Directors; assumed its current name in 2005. NASTD is concerned with providing a forum for the exchange of ideas and practices and the development of a unified position on matters of national telecommunications policy and regulatory issues. Administrative support provided by the Council of State Governments. Membership: $3,500/year.

Meetings/Conferences:
Annual Meetings: Fall/250

Publications:
State Telecommunications Reports. a.
Monitor - electronic. w.

NATCO - The Organization for Transplant Professionals *(1980)*
P.O. Box 15384
Lenexa, KS 66285-5384
Tel: (913)492-3600 *Fax:* (913)599-5340
E-Mail: natco-info@goamp.com
Web Site: www.natco1.org
Members: 1800 individuals
Staff: 4
Annual Budget: $500-1,000,000
Executive Director: Dede Gish Panjada
E-Mail: natco-info@goamp.com

Historical Note
NATCO's members are health professionals involved in obtaining and distributing human organs and tissues for transplant or working with transplant recipients. Membership: $150/year.

Meetings/Conferences:
Annual Meetings: July-August

Publications:
Progress In Transplantation. q. adv.
NATCO Newsletter. bi-m. adv.

National Abortion Federation *(1977)*
1755 Massachusetts Ave. NW, Suite 600
Washington, DC 20036
Tel: (202)667-5881 *Fax:* (202)667-5890
E-Mail: naf@prochoice.org
Web Site: www.prochoice.org
Members: 500institutions&individuals
Staff: 35
Annual Budget: $2-5,000,000
President and Chief Executive Officer: Vicki Saporta
E-Mail: naf@prochoice.org
Public Policy Director: Jennifer Blasdell
E-Mail: naf@prochoice.org

Historical Note
The National Abortion Federation is the professional association of abortion providers which works to ensure access to safe, legal abortion. NAF members include clinics, doctors' offices and hospital surgi-centers, and provide over half of all U.S. abortions.

Meetings/Conferences:
Annual Meetings: Spring

National Academic Advising Association *(1979)*
Kansas State University
2323 Anderson Ave., Suite 225
Manhattan, KS 66502-2912
Tel: (785)532-5717 *Fax:* (785)532-7732
E-Mail: nacada@k-state.edu
Web Site: www.nacada.k-state.edu
Members: 9200 individuals
Staff: 13
Annual Budget: $1-2,000,000
Executive Director: Roberta D. Flaherty
Associate Director: Charlie Nutt

Historical Note
Membership open to professionals, faculty, and students working through academic advising to ensure the educational development of students in educational institutions. Membership: $55/year (professional); $25/year (student).

Meetings/Conferences:
Annual Meetings: October
2007 - Baltimore, MD(Convention Center)/Oct. 18-21
2008 - Chicago, IL(Hyatt)/Oct. 1-4
2009 - San Antonio, TX
2010 - Orlando, FL

Publications:
NACADA Journal. semi-a. adv.
Academic Advising Today. q.

National Academies of Practice *(1981)*
P.O. Box 1037
Edgewood, MD 21040
Tel: (410)676-3390 *Fax:* (410)676-7980
E-Mail: naphdq@comcast.us
Web Site: www.napnet.us
Members: 700 individuals
Staff: 1
Annual Budget: $100-250,000

Historical Note
NAP is an indisciplinary health care policy forum addressing public policy, education, research, and inquiry issues. Represents nine professions including dentistry, medicine, nursing, optometry, osteopathic medicine, podiatric medicine, psychology, social work, and veterinary medicine. Membership: $150/year (individual).

Publications:
NAP Forum.
NAP Newsletter. q.

National Academy of Arbitrators *(1947)*
One N. Main St., Suite 412
Cortland, NY 13045
Tel: (607)756-8363 *Fax:* (607)756-8365
E-Mail: naa@naarb.org
Web Site: www.naarb.org
Members: 660 individuals
Staff: 3
Annual Budget: $100-250,000
Administrative Assistant: Suzanne Kelly

Historical Note
Founded in Chicago on September 14, 1947 to upgrade the professionalism of those engaged in the arbitration of labor-management disputes.

Publications:
The Chronicle. 3/year.
Membership Directory. a.

National Academy of Building Inspection Engineers *(1989)*
P.O. Box 522158
Salt Lake City, UT 84152
Toll Free: (800)294 - 7729
E-Mail: director@nabie.org
Web Site: www.nabie.org
Members: 165 individuals
Staff: 1
Annual Budget: $10-25,000
Executive Director: Michael Stotts

Historical Note
NABIE is a professional society that accepts State-registered Professional Engineers specializing in the practice of building inspections. The association advances the practice of professional engineering as it applies to the inspection, investigation and evaluation of buildings and homes.

Meetings/Conferences:
Annual Meetings: Winter

National Academy of Clinical Biochemistry *(1976)*
1850 K St. NW
Suite 625
Washington, DC 20006
Tel: (202)835-8746 *Fax:* (202)887-5093
Web Site: www.nacb.org
Members: 535 individuals
Annual Budget: $50-100,000
Director, Administrative: Penelope Jones

Historical Note
NACB is the official Academy of the American Association for Clinical Chemistry (AACC) and membership in AACC is required. Fellows and Associate Fellows are all doctoral level scientists who are actively engaged in research, education, or service of clinical biochemistry. Fellows of the Academy are either certified by the American Board of Clinical Chemistry or another board judged to be equivalent, or have at least 10 years experience as a clinical biochemist and sufficient publications or other activities to have been judged as distinguished. Associate Fellows lack Board certification or sufficient publications to be judged distinguished, but meet all other requirements. Has no paid officers or full time staff. Membership: $60/year.

Meetings/Conferences:
Annual Meetings: Summer
2007 - San Diego, CA/July 15-19

National Academy of Education *(1965)*
500 Fifth St. NW, Suite 333
Washington, DC 20001
Tel: (202)334-2341 *Fax:* (202)334-2350
Web Site: www.naeducation.org
Members: 150 institutions
Staff: 3
Annual Budget: $1-2,000,000
Executive Director: Gregory White
Program Officer: Jennifer Tinch

Historical Note
The mission of NAEd is the advancement of the highest quality education research and its use in policy formation and practice.

National Academy of Elder Law Attorneys *(1987)*
1604 N. Country Club Rd.
Tucson, AZ 85716
Tel: (520)881-4005 *Fax:* (520)325-7925
Web Site: www.naela.org
Members: 4800 individuals
Staff: 14
Annual Budget: $1-2,000,000

Historical Note
Members are private attorneys, law professors, judges, students and Title III interested in the provision of legal services to the elderly. Organization has grown from 35 to 4,800 members in 11 years. Membership: $175/year (individual).

Meetings/Conferences:
Semi-Annual Meetings: Spring and Fall

Publications:
NAELA Journal. semi-a.. adv.
NAELA News. 8/year. adv.

National Academy of Engineering of the United States of America *(1964)*
2101 Constitution Ave. NW
Washington, DC 20418
Tel: (202)334-3201 *Fax:* (202)334-2290
Web Site: www.nae.edu
Members: 2115 individuals
Staff: 38
Annual Budget: $10-25,000,000
President: William A. Wulf, Ph.D.
Director, Membership Office: Karen Spaulding

Historical Note
A private organization established in 1964 to share in the responsibility given the National Academy of Sciences under its Congressional charter of 1863 to examine questions of science and technology at the request of the federal government; to sponsor engineering programs aimed at meeting national needs; to encourage engineering research and to recognize distinguished engineers. Membership is by peer election only. Membership: $200/year.

Meetings/Conferences:
Annual Meetings: October/Washington, DC(Nat'l Academy of Sciences Bldg.)

Publications:
The Bridge. q.

National Academy of Neuropsychology *(1975)*
2121 S. Oneida St., Suite 550
Denver, CO 80224-2594
Tel: (303)691-3694 *Fax:* (303)691-5983

E-Mail: office@nanonline.org
Web Site: www.nanonline.org
Members: 3300 individuals
Staff: 3
Annual Budget: $100-250,000
Contact: Dorothy Shadrick

Historical Note

Formerly (1989) National Academy of Neuropsychologists. NAN members are neuropsychologists and other individuals who have interests in brain-behavior relationships and neuropsychology as a science and profession. Membership: $80/year (individual); $40/year (student).

Meetings/Conferences:

Annual Meetings: November

Publications:

Bulletin of NAN. q.
Archives of Clinical Neuropsychology. bi-m.
Membership Directory. bien.

National Academy of Opticianry *(1963)*
8401 Corporate Dr., Suite 605
Landover, MD 20785
Tel: (301)577-4828 *Fax:* (301)577-3880
Toll Free: (800)229 - 4828
E-Mail: info@nao.org
Web Site: www.nao.org
Members: 5300 individuals
Staff: 6
Annual Budget: $500-1,000,000
Executive Director: James E. Iciek
E-Mail: info@nao.org

Historical Note

An association of individual opticians who are state licensed or nationally certified, NAO's purpose is to promote continuing education through home study courses and seminars. Membership: $75/year.

Meetings/Conferences:

Annual Meetings: June-September

Publications:

Academy Programs. q.
ARCHIVES Newsletter. m.

National Academy of Recording Arts and Sciences *(1957)*
3402 Pico Blvd.
Santa Monica, CA 90405-2118
Tel: (310)392-3777 *Fax:* (310)399-3090
Web Site: www.grammy.com
Members: 20000 individuals
Staff: 100
Vice President, West Region: Angelia Bibbs-Sanders
Chief Financial Officer: Susan Leary
Vice President, Member Services: Kristen Madsen
Vice President, Central Region: Griff Morris
Vice President, Business Development: Mitch Roth
Vice President, South Region: Nancy Shapiro
Senior Vice President, Awards: Diane Theroit
Chief Operating Officer: Paul Tsuchiya

Historical Note

Singers, musicians, engineers, composers, arrangers and others engaged in producing commercial recordings. Presents the annual "Grammy" awards for outstanding recordings and grants the "Grammy Lifetime Achievement" to those who have contributed to the world of music during their lifetime. Membership: $100/year (individual).

Meetings/Conferences:

Annual Meetings: Spring

Publications:

Grammy Magazine. q.
Program Book. a.
NARAS Journal. bien.
The Grammy Winner's Book. a.

National Academy of Sciences *(1863)*
500 Fifth St. NW
Washington, DC 20001
Tel: (202)334-2000 *Fax:* (202)334-1684
Web Site: www.nas.edu
Members: 2300 individuals
Staff: 1100
Annual Budget: Over $100,000,000
President: Ralph J. Cicerone
Executive Director: Kenneth R. Fulton
E-Mail: kfulton@nas.edu
Chief Financial Officer: Archie Turner
E-Mail: aturner@nas.edu

Historical Note

Private honorary organization of scholars in scientific and engineering research, chartered by act of Congress March 3, 1863 to serve as an advisor to the federal government on questions of science and technology. Conducts studies in all disciplines of natural and social sciences and engineering, with special emphasis on science advisory role in public policy issues. Affiliated with the National Academy of Engineering and the Institute of Medicine. The National Research Council is the operating arm of the NAS. Has an annual budget of approximately $190 million.

Meetings/Conferences:

Annual Meetings: April in Washington, D.C.

Publications:

Proceedings of the National Academy of Sciences. bi-w.
News Report. q.
Issues in Science and Technology. q. adv.

National Academy of Television Arts and Sciences *(1957)*
111 W. 57th St., Suite 600
New York, NY 10019
Tel: (212)586-8424 *Fax:* (212)246-8129
Web Site: www.emmyonline.org
Members: 13000 individuals
Staff: 10
Annual Budget: $2-5,000,000
President: Peter Price
Contact: Luke E. Smith

Historical Note

Maintains an archival program library on the campus of UCLA. Members are writers, engineers, editors, musicians and others engaged in the creative aspects of the television industry. Presents the annual "Emmy" awards for excellence.

Publications:

The National Online.
Emmy Awards Directory. a.
Television Quarterly. q. adv.
NATAS News. q.

National Academy of Television Journalists *(1987)*
P.O. Box 289
Salisbury, MD 21083-0289
Tel: (410)543-1943 *Fax:* (410)543-0658
Web Site: http://angelfire.com/md/natj
Members: 400 individuals
Staff: 6
Executive Director: Neil F. Bayne

Historical Note

Members are television journalists and journalism students. Membership: $50/Year.

Meetings/Conferences:

Annual Meetings: always 2nd Saturday in May.

Publications:

NATJ Online.
Golden Viddy Award. a.

National Accounting and Finance Council *(1941)*
2200 Mill Road
Alexandria, VA 22314
Tel: (703)838-1915 *Fax:* (703)836-0751
Web Site: www.truckline.com
Members: 1000 individuals
Staff: 4
Annual Budget: $250-500,000
Executive Director: David Hershey

Historical Note

NAFC is a member organization of chief financial officers within the trucking industry and is a part of the American Trucking Association.

Meetings/Conferences:

Annual Meetings: June/500

Publications:

The Controller. m. adv.

National Active and Retired Federal Employees Association *(1921)*
606 N. Washington St.
Alexandria, VA 22314
Tel: (703)838-7760 *Fax:* (703)838-7785
Web Site: www.narfe.org
Members: 450000 individuals
Staff: 70
Annual Budget: $5-10,000,000
National President: Charles L. Fallis
E-Mail: natpres@narfe.org
Director, Membership Development: John Clements
E-Mail: mem@narfe.org
Director, Marketing and Meeting Planning: Juliet Harding
E-Mail: jharding@narfe.org
Director, Legislation: Judy Park
E-Mail: leg@narfe.org
Director, Office Operations: Wilbur Speer
E-Mail: ops@narfe.org

Historical Note

Formerly (1971) National Association of Retired Civil Employees. Sponsors and supports the National Association of Retired Federal Employees Political Action Committee. Has an annual budget of over $9 million. Membership: $20/year, plus chapter dues.

Meetings/Conferences:

Biennial Meetings: Even years/2,800

Publications:

NARFE Highlights. q.
Retirement Life. m. adv.

National Adult Day Services Association
2519 Connecticut Ave. NW
Washington, DC 20008-1520
Tel: (202)508-1205 *Fax:* (202)783-2255
Toll Free: (866)890 - 7357
E-Mail: info@nadsa.org
Web Site: www.nadsa.org
Members: 3500 adult day centers
Staff: 2
Executive Officer: Lauren Shaham

Historical Note

NADSA represents community-based group programs that provide care services for seniors in a non-residential setting.

Meetings/Conferences:

Annual Meetings: Winter

National Adult Education Professional Development Consortium *(1991)*
444 North Capitol St., Suite 422
Washington, DC 20001
Tel: (202)624-5250 *Fax:* (202)624-1497
E-Mail: dc1@naepdc.org
Web Site: www.naepdc.org
Members: 55 state/territorial agencies
Staff: 3
Annual Budget: $100-250,000
Executive Director: Dr. Lennox L. McLendon
E-Mail: lmclendon@naepdc.org

Meetings/Conferences:

Annual Meetings: July

Publications:

Stateline. 8/year.
Annual Report. a. adv.

National Aeronautic Association *(1905)*
1737 King St., #220
Alexandria, VA 22314
Tel: (703)527-0226 *Fax:* (703)527-0229
Toll Free: (800)644 - 9777
E-Mail: naa@naa.aero
Web Site: www.naa.aero
Members: 3000 individuals
Staff: 6
Annual Budget: $500-1,000,000
Director, Membership and Marketing: Shannon Chambers

Historical Note

Members include aerospace corporations, aero clubs, affiliates, and major national sporting aviation organizations such as the Academy of Model Aeronautics; the United States Parachute Association; the International Aerobatic Club; the Soaring Society of America; the Balloon Federation of America; the United States Ultralight Association; and the United States Hang Gliding Association. Absorbed the Aero Club of America in 1922; absorbed the National Aviation Club in 2003. NAA is the U.S. representative to the Federation Aeronautique Internationale

(Switzerland), the world organization for validating air and space records. Membership: $39/year (individual); $1,000-15,000/year (organization).

Publications:
Aero Magazine. bi-m. adv.
World and United States Aviation and Space Records. a.

National Aerosol Association *(1986)*
9142 Golden St.
Alta Loma, CA 91737
Tel: (909)989-9811 *Fax:* (909)989-7900
E-Mail: naa@nationalaerosol.com
Members: 30 individuals
Staff: 1
Annual Budget: $50-100,000
Executive Director: Sharon Rowson

Historical Note
Membership is open to individuals, firms, and agencies engaged in business related to the development, manufacture, packaging, sale or distribution of aerosol products.

Meetings/Conferences:
Annual Meetings: Winter

Publications:
Aerosol News. q.

National Affordable Housing Management Association *(1990)*
400 N. Columbus St., Suite 203
Alexandria, VA 22314
Tel: (703)683-8630 *Fax:* (703)683-8634
Web Site: www.nahma.org
Members: 2500 individuals
Staff: 5
Annual Budget: $1-2,000,000
Executive Director: Kristina C. Cook
Director, Meetings, Membership and Special Projects: Jessica L. Allen

Historical Note
Formerly the National Assisted Housing Management Association. NAHMA represents owners and managers of affordable housing and multifamily housing communities subject to the regulations of federal agencies. NAHMA was formed through a merger of the former National Advisory Council of HUD Management Agents and the National Federation of Associations of HUD Management Agents.

Meetings/Conferences:
Three Meetings Annually:

Publications:
NAHMA News. m. adv.
NAHP Update. q.

National Agri-Marketing Association *(1956)*
11020 King St., Suite 205
Overland Park, KS 66210
Tel: (913)491-6500 *Fax:* (913)491-6502
E-Mail: agrimktg@nama.org
Web Site: www.nama.org
Members: 2500 individuals
Staff: 12
Annual Budget: $1-2,000,000
Executive Vice President and Chief Executive Officer: Eldon White
Director, Communications and Operations: Jenny Pickett

Historical Note
Originated as the Chicago Area Agricultural Advertising Association with 39 charter members. In 1963 the name was changed to the National Agricultural Advertising and Marketing Association, and the present name was assumed in 1973. Membership: $100/year, average (individual).

Meetings/Conferences:
Annual Meetings: Spring/1,500

Publications:
Leader Newsletter. m.
Agri-Marketing Magazine. m.
Marketing Services Guide and NAM Directory. a.

National Agricultural Aviation Association *(1967)*
1005 E St. SE
Washington, DC 20003
Tel: (202)546-5722 *Fax:* (202)546-5726
E-Mail: information@agaviation.org
Web Site: www.agaviation.org
Members: 1200cropsprayers&alliedcompanies
Staff: 7
Annual Budget: $1-2,000,000
Executive Director: Andrew D. Moore
Assistant Executive Director: Peggy Knizner

Historical Note
Formerly (1971) National Aerial Applicators Association. Membership: $400/year (operator member).

Meetings/Conferences:
Annual Meetings: December

Publications:
Agricultural Aviation. 6/year. adv.

National Air Carrier Association *(1962)*
1000 Wilson Blvd., Suite 1700
Arlington, VA 22209
Tel: (703)358-8060 *Fax:* (703)358-8070
Web Site: www.naca.cc
Members: 15 companies
Staff: 4
Annual Budget: $500-1,000,000
President and Chief Executive Officer: Ronald N. Priddy
Director, Government Affairs: Paul H. Doell

Historical Note
Members are U.S.-certificated scheduled and charter airlines.

National Air Duct Cleaners Association *(1989)*
1518 K St. NW, Suite 503
Washington, DC 20005
Tel: (202)737-2926 *Fax:* (202)347-8847
E-Mail: info@nadca.com
Web Site: www.nadca.com
Members: 900 + companies
Staff: 4
Annual Budget: $1-2,000,000
Executive Director: John Schulte
Director, Publications: Jennifer Harbel
Director, Communications: Sara Wiltshire

Historical Note
NADCA, the trade association of the air duct cleaning industry, was established to raise the ethical standards and cleaning procedures within the industry and to educate the public on the need for clean indoor air. Has developed standards for the industry and a certification program. Membership: $495-695/year.

Publications:
NADCA Annual Buyers Guide. a. adv.
NADCA Annual Report. a.
Quality Through Knowledge Update. bi-m.
DucTales magazine. bi-m. adv.

National Air Filtration Association *(1980)*
P.O. Box 68639
Virginia Beach, VA 23471
Tel: (757)313-7400 *Fax:* (757)497-1895
E-Mail: nafa@nafahq.org
Web Site: www.nafahq.org
Members: 20 individuals
Staff: 7
Annual Budget: $250-500,000
Executive Director: Alan C. Veeck, CAFS

Historical Note
Members are companies selling and/or servicing air filtration equipment.

Meetings/Conferences:
Annual Meetings: early Fall

Publications:
Air Media. q. adv.
Yearbook. As needed.
Membership Directory. q.

National Air Traffic Controllers Association *(1987)*
1325 Massachusetts Ave. NW
Washington, DC 20005
Tel: (202)628-5451 *Fax:* (202)628-5767
Web Site: www.natca.org
Members: 15000 individuals
Staff: 43
Annual Budget: $10-25,000,000
Director, Strategic Planning/Policy: Jose Ceballos
President: Patrick Forrey
Chief of Staff: Adell Humphreys
Director, Political and Legislative Affairs: Ken Montoya
Director, Communications: Courtney Portner
Executive Vice President: Paul Rinaldi
Director, Labor Relations: Bob Taylor
Director, Membership: Lew Zietz

Historical Note
NATCA represents over 18,000 air traffic controllers, engineers and other safety aviation related professionals. NATCA is a federal sector labor union, and a direct affiliate of the AFL-CIO. Membership: $50/year (associate); 1.5% base pay/year (active); $500/year (company).

Meetings/Conferences:
Biennial Conventions: Even Years

Publications:
The Air Traffic Controller. bi-m.
ATC Safety Net. q.
Calendar. a.
Annual Report.
NATCA Insider. bi-w.
NATCA Facility Representative Bulletin. bi-w.

National Air Transportation Association *(1940)*
4226 King St.
Alexandria, VA 22302
Tel: (703)845-9000 *Fax:* (703)845-8176
Toll Free: (800)808 - 6282
E-Mail: info@nata.aero
Web Site: www.nata.aero/
Members: 2000 air carriers & airport service organizations
Staff: 20
Annual Budget: $2-5,000,000
President: James K. Coyne
Vice President, Membership, Marketing and Communications: David Almy
Vice President, Government and Industry Affairs: Eric Byer
Vice President and Chief Financial Officer: Alan Darrow
Manager, Meetings and Conventions: Diane Gleason

Historical Note
Established December, 1940 as the National Air Training Association and became the National Aviation Trades Association in 1946. In 1968 the Association of Commuter Airlines merged with the National Air Taxi Conference and changed its name to the National Air Transportation Conferences. In 1974 the National Aviation Trades Association merged with NATC and the association assumed its present name. Sponsors the National Air Transportation Foundation.

Meetings/Conferences:
Annual Meetings: Spring
2007 – Orlando, FL/March 20-

Publications:
Legislative Report. 20/yr.
Aviation Business Journal. q. adv.
Regulatory Report. 20/yr.
Aviation Businesses and the Services They Provide. a.
Industry Compensation Survey. a.
Annual Report. a.

National Aircraft Finance Association *(1969)*
P.O. Box 1570
Edgewater, MD 21037
Tel: (410)571-1740 *Fax:* (410)571-1780
E-Mail: info@nafa-us.org
Web Site: www.nafa-us.org
Members: 70 lendinginstitutions
Executive Director: Karen C. Griggs

Historical Note
NAFA members are lending institutions involved in aircraft financing. Membership: $500/yr.

Meetings/Conferences:
Annual Meetings: May

National Aircraft Resale Association
320 King St., Suite 250
Alexandria, VA 22314-4
Tel: (703)671-8273 *Fax:* (703)671-5848
E-Mail: nara@nara-dealers.com
Web Site: www.nara-dealers.com
Members: 105 companies
Staff: 2
President: Susan L. Sheets

Historical Note
NARA members are brokers and resellers specializing in pre-owned aircraft. Associate membership is available for firms who supply services or materials to the industry.

National Alarm Association of America *(1984)*
P.O. Box 3409
Dayton, OH 45401-3409
Toll Free: (800)283 - 6285
E-Mail: info@naaa.org
Web Site: www.naaa.org
Members: 300 companies; 50 associate companies
Staff: 2
Annual Budget: $10-25,000
President: Gene D. Riddlebaugh
Historical Note
Incorporated in Los Angeles, CA. Members are small alarm dealers. Membership: $100/year.
Publications:
Counterforce. a.

National Alcohol Beverage Control Association *(1938)*
4401 Ford Ave.
Suite 700
Alexandria, VA 22302-1473
Tel: (703)578-4200 *Fax:* (703)820-3551
Web Site: www.nabca.org
Members: 18 state agencies, 175 companies
Staff: 27
Annual Budget: $1-2,000,000
President and Chief Executive Officer: James M. Sgueo
Executive Assistant: Dixie Jamison
Vice President, Administration, and Chief Financial Officer: Patricia K. LaCava
Historical Note
Members include control jurisdictions, supplier members and industry trade associations.
Meetings/Conferences:
Annual Meetings: Spring
2007 - La Quinta, CA(La Quinta Resort)/May 16-20/850
Publications:
CONTACTS - Membership Directory. a.
NABCA NewsGram. bi-m.

National ALEC Association/ Prepaid Communications Association
3050 K St.
Suite 400
Washington, DC 20007-5108
Tel: (202)342-8812
E-Mail: info@nala-pca.org
Web Site: www.nala-pca.org
Office Administrator: Torian Meals
Historical Note
NALA/PCA represents local exchange carriers, long distance distributors, and other companies.

National Alfalfa Alliance *(2003)*
100 N. Fruitland, Suite B
Kennewick, WA 99336
Tel: (509)585-6798 *Fax:* (509)585-2671
E-Mail: agmgt@agmgt.com
Web Site: www.alfalfa.org
Members: 900 individuals
Staff: 3
Annual Budget: $100-250,000
Executive Director: Rod Christensen
Historical Note
Supersedes Alfalfa Council (1953-2003). Members are alfalfa seed growers, genetic suppliers, and university/extension, allied industries, and consumers.
Meetings/Conferences:
Annual Meetings: Winter/300-550
Publications:
Alfalfa Talk. q.

National Alliance for Hispanic Health *(1974)*
1501 16th St. NW
Washington, DC 20036-1401
Tel: (202)387-5000 *Fax:* (202)797-4353
E-Mail: alliance@hispanichealth.org
Web Site: www.hispanichealth.org
Members: 1200 organizations and individuals
Staff: 30
Annual Budget: $2-5,000,000
President and Chief Executive Officer: Jane L. Delgado, Ph.D.
Historical Note
Founded as National Coalition of Hispanic Mental Health and Human Services Organizations; became National Coalition of Hispanic Health and Human Services Organizations in 1986, and assumed its current name in 2000. Formed to expand and improve services, research, and training opportunities for the advancement of health status and quality of life of Hispanics in the U.S. Membership: $75/year (individual); $50-250/year (organization).
Publications:
The Reporter. q. adv.

National Alliance for Media Arts and Culture *(1980)*
145 Ninth St., Suite 250
San Francisco, CA 94103
Tel: (415)431-1391 *Fax:* (415)431-1392
E-Mail: namac@namac.org
Web Site: www.namac.org
Members: 350 media arts centers
Staff: 4
Annual Budget: $250-500,000
Co-Director: Helen DeMichiel
Co-Director: Jack Walsh
Historical Note
Members are non-profit media arts centers, institutions and individuals with an interest in media arts. Formerly (1992) the National Alliance of Media Arts Centers. Membership fees: assessed by organizational budget; range from $75-$450/year.
Meetings/Conferences:
Annual Meetings: 400
2007 - Austin, TX/Oct. 17-20
Publications:
MAIN journal. q.
BULLETin newsletter (online). m.
A Closer Look. a.

National Alliance for Musical Theatre *(1985)*
520 Eighth Ave., Suite 301
New York, NY 10018
Tel: (212)714-6668 *Fax:* (212)714-0469
E-Mail: info@namt.net
Web Site: www.namt.net
Members: 100 theatres and organizations
Executive Director: Kathy Evans
Historical Note
NAMT members are theatres and professional drama organizations with an interest in the development of stage musicals.
Meetings/Conferences:
Annual Meetings: Spring
Publications:
Directory. a.

National Alliance for Youth Sports *(1981)*
2050 Vista Pkwy.
West Palm Beach, FL 33411
Tel: (561)684-1141 *Fax:* (561)684-2546
Toll Free: (800)729 - 2057
E-Mail: nays@nays.org
Web Site: www.nays.org
Members: 150000 individuals
Staff: 25
Annual Budget: $1-2,000,000
President: Fred C. Engh
Vice President, Community Relations: Lisa Licata
Vice President, Membership Programs: Emmy Martinez
Historical Note
Formerly (1997) National Youth Sport Coaches Association, NAYS sponsors research and education programs to improve the quality of sports for youth. A national certification program is focused on giving coaches a clear understanding of the psychological, physical and social needs of children.
Meetings/Conferences:
Annual Meetings: August
Publications:
Youth Sports Coach. q. adv.

National Alliance of Black School Educators *(1970)*
310 Pennsylvania Ave. SE
Washington, DC 20003
Tel: (202)608-6310 *Fax:* (202)608-6319
Toll Free: (800)221 - 2654 Ext:
Web Site: www.nabse.org
Members: 4000 individuals
Staff: 6
Annual Budget: $2-5,000,000
Executive Director: Quentin Lawson
E-Mail: qlawson@nabse.org
Historical Note
Formerly (1970) the National Alliance of Black School Superintendents; assumed its current name in 1973. Membership: $100/year.
Meetings/Conferences:
Annual Meetings: Fall
Publications:
NABSE Research Journal. a.
NABSE News Briefs. 3/yr. adv.

National Alliance of Independent Crop Consultants *(1978)*
349 E. Nolley Dr.
Collierville, TN 38017
Tel: (901)861-0511 *Fax:* (901)861-0512
Web Site: www.naicc.org
Members: 500 individuals
Staff: 1
Annual Budget: $250-500,000
Executive Vice President: Allison Jones
Historical Note
Founded in 1978, NAICC is an outgrowth of the Southern Alliance of Independent Crop Consultants. Membership: $195/year (individual); $750-2,500/year (company).
Meetings/Conferences:
Annual Meetings: Winter
Publications:
Newsletter. m.
Membership Directory. a.

National Alliance of Nurse Practitioners *(1985)*
P.O. Box 40326
Washington, DC 20016
Tel: (202)675-6350
Members: 12 organizations
Staff: 1
Annual Budget: $10-25,000
Chairperson: Marie-Eileen Onieal
Historical Note
NANP is a coalition of national organizations with nurse practitioner constituencies. NANP promotes the public health through primary care, and promotes the visibility and unity of nurse practitioners as primary care providers. Has no paid officers or full-time staff. Membership: $750/year (organization); $500/year (associate); $1,000/year (sustaining).
Meetings/Conferences:
Semi-annual Meetings: April and November

National Alliance of Postal and Federal Employees *(1913)*
1628 11th St. NW
Washington, DC 20001
Tel: (202)939-6325 *Fax:* (202)939-6389
E-Mail: headquarters@napfe.org
Web Site: www.napfe.com
Members: 35000 individuals
Staff: 51
Annual Budget: $2-5,000,000
President: James M. McGee
Secretary: David Lage
Historical Note
Established as the National Alliance of Postal Employees in 1913 with the immediate purpose of preventing elimination of blacks from railway mail service; became the first industrial Union in the U.S. in 1923 when it opened its membership to any postal employee who desired to join; assumed its present name in 1965 when it expanded its membership eligibility requirements to include federal employees. Supports the National Alliance for Political Action.
Meetings/Conferences:
Biennial Meetings: even years/Summer/1,500-2,000

Publications:
National Alliance Magazine. m. adv.
Legislative Newsletter. q.
Credit Union Newsletter.

National Alliance of Preservation Commissions *(1983)*
P.O. Box 1605
Athens, GA 30603
Tel: (706)542-4731
E-Mail: napc@arches.uga.edu
Web Site: www.uga.edu/sed/pso/programs/napc/napc.htm
Members: 400 individuals
Staff: 1
Annual Budget: $50-100,000
Executive Director: Drane Wilkinson

Historical Note
NADC assists local preservation commissions and review boards through education, advocacy and training. Serves as a bridge between commissions and other preservation organizations. Membership fee: $25-125/year.

Publications:
Alliance Review. q.

National Alliance of State and Territorial AIDS Directors *(1992)*
444 N. Capitol St. NW, Suite 339
Washington, DC 20001
Tel: (202)434-8090 *Fax:* (202)434-8092
Web Site: www.nastad.org
Members: 59
Staff: 20
Annual Budget: $1-2,000,000
Executive Director: Julie M. Scofield
E-Mail: jscofield@nastad.org
Director, Operations: Patrick Blais
Director, Government Relations: Laura Hanen
E-Mail: lhanen@nastad.org

Historical Note
NASTAD provides support to directors of HIV/AIDS programs within the state and territorial health departments. Membership, composed of 59 individuals, consists of the individual AIDS directors of each of the 50 states and of the U.S. territories and the District of Columbia. Membership fee varies.

Meetings/Conferences:
Annual Meetings: *Spring/70*

Publications:
NASTAD HIV Prevention Update. bi-m.

National Alliance of Statewide Preservation Organizations *(1986)*
Historic Landmarks Foundation of Indiana
340 W. Michigan St.
Indianapolis, IN 46202-3204
Tel: (317)639-4534
Toll Free: (800)450 - 4534
Members: 48 organizations
Contact: Tina Connor

Historical Note
NASPO members are state historic preservation organizations. Has no permanent office or paid staff.

Meetings/Conferences:
Semi-annual Meetings: Fall and Winter

National AMBUCS *(1922)*
4285 Regency Ct.
High Point, NC 27265
Tel: (336)852-0052 *Fax:* (336)852-6830
E-Mail: ambucs@ambucs.org
Web Site: www.ambucs.org
Members: 5500 individuals
Staff: 6
Annual Budget: $500-1,000,000
Executive Director: J. Joseph Copeland

Historical Note
Founded as National Association of American Business Clubs, AMBUCS is a national service organization dedicated to creating opportunity and independence for people with disabilities. Programs include community service projects, scholarships for therapists, and Amtryke, the therapeutic tricycle for children with disabilities.

Meetings/Conferences:
Annual Meetings: *Summer*

Publications:
The AMBUC Leader. m.
The AMBUC Magazine. q. adv.

National American Indian Court Judges Association *(1968)*
3618 Reder St.
Rapid City, SD 57702
Tel: (605)342-4804 *Fax:* (605)719-9357
E-Mail: mail@naicja.org
Web Site: www.naicja.org
Members: 150 individuals
Staff: 1
Executive Director: Chuck Robertson
E-Mail: mail@naicja.org

Historical Note
The mission of NAICJA, as a national representative association, is to strengthen and enhance tribal justice systems.

Publications:
NAICJA News. q.

National American Indian Housing Council *(1974)*
50 F St. NW
Suite 3300
Washington, DC 20001
Tel: (202)789-1754 *Fax:* (202)789-1758
Toll Free: (800)284 - 9165
E-Mail: housing@naihc.net
Web Site: www.naihc.net
Members: 456 agencies
Staff: 35
Annual Budget: $5-10,000,000
Director, Communications: Jane DeMarines

Historical Note
NAIHC members are tribes on their tribally designated housing entities.

Meetings/Conferences:
Annual Meetings: *Summer*

Publications:
Native American Housing News. 6/year.
Quick Facts. bi-m.
Federal Monitor. bi-m.

National American Legion Press Association *(1923)*
P.O. Box 1184
Decatur, GA 30031-1184
Tel: (404)377-5602
Web Site: www.nalpa.legion.org
Members: 2000 individuals
Staff: 1
Annual Budget: under $10,000
Executive Director: George W. Hooten

Historical Note
Formerly (1973) American Legion Press Association.

Meetings/Conferences:
Annual Meetings: *With American Legion*

Publications:
NALPA News-Letter. q.

National Animal Control Association *(1978)*
P.O. Box 480851
Kansas City, MO 64148-0851
Tel: (913)768-1319 *Fax:* (913)768-1378
E-Mail: naca@interserv.com
Web Site: www.nacanet.org
Members: 4000 individuals
Staff: 5
Annual Budget: $100-250,000
Executive Director: John Mays

Historical Note
Members are animal shelters, public health organizations, government officials, humane societies, and individuals concerned with animal care and control. Membership: $35/year (individual); $125/year (organization).

Meetings/Conferences:
Annual Meetings: *May*

Publications:
NACA News. bi-m. adv.

National Antique and Art Dealers Association of America *(1954)*
220 E. 57th St.
New York, NY 10022
Tel: (212)826-9707 *Fax:* (212)832-9493
Web Site: www.NAADAA.org
Members: 40 individuals
Annual Budget: $10-25,000
Director: Mark A. Shaffer

Historical Note
A member of the Confederation Internationale des Negociants en Oeuvres d'Art. Formerly New York Antique and Art Dealers Association, Inc. NAADAA works to safeguard the interests of buyers, sellers, and collectors of antiques and art. Has no paid officers or full-time staff; officers change biennially.

Publications:
Membership Directory. bien.

National Apartment Association *(1939)*
201 N. Union St., Suite 200
Alexandria, VA 22314-2642
Tel: (703)518-6141 *Fax:* (703)518-6191
Web Site: www.naahq.org
Members: 32000 individuals
Staff: 36
Annual Budget: $5-10,000,000
Executive Vice President: Douglas S. Culkin, CAE
E-Mail: Doug@naahq.com
Director, Meetings and Expositions: Jeremy Figoten
Senior Vice President, Administration: Maureen Lambe
E-Mail: maureen@naahq.org
Director, Database Management: Rene Shonerd
Vice President, Government Affairs: Barbara Vassallo
E-Mail: barbara@naahq.org

Historical Note
Established as National Apartment Owners Association, it assumed its present name in 1967. A federation of local and state associations of owners, builders, investors and managers of rental property. Awards the CAS ("Certified Apartment Supplier"), CAMT ("Certified Apartment Maintenance Technician") and CAPS ("Certified Apartment Property Supervisor") designations. Sponsors the NAA Political Action Committee and the NAA Education Foundation.

Meetings/Conferences:
Annual Meetings: *Summer*
2007 – Las Vegas, NV(Mandalay Bay)/June 28-30

Publications:
Apartment Economics. m.
Leadership Directory. a.
Units magazine. m. adv.
Income and Expense Survey. a.

National Appliance Parts Suppliers Association *(1966)*
4015 W. Marshall Ave.
Longview, TX 75604
Tel: (903)759-3983
E-Mail: info@napsaweb.org
Web Site: www.napsaweb.org
Members: 250 companies
Staff: 4
Annual Budget: $100-250,000
Contact: Sherry Harrell

Historical Note
Provides distributors of replacement parts for major home appliances (both non-OEM and OEM) with information and services. Sponsors industry trade show. Emphasis on supplier relations/activities to promote mutual understanding.

Meetings/Conferences:
Annual Meetings: *Spring/400*

Publications:
NAPSA Results. q.

National Appliance Service Association *(1949)*
P.O. Box 2514
Kokomo, IN 46904
Tel: (765)453-1820 *Fax:* (765)453-1895
E-Mail: nasahq@abcglobal.net
Web Site: www.nasa1.org
Members: 200 companies
Staff: 1

Annual Budget: $50-100,000
Executive Director: Carrie Giannakos

Historical Note

Members are owners of portable small appliance repair centers. Appliance manufacturers and industry suppliers also participate. Membership: $250/year (company).

Meetings/Conferences:

Annual Meetings: June

Publications:

Annual Membership Directory. a. adv.
NASA Newsletter. m. adv.

National Aquaculture Council

Historical Note

An affiliate of National Fisheries Institute, which provides administrative support.

National Arborist Association

Historical Note

Became Tree Care Industry Association in 2003.

National Armored Car Association *(1929)*

9532 Stevebrook Rd.
Fairfax, VA 22032
Tel: (703)426-1976 *Fax:* (703)978-2399
Web Site: www.nationalarmoredcar.com
Members: 5 companies
Staff: 1
Annual Budget: $50-100,000
Executive Director: Larry Sabbath

Historical Note

Absorbed the Armored Transportation Institute in 1993. Membership: annual dues vary based on company size.

Publications:

Newsletter. q.

National Art Education Association *(1947)*

1916 Association Dr.
Reston, VA 20191-1590
Tel: (703)860-8000 *Fax:* (703)860-2960
E-Mail: thatfield@naea-reston.org
Web Site: www.naea-reston.org
Members: 18000 individuals
Staff: 15
Annual Budget: $1-2,000,000
Executive Director: Dr. Thomas A. Hatfield
Deputy Executive Director: Dr. Larry N. Peeno

Historical Note

Founded in 1947 by the merger of Eastern Arts Association, Pacific Arts Association, Southeastern Arts Association and Western Arts Association with the Art Department of the National Education Association. NAEA is a leading professional association for educators in the visual arts at all instructional levels. Purpose is to advance art education through professional development, service, advancement of knowledge and leadership. Membership: $50/year (affiliated states).

Meetings/Conferences:

Annual Meetings: Spring
2007 – New York, NY/March 14-18
2008 – New Orleans, LA/March 26-30
2009 – Minneapolis, MN/Apr. 17-21
2010 – Washington, DC/March 25-29

Publications:

NAEA Advisory. q.
Studies in Art Education. q.
NAEA News. bi-m. adv.
Art Education. bi-m. adv.

National Art Materials Trade Association *(1950)*

15806 Brookway Dr., Suite 300
Huntersville, NC 28078
Tel: (704)892-6244 *Fax:* (704)892-6247
E-Mail: info@namta.org
Web Site: www.namta.org
Members: 1200 companies
Staff: 6
Executive Director: Katharine Coffey

Historical Note

NAMTA is an international association of manufacturers, importers, publishers, manufacturer's representatives, distributors/wholesales, and retailers of fine and commercial art materials.

Meetings/Conferences:

Annual Meetings: May
2007 – Chicago, IL(Navy Pier)/Apr. 19-21/3500

Publications:

Convention Directory. a. adv.
News and Views. 10/yr. adv.
Membership Directory, Who's Who in Art Materials. a. adv.

National Asphalt Pavement Association *(1955)*

NAPA Bldg.
5100 Forbes Blvd.
Lanham, MD 20706
Tel: (301)731-4748 *Fax:* (301)731-4621
Toll Free: (888)468 - 6499
E-Mail: napa@hotmix.org
Web Site: www.hotmix.org
Members: 1100 companies
Staff: 23
Annual Budget: $2-5,000,000
President: Mike Acott
Vice President, Marketing and Public Affairs: Margaret Cervarich
Associate Director, Awards and Marketing: Tracy Christie
Director, Environmental and Safety Services: Una Connolly
Vice President, Environment, Health and Safety: Gary Fore
Vice President, Government Affairs: Jay Hansen
Vice President, Conventions and Meetings: Nancy Lawler, CMP
Vice President, Research and Technology: Dave Newcomb
Vice President, Finance and Operations: Carolyn Wilson

Historical Note

Founded as the National Bituminous Concrete Association; assumed its present name in 1965. Members are producers of hot mix asphalt for paving roads, airfields and other surfaces.

Meetings/Conferences:

Annual Meetings: Winter
2007 – San Francisco, CA(San Francisco Marriott)/Feb. 18-21
2009 – San Diego, CA

Publications:

HMAT. bi-m. adv.
Action News. bi-w.
Technical & Educational Publications. irreg.

National Assembly of Health and Human Services Organizations

Historical Note

Became National Human Services Assembly in 2005.

National Assembly of State Arts Agencies *(1974)*

1029 Vermont Ave. NW, Second Floor
Washington, DC 20005
Tel: (202)347-6352 *Fax:* (202)737-0526
E-Mail: nasaa@nasaa-arts.org
Web Site: www.nasaa-arts.org
Members: 55 agencies
Staff: 12
Annual Budget: $1-2,000,000
Chief Executive Officer: Jonathan Katz
Director, Policy, Research and Evaluation: Kelly J. Barsdate
Managing Director: W. Dennis Dewey
Manager, Meetings and Events: Sharon Gee

Historical Note

Founded June 1968 as the North American Assembly of State and Provincial Arts Agencies and affiliated with the Associated Councils of the Arts. The organization became independent and assumed its present name in 1976. Members are state agencies receiving appropriations from their states and designated by federal legislation to receive funding from the National Endowment for the Arts.

Meetings/Conferences:

Annual Meetings: Fall/500

Publications:

NASAA Membership Directory. m.
Legislative Appropriations Annual Survey. a.

National Assistance Management Association

Historical Note

See National Grants Management Association.

National Associated CPA Firms

136 S. Keowee St.
Dayton, OH 45402
Tel: (937)222-1024 *Fax:* (937)222-5794
E-Mail: email@nacpaf.com
Web Site: www.nacpaf.com
Members: 50 firms
Staff: 7
Executive Director: Kim Fantaci
E-Mail: email@nacpaf.com

Meetings/Conferences:

Annual Meetings: Summer
2007 – Minneapolis, MN(Radisson)/July 18-22/100

Publications:

Newsletter. q.

National Association for Armenian Studies and Research *(1955)*

395 Concord Ave.
Belmont, MA 02478-3049
Tel: (617)489-1610 *Fax:* (617)484-1759
E-Mail: hq@naasr.org
Web Site: www.naasr.org
Members: 1200 individuals
Staff: 3
Annual Budget: $100-250,000
Administrative Director: Sandra L. Jurigian

Historical Note

Founded in 1955 to sponsor and promote educational, cultural and other activities and projects to foster and promote Armenian studies, research, and publications. Membership: $50/year (individual); $40/year (senior citizen); $35/year (student); $75/year (family).

Meetings/Conferences:

Annual Meetings: Fall (3rd weekend in November at Nat'l Headquarters/75-100

Publications:

Journal of Armenian Studies. semi-a. adv.
NAASR Newsletter. q. adv.

National Association for Bilingual Education *(1975)*

1030 15th St. NW, Suite 470
Washington, DC 20005-1503
Tel: (202)898-1829 *Fax:* (202)789-2866
E-Mail: nabe@nabe.org
Web Site: www.nabe.org
Members: 5000 individuals
Staff: 10
Annual Budget: $2-5,000,000
Executive Director: James Crawford
Director, Public Affairs: Carmella Baccari

Historical Note

NABE is a professional association which represents the interests of non-English background children and families. Members are professional educators, concerned citizens and community leaders who wish to promote bilingual education. Membership: $60/year (individual); $125/year (organization/company).

Meetings/Conferences:

Annual Meetings: Winter

Publications:

NABE Journal of Research and Practice. q. adv.
NABE News Magazine. adv.

National Association for Biomedical Research *(1979)*

818 Connecticut Ave. NW, Suite 900
Washington, DC 20006
Tel: (202)857-0540 *Fax:* (202)659-1902
E-Mail: info@nabr.org
Web Site: www.nabr.org
Members: 300 organizations
Staff: 6
Annual Budget: $500-1,000,000
President: Frankie L. Trull

Historical Note

Founded as the Research Animal Alliance; became (1981) Association for Biomedical Research before absorbing the National Society for Medical Research and assuming its present name in 1985. Members are institutions, professional societies and companies that use animals in biomedical research and testing. The association's purpose is to keep members informed of legislative and regulatory activity in the field. Membership: $600-2,400/year (nonprofit institutions, dependent on budget); $600-40,000/year (industry, dependent on budget/sales).

Meetings/Conferences:
Annual Meetings: April

Publications:
NABR Update. 2/m.
NABR Alert. irreg.
Annual Report. a.
State Laws Concerning the Use of Animals in Research. bien.

National Association for Black Geologists and Geophysicists *(1981)*
4212 San Felipe, Suite 420
Houston, TX 77027-2902
E-Mail: nabgg_us@hotmail.com
Web Site: www.nabgg.com
Members: 250 individuals
Secretary: Aisha Ragas

Historical Note
NABGG members are geologists and geophysicists employed by major and independent oil companies, academics, students and others with an interest in the organization's goals.

Meetings/Conferences:
Annual Meetings: in conjunction with GSA annual meeting

Publications:
Newsletter. irreg.

National Association for Business Teacher Education *(1927)*

Historical Note
A division of the National Business Education Association.

National Association for Campus Activities *(1960)*
13 Harbison Way
Columbia, SC 29212-3401
Tel: (803)732-6222 *Fax:* (803)749-1047
Toll Free: (800)845 - 2338
E-Mail: info@naca.org
Web Site: www.naca.org
Members: 1100 schools, 600 agencies/bureaus
Staff: 24
Annual Budget: $2-5,000,000
Executive Director: Alan Davis
E-Mail: aland@naca.org
Manager, Member Services: Gordon Schell
E-Mail: gordons@naca.org
Director, Educational and Event Services: Dawn Thomas
E-Mail: dawnt@naca.org
Director, Communications and Marketing: Erin Wilson

Historical Note
NACA's members are colleges and universities. Its purpose is to assist in marketing entertainment services to educational institutions and providing student leadership development programs and services. Membership: $368-843/year (school); $314-632/year (associate).

Meetings/Conferences:
Annual Meetings: February/2,500
2007 – Nashville, TN(Gaylord Opryland)/Feb. 17-21/2500

Publications:
Campus Activities Programming. m. adv.

National Association for Check Safekeeping *(1981)*

Historical Note
An affiliate of the National Automated Clearing House Association, which provides administrative support.

National Association for Chicana and Chicano Studies *(1972)*
P.O. Box 720052
San Jose, CA 95172-0052
Tel: (408)924-5310
Web Site: www.naccs.org
Staff: 1
Executive Director: Julia Curry Rodriguez, Ph.D.

Historical Note
Founded as National Association for Chicano Studies; assumed its current name in 1995. NACCS members are academics with an interest in the study of Chicano culture. Membership: $45/year (individual); $100/year (organization).

Meetings/Conferences:
Annual Meetings: Spring

Publications:
Noticias de NACCS. q. adv.
Proceedings. a.

National Association for College Admission Counseling *(1937)*
1631 Prince St.
Alexandria, VA 22314-2818
Tel: (703)836-2222 *Fax:* (703)836-8015
Toll Free: (800)822 - 6285
E-Mail: info@nacac.com
Web Site: www.nacacnet.org
Members: 7050 individuals
Staff: 36
Annual Budget: $5-10,000,000
Executive Director: Joyce E. Smith
Deputy Executive Director: Anita Bollt
Director, National College Fairs: Gregory Ferguson
E-Mail: gferguson@nacac.com
Director, Government Relations: David Hawkins
E-Mail: dhawkins@nacac.com
Director, Communications, Publications and Technology: Shanda T. Ivory
E-Mail: sivory@nacac.com

Historical Note
Formerly (1995) National Association of College Admissions Counselors, (1968) Association of College Admissions Counselors, and (1939) Association of College Representatives. Membership: $60/year (individual); $160/year (high school); $285/year (college).

Meetings/Conferences:
Annual Meetings: Fall
2007 – Austin, TX(Austin Convention Center)/Sept. 27-29
2008 – Seattle, WA(Washington State Convention Center)/Sept. 25-27
2009 – Baltimore, MD(Baltimore Convention Center)/Sept. 24-26
2010 – St. Louis, MO(America's Center)/Sept. 30-Oct. 2
2011 – New Orleans, LA(Morial Convention Center)/Sept. 22-24
2012 – Denver, CO(Colorado Convention Center)/Oct. 4-6

Publications:
NACAC Membership Directory. a. adv.
Journal of College Admission. q.
NACAC Bulletin. m. adv.

National Association for Community Mediation *(1994)*
1527 New Hampshire Ave. NW
Washington, DC 20036
Tel: (202)667-9700 *Fax:* (202)667-8629
E-Mail: nafcm@nafcm.org
Web Site: www.nafcm.org
Members: 525 individuals
Staff: 4
Annual Budget: $500-1,000,000
Executive Director: Linda Baron
E-Mail: lbaron@nafcm.org
Manager, Membership and Programs: Erika Acerra
Associate Director: Joanne Galindo
E-Mail: jgalindo@nafcm.org

Historical Note
NAFCM supports the maintenance and growth of community-based mediation program and processes; presents a compelling voice in appropriate policy-making, legislative, professional, and other arenas; and encourages the development and sharing of resources for these efforts. Members are community mediation programs, volunteer mediators, and other organizations and individuals that support commmunity mediation. Membership: $30/year (individual); $25-300/year (organization/company).

Publications:
Face to Face Curriculum. a.
The State of Community Mediation. q. adv.
Community Mediation Center Self-Assessment Manual.
Community Mediation Center Start-up Packet.

National Association for Core Curriculum *(1953)*

Historical Note
An outgrowth of the National Conference of Core Teachers, first held in Morgantown, West Virginia on the campus of West Virginia University on October 30-31, 1953. The present name was adopted in 1966. Promotes integrative/interdisciplinary approaches to education at all levels, elementary school through college. Membership: $10/year.

Meetings/Conferences:
Annual Meetings: Fall, usually in conjuction with other educational organizations

National Association for County Community and Economic Development *(1978)*
2025 M St. NW, Suite 800
Washington, DC 20036-3309
Tel: (202)367-1149 *Fax:* (202)367-2149
E-Mail: john_murphy@nacced.org
Web Site: www.nacced.org
Members: 130 individuals
Staff: 3
Executive Director: John C. Murphy
Director, Community and Economic Development: Sarah Nusser

Historical Note
NACCED members are directors and staff members of county community and economic development agencies.

Meetings/Conferences:
Annual Meetings: Fall

Publications:
NACCED Insights Newsletter. bi-m.
NACCED Alert. bi-m.
NACCED Directory. semi-a.

National Association for Court Management *(1985)*
National Center for State Courts
300 Newport Ave.
Williamsburg, VA 23187
Tel: (757)259-1841 *Fax:* (757)259-1520
Toll Free: (800)616 - 6165
E-Mail: nacm@ncsc.dni.us
Web Site: www.nacmnet.org
Members: 2400 individuals
Annual Budget: $500-1,000,000
Executive Director: John Ramsey

Historical Note
NACM members are clerks of court, court administrators and others serving in a court management capacity. NACM's purpose is to increase the proficiency of judicial administrators through the exchange of information. Membership: $75/year (individual); $300/year (organization).

Meetings/Conferences:
Annual Meetings: Spring-Summer

Publications:
The Court Manager. q. adv.
Court Communique. q.

National Association for Developmental Education *(1976)*
2447 Tiffin Ave., Suite 207
Findlay, OH 45840
Tel: (877)233-9455 *Fax:* (567)202-4385
E-Mail: office@nade.net
Web Site: www.nade.net
Members: 3000 individuals
Staff: 5
Annual Budget: $100-250,000
Database Manager: Carol O'Shea

Historical Note
Executives change annually. Membership: $50/year (individual); $1,000/year (organization/company).

Meetings/Conferences:
Annual Meetings: February or March

Publications:
Journal of Developmental Education. 3/year. adv.
NADE Newsletter. 3/year. adv.

National Association for Drama Therapy *(1979)*
15 Post Side Lane
Pittsford, NY 14534
Tel: (585)381-5618 *Fax:* (585)383-1474

E-Mail: nadt.office@nadt.org
Web Site: www.nadt.org
Members: 400 individuals
Staff: 1
Annual Budget: $25-50,000
Office Manager: Sue Leo

Historical Note

Established and incorporated in New York. Members are professionals trained in theatre arts, psychology and psychotherapy making use of drama/theatre processes to achieve therapeutic goals. Awards the designation R.D.T. (Registered Drama Therapist) to individuals meeting professional standards. Membership: $55-115/year.

Meetings/Conferences:
Annual Meetings: November

Publications:
Monographs on Drama Therapy. a.
Dramascope Newsletter. bi-a.
Membership List. a.
Proceedings of Annual Conference. a.

National Association for Environmental Management *(1990)*
1612 K. St. NW, Suite 1102
Washington, DC 20006
Tel: (202)986-6616 *Fax:* (202)530-4408
Toll Free: (800)391 - 6236
E-Mail: programs@naem.org
Web Site: www.naem.org
Members: 1200 individuals
Staff: 3
Annual Budget: $250-500,000
Executive Director: Carol Singer Neuvelt
E-Mail: programs@naem.org

Historical Note

NAEM is dedicated to advancing the profession of environmental management and is the only national association created specifically to support the professional corporate and facility environmental manager. NAEM is composed of individuals who have responsibility for managing the environmental program of a corporation, institution, or individual facility. Primary activities include formal seminars and informal professional exchanges at the national and regional levels. NAEM focuses on information concerning emerging regulatory, technical and management issues which impact the professional environmental manager and the organizations they serve. Membership: $195/year (individual); $900-5,000/year, based on revenues (corporate); $750/year (non-profit & government).

Meetings/Conferences:
Annual Meetings: Fall

Publications:
Network News. bi-m.

National Association for Equal Opportunity in Higher Education *(1969)*
8701 Georgia Ave., Suite 200
Silver Spring, MD 20910
Tel: (301)650-2440 *Fax:* (301)495-3306
Web Site: www.nafeo.org/
Members: 118 institutions
Staff: 35
Annual Budget: $1-2,000,000
President and Chief Executive Officer: Lezli Baskerville, J.D.

Historical Note

Members are black colleges and universities united in an attempt to sensitize public policy makers and funders to the importance of enhancing the education of blacks. Membership: $10,000/year (organization).

Meetings/Conferences:
Annual Meetings: Spring/Washington, DC

Publications:
Profiles. a.
NAFEO Inroads. bi-m.
NAFEO Record-Calendar Directory. a. adv.
Black Excellence Magazine. bi-m. adv.
Proceedings of the National Conference. a.

National Association for Ethnic Studies *(1972)*
Western Washington University
516 High St., MS 9113
Bellingham, WA 98225
Tel: (360)650-2349 *Fax:* (360)650-2690
E-Mail: naes@www.edu
Web Site: www.ethnicstudies.org
Members: 225 individuals
Staff: 1
Annual Budget: $10-25,000
President: Larry Estrada

Historical Note

Promotes activities and scholarship in the field of ethnic studies. Formerly (1984) the National Association of Interdisciplinary Ethnic Studies. Membership: $35-85/year (individual, income contingent); $40/year (maximum-student/associate); $65/year (library/institution); $150/year (patron); $500 (lifetime).

Meetings/Conferences:
Annual Meetings: Spring

Publications:
Ethnic Studies Review. 2/year. adv.
Ethnic Reporter. 2/year. adv.

National Association for Family and Community Education *(1936)*
73 Cavalier Blvd., Suite 106
Florence, KY 41042
Tel: (859)525-6401 *Fax:* (859)525-6496
Toll Free: (877)712 - 4477
Web Site: www.nafce.org
Members: 20000 individuals
Staff: 1
Annual Budget: $500-1,000,000
Executive Secretary: Judith Jones
E-Mail: nafcehq@juno.com

Historical Note

FCE focuses on three major concerns: literacy, leadership, and the effects of television and other media on children.

Meetings/Conferences:
Annual Meetings: July

Publications:
Newsletter. 4/year.

National Association for Family Child Care *(1982)*
5202 Pinemont Dr.
Salt Lake City, UT 84123
Tel: (801)269-9338 *Fax:* (801)268-9507
E-Mail: nafcc@nafcc.org
Web Site: www.nafcc.org
Members: 7500 child care organizations
Staff: 13
Annual Budget: $250-500,000
Executive Director: Linda Geigle

Historical Note

Formerly (1993) the National Association for Family Day Care. Members are providers and users of family child care services. Operates an accreditation program for care providers. Membership: $25/year (individual); $50/year (association); $100/year (agency).

Meetings/Conferences:
Annual Meetings: Summer

Publications:
Perspective Newsletter. q. adv.

National Association for Girls and Women in Sport *(1899)*
1900 Association Dr.
Reston, VA 20191-1598
Tel: (703)476-3400
Toll Free: (800)213 - 7193 Ext: x450
E-Mail: nagws@aahperd.org
Web Site: www.nagws.org
Members: 4000 individuals
Staff: 3
Annual Budget: $250-500,000
Executive Director: Pamela Noakes

Historical Note

NAGWS is a member association of the American Alliance for Health, Physical Education, Recreation and Dance, and is the only national professional organization devoted exclusively to providing opportunities for girls and women in sport-related disciplines and careers. It is a non-profit, educational organization serving the needs of administrators, teachers, coaches, leaders and participants of sports programs for girls and women. Membership: $100/year.

Meetings/Conferences:
Annual Meetings: Spring, with AAHPERD

Publications:
GWS News. q. adv.

National Association for Government Training and Development *(1980)*
2516 Wertherson Lane
Raleigh, NC 27613-1700
Tel: (919)306-1787 *Fax:* (919)845-6922
E-Mail: go2nagtad@aol.com
Web Site: www.nagtad.org
Members: 78 individuals
Staff: 4
Annual Budget: $25-50,000
Executive Director: Jack Lemons

Historical Note

Founded as National Association of Government Training and Development Directors; assumed its current name in 1998. Membership: $150-$525/year (individual).

Meetings/Conferences:
Annual Meetings: Fall

National Association for Health and Fitness *(1979)*
c/o BANYS, 65 Niagara Sq., Room 607
Buffalo, NY 14202
Tel: (716)583-0521 *Fax:* (716)851-4309
E-Mail: wellness@city-buffalo.org
Web Site: www.physicalfitness.org
Members: 40 councils
Annual Budget: $250-500,000
Executive Director: Philip Haberstro

Historical Note

Founded as National Association of Governors' Councils on Physical Fitness and Sports; assumed its current name in 2000. Members are state and provincial governors' councils responsible for promoting physical fitness. Has no paid officers or full-time staff. Membership: $160/year (council); $125/year (corporate); $90/year (community organization); $45/year (individual).

Meetings/Conferences:
Annual Meetings: March
2007 – Anaheim, CA/Apr. 29-30

Publications:
National Employee Health-Fitness Day. adv.
State by State Newsletter. q. adv.

National Association for Health Care Recruitment *(1975)*
833 North Highland Ave., Suite 200
Orlando, FL 32803
Tel: (407)843-6981 *Fax:* (407)481-2825
E-Mail: fha@fha.org
Web Site: www.nahcr.com
Members: 1000 individuals
Staff: 2
Annual Budget: $500-1,000,000
Executive Director: Cathy Allman
Director, Marketing and Member Relations: Amy Allman

Historical Note

Established in 1975 as National Association for Nurse Recruiters; assumed its current name in 1984.

Meetings/Conferences:
Annual Meetings: Summer

Publications:
NAHCR Directions. bi-m. adv.
Recruitment Resources. a. adv.

National Association for Healthcare Quality *(1976)*
4700 W. Lake Ave.
Glenview, IL 60025-1485
Toll Free: (800)966 - 9392
E-Mail: info@nahq.org
Web Site: www.nahq.org
Members: 7000 individuals
Staff: 12
Annual Budget: $1-2,000,000
Executive Director: Diane Simmons, MPA
Manager, Education: Nicki LaCroix

Historical Note

Formerly (1992) National Association of Quality Assurance Professionals. NAHQ promotes continuous *improvement in quality in healthcare by providing educational and developmental opportunities for professionals at all management levels and within a variety of healthcare settings. Awards the CPHQ (Certified Professional in Healthcare Quality) designation to individuals who meet the requirements and pass an examiniation. Healthcare Quality Foundation and Healthcare Quality Certification Board are divisions of NAHQ. Membership: $100/year (individual); $325/year (institution).*

Meetings/Conferences:
Annual Meetings: Fall/2,500
2007 – Boston, MA/Sept. 9-12
2008 – Phoenix, AZ/Sept. 14-17

Publications:
Journal for Healthcare Quality. bi-m. adv.
NAHQ News Newsletter. q.
Directory. a.

National Association for Holistic Aromatherapy *(1990)*
3327 W. Indian Trail Rd., P.M.B 144
Spokane, WA 99208
Tel: (509)325-3419 *Fax:* (509)325-3479
E-Mail: info@naha.org
Web Site: www.naha.org
Members: 1600 individuals
Staff: 2
Annual Budget: $50-100,000
President: Michelle Miller

Historical Note
NAHA members are professional aromatherapists and others with an interest in the field. The organization's goals include maintaining high standards of aromatherapy education, establishing professional and ethical standards of practice, providing public education, and networking to stay abreast of current research. Membership: $45/year (friend); $100/year (professional); $100/year (business); $250/year (donor); $1000/year (grand donor).

Meetings/Conferences:
Biennial Meetings: even years/Fall

Publications:
Aromatherapy Journal. q. adv.
Source/Practitioner Directory Online. a. adv.

National Association for Home Care *(1982)*
228 Seventh St. SE
Washington, DC 20003
Tel: (202)547-7424 *Fax:* (202)547-3540
E-Mail: exec@nahc.org
Web Site: www.nahc.org
Members: 4000 agencies
Staff: 75
Annual Budget: $10-25,000,000
President: Val J. Halamandaris
Director, Publications: Margaret J. Cushman
E-Mail: pubs@nahc.org
Director, Meetings: Danielle Donaldson
E-Mail: meetings@nahc.org
Vice President, Exhibits: Ronald Everly
E-Mail: expo@nahc.org
Vice President, Operations: Kaliope Poulianos
E-Mail: membership@nahc.org
Vice President, Regulatory Affairs and Membership: Mary St. Pierre
E-Mail: regulatory@nahc.org

Historical Note
Members are concerned with the provision of health care and related services in the home and hospice services. Formerly (1982) National Association of Home Health Agencies. Merged with National Homecaring Council in 1986. Sponsors and supports the NAHC Congressional Action Committee.

Meetings/Conferences:
Annual Meetings: Fall

Publications:
Caring Magazine. m. adv.
NAHC Report Index and Archives. w. adv.
Health Care Reform Update. irreg.

National Association for Humanities Education *(1967)*
P.O. Box 777
Pacifica, CA 94044
Web Site: www.nahe.org
Members: 500 individuals
Annual Budget: under $10,000
President: Marcia Green

Historical Note
Growing out of a series of programs sponsored by the New York State Department of Education, NAHE is a multidisciplinary professional educational organization for teachers in colleges, schools and museums. Has no paid officers or full-time staff. Membership: $55/two years.

Meetings/Conferences:
Biennial Meetings: Odd years
2007 – San Francisco, CA

Publications:
Interdisciplinary Humanities. bi-a.

National Association for Information Destruction
3420 E. Shea Blvd., Suite 115
Phoenix, AZ 85028
Tel: (602)788-6243 *Fax:* (602)788-4144
Web Site: www.naidonline.org
Executive Director: Robert J. Johnson
E-Mail: exedir@naidonline.org

Historical Note
Members are document shredding firms and manufacturers of related equipment.

Meetings/Conferences:
Annual Meetings: Spring

National Association for Interpretation *(1988)*
P.O. Box 2246
Ft. Collins, CO 80522
Tel: (970)484-8283 *Fax:* (970)484-8179
Toll Free: (888)900 - 8283
E-Mail: memberassist@interpnet.com
Web Site: www.interpnet.com
Members: 5000 individuals
Staff: 10
Annual Budget: $1-2,000,000
Executive Director: Tim Merriman
Manager, Membership: Jamie King
E-Mail: membership@interpnet.com

Historical Note
Product of a merger (1988) of the Association of Interpretive Naturalists and the Western Interpreter's Association. NAI members are naturalists, historians, park rangers, educators, museum technicians and curators, administrators, recreation specialists, and others concerned with communicating the meanings and relationships between people and their natural, cultural and recreational world. Membership: $75/year (individual); $195/year (institution); $275/year (commercial); $30/year (student); $85/year (family professional); $50/year (senior professional).

Meetings/Conferences:
Annual Meetings: Fall

Publications:
Journal of Interpretation Research. semi-a.
Legacy magazine. bi-m. adv.
NAI News. q.
Jobs in Interpretation. bi-w.
Interpreter magazine. bi-m. adv.

National Association for Kinesiology and Physical Education in Higher Education *(1978)*
c/o Dept. KH, Box 3984
Georgia State University
Atlanta, GA 30302-3984
Tel: (404)463-2293 *Fax:* (404)651-4814
Web Site: www.nakpehe.org
Members: 500 individuals
Staff: 1
Annual Budget: $25-50,000
Executive Secretary-Treasurer: Jackie Lund

Historical Note
The result of a merger between the National Association for Physical Education of College Women and the National College Physical Education Association for Men (founded in 1907). A professional society of physical education instructors at the college level. Has no paid staff.

Meetings/Conferences:
Annual Meetings: January

Publications:
Quest Journal. q.
Chronicle of Physical Education in Higher Education. 3/year.

National Association for Law Placement *(1971)*
1025 Connecticut Ave. NW, Suite 1110
Washington, DC 20036-5413
Tel: (202)835-1001 *Fax:* (202)835-1112
E-Mail: info@nalp.org
Web Site: www.nalp.org
Members: 1100 law schools & employers
Staff: 11
Annual Budget: $2-5,000,000
Executive Director: James Leipold
Deputy Director: Fred Thrasher

Historical Note
An incorporated not-for-profit organization of American Bar Association-approved law schools and employers of lawyers. Representatives include hiring attorneys, legal administrators, professional development administrators, law school career services officials and deans. NALP is not a placement agency for individuals jobs. It deals with issues such as career planning and ethical and effective recruiting. Membership: $795/year (law schools and private employers); $150/year (government agencies and public interest groups).

Meetings/Conferences:
Annual Meetings: Spring
2007 – Keystone, CO(Keystone Resort)/Apr. 25-28

Publications:
Associate Salary Survey. a.
NALP Bulletin. m. adv.
NALP Directory of Law Schools. a.
NALP Directory of Legal Employers. a.
Comprehensive Fellowship Guide. a.
Jobs & J.D.'s: Employment and Salaries of New Graduates. m.
Starting Salaries: What New Law Graduates Earn. a.
Patterns & Practices: Measures of Law Firm Hiring, Leverage and Billable Hours. a.

National Association for Medical Direction of Respiratory Care
8618 Westwood Center Dr., Suite 210
Vienna, VA 22182-2222
Tel: (703)752-4359 *Fax:* (703)752-4360
E-Mail: execoffice@namdrc.org
Web Site: www.namdrc.org
Members: 700 individuals
Staff: 3
Annual Budget: $100-250,000
Executive Director: Phillip Porte

Historical Note
Formerly (1994) National Association of Medical Directors of Respiratory Care. Membership: $210/year.

Meetings/Conferences:
Annual Meetings: Spring
2007 – Monterey, CA(Monterey Plaza)/March 22-24

Publications:
Washington Watchline. m. adv.
Current Controversies. bi-m. adv.

National Association for Membership Development *(1941)*

Historical Note
Absorbed by American Chamber of Commerce Executives in 2003.

National Association for Multi-Ethnicity in Communications *(1980)*
336 W. 37th St., Suite 302
New York, NY 10018
Tel: (212)594-5986 *Fax:* (212)594-8391
E-Mail: info@namic.com
Web Site: www.namic.com
Members: 1200 individuals
Staff: 8
Executive Vice President: Kathy A. Johnson

Historical Note
Founded as National Association of Minorities in Cable; became National Association of Minorities in Communications in 1999, and assumed its current

name in 2003. NAMIC works for the cause of diversity in the telecommunications industry.

Meetings/Conferences:
Annual Meetings: Fall

Publications:
In Touch Newsletter. q.

National Association for Parish Coordinators and Directors of Religious Education

Historical Note
An affiliate of the National Catholic Educational Association which provides administrative support.

National Association for PET Container Resources *(1987)*

P.O. Box 1327
Sonoma, CA 95476-1327
Tel: (707)996-4207 *Fax:* (707)935-1998
E-Mail: information@napcor.com
Web Site: www.napcor.com
Members: 29 companies (corporate)
Staff: 7
Annual Budget: $1-2,000,000
Vice President, Technology: Michael F. Schedler

Historical Note
Represents polyethylene terephthalate (PET) resin producers and container manufacturers. It facilitates the economical recovery of plastic containers with emphasis on PET plastic bottles. Assists communities in promoting PET recycling and publicizes PET as an environmentally sound packaging material.

National Association for Poetry Therapy *(1981)*

525 S.W. Fifth St.
Suite A
Des Moines, IA 50309-4501
Tel: (515)282-8192 *Fax:* (515)282-9117
E-Mail: info@poetrytherapy.org
Web Site: www.poetrytherapy.org
Members: 350 individuals
Staff: 1
Annual Budget: under $10,000
Administrator: Sheila Dietz

Historical Note
NAPT members represent a wide range of professional experience, schools of therapy, educational affiliations, artistic disciplines, and other fields of training in both mental and physical health. Awards the designations Certified Poetry Therapist (CPT) and Registered Poetry Therapist (RPT). Membership: $115/year (regular); $250/year (institutional); $80/year (student/retiree).

Meetings/Conferences:
Annual Meetings: May

Publications:
Journal of Poetry Therapy. q.
Museletter. 3/year.

National Association for Practical Nurse Education and Service *(1941)*

P.O. Box 25647
Alexandria, VA 22313
Tel: (703)933-1003 *Fax:* (703)940-8089
E-Mail: jbova@napnes.org
Web Site: www.napnes.org
Members: 10000 individuals
Staff: 5
Annual Budget: $250-500,000
Executive Director: Patrick Mahan, L.P.N.

Historical Note
Membership: $75/year.

Meetings/Conferences:
Annual Meetings: Spring

Publications:
The Journal of Practical Nursing. q. adv.
eJPN-NAPNES (online newsletter). m.

National Association for Printing Leadership *(1933)*

75 W. Century Rd.
Paramus, NJ 07652-1408
Tel: (201)634-9600 *Fax:* (201)634-0324
Toll Free: (800)642 - 6275
Web Site: www.napl.org
Members: 3000 companies
Staff: 35
Annual Budget: $5-10,000,000
President and Chief Executive Officer: Joseph P. Truncale, CAE
E-Mail: jtruncale@napl.org
Vice President, Finance and Member Services: Timothy Fisher
Senior Director, Association Partnerships and Board Relations: Joan Kasper
Senior Director, Communications: Dawn A. Lospaluto
Vice President and Chief Economist: Andrew Paparozzi
Director, Professional Development: Susan Reif

Historical Note
Established as the National Association of Photo-Lithographers in 1933, became National Association of Printers and Lithographers in 1972, and assumed its present name in 1999. Absorbed the Research and Engineering Council of the Graphic Arts in 2002. NAPL works toward increasing printers' profitability via a full range of management and educational services for its worldwide membership. Services cover every aspect of profitable printing management including cost and finance, human resources, sales and marketing, quality, desktop, economics, the environment and more. Membership: $375-2975/year (company, based on number of employees); $225/year (educational members).

Meetings/Conferences:
2007 - Santa Barbara, CA(Four Season)/March 7-11/275
2008 - Orlando, FL(Ritz-Carlton)/March 5-8/275

Publications:
Marketing Action Planner (electronic). q.
Print Operations Under 20 Employees Blue Book. b. adv.
NAPL Business Review. q.
Print Profit (electronic). q.
Sales Focus (electronic). q.
Sheetfed Blue Book. b. adv.
Special Reports. 5/year.
Bindery Blue Book. b. adv.
Web Blue Book. b. adv.
On The Job (electronic). q.
Prepress Blue Book. semi-a. adv.
Tech Trends (electronic). q.
At Your Service (electronic). q.

National Association for Promotional and Advertising Allowances

Historical Note
Became Trade Promotion Management Association in 2005.

National Association for Proton Therapy *(1990)*

1301 Highland Dr.
Silver Spring, MD 20910
Tel: (301)587-6100
Web Site: www.proton-therapy.org
Members: 5 medical centers
Staff: 1
Annual Budget: $50-100,000
Executive Director: Leonard Arzt

Historical Note
NAPT members are medical centers operating proton beam radiation as a cancer therapy.

Publications:
Proton Treatment Newsletter. q.

National Association for Public Health Statistics and Information Systems *(1933)*

801 Roeder Rd., Suite 650
Silver Spring, MD 20910
Tel: (301)563-6001 *Fax:* (301)563-6012
E-Mail: jmarkowitz@naphsis.org
Web Site: www.naphsis.org
Members: 300 individuals
Staff: 4
Annual Budget: $2-5,000,000
Acting Executive Director: Jan Markowitz

Historical Note
Organized in 1933 as the American Association of Registration Executives. Became American Association for Vital Records and Public Health Statistics in 1958, Association for Public Health Statistics and Information Systems in 1995, and assumed its current name in 1997. Membership: based on state population (agency based).

Meetings/Conferences:
Annual Meetings: Spring/Summer

Publications:
The Journal. bi-m.

National Association for Pupil Transportation *(1974)*

1840 Western Ave.
Albany, NY 12203
Tel: (518)452-3611 *Fax:* (518)218-0867
Toll Free: (800)989 - 6278
E-Mail: info@napt.org
Web Site: www.napt.org
Members: 1651 individuals
Staff: 4
Annual Budget: $500-1,000,000
Executive Director: Michael J. Martin

Historical Note
Represents educators, administrators, and other professionals whose responsibilities include safe transit for students.

Meetings/Conferences:
Annual Meetings: November

Publications:
NAPT Newsletter. q. adv.

National Association for Rehabilitation Leadership

1020 W. 5th St.
Dickinson, ND 58601
Tel: (701)227-7415
Web Site: www.homestead.com/prosites-nraa/index.html
Members: 1000 individuals
President: Ray Feroz

Historical Note
Founded as National Rehabilitation Administration Association; assumed its current name in 2003. A professional division of the National Rehabilitation Association. Members are non-profit rehabilitation administrators, state agency vocational rehabilitation administrators and private rehabiliation administrators. NRAA supports professional training sessions on the state and regional levels and encourages professional development of rehabilitation administrators. Membership: $50/year, plus NRA dues (professional); $25/year, plus NRA dues (affiliate).

Publications:
Journal of Rehabilitation Administration.
NRAA Newsletter.

National Association for Research and Therapy of Homosexuality *(1992)*

16633 Ventura Blvd., Suite 1340
Encino, CA 91436-1801
Tel: (818)789-4440 *Fax:* (818)789-6452
E-Mail: narth@earthlink.net
Web Site: www.narth.com
Members: 900 individuals
Staff: 2
Administrative Assistant: Joan Mackenzie

Historical Note
Members are psychoanalysts, social workers and behavioral scientists who specialize in sexual reorientation therapies. Provides a referral service, discussion group, and other programs to its members.

Publications:
NARTH Bulletin. 3/year. adv.

National Association for Research in Science Teaching *(1928)*

University of Missouri - Columbia
303 Townsend Hall
Columbia, MO 65211-2400
Tel: (573)884-1401 *Fax:* (573)884-2917
E-Mail: narst@missouri.edu
Web Site: www.narst.org
Members: 1600 individuals
Staff: 2
Annual Budget: $100-250,000
Administrative Assistant: Marilyn Estes

Historical Note
A professional association of science educators. Affiliated with the National Science Teachers Association, the American Association for the Advancement of Science and the International Council

of Science Associations for Education. Membership: $100/year (individual).

Meetings/Conferences:
Annual Meetings: *Alternately with the National Science Teachers Association and the American Education Research Association*

Publications:
Newsletter (online).
Journal of Research in Science Teaching. 10/year.

National Association for Retail Marketing Services *(1995)*
P.O. Box 906
Plover, WI 54467
Tel: (715)342-0948 *Fax:* (715)342-1943
Toll Free: (888)526 - 2767
E-Mail: admin@narms.com
Web Site: www.narms.com
Members: 523 companies
Staff: 4
Annual Budget: $1-2,000,000
President and Chief Executive Officer: Daniel C. Borschke, CAE
Vice President: Ken McKenzie

Historical Note
NARMS conducts and publishes ongoing industry research and related information for its merchandising and marketing sales and service members. Absorbed Fluid Marketing Services Association in 2002. Membership: $595-4,500/year.

Meetings/Conferences:
Annual Meetings: *Spring*

Publications:
NARMS Today. 4/year.

National Association for Rural Mental Health *(1977)*
1756 74th Ave., Suite 101
St. Cloud, MN 56301
Tel: (320)202-1820 *Fax:* (320)202-1833
Toll Free: (800)809 - 5879
E-Mail: narmh@facts.ksu.edu
Web Site: www.narmh.org
Members: 500 individuals
Staff: 1
Annual Budget: $100-250,000
Administrative Assistant: LuAnn Rice

Historical Note
Members include social workers, psychiatrists, psychologists and others who work in rural community mental health settings. Membership fee varies, based on type.

Meetings/Conferences:
Annual Meetings: *Summer*

Publications:
Rural Mental Health. 4/year. adv.

National Association for Search and Rescue *(1974)*
4500 Southgate Place, Suite 100
Chantilly, VA 20151
Tel: (703)222-6277 *Fax:* (703)222-6277
Toll Free: (888)893 - 0702
E-Mail: info@nasar.org
Web Site: www.nasar.org
Members: 14000 individuals
Staff: 10
Annual Budget: $2-5,000,000
Executive Director: Megan Riccardi Bartlett
E-Mail: meganr@nasar.org
Manager, Member Services: Cyndi Mahler

Historical Note
Established as the National Association of Search and Rescue Coordinators; assumed its present name in 1975. Members belong to various emergency medical, fire or survival rescue services. Membership: $49/year (individual); $70/year (organization).

Meetings/Conferences:
Annual Meetings: *Spring/800*

Publications:
SAR Dog Alert. bi-m. adv.
SAR Dog Directory. a.
Search and Rescue Magazine. bi-m. adv.
Proceedings. a.

National Association for Sport and Physical Education *(1974)*
1900 Association Dr.
Reston, VA 20191-1599
Tel: (703)476-3410 *Fax:* (703)476-8316
E-Mail: naspe@aahperd.org
Web Site: www.naspeinfo.org
Members: 20000 individuals
Staff: 9
Annual Budget: $100-250,000
Executive Director: Charlene Burgeson

Historical Note
Created from the merger of the Division of Men's Athletics and the Physical Education Division of the American Association for Health, Physical Education, Recreation and Dance, NASPE is one of AAHPERD's six autonomous affiliates. Membership: fees vary.

Meetings/Conferences:
Annual Meetings: *in conjunction with the AAPHERD national convention*

Publications:
Right Moves. 3/yr.
Peak Performance. semi-a.
NASPE News. q.
Strategies-A Journal for Physical and Sport Educators. bi-m.

National Association for State Community Services Programs *(1968)*
400 North Capitol St. NW, Suite 395
Washington, DC 20001
Tel: (202)624-5866 *Fax:* (202)624-8472
E-Mail: nascsp@sso.org
Web Site: www.nascsp.org
Members: 50 states, Puerto Rico and the District of Columbia
Staff: 9
Annual Budget: $1-2,000,000
Executive Director: Timothy R. Warfield
E-Mail: nascsp@sso.org

Historical Note
Members are state administrators of federal Community Services Block Grant and Weatherization Assistance Programs.

Meetings/Conferences:
Semi-Annual Meetings: Mid-winter and fall
2007 – Washington, DC(Washington Marriott)/Feb. 12-16
2007 – Boise, ID(Red Lion Hotel)/Sept. 18-21

Publications:
NASCP Newsletter. m.
Community Services Block Grant Statistical Report. a.

National Association for Stock Car Auto Racing *(1947)*
P.O. Box 2875
Daytona Beach, FL 32120-2875
Tel: (386)253-0611
Web Site: www.nascar.com
Members: 50000 individuals
Staff: 40
Annual Budget: $1-2,000,000
President: Mike Helton
Managing Director, Corporate Communications: Ramsey Posten

Meetings/Conferences:
Annual Meetings: *Daytona Beach, FL/mid-February*

Publications:
NASCAR News. bi-m. adv.
NASCAR Yearbook. a. adv.

National Association for the Advancement of Psychoanalysis *(1972)*
80 Eighth Ave., Suite 1501
New York, NY 10011
Tel: (212)741-0515 *Fax:* (212)366-4347
E-Mail: info@naap.org
Web Site: www.naap.org
Members: 1500 individuals
Staff: 5
Annual Budget: $100-250,000
Executive Director: Margery Quackenbush, Ph.D.

Historical Note
NAAP monitors educational standards for the registration of individuals as certified psychoanalysts. Membership: $195/year (individual); $100/year (candidate-in-training); $300/year (organization).

Meetings/Conferences:
Annual Meetings: *Fall, usually in New York*

Publications:
NAAP News. q. adv.
National Registry of Psychoanalysts. a.

National Association for the Education of Young Children *(1926)*
1313 L St. NW
Suite 500
Washington, DC 20005
Tel: (202)232-8777 *Fax:* (202)328-1846
Toll Free: (800)424 - 2460
E-Mail: naeyc@naeyc.org
Web Site: www.naeyc.org
Members: 100000 individuals
Staff: 100
Annual Budget: $5-10,000,000
Executive Director: Mark Ginsberg
Associate Executive Director, Finance, Operations and Chief Financial Officer: Bill Harris
Senior Director, Marketing and Communications: Alan Simpson

Historical Note
Established as the National Association for Nursery Education, it assumed its present name in 1964. Members are administrators and teachers in schools for children (birth through age 8). Membership: $45-500/year.

Meetings/Conferences:
Annual Meetings: *Fall*

Publications:
Young Children. bi-m. adv.

National Association for the Practice of Anthropology *(1983)*

Historical Note
A section of the American Anthropological Association. Represents the practice of anthropology and the interests of practicing anthropologists.

National Association for the Self-Employed *(1981)*
1200 G St. NW, Suite 800
Washington, DC 20005
Tel: (202)466-2100
Toll Free: (800)232 - 6273
E-Mail: media@nase.org
Web Site: www.nase.org
Members: 200000 individuals
Staff: 5
Annual Budget: $10-25,000,000
President: Robert Hughes

Historical Note
NASE promotes small business growth and entrepreneurship. NASE is a leading resource for the self-employed and micro-businesses, bringing a broad range of resources to help entrepreneurs succeed and to drive continued growth of this segment of the American economy. NASE's member businesses represent over 600,000 micro-business employers and employees. Members are small businesses, usually with 10 or fewer employees. Membership: $96/year.

Publications:
Washington Watch E-newsletter (online). w.
Self-Employed America. bi-m.
Member Benefits Guide. a.

National Association for the Specialty Food Trade *(1951)*
120 Wall St., 27th Floor
New York, NY 10005-4001
Tel: (212)482-6440 *Fax:* (212)482-6459
E-Mail: custserv@nasft.org
Web Site: www.specialtyfoods.com
Members: 2800 companies
Staff: 40
Annual Budget: $10-25,000,000
Vice President, Media Development: Chris Crocker
President: Ann Daw
Vice President, Exhibition Management: Chris Nemchek

Vice President, Finance and Administration: Gerry Shamdosky
Vice President, Communications and Education: Ronald Tanner

Historical Note
Members are manufacturers, importers, distributors, chefs, caterers, catalogers, gift stores, of specialty gourmet foods, beverages and confections. Absorbed Specialty Food Distributors and Manufacturers association in 2002.

Publications:
Foodspring. q. adv.
NASFT Specialty Food Magazine. 9/year. adv.
NASFT Insider.
Specialty Food Newsletter. daily. adv.

National Association for the Support of Long-Term Care *(1989)*
1321 Duke St., Suite 304
Alexandria, VA 22314-3563
Tel: (703)549-8500 *Fax:* (703)549-8342
Web Site: www.nasl.org
Members: 120 companies
Staff: 4
Annual Budget: $500-1,000,000
Executive Vice President: Peter C. Clendenin, CAE

Historical Note
Members are providers to the long term care industry. NASL represents professional medical services, IT vendors, diagnostic testing providers, and products for the post-acute care industry; NASL represents these professional medical services by providing a national communication forum and legislative and regulatory representation for health care industry executives and their businesses. Membership: $3,700-25,000/year (organization).

National Association for Trade and Industrial Education *(1974)*
Box 1665
Leesburg, VA 20177-1655
Tel: (703)777-1740
E-Mail: info@natie.org
Members: 1500 individuals
Staff: 1
Annual Budget: $10-25,000
Executive Director: Don Esheley

Historical Note
Membership includes instructors, state supervisors, teacher educators, representatives from labor organizations, and companies concerned with vocational education and training. Affiliated with Skills USA and ACTE, et al. Membership: $10/year (professional); $200/year (industrial).

Meetings/Conferences:
Annual Meetings: Held in conjunction with Skills USA and the Association of Career and Technical Education (ACTE)

Publications:
NATIE News Notes. q. adv.

National Association for Treasurers of Religious Institutes *(1981)*
8824 Cameron St.
Silver Spring, MD 20910
Tel: (301)587-7776 *Fax:* (301)589-2897
E-Mail: natri@natri.org
Web Site: www.natri.org
Members: 600 individuals
Staff: 4
Annual Budget: $500-1,000,000
Executive Director: Laura Reicks
Associate Director, Finance: Lorelle Elcock

Historical Note
NATRI's mission is to address the fiscal, legal and administrative responsibilities specific to religious institutes in the U.S. Membership: $410/year (individual); $600/year (organization).

Meetings/Conferences:
Annual Meetings: Fall

Publications:
NATRI Newsletter. bi-m.
Membership Directory. a.
Service Directory. a. adv.

National Association for Uniformed Services and Society of Military Widows *(1968)*
5535 Hempstead Way
Springfield, VA 22151-4094
Tel: (703)750-1342 *Fax:* (703)354-4380
Toll Free: (800)842 - 3451
E-Mail: naus@ix.netcom.com
Web Site: www.naus.org
Members: 160000 individuals
Staff: 10
Annual Budget: $2-5,000,000
President: MG William M. Matz, Jr, USA (Ret.)
E-Mail: mmatz@naus.org
Treasurer/Director, Membership: Tamea A. Boone
E-Mail: taboone@naus.org

Historical Note
Promotes development and support of legislation to sustain the morale of the Armed Forces and provide fair and equitable consideration for all members of the uniformed services. NAUS affiliated with the Society of Military Widows in 1984. Sponsors the National Association for Uniformed Services Political Action Committee (NAUS-PAC). Membership: $15/year, $12/year (widows).

Meetings/Conferences:
Annual Meetings: Washington, DC area/last week of Oct.-1st week of Nov./200-300

Publications:
Uniformed Services Journal. bi-m. adv.

National Association for Variable Annuities *(1991)*
11710 Plaza America Dr., Suite 100
Reston, VA 20190
Tel: (703)707-8830 *Fax:* (703)707-8831
E-Mail: nava@navanet.org
Web Site: www.navanet.org
Members: 300 companies
Staff: 9
Annual Budget: $1-2,000,000
President and Chief Executive Officer: Mark J. Mackey
Vice President, Communications: Deborah Tucker
E-Mail: dtucker@navanet.org

Historical Note
Membership: $750/year (companies with less than 50 employees); $2,000/year (companies with more than 50 employees).

Meetings/Conferences:
2007 – Boston, MA(The Westin Copley Place)/Sept. 9-11

Publications:
NAVA Outlook Newsletter. bi-m.

National Association for Women's Health *(1987)*

Historical Note
Address unknown in 2004.

National Association for Year-Round Education *(1972)*
P.O. Box 711386
San Diego, CA 92171-1386
Tel: (619)276-5296 *Fax:* (858)571-5754
E-Mail: info@NAYRE.org
Web Site: www.NAYRE.org
Members: 1570 individuals
Staff: 5
Annual Budget: $500-1,000,000
Executive Director: Samuel J. Pepper
E-Mail: info@NAYRE.org

Historical Note
Formerly (1986) the National Council on Year-Round Education, NAYRE is a professional association of individuals with an interest in the concept of year round education. Membership: $45/year (individual); $350-$750/year, varies by enrollment (institution).

Publications:
Reference Directory of Year-Round Education Programs. a.

National Association Medical Staff Services *(1978)*
2025 M St. NW, Suite 800
Washington, DC 20036
Tel: (202)367-1196 *Fax:* (202)367-2196
E-Mail: info@namss.org
Web Site: www.namss.org
Members: 4200 individuals
Staff: 4
Annual Budget: $1-2,000,000
Executive Director: Steve Hartley

Historical Note
NAMSS promotes educational opportunities to enhance the skills and general competence of practicing medical staff services professionals. Serves to increase recognition of the role of the medical staff services professional and to assist its members in understanding and succeeding in the changing health care industry. Membership: $150/year (individual).

Meetings/Conferences:
Annual Meetings: October/1,000
2007 – New York, NY

Publications:
Synergy. bi-m. adv.

National Association of Academic Advisors for Athletes *(1976)*
P.O. Box A-7
College Station, TX 77844-9007
Tel: (979)862-4310 *Fax:* (979)862-2461
E-Mail: n4a@athletics.tamu.edu
Web Site: www.nfoura.org
Members: 800 individuals
Staff: 1
Annual Budget: $10-25,000
National Office Manager: Shanna O'Gilvie

Historical Note
N4A serves professional advisors giving guidance to student athletes at the college level. Membership: $50/year (non-voting/student); $100/year (individual).

Meetings/Conferences:
Annual Meetings: June

Publications:
N4A Newsletter. 3/year.
Athletic Academic Journal. semi-a.

National Association of Academies of Science *(1926)*
84918 King Richard Dr.
Annandale, VA 22003
Tel: (703)323-7810
Web Site: http://astro.physics.sc.edu/NAAS.html
Members: 44 academies
Staff: 1
Annual Budget: $50-100,000
President: Michael S. Strauss

Historical Note
Before 1919 various academies were informally associated with the American Association for the Advancement of Science (AAAS). In 1920, they were given the right of representation on the AAAS council and became known as the Affiliated Academies. In 1926, they became a more organized group known as the Academy Conference, and in 1969 became known as the Association of Academies of Science. Affiliated with AAAS. Until 1979, known as the Association of Academies of Science. Membership: $250/year (maximum).

Meetings/Conferences:
Annual Meetings: With American Association for the Advancement of Science

Publications:
NAAS Directory, Proceedings and Handbook. a.

National Association of Activity Professionals *(1981)*
P.O. Box 5530
Sevierville, TN 37864
Tel: (865)429-0717 *Fax:* (865)453-9914
E-Mail: THENAAP@aol.com
Web Site: www.thenaap.com
Members: 1800 individuals
Staff: 3
Annual Budget: $250-500,000
Executive Director: Charles T. Taylor

Historical Note
Active members are activity directors, coordinators, or consultants in long-term care facilities, senior retirement housing, senior centers, or adult day-care programs. Membership: $75/year.

Meetings/Conferences:
Annual Meetings: Annual/500+
2007 – Columbus, OH/Apr. 15-21
2008 – Orlando, FL/Apr. 30-May 3

Publications:
NAAP News. m. adv.

National Association of Addiction Treatment Providers *(1978)*
313 W. Liberty St., Suite. 129
Lancaster, PA 17603-2748
Tel: (717)392-8480 *Fax:* (717)392-8481
Web Site: www.naatp.org
Members: 300 organizations
Staff: 2
Annual Budget: $500-1,000,000
Chief Executive Officer: Dr. Ronald J. Hunsicker
Historical Note
Members are for-profit and non-profit treatment centers for alcoholism and drug dependency. Absorbed American College of Addictions Treatment Administrators in 2003.
Meetings/Conferences:
Annual Meetings: May
Publications:
NAATP Vision. 10/yr. adv.
NAATP Update. m. adv.

National Association of Advisors for the Health Professions *(1974)*
P.O. Box 1518
Champaign, IL 61824-1518
Tel: (217)355-0063 *Fax:* (217)355-1287
E-Mail: naahpja@aol.com
Web Site: www.naahp.org
Members: 1200 individuals
Staff: 4
Executive Director: Susan Maxwell
Office Manager: Jerolyn Atwood
Historical Note
Membership includes pre-health advisors in many of the country's undergraduate colleges and universities, who counsel students on careers in the health professions, and also includes representatives of national health associations and deans of professional schools' admissions/student affairs departments. Membership: $125/year (undergraduate institution); $300/year (health professionals school).
Meetings/Conferences:
Biennial Meetings: Even years/600-800 attendees
Publications:
Newsletter (online). q.
The Advisor. q. adv.
Directory. a. adv.

National Association of Affordable Housing Lenders *(1988)*
1300 Connecticut Ave. NW, Suite 905
Washington, DC 20036
Tel: (202)293-9850 *Fax:* (202)293-9852
E-Mail: naahl@naahl.org
Members: 200 organizations
Staff: 4
Annual Budget: $1-2,000,000
President and Chief Executive Officer: Judith A. Kennedy
Historical Note
The National Association of Affordable Housing Lenders (NAAHL) is the only association devoted to increasing private capital lending and investment in low and moderate income communities. NAAHL encompasses nearly 200 organizations, including 64 insured depository institutions, 45 non-profit providers and 800 individuals as members. Membership: $250-6,000/year.
Meetings/Conferences:
Annual Meetings: Winter-Spring
Publications:
Washington Update. m.
Directions in Affordable Housing Finance. q.

National Association of African American Studies *(1992)*
P.O. Box 6670
Scarborough, ME 04070-6670
Tel: (207)839-8004 *Fax:* (207)839-3776
E-Mail: naaasconference@earthlink.net
Web Site: www.naaas.org
Members: 372 individuals
Staff: 4
Annual Budget: $100-250,000
Executive Director: Lemuel Berry, Jr., Ph.D.
Historical Note
NAAAS represents scholars and educators exploring the full spectrum of cultural discourse. Affiliated organizations include National Association of Hispanic and Latino Studies, National Association of Native American Studies, and International Association of Asian Studies (same address). Membership: $125/year (individual); $500/year (organization).
Meetings/Conferences:
Annual Meetings: Winter
2007 – Baton Rouge, LA(Marriott)/Feb. 12-17
Publications:
NAAAS. a.
Journal of Interdisciplinary Studies. semi-a. adv.
NAAAS Newsletter. q. adv.

National Association of Agricultural Educators *(1948)*
300 Garrigus Bldg., University of Kentucky
Lexington, KY 40546-0215
Tel: (859)257-2224 *Fax:* (859)323-3919
Toll Free: (800)509 - 0204
E-Mail: naae@uky.edu
Web Site: www.naae.org
Members: 7500 individuals
Staff: 4
Annual Budget: $500-1,000,000
Executive Director: Wm. Jay Jackman, Ph.D.
Historical Note
Formerly (1998) National Vocational Agricultural Teachers Association. NAAE is a federation of affiliated state agricultural teacher associations. Membership: $60/year (educational member); $35/year (associate); $5/year (student).
Meetings/Conferences:
Annual Meetings: December, in conjunction with the Association for Career and Technical Education (ACTE)
Publications:
NAAE News and Views. q.

National Association of Agricultural Fair Agencies *(1966)*
Michigan State Dept. of Agriculture
P.O. Box 30017
Lansing, MI 48909
Tel: (517)373-9766 *Fax:* (517)373-9146
Members: 35 agencies
Staff: 1
Annual Budget: under $10,000
Secretary-Treasurer: Carol Carlson
Historical Note
U.S. and Canadian representatives of state/provincial agencies that are responsible for the support of educational and agricultural fairs. Affiliated with the National Association of State Departments of Agriculture. Membership: $35/year.
Meetings/Conferences:
Semi-Annual Meetings: Summer and Winter
Publications:
Newsletter. a.
Constitution and Membership Roster. a.

National Association of Agriculture Employees *(1954)*
9080 Torrey Rd.
Willis, MI 48191
Tel: (734)942-9005 *Fax:* (734)942-7691
Web Site: www.aginspectors.org
Members: 750 individuals
Annual Budget: $100-250,000
Secretary: Sarah Clore
Historical Note
Formerly (1981) the Federal Plant Quarantine Inspectors National Association. NAAE is an independent federal labor union which represents employees working for the U.S. Dept. of Agriculture, Animal and Plant Health Inspection Service, Plant Protection and Quarantine. Members are professional employees with college degrees in Biological Sciences. Bargaining unit consists of federal officers enforcing federal agricultural quarantines relating to foreign and domestic programs. Has no paid officers or full-time staff. Membership: $15/month.
Meetings/Conferences:
Biennial Meetings: Even years in April
Publications:
Newsletter. q.

National Association of Air Medical Communication Specialists
P.O. Box 28
Otis Orchards, WA 99027-0028
Tel: (877)396-2227
Web Site: www.naacs.org
Members: 200 individuals
Annual Budget: $10-25,000
President: Shelly Sholl
Historical Note
Formerly (2000) National Association of Air Communications Specialists. NAACS members are air medical communicatons specialists.

National Association of Air Traffic Specialists *(1960)*
P.O. Box 2550
Landover Hills, MD 20784-0550
Tel: (301)459-5595 *Fax:* (301)459-5597
E-Mail: naatshq@aol.com
Web Site: www.naats.org
Members: 2000 individuals
Staff: 4
Annual Budget: $500-1,000,000
President: Walter Pike
Historical Note
An independent labor union. Supports the NAATS Political Action Fund.
Meetings/Conferences:
Biennial Meetings: odd years in Fall
Publications:
NAATS News. m.

National Association of Aircraft and Communication Suppliers
4301 Connecticut Ave. NW, Suite 453
Washington, DC 20008
Tel: (202)237-0505 *Fax:* (202)237-7566
Members: 120 companies
Executive Director: John J. Fausti
Historical Note
NAACS is a national organization of small businesses who regularly purchase military surplus aircraft and electronics parts from the U.S. Department of Defense.

National Association of American Business Clubs
Historical Note
See National Ambucs.

National Association of Animal Breeders *(1947)*
401 Bernadette Dr.
P.O. Box 1033
Columbia, MO 65205-1033
Tel: (573)445-4406 *Fax:* (573)446-2279
E-Mail: naab-css@naab-css.org
Web Site: www.naab-css.org
Members: 23 organizations
Staff: 5
Annual Budget: $1-2,000,000
President: Gordon A. Doak, Ph.D.
Historical Note
Formerly the National Association of Artificial Breeders. Members are farmer co-ops and others interested in livestock improvement.
Meetings/Conferences:
Annual Meetings: Summer
2007 – St. Louis, MO(The Westin)/Aug. 23-23/30
Publications:
Proceedings. a.
Proceedings of Technical Conference. bien.

National Association of Architectural Metal Manufacturers *(1938)*
Eight S. Michigan Ave., Suite 1000
Chicago, IL 60603
Tel: (312)332-0405 *Fax:* (312)332-0706
E-Mail: naamm@gss.net
Web Site: www.naamm.org
Members: 90 companies

Staff: 2
Annual Budget: $250-500,000
Executive Vice President: August L. Sisco

Historical Note
Comprised of four divisions: Architectural Metal Products, Expanded Metal, Hollow Metal Doors and Frames, and Metal Bar Grating. Membership: $995-2,995/year (corporate).

Meetings/Conferences:
Annual Meetings: *Spring*

Publications:
Technical Standards.
Member Directory (online). a.

National Association of Area Agencies on Aging *(1974)*

1730 Rhode Island Ave. NW, Suite 1200
Washington, DC 20036
Tel: (202)872-0888 *Fax:* (202)872-0057
E-Mail: info@n4a.org
Web Site: www.n4a.org
Members: 885 agencies
Staff: 9
Annual Budget: $1-2,000,000
Chief Executive Officer: Sandra Markwood
Deputy Director: Adrienne Dern

Historical Note
Members include Area Agencies on Aging and Title VI - Native American Aging Programs. N4A's mission is to promote a national policy that enhances the ability of older Americans to remain independent in their communities and homes for as long as possible. Membership: $125-$7,000/year, based on total annual budget of agency.

Meetings/Conferences:
Annual Meetings: *Summer*

Publications:
In Touch with N4A. m.
National Directory for Eldercare Information and Referral. bien. adv.
Eldercare Directory.

National Association of Artists' Organizations *(1982)*

230 Vine St.
Philadelphia, PA 19106
Tel: (215)925-9951
E-Mail: info@naao.net
Web Site: www.naao.net
Members: 265 individuals
Staff: 1
Annual Budget: $2-5,000,000
Executive Director: Laurel Raczka

Historical Note
A service-oriented organization which promotes and protects artists within non-profit organizations. NAAO is dedicated to the presentation of alternative visual arts, media, literature, new music, and performing arts. Membership: $35/year (individual); $175-500/year (organization).

Publications:
eNews.
NAAO Field Guide. a.
Organizing Artist. bien. adv.

National Association of Assistant United States Attorneys *(1992)*

12427 Hedges Run Dr.
Suite 104
Lake Ridge, VA 22192
Tel: (703)426-4266 *Fax:* (800)528-3492
Toll Free: (800)455 - 5661
E-Mail: staff@naausa.org
Web Site: www.naausa.org
Members: 1600 individuals
Staff: 2
Annual Budget: $100-250,000
Executive Director: Dennis W. Boyd

Historical Note
NAAUSA is a professional association with the primary objective of promoting and protecting the careers and professional interests of Assistant U.S. Attorneys. Membership: $130/year (individuals); $25/year (former Assistant U.S. Attorneys).

Publications:
NAAUSA Brief. irreg.
NAAUSA Quarterly. q. adv.

National Association of Athletic Development Directors *(1993)*

P.O. Box 16428
Cleveland, OH 44116
Tel: (440)892-4000 *Fax:* (440)892-4007
Web Site: www.naadd.com
Members: 500 individuals
Staff: 2
Associate Executive Director: Pat Manak
Association Liaison/Assistant Administrator: Jason Galaska

Historical Note
NAADD is an affiliate of the National Association of Collegiate Directors of Athletics, which provides administrative support. Membership: $75-250/year.

Meetings/Conferences:
Annual Meetings: *June*

Publications:
Athletics Administration Magazine. bi-m. adv.

National Association of Attorneys General *(1907)*

750 First St. NE, Suite 1100
Washington, DC 20002
Tel: (202)326-6000 *Fax:* (202)408-7014
Web Site: www.naag.org
Members: 56 individuals
Staff: 40
Annual Budget: $2-5,000,000
Executive Director: Lynne M. Ross

Historical Note
NAAG fosters interstate cooperation on legal and law enforcement issues, conducts policy research and analysis, and provides for advocacy at all levels of government on behalf of the states' chief legal officers. Members are the Attorneys General of the 50 states, 5 territorial jurisdictions and the Corporation Counsel of the District of Columbia.

Meetings/Conferences:
Three Meetings Annually: March (Washington, DC), June, and December.

Publications:
Antitrust and Commerce Report. 10/year.
National Environmental Enforcement Journal. 11/year.
Consumer Protection Report. 10/year.
A-G Bulletin. 10/year.
State Constitutional Law Bulletin. 10/year.

National Association of Band Instrument Manufacturers

Historical Note
Became NABIM - the International Band and Orchestral Products Association in 2003.

National Association of Bankruptcy Trustees *(1981)*

One Windsor Cove, Suite 305
Columbia, SC 29223
Tel: (803)252-5646 *Fax:* (803)765-0860
Toll Free: (800)445 - 8629
E-Mail: info@nabt.com
Web Site: www.nabt.com
Members: 1200 individuals
Staff: 8
Annual Budget: $50-100,000

Historical Note
The majority of the members of the NABT are Chapter 7 trustees who primarily liquidate nonexempt assets for the benefit of creditors. Membership: $100/year.

Meetings/Conferences:
Semi-Annual Meetings:

Publications:
NABTalk. q. adv.

National Association of Baptist Professors of Religion *(1927)*

P.O. Box 1123
Anderson College
Anderson, SC 29621
Tel: (864)231-2000 *Fax:* (864)231-5676
Members: 350 individuals
Staff: 1
Annual Budget: $10-25,000
Executive Secretary - Treasurer: Danny Mynatt

Historical Note
Formerly (1983) the Association of Baptist Professors of Religion. Members are not required to be related to any Baptist group or denomination. Membership: varies with salary levels.

Meetings/Conferences:
Annual Meetings: in conjunction with AAR/SBL

Publications:
Festschriften Series. a.
NABPR News.
Perspectives in Religious Studies. q. adv.
Monograph Series. irreg.
Dissertation Series. irreg.

National Association of Bar Executives *(1953)*

Historical Note
An affiliate of American Bar Association, which provides administrative support.

National Association of Bar-Related Title Insurers

Historical Note
Became North American Bar-Related Title Insurers in 2005.

National Association of Barber Boards *(1935)*

2708 Pine St.
Arkadelphia, AR 71923
Tel: (501)682-2806 *Fax:* (501)682-5073
Web Site: www.nationalbarberboards.com
Members: 50 state licensing boards
Annual Budget: $50-100,000
Executive Officer: Charles Kirkpatrick

Historical Note
Formerly (1986) National Association of Boards of Barbers Examiners of America. Members are state licensing boards for barbers. Has no paid officers or full-time staff. Membership: $100/year.

National Association of Basketball Coaches *(1927)*

1111 Main St., Suite 1000
Kansas City, MO 64105-2136
Tel: (816)878-6222 *Fax:* (816)878-6223
Web Site: www.nabc.com
Members: 5000 individuals
Staff: 9
Annual Budget: $500-1,000,000
Executive Director: James A. Haney
Associate Executive Director: Kevin Henderson
Director, Association Affairs: Troy Hilton
Deputy Executive Director: Reggie Minton
Director, Business Operations: Debbie Page
Director, Membership: Dottie Yearout

Historical Note
Formerly National Association of Basketball Coaches of the United States (1998). NABC lobbies on the behalf of college coaches and serves as a resource for coaches. Membership: $70-350/year (individual).

Meetings/Conferences:
Annual Meetings: *Spring*

Publications:
Time Out. q. adv.

National Association of Beverage Importers-Wine-Spirits-Beer *(1934)*

932 Hungerford Dr., Unit 12A
Rockville, MD 20850
Tel: (240)453-9998 *Fax:* (240)453-9358
E-Mail: beverageimporters@nabi-inc.org
Web Site: www.nabi-inc.org
Members: 60 companies
Staff: 2
Annual Budget: $250-500,000
President: Robert J. Maxwell
Vice President: Bernadeen Emamali

Historical Note
Members are required to hold a Federal Basic Importer's Permit. Founded in New York City, January 12, 1934, by 18 charter members for the purpose of electing an NRA code authority. After the NRA was declared unconstitutional in 1935, the present organization was formed. Formerly (until 1979) known as the National Association of Alcoholic Beverage Importers, Inc.

Meetings/Conferences:
Annual Meetings: *Spring*

Publications:
Statistics. m.
Statistical Report. a.

National Association of Biology Teachers *(1938)*
12030 Sunrise Valley Dr., Suite 110
Reston, VA 20191
Tel: (703)264-9696 *Fax:* (703)264-7778
Toll Free: (800)406 - 0775
E-Mail: office@nabt.org
Web Site: www.nabt.org
Members: 7500 individuals
Staff: 12
Annual Budget: $1-2,000,000
Executive Director: Wayne W. Carley
E-Mail: wcarley@nabt.org
Historical Note
Founded in 1938 and incorporated in Illinois in 1956. NABT members are biology educators and administrators in elementary schools, middle/junior high schools, high schools and colleges. NABT also includes representatives from biology-related industries. NABT improves biology/life science education by introducing innovative classroom strategies as well as keeping teachers informed on developments in the biological sciences. Membership: $59/year (individual); $520/year (sustaining); $125/year (organization/company).
Meetings/Conferences:
Annual Meetings: Fall/1,500
Publications:
The American Biology Teacher. 9/year. adv.
News and Views. q.

National Association of Black Accountants *(1969)*
7249-A Hanover Pkwy.
Greenbelt, MD 20770-3653
Tel: (301)474-6222 *Fax:* (301)474-3114
E-Mail: nabaoffice@nabainc.org
Web Site: www.nabainc.org
Members: 5500 individuals
Staff: 8
Annual Budget: $2-5,000,000
Executive Director and Chief Operating Officer: Darryl R. Matthews, Sr.
Historical Note
Established and incorporated in New York. Membership: $120/year (professional); $20/year (undergraduate).
Meetings/Conferences:
Annual Meetings: Summer
2007 – Philadelphia, PA(Philadelphia Downtown Marriott)/June 19-23
2008 – Atlanta, GA(Hilton Atlanta)
Publications:
News Plus. q. adv.
Achieve. q. adv.
Spectrum. a. adv.

National Association of Black County Officials *(1984)*
Historical Note
An affiliate of National Association of Counties, which provides administrative support.

National Association of Black Journalists *(1975)*
8701-A Adelphi Rd.
Adelphi, MD 20783-1716
Tel: (301)445-7100 *Fax:* (301)445-7101
E-Mail: nabj@nabj.org
Web Site: www.nabj.org
Members: 4000 individuals
Staff: 10
Annual Budget: $2-5,000,000
Executive Director: Tangie Newborn
E-Mail: tangie@nabj.org
Director, Membership and Development: Germaine Ashton
E-Mail: germaine@nabj.org
Manager, Communications: Lisa Goodnight
Program Development Manager: Ryan Williams
E-Mail: ryan@nabj.org
Historical Note
Founded in 1975 by a group of journalists covering the Third National Institute for Black Elected Officials in Washington, DC. Works to strengthen ties among black journalists, to reward excellence in the field, and to expand job opportunities. Membership: $80/year; $50/year (associate); $25/year (student).
Meetings/Conferences:
Annual Meetings: Summer
Publications:
NABJ Journal. 4/yr. adv.

National Association of Black Professors *(1974)*
P.O. Box 526
Crisfield, MD 21817
Tel: (410)968-2393
Members: 135 individuals
President: S. Miles Woods, Ph.D.
Historical Note
NABP was formed to foster communication among Black professors and to sponsor activities to help minority students go on for advanced education.

National Association of Black Social Workers *(1968)*
1220 11th St. NW
Washington, DC 20001
Tel: (202)589-1850 *Fax:* (202)589-1853
E-Mail: nasbw.harambee@verizon.net
Web Site: www.nabsw.org
Members: 10000 individuals
Staff: 5
Annual Budget: $500-1,000,000
President: Judith Jackson
Historical Note
Membership: $100/year (individual); $400/year plus $20 per capita (organization).
Meetings/Conferences:
Annual: 2000
Publications:
Newsletter. q. adv.

National Association of Black Women Entrepreneurs *(1978)*
1 Ford Place
Detroit, MI 48202
Tel: (313)874-6284 *Fax:* (313)874-9582
E-Mail: info@nabwe.org
Web Site: www.nabwe.org
Members: 5500 individuals
Staff: 7
Annual Budget: $100-250,000
President: Dolores Ratcliffe
Historical Note
Provides professional support and networking to members.
Publications:
NABWE Newsletter. bi-m.

National Association of Black-Owned Broadcasters *(1976)*
1155 Connecticut Ave. NW, Sixth Floor
Washington, DC 20036
Tel: (202)463-8970 *Fax:* (202)429-0657
E-Mail: nabob@nabob.org
Web Site: www.nabob.org
Members: 102 companies
Staff: 2
Annual Budget: $500-1,000,000
Executive Director: James Winston
Historical Note
Founded in September, 1976 and incorporated in the District of Columbia in 1977. Members are African-Americans who own radio and/or television stations, cable television systems and related businesses.
Meetings/Conferences:
Semi-annual Meetings: Washington, D.C./Sept. and Spring

National Association of Blacks in Criminal Justice *(1974)*
North Carolina Central University
P.O. Box 19788
Durham, NC 27707-0099
Tel: (919)683-1801 *Fax:* (919)683-1903
Toll Free: (866)846 - 2225
Web Site: www.nabcj.org
Members: 5000 individuals
Staff: 2
Annual Budget: $250-500,000
Director, National Office Operations: Wilma J. Nichols-Franco
President: Fay Lessister
Historical Note
The National Association of Blacks in Criminal Justice is a multi-racial, non-partisan, non-profit association of criminal justice professionals and community leaders dedicated to improving the administration of justice. The association was founded as a vehicle by which criminal justice practitioners could initiate positive changes from within, while increasing opportunities for the average citizen to better understand the nature and the operation of our local, state, and federal criminal justice processes. Membership and participation in the activities of the association are open to all, irrespective of race, creed, or country of national origin.
Meetings/Conferences:
Annual Meetings: July
Publications:
NABCJ Journal. q. adv.
NABCJ Directory. a. adv.

National Association of Blacks In Government *(1975)*
3005 Georgia Ave. NW
Washington, DC 20001-3807
Tel: (202)667-3280 *Fax:* (202)667-3705
E-Mail: big@bignet.org
Web Site: www.bignet.org
Staff: 4
Office Staff Director: James Wilson
Historical Note
Incorporated in 1976 in the District of Columbia. Membership: $25/year.
Publications:
Newsletter. semi-a.

National Association of Blind Teachers *(1971)*
Historical Note
An affiliate of American Council of the Blind, which provides administrative support.

National Association of Boards of Examiners of Long Term Care Administrators *(1970)*
1444 I St. NW, Suite 700
Washington, DC 20005-2210
Tel: (202)712-9040 *Fax:* (202)216-9646
E-Mail: nab@bostrom.com
Web Site: www.nabweb.org
Members: 52 licensing boards/50 individuals
Staff: 5
Annual Budget: $1-2,000,000
Executive Director: Randy L. Lindner, CAE
Deputy Executive Director: Nancy Williams
Program Manager, Education, Marketing and Public Relations: Mark Wright
Historical Note
Purpose is to consider questions of common interest (i.e. educational and professional standards, uniformity of laws and regulations) to the long term care administrators' examination and licensing boards and authorities of the United States. Regular members are licensing boards; associate members are individuals; subscribing members are non-profit organizations and educational institutions. Membership: $1,100/year (regular); $70/year (associate/subscribing).
Meetings/Conferences:
Semi-annual Meetings: June and November
2007 – San Francisco, CA(Hotel Nikko)/June 13-15/80
Publications:
NAB NHA Study Guide. every 5 years.
NAB RC/AL Study Guide. every 5 years.
NAB Newsletter. q.

National Association of Boards of Pharmacy *(1904)*
1600 Feehanville Dr.
Mt. Prospect, IL 60056
Tel: (847)391-4406 *Fax:* (847)391-4502
E-Mail: custserv@nabp.net
Web Site: www.nabp.net
Members: 67 states or jurisdictions
Staff: 86
Annual Budget: $10-25,000,000

Executive Director and Secretary: Carmen A. Catizone

Historical Note

Serves all American boards of pharmacy in matters of interstate reciprocity of licensure, uniform examination and licensing as well as other matters of mutual concern. $250/state board.

Meetings/Conferences:

Annual Meetings: Spring/300

2007 – Portland, OR(Hilton Hotel and Executive Tower)/May 19-22/425

2008 – Baltimore, MD(Marriot Baltimore Waterfront Hotel)/May 17-20/425

Publications:

NABP Newsletter. 10/year.

NABP Survey of Pharmacy Law. a.

National Association of Boards, Commissions, and Councils of Catholic Education *(1972)*

Historical Note

An affiliate of National Catholic Educational Association, which provides administrative support.

National Association of Boat Manufacturers *(1945)*

Historical Note

An affiliate of National Marine Manufacturers Association, which provides administrative support.

National Association of Bond Lawyers *(1979)*

250 S. Wacker Dr., Suite 1550
Chicago, IL 60606-5886
Tel: (312)648-9590 *Fax:* (312)648-9588
E-Mail: nabl@nabl.org
Web Site: www.nabl.org
Members: 3000 individuals
Staff: 7
Annual Budget: $2-5,000,000
Executive Director: Kenneth J. Luurs, CAE
Director, Government Affairs: Elizabeth Wagner

Historical Note

Members are lawyers specializing in the legal problems of debt obligations of the various states and their political subdivisions. Membership: $275/year (over 3 years of practice); $150/year (less than 2 years of practice).

Meetings/Conferences:

2007 – Chicago, IL(Sheraton Chicago Hotel and Towers)/Sept. 26-28

2008 – Chicago, IL(Sheraton Chicago Hotel and Towers)/Sept. 17-19

Publications:

Directory. a.

The Bond Lawyer. q. adv.

National Association of Broadcast Employees and Technicians - Communications Workers of America *(1934)*

501 Third St. NW, Sixth Floor
Washington, DC 20001-2797
Tel: (202)434-1254 *Fax:* (202)434-1426
E-Mail: nabet-cwa@cwa-union.org
Web Site: www.nabetcwa.org
Members: 10000 individuals
Staff: 11
Annual Budget: $5-10,000,000
Sector President: John S. Clark
Administrative Secretary: Sherry King
Director, Membership and Information: Mike Tiglio

Historical Note

Organized as a company union in 1934 by the National Broadcasting Company under the title, Association of Technical Employees. Broke away from NBC in 1940 and changed its name to the National Association of Broadcast Engineers and Technicians. Chartered as an industrial union in 1951 by the Congress of Industrial Organizations under the name, National Association of Broadcast Employees and Technicians. Merged with the Communications Workers of America, AFL-CIO, January 1, 1994. Membership: 1.666% of gross wages.

Meetings/Conferences:

Quadrennial Meetings:

Publications:

NABET News. bi-m.

National Association of Broadcasters *(1922)*

1771 N St. NW
Washington, DC 20036
Tel: (202)429-5300 *Fax:* (202)429-4199
E-Mail: nab@nab.org
Web Site: www.nab.org
Members: 7500radio,tvstations&associates
Staff: 175
Annual Budget: $25-50,000,000
President and Chief Executive Officer: David K. Rehr, Ph.D.
Executive Vice President and Chief Financial Officer: Kenneth D. Almgren
Senior Vice President, Conventions and Exhibits: Chris Brown
Vice President, Science and Technology: Lynn Claudy
Senior Vice President, Finance: Mary P. Dickson
Senior Vice President, Meetings and Special Events: Joan Joffe
Executive Vice President, Law and Regulatory Policy: Marsha J. McBride
Executive Vice President, Corporate Communications: Dennis Wharton
Executive Vice President, Government Relations: Douglas S. Wiley

Historical Note

In 1951 NAB merged with the Television Broadcasters Association and changed its name to the National Association of Radio and Television Broadcasters; in 1958 the present name was reassumed. Absorbed the Daytime Broadcasters Association in 1985 and the National Radio Broadcasters Association in 1986. Connected with the Television and Radio Political Action Committee (TARPAC). The Television Information Office is an affliate of NAB. NAB upholds the American system of broadcasting, free from government censorship, and combats discriminatory legislative proposals against broadcasting and advertising. Maintains an annual budget of approximately $27 million.

Meetings/Conferences:

Semi-Annual Meetings: Spring and Fall(Radio Convention)

Publications:

At Your Service. bi-m.

RadioWeek. w. adv.

Engineering Conference Proceedings. a.

NAB Daily News. d.

TV Today. w. adv.

National Association of Business Consultants *(1984)*

P.O. Box 7345
Hudson, FL 34674
Tel: (727)838-1934 *Fax:* (561)423-8433
E-Mail: placeme@nabc-inc.com
Web Site: www.nabc-inc.com
Members: 10300 individuals
Staff: 25
Annual Budget: $5-10,000,000
Executive Officer: Jefferis H. Livingston, Ph.D.

Historical Note

NABC members are accountants, financial planners, information technologists and others offering business consulting services. Provides member referrals to companies seeking consultants. Services to members include web design/internet access and other professional services.

Publications:

Communicator Newsletter. q.

Membership Directory. a.

National Association for Business Economics *(1959)*

1233 20th St. NW, Suite 505
Washington, DC 20036-2304
Tel: (202)463-6223 *Fax:* (202)463-6239
E-Mail: nabe@nabe.com
Web Site: www.nabe.com
Members: 2600 individuals
Staff: 3
Annual Budget: $500-1,000,000
Executive Director: Susan Doolittle
E-Mail: doolittle@nabe.com

Historical Note

Founded as National Association of Business Economists; assumed its current name in 2000. A professional society of persons with an active interest in business economics who are employed by private, institutional or academic concerns in the area of business. Membership: $140/year (individual); $400/year (institution).

Meetings/Conferences:

Annual Meetings: Fall/300

Publications:

Business Economics. q. adv.

NABE News. 10/year. adv.

NABE Outlook. q.

Industry Survey. q.

Policy Survey. semi-a.

Salary Survey. bien.

Membership Directory. a. adv.

National Association of Business Political Action Committees *(1977)*

101 Constitution Ave. NW
#800-West
Washington, DC 20001
Tel: (202)341-3780 *Fax:* (202)478-0342
E-Mail: NABPAC@aol.com
Web Site: www.nabpac.org
Members: 130 corporate & trade association PACS
Staff: 2
Annual Budget: $250-500,000
Executive Director: Geoff Ziebart

Historical Note

Members are companies and trade associations sponsoring political action committees for their employees and members. Provides a forum for improving PAC management, solicitation and contributions. Lobbies on campaign finance legislation. Membership: $750-4,500/year (organization).

Publications:

The PAC Professional. w.

NABPAC News Memo. m.

National Association of Business Travel Agents *(1980)*

3699 Wilshire Blvd., Suite 700
Los Angeles, CA 90010-2726
Tel: (213)382-3335 *Fax:* (213)480-7712
Members: 1600 individuals
Staff: 6
Director: Stuart J. Faber

Historical Note

NABTA members are travel agents specializing in corporate and business travel.

Publications:

Adjourn Magazine. bi-m.

First Class Executive Travel. bi-m.

National Association of Case Management *(1990)*

7 Ebb Tide Ct.
Salem, SC 29676
Tel: (864)944-9788
E-Mail: lindanacm@aol.com
Web Site: www.yournacm.addr.com
Executive Officer: Linda Giesler

Historical Note

The NACM, a not-for-profit organization, provides case managers and other service coordination practitioners with an opportunity for professional growth and for the promotion of case management. Membership: $79/year (individual); $245/year (organizational).

Publications:

Case Management Reports.

National Association of Casino and Theme Party Operators *(1990)*

7815 S. 180th St.
Kent, WA 98032-1050
Tel: (425)272-0244 *Fax:* (425)272-0335
Toll Free: (800)355 - 8259
E-Mail: nactpo@aol.com
Web Site: www.casinoparties.com
Members: 50 companies
Annual Budget: under $10,000
Vice President, Technology: Geri Windecker
E-Mail: nactpo@aol.com

Historical Note

Founded as Casino and Theme Party Operators Association; assumed its current name in 2001. NACPO members are casino and theme party operators, planners, suppliers and others with an *interest in the industry. Membership: $300/year (organization/company).*

Publications:
Newsletter. q.
Membership Directory. a.
Suppliers & Manufacturers Directory. irreg.

National Association of Catastrophe Adjusters *(1976)*
P.O. Box 821864
North Richland Hills, TX 76182
Tel: (817)498-3466 *Fax:* (817)498-0480
E-Mail: nacatadj@aol.com
Web Site: www.nacatadj.org
*Members:*390 individuals
Staff: 1
Annual Budget: $25-50,000
Executive Administrator: Lori Ringo

Historical Note
NACA's mission is to be a professional organization focused on excellence in catastrophe insurance adjusting. NACA provides its members with education, shared resources and access to technology.

Meetings/Conferences:
Annual Meetings: January

Publications:
Roster. a. adv.
Naca News. q. adv.

National Association of Catering Executives *(1958)*
9881 Broken Land Pkwy., Suite 101
Columbia, MD 21046
Tel: (410)290-5410 *Fax:* (410)290-5460
Web Site: www.nace.net
*Members:*3500 individuals
Staff: 7
Annual Budget: $1-2,000,000
Interim Director: Joyce Summers

Historical Note
Founded as the Banquet Managers Guild in New York City on June 3, 1958; assumed its present name in 1977. Membership: $395/year (individual); $345/year renewing; $1,750-2,750/year (company).

Meetings/Conferences:
Annual Meetings: Summer
2007 - Houston, TX(Houston Marriott)/July 15-18

Publications:
NACE E-News (online). m.
The Professional Caterer. bi-m. adv.

National Association of Catholic Chaplains *(1965)*
P.O. Box 070473
Milwaukee, WI 53207-0473
Tel: (414)483-4898 *Fax:* (414)483-6712
E-Mail: nacc@nacc.org
Web Site: www.nacc.org
*Members:*3200 individuals
Staff: 9
Director, Operations: Kathy Eldridge
Director, Education and Professional Practice: Susanne Chawszczewski
Executive Director: Lawrence Seidl

Historical Note
Members are Catholic priests, sisters, permanent deacons, and laity engaged in professional health care and related institutional and parish ministries. Membership: $225/year.

Meetings/Conferences:
Annual Meetings: Annual conference, held in conjunction with Association of Professional Chaplains

Publications:
Vision. 10/year.

National Association of Catholic School Teachers *(1978)*
1700 Sansom St., Suite 903
Philadelphia, PA 19103
Tel: (215)568-4175 *Fax:* (215)568-8270
E-Mail: nacst@mail.idt.net
Web Site: www.nacst.com
*Members:*5000 individuals
Staff: 1
President: Rita C. Schwartz
Executive Vice President: Michael A. Milz

Historical Note
NACST members are teachers in Catholic schools. Membership: $60/year (individual).

Publications:
NACST Newsworthy. q.

National Association of Certified Valuation Analysts *(1990)*
1111 Brickyard Rd., Suite 200
Salt Lake City, UT 84106-5401
Tel: (801)486-0600 *Fax:* (801)486-7500
Toll Free: (800)677 - 2009
E-Mail: nacva1@nacva.com
Web Site: www.navca.com
*Members:*6000 individuals
Staff: 35
Executive Director: Pamela R. Bailey
Chief Executive Officer: Parnell Black, MBA, CPA, CVA
Senior Public Relations Manager: Jeffrey Chappell
Director, Education and Conferences: Brien K. Jones
Director, Marketing and Quality Assurance: Douglas Kirchner
Senior Financial Officer: Steve Marston
Director, Staff Support: Jackie Phillips
Director, Member Services: Sheila Travis

Historical Note
NACVA's membership of approximately 6,000 professionals is comprised of primarily CPAs and other valuation and consulting professionals, all of whom are pursuing business valuation, litigation forensics consulting, fraud deterrence and detection, and various other types of related services serving the legal and business communities. Of the total membership, about 80% have obtained the Certified Valuation Analyst (CVA), Accredited Valuation Analyst (AVA), Certified Forensic Financial Analyst (CFFA) or Certified Fraud Deterrence Analyst (CFD) designation. NACVA's membership comprises some of the most intelligent, dynamic, and innovative people in the professional financial/accounting community- who have completed rigorous certification programs requiring a complete understanding of the knowledge base and theory in the fields of valuation, litigation, fraud deterrence, and related disciplines. Membership: $430/year (Practitioner); $215/year (Professional/Academician); $195 (Associate/Student/Government).

Meetings/Conferences:
Annual Meetings: Spring
2007 - Washington, DC(Omni Shoreham)/June 6-9

Publications:
Speakers Bureau Directory. online.
KeyValueData.com - Quarterly National Economic Reports. q.
Writers' Guild Directory (Online).
The Association News (Online). q.
Mentor Support Group Directory (Online).
Technical Resources Directory. online.
The Value Examiner. bi-m (and online). adv.
Credentials Member Directory (Online).
The Valuation Compilation (Online).

National Association of Chain Drug Stores *(1933)*
413 N. Lee St.
P.O. Box 1417-D49
Alexandria, VA 22313
Tel: (703)549-3001 *Fax:* (703)836-4869
Web Site: www.nacds.org
*Members:*200 chains and 36,000 pharmacies
Staff: 115
Annual Budget: $25-50,000,000
Senior Vice President, Member Programs and Services: James A. Whitman
Vice President, Communications, Marketing and Production: Daniel Faoro
E-Mail: dfaoro@nacds.org
Chief Financial Officerand Senior Vice President, Finance and Administration: R. James Huber
Vice President, Membership Services: Rhonda L. Kelly
E-Mail: rkelly@nacds.org
Vice President, State Government Affairs: Cathy Polley
Vice President, Human Resources/Administration: Nancy Riegle

Historical Note
NACDS members are retail chain drugstore companies with four or more stores. In addition, NACDS membership includes includes over 1,400 suppliers of goods and services to the chain drug industry. Sponsors and supports the NACDS Political Action Committee. Has an annual budget of approximately $31 million. Membership: $1,500-50,000/year.

Meetings/Conferences:
Annual Meetings: Spring

Publications:
Issue Update. w.
The Practice Memo. m.
Monday Morning. w.
Membership Directory. a.
Industry Events Calendar. a.
NACDS Smart Brief. d.
Government Affairs Bulletin. w.
National Health and Community events Resource Guide. a.
Chain Pharmacy Industry Profile. a.
CEO Update. w.

National Association of Chain Manufacturers *(1932)*
P.O. Box 22681
Lehigh Valley, PA 18002-2268
Tel: (610)691-8708 *Fax:* (520)886-0695
E-Mail: dsayenga@aol.com
Web Site: www.nacm.info
*Members:*8 companies
Staff: 1
Annual Budget: under $10,000
Executive Director: Donald Sayenga

Meetings/Conferences:
Semi-Annual Meetings: Spring and Fall, Chicago, IL

Publications:
Specifications-Welded Chain. irreg.
Specifications-Weldless Chain. irreg.

National Association of Chapter 13 Trustees
3008 Millwood Ave.
Columbia, SC 29205
Tel: (803)252-5646 *Fax:* (803)765-0860
Toll Free: (800)445 - 8629
Web Site: www.nactt.com
Members: 1000 individuals
Executive Director: Carol H. Webster

Publications:
NACTT Quarterly. q.

National Association of Charterboat Operators *(1991)*
P.O. Box 2990
Orange Beach, AL 36561
Tel: (251)981-5136 *Fax:* (251)981-8191
Toll Free: (866)981 - 5136
E-Mail: info@nacocharters.org
Web Site: www.nacocharters.org/
*Members:*3600 individuals
Staff: 4
Annual Budget: $100-250,000
Executive Director: Bobbi Walker

Historical Note
NACO members are operators of sportfishing, diving and small excursion vessels. NACO provides group charterboat insurance and a drug testing consortium. Membership: $35/year (individual).

Publications:
NACO Report. q. adv.

National Association of Chemical Distributors *(1971)*
1560 Wilson Blvd., Suite 1250
Arlington, VA 22209-2409
Tel: (703)527-6223 *Fax:* (703)527-7747
E-Mail: nacdpublicaffairs@nacd.com
Web Site: www.nacd.com
*Members:*251 companies
Staff: 12
Annual Budget: $2-5,000,000
President and Chief Operating Officer: James L. Kolstad
E-Mail: jkolstad@nacd.com

Director, Regulatory Affairs: Bill Allmond
Vice President, Goverment and Public Affairs: Jennifer Gibson
Vice President, Operations: Mary Ann Hall
E-Mail: mahall@nacd.com
Vice President, Association Programs: Camille S. Iasiello

Historical Note
NACD is composed of distributors of industrial chemicals. Supports and houses the Chemical Educational Foundation (www.chemed.org). Membership: $1,525-26,940/year (company).

Meetings/Conferences:
Annual Meetings: November-December/800

Publications:
Membership Directory. a. adv.
Chemical Distributor. 10/year. adv.

National Association of Chiefs of Police *(1967)*
6350 Horizon Dr.
Titusville, FL 32780
Tel: (321)264-0911 *Fax:* (321)264-0033
E-Mail: policeinfo@aphf.org
Web Site: www.aphf.org
Members: 11000 individuals
Staff: 22
Annual Budget: $500-1,000,000
Executive Director: Donna M. Shepherd

Historical Note
Formerly National Police Museum. Maintains the American Police Hall of Fame and Museum. Membership: $50/year.

Meetings/Conferences:
Annual Meetings: With the American Federation of Police

Publications:
Chief of Police Magazine. bi-m. adv.

National Association of Child Advocates

Historical Note
Became Voices for America's Children in 2003.

National Association of Child Care Professionals *(1984)*
P.O. Box 90723
Austin, TX 78709-0723
Tel: (512)301-5557 *Fax:* (512)301-5080
Toll Free: (800)537 - 1118
E-Mail: admin@naccp.org
Web Site: www.naccp.org
Members: 2000 individuals
Staff: 6
Annual Budget: $250-500,000
Chief Executive Officer and Executive Director: Sherry Workman
Director, Accreditation: Lois Gamble
Director, Marketing: Ginger Meyners
Director, Administration: Dana Wadham

Historical Note
Professional association for supervisors and administrators of child care facilities. Membership: $120/year (individual); $100/year (associate); $349/year (vendor).

Meetings/Conferences:
Annual Meetings: Spring
2007 - Boston, MA(Seaport)/Apr. 25-28/500

Publications:
Caring for Your Children Newsletter. q. adv.
Professional Connections Newsletter. q. adv.
Teamwork Newsletter. q. adv.

National Association of Child Care Resource and Referral Agencies *(1987)*
1301 Wilson Blvd., #350
Arlington, VA 22210
Tel: (703)341-4100 *Fax:* (703)341-4101
E-Mail: info@naccrra.org
Web Site: www.naccrra.org
Members: 250 individuals
Staff: 30
Annual Budget: $10-25,000,000
Executive Director: Linda Smith
Chief of Operations: Ollie Smith

Historical Note
NACCRRA promotes the development, maintenance and expansion of quality community-based child care resource and referral services. Voting members are resource and referral organizations. Auxiliary members are organizations and individuals supporting NACCRRA's goals. Membership: $50-$350/year, varies by budget (voting); $50-5,000 (auxiliary).

Meetings/Conferences:
Annual Meetings: Winter

Publications:
Daily Parent. q.
CCR&R Issues. q. adv.

National Association of Children's Hospitals *(1968)*
401 Wythe St.
Alexandria, VA 22314
Tel: (703)684-1355 *Fax:* (703)684-1589
Web Site: www.childrenshospitals.net
Members: 168 hospitals
Staff: 70
Annual Budget: $5-10,000,000
President and Chief Executive Officer: Lawrence A. McAndrews
E-Mail: lmcandrews@nachri.org
Vice President, Education, M.I.S., and Operations: Mary Gorman
Senior Fellow and Vice President, Classification Research: John Muldoon
E-Mail: jmuldoon@nachri.org
Vice President, Public Affairs: Lisa M. Tate
Vice President, Public Policy: Peters D. Willson
E-Mail: pwillson@nachri.org

Historical Note
NACHRI promotes the well-being of children through support of children's hospitals and related institutions committed to excellence in treating, healing and nurturing children. Members are free standing hospitals providing a range of services from general acute care to specialty care. Other members include universities and medical centers specializing in the care of children.

Meetings/Conferences:
Annual Meetings: Fall

Publications:
Children's Hospitals Today. q.

National Association of Church Business Administration *(1957)*
100 N. Central Expy., Suite 914
Richardson, TX 75080-5326
Tel: (972)699-7555 *Fax:* (972)699-7617
Toll Free: (800)898 - 8085
E-Mail: info@nacba.net
Web Site: www.nacba.net
Members: 2900 individuals
Staff: 5
Annual Budget: $500-1,000,000
Chief Executive Officer: Simeon May
E-Mail: info@nacba.net

Historical Note
Business managers of local congregations, military chapels or other religious institutions. Provides training, resources, and support for managers of all Christian churches. Also provides a certification program in church administration. Membership: $150/year.

Meetings/Conferences:
Annual Meetings: July
2007 - Grapevine, TX(Gaylord Texan)/July 11-15
2008 - Nashville, TN(Gaylord Opryland)/July 4-8
2009 - Long Beach, CA(Long Beach Convention Center)/July 17-21
2010 - Orlando, FL(Gaylord Palms)/July 2-6

Publications:
NACBA Ledger. q. adv.
NACBA Gram. m.

National Association of Church Food Service *(1990)*
P.O. Box 550413
Atlanta, GA 30305
Tel: (404)240-8217 *Fax:* (404)240-8276
Web Site: www.nacfs.org
Members: 225 individuals
Staff: 1
Chief Executive Officer: Carolyn B. Clayton

Historical Note
NACFS members are directors of church food services. Offers certification program.

Publications:
Newsletter.
Membership Directory.

National Association of Church Personnel Administrators *(1971)*
100 E. Eighth St.
Cincinnati, OH 45202-2129
Tel: (513)421-3134 *Fax:* (513)421-3085
E-Mail: nacpa@nacpa.org
Web Site: www.nacpa.org
Members: 1200 individuals
Staff: 6
Annual Budget: $500-1,000,000
Executive Director: Mary Jo Moran, Ph.D.

Historical Note
Formed by the National Federation of Priests' Councils at the University of Notre Dame in October, 1971. Members are personnel administrators in church-related organizations. Membership: $160/year (individual); $600/year (company).

Meetings/Conferences:
Annual Meetings: Spring
2007 - St. Louis, MO(Hyatt Regency)/Apr. 22-26

Publications:
NACPA Newsletter. bi-m. adv.

National Association of Clean Water Agencies *(1970)*
1816 Jefferson Place NW
Washington, DC 20036-2505
Tel: (202)833-2672 *Fax:* (202)833-4657
E-Mail: info@nacwa.org
Web Site: www.nacwa.org
Members: 340 agencies
Staff: 18
Annual Budget: $2-5,000,000
Executive Director: Ken Kirk, CAE
Deputy Executive Director: Paula Dannenfeldt
Counsel: Alexandra Dunn

Historical Note
Founded as Association of Metropolitan Sewerage Agencies. Incorporated in the District of Columbia in 1970. Assumed tis current name in 2005. Membership consists of sewerage agencies. Formed to exchange technical data of mutual benefit and deal with the Federal Government on environmental and regulatory matters. Membership:$1,500-$25,000 for individual municipal utilities.

Meetings/Conferences:
Annual Meetings: Spring/300

Publications:
Wastewater Sector Security Link e-news. q.
Wet Weather Consent Decrees.
Legal Alert.
AMSA Clean Water News. m.
Year in Review Handbook. a.

National Association of Clinical Nurse Specialists *(1995)*
2090 Linglestown Rd., Suite 107
Harrisburg, PA 17110
Tel: (717)234-6799 *Fax:* (717)234-6798
Web Site: www.nacns.org
Members: 1750
Staff: 1
Executive Director: Christine C. Filipovich
E-Mail: christine@pronursingresources.com

Historical Note
NACNS regular members are nurses who are masters-prepared as clinical nurse specialists, masters-prepared in related areas practicing as clinical nurse specialists, or doctorally-prepared and involved in the education of clinical nurse specialists. Membership: $110/year (regular); $65/year (student).

Meetings/Conferences:
2007 - Phoenix, AZ(Hyatt Regency)/Feb. 28-March 3/400
2008 - Atlanta, GA(Westin Peachtree Plaza)/March 3-10/400

Publications:
Clinical Nurse Specialists. bi-m. adv.

NACNS News. bi-m.
Networking Membership Directory. bien.

National Association of College and University Attorneys *(1961)*
One Dupont Circle NW, Suite 620
Washington, DC 20036
Tel: (202)833-8390 *Fax:* (202)296-8379
E-Mail: nacua@nacua.org
Web Site: www.nacua.org
Members: 660 colleges and universities
Staff: 14
Annual Budget: $1-2,000,000
Chief Executive Officer: Kathleen Curry Santora
Director, Information Services: John R. Bishop
Director, Legal Resources: Karl Brevitz
Manager, Publications: Linda Henderson
Manager, Membership and Outreach Services: Miriam Miller

Historical Note
NACUA was established to improve the quality of legal assistance to colleges and universities by educating attorneys and administrators to the nature of campus legal issues. NACUA produces publications, sponsors seminars and operates a clearinghouse through which attorneys share knowledge and work-product on current legal problems. Members are accredited institutions of higher education in the U.S. and Canada; each institution may be represented by several attorneys. Membership: $270-3,155/year (organization).

Meetings/Conferences:
Annual Meetings: June/650

Publications:
New to Higher Education.
NACUA News.
NACUA Contract Formbook.
NACUA Handbook for Lawyers.

National Association of College and University Business Officers *(1956)*
2501 M St. NW, Suite 400
Washington, DC 20037-1308
Tel: (202)861-2500 *Fax:* (202)861-2583
Toll Free: (800)462 - 4916
Web Site: www.nacubo.org
Members: 2300 colleges and universites
Staff: 48
Annual Budget: $5-10,000,000
President and Chief Executive Officer: James E. Morley, Jr.
Vice President, Business Development: Bill Dillon
Vice President, Community Member Services: Jeff Shields
E-Mail: jeff.shields@nacubo.org

Historical Note
Formerly (1962) National Federation of College and University Business Officers Associations. Represents accredited, non-profit institutions of higher learning approved for membership by a regional business officers association. NACUBO members represent approximately two-thirds of all institutions of higher learning in the U.S. Has an annual budget of approximately $8 million. Membership: $494-3,705/year (organization).

Meetings/Conferences:
Annual Meetings: Summer/1,200
2007 - New Orleans, LA/July 21-24

Publications:
Business Officer Magazine. m. adv.

National Association of College and University Food Services *(1958)*
1405 S. Harrison, Suite 305
East Lansing, MI 48824-5242
Tel: (517)332-2494 *Fax:* (517)332-8144
Web Site: www.nacufs.org
Members: 600 institutions, 450 companies
Staff: 11
Annual Budget: $2-5,000,000
Executive Director: Joseph H. Spina, Ph.D., CAE
E-Mail: jspina@nacufs.org
Director, Education: Ellen Behrens
Financial Coordinator: Trish Collier
Education Planner: Morgan Lucero
E-Mail: mlucero@nacufs.org
Coordinator, Member Services: Mary O'Connor
E-Mail: moconnor@nacufs.org
Manager, Marketing: Jodi L. Smith
National Conference Planner: Sandra L. Smith

Meetings/Conferences:
Annual Meetings: Summer/900
2007 - Seattle, WA(Sheraton)/July 11-14
2008 - Washington, DC(Marriott Wardman Park)/July 9-12
2009 - Milwaukee, WI/July 8-11

Publications:
Campus Dining Today. q. adv.
NACUFS Directory. a. adv.

National Association of College Auxiliary Services *(1969)*
P.O. Box 5546
Charlottesville, VA 22905
Tel: (434)245-8425 *Fax:* (434)245-8453
E-Mail: info@nacas.org
Web Site: www.nacas.org
Members: 1400 individuals
Staff: 9
Annual Budget: $1-2,000,000
Executive Director: Dr. Bob Hassmiller
E-Mail: bob@nacas.org
Manager, Member Services: Cheryl Armstrong
E-Mail: cheryl@nacas.org
Coordinator, Member Services: Julie Arnatt
E-Mail: julie@nacas.org
Director, Education: Cathy Pales
Deputy Executive Director: Jeffery Perdue
E-Mail: jeff@nacas.org
Director, Media Services: David Rood
E-Mail: david@nacas.org

Historical Note
Founded as the Association of College Auxiliary Services; assumed its present name in 1973. Members are directors of college auxiliary services such as book stores, laundries, food services, housing, vending, printing, etc. Membership: $225-875/year (organization/company).

Meetings/Conferences:
Annual Meetings: Fall/650
2007 - Las Vegas, NV(MGM Grand)/Oct. 28-31

Publications:
College Services. bi-m. adv.
NACAS News/NACAS Online. q.

National Association of College Stores *(1923)*
500 E. Lorain St.
Oberlin, OH 44074-1298
Tel: (440)775-7777 *Fax:* (440)775-4769
Toll Free: (800)622 - 7498
Web Site: www.nacs.org
Members: 3200 college stores
Staff: 89
Annual Budget: $10-25,000,000
Chief Executive Officer: Brian Cartier, CAE
E-Mail: bcartier@nacs.org
Vice President, Association Services: Cynthia D'Angelo
E-Mail: cdangelo@nacs.org
Director, Education: Tony Ellis, CAE
E-Mail: tellis@nacs.org
Managing Director, PartnerShip: John Finucane
E-Mail: jfinucane@nacs.org
Chief Human Resources Officer: Sheila Giano
Vice President, Marketing and Member Services: Wendy Holliday
Director, Publications: Cynthia E. Ruckman
E-Mail: cruckman@nacs.org
Senior Vice President, Industry Services: Ed Schlichenmayer
E-Mail: eschlichenmayer@nacs.org
Director, Public Relations: Charlie Schmidt
Chief Operating Officer, NASCORP: Kurt Schoen
Chief Financial Officer: Frank Sulen
E-Mail: fsulen@nacs.org
Director, Planning and Research: Julie Traylor
E-Mail: jtraylor@nacs.org

Historical Note
NACS supports the collegiate retailing industry with education, services and advocacy. Organized in 1923, NACS now includes NACSCORP (a for-profit book and software distributor); NACS Foundation (a foundation providing research and education to college retailers); and PartnerShip (a for-profit provider of freight services). Membership fees vary based on store size.

Meetings/Conferences:
Annual Meetings: April

Publications:
CM Bulletin. w. adv.
Course Materials Resource Guide. bien.
NACS Schedule of College and University Dates. a.
NACS Directory of Colleges and College Stores. a. adv.
College Store. 6/yr. adv.
NACS Campus Marketplace. bi-w. adv.
College Store Monthly Planner. a.
NACS Book Buyers Manual. bien.

National Association of College Wind and Percussion Instructors *(1951)*
Division of Fine Arts
Truman State University
Kirksville, MO 63501
Tel: (660)785-4442 *Fax:* (660)785-7463
Web Site: www.nacwpi.org/
Members: 1400 individuals
Staff: 1
Annual Budget: $10-25,000
Executive Secretary-Treasurer: Richard Weerts

Historical Note
Associated with the Music Educators National Conference. Members are those responsible for teaching wind and percussion instruments in American colleges and universities. Membership: $30/year.

Meetings/Conferences:
Biennial Meetings: Even Years

Publications:
Bibliography of Papers Appearing in the NACWPI Journal. a.
Holdings of the NACWPI Research Library. a.
NACWPI Journal. q. adv.

National Association of Colleges and Employers *(1956)*
62 Highland Ave.
Bethlehem, PA 18017
Tel: (610)868-1421 *Fax:* (610)868-0208
Toll Free: (800)544 - 5272
Web Site: www.naceweb.org
Members: 3000 colleges and employers
Staff: 34
Annual Budget: $2-5,000,000
Executive Director: Marilyn F. Mackes, Ph.D.
Director, Information: Mimi Collins
Director, Membership Services: Sandra Dalious
Director, Finance and Facility: Thomas Homanick
Assistant Executive Director, Products and Services: Norita H. Rehrig

Historical Note
Formerly (1953) Association of School and College Placement and (1995) College Placement Council. NACE is a professional association for career services professionals and employers of college graduates. Membership: $360/year.

Publications:
Spotlight (Online). bi-w. adv.
NACE Journal. q. adv.
Salary Survey. q.
Job Choices. a. adv.

National Association of Collegiate Directors of Athletics *(1965)*
P.O. Box 16428
Cleveland, OH 44116-0428
Tel: (440)892-4000 *Fax:* (440)892-4007
Web Site: www.nacda.com
Members: 6100 individuals
Staff: 10
Annual Budget: $1-2,000,000
Executive Director: Michael J. Cleary
Liaison, Administration: Jason Galaska
Assistant Executive Director, Communications: Laurie Garrison
Membership Coordinator: Brian Horning
Associate Executive Director: Pat Manak
Meeting Coordinator: Dorothy A. Sikkila
Manager, Business: Terry Steirer

Senior Associate Executive Director: Bob Vecchione

Historical Note

Members are directors of athletics and athletic staff members at two- and four-year institutions. Membership: $50-1,250/year (based on NCAA division and size of school).

Meetings/Conferences:

Annual Meetings: June

2007 – Orlando, FL/June 7-10

Publications:

Athletics Administration. bi-m. adv.

National Association of Collegiate Marketing Administrators *(1990)*

P.O. Box 16428
Cleveland, OH 44116-0428
Tel: (440)892-4000 *Fax:* (440)892-4007
Web Site: www.nacda.coma
Members: 600 individuals
Staff: 2
Senior Associate Executive Director: Bob Varchione
E-Mail: bvarchione@nacda.com

Historical Note

NACMA members are public relations and marketing professionals in college and university athletics departments. NACMA promotes a standard of ethics and provides professional support to members. An affiliate of National Association of Collegiate Directors of Athletics, which provides administrative support. Membership: $50-75/year (individual); $125/year (affiliates).

Meetings/Conferences:

Annual Meetings: June

Publications:

NACMA Corner in Athletics Administration. bi-m. adv.
NACMA Ideas. q.

National Association of Collegiate Women Athletic Administrators *(1979)*

4701 Wrightsville Ave.
Oak Park D-1
Wilmington, NC 28403
Tel: (910)793-8244 *Fax:* (910)793-8246
E-Mail: nacwaa@nacwaa.org
Web Site: www.nacwaa.org/
Members: 1200 individuals
Staff: 5
Annual Budget: $500-1,000,000
Executive Director: Jennifer Alley
E-Mail: jalley@nacwaa.org
Director, Events and External Affairs: Sheree Gibson, CMP
Director, Education and Member Services: Annette Lynch

Meetings/Conferences:

Annual Meetings: October

Publications:

NACWAA Weekly Update. w.
NACWAA Newsletter. q.

National Association of Colored Women's Clubs *(1896)*

1601 R St. NW
Washington, DC 20009
Tel: (202)667-4080 *Fax:* (202)667-2754
Web Site: www.nacwc.org
Members: 1000 organizations
Staff: 3
Annual Budget: $50-100,000
Executive Secretary: Carole A. Early
President: Margaret J. Cooper

Historical Note

Formed through a merger of the National Colored Women's League and the National Federation of Afro-American Women. Sponsors the National Association of Youth Clubs.

Meetings/Conferences:

Biennial Meetings: Summer

Publications:

National Notes. 2/year.

National Association of Commissions for Women *(1970)*

401 N. Washington St., Suite 100
Rockville, MD 20850-1772
Tel: (240)777-8308 *Fax:* (301)279-1318
Toll Free: (800)338 - 9267
E-Mail: info@nacw.org
Web Site: www.nacw.org
Members: 240 member commissions
Associate Director: Judith Vaughan-Pratner

Meetings/Conferences:

Annual Meetings: Summer

Publications:

Breakthrough. 3/yr. adv.
Health. a. adv.
NACW Networking News. q.

National Association of Community Health Centers *(1970)*

7200 Wisconsin Ave., #210
Bethesda, MD 20814
Tel: (301)347-0400 *Fax:* (301)347-0459
Web Site: www.nachc.com
Members: 1200 community health centers
Staff: 65
President and Chief Executive Officer: Thomas Van Coverden
Director, Meetings: Cindy Cady
Chief Medical Officer: Tom Curtin, M.D.
Director, Membership: Maurice Denis
Executive Vice President: Claudia G. Gibson
Vice President, Finance and Administration: Mary Hawbecker
Vice President, Policy Research and Analysis: Daniel R. Hawkins, Jr.
Vice President, Programs and Planning: Malvise A. Scott
Chief Operating Officer: L. David Taylor

Historical Note

Formerly (1970) National Association of Neighborhood Health Center Directors and Administrators and (1977) National Association of Neighborhood Health Centers. NACHC is an organization which works to assure the continued growth and development of community-based health care programs by providing education, training, and technical assistance to health center staff and board members. Membership: $65/year (individual); organizational fee based on budget.

Meetings/Conferences:

Annual Meetings: Summer

Publications:

Community Health Forum Magazine. bi-m. adv.

National Association of Composers, USA *(1932)*

P.O. Box 49256, Barrington Station
Los Angeles, CA 90049
Tel: (310)838-4465
E-Mail: nacusa@music-usa.org
Web Site: www.music-usa.org/nacusa/
Members: 600 individuals
Annual Budget: under $10,000
President: Deon Nielson Price

Historical Note

Successor (1975) to the National Association of American Composers and Conductors headquartered in New York City. NACUSA members are composers, conductors and performers of music, and interested individuals. Membership: $20/year, except in New York, Los Angeles and San Fransisco; $40/year.

Publications:

Composer/USA. 3/year. adv.

National Association of Computer Consultant Businesses *(1987)*

1420 King St., Suite 610
Alexandria, VA 22314
Tel: (703)838-2050 *Fax:* (703)838-3610
E-Mail: staff@naccb.org
Web Site: www.naccb.org
Members: 450 companies
Staff: 8
Annual Budget: $100-250,000
Chief Executive Officer and General Counsel: Mark Roberts
Director of Programs and Public Policy: Susan Donohoe
Director, Membership and Services: Kimberly Grever
Director, Marketing and Communications: Julie Price-Shehan

Historical Note

NACCB members are companies providing technical support services to clients such as programming, systems analysis and software/hardware engineering.

Meetings/Conferences:

Annual Meetings: Fall

Publications:

NACCB Monitor. q.
Legislative & Legal Update. q.

National Association of Computerized Tax Processors *(1969)*

c/o Drake Software
235 East Palmer St.
Franklin, NC 28734
Tel: (828)524-8020 Ext: 8233 *Fax:* (828)349-5783
E-Mail: email@nactp.org
Web Site: www.nactp.org
Members: 65 companies
Annual Budget: $10-25,000
President: Jamie Stiles

Historical Note

Serves as a communications link with government agencies, facilitates dispersal of information affecting the industry, and coordinates solutions to industry-wide problems. Represents the computer tax industry affecting its general welfare. Members are companies developing products and services for the tax industry. Has no paid officers or full-time staff. Membership: $300/year.

Meetings/Conferences:

Annual Meetings: August

Publications:

Accounting Today Supplement. a.
Practical Accountant Supplement a.
Tax Form Design Guidelines. a.
Bylaws. irreg.
Membership Directory. a.
Supplement to Accounting Today Magazine. a.

National Association of Concessionaires *(1944)*

35 E. Wacker Dr., Suite 1816
Chicago, IL 60601
Tel: (312)236-3858 *Fax:* (312)236-7809
Web Site: www.naconline.org
Members: 1000 companies
Staff: 3
Annual Budget: $500-1,000,000
Executive Director: Charles A. Winans
E-Mail: cwinans@naconline.org
Manager, Membership Services: Barbara Aslan
Director, Communications: Susan Cross
E-Mail: scross@naconline.org

Historical Note

Founded as the National Association of Popcorn Manufacturers, it became the International Popcorn Association and then the Popcorn and Concessions Association before assuming its present name. Members are operators of food, vending and beverage concessions and their suppliers. Association activities include education and training opportunities, an annual convention in recreation and leisure venues, and trade shows. Membership: $215-545/year.

Meetings/Conferences:

Annual Meetings: Spring

Publications:

Concessionworks. q.
Concession Profession. semi-a. adv.

National Association of Conservation Districts *(1946)*

509 Capitol Ct. NE
Washington, DC 20002
Tel: (202)547-6223 *Fax:* (202)547-6450
E-Mail: washington@nacdnet.org
Web Site: www.nacdnet.org
Members: 3000 districts
Staff: 45
Annual Budget: $2-5,000,000
Chief Executive Officer: Krysta Harden
Director, Operations: Robert M. Doucette
E-Mail: bob-doucette@nacdnet.org
Director, Government Affairs: Rich Duesterhaus
Director, Communications: Darlene Robbins

Historical Note
Conservation districts are local subdivisions of state governments which work to conserve and develop land, water, forests, wildlife and related natural resources. Formerly (1970) National Association of Soil and Water Conservation Districts. Membership: $35-100/year (individual); $775-1,775/year (districts).

Meetings/Conferences:
Annual Meetings: First week in February/1,500

Publications:
Forester Notes.
Buffer Notes.
NACD News & Views. 6/year.

National Association of Consumer Advocates
(1994)
1730 Rhode Island Ave. NW, Suite 710
Washington, DC 20036
Tel: (202)452-1989 *Fax:* (202)452-0099
E-Mail: info@naca.net
Web Site: www.naca.net
Members: 700 individuals
Staff: 2
Annual Budget: $100-250,000
General Counsel: Ira Rheingold

Historical Note
Provides support to lawyers and other professionals who represent consumers seeking redress from unfair business practices. Membership: $100/year, minimum (individual).

Publications:
"The Consumer Advocate" Newsletter. 6/year.

National Association of Consumer Agency Administrators *(1976)*
Two Brentwood Commons, Suite 150
750 Old Hickory Blvd.
Brentwood, TN 37027
Tel: (615)371-6125 *Fax:* (615)369-6225
E-Mail: info@nacaa.net
Web Site: www.nacaa.net
Members: 165 consumer agencies and corporate offices
Staff: 2
Annual Budget: $100-250,000
Executive Director: Elizabeth Owen

Historical Note
Members are municipal, county or state supported consumer affairs agencies. Qualified individuals are eligible for associate membership. Membership: $100-450/year (varies by agency budget); $750/year (corporate member).

Meetings/Conferences:
Annual Meetings: Summer

Publications:
NACAA Forum. 10/year.

National Association of Consumer Credit Administrators *(1935)*
Office of the Commissioner of Banks
P.O. Box 20871
Columbus, OH 43220-0871
Tel: (614)326-1165 *Fax:* (614)326-1162
E-Mail: nacca2001@aol.com
Web Site: www.naccaonline.org
Members: 55 individuals
Annual Budget: $25-50,000
Executive Director: Raymond J. Sasala

Historical Note
Formerly Association of Small Loan Administrators and National Association of Small Loan Supervisors. Membership: $350/yr.

Meetings/Conferences:
2008 - Beverly Hills, CA(Beverly Hilton)/Sept. 30-Oct. 3

Publications:
NACCA Newsletter. q.

National Association of Consumer Shows *(1987)*
147 S.E. 102nd St.
Portland, OR 97216
Tel: (503)253-0832 *Fax:* (503)253-9172
Toll Free: (800)728 - 6227
E-Mail: info@publicshows.com
Web Site: www.publicshows.com
Members: 350 individuals
Staff: 3
Annual Budget: $100-250,000
Executive Director: Michael Fisher

Historical Note
Membership: $245/year (individual).

Meetings/Conferences:
Annual Meetings: June/July

Publications:
Membership Roster. a. adv.
Show Producer newsletter. bi-m. adv.

National Association of Container Distributors
(1925)
1601 N. Bond St., Suite 101
Naperville, IL 60563
Tel: (630)544-5052 *Fax:* (630)544-5055
E-Mail: info@nacd.net
Web Site: www.nacd.net
Members: 36 companies
Staff: 2
Annual Budget: $50-100,000

Historical Note
Formerly (1964) National Association of Glass Containers Distributors.

Meetings/Conferences:
Annual Meetings:

Publications:
Newsletter. q.

National Association of Convenience Stores
(1961)
1600 Duke St.
Alexandria, VA 22314
Tel: (703)684-3600 *Fax:* (703)836-4564
E-Mail: nacs@nacsonline.com
Web Site: www.nacsonline.com
Members: 2400retailcompanies,78,000outlets
Staff: 51
Annual Budget: $25-50,000,000
President and Chief Executive Officer: Henry O. Armour
Senior Vice President, Government Relations: Lyle Beckwith
Senior Vice President, Events, and Supplier Relations: Jane Berzan
Vice President, Retailer Services: Michael Davis
Senior Vice President, Finance and Systems: Brian Kimmel
Director, Communications: Jeff Lenard
Vice President, Research: Gray Taylor

Historical Note
Retail food stores carrying a more limited selection than supermarkets and usually open longer hours. Sponsors and supports the NACS Political Action Committee. Has an annual budget of approximately $12 million. Membership: $200-10,000/year (based on sales volume).

Meetings/Conferences:
Annual Meetings: Fall/25,000
2007 - Atlanta, GA(Georgia World Congressional Center)/Nov. 6-9/25000

Publications:
NACS Magazine. m. adv.
State of the Industry. a.
Compensation Survey. a.
Membership and Services Directory. a.
Washington Report. w.
Fact Book. a.
NACS Daily. d. adv.

National Association of Corporate Directors
(1977)
Two Lafayette Centre, Suite 700
1133 21st St. NW, Suite 700
Washington, DC 20036
Tel: (202)775-0509 *Fax:* (202)775-4857
E-Mail: info@nacdonline.org
Web Site: www.nacdonline.org
Members: 8000 individuals
Staff: 8
Annual Budget: $2-5,000,000
President and Chief Executive Officer: Roger W. Raber
E-Mail: rwraber@nacdonline.org
Vice President, Marketing: Doreen Kelly Ruyak

Historical Note
A not-for-profit educational association dedicated to ongoing information and education for corporate directors in board practices and corporate governance; focuses on issues such as Director's and Officer's liability, shareholder concerns, and responsible board decision making. Provides publications, seminars and in-house training, as well as a Register for filling board vacancies with qualified candidacies. Membership: $450/year (individual); $2,000-5,000/year (full board).

Meetings/Conferences:
Annual Meetings: Fall

Publications:
Governance Survey. bien.
Compensation Surveys. a.
Blue Ribbon Commission Reports. q.
Directors Monthly Newsletter. m.
Convention Program. a. adv.

National Association of Corporate Real Estate Executives International

Historical Note
See listing under NACORE.

National Association of Corporate Treasurers
(1982)
12100 Sunset Hills Rd., Suite 130
Reston, VA 20190
Tel: (703)437-4377 *Fax:* (703)435-4390
E-Mail: nact@nact.org
Web Site: www.nact.org
Members: 825 individuals
Staff: 1
Annual Budget: $250-500,000
Executive Director: Kathy Hoskins
Director, Finance: Glenn Beales

Historical Note
Established in Blacksburg, Virginia and incorporated in Washington, DC. NACT members are corporate chief financial officers, treasurers, or assistant treasurers. Membership: $400/year.

Meetings/Conferences:
Annual Meetings: Spring, plus technical seminars in the Winter and Fall
2007 - San Francisco(Hyatt Regency)/June 6-8

National Association of Cosmetology Schools

Historical Note
See American Association of Cosmetology Schools.

National Association of Councils on Developmental Disabilities *(1973)*
225 Reinekers Lane, #630B
Alexandria, VA 22314
Tel: (703)739-4400 *Fax:* (703)739-6030
E-Mail: info@nacdd.org
Web Site: www.nacdd.org
Members: 55 councils
Staff: 6
Annual Budget: $500-1,000,000
Executive Director: Karen Flippo

Historical Note
Provides technical support to State and territorial councils on the developmentally disabled. Founded as National Conference on Developmental Disabilities, became National Association of Developmental Disabilities Councils in 1978, and assumed its current name in 2003.

Publications:
Council Chronicles. q.
NACDD L.A.W. w.

National Association of Counsel for Children
(1977)
1825 Marion St., Suite 242
Denver, CO 80218
Toll Free: (888)828 - 6222
Web Site: www.nacchildlaw.org
Members: 2000 individuals
Staff: 4
Annual Budget: $500-1,000,000
President and Chief Executive Officer: Marvin R. Ventrell
E-Mail: ventrell.marvin@tchden.org
Policy Representative: Miriam Rollin

Historical Note
NACC members are lawyers, judges, mental health professionals, social services professionals and others with an interest in the legal status of children. Membership: $80/year (individual).

Meetings/Conferences:
Annual Meetings: Fall
2007 - Keystone, CO(Keystone Resort)/Aug. 15-18/500

Publications:
Children's Legal Rights Journal. q.
Children's Law Manual. a.
Guardian Newsletter. q. adv.

National Association of Counties *(1935)*
440 First St., NW
Eighth Floor
Washington, DC 20001
Tel: (202)393-6226 *Fax:* (202)393-2630
Web Site: www.naco.org
Members: 2064 counties
Staff: 80
Annual Budget: $10-25,000,000
Executive Director: Larry E. Naake
Director, Finance and Administration: Kathy Bosak
Director, Membership and Marketing: Andrew Goldschmidt, CAE
Director, Legislative Affairs: Edwin Rosado

Historical Note
Formerly National Association of County Officials. Founded in 1935, The National Association of Counties (NACo) provides services to the nation's 3,066 counties.
NACo represents its members before the federal government and assists counties in finding and sharing innovative solutions through education and research. Has an annual budget of approximately $19 million.

Meetings/Conferences:
Annual Meetings: Summer/5,000
2007 - Richmond, VA/July 13-17

Publications:
NACo Workforce Development. bi-w.
County News. bi-w. adv.

National Association of Counties Information Technology Administrators

Historical Note
An affiliate of National Association of Counties, which provides administrative support.

National Association of County Administrators *(1961)*

Historical Note
An affiliate of National Association of Counties, which provides administrative support.

National Association of County Aging Programs *(1978)*

Historical Note
An affiliate of National Association of Counties, which provides administrative support.

National Association of County Agricultural Agents *(1915)*
252 N. Park St.
Decatur, IL 62523
Tel: (217)876-1220 *Fax:* (217)877-5382
E-Mail: exec-dir@nacaa.com
Web Site: www.nacaa.com
Members: 4500 individuals
Staff: 1
Annual Budget: $250-500,000
Executive Director: Scott Hawbaker

Historical Note
Organized in Chicago in the old Livestock Record Building by a small group of county agents from 10 states. An association of associations, NACAA members are employees of the U.S. Department of Agriculture's Cooperative Extension Service and State Land Grant Universities.

Meetings/Conferences:
Annual Meetings: Summer/2,000

Publications:
The County Agent. q.

National Association of County and City Health Officials *(1966)*
1100 17th St. NW, Second Floor
Washington, DC 20036-4631
Tel: (202)783-5550 *Fax:* (202)783-1583
E-Mail: info@naccho.org
Web Site: www.naccho.org
Members: 3000 individuals
Staff: 45
Annual Budget: $5-10,000,000
Executive Director: Patrick Libbey
E-Mail: plibbey@naccho.org
Legislative Council: Donna Brown
Chief Financial Officer: John Mericsko
Senior Advisor, Membership and Administrative Services: Danielle Poux

Historical Note
An affiliate of the National Association of Counties. Incorporated in 1985. Founded as National Association of County Health Officials; assumed its current name in 1994. Absorbed the United States Conference of Local Health Officers in 1997. Membership: $45-1,250/year, based on size of jurisdiction population.

Meetings/Conferences:
Annual Meetings: With National Association of Counties in July and the American Public Health Association in Fall/10,000

Publications:
Public Health Dispatch. m.
Annual Report. a.
NACCHO Exchange. bi-m.

National Association of County Behavioral Health Directors *(1996)*

Historical Note
An affiliate of National Association of Counties, which provides administrative support.

National Association of County Civil Attorneys *(1963)*

Historical Note
An affiliate of National Association of Counties, which provides administrative support.

National Association of County Engineers *(1956)*
440 First St. NW
Washington, DC 20001-2028
Tel: (202)393-5041 *Fax:* (202)393-2630
E-Mail: nace@naco.org
Web Site: www.countyengineers.org
Members: 1700 individuals
Staff: 2
Annual Budget: $250-500,000
Executive Director: Anthony R. Giancola, P.E.

Historical Note
Members are county engineering professionals or road management authorities. NACE is an affiliate of the National Association of Counties. Membership: $110/year (individual); $500-5,000/year (organization/company).

Meetings/Conferences:
Annual Meetings: Late Winter/Early Spring

Publications:
Blading Unpaved Roads Video.
NACE News. m.
NACE Membership Directory. a.

National Association of County Health Facility Administrators *(1978)*
1523 W. US 2
Crystal Falls, MI 49920
Tel: (906)875-6671 *Fax:* (906)875-6573
Members: 240 individuals
Staff: 1
Annual Budget: under $10,000
President: Chester Pintarelli
E-Mail: cepicmcf@up.net

Historical Note
An affiliate of the National Association of Counties, which provides administrative support. NACHFA works to improve the quality of healthcare available from county nursing homes and other long-term care institutions. Membership: $25/year (individual); $250/year (organization).

Meetings/Conferences:
Semi-annual Meetings: with NACo in July and in March

National Association of County Human Services Administrators *(1935)*

Historical Note
An affiliate of National Association of Counties, which provides administrative support.

National Association of County Information Officers *(1965)*

Historical Note
An affiliate of National Association of Counties, which provides administrative support.

National Association of County Intergovernmental Relations Officials *(1966)*
440 First St. NW
Washington, DC 20001
Tel: (202)393-6226 Ext: 254 *Fax:* (202)942-4281
Web Site: www.naco.org
Members: 100 individuals
Staff: 1
Annual Budget: under $10,000
Staff Liaison: Dalen Harris

Historical Note
Established in 1966 as the National Association of County Development Coordinators to satisfy the need for a greater exchange of ideas in coordinating federal and state aid programs at the county level; became (1975) National Association of Counties Council of Intergovernmental Coordinators; assumed current name in 1991. An affiliate of the National Association of Counties.

Meetings/Conferences:
Annual Meetings: Fall in Washington, DC

National Association of County Park and Recreation Officials *(1964)*

Historical Note
An affiliate of National Association of Counties, which provides administrative support.

National Association of County Planners *(1965)*

Historical Note
An affiliate of National Association of Counties, which provides administrative support.

National Association of County Recorders, Election Officials and Clerks *(1949)*
P.O. Box 3159
Durham, NC 27715-3159
Tel: (919)384-8446 *Fax:* (919)383-0035
E-Mail: info@nacrc.org
Web Site: www.nacrc.org
Members: 1000 individuals
Staff: 2
Annual Budget: $100-250,000
Executive Director: Tracy Seabrook

Historical Note
Formerly the National Association of County Recorders and Clerks. An affiliate of the National Association of Counties. Members include county officials who are responsible for adminstration of land/property records, courts and elections. Membership: variable, depends on the size of the county.

Meetings/Conferences:
Annual Meetings: July, with National Association of Counties
2007 - Richmond, VA/July 12-16

Publications:
NACRC Bulletin. q. adv.

National Association of County Surveyors

Historical Note
An affiliate of National Association of Counties, which provides administrative support.

National Association of County Training and Employment Professionals *(1974)*

Historical Note
An affiliate of National Association of Counties, which provides administrative support.

National Association of County Treasurers and Finance Officers *(1950)*

Historical Note
An affiliate of National Association of Counties, which provides administrative support.

National Association of Credential Evaluation Services, Inc. *(1987)*

P.O. Box 514070
Milwaukee, WI 53203-3470
Tel: (414)270-3680 *Fax:* (414)289-3411
Web Site: www.naces.org
Members: 16 firms
Annual Budget: under $10,000
Membership Committee Past Chairman: James S. Frey

Historical Note

Members are companies specializing in the evaluation of foreign educational credentials for further education, professional licensure, employment, or immigration. Has no paid officers or full-time staff.

Meetings/Conferences:

Annual Meetings: *Spring*

Publications:

List of Members. a.

National Association of Credit Management *(1896)*
8840 Columbia 100 Pkwy.
Columbia, MD 21045
Tel: (410)740-5560 *Fax:* (410)740-5574
E-Mail: info@nacm.org
Web Site: www.nacm.org
Members: 25000 individuals
Staff: 35
Annual Budget: $2-5,000,000
President and Chief Operating Officer: Robin Schauseil, CMP
Director, Meetings: Jill Leimbach
Vice President, Secretary and Treasurer: James E. Vanghel

Historical Note

Founded June 23, 1896 in Toledo, Ohio by 82 charter member credit executives. Provides credit reports on business customers, collection service, assistance to creditors and commercial fraud detection and prevention. Sponsors the National Institute of Credit, which is a non-profit educational organization of the NACM. Conducts education and research programs dealing with the needs of current credit management.

Meetings/Conferences:

Annual Meetings: *Spring*

Publications:

Business Credit Magazine. 10/year. adv.
Credit Manual of Credit and Commercial Laws. a.

National Association of Credit Union Chairmen *(1977)*
P.O. Box 160
Del Mar, CA 92014-0160
Tel: (858)792-3883 *Fax:* (858)792-3884
Toll Free: (888)987 - 4247
E-Mail: nacuc@nacuc.org
Web Site: www.nacuc.org
Members: 250 individuals
Annual Budget: $100-250,000

Historical Note

Formerly (1993) the National Association of Credit Union Presidents. Conceived at Williamsburg in July 1976 at a conference of presidents of Southeast credit unions, the association was formally established the following year at the Hilton Inn in Albuquerque by 47 charter members representing credit unions with more than 20 million dollars in assets. It was incorporated in Alabama in 1978. Membership: $300/year.

Meetings/Conferences:

Annual Meetings: *Fall*

Publications:

Directory.
Exchange. q.

National Association of Credit Union Service Organizations *(1984)*
PMB 3419 Via Lido, Suite 135
Newport Beach, CA 92663
Tel: (949)645-5296 *Fax:* (949)645-5297
Toll Free: (888)462 - 2870
E-Mail: info@nacuso.org
Web Site: www.nacuso.org
Members: 412 individuals
Staff: 2
Annual Budget: $500-1,000,000
Interim Chief Executive Officer: Victor Pantea

Historical Note

NACUSO is a trade association for credit union service organizations (subsidiaries of credit unions). Membership: $375/year (CUSO); $625/year (CUSO sponsor company).

Meetings/Conferences:

Semi-Annual Meetings: Spring and Fall

Publications:

NACUSO Connection magazine. 3/year.
Nat'l CUSO Directory. a. adv.

National Association of Credit Union Supervisory and Auditing Committees *(1985)*
P.O. Box 160
Del Mar, CA 92014
Toll Free: (800)287 - 5949
E-Mail: nacusac@nacusac.org
Web Site: www.nacusac.org
Members: 500 individuals
Staff: 3
Annual Budget: $100-250,000
Executive Director: Katherine E. Clark
E-Mail: kathy@nacusac.org

Meetings/Conferences:

Annual Meetings: *Summer*

Publications:

NACUSAC News. q.

National Association of Crime Victim Compensation Boards *(1978)*
P.O. Box 16003
Alexandria, VA 22302
Tel: (703)313-9500
Web Site: www.nacvcb.org
Members: 52 state gov't programs
Staff: 1
Annual Budget: $50-100,000
Executive Director: Dan McLeod Eddy

Historical Note

NACVCB members are state and territory crime victim compensation programs.

Meetings/Conferences:

Annual Meetings: *Fall*

Publications:

Newsletter. q.

National Association of Criminal Defense Lawyers *(1958)*
1150 18th St. NW
Suite 950
Washington, DC 20036
Tel: (202)872-8600 *Fax:* (202)872-8690
Web Site: www.criminaljustice.org
Members: 10000 individuals
Staff: 18
Annual Budget: $2-5,000,000
Executive Director: Ralph E. Grunewald
E-Mail: ralph@nacdl.org
Director, Publications: Richard Bing
E-Mail: richard@nacdl.org
Director, Finance and Administration: Tom Chambers
E-Mail: tom@nacdl.org
Information Technology: Steven Frazier
E-Mail: steven@nacdl.org
Director, Meetings and Affiliates: Cecelia Hannon
E-Mail: cecelia@nacdl.org
Legislative Director: Kyle O'Dowd
E-Mail: kyle@nacdl.org

Historical Note

Formerly (1972) National Association of Defense Lawyers in Criminal Cases. NACDL's purpose is to assure justice and due process for persons accused of crime or wrongdoing. Provides continuing legal education and other activities in support of attorneys engaged in criminal defense practice. Membership: $250/year (full member); $125/year (new lawyer/allied non-lawyer); $110/year (public defender/judge/law professor/active military); $50/year (student).

Meetings/Conferences:

Annual Meetings: *Summer*

Publications:

The Champion. 10/yr. adv.
Members Handbook. a.

National Association of Cruise Oriented Agencies *(1985)*
7600 Red Rd.
Suite 126
South Miami, FL 33143
Tel: (305)663-5626
E-Mail: nacoafl@aol.com
Web Site: www.nacoaonline.com
Members: 800 agencies
Staff: 3
Annual Budget: $250-500,000
President: Donna Esposito

Historical Note

Formerly National Association of Cruise Only Agencies (1998). Members are travel agencies specializing in cruiseship bookings. Allied membership is available for cruise lines, suppliers to the industry, trade publications and other entities with an interest in the industry. Membership: $150/year (individual); $3,000-10,000/year (allied or cruise line).

Meetings/Conferences:

Semi-annual Meetings:

Publications:

'Now Hear This' Newsletter. q. adv.

National Association of Decorative Fabric Distributors *(1969)*
One Windsor Cove, Suite #305
Columbia, SC 29223
Tel: (803)252-5646 *Fax:* (803)765-0860
Toll Free: (800)445 - 8629
E-Mail: info@nadfd.com
Web Site: www.nadfd.com
Members: 60 companies
Annual Budget: $100-250,000
Executive Director: Mary Ann Crews
Director, Communications: Nancy Cooper

Historical Note

Established in 1969 as the National Association of Upholstery Fabric Distributors; assumed its present name in 1975.

National Association of Dental Assistants *(1974)*
900 S. Washington St., Suite G13
Falls Church, VA 22046-4020
Tel: (703)237-8616 *Fax:* (703)533-1153
Members: 4000 individuals
Staff: 4
Annual Budget: $50-100,000
Director, Membership: Ruth Ludeman

Historical Note

NADA's purpose is to assist its members in achieving their career goals by keeping them informed of advances and/or changes in their chosen professions, by offering continuing education opportunities, and by promoting the free exchange of ideas with their peers. Membership open to anyone employed by a dentist, including office personnel. Membership: $30/year, $55/year (2 year membership).

Meetings/Conferences:

Annual Meetings: *Summer*

Publications:

The Explorer. 11/year. adv.

National Association of Dental Laboratories *(1951)*
325 John Knox Rd., L103
Tallahassee, FL 32303
Tel: (850)205-5626 *Fax:* (850)222-0053
Toll Free: (800)950 - 1150
E-Mail: nadl@nadl.org
Web Site: www.nadl.org
Members: 2000 individuals
Staff: 12
Annual Budget: $2-5,000,000
Executive Director: Bennett E. Napier, CAE
E-Mail: bennett@nadl.org
Co-Executive Director: Ricki Braswell, C.A.E.
E-Mail: ricki@nadl.org
Director, Certification: Lance Rodan, CPM

Historical Note

A federation of state laboratory associations formed by a merger of the Dental Laboratory Institute of America and the American Dental Laboratory Association. From 1968-71 it was known as the National Association of Certified Dental Laboratories.

Affiliated with the National Board for Certification in Dental Laboratory Technology, granting the Certified Dental Technician (CDT) designation and the National Board for Certification of Dental Laboratories, granting the Certified Dental Laboratory (CDL) designation. Membership: $300/year (active members); $400/year (associate members).

Meetings/Conferences:
Semi-Annual Meetings: Winter and Fall
2007 – Las Vegas, NV(Bellagio)/Jan. 28-30/250

Publications:
Journal of Dental Technology. 9/yr. adv.

National Association of Dental Plans *(1989)*
8111 LBJ Fwy., Suite 935
Dallas, TX 75251-1347
Tel: (972)458-6998 *Fax:* (972)458-2258
E-Mail: info@nadp.org
Web Site: www.nadp.org
Members: 80 companies
Staff: 7
Annual Budget: $1-2,000,000
Executive Director: Evelyn F. Ireland, CAE
E-Mail: eireland@nadp.org
Director, Research and Information: Jerry Berggren
Deputy Executive Director: Tim Brown
E-Mail: tbrown@nadp.org
Director, Government Relations: Kris Hathaway

Historical Note
NADP provides legislative and regulation tracking and coordination of industry action, continuing education, industry research and other services to its members. Nonvoting memberships are available to dental benefit companies. Associate membership is available to dental practice management companies, companies providing services to the industry and individuals. Sponsors and supports the NADP Foundation.

Publications:
Annual Statistical Profile of Industry. a.
NADP News. m.

National Association of Development Companies *(1981)*
6764 Old McLean Village Dr.
McLean, VA 22101-3906
Tel: (703)748-2575 *Fax:* (703)748-2582
Web Site: www.nadco.org
Members: 350 companies
Staff: 4
Annual Budget: $500-1,000,000
President: Christopher L. Crawford

Historical Note
Organized to represent Certified Development Companies that participate in the Small Business Administration's "504" lending program. Through the program, CDCs provide long-term, fixed asset financing to eligible small businesses. Affiliate membership is open to lawyers, bankers, accountants and other participants recommended by an active CDC. Membership: $250/year or 0.1% of Sec. 504 debentures (up to $1,000).

Meetings/Conferences:
Annual Meetings: Spring

Publications:
Certified News. m.

National Association of Development Organizations *(1967)*
400 N. Capitol St. NW
Suite 390
Washington, DC 20001
Tel: (202)624-7806 *Fax:* (202)624-8813
Web Site: www.nado.org
Members: 360 organizations
Staff: 12
Annual Budget: $1-2,000,000
Executive Director: Matthew Chase
E-Mail: mchase@nado.org
Director, Meetings and Membership: Vicki Glass

Historical Note
Members are multi-county regional development organizations, mainly in small metropolitan and rural areas. NADO's primary concern is to promote economic development in non-metropolitan regions. Membership: $500/year (individual); $1,000/year (organization).

Meetings/Conferences:
Annual Meetings: Fall

Publications:
Economic Development Digest. 10/year.
Regional Transportation Connector. q.
EDFS Reporter. m.
NADO News. w.

National Association of Diaper Services *(1946)*
994 Old Eagle School Road, Suite 1019
Wayne, PA 19087-1802
Tel: (610)971-4850 *Fax:* (610)971-4859
E-Mail: nads@diapernet.com
Web Site: www.diapernet.com
Members: 350 companies
Staff: 2
Executive Director: John A. Shiffert, CAE

Historical Note
Established in 1946 as the Diaper Service Institute of America. Became the Diaper Service Industry Association in 1960. Merged in 1970 with the National Institute of Diaper Services (1938), and became the National Institute of Infant Services in 1971. It assumed its present name in 1985. Members are diaper rental and laundry services, whose existence is increasingly threatened by the growing use of disposable diapers. The Diaper Service Accreditation Council is its certification arm.

Meetings/Conferences:
Annual Meetings: May

Publications:
Newsletter. m.

National Association of Diocesan Ecumenical Officers *(1972)*
730 Washington Ave.
Carnegie, PA 15106
Tel: (412)279-4652 *Fax:* (412)279-5109
Web Site: www.nadeo.org/
Members: 200 individuals
Annual Budget: $10-25,000
Secretary: George Appleyard

Historical Note
NADEO members are officers in Roman Catholic dioceses responsbile for promoting Christian unity and interfaith cooperation. Has no paid officers or full-time staff. Membership: $200/year

Meetings/Conferences:
Annual Meetings: usually Spring

Publications:
Newsletter. q.

National Association of Directors of Nursing Administration in Long Term Care *(1986)*
10101 Alliance Rd.
Suite 140
Cincinnati, OH 45242
Tel: (513)791-3679 *Fax:* (513)791-3699
Toll Free: (800)222 - 0539
E-Mail: info@nadona.org
Web Site: www.nadona.org
Members: 6200 individuals
Staff: 6
Executive Director and Founder: Joan C. Warden-Saunders, RN
E-Mail: joan@nadona.org
Coordinator, Membership: Kathy Romano

Historical Note
Membership: $80/year, plus state chapter dues (individual).

Meetings/Conferences:
Annual Meetings: June

Publications:
Director Journal. q. adv.

National Association of Disability Evaluating Professionals *(1984)*
13801 Village Mill Dr.
Midlothian, VA 23113
Tel: (804)378-7275
Web Site: www.nadep.com
Members: 1000 individuals
Staff: 2
Annual Budget: $250-500,000
Director: Virgil Robert May, III

Historical Note
NADEP members are lawyers, medical doctors and other professionals involved in the evaluation and rehabilitation of persons with disabilities resulting from work or personal injuries. Membership: $150 (individual and organization)

Publications:
NADEP-Handbook of Practice Standards and Guidelines. a.
Disability Guide and Rehabilitation Review. q.
Newsletter. q.

National Association of Disability Examiners *(1963)*
2704 Frank St.
Lansing, MI 48911
Tel: (517)882-8073
E-Mail: mamarshall2704@aol.com
Web Site: www.nade.org
Members: 2000 individuals
Annual Budget: $50-100,000
President: Martha Marshall

Historical Note
Established and incorporated in 1963 as a division of the National Rehabilitation Association, NADE became autonomous in 1978. Members are doctors and examiners engaged in judging social security disability claims. Promotes disability evaluation as a science and a profession. Has no paid staff or permanent officers. Membership: $50/year (professional); $25/year (associate/retiree); $200/year (organization); $500/year (gold corporation).

Meetings/Conferences:
Annual Meetings: October

Publications:
NADE Advocate. 4/yr. adv.
Directory. a.

National Association of Display Industries *(1942)*
4651 Sheridan St., Suite 470
Hollywood, FL 33021
Tel: (954)893-7225 *Fax:* (954)893-8375
E-Mail: nadi@nadi-global.com
Web Site: www.nadi-global.com
Members: 100 businesses
Staff: 3
Annual Budget: $50-100,000
Executive Director: Klein S. Merriman

Historical Note
The visual merchandising division of NASFM.

Meetings/Conferences:
Annual Meetings: Spring at GlobalShop
2007 – Las Vegas, NV

Publications:
Newsletter. 6/yr.

National Association of Division Order Analysts *(1974)*
2805 Oak Trail Ct.
Suite 6312
Arlington, TX 76016
Tel: (405)749-6601
E-Mail: nadoa_org@hotmail.com
Web Site: www.nadoa.org
Members: 1000 individuals
Annual Budget: $100-250,000
President: Pamela Parrish

Historical Note
Division order analysts are petroleum and gas company employees or independent consultants responsible for royalty, working interset and overiding royalty payments. Offers a certification program providing education, training and testing for qualified applicants desiring to attain Certified Division Order Analyst credentials. Has no paid officers or full-time staff. Membership: $35/year (individual).

Publications:
NADOA Newsletter. q. adv.
Directory. a.
Annual Institute Journal. a.
Mergers and Acquisitions Handbook. a.

National Association of Document Examiners *(1979)*
3490 U.S. Rte. 1, Suite 3B

Princeton, NJ 08540-5920
Tel: (609)452-7030 *Fax:* (609)452-7003
E-Mail: forgerynet@aol.com
Web Site: www.forgery.net
Members: 165 individuals
Annual Budget: $25-50,000
Executive Officer: Renee C. Martin

Historical Note
NADE was organized for the education of document examiners. Promotes the interests of forensic document examiners specializing in handwriting identification through seminars, publications, and a certification program for professional members. Membership: $100/year (individual).

Meetings/Conferences:
Annual Meetings: May

Publications:
NADE Journal.
Communique Newsletter. bi-m. adv.

National Association of Dog Obedience Instructors *(1964)*

PMB 369, 729 Grapevine Hwy.
Hurst, TX 76054-2085
E-Mail: corrsec@nadoi.org
Web Site: www.nadoi.org
Members: 450 individuals
Corresponding Secretary: Camille Robinson
E-Mail: corrsec@nadoi.org

Historical Note
NADOI was founded to elevate the standards of the dog instructing profession, to aid both dog and human in the solution of the many problems associated with dog ownership, and to endorse its members as having attained the skills and knowledge necessary to serve those ends. Has no paid officers or full-time staff.

Meetings/Conferences:
Annual Meetings: Spring

Publications:
Forward. q. adv.
NADOI News Newsletter. m.

National Association of Ecumenical and Interreligious Staff *(1940)*

P.O. Box 7093
Tacoma, WA 98406-0093
Tel: (253)759-0141 *Fax:* (253)759-9689
E-Mail: naeisjan@aol.com
Web Site: www.haeis.org
Members: 375 individuals
Staff: 1
Annual Budget: $50-100,000
Membership Development: Janet E. Leng
E-Mail: naeisjan@aol.com

Historical Note
NAEIS is the product of a merger of the Employed Council Officers Association and the Association of Executive Secretaries. Formerly (1971) Association of Council Secretaries, and (1997) National Association of Ecumenical Staff. Membership: $125/year (executive); $75/year (associate); $50/year (introductory).

Meetings/Conferences:
Annual Meetings: Summer

Publications:
NAEIS News. 3/year.

National Association of Educational Buyers *(1920)*

5523 Research Park Dr.
Suite 340
Baltimore, MD 21228
Tel: (443)543-5540 *Fax:* (443)543-5550
Web Site: www.naeb.org
Members: 1900 institutions
Staff: 7
Annual Budget: $1-2,000,000
Chief Executive Officer: Doreen Murner

Historical Note
Founded as the Educational Buyers Association, it assumed its present name in 1947. Members are college and university purchasing directors and purchasing staff.

Meetings/Conferences:
Annual Meetings: Spring

Publications:
Journal. m. adv.
NAEB Bulletin. m. adv.

National Association of Educational Office Professionals *(1934)*

1841 S. Eisenhower Ct.
P.O. Box 12619
Wichita, KS 67209
Tel: (316)942-4822 Ext: 11 *Fax:* (316)942-7100
E-Mail: naeop@naeop.org
Web Site: www.naeop.org
Members: 4800 individuals
Staff: 4
Annual Budget: $250-500,000
Executive Director: Sharon Daggett Manner
E-Mail: sdmanner@naeop.org

Historical Note
Formerly (1979) the National Association of Educational Secretaries and (1995) National Association of Office Personnel. Members are office personnel in educational institutions. Sponsors a professional standards program which awards the designation Certified Educational Office Employee. Membership: $45/year.

Meetings/Conferences:
Annual Meetings: July
2007 - Seattle, WA/July 16-20

Publications:
The National Educational Staff Connector. q. adv.
The Beam. q.

National Association of Electrical Distributors *(1908)*

1100 Corporate Square Dr., Suite 100
St. Louis, MO 63132
Tel: (314)991-9000 *Fax:* (314)991-3060
Toll Free: (888)791 - 2512
E-Mail: info@naed.org
Web Site: www.naed.org
Members: 470 Companies
Staff: 28
Annual Budget: $5-10,000,000
President/Publisher: Tom Naber
E-Mail: tnaber@naed.org
Director, Marketing and Member Services: Anita Bauer
Director, Meetings and Conferences: Becky Burgess
Director, Publications: Sonia Crites
Controller: Tim Dencker
Director, Education: Michelle Jaworowski

Historical Note
NAED serves as a major resource for electrical distributors to gain business opportunities, education, industry knowledge, and information. Formerly (1928) Electrical Supply Jobbers Association and (1949) National Electric Wholesalers Association.

Meetings/Conferences:
Annual Meetings: May
2007 - Washington, DC(Marriott Wardman Park)/May 5-9
2008 - San Francisco, CA(San Francisco Marriott)/May 17-21
2009 - Ft. Lauderdale, FL(The Westin Diplomat Resort and Spa)/May 16-21

Publications:
The Electrical Distributor. m. adv.

National Association of Elementary School Principals *(1921)*

1615 Duke St.
Alexandria, VA 22314-3483
Tel: (703)684-3345 *Fax:* (800)396-2377
Toll Free: (800)386 - 2377
E-Mail: naesp@naesp.org
Web Site: www.naesp.org
Members: 30000 individuals
Staff: 52
Annual Budget: $2-5,000,000
Executive Director: Dr. Vincent L. Ferrandino
Associate Executive Director, Membership and Professional Outreach: Fred Brown
Deputy Executive Director: Gail C. Gross
Associate Executive Director, Government Relations: Dr. Sally N. McConnell

Historical Note
Founded in 1921 as a division of the National Education Association, it became autonomous in 1972. Represents the professional interests of elementary and middle school principals in the U.S., Canada, and abroad. Serves as advocate for high-quality educational and social programs to benefit children and youth. Membership: $175/year (individual), $215/year (institution).

Meetings/Conferences:
Annual Meetings: Spring
2007 - Anaheim, CA/Apr. 13-17
2008 - Nashville, TN/Apr. 4-8

Publications:
Before the Bell. irreg.
Leadership Compass. q.
Middle Matters. 5/year.
Research Roundup. q.
Student and Community News Today. 5/year.
International Bulletin. m.
Leaders Advantage. m.
Communicator. m.
Principal. 5/year. adv.
Report to Parents. m.

National Association of Elevator Contractors *(1951)*

1298 Wellbrook Circle, Suite A
Conyers, GA 30012
Tel: (770)760-9660 *Fax:* (770)760-9714
Toll Free: (888)847 - 7530
E-Mail: info@naec.org
Web Site: www.naec.org
Members: 650 companies
Staff: 5
Annual Budget: $500-1,000,000
Executive Director: Teresa M. Shirley

Historical Note
Members are installers and servicers of elevators and suppliers of equipment.

Meetings/Conferences:
Annual Meetings: Fall

Publications:
MainLine Newsletter. 10/year.

National Association of Elevator Safety Authorities International *(1969)*

8805 N. 23rd Ave., Suite 350
Phoenix, AZ 85021-4146
Tel: (602)266-9701 Ext: 11 *Fax:* (602)265-0093
Toll Free: (800)746 - 2372
E-Mail: info@naesai.org
Web Site: www.naesai.org
Members: 2200 individuals
Staff: 4
Annual Budget: $250-500,000
Executive Director: Dotty Stanlaske

Historical Note
Members are manufacturers, installers, servicers and inspectors of elevators. Membership: $75-350/year (individual); $500/year (organization/company).

Meetings/Conferences:
Annual Meetings: August

Publications:
Progress Newsletter. m.

National Association of Emergency Medical Technicians *(1975)*

132- A E. Northsider Dr.
Clinton, MS 39056
Tel: (601)924-7744 *Fax:* (601)924-7325
Toll Free: (800)346 - 2368
E-Mail: info@naemt.org
Web Site: www.naemt.org
Members: 14960 individuals
Staff: 5
Annual Budget: $250-500,000
Association Manager: Lisa Lindsay

Historical Note
Members are state certified and/or nationally registered emergency medical technicians (EMTs), paramedics, and other professionals working in prehospital emergency medicine. The association has six divisions for its members with specialized interests: Instructor/Coordinators; Paramedics; Administrators; Industrial.; Military and Special Operations.

Membership: $40/year (individual); $300/year (organization).

Meetings/Conferences:

Annual Meetings: Fall/1,500

Publications:

NAEMT News. bi-m. adv.

National Association of EMS Physicians *(1983)*

P.O. Box 15945-281
Lenexa, KS 66285-5945
Tel: (913)492-5858 *Fax:* (913)599-5340
Toll Free: (800)228 - 3677
E-Mail: info-naemsp@goamp.com
Web Site: www.naemsp.org
Members: 1200 individuals
Staff: 5
Annual Budget: $1-2,000,000
Executive Director: Dede Gish-Panjada

Historical Note

NAEMSP members are designated, medically-legally responsible medical directors of municipal and state emergency medical systems and programs, as well as key associates, including state directors, administrative heads, regular EMS personnel and legal experts from the United States and Canada. NAEMSP provides a national resource on EMS standards of care and a forum for EMS physicians and their associates to discuss the problems and responsibilities of EMS medical supervision, as well as to provide role models and consensus for various aspects of EMS care. Membership: $275/year (individual physician); $105/year (resident); $135/year (professional/fellow); $75/year (medical student).

Meetings/Conferences:

Semi-Annual Meetings: Winter and Summer

Publications:

Prehospital Emergency Care (PEC) Journal. q. adv.
NAEMSP News. bi-m. adv.

National Association of Energy Service Companies *(1983)*

1615 M St. NW
Suite 800
Washington, DC 20036
Tel: (202)822-0950 *Fax:* (202)822-0955
E-Mail: tes@dwgp.com
Web Site: www.naesco.org
Members: 140 companies
Staff: 6
Annual Budget: $250-500,000
Executive Director: Terry E. Singer
E-Mail: tes@dwgp.com

Historical Note

A non-profit corporation formed by energy service companies to meet the needs of the growing energy service industry. Represents the interests of the industry before legislative and administrative bodies; informs the public of the benefits of third party financing of energy conservation and alternative energy programs; educates members about the growth, development, and status of the energy service industry.

Meetings/Conferences:

Semi-annual Meeting: Spring and Fall

Publications:

NAESCO News newsletter. 2/yr.

National Association of Enrolled Agents *(1972)*

1120 Connecticut Ave. NW
Suite 460
Washington, DC 20036
Tel: (202)822-6232 *Fax:* (202)822-6270
E-Mail: info@naeahq.org
Web Site: www.naea.org
Members: 11400 individuals
Staff: 13
Annual Budget: $2-5,000,000
Executive Vice President: Susan Zuber, CAE
E-Mail: szuber@naeahq.org
Director, Finance and Operations: Bill Grutzkuhn
E-Mail: bgrutzkuhn@naea.org
Senior Director, Government Relations: Robert Kerr
Director, Membership and Communications: Sam Matilick

Historical Note

Membership consists of individuals who are enrolled to represent taxpayers before the Internal Revenue Service. Formed (1972) as the Association of Enrolled Agents; assumed its current name in 1978. Membership: $150/year.

Meetings/Conferences:

Annual Meetings: Summer/500

Publications:

EA Journal. bi-m. adv.
Membership Directory. a. adv.
EAlert. bi-w. adv.

National Association of Environmental Professionals *(1975)*

389 Main St.
Suite 202
Malden, MA 02148
Tel: (781)397-8870 *Fax:* (781)397-8870
Toll Free: (888)251 - 9902
E-Mail: office@naep.org
Web Site: www.naep.org
Members: 1600 individuals
Staff: 1
Annual Budget: $500-1,000,000
President: Brian R. Moyer

Historical Note

NAEP is a multidisciplinary, non-profit professional association dedicated to the promotion of a code of ethics and standards of practice in the enviromental field. NAEP's interdisciplinary focus brings together specialists from each of the major segments of the environmental profession. NAEP members represent government, consulting, industry, academia, and the private sector in the U.S. and abroad, working in all areas of air, water, noise, waste, ecology and education, and providing access to the latest trends in environmental research, technology, law and policy. Membership in NAEP provides access to the latest trends in research, technology, law, and policy. General membership: $125/year (individual).

Meetings/Conferences:

Annual Meetings: Spring

Publications:

Environmental Practice. q. adv.
Annual Conference Proceedings. a. adv.

National Association of Episcopal Schools *(1954)*

815 Second Ave., Suite 313
New York, NY 10017
Tel: (212)716-6134 *Fax:* (212)286-9366
Toll Free: (800)334 - 7626 Ext: 6134
E-Mail: info@episcopalschools.org
Web Site: www.naes.org
Members: 400 schools
Staff: 4
Annual Budget: $500-1,000,000
Executive Director: Rev. Peter G. Cheney
Coordinator, Conferences and Communications: David J. Schnabel

Historical Note

Founded as Episcopal School Association; incorporated as NAES in 1965. Membership includes pre-school through secondary level Episcopal schools. Membership fee varies, based on tuition income.

Meetings/Conferences:

Biennial Meetings:

Publications:

NAES Directory. a. adv.
Network (newsletter). m.

National Association of Equipment Leasing Brokers *(1990)*

304 W. Liberty St., Suite 201
Louisville, KY 40202
Toll Free: (800)996 - 2352
E-Mail: info@naelb.org
Web Site: www.naelb.org
Members: 800 companies
Staff: 3
Annual Budget: $100-250,000
Executive Administrator: Monica Harper

Historical Note

Broker-oriented association. Began in 1990 with conferences and workshops covering various areas of concern to the leasing industry. Funding sources join as non-voting members. Membership: $295/year (broker); $750/year (funding source); $600/year (associate).

Meetings/Conferences:

Annual Meetings: Spring
2007 – Nashville, TN(Gaylord Opryland Hotel)/May 17-19

Publications:

Leasing Logic (online). q.

National Association of Evangelicals *(1942)*

P.O. Box 23269
Washington, DC 20026
Tel: (202)789-1011 *Fax:* (202)842-0392
E-Mail: nae@nae.net
Web Site: www.nae.net
Members: 45000 churches
Staff: 5
Annual Budget: $250-500,000
President: Ted Haggard
Vice President, Government Affairs: Dr. Richard Cizik

Historical Note

NAE is a voluntary association of individuals, denominations, churches, schools and organizations dedicated to united action without theological compromise. NAE represents more than 45,000 local churches from 40 Protestant denominations and serves more than 30 million people through its subsidiary, affiliates and commissions. National Christian Education Association is a program of NAE. Membership: $30/year (individual); organizational fee based on size.

Meetings/Conferences:

Annual Meetings: March

Publications:

Bible Reading Guide. a.
NAE Washington Insight. m.

National Association of Executive Recruiters *(1984)*

1901 N. Roselle Rd.
Schaumburg, IL 60195
Tel: (847)885-1453 *Fax:* (847)885-8393
E-Mail: info@naer.org
Web Site: www.naer.org
Members: 30 companies
Staff: 2
Annual Budget: $25-50,000
Chair: Robert Zahra
E-Mail: info@naer.org

Historical Note

Incorporated in Illinois, NAER members are executive recruitment/search firms on a retainer or contingency basis. Membership: $750/year.

Meetings/Conferences:

Semi-Annual Meetings: Spring and Fall

National Association of Export Companies *(1965)*

Grand Central Station
P.O. Box 3949
New York, NY 10163
Toll Free: (877)291 - 4901
E-Mail: director@nexco.org
Web Site: www.nexco.org
Members: 300 companies
Staff: 2
Annual Budget: $50-100,000
Executive Director: Gerri Christantiello

Historical Note

Formerly (1983) National Association of Export Management Companies. Members are import and export trading and import and export management companies, international trade service vendors, and other international trade companies. Membership: $95-$1,000/year.

Meetings/Conferences:

Annual Meetings: Monthly Meetings, New York, NY

National Association of Extension 4-H Agents *(1946)*

1800 Camden Road, Suite 107, #213
Charlotte, NC 28203
Tel: (704)333-8445 *Fax:* (704)333-6927
E-Mail: 4h@themanagementoffice.com
Web Site: www.nae4ha.org
Members: 3300 individuals

Annual Budget: $500-1,000,000
Executive Services: Kay Chelena

Historical Note

Established as the National Association of County Club Agents, it became the National Association of County 4-H Club Agents and in 1969 asssumed its present name. NAE4-HA strives to promote, strengthen, enhance, and advocate the 4-H youth development profession. Membership: $35/year (individual).

Meetings/Conferences:

Annual Meetings: Fall
2007 – Atlanta, GA/Oct. 21-25
2008 – Indianapolis, IN

Publications:

News & Views. q. adv.
Journal of Extension. q.

National Association of Family Development Centers *(1960)*

1114 Ave. J
Brooklyn, NY 11230
Tel: (718)258-7767 *Fax:* (718)338-1043
Members: 400 individuals
Director: Dr. Alfred Schnell Kaplan

Historical Note

Has no paid officers or full-time staff.

Meetings/Conferences:

Annual Meetings:

National Association of Farm Broadcasting *(1944)*

P.O. Box 500
Platte City, MO 64079
Tel: (816)431-4032 *Fax:* (816)431-4087
Web Site: www.nafb.com
Members: 600 individuals
Staff: 5
Annual Budget: $500-1,000,000
Executive Director: Bill O'Neill
E-Mail: bill@nafb.com

Historical Note

Established as the National Association of Radio Farm Directors; became the National Association of Television-Radio Farm Directors in 1956 and assumed its present name in 1964. Membership: $100/year (individual).

Meetings/Conferences:

Annual Meetings: Kansas City, MO(Crown Center)/November/700
2007 – Kansas City, MO/Nov. 14-16

Publications:

eChats. m.
NAFB Directory. a.

National Association of Federal Credit Unions *(1967)*

3138 Tenth St. North
Arlington, VA 22201
Tel: (703)522-4770 *Fax:* (703)524-1082
Toll Free: (800)336 - 4644
Web Site: www.nafcu.org
Members: 804 federal credit unions
Staff: 65
Annual Budget: $5-10,000,000
President: Fred Becker
E-Mail: fbecker@nafcu.org
Director, Planning and Programming: Joseph M. Boyle
Director, Information Technology: James Chapman
Director, Membership: Lauren Corbin
Regulatory Compliance Counsel: Anthony Demangone
Senior Vice President, Communications: Jay Morris
Director, Education: Sara J. Romanick
Manager, Public Relations: Rebecca Somers
Executive Vice President: Diane Swenson
E-Mail: dswenson@nafcu.org
Director, Marketing: Peter Taylor
E-Mail: ptaylor@nafcu.org
Director, Legislative and Political Affairs: Bradford Thaler
Controller: Paul Weiler

Historical Note

Originated in Los Angeles in 1966 at a meeting of 56 credit union leaders to consider ways to shape the laws and regulations under which federal credit unions operate. Incorporated in the state of California in 1967. Supports the National Association of Federal Credit Unions Political Action Committee.

Meetings/Conferences:

Annual Meetings: July/1,500

Publications:

The Federal Credit Union. bi-m. adv.
Update. w.

National Association of Federal Education Program Administrators *(1975)*

P.O. Box 2084
Anniston, AL 36202
Tel: (256)741-7453 *Fax:* (256)237-5332
E-Mail: bburns@calhoun.k12.al.us
Web Site: www.nafepa.org
Members: 1500 individuals
Staff: 8
Annual Budget: $100-250,000
President: Bobby Burns

Historical Note

Organized in 1975 to represent those professional educators employed by local and intermediate school districts, state departments of education, non-public schools, and education-product suppliers who have responsibility for supervising, coordinating or administering federally funded education programs. Formerly (1984) the National Association of Administrators of State and Federal Education Programs and (1985) the National Association of Administrators of Federal Education Programs. Membership: $100/year (individual).

Publications:

Newsletter. bi-m.

National Association of Federal Veterinarians *(1918)*

1910 Sunderland Pl. NW
Washington, DC 20036-1608
Tel: (202)289-6334 *Fax:* (202)842-4360
E-Mail: vragan@nafv.org
Web Site: www.nafv.org
Members: 2200 individuals
Staff: 2
Annual Budget: $100-250,000
President: Dr. Christopher L. Bratcher

Historical Note

Affiliated with the American Veterinary Medical Association. Supports the National Association of Federal Veterinarians Political Action Committee. Sponsors American Academy of Veterinary Preventive Medicine. Sponsors the NAFV Memorial Scholarship Fund. Membership: $260/year.

Meetings/Conferences:

Semi-annual Meetings:: Summer and Fall

Publications:

The Federal Veterinarian. m. adv.

National Association of Federally Impacted Schools *(1973)*

444 N. Capitol St. NW
Suite 419
Washington, DC 20001-1606
Tel: (202)624-5455 *Fax:* (202)624-5468
Web Site: www.sso.org/nafis
Members: 600 school districts
Staff: 5
Annual Budget: $500-1,000,000
Executive Director: John B. Forkenbrock
E-Mail: johnfork@sso.org
Director, Communications: Bryan Jernigan
E-Mail: bjernigan@sso.org
Director, Government Relations: Gail McSpadden
E-Mail: mcspaddg@sso.org
Director, Information Systems: Lynn Watkins
E-Mail: watkinsl@sso.org

Historical Note

NAFIS is a non-profit, non-partisan corporation of school districts from throughout the United States, organized primarily to educate Congress on the importance of impact aid. The Association works to ensure that the needs of federally connected children are met with adequate federal funds. Membership: $350-9,000/year (based on amount of aid funds received).

Meetings/Conferences:

Semi-annual Meetings: Washington, DC(Hyatt Regency)/Spring and Fall

Publications:

Newsletter. m. adv.
Impact!Insider. irreg.
Blue Book. a. adv.

National Association of Federally Licensed Firearms Dealers *(1973)*

150 S.E. 12th St., Suite 200
Ft. Lauderdale, FL 33316
Tel: (954)467-9994 *Fax:* (954)463-2501
Web Site: www.amfire.com
Members: 25000 individuals
Staff: 11
President: Andrew Molchan
E-Mail: km@400bellsouth.net

Historical Note

Members are individuals licensed to sell firearms. Membership: $55/year; $65/2 years; $75/3 years (individual).

Publications:

American Firearms Industry. m. adv.
AFI Buying Directory & Who's Who. a. adv.

National Association of Fire Equipment Distributors *(1962)*

104 S. Michigan Ave., Suite 300
Chicago, IL 60603
Tel: (312)263-8100 *Fax:* (312)263-8111
Web Site: www.nafed.org
Members: 1200 companies
Staff: 6
Annual Budget: $1-2,000,000
Executive Director, Operations: Danny Harris
Manager, Communications and Marketing: Kristen McCullough

Historical Note

NAFED members sell, service and maintain fire equipment. NAFED is involved with state licensing of distributors and works with governmental agencies and fire services on other industry matters.

Meetings/Conferences:

Annual Meetings: Spring

Publications:

Firewatch. q. adv.
Firewire. q.

National Association of Fire Investigators *(1961)*

857 Tallevast Rd.
Sarasota, FL 34243
Tel: (941)359-2800 *Fax:* (941)351-5849
Toll Free: (877)506 - 6234
E-Mail: nafi_info@yahoo.com
Web Site: www.nafi.org
Members: 4200 individuals
Staff: 2
Annual Budget: $50-100,000
President: John Kennedy
Director, Membership Services: Heather Kennedy

Historical Note

Primary purposes are to increase the knowledge and improve the skills of persons engaged in the investigation and analysis of fires/explosions or in the litigation which ensues from such investigations. Awards the Certified Fire and Explosion Investigator (CFEI) and Certifed Fire Investigation Instructor (CFII) designations. Membership: $40/year (regular member); $50/year (certified member).

Meetings/Conferences:

Annual Meetings: Spring or Summer

Publications:

Nat'l Fire Investigator. irreg.

National Association of First Responders *(1984)*

5334 Armadillo Ave.
Orange Beach, AL 36561-4211
Tel: (334)981-3383
Members: 4561 individuals
Staff: 22
Annual Budget: $250-500,000
President: Henry S. Weir, Jr.

Historical Note

Members are Emergency Medical Response professionals with at least 40 hours of continuing professional education.

Meetings/Conferences:
2007 - Memphis, TN(Airport Marriott)/Sept. 2-5/1500

Publications:
Nat'l EMR Responder. m.

National Association of Flavors and Food-Ingredient Systems *(1917)*
3301 Rt. 66, Suite 205, Bldg. C
Neptune, NJ 07753
Tel: (732)922-3218 *Fax:* (732)922-3590
E-Mail: info@naffs.org
Web Site: www.naffs.org
Members: 140
Staff: 5
Executive Director: Bob Bauer
E-Mail: bobbauer@naffs.org

Historical Note
Founded as National Fruit and Syrup Manufacturers Association; became National Association of Fruits, Flavors and Syrups in 1974, and assumed its current name in 2003. NAFFS is a trade association for manufacturers, processors and suppliers of fruits, flavors, syrups, stabilizers, emulsifiers, colors, sweeteners, cocoa and related food ingredients. Associate membership is open to all companies that provides products and services to the food industry. Mission is to provide a forum for the exchange of technology and marketing information; to keep its membership informed of legislative and regulatory developments which impact the trade and commerce of that membership; to respond to the needs of the membership; and to take a proactive role that generally promotes, protects, and extends the welfare of the industries represented. Membership: fees vary, based on annual sales.

Meetings/Conferences:
Annual Meetings: 75

National Association of Fleet Administrators *(1957)*
100 Wood Ave. South, Suite 310
Iselin, NJ 08830-2709
Tel: (732)494-8100 *Fax:* (732)494-6789
Web Site: www.nafa.org
Members: 3900 individuals
Staff: 13
Annual Budget: $2-5,000,000
Executive Director: Phillip E. Russo
E-Mail: prusso@nafa.org
Director, Meetings: Pat Murtaugh

Historical Note
Organized at a luncheon meeting at the Congress Hotel in Chicago on March 12, 1957 and incorporated with 25 charter members in the State of Illinois, April 11, 1957. Members are individuals responsible for administration of a fleet of 25 or more motor vehicles not for hire commercially. Membership: $415/year.

Meetings/Conferences:
Annual Meetings: Spring/1,500
2007 - Houston, TX(Houston Americas)/May 7-10/3000

Publications:
NAFA Newsletter. bi-m.
NAFA's Fleet Executive. m. adv.

National Association of Fleet Resale Dealers *(1984)*
396 Clarkston Dr.
Smyrna, TN 37167
Tel: (615)355-5225 *Fax:* (615)825-7794
E-Mail: kimg@nafrd.com
Web Site: www.nafrd.com
Members: 100 wholesalers
Staff: 2
Annual Budget: $100-250,000
Executive Director: Kimberly W. Glasscock

Historical Note
NAFRD members are used car wholesalers who deal exclusively in fleet vehicles. Associate membership is available for those who provide goods or services to the industry. Industry partners are those who are potential suppliers of vehicles to dealers. Membership: $1,200/year (regular); $750/year (associate); $100/year (industry partner).

Meetings/Conferences:
Annual Meetings: Fall

Publications:
Tracks Newsletter. q. adv.
Annual Business Survey. a.
Resource Directory. a. adv.

National Association of Flight Instructors *(1966)*
P.O. Box 3086
Oshkosh, WI 54903-3086
Tel: (920)426-6801 *Fax:* (920)426-6865
E-Mail: nafi@eaa.org
Web Site: www.nafinet.org
Members: 5000 individuals
Staff: 2
Annual Budget: $100-250,000
Executive Director: Rusty Sachs

Historical Note
Members are flight instructors certified by the Federal Aviation Administration and others who support flight instruction. Seeks to raise the professonal standards for flight instruction through education and organization. Membership: $39/year (initial); $39/year (renewal).

Meetings/Conferences:
2007 - Oshkosh, WI/July 24-30

Publications:
NAFI Mentor. a.

National Association of Flood and Stormwater Management Agencies *(1978)*
1301 K St. NW
Suite 800 East
Washington, DC 20005
Tel: (202)218-4122 *Fax:* (202)478-1734
E-Mail: info@nafsma.org
Web Site: www.nafsma.org
Members: 102 agencies
Staff: 4
Annual Budget: $100-250,000
Executive Director: Susan Gilson
Director, Membership Services: Kerry Wilson

Historical Note
Members are state, county and municipal organizations concerned with the management of water resources in metropolitan areas. Formerly the National Association of Urban Flood Management Agencies, the Association assumed its present name in 1989. Membership: fees based on service population (regular); number of employees (subscribing).

Meetings/Conferences:
Annual Meetings: Fall

Publications:
Survey of Stormwater Phase II Communities.
NAFSMA News Bulletin. irreg.

National Association of Floor Covering Distributors *(1971)*
401 N. Michigan Ave., Suite 2400
Chicago, IL 60611-4703
Tel: (312)321-6836 *Fax:* (312)673-6962
Web Site: www.nafcd.org
Members: 300 individuals
Staff: 4
Annual Budget: $500-1,000,000
Executive Director: Maurice A. Desmarais, CAE

Historical Note
Membership: $795/year.

Publications:
News and Views. bi-m.

National Association of Flour Distributors *(1919)*
c/o Compass Group
P.O. Box 610
Montville, NJ 07045
Tel: (973)402-1801 *Fax:* (973)316-6668
Web Site: www.thenafd.com/
Members: 225 individuals
Staff: 2
Annual Budget: $50-100,000
Executive Director: Jean LaCorte

Historical Note
Members are brokers, distributors, manufacturers, and other professionals allied with the flour industry.

Meetings/Conferences:
Annual Meetings: Spring

Publications:
Newsletter. 2/year.
Membership Directory. a.
The Flour Distributor. 2/year.

National Association of Foreign-Trade Zones *(1973)*
1000 Connecticut Ave. NW
Suite 1001
Washington, DC 20036
Tel: (202)331-1950 *Fax:* (202)331-1994
Web Site: www.naftz.org
Members: 620 organizations
Staff: 4
Annual Budget: $500-1,000,000
Executive Director: William M. Berito

Historical Note
Foreign-Trade Zones are sites where foreign and domestic goods may be stored, tested, repackaged, assembled, etc. and where neither customs duty nor government excise tax is levied on exported products. Members are companies and organizations who are operators, grantees, and users of these sites. Membership: $100-950/year (company).

Publications:
Zones Report. m.

National Association of Forensic Accountants
2455 E. Sunrise Blvd., Suite 1201
Ft. Lauderdale, FL 33304
Tel: (954)535-5556 *Fax:* (954)537-4942
Toll Free: (800)523 - 3680
E-Mail: info@nafanet.com
Web Site: www.nafanet.com

Historical Note
Members are accountants who specialize in documentary analysis for legal proceedings and/or expert testimony.

National Association of Forensic Economics *(1986)*
P.O. Box 394
Mount Union, PA 17066
E-Mail: umkcnafe@umkc.edu
Web Site: www.nafe.net
Members: 750 individuals
Staff: 2
Annual Budget: $25-50,000
Executive Director: George A. Schieren, Ph.D.
E-Mail: schierenga@appstate.edu
Production Editor: Nancy Eldredge
E-Mail: nancy@nafe.net

Historical Note
Formerly (1992) National Association of Forensic Economists. NAFE fosters research and education in the application of economics to litigation. Has members in all 50 states and in 6 countries. Membership: $110/year.

Meetings/Conferences:
Annual Meetings: January

Publications:
NAFE Newsletter. q. adv.
Litigation Economics Review. semi-a.
Journal of Forensic Economics. 3/year. adv.
NAFE Membership Directory. bien.

National Association of Foster Grandparent Program Directors *(1971)*
c/o Foster Grandparent Program
3200 Wayne, Suite 123
Kansas City, MO 64109
Tel: (816)784-4519 *Fax:* (816)784-4529
Web Site: www.nafgpd.org
Members: 325 individuals
Annual Budget: $10-25,000
President: Brenda Lax
E-Mail: brenda_lax@kcmo.org

Historical Note
Created in 1971, NAFGPD serves as the principal advocate for Foster Grandparent Programs. The purpose of the NAFGPD is to provide a national focus for issues which directly affect both the quality of the services provided to volunteers and the children they serve, and the ability of directors to manage their programs effectively and to meet the changing needs of their communities. Professional membership is open to all directors, coordinators, and supervisors. Has no

paid officers or full time staff. Membership: $75/year (individual); $125/year (organization).

Publications:
NAFGPD Update. bi-m.

National Association of Fraternal Insurance Counsellors *(1950)*
211 Canal Rd.
Waterloo, WI 53594
Tel: (866)478-3880
E-Mail: office@nafic.org
Web Site: http://codewriters.com/asites/main-pub.cfm?usr=NAFIC
Members: 2750 individuals
Executive Secretary: Anna Maenner

Historical Note
Formerly (1966) Fraternal Insurance Counsellors Association. Affiliate of the Fraternal Field Managers Association. Professional organization of sales personnel for fraternal benefit life insurance societies.

Publications:
The Fraternal Monitor. m.

National Association of Fruits, Flavors and Syrups

Historical Note
Became National Association of Flavors and Food-Ingredient Systems in 2003.

National Association of FSA County Office Employees
P.O. Box 476
Bloomfield, MO 63625
Web Site: www.nascoe.org
Members: 10000 individuals
Annual Budget: $100-250,000
Contact: Steve Morrison

Historical Note
Formerly (1995) National Association of ASCS County Office Employees and (1997) National Association of FSA County Office. An independent labor association. Members are county office employees of the U.S. Department of Agriculture's Farm Service Agency. Has no paid officers or full-time staff. Membership: $40/year (individual).

Publications:
NASCOE Newsletter. bi-m.

National Association of Fundraising Ticket Manufacturers *(1983)*
1360 Energy Park Dr., Suite 210
St. Paul, MN 55108-5252
Tel: (651)644-4710 *Fax:* (651)644-5904
Web Site: www.naftm.org
Members: 5 manufacturers
Staff: 2
Annual Budget: $500-1,000,000
President: Roger Franke
Legal Counsel: Mary Magnuson
E-Mail: mary.magnuson@naftm.org

Historical Note
NAFTM is a trade association of companies that manufacture pull tabs, bingo paper, and related supplies for the North American charitable gaming industry.

Publications:
Charitable Guidebook.

National Association of Geoscience Teachers *(1938)*
31 Crestview Dr.
Napa, CA 94558
Tel: (707)427-8864
E-Mail: nagt@gordonvalley.com
Web Site: www.nagt.org
Members: 1900 individuals
Annual Budget: $100-250,000
Executive Director: Ian Macgregor

Historical Note
Founded in Rock Island, IL as the Association of College Geology Teachers; dropped "College" from name in 1946; became the National Association of Geology Teachers in 1958; and assumed present name in 1996. A member society of the American Geological Institute. Has no paid or full-time staff. Membership: $35/year (individual); $75/year (organization).

Meetings/Conferences:
Annual Meetings: Fall, with Geological Soc. of America

Publications:
Journal of Geoscience Education. 5/year. adv.

National Association of Golf Tournament Directors *(1996)*
212 S. Henry St.
Alexandria, VA 22314-3522
Tel: (703)549-3543 *Fax:* (703)549-9074
Toll Free: (888)899 - 2483
E-Mail: nagtd2@aol.com
Web Site: www.nagtd.com
Members: 500 individuals
Staff: 4
Annual Budget: $250-500,000
Executive Director: Walter E. Galanty, Jr.

Historical Note
NATGD members are professionals who develop and direct national association, celebrity, charity and corporate golf tournaments. Membership $175/year (individual); $450/year (individual golf tournament suppliers).

Meetings/Conferences:
Annual Meetings:

Publications:
Leaderboard newsletter. m. adv.

National Association of Government Archives and Records Administrators *(1984)*
90 State St., Suite 1009
Albany, NY 12207
Tel: (518)463-8644
E-Mail: nagara@caphill.com
Web Site: www.nagara.org
Members: 350 individuals
Annual Budget: $50-100,000
Membership Services Coordinator: Steve Grandin

Historical Note
Incorporated in New York State, NAGARA is a nationwide association of local, state and federal records administrators and others concerned with improving administration of government records. Membership: $600/program/year (records management & archival agencies); $40/year (individuals).

Meetings/Conferences:
Annual Meetings: Summer

Publications:
The Clearinghouse. q.

National Association of Government Communicators *(1976)*
10366 Democracy Ln., Suite B
Fairfax, VA 22030
Tel: (703)691-0377 *Fax:* (703)691-0866
E-Mail: info@nagc.com
Web Site: www.nagc.com
Members: 500 individuals
Staff: 3
Annual Budget: $100-250,000
Executive Director: Michael Sheward, APR
Director, Administration: Sherri Core

Historical Note
Product of a merger of the Federal Editors Association, the Government Information Organization, and the Armed Forces Writers' League. NAGC is a member of the Council of Communication Societies. Membership: $85/year (individual).

Meetings/Conferences:
Annual Meetings: May

National Association of Government Defined Contribution Administrators *(1980)*
201 E. Main St., Suite 1405
Lexington, KY 40507
Tel: (859)514-9161 *Fax:* (859)514-9188
E-Mail: InfoNAGDCA@AMRms.com
Web Site: www.nagdca.org
Members: 275governmentagenciescompanies
Staff: 2
Annual Budget: $500-1,000,000
Association Director: Tracy Tucker

Historical Note
Founded as National Association of Government Deferred Compensation Administrators; assumed its current name in 2000. NAGDCA's mission is to unite representatives from state and local governments along with private sector organizations that service and support defined contribution plans. Membership: $500/year (government member); $750/year (industry member), $350/year (associate).

Meetings/Conferences:
Annual Meetings: Fall
2007 - Indian Wells, CA(Hyatt Grand Champions Resort and Spa)/Sept. 15-19

Publications:
Guidebook. irreg..
Question & Answer Book. irreg..
Newsletter. q.
Survey of 457 Plans. bien.
Conference Report. a.
Membership Directory. a.

National Association of Government Employees *(1961)*
159 Burgin Pkwy.
Quincy, MA 02169
Tel: (617)376-0220 *Fax:* (617)376-0285
Web Site: www.nage.org
Members: 200000 individuals
Staff: 100
Annual Budget: $2-5,000,000
President: David Holway
Executive Vice President: James Farley
Executive Vice President: Barbara Osgood

Historical Note
NAGE, a labor union representing civilian government employees, which includes the National Association of Nurses, National Association of Health Care Workers, International Brotherhood of Correctional Officers, and International Brotherhood of Police Officers, became affiliated with the Service Employees International Union, AFL-CIO in 1982. Sponsors and supports the Government Employees' Political Research Institute and the National Association of Government Employees Political Action Committee.

Meetings/Conferences:
Quadrennial Meetings:

Publications:
Fednews. q.
NAGE Reporter. q.
Police Chronicle. q.

National Association of Government Guaranteed Lenders *(1984)*

Historical Note
No updated contact information as of 2006.

National Association of Government Labor Officials *(1914)*
444 N. Capitol St. NW
Suite 401
Washington, DC 20001
Tel: (202)624-5460 *Fax:* (202)624-5452
Web Site: www.naglo.org
Members: 50 individuals
Annual Budget: $25-50,000
Affiliate Director: Melinda Glazer

Historical Note
Founded as the International Association of Governmental Labor Officials; assumed its present name in 1979. NAGLO is dedicated to improving the protection of workers' rights, and to promoting safe and healthy workplaces. Members are directors and commissioners of state labor departments. Has no paid staff or permanent address. Membership: $500/year.

Meetings/Conferences:
Annual Meetings: Summer

Publications:
NAGLO Membership Directory. a.
NAGLO News. m.

National Association of Graduate Admissions Professionals *(1987)*
P.O. Box 14605
Lenexa, KS 66285-4605
Tel: (913)752-4977 *Fax:* (913)599-5340
E-Mail: info@nagap.org
Web Site: www.nagap.org
Members: 1500 individuals
Staff: 5

Annual Budget: $500-1,000,000
Executive Director: Michael P. Flanagan, CAE

Historical Note

Founded as New England Association of Graduate Admissions Professionals, NAGAP is the only professional organization in the United States devoted exclusively to the concerns of individuals working in the graduate admissions and recruitment environment. NAGAP is committed to serving the needs and interests of graduate admissions professionals throughout the United States and abroad. Has no paid officers or full-time staff; uses consultants and contract services. Membership: $125/year.

Meetings/Conferences:

Annual Meetings: Annual/Spring
2007 - Orlando, FL/Apr. 25-28/900
2008 - Denver, CO(Hyatt Regency Denver)/Apr. 23-26/900

Publications:

Electronic newsletter (online). m.
Perspectives of NAGAP. q.
Calendar of Grad & Professional School Fairs Online. a.
Membership Directory Online. a.

National Association of Graphic and Product Identification Manufacturers *(1951)*

P.O. Box 1237
Simpsonville, SC 29681
Tel: (864)962-2366 *Fax:* (864)962-2483
Members: 80 companies
Staff: 12
Annual Budget: $100-250,000
Executive Vice President: James A. Kinder
Meeting Planning: Dita Howell

Historical Note

Incorporated on July 24, 1951 in the State of Delaware as a result of meetings by manufacturers during World War II to discuss metal shortages. Established as the Metal Etching and Fabricating Association; became National Association of Metal Name Plate Manufacturers in 1967; then National Association of Name Plate Manufacturers in 1979, and assumed its current name in 1994. Publishes the only book of standards for the name plate industry.

Meetings/Conferences:

Semi-Annual Meetings: Spring and Fall

Publications:

Membership Directory. a. adv.
Newsletter. 3/yr. adv.

National Association of Health Care Workers

Historical Note

A unit of the National Association of Government Employees.

National Association of Health Data Organizations *(1986)*

448 East 400 South
Suite 301
Salt Lake City, UT 84111
Tel: (801)532-2299 *Fax:* (801)532-2228
E-Mail: nahdoinfo@nahdo.org
Web Site: www.nahdo.org
Members: 250 organizations
Staff: 6
Annual Budget: $250-500,000
Executive Director: Denise Love
E-Mail: dlove@nahdo.org
Project and Meeting Coordinator: Deana Clark

Historical Note

NAHDO members are federal and state health data organizations, software developers, consultants, hospital associations, health series researchers, insurers, managed care firms, cost containment companies, and health trade groups. Membership: $150/year (individual); $2,000-2,500/year (organization); $2,400/year (public/nonprofit); $3,000/year (corporate).

Meetings/Conferences:

Annual Meetings: Winter

Publications:

Annual Report. a. adv.
NAHDO News Newsletter. q. adv.
NAHDO News Update. m. adv.

National Association of Health Services Executives *(1968)*

8630 Fenton St., Suite 126
Silver Spring, MD 20910
Tel: (202)628-3953 *Fax:* (301)588-0011
E-Mail: nationalhq@nahse.org
Web Site: www.nahse.org
Members: 1700 individuals
Annual Budget: $250-500,000
Executive Director: Ozzie Jenkins, CMP

Historical Note

Members are African-American health care executives. Membership: $200/year (individual); $1,500/year (organization).

Meetings/Conferences:

Annual Meetings: April-May

Publications:

NAHSE Notes. q. adv.

National Association of Health Underwriters *(1930)*

2000 N. 14th St., Suite 450
Arlington, VA 22201
Tel: (703)276-0220 *Fax:* (703)841-7797
E-Mail: nahu@nahu.org
Web Site: www.nahu.org
Members: 20000 individuals
Staff: 26
Annual Budget: $5-10,000,000
Vice President, Meetings: Kathleen D. Cochran, CAE, CMP
Vice President, Communications: Jim Hostetler
Vice President, Public Relations: Kelly Loussedes
Senior Vice President, Membership and Development: Ilana Maze
Senior Vice President, Operations: Jennifer Murphy, CPA
Vice President, Education: Farren Ross
Vice President, Congressional Affairs: Pete Stein
Executive Vice President: Janet Trautwein

Historical Note

Formerly (1962) National Association of Accident & Health Underwriters, and (1978) International Association of Health Underwriters. Awards the Leading Producers Round Table (LPRT) Award and Harold R. Gordan Memorial Award. Membership: $145/year (individual).

Meetings/Conferences:

Annual Meetings: June
2007 - To Be Determined
2008 - San Diego, CA(Sheraton)/June 28-July 2

Publications:

Health Insurance Underwriter Magazine. m. adv.

National Association of Health Unit Coordinators *(1980)*

1947 Madron Rd.
Rockford, IL 61107-1716
Tel: (815)633-4351 *Fax:* (815)633-4438
Toll Free: (888)226 - 2482
E-Mail: office@nahuc.org
Web Site: www.nahuc.org
Members: 1900 individuals
Annual Budget: $100-250,000
Association Manager: Patricia Rice

Historical Note

Formerly (1990) National Association of Health Unit Clerks/Coordinators. Members are coordinators of non-clinical nursing unit activities, educators, supervisors, students and graduates in the field. Membership: $35/year (new); $30/year (renewal); $300/year (organization/company).

Meetings/Conferences:

Annual Meetings: Summer
2007 - Tampa, FL(Sheraton Suite Airport)/Aug. 8-11/200

Publications:

The Coordinator. q. adv.
NAHUC - Membership Directory. a.

National Association of Healthcare Access Management *(1974)*

2025 M St. NW
Suite 800
Washington, DC 20036
Tel: (202)367-1125 *Fax:* (202)367-2125
E-Mail: info@naham.org
Web Site: www.naham.org
Members: 1000 individuals
Staff: 3
Annual Budget: $250-500,000
Executive Director: Steve Kemp

Historical Note

Formerly (1990) the National Association of Hospital Admitting Managers. NAHAM was established and incorporated in New York. Membership: $140/year (individual); $1,000/year (corporate).

Meetings/Conferences:

Annual Meetings: May/500

Publications:

The NAHAM Management Journal q. adv. adv.
Connections. m.

National Association of Healthcare Consultants *(1992)*

1255 23rd St. NW
Suite 200
Washington, DC 20037-1174
Tel: (202)452-8282 *Fax:* (202)833-3636
E-Mail: consultants@healthcon.org
Web Site: www.healthcon.org
Members: 350 individuals
Staff: 3
Annual Budget: $250-500,000
Executive Director: Brian J. Mandrier

Historical Note

NAHC represents consultants who provide ethical, confidential, and professional advice to the health care industry. Membership $425/year (individual).

Meetings/Conferences:

Annual Meetings: Spring

Publications:

Roster "Membership Sourcebook". a. adv.
UPDATE Newsletter. q.
Statistics of Physician Practices. a.

National Association of Hispanic and Latino Studies *(1995)*

Historical Note

An affiliate of Nat'l Ass'n of African American Studies, which provides administrative support.

National Association of Hispanic County Officials

Historical Note

An affiliate of the National Association of Counties which provides administrative support.

National Association of Hispanic Federal Executives *(1984)*

P.O. Box 469
Herndon, VA 20172-0469
Tel: (703)787-0291 *Fax:* (703)787-4675
E-Mail: nahfe@cs.com
Web Site: www.nahfe.org
Members: 2000 individuals
Staff: 3
Annual Budget: $50-100,000
President: Manuel Oliverez

Historical Note

NAHFE promotes the federal government as a model employer, recruits qualified Hispanics for federal service and provides quality executive development training to Federal personnel. Its goal is to increase the number of Hispanic Americans in high level policy positions in the Federal executive departments and agencies. Membership: $36/year (individual); $1,000/year (organization/company).

Meetings/Conferences:

Annual Meetings: Fall

Publications:

Project Alpha Report: Employment Analysis of Federal Departments.
Hispanic Executive. q. adv.

National Association of Hispanic Journalists *(1982)*

529 14th St. NW
Suite 1000
Washington, DC 20045-2001
Tel: (202)662-7145 *Fax:* (202)662-7144

Toll Free: (888)346 - 6245
E-Mail: nahj@nahj.org
Web Site: www.nahj.org
Members: 1700 individuals
Staff: 4
Annual Budget: $1-2,000,000
Executive Director: Ivan Roman
E-Mail: iroman@najh.org
Coordinator, Membership: Claudio Araujo
E-Mail: caraujo@nahj.org
Deputy Director, Communications and Media Policy: Joseph Torres
E-Mail: jtorres@nahj.org

Historical Note

NAHJ's purposes are to increase educational and career opportunities in journalism for Hispanic Americans; to organize and provide mutual support of Hispanic journalists; and to promote fair treatment of Hispanics by the news media. Membership: $55/year (regular, academic and associate members); $25/year (students); $110/year (individuals); $1,100/year (corporate).

Meetings/Conferences:

Annual Meetings: Summer/1,200

Publications:

NAHJ Membership Newsletter. q. adv.
National Hispanic Media Directory. a. adv.

National Association of Hispanic Nurses *(1975)*
1501 16th St. NW
Washington, DC 20036
Tel: (202)387-2477 *Fax:* (202)483-7183
E-Mail: info@thehispanicnurses.org
Web Site: www.TheHispanicNurses.org
Members: 1000 individuals
Staff: 1
President: Rudy Valenzuela

Historical Note

NAHN strives to serve the nursing and healthcare delivery needs of the Hispanic community and the professional needs of Hispanic nurses. NAHN is designed and committed to work toward the improvement of the quality of health and nursing care for Hispanic consumers and toward providing equal access to educational, professional, and economic opportunities for Hispanic nurses. Membership fees vary.

Meetings/Conferences:

Annual Meetings: July/110

Publications:

Hispanic Health Care International. q. adv.

National Association of Hispanic Publications *(1982)*
52914th St. NW
Suite 1085
Washington, DC 20045
Tel: (202)662-7250 *Fax:* (202)662-7251
E-Mail: info@nahp.org
Web Site: www.nahp.org
Members: 234 publications
Staff: 4
Annual Budget: $250-500,000
Chief Operating Officer: Joseph Carrillo
Director, Communications: Alec Andrade

Historical Note

NAHP was founded in the belief that the most effective way to reach the more than 29 million Hispanic Americans in the country is their own language. Membership open to publications which serve or cover the Hispanic and/or Spanish speaking community in the U.S. Associate membership open to individuals, corporations, or news services who support the goals of the NAHP. National Hispanic Press Foundation is that NAHP's foundation. Membership: $100-500/year., depending on type of publication (weekly, monthly, magazine, etc.).

Meetings/Conferences:

Semi-Annual Meetings: Spring and Fall

Publications:

Hispanic Press. q. adv.
National Hispanic Media Directory. a. adv.

National Association of Home and Workshop Writers *(1973)*
8 Burma Road
Baker, NV 89311
Tel: (775)234-7167 *Fax:* (775)234-7361
E-Mail: danramsey@nahww.org
Web Site: www.nahww.org
Members: 100 individuals
Annual Budget: under $10,000
Secretary/Treasurer: Susan Geary

Historical Note

Writers of articles, books and video material on such subjects as home maintenance, repair and improvement, and on workshop projects. Has no paid officers or full-time staff. Membership: $36/year (individual); $220/year (organization).

Meetings/Conferences:

Annual Meetings: Summer

Publications:

Newsletter. q.
Directory of Members. a.

National Association of Home Builders *(1942)*
1201 15th St. NW
Washington, DC 20005
Tel: (202)266-8200 *Fax:* (202)266-8400
Toll Free: (800)368 - 5242
E-Mail: info@nahb.org
Web Site: www.nahb.org
Members: 235,000 individuals
Staff: 350
Annual Budget: $25-50,000,000
Executive Vice President and Chief Executive Officer: Jerry Howard
Manager, Public Relations: Niki M. Clark
E-Mail: nclark@nahb.org
First Vice President: David L. Pressly, Jr.
Staff Vice President, Media and Public Relations: Donna Reichle

Historical Note

Connected with the Builders Political Campaign Committee (BUILD-PAC). Also supports the Homeowners Warranty Corporation, the NAHB Research Center, the Home Builders Institute, the National Council of the Housing Industry, and the National Housing Endowment. The National Commercial Builders Council, National Council of the Multifamily Housing Industry, National Remodelors Council and the National Sales and Marketing Council are councils of NAHB. The National Council of Multifamily Housing is a division. Absorbed the National Association of Home Manufacturers in 1981 and the North American Log Homes Council in 1987.

Meetings/Conferences:

Annual Meetings: Winter

Publications:

Education Insider (online). q.
At Home with Concrete. bi-m.
Forecast of Housing Activity. m.
Builder Magazine (online). m. adv.
Housing Economics (online).
Housing Market Statistics. m.
Building Women Magazine. q.
Commercial Builder Magazine. q.
Land Development Magazine. q.
Sales and Marketing Ideas Magazine. bi-m.
Washington Hotline and Multifamily Outlook (online). m.

National Association of Home Inspectors *(1987)*
4248 Park Glen Road
Minneapolis, MN 55416
Tel: (952)928-4641 *Fax:* (952)929-1318
Toll Free: (800)448 - 3942
E-Mail: info@nahi.org
Web Site: www.nahi.org
Members: 2300 individuals
Staff: 4
Annual Budget: $500-1,000,000
Executive Director: Mallory C. Anderson
E-Mail: mallory@nahi.org

Historical Note

NAHI is a trade association established to promote and develop the home inspection industry. Membership: $295-345/year (individual); $395/year (affiliate); $500/year (corporate).

Meetings/Conferences:

2007 - Las Vegas, NV(The Riveria)/Feb. 18-21/400

Publications:

Membership Directory (online).
Standards of Practice Code of Ethics.
NAHI Forum Newsletter. bi-m. adv.

National Association of Hospital Hospitality Houses *(1986)*
P.O. Box 18087
Asheville, NC 28814-0087
Tel: (828)253-1188 *Fax:* (828)253-8082
Toll Free: (800)542 - 9730
E-Mail: helpinghomes@nahhh.org
Web Site: www.nahhh.org
Members: 200 organizations
Staff: 2
Annual Budget: $100-250,000
President: Phyllis Youngberg

Historical Note

NAHHH members are hospital hospitality house facilities providing temporary residential facilities for the use of patients and their families. Membership: $200/year (individual); $200-250/year (organization/company).

Meetings/Conferences:

Annual Meetings: Spring

Publications:

Inside Hospitality. q.
Nat'l Referral Directory. irreg.
NAHHH Newsletter. semi-a.

National Association of Housing and Redevelopment Officials *(1933)*
630 I St. NW
Washington, DC 20001-3736
Tel: (202)289-3500 *Fax:* (202)289-8181
Toll Free: (877)866 - 2476
E-Mail: nahro@nahro.org
Web Site: www.nahro.org
Members: 18000 individuals
Staff: 38
Annual Budget: $5-10,000,000
Executive Director: Saul N. Ramirez, Jr.
Director, Legislation, Program Development and Media: John Bohm
Director, Finance and Administration: L. Leon Durham, CAE
Director, Member Services: Mary L. Pike

Historical Note

Formerly (1953) National Association of Housing Officials. Members are housing and community development officials who administer local programs under the auspices of HUD. Has an annual budget of approximately $7 million.

Meetings/Conferences:

Annual Meetings: Spring

Publications:

NAHRO Monitor. semi-m.
Journal of Housing and Community Development. bi-m. adv.

National Association of Housing Cooperatives *(1950)*
1707 H St. NW
Suite 201
Washington, DC 20006
Tel: (202)737-0797 *Fax:* (202)783-7869
E-Mail: info@coophousing.org
Web Site: www.coophousing.org
Members: 1000coopsandprofessionalfirms
Staff: 5
Annual Budget: $500-1,000,000
Executive Director: Douglas M. Kleine, CAE

Historical Note

NAHC is a federation of regional or specialized associations of cooperatives. NAHC provides education for cooperative boards of directors and managers. Advocates creation of new cooperatives to provide home ownership for low and moderate income families. Membership: $1.25-$3.25 per co-op apartment in each building. Maxmimum $2500.

Meetings/Conferences:

Annual Meetings: Fall
2007 - Miami, FL/Sept. 26-29/600
2008 - Houston, TX/Sept. 17-20/600

Publications:

Cooperative Housing Bulletin. bi-m. adv.

Cooperative Housing Journal. a. adv.

National Association of Housing Information Managers *(1992)*
134 S. 13th St., Suite 701
Lincoln, NE 68508-1901
Tel: (402)476-9424 *Fax:* (402)420-1770
Toll Free: (800)379 - 3807
E-Mail: NAHIMEXEC@aol.com
Web Site: www.nahim.org
Members: 200 public housing authorities
Staff: 2
Annual Budget: $10-25,000
Executive Director: John E. Mooring
Historical Note
Established to focus on information technology issues affecting public housing authorities, NAHIM members are public housing authorities. Associate membership is available for private software firms. Membership: $75-$125/year (public housing agency); $250/year (associate).
Publications:
NAHIM News Newsletter. m.

National Association of Independent Colleges and Universities *(1976)*
1025 Connecticut Ave. NW
Suite 700
Washington, DC 20036-5405
Tel: (202)785-8866 *Fax:* (202)835-0003
E-Mail: geninfo@naicu.edu
Web Site: www.naicu.edu
Members: 1000 colleges and universities
Staff: 22
Annual Budget: $2-5,000,000
President: David L. Warren
Director, Finance and Administration: Linda S. Allison
Director, Student Aid Policy: Maureen Budetti
Vice President, Government Relations and Policy: Sarah A. Flanagan
Director, Publications: Jeffery E. Hume-Pratuch
Vice President, Public Affairs: Roland King
Director, Member Relations and Conference Planning: Deborah Sykes Reilly
Historical Note
Founded as Federation of State Associations of Colleges and Universities, a lobbying group for the Association of American Colleges, it became the National Council of Independent Colleges and Universities in 1971, and assumed independence under its present name in 1976. Promotes private and government support for the nation's 1200 private institutions of higher learning.
Meetings/Conferences:
Annual Meetings: Winter in Washington, DC(Hyatt Regency)/600
Publications:
Week In Review. w.

National Association of Independent Fee Appraisers *(1961)*
401 N. Michigan Ave., Suite 2200
Chicago, IL 60611
Tel: (312)321-6830 *Fax:* (312)673-6652
E-Mail: info@naifa.com
Web Site: www.naifa.com
Members: 3000 individuals
Staff: 16
Annual Budget: $1-2,000,000
Executive Vice President: Laura J. Rudzinski
Membership Coordinator: Maggie Haptas
Director, Marketing and Communications: Tracy Schorle
Historical Note
Founded in Phoenix, Arizona in 1961. Majority of members are self-employed appraisers specializing in the appraisal of real estate held in fee simple. Awards four designations: Independent Fee Appraiser (IFA), IFA Senior (IFAS), IFA Agricultural (IFAA), and IFA Counselor (IFAC). Sponsors and supports the IFA Good Government PAC and the Appraisal Foundation. Membership: $400/year.
Meetings/Conferences:
Annual Meetings: Fall

National Association of Independent Insurance Adjusters *(1937)*
825 West State St., Suite 117-C & B
Geneva, IL 60134
Tel: (630)397-5012 *Fax:* (630)397-5013
E-Mail: assist@naiia.com
Web Site: www.naiia.com
Members: 290 companies
Staff: 3
Annual Budget: $100-250,000
Executive Vice President: David F. Mehren
Historical Note
Members are independently-owned property and casualty claims adjusting companies.
Meetings/Conferences:
Annual Meetings: May
Publications:
Membership Directory. a.
Status Report Member Newsletter. q.
Claims Professional Newsletter. q.

National Association of Independent Insurance Auditors and Engineers *(1963)*
320 Cumberland St.
Lebanon, PA 84020
Toll Free: (800)544 - 2551
Web Site: www.naiiae.com
Members: 37 organizations
Annual Budget: $10-25,000
President: Russell DeLuca
Historical Note
NAIIAE members are independent companies providing audits, underwriting surveys, loss control services and other related services to the insurance industry. Has no paid staff; officers change annually. Membership: $250-1,500/year.
Meetings/Conferences:
Annual Meetings: Always October/50
Publications:
Directory. a.
NAI Letter. m.

National Association of Independent Life Brokerage Agencies *(1982)*
12150 Monument Dr., Suite 125
Fairfax, VA 22033
Tel: (703)383-3081 *Fax:* (703)383-6942
Web Site: www.nailba.org
Members: 300 agencies
Staff: 6
Annual Budget: $2-5,000,000
Executive Director: Joseph Normandy
E-Mail: jnormandy@nailba.org
Director, Member Services: Michelle Jones
Historical Note
Membership: $1195/year (agency).
Meetings/Conferences:
Annual Meetings: November
Publications:
NAILBA Magazine. o. adv.
NAILBA Directory (available to members only). a.

National Association of Independent Lighting Distributors *(1977)*
2207 Elmwood Ave.
Buffalo, NY 14216-1009
Tel: (716)875-3670 *Fax:* (716)875-0734
E-Mail: lmd@naild.org
Web Site: www.naild.org
Members: 150 companies
Staff: 2
Annual Budget: $100-250,000
Administrator: Linda M. Daniel
Historical Note
NAILD members are distributors of lighting products. Vendor members are manufacturers and suppliers. Membership: varies by category.
Publications:
NAILD Membership Directory. a. adv.
Today's Lighting Distributor. bi-m. adv.

National Association of Independent Public Finance Advisors *(1989)*
P.O. Box 304
Montgomery, IL 60538-0304
Tel: (630)896-1292 *Fax:* (209)633-6265
Toll Free: (800)624 - 7321
E-Mail: rmhoban@yahoo.com
Web Site: www.naipfa.com
Members: 71 individuals
Staff: 1
Annual Budget: $25-50,000
Executive Director: Roseanne M. Hoban
Historical Note
NAIPFA members are independent firms specializing in providing financial advice to public agencies regarding infrastructure financing, long-term capital improvement, marketing of debt issues, and other financial advisory engagements. Qualified employees of member firms may become Certified Independent Public Finance Advisors (Professional Members).
Meetings/Conferences:
Semi-Annual Meetings: Spring and Fall
Publications:
Directory. a.
CIPFA Newsletter. q.

National Association of Independent Publishers *(1985)*
P.O. Box 430
Highland City, FL 33846-0430
Tel: (863)648-4420
Web Site: www.publishersreport.com
Members: 500 companies
Staff: 3
Annual Budget: $10-25,000
Executive Director: Betsy Lampe
Historical Note
Established in Florida, NAIP members are small independent publishers and self-publishers. Purpose is to provide a clearinghouse for information about publishing and support in the field of publishing. Membership: $75/year (individual).
Meetings/Conferences:
Annual Meetings: Annual meeting held in conjunction with Florida Publishers Ass'n. Usually held first weekend in April and November/100
Publications:
Publisher's Report. w.

National Association of Independent Publishers Representatives *(1989)*
111 E.14th St., PMB 157
New York, NY 10003-4103
Tel: (646)414-2993 *Fax:* (212)217-0242
Toll Free: (888)624 - 7779
E-Mail: greatblue2@rcn.com
Web Site: www.naipr.org
Members: 350 individuals
Annual Budget: $50-100,000
Executive Director: Paul C. Williams
Historical Note
Members are individuals and companies acting as sales representatives for one or more independent publishers on contractual basis. Promotes continuing education and ethical standards for members. Has no paid officers or full-time staff. Membership: $50/year.
Meetings/Conferences:
Semi-Annual Meetings: May and December/50
Publications:
On-line Newsletter. m.
Membership Directory. a.

National Association of Independent Schools *(1962)*
1620 L St. NW
Suite 1100
Washington, DC 20036-5695
Tel: (202)973-9700 *Fax:* (202)973-9790
E-Mail: info@nais.org
Web Site: www.nais.org
Members: 1200 schools, 96 associations
Staff: 40
Annual Budget: $10-25,000,000
President: Patrick F. Bassett
E-Mail: bassett@nais.org
Vice President, Government Relations Team: Jefferson Burnett
E-Mail: burnett@nais.org
Director, Membership: Vivian Dandridge-Charles
Vice President, Professional Development: Claudia Gallant
E-Mail: gallant@nais.org
Director, Conferences and Meetings: John Hawkins
Vice President, Member Relations: Heather Hoerle

Chief Financial Officer: Thoai Hovanky
E-Mail: hovanky@nais.org
Vice President, Financial Aid Services: Mark Mitchell
E-Mail: mitchell@nais.org
Vice President, Strategic Initiatives: Donna Orem
E-Mail: orem@nais.org
Vice President, Communications: Nancy Raley
Director, Information Technologies: John Rodrigues
Director, Marketing: Shannon Spaeder
E-Mail: spaeder@nais.org
Director, Publications: Kitty Thuermer
E-Mail: thuermer@nais.org

Historical Note
The result of a merger in 1962 of the National Council of Independent Schools and the Independent Schools Education Board. Members are independent elementary and secondary schools, K-12, day, boarding and a combination of both.

Meetings/Conferences:
Annual Meetings: February-March/3,000-4,500

Publications:
Independent School Magazine. q. adv.
Directory. a. adv.

National Association of Industrial and Office Properties *(1967)*

2201 Cooperative Way, Third Floor
Herndon, VA 20171-3034
Tel: (703)904-7100 *Fax:* (703)904-7942
Toll Free: (800)666 - 6780
Web Site: www.naiop.org
Members: 10900 individuals
Staff: 31
Annual Budget: $5-10,000,000
President: Thomas J. Bisacquino
Vice President, Finance: Liz Greene
Senior Vice President: Shirley Maloney
Vice President, Government Affairs: Reba Raffaelli
Vice President, Marketing and Communications: Edward M. Remington
Vice President, Education: Karen Soyster

Historical Note
Formerly National Association of Industrial Parks, (1992) National Association of Industrial and Office Parks and then (1996) NAIOP, The Association for Commerical Real Estate before assuming its current name. Members are professionals involved in development, master planning, design and construction, financing, and/or management of office and industrial properties. Sponsors and supports the American Development Political Action Committee. Membership: $645/year (principal or associate).

Meetings/Conferences:
Annual Meetings: October/1,000

Publications:
Development Magazine. q. adv.

National Association of Industrial and Technical Teacher Educators *(1937)*

Illinois State University
210E Turner Hall, Campus Box 5100
Normal, IL 61790-5100
Tel: (309)438-2695 *Fax:* (309)438-8626
Web Site: www.coe.uga.edu/naitte
Members: 300 individuals
Annual Budget: $10-25,000,000
President: Danny C. Brown
E-Mail: dcbrown@ilstu.edu

Historical Note
NAITTE represents trade and industrial teacher educators, business and industrial trainers as well as persons in college and university trade and technical teacher education. Has no paid officers or full-time staff. Membership: $50/year.

Meetings/Conferences:
Annual Meetings: December with Ass'n for Career and Technical Education
2007 – San Antonio, TX

Publications:
NAITTE Mailings. 3/year.
Directory. a.
Journal of Industrial Teacher Education. q.

National Association of Industrial Technology *(1967)*

3300 Washtenaw Ave., Suite 220
Ann Arbor, MI 48104-4200
Tel: (734)677-0720 *Fax:* (734)677-0046
E-Mail: nait@nait.org
Web Site: www.nait.org
Members: 1500 individuals
Staff: 3
Annual Budget: $250-500,000

Historical Note
Membership consists of individuals and companies active in the field of industrial technology. Major purpose is to improve degree-level curricula in industrial technology. Membership: $80/year (individual); $240/year (organization).

Meetings/Conferences:
Annual Meetings: Fall
2007 – Panama City, FL(Edgewater Resort)/Oct. 24-27

Publications:
IT Insider. 3/yr. adv.
Journal of Industrial Technology. a. adv.
Program Directory - Industrial Technology. a. adv.

National Association of Installation Developers *(1978)*

734 15th St., NW
Suite 900
Washington, DC 20005
Tel: (202)822-5256 *Fax:* (202)822-8819
Web Site: www.naid.org
Members: 320 individuals
Staff: 2
Annual Budget: $250-500,000
Executive Director: Jeffrey A. Finkle
Editor, Newsletter: Dan Cohen
E-Mail: naid@urbandevelopment.com

Historical Note
Members are individuals, organizations and communities interested in the industrial development of closed military bases. NAID is managed by the National Council for Urban Economic Development.

Meetings/Conferences:
Annual Meetings: Summer

Publications:
NAID News Newsletter. bi-m. adv.

National Association of Institutional Linen Management *(1939)*

2161 Lexington Rd.
Suite Two
Richmond, KY 40475-7952
Tel: (859)624-0177 *Fax:* (859)624-3580
Toll Free: (800)669 - 0863
Web Site: www.nlmnet.org/index.cfm
Members: 1200 individuals
Staff: 5
Annual Budget: $500-1,000,000
Executive Director: Jim Thacker
Coordinator, Member Services: Barbara Withers

Historical Note
Founded as the National Association of Institutional Laundry Managers in 1939; assumed its present name in 1985. Represents a major portion of linen service employees working in hospitals, hotel/motels, Federal and State correctional facilities, retirement/nursing homes, and university/educational institutions. Mission of Association is to promote the professional development of its members and to advance and improve institutional textile management. Membership: $120/year (individual); $290-$410/year (institution).

Meetings/Conferences:
Annual Meetings: Spring/250

Publications:
AIDS/HIV Guide: An In-Service for Laundry and Linen Personnel. m.
NAILM News Magazine. bi-m. adv.
Roster. a.

National Association of Insurance and Financial Advisors *(1890)*

2901 Telestar Ct.
Falls Church, VA 22042-1205
Tel: (703)770-8100 *Fax:* (703)770-8352
Toll Free: (877)866 - 2482
E-Mail: communications@naifa.org
Web Site: www.naifa.org
Members: 6500 individuals
Staff: 60
Annual Budget: $10-25,000,000
Chief Executive Officer: David F. Woods
Vice President, Membership and Association Services: Matthew D'Uva
Chief Operating Officer: Francesca Dea
Director, Federal Relations: Jill Edwards
Vice President, Communications: John Phillips

Historical Note
Founded as National Association of Life Underwriters; assumed its current name in 2000. A federation of 850 state and local associations of financial service professionals, NAIFA is a professional and advocacy organization supporting members who specialize in the sale of life insurance and annuities, health insurance and employee benefits, mulitline insurance and financial advising and investment life insurance agents, general agents and managers. Has an annual budget of approximately $14 million. Sponsors and supports the NAIFA Political Action Committee. Membership: $57/per capita.

Meetings/Conferences:
Annual Meetings: Fall
2007 – Washington, DC/Sept. 8-12
2008 – San Diego, CA/Sept. 6-10

Publications:
Advisor Today. m. adv.

National Association of Insurance Commissioners *(1871)*

2301 McGee St., Suite 800
Kansas City, MO 64108-2662
Tel: (816)842-3600 *Fax:* (816)783-8175
Web Site: www.naic.org
Members: 55 state officials
Staff: 360
Annual Budget: $50-100,000,000
Executive Vice President and Chief Executive Officer: Catherine J. Weatherford
E-Mail: cweather@naic.org
Communications Manager: Scott Holeman
Director, Government Affairs: Brett Palmer

Historical Note
Members are the chief insurance regulatory officials of the 50 states, the District of Columbia, Guam, Puerto Rico and the Virgin Islands. Formerly National Conference of Insurance Commissioners. Has an annual budget of approximately $51 million.

Meetings/Conferences:
Three Meetings Annually: Spring, Summer, and Fall

Publications:
Proceedings. q.
NAIC News. m.

National Association of Insurance Women *(1940)*

6528 E. 101st St., PMB 750
Tulsa, OK 74182
Toll Free: (800)766 - 6249
E-Mail: joinnaiw@naiw.org
Web Site: www.naiw.org
Members: 13500 individuals
Staff: 7
Annual Budget: $1-2,000,000
Director, Communications: Causby Briscoe

Historical Note
Promotes insurance education and supports the professional advancement of its members; offers education programs through 400 local chapters in the United States, Western Canada, and Puerto Rico. Offers the Certified Professional Insurance Woman/Man (CPIW/CPIM) designation. Membership: $60/year (individual); $85/year (at-large).

Meetings/Conferences:
Annual Meetings: June

Publications:
Today's Insurance Woman. bi-m. adv.

National Association of Intercollegiate Athletics *(1940)*

P.O. Box 1325
Olathe, KS 66051
Tel: (913)791-0044 *Fax:* (913)791-9555
E-Mail: dharmon@naia.org

Web Site: www.naia.org
Members: 283 institutions
Staff: 25
Annual Budget: $2-5,000,000
President and Chief Executive Officer: James Carr
E-Mail: jcarr@naia.org
Vice President, Marketing and Corporate Sponsorships: Mike Campbell
Vice President, Membership: John Leavens

Historical Note
Formerly (1952) National Association of Intercollegiate Basketball. NAIA members are four-year colleges and universities.

Meetings/Conferences:
Annual Meetings: March
2007 – Kansas City, MO(Marriott)/March 17-20

Publications:
NAIA Membership Directory. a.
NAIA Official Records Book. a.
NAIA Handbook. a.
Media Guides (covering all NAIA sports). 3/yr.
NAIA News. m.

National Association of Investigative Specialists *(1984)*
P.O. Box 33244
Austin, TX 78764
Tel: (512)719-3595 *Fax:* (512)719-3594
E-Mail: naisbiz@aol.com
Web Site: www.pimail.com/nais
Members: 3000 individuals
Staff: 5
Annual Budget: $100-250,000
Director: Ralph D. Thomas
E-Mail: rthomas007@aol.com

Historical Note
NAIS promotes the private investigative profession; it provides members with case assignments from other members; provides training manuals for the investigative profession; trains new private investigators. Membership: $85/bien.

Meetings/Conferences:
Annual Meetings: Fall

National Association of Investment Companies *(1971)*
1300 Pennsylvania Ave. NW
Suite 700
Washington, DC 20004
Tel: (202)204-3001 *Fax:* (202)204-3022
Web Site: www.naicvc.com
Members: 47 companies
Staff: 3
Annual Budget: $250-500,000
President: Robert Greene
Chief Administrative Officer: Angela Johnson

Historical Note
NAIC is an industry association for venture capital firms that dedicate their resources to investing in an ethnically and socially diverse marketplace. Members include privately-owned Specialized Small Business Investment Companies (SSBICs) licensed and regulated by the Small Business Administration, privately-owned venture capital firms that manage investment partnerships, and quasi-private investment companies chartered by state and local government for minority-focused investing. Affiliate membership also available for individuals and for business entities with an interest in the minority marketplace. Membership: annual dues vary, based on committed capital for private equity funds, and on private paid-in capital and SBA leverage for SSBICs.

Meetings/Conferences:
Annual Meetings: October/125-150

Publications:
NAIC Journal. q.
NAIC Membership Directory. a.

National Association of Investment Professionals *(1996)*
12664 Emmer Pl.
Suite 201
St. Paul, MN 55124
Tel: (952)322-4322
E-Mail: tokeefe@naip.com
Web Site: www.naip.com
Members: 100 individuals
Staff: 2
Annual Budget: under $10,000
President: Tom O'Keefe
E-Mail: tokeefe@naip.com

Historical Note
NAIP members are individuals (stockbrokers, registered sales assistants, traders, investment advisors) and companies who provide financial planning services to individuals. Membership: $100/year (individual); $750/year (corporate).

Publications:
NAIP Forum. m.
Securities Industry Digest. q. adv.

National Association of Jai Alai Frontons *(1977)*
301 E. Dania Beach Blvd.
Dania, FL 33004
Tel: (954)927-2841 *Fax:* (954)927-0149
Members: 11 frontons
Annual Budget: $25-50,000
Director: Stephen F. Snyder

Historical Note
Established January 1, 1977 and incorporated in Florida. NAJAF represents the interests of fronton (venue) operators. Has no paid officers or full-time staff.

Meetings/Conferences:
Annual Meetings: Not held.

Publications:
NAJF Notes. q.
Tournament Programs. bi-m. adv.

National Association of Jewelry Appraisers *(1981)*
P.O. Box 18
Rego Park, NY 11374-0018
Tel: (718)896-1536 *Fax:* (718)997-9057
E-Mail: naja.appraisers@netzero.net
Web Site: www.najappraisers.com
Members: 750 individuals
Staff: 3
Annual Budget: $100-250,000
Executive Director: Gail B. Levine

Historical Note
Purpose is to maintain professional standards and education in the field of jewelry appraisal. Members include jewelers, jewelry appraisers, importers, brokers and other professionally interested trade members. Membership: $145/year (individual American member), $185/year (individual foreign member); plus a $25 one time initial fee.

Meetings/Conferences:
Semi-Annual Meetings: Winter and Summer
2007 – Tucson, AZ(Tuscon Convention Center)/Jan. 29-30/80
2008 – Atlanta, GA(The Galleria)/Aug. 11-14/100

Publications:
The Jewelry Appraiser. q. adv.
Membership Directory. a.

National Association of Judiciary Interpreters and Translators *(1978)*
603 Stewart St.
Suite 610
Seattle, WA 98101
Tel: (206)267-2300 *Fax:* (206)626-0392
E-Mail: headquarters@najit.org
Web Site: www.najit.org
Members: 1000 individuals
Staff: 3
Annual Budget: $100-250,000
Executive Director: Ann Macfarlane

Historical Note
Formerly Court Interpreters and Translators Association. NAJIT members are interpreters and translators working in federal, state or local courts, or in other capacities within the legal profession. Membership: $105/year (individual); $40/year (student); $110/year (organization); $85/year (associate).

Meetings/Conferences:
Annual Meetings: always 3rd week in May/200

Publications:
Proteus Newsletter. 6/yr. adv.

National Association of Juvenile Correctional Agencies *(1903)*
2290 S. Theobald Ln.
Vincennes, IN 47591
Tel: (812)886-3000 *Fax:* (812)886-3010
E-Mail: NJDAEKU@aol.com
Web Site: www.najca.org/index.html
Members: 300 individuals
Staff: 1
Annual Budget: $10-25,000
Executive Director: Charlotte A. Nesbitt

Historical Note
An affiliate of the American Correctional Association. Founded as the National Association of Training Schools and Juvenile Agencies, it assumed its present name in 1981. Merged with the Association of State Juvenile Justice Administrators in 1984. Members are executives and staff members of residential centers and agencies for the care and treatment of adjudicated delinquent youth. Membership: $25/year (individual); $50/year (organization).

Meetings/Conferences:
Semi-annual Meetings: Summer/In conjunction with American Correctional Ass'n

Publications:
Proceedings. a. adv.
NAJCA News. q. adv.

National Association of Latino Elected and Appointed Officials *(1976)*
1122 W. Washington Blvd., Third Floor
Los Angeles, CA 90015
Tel: (213)747-7606 *Fax:* (213)747-7664
E-Mail: info@naleo.org
Web Site: www.naleo.org
Members: 1000 individuals
Staff: 24
Annual Budget: $2-5,000,000
Executive Director: Arturo Vargas

Historical Note
NALEO is a non-profit, non-partisan civic affairs research organization which works to initiate public policies responsive to the Hispanic community and to inform that community of issues affecting them. While membership includes state representatives, mayors, and members of Congress, it is open to all who support NALEO's objectives. Membership: $50/year (active); $25/year (associate); $150/year (affiliate).

Meetings/Conferences:
Annual Meetings: June/500

Publications:
Latino Elected Officials. bi-m.

National Association of Legal Assistants *(1975)*
1516 S. Boston Ave., Suite 200
Tulsa, OK 74119-4013
Tel: (918)587-6828 *Fax:* (918)582-6772
E-Mail: nalanet@nala.org
Web Site: www.nala.org
Members: 6000 individuals
Staff: 8
Annual Budget: $2-5,000,000
Executive Director: Marge Dover, CAE
E-Mail: mdover@nala.org

Historical Note
Members are professional legal assistants. Awards the Certified Legal Assistant (CLA) designation, Certified Paralegal (CP) designation, and CLA Specialist designation. Membership: $99/year (individual); $200/year (organization/company).

Meetings/Conferences:
Annual Meetings: July

Publications:
Facts and Findings. q.

National Association of Legal Investigators *(1967)*
802 E. 19th Ave.
Denver, CO 80218
Tel: (303)825-2373 *Fax:* (303)825-2374
Toll Free: (800)266 - 6254
Members: 700 individuals
Staff: 1
Annual Budget: $50-100,000
National Director: H. Ellis Armistead

Historical Note
Members are investigators who are employed by attorneys or who are self-employed. NALI conducts a certification program for the legal investigator profession. Membership: $150/year.

Publications:
The Legal Investigator. q. adv.

National Association of Legal Search Consultants *(1984)*
1525 North Park Dr., Suite 102
Weston, FL 33326
Tel: (954)349-8081 *Fax:* (954)349-1979
E-Mail: info@nalsc.org
Web Site: www.nalsc.org
Members: 150 firms
Staff: 3
Annual Budget: $100-250,000
Executive Director: Joseph Ankus

Historical Note
Originally organized to establish a code of ethics for the legal recruiting industry, NALSC now provides a forum for dialogue between firms in the field. Members are either consulting/search firms or law offices. Membership: $595/year.

Publications:
Directory of Legal Search Consultants. a.
NALSC Newsletter. q.

National Association of Legal Secretaries

Historical Note
Became NALS in 2003.

National Association of Letter Carriers *(1889)*
100 Indiana Ave. NW
Washington, DC 20001
Tel: (202)393-4695 *Fax:* (202)737-1540
E-Mail: nalcinf@nalc.org
Web Site: www.nalc.org
Members: 312790 individuals
Staff: 160
Annual Budget: $50-100,000,000
President: William H. Young
Secretary-Treasurer: Jane E. Brodendel

Historical Note
A union representing city letter carriers throughout the U.S. Formerly the National Association of Letter Carriers of the United States of America, NALC was organized in Milwaukee, WI, August 30, 1889, and chartered by The American Federation of Labor in 1917. Has an annual budget of approximately $82.3 million.

Meetings/Conferences:
Biennial Convention: Even years
2008 – Boston, MA

Publications:
NALC Bulletin. bi-w.
The Postal Record. m.
The Activist. q.

National Association of Limited Edition Dealers *(1976)*
332 Hurst Mill North
Bremen, GA 30110
Tel: (770)537-1970 *Fax:* (770)824-5618
Toll Free: (800)446 - 2533
E-Mail: naledoffice@aol.com
Web Site: www.naled.org
Members: 414 companies
Staff: 1
Annual Budget: $50-100,000
Executive Director: Sharon Harper

Historical Note
Members are dealers, vendors, artists, sales representatives, and publishers involved with collectibles and gifts. Membership: $150/year (full member); $225-$750/year (associate).

Meetings/Conferences:
Annual Meetings: June

Publications:
NALED Bulletin. q.
Membership Directory. a.

National Association of Litho Clubs *(1946)*
P.O. Box 6190
Ocean Isle Beach, NC 28469
Tel: (910)575-0399
Web Site: www.graphicarts.org
Members: 3500 individuals
Staff: 1
Annual Budget: $50-100,000
Executive Vice President: Ed Riggs

Historical Note
NALC is a professional organization composed of litho clubs from all over the United States. Club members are supervisory personnel in lithographic plants, company owners and suppliers. Membership: $12/year (individual).

Meetings/Conferences:
Annual Meetings: June/125-150

Publications:
Litho Tips. bi-a. adv.

National Association of Local Boards of Health *(1992)*
1840 E. Gypsy Lane Rd.
Bowling Green, OH 43402
Tel: (419)353-7714 *Fax:* (419)352-6278
E-Mail: nalboh@nalboh.org
Web Site: www.nalboh.org
Members: 22000 individuals
Staff: 7
Annual Budget: $500-1,000,000
Executive Director: Marie M. Fallon, MHSA
E-Mail: Marie@nalboh.org

Historical Note
NALBOH represents local boards of health and similar organizations that oversee local public health service programs, providing members with a means of communication with each other and with the organizations who develop public health policy at the national level. Membership: $120/year (institutional); $60/year (associate); $300/year (affiliate).

Meetings/Conferences:
Annual Meetings: Summer

Publications:
News Brief. q.

National Association of Local Government Auditors *(1989)*
449 Lewis Hargett Circle
Suite 290
Lexington, KY 40503-3669
Tel: (859)276-0686
Web Site: www.nalga.org
Members: 350 organizations
Staff: 3
Contact Person: Joanne Norris

Historical Note
Membership: $100/year.

Meetings/Conferences:
Annual Meetings: May

Publications:
Local Government Auditing. q.

National Association of Local Government Environmental Professionals *(1993)*
1333 New Hampshire Ave. NW
Washington, DC 20036
Tel: (202)638-6254 *Fax:* (202)393-2866
E-Mail: nalgep@spiegelmcd.com
Web Site: www.nalgep.org
Members: 150 local governments
Staff: 4
Executive Director: Paul Connor

Historical Note
Founded in 1993, NALGEP is a national organization representing local government professionals responsible for environmental compliance and the development of local environmental policy. NALGEP brings together local environmental officials to share information on practices, conduct policy projects, promote environmental training and education, and communicate the view of local officials on national environmental issues. Membership: $175/year.

Meetings/Conferences:
Annual Meetings: regional workshops

Publications:
News Flash. bi-w.
Reports. semi-a.

National Association of Local Housing Finance Agencies *(1982)*
2025 M St. NW
Suite 800
Washington, DC 20036-3309
Tel: (202)367-1197 *Fax:* (202)367-2197
Web Site: www.nalhfa.org
Members: 275 organizations
Staff: 4
Annual Budget: $500-1,000,000
Executive Director: John C. Murphy
Deputy Director: Scott Lynch
Coordinator, Membership: Anna Watsey

Historical Note
Regular members of NALHFA are primarily county and city agencies which finance, directly or indirectly, affordable housing through a variety of means: tax-exempt and taxable bonds, federal grant programs, and state and local subsidies. Affiliate members are organizations providing technical assistance to local agencies. Serves as an advocate before Congress and the Executive branch on affordable housing issues. Provides a forum for information exchange and capacity building.

Meetings/Conferences:
Semi-annual Meetings: Spring and Fall

Publications:
NALHFA Conference Program. semi-a. adv.
NALHFA Membership Directory. a.
Newsletter. bi-m.

National Association of Managed Care Physicians *(1991)*
4435 Waterfront Dr., Suite 101
Glen Allen, VA 23060
Tel: (804)527-1905 *Fax:* (804)747-5316
Web Site: www.namcp.org
Members: 15000 individuals
Staff: 16
Annual Budget: $500-1,000,000
Executive Vice President: William C. Williams, III, M.D.

Historical Note
Provides continuing education and information resources to health care regarding managed care. Membership: $195/year (physicians); $250/year (other individuals); $1,500/year minimum (corporations).

Publications:
Managed Care Medicine. 6/year. adv.
American Journal of Integrated Healthcare.
NAMCP News. q. adv.

National Association of Manufacturers *(1895)*
1331 Pennsylvania Ave. NW
Washington, DC 20004-1790
Tel: (202)637-3000 *Fax:* (202)637-3182
E-Mail: manufacturing@nam.org
Web Site: www.nam.org
Members: 14000 companies
Staff: 180
Annual Budget: $10-25,000,000
President and Chief Executive Officer: John M. Engler
Senior Vice President and General Counsel: Jan Admundson
E-Mail: jadmundson@nam.org
Executive Vice President: Michael E. Baroody
E-Mail: mbaroody@nam.org
Senior Vice President, Communications: Patrick Cleary
E-Mail: pcleary@nam.org
Senior Vice President, Corporate Affairs: Donna Lee Cole
Vice President, Tax Policy: Dorothy Coleman
E-Mail: dcoleman@nam.org
Vice President, Communications and Media Relations: Hank Cox
Vice President, Human Resources.: Bob Cunningham
E-Mail: bcunningham@nam.org
Senior Director, Political Affairs and Government Relations: Teresa Cupit
E-Mail: tcupit@nam.org
Vice President, Legal and Regulatory Reform Policy: Larry Fineran
Senior Vice President, Chief Financial Officer and Treasurer: Rick Klein
Vice President, Member Communications: Doug Kurkul
Vice President, Energy and Resources Policy: Keith McCoy
Vice President, Accounting: Tim Rogers
E-Mail: trogers@nam.org

Senior Vice President, Policy: Jay Timmons
Vice President, International Economic Affairs: Franklin Vargo
E-Mail: fvargo@nam.org
Chief Operating Officer: LeeAnne Wilson

Historical Note

Established in Cincinnati in 1895 to promote America's economic growth and productivity, particularly in the manufacturing sector. Headquartered in Washington, DC with ten field offices, NAM's member companies produce more than 80% of the nation's manufactured goods. NAM is affiliated with 130 state and local business associations through its National Industrial Council, and with 230 manufacturing trade associations through its NAM Council of Manufacturing Associations. The Manufacturing Institute is its educational affiliate. Has an annual budget of approximately $24 million.

Publications:

Tax Bulletin. m.
Clearing the Air. m.
Trade Talk. m.
Plant Site Locations. a. adv.
Workplace Watch. m.
Capitol News by Email. d.
Eye on Manufacturing. q.
Just in Time. m.
Washington Fax Line. m.
Employer Association Group Network Notes. bi-m.
Briefing. w.
Congressional Directory. a.
Associations Council Connections. m.

National Association of Margarine Manufacturers *(1936)*

1101 15th St. NW
Suite 202
Washington, DC 20005
Tel: (202)785-3232 *Fax:* (202)223-9741
E-Mail: namm@kellencompany.com
Web Site: www.margarine.org
Members: 5 companies
Staff: 5
Annual Budget: $100-250,000
President: Richard E. Cristol

Historical Note

Members are manufacturers and distributors of margarine industry products.

Meetings/Conferences:

Annual Meetings: *Annual*

National Association of Marine Services *(1951)*

5458 Wagonmaster Dr.
Colorado Springs, CO 80917
Tel: (719)573-5946 *Fax:* (719)573-5952
E-Mail: nams@namsshipchandler.com
Web Site: www.namsshipchandler.com
Members: 60 firms
Staff: 2
Annual Budget: $100-250,000
Executive Director: William L. Robinson

Historical Note

Established as Associated Ship Chandlers, it became the National Associated Marine Suppliers in 1951 and assumed its present name in 1969. Members are purveyors of supplies and equipment to ocean-going commercial vessels.

Meetings/Conferences:

Annual Meetings: *May*

Publications:

Directory (online). a. adv.
NAMS Newsletter (online). q.

National Association of Marine Surveyors *(1962)*

P.O. Box 9306
Chesapeake, VA 23321-9306
Tel: (757)638-9638 *Fax:* (757)638-9639
Toll Free: (800)822 - 6267
E-Mail: nationaloffice@nams-cms.org
Web Site: www.nams-cms.org
Members: 400 individuals
Staff: 2
Annual Budget: $50-100,000
National Secretary: Chris LaBure

Historical Note

Incorporated in the State of New York, in September, 1962. Originally Corresponding Surveyors to the Yacht Safety Bureau. Founded to create an organization that would establish professional qualifications and generate an exchange of current information on approved and recommended practices relating to marine surveying. Offers Certified Marine Surveyor (CMS) distinction. Membership: $300/year.

Publications:

Conference Proceedings. semi-a.
Membership List. a.
NAMS News. semi-a.

National Association of Master Appraisers

(1982)
303 W. Cypress St.
San Antonio, TX 78212
Toll Free: (800)229 - 6262
Web Site: www.masterappraisers.org
Members: 3000 individuals
Staff: 20
Annual Budget: $500-1,000,000
Chief Executive Officer: Deborah J. Deane

Historical Note

NAMA members are professional real estate appraisers. Awards the designations Master Senior Appraiser (MSA), Master Farm & Land Appraiser (MFLA) and Master Residential Appraiser (MRA). Membership: $150/year (individual).

Publications:

Master Appraiser. m.
Membership Directory. a.
NAMA Alert. q.

National Association of Media and Technology Centers *(1979)*

P.O. Box 9844
Cedar Rapids, IA 52409-9844
Tel: (319)654-0608 *Fax:* (319)654-0609
Web Site: www.namtc.org
Members: 260 individuals
Annual Budget: $25-50,000
Executive Director: Betty Gorsegner Ehlinger

Historical Note

NAMTC members are regional, K-12 and higher education media centers which serve K-12, as well as commercial media and technology vendors. Has no paid officers or full-time staff. Membership: $55/year (individual); $250/year (institutional).

Meetings/Conferences:

Annual Meetings: *Fall*

Publications:

NARMC'etin. q. adv.
Directory. a.
NARMC Press. m.

National Association of Media Brokers *(1979)*

c/o Vincent Pepper, Womble, Carlyle Sandridge & Rice PLLC
1401 I St. NW, Seventh Floor
Washington, DC 20005
Tel: (202)467-6900 *Fax:* (202)467-6910
Web Site: www.nambonline.com
Members: 60 firms
Staff: 1
Annual Budget: $50-100,000
General Counsel: Vincent Pepper

Historical Note

Members are media brokerage firms.

Meetings/Conferences:

Semi-annual: Meetings held at NAB Convention.

Publications:

Membership Directory & Organization Brochure. a.

National Association of Medicaid Directors

810 First St. NE
Suite 500
Washington, DC 20002-4267
Tel: (202)682-0100 *Fax:* (202)289-6555
Web Site: www.nasmd.org
Members: 54 individuals
Annual Budget: $250-500,000
Director, Health Policy: Kathryn Kotula

Historical Note

Formerly (1996) State Medicaid Directors Association. Members are directors of state and territorial medical assistance programs. An affiliate of the American Public Welfare Association.

Meetings/Conferences:

Semi-annual Meetings: Spring and Fall

Publications:

MMI Bulletin.

National Association of Medical Examiners

(1966)
430 Pryor St. SW
Atlanta, GA 30312
Tel: (404)730-4781 *Fax:* (404)730-4420
Web Site: www.thename.org
Members: 900 individuals
Staff: 2
Annual Budget: $250-500,000
Executive Director: Denise McNally

Historical Note

NAME represents physician medical examiners, medical death investigators, and related professionals. Supports the professional development of its members in technical and administrative issues relating to the field. Membership: $300/year (physicians); $65/year (affiliates).

Meetings/Conferences:

Annual Meetings: *Fall*

Publications:

Journal of Forensic Medicine & Pathology. q. adv.

National Association of Medical Minority Educators *(1975)*

c/o Anderson Dental
P.O. Box 11277
Jackson, MS 39283
Web Site: www.namme-hpe.org
Staff: 1
Annual Budget: $50-100,000
President: Marc A. Nivet, MS

Historical Note

Membership: $125/year (individual); $1,000/year (company).

Meetings/Conferences:

Annual Meetings: *Fall*

Publications:

NAMME Edition Newsletter.

National Association of Men's Sportswear Buyers *(1953)*

Historical Note

Organization reported inactive in 2005.

National Association of Metal Finishers *(1955)*

1155 15th St. NW, Suite 500
Washington, DC 20005
Tel: (202)457-8403 *Fax:* (202)530-0659
E-Mail: info@namf.org
Web Site: www.namf.org
Members: 700 companies
Staff: 2
Annual Budget: $1-2,000,000
Executive Director: Carrie Hoffman

Historical Note

Product of a merger of the National Federation of Metal Finishers and the National Association of Plating. Members are executives of firms engaged in all methods of finishing metal, plastic and organic surfaces. Membership: $840/year (company).

Meetings/Conferences:

Annual Meetings: *Spring*

Publications:

(SFMRB)Statistics of the Metal Finishing Industry Report. y.
Directory. bien. adv.
Finishing Line. bi-m. adv.
Legislative Line. bi-m. adv.

National Association of Minorities in Communications

Historical Note

Became National Association for Multi-Ethnicity in Communications in 2003.

National Association of Minority Automobile Dealers *(1980)*
8201 Corporate Dr., Suite 190
Lanham, MD 20785
Tel: (301)306-1614 *Fax:* (301)306-1493
Web Site: www.namad.org
Members: 650 individuals
Staff: 6
Annual Budget: $1-2,000,000
President: Sheila Vaden-Williams

Historical Note
NAMAD is committed to increasing opportunities for minorities in the automobile industry. Membership: $250/year (individual).

Publications:
Commemorative Booklet. a. adv.
Resource Guide. a. adv.
Newsletter. q. adv.

National Association of Minority Contractors *(1969)*
1300 Pennsylvania Ave. NW, Suite 700
Washington, DC 20004
Tel: (202)347-8259 *Fax:* (202)789-7349
E-Mail: national@namcline.org
Web Site: www.namcline.org
Members: 5000 individuals
Staff: 3
Annual Budget: $250-500,000
Executive Director: Al Barber

Historical Note
Established in Washington, DC in 1969 and incorporated the same year. Membership consists of, but is not limited to, general contractors, subcontractors, construction managers, manufacturers, suppliers, local minority contractor associations, funded technical assistance organizations, state and local government agencies, attorneys and accountants. Regular Membership: $1,600/year (for companies with annual gross revenue over $5 million); $800/year (for companies with annual gross revenue of $1-4 million); $400/year (for companies with annual gross revenue of less than $1 million). Affiliate Membership: $15,000/year (Major Government Partner); $10,000/year (Major Corporate Sponsor); $5,000/year (Major Corporate Partner); $5,000/year (Surety Industrial Partner).

Meetings/Conferences:
Annual Meetings: Summer

Publications:
Building Concerns. q. adv.

National Association of Minority Engineering Program Administrators *(1979)*
1133 W. Morse Blvd., Suite 201
Winter Park, FL 32789
Tel: (407)647-8839 *Fax:* (407)629-2502
E-Mail: NAMEPA@nampea.org
Web Site: www.namepa.org
Members: 575 individuals
Staff: 2
Annual Budget: $250-500,000
Executive Vice President: Phil Pyster
E-Mail: phil@crowsegal.com

Historical Note
NAMEPA was established to provide a communication network among college level administrators of minority engineering programs and to provide a cohesive voice in the national minority engineering effort. Membership: $105/year (individual); $255/year (institution); $655/year (corporate).

Publications:
NAMEPA Newsletter. q. adv.
Brochure. a.
Report. semi-a.

National Association of Minority Media Executives *(1990)*
7950 Jones Branch Dr.
McLean, VA 22107
Tel: (703)854-7179 *Fax:* (703)854-7181
Toll Free: (888)968 - 7658
Web Site: www.namme.org
Members: 350 individuals
Staff: 3
Annual Budget: $100-250,000
Executive Director: Toni F. Lewis
E-Mail: tlaws@namme.org
Administrator: Nancy Osborn
Director, Programs: Carolyn Terry

Historical Note
NAMME members are minority media executives working in the mainstream media. Provides executive development opportunities for its members and works to improve minority representation among executives in print, broadcast, and emerging media. Membership: $400/year (individual); $1,750-3,750/year (corporate).

Meetings/Conferences:
2007 – Washington, DC(Ritz Carlton)/July 10-12/200

Publications:
NAMME Membership Directory. bien.

National Association of Miscellaneous, Ornamental and Architectural Products Contractors *(1969)*
10382 Main St., Box 280, Suite 200
Fairfax, VA 22038
Tel: (703)591-1870 *Fax:* (703)591-1895
Members: 950 companies
Staff: 3
Annual Budget: $100-250,000
Executive Vice President: Fred H. Codding

Historical Note
Members are companies fabricating and installing decking systems, ornamental iron, steel and aluminum sheathing and architectural motifs on building exteriors.

Publications:
Membership Roster. a.
Newsletter. m.

National Association of Mortgage Brokers *(1973)*
7900 Westpark Dr., Suite T-309
McLean, VA 22102
Tel: (703)342-5900 *Fax:* (703)342-5905
Web Site: www.namb.org
Members: 25000 individuals
Staff: 19
Annual Budget: $2-5,000,000
Vice President, Legislative and Regulatory Affairs: Roy DeLoach
Consultant: Rebecca Dopkin DeMattos

Historical Note
Formed to provide a focal point for mortgage brokers and a communications link with mortgage bankers and underwriters. Membership: $95/year, plus a $25 one-time application fee.

Publications:
National Mortgage Broker. m. adv.
Capitol Comment. m.

National Association of Mutual Insurance Companies *(1895)*
3601 Vincennes Rd.
P.O. Box 68700
Indianapolis, IN 46268
Tel: (317)875-5250 *Fax:* (317)879-8408
Web Site: www.namic.org
Members: 1400 companies
Staff: 82
Annual Budget: Over $100,000,000
President and Chief Executive Officer: Charles M. Chamness
Chief Administrative Officer: Gregg Dykstra

Historical Note
Founded in 1895, NAMIC is America's largest trade association for property and casualty insurance companies. The Association represents over 1,400 members which comprise over 40 percent of all property and casualty insurance premiums in the United States. NAMIC benefits member companies through government relations, educational services, and insurance and employee benefits programs. Membership consists of property and casualty mutual insurance companies. Sponsors and supports the NAMIC Political Action Comittee.

Meetings/Conferences:
Annual Meetings: Fall
2007 – Grapevine, TX(Gaylord Texan)/Sept. 16-19
2008 – Philadelphia, PA(Marriott)/Sept. 28-Oct. 1

Publications:
NAMIC Magazine. bi-m. adv.
NAMIC Forum. m.
NAMIC Government Affairs Insider. bi-w.

National Association of Native American Studies

Historical Note
An affiliate of National Association of African American Studies, which provides administrative support.

National Association of Negro Business and Professional Women's Clubs *(1935)*
1806 New Hampshire Ave. NW
Washington, DC 20009
Tel: (202)483-4206 *Fax:* (202)462-7253
E-Mail: nanbpwc@aol.com
Web Site: www.nanbpwc.org
Members: 10000 individuals
Staff: 4
Annual Budget: $100-250,000
Executive Director: Tylene Harrell
Director, Education: Twyla N. Whitby

Historical Note
Membership: $75/year.

Meetings/Conferences:
Annual Meetings: Summer

Publications:
Responsibility. q.

National Association of Neighborhoods *(1975)*
1300 Pennsylvania Ave. NW
Suite 700
Washington, DC 20004
Tel: (202)332-7766
E-Mail: staff@nanworld.org
Web Site: www.nanworld.org
Members: 2400 organizations
Staff: 4
Annual Budget: $250-500,000
Executive Director: Ricardo Byrd
Director, Finance Special Projects: Leon Townsend

Historical Note
Urban and rural organizations and coalitions working to strengthen neighborhood rights and responsibilities. Membership: $25/year (individual), $100/year (organization).

Meetings/Conferences:
Annual Meetings: Fall

National Association of Neonatal Nurses *(1984)*
4700 W. Lake Ave.
Glenview, IL 60025-1485
Tel: (847)375-3660 *Fax:* (888)477-6266
Toll Free: (800)451 - 3795
E-Mail: info@nann.org
Web Site: www.nann.org
Members: 5200 individuals
Staff: 12
Annual Budget: $2-5,000,000
Executive Director: Diane Simmons, MPA

Historical Note
NANN regular members are nurses specializing in neonatal care; memberships are also available to companies and individuals interested in neonatal care. Sponsors and supports a specialty interest group for advanced practice and management issues. Membership: $65/year (regular), plus $10/year specialty dues.

Meetings/Conferences:
Annual Meetings: September/1,000

Publications:
Central Lines Newsletter. 4/yr.
Advances in Neonatal Care. 6/yr. adv.

National Association of Nephrology Technologists and Technicians *(1982)*
P.O. Box 2307
Dayton, OH 45401-2307
Tel: (937)586-3705 *Fax:* (937)586-3699
Toll Free: (877)607 - 6268
E-Mail: nant@meinet.com

Web Site: www.dialysistech.org
Members: 1000 individuals
Staff: 2
Annual Budget: $250-500,000
Executive Director: Francine W. Rickenbach, C.A.E.

Historical Note
Added Technicians to their title in 1993. Membership: $50/year (individual).

Meetings/Conferences:
2007 - Atlanta, GA(Sheraton Downtown)/March 9-11/400

Publications:
Newsletter. bi-m. adv.
Annual Symposium Proceedings. a. adv.

National Association of Noise Control Officials *(1978)*

53 Cubberley Rd.
West Windsor, NJ 08550
Tel: (609)586-2684
Members: 70 individuals
Administrator: Edward J. Di Polvere

Historical Note
Incorporated in the State of New Jersey. Members are employees of the federal or state governments, consultants, scientists and students concerned with acoustical control of the environment. NANCO is an affiliate of the National Environmental Health Association.

Meetings/Conferences:
Annual Meetings: Fall, with the Nat'l Environmental Health Ass'n

Publications:
Vibrations. irreg.

National Association of Nurse Massage Therapists *(1990)*

6749 Willow Creek Dr.
P.O. Box 24004
Huber Heights, OH 45424
Tel: (937)235-0872 *Fax:* (937)235-0872
Toll Free: (800)262 - 4017
E-Mail: nanmtadmin@nanmt.org
Web Site: www.nanmt.org
Members: 1000 individuals
Annual Budget: $50-100,000
Manager: Barb Nichols
Education: Teresa Ramsey

Historical Note
NANMT members are licensed nurses who practice touch/massage therapy. Promotes the recognition of therapeutic touch within nursing practice, and acts as a source of information for members of the nursing profession. Membership: $85/year (active individual); $50/year (student/retired); $150/year (corporate); $75/year (all others).

Meetings/Conferences:
2007 - Phoenix, AZ(Hilton Garden Inn)/June 7-9/100
2008 - , VA/June 1- /100

Publications:
Membership directory. a.
NANMT News newsletter. q. adv.
Online Nurse Massage Referral Directory. a.

National Association of Nurse Practitioners in Women's Health *(1980)*

505 C St. NE
Washington, DC 20002
Tel: (202)543-9693 *Fax:* (202)543-9858
E-Mail: info@npwh.org
Web Site: www.npwh.org
Members: 3500 individuals
Staff: 5
Annual Budget: $500-1,000,000
President and Chief Executive Officer: Susan Wysocki
Vice President: Gay Johnson
E-Mail: gjohnson@npwh.org

Historical Note
Founded as the National Association of Nurse Practitioners in Reproductive Health; assumed its present name in 1999. Membership: $75/year (individual); $75-1,000/year (organization).

Publications:
Monthly Cycle. m. adv.
Women's Health Care: A Practical Journal for Nurse Practitioners. 6/year. adv.

National Association of Nurses

Historical Note
A unit of the National Association of Government Employees.

National Association of Nutrition and Aging Services Programs *(1976)*

1612 K St. NW
Suite 400
Washington, DC 20006
Tel: (202)682-6899 *Fax:* (202)223-2099
Toll Free: (800)999 - 6262
Web Site: www.nanasp.org
Members: 1000 individuals
Staff: 3
Annual Budget: $250-500,000
Executive Director: Laura Howard
Director, Conferences: Emily Ross

Historical Note
NANASP members are individuals and organizations involved with direct service provision under the Older Americans Act. Membership is open to individuals or group supportive of NANASP's work. Membership: $150/year (regular); $300/year (corporate).

Meetings/Conferences:
Annual Meetings: June

Publications:
Washington Bulletin. irreg.
NANASP Update. q. adv.

National Association of Off-Track Betting *(1973)*

700 Ellicot St.
Batavia, NY 14024
Tel: (716)343-1423
Members: 12 companies
Staff: 3
President: Donald Groth

Historical Note
Members are off-track betting companies.

Meetings/Conferences:
Semi-annual Meetings:

National Association of Oil Heating Service Managers *(1952)*

P.O. Box 67
East Petersburg, PA 17520-0067
Tel: (717)625-3076 *Fax:* (717)625-3077
Toll Free: (888)552 - 0900
E-Mail: info@naohsm.org
Web Site: www.naohsm.org
Members: 1400 individuals
Staff: 1
Annual Budget: $250-500,000
Executive Administrator: Judy Garber

Historical Note
Members are oil heat service managers and small business owners. NAOHSM provides members with technical tapes, books and speakers to train their employee technicians. Membership: $60/year.

Publications:
Newsletter. 3/year.

National Association of Older Worker Employment Services *(1980)*

Historical Note
A special interest group of the National Council on the Aging concerned with employment opportunities for older workers.

National Association of Optometrists and Opticians *(1959)*

P.O. Box 459
Marblehead, OH 43440
Tel: (419)798-2031 *Fax:* (419)798-8548
E-Mail: fdrozak@cros.net
Members: 15500 individuals
Staff: 2
Annual Budget: $100-250,000
Secretary-Treasurer: Frank Rozak

Historical Note
Formerly the National Optical Association. NAOO carries out continuing educational and public affairs programs of mutual importance to members and serves as a clearing house for retail optical information. Membership: $500/year (individual); $1,000 minimum/year (organization/company).

Meetings/Conferences:
Semi-annual Meetings: Spring and Fall

National Association of Orthopaedic Nurses *(1980)*

401 N. Michigan Ave., Suite 2200
Chicago, IL 60611
Toll Free: (800)289 - 6266
E-Mail: naon@smithbucklin.com
Web Site: www.orthonurse.org
Members: 6000 individuals
Annual Budget: $2-5,000,000
Executive Director: Kaye Englebrecht

Historical Note
Members are licensed registered nurses, LVN's or LPN's, and students associated with all facets of orthopaedic patient care. Membership: $85/year (individual).

Meetings/Conferences:
Annual Meetings: Spring/1,500
2007 - St. Louis, MO(America's Center)/May 19-23

Publications:
Orthopaedic Nursing. bi-m. adv.
NAON News. bi-m.

National Association of Orthopaedic Technologists *(1982)*

8365 Keystone Crossing, Suite 107
Indianapolis, IN 46240
Tel: (317)205-9484 *Fax:* (317)205-9481
E-Mail: naot@hp-assoc.com
Web Site: www.naot.org
Members: 1000 individuals
Staff: 2
Annual Budget: $100-250,000
Executive Director: Kent A. Lindeman, CMP

Historical Note
Membership: $75/year (individual); $1,050/year (organization).

Meetings/Conferences:
Annual Meetings: Summer
2007 - Charlotte, NC(Hilton City Center)/Aug. 1-4/300
2008 - Minneapolis, MN(Hilton Minneapolis)/June 27-30/450

Publications:
NAOT Journal. semi-a. adv.
Orthotech Professional. bi-m.

National Association of Osteopathic Foundations

P.O. Box 1245
Bettendorf, IA 52722-0021
Tel: (319)386-6030
Members: 30
Secretary-Treasurer: Eugene R. Holst, CFP

Historical Note
Members are professional staff executives at foundations who provide support and sponsor programs on behalf of osteopathic practitioners. Has no paid officers or full-time staff.

National Association of Parish Coordinators/Directors of Religious Education

Historical Note
A division of the National Catholic Educational Association.

National Association of Parliamentarians *(1930)*

213 S. Main St.
Independence, MO 64050-3850
Tel: (816)833-3892 *Fax:* (816)833-3893
Toll Free: (888)627 - 2929
E-Mail: hq@nap2.org
Web Site: www.parliamentarians.org
Members: 4000 individuals
Staff: 3
Annual Budget: $250-500,000
Executive Director: Sarah Nieft

Historical Note
Organized in 1930 for the purposes of studying, teaching and promoting the rules of deliberative assemblies.

Meetings/Conferences:
Annual Meetings: Fall

Publications:
National Parliamentarian. q.
NAP President Newsletter. q.

National Association of Pastoral Musicians
(1976)
962 Wayne Ave., Suite 210
Silver Spring, MD 20910
Tel: (240)247-3000 *Fax:* (240)247-3001
E-Mail: NPMSING@NPM.org
Web Site: www.npm.org
Members: 8900 individuals
Staff: 11
Annual Budget: $1-2,000,000
President: J. Michael McMahon
Editor: Dr. Gordon E. Truitt

Historical Note
NPM is a national Catholic membership organization for parish musicians and parish clergy. Membership: $89/year.

Meetings/Conferences:
Annual Meetings: Biennial Meetings/odd years
2007 – Indianapolis, IN(Indiana Convention Center)/July 9-13

Publications:
Liturgical Singer. 4/year. adv.
NPM Organist. 2/year.
Praxis. 3/year. adv.
Clergy Update. 4/year.
Catholic Music Educator. 5/year. adv.
Pastoral Music. 6/year. adv.
Pastoral Music Notebook. 6/year. adv.

National Association of Pediatric Nurse Practitioners *(1973)*
20 Brace Rd., Suite 200
Cherry Hill, NJ 08034-2633
Tel: (856)857-9700 *Fax:* (856)857-1600
Toll Free: (877)662 - 7627
E-Mail: info@napnap.org
Web Site: www.napnap.org
Members: 7000 individuals
Staff: 12
Annual Budget: $1-2,000,000
Executive Director: Karen Kelly Thomas
Director, Membership and Communications: Joseph G. Casey
E-Mail: jcasey@napnap.org
Director, Professional Affairs: Dolores C. Jones
E-Mail: djones@napnap.org
Director, Human Resource, Finance and Administration: Catherine Van Horn

Historical Note
The goals of NAPNAP are to provide continuing education and standards for pediatric nurse practitioners and to support certification for practice; and to support legislation designed to improve the quality of infant, child and adolescent health. Membership: $120/year.

Meetings/Conferences:
Annual Meetings: Spring

Publications:
The Journal of Pediatric Health Care. bi-m. adv.
The Pediatric Nurse Practitioner. bi-m.

National Association of Personal Financial Advisors *(1983)*
3250 N. Arlington Heights Rd.
Suite 109
Arlington Heights, IL 60004
Tel: (847)483-5400 *Fax:* (847)483-5415
Toll Free: (800)366 - 2732
E-Mail: info@napfa.org
Web Site: www.napfa.org
Members: 1400 individuals
Staff: 10
Annual Budget: $2-5,000,000
Chief Executive Officer: Ellen Turf

Historical Note
Members are financial planners who are compensated only by fees. NAPFA members are prohibited from receiving any type of product-related compensation, such as sales commissions. Members do not sell products nor do they direct sales to parties with whom they have financial interests. Membership: $425/year.

Meetings/Conferences:
Annual Meetings: Annual/700
2007 – Chicago, IL(Sheraton)/May 2-5

Publications:
NAPFA Newslink. q.
NAPFA Advisor Magazine. m. adv.
NAPFA Planning Prespectives. q.

National Association of Personnel Services
(1917)
P.O. Box 2128
Banner Elk, NC 28604
Tel: (828)898-4929 *Fax:* (828)898-8098
E-Mail: conrad.taylor@mindspring.com
Web Site: www.recruitinglife.com
Members: 1100 companies
Staff: 3
Annual Budget: $1-2,000,000
President: Conrad Taylor, CPC, CTS
Director, Member Services: John Sacerdote

Historical Note
Formerly (1992) the National Association of Personnel Consultants. Founded as the National Employment Board. Merged (1960) with Employment Agencies Association (1923) and National Association of Employment Agencies (1956), to become the National Employment Association, then the National Association of Personnel Consultants (1978). Membership: $400/year minimum. Awards the Certified Personnel Consultant (CPC) designation, the Certified Temporary Specialist (CTS) designation, and the Physician Recruiter Consultant (PRC) designation.

Meetings/Conferences:
Annual Meetings: Fall/1,100 companies

Publications:
National Directory of Personnel Consultants. a. adv.
Inside NAPS. 10/year.

National Association of Photo Equipment Technicians *(1973)*
3000 Picture Pl.
Jackson, MI 49201
Tel: (517)788-8100 *Fax:* (517)788-8371
Web Site: www.pmai.org
Members: 250 individuals
Staff: 1
Annual Budget: $10-25,000
Executive Director: Ted Fox

Historical Note
A division (1976) of the Photo Marketing Association International. Provides information on the photographic industry to those engaged in photographic repair. Membership $25/year (individual), $95/year (company).

Meetings/Conferences:
Annual Meetings: February

Publications:
Photo Marketing.
Digital Imager.
Editorial Bank.
NAPET News. q.
Who's Who in Photographic Management. semi-a.

National Association of Physician Nurses *(1973)*
900 S. Washington St., Suite G13
Falls Church, VA 22046-4020
Tel: (703)237-8616
Members: 2000 individuals
Staff: 3
Annual Budget: $100-250,000
Director, Membership: S. Young

Historical Note
Membership: $31/year.

Meetings/Conferences:
Annual Meetings: Spring/Summer

Publications:
The Nightingale. 11/year. adv.

National Association of Physician Recruiters
(1984)
P.O. Box 150127
Altamonte Springs, FL 32715-0127
Tel: (407)774-7880 *Fax:* (407)774-6440
Toll Free: (800)726 - 5613
E-Mail: napr@napr.org
Web Site: www.napr.org
Members: 300 companies
Staff: 14
Annual Budget: $250-500,000
Executive Vice President: Willard S. Kautter, CAE

Historical Note
Membership: $300-975/year.

Publications:
NAPR Business Report. q.
Newsletter. bi-m. adv.

National Association of Pipe Coating Applicators
(1965)
8570 Business Park Dr.
Shreveport, LA 71105
Tel: (318)227-2769 *Fax:* (318)222-0482
Web Site: www.napca.com
Members: 145 companies
Staff: 2
Annual Budget: $250-500,000
Managing Director: Merritt B. Chastain, Jr.

Historical Note
Members apply exterior and interior protective pipe coatings to steel pipe in permanently established facilities. NAPCA is the trade association for the plant pipe coating industry throughout the world. Membership: $1,500/year (full member); $500/year (associate); $750/year (foreign); $500/year (foreign associate).

Meetings/Conferences:
2007 – Indian Wells, CA(Renaissance)/Apr. 11-15/240
2008 – Orlando, FL(Hyatt)/Apr. 2-6/240

Publications:
Newsletter. q.

National Association of Pipe Fabricators *(1977)*
1901 N.W. 161st St.
Edmond, OK 73013
Toll Free: (888)798 - 1924
E-Mail: info@napf.com
Web Site: www.napf.com
Members: 40 individuals
Staff: 2
Annual Budget: $100-250,000
Executive Director/President: Ted Wright

Historical Note
NAPF members are fabricators of ductile iron pipe used in water and waste water treatment plants. Members must be in compliance with all phases of the the NAPF Quality Certification Program. Membership: $2,500/year (company).

Publications:
NAPF Pipeline. q. adv.

National Association of Pizza Operators *(1982)*
908 S. Eighth St.
Suite 200
Louisville, KY 40203
Tel: (502)736-9500 *Fax:* (502)736-9531
Toll Free: (800)489 - 8324
Web Site: www.napo.com
Members: 1600 companies
Staff: 3
Annual Budget: $500-1,000,000
Executive Program Manager: Angela Hoskins
Manager, Shows: Bill Oakley

Historical Note
Formerly (2003) National Association of Pizza Operators. Pizza equipment manufacturers, industry suppliers, franchise and independent pizza operators and frozen pizza producers. Provides liaison between pizza industry and governmental agencies. Researches industry data and statistics. Membership: $99/year.

Meetings/Conferences:
Two Meetings Annually: Spring and Fall
2007 – Las Vegas, NV/March 20-22/5000
2007 – Atlantic City, NJ/Sept. 12-13/850

Publications:
Pizza Today. m. adv.

National Association of Plant Patent Owners *(1939)*
1000 Vermont Ave. NW
Suite 300
Washington, DC 20005-4914
Tel: (202)789-2900 *Fax:* (202)789-1893
Web Site: www.anla.org
Members: 70 individuals
Staff: 1
Annual Budget: $10-25,000
Senior Director, Government Relations: Craig J. Regelbrugge

Historical Note
Members are owners of patents on newly propagated flowers, trees and plants. Affiliated with American Nursery and Landscape Association.

Meetings/Conferences:
Annual Meetings: July, with American Ass'n of Nurserymen

National Association of Police Organizations *(1979)*
750 First St. NE
Suite 920
Washington, DC 20002-4241
Tel: (202)842-4420 *Fax:* (202)842-4396
Toll Free: (800)322 - 6276
E-Mail: info@napo.org
Web Site: www.napo.org
Members: 236000 individuals
Staff: 7
Executive Director: William Johnson
Director, Events: Jill Cameron

Historical Note
Members are law enforcement officers.

Meetings/Conferences:
Annual Meetings: August

Publications:
Newsletter. q.

National Association of Postal Supervisors *(1908)*
1727 King St., Suite 400
Alexandria, VA 22314-2753
Tel: (703)836-9660 *Fax:* (703)836-9665
E-Mail: napshq@naps.org
Web Site: www.naps.org
Members: 34000 individuals
Staff: 7
Annual Budget: $2-5,000,000
President: Ted Keating
National Secretary/Treasurer: John B. Aceves
Executive Vice President: Louis M. Atkins

Historical Note
An independent professional association founded in Louisville, KY. Sponsors the Supervisors Political Action Committee. Membership: $91/year (individual).

Meetings/Conferences:
Biennial Meetings: even years in August/September
2008 – Louisville, KY/Sept. 7-11

Publications:
The Postal Supervisor Magazine. m.

National Association of Postmasters of the United States *(1898)*
Eight Herbert St.
Alexandria, VA 22305-2600
Tel: (703)683-9027 *Fax:* (703)683-6820
E-Mail: napusinfo@napus.org
Web Site: www.napus.org/index4.htm
Members: 43000 individuals
Staff: 9
Annual Budget: $2-5,000,000
Executive Director: Charlie Moser
Director, Government Relations: Bob Levi

Historical Note
NAPUS members are active and retired postmasters. Sponsors and supports the Political Education for Postmasters Political Action Committee. Membership: $36-$293/year (active individual).

Meetings/Conferences:
Annual Meetings: Summer/5,000
2007 – Albuquerque, NM/Sept. 8-13
2008 – St. Louis, MO/Aug. 23-28

Publications:
Postmaster's Gazette. 11/year. adv.
Update Newsletter. m.

National Association of Power Engineers *(1879)*
One Springfield St.
Chicopee, MA 01013-2624
Tel: (413)592-6273 *Fax:* (413)592-1998
E-Mail: napenatl@verizon.net
Web Site: www.powerengineers.com
Members: 3000 individuals
Staff: 3
Annual Budget: $250-500,000
Office Manager: William Judd

Historical Note
Members include those in power plant operation and maintenance responsible for supplying industry and service establishments with process power, heat, air conditioning, lighting, ventilation and related building and plant services. Membership: $80/year (individual); $500/year (corporation).

Meetings/Conferences:
Annual Meetings: Summer

Publications:
National Engineer. bi-m. adv.

National Association of Principals of Schools for Girls *(1921)*
23490 Caraway Lakes Dr.
Bonita Springs, FL 34135
Tel: (239)947-6196 *Fax:* (239)390-3245
E-Mail: naspg@mac.com
Web Site: www.napsq.org
Members: 600 individuals
Staff: 1
Annual Budget: $100-250,000
Executive Director: Bruce W. Galbraith
E-Mail: naspg@mac.com

Historical Note
NASPG addresses common concerns of administrators of American and Canadian independent schools and colleges which enroll women. Membership: $50/year (college); $250/year (school below college level).

Meetings/Conferences:
Annual Meetings: Winter
2007 – Tucson, AZ(Ventana Canyon)/Feb. 25-28/200

National Association of Printing Ink Manufacturers *(1917)*
581 Main St.
Woodbridge, NJ 07095
Tel: (732)855-1525 *Fax:* (732)855-1838
E-Mail: napim@napim.org
Web Site: www.ippic.org/napim.htm
Members: 51 ink companies, 78 suppliers
Staff: 5
Annual Budget: $1-2,000,000
Executive Director: James E. Coleman

Historical Note
Established as the National Association of Printing Ink Makers; assumed its present name in 1967. Sponsors the National Printing Ink Research Institute.

Meetings/Conferences:
Annual Meetings: Spring/350
2007 – Bermuda(Fairmont Hotel Southampton)March 24-28
2007 – Chicago, IL(Eaglewood)/Sept. 5-8/200

National Association of Private Special Education Centers *(1971)*
1522 K St. NW
Suite 1032
Washington, DC 20005
Tel: (202)408-3338 *Fax:* (202)408-3340
E-Mail: napsec@aol.com
Web Site: www.napsec.org
Members: 300 schools
Staff: 4
Annual Budget: $500-1,000,000
Executive Director and Chief Executive Officer: Sherry L. Kolbe
Communications Coordinator: Jonathan Cartagena

Historical Note
Formerly (2001) National Association of Private Schools for Exceptional Children. Founded to improve educational opportunities for children with disabilities, promote private special education as a vital component of the nation's educational system, and educate the public about the services provided and needed for these students. Member organizations are early intervention services, schools, residential treatment centers and adult living assistance programs serving children and adults with disabilities in an educational and/or therapeutic setting, as well as organizations and individuals supporting such institutions. Membership: $250/year (affiliate); $775-$1,675/year (private school); $750-$2,750/year (Council of State Affiliated Associations).

Meetings/Conferences:
Annual Meetings: Winter

Publications:
The NAPSEC News. q. adv.
Directory. bi-a. adv.
National Issues Service. m. adv.

National Association of Private, Nontraditional Schools and Colleges with Accrediting Commission for Higher Education *(1974)*
182 Thompson Rd.
Grand Junction, CO 81503
Tel: (970)243-5441 *Fax:* (970)242-4392
E-Mail: director@napnsc.org
Web Site: www.napnsc.org
Members: 4 institutions
Staff: 2
Annual Budget: $100-250,000
Executive Director: H. Earl Heusser, Ed.D.
Office Manager: Irene Dolly Heusser, Psy.D.

Historical Note
Formerly (1977) National Association of Schools and Colleges. Later (1998) National Association of Private, Nontraditional Schools and Colleges. Its Accrediting Commission for Higher Education is the only national institutional accrediting body which has developed criteria, standards and guidelines expressly for private, nontraditional or alternative education at all postsecondary levels.

Meetings/Conferences:
Annual Meetings: Winter or Spring

Publications:
Accreditation Fact Sheet. q.
General Information Brochure. a.
Accreditation Brochure. a.
Comparisons of Traditional & Nontraditional Education. a.
Founding History of the NAPNSC Accrediting Commission. a.
A Summary of NAPNSC Accrediting History. a.

National Association of Produce Market Managers *(1946)*
Eight Whithorn Way
Blythewood, SC 29016
Tel: (585)428-6770 *Fax:* (585)428-6021
Web Site: www.napmm.com
Members: 110 individuals
President: James Farr
E-Mail: farrj@cityofrochester.gov

Historical Note
Members are produce market managers and industrial produce dealers. Has no paid officers or full-time staff.

Publications:
Green Sheet. q.
Convention Proceedings. a.

National Association of Professional Background Screeners
P.O. Box 3159
Durham, NC 27715-3159
Tel: (919)433-0123 *Fax:* (919)383-0035
E-Mail: info@napbs.com
Web Site: www.nabps.com

National Association of Professional Band Instrument Repair Technicians *(1976)*
P.O. Box 51
Normal, IL 61761-0051
Tel: (309)452-4257 *Fax:* (309)452-4825
E-Mail: napbirt@napbirt.org
Web Site: www.napbirt.org
Members: 1300 individuals
Staff: 1

Executive Director: Bill Mathews

Historical Note

Dedicated to integrity and professionalism in the craft of repair, restoration, and maintenance of band instruments. Membership: $85/year.

Meetings/Conferences:

Annual Meetings: Spring

Publications:

Techni-Com. bi-m. adv.
Newsletter. m.
Directory. a.

National Association of Professional Baseball Leagues *(1901)*

201 Bayshore Dr. SE
P.O. Box A
St. Petersburg, FL 33731
Tel: (727)822-6937 *Fax:* (727)821-5819
E-Mail: media@minorleaguebaseball.com
Web Site: www.minorleaguebaseball.com
Members: 20 minor leagues
Staff: 30
President and Chief Executive Officer: Mike Moore
Manager, Exhibition Services and Alumni Association: Noreen Branter
Vice President, Administration and Chief Operating Officer: Pat O'Conner

Historical Note

NAPBL, d/b/d as Minor League Baseball, oversees the activity of minor league baseball, representing some 250 teams in the U.S. and abroad.

Meetings/Conferences:

Annual Meetings: Winter

Publications:

2006 Minor League Baseball Information Guide.
Baseball News.

National Association of Professional Employer Organizations *(1984)*

901 N. Pitt St., Suite 150
Alexandria, VA 22314
Tel: (703)836-0466 *Fax:* (703)836-0976
E-Mail: info@napeo.org
Web Site: www.napeo.org
Members: 600 companies
Staff: 15
Annual Budget: $2-5,000,000
Executive Vice President: Milan P. Yager

Historical Note

Formerly (1993) National Staff Leasing Association. Established in California and incorporated in Virginia. NAPEO members are firms providing professional employer services. Membership: $750-30,000/year (based on volume).

Publications:

NAPEO Directory. a. adv.
NAPEO PEO Insider Magazine. m. adv.
NAPEO Convention Program. a. adv.

National Association of Professional Geriatric Care Managers *(1987)*

1604 N. Country Club Rd.
Tucson, AZ 85716
Tel: (520)881-8008 *Fax:* (520)325-7925
Web Site: www.caremanager.org
Members: 1600 individuals
Staff: 16
Annual Budget: $250-500,000
Executive Director: Victoria Tobin
Publications Coordinator: Jonathan Boyle

Historical Note

Formerly (1994) the National Association of Private Geriatric Care Managers. GCM is an organization of practitioners whose goal is the advancement of dignified care for the elderly and their families. Emphasizes the autonomy of the elderly patient along with principles of appropriate and effective care. Membership: $195/year.

Publications:

GCM Journal. q.
Inside GCM. q. adv.

National Association of Professional Insurance Agents *(1931)*

400 N. Washington St.
Alexandria, VA 22314-2312
Tel: (703)836-9340 *Fax:* (703)836-1279
E-Mail: piainfo@pianet.org
Web Site: www.pianet.com
Members: 160000 individuals
Staff: 45
Annual Budget: $2-5,000,000
Executive Vice President: Leonard C. Brevik
Vice President, Communications and Public Relations: Ted Besesparis, Jr.
Senior Vice President, Government and Regulatory Affairs: Patricia A. Borowski, CAE

Historical Note

Formerly (1976) the National Association of Mutual Insurance Agents. Members are independent insurance agents/brokers and their employees representing over 160,000 individuals. Supports the Professional Insurance Agents Political Action Committee.

Meetings/Conferences:

Annual Meetings: Fall/2,000

Publications:

PIA Connection. m. adv.

National Association of Professional Mortgage Women *(1964)*

P.O. Box 2016
Edmonds, WA 98020-9516
Tel: (425)775-6589 *Fax:* (425)771-9588
Toll Free: (800)827 - 3034
E-Mail: info@napmw.org
Web Site: www.napmw.org
Members: 3400 individuals
Staff: 3
Annual Budget: $250-500,000
Executive Director: Patricia Hull

Historical Note

NAPMW is a network of more than 55 local associations in 25states. Members are individuals employed in mortgage banking and related fields. National Membership: varies from as low as $86 to $319 annually (individual).

Meetings/Conferences:

Annual Meetings: May

Publications:

National Mortgage Professional. m. adv.

National Association of Professional Organizers *(1985)*

35 Technology Pkwy. South, Suite 150
Norcross, GA 30092
Tel: (847)375-4746
E-Mail: hq@napo.net
Web Site: www.napo.net
Members: 1500 individuals
Staff: 2
Annual Budget: $500-1,000,000
Executive Director: Ed Jarboe

Historical Note

Members are time, productivity, and organization management consultants. Membership: $200/year (individual); $550/year (organization).

Meetings/Conferences:

Annual Meetings: Spring

Publications:

NAPO News Newsletter. bi-m. adv.
NAPO Membership Directory. a. adv.

National Association of Professional Pet Sitters *(1989)*

15000 Commerce Pkwy., Suite C
Mt. Laurel, NJ 08054
Tel: (856)439-0324 *Fax:* (856)439-0525
Toll Free: (800)296 - 7387
E-Mail: napps@ahint.com
Web Site: www.petsitters.org
Members: 1800 companies
Staff: 5
Annual Budget: $250-500,000
Executive Director: Felicia Lembesis
E-Mail: flembesis@ahint.com

Historical Note

Formerly (1994) National Association of Pet Sitters. Members are owners of pet-care services offering in-home pet care. Membership: $140/year.

Meetings/Conferences:

2007 - Houston, TX(Hyatt Regency)/Jan. 26-28/200

Publications:

The NAPPS Network. q. adv.

National Association of Professional Process Servers *(1982)*

P.O. Box 4547
Portland, OR 97208
Tel: (503)222-4180 *Fax:* (503)222-3950
Toll Free: (800)477 - 8211
E-Mail: administrator@napps.org
Web Site: www.napps.org
Members: 1600 individuals
Staff: 3
Annual Budget: $250-500,000
Administrator: Alan H. Crowe

Historical Note

Members are individuals and companies serving summonses, complaints, subpoenas, and other documents of the courts. Provides services to members including E&O and professional liability insurance. Membership: $150/year.

Meetings/Conferences:

Annual Meetings: Spring
2007 - Washington, DC(Capitol Marriott)/May 17-21/215

Publications:

Docket Sheet Newsletter. bi-m. adv.
Membership Directory. semi-a.

National Association of Professional Surplus Lines Offices *(1975)*

6405 N. Cosby Ave., Suite 201
Kansas City, MO 64151
Tel: (816)741-3910 *Fax:* (816)741-5409
E-Mail: info@napslo.org
Web Site: www.napslo.org
Members: 800 firms
Staff: 6
Annual Budget: $2-5,000,000
Executive Director: Richard M. Bouhan
Director, Communications and Technology: Mike Ardis
Director, Meetings and Conventions: Debbie Hill

Historical Note

Members are brokerage firms and companies writing excess and surplus insurance lines. Founded and incorporated in the State of New York. Membership: $2,750-5,500/year (company); $770/year (broker).

Meetings/Conferences:

Annual Meetings: Fall/2,000

Publications:

NAPSLO News. bi-m.

National Association of Professionals in Women's Health

Historical Note

Became Nat'l Ass'n for Women's Health in 2000.

National Association of Professors of Hebrew in American Institutions of Higher Learning *(1950)*

1342 Van Hise Hall, Univ. of Wisconsin
Madison, WI 53706-1558
Tel: (608)262-2968
Web Site: www.polyglot.lss.wisc.edu/naph/ebr.html
Members: 400 individuals
Annual Budget: under $10,000
Executive Vice President: Gilead Morahg

Historical Note

A service and information organization composed of professors in colleges, universities and seminaries who specialize in the area of Hebrew Language (from Biblical to Modern) and related subjects and non-academic associate members whose occupations or interests are related to Hebrew studies. Membership: $50/year.

Meetings/Conferences:

Annual Meetings: With the Soc. for Biblical Literature

Publications:

Iggeret. semi-a.
Hebrew Studies. a.
Bulletin of Higher Hebrew Education. a.

National Association of Program Information and Performance Measurement

Historical Note
An affiliate of the American Public Welfare Association, which provides administrative support.

National Association of Property Inspectors *(1993)*

Historical Note
An affiliate of National Association of Master Appraisers, which provides administrative support.

National Association of Property Tax Representatives - Transportation, Energy, Communications *(1963)*
175 E. Houston, Room 8-H-40
San Antonio, TX 78205
Tel: (210)351-2425 *Fax:* (210)351-3960
Members: 200 individuals
Staff: 7
Annual Budget: under $10,000
President: Bill Ware

Historical Note
Formerly National Association of Railroad and Public Utilities Tax Representatives; assumed its present name in 1999. Has no paid staff or permanent address; officers change annually. Membership: $25/year.

Meetings/Conferences:
Annual Meetings: Fall

Publications:
None.

National Association of Protection and Advocacy Systems

Historical Note
Became National Disability Rights Network in 2005.

National Association of Psychiatric Health Systems *(1933)*
701 13th St. NW
Suite 950
Washington, DC 20005
Tel: (202)393-6700 *Fax:* (202)783-6041
E-Mail: naphs@naphs.org
Web Site: www.naphs.org
Members: 400 behavioral systems of care
Staff: 7
Annual Budget: $1-2,000,000
Executive Director: Mark J. Covall
Director, Clinical Services and Regulatory Affairs: Kathleen McCann, RN, DNS.c
Director, Operations and Communications: Carole Szpak
E-Mail: comm@naphs.org
Director, Congressional Affairs: Nancy Trenti

Historical Note
Formerly (1993) National Association of Private Psychiatric Hospitals. An association of specialty psychiatric healthcare organizations for the treatment of mental illness, alcohol, and drug dependencies. Sponsors the National Association of Psychiatric Health Systems Political Action Committee. Membership: $1,000/year (individual); organization dues are based on net revenues.

Meetings/Conferences:
Annual Meetings: January/850
2007 - Washington, DC/May 5-9

Publications:
Membership Directory. a. adv.

National Association of Public Child Welfare Administrators *(1983)*
810 First St. NE
Suite 500
Washington, DC 20002-4267
Tel: (202)682-0100 *Fax:* (202)289-6555
E-Mail: jfriedman@aphsa.org
Members: 700 individuals
Staff: 5
Annual Budget: $250-500,000
Executive Director: Jerry W. Friedman

Historical Note
A constituent unit of the American Public Human Services Association. Members are primarily state or local administrators responsible for public child welfare agencies that provide child protective services, foster care, adoption, and family preservation services. Membership: $90/year (individual); $6,000-$11,000/year (organization).

Meetings/Conferences:
Annual Meetings: Held twice a year, usually in Washington, DC

National Association of Public Hospitals and Health Systems *(1980)*
1301 Pennsylvania Ave. NW
Suite 950
Washington, DC 20004
Tel: (202)585-0100 *Fax:* (202)585-0101
E-Mail: naph@naph.org
Web Site: www.naph.org
Members: 110 hospitals and hospital systems
Staff: 22
Annual Budget: $1-2,000,000
Executive Director: Christine Burch
E-Mail: cburch@naph.org
Conference Administrator: Pam Bradley
E-Mail: pbradley@naph.org
President: Larry S. Gage
Assistant Vice President, Communications: Brigette Settles Scott

Historical Note
Formerly (1996) National Association of Public Hospitals. Members provide primary care and public health services. Membership: $41,000/year (institution).

Meetings/Conferences:
Annual Meetings: Summer
2007 - Boston, MA(Westin Hotel)/June/225

Publications:
Newsline. m.
Safety Net. q.

National Association of Public Insurance Adjusters *(1951)*
21165 Whitfield Pl.
Suite 105
Potomac Falls, VA 20165
Tel: (703)433-9217 *Fax:* (703)433-0369
E-Mail: info@napia.com
Web Site: www.napia.com
Members: 120 companies
Staff: 4
Annual Budget: $100-250,000
Deputy Director: Marjorie Musick

Historical Note
NAPIA is dedicated to improving and maintaining the professional standards of the public insurance adjuster through a rigid code of professional conduct and ethics.

Meetings/Conferences:
Semi-Annual Meetings: June and December
2007 - San Diego, CA(Hotel del Coronado)/June 20-24

Publications:
NAPIA Bulletin. q. adv.
Membership Directory. a. adv.

National Association of Public Sector Equal Opportunity Officers
c/o Tallahassee Equal Opportunity Dept.
300 S. Adams St.
Tallahassee, FL 32301
Tel: (850)891-8290 *Fax:* (850)891-8733
Contact: Sharon Ofuani

Historical Note
NAPSEO members are equal opportunity professionals and other public sector professional with an interest in the field. Has no paid officers or full-time staff. Membership: $75/year (active/associate); $100/year (affiliate).

Meetings/Conferences:
Annual Meetings: August-September

National Association of Publishers' Representatives *(1952)*
54 Cove Rd.
Huntington, NY 11743
Tel: (631)223-2200 *Fax:* (631)351-0526
Toll Free: (866)288 - 0354
E-Mail: napr@naprassoc.com
Web Site: www.naprassoc.com
Members: 360 individuals
Staff: 2
Annual Budget: $50-100,000
Executive Director: Myron Charness

Historical Note
Members are independent magazine advertising salespeople who have their own firms. Formerly (1982) the Association of Publishers' Representatives. Membership: $185/year.

Meetings/Conferences:
Monthly Meetings: Chicago and New York City in various locations

Publications:
Newsletter. bi-m.
E-Zine.

National Association of Puerto Rican/Hispanic Social Workers *(1983)*
P.O. Box 651
Brentwood, NY 11717
Tel: (631)864-1536
Web Site: www.naprhsw.com
Members: 350 individuals
Annual Budget: $10-25,000
Newsletter Editor: Sonia Palacio-Grottola
E-Mail: sonia@naprhsw.com

Historical Note
Has no paid officers or full-time staff. Individual members are professionals. Membership: $50/year.

Meetings/Conferences:
Annual Meetings: Summer
2007 - Bront Brook, NY(SUNY- Stony Brook)/June 9- /400

Publications:
NAPRHSW Newsletter. tri-a. adv.

National Association of Pupil Services Administrators *(1966)*
P.O. Box 783
Pittsford, NY 14534-0783
Tel: (585)223-2018 *Fax:* (585)223-1497
E-Mail: napsa@rochester.rr.com
Web Site: www.napsa.com
Members: 800 individuals
Staff: 1
Annual Budget: $100-250,000
Executive Director: Lee Johnson

Historical Note
Members are public and private school administrative personnel with district or statewide responsibility for the development and supervision of student support programs and personnel including attendance and student accounting, guidance, nursing, school psychology, school social work, exceptional or special education, pupil appraisal, at-risk programs, discipline, gifted programs, and federal or state grants. Associate members are other professional administrators whose interests are compatible with the purposes of NAPSA. Formerly the National Association of Pupil Personnel Administrators, the group assumed its present name in 1989. Membership: $75/year; $55/year (associate); $37/year (student).

Meetings/Conferences:
Annual Meetings: October

Publications:
NAPSA Notes. 2/year.
NAPSA News. q.

National Association of Rail Shippers

Historical Note
Became North American Rail Shippers Association in 2003.

National Association of Railroad Trial Counsel *(1954)*
1430 E. Missouri
Suite B200
Phoenix, AZ 85014
Tel: (602)265-2700 *Fax:* (602)265-2705
E-Mail: info@nartc.org
Web Site: www.usnartc.org
Members: 1100 individuals
Staff: 4
Annual Budget: $250-500,000
Executive Director: Michelle Miller Thorpe

Historical Note
Membership: $285/year.
Meetings/Conferences:
Meetings: Winter/200, Fall/150, Summer/350
Publications:
NARTC Newsletter. irreg.

National Association of Real Estate Appraisers *(1966)*
1224 N. Nokomis Ave. NE
Alexandria, MN 56308
Tel: (320)763-7626 *Fax:* (320)763-9290
E-Mail: narea@iami.org
Web Site: www.iami.org/narea.cfm
Members: 23500 individuals
Staff: 23
Annual Budget: $2-5,000,000
Executive Director: Robert G. Johnson
Managing Director: Joe Alexander
Associate Director: Mike Andreas
Historical Note
Established in New York, members primarily specialize in residential appraisals. New members must have two years of experience in the field, submit two appraisal reports and pass an appraisal certification examination. Awards the Certified Real Estate Appraiser (CREA) and Certified Commercial Real Estate Appraiser (CCRA) designations. Mandatory continuing education/recertification of 60 hours every 5 years required. Membership: $195/year.
Meetings/Conferences:
Semi-annual Meetings: March-April in Atlantic City, NJ and Sept.-Oct. in Las Vegas, NV
Publications:
Real Estate Appraisal Newsletter. bi-m. adv.
Appraisal Guidelines. m.
Appraisal Report. 3/year. adv.
Annual Membership Directory. a.

National Association of Real Estate Brokers *(1947)*
9301 Greenbelt Rd.
Suite 309
Lanham, MD 20706
Tel: (301)552-9340 *Fax:* (301)552-9216
Web Site: www.nareb.com
Members: 13000 individuals
Staff: 5
Annual Budget: $250-500,000
Office Manager: Antonio Brown
Historical Note
Membership consists principally of minority real estate brokers. Certifies qualified members to use the title, "Realtists." The National Society of Real Estate Appraisers, Real Estate Management Brokers Institute and United Developers Council are affiliates of NAREB. Membership: $349/year (member-broker).
Meetings/Conferences:
Annual Meetings: August/800-900
Publications:
Communicator. q. adv.
The Realtist Today Newsletter. q.

National Association of Real Estate Companies *(1977)*
216 W. Jackson Blvd.
Chicago, IL 60606
Tel: (312)263-1755 *Fax:* (312)750-1203
Web Site: www.narec.org
Members: 205 individuals
Staff: 1
Administrator: Kim Klein
Historical Note
NAREC members are individuals concerned with the financial management and accounting practices of real estate companies. Membership: $295/year (individual); $725/year (company).
Meetings/Conferences:
Annual Meetings: Summer
2007 – Monterey, CA/
2008 – Williamsburg, VA/
Publications:
NAREC Newsletter. q.

National Association of Real Estate Editors *(1929)*
1003 N.W. Sixth Terrace
Boca Raton, FL 33486-3455
Tel: (561)391-3599 *Fax:* (561)391-0099
Web Site: www.naree.org
Members: 650 individuals
Staff: 1
Annual Budget: $100-250,000
Executive Director: Mary Doyle-Kimball
Historical Note
Founded as National Conference of Real Estate Editors; assumed its current name in 1936. Serves the interest of real estate journalist, including writers and editors, from all forms of media. Membership: $75/year (active); $150/year (associate).
Publications:
NAREE News. q. adv.
Directory. a. adv.
NAREE Sourcebook for Real Estate and Housing Journalists (online). adv.

National Association of Real Estate Investment Managers *(1990)*
11755 Wilshire Blvd., Suite 1380
Los Angeles, CA 90025-1506
Tel: (310)479-2219 Ext: 10 *Fax:* (310)445-2565
Web Site: www.nareim.org
Members: 79 corporate members
Staff: 2
Annual Budget: $500-1,000,000
President: Fredric Halperin
E-Mail: fredhalperin@nareim.org
Vice President: Penny Powell
E-Mail: pennypowell@nareim.org
Historical Note
Membership: $7,000/year (organization/company).

National Association of Real Estate Investment Trusts *(1960)*
1875 I St. NW
Suite 600
Washington, DC 20006
Tel: (202)739-9400 *Fax:* (202)739-9401
Toll Free: (800)362 - 7348
Web Site: www.nareit.com
Members: 200 REITS/2,000 affiliated organizations
Staff: 35
Annual Budget: $5-10,000,000
President and Chief Executive Officer: Steven A. Wechsler
Vice President, Meetings: Pamela Coleman
Vice President, Government Relations: Robert Dibblee
Vice President, Operations: Victor Dristas
Senior Vice President/General Counsel: Tony M. Edwards
Senior Vice President, Finance and Operations: Sheldon M. Groner
Senior Vice President, Research and Investment Affairs: Michael Grupe
Vice President, Investor Relations: Rob Valero
Vice President, Financial Standards: George Yungmann
Historical Note
Formerly National Association of Real Estate Investment Funds, it assumed its present name in 1972. Membership is open to qualified REITs and publicly traded real estate companies and other organizations and individuals in related fields such as law, accounting, financial advising, mortgage and investment banking, teaching and real estate services. NAREIT's primary purpose is to represent the REIT and publicly owned real estate industry before Congress and the Executive branch; it also provides education and information about the industry to the investment community and the financial media and holds three major conferences each year. Membership: $550-950/year (associate); REIT fee determined by assets; $200/year (academic and other institutions).
Publications:
Real Estate Portfolio. bi-m.
REIT Watch. m.
The REIT Report. q.
REIT Handbook Directory. a.
Executive Compensation Survey. a.
Insurance Issues. q.
Federal Tax REIT Compendium. bien.

National Association of REALTORS *(1908)*
430 N. Michigan Ave.
Chicago, IL 60611-4087
Toll Free: (800)874 - 6500
E-Mail: infocentral@realtors.org
Web Site: www.realtor.org
Members: 750000 individuals
Staff: 300
Annual Budget: $50-100,000,000
Executive Vice President and Chief Executive Officer: Dale A. Stinton, CAE
General Counsel: Laurene K. Janik
Senior Vice President and Chief Economist: David Lereah
Historical Note
Founded in Chicago as the National Association of Real Estate Exchanges by 120 representatives from 19 local boards and one state association. Became the National Association of Real Estate Boards in 1916 and assumed its present name in 1974. Today it is a federation of about 1,800 local boards and 50 state associations. Supports the National Realtors Political Action Committee and a number of state political action groups. Has a budget of approximately $54.1 million.
Meetings/Conferences:
Annual Meetings: Mid-November
Publications:
Today's Realtor. m.

National Association of Recording Merchandisers *(1958)*
Nine Eves Dr., Suite 120
Marlton, NJ 08053-3138
Tel: (856)596-2221 *Fax:* (856)596-3268
Web Site: www.narm.com
Members: 500 companies
Staff: 10
Annual Budget: $1-2,000,000
President: Jim Donio
E-Mail: donio@narm.com
Vice President, Communications and Marketing: Susan L'Ecuyer
E-Mail: lecuyer@narm.com
Historical Note
Established in 1958, the National Association of Recording Merchandisers (NARM) is a not-for-profit trade association that serves the music retailing community in the areas of networking, advocacy, information, education, and promotion. The Association's membership includes music and other entertainment retailers, wholesalers, distributors, record labels, multimedia suppliers, and suppliers of related products and services, as well as individual professionals and educators in the music business field. Our retail members operate 7,000 storefronts that account for almost 85 percent of the music sold in the $12 billion U.S. music market.
Meetings/Conferences:
Annual Meetings: Late Winter
2007 – Chicago, IL(Chicago Hilton)/Apr. 29-May 1
2008 – San Francisco, CA(San Francisco Marriott)/May 4-7
Publications:
Research Briefs. m.
Membership Directory and Buyers Guide. a. adv.
NewsBits Newsletter. q.
Convention Guide. a. adv.

National Association of Recreation Resource Planners *(1981)*
MSC-1777
P.O. Box 2430
Pensacola, FL 32513
Tel: (850)587-5916
E-Mail: info@narrp.org
Web Site: www.narrp.org
Members: 170 individuals
Annual Budget: $50-100,000
President: Jim DeLoney
Historical Note
Formerly known as the National Association of State Recreation Planners (1994). Established to promote the professionalization of outdoor recreation resource planning at the state and regional level. Has no permanent staff or address; officers change annually in the spring. Membership: $50/year (individual);

$145/year (institutional/affiliate); $25/year (student).

Meetings/Conferences:
Annual Meetings: *Spring/100-125*

Publications:
Membership Directory. a.
NARRP Newsletter. q. adv.

National Association of Regional Councils *(1967)*
1666 Connecticut Ave. NW
Suite 300
Washington, DC 20009
Tel: (202)986-1032 Ext: 213 *Fax:* (202)986-1038
Web Site: www.narc.org
Members: 250 councils
Staff: 12
Annual Budget: $1-2,000,000
Executive Director: Cameron Moore
Director, Policy: Fred Abousleman
Manager, Communications: Miko Neri

Historical Note
Established in 1967 by the National League of Cities and the National Association of Counties. Incorporated as a membership organization in 1968. Members are regional councils of local governments and governmental agencies. Annual regional council dues vary, based on budget and/or population. Corporate associate membership is $1,000/year.

Meetings/Conferences:
Annual Meetings: *Every 4 months*

Publications:
Regions Newsletter. bi-m. adv.
Directory of Regional Councils. a. adv.

National Association of Regulatory Utility Commissioners *(1889)*
1101 Vermont Ave. NW
Suite 200
Washington, DC 20005
Tel: (202)898-2200 *Fax:* (202)898-2213
E-Mail: admin@naruc.org
Web Site: www.naruc.org
Members: 360 individuals
Staff: 24
Annual Budget: $5-10,000,000
Executive Director: Charles D. Gray
E-Mail: cgray@naruc.org
Director, Meetings: Michelle Malloy
E-Mail: mmalloy@naruc.org
General Counsel: James Bradford Ramsay

Historical Note
State and Federal regulatory commissioners. Formerly (1918) National Association of Railway Commissioners; (1923) National Association of Railroad and Utilities Commissioners and (1967) National Association of Regulatory Utility Commissioners.

Meetings/Conferences:
Annual Meetings: *Fall/2,000*

Publications:
Blue Bulletin. bi-w.

National Association of Rehabilitation Instructors

Historical Note
A professional division of the National Rehabilitation Association, which provides administrative support.

National Association of Rehabilitation Providers and Agencies *(1978)*
12100 Sunset Hills Rd.
Suite 130
Reston, VA 20190
Tel: (703)437-4377 *Fax:* (703)435-4390
E-Mail: nara@naranet.org
Web Site: www.naranet.org
Members: 100 organizations
Staff: 2
Annual Budget: $100-250,000
Executive Director: Robin M. Turner

Historical Note
Formerly (2001) National Association of Rehabilitation Agencies. Members are government-certified rehabilitation agencies, non-certified rehabilitation agencies, multidisciplinary rehabilitation companies, and rehabilitation vendors. Membership: $750-1,250/year (varies according to number of people in member organization).

Meetings/Conferences:
Semi-annual Meetings: *Spring and Fall*

Publications:
NARA News. q. adv.

National Association of Rehabilitation Secretaries *(1971)*

Historical Note
An affiliate of National Rehabilitation Association, which provides administrative support.

National Association of Reinforcing Steel Contractors *(1969)*
10382 Main St., Box 280, Suite 200
Fairfax, VA 22038
Tel: (703)591-1870 *Fax:* (703)591-1895
Web Site: www.narsc.com
Members: 425 companies
Staff: 3
Annual Budget: $100-250,000
Executive Director: Fred H. Codding

Historical Note
NARSC members are involved with the placing and installation of reinforcing steel end post-tensioning in commercial, bridge, highway, industrial and public projects.

Meetings/Conferences:
Annual Meetings: *Winter*

Publications:
Membership Roster. a.
Newsletter. m.

National Association of Relay Manufacturers

National Association of Resale & Thrift Shops *(1984)*
P.O. Box 80707
St. Clair Shores, MI 48080-5707
Tel: (586)294-6700 *Fax:* (586)294-6776
Toll Free: (800)544 - 0751
E-Mail: info@narts.org
Web Site: www.narts.org
Members: 1100 individuals
Staff: 3
Annual Budget: $250-500,000
Executive Director: Adele R. Meyer
Director, Membership Services: Gail A. Siegel

Historical Note
Members are owners, managers, professionals and other individuals who represent both profit and non-profit resale and thrift shops. Membership: $120/year.

Meetings/Conferences:
Annual Meetings: *June/250-300*
2007 - San Antonio, TX(Sheraton Gunter Hotel)/June 22-25/300

Publications:
Membership Directory. a.
Your NARTS Network. m. adv.

National Association of Residential Property Managers *(1988)*

Historical Note
Founded to promote professionalism through education and publications for the single-family residential property manager. NARPM awards three professional designations to licensed real estate professionals. Membership $195/year.

Meetings/Conferences:
Annual Meetings: *Fall*

Publications:
Residential Resource. m. adv.

National Association of Retail Collection Attorneys *(1993)*
1620 I St. NW
Suite 615
Washington, DC 20006
Tel: (202)861-0706 *Fax:* (202)463-8498
Toll Free: (800)633 - 6069
E-Mail: narca@narca.org
Web Site: www.narca.org
Members: 600 law firms
Staff: 7
Annual Budget: $1-2,000,000
Executive Director: Cynthia White, JD, CAE

Historical Note
NARCA members are firms and attorneys engaged in the collection of consumer accounts. Membership: $500/year (law firms); $275/year (retail in-house counsel).

Meetings/Conferences:
Semi-Annual Meetings: *Spring and Fall*

Publications:
NARCA Newsletter. q. adv.
Membership Directory. a. adv.

National Association of Retired Senior Volunteer Program Directors *(1976)*
1527 4th St., Suite 250
Santa Monica, CA 90401
Tel: (310)394-9871 *Fax:* (310)260-1131
Web Site: http://narsvpd.com
Members: 800 individuals
Annual Budget: $100-250,000
President: Melodye Kleinman

Historical Note
NARSVPD members are directors of programs sponsored by the Retired Senior Volunteer Program. Has no paid officers or full-time staff. Membership: $75/year (professional).

Meetings/Conferences:
Semi-annual Meetings: *Spring and Fall*

Publications:
Newsletter. semi-a. adv.

National Association of Reunion Managers *(1986)*
P.O. Box 59713
Renton, WA 98058-5713
Toll Free: (800)654 - 2776
E-Mail: narm@reunions.com
Web Site: www.reunions.com
Members: 60 companies
Staff: 1
Annual Budget: $25-50,000
Administrative Assistant: Renee Mead

Historical Note
Formerly (1994) National Association of Reunion Planners. NARM members are individually owned, locally operated companies providing comprehensive reunion planning services for high schools, sororities, fraternities, military units and families. Membership: $395/year (corporate member).

Meetings/Conferences:
Annual Meetings: *Winter/60*
2007 - Cozumel, Mexico(Splendor of the Seas)/Jan. 10-15

Publications:
Reunion Reporter. q. adv.

National Association of Review Appraisers and Mortgage Underwriters *(1975)*
1224 N. Nokomis Ave. NE
Alexandria, MN 56308
Tel: (320)763-6870 *Fax:* (320)763-9290
E-Mail: nara@iami.org
Web Site: www.iami.org/nara
Members: 8000 individuals
Staff: 12
Annual Budget: $1-2,000,000
Executive Director: Robert G. Johnson

Historical Note
Members, mainly from financial institutions, are responsible for overseeing, reviewing or supervising the work of appraisers. Awards the CRA (Certified Review Appraisal) designation. Membership: $195/year.

Meetings/Conferences:
Annual Meetings: *Fall/350*

Publications:
NARA Newsletter. 6/year. adv.
Membership Directory. a.
Appraisal Review and Mortgage Underwriting Journal. q. adv.

National Association of Royalty Owners *(1980)*
P.O. Box 21888
Oklahoma City, OK 73156
Tel: (405)286-9400 *Fax:* (405)286-9402

Web Site: www.naro-us.org
Members: 5000 individuals
Staff: 3
Annual Budget: $100-250,000
President: Wana Dee Box
E-Mail: president@naro-us.org

Historical Note
Organized in Oklahoma City in June 1980 after the passage of the Windfall Profits Tax, members are mineral, surface and royalty (producing sub-surface interests) owners concerned with the tax aspects of federal and state legislation, and with the effective management of their mineral properties. Incorporated in the State of Oklahoma. Membership: $105/year (individual); $300/year (corporate).

Publications:
Royalty Owners Action Report (ROAR). m. adv.

National Association of RV Parks and Campgrounds *(1966)*
113 Park Ave.
Falls Church, VA 22046
Tel: (703)241-8801 *Fax:* (703)241-1004
E-Mail: info@arvc.org
Web Site: www.arvc.org
Members: 3800 businesses
Staff: 7
Annual Budget: $1-2,000,000
President and Chief Executive Officer: Linda Profaizer
E-Mail: lprofaizer@arvc.org
Director, Marketing and Communications: Traci Pasqualone
E-Mail: tpasqualone@arvc.org

Historical Note
Formerly (1992) the National Campground Owners Association, ARVC is only trade association exclusively representing the U.S. commercial RV park and campground industry. Members are campground owners and operators, manufacturers and suppliers of campground products and services. National Foundation for RVing and Camping is the non-profit educational arm of ARVC. The National Campground Institute is the promotional arm of the association.

Meetings/Conferences:
Annual Meetings: late Fall

Publications:
RV Park & Campground Report. m. adv.
ARVC Direct Line. m. adv.

National Association of Sales Professionals *(1992)*
11000 N. 130th Pl.
Scottsdale, AZ 85259
Tel: (480)951-4311
E-Mail: info@nasp.com
Web Site: www.nasp.com
Members: 3000 companies
Staff: 2
Annual Budget: $100-250,000
President: Donna Reagan

Historical Note
Association administers a sales certification program directed to career-oriented sales professionals.

National Association of School Music Dealers *(1962)*
13140 Coit Rd.
Suite 320/LB-120
Dallas, TX 75240-5737
Tel: (972)233-9107 Ext: 204 *Fax:* (972)490-4219
E-Mail: office@nasmd.com
Web Site: www.nasmd.com
Members: 300 dealers & manufacturers
Staff: 1
Annual Budget: $25-50,000
Executive Secretary: Madeleine Crouch

Historical Note
Formed by a charter group of music dealers during the 1962 Trade Show in Chicago. Has no paid staff. Membership: $225/year.

Meetings/Conferences:
Annual Meetings: Spring

Publications:
NASMD Newsletter. q.

National Association of School Nurses *(1968)*
P.O. Box 1300
Scarborough, ME 04070-1300
Tel: (207)883-2117 *Fax:* (207)883-2683
Toll Free: (866)627 - 6767
E-Mail: NASN@nasn.org
Web Site: www.nasn.org
Members: 12000 individuals
Staff: 20
Annual Budget: $2-5,000,000
Executive Director: Amy Garcia
Administrator: Gloria Durgin

Historical Note
Originally established as a department of the National Education Association, NASN set up its own office in 1978.

Meetings/Conferences:
Annual Meetings: Summer
2007 – Nashville, TN(Gaylord's Opryland Hotel)/June 28-July 1/1400

Publications:
Journal of School Nursing. 6/year. adv.
NASN Newsletter. 6/year. adv.

National Association of School Psychologists *(1969)*
4340 East West Hwy., Suite 402
Bethesda, MD 20814
Tel: (301)657-0270 *Fax:* (301)657-0275
Web Site: www.nasponline.org
Members: 25000 individuals
Staff: 27
Annual Budget: $2-5,000,000
Executive Director: Susan Gorin, CAE
Assistant Executive Director: Ted Feinberg
Chief Financial Officer: James N. May

Historical Note
Promotes educationally and psychologically healthy environments for all children and youth by implementing research-based, effective programs that prevent problems, enhance independence, and promote optimal learning. Membership: $37-$130/year.

Meetings/Conferences:
2007 – New York, NY(Hilton New York)/March 27-31
2008 – New Orleans, LA(Sheraton)/Feb. 5-9/4000
2009 – Boston, MA(Boston Marriott Copley Hotel)/Feb. 24-28

Publications:
SPAN Update. 3/year.
Communique. 8/year. adv.
School Psychology Review. q. adv.
Convention Program and Abstracts. a. adv.

National Association of School Resource Officers *(1989)*
1951 Woodlane Dr.
St. Paul, MN 55125
Tel: (651)769-8150 *Fax:* (651)457-5665
Toll Free: (888)316 - 2776
E-Mail: resourcer@aol.com
Web Site: www.nasro.org
Members: 13000 individuals
Staff: 4
Annual Budget: $500-1,000,000
Executive Director: Kevin Campana

Historical Note
NASRO members are school police, security officers, administrators and others law enforcement professionals with an interest in police-student relations. Membership fee: $30/year.

Meetings/Conferences:
Annual Meetings: July or August

Publications:
Resourcer. q. adv.

National Association of School Safety and Law Enforcement Officers *(1970)*
P.O. Box 3147
Sowego, NY 13126
Tel: (315)529-4858 *Fax:* (315)343-2935
E-Mail: nassleo@gmail.com
Web Site: www.nassleo.org
Members: 350 individuals
Annual Budget: $25-50,000
Executive Director: Rick Harvell

Historical Note
Founded (1970) as the National Association of School Security Directors. Members are persons engaged in school security and school policy operations. NASSLEO is committed to reduce personal risk and tax dollar losses from vandalism, burglary, theft, assault, and other disturbances. Has no paid officers or full-time staff. Membership: $50/year (individual); $50/year (organization).

Meetings/Conferences:
Annual Meetings: July

Publications:
Quarterly. 3-4/year. adv.
Membership Directory. a.

National Association of Schools of Art and Design *(1944)*
11250 Roger Bacon Dr., Suite 21
Reston, VA 20190-5248
Tel: (703)437-0700 *Fax:* (703)437-6312
E-Mail: info@arts-accredit.org
Web Site: http://nasad.arts-accredit.org
Members: 269 schools
Staff: 12
Executive Director: Samuel Hope

Historical Note
Established as the National Conference of Schools of Design; became (1948) National Association of Schools of Design and then (1961) National Association of Schools of Art before assuming its present name in 1981.

Meetings/Conferences:
Annual Meetings: October

Publications:
Directory. a.
Handbook. bien.

National Association of Schools of Dance *(1980)*
11250 Roger Bacon Dr., Suite 21
Reston, VA 20190-5248
Tel: (703)437-0700 *Fax:* (703)437-6312
E-Mail: info@arts-accredit.org
Web Site: http://nasd.arts-accredit.org
Members: 62 schools
Staff: 12
Executive Director: Samuel Hope
E-Mail: info@arts-accredit.org

Historical Note
An outgrowth of the Joint Commission on Dance and Theatre Accreditation. NASD is the recognized accrediting agency for education programs in dance.

Meetings/Conferences:
Annual Meetings: September

Publications:
Directory. a.
Handbook. bien.

National Association of Schools of Music *(1924)*
11250 Roger Bacon Dr., Suite 21
Reston, VA 20190-5248
Tel: (703)437-0700 *Fax:* (703)437-6312
E-Mail: info@arts-accredit.org
Web Site: www.nasm.arts-accredit.org
Members: 609 schools
Staff: 12
Executive Director: Samuel Hope

Historical Note
The accrediting agency for educational programs in music in the U.S. Membership: $65/year (individual).

Publications:
Directory. a.
Handbook. bien.
Proceedings of the Annual Meeting. a.

National Association of Schools of Public Affairs and Administration *(1970)*
1120 G St. NW
Suite 730
Washington, DC 20005
Tel: (202)628-8965 *Fax:* (202)626-4978
Web Site: www.naspaa.org
Members: 250 institutions
Staff: 8
Annual Budget: $500-1,000,000
Executive Director: Laurel McFarland
Conference Coordinator: Jacqueline Lewis
E-Mail: jlewis@naspaa.org

Historical Note
Concerned with public service education and research in public policy and administration Membership: $693-2,793/year (institution, based on total enrollment).
Meetings/Conferences:
Annual Meetings: *Fall*
2007 - Seattle, WA(The Westin)
Publications:
Journal of Public Affairs Education. q. adv.

National Association of Schools of Theatre
(1969)
11250 Roger Bacon Dr., Suite 21
Reston, VA 20190-5248
Tel: (703)437-0700 *Fax:* (703)437-6312
E-Mail: info@arts-accredit.org
Web Site: http://nast.arts.accredit.org
Members: 150 schools
Staff: 12
Executive Director: Samuel Hope
Historical Note
The outgrowth of a study committee set up by the American Theatre Association, NAST was established as a division of ATA but is now autonomous. Its primary purpose is accreditation. NAST is the recognized accrediting agency for educational programs in theatre.
Meetings/Conferences:
Annual Meetings: *Spring*
Publications:
Directory of Member Institutions. a.
Handbook of Accreditation Standards. bi-e.

National Association of Science Writers *(1934)*
P.O. Box 890
Hedgesville, WV 25427
Tel: (304)754-5077 *Fax:* (304)754-5076
Web Site: www.NASW.ORG
Members: 2400 individuals
Staff: 1
Annual Budget: $100-250,000
Executive Director: Diane McGurgan
E-Mail: diane@nasw.org
Historical Note
Journalists and others who convey information about scientific developments to the public. Organized September 14, 1934, by twelve science reporters. Incorporated in the State of New York in 1955. Membership: $60/year.
Meetings/Conferences:
Annual Meetings: *With the American Ass'n for the Advancement of Science*
Publications:
NASW Newsletter. q.

National Association of Scientific Materials Managers *(1974)*
Univ. of Houston/ Biology Dept.
4800 Calhoun
Houston, TX 77004
Tel: (713)743-2639 *Fax:* (713)743-3928
Web Site: www.naosmm.org
Members: 500 individuals
Staff: 1
Annual Budget: $100-250,000
President: Ed Glumac
Historical Note
Members are laboratory and stockroom managers, supervisors and other support personnel, mainly in university, industry, and commercial research laboratories, who purchase scientific equipment. Membership: $50/year (individual); $150/year (organization/company).
Meetings/Conferences:
Annual Meetings: *End of July-first of August.*
Publications:
Newsline. q. adv.
Directory. a.

National Association of Secondary School Principals *(1916)*
1904 Association Dr.
Reston, VA 20191-1537
Tel: (703)860-0200 *Fax:* (703)476-5432
E-Mail: principals@principals.org
Web Site: www.principals.org
Members: 41000 individuals
Staff: 110
Annual Budget: $10-25,000,000
Executive Director: Gerald N. Tirozzi
Historical Note
Administers 4 non-profit organizations: National Association of Student Councils, National Association of Student Activity Advisers, National Honor Society, and National Junior Honor Society Membership: $210/year (individual); $210/year (institution); $70/year (associate); $95/year (international); $40/year (retired).
Meetings/Conferences:
Annual Meetings: *Winter*
2007 - Las Vegas, NV/Feb. 23-25
Publications:
Principal Leadership. 9/year.
Bulletin. 9/year.
Legal Memorandum. 5/year.
NewsLeader. m.
Principals Research Review. 6/year.
Leadership for Student Activities. 9/year.

National Association of Secretaries of State
(1904)
444 North Capitol St. NW
Suite 401
Washington, DC 20001
Tel: (202)624-3525 *Fax:* (202)624-3527
Web Site: www.nass.org
Members: 54 individuals
Staff: 3
Annual Budget: $250-500,000
Executive Director: Leslie Reynolds
Executive Assistant: Rachel Baker
E-Mail: rbecker@sso.org
Director, Communications: Kay Stimson
E-Mail: nass@sso.org
Historical Note
Established at the St. Louis World's Fair in 1904 as the Association of American Secretaries of State, it is the oldest organization of major public officials in the U.S.; assumed its present name in 1921. Membership: assessed by state population and tied to the CPI.
Meetings/Conferences:
Annual Meetings: *Winter*
2007 - Washington, DC/Feb. 9-12
Publications:
NASS News. m.

National Association of Securities and Commerical Law Attorneys
Historical Note
Became Nat'l Ass'n of Shareholder and Consumer Attorneys in 2003.

National Association of Securities Dealers *(1938)*
1735 K St. NW
Washington, DC 20006-1506
Tel: (202)728-8000 *Fax:* (202)728-8075
Web Site: www.nasd.com
Members: 668000 individuals
Staff: 2600
Annual Budget: Over $100,000,000
Chairman and Chief Executive Officer: Mary L. Schapiro
Executive Vice President and General Counsel: T. Grant Callery
Senior Vice President and Corporate Secretary: Barbara J. Sweeney
Historical Note
Established as the Investment Bankers Conference, it assumed its present name in 1939. NASD is the self-regulatory organization of the securities industry responsible for the regulation of the NASDAQ securities exchange and other over-the counter securities market and related financial products. In 1998, NASD merged with the American Stock Exchange to form the NASDAQ-AmEx Market Group, under which the two stock exchanges operate. Has an annual budget of approximately $500 million.
Publications:
NASD Manual.
NASD Mediation.
NASD Sanction Guidelines.

National Association of Securities Professionals
(1985)
1212 New York Ave. NW
Suite 950
Washington, DC 20005-3987
Tel: (202)371-5535 *Fax:* (202)371-5536
E-Mail: info@nasphq.org
Web Site: www.nasphq.org
Members: 450 individuals
Staff: 1
Annual Budget: $500-1,000,000
Executive Director: Lucius Ashby, C.P.A.
Executive Office Manager: Michelle Chandler
Historical Note
NASP members are minority and women securities professionals. Membership: $25-325/year (individual).
Publications:
Bullseye. q. adv.

National Association of Security Companies
(1972)
1625 Prince St., Suite 225A
Alexandria, VA 22314
Tel: (703)518-1477 *Fax:* (703)706-3711
E-Mail: info@nasco.org
Web Site: www.nasco.org
Members: 17 companies
Staff: 3
Annual Budget: $100-250,000
Executive Director: Joseph Ricci
Historical Note
Formerly (1993) the Committee of National Security Companies. Incorporated in New York, NASCO members are major contract security guard firms concerned with industry standards, legislation and public education. Membership: varies, based on revenues.
Meetings/Conferences:
2007 - Washington, DC/May 15-16/100

National Association of Self-Instructional Language Programs *(1971)*
Univ. of Arizona, Critical Language Program
1717 E. Speedway, Suite 3312
Tucson, AZ 85721-0151
Tel: (520)626-5258 *Fax:* (520)626-8205
E-Mail: nasilp@u.arizona.edu
Web Site: www.nasilp.org
Members: 122 academic institutions
Staff: 3
Annual Budget: $10-25,000
Executive Director: Dr. Alexander Dunkel
E-Mail: Adunkel@u.arizona.edu
Executive Assistant: Irina Carrera
Historical Note
North America's oldest professional organization specifically devoted to the fostering of self-instructional academic programs in foreign language skills acquisition. At the secondary, college and university levels, NASILP provides ongoing assistance in materials selection and utilization, testing standardization, program design and operation, and multi-media orientation for coordinators, tutors, examiners and students. Membership: $250 first 3 years $100/year thereafter.
Meetings/Conferences:
Annual Meetings: *Fall*
Publications:
NASILP Journal. a.

National Association of Service and Conservation Corps *(1985)*
666 11th St. NW
Suite 1000
Washington, DC 20001-4542
Tel: (202)737-6272 *Fax:* (202)737-6277
Web Site: www.nascc.org
Members: 50 individuals
Staff: 8
Annual Budget: $1-2,000,000
President: Sally T. Prouty
E-Mail: sprouty@nascc.org
Vice President: Martin J. O'Brien
Director, Finance and Administration: Nancy L. Siegal

Historical Note
NASCC serves youth corps programs as a national advocate and information exchange network, and provides technical assistance and training to strengthen and expand new and existing youth corps programs. Membership: $100/year (individual); $250-$5616/year (organization).
Meetings/Conferences:
Annual Meetings: February

National Association of Service Dealers
Historical Note
A division of the North American Retail Dealers Association.

National Association of Service Managers *(1955)*
P.O. Box 250796
Milwaukee, WI 53225
Tel: (414)466-6060 *Fax:* (414)466-0840
E-Mail: kencook@kencook.com
Web Site: www.nasm.com
Members: 200 individuals
Staff: 2
Annual Budget: $25-50,000
Treasurer: Ken Cook
Historical Note
NASM is committed to the educational and professional advancement of service managers in all industries. Maintains a Product Safety and Liability Special Interest Group. Administers a certification board awarding the ASE (Associate Service Executive) and CSE (Certified Service Executive) designations. Membership: $225/year (regular); $112.50/year (chapter); $225/year (associate); corporate based on number of persons joining in group.
Publications:
Proceedings Manual. a. adv.
NASM Service Management. m. adv.
Membership Directory. a. adv.

National Association of Service Providers in Private Rehabilitation *(1989)*
Historical Note
A professional division of the National Rehabilitation Association, which provides administrative support.

National Association of Seventh-Day Adventist Dentists *(1944)*
P.O. Box 101
Loma Linda, CA 92354
Tel: (909)558-8187 *Fax:* (909)558-0209
E-Mail: nasdad@llu.edu
Web Site: www.llu.edu/llu/dentistry/nasdad/
Members: 600 individuals
Staff: 2
Annual Budget: $25-50,000
Executive Director: William Heisler
Historical Note
Affiliated with the American Dental Association. Membership: $85/year.
Meetings/Conferences:
Annual Meetings: Fall
Publications:
SDA Dentist Directory. a.

National Association of Sewer Service Companies *(1976)*
1314 Bedford Ave., Suite 201
Baltimore, MD 21208
Tel: (410)486-3500 *Fax:* (410)486-6838
E-Mail: director@nassco.org
Web Site: www.nassco.org
Members: 250 companies
Staff: 3
Annual Budget: $500-1,000,000
Executive Director: Irvin Gemora
President: Gerry Muenchmeyer
Historical Note
Members clean, inspect and rehabilitate sewer pipes and structures, and are manufacturers or dealers in products utilized or others interested in pipeline rehabilitation (e.g. municipalities, consulting engineers, etc.) NASSCO publishes guidelines and other professional resources for its members. Membership: $650/year (contractors); $300/year (dealers); $550/year (manufacturers); $200/year (municipalities & others)
Meetings/Conferences:
Annual Meetings: February-March
Publications:
NASSCO Times.

National Association of Shareholder and Consumer Attorneys *(1988)*
818 Connecticut Ave. NW, Suite 1100
Washington, DC 20006
Tel: (202)728-1010 *Fax:* (202)728-4044
E-Mail: hbiden@obblaw.com
Historical Note
Formerly (1988) National Association of Securities and Commercial Law Attorneys; assumed its current name in 2003.

National Association of Sign Supply Distributors *(1991)*
5024-R Campbell Blvd.
Baltimore, MD 21236-5974
Tel: (410)931-8100 *Fax:* (410)931-8111
E-Mail: nassd@clemonsmgmt.com
Web Site: www.nassd.org
Members: 23 distributors, 35 manufacturers
Staff: 3
Annual Budget: $100-250,000
Executive Director: Calvin K. Clemons, CAE, CMP
Historical Note
Members are full line sign supply distributors and manufacturers of commercial, neon, and electrical products.
Meetings/Conferences:
Annual Meetings: October

National Association of Small Business Investment Companies *(1958)*
666 11th St. NW
Suite 750
Washington, DC 20001
Tel: (202)628-5055 *Fax:* (202)628-5080
Web Site: www.nasbic.org
Members: 400 companies
Staff: 6
Annual Budget: $2-5,000,000
President: Lee W. Mercer
Director, Member Services: Jamie G. Blake
Director, Communications: Sam Freedenberg
Vice President: Jeanette D. Paschal
Historical Note
Members are companies licensed under the Small Business Investment Act of 1958. Sponsors the National Association of Small Business Investment Companies Political Action Committee.
Meetings/Conferences:
Annual Meetings: Fall
Publications:
NASBIC News. q.
Membership Directory. a.

National Association of Social Workers *(1955)*
750 First St. NE
Suite 700
Washington, DC 20002
Tel: (202)408-8600 *Fax:* (202)336-8331
Toll Free: (800)638 - 8799
E-Mail: membership@naswdc.org
Web Site: www.naswdc.org
Members: 155000 individuals
Staff: 120
Annual Budget: $10-25,000,000
Executive Director: Elizabeth J. Clark
Manager, Marketing and Membership: Susan Rubin
Historical Note
A professional association of social workers formed Oct. 1, 1955 through the merger of the American Association of Group Workers, the American Association of Medical Social Workers, the American Association of Psychiatric Social Workers, the American Association of Social Workers, Association for the Study of Community Organization, the National Association of School Social Workers and the Social Work Research Group. Administers the Academy of Certified Social Workers and awards the ACSW designation. 55 chapters. Supports PACE (a political action committee). Membership: $157.50/year (regular); $39.50/year (student); $47.75/year (retired/doctoral candidate); $126.00/year (associate). Has an annual budget of approximately $15.6 million.
Publications:
NASW News. m. adv.
NASW Register of Clinical Social Workers. bien.
Social Work. bi-m. adv.

National Association of Solar Contractors *(1977)*
P.O. Box 15240
Phoenix, AZ 85060-5240
Tel: (602)957-2365 *Fax:* (602)957-2365
Members: 500 individuals
Staff: 2
Annual Budget: $50-100,000
President: Edward A. Schein
Historical Note
Members are contractors, architects, engineers, manufacturers and others involved in the installation of solar equipment. Serves as a clearinghouse for technical information, and represents the industry before Congress and the Department of Energy. Absorbed the American Solar Energy Association in 1978.
Meetings/Conferences:
Annual Meetings: 50-150
Publications:
NASC News. q.
Tech Bulletin. irreg.

National Association of Special Needs State Administrators *(1983)*
c/o Illinois State Board of Education
100 N. First St., Suite C-421
Springfield, IL 62777
Tel: (217)782-3370 *Fax:* (217)782-9224
Members: 30 individuals
Annual Budget: under $10,000
Historical Note
NASNSA members are state administrators of programs for special populations and vocational education. Officers and address change annually. Membership: $15/year.
Meetings/Conferences:
Annual Meetings: September
Publications:
Newsletter. 3/year.

National Association of Sporting Goods Wholesalers *(1953)*
P.O. Box 881525
Port St. Lucie, FL 34988-1525
Tel: (772)621-7162 *Fax:* (772)264-3233
E-Mail: nasgw@nasgw.org
Web Site: www.nasgw.org
Members: 50 wholesalers, 200 manufacturers, 60 representative groups
Staff: 2
Annual Budget: $250-500,000
President: Wayne Smith
Operations and Administration: Tracy Kolojeski
Historical Note
Formerly the Sporting Goods Jobbers Association. Membership includes 50 wholesalers of primarily fishing and shooting sports equipment, and roughly 200 manufacturers and 60 representative groups of this equipment. Membership: $500/year (wholesalers); $300/year (manufacturers); $200/year (representative group).
Meetings/Conferences:
Annual Meetings: November
Publications:
Membership Directory. a.

National Association of Sports Officials *(1980)*
2017 Lathrop Ave.
Racine, WI 53405
Tel: (262)632-5448 *Fax:* (262)632-5460
Web Site: www.naso.org
Members: 19000 individuals
Staff: 21
Annual Budget: $1-2,000,000
President: Barry Mano
Vice President, Marketing and Business Development: Patrick Sharpe

Vice President, Publishing and Management Services: William Topp

Historical Note

A non-profit organization providing services and benefits to amateur sports officials and umpires. Membership: $94/year.

Meetings/Conferences:

Annual Meetings: Summer
2007 – Denver, CO/July 29-31

Publications:

Referee Magazine. m. adv.
NASO-ON Newsletter ONBOARD. m.

National Association of State Administrators and Supervisors of Private Schools *(1971)*
c/o Arizona State Board for Private Postsecondary Education
1400 W. Washington, Room 260
Phoenix, AZ 85007
Tel: (602)542-5709 Ext: 6 *Fax:* (602)542-1253
Web Site: www.nasasps.com
Members: 50 individuals
Annual Budget: under $10,000
President: Teri Candelaria

Historical Note

Members are state licensure staff for private, post-secondary vocational schools. Has no paid officers or full-time staff.

Meetings/Conferences:

Annual Meetings: April
2007 – Boston, MA(Hyatt Harborside)/Apr. 22-25

National Association of State Agencies for Surplus Property *(1947)*
601 W. McCarty St.
Indianapolis, IN 46225
Tel: (317)234-3688 *Fax:* (317)234-3699
E-Mail: dgraves@idoa.in.gov
Web Site: www.nasasp.org
Members: 56 state agencies
Annual Budget: $50-100,000
President: Dick Graves

Historical Note

Members are surplus property agencies in the states and territories. Has no paid officers or full-time staff.

Publications:

Surplus Makes Sense Newsletter. q.

National Association of State Alcohol and Drug Abuse Directors *(1972)*
808 17th St. NW
Suite 410
Washington, DC 20006
Tel: (202)293-0090 *Fax:* (202)293-1250
E-Mail: dcoffice@nasadad.org
Web Site: www.nasadad.org
Members: 57 state & territorial agencies
Staff: 14
Annual Budget: $1-2,000,000
Executive Director: Lewis E. Gallant, Ph.D.
E-Mail: lgallant@nasadad.org
Director, Prevention Services: Alan Moghul
E-Mail: amoghul@nasadad.org
Director, Public Policy: Robert Morrison
E-Mail: rmorrison@nasadad.org

Historical Note

Formerly (until 1978) known as the National Association of State Drug Abuse Program Coordinators. Composed of directors of State and Territorial Alcoholism and Drug Abuse Agencies. Basic purpose is to foster, support and share information on the development of effective alcohol and drug abuse prevention and treatment services; serves as a focal point for public and private agency contacts. Membership: dues based on size of state.

Publications:

NASADAD Alcohol and Drug Abuse Special Report. bi-m.
State Alcohol and Drug Abuse Profile (SADAP). a.

National Association of State Archaeologists *(1978)*
c/o Division of Archaeology, P.O. Box 44247
Baton Rouge, LA 70804-4247
Tel: (225)342-8170 *Fax:* (225)342-4480
E-Mail: teubanks@crt.state.la.us
Web Site: www.uiowa.edu/~osa/nasa/
Members: 58 individuals
Annual Budget: under $10,000
President: Thomas Eubanks
E-Mail: teubanks@crt.state.la.us

Historical Note

Membership in NASA is limited to the official State Archaeologist of each state in the U.S. Has no paid officers or full-time staff. Membership: $25/year (individual).

Meetings/Conferences:

Annual Meetings: Spring, with the Society for American Archaeology.

Publications:

NASA Newsletter. q.
NASA Directory.

National Association of State Auditors, Comptrollers and Treasurers *(1916)*
2401 Regency Rd.
Suite 302
Lexington, KY 40503-2914
Tel: (859)276-1147 *Fax:* (859)278-0507
Web Site: www.nasact.org
Members: 170 individuals
Staff: 11
Annual Budget: $1-2,000,000
Executive Director: Kinney Poynter

Historical Note

Membership consists of three individuals from each state who serve in the capacity of auditors, comptrollers and treasurers of each state.

Publications:

Newsletter. m.
Directory. a.

National Association of State Aviation Officials *(1931)*
1010 Wayne Ave., Suite 930
Silver Spring, MD 20910
Tel: (301)588-0587 *Fax:* (301)585-1803
Web Site: www.nasao.org
Members: 52 states and territories
Staff: 4
Annual Budget: $250-500,000
President and Chief Executive Officer: Henry M. Ogrodzinski

Historical Note

Incorporated an affiliated research arm in 1986, the NASAO Center for Aviation Research and Education.

Meetings/Conferences:

Annual Meetings: Fall/250

Publications:

State Aviation Directory. q.
NASAO Newsletter. bi-m.
Funding and Organizational Data Report. a.

National Association of State Boards of Accountancy *(1908)*
150 Fourth Ave., North, Suite 700
Nashville, TN 37219-2417
Tel: (615)880-4200 *Fax:* (615)880-4290
Toll Free: (800)272 - 3926
Web Site: www.nasba.org
Members: 54 state boards
Staff: 47
Annual Budget: $10-25,000,000
President and Chief Executive Officer: David A. Costello
Chief Financial Officer: Robert E. Brosky
Executive Vice President and Chief Operating Officer: Lorraine P. Sachs

Historical Note

Formerly (1967) Association of Certified Public Accountant Examiners. Has an annual budget of approximately $8.5 million. Membership: $100/year (individual); $100/year (organization).

Meetings/Conferences:

Annual Meetings: September/October

Publications:

The State Board Report. m.
CPA Candidate Performance on the Uniform CPA Examination. a.

National Association of State Boards of Education *(1959)*
277 S. Washington St., Suite 100
Alexandria, VA 22314
Tel: (703)684-4000 *Fax:* (703)836-2313
Web Site: www.nasbe.org
Members: 650 board members
Staff: 19
Annual Budget: $2-5,000,000
Executive Director: Brenda L. Welburn
Director, Conventions and Meetings and Membership Associate: Doris J. Cruel
Director, Government and Public Affairs: David Griffith
Director, Publications: David Kysilko
E-Mail: davidk@nasbe.org

Historical Note

Composed of state board of education members from the U.S. and Canada.

Meetings/Conferences:

Annual Meetings: Fall

Publications:

State Board Connection. q.
Issues in Brief. q.
State Education Standard. q.

National Association of State Boards of Geology *(1991)*
P.O. Box 11591
Columbia, SC 29211-1591
Tel: (803)739-5676 *Fax:* (803)739-8874
E-Mail: asbog@asbog.org
Web Site: www.asbog.org
Members: 12 boards
Executive Director: Sam Christiano
E-Mail: asbog@asbog.org

Historical Note

NASBG members are state boards of geology.

National Association of State Boating Law Administrators *(1959)*
1500 Leestown Rd.
Suite 330
Lexington, KY 40511-2047
Tel: (859)225-9487 *Fax:* (859)231-6403
Web Site: www.nasbla.org
Members: 56 state/territories, 100 assoc.
Staff: 8
Annual Budget: $500-1,000,000
Executive Director: John Johnson

Historical Note

NASBLA is a professional association of state, commonwealth, and provincial officials having responsibility for administering and/or enforcing state boating laws. Non-voting membership is open to others on an associate basis. Membership: $2,475/yr. (state territories); $300/yr (501c3's); $1,000/yr (for profit organizations).

Meetings/Conferences:

Annual Meetings: Fall/250-350
2007 – Burlington, VT(Wyndham)/Sept. 4-11/300

Publications:

Reference Guide to State Boating Laws. a.
Directory. a.
Small Craft Advisory. bi-m.

National Association of State Budget Officers *(1945)*
444 North Capitol St. NW
Suite 642
Washington, DC 20001
Tel: (202)624-5382 *Fax:* (202)624-7745
E-Mail: nasbo-direct@nasbo.org
Web Site: www.nasbo.org
Members: 160 individuals
Staff: 7
Annual Budget: $500-1,000,000
Executive Director: Scott Pattison
E-Mail: spattison@nasbo.org
Member Relations Manager: Lauren Cummings
E-Mail: lcummings@nasbo.org

Historical Note

Membership limited to three budget officers per state. Affiliated with the National Governors Association.

Meetings/Conferences:

Annual Meetings: Summer

2007 - Lexington, KY(Hyatt Regency)/July 16-19/250

Publications:
NASBO Newsletter.
Budget Processes in the States. bien.
State Expenditure Report. a.
Fiscal Survey of the States. semi-a.

National Association of State Catholic Conference Directors *(1967)*
3211 Fourth St. NE
Washington, DC 20017-1194
Tel: (202)541-3000 *Fax:* (202)541-3313
Web Site: www.nasccd.org
Members: 37 individuals
Staff: 1
Annual Budget: under $10,000
Director: Frank Monahan

Historical Note
Directors of State Catholic Conferences.

Meetings/Conferences:
Semi-annual Meetings: Summer and Winter

National Association of State Charity Officials *(1978)*
c/o Office of the Attorney General
120 Broadway
New York, NY 10125
Tel: (212)416-8400 *Fax:* (212)416-8393
Web Site: www.nasconet.org/
Members: 100 individuals
Annual Budget: under $10,000
President: Mark Pacella

Historical Note
NASCO members are state government officers responsible for the regulation of charities. Has no paid officers or full-time staff

Meetings/Conferences:
Annual Meetings: Fall, in conjunction with the Nat'l Ass'n of Attorneys General

National Association of State Chief Administrators *(1976)*
P.O. Box 11910
Lexington, KY 40578-1910
Tel: (859)244-8181 *Fax:* (859)244-8001
E-Mail: nasca@esg.org
Web Site: www.nasca.org
Members: 37 states
Staff: 2
Annual Budget: $50-100,000
Director: Marcia Stone

Historical Note
Formerly (1998) National Association of State Directors of Administration and General Services, assumed its present name in 1999. Members are usually governor appointed administrators charged with the administration of state general services and corporate partners. Membership: $2,000/year (state); $3,000/year (corporate).

Meetings/Conferences:
Annual Meetings: Spring

Publications:
NASCA News: Managing Administrative Services. m.

National Association of State Chief Information Officers *(1969)*
201 E. Main St., Suite 1405
Lexington, KY 40507
Tel: (859)514-9153 *Fax:* (859)514-9166
E-Mail: nascio@amrms.com
Web Site: www.nascio.org
Members: 50 states
Staff: 8
Annual Budget: $2-5,000,000
Assistant Director: Beth Roszman
Program Manager: Elizabeth Van Meter

Historical Note
Formerly (2001) National Association for State Information Resource Executives. NASCIO represents information resource executives and managers from the 50 states, six U.S. territories, and the District of Columbia. NASCIO provides a forum to exchange information and to address the opportunities and challenges related to information technology, while also providing a vehicle to identify information technology issues.

Meetings/Conferences:
Semi-Annual Meetings: Spring/Fall
2007 - Scottsdale, AZ(Camelback Marriott)/Sept. 30-Oct. 3

Publications:
NASCIO Connection. bi-m.
Digital Government in the States - Survey Compendium.

National Association of State Controlled Substances Authorities *(1984)*
72 Brook St.
Quincy, MA 02170
Tel: (617)472-0520 *Fax:* (617)472-0521
E-Mail: kathykeough@nascsa.org
Web Site: www.nascsa.org
Staff: 1
Annual Budget: $10-25,000
Executive Director: Katherine Keough

Historical Note
NASCSA members are state, commonwealth and territory government agencies responsible for implementing and administering controlled substance scheduling, regulation and diversion control. Membership: $150/year (state agency).

Meetings/Conferences:
Annual Meetings: Fall

Publications:
Controlled Substances Authorities. 3/year.

National Association of State Credit Union Supervisors *(1965)*
1655 N. Ft. Myer Dr., Suite 300
Arlington, VA 22209
Tel: (703)528-8351 *Fax:* (703)528-3248
Toll Free: (800)728 - 7927
E-Mail: offices@nascus.org
Web Site: www.nascus.org
Members: 900 individuals
Staff: 8
Annual Budget: $1-2,000,000
Director, Education, Programs, and Events: Jennifer Champagne
President and Chief Executive Officer: Mary Martha Fortney
Vice President, State Regulatory Affairs: Brian D. Knight
Executive Vice President, Government Relations: Sandra Troutman
E-Mail: sandra@nascus.org

Historical Note
State chartered credit unions and state credit union supervisors. Membership: $150-$4300/year.

Meetings/Conferences:
Annual Meetings: Fall

Publications:
Fax from Washington. m.
Regulatory Crier. a.
Facts About Us. q.
Stateline. m.
Annual Report. a.

National Association of State Departments of Agriculture *(1915)*
1156 15th St. NW
Suite 1020
Washington, DC 20005-1711
Tel: (202)296-9680 *Fax:* (202)296-9686
E-Mail: nasda@nasda.org
Web Site: www.nasda.org
Members: 54 departments
Staff: 1000
Annual Budget: $10-25,000,000
Executive Vice President and Chief Executive Officer: Richard W. Kirchhoff
Director, Trade Shows: L. DeWitt Ashby
E-Mail: dewitt@nasda.org
Chief Operating Officer: Stephen R. Cox
E-Mail: steve@nasda.org
Director, Legislative and Regulatory Affairs: Charles Ingram
E-Mail: charlie@nasda.org
Manager, Information Services: Betsy Maixner

Historical Note
NASDA is a nonpartisan association of public officials comprised of the executive heads of the fifty state Departments of Agriculture and those from the territories of Puerto Rico, Guam, American Samoa and the Virgin Islands. NASDA's mission is to support and promote the American agriculture industry, while protecting the environment, through the development, implementation and communication of sound policy and programs.

Publications:
NASDA News. w.

National Association of State Development Agencies *(1946)*
1156 Fifteenth St. NW
Suite 1020
Washington, DC 20005
Tel: (202)296-9680 *Fax:* (202)296-9686
E-Mail: spope@nasda.com
Web Site: www.nasda.com
Members: 50 state agencies
Staff: 15
Annual Budget: $500-1,000,000
President and Chief Executive Officer: Miles Friedman
Deputy Director: Sally Pope

Historical Note
Formerly (1970) Association of State Planning & Development Agencies. Membership: $2,500-9,500/year.

Publications:
Directory of Incentives for Business Investment in the U.S.A.. a.
NASDA Newsletter. w.
Expenditure & Salary Survey. bien.

National Association of State Directors of Career Technical Education Consortium *(1920)*
444 North Capitol St. NW
Suite 830
Washington, DC 20001
Tel: (202)737-0303 *Fax:* (202)737-1106
Web Site: www.careertech.org
Members: 250 individuals
Staff: 4
Annual Budget: $250-500,000
Executive Director: Kimberly A. Green

Historical Note
NASDCTEC is the professional leadership association for 59 career and technical education agency heads committed to outstanding performance in career technical education. Membership also includes business, labor and education officials who share this commitment to quality occupational education at the secondary, post-secondary and adult levels. Membership: $100/year (individual associate); $75/year (individual associate who is a state employee); $1500/year (organization).

Meetings/Conferences:
Annual Meetings: Fall

Publications:
Conference Programs. 2/year.
Directory of State Directors of Vocational-Technical Educators. irreg.
Position Papers. irreg.
Congressional Testimony. irreg.

National Association of State Directors of Developmental Disability Services *(1969)*
113 Oronoco St.
Alexandria, VA 22314
Tel: (703)683-4202 *Fax:* (703)684-1395
Web Site: www.nasddds.org
Members: 50 states and the District of Columbia
Staff: 7
Annual Budget: $1-2,000,000
Executive Director: Robert M. Gettings
Manager, Membership: Karol B. Snyder

Historical Note
Formerly the National Association of State Mental Retardation Program Directors.

Publications:
Perspectives. m.
Community Service Reporter. m.

National Association of State Directors of Migrant Education *(1968)*

1001 Connecticut Ave. NW
Suite 918
Washington, DC 20036
Tel: (202)775-7780 *Fax:* (202)775-7784
Web Site: www.nasdme.org
Members: 51 individuals
Annual Budget: $250-500,000
Executive Coordinator: Roger Rosenthal

Historical Note

Each member is the person in each state education agency who has responsibility for Chapter One Migrant Education Program operation. NASDME promotes interstate coordination and cooperation to further the education of children whose parents are migrant agriculture farm workers.

Meetings/Conferences:

Annual Meetings: Spring/1,500

Publications:

Chapter I Migrant Education Program State Directors. a.

National Association of State Directors of Special Education *(1938)*

1800 Diagonal Rd.
Suite 320
Alexandria, VA 22314-2840
Tel: (703)519-3800 *Fax:* (703)519-3808
Web Site: www.nasdse.org
Members: 250 individuals
Staff: 20
Annual Budget: $2-5,000,000
Executive Director: Bill East
Deputy Executive Director, Government Relations: Nancy Reder

Historical Note

Represents state personnel responsible for education of handicapped students with disabilities. Provides training and technical assistance to state education agency staff.

Meetings/Conferences:

Annual Meetings: October

Publications:

Counterpoint. q.

National Association of State Directors of Teacher Education and Certification *(1922)*

1225 Providence Rd.
PMD 116
Whitinsville, MA 01588
Tel: (508)380-1202 *Fax:* (508)278-5342
Web Site: www.nasdtec.org
Members: 60 gov't agencies, 100 colleges and universities
Staff: 2
Annual Budget: $250-500,000
Executive Director: Roy Einreinhofer
E-Mail: rje@nasdtec.com

Historical Note

NASDTEC's purpose is to exercise leadership in matters relating to the preparation and certification of professional school personnel. Full membership is open to government agencies; associate membership is open to other organizations, such as schools and companies, that are involved with the preparation and certification of professional school personnel. Membership: $3,500/year (state); $400/year (associate).
Membership: $3,500/year (state); $400/year (associate).

Meetings/Conferences:

Annual Meetings: June

Publications:

Newsletters. q.
Directory. a.
Certification Manual. a.

National Association of State Directors of Veterans Affairs *(1946)*

c/o KDVA, 1111 Louisville Rd.
Frankfort, KY 40601
Tel: (502)564-9203 *Fax:* (502)564-9240
E-Mail: nasdva@aol.com
Web Site: www.nasdva.com
Members: 56 individuals
Annual Budget: under $10,000
President: Leslie Beavers
E-Mail: nasdva@aol.com

Historical Note

NMASDVA exists to provide professional support to the administrators of each state's resepctive office for veteran affairs. Has no paid officers or full-time staff. Membership: $400/year.

Meetings/Conferences:

Semi-Annual Meetings: Spring and Fall

National Association of State Election Directors *(1990)*

12543 Westella
Suite 100
Houston, TX 77077-3929
Tel: (281)752-6200
E-Mail: services@nased.org
Web Site: www.nased.org
Members: 50 individuals
Staff: 1
President: Kevin Kennedy

Historical Note

NASED members are state, commonwealth or territorial election directors or directors of voter registration. Administrative support provided by the Council of State Governments.

Meetings/Conferences:

Semi-Annual Meetings: Winter and Summer

National Association of State Emergency Medical Services Officials *(1980)*

201 Park Washington Ct.
Falls Church, VA 22046-4527
Tel: (703)538-1799 Ext: 2 *Fax:* (703)241-5603
E-Mail: info@nasemsd.org
Web Site: www.nasemso.org
Members: 56 state directors
Staff: 4
Annual Budget: $500-1,000,000
Executive Director: Elizabeth B. Armstrong, CAE
Manager, Meetings and Exhibits: Susan A. Denston
Program Manager: Melissa Trumbull

Historical Note

Members are directors of state emergency medical services. Membership: $450/year.

Meetings/Conferences:

Annual Meetings: Fall
2007 – Minneapolis, MN(Hyatt)//220

Publications:

NASEMSO Washington Update (electronic). 2/month.

National Association of State Energy Officials *(1992)*

1414 Prince St., Suite 200
Alexandria, VA 22314-2853
Tel: (703)299-8800 *Fax:* (703)299-6208
E-Mail: dshea@nasea.org
Web Site: www.naseo.org
Members: 55
Staff: 4
Executive Director: Diane Shea
E-Mail: dshea@nasea.org

Meetings/Conferences:

Annual Meetings: Fall

Publications:

Energy Forum. q.
NASEO newsfax. m.

National Association of State Facilities Administrators *(1987)*

2760 Research Park Dr.
P.O. Box 11910
Lexington, KY 40578-1910
Tel: (859)244-8181 *Fax:* (859)244-8001
E-Mail: nasfa@nasfa.net
Web Site: www.nasfa.net
Members: 1200 individuals
Staff: 2
Annual Budget: $100-250,000
Association Director: Marcia Stone

Historical Note

NASFA is a professional organization whose mission is to provide leadership in the development and implementation of state facility administration practices. As a non-profit organization founded in 1987, NASFA has greatly expanded its activities and services to include a National Conference & Resource Expo, regular publications, many exclusive member services, and several standing committees.

Meetings/Conferences:

Annual Meetings: Summer
2007 – Lake Tahoe, CA(Montbleu)/June 10-14/150
2008 – Jackson, WY

Publications:

NASFA Building Commissioning Recommended Guidelines. adv.
NASFA Resource Guide to State Facilities Management.
NASFA Representatives Directory.
NASFA CM/GC Guidelines for Public Owners. adv.

National Association of State Fire Marshals *(1989)*

1319 F. St. NW
Suite 301
Washington, DC 20004
Tel: (202)737-1226 *Fax:* (202)393-1296
Toll Free: (877)996 - 2736
Web Site: www.firemarshals.org
Members: 51 fire marshals
Staff: 6
Annual Budget: $2-5,000,000
Secretary/Treasurer: Alan Shuman

Historical Note

NASFM members are state fire marshals and private industry supporters. Membership: $100/year (individual); $2500/year (organization/company).

Meetings/Conferences:

Annual Meetings: Annual

National Association of State Foresters *(1920)*

444 N. Capitol St. NW
Suite 540
Washington, DC 20001
Tel: (202)624-5415 *Fax:* (202)624-5407
E-Mail: nasf@stateforesters.org
Web Site: www.stateforesters.org
Members: 54 jurisdictions
Staff: 5
Annual Budget: $100-250,000
Executive Director: Anne E. Heissenbuttel
Communications Specialist: Robert McConnell
Business Manager: Joan O'Hara Wehner

Historical Note

Founded as the Association of State Foresters in 1920, nationwide successor to the Association of Eastern Foresters (1911), NASF assumed its present name in 1964. Membership: $3,500/year (state).

Meetings/Conferences:

Annual Meetings: Fall

Publications:

NASF State Forestry Statistics. bi- a.
NASF Washington Update. m.

National Association of State Land Reclamationists *(1973)*

510 Coal Research Center
Carbondale, IL 62901-4623
Tel: (618)536-5521 *Fax:* (618)453-7346
E-Mail: aharrington@crc.siu.edu
Web Site: www.crc.siu.edu/naslr.htm
Members: 140 individuals
Staff: 1
Annual Budget: under $10,000
Contact: Anna Harrington
E-Mail: aharrington@crc.siu.edu

Historical Note

Organized to bring together State reclamation officials for activities of mutual interest and to promote cooperation between the states, private mining groups and the federal government on matters affecting the reclamation of mined lands. Membership: $10/year (individual); $100/year (corporate); $200/year (state).

Meetings/Conferences:

Annual Meetings: Spring or Fall

Publications:

NASLR Newsletter. q.

National Association of State Mental Health Program Directors *(1963)*
66 Canal Center Plaza, Suite 302
Alexandria, VA 22314-1591
Tel: (703)739-9333 *Fax:* (703)548-9517
Web Site: www.nasmhpd.org
Members: 55 state & territorial agencies
Staff: 22
Annual Budget: $1-2,000,000
Executive Director: Robert W. Glover, Ph.D.
Director, Government Relations: Andrew Hyman

Historical Note
State commissioners in charge of the state government programs for persons with mental illness. Promotes cooperation and exchange of ideas in the administration of public mental health programs. A cooperating agency of the National Governors' Association and the Council of State Governments.

Meetings/Conferences:
Semi-Annual Meetings: Winter and Summer/100

Publications:
U.S. Congress Report.
State Report.
Federal Agencies Report.
Children & Youth Update.
Legal Issues.
Studies on State Mental Health Systems.
Human Resource Development Issues.
Aging Issues.
Forensic Issues.

National Association of State Outdoor Recreation Liaison Officers *(1967)*
3116 Woodbrook Pl.
Boise, ID 83706
Tel: (208)384-5421 *Fax:* (208)331-7757
Members: 56 state/territorial representative
Staff: 1
Annual Budget: $25-50,000
Executive Director: Yvonne Ferrell

Historical Note
NASORLO members are governor-appointed state administrators of outdoor recreational grant programs funded under the federal Land and Water Conservation Act. Membership: $750/year (organization/company).

National Association of State Park Directors *(1962)*
8829 Woodyhill Rd.
Raleigh, NC 27613
Tel: (919)676-8365 *Fax:* (919)676-8365
E-Mail: naspd@nc.rr.com
Web Site: www.naspd.org
Members: 50 states
Staff: 1
Annual Budget: $50-100,000
Executive Director: Philip K. McKnelly

Historical Note
Members are chief administrative officers of each state park agency. Officers are elected biennially. Membership: $1,400/year (state).

Meetings/Conferences:
Annual Meetings: Fall/200

Publications:
Annual Information Exchange. a.
Directory of State Park Directors. a.

National Association of State Personnel Executives *(1976)*
P.O. Box 11910
Lexington, KY 40578-1910
Tel: (859)244-8182 *Fax:* (859)244-8001
E-Mail: naspe@csg.org
Web Site: www.naspe.net
Members: 150 individuals
Staff: 3
Annual Budget: $50-100,000
Manager: Leslie Scott

Historical Note
An affiliate of the Council of State Governments which provides administrative support, NASPE members are the chief personnel executives in each of the United States; the territories of Guam, Virgin Islands and American Somoa; the Commonwealth of Puerto Rico and the District of Columbia. To provide a forum for state personnel executives to share information on human resource issues and to collectively influence those issues through the conduct of professional research and the participation in various regional and national committees, forums and meetings so that members can better achieve their state's mission and business objectives. Membership: $1,500/year (state).

Meetings/Conferences:
Annual Meetings: Summer

Publications:
State Personnel Office: Roles and Functions. trien.
State Personnel View Newsletter. q. adv.
State Personnel Representatives Directory. bien.

National Association of State Procurement Officials *(1947)*
201 E. Main St., Suite 1405
Lexington, KY 40507
Tel: (859)514-9159 *Fax:* (859)514-9188
E-Mail: lpope@AMRms.com
Web Site: www.naspo.org
Members: 80 individuals
Staff: 125
Annual Budget: $100-250,000
Executive Director: Jack Gallt

Historical Note
Founded as National Association of State Purchasing Officials. NASPO provides professional support to procurement officers in state and municipal government, and information on the procurement process to companies interested in that market. Membership: $1200/year (state members); $500/year (associate members).

Meetings/Conferences:
Annual Meetings: Fall

Publications:
Survey of State and Local Govt. Purchasing Principles and Priorities. bi-a.
State and Local Govt. Purchasing Principles and Practices. bi-a.

National Association of State Radio Networks *(1973)*
17911 Harwood Ave.
Homewood, IL 60430
Tel: (708)799-6676 *Fax:* (708)799-6698
Web Site: www.statenets.com
Members: 30 companies
Staff: 13
Annual Budget: $250-500,000
Executive Director: Tom Dobrez

Historical Note
Members are companies that broadcast news and other informational programming to affiliated radio stations via satelite transmission. Member networks serve over 1,800 such stations.

Meetings/Conferences:
Annual Meetings: Annual

Publications:
State Network Newsletter. m. adv.

National Association of State Retirement Administrators *(1956)*
P.O. Box 14117
Baton Rouge, LA 70898
Tel: (225)757-9558 *Fax:* (225)757-9765
Web Site: www.nasra.org
Members: 82 individuals
Staff: 4
Annual Budget: $500-1,000,000
Executive Director: Glenda Chambers

Historical Note
Represents the administrators of various public-sector retirement programs, providing legislative advocacy and public and professional education Membership: $2,400/year (administrator), $2,500/year (associate).

Meetings/Conferences:
Annual Meetings: Summer

Publications:
Survey of State and Local Government Retirement Systems. a.
Newsletter. irreg.

National Association of State Supervisors of Home Economics Education

Historical Note
A division of the American Vocational Association.

National Association of State Supervisors of Music *(1940)*

Historical Note
Address unknown in 2005.

National Association of State Supervisors of Trade and Industrial Education *(1925)*
1450 Energy Park Dr., Suite 300
St. Paul, MN 55108
Tel: (651)649-5772 *Fax:* (651)632-5008
Web Site: http://itednt.ited.uidaho.edu/nasstie/index.html
Members: 100 individuals
Annual Budget: under $10,000
Executive Director: Gary Langer
E-Mail: gary.langer@so.mnscu.edu

Historical Note
Has no paid officers or full-time staff. Membership: $20/year (individual).

Meetings/Conferences:
Annual Meetings: December and June Kansas City, MO/June

National Association of State Telecommunications Directors

Historical Note
Became NASTAD - Telecommunications and Technology Professionals Serving State Government in 2003.

National Association of State Textbook Administrators
c/o Ray Lindley, Oregon Department of Education
255 Capitol St., NE
Salem, OR 97310
Tel: (503)947-5701 *Fax:* (503)378-5156
E-Mail: ray.lindley@state.or.us
Web Site: www.nasta.org
Members: 26 state offices
Annual Budget: under $10,000
President: Ray Lindley

Historical Note
Has no paid officers or full-time staff. Membership: $25/year (individual).

Meetings/Conferences:
Semi-Annual Meetings: Winter and Summer
2007 – Austin, TX(Crowne Plaza)/Feb. 13-15
2007 – Portland, OR(Doubletree Lloyd Center)/July 21-24

Publications:
Newsletter. a.

National Association of State Treasurers *(1976)*
P.O. Box 11910
Lexington, KY 40578-1910
Tel: (859)244-8175 *Fax:* (859)244-8053
E-Mail: nast@csg.org
Web Site: www.nast.org
Members: 53 individuals
Staff: 9
Annual Budget: $500-1,000,000
Executive Director: Pamela Taylor

Historical Note
Membership consists of State Treasurers, their deputies and staffs. Membership: $1,500/year (state); $1,000-3,000/year (corporate).

Meetings/Conferences:
Annual Meetings: July/over 450

Publications:
State Treasury Activities and Functions. trien.
State Treasury Profiles. bien.
NAST Review. q.

National Association of State Units on Aging *(1964)*
1201 15th St. NW
Suite 350
Washington, DC 20005
Tel: (202)898-2578 *Fax:* (202)898-2583

E-Mail: info@nasua.org
Web Site: www.nasua.org
Members: 57 individuals
Staff: 16
Annual Budget: $2-5,000,000
Acting Executive Director: Theresa Lambert

Historical Note

Members are the state agencies on aging of the fifty states, the District of Columbia,and U.S. territories. Provides general and specialized information, technical assistance and professional development support to state units on aging. Serves as organized channel for officially designated state leadership in aging to exchange information and mutual experiences and to join together for appropriate action on behalf of the elderly.

Meetings/Conferences:
Annual Meetings: Washington, DC/Spring

National Association of State Universities and Land Grant Colleges *(1887)*

1307 New York Ave. NW
Suite 400
Washington, DC 20005-4722
Tel: (202)478-6040 *Fax:* (202)478-6046
Web Site: www.nasulgc.org
Members: 214 institutions
Staff: 35
Annual Budget: $2-5,000,000
President: C. Peter McGrath
Director, Public Affairs: Cheryl Fields
Director, Administration: Teresa Streeter

Historical Note

NASULGC's overriding mission is to support high quality public higher education and its member institutions as they perform their traditional teaching, research and public service roles. NASULGC provides a forum for the discussion and development of policies affecting higher education and the public interest.

Meetings/Conferences:
Annual Meetings: November

Publications:
Newsline. 10/year.

National Association of State Utility Consumer Advocates *(1979)*

8380 Colesville Rd.
Suite 101
Silver Spring, MD 20910
Tel: (301)589-6313 *Fax:* (301)589-6380
E-Mail: nasuca@nasuca.org
Web Site: www.nasuca.org
Members: 50 agencies and organizations
Staff: 3
Annual Budget: $100-250,000
Executive Director: Charles A. Acquard

Historical Note

Represents utility consumer advocacy agencies which operate independently from the regulatory commissions in their states. Officers change every two years.

Meetings/Conferences:
Semi-Annual Meetings: June and November
2007 - Anaheim, CA/Nov. 11-14

Publications:
Washington Report. m.
NASUCA News. m. adv.
Consultants Directory. a.
Membership Directory. a.

National Association of State Veterans Homes *(1953)*

c/o Veterans Home of Wyoming
700 Veterans Ln.
Buffalo, WY 82834
Tel: (307)684-5511 *Fax:* (307)684-7636
Web Site: www.nasvh.com
Members: 119 facilities
Annual Budget: $100-250,000
Secretary-Treasurer: John (Jack) R. Tarter
E-Mail: jtarte@state.wy.us

Historical Note

Encourages continued federal support for building state facilities and to provide care for veterans currently living in state homes. Has no paid officers or full-time staff.

Meetings/Conferences:
Annual Meetings: Summer

Publications:
Nat'l Ass'n of State Veterans Homes Newsletter. 3/year.
LINK. q.
Nat'l Ass'n of State Veterans Homes Directory. a.

National Association of State Workforce Agencies *(1937)*

444 North Capitol St. NW
Suite 142
Washington, DC 20001-1512
Tel: (202)434-8020 *Fax:* (202)434-8033
Web Site: www.naswa.org
Members: 53 state agencies
Staff: 10
Annual Budget: $1-2,000,000
Executive Director: Richard A. Hobbie
E-Mail: rhobbie@naswa.org
Director, Finance and Administration: James Black
E-Mail: jblack@naswa.org
Director, Information Technology and Training: Pam Gerrasimides
E-Mail: pgerassimides@naswa.org
Director, Congressional and Intergovernmental Affairs: Curt Harris
Manager, Office and Membership Services: Martina L. Pass
Director, Workforce Development: Bob Simoneau
Director, Labor Market Information and Research: Mary Susan Vickers

Historical Note

Founded as Interstate Conference of Unemployment Compensation Agencies; became Interstate Conference of Employment Security Agencies in 1939, and assumed its current name in 2000. Members are administrators of state agencies responsible for employment and training programs, unemployment insurance, and labor market information. Center for Employment Security Education and Research is the education and research arm of NASWA. Membership: $18,000/year.

Publications:
NASWA Bulletin (on-line). w.

National Association of Steel Pipe Distributors *(1975)*

1501 E. Mockingbird Ln.
Suite 307
Victoria, TX 77904
Tel: (361)574-7878 *Fax:* (832)201-9479
E-Mail: naspd@nc.rr.com
Web Site: www.naspd.com
Members: 250 companies
Staff: 3
Annual Budget: $100-250,000
Executive Director: Susannah F. Porr

Historical Note

Trade Association organized in San Antonio, TX, April 1975, and incorporated in the same state. Members are distributors and manufacturers of steel pipes and tubing, and allied businesses. Membership: $750-1,200/year, dependent on type and size of company.

Meetings/Conferences:
Three Meetings Annually: February, June, and October

Publications:
Pipeline. m. adv.
Tubular Products Manual. a.
Membership Directory. a. adv.
OSHA Compliance Manual.

National Association of Stock Plan Professionals *(1993)*

P.O. Box 21639
Concord, CA 94521-0639
Tel: (925)685-9271 *Fax:* (925)685-5402
E-Mail: naspp@naspp.com
Web Site: www.naspp.com
Members: 7000 individuals
Program Director: Barbara Baksa

Historical Note

NASPP is dedicated to providing its members, including compensation and human resource professionals, stock plan administrators and brokers, opportunities for professional growth and education advancement. Membership: $395/year (individual); $495/year (corporate, up to three individuals).

Publications:
The Stock Plan Advisor. bi-m. adv.

National Association of Student Activity Advisors *(1971)*

Historical Note

Administrative support is provided by the Division of Student Activities of the National Association of Secondary School Principals. Members are education professionals involved with student activity programs.

National Association of Student Affairs Professionals *(1954)*

Albany State Univ., Graduate School
Box 9217
Albany, GA 31705
Tel: (229)430-5118 *Fax:* (229)430-6398
E-Mail: diane.frink@asurams.edu
Web Site: www.nasap.net
Members: 150 individuals
Staff: 15
Annual Budget: $10-25,000
Treasurer: Diane Frink

Historical Note

Formerly (1994) National Association of Personnel Workers. Members are student affairs personnel in the fields of teaching, housing, financial aid and social services.

Meetings/Conferences:
Annual Meetings: In February in a college or university setting.

National Association of Student Anthropolgists

Historical Note

A section of the American Anthropological Society

National Association of Student Assistance Professionals

Historical Note

Became National Student Assistance Association in 2003.

National Association of Student Councils *(1932)*

Historical Note

An activity administered by the Office of Student Activities of the National Association of Secondary School Principals. Now includes more than 7,000 student councils and their advisers.

National Association of Student Financial Aid Administrators *(1966)*

1129 20th St. NW
Suite 400
Washington, DC 20036-3453
Tel: (202)785-0453 *Fax:* (202)785-1487
Web Site: www.nasfaa.org
Members: 3000 institutions
Staff: 32
Annual Budget: $2-5,000,000
President: A. Dallas Martin, Ph.D.
E-Mail: martind@nasfaa.org
Executive Vice President: Joan Crissman
E-Mail: crissmanj@nasfaa.org
Director, Communications: Jeffrey Sheppard
E-Mail: sheppardj@nasfaa.org
Director, Congressional Relations: Larry Zaglanicszny

Historical Note

NASFAA promotes the professional preparation, effectiveness, and mutual support of persons involved in student financial aid administration. NASFAA works with others in institutions of postsecondary education, government agencies, foundations, private and community organizations, and regional and state financial aid associations who are concerned with the support and administration of student financial aid. NASFAA promotes and encourages programs which remove financial barriers to student enrollment and retention.

Meetings/Conferences:
Annual Meetings: Summer

Publications:
Student Aid Transcript. 3/year. adv.
Journal of Student Financial Aid. 3/year.
NASFAA Membership Directory. a. adv.

National Association of Student Personnel Administrators *(1919)*
1875 Connecticut Ave. NW
Suite 418
Washington, DC 20009
Tel: (202)265-7500 *Fax:* (202)797-1157
E-Mail: office@naspa.org
Web Site: www.naspa.org
Members: 7500 individuals
Staff: 14
Annual Budget: $1-2,000,000
Executive Director: Gwendolyn Jordan Dungy

Historical Note
Established in 1919 as the National Association of Deans and Advisers of Men by a group of midwestern deans; assumed its current name in 1951. Works to improve practices in student affairs administration. Membership: $54-$175/year (individual); $297-$1,370/year (institution).

Meetings/Conferences:
Annual Meetings: Spring

Publications:
NASPA Forum (online). m. adv.
NASPA Monograph Series. irreg.
Net Results. w.
NASPA Journal. q.
Membership Handbook (online).

National Association of Substance Abuse Trainers and Educators *(1983)*
1521 Hillary St.
New Orleans, LA 70118
Tel: (504)861-4756
Members: 41 colleges and universities
Annual Budget: under $10,000
President: Dr. Thomas Lief

Historical Note
Participating institutions of higher education are accredited colleges, universities and professional schools which offer twelve or more hours of substance abuse or alcoholism courses.

Publications:
Directory of the NASATE. a.

National Association of Supervisors for Business Education *(1965)*
Mississippi Dept. of Education
P.O. Box 771
Jackson, MS 39205
Tel: (601)359-3940 *Fax:* (601)359-3481
Web Site: www.nasbe.us
Members: 125 individuals
Annual Budget: under $10,000
Treasurer: Sherry Franklin

Historical Note
Formerly (1981) National Association of State Supervisors of Business and Office Education. NASBE members are state supervisors of business education programs. Membership: $15/year (individual).

Meetings/Conferences:
Semi-Annual Meetings:: Spring in conjunction with Nat'l Business Education Ass'n and Winter with the American Vocational Ass'n

Publications:
NASBE Newsletter. 3/yr.
NABESS Directory. a.

National Association of Supervisors of Agricultural Education *(1962)*

Historical Note
A division of Nat'l Ass'n of Agricultural Educators, which provides administrative support.

National Association of Surety Bond Producers *(1942)*
1828 L St. NW
Suite 720
Washington, DC 20036
Tel: (202)686-3700 *Fax:* (202)686-3656
E-Mail: info@nasbp.org
Web Site: www.nasbp.org
Members: 550 bond producers
Staff: 10
Annual Budget: $2-5,000,000
Executive Vice President: Richard A. Foss
E-Mail: dfoss@nasbp.org
Director, Government Relations: Connie Lynch
E-Mail: clynch@nasbp.org

Historical Note
NASBP members are independent insurance agencies and brokerage firms that specialize in providing surety bonding and insurance programs to construction contractors. Membership: open only to firms who have produced a minimum of $200,000 in total surety premiums in one calenday year for more than one company.

Meetings/Conferences:
Annual Meetings: Spring/900

Publications:
Pipeline. m.

National Association of Swine Records *(1954)*
1769 U.S. Hwy. 52 West
P.O. 2417
West Lafayette, IN 47996-2417
Tel: (765)463-3594 *Fax:* (765)497-2959
Members: 8 companies and 8 associations
Staff: 2
Annual Budget: $100-250,000
Chairman: Mike Paul

National Association of Tax Professionals *(1979)*
720 Association Dr.
Appleton, WI 54914-1483
Tel: (800)558-3402 *Fax:* (800)747-0001
E-Mail: natp@natptax.com
Web Site: www.natptax.com
Members: 18000 individuals
Staff: 41
Annual Budget: $5-10,000,000
Chief Executive Officer: Kathy Stanek

Historical Note
Membership is open to any individual, group or business interested in the betterment of those engaged in the practice of preparing federal tax returns. Provides a tax research center and over 200 tax workshops. Membership: $128/year (new member); $110/year (renewal).

Meetings/Conferences:
Annual Meetings: August
2007 – Las Vegas, NV(Caesar's)/July 23-26/1000
2008 – Atlanta, GA(Atlanta Marriott Marquis)/July 7-10/1000

Publications:
TAXPRO Monthly. m.
TAXPRO Quarterly Journal. q. adv.
TAXPRO Weekly. w.

National Association of Teacher Educators for Family Consumer Sciences *(1949)*
East Carolina University
Greenville, NC 27835
Tel: (252)328-5714
Web Site: www.natefacs.org
Members: 150 individuals
Annual Budget: $10-25,000
Treasurer: Mary J. Pickard

Historical Note
Formerly (1995) National Association of Teacher Educators for Vocational Home Economics. NATEFACS members are teacher educators in family and consumer sciences. Has no paid officers or full-time staff.

Meetings/Conferences:
Annual Meetings: June, September, December

Publications:
Journal of Family and Consumer Sciences Education. semi-a.
Directory. a.

National Association of Teachers of Singing *(1944)*
4745 Sutton Park Ct.
Suite 201
Jacksonville, FL 32224
Tel: (904)992-9101 *Fax:* (904)992-9326
Web Site: www.nats.org
Members: 6200 individuals
Staff: 3
Annual Budget: $500-1,000,000

Historical Note
Members are teachers of singing and vocal instruction in private studios, conservatories, schools, colleges and community life. Membership: $80/year.

Meetings/Conferences:
2008 – Nashville, TN(Gaylord Opryland)/June 26-30

Publications:
Journal of Singing. 5/y.
Inter Nos Newsletter. 3/yr.

National Association of Teachers' Agencies *(1914)*
797 Kings Hwy.
Fairfield, CT 06825
Tel: (203)333-0611 *Fax:* (203)334-7224
E-Mail: info@jobsforteachers.com
Web Site: www.jobsforteachers.com
Members: 22 agencies
Annual Budget: under $10,000
Secretary: Mark King

Historical Note
Members are private employment agencies concentrating on the placement of teachers and administrators serving public and private schools. Absorbed the Association of Southern Teacher Agencies (1909). Membership: $225/year (organization).

Meetings/Conferences:
Annual Meetings: Fall

Publications:
NATA.
Membership List. a.

National Association of Telecommunications Officers and Advisors *(1980)*
1800 Diagonal Rd.
Suite 495
Alexandria, VA 22314
Tel: (703)519-8035 *Fax:* (703)519-8036
E-Mail: info@natoa.org
Web Site: www.natoa.org
Members: 800 agencies and individuals
Staff: 2
Annual Budget: $500-1,000,000
Executive Director: Libby Beaty
E-Mail: lbeaty@natoa.org
Manager, Association Services: Jennifer Harman
E-Mail: jharman@natoa.org

Historical Note
NATOA is a professional organization serving citizens through city and county governments and regional authorities in the development, regulation, and administration of cable television and other telecommunication systems.

Meetings/Conferences:
Annual Meetings: Fall

Publications:
Natoa Journal of Municipal Telecommunications Policy. q.
NATOA News Quarterly. q.

National Association of Television Program Executives *(1963)*
5757 Wilshire Blvd., Penthouse Ten
Los Angeles, CA 90036
Tel: (310)453-4440 *Fax:* (310)453-5258
E-Mail: info@napte.org
Web Site: www.natpe.org
Members: 4000 corporations
Staff: 15
President and Chief Executive Officer: Rick Feldman
Senior Vice President, Marketing: Beth Braen
Senior Vice President, Conference Operations and Sales: Nick Orfanopoulos

Historical Note
NATPE is dedicated to furthering excellence in television programming around the world. Represents executives involved in all sectors of the television industry. Sponsors and supports the NAPTE Educational Foundation. Membership: $675/year (organization/company/individual).

Meetings/Conferences:
Annual Meetings: Winter/8,000
2007 – Las Vegas, NV(Mandalay Bay)/Jan. 16-18

2009 – Las Vegas, NV(Mandalay Bay)/Jan. 27-29

Publications:
Guide to North America Media. a. adv.

National Association of Temple Administrators *(1941)*
P.O. Box 936
Ridgefield, WA 98642
Tel: (360)887-0464
Toll Free: (800)966 - 6282
E-Mail: nataoffice@natanet.org
Web Site: http://natanet.org/
Members: 400 individuals
Staff: 1
Annual Budget: $100-250,000
Administrative Officer: Katherine Small

Historical Note
Members are synagogue executive directors in the Reform Jewish movement. Affiliated with the Union of American Hebrew Congregations. Established as the National Association of Temple Secretaries, it assumed its present name in 1959. Has no paid officers or full-time staff.

Meetings/Conferences:
Annual Meetings: Fall-Winter

Publications:
NATA Journal. q.
Temple Management Manual. irreg.

National Association of Temple Educators *(1955)*
633 Third Ave., Seventh Floor
New York, NY 10017-6778
Tel: (212)452-6510 *Fax:* (212)452-6512
E-Mail: nateoff@aol.com
Web Site: www.rj.org/NATE
Members: 950 individuals
Staff: 2
Annual Budget: $100-250,000
Executive Director: Rabbi Stanley Schicker, R.J.E.

Historical Note
Affiliated with the Union of American Hebrew Congregations. Members are educational leaders associated with the Reform Jewish movement in the United States, Canada, England, Israel, Australia and South Africa.

Meetings/Conferences:
Annual Meetings: Winter/200

Publications:
Membership Directory. a.
Proceedings. a.
NATE News. m.

National Association of Test Directors *(1985)*
Everett Public Schools
4730 Caby Ave.
Everett, WA 98203
Tel: (425)385-4057 *Fax:* (425)385-4052
E-Mail: phendrickson@everett.wednet.edu
Web Site: www.natd.org
Members: 300 individuals
Annual Budget: under $10,000

Historical Note
NATD members are individuals administering educational testing programs (primarily in the public schools). Has no paid officers or full-time staff. Membership: $20/year (individual).

Meetings/Conferences:
Annual Meetings: in conjunction with AERA & NCME

Publications:
Annual Symposia Proceedings. a.
NATD Constitution.
Annual Meeting Summary. a.
NATD Newsletter. 3/year.
Membership List. a.

National Association of the Remodeling Industry *(1982)*
780 Lee St., Suite 200
Des Plaines, IL 60016-6459
Tel: (847)298-9200 *Fax:* (847)298-9225
Toll Free: (800)611 - 6274
E-Mail: info@nari.org
Web Site: www.nari.org
Members: 7100 companies, 60 chapters
Staff: 13
Annual Budget: $2-5,000,000
Executive Vice President: Mary Busey Harris, CAE
Director, Marketing and Communications: Gwen Biasi
Director, Finance and Operations: Elsie Itarralde
Director, Member Services: Tracy Spears
Manager, Education: Dan Taddei
Director, National Membership and Business Development: Don Vossburg

Historical Note
Manufacturers of building products, remodeling contractors, lending institutions and other firms in the home improvement industry. The result of a merger (1982) between the National Remodelers Association and the National Home Improvement Council. Membership: $125/year, plus local chapter dues, when within 50-mile radius.

Meetings/Conferences:
Annual Meetings: usually Spring
2007 – Austin, TX(Marriott Austin at The Capital)/March 21-24

Publications:
Remodeler's Journal. bi-m. adv.

National Association of Theatre Owners *(1948)*
750 First St., N.E., Suite 1130
Washington, DC 20002
Tel: (202)962-0054 *Fax:* (202)962-0307
E-Mail: nato@natodc.com
Web Site: www.natoonline.org
Members: 28000 screens
Staff: 11
Executive Director and Vice President: Mary Ann Anderson
President and Chief Executive Officer: John Fithian

Historical Note
Founded as Theatre Owners of America. Absorbed Allied Theatre Owners of America and assumed its current name in 1966.

Meetings/Conferences:
Semi-Annual Meetings: Fall(West Coast) and Spring(East Coast)

Publications:
In Focus. 11/year. adv.
Encyclopedia of Exhibition. a. adv.

National Association of Ticket Brokers *(1994)*
214 N. Hale St.
Wheaton, IL 60187
Tel: (630)510-4594 *Fax:* (630)510-4501
Web Site: www.natb.org
Members: 170 companies
Staff: 2
Annual Budget: $100-250,000
Executive Director: Terry Stevenson
General Counsel: Gary Adler
E-Mail: gadler@oconnorhannan.com

Historical Note
NATB represents businesses engaged in the reselling of tickets to entertainment and sporting events. Members must have a permanent business location and abide by the NATB code of ethics. Membership: $750-2,500/year.

Meetings/Conferences:
Semi-Annual Meetings:
2007 – Las Vegas, NV

Publications:
Membership Directory. a. adv.
Newsletter. q. adv.

National Association of Towns and Townships *(1976)*
1130 Connecticut Ave. NW, Suite 300
Washington, DC 20036
Tel: (202)454-3954 *Fax:* (202)331-1598
Toll Free: (866)830 - 0008
E-Mail: info@natat.org
Web Site: www.natat.org
Members: 11000 local governments
Staff: 5
Annual Budget: $500-1,000,000
Contact: Sharon Blanchard

Historical Note
Established as the National Association of Town and Township Officials. Assumed its present name and opened a Washington office in 1977. NATaT is a non-profit membership organization offering technical assistance, educational services and public policy support to local government officials from 11,000 small communities across the U.S. Created the National Association of Small Communities in 1984; incorporated the National Center for Small Communities in 1997. Membership: $100(individual), $250 (organization).

Meetings/Conferences:
Annual Meetings: Washington, DC(Hyatt Regency)/September/800

Publications:
NATaT's Washington Report. 10/year.
Small Community Quarterly. q.

National Association of Trade Exchanges *(1984)*
8836 Tyler Rd.
Mentor, OH 44060
Tel: (440)205-5378 *Fax:* (440)205-5379
E-Mail: bartertrainer@aol.com
Web Site: www.nate.org
Members: 80 individuals
Staff: 4
Annual Budget: $100-250,000
Executive Director: Thomas H. McDowell

Historical Note
Membership: $495/year (organization).

Meetings/Conferences:
Semi-Annual Meetings: Spring and Fall

Publications:
NATE Update. 3/year adv. adv.

National Association of Traffic Accident Reconstructionists and Investigators *(1984)*
P.O. Box 2588
Westchester, PA 19380
Tel: (610)696-1919
E-Mail: natari@natari.org
Web Site: www.natari.org/index2.html
Members: 200 individuals
Annual Budget: $25-50,000
President: William Comlin

Historical Note
Established to foster the exchange of information between professionals involved in motor vehicle traffic collision analysis. Has no paid officers or full-time staff. Membership: $50/year.

Meetings/Conferences:
Annual Meetings: Meeting times vary.

Publications:
Accident Investigation Formula Book. irreg.
NATARI Newsletter. q. adv.

National Association of Trailer Manufacturers *(1988)*
1320 S.W. Topeka Blvd.
Topeka, KS 66612-1817
Tel: (785)272-4433 *Fax:* (785)272-4455
E-Mail: natmhq@natm.com
Web Site: www.natm.com
Members: 834 companies
Staff: 9
Annual Budget: $1-2,000,000
Executive Director: Pam O'Toole

Historical Note
Formerly (1992) National Association of Livestock Trailer Manufacturers. Membership: Regular $700/year, Associate $600/year.

Meetings/Conferences:
Annual Meetings: usually Winter
2007 – Orlando, FL(Coronado Springs Resort)/Jan. 29-Feb. 2

Publications:
Guidelines for Trailers.
Membership Directory and Buyer's Guide. a. adv.
Tracks. bi-m. adv.

National Association of Tribal Court Personnel *(1980)*

Historical Note
Address unknown in 2006.

National Association of Unclaimed Property Administrators *(1962)*
c/o NAST, P.O. Box 11910
Lexington, KY 40578-1910

Tel: (859)244-8150 *Fax:* (859)244-8053
E-Mail: naupa@csg.org
Web Site: www.unclaimed.org
Members: 53 state offices
Staff: 1
Annual Budget: $100-250,000
Association Manager: David D. Milby

Historical Note
Formerly (1980) the Association of Unclaimed Property Administrators. NAUPA members are state officials who administer escheat and unclaimed property programs. Facilitates transfer of unclaimed properties to their appropriate jurisdictions. Administrative support for NAUPA is provided by Council of State Governments (same address). Membership: $200/year.

Meetings/Conferences:
Annual Meetings: Fall

Publications:
Quick Reference Packet. a.
NAUPA News Newsletter. q.

National Association of Underwater Instructors *(1960)*
P.O. Box 89789
Tampa, FL 33689-0413
Tel: (813)628-6284 *Fax:* (813)628-8253
Toll Free: (800)553 - 6284
E-Mail: nauihq@nauiww.org
Web Site: www.naui.org
Members: 10500 individuals
Staff: 30
Annual Budget: $2-5,000,000
President: Jim Bram
Vice President, Finance and Operations: Carolyn Robertson

Historical Note
Certified instructors of basic, advanced, and specialized courses in underwater diving. Offers instructor certification programs and training programs. Affiliated with the National Safety Council, National Boating Council, American Red Cross and Underwater Society of America. Membership: $120/year (individual).

Meetings/Conferences:
Semi-annual Meetings: Spring and Fall

Publications:
Sources: The Journal of Underwater Education. bi-m. adv.

National Association of Uniform Manufacturers and Distributors *(1932)*
16 E. 41st St.,
Suite 700
New York, NY 10017
Tel: (212)869-0670 Ext: 205 *Fax:* (212)575-2847
E-Mail: rjlerman@naumd.com
Web Site: www.naumd.com
Members: 475 companies
Staff: 4
Annual Budget: $500-1,000,000
President: Richard J. Lerman
E-Mail: rjlerman@naumd.com

Historical Note
Members are manufacturers of uniforms, mills, fibre producers, and dealers. Membership: $350-2,650/year (organization, depending on size).

Meetings/Conferences:
2007 – Atlanta, GA(Hilton)/Apr. 13-17
2008 – Nashville, TN(Opryland)/March 27-Apr. 1

Publications:
FYI NAUMD. m. adv.
Official Guide. a. adv.
This Month (Fax Burst). m. adv.

National Association of University Fisheries and Wildlife Programs *(1991)*
Clemson Univ., Forestry and Natural Resources Dept.
G08A Lehotsky Hall, P.O. Box 340362
Clemson, SC 29634-0362
Tel: (864)656-5333 *Fax:* (864)656-5332
Web Site: www.naufwp.iastate.edu
Members: 55 university programs
Annual Budget: $25-50,000
President: John R. Sweeney

Historical Note
NAUFWP members are administrators of fisheries and wildlife programs in colleges/universities. NAUFWP aims to strengthen fisheries and wildlife education, research, public service and outreach, and international programs at the university level. Has no paid officers or full-time staff. Membershp: $500/year (institution); $100/year (associate).

Meetings/Conferences:
Semi-Annual Meetings: Spring/Fall

National Association of Urban Hospitals *(1993)*
21351 Gentry Dr.
Suite 210
Sterling, VA 20166
Tel: (703)444-0989 *Fax:* (703)444-3029
E-Mail: ellen@nauh.org
Web Site: www.nauh.org
Executive Director: Ellen J. Kugler

Historical Note
Founded as National Association of Urban Critical Access Hospitals; assumed its current name in 1998. NAUH focuses on Medicare/Medicaid reimbursement and related issues on behalf of its member hospitals.

National Association of VA Physicians and Dentists *(1975)*
11 Canal Center Plaza, Suite 110
Alexandria, VA 22314
Tel: (703)548-0280 *Fax:* (703)683-7939
E-Mail: navapd@aol.com
Web Site: www.navapd.org
Members: 2000 individuals
Staff: 1
Annual Budget: $250-500,000
Executive Director: C. William Booher

Historical Note
Membership: $150/year.

Publications:
NAVAPD Notes. bi-m.
NAVAPD News. bi-m. adv.
Capitol Beat Online.

National Association of Vertical Transportation Professionals *(1990)*
2107 Pogue Ave.
Cincinnati, OH 45208
Tel: (513)533-3500 *Fax:* (513)533-3504
Web Site: www.navtp.org
Members: 100 companies
Annual Budget: $50-100,000

Historical Note
NAVTP members are engineers and other professionals specializing in elevator and escalator design. Membership: $250/year.

Publications:
View From the Penthouse. 3/year.

National Association of Veterans Program Administrators *(1975)*
2020 Pennsylvania Ave. NW
Suite 1975
Washington, DC 20006-1846
Tel: (202)392-6822
E-Mail: navpa@mnstate.edu
Web Site: www.navpa.org
Members: 500 individuals
Annual Budget: $25-50,000
Director, Membership: Jack Mordente
E-Mail: navpa@mnstate.edu

Historical Note
Members are coordinators of veterans programs on college campuses. Concerned with administering and preserving the educational benefits promised by the military to service persons upon their enlistment. Membership: $30/year (individual and associate) $50/year (organization).

Meetings/Conferences:
Annual Meetings: Last week in October/250

Publications:
NAVPA Newsletter. Semi-a.

National Association of Veterans' Research and Education Foundations *(1992)*
5480 Wisconsin Ave., Suite 214
Chevy Chase, MD 20815
Tel: (301)656-5005 *Fax:* (301)656-5008
E-Mail: navref@navref.org
Web Site: www.navref.org
Members: 85 organizations
Staff: 3
Annual Budget: $250-500,000
Executive Director: Barbara F. West

Historical Note
NAVREF is the national association of nonprofit research and education foundations affiliated with the U.S. Department of Veterans Affairs (DVA) Medical Centers. Membership: 0.5% of annual revenues (organization).

Publications:
NAVREF Newsletter. q.

National Association of Video Distributors *(1981)*
1092 N. Forest Oak
Henderson, KY 42420
Tel: (270)826-9423 *Fax:* (270)826-9424
Members: 35 companies
Staff: 2
Annual Budget: $250-500,000
Executive Director: Bill Burton

Historical Note
Members are wholesale distributors of home video software; associate members are manufacturers of such goods.

Meetings/Conferences:
Annual Meetings: April-May/300

National Association of Vision Professionals *(1976)*
1775 Church St. NW
Washington, DC 20036
Tel: (202)234-1010 *Fax:* (202)234-1020
Web Site: www.visionpros.org
Members: 100 individuals
Staff: 6
Annual Budget: $25-50,000
President: Michelle D. Hartlove

Historical Note
Formerly (1985) National Association of Vision Program Consultants. Members are professionals in the field of eye health and safety. Has no paid staff. Membership: $35/year.

Meetings/Conferences:
Annual Meetings: August

Publications:
Newsletter. q.

National Association of Wastewater Transporters *(1983)*
336 Chestnut Ln.
Ambler, PA 19002
Tel: (215)643-6798 *Fax:* (267)200-0279
Toll Free: (800)236 - 6298
E-Mail: info@nawt.org
Web Site: www.nawt.org
Members: 500 individuals
Staff: 3
Annual Budget: $50-100,000
Executive Director: Tom Ferrero
E-Mail: info@nawt.org

Historical Note
Membership: $150/year (individual member); $300/year (member company).

Meetings/Conferences:
Annual Meetings: Winter/usually Nashville, TN
2007 – Nashville, TN(Opryland)/Feb. 7-10

Publications:
NAWT News. q.

National Association of Water Companies *(1895)*
1725 K St. NW
Suite 200
Washington, DC 20006
Tel: (202)833-8383 *Fax:* (202)331-7442
Web Site: www.nawc.org
Members: 130 companies
Staff: 7
Annual Budget: $2-5,000,000
Executive Director: Peter L. Cook
Deputy Executive Director, State Relations: Sharon L. Gascon

Director, Administration and Membership: Michael J. Horner

Senior Director, Government and Public Relations: Louis J. Jenny

Historical Note

Established July 30, 1895, at a meeting in Cressona Springs, Pennsylvania, as the Pennsylvania Water Works Association. Became the Eastern Water Company Conference in 1959, and in 1963 the National Water Company Conference. Adopted its present name in 1971. Sponsors the National Association of Water Companies Political Action Committee (NAWC/PAC). Membership: dues vary by company.

Meetings/Conferences:

Annual Meetings: October

Publications:

Newsflow. q.
Water Currents.

National Association of Waterfront Employers *(1933)*

2011 Pennsylvania Ave. NW
Suite 301
Washington, DC 20006
Tel: (202)296-2810 *Fax:* (202)331-7479
Members: 25 companies
Staff: 3
Annual Budget: $250-500,000
Executive Director and General Counsel: Charles T. Carroll, Jr.
Assistant General Counsel: F.E. Froelich
Manager, Meetings: Elaine Tendler

Historical Note

Formerly (1993) National Association of Stevedores. Members are privately owned stevedore contractors, marine terminal operators, and other waterfront-activity employers.

National Association of Waterproofing and Structural Repair Contractors *(1981)*

8015 Corporate Dr., Suite A
Baltimore, MD 21236
Tel: (410)931-3332 *Fax:* (410)931-2060
Toll Free: (800)245 - 6292
E-Mail: info@nawsrc.org
Web Site: www.nawsrc.org
Members: 180 companies
Staff: 2
Annual Budget: $50-100,000
Executive Director: Claudia J. Clemons

Historical Note

Formerly (2000) National Association of Waterproofing Contractors. Established to promote ethical business standards and to improve communication in the waterproofing and structural repair industry. Membership $795/year.

Meetings/Conferences:

Annual Meetings: Fall

Publications:

NAWSRC Foundation News. m. adv.

National Association of Wheat Growers *(1950)*

415 Second St. NE
Suite 300
Washington, DC 20002
Tel: (202)547-7800 *Fax:* (202)546-2638
E-Mail: wheatworld@wheatworld.org
Web Site: www.wheatworld.org
Members: 25000 individuals
Staff: 6
Annual Budget: $1-2,000,000
Chief Executive Officer: Daren Coppock
Government Affairs: Mark Gaede

Historical Note

A non-profit federation of state wheat organizations. Sponsors and supports the National Association of Wheat Growers Foundation and the NAWG Political Action Committee (Wheat-PAC). Membership: $50/year (individual), $2,000/year (company).

Meetings/Conferences:

Annual Meetings: January

Publications:

Report from Washington. w.

National Association of Wholesaler-Distributors *(1946)*

1725 K St. NW
Suite 300
Washington, DC 20006-1419
Tel: (202)872-0885 *Fax:* (202)785-0586
E-Mail: naw@nawd.org
Web Site: www.nawd.org/
Members: 18536companies, 166associations
Staff: 40
Annual Budget: $5-10,000,000
President: Dirk Van Dongen
Senior Vice President, Corporate Relations: Carl Farr
Chief Information Officer: Ed Joynes
Senior Vice President, Strategic Directions: Ron Schreibman, CAE
Senior Vice President, Government Relations: Jade West

Historical Note

Established as the National Association of Wholesalers by a group of leading wholesaler-distributor trade associations that specialized in a particular product such as auto parts, drugs, lumber, food, or tobacco. Assumed its present name in 1970. A federation of national, state and local wholesaler associations, together with individual wholesalers. Supports the Wholesaler-Distributor Political Action Committe (WDPAC). Maintains the Distribution Research and Education Foundation and the NAW Service Corporation. Has an annual budget of approximately $6.0 million

Meetings/Conferences:

Annual Meetings: Winter

Publications:

NAW Report. 8/year.

National Association of Women Artists *(1889)*

80 Fifth St., Suite 1405
New York, NY 10011
Tel: (212)675-1616 *Fax:* (212)675-1616
E-Mail: info@nawanet.org
Web Site: www.nawanet.org
Members: 800 individuals
Staff: 3
Annual Budget: $50-100,000
Executive Director: Linda Pederson

Historical Note

Established in 1889 as the Women's Art Club of the City of New York. NAWA is a non-profit, non-political member-supported art association for women in the fine arts. Its purpose is to serve as a forum for members by seeking exhibition space and creating opportunities for its painters, printmakers and sculptors. Provides free cultural/educational programs to the public. Holds an annual exhibition of members' works in New York City in Spring. Sponsors group traveling art shows of works by members, shown both in the U.S. and abroad. Membership: $52/year (individual).

Meetings/Conferences:

Semi-annual Meetings: May and November/usually New York, NY

Publications:

Exhibition Catalog. a. adv.
Newsletter. 2/year.

National Association of Women Business Owners *(1974)*

8405 Greensboro Dr., Suite 800
McLean, VA 22102
Toll Free: (800)556 - 2926
E-Mail: national@nawbo.org
Web Site: www.nawbo.org
Members: 8000 individuals
Staff: 6
Annual Budget: $1-2,000,000
Executive Director: Erin M. Fuller, CAE

Historical Note

Established in Washington, D.C., as the Association of Women Business Owners; assumed its present name in 1976. NAWBO exists to provide education and training to its members, to promote business ownership by women and to serve as a forum through which women can establish themselves in the business world. An affiliate, National Foundation for Women Business Owners (same address), provides research, consulting, and leadership development programs. Membership: $75/year, plus chapter dues.

Meetings/Conferences:

Annual Meetings: Public Policy Days/250

Publications:

Leader Bulletin. bi-m.
NAWBO Time. bi-m.

National Association of Women Highway Safety Leaders *(1967)*

2743 N. Albany
Chicago, IL 60647
Tel: (773)384-2279 *Fax:* (773)278-7135
E-Mail: safety_leaders@yahoo.com
Web Site: www.nawhsl.org
Members: 100000 individuals
Staff: 2
Annual Budget: $100-250,000
Executive Director: Judy Keippel
E-Mail: safety_leaders@yahoo.com

Historical Note

Promotes safety belt usage, alcohol and drug education, child passenger seats, car care, gasoline saving tips, motorcycle safety, police enforcement, highway environment, traffic court improvement, mature driver safety, and high school driver education.

Publications:

President's Newsletter. q.
NAWHSL Newsletter. q.
Serving Safety. q.
News from NAWHSL. q.
Regional Director's Newsletter. m.
State Representatives Newsletter. irreg.
National News. q.

National Association of Women in Construction *(1955)*

327 S. Adams St.
Ft. Worth, TX 76104-1002
Tel: (817)877-5551 *Fax:* (817)877-0324
Toll Free: (800)552 - 3506
E-Mail: dedeh@nawic.org
Web Site: www.nawic.org
Members: 6200 individuals
Staff: 9
Annual Budget: $500-1,000,000
Executive Vice President: Dede Hughes
E-Mail: dedeh@nawic.org
Director, Conventions: Shelly Reeves
Director, Communications: Kara Roberson

Historical Note

NAWIC members hold diverse positions within the construction industry, including as architects, owners, estimators, accountants and tradeswomen. NAWIC encourages continuing education within the industry and for students to promote interest. Membership: $90/year (national dues plus additional chapter dues).

Meetings/Conferences:

Annual Meetings: Fall
2007 – Orlando, FL(Caribe Royale)/Sept. 5-8/600
2008 – New Orleans, LA(Hyatt Regency)/Sept. 3-6/600
2009 – Phoenix, AZ(JW Marriott Desert Ridge Resort)/Aug. 26-29/600

Publications:

NAWIC Image. bi-m. adv.

National Association of Women Judges *(1979)*

1112 16th St. NW
Suite 520
Washington, DC 20036
Tel: (202)393-0222 *Fax:* (202)393-0125
E-Mail: nawj@nawj.org
Web Site: www.nawj.org
Members: 1200 individuals
Staff: 5
Annual Budget: $500-1,000,000
Executive Director: Drucilla S. Ramey
Director, Operations: Jeffrey Groton

Historical Note

Organized in Los Angeles, October 28, 1979. Membership: $175/year (voting members); $150/year (first-time, associate, retired, and amicus judicii members).

Meetings/Conferences:

Annual Meetings: October/250

Publications:
NAWJ Counterbalance. 3/year.

National Association of Women Lawyers *(1899)*
321 N. Clark St.
Chicago, IL 60610
Tel: (312)988-6186 *Fax:* (312)988-5491
E-Mail: nawl@nawl.org
Web Site: www.nawl.org
Members: 2000 individuals
Staff: 4
Executive Director: Dr. Stacie I. Strong
E-Mail: strongs@nawl.org

Historical Note
Founded in 1899 as the Women Lawyers Club. Reorganized in 1911 as the National Association of Women Lawyers. Membership: $45-80/year (individual); no fee for students.

Meetings/Conferences:
Semi-Annual Meetings: February and August, with American Bar Ass'n
2007 – San Francisco, CA/August

Publications:
NAWL Newsletter. m.
Women Lawyers Journal. 4/year. adv.
Nat'l Directory of Women-Owned Law Firms & Women Lawyers. a. adv.

National Association of Workforce Boards *(1979)*
1701 K St. NW
Suite 1000
Washington, DC 20006
Tel: (202)775-0960 *Fax:* (202)775-0330
E-Mail: nawb@nawb.org
Web Site: www.nawb.org
Members: 500 councils
Staff: 10
Annual Budget: $250-500,000
Chief Executive Officer: Stephanie J. Powers

Historical Note
Founded as National Association of Private Industry Councils and assumed its current name in 1999. Private industry councils and private employers concerned with employment and training policies in the context of economic development and education. Membership: $150-600/year.

Meetings/Conferences:
Annual Meetings: February

Publications:
NAWB Reports To Workforce Advisor. q.

National Association of Workforce Development Professionals *(1989)*
810 First St. NE
Suite 525
Washington, DC 20002-4227
Tel: (202)589-1790
E-Mail: nawdp@aol.com
Web Site: www.nawdp.org
Members: 4500 individuals
Staff: 2
Annual Budget: $500-1,000,000
President: C. Paul Mendez
Manager, Membership and Certification: Tracy Holt
E-Mail: nawdp@aol.com

Historical Note
NAWDP is an national association for individual practitioners who work in workforce development programs. Mission is to be the national voice for the profession and meet the individual professional development needs of its membership. Membership: $50/year (individual).

Meetings/Conferences:
Annual Meetings: Spring
2007 – Reno, NV(Nuggett)/May 20-23
2008 – Virginia Beach, VA

Publications:
Journal of Workforce Development. 2/yr.
NAWDP Advantage. m. adv.

National Association of Youth Clubs *(1930)*

Historical Note
NAYC is the youth development arm of the Nat'l Ass'n of Colored Women's Clubs, which provides administrative support.

National Athletic Trainers' Association *(1950)*
2952 N. Stemmons Fwy., Suite 200
Dallas, TX 75247-6916
Tel: (214)637-6282 *Fax:* (214)637-2206
Web Site: www.nata.org
Members: 30000 individuals
Staff: 35
Annual Budget: $5-10,000,000
Executive Director: Eve Becker-Doyle, CAE
Director, External Affairs: Cate Brennan Lisak
Director, Internal Marketing: Larry Commons
Director, Accounting: Linda Tilley
Director, Membership/MIS: Sandy Ward
Assistant Executive Director: Teresa Foster Welch

Historical Note
NATA members are athletic trainers working in high schools, colleges, clinics, industry, hospitals and professional sports teams. Membership is also open to those individuals whose interests are related to sports medicine, such as doctors, and to corporations and businesses that sell or manufacture sports medicine products. Membership: $115/year, plus district; $65/year (student).

Meetings/Conferences:
Annual Meetings: During last two weeks in June

Publications:
Journal of Athletic Training. q. adv.
NATA News. m. adv.

National Auctioneers Association *(1949)*
8880 Ballentine St.
Overland Park, KS 66214-1985
Tel: (913)541-8084 *Fax:* (913)894-5281
Toll Free: (888)541 - 8084
E-Mail: hq@auctioneers.org
Web Site: www.auctioneers.org
Members: 5870 individuals
Staff: 13
Annual Budget: $500-1,000,000
C.A.E., Chief Executive Officer: Robert A. Shively
Director, Education: Harlan Rimmerman, Ph.D.

Historical Note
Provides continuing education and ethical standards for the practice of auctioneering. Absorbed Auction Marketing Institute in 2003. Membership: $250/year.

Meetings/Conferences:
Annual Meetings: July

Publications:
The Auctioneer. m. adv.
Auction World. m. adv.

National Auto Auction Association *(1945)*
5320-D Spectrum Dr.
Frederick, MD 21703
Tel: (301)696-0400 *Fax:* (301)631-1359
E-Mail: naaa@naaa.com
Web Site: www.naaa.com
Members: 365 companies, 105 associates
Staff: 6
Annual Budget: $2-5,000,000
Executive Director: Frank Hackett
E-Mail: hackett@naaa.com
Manager, Meetings: Kelly Beach

Historical Note
NAAA represents dealers auto auctions, held in a permanent location on a regular weekly schedule. Promotes exchange of ideas and works in public relations in the used car merchandising industry. Members are from 18 countries and handle approximately 15 million vehicles per year. Membership: $800-2,200/year (organization/company).

Meetings/Conferences:
Annual Meetings: September/October
2007 – Chicago, IL(Hilton Chicago)/Sept. 17-22/1400
2008 – Washington, DC(Wardman Park Marriott)/September/1400

Publications:
Industry Standards.
Auction Industry History.
On the Block. q.
Membership Directory. a.

National Automatic Merchandising Association *(1936)*
20 N. Wacker Dr., Suite 3500
Chicago, IL 60606-3102
Tel: (312)346-0370 *Fax:* (312)704-4140
Web Site: www.vending.org
Members: 2500 companies
Staff: 30
Annual Budget: $2-5,000,000
President and Chief Executive Officer: Richard M. Geerdes
E-Mail: rgeerdes@vending.org
Director, Tradeshows and Allied Membership: Stuart Aizenberq, CEM
E-Mail: saizenberg@vending.org
Director, Government Affairs and Counsel: Brian B. Allan
E-Mail: ballen@vending.org
Chief Financial Officer and Assistant Secretary/Treasurer: Patrick Caffarelli
E-Mail: pcaffarelli@vending.org
Manager, Sales and Sevices: Rachel E. Campbell
Senior Director, Technical Services: Larry M. Eils
E-Mail: leils@vending.org
Vice President, Membership: Dean R. Gilland
Senior Vice President and Chief Operating Officer: Dan Mathews
Manager, Meeting Services: Barbara M. Moll
Director, Education and Meeting Services: Lynae Schleyer, C.M.P.
E-Mail: lschleyer@vending.org

Historical Note
Members are makers and operators of automatic vending equipment, contract food service management, and office coffee service industry in collaboration with the providers of products and services to the vending industry. Programs in health, safety and standards, public relations, employee relations and training, education, accounting, and statistics comprise some of NAMA's other services. Sponsors and supports the NAMA Political Action Committee and the MSU Endowed Professorship.

Meetings/Conferences:
Semi-annual meetings: Spring and Fall

Publications:
In Touch Newsletter. q.
Security Newsletter. q.
Directory of Members. a.
Quarterly Labor Relations Report. q.

National Automobile Dealers Association *(1917)*
8400 Westpark Dr.
McLean, VA 22102
Tel: (703)821-7000 *Fax:* (703)821-7075
Toll Free: (800)252 - 6232
E-Mail: nadainfo@nada.org
Web Site: www.nada.org
Members: 19500 individuals
Staff: 450
Annual Budget: $10-25,000,000
President: Phillip D. Brady
Vice President and Chief Financial Officer: Joseph L. Cowden
Chief Public Affairs Officer: David F. Hyatt
Executive Vice President and Chief Administrative Officer: Bruce M. Kelliher
Vice President and General Counsel: Andrew Koblenz
Director, Human Resources: Lisa Maghraoui
Executive Director and Associate General Counsel: James Minnis
Executive Director, Conventions and Expositions: Stephen R. Pitt
Executive Director, Legislative Affairs: Ivette Rivera
Executive Director, Publications: Marc H. Stertz

Historical Note
Organized in Chicago, June 10-11, 1917 as the result of the U.S. entry into World War I and a proposed luxury tax of 5% on automobiles. Incorporated in Illinois the same year, NADA represents dealers franchised by manufacturers and importers to sell and service new cars and trucks. Affiliated with National Automobile Dealers Association Used Car Guide Company. Connected with the Dealers Election Action Committee and the National Automobile Dealers Charitable Foundation. The American Truck Dealers Association is a division of the NADA.

Meetings/Conferences:
Annual Meetings: Winter
2007 – Las Vegas, NV/Feb. 9-12

2008 – San Francisco, CA/Feb. 9-12

Publications:
Dealer's Resource Locator (online).
Auto Ex. m. adv.
NADA Official Used Car Guide. m.

National Automobile Transporters Association *(1934)*

Historical Note
NATA members transport motor vehicles from assembly plants, railheads and seaports to dealers in the U.S. and Canada by both "truckaway" and "driveaway." Administrative support provided by American Trucking Associations (same address).

National Automotive Finance Association *(1996)*
P.O. Box 383
Linthicum, MD 21090
Tel: (410)712-4036 *Fax:* (410)712-4038
Toll Free: (800)463 - 8955
E-Mail: information@nafassociation.com
Web Site: www.nafassociation.com
Members: 85
Staff: 2
Annual Budget: $250-500,000
Executive Director: Jack Tracey, CAE

Historical Note
NAF Association serves companies and professionals in the non-prime auto lending industry.

National Automotive Radiator Service Association *(1954)*
17000 Commerce Pkwy., Suite C
Mt. Laurel, NJ 08054
Tel: (856)439-1575 *Fax:* (856)439-9596
Toll Free: (800)551 - 3232
E-Mail: info@narsa.org
Web Site: www.narsa.org
Members: 1500 individuals
Staff: 10
Annual Budget: $1-2,000,000
Executive Director: Michael R. Dwyer

Historical Note
Founded to promote the interests of radiator repair shop owners, NARSA acts as an educational industry forum for cooling system specialists, shops, and allied industries. Headquarters street address: 2767 Geryville Pike, Pennsburg, PA 18073. Membership: $575-$2300/year (associate); $150-350/year (shop member); $35/year (retired).

Meetings/Conferences:
Annual Meetings: Spring/2,000

Publications:
NARSA Legal Reports. q.
Automotive Cooling Journal. m. adv.
NARSA Radiator Reporter. m.

National Ballroom and Entertainment Association *(1947)*
2799 Locust Rd.
Decorah, IA 52101-7600
Tel: (563)382-3871
E-Mail: nbea@oneota.net
Web Site: www.nbea.com
Members: 400 individuals
Staff: 1
Annual Budget: $10-25,000
Executive Director: John Matter

Historical Note
The NBEA's origins go back to the late 1930s when a state organization was formed to work out mutual problems of the ballroom industry. In 1941 this became the Midwestern Ballroom Operators Association and, in 1948, the National Ballroom Operators Association. In 1970 the name was changed to the Entertainment Operators of America; present name was adopted in 1976. Membership is open to anyone operating a ballroom or dance establishment featuring live music for public dancing. Members include band leaders, agents, and dance instructors. Membership: $125/year (individual).

Publications:
Newsletter. q. adv.

National Band Association *(1960)*
118 College Dr., Suite 5032
Hattiesburg, MS 39406
Tel: (601)297-8168 *Fax:* (601)266-6185
E-Mail: info@nationalbandassociation.org
Web Site: www.nationalbandassociation.org
Members: 3000 individuals
Staff: 1
Annual Budget: $50-100,000
Executive Secretary: Thomas V. Fraschillo

Historical Note
Members are band directors, music teachers, musical instrument makers and others interested in band development. Affiliated with the Music Educators National Conference. Membership: $45/year (individual), $55/year (institution & international); $120/year (corporate).

Meetings/Conferences:
Biennial Meetings: Even years

Publications:
Journal. 3/year.
NBA Newsletter. 3/year.

National Bankers Association *(1927)*
1513 P St. NW
Washington, DC 20005
Tel: (202)588-5432 *Fax:* (202)588-5443
Web Site: www.nationalbankers.org
Members: 52 banks
Staff: 4
Annual Budget: $500-1,000,000
President: Norma A. Hart

Historical Note
Formerly (1951) National Negro Bankers Association. Members are minority and women's banking institutions, minority individuals employed by majority banks and majority institutions. Membership: Institutional (minority bank) based on assets; Associate (minority individual employed in a majority bank) $250/year; Affiliate (majority institution) $2,000/year.

Publications:
NBA Monitor. q.
NBA Today. a. adv.

National Bar Association *(1925)*
1225 11th St. NW
Washington, DC 20001-4217
Tel: (202)842-3900 *Fax:* (202)289-6170
E-Mail: headquarters@nationalbar.org
Web Site: www.nationalbar.org
Members: 18000 individuals
Staff: 10
Annual Budget: $1-2,000,000
Executive Director: John L. Crump, CMP, CAE
E-Mail: jcrumpnba@aol.com

Historical Note
The National Bar Association is the oldest and largest organization consisting primarily of black attorneys in the U.S. It is the principal advocate for the interests of black lawyers, judges, and law students. Membership: $75-300/year.

Meetings/Conferences:
Annual Meetings: Summer

Publications:
NBA Magazine. 3/yr. adv.

National Barbecue Association *(1991)*
1306-A W. Anderson Ln.
Austin, TX 78757-1454
Tel: (512)454-8626 *Fax:* (512)454-3036
Toll Free: (888)909 - 2121
E-Mail: nbbqa@assnmgmt.com
Web Site: www.nbbqa.org
Members: 625 individuals and companies
Staff: 3
Annual Budget: $100-250,000
Executive Vice President: Don R. McCullough, CAE

Historical Note
Represents manufacturers of barbecue equipment, products, and supplies, as well as professional barbecuers, food industry professionals in barbecue, and barbecue enthusiasts. Membership: $50/year (individual); $150/year (company).

Meetings/Conferences:
Annual Meetings: Spring
2007 – Raleigh, NC(Hilton North)/Feb. 14-17/1500

Publications:
Barbecue Buyers Guide. a. adv.
Center Section National BBQ News. m.. adv.

National Barrel Horse Association
725 Broad St.
P.O. Box 1988
Augusta, GA 30903-1988
Tel: (706)722-7223 *Fax:* (706)828-3909
E-Mail: nbha@nbha.com
Web Site: www.nbha.com
Members: 24000
Executive Director: Sherry Fulmer
E-Mail: rhardy@nbha.com
Director, Member Services: Rick Hardy

National Basketball Association *(1946)*
645 Fifth Ave., 15th Floor
New York, NY 10022
Tel: (212)407-8000 *Fax:* (212)826-6197
E-Mail: bmcintyre@nba.com
Web Site: www.nba.com
Members: 29 clubs
Staff: 800
Annual Budget: $5-10,000,000
Commissioner: David Stern
E-Mail: bmcintyre@nba.com

Historical Note
The association that administers the principal professional basketball league in the United States.

Meetings/Conferences:
Annual Meetings: September

Publications:
NBA Encyclopedia. trien.
Hoop. m.
Guide. a.
Register. a.

National Basketball Athletic Trainers Association *(1974)*
400 Colony Square, Suite 1750
Atlanta, GA 30361
Tel: (404)875-4000 Ext: 1 *Fax:* (404)892-8560
Web Site: www.nbata.com
Members: 56 individuals
Annual Budget: $50-100,000
General Counsel: Rollin E. Mallernee, II

Historical Note
A satellite of the National Athletic Trainers' Association. NBTA is a professional association composed of all head and assistant athletic trainers in the NBA. Membership: $750/year.

Meetings/Conferences:
Annual Meetings: Always Orlando, FL/June, in conjunction with NBA combine

National Basketball Players Association *(1954)*
Two Penn Plaza, Suite 2430
New York, NY 10121
Tel: (212)655-0880 *Fax:* (212)655-0881
E-Mail: info@nbpa.com
Web Site: www.nbpa.com
Members: 420 individuals
Staff: 20
Annual Budget: $2-5,000,000
Executive Director: G. William Hunter

Historical Note
Independent labor union. Membership: $5,000/year.

Meetings/Conferences:
Semi-Annual Meetings: February and September

Publications:
Time out. q.

National Basketball Referees Association *(1977)*
c/o Perennial Strategy Group
1455 Pennsylvania Ave. NW, Suite 225
Washington, DC 20004
Tel: (202)638-5090 *Fax:* (202)638-5564
Web Site: http://probasketballrefs.com
Members: 60 individuals
Staff: 5
Annual Budget: $10-25,000
Spokesperson: Lamell J. McMorris

Historical Note
Formerly (1993) National Association of Basketball Referees. An independent union of professional basketball referees. Conducts basketball camps.

National Beauty Culturists' League *(1919)*
25 Logan Circle, NW
Washington, DC 20005
Tel: (202)332-2695 *Fax:* (202)332-0940
E-Mail: info@nbcl.org
Web Site: www.nbcl.org
Members: 10000 individuals
Staff: 2
President: Dr. Katie B. Catalon

Historical Note
Established as the National Hair System Culture League, it assumed its present name in 1920. Members are black beauticians and cosmetologists who embrace diversity.

Meetings/Conferences:
Annual Meetings: Summer

National Bed and Breakfast Association *(1981)*
P.O. Box 332
Norwalk, CT 06852
Tel: (203)847-6196 *Fax:* (203)847-0469
E-Mail: administrator@nbba.org
Web Site: www.nbba.com
Members: 2000 facilities
Staff: 11
Annual Budget: $10-25,000
President: Phyllis Featherston

Historical Note
Membership includes individual B & B homes and inns in the U.S., Canada, Bermuda, Puerto Rico, and the U.S. Virgin Islands. Membership: $155/year.

Meetings/Conferences:
Annual Meetings: None held.

Publications:
Official Bed and Breakfast Guide for the U.S., Canada and the Caribbean. bien. adv.

National Beer Wholesalers Association *(1938)*
1101 King St., Suite 600
Alexandria, VA 22314-2944
Tel: (703)683-4300 *Fax:* (703)683-8965
E-Mail: info@nbwa.org
Web Site: www.nbwa.org
Members: 1850 beer wholesalers
Staff: 23
Annual Budget: $5-10,000,000
President: Craig Purser, CAE
Director, Political Affairs: Linda Auglis
Director, Conventions and Meetings: Patricia Rouzie
Vice President, Public Affairs: Michelle Semones

Historical Note
Represents the independent wholesaling segment of the U.S. malt beverage industry. Sponsors and supports the National Beer Wholesalers Association Political Action Committee. Membership: fees proportional to member company's annual sales.

Meetings/Conferences:
Annual Meetings: Fall

Publications:
NBWA Beer Perspectives. bi-w.
NBWA Handbook. a.
Distributor Productivity Report. bi-a.
Compensation & Benefits Study. bi-a.

National Bicycle Dealers Association *(1946)*
777 W. 19th St., Suite O
Costa Mesa, CA 92627
Tel: (949)722-6909 *Fax:* (949)722-1747
E-Mail: info@nbda.com
Web Site: www.nbda.com
Members: 1200 dealers
Staff: 2
Executive Director: Fred Clements
Director, Marketing and Communications: Mike Baker

Historical Note
Trade association of independent bicycle dealers. Manufacturers and distributors are eligible for associate membership. Membership: $100/year (dealer); $225/year (associate).

Meetings/Conferences:
Semi-Annual Meetings:

Publications:
Outspokin'. m.

National Bio-Energy Industries Association *(1979)*

Historical Note
Absorbed by Solar Energy Industries Ass'n

National Bison Association
1400 W. 122nd Ave.
Westminster, CO 80234
Tel: (303)292-2833 *Fax:* (303)292-2564
Web Site: www.bisoncentral.com
Members: 1500 individuals
Staff: 4
Annual Budget: $500-1,000,000
Executive Director: Dave Carter
E-Mail: david@bisoncentral.com

Historical Note
Formerly (1965) the National Buffalo Association and (1975) American Bison Association. Members are producers and marketers of buffalo products; their purpose is to promote and preserve the American Bison. Absorbed National Buffalo Association in 1994. Membership: $150/year (full member), $125/year (associate).

Meetings/Conferences:
Annual Meetings: Winter

Publications:
Bison World Magazine. q. adv.

National Black Association for Speech, Language and Hearing *(1978)*
800 Perry Hwy., Suite Three
Pittsburgh, PA 15229
Tel: (412)366-1117 *Fax:* (412)366-8804
E-Mail: NBASLH@nbaslh.org
Web Site: http://nbaslh.org
Members: 400 individuals
Annual Budget: $50-100,000
Treasurer: Constance Dean Qualls, Ph.D.

Historical Note
Addresses the specific needs, concerns, and interests of African American students studying in the profession, practicing professionals, and consumers with communication disorders. Has no apid officers or full-time staff.Membership: $60/year (individual).

Publications:
Resound newsletter. semi-a.
Echo E-Journal. semi-a. adv.

National Black Caucus of Local Elected Officials *(1970)*

Historical Note
A affiliate of National League of Cities, which provides administrative support.

National Black Caucus of State Legislators *(1977)*
444 N. Capitol St. NW
Suite 622
Washington, DC 20001
Tel: (202)624-5457 *Fax:* (202)508-3826
E-Mail: staff@nbcsl.com
Web Site: www.nbcsl.com
Members: 600 individuals
Staff: 6
Annual Budget: $500-1,000,000
Executive Director: LaKimba D.S. Walker
E-Mail: staff@nbcsl.com

Historical Note
Promotes and sponsors training and education for its members on issues and potential legislation which may affect African-American constituencies within their jurisdictions. Membership includes individuals in the U.S. Virgin Islands and the District of Columbia. Membership: $100/year.

Meetings/Conferences:
Annual Meetings: Winter

Publications:
Legislator Newsletter. q. adv.
Directory of Black State Legislators. bien.
NBCSL Public Policy Document. a.

National Black Chamber of Commerce *(1993)*
1350 Connecticut Ave. NW
Suite 405
Washington, DC 20036
Tel: (202)466-6888 *Fax:* (202)466-4918
E-Mail: info@nationalbcc.org
Web Site: www.nationalbcc.org
Members: 62000 individuals
Staff: 12
Annual Budget: $1-2,000,000
President and Chief Executive Officer: Harry Alford
E-Mail: halford@nationalbcc.org

Historical Note
NBCC is dedicated to the economic empowerment of African American communities.

Publications:
State of Black Business. a.
How to Start A Chamber. a.
Financial Resources Guide. a.
Newsletter. q.

National Black Coalition of Federal Aviation Employees *(1976)*

Historical Note
Address unknown in 2004.

National Black MBA Association *(1970)*
180 N. Michigan Ave.
Chicago, IL 60601
Tel: (312)236-2622 *Fax:* (312)236-0390
E-Mail: mail@nbmbaa.org
Web Site: www.nbmbaa.org
Members: 7500 individuals
Staff: 25
Annual Budget: $5-10,000,000
President and Chief Executive Officer: Barbara L. Thomas
Director, Member/Partner Services: Jetaun Mallett

Historical Note
Composed of minority MBAs in both the private and public sectors, the NBMBAA seeks to improve the professional skills of the membership body and to focus its combined leverage towards achieving meaningful gains for minority MBA students and professionals. Membership: $100/year (individual); $2,500-12,500/year (organization).

Meetings/Conferences:
Annual Meetings: Fall

Publications:
Black MBA Magazine. 3/year. adv.
NBMBAA Newsletter. q. adv.

National Black Nurses Association *(1971)*
8630 Fenton St., Suite 330
Silver Spring, MD 20910-3803
Tel: (301)589-3200 *Fax:* (301)589-3223
E-Mail: nbna@erols.com
Web Site: www.nbna.org
Members: 3000 individuals
Staff: 4
Annual Budget: $500-1,000,000
Executive Director: Millicent Gorham

Historical Note
Functions as a non-profit membership association and as an advocate for the Black community and their health care. Assists Blacks and other minorities interested in pursuing a nursing career. Membership: $150/year (RN/LVN/LPN); $35/year (student).

Meetings/Conferences:
Annual Meetings: August

Publications:
NBNA Newsletter. q. adv.
Journal NBNA. semi-a. adv.

National Black Police Association *(1972)*
3251 Mount Pleasant St. NW, Second Floor
Washington, DC 20010-2103
Tel: (202)986-2070 *Fax:* (202)986-0410
Web Site: www.blackpolice.org
Members: 130 associations
Staff: 2
Annual Budget: $100-250,000
Executive Director: Ronald E. Hampton
E-Mail: nbpanatofc@worldnet.att.net

Historical Note
Established in November 1972 by 13 charter police associations and incorporated in the State of Maryland. A federation of police associations with about 35,000 individual members, NBPA serves as an advocate for minority police officers and provides training and education programs. Membership: $100/year (individual); $200/year (organization).

Meetings/Conferences:
Annual Meetings: Summer/400

Publications:
NBPA Advocate Newsletter. q. adv.

National Black Public Relations Society *(1982)*
4929 Wilshire Blvd., Suite 245
Los Angeles, CA 90010
Tel: (323)857-1171 *Fax:* (323)857-7210
E-Mail: bprsmail@nbprc.org
Web Site: www.nbprs.org
Members: 2500 individuals
Staff: 3
Annual Budget: under $10,000
President: Wynona Redmond
Historical Note
Established in Chicago, IL in 1982, NBPRS was formed to promote and expand the opportunites for people of color/African Americans in public relations. Chapters located in Atlanta, Chicago, Florida, Los Angeles, New York, Philadelphia and Washington. Membership: $75-100/year; $25/year (students).
Publications:
Beepers Newsletter. q.

National Blacksmiths and Weldors Association *(1875)*
P.O. Box 123
Arnold, NE 69120-0123
Tel: (308)848-2913
Members: 250 individuals
Staff: 1
Annual Budget: under $10,000
Director, Information: James E. Holman
Historical Note
NBWA members are blacksmiths, weldors, manufacturing machine shops and general repair shops. Has no paid staff or permanent headquarters; officers change annually. Membership principally in the Midwest. Membership: $40/year.
Meetings/Conferences:
Annual Meetings: *First week of December.*
Publications:
Black Smithing Today. q. adv.

National Block and Bridle Club *(1919)*
Dept. Animal Science, North Carolina State Univ.
Box 7621, 102 Polk Hall
Raleigh, NC 27695-7621
Tel: (919)515-4010 *Fax:* (919)515-8753
E-Mail: Jeannette_Moore@ncsu.edu
Web Site: www.blockandbridle.org
Members: 87 active chapters
Annual Budget: $100-250,000
President: Dr. Jeannette A. Moore
Historical Note
Professional fraternity of men and women working in animal husbandry and affiliated with the American Society of Animal Science.
Publications:
Newsletter. bien.
Annual Report. a.

National Blue Crab Industry Association *(1977)*
Historical Note
An affiliate of National Fisheries Institute, which provides administrative support.

National Board for Certified Clinical Hypnotherapists *(1991)*
1110 Fiddler Lane, Suite 1218
Silver Spring, MD 20910
Tel: (301)608-0123 *Fax:* (301)588-9535
Toll Free: (800)449 - 8144
E-Mail: nbcch@natboard.com
Web Site: www.natboard.com
Members: 2900 individuals
Staff: 5
Annual Budget: $100-250,000
Executive Director: Ron Klein, MCS, NBCCH
Historical Note
NBCCH provides professional credentials to mental health and counseling professionals who utilize hypnotherapy as a subspecialty. Provides two certification categories: NBCCH (National Board Certified Clinical Hypnotherapist) and NBCCH-PS (National Board Certified Clinical Hypnotherapist in Public Service). Requires a minimum of a master's degree in a mental health field, training and experience in hypnosis. Membership: $65/year.
Meetings/Conferences:
Annual Meetings: *Fall*
Publications:
Interlink Newsletter. q.

National Board for Certified Counselors
Three Terrace Way
Greensboro, NC 27403
Tel: (336)547-0607 *Fax:* (336)547-0017
Web Site: www.nbcc.org
Members: 37600 individuals
Staff: 42
Annual Budget: $2-5,000,000
President and Chief Executive Officer: Thomas Clawson
Executive Vice President: Susan H. Eubanks
E-Mail: eubanks@nbcc.org
Director of Financial Operations: Dana Walker
Historical Note
NBCC is a certification organization that provides testing and credentialing to professionals in counseling and mental health care.

National Board of Boiler and Pressure Vessel Inspectors *(1919)*
1055 Crupper Ave.
Columbus, OH 43229-1183
Tel: (614)888-8320 *Fax:* (614)888-0750
E-Mail: getinfo@nationalboard.org
Web Site: www.nationalboard.org
Members: 60 jurisdictions
Staff: 70
Annual Budget: $5-10,000,000
Executive Director: Donald E. Tanner
E-Mail: dtanner@nationalboard.org
Director, Public Affairs: Paul D. Brennan
E-Mail: pbrennan@nationalboard.org
Historical Note
Membership is composed of chief boiler inspectors of states, major U.S. cities and provinces of Canada having boiler laws.
Meetings/Conferences:
Annual Meetings: *Spring/1,000*
2007 – Grapevine, TX(Gaylord Texan Resort)/May 14-18
2008 – Vancouver, BC, Canada/Apr. 21-25
Publications:
Nat'l Board Synopsis. a.
Nat'l Board Inspection Code. trien.
Pressure Relief Device Certifications. a.
Bulletin. q.

National Book Critics Circle *(1974)*
c/o Library Journal
360 Park Ave., South
New York, NY 10010
Tel: (646)746-6725 *Fax:* (646)746-6734
E-Mail: miller@reedbusiness.com
Web Site: www.bookcritics.org
Members: 700 individuals
President: Rebecca Miller
Historical Note
NBCC encourages the advancement of book criticism in all media. Full membership is open to professional book reviewers and book review editors; associate membership is available to other professionals in publishing. Presents annual awards to recognize achievement in fiction, poetry, non-fiction, biography, and criticism. Has no paid officers or full-time staff. Membership: $40/year.
Meetings/Conferences:
Annual Meetings: *usually New York, NY/March*
Publications:
Journal of the National Book Critics Circle. q. adv.

National Border Patrol Council *(1965)*
P.O. Box 678
Campo, CA 91906-0678
Tel: (619)478-5145 *Fax:* (619)478-5716
E-Mail: nbpc-info@nbpc.net
Web Site: www.nbpc.net
Members: 6600 individuals
Staff: 3
Annual Budget: $500-1,000,000
President: T.J. Bonner
Historical Note
A labor union representing employees of the U.S. Border Patrol, affiliated with the AFL-CIO and the American Federation of Government Employees.
Meetings/Conferences:
Biennial Meetings: *odd years*
Publications:
The Educator. bi-m.

National Broadcast Association for Community Affairs *(1974)*
13502 Whittier Blvd., Suite H, PMB 341
Whittier, CA 90605
Tel: (562)698-6280 *Fax:* (562)698-9912
E-Mail: dysaisknx@yahoo.com
Web Site: www.nbaca.org
Members: 300 companies/organizations
Annual Budget: $50-100,000
President: David Ysais
Historical Note
NBACA is an organization for broadcast professionals dedicated to strengthening community affairs programming. NBACA acts as an advocate and resource for community affairs broadcasters seeking professional development. Has no paid officer or full-time staff.
Meetings/Conferences:
Annual Meetings: *Fall.*
Publications:
NBACA Membership Directory. a. adv.
NBACA News. q. adv.

National Building Granite Quarries Association *(1917)*
1220 L St. NW
Suite 100-167
Washington, DC 20005
Toll Free: (800)557 - 2848
Web Site: www.nbgqa.com
Members: 10 companies
Staff: 1
Annual Budget: $10-25,000
Secretary: Kurt Swenson
Historical Note
Members are producers of granite blocks and slabs for architectural applications. NBGDA provides current quarrying and fabrication specifications for member quarries. Membership fee varies, based on sales volume.
Meetings/Conferences:
Annual Meetings: *April*
Publications:
Specifications for Architectural Granite. a.

National Bulk Vendors Association *(1949)*
191 N. Wacker Dr.
Chicago, IL 60606-1615
Tel: (312)521-2400 *Fax:* (312)521-2300
E-Mail: nbva@muchelist.com
Web Site: www.nbva.org
Members: 330 individuals
Staff: 1
Annual Budget: $250-500,000
Counsel: Morrie Much
E-Mail: nbva@muchelist.com
Historical Note
Founded as the National Vendors Association; assumed its present name in 1977. Members are makers and operators of bulk vending equipment and supplies. Membership: $100/year (company).
Meetings/Conferences:
Annual Meetings: *Spring*
2007 – Las Vegas, NV(Caesar's Palace)/Apr. 19-22/700
2008 – Las Vegas, NV(Caesar's Palace)/Apr. 17-19/700
Publications:
Bulletin. bi-m.

National Bureau of Certified Consultants *(1989)*
Management Consulting Center
1850 Fifth Ave.
San Diego, CA 92101
Tel: (619)239-7076 *Fax:* (619)296-3580
Toll Free: (800)543 - 1114

E-Mail: mail@nbmbaa.org
Members: 3000 individuals
Staff: 7
Annual Budget: $250-500,000
Chairman: Vito A. Tanzi, CPCM
Director, Executive Board: Michael J. Barney
Director, Professional Services: Alma R. Gonzalez

Historical Note

Formerly National Bureau of Professional Management Consultants (1998). A national organization with an objective to secure legislative Certification in order to recognize the appellation of CPCM (Certified Professional Consultant to Management). NISCC is also working with the academic community to introduce MBA graduate courses in consultancy in the United States. The American Association of Professional Consultants became a professional division of NBPMC after merging in 1992. Membership: $225/year (individual).

Publications:

Consultant's Bulletin/NISCC. bi-m.
The Chairman Speaks. 6/year.

National Burglar and Fire Alarm Association *(1948)*

2300 Vally View Ln.
Suite 230
Irving, TX 75062
Tel: (214)260-5970 *Fax:* (214)260-5979
E-Mail: info@alarm.org
Web Site: www.alarm.org
Members: 3200 companies
Staff: 11
Annual Budget: $1-2,000,000
Executive Director: Merlin J. Guilbeau
Director, Business Development: Tonja Jenkins

Historical Note

Members provide installation, repair, and/or monitoring of burglar alarms, fire alarms, and other security systems. Houses the Alarm Industry Research and Education Foundation (AIREF), which sponsors industry and safety research programs. Membership: $125-33,800/year, based on number of employees and branch offices.

Meetings/Conferences:

Annual Meetings: Spring/Summer

Publications:

NBFAA Member Update. w.
NBFAA Newsline. q. adv.

National Business Association *(1982)*

P.O. Box 700728
Dallas, TX 75370
Tel: (972)458-0900 *Fax:* (972)960-9149
Toll Free: (800)456 - 0440
E-Mail: info@nationalbusiness.org
Web Site: www.nationalbusiness.org
Members: 30000 individuals
Staff: 11
Annual Budget: $2-5,000,000
President: Raj Nisankarao
E-Mail: raj.n@nationalbusiness.org
Editor/Manager, Communications/Marketing: Catherine Cale-Roberts
E-Mail: mag.editor@nationalbusiness.org

Historical Note

The NBA is a national nonprofit organization that assists the Self-Employed and Small Business community in achieving their professional and personal goals. Members are small-business owners, entrepreneurs, and professionals. Membership: $144/year (select); $420/year (premium).

Publications:

Boss Magazine. bi-m.

National Business Aviation Association

1200 18th St. NW
Suite 400
Washington, DC 20036-2527
Tel: (202)783-9000 *Fax:* (202)331-8364
E-Mail: info@nbaa.org
Web Site: www.nbaa.org
President and Chief Executive Officer: Edward M. Bolen
Senior Vice President, Conventions, Seminars and Forums: Kathleen Blovin
Vice President, Communications: Dan Hubbard
Senior Vice President, Government Affairs: Lisa Piccione

National Business Education Association *(1946)*

1914 Association Dr.
Reston, VA 20191
Tel: (703)860-8300 *Fax:* (703)620-4483
E-Mail: nbea@nbea.org
Web Site: www.nbea.org
Members: 11000 individuals
Staff: 5
Annual Budget: $1-2,000,000
Executive Director: Janet M. Treichel
Controller: Leslie Stanfield

Historical Note

Formed in Buffalo, NY as the United Business Education Association through a merger of the Dept. of Business Education of the National Education Association (founded in 1892) and the National Council for Business Education. Absorbed the National Business Teachers Association (formerly the National Commercial Teachers Federation) and assumed its present name in 1962. The National Association for Business Teacher Education is a division. Membership: $65/year.

Meetings/Conferences:

Annual Meetings: Spring/2,000
2007 – New York, NY(Marriott)/Apr. 4-7/1500

Publications:

Business Education Forum. q. adv.
NBEA Yearbook. a.
Keying In Newsletter. q.

National Business Incubation Association *(1985)*

20 E. Circle Dr., Suite 37198
Athens, OH 45701-3571
Tel: (740)593-4331 *Fax:* (740)593-1996
E-Mail: info@nbia.org
Web Site: www.nbia.org
Members: 1200 individuals
Staff: 21
Annual Budget: $1-2,000,000
President and Chief Executive Officer: Dinah Adkins
Manager, Business Administration: Cheryl Brink
Director, Publications: Meredith Erlewine
Vice President and Chief Operating Officer: Tracy Kitts
Manager, Communications: Linda Knopp

Historical Note

An organization of small business incubator managers and developers, as well as those interested in tracking the industry. Business incubators are business assistance programs that provide support and business development services to start-up and fledgling firms. Membership: $225/year (individual); $350/year (organization).

Meetings/Conferences:

Annual Meetings: Spring

Publications:

The Incubation Edge.
NBIA Conference (CD-ROM).
Conference 2004 Session Material.

National Business Owners Association *(1987)*

P.O. Box 111
Stuart, VA 24076
Tel: (276)251-7500 *Fax:* (276)251-2217
E-Mail: membershipservices@nboa.org
Web Site: www.nboa.org
Members: 4000 companies
Staff: 4
Annual Budget: $1-2,000,000
Executive Director: Paul Labarr
Vice President, Government Affairs: Brendan Quinn

Meetings/Conferences:

Annual Meetings: Not held

Publications:

Members Talk. q. adv.

National Business Travel Association *(1968)*

110 N. Royal St., Fourth Floor
Alexandria, VA 22314
Tel: (703)684-0836 *Fax:* (703)684-0263
Web Site: www.nbta.org
Members: 1800 individuals
Staff: 15
Annual Budget: $2-5,000,000
President and Chief Executive Officer: Suzanne Fletcher
Vice President, Domestic and Global Operations: Bill Connors, CTC
Senior Director, Education and Research: Kristi Long
E-Mail: klong@nbta.org
Director, Meetings and Conventions: Henry J. Roeder
E-Mail: hroeder@nbta.org

Historical Note

A professional non-profit association of business travel managers and business travel service/product suppliers, NBTA serves as the voice of business travel management. Formerly (1989) National Passenger Traffic Association. Membership: $310/first year, $260/year thereafter (travel managers); $1,260/first year, $260/year thereafter (suppliers).

Meetings/Conferences:

Annual Meetings: July/2,700

Publications:

Conference Journal. a. adv.
Membership Directory. a. adv.
Business Travel Quarterly. q.

National Cable & Telecommunications Association *(1952)*

25 Massachusetts Ave. NW
Suite 100
Washington, DC 20001
Tel: (202)222-2376 *Fax:* (202)222-2300
Web Site: www.ncta.com
Members: 2713 cable systems, 476 associates
Staff: 85
Annual Budget: $25-50,000,000
President and Chief Executive Officer: Kyle E. McSlarrow
Senior Vice President, Law and Regulatory Policy: Daniel Brenner
Senior Vice President, Finance and Administration: Bruce Carnes
Executive Vice President: David Krone
Senior Vice President, Government Relations: Gail MacKinnon
Senior Vice President, Communications and Public Affairs: Rob Stoddard
Senior Vice President, Special Projects: Eleanor Winter

Historical Note

Formerly National Cable Television Association. Members are cable TV systems; associate members are manufacturers, distributors, suppliers of hardware, programmers and other services. Has an annual budget of approximately $29.7 million. Sponsors and supports the Cable Television Political Action Committee (Cable-PAC). NCTA's mission is to advance the public policies of the cable television industry before Congress, the executive branch, the courts and the American public.

Meetings/Conferences:

Annual Meetings: Spring

Publications:

Convention Newsletter. a.

National Cable Television Association

Historical Note

Became National Cable & Telecommunications Association in 2005.

National Campground Institute *(1974)*

Historical Note

Promotional arm of the National Association of RV Parks and Campgrounds.

National Campus Ministries Association *(1964)*

Two Ocean Dune Circle
Palm Coast, FL 32137-2266
Tel: (386)446-8066
Web Site: www.campusministry.net
Members: 350 individuals
Annual Budget: $10-25,000
Membership Secretary and Newsletter Editor: Robert T. Thomason
E-Mail: thomason@pcfl.net

Historical Note

Membership: $75/year (full time staff); $95/year (part time staff); $30/year (student).

Meetings/Conferences:

Annual Meetings: Summer

Publications:

NCMA Newsletter. q.

National Cancer Registrars Association *(1974)*

COLUMBIA BOOKS ORDER FORM

Wash Reps and NDCPA: Power In Print

Washington Representatives

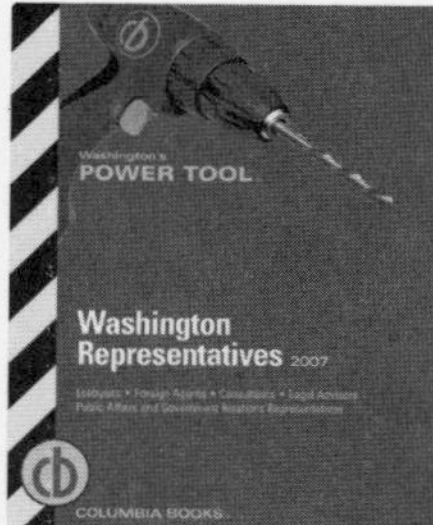

Includes over 18,000 lobbyists, public and government affairs representatives, and special interest advocates in the nation's capital, and the causes they represent. Includes contact information and foreign agent and federal lobbyist indicators. Listings organized by client and by representative. Indexed by subject/industry and foreign interest.

Spring, 2007: $249
Fall, 2007: $249
Both 2007 Editions: $399

National Directory of Corporate Public Affairs

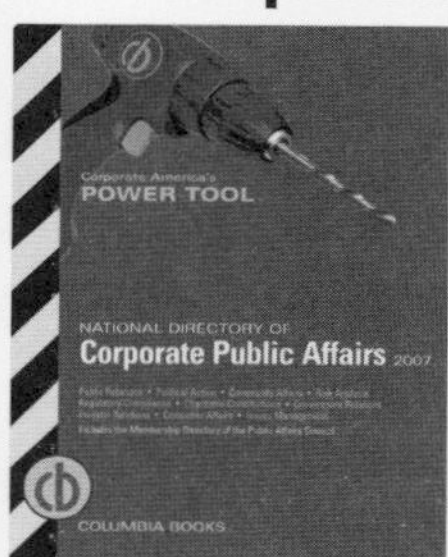

Tracks the public/government affairs programs of over 1,700 major U.S. corporations and lists the 13,000 people who run them. It also lists: Washington area offices, corporate foundations/giving programs, corporate PACs, and federal lobbyists. Indexed by subject and geographic area. Includes membership directory of the Public Affairs Council.

Cover Price: $249

NTPA and SRA: Your Key In Print

National Trade and Professional Associations of the United States

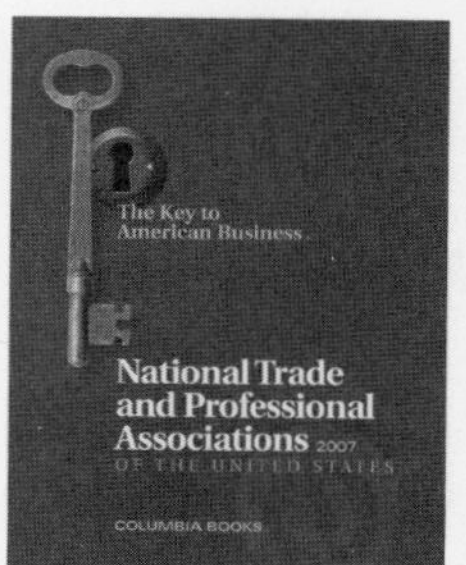

Lists 8,000 national trade associations, professional societies and labor unions. Five convenient indexes enable you to look up associations by subject, budget, geographic area, acronym and executive director. Other features include: contact information, serial publications, upcoming convention schedule, membership/ staff size, budget figures, and background information.

Pre-Publication Price: $249 (by 12/11/06)
Cover Price: $299

State and Regional Associations of the United States

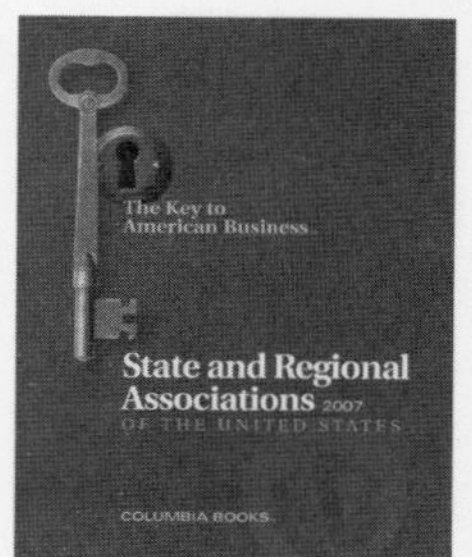

Lists 8,000 of the largest and most significant state and regional trade and professional organizations in the U.S. Look up associations by subject, budget, state, acronym, or chief executive. Also lists contact information, serial publications, upcoming convention schedule, membership/ staff size, budget figures, and background information.

Pre-Publication Price: $179 (by 1/19/07)
Cover Price: $199

TO ORDER: **WEB:** www.columbiabooks.com **FAX this form to:** 202.464.1775 **PHONE:** 1.888.265.0600
MAIL this form to: Columbia Books, 8120 Woodmont Ave, Suite 110, Bethesda, MD 20814

National Directory of Corporate Public Affairs 2007 QUANTITY
Cover Price: _____ @ $249 each $_______

National Trade and Professional Associations 2007
Pre-Publication Price *(payment must be received by 12/11/06)*: _____ @ $249 each $_______
Cover Price: _____ @ $299 each $_______

State and Regional Associations 2007
Pre-Publication Price *(payment must be received by 01/19/07)*: _____ @ $179 each $_______
Cover Price: _____ @ $199 each $_______

Washington Representatives
Spring 2007 *(No Pre-Publication Price Available)* Cover Price: _____ @ $249 each $_______
Fall 2007 *(No Pre-Publication Price Available)* Cover Price: _____ @ $249 each $_______
Both 2007 Editions *(No Pre-Publication Price Available)*: _____ @ $399 $_______

Tax (5.75% if DC resident, 5% if MD resident) $_______

TOTAL $_______

PAYMENT METHOD

☐ **Check enclosed OR** ☐ **Credit Card**

☐MasterCard ☐ Visa ☐AMEX EXPIRATION DATE: ____________

CREDIT CARD # ____________

P.O.#, if applicable ____________

NAME ____________

TITLE ____________ E-MAIL ____________

ORGANIZATION ____________

ADDRESS ____________

CITY/STATE/ZIP ____________

TELEPHONE (required) ____________ FAX ____________

SIGNATURE (required) ____________ DATE ____________

PRAISE FOR COLUMBIA BOOKS DIRECTORIES

Columbia Books reference products are:

RELEVANT...focused on subjects of interest and importance

TIMELY...updated every year and throughout the year

ACCURATE...compiled from reliable sources, confirmed with each organization listed via questionnaire and/or phone interview

CONCISE...providing the significant, omitting the trivial

CONVENIENT...attractively bound in volumes of manageable size and weight, or a click away on your browser.

AFFORDABLE...reasonably priced with the individual as well as the institution in mind.

But don't just take our word for it!
HERE'S WHAT OTHERS HAVE SAID:

National Directory of Corporate Public Affairs

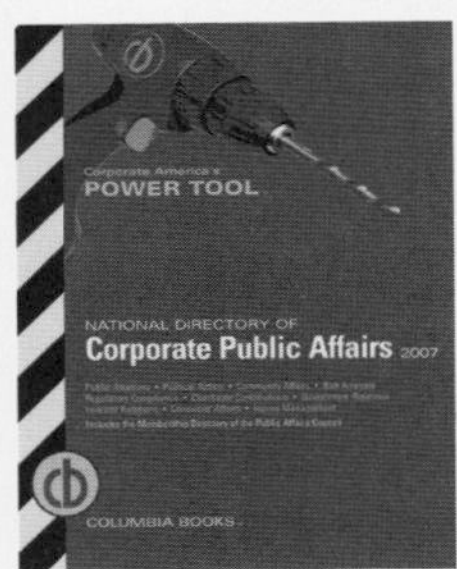

"...a vital resource that provides me with much-needed, up to date information..."

—Stephen E. Chaudet, Lockheed Martin Corp.

Washington Representatives

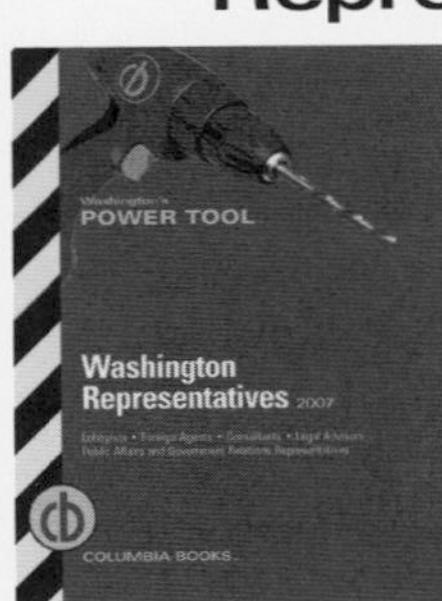

"I use it all the time!"

—Judy Sarasohn, "Special Interests," The Washington Post

National Trade and Professional Associations of the U.S.

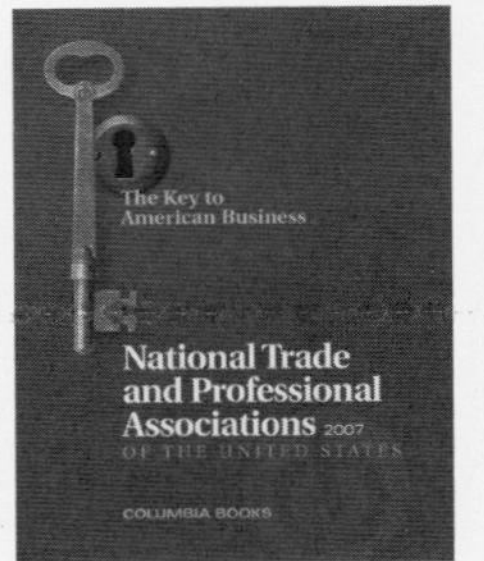

"...NTPA is one of the most used books in our library... it has the information needed by business people."

—Ken Davis, Manager, Los Angeles SBA Business Information Center

State and Regional Associations of the U.S.

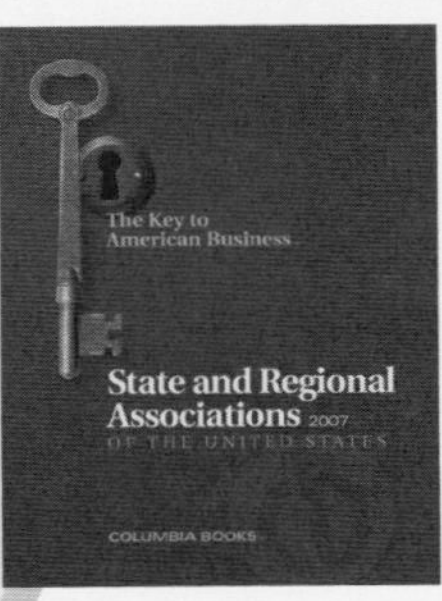

"This fine product will be an important addition to our business library."

—LA Business Information Center

1340 Braddock Pl.
Suite 203
Alexandria, VA 22314
Tel: (703)299-6640 *Fax:* (703)299-6620
E-Mail: info@ncra-usa.org
Web Site: www.ncra-usa.org
Members: 4000 individuals
Staff: 5
Annual Budget: $500-1,000,000
Executive Director: Lori Swain

Historical Note
Formerly (1993) National Tumor Registrars Association. NCRA represents Cancer Registrars who capture a complete summary of patient history, diagnosis, treatment, and status for every cancer patient in the United States. Membership: $80/year (individual); $150/year (organization).

Meetings/Conferences:
Annual Meetings: May/June

Publications:
Journal of Registry Management. q. adv.
The Connection. q. adv.

National Candle Association *(1974)*
1156 15th St. NW
Suite 900
Washington, DC 20005
Tel: (202)393-2210 *Fax:* (202)223-9741
E-Mail: nca@kellencompany.com
Web Site: www.candles.org
Members: 180 companies
Staff: 6
Annual Budget: $500-1,000,000
Executive Vice President: Valerie B. Cooper, CAE
Executive Director: Kathy Prunty

Historical Note
Founded in 1974. Proponent of safe candle usage. Maintains a technical committee, providing research on topics relevant to the industry.

Meetings/Conferences:
Semi-annual Meetings: Spring/Fall

Publications:
Illuminations. q.

National Career Development Association *(1913)*
305 N. Beech Circle
Broken Arrow, OK 74012
Tel: (918)663-7060 *Fax:* (918)663-7058
Toll Free: (866)367 - 6232
Web Site: www.ncda.org
Members: 4500 individuals
Staff: 4
Annual Budget: $500-1,000,000
Executive Director: Deneen Pennington

Historical Note
Founded as the National Vocational Guidance Association; assumed its present name in 1985. Members are counselors and career development professionals who work in education, business/industry, community agencies, military installations and private practice. NCDA is a division of the American Counseling Association. Membership: $55/year.

Meetings/Conferences:
Annual Meetings: Annual/1200
2007 - Seattle, WA(Sheraton)/July 6-8/1000
2008 - Washington, DC(Hyatt Capitol Hil)/July 8-10/1000

Publications:
Career Development Newsletter. q. adv.
Career Development Quarterly. q. adv.

National Cargo Bureau *(1952)*
17 Battery Pl.
Suite 1232
New York, NY 10004-1110
Tel: (212)785-8300 *Fax:* (212)785-8333
E-Mail: ncbnyc@natcargo.org
Web Site: www.natcargo.org
Members: 205 businesses
Staff: 105
Annual Budget: $10-25,000,000
President: Captain James J. McNamara
Vice President and Corporate Secretary: Ian Lennard

Historical Note
Formed by the merger of the Bureau of Inspection of the Board of Underwriters of New York (founded in 1820) and the Board of Marine Underwriters of San Francisco (founded in 1886). Promotes the safe loading, stowage, securing and unloading of cargo on all vessels. Has an annual budget of approximately $10 million.

Meetings/Conferences:
Annual Meetings: New York, NY/first Monday in March

Publications:
Correspondence Course: Ship's Stability.
Correspondence Course: Hazardous Cargo.
Correspondence Course: Stability for Fishermen.

National Cartoonists Society *(1946)*
1133 W. Morse Blvd., Suite 201
Winter Park, FL 32789
Tel: (407)647-8839 *Fax:* (407)629-2502
Web Site: www.reuben.org
Members: 600 individuals
Staff: 4
President: Rick Stromoski

Historical Note
A professional organization of cartoonists, editors, writers, and others interested in cartooning are accepted as associate members.

Publications:
The Cartoonist. q.
NCS Album.

National Catalog Managers Association *(1974)*
7101 Wisconsin Ave., Suite 1300
Bethesda, MD 20814-3415
Tel: (301)654-6664 *Fax:* (301)654-3299
E-Mail: ncma@aftermarket.org
Web Site: www.ncmacat.org
Members: 150 individuals
Staff: 1
Annual Budget: $50-100,000
Executive Director: Scott Luckett

Historical Note
Members are producers of automotive products catalogues. An affiliate of Automotive Aftermarket Industry Association, which provides administrative support. Membership: $200/year (individual).

Meetings/Conferences:
Annual Meetings: April/May
2007 - Savannah, GA(Hyatt Regency)/May 5-8

Publications:
Membership Book. adv. adv.
Newsletter. q.

National Catholic Band Association *(1953)*
3334 N. Normandy Ave.
Chicago, IL 60634
Tel: (773)282-9153
E-Mail: info@catholicbands.org
Web Site: www.catholicbands.org
Members: 150 individuals
Annual Budget: under $10,000
Secretary-Treasurer: John Badsing

Historical Note
Formerly (1993) National Catholic Bandmasters' Association. Active membership open to any qualified band director who teaches in a Catholic grammar school, high school or college, and to woodwind, brass or percussion instructors in a Catholic band program. Membership: $40/year (individual/retail); $50/year (commercial).

Meetings/Conferences:
Annual Meetings: July or August Chicago, IL/December/Board of Directors Meeting

Publications:
Update. irreg.
Proceedings. a.
Directory. a.
Newsletter. bi-m.

National Catholic Cemetery Conference *(1949)*
710 N. River Rd.
Des Plaines, IL 60016-1296
Tel: (847)824-8131 *Fax:* (847)824-9608
E-Mail: webmaster@ntriplec.com
Web Site: www.ntriplec.com
Members: 1800 businesses
Staff: 4
Annual Budget: $500-1,000,000
Executive Director: Irene K. Pesce, CAE

Meetings/Conferences:
Annual Meetings: Fall/500

Publications:
The Catholic Cemetery. m. adv.
Membership Directory. a.

National Catholic Development Conference *(1968)*
86 Front St.
Hempstead, NY 11550-3667
Tel: (516)481-6000 *Fax:* (516)489-9287
Toll Free: (888)879 - 6232
Web Site: www.ncdcusa.org
Members: 500 organizations
Staff: 6
Annual Budget: $500-1,000,000
President and Chief Executive Officer: Georgette Lehmuth
Coordinator, Communications and Public Relations: Ryan Gates Gold

Historical Note
NCDC members are religious fund raising organizations including development officers and key fund raisers of charitable institutions and agencies, religious orders, dioceses, hospitals and educational institutions. While active membership is restricted to Catholic organizations, non-Catholic groups may apply for associate memberships. Membership fee varies, $200-3,200/year.

Meetings/Conferences:
Annual Meetings: Fall/600

Publications:
Resource Guide. a. adv.
Dimensions. m. adv.
Member Resource Directory. a. adv.

National Catholic Educational Association *(1904)*
1077 30th St. NW
Suite 100
Washington, DC 20007-3852
Tel: (202)337-6232 *Fax:* (202)333-6706
E-Mail: nceaadmin@ncea.org
Web Site: www.ncea.org
Members: 24000individualsandinstitutions
Staff: 56
Annual Budget: $5-10,000,000
Director, Conventions and Expositions: Sue Arvo
Director, Communications: Barbara A. Keebler
E-Mail: keebler@ncea.org
Controller: George W. Kirby
E-Mail: mcdaniel@ncea.org
Director, Member and Information Services: Wade Marshall
Director, Public Policy and Educational Research: Sr. Dale McDonald, PBVM
E-Mail: mcdonald@ncea.org
President: Karen Ristau, Ed.D.

Historical Note
Founded in St. Louis June 12-14, 1904 as the Catholic Education Association through the merger of the Association of Catholic Colleges (1899), the Parish School Conference (1902) and the Educational Conference of Seminary Faculties (1898). Within NCEA are several entities including the Association of Catholic Colleges and Universities (ACCU); Chief Administrators of Catholic Education and the National Association for Parish Coordinators and Directors of Religion Education (NPCD). Members are Catholic educators involved at all levels from preschool through universities and seminaries. Membership: $105-115/year (individual); $100-4,590/year (institution).

Meetings/Conferences:
Annual Meetings: Week after Easter

Publications:
Momentum. q. adv.
NCEA Notes. q.

National Catholic Educational Exhibitors *(1950)*
2621 Dryden Rd.
Suite 300
Dayton, OH 45439
Tel: (937)293-1415 *Fax:* (937)293-1310

Toll Free: (888)555 - 8512
E-Mail: ccostello@peterli.com
Members: 500 individuals
Staff: 2
Annual Budget: $25-50,000
Executive Director: Bret Thomas
E-Mail: bthomas@peterli.com

Historical Note

Members are companies and individuals who exhibit at Catholic shows. Associate members are 150 Catholic school superintendents and administrators. Membership: $25/year (individual); $150/year (organization).

Meetings/Conferences:

Annual Meetings: In conjunction with the Nat'l Catholic Educational Ass'n
2007 - Baltimore, MD/Apr. 10-13

Publications:

Membership Directory. a.
NCEE Bulletin. q.

National Catholic Pharmacists Guild of the United States *(1962)*
1012 Surrey Hills Dr.
St. Louis, MO 63117-1438
Tel: (314)645-0085
Members: 375 individuals
Staff: 1
Annual Budget: under $10,000
Co-President, Executive Director and Editor: John Paul Winkelmann

Historical Note

Founded on September 19, 1962 in New York City through the auspices of the National Catholic Welfare Conference (currently known as the United States Catholic Conference). Affiliated with the National Council of Catholic Laity and the International Federation of Catholic Pharmacists. Membership: $20/year.

Publications:

The Catholic Pharmacist. q. adv.

National Cattlemen's Beef Association *(1898)*
9110 E. Nichols Ave
Suite 300
Centennial, CO 80112
Tel: (303)694-0305 *Fax:* (303)694-2851
Web Site: www.beefusa.org
Members: 36000 individuals
Staff: 120
Annual Budget: $50-100,000,000
Chief Executive Officer: Terry Stokes
Vice President, Planning and Administration: Tim Downey
Vice President, Public Opinon and Issues Management: Kendal Frazier
Director, Conventions and Meetings: Debbie Kaylor
Chief Financial Officer: Susan Lambert
Vice President, Public Policy: Jay Truitt

Historical Note

Formed as National Cattlemen's Association as the result of a merger of American National Cattlemen's Association (founded 1898) and National Livestock Feeders Association (founded 1943). Absorbed National Livestock Tax Committee in 1978; consolidated with National Live Stock and Meat Board and Beef Industry Council and assumed its current name in 1995. NCBA provides unified efforts on behalf of the beef industry to increase market share and provide quality meat. Supports the Public Lands Council and sponsors the NCBA Political Action Committee. Has an annual budget of approximately $11.5 million. Membership: $60/year (individual).

Meetings/Conferences:

Annual Meetings: Winter/5,500-6,000
2007 - Nashville, TN/Jan. 31-Feb. 3

Publications:

Beef Business Bulletin. m. adv.
National Cattlemen. q. adv.

National Caves Association *(1965)*
P.O. Box 280
Park City, KY 42160
Toll Free: (866)552 - 2837
E-Mail: info@cavern.com
Web Site: www.cavern.com
Members: 95 cave operators
Staff: 1
Annual Budget: $25-50,000
Secretary-Treasurer: Susan Berdeaux

Historical Note

NCA is a non-profit organization which sets and maintains standards for show caves throughout the country. NCA's Legislative Program is designed to protect caves being operated as attractions. Membership: $300-650/year.

Meetings/Conferences:

Annual Meetings: Fall

Publications:

NCA Cave Talk Newsletter. bi-m.
Caves and Caverns Directory. a.

National Center for Advanced Technologies

Historical Note

The non-profit foundation of the Aerospace Industries Association.

National Center for Homeopathy *(1974)*
801 N. Fairfax St., Suite 306
Alexandria, VA 22314
Tel: (703)548-7790 *Fax:* (703)548-7792
Toll Free: (877)624 - 0613
E-Mail: info@homeopathic.org
Web Site: www.homeopathic.org
Members: 6000 individuals
Staff: 6
Annual Budget: $250-500,000
Executive Director: Sharon Stevenson

Historical Note

Formerly associated with the American Foundation for Homoeopathy, but now independent. Membership: $40/year.

Meetings/Conferences:

Annual Meetings: Spring

Publications:

Directory of Homeopathy Practitioners On-Line.
Homoeopathy Today. m.

National Center on Rural Aging *(1978)*

Historical Note

A special interest group of the National Council on the Aging concerned with the interests of older persons living in rural America.

National Certification Commission *(1993)*
P.O. Box 15282
Chevy Chase, MD 20825-0282
Tel: (301)847-0102 *Fax:* (301)847-0103
E-Mail: certification@usa.com
Web Site: http://pages.zdnet.com/washdc/certification
Members: 150 organizations
Staff: 3
Annual Budget: $100-250,000
Executive Director: Richard C. Jaffeson, AICP, ACA

Historical Note

Members are associations and individuals with interests in certification program development and implementation. Operates the Approved Certification Administrator (ACA), Basic Certification Administrator (BCA), Certification Committee Administrator (CCA) and Distinguished Certification Administrator (DCA) programs, and national registration for certification programs, and offers educational seminars on development and legal issues. Membership: $75 application fee, then $25/year renewal (ACA);
$50 application fee, then $25/year, renewal (BCA); $100/year (national registration); $100/year (association members).

Meetings/Conferences:

Annual Meetings: Bethesda, MD/Fall

Publications:

Certification Census. a.
Question and Comment. w.
Program Profiles. w.
Career Captions. w.
Certification Communications. m.

National Certification Council for Activity Professionals *(1986)*
P.O. Box 62589
Virginia Beach, VA 23466-2589
Tel: (757)552-0653 *Fax:* (757)552-0491
E-Mail: info@nccap.org
Web Site: www.nccap.org
Members: 6600 individuals
Staff: 3
Annual Budget: $100-250,000
President: Kathy Hughes
E-Mail: info@nccap.org
Executive Director: Cindy Bradshaw

Historical Note

NCCAP is the only national organization that exclusively certifes activity professionals who work with the elderly. Certifications are: Activity Assistant Certified (AAC), Activity Director Provisionally Certified (ADPC); Activity Director Certified (ADC); and Activity Consultant Certified (ACC).

Meetings/Conferences:

Annual Meetings: in conjuntion with the Nat'l Ass'n of Activity Professionals
2007 - Columbus, OH/April

Publications:

NCCAP Newsletter. q. adv.

National Certified Pipe Welding Bureau *(1944)*
1385 Piccard Dr.
Rockville, MD 20850-4340
Tel: (301)869-5800 *Fax:* (301)990-9690
Toll Free: (800)556 - 3653
Web Site: www.mcaa.org/ncpwb
Members: 600 companies
Staff: 2
Annual Budget: $250-500,000
Communications Coordinator: Stephanie Mills

Historical Note

A department of the Mechanical Contractors Association of America. Membership: $400/year.

Meetings/Conferences:

Annual Meetings: Spring/60

Publications:

Membership Directory. a. adv.
The Reporter. m.

National Cheese Institute *(1927)*
1250 H St. NW
Suite 900
Washington, DC 20005-3952
Tel: (202)220-3509 *Fax:* (202)331-7820
Members: 70 manuf., distributors, & proc.
Staff: 55
Annual Budget: $1-2,000,000
President and Chief Executive Officer: Constance E. Tipton

Historical Note

NCI represents manufacturers, processors and distributors of natural and processed cheese and cheese products. NCI's activities range from legislative and regulatory advocacy to market research, industry training and education. Administrative support provided by International Dairy Foods Association. Membership: annual dues based on volume.

Meetings/Conferences:

Annual Meetings: in conjunction with Internat'l Dairy Foods Ass'n/Fall

Publications:

Dairy Facts. a.
Cheese Labeling Manual. irreg.
Cheese Varieties and Descriptions Booklet. irreg.

National Chemical Credit Association *(1936)*
1100 Main St.
Buffalo, NY 14209-2356
Tel: (716)887-9527 *Fax:* (716)878-2866
Web Site: www.ncca1.org
Members: 100 companies
Staff: 3
Annual Budget: $250-500,000
Contact: Don Peters

Historical Note

Members are major producers of basic chemicals and allied products.

Publications:

Roster. a.

National Cherry Growers and Industries Foundation *(1946)*
P.O. Box 271
Hood River, OR 97031
Tel: (541)386-5761 *Fax:* (541)386-3191
Web Site: www.nationalcherries.com
Members: 1500 growers and industries
Staff: 2
Annual Budget: $100-250,000
Secretary: Dana Branson
Historical Note
NCGIF members are growers and processors of canned, frozen and brined cherries. Provides funds for promotional campaigns on behalf of the cherry industry.
Meetings/Conferences:
Annual Meetings:
2007 – San Diego, CA/Jan. 25
Publications:
NCGIF Statistical Summary. a.

National Chicken Council *(1954)*
1015 15th St. NW
Suite 930
Washington, DC 20005
Tel: (202)296-2622 *Fax:* (202)293-4005
E-Mail: rlobb@ichickenusa.org
Web Site: www.nationalchickencouncil.com
Members: 225 companies
Staff: 11
Annual Budget: $2-5,000,000
President: George B. Watts
E-Mail: gwatts@chickenusa.org
Director, Government Relations: Mary Colville
Director, Meetings and Member Communications: Margaret Ernst
Director, Communications: Richard Lobb
Director, Science and Technology: Stephen Pretanik
Senior Vice President and Chief Economist: William P. Roenigk
Historical Note
Organized at a meeting in Atlanta, Georgia, sponsored by the Broiler Institute in May, 1954; incorporated in 1955 as National Broiler Council. Assumed its current name in 2000. Members are producers and processors of broiler chickens, and their suppliers. Absorbed the National Broiler Association in 1956. Supports the NCC Political Action Committee. Membership: Processors - fee based on liveweight production; Allied - supplies to broiler trade industry $2,000-10,000/year; Distributor - $275/year.
Meetings/Conferences:
Annual Meetings: Washington, DC/October
Publications:
NCC Washington Report. w.
Broiler Marketing Practices Survey. bien.

National Chief Petty Officers' Association *(1988)*
1014 Ronald Dr.
Corpus Christi, TX 78412-3548
Tel: (361)991-2383 *Fax:* (361)991-6870
Web Site: http://members.tripod.com/NCPOA/
Members: 2900 individuals
Tresurer: Marjorie L. Hays
E-Mail: ncpoahays@aol.com
Historical Note
NCPOA members are active duty, reserve and retired chief petty officers of the U.S. Navy and Coast Guard. Has no paid officers or full-time staff. Membership: $15/year.
Publications:
Chiefs Newspaper. q. adv.

National Child Care Association *(1988)*
2025 M St. NW
Suite 800
Washington, DC 20036-3309
Tel: (202)367-1133 *Fax:* (202)367-2133
Toll Free: (800)543 - 7161
E-Mail: info@nccanet.org
Web Site: www.nccanet.org
Members: 7000 company sites
Staff: 12
Annual Budget: $1-2,000,000
Executive Director: Dawn Hatzer
Director, Membership: Sarah Luczyk
E-Mail: sluczyk@nccanet.org
Director, Annual Conference: John Rubseman
Historical Note
NCCA is a professional trade association representing licensed private child care centers. Membership: $75/year.
Meetings/Conferences:
Annual Meetings: March
Publications:
NCCA's National Focus. q.

National Child Support Enforcement Association *(1952)*
444 N. Capitol St. NW
Suite 414
Washington, DC 20001-1512
Tel: (202)624-8180 *Fax:* (202)624-8828
E-Mail: ncsea@ncsea.org
Web Site: www.ncsea.org
Members: 1800 individuals
Staff: 8
Annual Budget: $500-1,000,000
Director, Communications: Kay Cullen
Historical Note
Formerly National Conference on Uniform Reciprocal Enforcement of Support and National Reciprocal and Family Support Enforcement Association. Assumed its present name in 1984. Members are child support professionals at all levels of government. Membership: $50/year (individual); $300/year local agency, and $300-1,500/year, varies based on population (state agency); $600-5,000/year (private sector corporate membership).
Meetings/Conferences:
Annual Meetings: August/1,500
2007 – Orlando, FL(Marriot Orlando World Center Resort)/Aug. 5-9
2008 – San Francisco, CA(San Francisco Marriott)/Aug. 3-7
Publications:
Child Support Quarterly. q. adv.
NCSEA Membership Directory and Buyer's Guide. a. adv.
NCSEA Rapid Read. m.

National Chimney Sweep Guild *(1976)*
2155 Commercial Dr.
Plainfield, IN 46168
Tel: (317)837-1500 *Fax:* (317)837-5365
E-Mail: office@ncsg.org
Web Site: www.ncsg.org
Members: 1000 service companies, 45 additional
Staff: 10
Annual Budget: $250-500,000
Executive Director: Mark McSweeney
E-Mail: office@ncsg.org
Director, Finance: Judy Thompson
Historical Note
Members are professional chimney service companies and their suppliers. Membership: $405/year (company); $610/year (supplier).
Publications:
Sweeping Magazine. m. adv.
News/Link. m.

National Christian College Athletic Association *(1966)*
302 W. Washington St.
Greenville, SC 29601
Tel: (864)250-1199 *Fax:* (864)250-1141
E-Mail: info@thenccaa.org
Members: 105 colleges
Staff: 4
Annual Budget: $500-1,000,000
Executive Director: Dan Wood
Director, Member Relations: Vern Howard
Director, Community Relations: Kelly Wood
Historical Note
NCCAA members are evangelical Christian colleges.
Meetings/Conferences:
Annual Meetings: Spring-Summer
Publications:
NCCAA Directory. a. adv.
NCCAA News Update. q. adv.
NCCAA Official Handbook. a. adv.

National Christian Education Association *(1942)*
Historical Note
A program of the National Association of Evangelicals.

National Christmas Tree Association *(1955)*
16020 Swingley Ridge Rd.
Suite 300
Chesterfield, MO 63017
Tel: (636)449-5070 *Fax:* (636)449-5057
E-Mail: info@realchristmastrees.org
Web Site: www.realchristmastrees.org
Members: 1800 individuals
Staff: 6
Annual Budget: $500-1,000,000
Executive Director: Pam Helmsing
E-Mail: helmsing@realchristmastrees.org
Historical Note
Formerly (1974) the National Christmas Tree Growers' Association. Membership: $169/year (minimum).
Meetings/Conferences:
Semi-Annual Meetings: Summer and Winter
Publications:
NCTA Intelligencer. semi-a.
Membership Directory. a. adv.
American Christmas Tree Journal. q. adv.

National Church Goods Association *(1904)*
800 Roosevelt Rd., Bldg. C
Suite 312
Glen Ellyn, IL 60137
Tel: (630)942-6599 *Fax:* (630)790-3095
E-Mail: ncga@ncgaweb.com
Web Site: www.ncgaweb.com
Members: 300 companies
Staff: 1
Annual Budget: $100-250,000
Executive Director: Rick Church
Historical Note
Membership fee varies, based on sales volume.
Meetings/Conferences:
Annual Meetings: usually January/200
2007 – Grand Bahama Island, Bahamas(Westin Sheraton Our Lucaya Resort)/Jan. 4-10
2008 – Honolulu, HI(Wakiki Beach Marriott)/Jan. 5-9
Publications:
Directory. a.
Association News. 3/year.

National Church Library Association *(1958)*
275 Third St. South, Suite 101
Stillwater, MN 55082-4987
Tel: (651)430-0776
E-Mail: info@churchlibraries.org
Web Site: www.lclahq.org
Members: 125 individuals
Staff: 3
Annual Budget: $50-100,000
Executive Director: Susan Benish
Historical Note
Formerly the Lutheran Church Library Association; Renamed the National Church Library Association in 2004. Founded in 1958 in Minneapolis. NCLA provides support to churches that maintain libraries. Membership: $28/year (individual); $28-70/year (churches).
Meetings/Conferences:
Annual Meetings: Fall
Publications:
Lutheran Libraries. q.

National Civic League
1445 Market St., Suite 300
Denver, CO 80202
Tel: (303)571-4343 *Fax:* (303)571-4404
E-Mail: ncl@ncl.org
Web Site: www.ncl.org
President: Christopher T. Gates
Director, Communications and Marketing: Gary R. Chandler
Historical Note
NCL members are politicians, activists, and other citizens concerned with improving local governments.

Provides training, representation, and other services to members.

National Classification Management Society *(1964)*
994 Old Eagle School Rd.
Suite 1019
Wayne, PA 19087-1802
Tel: (610)971-4856 *Fax:* (610)971-4859
E-Mail: info@classmgmt.com
Web Site: www.classmgmt.com
Members: 1600 individuals
Annual Budget: $100-250,000
Executive Director: Sharon K. Tannahill
E-Mail: sharont@multiservicemgmt.com
Historical Note
Members consist of information security professionals concerned with identifying and assigning a security classification to information and materials needing protection in the national interest. Membership: $75/year, plus $30 entrance fee.
Meetings/Conferences:
Annual Meetings: *Summer/300-400*
Publications:
C M Bulletin. bi-m.
Directory. a.

National Clay Pipe Institute *(1942)*
N3219 County Hwy H
P.O. Box 759
Lake Geneva, WI 53147
Tel: (262)248-9094 *Fax:* (262)248-1564
E-Mail: info@ncpi.org
Web Site: www.ncpi.org
Members: 6 companies
Staff: 6
Annual Budget: $100-250,000
Corporate Engineer: Michael VanDine
Historical Note
Formerly National Clay Pipe Manufacturers. Members are makers of vitrified clay sewer pipes and fittings.
Publications:
Sewer Sense. q.

National Clay Pottery Association *(1956)*
Drawer 485
Jackson, MO 63755-0485
Tel: (573)243-3138 *Fax:* (573)243-3130
Members: 8 companies
Annual Budget: under $10,000
President: Stone Manes
Historical Note
Formerly National Clay Pot Manufacturers Association. NCPMA acts to stimulate the professional and public interest in the uses and advantages of clay flower pots and in the modern techniques employed in their manufacture and production. Members are makers of flower pots. Has no paid officers or full-time staff. Membership: $400/year.
Meetings/Conferences:
Annual Meetings: *Caribbean Cruise*

National Cleaners Association *(1946)*
252 W. 29th St., Second Floor
New York, NY 10001-5201
Tel: (212)967-3002 *Fax:* (212)967-2240
E-Mail: ncaiclean@aol.com
Web Site: www.nca-i.com
Members: 4200 companies
Staff: 26
Annual Budget: $2-5,000,000
Executive Director: Nora Nealis
Historical Note
Formerly Neighborhood Cleaners Association; assumed current name in 2004. Membership: $410/year (minimum), based on number of employees.
Meetings/Conferences:
Annual Meetings: *TexCare Convention/Spring*
2007 – Secaucus, NJ(Meadowlands Exposition Center)/
Publications:
NCA Bulletin. bi-m. adv.

National Club Association *(1961)*
1201 15th St. NW
Suite 450
Washington, DC 20005
Tel: (202)822-9822
Toll Free: (800)625 - 6221
E-Mail: natlclub@natlclub.org
Web Site: www.natlclub.org
Members: 1000 private clubs
Staff: 11
Annual Budget: $1-2,000,000
President and Chief Executive Officer: Susanne R. Wegrzyn
Vice President, Legal and Government Relations: Andrew Fortin
Historical Note
Members are private golf, country, city, tennis, and yacht clubs. Membership: dues vary according to membership size.
Meetings/Conferences:
Annual Meetings: Not held.
Publications:
Clubhouse. 6/yr. adv.
Reference Series. m.
Club Director. 6/yr. adv.

National Coalition of Abortion Providers *(1990)*
1718 Connecticut Ave. NW
Suite 700
Washington, DC 20009
E-Mail: info@ncap.com
Web Site: www.ncap.com
Members: 200 clinics
Staff: 3
Annual Budget: $100-250,000
Historical Note
Members are independently owned clinics providing abortion services. Membership: $2,000/year.
Publications:
Newsletter. q. adv.

National Coalition of Alternative Community Schools *(1978)*
P.O. Box 6009
Ann Arbor, MI 48106-6009
Tel: (734)883-7040 *Fax:* (734)482-1567
Toll Free: (888)771 - 9171
E-Mail: ncacs1@earthlink.net
Web Site: www.ncacs.org
Members: 250 schools
Staff: 1
Annual Budget: $50-100,000
Treasurer: Terri Wheeler
Historical Note
NCACS is composed of individuals, schools, home schools, foreign schools and resources supporting alternatives to traditional educational systems including educating children at home and developing tools and skills to work for social justice. Programs include teacher education. Membership: $75/year (individual); $75-$250/year, varies by enrollment (school).
Meetings/Conferences:
Annual Meetings: *Spring*
Publications:
Nat'l Coalition News. q. adv.
Nat'l Directory of Alternative Schools. a. adv.

National Coalition of Black Meeting Planners *(1983)*
8630 Fenton St., Suite 126
Silver Spring, MD 20910-3803
Tel: (202)628-3952 *Fax:* (301)588-0011
E-Mail: ncbmp@compuserve.com
Web Site: www.ncbmp.com
Members: 625 individuals
Staff: 4
Annual Budget: $100-250,000
Executive Director: Ozzie Jenkins
Historical Note
Formerly (1984) the National Black Meeting Planners Coalition. Membership: $125/year (meeting planners); $250/year (suppliers).
Meetings/Conferences:
Semi-annual Meetings: *Spring and Fall/350*
Publications:
NCBMP Newsletter. q. adv.

National Coalition of Creative Arts Therapies Associations *(1979)*
8455 Colesville Rd.
Suite 1000
Silver Spring, MD 20910
E-Mail: dianne.dulicai@cox.net
Web Site: www.nccata.org
Members: 6 associations
Contact: Dianne Dulicai
Meetings/Conferences:
Quinquennial Conference:

National Coalition of Girls Schools *(1991)*
57 Main St.
Concord, MA 01742
Tel: (978)287-4485 *Fax:* (978)287-6014
E-Mail: ncgs@ncgs.org
Web Site: www.ncgs.org
Members: 90 schools
Staff: 3
Annual Budget: $100-250,000
Executive Director: Whitney Ransome
Co Executive Director: Meg Moulton
Historical Note
Represents boarding, day, public and private schools for girls in the U.S., Canada, and Australia. Membership: $1,500-5,200/year.
Publications:
Choosing a Girls School.

National Coffee Association of the U.S.A. *(1911)*
15 Maiden Ln.
Suite 1405
New York, NY 10038
Tel: (212)766-4007 *Fax:* (212)766-5815
E-Mail: info@ncausa.org
Web Site: www.coffeescience.org
Members: 185 companies
Staff: 5
Annual Budget: $1-2,000,000
President and Chief Executive Officer: Robert F. Nelson
E-Mail: rfnelson@ncausa.org
Director, Public Relations and Communications: Joe DeRupo
Director, Membership Development and Marketing: Steve Wolfe
E-Mail: smwolfe@ncausa.org
Historical Note
Founded in 1911, the NCA was one of the first trade associations organized in the U.S. NCA membership is composed of coffee producers, exporters, importers, roasters, wholesalers/distributors, retailers and allied trade professionals. Formerly (1939) Associated Coffee Industries of America.
Meetings/Conferences:
Annual Meetings: *Spring*
Publications:
CoffeeTrax. q.
National Coffee Drinking Trends. a.
Coffee Reporter Newsletter. m.

National Coil Coating Association *(1962)*
1300 Sumner Ave.
Cleveland, OH 44115-2851
Tel: (216)241-7333 *Fax:* (216)241-0105
E-Mail: ncca@coilcoating.org
Web Site: www.coilcoating.org
Members: 115 companies
Staff: 4
Annual Budget: $1-2,000,000
Executive Director: John H. Addington
Historical Note
Formerly (2000) National Coil Coaters Association. Members are manufacturers of continuously coated metal coil and suppliers of materials or services used in coil coating.
Meetings/Conferences:
Annual Meetings: *Semi-Annual*
2007 – Marco Island, FL(Marco Island Marriott)/Apr. 14-17
2007 – Nashville, TN(Gaylord Opryland Resort)/Sept. 25-28
Publications:
Coil Lines. q.

National College of Foot Surgeons *(1960)*
P.O. Box 261024

Encino, CA 91426
Tel: (818)340-0616
Annual Budget: $1-2,000,000
Secretary, Director and Chief Executive Officer: Dr. Albert Apkarian

Meetings/Conferences:
Semi-annual Meetings:

Publications:
Journal. a.

National Collegiate Athletic Association *(1906)*
700 W. Washington St.
P.O. Box 6222
Indianapolis, IN 46206-6222
Tel: (317)917-6222 *Fax:* (317)917-6888
Web Site: http://www2.ncaa.org
Members: 1060 institutions and organizations
Staff: 350
Annual Budget: Over $100,000,000
President: Myles Brand
Managing Director of Government Relations: Abe Frank
Managing Director of Public and Media Relations: Bob Williams

Historical Note
NCAA members are colleges, universities and related educational athletic organizations. Annual Budget: $160 million.

Meetings/Conferences:
Annual Meetings: January
2007 - Orlando, FL/Jan. 5-9

Publications:
NCAA Convention Proceedings. a.
NCAA Directory. a.
NCAA Manual. a.
NCAA News. 46/yr.
NCAA Annual Report. a.

National Collegiate Honors Council *(1966)*
1100 Neihardt Residence Center, University of Nebraska - Lincoln
540 N. 16th St.
Lincoln, NE 68588-0627
Tel: (402)472-9150 *Fax:* (402)472-9152
E-Mail: nche@unlserve.unl.edu
Web Site: www.nchchonors.org
Members: 167 individuals
Staff: 2
Annual Budget: $500-1,000,000
Executive Director: Patricia A. Speelmon

Historical Note
An outgrowth of the Inter-University Committee on the Superior Student (ICSS) which was funded by the Carnegie Foundation from 1958 to 1965. A professional organization composed of faculty, administrators, and students committed to serving as a voice for excellence in undergraduate education; includes both public and private universities and colleges. Membership: $100/year (individual); $500/year (institution); $350/year (non-member); $35/year (student).

Meetings/Conferences:
Annual Meetings: Fall
2007 - Denver, CO(Hyatt)/Oct. 29-Nov. 5/1800

Publications:
Journal of the National Collegiate Honors Council. 2/year.
Honors in Practice. a.

National Collegiate Wrestling Association *(1997)*
9500 Forest Ln.
Suite 435
Dallas, TX 75243
Tel: (214)378-8700 Ext: 107 *Fax:* (214)378-9900
Web Site: www.ncwa.net
Members: 110 colleges
Staff: 6
Annual Budget: $100-250,000
Executive Director: Jim Giunta
E-Mail: jim@ncwa.net

Meetings/Conferences:
2007 - Dallas, TX(Renaissance)/March 8-11/600

Publications:
NCWA Coaches Hand Book. a. adv.
NCWA Nationals Program. a. adv.
NCWA/Sport Source - Official Athletic College Guide - Wrestling. a. adv.

National Commercial Builders Council

Historical Note
A council of the National Association of Home Builders of the United States.

National Committee for Quality Assurance *(1979)*
2000 L St. NW
Suite 500
Washington, DC 20036
Tel: (202)955-3500 *Fax:* (202)955-3599
Toll Free: (888)275 - 7585
E-Mail: webmaster@ncqa.org
Web Site: www.ncqa.org
Staff: 150
Annual Budget: $10-25,000,000
President: Margaret E. O'Kane
General Counsel: Sharon King Donohue
Chief Operating Officer: Esther Emard
Chief Financial Officer: Scott Hartranft
Executive Vice President: Greg Pawlson
Vice President, Public Policy and External Relations: Richard Sorian

Historical Note
Founded as a subdivision of Group Health Association of America; became an autonomous organization in 1990. Reviews performance and qualifications of health maintenance organizations and other managed health care providers in the U.S., and confers accreditation on organizations meeting standards in several categories.

National Committee on Planned Giving *(1988)*
233 McCrea St., Suite 400
Indianapolis, IN 46225-1030
Tel: (317)269-6274 *Fax:* (317)269-6276
E-Mail: ncpg@ncpg.org
Web Site: www.ncpg.org
Members: 11500 individuals
Staff: 16
Annual Budget: $1-2,000,000
President and Chief Executive Officer: Tanya Howe Johnson, CAE
E-Mail: thjohnson@ncpg.org
Director, Membership and Manager, Human Resources: Barbara Owens
E-Mail: bowens@ncpg.org
Director, Meetings: Kathryn J. Ramsey
E-Mail: kramsey@ncpg.org
Manager, Education and Technology: Kurt Reusze
E-Mail: kreusze@ncpg.org
Communications Services Manager: Ron Tellmann
E-Mail: rtellmann@ncpg.org
Manager, Finance: Staci Tingley
E-Mail: stingley@ncpg.org
Director, Operations: Barbara Yeager
E-Mail: byeager@ncpg.org

Historical Note
Members are professionals involved in the process of planning and cultivating charitable gifts.

Meetings/Conferences:
Annual Meetings: Typical Attendance: 1700
2007 - Grapevine, TX(Gaylord Texan on Lake Grapvine)/Oct. 10-13
2008 - Denver, CO(Hyatt Regency Denver)/Oct. 22-25
2009 - Prince George's County, MD(Gaylord National Resort)/Oct. 14-17
2010 - Nashville, TN(Gaylord Opryland)/Oct. 13-16

Publications:
Journal of Gift Planning. q.
Proceedings of the Nat'l Conference on Planned Giving. a.
Research Reports. irreg.
Gift Planner Update (e-newsletter).

National Communication Association *(1914)*
1765 N St. NW
Washington, DC 20036
Tel: (202)464-4622 *Fax:* (202)464-4600
Web Site: www.natcom.org
Members: 7400 individuals
Staff: 15
Annual Budget: $2-5,000,000
Executive Director: Roger Smitter

Historical Note
Founded in 1914 as the National Association of Academic Teachers of Public Speaking. Became the National Association of Teachers of Speech in 1923, the Speech Association of America in 1946, the Speech Communication Association in 1970, and the National Communication Association in 1998. Incorporated in Missouri in 1950. A constituent of the American Council on Education. Members are teachers at all levels and in all aspects of communication arts and sciences; media and communications consultants; students; libraries; and persons in theatre production. SCA promotes the study, criticism, research, educating, and application of the artistic, humanistic, and scientific principles of communication. Membership: $110/year (individual); $150/year (organization).

Meetings/Conferences:
Annual Meetings: November

Publications:
Journal of Applied Communication Research. q.
Communication Education. q. adv.
Communication Monographs. q.
Quarterly Journal of Speech. q.
Text and Performance Quarterly. q.
The Review of Communication. q.
Critical Studies in Media Communication. q.
Communication Techer. q.
Communication and Critical/Cultural Studies. q.

National Community Development Association *(1973)*
522 21st St. NW
Suite 120
Washington, DC 20006
Tel: (202)293-7587 *Fax:* (202)887-5546
E-Mail: ncda@ncdaonline.org
Web Site: www.ncdaonline.org
Members: 550 local governments
Staff: 5
Executive Director: Chandra Western

Historical Note
Formerly (1977) National Model Cities Community Development Directors Association. NCDA members are community development program administrators.

National Community Education Association *(1966)*
3929 Old Lee Hwy., Suite 91-A
Fairfax, VA 22030-2401
Tel: (703)359-8973 *Fax:* (703)359-0972
E-Mail: ncea@ncea.com
Web Site: www.ncea.com
Members: 1400 individuals
Staff: 4
Annual Budget: $500-1,000,000
Executive Director: Steve Parson
Director, Member Services: Kerry Loughney

Historical Note
Established as the National Community School Education Association, it assumed its present name in 1974. Members are primarily school administrators. NCEA sponsors and supports community involvement in public education and lifelong learning opportunities. Membership: $149/year (individual); $315/year (organization).

Publications:
Community Education Journal. q. adv.
Community Education Today. m.

National Community Pharmacists Association *(1898)*
100 Daingerfield Road
Alexandria, VA 22314
Tel: (703)683-8200 *Fax:* (703)683-3619
Toll Free: (800)544 - 7447
E-Mail: info@ncpanet.org
Web Site: www.ncpanet.org
Members: 36000 individuals
Staff: 40
Annual Budget: $5-10,000,000
Executive Vice President and Chief Executive Officer: Bruce T. Roberts

Director, Membership: Colleen Agan
Senior Vice President, Communications: Robert Appel
Senior Vice President, Strategic Initiatives: Todd Dankmeyer
Senior Vice President, Pharmacy Programs and Executive Director, NIPCO: Kathryn Kuhn
Vice President, Operations: Beverly Martin
Senior Vice President, Legislative Affairs: John M. Rector, Esq.
Director, Meetings and Conventions: Glenn M. Reighart, CMP, CMM, CAE

Historical Note
Formerly the National Association of Retail Druggists, adopted its acronym (NARD) as its official name in 1987 before assuming its current name in 1996. NCPA promotes the needs of the independent pharmacist. Sponsors and supports the NCPA Political Action Committee.

Meetings/Conferences:
Annual Meetings: Fall
2008 - Tampa, FL(Tampa Convention Center)/Oct. 11-15

Publications:
America's Pharmacists. m.
Pharmacist (online). w. adv.

National Computer Dealer Forum

Historical Note
A forum of the Business Products Industry Association.

National Concrete Burial Vault Association *(1929)*
195 Wekiva Springs Rd.
Suite 200
Longwood, FL 32779
Tel: (407)788-1996 *Fax:* (407)774-6751
Toll Free: (800)538 - 1423
E-Mail: tom@camco.biz
Web Site: www.ncbva.org
Members: 350 companies
Staff: 4
Annual Budget: $50-100,000
Executive Director: Thomas A. Monahan, CAE

Historical Note
Members are companies seeking recognition and uniformity in the industry. Membership: $125-500/year (organization).

Meetings/Conferences:
Annual Meetings: June/200

Publications:
Newsletter. bi-m.

National Concrete Masonry Association *(1918)*
13750 Sunrise Valley Dr.
Herndon, VA 20171
Tel: (703)713-1900 *Fax:* (703)713-1910
E-Mail: ncma@ncma.org
Web Site: www.ncma.org
Members: 400 companies
Staff: 30
Annual Budget: $2-5,000,000
President: Mark Hogan
E-Mail: mhogan@ncma.org
Communications Manager: Rick Ardalan
Vice President, Research and Development: Jeffrey Greenwald
E-Mail: mhogan@ncma.org
Vice President, Marketing: Jerry R. Harke, APR
Director, Meetings and Conventions: Deborah W. Morris
Consultant, Government Affairs: Randall G. Pence
Vice President, Engineering: Robert D. Thomas

Historical Note
Membership consists of manufacturers of concrete masonry products, and suppliers to the industry. Sponsors the NCMA Political Action Committee.

Meetings/Conferences:
Annual Meetings: Winter/2,800

Publications:
Concrete Masonry Designs. m. adv.
TEK - Technical Information Services. m.
Wage and Benefit Survey. a.
Membership Directory. a. adv.
CM News. m. adv.
Market Planning Statistical Survey. a.

National Confectioners Association of the United States *(1883)*
8320 Old Courthouse Rd.
Suite 300
Vienna, VA 22182
Tel: (703)790-5750 *Fax:* (703)790-5752
E-Mail: info@candyusa.org
Web Site: www.candyusa.com
Members: 700 manufacturers and suppliers
Staff: 22
Annual Budget: $2-5,000,000
President: Lawrence T. Graham
Vice President, Trade Relations: Jim Corcoran
Director, Public Affairs: Susan Fussell
Director, Trade Relations: Dave Klabunde
Vice President, Legislative Affairs: Stephen G. Lodge
Vice President, Federal Government Affairs: Melane Rose
Senior Vice President, Public Affairs: Susan Snyder Smith

Historical Note
Manufacturers of confectionery products and their suppliers. NCA is connected with the National Confectioners Association of the United States Political Action Committee.

Meetings/Conferences:
Semi-annual: Winter and Spring

National Confectionery Sales Association *(1899)*
10225 Berea Rd.
Suite B
Cleveland, OH 44102
Tel: (216)631-8200 *Fax:* (216)631-8210
Web Site: www.candyhalloffame.com
Members: 365 individuals
Staff: 2
Annual Budget: under $10,000
Executive Director: Teresa Tarantino
E-Mail: ttarantino@propressinc.com

Historical Note
Formerly known as the National Confectionery Salesmen's Association of America (1992). Founded in 1899 and incorporated in 1912. Sponsors the Candy Hall of Fame, established in 1971. Membership: $50/year (individual).

Meetings/Conferences:
Annual Meetings: Summer

Publications:
NCSA Journal. a. adv.

National Conference of Appellate Court Clerks *(1974)*
c/o Nat'l Center for State Courts, 300 Newport Ave.
Williamsburg, VA 23187-8798
Tel: (757)259-1841 *Fax:* (757)259-1520
E-Mail: inquiries@appellatecourtclerks.org
Web Site: www.appellatecourtclerks.org
Members: 230 individuals
Staff: 1
Annual Budget: under $10,000
Executive Director: John Ramsey

Historical Note
NCACC's mission is to improve the appellate process. Officers are elected annually; administrative support is provided by the National Center for State Courts. Membership: $100/year (individual).

Meetings/Conferences:
Annual Meetings: August

Publications:
NCACC Newsletter. q.

National Conference of Bankruptcy Judges *(1926)*
235 Secret Cove Dr.
Lexington, SC 29072-8854
Tel: (803)957-6225 *Fax:* (803)957-8890
Web Site: www.ncbj.org
Members: 350 individuals
Annual Budget: $1-2,000,000
Executive Director: Christine J. Molick

Historical Note
An organization of bankruptcy judges and former judges organized to further the administration of bankruptcy laws. Established as the National Association of Referees in Bankruptcy, it became the National Conference of Referees in Bankruptcy in 1969 and assumed its present name in 1973. Has no permanent address or paid staff.

Meetings/Conferences:
Annual Meetings: Fall
2007 - Orlando, FL/Oct. 10-13
2008 - Scottsdale, AZ/Sept. 24-27
2009 - Las Vegas, NV/Oct. 18-21
2010 - New Orleans, LA/Oct. 21-24
2011 - Tampa, FL/Oct. 12-15

Publications:
American Bankruptcy Law Journal. q.

National Conference of Bar Examiners *(1931)*
402 W. Wilson St.
Madison, WI 53703
Tel: (608)280-8550 *Fax:* (608)280-8552
Web Site: www.ncbex.org
Staff: 45
Annual Budget: $5-10,000,000
President: Erica Moeser

Historical Note
Conducts character investigations pertinent to admission to the practice of law at the request of state bar examiners boards, principally in cases of lawyers moving across state lines. An affiliated organization of the American Bar Association.

Meetings/Conferences:
Annual Meetings: With American Bar Ass'n in August

Publications:
The Bar Examiner. q.

National Conference of Bar Foundations *(1977)*

Historical Note
An affiliate of American Bar Association, which provides administrative support.

National Conference of Bar Presidents *(1950)*

Historical Note
An affiliate of American Bar Association, which provides administrative support.

National Conference of Black Lawyers *(1968)*
116 W. 111th St.
New York, NY 10027
Tel: (212)864-4000 *Fax:* (212)222-2680
Toll Free: (866)266 - 5091
Web Site: www.ncbl.org
Members: 1500 individuals
Staff: 1
Annual Budget: $100-250,000
Co-Chair: Thomas Ruffin

Historical Note
Membership in the U.S., Canada, and the Virgin Islands. A progressive organization of lawyers, law students, judges and lay people committed to utilizing legal remedies to eliminate institutional racism and aid in the development of the black community. Membership: $25-100/year (individual).

Publications:
NCBL Notes. q.

National Conference of Black Mayors *(1974)*
1151 Cleveland Ave., Suite D
East Point, GA 30344
Tel: (404)765-6444 *Fax:* (404)765-6430
Web Site: www.ncbm.org
Members: 544 individuals
Staff: 8
Annual Budget: $500-1,000,000
Executive Director: Vanessa R. Williams
E-Mail: vwilliams@ncbm.org
Deputy Director, Convention Coordinator: Carol Crawford

Historical Note
Organized in 1974 as the Southern Conference of Black Mayors. Changed to its present name in January, 1977. Membership fee based on sliding scale according to population.

Publications:
Municipal Watch Newsletter. q.
Membership Roster. a.
Convention Program and Journal. a.

National Conference of Black Political Scientists *(1969)*
Mississippi Valley State Univ.
Itta Bena, MS 38941
Tel: (662)254-3794 *Fax:* (662)254-3844

E-Mail: info@ncobps.org
Web Site: www.ncobps.org
Members: 400 individuals
Staff: 1
Executive Director: Kathie S. Golden

Historical Note

The NCOBPS is a professional organization of political scientists and other scholars committed to the study and research of those aspects of political science and political institutions which clarify the problems of black people, suggest useful remedies for solutions and mobilize needed resources. Membership: $65/year (professional); $35/year (student); $200/year (institutional).

Meetings/Conferences:
Annual Meetings: Spring

Publications:
NCOBPS Newsletter. q.
Nat'l Political Science Review. a.

National Conference of Brewery and Soft Drink Workers - United States and Canada *(1886)*
25 Louisiana Ave. NW
Washington, DC 20001
Tel: (202)624-6921 *Fax:* (202)624-8137
Members: 75 individuals
Staff: 12
Director: Jack Cipriani

Historical Note

Formerly the International Union of United Brewery, Flour, Cereal, Soft Drink and Distillery Workers of America, it became a conference of the International Brotherhood of Teamsters in 1976.

National Conference of Catechetical Leadership *(1905)*
125 Michigan Ave. NE
Washington, DC 20017
Tel: (202)884-9754 *Fax:* (202)884-9756
E-Mail: nccl@nccl.org
Web Site: www.nccl.org
Members: 3000 individuals
Staff: 6
Annual Budget: $250-500,000
Executive Director: Neil Parent
Associate Director: Joyce Crider

Historical Note

Formerly (1966) Confraternity of Christian Doctrine. Members are directors of religious education for Catholic Dioceses. Formerly (1992) the National Conference of Diocesan Directors of Religious Education (CCD). Membership has been expanded to include academicians in religious education, publishers, and those in ministry or religious education. Membership: $50/year (individual); $250-650/year (organization).

Meetings/Conferences:
2007 – Columbus, OH(Hyatt)/Apr. 8-12
2008 – Houston, TX(Hyatt)/Apr. 6-10

Publications:
Directory. a.
Catechetical Leader. bi-m. adv.

National Conference of Commissioners on Uniform State Laws *(1892)*
211 E. Ontario St., Suite 1300
Chicago, IL 60611
Tel: (312)915-0195 *Fax:* (312)915-0187
E-Mail: nccusl@nccusl.org
Web Site: www.nccusl.org
Members: 335 individuals
Staff: 6
Annual Budget: $1-2,000,000
Executive Director: William H. Henning
Legislative Director and Legal Counsel: John M. McCabe
Communications Officer: Katie Robinson

Historical Note

NCCUSL, one of the oldest state organizations designed to encourage interstate cooperation, was organized in 1892 to promote uniformity by voluntary action of each state government. Since its organization the Conference has drafted over two hundred uniform laws on numerous subjects in various fields of law, many of which have been widely enacted.

Meetings/Conferences:
Annual Meetings: Last week in July

Publications:
Drafting Manual.
Handbook and Proceedings. a.

National Conference of CPA Practitioners *(1979)*
22 Jericho Tpk., Suite 106
Mineola, NY 11501
Tel: (516)333-8282 *Fax:* (516)333-4099
Toll Free: (888)488 - 5400
E-Mail: office@nccpap.org
Web Site: www.nccpap.org
Members: 1200 firms
Staff: 2
Annual Budget: $250-500,000
Director, Membership: Holly Coscetta

Historical Note

NCCPAP represents independent, medium sized regional and local CPA firms. Membership: $200-650/year (depending on number of professional personnel in firm).

Meetings/Conferences:
Annual Meetings: October

Publications:
NCCAP News & Views. m. adv.

National Conference of Diocesan Vocation Directors *(1962)*
5400 Roland Ave.
Baltimore, MD 21210
Tel: (715)254-0830 *Fax:* (715)254-0831
E-Mail: office@ncdvd.org
Web Site: www.ncdvd.org
Members: 500 individuals
Staff: 3
Executive Director: Randall Cirner
E-Mail: office@ncdvd.org

Historical Note

NCDVD promotes the priesthood by providing training, support and advocacy to diocesan vocation directors.

Meetings/Conferences:
Annual Meetings: Fall
2007 – Baltimore, MD(Tremont)/Sept. 22-27

Publications:
NCDVD News. q.
Vocation Journal. a.

National Conference of Directors of Religious Education

Historical Note

A division of the National Catholic Educational Association.

National Conference of Editorial Writers *(1947)*
3899 N. Front St.
Harrisburg, PA 17110
Tel: (717)703-3015 *Fax:* (717)703-3014
E-Mail: ncew@pa-news.org
Web Site: www.ncew.org
Members: 545 individuals
Staff: 1
Annual Budget: $100-250,000
Director, Administration: Sherid Virnig

Historical Note

Membership open to professional editorial writers who prepare institutional opinion on a regular basis for newspapers or magazines of general circulation or radio or television stations, or online outlets; to columnists; to teachers of journalism; to college students who profess a serious interest in editorial writing; and to others who play an active role in editorial operations. Membership is not extended to representatives of trade journals or party organs, to public relations personnel, or to writers of opinion for nonprofit advocacy organizations. Membership: $50/year (retirees); $25/year (students); $100/year (academics); $90-$200/year (regular).

Meetings/Conferences:
Annual Meetings: Fall/200
2007 – Kansas City, MO(Fairmont Hotel)/Sept. 26-29

Publications:
The Masthead. q.

National Conference of Executives of The ARC *(1964)*
1010 Wayne Ave., Suite 650
Silver Spring, MD 20910
Tel: (301)565-5475 *Fax:* (301)565-3843
E-Mail: ncearc@thearc.org
Web Site: www.ncearc.org
Members: 450 individuals
Annual Budget: $100-250,000
Staff Liaison: Darcy Littlefield

Historical Note

Formerly the National Conference of Executives of Associations for Retarded Citizens. Membership: $99-199/year (individual).

Meetings/Conferences:
Annual Meetings: Fall

Publications:
The Executive. bi-m. adv.

National Conference of Federal Trial Judges *(1972)*

Historical Note

An affiliate of American Bar Association, which provides administrative support.

National Conference of Firemen and Oilers, SEIU *(1898)*
1023 15th St. NW, 10th Floor
Washington, DC 20005
Tel: (202)962-0981 *Fax:* (202)872-1222
E-Mail: mail@ncfo.org
Web Site: www.ncfo.org
Members: 25000 individuals
Staff: 10
Annual Budget: $25-50,000
International President: George G. Francisco, Jr.
International Secretary-Treasurer: Daniel S. Anderson, Jr.

Historical Note

Formerly (1995) International Brotherhood of Firemen and Oilers. Organized in Kansas City December 18, 1898 as the International Brotherhood of Stationary Firemen and chartered by the American Federation of Labor the following year. In 1919 the charter was expanded to include oilers and boiler room helpers and the name was changed to its present form. An affiliate of Service Employees International Union. Sponsors and supports the International Brotherhood of Firemen and Oilers Political League.

Meetings/Conferences:
Quadrennial Meetings: 2008

Publications:
Journal of the NCFO. q.

National Conference of Insurance Legislators *(1969)*
385 Jordan Rd.
Troy, NY 12180
Tel: (518)687-0178 *Fax:* (518)687-0401
E-Mail: info@ncoil.org
Web Site: www.ncoil.org
Members: 36 states
Staff: 7
Annual Budget: $50-100,000
Executive Director: Susan F. Nolan

Historical Note

A national organization of state legislators working toward a better understanding of insurance, state insurance regulation and legislation and against federal intervention into the rights of states to regulate and legislate insurance matters. Added "National" to its name in 1987. Liasons with the National Association of Insurance Commissioners. Membership: $3,000/year (state).

Meetings/Conferences:
Annual Meetings: November/400
2007 – Las Vegas, NV(Renaissance Las Vegas Hotel)/Nov. 15-18
2008 – Duck Key, FL(Hawk's Cay Resort)/Nov. 20-23
2009 – New Orleans, LA(Royal Sonesta)/Nov. 19-22

Publications:
NCOIL Legislative Fact Book and Almanac. a.
NCOILetter. m.

National Conference of Local Environmental Health Administrators *(1938)*
c/o NEHA, 720 S. Colorado Blvd.
South Tower, Suite 970

Denver, CO 80246-1925
Tel: (303)756-9090 *Fax:* (303)691-9490
Members: 300 individuals
Staff: 1
Annual Budget: under $10,000
Executive Director: Nelson E. Fabian
E-Mail: nfabian@neha.org

Historical Note

Formerly (1966) the Conference of Municipal Public Health Engineers and (1983) Conference of Local Environmental Health Administrators. An organization of environmental health administrators employed at the local level, at universities, and in industry. Purpose is to promote efficient and effective local environmental health programs. Affiliated with the National Environmental Health Association. Membership: $15/year.

Meetings/Conferences:
Annual Meetings: June, with the Nat'l Environmental Health Ass'n
2007 - Atlantic City, NJ/100

Publications:
Newsletter. 3/year. adv.

National Conference of Personal Managers *(1942)*
P.O. Box 50008
Henderson, NV 89016
Tel: (702)837-1170
E-Mail: ncopm@earthlink.net
Web Site: www.ncopm.com
Members: 220 individuals
Staff: 6
Annual Budget: $10-25,000
National President: Clinton Ford Billups, Jr.

Historical Note

Members are personal managers for artists in the entertainment industry.

Meetings/Conferences:
Annual Meetings: Meetings held quarterly at Friar's Club in New York City.

Publications:
NCOPM Newsletter. q.

National Conference of Regulatory Utility Commission Engineers *(1922)*
Federal Communications Commission
445 12th St. NW
Washington, DC 20554
Tel: (202)418-0840 *Fax:* (202)418-0167
Web Site: www.ai.org/iurc
Members: 125 individuals
Annual Budget: $10-25,000
Secretary: Fatina Franklin
E-Mail: ffrankli@fcc.gov

Historical Note

Formerly (1972) Conference of State Utility Commission Engineers. Affiliated with the National Association of Regulatory Utility Commissioners.

Meetings/Conferences:
Annual Meetings: June

Publications:
Proceedings. a.

National Conference of Specialized Court Judges *(1969)*

Historical Note

An affiliate of American Bar Association, which provides administrative support.

National Conference of State Fleet Administrators *(1987)*
P.O. Box 159
Litchfield Park, AZ 85340-0159
Tel: (623)772-9096 *Fax:* (623)772-9098
E-Mail: ncsfa@qwest.net
Web Site: http://ncsfa.state.ut.us
Members: 120 individuals
Staff: 2
Annual Budget: $100-250,000
Executive Director: Joe O'Neill

Historical Note

NCFSA members are state goverment administrators responsible for vehicle fleet management. Associate membership is available to municipal or local government entities. Corporate membership is available for private sector representatives. Membership: $480/year (1st member from state agency); $240/year (2nd member from state agency/associate); $1,000/year (corporate).

Meetings/Conferences:
Annual Meetings: Fall/150

Publications:
Annual Survey Report. a.
Fleet Administration News Newsletter. q.
NCSFA Roster. irreg.

National Conference of State Historic Preservation Officers *(1969)*
444 N. Capitol St. NW
Suite 342
Washington, DC 20001
Tel: (202)624-5465 *Fax:* (202)624-5419
Web Site: www.ncshpo.org
Members: 59 states and territories
Staff: 4
Annual Budget: $250-500,000
Executive Director: Nancy Schamu
Assistant Director: Elizabeth A. Szufnar

Historical Note

Professional organization of the gubernatorially appointed State Historic Preservation Officers who carry out the national preservation program as delegates of the Secretary of the Interior under the National Historic Preservation Act of 1966, as amended.

National Conference of State Legislatures *(1975)*
7700 E. First Pl.
Denver, CO 80230
Tel: (303)364-7700 *Fax:* (303)364-7800
E-Mail: info@ncsl.org
Web Site: www.ncsl.org
Members: 37000 individuals
Staff: 200
Annual Budget: $10-25,000,000
Executive Director: William T. Pound
Public Affairs Manager: Nicole Casal Moore

Historical Note

Formed by a merger of the National Legislative Conference (founded in 1947), the National Conference of State Legislative Leaders (founded 1959) and the National Society of State Legislators (founded in 1965). An organization of state legislators, legislative staffs, territories, and commonwealths. Supported by state dues; the Foundation for State Legislatures, a center for public/private sector interaction; private foundations, grants and contracts. Affiliated with the Council of State Governments and the National Governors' Association. Has an annual budget of $13 million.

Meetings/Conferences:
Annual Meetings: Summer

Publications:
State Budget and Tax Notes. bi-m.
LegisBrief. 48/yr.
Fiscal Letter. bi-m.
State Legislatures Magazine. 10/yr.

National Conference of State Liquor Administrators *(1934)*
6183 Beau Douglas Ave.
Gonzales, LA 70737
Tel: (225)473-7209
Web Site: www.ncsla.org
Members: 41 government and state agencies
Annual Budget: $50-100,000
Executive Director: Pamela D. Salario
E-Mail: pamsalario@cox.net

Historical Note

NCSLA was formed to provide opportunities for state-licensed administrators to meet and exchange ideas and information and to formulate uniform regulations, statute and laws affecting the sales of alcoholic beverages. Has no paid officers or full-time staff. Membership: $225/year (state).

Publications:
Directory. a.

National Conference of State Retail Associations *(1968)*

Historical Note

A federation of 50 state retail associations meeting annually in Washington in May under the auspices of the National Retail Federation.

National Conference of State Social Security Administrators *(1952)*
c/o Colorado Public Employees Social Security Program
633 17th St., Suite 700
Denver, CO 80202-3660
Tel: (303)318-8060 *Fax:* (303)318-8069
E-Mail: info@ncsssa.org
Web Site: www.ncsssa.org
Members: 115 individuals
Staff: 1
Annual Budget: $10-25,000
President: Dean Conder

Historical Note

Founded in January 1952 in Bloomington, Indiana. Formerly (1963) Conference of State Social Security Administrators. NCSSSA acts as the administrator for state government and political subdivisions within each state. Membership: $125/year (organization).

Meetings/Conferences:
Annual Meetings: Fall

Publications:
Newsletter. q.

National Conference of States on Building Codes and Standards *(1967)*
505 Huntmar Park Dr., Suite 210
Herndon, VA 20170
Tel: (703)437-0100 Ext: 238 *Fax:* (703)481-3596
E-Mail: cfitch@ncsbs.org
Web Site: www.ncsbcs.org
Members: 500 individuals and organizations
Staff: 7
Annual Budget: $250-500,000
Executive Director: Robert C. Wible
Membership Coordinator: Carolyn Fitch

Historical Note

Serves the building code and public safety interests of the 50 states and territories. Provides a forum for the discussion and solution of problems of state building codes and regulations and coordinates intergovernmental reforms in the area of building codes and standards. Executive branch agreement with the National Governors' Association. Works closely with the Center for Building Technology of the National Institute of Standards and Technology. Membership: $100/year (associate); $400/year (organization); $100/year (affiliate); $75/year (state).

Meetings/Conferences:
Annual Meetings: October

Publications:
Directory of Building Codes & Regulations (online).
Introduction to Building Codes & Effective Codes Administration.
Member Bulletin. m.

National Conference of Women's Bar Associations *(1981)*
P.O. Box 82366
Portland, OR 97282-0366
Tel: (503)657-3813 *Fax:* (503)657-3932
E-Mail: ncwba@aol.com
Web Site: www.ncwba.org
Members: 300 individuals
Staff: 1
Executive Director: Pamela Ly Nicholson

Historical Note

Members are state and local women's bar associations, sections, special interest groups and individuals serving as a resource for members and offering them support, guidance and information. Membership: $50/year (individual); $75-350/year (based upon bar association).

Meetings/Conferences:
Annual Meetings: In conjuction with the American Bar Ass'n

Publications:
Directory of Members. a.
NCWBA Newsletter. q.

National Conference of Yeshiva Principals *(1947)*
160 Broadway
New York, NY 10038
Tel: (212)227-1000 *Fax:* (212)406-6934
E-Mail: umesorah@aol.com
Members: 380 individuals
Staff: 2
Annual Budget: $25-50,000
Executive Vice President: Rabbi A. Moshe Possick

Historical Note
Affiliated with the National Society for Hebrew Day Schools.

Meetings/Conferences:
Annual Meetings: May in New York, NY

Publications:
Educational Newsletter. 5/year.

National Conference on Public Employee Retirement Systems *(1941)*
444 N. Capitol St. NW
Suite 221
Washington, DC 20001-4005
Tel: (202)624-1456 *Fax:* (202)624-1439
Toll Free: (877)202 - 5706
Web Site: www.ncpers.org
Members: 1300 individuals
Staff: 4
Annual Budget: $250-500,000
Executive Director and Legislative Council: Fred Nesbitt
E-Mail: fred@ncpers.org
Director, Government Relations and Counsel: Hank H. Kim
Director, Programs and Research: Cassandra Smoot

Historical Note
NCPERS represents administrators and trustees of public pension funds. Membership: $100-400/year (pension funds); $6,000/year (sponsors).

Meetings/Conferences:
Annual Meetings: Spring

Publications:
Monitor. m.
Legislative Alert. w.
Sponsoring Member Services Directory. a.
Persist newsletter. q.
Proceedings. a.

National Conference on Research in Language and Literacy *(1937)*
MSC 05 3040, Univ. of New Mexico
Albuquerque, NM 87131
Members: 450 individuals
Annual Budget: $25-50,000
Newsletter Editor: Betsy Noll

Historical Note
Formerly the National Conference on Research in English(1996). Members are teachers and researchers in English. Has no paid officers or full-time staff; the secretariat changes bienially. Membership by invitation only. Membership: $10/year.

Meetings/Conferences:
Annual Meetings: Spring, with Internat'l Reading Ass'n and Fall, with Nat'l Council of Teachers of English

Publications:
Newsletter. semi-a.
Directory.

National Conference on Weights and Measures *(1905)*
15245 Shady Grove Rd.
Suite 130
Rockville, MD 20850-3222
Tel: (240)632-9454 *Fax:* (301)990-9771
E-Mail: ncwm@mgmtsol.com
Web Site: www.ncwm.net
Members: 3500 individuals
Staff: 5
Annual Budget: $500-1,000,000
Executive Director: Beth W. Palys, CAE

Historical Note
Members are weights and measures enforcement officials from federal, state, county and local governments; associate members from industry. Sponsored by the National Institute of Standards & Technology. Membership: $50/year (state or government); $65/year (associate member).

Meetings/Conferences:
Annual Meetings: July/450

Publications:
Newsletter. 3/year.
Annual Report. a.
Handbook 44. a.
Handbook 130. a.
Proceedings of Annual Meeting. a.

National Congress for Community Economic Development *(1970)*
1030 15th St. NW
Suite 325
Washington, DC 20005
Tel: (202)289-9020 *Fax:* (202)289-7051
Toll Free: (877)446 - 2233
Web Site: www.ncced.org
Members: 3600 CDCs
Staff: 12
Annual Budget: $2-5,000,000
Interim President and Chief Executive Officer: Pamela McKee
Fiscal Manager: Robin Essandoh

Historical Note
The National Congress for Community Economic Development (NCCED) is the association and advocate for the community-based development industry.

Meetings/Conferences:
Annual Meetings: Spring

National Congress of Animal Trainers and Breeders *(1975)*
23675 W. Chardon Rd.
Grayslake, IL 60030
Tel: (847)546-0717 *Fax:* (847)546-3454
Members: 300 individuals
Staff: 2
President: John F. Cuneo, Jr.

Historical Note
NCATB members are individuals and organizations involved in the breeding and training of rare animals for display in circuses, fairs and parks.

National Congress of Inventor Organizations *(1977)*
P.O. Box 931881
Los Angeles, CA 90093-1881
Tel: (323)878-6952
Toll Free: (888)695 - 4495
E-Mail: ncio@inventionconvention.com
Web Site: www.inventionconvention.com/ncio
Staff: 1
Executive Director: Stephen Paul Gnass

Historical Note
NCIO is the central umbrella organization representing inventors' groups and collegiate inventors' programs in the U.S. Membership: $75/year (individual); $200/year (organization); $600/year (company).

Meetings/Conferences:
Annual Meetings: usually Labor Day weekend/Pasadena, CA

Publications:
America's Inventor. q.
Invention Resource Directory. bien.

National Constables Association *(1973)*
16 Stonybrook Dr.
Levittown, PA 19055-2217
Tel: (215)547-6400 *Fax:* (215)943-0979
Toll Free: (800)272 - 1775
Members: 15000 individuals
Staff: 3
Annual Budget: $50-100,000
Executive Director: Hal Lefcourt

Historical Note
Founded in New Jersey in 1973 as the National Police Constables Association and incorporated in Pennsylvania in 1976. The present name was assumed in 1981. A non-profit, professional fraternal organization of constables, geared to a rebirth of the constable system and dedicated to upgrading their quality of performance. Membership: $60/year.

Meetings/Conferences:
Annual Meetings: March

Publications:
All Points Bulletin. q. adv.
NCA Program Booklet. a. adv.
Constable News. q. adv.
Buyer's Guide. semi-a. adv.
Newsletter. q. adv.

National Consumers League *(1899)*
1701 K St. NW
Suite 1200
Washington, DC 20006
Tel: (202)835-3323 *Fax:* (202)835-0747
Web Site: www.nclnet.org
Staff: 20
Annual Budget: $1-2,000,000
President and Chief Executive Officer: Linda F. Golodner
E-Mail: lindag@nclnet.org
Vice President, Fair Labor Standards: Darlene Adkins
E-Mail: darlenea@nclnet.org
Vice President, Development: Larry Bostian
E-Mail: larryb@nclnet.org
Director, Health Policy: Rebecca Burkholder
E-Mail: rebeccab@nclnet.org
Executive Vice President: Sara Cooper
E-Mail: sarac@nclnet.org
Program Director, Life Smarts: Liza Hertzberg
E-Mail: lisah@nclnet.org
Vice President, Communications: Carol McKay
Director, Information and Special Services: Faith Silvers
E-Mail: faiths@nclnet.org
Office Manager: Theresa E. Smith
E-Mail: theresas@nclnet.org

Historical Note
A non-profit membership organization, the League's mission is to identify, protect, represent, and advance the economic and social interests of consumers and workers. Absorbed the National Consumers Congress in 1978. Absorbed the National Coalition for Consumer Education in 2000. Membership: $20/year (individual); $25-250/year (organization).

Meetings/Conferences:
Annual Meetings: April or May

Publications:
Online Child Labor Monitor. m.
Focus on Fraud (online). q.
Bulletin. bi-m.

National Contact Lens Examiners *(1976)*
6506 Loisdale Rd.
Suite 209
Springfield, VA 22150
Tel: (703)719-5800 *Fax:* (703)719-9144
Toll Free: (800)296 - 1379
E-Mail: mail@abo-ncle.org
Web Site: www.abo-ncle.org
Members: 7500 individuals
Staff: 8
Annual Budget: $250-500,000
Executive Director: Michael H. Robey

National Contract Management Association *(1959)*
8260 Greensboro Dr., Suite 200
McLean, VA 22102
Tel: (571)382-0082 *Fax:* (703)448-0939
Toll Free: (800)344 - 8096 Ext:
E-Mail: memberservices@ncmahq.org
Web Site: www.ncmahq.org
Members: 21500 individuals
Staff: 28
Annual Budget: $2-5,000,000
Executive Director: Neal J. Couture
Director, Meetings: Michelle Bourke
E-Mail: bourke@ncmahq.org
Director, Communications: Amy Miedema
E-Mail: miedema@ncmahq.org
Manager, Chapter Relations: Wendy Murrah
E-Mail: murrah@ncmahq.org
Chief Financial Officer: Sam Smith, CPA
E-Mail: ssmith@ncmahq.org

Historical Note
Members are concerned with various forms of contracting with federal, state and local governments and industry. Formerly (1965) National Association of Professional Contracts Administrators. Absorbed Gov't Contract Management Association of America in 1965. Membership: $100/year, $20/initiation fee.

Publications:
Contract Management Journal. semi-a. adv.
Contract Management Magazine. m. adv.
Buyers Guide. a.

National Cooperative Business Association *(1916)*
1401 New York Ave. NW
Suite 1100
Washington, DC 20005
Tel: (202)638-6222 *Fax:* (202)638-1374
E-Mail: ncba@ncba.org
Web Site: www.ncba.coop
Members: 385 individuals
Staff: 35
Annual Budget: $5-10,000,000
President and Chief Executive Officer: Paul Hazen
Director, Communications and Marketing: Art Jaeger
Historical Note
Founded as the Cooperative League of the U.S.A.; NCBA assumed its present name in 1985. Represents American cooperatives in International Cooperative Alliance. Supports and represents all types of cooperatives. Sponsors and supports the Cooperative Action for Congressional Trust (CO-ACT). Has an annual budget of approximately $9.3 million. Membership: $50/year (individual); varies for organizations.
Meetings/Conferences:
Annual Meetings: *Spring in Washington, DC*
Publications:
Cooperative Business Journal. 10/year.

National Corn Growers Association *(1957)*
632 Cepi Drive
Chesterfield, MO 63005
Tel: (636)733-9004 *Fax:* (636)733-9005
E-Mail: corninfo@ncga.com
Web Site: www.ncga.com
Members: 30000 individuals
Staff: 30
Annual Budget: $2-5,000,000
Chief Executive Officer: S. Richard Tolman
E-Mail: tolman@ncga.com
Director, Administration: Rodger Mansfield
Director, Marketing Communications: Mimi Ricketts
E-Mail: ricketts@ncga.com
Vice President, Marketing: Fred O. Stemme
Historical Note
NCGA represents U.S. corn growers. Membership: $20-50/year (varies by state).
Meetings/Conferences:
2007 - Tampa, FL
Publications:
Corn Grower Newsletter. m.

National Correctional Industries Association *(1941)*
1202 N. Charles St.
Baltimore, MD 21201
Tel: (410)230-3972 *Fax:* (410)230-3981
E-Mail: info@nationalncia.org
Web Site: www.nationalcia.org
Members: 8000 individuals
Staff: 5
Annual Budget: $50-100,000
Executive Director: Gina Honeycutt
E-Mail: info@nationalncia.org
Historical Note
Members are personnel in correctional industries. Affiliated with the American Correctional Association and Jail Industries Association Representatives. Membership: $30/year (individual); $700/year (organization).
Meetings/Conferences:
2007 - Jacksonville, FL(Hyatt Regency)/March 25-28/600
Publications:
NCIA Newsletter. q. adv.
NCIA Directory. a. adv.

National Corrugated Steel Pipe Association *(1956)*
13140 Coit Rd.
Suite 320, LB 120
Dallas, TX 75240-5737
Tel: (972)850-1907 *Fax:* (972)490-4219
E-Mail: csp@ncspa.org
Web Site: www.ncspa.org
Members: 90 manufacturers
Staff: 3
Annual Budget: $500-1,000,000
Director, Operations and Member Services: Jennifer Raney
Chief Engineer: Dan Edwards, PE
Historical Note
NCSPA's mission is to promote sound public policy relating to the use of corrugated steel drainage structures in private and public construction. Formerly National Corrugated Metal Pipe Association. Membership: $550-$5,500/year (company); $660-$1,320/year (affiliate).
Meetings/Conferences:
Annual Meetings: March
Publications:
NCSPA News. q.
Pipeline. q.

National Cosmetology Association *(1921)*
401 N. Michigan Ave., Suite 2200
Chicago, IL 60601
Tel: (312)527-6765 *Fax:* (312)464-6118
Web Site: www.salonprofessionals.org
Members: 40000 individuals
Staff: 2
Annual Budget: $2-5,000,000
Executive Director: Gordon Miller
Historical Note
Members are owners and operators of hair, skin and nail salons. Formerly (1986) National Hairdressers and Cosmetologists Association. Sponsors and supports the NCA Political Action Committee. Membership: dues vary by state.
Meetings/Conferences:
Semi-Annual Meetings: Winter and Summer
Publications:
CB Journal.
Salon Ovations Magazine. m. adv.
Leadership Newsletter. q.
American Looks. semi-a.
American Salons Magazine.

National Costumers Association *(1923)*
121 N. Bosart Ave.
Indianapolis, IN 46201
Tel: (317)351-1940 *Fax:* (317)351-1941
Toll Free: (800)622 - 1321
E-Mail: office@costumers.org
Web Site: www.costumers.org
Members: 525 theatrical costumers & suppliers
Staff: 2
Annual Budget: $250-500,000
Secretary-Treasurer: Jennifer Skarstedt
Historical Note
Membership: $285/year (organization/company).
Meetings/Conferences:
2007 - Sunnyvale, CA/July 6-12
Publications:
The Costumers Magazine. bi-m. adv.

National Cotton Batting Institute *(1954)*
4322 Bloombury St.
Southaven, MS 38672
E-Mail: info@natbat.com
Web Site: www.natbat.com
Members: 40 individuals
Staff: 2
Annual Budget: $10-25,000
Executive Secretary: Fred Middleton
Historical Note
Administrative support provided by National Cotton Council.
Meetings/Conferences:
Annual Meetings: Spring

National Cotton Council of America *(1939)*
1918 N. Parkway
Memphis, TN 28112-5000
Tel: (901)274-9030 *Fax:* (901)725-0510
E-Mail: info@cotton.org
Web Site: www.cotton.org
Members: 35000 individuals
Staff: 78
Annual Budget: $5-10,000,000
President: Dr. Mark D. Lange
Vice President, Policy Analysis and Information Services/Program Coordinator: Dr. Gary Adams
Vice President, Producer Affairs: Craig Brown
Director, Meetings and Travel Services: Ellen Carpenter
Director, Member Services: John Gibson
Vice President, Technical Services: Dr. Andrew G. Gordon
Vice President, Administration and Program Coordination: Fred Johnson
Historical Note
Members are individuals and companies in seven segments of the cotton industry: producers, ginners, crushers, warehousemen, shippers, cooperatives and textile mills.
Meetings/Conferences:
Annual Meetings: Winter
Publications:
Journal of Cotton Science. q.
Cotton Economic Review. m.
Cotton's Week. w.

National Cotton Ginners' Association *(1938)*
P.O. Box 820285
Memphis, TN 38182-0285
Tel: (901)274-9030 *Fax:* (901)725-0510
E-Mail: bnorman@cotton.org
Web Site: http://ncga.cotton.org
Members: 8 organizations
Staff: 2
Annual Budget: $100-250,000
Executive Vice President: Bill M. Norman, D.Engr.
Historical Note
Members are state and regional associations representing cotton ginners and processors. Administrative support provided by National Cotton Council.
Meetings/Conferences:
Annual Meetings: Winter with Nat'l Cotton Council
2007 - Austin, TX(Hilton Austin)/Feb. 1-5/100

National Cottonseed Products Association *(1897)*
104 Timber Creek Dr.
Suite 200
Cordova, TN 38018-4234
Tel: (901)682-0800 *Fax:* (901)682-2856
E-Mail: info@cottonseed.com
Web Site: www.cottonseed.com
Members: 300 businesses
Staff: 2
Annual Budget: $500-1,000,000
Executive Vice President: Ben Morgan
Treasurer: Sandra Stine
Historical Note
Founded as the Interstate Cottonseed Crushers Association, it assumed its present name in 1929. NCPA is the trade association of the cottonseed processing industry in the United States and represents the industry's interests in many fora. Major services include administration of a set of trading rules, providing information to individuals and groups, and promoting the culinary value of cottonseed oil and the animal feed value of cottonseed meal.
Meetings/Conferences:
Annual Meetings: May
Publications:
Proceedings. a.
Newsletter. bi-w.
Trading Rules. a.
Statistical Handbook. a.

National Council for Advanced Manufacturing *(1989)*
2000 L St. NW
Suite 807
Washington, DC 20036
Tel: (202)429-2220 *Fax:* (202)429-2422
E-Mail: nacfam@nacfam.org
Web Site: www.nacfam.org
Members: 300companiesandorganizations
Staff: 12
Annual Budget: $1-2,000,000
Chief Executive Officer: Eric Mittelstadt

Manager, Membership: Neil Reddy

Historical Note

NACFAM members are manufacturers, non-profit organizations and educational institutions with an interest in advanced manufacturing technology and workforce development. NACFAM promotes the interests of United States manufacturers by improving their product quality, market share and productivity through the deployment of advanced manufacturing processes, related management strategies, and technical training. Membership: $1,000-15,000/year, varies by type and size of organization.

Meetings/Conferences:

Annual Meetings: Spring

Publications:

Policy Insights. m.
NACFAM Manufacturing Metrics. q.
NACFAM White Papers. irreg.
NACFAM Reports. irreg.
NACFAM Weekly. w.
NACFAM Issue Briefs. q.

National Council for Agricultural Education *(1983)*

1410 King St., Suite 400
Alexandria, VA 22314
Tel: (703)838-5881 *Fax:* (703)838-5888
Toll Free: (800)772 - 0939 Ext: 4241
E-Mail: council@teamaged.org
Web Site: www.teamaged.org
Staff: 2
Executive Secretary: C. Coleman Harris

Publications:

Monday Morning Monitor (online). w.

National Council for Air and Stream Improvement *(1943)*

P.O. Box 13318
Research Triangle Park, NC 27709-3318
Tel: (919)941-6400 *Fax:* (919)941-6401
Web Site: www.ncasi.org
Members: 70 companies
Staff: 86
Annual Budget: $10-25,000,000
President: Ronald Yeske, Ph.D.

Historical Note

A technical organization devoted to finding solutions to environmental protection problems related to the manufacture of pulp, paper and wood products and industrial forestry. Formerly (1968) National Council for Stream Improvement. Has an annual budget of over $10 million. Membership: dues based on production.

Meetings/Conferences:

Biennial Meetings:

Publications:

Bulletin Board. bi-w.
Technical Bulletins. irreg.
Forestry Environmental Program News. bi-w.

National Council for Community Behavioral Healthcare *(1970)*

12300 Twinbrook Pkwy., Suite 320
Rockville, MD 20852
Tel: (301)984-6200 *Fax:* (301)881-7159
Web Site: www.nccbh.org
Members: 1200 companies
Staff: 14
Annual Budget: $2-5,000,000
President and Chief Executive Officer: Linda Rosenberg
Executive Vice President: Jeannie Campbell
Director, Marketing and Communications: Meena Dayak
Director of Government Relations: Charles Ingoglia
Senior Vice President: Tom Willis

Historical Note

Founded as National Council of Community Mental Health Centers; became National Community Mental Healthcare Council in 1993, and assumed its current name in 1997. Absorbed Association of Mental Health Administrators in 1998. Promotes a unified network of community behavioral health care providers, authorities, state associations, integrated service networks on the national, state and local level. Membership fee based on budget.

Meetings/Conferences:

Annual Meetings: Spring
2007 – Las Vegas, NV(MGM Grand)/March 26-27/1300

Publications:

National Council News. q. adv.

National Council for Geographic Education *(1915)*

Jacksonville State University
206A Martin Hall
Jacksonville, AL 36265-1602
Tel: (256)782-5293 *Fax:* (256)782-5336
E-Mail: ncge@jsu.edu
Web Site: www.ncge.org
Members: 2500 individuals
Staff: 4
Annual Budget: $250-500,000
Executive Director: Michal LeVasseur
Associate Director: Allison L. Newton

Historical Note

Formerly National Council of Geography Teachers. Seeks to enhance the status, quality, and effectiveness of geography teaching in North America. Membership: $45-$75/year (individual), $80/year (institution).

Meetings/Conferences:

Annual: Fall

Publications:

Perspective. bi-m. adv.
Journal of Geography. bi-m. adv.

National Council for Marketing and Public Relations *(1974)*

P.O. Box 336039
Greeley, CO 80633
Tel: (970)330-0771 *Fax:* (970)330-0769
Web Site: www.ncmpr.org
Members: 1550 individuals
Staff: 2
Annual Budget: $100-250,000
Executive Director: Rebecca Olson

Historical Note

Formerly (1988) the National Council for Community Relations. Affiliated with the American Association of Community Colleges. NCMPR was created to focus on the responsibilities of officers of junior community and technical colleges as communicators. Membership: $150/year (individual); $325/year (college institution).

Meetings/Conferences:

Annual Meetings: Spring

Publications:

Counsel. q.

National Council for Prescription Drug Programs *(1977)*

9240 E. Raintree Dr.
Scottsdale, AZ 85260
Tel: (480)477-1000 *Fax:* (480)767-1042
E-Mail: dkitterman@ncpdp.org
Web Site: www.ncpdp.org
Members: 1510 individuals
Staff: 21
Annual Budget: $2-5,000,000
President: Lee Ann C. Stember
Director, Standards Development: Lynne Gilbertson
Senior Vice President, Communications and Industry Relations: Catherine Graeff
Director, Marketing Communications: Dennis Kitterman
Vice President, Operations: Joanne Longie
Senior Vice President, Sales and Marketing: Phillip Scott

Historical Note

NCPDP members are chain and independent pharmacies, consulting companies, pharmacists, database management organizations, federal/state agencies, health insurers, health maintenance organizations, mail service pharmacy companies, pharmaceutical manufacturers, pharmaceutical services administration organizations, prescription service organizations, pharmacy benefit management companies, professional and trade associations, telecommunications and systems vendors, wholesale drug distributors, and other parties interested in electronic standardization within the pharmacy services sector of the health care industry. Membership: $650/year (individual).

Meetings/Conferences:

Annual Meetings: Spring

Publications:

Council Connection. q. adv.

National Council for Textile Education *(1933)*

Historical Note

An affiliate of American Textile Manufacturers Institute, which provides administrative support.

National Council for the Social Studies *(1921)*

8555 16th St., Suite 500
Silver Spring, MD 20910
Tel: (301)588-1800 *Fax:* (301)588-2049
E-Mail: ncss@ncss.org
Web Site: www.socialstudies.org
Members: 23000 individuals
Staff: 20
Annual Budget: $2-5,000,000
Executive Director: Susan Griffin
Communications and Government Relations Director: Albert Frascella
Director, Meetings: Ella McDowell
Director, Membership Processing: Cassandra Roberts
Director, Publications: Michael Simpson

Historical Note

Formed by a group of college and public school educators in 1921 in Atlantic City, NJ as the National Council of Teachers of the Social Studies, it was transformed into the National Council for the Social Studies a year later with a new constitution. This subsequently became a department of the National Education Association in 1925 and completely independent in 1973. NCSS includes elementary and secondary teachers of history, geography, economics, political science, sociology, psychology, anthropology and law-related education, as well as college and university professors involved in teacher education and social studies research. NCSS provides leadership in the field of social studies education, assists in the professional development for social studies educators, and fosters and strengthens the advancement of social studies education. Membership: $55/year (individual); $75/year (institution).

Meetings/Conferences:

Annual Meetings: November
2007 – San Diego, CA
2008 – Houston, TX
2009 – Atlanta, GA
2010 – Denver, CO
2011 – Washington, DC

Publications:

Social Studies Professional. bi-m. adv.
NCSS Bulletin. bi-a..
Social Education. 4/yr. adv.
Theory and Research in Social Education. 4/yr.
Social Studies and the Young Learner. 4/yr. adv.
Middle Level Learning. 3/year.

National Council for Therapeutic Recreation Certification *(1981)*

Seven Elmwood Dr.
New City, NY 10956
Tel: (845)639-1439 *Fax:* (845)639-1471
E-Mail: nctrc@nctrc.org
Web Site: www.nctrc.org
Members: 18000 individuals
Staff: 15
Annual Budget: $1-2,000,000
Executive Director: Bob Riley, Ph.D.

Historical Note

Founded in 1981, NCTRC is the recognized certifying body for recreation therapy personnel in the United States, awarding the Certified Therapeutic Recreation Specialist (CTRS) designation. Certification renewal: $75.

Meetings/Conferences:

Semi-Annual: April and November in New York, NY

Publications:

NCTRC Newsletter. 2/year.

National Council for Workforce Education

410 Oak Street, ALU 113
Big Rapids, MI 49307
Tel: (231)591-3534 *Fax:* (231)591-3539
Toll Free: (800)562 - 9130
E-Mail: ncwe@ncwe.org

Web Site: www.ncwe.org
Members: 650 individuals
Staff: 1
Annual Budget: $100-250,000
President: Dr. Lydia Tena-Perez
E-Mail: lydiap@epcc.edu

Historical Note

NCWE members are occupational, vocational, technical and career educators; economic development professionals; and business, labor, military and government representatives. An affiliate council of the American Association of Community Colleges, NCWE provides a national forum for workforce and economic development professionals to affect and direct the future of work-related education. Membership: $125/year (individual); $295/year (3 institutional members); $495 (5 institutional members).

Meetings/Conferences:

Annual Meetings: 45
2007 - Savannah, GA(Marriott)/Oct. 27-30/450

Publications:

Mongraphs.
Workplace Newsletter. q.
Membership Directory. a.

National Council of Acoustical Consultants *(1962)*

7150 Winston Dr., Suite 300
Indianapolis, IN 46268
Tel: (317)328-0642 *Fax:* (317)328-4629
E-Mail: info@ncac.com
Web Site: www.ncac.com
Members: 116 companies
Staff: 2
Annual Budget: $10-25,000
Executive Director: Jackie Williams

Historical Note

Dedicated to management and related concerns of professional acoustical consulting firms and to safeguarding the interests of the clients and public which they serve. Membership: $180/year (one person firm).

Meetings/Conferences:

Semi-annual Meetings: May/November

Publications:

Directory. a.
NCAC Newsletter. q. adv.

National Council of Administrative Women in Education *(1915)*

Lakeside Union School District
P.O. Box 578
Lakeside, CA 92040
Tel: (619)390-2606 *Fax:* (619)561-7929
Members: 1500 individuals
Annual Budget: $10-25,000
President: Carol Leighty
E-Mail: Cleighty@sdcoe.k12.ca.us

Historical Note

Founded in 1915 at the National Education Association convention in Oakland, California. Became an accredited department of the NEA in 1932, and an autonomous organization in 1973. Main purpose is to encourage women to prepare for and accept administrative and executive positions in education. Has no paid officers or full-time staff; officers change annually in June. Membership: $15/year.

Meetings/Conferences:

Annual Meetings: Spring

Publications:

NCAWE News. 2/year. adv.
Leadership in Education Journal. bien.

National Council of Agricultural Employers *(1964)*

1112 16th St. NW
Suite 920
Washington, DC 20036-4823
Tel: (202)728-0300 *Fax:* (202)728-0303
E-Mail: info@ncaeonline.org
Web Site: www.ncaeonline.org
Members: 300 individuals
Staff: 3
Annual Budget: $250-500,000
Executive Vice President: Sharon M. Hughes, CAE
Administrative Manager: Jason Rios

Historical Note

Members are growers and producers who employ agricultural laborers, as well as processors and organizations related to the agriculture business. Strictly an information and government relations center; does not negotiate contracts. Membership: $400/year minimum.

Meetings/Conferences:

Semi-Annual Meetings: February; Summer and Winter

Publications:

NCAE Field Report. m.

National Council of Architectural Registration Boards *(1919)*

1801 K St. NW
Suite 1100-K
Washington, DC 20006
Tel: (202)783-6500 *Fax:* (202)783-0290
Web Site: www.ncarb.org
Members: 54 state registration boards
Staff: 75
Annual Budget: $10-25,000,000
Executive Vice President: Lenore M. Lucey, FAIA
Director, Educational and International Services: Michiel M. Bourdrez
Director, Finance and Administration: Mary de Sousa
Director, Corporate Affairs: Susan L. Wise

Historical Note

Assists state regulatory agencies in developing regulations for the practice of architecture and the licensing of persons wishing to practice. Membership: $4,500/year (state regulatory boards).

Meetings/Conferences:

Annual Meetings: Summer/400
2007 - Denver, CO

Publications:

Direct Connection. 2/year.
Annual and Pre-Annual Reports. a.
Examination Handbooks. a.

National Council of Area and Regional Travel Organizations

Historical Note

A division of the Travel Industry Association of America, which provides administrative support.

National Council of Art Administrators *(1972)*

College of Fine Arts
Univ. of Kentucky
Louisville, KY 40506-0022
Tel: (859)257-1707 *Fax:* (859)323-1050
Web Site: www.ncaaarts.org
Members: 200 individuals
Administrative Coordinator: Robert Shay
E-Mail: rshay@uky.edu

Historical Note

NCAA members are visual arts administrators in higher education. Has no paid officers or full-time staff. Membership: $30/year (individual).

Publications:

Newsletter.
Directory.

National Council of Athletic Training *(1976)*

Historical Note

An affiliate of National Association for Sport and Physical Education, which provides administrative support.

National Council of Black Engineers and Scientists *(1977)*

1525 Aviation Blvd., Suite C424
Redondo Beach, CA 90278
Tel: (213)896-9779
Annual Budget: $100-250,000
President: Paula Gray

Historical Note

Created to establish a link between individual technical organizations in order to maintain communications between such groups and improve the ability of these organizations to voice their concerns on a national level. Membership: $50/year (national dues).

Meetings/Conferences:

Annual Meetings: October

Publications:

Technews. q. adv.
Technet Conference Program Book. a. adv.
NCBES Magazine. a. adv.

National Council of Catholic Women *(1920)*

200 N. Glebe Rd.
Suite 703
Arlington, VA 22203
Tel: (703)224-0990 *Fax:* (703)224-0991
Toll Free: (800)506 - 9407
E-Mail: nccw01@algxmail.com
Web Site: www.nccw.org
Members: 5000 organizations
Staff: 9
Annual Budget: $500-1,000,000
Executive Director: Sheila McCarron
E-Mail: smccarron.nccw@algxmail.com
Assistant to Director, Meetings and Member Services: Sheila Bostick-Dobbs
E-Mail: meetings.nccw@algxmail.com

Historical Note

A federation of national, state, diocesan, inter-parochial, and parochial organizations of Catholic women. Membership fee based upon type of organization.

Meetings/Conferences:

Annual Meetings: Fall

Publications:

Catholic Woman. bi-m.

National Council of Chain Restaurants *(1965)*

325 Seventh St. NW
Suite 1100
Washington, DC 20004
Tel: (202)626-8183 *Fax:* (202)626-8185
Members: 40 companies
Staff: 3
Annual Budget: $250-500,000
Vice President, Government Relations: Scott Vinson

Historical Note

Formerly (1973) American Restaurant Institute and (1990) Foodservice and Lodging Institute. Membership limited to major multi-unit, multi-state operators. The principal objective of NCCR is to monitor and lobby the government on legislative and regulatory initiatives of general significance to its membership. NCCR also litigates issues of common interest to the majority of its membership. Membership fees vary, based on sales.

Meetings/Conferences:

Three Meetings Annually: two in Washington, DC, one elsewhere

National Council of Coal Lessors *(1951)*

300 Summers St., Suite 1050
Charleston, WV 25301
Members: 50 companies
Staff: 1
Assistant Secretary: Lynn Lawson

Historical Note

Supports the National Council of Coal Lessors Political Action Committee. Members are owners of coal-bearing land concerned with taxes, depletion allowances, black lung payments, etc.

National Council of Commercial Plant Breeders *(1954)*

225 Reinekers Lane, Suite 650
Alexandria, VA 22314
Tel: (703)837-8140 *Fax:* (703)837-9365
Toll Free: (888)890 - 7333
Web Site: www.nccpb.org
Members: 63 companies
Staff: 1
Annual Budget: $25-50,000
Secretary/ Treasurer: Ann Jorss

Historical Note

Founded in 1954 by representatives of thirteen commercial firms as a non-profit organization to promote the achievement and interest of American plant breeders both in the United States and abroad.

Meetings/Conferences:

Annual Meetings: June/100

National Council of Erectors, Fabricators and Riggers *(1969)*

10382 Main St., Suite 200
Box 280
Fairfax, VA 22038
Tel: (703)591-1870 *Fax:* (703)591-1895
Members: 3 organizations
Staff: 3
Annual Budget: $50-100,000
Executive Vice President: Fred H. Codding

Historical Note
Members are the Specialized Carriers and Rigging Association, the National Association of Reinforcing Steel Contractors, and the National Association of Miscellaneous Ornamental and Architectural Products Contractors. Serves as interface with construction unions.

National Council of Examiners for Engineering and Surveying *(1920)*
P.O. Box 1686
Clemson, SC 29633-1686
Tel: (864)654-6824 *Fax:* (864)654-6033
Toll Free: (800)250 - 3196
Web Site: www.ncees.org
Members: 70 member boards
Staff: 60
Annual Budget: $10-25,000,000
Executive Director: F. Elizabeth Brown
Manager, Corporate Communications: Keri Anderson
Associate Executive Director: Jerry Carter
Director, Information Technology: Phyllis Fenno
Manager, Meetings and Marketing Communications: Nina Norris
Director, Finance: Jeannie VanderZalm
Director, Exam Development: Chuck Wallace
Director, ELSES: Susan Whitfield

Historical Note
Formerly (1967) National Council of State Boards of Engineering Examiners, and (1989) National Council of Engineering Examiners. Coordinates examination and registration of professional engineers and land surveyors. Has an annual budget of approximately $10 million. Membership: $5,000/year (company).

Meetings/Conferences:
Annual Meetings: August/350
2007 – Philadelphia, PA/Aug. 22-25

Publications:
Licensure Exchange. 6/year.
Convention Reports. a.

National Council of Exchangors *(1975)*
P.O. Box 3658
Prescott, AZ 86302
Tel: (928)771-2300 *Fax:* (928)771-2323
E-Mail: nb@infoville.com
Web Site: www.infoville.com
Members: 400 individuals
Staff: 2
Annual Budget: $50-100,000
Past President: Ken Kisner
E-Mail: nb@infoville.com

Historical Note
The National Council of Exchangors, a non-profit association, is a nationwide network of real estate professionals who specialize in marketing real estate equities primarily through the medium of the real estate exchange. This network is comprised of local Groups organized into Regional Chapters. Membership: $150/year (indvidual).

Publications:
NCE Marketing Conference Publication.
NCEmail Newsletter.
NCE Membership Networking Directory. a.

National Council of Farmer Cooperatives *(1929)*
50 F St. NW
Suite 900
Washington, DC 20001-1530
Tel: (202)626-8700 *Fax:* (202)626-8722
Web Site: www.ncfc.org
Members: 3000 local co-ops; 27 state and reg'l councils
Staff: 14
Annual Budget: $2-5,000,000
President and Chief Executive Officer: Jean-Mari Peltier
Director, Meetings: Christina Cooper
Senior Vice President: Randall T. Jones
Director, Finance/Administration: Catherine Wilson

Historical Note
NCFC is a nationwide association of cooperative businesses which are owned and controlled by farmers. Absorbed National Federation of Grain Cooperatives (1973) and American Institute of Cooperation (1991). Sponsors and supports the National Council of Farmer Cooperatives Political Action Committee (Co-op PAC). Affiliated with Farm Credit Council and the Agricultural Cooperative Development International.

Meetings/Conferences:
2007 – Jan. 22-24

Publications:
American Cooperation. a.
Journal of Agricultural Cooperation. a.

National Council of Health Facilities Finance Authorities *(1987)*
330 S. Poplar
Pierre, SD 57501
Tel: (605)224-9200 *Fax:* (605)224-7177
E-Mail: don.templeton@sdhefa.com
Web Site: www.nchffa.com
Members: 30 member states, 3 associates
Annual Budget: $100-250,000
President: Don A. Templeton

Historical Note
NCHFFA's mission is to preserve, promote and enhance common interests and effectiveness of its member organizations, through communication, education and advocacy. NCHFFA focuses its efforts on issues which directly influence the availability of and access to tax-exempt financing for health care facilities. Membership: $500/year.

Meetings/Conferences:
Annual Meetings: Fall

Publications:
Nat'l Council of Health Facilities Finance Authorities Newsletter. q.
Council Report. bien.

National Council of Higher Education Loan Programs *(1961)*
1100 Connecticut Ave. NW
Suite 1200
Washington, DC 20036-4110
Tel: (202)822-2106 *Fax:* (202)822-2143
Web Site: www.nchelp.org
Members: 175 organizations
Staff: 11
Annual Budget: $500-1,000,000
President: Brett E. Lief
Federal Relations and Industry Operations: Mike Balough
Vice President, Communications and Research: Karen Lanning
Membership Services: Chris Martin
Vice President, Counsel for Regulation and Legislation: Bart Stevens

Historical Note
Formerly (1969) National Conference of Executives of Higher Education Loan Plans. Members are private and state non-profit corporations that guarantee student loans under the Higher Education Act of 1965, secondary markets, lenders, servicers, collectors, institutions of higher education and other organizations involved in the administration of the Federal Family Education Loan Program.

Meetings/Conferences:
Semi-Annual Meetings: Spring and Fall

National Council of Industrial Naval Air Stations *(1957)*
P.O. Box 1239
Jacksonville, FL 32230
Tel: (904)542-2617 Ext: 101 *Fax:* (904)542-2610
Members: 7 organizations
Staff: 2
Annual Budget: $10-25,000
President: Barry K. Adams
E-Mail: adamsbk@navair.navy.mil

Historical Note
Formerly (1980) National Council of Naval Air Station Employee Organizations. NCINAS is an umbrella organization composed of regional organizations representing 20,000 civilian employees of naval air stations.

National Council of Investigation and Security Services *(1975)*
7501 Sparrows Point Blvd.
Baltimore, MD 21219-1927
Toll Free: (800)445 - 8408
E-Mail: nciss@aol.com
Web Site: www.nciss.org
Members: 525 state associations and firms
Staff: 1
Annual Budget: $50-100,000
Executive Director: Carolyn Ward
E-Mail: nciss@aol.com

Historical Note
State associations and firms providing contract security services and investigative services. Membership: $125/year (organization/company).

Meetings/Conferences:
Annual Meetings: Spring

Publications:
NCISS Report. q.

National Council of Juvenile and Family Court Judges *(1937)*
P.O. Box 8970
Reno, NV 89507
Tel: (775)784-6012 *Fax:* (775)784-6628
E-Mail: staff@ncjfcj.org
Web Site: www.ncjfcj.org
Members: 2500 individuals
Staff: 110
Annual Budget: $10-25,000,000
Executive Director: Mary Mentaberry
Director, Conference Planning: Diane Barnette
Director, Finance: Cheryl Dailey
Director, Administration: Cheryl Davidek
Manager, Membership: Dorothy Hall
Director, Human Resources: Kim Studebaker
Manager, Information Technology: Robyn Whyms

Historical Note
NCJFCJ is located on the campus of the University of Nevada, Reno, with a mission to improve the standards, practices, and effectiveness of the Nation's juvenile and family courts and related systems while acknowledging and upholding victims' rights, the safety of all family members, and the safety of the community. Provides continuing education opportunities, practice-based resources, research, and policy development in juvenile and family justice. Membership: $150/year (judicial); $100/year (associate); $40/year (student).

Meetings/Conferences:
Annual Meetings: July

Publications:
Juvenile and Family Justice Today. q. adv.
Juvenile and Family Law Digest. m.
Juvenile and Family Court Journal. q.

National Council of Legislators from Gaming States *(1995)*
385 Jordan Rd.
Troy, NY 12180
Tel: (518)687-0615 *Fax:* (518)687-0401
E-Mail: info@nclgs.org
Web Site: www.nclgs.org
Members: 12 member states
Staff: 2
Executive Director: Susan F. Nolan

Historical Note
NCLGS is the only organization of state lawmakers that meet on a regular basis to discuss issues in regard to gaming. Members of NCLGS chair are members of committees responsible for the regulation of gaming in their state legislative house. NCLGS does not promote or oppose gaming but is primarily concerned with the proper regulation of the industry.

Meetings/Conferences:
2007 – Duck Key, FL(Hawk's Cay Resort)/Jan. 12-14/110

National Council of Local Human Service Administrators *(1940)*
810 1st St. NE
Suite 500
Washington, DC 20002-4267
Tel: (202)682-0100 *Fax:* (202)289-6555
Members: 150 local agencies

Staff: 1
Annual Budget: $50-100,000
Deputy Executive Director, Communications and Member Services: Gary Cyphers

Historical Note
Formerly National Council of Local Public Welfare Administrators. NCLHSA is a council of the American Public Welfare Association. NCLHSA assumed its current name in 2002, when its parent organization, APWA, assumed its current name; represents local agencies and their policy practice and leadership issues.

Meetings/Conferences:
Three Annual:

National Council of Multifamily Housing

Historical Note
A division of the National Association of Home Builders of the U.S.

National Council of Music Importers and Exporters *(1966)*

Historical Note
Address unknown in 2006.

National Council of Nonprofit Associations *(1989)*

1030 15th St. NW
Suite 870
Washington, DC 20005-1525
Tel: (202)962-0322 *Fax:* (202)962-0321
E-Mail: ncna@ncna.org
Web Site: www.ncna.org
Members: 38 state ass'ns of non-profits
Staff: 9
Annual Budget: $500-1,000,000
Executive Director: Audrey Alvarado
E-Mail: aalvarado@ncna.org
Director, Strategic Public Policy Planning: Erica Greeley
E-Mail: egreeley@NCNA.org
Director, Marketing and Communications: Jocelyn Harmon
E-Mail: jharmon@NCNA.org

Historical Note
NCNA is an umbrella of state/regional associations of nonprofits. The mission is to advance the vital role and capacity of nonprofits. Current programming initiatives include ethics and accountability, public policy and public education on the nonprofit sector. Membership: $300/year (supporter member), and based on budget for regular members.

Meetings/Conferences:
Annual Meetings: June

Publications:
What You Need to Know. m..
SPARC Change. q.. adv.

National Council of Postal Credit Unions *(1984)*

P.O. Box 160
Del Mar, CA 92014-0160
Tel: (858)792-3883 *Fax:* (858)792-3884
E-Mail: ncpcu@ncpcu.org
Web Site: www.ncpcu.org
Members: 160 credit unions
Staff: 2
Annual Budget: $100-250,000
Executive Director: Robert P. Spindler

Publications:
Postal Courier. q.

National Council of Real Estate Investment Fiduciaries *(1982)*

Two Prudential Plaza, 180 North Stetson Ave., Suite 2515
Chicago, IL 60601
Tel: (312)819-5890 *Fax:* (312)819-5891
E-Mail: info@ncreif.org
Web Site: www.ncreif.org
Members: 300 companies
Staff: 7
Annual Budget: $500-1,000,000
Chief Executive Officer: Blake Eagle

Historical Note
Members are real estate investment managers, including insurance companies, banks and independent investment advisors, serving the pension fund real estate industry. Membership: $4,500/year (voting membership), $3,500/year (professional membership), $250/year (academic). Subscriptions for NCREIF Report available to non-members for $1,000/year.

Meetings/Conferences:
Three Meetings Annually: March, June and October

Publications:
NCREIF Real Estate Performance Report. q.

National Council of Secondary School Athletic Directors *(1968)*

Historical Note
An affiliate of National Association for Sport and Physical Education, which provides administrative support.

National Council of Self-Insurers *(1946)*

1253 Springfield Ave.
PMB 345
New Providence, NJ 07974
Tel: (908)665-2152 *Fax:* (908)665-4020
E-Mail: natcouncil@aol.com
Web Site: www.natcouncil.com/
Members: 3500 companies
Staff: 2
Annual Budget: $50-100,000
Executive Director: Lawrence J. Holt

Historical Note
Formerly (1973) National Council of State Self-insurers Associations. Members are organizations and individuals concerned with self-insurance under the workmen's compensation laws. Membership: $200/year (individual); $475/year (organization/company).

Meetings/Conferences:
Annual Meetings: Spring

Publications:
State Self-Insurance Requirements. 3/year.
Membership Directory. a.

National Council of Social Security Management Associations *(1970)*

418 C St. NE
Washington, DC 20002
Tel: (202)547-8530 *Fax:* (202)547-8532
E-Mail: president@ncssma.org
Web Site: www.ncssma.org
Members: 3000 individuals
Annual Budget: $100-250,000
President: Rick Warsinskey

Historical Note
Members are managers and supervisors of Social Security field offices and teleservice centers in the U.S. and Puerto Rico. Has no paid officers or full-time staff. Membership: $52-104/year (individual).

Meetings/Conferences:
Annual Meetings: Fall

Publications:
FrontLine. q.

National Council of State Agencies for the Blind

4733 Bethesda Ave., Suite 300
Bethesda, MD 20814
Tel: (301)654-4885 *Fax:* (301)654-5542
Web Site: www.ncsab.org
Members: 54 agencies
Annual Budget: $50-100,000
President: Allen Harris

Meetings/Conferences:
Semi-annual Meetings:

National Council of State Boards of Nursing *(1978)*

111 E. Wacker Dr., Suite 2900
Chicago, IL 60601
Tel: (312)525-3600 *Fax:* (312)279-1032
Toll Free: (866)293 - 9600
E-Mail: info@ncsbn.org
Web Site: www.ncsbn.org
Members: 61 boards
Staff: 60
Annual Budget: $10-25,000,000
Executive Director: Kathy Apple, MS, RN
Director, Member Relations: Alicia Byrd
Manager, Executive Office Administration: Kristin Garcia
Associate Director, Policy and Government Relations: Kristin Hellquist
Director, Marketing and Communications: Dawn Kappel
Director, Information Technology: Nur Rajwany
Director, Education: Nancy Spector

Historical Note
Members are state boards of nursing. Provides members with programs and services related to the regulation of nursing practice, including research, the collection and analysis of data, communications, and consulting services. The NCSBN has developed licensure examinations used by its members to test the entry-level nursing competence of candidates for licensure as registered nurses, practical nurses and nurse aides. Membership: $3,000/year.

Meetings/Conferences:
Annual Meetings: Summer
2007 – Chicago, IL(Chicago Marriott)/Aug. 7-10
2008 – Nashville, TN(Sheraton Music City)/Aug. 5-8

National Council of State Directors of Community Colleges *(1969)*

Historical Note
An affiliate of American Association of Community and Junior Colleges, which provides administrative support.

National Council of State Education Associations *(1966)*

Historical Note
A program of Nat'l Education Ass'n, which provides administrative support.

National Council of State Emergency Medical Services Training Coordinators *(1977)*

201 Park Washington Ct.
Falls Church, VA 22046
Tel: (703)538-1794 *Fax:* (703)241-5603
E-Mail: info@ncsemstc.org
Web Site: www.ncsemstc.org
Members: 56 individuals
Staff: 5
Annual Budget: $50-100,000
Executive Director: Laurence Gration, CAE

Historical Note
Members are supervisors or coordinators of state EMS training programs (limited to three members from each state). Affiliated with the American College of Emergency Physicians, National Association of State Emergency Medical Service Directors, National Association of Emergency Technicians, and the National Registry of Emergency Medical Technicians. Purpose is to improve EMS education and promote standardized training and licensure. No membership fee.

Meetings/Conferences:
Annual Meetings: Fall

National Council of State Housing Agencies *(1970)*

444 N. Capitol St. NW
Suite 438
Washington, DC 20001
Tel: (202)624-7710 *Fax:* (202)624-5899
Web Site: www.ncsha.org
Members: 55 agencies, 360 affiliates
Staff: 21
Annual Budget: $2-5,000,000
Executive Director: Barbara J. Thompson
Manager, Meetings: Maury Edwards
Director, Administration: Peggy Meehan
Director, Policy and Government Affairs: Garth Rieman

Historical Note
Formerly (1987) the Council of State Housing Agencies. Members are the housing finance agencies of the 50 states, Washington, DC, Virgin Islands, Puerto Rico, and New York City. Sponsors workshops and other opportunities for members.

Meetings/Conferences:
Annual Meetings: October

Publications:
Directory of State Housing Finance Agencies. a.
Developer's Guide to the Low Income Housing Credit.
State Housing Finance Agencies Factbook. a.

National Council of State Human Service Administrators *(1939)*

Historical Note

An affiliate of the American Public Welfare Association, which provides administrative support.

National Council of State Pharmacy Association Executives *(1929)*

5501 Patterson Ave., Suite 200
Richmond, VA 23226
Tel: (804)285-4413 *Fax:* (804)285-4227
Web Site: www.ncspae.org
Members: 52 individuals
Staff: 1
Annual Budget: $10-25,000
Administrative Manager: Rebecca P. Snead

Historical Note

Formerly (1993) National Council of State Pharmaceutical Association Executives. Membership: $100-$300/year.

Meetings/Conferences:

Annual Meetings: *With American Pharmaceutical Ass'n and Nat'l Ass'n of Retail Druggists*

National Council of State Supervisors for Languages *(1960)*

Maine Department of Education
23 State House Station
Augusta, ME 04333-0023
Tel: (207)624-6826 *Fax:* (207)624-6821
E-Mail: don.reutershan@maine.gov
Web Site: www.ncssfl.org
Members: 50 individuals
Annual Budget: under $10,000
President: Donald Reutershan

Historical Note

Provides state level leadership and support for world language programs, and liaison with other agencies and the federal government. Has no paid officers or full-time staff. Membership: $40/year (regular); $20/year (retired).

Meetings/Conferences:

Annual Meetings: *November, with the American Council on the Teaching of Foreign Languages/50*

Publications:

State Reports on Website. a..

National Council of State Tourism Directors *(1969)*

Historical Note

A council of the Travel Industry Association of America, which provides administrative support.

National Council of Supervisors of Mathematics *(1968)*

P.O. Box 150368
Lakewood, CO 80215-0308
Tel: (303)274-5932
E-Mail: ncsm@mathforum.org
Web Site: www.ncsmonline.org
Members: 2900 individuals
Staff: 1
Annual Budget: $100-250,000
President: Linda Gojak

Historical Note

Members are leaders in mathematics education at all levels of the educational system. Membership: $55/year (individual).

Meetings/Conferences:

Annual Meetings: *Early Spring/1,500*

Publications:

NCSM Journal of Mathematics Education Leadership. bi-a.
Sourcebook. irreg.
NCSM Newsletter. q.
Membership Directory. a.

National Council of Teachers of English *(1911)*

1111 W. Kenyon Rd.
Urbana, IL 61801-1096
Tel: (217)328-3870 *Fax:* (217)328-0977
Toll Free: (800)369 - 6283
Web Site: www.ncte.org
Members: 80000 individuals
Staff: 90
Annual Budget: $2-5,000,000
Executive Director: Kent D. Williamson
Assistant, Public Affairs: Lori Bianchini
Conventions: Jacqui Joseph-Biddle
Director, Finance Division: Peggy Weaver

Historical Note

An educational association devoted to improving the teaching of English and language arts, serves as a forum for the profession providing opportunities for teachers to continue their professional growth and is a forum for dealing with relevant issues. Publishes 20-25 books for teachers of English and the language arts at the elementary, secondary and college levels. Membership: $40/year (individual).

Meetings/Conferences:

Annual Meetings: *November*

Publications:

Council Chronicle Newspaper. 4/year. adv.
Language Arts. 6/year. adv.
Talking Points. 2/year.
Voices from the Middle. q. adv.
Primary Voices, K-6. q. adv.
College Composition and Communication. q. adv.
College English. 6/year. adv.
English Education. q. adv.
English Journal. 6/year. adv.
English Leadership Quarterly. q. adv.
Research in the Teaching of English. q. adv.
SLATE Newsletter. 3/year.
Teaching English in the Two-Year College. q. adv.

National Council of Teachers of Mathematics *(1920)*

1906 Association Dr.
Reston, VA 20191-1502
Tel: (703)620-9840 *Fax:* (703)476-2970
Toll Free: (800)235 - 7566
E-Mail: ntcm@ntcm.org
Web Site: www.nctm.org
Members: 100000 individuals
Staff: 105
Annual Budget: $10-25,000,000
Executive Director: James M. Rubillo
Director, Information Services and Systems: Richard Aldridge
Director, Member Services and Marketing: Krista Barnes
Director, Public Affairs: Ken Krehbiel
Director, Human Resources and Development: Melanie Ott
Associate Executive Director and Chief Financial Officer: David Shayka
E-Mail: dshayka@nctm.org
Director, Publications: Harry Tunis
Director, Conference Services: Mark E. Workman

Historical Note

NTCM is a public voice of mathematics education. Providing vision, leadership and professional development to support teachers in working to ensure the highest quality mathematics learning for all students. Membership: $72/year (individual); $46/year
(electronic membership); $99/year (institution).

Meetings/Conferences:

Annual Meetings: *Spring*
2007 – Atlanta, GA/March 21-24
2008 – Salt Lake City, UT/Apr. 9-12
2009 – Washington D.C., DC/Apr. 22-25
2010 – San Diego, CA/Apr. 21-24

Publications:

Journal for Research in Mathematics Education. 5/year. adv.
Mathematics Teacher. 9/year. adv.
Mathematics Teaching in the Middle School. 9/year. adv.
NCTM News Bulletin. 9/year. adv.
Teaching Children Mathematics. 9/yr. adv.

National Council of Textile Organizations

910 17th St. NW, Suite 1020
Washington, DC 20006
Tel: (202)822-8028 *Fax:* (202)822-8029
Web Site: www.ncto.org
Annual Budget: $1-2,000,000
President: Cass Johnson

National Council of the Churches of Christ in the U.S.A. *(1950)*

475 Riverside Dr., Room 880
New York, NY 10115-0050
Tel: (212)870-2025 *Fax:* (212)870-2817
E-Mail: news@ncccusa.org
Web Site: www.ncccusa.org
Members: 36 communions
Staff: 50
Annual Budget: Over $100,000,000
General Secretary: Rev.Dr. Robert Edgar
E-Mail: redgar@ncccusa.org
Associate General Secretary, Administration and Finance: Leora Landmesser
Associate General Secretary, Public Policy: Brenda G. Mitchell
Associate General Secretary, Communications: Wesley M. "Pat" Pattillo
E-Mail: wpatillo@ncccusa.org
Director, Education Leadership Ministries Commission: Patrice Rosner
E-Mail: prosner@ncccusa.org

Historical Note

Founded in 1950 by representatives of 29 major Protestant and Orthodox denominations who met to unite 12 nationwide interchurch agencies and form the National Council of Churches. NCC is now the primary expression of the ecumenical movement in the United States, with 36 communions - Protestant, Orthodox and Anglican church bodies with a combined membership of 52 million Christians.

Meetings/Conferences:

Annual Meetings: *November*

Publications:

EcuLink, NCC Newsletter. q.
Yearbook of American and Canadian Churches. a.

National Council of the Housing Industry

Historical Note

A subsidiary of the National Association of Home Builders of the U.S.

National Council of the Multifamily Housing Industry

Historical Note

A council of the National Association of Home Builders of the United States.

National Council of Travel Attractions

Historical Note

A division of the Travel Industry Association of America, which provides administrative support.

National Council of University Research Administrators *(1959)*

One Dupont Circle NW
Suite 220
Washington, DC 20036
Tel: (202)466-3894 *Fax:* (202)223-5573
E-Mail: info@ncura.edu
Web Site: www.ncura.edu
Members: 3100 individuals
Staff: 6
Annual Budget: $250-500,000
Executive Director: Kathleen M. Larmett
Associate Executive Director: Tara Bishop
E-Mail: bishop@ncura.edu

Historical Note

Members are individuals with professional interests in problems and policies relating to the administration of sponsored research, education and training activities at colleges and universities. Membership: $120/year.

Meetings/Conferences:

Annual Meetings: *Fall*

Publications:

ENews.
NCURA Newsletter. 5/year.
Research Management Review. semi-a.

National Council of Urban Tourism Organizations

Historical Note

A division of the Travel Industry Association of America, which provides administrative support.

National Council of Writing Program Administrators *(1975)*
Department of English
Miami University
Oxford, OH 45056
Tel: (513)529-1393 *Fax:* (513)529-1392
E-Mail: tassonjp@muohio.edu
Web Site: www.wpacouncil.org
Members: 600 individuals
Staff: 10
Annual Budget: $10-25,000
Secretary: John Paul Tassoni

Historical Note
Also known as Council of Writing Program Administrators. A national organization that fosters professional development, communication and community among college and university writing program administrators and other interested faculty. WPA provides institutions with consultant-evaluators to assess activities. Affiliated with Association of American Colleges. Membership: $30/year (individual); $40/year (institution).

Publications:
WPA News. q.
WPA: Writing Program Administration. semi-a.

National Council on Compensation Insurance *(1922)*
901 Peninsula Corp. Circle
Boca Raton, FL 33487
Tel: (561)893-1000 *Fax:* (561)893-1191
Toll Free: (800)622 - 4123
E-Mail: customer_service@ncci.com
Web Site: www.ncci.com
Members: 750insurancecompaniesandcarriers
Staff: 1000
Annual Budget: Over $100,000,000
President and Chief Executive Officer: Stephen J. Klingel
Chief Communications Officer: Cheryl Budd
Chief Financial Officer: Alfredo Guerra
Director, Community Relations: Judy Joffe

Historical Note
NCCI is a statistical research and ratemaking organization for the worker's compensation industry. Supported by the insurance industry, NCCI's primary functions are the preparation and administration of rates, rating plans, and services for workers compensation insurance in 36 states. Members include stock companies, mutual companies, competitive state funds and reciprocals. Membership: based on sliding scale. Has an annual budget of approximately $140 million.

Meetings/Conferences:
Annual Meetings: May
2007 - Orlando, FL(Portofino Bay Hotel)/May 10-11/650

Publications:
Annual Statistical Bulletin. a.
Scopes. a.
Issues Report. a.

National Council on Crime and Delinquency *(1907)*
1970 Broadway, Suite 500
Oakland, CA 94612
Tel: (510)208-0500 *Fax:* (510)208-0511
Web Site: www.nccd-crc.org
Members: 500 individuals
Staff: 65
Annual Budget: $5-10,000,000
President: Barry Krisberg, Ph.D.
Director, Communications: Susan Marchionna

Historical Note
Established in 1907 as the National Probation Association., NCCD is concerned with upgrading criminal justice practices. Membership: $200/year (institutional); $50/year (charter); $130/year (advocate); $40/year (subscriber).

Meetings/Conferences:
Meetings: three or four per year

Publications:
NCCD FOCUS. irreg.
NCCD Policy Papers. irreg.
Perspectives newsletter. semi-a.

National Council on Education for the Ceramic Arts *(1967)*
77 Erie Village Square, Suite 280
Erie, CO 80516
Toll Free: (866)266 - 2322
E-Mail: office@nceca.net
Web Site: http://nceca.net
Members: 4000 individuals
Staff: 3
Annual Budget: $500-1,000,000
Conference Manager: Dori Nielsen
E-Mail: dori@nceca.net

Historical Note
Members are faculty, professional studio artists, students and others concerned with the ceramic arts. NCECA became an independent organization in 1967 after several years of affiliation with the Ceramic Educational Council of the American Ceramic Society. Purpose is to promote and improve education in the ceramic arts. Membership: $70/year (United States member); $75/year (Canadian member); $85/year (overseas member), $40/year (U.S. student); $45/year (Canadian student); $55/year (other student).

Meetings/Conferences:
Annual Meetings: Spring
2007 - New Orleans, LA(Hyatt)/March 28-31

Publications:
NCECA Newsletter. 3/year.
NCECA Journals. a.

National Council on Family Relations *(1938)*
3989 Central Ave. NE, Suite 550
Minneapolis, MN 55421
Tel: (763)781-9331 Ext: 15 *Fax:* (763)781-9348
Toll Free: (888)781 - 9331 Ext: 15
E-Mail: info@ncfr.org
Web Site: www.ncfr.org
Members: 3500 individuals
Staff: 10
Annual Budget: $1-2,000,000
Director, Conference: Cynthia Winter

Historical Note
Professionals, academics and others interested in education and research about the family, development of community services for and government policies concerning families, and related issues. Provides a forum for family researchers, educators, practitioners and policy makers to share in the development and dissemination of knowledge about families and family relationships, establishes professional standards, and works to promote family well-being. Membership: $143/year (colleague); $450/year (organization); $200/year (benefactor); $50-$75/year (student).

Meetings/Conferences:
Annual Meetings: Fall
2007 - Pittsburgh, PA(Hilton)/Nov. 5-10
2008 - Little Rock, AR(Peabody)/Nov. 3-8
2009 - San Francisco, CA(Hyatt Regency)/Nov. 10-14

Publications:
National Report. q. adv.
Family Relations. q. adv.
Journal of Marriage and Family. q. adv.

National Council on International Trade Development *(1967)*
818 Connecticut Ave. NW, 12th Floor
Washington, DC 20006
Tel: (202)872-9280 *Fax:* (202)872-8324
E-Mail: cu@ncitd.org
Web Site: www.ncitd.org
Members: 100 individuals
Staff: 1
Annual Budget: $50-100,000
Executive Director: Mary O. Fromyer
E-Mail: mfromyer@ibqc.com
Deputy Director: Rose Flores

Historical Note
Formerly (1988) National Council on International Trade Documentation and (1995) NCITD-International Trade Facilitation Council. Members are exporters and importers and other professionals serving the international trade industry. Emphasis is on export, import and e-commerce compliance. Membership: $500-3,000/year (corporate).

Publications:
NCITD Newsletter. m.

National Council on Measurement in Education *(1938)*

Historical Note
An affiliate of American Educational Research Association, which provides administrative support.

National Council on Public History *(1979)*
327 Cavanaugh Hall - IUPUI
425 University Blvd.
Indianapolis, IN 46202-5140
Tel: (317)274-2716 *Fax:* (317)278-5230
Web Site: www.ncph.org
Members: 1700 individuals
Staff: 2
Annual Budget: $50-100,000
Executive Director: David G. Vanderstel
E-Mail: dvanders@iupui.edu

Historical Note
NCPH members are professionals and others concerned with the presentation of history in non-academic settings. Membership: $65 (individual); $100 (associate); $35 (new professionals); $25 (students); $140 (US institution); $160 (electronic only). Canada resident add 7% GST (#R122058662). Outside North America? Please add $20 to cover postage.

Meetings/Conferences:
Annual Meetings: Spring

Publications:
Careers for Students of History. irreg.
Public History News Newsletter. q. adv.
Guide to Graduate Programs in Public History. irreg.
Public Historian. q. adv.

National Council on Public Polls *(1969)*
Inst. for Public Opinion, Marist Coll.
Poughkeepsie, NY 12601
Tel: (845)575-5050 *Fax:* (845)575-5111
E-Mail: info@ncpp.org
Web Site: www.ncpp.org
Members: 40 companies
Annual Budget: under $10,000
Secretary/Treasurer: Barbara Carvalho

Historical Note
Formerly National Committee on Public Polls. Members are public opinion polling organizations. Has no paid staff. Membership: $125/year.

National Council on Qualifications for the Lighting Professions *(1992)*
P.O. Box 142729
Austin, TX 78714-2729
Tel: (512)973-0042 *Fax:* (512)973-0043
E-Mail: info@ncqlp.org
Web Site: www.ncqlp.org
Members: 972 individuals
Staff: 3
Annual Budget: $250-500,000
Executive Director: Mary Jane Kolar, CAE

Historical Note
NCQLP provides certification to professionals in the lighting industry.

National Council on Radiation Protection and Measurements *(1964)*
7910 Woodmont Ave., Suite 400
Bethesda, MD 20814-3095
Tel: (301)657-2652 *Fax:* (301)907-8768
Toll Free: (800)229 - 2652
Web Site: www.ncrponline.org
Members: 100 individuals
Staff: 12
Annual Budget: $1-2,000,000
Executive Director: David A. Schauer

Historical Note
Formerly (1929) Advisory Committee on X-ray and Radium Protection; (1947) National Committee on Radiation Protection; (1957) National Committee on Radiation Protection and Measurements.

Meetings/Conferences:
Annual Meetings: Washington, DC/Spring

Publications:
NCRP Reports. irreg.

Proceedings. a.
Commentaries. irreg.
Statements. irreg.
Annual Report. a.

National Council on Rehabilitation Education
(1961)
2012 W. Norwood Dr.
Carbondale, IL 62901
Tel: (618)549-3267 *Fax:* (618)457-3632
E-Mail: sbenshoff@ncre-admin.org
Web Site: www.rehabeducators.org
Members: 800 individuals
Staff: 1
Annual Budget: $100-250,000
Administrative Secretary: Sharon Benshoff
E-Mail: sbenshoff@ncre-admin.org

Historical Note
Members are professional educators and researchers with expertise in numerous facets of vocational rehabilitation, and eduational institutions offering academic training programs and conducting research related to rehabilitation education and improved services to consumers. Membership: $50/year (individual); $450/year (organization).

Meetings/Conferences:
Annual Meetings: Semi-Annual Meetings
2007 - San Diego, CA(Marriott Mission Valley)/Feb. 22-25/325

Publications:
Rehabilitation Education Journal. q.
Report Newsletter. q.
Membership Directory. a.

National Council on Student Development
(1960)
51 Gerty Dr., Room 129
Univ. of Illinois
Champaign, IL 61820
Tel: (217)333-9230 *Fax:* (217)244-0851
E-Mail: ncsd@uiuc.edu
Web Site: www.nationalcouncilstudentdevelopment.org
Members: 700 individuals
Staff: 2
Annual Budget: $10-25,000
Director, National Office: Debra Bragg

Historical Note
A council of the American Association of Community Colleges. Members are student affairs, student development and personnel management professionals at two-year colleges. Has no paid officers or full-time staff. Membership: $50/year (individual); $200/year (institution); $25/year (graduate student); $50/year (faculty).

Meetings/Conferences:
Annual Meetings: April, with American Ass'n of Community and Junior Colleges

National Council on Teacher Retirement *(1924)*
7600 Greenhaven Dr.
Suite 302
Sacramento, CA 95831
Tel: (916)394-2075 *Fax:* (916)392-0295
Web Site: www.nctr.org
Members: 284 organizations
Staff: 2
Annual Budget: $1-2,000,000
Executive Director: Jim Mosman
E-Mail: jmosman@nctr.org

Historical Note
Members are 50 state and 12 local retirement systems, 20 education associations, 10 state departments and agencies and 192 commercial firms.

Meetings/Conferences:
Annual: Fall
2007 - Scottsdale, AZ(Westin)/Oct. 7-11
2008 - Washington, DC(Omni)/Oct. 11-16
2009 - Palm Springs, CA(Renaissance)/Oct. 8-16/750

Publications:
Proceedings and Membership Directory. a.
Newsletter. m.

National Council on the Aging *(1950)*
1901 L St. NW
Fourth Floor
Washington, DC 20036
Tel: (202)479-1200 *Fax:* (202)479-0735
E-Mail: info@ncoa.org
Web Site: www.ncoa.org
Members: 3800 individuals
Staff: 90
Annual Budget: $25-50,000,000
President and Chief Executive Officer: James Firman
Vice President, Public Policy and Advocacy: Howard Bedlin
Vice President, Workforce Development: Donald Davis
Executive Vice President, Business Development and Decision Support Services: Jay Greenberg
Vice President, Communications: Scott L. Parkin
Vice President, Member Relations and Network Services: Donna Phillips
Chief Financial Officer and General Counsel: Todd Rathbun
Director, Access to Benefits Coalition: Wendy Zenker

Historical Note
A nonprofit voluntary organization in the field of aging, NCOA is also a central national resource for planning information, technical consultation, advocacy, and materials for professionals in the field. Supports the Health Promotion Institute; the National Association of Older Worker Employment Services; the National Center on Rural Aging; the National Institute of Senior Centers; the National Institute of Senior Housing; the National Adult Day Services Association; the National Institute on Community-Based Long-Term Care; the National Institute on Financial Issues and Services for Elders; and National Interfaith Coalition on Aging. Membership: $125/year (individual).

Meetings/Conferences:
Annual Meetings: Spring/1,800

Publications:
Innovations in Aging. q.
NCOA Networks. bi-m.

National Counter Intelligence Corps Association
(1947)
6198 Morris Rd.
Geneseo, NY 14454
Tel: (585)243-0819
E-Mail: malmeju@aol.com
Web Site: www.ncica.org
Members: 700 individuals
Annual Budget: $10-25,000
Chairman of the Board: Jerry Malme

Historical Note
Members are veteran Special Agents of the Counter Intelligence Corps of the U.S. Armed Forces. Has no paid officers or full-time staff. Membership: $15/year; $25/2 years.

Meetings/Conferences:
Annual Meetings: Fall

Publications:
Golden Sphinx. q.

National Court Reporters Association *(1899)*
8224 Old Courthouse Rd.
Vienna, VA 22182-3808
Tel: (703)556-6272 *Fax:* (703)556-6291
Toll Free: (800)272 - 6272
E-Mail: msic@ncrahq.org
Web Site: www.ncraonline.org
Members: 26000 individuals
Staff: 57
Annual Budget: $5-10,000,000
Chief Executive Officer and Executive Director: Mark J. Golden, CAE
E-Mail: mgolden@ncrahq.org
Director, Membership and Information Systems: Irene Cahill
E-Mail: icahill@ncrahq.org
Senior Director, Finance and Operations: Melanie Dixon
E-Mail: mdixon@mcrahq.org
Director, Communications: Marshall S. Jorpeland
E-Mail: mjorpeland@ncrahq.org
Director, Professional Development and Certification: Patrick Magnan
Senior Director, Communications and Public Affairs: Pete Wacht
E-Mail: pwacht@ncrahq.org
Director, Government Relations and Public Policy: Dave Wenhold
E-Mail: dwenhold@ncrahq.org
Senior Director, Membership Programs and Services: Sue Wolk
E-Mail: swolk@ncrahq.org

Historical Note
Formerly (1991) National Shorthand Reporters Association. Merged (1970) with Associated Stenotypists of America. Sponsors and supports the National Court Reporters Association Political Action Committee. Members are individuals "skilled in the art of verbatim reporting of proceedings by the use of shorthand symbols, manually or by machine". Membership: $200/year. Has an annual budget of $8.1 million.

Meetings/Conferences:
Annual Meetings: 1500

Publications:
Journal of Court Reporting. 10/year. adv.
Court Reporter Source Book/Membership Directory. a. adv.
Annual Report & Convention Proceedings. a.

National CPA Health Care Advisors Association
(1992)
10831 Old Mill Rd.
Suite 400
Omaha, NE 68154
Tel: (402)778-7922 *Fax:* (402)778-7931
Toll Free: (888)475 - 4476
E-Mail: info@hcaa.com
Web Site: www.hcaa.com
Members: 48 firms
Staff: 6
Executive Director: Nancy Drennen

Historical Note
HCAA is an association of CPA firms that provide services to health care providers beyond traditional compliance work, particularly to firms that specialize in providing accounting services beyond traditional tax and audit work. Members are admitted on a territorial exclusive basis.

Meetings/Conferences:
Semi-Annual Meetings:

Publications:
Members' Newsletter. q.

National Credit Reporting Association *(1992)*
125 E. Lake St., Suite 200
Bloomingdale, IL 60108
Tel: (630)539-1525 *Fax:* (630)539-1526
Web Site: www.ncrainc.org
Members: 150 companies
Staff: 2
Annual Budget: $250-500,000
Executive Director: Terry W. Clemans
E-Mail: tclemans@ncrainc.org

Historical Note
Formerly (1997) National Association of Independent Credit Reporting Agencies. NCRA's membership includes mortgage credit reporting agencies, employment screening services, tenant screening companies, consultants and a variety of affiliate vendors. Membership: $650-$3,500/year.

Publications:
The Credit Reporter. bi-m. adv.
The Advocate. m.

National Credit Union Management Association
(1949)
4989 Rebel Trail NW
Atlanta, GA 30327
Tel: (404)255-6828
Web Site: www.ncuma.com
Members: 7200internationalcreditunions
Annual Budget: $250-500,000
President: Kathy Anchors

Historical Note
Members are credit unions whose assets total more than $10 million.

National Criminal Justice Association *(1971)*
720 7th St. NW, Third Floor
Washington, DC 20001-3716
Tel: (202)628-8550 *Fax:* (202)628-0080
E-Mail: info@ncja.org
Web Site: www.ncja.org
Members: 900 individuals

Staff: 10
Annual Budget: $1-2,000,000
Executive Director: Cabell C. Cropper
Deputy Executive Director: Kay Chopard

Historical Note

Membership open to all criminal justice system practitioners and others with interest in crime prevention and control, law enforcement, the courts, corrections or other aspects of the administration of justice. Incorporated in the District of Columbia in 1974. Formerly (until 1979) known as the National Conference of State Criminal Justice Planning Administrators. Membership dues information is available on web site.

Meetings/Conferences:

Annual Meetings: Summer

Publications:

Justice Bulletin. m.

National Crop Insurance Services *(1915)*
8900 Indian Creek Pkwy, Suite 600
Overland Park, KS 66210
Tel: (913)685-2767 *Fax:* (913)685-3080
Web Site: www.agrisk.org
Members: 135 companies
Staff: 45
Annual Budget: $2-5,000,000
President: Robert W. Parkerson
E-Mail: bobp@ag-risk.org
Director, Public Relations: Laura A. Langstraat
E-Mail: lauriel@ag-risk.org

Historical Note

Formed in 1989 by the merger of the Crop Hail Insurance Actuarial Association and the National Crop Insurance Association. NCIS is an association of insurance companies writing insurance for damage by hail, fire and other weather perils to growing crops. Membership: dues based upon crop insurance writings.

Meetings/Conferences:

Annual Meetings: February/March

Publications:

Crop Insurance Today. q. adv.
CropTalk. m.

National Customs Brokers and Forwarders Association of America *(1897)*
1200 18th St. NW
Suite 901
Washington, DC 20036
Tel: (202)466-0222 *Fax:* (202)466-0226
E-Mail: staff@ncbfaa.org
Web Site: www.ncbfaa.org
Members: 800 companies
Staff: 5
Annual Budget: $1-2,000,000
Executive Vice President: Barbara Reilly
E-Mail: br@ncbfaa.org
Director, Conferences and Meetings: Kim O' Beirne
E-Mail: kim@ncbfaa.org

Historical Note

Founded (1897) as the Customs-Clerks Association of the Port of New York. Became the New York Customs Brokers Association (1922) and was incorporated under the same name in 1933. Accepted national membership in 1945, and was incorporated as the Customs Brokers and Forwarders Association of America, Inc., in 1948. Name changed to National Customs Brokers and Forwarders Association of America, Inc., in 1962. NCBFAA represents licensed customs brokers, international freight forwarders, international air cargo agents and non-vessel operating common carriers (NVOCCs) located throughout the United States. Internationally, NCBFAA represents its membership at the International Federation of Customs Brokers Association, which represents many foreign countries and maintains ties with APEC and the World Customs Organization. Membership dues vary, based on the size of the firm.

Meetings/Conferences:

Annual Meetings: March

Publications:

Monday Morning Briefing. w.
Membership Directory. a. adv.
NCBFAA Bulletin Newsletter. m. adv.

National Cutting Horse Association *(1946)*
260 Bailey Ave.
Ft. Worth, TX 76107
Tel: (817)244-6188 *Fax:* (817)244-2015
Web Site: www.nchacutting.com
Members: 16400 individuals
Staff: 35
Annual Budget: $2-5,000,000
Executive Director: Jeff Hooper

Historical Note

Members are individuals, firms, organizations and riding clubs interested in the development of superior horses and the refinement of true cutting horse competition. Membership: $50/year.

Publications:

NCHA Rule Book. a.
The Cutting Horse Chatter. m. adv.
Annual Yearbook. a.

National Dairy Council *(1915)*

Historical Note

A wholly-owned subsidiary of Dairy Management Inc., which provides administrative support.

National Dairy Herd Improvement Association
P.O. Box 930398
Verona, WI 53593
Tel: (608)848-6455 *Fax:* (608)848-7675
E-Mail: dhia@dhia.org
Web Site: www.dhia.org
Members: 4500 individuals
Staff: 2
Annual Budget: $250-500,000
Administrator: Jay Mattison

Historical Note

Dairy industry association provides sample analysis data processing and communications services to 48% of U.S. dairy farmers.

Publications:

DHIA Connection. 10/year.

National Dance Association *(1932)*
1900 Association Dr.
Reston, VA 20191-1599
Tel: (703)476-3421 *Fax:* (703)476-9527
Toll Free: (800)213 - 7193 Ext: 421
E-Mail: nda@aahperd.org
Web Site: www.aahperd.org/nda
Members: 2000 individuals
Staff: 2
Annual Budget: $100-250,000
Program Coordinator: Colleen Dean

Historical Note

An association of the American Alliance for Health, Physical Education, Recreation and Dance (AAHPERD). NDA is dedicated to promoting the development and implementation of sound philosophies and policies in all forms of dance and in dance education at all levels. In cooperation with other arts and education organizations, NDA strives to cultivate, facilitate, and promote the understanding and practice of dance. Membership in NDA includes dancers, choreographers, dance educators, therapists, dance science and medicine specialists, and arts administrators. Membership: $125/year.

Meetings/Conferences:

Annual Meetings: Spring, with AAHPERD

Publications:

Journal of Physical Education, Recreation and Dance. 9/year. adv.
Spotlight on Dance (online). 4/year.

National Dance Council of America *(1948)*
1077 Ponce De Leon Blvd.
Coral Gables, FL 33134
Tel: (609)466-8737 *Fax:* (305)445-0451
Toll Free: (888)390 - 4833
Web Site: www.ndca.org
Members: 15 organizations
Executive Secretary: Tom Murdock

Historical Note

Membership: $60/year (professional competitors); $75/year (scrutineers).

Publications:

Dance Events Bulletin. 3/year.

National Dance-Exercise Instructor's Training Association

Historical Note

Became National Exercise Trainers Association in 2004.

National Defender Investigator Association
460 Smith St.
Suite K
Middletown, CT 06457
Tel: (860)635-5533 *Fax:* (860)613-1650
E-Mail: ndia@cox.net
Web Site: www.ndia.net
Members: 1200 individuals
Staff: 1
Executive Secretary: Beverly Davidson
Director, Meetings and Conventions: Mark Neer
Director, Finance: John Townley
President: Matt Whalen
Publications: Dave Young

Historical Note

Members are criminal defense investigators, paralegals and others in the criminal justice system dedicated to providing services to indigent persons. Membership: $35/year.

Meetings/Conferences:

Semi-Annual Meetings: Spring and Fall
2007 – Myrtle Beach, SC/Apr. 18-20

Publications:

Newsletter. q.

National Defense Industrial Association *(1919)*
2111 Wilson Blvd., Suite 400
Arlington, VA 22201-3061
Tel: (703)522-1820 *Fax:* (703)522-1885
E-Mail: info@ndia.org
Web Site: www.ndia.org
Members: 38000 individuals
Staff: 70
Annual Budget: $10-25,000,000
President and Chief Executive Officer: Lt. Gen. Lawrence P. Farrell, USAF (Ret.)
Vice President, Operations: Maj. Gen. Barry Bates, USA (Ret.)
Vice President, Membership: Maj. Gen. Jim McInerney, USAF (Ret.)
Vice President, Business Operations: B. Prokuski
Vice President, Government Policy: Peter Steffes

Historical Note

NDIA was formed by a merger of the National Security Industrial Association and the American Defense Preparedness Association in 1997. Members are industrial, research, legal and educational organizations of all sizes, drawn from all segments of the industrial community interested in and related to the national security. NDIA fosters an effective working relationship between government and industry in the interest of national security. Membership: $500-41,750/year, based on sales to the federal government.

Meetings/Conferences:

Annual Meetings: Tysons Corner Ritz Carlton, April/800

Publications:

National Defense Magazine. m. adv.

National Defense Transportation Association *(1944)*
50 S. Pickett St., Suite 220
Alexandria, VA 22304-7296
Tel: (703)751-5011 *Fax:* (703)823-8761
E-Mail: info@ndtahq.com
Web Site: www.ndtahq.com
Members: 8300 individuals
Staff: 8
Annual Budget: $1-2,000,000
President: Lt. Gen. Kenneth R. Wykle, USA (Ret.)
Executive Assistant: Col. Mark Victorson, USA (Ret.)
E-Mail: mark@ndtahq.com

Historical Note

Established October 11, 1944 as the Army Transport Association by seven officers from the Army Transportation Corps; assumed its present name in 1949. Originally intended as a liaison between government and private transportation officials, NTDA has evolved into a major facilitator of interaction between government and commercial *transportation interests. Sustaining members are air, sea and land transportation industry and private enterprise. Membership: $35/year (individual); $1,200/year (company).*

Meetings/Conferences:
Annual Meetings: September-October

Publications:
NDTA Gram. m.
Defense Transportation Journal. bi-m. adv.

National Defined Contribution Council *(1995)*
714 Hopemeadow St., Suite 3
Simsbury, CT 06070
Tel: (860)658-5161 *Fax:* (860)658-5068
E-Mail: info@ndcconline.org
Web Site: www.ndcconline.org
Members: 300 individuals
Staff: 3
Annual Budget: $250-500,000
Contact: Glenna Best

Historical Note
NDCC is dedicated to the promotion and protection of the defined contribution industry and the public it serves. The Council specifically addresses the legislative needs of the defined contribution industry's plan service providers. Membership: $5,000/year.

Meetings/Conferences:
Semi-Annual Symposia: Spring and Fall

Publications:
Defined Contribution Market Insights. a.
DC Advocate. q.

National Demolition Association *(1972)*
16 N. Franklin St., Suite 203
Doylestown, PA 18901-3536
Tel: (215)348-4949 *Fax:* (215)348-8422
Toll Free: (800)541 - 2412
Web Site: www.demolitionassociation.com
Members: 1000 contractors
Staff: 3
Annual Budget: $1-2,000,000
Executive Director: Michael R. Taylor, CAE
E-Mail: mtaylor@demolotionassociation.com

Historical Note
Formerly National Association of Demolition Contractors; assumed its current name in 2004. Members are demolition contractors and equipment manufacturers. Membership: $500-750/year, based on revenues.

Meetings/Conferences:
2007 – Las Vegas, NV(Mirage)/Apr. 1-4/1700
2008 – Las Vegas, NV(Mirage)/Feb. 24-27/1700

Publications:
Membership List. a.
Demolition. bi-m. adv.

National Dental Assistants Association *(1964)*

Historical Note
An auxillary of the Nat'l Dental Ass'n, which provides administrative support.

National Dental Association *(1913)*
3517 16th St. NW
Washington, DC 20010
Tel: (202)588-1697 Ext: 15 *Fax:* (202)588-1244
E-Mail: admin@ndaonline.org
Web Site: www.ndaonline.org
Members: 7000 individuals
Staff: 4
Annual Budget: $500-1,000,000
Executive Director: Robert Johns
Manager, Meetings and Conferences: Lavette Henderson

Historical Note
Founded in Hampton, VA. Members are minority dentists dedicated to providing quality dental care to the unserved and underserved. Membership: $395/year.

Meetings/Conferences:
Annual Meetings: Summer/1,000
2007 – Atlanta, GA(Marriott)/July 27-Aug. 1/2000

Publications:
Flossline Newsletter. bi-m. adv.

National Dental Hygienists' Association *(1932)*
3517 16th St. NW
Washington, DC 20010-3041
Members: 200 individuals
Executive Director: Robert Johns

Historical Note
Members are minority dental hygienists. An affiliate of National Dental Association, which provides administrative support.

Meetings/Conferences:
Annual Meetings: In conjunction with the Nat'l Dental Ass'n

Publications:
Newsletter. q.

National Directory Publishing Association *(1987)*
4701 Sangamore Rd.
Suite S-155
Bethesda, MD 20816
Tel: (301)229-5561 *Fax:* (301)229-6133
Members: 400 individuals
Annual Budget: under $10,000
President: Tom Johnson
E-Mail: tojo@att.net

Historical Note
Formerly the Washington Directory Association. NDPA members are professionals involved in the publishing of directories and information products. Has no paid officers or full-time staff. Membership: $40/year (individual); $80/year (corporate); $140/year (supplier); $20/year (student).

National Disability Rights Network *(1978)*
900 Second St. NE, Suite 211
Washington, DC 20002
Tel: (202)408-9514 *Fax:* (202)408-9520
E-Mail: info@ndrn.org
Members: 96 programs
Staff: 23
Annual Budget: $1-2,000,000
Executive Director: Curtis L. Decker
E-Mail: www.ndrn.org

Historical Note
Formerly (1978) National Association of Protection and Advocacy Systems; assumed current name in 2005. NDRN members are disability rights agencies, protection and advocacy systems (P&As), and client assistance programs (CAPs) assisting the disabled and mentally ill.

Meetings/Conferences:
Annual: Washington, DC area

Publications:
Protection and Advocacy News. q. adv.
State Protection and Advocacy Agencies Directory. a. adv.

National District Attorneys Association *(1950)*
99 Canal Center Plaza, Suite 510
Alexandria, VA 22314
Tel: (703)549-9222 *Fax:* (703)836-3195
E-Mail: jean.holt@ndaa-apri.org
Web Site: www.ndaa-apri.org
Members: 6800 individuals
Staff: 14
Annual Budget: $2-5,000,000
Executive Director: Thomas J. Charron
E-Mail: shirley.sarni@ndaa-apri.org
Chief of Staff: Roger Floren
Director, Publications: Jean Holt
E-Mail: jean.holt@ndaa-apri.org
Media Relations: Velva Walter
E-Mail: velva.walter@ndaa-apri.org

Historical Note
Established as the National Association of County and Prosecuting Attorneys; assumed its present name in 1959. Membership: $75-975/year, varies by size of jurisdiction (individual).

Meetings/Conferences:
Annual Meetings: May, July

Publications:
National Directory of Prosecuting Attorneys. bien. adv.
The Prosecutor. 6/year. adv.

National Dog Groomers Association of America *(1969)*
P.O. Box 101
Clark, PA 16113
Tel: (724)962-2711 *Fax:* (724)962-1919
E-Mail: ndga@nationaldoggroomers.com
Web Site: www.nationaldoggroomers.com
Members: 2500 individuals
Staff: 2
Annual Budget: $100-250,000
Executive Director: Jeffrey L. Reynolds

Historical Note
Established to provide professional indentification and continuing education. Awards the designation NCMG (National Certified Master Groomer) and holds 20 certification workshops every year throughout the U.S. Membership: $85/first year; $40/year (renewal).

Meetings/Conferences:
Semi-Annual Meetings: Spring and Fall

Publications:
Groomers Voice. q. adv.

National Drilling Association *(1972)*
11001 Danka Way North
Suite One
St. Petersburg, FL 33716
Tel: (727)577-5006 *Fax:* (727)577-5012
E-Mail: info@nda4u.com
Web Site: www.nda4u.com
Members: 250 companies
Staff: 2
Annual Budget: $100-250,000
Executive Director: Patrick A. O'Brien

Historical Note
Formerly National Drilling Contractors Association; merged with Drilling Equipment Manufacturers Association and International Drilling Federation and assumed its current name in 1995. NDA represents the geotechnical, environmental and mineral exploration sectors of the drilling industry. Members are exploratory, ground water monitoring well, and ground water recovery well drillers. NDA's mission is to promote the use of professional drilling contractors and their methods. Incorporated in the State of Pennsylvania.

Meetings/Conferences:
Annual Meetings: Fall

Publications:
Drill Bits. 2/yr. adv.

National Dry Bean Council *(1950)*

Historical Note
Address unknown in 2006.

National Earth Science Teachers Association *(1982)*
4784 Four Seasons Dr.
Liverpool, NY 13088
Tel: (315)451-1590
Web Site: www.nestanet.org
Members: 1000 individuals
Annual Budget: $10-25,000
Treasurer: Bruce Hall

Historical Note
NESTA members are earth science teachers concerned with teaching in grades K-12. Has no paid officers or full-time staff. Membership: $15/year (individual).

Meetings/Conferences:
Annual Meetings: in conjunction with the Nat'l Science Teachers Ass'n

Publications:
Earth Scientist, The. q. adv.
NESTANet News. bi-m.
Summer School Oportunities. a.

National Economic Association *(1969)*
Optimal Solutions Group
3225 Ellersville Ave., Suite E-303
Baltimore, MD 21218-3554
Tel: (443)451-7060 *Fax:* (443)451-7069
Web Site: www.ncat.edu/~neconasc/
Members: 150 individuals
Annual Budget: under $10,000
Secretary and Web Administrator: Dr. Mark D. Turner

Historical Note
Formerly (1975) Caucus of Black Economists. NEA promotes black representation in the economics profession, acts as a job clearing house and gives financial assistance to black students of economics. Membership: $40/year; $15/year (student).

Meetings/Conferences:
Annual Meetings: In conjunction with the American Economic Ass'n

Publications:
Newsletter. q.
Review of Black Political Economy. q.

National Education Association *(1857)*
1201 16th St. NW
Washington, DC 20036
Tel: (202)833-4000 *Fax:* (202)822-7974
Web Site: www.nea.org
Members: 2500000 individuals
Staff: 600
Annual Budget: Over $100,000,000
Executive Director: John I. Wilson
General Counsel: Robert Chanin
Manager, Federal Affairs and Politics: Randall Moody
Director, Government Relations: Diane Schust
Manager, Publishing Systems: Lorraine Wilson

Historical Note
Formerly (1870) National Teachers Association. Merged with American Teachers Association in 1966. Supports the National Education Association Political Action Committee. Strives to enhance and strengthen public education in America in order to further equity and excellence for all Americans. Also works to advance human and civil rights. Has an annual budget of approximately $190 million. Membership: $107/year.

Meetings/Conferences:
Annual Meetings: June/July

Publications:
NEA Now. m.
Today's Education. a.
NEA Addresses and Proceedings. a.
NEA Handbook. a.
NEA Today. 10/year.
NEA Advocate. q.
Almanac of Higher Education. a.
The Best Years. q.
ESP Progress. q.

National Education Knowledge Industry Association *(1971)*
1718 Connecticut Ave. NW
Suite 700
Washington, DC 20009-1162
Tel: (202)518-0847 *Fax:* (202)785-3849
E-Mail: info@nekia.org
Web Site: www.nekia.org
Members: 35 companies
Staff: 3
Annual Budget: $250-500,000
President: James W. Kohlmoos

Historical Note
Founded as Council for Educational Development and Research; assumed its current name in 1997. Members are companies and institutions interested in continuing research and development that contributes to cost-effective education innovation.

Meetings/Conferences:
Annual Meetings: Fall

National Educational Telecommunications Association *(1997)*
P.O. Box 50008
Columbia, SC 29250
Tel: (803)799-5517 *Fax:* (803)771-4831
Toll Free: (800)507 - 7322
Web Site: www.netaonline.org
Members: 86 individuals
Staff: 33
President: Wilbur H. "Skip" Hinton
E-Mail: skip@netaonline.org

Historical Note
Founded as Southern Educational Communications Association; assumed its current name in 1997 to reflect its national constituency. Members are public television licensees.

National Electrical Contractors Association *(1901)*
Three Bethesda Metro Center, Suite 1100
Bethesda, MD 20814-5330
Tel: (301)657-3110 *Fax:* (301)215-4500
E-Mail: webmaster@necanet.org
Web Site: www.necanet.org
Members: 4500 companies and 120 local chapts
Staff: 75
Annual Budget: $10-25,000,000
Chief Executive Officer: John M. Grau
Editor: Bonnie N. Duncan
Convention and Exposition Director: Bettie Luckman
Public Relations Director: Beth Marguilies
Vice President and Chief Operating Officer: Daniel G. Walter
Director, Government Affairs: Robert White

Historical Note
Members are electrical contruction companies. Sponsors and supports the Electrical Construction Political Action Committee (ECPAC). Has an annual budget of approximately $22 million.

Meetings/Conferences:
Annual Meetings: October/8,000

Publications:
Electrical Contractor. m. adv.
NECA News. w.

National Electrical Manufacturers Association *(1926)*
1300 N. 17th St.
Suite 1752
Rosslyn, VA 22209
Tel: (703)841-3200 *Fax:* (703)841-5900
E-Mail: webmaster@nema.org
Web Site: www.nema.org
Members: 400 companies
Annual Budget: $10-25,000,000
President: Evan R. Gaddis
Vice President, Communications: Rae Hamilton
Vice President, Finance/Administration: Thomas E. Hixon
Director, Information Systems: Paul Hou
Vice President and Chief Economist: Donald Leavens
Legal Counsel: Clark R. Silcox

Historical Note
The largest trade organization for manufacturers of electrical products in the U.S. Organized in 1926 through the merger of several organizations, the oldest of which, Electrical Manufacturers Club, was formed in 1905. Has an annual budget of approximately $8.4 million.

Meetings/Conferences:
Annual: Held alternately in Washington, D.C. and Chicago, IL

Publications:
Electroindustry. m. adv.

National Electrical Manufacturers Representatives Association *(1969)*
660 White Plains Rd.
Suite 600
Tarrytown, NY 10591-5104
Tel: (914)524-8650 *Fax:* (914)524-8655
Web Site: www.NEMRA.org
Members: 1150 companies
Staff: 11
Annual Budget: $1-2,000,000
President: Henry P. Bergson
E-Mail: hank@nemra.org
Vice President, Operations: Nancy J. Sciotto
E-Mail: nancy@nemra.org

Historical Note
Members are independent electrical sales representatives. Membership: $595/year (company); $75/year (employee).

Meetings/Conferences:
Annual Meetings: Spring

Publications:
NEMRA Locator. a.
Repconnections. m.
The Insider. irreg.

National Electrical Testing Association

Historical Note
Became International Electrical Testing Association in 2005.

National Electronic Distributors Association *(1937)*
1111 Alderman Dr., Suite 400
Alpharetta, GA 30005-4175
Tel: (678)393-9990 *Fax:* (678)393-9998
Web Site: www.nedaassoc.org
Members: 400distributorsandmanufacturers
Staff: 7
Annual Budget: $1-2,000,000
Executive Vice President: Robin B. Gray, Jr.
Director, Marketing: Debbie Conyers
Director, Meetings: Michelle Meyer
Vice President, Administration: Janet Wood

Historical Note
Formerly National Radio Parts Distributors Association. Members are distributors and manufacturers of electronics and high technology components and systems to industry.

Meetings/Conferences:
Semi-Annual Meetings: Spring/Fall

Publications:
NEDA News. m. adv.

National Electronic Service Dealers Association *(1963)*
3608 Pershing Ave.
Ft. Worth, TX 76107
Tel: (817)921-9061 *Fax:* (817)921-3741
E-Mail: info@nesda.com
Web Site: www.nesda.com
Members: 800 individuals
Staff: 7
Annual Budget: $500-1,000,000
Executive Director: Mack Blakely
ISCET Administrator: Ed Clingman
Director, Communications: Sheila Fredrickson

Historical Note
Formerly National Electronic Association; became (1974) National Electronic Service Dealers Association and (1983) National Electronic Sales and Service Dealers Association; became National Electronic Service Dealers Association again in 1992. Absorbed National Association of Television and Electronic Servicers of America in 1986. Members are electronics service centers. Sponsors International Society of Certified Electronics Technicians. Membership: $240/year.

Meetings/Conferences:
Annual Meetings: Winter

Publications:
Newsletter. q. adv.
ProService Yearbook. a. adv.

National Elevator Industry *(1934)*
1677 County Rod. 64
P.O. Box 838
Salem, NY 12865-0838
Tel: (518)854-3100 *Fax:* (518)854-3257
E-Mail: info@neii.org
Web Site: www.neii.org
Members: 35 companies
Staff: 1
Annual Budget: $500-1,000,000
Secretary: Edward A. Donoghue, CPCA

Historical Note
Formerly (1969) National Elevator Manufacturing Industry, Inc. Membership: fees based on level of membership and annual sales.

Meetings/Conferences:
2007 – Sarasota, FL/March 28/45

Publications:
Building Transportation Standard and Guidelines, NEII-1. online.

National Emergency Equipment Dealers Association *(1996)*
P.O. Box 220
Annandale, VA 22003
Tel: (703)280-4622 *Fax:* (703)532-1798
Web Site: www.needa.org
Members: 60 dealers
Staff: 1
Annual Budget: $10-25,000
Executive Director: Kenton Pattie
E-Mail: KentonP1@aol.com

Historical Note
NEEDA represents dealers and distributors who sell fire trucks, ambulances, rescue vehicles and all related equipment, parts, maintenance and repair services. Membership: $600/year (company).

Meetings/Conferences:
Annual Meetings: January
Publications:
Needa News (online).
Congressional Directory. a.

National Emergency Management Association
(1950)
P.O. Box 11910
Lexington, KY 40578-1910
Tel: (859)244-8000 *Fax:* (859)244-8239
E-Mail: nemaadmin@csg.org
Web Site: www.nemaweb.org
Members: 300 individuals
Staff: 4
Annual Budget: $100-250,000
Executive Director: Trina Hembree Sheets
E-Mail: thembree@csg.org
Administrative Assistant: Leah Baldwin
E-Mail: lbaldwin@csg.org
Coordinator, Meetings and Marketing: Karen Cobuluis
E-Mail: kcobuluis@csg.org
Historical Note
Founded as the National Association of State Civil Defense Directors; became the National Association of State Directors for Disaster Preparedness in 1974 and assumed its present name in 1980. Members include State Directors of Emergency Management, while associate members include federal agencies, local emergency management representatives and interested individuals, associations, and corporations. Affiliated with the Council of State Governments in 1990. Officers change annually. Membership: $200/year (individual); $250/year (association); $1200/year (state); $400-1000/year (corporate); $300/year (key state staff).
Meetings/Conferences:
Semi-annual Meetings: Washington, DC/Spring and Fall

National Emergency Number Association *(1982)*
4350 N. Fairfax Dr., Suite 750
Arlington, VA 22203-1695
Tel: (703)812-4600 *Fax:* (703)812-4675
Toll Free: (800)332 - 3911
Web Site: www.nena.org
Members: 7500 individuals
Staff: 10
Executive Director: Robert L. Martin
E-Mail: rmartin@nena.org
Manager, Conferences and Events: Deborah Shields
Historical Note
NENA is the only organization dedicated solely to the promotion and implementation of 9-1-1 as America's universal emergency number. Membership: $95/year (individual in public sector); $125/year (individual in private sector).
Meetings/Conferences:
Annual Meetings: June
2007 – Ft. Worth, TX/June 9-14
Publications:
Emergency Number Professional. bi-m. adv.
Membership Directory. a. adv.

National Employment Counseling Association
(1964)
Historical Note
A division of the American Counseling Association, which provides administrative support.

National Employment Lawyers Association
(1985)
44 Montgomery St., Suite 2080
San Francisco, CA 94104
Tel: (415)296-7629 *Fax:* (415)677-9445
E-Mail: nelahq@nelahq.org
Web Site: www.nela.org
Members: 3000 individuals
Staff: 8
Annual Budget: $1-2,000,000
Executive Director: Terisa E. Chaw
E-Mail: nelahq@nelahq.org
Historical Note
Founded to provide assistance and support to lawyers in protecting the rights of employees against the greater resources of their employers and the defense bar. NELA is the country's only professional organization that is exclusively comprised of lawyers who represent individual employees in cases involving employment discrimination, wrongful termination, employee benefits and other employment-related matters. Membership: $20-1000/year.

Meetings/Conferences:
Annual Meetings: June/350-400
2007 – San Juan, PR(Westin Rio Mar Resort and Golf Club)/June 27-30
2008 – Atlanta, GA(Omni Hotel at CNN Center)/June 25-28
2009 – Rancho Mirage, CA(Westin Mission Hills Resort)/June 24-27
Publications:
Employee Rights Litigation: Pleading & Practice.
Employee Advocate Magazine. q. adv.
Membership Directory. a. adv.

National EMS Pilots Association *(1984)*
526 King St., Suite 415
Alexandria, VA 22314-3143
Tel: (703)836-8930 *Fax:* (703)836-8920
E-Mail: mporter@aams.org
Web Site: www.nemspa.org
Members: 143 individuals and organizations
Staff: 4
Annual Budget: $100-250,000
Membership: Melissa Porter, CME
Historical Note
NEMSPA is a professional organization serving both helicopter and fixed-wing aircraft pilots involved in emergency medical service. Membership: $38/year (active/affiliate); $250/year (junior corporate member); $500/year (senior corporate member); $1000/year (corporate benefactor).
Meetings/Conferences:
Annual Meetings: Fall
Publications:
Air Medical Journal. bi-m. adv.
AirNet Newsletter. q. adv.

National Energy Assistance Directors Association *(1983)*
1615 M St. NW
Suite 800
Washington, DC 20036
Tel: (202)237-5199 *Fax:* (202)237-7316
E-Mail: info@naeda.org
Web Site: www.neada.org
Executive Director: Mark Wolfe
Historical Note
NEADA support states in the development of Low-Income Home Energy Assistance(LIHEAP) policies. The association coordinates and cooperates in the collection and dissemination of information and proposes energy policies.

National Energy Services Association
6430 FM 1960 West, Suite 213
Houston, TX 77069
Tel: (713)856-6525 *Fax:* (713)856-6199
Web Site: www.nesanet.org
Members: 2200 industries
Staff: 3
Annual Budget: $1-2,000,000
President: Teresa Rice
Historical Note
Formerly the National Gas Transportation Association (NGTA); assumed its current name in 1996. Membership: $75/year (individual).
Meetings/Conferences:
Annual Meetings: September

National Environmental Balancing Bureau
(1971)
8575 Grovemont Circle
Gaithersburg, MD 20877
Tel: (301)977-3698 *Fax:* (301)977-9589
E-Mail: miked@nebb.org
Web Site: www.nebb.org
Members: 600 companies
Staff: 9
Annual Budget: $1-2,000,000
Executive Vice President: Michael P. Dolim
Director, Education and Certification: Margaret Andrews
E-Mail: margaret@nebb.org
Historical Note
NEBB members are contractors in the heating, ventilating and air conditioning (HVAC) industry. NEBB establishes and maintains industry standards, procedures and specifications for work in its various disciplines. Membership: $650/year.
Meetings/Conferences:
Annual Meetings: Fall
Publications:
The Balance Sheet Newsletter. q.

National Environmental Development Association *(1973)*
Historical Note
NEDA members are companies and other organizations concerned with balancing environmental and economic interests to obtain both a clean environment and a strong economy.

National Environmental Health Association
(1937)
720 S. Colorado Blvd.
North Tower, Suite 1000-N
Denver, CO 80246-1926
Tel: (303)756-9090 *Fax:* (303)691-9490
E-Mail: staff@neha.org
Web Site: www.neha.org
Members: 5700 individuals
Staff: 30
Annual Budget: $2-5,000,000
Executive Director: Nelson E. Fabian
Manager, Research and Development: Larry Marcum
Human Resources and Office Manager: Dawn Parks
Historical Note
Incorporated in California in 1937 as the National Association of Sanitarians; became the National Environmental Health Association in 1970. NEHA members represent virtually all environmental health and protection professionals. NEHA administers certification programs concerning environmental health, hazardous waste and food protection. NEHA also conducts continuing education programs and special seminars. Membership rates vary for individuals, students, institutions, and companies.
Meetings/Conferences:
Annual Meetings: June/1,500
2007 – Atlantic City, NJ/1500
2008 – Tuscon, AZ/1500
Publications:
Journal of Environmental Health. 10/year. adv.

National Environmental Training Association
Historical Note
Beacame National Environmental, Safety and Health Training Association in 2003.

National Environmental, Safety and Health Training Association *(1977)*
P.O. Box 10321
Phoenix, AZ 85064-0321
Tel: (602)956-6099 *Fax:* (602)956-6399
E-Mail: info@neshta.org
Web Site: www.neshta.org
Members: 1100 individuals
Staff: 3
Annual Budget: $500-1,000,000
Executive Director: Charles L. Richardson
Manager, Certification and Membership Services: Suzanne Lanctot
Historical Note
Founded as National Environmental Training Association; assumed its current name in 2003. Members are trainers of personnel in the field of air and noise pollution, solid and hazardous waste control, water supply and waste-water treatment, and occupational safety and health. Membership: $90/year (individual); $360/year (organization).
Meetings/Conferences:
2007 – Atlantic City, NJ/June/1200
Publications:
NETAnews. m.

National Exchange Carrier Association *(1983)*
80 S. Jefferson Rd.
Whippany, NJ 07981-1009

Tel: (973)884-8000 *Fax:* (973)884-8469
Toll Free: (800)228 - 8597
E-Mail: dlauerm@neca.org
Web Site: www.neca.org
Members: 1250localtelephonecompanies
Staff: 250
President: Bill Hegmann
Vice President, Chief Financial Officer: Paul Dunbar
Vice President, Operations: James W. Frame
E-Mail: jframe@neca.org
Director, Corporate Communications: David P. Lauerman
Vice President, General Counsel and Corporate Secretary: Regina McNeil

Historical Note
NECA members are local telephone companies.

Meetings/Conferences:
Annual Meetings: Fall
2007 – San Francisco, CA(Hyatt Regency)/Sept. 23-27

Publications:
Washington Watch online newsletter. d. Access. 7/year.

National Exercise Trainers Association *(1977)*
5955 Golden Valley Rd., Suite 240
Minneapolis, MN 55422
Tel: (763)545-2505 *Fax:* (763)545-2524
Toll Free: (800)237 - 6242
E-Mail: neta@netafit.org
Web Site: www.netafit.org
Members: 14000 individuals
Staff: 50
President: Mario Crespo

Historical Note
Formerly (1977) National Dance-Exercise Instructor's Training Association; assumed current name in 2004. Members are aerobic exercise instructors and personal trainers.

Publications:
Fitness Professionals Manual. semi-a.

National Export Traffic League *(1946)*

Historical Note
Address unknown in 2006.

National Extension Association of Family and Consumer Sciences *(1933)*
P.O. Box 849
Winchester, VA 22604
Tel: (540)678-9955 *Fax:* (540)678-9940
E-Mail: info@neafcs.org
Web Site: www.neafcs.org
Members: 3300 individuals
Staff: 3
Annual Budget: $250-500,000
Executive Director: Michele Grassley Franklin

Historical Note
Formerly National Home Demonstration Agents' Association and National Association of Extension Home Economists; assumed its current name in 1996. Extension Family and Consumer Sciences Educators are employees of the Cooperative Extension Service, a joint venture of the U.S. Department of Agriculture, county government and State Land Grand Universities. NEAFCS is a professional organization providing encouragement and opportunities for members to improve their skills as extension educators. Membership: $40/year (individual).

Meetings/Conferences:
Annual Meetings: September-October

Publications:
Communique. a. adv.
The Reporter. a.
eNEAFCS (online). m.

National Family Business Council *(1969)*
1640 W. Kennedy Rd.
Lake Forest, IL 60045
Tel: (847)295-1040 *Fax:* (847)295-1898
E-Mail: lmsnfbc@msn.com
Members: 1000familybusinesses
Staff: 4
Annual Budget: $1-2,000,000
President: John E. Messervey
Director, Client Services: Lynn Smith

Historical Note
NFBC serves as a resource center for closely held and family owned businesses. The Council was formed in 1969 by a group of concerned successors to family business as the Sons of Bosses (SOB's) and assumed it present name in 1976. Provides research, consulting, and other services to client members.

Meetings/Conferences:
Semi-Annual Meetings: Spring and Winter

Publications:
Conference Proceedings & Audio Tapes. irreg.

National Family Caregivers Association *(1992)*
10400 Connecticut Ave., Suite 500
Kensington, MD 20895-3944
Toll Free: (800)896 - 3650
E-Mail: info@thefamilycaregiver.org
Web Site: www.thefamilycaregiver.org
Members: 9000 individuals
Staff: 4
Annual Budget: $100-250,000
President: Suzanne Mintz
Director, Administration and Finance: Christal Willingham

Historical Note
NFCA members are family caregivers, health professionals and organizations with an interest in the provision of home health care. Membership: Free (family caregivers); $20/year (family/friend); $40/year (professional); $60/year (non-profit group); $100/year (for-profit group).

Publications:
Take Care! Newsletter. q. adv.

National Family Planning and Reproductive Health Association *(1971)*
1627 K St. NW, 12th Floor
Washington, DC 20006-1702
Tel: (202)293-3114 *Fax:* (202)293-1990
E-Mail: info@nfprhq.org
Web Site: www.nfprha.org
Members: 700 organizations and individuals
Staff: 10
Annual Budget: $1-2,000,000
President and Chief Executive Officer: Judith M. DeSarno
Vice President, Business and Internal Affairs: Megan Jackson
Vice President, Public Policy: Marilyn Keefe

Historical Note
A professional membership group concerned with the delivery and availability of family planning services in the United States. Its members are primarily government-funded agencies involved in the provision of family planning and related health services. NFPRHA follows legislative and administrative developments affecting reproductive health issues, conducts policy research analysis and provides technical assistance. Funding sources include private donations, membership dues and foundation grants. Until 1979 known as the National Family Planning Forum. Membership: $75-250/year (individual), $500-3,000/year (organization).

Meetings/Conferences:
Annual Meetings: Washington, DC/June

Publications:
Reproductive Health Watch (online). w.
NFPRHA Annual Report. a.
NFPRHA ALERT (online). irreg.
NRPRHA REPORT. bi-m.

National Farmers Organization *(1955)*
528 Billy Sunday Rd.
Ames, IA 50010
Tel: (515)292-2000 *Fax:* (515)292-7106
Toll Free: (800)247 - 2110
E-Mail: nfo@nfo.org
Web Site: www.nfo.org
Staff: 250
Communications Director: Perry Garner

Historical Note
An agricultural marketing company utilizing group marketing concepts to achieve higher returns for its member producers.

Meetings/Conferences:
Annual Meetings: December/2,000

Publications:
NFO Reporter.

National Farmers Union

Historical Note
Official name is the Farmers Educational and Co-operative Union of America.

National Fashion Accessories Association *(1916)*
350 Fifth Ave., Suite 2030
New York, NY 10118
Tel: (212)947-3424 *Fax:* (212)629-0361
Web Site: www.accessoryweb.com
Members: 100 individuals
Staff: 4
Annual Budget: $100-250,000
Executive Director: Harold Sachs

Historical Note
Formerly (1966) National Authority for the Ladies Handbag Industry. Added the title National Fashion Accessories Association, in 1986. Formerly (1987) National Association of Handbag Makers/National Fashion Accessories Association.

Meetings/Conferences:
Annual Meetings: None held.

Publications:
Newsletter. m.

National Fastener Distributors Association *(1968)*
401 N. Michigan Ave., Suite 2200
Chicago, IL 60611
Tel: (312)527-6671 *Fax:* (312)673-6740
E-Mail: nfda@nfda-fastener.org
Web Site: www.nfda-fastener.org
Members: 247 companies
Staff: 3
Annual Budget: $250-500,000
Executive Vice President: Karen A. Hurley
E-Mail: khurley@nfda-fastener.org

Historical Note
Absorbed the Southern Association of Industrial Fastener Distributors in 1972. Membership: $500-$1,000/year, plus $1000 initiation (organization).

Meetings/Conferences:
Semi-Annual Meetings: Spring and Fall/300

Publications:
Inside NFDA. m.
Roster/Source Guide.

National Federation Coaches Association *(1981)*
P.O. Box 690
Indianapolis, IN 46206
Tel: (317)792-6900 *Fax:* (317)822-5700
Web Site: www.nfhs.org/nfca.htm
Members: 30000 individuals
Staff: 2
Annual Budget: $500-1,000,000
Director: Tim Flannery

Historical Note
An affiliate of National Federation of State High School Associations (same address), NFCA members are secondary school athletic coaches. Membership: $16/year.

Meetings/Conferences:
Annual Meetings: in conjunction with Alabama Coaches and Athletic Director's Conference

Publications:
Coaches Quarterly Magazine. 4/year. adv.
Nat'l Federation News. 5/year. adv.

National Federation of Abstracting and Information Services *(1958)*
1518 Walnut St., Suite 1004
Philadelphia, PA 19102-3403
Tel: (215)893-1561 *Fax:* (215)893-1564
E-Mail: nfais@nfais.org
Web Site: www.nfais.org
Members: 60 organizations
Staff: 3
Annual Budget: $250-500,000
Executive Director: Bonnie Lawler
Director, Planning and Communications: Jennifer O'Neill
E-Mail: jilloneill@nfais.org

Historical Note
Formerly (1972) National Federation of Science Abstracting and Indexing Services and (1982) National Federation of Abstracting and Indexing Services. Cooperates with the American Society for

Information Science, the American Library Association and other national and international organizations concerned with information science. Members are private organizations and government offices here and abroad which abstract and index popular and professional literature in print and machine-readable form, plus online vendors, CD-ROM vendors and others in related fields. Membership fee varies with revenues.

Meetings/Conferences:
Annual Meetings: February
2007 - Philadelphia, PA(Ritz Carlton)/Feb. 25-27

Publications:
Membership Directory. a.
NFAIS Newsletter. m.

National Federation of Community Broadcasters *(1975)*
1970 Broadway, Suite 1000
Oakland, CA 94612
Tel: (510)451-8200 *Fax:* (510)451-8208
E-Mail: NFCB@nfcb.org
Web Site: www.nfcb.org
Members: 250 stations
Staff: 8
Annual Budget: $500-1,000,000
President and Chief Executive Officer: Carol Pierson
E-Mail: carol@nfcb.org
Vice President: Ginny Z. Berson

Historical Note
Members are non-commercial public radio stations licensed to community organizations, as well as university and other licensees, independent producers and production groups. NFCB's purpose is to advance community-oriented non-commercial broadcasting; provide services and resources to community licensees; foster cooperation among broadcasting organizations; and participate at the national level in the development of public broadcasting policy. Membership: $100/year (individual); $200-3,000/year (company).

Meetings/Conferences:
Annual Meetings: Spring
2007 - New Orleans, LA(Sheraton)/Apr. 11-14/500

Publications:
Community Radio News. m. adv.

National Federation of Community Development Credit Unions *(1974)*
120 Wall St., 10th Floor
New York, NY 10005
Tel: (212)809-1850 *Fax:* (212)809-3274
E-Mail: info@natfed.org
Web Site: www.natfed.org
Members: 200 credit unions
Staff: 10
Annual Budget: $1-2,000,000
Executive Director: Clifford N. Rosenthal

Historical Note
Established in 1974 to serve and represent financial cooperatives in low-income communities. Members are community-based credit unions. The Federation provides training and management support to CDCU's and assists groups in organizing new credit unions. NFCDCU has an annual budget of $1.5 million. Membership: $50-$3,500/year depending on assets.

Meetings/Conferences:
Annual Meetings: Spring

National Federation of Federal Employees *(1917)*
1016 16th St. NW
Washington, DC 20036
Tel: (202)862-4400 *Fax:* (202)862-4432
Web Site: www.nffe.org
Members: 30000 individuals
Staff: 30
Annual Budget: $2-5,000,000
President: Richard G. Brown
Secretary-Treasurer: John Paolino

Historical Note
Chartered by the American Federation of Labor in 1917, NFFE withdrew from the AFL in 1931 objecting to the AFL's position that civil service classification should not be extended to skilled crafts. It is now an independent labor union in competition with the American Federation of Government Employees (AFL-CIO). Sponsors the Public Affairs Council (NFFE), a political action committee.

Meetings/Conferences:
Biennial meetings: Even years

Publications:
The Federal Employee. q.

National Federation of Hispanic Owned Newspapers *(1982)*
c/o La Informacion
6065 Hill Croft, Suite 400-B
Houston, TX 77081
Tel: (713)272-0100 *Fax:* (713)272-0011
Members: 100 publications
Annual Budget: $50-100,000
President: Lina Martinez

Historical Note
NFHON is a network of Hispanic newspapers in the U.S. and Puerto Rico. Has no paid officers or full-time staff. Membership: $125/year (individual).

Meetings/Conferences:
Annual Meetings: Fall

Publications:
Ultima Hora Newsletter. q. adv.
Hispanic Print Media Directory. a.

National Federation of Housing Counselors *(1973)*
P.O. Box 5607
Savannah, GA 31414
Tel: (912)236-9670 *Fax:* (912)238-2977
Members: 1600 individuals
Staff: 1
Annual Budget: $50-100,000
President: Terry Tolbert

Historical Note
Members are individuals who assist families with the acquisition and management of rented or privately owned homes. NFHC maintains a certification program to develop standards of competency and efficiency, provides technical assistance in the development of counseling programs, provides legislative representation, and operates a clearinghouse for housing information. Membership: $35/year (individual); $50/year (organization/company).

Meetings/Conferences:
Annual Meetings: usually June

Publications:
Training Manual. a. adv.
Housing Pipeline. q. adv.

National Federation of Independent Business *(1943)*
1201 F St. NW
Suite 200
Washington, DC 20004
Tel: (202)554-9000 *Fax:* (202)554-0496
Toll Free: (800)552 - 6342
Web Site: www.nfib.com
Members: 600000 businesses
Staff: 1000
Annual Budget: $50-100,000,000
President and Chief Executive Officer: Todd Stottlemyer
Vice President and Chief Technology Officer: Jeff Cantwell
Executive Vice President, Policy: Dan Danner

Historical Note
Established as the National Federation of Small Business, it assumed its present name about 1950. In addition to the Washington and Nashville offices, it maintains offices in all 50 state capitals. Its principal focus is legislative relations and research. Sponsors the NFIB S.A.F.E. Trust and NFIB Research Foundation. Has an annual budget of approximately $70 million. Membership: $100-1,000/year.

Publications:
Member Ballot. 3/year.
Small Business Economic Trends. m.
State Reports. a.
Action Report. a.
How Congress Voted. a.
Capitol Coverage. bi-m.
IB Magazine. bi-m. adv.

National Federation of Independent Unions *(1963)*
1166 S. 11th St.
Philadelphia, PA 19147
Tel: (215)336-3300 *Fax:* (215)755-3542
Toll Free: (888)595 - 6388
Web Site: www.nfiu.org
Members: 57000 individuals
Staff: 2
Annual Budget: $25-50,000
President: F.J. Chiappardi
E-Mail: fjcnfiu@aol.com
Secretary/Treasurer: Alonzo Wheeler
E-Mail: awheeler@nfiu.org

Historical Note
Independent labor federation. Product of a merger of National Independent Union Council and Confederated Unions of America.

National Federation of Interscholastic Speech and Debate Association

Historical Note
Beacame NFHS Speech Debate and Theatre Association in 2003.

National Federation of Licensed Practical Nurses *(1949)*
605 Poole Dr.
Garner, NC 27529
Tel: (919)779-0046 *Fax:* (919)779-5642
Toll Free: (800)948 - 2511
Web Site: www.nflpn.org
Members: 6000 individuals
Staff: 3
Annual Budget: $250-500,000
Executive Director: Charlene B. Barbour
Director, Convention Services: Diana Mills

Historical Note
Independent professional association. Membership: $55/year and up.

Meetings/Conferences:
Annual Meetings: Fall/500

Publications:
Advance for LPNS. q. adv.

National Federation of Modern Language Teachers Associations *(1916)*
7841 E. Camino Montaraz
Tucson, AZ 85715
Tel: (520)885-2509
E-Mail: ervin7841@earthlink.net
Members: 15 associations
Staff: 2
Annual Budget: $100-250,000
Treasurer: Gerard L. Ervin, Ph.D.

Historical Note
Provides a forum for the exchange of information of interest to organizations of modern language teachers.

Meetings/Conferences:
Annual Meetings: With the American Council on the Teaching of Foreign Languages

Publications:
The Modern Language Journal. q. adv.

National Federation of Municipal Analysts *(1983)*
P.O. Box 14893
Pittsburgh, PA 15234
Tel: (412)341-4898 *Fax:* (412)341-4894
Web Site: www.nfma.org
Members: 900 individuals
Executive Director: Lisa S. Good

Historical Note
Founded by four regional organizations of municipal analysts, NFMA now promotes the profession of municipal credit analyst, through educational programs, industry communications, and related programming. Membership: $20-35/year.

Meetings/Conferences:
Annual Meetings: Spring/175

Publications:
Municipal Analysts Bulletin. 3-4/year.

National Federation of Music Clubs *(1898)*
1336 N. Delaware St.
Indianapolis, IN 46202-2481
Tel: (317)638-4003 *Fax:* (317)638-0503

E-Mail: info@nfmc-music.org
Web Site: www.NFMC-music.org
Members: 200000 individuals
Staff: 2
Annual Budget: $100-250,000
Administrative Manager: Jennifer Keller

Historical Note
NFMC supports professional and amateur musicians and composers. Through its own programming and the programs of its member clubs, it strives to recognize musical talent, promote American music, and enhance music education and music therapy programs.

Meetings/Conferences:
Biennial Meetings: odd years

Publications:
Junior Keynotes. q. adv.
Music Clubs Magazine. q. adv.

National Federation of Nonpublic School State Accrediting Associations
c/o ANSAA, 6300 Fr. Tribou St.
Little Rock, AR 72205
Tel: (501)664-3939 *Fax:* (501)664-9075
Members: 5 state agencies
Annual Budget: under $10,000
President: Dr. Michael M. Rockers

Historical Note
A federation of state accrediting associations serving non-public schools. Through its state chapters, NF accredits over 800 elementary and secondary schools in the U.S. Has no paid officers or full-time staff. Membership: $200/year.

National Federation of Officials Association *(1981)*
P.O. Box 690
Indianapolis, IN 46206
Tel: (317)972-6900 *Fax:* (317)822-5700
Web Site: www.nfhs.org/nfoa
Members: 118000 individuals
Staff: 5
Annual Budget: $500-1,000,000
Director: Tim Flannery
E-Mail: tflannery@nfhs.org

Historical Note
Formed through the National Federation of State High School Associations, NFOA members are secondary school, college and youth league sports officials. Membership: $16/year (individual).

Meetings/Conferences:
Annual Meetings: in conjunction with Nat'l Federation Interscholastic Coaches Ass'n

Publications:
NFHS Coaches' Quarterly. q.
NFHS Officials' Quarterly. q.
Interscholastic Athletic Administration. q.
Nat'l Federation News. 9/yr. adv.

National Federation of Paralegal Associations *(1974)*
P.O. Box 2016
Edmonds, WA 98020
Tel: (425)967-0045 *Fax:* (425)771-9588
E-Mail: info@paralegals.org
Web Site: www.paralegals.org
Members: 50 state and local associations
Staff: 4
Annual Budget: $500-1,000,000
Managing Director: Jane E. Kennedy

Historical Note
NFPA is a non-profit professional organization representing more than 11,000 paralegals and is headquartered in Edmonds, Washington. NFPA's core purpose is the advancement of the paralegal profession. NFPA promotes a global presence for the paralegal profession, and leadership in the legal community. Individual Sustaining Membership $85, Student Sustaining Membership $50, Organization Sustaining Membership $200.

Meetings/Conferences:
Annual Meetings: Tech Institute, July 2007; Annual Convention, October 2007
2007 – Pittsburgh, PA(Omni William Penn)/July 19-20/300
2007 – Tampa, FL(Hyatt Regency)/Oct. 18-21/250

Publications:
National Paralegal Reporter. bi-m. adv.

National Federation of Press Women *(1937)*
P.O. Box 5556
Arlington, VA 22205
Tel: (703)534-2500 *Fax:* (703)812-4555
Toll Free: (800)780 - 2715
E-Mail: presswomen@aol.com
Web Site: www.nfpw.org
Members: 2000 individuals
Staff: 1
Annual Budget: $100-250,000
President: Rishi Hingoraney

Historical Note
NFPW members are writers, editors and other communications professionals for newspapers, magazines, radio-TV, corporations, wire services, agencies and freelance. Organized at the Chicago Women's Club on May 6, 1937 under the leadership of Helen Miller Malloch as a federation of state affiliates of working press women. Membership: $51.50/year, plus affiliate dues.

Publications:
NFPW Agenda. q. adv.

National Federation of Priests' Councils *(1968)*
333 N. Michigan Ave., Suite 1205
Chicago, IL 60601-4002
Tel: (312)442-9700 *Fax:* (312)442-9709
Toll Free: (888)271 - 6372
E-Mail: nfpc@nfpc.org
Web Site: www.nfpc.org
Members: 110 councils
Staff: 3
Annual Budget: $250-500,000
Director, Programs and Publications: Vic Doucette

Historical Note
Members are priests' councils, no individual membership.

Meetings/Conferences:
Annual Meetings: April/250-275
2007 – Tampa, FL(Hyatt Regency)/Apr. 23-26

Publications:
Touchstone Newsletter. q.

National Federation of State High School Associations *(1920)*
P.O. Box 690
Indianapolis, IN 46206
Tel: (317)972-6900 *Fax:* (317)822-5700
Web Site: www.nfhs.org
Members: 51 stateass'ns/18,000highschools
Staff: 48
Annual Budget: $2-5,000,000
Executive Director: Robert F. Kanaby

Historical Note
Established as the National Federation of State High School Athletic Associations, it assumed its present name in 1970. The governing body for the interscholastic athletic activity of more than 18,000 high schools in the United States, Canada, the Philippines, Bermuda, Guam and the Virgin Islands.

Publications:
Coaches Quarterly. q.
Officials Quarterly. q.
National Federation News. 9/year.
Interscholastic Athletic Administration Magazine. q.

National Federation of Temple Brotherhoods *(1923)*
633 Third Ave.
New York, NY 10017
Tel: (212)650-4100 *Fax:* (212)650-4189
Toll Free: (800)765 - 6200
E-Mail: contact@nftb.org
Web Site: www.nftb.org
Staff: 3
Executive Director: Doug Barden

Historical Note
NFTB members are organizers of Reform synagogues. Through its association with affliated organizations, NFTB promotes social action, youth activities and other programs that contribute to temple and community life.

Meetings/Conferences:
Biennial Meetings: Summer

National Fellowship of Child Care Executives *(1954)*
Auberle Foundation, 1101 Hartman St.
McKeesport, PA 15132
Tel: (412)673-1992
Web Site: www.nfcce.org
Members: 48 organizations
Annual Budget: $25-50,000
Executive Secretary: Ray Niedenberger

Historical Note
Members are administrators of homes maintaining group residential care for children. Established as the National Association of Homes for Boys, it assumed its present name in 1981. Membership: $250/year.

Publications:
Book of Proceedings. a.

National FFA Organization *(1928)*
National FFA Center
P.O. Box 68960
Indianapolis, IN 46268
Tel: (317)802-6060 *Fax:* (317)802-6061
E-Mail: info@ffa.org
Web Site: www.ffa.org
Members: 476732 individuals
Staff: 90
Annual Budget: $2-5,000,000
National Advisor and Chief Executive Officer: Larry D. Case, Ed.D.
Chief Operating Officer: Doug Loudenslager

Historical Note
Formerly the Future Farmers of America, adopted its present name in 1989. A vocational student organization organized under the National Vocational Education Act to foster character, leadership and good citizenship. Absorbed the New Farmers of America in 1965. Membership: $5/year.

Publications:
FFA New Horizons. bi-m. adv.
Update. m.

National Field Selling Association *(1987)*
100 N. 20th St., Fourth Floor
Philadelphia, PA 19103-1443
Tel: (215)564-1627 *Fax:* (215)564-2175
E-Mail: nfsa@fernley.com
Web Site: www.nfsa.com
Staff: 3
Annual Budget: $100-250,000
Director, Administration: Ellen R. Buckley
E-Mail: ebuckley@fernley.com

Historical Note
Promotes professional excellence in the door-to-door direct selling industry.

Meetings/Conferences:
2007 – Bloomingdale, IL(Indian Lake)/

Publications:
Newsletter. q. adv.
Directory. a. adv.

National Finance Adjusters *(1947)*
1370 W. North Ave.
Baltimore, MD 21217
Tel: (410)728-2400 *Fax:* (410)523-8336
Toll Free: (800)253 - 7376
E-Mail: homeoffice@nfa.org
Web Site: www.nfa.org
Members: 210 individuals
Staff: 2
Annual Budget: $500-1,000,000
Central Office Manager: Helen M. Mullaney

Historical Note
The NFA is the largest association of professional collateral recovery specialists.

Meetings/Conferences:
Annual Meetings: Summer

Publications:
Director of Members. a.
The Repossession Process.
NFA Newsletter. 4/year.

National Fire Protection Association *(1896)*
One Batterymarch Park
Quincy, MA 02169-7471

Tel: (617)770-3000 *Fax:* (617)770-0700
Toll Free: (800)344 - 3555
Web Site: www.nfpa.org
Members: 79,000
Staff: 300
Annual Budget: $50-100,000,000
President and Chief Executive Officer: James M. Shannon
Associate Vice President, Conferences and Meetings: Linda Bailey
Assistant Vice President, Communications: Lorraine Carli
E-Mail: public_affairs@nfpa.org
Executive Vice President: Arthur E. Cote
Vice President, Marketing and Sales: Paul Crossman

Historical Note

NFPA promotes fire protection through the promulgation of codes and standards, research, technical advisory sources and public education. Has an annual budget of approximately $75 million. Membership: $135/year.

Meetings/Conferences:

2007 - Boston, MA(Boston Convention & Exhibition Center)/June 3-7
2007 - Miami Beach, FL(Miami Beach Convention Center)/July 24-26

Publications:

Buyers' Guide. a. adv.
NFPA Journal. bi-m. adv.
NFPA Update. bi-m.
Fire Technology. q.
National Fire Codes. a.

National Fire Sprinkler Association *(1905)*

P.O. Box 1000
Patterson, NY 12563
Tel: (845)878-4200 Ext: 133 *Fax:* (845)878-4215
Web Site: www.nfsa.org
Members: 2600 individuals
Staff: 30
Annual Budget: $2-5,000,000
President: John A. Viniello
E-Mail: viniello@nfsa.org
Director, Communications: David J. Vandeyar
E-Mail: vandeyar@nfsa.org

Historical Note

Founded as the National Automatic Sprinkler Association; became the National Automatic Sprinkler and Fire Control Association in 1958 and assumed its present name in 1983. Members are makers and installers of automatic fire sprinklers and related equipment. Membership: $85-165/year (individual); $750/minimum (contractor company); $1,100/minimum (supplier company).

Meetings/Conferences:

Annual Meetings: Spring
2007 - Las Vegas, NV(Red Rock Resort)/May 3-6/1200
2008 - Bahamas(Atlantis)March 14-17
2009 - Orlando, FL(Omni Champions Gate)/Apr. 29-May 2

Publications:

Sprinkler Scene. 3/yr.
Code Watch. q.
SQ. 6/year. adv.
Sprinkler Technotes. bi-m.
NFSA Grassroots. m.
Labor Line. bi-m.

National Fisheries Institute *(1945)*

7918 Jones Branch Dr., Suite 700
McLean, VA 22102
Tel: (703)752-8880 *Fax:* (703)752-7583
E-Mail: contact@nfi.org
Web Site: www.nfi.org
Members: 380 Companies
Staff: 12
Annual Budget: $2-5,000,000
President: John P. Connelly
Vice President, Membership and Marketing: Judy Dashiell

Historical Note

Absorbed (1970) American Seafood Distributors Association, (1983) the Shellfish Institute of North American and (1983) the National Blue Crab Industry Association. Divisions include National Aquaculture Council, Molluscan Shellfish Institute and Shrimp Council. Sponsors the NFI Political Action Committee.

Publications:

Buyer's Guide. a. adv.
NFInsider. w.

National Flight Paramedics Association *(1986)*

Historical Note

A professional association for flight paramedics involved with the air-medical industry. Membership: $45/year (individual, active or associate).

National Fluid Power Association *(1953)*

3333 N. Mayfair Rd.
Suite 211
Milwaukee, WI 53222-3219
Tel: (414)778-3344 *Fax:* (414)778-3361
Web Site: www.nfpa.com
Members: 275 companies
Staff: 12
Annual Budget: $1-2,000,000
Executive Director: Linda Western
E-Mail: lwestern@nfpa.com
Director, Member Services and Development: Peter Alles
E-Mail: palles@nfpa.com
International Standards Manager: Karen Boehme
E-Mail: kboehme@nfpa.com
Financial Director: Sue Chase
E-Mail: schase@nfpa.com
Membership Manager: Dawn Krueger
Publications Manager: Erin Tull
E-Mail: ctschwartz@nfpa.com

Historical Note

NFPA is an organization that serves as a forum for all interested stakeholders in the fluid power industry, including manufacturers, distributors, suppliers, educators and customers.

Meetings/Conferences:

Semi-Annual Meetings: Spring/Fall

Publications:

NFPA Reporter. bi-m.

National Flute Association *(1973)*

26951 Reuther Ave., Suite H
Santa Clarita, CA 91351
Tel: (661)299-4632 *Fax:* (661)299-6681
E-Mail: nationalflute@aol.com
Web Site: www.nfaonline.org
Members: 5500 individuals
Staff: 2
Annual Budget: $100-250,000
Executive Director: Phyllis Pemberton
Convention Manager: Madeline Neumann
E-Mail: nfaconvention@aol.com
Membership Services: Maria Stibelman

Historical Note

Members are flutists and individuals interested in the flute. Membership: $45/year.

Meetings/Conferences:

Annual Meetings: August

Publications:

Flutist Quarterly magazine. q. adv.
Membership Roster. a.

National Food and Energy Council *(1957)*

P.O. Box 309
Wilmington, OH 45177-0309
Tel: (937)383-0001 *Fax:* (937)383-0003
E-Mail: info@nfec.org
Web Site: www.nfec.org
Members: 250 companies
Staff: 2
Annual Budget: $100-250,000
President and Executive Manager: Richard S. Hiatt

Historical Note

Formerly (1957) Inter-Industry Farm Electric Utilization Council, (1962) Farm Electrification Council and then (1977) Food and Energy Council before assuming its present name in 1982. Members are electric utilities, agricultural cooperatives and related organizations.

Publications:

Current Marketing. bi-m.

National Food Processors Association

Historical Note

Became Food Products Association in 2004.

National Food Processors Institute *(1973)*

Historical Note

An educational organization established and managed by the National Food Processors Association. Also known as the Food Processors Institute.

National Football League *(1920)*

280 Park Ave., Suite 12-West
New York, NY 10017-1216
Tel: (212)450-2000 *Fax:* (212)681-7599
Web Site: www.nfl.com
Members: 30 teams
Staff: 100
Annual Budget: $5-10,000,000
Executive Vice President, Communications and Government Affairs: Joe Browne
Commissioner: Roger Goodell
Executive Vice President, Labor: Harold Henderson

Historical Note

Founded as the American Professional Football Association on September 17, 1920 in the showroom of the Huppmobile agency in Canton, Ohio with Jim Thorpe as President. Assumed its present name in 1922 and merged with the American Football League on February 1, 1970.

Meetings/Conferences:

Annual Meetings: March

Publications:

NFL Record and Fact Book. a.

National Football League Players Association *(1970)*

2021 L St. NW
Suite 600
Washington, DC 20036
Tel: (202)463-2200 *Fax:* (202)835-9775
Toll Free: (800)372 - 2000
Web Site: www.nflpa.org
Members: 1800 individuals
Staff: 90
Annual Budget: $1-2,000,000
Executive Director: Gene Upshaw
General Counsel: Richard Berthelsen
Director, Retired Players: Andre Collins
Assistant Executive Director: Allen Doug
Director, Communications: Carl Francis
Controller: William Garner
Director, Membership Services: Marie Snyder

Historical Note

The result of a merger on January 8, 1970 of the National Football League Players Association (formed in 1956) and the American Football League Players Association (formed about 1959). Originally a labor union affiliated with AFL/CIO under the umbrella of the Federation of Professional Athletes, NFLPA decertified itself in 1989 and acted solely as a professional association representing players in such areas as group licensing, insurance services and salary information. In 1993, NFPLA was again certified as the players' collective bargaining agent with the National Football League.

Meetings/Conferences:

Annual Meetings: March

Publications:

The Playbook. w.

National Foreign Trade Council *(1914)*

1625 K St. NW
Suite 200
Washington, DC 20006
Tel: (202)887-0278 *Fax:* (202)452-8160
E-Mail: nftcinformation@nftc.org
Web Site: www.nftc.org
Members: 300 companies
Staff: 15
Annual Budget: $2-5,000,000
President: William Reinsch
Senior Vice President: Anne Alonzo

Historical Note

Established in New York City pursuant to a resolution of the First National Foreign Trade Convention in 1914, as a private non-profit organization for the promotion and protection of U.S. international trade and investment.

Meetings/Conferences:

Annual Meetings: December

Publications:

Council Highlights. m.

National Forensic Association *(1972)*
107 Agency Road
Mankato, MN 56001
Tel: (507)387-3010 *Fax:* (507)387-3068
E-Mail: lschoor@hickorytech.net
Web Site: www.bethel.edu/Majors/Communication/nfa
Members: 300 colleges
Staff: 1
Annual Budget: $10-25,000
President: Larry Schoor

Historical Note
An affiliate of American Forensics Association, NFA promotes forensics competition at the collegiate level. Has no paid officers or full-time staff.

Meetings/Conferences:
Semi-annual Meetings: Spring and Fall

Publications:
Newsletter. 3/year.
NFA Journal. semi-a.

National Forest Recreation Association *(1948)*
P.O. Box 488
Woodlake, CA 93286
Tel: (559)564-2365 *Fax:* (559)564-2048
E-Mail: info@nfra.org
Web Site: www.nfra.org
Members: 300 individuals
Staff: 2
Annual Budget: $50-100,000
Executive Director: Marily Reese
E-Mail: info@nfra.org

Historical Note
NFRA is an organization assisting owners and operators of recreational and commercial facilities on National Forest, Bureau of Land Management and National Park Service lands, in their relationship with their respective agencies. Members include resorts, youth camps, campgrounds, pack stations, outfitters, tour and shuttle services, marinas, stores and restaurants. Memberships are based upon revenue scale of the applicant.

Meetings/Conferences:
Annual Meetings: March

Publications:
NFRA Report. q. adv.

National Forum for Black Public Administrators *(1983)*
777 North Capitol St. NE
Suite 807
Washington, DC 20002
Tel: (202)408-9300 *Fax:* (202)408-8558
E-Mail: webmaster@nfbpa.org
Web Site: www.nfbpa.org
Members: 2800 individuals
Staff: 7
Annual Budget: $1-2,000,000
Executive Director: John E. Saunders, III
E-Mail: webmaster@nfbpa.org

Historical Note
NFBPA members are city and county managers; chief administrative officers; agency and department directors; rank-and-file professionals; and deans, faculty members and graduate students at schools of public administration. NFBPA was established to strengthen the position of blacks within the field of public administration, to correct the inequity which exists with respect to the representation of blacks at the executive level, and to groom younger, aspiring administrators for top level public administrative posts. Membership: $150/year (individual); $1000-$5000/year (organization/company).

Meetings/Conferences:
Annual Meetings: April/1,400
2007 – Phoenix, AZ(Phoenix Civic Plaza)/Apr. 21-25/1100

Publications:
Membership Directory. a. adv.
Career Link. m. adv.
Forum Newsletter. q. adv.

National Foundation for Credit Counseling *(1951)*
801 Roeder Road, Suite 900
Silver Spring, MD 20910
Tel: (301)589-5600 *Fax:* (301)495-5623
Toll Free: (800)388 - 2227
E-Mail: info@nfcc.org
Web Site: www.nfcc.org
Members: 1000 member offices
Staff: 13
Annual Budget: $5-10,000,000
Chief Executive Officer and President: Susan Kealing
Senior Vice President, Legislative Affairs and Chief Counsel: William Binzel
Senior Vice President, Marketing and Communications: Robert Ensinger
Senior Vice President, Creditor Relations: Sally Parker
Senior Vice President and Chief Financial Officer: Paul Weiss

Historical Note
Founded as National Foundation for Consumer Credit; assumed its current name in 2000. Members are non-profit community Consumer Credit Counseling Services and creditors. The purpose is to educate the public to the proper and wise use of credit and to provide budget and debt management counseling to families in financial difficulty. Absorbed the Retail Credit Institute of America in 1951.

Meetings/Conferences:
Annual Meetings: Fall

Publications:
Guide Book- Keys to Homeownership. a.
Newsletter. m.
Bankruptcy Publications.

National Foundation for Women Business Owners

Historical Note
NFWBO is a research and development affiliate of National Association of Women Business Owners.

National Foundation for Women Legislators *(1938)*
910 16th St. NW, Suite 100
Washington, DC 20006-2903
Tel: (202)293-3040 *Fax:* (202)293-5430
E-Mail: nfwl@womenlegislators.org
Web Site: http://womenlegislators.org
Members: 3300 individuals
Staff: 9
Annual Budget: $500-1,000,000
President and Chief Executive Officer: Robin Read
Director, Public Policy and Operations: Julie Swaney

Historical Note
NFWL is a non-partisan, nonprofit educational foundation consisting of members of National Order of Women Legislators (current and former women legislators), and corporate and associate members (women and men) who, with funds and participation, support women legislators. Mission of the foundation is to provide a stepping stone for women legislators as they become comfortable in the positions of leadership and authority to climb into higher state or federal office, commissions, or appointed positions on the political ladder. Membership: varies.

Meetings/Conferences:
Annual Meetings: Fall

Publications:
Connection Newsletter. q. adv.

National Frame Builders Association *(1970)*
4840 Bob Billings Pkwy., Suite 1000
Lawrence, KS 66049-3862
Tel: (785)843-2444 *Fax:* (785)843-7555
Toll Free: (800)557 - 6957
E-Mail: www.nfba.org
Members: 700 companies
Staff: 12
Annual Budget: $250-500,000
President: Tom Knight
E-Mail: nfba@nfba.org
Vice President: John Fullerton

Historical Note
Members are building contractors, suppliers, design and code professionals and academic personnel specializing in the post-frame construction industry. Largest portion of membership consists of post-frame building contractors. Membership fee varies for each membership type.

Meetings/Conferences:
Annual Meetings: Winter

Publications:
Frame Building News Magazine. 6/year. adv.
Builders Newsletter. q.
Suppliers Newsletter. q.
Membership Directory. a. adv.

National Fraternal Congress of America *(1886)*
1315 W. 22nd St., Suite 400
Oak Brook, IL 60523
Tel: (630)522-6322 *Fax:* (630)522-6326
E-Mail: nfca@nfcanet.org
Web Site: www.nfcanet.org
Members: 75 societies
Staff: 10
Annual Budget: $1-2,000,000
President and Chief Executive Officer: Frederick H. Grubbe
Manager, Administrative Services: Joan A. Barngrover
E-Mail: jbarngrover@nfcanet.org
Director, Government Affairs: Robert Huxel
Director, Communications and Marketing: Rose Riccetti

Historical Note
Membership open to any fraternal benefit organization which is without capital stock, is carried on solely for the mutual benefit of its members and their beneficiaries, having a lodge system and a representative form of government which provides for the payment of death, sickness or disability benefits.

Meetings/Conferences:
Annual Meetings: September/350
2007 – Pittsburgh, PA/Sept. 6-8

Publications:
Fraternal Advantage. m.
Manual and Directory. a.
Report of Annual Meeting. a.
Statistics of Fraternal Benefit Societies. a.

National Fraternal Order of Police *(1915)*
1410 Donelson Pike, Suite A-17
Nashville, TN 37217-2933
Tel: (615)399-0900 *Fax:* (615)399-0400
E-Mail: glfop@grandlodgefop.org
Web Site: www.grandlodgefop.org
Members: 230000 individuals
Staff: 13
Annual Budget: $500-1,000,000
National Secretary: Patrick Yoes

Historical Note
Formerly (1988) the Fraternal Order of Police. Members are full time law enforcement officers seeking economic benefits and professional advancement. Membership: $3.50/year.

Meetings/Conferences:
Biennial Meetings: odd years in Summer

Publications:
National FOP Journal. q. adv.
Fair Labor Standards Handbook and FLSA Update. a.
Corporate and Tax Affairs of a Lodge.
Collective Bargaining and Dispute Resolution.

National Fraternity of Student Musicians *(1927)*

Historical Note
NFSM is a division of the American College of Musicians, representing students whose teachers are members of the National Guild of Piano Teachers, another division of ACM. For more information see American College of Musicians.

National Freight Transportation Association *(1905)*
P.O. Box 1321
Exton, PA 19341
Tel: (610)363-7747 *Fax:* (610)363-2971
E-Mail: nfta2000@aol.com
Web Site: www.nftahq.org
Members: 410 individuals
Staff: 2
Annual Budget: $100-250,000
Executive Director: George Turner

Historical Note
Provides information on rules and regulations to members.

Meetings/Conferences:
Semi-Annual Meetings: Spring and Fall

National Frozen and Refrigerated Foods Association *(1945)*
4755 Linglestown Road, Suite 300
P.O. Box 6069
Harrisburg, PA 17112-0069
Tel: (717)657-8601 *Fax:* (717)657-9862
E-Mail: info@nfraweb.org
Web Site: www.nfraweb.org
Members: 430 companies
Staff: 9
Annual Budget: $2-5,000,000
President and Chief Executive Officer: Nevin B. Montgomery
E-Mail: nevin@nfraweb.org
Director, Finance: Winifred E. Ethridge
E-Mail: winnie@nfraweb.org
Vice President, Communications: Julie Henderson
E-Mail: julie@nfraweb.org
Vice President, Foodservice and Membership: Marlene Redden
E-Mail: marlene@nfraweb.org
Executive VIce President and Chief Operating Officer: H.V. "Skip" Shaw
E-Mail: skip@nfraweb.org
Historical Note
Founded as National Frozen Food Association; assumed its current name in 2002. Sponsors National Frozen Food Month and annual NFRA convention. Membership fee based on volume of frozen food sales.
Meetings/Conferences:
Annual Meetings: Fall/1,200
2007 – San Antonio, TX(Marriott)/Oct. 13-16/1100
2008 – San Diego, CA(Marriott)/Oct. 11-15/1100
Publications:
Frozen Food Directory. q. adv.

National Frozen Dessert and Fast Food Association *(1961)*
P.O. Box 510
Millbrook, NY 12545-0510
Tel: (845)677-9301
Toll Free: (800)535 - 7748
Web Site: www.nfdffa.org
Members: 400 stores; 75 suppliers
Staff: 2
Annual Budget: $25-50,000
Executive Director: David E. Roberts
E-Mail: director@nfdffa.org
Historical Note
Formerly (1996) National Soft Serve and Fast Food Association. NFD & FFA was established as a medium through which operators and suppliers of frozen desserts and fast food establishments may promote their industry and speak with a unified voice. Membership: $75/year (operator); $90/year (distributor); $140/year (supplier).
Meetings/Conferences:
Annual Meetings: January
Publications:
Tidbits. bi-m. adv.

National Frozen Pizza Institute *(1975)*
2000 Corporate Ridge, Suite 1000
McLean, VA 22102
Tel: (703)821-0770 *Fax:* (703)821-1350
Web Site: www.affi.com/nfpi/nfpihomepage.htm
Staff: 3
Executive Director: Robert Garfield
Historical Note
Managed by American Frozen Food Institute.
Meetings/Conferences:
Annual Meetings: Fall/Washington, DC or Chicago, IL

National Fruit and Syrup Manufacturers Association *(1917)*
Historical Note
Became National Association of Flavors and Food Ingredient Systems in 2003.

National Funeral Directors and Morticians Association *(1924)*
3951 Snapfinger Pkwy., Suite 570
Decatur, GA 30035
Tel: (404)286-6680 *Fax:* (404)286-6573
Toll Free: (800)434 - 0958
E-Mail: nfdma@nfdma.org
Web Site: www.nfdma.com/
Members: 1500 individuals
Staff: 4
Annual Budget: $250-500,000
Executive Director: Sharon L. Seay
Historical Note
NFDMA is an organization of professional funeral directors and morticians. Membership in respective state association required.
Meetings/Conferences:
Annual Meetings: August
Publications:
Directory. bien. adv.

National Funeral Directors Association *(1882)*
13625 Bishop's Dr.
Brookfield, WI 53005
Tel: (262)789-1880 *Fax:* (262)789-6977
Toll Free: (800)228 - 6332
E-Mail: nfda@nfda.org
Web Site: www.nfda.org
Members: 14000 individuals
Staff: 47
Annual Budget: $5-10,000,000
Chief Executive Officer: Christine Reichelt-Pepper, CAE
E-Mail: cpepper@nfda.org
Convention and Meetings Manager: Jane Marie Alberti
Senior Vice President, Marketing and Communications Division: Laura Porfilio Glawe
Historical Note
NFDA sponsors and supports the NFDA Political Action Committee. Members are licensed funeral directors. Membership: fees vary, $290/year minimum.
Meetings/Conferences:
Annual Meetings: October-early November
Publications:
NFDA Bulletin E-Newsletter. bi-w.
The Director. m. adv.

National Futures Association *(1982)*
200 W. Madison St., Suite 1600
Chicago, IL 60606-3447
Tel: (312)781-1300 *Fax:* (312)781-1467
Toll Free: (800)621 - 3570
E-Mail: information@nfa.futures.org
Web Site: www.nfa.futures.org
Members: 4216 firms
Staff: 250
Annual Budget: $25-50,000,000
President and Chief Executive Officer: Daniel J. Roth
Manager, Membership and Registration: Yvette Christman
Executive President and Chief Operating Officer: Daniel A. Driscoll
Director, Communications and Education: Larry Dyekman
Senior Vice President, Information Systems: Ken Haase
Vice President, Chief Financial and Treasurer: David Hawrysz
Vice President, Registration: Gregory C. Prusik
Vice President, General Counsel and Secretary: Thomas W. Sexton, III
E-Mail: information@nfa.futures.org
Senior Vice President, Compliance: Regina G. Thoele
Senior Vice President, Strategic Planning and Communications: Karen Wuertz
Historical Note
Registered as a futures association under the Commodity Exchange Act in the Fall of 1981 and began operations October 1, 1982 as an industry-wide self-regulatory organization for the futures industry. Members are futures commission merchants (FCMs), commodity trading advisors (CTAs), commodity pool operators (CPOs), introducing brokers (IBs), exchanges and associated personnel. Maintains a separate toll-free number for Illinois residents: (800) 572-9400. Has an annual budget of approximately $32 million. Membership: $1,000-5,000/year (FCM); $500/year (CPO, CTA, or IB).
Meetings/Conferences:
Annual Meetings: Third or Fourth Thursday in February
Publications:
Annual Review. a.
Report of Quarterly Actions.

National Garden Clubs *(1929)*
4401 Magnolia Ave.
St. Louis, MO 63110
Tel: (314)776-7574 *Fax:* (314)776-5108
E-Mail: headquarters@gardenclub.org
Web Site: www.gardenclub.org
Members: 217233 individuals
Staff: 15
Executive Director: Francis Mantler
Historical Note
Formerly (2001) National Council of State Garden Clubs. A federation of garden clubs united to protect and conserve natural resources through teacher training and environmental workshops. Supported by dues of 25 cents per person from its member clubs. Sponsors the National Garden Week.
Meetings/Conferences:
Annual Meetings: May/1,000
Publications:
The National Gardener. bi-m. adv.

National Genealogical Society *(1903)*
3108 Columbia Pike
Arlington, VA 22204-4304
Tel: (703)525-0050 *Fax:* (703)525-0052
Toll Free: (800)473 - 0060
E-Mail: ngs@ngsgenealogy.org
Web Site: www.ngsgenealogy.org
Members: 18300 individuals
Staff: 14
Annual Budget: $1-2,000,000
President: Barbara Vines Little
Historical Note
Established April 24, 1903 at 920 S St. NW, Washington, DC, by Newton L. Collamer and other genealogists. Absorbed the Association for Genealogical Education in 1981. Incorporated as a nonprofit organization under the laws of the District of Columbia in 1904 to collect and preserve genealogical, historical and heraldic data; inculcate and promote interest in research; foster careful documentation and scholarly writing; and issue publications relating to the field of genealogy. Membership: $35/year.
Meetings/Conferences:
Annual Meetings: Spring
Publications:
NGS Quarterly. q. adv.
Newsmagazine. bi-m. adv.
Upfront with NGS. 2/m.
Conference Syllabus. a.

National Gerontological Nursing Association *(1984)*
7794 Grow Dr.
Pensacola, FL 32514
Tel: (850)473-1174 *Fax:* (850)484-8762
Toll Free: (800)723 - 0560
E-Mail: ngna@puetzamc.com
Web Site: www.ngna.org
Members: 1600 individuals
Staff: 5
Annual Budget: $50-100,000
Nurse Consultant: Belinda E. Puetz, Ph.D., RN
E-Mail: ngna@puetzamc.com
Historical Note
NGNA is a professional organization of registered nurses, licensed practical nurses and allied health professionals working in, or with an interest in, the field of gerontology. Membership: $95/year.
Meetings/Conferences:
Annual Meetings: October
2007 – Orlando, FL(Doubletree Hotel at Entrance to Universal Orlando)/Oct. 19-21
Publications:
SIGN Newsletter. bi-m. adv.
Geriatric Nursing Magazine. bi-m. adv.

National Glass Association *(1948)*
8200 Greensboro Dr., Suite 302
McLean, VA 22102-3881
Tel: (703)442-4890 *Fax:* (703)442-0630

Toll Free: (866)342 - 5642
E-Mail: info@glass.org
Web Site: www.glass.org
Members: 1900 individuals
Staff: 30
Annual Budget: $5-10,000,000
President and Chief Executive Officer: Philip J. James, CAE
Vice President, Publications: Nicole Harris, CAE
Vice President, Meetings and Expositions: Denise Sheehan

Historical Note
Formerly the National Auto & Flat Glass Dealers Association and the National Glass Dealers Association (until 1984). Incorporated in the State of Michigan in 1948. Reincorporated in the District of Columbia in 1978. Members are architectural and automobile glass manufacturers, wholesalers, fabricators, distributors, installers and companies that do work related to the industry, such as companies that manufacture and/or are otherwise concerned with windows, mirrors, sealants, tools, and material handling equipment. Absorbed the Auto Glass Industry Council in 1990.

Meetings/Conferences:
Annual Meetings: Glass Build America: The Glass, Window & Door Expo

Publications:
AutoGlass Magazine. 7/yr. adv.
NGA Members Update (online). m.
Window & Door Magazine. 11/year. adv.
Glass Magazine. m. adv.

National Golf Car Manufacturers Association *(1984)*

Two Ravinia Dr., Suite 1200
Atlanta, GA 30346
Tel: (770)394-7200 *Fax:* (770)454-0138
Staff: 1
General Counsel and Secretary-Treasurer: Fred L. Somers, Jr.
E-Mail: somersf@abanet.org

Meetings/Conferences:
Semi-Annual Meetings:

National Golf Course Owners Association *(1976)*

291 Seven Farms Dr.
Charleston, SC 29492
Tel: (800)933-4262 *Fax:* (843)881-9958
E-Mail: info@ngcoa.org
Web Site: www.ngcoa.org
Members: 4000 clubs
Staff: 20
Annual Budget: $1-2,000,000
Executive Director: Mike Hughes
E-Mail: mhughes@ngcoa.org
Director, Membership: Jay Karen

Historical Note
Established as the National Association of Public Golf Courses under the aegis of the National Golf Foundation, it became fully independent as Golf Course Association in 1982 and assumed its present name in 1991. Members are privately-owned golf courses. Membership: $325/year.

Meetings/Conferences:
Annual Meetings: Winter

Publications:
Golf Business Magazine. m. adv.

National Golf Foundation *(1936)*

1150 South U.S. Hwy. 1, Suite 401
Jupiter, FL 33477
Tel: (561)744-6006 *Fax:* (561)744-6107
Toll Free: (800)275 - 4643
E-Mail: general@ngf.org
Web Site: www.ngf.org
Members: 4625 organizations
Staff: 27
Annual Budget: $1-2,000,000
President and Chief Executive: Dr. Joseph Beditz
Director, Membership and Marketing: Barbara Divver
Director, Reseach: Jim Kass
Director, Consulting: Richard Singer

Historical Note
The National Golf Foundation is a membership-based organization comprised of 4,500 members that provides information and insights on the business of golf. Founded in 1936, the NGF now has over 6,000 member organizations representing a broad cross-section of the industry. Members include equipment manufacturers, media, facilities and ranges, golf course architects, builders and developers, retailers, associations and turf maintenance suppliers.

Meetings/Conferences:
Biennial Meetings:
2007 – Wheeling, WV(Ogelbay Resort)/Jan. 14-19

Publications:
Golf Participation In The U.S. a.
Golf Facilities In The U.S. a.
Golf Industry Report. q.
NGF Research Publications. a.

National Goose Council *(1971)*

Historical Note
Address unknown in 2006.

National Government Publishing Association *(1977)*

207 Third Ave.
Hattiesburg, MS 39401
Tel: (601)582-3330 *Fax:* (601)582-3354
E-Mail: info@govpublishing.org
Web Site: www.govpublishing.org
Members: 125 jurisdictions
Staff: 2
Annual Budget: $50-100,000
Executive Director: F. Lamar Evans
E-Mail: info@govpublishing.org

Historical Note
An association of various states and other related political jurisdictions, NSPA is concerned with improving the management of printing programs, exchanging information, cooperating for more effective production and procurement of printing products. Membership: $400/year (individual); $750/year (company); $225/year (associate).

Meetings/Conferences:
Annual Meetings: Fall

Publications:
NSPA Newsletter. q.

National Governors Association *(1908)*

444 North Capitol St., NW
Suite 267
Washington, DC 20001-1512
Tel: (202)624-5300 *Fax:* (202)624-5313
E-Mail: webmaster@nga.org
Web Site: www.nga.org
Members: 55 governors
Staff: 87
Annual Budget: $10-25,000,000
Executive Director: Raymond C. Scheppach, Ph.D.
Director, Communications: Jay Hyde

Historical Note
Formerly (1977) National Governors Conference. Members are the Governors of the 50 states and five territories of the U.S. Funded by individual states and grants, NGA informs members of federal legislation that will have an impact on their states. Influences the development of national policy. Includes an Office of Management Services which offers technical and consultant services, as well as a Center for Best Practices, which handles demonstration projects.

Meetings/Conferences:
Semi-annual Meetings: Winter and Summer

Publications:
Current Developments in Employment and Training. bi-w.
Governors Executive Report. w.
Directory of Governors of the American States, Commonwealths and Territories. a.
Fiscal Survey of the States. semi-a.

National Grain and Feed Association *(1896)*

1250 I St. NW
Suite 1003
Washington, DC 20005-3922
Tel: (202)289-0873 *Fax:* (202)289-5388
E-Mail: ngfa@ngfa.org
Web Site: www.ngfa.org
Members: 900 companies
Staff: 13
Annual Budget: $2-5,000,000
President: Kendell W. Keith
Counsel for Public Affairs: Charles Delacruz
Director, Legislative Affairs: Christopher Holdgreve
Director, Marketing and Treasurer: Todd E. Kemp

Historical Note
Formerly (1970) Grain and Feed Dealers National Association. Represents firms that store, handle, merchandise, mill, process, and/or export grains and oilseeds for domestic and international markets.

Meetings/Conferences:
2007 – San Francisco, CA(Westin St. Francis)/March 18-20

Publications:
Insurance, Loss Control and Employee Protection. a.
NGFA Trade Rules and Arbitration Rules. a.
Feed Quality Assurance Manual.
NGFA Directory Yearbook. a. adv.
NGFA Newsletter. bi-w.
Directory of River Barge Shipping Points. irreg.

National Grain Sorghum Producers *(1985)*

4201 N. I-27
Lubbock, TX 79403
Tel: (806)749-3478
Toll Free: (800)749 - 3478
E-Mail: ngsp@sorghumgrowers.com
Web Site: www.sorghumgrowers.com
Members: 4000 individuals
Staff: 8
Annual Budget: $250-500,000
Executive Director: Tim Lust

Historical Note
Founded as the Grain Sorghum Producers Association in 1955; assumed its present name in 1985. Affiliated with the Texas Grain Sorghum Producers Board and the U.S. Feed Grains Council. Membership: $40/year.

Meetings/Conferences:
Annual Meetings: February

Publications:
Grain Sorghum News. q.
Utilization Conference Proceedings. bien.

National Grain Trade Council *(1936)*

1300 L St. NW
Suite 1020
Washington, DC 20005-4113
Tel: (202)842-0400 *Fax:* (202)789-7223
Web Site: www.ngtc.org
Members: 40 companies and organizations
Staff: 2
Annual Budget: $250-500,000
President: Jula J. Kinnaird
E-Mail: jkinnaird@ngtc.org

Historical Note
NGTC members are commodity exchanges, boards of trade, national grain marketing associations and grain related businesses.

Meetings/Conferences:
Annual Meetings: February

National Grange *(1867)*

1616 H St. NW
Washington, DC 20006
Tel: (202)628-3507 *Fax:* (202)347-1091
Toll Free: (888)447 - 2643
E-Mail: info@nationalgrange.org
Web Site: www.nationalgrange.org
Members: 300000 individuals
Staff: 20
National Master: William Steel
E-Mail: bsteel@nationalgrange.org
Chief Operating Officer: Richard H. Weiss

Historical Note
Fraternal organization of rural families.

Publications:
Journal of Proceedings. a.
NPW Grange. q.

National Grants Management Association *(1978)*

11654 Plaza America Dr., Suite 609
Reston, VA 20190-4700
Tel: (703)648-9023 *Fax:* (703)648-9024
E-Mail: info@ngma.org
Web Site: www.ngma.org
Members: 9500 individuals

Staff: 3
Annual Budget: $250-500,000
Executive Director: Torryn Brazell, CAE, CMP

Meetings/Conferences:
2007 - Washington, DC(Reagan International Center)/Apr. 24-26/450
2008 - Washington, DC(Reagan International Center)/Apr. 22-24/500

Publications:
NGMA E-Bulletin. 6/yr. adv.
NGMA News Brief. q. adv.
Membership Directory. a. adv.
Journal of NGMA. semi-a.

National Grape Cooperative Association
1223 Potomac St. NW
Washington, DC 20007
Tel: (202)333-8578 *Fax:* (202)337-3809
E-Mail: kkormondy@mindspring.com
Members: 1390
Government Relations: Nicholas A. Pyle
Contact: Karen Kormondy

National Greenhouse Manufacturers Association *(1958)*
4305 N. Sixth St.
Suite A
Harrisburg, PA 17110
Tel: (717)238-4530 *Fax:* (717)238-9985
Toll Free: (800)792 - 6462
E-Mail: ngma@ngma.org
Web Site: www.ngma.com
Members: 80 companies
Staff: 5
Annual Budget: $100-250,000
Executive Director: Melanie K. Hughes

Historical Note
Founded to foster and advance the interests of the greenhouse industry. Serves various segments of the industry: growers, consumers, and manufacturers or suppliers of materials and equipment, or related services. Membership: $600-800/year.

Meetings/Conferences:
Semi-Annual Meetings: Spring and Fall

National Grocers Association *(1982)*
1005 N. Glebe Road, Suite 250
Arlington, VA 22201-5758
Tel: (703)516-0700 *Fax:* (703)516-0115
E-Mail: info@nationalgrocers.org
Web Site: www.nationalgrocers.org
Members: 2000 retailers and wholesalers
Staff: 32
Annual Budget: $2-5,000,000
President and Chief Executive Officer: Thomas K. Zaucha
Director, Government Affairs: Gregory B. Ferrara
Director, Membership and MIS: Larry Gibson
Senior Vice President and General Counsel: Thomas F. Wenning

Historical Note
The National Grocers Association was formed in 1982 as the result of the merger of the National Association of Retail Grocers of the U.S. (1893) and the Cooperative Food distributors of America (1937). It is the only national trade association representing the retail and wholesale grocers who comprise the independent sector of the food industry which accounts for nearly one-half of all food store sales in the U.S. Retail and wholesale grocers hold membership in NGA as well as state and local associations and manufacturers/service suppliers. NGA services include legislative and regulatory advocacy, trade relations and labor relations, as well as educational programs and operational research through the Grocers Research and Education Foundation (GREF); and central buying and marketing through its subsidary, the NGA Service Corporation (NGASC).

Meetings/Conferences:
Annual Meetings: Winter/6,000

Publications:
Employee & Labor Relations. q.
Advocate. m.
Express Lane. m.

National Ground Water Association *(1948)*
601 Dempsey Road
Westerville, OH 43081-8978
Tel: (614)898-7791 *Fax:* (614)898-7786
Toll Free: (800)551 - 7379
E-Mail: ngwa@ngwa.org
Web Site: www.ngwa.org
Members: 15000 individuals and companies
Staff: 40
Annual Budget: $5-10,000,000
Executive Director: Kevin McCray
Director, Education: Kathy Butcher
Director, Finance: Paul Humes
Expositions Director: Greg Phelps
Government Affairs: Chris Reimer

Historical Note
Formerly (1991) the National Water Well Association. NGWA members are ground water contractors, makers and suppliers of well drilling/water systems equipment, and scientists/engineers interested in the problems of locating, using and protecting underground water. Mission of NGWA is to enchance the skills and credibility of all ground water professionals, to develop and exchange industry knowledge, and to promote the ground water industry and understanding of ground water resources. The Association of Ground Water Scientists and Engineers, and the Manufacturers and Suppliers, are divisions of NGWA. Provides education, information, and leadership to an international membership, and sponsors the National Ground Water Information Center. Membership: dues vary, based on membership division and category.

Meetings/Conferences:
Annual Meetings: Fall/4,000

Publications:
Ass'n of Ground Water Scientists and Engineers Newsletter (online). m.
Ground Water Monitoring & Remediation. q. adv.
Water Well Journal. m. adv.
Journal of Ground Water. bi-m. adv.
The Well Log (online). m.

National Guard Association of the U.S. *(1878)*
One Massachusetts Ave. NW
Washington, DC 20001
Tel: (202)789-0031 *Fax:* (202)682-9358
Toll Free: (888)226 - 4287
Web Site: www.ngaus.org
Members: 52000 individuals
Staff: 30
Annual Budget: $2-5,000,000
President: Stephen Koper
Director, Communications: John Goheen
E-Mail: jgoheen@ngaus.org

Historical Note
Founded in 1878. Membership is open to any officer or warrant officer who serves or has served in the Army or Air National Guard and association members. Membership fee: scaled according to rank.

Meetings/Conferences:
Annual Meetings: Fall
2007 - San Juan, PR/Aug. 25-27
2008 - Baltimore, MD/Sept. 20-22

Publications:
The National Guard. m. adv.

National Guard Executive Directors Association
3706 Crawford
P.O. Box 10045
Austin, TX 78766-1045
Tel: (512)454-7300 *Fax:* (512)467-6803
E-Mail: dpyeatt@ngat.org
Web Site: www.ngeda.org
Members: 200 individuals
Staff: 7
Annual Budget: $25-50,000
Secretary-Treasurer: Dale M. Pyeatt

Historical Note
Membership: $50/year (individual).

Publications:
Directory. a. adv.

National Guardianship Association *(1988)*
1604 N. Country Club Road
Tucson, AZ 85716-3102
Tel: (520)881-6561 *Fax:* (520)325-7925
Web Site: www.guardianship.org
Members: 700 individuals
Staff: 16
Annual Budget: $10-25,000
Executive Director: Laury A. Gelardi
Administrator: Maggie Rodeffer

Historical Note
Incorporated in 1988. NGA's mission is to establish and promote a nationally recognized standard of excellence in guardianship. NGA works to strengthen guardianship and related services through networking, education, and tracking and commenting on legislation. Composed of individuals and organizations in the United States, Canada and Australia; includes guardians, conservators, fiduciaries, representative payees, physicians, hospitals, others interested in guardianship and surrogacy, attorneys, social workers, bankers and advocates. Membership: $50/year (family); $170/year (professional).

Meetings/Conferences:
Annual Meetings: October

Publications:
National Guardian. q. adv.
Membership Directory. a. adv.

National Guild of Community Schools of the Arts *(1937)*
520 Eighth Ave., Suite 302
New York, NY 10018
Tel: (212)268-3337 *Fax:* (212)268-3995
E-Mail: info@natguild.org
Web Site: www.nationalguild.org
Members: 80 individuals
Staff: 4
Annual Budget: $500-1,000,000
Executive Director: Jonathan Herman
Director, Programs: Kenneth Cole

Historical Note
NACSA is an association of non-profit, non-degree granting arts schools. Mission is to foster and promote broad access to the arts in all our communities, by providing service, advocacy and leadership for community arts education organizations. NACSA's affiliate members are all businesses. Membership: $100/year (Individual); $250/year (Business Affiliate); $185-2,500/year (Institution).

Meetings/Conferences:
Annual Meetings: Fall

Publications:
Annual Report. a.
Guildnotes. bi-m. adv.
Membership Directory. a. adv.
Employment Opportunities. m.

National Guild of Piano Teachers *(1929)*
808 Rio Grande St., Box 1807
Austin, TX 78767-1807
Tel: (512)478-5775 *Fax:* (512)478-5843
E-Mail: ngpt@pianoguild.com
Web Site: www.pianoguild.com
Members: 115000 individuals
Staff: 10
Annual Budget: $1-2,000,000
President: Richard Allison

Historical Note
A division of the American College of Musicians. NGPT is a professional society of piano teachers and music faculty members. Sponsors national examinations.

Publications:
Piano Guild Notes. q. adv.

National Guild of Professional Paperhangers *(1974)*
136 S. Keowee St.
Dayton, OH 45402
Tel: (937)222-6477 *Fax:* (937)222-5794
Toll Free: (800)254 - 6477
E-Mail: ngpp@ngpp.org
Web Site: www.ngpp.org
Members: 1000 individuals
Staff: 7
Annual Budget: $250-500,000
Executive Vice President: Kim Fantaci
E-Mail: ngpp@ngpp.org

Historical Note
Founded at Hicksville, NY in 1974, incorporated in Pennsylvania in 1982. NGPP's main objective is to promote the wallcovering industry. Membership is made up of professionals in the wallcovering industry. Membership: $150/year (individual); $360/year (organization/company); chapter member and chapter associate - varies, depending on chapter.

Meetings/Conferences:
2007 - San Diego, CA(Sheraton)/Sept. 4-7

Publications:
National Membership Directory. a. adv.
NGPP Wallcovering Installer. bi-m. adv.

National Gymnastics Judges Association *(1969)*
2302 San Point
Champaign, IL 61822
Tel: (217)384-8517
Web Site: www.NGJA.org
Members: 800 individuals
Annual Budget: $25-50,000
President: Butch Zunich
E-Mail: zunich@urbana.css.mot.com

Historical Note
Founded in 1969 and incorporated in 1980, the NGJA acts as a professional service organization, providing technical and educational knowledge, training and certification for men's gymnastics officials. Affiliated with USA Gymnastics. Assigns officials for men's gymnastic competitions at junior, national and international levels. NGJA President serves on the USA Gymnastics Board of Directors. Provides officials for men's gymnastic competitions. Organization has National Hall of Fame. Officials certify at three levels: JO, National and FIG (international). Officials take national examiniation annually. Membership: $25/year.

Meetings/Conferences:
Semi-annual Meetings: Fall, with USA Gymnastics and Spring, in conjunction with major gymnastics championships

Publications:
NGJA Newsletter. a.
NGJA Directory. a.
Men's Rules Interpretations Book. quadren. adv.
Men's Rules Interpretations Book Update. a. adv.

National Hardwood Lumber Association *(1898)*
P.O. Box 34518
Memphis, TN 38184-0518
Tel: (901)377-1818 *Fax:* (901)382-6419
E-Mail: info@nhla.com
Web Site: www.nhla.com
Members: 1700 companies
Staff: 50
Annual Budget: $2-5,000,000
Executive Manager: Paul Houghland, Jr., CAE

Historical Note
Trade association of the hardwood lumber industry. Establishes offical grading rules for hardwood lumber and provides lumber inspection service in the U.S. and Canada. Operates school for teaching hardwood lumber grading rules. Helps maintain order, structure and ethics in the hardwood market place.

Meetings/Conferences:
Annual Meetings: Fall/1,100
2007 - Washington, DC(Washington Hilton)/Sept. 12-15/1100
2008 - San Francisco, CA(San Francisco Marriott)/Oct. 8-11/1100

Publications:
Hardwood Matters. m. adv.
Exporter's Directory. a. adv.
Membership Directory. a. adv.

National Hay Association *(1895)*
102 Treasure Island Causeway
Treasure Island, FL 33706-4716
Tel: (727)367-9702 *Fax:* (727)367-9608
Toll Free: (800)707 - 0014
Web Site: www.nationalhay.org
Members: 660 individuals
Staff: 2
Annual Budget: $100-250,000
Executive Director: Donald Kieffer

Historical Note
Represents the interests of both companies and individuals which make up the hay industry as it moves hay and straw from surplus to deficit areas. Membership: $260/year.

Meetings/Conferences:
Annual Meetings: Fall

Publications:
Yearbook and Membership Directory. a. adv.
Hay There. m. adv.

National Head Start Association *(1973)*
1651 Prince St.
Alexandria, VA 22314-2818
Tel: (703)739-0875 *Fax:* (703)739-0878
Web Site: www.nhsa.org
Members: 133000 individuals
Staff: 36
Annual Budget: $5-10,000,000
Chief Executive Officer: Sarah M. Greene
Director, Research and Evaluations: Ben Allen
Director, Publishing and Marketing: Bridget Boel
Director, Office Operations: Laurie Byers
Director, Field Operations: Charles Marcy
Director, Technology Services: Gregg Porter
Director, Government Affairs: Joel Ryan
Conference Director: Cheryl Thompson
Director, Program Development: Diane Whitehead

Historical Note
NHSA members include staff, parents, directors, agencies and other organizations concerned with the Head Start program. NHSA provides professional, statistical and technical assistance to encourage and promote the development of children, youth, families and communities. Membership: $40/year (individual); $100/year (affiliate); $200-2500/year (agency); $350/year (corporation).

Meetings/Conferences:
Annual Meetings: Spring

Publications:
Children and Families. 3/year. adv.

National Health Association *(1948)*
P.O. Box 30630
Tampa, FL 33630-3630
Tel: (813)855-6607 *Fax:* (813)855-8052
E-Mail: info@healthscience.org
Web Site: www.anhs.org
Members: 7000 individuals
Staff: 2
Executive Director: Lynn Grudnik

Historical Note
Founded as American Natural Hygiene Society; assumed its current name in 1998.

Publications:
Health Science Magazine. 6/year.

National Health Care Anti-Fraud Association *(1985)*
1201 New York Ave. NW
Suite 1120
Washington, DC 20005
Tel: (202)659-5955 *Fax:* (202)785-6764
E-Mail: fraud@nhcaa.org
Web Site: www.nhcaa.org
Members: 800 individuals
Staff: 7
Annual Budget: $1-2,000,000
Executive Director: Lou Saccoccio
Director, Administration: Tia Theriaque, CAP

Historical Note
NHCAA's mission is to improve the detection, investigation, prosecution and prevention of health care fraud. It seeks to help control health care costs through an aggressive and coordinated anti-fraud effort employing public awareness, national communications, information systems and private/public sector cooperation. Membership: $100/year (individual); $6,500-25,000/year (organization/company).

Meetings/Conferences:
Annual Meetings: November

National Health Club Association *(1988)*
640 Plaza Dr., Suite 300
Highlands Ranch, CO 80129
Tel: (303)986-9563 *Fax:* (303)986-6813
Web Site: www.asfinternational.com
Members: 3000 health clubs
Staff: 20
Executive Vice President: Robert Riches

Historical Note
Absorbed the Fitness Trade Association in 1990. NHCA members are fitness centers.

Meetings/Conferences:
Annual Meetings: Fall

Publications:
Nat'l Fitness Trade Journal. bi-m. adv.

National Health Council *(1920)*
1730 M St. NW
Suite 500
Washington, DC 20036
Tel: (202)785-3910 *Fax:* (202)785-5923
E-Mail: info@nhcouncil.org
Web Site: www.nhcouncil.org
Members: 115 national organizations
Staff: 7
Annual Budget: $1-2,000,000
President: Myrl Weinberg, CAE
Vice President, Policy Development and Advocacy: Marc Boutin

Historical Note
A federation of voluntary health agencies, professional societies, business groups, and other organizations concerned with the nation's health. Membership: $1,200-35,000/year, dues vary as a percentage of total income (voluntary health agencies); $900-7600/year, dues vary by gross income (professional and membership associations); $1,200-$2,400/year, dues vary by total income (nonprofit organizations; $8,800/year (companies).

Meetings/Conferences:
Annual Meetings: Spring

Publications:
Council Currents. bi-m.
Washington Health Groups Directory. a. adv.
Report on Voluntary Health Agency Revenue and Expenses. a.

National Hearing Conservation Association *(1976)*
7995 E. Prentice Ave., Suite 100
Greenwood Village, CO 80111
Tel: (303)224-9022 *Fax:* (303)770-1614
E-Mail: nhca@gwami.com
Web Site: www.hearingconservation.org
Members: 450 companies and individuals
Staff: 2
Annual Budget: $100-250,000
Executive Director: Karen Wojdyla

Historical Note
Established and incorporated in Colorado. Reincorporated in Iowa. Members are groups providing hearing conservation program services, companies manufacturing occupational noise or hearing loss products, and individuals holding advanced degress in disciplines dealing with hearing and hearing loss. Membership: $152/year (individual/associate); $357/year (service organization); $890/year (commercial); .

Meetings/Conferences:
Annual Meetings: Winter
2007 - Savannah, GA(Hyatt Regency)/Feb. 15-17/250

Publications:
Spectrum. q. adv.
Membership Directory. a.

National Hemophilia Foundation *(1948)*
116 W. 32nd St.
11th Floor
New York, NY 10001
Tel: (212)328-3700 *Fax:* (212)328-3777
Web Site: www.hemophilia.org
Members: 3000 individuals
Staff: 40
Annual Budget: $5-10,000,000
Director, Research: Neil Frick, MS

Historical Note
The National Hemophilia Foundation is dedicated to finding the cures for inherited bleeding disorders and

to preventing and treating the complications of these diseases-through education, advocacy, and research.

Meetings/Conferences:
Annual Meetings: *Fall*

Publications:
NHF e*Notes. m.
HemAware. bi-m.

National Hereford Hog Record Association *(1933)*
22405 480th Ave.
Flandreau, SD 57028-7004
Tel: (605)997-2116
Members: 150 individuals
Staff: 1
Annual Budget: under $10,000
Secretary-Treasurer: Ruby Schrecengost

Historical Note
Established and incorporated in Iowa. Maintains registry of pedigrees. Membership: $10/lifetime (individual); $100/lifetime (organization/company)

Meetings/Conferences:
2007 – Aledo, IL/Aug. 25- /50

Publications:
Newsletter. a. adv.
Advertiser. q. adv.

National High School Athletic Coaches Association *(1965)*
P.O. Box 10065
Fargo, ND 58106
E-Mail: office@hscoaches.org
Web Site: www.hscoaches.org
Members: 55000 individuals
Staff: 4
Annual Budget: $500-1,000,000
Executive Director: Gelaine Orvik
E-Mail: office@hscoaches.org

Historical Note
NHSACA sponsors programs of recognition (High School Coach of the Year Awards for 16 different sports), education and competition. It is involved in varied activities in the commmercial, educational, governmental and communications fields and serves as a source of information and counsel to individuals and organizations. Members number 55,000 men and women coaches and athletic directors from 40 affiliated state coaches organizations. Membership: $35/year (individual).

Meetings/Conferences:
Annual Meetings: *June/1,000*

National Hispanic Corporate Council *(1985)*
1530 Wilson Blvd., Suite 110
Arlington, VA 22209
Tel: (703)807-5137 *Fax:* (703)842-7924
Web Site: www.nhcc-hq.org
Members: 60 companies
President and Chief Executive Officer: Carlos Soto
E-Mail: csoto@nhcc-hq.org
Vice President: Helen Trinidad

Publications:
NHCC Fastread. m.
Annual Report. a.

National Hispanic Medical Association *(1994)*
1411 K St. NW
Suite 1100
Washington, DC 20005
Tel: (202)628-5895 *Fax:* (202)628-5898
E-Mail: nhma@nhmamd.org
Web Site: www.nhmamd.org
Members: 500 individuals
Staff: 7
Annual Budget: $1-2,000,000
President and Chief Executive Officer: Dr. Elena V. Rios

Publications:
NHMA Net. bi-m. adv.

National Hockey League *(1917)*
1251 Ave. of the Americas
47th Floor
New York, NY 10020-1104
Tel: (212)789-2000 *Fax:* (212)789-2020
Web Site: www.nhl.com
Members: 30 teams
Staff: 160
Annual Budget: $5-10,000,000
Commissioner: Gary B. Bettman
Vice President, Media Relations: Frank Brown
Deputy Commissioner: William Daly
Executive Vice President and Chief Financial Officer: Craig Harnett
Group Vice President, Communications: Bernadette Mansur

Historical Note
Professional ice hockey league based in Canada and the United States.

Meetings/Conferences:
Annual Meetings: *Summer*

Publications:
NHL This Week. w.
All-Star Magazine. a.
Official Guide and Record Book. a.
Rule Book. a.
Club Media Guides. a.

National Hockey League Players' Association *(1967)*
20 Bay St., Suite 1700
Toronto, ON M5J 2-N8
Tel: (416)313-2300 *Fax:* (416)313-2301
Web Site: www.nhlpa.com
Members: 750 individuals
Staff: 35
Annual Budget: $2-5,000,000
Executive Director: Ted Saskin
Manager, Communications: Tyler Currie

Historical Note
Independent labor union established in Montreal in June, 1967. Membership: $2,880/year.

Meetings/Conferences:
Annual Meetings: *Summer*

Publications:
Power Play Magazine. 4/year.

National Home Equity Mortgage Association *(1974)*
1301 Pennsylvania Ave. NW
Suite 500
Washington, DC 20004
Tel: (202)347-1210 *Fax:* (202)347-1171
Toll Free: (800)342 - 1121
Web Site: www.nhema.org
Members: 250 companies
Staff: 3
Annual Budget: $2-5,000,000
Executive Director: Jeffrey L. Zeltzer

Historical Note
Formerly (1995) National Second Mortgage Association. Active members include banks, bank holding companies, national and regional finance companies, savings associations, mortgage bankers and brokers, and a full array of mortgage product and service providers. NHEMA's mission is to promote the growth and recognition of the home equity lending industry. Membership: $1,500/year.

Meetings/Conferences:
Annual Meetings: *April/330*

Publications:
Equity:The Journal of the Home Equity Lending Professional. bi-m. adv.
Membership Roster. semi-a.
Equity Update. w.
Media Update. bi-w.

National Home Furnishings Association *(1920)*
3910 Tinsley Dr., Suite 101
High Point, NC 27265
Tel: (336)886-6100 *Fax:* (336)801-6102
Toll Free: (800)888 - 9590
E-Mail: mail@nhfa.org
Web Site: www.nhfa.org
Members: 3000 corporations
Staff: 44
Annual Budget: $2-5,000,000
Executive Vice President: Steve DeHaan
Senior Director, Membership and Member Services: Jerry Alderman
System Administrator: Connie Cramer
Director, Industry Relations: Sheryl Johnson
Senior Director, Education and Communications: Karin Mayfield, CMP
Controller: Trishonda Patrick
Director, Communications: Mike Pierce
Director, Marketing: Tim Timmons

Historical Note
Formerly (1970) National Retail Furniture Association. NHFA's corporate members represent 10,000 retail stores. Membership fee determined by volume.

Meetings/Conferences:
Annual Meetings: *Spring*
2008 – Paradise Islands, Bahamas(The Atlantis Hotel)/May 2-4/750

Publications:
Home Furnishings Retailer (Magazine). m. adv.
Currents (Newsletter). m.

National Honey Packers and Dealers Association *(1952)*
3301 Route 66
Suite 205, Building C
Neptune, NJ 07753
Tel: (732)922-3008 *Fax:* (732)922-3590
E-Mail: info@nhpda.org
Web Site: www.nhpda.org
Members: 35 companies
Staff: 5
Annual Budget: $50-100,000
Executive Vice President: Bob Bauer
E-Mail: bobbauer@afius.org

Historical Note
NHPDA, a section of the Association of Food Industries (see separate listing), is a trade association for packers and dealers of honey. NHPDA is committed to an industry quality and to the welfare of packers and importers of honey.

Publications:
AFI Newsletter. bi-m.
AFI Annual. a. adv.
NHPDA Bulletins. 2-4/month.

National Horsemen's Benevolent and Protective Association *(1940)*
4063 Iron Works Pkwy., Suite Two
Lexington, KY 40511
Tel: (859)259-0451 *Fax:* (859)259-0452
Toll Free: (866)245 - 1711
E-Mail: racing@hbpa.org
Web Site: www.hbpa.org
Members: 30000 individuals
Staff: 2
Annual Budget: $100-250,000
Chief Executive Officer: Remi Bellocq

Historical Note
Members are owners and trainers of thoroughbred race horses.

Meetings/Conferences:
Semi-annual meetings: *Summer and Winter*

Publications:
Horseman's Journal. q.

National Hospice and Palliative Care Organization *(1978)*
1700 Diagonal Road, Suite 625
Alexandria, VA 22314
Tel: (703)837-1500 *Fax:* (703)837-1233
Toll Free: (800)658 - 8898
Web Site: www.nhpco.org
Members: 4100 individuals
Staff: 30
Annual Budget: $2-5,000,000
President and Chief Executive Officer: J. Donald Schumacher
E-Mail: pbouchard@nhpco.org
Vice President, Administration: Pam Bouchard
Executive Vice President: Galen Miller
Vice President, Communications: Jon Radulovic

Historical Note
Founded as National Hospice Organization. The hospice concept cares for terminally ill people and their families by centering the caring process in the home backed up by in-patient facilities when needed and appropriate.

Meetings/Conferences:
2007 – Washington, DC(Omni Shoreham)/Apr. 19-21

2008 - Washington, DC(Omni Shoreham)/Apr. 10-12

Publications:
NewsLine. m. adv.
Insights. q. adv.
NewsBriefs. w.

National Housing and Rehabilitation Association *(1971)*
1400 16th St. NW
Suite 420
Washington, DC 20036
Tel: (202)939-1750
Web Site: www.housingonline.com
Members: 350 individuals
Staff: 7
Annual Budget: $250-500,000
Executive Director: Peter H. Bell

Historical Note
Formerly (1985) National Housing Rehabilitation Association. NH&RA promoted partnerships among professionals with an interest in affordable multi-family housing. Members include organizations and individuals in construction, finance, property management and real estate development. Membership: $1,500/year (full); $1,000/year (associate); $350/year (public).

Meetings/Conferences:
Annual Meetings: March

Publications:
Multifamily Advisor Newlsetter. 6/year.
First of the Month Bulletin. m.

National Housing Conference *(1931)*
1801 K St. NW
Suite M-100
Washington, DC 20006-1301
Tel: (202)466-2121 *Fax:* (202)466-2122
E-Mail: nhc@nhc.org
Web Site: www.nhc.org
Members: 800individualsandorganizations
Staff: 11
Annual Budget: $2-5,000,000
President and Chief Executive Officer: Conrad E. Egan
Director, Communications: Michele Anapol
Director, Policy: Maria Fiore
Director, Development: Maria J. Sayers
E-Mail: msayers@nhc.org

Historical Note
The mission of the National Housing Conference is to see that every American, regardless of income, has the opportunity to live in decent housing, in a safe and stable neighborhood. Formerly the National Public Housing Conference. Membership: $500-$4,000/year organization).

Meetings/Conferences:
Annual Meetings: Spring

Publications:
NHC At Work. m.
New Century Housing. bien.
Washington Wire. w.

National Human Resources Association *(1950)*
P.O. Box 7326
Nashua, NH 03060-7326
Toll Free: (866)523 - 4417
E-Mail: info@humanresources.org
Web Site: www.humanresources.org
Members: 2000 individuals
Staff: 1
Annual Budget: $100-250,000
Association Manager: Sue Murphy

Historical Note
Formerly (1992) International Association for Personnel Women. Membership: $70/year.

Meetings/Conferences:
Annual Meetings: Spring

Publications:
Annual Roster (online). a.
Human Resources: Journal of IAPW. q. adv.
Connections. q.

National Human Services Assembly *(1923)*
1319 F St. NW
Suite 402
Washington, DC 20004
Tel: (202)347-2080 *Fax:* (202)393-4517
Web Site: www.nassembly.org
Members: 70 organizations
Staff: 10
Annual Budget: $1-2,000,000
President and Chief Executive Officer: Irv Katz
E-Mail: irv@nassembly.org
Web/IT Manager: Todd Christensen
E-Mail: todd@nassembly.org

Historical Note
Established as the National Social Work Council, it became the National Social Welfare Assembly in 1945, the National Assembly for Social Policy and Development in 1967, National Assembly of Health and Human Services Organizations in 1974, and assumed its present name in 2005. Advances the effectiveness of each member and provides collective leadership in the areas of health and human services. As members face organizational challenges, the National Assembly provides a forum for them to focus on both operational and policy issues and work toward mutual goals.

Meetings/Conferences:
Annual Meetings: Fall

Publications:
Newsbytes. m.

National Humanities Alliance *(1981)*
21 Dupont Circle NW
Suite 800
Washington, DC 20036
Tel: (202)296-4994 *Fax:* (202)872-0884
Web Site: www.nhalliance.org
Members: 90 associations
Staff: 2
Annual Budget: $100-250,000
Director: Jessica Jones Irons
E-Mail: jessica@cni.org

Historical Note
NHA, made up of associations, organizations and institutes in the humanities, is a representation of the interests in the humanities - scholarly, higher education, museums, libraries, state and local organizations. NHA also speaks on behalf of the interests of individuals engaged in research, writing, teaching, and public presentations of the humanities. Membership: $1,000-$25,000 (active); $500-$999 (associate).

Meetings/Conferences:
Annual Meetings: April

National Hydrogen Association *(1989)*
1800 M St. NW
Suite 300-North
Washington, DC 20036-5802
Tel: (202)223-5547 *Fax:* (202)223-5537
E-Mail: info@hydrogenassociation.org
Web Site: www.hydrogenassociation.org
Members: 86 companies and universities
Staff: 7
Annual Budget: $250-500,000

Historical Note
NHA members are industrial companies, university and other research organizations with an interest in hydrogen production, storage, transport or utilization. NHA was established to foster the development of hydrogen technologies and their utilization in industrial and commercial applications and promote the transition role of hydrogen in the energy field. $2,000/year (small business); $900/year (univesity/research). Membership: $12,000/year (sustaining); $5,500/year (industry).

Meetings/Conferences:
Annual Meetings: March

Publications:
Hydrogen Safety Report. m.
H2 Digest. bi-m.
Annual U.S. Hydrogen Meeting Proceedings. a.
NHA News. q.
H2 Legislative Update. q.

National Hydropower Association *(1983)*
One Massachusetts Ave., Suite 850
Washington, DC 20001
Tel: (202)682-1700 *Fax:* (202)682-9478
E-Mail: info@hydro.org
Web Site: www.hydro.org
Members: 140 organizations
Staff: 6
Annual Budget: $500-1,000,000
Executive Director: Linda Church Ciocci
E-Mail: linda@hydro.org
Manager, Finance and Administration: Stephanie Knox
E-Mail: stephanie@hydro.org

Historical Note
Provides regulatory and legislative advocacy for hydropower industry. Members include all segments of industry, public and private utilities, developers, equipment manufacturers, engineering and design firms, environmental and hydro licensing consultants, legal and financial firms. Membership: $1,000/year (individual); $3,250-$6,000/year (service/industry) corporate membership fee based on megawatts produced.

Meetings/Conferences:
Annual Meetings: Spring/400

Publications:
NHA Today. bi-m.

National Ice Cream Mix Association *(1945)*
2101 Wilson Blvd., Suite 400
Arlington, VA 22201
Tel: (703)243-5630 *Fax:* (703)841-9328
Members: 115 companies
Staff: 2
Annual Budget: $10-25,000
Executive Director: Thomas M. Balmer

Historical Note
Provides technical and business support to ice cream mix manufacturers. Administrative support provided by the Nat'l Milk Producers Federation.

Publications:
Bulletin. q.
Membership Directory. bien.

National Ice Cream Retailers Association *(1933)*
1028 W. Devon Ave.
Elk Grove Village, IL 60007
Tel: (847)301-7500 *Fax:* (847)301-8402
E-Mail: info@nicra.org
Web Site: www.nicra.org
Members: 400 companies
Staff: 2
Annual Budget: $100-250,000
Executive Director: Lynda Utterback

Historical Note
Established as the National Association of Retail Ice Cream Manufacturers, it became National Ice Cream Retailers Association in the mid-1960s and National Ice Cream and Yogurt Retailers Association in 1989; resumed its present name in 2003. Membership: $200-350/year (company, based on number of retail locations operated).

Meetings/Conferences:
Annual Meetings: Fall/250
2007 - San Antonio, TX(Crowne Plaza)/Nov. 7-10
2008 - St. Petersburg, FL(Hilton)/Nov. 12-15/350

Publications:
Bulletin. m. adv.
NICRA Yearbook. a. adv.

National Independent Automobile Dealers Association *(1946)*
2521 Brown Blvd.
Arlington, TX 76006-5203
Tel: (817)640-3838 *Fax:* (817)649-5866
Toll Free: (800)682 - 3837
E-Mail: gail@niada.com
Web Site: www.niada.com
Members: 19000 companies
Staff: 18
Annual Budget: $2-5,000,000
Executive Vice President and Chief Executive Officer: Michael R. Linn
E-Mail: mike@niada.com

Historical Note
Founded as the National Used Car Dealers Association, it assumed its present name in 1955. Regular membership is open to any organization, company or corporation licensed through the state to buy, sell or auction used motor vehicles, and who are

members of the affiliated state association. Regular membership: through affiliated state association, or $60/year in states without an affiliated state association.

Meetings/Conferences:
Annual Meetings: Summer

Publications:
Used Car Dealer. m. adv.

National Independent Fire Alarm Distributors
1001 Office Park Road, Suite 105
West Des Moines, IA 50265
Tel: (515)440-6057 *Fax:* (515)440-6055
Web Site: www.nifad.org
Staff: 1
Executive Director: Beverly V. Thomas
E-Mail: apmsthomas@aol.com

Historical Note
Provides marketing, safety, promotional and other materials to its members. Membership: $250/year.

National Independent Flag Dealers Association
214 N. Hale St.
Wheaton, IL 60187
Tel: (630)510-4521 *Fax:* (630)510-4501
Toll Free: (877)544 - 3524
E-Mail: info@nifda.org
Web Site: www.nifda.org
Members: 120flagdealersandmanufacturers
Staff: 2
Annual Budget: $100-250,000
Executive Director: Terry Stevenson

Historical Note
Membership: $465/year.

Meetings/Conferences:
Annual Meetings: Semi-Annual Meetings

Publications:
NIFDA News. q. adv.

National Independent Living Association *(1980)*
4203 Southpoint Blvd.
Jacksonville, FL 32216
Tel: (904)296-1038 *Fax:* (904)296-1953
E-Mail: info@nilausa.org
Web Site: www.nilausa.org
Members: 200 individuals
Executive Director: Susan Alevy

Historical Note
Members are individuals and organizations providing services to youth and adolescents in child welfare programs.

Publications:
NILA News. q.
Newsletter (online). bi-w.

National Independent Nursery Furniture Retailers Association *(1973)*
12302 Hart Ranch
San Antonio, TX 78249
Tel: (210)699-1133 *Fax:* (210)699-3232
E-Mail: info@ninfra.com
Web Site: www.ninfra.com
Members: 90 individuals
Staff: 2
Annual Budget: under $10,000
Executive Director: Larry Schur

Historical Note
NINFRA members are independent retailers of juvenile products. NINFRA participates in buying programs and trade shows, publishes a catalog, maintains a presence on the Internet, and provides networking opportunities for its members.

Meetings/Conferences:
Semi-annual Meetings: Annual meetings held in conjuction with ABC Kids Expo in November, at Convention Center in Las Vegas, NV. Informal meetings may also be held in conjunction with Juvenile Products Manufacturers Ass'n.

Publications:
Newsletters. m.
Catalog. a. adv.

National Indian Education Association *(1970)*
110 Maryland Ave. NE
Suite 104
Washington, DC 20002-5626
Tel: (202)544-7290 *Fax:* (202)544-7293
E-Mail: niea@niea.org
Web Site: www.niea.org
Members: 3000 individuals
Staff: 4
Annual Budget: $500-1,000,000
Executive Director: Lillian Sparks
NIEA Fellow: Brandon Ashely
Events Planner and Office Manager: D. Wanda Johnson

Historical Note
Members are American Indian teachers and school administrators. Membership: $75/year (professional); $20/year (student).

Meetings/Conferences:
Annual Meetings: Fall

Publications:
NIEA Newsletter. 4/year. adv.

National Indian Gaming Association *(1985)*
224 Second St. SE
Washington, DC 20003-1943
Tel: (202)546-7711 *Fax:* (202)546-1755
Toll Free: (800)286 - 6442
E-Mail: info@indiangaming.org
Web Site: www.indiangaming.org
Members: 170Tribes; 75AssociateMembers
Staff: 14
Annual Budget: $1-2,000,000
Executive Director: Mark Van Norman
E-Mail: MVanNorman@indiangaming.org
Public Relations: Victoria Wright
Director, Casino and Industry Relations: Dianne Wyss
E-Mail: dwyss@indiangaming.org

Historical Note
NIGA is an organization representing Indian Nations, with other non-voting associate members representing organizations, tribes and businesses engaged in tribal gaming enterprises from around the country. NIGA operates as a clearinghouse and educational, legislative and public policy resource for tribes, policymakers and the public on Indian gaming issues and tribal community development.

Meetings/Conferences:
Annual Meetings: Spring

Publications:
Indian Gaming Studies. a.
Directory. a. adv.
Seminar Manuals. a. adv.

National Industrial Belting Association

Historical Note
Became NIBA - The Belting Association in 2001.

National Industrial Council - Employer Association Group *(1907)*
1331 Pennsylvania Ave. NW
Sixth Floor
Washington, DC 20004-1703
Tel: (202)637-3052 *Fax:* (202)637-3182
Members: 75 organizations
Staff: 3
Annual Budget: $100-250,000
Executive Director: Mark Stuart

Historical Note
A federation of state and local manufacturers' associations. Affiliated with National Association of Manufacturers. Founded as the Nat' Council for Industrial Defense by the National Association of Manufacturers in 1907; became the National Industrial Council in 1918. Known as the National Industrial Council - Industrial Relations Group until 1990. Composed of two groups of employer associations, each with its own executive director: the Employer Association Group and the State Associations Group (see separate entry). Primarily interested in labor relations and employment law issues. Membership: $300-1,500/year. (association).

Meetings/Conferences:
Semi-annual Meetings: Spring and Fall

Publications:
EAG Network Notes. bi-m.
Annual Executive Compensation Survey. a.
Annual Succesful Programs/Services Survey. a.

National Industrial Council - State Associations Group *(1907)*
1331 Pennsylvania Ave. NW
Sixth Floor
Washington, DC 20004-1703
Tel: (202)637-3054 *Fax:* (202)637-3182
Members: 49 state associations
Staff: 3
Annual Budget: $100-250,000
Executive Director: Barry Buzby

Historical Note
The NIC is composed of two groups of industrial employer associations: NIC State Associations Group and NIC Employer Association Group (see listing). Forty-eight states plus the Commonwealth of Puerto Rico are represented in the SAG. While associations vary in size, structure and primary activities, their goals are to maintain and strengthen the private enterprise system in the U.S., to encourage individual initiative, progress and freedom. SAG represents a business constituency interested in federal and state legislation. Membership: $400-$2,000/year (organization).

Meetings/Conferences:
Annual Meetings: May

Publications:
Nat'l Industrial Council Member Directory. a.

National Industrial Glove Distributors Association *(1959)*

Historical Note
Merged with Internat'l Hand Protection Ass'n in 2003 to form Internat'l Glove Ass'n.

National Industrial Sand Association *(1936)*
2011 Pennsylvania Ave.
Suite 301
Washington, DC 20006
Tel: (202)457-0200 *Fax:* (202)457-0287
E-Mail: info@sand.org
Web Site: www.sand.org
Members: 22 businesses
Staff: 3
Annual Budget: $500-1,000,000
Vice President: Gerald C. Hurley

Historical Note
NISA provides member companies with programs including silicosis prevention and other safety and health initiatives, government relations, and technical support. Membership fee varies, based on sales.

Meetings/Conferences:
Annual Meetings: Spring/80

National Industrial Transportation League *(1907)*
1700 N. Moore St., Suite 1900
Arlington, VA 22209-1904
Tel: (703)524-5011 *Fax:* (703)524-5017
Web Site: www.nitl.org
Members: 1500 individuals
Staff: 4
Annual Budget: $2-5,000,000
President: John B. Ficker
Vice President, Finance, Administration and Membership: Ellie Gilanshah
E-Mail: gilanshah@nitt.org

Historical Note
Founded as National Industrial Traffic League; assumed its current name in 1982. Represents industrial and commercial shippers, boards of trade, chambers of commerce, and similar groups. Its members use all modes of transportation, and directly or indirectly represent an estimated eighty percent of the nation's commercial freight. Membership: $400-3,500/year (regular); $350-2,000/year (associate).

Meetings/Conferences:
Annual Meetings: November/3,000

Publications:
Notice. w. adv.

National Industries for the Blind *(1938)*
1310 Braddock Place
Alexandria, VA 22314-1691
Tel: (703)310-0500
Web Site: www.nib.org
Members: 118 agencies
Staff: 100
Annual Budget: $5-10,000,000
President and Chief Executive Officer: James Gibbons
Director, Finance and Administration: Steve Brice

Vice President, Communications and Public Affairs: Angela Hartley
Vice President, Marketing and Operations: Kevin Lynch
Senior Vice President, New Business Development: J.A. "Yogi" Mangual
Director, Human Resoures: Lynn Millar
Vice President, Strategic Business Issues: Arun Shimpi

Historical Note
Congress passed the Wagner-O'Day Act in 1938 directing the Federal Government to purchase, under certain conditions, products from agencies employing people who are blind. To carry the provisions of the Act, the Committee for Purchase from the Blind (now known as the Committee for Purchase From People who are Blind or Severly Disabled) was established; it designated National Industries for the Blind as a central non-profit agency to facilitate equitable distribution of Federal Government contracts to its associated agencies throughout the country. In 1971, the Act was amended to include the purchase of services as well as products from industries employing people who are blind. It also provided that agencies employing people who are severely disabled participate in the Act, which became known as the Javits-Wagner-O'Day Act. Has an annual budget of $9 million.

Meetings/Conferences:
Semi-annual Meetings: Spring and Fall

Publications:
NIB Now. m.
Annual Report. a.

National Information Standards Organization *(1939)*

4733 Bethesda Ave., Suite 300
Bethesda, MD 20814
Tel: (301)654-2512 *Fax:* (301)654-1721
E-Mail: nisohq@niso.org
Web Site: www.niso.org
Members: 70 organizations
Staff: 2
Annual Budget: $500-1,000,000
Interim Executive Director: Patricia Stevens

Historical Note
NISO, a non-profit association accredited by the American National Standards Institute (ANSI), identifies, develops, maintains, and publishes technical standards to manage information. NISO standards apply both traditional and new technologies to the full range of imformation-related needs, including retrieval, re-purposing, storage, megadata, and preservation. Founded in 1939, incorporated asa not-for-profit education association in 1983, and assuming its current name the following year, NISO draws its support from the communities and as officers of the association. NISO is designated by ANSU to represent U.S. interests to the International Organization for Standardization's (ISO) Technical Committee 46 on Information and Documentation.

Publications:
Information Standards Quarterly. q.

National Institute for Animal Agriculture *(1916)*

1910 Lyda Ave.
Bowling Green, KY 42104-5809
Tel: (270)782-9798 *Fax:* (270)782-0188
E-Mail: niaa@animalagriculture.org
Web Site: www.animalagriculture.org
Members: 200 organizations
Staff: 4
Annual Budget: $250-500,000
President and Chief Executive Officer: Glenn N. Slack
E-Mail: gslack@animalagriculture.org
Director, Communications: Benjamin Richey
Director, Member Relations: Michele Vise-Brown

Historical Note
Formed by a merger of the National Livestock Sanitary Committee and the National Livestock Loss Prevention Board (founded in 1916). Formerly (1976) Livestock Conservation Inc. and (2000) Livestock Conservation Institute. NIAA provides a forum for diverse segments of the livestock industry to discuss common issues, build consensus, and offer solutions to the challenges facing meat animal production in North America. Membership includes producers, industry professionals, state and federal regulators and the research community. The organization specializes in producing educational materials and enhancing the industry's communications efforts. Issues addressed by NIAAI include animal health, livestock care and handling, food safety, and uniform livestock identification.Membership: dues based on type of organization or corporation.

Meetings/Conferences:
Annual Meetings: Spring

Publications:
Equine Health Report. q.
Poultry Health Report. q.
Animal Agriculture Quarterly. q.
Sheep Health Report. q.
Swine Health Report. q.
Food Safety Digest. q.
Cattle Health Report. q.

National Institute for Electromedical Information *(1984)*

P.O. Box 4633
Bay Terrace, NY 11360
Tel: (212)410-8498 *Fax:* (718)225-1041
E-Mail: sniei@aol.com
Web Site: www.niei.org
Members: 1356 individuals
Staff: 5
Annual Budget: $100-250,000
President: Dr. Stanley H. Kornhauser, Ph.D.
E-Mail: sniei@aol.com

Meetings/Conferences:
Annual Meetings: January

Publications:
American Journal of Electromedicine in Medical Electronics. 6/year.
NIEI Newsletter. m.

National Institute for Farm Safety *(1962)*

895 Smith Road
Charles Town, WV 25414
Tel: (304)728-0011
E-Mail: ghetzel@citilink.net
Web Site: www.ag.ohio-state.edu/~agsafety/NIFS/nifs.htm
Members: 200 individuals
Staff: 1
Annual Budget: $10-25,000
Interim Treasurer: Glen Hetzel

Historical Note
Members professionals concerned with agricultural safety. Membership: $75-100/year (individual), $100+/year (organization /company).

Meetings/Conferences:
Annual Meetings: Summer
2007 – Penticton, BC, Canada/June 24-26

Publications:
Newsletter. q.

National Institute of American Doll Artists *(1963)*

3592 Cherokee Road
Atlanta, GA 30340-2749
Tel: (770)936-9851
E-Mail: nonicely@gmail.com
Web Site: www.niada.org
Members: 200 individuals
Staff: 1
Annual Budget: $25-50,000
President: Antonette Cely

Historical Note
Professional doll artists creating original dolls. Has no paid officers or full-time staff. Membership is by election. Membership: $100/year. Patron membership is open to anyone at $50/yr.

Meetings/Conferences:
Annual Meetings: Summer

Publications:
Newsletter. q.
Directory.
Yearbook. a. adv.

National Institute of Building Sciences *(1976)*

1090 Vermont Ave. NW, Suite 700
Washington, DC 20005-4905
Tel: (202)289-7800 *Fax:* (202)289-1092
E-Mail: nibs@nibs.org
Web Site: www.nibs.org
Members: 800individualsandorganizations
Staff: 30
Annual Budget: $5-10,000,000
President: David A. Harris, FAIA
Vice President, Development and NCEF: William Brenner, AIA
Vice President, BSSC and MMC: Claret M. Heider
Vice President, Technical Programs/CCB: Earle Kennett
Vice President, Financea nd Administration: John Lloyd
Editor and Director, Communications: Robert L. Miller, FAIA

Historical Note
A public-private partnership created by Congress to improve regulation of the building process, facilitate the introduction of new and innovative building technology, and disseminate technical and regulatory information. Major NIBS activities include: Building Enclosure Technology and Environment Council (BETEC), Multihazard Mitigation Council (MMC), the Facility Maintenance and Operations Committee (FMOC), the National Clearinghouse for Educational Facilities (NCEF), Building Seismic Safety Council (BSSC), and CADD Council. Membership includes individuals, companies, associations, government bodies and unions. Membership: $75-150/year. (individual); $1,000-$25,000/year (company).

Meetings/Conferences:
Annual: June and October

Publications:
Annual Report to the President of the U.S. a.
Building Sciences Newsletter. bi-m.
CCB Bulletin Newsletter. q.
Membership Directory. a.
Construction Criteria Base on CD-ROM. q.

National Institute of Business and Industrial Chaplaincy

1770 St. James Place, Suite 550
Houston, TX 77056
Tel: (713)266-2456 *Fax:* (713)266-0845
E-Mail: info@nibic.com
Web Site: www.nibic.com

Historical Note
NIBIC members are ministers, priests, rabbis, and other religious professionals employed in the private sector. Membership: $85/year (certified chaplain/clinician); other memberships available.

Publications:
Newsletter.

National Institute of Ceramic Engineers *(1938)*

c/o Virginia Tech, Dept. of Materials Science & Engrg
213 Holden Hall
Blacksburg, VA 24061
Tel: (540)231-3897 *Fax:* (540)231-8919
Web Site: www.ceramics.org
Members: 1291 individuals
Annual Budget: $50-100,000
Executive Director: Diane Folz
E-Mail: dfolz@vt.edu

Historical Note
Professional society of ceramic engineers, dedicated to the development, promotion and advancement of ceramic engineering interests. Founded by the American Ceramic Society, of which it remains a class. Also affiliated with the American Association of Engineering Socs., the Accreditation Board for Engineering and Technology, the National Society of Professional Engineers and the National Council of Engineering Examiners. Membership: $20/year. (Applicants must be members of the ACerS and approved for admission.) ACerS provides administrative support.

Meetings/Conferences:
Annual Meetings: Spring, with MS&T Materials Science and Technology Conference and Exhibition (ACerS, TMS, ASM, AIST); January, Cocoa Beach, FL

National Institute of Governmental Purchasing *(1944)*

151 Spring St.
Herndon, VA 20170-5223
Tel: (703)736-8900 *Fax:* (703)736-9644
Toll Free: (800)367 - 6447
E-Mail: chodes@nigp.org
Web Site: www.nigp.org
Members: 2200 agencies

Staff: 24
Annual Budget: $2-5,000,000
Chief Executive Officer: Rick Grimm
E-Mail: rgrimm@nigp.org
Director, Education and Professional Development: Carol Hodes

Historical Note
Members are government purchasing agencies at local, state and federal levels in the U.S. and Canada. Promotes professional development, uniform purchasing laws and procedures. Affiliated with the United States Conference of Mayors, the Chartered Institute of Purchasing & Supply of Great Britain and the International Federation of Purchasing and Supply Management. Conducts a two-tier certification program awarding CPPO (Certified Public Purchasing Officer) and CPPB (Certified Professional Public Buyer) designations. Sponsors seminars and distance learning opportunities in public purchasing. Membership leves: $315 + year (based on number of agency participants).

Meetings/Conferences:
Annual Meetings: Summer
2007 - Hartford, CT/Aug. 4-8

Publications:
NIGP BuyWeekly online. bi-w.
The NIGP Source e-zine. q. adv.

National Institute of Management Counsellors *(1954)*
P.O. Box 193
Great Neck, NY 11022-0193
Tel: (516)482-5683
Members: 250 individuals
Staff: 2
Executive Director: Willard Warren

National Institute of Oilseed Products *(1934)*
1156 15th St. NW
Suite 900
Washington, DC 20005
Tel: (202)785-8450 *Fax:* (202)223-9741
E-Mail: niop@kellencompany.com
Web Site: www.oilseeds.com
Members: 155 companies
Staff: 4
Annual Budget: $100-250,000
Executive Director: Richard E. Cristol
Executive Secretary: Carol Freysinger

Historical Note
Members are importers, exporters, storage tank operators, and brokers in copra, palm, coconut, soybean and other edible oils and related raw material.

Meetings/Conferences:
Annual Meetings: March
2007 - Palm Springs, CA(Marriott Rancho Las Palmas Resort & Spa)/March 21-25

Publications:
Washington Correspondence. irreg.
Trading Rules. a.

National Institute of Packaging, Handling and Logistics Engineers *(1956)*
177 Fairson Court
Lewisburg, PA 17837-6844
Tel: (570)528-6475
E-Mail: niphle@dejazzd.com
Web Site: www.niphle.com
Members: 660 individuals
Staff: 1
Annual Budget: $10-25,000
Executive Director: Richard D. Owen

Historical Note
Originally the DC chapter of the Society of Packaging and Handling Engineers, the Institute became independent in an effort to give more emphasis to the government liaison responsibilities of its members. Membership: $80/year (individual); $225 or $600/year (company).

Meetings/Conferences:
Semi-annual meetings: Spring and Fall

Publications:
PHL Bulletin. m. adv.
Membership Directory. a. adv.

National Institute of Pension Administrators *(1983)*
401 N. Michigan Ave., Suite 2200
Chicago, IL 60611-4267
Toll Free: (800)999 - 6472
E-Mail: nipa@nipa.org
Web Site: www.nipa.org
Members: 1000 individuals
Staff: 8
Annual Budget: $1-2,000,000
Executive Director: Laura J. Rudzinski

Historical Note
The Institute is responsible for the formation of professional standards, an ongoing education program consisting of workshops and home study courses, and awards the APA (Accredited Pension Adminstrator) and the APR (Accredited Pension Representative) designations by examination and experience. Membership: $295/year (individual); $750-1,500/year (firm).

Meetings/Conferences:
Semi-annual: Winter/Spring

Publications:
Plan Horizons. q. adv.

National Institute of Senior Centers *(1970)*

Historical Note
An affiliate of National Council on the Aging, which provides administrative support.

National Institute of Senior Housing *(1979)*

Historical Note
A special interest group of the National Council on the Aging.

National Institute of Steel Detailing *(1969)*
7700 Edgewater Dr., Suite 670
Oakland, CA 94621-3022
Tel: (510)568-3741 *Fax:* (510)568-3781
E-Mail: nisd@sbcglobal.net
Web Site: www.nisd.org
Members: 400 firms and individuals
Staff: 1
Annual Budget: $100-250,000
Administrator: Stephanie Andrew
E-Mail: nisd@sbcglobal.net

Historical Note
Steel detailing is the production, from architectural and engineering drawings, of fabrication drawings that can be read by workers in a fabrication shop, where designs for steel skeletons of buildings are created. NISD was founded May 10, 1969 in Houston by thirty-eight detailing firms. Membership: $65-450/year (individual/company).

Meetings/Conferences:
2007 - Myrtle Beach, SC(Hilton)/March 15-17/100

Publications:
The Connection. q. adv.
Membership Directory. a.

National Institute on Adult Daycare *(1979)*

Historical Note
A special interest group of the National Council on the Aging concerned with meeting the needs of day care practitioners.

National Institute on Community-based Long-term Care *(1983)*

Historical Note
A special interest group of the Nat'l Council on the Aging, which provides administrative support.

National Institute on Park and Grounds Management *(1975)*
P.O. Box 5162
De Pere, WI 54115-5162
Tel: (920)339-9057 *Fax:* (920)339-9057
E-Mail: nipgm@nipgm.org
Web Site: www.nipgm.org
Members: 350 individuals
Staff: 2
Annual Budget: $50-100,000
Co-Executive Director: Laura Sinclair
Co-Executive Director: Steve Sinclair

Historical Note
Seeks to improve grounds management through education and exchange of information within its membership. Members include managers of parks, campuses and other large outdoor areas. Membership: $145/year (individual); $190/year (company).

Meetings/Conferences:
Annual Meetings: Fall/Late Winter

Publications:
Roster. a. adv.
Park and Grounds Messenger. 10/yr. adv.

National Institutes for Water Resources *(1974)*
47 Harkness Road
Pelham, MA 10002
Tel: (413)253-5686 *Fax:* (413)253-1309
Members: 54 individuals
Staff: 2
Annual Budget: $100-250,000
Executive Director: Paul Joseph Godfrey, Ph.D.
E-Mail: godfrey@tei.umass.edu

Historical Note
Formed in 1974 to coordinate the institute program both internally and externally. Membership consists of the directors of 54 institutes. Has no paid staff. Formerly (1992) the National Association of Water Institute Directors. Membership: $2,700/year.

Meetings/Conferences:
Annual Meetings: Spring in Washington, DC/50

Publications:
NIWR Publications: An Electronic Database. bi-a.
Directory of Institute Programs. bi-a.
Annual Research Program Report. a.

National Insulation Association *(1954)*
99 Canal Center Plaza, Suite 222
Alexandria, VA 22314-1538
Tel: (703)683-6422 *Fax:* (703)549-4838
E-Mail: niainfo@insulation.org
Web Site: www.insulation.org
Members: 450 headquarter company members
Staff: 10
Annual Budget: $1-2,000,000
Executive Vice President: Michele M. Jones, CMP
E-Mail: mjones@insulation.org
Director, Publications: Julie McLaughlin
Director, Programs and Marketing: Wendy Santantonio

Historical Note
Formerly (1970) Insulation Distributor-Contractors National Association, (1989) National Insulation Contractors Association and (1995) National Insulation and Abatement Contractors Association. Members are industrial and commercial insulation contractors, manufacturers and distributors. Membership fee based on volume of business.

Meetings/Conferences:
Annual Meetings: Spring

Publications:
Insulation Outlook Magazine. m. adv.
Manufacturers Technical Literature. a. adv.
Industry Directory and Buyers Guide. a. adv.

National Insurance Association *(1921)*
411 W. Chapel Hill Dr., Suite 633
Durham, NC 27701
Tel: (919)683-5328
Web Site: www.national-ins-assoc.org/
Members: 13 companies
Staff: 2
Annual Budget: $50-100,000
Secretary: Glenda Small

Historical Note
Formerly (1954) National Negro Insurance Association. NIA is an organization of black-owned and operated life insurance companies cooperating to raise standards and promote efficiency in practices among participating members, to contribute to the total health and insurance education of the nation, and to build confidence in insurance companies owned and controlled by its members. Membership: $700/year, minimum (company).

Meetings/Conferences:
Annual Meetings: June

Publications:
Membership Roster. a.

National Insurance Crime Bureau *(1992)*
1111 E. Touhy Ave.
Suite 400
Des Plaines, IL 60018
Tel: (847)544-7000 *Fax:* (847)544-7100
Toll Free: (800)447 - 6282
Web Site: www.nicb.org
Members: 1000 insurance companies
Staff: 320
Annual Budget: $25-50,000,000
Chief Executive Officer: Robert M. Bryant
Senior Vice President, Government Relations: Judy Fitzgerald
Vice President and Chief Financial Officer: Robert J. Jachnicki
Vice President, General Counsel: Robert Mason
Director, Public Affairs: Frank G. Scafidi
Vice President, Training: Thomas F. Welch
Historical Note
Formed in 1992 by the merger of Insurance Crime Prevention Institute (founded 1970) and National Automobile Theft Bureau (founded 1912). Members are insurance companies interested in the detection, prevention and prosecution of fraud.
Publications:
Spotlight on Insurance Crime. q.

National Intercollegiate Soccer Officials Association *(1964)*
541 Woodview Dr.
Longwood, FL 32779-2614
Tel: (407)862-3305 *Fax:* (407)862-8545
Members: 5000 individuals
Annual Budget: $100-250,000
Executive Director: Raymond Bernabei
Historical Note
Their mission is to provide qualified and certified soccer officials for colleges and high schools. NISOA has a nationwide volunteer staff of approximately 225 individuals. Membership: $75/year.
Meetings/Conferences:
Annual Meetings: Summer
2007 – Oneonta, NY/July 13-16
Publications:
Newsletter. 3/year. adv.
Pre-Season Guide. a.

National Interfaith Coalition on Aging *(1972)*
Historical Note
A special interest group of the National Council on the Aging.

National Interscholastic Athletic Administrators Association *(1977)*
P.O. Box 690
Indianapolis, IN 46206
Tel: (317)822-5715 *Fax:* (317)822-5700
E-Mail: bwhitehead@niaaa.org
Web Site: www.niaaa.org
Members: 51 state associations
Staff: 4
Annual Budget: $1-2,000,000
President: Larry Munksgaard
Executive Director: Bruce Whitehead
E-Mail: bwhitehead@niaaa.org
Historical Note
Members are high school and middle school athletic administrators. Membership: $60/year (individual); $50-250/year (organization).
Meetings/Conferences:
2007 – Nashville, TN(Opryland)/Dec. 14-18/2500
Publications:
Conference Proceedings.
Interscholastic Athletic Administration. q. adv.
State Athletic Director Ass'n Directory. a.
Nat'l Conference Proceedings. a.

National Interscholastic Swimming Coaches Association *(1934)*
c/o Arvel McElory, Olathe South High School
1640 E. 151st St.
Olathe, KS 66062
Tel: (913)780-7160 *Fax:* (913)780-7170
Web Site: www.nisca.net
Members: 1800 individuals
President: Mark P. Onstott
Secretary: Arvel McElroy
Historical Note
NISCA represents interscholastic swimming, diving and water polo coaches.
Publications:
NISCA Journal. bi-m. adv.
NISCA Newsletter (on-line). adv.
High School Academic All-America. a.
High School Diving All-America. a.
High School Swimming All-America. a.
High School Water Polo All-America. a.

National Interstate Council of State Boards of Cosmetology *(1936)*
7622 Briarwood Circle
Little Rock, AR 72205
Tel: (501)227-8262 *Fax:* (501)227-8212
E-Mail: dnorton@nictesting.org
Web Site: www.nictesting.org
Members: 250 individuals
Staff: 2
Annual Budget: $500-1,000,000
Executive Director: Debra Norton
E-Mail: dnorton@nictesting.org
Historical Note
Merger (1956) of National Council of State Boards of Cosmetology and Interstate Council of State Boards of Cosmetology. Persons commissioned by state governments to administer cosmetology laws and examine applicants for cosmetology licenses.
Publications:
NIC Bulletin. bi-m.
NIC Directory. a.

National Intramural-Recreational Sports Association *(1950)*
4185 S.W. Research Way
Corvallis, OR 97333-1067
Tel: (541)766-8211 *Fax:* (541)766-8284
E-Mail: nirsa@nirsa.org
Web Site: http://nirsa.org
Members: 2500 individuals
Staff: 23
Annual Budget: $2-5,000,000
Executive Director: Kent J. Blumenthal
Chief Operating Officer: Karen Bach
Director, Publications and Educational Resources: Mary Callender
E-Mail: mary@nirsa.org
Education Director: Carole Hobrock
Chief Financial Officer: Mark Jacobson
Membership Operations Coordinator: Mary Martin
Director, National Sport Programs: Valerie McCutchan
E-Mail: Valerie@nirsa.org
Historical Note
Formerly (1973) National Intramural Association. NIRSA members include recreational sports professionals, institutions, and students. Promotes the advancement of recreational sports programs and the professional growth of individuals. Membership: $104-129/year (individual).
Meetings/Conferences:
Annual Meetings: April
2007 – Minneapolis, MN(Conventin Center)/Apr. 18-21/2000
2008 – Austin, TX(Convention Center)/Apr. 2-5/3000
Publications:
Recreational Sports Journal. 2/year. adv.
NIRSA Proceedings. a.
Recreational Sports Directory. a. adv.
NIRSA Newletter. 10/year.
Flag & Touch Football Rules & Official's Manual. bien. adv.

National Investment Banking Association *(1994)*
P.O. Box 6625
Athens, GA 30604
Tel: (706)208-9620 *Fax:* (706)208-1033
E-Mail: admin@nibanet.org
Web Site: www.nibanet.org
Members: 250 companies
Staff: 2
Managing Director: Emily Foshee
Historical Note
NIBA members are regional and independent broker-dealer and investment banking firms, and related capital market service providers.

National Investment Company Service Association *(1962)*
2 Mount Royal Ave., Suite 320
Marlborough, MA 01752
Tel: (508)485-1500 *Fax:* (508)485-1560
E-Mail: info@nicsa.org
Web Site: www.nicsa.org
Members: 10000 individuals
Staff: 7
Annual Budget: $1-2,000,000
President: Barbara V. Weidlich
Vice President: Keith Dropkin
Registrar: Doris Jaimes
Events Manager: Sheila Kobaly
Information Technology Manager: Chris Ludena
Director, Education: Kathleen O'Halloran
Director, Marketing: Ellen Weinraub
Historical Note
NICSA works to facilitate and promote leadership and innovation within the operations sector of the mutual fund industry. Membership: $3,000/year.
Publications:
TA Guide & Checklist. a.
NICSA News. q.
Membership Directory (online). a.
Shareholder Satisfaction Survey. a.

National Investor Relations Institute *(1969)*
8020 Towers Crescent Dr., Suite 250
Vienna, VA 22182
Tel: (703)506-3570 *Fax:* (703)506-3571
E-Mail: info@niri.org
Web Site: www.niri.org
Members: 3000 individuals
Staff: 10
Annual Budget: $1-2,000,000
President and Chief Executive Officer: Louis M. Thompson, Jr.
E-Mail: lthompson@niri.org
Vice President, Professional Development: Linda Kelleher
Vice President, Member Development: Michael McGough
Vice President, Communications: Heather Sieber
Historical Note
A professional association of corporate officers and investor relations consultants. Membership: $375/year.
Meetings/Conferences:
Annual Meetings: Spring
Publications:
Director of Meeting Information. a.
Who's Who in Investor Relations. a.
Legislative Bulletin. irreg.
Investor Relations Resource Guide. a.
Investor Relations Update. m.
Emerging Trends in Investor Relations. trien.
Investor Relations Job Descriptions. a.
Practice Guides. irreg.
IR Bibliography. irreg.

National Judges Association *(1979)*
P.O. Box 160
Maud, OK 74854-0160
Tel: (405)374-1213 *Fax:* (405)374-2316
Toll Free: (888)366 - 3652
E-Mail: rjzjd@sbcglobal.net
Web Site: www.nationaljudgesassociation.org
Members: 400 individuals
Staff: 1
Annual Budget: $10-25,000
Executive Director: Ralph J. Zeller
E-Mail: rjzjd@sbcglobal.net
Historical Note
Incorporated in Nevada, NJA members are non-lawyer judges and judicial officers. Works to publicize the contributions of non-lawyer judges to the court system, fosters the exchange of information among members, and encourages further education to enhance members' judicial performance. Conducts a judicial training program. Membership: $35-50/year, based on salary.

Meetings/Conferences:
Annual Meetings: Spring/200

Publications:
The Gavel. q. adv.

National Juice Products Association

Historical Note
Became Juice Products Association in 2003.

National Junior College Athletic Association *(1938)*

1755 Telstar Dr., Suite 103
Colorado Springs, CO 80920
Tel: (719)590-9788 *Fax:* (719)590-7324
Web Site: www.njcaa.org
Members: 520 junior colleges
Staff: 8
Annual Budget: $1-2,000,000
Executive Director: Wayne Baker
E-Mail: wbaker@njcaa.org

Historical Note
NJCAA members are two year institutions recognized by the American Association of Community and Junior Colleges.

Meetings/Conferences:
Annual Meetings: March-April

Publications:
Juco Review Magazine. 9/year. adv.
NJCAA Handbook & Casebook. a. adv.
Eligibility Rules of NJCAA. a.

National Juvenile Court Services Association *(1970)*

University of Nevada
P.O. Box 9870
Reno, NV 89507
Tel: (775)784-6895
E-Mail: icurley@ncjfcj.org
Web Site: www.njcsa.org/
Members: 678 individuals
Staff: 2
Annual Budget: $10-25,000
Executive Director: Ian Curley

Historical Note
Formed in 1970 and chartered in 1972, NJCSA members are individuals operating in the juvenile justice systems of the United States and Canada. In 1992 NJCSA absorbed the membership from the International Conference of Administrators of Residential Agencies. Administrative support provided by National Council of Juvenile and Family Court Judges (same address). Membership: $30-92/year (individual); $138-200/year (organization).

Meetings/Conferences:
Semi-annual Meetings: Spring and Summer

Publications:
eRapport Newsletter (online). m. adv.

National Juvenile Detention Association *(1968)*

Eastern Kentucky Univ., 1301 Perkins Blvd.
521 Lancaster Ave.
Richmond, KY 40475-3102
Tel: (859)622-6259
E-Mail: njdaeku@aol.com
Web Site: www.njda.com
Members: 900 individuals
Staff: 6
Annual Budget: $100-250,000
Executive Director: Earl Dunlap
Manager, Finance: Kristin Bratcher
Assistant Executive Director: Michael A. Jones
Director, Conferences and Communications: Sherry L. Scott

Historical Note
An affiliate of the American Correctional Association, NJDA was incorporated in Illinois in 1971. Members include professionals from detention facilities, the justice system, detention education, and other programs and services related to promoting adequate detention services for juveniles. NJDA reviews standards and practices, encourages training programs for detention staffs, conducts research, and provides a forum for the exchange of ideas between members as well as with other organizations interested in the field of juvenile detention. Membership: $25-$395/year.

Meetings/Conferences:
Semi-Annual Meetings: June and October/300-500

Publications:
Directory. a.
Journal for Juvenile Justice and Detention Services. semi-a.
NJDA News. q. adv.

National Kerosene Heater Association *(1981)*

1816 Old Natchez Trace
Franklin, TN 37069-4785
Tel: (615)790-0770
Members: 6 companies
Annual Budget: $250-500,000
Contact: J. Thomas Smith

Historical Note
Members are individuals, partnerships and corporations involved in the manufacturing and marketing of kerosene heaters.

Publications:
Bulletins. irreg.

National Kidney Foundation *(1950)*

30 E. 33rd St.
New York, NY 10016
Tel: (212)889-2210 *Fax:* (212)779-0068
Toll Free: (800)622 - 9010
Web Site: www.kidney.org
Members: 45 affiliates, 200 chapters
Staff: 125
Annual Budget: $25-50,000,000
Chief Executive Officer: John Davis
Vice President, Health Policy and Research: Dolph Chianchiano
Director, Government Relations: Troy Zimmerman

Historical Note
A major voluntary health organization, the NKF works to prevent kidney and urinary tract diseases, improve the health and well-being of individuals and families affected by these disases, and increase the availability of all organs for transplantation. Through its nationwide affiliates, NKF conducts programs in research, professional education, patient and community services, public education and organ donation. Professional NKF members can join one of three Professional Councils: Nephrology Nurses and Technicans, Nephrology Social Workers, or Renal Nutrition. NKF's work is funded by public donations.

Meetings/Conferences:
Annual Meetings: Spring
2007 – Orlando, FL(Dolphin Resort)/Apr. 10-14/2000

Publications:
Journal of Nephrology Social Work. q.
Advances in Chronic Kidney Disease Journal. q. adv.
Best Practice newsletter. bi-m.
Capital Kidney Connection. q.
Renalink.
Kidney Care. q. adv.
American Journal of Kidney Diseases. q. adv.
Journal of Nephrology Social Work. a.
NKF Family Focus newspaper. q.
Journal of Renal Nutrition. q. adv.
For Those Who Give - Grieve (newsletter). q.
Transplant Chronicles. q.

National Kitchen and Bath Association *(1963)*

687 Willow Grove St.
Hackettstown, NJ 07840
Tel: (877)652-2776 *Fax:* (908)852-1695
Toll Free: (800)843 - 6522
Web Site: www.nkba.org
Members: 7000 companies
Staff: 40
Annual Budget: $5-10,000,000
Chief Executive Officer: Michael Kelly
General Counsel and Director, Legislative Affairs: Edward Nagorsky
Media Contact: Sean Ruck

Historical Note
Kitchen equipment manufacturers, suppliers, wholesalers, retail dealers, distributors and designers. Awards the designations Certified Kitchen Designer (CKD), Certified Bath Designer (CBD), and Certified Kitchen and Bath Installer. Formerly (1982) the American Institute of Kitchen Dealers. Membership: $300/year.

Publications:
NKBA Today. bi-m.
Profiles. q.
Directory. a.

National Labor Relations Board Professional Association *(1962)*

1099 14th St. NW
Suite 8824
Washington, DC 20570-0001
Tel: (202)273-1749 *Fax:* (202)273-4283
Members: 160 individuals
Annual Budget: $10-25,000
President: Leslie E. Rossen
Vice President: Eric C. Marx

Historical Note
Independent union of lawyers working for the N.L.R.B. in Washington. In additon to representing attorneys, the association also represents law clerks and law students employed by the Board's Division of Administrative Law Judges. Has no headquarters or paid staff. Officers are elected annually. Membership: $78/year.

National Lamb Feeders Association *(1950)*

1270 Chemeketa St. NE
Salem, OR 97301
Tel: (503)370-7024 *Fax:* (503)585-1921
E-Mail: info@nlfa-sheep.org
Web Site: www.nlfa-sheep.org
Members: 300 individuals
Staff: 1
Annual Budget: $50-100,000
Administrator: Richard Kosesan

Meetings/Conferences:
Semi-annual meetings: February and July

Publications:
Feeder News Newsletter. bi-m.

National Landscape Association

Historical Note
A division of American Nursery and Landscape Association.

National Lawyers Guild *(1937)*

132 Nassau St., #922
New York, NY 10038
Tel: (212)679-5100 *Fax:* (212)679-2811
E-Mail: nlgno@nlg.org
Web Site: www.nlg.org
Members: 6000 individuals
Staff: 6
Annual Budget: $500-1,000,000
Executive Director: Heidi Boghosian

Historical Note
Funded as a progressive, anti-racist alternative to the American Bar Association. The Guild is open to lawyers, law students, legal workers and jailhouse lawyers, supporting the movement for social change in the U.S. Progressive membership fee schedule.

Meetings/Conferences:
Annual Meetings: Late Summer-Fall
2007 – Washington, DC/

Publications:
Guild Notes. q. adv.
Guild Practitioner. q.
Referral Directory. a.

National Lead Burning Association *(1945)*

c/o New England Lead Burning Co. - NELCO
98 Baldwin Ave., Box 607
Woburn, MA 01801
Tel: (781)933-1940 *Fax:* (781)933-4763
Members: 6 companies
Annual Budget: under $10,000
President: Karl E. Weiss
E-Mail: karl_weiss@nelco-usa.com

Historical Note
Fabricators of lead-lined equipment for handling corrosive chemicals and radiation shielding. Primarily exists to negotiate labor agreements on behalf of member companies.

Meetings/Conferences:
Annual Meetings: New York, NY in Spring

National League for Nursing *(1952)*

61 Broadway, 33rd Fl.

New York, NY 10006
Tel: (212)812-0376 *Fax:* (212)812-0393
Toll Free: (800)669 - 1656
E-Mail: generalinfo@nln.org
Web Site: www.nln.org
Members: 15000 individuals
Staff: 35
Annual Budget: $5-10,000,000
Chief Executive Officer: Beverly Malone

Historical Note

Originally founded in 1893 as the American Society of Superintendents of Training Schools for Nurses, the first organization for nursing. In 1912, the society was renamed the National League for Nursing Education (NLNE) and in 1952, NLNE, the National Organization for Public Health Nursing, and the Association for Collegiate Schools of Nursing combined to establish the National League of Nursing (NLN). Has an annual budget of approximately $10 million. Membership: $90/year (individual); $75/year (graduate); $35/year (student); $935-1375/year (agency).

Meetings/Conferences:

Annual Meetings: Fall

Publications:

Professional Development Bulletin. bi-w.
Shaping the Future. q.
NLN Journal, Nursing Education Perspectives. bi-m. adv.
NLN Update. bi-w.
Nursing Education Policy. m.

National League of American Pen Women *(1897)*
1300 17th St. NW
Washington, DC 20036-1973
Tel: (202)785-1997 *Fax:* (202)452-6868
E-Mail: info@americanpenwomen.org
Web Site: www.americanpenwomen.org
Members: 4 individuals
Staff: 4
Annual Budget: $100-250,000
National President: Anna Di Bella

Historical Note

Organized June 26, 1897 in Washington, DC as the League of American Pen Women; assumed its present name and was incorporated in 1926. Promotes the development of the creative talents of professional women artists, writers, dramatists, lecturers and composers. Membership: $30/year (individual).

Publications:

Roster for Membership and Bylaws. bien.
The Pen Woman. bi-m. adv.

National League of Cities *(1924)*
1301 Pennsylvania Ave. NW
Suite 550
Washington, DC 20004-1701
Tel: (202)626-3000 *Fax:* (202)626-3043
Web Site: www.nlc.org
Members: 1620 municipalities; 49 leagues
Staff: 100
Annual Budget: $10-25,000,000
Executive Director: Donald J. Borut
E-Mail: borut@nlc.org
Director, Media Relations: Sherry Conway Appel
Director, Research and Municipal Programs: Bill Barnes
E-Mail: barnes@nlc.org
Director, Information Technology: David Bean
E-Mail: bean@nlc.org
Deputy Executive Director: Christine Becker
E-Mail: becker@nlc.org
Director, Federal Relations: Carolyn Coleman
Director, Communications and Corporate Programs: Amy Elsbree
E-Mail: elsbree@nlc.org
Director, Administrative Services: Bernard Ford
E-Mail: ford@nlc.org
Director, Financial Management: Carlsen Griffith
E-Mail: griffith@nlc.org
Director, Institute for Youth, Education and Families: Clifford Johnson
E-Mail: cjohnson@nlc.org
Director, Human Resources: Anna Langham
Director, Conference and Seminar Management: Janice Pauline
E-Mail: pauline@nlc.org
Director, Member Programs: Cathy Spain
E-Mail: spain@nlc.org

Historical Note

Known until 1964 as the American Municipal Association, the National League of Cities was founded in 1924 by reform-minded state municipal leagues to represent the interests of its members to the federal and state governments. Has an annual budget of approximately $19 million. Membership: $208-73,521/year (city), based on city population.

Meetings/Conferences:

Annual Meetings: Winter - Annual Congress, Business Meeting, and Exhibition Spring - Annual Congressional Conference
2007 – New Orleans, LA/Nov. 13-17/6000

Publications:

Nation's Cities Weekly. w. adv.

National League of Postmasters of the U.S. *(1887)*
5904 Richmond Hwy.
Suite 500
Alexandria, VA 22303-1864
Tel: (703)329-4550 *Fax:* (703)329-0466
E-Mail: information@postmasters.org
Web Site: www.postmasters.org
Members: 30000 individuals
Staff: 30
Annual Budget: $2-5,000,000
President: Charles W. Mapa
Legislative Consultant: Robert Brinkmann
Director, Conventions and Meetings: Barbara Veech

Historical Note

Organized in Wasington, DC in December 1887 by about 200 Third and Fourth Class Postmasters to represent the interests of professional postmasters. Sponsor of Postmasters Benefit Plan, a health insurance program operated under the Federal Employees Health Benefits Program. Membership fee varies according to level of Postmaster.

Meetings/Conferences:

Annual Meetings: Summer

Publications:

Postmasters Advocate. m. adv.

National Leased Housing Association *(1972)*
1818 N St. NW
Suite 405
Washington, DC 20036
Tel: (202)785-8888 *Fax:* (202)785-2008
E-Mail: info@hudnlha.com
Web Site: www.hudnlha.com
Members: 600 organizations
Staff: 5
Annual Budget: $250-500,000
Executive Director: Denise Muha

Historical Note

Founded by developers and financers of federally funded housing under the government's Section 8 rent subsidy program for the poor. With the demise of the Section 8 new construction/substantial rehabilitation program, NLHA has broadened its purview to all government-related rental housing programs. Membership: $300-550/year (organization).

Meetings/Conferences:

Annual Meetings: Summer

Publications:

NLHA Bulletin. m.
Membership Directory. a.

National Legal Aid and Defender Association *(1911)*
1140 Connecticut Ave. NW
Suite 900
Washington, DC 20036
Tel: (202)452-0620 *Fax:* (202)872-1031
Web Site: www.nlada.org
Members: 1200 individuals
Staff: 29
Annual Budget: $1-2,000,000
President and Chief Executive Officer: Clinton Lyons
E-Mail: c.lyons@nlada.org

Historical Note

Organized in 1911 by fifteen legal assistance programs as the National Alliance of Legal Aid Socs., it became the National Association of Legal Aid Organizations in 1949 and assumed its present name in 1958. The only private, non-profit organization devoting all its resources to the support and development of quality legal assistance to the poor. Membership: $60/year (individual); .137%/budget/year (organization).

Meetings/Conferences:

Annual Meetings: Fall/800

Publications:

Directory of Legal Aid and Defender Offices. bien.
Corporate Counsel News. q.
Indigent Defense. 6/year.
Cornerstone. q. adv.
Capital Report. bi-m.

National Lesbian and Gay Journalists Association *(1990)*
1420 K St. NW
Suite 910
Washington, DC 20005
Tel: (202)588-9888 *Fax:* (202)588-1818
Web Site: www.nlgja.org
Members: 1300 individuals
Staff: 7
Annual Budget: $1-2,000,000
Executive Director: Pamela Strother, CAE
E-Mail: info@nlgja.org

Historical Note

NLGJA works within the news industry to foster fair and accurate coverage of gay and lesbian issues, and opposes newsroom bias against gay men, lesbians and other minorities. Membership : $55/year (individual); $750/year (organization)

Meetings/Conferences:

Annual Meetings: Fall
2007 – San Diego, CA(Westin Horton Plaza)/Aug. 30-Sept. 2/650

Publications:

NLGJA: Outlook. 4/year. adv.

National Lesbian and Gay Law Association *(1988)*
601 13th St. NW
Suite 1170 South
Washington, DC 20005-3807
Tel: (202)637-6384 *Fax:* (202)639-6066
E-Mail: info@nlgla.org
Web Site: www.nlgla.org
Members: 7500 individuals
Staff: 1
Annual Budget: $100-250,000
Executive Director: D'Arcy Kemnitz

Historical Note

Founded as National Lesbian and Gay Lawyers Association; assumed its current name in 1999. Membership: based on annual income.

Meetings/Conferences:

2007 – Chicago, IL(Chicago Hilton)/Sept. 6-8

Publications:

E-Newsletter. m.

National Lieutenant Governors Association *(1962)*
71 Cavalier Blvd.
Suite 124
Florence, KY 41042
Tel: (859)283-1400 *Fax:* (859)244-8001
E-Mail: jhurst@csg.org
Web Site: www.nlga.us
Members: 55 individuals
Staff: 1
Annual Budget: $100-250,000
Director: Julia Hurst

Historical Note

Formerly (1962) National Conference of Lieutenant Governors; assumed its current name in 2002. Affiliated with the Council of State Governments. Promotes the exchange of information, fosters interstate cooperation, and seeks to improve the efficiency and effectiveness of the office of the lieutenant governor. Membership: $600-800/year (state).

Meetings/Conferences:

Semi-annual Meetings: Late Summer & State-Fed/Washington, DC/Feb-March

2007 – Washington, DC(Westin Embassy Row)/March 14-16
2007 – Williamsburg, VA(Kingsmill Resort)/July 25-27
2008 – Washington, DC(The Hamilton)/125

Publications:
NLGA Focus. q. adv.

National Lime Association *(1902)*
200 N. Glebe Road, Suite 800
Arlington, VA 22203
Tel: (703)243-5463 *Fax:* (703)243-5489
Web Site: www.lime.org
Members: 21 manufacturers
Staff: 5
Annual Budget: $500-1,000,000
Executive Director: Arline Seeger
E-Mail: aseeger@lime.org
Director, Administration and Member Services: Deborah Cummings-Gaghan
Director, Regulatory Issues: Eric Males
E-Mail: emales@lime.org
Director, Government Affairs: Hunter Prillaman
E-Mail: hprillaman@lime.org

Historical Note
Members are manfacturers of quicklime and hydrated lime for environmental, industrial, construction, and other purposes.

Publications:
Lime-Lites. q.

National Limousine Association *(1985)*
49 S. Maple Ave.
Marlton, NJ 08053
Tel: (856)596-3344 *Fax:* (856)596-2145
Toll Free: (800)652 - 7007
E-Mail: info@limo.org
Web Site: www.limo.org
Members: 1750 individuals
Staff: 4
Annual Budget: $500-1,000,000
Executive Director: Francis J. Shane

Historical Note
Members are manufacturers, owners and operators of limousines. Provides legislative representation on issues including fuel tax, worker's compensation, and transportation infrastructure funding. Membership: $150-1,500/year (operator); $995/year (manufacturer).

Meetings/Conferences:
2007 – Las Vegas, NV(Venetian Resort and Casino)/Jan. 28-30

Publications:
Limo Scene. m.
Membership Directory. a.

National Lincoln Sheep Breeders Association *(1889)*
15603 173rd Ave.
Milo, IA 50166
Tel: (641)942-6402
E-Mail: kclaghorn@earthlink.net
Web Site: www.lincolnsheep.org
Members: 85 individuals
Staff: 1
Annual Budget: under $10,000
Secretary/Treasurer: Roger Watkins

Historical Note
Members are breeders and fanciers of Lincoln sheep. Membership: $10/year, plus $10 initiation fee.

Publications:
The Lincoln Letter. 4/year.

National Lipid Association *(2002)*
8833 Perimeter Park Blvd., Suite 301
Jacksonville, FL 32216
Tel: (904)998-0854 *Fax:* (904)998-0855
Web Site: www.lipid.org
Staff: 5
Executive Director: Christopher R. Seymour

Historical Note
NLA members are medical and scientific professionals who manage patients with lipid disorders and increased cardiovascular risk. Membership: $50/year.

National Litigation Support Services Association *(1991)*
60 Bristol Road East, Suite 248
Mississauga, ON L4Z 3-K8
Tel: (905)502-7890 *Fax:* (905)502-5418
E-Mail: webmaster@nlssa.com
Web Site: www.nlssa.com
Members: 36 firms
Staff: 10
Contact: Eve Horvath

Historical Note
NLSSA is a not-for-profit association of CPA firms that provide litigation support services. Member firms are accepted on a territorially exclusive basis, and are approved for membership based on their experience and reputation in, and commitment to, providing litigation consulting and support.

Meetings/Conferences:
Annual Meetings: Semi-Annual Meetings

Publications:
Members Bulletin. q.
The Expert. q.

National Livestock Producers Association *(1921)*
660 Southpointe Court, Suite 314
Colorado Springs, CO 80906-3874
Tel: (719)538-8843 *Fax:* (719)538-8847
Toll Free: (800)237 - 7193
E-Mail: maschneider@nlpa.org
Web Site: www.nlpa.org
Members: 28392 livestock producers
Staff: 3
Annual Budget: $250-500,000
President and Chief Executive Officer: Scott Stewart

Historical Note
Formerly (1943) National Live Stock Marketing Association. A federation of cooperative livestock marketing agencies and regional credit corporations.

Publications:
Annual Report. a.
Yearbook. a.

National Lubricating Grease Institute *(1933)*
4635 Wyandotte St., Suite 202
Kansas City, MO 64112-1542
Tel: (816)931-9480 *Fax:* (816)753-5026
E-Mail: nlgi@nlgi.com
Web Site: www.nlgi.com
Members: 280 companies
Staff: 2
Annual Budget: $250-500,000
General Manager: Chuck Hitchcock
E-Mail: nlgi@nlgi.com

Historical Note
Incorporated as the National Association of Lubricating Grease Manufacturers; assumed its present name in 1937. Members are companies that manufacture and market all types of lubricating greases, additive or equipment suppliers, and research and educational groups whose interests are primarily technical.

Meetings/Conferences:
2007 – Scottsdale, AZ(Fairmont Scottsdale Princess)/June 10-12/300

Publications:
NLGI Spokesman. m. adv.

National Luggage Dealers Association *(1925)*
1817 Elmdale Ave.
Glenview, IL 60025
Tel: (847)998-6869 *Fax:* (847)998-6884
E-Mail: inquiry@nlda.com
Web Site: www.nlda.com
Members: 75 individuals
Staff: 13
Annual Budget: $500-1,000,000
Executive Administrator: Marrilyn Murray
E-Mail: inquiry@nlda.com

Historical Note
Members are retailers of luggage, leather goods, gifts and handbags with over 300 stores nationally. NLDA acts as a purchasing office for membership. Membership fee based on retail volume.

Meetings/Conferences:
Semi-annual Meetings: Annual Meeting in June held in Chicago, IL.

Publications:
Retail Christmas Catalogue. a.

National Lumber and Building Material Dealers Association *(1916)*
900 Second St. NE, Suite 305
Washington, DC 20002
Tel: (202)547-2230 *Fax:* (202)547-7640
Toll Free: (800)634 - 8645
E-Mail: industrynews@dealer.org
Web Site: www.dealer.org
Members: 8000 companies
Staff: 8
Annual Budget: $1-2,000,000
President: Shawn Conrad

Meetings/Conferences:
Annual Meetings: Fall: Industry Summit
Spring: Legislative Conference
2007 – Washington, DC(Ritz Carlton)/Apr. 14-16
2007 – Las Vegas, NV(JW Marriot and Spa)/Oct. 4-6

National Magazine, Book, and Film Carriers *(1932)*

Historical Note
An affiliate of International Digital Enterprise Alliance, which provides administrative support.

National Mail Order Association *(1972)*
2807 Polk St. NE
Minneapolis, MN 55418-2954
Tel: (612)788-1673 *Fax:* (612)788-1147
E-Mail: info@nmoa.org
Web Site: www.nmoa.org
Members: 7500 individuals and companies
Staff: 5
Annual Budget: $100-250,000
Chief Manager: John Schulte
Director, Publications: Brad Lee
Director, Membership: Cindy Schulte

Historical Note
Founded to help small-to-midsize firms in mail order and other direct marketing areas. Membership: $199-365/year (organization).

Publications:
Mail Order Digest. m. adv.
Washington Newsletter. m. adv.

National Management Association *(1925)*
2210 Arbor Blvd.
Dayton, OH 45439
Tel: (937)294-0421 *Fax:* (937)294-2374
E-Mail: nma@nma1.org
Web Site: www.nma1.org
Members: 30000 individuals
Staff: 15
Annual Budget: $2-5,000,000
President: Stephen Bailey
Vice President, Professional Development: Karen Tobias

Historical Note
Formerly (1956) National Association of Foremen. Absorbed International Management Council in 2004. Members are middle level and supervisory management personnel united to professionalize management and promote American competitive enterprise. Membership: $35/year (individual); $30/year (chapter member).

Meetings/Conferences:
Annual Meetings: Fall

Publications:
Manage. q. adv.

National Marine Bankers Association *(1979)*
200 E. Randolph Dr., Suite 5100
Chicago, IL 60601-6436
Tel: (312)946-6260 *Fax:* (312)946-0388
Web Site: www.marinebankers.org
Members: 80 companies
Staff: 1
Annual Budget: $25-50,000
Association Manager: Bernice McArdle

Historical Note
Any bank, savings institution or credit union which holds marine loans directly in its portfolio is eligible for membership. Membership: $445/year, plus $100 initiation fee.

Publications:
Annual Marine Lending Survey. a.
The Business of Pleasure Boats. q.

National Marine Distributors Association *(1965)*
37 Pratt St.
Essex, CT 06426-1159
Tel: (860)767-7898 *Fax:* (860)767-7932
E-Mail: info@nmdaonline.com
Web Site: www.nmdaonline.com
Members: 225 individuals
Staff: 2
Annual Budget: $250-500,000
Executive Director: Nancy Cueroni
Historical Note
Wholesalers of marine accessories and hardware.
Meetings/Conferences:
Annual Meetings: Spring
Publications:
The Journal. bi-m.

National Marine Educators Association *(1976)*
P.O. Box 7000
Ocean Springs, MS 39566-1470
Tel: (228)374-7557
E-Mail: nmea@usm.edu
Web Site: www.marine-ed.org
Members: 1200 individuals
Staff: 1
Annual Budget: $25-50,000
Contact: Johnette Bosarge
Historical Note
Members are interested in all types of marine education at the K-12 and college levels as well as continuing education and informal instruction in the marine environment. NMEA's primary goal is to promote a "marine literate" society. Membership: $40/year.
Meetings/Conferences:
Annual Meetings: Summer
Publications:
Current: The Journal of Marine Education. q.
NMEA News. q.

National Marine Electronics Association *(1957)*
Seven Riggs Ave.
Severna Park, MD 21146
Tel: (410)975-9425 *Fax:* (410)975-9450
E-Mail: info@nmea.org
Web Site: www.nmea.org/
Members: 550 companies
Staff: 3
Annual Budget: $1-2,000,000
President and Executive Director: Bonnie J. Barsa
E-Mail: bbarsa@nmea.org
Historical Note
A national trade association for manufacturers and dealer/distributors in the marine electronics industry. Supports education, industry standards and government regulations for the industry and acts as an information clearinghouse. Membership: $100/year (individual); $200-$800/year (organization/company).
Publications:
NMEA News Newsletter. bi-m.
Marine Electronics Journal. bi-m. adv.

National Marine Manufacturers Association *(1979)*
200 E. Randolph Dr., Suite 5100
Chicago, IL 60601
Tel: (312)946-6200 *Fax:* (312)946-0388
Web Site: www.nmma.org
Members: 1515 companies
Staff: 130
Annual Budget: $25-50,000,000
President: Thomas J. Dammrich
Vice President, Marketing and Communications: Carl Blackwell
VIce President, Finance and Chief Financial Officer: Craig Boskey
Vice President, Government Relations: Monita Fontaine
Vice President, Engineering Standards: Tom Marhevko
Executive Vice President: Ben Wold
Historical Note
Represents companies that manufacture products or provide services to the recreational boating industry, including boats, engines, trailers, and electronic marine accessories. Promotes recreational boating to the public and industry interests in government regulation and legislation.
Meetings/Conferences:
Annual Meetings: Fall
Publications:
Innerport. 2/yr.
Currents. w.

National Marine Representatives Association *(1960)*
P.O. Box 360
Gurnee, IL 60031
Tel: (847)662-3167 *Fax:* (847)336-7126
E-Mail: info@nmraonline.org
Web Site: www.nmraonline.org/
Members: 530 individuals
Staff: 1
Annual Budget: $50-100,000
Executive Director: Kelly Flory
Historical Note
Members are independent boat and marine accessory sales representatives. Membership: $300/year (full member); $75/year (associate); $125/year (affiliate).
Publications:
Tidings. q. adv.
NMRA Membership Directory. a. adv.

National Maritime Alliance *(1988)*
East Carolina Univ., Maritime Studies Program
Adm. Ernest Eller House
Greenville, NC 27858-4353
Tel: (252)328-6097 *Fax:* (252)328-6754
Staff: 2
Annual Budget: $100-250,000
Contact: Karen Underwood
Historical Note
Represents individuals and organizations involved in preserving and promoting America's maritime heritage.
Publications:
Maritime America. q.

National Marrow Donor Program *(1986)*
3001 Broadway St. NE
Suite 500
Minneapolis, MN 55413-2197
Tel: (612)627-5800 *Fax:* (612)627-8125
Toll Free: (800)627 - 7692
Web Site: www.marrow.org
Members: 350 medical centers
Staff: 500
Annual Budget: Over $100,000,000
Chief Executive Officer: Jeffrey W. Chell, MD
E-Mail: jchell@nmdp.org
Director, Marketing and Communications: JoAnne Al Kire
E-Mail: jalkire@nmdp.org
Chief Financial Officer: Gordon C. Bryan
E-Mail: questions@nmdp.org
Legislative Policy Analyst: Isaac Fordjour
E-Mail: questions@nmdp.org
Director, Quality Systems and Membership Services: Kathy Welte, RN
E-Mail: questions@nmdp.org
Director, Information Systems: Paul Zyla
E-Mail: questions@nmdp.org
Historical Note
NMDP is a national registry of volunteer unrelated marrow and blood stem cell donors, and the international coordinating body for medical centers performing marrow transplants. Maintains database on transplant outcomes. NMDP advocates for patients seeking marrow or blood stem cell transplants and coordinates and sponsors research on patient outcomes.
Meetings/Conferences:
Annual Meetings: Annual; 850
Publications:
Transplant Center Access Directory. a.
Data and Scientific Report. a.
The Networker. q.
Marrow Messenger. a.

National Mastitis Council *(1961)*
421 S. Nine Mound Road
Madison, WI 53593
Tel: (608)848-4615 *Fax:* (608)848-4671
Web Site: www.nmconline.org
Members: 2000 individuals
Staff: 1
Annual Budget: $100-250,000
Executive Director: Anne Saeman
E-Mail: anne@nmconline.org
Historical Note
Members are dairy industry professionals. Membership: $50/year (individual); $150-550/year (organization).
Meetings/Conferences:
Annual Meetings: February
Publications:
Regional Meetings Proceedings. a.
Udder Topics Newsletter. bi-m.
Annual Meeting Proceedings. a.

National Meat Association *(1946)*
1970 Broadway, Suite 825
Oakland, CA 94612
Tel: (510)763-1533 *Fax:* (510)763-6186
E-Mail: staff@nmaonline.org
Web Site: www.nmaonline.org
Members: 600 companies
Staff: 6
Annual Budget: $500-1,000,000
Executive Director: Rosemary M. Mucklow
Director, Communications: Kirn Kernelli
Government Relations Liaison: Shawna Thomas
Historical Note
Originally the Western States Meat Association formed in 1982 by a merger of the Western States Meat Packers Association and the Pacific Coast Meat Association; assumed its current name to reflect its national membership in 1995. General members are persons or companies engaged in the slaughtering of livestock or the processing, sale and distribution of meat and meat products. Allied members are persons or firms engaged primarily in buying and selling meat and poultry products; associate members are persons or companies supplying non-meat supplies and equipment to the meat processing industry. Membership fee varies, based on classification: $600-26,500/year.
Meetings/Conferences:
Annual Meetings: WInter-Spring
Publications:
Herd on the Hill. w.
NMA Membership Directory. a. adv.
NMA Resource. m.
Lean Trimmings Bulletin. w.

National Meat Canners Association *(1923)*
1150 Connecticut Ave. NW
12th Floor
Washington, DC 20036
Tel: (202)587-4273 *Fax:* (202)587-4303
E-Mail: nmca@meatami.com
Web Site: www.meatami.com
Members: 35 companies
Staff: 4
Annual Budget: $25-50,000
President and Executive Secretary: James H. Hodges
Director, Research: Susan Backus
Historical Note
Promotes the interests of packers of commercially sterile canned meats, can equipment suppliers, and encourages scientific and practial research. Manageed by the American Meat Institute. Membership: $750/year.
Meetings/Conferences:
Annual Meetings: Spring

National Medical Association *(1895)*
1012 10th St. NW
Washington, DC 20001
Tel: (202)898-2510 *Fax:* (202)842-3293
Toll Free: (800)662 - 0554
Web Site: www.nmanet.org
Members: 16000 individuals
Staff: 30
Annual Budget: $5-10,000,000
Executive Director: James G. Barnes
Director, Grants Management: Ivonne Fuller
Editor, Journal of the National Medical Association: Eddie Hoover, MD

Director, Convention Services: Patricia Norman
Director, External Affairs: Reese J. Stone
Manager, Publications: Kimberly Taylor
Director, Membership: Jennifer Wilson

Historical Note

Professional society of black physicians. Represents 30,000 African American physicians. Membership: $445/year.

Meetings/Conferences:

Annual Meetings: Summer
2007 – Honolulu, HI/Aug. 3-9
2008 – Atlanta, GA

Publications:

NMA Healthy Living. q. adv.
Journal of the National Medical Association. m. adv.

National Mental Health Association *(1909)*
2000 N. Beauregard St., Sixth Floor
Alexandria, VA 22311
Tel: (703)684-7722 *Fax:* (703)684-5968
Toll Free: (800)969 - 6642
E-Mail: infoctr@nmha.org
Web Site: www.nmha.org
Members: 1000 individuals
Staff: 70
Annual Budget: $5-10,000,000
Senior Vice President, Public Affairs: James Radack

Historical Note

Formed by a merger of the National Committee for Mental Hygiene, the National Mental Health Foundation and the Psychiatric Foundation. Absorbed the National Organization for Mentally Ill Children. Formerly (1978) the National Association for Mental Health and (1980) the National Mental Health Association.

Publications:

Consumer Supporter News. m.
Executive Update. m.
Bell. m.
Legislative Alert.
MMHA News Release.

National Middle School Association *(1973)*
4151 Executive Pkwy., Suite 300
Westerville, OH 43081
Tel: (614)895-4730 *Fax:* (614)895-4750
Toll Free: (800)528 - 6672
E-Mail: info@nmsa.org
Web Site: www.nmsa.org
Members: 30000 individuals
Staff: 29
Annual Budget: $1-2,000,000
Executive Director: Sue Swaim
Assistant Executive Director: Jack Berckmeyer
Deputy Executive Director: Jeff Ward

Historical Note

Formerly (1973) Midwest Middle School Association. Educators and parents interested in middle school education. Membership: $45-55/year (individual); $175/year (organization).

Meetings/Conferences:

Annual Meetings: Fall/8,000-10,000

Publications:

Middle School Journal. 5/year. adv.
Middle Ground. 2/year.
Target. 4/year.

National Military Intelligence Association *(1974)*
P.O. Box 470
Hamilton, VA 20159
Tel: (540)338-1143 *Fax:* (703)738-7487
E-Mail: nmia@adelphia.net
Web Site: www.nmia.org
Members: 2500 individuals
Staff: 1
Annual Budget: $100-250,000
Director: Zhi Hamby
E-Mail: zhi@zgram.net

Historical Note

NMIA is a professional association focusing on defense intelligence, including strategic, tactical and counter intelligence affecting the security of the United States. Members are current and former U.S. intelligence professionals and U.S. citizens interested in supporting defense intelligence through educational efforts. Membership: $15-35/year (individual, based on rank), $600-$1,200/year (corporate).

Meetings/Conferences:

Awards Banquet: June

Publications:

NMIA Z-GRAM. 5/wk. adv.
American Intelligence Journal. semi-a. adv.
NMIA Newsletter. irreg.. adv.

National Milk Producers Federation *(1916)*
2101 Wilson Blvd., Suite 400
Arlington, VA 22201
Tel: (703)243-6111 *Fax:* (703)841-9328
E-Mail: info@nmpf.org
Web Site: www.nmpf.org
Members: 29 dairy cooperatives
Staff: 18
Annual Budget: $2-5,000,000
Chief Executive Officer: Jerome J. Kozak
Executive Vice President: Thomas M. Balmer
Vice President, Government Relations: Roger Eldridge

Historical Note

Established as the National Cooperative Milk Producers Federation, it assumed its present name in 1966 and absorbed the National Creameries Association in 1966. Membership fee varies based on production.

Meetings/Conferences:

Annual Meetings: November/1,200

Publications:

News for Dairy Co-ops. w.
Dairy Market Report. m.

National Miniature Donkey Association *(1990)*
6450 Dewey Road
Rome, NY 13440
Tel: (315)336-0154 *Fax:* (315)339-4414
E-Mail: nmdaasset@aol.com
Web Site: www.nmdaasset.com
Executive Director: Lynn Gattari

Historical Note

Established to protect and promote the miniature donkey breed. Membership: $35/year (domestic); $45/year (international).

Publications:

Asset. q.

National Mining Association *(1995)*
101 Constitution Ave., N.W., Suite 500-East
Washington, DC 20001-2133
Tel: (202)463-2600 *Fax:* (202)463-2666
Web Site: www.nma.org
Members: 400 companies
Staff: 40
Annual Budget: $10-25,000,000
President and Chief Executive: Kraig Naasz
Senior Vice President, Government and Political Affairs: Daniel R. Gerkin
Senior Vice President, Administration and Finance: Moya Phelleps
Vice President, External Communications: Luke Popovich
Senior Vice President: Harold P. Quinn, Jr.
Senior Vice President, Communications: Carol Raulston

Historical Note

Product of the merger (1995) of the American Mining Congress and the National Coal Association. Absorbed Gold Institute in 2003. NMA is an industry association that encompasses producers of most of America's metals, coal, industrial and agricultural minerals; manufacturers of mining and mineral processing machinery, equipment and supplies; and engineering and consulting firms and financial institutions that serve the mining industry. The NMA is both a clearinghouse for information and coordinator for action on behalf of the mining industry. The political action committees of the NMA are CoalPAC and MinePAC. Has an annual budget of approximately $12 million.

Meetings/Conferences:

Quadrennial Meetings: Fall
2008 – Las Vegas, NV/Sept. 22-24

Publications:

Mining Week. w.

National Minority Business Council *(1972)*
25 W. 45th St., Suite 301
New York, NY 10036
Tel: (212)997-4753 *Fax:* (212)997-5102
E-Mail: nmbc@msn.com
Web Site: www.nmbc.org
Members: 350 vendor firms
Staff: 5
Annual Budget: $250-500,000
President and Chief Executive Officer: John F. Robinson

Historical Note

NMBC is dedicated to providing business assistance, educational opportunities, seminars, purchasing exchanges, mentoring, business listings and related services to small, minority and women-owned businesses. Membership: $350/year.

Publications:

NMBC Business Report. q.

National Minority Supplier Development Council *(1972)*
1040 Ave. of the Americas
Second Floor
New York, NY 10018
Tel: (212)944-2430 *Fax:* (212)719-9611
Web Site: www.nmsdc.org
Members: 3500 Corporate Members
Staff: 22
Annual Budget: $10-25,000,000
President: Harriet R. Michel
Vice President, Finance and Administration: Casilda Del Valle

Historical Note

Formerly (1980) the National Minority Purchasing Council. Founded to expand business opportunities for minority-owned companies and to encourage mutually beneficial economic links between minority suppliers and the public and private sector. Network includes 39 Regional Councils across the country. There are 3,500 corporate members throughout the network, including more than 170 of the top Fortune 500 companies. Regional councils certify and match more than 15,000 minority-owned businesses with member corporations which want to purchase goods and services. Membership fee based on a sliding scale.

Meetings/Conferences:

Annual Meetings: Fall

Publications:

Minority Supplier News. q.
Annual Report. a.

National Mobility Equipment Dealers Association *(1988)*
3327 W. Bearss Ave.
Tampa, FL 33618
Tel: (813)264-2697 *Fax:* (813)962-8970
Toll Free: (800)833 - 0427
E-Mail: nmeda@aol.com
Web Site: www.nmeda.org
Members: 700 individuals
Staff: 5
Annual Budget: $500-1,000,000
Executive Director: Dana L. Roeling

Historical Note

A trade association of dealers and merchants who convert vehicles for use by people with disabilities.

Meetings/Conferences:

2007 – Daytona Beach, FL(Hilton)/Feb. 7-10

Publications:

Circuit Breaker. q. adv.

National Motor Freight Traffic Association *(1956)*
2200 Mill Road
Alexandria, VA 22314
Tel: (703)838-1810 *Fax:* (703)683-1094
Web Site: www.erols.com/nmfta
Members: 1700 individuals
Staff: 19
Annual Budget: $2-5,000,000
Executive Director and Secretary: William W. Pugh
E-Mail: PUGH@NMFTA.ORG

Historical Note

NMFTA is a trade association representing motor common carriers (trucking companies) of every kind of product which moves via less than truckload service. Membership: $265-$13,314/year.

Meetings/Conferences:

Quarterly Meetings: various locations

Publications:
National Motor Freight Classification Tariff. a.
Directory of Standard Carrier Agent Codes. a.
Continental Directory of Standard Point Location Codes. a.

National Motorsports Press Association *(1959)*
P.O. Box 500
Darlington, SC 29540
Tel: (843)395-8900 *Fax:* (843)393-3911
Members: 300 individuals
Staff: 1
Executive Secretary: Bridget Holloman

Historical Note
Formerly Southern Motorsports Press Association. Membership: $35/year (full member); $75/year (associate).

National Multi Housing Council *(1978)*
1850 M St. NW
Suite 450
Washington, DC 20036-5803
Tel: (202)974-2300 *Fax:* (202)775-0112
E-Mail: info@nmhc.org
Web Site: www.nmhc.org
Members: 700 individuals
Staff: 30
Annual Budget: $2-5,000,000
President: Douglas M. Bibby
E-Mail: dbibby@nmhc.org
Director, Meetings, Marketing and Exhibits: Jennifer M. Angebrandt
E-Mail: jangebrandt@nmhc.org
Senior Vice President, Government Affairs: Jim Arbury
E-Mail: jarbury@nmhc.org
Director, Membership: Doris D. Collins
E-Mail: dcollins@nmhc.org
Vice President, Communications: Kimberly D. Duty
E-Mail: kduty@nmhc.org
Vice President, Operations: Susan Guthrie
E-Mail: sguthrie@nmhc.org

Historical Note
NMHC represents the interests of the nation's larger and most prominent firms participating in the apartment industry. Members are engaged in all aspects of the development and operation of apartment housing, including ownership, construction, management, and finance of such communities. Also concentrates on public policies related to finance, tax, property management, the environment, building codes, seniors' housing, and technology issues. Membership: $1,000-20,000/year (company).

Meetings/Conferences:
Annual Meetings: January

Publications:
Research Notes. q.
Market Trends. q.
Tax Update. q.
Washington Update. semi-m.
Building Codes Update. q.
Technology Update. q.
Environmental Update. q.

National Multiple Sclerosis Society *(1946)*
733 Third Ave.
New York, NY 10017-3288
Tel: (212)986-3240 *Fax:* (212)986-7981
Toll Free: (800)344 - 4867
E-Mail: net@nmss.org
Web Site: www.nationalmssociety.org
Members: 500000 individuals
Staff: 1250
Annual Budget: $50-100,000,000
President and Chief Executive Officer: Joyce Nelson
Vice President, Research Programs: Dr. John Richert
Director, Communications: Arney Rosenblat
Vice President, Advocacy Programs: Susan Sanabria
E-Mail: susan.sanabria@nmss.org

Historical Note
Founded in 1946, the mission of NMSS is to end the devastating effects of multiple schlerosis (MS), a nerological disorder affecting both young and middle-aged adults. NMSS funds MS research, offers services to people with MS, provides professional education programs and advances advocacy efforts. Membership: $25/year.

Publications:
Inside MS. q. adv.

National Music Council *(1940)*
425 Park St.
Upper Montclair, NJ 07043
Tel: (973)655-7974 *Fax:* (973)655-5432
E-Mail: sandersd@mail.montclair.edu
Web Site: www.musiccouncil.org
Members: 50 organizations
Staff: 1
Annual Budget: $25-50,000
Director: David Sanders, Ph.D.
E-Mail: sandersd@mail.montclair.edu

Historical Note
Association of music organizations chartered by the U.S. Congress as a forum for discussion of national music problems. Composed of organizations of national scope and activity which are interested in the development of music and in the purposes for which the National Music Council was formed. Council has no individual members; however, individuals associated with member organizations are encouraged to attend the Council's Music Leadership Meetings and Symposia.

Meetings/Conferences:
Annual Meetings: New York/June

Publications:
Membership Directory. a.

National Music Publishers' Association *(1917)*
101 Constitution Ave. NW
Suite 705 East
Washington, DC 20001
Tel: (202)742-4375 *Fax:* (202)742-4377
E-Mail: pr@nmpa.org
Web Site: www.nmpa.org
Members: 700 companies
Staff: 5
Annual Budget: $1-2,000,000
President and Chief Executive Officer: David Israelite
Senior Vice President, International Affairs and Legal: Charles Sanders

Historical Note
Established as the Music Publishers Protective Association; assumed its present name in 1966. Members are publishers of music concentrated principally around New York, Los Angeles and Nashville. A separate staff presides over a subsidiary, the Harry Fox Agency, which is a licensing group for the members' product. Membership: $100.00/year.

Publications:
NMPA News & Views. q.

National Naval Officers Association *(1972)*
P.O. Box 10871
Alexandria, VA 22310-0871
E-Mail: nnoa@nnoa.org
Web Site: www.nnoa.org
National President: Manson Brown

Historical Note
NNOA promotes the ideal of diversity in the naval services and provides a forum for professional development, mentoring, and support of its member officers. Has no paid officers or full-time staff.

The National NeedleArts Association *(1974)*
P.O. Box 3388
Zanesville, OH 43702-3388
Tel: (740)455-6773 *Fax:* (740)452-2552
Toll Free: (800)889 - 8662
Web Site: www.tnna.org
Members: 2600 businesses
Staff: 4
Annual Budget: $500-1,000,000
Executive Director: Patty Parrish
E-Mail: pparrish@offinger.com
Association Event Manager: Rise Fulmer

Historical Note
Originally (1974) National Needwork Association; assumed its current name in 2004. Formed by 34 companies to advance needlework quality, understanding and marketing in the United States. Members are needlework manufacturers, designers, retailers, and distributors. Holds both national and regional shows. Membership: $60/year (buyers); $275-850/year (exhibitors).

Publications:
Membership Directory. a.
Show Directory. a.
TNNA Today. q.

National Network for Social Work Managers *(1985)*
c/o JACSW, M/C 309
1040 W. Harrison St., Fourth Floor
Chicago, IL 60607-7134
Tel: (312)413-2302 *Fax:* (312)996-2770
E-Mail: info@socialworkmanager.org
Web Site: www.socialworkmanager.org
Members: 300 individuals
Staff: 1
Annual Budget: $50-100,000
Executive Director: Glynne Gervais

Historical Note
The mission of NNSWM is to enhance and promote effective, values-based social work management. NNSWM members are administrators and managers of human services with degrees in social work. NNSWM works to improve the management of social programs by connecting social work-degreed professionals engaged in or interested in management, by positioning and enhancing social work managers' careers, and by acting as a professional forum for social work manager concerns. Awards the designation CSWM (Certified Social Work Manager). Membership: $130/year (individual); membership fee per organizations varies (contact NNSWM); $55/year (student).

Meetings/Conferences:
2007 – Chicago, IL(University of Illinois, Chicago)/Apr. 13-14/100

Publications:
electronic newsletter. m. adv.
Membership Directory. a.
Monographs. a.
Journal of Administration in Social Work. q.

National Network of Estate Planning Attorneys *(1989)*
10831 Old Mill Road, Suite 400
Omaha, NE 68154
Toll Free: (800)638 - 8681
E-Mail: info@nnepa.com
Web Site: http://the.nnepa.com/public
Members: 400 individuals
Staff: 10
Annual Budget: $1-2,000,000
Chief Executive Officer: Richard Randall
Executive Director: Dan Stuenzi

Historical Note
An interactive alliance of about 400 estate planning attorneys nationwide which provides leadership in innovative estate planning techniques to assist families from various income levels in preserving their assets and perpetuating philanthropy.

Meetings/Conferences:
Biennial Meetings: odd years

National Network of Grantmakers *(1980)*
2801 21st Ave. South, Suite 132
Minneapolis, MN 55407
Tel: (612)724-0702 *Fax:* (612)724-0705
E-Mail: nng@nng.org
Web Site: www.nng.org
Members: 450 individuals
Staff: 2
Annual Budget: $500-1,000,000
Executive Director: Ron McKinley

Historical Note
NNG members are staff or trustees of private, public and corporate philanthropic organizations dedicated to social and economic justice. Membership:$200/year (individual); $1000/year (organization).

Meetings/Conferences:
Annual Meetings: Fall/500

Publications:
Grantmakers Directory. a.
Network Newsletter. q.

National Newspaper Association *(1885)*
P.O. Box 7540
Columbia, MO 65205-7540

Tel: (573)882-5800 *Fax:* (573)884-5490
Toll Free: (800)829 - 4662
E-Mail: info@nna.org
Web Site: www.nna.org
Members: 2500 newspapers
Staff: 5
Annual Budget: $1-2,000,000
Executive Director: Brian Steffens

Historical Note
Founded as the National Editorial Association; assumed its present name in 1960. Members comprise about 45% of the country's weeklies and one-third of the nation's dailies. In addition to its National Convention, NNA sponsors a Government Affairs Conference in the spring. Membership fee based on individual paper plus circulation.

Meetings/Conferences:
Semi-annual Meetings: Spring and Fall

Publications:
Publishers' Auxiliary. m. adv.

National Newspaper Publishers Association *(1940)*

3200 13th St. NW
Washington, DC 20010
Tel: (202)588-8764
Web Site: www.nnpa.org
Members: 215 newspaper publishers
Staff: 7
Annual Budget: $500-1,000,000
Acting Executive Director: George E. Curry

Historical Note
Formerly National Negro Publishers Association, also known as The Black Press of America. Membership: $150-660/year (based on circulation).

Publications:
Convention Journal. a.

National Notary Association *(1957)*

President: Milton G. Valera
E-Mail: nna@nationalnotary.org
Vice President and Executive Director: Tim Reininger

Historical Note
Established in 1957 as the California Notary Association; assumed its present name in 1965. Membership: $45/year.

Meetings/Conferences:
Annual Meetings: Spring-Summer
2007 - Los Angeles, CA(Westin Bonaventure Hotel)/June 2-

Publications:
Notary Bulletin. bi-m. adv.
The National Notary. bi-m. adv.

National Nursing Staff Development Organization *(1989)*

7794 Grow Dr.
Pensacola, FL 32514
Tel: (850)474-0995 *Fax:* (850)484-8762
Toll Free: (800)489 - 1995
E-Mail: nnsdo@puetzamc.com
Web Site: www.nnsdo.org
Members: 3000 individuals
Staff: 5
Annual Budget: $250-500,000
Account Executive: Patricia Barlow

Historical Note
NNSDO provides training and networking opportunities for professionals specializing in staff development in a variety of medical settings. Membership: $95/year.

Meetings/Conferences:
Annual Meetings: Summer
2007 - Atlanta, GA(Sheraton Atlanta)/July 26-29
2008 - Minneapolis, MN(Hilton Minneapolis)/July 10-13/800

Publications:
Trendlines. bi-m. adv.
Journal for Nurses in Staff Development. bi-m. adv.

National Nutritional Foods Association *(1936)*

2112 E. Fourth St., Suite 200
Santa Ana, CA 92705
Tel: (714)460-7732 *Fax:* (714)460-7444
Toll Free: (800)966 - 6632 Ext: 226
E-Mail: nnfa@nnfa.org
Web Site: www.nnfa.org
Members: 8000 retailers and manufacturers
Staff: 16
Annual Budget: $2-5,000,000
Senior Vice President and Chief Financial Officer: Brent Weickert
E-Mail: bweickert@nnfa.org
Vice President, Membership Services: Adam Finney

Historical Note
Organized in 1936 as the National Dietary Foods Association. Absorbed the American Dietary Retailers Association in 1969 and assumed its present name in 1970. Members are natural, nutritional, and dietary food retailers, distributors and producers. Supports the National Nutritional Foods Political Action Committee.

Meetings/Conferences:
Annual Meetings: Summer/10,000

Publications:
NNFA Today. m. adv.

National Ocean Industries Association *(1972)*

1120 G St. NW
Suite 900
Washington, DC 20005
Tel: (202)347-6900 *Fax:* (202)347-8650
E-Mail: noia@noia.org
Web Site: www.noia.org
Members: 300 companies
Staff: 9
Annual Budget: $1-2,000,000
President: Thomas A. Fry, III
Director, Government Affairs: Kim Harb
Director, Public Affairs: Michael Kearns
C.A.O. and Director, Member Development: Franki K. Stuntz
Director, Congressional Affairs: Nolty J. Thuriot

Historical Note
NOIA members are oil and gas companies, their suppliers, and support companies drilling and exploring on the outer continental shelf. Membership: fees based on gross allocated sales to U.S. offshore operations.

Meetings/Conferences:
Semi-annual Meetings: Spring/Fall/ Washington, DC

Publications:
Washington Report. bi-w. adv.
NOIA Membership Directory. a.
NOIA Leaders. a.
NOIA Annual Report. a.

National Oilseed Processors Association *(1929)*

1300 L St. NW, Suite 1020
Washington, DC 20005-4168
Tel: (202)842-0463 *Fax:* (202)842-9126
Web Site: www.nopa.org
Members: 13 companies
Staff: 5
Annual Budget: $1-2,000,000
President: Thomas A. Hammer

Historical Note
Formerly (1988) National Soybean Processors Association.

Meetings/Conferences:
2007 - Naples, FL(Ritz Golf Resort)/Feb. 4-8/200

National Onion Association *(1913)*

822 Seventh St.
Suite 1020
Greeley, CO 80631-3277
Tel: (970)353-5895 *Fax:* (970)353-5897
Web Site: www.onions-usa.org
Members: 600 individuals and companies
Staff: 3
Annual Budget: $250-500,000
Executive Vice President: Wayne Mininger

Historical Note
Represents interests of U.S. onion producers. Informational, lobbying, and generic promotional headquarters for fresh and storage dry bulb onion growers shippers and handlers. Provides conventions for networking and education exchange. Voluntary contributions (dues/assessments) are sole means of support.

Meetings/Conferences:
Semi-Annual Meetings: Summer and Fall
2007 - Fresno, CA/July 18-21
2007 - Wailea, HI/Nov. 28-Dec. 2

Publications:
News Letter. m. adv.
Statistical Report. m.
Membership Directory. a. adv.
Legislative Outlook. a.

National Onsite Wastewater Recycling Association *(1991)*

P.O. Box 1270
Edgewater, MD 21037
Tel: (410)798-1697 *Fax:* (410)798-5741
Toll Free: (800)966 - 2942
Web Site: www.nowra.org
Members: 75000
Staff: 3
Annual Budget: $250-500,000
Executive Director: Linda Hanifin Bonner

Meetings/Conferences:
Annual Meetings: 600

Publications:
Onsite Journal. bi-m. adv.

National Opera Association *(1955)*

P.O. Box 60869
Canyon, TX 79016-0869
Tel: (806)651-2857 *Fax:* (806)651-2958
E-Mail: rhansen@mail.wtamu.edu
Web Site: www.noa.org
Members: 550 individuals
Staff: 1
Annual Budget: $50-100,000
Executive Director: Robert Hansen
President: Jo Elyn Wakefield Wright

Historical Note
Members are opera companies, schools of music, opera directors, composers, conductors, librettists, teachers, and other professionals whose work is opera-related. Sponsors the nationwide Opera Production Competition, the New Opera Competition, and the NOA Voice Competition. Membership: $60/year (individual); $75/year (organization); $45/year (libraries). Has 160 library subscription members in addition to regular members.

Publications:
NOA Newsletter. bi-m. adv.
Opera Journal. q. adv.

National Optometric Association *(1969)*

3723 Main St.
P.O. Box F
East Chicago, IN 46312
Toll Free: (877)394 - 2020
Web Site: www.natoptassoc.org
Members: 600 individuals
Staff: 1
Annual Budget: $100-250,000
Manager/Meeting Planner: Dr. Charles Comer

Historical Note
Established and incorporated in Atlanta, NOA is a professional society of predominantly minority optometrists especially concerned with the delivery of vision/eye health care to the minority community. Affiliated with the American Optometric Association, American Public Health Association, Association of Schools and Colleges of Optometry and National Health Council. Membership: $150/year.

Meetings/Conferences:
Annual Meetings: Summer
2007 - Ft. Lauderdale, FL(Harbor Beach Marriott)/July 8-13

Publications:
NOA Newsletter. biennial. adv.

National Organization for Associate Degree Nursing *(1984)*

7794 Grow Dr.
Pensacola, FL 32514
Tel: (850)484-0514 *Fax:* (850)484-8762
E-Mail: noadn@noadn.org
Web Site: www.noadn.org

Members: 900 individuals
Staff: 5
Annual Budget: $250-500,000
Account Executive: Patricia Barlow

Historical Note
NOADN is a professional network and forum for ideas concerning associate degree nursing recruitment, education and practice. Membership: $95/year (individual); $400/year (organization/company).

Meetings/Conferences:
Annual Meetings: Fall
2007 – Las Vegas, NV(Flamingo)/Nov. 5-12/300
2008 – Myrtle Beach, SC(Marriott)/Nov. 14-16/300

Publications:
Teaching and Learning in Nursing. q. adv.
NOADN Newsletter. q. adv.

National Organization for Competency Assurance *(1977)*
2025 M St. NW
Suite 800
Washington, DC 20036-3309
Tel: (202)367-1165 *Fax:* (202)367-2165
E-Mail: info@noca.org
Web Site: www.noca.org
Members: 300 organizations
Staff: 2
Annual Budget: $250-500,000
Executive Director: Wade Delk

Historical Note
Established and incorporated in the District of Columbia, NOCA members are primarily organizations interested in encouraging the establishment and implementation of methods to insure the competency of practitioners whose services directly affect public health, safety, and welfare. Many members are certifying programs that have been acrredited by the National Commission for Certifying Agencies, an accreditation division of NOCA. Membership: $500-3,000/year.

Meetings/Conferences:
Annual Meetings: November

Publications:
NOCA News. q. adv.

National Organization for Human Service Education *(1975)*
5601 Brodie Lane, Suite 625-215
Austin, TX 78745
Tel: (512)692-9361 *Fax:* (512)692-9445
Web Site: www.nohse.org
Members: 600 individuals
Staff: 1
Annual Budget: $25-50,000

Historical Note
NOHSE members are drawn from diverse educational and professional backgrounds including educators, students, direct care professionals, administrators as well as organizations in both the U.S. and Canada. NOHSE's focus includes supporting and promoting improvements in direct service, public education, program development, planning and evaluation, administration and public policy. Membership: $50/year (individual); $100/year (organization); $15/year (student).

Meetings/Conferences:
Annual Meetings: October

Publications:
The Link Newsletter. q. adv.
Journal of Human Service Education. a. adv.

National Organization for the Professional Advancement of Black Chemists and Chemical Engineers *(1972)*
P.O. Box 77040
Washington, DC 20012
Tel: (202)667-1699 *Fax:* (202)667-1705
Toll Free: (800)776 - 1419
Web Site: www.nobcche.org
Members: 1000 individuals
Annual Budget: $250-500,000
President: Damon Larry

Historical Note
NOBCChE was founded as an ad hoc group in 1972, and incorporated in 1975. Provides a forum for African-Americans in chemistry to exchange professional and technical information. Membership: $75/year.

Meetings/Conferences:
Annual Meetings: Spring
2007 – Orlando, FL(JW Marriott Grande Lakes Resort)/Apr. 1-7
2008 – Philadelphia, PA(Marriott)/March 24-29
2009 – St. Louis, MO(Renaissance Grand Hotel)/Apr. 13-18
2010 – Atlanta, GA(Marriott Marquis Atlanta Downtown)/March 29-Apr. 3

Publications:
Proceeding of Annual Meeting. a.
NOBCChE News. q.

National Organization of Bar Counsel *(1964)*

Historical Note
Address unknown in 2006.

National Organization of Black County Officials *(1984)*

Historical Note
An affiliate of National Association of Counties, which provides administrative support.

National Organization of Black Law Enforcement Executives *(1976)*
4609 Pinecrest Office Park Dr.
Second Floor, Suite F
Alexandria, VA 22312
Tel: (703)658-1529 *Fax:* (703)658-9479
E-Mail: noble@noblenatl.org
Web Site: www.noblenatl.org
Members: 2300 individuals
Staff: 17
Annual Budget: $1-2,000,000
Executive Director: Jessie Lee, Jr.

Historical Note
NOBLE members are minority law enforcement executives including police chiefs, command-level officers and others. Membership: $75/year (individual).

Meetings/Conferences:
Annual Meetings: Summer
2007 – Ft. Lauderdale, FL

Publications:
NOBLE Actions. bi-m. adv.
NOBLE National. q. adv.

National Organization of Industrial Trade Unions *(1954)*
148-06 Hillside Ave.
Jamaica, NY 11435
Tel: (718)291-3434 *Fax:* (718)526-2920
Web Site: www.noitu.org
Members: 10000 individuals
Staff: 100
Annual Budget: $1-2,000,000
National President-Emeritus Elect: Daniel Lasky

Historical Note
NOITU is an independent labor union.

Meetings/Conferences:
Annual Meetings: Winter/New York, NY

Publications:
NOITU Reporter. q.

National Organization of Legal Services Workers *(1972)*
113 University Place
Fifth Floor
New York, NY 10003
Tel: (212)228-0992 *Fax:* (212)228-0097
Toll Free: (800)829 - 2320
Members: 4800 individuals
Staff: 7
President: Ellen N. Wallace
Union Administrator: Diane Lanigan

Historical Note
Labor union affiliated with the AFL-CIO.

Meetings/Conferences:
Annual Meetings: 300

Publications:
Newsletter. irreg.

National Organization of Life and Health Insurance Guaranty Associations *(1983)*
13873 Park Center Road, Suite 329
Herndon, VA 20171
Tel: (703)481-5206 *Fax:* (703)481-5209
E-Mail: info@nolhga.com
Web Site: www.nolhga.com
Members: 52 associations
Staff: 20
Annual Budget: $2-5,000,000
President: Peter G. Gallanis
Executive Vice President and Chief Operating Officer: Richard Klipstein
Senior Vice President and General Counsel: William P. O'Sullivan
Vice President, Administrative Services: Holly L. Wilding

Historical Note
NOLHGA members are state life and health insurance guaranty associations. Members are located in 50 states as well as Washington D.C. and Puerto Rico.

Meetings/Conferences:
Annual Meetings: Fall

Publications:
NOLHGA Journal. q.
Weekly Wire. w.

National Organization of Nurse Practitioner Faculties *(1980)*
1522 K St. NW
Suite 7072
Washington, DC 20005
Tel: (202)289-8044 *Fax:* (202)289-8046
E-Mail: nonpf@nonpf.org
Web Site: www.nonpf.org
Members: 1200 individuals
Staff: 2
Annual Budget: $250-500,000
President: Annie O'Sullivan

Historical Note
NONPF is committed to leadership in the development, implementation and evaluation of nurse practitioner education at the regional, national and international levels. Membership: $100/year (individual); $75/year (associate); $400/year (group); $50/year (student; retired).

Meetings/Conferences:
Annual Meetings: April

Publications:
Directory of Nurse Practitioner Primary Care Competencies in Specialty Areas.
New Paradigms in Advanced Nursing Practice.
NONPF Quarterly Newsletter. q. adv.
Directory of Nurse Practitioner Programs. bien.
Grantmanship: Developing a Program of Research.

National Organization of Social Security Claimants' Representatives *(1979)*
560 Sylvan Ave.
Englewood Cliffs, NJ 07632
Toll Free: (800)431 - 2804
E-Mail: nosscr@worldnet.att.net
Web Site: www.nosscr.org
Members: 3500 individuals
Staff: 6
Annual Budget: $50-100,000
Executive Director: Nancy G. Shor

Historical Note
Members are lawyers and related professionals representating clients in federal and/or state adjudication.

Meetings/Conferences:
Semi-annual Meetings: Spring and Fall
2007 – Baltimore, MD(Baltimore Marriott Waterfront)/Apr. 18-21
2007 – St. Louis, MO(Hyatt Regency Union Station)/Oct. 17-21

Publications:
NOSSCR Forum. m.

National Orientation Directors Association *(1947)*

375 University Center
Flint, MI 48502-1950
Tel: (810)424-5513 *Fax:* (810)762-3023
E-Mail: nodahomeoffice@umflint.edu
Web Site: www.nodaweb.org
Members: 1200 individuals
Staff: 2
Annual Budget: $50-100,000
Director, Membership Services: Becky Armour

Historical Note
NODA members are college personnel professionals, graduate and undergraduate students who are responsible for student orientation programs. Has no paid officers or full-time staff. Membership: $100/year.

Meetings/Conferences:
Annual Meetings: October

Publications:
Orientation Review Newsletter. q.
NODA Membership Directory. a.
Orientation Director's Manual. bien.
NODA First Timers Handbook. a.

National Ornamental and Miscellaneous Metals Association *(1958)*
1535 Pennsylvania Ave.
McDonough, GA 30253
Toll Free: (888)516 - 8585
E-Mail: nonmainfo@nomma.org
Web Site: www.nomma.org
Members: 1000 companies
Staff: 6
Annual Budget: $500-1,000,000
Executive Director: Barbara H. Cook
Communications Manager: J. Todd Daniel
Meetings and Exposition Manager: Martha Pennington

Historical Note
Organized at the Claridge Hotel in Memphis, Tennessee in January, 1958 as the National Ornamental Iron Manufacturers Association. Changed its name to National Ornamental Metal Manufacturers Association (1961) and adopted present name in 1977. Membership: $365/year (company).

Meetings/Conferences:
Annual Meetings: Winter

Publications:
NOMMA Ornamental/Miscellaneous Metal Fabricator. bi-m. adv.

National Ornamental Goldfish Growers Association *(1981)*
6916 Black's Mill Road
Thurmont, MD 21788
Tel: (301)271-7475 *Fax:* (301)271-7059
Members: 6 companies
Annual Budget: under $10,000
Executive Secretary: Raymond W. Klinger

Historical Note
NOGGA was established by professional goldfish growers in the U.S. to fund research on goldfish, principally disease research.

Meetings/Conferences:
Annual Meetings: Winter

National Paint and Coatings Association *(1933)*
1500 Rhode Island Ave. NW
Washington, DC 20005
Tel: (202)462-6272 *Fax:* (202)462-8549
E-Mail: npca@paint.org
Web Site: www.paint.org
Members: 400 manufacturers
Staff: 31
Annual Budget: $5-10,000,000
President and Chief Operating Officer: J. Andrew Doyle
Vice President, General Counsel and Corporate Secretary: Thomas J. Graves
Vice President, Meetings and Conventions: Cheryl Matthews
E-Mail: cmatthews@paint.org
Director, Industry Affairs: Ken Zacharias
E-Mail: kzacharias@paint.org

Historical Note
Manufacturers of paints and industrial coatings, and suppliers to the industry. Formed in 1933 as the National Paint, Varnish and Lacquer Association through a merger of the American Paint Manufacturers Association and the National Paint, Oil and Varnish Association, the name was changed to the National Paint and Coatings Association in 1972.

Meetings/Conferences:
Annual Meetings: Fall

Publications:
Coatings. 10/year.
Member/Services Directory. a. adv.
Trade Mark Directory.

National Pan-Hellenic Council *(1930)*
Indiana University, Eigenmann Center 635
1900 E. 10th St.
Bloomington, IN 47406
Tel: (812)855-8820
E-Mail: info@nphchq.org
Web Site: www.nphchq.org
Members: 9 fraternities & sororities
Staff: 1
Annual Budget: $50-100,000
Executive Director and Chief Executive Officer: Virginia LeBlanc
Executive Assistant and Financial Secretary: Tykia Rodgers

Historical Note
NPHC is the umbrella organization coordinating activities among nine predominately African-American fraternities and sororities.

Meetings/Conferences:
Biennial Meetings: odd years in Oct.
2007 – Detroit, MI(Hyatt Dearborn)/Oct. 17-21

Publications:
The Summit. q.

National Panhellenic Conference *(1902)*
877 Purdue Road, Suite 117
Indianapolis, IN 46268
Tel: (317)872-3185 *Fax:* (317)872-3192
E-Mail: npccentral@npcwomen.org
Web Site: www.npcwomen.org
Members: 26 national sororities
Staff: 4
Annual Budget: $50-100,000
Administrative Director: Carol Armstrong

Historical Note
Organized in Chicago, May 24, 1902.

Publications:
NPC Directory. a.
PH Factor. bien.
Chapter & Campus Listing. a.

National Paperbox Association *(1918)*
113 S. West St.
Alexandria, VA 22314
Tel: (703)684-2212 *Fax:* (703)683-6920
E-Mail: npahq@paperbox.org
Web Site: www.paperbox.org
Members: 250 companies
Staff: 4
Annual Budget: $500-1,000,000
Executive Vice President and Membership: Scott Miller
Meetings and Conventions: Joan Griffith

Historical Note
Formed (1918) as the National Federation of Paper Box Manufacturers; developed into the National Paper Box Manufacturers Association in 1919; changed name to (1972) the National Paper Box Association, then (1981) National Paperbox and Packaging Association and assumed its present name in 1992. In 1982, NPPA opened membership to all independent manufacturers of packaging including rigid paper boxes, folding cartons and thermoform materials and their suppliers. Membership: fee based upon sales volume.

Meetings/Conferences:
Annual Meetings: April-May/300
2007 – Orlando, FL(Marriott Grande Lake)/Apr. 18-21/200

Publications:
Benefits and Wage Rates of the Rigid Box and Folding Carton Industries. bien.
Key Ratios of the Rigid Box Industry. bien.
Packet Update. m.
Packet Magazine. q.
Key Ratios of the Folding Carton Industry. bien.
Monthly Billing Reports for Rigid Box and Folding Carton Industries.
Membership Directory. a.

National Paralegal Association *(1982)*
P.O. Box 406
Solebury, PA 18963-0406
Tel: (215)297-8333 *Fax:* (215)297-8358
E-Mail: admin@nationalparalegal.org
Web Site: www.nationalparalegal.org
Members: 24500 individuals, schools and firms
Staff: 6
Executive Director: H. Jeffrey Valentine

Historical Note
Members are paralegals, paralegal educators, independent paralegals, paralegal schools, corporate law departments, law libraries, law firms, paralegal students, and others with an interest in the advancement of the profession. Maintains mailing lists of over 170,000 paralegals, available for rental. Membership: $70/first year; $45/year (full member); $70/year (associate); $30/year (student); $20/year (pre-student).

Publications:
Legal Publishers Directory. adv.
National Legal Placement Agency Directory. adv.
The Paralegal. irreg. adv.
NPA News. m.
Directory of Corporate Legal Departments.
Annual Nat'l Salary & Employment Survey. a. adv.
Nat'l School & Institute Directory. a. adv.
Paralegal Career Booklet. a. adv.
Directory of Local Paralegal Clubs. a. adv.

National Park and Recreation Society *(1932)*

Historical Note
Formerly the American Park and Recreation Association, it is now a branch of the National Recreation and Park Association. Members are professional recreation directors in towns and cities throughout the country.

National Park Hospitality Association *(1919)*
129 Park St. NE
Suite B
Vienna, VA 22180
Tel: (703)242-1999 *Fax:* (703)242-1992
E-Mail: info@nphassn.org
Web Site: www.nphassn.org
Members: 125 companies and individuals
Staff: 1
Annual Budget: $250-500,000

Historical Note
Members are individuals and companies holding contracts with the Department of the Interior to provide goods and services to visitors to U.S. national parks. Established in 1919. Incorporated in 1975. Supports the Concessioners Political Action Committee. Formerly the Conference of National Park Concessioners. Membership: $200/year plus % of Annual Budget.

Meetings/Conferences:
Semi-annual Meetings: Washington, DC/March & National Park/Oct.
2007 – Washington, DC(Madison Hotel)/March 4-6

Publications:
newsletter. q.
National Parks Visitor Facilities & Services Guide.
Membership Roster. semi-a.

National Parking Association *(1951)*
1112 16th St. NW
Suite 300
Washington, DC 20036
Tel: (202)296-4336 *Fax:* (202)331-8523
Toll Free: (800)647 - 7275
E-Mail: info@npapark.org
Web Site: www.npapark.org
Members: 1200 organizations
Staff: 5
Annual Budget: $1-2,000,000

Executive Director: Martin L. Stein
Director, Communications: Barbara Darraugh
E-Mail: bdarraugh@npapark.org
Director, Finance: Barbara Krone
E-Mail: krone@npapark.org
Director, Marketing and Business Development: Patricia Langfeld

Historical Note

Sponsors the National Parking Association Political Action Committee and the Parking Industry Institute. Membership fees vary.

Meetings/Conferences:

2007 – Los Angeles, CA(Renaissance Hollywood)/Oct. 22-25/1000
2008 – Las Vegas, NV(Caesar's Palace)/Sept. 15-18/1000

Publications:

Convention Directory. a. adv.
Products & Services Directory. a. adv.
Parking Magazine. 10/year. adv.

National Parks Conservation Association *(1919)*

1300 19th St. NW
Suite 300
Washington, DC 20036
Tel: (202)223-6722 *Fax:* (202)659-0650
Toll Free: (800)628 - 7275
E-Mail: npca@npca.org
Web Site: www.eparks.org
Members: 400000 individuals
Staff: 100
Annual Budget: $10-25,000,000
President: Thomas C. Kiernan
Vice President, Government Affairs: Craig Obey
VicePresident, Communication: Linda M. Rancourt
Vice President, Membership: Mina Stanard

Historical Note

Established as the National Parks Association; became National Parks and Conservation Association in 1970 and assumed its current name in 1999. Members are individuals interested in conservation, protection of National Parks, wildlife and the wilderness. Has an annual budget of $16 million. Membership: $25/year (individual).

Publications:

National Parks Magazine. bi-m. adv.

National Party Boat Owners Alliance *(1952)*

181 Thames St.
Groton, CT 06340
Tel: (860)535-2066 *Fax:* (860)535-8389
Members: 500 individuals
Annual Budget: under $10,000
President and Executive Director: Bradley J. Glas

Historical Note

Established in 1952 in response to increased federal legislation affecting the industry, NPBOA members are Coast Guard licensed Operators or Masters of passenger-for-hire charter/party boats. NPBOA's principal activity is monitoring proposed and new laws or regulations that might be detrimental to its segment of the maritime industry. Membership: $30/year (individual).

Publications:

Newsletter. 6/yr.

National Pasta Association *(1904)*

1156 15th St. NW
Suite 900
Washington, DC 20005
Tel: (202)785-8540 *Fax:* (202)223-9741
E-Mail: npa@kellencompany.com
Web Site: www.ilovepasta.org
Members: 80 businesses
Staff: 4
Annual Budget: $100-250,000
Executive Director: Richard E. Cristol

Historical Note

Established as the National Macaroni Manufacturers Association. Absorbed the National Macaroni Institute in 1979 and assumed its present name in 1981. NPA member manufacturers provide a wide variety of pasta products for the retail and foodservice markets.

National Patio Enclosure Association *(1952)*

Historical Note

Formerly (1990) Western Awning Association. Sellers and manufacturers of patio structures, screen enclosures and sun rooms. Member of The International Conference of Building Officials.

Publications:

News Bulletin. q.

National Pawnbrokers Association *(1988)*

P.O. Box 1040
Roanoke, TX 76262
Tel: (817)491-4554 *Fax:* (817)491-8770
E-Mail: info@nationalpawnbrokers.org
Web Site: www.nationalpawnbrokers.org
Members: 2000 individuals
Staff: 3
Annual Budget: $1-2,000,000
Executive Director: Dana Meinecke
E-Mail: info@nationalpawnbrokers.org

Historical Note

NPA was founded to unite all pawnbrokers in their common efforts to improve the image of the industry, educate the public, and disseminate professional information and assistance. Provides numerous membership benefits. Membership: $250/year (individual).

Meetings/Conferences:

Annual Meetings: Summer

Publications:

Pawnbroker News. m. adv.
National Pawnbroker Magazine. q. adv.

National Peach Council *(1942)*

12 Nicklaus Lane, Suite 101
Columbia, SC 29229
Tel: (803)788-7101 *Fax:* (803)865-8090
Members: 2000 individuals
Staff: 2
Annual Budget: $50-100,000
Managing Director: Charles Walker
E-Mail: charleswalker@worldnet.att.net

Historical Note

Formed in 1942 and incorporated in 1945 in West Virginia. Purpose is to promote the fresh market peach industry and U.S. fresh market peach growers.

Publications:

Peach Statistical Yearbook. a.
Peach Times Newsletter. q. adv.

National Pecan Shellers Association *(1943)*

1100 Johnson Ferry Rd., Suite 300
Atlanta, GA 30342
Tel: (404)252-3663 *Fax:* (404)252-0774
E-Mail: info@ilovepecans.org
Web Site: www.ilovepecans.org
Members: 60 companies
Staff: 4
Annual Budget: $50-100,000
Executive Director: Vickie Mabry

Historical Note

Formerly (1985) the National Pecan Shellers and Processors Association. NPSA members are pecan shellers and processors; brokers; accumulators; growers; and packaging, equipment and ingredient suppliers to the industry.

Meetings/Conferences:

Semi-Annual Meetings: Winter/Fall

Publications:

In A Nutshell. q.
Perfect Performance with Pecans.

National Perinatal Association *(1976)*

2090 Linglestown Road, Suite 107
Harrisburg, PA 17110
Toll Free: (888)971 - 3295
E-Mail: npa@nationalperinatal.org
Web Site: www.nationalperinatal.org
Members: 1100 individuals
Staff: 3
Annual Budget: $250-500,000
President: Dr. Albert Pizzica

Historical Note

Members are individuals providing health care with particular emphasis on care for the pregnant woman, fetus and newborn. Membership: $75/year (individual); $200/year (organization); $5,000/year (corporate).

Meetings/Conferences:

Annual Meetings: Fall

Publications:

NPA Bulletin. q. adv.
Journal of Perinatology. m. adv.

National Pest Management Association *(1933)*

9300 Lee Hwy., Suite 301
Fairfax, VA 22031
Tel: (703)352-6762 *Fax:* (703)352-3031
Toll Free: (800)678 - 6722
E-Mail: jbevard@pestworld.org
Web Site: www.pestworld.org
Members: 5000 companies
Staff: 18
Annual Budget: $2-5,000,000
Executive Vice President: Robert F Lederer, Jr.
E-Mail: lederer@pestworld.org
Executive Assistant: Jill Bevard
E-Mail: lederer@pestworld.org
Chief Financial Officer and Director, Finance: Gary McKenzie
E-Mail: mckenzie@pestworld.org
Senior Vice President, Government Affairs: Robert Rosenberg
E-Mail: rosenberg@pestworld.org
Director, Conventions and Meetings: Dominique Stumpf
E-Mail: dstumpf@pestworld.org

Historical Note

Founded as National Association of Exterminators and Fumigators; became National Pest Control Association in 1937, and assumed its current name in 2000. Members are companies engaged in the integrated management of insects, rodents, birds and other pests which inhabit buildings or structures of any kind. Produces educational and training materials and conducts workshops. Supports the National Pest Management Association Political Action Committee.

Meetings/Conferences:

Annual Meetings: Late October
2007 – Kissimmee, FL(Gaylord Palms Resort)/Oct. 17-20

Publications:

Divisional ePestworld. bi-w.
ePestworld. bi-w. adv.
Pestworld. 6/year. adv.

National Petrochemical & Refiners Association *(1902)*

1899 L St. NW
Suite 1000
Washington, DC 20036
Tel: (202)457-0480 *Fax:* (202)457-0486
E-Mail: info@npra.org
Web Site: www.npra.org
Members: 450 companies
Staff: 30
Annual Budget: $1-2,000,000
President: Bob Slaughter
Business Manager/Petrochemcial Director: Richard W. Brown
Director, Environmental Affairs: Norbert Dee, Ph.D.
Director, Public Policy and Communications: Sharon Dey
Director, Technical Advocacy: Charles Drevna
Director, Environmental Advocacy: David Friedman
Technical Director: Jeff Hazle
Director, Congressional Affairs: Sharon Kirk
Director, Convention Services: Helen Kutska
Secretary and Attorney: Maurice H. McBride, CAE
Director, Administration: Pamela Neuman
Director, Government Relations: June M. Whelan

Historical Note

Product of a merger in 1961 of the National Petroleum Association (1902) and the Western Petroleum Refiners Association (1912). Became National Petroleum Refiners Association and assumed its present name in 1999. Members include virtually all U.S. petroleum refiners and petrochemical manufacturers.

Meetings/Conferences:

Annual Meetings: Spring/4,000

National Petroleum Council *(1946)*

1625 K St. NW, Suite 600
Washington, DC 20006
Tel: (202)393-6100 *Fax:* (202)331-8539
E-Mail: info@npc.org

Web Site: www.npc.org
Members: 175 individuals
Staff: 12
Annual Budget: $1-2,000,000
Executive Director: Marshall W. Nichols

Historical Note
Established in 1946 at the request of President Truman, the NPC is a self-supporting federal advisory body to the Secretary of Energy.

Meetings/Conferences:
Semi-annual Meetings: Washington, DC

National Pharmaceutical Alliance

Historical Note
Merged with Generic Pharmaceutical Ass'n in 2000. Address unknown in 2006.

National Pharmaceutical Council *(1953)*

1894 Preston White Dr.
Reston, VA 20191
Tel: (703)620-6390 *Fax:* (703)476-0904
Web Site: www.npcnow.org
Members: 21 companies
Staff: 21
Annual Budget: $2-5,000,000
President: Karen Williams
E-Mail: kwilliams@npcnow.com
Vice President, Business Operations and External Affairs: Patricia L. Adams
E-Mail: padams@npcnow.com
Director, Scientific Affairs: Jeann Lee Gillespie, PharmD
E-Mail: jgillespie@npcnow.com
Manager, Member Services: Kathryn Gleason
E-Mail: kgleason@npcnow.com
Vice President, Health Care Systems: Gary S. Persinger
E-Mail: gpersinger@npcnow.com

Historical Note
Members are reserach-intensive companies producing brand name prescription medicines. NPC communicates the economic, clinical and societal value of pharmaceuticals for the betterment of human health.

Publications:
Pharmaceutical Benefits Under State Medical Assistance Programs. a.

National Phlebotomy Association *(1978)*

1901 Brightseat Road
Landover, MD 20785
Tel: (301)386-4200 *Fax:* (301)386-4203
E-Mail: naltphle@aol.com
Web Site: www.nationalphlebotomy.org
Members: 7800 individuals
Staff: 5
Annual Budget: $250-500,000
Chief Executive Officer: Diane C. Crawford

Historical Note
NPA's primary focus is on education and research in phlebotomy; provides certification to individuals through school programs. Has an accreditation mechanism for phlebotomy training programs. Membership: $100 (certification); $65/year (renewal fee).

Meetings/Conferences:
Annual Meetings: August

National Plant Board *(1925)*

Michigan Department of Agriculure
P.O. Box 30017
Lansing, MI 48909
Tel: (517)373-4087 *Fax:* (517)335-4540
E-Mail: rauscherk@michigan.gov
Web Site: www.nationalplantboard.org
Members: 51 individuals
Annual Budget: $10-25,000
President: Ken Rauscher

Historical Note
Representatives from each state and Puerto Rico interested in protecting agriculture, forestry and horticulture throughout the U.S. by pest control and plant quarantine. Affiliated with the National Association of State Departments of Agriculture.

Meetings/Conferences:
Annual Meetings: Third week of August/75
2007 - , HI/Aug. 19-23

Publications:
Minutes of Annual Meeting. a.

National Plasterers Council

2811-D Tamiami Trail
Port Charlotte, FL 33952
Toll Free: (866)483 - 4672
Web Site: www.npconline.org/mc/page.do
Executive Director: Mitch Brooks

National Police and Security Officers Association of America *(1955)*

P.O. Box 663
South Plainfield, NJ 07080-0663
Toll Free: (800)467 - 6762
E-Mail: npsoaa@usacops.com
Web Site: http://npoaa.tripod.com
Members: 620 individuals
Staff: 2
Annual Budget: $50-100,000

Historical Note
Founded as National Police Officers Association of America; assumed its current name in 2003. NPOA active members are law enforcement, corrections, security, and military officers. Promotes training through scholarships, seminars, and a yearly conference. Membership: $35/year.

Publications:
NPSOAA Review. q.

National Police Officers Association of America

Historical Note
Became National Police and Security Officers Association of America in 2003.

National Pork Producers Council *(1954)*

10664 Justin Dr.
Urbandale, IA 50322
Tel: (515)278-8012 *Fax:* (515)278-8011
Web Site: www.nppc.org
Members: 85000 individuals
Staff: 100
Annual Budget: $25-50,000,000
Chief Executive Officer: Neil Dierks
Director, Government Relations: Audrey Adamson
Vice President, State Relations and Resource Development: Pat Mcgonegle
Director, Communications: Dave Warner

Historical Note
Established as the National Swine Growers Council, NPPC assumed its present name in 1967 and is now a federation of 44 state associations.

Meetings/Conferences:
Annual Meetings: March, during the Nat'l Pork Industry Forum

National Postal Mail Handlers Union

1101 Connecticut Ave NW
Suite 500
Washington, DC 20036
Tel: (202)833-9095 *Fax:* (202)833-0008
Web Site: www.npmhu.org
Members: 52000 individuals
Manager: William J. Flynn

Historical Note
A division of the Laborers' International Union of North America, AFL-CIO.

Meetings/Conferences:
Quadrennial Meetings: (2008)

Publications:
Mail Handlers Magazine. q.

National Postsecondary Agriculture Student Organization *(1979)*

6060 FFA Dr.
P.O. Box 68960
Indianapolis, IN 48268-0960
Tel: (317)802-4220 *Fax:* (317)802-5220
Web Site: www.nationalpas.org/
Members: 1200 individuals
Staff: 2
Annual Budget: $100-250,000
Program Coordinator: Michelle Foley
E-Mail: mfoley@nationalpas.org

Historical Note
Members are institutions educating agricultural students on the college level. Membership: $15/year (individual); $50/year (instutution).

Meetings/Conferences:
Annual Meetings: March

Publications:
Newsletter-Pastimes. trien.

National Potato Council *(1948)*

1300 L St. NW
Suite 910
Washington, DC 20005
Tel: (202)682-9456 *Fax:* (202)682-0333
E-Mail: spudinfo@nationalpotatocouncil.org
Web Site: www.nationalpotatocouncil.org
Members: 8000 individuals
Staff: 5
Annual Budget: $500-1,000,000
Executive Vice President and Chief Executive Officer: John R. Keeling
Manager, Administrative Services: Otelia Quarles
Manager, Communications: Hollee Stubblebine

Historical Note
Represents all U.S. potato growers on federal legislative and regulatory issues. Membership: $50/year (individual); $200/year (associate).

Meetings/Conferences:
Annual Meetings: Winter

Publications:
Insider Report. w.
Potato Statistical Year Book. a. adv.

National Potato Promotion Board *(1971)*

7555 E. Hampden Ave., Suite 412
Denver, CO 80231-4835
Tel: (303)369-7783 *Fax:* (303)369-7718
E-Mail: info@uspotatoes.com
Web Site: www.uspotatoes.com/pressroom.htm
Members: 10000 individuals
Staff: 17
Annual Budget: $5-10,000,000
President and Chief Executive Officer: Timothy O'Connor
Vice President, Marketing: Mac Johnson
Manager, Accounting and Information Technology: Diana LeDoux
Vice President, Public Relations: Linda McCashion
Vice President, International Marketing: John Toaspern
Administrator, Executive Office: Karen Tromly

Historical Note
Also known as The Potato Board. Founded in 1972 by federal law and a grower referendum. The Board was organized to operate a national promotion plan for potatoes, to position the potato as a low-calorie, nutritious vegetable and to facilitate market expansion into such areas as domestic and export sales.

Publications:
Tuber News.

National Poultry and Food Distributors Association *(1967)*

958 McEver Road Ext., Suite B-8
Gainesville, GA 30504
Tel: (770)535-9901 *Fax:* (770)535-7385
Toll Free: (877)845 - 1545
E-Mail: info@nfpda.org
Web Site: www.nfpda.org
Members: 250 companies
Staff: 2
Annual Budget: $100-250,000
Executive Director: Kristin McWhorter
E-Mail: info@nfpda.org

Historical Note
Formerly (1992) the National Independent Poultry and Food Distributors Association. Established to represent the varied voices of independent poultry distributors, processors, marketing firms and allied suppliers. Provides members with cost saving programs. Sponsor of NPFDA Poultry Suppliers Showcase/Food Show. Membership: $450/year (corporate).

Meetings/Conferences:
Semi-annual Meetings: Winter and Spring
2007 - Lake Tahoe, NV(Hyatt Lake Tahoe)/July 15-18/240

Publications:
NPFDA News Newsletter. m. adv.
NIPFDA Handbook/Directory. a. adv.

National Precast Concrete Association *(1965)*
10333 N. Meridian St., Suite 272
Indianapolis, IN 46290-1
Tel: (317)571-9500 *Fax:* (317)571-0041
Toll Free: (800)366 - 7731
Web Site: www.precast.org
Members: 920 companies
Staff: 26
Annual Budget: $5-10,000,000
President: Ty E. Gable, CAE
E-Mail: tgable@precast.org
Director, Meetings: Danielle Bowman, CMP
Director, Technical Services: Dean Frank
E-Mail: dfrank@precast.org
Director, Finance and Human Resources: Claudia Hunter
Director, Development and Member Services: Brenda Ibitz
E-Mail: bibitz@precast.org
Director, Technical Education: Alex Morales
Director, Membership, Marketing and Quality Assurance: Alan Siebenthaler
E-Mail: asiebenthaler@precast.org
Director, Communications: Bob Whitmore
E-Mail: rwhitmore@precast.org
Historical Note
Membership: $1,000-$2,250/year (company).
Meetings/Conferences:
Annual Meetings: February-March
Publications:
MC Magazine. bi-m. adv.
Annual Directory. a. adv.
Precast Solutions magazine. q. adv.
Update newsletter. bi-m. adv.

National Prehealth Student Association
Historical Note
The student support division of National Association of Advisors for the Health Professions, which provides administrative support.

National Press Photographers Association *(1946)*
3200 Croasdaile Dr., Suite 306
Durham, NC 27705
Tel: (919)383-7246 *Fax:* (919)383-7261
Web Site: www.nppa.org
Members: 10000 individuals
Staff: 4
Annual Budget: $1-2,000,000
Executive Director: Greg Garneau
E-Mail: director@nppa.org
Director, Membership: Jim Haverkamp
Historical Note
Membership: $55/year (student); $90/year (professional).
Meetings/Conferences:
Annual Meetings: Summer
Publications:
NPPA Membership Directory (online). a. adv.
News Photographer. m. adv.

National Prison Hospice Association *(1991)*
P.O. Box 4623
Boulder, CO 80306-4623
Tel: (303)447-8051 *Fax:* (303)447-8055
E-Mail: npha@npha.org
Web Site: www.npha.org
Members: 10 hospice care organizations
Staff: 1
Annual Budget: $25-50,000
Historical Note
Mission is to promote hospice care for terminally ill inmates and those facing the prospect of dying in prison. Goal is to assist and support corrections professionals in their continuing efforts to develop high-quality patient care procedures and management programs.
Publications:
NPHA Newsletter. q.

National Private Truck Council *(1988)*
2200 Mill Road, Suite 350
Alexandria, VA 22314
Tel: (703)683-1300 *Fax:* (703)683-1217
E-Mail: gpetty@nptc.org
Web Site: www.nptc.org
Members: 700 companies
Staff: 6
Annual Budget: $2-5,000,000
President and Chief Executive Officer: Gary Frank Petty, Ph.D., CAE
Senior Vice President: George Mundell
Historical Note
Formed in 1988 in a consolidation of Private Carrier Conference with Private Truck Council of America. In 1990, NPTC formed the Institute for Track Transportation Management.
Meetings/Conferences:
Annual Meetings: Spring
2007 – Indianapolis, IN(Indiana Convention Center)/Apr. 29-May 1/900
Publications:
Annual Membership Directory and Buyer's Guide. y. adv.
Weekly News Update. w.
Annual Yearbook. y. adv.

National Propane Gas Association *(1931)*
1150 17th St. NW
Suite 310
Washington, DC 20036-4623
Tel: (202)466-7200 *Fax:* (202)466-7205
E-Mail: info@npga.org
Web Site: www.npga.org
Members: 3500 marketers, producers & suppliers
Staff: 24
Annual Budget: $5-10,000,000
President and Chief Executive Officer: Richard R. Rolden
Director, Communications: Robert Baylor
Director, Legislative Affairs: Brian Cavdill
Vice President, Administration: Brian Dunlap
Manager, Membership Services: Miriam Hankins
Manager, Propane PAC: Helen Kim
Senior Vice President, Regulatory and Technical Services: Philip Squair
Vice President, Legislative Affairs: Michael Troop
Historical Note
Formerly (1988) National LP-Gas Association. Members are producers and distributors of liquefied petroleum gas and propane and manufacturers of equipment for its use. Supports the Propane Industry Political Action Committee and the National Propane Gas Foundation.
Meetings/Conferences:
Annual Meetings: Spring/3,000
Publications:
NPGA Reports. w.

National Property Management Association *(1970)*
1102 Pinehurst Road
Dunedin, FL 34698-5427
Tel: (727)736-3788 *Fax:* (727)736-6707
E-Mail: hq@npma.org
Web Site: www.npma.org
Members: 4200 individuals
Staff: 3
Annual Budget: $500-1,000,000
Executive Director: Paul Nesbitt
Historical Note
Formed by a merger of the National Industrial Property Management Association and the Property Administration Association. NPMA members specialize in asset management for federal, state and local government agencies; industry; educational institutions, hospitals and non-profit organizations. Membership: $75/year (individual).
Meetings/Conferences:
Annual Meetings: Summer
2007 – Seattle, WA/June 3-7
Publications:
Property Professional. bi-m. adv.

National Psychological Association for Psychoanalysis *(1948)*
150 W. 13th St.
New York, NY 10011-7891
Tel: (212)924-7440 *Fax:* (212)989-7543
E-Mail: info@npap.org
Web Site: www.npap.org
Members: 365 individuals
Staff: 2
Administrator: Doris Mare
E-Mail: info@npap.org
Historical Note
NPAP promotes advancements in the science of psychoanalysis as a distinct discipline separate from the practice of medicine.
Meetings/Conferences:
Annual Meetings: December
Publications:
NPAP Bulletin. bien.
News and Reviews. 3/year.
The Psychoanalytic Review. bi-m. adv.

National Public Employer Labor Relations Association *(1970)*
1012 South Coast Hwy., Suite M
Oceanside, CA 92054
Tel: (760)433-1686 *Fax:* (760)433-1687
E-Mail: info@npelra.org
Web Site: www.npelra.org
Members: 2000 individuals
Staff: 4
Annual Budget: $250-500,000
Executive Director: Michael D. Suppan
Historical Note
Members are federal, state, county and municipal labor and employee relations professionals. Membership: $125/year (individual).
Meetings/Conferences:
Annual Meetings: March-April
Publications:
NPELRA Newsletter. 11/yr.

National Purchasing Institute *(1968)*
65 Enterprise
Aliso Viejo, CA 92656
Tel: (949)715-7857 *Fax:* (949)715-6931
Toll Free: (800)246 - 7143
E-Mail: executivedirector@nationalpurchasinginstitute.com
Web Site: www.nationalpurchasinginstitute.com
Members: 600 individuals
Staff: 1
Annual Budget: $100-250,000
Executive Director: Fred Droz
E-Mail: executivedirector@nationalpurchasinginstitute.com
Historical Note
Established in 1968 in Galveston, Texas as Southern Purchasing Institute; assumed its present name in 1973. Members are educational, government, and institutional purchasing administrators. Membership: $150/year (individual).
Publications:
Purchasing News. bi-m.
Membership Directory. a. adv.
Conference Program. a. adv.

National Quartz Producers Council *(1967)*
P.O. Box 1719
Wheat Ridge, CO 80034-1719
Tel: (303)432-0044 *Fax:* (303)467-0107
Members: 10 producers
Staff: 1
Annual Budget: under $10,000
President: Marc R. Busley
Historical Note
Members are producers of crushed quartz for use in decorative architectural concrete.

National Railroad Construction and Maintenance Association *(1967)*
122 C St. NW
Suite 850
Washington, DC 20001-2109
Tel: (202)638-7790 *Fax:* (202)638-1045
Toll Free: (800)883 - 1557
E-Mail: info@nrcma.org
Web Site: www.nrcma.org
Members: 150 companies
Staff: 2
Annual Budget: $250-500,000

President: Ray Chambers
E-Mail: info@nrcma.org
Executive Director: Chuck Baker
E-Mail: info@nrcma.org

Historical Note
Founded as Railroad Construction and Maintenance Association. Incorporated, affiliated with Laborers' International Union of North America and the International Union of Operating Engineers, and assumed its current name in 1978. Members are private railroad construction and maintenance contractors, engineers, manufacturing, supply and service firms. Membership: $630-2,625/year (contractors); $788/year (suppliers).

Meetings/Conferences:
Annual Meetings: Winter

Publications:
Model Contractor Safety Program. a.
E-Newsletter. m.
Worker Bi-Lingual Safety Handbooks. a.
Web-based Safety Training Program. a.
Membership Directory. a. adv.

National Reading Conference *(1950)*

7044 S. 13th St.
Oak Creek, WI 53154-1429
Tel: (414)908-4924 *Fax:* (414)768-8001
E-Mail: nrc@smtp.bmai.com
Web Site: www.nrconline.org
Members: 1100 individuals
Annual Budget: $100-250,000
Executive Director: Tracy Burr

Historical Note
Teachers involved in college and adult education literacy programs and research. Membership: $70/year (regular); $115/year (family); $35/year (student); $50/year (emeritus).

Meetings/Conferences:
Annual Meetings: Winter

Publications:
Journal of Literacy Research. q. adv.
NRC Yearbook. a.

National Ready Mixed Concrete Association *(1930)*

900 Spring St.
Silver Spring, MD 20910
Tel: (301)587-1400 *Fax:* (301)585-4219
Toll Free: (888)846 - 7622
Web Site: www.nrmca.org
Members: 1200 producers
Staff: 38
Annual Budget: $5-10,000,000
President: Robert Garbini
E-Mail: bgarbini@nrmca.org

Historical Note
Sponsors the National Ready Mixed Concrete Association Political Action Committee.

Meetings/Conferences:
Annual Meetings: April

Publications:
Concrete in Focus. m.

National Real Estate Forum *(1978)*

P.O. Box 598
Ticonderoga, NY 12883
Tel: (518)585-2746 *Fax:* (518)585-3206
Members: 70 individuals
Staff: 1
Executive Director: Edwin A. Howe, Jr.
E-Mail: eahowe@rosevilleco.com

Historical Note
Formerly (1998) National Society for Real Estate Finance. Incorporated in Delaware in 1978 as the National Association of Certified Mortgage Bankers, it began functioning in the spring of 1979 and was rechartered as NSREF in 1982, and as NREF in 1998. Membership consists of individuals who have achieved distinction in one or more areas of real estate/real estate finance.

National Real Estate Investors Association *(1985)*

525 W. Fifth St., Suite 230
Covington, KY 41011
Toll Free: (888)762 - 7342
E-Mail: info@nationalreia.com
Web Site: www.nationalreia.com
Members: 72 organizations
Staff: 2
Annual Budget: $10-25,000
Executive Director: Rebecca McLean

Historical Note
Founded as Real Estate Leadership Conference; assumed its current name in 1993. Members are realtors and investment professionals who emphasize real estate as an investment strategy.

Publications:
Newsletter. q. adv.

National Recreation and Parks Association *(1965)*

22377 Belmont Ridge Road
Ashburn, VA 20148-4501
Tel: (703)858-0784 *Fax:* (703)858-0794
E-Mail: info@nrpa.org
Web Site: www.nrpa.org
Members: 24000 individuals
Staff: 52
Annual Budget: $5-10,000,000
Executive Director: John Thorner
Director, Information Technology: Ed Zier

Historical Note
Formed by a merger of the American Association of Zoological Parks and Aquariums (founded in 1924), the American Institute of Park Executives (formed in 1898), the American Recreation Society (formed in 1938), the National of State Parks (founded in 1921) and the National Recreation Association (founded in 1906). Has an annual budget of approximately $9.6 million.

Meetings/Conferences:
Annual Meetings: Fall/4,000

Publications:
Journal of Leisure Research. q.
Parks and Recreation. m. adv.
Therapeutic Research Journal. q.

National Register of Health Service Providers in Psychology *(1974)*

1120 G St. NW
Suite 300
Washington, DC 20005-3801
Tel: (202)783-7663 *Fax:* (202)347-0550
Web Site: www.nationalregister.org
Members: 14000 individuals
Staff: 16
Annual Budget: $1-2,000,000
Executive Officer: Judy E. Hall, Ph.D.
E-Mail: judy@nationalregister.org
Director, Finance and Administration: Claire M. Long

Historical Note
Established to identify licensed psychologists who are qualified to deliver health care services. Provides credential verification to the health care industry through its subsidiary, HSP Verified. Membership: $115/year.

Meetings/Conferences:
Annual Meetings: None held.

Publications:
Register Report. 3-4/year.
Legal Update. irreg.
Nat'l Register of Health Service Providers in Psychology. bi-a.

National Registry of Environmental Professionals *(1983)*

P.O. Box 2099
Glenview, IL 60025
Tel: (847)724-6631 *Fax:* (847)724-4223
E-Mail: nrep@nrep.org
Web Site: www.nrep.org
Members: 17000 individuals
Staff: 8
Annual Budget: $500-1,000,000
Executive Director: Richard A. Young, Ph.D.
Senior Director: Edward Beck, Ph.D.
Director: Carol Schellinger
Director, Operations: Chris Young

Historical Note
The mission of NREP is to promote legal and professional recognition of individuals possessing education, training and experience as environmental managers, engineers, technologists, scientists and technicians; and to consolidate that recognition in one centralized source so that the public, government, employers and insurers can justify the importance and acceptance of such individuals to carry out operation and management of environment activities. Membership: $90/year.

Meetings/Conferences:
Annual Meetings: Semi-Annual meetings
2007 – Dallas, TX(Marriott)/Oct. 16-19

Publications:
Code of Professional Practice. a.
Registry Report. bi-m. adv.

National Rehabilitation Administration Association

Historical Note
Became National Association for Rehabilitation Leadership in 2003.

National Rehabilitation Association *(1925)*

633 S. Washington St.
Alexandria, VA 22314-4109
Tel: (703)836-0850 *Fax:* (703)836-0848
Members: 11000 individuals
Staff: 10
Annual Budget: $1-2,000,000
Executive Director: Ann Marie Hoffman
Director, Government Affairs: Patricia Leahy

Historical Note
Founded in 1925 and incorporated in the District of Columbia in 1963. Membership consists of those concerned with the rehabilitation of the physically and mentally impaired. Professional divisions include the National Association for Independent Living, National Association of Rehabilitation Instructors, National Association of Rehabilitation Secretaries, National Association of Service Providers in Private Rehabilitation, National Association on Multi-cultural Rehabilitation Concerns, National Rehabilitation Administration Association, National Rehabilitation Counseling Association, and Vocational Evaluation and Work Adjustment Association (see separate listings). Membership: $110/year (individual).

Meetings/Conferences:
Annual Meetings: Fall/800

Publications:
Contemporary Rehabilitation. 7/year. adv.
Journal of Rehabilitation. q. adv.
Mary Switzer Monograph. a. adv.

National Rehabilitation Counseling Association *(1958)*

P.O. Box 4480
Manassas, VA 20108
Tel: (703)361-2077 *Fax:* (703)361-2489
E-Mail: ncraoffice@aol.com
Web Site: http://nrca-net.org
Members: 1800 individuals
Staff: 2
Annual Budget: $100-250,000
Administrator: Dr. Betty Hedgeman
E-Mail: ncraoffice@aol.com

Historical Note
Founded as a professional division of National Rehabilitation Association; became an independent organization in 2005. Membership: $70/year.

Publications:
Journal of Applied Rehabilitation Counseling. q. adv.

National Reining Horse Association *(1966)*

3000 N.W. Tenth St.
Oklahoma City, OK 73107-5302
Tel: (405)946-7400 *Fax:* (405)946-8425
E-Mail: nrha@nrha.com
Web Site: www.nrha.com
Members: 12000 individuals
Staff: 25
Annual Budget: $2-5,000,000
Executive Director: Dan Wall

Historical Note
Membership: $40/year.

Meetings/Conferences:
Annual Meetings: Winter

Publications:
Reiner. 11/year. adv.

National Religious Broadcasters *(1944)*
9510 Technology Dr.
Manassas, VA 20110
Tel: (703)330-7000 *Fax:* (703)330-7100
E-Mail: info@nrb.org
Web Site: www.nrb.org
President: Dr. Frank Wright
Vice President, Operations: David Keith
Vice President, Communications: Robert McFarland
Historical Note
The oldest and most comprehensive association in the field of religious broadcasting, representing about 75% of those in the field in the country. Strives to maintain free access to the U.S. airwaves for religious broadcasters and to improve quality of religious media. Individual members are program producers. Membership: based on income.
Meetings/Conferences:
Annual Meetings: Winter
2007 – Orlando, FL(Rosen Hotel & Convention Center)/Feb. 16-21
Publications:
Membership Newsletter. w. adv.
NRB Magazine. m. adv.
NRB Convention Program/News. a. adv.

National Reloading Manufacturers Association *(1958)*
One Centerpointe Dr., Suite 350
Lake Oswego, OR 97035-8613
Web Site: www.reload-nrma.com
Members: 25 individuals
Staff: 3
Annual Budget: $10-25,000
Executive Secretary: Greg Chevalier
Historical Note
Manufacturers of tools and components for reloading ammunition.

National Remodelers Council
Historical Note
A division of the National Association of Home Builders of the United States.

National Remotivation Therapy Organization *(1972)*
P.O. Box 5
New Tripoli, PA 18066
Tel: (610)767-5028 *Fax:* (610)767-5034
E-Mail: lowhill@rcn.com
Web Site: www.remotivation.com
Members: 400 individuals
Staff: 1
Annual Budget: $10-25,000
Executive Secretary: Beverly Gruber
E-Mail: lowhill@rcn.com
Historical Note
Established in Philadelphia. NRTO members are certified remotivation therapists. Remotivation is a collaborative group therapy procedure emphasizing objective or shared aspects of personal experience. Membership: $30/year (individual).
Meetings/Conferences:
Annual Meetings: Fall
Publications:
Remotivator Newsletter. q. adv.

National Renal Administrators Association *(1977)*
1904 Naomi Place
Prescott, AZ 86303-5061
Tel: (928)717-2772 *Fax:* (928)441-3857
E-Mail: nraa@nraa.org
Web Site: www.nraa.org
Members: 800 individuals
Staff: 3
Annual Budget: $500-1,000,000
Executive Director: Michael Paget
Historical Note
NRAA was formed to provide a vehicle for the development of educational and informational services for administrative personnel involved in the ESRD program. Membership: $300/year (professional); $1,000/year (corporate).
Meetings/Conferences:
Semi-Annual Meetings: Fall and Spring
Publications:
Renal Watch newsletter (online). w. adv.
NRAA Membership Directory (online).

National Renderers Association *(1933)*
801 N. Fairfax St., Suite 205
Alexandria, VA 22314
Tel: (703)683-0155 *Fax:* (703)683-2626
Web Site: www.renderers.org
Members: 260 companies and plants
Staff: 12
Annual Budget: $2-5,000,000
President and Chief Executive Officer: Tom Cook
E-Mail: tcook@nationalrenderers.com
Historical Note
NRA is a trade organization representing companies which are producers of animal byproducts and supplier firms servicing the industry. Membership: varies.
Meetings/Conferences:
Annual Meetings: October-November/600
2007 – Miami, FL(Ritz Carlton)/Oct. 23-26/400
Publications:
Render. bi-m. adv.
Renditions. bi-m.

National Research Council *(1916)*
Historical Note
Established by the National Academy of Sciences in 1916 and perpetuated at the request of the President of the United States to serve as the operating arm of the National Academy of Sciences and the National Academy of Engineering for providing scientific and technical advice to the government, the public and the scientific and engineering communities. Administered by the National Academy of Sciences, the National Academy of Engineering and the Institue of Medicine. Not a membership organization.

National Restaurant Association *(1919)*
1200 17th St. NW
Washington, DC 20036-3097
Tel: (202)973-3677 *Fax:* (202)973-3961
E-Mail: media@dineout.orrg
Web Site: www.restaurant.org
Members: 300000 individuals
Staff: 225
Annual Budget: $25-50,000,000
President and Chief Executive Officer: Steven C. Anderson, CAE
Vice President, State Relations and Grassroots: Tim Foulkes
Senior Vice President, Conventions: Mary P. Heftman
Senior Vice President, Marketing, Communications and Media Relations: Sue Hensely
Director, Legislative Affairs: Michael Shutley
Historical Note
NRA is the foodservice industry's leading trade group with a membership representing more than 220,000 establishments. Maintains a Chicago office. Sponsors the National Restaurant Association Political Action Committee (NRA PAC). Has an annual budget of approximately $46 million. Membership: $125-20,000/year (company, based on sales volume).
Meetings/Conferences:
Annual Meetings: Chicago, IL/Spring
Publications:
Research News and Numbers (online). m.
Buyers Guide.
Restaurants U.S. q.
SmartBrief. d.
Washington Weekly. w.

National Retail Federation *(1911)*
325 Seventh St. NW
Suite 1100
Washington, DC 20004-2802
Tel: (202)783-7971 *Fax:* (202)737-2849
Toll Free: (800)673 - 4692
E-Mail: mullint@nrf.com
Web Site: www.nrf.com
Staff: 65
Annual Budget: $5-10,000,000
President and Chief Executive Officer: Tracy Mullin
Vice President, Membership: Denise Brasse
Senior Vice President and General Counsel: Mallory B. Duncan
Senior Vice President and Chief Information Officer: David Hogan
Senior Vice President and Chief Financial Officer: Carleen C. Kohut
Vice President, Industry Public Relations: Scott Krugman
Vice President, Conferences: Susan Newman
Senior Vice President, Government Relations: Steve Pfister
Historical Note
Founded as National Retail Dry Good Association; became the National Retail Merchants Association in 1958. Assumed its present name after merging with the American Retail Federation in 1990. Absorbed the Apparel Retailers of America in 1995. NRF is the world's largest retail trade association, with membership that includes the leading department, specialty, discount, mass merchandise and independent stores, as well as 32 national and 50 state associations. NRF members represent an industry that encompasses over 1.4 million U.S. retail establishments, employs more than 20 million people (1 in 5 American workers), and registered sales in 1996 of more than $2.6 trillion. NRF's international members operate stores in more than 50 nations.
Meetings/Conferences:
Annual Meetings: Winter
Publications:
NRF Weekly Tax Update. w.
Washington Retail Insight. w.
Retail Trade Bulletin. m.
Stores. m. adv.
Retail Sales Outlook. q.

National Retail Hobby Stores Association *(1992)*
214 N. Hale St.
Wheaton, IL 60187
Tel: (630)510-4596 *Fax:* (630)510-4501
E-Mail: info@nrhsa.org
Web Site: www.nhrsa.org
Members: 350 companies
Staff: 5
Annual Budget: $100-250,000
Executive Director: Janet Svazas
Historical Note
Members are hobby store operators and suppliers to the retail hobby trade. Provides marketing and operating information to members. Membership: $50/year.
Meetings/Conferences:
Annual Meetings: Quarterly Meetings.
2007 – Las Vegas, NV(Hilton)/May 29-June 2
Publications:
Newsletter. bi-m.

National Retired Teachers Association
Historical Note
A division of American Association of Retired Persons, which provides administrative support.

National Reverse Mortgage Lenders Association *(1997)*
1400 16th St. NW
Suite 420
Washington, DC 20036
Tel: (202)939-1760 *Fax:* (202)265-4435
Web Site: www.nrmlaonline.org
Members: 125 companies
Staff: 7
Annual Budget: $250-500,000
Executve Director: Peter H. Bell
Publications:
Reverse Mortgage Advisor. q.

National Rifle Association of America *(1871)*
11250 Waples Mill Road
Fairfax, VA 22030
Tel: (703)267-1000 *Fax:* (703)267-3918
E-Mail: nra-contact@nra.org
Web Site: www.nra.org
Members: 4000000 individuals
Staff: 550
Annual Budget: Over $100,000,000
Executive Vice President: Wayne R. LaPierre, Jr.
E-Mail: nra-contact@nra.org

Historical Note

Formed August 19, 1871 in New York City "to promote and encourage rifle shooting on a scientific basis" and incorporated in the State of New York November 20, 1871 with General Ambrose Burnside as first President. It is the oldest sportsmen's organization in the U.S. Maintains the NRA Political Victory Fund and supports the Institute for Legislative Action (founded in 1975), its political action arm. Has an annual budget over $140 million. Membership: $35/year.

Meetings/Conferences:

Annual Meetings: Spring

Publications:

America's First Freedom. m. adv.
Woman's Outlook. m. adv.
Shooting Education Update. q. adv.
The American Hunter. m. adv.
American Rifleman. m. adv.
InSights. m. adv.
Shooting Sports USA. m. adv.

National Risk Retention Association *(1987)*

4248 Park Glen Road
Minneapolis, MN 55416
Tel: (952)928-4656 *Fax:* (952)929-1318
Toll Free: (800)999 - 4505
E-Mail: info@nrra-usa.org
Web Site: www.nrra-usa.org
Members: 44 individuals
Staff: 2
Annual Budget: $100-250,000
Executive Director: Patrick E. Winters, CAE
E-Mail: pwinters@nrra-usa.org

Meetings/Conferences:

Annual Meetings: Spring
2007 - Washington, DC/Sept. 26-28

Publications:

NRRA Newsletter. q. adv.
Membership Directory. a. adv.

National Roadside Vegetation Management Association *(1984)*

5616 Lynchburg Circle
Hueytown, AL 35023
Tel: (205)491-7574 *Fax:* (205)491-2725
E-Mail: jreynoldsnrvma@aol.com
Web Site: www.nrvma.org
Members: 750 individuals
Staff: 1
Annual Budget: $25-50,000
Executive Director: John R. Reynolds, CAE

Historical Note

NRVMA members are individuals concerned with the management, beautification, and maintenance of roadside vegetation. Membership: $110/year (individual).

Publications:

Newsletter. q.
Proceedings. a.

National Roof Deck Contractors Association *(1959)*

P.O. Box 1582
Westford, MA 01886-4996
Toll Free: (800)217 - 7944
E-Mail: nrdca@nrdca.org
Web Site: http://nrdca.org
Members: 60 companies
Staff: 2
Annual Budget: $50-100,000
Executive Director: Hubert T. Dudley

Historical Note

Members are contractors installing poured gypsum, lightweight insulating concrete and cementitious wood fiber structural roof deck systems. Formerly (until 1980) known as the Gypsum Roof Deck Foundation.

National Roofing Contractors Association *(1886)*

O'Hare International Center
10255 W. Higgins Road, Suite 600
Rosemont, IL 60018-5607
Tel: (847)299-9070 *Fax:* (847)299-1183
E-Mail: nrca@nrca.net
Web Site: www.nrca.net
Members: 5000 firms
Staff: 50
Annual Budget: $10-25,000,000
Executive Director: William Good, CAE
Associate Executive Director, Information Technology: Paul Apostolos
Vice President, Government Relations: Craig Brightup
E-Mail: cbrightup@nrca.net
Associate Executive Director, Operations: Jacki Golike
Associate Executive Director, Communications, Membership Development and International Relations: Carl Good
E-Mail: cgood@nrca.net
Associate Executive Director, Technical Services: Mark Graham
E-Mail: mgraham@nrca.net
Associate Executive Director, Meeting Services and Executive Director, National Roofing Foundation: Bennett Judson, CMP
E-Mail: bjudson@nrca.net
Associate Executive Director, Marketing/Express Info/Affiliate Relations/NRLRC: Alison LaValley, CAE
E-Mail: alavalley@nrca.net
Associate Executive Director, Finance and Information Management: Harry Ryder, CPA
E-Mail: hryder@nrca.net
Associate Executive Director, Education and Risk Management: Thomas Shanahan, CAE
E-Mail: tshanahan@nrca.net

Historical Note

NRCA is a non-profit, tax exempt association of roofing, roof deck, sheet metal and waterproofing contractors and industry-related associates.

Meetings/Conferences:

Annual Meetings: Late Winter

Publications:

NRCA Annual Membership Directory. a. adv.
Professional Roofing. m. adv.
Material Reference Guide.

National Rural Economic Developers Association

431 E. Locust St., Suite 300
Des Moines, IA 50309
Tel: (515)284-1421 *Fax:* (515)243-2049
E-Mail: director@nreda.org
Web Site: www.nreda.org
Executive Director: Molly Lopez, CAE

Historical Note

NREDA members are economic development professionals with a special interest in rural utility and telecommunications projects. Membership: $225/year (individual); $350/year (company).

Meetings/Conferences:

Annual Meetings: Fall

National Rural Education Association *(1907)*

820 Van Vleet Oval, Room 227
University of Oklahoma
Norman, OK 73019
Tel: (405)325-7959
Web Site: www.nrea.net
Members: 1400individualsandorganizations
Staff: 2
Annual Budget: $100-250,000
Executive Director: Bob Mooneyham

Historical Note

Established as the Department of Rural and Agricultural Education of the National Education Association, it became the Rural Education Association in 1959, the Rural Regional Education Association in 1975, the Rural Education Association in 1986 and assumed its present name in 1987. Purpose is to improve and expand public education in rural areas. Membership: $85/year (individual); $35/year (teachers); $30/year (libraries); $225/year (institution); and $250/year (affiliate).

Meetings/Conferences:

Annual Meetings: Fall
2007 - Oklahoma City, OK/

Publications:

The NREA News. 4/year. adv.
The Rural Educator. 3/year. adv.

National Rural Electric Cooperative Association *(1942)*

4301 Wilson Blvd.
Arlington, VA 22203-1860
Tel: (703)907-5500 *Fax:* (703)907-5511
Web Site: www.nreca.coop
Members: 1000 cooperatives
Staff: 500
Annual Budget: Over $100,000,000
Chief Executive Officer: Glenn L. English
Vice President, Education, Training and Consulting: James Collins
Editor, Rural Electric Magazine: Frank Galant
Executive Vice President, Internal Services: Patrick Gioffre
Vice President, Marketing: Lauren E. Haywood
Director, Media and Public Relations: Patrick Lavigne
Executive Vice President, External Affairs: Martin Lowery
Vice President, Communications: Zan McKelway
Director, Meetings and Conventions: Russell McKinnon
Vice President, Government Relations: Dena Stoner
Chief Counsel and Vice President, Energy Policy: Wallace F. Tillman

Historical Note

NRECA's membership consists of cooperative systems, public power and public utility districts. Has an annual budget of approximately $140 million. Sponsors and supports the Action for Rural Electrification Political Action Committee (ACRE PAC).

Meetings/Conferences:

Annual Meetings: Late Winter/14,000

Publications:

Management Quarterly. m.
Rural Electric Magazine. m. adv.
Electric Co-Op Today. w.

National Rural Health Association *(1977)*

One W. Armour Blvd., Suite 203
Kansas City, MO 64111-2087
Tel: (816)756-3140 *Fax:* (816)756-3144
E-Mail: mail@nrharural.org
Web Site: www.NRHArural.org
Staff: 15
Annual Budget: $2-5,000,000
Chief Executive Officer: Alan Morgan

Historical Note

Formerly (1984) National Rural Primary Care Association and (1987) National Rural Health Care Association. Absorbed the American Rural Health Association and the American Small and Rural Hospital Association in 1986. Members are rural health professionals and institutions involved in rural health care. Has a government affairs office in Washington, DC. Membership: $200/year (individual); $660-1,980/year (organization); $3,500/year (supporting); $35/year (advocate); $35/year (student).

Meetings/Conferences:

Annual Meetings: Spring

Publications:

Rural Roads Magazine. q. adv.
NRHA eNews. bi-w. adv.
Journal of Rural Health. q. adv.

National Rural Letter Carriers' Association *(1903)*

1630 Duke St.
Fourth Floor
Alexandria, VA 22314-3465
Tel: (703)684-5545 *Fax:* (703)548-8735
Web Site: www.nrlca.org
Members: 106000 individuals
Staff: 25
Annual Budget: $10-25,000,000
President: Donnie Pitts
Vice President: Don Cantriel
Secretary-Treasurer: Clifford D. Dailing
Office Manager: Mary Doherty
Accountant: Monica J. Felder
Senior Advisor, Government Affairs: Ken Parmelee
Coordinator, Convention: Ruth C. Pugh
Managing Editor: Melissa Ray

Historical Note

Independent labor union organized in Chicago in 1903 and composed of 48 state associations. NRLCA is the exclusive bargaining representative for rural carriers. Sponsors and supports the National Rural Letter Carriers Association Political Action Committee. Membership: fees vary by state.

Meetings/Conferences:

2007 - Grand Rapids, MI
2008 - Lexington, KY

2009 – Grapevine, TX

Publications:
The National Rural Letter Carrier. m. adv.

National Rural Water Association *(1976)*
2915 S. 13th St.
Duncan, OK 73533
Tel: (580)252-0629 *Fax:* (580)255-4476
E-Mail: info@nrwa.org
Web Site: www.nrwa.org
Members: 900 individuals
Staff: 39
Annual Budget: $25-50,000
Chief Executive Officer: Robert K. Johnson
Deputy Chief Executive Officer: Sam Wade

Historical Note
NRWA is a water, wastewater and groundwater public utility membership organization representing over 25,000 utilities through state rural water affiliates. NRWA provides training, technical assistance, retirement and legislative representation services, and sponsors and supports the NRWA Political Action Committee (Water PAC). Has an annual budget of approximately $46 million. Membership: $25/year (individual).

Meetings/Conferences:
Annual Meetings: October-November

Publications:
Rural Water Magazine. q. adv.
Educational Materials. irreg.

National Safety Council *(1913)*
1121 Spring Lake Dr.
Itasca, IL 60143-3201
Tel: (630)285-1121 *Fax:* (630)285-1315
Web Site: www.nsc.org
Members: 15000 companies
Staff: 250
Annual Budget: $25-50,000,000
President: Alan McMillan
Vice President, Safety and Health Programs: Paulette Moulos
Executive Director, Publications: Suzanne Powills

Historical Note
Founded September 24, 1913 in Chicago as the National Council for Industrial Safety. Became the National Safety Council in 1914 and was granted a charter by Congress August 13, 1953 to arouse and maintain the interest in safety and accident prevention, and to encourage the adoption and institution of safety methods by all persons, corporations and other organizations. Has an annual budget of $46 million.

Meetings/Conferences:
Annual Meetings: Fall, Nat'l Safety Congress & Exposition/20,000

Publications:
Family Safety and Health. q.
Journal of Safety Research. q.
Safety and Health. m. adv.

National Safety Management Society *(1966)*
P.O. Box 4460
Walnut Creek, CA 94596-0460
Toll Free: (800)321 - 2910
E-Mail: info@nsms.us
Web Site: www.nsms.us
Members: 800 individuals
Staff: 1
Annual Budget: $25-50,000
Executive Director: Jeffrey Chung, Ph.D., CSHM

Historical Note
A professional society dedicated to the advancement of new concepts of accident prevention and loss control, promoting the role of safety management as an indispensable tool for management improvement, and providing the individual member an opportunity for professional growth. Membership is open to anyone with safety program and/or management responsibilities. NSMS also offers several nat'l certifications: Certified Safety Technician (CST) and Certified Safety Supervisor (CSS). Membership: $70/year; $40/year (new member application fee).

Meetings/Conferences:
Annual Meetings: Summer/Fall

Publications:
NSMS Digest (online). m. adv.
Journal of Safety Management. irreg. adv.

National Sailing Industry Association

Historical Note
A promotional council comprised of National Marine Manufacturers Association members interested in promoting amateur sailing.

National Sales and Marketing Council

Historical Note
A council of the National Association of Home Builders of the United States.

National Scholastic Press Association

Historical Note
See Associated Collegiate Press, National Scholastic Press Association.

National School Boards Association *(1940)*
1680 Duke St.
Alexandria, VA 22314-3407
Tel: (703)838-6722 *Fax:* (703)683-7590
E-Mail: info@nsba.org
Web Site: www.nsba.org
Members: 53 state level organizations
Staff: 140
Annual Budget: $10-25,000,000
Executive Director: Anne L. Bryant, Ed.D., CAE
E-Mail: abryant@nsba.org
Associate Executive Director, Federation Member Services and Outreach: Richard Anderson
Associate Executive Director, Constitutent Services, Publications and Marketing: Don Blom
Director, Council of School Attorneys: Susan R. Butler, CAE
Associate Executive Director, Finance, Technology and Management: Susan Merry
Associate Executive Director and General Counsel: Francisco Negron, Jr.
Associate Executive Director, Advocacy and Issues Management: Michael Resnick
Deputy Executive Director: Joseph Villani

Historical Note
Formerly (1940) National Council of State School Boards Assn's. NSBA Has an annual budget of approximately $25 million.

Meetings/Conferences:
Annual Meetings: Spring/20,000

Publications:
American School Board Journal. m. adv.
School Board News. bi-w. adv.
Action Alert. irreg.

National School Public Relations Association *(1935)*
15948 Derwood Road
Rockville, MD 20855-2123
Tel: (301)519-0496 *Fax:* (301)519-0494
E-Mail: nspra@nspra.org
Web Site: www.nspra.org
Members: 1997 individuals
Staff: 9
Annual Budget: $1-2,000,000
Executive Director: Richard Bagin, APR
Business Coordinator: Tom Jones
Associate Director: Karen Kleinz

Historical Note
Formerly (1950) School Public Relations Association. Individuals from school districts, national, state and local associations, state education agencies, school-community relations programs, and information agencies. Membership: $225/year (professional); $485/year (institutional).

Meetings/Conferences:
Annual Meetings: July/600
2007 – Phoenix, AZ(South Point Resort)/July/750

Publications:
NSPRA This Week. w.
NSPRA Alert Newsletter. 6/year.
Principal Communicator. m.
NSPRA Opportunities Newsletter. 6/year. adv.
NSPRA Counselor Newsletter. 4/year.
NSPRA Website. w. adv.
NSPRA Network. m.
Communication Matters for Leading Superintendants. 6/yr. adv.

National School Supply and Equipment Association *(1916)*
8380 Colesville Road, Suite 250
Silver Spring, MD 20910
Tel: (301)495-0240 *Fax:* (301)495-3330
Toll Free: (800)395 - 5550
E-Mail: nssea@nssea.org
Web Site: www.nssea.org
Members: 1500 companies
Staff: 14
Annual Budget: $1-2,000,000
President and Chief Executive Officer: Tim Holt
Vice President, Operations: William T. Duffy
E-Mail: bduffy@nssea.org
Coordinator, Meetings: Monique Ferguson
E-Mail: mferguson@nssea.org
Information Technology Manager: Alice Frazier
E-Mail: afrazier@nssea.org
Membership Manager: Karen Price
Vice President, Marketing: Adrienne Watts
E-Mail: awatts@nssea.org

Historical Note
Formerly (1958) National School Service Institute. Members are manufacturers, distributors, retailers and independent manufacturers representatives of school supplies, instructional materials and equipment. Absorbed the Education Industries Association in 1978.

Meetings/Conferences:
Semi-Annual Meetings: Spring and Fall/1,500-2,300
2007 – Atlanta, GA(Georgia World Congress Center)/March 1-3
2008 – Orlando, FL(Orlando Convention Center)/March 6-8
2009 – Dallas, TX(Dallas Convention Center)/March 5-7

Publications:
Membership Directory. a. adv.
State of the School Market. a.
Essentials. a. adv.

National School Transportation Association *(1964)*
113 S. West St., Suite 400
Alexandria, VA 22314
Tel: (703)684-3200 *Fax:* (703)684-3212
E-Mail: info@schooltrans.com
Web Site: www.yellowbuses.org
Members: 1500 companies and individuals
Staff: 2
Annual Budget: $250-500,000
Executive Director: Jeffrey Kulick

Historical Note
Formerly (1975) National Association of School Bus Contract-Operators. Founded in 1964 to represent the interests of school bus contractors, NSTA works with government officials, parents, teachers and all others interested in school bus safety. Supports the Non-Partisan Transportation Action Committee (political action). Membership: $115-7,600/year ($18.50 per vehicle/year).

Meetings/Conferences:
Annual Meetings: July/400

Publications:
NSTA Newsletter. bi-w.
NSTA Washington Update Fax. bi-w.

National Science Education Leadership Association *(1960)*
P.O. Box 99381
Raleigh, NC 27624-9381
Tel: (919)848-8171 *Fax:* (919)848-0496
Web Site: www.nsela.org
Members: 900 individuals
Staff: 1
Annual Budget: $25-50,000
Executive Director: Peggy W. Holliday
E-Mail: pegholli@bellsouth.net

Historical Note
Formerly (1994) National Science Supervisors Association. An affiliate of the National Science Teachers Association and the American Association for the Advancement of Science, NSELA members include department heads, supervisors, consultants, administrators, coordinators and directors of science

programs in public and private educational institutions. Membership: $35/year (individual or company).

Meetings/Conferences:
Annual Meetings: usually in conjunction with Nat'l Science Teachers Ass'n meeting

Publications:
The Navigator. q. adv.
Membership Directory. a. adv.
Science Educator Journal. a. adv.

National Science Teachers Association
1840 Wilson Blvd.
Arlington, VA 22201-3000
Tel: (703)243-7100 *Fax:* (703)243-7177
Toll Free: (800)722 - 6782
Web Site: www.nsta.org
Members: 53000 individuals
Staff: 110
Annual Budget: $10-25,000,000
Executive Director: Gerald F. Wheeler, Ph.D.
Associate Director, Publications: David Beacom
Associate Director, Operations: Moira Fathy

Historical Note
NSTA is committed to promoting excellence and innovation in science teaching and learning for all. The association provides many programs and services to science educators, including awards and professional development workshops. NSTA also serves as an advocate for science educators through its programs and legislative campaigns. Membership includes science teachers, scientists, and others involved in science education.

Meetings/Conferences:
Annual Meetings: Spring
2007 - TBA/Apr. 12-15
2008 - Boston, MA/March 27-30
2009 - Indianapolis, IN/Apr. 2-5
2010 - Washington, DC/March 18-21
2011 - San Francisco, CA/Apr. 7-10

Publications:
Journal of College Science Teaching. 6/year. adv.
NSTA Reports. 6/year. adv.
Science and Children. 8/year. adv.
Science Scope. 8/year. adv.
The Science Teacher. 9/year.
Quantum. 6/year.

National Sculpture Society *(1893)*
237 Park Ave.
New York, NY 10017
Tel: (212)764-5645 *Fax:* (212)764-5651
E-Mail: info@nationalsculpture.org
Web Site: www.nationalsculpture.org
Members: 4000 individuals
Staff: 4
Annual Budget: $500-1,000,000
Executive Director: Gwen Pier

Historical Note
Mission is to promote excellence in sculpture throughout the United States, to which end its programs are directed. Programs include exhibitions, publications, educational scholarships, and awards for sculptors.

Meetings/Conferences:
Annual Meetings: always at headquarters New York, NY/January/65-80

Publications:
Sculpture Review. q. adv.
News Bulletin. bi-m.

National Seasoning Manufacturers Association *(1973)*
8905 Maxwell Dr., Suite 200
Potomac, MD 20854-3125
Tel: (301)765-9675 *Fax:* (301)299-7523
E-Mail: alsmeyerfood@isp.com
Members: 28 companies
Staff: 1
Annual Budget: $10-25,000
Executive Director: Dr. Richard H. Alsmeyer

Historical Note
Established as the Industrial Meat Seasoning Manufacturers Association; later became the National Association of Meat Seasoning Manufacturers. In 1981, became the National Association of Meat and Food Seasoning Manufacturers; assumed its present name in 1984. Promotes scientific study and research in the seasoning industry. Membership: $750/year.

Meetings/Conferences:
Annual Meetings: With the Institute of Food Technologists

Selected Independent Funeral Homes *(1917)*
500 Lake Cook Road, Suite 205
Deerfield, IL 60015
Toll Free: (800)323 - 4219
E-Mail: info@selectedfuneralhomes.org
Web Site: www.selectedfuneralhomes.org
Members: 950 firms
Staff: 10
Annual Budget: $500-1,000,000
Executive Director: George Clarke
E-Mail: info@selectedfuneralhomes.org

Meetings/Conferences:
Annual Meetings: Fall/900

Publications:
NSM Bulletin. m.

National Shellfisheries Association *(1908)*
c/o U.S. EPA, Atlantic Ecology Div.
27 Tazewell Dr.
Narragansett, RI 02880
Tel: (401)782-3155 *Fax:* (401)782-3030
E-Mail: news@shellfish.org
Web Site: www.shellfish.org
Members: 1000 individuals
Annual Budget: $50-100,000
Secretary: Maureen K. Krause

Historical Note
Organized as National Association of Shellfish Commissioners; assumed its present name in 1930 and was incorporated in Maryland in 1968. Members are individuals interested in research on that group of mollusks and crustaceans of economic importance known as shellfish. Has no paid officers or full-time staff. Membership: $65/year (full member); $35/year (student).

Meetings/Conferences:
Annual Meetings: late Spring

Publications:
Journal of Shellfish Research. semi-a.
Newsletter. q.

National Sheriffs' Association *(1940)*
1450 Duke St.
Alexandria, VA 22314-3490
Tel: (703)836-7827 *Fax:* (703)683-6541
Toll Free: (800)424 - 7827
E-Mail: nsamail@sheriffs.org
Web Site: www.sheriffs.org
Members: 25000 individuals
Staff: 45
Annual Budget: $2-5,000,000
Executive Director: Thomas N. Faust
Director, Membership: Yanecia Green
Director, Meetings: Ross F. Mirmelstein
Legislative Liaison: Matt Socknat
Director, Publications: Michael Terault

Historical Note
The NSA is dedicated to assisting sheriffs and other law enforcement practitioners to perform their duties in the most professional manner possible. Membership: $25-100/year (individual); $1,000/year (organization).

Meetings/Conferences:
Annual Meetings: June/3,500

Publications:
Sheriff Magazine. bi-m. adv.

National Shoe Retailers Association *(1912)*
7150 Columbia Gateway Dr., Suite G
Columbia, MD 21046-1151
Tel: (410)381-8282 *Fax:* (410)381-1167
E-Mail: info@nsra.org
Web Site: www.nsra.org
Members: 1800 companies
Staff: 12
Annual Budget: $500-1,000,000
President: James F. Hollan, II
Meetings and Conventions Planner: Deb Martinez
E-Mail: deb@nsra.org
Director, Education: Cynthia Mullaly

Historical Note
NSRA members are owners and managers of independent shoe stores. NSRA provides its members with business services, educational programs and business consulting services.

Meetings/Conferences:
Semi-Annual Meetings: Las Vegas, NV/February and August/300
2007 - Las Vegas, NV
2008 - Las Vegas, NV

Publications:
Shoe Retailing Today. bi-m.
Business Performance Report. bien.

National Shooting Sports Foundation *(1961)*
11 Mile Hill Road
Newtown, CT 06470-2359
Tel: (203)426-1320 *Fax:* (203)426-1087
E-Mail: info@nssf.org
Web Site: www.nssf.org
Members: 2000 businesses
Staff: 40
Annual Budget: $10-25,000,000
President: Doug Painter
Senior Vice President: Chris Doluak
Senior Vice President and General Counsel: Lawrence Keane

Meetings/Conferences:
Annual Meetings: January/February; annual Shot Show
2007 - Orlando, FL(Orange County Convention Center)/Jan. 11-14

Publications:
Range Report. q. adv.
NSSF Reports. 11/yr.
Shot Business. 7/yr. adv.

National Show Horse Registry *(1982)*
10368 Bluegrass Pkwy.
Louisville, KY 40299-2221
Tel: (502)266-5100 *Fax:* (502)266-5806
E-Mail: nshowhorse@aol.com
Web Site: www.nshregistry.org
Members: 1400 individuals
Staff: 2
Annual Budget: $500-1,000,000
Manager: Brenda Jett
E-Mail: nshowhorse@aol.com

Historical Note
The purpose of the Registry is to create a high performance, low maintenance show horse and to encourage the amateur as well as the professional competitor. Membership: $60/year (adult member, farm or corporation); $25/year (youth member).

Meetings/Conferences:
Annual Meetings: Fall

Publications:
National Show Horse. bi-m. adv.

National Shrimp Industry Association *(1957)*
1520 Berkeley Road
Highland Park, IL 60035
Tel: (847)831-2030 *Fax:* (847)831-2343
E-Mail: info@nsiaonline.org
Web Site: www.nsiaonline.org
Members: 40 processors
Annual Budget: $10-25,000
Coordinator: Beth Dancy
E-Mail: info@nsiaonline.org

Historical Note
Founded as National Shrimp Breeders and Processors Association; became National Shrimp Processors Association in 1984 and assumed its current name in 2001. Membership: $500/year (corporate).

Meetings/Conferences:
Annual Meetings: February/100

Publications:
Newsnet. q.

National Ski and Snowboard Retailers Association *(1987)*
1601 Feehanville Dr., Suite 300
Mt. Prospect, IL 60056
Tel: (847)391-9825 *Fax:* (847)391-9827
Web Site: www.nssra.com
Members: 400 companies

Staff: 1
Annual Budget: $10-25,000
President: Thomas B. Doyle

Historical Note

Formerly National Ski Retailers Association (1996). Retail association providing ski and snowboard shops with business-related services and representation. Administrative support for NSSRA is provided by ASMI, a subsidiary of National Sporting Goods Association (same location). Membership: $115-300/year.

Meetings/Conferences:

Annual Meetings: January/50
2007 – Las Vegas, NV(Convention Center)/Jan. 23- /50

Publications:

NSSRA Newsletter. q.
NSSRA Cost of Doing Business Survey. bi-a.

National Ski Areas Association *(1962)*

133 S. Van Gordon St., Suite 300
Lakewood, CO 80228
Tel: (303)987-1111 *Fax:* (303)986-2345
E-Mail: nsaa@nsaa.org
Web Site: www.nsaa.org
Members: 332 ski areas and 428 suppliers
Staff: 15
Annual Budget: $1-2,000,000
President: Michael Berry
Director, Member Services: Kate Powers
Director, Education: Tim White

Historical Note

NSAA is a trade association for ski area owners and operators. The association's member areas represent about 90 percent of the skier visits nationwide. For its members, NSAA develops educational programs and employee training materials, and provides information on important industry issues including: OSHA, ADA, NEPA, environmental laws, state regulatory industries, aerial tramway safety and area operations. NSAA also analyzes and provides industry statistics for members and participates in state and federal lobbying efforts.

Meetings/Conferences:

Annual Meetings: Spring

Publications:

NSAA Journal.

National Ski Patrol System *(1938)*

133 S. Van Gordon St., Suite 100
Lakewood, CO 80228-1706
Tel: (303)988-1111 *Fax:* (303)988-3005
E-Mail: nsp@nsp.org
Web Site: www.nsp.org
Members: 24500 individuals
Staff: 20
Annual Budget: $500-1,000,000
Administrative Director: Frankie Jean Barr
Director, Communications: Rebecca Ayers

Historical Note

Started in 1938 by Minot Dole. Chartered in 1980 by Act of Congress to promote ski safety and the sport of skiing and, under the direction of ski area management, to render immediate first aid to injured skiers and evacuate them from slopes for further attention. Members are trained in all phases of ski patrolling, including W.E.C. first aid, ski mountaineering, avalanche patrol and lift evacuation.

Meetings/Conferences:

Annual Meetings: June

Publications:

Ski Patrol Magazine. q.

National Slag Association *(1918)*

25 Stevens Ave., Bldg. A
West Lawn, PA 19609
Tel: (610)670-0701 *Fax:* (610)670-0702
E-Mail: info@nationalslagassoc.org
Web Site: www.nationalslagassoc.org
Members: 35 processors
Staff: 2
Annual Budget: $100-250,000
President: Terry R. Wagaman
E-Mail: info@nationalslagassoc.org

Historical Note

Members are processors of iron and steel slags for use as a mineral aggregate in construction and manufacturing applications.

Publications:

NSA Bulletin.
The Slag Runner.

National Small Business Association *(1937)*

1156 15th St. NW, Suite 1100
Washington, DC 20005
Tel: (202)293-8830 *Fax:* (202)872-8543
Web Site: www.nsba.biz
Members: 65000 individuals
Staff: 16
President: Todd O. McCracken
E-Mail: tmccracken@nsba.biz
Vice President, Membership Development: Patrick Post
Director, Administration: Rosa Wright
Director, Communications: Rob Yunich

Historical Note

Founded and incorporated in Ohio in 1937, the NSBA is a volunteer directed association. Originally the National Small Business Men's Association, it became the National Small Business Association in 1962, the same year in which the American Association of Small Business was absorbed. Merged with Small Business United in 1986 and changed its name to National Small Business United; reverted to the NSBA name in 2003. Sponsors and supports the NSBU Political Action Committee. Acts as an advocate for the small business community. The primary mission of the NSBA is to advocate state and federal policies which are beneficial to small business, the state, and the nation and to promote the growth of free enterprise.

Meetings/Conferences:

Semi-Annual Meetings: Winter and Spring

Publications:

NSBA Advocate. bi-m. adv.

National Small Shipments Traffic Conference *(1952)*

380 Industrial Blvd.
Waconia, MN 55387
Tel: (952)442-8850 *Fax:* (952)442-3941
Web Site: www.nasstrac.org
Members: 400 companies
Staff: 2
Annual Budget: $500-1,000,000
Executive Director: Brian Everett

Historical Note

Founded in 1952 by former members of The National Industrial Traffic League, making LTL ("less than truckload") shipments. Members are truck, air, rail and sea shippers of freight weighing less than 10,000 pounds. Membership fee based on gross annual sales.

Meetings/Conferences:

Semi-annual meetings: Spring and Fall/175

Publications:

NASSTRAC Newslink. m. adv.

National Soccer Coaches Association of America *(1941)*

6700 Squibb Road, Suite 215
Mission, KS 66202
Tel: (913)362-1747 *Fax:* (913)362-3439
Toll Free: (800)458 - 0678
Web Site: www.nscaa.com
Members: 17000 individuals
Staff: 11
Annual Budget: $2-5,000,000
Executive Director: Jim Sheldon
E-Mail: jsheldon@nscaa.com
Assistant Executive Director, Communications: Craig Bohnert
E-Mail: cbohnert@nscaa.com
Director, Coaching Education: Jeff Tipping
E-Mail: jtipping@nscaa.com
Associate Executive Director, Administration: Steve Veal
E-Mail: sveal@nscaa.com
Membership Coordinator: Sandy Williamson
E-Mail: swilliamson@nscaa.com
Assistant Executive Director, Marketing: Chris Wyche

Historical Note

NSCAA's purpose is to educate coaches and promote the game of soccer. Has an annual budget of approximately $4.2 million. Membership: $70/year (regular); $50/year (youth coach).

Meetings/Conferences:

Annual Meetings: January/5,000

Publications:

Soccer Journal. bi-m. adv.

National Society for Experiential Education *(1971)*

515 King St., Suite 420
Alexandria, VA 22314
Tel: (703)706-9552 *Fax:* (703)684-6048
E-Mail: staff@nsee.org
Web Site: www.nsee.org
Members: 1500 individuals
Staff: 2
Annual Budget: $250-500,000
Executive Director: Carole M. Rogin
E-Mail: staff@nsee.org
Director, Operations: Haley J. Brust

Historical Note

NSEE is an education membership association and acts as a clearinghouse for information on experiential and service learning. Members are college and K-12 faculty; directors of internship, service-learning, school to work, and cooperative education programs; principals, superintendents, and deans; career counselors; and employers who sponsor interns who all have an interest in fostering the effective use of experience as an integral part of education. Experiential Education includes internships, service-learning, school-to-work, cooperative education, field studies, cross-cultural education, leadership development, and active learning in the classroom. Formerly (1992) the National Society For Internships and Experiential Education. Membership: $95/year (individual); $375-1,000/year (institution).

Meetings/Conferences:

Annual Meetings: Fall

Publications:

NSEE Quarterly. q.

National Society for Graphology *(1972)*

250 W. 57th St., Suite 1228-A
New York, NY 10107
Tel: (212)265-1148
Web Site: www.handwriting.org/nsg/nsgmain.htm l
Members: 300 individuals
Staff: 1
Annual Budget: under $10,000
President: Ada Gilman

Historical Note

Members are professional graphologists and individuals interested in graphology. NSG promotes the study and practice of gestalt graphology. Membership $65/year (individual).

Meetings/Conferences:

Eight Meetings Annually: usually New York, NY (Warwick Hotel)

Publications:

Write-Up Newsletter. bi-m.

National Society for Healthcare Foodservice Management *(1990)*

355 Lexington Ave., 17th Floor
New York, NY 10017
Tel: (212)297-2166 *Fax:* (212)370-9047
E-Mail: info@hfm.org
Web Site: www.hfm.org
Members: 3500 individuals
Staff: 6
Annual Budget: $250-500,000
Executive Director: Carolynn Jennings

Historical Note

HFM members are independent, self-operated healthcare foodservice managers and suppliers to the industry. Membership: $175/year (individual); $700/year (corporate); $50/year (student); $150/year (educational institution).

Meetings/Conferences:

Annual Meetings: Summer-Fall

Publications:

Innovator. q. adv.
Membership & Networking Directory. a. adv.

National Society for Hebrew Day Schools *(1944)*
160 Broadway
New York, NY 10038
Tel: (212)227-1000 *Fax:* (212)406-6934
E-Mail: umesorah@aol.com
Members: 675 organizations
Staff: 25
Annual Budget: $500-1,000,000
Executive Vice President: Rabbi Joshua Fishman
E-Mail: umesorah@aol.com

Historical Note
Torah Umesorah was originally organized by Rabbinical leaders of Eastern Europe who found haven in America and who wished to re-establish Jewish centers of learning on this continent. NSHDS is the North American organization for Torah Umesorah, supporting the religious and secular learning traditions of the Hebrew Day School. Provides a range of services to member schools.

National Society for Histotechnology *(1973)*
4201 Northview Dr., Suite 502
Bowie, MD 20716-2604
Tel: (301)262-6221 *Fax:* (301)262-9188
E-Mail: histo@nsh.org
Web Site: www.nsh.org
Members: 4500 individuals
Staff: 5
Annual Budget: $500-1,000,000
Executive Director: Carrie Diamond

Historical Note
Members are laboratory personnel who study tissues and prepare slides for diagnosis by a pathologist. Membership: $60/year (individual); $250/year (organization/company).

Meetings/Conferences:
Annual Meetings: Fall
2007 – Denver, CO/Oct. 26-31

Publications:
Journal of Histotechnology. q. adv.
NSH in Action newsletter. q.

National Society for Park Resources *(1921)*

Historical Note
An affiliate of National Recreation and Park Association (same address), which provides administrative support.

National Society for the Study of Education *(1901)*
Univ. of Illinois, College of Education
1040 W. Harrison St., M/C 147
Chicago, IL 60607-7133
Tel: (312)996-4529
E-Mail: nsse@uic.edu
Web Site: www.nsse-chicago.org
Members: 1500 individuals
Staff: 2
Annual Budget: $100-250,000
Program Director: Debra Miretzky
E-Mail: dmiret1@uic.edu

Historical Note
A professional society of professors, administrators, and teachers established as the National Herbart Society for the Scientific Study of Education; assumed its present name in 1910. Membership: $40/year (regular).

Publications:
Yearbooks of The NSSE. a.

National Society of Accountants *(1945)*
1010 N. Fairfax St.
Alexandria, VA 22314-1574
Tel: (703)549-6400 *Fax:* (703)549-2984
Toll Free: (800)966 - 6679
Web Site: www.nsacct.org
Members: 30000 individuals
Staff: 21
Annual Budget: $2-5,000,000
Executive Vice President: John G. Ams
E-Mail: jams@nsacct.org
Director, Marketing and Member Services: Jodi Goldberg

Historical Note
Formerly (1996) National Society of Public Accountants. NSA is a professional society of practicing accountants and tax practitioners. Sponsors the Accreditation Council for Accountancy and Taxation. Supports the National Society of Public Accountants Political Action Committee and NSPA Scholarship Foundation. Membership: $159/year (individual).

Meetings/Conferences:
Annual Meetings: August/1000

Publications:
MemberLink. bi-w. adv.
NSAlert. bi-w.
NSA Technology Advisor. 8/year.

National Society of Accountants for Cooperatives *(1936)*
136 S. Keowee St.
Dayton, OH 45402
Tel: (937)222-6707 *Fax:* (937)222-5794
E-Mail: info@nsacoop.org
Web Site: www.nsacoop.org
Members: 1650 individuals
Staff: 10
Annual Budget: $250-500,000
Executive Director: Kim Fantaci

Historical Note
Members are accountants, attorneys, financial officers and other professionals actively involved in the financial planning and management of cooperative businesses. Membership: $150/year (indvidual).

Meetings/Conferences:
Annual Meetings: August/400
2007 – Minneapolis, MN(Marriott)/Aug. 8-10

Publications:
The Cooperative Accountant. q.

National Society of Appraiser Specialists *(1969)*

Historical Note
An affiliate of National Association of Master Appraisers, which provides administrative support.

National Society of Black Physicists *(1977)*
6704G Lee Hwy.
Arlington, VA 22205
Tel: (703)536-4207 *Fax:* (703)536-4203
E-Mail: headquarters@nspb.org
Web Site: www.nsbp.org
Members: 300 individuals
Annual Budget: under $10,000
Executive Officer: Dr. David Beam
E-Mail: headquarters@nspb.org

Historical Note
NSBP recognizes the contributions of African-Americans to advances in the sciences in general and particularly in the field of physics. Promotes education in the sciences. Has no paid officers or full-time staff. Membership: $45/year (individual); $15/year (student); $2,500/year (organization).

Meetings/Conferences:
Annual Meetings: April
2007 – Boston, MA(Sheraton)/Feb. 21-25
2008 – Washington, DC(Omni Shoreham Hotel)/Feb. 20-24
2009 – Nashville, TN(Renaissance Hotel)/Feb. 15-19

Publications:
Newsletter. irreg.

National Society of Compliance Professionals *(1987)*
22 Kent Road
Cornwall Bridge, CT 06754
Tel: (860)672-0843 *Fax:* (860)672-3005
E-Mail: info@nscp.org
Web Site: www.nscp.org
Members: 1750 individuals
Staff: 8
Annual Budget: $1-2,000,000
President, Chief Executive Officer and Executive Director: Joan Hinchman
E-Mail: jhinchman@nscp.org
Manager, Membership Development Marketing: Georgette Mercado
E-Mail: gmercado@nscp.org
Certification Program Director: Lisa Nepi
Director, Publishing and Information Technology: Fred Vorck
Meeting Planner: Liza Wentworth

Historical Note
NSCP members are individuals responsible for insuring their company's compliance with securities laws and government regulations. Membership: $350/year (individual).

Meetings/Conferences:
Annual Meetings: Fall
2007 – Washington, DC(J. W. Marriott)/Oct. 17-19

Publications:
NSCP Hotline Memo. m.
NSCP Currents. bi-m.

National Society of EMS Administrators

Historical Note
A division of the National Association of Emergency Medical Technicians.

National Society of EMS Instructor/Coordinators

Historical Note
A division of the National Association of Emergency Medical Technicians.

National Society of EMT Paramedics

Historical Note
A division of the National Association of Emergency Medical Technicians.

National Society of Environmental Consultants *(1992)*

Historical Note
An affiliate of National Association of Master Appraisers, which provides administrative support.

National Society of Film Critics
c/o New York Metro
444 Madison Ave., Fourth Floor
New York, NY 10022
Annual Budget: under $10,000
Chairman: Peter Rainer

Historical Note
NFSC members are film critics working in print and broadcast. Has no paid officers or full-time staff.

National Society of Genetic Counselors *(1978)*
401 N. Michigan Ave.
Chicago, IL 60611
Tel: (312)321-6834 *Fax:* (312)673-6972
E-Mail: nsgc@nsgc.org
Web Site: www.nsgc.org
Members: 2100 individuals
Staff: 3
Annual Budget: $500-1,000,000
Executive Director: Kristen Smith
E-Mail: nsgc@nsgc.org

Historical Note
Incorporated in New York, NSGC was formed to further the professional interests of those with advanced education and experience in the areas of medical genetics and counseling separate from the concerns of any particular genetic disorder. Membership: $110/year (full); $90/year (associate); $60/year (student).

Meetings/Conferences:
Annual Meetings: Fall

Publications:
Journal of Genetic Counseling. q.
Perspectives in Genetic Counseling. q.
Membership Directory. a.

National Society of Hispanic MBAs *(1988)*
1303 Walnut Hill Lane, Suite 300
Irving, TX 75038
Tel: (214)596-9338 *Fax:* (214)596-9325
Toll Free: (877)467 - 4622
E-Mail: mraczynski@nshmba.org
Web Site: www.nshmba.org
Members: 6500 individuals
Staff: 11
Annual Budget: $2-5,000,000
Chapter Manager: Esther Gonzales Smith
E-Mail: egsmith@nshmba.org
Communications Specialist: Michelle Raczynski

Historical Note
Formed by a group of Hispanic MBAs in order to address the declining enrollment of Hispanics in graduate business programs and to promote the

growth of Hispanic MBAs in the private and public environments. Membership: $65/year (individual); $20/year (student).

Publications:
Bottom Line. m. adv.
Hispanic Professional. bien. adv.

National Society of Hypnotherapists *(1984)*
612 S. Jones Blvd.
Las Vegas, NV 89107
Tel: (702)395-0588 *Fax:* (702)386-2851
E-Mail: email@thensh.com
Web Site: ww.thensh.com
Members: 250 individuals
Staff: 1
Annual Budget: $25-50,000
Executive Director: Layne C. Keck
E-Mail: email@thensh.com
Meetings/Conferences:
Annual Meetings: September
Publications:
NSH Newsletter. m.

National Society of Insurance Premium Auditors *(1975)*
P.O. Box 1896
Columbus, OH 43216-1896
Tel: (614)221-9266 *Fax:* (614)221-2335
Toll Free: (888)846 - 7472
E-Mail: nsipa@nsipa.org
Web Site: www.nsipa.org
Members: 880 individuals
Annual Budget: $100-250,000
Executive Director: Brad L. Feldman, MPA
Historical Note
A professional society of auditors from insurance or fee service insurance auditing companies. Membership: $95/year.
Publications:
Newsline. q. adv.

National Society of Military EMTs
Historical Note
A division of the National Association of Emergency Medical Technicians.

National Society of Mural Painters *(1895)*
c/o American Fine Arts Soc.
215 W. 57th St.
New York, NY 10019
Tel: (212)941-0130
Web Site: www.anny.org/2/orgs/0041/mural.htm
Members: 120 individuals
Annual Budget: under $10,000
Executive Director: Regina Stewart
E-Mail: reginas@anny.org
Historical Note
Founded in 1895. NSMP members are muralists from all over the world chosen by a majority vote of the organization after a review of slides and biographical material. Membership: $45/yea (within NYC boundary); $25/year (outside NYC boundary).
Meetings/Conferences:
Annual Meetings: Spring/New York, NY
Publications:
National Society of Mural Painters Newsletter. q.

National Society of Newspaper Columnists *(1978)*
P.O. Box 156885
San Francisco, CA 94115
Tel: (415)541-5636 *Fax:* (415)563-5403
E-Mail: director@columnists.com
Web Site: www.columnists.com
Members: 510 individuals
Staff: 3
Annual Budget: $25-50,000
Executive Director: Luenna H. Kim
Historical Note
Members are columnists on daily newspapers. Membership: $50/year (individual); $50/year (foreign individual).
Meetings/Conferences:
Annual Meetings: June
Publications:
The Columnist. bi-m.

National Society of Painters in Casein and Acrylic *(1952)*
969 Catasauqua Road
Whitehall, PA 18052
Web Site: www.bright.net/~paddy-o/art/nspca.htm
Annual Budget: $10-25,000
President: Douglas Wiltraut
Historical Note
Established to give artists opportunity to exhibit works regardless of style, school, or subject matter. Membership limited to 150 professional artists (by invitation). Sponsors exhibitions and demonstrations of painting in casein, acrylic and polymer watercolor. Has no paid staff. Membership: $40/year (individual).
Publications:
Catalog. bien.

National Society of Professional Engineers *(1934)*
1420 King St.
Alexandria, VA 22314-2794
Tel: (703)684-2800 *Fax:* (703)836-4875
Toll Free: (888)285 - 6773
E-Mail: customer.service@nspe.org
Web Site: www.nspe.org
Members: 55000 individuals
Staff: 47
Annual Budget: $5-10,000,000
Executive Director: Albert C. Gray, CAE
E-Mail: agray@nspe.org
Director, Membership Development and Membership Services: Rob Bergeron
E-Mail: rbergeron@nspe.org
Director, Meetings: Polly P. Collins
E-Mail: pcollins@nspe.org
Senior Director, Strategic Planning: Stefan Jaeger
E-Mail: sjaeger@nspe.org
Director, Government Relations: Leland White
E-Mail: pcollins@nspe.org
Historical Note
Founded in New York City in 1934 and incorporated the same year in South Carolina. Consists of 54 state societies and more than 500 chapters. The National Institute for Certification in Engineering Technologies is a part of NSPE. Affiliated with the Accreditation Board for Engineering and Technology. Sponsors and supports the NSPE Political Action Committee, the NSPE Education Foundation, and the National Institute for Engineering Ethics.
Meetings/Conferences:
Semi-Annual Meetings: Winter and Summer
Publications:
Engineering Times. 11/year. adv.

National Society of Professional Surveyors *(1981)*
Six Montgomery Village Ave., Suite 403
Gaithersburg, MD 20879
Tel: (240)632-9716 Ext: 113 *Fax:* (240)632-1321
Web Site: www.nspsmo.org
Members: 4500 individuals
Staff: 1
Annual Budget: $250-500,000
Executive Administrator: Pat Canfield
Historical Note
A member organization of the American Congress on Surveying and Mapping. Membership is concurrent. Called the Land Surveys Division of ACSM until 1981 when it became a self-governing organization as the National Society of Professional Surveyors; assumed its present name in 1983.
Meetings/Conferences:
Annual Meetings: With the American Congress on Surveying and Mapping.
Publications:
Surveying and Land Information Science. q.
Membership Directory. irreg.

National Society of Real Estate Appraisers
Historical Note
An affiliate of the National Association of Real Estate Brokers.

National Soft Drink Association
Historical Note
Became American Beverage Association in 2004.

National Solid Wastes Management Association *(1982)*
4301 Connecticut Ave. NW
Suite 300
Washington, DC 20008
Tel: (202)244-4700 *Fax:* (202)966-4824
Toll Free: (800)424 - 2869
E-Mail: membership@envasns.org
Web Site: www.nswma.org
Members: 2000 companies
Staff: 35
Annual Budget: $250-500,000
President and Chief Executive Officer: Bruce J. Parker
Historical Note
A constituent group of the Environmental Industries Associations.
Meetings/Conferences:
Annual Meetings: with the Environment Industry Ass'ns.

National Speakers Association *(1973)*
1500 S. Priest Dr.
Tempe, AZ 85281
Tel: (480)968-2552 *Fax:* (480)968-0911
Web Site: www.nsaspeaker.org
Members: 4000 individuals
Staff: 20
Annual Budget: $2-5,000,000
Chief Executive Officer: Stacy Tetschner, CAE
Director, Communications: Marsha Mardock, APR, CAE
Director, Professional Development: Cara Tracy, CMP
E-Mail: cara@nsaspeaker.org
Historical Note
NSA is a leading organization for professional speakers. Since 1973, NSA has provided resources and education designed to advance the skills, integrity and value of its members and the speaking profession. Membership: $325/year.
Meetings/Conferences:
Annual Meetings: Summer
Publications:
Professional Speaker Magazine. m. adv.

National Speleological Society *(1941)*
2813 Cave Ave.
Huntsville, AL 35810-4431
Tel: (256)852-1300 *Fax:* (256)851-9241
Web Site: www.caves.org/~nss
Members: 12315 individuals
Staff: 4
Annual Budget: $500-1,000,000
Operations Manager: Stephanie Cothron-Searles
E-Mail: manager@caves.org
Historical Note
Founded and incorporated in the District of Columbia in January 1941. Affiliated with the American Association for the Advancement of Science, the National Parks and Conservation Association and the International Union of Speleology. Dedicated to the exploration, study and conservation of caves and caverns. Membership: $36/year (individual); $75/year (company); $7/year (family members); $15/year (general); $720/year (life).
Meetings/Conferences:
Annual Meetings: Summer
Publications:
American Caving Accidents. bien. adv.
NSS Members Manual. a. adv.
Journal of Cave and Karst Studies. 3/year. adv.
NSS News. m. adv.

National Spinal Cord Injury Association *(1948)*
6701 Democracy Blvd., Suite 300-9
Bethesda, MD 20817
Toll Free: (800)962 - 9629
E-Mail: info@spinalcord.org
Web Site: www.spinalcord.org
Members: 8000 individuals
Staff: 6
Annual Budget: $250-500,000
Executive Director: Marcie Roth

Historical Note

Founded by the Paralyzed Veterans of America in response to the medical and social problems arising from spinal cord injury within the civilian population. Focuses on information, referral and health maintenance. Members are individuals with spinal cord injuries, their families, health professionals, and others. Membership: $25/year (individual); $50/year (professional); $100/year, minimum (organization).

Publications:

SCI Life. q. adv.
SCI e-News. m.

National Sporting Goods Association *(1929)*
1601 Feehanville Dr., Suite 300
Mt. Prospect, IL 60056
Tel: (847)296-6742 *Fax:* (847)391-9827
Toll Free: (800)815 - 5422
Web Site: www.nsga.org
Members: 22000retailoutlets&500suppliers
Staff: 17
Annual Budget: $2-5,000,000
President and Chief Executive Officer: James L. Faltinek, Ph.D., CAE
Vice President, Information and Research: Thomas B. Doyle
Director, Membership: Rhonda Onuszko
Vice President, Business Development: Paul M. Prince
Director, Marketing and Education: Chuck Suritz
Vice President and Chief Financial Officer: William H. Webb, Jr.
E-Mail: bwebb@nsga.org
Director, Communications: Larry Weindruch
E-Mail: lweindruch@nsga.org
Vice President, Membership and Adminstration: Susan L. Wenderski
E-Mail: swenderski@nsga.org

Historical Note

NSGA is the largest sporting goods trade association in the world. Membership consists of manufacturers, retailers, dealers, wholesalers, sales agents and media in the sporting goods industry; Divisions of membership include Team Dealer, Specialty Fitness, Specialty Golf and Independent Retailer. Association and Show Management, Inc. (ASMI) is a trade show and association management subsidiary. Organizes and hosts the NSGA Annual Management Conference and Team Dealer Summit. Membership fee: $125-535/year (company).

Meetings/Conferences:

Annual Meetings: *Spring-Summer*
2007 – Bonita Springs, FL(Hyatt Regency Coconut Pointe Resort and Spa)/May 20-23/400

Publications:

NSGA Athletic Footwear newsletter. m. adv.
NSGA Research newsletter. bi-m. adv.
NSGA Specialty Golf newsletter. m. adv.
NSGA Sporting Goods Alert newsletter. w. adv.
NSGA Specialty Fitness newsletter. m. adv.
NSGA Retail Focus magazine. 6/yr. adv.
Sporting Goods Market. a.
NSGA Cost of Doing Business Survey. bi-a.
NSGA Buying Guide. a. adv.
NSGA Sports Participation Study. a.

National Sports and Fitness Association *(1987)*
1945 Palo Verde Ave., Suite 202
Long Beach, CA 90815-3445
Tel: (562)652-3559
Members: 2000 individuals
Staff: 5
Annual Budget: $50-100,000
President: Dr. John Russell

Historical Note

National Sports and Fitness is a division of the American Fitness Association. Founded as American Fitness Association; assumed its present name in 1999. A national association of health, sports and fitness enthusiasts and professionals. Membership: $25/year (student); $45/year (general); $55/year (professional); $35/year (senior); $250/year (organization).

Publications:

Newsletter. q.

National Sportscasters and Sportswriters Association *(1959)*
323 North Main St.
Salisbury, NC 28144
Tel: (704)633-4275 *Fax:* (704)633-2027
E-Mail: nssa@nssahalloffame.com
Web Site: http://nssahalloffame.com/
Members: 1000 individuals
Staff: 1
Annual Budget: $50-100,000
Executive Director: Glen Hudson
Contact: Barbara Lockert

Historical Note

Operates the National Sportscasters and Sportswriters Hall of Fame (same address). Membership: $25/year.

Meetings/Conferences:

Annual Meetings: *Always Salisbury, NC/April*

Publications:

NSSA News. semi-a.

National Spotted Saddle Horse Association *(1979)*
P.O. Box 898
Murfreesboro, TN 37133-0898
Tel: (615)890-2864 *Fax:* (615)890-2864
E-Mail: nssha898@aol.com
Web Site: www.nssha.com
Members: 4000 individuals
Staff: 2
Annual Budget: $100-250,000
Manager: Donna Fletcher
E-Mail: nssha898@aol.com

Historical Note

NSSHA is a breed registry for spotted, gaited horses.

Meetings/Conferences:

Annual Meetings: *Murfreesboro, TN on the last Saturday in January.*

Publications:

Nat'l Spotted Saddle Horse Journal. q. adv.
Newsletter. m. adv.

National Spotted Swine Record *(1914)*
P.O. Box 9758
Peoria, IL 61612-9758
Tel: (309)693-1804 *Fax:* (309)691-0168
E-Mail: cpspeoria@mindspring.com
Web Site: www.cpsswine.com/spots/spotted.htm
Members: 565 individuals
Staff: 3
Annual Budget: $100-250,000
Director: Jack Wall

Meetings/Conferences:

Annual Meetings: *July*

Publications:

Spotted News. 10/year. adv.

National Staff Development and Training Association *(1930)*

Historical Note

An affiliate of the American Public Welfare Association, which provides administrative support.

National Staff Development Council *(1978)*
5995 Fairfield Road, Suite Four
Oxford, OH 45056
Tel: (513)523-6029 *Fax:* (513)523-0638
Toll Free: (800)727 - 7288
E-Mail: nsdcoffice@aol.com
Web Site: www.nsdc.org
Members: 10000 individuals
Staff: 19
Annual Budget: $2-5,000,000
Executive Director: Dennis Sparks, Ph.D.
Business Manager: Leslie Miller

Historical Note

NSDC members are local school district administrators responsible for staff development. Membership fees vary, based on number of publications received: $79 or $119/year (individual); $149/year (organization).

Meetings/Conferences:

Annual Meetings: *Winter/1,500-2,000*
2007 – Dallas, TX/Dec. 1-5

Publications:

JSD. q. adv.
The Learning System. 8/year.
Tools for Schools. q.
The Learning Principal. 8/year.

National Star Route Mail Contractors Association *(1933)*
324 E. Capitol St. NE
Washington, DC 20003-3897
Tel: (202)543-1661 *Fax:* (202)543-8863
E-Mail: info@starroutecontractors.org
Web Site: www.starroutecontractors.org
Members: 4500 individuals
Staff: 4
Annual Budget: $500-1,000,000
Executive Director: John V. "Skip" Maraney
E-Mail: info@starroutecontractors.org

Historical Note

Members have mail delivery contracts with the U.S. Postal Service to transport mail over the highways on authorized schedules. Formerly (1982) National Star Route Mail Carriers Association.

Meetings/Conferences:

Annual Meetings: *August*

Publications:

Star Carrier. m.

National Stone, Sand and Gravel Association *(1916)*
1605 King St.
Alexandria, VA 22314
Tel: (703)525-8788 *Fax:* (703)525-7782
Toll Free: (800)346 - 1415
Web Site: www.nssga.org
Members: 650 manufacturers
Staff: 30
Annual Budget: $5-10,000,000
President and Chief Executive Officer: Jennifer Joy Wilson
Executive Vice President and Chief Operating Officer: Charles E. Hawkins, III, CAE

Historical Note

Founded as National Sand and Gravel Association; became National Aggregates Association in 1987. Merged with National Stone Association and assumed its current name in 2000. Sponsors the National Sand and Gravel Association Political Action Committee (Rock Pac).

Meetings/Conferences:

Annual Meetings: *Winter*
2007 – San Francisco, CA(The Westin St. Francis Hotel)/Feb. 28-March 2

Publications:

Stone, Sand & Gravel Review. 6/year. adv.

National Strength and Conditioning Association *(1978)*
1885 Bob Johnson Dr.
Colorado Springs, CO 80906
Tel: (719)632-6722 Ext: 113 *Fax:* (719)632-6367
Toll Free: (800)815 - 6826
E-Mail: nsca@nsca-lift.org
Web Site: www.nsca-lift.org
Members: 33000 individuals
Staff: 34
Annual Budget: $2-5,000,000
Executive Director: Robert Jursnick
E-Mail: nsca@nsca-lift.org

Historical Note

Formerly (1981) National Strength Coaches Association. Members are professionals involved in all aspects of strength training. Provides certification and other opportunities to members. Membership: $80/year (professional level).

Meetings/Conferences:

Annual Meetings: *Summer*
2007 – Atlanta, GA(Hilton Hotel)/July 11-14

Publications:

Strength and Conditioning Journal. bi-m. adv.
Journal of Strength & Conditioning Research. q. adv.
NSCA Bulletin. bi-m. adv.
NSCA Performance and Training Journal - online.

National Stripper Well Association *(1934)*

Historical Note
A program of Independent Petroleum Ass'n of America, which provides administrative support.

National Stroke Association *(1984)*
9707 E. Easter Lane
Englewood, CO 80112-3747
Tel: (303)649-9299 *Fax:* (303)649-1328
Toll Free: (800)787 - 6537
E-Mail: info@stroke.org
Web Site: www.stroke.org
Members: 10000 individuals
Staff: 15
Annual Budget: $2-5,000,000
Chief Executive Officer: Jim Baranski
Vice President, National Communications: Diane Mulligan-Fairfield

Historical Note
NSA is a national voluntary health care organization focusing exclusively on stroke prevention, treatment, rehabilitation, and support of stroke survivors and their families. NSA's professional society is open to all health care professionals, including physicians, therapists, nurses and others involved in preventing and treating stroke. Membership: $125/year (professional); $200/year(organization).

Publications:
Magazine-Stoke Smart. bi-m. adv.
Journal of Stroke and Cerebrovascular Disease. q. adv.
Newsletter-Stroke Clinical Update. bi-m.

National Structured Settlements Trade Association *(1985)*
1800 K St. NW
Suite 718
Washington, DC 20006
Tel: (202)466-2714 *Fax:* (202)466-7414
E-Mail: info@nssta.com
Web Site: www.nssta.com
Members: 700 individuals
Staff: 5
Annual Budget: $1-2,000,000
Executive Vice President: Randy Dyer, CAE

Historical Note
Provides long-term periodic payment of settlements on personal injury lawsuits. Membership fee varies by category.

Meetings/Conferences:
Annual Meetings: Spring/300

National Student Assistance Association *(1987)*
4200 Wisconsin Ave. NW
Suite 106-118
Washington, DC 20016
Toll Free: (800)257 - 6310
E-Mail: info@nsaa.us
Web Site: www.nsaa.us
Members: 500individualsandinstitutions
Staff: 2
Annual Budget: $100-250,000
Executive Director: Lee Rush

Historical Note
NSAA members represent a full spectrum of individuals and organizations involved with student assistance programs for students at risk. Members include teachers, counselors, psychologists, social workers, nurses, program coordinators, administrators and others with an interest in student assistance programs. Membership: $85/year (individual).

Publications:
Legislative Update. 3/year.
Student Assistance Today Newsletter. 2/year.
Student Assistance Journal. 5/year.
NASAP Membership Directory. a.

National Student Employment Association *(1976)*
P.O. Box 23606
Eugene, OR 97402
Tel: (541)484-6935 *Fax:* (541)484-6935
E-Mail: nsea@nsea.info
Web Site: www.nsea.info
Members: 500 individuals
Staff: 1
Annual Budget: $50-100,000
Office Manager: Joan Adams
E-Mail: nsea@nsea.info

Historical Note
Formerly (1975) National Association on Work and the College Student and (1997) National Association of Student Employment Administrators. NSEA members are professionals involved with programs for students who work while attending college. Membership: $100/year (individual); $300/year (organization, minimum); $750/year (company).

Meetings/Conferences:
Annual Meetings: Fall/200-250

Publications:
Workbook.
Bibliography. a.
NASEA News. q.
Membership Directory. a.
Annual Report. a.
Student Employment Journal. a.

National Student Nurses Association *(1952)*
45 Main St., Suite 606
Brooklyn, NY 11201
Tel: (718)210-0705 *Fax:* (718)210-0710
E-Mail: nsna@nsna.org
Web Site: www.nsna.org
Members: 45,000 individuals
Staff: 12
Annual Budget: $2-5,000,000
Executive Director: Diane J. Mancino, Ed.D., RN, CAE
Controller: Dev Persaud
Director, Programs: Judith Tyler, MA, RN
Director, Membership Development: Susan Wong, BS, CAE

Historical Note
Provides education, representation, and a forum in which to further the current professional interests and concerns of student nurses. Membership: $30/year (individual); $250-2000/year (organization/company).

Meetings/Conferences:
Annual Meetings: April
2007 – Anaheim, CA(Convention Center)/Apr. 11-15/3000
2008 – Grapevine, TX(The Texan)/March 26-30/3500
2009 – Nashville, TN(Opryland)/Apr. 15-19/3500

Publications:
Pieces-"Getting the Pieces to Fit". a.
Imprint. 5/year. adv.
Deans Notes.
NSNA News. bi-m. adv.

National Student Osteopathic Medical Association *(1970)*
142 E. Ontario St.
Chicago, IL 60611
Tel: (312)202-8193 *Fax:* (312)202-8224
E-Mail: somanat@aol.com
Web Site: www.studentdo.com
Members: 7000 individuals
Staff: 1
Annual Budget: $50-100,000
Administrator: Marie Perone
E-Mail: somanat@aol.com

Historical Note
Affiliated with the American Osteopathic Association (Chicago, IL), SOMA was founded in 1970 and is a professional association of osteopathic medical students from the 19 colleges of osteopathic medicine. Membership: $60/quadrennially.

Meetings/Conferences:
Annual Meetings: Semi-Annual Meetings

National Student Speech Language Hearing Association *(1972)*
10801 Rockville Pike
Rockville, MD 20852
Toll Free: (800)498 - 2071
E-Mail: nsslha@hsslha.org
Web Site: www.nsslha.org
Members: 15000 individuals
Staff: 2
Annual Budget: $500-1,000,000
Director, Operations: Dawn D. Dickerson

Historical Note
Formed as National Student Speech and Hearing Association through a merger of Sigma Alpha Eta and the Student Journal Group of American Speech and Hearing Association; assumed its present name in 1980. Members are undergraduates and master's degree candidates working in the field of speech-language pathology and audiology. Recognized by the American Speech-Language-Hearing Association as the only official national student association in speech and hearing. Membership: $35/year.

Meetings/Conferences:
Annual Meetings: With the American Speech-Language-Hearing Ass'n.

Publications:
Contemporary Issues in Communication Science and Disorders. semi-a. adv.

National Subacute and Postacute Care Association *(1992)*
P.O. Box 65085
Washington, DC 20035
Tel: (202)481-7501 *Fax:* (202)481-7502
Toll Free: (888)758 - 8970
E-Mail: naspac@naspac.net
Web Site: www.naspac.net
Members: 1200 individuals
Staff: 4
Annual Budget: $1-2,000,000
Executive Director: Lyle Williams

Historical Note
Founded as National Subacute Care Association; assumed its current name in 2002. Seeks to develop standards for the subacute and transitional healthcare industry so that the public, payers and healthcare personnel can clearly identify quality providers. Represents the industry to the federal government. Provides education and information to those interested in subacute healthcare. Changed its name to National Subacute and Post-Acute Care from National Subacute Care Association in 2001. Supersedes Association for Advancement of Rehabilitation, which disbanded in 1991. Membership: $300/year (individual); $750-$7,500/year (organization).

Meetings/Conferences:
Annual Meetings: Spring/800

Publications:
Nursing Home Magazine. m.
NASPAC Newsletter. m. adv.
Friday Report Fax. w.

National Submetering and Utility Allocation Association *(1998)*
1866 Sheridan Road, Suite 201
Highland Park, IL 60035-2545
Tel: (847)681-8475 *Fax:* (847)681-1869
E-Mail: nsuaa@netzero.com
Web Site: www.nsuaa.org
Members: 75 companies
Staff: 5
Annual Budget: $100-250,000
Executive Director: Charles G. Stolberg

Historical Note
NSUAA's members are service providers, producers of submetering and utility allocation equipment, and multifamily and manufactured housing property owners and managers who utilize utility submetering and allocation programs.

Meetings/Conferences:
Semi-Annual Meetings: usually February and June

Publications:
Membership Roster & Product Reference Guide. a. adv.

National Sugar Brokers Association *(1903)*
3000 Chestnut Ave., Suite 100-A
Baltimore, MD 21211
Tel: (410)366-7400 *Fax:* (410)467-9552
E-Mail: semisweet@chesa.com
Members: 47 sugar brokers
Staff: 2
Annual Budget: $10-25,000
Executive Secretary: Susan Ladner
E-Mail: semisweet@chesa.com

Historical Note
Members are brokers of refined sugar.

Meetings/Conferences:
Annual Meetings: August/70

Publications:
Bulletin. q.

National Sunflower Association *(1975)*
4023 State St.
Bismarck, ND 58503-0690
Tel: (701)328-5100 *Fax:* (701)328-5101
Toll Free: (888)718 - 7033
E-Mail: info@sunflowernsa.com
Web Site: www.sunflowernsa.com
Members: 38315 individuals
Staff: 4
Annual Budget: $250-500,000
Executive Director: Larry Kleingartner
Coordinator, Events and Advertising Sales: Lerrene Kroh
Manager, Business and Office: Tina Mittelsteadt
Director, Marketing: John SandBakken

Historical Note
Companies associated with sunflower products, including growers' councils, seed companies, processors, exporters, researchers, chemical firms, shippers, commission firms and merchandisers. Established as the Sunflower Association of America, it assumed its present name in 1981. Membership: $40/year (individual); $325-500/year (company).

Meetings/Conferences:
Annual Meetings: Summer
2007 – Medora, MN(Medora Community Center)/Jan. 27-28/150

Publications:
The Sunflower Magazine. 6/year. adv.
Sunflower Week in Review. bi-w.

National Sunroom Association *(1997)*
2945 S.W. Wanamaker Dr., Suite A
Topeka, KS 66614-5321
Tel: (785)271-0208 *Fax:* (785)271-0166
E-Mail: info@nationalsunroom.org
Web Site: www.nationalsunroom.org
Members: 45
Staff: 7
Executive Director: Stanley L. Smith

Historical Note
Established in 1997. Members are manufacturers and producers of sunrooms, patio rooms, solariums and related structures.

Meetings/Conferences:
Semi-annual Meetings: Spring and Fall

National Surgical Assistant Association *(1983)*
2615 Amesbury Road
Winston-Salem, NC 27103
Tel: (336)768-4448 *Fax:* (336)768-4445
Toll Free: (888)633 - 0479
E-Mail: ruth@namgmt.com
Web Site: www.nsaa.net
Members: 800 individuals
Staff: 1
Annual Budget: $100-250,000
Executive Director: Ruth Helein
E-Mail: ruth@namgmt.com

Meetings/Conferences:
Annual Meetings: October

Publications:
CSA Node. q. adv.

National Swine Improvement Federation *(1975)*
109 Kildee Hall, Iowa State Univ.
Ames, IA 50011
Tel: (515)294-4683 *Fax:* (515)294-5698
E-Mail: stalder@iastate.edu
Web Site: www.nsif.com
Members: 60 individuals
Annual Budget: under $10,000
Contact: Ken Stalder, Ph.D.

Historical Note
Established in Kansas City, MO and incorporated in Nebraska. Members are central testing stations, field performance testing programs, purebred breed associations and the National Pork Producers Council. Membership: $100/year.

Meetings/Conferences:
Annual Meetings: December

Publications:
Proceedings of the Annual Conference. a.
Swine Genetics Handbook.
Guidelines for Uniform Swine Improvement Programs.

National Swine Registry
P.O. Box 2417
West Lafayette, IN 47996-2417
Tel: (765)463-3594 *Fax:* (765)497-2959
E-Mail: nsr@nationalswine.com
Web Site: www.nationalswine.com
Members: 2500
Staff: 15
Annual Budget: $1-2,000,000
Chief Executive Officer: Darrell D. Anderson
E-Mail: nsr@nationalswine.com

Historical Note
Product of a merger (1996) of the American Yorkshire Club, Hampshire Swine Registry, American Landrace Association and United Duroc Swine Registry. Membership: $50/year (individual).

Publications:
Seedstock Edge. m. adv.

National Systems Contractors Association *(1980)*
625 First St. SE
Suite 420
Cedar Rapids, IA 52401
Tel: (319)366-6722 *Fax:* (319)366-4164
Toll Free: (800)446 - 6722
Web Site: www.nsca.org
Members: 2800 companies
Staff: 15
Annual Budget: $2-5,000,000
Executive Director: Chuck Wilson
E-Mail: cwilson@nsca.org
Director, Marketing and Communications: Leslie George
Executive Vice President: Jeff Quint
E-Mail: jquint@nsca.org

Historical Note
Formerly (1994) National Sound and Communications Association. Members are installers and servicers of electronic communications equipment.

Publications:
Building Connections. bi-m.

National Tank Truck Carriers Conference *(1945)*
2200 Mill Road
Alexandria, VA 22314-4677
Tel: (703)838-1960 *Fax:* (703)684-5753
E-Mail: nttcstaff@tanktruck.org
Web Site: www.tanktruck.org
Members: 500 carriers, 2 associates
Staff: 7
Annual Budget: $2-5,000,000
President: John Conley
E-Mail: jconley@tanktruck.org
Vice President: Tom Lynch
E-Mail: tlynch@tanktruck.org

Historical Note
Represents the for-hire tank truck industry. Membership: $500-6,600/year; $600/year (associate).

Meetings/Conferences:
Annual Meetings: May
2007 – Las Vegas, NV(Mandalay Bay)/May 7-9/550

Publications:
Directory. a. adv.
Newsletter. m.
Regulations. a.

National Tax Association *(1907)*
725 15th St. NW
Suite 600
Washington, DC 20005-2109
Tel: (202)737-3325 *Fax:* (202)737-7308
E-Mail: natltax@aol.com
Web Site: www.ntanet.org
Members: 1400 individuals and institutions
Staff: 3
Annual Budget: $250-500,000
Executive Director: J. Fred Giertz
E-Mail: natltax@aol.com

Historical Note
Merged in 1973 with the Tax Institute of America (formed 1932). NTA provides the taxpayer, tax administrator, practitioner, educator, and student with a vehicle for national research, discussion, and dissemination of information. Membership: $95-135/year (individual); $365/year (organization).

Meetings/Conferences:
Annual Meetings: Fall/350

Publications:
National Tax Journal. q.
Proceedings. a.

National Tax Lien Association *(1997)*
306 W. Chase St.
Pensacola, FL 32502
Tel: (850)470-9974 *Fax:* (850)470-9522
Toll Free: (877)470 - 9007
Web Site: www.ntlainfo.org
Members: 100 individuals
Staff: 3
Executive Director: Howard C. Liggett

Meetings/Conferences:
Annual Meetings: Spring

National Taxidermists Association *(1970)*
108 Branch Dr.
Slidell, LA 70461
Tel: (985)641-4682 *Fax:* (985)641-9463
Toll Free: (866)662 - 9054
E-Mail: ntah@aol.com
Web Site: www.nationaltaxidermist.com
Members: 2500 individuals
Staff: 5
Annual Budget: $100-250,000
Executive Director: Greg Crain

Historical Note
Membership: $50/year (individual).

Meetings/Conferences:
2007 – Louisville, KY(Clarion Hotel and Conference Center)/July 18-21
2008 – Lubbock, TX(Holiday Inn Towers and Lubbock Civic Center)/July 9-12
2009 – Huntsville, AL(Holiday Inn Select and Von Braun Center)/July 8-11

Publications:
Annual Directory of Membership. a. adv.
Outlook Magazine. bi-m.

National Tay-Sachs and Allied Diseases Association *(1957)*
2001 Beacon St.
Brighton, MA 02135
Tel: (617)277-4463 *Fax:* (617)277-0134
Toll Free: (800)906 - 8723
E-Mail: info@ntsad.org
Web Site: www.ntsad.org
Members: 350 affected families
Staff: 2
Annual Budget: $250-500,000
Executive Director: Jayne C. Gerrshkowitz
E-Mail: jayne@ntsad.org

Historical Note
NTSAD is the nation's oldest genetic disease organization. Tay-Sachs disease is an inherited genetic disorder, caused by the absence of a vital enzyme and resulting in the destruction of the Central nervous system and death in young children. NTSAD's purpose is public and professional education, prevention, family support service and research advocacy. Membership: $50/year.

Publications:
Breakthrough. semi-a. adv.
Lifeline. q. adv.

National Technical Association *(1925)*
26100 Brush Ave., Suite 31
Cleveland, OH 44132
Tel: (216)289-4682 *Fax:* (216)289-4683
E-Mail: info@ntaonline.org
Web Site: www.ntaonline.org
Members: 2,000 individuals
Staff: 1
President: Willie B. Williams

Historical Note
NTA is America's first and oldest professional association for minorities in science, technology, and engineering. Membership: varies by classification.
Publications:
Journal of the NTA. a. adv.
National Technical Newsletter. q.

National Technical Association of Scientists
Historical Note
Became National Technical Association in 2003.

National Technical Services Association *(1966)*
P.O. Box 846
Edison, NJ 08818-0846
Members: 300 firms
Staff: 5
Annual Budget: $1-2,000,000
Executive Director: Toby J. Malara
Manager, Operations: Vera Johnson
Manager, Membership: Ruth Seyler
Coordinator, Meetings and Production: Sarah Stacy
Historical Note
Formerly the Technical Services Industry Association. NTSA represents contract technical services firms (engineering, designing and drafting, and information service companies).
Meetings/Conferences:
Annual Meetings: October
Publications:
Weekly Fast Facts. w. adv.
NTSA Reporter. m. adv.

National Telecommunications Cooperative Association *(1954)*
4121 Wilson Blvd., Tenth Floor
Arlington, VA 22203
Tel: (703)351-2000 *Fax:* (703)351-2001
E-Mail: pubrelations@ntca.org
Web Site: www.ntca.org
Members: 560 phone companies and cooperatives
Staff: 120
Chief Executive: Michael E. Brunner, CAE
Vice President, Government Affairs and Association Services: Shirley Bloomfield
Public Affairs Manager: Caitlin Colligan
Director, Communications: Wendy Mann
Director, Training and Development and Member Services: Ronald D. Precourt, CAE
Vice President, Finance and Internal Operations: Lisa T. Schweitzer
Historical Note
Represents both cooperative and commercial, independent rural communications providers throughout America.
Meetings/Conferences:
Annual Meetings: First Quarter/2,500 and Conference/Fall
2007 – Orlando, FL(Swan and Dolphin)/Feb. 4-7
Publications:
Rural Telecommunications. bi-m. adv.
NTCA Exchange. bi-m.
Washington Report. w.
Compensation & Benefits in the Independent Telephone Industry. a.

National Terrazzo and Mosaic Association *(1924)*
201 N. Maple Ave., Suite 208
Purcellville, VA 20132
Tel: (540)751-0930 *Fax:* (540)751-0935
Toll Free: (800)323 - 9736
E-Mail: info@ntma.com
Web Site: www.ntma.com
Members: 200 individuals
Staff: 2
Annual Budget: $250-500,000
Executive Director: George D. Hardy
E-Mail: info@ntma.com
Historical Note
Membership: $1,932/year.
Meetings/Conferences:
Annual Meetings: March/April
Publications:
NTMA Newsletter. q.
Convention Program Journal. a. adv.
Terrazzo Information Guide.
Terrazo Design Guide.
Catalog - Terrazzo Systems.
Technical Brochures on Terrazzo Systems.

National Textile Association *(1854)*
Six Beacon St., Suite 1125
Boston, MA 02108-3812
Tel: (617)542-8220 *Fax:* (617)542-2199
E-Mail: info@nationaltextile.org
Web Site: www.textilenta.org
Members: 200 companies
Staff: 3
Annual Budget: $250-500,000
President: Karl H. Spilhaus
Historical Note
Established as the Nation Council of Cotton Manufacturing, later became the Northern Textile Association and then (2002) merged with the Knitted Textile Ass'n to form the present organization. Members are companies that work in a number of sectors of the textile industry and in supplier industries.
Publications:
Resources Guide. a.

National Therapeutic Recreation Society *(1966)*
Historical Note
A branch of National Recreation and Park Association, which provides administrative support.

National Tile Contractors Association *(1947)*
626 Lakeland East Dr.
Jackson, MS 39232
Tel: (601)939-2071 *Fax:* (601)932-6117
Web Site: www.tile-assn.com
Members: 800 companies
Staff: 6
Annual Budget: $1-2,000,000
Executive Director: Bart A. Bettiga
E-Mail: bart@tile-assn.com
Membership Director: Bob Brown
Director, Training and Education: Justin Woelfer, Jr.
E-Mail: justin@tile-assn.com
Historical Note
Formerly (1988) the Association of Tile Terrazzo, Marble Contractors and Affiliates and the Southern Tile, Terrazzo, Marble Contractors Association. Membership is limited to individuals, firms, and corporations engaged in the installation, manufacture, or sale of ceramic tile, terrazzo, marble and allied products. Membership: $425/year.
Meetings/Conferences:
Annual Meetings: in conjunction with the Internat'l Tile Exposition
Publications:
Tileletter. m. adv.

National Time Equipment Association *(1978)*
P.O. Box 27399
Memphis, TN 38167-0399
Toll Free: (800)235 - 6832
E-Mail: info@thentea.net
Web Site: www.thentea.net
Members: 350 manufacturers
Staff: 1
Annual Budget: $50-100,000
Executive Secretary: Janet George
E-Mail: info@thentea.net
Historical Note
NTEA members are manufacturers and distributors of time keeping devices such as time clocks, computerized time systems and peripherals.
Meetings/Conferences:
Semi-annual Meetings:
Publications:
The Times Newsletter. bi-m.

National Tooling and Machining Association *(1943)*
9300 Livingston Road
Ft. Washington, MD 20744
Tel: (301)248-6200 *Fax:* (301)248-7104
Toll Free: (800)248 - 6862
E-Mail: matt@ntma.org
Web Site: www.ntma.org
Members: 2700 companies
Staff: 31
Annual Budget: $2-5,000,000
President and Chief Executive Officer: Matthew B. Coffey
E-Mail: matt@ntma.org
Manager, Marketing and Meetings: Thomas Garcia
Historical Note
Established as the National Tool and Die Manufacturers Association, it became the National Tool, Die and Precision Machining Association in 1960, and assumed its present name in 1980. Members are makers of jigs, molds, tools, gages, dies and fixtures for companies doing precision machining. Supports the NTMA - Committee for A Strong Economy (CFASE).
Meetings/Conferences:
Annual Meetings: January
Publications:
The Record. m. adv.
Business and Customer Market Forecast Reports. q.
Membership Directory. a.

National Tour Association *(1951)*
546 E. Main St.
Lexington, KY 40508-2300
Tel: (859)226-4444 *Fax:* (859)226-4414
Toll Free: (800)682 - 8886
E-Mail: questions@nta.travel
Web Site: www.nta.travel
Members: 4000
Staff: 30
Annual Budget: $5-10,000,000
Vice President, Operations: Tonya Cummings
Manager, Public Relations: Sara Morton
Vice President, Communications: Catherine Prather
Historical Note
Founded as National Tour Brokers Association; became (1983) National Tour Association. NTA is a non-profit organization whose membership consists of package travel companies, suppliers, and destinations.
Meetings/Conferences:
2007 – Kelowna, BC, Canada/Apr. 26-28
2007 – Kansas City, MO/Nov. 2-6
Publications:
NTA Courier. m. adv.
Annual Membership Directory. a. adv.
Tuesday. bi-w.

National Tractor Parts Dealer Association
P.O. Box 1181
Gainesville, TX 76241
Tel: (940)668-0900 *Fax:* (940)668-1627
Toll Free: (877)668 - 0900
E-Mail: phyllis@ntpda.com
Web Site: www.ntpda.com
Members: 186 companies
Staff: 3
Executive Director: Phyllis Cox
Historical Note
NTPDA is an international association with members across the U.S. and Canada. NTPDA members serve the agricultural and industrial industries by buying and selling repair parts and related equipment via direct communication among their membership.
Meetings/Conferences:
Annual Meetings: Winter
Publications:
Bulletin. q. adv.

National Tractor Pullers Association *(1970)*
6155-B Huntley Road
Columbus, OH 43229
Tel: (614)436-1761 *Fax:* (614)436-0964
E-Mail: gregg@ntpapull.com
Web Site: www.ntpapull.com
Members: 5600 individuals
Staff: 12
Annual Budget: $500-1,000,000
Manager, Operations: Gregg Randall
E-Mail: gregg@ntpapull.com
Historical Note
NTPA is the sanctioning body for truck and tractor pulling, setting safety and equipment standards.
Publications:
Puller Magazine. m. adv.

Pulling Rules: Official Rule Book. a. adv.
Pull! Program & Yearbook. a. adv.

National Trade Circulation Foundation *(1948)*
c/o PTM Communications
352 Seventh Ave. Suite 211
New York, NY 10001-0832
Tel: (212)210-0286
Web Site: www.ntcfi.org
Members: 125 publications
Annual Budget: $25-50,000
President: Philip Scarano

Historical Note
Founded as National Business Circulation Association; assumed its current name in 1999. Members are executives in charge of business-to-business circulation at magazines, newspapers, and other publications. Has no paid officers or full-time staff.

Meetings/Conferences:
Annual Meetings: Meetings held six times a year at the Penn Club in New York City

Publications:
Membership Directory. a. adv.
Newsletter. q. adv.

National Trailer Dealers Association *(1990)*
37400 Hills Tech Dr.
Farmington, MI 48331-3414
Toll Free: (800)800 - 4552
E-Mail: info@ntda.org
Web Site: www.ntda.org
Members: 300 companies
Staff: 4
Annual Budget: $50-100,000
Executive Director: Steve Carey
E-Mail: steve@ntda.org

Historical Note
NTDA members are companies with interests in all aspects of the semi-trailer industry. Membership: $250-300/year.

Meetings/Conferences:
Annual Meetings: Fall/160

Publications:
Trailer Talk Hotline. 10/year. adv.

National Training Systems Association *(1988)*
2111 Wilson Blvd., Suite 400
Arlington, VA 22201-3061
Tel: (703)247-2569 *Fax:* (703)243-1659
E-Mail: bmcdaniel@ndia.org
Web Site: www.trainingsystems.org
Members: 800 individuals
Staff: 4
Annual Budget: $1-2,000,000
President: Frederick L. Lewis

Historical Note
Merged with NDIA in 1992; represents companies in the simulation and training industry and training support services. Provides industry forums, market surveys, business development information and other services to members. Membership: $500-$5,000/year (companies); $125/year (individuals).

Meetings/Conferences:
Annual Meetings: Fall-Winter

Publications:
Training Survey - NTSA Training 2012. bi-a.
Training and Technology Yearbook. a. adv.
NTSA Newsletter. bi-m.

National Translator Association *(1962)*
5611 Kendell Court #2
Arvada, CO 80002
Tel: (303)465-5742 *Fax:* (303)465-4067
Web Site: www.tvfmtranslators.com
Members: 250 translator stations
Annual Budget: $100-250,000
President: Byron St. Clair

Historical Note
Translator FM and TV stations boost normal signals over mountains into rural areas. Membership: $150/year (individual or organization/company).

Meetings/Conferences:
Annual Meetings: Spring

Publications:
The Translator. q. adv.

National Trappers Association *(1959)*
524 Fifth St.
Bedford, IN 47421-2247
Tel: (812)277-9670 *Fax:* (812)277-9672
E-Mail: info@nationaltrappers.com
Web Site: www.nationaltrappers.com
Members: 20000 individuals
Staff: 1
Annual Budget: $250-500,000
Executive Administrator: David Sollman

Historical Note
Formerly (1969) National Trappers Association of America. Promotes wildlife management programs and education for trappers and the general public, helps maintain trapper rights and preserve their heritage, and provides youth scholarships. Membership: $25/year.

Meetings/Conferences:
Annual Meetings: Summer

Publications:
American Trapper. bi-m. adv.

National Treasury Employees Union *(1938)*
1750 H St. NW
Suite 600
Washington, DC 20006
Tel: (202)572-5500 *Fax:* (202)572-5644
E-Mail: nteu-pr@inteu.org
Web Site: www.nteu.org
Members: 150000 individuals
Staff: 130
Annual Budget: $10-25,000,000
National President: Colleen M. Kelley
E-Mail: nteu-pr@inteu.org

Historical Note
An independent labor union. Founded as National Association of Collectors of Internal Revenue; became National Association of Internal Revenue Employees in 1970, and assumed its current name in 1973. Absorbed National Association of Alcohol and Tobacco Tax Officers in 1970.Absorbed the National Custom Service Association in 1975. Sponsors and supports the National Treasury Employees Union Political Action Committee. Has an annual budget of approximately $18 million.

Meetings/Conferences:
Biennial Meetings: odd years in August

Publications:
NTEU Bulletin. m.
Stewards Update. m.
Capitol Report. m.

National Troubleshooting Association *(1996)*
2996 Point Dr.
St. Louis, MO 63129-5340
Tel: (314)846-2665 *Fax:* (314)846-9950
E-Mail: nta-usa@charter.net
Staff: 1
Annual Budget: under $10,000
Director: Ronald J. Montplaisir
E-Mail: nta-usa@charter.net

Historical Note
Members are industrial machinery manufacturers, users of industrial machinery systems, and other interested individuals and companies. NTA develops standards and conducts programs on troubleshooting industrial machinery.

National Truck and Heavy Equipment Claims Council *(1961)*
18504 Bothell Way NE
Bothell, WA 98011
Tel: (425)481-2800 *Fax:* (425)481-0817
Web Site: www.nthecc.org
Members: 55 individuals
Staff: 1
Annual Budget: $10-25,000
Administrator: Tom Fergus

Historical Note
Formerly (1995) Truck and Heavy Equipment Claims Council. Established Oct. 3, 1961, in Chicago, to consider common problems of the members in the handling of insurance claims in trucks and heavy equipment. Membership: $150/year.

Meetings/Conferences:
Annual Meetings: October/250
2007 - San Antonio, TX(Hyatt Regency)/Oct. 4-7

National Truck Equipment Association *(1964)*
37400 Hills Tech Dr.
Farmington Hills, MI 48331-3414
Tel: (248)489-7090 *Fax:* (248)489-8590
Toll Free: (800)441 - 6832
E-Mail: info@ntea.com
Web Site: www.ntea.com
Members: 1600 companies
Staff: 23
Annual Budget: $2-5,000,000
Executive Director: James D. Carney
E-Mail: jim@ntea.com
Director, Marketing and Communications: Gwendolyn Brown
Director, Meetings and Member Services: Steve Carey
Director, Government Relations: Michael E. Kastner
Director, Information Technology: David C. Lee
E-Mail: davidlee@ntea.com
Director, Technical Services: Bob Raybuck

Historical Note
Formerly (1979) Truck Equipment and Body Distributors Association. Members are companies engaged in the manufacture, distribution and repair of commercial trucks, truck bodies, accessories and equipment. NTEA affiliates include the Ambulance Manufacturers Division, American Institute of Service Body Manufacturers, Articulating Crane Council of North America, Body and Hoist Manufacturers Committee, Manufacturers Council of Small School Buses, Mid-Size Bus Manufacturers Association, Snow Control Equipment Manufacturers Committee, Towing Equipment Manufacturers Association, and Van Body Manufacturers Division. Sponsors and supports The Work Truck Show. Membership: $450-1,600/year, based on sales volume.

Meetings/Conferences:
Annual Meetings: Spring
2007 - Indianapolis, IN/March 6-9

Publications:
Truck Equipment Outlook. q.
Excise Tax Quarterly. q.
Washington Update. m.
Membership Roster and Product Directory. a. adv.
Technical Report. irreg.
NTEA News. m. adv.

National Truck Leasing System *(1944)*
One S. 450 Summit Ave., Suite 300
Oakbrook Terrace, IL 60181
Tel: (630)953-8878 *Fax:* (630)953-0040
Toll Free: (800)729 - 6857
E-Mail: Info@NationaLease.com
Web Site: www.nationalease.com
Members: 124 companies
Staff: 29
Annual Budget: $1-2,000,000
President and Chief Executive Officer: John Grainger
Vice President and Chief Financial Officer: Stan Boris

Historical Note
Members are independent truck leasing companies. Membership: based on size of company.

Meetings/Conferences:
Annual Meetings: Fall

Publications:
NationaLease Newsletter. w.

National Tunis Sheep Registry *(1929)*
819 Lyons St.
Ludlow, MA 01056
Tel: (413)589-9653
Web Site: www.tunissheep.org
Members: 187 individuals
Staff: 1
Annual Budget: under $10,000
Clerk: Judy Harris

Historical Note
Membership: $10/year (individual).

Publications:
Tunis Shepherd Newsletter. 3-4/yr. adv.

National Turf Writers Association *(1960)*
1244 Meadow Lane
Frankfort, KY 40601

Tel: (502)875-4864
E-Mail: info@turfwriters.org
Web Site: www.turfwriters.org
Members: 225 individuals
Staff: 1
Annual Budget: $10-25,000
Secretary-Treasurer: Dan Liebman
E-Mail: info@turfwriters.org

Historical Note
Membership: $40/year.

Meetings/Conferences:
Semi-Annual Meetings: usually in conjunction with the Kentucky Derby and the Breeders' Cup

Publications:
Roster of Membership. a.
NTWA News Newsletter. m.
NTWA Awards Dinner Journal. a.

National Turkey Federation *(1939)*
1225 New York Ave. NW
Suite 400
Washington, DC 20005
Tel: (202)898-0100 *Fax:* (202)898-0203
Web Site: www.eatturkey.com
Members: 4000 individuals
Staff: 9
Annual Budget: $1-2,000,000
President: Dr. Alice L. Johnson
E-Mail: ajohnson@turkeyfed.org
Senior Vice President, Legislative Affairs: Joel Brandenberger
E-Mail: jbrandenberger@turkeyfed.org
Senior Director, Marketing and Communications: Sherrie Rosenblatt
E-Mail: srosenblatt@turkeyfed.org
Membership and Convention Services Manager: Brie Wilson

Historical Note
Provides support to the U.S. turkey industry in marketing and government relations.

Meetings/Conferences:
Annual Meetings: January

Publications:
NTF Newsletter. m.

National Tutoring Association *(1991)*
P.O. Box 6840
Lakeland, FL 33807-6840
Tel: (863)529-5206 *Fax:* (863)644-9621
E-Mail: ntatutor@aol.com
Web Site: www.ntatutor.org
Members: 3900 individuals
Annual Budget: $50-100,000
Executive Director: Sandi Ayaz

Historical Note
Founded as National Organization of Tutoring and Mentoring Centers; became National Association of Tutoring in 1993 and assumed its current name in 1995. NTA members are individuals who are actively engaged in tutoring or tutoring program administration, and others with an interest in the field. Membership: $45/year (individual); $80/year (program); $400/year (institution).

Meetings/Conferences:
Annual Meetings: Spring

Publications:
NTA Newsletter. 3/year. adv.
Journal. irreg.

National U.S.-Arab Chamber of Commerce *(1987)*
1023 15th St. NW
Fourth Floor
Washington, DC 20005
Tel: (202)289-5920 *Fax:* (202)289-5938
E-Mail: nusaac@aol.com
Web Site: www.nusacc.org
Members: 1000 companies and organizations
Staff: 15
Annual Budget: $1-2,000,000
President: David Hamod
E-Mail: nusaac@aol.com
Director, Operations: Marleine Davis

Historical Note
A trade association chartered in Washington DC with branch offices in Houston, New York, and Chicago. Membership includes corporations, associations, and individuals with interests in US-Arab business. Provides extensive research, programs, and information services. Membership: $250/year (individual); $500-1,000/year (corporation).

Publications:
U.S. Arab Tradeline. m.

National United Merchants Beverage Association *(1979)*
609 Ann St.
Homestead, PA 15120
Tel: (412)678-9583 *Fax:* (412)678-9584
Web Site: www.numba.org
Members: 5000 individuals
Staff: 2
President: Melvin Cornelious

Historical Note
Founded as National United Affiliated Beverage Association; assumed its current name in 1991. Members are minority beverage distributors.

National Utility Contractors Association *(1964)*
4301 N. Fairfax Dr., Suite 360
Arlington, VA 22203
Tel: (703)358-9300 *Fax:* (703)358-9307
Web Site: www.nuca.com
Members: 1500 companies
Staff: 14
Annual Budget: $2-5,000,000
Chief Executive Officer: Bill Hillman
Vice President, Member and Chapter Relations: Heather Caldwell
Vice President, Safety: George Kennedy, CSP
Chief Executive Officer: Linda Kinnecome
Director, Communications: Susan Williams
Vice President, Government Relations: Eben Wyman

Historical Note
NUCA is comprised of 1700 member companies and 44 groups of local underground utility construction contractors and suppliers thoughout the United States. Membership: $1000/year (contractor); $600/year (associate); $400/year (institutional).

Meetings/Conferences:
Annual Meetings: late Winter
2007 – Las Vegas, NV(Caesar's Palace)/Feb. 11-14

Publications:
Washington Report. bi-w.
Directory of Members. a. adv.
Utility Contractor. m. adv.
NUCA Safety News. bi-m.

National Vehicle Leasing Association *(1968)*
100 N. 20th St.
Fourth Floor
Philadelphia, PA 19103-1443
Tel: (215)564-3484 *Fax:* (215)963-9785
E-Mail: info@nvla.org
Web Site: www.nvla.org
Members: 300 companies
Staff: 2
Annual Budget: $250-500,000
Executive Director: Kenneth R. Hutton

Historical Note
Founded as an amalgamation of two separate groups of pioneer lessors in 1968 in San Francisco as the Automotive Leasing Association; merged with the Southern California Leasing Association to become the California Vehicle Leasing Association; expanded its membership in 1981 to become the Western Vehicle Leasing Association; and in 1984 voted to act as a national body under the name National Vehicle Leasing Association. As the central representative body for all members of the vehicle leasing industry in the U.S., NVLA's activities include: governmental affairs, education, publishing, conferences, legal and other member services, industry relations and certification. Membership: $695-$2,495/year (organization).

Meetings/Conferences:
Annual Meetings: Spring

Publications:
Foundations of Leasing. irreg. adv.
A Consumer Education Guide to Leasing vs. Buying.
Vehicle Leasing Today. q. adv.
Lifeline. q.
Leasing News. q.

National Venture Capital Association *(1973)*
1655 N. Ft. Myer Dr., Suite 850
Arlington, VA 22209
Tel: (703)524-2549 *Fax:* (703)524-3940
Web Site: www.nvca.org
Members: 450 companies
Staff: 11
Annual Budget: $2-5,000,000
President: Mark Heesen
E-Mail: mheesen@nvca.org
Vice President, Federal Policy: Jennifer Dowling
Vice President, Marketing: Jeanne Metzger
E-Mail: jmetzger@nvca.org
Vice President, Administration and Program Development: Molly M. Myers
E-Mail: mmyers@nvca.org
Vice President, Research: John S. Taylor, Sr.
E-Mail: research@nvca.org

Historical Note
Membership by invitation only. Members consist of corporations, financiers and private partnerships who are responsible for investing private capital in young companies on a professional basis. Sponsors and supports the NVCA Political Action Committee.

Meetings/Conferences:
Annual Meetings: Spring

Publications:
The Venture Capital Review. semi-a.
Membership Directory. a. adv.
NVCA Today. bi-m. adv.
Annual Statistical Report. a.

National Verbatim Reporters Association *(1967)*
207 Third Ave.
Hattiesburg, MS 39401
Tel: (601)582-4345 *Fax:* (601)582-3354
E-Mail: nvra@nvra.org
Web Site: http://nvra.org
Annual Budget: $25-50,000
Associate Administrator: Kelly Evans
E-Mail: nvra@nvra.org

Historical Note
Membership: $100/year (individual).

Publications:
eVoice. w.
The Verbatim Record. q. adv.
The Voice. 8/yr. adv.

National Voluntary Organizations for Independent Living for the Aging *(1971)*

Historical Note
A special interest group of the National Council of the Aging.

National Volunteer Fire Council *(1976)*
1050 17th St. NW
Suite 490
Washington, DC 20036
Tel: (202)887-5700 *Fax:* (202)887-5291
Toll Free: (888)275 - 6832
E-Mail: nvfcoffice@nvfc.org
Web Site: www.nvfc.org
Members: 1000 individuals
Staff: 5
Annual Budget: $500-1,000,000
Executive Director: Heather Schafer
E-Mail: hschaefer@nvfc.org
Director, Administration: Alicia Hawkins
Director, Government Relations: Craig Sharman
E-Mail: csharman@nvfc.org

Historical Note
NVFC members include state level organizations that represent volunteer firefighters and EMS personnel, volunteer fire departments, individual firefighters, corporate members, and a number of allied organizations. Membership: $300/year (organization); $25/year (individual).

Meetings/Conferences:
Semi-annual Meetings: Spring and Fall.

Publications:
Dispatch. q. adv.

National Water Resources Association *(1932)*
3800 N. Fairfax Drive, Suite Four
Arlington, VA 22203

Tel: (703)524-1544 *Fax:* (703)524-1548
E-Mail: nwra@nwra.org
Web Site: www.nwra.org
Members: 5000 individuals
Staff: 3
Annual Budget: $500-1,000,000
Executive Vice President: Thomas F. Donnelly
Vice President, Government Relations: Kris D. Polly

Historical Note

Formerly (1970) National Reclamation Association. Operates in 16 western states. Members are directors of water resource development projects such as irrigation districts, canal companies, conservancy districts and water users in general. Memberships available through state associations and the Professional Services Council.

Meetings/Conferences:

Annual Meetings: Fall

Publications:

Water Report. w.
Nat'l Water Line. m. adv.

National Watercolor Society *(1920)*

915 S. Pacific Ave.
San Pedro, CA 90731
Toll Free: (800)486 - 8670
E-Mail: nws-website@cox.net
Web Site: www.nws-online.org
Members: 1700 individuals
Staff: 15
Annual Budget: $50-100,000
Director, Membership: Lowrie Sprung
E-Mail: nws-website@cox.net

Historical Note

NWS is dedicated to the exhibition and promotion of excellence in water media painting. Membership: $40/year (signature juried member); $35/year (associate).

Meetings/Conferences:

Annual Meetings: January, with an Exhibition in Fall or early Winter

Publications:

Newsletter/Periodical. q.
NWS Catalogue. a.

National Watermelon Association *(1914)*

1305 West Dr. MLK JR. Blvd.
Suite One, Box Four
Plant City, FL 33563-3311
Tel: (813)754-7575 *Fax:* (813)754-1118
E-Mail: nwa@tampabay.rr.com
Web Site: www.nationalwatermelonassociation.co m
Members: 700 individuals
Staff: 3
Annual Budget: $250-500,000
Executive Director: Bob Morrissey

Historical Note

NWA members are producers, distributors and sellers of watermelons and related support industries. Membership: $150/year (individual).

Meetings/Conferences:

2007 - Asheville, NC(Grove Park Inn)/Feb. 21-25/400
2008 - Orange Beach, CA(Perdido Beach Resort)/Feb. 20-24/400

Publications:

Convention Program Book. a. adv.
The Vineline Magazine. bi-m. adv.
Convention Proceedings. a.

National Waterways Conference *(1960)*

4650 Washington Blvd., #608
Arlington, VA 22201
Tel: (703)243-4090 *Fax:* (703)243-4155
E-Mail: info@waterways.org
Web Site: www.waterways.org
Members: 350 businesses
Staff: 4
Annual Budget: $250-500,000
President: Worth Hager
E-Mail: info@waterways.org

Historical Note

An umbrella group of shippers, barge lines and local port authorities working to promote a better understanding of the public value of the American waterways system. Membership: $100/year (individual); $1000/year (organization/company).

Meetings/Conferences:

Annual Meetings: September/350

Publications:

Washington Watch. m.

National Weather Association *(1975)*

1697 Capri Way
Charlottesville, VA 22911-3534
Tel: (434)296-9966 *Fax:* (434)296-9966
E-Mail: natweaasoc@aol.com
Web Site: www.nwas.org
Members: 3000 individuals
Staff: 2
Annual Budget: $100-250,000
Executive Director: J. Kevin Lavin
E-Mail: natweaasoc@aol.com

Historical Note

NWA is a member-led professional association supporting and promoting excellence in operational meteorology and related activities for over 25 years. Awards Radio-Television Weathercaster Seal of Approval through testing and a continuing education requirement. Sponsors an annual awards program; provides grants to teachers to help improve teaching of meteorology in grades K-12; and has recently started a college scholarship program. Membership: $42year (individual); $21/year (student); $125/year (organization/company).

Meetings/Conferences:

Annual Meetings: mid October/300-450

Publications:

National Weather Digest. semi-a. adv.
Newsletter. 12/year.
Meeting Program. a. adv.

National Weather Service Employees Organization *(1976)*

601 Pennsylvania Ave. NW
Suite 900
Washington, DC 20004-2612
Tel: (703)293-9651 *Fax:* (703)293-9653
Web Site: www.nwseo.org
Members: 1200 individuals
Staff: 2
Annual Budget: $250-500,000
Director, Membership Services: Peter Nuhn

Meetings/Conferences:

Annual Meetings: Fall

Publications:

Four Winds. q.

National Wellness Institute *(1977)*

1300 College Court
P.O. Box 827
Stevens Point, WI 54481-0827
Tel: (715)342-2969 *Fax:* (715)342-2979
Toll Free: (800)243 - 8694
E-Mail: nwi@nationalwellness.org
Web Site: www.nationalwellness.org
Members: 2400 individuals
Staff: 3
Annual Budget: $250-500,000
Executive Director: Derrick Bell

Historical Note

NWI is composed of professionals working in all areas of health and wellness promotion. Its mission is to meet the growing need of these professionals for information, services and networking. Membership: $179/year (deluxe individual); $399/year (deluxe organization); $89/year (basic individual); $209/year (basic organization).

Meetings/Conferences:

Annual Meetings: With Nat'l Wellness Conference in July at Univ. of WI - Stevens Pt.

Publications:

Health Issues Update. bi-m.
Wellness Management (newsletter). q.

National Wheel and Rim Association *(1924)*

5121 Bowden Road, Suite 303
Jacksonville, FL 32216-5950
Tel: (904)737-2900 *Fax:* (904)636-9881
E-Mail: nwra@bellsouth.net
Web Site: www.nationalwheelandrim.org
Members: 34 with over 245 locations
Staff: 3
Annual Budget: $250-500,000
Executive Vice President: Angelo Volpe

Historical Note

Organized in Chicago in 1924 at the Metropole Hotel. Members are warehouse distributors of wheels, rims and related parts. NWRA is affiliated with the National Association of Wholesaler-Distributors.

Meetings/Conferences:

Annual Meetings: September/200

Publications:

Wheel and Rim Manual. irreg.
Membership Directory/Roster. a.

National WIC Association *(1983)*

2001 S St. NW
Suite 580
Washington, DC 20009-1165
Tel: (202)232-5492 *Fax:* (202)387-5281
Web Site: www.nwica.org
Members: 19 companies, 711 individuals
Staff: 5
Annual Budget: $500-1,000,000
Executive Director: Douglas A. Greenaway
E-Mail: douglasg@nwica.org
Director, Nutritional Programs: Cecilia Richardson, MS, RD, LD
E-Mail: crichard@nwica.org

Historical Note

NWA members are state and local agency directors and nutrition coordinators of the Special Supplemental Nutrition Program for Women, Infants and Children.

Meetings/Conferences:

Annual Meetings: Spring
2007 - Washington, DC(The Sofitel)/March 10-14/150
2007 - Pittsburgh, PA(The David Lawrence Convention Center)/Apr. 27-May 2/1304

Publications:

WIC for a Healthier America. a.
Washington Update. w.
Legislative Agenda. a.
Monday Morning Report. w.

National Wildlife Rehabilitators Association *(1982)*

2625 Clearwater Road, Suite 110
St. Cloud, MN 56301
Tel: (320)230-9920 *Fax:* (320)230-3077
E-Mail: nwra@nwra.wildlife.org
Web Site: www.nwrawildlife.org
Members: 1500 individuals
Staff: 3
Annual Budget: $250-500,000
Office Manager: Debra Duffy
E-Mail: nwra@nwra.wildlife.org

Historical Note

NWRA members are professional wildlife rehabilitators and others with an interest in wild animal care. NWRA provides information, education and training to persons involved with helping injured, orphaned and displaced wild animals grow, heal and return to the wild. Membership: $40/year (individual); 20/year (student); $70/year (family); $1500 (life membership).

Meetings/Conferences:

Annual Meetings: Spring
2007 - Chicago, IL(Indian Lakes Resort)/March 13-17/500

Publications:

Newsletter. semi-a. adv.
Wildlife Rehabilitation Bulletin. semi-a. adv.
Wildlife Rehabilitation Proceedings. a.
NWRA Membership Directory. a.

National Women's Studies Association *(1977)*

7100 Baltimore Ave., Suite 502
College Park, MD 20740
Tel: (301)403-0524 *Fax:* (301)403-4137
E-Mail: nwsa@umail.umd.edu
Web Site: www.nwsa.org
Members: 3000 individuals
Staff: 1
Annual Budget: $100-250,000

Executive Director: Allison Kimmich

Historical Note

NWSA members are teachers, students, independent scholars, program administrators, and community activists. Membership: $75/year (individual); $185/year (institution).

Meetings/Conferences:

Annual Meetings: June

Publications:

NWSAction Newsletter. irreg.
NWSA Journal. q. adv.
Women's Studies Program Directory. bien.

National Wood Flooring Association *(1986)*

111 Chesterfield Ind. Blvd.
Chesterfield, MO 63005
Tel: (636)519-9663 *Fax:* (636)519-9664
Toll Free: (800)422 - 4556
E-Mail: edk@nwfa.org
Web Site: www.woodfloors.org
Members: 3500 companies
Staff: 15
Annual Budget: $2-5,000,000
Chief Executive Officer and Executive Director: Edward S. Korczak, CAE
E-Mail: edk@nwfa.org
Executive Assistant: Jan Kuehn
E-Mail: jank@nwfa.org
Director, Technical Services: Steve Seabaugh
E-Mail: steves@nwfa.org

Historical Note

An international Trade association for the wood flooring industry, providing technical training, publications, educational videos, certification programs, management education programs, and membership services that assist members in operating their businesses more successfully. NWFA's worldwide membership includes wood flooring manufacturers, dealers, contractors and wholesale distributors.

Meetings/Conferences:

Annual Meetings: Spring
2007 – Denver, CO(Denver Convention Center)/Apr. 11-14/4000
2008 – Ft. Lauderdale, FL

Publications:

Installation Guidelines.
Technical Reference Manual. m.
Hardwood Floors Magazine. 7/yr. adv.
The Log. bi-m.

National Wood Tank Institute *(1942)*

P.O. Box 2755
Philadelphia, PA 19120
Tel: (215)329-9022 *Fax:* (215)329-1177
E-Mail: jhillman@woodtank.com
Web Site: www.woodtank.com
Members: 8 companies
Annual Budget: under $10,000
Secretary: Harrison W. Rippen
E-Mail: jhillman@woodtank.com

Historical Note

NWTI members are companies and individuals in the U.S. and Canada involved in the manufacture of wood tanks, vats and pipes.

National Wooden Pallet and Container Association *(1947)*

329 S. Patrick St.
Alexandria, VA 22314-3501
Tel: (703)519-6104 *Fax:* (703)519-4720
E-Mail: palletinfo@palletcentral.com
Web Site: www.palletcentral.com
Members: 630 companies
Staff: 9
Annual Budget: $1-2,000,000
President and Chief Executive Officer: Bruce N. Scholnick
Director, Technical: Edgar Deomano, Ph.D.
Director, Meetings and Education: Isabel "Mimi" Sullivan

Historical Note

Represents manufacturers, recyclers and distributors of pallets, containers and reels, and companies that supply products, equipment, and services to the industry. Membership fee varies, based on annual volume of sales.

Meetings/Conferences:

Annual Meetings: Winter

Publications:

PalletCentral newsletter. m. adv.

National Woodland Owners Association *(1983)*

374 Maple Ave. East, Suite 310
Vienna, VA 22180-4751
Tel: (703)255-2700 *Fax:* (703)281-9200
Toll Free: (800)476 - 8733
E-Mail: info@woodlandowners.org
Web Site: www.woodlandowners.org
Members: 25000 individuals
Staff: 3
Annual Budget: $100-250,000
President: Keith A. Argow

Historical Note

Founded with the purpose of uniting non-industrial private woodland owners in America; membership includes landowners in all 50 states. Although independent of the forest products industry and public agencies, NWOA works with all organizations to promote non-industrial forestry and the interests of woodland owners. Has 34 state affiliates. Membership: $25/year (individual); $75-1000/year (state association).

Meetings/Conferences:

Annual Meetings: None held.

Publications:

Woodland Report. q.
National Woodlands Magazine. q. adv.

National Writers Association *(1937)*

10940 S. Parker Rd. #508
Parker, CO 80134-7440
Tel: (303)841-0246 *Fax:* (303)841-2607
Web Site: www.nationalwriters.com
Members: 3000 individuals
Staff: 1
Annual Budget: $50-100,000
Executive Director: Sandy Whelchel

Historical Note

Founded in 1937 by David Raffelock to serve freelance writers. Membership: $65/year; $85/year (professional); $35/year (student).

Meetings/Conferences:

Annual Meetings: June, with the Associated Business Writers of America

Publications:

Authorship. q. adv.

National Writers Union *(1983)*

113 University Place
Sixth Floor
New York, NY 10003-4527
Tel: (212)254-0279 *Fax:* (212)254-0673
E-Mail: nwu@nwu.org
Web Site: www.nwu.org
Members: 3600 individuals
Staff: 8
Annual Budget: $500-1,000,000
President: Gerald Colby
Operations Manager: Juliet Sandford
E-Mail: eng-wachsber@online.emich.edu

Historical Note

An independent union established to improve the working conditions of freelance writers through the collective strength of its members. NWU members include journalists, novelists, biographers, historians, poets, children's book authors, textbook authors, commercial writers, technical writers and cartoonists. Originated in New York City in October, 1981 in connection with the American Writers Congress. Membership: $90-$195/year (based on income).

Meetings/Conferences:

Monthly Meetings: based on local area

Publications:

The American Writer. q. adv.

National Yogurt Association *(1987)*

2000 Corporate Ridge, Suite 1000
McLean, VA 22102
Tel: (703)821-0770 *Fax:* (703)821-1350
Web Site: www.aboutyogurt.com
Members: 5 companies
Staff: 3
Annual Budget: $500-1,000,000
President and Chief Executive Officer: Leslie G. Sarasin, CAE

Historical Note

Members are manufacturers and marketers of live and active culture yogurt products, and the suppliers to the industry.

Nationwide Alternate Delivery Alliance

P.O. Box 70244
Washington, DC 20024
Tel: (202)678-8350 *Fax:* (202)889-9209
Toll Free: (800)969 - 2258
President: Clyde Northrop

Historical Note

Members are private, regional delivery companies united to provide publishers with an alternative to postal delivery.

Native American Journalists Association *(1984)*

Al Neuharth Media Center
555 Dakota St.
Vermillion, SD 57069
Tel: (602)677-5282 *Fax:* (866)694-4264
E-Mail: info@naja.com
Web Site: www.naja.com
Members: 600 individuals
Staff: 2
Annual Budget: $250-500,000
Interim Executive Director: Kim Boca
E-Mail: info@naja.com

Publications:

Newsletter. bi-m.

NATSO, Representing America's Travel Plazas and Truckstops *(1960)*

1737 King St., Suite 200
Alexandria, VA 22314
Tel: (703)549-2100 *Fax:* (703)684-4525
Web Site: www.natso.com
Members: 1100 locations
Staff: 29
Annual Budget: $2-5,000,000
President and Chief Executive Officer: Lisa Mullings
E-Mail: lmullings@natso.com
Vice President, Public Affairs: Linda Arsdale
Director, Finance: Kimberly Roberts

Historical Note

Formerly (1993) the National Association of Truck Stop Operators. Members are owners and operators of large fully-equipped truck stops and travel plazas. Allied members include oil companies and other suppliers. Sponsors the Political Action Committee (NATSO/PAC). Headquarters for the American Truck Stop Foundation, dba The NATSO Foundation.

Meetings/Conferences:

Annual Meetings: Winter

Publications:

Stopwatch Magazine. bi-m. adv.
Checklink Directory. m.
Membership Directory. a.

Natural Colored Wool Growers Association *(1977)*

429 W. U.S. 30
Valparaiso, IN 46385-9207
Tel: (219)759-9665
E-Mail: kloese@gte.net
Web Site: www.ncwga.org
Members: 640 individuals
Staff: 4
Annual Budget: $10-25,000
Registrar: Barbara Kloese
E-Mail: kloese@gte.net

Historical Note

NCWGA members are breeders and owners of colored sheep as well as those who use or otherwise have an interest in colored wool. In addition to assisting members in the development, improvement and promotion of colored sheep and colored wool, the NCWGA maintains a registration program. Membership: $20/year (individual); $15/year (organization/company); $5/year (junior).

Publications:

Marker. q. adv.

Natural Gas Supply Association *(1965)*

805 15th St. NW

Suite 510
Washington, DC 20005
Tel: (202)326-9300 *Fax:* (202)326-9330
Web Site: www.ngsa.org
Members: 90 companies
Staff: 10
Annual Budget: $2-5,000,000
President and Chief Executive Officer: R. Skip Horvath
Vice President, Regulatory Affairs: Patricia W. Jagtiani
E-Mail: pjagtiani@ngsa.org
Director, Public Affairs: Mark Stultz

Historical Note
Members are domestic natural gas producers and marketers. Formerly (1979) known as the Natural Gas Supply Committee.

Meetings/Conferences:
Annual Meetings: First Quarter of the Year

Natural Gas Vehicle Coalition *(1988)*

400 N. Capitol St. NW
Washington, DC 20001
Tel: (202)824-7360 *Fax:* (202)824-7087
Web Site: www.ngvc.org
Members: 180 companies
Staff: 6
Annual Budget: $1-2,000,000
President: Richard R. Kolodziej
E-Mail: rkolodziej@ngvc.org
Director, Government Affairs: Paul Kerkhoven
E-Mail: pkerkhoven@ngvc.org

Historical Note
NGVC members are organizations with an interest in encouraging the development of natural gas powered vehicles. Membership fee varies, $500-$25,200/year, based on type of company and business volume.

Meetings/Conferences:
Annual Meetings: Fall

Publications:
NGV Purchasing Guide. a.
NGVCommunications. w.
Member Business Guide. a. adv.

Natural Science Collections Alliance *(1972)*

P.O. Box 44095
Washington, DC 20026-4095
Tel: (202)633-2772 *Fax:* (202)633-2821
E-Mail: general@nscalliance.org
Web Site: www.nscalliance.org
Members: 83 institutions, 25 societies
Staff: 2
Annual Budget: $100-250,000
Manager: Karen Kajiwara

Historical Note
Founded as Association of Systematics Collections; assumed its current name in 2001. NSC Alliance is a nonprofit assocation that supports natural science collections, their human resources, the institutions that house them, and their activities. Members are museums, zoos, botanic gardens and other systematic collections housed at universities, non-profit research institutions, state-funded institutions, governmental agencies, and professional societies of individuals interested in the systematics of organisms. Membership: $750, $2300, or $6000/year (based on size of organization). Affiliate Membership: $100-$1000/year (based on size).

Meetings/Conferences:
Annual Meetings: Summer
2007 – Washington, DC(Capital Hilton)/May 14-15

Naval Enlisted Reserve Association *(1957)*

6703 Farragut Ave.
Falls Church, VA 22042-2189
Tel: (703)534-1329 *Fax:* (703)534-3617
Toll Free: (800)776 - 9020
E-Mail: members@nera.org
Web Site: www.nera.org
Members: 15000 individuals
Staff: 3
Annual Budget: $250-500,000
Executive Director: Joanne Elliott

Historical Note
Members are the enlisted personnel in the Navy, Marine Corps and Coast Guard Reserve. Membership: $20/year (individual).

Meetings/Conferences:
Annual Meetings: October

Publications:
Mariner. q. adv.

Naval Reserve Association *(1954)*

1619 King St.
Alexandria, VA 22314
Tel: (703)548-5800 *Fax:* (703)683-3647
Toll Free: (866)672 - 4968
E-Mail: membership@navy-reserve.org
Web Site: www.navy-reserve.org
Members: 25000 individuals
Staff: 8
Annual Budget: $1-2,000,000
Executive Director: RADM Casey Coane
Chief Financial Officer: Bob Lyman
Director, Legislation: CAPT Ike Puzon
Director, Membership and Professional Development: CAPT Art Schultz

Historical Note
NRA is a professional organization of reservists joined together to support the Navy and to provide services to Naval Reservists. Membership: $35/year (individual).

Meetings/Conferences:
Semi-annual Meetings: Spring and Fall
2007 – Washington, DC(Sheraton Crystal City)/Apr. 26-28
2007 – Chicago, IL(Oak Brook Marriott Hotel)/Oct. 4-6
2008 – Honolulu, HI/April
2008 – Norfolk, VA/September

Publications:
Naval Reserve Association News. m. adv.

NCSL International *(1961)*

2995 Wilderness Place, Suite 107
Boulder, CO 80301-5404
Tel: (303)440-3339 *Fax:* (303)440-3384
E-Mail: info@ncsli.org
Web Site: www.ncsli.org
Members: 1500 laboratories
Staff: 3
Annual Budget: $500-1,000,000
Business Manager: Craig Gulka
E-Mail: cgulka@ncsli.org

Historical Note
Founded as National Conference of Standards Laboratories; assumed its current name in 2001. NCSL is an independent non-profit association of academic, scientific, industrial, commercial and governmental laboratories concerned with the measurement of physical quantities, the calibration of standards and instruments, and the development of standards of practice. Membership: $400/first year, $325/annually.

Meetings/Conferences:
Annual Meetings: Summer

Publications:
NCSL Newsletter. q.
NCSL Directory of Standards Laboratories. online.
Conference Proceedings (online). a.

NEA - the Association of Union Constructors *(1969)*

1501 Lee Hwy., Suite 202
Arlington, VA 22209
Tel: (703)524-3336 *Fax:* (703)524-3364
Web Site: www.nea-online.org
Members: 150 companies
Staff: 8
Annual Budget: $1-2,000,000
Executive Vice President: Noel C. Borck
Vice President, Industrial Relations: Kevin J. Hilton
Manager, Communications: Todd Mustard
Vice President, Association Services: Wayne Rice

Historical Note
Formerly National Steel Erectors Association and National Erectors Association; assumed its current name in 2001. A construction employers trade association consisting of steel erectors, general contractors, and industrial maintenance firms. Primary functions are labor relations and safety/information services.

Meetings/Conferences:
Annual Meetings: Spring

Publications:
NEA Contractor Safety Guide.
NEA Craft Jurisdiction Guide. a.
NEA Notes. q.
The Construction Use magazine.

Neckwear Association of America *(1946)*

151 Lexington Ave., #2F
New York, NY 10016
Tel: (212)683-8454 *Fax:* (212)686-7382
Web Site: www.apparel.net
Members: 100 companies
Staff: 2
Annual Budget: $100-250,000
Executive Director: Gerald Andersen, CAE
E-Mail: geralda476@aol.com

Historical Note
Formerly (1979) the Men's Tie Foundation.

Meetings/Conferences:
Semi-annual Meetings: June and October in New York, NY

Publications:
Neckwear News.
Washington Updates.
Neckwear Industry Directory. bien.

Netherlands Chamber of Commerce in the United States *(1903)*

267 Fifth Ave., Suite 301
New York, NY 10016
Tel: (212)265-6460 *Fax:* (212)265-6402
E-Mail: newyork@nlcoc.com
Web Site: www.nlcoc.com
Members: 400 businesses
Staff: 3
Administrator: R. Van Heche
E-Mail: newyork@nlcoc.com

Historical Note
The mission of The Netherlands Chamber of Commerce in the United States is to expand business relations between the Netherlands and the United States, to assist Dutch companies in starting or expanding their business in the United States, and to assist American companies in starting or expanding their business in the Netherlands. Membership: $775/year (corporate); $1,550/year (sustaining).

Meetings/Conferences:
Annual Meetings: November/New York, NY

Network of Executive Women in Hospitality *(1984)*

P.O. Box 322
Shawano, WI 54166
Tel: (715)526-5267 *Fax:* (715)526-5179
E-Mail: office@newh.org
Web Site: www.newh.org
Members: 1000 individuals
Executive Director: Sheila Lohmiller
E-Mail: office@newh.org

Historical Note
NEWH is a professional association for women involved in hotel and restaurant management or having an interest in the industry. Membership: $100/year (individual); $90/year (associate).

Publications:
Membership Directory. a.

Network of Ingredient Marketing Specialists *(1981)*

304 W. Liberty St., Suite 201
Louisville, KY 40202
Tel: (502)589-3783 *Fax:* (502)589-3602
E-Mail: nims@hqtrs.com
Web Site: www.nimsgroup.com
Members: 18 companies
Staff: 1
Annual Budget: $50-100,000

Historical Note
Founded as North American Ingredient Marketing Specialists; assumed its current name in 1998. NIMS members are food ingredient brokers.

Meetings/Conferences:
Semi-Annual Meetings: Summer and Winter

Network on Ministry in Specialized Settings *(1987)*
P.O. Box 2409
Poquosou, VA 23662
Tel: (757)728-3180 *Fax:* (757)728-3179
E-Mail: info@comissnetwork.org
Web Site: www.comissnetwork.org
Members: 40 organizations
Annual Budget: $10-25,000
Chair: Chaplain Will Kinnaird
E-Mail: info@comissnetwork.org

Historical Note
Founded in 1979 as the Council on Ministry in Specialized Settings, this organization successively became the Council, Congress, and Coalition before becoming the Network. Informally known as the COMMISS Network. Providing advice and discussion to chaplains and ministers serving congregations in institutional settings, the Network is a division of the American Association of Pastoral Counselors. Membership: $100/year.

Meetings/Conferences:
Annual Meetings: Always Washington, DC/first weekend in December/100

Publications:
Journal of Pastoral Care. q. adv.

Network Professional Association *(1990)*
17 S. High St., Suite 200
Columbus, OH 43215
Tel: (614)221-1900 Ext: 227 *Fax:* (614)221-1989
Toll Free: (888)672 - 6726
E-Mail: npa@npa.org
Web Site: www.npanet.org
Staff: 1
Executive Director: Lori Landry

Historical Note
Members are network administrators and other professionals involved in computer network deployment, maintenance and administration. Membership: $175/year.

Neural Networks Council

Historical Note
A subsidiary of the Institute of Electrical and Electronics Engineers (IEEE). Membership in the Council, open only to IEEE members, includes subscription to a technical periodical in the field published by IEEE. Administrative support is provided by IEEE.

Neurodevelopmental Treatment Association *(1967)*
1540 S. Coast Hwy., Suite 203
Laguna Beach, CA 92651
Toll Free: (800)869 - 9295
E-Mail: info@ndta.org
Web Site: www.ndta.org
Members: 1600 individuals
Staff: 4
Annual Budget: $100-250,000
Executive Director: Brad Lund

Historical Note
NDTA members include physical therapists, occupational therapists, speech-language pathologists, special education professionals, physicians and others using an interdisciplinary approach in treating individuals with central nervous system dysfunction. Membership: $95/year (individual); $55/year (student/retired); $250/year (corporate).

Meetings/Conferences:
Annual Meetings: October

Publications:
NDTA Network Newsletter. bi-m. adv.

Neurosurgical Society of America *(1948)*
P.O. Box 208082
New Haven, CT 06520
Tel: (203)785-2791
Web Site: www.neurosurgicalsociety.com
Members: 210 individuals
Annual Budget: $50-100,000
Secretary: Dr. Nicholas M. Barbaro

Historical Note
Membership by invitation only. Has no paid officers or full-time staff.

Meetings/Conferences:
Annual Meetings: Spring-Summer

New York Academy of Sciences *(1817)*
Seven World Trade Center
250 Greenwich St., 40th Floor
New York, NY 10007
Tel: (212)838-0230 *Fax:* (212)888-2894
Toll Free: (800)843 - 6927
E-Mail: info@nyas.org
Web Site: www.nyas.org
Members: 23000 individuals
Staff: 76
Annual Budget: $5-10,000,000
President: Ellis Rubinstein
Chief Financial Officer: Thomas J. Kelly
Director, Programs: Rashid Shaikh, Ph.D.
Director, Human Rights: Svetlana Stone-Wachtel

Historical Note
The Academy, founded in 1817, is the oldest scientific organization in New York and the third oldest in the nation. Its initiatives include disseminating scientific information, advancing science education, protecting the human rights of scientists, and applying science and technology to achieve economic and social goals. Has an annual budget of $8.5 million. Membership: $95/year (domestic); $115/year (overseas).

Publications:
Annals of NYAS. 28/yr.
Academy Update Magazine. 6/yr.

New York Board of Trade *(1870)*
One N. End Ave.
New York, NY 10282
Tel: (212)748-4090 *Fax:* (212)748-4088
E-Mail: reginarocker@nybot.com
Web Site: www.nybot.com
Members: 975 individuals
Staff: 250
Annual Budget: $50-100,000,000
President and Chief Executive: Charles H. Falk
Group Vice President, Information Technology: Steve Bass
Vice President, Administration: Richard M. Foster
Executive Vice President, Operations: Patrick L. Gambaro
Senior Vice President, Market Development: Joseph O'Neill
Vice President, eCops Marketing and Administration: Regina Rocker
E-Mail: reginarocker@nybot.com

Historical Note
Formerly (1998) the New York Cotton Exchange and The Coffee, Sugar and Cocoa Exchange, Inc. Oldest of the New York commodity futures exchanges. Formed Citrus Associates in 1966 and Finex Division in 1985. Purchased the New York Futures Exchange, a wholly-owned subsidiary, in 1993.

Publications:
Member Newsletter. m. adv.
Daily Market Report. d. adv.
Weekly Trade Report. w. adv.

New York Mercantile Exchange *(1872)*
World Financial Center
One North End Ave.
New York, NY 10282-1101
Tel: (212)299-2000 *Fax:* (212)301-4700
E-Mail: exchangeinfo@nymex.com
Web Site: www.nymex.com
Members: 816 individuals
Staff: 245
Annual Budget: $10-25,000,000
President: James E. Newsome
General Counsel and Chief Administrative Officer: Christopher Bowen
Chief Information Officer: Samuel Gaer
Vice President, Membership Services: M. Dawn Lowe

Historical Note
Formerly (1880) Butter, Cheese, and Egg Exchange of the City of New York. Concerned with the trading of futures in heating and crude oil, unleaded gasoline and heating options, platinum, and palladium. Also known as the Commodity Exchange. Has an annual budget of approximately $10 million.

Publications:
Energy in the News. q.
Membership Directory. a.
Metals in the News. bi-a.

New York Stock Exchange *(1792)*
11 Wall St.
New York, NY 10005
Tel: (212)656-3000
Web Site: www.nyse.com
Members: 1366 companies
Staff: 1450
Annual Budget: $5-10,000,000
Chief Executive Officer: John A. Thain
Senior Vice President, Communications: Richard C. Adamonis
Executive Vice President and General Counsel: Richard P. Bernard

Historical Note
NYSE is the one of the oldest U.S. markets for the securities industry. More than 2,500 major U.S. and foreign corporations are traded on the Exchange. NYSE also provides a marketplace to trade options through the NYSE composite index, NYSE utility index, and more than 160 stock options.

Publications:
NYSE Magazine. bi-m. adv.

Newspaper Association Managers *(1923)*
c/o New England Newspaper Ass'n
70 Washington St., Suite 214
Salem, MA 01970
Tel: (978)744-8940 *Fax:* (978)744-0333
Web Site: www.nammanagers.com
Members: 70 individuals
Staff: 1
Annual Budget: $25-50,000
Clerk: Morley Piper

Historical Note
An association of managers of state, regional, national and international press associations.

Meetings/Conferences:
Annual Meetings: August, and Legislative Conference in December

Publications:
The Round-Table. m.

Newspaper Association of America *(1992)*
1921 Gallows Road, Suite 600
Vienna, VA 22182-3900
Tel: (703)902-1600 *Fax:* (703)917-0636
Web Site: www.naa.org
Members: 1700 individuals
Staff: 140
Annual Budget: $25-50,000,000
President and Chief Executive Officer: John F. Sturm
Senior Vice President, Public Policy: Paul Boyle
Senior Vice President, Association Sales and Marketing: Reggie R. Hall
Senior Vice President, Marketing: John Kimball
Senior Vice President and Chief Financial Officer: Margaret Vassilikos

Historical Note
Formed in 1992 by the American Newspaper Publishers Association, Association of Newspaper Classified Advertising Managers, International Circulation Managers Association, International Newspaper Advertising and Marketing Executives, Newspaper Advertising Bureau, Newspaper Advertising Co-op Network and the Newspaper Research Council. Members include 1,700 newspapers in the United States and Canada and 63 international newspapers. Has an annual budget of approximately $30 million.

Meetings/Conferences:
Annual Meetings: Spring

Publications:
Digital Edge.
Big Ideas for Smaller-Market Newspapers.
Presstime Magazine. m.
Foundation Update. Q.
Fusion.
Labor and Employment Law Letter.

Newspaper Guild - CWA *(1933)*
501 Third St. NW
Suite 250
Washington, DC 20001-2760
Tel: (202)434-7177 *Fax:* (202)434-1472
Toll Free: (800)585 - 5864
E-Mail: guild@cwa-union.org

Web Site: www.newsguild.org
Members: 34000 individuals
Staff: 32
Annual Budget: $2-5,000,000
President: Linda K. Foley
E-Mail: lfoley@cwa-union.org
Secretary-Treasurer: Bernard J. Lunzer
E-Mail: blunzer@cwa-union.org
Editor, Guild Reporter: Andrew Zipser
E-Mail: azipser@cwa-union.org

Historical Note

A labor union representing editorial and commercial department employees of newspapers, wire and news services, magazines and related enterprises in the U.S., Canada and Puerto Rico. Established as the American Newspaper Guild in Washington, DC, December 15, 1933. Assumed its present name in 1971. Affiliated with AFL-CIO, the Canadian Labour Congress, and the International Federation of Journalists. In 1997, TNG became a sector of the Communications Workers of America. TNG membership: 6% of 1 weeks pay/month.

Publications:

Guild Reporter. m.

Newspaper Purchasing Management Association *(1958)*
c/o New York Times Co.
101 W. Main St., Suite 7000
Norfolk, VA 23510
Tel: (757)628-2079 *Fax:* (757)628-1919
Web Site: www.npma.net
Members: 100 individuals
Annual Budget: $25-50,000
President: Bob Steinmetz

Historical Note

Members are purchasing officers at daily newspapers and newspaper publishing companies. Has no paid officers or full-time staff. Membership: $150/year (regular); $100/year (associate).

Meetings/Conferences:

Annual Meetings: Spring

Publications:

NPMA Newsletter. bi-m.
Roster. q.

NFHS Music Association *(1983)*
P.O. Box 690
Indianapolis, IN 46206
Tel: (317)972-6900 *Fax:* (317)822-5700
E-Mail: ksummers@nfhs.org
Web Site: www.nfhs.org
Members: 850 individuals
Staff: 2
Annual Budget: under $10,000
Assistant Director: Kent Summers

Historical Note

Founded as NFHS Music Association; assumed its current name in 2003. NFHSMA members are secondary school and college music directors. Membership: $20/year (individual).

Meetings/Conferences:

2007 – Indianapolis, IN/Nov. 9-10

Publications:

NFHS News. bi-m. adv.
NFHSMA Journal. irreg.

NFHS Speech Debate and Theatre Association *(1986)*
P.O. Box 690
Indianapolis, IN 46206
Tel: (317)972-6900 *Fax:* (317)822-5700
E-Mail: ksummers@nfhs.org
Web Site: www.nfhs.org/sdta.htm
Members: 1250 individuals
Staff: 2
Annual Budget: under $10,000
Executive Director: Kent Summers

Historical Note

Founded as NFHS Speech, Debate and Theatre Association; assumed current name in 2003. Members are secondary and post-secondary speech, drama and debate coaches. Affiliated with the National Federation of State High School Associations. Membership: $20/year (individual).

Meetings/Conferences:

2007 – Indianapolis, IN/October

Publications:

Newsletter. bi-m. adv.
Forensic Educator. a.

NIBA - The Belting Association *(1920)*
N19 W24400 Riverwood Dr.
Waukesha, WI 53188
Tel: (262)523-9090 *Fax:* (262)523-9091
E-Mail: staff@niba.org
Web Site: www.niba.org
Members: 300 companies
Staff: 2
Annual Budget: $500-1,000,000
Executive Vice President and Chief Executive Officer: Randall E. Rakow
Manager, Association Services: Cie Motelet
E-Mail: randyr@mranet.org

Historical Note

Founded as American Leather Belting Association; became National Industrial Leather Association in 1926, National Industrial Belting Association in 1977, and assumed its current name in 2001. Composed of distributors and manufacturers of flat industrial belting used for conveying, elevating and power transmission. Membership: $675-975/year.

Meetings/Conferences:

Annual Meetings: Fall/500
2007 – Baltimore, MD(Marriott Waterfront)/Sept. 19-22/500

Publications:

Technical Bulletins. irreg.
Beltline. q.

Nine to Five, National Association of Working Women *(1973)*
152 W. Wisconsin Ave., Suite 408
Milwaukee, WI 53203-2508
Tel: (414)274-0925 *Fax:* (414)272-2870
Toll Free: (800)522 - 0925
E-Mail: 9to5@9to5.org
Web Site: www.9to5.org
Members: 15000 individuals
Staff: 25
Annual Budget: $1-2,000,000
Director: Ellen Bravo
E-Mail: 9to5@9to5.org

Historical Note

Established in Boston, MA, 9 to 5 is a research and advocacy group concerned with working women's issues. Membership: $25/year (individuals); $40/year (institutions).

Publications:

Newsline. 5/year. adv.

NOFMA: the Wood Flooring Manufacturers Association *(1909)*
P.O. Box 3009
Memphis, TN 38173-0009
Tel: (901)526-5016 *Fax:* (901)526-7022
Web Site: www.nofma.org
Members: 27 manufacturers
Staff: 6
Annual Budget: $1-2,000,000
Executive Vice President: Timm Locke

Historical Note

Formerly (2002) National Oak Flooring Manufacturers Association. Main purpose is to establish manufacturing and grading standards for the industry and to see that these standards are observed by a continuous inspection service. Open to manufacturers in the U.S., Canada, Central and South America who make solid and engineered hardwood flooring, and also to associate members who provide allied services, make allied products, or are distributors. Formerly the Oak Flooring Manufacturers of the United States and Southern Oak Flooring Industries. NOFMA sponsors the Hardwood Flooring Installation School (since 1979) with the Maple Flooring Manufacturers Association and the National Wood Flooring Association. The Wood Flooring Institute is the promotional arm of NOFMA.

Meetings/Conferences:

Semi-Annual Meetings: Summer & first week of December Memphis, TN(Peabody)

Publications:

Advocate. q.

Non Commissioned Officers Association of the U.S.A. *(1960)*
610 Madison St.
Alexandria, VA 22314
Tel: (703)549-0311 *Fax:* (703)549-0245
Toll Free: (800)662 - 2620
E-Mail: membersuc@ncoausa.org
Web Site: www.ncoausa.org
Members: 65000 individuals
Staff: 25
Annual Budget: $10-25,000,000
Contact: Richard Schneider

Historical Note

Individuals who serve or have served in U.S. Military forces in grades E1 through E9. Membership: $30/year (full member); $20 (auxiliary), $20/year (apprentice); $55/year (dual); $45/year (joint).

Publications:

NCOA Journal. bi-m. adv.
NCOA Newsbrief. bi-w.
NCOA Inside Update. m.

Non-Ferrous Founders' Society *(1943)*
1480 Renaissance Dr., Suite 310
Park Ridge, IL 60068
Tel: (847)299-0950 *Fax:* (847)299-3598
Web Site: www.nffs.org
Members: 160 companies
Staff: 4
Annual Budget: $500-1,000,000
Executive Director: James L. Mallory, CAE
E-Mail: jlm@nffs.org
Director, Membership: Ryan J. Moore
Director, Education and Training: Jerrod A. Weaver
E-Mail: NQS9000@nffs.org

Historical Note

Members are manufacturers of bronze, brass and aluminum castings. Absorbed the Cast Bronze Institute in 1988. Introduced NQS 9000 Quality System for Metalcasting in 1996. Membership: $800-3700/year (company).

Meetings/Conferences:

Annual Meetings: Fall

Publications:

Crucible. bi-m. adv.
NFFS Notes. m.
NFFScene. bi-m.

Non-Powder Gun Products Association *(1975)*

Historical Note

Affiliated with the Sporting Goods Manufacturers Association which provides administrative support.

NORA: An Association of Responsible Recyclers *(1984)*
5965 Amber Ridge Road
Haymarket, VA 20169
Tel: (703)753-4277 *Fax:* (703)753-2445
Web Site: www.noranews.org
Members: 200 companies
Staff: 3
Annual Budget: $250-500,000
Executive Director: Scott D. Parker
E-Mail: sparker@noranews.org

Historical Note

Founded as National Oil Recyclers Association; absorbed National Association of Chemical Recyclers in 2000, and assumed its current name in 2001. NORA is a trade association representing the interests of companies in the United States engaged in the safe recycling of used oil, antifreeze, waste water and oil filters. Membership: $1,000-5,000/year (company).

Publications:

Liquid Recycling. 6/year. adv.

North America Colleges and Teachers of Agriculture *(1955)*
151 W. 100 South
Rupert, ID 83350
Tel: (208)436-1384
E-Mail: ricpar@pmt.org
Web Site: www.nactateachers.org
Members: 1000 individuals
Staff: 5

Annual Budget: $25-50,000
Editor, NACTA Journal: Rick Parker
E-Mail: ricpar@pmt.org

Historical Note
Formerly (2002) National Association of Colleges and Teachers of Agriculture. NACTA promotes excellence in the teaching of agriculture and related disciplines at the postsecondary level. Membership: $50/year (individual); $100/year (institution).

Meetings/Conferences:
Annual Meetings: Summer

Publications:
NACTA Journal. q. adv.

North American Academy of Ecumenists *(1957)*
5025 Southampton Circle
Tampa, FL 33647-2031
Tel: (813)910-1532
Web Site: www.naae.net
Members: 300 individuals
Annual Budget: under $10,000
Treasurer: Rev. Russell L. Meyer
E-Mail: russellm@fbsynod.org

Historical Note
Formerly Association of Professors of Ecumenics. Membership includes ecumenically active clergy and laity as well as professors and students. Affiliated with the Journal of Ecumenical Studies. Has no paid officers or full-time staff. Membership: $25/year (student); $50/year (regular).

Meetings/Conferences:
Annual Meetings: September

Publications:
Journal of Ecumenical Studies. 3/year.

North American Academy of Liturgy
2127 N.W. Irving, #301
Portland, OR 97210
Tel: (877)737-0822 *Fax:* (877)348-1429
Web Site: www.naal-liturgy.org
Treasurer: Dr. Glenn CJ Byer
E-Mail: gcjb@aol.com

Historical Note
Members of the association are Christian and Jewish specialists in liturgy and related art disciplines. Has no paid officers or full-time staff.

Meetings/Conferences:
Annual Meetings: Winter
2007 - Toronto, ON, Canada(Park Hyatt)/Jan. 4-7
2008 - Savannah, GA(Hyatt)/Jan. 3-6
2009 - Baltimore, MD(Hyatt)/Jan. 2-5

Publications:
Proceedings. a.

North American Agricultural Marketing Officials *(1920)*
c/o Wyoming Business Council
214 W. 15th St.
Cheyenne, WY 82002
E-Mail: info@naamo.org
Web Site: www.naamo.org
Members: 45 individuals
Annual Budget: $10-25,000
Vice President: Linda MacDonald

Historical Note
Formerly (1977) National Association of Marketing Officials and (1992) National Agricultural Marketing Officials. Has no paid staff or permanent address. Officers change annually. Members are state and provincial officials responsible for agricultural products marketing programs in the United States, Canada and ultimately Mexico. Membership: $150/year (individual); $30/year (associate).

Meetings/Conferences:
Annual Meetings: mid-July

Publications:
Directory and Report. a.
Newsletter. irreg.

North American Association For Ambulatory Care *(1981)*
4019 Quayle Briar Dr.
Valrico, FL 33594
Toll Free: (866)793 - 1396
E-Mail: tomc@nafac.com
Web Site: www.nafac.com
Members: 700 individuals
Annual Budget: $500-1,000,000
Executive Director: Tom Charland
E-Mail: tomc@nafac.com

Historical Note
Founded as National Association of Centers for Urgent Treatment; became (1982) National Association of Freestanding Emergency Centers and (1984) National Association for Ambulatory Care. Assumed its current name in 2001 NAFAC represents the operational, economic, and legislative interests of 8,500 ambulatory care centers (ACC) in the United States; and provides services and information to individuals and corporations planning to open ambulatory care centers. Membership: $150/year (individual); $250/year (corporate/business).

North American Association for Environmental Education *(1971)*
2000 P St. NW
Suite 540
Washington, DC 20036
Tel: (202)419-0412 *Fax:* (202)419-0415
E-Mail: email@naaee.org
Web Site: www.naaee.org
Members: 2000 individuals
Staff: 9
Annual Budget: $500-1,000,000
Executive Director: William H. Dent, Jr.
Chief Operating Officer: Teresa Mourad

Historical Note
Formerly (1985) the National Association for Environmental Education. Merged with the Conservation Education Association in 1990. Purpose is to assist and support the work of individuals and groups engaged in environmental education, research and service. NAAEE is organized into four interactive sections: Elementary and Secondary Education Section; Environmental Studies Section; the Non-Formal Section; and the Conservation Education Section. Membership: $45/year (individual), $200/year (institution).

Meetings/Conferences:
Annual Meetings: Fall

Publications:
Communicator. q.
Monographs. 1-3/year.
Conference Proceedings. a.

North American Association for the Study of Religion *(1987)*
211 Manly Hall, Univ. of Alabama
Tuscaloosa, AL 35487-0264
Tel: (205)348-8512
Members: 75 individuals
Executive Secretary: Russell T. McCutcheon

Historical Note
NAASR encourages the historical, comparative and structural study of religion in North America. Membership: $28/year (individual); $10/year (graduate student).

Meetings/Conferences:
Annual Meetings: held in conjunction with the American Academy of Religion.

North American Association of Christians in Social Work *(1954)*
P.O. Box 121
Botsford, CT 06404-0121
Tel: (203)270-8780
Toll Free: (888)426 - 4712
E-Mail: info@nacsw.org
Web Site: www.nacsw.org
Members: 1950 individuals
Staff: 1
Annual Budget: $100-250,000
Executive Director: Rick Chamiec-Case

Historical Note
NACSW assists its members in integrating their Christian faith with their social work practice and in representing a Christian presence in the social work profession and a social work presence in the Christian church. Membership: $71/year (individual); $22/year (student).

Meetings/Conferences:
Annual Meetings: Fall
2007 - Tampa, FL

Publications:
Social Work and Christianity. 3/year. adv.
Catalyst newsletter. bi-m. adv.
Practice Monograph Series. irreg.

North American Association of Educational Negotiators *(1970)*
c/o OSBA
P.O. Box 1068
Salem, OR 97308
Tel: (503)588-2800 *Fax:* (503)588-2813
E-Mail: naen@osba.org
Web Site: www.naen.org
Members: 500 individuals
Staff: 1
Annual Budget: $50-100,000
Executive Director: Ron Wilson
E-Mail: naen@osba.org

Historical Note
NAEN members are individuals who negotiate on the behalf of college and school administrations, and school boards. Established as the Association of Educational Negotiators; later became the National Association of Educational Negotiators and assumed its present name in 1991. Membership: $80/year (individual); $200/year (institution, up to four members); $60/year (each add'l member).

Meetings/Conferences:
Annual Meetings: Spring
2007 - San Diego, CA(Catamaran Resort)/March 11-14

Publications:
The NAEN Bulletin. bi-m. adv.

North American Association of Food Equipment Manufacturers *(1948)*
161 N. Clark St., Suite 2020
Chicago, IL 60601
Tel: (312)821-0201 *Fax:* (312)821-0202
E-Mail: info@nafem.org
Web Site: www.nafem.org
Members: 700 manufacturers
Staff: 20
Annual Budget: $2-5,000,000
Executive Vice President: Deirdre Flynn

Historical Note
Formerly (1994) National Association of Food Equipment Manufacturers. Membership: dues vary, based on company sales volume.

Publications:
NAFEM in print. q.. adv.
NAFEM for operators. q..

North American Association of Professors of Christian Education *(1947)*
c/o Southern Baptist Theological Seminary
2825 Lexington Road
Louisville, KY 40280
Tel: (502)649-3726 *Fax:* (502)339-9692
E-Mail: mail@napce.org
Web Site: www.napce.org
Members: 275 individuals
Staff: 1
Annual Budget: $25-50,000
Executive Administrator: Dennis E. Williams, Ph.D.
E-Mail: dwilliams@sbts.edu

Historical Note
Formerly (1992) National Association of Professors of Christian Education. NAPCE is a professional society for teachers of Christian education in post-secondary institutions. Has no paid officers or full-time staff. Membership: $55/year.

Meetings/Conferences:
Annual Meetings: fourth weekend in October
2007 - San Jose, CA(Marriott)/Oct. 18-20

Publications:
NAPCE Newsletter. 2/year.
Christian Education Journal. semi-a.

North American Association of State and Provincial Lotteries *(1971)*
2775-B Bishop Road
Willoughby Hills, OH 44092
Tel: (216)241-2310 *Fax:* (216)241-4350
E-Mail: nasplhq@aol.com
Web Site: www.naspl.org
Members: 47 organizations

Staff: 5
Annual Budget: $500-1,000,000
Executive Director: David B. Gale
E-Mail: dgale@nasplhq.org
Conference Coordinator: Tamika Ligon
Director, Administration: Thomas C. Tulloch
E-Mail: ttulloch@nasplhq.org
Publications and Tradeshow Coordinator: Andrew White

Historical Note
NASPL evolved from an informal exchange of information among three pioneering lottery directors, and has now grown into an active association of state and provincial lotteries representing 46 lottery organizations throughout North America. The Association works to assemble and disseminate information and benefits of state and provincial lottery organizations through education and communications and, when appropriate, publicly advocates the positions of the Association on matters of general policy. Membership: $12,000/year.

Meetings/Conferences:
Semi-annual Meetings: Spring and Fall
2007 – Louisville, KY(Louisville Marriott)/Oct. 3-6

Publications:
Lottery Insights. m. adv.
Lottery Resource Handbook. a.

North American Association of Summer Sessions *(1964)*
43 Belanger Dr.
Dover, NH 03820-4602
Tel: (603)740-9880 *Fax:* (603)742-7085
E-Mail: naass@aol.com
Web Site: www.naass.org
Members: 450 schools
Staff: 1
Annual Budget: $50-100,000
Executive Secretary: Michael U. Nelson
E-Mail: naass@aol.com

Historical Note
Established as the National Association of College and University Summer Sessions, it became the National Association of Summer Sessions in 1968, and assumed its present name in 1975. Membership: $35/year (individual); $100/year (institution).

Meetings/Conferences:
Annual Meetings: Fall
2007 – Maui, HI(Sheraton Maui)/Nov. 11-14/185

Publications:
Newsletter. q.
Summer Academe. bi-a.
Joint Statistical Report. a.
Membership Directory. a.

North American Association of Wardens and Superintendents *(1970)*
P.O. Box 11037
Albany, NY 12211-0037
Tel: (518)429-1923
Web Site: www.corrections.com/naaws/index.htm
Members: 950 individuals
Annual Budget: $10-25,000
Executive Director: Arthur A. Leonardo
Executive Treasurer: Gloria Hultz
E-Mail: elart26@aol.com

Historical Note
Formerly (1971) Wardens' Association of America and (1980) American Association of Wardens and Superintendants. Has no paid officers or full-time staff. An affiliate of the American Correctional Association. Membership: $25/year (new); $45/year (renewal, one year); $65/three years.

Meetings/Conferences:
Semi-Annual Meetings: Winter/Summer With American Correctional Ass'n

Publications:
The Grapevine. q.

North American Bar-Related Title Insurers *(1965)*
1430 Lee St.
Des Plaines, IL 60018
Tel: (847)298-8300 *Fax:* (847)298-8388
Web Site: www.nabrti.com
Members: 10 companies
Staff: 2
Annual Budget: $25-50,000
Executive Vice President: Joanne P. Elliot

Historical Note
Formed (1965) as the National Conference of Bar-Related Title Insurers; became National Association of Bar-Related Title Insurers in 1979 and assumed current name in 2005. Members are title insurance companies "bar-related" as registered as a service mark with the U.S. Patent Office.

Meetings/Conferences:
Annual Meetings: In conjunction with the ABA.

Publications:
Newsletter. q.
Membership Directory. a.

North American Benthological Society *(1953)*
3206 Maple Leaf Dr.
Glenview, IL 60026
Tel: (847)564-9905
E-Mail: ipolls@comcast.net
Web Site: www.benthos.org
Members: 1800 individuals
Staff: 1
Annual Budget: $100-250,000
Business Manager: Irwin Polls
E-Mail: ipolls@comcast.net

Historical Note
Founded as Midwest Benthological Society, NABS now serves an international membership. Members are scientists concerned with freshwater-habitat ecology. Has no paid officers. Membership: $70/year (individual); $35/year (student). Membership benefits include an electronic subscription to Journal of North American Benthological Society.

Meetings/Conferences:
Annual Meetings: Spring-Summer
2007 – Columbia, SC(Columbia Metropolitan Convention Center)/June 3-7/800

Publications:
NABS Bulletin. 3/year.
NABS Bibliography. a.
Journal of NABS. q.

North American Blueberry Council *(1965)*
2390 E. Bidwell St., Suite 300
Folsom, CA 95630
Tel: (916)983-2279 *Fax:* (916)983-9022
Web Site: www.nabcblues.org
Members: 60 grower organizations
Staff: 3
Annual Budget: $50-100,000
Executive Director: Mark Villata

Historical Note
Members are blueberry growers and marketers from the U.S. and Canada. Membership fee varies, based on annual production (full member); $700/year (associate).

Meetings/Conferences:
Annual Meetings: Winter

North American Bramble Growers Association

Historical Note
NABGA members are growers and processors of raspberries, blackberries and similar fruits. An affiliate of North American Strawberry Growers Association (same address).

North American Building Material Distribution Association *(1952)*
401 N. Michigan Ave.
Chicago, IL 60611-4274
Tel: (312)321-6845 *Fax:* (312)644-0310
Toll Free: (888)747 - 7862
E-Mail: nbmda@smithbucklin.com
Web Site: www.nbmda.org
Members: 500 companies
Staff: 5
Annual Budget: $1-2,000,000
Executive Vice President: Kevin Gammonley
E-Mail: kgammonsley@sba.com
Manager, Education and Product Development: Gretchen Fox
Director, Marketing: Chris Mundschenk
Member Services Manager: Judi Nosal
Convention Manager: Michelle Omansky

Historical Note
Absorbed (1964) National Plywood Distributors Association. Formerly (1994) National Building Material Distributors Association. Merged (1994) with the Canadian National Building Materials Distributors Association. NBMDA is one of the largest association of building products distributors and manufacturers in North America representing over 1,200 locations with distributor sales in excess of $20 billion. Membership: dues vary, based on annual sales.

Meetings/Conferences:
2007 – Colorado Springs, CO(The Broadmoor)/Nov. 3-4

Publications:
Channels. bi-m. adv.
Membership Directory (online).
Sales Trainer. bi-m.

North American Canon Law Society *(1986)*
P.O. Box 16201
Duluth, MN 55816-1612
Tel: (218)733-0345
E-Mail: rbsocc@juno.com
Members: 100 individuals
Staff: 3
Annual Budget: under $10,000
Vicar: Rev. Timothy A. Kiera, JCB, MDiv
Canonical Auditor: Rev. Thomas Dillon, JCD

Historical Note
Established in Indiana as a professional organization dedicated to canon and church lawyers trained in the canon laws accepted by the Orthodox Catholic Church. Membership: $175/year.

Meetings/Conferences:
Biennial Meetings: Summer

Publications:
Orthodox Christian Herald. bi-m. adv.
Legal Notes. q.

North American Cartographic Information Society *(1980)*
c/o AGS Collection
P.O. Box 399
Milwaukee, WI 53201
Tel: (414)229-6282 *Fax:* (414)229-3624
Web Site: www.nacis.org/
Members: 450 individuals
Annual Budget: under $10,000
Executive Director: Louis Cross
E-Mail: director@nacis.org

Historical Note
Incorporated in Wisconsin. Members are cartographers and others interested in the creation and use of accurate maps. Membership: $42/year (individual); $20/year (student); $72/year (organization).

Meetings/Conferences:
Annual Meetings: October/100

Publications:
Cartographic Perspectives. 3/year.

North American Case Research Association *(1958)*
3719 Meadow Lane
Saline, MI 48176
Tel: (734)429-5032
E-Mail: rpcnacra@worldnet.att.net
Web Site: www.nacra.net
Members: 350 individuals
Staff: 1
Treasurer: Robert Crowner
E-Mail: rpcnacra@worldnet.att.net

Historical Note
Founded as Southern Case Writers; became Southern Case Research Association in 1971, and assumed its current name in 1981. Sponsors and supports case research in a number of areas in business, management, and academia. Membership: $50/year.

Meetings/Conferences:
Annual Meetings: Fall

Publications:
Case Research Journal. q. adv.
Newsletter. 2-3/year.

North American Catalysis Society *(1956)*
P.O Box 80262

Wilmington, DE 19880-0262
Tel: (302)695-2488
Web Site: www.nacatsoc.org
Members: 2000 individuals
Staff: 1
Annual Budget: $10-25,000
Editor: Michael D'Amore, Ph.D.
E-Mail: michael.b.damore@usa.dupont.com

Historical Note

Formerly (1995) The Catalysis Society (North America). Fosters an interest in heterogeneous and homogeneous catalysis in the U.S., Mexico, and Canada. Organizes national meetings for the purpose of discussing the latest developments in the field. Members are chemists and chemical engineers engaged in the study and use of reactions involving catalysts, substances used to accelerate reactions and which may be recovered virtually unchanged. Membership: $5/year and a prerequiste of local affiliate membership.

Meetings/Conferences:

Biennial Meetings: Spring
2007 - Houston, TX/June 17-21

Publications:

North American Catalysis Society Newsletter. 3/year.

North American Clinical Dermatological Society *(1959)*

12613 133rd Ave. East
Puyallup, WA 98374
Tel: (253)770-8785 *Fax:* (253)840-5519
Web Site: www.nacds.com
Members: 180 individuals
Annual Budget: $100-250,000
Secretary-General: Mark A. Crowe, M.D.

Historical Note

NACDS provides continuing education to is members through its program of organized visits to dermatology clinics and related institutions around the world. Has no paid officers or full-time staff.

Meetings/Conferences:

Annual Meetings: Spring, for members only

Publications:

Cutis. a.
Program. a.

North American Clun Forest Association *(1973)*

21727 Randall Dr.
Houston, MN 55943-9801
Tel: (507)864-7585
Web Site: www.clunforestsheep.org
Members: 60 individuals
Staff: 1
Annual Budget: under $10,000
Executive Secretary: Elizabeth Reedy

Meetings/Conferences:

Annual Meetings: Fall

North American Conference on British Studies *(1950)*

Department of History
University of California, Irvine
Irvine, CA 92697
Tel: (949)824-3275 *Fax:* (949)824-2865
Toll Free: (877)705 - 1878
Web Site: www.nacbs.org
Members: 673 individuals
Associate Executive Secretary: Douglas Haynes
E-Mail: dhaynes@uci.edu

Historical Note

NACBS welcomes scholars from all fields dealing with the history and culture of the British Isles. Membership: $38/year (regular); $22/year (student); $40/year (foreign); $22/year (foreign/student); $50/year (sustaining); $400/year (life member).

Meetings/Conferences:

Annual Meetings: October-November

Publications:

Albion. q. adv.
British Studies Intelligencer Newsletter. semi-a.
Current Research in British History in the US & Canada. quad.
Journal of British Studies. q. adv.

North American Contractors Association *(1947)*

1702 W. Market St.
Greensboro, NC 27403
Tel: (336)370-4979
E-Mail: infonaca@aol.com
Members: 14 companies
Staff: 4
Annual Budget: $250-500,000
Contact: Todd Zepke
E-Mail: infonaca@aol.com

Historical Note

Founded as National Constructors Association; assumed its current name in 2000. Large, unionized engineering and construction companies. Deals in labor relations, safety issues, and government relations. Membership: $27,000/year (company).

Publications:

Newsletter. bi-m.

North American Corriente Association *(1982)*

P.O. Box 12359
North Kansas City, MO 64116
Tel: (816)421-1992 *Fax:* (816)421-1991
E-Mail: info@corrientecattle.org
Web Site: www.corrientecattle.org
Members: 675 individuals
Staff: 2
Annual Budget: $100-250,000
Executive Director: James A. Spawn

Historical Note

The NACA promotes the use of Corriente cattle and has instituted and monitors a registered breeding program to preserve the true breed and make it available for the fast-growing rodeo circuit. Membership: $350/life; $35/year (active member); $15/year (associate).

Meetings/Conferences:

Annual Meetings: Spring

Publications:

The Corresponder. q. adv.

North American Council of Automotive Teachers *(1974)*

P.O. Box 80010
Charleston, SC 29416
Tel: (843)556-7068 *Fax:* (843)556-7068
E-Mail: office@nacat.com
Web Site: www.nacat.com
Members: 750 individuals
Staff: 1
Annual Budget: $25-50,000
Executive Manager: Dan Perrin
E-Mail: office@nacat.com

Historical Note

Formerly (1991) National Association of College Automotive Teachers. NACAT is an organization of automotive teachers and supporting companies in the automotive industry. The purpose of the organization is to advance all levels of automotive education. Operates the NACAT Foundation to provide funding for scholaships and other worthy causes. Membership: $40/year.

Meetings/Conferences:

Annual Meetings: Third week in July.
2007 - Long Beach, CA

Publications:

NACAT News. 3/year. adv.

North American Deer Farmers Association *(1983)*

1215 N. 77th St., Suite 104
Lake City, MN 55041-1264
Tel: (651)345-5600 *Fax:* (651)345-5603
E-Mail: info@nadefa.org
Web Site: www.nadefa.org
Members: 650 individuals
Staff: 2
Annual Budget: $100-250,000
Executive Director: Holly Johnson

Historical Note

NADeFA members are commercial deer farmers, producing venison for public consumption. Membership: $100/year (individual)

Meetings/Conferences:

Annual Meetings: Spring

Publications:

North American Deer Farmer Journal. 4/yr. adv.

North American Die Casting Association *(1989)*

241 Holbrook Dr.
Wheeling, IL 60090
Tel: (847)279-0001 *Fax:* (847)279-0002
E-Mail: nadca@diecasting.org
Web Site: www.diecasting.org
Members: 3700 individuals
Staff: 15
Annual Budget: $5-10,000,000
President: Daniel Twarog
E-Mail: nadca@diecasting.org
Director, Membership and Marketing: Leo J. Baran

Historical Note

The mission of the North American Die Casting Associaton is to be the world wide leader of and resource for stimulating continuous improvement in the die casting industry. Membership: $85/year, renewal (individual); $1,975-$12,000/year, (corporate).

Meetings/Conferences:

Biennial Meetings: Odd years in Fall

Publications:

Die Casting Engineer. bi-m. adv.

North American Electric Reliability Council *(1968)*

116-390 Village Blvd.
Princeton, NJ 08540-5731
Tel: (609)452-8060 *Fax:* (609)452-9550
E-Mail: info@nerc.com
Web Site: www.nerc.com
Members: 10 regional councils
Staff: 60
Annual Budget: $10-25,000,000
President and Chief Executive Officer: Richard P. Sergel
Director, Communications and Government Affairs: Ellen P. Vancko
E-Mail: ellen.vancko@nerc.net

Historical Note

Founded in 1968 as the National Electric Reliability Council, it assumed its current name in 1981. NERC is the principal organization for coordinating, promoting, and communicating about the reliability and security of North America's bulk electric systems

Meetings/Conferences:

Three Meetings Annually:

Publications:

Winter Assessment. a.
Summer Assessment. a.
Annual Report. a.
Reliability Assessment. a.
System Disturbances. a.
Generating Availability Data Report. a.

North American Elk Breeders Association *(1990)*

P.O. Box 1640
Platte City, MO 64079
Tel: (816)431-3605 *Fax:* (816)431-2705
E-Mail: info@naelk.org
Web Site: www.naelk.org
Members: 1800 individuals
Staff: 10
President: Ted Winters
Membership Services: Jonnie Boone
E-Mail: jonnie@naelk.org

Historical Note

Maintains a registry of purebred Wapiti (North American Elk), and provides education and support to member breeders. An affiliate of the U.S. Animal Health Association.

Publications:

North American Elk Journal. bi-m. adv.
NAEBA Newsletter. bi-m. adv.

North American Equipment Dealers Association *(1900)*

1195 Smizer Mill Road
Fenton, MO 63026-3480
Tel: (636)349-5000 *Fax:* (636)349-5443
E-Mail: naeda@naeda.com
Web Site: www.naeda.com
Members: 4500 retail dealers
Staff: 8

Annual Budget: $250-500,000
Chief Executive Officer: Paul E. Kindinger
Director, Communications and Credit Services: Mike Kraemer
Director, Administration and Finance: Kim White
Director, Professional Development: Michael C. Williams

Historical Note
Founded as the National Retail Farm Equipment Association; became the National Farm and Power Equipment Dealers Association in 1962 and assumed its present name in 1988. Members are retail dealers of agricultural, industrial and outdoor power equipment in the U.S. and Canada.

Meetings/Conferences:
Annual Meetings: March and September Meetings

North American Export Grain Association *(1920)*
1250 Eye St. NW, Suite 1003
Washington, DC 20005
Tel: (202)682-4030 *Fax:* (202)682-4033
E-Mail: info@naega.org
Web Site: www.naega.org
Members: 36 companies
Staff: 3
Annual Budget: $500-1,000,000
President: Gary C. Martin
Director, Operations: Dianna Firtu

Historical Note
Incorporated in 1920, NAEGA represents North American grain and oilseed exporters.

Publications:
Bulletins. irreg.

North American Farm Show Council *(1972)*
11240 Beacom Road
Sunbury, OH 43074
Tel: (740)524-0658
Web Site: www.farmshows.org
Members: 30 membershows, 12 associates
Staff: 1
Annual Budget: $25-50,000
Executive Coordinator: Craig Fendrick
E-Mail: fendrick.1@osu.edu

Historical Note
Established in Chicago and incorporated in Ohio, NAFSC members are agricultural equipment trade shows. Suppliers of services to shows can obtain an associate membership. Membership: $700/year (regular); $100/year (associate).

Meetings/Conferences:
Annual Meetings: May

Publications:
NAFSC Brochure. bien.

North American Flowerbulb Wholesalers Association *(1983)*
c/o Marlboro Bulb Co.
2424 Hwy. 72/221 East
Greenwood, SC 29649
Tel: (864)229-1618 *Fax:* (864)229-5719
E-Mail: nafwa@emeraldis.com
Web Site: www.nafwa.com
Members: 50 companies
Staff: 1
Annual Budget: $25-50,000
Executive Director: Jack DeVroomen
E-Mail: nafwa@emeraldis.com

Historical Note
Absorbed the Horticultural Dealers Association in 1984.

Meetings/Conferences:
Annual Meetings: Spring

Publications:
NAFWA News. q.

North American Folk Music and Dance Alliance *(1989)*
510 South Main, Suite B
Memphis, TN 38103-4488
Tel: (901)522-1170 *Fax:* (901)522-1172
E-Mail: fa@folk.org
Web Site: www.folk.org
Members: 1750 individuals
Staff: 5
Annual Budget: $500-1,000,000
Executive Director: Louis J. Meyers
Administrative Director: Cindy Cogbill
Director, Member Services: Randi Lynn

Historical Note
The Folk Alliance fosters and promotes multi-cultural, traditional and contemporary folk music, dance and related performing arts in the United States and Canada. Membership: $70/year (individual); $150-505/year (organization/company).

Meetings/Conferences:
Annual Meetings: February/1,500

Publications:
Folk Music Business Directory.
Annual Report. a.
Newsletter. bi-m. adv.
Membership Directory. a. adv.

North American Fuzzy Information Processing Society *(1981)*
321 E. 43rd St., #209
New York, NY 10017
E-Mail: secretary@nafips.org
Web Site: www.nafips.org
Members: 120 individuals
Annual Budget: under $10,000
Treasurer: Dr. Joseph Barone
E-Mail: secretary@nafips.org

Historical Note
Affiliated with the International Fuzzy Systems Association, NAFIPS was established to promote and disseminate studies related to theories of fuzzy sets and related topics and to the study of their application in such fields as artificial intelligence, medicine, image processing, speech, linguistics, control theory, operations research, economics, and decision theory. Membership: $19/year (individual).

Meetings/Conferences:
Annual Meetings: Summer
2007 – San Diego, CA/June 24-27

Publications:
Int'l Journal of Approximate Reasoning. bi-m. adv.

North American Gamebird Association *(1931)*
1214 Brooks Ave.
Raleigh, NC 27607
Tel: (919)782-6758 *Fax:* (919)515-7070
E-Mail: gamebird@naga.org
Web Site: www.naga.org
Members: 1500 individuals
Staff: 2
Annual Budget: $50-100,000
Executive Director: Dr. Gary S. Davis
E-Mail: gamebird@naga.org

Historical Note
Formerly (1981) North American Game Breeders and Shooting Preserve Operators Association. Membership: $60/year (U.S.); $65/year (foreign).

Meetings/Conferences:
Annual Meetings: Winter

Publications:
Wildlife Harvest. m. adv.
Membership Directory.

North American Gaming Regulators Association *(1984)*
1000 Westgate Dr., Suite 252
St. Paul, MN 55114
Tel: (651)203-7244 *Fax:* (651)290-2266
E-Mail: info@nagra.org
Web Site: www.nagra.org
Members: 170 agencies
Staff: 1
Annual Budget: $100-250,000
Executive Director: Eric Ewald

Historical Note
Members are government entities involved in local, state, federal, and provincial regulation of gambling activities. Membership: $350-525/year (organization).

Meetings/Conferences:
Semi-Annual Meetings: Spring and Fall

Publications:
NAGRA News. q.

North American Heating, Refrigeration and Airconditioning Wholesalers Association

Historical Note
Became Heating, Airconditioning and Refrigeration Distributors International in 2003.

North American Horticultural Supply Association *(1988)*
100 N. 20th St., Fourth Floor
Philadelphia, PA 19103-1443
Tel: (215)564-3484 *Fax:* (215)963-9784
E-Mail: nahsa@fernley.com
Web Site: www.nahsa.org
Members: distributors
Staff: 3
Annual Budget: $50-100,000
Executive Director: Trudie Rowello

Historical Note
NAHSA promotes the role of the full service distributors in the greenhouse and nursery hard good supply market. NAHSA serves as liaison between industry distributors and manufacturers.

Meetings/Conferences:
2007 – Palm Beach Gardens, FL(PGA National Resort)/June 3-6

Publications:
NAHSA Newsletter. m.
Membership Directory. a.

North American Hyperthermia Society

Historical Note
Became Society for Thermal Medicine in 2004.

North American Insulation Manufacturers Association *(1933)*
44 Canal Center Plaza, Suite 310
Alexandria, VA 22314
Tel: (703)684-0084 *Fax:* (703)684-0427
E-Mail: insulation@naima.org
Web Site: www.naima.org
Members: 16 companies
Staff: 10
Annual Budget: $2-5,000,000
President and Chief Executive Officer: Kenneth D. Mentzer
Director, Communications: Robin M. Bectel
Director, Administration: Michelle Bunch
Vice President, General Counsel, and Secretary: Angus Crane
Director, Federal and State Programs: Kate Offringa
Vice President, Government and Industry Affairs: George R. Phelps

Historical Note
Formerly the National Rock and Slag Wool Association, the National Mineral Wool Association, (1980) the National Mineral Wool Insulation Association, and (1992) the Mineral Insulation Manufacturers Association.

Meetings/Conferences:
Annual Meetings: Fall

North American Interfraternity Conference *(1909)*
3901 W. 86th St., Suite 390
Indianapolis, IN 46268-1791
Tel: (317)872-1112 *Fax:* (317)872-1134
E-Mail: nic@nicindy.org
Web Site: www.nicindy.org
Members: 64 fraternities
Staff: 7
Annual Budget: $500-1,000,000
Executive Vice President: John Williamson, CAE

Historical Note
Formerly National Interfraternity Conference; assumed current name in 1999. An association of men's national social fraternities. Membership includes national social fraternities in the U.S. and Canada. NIC's original membership first convened November 27, 1909 at the University Club in New York City. Membership: $400/year (organization).

Meetings/Conferences:
Annual Meetings: Always week after Thanksgiving.

Publications:
Campus Commentary. 8/yr.
Foundation Focus. 3/yr.
Interfraternity Directory. semi-a.

North American Lake Management Society *(1980)*

P.O. Box 5443
Madison, WI 53705-0443
Tel: (608)233-2836 *Fax:* (608)233-3186
Web Site: www.nalms.org
Members: 2500 individuals
Staff: 3
Business Manager: Carol Winge
E-Mail: winge@nalms.org

Historical Note

Members are academics, lake managers and others having an interest in furthering the understanding of lake ecology. Awards the CLM (Certified Lake Manager) designation to members meeting program requirements. Membership: $35/year (student); $45/year (individual); $60/year (non-profit organizations/company); $85/year (library); $325/year (corporate).

Publications:

Lake & Reservoir Management. q. adv.
LakeLine Magazine. q. adv.

North American Limousin Foundation *(1968)*
P.O. Box 4467
Englewood, CO 80155
Tel: (303)220-1693 *Fax:* (303)220-1884
E-Mail: limousin@nalf.org
Web Site: www.nalf.org
Members: 4500 individuals
Staff: 13
Annual Budget: $1-2,000,000
Executive Vice President: Dr. Kent Andersen
E-Mail: kent@nalf.org
Director, Communications: Brad Parker
E-Mail: brad@nalf.org

Historical Note

Registers and promotes Limousin beef cattle, a French breed introduced into the U.S.A. in 1968.

Meetings/Conferences:

Annual Meetings: Annual
2007 – Denver, CO(Doubletree Hotel)/Jan. 8
2008 – Denver, CO(Doubletree Hotel)/Jan. 7

Publications:

Limousin World. m. adv.

North American Manufacturing Research Institution of SME *(1981)*
One SME Dr.
P.O. Box 930
Dearborn, MI 48121-0930
Tel: (313)425-3307 *Fax:* (313)425-3415
Web Site: www.sme.org/namri
Members: 200 individuals
Staff: 1
Annual Budget: $25-50,000
Manager: Mark Stratton
E-Mail: mstratton@sme.org

Historical Note

Founded and supported by the Society of Manufacturing Engineers. Members are individuals engaged in manufacturing research and technology development. Membership: $99/year, plus $10 initial fee for first year members.

Meetings/Conferences:

Annual Meetings: May
2007 – Ann Arbor, MI(University of Michigan)/May 22-25

Publications:

Transactions of NAMRI/SME. a.
Manufacturing Engineering. m. adv.

North American Maple Syrup Council *(1959)*
c/o Joe Polak
W. 1887 Robinson Dr.
Merrill, WI 54452
Tel: (715)536-7251
Members: 16 associations
Staff: 1
Annual Budget: under $10,000
Secretary/Treasurer: Joe Polak

Historical Note

Members are state and provincial maple syrup associations.

Meetings/Conferences:

Annual Meetings: October

Publications:

Maple Syrup Digest. q. adv.

North American Meat Processors Association *(1942)*
1910 Association Dr.
Reston, VA 20191
Tel: (703)758-1900 *Fax:* (703)758-8001
Toll Free: (800)368 - 3043
Web Site: www.namp.com
Members: 400 purveyors
Staff: 4
Annual Budget: $500-1,000,000
Executive Vice President: Devon Scott
Director, Communications and Membership: Jane Jacobs
Director, Meetings, Marketing, and Accounting: Sabrina Moore

Historical Note

Formerly (1966) National Association of Hotel & Restaurant Meat Purveyors and (1996) National Association of Meat Purveyors. Represents processors and distributors of meat, poultry, seafood, and game to the food-service industry. Membership: $500-2500/year, varies according to sales.

Meetings/Conferences:

Semi-Annual Meetings:

Publications:

Newsletter. m.
The Meat Buyers Guide. a. adv.

North American Membrane Society *(1985)*
Dept. of Chemical and Environmental Engineering
The University of Toledo, MS 305
Toledo, OH 43606-3390
Tel: (419)530-3469 *Fax:* (419)530-8086
E-Mail: nams@eng.utoledo.edu
Web Site: www.membranes.org
Members: 600 individuals
Annual Budget: $50-100,000
Office Manager: Renee Norrils
E-Mail: nams@eng.utoledo.edu

Historical Note

NAMS members are scientists, engineers, academics and businessmen interested in promoting research and development in the membrane separations area. Membership: $50/year (individual); $20/year (student); an additional $10/year (members outside the United States).

Publications:

Membrane Quarterly. q. adv.

North American Menopause Society *(1989)*
P.O. Box 94527
Cleveland, OH 44101-4527
Tel: (440)442-7550 *Fax:* (440)442-2660
Toll Free: (800)774 - 5342
E-Mail: info@menopause.org
Web Site: www.menopause.org
Members: 2000 health professionals
Staff: 9
Annual Budget: $2-5,000,000
Executive Director: Wulf H. Utian, M.D., Ph.D
E-Mail: utian@menopause.org
Director, Education and Development: Pamela Boggs, M.B.A.
E-Mail: info@menopause.org
Director, Administration: Carolyn Develen
E-Mail: carolyn@menopause.com

Historical Note

Members are health professionals interested in human menopause. NAMS promotes the understanding of menopause among health professionals and the general public. Membership: $215/year.

Meetings/Conferences:

Annual Meetings: September or October
2007 – Dallas, TX(Gaylord Texan)/Oct. 3-7

Publications:

Menopause. 6/year. adv.
Flashes Newsletter (for members). 2/year.
Menopause e-consult (e-newsletter for members). 4/yr.
Federal Funds Alert (e-newsletter for members). 4/yr.
Editorial review for Menopause Management (for physicians). 6/yr. adv.
Editorial review for Changes (for consumers). a. adv.
Menopause Flashes (e-newsletter for consumers). 12/yr.

North American Millers Association *(1902)*
600 Maryland Ave. SW
Suite 450-E
Washington, DC 20024-2519
Tel: (202)484-2200 *Fax:* (202)488-7416
Web Site: www.namamillers.org
Members: 48 companies
Staff: 6
Annual Budget: $1-2,000,000
President: Betsy Faga
E-Mail: bfaga@namamillers.org
Vice President: James Bair
E-Mail: jbair@namamillers.org
Treasurer/Secretary: Terri Todd
E-Mail: ttodd@namamillers.org

Historical Note

Formerly (1998) Millers' National Federation. Absorbed the National Soft Wheat Association in 1976, the Durum Wheat Institute in 1982, the American Corn Millers Federation and Protein Grain Products International in 1998, and the American Oat Association in 1999. Represents the dry milling of wheat, corn, oats and rye. Membership is based on hudredweights of production.

Meetings/Conferences:

Annual Meetings: Fall

Publications:

Newsletter. m.
Handbook. a.

North American Mycological Association *(1959)*
6615 Tudor Court
Gladstone, OR 97027-1032
Tel: (503)657-7358
E-Mail: execsec@namyco.org
Web Site: www.namyco.org
Members: 2000 individuals & local clubs
Staff: 1
Annual Budget: $25-50,000
Executive Secretary: Judy Roger
E-Mail: execsec@namyco.org

Historical Note

Originated at Ohio State University in November 1959 as the Committee on Fungi and incorporated in Ohio as the North American Mycological Association in 1967. Membership: $35/year (individual).

Meetings/Conferences:

Annual Meetings: July-November
2007 – Pipestem, WV(TBD)/Aug. 16-19/300

Publications:

McIlvainea. a.
The Mycophile. bi-m.

North American Natural Casing Association *(1990)*
494 Eighth Ave., Suite 804
New York, NY 10001
Tel: (212)695-4980 *Fax:* (212)695-7153
E-Mail: info@nanca.org
Web Site: www.nanca.org
Members: 31 companies
Staff: 1
Annual Budget: $100-250,000
President: Barbara Negron
E-Mail: info@nanca.org

Historical Note

An outgrowth of the International Natural Sausage Casing Association, NANCA was formed to confront trade issues that affect North American suppliers, producers and distributors of natural casings.

Meetings/Conferences:

Annual Meetings: Spring

Publications:

NANCA News. bi-m.

North American Nature Photography Association *(1994)*
10200 W. 44th Ave., Suite 304
Wheat Ridge, CO 80033-2840
Tel: (303)422-8527 *Fax:* (303)422-8894
Web Site: www.nanpa.org
Members: 2600 individuals
Staff: 5
Annual Budget: $500-1,000,000

Executive Director: Francine Bulter, PhD
Director, Meetings: Christy Powers
E-Mail: cpowers@resourcecenter.com

Historical Note

NANPA represents photographers, editors, publishers, educators, and students interested in photography of nature and the environment. Provides educational opportunities and promotes standards of ethical conduct. Membership: $90/year (general); $25/year (student); $100/year (joint); $250-5,000/year (corporate).

Meetings/Conferences:

Annual Meetings: Winter

Publications:

Currents. 6/year. adv.
Membership Directory. a. adv.

North American Neuro-Ophthalmology Society

5841 Cedar Lane Rd., #204
Minneapolis, MN 55416
Tel: (952)646-2037 *Fax:* (952)545-6073
Web Site: www.nanosweb.org
Members: 450 individuals
Staff: 2
Annual Budget: $250-500,000
Executive Director: Lori J. Anderson

Historical Note

NANOS sponsors continuing education and professional advancement opportunities for medical doctors specializing in treatment of the eye. Membership: $325/year, plus $50 initiation fee.

Meetings/Conferences:

Annual Meetings: early Spring

Publications:

Journal of Neuro-Ophthalmology. q. adv.

North American Neuromodulation Society

(1994)

4700 W. Lake Ave.
Glenview, IL 60025
Tel: (847)375-4714 *Fax:* (877)594-6704
Web Site: www.neuromodulation.org
Executive Director: Kris Haskin

Historical Note

Formerly (2004) American Neuromodulation Society.

Publications:

ANS Newsletter. q.
ANS Economic Newsletter. bi-m.

North American Nursing Diagnosis Association

Historical Note

Became NANDA International in 2003.

North American Olive Oil Association

3301 Route 66, Bldg. C, Suite 205
Neptune, NJ 07753
Tel: (732)922-3008 *Fax:* (732)922-3590
E-Mail: info@naooa.org
Web Site: www.naooa.org
Members: 110
Staff: 5
President: Bob Bauer
E-Mail: bobbauer@afius.org

Historical Note

NAOOA is a trade association for importers and distributors of olive oil, and for their suppliers abroad. NAOOA is committed to supplying North American consumers with quality olive oil products in a fair and competitive environment, to fostering a clear understanding of the different grades of olive oil, and to expounding the benefits of olive oil in nutrition, health and the culinary arts.

Meetings/Conferences:

Semi-Annual Meetings: Attendance: 30-60

North American Performing Arts Managers and Agents *(1979)*

459 Columbus Ave., Suite 133
New York, NY 10024
Toll Free: (888)745 - 8759
E-Mail: info@napama.org
Web Site: www.napama.org
Members: 125 companies
Annual Budget: $25-50,000
Treasurer: Jennifer Morris

Historical Note

Formerly (2000) National Association of Performing Arts Managers and Agents. Incorporated in New York, NY. Organization of professionals who serve artists in the development of their performing careers. Members are professional managers, agents, or personal representatives, and businesses and individual related to the industry. Membership: fees based on annual contract fees.

Publications:

NAPAMA News. 3/year.
Notes from NAPAMA. m.

North American Plant Preservation Council

(1990)

HC 67, Box 539-B
Renick, WV 24966
Tel: (304)497-2208 *Fax:* (304)497-2698
Web Site: www.gardenweb.com/orgs/nappc/nappc.html
Members: 3500 individuals
Annual Budget: $25-50,000
Executive Director: Barry Glick
E-Mail: barry@sunfarm.com

Historical Note

NAPPC is dedicated to establishing plant collections in a range of areas and climate zones on the North American continent. These collections will be used to preserve plants in danger of extinction, for research, for horticultural study, education and dissemination. Membership $10/year (individual).

Publications:

Directory of Collections. a.

North American Polyelectrolyte Producers Association *(1996)*

1250 Connecticut Ave. NW
Suite 700
Washington, DC 20036
Tel: (202)419-1500 *Fax:* (202)659-8037
E-Mail: info@regnet.com
Members: 5 companies
Staff: 2
Executive Director: Robert J. Fensterheim

Historical Note

Founded as Acrylamide Monomer Producers Association; assumed its current name in 2003. NAPPA represents the major manufacturers and importers of synthetically produced coagulants and flocculants, which are generically referred to as polyelectrolytes. Monitors regulatory issues affecting manufacturers in the chemical industry.

North American Private Truck Council

Historical Note

NAPTC is an umbrella organization supported by the National Private Truck Council to coordinate activities between NPTC and Private Motor Truck Council of Canada, NPTC's Canadian counterpart.

North American Professional Driver Education Association *(1958)*

P.O. Box 27
Glenview, IL 60025-0027
Tel: (773)777-9605
Members: 280 schools
Staff: 2
Annual Budget: $50-100,000
President: Charles Rumsfield

Historical Note

Formerly (1970) National Professional Driver Education Association, Inc., and (1960) National Association of Driving Schools. Members are individuals and companies involved in driver education. Awards the "Qualified Driving School" designation. Membership: $200/year (full member); $50/year (associate).

Meetings/Conferences:

Annual Meetings: Spring

Publications:

NAPDEA News. q. adv.
Driver Training Bulletin.

North American Punch Manufacturers Association *(1963)*

21 Turquoise Ave.
Naples, FL 34114-8239
Tel: (239)775-7245 *Fax:* (239)775-7245
Web Site: www.napma.org
Members: 15 companies
Staff: 1
Annual Budget: $10-25,000
Executive Secretary: Robert May

Historical Note

Formerly (1996) the National Association of Punch Manufacturers. Membership: $1,000/year (full membership) and $350/year (associate membership).

Meetings/Conferences:

Annual Meetings: March

North American Rail Shippers Association *(1927)*

2115 Portsmouth Dr.
Richardson, TX 75082-4839
Tel: (972)690-4740 *Fax:* (972)644-8208
E-Mail: nars@railshippers.com
Web Site: www.railshippers.com
Members: 1500 individuals
Staff: 1
Annual Budget: $50-100,000
Executive Director: E. Leo Mountjoy

Historical Note

Members are industrial traffic executives using rail transportation. An umbrella association for six regional associations. NARS has no dues. Administrative support provided by Association of American Railroads. Formerly (1984) National Association of Shippers Advisory Boards, National Association of Rail Shippers Advisory Board (1985), and (2003) National Association of Rail Shippers.

Meetings/Conferences:

Annual Meetings: May

North American Retail Dealers Association

(1943)

4700 W. Lake Ave.
Glenview, IL 60025-1468
Tel: (847)375-4711 *Fax:* (866)879-7505
Toll Free: (800)621 - 0298
E-Mail: rjacobshagen@narda.com
Web Site: www.narda.com
Members: 1000 dealers
Staff: 8
Annual Budget: $2-5,000,000
President and Chief Executive Officer: Thomas G. Drake, CAE
Vice President, Membership Marketing: Larry Forssberg
Executive Vice President: Rosemary Jacobshagen, CAE

Historical Note

Formerly (until 1979) the National Appliance and Radio TV Dealers Association and (1994) National Association of Retail Dealers of America. The National Association of Service Dealers is a division. Membership: $295/year (individual).

Meetings/Conferences:

Annual Meetings:

Publications:

NARDA Independent Retailer. m. adv.
NARDA E-Newsletter. w.

North American Retail Hardware Association

(1900)

5822 W. 74th St.
Indianapolis, IN 46278-1756
Tel: (317)290-0338 *Fax:* (317)328-4354
E-Mail: nrha@nrha.org
Web Site: www.nrha.org
Members: 15000 individuals
Staff: 47
Annual Budget: $50-100,000
Managing Director: John Hammond
Director, Conventions and Meetings: Dianne Allen
Chief Executive Officer: Thomas W. Smith
E-Mail: tsmith@nrha.org

Historical Note

Founded in 1900, NARHA was known as National Retail Hardware Association before assuming current name in 2005. Serves more than 15,000 hardware retailers through its 15 state and regional affiliates in the U.S. and Canada. Has an annual budget of approximately $6 million. Services include more than 100 educational products, business consultation, industry research and statistics, and a wide range of *store management aids. Membership: $140/year (company average).*

Meetings/Conferences:
Annual Meetings: Summer
2007 – Orlando, FL(Hyatt Grand Cypress)/June 11-13/350

Publications:
Hardware Retailing. m. adv.

North American Sawing Association *(1959)*
1300 Sumner Ave.
Cleveland, OH 44115-2851
Tel: (216)241-7333 *Fax:* (216)241-0105
E-Mail: nasa@sawingassociation.com
Web Site: www.sawingassociation.com
Members: 7 companies
Staff: 3
Secretary-Treasurer: Charles M. Stockinger

Historical Note
Formerly (2001) Hack and Band Saw Manufacturers Association of America. Formed by a merger of the Hack Saw Association and Metal Cutting Band Saw Association.

North American Saxophone Alliance
c/o University of Iowa School of Music
2046 Voxman Music Bldg.
Iowa City, IA 52242
Web Site: www.saxalliance.org
Members: 900 individuals
Annual Budget: $10-25,000
Contact: Kenneth Tse

Historical Note
NASA members are professional musicians, teachers and amateur players of the saxophone. Membership: $35/year (professional); $25/year (student).

Meetings/Conferences:
Annual Meetings: Spring-Summer

Publications:
NASA Update Newsletter. bi-m. adv.
Saxophone Symposium. a. adv.

North American Securities Administrators Association *(1917)*
750 First St., Suite 1140
Washington, DC 20002
Tel: (202)737-0900 *Fax:* (202)783-3571
Web Site: www.nasaa.org
Members: 66 individuals
Staff: 16
Annual Budget: $2-5,000,000
Interim Executive Director: John H. Lynch
E-Mail: jhl@nassa.org

Historical Note
Formerly (1945) National Association of Securities Administrators. NASAA members are the 66 state, provincial and territorial securities regulators in the United States, Canada, Mexico and Puerto Rico. In the U.S., NASAA is the national voice of the fifty state agencies responsible for investor protection and regulatory oversight of the securities industry. The jurisdiction of state governments over securities regulation is co-extensive with that of the U.S. Securities and Exchange Commission. As industry co-regulators, state securities commissioners play a key role in assuring fairness in the securities markets, particularly in regard to the treatment of individual small investors. Membership: $600/year.

Meetings/Conferences:
Annual Meetings: Fall

Publications:
NASAA Reports. m.
Investor Alert. q.
NASAA Investor Bulletin. q.

North American Serials Interest Group *(1985)*
P.O. Box 438
New Hampton, NY 10958-0438
E-Mail: info@nasig.org
Web Site: www.nasig.org
Members: 1200 individuals
Annual Budget: $100-250,000
Treasurer: Rose Robischon
E-Mail: info@nasig.org

Historical Note
NASIG promotes communication and sharing of ideas among all members of the serials information chain, including any interested individuals working with or concerned about serial publication. Membership: $25/year (U.S. and Mexico); $35/year (outside North America).

Meetings/Conferences:
Annual Meetings: June

Publications:
NASIG Newsletter (online only). 5/year.
Directory (online only). a.
Proceedings. a.

North American Simulation and Gaming Association *(1961)*
4019 Ave. Hingston
Montreal, QC H4A -2J6
Tel: (317)512-0920 *Fax:* (815)346-4032
Toll Free: (888)432 - 4263
E-Mail: info@nasaga.org
Web Site: www.nasaga.org
Members: 1,000 individuals
Staff: 15
Annual Budget: under $10,000
Membership Administrator: Brett Atkin
E-Mail: info@nasaga.org

Historical Note
Established as National Gaming Council, it assumed its present name in 1974. Members are teachers, trainers and others interested in the concept of using simulated situations and games as educational and planning tools. Has no paid staff. Membership: $85/year.

Meetings/Conferences:
Annual Meetings: Fall

Publications:
Simages Newsletter. irreg.
Simulation and Gaming: An Internat'l Journal. q. adv.

North American Skull Base Society *(1989)*
12100 Sunset Hills Road, Suite 130
Reston, VA 20190-3221
Tel: (703)437-4377 *Fax:* (703)435-4390
E-Mail: info@nasbs.org
Web Site: www.nasbs.org
Members: 500 individuals
Staff: 2
Annual Budget: $250-500,000

Historical Note
NASBS is a medical subspecialty society with representation from many disciplines with an interest in diseases involving the base of the skull. Members include neurosurgeons, otolaryngologists, plastic surgeons, ophthalmologists, pathologists, anesthesiologists and radiologists. Membership: $220/year (individual).

Publications:
Skull Base Surgery. q. adv.
Petrous Pulse Newsletter. semi-a. adv.

North American Small Business International Trade Educators *(1988)*
Rawls Coll., Executive Ed. Division, Box 42102
Lubbock, TX 79409-2102
Tel: (806)742-1963 *Fax:* (806)742-1826
E-Mail: info@nasbite.org
Web Site: www.nasbite.org/
Members: 300individualsandorganizations
Staff: 1
Annual Budget: $50-100,000
Executive Officer: Alan Whitebread

Historical Note
Founded as National Association of Small Business International Trade Educators; assumed its current name in 1999. NASBITE works to promote and enhance the involvement and competitiveness of small businesses in international trade. Its mission is to improve global competitiveness through effective education and training. NASBITE members include U.S. Dept. of Education, Commerce, State and U.S. Small Business Administration officials. Membership: $75/year (individual), $225/year (institutional).

Publications:
Membership Directory. a.
Resource Directory. a.

North American Snowsports Journalists Association *(1963)*
460 Sarsons Road
Kelowna, BC V1WIC-2
Tel: (250)764-2143 *Fax:* (250)764-2145
E-Mail: nasja@shaw.ca
Web Site: www.nasja.org
Members: 400 individuals
Annual Budget: $25-50,000
Executive Secretary: Steve Threndyle
E-Mail: nasja@shaw.ca

Historical Note
Founded as United States Ski Writers Association; became North American Ski Journalists Association in 1990, and assumed its current name in 1998. NASJA is a professional group of writers, photographers, film-makers and broadcasters who present ski-related news, information and features throughout the United States and Canada, via the various media. Corporate members include media contacts, employees of ski-related businesses, and others who have a commercial interest in the journalistic coverage of the sport. Membership: $75 initiation, $25/year (individual); $100/year (coprorate).

Meetings/Conferences:
Annual Meetings: March-April/300-400

Publications:
Inside Edge Newsletter. q.
NASJA Directory. a. adv.

North American Society for Cardiac Imaging *(1973)*
203 Washington St., PMB 311
Salem, MA 01970
Tel: (978)744-5005 *Fax:* (978)744-5029
Web Site: www.nasci.org
Members: 170 individuals
Annual Budget: $50-100,000
Executive Director: Lorraine J. Bell

Historical Note
NASCI members are radiologists with an interest in cardiac imaging and the application of imaging methods to the study of heart disease in both research laboratory and clinical settings. Membership: $160/year (individual; includes journal subscription).

Meetings/Conferences:
Annual Meetings: Fall

Publications:
International Journal of Cardiovascular Imagery. 6/year. adv.
NASCI Beat Newsletter. 2/year.

North American Society for Dialysis and Transplantation *(1981)*
4010 Bentley Dr.
Pearland, TX 77584
Tel: (281)997-1944
Web Site: www.nasdat.org
Members: 200 individuals
Staff: 1
Executive Director: Laura Brazil-Nichols
E-Mail: lbrazil@nasdat.org

Historical Note
NASDT members are health professional concerned with kidney dialysis and transplantation procedures.

Meetings/Conferences:
Annual Meetings: Summer

North American Society for Oceanic History *(1974)*
P.O. Box 18108
Washington, DC 20036-8108
Tel: (202)707-1409
E-Mail: nasoh@mail.ecu.edu
Web Site: www.theaha.org/affiliates/nasoh.htm
Members: 220 individuals
Secretary: Virginia Steele Wood
E-Mail: nasoh@mail.ecu.edu

Historical Note
NASOH members are academics and others with an interest in the study of seafaring and inland waterways. Has no paid officers or full-time staff. Membership: $25/year (individual); $15/year (student).

Meetings/Conferences:
Annual Meetings: Spring

Publications:
NASOH Newsletter. 3/year.
Proceedings. irreg.

Membership Roster. irreg.

North American Society for Pediatric Gastroenterology, Hepatology and Nutrition *(1971)*
P.O. Box 6
Flourtown, PA 19031
Tel: (215)233-0808 *Fax:* (215)233-3918
E-Mail: naspghan@naspghan.org
Web Site: www.naspghan.org
Members: 800 individuals
Staff: 3
Annual Budget: $250-500,000
Executive Director: Margaret Stallings
E-Mail: naspghan@naspghan.org

Historical Note
Founded as North American Society for Pediatric Gastroenterology; became North American Society for Pediatric Gastroenterology and Nutrition in 1988, and assumed its current name in 2002 . NASPGHAN promotes excellence in training, education, research and patient care in the area of pediatric intestinal and liver disease. Membership: $352/year (individual).

Meetings/Conferences:
Annual Meetings: Fall

Publications:
NASPGHAN Membership Directory. a.
Journal of Pediatric Gastroenterology and Nutrition. m.
Newsletter. q.

North American Society for Social Philosophy *(1983)*
Queen's University at Kingston Dept. of Philosophy
Watson Hall, Room 313
Kingston, ON K7L3N-6
Tel: (413)533-2182
Web Site: www.pitt.edu/~nassp/nassp.html
Members: 200 individuals
President: Alistair MacLeod
Secretary and Archivist: Matthew Silliman

Historical Note
NASSP members are academics drawn from a wide range of disciplines with an interest in social philosophy. Has no paid officers or full-time staff. Membership: $40/year (individual). Membership benefits include receiving each annual volume in the series
Proceedings: Social Philosophy Today.

Meetings/Conferences:
Annual Meetings: Summer

Publications:
Proceedings: Social Philosophy Today. 1/year.
Journal of Social Philosophy. 4/year.

North American Society for Sport History *(1972)*
P.O. Box 1026
Lemont, PA 16851-1026
Tel: (814)238-1288 *Fax:* (814)238-1288
Web Site: www.nassh.org
Members: 950 individuals and institutions
Annual Budget: $25-50,000
Secretary-Treasurer: Ronald A. Smith
E-Mail: secretary-treasurer@nassh.org

Historical Note
Has no paid officers or full-time staff. Membership: $55/year(foreign); $50/year (regular); $25/year (student); $70/year (institution); $75/year (foreign institution).

Meetings/Conferences:
Annual Meetings: May
2007 - Lubbock, TX(Texas Technical University)/May 25-27

Publications:
Directory of Scholars Identifying with the History of Sport. irreg.
Proceedings. a.
Journal of Sport History. 3/year.
Newsletter. irreg.

North American Society for Sport Management *(1985)*
West Gym 014, Slippery Rock Univ.
Slippery Rock, PA 16057
Tel: (724)738-4812 *Fax:* (724)738-4858
Web Site: www.nassm.org
Members: 475 individuals
Contact: Dr. Rob Ammon

Historical Note
NASSM members are academics with an interest in sport management.

Meetings/Conferences:
Annual Meetings: Spring

Publications:
Journal of Sport Management. q.

North American Society for the Psychology of Sport and Physical Activity *(1966)*
244 Forker Blvd.
Iowa State University
Ames, IA 50011
Tel: (515)294-8261
E-Mail: naspspa@hotmail.com
Web Site: www.naspspa.org
Members: 600 individuals
Annual Budget: $10-25,000
Secretary-Treasurer: Ann L. Smiley-Oyen

Historical Note
Members are kinesiologists, physical education and physical therapy professionals and others with an interest in motor skills development, motor/learning control, and sport and exercise psychology. Has no paid officers or full-time staff.

Meetings/Conferences:
Annual Meetings: May-June

Publications:
NASPSPA Newsletter. 3/year.
NASPSPA Directory. a.

North American Society for the Sociology of Sport *(1980)*
Conference Consulting
P.O. Box 291
Bowling Green, OH 43402
Tel: (419)352-1928 *Fax:* (419)354-2957
E-Mail: treasurer@nasss.edu
Members: 400 individuals
Annual Budget: $10-25,000
Treasurer: Dean Purdy, Ph.D.

Historical Note
NASSS members are academics concerned with the sociology of sport. Has no paid officers or full-time staff. Membership: $75/year (individual); $150/year (company); $35/year (student).

Meetings/Conferences:
Annual Meetings: early November
2007 - Pittsburgh, PA(Marriott)/Nov. 2-8

Publications:
Newsletter. 3/year.
Sociology of Sport Journal. q. adv.

North American Society for Trenchless Technology *(1990)*
1655 N. Fort Myer Dr., Suite 700
Arlington, VA 22209
Tel: (703)351-5252 *Fax:* (703)739-6672
E-Mail: Nastt@nastt.org
Web Site: www.nastt.org
Members: 950individualsandcompanies
Staff: 3
Annual Budget: $500-1,000,000
Executive Director: John Hemphill

Historical Note
Members are individuals and organizations interested in the construction, maintenance and rehabilitation of utility service lines without the use of trenches. An affiliate of the International Society for Trenchless Technology. Membership: $150/year (individual); $500/year (company); $300/year (governmental/educational institutions).

Meetings/Conferences:
Annual Meetings: Spring

Publications:
Conference Proceedings. a. adv.
Newsletter. q. adv.
Membership Directory. a. adv.

North American Society of Adlerian Psychology *(1952)*
614 W. Chocolate Ave.
Hershey, PA 17033
Tel: (717)579-8795 *Fax:* (717)533-8616
E-Mail: info@alfredadler.org
Web Site: www.alfredadler.org
Members: 1000 individuals
Staff: 2
Annual Budget: $100-250,000
Executive Director: Becky LaFountain
E-Mail: info@alfredadler.org

Historical Note
Formerly (1976) American Society of Adlerian Psychology. Members are individuals interested in the teachings of the Austrian psychiatrist, Alfred Adler (1870-1937). His system emphasizes the uniqueness of each individual and that individual's relationships with society. Membership: $125/year.

Meetings/Conferences:
Annual Meetings: Spring

Publications:
NASAP Newsletter. 6/year.
Membership Directory. bien. adv.
Journal of Individual Psychology. q.

North American Society of Pacing and Electrophysiology

Historical Note
Became NASPE - Heart Rhythm Soc. in 2003.

North American Society of Scaffold Professionals

Historical Note
Address unknown in 2006.

North American South Devon Association *(1974)*
19590 E. Main St., Suite 202
Parker, CO 80138
Tel: (303)770-3130 *Fax:* (303)770-9302
E-Mail: southdevoninfo@aol.com
Web Site: www.southdevon.com
Members: 220 individuals
Staff: 3
Annual Budget: $100-250,000
Administrator: Sherry Doubet

Historical Note
Members are owners and breeders of purebred South Devon cattle, a breed originating in England and now used as a maternal beef bloodstock. Maintains breed registry. Membership: $75/year (active member); $25/year (associate); $15/year (junior member).

Meetings/Conferences:
Annual Meetings: Always in conjunction with Nat'l Western Stock Show/Denver, CO

Publications:
North American South Devon. q.
Sire Summary. a.

North American Spine Society *(1985)*
22 Calendar Court, Second Floor
La Grange, IL 60525
Tel: (708)588-8080 *Fax:* (708)588-1080
Toll Free: (877)774 - 6337
E-Mail: info@spine.org
Web Site: www.spine.org
Members: 2700 individuals
Staff: 20
Annual Budget: $2-5,000,000
Executive Director: Eric J. Muehlbauer, CAE
E-Mail: muehlbauer@spine.org
Director, Communications: Phyllis Anderson
E-Mail: anderson@spine.org
Director, Meeting Services: Amy K. Hedland
Manager, Information Technology: Brad Repsold
Director, Educational Programming: Christina Wolf

Historical Note
Formed by the merger of the American College of Spine Surgeons and the North American Lumbar Spine Association. NASS members are physicians, orthopedists, osteopaths and other health professionals with an interest in the treatment of the spine. Membership: $250/year (individual).

Meetings/Conferences:
Annual Meetings: Fall
2007 - Austin, TX(Austin Convention Center)/Oct. 23-27/6250
2008 - Toronto, ON, Canada/Oct. 14-18
2009 - San Francisco, CA/Oct. 13-17
2011 - Chicago, IL/Oct. 11-15
2012 - San Francisco, CA/Nov. 14-18

Publications:
Spineline. bi-m. adv.
The Spine Journal. bi-m. adv.

North American Strawberry Growers Association *(1978)*
526 Brittany Dr.
State College, PA 16803
Tel: (814)238-3364 *Fax:* (814)238-7051
E-Mail: info@nasga.org
Web Site: www.nasga.org
Members: 500 individuals
Staff: 2
Annual Budget: $50-100,000
Executive Director: Patricia E. Heuser
Historical Note
NASGA members are growers, nurserymen and academics interested in strawberry production and development. North American Bramble Growers Association (same address) is an affiliate of NASGA. Membership: $55/year (professional); $175/year (grower/organization/ company).
Meetings/Conferences:
Annual Meetings: February
Publications:
Quarterly Newsletter. q. adv.
Proceedings. a.
Advances in Strawberry Production. a.

North American Technician Excellence *(1997)*
4100 N. Fairfax Dr., Suite 210
Arlington, VA 22203
Tel: (703)276-7247 *Fax:* (703)527-2316
Toll Free: (877)420 - 6283
E-Mail: mail@natex.org
Web Site: www.natex.org
Members: 20000 certificants
Staff: 6
Annual Budget: $2-5,000,000
President: Rex P. Boynton
E-Mail: rboynton@natex.org
Vice President, Certifications: Pat Murphy
Director, Marketing and Public Relations: Carl Smith
Historical Note
In order to develop and promote excellence in the installation and service of HVACR equipment, NATE provides a national certification program with broad based industry support to recognize high quality industry technicians through voluntary testing and certification.

North American Transportation Employee Relations Association *(1987)*
1300 19th St. NW
Suite 700
Washington, DC 20036
Tel: (202)719-2020 *Fax:* (202)719-2077
Web Site: www.natera.org
Members: 128 individuals
Staff: 2
Annual Budget: $25-50,000
Executive Director: Herve H. Aitken
E-Mail: haitken@fordharrison.com
Historical Note
Founded as National Trucking Industrial Relations Association, became North American Trucking Industrial Relations Association in 1997 and assumed its current name in 2001. NATERA members are trucking executives and lawyers concerned with personnel and labor relations issues. Membership: $175/year.
Meetings/Conferences:
Semi-annual Meetings:
Publications:
Newsletter. q.

North American Transportation Management Institute *(1944)*
2460 W. 26th Ave., Suite 17C
Denver, CO 80211
Tel: (303)952-4013 *Fax:* (775)370-4055
E-Mail: info@natmi.org
Web Site: www.natmi.org
Members: 1050individualsandorganizations
Staff: 3
Annual Budget: $250-500,000
Executive Director: Jeff Arnold
E-Mail: jeff@natmi.org
Member Services Manager: Chydie Crandall
Historical Note
Founded as National Committee for Motor Fleet Supervisor Training; assumed its current name in 1997. Provides certification which designates competence in the fleet industry's universal standards. Members are those in the industry and related organizations concerned with training and certification. Membership: $250/year.
Publications:
Guardrail Magazine. q. adv.
Motor Fleet Monthly. m.

North American Wensleydale Sheep Association *(1999)*
4589 Fruitland Road
Loma Rica, CA 95901
Tel: (530)743-5262
E-Mail: info@wensleydalesheep.org
Web Site: www.wensleydalesheep.org
Members: 34 herds
Secretary: Sherry Carlson
E-Mail: info@wensleydalesheep.org
Historical Note
NAWSA maintains a pedigree registry on behalf of its member breeders. The Wensleydale is a longwool breed indigeonous to Britain. Has no paid officers or full-time staff. Membership: $25/year (active); $15/year (associate).

North American Wholesale Lumber Association *(1893)*
3601 Algonquin Road, Suite 400
Rolling Meadows, IL 60008
Tel: (847)870-7470 *Fax:* (847)870-0201
E-Mail: info@lumber.org
Web Site: www.lumber.org
Members: 650 companies
Staff: 9
Annual Budget: $1-2,000,000
President and Chief Executive Officer: Nicholas Kent
E-Mail: nrkent@lumber.org
Director, Meetings and Information: Pam Baker
E-Mail: pbaker@lumber.org
Programs and Administration: Mark Palmer
E-Mail: mpalmer@lumber.org
Historical Note
Formerly (1972) National American Wholesale Lumber Association. Membership: $595-1,900/year (organization/company), depending on membership category and size.
Meetings/Conferences:
Annual Meetings: Spring/500
Publications:
NAWLA Bulletin. m.

North American-Chilean Chamber of Commerce *(1977)*
30 Vesey St., Suite 506
New York, NY 10007
Tel: (212)233-7776 *Fax:* (212)233-7779
E-Mail: andean@nyct.net
Members: 120 businesses
Staff: 1
Annual Budget: $10-25,000
President: David Spencer
E-Mail: andean@nyct.net
Historical Note
Founded in 1977 by the merger of Chile-American Association with North American-Chile Chamber of Commerce. Members are United States, Canadian and Chilean executives interested in fostering improved trade and commerce between their repective countries. Membership: $100/year (individual); $250/year (corporate).
Meetings/Conferences:
Annual Meetings: January in New York

North-American Association of Telecommunications Dealers *(1987)*
131 N.W. First Ave.
Delray Beach, FL 33444
Tel: (561)266-9440 *Fax:* (561)266-9017
Web Site: www.natd.com
Members: 175 companies
Staff: 3
Annual Budget: $100-250,000
Executive Director: Joseph Marion
E-Mail: jmarion@natd.com
Historical Note
Formerly (1994) the National Association of Telecommunications Dealers, NAATD members are secondary marketers of telecommunications equipment and major PBX installations. Membership: $600-2,000/year.
Meetings/Conferences:
Semi-Annual Meetings: January and June/300
Publications:
NATD-Network. q.

Northern Nut Growers Association *(1910)*
654 Beinhower Road
Etters, PA 17319-9774
Tel: (717)938-6090 *Fax:* (717)938-6090
Web Site: www.nutgrowing.org
Members: 825 individuals
Staff: 1
Annual Budget: $25-50,000
Secretary: Tucker Hill
E-Mail: tuckerh@epix.net
Historical Note
Promotes interest in nut-bearing trees, their culture and products. Mainly concerned with 14 different species of nut trees grown in the northern U.S. and southern Canada. Membership: $25/year (U.S. members); $27/year (Canadian); $30/year (foreign).
Meetings/Conferences:
Annual Meetings: Summer
Publications:
Nutshell. q. adv.
Proceedings. a.

Northwest Fruit Exporters *(1980)*
105 S. 18th St., Suite 227
Yakima, WA 98901
Tel: (509)453-3193 *Fax:* (509)457-7615
E-Mail: nfe@goodfruit.com
Members: 17 companies
Staff: 3
Annual Budget: $250-500,000
Manager: Jim Archer
E-Mail: nfe@goodfruit.com
Historical Note
A Webb-Pomerene Act association. Membership: $1500 (organization/company).

Norwegian-American Chamber of Commerce *(1915)*
800 Third Ave., 38th Floor
New York, NY 10022
Tel: (212)421-1655 *Fax:* (212)838-0374
E-Mail: nacc@ntcny.org
Web Site: www.nacc.no
Members: 800 national membership
Staff: 2
Annual Budget: $50-100,000
General Manager: Inger M. Tallaksen
E-Mail: nacc@ntcny.org
Historical Note
Membership: $475/year.
Meetings/Conferences:
Annual Meetings: New York City, in March/150-200
Publications:
NACC NEWS. q. adv.

Not-for-Profit Services Association *(1995)*
One Valmont Plaza
Fourth Floor
Omaha, NE 68154
Tel: (402)778-7922 *Fax:* (402)778-7931
Toll Free: (888)475 - 4476
E-Mail: info@nonprofitcpas.com
Web Site: www.nonprofitcpas.com
Members: 17 firms
Staff: 6
Executive Director: Nancy Drennen
Historical Note
NSA members are CPA firms who provide services to not-for-profit organizations, particularly firms who specialize in providing accounting services beyond traditional tax and audit services. Membership is on a territorially protected basis.

Meetings/Conferences:
Semi-Annual Meetings:

Publications:
Members' E-Bulletin (online). m.

NPES, The Association for Suppliers of Printing, Publishing and Converting Technologies *(1933)*
1899 Preston White Dr.
Reston, VA 20191-4367
Tel: (703)264-7200 Fax: (703)620-0994
E-Mail: npes@npes.org
Web Site: www.npes.org
Members: 400 suppliers
Staff: 30
Annual Budget: $2-5,000,000
Vice President, Member Services: William K. Smythe
Director, Government Affairs: Mark J. Nuzzaco
Director, Communications and Marketing: Douglas Sprei

Historical Note
Established as the National Printing Equipment Association; became the National Printing Equipment and Supply Association in 1979 and assumed its present name in 1998. Members are manufacturers and distributors of equipment, systems, software, and supplies. The purpose of the association is to strengthen the entire industry and aid member firms in the areas of statistics and marketing, safety and industry standards, international trade, and government relations.

Meetings/Conferences:
Annual Meetings: Fall/100 and Spring
2007 – Chicago, IL(Fairmont Hotel Chicago)/March 27-28

Publications:
NPES News. m.
NPES Directory-Internat'l Suppliers of Printing and Publishing Technologies. irreg.

NPTA Alliance *(1903)*
500 Bi-County Boulevard
Farmingdale, NY 11735
Tel: (631)777-2223 Fax: (631)777-2224
Web Site: www.gopta.com
Members: 850 wholesalers
Staff: 13
Annual Budget: $2-5,000,000
President: William H. Frohlich

Historical Note
Formerly National Paper Trade Association; assumed current name in 2001. NPTA serves the paper, packaging and supplies distribution channel. Mission is to promote the success of its member companies by providing valuable service though which they can better serve their customers.

Meetings/Conferences:
Annual Meetings: Fall

Publications:
Distribution Sales and Management. m.

Nuclear Energy Institute *(1981)*
1776 I St. NW
Suite 400
Washington, DC 20006-3708
Tel: (202)739-8079 Fax: (202)785-4019
Web Site: www.nei.org
Members: 249 organizations
Staff: 138
Annual Budget: $25-50,000,000
President and Chief Executive Officer: Frank Bowman
Senior Vice President and Chief Nuclear Officer: Marvin Fertel
Senior Vice President, Government Affairs: Alex Flint
Vice President, Legal, General Counsel, and Secretary: Ellen Ginsberg
Vice President, Office of the President and Executive Advisor to the President: Angelina Howard
Executive Director and Special Assistant to the President, Policy Development: Richard Myers
Vice President, Communications: Scott Peterson
Vice President, Regulatory Affairs: Anthony Pietrangelo
Vice President, Member Relations and Corporate Services: Phyllis Rich
Senior Director, Member Services and Assistant Secretary: Lisa Steward
Vice President, Nuclear Operations: Jay Thayer

Historical Note
Established as the Committee for Energy Awareness, it became the U.S. Council for Energy Awareness in 1987. Absorbed the American Nuclear Energy Council and the Nuclear Management and Resources Council and assumed its present name in 1994. In July 1987, the Atomic Industrial Forum was merged with the Council. Members consist of utilities, manufacturers of electrical generating equipment, researchers, architects, engineers, labor unions, milling and mining companies, constructors, laboratories, educational institutions and government agencies with interest in the generation of electricity by nuclear power. Has an annual budget of approximately $31 million. Membership dues vary, based on type of company.

Meetings/Conferences:
Annual Meetings: May/500

Publications:
Nuclear Energy Insight. m.
Nuclear Energy Overview. w.
Nuclear Energy Outlook. q.
Energy Information Digest. bi-m.

Nuclear Information and Records Management Association *(1978)*
Ten Almas Road
Windham, NH 03087
Tel: (603)432-6476 Fax: (603)432-3024
E-Mail: jnirma@nirma.mv.com
Web Site: www.nirma.org
Members: 350 individuals
Staff: 1
Annual Budget: $50-100,000
Administrator: Jane Hannum
E-Mail: jnirma@nirma.mv.com

Historical Note
Purpose is to improve the management of corporate information and records relating to nuclear facilities. Membership includes utility company employees, architectural engineers and industrial consultants. Formerly (1985) the Nuclear Records Management Association. Membership: $60/year.

Meetings/Conferences:
Annual Meetings: Fall

Publications:
Newsletter. q.

Nuclear Suppliers Association *(1984)*
P.O. Box 2038
Springfield, VA 22152
Tel: (703)451-1912 Fax: (703)451-2334
E-Mail: nsanews@aol.com
Web Site: www.nuclearsuppliers.org
Members: 60 companies
Annual Budget: $25-50,000
Director, Meetings: R. Travis
E-Mail: nsanews@aol.com

Historical Note
Members are companies which specialize in the manufacture and distribution of products and services for the nuclear industry. Membership: $150/year (organization).

Nurse Healers - Professional Associates International *(1978)*
P.O. Box 158
Warnerville, NY 12187-0158
Tel: (518)325-1185 Fax: (509)693-3537
Toll Free: (877)325 - 4724
E-Mail: nh-pai@therapeutic-touch.org
Web Site: www.therapeutic-touch.org
Members: 700 individuals
Staff: 1
Annual Budget: $25-50,000
Treasurer: Sue Conlin
E-Mail: nh-pai@therapeutic-touch.org

Historical Note
NH-PAI is the official organization of Therapeutic Touch. Develops standards of practice and teaching for TT and offers credentialing for Qualified Teachers and Practitioners of Therapeutic Touch. Has no paid officers or full-time staff. Membership: $75/year.

Meetings/Conferences:
Annual Meetings: October

Publications:
Cooperative Connection. q. adv.

Nursery and Landscape Association Executives of North America *(1947)*
968 Trinity Road
Raleigh, NC 27607
Tel: (919)816-9120 Fax: (919)816-9118
Members: 70 associations
Staff: 1
Annual Budget: $10-25,000
Executive Director: Beverly Gelvin, CMP
E-Mail: bgelvin@ncan.com

Historical Note
Formerly (1972) Nursery Association Secretaries, (1987) Nursery Association Executives, and (2000) Nursery Association Executives of North America. Members are chief executives of nursery associations of the U.S. and Canada. The association was formed primarily for educational purposes.

Meetings/Conferences:
Semi-annual Meetings: Winter and Summer, with American Ass'n of Nurserymen

Publications:
Newsletter. q.

Nurses Organization of Veterans Affairs *(1980)*
1726 M St. NW
Suite 1101
Washington, DC 20036
Tel: (202)296-0888 Fax: (202)833-1577
E-Mail: nova@vanurse.org
Web Site: www.vanurse.org
Members: 2600 individuals
Staff: 2
Annual Budget: $250-500,000
Executive Director: Deborah Beck

Historical Note
Formerly (1989) Nurses Organization of the Veterans Administration. Membership: $80/year.

Meetings/Conferences:
Annual Meetings: April

Publications:
News from NOVA. q. adv.

NYSE Arca *(1957)*
100 South Wacker Drive
Suite 1800
Chicago, IL 60606
Tel: (888)514-7284
Web Site: www.archipelago.com
Members: 551 companies and brokers
Staff: 400
Chairman and Chief Executive Officer: Philip D. DeFeo

Historical Note
Formed for the merger of Archipelago Exchange, or ArcaExÆ, and the Pacific Stock Exchange

Publications:
Directory of Member Firms. semi-a.
Pit Stop. bi-m.
Coast Lines. q.
Directory of Securities. q.

Object Management Group *(1989)*
250 First Ave., Suite 100
Needham, MA 02494
Tel: (781)444-0404 Fax: (781)444-0320
E-Mail: info@omg.org
Web Site: www.omg.org
Members: 450 companies
Staff: 21
Chairman and Chief Executive Officer: Dr. Richard Soley
E-Mail: soley@omg.org
Director, Business Development: Kenneth Berk
President and Chief Operating Officer: Bill Hoffman
E-Mail: hoffman@omg.org
Director, Event Management: Kevin Loughry
Vice President, Marketing: Dana Morris

Historical Note
OMG is an open membership, not-for-profit consortium that produces and maintains computer inventory specifications for interoperable business applications. Membership includes many large and smaller companies in the computer industry. All of OMG's adopted specifications are available for free download from OMG's web site.

Oceanic Engineering Society

Historical Note
A technical society of the Institute of Electrical and Electronics Engineers (IEEE). Membership in the Society, open only to IEEE members, includes subscription to a technical periodical in the field published by IEEE. All administrative support is provided by IEEE.

Oceanography Society *(1988)*
P.O. Box 1931
Rockville, MD 20849-1931
Tel: (301)251-7708 *Fax:* (301)251-7709
E-Mail: info@tos.org
Web Site: www.tos.org
Members: 1500 individuals
Executive Director: Jenny Ramarui
E-Mail: info@tos.org
Historical Note
TOS members are oceanographers, scientists and engineers with a professional interest in oceanography and related fields. Membership: $50/year (individual); $25/year (student); $135/year (library subscription); $500/year (corporate/institution).
Publications:
Oceanography Magazine. 3/year.

Office and Professional Employees International Union *(1945)*
265 W. 14th St., Suite 610
New York, NY 10011
Tel: (212)675-3210 *Fax:* (212)727-3466
Toll Free: (800)346 - 7348
E-Mail: opeiu@opeiu.org
Web Site: www.opeiu.org
Members: 140000 individuals
Staff: 50
Annual Budget: $2-5,000,000
President: Michael Goodwin
E-Mail: opeiu@opeiu.org
Historical Note
Organized in Cincinnati, Ohio January 8, 1945 as the Office Employees International Union and chartered by the American Federation of Labor at the same time. Absorbed the Associated Unions of America in 1972. Sponsors and supports the Voice of the Electorate Political Action Committee. Absorbed the Leather Workers International Union (previously in Peabody, MA) in 1992. Membership fee varies by local union.
Publications:
White Collar. q.
Steward's Update. bi-m.

Office Business Center Association International *(1986)*
1500 Commerce Pkwy.
Suite C
Mt. Laurel, NJ 08054
Tel: (856)237-4741 *Fax:* (856)439-0525
Toll Free: (800)237 - 4741
E-Mail: info@officebusinesscenters.com
Web Site: www.officebusinesscenters.com
Members: 9807 companies
Staff: 5
Annual Budget: $250-500,000
Historical Note
Founded as Executive Suite Network; became Executive Suite Association in 1993, and assumed its current name in 2001. OBCAI is a member-owned trade association for owners and operators of office business centers worldwide. OBCAI provides professional development and education to its members. Membership: based upon total square footage of all office business center locations.
Meetings/Conferences:
Annual Meetings: Fall
Publications:
ESA World. m.

Office Furniture Dealers Alliance
Historical Note
An alliance of the Business Products Industry Association.

Office Furniture Distribution Association *(1976)*
739 Daniel Shays Hwy., Suite D-16
Athol, MA 01331
Tel: (978)249-0303 *Fax:* (978)249-5937
E-Mail: kmiller@mass.rr.com
Web Site: www.theofda.org
Members: 63 individuals
Staff: 3
Managing Director: Kenneth E. Miller
E-Mail: kmiller@mass.rr.com
Historical Note
Membership: $250/year (individual).
Meetings/Conferences:
2007 – Ft. Lauderdale, FL(Lago Mar)/May 2-4
2008 – Grand Rapids, MI(Amway Grand Plaza Hotel)/Sept. 19-20
Publications:
Office Furniture Logistics newsletter. m.

Office Products Dealers Alliance *(1983)*
Historical Note
A subsidiary of Business Products Industry Ass'n, which provides administrative support

Office Products Manufacturers Association *(1970)*
Historical Note
An alliance of the Business Products Industry Association.

Office Products Representatives Association *(1973)*
Historical Note
An alliance of the Business Products Industry Association.

Office Products Wholesalers Association *(1995)*
5024-R Campbell Blvd.
Baltimore, MD 21236-5974
Tel: (410)931-8100 *Fax:* (410)931-8111
E-Mail: opwa@clemonsmgmt.com
Web Site: www.opwa.org
Members: 20 wholesalers, 85 manufacturers
Staff: 3
Annual Budget: $500-1,000,000
Executive Vice President: Calvin K. Clemons, CAE, CMP
Historical Note
Formed (1995) by the consolidation of National Association of Wholesale Independent Distributors (formerly National Association of Writing Instrument Distributors) and Wholesale Stationers Association. OPWA members are chief executives of office product wholesalers and manufacturers who affirm the concept of wholesale distribution in the office products industry.
Publications:
Member Directory (online).
OPWA Magazine. a. adv.

Offshore Marine Service Association *(1957)*
990 N. Corporate Dr., Suite 210
Harahan, LA 70123-3324
Tel: (504)734-7622 *Fax:* (504)734-7134
E-Mail: kenwells@offshoremarine.org
Web Site: www.offshoremarine.org
Members: 270 corporations
Staff: 4
Annual Budget: $500-1,000,000
President: Ken Wells
E-Mail: kenwells@offshoremarine.org
Manager, Administration and Finance: Ragen Brown
Executive Secretary: Lillie Licciardi
Vice President: Ken Parris
E-Mail: ken@offshoremarine.org
Historical Note
Members are owners and operators of offshore installations or of vessels servicing such installations, and suppliers to the industry. Provides regulatory input on issues of concern to the offshore business community. Membership: $885-56,800/year (company).
Meetings/Conferences:
Quarterly Meetings: usually New Orleans, LA/300
Publications:
OMSA Newsletter. q.

Ombudsman Association, The *(1982)*
203 Towne Center Dr.
Hillsborough, NJ 08844
Tel: (908)359-0246 *Fax:* (908)359-7619
E-Mail: info@ombudsassociation.org
Web Site: www.ombuds-toa.org/
Members: 400 individuals
Annual Budget: $100-250,000
President: Janis Schonauer
Historical Note
Formerly (1992) the Corporate Ombudsman Association. Incorporated as an association of individuals actively engaged in the practice of ombudsmanry, as designated neutrals. TOA works to enhance the quality and value of the ombudsman profession. Membership: $175.
Meetings/Conferences:
Annual Meetings: May
2007 – St. Louis, MO/Apr. 11-14
Publications:
Booklets. irreg.
Bulletin. irreg.
Ombuds News Newsletter. q. adv.
Ombudsman Handbook. irreg.

Omega Delta *(1917)*
Southern College of Optometry
1245 Madison Ave.
Memphis, TN 38104
Members: 90 individuals
Annual Budget: under $10,000
President: Nicole Irick
Historical Note
Professional fraternity serving optometry.
Publications:
Membership Directory. irreg.

Omega Tau Sigma *(1906)*
9947 E. Bloomfield Hills Dr.
Effingham, IL 62401
Tel: (217)868-5095 *Fax:* (217)868-5080
E-Mail: kentuckyauburn@yahoo.com
Members: 8054 individuals
Staff: 8
Annual Budget: under $10,000
President: Mark Ballman, DVM
Secretary: John Gordan, D.V.M.
Historical Note
Professional veterinary medical fraternity, established at the University of Pennsylvania School of Veterinary Medicine. Member of the Professional Fraternity Association. Has no paid officers or full-time staff.
Meetings/Conferences:
Annual Meetings: Fall, on a college campus hosted by local chapter/100
Publications:
Inner Square. semi-a.
OTS Directory. irreg.

Omicron Kappa Upsilon *(1914)*
Univ. of Medicine & Dentistry of New Jersey
110 Bergen St., Suite D-860
Newark, NJ 07103
Tel: (973)972-4635 *Fax:* (973)972-3164
Web Site: www.oku.org
Members: 17000 individuals
Staff: 2
Annual Budget: $25-50,000
Bulletin Editor: James L. Delahanty
Historical Note
Honorary dental society. Organized May 21, 1914 by the faculty of Northwestern University Dental School.
Meetings/Conferences:
Annual Meetings: Spring, in conjunction with the American Ass'n of Dental Schools

Oncology Nursing Society *(1975)*
125 Enterprise Dr.
Pittsburgh, PA 15275-1214
Tel: (412)859-6100 *Fax:* (877)369-5497
Toll Free: (866)257 - 4066
E-Mail: customer.service@ons.org
Web Site: www.ons.org
Members: 30,000 individuals
Staff: 114
Annual Budget: $10-25,000,000
Executive Director: Bridget Culhane
E-Mail: bridget@ons.org
Chief Operating Officer: Layla Ballon
E-Mail: layla@ons.org
Director, Meeting Services: Nancy Berkowitz

E-Mail: nancy@ons.org
Director, Information Technology: Kristine Burns
E-Mail: kristine@ons.org
Director, Finance: Jeff Dewalt
E-Mail: jeff@ons.org
Director, Education: Laura Fennimore
E-Mail: lfennimore@ons.org
Director, Marketing: Jon Galatis
E-Mail: jgalatis@ons.org
Associate, Health Policy: Ilisa Halpern
E-Mail: halperni@arentfox.com
Executive Director, Communications and Publisher: Leonard Mafrica
E-Mail: len@ons.org
Director, Research: Gail Mallory
E-Mail: gmallory@ons.org
Executive Director, Oncology Education Services: Michele McCorkle
E-Mail: michele@ons.org
Chief Executive Officer: Pearl Moore, R.N.
E-Mail: pearl@ons.org
Executive Director, Oncology Nursing Certificate Corporation: Cynthia Miller Murphy
E-Mail: cyndi@ons.org
Director, Periodical Publications: Vicki Newton
E-Mail: vikki@ons.org
Director, Membership and Leadership: Angela Stengel
E-Mail: astengel@ons.org

Historical Note

Members are nurses and other health care professionals involved in the treatment and care of cancer patients. Has an annual budget of approximately $24 million. Membership: $85/year (individual); $2,000/year (organization); $25,000 (lifetime organization).

Meetings/Conferences:

Annual Meetings: Spring/5,000

Publications:

Oncology Nursing Forum. bi-m. adv.
Clinical Journal of Oncology Nursing. bi-m. adv.
ONS News. m. adv.

Online Audiovisual Catalogers *(1980)*

110 Olin Library
Cornell University
Ithaca, NY 14853
Tel: (607)255-5752 *Fax:* (607)255-6110
E-Mail: ilw2@cornell.edu
Web Site: www.olacinc.org
Members: 700 individuals
Annual Budget: under $10,000
Archivist: Iris Wolley
E-Mail: ilw2@cornell.edu

Historical Note

OLAC represents catalogers of audiovisual materials and computer files. Provides a means of exchange of information, opportunities for continuing education, and a unified voice for its members, and works toward a common understanding of practices and standards. Membership: $12/year (individual); $18/year (institution).

Publications:

OLAC Newsletter. q.

Open Applications Group *(1995)*

P.O. Box 4897
Marietta, GA 30061
Tel: (678)715-7588 *Fax:* (678)234-6036
E-Mail: oagis@openapplications.org
Web Site: www.openapplications.org
Staff: 4
President: David Connelly

Historical Note

The OAGI sets specifications that define the business object interoperability between enterprise business applications. Members are enterprise application software developers. Membership: $25,000/year (corporate); $12,000/year (associate).

Open Group *(1983)*

44 Montgomery St., Suite 960
San Francisco, CA 94104-4704
Tel: (415)374-8280 *Fax:* (415)374-8293
Web Site: www.opengroup.org
Members: 550 companies
Staff: 50
Annual Budget: $2-5,000,000
President and Chief Executive Officer: Allen Brown
Vice President, Marketing: Graham Bird
Vice President and Chief Operating Officer: Steve Nunn

Historical Note

Founded as the Electronic Messaging Association; became EMA - The E-Business Forum in 1999, and assumed its present name in 2002. Members are corporate users plus telecommunications carriers, computer equipment and software manufacturers, and consultants. Membership: $1000-10,000/year.

Meetings/Conferences:

Annual Meetings: No Meetings Held

OPERA America *(1970)*

330 Seventh Ave.
16th Floor
New York, NY 10001
Tel: (212)796-8620 *Fax:* (212)796-8631
E-Mail: frontdesk@operaamerica.org
Web Site: www.operaamerica.org
Members: 1500 individuals
Staff: 17
Annual Budget: $2-5,000,000
President and Chief Executive Officer: Marc A. Scorca
Director, Finance and Operations: Debra Harrison
Managing Director: Diana Hossack
Director, Public Affairs: Elizabeth Rocca
Director, Publications and Research: Kelly Rourke

Historical Note

Established to facilitate communication and cooperation among opera producing companies in the U.S., Canada, and abroad. Purpose is to: promote the growth and expansion of opera; assist in development of resident professional opera companies through cooperative artistic management services to its members; assist improvement of operatic presentations; encourage the appreciation and enjoyment of opera by all segments of society; and to foster the education, training and development of operatic composers, singers and allied talents. Membership: sliding scale based on budget (professional companies); $200/year (affiliate organizations); $50-1000/year (individuals); $250/year (businesses); $40/year (singer), $150/year (library).

Meetings/Conferences:

Annual: 500

Publications:

Standing Ovations. 3/year.
Membership Register. a.
Audition Connection. bi-m.
Voices. 3/year.
OPERA America Newsline. 10/year. adv.
Annual Field Report. a.
Career Guide for Singers. bien.
Perspectives Series.

Operations Security Professionals Society *(1990)*

P.O. Box 489
Hamilton, VA 20159
Tel: (540)338-3048 *Fax:* (703)738-7145
E-Mail: opsec@adelphia.net
Web Site: www.opsec.org
Members: 780 individuals
Annual Budget: $100-250,000
Contact: Deb Davis

Historical Note

Also known as OPSEC Professionals Society OPS members are are operations security professionals from both government and the private sector. Awards the designation OCP (OPSEC Certified Professional). Membership: $40/year (individual); $200/year (corporate).

Meetings/Conferences:

Annual Meetings: Spring

Publications:

OPS ZGram. d.
OPS News Newsletter. q.
Operations Security Journal. irreg. adv.

Operative Plasterers' and Cement Masons' International Association of the United States and Canada *(1864)*

14405 Laurel Place, Suite 300
Laurel, MD 20707
Tel: (301)470-4200 *Fax:* (301)470-2502
E-Mail: opcimiaintl@opcmia.org
Web Site: www.opcmia.org
Members: 55000 individuals
Staff: 43
Annual Budget: $2-5,000,000
General President: John J. Dougherty
E-Mail: opcimiaintl@opcmia.org

Historical Note

Founded in 1864 as the National Plasterers' Organization of the United States, it was renamed the Operative Plasterers International the United States and Canada in 1889. Affiliated with the American Federation of Labor in 1908, it absorbed the cement finishers of the United Brotherhood of Cement Workers in 1915 and changed its name to the Operative Plasterers' and Cement Finishers' International Association of the United States and Canada. The present name was adopted in 1950. Sponsors and supports the Plasterers' and Cement Masons' Political Action Committee.

Publications:

The Plasterer and Cement Mason. bi-m.

Ophthalmic Photographers' Society *(1969)*

1869 Ranch Road
Nixa, MO 65714-8262
Tel: (417)725-0181 *Fax:* (417)724-8450
Toll Free: (800)403 - 1677
E-Mail: ops@opsweb.org
Web Site: www.opsweb.org
Members: 1200 individuals
Staff: 1
Annual Budget: $50-100,000
Executive Director: Barbara McCalley
E-Mail: ops@opsweb.org

Historical Note

OPS members are health professionals actively engaged in ophthalmic photography including ophthalmic photographers, ophthamologists, ophthalmic technicians, and basic scientific researchers. Provides continuing education opportunities and certification as Certified Retinal Angiographer (CRA). Membership: $80/year (individual); $250/year (sustaining membership).

Meetings/Conferences:

Annual Meetings: Fall/450

Publications:

OPS Newsletter. bi-m.
Journal of Ophthalmic Photography. semi-a. adv.
OPS Directory. a.

Opportunity Finance Network *(1986)*

Public Ledger Bldg., Suite 572
620 Chestnut St.
Philadelphia, PA 19106
Tel: (215)923-4754 *Fax:* (215)923-4755
E-Mail: info@opportunityfinance.net
Web Site: www.opportunityfinance.net
Members: 170 funds
Staff: 27
Annual Budget: $5-10,000,000
President and Chief Executive Officer: Mark Pinsky
Executive Vice Preisdent and Chief Lending and Investment Officer: Arthur Fleming
Executive VIce President and Chief Financial Officer: Geoffrey Kent

Historical Note

Founded as National Association of Community Development Loan Funds; assumed its current name in 2006. OFN provides support for non-profit revolving loan funds that lend capital and provide technical assistance and training in distressed and disenfranchised communities. Formerly known as National Community Capital Association.

Publications:

Left Click/Right Click. q.
Policy Update. q.

OPSEC Professionals Society *(1990)*

Historical Note

See Operations Security Professionals Society

Optical Imaging Association

225 Reinekers Lane, Suite 625
Alexandria, VA 22314
Tel: (703)836-1360 Ext: 27 *Fax:* (703)836-6644

Web Site: www.opia.org
Members: 25 companies
Staff: 1
Annual Budget: $50-100,000
Executive Director: William C. Strackbein

Historical Note
Founded as the Opto-Precision Instruments Association; assumed its present name in 1999. OPIA is an affiliate of the SAMA Group of Associations.

Optical Laboratories Association *(1894)*
11096 Lee Hwy., #A-01
Fairfax, VA 22030-5039
Tel: (703)359-2830 *Fax:* (703)359-2834
Toll Free: (800)477 - 5652
E-Mail: ola@ola-labs.org
Web Site: www.ola-labs.org
Members: 360 companies
Staff: 8
Annual Budget: $1-2,000,000
Executive Director: Robert L. Dziuban, CAE
E-Mail: ola@ola-labs.org

Historical Note
Formerly the Optical Wholesalers Association, it adopted its present name in 1977. Independent ophthalmic laboratories and supply houses making prescription glasses to requirements of ophthalmologists, optometrists and opticians.

Meetings/Conferences:
Annual Meetings: November/2,400
2007 – Indianapolis, IN(Convention Center)/Nov. 15-17/1500

Publications:
Member news. m.
Swap Shop. irreg.
Technical Topics. q.
Clear Visions. bi-m.
Special Bulletin. irreg.

Optical Society of America *(1916)*
2010 Massachusetts Ave. NW
Washington, DC 20036-1023
Tel: (202)223-8130 *Fax:* (202)223-1096
E-Mail: info@osa.org
Web Site: www.osa.org
Members: 15000 individuals
Staff: 100
Annual Budget: $10-25,000,000
Executive Director: Elizabeth Rogan
Senior Director, Publications: John Childs
Manager, Human Resources: Amy Dufane
Chief Marketing Officer: Beth T. Hampton
Chief Operating Officer: John R. Heberlein
Senior Director, Information Technology: Deborah C. Herrin
Senior Director, Conventions and Meetings: William Ryan

Historical Note
OSA is a professional society of optical engineers and scientists concerned with the fields of optics and photonics. A member of the American Institute of Physics. Has an annual budget of $10 million. Membership: $75/year (regular); $30/year (student); $550/year (corporation); $24/year (teachers).

Meetings/Conferences:
Annual Meetings: Fall

Publications:
Applied Optics. 3/m. adv.
Journal A of the Optical Society of America. a.
Journal B of the Optical Society of America. a.
Optics and Spectroscopy. m.
Optics Letters. bi-w.
Optics & Photonics News. m. adv.
Journal of Optical Technology. m.
Journal of Lightwave Technology. m.
Journal of Optical Networking. m.

Opticians Association of America *(1926)*
441 Carlisle Dr.
Herndon, VA 20170
Tel: (703)437-8780 *Fax:* (703)437-0727
E-Mail: oaa@oaa.org
Web Site: www.oaa.org
Members: 7500 individuals
Staff: 15
Annual Budget: $1-2,000,000
Executive Director: Catherine Langley

Historical Note
Formerly (1972) Guild of Prescription Opticians of America. Provides legislative advocacy ans professional support to dispensing opticians. Membership: $50/year (individual); company memberships vary, based on number of locations.

Meetings/Conferences:
Annual Meetings: Summer/1,000

Publications:
State Leaders Bulletin.
Membership Directory. a.
Guild Quarterly. q.
OAA News.
American Optician.

Oral History Association *(1966)*
P.O. Box 1773
Dickinson College
Carlisle, PA 17013
Tel: (717)245-1036 *Fax:* (717)245-1046
E-Mail: oha@dickinson.edu
Web Site: www.dickinson.edu/oha
Members: 1200 individuals
Staff: 1
Annual Budget: $50-100,000
Executive Secretary: Madelyn Campbell
E-Mail: oha@dickinson.edu

Historical Note
Historians and others involved in recording, transcribing, and preserving conversations with persons who have participated in seminal developments of history. Membership: $500 (lifetime individual), $50/year (regular individual), $75-120/year (institutional), $50/year (library), $25/year (student).

Meetings/Conferences:
Annual Meetings: Fall

Publications:
Oral History Evaluation Guidelines.
Oral History Review. 2/year. adv.
Oral History Association Newsletter. 3/year.
Pamphlet Series. irreg.
Annual Report & Membership Directory. a.

Order Selection, Staging and Storage Council *(1986)*

Historical Note
An affiliate of Material Handling Industry of America, which provides administrative support.

Organic Crop Improvement Association International *(1985)*
6400 Cornhusker Hwy., Suite 125
Lincoln, NE 68507-3160
Tel: (402)477-2323 *Fax:* (402)477-4325
E-Mail: info@ocia.org
Web Site: www.ocia.org
Members: 50000 growers/processors/mfgs.
Staff: 30
Annual Budget: $1-2,000,000
Executive Director: Jeff See
Manager, Marketing and Communications: Patricia Saldana

Historical Note
OCIA members are farmers, processors, manufacturers and traders of organic crops from different parts of the world. The association aims to expand organic cultivation by ensuring organic production is economically and environmentally viable.
Membership: $250/year (member); $15/year (chapter member).

Publications:
The Communicator. q. adv.
Organic Crop Improvement Newsletter. bi-m. adv.

Organic Reactions Catalysis Society *(1966)*
c/o Johnson-Matthey
25 Patton Road
Devens, MA 01434
Tel: (978)784-5403 *Fax:* (978)784-5200
E-Mail: treasurer@orcs.org
Web Site: www.orcs.org
Members: 250 individuals
Annual Budget: $50-100,000
Secretary-Treasurer: Helene Shea

Historical Note
Members are chemists and researchers interested in reagents that increase or provoke chemical reactions. Has no paid officers or full-time staff.

Meetings/Conferences:
Biennial Conference: Spring
2008 – Richmond, VA(Jefferson Hotel)/March 30-Apr. 3

Publications:
Catalysis in Organic Reactions. bien. adv.

Organic Trade Association *(1984)*
P.O. Box 547
Greenfield, MA 01302
Tel: (413)774-7511
Web Site: www.ota.com
Members: 1500 businesses
Staff: 15
Annual Budget: $1-2,000,000
Executive Director: Katherine Dimatteo
E-Mail: info@ota.com
Director, Operations: David Gagnon
E-Mail: dgagnon@ota.com
Director, Communications: Holly Givens
E-Mail: hgivens@ota.com
Director, Membership and Special Events: Laura Stravino
E-Mail: lstravino@ota.com

Historical Note
Formerly (1994) Organic Foods Production Association of America. Members are businesses involved in the organic products industry. The association seeks to promote the industry and establish production and marketing standards. Absorbed (1991) Organic Food Alliance. Membership: $100/year (minimum).

Meetings/Conferences:
Annual Meetings: Spring

Publications:
The Organic Report. q. adv.
Organic Export Directory. a.
News Flash. bi-w.

Organization Development Institute *(1968)*
11234 Walnut Ridge Road
Chesterland, OH 44026-1299
Tel: (440)729-7419 *Fax:* (440)729-9319
E-Mail: don@odinstitute.org
Web Site: www.odinstitute.org
Members: 455 individuals
Staff: 1
Annual Budget: $25-50,000
President: Dr. Donald W. Cole, RODC

Historical Note
The OD Institute is an International, educational association organized to disseminate information about organization development and training in conflict resolution technologies for effective management. Seeks to build the field of organization development into a respected profession and establish a worldwide network of organization development professionals and networks. Awards the RODC (Registered Organization Development Consultant) to professional consultant members who demonstrate minimum experience and educational credentials and pass the Institute's written exam; and accredits relevant academic programs. The OD Institute has written an international Organization Development Code of Ethics for the field. Membership: $110/year (regular); $150/year (professional/consultant); $80/year (full time student or otherwise not working full-time).

Meetings/Conferences:
Semi-annual Meetings: Spring in the U.S. and Summer or Fall abroad.

Publications:
Internat'l Registry of Organizational Development Institute. a.
The Organization Development Journal. q. adv.
Organizations and Change. m. adv.

Organization Development Network *(1964)*
71 Valley St., Suite 302
South Orange, NJ 07079-2825
Tel: (973)763-7337 *Fax:* (973)763-7488
E-Mail: odnetwork@odnetwork.org

Web Site: www.odnetwork.org
Members: 4000 individuals
Staff: 6
Annual Budget: $500-1,000,000
Executive Director: Maggie Hoyer

Historical Note
Members are scholars, practitioners and others with an interest in human, organizational, and systems development. Membership: $110/year (individual).

Publications:
ODN Network Briefs (e-mail to members only). m.
Membership Roster (members only). a.
OD Practitioner. q.

Organization for International Investment *(1991)*
1225 19th St. NW
Suite 501
Washington, DC 20036
Tel: (202)659-1903 *Fax:* (202)659-2293
Web Site: www.ofii.org
Members: 136 companies
Staff: 6
Annual Budget: $1-2,000,000
Executive Director: Todd M. Malan
E-Mail: tmalan@ofii.org
Director, Program: Monica L. Coates
Manager, Government Affairs: Alex Kaplan
Senior Vice President: Nancy McLennon
Manager, Business Development: Philip L. Rice

Historical Note
The Organization for International Investment (OFII) is a Washington, DC-based association representing the US subsidiaries of overseas parent companies. OFII's member companies range from medium-sized enterprises to some of the largest firms in the United States. OFII's members employ hundreds of thousands of workers in thousands of plants and locations throughout America. OFII is dedicated to ensuring that US subsidiaries receive nondiscriminatory treatment under US federal and state law.

Meetings/Conferences:
Annual Meetings: November

Organization for the Promotion and Advancement of Small Telecommunications Companies *(1963)*
21 Dupont Circle NW
Suite 700
Washington, DC 20036-1109
Tel: (202)659-5990 *Fax:* (202)659-4619
Web Site: www.opastco.org
Members: 560 companies, 175 associate members
Staff: 22
Annual Budget: $1-2,000,000
President: John N. Rose
Director, Membership: Lora Magruder
E-Mail: lam@opastco.org
Director, Education and Events: Kathleen Kelley Riesett
E-Mail: kkr@opastco.org
Director, Public Relations: Martha Silver
Director, Finance: Michael Viands

Historical Note
Formerly (1996) the Organization for the Protection and Advancement of Small Telephone Companies. OPASTCO protects the interests of small, rural, independent commercial telephone companies and cooperatives that have less than 50,000 access lines. Has an annual budget of $1.9 million.

Publications:
OPASTCO 411 newsletter. bi-w.
OPASTCO Roundtable. 6/yr. adv.
Convention Wrap-up. semi-a. adv.
Membership Directory (online). adv.

Organization for Tropical Studies *(1963)*
P.O. Box 90630
Durham, NC 27708-0630
Tel: (919)684-5774 *Fax:* (919)684-5661
E-Mail: ots@duke.edu
Web Site: www.ots.duke.edu
Members: 64 institutions
Staff: 30
Annual Budget: $5-10,000,000
Interim Chief Executive Officer: Don Stone
E-Mail: ghartsho@duke.edu

Historical Note
Universities and research institutions with graduate and undergraduate programs in tropical ecology studies. Maintains an office and three research stations in Costa Rica. Membership: $35/year (individual); $8,800/year (organization).

Publications:
OTS Newsletter. q.
LIANA. 2/year.

Organization of American Historians *(1907)*
112 N. Bryan Ave.
P.O. Box 5457
Bloomington, IN 47408-5457
Tel: (812)855-7311 *Fax:* (812)855-0696
E-Mail: oah@oah.org
Web Site: www.oah.org
Members: 9200 individuals
Staff: 18
Annual Budget: $2-5,000,000
Executive Director: Lee W. Formwalt
E-Mail: lee@oah.org
Deputy Director: John Dichtl
E-Mail: john@oah.org

Historical Note
Formerly (1964) Mississippi Valley Historical Association. Members are specialists in United States history who are concerned with the promotion of historical study and research in American history. Membership Fee: $40-130/year (individual historian; varies by income); $110-275/year (institution; varies by size).

Meetings/Conferences:
2007 – Minneapolis, MN(Hilton)/March 29-Apr. 1
2008 – New York, NY(Hilton)/March 28-31

Publications:
Journal of American History. q. adv.
OAH Magazine of History. bi-m. adv.
OAH Annual Program. a. adv.
OAH Newsletter. q. adv.

Organization of American Kodaly Educators *(1976)*
1612 29th Ave. South
Moorhead, MN 56560
Tel: (218)227-6253 *Fax:* (218)227-6254
E-Mail: oakeoffice@oake.org
Web Site: www.oake.org
Members: 1700 individuals
Staff: 1
Annual Budget: $250-500,000
Administrative Director: Joan Dahlin
E-Mail: oakeoffice@oake.org

Historical Note
Members are music teachers and others interested in the Kodaly approach to music education. Membership: $75/year.

Meetings/Conferences:
Annual Meetings: early Spring and Fall
2007 – Chicago, IL(The Palmer House Hilton)/March 20-25/1200

Publications:
Kodaly Envoy. q. adv.

Organization of Black Airline Pilots *(1976)*
8630 Fenton St., Suite 126
Silver Spring, MD 20910
Toll Free: (800)538 - 6227
E-Mail: president@obap.org
Web Site: www.obap.org
Members: 1000 individuals
Staff: 3
Annual Budget: $250-500,000
President and Chief Executive Officer: Karl Minter

Historical Note
Seeks to enhance the participation of minorities in the aerospace industry. Provides a communication network and job search assistance. Regular membership is open to cockpit crewmembers of commercial air carriers including corporate pilots. Sponsors a summer flight academy for youth at Tuskegee, Alabama. Membership: $100/year (individual); $1,000/year (organization).

Meetings/Conferences:
Semi-annual Meetings: Spring and August

Publications:
OBAP Newsletter. q. adv.

Organization of Black Designers *(1994)*
300 M St. SW
Suite N-110
Washington, DC 20024
Tel: (202)659-3918 *Fax:* (202)488-3838
E-Mail: OBDesign@aol.com
Web Site: www.obd.org
Members: 6700 individuals
Staff: 6
Annual Budget: $250-500,000
Executive Director: Shauna D. Stallworth
Director, Communications: Bill Browne
Director, Membership Development: Kathy Johnson

Historical Note
OBD members are African-Americans working as fashion, graphic, product, interior or industrial designers. Membership: $175/year (professional); $150/year (affiliate); $75/year (student); $500/year (corporate).

Meetings/Conferences:
Annual Meetings: Annual

Publications:
DesigNation Journal. a. adv.
Newsletter. bi-a. adv.

Organization of Flying Adjusters *(1958)*
1501 Bluff Dr.
Round Rock, TX 78681
Tel: (512)255-2740 *Fax:* (512)246-1066
E-Mail: dh2729@sbcglobal.net
Web Site: www.ofainc.com
Members: 50 companies
Staff: 1
Annual Budget: $10-25,000
Executive Secretary: Donald Hendricks
E-Mail: dh2729@sbcglobal.net

Historical Note
Members are insurance adjusters who process aviation insurance claims and investigate causes of aircraft accidents. Membership: $175/year (regular).

Meetings/Conferences:
Annual Meetings: October

Publications:
OFA Newsletter. q.
Membership Directory. a.

Organization of News Ombudsmen *(1980)*
San Diego Union-Tribune
P.O. Box 120191
San Diego, CA 92112-0191
Tel: (619)293-1525
E-Mail: ono@uniontrib.com
Web Site: www.newsombudsmen.org
Members: 100 individuals
Annual Budget: $10-25,000
Executive Secretary: Gina Lubrano
E-Mail: ono@uniontrib.com

Historical Note
Formerly (1983) Organization of Newspaper Ombudsmen. ONO members are ombudsmen from both the print and broadcast news media. Has no paid officers or full-time staff. Membership: $75/year (individual).

Meetings/Conferences:
Annual Meetings: Spring

Publications:
ONO Newsletter. m.

Organization of Professional Employees of the U.S. Department of Agriculture *(1929)*
P.O. Box 381
Washington, DC 20044
Tel: (202)720-4898 *Fax:* (202)720-6692
E-Mail: opeda@usda.gov
Web Site: www.usda.gov/opeda
Members: 4000 individuals
Staff: 3
Annual Budget: $100-250,000
Executive Director: Otis N. Thompson
E-Mail: otis.thompson@usda.gov

Historical Note
OPEDA works for the economic and professional interests of its members. Membership: $52/year (active employees); $25/year (retired).

Meetings/Conferences:
Annual Meetings: May

Publications:
OPEDA News. m.

Organization of State Broadcasting Executives *(1986)*
P.O. Box 50008
Columbia, SC 29250
Tel: (803)799-5517 *Fax:* (803)771-4831
Web Site: www.osbe.org
Members: 30 agencies and organizations
Staff: 1
Contact: Skip Hinton

Historical Note
OSBE members are chief executive officers of state public broadcasting networks and directors of state agencies responsible for statewide public broadcasting.

Organization of Teachers of Oral Diagnosis *(1963)*
Univ. of Michigan, School of Dentistry
Dept. of Oral Medicine/Pathology, Room 2029
Ann Arbor, MI 48109
Tel: (734)615-6948
Web Site: www.otod.org
Members: 1100 individuals
Annual Budget: under $10,000
President: Carol Anne Murdoch-Kinch, Ph.D.
E-Mail: camurdoc@umich.edu

Historical Note
Conceived at a workshop for oral diagnosis teachers in 1963 at Iowa State University. Has no paid officers or full-time staff. Membership: $90/year.

Meetings/Conferences:
Annual Meetings: March, with American Ass'n of Dental Schools

Publications:
OTOD Newsletter. q.

Organization of Wildlife Planners *(1978)*
1919 Creekwood Dr.
Ft. Collins, CO 80525-1328
Tel: (970)221-2823
Web Site: www.owpweb.org
Members: 100 individuals
Annual Budget: $10-25,000
Newsletter Editor: Cheryl Kolus
E-Mail: ckolus@juno.com

Historical Note
Provides resources to improve management of fish and wildlife resources. Has no paid officers or full-time staff. Membership: $25/year (individual), $50/year (company).

Meetings/Conferences:
Annual Meetings: May-June

Publications:
Tomorrow's Management. semi-a.
OWP Annual Proceedings. a.
President's Report. q.

Organization of Women in International Trade *(1989)*
c/o Reed Smith, LLP
1301 K St. NW, East Tower, Suite 1100
Washington, DC 20005
Web Site: www.owit.org
Members: 200 individuals
Annual Budget: $10-25,000
Counsel and Secretary: Marian Ladner

Historical Note
Founded as Organization of Women in International Trade, WIIT is a federation of nineteen organizations of women in international trade whose purpose is to enhance the role of women in the profession. Has no paid officers or full-time staff. Membership: $250/year (organization).

Meetings/Conferences:
Annual Meetings: Spring and Fall

Publications:
Directory Report. a. adv.

Organizational Behavior Teaching Society *(1973)*
Mount Saint Mary's College
330 Powell Ave.
Newburgh, NY 12550
Web Site: www.obts.org
Members: 450 individuals
Annual Budget: $100-250,000
Treasurer: Cynthia L. Krom

Historical Note
Members are academics, consultants and other teaching professionals with an interest in management education training. Membership: $55/year.

Meetings/Conferences:
Annual Meetings: May-June
2007 – Malibu, CA(Pepperdine University)/June 1-

Publications:
Journal of Management Education. 6/year.
OTBS Exchange newsletter. bi-a.

Organizational Systems Research Association *(1981)*
Morehead State University
150 University Blvd., Box 2478
Morehead, KY 40351-1689
Tel: (606)783-2718 *Fax:* (606)783-5025
Web Site: www.osra.org
Members: 150 individuals
Staff: 1
Annual Budget: $10-25,000
Executive Director: Donna R. Everett

Historical Note
Organized as Office Systems Research Association in 1980 and officially chartered in the State of Ohio in June 1981. Assumed its current name in 2000. Members are individuals from business, government or education interested in a professional approach to the planning of office systems. Absorbed (1995) Office Automation Society International. Membership: $55/year (individual); $300/year (corporate).

Meetings/Conferences:
Annual Meetings: Winter

Publications:
Newsletter. q. adv.
Information Technology, Learning, and Performance Journal. semi-a. adv.

Oriental Rug Importers Association of America *(1958)*
100 Park Plaza Dr.
Secaucus, NJ 07094-3606
Tel: (201)866-5054 *Fax:* (201)866-6169
E-Mail: oria@oria.org
Web Site: www.oria.org
Members: 90 companies
Staff: 1
Annual Budget: $10-25,000
Executive Director: Lucille J. Laufer

Historical Note
Membership is concentrated in the New York area.

Meetings/Conferences:
Quarterly Meetings: New York, NY

Publications:
Oriental Rug Magazine. q. adv.

Oriental Rug Retailers of America *(1969)*
P.O. Box 71831
Richmond, VA 23255
Tel: (804)270-3195 *Fax:* (804)270-3196
E-Mail: orra@orrainc.com
Web Site: www.orrainc.com
Members: 338 individuals
Staff: 4
Annual Budget: $250-500,000
Executive Director: Elizabeth Arnold

Historical Note
Members represents over 500 store locations. Membership: $250/year.

Meetings/Conferences:
Annual Meetings:

Publications:
Membership Directory.
Newletter. q. adv.

Original Equipment Suppliers Association
2950 W. Square Lake Road, Suite 101
Troy, MI 48098-5724
Tel: (248)952-6401 *Fax:* (248)952-6404
E-Mail: info@oesa.org
Web Site: www.oesa.org
Members: 355 companies
Staff: 8
Annual Budget: $2-5,000,000
President: Neil DeKoker
E-Mail: ndekoker@oesa.org
Vice President, Business Development: Dave Andrea
Vice President, Policy: Margaret Baxter
E-Mail: mbaxter@oesa.org
Vice President, Marketing: Noelle Schiffer
E-Mail: nschiffer@oesa.org

Historical Note
An affiliate of Motor and Equipment Manufacturers Association. OESA represents manufacturers who specialize in original equipment parts and accessories for motor vehicles.

Publications:
Automotive OE Industry Review. a. adv.

Ornamental Concrete Producers Association *(1991)*
502 Kay Ave. SE
Bemidji, MN 56601
Tel: (218)751-1982 *Fax:* (218)751-2186
Web Site: www.ornamentalconcrete.org
Members: 500 individuals
Staff: 1
Annual Budget: $250-500,000
Executive Director: Del R. Preuss
E-Mail: delpreus@paulbunyan.net

Historical Note
Primarily concerned with education. Membership: $50/year.

Meetings/Conferences:
Semi-Annual: October/January

Publications:
Ornamental Observer. bi-m. adv.

Orthodox Theological Society in America *(1968)*
50 Goddard Ave.
Brookline, MA 02445
Members: 135 individuals
Annual Budget: under $10,000
Treasurer: Demetrios Katos

Historical Note
Members are Orthodox Christian theologians. Has no paid staff. Membership: $10/year.

Meetings/Conferences:
Annual Meetings: Spring, usually alternates between Hellenic College/Holy Cross Greek Orthodox Seminary in Brookline, MA and St.Vladimir's Orthodox Seminary in Crestwood, NY.

Publications:
Bulletin. semi-a.
Directory. a.

Orthopaedic Research Society *(1954)*
6300 N. River Road, Suite 727
Rosemont, IL 60018-4226
Tel: (847)384-4242 *Fax:* (847)823-4921
E-Mail: ors@aaos.org
Web Site: www.ors.org
Members: 1800 individuals
Staff: 3
Annual Budget: $250-500,000
Executive Director: Brenda Welborn

Historical Note
Founded in 1954, ORS is an international society of orthopaedic researchers. ORS's purpose is to improve the care of patients with musculoskeletal diseases and injuries. Membership: $220/year.

Meetings/Conferences:
Annual Meetings: Winter

Publications:
Journal of Orthopaedic Research. q. adv.

Orthopaedic Section - American Physical Therapy Association *(1974)*
2920 East Ave., South, Suite 200
La Crosse, WI 54601-7202
Tel: (608)788-3982 *Fax:* (608)788-3965
E-Mail: tdeflorian@orthopt.org

Web Site: http://orthopt.org
Members: 15000 individuals
Staff: 5
Annual Budget: $1-2,000,000
Executive Director: Terri A. DeFlorian
E-Mail: tdeflorian@orthopt.org

Historical Note
Members are orthopaedic physical therapists. Membership: $50/year.

Publications:
Journal of Orthopaedic and Sports Physical Therapy. m.
Orthopaedic Physical Therapy Practice. q.

Orthopaedic Trauma Association
6300 N. River Road, Suite 727
Rosemont, IL 60018-4226
Tel: (847)698-1631 *Fax:* (847)823-0536
Web Site: www.ota.org
Members: 380 individuals
Staff: 3
Executive Director: Nancy Franzon

Meetings/Conferences:
2007 - Boston, MA(Sheraton)/Oct. 18-20

Orthopedic Surgical Manufacturers Association *(1955)*
325 Paramount Dr.
Raynham, MA 02767
Tel: (508)828-3769 *Fax:* (508)828-3727
Web Site: www.osma.cc
Members: 21 companies
Staff: 1
Annual Budget: $50-100,000
President: Bill Christianson

Historical Note
OSMA member companies are manufacturers and distributors of orthopedic devices, instrumentation and biological materials used to treat orthopedic conditions. Meetings are attended primarily by regulatory affairs professionals to interface with government agencies and professional health associations, develop guidelines and standardize orthopedic device materials and sizes, foster research, and promote ethical conduct in all phases of the surgical supply industry. Membership: $800-$5,000/year, varies by size (corporate).

Meetings/Conferences:
Quarterly Meetings:

Osborne Association *(1932)*
36-31 38th St.
Long Island City, NY 11101
Tel: (718)707-2600 *Fax:* (718)707-3103
E-Mail: info@osborneny.org
Web Site: www.osborneny.org
Staff: 160
Annual Budget: $5-10,000,000
Executive Director: Elizabeth Gaynes
E-Mail: egaynes@osborneny.org

Historical Note
Formed by merger of the National Society of Penal Information and the Welfare League Association of New York. Named after Thomas Mott Osborne (1859-1926), pioneer prison reformer and founder of the Welfare League Association to assist persons discharged from prison. The Association relies on government funding and private donors for a variety of programs, including El Rio, an intensive all-day treatment program for substance abusers involved with the criminal justice system; LIVING-Well, HIV/AIDS services; social work advocacy programs through which staff work with defendants' attorneys to develop non-prison alternatives; job placement; and FamilyWorks, a model parenting program for incarcerated fathers. Has an annual budget of approximately $7 million.

Meetings/Conferences:
Annual Meetings: July

Publications:
Newsletter. q.

Osteoarthritis Research Society International
15000 Commerce Pkwy., Suite C
Mt. Laurel, NJ 08054
Tel: (856)439-1385 *Fax:* (856)439-0525
E-Mail: oarsi@oarsi.org
Web Site: www.oarsi.org
Members: 630
Staff: 6
Executive Director: Victoria E. Elliott, RPh, MBA, CAE

Meetings/Conferences:
Annual Meetings: Fall

Outdoor Advertising Association of America *(1891)*
1850 M St. NW, Suite 1040
Washington, DC 20036-5803
Tel: (202)833-5566 *Fax:* (202)833-1522
Web Site: www.oaaa.org
Members: 1100 companies
Staff: 12
Annual Budget: $2-5,000,000
President and Chief Executive Officer: Nancy J. Fletcher
E-Mail: nfletcher@oaaa.org
Chief Marketing Officer: Stephen Freitas
E-Mail: sfreitas@oaaa.org
Executive Vice President, Government Relations: Ken Klein
E-Mail: kklein@oaaa.org
Vice President, State, Local, Regulatory Affairs: Myron Laible
Vice President, Membership and Administration: Marci Werlinich
E-Mail: mwerlinich@oaaa.org

Historical Note
OAAA works to protect and promote outdoor advertising. Recommends standards for outdoor display structures and disseminates information on the industry. Sponsors and supports the Outdoor Advertising Political Action Committee (OA-PAC).

Meetings/Conferences:
Biennial meetings: odd years

Publications:
Outdoor Outlook. w.

Outdoor Amusement Business Association *(1965)*
1035 S. Semoran Blvd., Suite 1045A
Winter Park, FL 32792
Tel: (407)681-9444 *Fax:* (407)681-9445
Toll Free: (800)517 - 6222
E-Mail: oaba@aol.com
Web Site: www.oaba.org
Members: 5000 companies
Staff: 5
Annual Budget: $500-1,000,000
President: Robert W. Johnson
E-Mail: oaba@aol.com

Historical Note
Formed in 1965, the OABA has since represented circuses, carnivals and concessionaires in the mobile amusement industry. Membership consists of road shows, food and beverage and games suppliers, carnivals and equipment suppliers.

Meetings/Conferences:
Semi-Annual Meetings: Tampa, FL/February and Las Vegas, NV/November

Publications:
Showtime. m. adv.
Midway Marquee. a. adv.

Outdoor Power Equipment Aftermarket Association *(1986)*
1726 M St. NW
Suite 1101
Washington, DC 20036
Tel: (202)775-8605 *Fax:* (202)833-1577
E-Mail: opeaa@opeaa.org
Web Site: www.opeaa.org
Members: 75 companies
Staff: 3
Annual Budget: $250-500,000
Executive Vice President: William S. Bergman, CAE
E-Mail: wsb@opeaa.org
Director, Administration: Susan Dove
Director, Membership Services: Joy Ross

Historical Note
OPEAA is a group whose membership is composed of small to medium-sized businessmen dedicated to promoting the use of aftermarket (spare) parts in outdoor power equipment (lawnmowers, chain saws, etc.), as well as ensuring an atmosphere of free and unrestrained trade in the industry. Membership: $400-$4,200/year (based on sales volume).

Meetings/Conferences:
Annual Meetings: February
2007 - Charleston, SC/Feb. 22-25

Publications:
The Business Owner. bi-m.
Cutting Edge. q. adv.

Outdoor Power Equipment and Engine Service Association *(1980)*
37 Pratt St.
Essex, CT 06426
Tel: (860)767-1770 *Fax:* (860)767-7932
E-Mail: info@opeesa.com
Web Site: www.opeesa.com
Members: 200 companies
Staff: 3
Annual Budget: $100-250,000
Executive Director: Nancy Cueroni

Historical Note
Formerly (2002) Outdoor Power Equipment Distributors Association. Absorbed Engine Service Association in 2002. OPEESA members are distributors of outdoor power equipment to retailers with a minimum of $1 million gross sales. Associate membership is available for suppliers and finance companies associated with the industry.

Meetings/Conferences:
Annual Meetings: February

Publications:
Membership Directory. a.

Outdoor Power Equipment Institute *(1952)*
341 S. Patrick St.
Alexandria, VA 22314
Tel: (703)549-7600 *Fax:* (703)549-7604
E-Mail: mroach@opei.org
Web Site: http://opei.mow.org
Members: 81 companies
Staff: 9
Annual Budget: $2-5,000,000
President and Chief Executive Officer: William G. Harley
Vice President, Finance and Administration: Jean Hawes

Historical Note
Established as the Lawn Mower Institute, OPEI assumed its present name in 1960. Members are manufacturers of all types of mechanized lawn and garden equipment and industry suppliers of major components.

Meetings/Conferences:
Annual Meetings: Summer

Publications:
Association Newsletter.
HR Newsline. m.

Outdoor Writers Association of America *(1927)*
121 Hickory St., Suite One
Missoula, MT 59801
Tel: (406)728-7434 *Fax:* (406)728-7445
Toll Free: (800)692 - 2477
E-Mail: owaa@montana.com
Web Site: www.owaa.org
Members: 1400 individuals
Staff: 4
Annual Budget: $250-500,000
Executive Director: Kevin Rhoades
Coordinator, Conference and Contests: Eileen N. King

Historical Note
OWAA was formed at a meeting April 9, 1927 in Chicago by a group of writers attending an Izaak Walton League of America convention. Members are broadcasters, writers and editors, authors, photographers and artists who communicate about outdoor recreation and related topics. Sponsors the North American Outdoor Film/Video Awards annually. Membership: $100/year (individual); $300/year (organization).

Meetings/Conferences:
Annual Meetings: June

Publications:
Outdoors Unlimited. m.

Outpatient Ophthalmic Surgery Society *(1981)*
16731 E. Iliff Ave.
Box 189
Aurora, CO 37602

Tel: (303)362-0187
E-Mail: info@ooss.org
Web Site: www.ooss.org
Members: 1000 individuals
Staff: 1
Executive Director: Claudia A. McDougal

Historical Note
OOSS members are ophthalmic surgeons.

Publications:
Washington Update (online). adv.
Outlook Magazine (online). m. adv.

Overseas Automotive Council *(1923)*
P.O. Box 13966
Research Triangle Park, NC 27709-3966
Tel: (919)406-8810 Fax: (919)549-4824
E-Mail: oac@mema.org
Web Site: www.oac-intl.org
Members: 700 individuals
Staff: 2
Annual Budget: $100-250,000
Executive Secretary: Anthony Cardez

Historical Note
Formerly the Overseas Automotive Club (1996). An international organization whose membership includes both domestic and international companies. Members export U.S. automotive parts, chemicals, tools, accessories and other automotive products. International members are importers of these products into their countries. Membership: $300/year (domestic); $150/year (international).

Publications:
OAC Update Newsletter. m.
Personal Insight. m.
OAC Roster. a.

Overseas Press Club of America *(1939)*
40 W. 45th St.
New York, NY 10036-4202
Tel: (212)626-9220 Fax: (212)626-9210
Web Site: www.opcofamerica.org
Members: 600 individuals
Staff: 2
Executive Director: Sonya K. Fry

Historical Note
Members are professional journalists. Membership: $375/year (resident members); $175/year (non-resident members).

Meetings/Conferences:
Annual Meetings: *Awards Dinner in April (New York, NY)*

Publications:
Dateline. a. adv.
Overseas Press Club Bulletin. m.

Owner Operators of America *(1982)*
3 Brompton Woods
Buffalo, NY 14221-5932
Members: 250 individuals
Staff: 1
Annual Budget: $50-100,000
Executive Secretary: Chuck DeVaul

Historical Note
Provides business and legislative information to self-employed truckers; represents self-employed truckers on Capitol Hill; and provides discounts on services and supplies for self-employed members.

Meetings/Conferences:
Annual Meetings: *Not held.*

Publications:
Owner Operators News. q.

Owner-Operator Independent Drivers Association *(1973)*
One N.W. OOIDA Dr.
Grain Valley, MO 64029
Tel: (816)229-5791 Fax: (816)229-0518
Toll Free: (800)444 - 5791
E-Mail: ooida@ooida.com
Web Site: www.ooida.com
Members: 114000 individuals
Staff: 270
Annual Budget: $2-5,000,000
President: James J. Johnston
Treasurer: Rick Craig
Executive Vice President: Todd Spencer

Historical Note
OOIDA is a national association lobbying on behalf of the interests of small business truckers. Membership: $45/year (driver); $45 plus $10/truck/year (owner/operator).

Meetings/Conferences:
Annual Meetings: *Open Board of Directors Meeting*

Publications:
Land*Line Magazine. 9/year. adv.

Packaging Machinery Manufacturers Institute *(1933)*
4350 N. Fairfax Dr., Suite 600
Arlington, VA 22203
Tel: (703)243-8555 Fax: (703)243-8556
Toll Free: (888)275 - 7664
E-Mail: pmmi@pmmi.org
Web Site: www.pmmi.org
Members: 500+ companies
Staff: 30
Annual Budget: $2-5,000,000
President and Chief Executive Officer: Charles D. Yuska
Director, Web Services: Jacquelyn Bradshaw
Director, Member Services: Matt Croson
Vice President, Meetings and Facilities Management: Patricia Fee
Director, Workforce Development: Maria Ferrante
Director, Expositions: Jim Pittas
Vice President, Finance: Craig Silverio
General Counsel: Hugh Webster

Historical Note
PMMI members are manufacturers of packaging and packaging-related converting equipment. Owns and manages PACK EXPO International and PACK EXPO Las Vegas; these are expositions of packaging machinery and materials. Membership: $1,000/year (company).

Meetings/Conferences:
Semi-Annual Meetings: *Spring and Fall*

Publications:
Packaging Machinery Technology. 6/year. adv.
PMMI Reports Newsletter. m.
Packaging Machinery Directory. bi-a.

Paint and Decorating Retailers Association *(1947)*
403 Axminister Dr.
Fenton, MO 63026-2941
Tel: (636)326-2636 Fax: (636)326-1823
E-Mail: info@pdra.org
Web Site: www.pdra.org
Members: 3500 individuals
Staff: 11
Annual Budget: $2-5,000,000
Managing Editor: Michael Austin

Historical Note
Formerly Retail Paint & Wallpaper Distributors of America, (1972) Paint and Wallpaper Association of America, and (1996) National Decorating Products Association. Members are independent dealers and interior designers selling decorating products. Has an annual budget of approximately $10 million. Membership: $125/year (company).

Publications:
Paint & Decorating Retailer's Registry Directory. a. adv.
Paint & Decorating Retailer Gold Book Directory. a. adv.
Paint & Decorating Retailer Magazine. m. adv.
The Faux Finisher Magazine. q. adv.

Painting and Decorating Contractors of America *(1884)*
11960 Westline Industrial Dr., Suite 201
St. Louis, MO 63146-3209
Tel: (314)514-7322 Fax: (314)514-9417
Toll Free: (800)332 - 7322
E-Mail: ihoren@pdca.org
Web Site: www.pdca.org
Members: 10,000 individuals; 3,000 firms
Staff: 13
Annual Budget: $2-5,000,000
Chief Executive Officer: Ian Horen, Ph.D.
E-Mail: ihoren@pdca.org

Historical Note
PDCA is the trade association of the coatings applications industry. Members are professional painting and decorating contractors. Membership: $235-500/year, varies by sales volume; plus council and chapter dues.

Publications:
Membership Directory. a. adv.
Painting and Wallcovering Contractor Magazine. bi-m. adv.
PDCA Briefer Newsletter. m.

Paleontological Research Institution *(1932)*
1259 Trumansburg Road
Ithaca, NY 14850
Tel: (607)273-6623 Fax: (607)273-6620
Web Site: www.priweb.org
Members: 1100 individuals
Staff: 9
Annual Budget: $250-500,000
Director: Dr. Warren D. Allmon

Historical Note
Founded in Ithaca in 1932 and incorporated in New York in 1933. Affiliated with the American Association for the Advancement of Science and the Association of Systematics Collections.

Meetings/Conferences:
Annual Meetings: *Ithaca, NY/May*

Publications:
Bulletins of American Paleontology. 2-5/year.
Paleontographica Americana. irreg.

Paleontological Society *(1908)*
Allen Marketing and Management
P.O. Box 1897
Lawrence, KS 66044-1897
Toll Free: (800)627 - 0629 Ext: 297
E-Mail: paleosoc@allenpress.com
Web Site: www.paleosoc.org
Members: 1700 individuals
Staff: 1
Annual Budget: $250-500,000
Association Manager: Derek Gates
E-Mail: paleosoc@allenpress.com

Historical Note
Affiliated with the Geological Society of America. Membership: $59/year.

Meetings/Conferences:
Annual Meetings: *Fall, with the Geological Soc. of America.*

Publications:
Paleobiology. q.
Journal of Paleontology. bi-m.

Palomino Horse Association *(1936)*
Route One, Box 125
Nelson, MO 65347
Tel: (660)859-2064
Web Site: www.palominohorseassoc.com
Members: 500 individuals
Staff: 2
Annual Budget: under $10,000
Contact: Patricia Rebuck

Historical Note
PHA is the original registry for the Palomino horse. Members are owners and breeders of Palomino horses. Membership: $25/year (individual).

Publications:
Palomino Parade. q. adv.

Palomino Horse Breeders of America *(1941)*
15243 E. Skelly Dr.
Tulsa, OK 74116-2637
Tel: (918)438-1234 Fax: (918)438-1232
E-Mail: yellahrses@palominohba.com
Web Site: www.palominohba.com
Members: 12011 individuals
Staff: 6
General Manager: Cindy Chilton
E-Mail: yellahrses@palominohba.com

Historical Note
Members are owners and breeders of Palomino horses. Maintains a registry as well as show records. Membership: $40/year.

Meetings/Conferences:
Semi-annual Meetings: *June - varying locations, July - Tulsa, OK.*
2007 - Lexington, KY/March 15-17/250
2008 - Jacksonville, FL/March 12-15/250

Publications:
Palomino Horses. m. adv.

Panelized Building Systems Council *(1942)*
Historical Note
A division of the Building Systems Councils of the National Association of Home Builders.

Paper and Plastic Representatives Management Council *(1995)*
P.O. Box 150229
Arlington, TX 76015
Tel: (682)518-6008 *Fax:* (682)518-6476
E-Mail: assnhqtrs@aol.com
Web Site: www.pprmc.com
Members: 20 companies
Staff: 2
Annual Budget: $25-50,000
Executive Director: Pamela L. Bess
Historical Note
Membership: $1,800/year.

Paper Distribution Council *(1958)*
c/o NPTA Alliance
500 Bi-County Blvd., Suite 200E
Farmingdale, NY 11735-3931
Tel: (631)777-2223 *Fax:* (631)777-2224
Toll Free: (800)355 - 6782
Web Site: www.gonpta.com
Members: 40 companies
Staff: 1
Annual Budget: under $10,000
Secretary: William H. Frohlich
Historical Note
Members are manufacturers and distributors concerned with the problems of wholesale paper distribution. Affiliated with the American Paper Institute and the NPTA Alliance, (same address) which provides administrative support.
Meetings/Conferences:
Annual Meetings: 50-75

Paper Industry Management Association *(1919)*
4700 W. Lake Ave.
Glenview, IL 60025-1485
Tel: (847)375-6860 *Fax:* (877)527-5973
E-Mail: info@pimaweb.org
Web Site: www.pimaweb.org
Members: 1500 individuals
Staff: 10
Annual Budget: $500-1,000,000
Executive Vice President and Chief Operating Officer: James M. Weir
Historical Note
Founded as the American Pulp and Paper Mill Superintendents Association; assumed its present name in 1959. PIMA provides networking and education opportunities to its members, who are typically managers in paper mills.
Meetings/Conferences:
Annual Meetings: June
Publications:
PIMA Online Buyers Guide. a. adv.
PIMA Post. q.

Paper Machine Clothing Council *(1924)*
c/o Conlon, Frantz
1818 N St. NW, Suite 700
Washington, DC 20036
Tel: (202)331-7050 *Fax:* (202)331-9306
Members: 7 companies
Staff: 2
Annual Budget: $50-100,000
Secretary-Treasurer/General Counsel: David Frantz
Historical Note
Formerly Paper Mill Fourdrinier Wire Cloth Manufacturers Association (1965) and Fourdrinier Wire Council (1996). PMCC member manufacturers produce transfer roller covers and similar fabric products used in commercial paper production.
Meetings/Conferences:
Annual Meetings: None held.
Publications:
None.

Paper Shipping Sack Manufacturers Association *(1933)*
520 E. Oxford St.
Coopersburg, PA 18036-1537
Tel: (610)282-6845 *Fax:* (610)282-6921
E-Mail: pssma@mindspring.com
Web Site: www.pssma.com
Members: 12 companies
Staff: 2
Annual Budget: $250-500,000
President: Richard Storat
Publications:
Industry Reference Guide. irreg.

Paper, Allied-Industrial, Chemical and Energy Workers International Union *(1884)*
Historical Note
Merged with United Steel Workers in 2005 to form a new union, the United Steel, Paper and Forestry, Rubber, Manufacturing, Energy, Allied Industrial and Service Workers International Union, as known by the acronymn USW.

Paperboard Packaging Council *(1964)*
201 N. Union St., Suite 220
Alexandria, VA 22314-2642
Tel: (703)836-3300 *Fax:* (703)836-3290
Web Site: www.ppcnet.org
Members: 55 principal members, 35 associate
Staff: 5
Annual Budget: $1-2,000,000
President: Jerome Van de Water
E-Mail: van@ppcnet.org
Director, Business Services: James P. Brown, Jr.
E-Mail: jbrown@ppcnet.org
Director, Communications and Marketing: Laura Bynum
Director, Industry Information: Melissa Teates
Historical Note
Formed in 1964 by a merger of the Folding Paper Box Association of America (est. 1929) and the Institute for Better Packaging (est. 1929), PPC thus has antecedents dating back to 1929. PPC is the leading trade association serving suppliers and converters of all forms of paperboard packaging, including folding cartons, rigid boxes, paper cylinders and laminated small-flute containers. Mission is to grow, promote and protect the paperboard packaging industry, and to provide tools to help members compete effectively in the marketplace. Provides a range of publications and instructional materials on aspects of the paper industry, recycling, and other pertinent issues. Membership fee varies, based on annual sales.
Meetings/Conferences:
Semi-Annual Meetings: Spring and Fall
Publications:
PPC Today. q. adv.
Trends. a.
Exempt Compensation Report. bien.
Labor Data Survey (Hourly Wage Compensation). a.
Boxscore Safety Program Report. m.
Marketflash. m.
Directory of Members. a.
PPC Live! e-newsletter. m.

Parapsychological Association *(1957)*
2474-342 Walnut St.
Cary, NC 27511
Tel: (202)318-2364
E-Mail: business@parapsych.org
Web Site: www.parapsych.org
Members: 271 individuals
Staff: 1
Annual Budget: $10-25,000
Business Manager: Cheryl Alexander
E-Mail: business@parapsych.org
Historical Note
Membership open to persons doing research or scholarly work of publishable quality in the field, also professionals and students in other academic disciplines with a serious interest in this field. Affiliated with the American Association for the Advancement of Science, PA strives to promote and advance rigorous scientific inquiry into anomalous areas of human communication processes, disseminate such information to the wider scientific community, and integrate this information with findings from other scientific disciplines. Membership: $55/year.

Meetings/Conferences:
Annual Meetings: August
Publications:
PA Newsletter. q.

Parcel Shippers Association *(1953)*
1211 Connecticut Ave. NW
Suite 610
Washington, DC 20036-2701
Tel: (202)296-3690 *Fax:* (202)296-0343
E-Mail: psa@parcelshippers.org
Web Site: www.parcelshippers.org
Members: 200 companies
Staff: 2
Annual Budget: $100-250,000
Executive Vice President: Pierce Myers
Historical Note
Formerly (1977) the Parcel Post Association. Sponsors and supports the Parcel Shippers Association Political Action Committee. Membership: fees based upon annual parcel shipping expense.
Meetings/Conferences:
Annual Meetings: Spring and Biennial Operations Workshop
Publications:
Newsletter. m.

Parenting Publications of America *(1988)*
4929 Wilshire Blvd., Suite 428
Los Angeles, CA 90010
Tel: (323)937-5514 *Fax:* (323)937-0959
Web Site: www.parentingpublications.org
Members: 120 publications
Staff: 2
Annual Budget: $100-250,000
Executive Director: C. James Dowden
Historical Note
PPA members are regional free controlled-circulation periodicals, published monthly or bi-monthly that serve as resource guides for parents and children and provide information on trends and issues relevant to contemporary parenting. Member publications have a combined circulation of over 5 million. Membership: $700/year (initial); varies based on total revenues (renewal).
Meetings/Conferences:
Annual Meetings: late January-early February

Parliamentary Associates *(1990)*
P.O. Box 1102
Independence, MO 64051-0602
Toll Free: (800)572 - 8328
E-Mail: info@parliassoc.com
Web Site: www.parliassoc.com
Members: 40 individuals
Staff: 2
Annual Budget: $10-25,000
Administrative Assistant: Helene Goldsmith
E-Mail: info@parliassoc.com
Historical Note
Members are credentialed professional parliamentarians.

Parthenais Cattle Breeders Association of America *(1995)*
P.O. Box 788
Arp, TX 75750-0788
Toll Free: (800)762 - 0164
E-Mail: parthenais@dctexas.net
Web Site: www.parthenaiscattle.org
Members: 30 breeders
Secretary: Jimmy C. Williams
E-Mail: parthenais@dctexas.net
Historical Note
Maintains a breed registration and distributes information on best practices to breeders who use Parthenais cattle stock in the beef and bloodline production. Has no paid officers or full-time staff.
Publications:
President's Newsletter. q.
Breeders Directory and Membership List. a. adv.

Partnership for Air-Conditioning, Heating Refrigeration Accreditation *(2000)*
4100 N. Fairfax Dr., Suite 200
Arlington, VA 22203

Tel: (703)524-8800 *Fax:* (703)528-3816
E-Mail: pahra@pahrahvacr.org
Web Site: www.pahrahvacr.org
Staff: 1
Annual Budget: $25-50,000
President: Patrick Murphy
Secretary: Ray Mach

Historical Note
PAHRA is an industry consortium promoting educational standards in technical training for HVACR professionals.

Partnership in Print Production *(1977)*
276 Bowery
New York, NY 10012
Tel: (212)334-2106 *Fax:* (212)431-5786
E-Mail: admin@p3-ny.org
Web Site: www.p3-ny.org
Members: 500 individuals
Annual Budget: $100-250,000
Executive Officer: Katerina Caterisano

Historical Note
Founded as Women in Production; absorbed Association of Publication Production Managers and assumed its current name in 2003. Members are individuals involved in all phases of print, graphics and digital production. Membership: $95/year.

Publications:
WIPWatch. m.
WIP Roster. a.

Paso Fino Horse Association *(1972)*
101 N. Collins St.
Plant City, FL 33563-3311
Tel: (813)719-7777 *Fax:* (813)719-7872
E-Mail: execdir@pfha.org
Web Site: www.pfha.org
Members: 8500 individuals
Staff: 12
Annual Budget: $1-2,000,000
Executive Director: C.J. Marcello, Jr.
Director, Marketing: Tarah Malek
E-Mail: dirmkt@pfha.org

Historical Note
Formerly (1986) Paso Fino Owners and Breeders Association. Members are owners and breeders of Paso Fino horses. Incorporated in Tennessee. Membership fee varies.

Meetings/Conferences:
2007 – New Orleans, LA/Jan. 19-21

Publications:
Paso Fino Horse World. m. adv.

Passenger Vessel Association *(1971)*
901 N. Pitt St.
Suite 100
Alexandria, VA 22314
Tel: (703)518-5005 *Fax:* (703)518-5151
Toll Free: (800)807 - 8360
E-Mail: pvainfo@passengervessel.com
Web Site: www.passengervessel.com
Members: 600 companies
Staff: 7
Annual Budget: $500-1,000,000
Executive Director: John Groundwater
Director, Membership: Jennifer Williams

Historical Note
Formerly (1993) the National Association of Passenger Vessel Owners. PVA represents operators of tours, excursions, ferries, charter vessels, dinner boats, and other small passenger vessels.

Meetings/Conferences:
Annual Meetings: January

Publications:
Foghorn Newsletter. m. adv.
Passenger Vessel Directory. a.
PVA Member Update. bi-w.

Passive Solar Products Association *(1979)*

Historical Note
A division of the Industrial Fabrics Association International. Members are makers of screens, awnings, movable insulation, window glazings and thermal storage units.

Patent and Trademark Office Society *(1963)*
P.O. Box 2600
Arlington, VA 22202
Tel: (703)408-2900
Web Site: www.ptos.org
Members: 230 individuals
Annual Budget: under $10,000
Business Manager: Thomas Beach

Historical Note
Labor union of Patent Office Trademark examiners. Affiliated with the National Treasury Employees Union, Chapter 245. All members are attorneys. Has no paid officers or full-time staff.

Meetings/Conferences:
Annual Meetings: Not held.

Publications:
Journal of the PTOS. m. adv.

Patent Office Professional Association *(1962)*
P.O. Box 2745
Arlington, VA 22202
Tel: (703)571-2322
Web Site: www.popa.org
Members: 2800 individuals
Staff: 7
Annual Budget: $100-250,000
President: Ronald J. Stern
E-Mail: Ronald.Stern@uspto.gov

Historical Note
Independent labor union representing all non-managerial professionals (other than trademark professionals) in the U.S. Patent and Trademark Office. Affiliated with Public Employees Roundtable, Federal Employees Coordinating Committee and Fund for Assuming an Independent Retirement Membership: $130/year.

Meetings/Conferences:
Annual Meetings: First Thursday in December near Washington, DC

Publications:
POPA Newsletter. m.

Pattern Recognition Society *(1966)*

Historical Note
Address unknown in 2006.

PCIA - the Wireless Industry Association *(1949)*
500 Montgomery St., Suite 700
Alexandria, VA 22314-1561
Tel: (703)739-0300 *Fax:* (703)836-1608
Toll Free: (800)759 - 0300
E-Mail: foundation@pcia.com
Web Site: www.pcia.com
Members: 3000 companies
Staff: 95
Annual Budget: $5-10,000,000
President and Chief Executive Offier: Michael T.N. Fitch
E-Mail: foundation@pcia.com
Director, Government Relations: Andrea Bruns
Senior Director, Industry and Government Relations: Connie Durcksak
Manager, Industry Affairs: Anne Perkins

Historical Note
Formerly (2003) Personal Communications Industry Association. Absorbed (1994) National Association of Business and Educational Radio. PCIA represents the wireless communications industry, particularly in the areas of regulatory policy, legislation, and technological standards. PCIA members include PCS licensees and those in paging and messaging, ESMR, mobile data, fixed wireless, manufacturing, and others providing goods and servcies to the wireless communications industry.

Publications:
Inside PCIA. q.
Bulletin. w.

PDA - an International Association for Pharmaceutical Science and Technology *(1946)*
Three Bethesda Metro Center, Suite 1500
Bethesda, MD 20814-6133
Tel: (301)656-5900 *Fax:* (301)986-0296
E-Mail: info@pda.org
Web Site: www.pda.org
Members: 9100 individuals
Staff: 25
Annual Budget: $2-5,000,000
President: Richard Myers
Director, Membership and Chapter and Marketing Services: Matthew Clark
Vice President, Finance and Strategic Planning: Lance K. Hoboy
Director, Meetings and Programs: Wanda Neal Ballard
Vice President, Education: Gail Sherman

Historical Note
Formerly (2000) Parenteral Drug Association. Members are makers of parenteral (injectable) drugs and other pharmaceuticals, as well as suppliers, academia, regulatory and compendial bodies, and other interested parties. Membership: $195/year (private sector); $80/year (government employee).

Publications:
PDA Letter. m. adv.
PDA Journal.

Peanut and Tree Nut Processors Association *(1969)*
P.O. Box 59811
Potomac, MD 20859-9811
Tel: (301)365-2521 *Fax:* (301)365-7705
E-Mail: ptnpa@mindspring.com
Web Site: www.ptnpa.org
Members: 156 companies
Staff: 3
Annual Budget: $100-250,000
Executive Vice President: Russell E. Barker
E-Mail: rbarker@ptnpa.org

Historical Note
Formed by a merger of The Peanut Butter Manufacturers Association (1939) and The Peanut and Nut Salters Association (1941). Absorbed the Peanut Butter Sandwich and Cookie Manufacturers Association. Formerly (1978) Peanut Butter Manufacturers and Nut Salters Association, and (1995) Peanut Butter and Nut Processors Association. Sponsors and supports the Peanut Butter and Nut Processors Association Political Action Committee.

Meetings/Conferences:
Annual Meetings: January

Publications:
Newsletter. w.
Membership Directory. a.

Pediatric Orthopedic Society of North America *(1982)*
6300 N. River Road, Suite 727
Rosemont, IL 60018-4226
Tel: (847)698-1692 *Fax:* (847)823-0536
Web Site: www.posna.org
Members: 769 individuals
Staff: 2
Annual Budget: $250-500,000
Executive Director: Sharon C. Goldberg

Historical Note
Formerly (1985) the Society of Pediatric Orthopedics. POSNA members are pediatric orthopedic surgeons who support the highest quality of education to assure the best possible care of children with musculoskeletal disorders. Membership: $300/year (individual).

Meetings/Conferences:
2007 – Hollywood, FL(Diplomat)/May 23-26

Publications:
Abstracts of Annual Meeting.
Newsletter. q.
Membership Directory. a.

Pedorthic Footwear Association *(1958)*
7150 Columbia Gateway Dr.
Columbia, MD 21046-1151
Tel: (410)381-7278 *Fax:* (410)381-1167
Web Site: www.pedorthics.org
Members: 2100 companies and individuals
Staff: 13
Annual Budget: $1-2,000,000
Executive Director: Brian Lagana
Director, Communications: Nancy Hultquist
Director, Education: Cynthia Mullaly
E-Mail: cindi@pedorthics.org

Historical Note
PFA is the membership organization for people engaged in pedorthics: the design, manufacture, modification and fitting of footwear, including foot orthoses, to alleviate problems caused by disease, congenital conditions, overuse or injury. Members include individuals and companies. PFA provides

educational programs, publications, legislative monitoring, marketing materials, professional liaison and business operations services to members. Membership: dues range from $90-750/year, depending on individual or company category.

Meetings/Conferences:
Annual Meetings: Late Fall/400

Publications:
Current Pedorthics. bi-m. adv.

Pellet Fuels Institute *(1982)*
1901N. Moore St., Suite 600
Arlington, VA 22209-2105
Tel: (703)522-6778 *Fax:* (703)522-0548
E-Mail: pfimail@pelletheat.org
Web Site: www.pelletheat.org
Members: 110 companies
Staff: 3
Annual Budget: $100-250,000
Executive Director: Don Kaiser
E-Mail: kaiser@pelletheat.org

Historical Note
Formerly Fiber Fuels Institute. Members are manufacturers of pellet and briquette fuel, suppliers and others with an interest in the industry. Membership: $600-$5,000/year (organization/company).

Meetings/Conferences:
Annual Meetings: Annual; 100

Publications:
PFI Newsletter. q. adv.

Pension Real Estate Association *(1979)*
100 Pearl St., 13th Floor
Hartford, CT 06103
Tel: (860)692-6341
E-Mail: prea@prea.org
Web Site: www.prea.org
Members: 1400 individuals
Staff: 7
Annual Budget: $2-5,000,000
President: Gail C. Haynes
Director, Meetings and Events: Amy Laffarque

Historical Note
Industry trade association whose members share a interest in investment practices for pension funds (public, private and Taft-Hartley) participating in institutional real estate investment. Memberhip open to qualified pension funds, endowments, foundations, asset managers and other supportive firms. Membership: fee varies.

Meetings/Conferences:
Semi-Annual: Conferences

Publications:
Research Review. a.
PREA Quarterly. q.
Membership Directory. a.

Percheron Horse Association of America *(1876)*
10330 Quaker Road
P.O. Box 141
Fredericktown, OH 43019-0141
Tel: (740)694-3602 *Fax:* (740)694-3604
E-Mail: percheron@percheronhorse.org
Web Site: www.percheronhorse.org
Members: 900 individuals
Staff: 3
Annual Budget: $50-100,000
Secretary-Treasurer: Alex T. Christian
E-Mail: percheron@percheronhorse.org

Historical Note
Formerly Percheron Society of America, it assumed its present name in 1934. Members are owners and breeders of Percheron horses. Membership: $20/yr.

Meetings/Conferences:
Annual Meetings: First Saturday in November

Publications:
Percheron News. q. adv.

Percussion Marketing Council *(1995)*
P.O. Box 33252
Cleveland, OH 44133
Tel: (440)582-7006 *Fax:* (440)230-1346
Web Site: www.playdrums.com
Members: 35 individuals
Staff: 1
Executive Director: Karl Dustman

Historical Note
Members are individuals representing firms in or related to the industry.

Meetings/Conferences:
Annual Meetings: Winter

Percussive Arts Society *(1961)*
701 N.W. Ferris Ave.
Lawton, OK 73507-5442
Tel: (580)353-1455 *Fax:* (580)353-1456
E-Mail: percarts@pas.org
Web Site: www.pas.org
Members: 8000 individuals
Staff: 10
Annual Budget: $1-2,000,000
Executive Director: Michael Kenyon
E-Mail: percarts@pas.org

Historical Note
PAS is a music service organization that promotes percussion music education, research, performance and appreciation around the world. Members are teachers and performers on drums and other percussion instruments. Membership: $90/year (professional); $60/year (student/senior citizen); $400-2000 (company); $50/year (online access to ePAS).

Meetings/Conferences:
Annual Meetings: Fall
2007 – Columbus, OH(Columbus Convention Center)/Oct. 31-Nov. 3/7000
2008 – Austin, TX(Austin Convention Center)/Nov. 5-8/7000

Publications:
Percussive Notes. bi-m. adv.
Percussion News. bi-m. adv.

Perennial Plant Association *(1983)*
3383 Schirtzinger Road
Hilliard, OH 43026
Tel: (614)771-8431 *Fax:* (614)876-5238
E-Mail: ppa@perennialplant.org
Web Site: www.perennialplant.org
Members: 2200 firms and individuals
Staff: 2
Annual Budget: $250-500,000
Executive Director: Steven M. Still, Ph.D.
E-Mail: ppa@perennialplant.org

Historical Note
Voting membership in PPA is open to firms or individuals who are actively engaged in the growing, landscape planting, landscape designing or merchandising of perennials. Membership: Based upon gross volume of business in perennials.

Meetings/Conferences:
Annual Meetings: August

Publications:
Newsletter. bi-m.
Proceedings of Herbaceous Perennial Plant Symposium. a.
Journal. q. adv.

Performance Warehouse Association *(1971)*
41-701 Corporate Way, Suite 1
Palm Desert, CA 92260
Tel: (760)346-5647 *Fax:* (760)346-5847
E-Mail: info@pwa-par.org
Web Site: www.pwa-par.com
Members: 600 individuals
Staff: 2
Annual Budget: $250-500,000
Executive Director: John M. Towle

Historical Note
PWA members are distributors of specialty automotive parts and suppliers.

Meetings/Conferences:
2007 – Phoenix, AZ(Pointe South Mountain)/Sept. 24-26

Publications:
PWA Newsletter. a. adv.
PWA Membership Directory. a.

Periodical and Book Association of America *(1965)*
481 Eighth Ave., Suite 826
New York, NY 10001
Tel: (212)563-6502 *Fax:* (212)563-4098
E-Mail: info@pbaa.org
Web Site: www.pbaa.net
Members: 150 individuals
Staff: 1
Annual Budget: $100-250,000
Executive Director: Lisa Scott
Associate Director: Jose Concio

Historical Note
Membership: $2500/year.

Meetings/Conferences:
Annual Meetings: Regular member meetings held in New York City

Publications:
PBAA Annual magazine. a. adv.

Periodical Publications Association *(1964)*
P.O. Box 10669
Rockville, MD 20849-0669
Tel: (301)260-1646
E-Mail: periodicalpubs@yahoo.com
Staff: 1
Annual Budget: $10-25,000
Executive Director: Kimberly Scott

Historical Note
Established in 1964 as the Paid Circulation Committee, it changed its name in 1965 to the Paid Circulation Council. In 1974 it became the Association of Second Class Mail Publications, in 1979 the Association of Second Class Mail Publishers, and in 1982 the Association of Paid Circulation Publications. Assumed its current name in 2005. Members are national periodical publishers and associated businesses.

Publications:
Washington Report. m.

Perishable Agricultural and Foodstuffs Conference

Historical Note
A conference of the Transporation Intermediaries Association.

Perlite Institute *(1949)*
4305 N. Sixth St., Suite A
Harrisburg, PA 17110
Tel: (717)238-9723 *Fax:* (717)238-9985
E-Mail: info@perlite.org
Web Site: www.perlite.org
Members: 40 companies
Staff: 4
Executive Director: Denise Calabrese

Historical Note
Members include mining firms; processors of expanded perlite; roof deck applicators; furnace manufacturers; and other processors of perlite. Perlite is a volcanic rock used for horticultural applications, building and industrial insulation, plaster and concrete aggregate, and in fillers and filter aid applications. Membership: $2000/year (organization/company).

Meetings/Conferences:
2007 – Shangai, China/May 5-9/25

Publications:
Perlite Today Newsletter. 4/year.

Personal Communications Industry Association

Historical Note
Became PCIA - the Wireless Industry Association in 2003.

Personal Computer Memory Card International Association *(1989)*
2635 N. First St., Suite 218
San Jose, CA 95134
Tel: (408)433-2273 *Fax:* (408)433-9558
E-Mail: office@pcmcia.org
Web Site: www.pcmda.org
Members: 350 companies
Staff: 8
Annual Budget: $500-1,000,000
Executive Director: Patrick Maher

Historical Note
Members are manufacturers, distributors, and suppliers of laptop personal computers and software and other products for laptops. Promotes standards and specifications for laptop peripherals and other computer hardware items. PCMCIA establishes standards and promotes interoperability of PC cards

in mobile and a variety of other products. Membership: $1,500/year (affiliate); $3,500/year (associate); $10,000/year (executive).

Publications:
PC Card Developers Standard Guide.
PC Card Standard. a.
PC Express Standard. a.

Personal Watercraft Industry Association *(1987)*
444 North Capitol St. NW
Suite 645
Washington, DC 20001
Tel: (202)737-9768 *Fax:* (202)628-4716
E-Mail: info@pwia.org
Web Site: www.pwia.org
Members: 5 companies
Staff: 4
Annual Budget: $1-2,000,000
Executive Director: Maureen Healey
Public Relations Manager: Elinore Boeke
Regulatory Affairs Manager: Jeff Ludwig
Historical Note
An affiliate of the National Marine Manufacturers Association. PWIA members are manufacturers of jet drive personal watercraft.
Meetings/Conferences:
Annual Meetings: Not held.

Peruvian Paso Horse Registry of North America *(1970)*
3077 Wiljan Court, Suite A
Santa Rosa, CA 95407-5764
Tel: (707)579-4394 *Fax:* (707)579-1038
E-Mail: info@pphrna.org
Web Site: www.pphrna.org
Members: 1100 individuals
Staff: 3
Annual Budget: $100-250,000
Executive Director: Janetta Michael
Historical Note
Members breed and own Peruvian Paso horses. Maintains the stud book for purebred Peruvian Pasos, formulates rules and regulations for showing, and promotes shows and exhibitions. Membership: $65/year (individual).
Meetings/Conferences:
Semi-annual Meetings:
Publications:
Nuestro Caballo (newsletter). irreg.
Membership Directory. a.

Pet Food Institute *(1958)*
2025 M St. NW
Suite 800
Washington, DC 20036
Tel: (202)367-1120 *Fax:* (202)367-2120
E-Mail: info@petfoodinstitute.org
Web Site: www.petfoodinstitute.org
Members: 100 companies
Staff: 5
Annual Budget: $1-2,000,000
Vice President, Technology and Regulatory Affairs: Nancy K. Cook
Vice President, Communications: Stephen Payne
Historical Note
PFI represents dog and cat food manufacturers.
Meetings/Conferences:
Annual Meetings: Fall

Pet Industry Distributors Association *(1968)*
2105 Laurel Bush Road, Suite 200
Bel Air, MD 21015
Tel: (443)640-1060 *Fax:* (443)640-1031
E-Mail: marci@ksgroup.org
Web Site: www.pida.org
Members: 300 companies
Staff: 5
Annual Budget: $500-1,000,000
Executive Director: Steven T. King, CAE
Historical Note
Affiliated with the National Association of Wholesaler-Distributors and the Pet Industry Joint Advisory Council. Membership: $500-1,200/year (company). PIDA represents distributors and manufacturers of pet products.
Meetings/Conferences:
Annual Meetings: Winter
2007 – Dana Point, CA(St. Regis Monarch Beach)/Jan. 31-Feb. 3/225
Publications:
Profit Report. a.
PIDA News Bulletin. bi-m.

Pet Industry Joint Advisory Council *(1971)*
1220 19th St. NW
Suite 400
Washington, DC 20036
Tel: (202)452-1525 *Fax:* (202)293-4377
Toll Free: (800)553 - 7387
E-Mail: info@pijac.org
Web Site: www.pijac.org
Members: 2000 firms & associations
Staff: 7
Annual Budget: $1-2,000,000
Executive Vice President and General Counsel: N. Marshall Meyers
Historical Note
Monitors federal and state legislation affecting the industry; sponsors research; publishes management and training manuals for pet shops; and disseminates information on pet ownership responsibility, and on the pet industry. Members are pet shop retailers, companion animal breeders and importers, product manufacturers, and distributors.
Publications:
Pet Letter. m.
Pet Alert. irreg.

Pet Sitters International *(1994)*
201 E. King St.
King, NC 27021-9163
Tel: (336)983-9222 *Fax:* (336)983-5266
E-Mail: info@petsit.com
Web Site: www.petsit.com
Members: 7200 companies
Staff: 12
Annual Budget: $500-1,000,000
President: Patti Moran
Historical Note
PSI is an educational organization for professional pet sitters. Membership benefits include subscription to PSI's monthly magazine. PSI conducts an accreditation program and awards the annual Pet Sitter of the Year Award. Membership: $129/year (U.S. member); $104/year (Canadian).
Meetings/Conferences:
Annual Meetings: mid-September to mid-October
Publications:
The World of Professional Pet Sitting. bi-m. adv.

Petroleum Equipment Institute *(1951)*
P.O. Box 2380
Tulsa, OK 74101-2380
Tel: (918)494-9696 *Fax:* (918)491-9895
E-Mail: info@pei.org
Web Site: www.pei.org
Members: 1650 individuals
Staff: 12
Annual Budget: $2-5,000,000
Executive Vice President and General Counsel: Robert N. Renkes
E-Mail: rrenkes@pei.org
Coordinator, Membership: Carletta Denison
Director, Administration: Connie Dooley
E-Mail: cdooley@pei.org
Historical Note
Established as the National Association of Oil Equipment Jobbers; assumed its present name in 1966. Members are makers and distributors of equipment used in service stations, bulk plants and other petroleum marketing facilities.
Publications:
Petroleum Equipment Directory. a. adv.
Tulsa Letter. semi-m.

Petroleum Equipment Suppliers Association *(1933)*
9225 Katy Fwy., Suite 310
Houston, TX 77024
Tel: (713)932-0168 *Fax:* (713)932-0497
Web Site: www.pesa.org
Members: 175 individuals
Staff: 6
Annual Budget: $1-2,000,000
President: Sherry A. Stephens
Historical Note
Founded as American Petroleum Equipment Suppliers; assumed its current name in 1938. Members are makers of oil field production and drilling equipment, well site services and supplies.
Meetings/Conferences:
Annual Meetings: Spring
Publications:
PESA News. 8/year.
Service Point Directory. bi-a. adv.

Petroleum Investor Relations Association *(2000)*
c/o Unocal Corporation, Suite 4000
2141 Rosecrans Ave.
El Segundo, CA 90245
Web Site: www.pira.org
Members: 100 companies
Secretary-Treasurer: Robert E. Wright
Historical Note
PIRA represents investor communications professionals in the petroleum and natural gas industry. Has no paid officers or full-time staff. Membership: $300/year.

Petroleum Marketers Association of America *(1941)*
1901 N. Fort Myer Dr., Suite 500
Arlington, VA 22209
Tel: (703)351-8000 *Fax:* (703)351-9160
Toll Free: (800)300 - 7622
E-Mail: info@pmaa.org
Web Site: www.pmaa.org
Members: 45 associations
Staff: 9
Annual Budget: $2-5,000,000
President: Daniel Gilligan
Director, Legislative Affairs: Sarah Dodge
E-Mail: srdodge@pmaa.org
Director, Administration: Patricia Murrey
E-Mail: pmurrey@pmaa.org
Manager, Communications and Conferences: Laura Stewart
Vice President: Holly Tuminello
E-Mail: htuminello@pmaa.org
Historical Note
PMAA is the national organization representing the nation's independent petroleum marketers. PMAA is a federation of 45 state and regional petroleum marketing trade associations; these associations represent 7,850 independent petroleum marketers. PMAA's origins date back to 1909, when the Independent Petroleum Marketers Association of the United States was formed. This association became defunct, but in 1940, the President's Council of Petroleum Marketers Association was formed. In 1948, that group became the National Oil Jobbers Council; assumed its current name in 1984.

Meetings/Conferences:
Annual Meetings: Fall (Conference and Trade Show)
Publications:
PMAA Journal. q.
Weekly Review. w.
Directory. a.

Petroleum Product Stewardship Council
Historical Note
An affiliate of the Synthetic Organic Chemical Manufacturers Association which provides administrative support.

Petroleum Technology Transfer Council *(1994)*
16010 Barkers Point Lane, Suite 220
Houston, TX 77079
Tel: (281)921-1720 *Fax:* (281)921-1723
Toll Free: (888)843 - 7882
E-Mail: hq@pttc.org
Web Site: www.pttc.org
Staff: 4
Annual Budget: $2-5,000,000
Executive Director: Don Duttlinger
E-Mail: hq@pttc.org

Historical Note
PTTC is a national non-profit organization formed to foster the effective transfer of exploration and production technology to U.S. petroleum producers. The technical information that the PTTC transfers to producers comes from the research and development community and intermediary providers of technology including: government, universities, professional and trade societies, national labs, major companies, the service industry, etc. Although the PTTC is not involved directly with any research and development efforts, it identifies the best mechanisms for improving near-term and long-term technology transfer to domestic operators.

Publications:
PTTC Network News. q. adv.
Petroleum Technology Digest. semi-a. adv.

PGA TOUR Tournaments Association *(1969)*
13000 Sawgrass Village Circle, Suite 36
Ponte Vedra Beach, FL 32082-5023
Tel: (904)285-4222 *Fax:* (904)273-5726
Web Site: www.pgatta.org
Members: 50 individuals
Staff: 2
Annual Budget: $500-1,000,000
Executive Director: Suzanne Bohle
Manager, Member Services: Erin LaPorte

Historical Note
PGATTA members are sponsors of PGA Tour Golf tournaments. Formerly (1970) International Golf Sponsors Association and (1997) American Golf Sponsors Association. Membership: $3,000/year (organization).

Meetings/Conferences:
Annual Meetings: Winter

Publications:
PGATTA Quarterly. q.
Bulletin Board. m.

Pharmaceutical Care Management Association *(1975)*
601 Pennsylvania Ave. NW
Seventh Floor
Washington, DC 20004
Tel: (202)207-3610 *Fax:* (202)207-3623
E-Mail: info@pcmanet.org
Web Site: www.pcmanet.org
Members: 75 companies
Staff: 17
Annual Budget: $5-10,000,000
President and Chief Executive Officer: Mark Merritt
Director, Public Affairs: Charles Cote
Vice President, Federal Affairs: Missy Jenkins
Vice President and Chief Executive Officer: John Murray

Historical Note
Formerly (1989) National Association of Mail Service Pharmacies and then (1996) American Managed Care Pharmacy Association before assuming its current name. PCMA is the national association representing Pharmaceutical Benefits Managers. PCMA is dedicated to enhancing the proven tools and techniques that PBMs have pioneered in the marketplace, and to working to lower the cost of prescription drugs for all Americans.

Meetings/Conferences:
Annual Meetings: October

Pharmaceutical Printed Literature Association *(2001)*
131 E. Broad St., #206
Falls Church, VA 22046
Tel: (703)538-5799 *Fax:* (703)538-6305
E-Mail: info@pplaonline.org
Web Site: www.pplaonline.org
Members: 25 Corporate Members
Staff: 4
Annual Budget: $100-250,000
Executive Director: Peter G. Mayberry

Historical Note
PPLA represents companies involved in the production of printed instructional matter for pharmacists, other health professionals, and consumers.

Meetings/Conferences:
Annual Meetings: Spring

Pharmaceutical Research and Manufacturers of America *(1958)*
950 E St. NW
Washington, DC 20004
Tel: (202)835-3400 *Fax:* (202)835-3414
Web Site: www.phrma.org
Members: 110 companies
Staff: 100
Annual Budget: $10-25,000,000
President and Chief Executive Officer: W.J. "Billy" Tauzin
Senior Vice President, Communications: Ken Johnson
Senior Vice President, External Affairs: Mimi Simoneaux

Historical Note
Formed by merger of the American Drug Manufacturers Association and the American Pharmaceutical Manufacturers Association. Formerly (1994) Pharmaceutical Manufacturers Association. Non-profit trade association of over 100 research-based pharmaceutical companies. To qualify for membership, a company must manufacture and market finished dosage-form pharamaceuticals under their own brand name. In addition, they must conduct a significant amount of R&D within the United States. Together, PhRMA member companies account for 90 percent of sales within the United States and a substantial portion of the world's supply.

Meetings/Conferences:
Annual Meetings: Spring

Phi Alpha Delta *(1902)*
345 N. Charles St.
Baltimore, MD 21201-4300
Tel: (410)347-3118 *Fax:* (410)347-3119
Members: 265000 individuals
Staff: 9
Annual Budget: $1-2,000,000
Executive Director: Frank Patek
E-Mail: frank@pad.org

Historical Note
Professional and international law fraternity formed in Chicago, Nov. 8, 1902. Absorbed Phi Delta Delta, a women's professional law sorority, in 1972. Membership: $70/year (individual).

Meetings/Conferences:
Biennial Meetings: August, even years
2008 – Scottsdale, AZ(Doubletree Paradise Valley)/August/350
2010 – Orlando, FL(Sheraton World Resort)/August/250

Publications:
The Reporter. q. adv.

Phi Alpha Theta *(1921)*
University of South Florida SOC107
4202 E. Fowler Ave.
Tampa, FL 33620
Tel: (813)974-8212 *Fax:* (813)974-8215
Toll Free: (800)394 - 8195
E-Mail: phialpha@phialphatheta.org
Web Site: www.phialphatheta.org
Members: 275000 individuals
Staff: 3
Annual Budget: $500-1,000,000
Executive Director: Graydon A. Tunstall, Jr.

Historical Note
Phi Alpha Theta is the college-level honor society promoting the study of history through the encouragement of research, teaching, publication, and the exchange of learning and ideas among historians. Membership: $40/life (individual).

Meetings/Conferences:
Biennial Convention: Odd Years

Publications:
Historian. q. adv.
News Letter. 3/year.

Phi Beta *(1912)*
5481-D Millwood Lane
Willoughby, OH 44094
Tel: (440)942-7337
E-Mail: ringleader@peoplepc.com
Members: 400 individuals
Staff: 5
Treasurer: Nancy Schuman, Ph.D.
E-Mail: ringleader@peoplepc.com

Historical Note
Professional fraternity in the creative and performing arts. Membership: $45/year (individual).

Meetings/Conferences:
Biennial Conventions: even years

Publications:
Rosepetal. q. adv.

Phi Beta Lambda

Historical Note
See Future Business Leaders of America.

Phi Chi Theta *(1924)*
1508 E. Belt Line Road, Suite 104
Carrollton, TX 75006
Tel: (972)245-7202
E-Mail: executivedirector@phichitheta.org
Web Site: www.phichitheta.org
Members: 47000 individuals
Staff: 1
Annual Budget: $50-100,000
Executive Director: Saundra Finley
E-Mail: executivedirector@phichitheta.org

Historical Note
A co-ed professional fraternity in business and economics which seeks to promote the cause of higher business education and training for all individuals. Membership: $60/year (individual).

Meetings/Conferences:
Triennial Meetings:

Publications:
Iris. semi-a.

Phi Delta Chi *(1883)*
P.O. Box 83250
Conyers, GA 30013
Tel: (800)732-1883
Executive Director: Anthony Chaffee
E-Mail: pdc_executive_director@hotmail.com

Historical Note
A professional fraternity in pharmacy. Membership: $60/year.

Meetings/Conferences:
Biennial Meetings: August

Publications:
The Communicator. q. adv.

Phi Delta Epsilon Medical Fraternity *(1904)*
2655 Collins Ave., Suite 912
Miami, FL 33140
Tel: (305)531-1929 *Fax:* (305)531-7483
E-Mail: phide@phide.org
Web Site: www.phide.org
Members: 35000 individuals
Staff: 1
Executive Director: George S. Craft, M.D.
E-Mail: phide@phide.org

Historical Note
Professional fraternity serving the medical profession.

Publications:
Phi Delta Epsilon News & Scientific Journal. q. adv.

Phi Delta Kappa *(1906)*
408 N. Union Ave.
P.O. Box 789
Bloomington, IN 47402-0789
Tel: (812)339-1156 *Fax:* (812)339-0018
Toll Free: (800)766 - 1156
E-Mail: information@pdkintl.org
Web Site: www.pdkintl.org
Members: 60000 individuals
Staff: 65
Annual Budget: $2-5,000,000
Executive Director: William Bushaw
E-Mail: information@pdkintl.org

Historical Note
Phi Delta Kappa is a professional education association concerned with providing leadership and research in the field. Members include classroom teachers, school administrators, college and university professors, and educational specialists of many types. The primary focus of PDK is to promote quality publicly-supported education. Membership: $70/year (international dues) and local dues and initiation fee.

Publications:
Phi Delta Kappan. 10/year. adv.

PDK Connection. 3/year.
PDK Edge.

Phi Epsilon Kappa *(1913)*
901 W. New York St.
Indianapolis, IN 46202
Tel: (317)637-8431 *Fax:* (317)278-2041
Web Site: http://www2.truman.edu/pek/
Members: 3000 individuals
Staff: 1
Annual Budget: $50-100,000
Executive Director: Jeffery Vessely, Ed.D.
E-Mail: jvessel@iupui.edu

Historical Note
Phi E K is a professional fraternity in physical education. Membership: $30/year.

Meetings/Conferences:
Triennial Meetings: (2005)

Publications:
Black and Gold Bulletin. semi-a.
Physical Educator. q.

Phi Gamma Nu *(1924)*
6745 Cheryl Ann Dr.
Seven Hills, OH 44131
Tel: (216)524-0934
Members: 30000 individuals
Executive Director: Lorraine A. Scott

Meetings/Conferences:
Triennial Meetings: (1998)

Publications:
Magazine of Phi Gamma Nu. semi-a.
Nat'l Headquarters Bulletin. bi-m.
Alumni Newsletter. a.
Directory. irreg.

Phi Mu Alpha Sinfonia *(1898)*
Lyrecrest, 10600 Old State Road
Evansville, IN 47711
Tel: (812)867-2433 *Fax:* (812)867-0633
Toll Free: (800)473 - 2649
Web Site: www.sinfonia.org
Members: 14000 individuals
Staff: 9
Annual Budget: $250-500,000
Executive Director: Ryan T. Ripperton
E-Mail: ripperton@sinfonia.org

Historical Note
A fraternity for men in music. Formerly (1934) The Sinfonia Fraternity. Membership: $100/year (individual).

Publications:
The Red and Black Newsletter. m.
Sinfonian Magzine. q.
National Directory. a.

Phi Rho Sigma Medical Society *(1890)*
P.O. Box 90264
Indianapolis, IN 46290-0264
Tel: (317)334-8720 *Fax:* (317)334-8721
Web Site: www.phirhosigma.org
Members: 31000 individuals
Staff: 1
Annual Budget: $50-100,000
Central Office Director: Harriet Rodenberg

Historical Note
A professional fraternity in medicine, stressing professional development, high scholarship and community service. Membership: $35/year (voluntary dues).

Meetings/Conferences:
Annual Meetings: Fall

Publications:
Journal of Phi Rho Sigma. q.

Philanthropy Roundtable *(1991)*
1150 17th St. NW
Suite 503
Washington, DC 20036
Tel: (202)822-8333 *Fax:* (202)822-8325
Web Site: www.philanthropyroundtable.org
Members: 650 individuals
Staff: 9
President: Adam Myerson
E-Mail: ameyerson@philanthropyroundtable.org

Historical Note
The Roundtable is a national organization whose members include corporate giving representatives, foundation staff, estate officers and individual donors.

Meetings/Conferences:
Annual Meetings: Fall

Publications:
Philanthropy Magazine. bi-m.

Philippine-American Chamber of Commerce *(1920)*
317 Madison Ave., Suite 520
New York, NY 10017
Tel: (212)972-9326 *Fax:* (212)687-5844
E-Mail: philamcham@prodigy.net
Web Site: www.thepinoy.com/philamchamber
Members: 105 individuals
Staff: 4
Annual Budget: $100-250,000
Executive Director: Ellison M. Quijano
E-Mail: philamcham@prodigy.net

Historical Note
Non-profit organization working with the public and private sector in the United States and the Philippines to promote trade and investment between the two countries. Assists U.S. companies seeking business opportunities in the Philippines and Philippine companies seeking U.S. markets.

Publications:
Philippine Business. m.
PHILAMCHAM News Briefs. q.

Philosophy of Education Society *(1941)*
Southern Illinois University
College of Education
Carbondale, IL 62901-4606
Tel: (618)536-4434 *Fax:* (618)453-4338
E-Mail: help@philosophyofeducation.org
Web Site: www.philosophyofeducation.org
Members: 500 individuals
Annual Budget: $25-50,000
Executive Secretary: Kathy Hytten

Historical Note
PES addresses philosophic issues in education, particularly those which focus on professional ethics. Has no paid staff. Membership: $30-85/year.

Meetings/Conferences:
Annual Meetings: Spring

Publications:
Educational Theory. q.
Philosophy of Education (Yearbook). a.
Newsletter. 3/yr.

Philosophy of Science Association *(1934)*
University of Missouri-Kansas City,
Department of Philosophy
5100 Rockhill Road
Kansas City, MO 64110-2499
Tel: (816)235-2816 *Fax:* (816)235-2819
E-Mail: galeg@umkc.edu
Web Site:
http://philosophy.wisc.edu/PSA/Default.htm
Members: 950 individuals
Staff: 1
Annual Budget: $50-100,000
Executive Secretary: George D. Gale, Ph.D.
E-Mail: galeg@umkc.edu

Historical Note
PSA is a member of the International Union of History and Philosophy of Science and an affiliate of the American Association for the Advancement of Science. Membership: $40-$60/year based on income.

Meetings/Conferences:
Biennial Meetings: even years in Fall

Publications:
Newsletter. q.
Philosophy of Science. q. adv.
Proceedings of Biennial Meetings. bien.

Phlebology Society of America *(1962)*
Five Daremy Court
Nesconset, NY 11767-1547
Tel: (631)366-1429 *Fax:* (631)366-3609
Members: 260 individuals
Staff: 1
Annual Budget: $100-250,000
Executive Director: Denise Rossignol
E-Mail: deniserossignol@cs.com

Historical Note
Established and incorporated in New York in 1962 as a professional membership society for the purpose of exchanging scientific information, nationally, in the field of peripheral vascular disease. Members are designated as Fellows, Associate Fellows, and Clinical Members, depending upon the extent of their involvement in the research or clinical practice in phlebology. Membership: $150/year.

Meetings/Conferences:
Annual Meetings: Spring/200

Publications:
Internat'l Journal of Angiology. q. adv.
Proceedings of the Annual Meeting. a. adv.

Phosphonates Task Force

Historical Note
An affiliate of the Synthetic Organic Chemical Manufacturers Association which provides administrative support.

Photo Chemical Machining Institute *(1968)*
38 Strawberry Lane
P.O. Box 739
East Dennis, MA 02641
Tel: (508)385-0085 *Fax:* (508)385-0086
E-Mail: info@pcmi.org
Web Site: www.pcmi.org
Members: 210 companies
Annual Budget: $100-250,000
Executive Director: Betty Berndt Brown
E-Mail: info@pcmi.org

Historical Note
PCMI members are companies producing metal products through photo chemical machining. In addition, the Institute includes companies that service the PCM industry and supply its needs. Membership: $500/year (organization).

Meetings/Conferences:
Semi-annual Meetings: April and September
2007 – Cambridge, MA(Massachusetts Institute of Technology)/Apr. 23-25

Publications:
Membership Directory. a. adv.
Journal. q. adv.

Photo Marketing Association-International *(1924)*
3000 Picture Place
Jackson, MI 49201-8853
Tel: (517)788-8100 *Fax:* (517)788-8371
E-Mail: pma_information_central@pmai.org
Web Site: www.pmai.org
Members: 20000 individuals
Staff: 95
Annual Budget: $5-10,000,000
Executive Director: Ted Fox
Corp. Communications Executive: Tom Crawford

Historical Note
Created by a merger of National Photo Dealers Association (1946) and Master Photo Finishers of America. Formerly (1974) Master Photo Dealers and Finishers' Association. Maintains branches in Australia, Brazil, Canada, a number of European countries including Italy and the United Kingdom, and New Zealand. The Association of Photo CD Imagers, the Association of Professional Color Laboratories, the Digital Imaging Marketing Association, Professional School Photographers, and the Professional Picture Framers Association are sections of PMA-I. Has an annual budget of approximately $8.1 million.

Meetings/Conferences:
Semi-Annual Meetings: Spring and Fall

Publications:
Photo Marketing Magazine. m. adv.
Newsline Internat'l. w.

Photographic Materials Specialty Group *(1979)*

Historical Note
A special interest group of the American Institute for Conservation of Historic and Artistic Works concerned with the conservation and preservation of photographic materials.

Photoimaging Manufacturers and Distributors Association *(1939)*

109 White Oak Lane, Suite 72F
Old Bridge, NJ 08857
Tel: (732)679-3460 *Fax:* (732)679-2294
Web Site: www.pmda.com
Members: 78 companies
Staff: 2
Annual Budget: $250-500,000
Executive Director: Robert H. Nunn

Historical Note

Founded as Photographic Merchandising and Distributing Association and became Photographic Manufacturers and Distributors Association before assuming its present name in 1999. Membership: $500/year (associate members); $1,000/year (voting members).

Publications:

PMDA Today-Newsletter. 6/year.
PMDA Awards Dinner Journal. a. adv.
Membership Directory. a.

Phycological Society of America *(1946)*

c/o Blackwell Science, Inc.
350 Main St., Commerce Place
Malden, MA 02148
Tel: (781)388-8250 *Fax:* (781)388-8270
Web Site: www.psaalgae.org
Members: 1200 individuals
Annual Budget: $250-500,000
Communications Director: Dr. Morgan L. Vis

Historical Note

Established in 1946 to promote basic and applied research of algae. Affiliated with the American Association for the Advancement of Science and the American Institute of Biological Sciences. Membership: $65/year (individual), $195/year (institution).

Meetings/Conferences:

Annual Meetings: Summer, at a university environment.

Publications:

Phycological Newsletter. semi-a.
Journal of Phycology. bi-m.

Physician Insurers Association of America *(1977)*

2275 Research Blvd., Suite 250
Rockville, MD 20850-6213
Tel: (301)947-9000 *Fax:* (301)947-9090
Web Site: www.piaa.us
Members: 65 companies
Staff: 17
Annual Budget: $2-5,000,000
President: Lawrence E. Smarr
Director, Loss Prevention and Research: Lori Bartholomew
Director, Communications: Lisa A. Cole
Director, Finance and Accounting: Betty Heng
Director, Business Development and Membership: Ann Horwich
Director, Meetings and Education: Kimberley Jacques
Director, Administration Services: Jill K. Kerr
Director, Government Relations: Bruce A. Wilson

Historical Note

Represents domestic and international medical and dental malpractice insurance companies which are physician or dentist owned or controlled. Membership fee varies; approximately $23,000/year (company).

Meetings/Conferences:

Annual Meetings: Spring/1,200
2007 – Seattle, WA(Westin)/May 23-26
2008 – Philadelphia, PA(Loews)/May 21-24
2009 – Hawaii, HI(Hilton)/May 13-16

Publications:

PIAA Newsbriefs. w.
Physician Insurer. q. adv.

Pi Lambda Theta *(1910)*

P.O. Box 6626
Bloomington, IN 47407-6626
Tel: (812)339-3411 *Fax:* (812)339-3462
Toll Free: (800)487 - 3411
E-Mail: office@pilamda.org
Web Site: www.pilambda.org
Members: 17000 individuals
Staff: 6
Annual Budget: $500-1,000,000
Executive Director: J. Ogden Hamilton, Ph.D.
E-Mail: joh@pilambda.org

Historical Note

Phi Lambda Theta was founded in 1910. Its mission is twofold: to honor outstanding educators and to inspire their leadership on critical education issues. The most selective society of its kind, PLT extends membership to students and professionals who satisfy academic eligibility requirements, as well as to professional educators who have earned a PLT-recognized award or certification by the National Board for Professional Teaching Standards. Membership: $40/year (professional); $30/year (student).

Meetings/Conferences:

Biennial meetings: uneven years in summer.
2007 – Richmond, VA(Omni)/July 26-29/30

Publications:

Educational Horizons. q.
Pi Lambda Theta Newsletter. bi-m.

Pi Sigma Epsilon

Historical Note

Professional fraternity affiliated with Sales and Marketing Executives, International.

Piano Manufacturers Association International *(1891)*

590 W. Parker Road
Suite 278, #233
Plano, TX 75093-7792
Tel: (972)625-0110 *Fax:* (972)625-0110
Web Site: www.pianonet.com
Members: 20 piano manufacturers
Annual Budget: $250-500,000
Executive Director: Donald W. Dillon
E-Mail: don@dondillon.com

Historical Note

Formerly (1986) the National Piano Manufacturers Association. Supports the National Piano Foundation (same address) as its educational arm.

Meetings/Conferences:

Semi-annual Mtgs: Winter & Summer with Nat'l Ass'n of Music Merchants
2007 – Anaheim, CA(Convention Center)/Jan. 18-21

Publications:

NPF Piano Notes. q.

Piano Technicians Guild *(1957)*

4444 Forest Ave.
Kansas City, KS 66106
Tel: (913)432-9975 *Fax:* (913)432-9986
E-Mail: info@ptg.org
Web Site: www.ptg.org
Members: 4100 individuals
Staff: 7
Annual Budget: $1-2,000,000
Executive Director: Barbara Cassaday

Historical Note

Formed in 1957 by a consolidation of the American Society of Piano Technicians and the National Association of Piano Tuners. Membership as Registered Technician acquired by examination.

Meetings/Conferences:

Annual Meetings: Summer
2007 – Kansas City, MO(Hyatt Crown Center)/June 20-24

Publications:

Membership Directory & Resource Guide. a. adv.
The Piano Technician's Journal. m. adv.

Pickle Packers International *(1893)*

1620 I St. NW
Suite 925
Washington, DC 20006
Tel: (202)331-2456
E-Mail: bbursjek@therobertsgroup.net
Web Site: www.ilovepickles.org
Members: 160 companies
Staff: 3
Annual Budget: $500-1,000,000
Executive Director: Brian Bursjek

Historical Note

Formerly (1963) National Pickle Packers Association. Members are manufacturers of pickles and other fermented or acidified vegetables, suppliers of salt, salt stock brokers, and other suppliers to the industry. The objectives of the PPI are to perfect the pickling process from seed to finished product and to increase consumption of pickled vegetables. Membership: annual dues vary.

Meetings/Conferences:

2007 – Milwaukee, WI(Hilton City Center)/Apr. 17-19
2007 – Memphis, TN(The Peabody Hotel)/Oct. 2-4/250

Picture Agency Council of America

c/o Robertstock/Retrofile
P.O. Box 301
Chatham, NY 12037
Tel: (518)392-6967 *Fax:* (518)392-9131
E-Mail: pacanews@pacaoffice.org
Web Site: www.stockindustry.org
Members: 170 firms
Staff: 1
Annual Budget: $250-500,000
President: Chris Ferrone
E-Mail: president@pacaoffice.org

Historical Note

PACA is the trade association for stock picture agencies in North America. Membership: dues vary by staff size and membership category.

Meetings/Conferences:

Annual Meetings:

Publications:

PACA update. w.

Piedmontese Association of the United States *(1984)*

343 Barrett Road
Elsberry, MO 63343-4137
Tel: (573)384-5685 *Fax:* (573)384-5567
Web Site: http://pauscattle.org
Members: 400 individuals
Staff: 1
Annual Budget: $50-100,000
Secretary: Jerold Brocker

Historical Note

PAUS members are breeders of Piedmontese cattle. Membership: $25/year.

Meetings/Conferences:

Annual Meetings: January/150

Publications:

Magazine. q. adv.

Pierre Fauchard Academy *(1936)*

P.O. Box 80330
Las Vegas, NV 89180-0330
Tel: (702)651-5013 *Fax:* (702)651-5537
Toll Free: (800)232 - 0099
E-Mail: rkozal@aol.com
Web Site: www.fauchard.org
Members: 6000 individuals
Staff: 2
Annual Budget: $100-250,000
Secretary/General: Dr. Richard A. Kozal
E-Mail: rkozal@aol.com

Historical Note

Academy members are dentists. Membership: $100/year, plus $150 initiation fee.

Publications:

Dental Abstracts. bi-m. adv.
Dental World. bi-m. adv.
Membership Roster (online). irreg.

Pile Driving Contractors Association *(1996)*

P.O. Box 66208
Orange Park, FL 32065
Tel: (904)215-4771 *Fax:* (904)264-9531
Toll Free: (888)440 - 7453
E-Mail: execdir@piledrivers.org
Web Site: www.piledrivers.org
Members: 300 companies
Staff: 1
Annual Budget: $100-250,000
Executive Director: Tanya Goble
E-Mail: execdir@piledrivers.org

Historical Note

PDCA is an organization of pile driving contractors that seeks to increase the use of driven piles for deep foundations and earth retention systems. Membership: $700/year (company).

Publications:
Pile Driver. 4/yr. adv.

Pine Chemicals Association *(1947)*
3350 Riverwood Pkwy. SE
Suite 1900
Atlanta, GA 30339
Tel: (770)984-5340 *Fax:* (770)984-5341
Web Site: www.pinechemicals.org
Members: 60 companies
Staff: 2
Annual Budget: $250-500,000
President and Chief Operating Officer: Walter L. Jones
Office Administrator: Cheryl Morgan

Historical Note
Membership consists of international manufacturers of chemical products (other than pulp and paper) produced by or from products of the wood pulp industry.

Meetings/Conferences:
Annual Meetings: Fall/300

Publications:
Conference Proceedings. bien.

Pinto Horse Association of America *(1956)*
7330 N.W. 23rd St.
Bethany, OK 73008
Tel: (405)491-0111 *Fax:* (405)787-0773
E-Mail: membership@pinto.org
Web Site: www.pinto.org
Members: 12000 membership units
Staff: 15
Annual Budget: $1-2,000,000
Executive Vice President and Chief Operating Officer: Darrell Bilke
E-Mail: membership@pinto.org

Historical Note
Members are breeders and owners of Pinto horses. Maintains the registry for the Pinto breed, sets standards for conformation, color, and performance, and encourages the showing of the Pinto breed. Membership: $30/year.

Meetings/Conferences:
Annual Meetings: Spring

Publications:
The Pinto Horse Magazine. 6/yr. adv.

Pipe Fabrication Institute *(1913)*
666 Fifth Ave., #325
New York, NY 10103
Tel: (514)634-3434 *Fax:* (514)634-9736
Toll Free: (866)913 - 3434
E-Mail: pfi@pfi-institute.org
Web Site: www.pfi-institute.org
Members: 54 companies
Staff: 1
Annual Budget: $50-100,000
Executive Director: Guy Fortin
E-Mail: guy.fortin@pfi-institute.org

Historical Note
PFI members are companies producing sophisticated high-temperature, high-pressure piping systems installed throughout the U.S. and Canada. PFI member companies employ specialists from the ranks of the United Association of Journeymen and Apprentices of the Plumbing and Pipe Fitting Industry, and are signatories to the Pipe Fabrication Agreement with the United Association.

Meetings/Conferences:
Semi-annual Meetings:

Pipe Line Contractors Association *(1948)*
1700 Pacific Ave., Suite 4100
Dallas, TX 75201-4675
Tel: (214)969-2700 *Fax:* (214)969-2705
E-Mail: plca@plca.org
Web Site: www.plca.org
Members: 130 companies
Staff: 3
Managing Director and General Counsel: J. Patrick Tielborg
E-Mail: jptielborg@plca.org

Historical Note
Members are builders of cross-country pipelines and their suppliers.

Meetings/Conferences:
Annual Meetings: February
2007 - Aventura, FL(Turnberry)/

Publications:
Newsletter. w.

Pipe Tobacco Council *(1988)*
1707 H St. NW, Suite 800
Washington, DC 20006
Tel: (202)223-8207 *Fax:* (202)833-0379
Members: 11 companies
Staff: 1
Annual Budget: $100-250,000
President: Norman F. Sharp

Historical Note
Formed in 1988 "to advance and foster the economic interests of its members, the general welfare of the pipe and smoking tobacco industry, and the nation's economy and society."

Meetings/Conferences:
Annual Meetings: Fall

Publications:
Bulletin. m.
Import Export Report. m.

Pipeline Research Council International *(1952)*
1401 Wilson Blvd., Suite 1101
Arlington, VA 22209
Tel: (703)387-0190 *Fax:* (703)387-0192
E-Mail: gtenley@prci.org
Web Site: www.prci.com
Members: 24 corporations
Staff: 2
President: George W. Tenley, Jr.

Historical Note
Founded as Pipeline Research Committe, an autonomous program of the American Gas Association. PRC International sponsors research on technical issues facing the natural gas transmission industry. Members are companies operating pipeline systems.

PKF North American Network *(1969)*
3700 Crestwood Pkwy., Suite 350
Duluth, GA 30096
Tel: (770)279-4560 *Fax:* (770)279-4566
E-Mail: rbeilfuss@pkfnan.org
Web Site: www.pkfnan.org/www/ARAF-NET/ARAF/signin.aspx
Members: 93 firms
Staff: 15
Annual Budget: $1-2,000,000
President: Rudolf Beilfuss
E-Mail: rbeilfuss@pkfnan.org

Historical Note
Formerly (1998) Associated Regional Accounting Firms. Polaris is an association of independently owned and operated accounting and consulting firms with offices throughout North America.

Publications:
Management Services Update. m.
Marketing Services Update. m.
Membership Directory. a.
Pictorial Directory. a.
Resource Guide. a.
Technical Services Update. m.
Resource Directory. a.

Plant Growth Regulators Society of America *(1973)*
P.O. Box 2945
LaGrange, GA 30241-2945
Tel: (706)845-9085 *Fax:* (706)883-8215
Web Site: www.griffin.peachnet.edu/pgrsa/
Members: 300 individuals
Annual Budget: $25-50,000
Executive Secretary: Charles T. Hall, Jr.

Meetings/Conferences:
Annual Meetings: Summer

Publications:
PGRSA Quarterly. q.
Annual Meeting Proceedings. a.

Plasma Protein Therapeutics Association *(1971)*
147 Old Solomons Island Rd., Suite 100
Annapolis, MD 21401
Tel: (410)263-8296 *Fax:* (410)263-2298
E-Mail: ppta@pptaglobal.org
Web Site: www.pptaglobal.org
Members: 95 companies
Staff: 20
Annual Budget: $1-2,000,000
Executive Director: Julie Birkofer
E-Mail: ppta@pptaglobal.org

Historical Note
Founded as American Blood Resources Association; became ABRA - the International Authority for the Source Plasma Collection Industry in 2000, and assumed its current name in 2004. Members are commercial plasma product processors, blood component collectors, distributors and manufacturers. Membership: $1,350/year (company, per each operating location).

Publications:
FAX Letter. 10/year.
Annual Report. a.
The Journal of the ABRA. q. adv.

Plastic Pipe and Fittings Association *(1978)*
800 Roosevelt Rd., Bldg. C
Suite 312
Glen Ellyn, IL 60137
Tel: (630)858-6540 *Fax:* (630)790-3095
E-Mail: info@ppfahome.org
Web Site: www.ppfahome.org
Members: 77 companies
Staff: 5
Annual Budget: $500-1,000,000
Executive Secretary: Richard Church

Historical Note
PPFA is the national trade association of manufacturers of plastic piping products used for plumbing applications. Members include pipe and fitting processors, prime resin suppliers, equipment suppliers, solvent cement manufacturers and suppliers of compounding ingredients.

Meetings/Conferences:
Semi-annual Meetings: Spring/Fall
2007 - Indian Wells, CA(Renaissance Esmeralda)/March 3-7
2007 - Naples, FL(Ritz Carlton Golf Resort)/Oct. 6-10

Plastic Shipping Container Institute *(1976)*
1920 N St. NW
Washington, DC 20036
Tel: (202)973-2709 *Fax:* (202)331-8330
E-Mail: info@pscionline.org
Web Site: www.pscionline.org
Members: 45 companies
Staff: 1
Annual Budget: $100-250,000
General Counsel: David H. Baker

Historical Note
Members are manufacturers of open head plastic shipping containers. Associate members are companies producing virgin high density polyethylene, component parts for shipping containers and companies manufacturing machines capable of producing a finished plastic shipping container, and all companies which provide a performance evaluation service on the finished plastic shipping container. Membership: $5,000/year; $2,000/year (associate).

Meetings/Conferences:
Semi-annual Meetings: Winter and Fall

Plastic Soft Materials Manufacturers Association *(1937)*
145 W. 45th St., Suite 800
New York, NY 10036
Tel: (212)489-5400
E-Mail: joey5400@aol.com
Members: 20 companies
Staff: 2
Annual Budget: $50-100,000
Executive Director: Sheldon M. Edelman

Publications:
The Association. q.

Plastic Surgery Admininstrative Association *(1974)*
6324 Fairview Ave. North
Minneapolis, MN 55428
Tel: (952)767-3170 *Fax:* (952)925-1579
Toll Free: (800)373 - 0302
E-Mail: psaa@mindspring.com

Web Site: www.plasticadmin.org
Members: 250 individuals
Staff: 1
Annual Budget: $50-100,000
Executive Director: Orla McClure

Historical Note
Membership: $130/year (individual).

Meetings/Conferences:
Annual Meetings: Fall

Publications:
The Administrator. q. adv.

Plastic Surgery Research Council *(1955)*
45 Lyme Rd., Suite 304
Hanover, NH 03755
Tel: (603)643-2325 *Fax:* (603)643-1444
E-Mail: psrc@sover.net
Web Site: www.ps-rc.org
Members: 598 individuals
Staff: 4
Annual Budget: $50-100,000
Executive Director: Catherine B. Foss
E-Mail: psrc@sover.net

Historical Note
Purpose of PSRC is to promote basic research in plastic and reconstructive surgery. Membership: $175/year (full member); $75/year (associate); $25/year (resident).

Meetings/Conferences:
2007 – Palo Alto, CA(Stanford Park)/June 18-23

Plastics Molders and Manufacturers Association of SME

Historical Note
Part of Engineering Materials Applications Community of SME, a program of Society of Manufacturing Engineers, which provides administrative support.

Plastics Pipe Institute *(1950)*
105 Decker Ct.
Suite 825
Irving, TX 75062
Tel: (469)499-1044 *Fax:* (469)499-1063
E-Mail: info@plasticpipe.org
Web Site: www.plasticpipe.org
Members: 125 corporate members
Staff: 7
Annual Budget: $1-2,000,000
President: Rich Gottwald
Executive Director: Tony Radoszewski

Historical Note
PPI promotes the effective use of plastic piping systems, contributes to the development of standards, publishes technical reports and statistics, educates designers, installers, users and officials and maintains liaison with other groups. Membership: varies by sales level (corporate).

Meetings/Conferences:
Semi-annual Meetings: Spring and Fall

Publications:
Annual Statistics for Industry. a.

Pleaters, Stitchers and Embroiderers Association *(1920)*
145 W. 45th St., Suite 800
New York, NY 10036
Tel: (212)489-5400
Members: 90 companies
Staff: 6
Executive Director: Sheldon M. Edelman

Historical Note
Absorbed (1988) National Hand Embroidery and Novelty Manufacturers Association, and (1996) Artificial Flower Manufacturers Board of Trade. Major activity is labor negotiations with the International Ladies Garment Workers Union.

Plumbing and Drainage Institute *(1928)*
800 Turnake St., Suite 300
North Andover, MA 01845
Tel: (978)557-0721 *Fax:* (978)557-0721
Toll Free: (800)589 - 8956
E-Mail: bill@pdionline.org
Web Site: www.pdionline.org
Members: 15 companies, 5 licensees
Staff: 1
Executive Director: William C. Whitehead

Historical Note
Formerly (1949) Plumbing and Drainage Manufacturers Association. Incorporated in 1954 in the State of Illinois. Members are manufacturers of engineered plumbing products, including drains, cleanouts, backwater valves, and other drainage specialties. PDI is active in the development and implementation of engineering standards for the industry.

Meetings/Conferences:
Annual Meetings: April

Plumbing Contractors of America *(1989)*
1385 Piccard Dr.
Rockville, MD 20850
Tel: (301)869-5800 *Fax:* (301)990-9690
Toll Free: (800)556 - 3653
E-Mail: smcguire@mcaa.org
Web Site: www.mcaa.org/pca
Members: 1300 firms
Staff: 1
Annual Budget: $2-5,000,000
Communications Coordinator: Stephanie Mills
Associate Director, Communications MCAA: Sean McGuire

Historical Note
Founded as the National Plumbing Bureau; assumed its present name in 1999. A department of the Mechanical Contractors Association of America, NCPWB assists plumbing contractors in becoming better equipped to conduct business.

Meetings/Conferences:
Annual Meetings: In conjunction with the MCAA national convention.

Publications:
Reporter. m.

Plumbing Manufacturers Institute *(1975)*
1340 Remington Rd., Suite A
Schaumburg, IL 60173
Tel: (847)884-9764 *Fax:* (847)884-9775
E-Mail: bhiggens@pmihome.org
Web Site: www.pmihome.org
Members: 40 companies
Staff: 4
Annual Budget: $500-1,000,000
Executive Director: Barbara C. Higgins

Historical Note
The national trade association of plumbing products manufacturers. It has been, successively, the Sanitary Brass Institute, the Brass Gas Stop Institute, the Tubular Brass Institute and, most recently, in 1975, the Plumbing Brass Institute.

Meetings/Conferences:
Semi-Annual Meetings: Spring and Fall

Publications:
PMI News. bi-m.

Plumbing-Heating-Cooling Contractors - National Association *(1883)*
180 S. Washington St.
Falls Church, VA 22042
Tel: (703)237-8100 *Fax:* (703)237-7442
Toll Free: (800)533 - 7694
E-Mail: naphcc@naphcc.org
Web Site: www.phccweb.org
Members: 3700 individuals
Staff: 22
Annual Budget: $2-5,000,000
Executive Vice President: Dwight L. Casey
E-Mail: casey@naphcc.org
Vice President, Government Relations: Lake A. Coulson
Vice President, Education: Gerald J. Kennedy, Jr.
E-Mail: kennedy@naphcc.org
Director, Communications: Charlotte Perham
E-Mail: perham@naphcc.org
Director, Membership: Cynthia Sheridan
E-Mail: sheridan@naphcc.org
Director, Creative Production: Julie A. Turner
E-Mail: turner@naphcc.org
Director, Finance: Penny L. Young
E-Mail: young@naphcc.org

Historical Note
Established as the National Association of Master Plumbers; became (1953) the National Association of Plumbing Contractors and (1962) National Association of Plumbing-Heating-Cooling Contractors before assuming its present name in 1997. Sponsors and supports the PHCC-NA Political Action Committee, Education Techshow, Foundation, Scholarship Trust, and Legal Action Trust. Membership: $365/year.

Meetings/Conferences:
Annual Meetings: Fall

Publications:
Connection. bi-m. adv.
PHCC Online. m.
Who's Who in PHCC. a. adv.

PMA, the Independent Book Publishers Association *(1983)*
627 Aviation Way
Manhattan Beach, CA 90266-7107
Tel: (310)372-2732 *Fax:* (310)374-3342
E-Mail: info@pma-online.org
Web Site: www.pma-online.org
Members: 4200 publishers
Staff: 9
Annual Budget: $2-5,000,000
Executive Director: Jan Nathan
Director: Terry Nathan

Historical Note
Formerly (1983) the Publishing Marketing Association; assumed current name in 2005. PMA is a non-profit trade association of independent publishers who cooperatively market their titles to the trade. Membership $109/year.

Meetings/Conferences:
Annual Meetings: May
2007 – New York, NY/May 29-31

Publications:
Independent. m. adv.
PMA Annual Resource Directory. a. adv.

Poetry Society of America *(1910)*
15 Gramercy Park
New York, NY 10003
Tel: (212)254-9628 *Fax:* (212)673-2352
Toll Free: (888)872 - 7636
Web Site: www.poetrysociety.org
Members: 3000 individuals
Staff: 6
Annual Budget: $250-500,000
Executive Director: Alice Quinn
Director, Development: Maryann Jacob

Historical Note
A non-profit cultural organization in support of poetry and poets, PSA's mission is to secure a wider recognition for poetry as one of the important forces making for a higher cultural life, to kindle a more intelligent appreciation of poetry, and to assist poets. PSA offers readings, lectures and symposia open to the public and conducts an extensive awards program. Membership: $40/year (individual).

Publications:
Poetry Society of America Journal. semi-a. adv.

Point-of-Purchase Advertising International

Historical Note
Became POPAI The Global Assocaition for Marketing at Retail in 2005.

Poland China Record Association *(1876)*
P.O. Box 9758
Peoria, IL 61612-9758
Tel: (309)691-6301 *Fax:* (309)691-0168
E-Mail: cpspeoria@mindspring.com
Web Site: www.cpsswine.com/poland/polands.htm
Members: 275 individuals
Staff: 3
Annual Budget: under $10,000
Executive Secretary: Jack Wall

Historical Note
Breeders and fanciers of Poland China swine. Member of the National Society of Livestock Record Associations. Membership: $10 (first year); $75/year (thereafter - includes magazine subscription, listing in breeders directory, and maintenance fee).

Meetings/Conferences:
Annual Meetings: Semi-annual Meetings
Publications:
Purebred Picture. 10/year. adv.

Police Executive Research Forum *(1977)*
1120 Connecticut Ave. NW, Suite 930
Washington, DC 20036
Tel: (202)466-7820 *Fax:* (202)466-7826
E-Mail: khartwick@policeforum.org
Web Site: www.policeforum.org
Members: 1100 individuals
Staff: 30
Annual Budget: $2-5,000,000
Executive Director: Chuck Wexler
E-Mail: cwexler@policeforum.org
Director, Finance: Ken Hartwick
E-Mail: khartwick@policeforum.org
Assistant Director, Membership: Rebecca Neuburger
Historical Note
A national organization of chief executives of city, county, and state police agencies. Membership is limited to nominated leaders of large police departments -- those with more than one hundred members or which are the principal police agency for a jurisdiction of at least 50,000 people. Originated in January, 1975; officially established in July, 1976; incorporated in the District of Columbia in May, 1977. Membership $300/year.
Publications:
Police Quarterly. q.
Subject of Debate. m.

Polish-U.S. Business Council *(1974)*
Historical Note
A program of U.S. Chamber of Commerce, which provides administrative support.

Political Products Manufacturers Association *(1972)*
Historical Note
Address unknown in 2006.

Polyisocyanurate Insulation Manufacturers Association *(1986)*
515 King St., Suite 420
Alexandria, VA 22314
Tel: (703)684-1136 *Fax:* (703)684-6048
E-Mail: pima@pima.org
Web Site: www.pima.org
Members: 27 companies
Staff: 2
Annual Budget: $500-1,000,000
President: Jared O. Blum
Director, Member Services: Rene LaMura
Historical Note
PIMA represents the interests of polyisocyanurate (polyiso) manufacturers and suppliers to the industry. PIMA's efforts center around four principal activities: product education, environmental responsibility, government partnerships, and energy conservation.

Polystyrene Packaging Council *(1988)*
1300 Wilson Blvd.
Eighth Floor
Arlington, VA 22209
Tel: (703)741-5649 *Fax:* (703)741-5651
E-Mail: pspc@plastics.org
Web Site: www.polystyrene.org
Members: 9 companies
Staff: 2
Annual Budget: $500-1,000,000
Executive Director: Michael Levy
E-Mail: pspc@plastics.org
Historical Note
PSPC, a business unit of the American plastics council, creates and implements programs designed to educate the public about the importance and benefits of polystyrene food packaging.
Publications:
Polystyrene News. q.

Polyurethane Foam Association *(1980)*
9724 Kingston Pike, Suite 503
Knoxville, TN 37922
Tel: (865)690-4648 *Fax:* (865)690-4649
E-Mail: rluedeka@pfa.org
Web Site: www.pfa.org
Members: 50 companies
Staff: 1
Annual Budget: $250-500,000
Executive Director: Robert J. Luedeka
E-Mail: rluedeka@pfa.org
Historical Note
Formerly (1981) Flexible Polyurethane Foam Manufacturers Association. Members are manufacturers of flexible polyurethane foam. Suppliers of raw material and equipment to the industry are eligible for associate membership.
Meetings/Conferences:
Semi-Annual Meetings: Spring and Fall

Polyurethane Manufacturers Association *(1971)*
1123 N. Water St.
Milwaukee, WI 58202
Tel: (414)431-3094 *Fax:* (414)276-7704
E-Mail: info@pmahome.org
Web Site: www.pmahome.org
Members: 80 companies
Annual Budget: $250-500,000
Associate Executive: Jennifer Gelinskey
Associate Executive: Jane A. Svinicki, CAE
Historical Note
Membership includes processors of solid cast, microcellular, RIM and thermoplastic urethane elastomers; manufacturers, suppliers, distributors and sales agents of raw materials, additives or processing equipment; and individuals or companies providing publishing, education, research, or consulting services to the industry. Membership: $750 processors/$1000-5000 suppliers.
Meetings/Conferences:
2007 – Las Vegas, NV/Apr. 22-24
Publications:
Polytopics. q.
Membership Directory. a.

Pony of the Americas Club
5240 Elmwood Ave.
Indianapolis, IN 46203
Tel: (317)788-0107 *Fax:* (317)788-8974
E-Mail: poac@poac.org
Web Site: www.poac.org
Members: 2300 individuals
Staff: 4
Annual Budget: $250-500,000
Executive Secretary: Sid Hutchcraft
Office Manager: Missy Corn
Historical Note
Members are breeders and fanciers of the Pony of the Americas breed, an Appaloosa-type pony used in pleasure, performance, and halter competitions. Membership: $20/year.
Publications:
PoA. a. adv.

POPAI The Global Association for Marketing at Retail *(1938)*
1660 L St. NW, Tenth Floor
Washington, DC 20036-5603
Tel: (703)373-8800
E-Mail: info@popai.com
Web Site: www.popai.com
Members: 1700 companies
Staff: 19
Annual Budget: $5-10,000,000
President and Chief Executive Officer: Dick Blatt
Vice President, Corporate Communications: Tim Bucholz
Historical Note
Formerly Point-of-Purchase Advertising International; assumed current name in 2005. Members are producers, buyers and users of signs and displays at retail.
Meetings/Conferences:
Annual Meetings:
Publications:
Research Bulletins. m.
The POPAI Post. m.

Popcorn Institute *(1943)*
401 N. Michigan Ave.
Chicago, IL 60611-4267
Tel: (312)644-6610 *Fax:* (312)321-5150
Web Site: www.popcorn.org
Members: 86 companies
Staff: 2
Annual Budget: $10-25,000
Manager: Genny Bertalmio
Historical Note
Trade association of popcorn processing, dedicated to improving the popcorn industry through education and cooperation. Absorbed the Popcorn Processors Association in 1960.

Population Association of America *(1931)*
8630 Fenton St., Suite 722
Silver Spring, MD 20910-3812
Tel: (301)565-6710 *Fax:* (301)565-7850
E-Mail: info@popassoc.org
Web Site: www.popassoc.org
Members: 3000 individuals
Staff: 3
Annual Budget: $500-1,000,000
Executive Director: Stephanie D. Dudley
E-Mail: info@popassoc.org
Historical Note
Established in 1931 and incorporated in New York in 1937. Promotes research in human population. Membership: $100/year (individual); $275/year (company).
Meetings/Conferences:
Annual Meetings: Spring
2007 – New York, NY(Marriott Marquis)/March 28-31/1700
2008 – New Orleans, LA(Sheraton)/Apr. 17-19/1600
2009 – Detroit, MI(Marriott)/Apr. 30-May 2/1600
2010 – Dallas, TX(Hyatt)/Apr. 15-17/1600
2011 – Washington, DC(Marriott Wordman)/March 31-Apr. 2/1800
Publications:
Demography. q. adv.
PAA Affairs. q.
Applied Demography. semi-a.

Porcelain Enamel Institute *(1930)*
P.O. Box 920220
Norcross, GA 30010
Tel: (770)281-8980 *Fax:* (770)281-8981
E-Mail: penamel@aol.com
Web Site: www.porcelainenamel.com
Members: 90 companies
Staff: 3
Annual Budget: $500-1,000,000
Executive Vice President: Cullen L. Hackler
Historical Note
PEI broke away from the American Ceramic Society in 1930. From then until 1994, it represented the porcelain enamel industry in the United States, when it expanded its scope to include suppliers and makers of porcelain enamel products and raw materials in all of North America. Membership: annual dues based on sales volume.
Publications:
First Firing. m.
Newsletter. bi-m. adv.
Proceedings. a.

Portable and Stationary Crushing Bureau
Historical Note
A bureau of the Construction Industry Manufacturers Association.

Portable Computer and Communications Association
P.O. Box 680
Hood River, OR 97031
Tel: (541)490-5140
Web Site: www.pcca.org
Members: 65 firms and organizations
Annual Budget: $50-100,000
Director: Gloria Kowalski
Historical Note
Represents firms, organizations, and individuals interested in mobile communications. PCCA publishes and disseminates information, standards, software, and other materials to facilitate the synthesis of computing and communications technologies. Membership: dues $100-5,000/year.

Portable Rechargeable Battery Association *(1991)*
1000 Parkwood Circle, Suite 430
Atlanta, GA 30339
Tel: (770)612-8826 *Fax:* (770)612-8841
E-Mail: n.england@att.net
Web Site: www.prba.org
Members: 130 companies
Staff: 2
Annual Budget: $1-2,000,000
President and Chief Executive Officer: Norm England
Historical Note
Incorporated in the District of Columbia in 1991. Members are manufacturers, distributors, users, and sellers of small rechargeable batteries and battery-powered products. Works to facilitate the collection and recycling of small sealed rechargeable batteries. Membership fee varies, based on sales volume.
Publications:
Recharger Newsletter. q.
Recharger Update. irreg.
Battery Reclamation Manual.

Portable Sanitation Association International *(1971)*
7800 Metro Pkwy., Suite 104
Bloomington, MN 55425
Tel: (952)854-8300 *Fax:* (952)854-7560
Toll Free: (800)822 - 3020
E-Mail: portsan@aol.com
Web Site: www.psai.org
Members: 700 companies
Staff: 4
Annual Budget: $250-500,000
Executive Director: William F. Carroll
E-Mail: portsan@aol.com
Historical Note
PSAI members are makers of chemical toilets, supplies and services and companies that rent and service them. Representation is expanding to include site services on constuction and special events. Membership: $300/year (company, average).
Publications:
PSAI In Action. bi-m. adv.
Industry Catalog. a. adv.

Portfolio Management Institute
11166 Huron St., Suite 27
Denver, CO 80234
Tel: (303)433-4446 *Fax:* (303)458-0002
E-Mail: pmi@pminstitute.org
Web Site: www.pminstitute.org
Members: 100
Annual Budget: $250-500,000
Contact: Gary E. Leeper
Historical Note
PMI members are investment managers. PMI provides educational opportunities and professional development opportunities.

Portland Cement Association *(1916)*
5420 Old Orchard Rd.
Skokie, IL 60077
Tel: (847)966-6200 *Fax:* (847)966-8389
E-Mail: info@cement.org
Web Site: www.cement.org
Members: 55 cement companies
Staff: 250
Annual Budget: $25-50,000,000
President: John P. Gleason, Jr.
Senior Vice President, Development and Technical Services: George B. Barney
Corporate Secretary: Jan E. Farnsworth
Staff Vice President, Communications: Bruce D. McIntosh
Senior Vice President/Finance and Administration: James F. Rappel
Historical Note
Absorbed American Portland Cement Alliance in 2002. PCA sponsors market development, education, research, technical services, and government affairs on behalf of member cement companies in the United States and Canada. Has an annual budget of approximately $25 million.
Meetings/Conferences:
Annual Meetings: November
Publications:
Executive Report. w.

Portugal-United States Chamber of Commerce *(1979)*
590 Fifth Ave.
New York, NY 10036
Tel: (212)354-4627 *Fax:* (212)575-4737
E-Mail: poruguesecham@aol.com
Web Site: www.portugal-us.com
Members: 150 businesses
Staff: 1
Annual Budget: $25-50,000
Executive Director: Thomas E. Dierson
E-Mail: poruguesecham@aol.com
Historical Note
A bilateral Chamber of Commerce, PUSCC exists to promote trade, investment and joint ventures between the two countries. Membership: $200/year (individual); $500/year (corporation); $1,000/year (sustaining).
Publications:
Newsletter. w.
Directory. a. adv.

Post-Print Manufacturers Association *(1999)*
218 E. North Ave.
Lake Bluff, IL 60044
Tel: (847)283-0970 *Fax:* (847)295-0489
Web Site: www.printfinish.org
Members: 21 companies
Staff: 2
Executive Director: Albert B. Boese
Historical Note
PPMA promotes print finishing, lamination, binding, packaging, and other processes that add value to printed matter. Members are manufacturers of equipment and products used in print production.

Post-Tensioning Institute *(1976)*
8601 N. Black Canyon Hwy., Suite 103
Phoenix, AZ 85021
Tel: (602)870-7540 *Fax:* (602)870-7541
E-Mail: info@post-tensioning.org
Web Site: www.post-tensioning.org
Members: 700 individuals
Staff: 6
Annual Budget: $1-2,000,000
Executive Director: Theodore L. Neff
E-Mail: tedneff@post-tensioning.org
Historical Note
PTI provides research, technical development, marketing and promotional activities for companies engaged in post-tensioned, prestressed construction. Members of the institute include major post-tension materials fabricators and manufacturers of prestressing materials. Membership: $80/year (individual); corporate dues vary.
Meetings/Conferences:
Semi-annual Meetings: Fall and Spring
Publications:
PTI Journal. 2/year. adv.
PTI Newsletter. q.
Technical Notes. q.

Postcard and Souvenir Distributors Association *(1973)*
2105 Laurel Bush Road, Suite 200
Bel Air, MD 21015
Tel: (443)640-1055 *Fax:* (443)640-1031
E-Mail: info@ksgroup.org
Web Site: www.postcardcentral.org
Members: 110 companies
Staff: 2
Annual Budget: $100-250,000
Executive Director: Steven T. King, CAE
Historical Note
PCDANA members are companies distributing local view scenic post cards and souvenirs in North America and the Caribbean. Membership $350/year (company).
Meetings/Conferences:
Annual Meetings: Fall
2007 – Myrtle Beach, SC(Myrtle Beaceh Sheraton)/Sept. 25-29/250
Publications:
Post Card Letter. q. adv.

Potash & Phosphate Institute *(1935)*
655 Engineering Dr., Suite 110
Norcross, GA 30092
Tel: (770)447-0335 *Fax:* (770)448-0439
E-Mail: ppi@ppi-ppic.org
Web Site: www.ppi-ppic.org
Members: 7 companies
Staff: 50
Annual Budget: $5-10,000,000
President: Terry L. Roberts
Historical Note
Formerly (1971) American Potash Institute, Inc., and then (1975) Potash Institute of North America before assuming its current name in 1977.
Meetings/Conferences:
Annual Meetings: October
Publications:
Better Crops with Plant Food. q.

Potato Association of America *(1913)*
University of Maine
5715 Coburn Hall, Rm. 6
Orono, ME 04469-5715
Tel: (207)581-3042 *Fax:* (207)581-3015
E-Mail: umpotato@maine.edu
Web Site: www.umaine.edu/paa/
Members: 1000 individuals
Staff: 4
Annual Budget: $50-100,000
Administrative Assistant: Lori Wing
Historical Note
Founded in New York, NY in 1912 as the National Potato Association of America and incorporated in New Jersey in 1913; became the Potato Association of America, Inc. in 1917. PAA is a professional society for potato research, extension, utilization and technical workers in all aspects of the American potato industry. Membership: $75/year (individual); $75/year (organization), $15/year (student), $400/year (sustaining).
Meetings/Conferences:
Annual Meetings: Summer
Publications:
American Journal of Potato Research. bi-m.

Poultry Breeders of America *(1959)*
c/o U.S. Poultry and Egg Ass'n
1530 Cooledge Road
Tucker, GA 30084-7303
Tel: (770)493-9401 *Fax:* (770)493-9257
Web Site: www.poultryegg.org/
Members: 20 companies
Annual Budget: under $10,000
President: Don Dalton
Historical Note
An affiliate of U.S. Poultry and Egg Association, PBA conducts an annual Poultry Breeders Roundtable and monitors legislative developments affecting the poultry industry. Membership: $300/year.
Meetings/Conferences:
Annual Meetings: January, in Atlanta, GA

Poultry Science Association *(1908)*
1111 N. Dunlap Ave.
Savoy, IL 61874-9510
Tel: (217)356-5285 *Fax:* (217)398-4119
Web Site: www.poultryscience.org
Members: 1500 individuals
Staff: 2
Annual Budget: $500-1,000,000
Executive Director: Dr. James W. Kessler
E-Mail: jamesk@assochq.org
Historical Note
Originated in 1908 as the International Association of Instructors and Investigators in Poultry Husbandry. Became the American Association of Instructors and Investigators in Poultry Husbandry in 1912 and the Poultry Science Association, Inc. 1926. Members are university and industry researchers involved in poultry, avian science, and related disciplines. Membership: $120/year (individual); $450/year Institution); $1,000/year (company).
Meetings/Conferences:
Annual Meetings: Summer
2007 – San Antonio, TX/July 8-12

Publications:
Abstracts. a.
Poultry Science. m.
Journal of Applied Poultry Research. q.
PSA Newsletter. bi-a.

Powder Actuated Tool Manufacturers Institute *(1952)*
1603 Boone's Lick Road
St. Charles, MO 63301
Tel: (636)947-6610 *Fax:* (636)946-3336
E-Mail: info@patmi.org
Web Site: www.patmi.org
Members: 7 companies
Staff: 2
Annual Budget: $50-100,000
Executive Director: James A. Borchers
E-Mail: jborchers@patmi.org
Historical Note
Represents manufacturers of construction tools used to fasten to and into steel and concrete. PATMI is a member of the National Safety Council and the American National Standards Institute. Membership: $5,500/year.
Meetings/Conferences:
Semi-annual Meetings:
Publications:
PATMI Basic Training Manual. irreg.

Powder Coating Institute *(1981)*
2121 Eisenhower Ave., Suite 401
Alexandria, VA 22314
Tel: (703)684-1770 *Fax:* (703)684-1771
E-Mail: pci-info@powdercoating.org
Web Site: www.powdercoating.org
Members: 320 companies
Staff: 4
Annual Budget: $1-2,000,000
Executive Director: Gregory J. Bocchi
Director, Communications: Jeff Palmer
Historical Note
Members are companies producing powder coatings, application equipment, and related materials and services for finishing a wide range of products.
Meetings/Conferences:
Annual Meetings: Fall
2008 – Indianapolis, IN(Convention Center)/Sept. 23-25/5000
Publications:
PCI Newsletter. bi-m.
Powder Coated Tough Magazine. 3/yr.
PCI News Bulletin. bi-m.

Powder Metallurgy Equipment Association *(1958)*
Historical Note
A constituent part of the Metal Powder Industries Federation. Equipment suppliers for powder metallurgy parts and products.

Powder Metallurgy Parts Association *(1957)*
Historical Note
A constituent part of the Metal Powder Industries Federation. Manufacturers of powder metallurgy parts and products. Formerly (1967) Powder Metallurgy Parts Manufacturers Association.

Power and Communication Contractors Association *(1945)*
103 Oronoco St., Suite 200
Alexandria, VA 22314
Tel: (703)212-7734 *Fax:* (703)548-3733
Toll Free: (800)542 - 7222
E-Mail: info@pccaweb.org
Web Site: www.pccaweb.org
Members: 550 companies
Staff: 5
Annual Budget: $500-1,000,000
Executive Vice President: Tim Wagner
E-Mail: info@pccaweb.org
Historical Note
Contractors and suppliers specializing in electric power line, telephone, cable television construction, directional drilling and their suppliers. Formerly (1950) Rural Electrical Contractors Association. Membership: $500/year (company).
Publications:
Power & Communications Contractor. m. adv.

Power Crane and Shovel Association *(1945)*
Historical Note
A bureau of the Construction Industry Manufacturers Association.

Power Electronics Society *(1987)*
Historical Note
See IEEE Power Electronics Society

Power Engineering Society
Historical Note
See IEEE Power Engineering Society

Power Sources Manufacturers Association *(1985)*
P.O. Box 418
Mendham, NJ 07945-0418
Tel: (973)543-9660 *Fax:* (973)543-6207
E-Mail: power@psma.com
Web Site: www.psma.com
Members: 160 companies
Staff: 2
Annual Budget: $100-250,000
Executive Director: Joseph Horzepa
E-Mail: power@psma.com
Historical Note
Worldwide membership consists of manufacturers and users of AC and DC power source systems and related components. Publishes technical standards and other information for the industry. Co-sponsors the Applied Power Electronics Conference annually each Spring. Regular membership: $650-2,250/year, based on revenue.
Meetings/Conferences:
Annual Meetings: February-March/600
2007 – Anaheim, CA(Disneyland Hotel)/Feb. 25-March 1
Publications:
Battery Reports. irreg.
Capacitors Reports. irreg.
Power Technology Roadmap. trien.
Update Newsletter. q.
Handbook of Terminology. irreg.

Power Tool Institute *(1937)*
1300 Sumner Ave.
Cleveland, OH 44115-2851
Tel: (216)241-7333 *Fax:* (216)241-0105
E-Mail: pti@powertoolinstitute.com
Web Site: www.powertoolinstitute.com
Members: 11 companies
Staff: 3
Executive Manager: Charles M. Stockinger
Historical Note
Formerly (1969) Electric Tool Institute. PTI works to harmonize global product listing standards and develops educational programs on the safe use of power tools.
Meetings/Conferences:
Annual Meetings: second or third week of October, alternating west coast-east coast.
Publications:
Directory. a.

Power Transmission Distributors Association *(1960)*
230 W. Monroe St., Suite 1410
Chicago, IL 60606-4703
Tel: (312)516-2100 *Fax:* (312)516-2101
E-Mail: ptda@ptda.org
Web Site: www.ptda.org
Members: 425 companies
Staff: 7
Annual Budget: $1-2,000,000
Executive Vice President: Mary Sue Lyon
Director, Membership Services: Brenda Holt
Director, Marketing and Communications: Stephanie Kaplan
Historical Note
Established as Mechanical Power Transmission Equipment Distributors Association, it assumed its present name in 1966. Members are industrial power transmission/motion control distributor firms representing locations throughout North America and several other countries, and manufacturing firms. Membership: based on annual sales volume.
Meetings/Conferences:
2007 – Palm Desert, CA(Marriott Desert Springs Resort & Spa)/Oct. 18-20/800
2008 – Miami Beach, FL(Loews)/Oct. 30-Nov. 1/800
Publications:
PTDA Spotlight. m.
Membership Directory. a. adv.
Transmissions. q.
Convention Guide. a. adv.

Power Washers of North America *(1988)*
P.O. Box 2296
Vincentown, NJ 08088
Tel: (609)268-9776 *Fax:* (609)268-9778
Toll Free: (800)393 - 7962
E-Mail: pwnahq@aol.com
Web Site: www.pwna.org
Members: 450 companies
Staff: 2
Annual Budget: $250-500,000
Operations Manager: Regina A. Dudley
Historical Note
Membership: $200-400/year (company).
Publications:
Waterworks. q.

Power-Motion Technology Representatives Association *(1972)*
One Spectrum Pointe, Suite 150
Lake Forest, CA 92630
Tel: (949)859-2885 *Fax:* (949)855-2973
Toll Free: (888)817 - 7872
E-Mail: info@ptra.org
Web Site: www.ptra.org
Members: 195 companies, 75 allied
Staff: 2
Annual Budget: $100-250,000
Executive Director: Pamela L. Bess
Historical Note
Formerly Power Transmission Representatives Association (1994). PTRA's purpose is three-fold: 1) to promote the science of power transmission/motion control engineering, 2) to promote educational programs and activities, and 3) to promote representatives placed in the industry.
Meetings/Conferences:
Annual Meetings: Spring/300
Publications:
Focus Newsletter. q.

Practising Law Institute *(1933)*
810 Seventh Ave.
New York, NY 10019-5818
Tel: (212)824-5710
Toll Free: (800)260 - 4754
E-Mail: info@pli.edu
Web Site: www.pli.edu
Members: 60000 individuals
Staff: 100
Annual Budget: $10-25,000,000
Executive Director: Victor J. Rubino
Historical Note
Has an annual budget of approximately $16 million. Membership: $100-$975/year, on a sliding scale based on the number of practicing attorneys in the firm.
Publications:
PLI News. bi-w.
Business Accounting for Lawyers. 8/year.

Precast/Prestressed Concrete Institute *(1954)*
209 W. Jackson Blvd., Suite 500
Chicago, IL 60606
Tel: (312)786-0300 *Fax:* (312)786-0353
E-Mail: info@pci.org
Web Site: www.pci.org
Members: 2550 firms, engineers & architects
Staff: 26
Annual Budget: $5-10,000,000
President: James G. Toscas
Managing Director, Marketing and Communications: Chuck Merydith
President: James G. Toscas

Historical Note
PCI is a non-profit association for the advancement of the design, manufacture and use of precast prestressed concrete, plant-produced building and bridge components. Members are producer companies, suppliers, engineers and architects. Formerly (1989) Prestressed Concrete Institute.

Publications:
Ascent. q. adv.
Publications Catalog. a. adv.
PCI Journal. bi-m. adv.
Membership Directory. a. adv.

Precision Machined Products Association *(1933)*
6700 W. Snowville Road
Brecksville, OH 44141
Tel: (440)526-0300 *Fax:* (440)526-5803
Web Site: www.pmpa.org
Members: 500 companies
Staff: 14
Annual Budget: $1-2,000,000
Executive Director: Michael B. Duffin
Director, Marketing and Membership Communication: Robert C. Kiener
E-Mail: rkiener@pmpa.org

Historical Note
Formerly (1995) National Screw Machine Products Association. PMPA member companies are producers of high precision component products. Produces several educational opportunities for members, emphasizing quality assurance and emerging technologies. Sponsors the PMPA Political Action Committee.

Publications:
Internet Weekly. w.
Production Machining. m. adv.

Precision Metalforming Association *(1942)*
6363 Oak Tree Blvd.
Independence, OH 44131-2500
Tel: (216)901-8800 *Fax:* (216)901-9190
E-Mail: pma@pma.org
Web Site: www.pma.org
Members: 1200 companies
Staff: 40
Annual Budget: $5-10,000,000
President: William E. Gaskin, CAE
Education Director, PMAEF: Bruce Broman
Meetings Manager: Judi Campobenedetto
Manager, Government, Safety and Public Affairs: Christie Carmigiano
Controller: Marcia C. Daniels
Publisher, Metal Forming Magazine: Kathy M. Delollis
Vice President: Daniel E. Ellashek, CAE
Membership Sales: Allen Grant
Editor, Metal Forming Magazine: Brad F. Kuvin
Manager, Exposition Services: Amy Primiano
Executive Director, PMAEF: David C. Sansone, CAE

Historical Note
Established in 1942 as the Pressed Metal Institute, it became the American Metal Stamping Association in 1961, and assumed its present name in 1987. Custom Roll Forming Institute was merged into PMA in August, 1992. PMA is the trade association representing the metalforming industry of North America. Members include producers of metal stampings, spinnings, washers and precision sheet metal fabrications as well as suppliers of equipment, materials and services to the metalforming industry. Sponsors and supports the PMA Voice of the Industry Committee. Membership: dues based on member company's annual sales.

Meetings/Conferences:
Semi-Annual Meetings: Spring and Fall

Publications:
Update. m.
Metal Forming Magazine. m. adv.

Preferred Funeral Directors International *(1937)*
P.O. Box 335
Indian Rocks Beach, FL 33785
Tel: (727)524-8100 *Fax:* (727)524-8200
E-Mail: info@pdfi.org
Web Site: www.pfdi.org
Members: 50 companies
Staff: 2
Annual Budget: $100-250,000
Administrator: Glenn Gould
E-Mail: info@pdfi.org

Historical Note
Established as the Advertising Funeral Directors of America; assumed its present name in the mid-1950s. Members are larger-volume independent funeral homes. Membership: $600/year.

Meetings/Conferences:
Semi-Annual Meetings: Spring and Fall.

Publications:
PFDI Newsletter. q.

Presbyterian Health, Education and Welfare Association *(1956)*
100 Witherspoon St., Room 4617
Louisville, KY 40202-1396
Tel: (502)569-5794 *Fax:* (502)569-8034
Toll Free: (888)728 - 7228
Web Site: www.pcusa.org/phewa
Members: 1500 individuals
Staff: 2
Annual Budget: $50-100,000
Executive Director: Rev. Nancy K. Troy
E-Mail: ntroy@ctr.pcusa.org

Historical Note
Formerly National Presbyterian Health and Welfare Association. Became the United Presbyterian Health, Education and Welfare Association in 1969 and assumed its present name in 1989. PHEWA is an organization for Presbyterians dedicated professionally and personally to the enactment of social justice. Eight networks are organized under the PHEWA aegis: Community Ministries and Neighborhood Organizations, Presbyterian AIDS Network, Presbyterians Affirming Reproductive Options, Presbyterian Association of Specialized Pastoral Ministries, Presbyterians for Disability Concerns, Presbyterian Health Network, Presbyterian Network on Alcohol and Other Drug Abuse, and Presbyterian Serious Mental Illness Network. Membership: $35/year (individual); $100-250/year (organization).

Meetings/Conferences:
Biennial Meetings: Uneven years

Publications:
Newsletter. q.

Pressure Sensitive Tape Council *(1953)*
P.O. Box 609
Northbrook, IL 60062
Tel: (847)562-2630 *Fax:* (847)562-2631
Toll Free: (877)523 - 7782
E-Mail: info@pstc.org
Web Site: www.pstc.org
Members: 25 companies
Staff: 3
Annual Budget: $500-1,000,000
Executive Vice President: Glen R. Anderson
E-Mail: info@pstc.org

Historical Note
Members are manufacturers of pressure sensitive tape located in North America. Membership: dues based on volume of tape sales.

Publications:
Pressure Sensitive Adhesive Tapes: A Guide.
Pressure Sensitive Tape Products Directory. a.
Technical Seminar Proceedings. a.
Test Methods For Pressure Sensitive Adhesive Tape. q.

Pressure Vessel Manufacturers Association *(1975)*
Eight S. Michigan Ave., Suite 1000
Chicago, IL 60603
Tel: (312)456-5590 *Fax:* (312)580-0165
E-Mail: pvma@gss.net
Web Site: www.pvma.org
Members: 31 companies
Staff: 2
Annual Budget: $50-100,000
Executive Director: August L. Sisco

Historical Note
Members are manufacturers and suppliers for the pressure vessel fabricating industry. Membership: $1,500-4,500/year (based on sales).

Meetings/Conferences:
Annual Meetings: Spring

Pressure Washer Manufacturers Association *(1997)*
1300 Sumner Ave.
Cleveland, OH 44115-2851
Tel: (216)241-7333 *Fax:* (216)241-0105
E-Mail: pwma@pwma.org
Web Site: www.pwma.org
Members: 2 companies
Staff: 3
Annual Budget: $50-100,000
Executive Director: John H. Addington

Prevent Blindness America *(1908)*
211 W. Wacker Dr., Suite 1700
Chicago, IL 60606
Tel: (312)363-6001 *Fax:* (312)363-6052
Toll Free: (800)331 - 2020
E-Mail: info@preventblindness.org
Web Site: www.preventblindness.org
Members: 18928individualsandcompanies
Staff: 125
Annual Budget: $2-5,000,000
Director, Media Relations: Sarah Hecker
President and Chief Executive Officer: Hugh Parry
Senior Vice President and Chief Financial Officer: Gloria Bozans
Senior Vice President: Daniel D. Garrett
Director, Media Relations: Sarah Hecker

Historical Note
Founded in 1908, Prevent Blindness America is the nation's leading volunteer eye health and safety organization dedicated to fighting blindness and saving sight. Formerly known as National Society to Prevent Blindess; assumed current name in 2004. BPA focuses on promoting a continuum of vision care, and touches the lives of million of people each year through public and professional education, certified vision screening training, community and patient service programs and research. These services are made possible through the generous support of the American public. Together with a network of affiliates, division and chapters, PBA is committed to eliminating preventable blindness in America.

Meetings/Conferences:
Annual Meetings: Fall/400

Publications:
Catalogue of Publications. bi-a.
Prevent Blindness News. q.
Annual Report. a.

Preventive Cardiovascular Nurses Association *(1993)*
613 Williamson St., Suite 205
Madison, WI 53703
Tel: (608)250-2440 *Fax:* (608)250-2410
E-Mail: info@pcna.net
Web Site: www.pcna.net
Members: 1500 individuals
Staff: 4
Annual Budget: $500-1,000,000
Executive Director: Susan Koob, MPA
E-Mail: skoob@pcna.net
Director, Membership: Carmen Hellenbrand
Planner, Meetings: Stacey Phelps

Historical Note
Fopunded as Lipid Nurse Task Force; assumed its current name in 2000. PCNA is committed to developing and promoting the role of nurses in the management of patients for greater cardiovascular health. Membership: $60/year (individual).

Meetings/Conferences:
Annual Meetings: Fall

Publications:
The Bulletin (email newsletter). m. adv.
Membership Directory. a.
Journal of Cardiovascular Nursing. a.

Print Council of America *(1956)*
Spencer Museum of Art
University of Kansas
Lawrence, KS 66045
Tel: (785)864-4710 *Fax:* (785)864-3112
Web Site: www.printcouncil.org
Members: 200 individuals
Annual Budget: under $10,000
Project Coordinator: Stephen Goddard

Historical Note
Professional organization of museum curators of prints, drawings, and photographs. Has no paid officers or full-time staff. Membership: $40/year.

Meetings/Conferences:
Annual Meetings: Spring

Publications:
Newsletter. a.

Print Information Center

Historical Note
A special industry group of Printing Industries of America.

PrintImage International *(1975)*

2250 E. Devon Ave., Suite 245
Des Plaines, IL 60018
Tel: (847)298-8680 *Fax:* (847)298-8705
Toll Free: (800)234 - 0040
E-Mail: info@printimage.org
Web Site: www.printimage.org
Members: 1000 companies
Staff: 2
Annual Budget: $1-2,000,000
President: Steven D. Johnson
Vice President: Christina Vargas

Historical Note
Founded in 1975 as National Association of Quick Printers (NAQP); assumed its current name in 1998. PrintImage International furthers the business of quick printers, copy shops, and small format commercial printers. Also welcomes manufacturers and suppliers of equipment and consumables, trade publications, and consultants to the quick print industry. Membership: $465-969/year.

Meetings/Conferences:
Semi-Annual Meetings: Winter/Fall

Publications:
Special Interest Group Newsletter (Sales & Marketing Group). bi-m.
Special Interest Group Newsletter (Mailing Services Group). bi-m.
PrintImage Network Newsletter. m. adv.
Special Interest Group Newsletter (Digital Imaging Applications Network). m.

Printing Brokerage/Buyers Association International *(1985)*

P.O. Box 744
Palm Beach, FL 33480
Tel: (561)585-7141 *Fax:* (561)845-7130
Toll Free: (877)585 - 7141
E-Mail: info@pbbai.org
Web Site: www.pbbai.net
Members: 1000 individuals
Staff: 3
Annual Budget: $1-2,000,000
President and Chief Financial Officer: Merry Francen
E-Mail: info@pbbai.org

Historical Note
Formerly (1993) Printing Brokerage Association. PBBA promotes business relationships between brokers, buying groups, manufacturers and related companies in the printing industry; sets standards and codes of ethical conduct and acts as a source of information and referral. Membership: $595/year (individual); $1650/year (organization).

Meetings/Conferences:
Annual Meetings: Spring

Publications:
The Law V. Printing. a.
Broker-Age. q. adv.
Directory and Sourcebook. a. adv.
Hot Markets Survey. a.
Printing Markets Census. a.

Printing Industries of America *(1887)*

200 Deer Run Road
Sewickley, PA 15143
Tel: (412)741-6860 *Fax:* (412)741-2311
Toll Free: (800)910 - 4283
E-Mail: piagaft@piagatf.org
Web Site: www.gain.net
Members: 13000 companies
Staff: 45
Annual Budget: $10-25,000,000
President and Chief Executive Officer: Michael Makin
E-Mail: mmakin@piagatf.org
Executive Vice President: Mary Garnett
E-Mail: mgarnett@piagatf.org
Director, Human Resources: Jim Kyger
E-Mail: jkyger@piagatf.org
Director, Marketing: Nancy Shafranski-Campobello
E-Mail: ncampobelloe@piagatf.org
Chief Financial Officer: Nicholas G. Stratigos
Administrator, Database: Kenneth Williams
E-Mail: kwilliams@piagatf.org

Historical Note
The umbrella organization of the graphic arts industry. PIA is a federation of national, regional, state, and city associations incorporated under the laws of the District of Columbia. Established as United Typothetae of America; became Printing Industry of America in 1945 and assumed its present name in 1965. Sections include Binding Industries of America, Graphic Arts Marketing Information Service, International Thermographers Association, Label Printing Industries of America, Magazine Printers Section, Non-Heatset Web Section, Printing Industry Financial Executives, Print Information Center, and Web Offset Association. Supports the Printing Industries of America Political Action Committee (PRINT-PAC). Has an annual budget of approximately $12.0 million.

Meetings/Conferences:
Annual Meetings: Fall

Publications:
Vision 21 Study.
Gate World.
Print Market Atlas.
PIA Ratios.
Benchmark Technologies.
Printer's Resource Catalog.
The Managment Portfolio. m.

Printing Industry Credit Executives *(1977)*

80 Broad St., Fifth Floor
New York, NY 10004
Tel: (212)964-8600 *Fax:* (212)964-0527
Toll Free: (866)964 - 8600
E-Mail: info@pice.com
Web Site: www.pice.com
Members: 125 individuals
Staff: 4
Annual Budget: $100-250,000
Administrator: Lee Berkowitz

Historical Note
Membership: $900/year (organization).

Meetings/Conferences:
Semi-annual Meetings: March/September
2007 – St. Louis, MO/Sept. 18-20

Publications:
Price Update Newsletter. semi-a.

Printing Industry Financial Executives

Historical Note
A special industry group of Printing Industries of America.

Private Art Dealers Association *(1990)*

P.O. Box 872, Lenox Hill Station
New York, NY 10021
Tel: (212)572-0772 *Fax:* (212)572-8398
E-Mail: pada99@msn.com
Web Site: www.pada.net
Members: 60 individuals
Administrator: Daisy Walker

Historical Note
PADA represents professional art dealers in the private market. Services include appraisals for estate purposes and donations. Membership (by invitiation only): $650/year (individual).

Publications:
Directory. a.

Private Label Manufacturers Association *(1979)*

369 Lexington Ave., Third Floor
New York, NY 10017
Tel: (212)972-3131 *Fax:* (212)983-1382
E-Mail: info@plma.com
Web Site: www.plma.com
Members: 2500 companies
Staff: 45
Annual Budget: $5-10,000,000
President: Brian Sharoff
Vice President, Administration: Myra Rosen

Historical Note
Promotes the purchase of private label or store brand products by consumers. Has an annual budget of approximately $6 million.

Publications:
Newsletter. q.

Process Equipment Manufacturers' Association *(1960)*

201 Park Washington Ct.
Falls Church, VA 22046
Tel: (703)538-1796 *Fax:* (703)241-5603
E-Mail: info@pemanent.org
Web Site: www.pemanet.org
Members: 50 companies
Staff: 12
Annual Budget: $100-250,000
Management Counsel: Harry W. Buzzerd, Jr. CAE
Manager, Meetings and Travel: Judith O. Buzzerd
Executive Director: Sue Denston

Historical Note
Companies engaged in the manufacture and supply of equipment for food, chemical, pulp and paper, water and wastewater processing, air pollution control, liquids-solids separation, etc.

Meetings/Conferences:
Biennial: Odd years-February
2007 – Tucson, AZ(Loews)/Feb. 28-March 4/90

Publications:
PEMA Press (online). bi-m.

Produce Marketing Association *(1949)*

1500 Casho Mill Rd.
P.O. Box 6036
Newark, DE 19714-6036
Tel: (302)738-7100 *Fax:* (302)731-2409
E-Mail: pma@mail.pma.com
Web Site: www.pma.com
Members: 2100 companies & individuals
Staff: 78
Annual Budget: $10-25,000,000
President: Bryan E. Silbermann, CAE
Senior Vice President, Industry Products and Services: Lorna Christie
Senior Vice President, Association Services: Duane Eaton, CAE

Historical Note
Founde in 1949 as Produce Prepackaging Association; became Produce Packaging Association in 1956, Produce Packaging and Marketing Association in 1967, and assumed its current name in 1971. Members are companies, corporations, organizations, or individuals engaged in any facet of marketing fresh produce and floral products, or providing equipment, supplies, transportation, or other services to the fresh produce and floral industry. Sponsors and supports the Produce for Better Health Foundation.

Meetings/Conferences:
2007 – Houston, TX/Oct. 12-15

Publications:
Floraline.
PMA Floral Marketing Directory and Buyer's Guide. a. adv.
PMA Membership Directory. a. adv.
Freshline. m.

Producer's Guild of America *(1950)*

8530 Wilshire Blvd., Suite 450
Beverly Hills, CA 90211
Tel: (310)358-9020 *Fax:* (310)358-9520
E-Mail: info@producersguild.org
Web Site: www.producersguild.org
Members: 2600 individuals
Staff: 6
Annual Budget: $2-5,000,000
Executive Director: Vance Van Petten
Director, Communications: Chris Green
Director, Member Services: Kyle Katz
Director, Operations: Audra Whaley

Historical Note
Formerly (1967) Screen Producers Guild. Members are members of the "producing team" (from Producers

to Production Coordinators) of motion pictures, television and new media. Membership: Producers Council $300/year; AP Council $150/year (individual); New Media Council $300/year.

Publications:
PGA Networker. q. adv.
"Produced by" Magazine. q. adv.

Product Development and Management Association *(1976)*
15000 Commerce Pkwy., Suite C
Mt. Laurel, NJ 08054
Tel: (856)439-9052 *Fax:* (856)439-0525
Toll Free: (800)232 - 5241
E-Mail: pdma@pdma.org
Web Site: www.pdma.org
Members: 2600 individuals
Staff: 3
Annual Budget: $500-1,000,000
Chief Executive Officer: Robin Karol

Historical Note
PDMA is an international association designed to serve people with a professional interest in improving the management of product innovation. Membership: $225/year or $400/2 years (regular/for profit); $135/year or $250/2years (academic/nonprofit).

Publications:
Journal of Product Innovation Management. 6/year.
Visions Magazine. q.

Production and Operations Management Society *(1989)*
11200 S.W. Eighth St., University Park, RB 250
Miami, FL 33199
Tel: (305)348-3248 *Fax:* (305)348-6890
E-Mail: poms@fiu.edu
Web Site: www.poms.org
Members: 1200 individuals
Annual Budget: $100-250,000
Executive Director: Sushil K. Gupta, Ph.D.
E-Mail: poms@fiu.edu

Historical Note
POMS members are professionals and academics with an interest in production and operations management. Membership: $95/year (individual).

Publications:
Production and Operations Management Journal. q.
POM Chronicle Newsletter. q.

Production Engine Remanufacturers Association *(1946)*
4215 Lafayette Center Dr., Suite Three
Chantilly, VA 20151-1243
Tel: (703)968-2772 Ext: 103 *Fax:* (703)968-2878
E-Mail: gager@bayreman.com
Web Site: www.pera.org
Members: 150 companies
Staff: 2
Annual Budget: $250-500,000
Executive Vice President: William C. Gager

Historical Note
Formerly (1970) Western Engine Rebuilders Association and (1973) Production Engine Rebuilders Association. Members are manufacturers, remanufacturers and parts suppliers to the production line combustion engine industry. Membership: $800/year.

Meetings/Conferences:
Annual Meetings: Fall/500

Publications:
Enginews (Electronic Newsletter). m.
Membership Directory. a. adv.
Engine Application & Identification Catalog. a.

Production Equipment Rental Association *(1992)*
P.O. Box 55515
Sherman Oaks, CA 91413-0515
Tel: (818)906-2467 *Fax:* (818)906-1720
E-Mail: eclare@pera.ws
Web Site: www.productionequipment.com
Members: 200 companies
Staff: 1
Annual Budget: $50-100,000
Executive Director: Edwin S. Clare
E-Mail: eclare@pera.ws

Historical Note
Members are rental companies who supply production equipment to the entertainment industry. Membership is international, with roughly half concentrated in southern California. Membership: $265-1,600/year (company).

Meetings/Conferences:
Annual Meetings: None held.

Publications:
PERA Scope. m.
Rental Resource Guide. a.

Professional Landscape Network *(1961)*

Historical Note
In 2004, ALCA announced plans to merge with Professional Lawn Care Association of America.

Professional Airways Systems Specialists *(1977)*

Historical Note
PASS is a division of the National Marine Engineers Beneficial Association/National Maritime Union of America.

Professional and Organizational Development Network in Higher Education *(1975)*
P.O. Box 3318
Nederland, CO 80466
Tel: (303)258-9521 *Fax:* (303)258-7377
E-Mail: podnetwork@podweb.org
Web Site: www.podnetwork.org
Members: 1500 individuals
Staff: 2
Annual Budget: $100-250,000
Executive Director: Hoag Holmgren

Historical Note
POD Network members are academics and other educational professionals with an interest in the improvement of teaching and learning. Membership: $72/year (individual); $85/year (individual outside U.S., Mexico and Canada); $180/year (institution); $215/year (institution outside the U.S., Mexico and Canada).

Meetings/Conferences:
Annual Meetings: Fall

Publications:
Essays on Teaching Excellence. 8/year.
To Improve the Academy (monograph). a.

Professional and Technical Consultants Association *(1975)*
543 Vista Mar Ave.
Pacifica, CA 94044
Tel: (408)971-5902 *Fax:* (650)359-3089
Toll Free: (800)747 - 2822
E-Mail: info@patca.org
Web Site: www.patca.org
Members: 400 individuals
Annual Budget: $100-250,000
Executive Director: Jim Saunders
E-Mail: info@patca.org

Historical Note
PATCA members are independent technical consultants and small consulting firms. Members are concentrated in northern California. Membership: $395/year.

Publications:
PATCA Journal. q.
PATCA Newsletter. m. adv.
PATCA Rate Survey. bien.

Professional Apparel Association *(1980)*
994 Old Eagle School Rd., Suite 1019
Wayne, PA 19087-1866
Tel: (610)971-4850 *Fax:* (610)971-4859
Toll Free: (800)722 - 7712
E-Mail: info@proapparel.com
Web Site: www.proapparel.com
Members: 30 companies
Staff: 2
Annual Budget: $250-500,000
Director, Marketing: Hope Silverman
E-Mail: info@proapparel.com

Historical Note
PAA is a trade association representing manufacturers of uniforms, shoes and accessories for the medical and hospitality industries. Members also manufacture career apparel. Membership: $1,500-$5,000/year.

Meetings/Conferences:
Annual Meetings: Bi-Annual, Fall

Publications:
Uniformer Newsletter. q.

Professional Association for Childhood Education *(1955)*
114 Sansome St., Suite 300
San Francisco, CA 94104
Tel: (415)749-6851 *Fax:* (415)397-7223
Toll Free: (800)924 - 2460
E-Mail: info@pacenet.org
Web Site: www.pacenet.org
Members: 800 child care centers
Staff: 3
Annual Budget: $100-250,000
Executive Director: Gina Aylion

Meetings/Conferences:
Semi-Annual Meetings: Spring and Fall

Publications:
PACESETTER. q. adv.

Professional Association of Christian Educators *(1959)*
P.O. Box 140284
Dallas, TX 75214
Tel: (214)841-3566 *Fax:* (214)841-3773
Toll Free: (800)829 - 9410
E-Mail: jharris@dts.edu
Web Site: www.PACEinc.org
Members: 200 individuals
Staff: 10
Annual Budget: $100-250,000
President: Dr. Michael S. Lawson
E-Mail: jharris@dts.edu

Historical Note
Formerly (1959) National Association of Directors of Christian Education. PACE members are Christian educators. PACE represents church-based associate ministries; its mission is to promote and strengthen Christian education around the world. Membership: $75/year.

Professional Association of Custom Clothiers *(1991)*
7722 Old Woodstock Lane
Ellicott City, MD 21043
Tel: (877)755-0303 *Fax:* (410)379-5698
E-Mail: info@paccprofessionals.org
Web Site: www.paccprofessionals.org
Members: 750 individuals
Annual Budget: $100-250,000
National Administrator: Doralee Billings
E-Mail: admin@paccprofessionals.org

Historical Note
PACC serves the needs of professionals in a home-based business or commercial setting through elevating the professional status of custom clothiers, setting professional standards, keeping members informed of industry developments, offering opportunities for continuing education and promoting the general use of custom clothing services. Membership: $65/year (individual).

Meetings/Conferences:
Annual Meetings: Spring

Publications:
PACC News. q. adv.

Professional Association of Diving Instructors *(1966)*
30151 Tomas St.
Rancho Santa Margarita, CA 92688-2125
Tel: (949)858-7234 *Fax:* (949)267-1267
Toll Free: (800)729 - 7234
E-Mail: webmaster@padi.com
Web Site: www.padi.com
Members: 80000 individuals
Staff: 220
Annual Budget: $25-50,000,000
Senior Vice President: Brian P. Cronin

Historical Note
PADI is a professional diving organization that certifies scuba diving instructors. Almost 100,000 PADI instructor members and 4,500 dive store members (PADI Dive Centers) conduct training in over 175 countries. PADI provides educational/training materials and retail support to its members.

Meetings/Conferences:
Semi-Annual Meetings:

Publications:
Fellow Diver Newsletter. m. adv.
Sport Diver Magazine. m. adv.
Undersea Journal. q. adv.

Professional Association of Health Care Office Management *(1988)*

461 E. Ten Mile Rd.
Pensacola, FL 32534-9712
Tel: (850)474-9460 *Fax:* (850)474-6352
Toll Free: (800)451 - 9311
E-Mail: pahcom@pahcom.com
Web Site: www.pahcom.com
Members: 3300 individuals
Staff: 8
Annual Budget: $500-1,000,000
Executive Director: Roger Landers
E-Mail: roger@pahcom.com
Special Projects and Web Services: Carol Potter
E-Mail: carol@pahcom.com
Manager, Business: Karen Williams
E-Mail: karen@pahcom.com

Historical Note
PAHCOM was founded in January 1988 as the Professional Association of Health Care Office Managers, with the explicit purpose of providing a networking system to managers of medical practices. Assumed its current name in 2002. Offers a certification exam leading to the designation CCM. Membership: $125/year (individual); $250/year (company).

Meetings/Conferences:
Annual Meetings: September

Publications:
Medical Office Management Newsletter. bi-m. adv.

Professional Association of Innkeepers International *(1988)*

207 White Horse Pike
Hadden Heights, NJ 08035
Tel: (856)310-1102 *Fax:* (856)310-1105
Toll Free: (800)468 - 7244
E-Mail: membership@paii.org
Web Site: www.paii.org
Members: 3500 individuals
Staff: 6
Annual Budget: $500-1,000,000
Chief Executive Officer: Pamela Horovitz

Historical Note
North American trade association for bed and breakfast/country inns. Membership: $189-549/year.

Publications:
Industry Study of Bed and Breakfast and Country Inns. bien.
Innkeeping, Newsletter. m. adv.

Professional Association of Resume Writers and Career Coaches *(1990)*

1388 Brightwaters Blvd. NE
St. Petersburg, FL 33704
Tel: (727)821-2274 *Fax:* (727)894-1277
Toll Free: (800)822 - 7279
E-Mail: parwhq@aol.com
Web Site: www.parw.com
Members: 950 companies
Staff: 2
Annual Budget: $250-500,000
Executive Director: Frank X. Fox
E-Mail: parwhq@aol.com

Historical Note
PARW members are companies offering resume writing services. Membership: $150/year.

Publications:
Membership Directory (online).
Spotlight. m.

Professional Association of Volleyball Officials

P.O. Box 780
Oxford, KS 67119
Toll Free: (888)791 - 2074
Web Site: www.pavo.org
Members: 1900 individuals
Staff: 2
Annual Budget: $250-500,000
Executive Director: Marcia Alterman
E-Mail: rules.interpreter@pavo.org
Assistant, Program: Miki Kennedy
E-Mail: pavo@pavo.org

Historical Note
Founded as the Affiliated Boards of Officials, assumed its present name in 1999. Certifies and trains officials for girls' and women's volleyball programs and promotes the involvement of women in the governing bodies of other sport officiating groups. Formerly (1992) a sub-section of National Association for Girls and Women in Sport. Membership: $35/year.

Publications:
The Official Word. q.

Professional AudioVideo Retailers Association *(1979)*

Historical Note
Merged with Consumer Electronics Association in 2004.

Professional Aviation Maintenance Association *(1972)*

717 Princess St.
Alexandria, VA 22314
Tel: (703)683-3171 *Fax:* (703)683-0018
Toll Free: (866)865 - PAMA
E-Mail: hq@pama.org
Web Site: www.pama.org
Members: 4500 individuals
Staff: 6
Annual Budget: $500-1,000,000
President: Brian Finnegan
E-Mail: hq@pama.org
Director, Administration: Carol Montoya

Historical Note
Members are technicians holding an A&P (Airframe and Power Plant) license, aviation maintenance companies and institutions. Membership: $20/year (student and active military); $49/year (individual); $650/year (company); $200/year (education).

Meetings/Conferences:
Annual Meetings: March

Publications:
PAMA Mx in AMT Magazine. q. adv.

Professional Bail Agents of the United States *(1981)*

1301 Pennsylvania Ave. NW, Suite 925
Washington, DC 20004
Tel: (202)783-4120 *Fax:* (202)783-4125
Toll Free: (800)883 - 7287
E-Mail: info@pbus.com
Web Site: www.pbus.com
Members: 1350 individuals
Staff: 3
Annual Budget: $100-250,000
Executive Director: Stephen H. Kreimer
Planner, Meetings: Kathie Bauerle-Berg

Historical Note
PBUS promotes the bail bond industry throughout the United States, educates members of changes, serves as a forum for the interchange of ideas, and serves as industry spokesman. Membership: $300/year (individual), $675/year (organization/company).

Publications:
Bail Agent's Prespective Magazine. q. adv.

Professional Baseball Athletic Trainers Society *(1983)*

400 Colony Square, Suite 1750
Atlanta, GA 30361
Tel: (404)875-4000 *Fax:* (404)892-8560
E-Mail: rmallernee@mallernee-branch.com
Web Site: www.pbats.com
Members: 60 individuals
Annual Budget: $50-100,000
General Counsel: Rollin E. Mallernee, II

Historical Note
A satellite organization of the National Athletic Trainers Association. PBATS is professional society composed of all athletic trainers in major league baseball. Membership: $100/year.

Meetings/Conferences:
Annual Meetings: First weekend in Dec., in conjunction with Baseball Winter Meetings

Publications:
Media Guide. a.
PBATS Newsletter. a.

Professional Basketball Writers' Association *(1972)*

P.O. Box 4744
Baltimore, MD 21211
Tel: (410)523-0635
E-Mail: richdubroff@aol.com
Members: 150 individuals
Staff: 1
Annual Budget: under $10,000
Treasuer: Rich Dubroff
E-Mail: richdubroff@aol.com

Historical Note
Members are sports editors and reporters who cover professional basketball. Membership: $20/year.

Meetings/Conferences:
Annual Meetings: Meetings held during the NBA All Star Game and the NBA Finals.

Professional Beauty Association *(1904)*

15825 N. 71st St., Suite 100
Scottsdale, AZ 85254
Tel: (480)281-0424 *Fax:* (480)905-0708
Toll Free: (800)468 - 2274 Ext:
Web Site: www.probeautyassociation.org
Members: 1400 firms
Staff: 21
Annual Budget: $2-5,000,000
Executive Director: Steve Sleeper
Senior Director, Member Services: Maya Brand
Senior Director, Marketing and Creative Services: Michael Toth

Historical Note
Formerly (1904) the Barber Supply Dealers of America and then the Beauty and Barber Supply Institute; assumed current name in 2004. Maximizes the potential of the professional salon industry. Membership: $400/year.

Meetings/Conferences:
Semi-annual Meetings: Winter and Summer

Professional Bowlers Association of America *(1958)*

719 Second Ave., Suite 701
Seattle, WA 98104
Tel: (206)332-9688 *Fax:* (206)332-9722
E-Mail: info@pba.com
Web Site: www.pba.com
Members: 3800 individuals
Staff: 37
Annual Budget: $5-10,000,000
Commissioner and Chief Executive Officer: Fred Schreyer
Vice President, Brand Communications: Lisa Gil
E-Mail: lisa.gil@pba.com

Historical Note
Members must have a minimum average of 200 established for 66 or more games per season for the 2 most recent seasons prior to applying for membership. Hosts regional, national, and senior tournaments throughout the year. Has an annual budget of approximately $9.5 million. Membership: $200/year (regional membership).

Publications:
Tournament Annual. a. adv.
Newsletter. q.
Press-Radio-TV Guide. a.
Senior Tour Program. a.

Professional Communications Society *(1957)*

Historical Note
A technical society of the Institute of Electrical and Electronics Engineers (IEEE). Membership in the Society, open only to IEEE members, includes subscription to a technical periodical in the field published by IEEE. All administrative support is provided by IEEE.

Professional Construction Estimators Association of America *(1956)*

P.O. Box 680336
Charlotte, NC 28216

Tel: (704)987-9978 *Fax:* (704)987-9979
Toll Free: (877)521 - 7232
E-Mail: pcea@pcea.org
Web Site: www.pcea.org
Members: 800 individuals
Staff: 1
Annual Budget: $100-250,000
Office Manager: Kim Ellis

Historical Note

PCEA's goal is to promote construction estimating as a profession by upholding the code of ethics, expanding public awareness through charity projects and supporting education programs and scholarships.

Meetings/Conferences:

Annual Meetings: Spring

Publications:

PCEA Nat'l Directory. a. adv.
Nat'l Estimator. q.

Professional Convention Management Association *(1958)*

2301 S. Lake Shore Dr., Suite 1001
Chicago, IL 60616-1419
Tel: (312)423-7267 *Fax:* (312)423-7222
Toll Free: (877)827 - 7262
Web Site: www.pcma.org
Members: 5700 individuals
Staff: 40
Annual Budget: $10-25,000,000
President and Chief Executive Officer: Deborah Sexton, CAE
Chief Financial Officer: Robert Cowan, CAE
Executive Vice President: Sian Moynihan
Vice President, Education: John Nawn
Vice President, Meetings and Events: Kelly Peacy

Historical Note

Incorporated in Illinois, February 28, 1958. Membership consists of convention managers, CEOs, meeting planners, and suppliers representing 1,000 organizations. Member of the Center for Exhibition Industry Research. Membership: $350-475/year.

Meetings/Conferences:

Annual Meetings: Winter
2007 - Toronto, ON, Canada/Jan. 7-10/3000
2008 - Seattle, WA/Jan. 13-16/3000
2009 - New Orleans, LA/Jan. 11-14/3000

Publications:

Convene. 11/yr. adv.

Professional Currency Dealers Association *(1985)*

P.O. Box 7157
Westchester, IL 60154
Tel: (630)889-8207
E-Mail: nge3@comcast.net
Web Site: www.pcdaonline.com
Members: 75 individuals
Staff: 1
Annual Budget: $25-50,000
Secretary: James A. Simek
E-Mail: nge3@comcast.net

Historical Note

A trade association composed of the leading dealers in rare currency, the PCDA's primary objective is to promote interest in the collecting of rare currency. Membership: $250/year.

Meetings/Conferences:

Annual Meetings: Fall

Professional Engineers in Private Practice *(1955)*

1420 King St.
Alexandria, VA 22314-2794
Tel: (703)684-2862 *Fax:* (703)836-4875
Web Site: www.nspe.org/pepp/home.asp
Members: 24000 individuals
Staff: 2
Annual Budget: $1-2,000,000

Historical Note

Formed in 1955 as an autonomous division of the National Society of Professional Engineers to address concerns of individual consulting professional engineers; reorganized in 1965 with independent dues structure. Provides information and lobbying efforts on practice management, professional liability, and career development interests of members.

Publications:

PEPP Talk. m. adv.

Professional Football Athletic Trainers Society *(1982)*

400 Colony Square, Suite 1750
Atlanta, GA 30361
Tel: (404)875-4000 Ext: 1 *Fax:* (404)892-8560
Web Site: www.pfats.com
Members: 120 individuals
Annual Budget: $50-100,000
General Counsel: Rollin E. Mallernee, II

Historical Note

An affiliate organization of the National Athletic Trainers Association. PFATS is a professional society composed of all the athletic trainers in the NFL. Promotes the professional interests of NFL athletic trainers.

Meetings/Conferences:

Annual Meetings: February, in conjuction with NFL Combine in Indianapolis, IN.

Publications:

Pro Football Athletic Trainer. a.

Professional Football Writers of America *(1962)*

11345 Frontage Ave.
Maryland Heights, MO 63043
Tel: (314)453-0755
Web Site: www.pfwa.org
Members: 400 individuals
Annual Budget: $10-25,000
Secretary-Treasurer: Howard Balzer

Historical Note

Members are sportswriters and columnists who cover professional football regularly. Promotes good working relationships between writers and leagues, and clubs and players' associations. Membership: $50/year.

Meetings/Conferences:

Annual Meetings: Friday preceding Super Bowl.

Publications:

Newsletter. bi-m.

Professional Fraternity Association *(1977)*

345 N. Charles St., Third Floor
Baltimore, MD 21201
Tel: (410)347-3118 *Fax:* (410)347-3119
Toll Free: (888)771 - 4732
E-Mail: info@pad.org
Web Site: www.profraternity.org
Members: 37 fraternities & sororities
Staff: 1
Annual Budget: $25-50,000
Executive Director: Andrew Sagan
E-Mail: andrew@pad.org

Historical Note

Established October 22, 1977, through a merger of the Professional Panhellenic Association (established 1925) and the Professional Interfraternity Conference (established 1928). Membership: $200/year (organization).

Publications:

PFA Today. 4-6/year.
Membership Directory. a.

Professional Golfers Association of America *(1916)*

P.O. Box 109601
Palm Beach Gardens, FL 33410-9601
Tel: (561)624-8400 *Fax:* (561)624-8448
Web Site: www.pga.com
Members: 24000 individuals
Staff: 115
Annual Budget: $2-5,000,000
Director, Communications and Publications: Kelly Elbin
Senior Director, Education: Chris Hunkler
Chief Executive Officer: Joe Steranka

Historical Note

Founded in New York City in 1916. Runs local, national and international tournaments. Most members are golf professionals managing golf courses.

Publications:

PGA Magazine. m. adv.

Professional Grounds Management Society *(1911)*

720 Light St.
Baltimore, MD 21230-3816
Tel: (410)752-3318 *Fax:* (410)752-8295
Toll Free: (800)609 - 7467
E-Mail: pgms@assnhqtrs.com
Web Site: www.pgms.org
Members: 1500 individuals
Annual Budget: $250-500,000
Executive Director: Thomas C. Shaner, CAE

Historical Note

Formerly (1971) National Association of Professional Gardeners. Members are professionals involved in the care and maintenance of schools, universities, parks, office parks, shopping malls, municipalities, sports grounds, etc. Awards the CGM (Certified Grounds Manager) and CGK (Certified Grounds Keepers) designation. Membership: $150/year (individual); $400/year (organization/company).

Meetings/Conferences:

Annual Meetings: Fall

Publications:

PGMS Membership Directory. a. adv.
Grounds Management Forum. bi-m. adv.
Grounds Maintenance Estimating Guidelines. bi-a.
Grounds Maintenance Management Guidelines. bi-a.
Grounds Management Forms and Job Descriptions Guide. bi-a.

Professional Handlers Association *(1926)*

17017 Norbrook Dr.
Olney, MD 20832
Tel: (301)924-0089
Web Site: www.phadoghandlers.com
Members: 250 individuals
Staff: 1
Executive Vice President: Kathleen Bowser

Historical Note

Members are individuals who show purebred dogs professionally as well as others interested in improving the stature of professional dog handling.

Publications:

Newsletter. q.

Professional Hockey Writers' Association *(1967)*

1480 Pleasant Valley Way, Suite 44
West Orange, NJ 07052
Tel: (973)669-8607
Members: 350 individuals
Annual Budget: under $10,000

Historical Note

Formerly (1971) National Hockey League Writers' Association. PHWA members are journalists covering the teams of the National Hockey League. Has no paid officers or full-time staff. Membership: $15/year (individual).

Publications:

PHWA Newsletter. q.

Professional Housing Management Association *(1973)*

154 Ft. Evans Road, NE
Leesburg, VA 20716
Tel: (703)771-1888 *Fax:* (703)771-0299
E-Mail: phmainfo@earthlink.net
Web Site: www.phma.com
Members: 3000 individuals
Staff: 4
Annual Budget: $1-2,000,000
Executive Director: Jon Moore

Historical Note

PHMA members are federal government employees, civilian or military, who are directly involved in the profession of housing management; or whose responsibility provides direct support to the field of housing management. Membership: $30/year.

Meetings/Conferences:

Annual Meetings: Winter

Publications:

Defense Communities. bi-m. adv.

Professional Insurance Communicators of America *(1955)*

P.O. Box 68700
Indianapolis, IN 46268

Tel: (317)875-5250 *Fax:* (317)879-8408
Web Site: www.pro-ins-coa.org
Members: 70 individuals
Staff: 1
Annual Budget: under $10,000
Secretary-Treasurer: Janet Wright
E-Mail: jwright@namic.org

Historical Note
Founded as the Mutual Insurance Council of Editors, it became the Mutual Insurance Communicators in 1969 and assumed its present name in 1981. An affiliate of the National Association of Mutual Insurance Companies. Members are editors of insurance company newsletters.

Meetings/Conferences:
Annual Meetings: Spring

Publications:
Communique. q.

Professional Insurance Marketing Association *(1975)*
6300 Ridgelea Pl., Suite 1008
Ft. Worth, TX 76116
Tel: (817)569-7462 *Fax:* (817)569-7461
Web Site: www.pima-assn.org
Members: 140 companies
Staff: 4
Annual Budget: $500-1,000,000
Chief Executive Officer: Mona Buckley
E-Mail: mona@pima-assn.org
Chief of Staff and Director, Membership Development: Gail Cannon
E-Mail: gail@pima-assn.org
Director, Communications: Ralph M. Gill

Historical Note
Formerly (1982) the Professional Independent Mass-Marketing Administrators and (1999) the Professional Insurance Mass-Marketing Administrators; assumed its present name in 1999. PIMA is the national association of leading third-party insurance administrators, carriers and allied business partners involved in association or affinity group marketing for all lines of insurance. The association was formed in 1975 to protect the interests of consumers and advance the professional quality of the independent mass marketer in business today. Membership dues for companies and agencies are based upon annual mass-marketed premium volume. Membership: $800 to $4,200/year (agency); $5,600 to $9,700/year (company); $200/year (employees of members agencies); $1,500/year (allied members).

Meetings/Conferences:
Semi-Annual Meetings:: Winter and Summer

Publications:
PIMA Membership Directory & Buyers' Resource Guide. a. adv.
PIMA News. q. adv.
PIMA-in-the-Loop. bi-m. adv.

Professional Landscape Network *(1979)*
950 Herndon Pkwy.
Suite 450
Herndon, VA 20170
Tel: (703)736-9666 *Fax:* (703)736-9668
Toll Free: (800)395 - 2522
E-Mail: plcaa@plcaa.org
Web Site: www.plcaa.org
Members: 4,000 firms
Staff: 26
Annual Budget: $1-2,000,000
Chief Operating Officer: Tanya Tolpegin
E-Mail: tanyatolpegin@landcarenetwork.org

Historical Note
PLANET emerged on January 1, 2005, when the Associated Landscape Contractors of America (ALCA) and the Professional Lawn Care Association of America (PLCAA) joined forces. Members are lawn care operators and manufacturers/suppliers of associated products. Membership: based on gross sales volume.

Meetings/Conferences:
Annual Meetings: Fall

Publications:
ProSource Newsletter. bi-m.

Professional Liability Agents Network *(1984)*
P.O. Box 1632
Monterey, CA 93942
Tel: (831)372-3706 *Fax:* (831)372-6647
Toll Free: (877)960 - 7526
E-Mail: info@plan.org
Web Site: www.plan.org
Members: 48 insurance agencies
Staff: 1
Executive Director: Tom Owens
E-Mail: info@plan.org

Historical Note
PLAN members are insurance agencies specializing in risk management and loss prevention programs for architects, engineers and environmental consultants.

Professional Liability Underwriting Society *(1986)*
5353 Wayzata Blvd., Suite 600
Minneapolis, MN 55416
Tel: (952)746-2580 *Fax:* (952)746-2599
Toll Free: (800)845 - 0778
Web Site: www.plusweb.org
Members: 6000 individuals
Staff: 9
Annual Budget: $2-5,000,000
Executive Director: Derek Hazeltine, CAE
Director, Operations: Scott A. Billey
Chapter and Events Planner: Diane Dukes
Director, Communications: Kimberly Holland
Director, Education: Deb Ropelewski, CPCU, AU, ARM, CPIW

Historical Note
Membership: $150/year (individual); $1,000/year (organization/company).

Meetings/Conferences:
Annual Meetings: Fall
2007 – Washington, DC/Nov. 7-9
2008 – San Francisco, CA/Nov. 12-14
2009 – Chicago, IL/Nov. 11-13
2010 – San Antonio, TX/Nov. 10-12
2011 – San Diego, CA/Nov. 1-3

Publications:
Resource Directory. a.
Monthly Newsletter. m.
Educational Program. a.

Professional Managers Association *(1981)*
P.O. Box 77235
Washington, DC 20013-0235
Tel: (202)874-1508 *Fax:* (202)874-1739
E-Mail: pmaoffice@aol.com
Web Site: www.promanager.org
Members: 2000
Staff: 5
Annual Budget: $100-250,000
National President and Executive Director: Tom Burger
E-Mail: pmaoffice@aol.com

Historical Note
Members are federal employees in management positions and management officials. Chapters established throughout the country. Membership: $65/year.

Publications:
The Public Manager. q.

Professional Numismatists Guild *(1955)*
3950 Concordia Ln.
Fallbrook, CA 92028
Tel: (760)728-1300 *Fax:* (760)728-8507
E-Mail: info@pngdealers.com
Web Site: www.pngdealers.com
Members: 300 individuals
Staff: 2
Annual Budget: $250-500,000
Executive Director: Robert Brueggeman
E-Mail: info@pngdealers.com

Historical Note
Members are individuals who have been full-time coin dealers for at least five years. Associate members have been full-time for 2 years. Promotes high standards of ethics in the hobby of numismatics. Affiliated with the American Numismatic Association and the American Numismatic Society Incorporated in 1955 as the Professional Numismatists Guild. Membership: $1,000/yr. (regular); $300/yr. (associate).

Meetings/Conferences:
Annual Meetings: Spring

Publications:
The Guild. bi-m. adv.
Membership Directory. a.

Professional Paddlesports Association *(1979)*
7432 Alban Station Blvd., Suite B-232
Springfield, VA 22150
Tel: (703)451-3864 *Fax:* (703)451-1015
Toll Free: (800)789 - 2202
E-Mail: paa@propaddle.com
Web Site: www.propaddle.com
Members: 450 companies
Staff: 4
Annual Budget: $100-250,000
Executive Director: Matt Menashes
E-Mail: matt@propaddle.com
Communications: Julie Phillips-Turner

Historical Note
Established as National Association of Canoe Liveries and Outfitters; assumed its current name in 1996. Incorporated in the state of Michigan. Promotes canoeing and related sports, works to preserve waterways for human-powered recreation, and protects the interests of professional outfitters and outfitting firms. Membership: $149-499/year.

Publications:
Paddler Magazine.
Pen and Paddle. m. adv.
Let's Go Paddling. a. adv.

Professional Photographers of America *(1880)*
229 Peachtree St. NE, Suite 2200
Atlanta, GA 30303
Tel: (404)522-8600 *Fax:* (404)614-6400
E-Mail: csc@ppa.com
Web Site: www.ppa.com
Members: 14000 individuals
Staff: 40
Annual Budget: $5-10,000,000
Chief Executive Officer: David Trust
Director, Membership, Copyright and Government Affairs: J. Alexander Hopper, CAE
Chief Financial Officer: Scott Kurkian

Historical Note
Professional society of portrait, commercial, wedding, industrial and specialized photographers and photographic artists. Grants the Master of Photography, Photographic Craftsman, Master of Electronic Imaging and Photographic Artist degrees in recognition of exceptional ability and service. Sponsors the Winona International School of Professional Photography. Formerly (1958) the Photographers' Association of America.

Meetings/Conferences:
Annual Meetings: Summer
2007 – San Antonio, TX(Convention Center)/Jan. 14-16

Publications:
Marketing Guide. q.
Photo Electronic Imaging. semi-m. adv.
PPA Today. m. adv.

Professional Picture Framers Association *(1971)*
3000 Picture Pl.
Jackson, MI 49201
Tel: (517)788-8100 *Fax:* (517)788-8371
E-Mail: ppfa@ppfa.com
Web Site: www.ppfa.com
Members: 3400 retailers, suppliers & instit.
Staff: 12
Annual Budget: $1-2,000,000
Secretary and Executive Director: Ted Fox

Historical Note
A section of Photo Marketing Association Internat'l, PPFA is a trade association of manufacturers, wholesalers, print publishers, importers and retailers selling art, framing, and related supplies. Sponsors an educational program and professional certification. Membership: $95-1800/year.

Publications:
Who's Who Directory. a. adv.
For Members Only newsletter. m. adv.

Professional Putters Association *(1959)*
6350 Quadrangle Dr., Suite 210
Chapel Hill, NC 27517
Tel: (919)493-9999

Toll Free: (866)788 - 8788
Web Site: www.proputters.com/
Members: 1117 individuals
Staff: 25
Annual Budget: $100-250,000
Executive Director: Jim Evans

Historical Note

Members are individuals over the age of 18 who compete in national putting tournaments as well as golf course owners, managers and suppliers. Membership: $20/year.

Publications:

Official Rules and Regulations of the PPA. a.
Facts and Membership. a.
Putt-Putt World. q.

Professional Reactor Operator Society *(1981)*

P.O. Box 484
Byron, IL 61010-0484
Tel: (815)234-8140
E-Mail: theprosoffice@nucpros.com
Web Site: http://nucpros.com
Members: 500 individuals
Annual Budget: $25-50,000
Manager: Mark Rasmussen
E-Mail: theprosoffice@nucpros.com

Historical Note

Members are operators of nuclear power facilities. Membership: $35/year (individual).

Meetings/Conferences:

Annual Meetings: Summer

Publications:

The Communicator. q. adv.

Professional Records and Information Services Management International *(1980)*

131 US 70
West Garner, NC 27529
Tel: (919)771-0657 *Fax:* (919)771-0457
Toll Free: (800)336 - 9793
E-Mail: staff@prismintl.org
Web Site: www.prismintl.org
Members: 500 individuals
Staff: 4
Annual Budget: $500-1,000,000
Executive Director: James Booth
E-Mail: jim@prismintl.org

Historical Note

PRISM International is a trade association providing educational and advocacy resources to promote smart records and information management solutions for its members and the business public.

Meetings/Conferences:

Annual Meetings: Spring

Publications:

In Focus. q.

Professional Retail Store Maintenance Association

14285 Midway Rd.
Suite 160
Addison, TX 75001
Tel: (972)231-9810 *Fax:* (972)231-4081
E-Mail: info@prsm.com
Web Site: www.prsm.com

Professional Rodeo Cowboys Association *(1936)*

101 ProRodeo Dr.
Colorado Springs, CO 80919
Tel: (719)593-8840 *Fax:* (719)548-4876
E-Mail: prca@prorodeo.com
Web Site: www.prorodeo.org
Members: 11375 individuals
Staff: 90
Annual Budget: $25-50,000,000
Commisioner: Troy Ellerman
Director, Rodeo Administration: Jim Nichols

Historical Note

Founded as Cowboys Turtle Association. Became Rodeo Cowboys Association in 1945 and Professional Rodeo Cowboys Association in 1975.

Publications:

Prorodeo Sports News. bi-m. adv.
Media Guide. a.

Professional School Photographers *(1951)*

Historical Note

A division of Photo Marketing Ass'n-Internat'l, which provides administrative support.

Professional Service Association *(1989)*

71 Columbia St.
Cohoes, NY 12047
Tel: (518)237-7777 *Fax:* (518)237-0418
Toll Free: (888)777 - 8851
E-Mail: psanet@compuserve.com
Web Site: www.psaworld.com
Members: 712 companies
Staff: 2
Annual Budget: $50-100,000
Executive Director: Ron Sawyer

Historical Note

PSA members are companies servicing and repairing electonics and appliances. Membership: $75/year.

Publications:

PSA Update. m. adv.
Professional Service Ass'n News. q. adv.

Professional Services Council *(1972)*

2101 Wilson Blvd., Suite 750
Arlington, VA 22201
Tel: (703)875-8059 *Fax:* (703)875-8922
Web Site: www.pscouncil.org
Members: 196 companies, 4 associations
Staff: 10
Annual Budget: $1-2,000,000
President: Stan Z. Soloway
Senior Vice President and Counsel: Alan L. Chvotkin
Director, Finance: Robert Piening

Historical Note

Formerly (1972) the National Council of Professional Services Firms; assumed its current name in 1982. Members are companies that provide professional and technical services to the government and private industry. Sponsors and supports the Professional Services Council Political Action Committee. Membership: $100/year (trade associations); $750-33,000/year (company); $2,650-5,300/year (associate).

Meetings/Conferences:

Annual Meetings: Fall

Publications:

Executive Report. m.

Professional Services Management Association *(1975)*

99 Canal Center Plaza, Suite 330
Alexandria, VA 22314
Tel: (703)739-0277 *Fax:* (703)549-2498
Toll Free: (866)739 - 0277
Web Site: www.psmanet.org
Members: 350 individuals
Staff: 12
Annual Budget: $100-250,000
Chief Executive Officer: Ronald Worth, FSMPS

Historical Note

Members are business managers, owners and principals of professional service firms (i.e. engineering, architecture, landscape architecture, interior design, management consultants, etc.) seeking to promote the exchange of ideas and information and to establish guidelines in the field of professional service firm management. Membership: $450/year.

Meetings/Conferences:

Annual Meetings: Fall
2007 – Washington, DC(Grand Hyatt)/Aug. 22-25/900
2008 – Denver, CO(Hyatt)/Aug. 6-9/1000

Publications:

PSMA Member Directory. a. adv.

Professional Show Managers Association

One Regency Dr.
P.O. Box 30
Bloomfield, CT 06002-0030
Tel: (860)243-3977 *Fax:* (860)286-0787
Web Site: www.psmashows.org
Members: 180 individuals
Staff: 1
Executive Director: C. Mitchell Sorensen, CAE

Publications:

newsletter. q.

Professional Skaters Association *(1938)*

3006 Allegro Park. SW
Rochester, MN 55902
Tel: (507)281-5122 *Fax:* (507)281-5491
Web Site: www.skatepsa.com
Members: 6000 individuals
Staff: 8
Annual Budget: $2-5,000,000
Executive Director: Carole K. Shulman
E-Mail: cshulman@skatepsa.com

Historical Note

PSA members are ice skaters, coaches, judges and others interested in the sport. Membership: $30-120/year.

Meetings/Conferences:

Annual Meetings: Spring

Publications:

Moves in the Field. irreg.
Dance Booklet. irreg.
Skating Handbook. irreg.
PSA Membership Directory. a. adv.
Coaches Manual. irreg.
Professional Skater Magazine. bi-m. adv.
PSA Ratings Systems Manual. irreg.

Professional Ski Instructors of America *(1961)*

133 S. Van Gordon St., Suite 101
Lakewood, CO 80228-1700
Tel: (303)987-9390 *Fax:* (303)988-3005
Toll Free: (800)222 - 4754
E-Mail: psia@psia.org
Web Site: www.psia.org
Members: 20000 individuals
Staff: 14
Annual Budget: $500-1,000,000
Executive Director: Stephen M. Over

Historical Note

Provides on-going education for certified ski instructors and international educational training.

Meetings/Conferences:

Semi-annual Meetings: Spring and Fall

Publications:

The Professional Skier. 3/year. adv.

Professional Soccer Reporters Association *(1975)*

Historical Note

Organization defunct in 2004.

Professional Society for Sales and Marketing Training *(1940)*

5905 N.W. 54th Cir.
Coral Springs, FL 33067
Tel: (800)219-0096 *Fax:* (800)219-0096
Web Site: www.smt.org
Members: 170 individuals
Staff: 1
Annual Budget: $250-500,000
Executive Director: Karen Bednarski

Historical Note

Formerly (1993) National Society of Sales Training Executives.

Meetings/Conferences:

Annual Meetings: Fall

Professional Tattoo Artists Guild *(1975)*

27 Mt. Vernon Ave.
P.O. Box 1374
Mt. Vernon, NY 10551-1374
Tel: (914)422-2727 *Fax:* (914)422-2692
E-Mail: bigjoe@tattooequipment.com
Members: 7500 individuals
President: Joe Kaplan

Professional Tennis Registry *(1976)*

P.O. Box 4739
Hilton Head, SC 29938
Tel: (843)785-7244 *Fax:* (843)686-2033
Toll Free: (800)421 - 6289
E-Mail: ptr@ptrtennis.org
Web Site: www.ptrtennis.org
Members: 11700 individuals
Staff: 10
Annual Budget: $1-2,000,000
Chief Executive Officer and Executive Director: Daniel Santorum

Director, Communications: Peggy Edwards
Vice President, Operations: Julie Jilly

Historical Note
Formerly United States Professional Tennis Registry; assumed its current name in 2002. An international association of officially recognized, certified and registered tennis teaching professionals in 120 countries. Developed the Official Standard Method of instruction to certify tennis professionals. Membership: $100 (application fee/initial dues); $110/year (renewal, minimum).

Publications:
Tennis Pro. bi-m. adv.
Membership Directory. a. adv.
Convention Program. a. adv.

Professional Women Controllers

P.O. Box 950085
Oklahoma City, OK 73195-0085
Toll Free: (800)232 - 9792
E-Mail: info@pwcinc.org
Web Site: www.pwcinc.org
Members: 1000 individuals
Staff: 1
President: Sallyanne Rice

Historical Note
PWC members are professional air traffic controllers. Membership: $65/year (active); $32.50/year (associate); $200/year (corporate).

Meetings/Conferences:
Annual Meetings: Annual

Publications:
The WATCH Newsletter. q. adv.
Membership Directory. irreg. adv.

Professional Women in Construction *(1980)*

315 E. 56th St.
New York, NY 10022
Tel: (212)486-7745 Fax: (212)486-0228
E-Mail: pwcusa1@aol.com
Web Site: www.pwcusa.org
Members: 500 individuals
Staff: 4
Annual Budget: $250-500,000
President: Lenore Janis
E-Mail: pwcusa1@aol.com
Executive Vice President: Theresa Vigilante
E-Mail: teevigi@aol.com

Historical Note
Founded in 1980. Formerly (1982) the Association of Business and Professional Women in Construction. PWC was incorporated in 1983 as a 501 (c) 3 organization, with the purpose of assisting the mainstreaming of women business owners, professionals and managers into the construction industry and related fields. Membership is open to individual women and men, companies and government agencies engaged in construction and related fields and industries. Monthly mailings reach a readership of 8,000. Membership: $175/year (individual); $225/year (consultant); $375/year or $600/year (company, depending on size).

Publications:
PWC Newsletter. q. adv.
Bulletin. m.

Professional Women Photographers *(1975)*

511 Avenue of the Americas #138
New York, NY 10011
Tel: (212)330-8225
E-Mail: president@pwponline.org
Web Site: www.pwponline.org
Members: 200 individuals
Annual Budget: $25-50,000
President: Fran Dickson
E-Mail: president@pwponline.org

Historical Note
Formed in 1975, PWP is a not-for-profit organization of professional women photographers with no paid staff. Works to support and promote the work of women photographers through the sharing of ideas, resources and experiences; to provide various educational forums that encourage artistic growth and photographic development; and to stimulate public interest and support for the art of photography. Membership: $95/year (general member); $35/year (student); $125/year (institution).

Meetings/Conferences:
Monthly Meetings: New York, NY/1st Thursday every month

Publications:
PWP Magazine. 3/year. adv.

Professional Women Singers Association *(1982)*

P.O. Box 884
New York, NY 10024
Tel: (212)969-0590 Fax: (928)395-2560
E-Mail: info@womensingers.org
Web Site: www.womensingers.org
Members: 50 individuals
Annual Budget: under $10,000
President: Elissa Weiss

Historical Note
PWSA serves as an information resource and referral network for professional women in opera, oratorio, musical theater, and related genres. Has no paid officers or full-time staff. Membership: $85/year (individual).

Publications:
PWSA Works. q.

Professional Women's Appraisal Association *(1986)*

1224 N. Nokomis Ave. NE
Alexandria, MN 56308
Tel: (320)763-7626 Fax: (320)763-9290
Members: 1250 individuals
Staff: 6
Annual Budget: $100-250,000
Executive Director: Deborah S. Johnson
Contact: Keith Starkey

Historical Note
PWAA provides professional recognition to women involved in real estate valuation. Membership: $75/year (individual).

Meetings/Conferences:
Annual Meetings: in conjunction with the NAREA

Publications:
Woman Appraiser Newsletter. m.

Professional Women's Bowlers Association *(1981)*

Historical Note
Ceased non-profit operations in 2003.

Profit Sharing/401(k) Council of America *(1947)*

20 N. Wacker Dr., Suite 3700
Chicago, IL 60606
Tel: (312)419-1863 Fax: (312)419-1864
E-Mail: psca@psca.org
Web Site: www.psca.org
Members: 1200 companies
Staff: 6
Annual Budget: $500-1,000,000
President: David L. Wray
E-Mail: davidw@psca.org
Coordinator, Membership: Georgianne Mudie
E-Mail: georgianne@psca.org
Vice President, Marketing and Communications: Connie Mullis

Historical Note
Formerly (1973) Council of Profit Sharing Industries. Members are companies with profit-sharing and 401(k) plans. Membership dues are based on size of company. PSCA represents its members' interests to federal policymakers and offers practical assistance with plan implementation, administration, and communications.

Meetings/Conferences:
Annual Meetings: October

Publications:
PSCA Executive Report and Compliance Bulletin. m.
Profit Sharing. m.

Project Management Institute *(1969)*

Four Campus Blvd.
Newtown Square, PA 19073-3299
Tel: (610)356-4600 Fax: (610)356-4647
E-Mail: pmihq@pmi.org
Web Site: www.pmi.org
Members: 207428 individuals
Staff: 175
Annual Budget: $50-100,000,000
Chief Executive Officer: Gregory Balestrero
E-Mail: gregory.balestrero@pmi.org
Director, Customer Care and Technology: Josephine Day
Director, Integrated Services: Mark Emery
Member and Organization Relations: John Engman
Director, Knowledge Delivery: Steve Fahrenkrog
Director, Governance and Executive Programs: Lewis Gedansky
E-Mail: lew.gedansky@pmi.org
Manager, Governance and Executive Administration: Dorothy Hamilton
Chief Operating Officer: Mark Langley
E-Mail: mark.langley@pmi.org
Manager, Public Relations: James D. McGeehan
Director, Organization Resources and Development: Dorothy McKelvy
E-Mail: dorothy.mckelvy@pmi.org
Director, Brand Management: Mahala Renkey
General Counsel: William Scarborough
E-Mail: william.scarborough@pmi.org
Director, Market and Business Development: Harry Stefanou

Historical Note
PMI sets professional standards, conducts research and provides access to information and resources in the field of project program and portfolio management. Also promotes career and professional development and organizational maturity in the field and offers certification, networking and community involvement opportunities. Membership: $119/year (individual); plus $10 application fee for all new members.

Meetings/Conferences:
Annual Meetings: Global Congresses

Publications:
PM Network. m. adv.
PMI Today. m.
Project Management Journal. q. adv.

PROMAX International *(1956)*

9000 W. Sunset Blvd., Suite 900
Los Angeles, CA 90069
Tel: (310)788-7600 Fax: (310)788-7616
Web Site: www.promax.tv
Members: 4300 companies
Staff: 25
Annual Budget: $1-2,000,000
President and Chief Executive Officer: James Chabin

Historical Note
PROMAX is an international association of promotion and marketing professionals in the electronic media, dedicated to advancing the role and increasing the effectiveness of promotion and marketing within the industry, related industries, and the academic community. Broadcast Designers Association (BDA) is the sister organization of PROMAX and represents broadcast designers. Membership: $45-345/year.

Meetings/Conferences:
Annual Meetings: June

Publications:
PROMAX Magazine. a. adv.
BDA News. w.
BDA Awards Annual. a.
PROMO Fax. w. adv.
PROMAX Directory. a. adv.

Promotion Marketing Association *(1911)*

257 Park Ave. South, 11th Fl.
New York, NY 10010-7304
Tel: (212)420-1100 Fax: (212)533-7622
E-Mail: pma@pmalink.org
Web Site: www.pmalink.org
Members: 700 companies
Staff: 12
Annual Budget: $2-5,000,000
President and Chief Operating Officer: Claire Rosenzweig, CAE

Historical Note
Formerly (1998) Promotion Marketing Association of America. Founded in 1911 as American Manufacturers Premiums Association, it became Premium Advertising Association of America in 1934

and Promotion Marketing Association of America, Inc. (PMAA) in 1977. PMA represents the promotion marketing profession. PMA's mission is to encourage the highest standards of excellence in promotion marketing. It represents member interests and promotes better understanding of the importance of promotion in the marketing mix. Membership: $1,300/year (organization).

Meetings/Conferences:
Annual Meetings: March

Publications:
Legislative Bulletin. m.
Outlook. q.
Promotion Marketing Abstracts. q.

Promotional Products Association International *(1904)*
3125 Skyway Circle North
Irving, TX 75038-3526
Tel: (972)258-3090 *Fax:* (972)258-3016
Web Site: www.ppa.org
Members: 7500 companies
Staff: 70
Annual Budget: $10-25,000,000
President and Chief Executive Officer: G. Stephen Slagle, CAE
E-Mail: steves@ppa.org
Vice President, Marketing and Business Development: Paul Bellantone
E-Mail: paulb@ppa.org
Director, Expositions and Meetings: Darel Cook
Director, Finance Affairs: Dennis Cormany
E-Mail: dennisc@ppa.org
Editor: Lisa Horn
E-Mail: lisah@ppa.org
Director, Education and Certification: Rick Merrill
E-Mail: rickm@ppa.org

Historical Note
Formed by a merger of the Specialty Advertising National Association (1904) and the Specialty Advertising Guild International (1953) as the Specialty Advertising Association in 1964. Became the Specialty Advertising Association International in 1970 and assumed its present name in 1994. Represents the specialty advertising, premium, incentive and gift industry. Members are suppliers or distributors of decorated promotional advertising products. Annual budget reported at $15 million. Membership: $330/year (minimum) for distributors; $641/year (minimum) for suppliers.

Meetings/Conferences:
2007 – Las Vegas, NV(Mandalay Bay)/Jan. 3-6
2008 – Las Vegas, NV(Mandalay Bay)/Jan. 14-18

Publications:
Membership Directory. a. adv.
Promotional Products Business. m. adv.
Promotional Consultant. bi-m. adv.

Propeller Club of the United States *(1927)*
3927 Old Lee Hwy., Suite 101A
Fairfax, VA 22030
Tel: (703)691-2777 *Fax:* (703)691-4173
E-Mail: info@propellerclubhq.com
Web Site: www.propellerclubhq.com
Members: 54 local clubs
Staff: 4
Annual Budget: $250-500,000
International Executive Vice President: Bart A. Goedhard

Historical Note
Promotes and supports American water-borne commerce and the development of river, Great Lakes and harbor improvements. Founded in 1923 as The Propeller Club of New York, it became a multi-club national organization and assumed its present name in 1927.

Meetings/Conferences:
Annual Meetings: Fall

Publications:
The Proceeding (online; accessible thru PCUS's URL). a.
The Propeller Club Quarterly. q. adv.

Property Casualty Conferences *(1930)*
P.O. Box 681098
3601 Vincennes Rd.
Indianapolis, IN 46268
Tel: (317)872-4061 *Fax:* (317)879-8408
Members: 152 companies
Staff: 1
Annual Budget: $100-250,000
Executive Vice President: Larry L. Forrester, CAE

Historical Note
Formerly (1977) Conference of Mutual Casualty Companies. Changed name to Conference of Casualty Insurance Companies and is now the Property Casualty Conferences. Members are insurance companies active in writing casualty coverages. CCIC is an education organization only: sponsors seven departmental and one management seminar each year and a "Claim Arbitration Program." Management and offices provided by the National Association of Mutual Insurance Companies. Membership Fee: Based on premiums written.

Meetings/Conferences:
Annual Meetings: June

Publications:
Directory.

Property Casualty Insurers Association of America *(1945)*
2600 River Rd.
Des Plaines, IL 60018-3286
Tel: (847)297-7800 *Fax:* (847)297-5064
Web Site: www.pciaa.net
Members: 1000 companies
Staff: 190
Annual Budget: $10-25,000,000
President and Chief Executive Officer: Ernie Csiszar
Senior Vice President, Public Affairs: Joseph Annotti
Senior Vice President, Treasurer: June T. Holmes
Senior Vice President, State Government Affairs: John Loberret

Historical Note
Formerly National Association of Independent Insurers; merged with Alliance of American Insurers and assumed its current name in 2004. Membership consists of property-liability companies. Has an annual budget of approximately $21 million.

Meetings/Conferences:
Annual Meetings: Fall

Publications:
Update. m.
Weekly Digest. w.
Fast Track Monitoring System. q.
Legislative Reporter. bi-w.

Property Loss Research Bureau *(1947)*
3025 Highland Pkwy., Suite 800
Downers Grove, IL 60515-1291
Tel: (630)724-2200 *Fax:* (630)724-2260
Toll Free: (888)711 - 7572
E-Mail: plrb@plrb.org
Web Site: www.plrb.org
Members: 800 insurance companies
Staff: 28
Annual Budget: $5-10,000,000
President and Chief Executive Officer: Thomas W. Mallin
E-Mail: tmallin@plrb.org

Historical Note
Founded as the Mutual Loss Research Bureau, it assumed its present name in 1972. Members are mutual and stock property and casualty insurance companies. Membership: $220/year. per million assessable premiums, with declining marginal rates as size increases.

Publications:
Law Reviews. w.
Educational Program. w.
Newsletter. w.

Property Owners Association *(1949)*
1250 Route Nine South
Howell, NJ 07731
Tel: (732)780-1966 *Fax:* (732)780-1611
E-Mail: info@poanj.org
Web Site: www.poanj.org
Members: 550 individuals
Staff: 2
Annual Budget: $100-250,000
Executive Director: Kelly Voicheck
E-Mail: poanj@worldnet.att.net

Historical Note
Membership: $185/year (individual).

Publications:
POA News & Views. m. adv.

Property Records Industry Association
P.O. Box 3519
Durham, NC 27715-3159
Tel: (919)433-0121 *Fax:* (919)383-0035
E-Mail: coordinator@pria.us
Web Site: www.pria.us

The Protein Society *(1986)*
9650 Rockville Pike
Bethesda, MD 20814-3998
Tel: (301)634-7277 *Fax:* (301)634-7271
Toll Free: (800)992 - 6466
Web Site: www.proteinsociety.org
Members: 3200 individuals
Staff: 3
Annual Budget: $1-2,000,000
Executive Officer: Cynthia A. Yablonski

Historical Note
The Protein Sociey is an international society dedicated to furthering research and development in protein science. Purpose of the Society is to provide national and international forums to facilitate communication, cooperation and collaboration regarding all aspects of the study of proteins. Members are scientists, students and research organizations interested in proteins. Affiliated with the Federation of American Societies for Experimental Biology. Membership: $220/year (full); $120/year (post doc); $62/year (edit board member); $60/year (grad student); $25/year (undergrad); $25/year (emeritus member).

Meetings/Conferences:
Annual Meetings: Spring and Summer
2007 – Stockholm, Sweden/May 12-16
2007 – Boston, MA/July 21-25
2008 – San Diego, CA/July 19-23

Publications:
Membership Directory (online).
Newsletter. q.
Protein Science Journal. m. adv.

Protestant Church-Owned Publishers Association *(1951)*
2850 Kalamazoo Ave. SE
Grand Rapids, MI 49560
Tel: (616)224-0795
Web Site: www.pcpanews.org
Members: 48 publishing houses/suppliers
Staff: 2
Annual Budget: $50-100,000
Association Director: Gary Mulder
E-Mail: mulder@pcpaonline.org

Historical Note
PCPA is a trade association of protestant church-owned publishing houses, incorporated in Pennsylvania. Membership: dues vary as a percentage of sales.

Meetings/Conferences:
Biennial Convention: Febuary-March, even years/Board Meeting: odd years

Publications:
PCPA Roundtable. q.

Psi Omega *(1892)*
1040 Savannah Hwy.
Charleston, SC 29407
Tel: (843)556-0573 *Fax:* (843)556-6311
E-Mail: psiomega@bellsouth.net
Web Site: www.psiomegafraternity.org
Members: 24500 individuals
Staff: 3
Annual Budget: $100-250,000
Co-Executive Director: B. Thomas Kays
Co-Executive Director: James A. Rivers

Historical Note
Professional dental fraternity. Organized at the Baltimore College of Dental Surgery in 1892. Affiliated with the Professional Fraternity Association.

Meetings/Conferences:
Annual Meetings: With American Dental Ass'n

Publications:
The Frater of Psi Omega. 3/year.

Psychoanalytic Research Society

Historical Note

A section of the American Psychological Association - Division of Psychoanalysis.

Psychology Society *(1960)*

100 Beekman St., #25D
New York, NY 10038-1810
Tel: (212)285-1872 *Fax:* (212)285-1872
Members: 3500 individuals
Staff: 5
Annual Budget: $250-500,000
Director: Pierre C. Haber, Ph.D.

Historical Note

Psychology as a science has three components: research, teaching, and the application of these two components. The Society seeks the membership of practitioners who treat people, i.e. clinical psychologists exclusively. In turn, it seeks to promote the use of psychology in the treatment of human ills, social and political discord and other problems involving humanity. In 2004, the society added financial advisory service for members who seek help in selecting investments and retirement planning. Membership: $200/year (individual).

Meetings/Conferences:

2007 - Washington, DC(The Willard)/November/300

Publications:

PS Quarterly. q.
PS: It Is News. bi-m.

Psychometric Society *(1935)*

Univ. of North Carolina, 207 Curry Bldg.
P.O. Box 26171
Greensboro, NC 27402
Tel: (336)334-3474 *Fax:* (336)334-4120
Web Site: www.psychometricsociety.org
Members: 600 individuals
Staff: 1
Annual Budget: $50-100,000
Secretary: Terry A. Ackerman

Historical Note

Founded in Chicago in 1935 and incorporated in New Jersey in 1962. Promotes the use of quantitative models for psychological phenomena and quantitative methodology in the social and behavioral sciences. Membership: $60/year .

Meetings/Conferences:

Annual Meetings: *Spring and Biennial European Meeting (Odd years)*

Publications:

Psychometrika. q.

Psychonomic Society *(1959)*

1710 Foxview Rd.
Austin, TX 78704
Tel: (512)462-2442 *Fax:* (512)462-1101
Web Site: www.psychonomic.org
Members: 2500 individuals
Staff: 6
Annual Budget: $100-250,000
Secretary-Treasurer: Robert Lorch

Historical Note

Members are psychologists conducting or supervising research. Membership: $55/year (individual).

Publications:

Cognitive, Affective & Behavioral Neuroscience. q. adv.
Animal Learning and Behavior. q. adv.
Behavior Research Methods, Instruments and Computers. bi-m. adv.
Bulletin of The Psychonomic Society. bi-m. adv.
Memory and Cognition. bi-m. adv.
Perception and Psychophysics. m. adv.

Public Affairs Council *(1954)*

2033 K St. NW, Suite 700
Washington, DC 20006
Tel: (202)872-1790 *Fax:* (202)835-8343
E-Mail: pac@pac.org
Web Site: www.pac.org
Members: 600corporationsandorganizations
Staff: 17
Annual Budget: $2-5,000,000
President: Douglas G. Pinkham
Director, Administration: Sameira Fernandes
Director, Center for Public Affairs Management: Brian P. Hawkinson
Senior Director, Public Affairs Programs: Caryn Pawliger
Director, Communications and Public Relations: Wes Pedersen

Historical Note

Formed as the Effective Citizens Organization, it assumed its present name in 1965. The Public Affairs Council is the leading association for public affairs professionals. Its mission is to advance the field of public affairs and to provide tools and resources that enable public affairs executives and managers to achieve their business and professional goals. Membership is by company. Affiliated with the Foundation for Public Affairs. Membership: $1,800-12,000/year.

Meetings/Conferences:

Annual Meetings: *October*

Publications:

Public Affairs Review. a.
IMPACT. m.

Public Agency Risk Managers Association *(1974)*

P.O. Box 6810
San Jose, CA 95150
Tel: (408)979-8031 *Fax:* (888)412-5913
Toll Free: (888)907 - 2762
E-Mail: brenda.reisinger@parma.com
Web Site: www.parma.com
Members: 750publicandprivateagencies
Annual Budget: $250-500,000
Contact Person: Brenda Reisinger

Historical Note

A forum for public agencies (cities, counties, universities, school districts, special districts) and associate members to discuss and exchange ideas for the improvement and functioning of risk management within governmental agencies. Membership: $100/year (regular); $275/year (associate).

Meetings/Conferences:

Annual Meetings: *Winter*

Publications:

Parmafacts. bi-m.

Public Broadcasting Management Association *(1981)*

P.O. Box 50008
Columbia, SC 29250
Tel: (803)799-5517 *Fax:* (803)771-4831
Web Site: www.pbma.org
Members: 300 stations
Staff: 2
Annual Budget: $100-250,000
Executive Director: Chuck McConnell

Historical Note

Formerly (1997) Public Telecommunications Financial Management Association. PBMA members are public broadcasting stations and others with an interest in financial management applications.

Meetings/Conferences:

Annual Meetings: *Spring-Summer*

Publications:

Bottom Line. w.

Public Employees Roundtable *(1982)*

1301 K St. NW, Suite 450 West
Washington, DC 20005
Tel: (202)728-0418 *Fax:* (202)728-0422
E-Mail: per@excelgov.org
Web Site: www.excelgov.org/index.php?keyword=a43bdb9358e756
Members: 50organizations&institutions
Staff: 5
Annual Budget: $500-1,000,000

Historical Note

The Roundtable is composed of 32 associations, 16 government agencies, and 5 corporations representing nearly two million public employees. Its purposes are to better inform American citizens about the quality of people in government and the services they provide; develop a stronger espirit de corps among public service employees; and encourage interest in public service careers. Membership: $50/year (individual); $1000/year (government agencies).

Meetings/Conferences:

Annual Meetings: *Spring*

Publications:

Teachers Kit. a.
How to Celebrate. a.
Unsung Heroes. q.

Public Housing Authorities Directors Association *(1979)*

511 Capitol Court NE, Suite 200
Washington, DC 20002-4937
Tel: (202)546-5445 *Fax:* (202)546-2280
Web Site: www.phada.org
Members: 1850 individuals
Staff: 8
Annual Budget: $500-1,000,000
Executive Director: Timothy G. Kaiser
E-Mail: tkaiser@phada.org
Director, Government Affairs: Katherine Senzee

Historical Note

Association of public housing agency executive directors. Membership: $60-2,280/year (based on agency size).

Meetings/Conferences:

Annual Meetings: *May/June*

Publications:

Advocates. semi-m. adv.
Legislative Update. bi-w.
PHADA Alert. w.

Public Library Association *(1944)*

50 E. Huron St.
Chicago, IL 60611
Tel: (312)280-5752 *Fax:* (312)280-5029
Toll Free: (800)545 - 2433
E-Mail: pla@pla.org
Web Site: www.pla.org
Members: 7800 individuals
Staff: 8
Annual Budget: $500-1,000,000
Executive Director: Greta Southard
E-Mail: gsouthar@ala.org
Manager, Communications and Managing Editor: Kathleen M. Hughes
E-Mail: khughes@ala.org

Historical Note

A division of the American Library Association, membership in which is a prerequisite. Provides continuing education to public librarians and library trustees. Membership: $50/year.

Meetings/Conferences:

2008 - Minneapolis, MN/March 25-29

Publications:

Statistical Report of the Public Library Data Service. a.
Public Libraries. bi-m. adv.

Public Radio News Directors *(1985)*

P.O. Box 8372
Grand Forks, ND 58202-8372
Tel: (701)777-6505 *Fax:* (701)777-2339
Web Site: www.prndi.org
Members: 125 individuals
Staff: 1
Annual Budget: $50-100,000
Executive Assistant: Christine Paige Diers

Historical Note

Formerly (1994) Public Radio News Directors Association. PRND provides a network for news directors; training for news personnel; a channel for the flow of information; and liaison with National Public Radio. Membership: $90-150/year, varies by size of news staff.

Meetings/Conferences:

2007 - New Orleans, LA(Royal Sonesta)/July 19-June 21

Publications:

PRNDI Newsletter. bi-m.

Public Radio Program Directors Association *(1987)*

517 Ocean Front Walk, Suite 10
Venice, CA 90291-2428
Tel: (310)664-1591 *Fax:* (310)664-1592
E-Mail: info@prpd.org
Web Site: www.prpd.org

Members: 200 stations, networks, producers,
Staff: 1
Annual Budget: $100-250,000
President: Marcia Alvar
E-Mail: info@prpd.org

Historical Note

PRPD sponsors an annual conference and provides other networking opportunities for programmers and program directors at public radio stations in the U.S. Membership: $300/year (individual); $775/year (organization); stations (based on size/ranking in metro area).

Meetings/Conferences:

Annual Meetings: September
2007 – Minneapolis, MN(Marriott City Center)/Sept. 26-29
2008 – Hollywood, CA(Renaissance Hollywood)/Sept. 17-20

Publications:

PRPD Newsletter (online). m.

Public Relations Society of America *(1947)*

33 Maiden Ln., 11th Floor
New York, NY 10038-5150
Tel: (212)460-1400 *Fax:* (212)995-0757
Web Site: www.prsa.org
Members: 18000 individuals
Staff: 58
Annual Budget: $5-10,000,000
Director, Public Relations: Cedric Boss
President and Chief Executive Officer: Cheryl Procter-Rogers
Director, Public Relations: Cedric Boss
Chief Financial Officer: John Colletti
Vice President, Member Services: Jennifer Ian
Chief Marketing and Sales Officer: John D. Robinson

Historical Note

The major professional association of public relations practitioners in the U.S. Absorbed the American Public Relations Association in 1961, the National Communication Council for Human Services in 1976, and the Academy of Hospital Public Relations in 1986. Has an annual budget of approximately $5.6 million. Membership: $225/year.

Meetings/Conferences:

Annual Meetings: Fall/1,500

Publications:

Strategist. m. adv.
Tactics.

Public Risk Management Association *(1978)*

500 Montgomery St., Suite 750
Alexandria, VA 22314
Tel: (703)528-7701 *Fax:* (703)739-0200
E-Mail: info@primacentral.org
Web Site: www.primacentral.org
Members: 1800 government entities
Staff: 12
Annual Budget: $2-5,000,000
Executive Director: Lisa Lopinsky
E-Mail: llopinsky@primacentral.org
Deputy Executive Director: Marshall Davies
Manager, Education and Training: Heather Ripley

Historical Note

Formerly (1989) Public Risk and Insurance Management Association. PRIMA promotes and encourages effective public risk management and risk management professionalism in the public sector. Members are local and state government entities, including intergovernmental risk pools. Member representatives include risk managers and other public servants who fulfill the risk management function including loss control, litigation and claims management, contract management, employee benefits, occupational safety and health insurance and risk financing. Membership: $310/year (government members).

Meetings/Conferences:

Annual Meetings: May/June
2007 – Boston, MA(Hynes Convention Center)/June 10-13/2000
2008 – Anaheim, CA(Convention Center)/June 1-4/2000
2009 – Dallas, TX(Wyndham Anatole)/May 31-June 3/2000

Publications:

Public Risk Magazine. m. adv.

Public Works Historical Society *(1975)*

Historical Note

A division of American Public Works Ass'n, which provides administrative support.

Publishers Marketing Association

Historical Note

Became PMA, the Independent Book Publishers Association in 2005.

Publishers Publicity Association *(1957)*

c/o Crown Publishing
1745 Broadway
New York, NY 10019
Web Site: www.publisherspublicity.org
Members: 250 individuals
Annual Budget: $10-25,000
President: Tina Constable

Historical Note

Founded as the Publishers' Adclub, it assumed its present name in 1963. Membership: $75-110/year.

Meetings/Conferences:

Monthly Meetings: except July and August

Publications:

Newsletter. 10/year.

Pulp and Paper Safety Association *(1942)*

1370 N. Nealon Dr.
Portago, IN 46368
Tel: (219)764-4787 *Fax:* (219)764-4307
E-Mail: ppsa.org@verizon.net
Web Site: www.ppsa.org
Members: 300 individuals
Staff: 1
Annual Budget: $50-100,000
Executive Director: Pamela J. Cordier
E-Mail: ppsa.org@verizon.net

Historical Note

Formerly (1992) Southern Pulp and Paper Safety Association. PPSA members are safety and health professionals in the industry.

Meetings/Conferences:

Annual Meetings: May/June
2007 – Portland, OR(Jantzen Beach)/June 10-13

Publications:

PPSA Statistical Report. q.

Purebred Dairy Cattle Association *(1940)*

3310 Latham Dr.
Madison, WI 53713
Tel: (608)224-0400 *Fax:* (608)224-0300
E-Mail: wde@wdexpo.com
Members: 7 cattle breeders associations
Staff: 3
Annual Budget: $10-25,000
General Manager: Tom McKittrick
E-Mail: wde@wdexpo.com

Historical Note

Members are breeders of Ayrshire, Brown-Swiss, Guernsey, Holstein, Milking Shorthorn, Red and White and Jersey breed registry associations.

Meetings/Conferences:

Annual Meetings: February

Purebred Dexter Cattle Association of North America *(2004)*

25979 Highway EE
Prairie Home, MO 65068
Tel: (660)841-9502
Members: 250 members
Staff: 1
Annual Budget: $25-50,000
Executive Secretary-Treasurer: Rosemary Fleharty

Historical Note

PDCA maintains a breed registry and operates an annual show and sale for the benefit of its member breeders.

Purebred Hanoverian Association of America Breeders and Owners *(1983)*

P.O. Box 429
Rocky Hill, NJ 08553
Tel: (609)466-1383 *Fax:* (609)466-9543
Members: 300 individuals
Registrar: Barbara Dressler

Historical Note

Members are breeders and owners of purebred and halfbreed Hanoverian horses. Maintains breed registry.

Publications:

News of the Hanoverian Horse. q.
Annual Report.

Purebred Morab Horse Association *(1984)*

P.O. Box 203
Hodgenville, KY 42776
Tel: (270)358-8727
E-Mail: pmha@puremorab.com
Web Site: www.puremorab.com
Members: 150 individuals
Staff: 1
Annual Budget: under $10,000
Executive Director: Patricia Fochs
E-Mail: pmha@puremorab.com

Historical Note

Founded as North American Horse Association; assumed its current name in 1998. Members are owners and breeders of Morab horses, a crossbreed of Arabian and Morgan horses. Absorbed the Hearst Memorial Morab Horse Registry in 1985. Maintains the North American Morab Horse Registry. Membership: $20/year (individual); $50/year (company).

Meetings/Conferences:

Annual Meetings: October

Publications:

Morab Visions. q. adv.

Pyrotechnics Guild International *(1969)*

304 West Main St.
Titusville, PA 16354
Tel: (814)827-0485
Web Site: www.pgi.org
Members: 1700 individuals
Annual Budget: $50-100,000
Secretary-Treasurer: Frank Kuberry

Historical Note

PGI promotes the safe and sane display and use of pyrotechnics and encourages the display of pyrotechnics in conjunction with local and national events. Members are amateur and professional fireworks enthusiasts. Has no paid officers or full-time staff. Membership: $25/year.

Meetings/Conferences:

Annual Meetings: August

Publications:

PGI Bulletin. 5/year. adv.

Qualitative Research Consultants Association *(1983)*

1000 Westgate Dr.
Suite 252
St. Paul, MN 55114
Tel: (651)290-7491 *Fax:* (651)290-2266
Toll Free: (888)674 - 7722
E-Mail: info@qrca.org
Web Site: www.qrca.org
Members: 700 individuals
Staff: 3
Annual Budget: $1-2,000,000
Executive Director: Shannon Pfarr Thompson
E-Mail: exdir@qrca.org

Historical Note

Members are owners and employees of independent marketing and social research firms conducting qualitative research. Membership: $245/year (individual).

Meetings/Conferences:

Annual Meetings: Fall
2007 – Vancouver, BC, Canada/Oct. 27-30/350

Publications:

The City List. a.
QRCA Facilities and Services Directory. a.
QRCA Membership Directory. a.
QRCA Views and Newsletter. q.
QRCA Code of Ethical Standards & Recommended Practices. a.

Quality Bakers of America Cooperative *(1922)*
1055 Parsippany Blvd., Suite 201
Parsippany, NJ 07054
Tel: (973)263-6970 *Fax:* (973)263-0937
Web Site: www.qba.com
Members: 35 companies
Staff: 25
Annual Budget: $1-2,000,000
Executive Vice President: Ernie Stolzer
E-Mail: info@qba.com

Historical Note
Members are independent wholesale bakeries and their suppliers. QBA and its member bakers market their products under the Sunbeam brand.

Meetings/Conferences:
Annual Meetings: October

Quarters Furniture Manufacturers Association *(1995)*
8425 Progress Dr., Suite BB
Frederick, MD 21701
Tel: (240)215-9700 *Fax:* (240)215-9721
Web Site: www.qfma.net
Members: 20 companies
Annual Budget: $50-100,000
President: Matt Yanson

QVM/CMC Vehicle Manufacturers Association *(1989)*
P.O. Box 3070
Warrenton, VA 20188
Tel: (540)347-0743 *Fax:* (540)347-0742
Members: 7 companies
Staff: 1
Annual Budget: $25-50,000
General Counsel: Jerome C. Loftus

Historical Note
Formerly (2003) Limousine Industry Manufacturers Organization. GVM/CMC/VMA is the trade association of the limousine manufacturing industry. Non-voting Supplier-Service Firm and Associate Member memberships are available for companies or individuals involved in the industry in a non-manufacturing capacity. Membership: $1,500/year (organization/company).

Meetings/Conferences:
Annual Meetings: Winter

Rabbinical Assembly *(1901)*
3080 Broadway
New York, NY 10027
Tel: (212)280-6000 *Fax:* (212)749-9166
E-Mail: info@rabbinicalassembly.org
Web Site: www.rabbinicalassembly.org
Members: 1500 individuals
Staff: 10
Annual Budget: $1-2,000,000
Executive Vice President: Rabbi Joel H. Meyers

Historical Note
Members are rabbis serving Conservative Jewish congregations and educational institutions.

Meetings/Conferences:
Annual Meetings: Spring

Publications:
Rabbinical Assembly Newsletter. m.
Conservative Judaism. q.
Proceedings. a.

Rack Manufacturers Institute *(1958)*

Historical Note
An affiliate of Material Handling Industry of America, which provides administrative support.

Racking Horse Breeders Association of America *(1971)*
67 Horse Center Road
Decatur, AL 35603
Tel: (256)353-7225 *Fax:* (256)353-7266
E-Mail: rhbaa67horse@aol.com
Web Site: www.rackinghorse.com
Members: 3000 individuals
Staff: 10
Annual Budget: $500-1,000,000
Executive Director: Melissa Taylor
E-Mail: rhbaa67horse@aol.com
Bookkeeper: Kim Johnson
E-Mail: rhbaa67horse@aol.com

Historical Note
Members are persons directly connected with Racking horses and the Racking horse industry. Membership: $25/year or $500 (lifetime).

Meetings/Conferences:
Annual Meetings: Winter

Publications:
Racking News. q.

Radiant Panel Association *(1994)*
P.O. Box 717
Loveland, CO 80539-0717
Tel: (970)613-0100 *Fax:* (970)613-0098
Toll Free: (800)660 - 7187
Web Site: www.rpa-info.com
Members: 1000 companies
Staff: 6
Annual Budget: $500-1,000,000
Executive Director: Lawrence Drake
E-Mail: ldrake@rpa-info.com

Historical Note
RPA is a trade association of manufacturers, distributors, designers, dealers and installers of radiant panel heating and cooling systems and components. Membership: $1,000-$2,000/year (manufacturer); $250/year (distributor); $150/year (trade associate); $150/year (architect/engineer); $200/year (contractor).

Meetings/Conferences:
Annual Meetings: Spring

Publications:
Radiant Showcase Magazine. a. adv.
Radiant Panel Report. m.
Membership Directory. bi-m.
Radiant Living Magazine. a. adv.

Radiation Research Society *(1791)*
810 E. 10th St.
Lawrence, KS 66044
Toll Free: (800)627 - 0629
E-Mail: info@radres.org
Web Site: www.radres.org
Members: 2025 individuals
Staff: 3

Historical Note
Founded in 1952 and incorporated in the District of Columbia. RRS is a professional society of individuals studying radiation and its effects. Affiliated with the International Association for Radiation Research. Membership: $115/year (members); $100/year (associate members); $15/year (student members); $1000/year (institution); $1250/year (corporate).

Publications:
Radiation Research Newsletter online.
Radiation Research: An International Journal. m. adv.

Radiation Therapy Oncology Group
1818 Market St., Suite 1600
Philadelphia, PA 19103
Tel: (215)574-3189 *Fax:* (215)928-0153
Toll Free: (800)227 - 5463
Web Site: www.rtog.org
Administrative Assistant: David Corrie

Historical Note
RTOG is a cooperative research organization. Members are medical and research institutions. RTOG conducts clinical trials and compiles information on cancer treatment outcomes. An affiliate of American College of Radiology.

Meetings/Conferences:
2007 – Tampa, FL(Marriott Waterside)/Feb. 1-4

Radical Philosophy Association *(1982)*

Historical Note
RPA is an international nonsectarian forum for philosophical discussion of fundamental change. Has no paid officers or full- time staff. Membership: $35/year.

Publications:
Radical Philosophy Review. semi-a.
RPA Newsletter. q.

Radio Advertising Bureau *(1951)*
22 Cortlandt St., 17th Floor
New York, NY 10007
Tel: (212)681-7200 *Fax:* (212)681-7223
Toll Free: (800)252 - 7234
Web Site: www.rab.com
Members: 6000 individuals
Staff: 50
Annual Budget: $5-10,000,000
Executive Vice President and Chief Financial Officer: Van Allen
President and Chief Executive Officer: Jeff Haley

Historical Note
Established originally as the Department of Radio Advertising of the National Association of Broadcasters, it became independent in 1951 as the Broadcast Advertising Bureau and assumed its present name in 1955. Members seek to increase national and local radio advertising, build the skills and professionalism of marketing personnel, and raise awareness of radio among advertising and business communities. Awards the CRMC (Certified Radio Marketing Consultant) designation. Has an annual budget of approximately $6.5 million.

Meetings/Conferences:
Annual Meetings: Winter
2007 – Dallas, TX/Feb. 8-11

Publications:
Radio Marketing Guide and Fact Book for Advertisers. a. adv.
Radio Co-op Directory. a.

Radio and Television Correspondents Association *(1939)*
U.S. Capitol, Room S-325
Washington, DC 20510
Tel: (202)224-6421
Members: 2400 individuals
Annual Budget: $10-25,000
President: Joe Johns

Historical Note
Formerly (1949) Radio Correspondents Association. Members are correspondents covering Congress. Its sole purpose is to oversee the work of the Senate and House press galleries. Has no paid staff; officers change annually. Membership: $15/year (individual).

Radio-Television News Directors Association *(1946)*
1600 K St. NW, Suite 700
Washington, DC 20006-2838
Tel: (202)659-6510 *Fax:* (202)223-4007
E-Mail: rtnda@rtnda.org
Web Site: www.rtnda.org
Members: 3000 individuals
Staff: 24
Annual Budget: $2-5,000,000
President: Barbara Cochran
E-Mail: barbarac@rtnda.org
Vice President, Finance and Administration: Jane Nassiri
E-Mail: janen@rtnda.org
Vice President, Conventions and Special Projects: Rick Osmanski, CMP
Vice President, Communications, Marketing and Membership: Noreen Welle
E-Mail: noreenw@rtnda.org

Historical Note
Membership open to all broadcast journalists, suppliers and educators. Administers the Edward R. Murrow Awards, given in recognition of excellence in broadcast news in radio and television. Membership: $95-$145/year (individual).

Meetings/Conferences:
Annual Meetings: Fall

Publications:
RTNDA Communicator. m. adv.

Radiological Society of North America *(1915)*
820 Jorie Blvd.
Oak Brook, IL 60523-2251
Tel: (630)571-2670 *Fax:* (630)571-7837
Toll Free: (800)381 - 6660
E-Mail: membership@rsna.org
Web Site: www.rsna.org
Members: 39000 individuals
Staff: 150
Annual Budget: $25-50,000,000
Executive Director: Dave Fellers, CAE
Assistant Executive Director, Publications and Communications: Roberta E. Arnold, MA, MHPE

E-Mail: rarnold@rsna.org
Director, Marketing and Communications: Natalie Boden
Assistant Executive Director, Research and Education: Linda Bresolin, Ph.D.
Assistant Executive Director, Scientific Assembly and Informatics: Steve Drew
E-Mail: sdrew@rsna.org
Director, Meetings and Conventions: Robert Hope
E-Mail: bhope@rsna.org
Director, Membership and Subscription Records: Kolleen Klein
E-Mail: kklein@rsna.org
Managing Director, Administration and Human Resources: Mark Lichtenberger
E-Mail: mlichtenb@rsna.org
Assistant Executive Director, Finance and Administration: Mark Watson

Historical Note
Founded as the Western Roentgen Society; assumed its present name in 1915. Members are individuals interested in the application of radiology to medicine. Membership: $355/year (individual).

Meetings/Conferences:
Annual Meetings: usually Chicago, IL(McCormick Place)/November/55,000
2007 – Chicago, IL(McCormick Place)/Nov. 25-30
2008 – Chicago, IL(McCormick Place)/Nov. 30-Dec. 5

Publications:
Directory of Members. a. adv.
Scientific Assembly Program. a. adv.
RSNA News. m.
Radiology. m. adv.
RadioGraphics. bi-m. adv.

Radiology Business Management Association *(1968)*
8001 Irvine Center Dr., Suite 1060
Irvine, CA 92618
Tel: (949)340-5000 *Fax:* (949)340-5001
E-Mail: info@rbma.org
Web Site: www.rbma.org
Members: 1600 individuals
Staff: 5
Annual Budget: $1-2,000,000
Executive Director: Peggy Wagner

Historical Note
RBMA promotes the improvement of radiology practice management through legislative action and business management. Membership: $375/year (individual); $550/year (corporation).

Meetings/Conferences:
Annual Meetings: Semi-Annual Meetings

Publications:
HIPAA Bulletin. m. adv.
RBMA Bulletin. m. adv.

Railway Engineering-Maintenance Suppliers Association *(1965)*
417 West Broad St., Suite 203
Falls Church, VA 22046
Tel: (703)241-8514 *Fax:* (703)241-8589
Toll Free: (888)33 - REMS
Web Site: www.remsa.org
Members: 216 individuals
Staff: 2
Annual Budget: $250-500,000
Executive Director: J.A. Meyerhoeffer
E-Mail: meyerhoeffer@remsa.org

Historical Note
Product of a merger (1965) of National Railway Appliance Association (1894) and Association of Track and Structures Suppliers (1914). Members are distributors and manufacturers of railway maintenance-of-way equipment, products and services. Membership: $675/year (organization).

Meetings/Conferences:
Annual Meetings: World Rail Expo/Spring

Publications:
Mainline. q.

Railway Industrial Clearance Association of North America *(1969)*
c/o TGX Co.
101 N. Wacker Dr.
Chicago, IL 60606
Tel: (312)984-3776 *Fax:* (312)984-3781
E-Mail: admin@rica.org
Web Site: www.rica.org
Members: 245 companies
Annual Budget: $10-25,000

Historical Note
Members are railroads and shippers of dimensional loads (loads which require shipping clearance because they exceed railway size/weight standards). Has no paid officers or full-time staff. Membership: $25/year (individual).

Publications:
Newsletter. 3/year.

Railway Supply Institute *(1962)*
50 F St. NW, Suite 7030
Washington, DC 20001
Tel: (202)347-4664 *Fax:* (202)347-0047
E-Mail: rpi@rpi.org
Web Site: www.rsiweb.org/
Members: 370 Companies
Staff: 2
Annual Budget: $500-1,000,000
Executive Director: Thomas D. Simpson

Historical Note
The Railway Supply Institute formally came into existence on Jan. 1, 2003, with a consolidation of the Railway Supply Assn. and the Railway Progess Institute. The Railway Progress Institute was organized as the Railway Business Assn in 1908, and the name was changed to Railway Progress Institute in 1955. The Railway supply Assn was organized in 1938 under the name Allied Mechanical Assn., and changed its name to the Railway Supply Assn. in 1982. The RSI is the internat'l assn of suppliers to the railraods and to rail mass tansit systems.

Meetings/Conferences:
Annual Meetings: Fall

Railway Systems Suppliers *(1906)*
9304 New LaGrange Rd., Suite 200
Louisville, KY 40242
Tel: (502)327-7774 *Fax:* (502)327-0541
E-Mail: rssi@rssi.org
Web Site: www.rssi.org
Members: 250 companies
Staff: 2
Annual Budget: $250-500,000
Executive Director: Donald F. Remaley
E-Mail: rssi@rssi.org

Historical Note
Product of a merger (1961) of the Railway Communications Suppliers Association and Signal Appliance Association. Formerly (1971) Railway Signal and Communications Suppliers Association and then (1977) Railway Systems Suppliers Association, Inc. RSSI is a trade association serving the communication and signal segment of the rail transportation industry. Primary activity is organizing and managing a trade show for its members to exhibit their products and services. Membership: $200-$600/year.

Publications:
Progressive Railroading. a. adv.
RSSI Newsletter. bi-a.
Mass Transit. a. adv.
Railway Age. m. adv.
International Railway Journal.

Railway Tie Association *(1919)*
115 Commerce Dr., Suite C
Fayetteville, GA 30214
Tel: (770)460-5553 *Fax:* (770)460-5573
E-Mail: ties@rta.org
Web Site: www.rta.org
Members: 3200 companies
Staff: 2
Annual Budget: $250-500,000
Executive Director: Jim Gauntt
E-Mail: ties@rta.org

Historical Note
Formerly (1929) the National Association of Railroad Tie Producers. Membership is comprised of crosstie producers, sawmill owners, chemical manufacturers, wood preservation companies railroad maintenance engineers, purchasing officials and others interesed in the manufacture and procurement of wood railroad ties. Membership: annual dues based on size and volume of production.

Meetings/Conferences:
Annual Meetings: Fall

Publications:
Crossties Magazine. bi-m. adv.

Rapid Prototyping Association of SME

Historical Note
Became Rapid Technologies & Additive Manufacturing Community of SME in 2004.

Rapid Technologies & Additive Manufacturing Community of SME

Historical Note
Part of Engineering Materials Applications Community of SME, a program of Society of Manufacturing Engineers, which provides administrative support.

RCI, Inc. *(1983)*
1500 Sunday Dr., Suite 204
Raleigh, NC 27607-5041
Tel: (919)859-0742 *Fax:* (919)859-1328
Toll Free: (800)828 - 1902
E-Mail: rci@rci-online.org
Web Site: www.rci-online.org
Members: 2300 individuals
Staff: 10
Annual Budget: $2-5,000,000
Executive Vice President: James R. Birdsong

Historical Note
Assumed current named in 2006. RCI members are professional building analysis consultants (those who derive their income from building analysis consulting) and industry members (individuals involved in contracting, sales or manufacturing). RCI provides educational programs for members. Membership: $372/year (professional); $426/year (industry).

Meetings/Conferences:
Annual Meetings: Spring
2007 – Orlando, FL(Rosen Shingle Creek Resort)/March 1-6

Publications:
RCItems Newsletter. 11/year. adv.
Interface Journal. 11/year. adv.
Internat'l Directory of Roofing Professionals. a. adv.

Real Estate Buyers Agent Council *(1988)*
430 N. Michigan Ave.
Chicago, IL 60611
Tel: (312)329-8656 *Fax:* (312)329-8632
Toll Free: (800)648 - 6224
E-Mail: rebac@realtors.org
Web Site: www.rebac.net
Members: 50000 individuals
Staff: 7
Executive Director: Janet Branton

Historical Note
REBAC represents professional real estate agents who act as buyer's agents, as opposed to representing the seller of a property. Became an affiliate of National Association of Realtors in 1996. Membership: $110/year.

Meetings/Conferences:
Annual Meetings: usually in conjunction with NAR

Publications:
Membership Directory. a. adv.
Newsletter. m.

Real Estate Educators Association *(1979)*
19 Mantua Road
Mt. Royal, NJ 08061
Tel: (856)423-3215 *Fax:* (856)423-3420
E-Mail: info@reea.org
Web Site: www.reea.org
Members: 1400 individuals
Staff: 2
Annual Budget: $250-500,000
Executive Director: Meridyth M. Senes

Historical Note
Members are individuals involved in all types of real estate training and education. Membership: $129/year (individual), $329/year (institutional).

Meetings/Conferences:
Annual Meetings: Spring
2007 – St. Louis, MO(Hyatt Regency)/June 10-13

Publications:
E-News. q. adv.
Proceedings. a.
REEA Journal. q. adv.

Real Estate Information Professionals Association *(1995)*
P.O. Box 3159
Durham, NC 27715-3159
Tel: (919)383-0044 *Fax:* (919)383-0035
E-Mail: mikeb@reipa.org
Web Site: www.reipa.org
Members: 110 individuals
Staff: 2
Annual Budget: $100-250,000
Executive Director: Mike Borden
E-Mail: mikeb@reipa.org

Historical Note
REIPA supports professional information providers in the real estate industry. Membership fee varies based on sales. $375-3,000/year.

Meetings/Conferences:
Annual Meetings: Fall

Publications:
Newsletter. m.

Real Estate Management Brokers Institute

Historical Note
An affilaite of the National Association of Real Estate Brokers.

Real Estate Round Table *(1969)*
1420 New York Ave. NW, Suite 1100
Washington, DC 20005
Tel: (202)639-8400 *Fax:* (202)639-8442
Web Site: www.rer.org
Members: 200 firms
Staff: 11
Annual Budget: $2-5,000,000
President and Chief Executive Officer: Jeffrey D. DeBoer
E-Mail: jdeboer@rer.org
Executive Assistant and Director, Meetings: Michelle M. Reid
E-Mail: mreid@rer.org
Senior Vice President and Counsel: Steve Renna
E-Mail: srenna@rer.org
Senior Vice President: Clifton E. Rodgers, Jr.
E-Mail: crodgers@rer.org
Director, Public Affairs: Scott Sherwood

Historical Note
Founded as the National Realty Committee; assumed its present name in 1999. Actively involves America's leading public and private real estate owners, advisors, builders, investors, lenders and managers on key tax, capital and credit, environmental and technology issues in Washington. Members are senior principals from every spectrum of the commercial real estate industry and leaders of major national real estate trade associations.

Meetings/Conferences:
Annual Meetings: Held in Washington, DC.

Publications:
Bulletins. irreg.
News Fax. w.
Policy Agenda. a.

REALTORS Land Institute *(1944)*
430 N. Michigan Ave.
Chicago, IL 60611
Tel: (312)329-8440 *Fax:* (312)329-8633
Toll Free: (800)441 - 5263
E-Mail: rli@realtors.org
Web Site: www.rliland.com
Members: 1600 individuals
Staff: 3
Annual Budget: $250-500,000
Executive Vice President: Jan Hope

Historical Note
Formerly (1975) National Institute of Farm and Land Brokers and (1986) Farm and Land Institute, RLI is an affiliate of the National Association of REALTORS. Members are those interested in the development and sale of all types of land. Offers the Accredited Land Consultant (ALC) designation. Membership: $185/year, plus chapter dues.

Publications:
Membership Roster. a. adv.
Realtors Land Institute Newsletter. q. adv.

Receptive Services Association of America *(1990)*
17000 Commerce Pkwy., Suite C
Mt. Laurel, NJ 08054
Tel: (856)638-0423 *Fax:* (856)439-0525
E-Mail: rsa@ahint.com
Web Site: www.rsana.com
Members: 400 companies
Staff: 3
Annual Budget: $250-500,000

Historical Note
Founded as Receptive Services Association of New York and New Jersey in 1990, RSA became a national organization in 1995. Members are companies who provide tour and travel related services to groups visiting the U.S. from overseas. Membership: $350/year (full member), $300/year (associate), plus $100 initiation fee.

Publications:
RSAdvisor. q. adv.

Recording Industry Association of America *(1952)*
1330 Connecticut Ave. NW, Suite 300
Washington, DC 20036
Tel: (202)775-0101 *Fax:* (202)775-7253
E-Mail: webmaster@riaa.com
Web Site: www.riaa.com
Members: 350 companies
Staff: 70
Annual Budget: $10-25,000,000
Chairman and Chief Executive Officer: Mitch Bainwol
Senior Vice President, Government and Industry Relations, Senior Leg. Counsel: Mitch Glazier
Senior Vice President, Communications: Jonathan Lamy
Vice President, Business and Legal Affairs: Stanley Pierre-Louis
President: Cary Sherman
Chief Financial Officer: Michael Williams

Historical Note
Formerly (1970) Record Industry Association of America. RIAA is the non-profit trade association representing the U.S. sound recording industry. RIAA member companies create, manufacture and market approximately 90% of all legitimate recordings produced and sold in the U.S. The principal goal of RIAA is to serve the common interests of recording companies and address their needs worldwide in the face of modern technology. A major concern is the unauthorized copying ("piracy") of recorded material and censorship issues. Has an annual budget of approximately $11 million.

Publications:
Fast Tracks. bi-w.

Recreation Vehicle Dealers Association of North America *(1968)*
3930 University Dr.
Fairfax, VA 22030-2515
Tel: (703)591-7130 *Fax:* (703)591-0734
E-Mail: info@rvda.org
Web Site: www.rvda.org
Members: 1500 companies
Staff: 15
Annual Budget: $2-5,000,000
President: Michael A. Molino, CAE
Vice President, Administration: Ronnie Hepp
E-Mail: rhepp@rvda.org
Vice President, Communications: Phil Ingrassia
E-Mail: pingrassia@rvda.org

Historical Note
Absorbed (1969) Recreational Dealer Association; formerly (1970) Recreation Vehicle Dealers Institute, and (1976) the Recreational Vehicle Dealers of America, Inc. Absorbed Recreation Vehicle Rental Association in 1982 and Recreation Vehicle After Market Association in 1986.

Publications:
Legislative Reports. m.
RV Executive Today. m. adv.

Recreation Vehicle Industry Association *(1963)*
1896 Preston White Dr.
P.O. Box 2999
Reston, VA 20195-0999
Tel: (703)620-6003 *Fax:* (703)620-5071
E-Mail: rvia@rvia.org
Web Site: www.rvia.org
Members: 520 companies
Staff: 60
Annual Budget: $5-10,000,000
President: Richard A. Coon
E-Mail: rvia@rvia.org
Vice President, Publics Relations and Advertising: Gary LaBella
Manager, Public Relations: Rachel Parsons

Historical Note
Established in 1963 as the Recreational Vehicle Institute, Inc. Merged in 1968 with Camping Trailer Manufacturers Association and American Institute of Travel Trailer and Camper Manufacturers, Inc. The name was changed in 1975 to Recreation Vehicle Industry Association. Members are manufacturers of motor homes, travel trailers, truck campers, folding camping trailers, and conversion vehicles, as well as suppliers of RV component parts. Has an annual budget of $6.8 million.

Meetings/Conferences:
Annual Meetings: Summer

Publications:
RVIA Marketing Report. m.
RV Road Signs. q.
Directory. a.
Year End Report. a.
RV Financing. a.
RVIA Today. m.

Recreation Vehicle Rental Association *(1982)*

Historical Note
A division of the Recreation Vehicle Dealers Association of North America, which provides staff support and to which all members of RVRA belong.

Recreational Park Trailer Industry Association *(1993)*
30 Greenville St., Second Floor
Newnan, GA 30263-2602
Tel: (770)251-2672 *Fax:* (770)251-0025
E-Mail: info@rptia.com
Web Site: www.rptia.com
Members: 150 firms and organizations
Staff: 4
Annual Budget: $500-1,000,000
Executive Director: William R. Garpow
E-Mail: wgarpow@rptia.com
Assistant to the Director: Laraine Ayers
E-Mail: layers@rptia.com
Administrator, Standards: Kathy Rook
E-Mail: standards@rptia.com

Historical Note
Formerly a division of Recreation Vehicle Industry Association; became an independent organization in 1993. RPTIA represents manufacturers and service firms producing park trailers as well as dealers and RV Parks. Other members include associations representing retailers, RV parks and resorts. RPTIA works to unite all segments of the industry so they may, in consort, have effective influence upon matters of public interest involving the betterment of the industry. Membership: $75-$10,000/year.

Publications:
RPTIA Flash Report. m.

Recreational Vehicle Aftermarket Association *(1967)*
54 Westerly Rd.
Camp Hill, PA 17011
Tel: (717)730-0300 *Fax:* (717)730-0544
E-Mail: karl@rvaahq.com
Web Site: www.rvaftermarket.org/
Members: 150 companies
Staff: 4
Annual Budget: $100-250,000
Executive Director: Karl J. Etshied

Historical Note
Founded as Warehouse Distributors Association; assumed its current name in 2001. Members are wholesale distributors of parts for manufactured

housing and recreational vehicles. Membership: $775/year.

Meetings/Conferences:
Annual Meetings: *Fall*

Publications:
Newsletter. q. adv.
Communicator. m.

Recreational Vehicle Manufacturer's Clubs Association *(1973)*
Holiday Rambler RV Club, Inc.
600 E. Wabash
Wakarusa, IN 46573
Tel: (219)862-7330 *Fax:* (574)862-7390
Toll Free: (877)702 - 5415
Members: 27 organizations
Annual Budget: under $10,000
Administrative Assistant: Stacy Peterson
E-Mail: stpeterson@monacohr.com

Historical Note
Members are managers/directors of manufacturer-sponsored travel clubs. Has no paid officers or full-time staff. Membership: $25/year.

Meetings/Conferences:
Annual Meetings: *November, usually Louisville, KY(Executive West)*

Recycled Paperboard Technical Association *(1953)*
920 Davis Road, Suite 306
Elgin, IL 60123-1390
Tel: (847)622-2544 *Fax:* (847)622-2546
E-Mail: rpta@rpta.org
Web Site: www.rpta.org/
Members: 28 companies
Staff: 4
Annual Budget: $250-500,000
Executive Director: David G. Ruby

Historical Note
Formerly (1991) the Boxboard Research and Development Association. An association of U.S., Canadian and other foreign companies interested in cooperative research and development in technical and operational aspects of the recycled paperboard industry.

Meetings/Conferences:
Annual Meetings: *Chicago, first week in May.*

Red and White Dairy Cattle Association *(1964)*
3085 S. Valley Road
Crystal Spring, PA 15536
Tel: (814)735-4221 *Fax:* (814)735-3473
E-Mail: rwdca@frontiernet.net
Web Site: www.redandwhitecattle.com
Members: 1400 individuals
Annual Budget: $500-1,000,000
Secretary-Treasurer: Joan Carpenter
E-Mail: rwdca@frontiernet.net

Historical Note
Founded as American Red and White Dairy Cattle Society; assumed its current name in 1966. Members are owners and breeders of Red and White dairy cattle, a hybrid of Red Holstein and Milking Shorthorn. Maintains breed registry. Membership: $30/year.

Meetings/Conferences:
Annual Meetings: *Fall*

Publications:
Red Bloodlines. 9/year.
Bull Briefs. 8-10/year.

Red Angus Association of America *(1954)*
4201 N. Interstate 35
Denton, TX 76207
Tel: (940)387-3502 *Fax:* (940)383-4036
E-Mail: info@redangus.org
Web Site: www.redangus.org
Members: 2200 individuals
Staff: 18
Annual Budget: $1-2,000,000
Executive Secretary: Robert Hough
E-Mail: bob@redangus.org
Director, Communications: Ben Spitzer
E-Mail: ben@redangus.org

Historical Note
Members are breeders and improvers of Red Angus Beef Cattle. Member of: National Pedigree Livestock Council; National Cattlemen's Association; U.S. Beef Breeds Council; and Beef Improvement Federation. Membership: $60/year.

Meetings/Conferences:
Annual Meetings: *Fall*
2007 – Dodge City, KS/Sept. 25-29

Publications:
American Red Angus. 10/year. adv.

Red Tag News Publications Association *(1971)*
1415 N. Dayton
Chicago, IL 60622
Tel: (312)274-2215 *Fax:* (312)266-3363
Toll Free: (800)460 - 4434
Web Site: www.redtag.org
Members: 57 publications
Staff: 3
Annual Budget: $50-100,000
Executive Director: Jim Franklin

Historical Note
RTNPA members are publications classified by the U.S. Postal Service as newspapers. Membership: based on circulation. Membership fee varies.

Meetings/Conferences:
Annual Meetings: *always in Washington, DC/September*

Publications:
Newsletter.
Bulletin. irreg.

Refractories Institute *(1951)*
650 Smithfield St., Suite 1160
Pittsburgh, PA 15222-3907
Tel: (412)281-6787 *Fax:* (412)281-6881
Web Site: www.refractoriesinstitute.com
Members: 60 companies
Staff: 1
Annual Budget: $500-1,000,000
President: Robert W. Crolius
E-Mail: rcrolius@aol.com

Historical Note
Incorporated in 1951 as the national trade association for refractory manufacturers, suppliers of equipment, raw material, and contractors/installers. Refractories are heat-resistant materials that are used for lining high-temperature furnaces and reactors. Membership: $3,000-$38,000/year.

Meetings/Conferences:
Annual Meetings: *Spring*

Publications:
Directory of the Refractories Industry. quadren. adv.
Refractory News Online.
Refractories.

Refractory Ceramic Fibers Coalition *(1992)*
c/o Dana Bishop, 2300 N St. NW
Washington, DC 20037
Tel: (202)663-9188 *Fax:* (202)354-5230
E-Mail: dana.bishop@pillsburylaw.com
Web Site: www.rcfc.net
Members: 3 companies
Staff: 1
Administrator: Dana Bishop
E-Mail: dana.bishop@pillsburylaw.com

Historical Note
Formed by refractory ceramic fiber manufacturers after the dissolution of TIMA (Thermal Insulation Manufacturers Association) in 1992.

Refractory Metals Association *(1970)*

Historical Note
Producers of powders and products made from tungsten, molybdenum, tatalum and niobium. Formerly (1975) Refractory and Reactive Metals Association. A constituent member of the Metal Powder Industries Federation.

Refrigerated Foods Association *(1980)*
2971 Flowers Road South, Suite 266
Atlanta, GA 30341
Tel: (770)452-0660 *Fax:* (770)455-3879
E-Mail: info@refrigeratedfoods.org
Web Site: www.refrigeratedfoods.org
Members: 150 companies
Staff: 3
Annual Budget: $100-250,000
Executive Director: Terry Dougherty, CMP
E-Mail: info@refrigeratedfoods.org
Director, Communications: Stephanie Cooke
E-Mail: info@refrigeratedfoods.org

Historical Note
Concerned with the manufacture and sale of refrigerated foods. Formerly (1991) Salad Manufacturers Association. Membership: $700-4150/year, based on gross sales (full member); $700/year (associate member).

Meetings/Conferences:
Annual Meetings: *January-March; Biennial Exhibition also held/odd years*

Publications:
Directory. a.
Chilled News Review. q.
Technical Newsletter. q.

Refrigerating Engineers and Technicians Association *(1910)*
P.O. Box 1819
Salinas, CA 93902
Tel: (831)455-8783 *Fax:* (831)455-7856
E-Mail: info@reta.com
Web Site: www.reta.com
Members: 2300 individuals
Annual Budget: $100-250,000

Historical Note
Formerly National Association of Practical Refrigerating Engineers. Members are designers, installers, operators and maintainers of central refrigeration and air conditioning equipment. Membership: $75/year (individual); $500/year (company); $50/year (student).

Meetings/Conferences:
Annual Meetings: *Fall*

Publications:
RETA Breeze. 6/year. adv.
Technical Report. q.

Refrigeration Service Engineers Society *(1933)*
1666 Rand Rd.
Des Plaines, IL 60016-3552
Tel: (847)297-6464 *Fax:* (847)297-5038
Toll Free: (800)297 - 5660
Web Site: www.rses.org
Members: 18,418 individuals
Staff: 23
Executive Vice President: Elaine Katsoris
E-Mail: risaacs@rses.org

Historical Note
Membership: $96/year.

Meetings/Conferences:
Annual Meetings: *Fall*

Publications:
RSES Journal. m. adv.

Regional Airline Association *(1975)*
2025 M St. NW, Suite 800
Washington, DC 20036-3309
Tel: (202)367-1170 *Fax:* (202)367-2170
Web Site: www.raa.org
Members: 300 companies and organizations
Staff: 5
Annual Budget: $1-2,000,000
President: Deborah C. McElroy
E-Mail: mcelroy@raa.org
Director, Legislative Affairs: Faye A. Malarkey
E-Mail: malarkey@raa.org

Historical Note
In 1968 the Association of Commuter Airlines merged with the National Air Taxi Conference to form what became the National Air Transportation Conferences and later, the National Air Transportation Associations. In 1975, this group again became independent under the name Commuter Airline Association of America until 1981, when it assumed its present name. Regional airlines provide short haul air transportation, primarily connecting small and medium sized communities with larger cities and connecting hubs. Membership consists of more than 40 airlines, plus 250 associate members who provide goods and services.

Meetings/Conferences:
Semi-Annual Meetings: *Spring and Fall*
2007 – Memphis, TN(Memphis Convention Center)/May 21-24/1400

2008 – Indianapolis, TN(Indiana Convention Center)/May 5-8

Publications:

Annual Report of the RAA. a. adv.

Regional Orchestra Managers Association

Historical Note

A sub-group of the American Symphony Orchestra League without dues structure or separate headquarters.

Register of Professional Archeologists *(1976)*

5024-R Campbell Blvd.
Baltimore, MD 21236
Tel: (410)933-3486 *Fax:* (410)931-8111
E-Mail: info@rpanet.org
Web Site: www.rpanet.org
Members: 1800 individuals
Staff: 1
Annual Budget: $25-50,000
Management Executive: Calvin K. Clemons, CAE

Historical Note

Formerly (1976) Society of Professional Archeologists; assumed current name in 1998. Established to speak for professional archeologists and develop professional standards in training, conduct and research. Promulgates a Code of Ethics and certifies the qualifications of its members. Membership fee varies, based on income.

Meetings/Conferences:

Annual Meetings: With the Soc. for American Archaeology

Publications:

SOPAnews. m.
Directory of Professional Archeologists. a.

Registry of Interpreters for the Deaf *(1964)*

333 Commerce St.
Alexandria, VA 22314
Tel: (703)838-0030 *Fax:* (703)838-0454
E-Mail: admin@rid.org
Web Site: www.rid.org
Members: 12000 individuals
Staff: 15
Annual Budget: $500-1,000,000
Executive Director: Clay Nettles
E-Mail: admin@rid.org

Historical Note

It is the mission of RID to provide international, national, regional, state and local forums and an organizational structure for the continued growth and development of the professions of interpretation and transliteration of American Sign language and English. Membership: $115/year (certified); $65/year (associate); $25/year (student); $24/year (supporting); $62/year (senior citizen); $24/year (certified inactive-retired).

Meetings/Conferences:

Annual Meetings: Summer

Publications:

VIEWS Newsletter. m. adv.

Regulatory Affairs Professionals Society *(1976)*

11300 Rockville Pike, Suite 1000
Rockville, MD 20852-3048
Tel: (301)770-2920 *Fax:* (301)770-2924
E-Mail: raps@raps.org
Web Site: www.raps.org
Members: 10000 individuals
Staff: 24
Annual Budget: $2-5,000,000
Executive Director: Sherry Keramidas, Ph.D., CAE
E-Mail: skeramidas@raps.org
Director, Conventions and Meetings: Adena Bryant
E-Mail: abryant@raps.org
Director, Member and Component Relations: A. Cedric Calhoun
E-Mail: ccalhoun@raps.org
Director, Communications and Public Relations: Jennifer Gibson
Director, Information Techology: Tim Maxey
Vice President, Administration: Iris Rush, CAE
E-Mail: irush@raps.org
Vice President, Education and Knowledge Services: Linda Temple, CAE
E-Mail: ltemple@raps.org

Historical Note

Members are regulatory affairs professionals, lawyers and consultants from drug, medical device, biologic and health care related industries who work with the Food and Drug Administration and other regulatory agencies worldwide. Membership: $185/year (new members).

Meetings/Conferences:

Annual Meetings: Fall

Publications:

Fundamentals of US Regulatory Affiars. a.
Annual Conference Update & Onsite Book. a. adv.
Regulatory Affairs Focus. m. adv.
Fundamentals of EU Regulatory Affiars. a.

Rehabilitation Engineering and Assistive Technology Society of North America *(1979)*

1700 N. Moore St., Suite 1540
Arlington, VA 22209-1903
Tel: (703)524-6686 *Fax:* (703)524-6630
E-Mail: info@resna.org
Web Site: www.resna.org
Members: 1300 individuals
Staff: 7
Executive Director: Thomas A. Gorski, CAE
Director, Communications and Membership Services: Mary Beth Leongini
Meetings Coordinator: Rosina Romano

Historical Note

Formerly (1995) RESNA, the Association for the Advancement of Rehabilitation Technology. Established in Chicago, IL in 1979. Formerly (1986) Rehabilitation Engineering Society of North America. A professional organization of the rehabilitation technology community, the society brings together a diverse group of individuals whose credentials, activities and interests vary widely but who are all committed to designing, developing, evaluating and providing external and internal devices that will put the benefits of technology to work for disabled persons. A member society of the American Institute for Medical and Biological Engineering. Membership: $150/year (regular); $500-$800/year (profit/not for profit).

Meetings/Conferences:

Annual Meetings: Summer

Publications:

Assistive Technology Journal. semi-a. adv.
Proceedings of the RESNA Annual Conference. a. adv.
RESNA News. q. adv.

Rehabilitation Nursing Foundation

Historical Note

The educational and research arm of the Association of Rehabilitation Nurses.

Reinsurance Association of America *(1968)*

1301 Pennsylvania Ave. NW, Suite 900
Washington, DC 20004
Tel: (202)638-3690 *Fax:* (202)638-0936
E-Mail: infobox@reinsurance.org
Web Site: www.reinsurance.org
Members: 28 companies
Staff: 25
President: Franklin W. Nutter
Senior Vice President, State Government Affairs: Marsha A. Cohen
Vice President and Director, Education: Sandra L. LaFevre
Senior Vice President and General Counsel: Tracey Laws
Vice President, Finance and Business Operations: Robyn L. Morriss
Senior Vice President and Director, Financial Services: Joseph Selverling
Office Manager: Sonya Tucker
Vice President, Federal Affairs: Mary B. Zetwick

Historical Note

Incorporated in the District of Columbia as the National Association of Property and Casualty Reinsurers. Became the Reinsurance Association of America in 1970.

Meetings/Conferences:

Annual Meetings: April

Publications:

Profitability Measures.
Line of Business Review.
Market Share Studies.
Leverage and Liquidity Reports.
Balance Sheet Analysis.
Quarterly Reinsurance Underwriting Report. q.
Loss and Reserve Development Study.

Reliability Society

Historical Note

A technical society of the Institute of Electrical and Electronics Engineers (IEEE). Membership in the Society, open only to IEEE members, includes a subscription to a technical periodical in the field published by IEEE. All administrative support is provided by IEEE.

Religion Communicators Council *(1929)*

475 Riverside Dr., Room 1355
New York, NY 10115
Tel: (212)870-2402 *Fax:* (212)870-2171
E-Mail: rccrprc@interport.net
Web Site: www.religioncommunicators.org
Members: 500 individuals
Staff: 1
Annual Budget: $100-250,000
Executive Director: Shirley Struchen

Historical Note

Founded as Religious Publicity Council; later became Religious Public Relations Council, and assumed its current name in 1999. RCC is an interfaith association of individuals working in public relations or communications for any religious communion, organization or related agency. Membership: $85/year.

Meetings/Conferences:

Annual Meetings: Spring
2007 – Louisville, KY(Marriott Downtown)/Apr. 26-28
2008 – Washington, DC

Publications:

Counselor. q.
Speaking Faith: The Essential Handbook for Religious Communicators.
Membership Directory Online.

Religion Newswriters Association *(1949)*

P.O. Box 2037
Westerville, OH 43086-2037
Tel: (614)891-9001 *Fax:* (614)891-9774
E-Mail: mason@rna.org
Web Site: www.rna.org
Members: 500 individuals
Staff: 2
Annual Budget: $100-250,000
Executive Director: Debra L. Mason
Associate Director: Tiffany McCallen

Historical Note

A professional association of journalists covering religion for the general circulation news media. Membership: $25-$100/year.

Meetings/Conferences:

Annual Meetings: Fall
2007 – San Antonio, TX/Sept. 27-30/250
2008 – Washington, DC/Sept. 25-28/250

Publications:

Conference Program. a. adv.
RNA Extra. bi-m.

Religious Communication Association *(1973)*

Communications Dept., Univ. of Texas
3900 University Blvd.
Tyler, TX 75799
Tel: (903)566-7093 *Fax:* (903)566-7287
Web Site: www.americanrhetoric.com/rca
Members: 210 individuals
Staff: 1
Annual Budget: under $10,000
Executive Secretary: Michael Eidenmuller

Historical Note

Formerly (1998) Religious Speech Communication Association, RCA is an academic society of individuals interested in the study of all aspects of public religious communication. RSCA members include teachers, students, clergy, broadcasters and other scholars and professionals. Until 1973 was the Religious Speech Division of the Speech

Communication Association. Membership: $20/year (individual); $50/year (institution).

Meetings/Conferences:
Annual Meetings: Fall

Publications:
RCA Newsletter. 3/year. adv.
Homiletic. semi-a.
Journal of Communication and Religion. semi-a. adv.

Religious Conference Management Association *(1972)*

One RCA Dome, Suite 120
Indianapolis, IN 46225
Tel: (317)632-1888 *Fax:* (317)632-7909
E-Mail: rcma@rcmaweb.org
Web Site: www.rcmaweb.org
Members: 3314 individuals
Staff: 5
Annual Budget: $500-1,000,000
Executive Director and Chief Executive Officer: DeWayne S. Woodring, D.Div.
Director, Administration: Judy Valenta
Director, Finance: Donna Woodring

Historical Note
A non-profit, professional international organization of men and women who have responsibility for planning and/or managing meetings, seminars, conferences, conventions, assemblies, or other gatherings for religious organizations. Formerly (1982) the Religious Convention Managers Association. Membership: $50/year (regular); $100/year (associate).

Meetings/Conferences:
Annual Meetings: January or February
2007 – Louisville, KY(Convention Center)/Jan. 30-Feb. 2/1390
2008 – Orlando, FL(Convention Center)/Feb. 5-8/1390
2009 – Grand Rapids, MI(Convention Center)/Jan. 27-30/1390

Publications:
Religious Conference Manager. bi-m. adv.
Who's Who in Religious Conference Management. a. adv.
RCMA Highlights. d. adv.

Religious Education Association *(1903)*

P.O. Box 12576
Alexandria, LA 71315
Tel: (318)442-4327
E-Mail: rea-appre@cox.net
Web Site: www.religiouseducation.net
Members: 1500 individuals
Staff: 1
Annual Budget: $100-250,000
President and Chair: Robert O'Gorman

Historical Note
REA is an association of professors, practitioners and researchers in the field of religious education. Merged with Association of Professors and Researchers in Religious Education in 2005. Provides support and networking opportunities to its members.

Meetings/Conferences:
Biennial Meetings:: usually Fall (2005)

Publications:
REACH. q.
Religious Education. q. adv.

Religious Research Association *(1959)*

618 S.W. Second Ave.
Galva, IL 61434-1912
Tel: (309)932-2727 *Fax:* (309)932-2282
Web Site: http://rra.hartsem.edu
Members: 500 individuals
Staff: 1
Annual Budget: $50-100,000
Executive Officer: William H. Swatos, Jr., Ph.D.

Historical Note
RRA is a professional society of individuals engaged in religious behavior research including social scientists, church researchers and planners, theologians, teachers, administrators, members of the clergy, editors and religious educators. Membership: $30/year (individual); $70/year (organization); $14/year (student).

Meetings/Conferences:
Annual Meetings: Fall, in conjunction with Soc. for the Scientific Study of Religion
2007 – Tampa, FL(Hyatt Regency)/Nov. 2-4
2008 – Louisville, KY
2009 – Denver, CO
2010 – Baltimore, MD

Publications:
Review of Religious Research. q. adv.
Context of Religious Research. semi-a.

Remanufacturing Institute, The *(1995)*

4215 Lafayette Center Dr., Suite Three
Chantilly, VA 20151-1243
Tel: (703)968-2772 Ext: 103 *Fax:* (703)968-2878
Web Site: www.reman.org
Annual Budget: $50-100,000
Chairman: William C. Gager

Historical Note
Founded as Remanufacturing Industries Council International; assumed its current name in 2000. TRI represents companies in the utomotive, furniture, electronics, and other industries who specialize in remanufacturing. Membership: $50/year (individual); $500/year (organization).

Publications:
TRI Newsletter (electronic).

Renaissance Society of America *(1954)*

c/o Graduate School and Univ. Center, City Univ. of New York
365 Fifth Ave., Room 5400
New York, NY 10016-4309
Tel: (212)817-2130 *Fax:* (212)817-1544
E-Mail: rsa@rsa.org
Web Site: www.rsa.org
Members: 3400 individuals
Staff: 1
Annual Budget: $100-250,000
Executive Director: John Monfasani
Office Manager: Laura Schwartz

Historical Note
A professional society of scholars of the Renaissance, RSA is a member of the American Council of Learned Societies and an affiliate of the American Historical Association. Membership: $60/year (individual); $100/year (library).

Meetings/Conferences:
Annual Meetings: March
2007 – Miami, FL/March 22-24
2008 – Chicago, IL/Apr. 3-5
2009 – Los Angeles, CA/March 26-28

Publications:
Renaissance News & Notes newsletter. 2/yr. adv.
Renaissance Quarterly. q. adv.

Renal Physicians Association *(1973)*

1700 Rockville Pike, Suite 220
Rockville, MD 20852
Tel: (301)468-3515 *Fax:* (301)468-3511
E-Mail: rpa@renalmd.org
Web Site: www.renalmd.org
Members: 2800 individuals
Staff: 8
Annual Budget: $1-2,000,000
Executive Director: Dale Singer, MHA
E-Mail: rpa@renalmd.org

Historical Note
Members are physicians, practice managers, advanced practice nurses and physician assistants specializing in treatment of renal disease. Membership: $350/year.

Meetings/Conferences:
Annual Meetings: February

Publications:
RPA News. 6/year.

Renewable Fuels Association *(1981)*

One Massachusetts Ave. NW, Suite 820
Washington, DC 20001-1431
Tel: (202)289-3835 *Fax:* (202)289-7519
E-Mail: info@ethanolrfa.org
Web Site: www.ethanolrfa.org
Members: 75 companies
Staff: 8
Annual Budget: $1-2,000,000
President: Robert Dinneen
Director, Congressional and Public Affairs: Mary Giglio
Director, Communications: Matt Hartwig
Office Manager: Holly Hewry
Vice President: Larry Schafer

Historical Note
Members are companies and individuals involved in the production and use of ethanol. Membership: based on capacity for producers.

Meetings/Conferences:
Annual Meetings: No regularly scheduled meetings.

Publications:
Changes in Gasoline Manual for Auto Technicians.
Ethanol Report Newsletter. bi-w..
Ethanol Industry Outlook. a.
Industry Guidelines, Specifications and Procedures for Ethanol.

Renewable Natural Resources Foundation *(1972)*

5430 Grosvenor Lane
Bethesda, MD 20814-2193
Tel: (301)493-9101 *Fax:* (301)493-6148
Web Site: www.rnrf.org
Members: 14 societies
Staff: 5
Annual Budget: $1-2,000,000
Executive Director: Robert D. Day
E-Mail: day@rnrf.org

Historical Note
Incorporated in the District of Columbia in 1972, RNRF is a consortium of professional and scientific societies whose members are concerned with the advancement of research, education, scientific practice and policy formulation for the conservation, replenishment and use of the earth's renewable natural resources. The member societies are: American Fisheries Society; American Geophysical Union; American Meteorological Society; American Society of Civil Engineers; American Society of Landscape Architects; American Water Resources Association; Estuarine Research Federation; Society for Range Management; Society of Env. Toxicology Chemistry; Society of Wood Science and Technology; Soil and Water Conservation Society; Universities Council on Water Resources; International Society of Arboriculture; and The Wildlife Society. Membership: $50/year (individual); $750-2250/year (organization).

Meetings/Conferences:
Annual Meetings: Fall

Publications:
Renewable Resources Journal. q.

Reprographic Services Association

8120 Sheridan Blvd., Suite B-106
Westminster, CO 80003
Tel: (303)428-0479 *Fax:* (303)428-0481
Toll Free: (800)445 - 8629
E-Mail: info@rsacorporation.com
Web Site: www.rsacorporation.com/
Executive Director: Mark Beilman

Research and Development Associates for Military Food and Packaging Systems *(1946)*

16607 Blanco Road, Suite 1506
San Antonio, TX 78232-1940
Tel: (210)493-8024 *Fax:* (210)493-8036
E-Mail: hqs@militaryfood.org
Web Site: www.militaryfood.org
Members: 1100 individuals
Staff: 3
Annual Budget: $500-1,000,000
Executive Director: James F. Fagan

Historical Note
Founded as a forum for the interchange of technical data on food products, feeding systems, food and feeding equipment and food packaging between industry and professors of Food Science and Technology on one hand and the U.S. Armed Forces and Government on the other. Membership: $125/year (individual), $400/year (corporate).

Meetings/Conferences:
2007 – Tucson, AZ(Ventana Canyon Resort)/260

Publications:
Activities Report. a. adv.

Newsletter - "The Link". q. adv.

Research and Engineering Council of the NAPL
(1950)
P.O. Box 1086
White Stone, VA 22578-1086
Tel: (804)436-9922 *Fax:* (804)436-9511
Toll Free: (800)642 - 6275 Ext: 1397
E-Mail: recouncil@rivnet.net
Web Site: www.recouncil.org
Members: 250 companies
Staff: 1
Annual Budget: $500-1,000,000
Managing Director: Ronald Mihills
E-Mail: recouncil@rivnet.net

Historical Note
Formerly (1950) Research and Engineering Council of the Graphics Arts; assumed current name in 2002 when became a member of the National Association for Printing Leadership. The Research and Engineering Council of the National Association for Printing Leadership is a technical trade association established to identify and address technical issues in the graphic arts industry. Has international membership, including companies, organizations, and individuals involved in all segments of the printing and publishing industries. Membership: $200/year (individual); $700/year (company).

Meetings/Conferences:
Annual Meetings: Spring/150

Research Association of Minority Professors
(1976)
Prairie View A&M Univ.
Drawer 67
Prairie View, TX 77446
Tel: (936)857-3425 *Fax:* (936)857-3425
E-Mail: mrh38@academicplanet.com
Members: 985
Staff: 1
Annual Budget: $10-25,000
Executive Director: Dr. Frank T. Hawkins
E-Mail: mrh38@academicplanet.com

Historical Note
Membership: $45/year (individual); $150/year (organization/company).

Publications:
RAMP journal. semi-a. adv.

Research Chefs Association *(1996)*
5775 Peachtree-Dunwoody Road, Suite 500-G
Atlanta, GA 30342
Tel: (404)252-3663 *Fax:* (404)252-0774
E-Mail: rca@kellencompany.com
Web Site: www.researchchef.com
Members: 2,000 individuals
Staff: 3
Executive Vice President: Mardi K. Mountford

Research Council on Structural Connections
(1946)
P.O. Box 663
Canton, MA 02021
Tel: (781)828-9408 *Fax:* (781)828-2557
E-Mail: steelstruck@aol.com
Web Site: www.boltcouncil.org
Members: 65 companies, associations and individuals
Annual Budget: $10-25,000
Secretary-Treasurer: Emile W.J. Troup
E-Mail: steelstruck@aol.com

Historical Note
Researches the effects of stress on bolted structural joints for its member companies and institutions. Formed (1946) as the Research Council on Riveted and Bolted Structural Joints; assumed current name in 1980. Has no paid officers or full-time staff.

Research Society on Alcoholism *(1976)*
7801 N. Lamar Blvd., Suite D-89
Austin, TX 78752
Tel: (512)454-0022 *Fax:* (512)454-0812
Web Site: www.rsoa.org
Members: 1600 individuals
Staff: 3
Annual Budget: $50-100,000
Executive Director: Debra Sharp

Historical Note
RSA provides a forum for communication among scientists conducting research that may contribute to the prevention and treatment of alcoholism. RSA members are qualified scientists interested in alcohol research, including all biomedical sciences, clinical fields and psychosocial sciences. Membership: $150/year (individual).

Meetings/Conferences:
Annual Meetings: Summer
2007 - Chicago, IL(Hyatt Regency)/July 7-13/1500
2008 - Washington, DC(Hyatt)/June 28-July 2/1500
2009 - San Diego, CA(Hyatt)/June 20-24/1500

Publications:
Alcoholism: Clinical & Experimental Research. m.

Reserve Officers Association of the U.S. *(1922)*
One Constitution Ave. NE
Washington, DC 20002
Tel: (202)479-2200 *Fax:* (202)479-0416
Toll Free: (800)809 - 9448
Web Site: www.roa.org
Members: 75000 individuals
Staff: 38
Annual Budget: $2-5,000,000
Executive Director: Lt. Gen. Dennis McCarthy, (Ret.)
Comptroller: Christina Antonelos
Director, Army Affairs and Deputy Executive Director: Maj. Gen. David R. Bockel, USAR (Ret.)
Legislative Director: Capt. Marshall A. Hanson, USNR
Director, Membership Services: Lt. Col. William Holehan
Director, Public Affairs: Lt. Col. Louis Leto
Coordinator, Conventions: Diane Markham
Webmaster: Kelly Matthews
Editor: Eric Minton

Historical Note
Membership is open to any regular, reserve or former officer of the Army, Navy, Air Force, Marine Corps, Coast Guard, Public Health Service, or National Oceanic and Atmospheric Administration. Membership: $40/year.

Meetings/Conferences:
Annual Meetings: Late June/1,200
2007 - San Francisco, CA(Marriott)/June 27-30/1000

Publications:
The Officer Magazine (online). m. adv.
ROA National Security Report. m.

Residential Space Planners International *(1985)*
P.O. Box 14393
Scottsdale, AZ 85267-4393
Tel: (480)473-0986 *Fax:* (480)473-0757
Toll Free: (800)548 - 0945
E-Mail: maryfisherdesigns1@cox.net
Web Site: www.maryfisherdesigns.com
Members: 30
Staff: 2
Executive Director: Mary Knott
E-Mail: maryfisherdesigns1@cox.net

Historical Note
RSPI members are architects and interior designers specializing in planning residential interiors and kitchen design. Membership: $85/year.

Resilient Floor Covering Institute *(1929)*
401 E. Jefferson St., Suite 102
Rockville, MD 20850
Tel: (301)340-8580 *Fax:* (301)340-7283
E-Mail: info@rfci.com
Web Site: www.rfci.com
Members: 19 companies
Staff: 3
Annual Budget: $500-1,000,000
Managing Director: Douglas Wiegand
E-Mail: info@rfci.com

Historical Note
Formerly (1973) Asphalt and Vinyl Asbestos Tile Institute and (1976) the Resilient Tile Institute.

Meetings/Conferences:
Semi-annual Meetings: May and October

Resistance Welder Manufacturers' Association
(1935)
550 N.W. LeJeune Road
Miami, FL 33126
Tel: (305)443-9353 *Fax:* (305)442-7421
E-Mail: rwma@aws.com
Web Site: www.rwma.org
Members: 100 companies
Staff: 3
Annual Budget: $100-250,000
Contact: Ray Shook
E-Mail: rwma@aws.com

Historical Note
Incorporated in Pennsylvania. RWMA strives to create widespread awareness and use of the various resistance welding processes and equipment; improve relations between individual manufacturers; foster higher ethical standards throughout the industry; develop industry standards to assist users of resistance welding equipment. Membership: sliding scale based on previous year's sales.

Publications:
RWMA Bulletins.
Newsletter. q.
Membership Directory.

Resort and Commercial Recreation Association
(1981)
6240 Topaz Court
Ft. Myers, FL 33912
Tel: (239)936-0233
E-Mail: info@r-c-r-a.org
Web Site: www.R-C-R-A.org
Members: 1500 individuals
Annual Budget: $50-100,000
Vice President: Mike DiBenedetto

Historical Note
RCRA seeks to provide appropriate services to professionals, educators and students in the commercial recreation field. RCRA also works to increase the profitability and efficiency of commercial enterprises. Has no paid officers or full-time staff.

Meetings/Conferences:
Annual Meetings: November

Publications:
Membership Directory (online). o.
Management Strategy. q. adv.
RCRA Job Bulletin (online). m. adv.
RCRA Update (online). bi-m. adv.

Respiratory Nursing Society *(1990)*
c/o N.Y. State Nurses Ass'n
11 Cornell Road
Latham, NY 12110
Tel: (518)782-9400 Ext: 286
E-Mail: rns@nysna.org
Web Site: www.respiratorynursingsociety.org
Members: 200 individuals
Staff: 6
Annual Budget: $25-50,000
Contact: Linda Degen
E-Mail: rns@nysna.org

Historical Note
RNS is the professional association for nurses who care for clients with pulmonary dysfunction and who are interested in the promotion of pulmonary health. The Society was created to promote coordinated, comprehensive, high-level nursing care for these clients by fostering respiratory nurses' personal and professional development; providing educational opportunities through which nurses can enhance their knowledge and skills; and conducting, participating in, and disseminating research. Also serves as a formal network for communications in the field. Membership open to all registered professional nurses interested in respiratory nursing from a research, practice, and/or educational perspective. Associate membership available to persons other than registered nurses who are concerned with or engaged in the practice of respiratory care. Membership: $75/year (individual); $1,500/year (corporate).

Publications:
Respiratory Exchange (newsletter). q.

Restaurant Facility Management Association

PMB 193
5960 W. Parker Road, Suite 278
Plano, TX 75093
Tel: (214)912-2266 *Fax:* (972)608-8703
Web Site: www.rfma.info
Managing Director: Tracy Tomson

Retail Advertising and Marketing Association International *(1952)*
325 Seventh St. NW, Suite 1100
Washington, DC 20004-2802
Tel: (202)661-3052 *Fax:* (202)737-2849
E-Mail: perweilerp@rama-urf.com
Web Site: www.rama-nrf.com
Members: 2000 individuals
Staff: 5
Annual Budget: $500-1,000,000
President and Chief Executive Officer: Tom Holliday
E-Mail: hollidayt@rama-nrf.com
Historical Note
Formerly (1991) the Retail Advertising Conference. International association of marketing and advertising executives. Membership: $125/year (company and individual); $875/year (corporation).
Meetings/Conferences:
Annual Meetings: *Late Winter in Chicago, IL/1,100*
Publications:
Excellence in Advertising/RAMA Membership Directory. a.

Retail Confectioners International *(1917)*
1807 Glenview Road
Glenview, IL 60025
Tel: (847)724-6120 *Fax:* (847)724-2719
Toll Free: (800)545 - 5381
Web Site: www.retailconfectioners.org
Members: 520 companies
Staff: 3
Annual Budget: $500-1,000,000
Executive Director: Van Billington
Historical Note
Founded in 1918 as Associated Retail Confectioners of the United States. In 1960 name was changed to Associated Retail Confectioners of North America to recognize members in Canada and Mexico. In 1969 changed to Retail Confectioners International to recognize membership in Europe, Australia and Japan.
Meetings/Conferences:
Annual Meetings: Summer/1,500
Publications:
Kettletalk. m. adv.
RCI Convention Buyers Guide. a. adv.

Retail Industry Leaders Association *(1965)*
1700 N. Moore St., Suite 2250
Arlington, VA 22209
Tel: (703)841-2300 *Fax:* (703)841-1184
E-Mail: info@retail-leaders.org
Web Site: www.retail-leaders.org
Members: 600 member companies
Staff: 25
Annual Budget: $5-10,000,000
President: Sandra Kennedy
Vice President, Government Affairs: Shannon Campagna
Senior Vice President, Government Affairs: Paul T. Kelly
Senior Vice President, Industry Affairs: Britt Wood
Historical Note
Formerly (1969) Mass Merchandising Research Foundation, (1976) Mass Retailing Institute, (1988) International Mass Retailing Institute. Absorbed the Association of General Merchandise Chains in 1987. Membership fee based on sales volume.
Publications:
News@IMRA.ORG. w.

Retail Packaging Manufacturers Association *(1990)*
P.O. Box 17656
Covington, KY 41017-0656
Tel: (859)341-9623 *Fax:* (859)341-9624
E-Mail: info@retailpackaging.org
Web Site: www.rpma.org
Members: 150 individuals
Staff: 2
Annual Budget: $500-1,000,000
Executive Director: Nancy Coons
Historical Note
RPMA provides comprehensive educational and networking services and organizes an annual trade show for its members. Members of the association include manufacturers, manufacturer representatives and distributors of retail packaging.
Meetings/Conferences:
Annual Meetings: Annual Meetings

Retail Print Music Dealers Association *(1976)*
13140 Coit Road, Suite 320, LB 120
Dallas, TX 75240-5737
Tel: (972)233-9107 Ext: 204 *Fax:* (972)490-4219
E-Mail: office@printmusic.org
Web Site: www.printmusic.org
Members: 295 businesses
Annual Budget: $50-100,000
Executive Director: Madeleine Crouch
Historical Note
Membership: $195/year.
Meetings/Conferences:
Annual Meetings: *Spring*
Publications:
The Measure. q.

Retail Solutions Providers Association *(1948)*
4115 Taggart Creek Road
Charlotte, NC 28208
Tel: (704)357-3124 *Fax:* (704)357-3127
E-Mail: bbussard@rspassn.org
Web Site: www.rspassn.org
Members: 480 companies
Staff: 29
Annual Budget: $10-25,000,000
Executive Director: William K. Bussard
E-Mail: bbussard@rspassn.org
Historical Note
Established in 1948 in Dayton, OH in protest to an arbitrary ceiling on prices of used cash registers. Formerly the Independent Cash Register Dealers Assn; assumed its current name in 2004. Membership: $300/year.
Publications:
Data Link Newsletter. m. adv.

Retail Stores Forum
Historical Note
A division of the Business Products Industry Association.

Retail Tobacco Dealers of America *(1932)*
Four Bradley Park Ct.
Suite 2-H
Columbus, GA 31904-3637
Tel: (706)494-1143 *Fax:* (706)494-1893
E-Mail: info@rtda.org
Web Site: www.rtda.org
Members: 3000 tobacco retailers
Staff: 4
Annual Budget: $2-5,000,000
Executive Director: Joe Rowe
Historical Note
Membership: $125/year (individual); $500/year (organization).
Publications:
Tobacco Retailers' Almanac. a. adv.
Newsletter. m.

Retail, Wholesale and Department Store Union *(1937)*
30 E. 29th St.
Fourth Floor
New York, NY 10016
Tel: (212)684-5300 *Fax:* (212)779-2809
Web Site: www.rwdsu.org
Members: 100000 individuals
Staff: 40
Annual Budget: $5-10,000,000
President: Steward Applebaum
Historical Note
Established in 1937 by dissidents from the Retail Clerks International Union and chartered by the Congress of Industrial Organizations as the United Retail Employees of America. Became the United Retail, Wholesale and Department Store Employees of America in 1940, a title that was later shortened to its present form. Absorbed the Distributive, Processing and Office Workers of America as well as the Playthings, Jewelry and Novelty Workers International Union in 1954 and the Cigar Makers International Union of America in 1974.
Meetings/Conferences:
Quadrennial Meetings:
Publications:
RWDSU Record. m.

Retailer's Bakery Association *(1918)*
8201 Greensboro Dr., Suite 300
McLean, VA 22102
Tel: (703)610-9035 *Fax:* (703)610-9005
Toll Free: (800)638 - 0924 Ext:
Web Site: www.rbanet.com
Members: 3500 companies
Staff: 4
Annual Budget: $1-2,000,000
Executive Vice President: Bernard D. Reynolds
E-Mail: breynolds@rbanet.com
Historical Note
Formerly (2004) Retail Bakers of America; (1994) Retail Bakers of America and (1996) Retailer's Bakery-Deli Association. RBA produces conventions and training programs for the retail baking industry. RBA also promotes the baking profession. Membership: $700/year (golden circle club); $250/year (basic); $200/year (corporate).
Meetings/Conferences:
Annual Meetings: *Spring*
2007 – Las Vegas, NV(Mandalay Bay Resort and Casino)/Sept. 8-10
Publications:
Insight Newsletter. m.

Retired Officers Association
Historical Note
Became Military Officers Association of America in 2003.

Retirement Industry Trust Association *(1987)*
c/o American Church Trust Co,
14615 Benfer Road
Houston, TX 77069
Tel: (281)444-5600
Web Site: www.r-i-t-a.org
Members: 11 companies
Annual Budget: $10-25,000
Historical Note
RITA members are trust and custodian companies providing professional guidance for self-directed retirement savings plans and related instruments. Has no paid officers or full-time staff. Membership: $350/year.

Reusable Industrial Packaging Association *(1942)*
8401 Corporate Dr., Suite 450
Landover, MD 20785-2224
Tel: (301)577-3786 *Fax:* (301)577-6476
Web Site: www.reusablepackaging.org
Members: 160 individuals
Staff: 3
Annual Budget: $500-1,000,000
President: Paul W. Rankin
E-Mail: prankin@igc.org
Office Administrator: Joan Hunnam
Vice President, Regulatory and Technical Affairs: C.L. Pettit
E-Mail: cpettit@igc.org
Historical Note
Formerly (1987) National Barrel and Drum Association and (1999) Association of Container Reconditioners. RIPA members are reconditioners and dealers of steel and plastic drums, as well as intermediate bulk containers. Founding member of the International Confederation of Drum Reconditioners.
Meetings/Conferences:
Annual Convention: Fall
Publications:
Membership and Industrial Supply Directory. a. adv.
Responsible Packaging Management. a. adv.
Reusable Packaging Newsletter. m. adv.

Rhetoric Society of America *(1968)*
c/o D. Hawhee, Membership Officer,
University of Illinois

244 Lincoln Hall, 702 S. Wright St.
Urbana, IL 61801
Tel: (217)265-6802
E-Mail: hawhee@uiuc.edu
Web Site: http://rhetoricsociety.org/
Members: 1000 individuals
Annual Budget: $25-50,000
Officer, Membership: D. Hawhee
E-Mail: hawhee@uiuc.edu

Historical Note
Teachers and students interested in promoting the development and dissemination of research and theory about the production and analysis of rhetorical discourse.

Meetings/Conferences:
2007 - Memphis, TN(Peabody Hotel)/May 26-29/600

Publications:
Rhetoric Society Quarterly. q. adv.

Rice Millers' Association *(1899)*
4301 N. Fairfax Dr., Suite 425
Arlington, VA 22203-1616
Tel: (703)236-2300 *Fax:* (703)236-2301
E-Mail: riceinfo@usarice.com
Web Site: www.usarice.com
Members: 29 mills and cooperatives
President and Chief Executive Officer: Stuart E. Proctor, Jr.

Historical Note
The national trade association of the United States' rice milling industry, RMA is among the nation's oldest agricultural organizations. Membership includes both independent rice milling companies and farmer-owned cooperative rice milling firms which, together, mill virtually all rice produced in the United States. RMA is a private, non-profit, non-stock organization and does not engage in rice trading. RMA is a charter member of the USA Rice Federation, which provides administrative support.

Meetings/Conferences:
Annual Meetings: June

Risk and Insurance Management Society *(1950)*
655 Third Ave.
New York, NY 10017
Tel: (212)286-9292 *Fax:* (212)986-9716
E-Mail: info@rims.org
Web Site: www.rims.org
Members: 8800 individuals
Staff: 50
Annual Budget: $5-10,000,000
Executive Director: Mary Roth
E-Mail: mroth@rims.org
General Counsel: Ellen Dunkin
E-Mail: edunkin@rims.org
Chief Marketing Officer: Stephanie Orange
E-Mail: sorange@rims.org

Historical Note
Founded as the National Insurance Buyers Association; it became the American Society of Insurance Management in 1954 and assumed its present name in 1975. Membership consists of corporations, municipalities, universities and other entities that plan and purchase insurance or insurance services. Has an annual budget of approximately $8.4 million. Membership: $440/year (company).

Meetings/Conferences:
Annual Meetings: Spring
2007 - New Orleans, LA/Apr. 29-May 3
2008 - San Diego, CA/Apr. 27-May 1

Publications:
Rimscope. bi-w.
Risk Management Magazine. m. adv.

River Management Society *(1988)*
P.O. Box 9048
Missoula, MT 59807
Tel: (406)549-0514 *Fax:* (406)542-6208
E-Mail: rms@river-management.org
Web Site: www.river-management.org
Members: 500 individuals
Staff: 1
Annual Budget: $50-100,000
Program Director: Caroline Tan
E-Mail: rms@river-management.org

Historical Note
The product of a merger of the American River Management Society and the River Federation in 1996. RMS serves as a forum for information on the appropriate use and management of river resources. Members are government agency employees, companies and organizations, and other private- and public-sector individuals concerned with holistic and ecosystem approaches to water quality, riparian health, and watershed management. Membership: $30/year (professional); $15/year (student); $50/year (organization); $20/year (associate).

Meetings/Conferences:
Biennial Meetings: Summer/300

Publications:
RMS News. q. adv.

RMA - The Risk Management Association *(1914)*
1801 Market St., Suite 300
Philadelphia, PA 19103
Tel: (215)446-4000 *Fax:* (215)446-4101
Toll Free: (800)677 - 7621
Web Site: www.rmahq.org
Members: 17500 individuals
Staff: 80
Annual Budget: $10-25,000,000
President and Chief Executive Officer: Maurice H. Hartigan, II
Director, Member Relations/Chapters/Credit Risk Management: William F. Githens
Director, Securities Lending: Curtis Knight
Director, Regulatory Relations and Communications: Pam Martin
Director, Marketing: Valerie Morris
Director, Credit Risk: Jim Nelson
Chief Financial and Information Technology Officer: Dwight Overturf
Director, Operational Risk: Charles Taylor
Chief Operations and Administrative Officer: Florence J. Wetzel
Director, Strategic Learning: Mark Zmiewski

Historical Note
Formerly (1994) Robert Morris Associates, the National Association of Bank Loan and Credit Officers, and (2000) Robert Morris Associates the Association of Lending and Risk Professionals. Seeks to improve the risk management capabilities and principles of commercial lending and credit functions, loan administration and asset management in commercial banks and other financial industires. Membership dues vary by asset size of institution. Has an annual budget of approximately $16 million.

Publications:
The RMA Journal. m.
Annual Statement Studies. a.

RNA Society *(1993)*
9650 Rockville Pike
Bethesda, MD 20814-3998
Tel: (301)634-7120 *Fax:* (301)634-7420
E-Mail: rna@faseb.org
Web Site: www.rnasociety.org
Members: 1000 individuals
Staff: 4
Executive Officer: Dr. Chris L. Greer
E-Mail: rna@faseb.org

Historical Note
RNA members are scientists engaged in research on ribonucleic acid. Membership: Fees vary $25/year to $150/year.

Meetings/Conferences:
Annual Meetings: early Summer

Publications:
RNA Journal. bi-m.
RNA Directory. a.
Proceedings. a.

Robotic Industries Association *(1974)*
900 Victors Way, Box 3724
Ann Arbor, MI 48106
Tel: (734)994-6088 *Fax:* (734)994-3338
E-Mail: ria@robotics.org
Web Site: www.roboticsonline.com
Members: 250 companies
Staff: 12
Annual Budget: $1-2,000,000
Executive Vice President: Donald A. Vincent, CAE
Director, Marketing and Public Relations: Brian Huse

Historical Note
Established in 1974 as Robot Institute of America, incorporated in Washington, DC; became Robotic Industries Association in 1983. RIA represents the robotics automation industry in North America. Concerned with developing industry guidelines and collecting and dispensing accurate information on research and applications.

Meetings/Conferences:
Semi-Annual Meetings: Spring and Fall

Publications:
Robotics Supplier Directory. a.
RIA Robotics Statistics Report. q. adv.
Robotics Online e-newsletter. bi-w. adv.
The Robot Files CD-Rom. a.

Robotics and Automation Society *(1989)*

Historical Note
A technical society of the Institute of Electrical and Electronics Engineers (IEEE). Membership in the Society, open only to IEEE members, includes subscription to a technical periodical in the field published by IEEE. All administrative support is provided by IEEE.

Robotics International of SME *(1980)*

Historical Note
Part of Engineering Materials Applications Community of SME, a program of Society of Manufacturing Engineers, which provides administrative support.

Rolf Institute *(1971)*
5055 Chaparral Court
Boulder, CO 80301
Tel: (303)449-5903 *Fax:* (303)449-5978
Toll Free: (800)530 - 8875
E-Mail: info@rolf.org
Web Site: www.rolf.org
Members: 1200 individuals
Staff: 8
Annual Budget: $1-2,000,000
Executive Director: G. Thomas Manzione, Ph.D.
Director, Membership Services: Karna Knapp

Historical Note
Established and incorporated in California. Members are practioners of the technique of connective tissue manipulation developed by Dr. Ida P. Rolf. Membership: $450/year.

Meetings/Conferences:
Annual Meetings: August

Publications:
Structural Integration: Journal of the Rolf Institute. a. adv.
Membership Directory. a.

Roller Skating Association International *(1937)*
6905 Corporate Dr.
Indianapolis, IN 46278
Tel: (317)347-2626 *Fax:* (317)347-2636
E-Mail: rsa@rollerskating.com
Web Site: www.rollerskating.org
Members: 2500 individuals
Staff: 10
Annual Budget: $1-2,000,000
Executive Director: Robin O. Brown
Membership Coordinator: Jason Cline
Coordinator, Convention Planning and Education: Kimberly Kissel
Director, Communications: Ingrid Thorson
Coordinator, Coaches: Jennifer Wendel

Historical Note
Formerly (1991) Roller Skating Rink Operators Association of America. RSA was originated by and exists for private businessmen and women engaged in the gainful enterprise of roller skating. Members either own or lease a roller skating facility. The RSA itself does not own or franchise any of the facilities enrolled in the association. Affiliated organizations: Speed Coaches Associations, Society of Roller Skating Teachers of America, Roller Hockey Coaches Association, and the Roller Skating Manufacturers. Membership: $350/year (facility), $350/year (company).

Meetings/Conferences:
Annual Meetings: May

2007 – Las Vegas, NV(Riviera)/Aug. 27-30

Publications:
RSA Today Newsletter. m.
RSA Today Coaches' Edition Newsletter. m.
RSM News Newsletter. bi-m. adv.
Roller Skating Business Magazine. bi-m. adv.

Romance Writers of America *(1980)*
16000 Stuebner Airline, Suite 140
Spring, TX 77379
Tel: (832)717-5200 *Fax:* (832)717-5201
E-Mail: info@rwanational.org
Web Site: www.rwanational.org
Members: 9500 individuals
Staff: 8
Annual Budget: $1-2,000,000
Executive Director: Allison Kelley

Historical Note
Promotes excellence in the genre of romance fiction and provides networking opportunities to writers, published and unpublished, who are seriously pursuing a career in the romance fiction industry. Conducts workshops, sponsors national and regional conferences and awards accomplishments. Membership: $75/year.

Meetings/Conferences:
Annual Meetings: Summer/1,700
2007 – Dallas, TX(Hyatt Regency)/July 11-14/2100
2008 – San Francisco, CA(San Francisco Marriott)/July 30-Aug. 2/2100

Publications:
Romance Writers Report. m. adv.

Romanian Studies Association of America *(1973)*
214 Centennial Hall, Texas State Univ.
San Marcos, TX 78666
Tel: (512)245-3073
Web Site: www.uwo.ca/modlang/RSAA/
Members: 55 individuals
Annual Budget: under $10,000
President: Dr. Valentina Glajar

Historical Note
RSAA's purpose is to foster and to advance Romanian studies on the American continent, particularly in the U.S.A. and Canada. An "allied" organization of the Modern Language Association. Has no paid staff. Membership: $12/year.

Meetings/Conferences:
Annual Meetings: December, with the Modern Language Ass'n

Publications:
RSAA Newsletter. semi-a.
Yearbook of Romanian Studies. a.

Romanian-American Chamber of Commerce *(1990)*
5530 Wisconsin Ave., Suite 920
Chevy Chase, MD 20815-7003
Tel: (301)656-9022 *Fax:* (301)657-1051
E-Mail: racc@racc.ro
Web Site: www.racc.ro
Members: 150 businesses
Annual Budget: $50-100,000
Managing Director: Jay McCrensky

Historical Note
Bilateral trade association dealing with Romania. Membership: $50/year (student); $100/year (individual); $250/year (small business, non-profit); $500/year (corporate); $2,500/year (corporate council).

Publications:
RACC Business Report. q. adv.
Romanian American Cultural Review.

Romanian-U.S. Business Council *(1974)*

Historical Note
A program of U.S. Chamber of Commerce, which provides administrative support.

Roof Coatings Manufacturers Association *(1982)*
1156 15th St. NW, Suite 900
Washington, DC 20005
Tel: (202)207-0919 *Fax:* (202)223-9741
E-Mail: info@roofcoatings.org
Web Site: www.roofcoatings.org
Members: 70 companies
Staff: 8
Annual Budget: $100-250,000
General Manager: Reed Hitchcock

Historical Note
RCMA represents the interests of manufacturers of cold applied roof coatings, cements, and waterproofing agents. Membership: annual dues vary by number of manufacturing plants and suppliers.

Meetings/Conferences:
Annual Meetings: January

Publications:
Regulatory/Legislative Member Alert Bulletin Svc..
Industry Newsletter. q.
Industry Shipment Report. q.
Government Issues Newsletter. q.

Rough Terrain Forklifts Council

Historical Note
A council of the Equipment Manufacturers Institute.

Roundtable for Women in Foodservice *(1983)*

Historical Note
Organization defunct in 2003.

Rubber and Plastics Industry Conference of the United Steelworkers of America *(1935)*
Five Gateway Center
Pittsburgh, PA 15222
Tel: (412)562-2400
Web Site: www.uswa.org
Members: 90000 individuals
Staff: 3
Annual Budget: $10-25,000,000
Secretary: Brenda Blake

Historical Note
Organized in Akron, Ohio September 12, 1935 as the United Rubber Workers of America and chartered as an industrial union the following year by the Congress of Industrial Organization. Became United Rubber, Cork, Linoleum and Plastic Workers of America in 1945; Merged with United Steelworkers of America and assumed its current name in 1995. Has an annual budget of approximately $12.5 million.

Meetings/Conferences:
Triennial Conference: (2005)

Rubber Manufacturers Association *(1900)*
1400 K St. NW, Suite 900
Washington, DC 20005
Tel: (202)682-4800 *Fax:* (202)682-4854
E-Mail: info@rma.org
Web Site: www.rma.org
Members: 130 companies
Staff: 24
Annual Budget: $2-5,000,000
President and Chief Executive Officer: Donald B. Shea, CAE
General Counse and Senior Vice President, Government Affairs: Laurie Baulig
Vice President, Technical and Standards: Steven Butcher
Treasurer and Chief Financial Officer: Lisa I. Murphy

Historical Note
Founded in 1900 as the New England Rubber Club. Incorporated in 1915 as the Rubber Club of America and became the Rubber Association of America in 1917. Name changed to Rubber Manufacturers Association in 1919. Members are manufacturers of rubber products of all types. Dues: based on gross sales to the rubber products industry.

Meetings/Conferences:
Annual Meetings: Winter

Publications:
InfoRMAtion. m.

Rubber Pavements Association *(1985)*
1801 S. Jentilly Lane, Suite A-2
Tempe, AZ 85281-5738
Tel: (480)517-9944 *Fax:* (480)517-9959
Web Site: www.rubberpavements.org
Members: 34 companies
Staff: 3
Annual Budget: $250-500,000
Executive Director: Douglas Carlson
E-Mail: dougc@rubberpavements.org
Director, Communications: Donna J. D. Carlson
Executive Assistant: Linda Kyle
E-Mail: linda@rubberpavements.org

Historical Note
Formerly (1993) the Asphalt Rubber Producers Group. RPA members are companies involved in the manufacture or application of asphalt-rubber or in the rubber recycling business. Membership: $2,000/year (producers/users); $550/year (associate).

Meetings/Conferences:
Annual Meetings: Winter

Publications:
RPA News. q.

Rubber Tired Backhoe Loader and Attachments Council

Historical Note
A council of the Equipment Manufacturers Institute.

Rubber Trade Association of North America *(1914)*
165 Muirfield Rd.
P.O. Box 196
Rockville Center, NY 11571
Tel: (516)536-7228 *Fax:* (516)536-3771
Members: 40 companies
Staff: 2
Secretary: Fred B. Finley

Historical Note
The purpose of the organization is to foster and promote the common business interests of the rubber trade as a whole for the benefit of all concerned; importers, brokers, dealers, agents, consumers and those servicing the natural rubber trade.

Meetings/Conferences:
Annual Meetings: always New York, NY/2nd Tuesday in December

Rural Sociological Society *(1937)*
Univ. of Missouri
104 Gentry
Columbia, MO 65211-7040
Tel: (573)882-9065 *Fax:* (573)882-1473
E-Mail: ruralsoc@missouri.edu
Web Site: www.ruralsociology.org
Members: 1020 individuals
Staff: 2
Annual Budget: $100-250,000
Treasurer: Kenneth E. Pigg
E-Mail: piggk@missouri.edu
Business Manager: Edie Pigg
E-Mail: piggk@missouri.edu

Historical Note
Originally a section of the American Sociological Society, the Rural Sociological Society became independent in 1937. Membership: dues based on salary.

Meetings/Conferences:
Annual Meetings: August/500

Publications:
Rural Sociology. q. adv.
The Rural Sociologist. q. adv.

Ruth Jackson Orthopaedic Society *(1983)*
6300 N. River Road, Suite 727
Rosemont, IL 60018-4226
Tel: (847)698-1637 *Fax:* (847)823-0536
Web Site: www.rjos.org
Members: 470 individuals
Staff: 2
Annual Budget: under $10,000

Historical Note
Formerly the Ruth Jackson Society; assumed present name in 1990. Members are women engaged in the practice of orthopaedic surgery. All active members are certified by the American Board of Orthopaedic Surgery, belong to the American Academy of Orthopaedic Surgeons, or are in training programs leading to these two qualifications. Membership also includes women orthopaedic surgeons in foreign countries. Membership: $250/year (post-resident); $50/year (resident); $25/year (medical student).

Meetings/Conferences:
Annual Meetings: With the American Academy of Orthopaedic Surgeons. Mid-winter/100.

Publications:
Membership List. a.
Ruth Jackson Orthopaedic Society newsletter. q.

Saddle, Harness, and Allied Trade Association *(1993)*
P.O. Box 818
Harrisonburg, VA 22803
Tel: (540)434-9845 *Fax:* (540)434-5298
E-Mail: shoptalk@proleptic.net
Members: 420 individuals
Staff: 2
Annual Budget: under $10,000
Executive Director: Daniel S. Preston
E-Mail: shoptalk@proleptic.net

Historical Note
SHATA represents professionals in the leather and nylon trade separate from the fashion industry. Serves as an information resource, providing technical information, networking, business expertise, and continuing education. Membership: $75/year.

Publications:
Shop Talk!. m. adv.
Manufacturers' Retailers' Buyers Guide. a. adv.

SAE International *(1905)*
400 Commonwealth Dr.
Warrendale, PA 15096-0001
Tel: (724)776-4841 *Fax:* (724)776-0790
E-Mail: customerservice@sae.org
Web Site: www.sae.org
Members: 90000 individuals
Staff: 254
Annual Budget: $50-100,000,000
Executive Vice President and Chief Operating Officer: Raymond A. Morris
General Manager Corporate Sales and Publisher: Thomas Drozda
Director, Commercial Vehicle Business and Chief Technology Officer: Herb Kaufman
Chief Financial Officer: Dana M. Pless

Historical Note
Originated in 1905 as the Society of Automobile Engineers, became the Society of Automotive Engineers in 1916, and assumed its current name in 2001. SAE is a network of engineers, business executives, educators and students from more than 80 countries who come together to share information and exchange ideas for advancing the engineering of mobility systems. Advances all aspects of the design, construction and use of self-propelled mechanisms, prime movers, their components and related equipment. Service Technicians Society is a division of SAE. Has an annual budget of approximately $50 million. Membership: $90/year (individual).

Meetings/Conferences:
Annual Meetings: February in Detroit, MI(Cobo Hall)/50,000

Publications:
SAE Off Highway Engineering. q. adv.
Automotive Engineering International. m. adv.
Aerospace Engineering. m. adv.
SAE Transactions. a.
SAE Update. m. adv.

Safe and Vault Technicians Association *(1986)*
3500 Easy St.
Dallas, TX 75247
Tel: (214)819-9771 *Fax:* (214)819-9736
Toll Free: (800)532 - 2562
E-Mail: savta@savta.org
Web Site: www.savta.org
Members: 2000 individuals
Staff: 3
Executive Director: Charles W. Gibson, Jr., CAE
Manager, Meetings: Kelly Carr, CMD
Editor: Jim DeSimone
Comptroller: Kathy Romo

Historical Note
SAVTA members are retail locksmiths. Associate membership is available for manufacturers, distributors and others with an interest in the industry. Membership: $161/year (individual); $500/year (company).

Publications:
Membership Directory (online).
Safe and Vault Technology Journal. m. adv.

SAFE Association *(1957)*
P.O. Box 130
Creswell, OR 97426-0130
Tel: (541)895-3012 *Fax:* (541)895-3014
E-Mail: safe@peak.org
Web Site: www.safeassociation.org
Members: 950 individuals
Staff: 1
Annual Budget: $100-250,000
Business Administrator: Jeani Benton
E-Mail: safe@peak.org

Historical Note
Established as the Space and Flight Equipment Association at Edwards Air Force Base in 1957 and moved to Los Angeles in 1960. Incorporated in California in 1964 as the Survival and Flight Equipment Association and became the SAFE Association in 1977. Promotes the science of survival and the development of air safety in all forms of transportation. Membership: $60/year (individual); $500/year (organization/company).

Meetings/Conferences:
Annual Meetings: October

Publications:
SAFE Journal. semi-a. adv.
Symposium Proceedings. a.

Safety and Loss Prevention Management Council *(1937)*
2200 Mill Road
Alexandria, VA 22314-4677
Tel: (703)838-1861 *Fax:* (703)838-8468
Toll Free: (888)333 - 1759
E-Mail: slpmc@trucking.org
Web Site: www.truckline.com/aboutata/councils/slpmc
Members: 400 individuals
Annual Budget: $1-2,000,000
Executive Director: Jai Kundu
E-Mail: slpmc@trucking.org

Historical Note
Founded as Transportation Loss Prevention and Security Council; assumed its current name in 2000. An autonomous part of the American Trucking Associations. Works to establish uniform standards of loss and damage claims, as well as ajudication of claims. TLP&SC members are claims and security professionals from motor carriers representing every segment of the industry. Allied membership is available for industry suppliers and associate membership for shipper/receivers. Membership: $160-450/year, varies by gross revenue (motor carrier); $300/year (supplier); $300/year (associate).

Meetings/Conferences:
Annual Meetings: June/200

Publications:
The Informer. q. adv.
Security News. bi-m.
Safety Bulletin. m.

Safety Equipment Distributors Association *(1968)*
2105 Laurel Bush Road, Suite 200
Bel Air, MD 21015
Tel: (443)640-1065 *Fax:* (443)640-1031
E-Mail: jackie@ksgroup.org
Web Site: www.safetycentral.org
Members: 130 companies
Staff: 3
Annual Budget: $250-500,000
Executive Director: Jackwelyn Raley-King
Director, Meetings and Membership Services: Kaymie T. Owen

Historical Note
SEDA represents wholesaler-distributors of safety equipment and works to enhance and improve distribution through excellence in communications, training, education and services.

Meetings/Conferences:
Annual Meetings: Summer

Publications:
Profit Report. a.
The SEDA Scene. bi-m.
SEDA Catalog Program. irreg.

Safety Equipment Manufacturers' Agents Association *(1986)*

Historical Note
A division of North American Industrial Representatives Ass'n, which provides administrative support.

Safety Glazing Certification Council *(1971)*
P.O. Box Nine
Henderson Harbor, NY 13651
Tel: (315)646-2234 *Fax:* (315)646-2297
E-Mail: staff@amscert.com
Web Site: www.sgcc.org
Members: 160 companies
Staff: 3
Annual Budget: $250-500,000
Manager, Administration: John G. Kent
E-Mail: staff@amscert.com

Historical Note
SGCC members are manufacturers of safety glazing products and others concerned with the manufacture and application of safety glazing.

Publications:
SGCC Certified Products Directory. semi-a.

Sailmakers' Institute *(1969)*

Historical Note
A division of the Industrial Fabrics Association International.

Sales and Marketing Executives International *(1935)*
P.O. Box 1390
Sumas, WA 98295-1390
E-Mail: admin@smei.org
Web Site: www.smei.org
Members: 10000 individuals
Staff: 5
Annual Budget: $1-2,000,000
President and Chief Executive Officer: Willis Turner, CSE
E-Mail: admin@smei.org

Historical Note
Established as National Federation of Sales Executives, it became National Sales Executives International in 1949 and assumed its present name in 1961. Members are most commonly professionals in the fields of sales and marketing management, market research management, sales training, distribution management and other senior executives in small and medium businesses. Offers many career development services including: Graduate School of Sales Management and Marketing (with Syracuse Univ.) and professional certification. Pi Sigma Epsilon (PSE), a professional fraternity, is an affiliate. Membership: $195/year.

Meetings/Conferences:
Annual Meetings: Fall

Publications:
Leadership Directory. a.
Marketing Times. q. adv.

Sales Association of the Chemical Industry *(1921)*
66 Morris Ave., Suite 2A
Springfield, NJ 07081-1409
Tel: (973)379-1100 *Fax:* (973)379-6507
E-Mail: bonnietaamc@earthlink.net
Members: 300 individuals
Staff: 1
Annual Budget: $100-250,000
Executive Director: Richard J. Alampi

Historical Note
Founded as the Salesmen's Association of the American Chemical Industry by 96 charter members September 7, 1921 at the Chemists' Club, New York City. Membership is concentrated in New York, New Jersey and Connecticut. Incorporated 1944 in the State of New York. Membership: $105/year (active); $55/year (associate).

Meetings/Conferences:
Annual Meetings: March

Publications:
SACI Slants. 3/year.

Sales Association of the Paper Industry *(1919)*
500 Bi-County Blvd., Suite 200E
Farmingdale, NY 11735
Toll Free: (866)307 - 7274
Web Site: www.sapil.org
Members: 500 individuals and companies

Staff: 2
Annual Budget: $250-500,000
Executive Director: Jack A. Vaccaro

Historical Note
Formerly (1972) Salesmen's Association of the Paper Industry. Membership: $95/year.

Meetings/Conferences:
Annual Meetings: New York, NY(Waldorf Astoria)/March

Publications:
E-Newsletter. m.

Salon Association, The *(1995)*
15825 N. 71st St., Suite 100
Scottsdale, AZ 85254
Tel: (480)281-0424 *Fax:* (480)905-0708
Toll Free: (800)211 - 4872
Web Site: www.salons.org
Members: 7000 salons and spas
Staff: 20
Annual Budget: $2-5,000,000
Executive Director: Steve Sleeper

Historical Note
TSA members are owners of salons. TSA offers bankcard and insurance programs, information networking and opportunities for continued professional business development. Membership: $125/year.

Meetings/Conferences:
Annual Meetings: late January/location alternates between east coast(even years) and west coast(odd years)

Publications:
Change. q.

Salt Institute *(1914)*
700 N. Fairfax St., Suite 600
Alexandria, VA 22314-2040
Tel: (703)549-4648 *Fax:* (703)548-2194
E-Mail: info@saltinstitute.org
Web Site: www.saltinstitute.org
Members: 35 companies
Staff: 4
Annual Budget: $1-2,000,000
President: Richard L. Hanneman
Director, Technical: Susan Feldman

Historical Note
Founded in 1914 as the Salt Producers Association; assumed its current name in 1963. Supported by major salt producers worldwide.

Meetings/Conferences:
Annual Meetings: Spring

Publications:
Salt and Highway Deicing. q.
Salt and Trace Minerals. q.
SI Report. m.

SAMA Group of Associations *(1918)*
225 Reinekers Lane, Suite 625
Alexandria, VA 22314-2875
Tel: (703)836-1360 *Fax:* (703)836-6644
Members: 200 companies
Staff: 2
Annual Budget: $1-2,000,000
President: William C. Strackbein

Historical Note
Formerly (1991) the Scientific Apparatus Makers Association, the SAMA Group of Associations is a non-profit industry trade association composed of three affiliated associations. The three are the Geomatics Industry Association; the Laboratory Products Association, and the Optical Imaging Association. The affiliated associations are composed of manufacturers, suppliers and distributors of analytical instruments and life science systems used for chemical and life science analysis, measurement, systems, and laboratory products, equipment, and supplies marketed worldwide to industry, government, education and research organizations.

Meetings/Conferences:
Annual Meetings: None held.

Sanitary Supply Wholesaling Association *(1981)*
P.O. Box 98
Swanton, OH 43558
Tel: (419)825-3055 *Fax:* (419)825-1815
E-Mail: info@sswa.com
Web Site: www.sswa.com
Members: 75 companies
Staff: 1
Annual Budget: $50-100,000
Executive Director: Donna Frendt
E-Mail: dfrendt@sswa.com

Historical Note
SSWA is comprosed of over 75 manufacturers and wholesalers in the sanitary supply industry who are interested in increasing the efficiencies and quality of distribution. Membership: $745/year.

Meetings/Conferences:
Annual Meetings: Summer
2007 – Charleston, SC(Charleston Place)/June 25-28/70

Publications:
Wholesaler. q.
Membership Directory. a.

Sanitation Suppliers and Contractors Institute *(1957)*

Historical Note
A component of the Environmental Management Association.

Santa Gertrudis Breeders International *(1951)*
Hwy. 141 West
P.O. Box 1257
Kingsville, TX 78364
Tel: (361)592-9357 *Fax:* (361)592-8572
E-Mail: sgbi@sbcglobal.net
Web Site: www.santagertrudis.ws
Members: 1000 individuals
Staff: 6
Annual Budget: $500-1,000,000
Executive Director: Ervin Kaatz

Historical Note
Incorporated April 9, 1951 with 169 charter members to standardize and certify those animals designated as "purebred" and to establish rigorous controls for grading-up to purebred herds. Membership: $100year (active).

Meetings/Conferences:
Annual Meetings: Spring

Publications:
Directory. bien. adv.

Satellite Broadcasting and Communications Association *(1986)*
1730 M St. NW, Suite 600
Washington, DC 20036
Tel: (202)349-3620 *Fax:* (202)349-3621
Toll Free: (800)541 - 5981
E-Mail: info@sbca.org
Web Site: www.sbca.com
Members: 1400 companies
Staff: 16
Annual Budget: $5-10,000,000
President: Richard DalBello
Director, Communications: Camille Osborne

Historical Note
Formerly (1985) the Society for Private and Commercial Earth Stations and (1986) Satellite Television Industry Association. SBCA Represents all segments of the satellite television industry, including manufacturers, distributors, dealers, programmers, and satellite service providers. SBCA provides data and representation on legislative and regulatory actions affecting its members. Membership: $70-$1,100/year (individual), corporate rate varies.

Meetings/Conferences:
Annual Meetings: Summer

Publications:
Membership/Buyers Guide. a.

SAVE International *(1959)*
136 S. Keowee St.
Dayton, OH 45402
Tel: (937)224-7283 *Fax:* (937)222-5794
E-Mail: info@value-eng.org
Web Site: www.value-eng.org
Members: 1100 individuals
Staff: 10
Annual Budget: $100-250,000
Executive Director: Kim Fantaci
E-Mail: info@value-eng.org

Historical Note
Formerly Society of American Value Engineers (1998). Awards the Certified Value Specialist (CVS) designation. Membership: $125/year (individual); $1,000/year (organization).

Meetings/Conferences:
Annual Meetings: Spring-Summer
2007 – Houston, TX(Westin)/May 1-

Publications:
Interactions. m. adv.
Value World. q. adv.

SB Latex Council *(1988)*
1250 Connecticut Ave. NW, Suite 700
Washington, DC 20036
Tel: (202)419-1500 *Fax:* (202)659-8037
E-Mail: info@regnet.com
Web Site: www.regnet.com/sblc
Members: 4 manufacturers
Staff: 2
Annual Budget: $100-250,000
Executive Director: Robert J. Fensterheim

Historical Note
Members are manufacturers of styrene/butadiene latex for carpet manufacturing and paper coating.

Scaffold Industry Association *(1972)*
P.O. Box 20574
Phoenix, AZ 85036
Tel: (602)257-1144 *Fax:* (602)257-1166
Toll Free: (888)310 - 0320
E-Mail: info@scaffold.org
Web Site: www.scaffold.org
Members: 925 companies
Staff: 4
Annual Budget: $1-2,000,000
Executive Vice President: Linda Tweten
E-Mail: linda@scaffold.org

Historical Note
Formerly (1972) the Scaffold Industry Association. Membership: $200-700/year (depending on type of company).

Meetings/Conferences:
Annual Meetings: Summer
2007 – San Francisco, CA/July

Publications:
SIA magazine. m. adv.
Directory/Handbook. a. adv.

Scaffolding, Shoring and Forming Institute *(1960)*
1300 Sumner Ave.
Cleveland, OH 44115-2851
Tel: (216)241-7333 *Fax:* (216)241-0105
E-Mail: ssfi@ssfi.org
Web Site: www.ssfi.org
Members: 17 companies
Staff: 2
Annual Budget: $25-50,000
Managing Director: John H. Addington

Historical Note
Formerly (1969) Steel Scaffolding and Shoring Institute and (1980) Scaffolding and Shoring Institute. SSFI members are companies manufacturing scaffolding, shoring and forming products.

Scale Manufacturers Association *(1945)*
6724 Lone Oak Blvd.
Naples, FL 34109-6834
Tel: (239)514-3441 *Fax:* (239)514-3470
Web Site: www.scalemanufacturers.org
Members: 17 companies
Staff: 4
Annual Budget: $100-250,000
Executive Director: Robert A. Reinfried

Historical Note
SMA members are manufacturers of general industrial scales, load cell weighing devices, retail scales, and vehicle and livestock scales. Purpose is to advance the science of weighing and force measuring, and the engineering and manufacturing of instruments, apparatus, equipment and facilities.

Meetings/Conferences:
Annual Meetings: April/60
2007 – Hilton Head, SC(Crowne Plaza)/Apr. 17-19/35

Publications:
Directory. a.
Weighlog. semi-a.

Scenic, Title and Graphic Artists

Historical Note
See Art Directors Guild/Scenic, Title and Graphic Artists.

Schiffli Lace and Embroidery Manufacturers Association *(1937)*

22 Industrial Ave.
Fairview, NJ 07022-1614
Tel: (201)943-7757 *Fax:* (201)943-7793
E-Mail: info@schiffli.org
Web Site: http://ww.schiffli.org
Members: 150 companies
Staff: 2
Annual Budget: $50-100,000
President: Larry Squiccimari

Historical Note
Formerly Embroidery Manufacturers Bureau. Members are manufacturers of machine-made embroideries and laces, or firms in allied trades (concentrated principally in northern New Jersey and New York City). Membership: $125/year (machine); $125/year (allied trade).

Meetings/Conferences:
Annual Meetings: October-November

Publications:
Embroidery Directory. a. adv.
Embroidery News. bi-m. adv.

School Management Study Group *(1969)*

4948 Rebecca Dr.
Pocatello, ID 83202-1666
Tel: (208)238-1695
Members: 350 individuals
Staff: 5
Annual Budget: $100-250,000
Chief Financial Officer: Gene Davis

Historical Note
School and college administrators interested in improving educational institutions. Membership: $20/year.

Meetings/Conferences:
Annual Meetings: In conjunction with the American Ass'n of School Administrators

School Nutrition Association *(1946)*

700 S. Washington St., Suite 300
Alexandria, VA 22314-3436
Tel: (703)739-3900 *Fax:* (703)739-3915
Toll Free: (800)877 - 8822
E-Mail: bbelmont@schoolnutrition.org
Web Site: www.schoolnutrition.org
Members: 55000 individuals
Staff: 48
Annual Budget: $5-10,000,000
Executive Director: Barbara Belmont, CAE
E-Mail: bbelmont@schoolnutrition.org
Washington Counsel: Marshall Matz
Chief Operating Officer: Patti Montague
Staff Vice President, Communications: Maria Robertson
Staff Vice President, Government Affairs and Public Awareness: Cathy Schuchart

Historical Note
Formerly American School Food Service Association; assumed its current name in 2004. Organized in 1946 when the school meals program was officially recognized and implemented through the National School Lunch Act. Members are individuals working in food services in elementary and secondary non-profit schools, state programs, CNP, and other non-profit community child nutrition programs. Seeks to encourage and promote children's health and nutrition, to promote united efforts between school personnel and the public and encourage nutrition projects and research development. Membership: $75/year (individual); $550/year (corporate sustaining).

Meetings/Conferences:
Annual Meetings: July/6,500
2007 - Chicago, IL(Convention Center)/July 15-18/65000

Publications:
Journal of Child Nutrition and Management (online). bi-a.
School Foodservice and Nutrition. 11/year. adv.

School Science and Mathematics Association *(1901)*

Texas Tech Univ.
3008 18th St., Box 41071
Lubbock, TX 79409-1071
Tel: (806)742-1997 Ext: 313 *Fax:* (806)742-2179
Web Site: www.ssma.org
Members: 500 individuals
Staff: 3
Annual Budget: $100-250,000
Executive Director: Arthur L. White

Historical Note
Incorporated in Illinois in 1901 as the Central Association of Science and Mathematics Teachers, Inc. Affiliated with the American Association for the Advancement of Science. Membership: $50/year (individual), $100/year (institution), $60/year (foreign), $125/year (foreign institution).

Meetings/Conferences:
Annual Meetings: Fall

Publications:
Math-Science Connector. 3/year.
School Science and Mathematics. 8/year. adv.

School, Home and Office Products Association *(1991)*

3131 Elbee Road
Dayton, OH 45439-1900
Tel: (937)297-2250 *Fax:* (937)297-2254
Toll Free: (800)854 - 7467
E-Mail: info@shopa.org
Web Site: www.shopa.org
Members: 2000 organizations
Staff: 30
Annual Budget: $5-10,000,000
President: Steven L. Jacober
E-Mail: stevej@shopa.org

Historical Note
Formed to sponsor an annual trade show (SHOPA SHOW) and conduct industry activities for the manufacturers, wholesalers, distributors, service merchandisers, manufacturing representatives and retailers, and commerical/contract stationers of school and home office products through mass retail and commercial channels. Membership: $250/year (domestic); $350/year (foreign).

Meetings/Conferences:
Annual Meetings: Fall

Publications:
Distribution Trends Report. a.
State of the Industry. a.
SHOPA Show Daily. a. adv.
SHOPTALK. m.
Membership Directory. a.

Science Fiction and Fantasy Writers of America *(1965)*

P.O. Box 877
Chestertown, MD 21620
Tel: (410)778-2211
E-Mail: execdir@sfwa.org
Web Site: www.sfwa.org
Members: 1428 individuals
Annual Budget: $50-100,000
Executive Director: Jane Jewell
E-Mail: execdir@sfwa.org

Historical Note
An organization of professional writers in the science fiction and fantasy field. Formerly (1992) Science Fiction Writers of America. Membership: $35 (affiliate); $50 (active/associate); $60 (institutional).

Meetings/Conferences:
Annual Meetings: April

Publications:
SFWA Handbook.
Nebula Awards Report.
The Bulletin. q.
SFWA Forum. bi-m.

Scientific Equipment and Furniture Association *(1988)*

1205 Franklin Ave., Suite 320
Garden City, NY 11530
Tel: (516)294-5424 *Fax:* (516)294-2758
E-Mail: sefalabs@aol.com
Web Site: www.sefalabs.com
Members: 83 companies
Staff: 2
Annual Budget: $100-250,000
Executive Director: David J. Sutton
E-Mail: sefalabs@aol.com

Historical Note
SEFA represents designers and manufacturers of equipment and furniture for laboratories and other scientific installations. Provides standards for safe practice and planning. Membership fee varies, based on revenues.

Meetings/Conferences:
Semi-Annual Meetings: Spring and Fall

Publications:
SEFA Scope. semi-a.

Scoliosis Research Society *(1966)*

555 E. Wells St., Suite 1100
Milwaukee, WI 53202
Tel: (414)289-9107 *Fax:* (414)276-3349
Web Site: www.srs.org
Members: 850 individuals
Staff: 5
Annual Budget: $500-1,000,000
Executive Director: Tressa Goulding
E-Mail: tgoulding@execinc.com

Historical Note
SRS members are physicians with an interest in spinal deformities.

Meetings/Conferences:
Annual Meetings: Fall
2007 - Edinburgh, United Kingdom/Sept. 4-8
2008 - Salt Lake City, UT/Sept. 9-13

Scottish Blackface Sheep Breeders Association *(1982)*

1699 HH Hwy.
Willow Springs, MO 65793
Tel: (417)962-5466
E-Mail: sbsba@pcis.net
Members: 90 individuals
Annual Budget: under $10,000
Secretary: Richard J. Harward
E-Mail: sbsba@pcis.net

Historical Note
Aids breeders in finding and perpetuating new blood lines. Membership fee: $10/year.

Meetings/Conferences:
Biennial Meetings: Late Summer

Publications:
Breed Specs. a.
Membership List. irreg.

Scrap Tire Management Council *(1990)*

Historical Note
STMC, an advocacy organization within the Rubber Manufacturers Association, was created to identify and promote environmentally and economically sound markets for scrap tires.

Screen Actors Guild *(1933)*

5757 Wilshire Blvd.
Los Angeles, CA 90036-3600
Tel: (323)954-1600
E-Mail: saginfo@sag.org
Web Site: www.sag.org
Members: 96000 individuals
Staff: 400
Annual Budget: $25-50,000,000
Interim National Executive Director and Chief Executive Officer: Peter C. Frank
Deputy National Executive Director, Policy and Strategic Planning: Pamm Fair
Chief Information Officer: Liam Mennis

Historical Note
Labor union affiliated with AFL-CIO. An autonomous branch union of Associated Actors and Artistes America representing actors in film, television, commercials, interactive multimedia

Publications:
Screen Actor. bi-m.

Screen Manufacturers Association *(1955)*
2850 S. Ocean Blvd., Suite 114
Palm Beach, FL 33480-6205
Tel: (561)533-0991 *Fax:* (561)533-7466
Web Site: www.smacentral.org
Members: 35 companies
Staff: 2
Annual Budget: $50-100,000
Executive Vice President: Frank S. Fitzgerald, CAE, DABFE, FACFE

Historical Note
Formerly (1957) Frame Screen Manufacturers Association.

Meetings/Conferences:
Annual Meetings: Spring

Publications:
Directory. a.

Screenprinting and Graphic Imaging Association International

Historical Note
Became Specialty Graphic Imaging Association in 2003.

Scribes *(1953)*
c/o Barry Univ. School of Law
6441 E. Colonial Dr.
Orlando, FL 32807-3650
Tel: (321)206-5701 *Fax:* (321)206-5730
Web Site: www.scribes.org
Members: 900 individuals
Staff: 2
Annual Budget: $10-25,000
Executive Director: Glen-Peter Ahlers, Sr.
E-Mail: gahlers@mail.barry.edu

Historical Note
Also known as the American Society of Writers on Legal Subjects. Members are judges, editors of legal publications, writers on legal topics, law professors and others with an interest in legal writing. Membership: $65/year (individual); $650/year (institution).

Meetings/Conferences:
Annual Meetings: in conjunction with the ABA and the AALS.

Publications:
The Scribes Journal of Legal Writing. a.
The Scrivener. q.

SCSI Trade Association *(1995)*
P.O. Box 29920
San Francisco, CA 94129
Tel: (415)561-6273 *Fax:* (415)561-6120
E-Mail: info@scsita.org
Web Site: www.scsita.org
Members: 20 individuals

Historical Note
STA develops and disseminates information about the SCSI (Small Computer System Interface) technology for member OEMs, resellers, and IT professionals.

Sculptors Guild *(1937)*
110 Greene St., Suite 601
New York, NY 10012
Tel: (212)431-5669
E-Mail: sculptorsguild@earthlink.net
Web Site: www.sculptorsguild.org
Members: 123 individuals
Staff: 1
Annual Budget: $10-25,000
President: Michael Rees
E-Mail: sculptorsguild@earthlink.net

Historical Note
The Guild features work by member artists in exhibitions held in corporate and other public spaces throughout the year. Membership: $150-175/year.

Meetings/Conferences:
Annual Meetings: always New York, NY/April-May

Publications:
Guild Reporter. 3/year. adv.

Seafarers' International Union *(1938)*
5201 Auth Way
Camp Springs, MD 20746-4275
Tel: (301)899-0675 *Fax:* (301)899-7355
Web Site: www.seafarers.org
Members: 80000 individuals
Staff: 125
Annual Budget: $2-5,000,000
President: Michael Sacco

Historical Note
Composed of 18 autonomous affiliated unions of seamen, fishermen, fish cannery workers, inland boatmen, transportation workers and industrial workers in the U.S., Canada, U.S. Virgin Islands and Puerto Rico. SIU was chartered by the American Federation of Labor October 14, 1938 as an outgrowth of the Sailor's Union of the Pacific.

Meetings/Conferences:
Quinquennial Meetings: (2007)

Publications:
Seafarers Log. m.

Sealant, Waterproofing and Restoration Institute *(1976)*
14 W. Third, Suite 200
Kansas City, MO 64105
Tel: (816)472-7974 *Fax:* (816)472-7765
E-Mail: info@swrionline.org
Web Site: www.swrionline.org
Members: 250 companies
Staff: 3
Annual Budget: $250-500,000
Executive Vice President: Kenneth R. Bowman
Vice President: Debra Nemec
Membership Director: Erin Nied
E-Mail: erin@robstan.com

Historical Note
Formerly the Sealant and Waterproofers Institute; adopted its present name in 1989. Regular members are sealant, waterproofing and restoration contractors; associate members are suppliers to the industry.

Meetings/Conferences:
Semi-Annual Meetings: Spring/Fall
2007 – Maui, HI(Hyatt Regency Maui)/Feb. 25-28
2007 – San Diego, CA(Rancho Bernardo Inn)/Oct. 14-16/200

Publications:
The Applicator. q. adv.

Seaplane Pilots Association *(1972)*
4315 Highland Park Blvd., Suite C
Lakeland, FL 33813-1639
Tel: (863)701-7979 *Fax:* (863)701-7588
Toll Free: (888)772 - 8923
Web Site: www.seaplanes.org
Members: 8000 individuals
Staff: 2
Annual Budget: $250-500,000
Executive Administrative Assistant: Ann Gaines
E-Mail: anng@seaplanes.org
Executive Editor: James McManus

Historical Note
Established in Little Ferry, NJ as the U.S. Seaplane Pilots Association. Seeks to protect right of access for seaplanes to waterways in the U.S. and Canada, to promote seaplane flying and to disseminate information to seaplane pilots. Membership: $36/year.

Meetings/Conferences:
Annual Meetings: Usually September (1st weekend after Labor Day), Greenville, ME

Publications:
Water Flying. bi-m. adv.
SPA Water Landing Directory. bien. adv.

Secondary Materials and Recycled Textiles Association *(1932)*
7910 Woodmont Ave., Suite 1130
Bethesda, MD 20814-3015
Tel: (301)656-1077 *Fax:* (301)656-1079
Web Site: www.smartasn.org
Members: 300 companies
Staff: 3
Annual Budget: $250-500,000
Executive Vice President: Bernard D. Brill

Historical Note
Founded as the Sanitary Institute of America, it became the National Association of Wiping Cloth Manufacturers, (1977) the International Association of Wiping Cloth Manufacturers, and (1993) Secondary Materials and Recycled Textiles Association. SMART members are manufacturers and distributors of industrial wiping cloths, used clothing, mill ends, remnants, and recycled textiles. Membership: $1,200/year (company).

Meetings/Conferences:
Annual Meetings: Spring

Publications:
SMART Talk Newsletter. m. adv.
Wiper Disposability Brochures.
SMART Membership & Buyers Guide. a. adv.

Section for Women in Public Administration *(1982)*

Historical Note
An affiliate of American Society for Public Administration, whioch provides administrative support.

Securities Industry and Financial Markets Association *(2006)*
Co-Chief Executive Officer: Micah S. Green
Co-Chief Executive Officer: Marc E. Lackritz
E-Mail: info@sia.com

Historical Note
Formed in 2006 from the merger of the Securities Industry Association and the Bond Market Association.

Securities Industry Association

Historical Note
Merged with the Bond Market Association in 2006 to form the Securities Industry and Financial Markets Association (SIFMA).

Securities Transfer Association *(1911)*
P.O. Box 5067
Hazlet, NJ 07730-5067
Tel: (732)888-6040 *Fax:* (732)888-2121
E-Mail: cgaffney@stai.org
Web Site: www.stai.org
Members: 200 companies
Staff: 2
Annual Budget: $250-500,000
Administrator: Carol Gaffney
E-Mail: cgaffney@stai.org

Historical Note
An association of representatives from banks and corporations in the U.S. and Canada who are involved in the issuance, transfer and registration of corporate securities or related duties. Membership: $500/year (minimum).

Meetings/Conferences:
Annual Meetings: Fall/300-350

Publications:
STA Rule Booklet. irreg.
Newsletter. q.

Security Hardware Distributors Association *(1940)*
100 N. 20th St.
Fourth Floor
Philadelphia, PA 19103-1443
Tel: (215)564-3484 *Fax:* (215)963-9784
E-Mail: shda@fernley.com
Members: 150manufacturersanddistributors
Staff: 3
Annual Budget: $100-250,000
Executive Director: Talbot M. Gee

Historical Note
Formerly (1997) National Locksmith Suppliers Association. Distributors and manufacturers of security hardware. Membership fee varies, based on sales volume.

Meetings/Conferences:
Annual Meetings: Spring

Security Industry Association *(1969)*
635 Slaters Lane, Suite 110
Alexandria, VA 22314
Tel: (703)683-2075 *Fax:* (703)683-2469
Web Site: www.siaonline.org
Members: 650 firms
Staff: 15
Annual Budget: $2-5,000,000
Executive Director: Richard Chace
Manager, Communications: Jennifer Hart Ackerman

Manager, Marketing and Meetings: Leigh A. McGuire
Director, Government Relations: Cathryn A. Mrosko
Director, Finance, Human Resources, and Administration: Stephanie Smith
Director, Research and Technology: Mark A. Visbal

Historical Note
The product of a merger of the Security Equipment Manufacturers Association and the Security Equipment Distributors Association, both founded in 1969. Membership: sliding scale based on annual sales. Formerly Security Equipment Industry Association (1988).

Meetings/Conferences:
Annual Meetings: *Fall*

Publications:
Market Research Reports. q.
SIA News. m. adv.

Security Traders Association *(1934)*
420 Lexington Ave., Suite 2334
New York, NY 10170
Tel: (212)867-7002 *Fax:* (212)867-7030
Web Site: www.securitytraders.org
Members: 6000 individuals
Staff: 3
Annual Budget: $2-5,000,000
President and Chief Executive Officer: John C. Giesea
E-Mail: jgiesea@securitytraders.org

Historical Note
Formerly (1988) National Security Traders Association. Members are security traders and others involved in the securities industry. Members are located in the U.S., Canada and Western Europe. STA, composed of 35 affiliate organizations, maintains communications with self-regulatory organizations, local and national governments, and their agencies, and fosters cooperation among all segments of the worldwide securities industry. Membership: $50/year, plus local affiliate membership (individual).

Meetings/Conferences:
Annual Meetings: *Fall/800*

Publications:
Newsletter. q.
Traders Annual. a. adv.
Pre-Convention Guide. a. adv.

Seismological Society of America *(1906)*
201 Plaza Professional Bldg.
El Cerrito, CA 94530
Tel: (510)525-5474 *Fax:* (510)525-7204
E-Mail: info@seismosoc.org
Web Site: www.seismosoc.org
Members: 1900 individuals
Staff: 4
Annual Budget: $500-1,000,000
Executive Director: Susan B. Newman
E-Mail: snewman@seismosoc.org

Historical Note
Established in San Francisco, CA in August 1906, and incorporated in California the same year. A member society of the American Geological Institute. Membership: $120/year (individual); $130/year (foreign); $1000/year (company).

Meetings/Conferences:
Annual Meetings: *Spring*

Publications:
Bulletin. bi-m.
Seismological Research Letters. bi-m.

Select Registry/Distinguished Inns of North America *(1971)*
P.O. Box 150
Marshall, MI 49068
Tel: (269)789-0393 *Fax:* (269)789-0970
Toll Free: (800)344 - 5244
E-Mail: maincontact@selectregistry.com
Web Site: www.selectregistry.com
Members: 411 inns and establishments
Staff: 6
Annual Budget: $1-2,000,000
Executive Director: Keith Kehlbeck
Director, Finance and Operations: Judy Baker
Director, Membership and Quality Assurance: Carol Riggs

Historical Note
Founded as Independent Innkeepers Association; assumed its current name in 2000. Members are independent, full-service inns and B&Bs in the U.S. and Canada.

Meetings/Conferences:
Annual Meetings: *Annual/ 200-300*
2007 - Coeur D'Alene, ID(Coeur D'Alene Resort)/May 6-9

Publications:
Select Registry. a. adv.

Self Insurance Institute of America, Inc. *(1981)*
883 N.E. Main St.
Simpsonville, SC 29681
Tel: (864)962-2208 *Fax:* (864)962-2483
Toll Free: (800)851 - 7789
Web Site: www.siia.org
Members: 1000 companies
Staff: 15
Annual Budget: $2-5,000,000
Chief Executive Officer: James A. Kinder
E-Mail: jkinder@siia.org
Executive Director: Mike W. Ferguson
E-Mail: mferguson@siia.org
Marketing Manager: Raquel Horton
Communications: Tom Mather
E-Mail: tmather@siia.org
Washington Counsel: George J. Pantos
Director, Finance: Mieka Scholten
Director, Government Relations and Public Affairs: Ashley Williams

Historical Note
Established in Santa Ana, CA in 1981 in order to bring the three principal entities of the self-insurance industry - consumer employers, third party administrators and reinsurance companies - and other interested parties together for dialogue; incorporated in California. Members are companies involved or interested in self-funding risk for workers compensation insurance programs, employee benefit plans or property and casualty protection. Membership: $695/year (associate); $1295/year (company).

Meetings/Conferences:
Annual Meetings: *October*

Publications:
Who's Who Directory. a. adv.
The Self Insurer Magazine. m. adv.
The Source. m.

Self Storage Association *(1975)*
1900 N. Beauregard St., Suite 110
Alexandria, VA 22311
Tel: (703)575-8000 *Fax:* (703)575-8901
E-Mail: info@selfstorage.org
Web Site: www.selfstorage.org
Members: 6500 member facilities
Staff: 17
Annual Budget: $2-5,000,000
President and Chief Executive Officer: Mike Scanlon, Jr.
Vice President, Education: Lyn Brackett
E-Mail: mkidd@selfstorage.org
Vice President, Communications and Government Relations: Tim Dietz
Vice President, Conferences and Tradeshows: Martha M. Morrison
E-Mail: martham@selfstorage.org
Vice President, Membership: Ginny Stengel
E-Mail: gstengel@selfstorage.org

Historical Note
Formerly (1989) Self-Service Storage Association. Self storage owners, operators, investors, managers, and vendor-suppliers to the industry. Membership: $395/year, plus $75 per facililty (regular); $195/year (small).

Meetings/Conferences:
Semi-Annual Meetings: *Spring and Fall*

Publications:
SSA Membership Directory and Resource Guide. a..
SSA Globe magazine. bi-m.
Self Storage Legal Review. bi-m.
SSA Monday Morning Memo (electronic). w.
SSA Facility Managers' Memo. m.

Semiconductor Environmental Safety and Health Association *(1978)*
1313 Dolley Madison Blvd., Suite 402
McLean, VA 22101-3926
Tel: (703)790-1745 *Fax:* (703)790-2672
E-Mail: sesha@burkinc.com
Web Site: www.seshaonline.org
Members: 1200 individuals
Staff: 12
Annual Budget: $250-500,000
Executive Director: Brett J. Burk

Historical Note
Formerly (2002) Semiconductor Safety Association. SESHA members are individuals employed within the electronics and related high technology industries with an interest in environmental, health and safety issues. Membership: $100/year (individual).

Meetings/Conferences:
Annual Meetings: *Spring*

Publications:
SSA Journal. q. adv.
SESHA E-Journal. q. adv.

Semiconductor Equipment and Materials International *(1970)*
3081 Zanker Road
San Jose, CA 95134
Tel: (408)943-6900 *Fax:* (408)428-9600
E-Mail: semihq@semi.org
Web Site: www.semi.org
Members: 150 individuals
Staff: 126
Annual Budget: $25-50,000,000
Senior Manager, Marketing Communications: Michael Droeger
Director, Media Relations: Jennifer Blatt
E-Mail: semihq@semi.org

Historical Note
Formerly (1988) Semiconductor Equipment and Materials Institute. SEMI is an international trade association representing firms supplying equipment, materials and services to the semiconductor industry. Maintains regional offices in Brussels, Tokyo, Seoul, Moscow, Washington, D.C. and Singapore. Has an annual budget of approximately $45 million. Membership: $100/year (individual), $1,200-5,200/year (corporate), $250/year (business affiliate).

Publications:
Forecast.
SEMI Membership Directory.
SEMI Standards.
Semiconductor Manufacturing Magazine. 9/year. adv.

Semiconductor Industry Association *(1977)*
181 Metro Dr., Suite 450
San Jose, CA 95110
Tel: (408)436-6600 *Fax:* (408)436-6646
E-Mail: mailbox@sia.online.org
Web Site: www.sia-online.org
Members: 125 companies
Staff: 14
Annual Budget: $5-10,000,000
President: George Scalise
Director, Communications: John Greenagel
E-Mail: mailbox@sia.online.org
Director, Marketing and Member Relations: Kirsten Romer

Historical Note
Represents U.S. producers of all semiconductor products, such as discrete components, integrated circuits and microprocessors.

Publications:
Statistical Report. a.
Annual Directory. a.

Semiotic Society of America *(1975)*
Univ. of St. Thomas, Houston
3800 Montrose Blvd.
Houston, TX 77006
Tel: (713)942-3449 *Fax:* (713)942-3452
E-Mail: SSA_Houston@stthom.edu
Web Site: www.uwf.edu/tprewitt/ssa.html
Members: 600individualsandinstitutions
Secretary: John Deely
E-Mail: SSA_Houston@stthom.edu

Historical Note
SSA members are academics and institutions with an interest in the function of signs and symbols.

Membership: $50/year (individuals); $25/year (student); $50/year (institution).

Meetings/Conferences:
Annual Meetings: October

Publications:
American Journal of Semiotics. q. adv.
Semiotic Scene Newsletter. q.

Senior Army Reserve Commanders Association *(1949)*
P.O. Box 5050
Springfield, VA 22150
Web Site: www.sarca.us
Members: 600 individuals
Staff: 3
Annual Budget: $100-250,000
National Secretary: William D.R. Waff

Historical Note
SARCA is a professional association of Army Reserve leadership formed to assure that the Army Reserve plays a major role in the defense of the United States. Membership: $125-175/year (active).

Meetings/Conferences:
Semi-annual Meetings:

Publications:
Washington Update. a.

Senior Executives Association *(1980)*
P.O. Box 44808
Washington, DC 20026
Tel: (202)927-7000 *Fax:* (202)927-5192
E-Mail: action@seniorexecs.org
Web Site: www.seniorexecs.org
Members: 2500 individuals
Staff: 8
Annual Budget: $500-1,000,000
President: Carol A. Bonosaro
Director, Communications: Lindsey Mikal
Director, Membership and Agency Liaison: Berton Subrin

Historical Note
Founded in 1980 as a tax-exempt, non-profit professional association representing career Federal executives, SEA is committed to effective and productive leadership in government. Seeks to advance the professionalism and advocate the interests of member executives who manage the government's departments and agencies. Membership: $281/year; $1,500 (lifetime).

Meetings/Conferences:
Annual Meetings: Fall/300

Publications:
Action. m. adv.

SEPM - Society for Sedimentary Geology *(1926)*
6128 E. 38th St., Suite 308
Tulsa, OK 74135-5814
Tel: (918)610-3361 *Fax:* (918)621-1685
Toll Free: (800)865 - 9765
E-Mail: hharper@sepm.org
Web Site: www.sepm.org
Members: 5000 individuals
Staff: 7
Annual Budget: $1-2,000,000
Executive Director: Howard Harper
E-Mail: hharper@sepm.org
Business Manager: Theresa L. Scott
E-Mail: tscott@sepm.org
Membership Coordinator: Michele Woods

Historical Note
Formerly Society of Economic Paleontologists and Mineralogists, it assumed its present name in 1989. Originated in Fort Worth in 1926 and became an affiliated society of the American Association of Petroleum Geologists in 1927. Later became a section, and in 1930 a technical division, of the AAPG. Membership: $70-115/year (individual).

Meetings/Conferences:
Semi-Annual Meetings: Annual with AAPG and Mid-Year

Publications:
Newsletter. q. adv.
Membership Directory. bien. adv.
Journal of Sedimentary Research. bi-m. adv.
PALAIOS. bi-m.

Service Dealers Association *(1986)*
P.O. Box 151389
Austin, TX 78715
Tel: (512)292-1260 *Fax:* (512)292-1221
Web Site: www.psd.info
Members: 2400 individuals
Staff: 1
Annual Budget: $100-250,000
President: Oscar Cavazos

Historical Note
SDA represents dealers and distributors of power equipment. Membership: $95/year (individual); $250/year (company).

Publications:
TSDA Newsletter. q. adv.
Membership Directory. a. adv.

Service Employees International Union *(1921)*
1800 Massachusettes Ave. NW
Washington, DC 20036
Tel: (202)898-3200 *Fax:* (202)898-3438
Toll Free: (800)424 - 8592
Web Site: www.seiu.org
Members: 1800000 individuals
Staff: 750
Annual Budget: Over $100,000,000
President: Andrew L. Stern
Director, Communications and Assistant to the President: Ben Boyd
Secretary-Treasurer: Anna Burger

Historical Note
Chartered by the American Federation of Labor on April 23, 1921 as a union of custodial and building service employees, SEIU now represents building service workers, healthcare workers, public employees and office workers. Originally, the Building Service Employees International Union, it assumed its present name in 1968. Absorbed International Leather Goods, Plastics, Novelty, and Service Workers' Union in 2000. Affiliated with AFL-CIO and CLC. Sponsors and supports the COPE Political Action Committee.

Meetings/Conferences:
Quadrennial Meetings:

Publications:
SEIU Action. m.
SEIU Uniting Our Strength e-news (online).

Service Industry Association *(1985)*
2164 Historic Decatur Road, Villa 19
San Diego, CA 92106
Tel: (619)221-9200 *Fax:* (619)221-8201
E-Mail: cbetzner@aol.com
Web Site: www.servicenetwork.org
Members: 250 companies
Staff: 3
Annual Budget: $100-250,000
Executive Director: Claudia J. Betzner
E-Mail: cbetzner@aol.com

Historical Note
SIA members are high tech service companies. Membership: dues based on number of employees.

Meetings/Conferences:
Annual Meetings: Spring

Publications:
Membership List. a. adv.
Network News Newsletter. q. adv.

Service Specialists Association *(1981)*
4015 Marks Road, Suite 2B
Medina, OH 44256
Tel: (330)725-7160 *Fax:* (330)722-5638
Toll Free: (800)763 - 5717
E-Mail: trucksvc@aol.com
Web Site: www.truckservice.org
Members: 140 companies
Staff: 1
Annual Budget: $100-250,000
Executive Vice President: Cara R. Giebner

Historical Note
Formerly (1990) the Spring Service Association and The Suspension Specialists Association (1996). Members are persons, firms, or corporations who have operated a full line heavy duty repair service shop for at least one year with sufficient inventory to service market area, have rebuilding department capable of making all necessary repairs. Membership: $600/year.

Meetings/Conferences:
Annual Meetings: October

Publications:
The Leaf Newsletter. m.

Service Station Dealers of America and Allied Trades *(1947)*
1532 Pointer Ridge Place, Suite E
Bowie, MD 20716
Tel: (301)390-4405 *Fax:* (301)390-3161
E-Mail: ssda-at@mindspring.com
Web Site: www.ssda-at.org
Members: 20000 individuals
Staff: 2
Annual Budget: $100-250,000
Executive Vice President: Paul Fiore
E-Mail: ssda-at@mindspring.com

Historical Note
Members are independent gasoline dealers who sell gasoline under the brand name of their supplier. Sponsors the SSDA Political Action Committee. Known as National Congress of Petroleum Retailers, Inc. until 1980. Membership: $99/year (regular); $300/year (associate).

Publications:
Membership Directory.
SSDA Newsletter. m.
Legislative/Legal Update. irreg.

Service Technicians Society

Historical Note
A division of Society of Automotive Engineers, which provides administrative support.

Sewn Products Equipment and Suppliers of the Americas *(1990)*
5107 Falls of Neuse Road, Suite B15
Raleigh, NC 27609-4871
Tel: (919)872-8909 *Fax:* (919)872-1915
Toll Free: (888)447 - 7372
E-Mail: spesa@spesa.org
Web Site: www.spesa.org
Members: 110 companies
Staff: 8
Annual Budget: $100-250,000
Executive Vice President and Secretary: Benton W. Gardner

Historical Note
Founded as Sewn Products Equipment Suppliers Association; assumed its currrent name in 2002. Members are companies engaged in or connected with supplying equipment, including replacement parts and computer software, to the sewn products industry. Associate membership is available to non-qualifying individuals and corporations; affiliate membership is available to individuals and corporations organizing trade shows, trade press or allied trade associations. Membership: $850-5,000/year, based on U.S. gross revenues (regular U.S. member); $750/year (associate or affiliate U.S. member).

Meetings/Conferences:
Annual Meetings: Spring

Publications:
Online News Service - Behind the Seams. bi-w. adv.
SPESA Speaks newsletter. bi-m.
Membership Directory.

Shareholder Services Association *(1946)*
1947 Wynnton Road
Columbus, GA 31999-0001
Tel: (706)596-3385 *Fax:* (706)596-3488
Web Site: www.shareholderservices.org
Members: 240 individuals
Annual Budget: $50-100,000
President: James Alden
Secretary: Joan M. DiBlasi
E-Mail: jdiblasi@aflac.com

Historical Note
Members are corporate employees responsible for the transfer of stock, shareholder services and related functions. Has no paid officers or full-time staff. Membership: $325/year (organization/company).

Meetings/Conferences:
Annual Meetings:
2007 – Hilton Head, SC

Publications:
CTAA Roster & Bylaws. irreg.

Sheet Metal and Air Conditioning Contractors' National Association *(1943)*
4201 Lafayette Center Dr.
Chantilly, VA 20151-1209
Tel: (703)803-2980 *Fax:* (703)803-3732
E-Mail: info@smacna.org
Web Site: www.smacna.org
Members: 1,966 companies, 94 chapters
Staff: 42
Annual Budget: $5-10,000,000
Executive Vice President and Chief Executive Officer: John W. Sroka
Executive Director, Technical Services: Eli Howard, III
Director, Government Relations: Stanley Kolbe
Controller: Jerrold Marans
Director, Communications and Public Relations: Rosalind Raymond
Executive Director, Operations: Robert Roach
Executive Director, Market Sectors: Thomas J. Soles
Director, Meetings and Conventions: Mary Lou Taylor

Historical Note
Formerly (1956) Sheet Metal Contractors National Association. Sponsors and supports the Sheet Metal and Air Conditioning Political Action Committee (SMAC PAC). Members are contractors in commercial and industrial heating, ventilation and air conditioning, architectural and industrial sheet metal, manufacturing, testing and balancing, and siding and decking. Has an annual budget of approximately $9 million.

Meetings/Conferences:
Annual Meetings: Fall/2,500
2007 – Las Vegas, NV(Mandaly Bay)/Oct. 21-25

Publications:
Architectural Metal (E-Mail). 2/year.
Industrial Insights (E-Mail). 2/year.
Residential Report (E-Mail). 2/year.
SMACNews (E-Mail). m.
Membership Directory. a.
Annual Report. a.

Sheet Metal Workers' International Association *(1888)*
1750 New York Ave. NW
Washington, DC 20006
Tel: (202)783-5880
E-Mail: info@smwia.org
Web Site: www.smwia.org
Members: 150000 individuals
Staff: 125
Annual Budget: $5-10,000,000
General President: Michael J. Sullivan
E-Mail: info@smwia.org
General Secretary-Treasurer: Joseph J. Nigro

Historical Note
Established in Toledo, Ohio on January 25, 1888 as the Tin, Sheet Iron and Cornice Workers' International Association. Chartered by the American Federation of Labor in 1899. Became the Amalgamated Sheet Metal Workers' International Association in 1897 and merged with the Sheet Metal Workers' National Alliance in 1903 to become the Amalgamated Sheet Metal Workers' International Alliance. Sponsors and supports the Sheet Metal Workers International Association Political Action Committee.

Meetings/Conferences:
Annual Meetings: August/600

Publications:
Sheet Metal Workers' Journal. bi-m.

Shipbuilders Council of America *(1920)*
1455 F St. NW, Suite 225
Washington, DC 20005
Tel: (202)347-5462 *Fax:* (202)347-5464
Web Site: www.shipbuilders.org
Members: 75 Shipyards
Staff: 2
Annual Budget: $250-500,000
Contact: Mary Allen

Historical Note
Formerly National Council of American Shipbuilders. Absorbed Atlantic and Gulf Coasts Drydock Association. Merged with National Shipyard Association in 1998. SCA members are private shipbuilding and repair companies and related firms such as manufacturers of marine equipment and supplies, many of which do work for the federal government. Membership: (dues vary according to sales to the industry).

Publications:
Shipyard Chronicle. m.

Shipowners Claims Bureau *(1917)*
60 Broad St., 37th Fl.
New York, NY 10004
Tel: (212)847-4500 *Fax:* (212)847-4599
E-Mail: info@american-club.net
Web Site: www.american-club.com
Members: 31 companies
Staff: 30
President and Chief Executive Officer: Joseph E.M. Hughes
E-Mail: info@american-club.net

Historical Note
Members are claim managers and adjusters for shipping lines and protection and indemnity clubs. The American Club, a mutual P&I association for the shipping industry, is managed by SCB.

Meetings/Conferences:
Annual Meetings: June

Shippers of Recycled Textiles *(1988)*
7910 Woodmont Ave., Suite 1130
Bethesda, MD 20814-3015
Tel: (301)656-1077 *Fax:* (301)656-1079
E-Mail: smartasn@erols.com
Web Site: www.sorti.com
Members: 50 companies
Staff: 1
Annual Budget: $10-25,000
Executive Vice President: Bernard D. Brill

Meetings/Conferences:
Annual Meetings: In conjunction with the Internat'l Ass'n of Wiping Cloth Manufacturers

Shock Society *(1978)*
c/o North Shore University Hospital, Dept. of Surgery
300 Community Dr.
Manhasset, NY 11030-3878
Tel: (516)562-2870 *Fax:* (516)562-4821
Web Site: www.shocksocieties.org
Members: 800 individuals
Staff: 2
Annual Budget: $100-250,000
Contact Person: Geri Ferruggio

Historical Note
Membership composed of individuals interested in extending basic and clinical knowledge of the nature and treatment of shock and trauma. Membership: $220/year (full); $50/year (student).

Meetings/Conferences:
Annual Meetings: June

Publications:
Directory. a.
Shock. m. adv.

Showmen's League of America *(1913)*
300 W. Randolph St.
Chicago, IL 60609
Tel: (312)332-6236 *Fax:* (312)332-6237
Toll Free: (800)350 - 9906
E-Mail: rickh@showmensleague.org
Web Site: www.showmensleague.org
Members: 1500 individuals
Staff: 2
Annual Budget: $250-500,000
Executive Secretary: Rick Haney

Historical Note
A fraternal and benevolent organization of indoor and outdoor amusement operators and showmen. Membership: $25/year.

Publications:
Newsletter. 10/year.
Yearbook. a. adv.

Shrimp Council

Historical Note
An affiliate of National Fisheries Institute, which provides administrative support.

SHRM Global Forum *(1991)*
1800 Duke St.
Alexandria, VA 22314-3409
Tel: (703)548-3440 *Fax:* (703)535-6497
E-Mail: shrm@shrm.org
Web Site: www.shrmglobal.org
Members: 6100 individuals
Staff: 5
Annual Budget: $1-2,000,000
Vice President, International Programs: Brian J. Glade
E-Mail: bglade@shrm.org

Historical Note
Founded as Institute for International Human Resources; assumed its current name in 2000. Members are individuals responsible for international personnel administration. A division of the Society for Human Resource Management. Membership: $95/year (regular); $20/year (student).

Meetings/Conferences:
Annual Meetings: Spring

Publications:
HR Magazine.
Visions. bi-m.

Sigma Delta Kappa *(1914)*

Historical Note
Address unknown in 2004.

Sigma Epsilon Delta Dental Fraternity *(1901)*
P.O. Box 278
Great Neck, NY 11022-0278
Tel: (516)482-0679
Staff: 1
Annual Budget: $25-50,000
Executive Director: Mrs. Nathan Massoff

Historical Note
The oldest dental fraternity in the United States. Membership: $40/year (individual).

Publications:
Sedeltan Journal. a.

Sigma Phi Delta *(1924)*
P.O. Box 5260
Toms River, NJ 08754
Toll Free: (877)744 - 7447
Web Site: www.sigmaphidelta.org/
Members: 7500 individuals
Staff: 1
Executive Director: Robert R. Featheringham

Historical Note
A professional and social fraternity in engineering.

Meetings/Conferences:
Biennial Meetings: odd years

Publications:
Star. 2/year.
Sigma Phi Delta Castle. semi-a.
Directory. a.

Signal Processing Society *(1948)*

Historical Note
See IEEE Signal Processing Society

Silicones Environmental, Health and Safety Council of North America *(1971)*
2325 Dulles Corner Blvd., Suite 500
Herndon, VA 20171
Tel: (703)788-6570 *Fax:* (703)788-6545
E-Mail: sehsc@sehsc.com
Web Site: www.sehsc.com
Members: 7 companies
Staff: 3
Annual Budget: $2-5,000,000
Executive Director: Reo Menning

Historical Note
For more than 30 years, SEHSC has promoted the safe use of silicones through product stewardship and envivronmental, health and safe research. The organization also is involved in legislative and regulatory issues relating to silicone materials.

Silver Council

Historical Note
A coalition of industrial silver users. Administrative support provided by Photographic and Imaging Manufacturers Association

Silver Institute *(1971)*
1200 G St. NW, Suite 800
Washington, DC 20036
Tel: (202)835-0185 *Fax:* (202)835-0155
E-Mail: info@silverinstitute.org
Web Site: www.silverinstitute.org
Members: 35 companies
Staff: 5
Annual Budget: $500-1,000,000
Executive Director: Michael D. Rienzo
Special Projects and Information Systems: Malissa Freese
Manager, Meetings and Membership: Joan Rinaldi
E-Mail: jrinaldi@silverinstitute.org
Historical Note
Members, drawn from 14 foreign countries as well as the U.S., are companies which mine and refine silver, fabricators and manufacturers of products containing silver.
Publications:
Silver Institute News. q.
World Silver Survey. a.

Silver Users Association *(1947)*
11240 Waples Mill Road, Suite 200
Fairfax, VA 22030
Tel: (703)930-7790 *Fax:* (703)359-7562
E-Mail: pmiller@mwcapitol.com
Web Site: www.silverusersassociation.org/
Members: 28 companies
Staff: 1
Annual Budget: $100-250,000
Executive Director: Paul A. Miller
E-Mail: pmiller@mwcapitol.com
Historical Note
Founded in 1947 and incorporated in Washington, DC in April, 1971, the Silver Users Association represents manufacturers and distributors of products in which silver is an essential element, such as photographic materials, medical and dental supplies, batteries and electronic and electrical equipment, silverware, mirrors, commemorative art and jewelry. SUA works for the recognition of silver as a commodity and the removal of governmental regulations which retard its free exchange in commerce both foreign and domestic. To help provide a stable trading climate in the metal, it monitors the silver market to insure that silver information available to the industry and public is accurate.
Meetings/Conferences:
Semi-Annual Meetings: Spring and Fall
Publications:
U.S. Silver Summary. a.

Single Ply Roofing Institute
Historical Note
See listing under SPRI.

Skills USA *(1965)*
P.O. Box 3000
Leesburg, VA 20177-3000
Tel: (703)777-8810 *Fax:* (703)777-8999
Toll Free: (800)321 - 8422
E-Mail: tholdsworth@skillsusa.org
Web Site: www.skillsusa.org
Members: 280,000 individuals
Staff: 28
Annual Budget: $2-5,000,000
Executive Director: Timothy W. Lawrence
Director, Training, Membership and Program Development: Marsha Daves
E-Mail: mdaves@skillsusa.org
Associate Executive Director and Corporate Treasurer: Gary M. Diehl
Director, Business and Industry Partnerships: Eric V. Gearhart
Director, Publications: E. Thomas Hall
Director, Communications and Government Relations: Thomas W. Holdsworth
Historical Note
Founded in 1965 as the national organization for students in trade, skilled and service careers. Members are students in high schools, area career and technical schools and in community college training. Sponsors an annual National Leadership and Skills Conference. Membership: $8.00/year (student); $14/year (professional/associate).
Meetings/Conferences:
Annual Meetings: June
2007 – Kansas City, MO(Bartle Hall)/June 24-29/14000
Publications:
Skills USA Champions. q. adv.

Sleep Research Society *(1961)*
One Westbrook Corporate Center, Suite 920
Westchester, IL 60154
Tel: (708)492-1093 *Fax:* (708)492-0943
E-Mail: info@aasmnet.org
Web Site: www.srssleep.org/
Members: 1500 individuals
Staff: 1
Annual Budget: $250-500,000
Society Coordinator: John Slater
E-Mail: info@aasmnet.org
Historical Note
Founded as Association for the Psychophysiological Study of Sleep; assumed its present name in 1983. SRS provides a forum for dialogue and cross-fertilization among sleep researchers. A constituent society of the Association of Professional Sleep Socs. Membership: $125/year (individual).
Meetings/Conferences:
Annual Meetings: In conjunction with the Ass'n of Professional Sleep Socs.
Publications:
SRS Bulletin. 3/year. adv.
Sleep. 8/year.

Slovak Studies Association *(1977)*
c/o Methodist College Social Science Div.
5400 Ramsey St.
Fayetteville, NC 28304
Tel: (910)907-3653
E-Mail: bertaj@soc.mil
Web Site: www.as.uky.edu/ssa
Members: 80 individuals
Annual Budget: under $10,000
Secretary: John A. Berta
E-Mail: bertaj@soc.mil
Historical Note
SSA is an international society of scholars promoting inter-disciplinary research, publication and teaching related to the Slovak experience. Affiliated with American Society for the Advancement of Slavic Studies. Membership: $5/year.
Meetings/Conferences:
Annual Meetings: with the American Ass'n for the Advancement of Slavic Studies
Publications:
Newsletter of the SSA. 2/year.

Small Business Council of America *(1979)*
P.O. Box 1229
Wilmington, DE 19899
Tel: (302)691-7222
Toll Free: (877)404 - 1329
Web Site: www.sbca.net
Members: 700 businesses
Staff: 1
Chief Executive Officer: Peter J. Shanley
Historical Note
SBCA is a national organization exclusively representing the federal tax and employee benefit interests of small business. SBCA's primary goals are to prevent federal tax laws from becoming more burdensome on small businesses and their owners and to support legislation which creates needed economic incentives. Membership: $150/year (individual).
Meetings/Conferences:
Annual Meetings:
Publications:
SBCA Alert. q.
SBCA Member and Congressional Directory. a.
News Flashes. irreg.
Washington Audio Hotline. bi-m.

Small Business Exporters Association of the United States *(1990)*
1156 15th St. NW, Suite 1100
Washington, DC 20005-1755
Tel: (202)659-9320 *Fax:* (202)872-8543
Toll Free: (800)345 - 6728 Ext: 211
E-Mail: info@sbea.org
Web Site: www.sbea.org
President and Chief Executive Officer: James Morrison
Historical Note
Members are exporters with fewer than 500 employees and servicers of the industry. Membership: $250-2100/year.
Publications:
SBEA Update newsletter. irreg.

Small Business Legislative Council *(1976)*
1100 H St. NW, Suite 540
Washington, DC 20005
Tel: (202)639-8500 *Fax:* (202)296-5333
E-Mail: email@sblc.org
Web Site: www.sblc.org
Members: 106 small business associations
Staff: 2
Annual Budget: $100-250,000
President and General Counsel: John Satagaj
E-Mail: email@sblc.org
Historical Note
SBLC is a coalition of trade and professional associations who share a common concern with advancing the interests of small business. Membership: fees based on member associations budget.
Meetings/Conferences:
Annual Meetings: Late Winter in Washington, DC
Publications:
SBLC Journal. m.

Small Luxury Hotels of the World *(1985)*
370 Lexington Ave., Suite 1506
New York, NY 10017
Tel: (212)953-2064 *Fax:* (212)953-0576
Web Site: www.slh.com
Members: 350 hotels
Staff: 60
Vice President, Marketing: Edward Donaldson
Historical Note
Founded as Small Luxury Hotels and Resorts in 1985, the organization became Small Luxury Hotels following a merger with Prestige Hotels, and assumed its current name in 1991. Members are independently owned and managed deluxe hotels with less than 200 rooms.
Publications:
Annual Membership Directory. a.

Small Motors and Motion Association
Historical Note
Became Motor and Motion Association in 2001.

Small Publishers Association of North America *(1996)*
1618 W. Colorado Ave
Colorado Springs, CO 80904
Tel: (719)475-1726 *Fax:* (719)471-2182
E-Mail: scott@spannet.org
Web Site: www.SPANnet.org
Members: 1300 individuals
Staff: 6
Annual Budget: $100-250,000
Executive Director: Scott Flora
Historical Note
SPAN members are small presses, self-publishers, authors and vendors offering products or services to the industry. Provides education and marketing opportunities to members, and discounts on freight and a variety of services. Membership: $105/year (U.S./Canada).
Meetings/Conferences:
Annual Meetings: Fall
Publications:
SPAN Connection. m. adv.
Membership Directory. a. adv.

Smart Card Alliance *(2001)*
191 Clarksville Road
Princeton Junction, NJ 08850
Tel: (609)799-5654 *Fax:* (609)799-7032
Toll Free: (800)556 - 6828
E-Mail: info@smartcardalliance.org

Web Site: www.smartcardalliance.org
Members: 103 companies
Staff: 3
Annual Budget: $100-250,000
Executive Director: Randy Vanderhoof
E-Mail: info@smartcardalliance.org

Historical Note
Founded as Smart Card Industry Association; absorbed Smart Card Forum and assumed its current name in 2001. SCA represents manufacturers of electronic transaction systems. Associate members are resellers, card issuers, and other interested companies. Supersedes Associated Users of Smart Cardsystems and Technologies. Membership: $500-2,000/year.

Meetings/Conferences:
Annual Meetings: February

Publications:
Smart Link. bi-m.

SMMA - The Motor and Motion Association *(1975)*
P.O. Box P182
South Dartmouth, MA 02748
Tel: (508)979-5935 *Fax:* (508)979-5845
E-Mail: info@smma.org
Web Site: www.smma.org
Members: 110 companies
Staff: 2
Annual Budget: $100-250,000
Executive Director: Elizabeth B. Chambers
Director, Operations: Bill H. Chambers

Historical Note
Founded as Small Motor Manufacturers Association; became Small Motors and Motion Association in 1993, and assumed its current name in 2001. Members are users, suppliers, and manufacturers of fractional and sub-fractional horsepower motors and controls; membership also includes consulting firms in the industry. Serves as a principal voice of the industry and provides a forum to develop, collect and disseminate technical and management knowledge.

Meetings/Conferences:
Semi-annual Meetings: Spring and Fall
2007 – San Diego, CA(Rancho Bernardo Inn)/May 9-11/80
2007 – Louisville, KY/October/80

Publications:
Membership Directory. online.
Member Company Product Index. online.

Smocking Arts Guild of America *(1979)*
P.O. Box Five
Flushing, MI 48433
Toll Free: (800)520 - 3101
E-Mail: manager@smocking.org
Web Site: www.smocking.org
Members: 2700 individuals
Staff: 3
Annual Budget: $250-500,000
Executive Director: Jimmy Broyles
E-Mail: manager@smocking.org
Business Manager: Karen VanWert
E-Mail: manager@smocking.org

Historical Note
The purpose of SAGA is to preserve and foster the art of smocking and related needlework for future generations through education, communication, and quality workmanship. Membership: $30/year (domestic); $34/year (foreign & Canada).

Meetings/Conferences:
Annual Meetings: Fall

Publications:
SAGA News. q.

Snack Food Association *(1937)*
1711 King St., Suite One
Alexandria, VA 22314-2720
Tel: (703)836-4500 *Fax:* (703)836-8262
Toll Free: (800)628 - 1334
Web Site: www.sfa.org
Members: 700 companies
Staff: 10
Annual Budget: $2-5,000,000
President and Chief Executive Officer: James A. McCarthy
E-Mail: jmccarthy@sfa.org
Vice President, Marketing and Member Programs: Judith Barth
E-Mail: jbarth@sfa.org
Senior Vice President, Government and Public Affairs: David Dexter
E-Mail: ddexter@sfa.org
Director, Administration: Colleen Robinson
E-Mail: crobinson@sfa.org
Director, Meetings: Elizabeth Wells
E-Mail: lwells@sfa.org
Vice President, Communications: Ann Wilkes
E-Mail: awilkes@sfa.org

Historical Note
Formerly (1976) the Potato Chip Institute International and (1985) the Potato Chip/Snack Food Association. Represents manufacturers of snacks made from vegetables, grains, fruits, meats and nuts. Supports the Snack Political Action Committee (SnackPAC). Membership: annual dues vary, based on sales (company).

Meetings/Conferences:
Annual Meetings: February-March

Publications:
Who's Who Membership Directory. bien. adv.

Snow Control Equipment Manufacturers Committee

Historical Note
An affiliate of the National Truck Equipment Council.

SnowSports Industries America *(1954)*
8377-B Greensboro Dr.
McLean, VA 22102-3529
Tel: (703)556-9020 *Fax:* (703)821-8276
E-Mail: siamail@thesnowtrade.org
Web Site: www.thesnowtrade.org
Members: 650 companies
Staff: 30
Annual Budget: $2-5,000,000
President: David J. Ingemie
Director, Trade Shows and Membership Services: Debbie Brown Des Roches
Director, Education and Special Projects: Mary Jo Tarallo

Historical Note
Formerly (1997) Ski Industries of America. SIA is the national trade association of snow and winter sports companies. Merged with the National Ski Areas Association in 1989 to form the United Ski Industries Association. In 1992 SIA again became an independent trade association upon the dissolution of USIA. Membership: dues based on sales volume.

Meetings/Conferences:
Annual Meetings: Winter

Publications:
SIA Snow Trade Directory. m.
SIA Trade Show Directory. a.

Soap and Detergent Association *(1926)*
1500 K St. NW, Suite 300
Washington, DC 20005
Tel: (202)347-2900 *Fax:* (202)347-4110
E-Mail: info@cleaning101.com
Web Site: www.cleaning101.com
Members: 130 companies
Staff: 20
Annual Budget: $2-5,000,000
President: Ernie Rosenberg
Vice President, Government Affairs: Dennis C. Griesing
E-Mail: dgriesing@sdahq.org
General Counsel and Vice President, Administration: Beth Olson
Manager, Membership and Meeting Services: Billie Robinson
Vice President, Communications and Membership: Brian Sansoni
E-Mail: bsansoni@cleaning101.com
Vice President, Technical and International Affairs: Richard I. Sedlack
E-Mail: rsedlack@sdahq.org

Historical Note
Founded as Association of American Soap & Glycerine Producers. SDA represents manufacturers of cleaning products and product ingredients, providing research and publishing technical information on behalf of the industry.

Meetings/Conferences:
Annual Meetings: usually Boca Raton, FL/January

Publications:
SDA Newsletter. m.

Soaring Society of America *(1932)*
P.O. Box 2100
Hobbs, NM 88241-2100
Tel: (505)392-1177 *Fax:* (505)392-8154
E-Mail: info@ssa.org
Web Site: www.ssa.org
Members: 16000 individuals
Annual Budget: $1-2,000,000
Executive Director: Dennis Wright
Chief Financial and Administrative Officer: Alan Gleason
E-Mail: info@ssa.org

Historical Note
SSA promotes all phases of soaring and gliding for its members.

Meetings/Conferences:
Annual Meetings: Winter

Publications:
Soaring magazine. m. adv.

SOCAP International *(1973)*
675 N. Washington St., Suite 200
Alexandria, VA 22314-1939
Tel: (703)519-3700 *Fax:* (703)549-4886
E-Mail: socap@socap.org
Web Site: www.socap.org
Members: 3000 individuals
Staff: 10
Annual Budget: $2-5,000,000
President: Louis Garcia, CAE
E-Mail: socap@socap.org

Historical Note
Founded as Society of Consumer Affairs Professionals in Business; assumed its current name in 2002. Members are individuals responsible for the management of consumer affairs or customer service in all types of businesses. Membership: $295/year (individual).

Meetings/Conferences:
Annual Meetings: Fall/600

Publications:
Customer Relationship Management. bi-m. adv.
SOCAP Training Resource Guide. a.
Update. bi-m.
Membership Directory. a.

Soccer Industry Council of America *(1985)*
1150 17th St., NW, Suite 850
Washington, DC 20036
Tel: (202)775-1762 *Fax:* (202)296-7462
E-Mail: info@sgma.com
Web Site: www.sgma.com
Members: 110 individuals
Staff: 2
Annual Budget: $100-250,000
President: Tom Cove
Director, Media Relations: Mike May

Historical Note
SICA members are soccer goods manufacturers, distributors, representatives, sales agents, retailers and other soccer related businesses. SICA is a committee of the Sporting Goods Manufacturers Association, which provides administrative support. Membership: $550-5,000/year (full member); $100/year (contributing).

Meetings/Conferences:
Semi-Annual Meetings: January and Sept. /125

Publications:
Community Soccer Center Planning Guide.
Overview of the American Soccer Market. a.
National Soccer Participation Survey. a.
Retail Soccer USA Directory a.
Soccer in the USA (statistical abstract). a.

Social Science History Association *(1976)*
Univ. of Michigan, Institute for Social Research
Ann Arbor, MI 48106
E-Mail: erik@icpsr.umich.edu
Web Site: www.ssha.org
Members: 1100 individuals
Annual Budget: $50-100,000

Executive Director: Erik W. Austin
E-Mail: erik@icpsr.umich.edu
Historical Note
SSHA members are historians and social scientists with an interest in interdisciplinary applications. Membership: $50/year (individual); $75/year (organization); $15/year (student).
Meetings/Conferences:
2007 – Chicago, IL/Nov. 15-19
2008 – Miami, FL/Oct. 23-26
2009 – Long Beach, CA/Nov. 12-15
2010 – Chicago, IL/Nov. 18-21
Publications:
Social Science History Journal. q. adv.
SSHA Newsletter. semi-a. adv.

Social Science Research Council *(1923)*
810 Seventh Ave., 31st Fl.
New York, NY 10019-5818
Tel: (212)377-2700 *Fax:* (212)377-2727
E-Mail: info@ssrc.org
Web Site: www.ssrc.org
Members: 7 societies
Staff: 50
Annual Budget: $10-25,000,000
Executive Director: Mary McDonnell
President: Craig Calhoun
Historical Note
The SSRC is an independent, not-for-profit organization composed of social and behavioral scientists and humanists from all over the world. The Council advances the quality and usefulness of research in the social sciences. It encourages scholars in different disciplines to work together on topical, conceptual and methodical issues that can benefit from interdisciplinary and international collaboration. A central task of the Council is to be a resource for international scholarship. It does this thorugh international conferences and meetings, collaborative work, with institutional partners around the world and cross-regional structures for research and training.
Meetings/Conferences:
Semi-Annual Meetings: June and December/New York, NY (SRCC Headquarters)
Publications:
Items & Issues. q.
Annual report. a.

Society for a Science of Clinical Psychology
Historical Note
A section of the American Psychological Association - Clinical Psychology Division.

Society for Academic Emergency Medicine *(1970)*
901 N. Washington Ave.
Lansing, MI 48906-5137
Tel: (517)485-5484 *Fax:* (517)485-0801
E-Mail: saem@saem.org
Web Site: www.saem.org
Members: 5000 individuals
Staff: 5
Annual Budget: $1-2,000,000
Executive Director: Mary Ann Schropp
E-Mail: saem@saem.org
Historical Note
Formerly (1977) the University Association for Emergency Medicine. Merged with the Society of Teachers of Emergency Medicine in 1988. Dedicated to promoting research and education in emergency medicine. Membership open to physicians, nurses, allied health professionals, and those interested in academic emergency medicine. Membership: $60-365/year.
Meetings/Conferences:
Annual Meetings: May
2007 – Chicago, IL(Sheraton)/May 16-19/1800
Publications:
Academic Emergency Medicine journal. m. adv.
SAEM Newsletter. bi-m. adv.

Society for Adolescent Medicine *(1968)*
1916 N.W. Copper Oaks Circle
Blue Springs, MO 64015-8300
Tel: (816)224-8010 *Fax:* (816)224-8009
E-Mail: sam@adolescenthealth.org
Web Site: www.adolescenthealth.org
Members: 1300 individuals
Staff: 3
Executive Director: Edie Moore
E-Mail: sam@adolescenthealth.org
Historical Note
SAM members are health professionals throughout the world who are involved in service, teaching, or research concerned with the health and well-being of adolescents including physicians, nurses, social workers, and psychologists. Membership: $250/year, doctoral level (individual); $200/year non-doctoral level (individual); reduced fees for those in full-time school and in training.
Meetings/Conferences:
Annual Meetings: Spring
2007 – Denver, CO(Marriott)/March 28-31/700
2008 – Greensboro, NC(Sheraton)/March 26-29/700
2009 – Los Angeles, CA(Park Hyatt)/March 25-28/700
Publications:
Journal of Adolescent Health. m. adv.
SAM Newsletter. q.

Society for Advancement of Management *(1912)*
Texas A&M University, College of Business
6300 Ocean Dr., FC111
Corpus Christi, TX 78412-5807
Tel: (361)825-6045 *Fax:* (361)825-2725
Toll Free: (888)827 - 6077
Web Site: www.cob.tamucc.edu/sam
Members: 5000 individuals
Staff: 2
Annual Budget: $100-250,000
President and Chief Executive Officer: Dr. Moustafa H. Abdelsamad
Historical Note
SAM is a professional organization of management executives. Formed by a merger of the Taylor Society and the Society of Industrial Engineers; absorbed the Industrial Methods Society in 1946. Merged in 1973 with the American Management Association, Inc. (1923), the American Foundation for Management Research, Inc. (1960), the International Management Association, Inc., and the Presidents Association, Inc. (1961), to form the American Management Associations, of which it was a semi-autonomous division. SAM returned to independent status on July 1, 1983 and is no longer affiliated with American Management Associations. Membership: $75/year (individual).
Meetings/Conferences:
2007 – Las Vegas, NV(Harrah's Hotel)/March 25-28/500
Publications:
SAM News Internat'l. 3/year.
Conference Program Book. a. adv.
SAM Advanced Management Journal. q.
Management in Practice. q.

Society for American Archaeology *(1934)*
900 Second St. NE, Suite 12
Washington, DC 20002
Tel: (202)789-8200 *Fax:* (202)789-0284
Web Site: www.saa.org
Members: 7000 individuals
Staff: 8
Annual Budget: $1-2,000,000
Executive Director: Tobi A. Brimsek, CAE
E-Mail: tobi_brimsek@saa.org
Manager, Membership and Marketing: Kevin Fahey
E-Mail: kevin_fahey@saa.org
Manager, Government Affairs: David Lindsay
Manager, Public Education: Maureen Malloy
E-Mail: maureen_malloy@saa.org
Manager, Publications: John Neirkirk
E-Mail: john_neirkirk@saa.org
Historical Note
SAA is an international organization dedicated to the research, interpretation and protection of the archaeological heritage of the Americas. SAA members include student, avocational and professional archaeologists working in a variety of settings including government agencies, colleges and universities, museums and the private sector. Membership: $125/year (regular); $65/year (student); $72/year (retired); $49/year (associate); $38/year (joint).
Meetings/Conferences:
Annual Meetings: Spring
2007 – Austin, TX/Apr. 25-29
2008 – Vancouver, BC, Canada/March 26-30
2009 – Atlanta, GA/Apr. 22-26
2010 – St. Louis, MO/Apr. 14-18
Publications:
American Antiquity. q. adv.
The SAA Archaeological Record. 5/year. adv.
Latin American Antiquity. q. adv.
Archaeology and Public Education (internet news).

Society for American Baseball Research *(1971)*
812 Huron Road East, Suite 719
Cleveland, OH 44115
Tel: (216)575-0500 *Fax:* (216)575-0502
E-Mail: info@sabr.org
Web Site: www.sabr.org
Members: 7000 individuals
Staff: 4
Annual Budget: $250-500,000
Executive Director: John Zajc
Historical Note
Membership: $60/year (individual); $500/year (organization/company).
Meetings/Conferences:
Annual Meetings: Summer
2007 – St. Louis, MO(Adams Mark)/July 26-29
2008 – Cleveland, OH
Publications:
The SABR Bulletin. 6/year. adv.
The National Pastime. a.
Baseball Research Journal. a.

Society for Ancient Greek Philosophy *(1953)*
Binghamton Univ., Dept. of Philosophy
Binghamton, NY 13902-6000
Tel: (607)777-2886 *Fax:* (607)777-2734
E-Mail: apreus@binghamton.edu
Web Site: www.philosophy.binghamton.edu/sagp/
Members: 500 individuals
Annual Budget: under $10,000
Secretary-Treasurer: Anthony Preus
E-Mail: apreus@binghamton.edu
Historical Note
SAGP members are academics and others with an interest in classical philosophy. Membership: $10/year (domestic); $15/year (international).
Publications:
Newsletter. q. adv.

Society for Anthropology in Community Colleges *(1978)*
Historical Note
A section of the American Anthropological Association. Established to stimulate communication among anthropologists and teachers of anthropology in community colleges, colleges and pre-collegiate institutions.

Society for Applied Anthropology *(1941)*
P.O. Box 2436
Oklahoma City, OK 73101
Tel: (405)843-5113 *Fax:* (405)843-8553
E-Mail: info@sfaa.net
Web Site: www.sfaa.net
Members: 2500 individuals
Staff: 3
Annual Budget: $250-500,000
Executive Director: J. Thomas May
Historical Note
Promotes the interdisciplinary scientific study of the principles controlling the relations of human beings to one another, and the wide application of those principles to practical problems. Membership: $50/year (individual);
Meetings/Conferences:
Annual Meetings: Spring
2007 – Tampa, FL(Hyatt Downtown)/March 27-31

2008 - Memphis, TN
Publications:
Human Organization. q. adv.
Newsletter. q. adv.
Practicing Anthropology. q. adv.

Society for Applied Learning Technology *(1972)*
50 Culpeper St.
Warrenton, VA 20186
Tel: (540)347-0055 *Fax:* (540)349-3169
Web Site: www.salt.org
Members: 300 individuals
Staff: 5
Annual Budget: $5-10,000,000
Executive Director: John G. Fox
Historical Note
Founded in Washington, DC in 1972. Members include industrial, military and academic managers involved in the design production or use of technology-based educational systems. Membership: $55/year.
Meetings/Conferences:
Semi-Annual Meetings: Winter/Summer
2007 - Orlando, FL(Int'l Plaza Resort and Spa)/Jan. 31-Feb. 2
Publications:
Journal of Instruction Delivery Systems On-line. q.
SALT Newsletter On-line. q.
Journal of Educational Technology Systems. q.
Journal of Interactive Instruction Development On-line. q.

Society for Applied Spectroscopy *(1958)*
201-B Broadway St.
Frederick, MD 21701-6501
Tel: (301)694-8122 *Fax:* (301)694-6860
E-Mail: sasoffice@aol.com
Web Site: www.s-a-s.org
Members: 2600 individuals
Staff: 3
Annual Budget: $500-1,000,000
Executive Director: Bonnie Saylor
Director, Administrative Affairs: Victor Hutcherson
Historical Note
The Federation of Spectroscopic Societies was founded in Pittsburgh in March 1956. From this grew the Society for Applied Spectroscopy established in New York in November 1958 and incorporated in Pennsylvania in 1960. Membership: $70/year (U.S. individual), $500-5,000/year (corporate sponsors), $110/year (foreign).
Meetings/Conferences:
Annual Meetings: Fall
Publications:
Directory. a. adv.
Applied Spectroscopy. 12/year. adv.
Newsletter. semi.

Society for Archaeological Sciences *(1977)*
c/o Department of Geosciences
Franklin & Marshall College
Lancaster, PA 17604-3003
Tel: (717)291-4134 *Fax:* (717)291-4186
E-Mail: rob.sternberg@fandm.edu
Web Site: www.socarchsci.org
Members: 600 individuals
Annual Budget: $10-25,000
General Secretary: Rob Sternberg
E-Mail: rob.sternberg@fandm.edu
Historical Note
SAS was founded to provide for communication between scholars applying methods from the physical sciences to archaeological questions. Members are archaeological scientists working in business, academic, and government settings. Membership: $20/year.
Meetings/Conferences:
Annual Meetings: Meetings held with Soc. for American Achaeology
Publications:
Advances in Archaeological and Museum Science. m.
Journal of Archaeological Science. 6/year.
SAS Bulletin. q.

Society for Asian Music *(1959)*
Cornell Univ., Dept. of Music
Lincoln Hall
Ithaca, NY 14853
Tel: (607)255-5049 *Fax:* (607)254-2877
Web Site: www.skidmore.edu/academics/asianmusic/
Members: 500 individuals
Staff: 1
Annual Budget: $10-25,000
Treasurer: Marty Hatch
E-Mail: mfh2@cornell.edu
Historical Note
SAM members are academics and others with an interest in the music of the middle and far east. Has no paid officers or full-time staff. Membership: $30/year (individual). Available through University of Texas Press, Austin, Texas.
Publications:
Asian Music Journal (Published by U. Texas Press, Austin TX). semi-a.

Society for Assisted Reproductive Technology *(1987)*
1209 Montgomery Hwy.
Birmingham, AL 35216-2809
Tel: (205)978-5000 Ext: 109 *Fax:* (205)978-5015
Web Site: www.sart.org
Members: 1500 individuals, 370 art practices
Staff: 2
Annual Budget: $500-1,000,000
Executive Administrator: Joyce G. Zeitz
Historical Note
Members are practice facilities offering assisted reproductive procedures and all members of the ART team. Administrative support provided by the American Society of Reproductive Medicine. Membership:$25/year (individual); $800/year (organization).
Meetings/Conferences:
Annual Meetings: With the American Soc. for Reproductive Medicine.
2007 - Washington, DC/Oct. 13-17

Society for Biomaterials *(1974)*
15000 Commerce Pkwy., Suite C
Mt. Laurel, NJ 08054
Tel: (856)439-0826 *Fax:* (856)439-0525
Web Site: www.biomaterials.org
Members: 1000 individuals
Staff: 8
Annual Budget: $1-2,000,000
Executive Director: Victoria E. Elliott, RPh, MBA, CAE
Historical Note
Incorporated as a non-profit organization in 1974, SFB serves to promote research, development, and education in the biomaterial sciences. Seeks to cooperate with scientific organizations, private industry, government agencies and other interested parties, to establish the standards and terms for biomaterials. Members are scientists, surgeons, dentists and others interested in the problems of developing replacements for living tissue. A member society of the American Institute for Medical and Biological Engineering. Membership: $250/year (individual).
Meetings/Conferences:
Annual Meetings: Spring
Publications:
Journal of Biomedical Materials Research. 16/year. adv.
Journal of Applied Biomaterials. q. adv.
BioMaterials Forum. bi-m. adv.

Society for Biomolecular Sciences *(1994)*
36 Tamarack Ave., #348
Danbury, CT 06811
Tel: (203)743-1336 *Fax:* (203)748-7557
E-Mail: email@sbsonline.org
Web Site: www.sbsonline.org
Members: 2000 individuals
Staff: 13
Annual Budget: $2-5,000,000
Executive Director: Christine Giordano
Manager, Meetings and Exhibitions: Marietta Manoni
Managing Director: Betty Soltesz
Historical Note
Supports research and discovery in pharmaceutical biotechnology and the agrichemical industry that utilize chemical screening procedures. Membership: $150/year.
Meetings/Conferences:
Annual Meetings: Fall, changing to Spring in 2007
2007 - Montreal, QC, Canada/Apr. 15-19
Publications:
Journal of Biomolecular Screening. q. adv.
e-newsletter (online). m.
Member newsletter. q. adv.

Society for Buddhist-Christian Studies
Historical Note
A program of Council of Societies for the Study of Religion, which provides administrative support. President of SBCS is Ruben L.F. Wells.

Society for Business Ethics *(1980)*
College of St. Benedict/St. John's University
College Ave.
St. Joseph, MN 56374
Tel: (320)363-5915
Web Site: www.societyforbusinessethics.org
Members: 600 individuals
Staff: 1
Annual Budget: $25-50,000
Executive Director: Joe DesJardins
Historical Note
SBE members are academics and practitioners (such as ethics and compliance officers) and other interested in the field. Membership: $60/year (individual); $135/year (organization/company); $30/year (students and retirees).
Meetings/Conferences:
Annual Meetings: August, in conjunction with the Academy of Management
Publications:
SBE Newsletter. q.
Business Ethics Quarterly. q.

Society for Cardiovascular Angiography and Interventions *(1976)*
2400 N St. NW
Washington, DC 20037
Tel: (202)375-6195 *Fax:* (202)375-6837
Toll Free: (800)992 - 7224
E-Mail: info@scai.org
Web Site: www.scai.org
Members: 3000 individuals
Staff: 6
Annual Budget: $500-1,000,000
Executive Director: Norm Linsky
E-Mail: nlinsky@scai.org
Historical Note
Membership: $375/year.
Meetings/Conferences:
Annual Meetings: May
2007 - Orlando, FL/March 9-12
Publications:
Catheterization and Cardiovascular Interventions. m. adv.
Guidelines Newsletter. q.
A Guide to Catheterization Labs in the United States.
Membership Directory.

Society for Cardiovascular Magnetic Resonance *(1994)*
19 Mantua Road
Mt. Royal, NJ 08061
Tel: (856)423-8955 *Fax:* (856)423-3420
E-Mail: hq@scmr.org
Web Site: www.scmr.org
Members: 1300 individuals
Staff: 2
Annual Budget: $500-1,000,000
Director: Kent Van Amborg
Historical Note
SCMR ias an organization for medical practitioners who are interested in applications of magnetic resonance in diagnosis of heart and circulatory

conditions. Membership: $160/year (full member); $50/year (associate); $160/year (industrial member).

Meetings/Conferences:
Semi-Annual Meetings: Spring and Fall

Publications:
Journal of Cardiovascular Magnetic Resonance. q. adv.
SCMR News. q.

Society for Chaos Theory in Psychology and Life Sciences *(1991)*
P.O. Box 484
Pewaukee, WI 53072
Web Site: www.societyforchaostheory.org
Members: 300 individuals
Staff: 23
Annual Budget: under $10,000
Secretary: David Pincus

Historical Note
An international forum. Membership: $60/year; $50/year (students).

Meetings/Conferences:
Annual Meetings: Summer

Publications:
Nonlinear Dynamics, Psychology and Life Sciences. q. adv.

Society for Cinema and Media Studies *(1959)*
Univ. of Oklahoma
640 Parrington Oval, Room 302
Norman, OK 73019
Tel: (405)325-8075 *Fax:* (405)325-7135
E-Mail: office@cmstudies.org
Web Site: www.cmstudies.org
Members: 2050 individuals
Staff: 1
Coordinator, Administrative: Jane Dye
E-Mail: office@cmstudies.org

Historical Note
Founded as Society for Cinema Studies; assumed its current name in 2003. An association of scholars and teachers devoted to the study of film, television and related media. SCMS's main activity is scholarly interchange through its quarterly journal and annual conference. Membership: $55-75/year (individual); $25/year (underemployed individual); $30/year (student).

Meetings/Conferences:
Annual Meetings: Spring

Publications:
Cinema Journal. q. adv.

Society for Clinical and Experimental Hypnosis *(1949)*
c/o MA School of Prof. Psychology
221 Rivermoor Street
Boston, MA 02132
Tel: (617)469-1981 *Fax:* (617)469-1889
E-Mail: sceh@mspp.edu
Web Site: www.sceh.us
Members: 400 individuals
Staff: 7
Annual Budget: $100-250,000
Executive Director: Dean R. Abby
E-Mail: sceh@mspp.edu

Historical Note
Founded June 12, 1949 and incorporated in New York in 1963. Affiliated with the American Association for the Advancement of Science, the World Federation for Mental Health and the International Society of Hypnosis. Membership: $139/year (regular member); $45/year (student member).

Meetings/Conferences:
Annual Meetings:
2007 - Dallas, TX(Adam's Mark Hotel)/Jan. 19-23/250

Publications:
SCEH Newsletter "Focus". 3/year.
International Journal of Clinical and Experimental Hypnosis. q. adv.

Society for Clinical Data Management *(1994)*
555 E. Wells St.
Suite 1100
Milwaukee, WI 53202-3823
Tel: (414)226-0362 *Fax:* (414)276-3349
E-Mail: info@scdm.org
Web Site: www.scdm.org
Members: 1877 Members
Staff: 3
Annual Budget: $100-250,000
Executive Director: Kim Breitback

Historical Note
Founded in 1994, SCDM has grown to be a premier data management organization which embodies upwards of 1500 domestic and international members who represent the biotechnology, medical device, and pharmaceutical industries as well as members of the academic, regulatory and scientific research communities. Third party organizations that support these groups: Contract Research Organizations, consultants, hardware and software vendors and placement firms, also represent an important portion of the Society's membership. Membership: $90/year.

Meetings/Conferences:
Annual Meetings: Fall
2007 - Chicago, IL(Hyatt Regency)/Sept. 16-19

Publications:
Data Connections (online newsletter). m. adv.
Databasics. q. adv.

Society for Clinical Trials *(1978)*
600 Wyndhurst Ave., Suite 112
Baltimore, MD 21210-2425
Tel: (410)433-4722 *Fax:* (410)435-8631
E-Mail: sctbalt@aol.com
Web Site: www.sctweb.org
Members: 2200 individuals
Staff: 2
Annual Budget: $50-100,000
Executive Director: Mary Karpers-Burke
E-Mail: sctbalt@aol.com

Historical Note
Incorporated in the State of Maryland. SCT members are involved in the controlled medical testing of procedures, drugs and other therapeutic agents. Membership: $110/year (individual); $50/year (student).

Meetings/Conferences:
Annual Meetings: Spring
2007 - Montreal, QC, Canada(Hyatt)/May 20-23
2008 - St. Louis, MO(Hyatt)/May 18-21

Publications:
Newsletter. bi-a.
Clinical Trials: Journal of the Society for Clinical Trials. bi-m. adv.

Society for Clinical Vascular Surgery *(1970)*
900 Cummings Center, Suite 221-U
Beverly, MA 01915
Tel: (978)927-8330 *Fax:* (978)524-8890
Members: 860 individuals
Annual Budget: $100-250,000
Executive Director: Pamela Wilson

Historical Note
Membership: $175/year.

Meetings/Conferences:
Annual Meetings: March/450

Publications:
American Journal of Surgery. q. adv.

Society for College and University Planning *(1965)*
339 E. Liberty St., Suite 300
Ann Arbor, MI 48104
Tel: (734)998-7832 *Fax:* (734)998-6532
E-Mail: info@scup.org
Web Site: www.scup.org
Members: 5000 individuals
Staff: 15
Annual Budget: $2-5,000,000
Executive Director: Jolene Knapp, CAE
Director, Communications and Publications: Terry Calhoun
Director, Planning and Education: Phyllis Grummon
Director, Member Relations and Marketing: Susan K. Rogers
Director, Administrative Services: Karen Verhey

Historical Note
SCUP provides higher education professionals with planning, knowledge, resources and connections to achieve institutional goals. Within higher education, SCUP focuses on the areas of academics, facilities, resources and strategic matters. Represents college and university administrators and faculty, corporate executives, and government officials involved in planning. Membership: $235/year (individual); $70/year (student); $95/year (retired); $530-1,265/year, based on enrollment (postsecondary institution); $1,065/year (nonuniversity organization).

Meetings/Conferences:
Annual Meetings: July
2007 - Chicago, IL(Sherton Hotel & Towers)/July 7-11/1800

Publications:
Planning for Higher Education. q. adv.
Membership Directory. a. adv.

Society for Community Research and Action

Historical Note
The Division of Community Psychology of the American Psychological Association.

Society for Computer Simulation *(1952)*
P.O. Box 17900
San Diego, CA 92177-7900
Tel: (858)277-3888 *Fax:* (858)277-3930
E-Mail: info@scs.org
Web Site: www.scs.org
Members: 1900 individuals
Staff: 6
Annual Budget: $1-2,000,000
Executive Director: Steve Branch

Historical Note
Founded in Oxnard, CA in 1952 as the Simulation Council and incorporated in California in 1957 as Simulation Councils, Inc. Became Society for Computer Simulation in 1973. A sponsoring society of the American Automatic Control Council. SCS is a multidisciplinary organization dedicated to advancing the use of computer simulation to solve real world problems.

Meetings/Conferences:
Quarterly Conferences:

Publications:
Modeling and Simulation Magazine. m. adv.
Simulation Series. q.

Society for Computers in Psychology *(1971)*
c/o Katja Wiemer-Hastings, Department of Psychology
Northern Illinois University
DeKalb, IL 60115
Tel: (815)753-5227 *Fax:* (815)753-8088
Web Site: www.scip.ws
Members: 70
Secretary-Treasurer: Katja Wiemer-Hastings
E-Mail: katja@niu.edu

Historical Note
Formerly (1982) the Society for the Use of On-Line Computers in Psychology. SCiP members are psychologists and others with an interest in the application of computers in psychological research. Membership: $50/year.

Meetings/Conferences:
Annual Meetings: 70

Publications:
Behavior Research Methods, Instruments and Computers. a.

Society for Conservation Biology *(1985)*
4245 N. Fairfax Dr., Suite 400
Arlington, VA 22203-1651
Tel: (703)276-2384 *Fax:* (703)995-4633
E-Mail: info@conbio.org
Web Site: www.conbio.org
Members: 9000 individuals
Staff: 14
Annual Budget: $2-5,000,000
Executive Director: Alan Thornhill

Historical Note
SCB is an international professional organization dedicated to advancing the science and practice of conserving the Earth's biological diversity. The Society's membership comprises a wide range of people interested in the conservation and study of biological diversity: resource managers, educators,

government and private conservation workers, and students. SCB is organized internationally by seven Regional Sections, and these Sections initiate activities relevant to conservation needs on their continents or in their oceans. Benefits of membership include free online access to publications in developing countries; global and regional conferences; and a job board. Also administers the David H. Smith Conservation Research Fellowship Program, sponsored by the Cedar Tree Foundation.

Meetings/Conferences:
Annual Meetings: *Summer*
2007 – Port Elizabeth, South Africa/July 1-5/1500
2008 – Chatanooga, TN/July 13-18/1500

Publications:
Neotropical Conservation. q. adv.
Conservation In Practice. q. adv.
Newsletter. q. adv.
Conservation Biology Journal. bi-m. adv.

Society for Consumer Psychology

Historical Note
A division of the American Psychological Association.

Society for Cross-Cultural Research *(1965)*

43 O'Connell Road
Colchester, CT 06415
Tel: (860)570-9155 *Fax:* (860)570-9404
Web Site: www.sccr.org
Members: 200 individuals
Annual Budget: under $10,000
Secretary-Treasurer: David Cournoyer

Historical Note
An interdisciplinary organization whose primary goal is to support and encourage comparative research which will aid in the establishment of scientifically derived generalizations about human behavior. Members come from a wide variety of social, behavioral and scientific professions. Has no paid staff. Membership fee: $50/year (individual).

Meetings/Conferences:
Annual Meetings: *February*

Publications:
SCCR Newsletter. semi-a. adv.
Cross-Cultural Research. q. adv.

Society for Cryobiology *(1964)*

c/o Georgia Inst. of Technology, MC 0405
Atlanta, GA 30332-0405
Tel: (404)385-4157 *Fax:* (404)385-1397
Web Site: www.societyforcryobiology.org
Members: 300 individuals
Annual Budget: $50-100,000
Secretary: Jens Karlsson

Historical Note
Organized March 20, 1964 and incorporated the same year in Maryland. Concerned with all aspects of low temperature biology and medicine including studies of freezing, freeze-drying, cryoprotective additives and their pharmacological actions, medical applications of reduced temperature, cryosurgery, hypothermia, perfusion of organs, hibernation, frost hardiness in plants, and all pertinent methodologies. Has no paid officers or full-time staff. Membership: $130/year, with subscription (individual); $60/year, without subscription (individual); $275/year (institution); $800/year (corporation); $40/year, with subscription (student); Free, without subscription (student).

Meetings/Conferences:
Annual Meetings: *Summer in a university setting.*
2007 – Banff, Canada/July 28-Aug. 1

Publications:
Cryobiology. bi-m. adv.
News Notes. semi-a. adv.

Society for Cultural Anthropology *(1983)*

Historical Note
A section of the American Anthropological Association. SCA is a broad, multidisciplinary organization of individuals interested in cultural, psychological, and social interrelations at all levels.

Society for Developmental and Behavioral Pediatrics *(1982)*

15000 Commerce Pkwy., Suite C
Mt. Laurel, NJ 08054
Tel: (856)439-0500 *Fax:* (856)439-0525
E-Mail: sdbp@ahint.com
Web Site: www.sdbp.org
Members: 750 individuals
Staff: 2
Annual Budget: $100-250,000

Historical Note
Formerly (1995) Society for Behavioral Pediatrics. Members are pediatricians, child psychologists and other professionals with an interest in developmental and behavioral pediatrics. Aim of SDBP is to improve the health care of infants, children, and adolescents by promoting research and teaching in developmental and behavioral pediatrics. Membership: $155/year (regular); $100/year (trainee & non-doctorate).

Publications:
Journal of Developmental and Behavioral Pediatrics. bi-m. adv.

Society for Developmental Biology *(1939)*

9650 Rockville Pike
Bethesda, MD 20814-3998
Tel: (301)634-7815 *Fax:* (301)634-7825
E-Mail: sdb@sdbonline.org
Web Site: www.sdbonline.org
Members: 2200 individuals
Staff: 2
Annual Budget: $250-500,000
Executive Officer: Ida Chow, Ph.D.
E-Mail: ichow@sdbonline.org

Historical Note
Formerly (1939-1965) the Society for the Study of Development and Growth. Membership: $70/year (full); $35/year (postdoctoral); $15/year (student).

Meetings/Conferences:
Annual Meetings: *Summer*
2007 – Cancun, Mexico(Hotel Gran Melia)/June 16-20

Publications:
Developmental Biology. bi-w. adv.

Society for Disability Studies *(1986)*

Dept. of Disability and Human Development, U. of Illinois at Chicago
1640 W. Roosevelt Road, Room 205D
Chicago, IL 60608-6904
Tel: (312)996-4664 *Fax:* (312)996-7743
Web Site: www.uic.edu/orgs/sds
Members: 350 individuals
Staff: 1
Annual Budget: $25-50,000
Executive Officer: Joy Hammel, Ph.D.

Historical Note
SDS is an international scientific and educational organization with a multidisciplinary membership, composed of scholars in the social sciences and humanities who study the problems of disabled people in society. Membership: $30-95/year, based on income (individual).

Meetings/Conferences:
Annual Meetings: *June/200*

Publications:
Disability Studies Quarterly. q.
Proceedings. a.

Society for Ear, Nose and Throat Advances in Children *(1973)*

c/o Cincinnatti Children's Hospital Medical Center
3333 Burnett Ave., ML 2018
Cincinnati, OH 45229-3039
Tel: (513)636-2287 *Fax:* (513)636-8133
Web Site: www.sentac.org
Members: 300 individuals
Annual Budget: $25-50,000
Secretary: Sally R. Scott

Historical Note
SENTAC members are physicians and other health professionals with an interest in pediatric speech, hearing, and otorhinolaryngology. Has no paid officers or full-time staff.

Meetings/Conferences:
Annual Meetings: *December*

Publications:
Directory and Meeting Abstracts. a.

Society for Ecological Restoration *(1988)*

285 W. 18th St., #1
Tucson, AZ 85701
Tel: (520)622-5485 *Fax:* (520)622-5491
E-Mail: info@ser.org
Web Site: www.ser.org
Members: 2500 individuals
Staff: 3
Executive Director: Mary Kay C. LeFevour
E-Mail: mkl@ser.org
Membership Coordinator: Jana Franz

Historical Note
Formerly Society for Ecological Restoration and Management. SER members are academics, scientists, environmental consultants, government agencies and others with an interest in ecological restoration.

Meetings/Conferences:
Annual Meetings: *Fall*

Publications:
Restoration Ecology Journal. q.
Restoration and Management Notes. semi-a.
SER News Newsletter. q.

Society for Economic Anthropology

California State U., Anthropology Dept.
18111 Nordhoff St.
Northridge, CA 91330-8244
Web Site: http://anthropology.tamu.edu/sea/
Members: 500 individuals
Secretary-Treasurer: Judith E. Marti, Ph.D.
E-Mail: judith.marti@csun.edu

Historical Note
Members are scientists and academics interested in economic systems and their relevance to human and cultural development. Membership: $40/year.

Meetings/Conferences:
Annual Meetings: *Spring*

Publications:
SEA Volumes.
SEA Newsletter. 2/year.

Society for Economic Botany *(1959)*

P.O. Box 61788
Honolulu, HI 96839
E-Mail: info@econbot.org
Web Site: www.econbot.org
Members: 1500 members
Annual Budget: $50-100,000
Secretary: Michael B. Thomas
E-Mail: secreatry@econbot.org

Historical Note
Promotes research on the past, present and future uses of plants. Has no paid officers or full-time staff. Membership: $65/year (individual); $75/year (family); $35/year (student/retired).

Meetings/Conferences:
Annual Meetings: *Summer*
2007 – Chicago, IL/June 4-7
2008 – Durham, NC/June 1-5

Publications:
People and Plants. semi-a.
Economic Botany. q. adv.

Society for Education and Research in Psychiatric Mental Health Nursing *(1983)*

Historical Note
Superseded by Internat'l Soc. of Psychiatric-Mental Health Nurses.

Society for Education in Anesthesia *(1984)*

520 N. Northwest Hwy.
Park Ridge, IL 60068-2573
Tel: (847)825-5586 *Fax:* (847)825-5658
Web Site: www.seahq.org
Members: 600 individuals
Staff: 4
Annual Budget: $25-50,000
Executive Director: Gary W. Hoorman
E-Mail: g.hoorman@asahq.org

Historical Note
Formerly (1994) Society of Education in Anesthesia. SEA members are individuals within anesthesia departments responsible for direct involvement in teaching, administration and planning educational programs for residents and medical students. Membership: $100/year.

Meetings/Conferences:
Semi-annual Meetings: Spring and October
Publications:
Anesthesia Education. 3/year.
Journal of Clinical Anesthesia.

Society for Environmental Geochemistry and Health *(1971)*
4698 S. Forrest Ave.
Springfield, MO 65810
Tel: (417)885-1166 *Fax:* (417)881-6920
Web Site: www.segh.net
Members: 400 individuals
Staff: 1
Annual Budget: under $10,000
Secretary: Bobby Wixson
Historical Note
SEGH was formed to promote a multi-disciplinary approach to research in fields of geochemistry and health, to facilitate and expand communication among scientists within these disciplines and to advance knowledge in the area. Membership: $50/year.
Meetings/Conferences:
Annual Meetings: Summer-Fall
Publications:
Environmental Geochemistry and Health. q. adv.
Interface newsletter. irreg.

Society for Environmental Graphic Design *(1973)*
1000 Vermont Ave., Suite 400
Washington, DC 20008
Tel: (202)638-5555 *Fax:* (202)638-0891
E-Mail: segd@segd.org
Web Site: www.segd.org
Members: 1100 individuals
Staff: 4
Annual Budget: $5-10,000,000
Executive Director: Leslie Gallery Dilworth
E-Mail: leslie@segd.org
Director, Conference and Meetings: Nazie Dana
Director, Membership and Communications: Ann Makowski
Historical Note
Formerly (1992) Society of Environmental Graphic Designers. SEGD members are individuals and corporations engaged in or affiliated with environmental graphic design including individuals from the fields of graphic design, architecture, interior and industrial design, education, research and sign manufacturing. Membership: $250/year (individual); $155/year (design associate); $250/year (allied/professional); $1,000/year (design studio); $45/year (student).
Meetings/Conferences:
Annual Meetings: Spring
Publications:
Messages Newsletter. bi-m. adv.
SEGDesign Magazine. q. adv.
Dimension. semi-a.
Membership Directory. a.

Society for Epidemiologic Research *(1967)*
P.O. Box 990
Clearfield, UT 84098
Tel: (801)525-0231 *Fax:* (801)774-9211
Web Site: www.epiresearch.org
Members: 2500 individuals
Staff: 1
Annual Budget: $50-100,000
Secretary-Treasurer: Joseph L. Lyon, M.D., M.P.
E-Mail: jlyon@dfpm.utah.edu
Manager, Membership: Jacqueline Brakey
E-Mail: membership@epiresearch.org
Historical Note
Established in Baltimore, MD. Membership: $130/year (domestic); $135/year (foreign); $80/year (domestic student); $85/year (foreign student).
Meetings/Conferences:
Annual Meetings: Summer
Publications:
Epidemiologic Reviews.
American Journal of Epidemiology. bi-m. adv.

Society for Ethnomusicology *(1956)*
Morrison Hall 005
1165 E. Third St.
Bloomington, IN 47405-3700
E-Mail: semexec@indiana.edu
Web Site: www.ethnomusicology.org
Members: 2400 individuals
Staff: 2
Annual Budget: $50-100,000
Executive Director: Alan Burdette
E-Mail: semexec@indiana.edu
Office Coordinator: Lyn Pittman
E-Mail: semexec@indiana.edu
Historical Note
Member of American Council of Learned Societies. Has an international membership. The Society promotes the research, study, and performance of music of all historical periods and cultural contexts. Membership: varies.
Meetings/Conferences:
Annual Meetings: Fall
2007 - Columbus, OH(Hyatt Capital Square)/Oct. 24-28
2008 - Middleton, CT(Wesleyan University)/Oct. 25-28
Publications:
Newsletter. q. adv.
Ethnomusicology. 3/year. adv.

Society for Excellence in Eyecare *(1989)*
P.O. Box 6139
Palm Harbor, FL 34684
Tel: (630)699-1929 *Fax:* (727)786-6622
E-Mail: info@excellenteyesurgery.com
Web Site: www.excellenteyesurgery.com
Members: 100 individuals
Staff: 3
Annual Budget: $250-500,000
Executive Director: Trent Roark
Historical Note
Membership: $1,000/year (individual).
Meetings/Conferences:
Annual Meetings: Usually early March
Publications:
Viewpoints Newsletter. q.

Society for Experimental Biology and Medicine *(1903)*
197 W. Spring Valley Ave.
Maywood, NJ 07607-1727
Tel: (201)291-9080 *Fax:* (201)291-2988
E-Mail: sebm@inch.com
Web Site: www.sebm.org
Members: 1500 individuals
Staff: 2
Annual Budget: $250-500,000
Executive Director: Felice O'Grady
E-Mail: sebm@inch.com
Historical Note
Established February 25, 1903 to promote investigation in the biomedical sciences. Membership: $60/year (regular member); $50/year (associate member); $20/year (student); $545/year (institutional subscription).
Meetings/Conferences:
2007 - Washington, DC/Apr. 28-May 2
Publications:
Experimental Biology and Medicine. 11/year. adv.

Society for Experimental Mechanics *(1943)*
Seven School St.
Bethel, CT 06801-1405
Tel: (203)790-6373 *Fax:* (203)790-4472
Web Site: www.sem.org
Members: 2000 individuals
Staff: 7
Annual Budget: $500-1,000,000
Executive Director: Thomas Proulx
Manager, Meetings: Katherine Ramsay
E-Mail: sem@sem1.com
Historical Note
Founded in 1943 and incorporated in Delaware in 1961. Formerly (1984) the Society for Experimental Stress Analysis. Promotes research in experimental mechanics. Membership: $72/year (individual); $450-1,000/year (organization/company).
Meetings/Conferences:
Semi-annual Meetings: Spring and Fall/500
Publications:
Mechanics of Time Dependent Materials. q.
Experimental Mechanics. bi-m.
Experimental Techniques. bi-m. adv.

Society for Foodservice Management *(1979)*
304 W. Liberty St., Suite 201
Louisville, KY 40202
Tel: (502)583-3783 *Fax:* (502)589-3602
E-Mail: sfm@hqtrs.com
Web Site: www.sfm-online.org
Members: 1971 individuals
Staff: 4
Annual Budget: $250-500,000
Executive Director: Greg Hobby
Director, Programs: Nick Hall
Director, Member Services: Amanda Reeves
Historical Note
Members are executives who are responsible for non-commercial food service, such as employee cafeterias, colleges and universities and healthcare facilities. Formed as the result of a merger of the Association for Food Service Management (established 1970) and the National Industrial Cafeteria Managers' Association (established 1949) on July 1, 1979. Membership: $225/year (active); $425/year (associate).
Meetings/Conferences:
Annual Meetings: Fall
Publications:
FastFacts email newsletter. bi-w.
Membership Roster. a.

Society for Free Radical Biology and Medicine *(1988)*
8365 Keystone Crossing, Suite 107
Indianapolis, IN 46240
Tel: (317)205-9482 *Fax:* (317)205-9481
E-Mail: info@sfrbm.org
Web Site: www.sfrbm.org
Members: 1400 individuals
Staff: 2
Annual Budget: $250-500,000
Executive Director: Kent A. Lindeman, CMP
Historical Note
SFRBM promotes interaction between the various disciplines involved in oxygen related research. Membership: $125/year (individual); $85/year (postdoctoral); $20/year (student).
Meetings/Conferences:
Annual: Typical Attendence: 600-650
2007 - Washington, DC(Renaissance Hotel)/Nov. 14-18/650
2008 - Indianapolis, IN(Marriott)/Nov. 19-23/650
Publications:
Free Radical Biology & Medicine. semi-m. adv.

Society for French Historical Studies *(1955)*
Univ. of Kentucky
Dept. of History
Lexington, KY 40506
Tel: (859)257-1731 *Fax:* (859)323-3885
Members: 1450 individuals
Annual Budget: under $10,000
Executive Director: Jeremy Popkin
E-Mail: popkin@uky.edu
Historical Note
A professional society concerned with scholarly research and teaching on French History. Membership: $40/year (individual).
Meetings/Conferences:
Annual Meetings: Spring
Publications:
French Historical Studies. q.

Society for General Music *(1982)*
Historical Note
A council of the Music Educators National Conference.

Society for German-American Studies *(1968)*
Scott Community College
500 Belmont Road
Bettendorf, IA 52722-6804
Tel: (319)441-4319

Web Site: www.ulib.iupui.edu/kade/sgasin.html
*Members:*600 individuals
Treasurer and Membership Coordinator: William Roba

Historical Note
SGAS members are academics and others with an interest in German-American studies. Membership: $25/year (individual); $10/year (student).

Publications:
Newsletter of SGAS. q.
Yearbook of German-American Studies. a.

Society for Gynecologic Investigation *(1952)*
409 12th St. SW
Washington, DC 20024-2188
Tel: (202)863-2544 *Fax:* (202)863-0739
Web Site: www.sgionline.org
Members: 1000 individuals
Staff: 9
Annual Budget: $500-1,000,000
Executive Director: Ava Ann Tayman
Executive Vice President: John H. Grossman, M.D.
E-Mail: jgrossman@icnt.net

Historical Note
Membership: $160/year (U.S.); $174/year (international).

Meetings/Conferences:
Annual Meetings: March

Publications:
Journal of the SGI. bi-m.

Society for Healthcare Consumer Advocacy *(1972)*
One N. Franklin, Suite 2800
Chicago, IL 60606
Tel: (312)422-3700 *Fax:* (312)422-4577
E-Mail: shca@aha.org
Web Site: www.shca-aha.org
Members: 1000 individuals
Staff: 5
Annual Budget: $250-500,000
Executive Director: Virginia Sylvestri

Historical Note
Affiliated with the American Hospital Association. Formerly (1997) the National Society for Patient Representation and Consumer Affairs, (1988) the National Society of Patient Representatives, and (1981) the Society of Patient Representatives. Membership: $125/year.

Meetings/Conferences:
Annual Meetings: Spring

Publications:
Healthcare Consumer Advocacy. q. adv.

Society for Healthcare Epidemiology of America *(1980)*
66 Canal Center Plaza, Suite 600
Alexandria, VA 22314
Tel: (703)684-1006 *Fax:* (703)684-1009
E-Mail: sheahq@shea-online.org
Web Site: www.shea-online.org
Members: 1200 individuals
Staff: 6
Annual Budget: $500-1,000,000
Executive Director: Kenneth Cleveland
E-Mail: sheahq@shea-online.org

Historical Note
Formerly (1994) Society for Hospital Epidemiology of America. Purpose is to advance expertise and education in hospital epidemiology and quality assurance.

Meetings/Conferences:
Annual Meetings: Spring
2007 – Baltimore, MD(Marriott)/Apr. 14-17/1000

Publications:
Infection Control and Hospital Epidemiology. m.

Society for Healthcare Strategy and Market Development *(1996)*
One N. Franklin, 28th Fl.
Chicago, IL 60606
Tel: (312)422-3888 *Fax:* (312)422-4579
E-Mail: stratsoc@aha.org
Web Site: www.stratsociety.org
*Members:*4000 individuals
Staff: 5
Annual Budget: $1-2,000,000
Executive Director: Lauren A. Barnett
E-Mail: stratsoc@aha.org
Associate Director: Susan Gergeley
E-Mail: stratsoc@aha.org

Historical Note
Founded in 1996 as the result of a merger between Society for Healthcare Planning and Marketing (founded 1977) and American Society for Health Care Marketing and Public Relations (founded 1964). An affiliate of American Hospital Association (same address). SHSMD's membership includes healthcare executives specializing in strategic planning, marketing, public relations, and other business and development functions. Membership: $195/year (individual).

Meetings/Conferences:
Annual Meetings: Fall/800
2007 – San Francisco, CA(San Francisco Marriott)/Sept. 17-21/1200
2007 – Washington, DC(Marriott Wardman Park)/Oct. 3-6/1200

Publications:
Futurescan/Environmental Assessment. a.
e-Connect Newsletter. w.
Newsletter. bi-m.

Society for Hematopathology *(1981)*
3643 Walton Way Extension
Augusta, GA 30909
Tel: (706)733-7550 *Fax:* (706)733-8033
E-Mail: sh@uscap.org
Web Site: http://socforheme.org
*Members:*500 individuals
Staff: 1
Coordinator: Carolyn Lane
E-Mail: sh@uscap.org

Historical Note
The society was created for the promotion and exchange of knowledge and the stimulation of clinical, morphologic, and functional investigation of the hematopoietic and lymphoreticular systems as its primary objectives.

Meetings/Conferences:
Annual Meetings: Annual/March

Publications:
Newsletter.

Society for Historians of American Foreign Relations *(1967)*
Department of History, Ohio State University
106 Dulles Hall, 230 W. 17th Ave.
Columbus, OH 43210
Tel: (614)292-7200 *Fax:* (614)292-2282
E-Mail: shafr@osu.edu
Web Site: www.shafr.org
*Members:*1700 individuals
Staff: 1
Annual Budget: $10-25,000
Executive Director: Peter Hahn
E-Mail: shafr@osu.edu

Historical Note
Affiliated with the American Historical Association and the Organization of American Historians. Promotes the study of diplomatic history in cooperation with the National Archives and other government agencies. Membership: $40/year (regular); $20/year (student).

Meetings/Conferences:
Annual Meetings: Summer

Publications:
Roster and Research List. irreg.
Diplomatic History. q. adv.
Newsletter. q. adv.

Society for Historians of the Early American Republic *(1978)*
3619 Locust Walk
Third Floor
Philadelphia, PA 19104-6213
Tel: (215)746-5393 *Fax:* (215)573-3391
E-Mail: info@shear.org
Web Site: www.shear.org
Members: 1500individualsandorganizations
Staff: 3
Annual Budget: $10-25,000
Executive Coordinator: Amy L. Baxter-Bellamy
E-Mail: info@shear.org

Historical Note
SHEAR members are academic and others with an interest in American history in the period of the early republic. Membership: $20-100/year (individual); $60/year (organization).

Publications:
Journal of the Early Republic. q. adv.

Society for Historians of the Gilded Age and Progressive Era *(1988)*
Hayes Presidential Center
Spiegel Grove
Fremont, OH 43420-2796
Tel: (419)332-2081 Ext: 21 *Fax:* (419)332-5424
*Members:*300 individuals
Annual Budget: under $10,000

Historical Note
SHGAPE members are academics and others with an interest in American history during the years 1865-1917. Membership: $40/year (individual); $15/year (student); $80/year (institutional/library).

Meetings/Conferences:
Annual Meetings: in conjunction with OAH annual meeting

Publications:
Newsletter. semi-a. adv.
Journal of the Gilded Age and Progressive Era. q. adv.

Society for Historical Archaeology *(1967)*
15245 Shady Grove Road, Suite 130
Rockville, MD 20850
Tel: (301)990-2454 *Fax:* (301)990-9771
E-Mail: hq@sha.org
Web Site: www.sha.org
Members: 1950 individuals
Annual Budget: $250-500,000
Executive Director: Karen Hutchison

Historical Note
SHA is concerned with the identification, excavation, interpretation and conservation of sites and materials, and applies archaeological methods to the study of history. Has no paid officers or full-time staff. Membership: 125/year (individual); $200/year (organization).

Meetings/Conferences:
Annual Meetings: Winter

Publications:
Underwater Archaeology. irreg.
Historical Archaeology. q.
SHA Newsletter. q.
Special Publications. irreg.

Society for History Education *(1972)*
P.O. Box 1578
Borrego Springs, CA 92004
Tel: (760)767-5938
E-Mail: conniegeorge@thehistoryteacher.org
Web Site: www.thehistoryteacher.org/
*Members:*2000 individuals
Staff: 12
Annual Budget: $50-100,000
General Manager: Connie George
E-Mail: conniegeorge@thehistoryteacher.org

Historical Note
Formerly (1972) History Teachers Association. Supports the improvement of history teaching at secondary and post-secondary levels. Membership: $31/year (individual); $61/year (institution); $21/year (student); $30/year (foreign student); $70/year (Canada and Mexico); $79/year (all other foreign institutions).

Meetings/Conferences:
Annual Meetings: Cal State Univ., Long Beach, CA/June

Publications:
The History Teacher. q. adv.

Society for History in the Federal Government *(1979)*
Ben Franklin Station
P.O. Box 14139
Washington, DC 20044-4139
Tel: (202)354-2009
Web Site: www.shfg.org
*Members:*500 individuals

Annual Budget: under $10,000

Historical Note

Promoting study and broad understanding of the history of the U.S. government, SHFG is a professional society of historians, archivists, curators and others with an interest in the historical and archival activities of the U.S. government. Affiliated with the American Historical Association. Has no paid officers or full-time staff. Membership: $35/year.

Meetings/Conferences:

Annual Meetings: Spring

2007 - College Park, MD(National Archives)/March 8-8

Publications:

Roster. a.
Directory of Federal Historical Programs and Activities. irreg.
The Federalist. irreg.

Society for Human Ecology *(1981)*

College of the Atlantic
105 Eden St.
Bar Harbor, ME 04609
Tel: (207)288-5015 Ext: 301 *Fax:* (207)288-3780
E-Mail: carter@coa.edu
Web Site: www.societyforhumanecology.org
Members: 250 individuals
Annual Budget: under $10,000
Assistant to the Executive Director: Barbara Carter
E-Mail: carter@coa.edu

Historical Note

SHE members are academics, scientists, health professionals and others with an interest in studying the interrelationship of man's actions and his environment. Has no paid officers or full-time staff. Membership: $60/year (individual); $35/year (student).

Meetings/Conferences:

Biennial Meetings:

Publications:

Human Ecology Review. semi-a. adv.
Convention Proceedings. 1/18 months. adv.
Internat'l Directory of Human Ecologists. irreg.

Society for Human Resource Management *(1948)*

1800 Duke St.
Alexandria, VA 22314-3499
Tel: (703)548-3440 *Fax:* (703)535-6490
Toll Free: (800)283 - 7476
E-Mail: shrm@shrm.org
Web Site: www.shrm.org
Members: 500 Affiliated Chapters
Staff: 185
Annual Budget: $50-100,000,000
President and Chief Executive Officer: Susan R. Meisinger, SPHR
E-Mail: shrm@shrm.org
Senior Vice President, Member Services: Gail Aldrich, SPHR
E-Mail: shrm@shrm.org
Manager, Media Affairs: Frank Scanlan

Historical Note

Formerly (1989) American Society for Personnel Administration. A professional society of human resource management professionals and others involved in human resources management. Institute for International Human Resources is a division of SHRM. The Human Resource Certification Institute is the certification arm of SHRM. The SHRM Foundation sponsors research and develops educational programs for its members. Has an annual budget of over $60 million. Membership: $160/year.

Meetings/Conferences:

Annual Meetings: Spring/9,000

Publications:

HR Magazine. m. adv.
Research Quarterly. q.
Hiring Source Book.

Society for Humanistic Anthropology *(1974)*

Historical Note

A section of the American Anthropological Association. Members are interested in the human meaning of anthropological inquiry and the anthropologist's commitment to experience and evaluation.

Society for Humanistic Judaism *(1969)*

28611 W. 12 Mile Road
Farmington Hills, MI 48334
Tel: (248)478-7610 *Fax:* (248)478-3159
E-Mail: info@shj.org
Web Site: www.shj.org
Members: 2500 individuals
Staff: 4
Annual Budget: $100-250,000
Executive Director: M. Bonnie Cousens

Historical Note

Creates, publishes and shares holiday and life cycle materials for secular humanistic Jews. Helps to organize communities of secular humanistic Jews. Membership: $65/year.

Meetings/Conferences:

Annual Meetings: Spring

Publications:

Humanorah. 4/year.
Humanistic Judaism. 4/year.

Society for Imaging Informatics in Medicine *(1980)*

19440 Golf Vista Plaza, Suite 330
Leesburg, VA 20176
Tel: (703)723-0432 *Fax:* (703)723-0415
Web Site: www.siimweb.org
Members: 2500 individuals
Staff: 8
Annual Budget: $2-5,000,000
Executive Director: Anna Marie Mason
E-Mail: amason@siimweb.org

Historical Note

Formerly the Society of Computer Applications in Radiology; assumed its current name in 2006. SIIM members are physicians and other health care professionals with an interest in the application of computers in medical imaging and designers/manufacturers of equipment. Membership: $150/year (individual); $100/year (student); $2,000/year (corporate member); $600/year (institutional member).

Meetings/Conferences:

Annual Meetings: Spring-SUmmer

2007 - Providence, RI(Rhode Island Convention Center)/June 7-10
2008 - Seattle, WA(Washington State Convention Center)/May 15-18

Publications:

SIIM University Primers.
Proceedings & Syllabus. a.
Journal of Digital Imaging. q. adv.
SIIM News Newsletter. q. adv.
Directory (online).

Society for Imaging Science & Technology *(1947)*

7003 Kilworth Lane
Springfield, VA 22151
Tel: (703)642-9090 *Fax:* (703)642-9094
E-Mail: info@imaging.org
Web Site: www.imaging.org
Members: 2000 individuals
Staff: 8
Annual Budget: $1-2,000,000
Executive Director: Suzanne E. Grinnan
E-Mail: info@imaging.org
Secretary, Membership: Jennifer Potter

Historical Note

Originated in 1947 as the Society of Photographic Engineers. In 1957 merged with the Technical Division of the Photographic Society of America to form the Society of Photographic Scientists and Engineers. Became (1986) Society for Imaging Science and Technology. Incorporated in the District of Columbia in 1966. Members are persons who engage in imaging science or engineering or teachers of photography or imaging science. Membership: $90/year (domestic); $100/year (foreign); $750-5,000/year (organization).

Meetings/Conferences:

Annual Meetings: Fall

Publications:

Journal of Imaging Science and Technology. bi-m. adv.
Journal of Electronic Imaging. q.
IS&T Reporter. q.

Society for In Vitro Biology *(1946)*

514 Daniels St. #411
Raleigh, NC 27605
Tel: (919)420-7940 *Fax:* (919)420-7939
Toll Free: (888)588 - 1923
E-Mail: sivb@sivb.org
Web Site: www.sivb.org
Members: 1,500 individuals
Staff: 3
Annual Budget: $500-1,000,000
Managing Director: Marietta Wheaton Ellis
Manager, Publications: Michele Schultz
E-Mail: michele@sivb.org

Historical Note

Founded in 1946 as the Tissue Culture Commission; became the Tissue Culture Association in 1950 and assumed its current name in 1994. The society fosters exchange, publication and teaching of knowledge related to in vitro biology of cells, tissues and organs. Focuses on biological problems of significance to science and society. Membership: $155/year (individual); $500/year (company).

Meetings/Conferences:

2007 - Indianapolis, IN(Westin)/June 9-13/600

Publications:

In Vitro Report Newsletter. 4/year. adv.
In Vitro Cellular & Developmental Biology-Plant. 7/year. adv.
In Vitro Cellular & Developmental Biology-Animal. 11/year. adv.
Meeting Program. a. adv.

Society for Industrial and Applied Mathematics *(1952)*

3600 University City Science Center
Philadelphia, PA 19104-2688
Tel: (215)382-9800 *Fax:* (215)386-7999
Toll Free: (800)447 - 7426
Web Site: www.siam.org
Members: 9000 individuals
Staff: 60
Annual Budget: $5-10,000,000
Executive Director: James M. Crowley
E-Mail: crowley@siam.org
Director, Information Management Systems: Ted Kull
Manager, Customer Svc.: Arlette Liberatore
E-Mail: liberatore@siam.org
Director, Conferences: Coley Lyons
E-Mail: lyons@siam.org
Director, Finance and Administration: Susan A. Palantino
E-Mail: palantino@siam.org

Historical Note

Organized in Philadelphia in Nov. 1951 and incorporated in Delaware in April 1952. Member of the American Association for the Advancement of Science, the Conference Board of the Mathematical Sciences, the Council of Engineering and Scientific Society Executives, and the Council of Scientific Society Presidents and Joint Policy Board for Mathematics. SIAM was formed to further the application of mathematics to industry and science, promote basic research in mathematics leading to new methods and techniques useful to industry and science and to provide media for the exchange of information and ideas between mathmeticians and other technical as well as scientific personnel. Annual Budget: $5.6 million. Membership: $105/year (individual); $270-$3,752/year (academic); $3900/year (corporate).

Meetings/Conferences:

Annual Meetings: Summer

Publications:

SIAM News. 10/year. adv.
SIAM Journal on Applied Mathematics. bi-m. adv.
SIAM Journal on Computing. bi-m. adv.
SIAM Journal on Control and Optimization. bi-m. adv.
SIAM Journal on Discrete Mathematics. q. adv.
SIAM Journal on Mathematical Analysis. bi-m. adv.
SIAM Journal on Matrix Analysis and Applications. q. adv.
SIAM Journal on Numerical Analysis. bi-m. adv.

SIAM Journal on Scientific Computing. bi-m. adv.
SIAM Review. q. adv.
SIAM Journal on Optimization. q. adv.
Theory of Probability and its Applications. q. adv.

Society for Industrial and Organizational Psychology *(1946)*
P.O. Box 87
Bowling Green, OH 43402-0087
Tel: (419)353-0032 *Fax:* (419)352-2645
E-Mail: siop@siop.org
Web Site: www.siop.org
Members: 6600 individuals
Staff: 6
Annual Budget: $1-2,000,000
Executive Director, Administration Office: Dave Nershi

Historical Note
Affiliated with the American Psychological Association and the American Psychological Society, SIOP is concerned with the scientific application of psychology to all types of organizations providing goods or services, such as manufacturing concerns, commercial enterprises, labor unions, trade associations and public agencies. Members must be engaged in professional activites as demonstrated by research, teaching and practice related to the purpose of the society. Membership: $55/year (individual).

Meetings/Conferences:
Annual Meetings: Spring/3,700
2007 – New York, NY(Marriott Marquis)/Apr. 27-29
2008 – San Francisco, CA(Hilton)/Apr. 11-13
2009 – New Orleans, LA(Sheraton)/Apr. 3-5

Publications:
TIP: The Industrial-Organizational Psychologist. q.

Society for Industrial Archeology *(1971)*
Dept. of Social Sciences/ MI Technological Univ.
1400 Townsend Dr.
Houghton, MI 49931-1295
Tel: (906)487-1889 *Fax:* (906)487-2468
Web Site: www.sia-web.org
Members: 1700 individuals
Staff: 1
Annual Budget: $50-100,000
Executive Secretary and Editor: Patrick Martin
E-Mail: pem-194@mtu.edu

Historical Note
Founded to promote the study of the physical survival of our technical and industrial past. Officers change biennially. Membership: $35/year (individual); $40/year (organization).

Meetings/Conferences:
Annual Meetings: Spring

Publications:
SIA Newsletter. q. adv.
IA. semi-a. adv.

Society for Industrial Microbiology *(1949)*
3929 Old Lee Hwy., Suite 92-A
Fairfax, VA 22030-2421
Tel: (703)691-3357 *Fax:* (703)691-7991
E-Mail: info@simhq.org
Web Site: www.simhq.org
Members: 1300 individuals
Staff: 5
Annual Budget: $50-100,000
Executive Director: Christine Lowe
Director, Membership: Maura Loughney

Historical Note
Founded in 1949 and incorporated in 1960. Promotes the advancement of the microbiological sciences especially as applied to industry. The Society is an Adherent Society member of the American Institute of Biological Sciences, Inc. Membership: $30/year (student for SIM news only); $55/year (Student SIM news and journal); $100/year (U.S.); $115/year (foreign), various levels/year (corporate).

Meetings/Conferences:
Annual Meetings: August
2007 – Denver, CO(Denver Hyatt Regency)/July 29-Aug. 2/650

Publications:
Journal of Industrial Microbiology. m. adv.
SIM News. bi-m. adv.

Society for Information Display *(1962)*
610 S. Second St.
San Jose, CA 95112
Tel: (408)977-1013 *Fax:* (408)977-1531
Web Site: www.sid.org
Members: 6000 individuals
Staff: 2
Annual Budget: $2-5,000,000
Office Manager: Jenny Needham
E-Mail: jenny@sid.org
Contact: Linda Lippin

Historical Note
SID is an international society dedicated to the advancement of display technology, manufacturing, and applications. Membership: $75/year (individual); $950/year (company).

Meetings/Conferences:
Semi-Annual Meetings: Spring and Summer

Publications:
Journal of the SID. q.
Information Display Magazine. m. adv.
Digest of Technical Papers. a.
Seminar Lecture Notes. a.
IDRC Conference Record. a.

Society for Information Management *(1969)*
401 N. Michigan Ave.
Chicago, IL 60611
Tel: (312)527-6734 *Fax:* (312)245-1081
E-Mail: sim@simnet.org
Web Site: www.simnet.org
Members: 3000 individuals
Staff: 10
Annual Budget: $1-2,000,000
Executive Director: Jim Luisi

Historical Note
SIM was formed to enhance international recognition of information as a basic organizational resource and to promote the effective utilization and management of this resource towards the improvement of management performance. It attempts to enhance communications between IS executives and the senior executives responsible for management of the business enterprise. Formerly (until 1982) the Society for Management Information Systems. Membership: $250/year (corporate at-large); $125/year (academic at-large); $125/year (corporate chapter); $62.50/year (academic at-large).

Meetings/Conferences:
Annual Meetings: Fall

Publications:
Network Newsletter. bi-m.
MIS Quarterly Journal. q.
Executive Brief. q.
Conference Executive Summaries. semi-a.

Society for Integrative and Comparative Biology *(1890)*
1313 Dolley Madison Blvd., Suite 402
McLean, VA 22101
Tel: (703)790-1745 *Fax:* (703)790-2672
Toll Free: (800)955 - 1236
E-Mail: sicb@burkinc.com
Web Site: www.sicb.org
Members: 2400 individuals
Staff: 6
Annual Budget: $500-1,000,000
Executive Director: Brett J. Burk

Historical Note
Formerly (1996) the American Society of Zoologists. The Eastern Branch of the American Society of Zoologists was founded in 1890 as the American Morphological Association; the Central Branch developed from the Central Naturalists, founded in 1899; the two merged in 1901-3 and the American Society of Zoologists emerged from a joint meeting in Philadelphia in 1913. Incorporated in Illinois in 1964. Membership is open to individuals who are actively engaged in the field of zoology. Membership: $85/year (full member, with Ph.D.); $36/year (student).

Meetings/Conferences:
Annual Meetings: Winter/800

Publications:
Integrative and Comparative Biology. bi-m. adv.

Society for Intercultural Education, Training and Research - USA *(1974)*
8835 S.W. Canyon Lane, Suite 110
Portland, OR 97225
Tel: (503)297-4622 *Fax:* (503)297-4695
Web Site: www.seitarusa.org
Members: 600 individuals
Staff: 1
Annual Budget: $100-250,000
Executive Director: Margaret D. "Peggy" Pusch
E-Mail: mdpusch@intercultural.org

Historical Note
Founded as the Society for Intercultural Education, Training and Research in 1974, it added "International" to its name in 1985, and reverted to its original name in 2000. SIETAR is part of a global network of individuals concerned with understanding the interaction between peoples of different national, cultural, racial and ethnic backgrounds. Membership: $125/year (individual); $500/year (organization/company); $70/year (student); $70/year (senior).

Meetings/Conferences:
Annual Meetings: Fall

Publications:
SUSA News. bi-m.
The Slate. irreg.

Society for Invertebrate Pathology *(1967)*
8904 Straw Flower Dr.
Knoxville, TN 37922
Toll Free: (888)486 - 1505
E-Mail: sip@sipweb.org
Web Site: www.sipweb.org
Members: 1100 individuals
Staff: 1
Annual Budget: $10-25,000
Executive Secretary: Margaret Rotstein
E-Mail: sip@sipweb.org

Historical Note
SIP is an interdisciplinary organization that promotes research and scietific inquiry into invertebrate pathology.

Meetings/Conferences:
Annual Meetings: Late Summer Ithaca, NY(Cornell Univ.)

Publications:
Newsletter. 3/year.

Society for Investigative Dermatology *(1937)*
820 W. Superior Ave., Seventh Floor
Cleveland, OH 44113-1800
Tel: (216)579-9300 *Fax:* (216)579-9333
E-Mail: sid@sidnet.org
Web Site: www.sidnet.org
Members: 2600 individuals
Staff: 10
Annual Budget: $2-5,000,000
Executive Director: Angela Welsh
E-Mail: welsh@sidnet.org
Director, Meetings and Educational Programs: Viveca Kimble

Historical Note
Founded and incorporated in New York, April 24, 1937. Membership: $200/year (individual); $1,500/year (corporate).

Meetings/Conferences:
Annual Meetings: Spring/1,000
2007 – Los Angeles, CA(Century Plaza Hotel)/May 9-12

Publications:
Journal of Investigative Dermatology. m. adv.

Society for Iranian Studies *(1967)*
Northeastern Illinois University
5500 N. St. Louis Ave.
Chicago, IL 60625
Tel: (773)442-6126
E-Mail: h-akbari@neiu.edu
Web Site: www.iranian-studies.com/
Members: 539 individuals
Staff: 1
Annual Budget: $10-25,000

Executive Director: Hamid Akbari
E-Mail: h-akbari@neiu.edu

Historical Note

Formerly (1969) Society for Iranian Cultural and Social Studies. Mmembership: $35/year (individual), $40/year institution.

Meetings/Conferences:

Annual Meetings: in conjunction with the MESA conference/Fall

Publications:

SIS Newsletter. 3/year.
Iranian Studies. q.

Society for Italian Historical Studies *(1955)*

Department of History, Boston College
Chestnut Hill, MA 02467
Tel: (617)552-3814
Web Site: http://faculty.valenciacc.edu/ckillinger/sihs/
Members: 350 individuals
Staff: 1
Annual Budget: under $10,000
Executive Secretary-Treasurer: Alan J. Reinerman

Historical Note

Members are professors and students of Italian history. Encourages the study and teaching of Italian history, promotes research, and awards prizes. Membership: $10/year (individual); $25/year (organization).

Meetings/Conferences:

Annual Meetings: December, with the American Historical Ass'n

Publications:

Newsletter. a.

Society for Latin American Anthropology *(1969)*

Historical Note

A section of the American Anthropological Association. Founded as the Ad Hoc Group on Latin American Anthropology, it became the Latin American Anthropology Group in 1971 and assumed its present name in 1982. Members are professional anthropologists interested in Latin America.

Society for Leukocyte Biology *(1954)*

c/o FASEB
9650 Rockville Pike
Bethesda, MD 20814-3998
Tel: (301)634-7810 *Fax:* (301)634-7813
E-Mail: slb@faseb.org
Web Site: www.leukocytebiology.org/
Members: 1300 individuals
Staff: 2
Annual Budget: $250-500,000
Executive Manager: Debra Weinstein, Ph.D.
E-Mail: dweinstein@faseb.org

Historical Note

Founded in 1954 and incorporated in 1965. Membership consists of those interested in phagocytic cells of the body, especially as relating to host defense, immunity and cancer. Membership: $60/year (students); $92/year (full); $849/year (institution).

Meetings/Conferences:

Annual Meetings: October

Publications:

The Journal of Leukocyte Biology Online. m. adv.
SLB Newsletter. 3/year.

Society for Light Treatment and Biological Rhythms *(1988)*

4648 Main St.
Chincoteague, VA 23336
Tel: (415)876-0716 *Fax:* (757)336-5777
E-Mail: sltbrinfo@aol.com
Web Site: www.sltbr.org
Members: 200 individuals
Staff: 1
Annual Budget: $25-50,000
Executive Director: Kathleen Matikonis

Historical Note

SLTBR fosters communication between scientists, clinicians, manufacturers, and others interested in the therapeutic use of lighting devices.

Meetings/Conferences:

Annual Meetings: Spring-Summer

Publications:

Light Treatment and Biological Rhythms. q.

Society for Linguistic Anthropology *(1983)*

Historical Note

A section of the American Anthropological Association. Established to advance the study of language in its social and cultural context.

Society for Maintenance Reliability Professionals *(1995)*

P.O. Box 51787
Knoxville, TN 37950-1787
Tel: (865)212-0111 *Fax:* (865)558-3060
Toll Free: (800)950 - 7354
E-Mail: admin@smrp.org
Web Site: www.smrp.org
Members: 1700 individuals
Staff: 5
Annual Budget: $500-1,000,000
Executive Director: Pat Winters
Manager, Business: Joe Petersen

Historical Note

Membership: $125/year (individual); $1,250/year (organization).

Meetings/Conferences:

Annual Meetings: Fall

Publications:

SMRP Solutions. q. adv.
Annual Conference Proceedings. a.

Society for Marketing Professional Services *(1973)*

99 Canal Center Plaza, Suite 330
Alexandria, VA 22314-1588
Tel: (703)549-6117 *Fax:* (703)549-2498
Toll Free: (800)292 - 7677
E-Mail: info@smps.org
Web Site: www.smps.org
Members: 5,800 individuals
Staff: 14
Annual Budget: $2-5,000,000
Chief Executive Officer: Ronald Worth, FSMPS
Senior Vice President: Lisa S. Bowman
E-Mail: lisa@smps.org
Vice President, Finance and Administration: Earl Klinger
E-Mail: earl@smps.org
Vice President, Membership Services: Tina Myers
E-Mail: tina@smps.org
Vice President, Education: William E. Scott

Historical Note

SMPS members are marketing and business development professionals who represent of architectural, engineering, planning, landscape architectural, interior design and construction management firms who are responsible for marketing their organizations' services. Membership: $295/year.

Meetings/Conferences:

Annual Meetings: August
2007 – Washington, DC(Grand Hyatt)/Aug. 22-25/1000

Publications:

SMPS News. bi-m. adv.
SMPS Marketer. bi-m. adv.

Society for Maternal Fetal Medicine *(1977)*

409 12th St. SW
Washington, DC 20024-2188
Tel: (202)863-2476 *Fax:* (202)554-1132
E-Mail: info@smfm.org
Web Site: www.smfm.org
Members: 2000 individuals
Staff: 3
Executive Director: Patricia D. Stahr
Project Specialist: Julie Miller

Historical Note

Formerly Society of Perinatal Obstetricians (1998). SMFM members are obstetrician-gynecologists specializing in maternal-fetal medicine. Membership: $425/year (regular); $375/year (associate/affiliate); $50/year (fellow in training).

Meetings/Conferences:

Annual Meetings: late January-early February

Publications:

American Journal of Obstetrics and Gynecology. irreg.
Directory of Maternal-Fetal Fellowships. a.
Abstracts/Proceedings of Annual Meeting. a.

Society for Mathematical Biology

P.O. Box 11283
Boulder, CO 80301
Tel: (303)661-9942 *Fax:* (303)665-8264
E-Mail: smbnet@smb.org
Web Site: www.smb.org
Members: 500 individuals
Treasurer: Dr. Torcom Chorbajian

Historical Note

Members are academics and others with an interest in the application of mathematics in biological research. Membership; $50/year (individual); $20/year (student).

Publications:

Bulletin of Mathematical Biology. irreg.

Society for Medical Anthropology *(1968)*

Historical Note

A section of the American Anthropological Association. Members are interested in the anthropological aspects of health, illness, health care and related topics.

Society for Medical Decision Making *(1978)*

100 N. 20th St., Fourth Floor
Philadelphia, PA 19103
Tel: (215)545-7697 *Fax:* (215)545-8107
E-Mail: smdm-office@lists.smdm.org
Web Site: www.smdm.org
Members: 1000 individuals
Staff: 2
Annual Budget: $250-500,000
Administrative Director: Tim Bower

Historical Note

SMDM is an international society promoting the theory and practice of medical decision making through the application of analytical methods. Membership: $110-185/year (individual).

Meetings/Conferences:

Annual Meetings: Fall

Publications:

Medical Decision Making Journal. bi-m. adv.
Listserve. adv.
Newsletter. q.

Society for Medieval and Renaissance Philosophy *(1979)*

Department of Philosophy, University of South Carolina
Columbia, SC 29208
Tel: (803)777-6903 *Fax:* (803)777-9178
E-Mail: hackettj@gwm.sc.edu
Members: 325 individuals
Annual Budget: under $10,000
Secretary/Treasurer: Jeremiah Hackett

Historical Note

SMRP members are academics with an interest in medieval or renaissance philosophy.

Meetings/Conferences:

Annual Meetings: in conjunction with the American Philosophical Ass'n

Publications:

Online Newsletter. semi-a.

Society for Menstrual Cycle Research *(1979)*

10559 N. 104th Place
Scottsdale, AZ 85258
Tel: (480)451-9731
Web Site: www.menstruationresearch.org
Members: 150 individuals
Annual Budget: under $10,000
Secretary-Treasurer: Mary Anna Friederich, M.D.

Historical Note

SMCR is an organization formed to meet the special needs of an interdisciplinary group of researchers, health care providers, students and others who share an interest in women's lives and health needs as these are related to the menstrual cycle. Membership is open to individuals who have demonstrated an interest in research on the menstrual cycle or related issues, and who support the purposes of the Society. Has no paid officers or full-time staff. Membership: $50/year.

Meetings/Conferences:
20077 - Vancouver, BC, Canada/

Publications:
SMRC Newsletter. 3/year.

Society for Military History *(1938)*
3119 Lakeview Circle
Leavenworth, KS 66048
Tel: (913)682-0035
Web Site: www.smh-hq.org
Members: 2300 individuals
Staff: 11
Annual Budget: $50-100,000
Executive Director: Robert H. Berlin
E-Mail: rhberlin@aol.com

Historical Note
SMH members are scholars and others with an interest in the study of military history. Membership: $50/year (individual); $25/year (student); $75/year (institution).

Meetings/Conferences:
Annual Meetings: April
2007 - Frederick, MD/Apr. 19-22/500
2008 - Ogden, UT/Apr. 17-20/400

Publications:
Journal of Military History. q.
Headquarters Gazette Newsletter. q.
Directory of Members (online).

Society for Mining, Metallurgy, and Exploration *(1957)*
8307 Shaffer Parkway
Littleton, CO 80127-4102
Tel: (303)973-9550 *Fax:* (303)973-3845
E-Mail: sme@smenet.org
Web Site: www.smenet.org/
Members: 12000 individuals
Staff: 28
Annual Budget: $2-5,000,000
Executive Director: David L. Kanagy
Manager, Meetings: Carol Cudworth
Manager, Publicity and Programming: Tara Davis
E-Mail: davis@smenet.org
Editor: Tim O'Neil
E-Mail: oneil@smenet.org
Education Assistant: Sharon Schwartz
E-Mail: schwartz@smenet.org
Manager, Membership Services: Connie Solfermoser

Historical Note
Member of the American Institute of Mining, Metallurgical, and Petroleum Engineers (1871). Formerly the Society of Mining Engineers, the Society adopted its present name in 1989. Membership: $113/year.

Meetings/Conferences:
Annual Meetings: 6,000
2007 - Denver, CO(Convention Center)/Feb. 25-28/4500

Publications:
Minerals and Metallurgical Processing Journal. q.
Mining Transactions, AIME. a.
Mining Engineering. m. adv.

Society for Mucosal Immunology
5272 River Road, Suite 630
Bethesda, MD 20816
Tel: (301)718-6516 *Fax:* (301)656-0989
E-Mail: smi@paimgmt.com
Web Site: www.socmucimm.org
Members: 700 individuals
Staff: 2
Executive Director: Mark Epstein, Sc.D.

Historical Note
SMI is an international professional society of medical researchers and physicians in mucosal immunology.

Meetings/Conferences:
Annual Meetings: Summer

Publications:
Mucosal Immunology Update. q.

Society for Natural Philosophy *(1963)*
Cornell University
Kimball Hall - TAM
Ithaca, NY 14853
Tel: (607)255-3738 *Fax:* (607)255-2011
Web Site: http://tam.cornell.edu/SNP/society.htm
Members: 300 individuals
Annual Budget: under $10,000
Treasurer: Tim Healey

Historical Note
Members are mathematicians, chemists, engineers, physicists, and other scientists interested in the foundations of mathematical sciences in nature. Has no paid officers or full-time staff. Membership: $15/year. (individual).

Meetings/Conferences:
Annual Meetings: Usually in a university setting

Society for Neuroscience *(1969)*
1121 14th St.
Suite 1010
Washington, DC 20005
Tel: (202)962-4000 *Fax:* (202)462-9740
E-Mail: info@sfn.org
Web Site: www.sfn.org
Members: 34000 individuals
Staff: 45
Annual Budget: $5-10,000,000
Executive Director: Marty Saggese
Senior Director, Communications and Public Affairs: Joseph Carey

Historical Note
Membership: $125/year (individual); $35/year (student); $2,500/year (company).

Meetings/Conferences:
Annual Meetings: Fall/22,000
2007 - San Diego, CA/Nov. 3-7
2008 - Washington, DC/Nov. 15-19

Publications:
Neuroscience Quarterly. q.
Neuroscience Nexus. m.
Brain Backgrounder.
Brain Briefings. q.
Brain Waves. q.
Journal of Neuroscience. m. adv.
Membership Directory. a.

Society for New Language Study *(1972)*
P.O. Box 326
Concord, VT 05824-0326
Tel: (802)695-8115 *Fax:* (802)695-1118
E-Mail: sakana@together.net
Members: 15 individuals
Staff: 1
Annual Budget: under $10,000
Treasurer: Raymond P. Tripp, Jr.
E-Mail: sakana@together.net

Historical Note
To stimulate consideration, evaluation and cultivation of the study of language, literature and philosophy from new perspectives.

Meetings/Conferences:
Annual Meetings: Fall, with the Rocky Mountain Modern Language Ass'n

Publications:
In Geardagum. a.

Society for News Design *(1979)*
1130 Ten Rod Road, F-104
North Kingstown, RI 02852-4177
Tel: (401)294-5233 *Fax:* (401)294-5238
E-Mail: snd@snd.org
Web Site: www.snd.org
Members: 2600 individuals
Staff: 3
Annual Budget: $500-1,000,000
Executive Director: Elise S. Burroughs
E-Mail: snd@snd.org

Historical Note
Originally the Society of Newspaper Designers; became Society of Newspaper Design in 1981 and assumed its current name in 1998. Membership is international and open to anyone interested in newspaper design. Members include designers, publishers, graphics artists, editors, illustrators, photographers, art directors, paginators, advertising artists, students and faculty who design newspapers, magazines and Web pages. The Society for News Design Foundation is its educational arm. Membership: $95/year; $65/year Small Newspapers; $45/year Students; $20 surcharge for members outside U.S.

Meetings/Conferences:
Annual Meetings: Fall/800

Publications:
Design. q. adv.
The Best of Newspaper Design. a.
SND Update Newsletter. 8/year. adv.

Society for Nutrition Education *(1967)*
7150 Winton Dr., Suite 300
Indianapolis, IN 46268
Tel: (317)328-4627 *Fax:* (317)280-8527
E-Mail: info@sne.org
Web Site: www.sne.org
Members: 1400 individuals
Staff: 4
Annual Budget: $500-1,000,000
Executive Director: Mary Ann Passi, CAE

Historical Note
Membership: $170/year (professional); $85/year (international); $94/year (retired); $69/year (students).

Meetings/Conferences:
Annual Meetings: Summer/750

Publications:
Journal of Nutrition Education. bi-m. adv.
Abstracts. a. adv.
Directory. adv.
Proceedings.
SNE Communicator. bi-m. adv.
SNE Supplement. a. adv.

Society for Obstetric Anesthesia and Perinatology *(1969)*
Two Summit Park Dr., Suite 140
Cleveland, OH 44131
Tel: (216)447-7863 *Fax:* (216)642-1127
E-Mail: soaphq@soap.org
Web Site: www.soap.org
Members: 1200 individuals
Staff: 10
Annual Budget: $250-500,000
Executive Director: Pamela R. Happ

Historical Note
The Society is a recognized subspecialty organization of the American Society of Anesthesiologists. SOAP was formed to provide a forum for the discussion of problems unique to the peripartum period, which includes the clinical practice of medicine, basic research, practical business and public health aspects of the field. Membership: $110/year.

Meetings/Conferences:
Annual Meetings: Spring
2007 - Banff, AB, Canada(Fairmont Banff Springs)/May 16-19/500

Publications:
SOAP Newsletter. q.

Society for Occupational and Environmental Health *(1972)*
6728 Old McLean Village Dr.
McLean, VA 22101
Tel: (703)556-9222 *Fax:* (703)556-8729
E-Mail: soeh@degnon.org
Web Site: www.soeh.org
Members: 300 individuals
Staff: 3
Annual Budget: $50-100,000
Executive Director: George K. Degnon, CAE

Historical Note
Founded at the New York Academy of Sciences on November 12, 1972. Incorporated in the District of Columbia. Members include physicians, hygienists, economists, laboratory scientists, academicians, labor and industry representatives, or anyone interested in occupational and/or environmental health. Serves as a forum for the presentation of scientific data and the exchange of information among members; sponsors conferences and meetings which address specific problem areas and policy questions. Officers are elected biennially; governing councilors triennially. Membership: $75/year (individual); $30/year (student).

Meetings/Conferences:
Annual Meetings: Spring
Publications:
SOEH Letter. q.
Archives of Environmental Health. bi-m.

Society for Organic Petrology *(1984)*
c/o U.S. Geological Survey
956 National Center, 12201 Sunrise Valley Dr.
Reston, VA 20192
Tel: (703)648-6469 *Fax:* (703)648-6419
E-Mail: pwarwick@usgs.gov
Web Site: www.tsop.org
Members: 250 individuals
Annual Budget: $10-25,000
Contact: Peter D. Warwick
E-Mail: pwarwick@usgs.gov
Historical Note
TSOP are scientists and engineers with an interest in coal petrology, kerogen petrology, organic geochemistry, and related fields. Has no paid officers or full-time staff. Membership: $25/year (individual); $15/year (student).
Meetings/Conferences:
Annual Meetings: Fall
2007 – Victoria, BC, Canada(University of Victoria)/Aug. 19-25
2008 – Oviedo, Spain(Prince Felipe Auditorium)/Sept. 21-28
Publications:
International Journal of Coal Geology. q. adv.
TSOP Newsletter. q. adv.
TSOP Annual Meeting Abstracts and Program. a. adv.

Society for Pediatric Anesthesia *(1956)*
P.O. Box 11086
Richmond, VA 23230-1086
Tel: (804)282-9780 *Fax:* (804)282-0090
E-Mail: spa@societyhq.com
Web Site: www.pedsanesthesia.org
Members: 4000 individuals
Staff: 10
Annual Budget: $250-500,000
Executive Director: Stewart A. Hinckley, CMP
Historical Note
The Society is a recognized subspecialty organization of the American Society of Anesthesiologists. Membership: $125/year.
Publications:
Newsletter. 3/year.
Anesthesia & Analgesia. m. adv.

Society for Pediatric Dermatology *(1976)*
8365 Keystone Crossing
Suite 107
Indianapolis, IN 46240
Tel: (317)202-0224 *Fax:* (317)205-9481
E-Mail: spd@hp-assoc.com
Web Site: www.pedsderm.net
Members: 500 individuals
Staff: 2
Annual Budget: $250-500,000
Historical Note
Members are physicians with an interest in pediatric dermatology. Membership: $250/year.
Meetings/Conferences:
Annual Meetings: Summer
2007 – Chicago, IL(Westin Chicago)/July 12-15/300
2008 – Snowbird, VT(Snowbird Ski Resort)/July 9-12/300
Publications:
Pediatric Dermatology. bi-m. adv.
SPD Newsletter. 4/yr.

Society for Pediatric Pathology *(1965)*
c/o U.S. and Canadian Academy of Pathology
3643 Walton Way Extension
Augusta, GA 30909
Tel: (706)364-3375 *Fax:* (706)733-8033
Web Site: www.spponline.org
Members: 650 individuals
Staff: 2
Annual Budget: $100-250,000
Administrator: James Crimmins
E-Mail: jim@uscap.org
Historical Note
Promotes continuing education, training and standards for specialists in the field. Full members are pathologists and other physicians substantially involved in pathology as it relates to pediatric medicine. Membership: $200/year (full member); $100/year (junior member).
Meetings/Conferences:
Semi-Annual Meetings: Spring and Fall
2007 – San Diego, CA(Hyatt)/March 24-25/225
2008 – Atlanta, GA(Hyatt)/March 8-9
Publications:
SPP Newsletter. 3/year.
Pediatric and Developmental Pathology. bi-m.

Society for Pediatric Psychology *(1968)*
P.O. Box 170231
Atlanta, GA 30317
Tel: (404)373-1099 *Fax:* (404)373-8251
E-Mail: pedpsychol@aol.com
Web Site: www.apa.org/divisions/div54/homepage.html
Members: 1400 individuals
Staff: 1
Annual Budget: $100-250,000
Administrative Officer: Martha Hagan
E-Mail: pedpsychol@aol.com
Meetings/Conferences:
Annual Meetings: in conjunction with the American Psychological Ass'n
2007 – San Francisco, CA/Aug. 17-20
Publications:
Newsletter Progress Notes. 3/year. adv.
Journal of Pediatric Psychology. 10/year. adv.

Society for Pediatric Radiology *(1958)*
4550 Post Oak Place, Suite 342
Houston, TX 77027
Tel: (713)965-0566 *Fax:* (713)960-0488
E-Mail: spr@meetingmanagers.com
Web Site: www.pedrad.org
Members: 1000 individuals
Staff: 2
Annual Budget: $250-500,000
Executive Director: Jennifer K. Boylan
Historical Note
Members are pediatric radiologists interested in pediatric imaging. Membership: $278/year (individual).
Meetings/Conferences:
Annual Meetings: Spring/225
2007 – Montreal, QC, Canada/May 17-20
Publications:
Pediatric Radiology. m.
Membership Directory. a.

Society for Pediatric Research *(1929)*
3400 Research Forest Dr., Suite B-7
The Woodlands, TX 77381-4259
Tel: (281)419-0052 *Fax:* (281)419-0082
E-Mail: info@aps.spr.org
Web Site: www.aps-spr.org
Members: 3000 individuals
Staff: 3
Annual Budget: $250-500,000
Executive Director: Debbie Anagnostelis
E-Mail: debbiea@aps-spr.org
Historical Note
Purpose is to provide a forum for pediatric researchers to present and receive information currently available in all fields of pediatric research. Membership: $295/year (active); $95/year (senior).
Meetings/Conferences:
Annual Meetings: Spring/7,000
2007 – Toronto, ON, Canada(Metro Convention Center)/May 5-8
Publications:
Pediatric Research. m. adv.

Society for Pediatric Urology
900 Cummings Center, Suite 221-U
Beverly, MA 01915
Tel: (978)927-8330 *Fax:* (978)524-8890
Web Site: www.spuonline.org
Members: 350 individuals
Staff: 1
Annual Budget: under $10,000
Executive Director: Aurelie M. Alger
Historical Note
An invitational professional society whose secretary changes every three years. Membership: $100/year (individual).
Publications:
Newsletter.
Society for Pediatric Urology. w.

Society for Personality Assessment *(1938)*
6109 Arlington Blvd., Suite H
Falls Church, VA 22044
Tel: (703)534-4772 *Fax:* (703)534-6905
Web Site: www.personality.org
Members: 2100 individuals
Staff: 2
Annual Budget: $250-500,000
Administrative Director: Paula J. Garber
E-Mail: manager@spaonline.org
Historical Note
Founded and incorporated in Newark, New Jersey in 1938 as the Rorschach Research Exchange. The name changed to the Society for Projective Techniques and then the Society for Projective Techniques and Personality Assessment; assumed its current name in 1971. Membership: $90/year (fellow/member/associate); $20/year (student).
Meetings/Conferences:
Annual Meetings: March
2007 – Arlington, VA(Sheraton National)/March 7-11/400
Publications:
SPA Exchange. semi-a. adv.
Journal of Personality Assessment. bi-m. adv.

Society for Philosophy and Technology *(1975)*
Sonoma State University, Department of Philosophy
1801 E. Cotati Ave.
Rohnert Park, CA 94928-3613
Tel: (707)664-2277 *Fax:* (707)664-4400
Web Site: www.spt.org
Members: 300 individuals
Secretary: John Sullins
E-Mail: john.sullins@sonoma.edu
Historical Note
SPT members are academics and other researchers studying the philosophical ramifications of techological innovation. Membership: $15/year (individual); $5/year (student).
Meetings/Conferences:
Annual Meetings: in conjunction with the American Philosophical Ass'n
Publications:
Techne: Journal of the Society for Philosophy and Technology. a.
Newsletter. q.

Society for Philosophy of Religion *(1940)*
Dept. of Philosophy, Univ. of Georgia
Athens, GA 30602
Tel: (706)542-2823
Members: 100 individuals
Annual Budget: under $10,000
Secretary-Treasurer: Frank R. Harrison, III
E-Mail: harrison@uga.edu
Historical Note
Members are leading scholars in the philosophy of religion who must be nominated and voted upon. Sponsors the Southern Humanities Conference. Has no paid officers or full-time staff. Membership: $20/year.
Meetings/Conferences:
Annual Meetings: February-March
Publications:
International Journal for Philosophy of Religion. bi-m.

Society for Photographic Education *(1963)*
126 Peabody Hall
Miami University
Oxford, OH 45056-1988
Tel: (513)529-8328 *Fax:* (513)529-9301

E-Mail: speoffice@spenational.org
Web Site: www.spenational.org
Members: 1900 individuals
Staff: 3
Annual Budget: $100-250,000
Executive Director: Jennifer Yamashiro

Historical Note

Members are college and university teachers of photography, photographers, museum curators and students of photography. Membership: $90/year (professional/instructor); $50/year (student); $65/year (senior citizen); $150/year (sustaining member).

Meetings/Conferences:

Annual Meetings: *Spring*
2007 - Miami, FL(Radisson)/March 15-18

Publications:

Exposure. semi-a. adv.
Membership Directory and Resource Guide. a. adv.
Newsletter. q. adv.

Society for Physical Regulation in Biology and Medicine *(1980)*

2412 Cobblestone Way
Frederick, MD 21702-2626
Tel: (301)663-4556 *Fax:* (301)694-4948
Web Site: www.sprbm.org
Members: 300 individuals
Staff: 1
Annual Budget: $25-50,000
Executive Director: Gloria Parsley

Historical Note

Founded as Bioelectrical Repair and Growth Society; assumed its current name in 1994. SPRBM members are persons conducting research relevant to electric or magnetic field effects on repair, growth, regeneration or other activity of living tissue and related fields including biologists, physical scientists, physicians, surgeons, engineers and members of industry. Membership: $75/year (individual).

Publications:

Transactions. a.

Society for Physician Assistants in Pediatrics *(1994)*

Historical Note

An affiliate of American Academy of Physician Assistants, which provides administrative support.

Society for Psychological Anthropology *(1977)*

Historical Note

A section of the American Anthropological Association. SPA is a broad, multidisciplinary organization of individuals interested in cultural, psychological and social interrelations at all levels.

Society for Psychophysiological Research *(1960)*

2810 Crossroads Dr.
Madison, WI 53718
Tel: (608)443-2472 *Fax:* (608)443-2474
E-Mail: spr@reesgroupinc.com
Web Site: www.sprweb.org
Members: 2000 individuals
Annual Budget: $25-50,000
Executive Director: Susan M. Rees

Historical Note

A multidisciplinary society of physicians, psychologists, and engineers.

Publications:

Psychophysiology. bi-m.

Society for Public Health Education *(1950)*

750 First St. NE, Suite 910
Washington, DC 20002
Tel: (202)408-9804 *Fax:* (202)408-9815
E-Mail: info@sophe.org
Web Site: www.sophe.org
Members: 2200 individuals
Staff: 6
Annual Budget: $500-1,000,000
Executive Director: Elaine Auld, MPH, CHES
Director, Professional Development: Eleanor Dixon-Terry

Historical Note

Formerly (1950) Society of Public Health Educators, Inc. Membership: $90/year (new member); $130/year (renewal); $60/year (full-time student).

Meetings/Conferences:

Semi-Annual Meetings: Fall, with American Public Health Ass'n & June
2007 - Seattle, WA(Renaissance Hotel)/June 6-9/600
2007 - Washington, DC/Oct. 31-Nov. 2

Publications:

Health Promotion Practice. q. adv.
Health Education & Behavior. bi-m. adv.
News and Views. bi-m.
News U Can Use. w.

Society for Radiation Oncology Administrators *(1984)*

P.O. Box 51687
Albuquerque, NM 87181-1687
Toll Free: (866)458 - 7762
E-Mail: sroa@asrt.org
Web Site: www.sroa.org
Members: 500 individuals
Staff: 2
Annual Budget: $100-250,000
Account Executive: Joan Parsons
E-Mail: sroa@asrt.org

Historical Note

Established in Philadelphia, SROA is concerned with the administration of the business and non-medical management aspects of radiation oncology. Membership: $175/year (active); $250/year (corporate).

Meetings/Conferences:

Annual Meetings: *Annual meetings held in conjunction with ASTRO.*
2007 - Los Angeles, CA/Oct. 27-Nov. 1

Publications:

Radiation Oncology News For Administrators Online. q. adv.
SROA Monograph Series.
SROA Membership Directory. a.

Society for Range Management *(1947)*

10030 W. 27th Ave.
Wheat Ridge, CO 80215
Tel: (303)986-3309 *Fax:* (303)986-3892
Web Site: www.rangelands.org
Members: 4200 individuals
Staff: 7
Annual Budget: $500-1,000,000
Executive Vice President: Jason Campbell
Director, Administration: Ann Harris

Historical Note

Founded in Salt Lake City in January 1947 as the American Society of Range Management and incorporated in Wyoming in 1949. Became the Society for Range Management in 1971. Studies rangeland ecosystems and the principles of managing range resources. Membership: $55-$70/year (individual); $205/year (organization/company).

Meetings/Conferences:

Annual Meetings: *Winter/1,500*

Publications:

Rangelawn Ecology and Management. bi-m. adv.
Abstracts. a. adv.
Rangelands. bi-m. adv.
Member Resource News. m. adv.

Society for Reformation Research *(1947)*

Dept. of History, Hope Coll.
P.O. Box 900
Holland, MI 49422-9000
Tel: (616)395-7591 *Fax:* (616)395-7447
Web Site: www.reformationresearch.org/
Members: 250 individuals
Annual Budget: under $10,000
Treasurer: Dr. Janis Gibbs

Historical Note

Affiliated with the American Historical Association and the American Society of Church History. Formerly (1985) the American Society for Reformation Research. Member of the Council on the Study of Religion. Has no paid officers or full-time staff. Membership: $20/year (regular member); $10/year (student).

Meetings/Conferences:

Annual Meetings: With the American Historical Ass'n

Publications:

Archive for Reformation History. a.

Society for Reproductive Endocrinology and Infertility *(1983)*

1209 Montgomery Hwy.
Birmingham, AL 35216-2809
Tel: (205)978-5000 Ext: 115 *Fax:* (205)978-5005
E-Mail: sgoldman@asrm.org
Web Site: www.socrei.org
Members: 936 individuals
Staff: 1
Administrative Coordinator: Senta Goldman
E-Mail: sgoldman@asrm.org

Historical Note

Formerly Society of Repoductive Endocrinologists (1998). Members are physicians, both in private practice and academia, who are certified by the American Board of Obstetrics and Gynecology as reproductive endocrinologists. Administrative support provided by the American Society for Reproductive Medicine.

Meetings/Conferences:

Annual Meetings: *Annual meeting held with the American Soc. for Reproductive Medicine.*
2007 - Washington, DC/October

Publications:

Sexuality, Reproduction and Menopause. q. adv.
Fertility and Sterility. m. adv.

Society for Research in Child Development *(1933)*

Univ. of Michigan
3131 S. State St., Suite 302
Ann Arbor, MI 48108-1623
Tel: (734)998-6578 *Fax:* (734)998-6569
E-Mail: info@srcd.org
Web Site: www.srcd.org/
Members: 5,721 individuals
Staff: 10
Annual Budget: $2-5,000,000
Deputy Executive Director: Susan Custer

Historical Note

Founded in 1933 in the District of Columbia as an outgrowth of the Committee on Child Development of the National Research Council. The Committee, formed in 1925, was the successor to a subcommittee on Child Development under the Division of Anthropology and Psychology of the National Research Council, which began in 1922. Incorporated in Illinois in 1950, in Indiana in 1956 and in Wisconsin in 1970. Affiliated with the American Association for the Advancement of Science. Membership: $150/year.

Meetings/Conferences:

Biennial meetings: odd years in Spring
2007 - Boston, MA/March 29-Apr. 1
2009 - Denver, CO/Apr. 1-5

Publications:

Newsletter. q.
Child Development. bi-m. adv.
Monographs of the SRCD. 4-5/year.
Social Policy Reports. q.
Child Development Abstracts.

Society for Research in Music Education

Historical Note

A council of the Music Educators National Conference.

Society for Research on Adolescence *(1984)*

University of Michigan
3131 S. State St., Suite 302
Ann Arbor, MI 48108-1623
Tel: (734)998-6578 *Fax:* (734)998-9586
E-Mail: socresadol@umich.edu
Web Site: www.s-r-a.org
Members: 1400 individuals
Staff: 7
President: Elizabeth Susman
E-Mail: socresadol@umich.edu

Historical Note
SRA is a dynamic, multidisciplinary, international organization dedicated to understanding adolescence through research. Its members conduct theoretical studies, basic and applied research, and policy analyses to understand and enhance adolescent development. Membership: $105/year (individual); $53/year (student).

Meetings/Conferences:
Biennial Meetings: even years/Spring

Publications:
Newsletter. bi-a.
SRA Directory of Members.
Journal of Research on Adolescence. q.

Society for Research on Nicotine and Tobacco *(1994)*
2810 Crossroads Dr., Suite 3800
Madison, WI 53718
Tel: (608)443-2462 *Fax:* (608)443-2474
E-Mail: info@srnt.org
Web Site: www.srnt.org
Members: 600 individuals
Staff: 7
Annual Budget: $250-500,000
Executive Director: Beth Klipping

Historical Note
Members are international scientists and other researchers interested in societal, biobehavioral, and political aspects of tobacco and tobacco use. Membership: $120/year (full member/affiliate); $35/year (student).

Meetings/Conferences:
Annual Meetings: Spring

Publications:
Nicotine and Tobacco Research Journal. q. adv.
SRNT Newsletter. q. adv.

Society for Risk Analysis *(1982)*
1313 Dolley Madison Blvd., Suite 402
McLean, VA 22101-3926
Tel: (703)790-1745 *Fax:* (703)790-2672
E-Mail: sra@burkinc.com
Web Site: www.sra.org
Members: 2090 individuals
Staff: 15
Annual Budget: $250-500,000
Executive Secretary: Richard J. Burk, Jr.

Historical Note
Founded to study and understand, on a scientific basis, the risks posed by technological development. Membership: $105/year.

Meetings/Conferences:
Annual Meetings: Fall

Publications:
Risk Analysis Journal. bi-m. adv.
Risk Newsletter. q. adv.

Society for Romanian Studies *(1973)*
Dept. of History, Huntington University
Huntington, IN 46750
Tel: (260)359-4242 *Fax:* (260)359-4086
Web Site: www.huntington.edu/srs
Members: 200 individuals
Annual Budget: under $10,000
Secretary: Paul Michelson
E-Mail: pmichelson@huntington.edu

Historical Note
Has no paid officers or full-time staff. Annual meetings held in conjunction with the AAASS. Membership: $15/year (full member); $10/year (student).

Publications:
SRS Newsletter. 2/year.

Society for Scholarly Publishing *(1978)*
10200 W. 44th Ave., Suite 304
Wheat Ridge, CO 80033-2840
Tel: (303)422-3914 *Fax:* (303)422-8894
Web Site: www.sspnet.org
Members: 800 individuals
Staff: 2
Annual Budget: $100-250,000
Executive Director: Francine Butler, Ph.D., CAE
Director, Member Services: Ruth Gleason

Historical Note
Established on June 16, 1978, in Washington, DC. Members are individuals, publishing companies and professional societies involved in the production of scholarly books and periodicals. Membership: $85/year.

Meetings/Conferences:
Annual Meetings: late Spring/450

Publications:
SSP E-Bulletin. irreg.
Directory of Members. a.

Society for Sedimentary Geology

Historical Note
See SEPM - Society for Sedimentary Geology.

Society for Sex Therapy and Research *(1974)*
409 12th St. SW
P.O. Box 96920
Washington, DC 20090-6920
Tel: (202)863-1648 *Fax:* (202)554-0453
Web Site: www.sstarnet.org
Members: 200 individuals
Annual Budget: $25-50,000
Administrative Director: Cassandra Larkins
Administrator: Yvonne Cousins

Historical Note
Formerly the Eastern Association of Sex Therapy, SSTAR is a professional society formed to enhance communication between clinicians and clinical investigators interested in the treatment of human sexual disorders. Membership is multidisciplinary with the criteria that members are actively involved in the treatment or clinical investigation of sexual disorders, possess superior clinical competence and high ethical standards. Membership: $85/year.

Meetings/Conferences:
Annual Meetings: Spring

Publications:
Newsletter. semi-a.

Society for Slovene Studies *(1973)*
3030 64th Ave., Unit C
Seattle, WA 98116
Tel: (206)937-1250
E-Mail: wwdslovene@aol.com
Web Site: www.arts.ualberta.ca/~ljubljan/sss.html
Members: 350 individuals
Staff: 1
Annual Budget: under $10,000
President: Dr. Metod M. Milac
E-Mail: wwdslovene@aol.com

Historical Note
An affiliate of American Association for the Advancement of Slavic Studies and American Association of Teachers of Slavic and East European Languages, SSS is a non-profit association of scholars dedicated to the research of Slovene culture. Its purpose is to promote the dissemination of scholarly information on Slovene studies through meetings, conferences, and the preparation of scholarly works for publication. Has no paid officers or full-time staff. Membership: $20/year (regular or sustaining); $5/year (students).

Meetings/Conferences:
Annual Meetings: September, with the American Ass'n for the Advancement of Slavic Studies

Publications:
SSS Letter.
Slovene Studies. semi-a. adv.

Society for Social Studies of Science *(1975)*
Dept. of Sociology, 126 Stubbs Hall
Louisiana State University
Baton Rouge, LA 70803
Tel: (225)578-5311
Web Site: www.its2.ocs.lsu.edu/guests/ssss
Members: 550 individuals
Staff: 1
Annual Budget: $25-50,000
Secretary: Wesley Shrum
E-Mail: shrum@lsu.edu

Historical Note
Affiliated with American Association for the Advancement of Science. Also known as 4S. Membership: $45/year (individual); $22/year (student and developing country).

Publications:
Handbook of Science and Technology Studies.
Science, Technology & Human Values. q.
Technoscience Newsletter. bi-a.

Society for Social Work Leadership in Health Care *(1965)*
100 N. 20th St.
Fourth Floor
Philadelphia, PA 19103
Toll Free: (866)237 - 9542
E-Mail: info@sswlhc.org
Web Site: www.sswlhc.org
Members: 1200 individuals
Staff: 5
Annual Budget: $250-500,000
Account Executive: Tim Bower

Historical Note
Formerly (1993) the Society for Hospital Social Work Directors, (1994) Social Work Administrators in Health Care and (1998) Society for Social Work Administrators in Health Care. Full membership is open to social workers with a BSW, MSW or doctoral degree in social work, employed in a health care setting as an administrator, manager, supervisor, or leader. Membership is also open to health care professionals, consultants, educators, students, retirees, or other individuals with an interest or involvement in health care social work administration. The Society is affiliated with the American Hospital Association.

Publications:
Social Work Administration/Career Opportunities. q.
Social Work Leader. q. adv.

Society for Software Quality *(1984)*
P.O. Box 86958
San Diego, CA 92138-6958
Tel: (858)675-1713
Web Site: www.ssq.org
Members: 250 individuals
Annual Budget: $50-100,000
President: Pete Miller

Historical Note
SSQ members are professionals interested in producing quality software. Membership: $45/year (individual).

Publications:
Journal. 11/year.

Society for Spanish and Portuguese Historical Studies *(1969)*
Department of History
University of Florida
Gainesville, FL 32611
Tel: (707)664-2489 *Fax:* (707)664-3920
Web Site: www.ssphs.org
Members: 500 individuals
Staff: 1
Annual Budget: $10-25,000

Historical Note
Founded to promote research in all aspects and epochs of Iberian historical studies. Membership: $20/year (individual); $7/year (student); $23 (overseas); $25/year (institutions).

Meetings/Conferences:
Annual Meetings: Spring
2007 – Miami Beach, FL/Apr. 19-22

Publications:
Bulletin of the SSPHS. 3/year. adv.

Society for Surgery of the Alimentary Tract *(1960)*
900 Cummings Center, Suite 221-U
Beverly, MA 01915
Tel: (978)927-8330 *Fax:* (978)524-8890
E-Mail: ssat@prri.com
Web Site: www.ssat.com
Members: 2700 individuals
Staff: 6
Executive Director: Robert P. Jones, Jr., Ed.D.
Director, Administration: Jon Blackstone
E-Mail: ssat@prri.com

Historical Note
Formerly Association of Colon Surgery. Membership: $155/year (active individual).

Meetings/Conferences:
Annual Meetings: Spring
2007 – Washington, DC/May 19-23
2008 – San Diego, CA/May 17-21

Publications:
Journal of Gastrointestinal Surgery. 10/year. adv.

Society for Technical Communication *(1953)*
901 N. Stuart St., Suite 904
Arlington, VA 22203-1822
Tel: (703)522-4114 *Fax:* (703)522-2075
E-Mail: stc@stc.org
Web Site: www.stc.org
Members: 18000 individuals
Staff: 14
Annual Budget: $2-5,000,000
Executive Director: Peter R. Herbst

Historical Note
In 1953, two organizations interested in improving the practice of technical communication, the Society of Technical Writers and the Association of Technical Writers and Editors, were founded simultaneously on the East Coast. These organizations merged in 1957 to form the Society of Technical Writers and Editors. This organization grew rapidly and, in 1960, merged with a Pacific Coast group, the Technical Publishing Society, founded in 1954. This merger resulted in the Society of Technical Writers and Publishers. In 1971, the name was changed to Society for Technical Communication. Today, STC is the largest professional society in the world concerned primarily with all phases of technical communication. Incorporated in New York in 1958. Member of the International Council of Communication Societies. Membership: $140/year (individual).

Meetings/Conferences:
Annual Meetings: Spring/Internat'l Technical Communication Conference/1,400
2007 – Minneapolis, MN/May 13-16

Publications:
Conference Proceedings. a.
INTERCOM. m. adv.
Technical Communication. q. adv.

Society for Technological Advancement of Reporting
222 S. Westmonte Dr., Suite 101
Altamonte Springs, FL 32714
Tel: (407)774-7880 *Fax:* (407)774-6440
Toll Free: (800)565 - 6054
E-Mail: star@kmgnet.com
Web Site: www.staronline.org
Members: 700 companies
Staff: 3
Executive Director: Tina Kautter, CAE

Meetings/Conferences:
2007 – La Jolla, CA(Hilton Torrey Pines)/Apr. 26-28
2008 – Boston, MA(Radisson)/Oct. 11-13

Publications:
Newsletter. a.

Society for Textual Scholarship *(1979)*
Dept. of English, University of Michigan
3224 Angell Hall
Ann Arbor, MI 48109
E-Mail: tinkle@umich.edu
Web Site: www.textual.org
Members: 600 individuals
Staff: 1
Annual Budget: under $10,000
Secretary: Theresa Tinkle

Historical Note
STS was founded to overcome the disciplinary isolation of textual scholarship in various fields. It aims to discover common theories and procedures which could be of value to researchers in all areas of textual study. Membership: $15/year.

Meetings/Conferences:
Annual Meetings: Biennial Meetings in April

Publications:
TEXT. a.
Newsletter. irreg.
Bulletin. irreg.

Society for the Advancement of American Philosophy *(1972)*
Southern Illinois Univ., MC 4505
Carbondale, IL 62901
Tel: (618)536-6641
Web Site: www.american-philosophy.org
Members: 900 individuals
Secretary-Treasurer: Dr. Kenneth W. Stikkers
E-Mail: kstikker@siu.edu

Historical Note
SAAP members are academics and others with an interest in the field of American Philosophy. Has no paid officers or full-time staff. Membership: based on annual income.

Meetings/Conferences:
Annual Meetings: usually Spring

Publications:
Journal of Speculative Philosophy. q. adv.
SAAP Newsletter. 3/year. adv.
Membership Directory. quad.

Society for the Advancement of Behavior Analysis *(1980)*

Historical Note
SABA is the fundraising arm of Association for Behavior Analysis, which provides administrative support.

Society for the Advancement of Economic Theory *(1990)*
330 Wohlers Hall, Univ. of Illinois
1206 S. Sixth St.
Champaign, IL 61820
Tel: (217)333-0120 *Fax:* (217)244-6678
Web Site: www.mgmt.purdue.edu/events/saet/main.html
Members: 170 individuals
President: Nicholas Yannelis
Secretary: Carol Froeschl

Historical Note
SAET members are individuals with an interest in theoretical economics. membership: $69/year (individual); $39/year (student).

Publications:
Economic Theory Journal. bi-m.

Society for the Advancement of Education *(1939)*
500 Bi-County Blvd., Suite 203
Farmingdale, NY 11735-3931
Tel: (631)293-4343
Members: 1900 individuals
Staff: 5
Annual Budget: $500-1,000,000
Managing Editor: Wayne Barrett

Historical Note
Membership: $29/year.

Publications:
USA Today Magazine. m. adv.

Society for the Advancement of Material and Process Engineering *(1944)*
1161 Park View Dr.
Suite 200
Covina, CA 91724-3751
Tel: (626)331-0616 *Fax:* (626)332-8929
Toll Free: (800)562 - 7360
E-Mail: sampeibo@sampe.org
Web Site: www.sampe.org
Members: 5000 individuals
Staff: 14
Annual Budget: $1-2,000,000
Executive Director: Gregg B. Balko
Registration: Priscilla Heredia
Office Manager: Sylvia Smith

Historical Note
Founded in Hawthorne, CA as the Society of Aircraft Material and Process Engineers. Incorporated in California in 1960 as the Society of Aerospace Material and Process Engineers and assumed its present name in 1973. Membership: $93/year (professional/ associate); $25/year (student). Dues include subscription cost to the SAMPE Journal.

Meetings/Conferences:
Semi-Annual Meetings: Spring and Fall
2007 – Baltimore, MD(Baltimore Convention Center)/June 4-8
2007 – Cincinnati, OH(Hilton Cincinnati Netherland Plaza)/Oct. 29-Nov. 1

Publications:
Conference Proceedings. semi-a.
SAMPE Journal. bi-m. adv.

Society for the Advancement of Scandinavian Study *(1911)*
Scandinavian Studies - Brigham Young Univ.
HRCB
Provo, UT 84602-4538
Tel: (801)422-5598 *Fax:* (801)422-0307
E-Mail: sass@byu.edu
Web Site: www.scandinavianstudy.org
Members: 800 individuals
Annual Budget: $25-50,000
Managing Editor: Steven P. Sondrup

Historical Note
Members are scholars, teachers, and researchers of Scandinavian language, literature and culture. Regular membership: $55/year (individual); $60/year (organization).

Meetings/Conferences:
Annual Meetings: May

Publications:
SASS News & Notes. semi-a.
Scandinavian Studies. q. adv.

Society for the Advancement of Socio-Economics *(1989)*
P.O. Box 39008
Baltimore, MD 21212
Tel: (410)435-6617 *Fax:* (410)377-7965
E-Mail: office@sase.org
Web Site: www.sase.org
Members: 900 individuals
Staff: 1
Annual Budget: $50-100,000
Executive Director: Mary Grossman

Historical Note
Academic disciplines represented in SASE includes economics, sociology, political science, psychology, anthropology, philosophy, history, law, and management. The membership of SASE includes business people and policy makers working in governmental and international organizations. Membership: $40/year (individual); $15/year (student).

Meetings/Conferences:
Annual Meetings: Summer

Publications:
Socio-Economic Review.

Society for the Advancement of Women's Health Research *(1990)*
1025 Connecticut Ave. NW, Suite 701
Washington, DC 20036
Tel: (202)223-8224 *Fax:* (202)833-3472
E-Mail: info@womenshealthresearch.org
Web Site: www.womenshealthresearch.org
Members: 40 individuals
Staff: 18
President and Chief Executive Officer: Phyllis M. Greenberger
Finance and Administrative Coordinator: Danielle Kyes

Historical Note
Formerly (1990) Society for the Advancement of Women's Health Research. SWHR seeks to improve the health of women through research. Membership: $25/year.

Meetings/Conferences:
Annual Meetings: Winter

Publications:
Sexx Matters. q.

Society for the Anthropology in Consciousness *(1980)*

Historical Note
A section of the American Anthropological Association. Established as a multidisciplinary organization designed to provide a forum for the study

of consciousness for cross-cultural, experimental, experiential, and theoretical perspectives.

Society for the Anthropology of Europe *(1986)*

Historical Note

A section of the American Anthropological Association.

Society for the Anthropology of Food and Nutrition *(1974)*

Historical Note

Formerly the Council on Nutritional Anthropology; a section of the American Anthropological Association. SAFN promotes interest and research in the anthropological study of food and nutrition.

Society for the Anthropology of North America

Historical Note

A section of the American Anthropological Association.

Society for the Anthropology of Work

Historical Note

A section of the American Anthropological Association. Provides a forum for discussing the study of work from a variety of perspectives, including those of archaeologists, linguists, and physical, cultural and practicing anthropologists.

Society for the Exploration of Psychotherapy Integration *(1984)*

3100 N. Leisure World Blvd., Apt. 1021
Silver Spring, MD 20906
Tel: (703)247-2199 *Fax:* (301)598-2436
E-Mail: geostricker@comcast.net
Web Site: www.cyberpsych.org/sepi
Members: 750 individuals
Staff: 1
Annual Budget: $10-25,000
Treasurer: George Stricker, Ph.D.

Historical Note

SEPI is an interdisciplinary organization of professionals interested in approaches to psychotherapy that are not limited by a single orientation. Members are mental health professionals with an interest in integrating theories and techniques in psychotherapy. Membership: $48/year (individual); $24/year (student).

Meetings/Conferences:

Annual Meetings: Spring
2007 - Lisbon, Portugal/July 5-8
2008 - Boston, MA

Publications:

Journal of Psychotherapy Integration. q. adv.
Directory. a.

Society for the History of Authorship, Reading and Publishing *(1991)*

P.O. Box 30
Wilmington, NC 28402-0030
Tel: (910)254-0399 *Fax:* (910)254-0308
E-Mail: brannonb@sc.edu
Web Site: www.sharpweb.org/
Members: 1000 individuals
Annual Budget: $10-25,000
Secretary: Barbara A. Brannon

Historical Note

SHARP promotes research and education in the historical sociology of literature, i.e., the creation, diffusion, and reception of the written and printed word. Has no paid officers or full-time staff. Membership: $45/year (individual).

Meetings/Conferences:

Annual Meetings: Summer

Publications:

SHARP News. q.
Membership & Periodicals Directory. a.
Book History. a.

Society for the History of Discoveries *(1960)*

1701 Silver Leaf Dr.
Arlington, TX 76013
Tel: (817)861-1425
E-Mail: goodwin@uta.edu
Web Site: www.sochistdisc.org
Members: 300 individuals
Annual Budget: $10-25,000
Executive Secretary: Katherine Goodwin
E-Mail: goodwin@uta.edu

Historical Note

Affiliated with the American Historical Association. Established as a result of the International Congress for the History of Discoveries, held in Lisbon in 1960. Has no paid officers or full-time staff. Membership: $30/year.

Meetings/Conferences:

Annual Meetings: Fall

Publications:

Newsletter. a.
Terrae Incognitae. a. adv.
Annual Report. a.

Society for the History of Technology *(1958)*

633 Ross Hall, History Department
Iowa State University
Ames, IA 50011
Tel: (515)294-8469 *Fax:* (515)294-6390
E-Mail: shot@instate.edu
Web Site: http://shot.press.jhu.edu
Members: 2000 individuals
Staff: 1
Annual Budget: $10-25,000
Secretary: Amy Bix

Historical Note

Formed in Cleveland in 1958 and incorporated in Ohio in 1959. Affiliated with the American Association for the Advancement of Science and the American Historical Association. SHOT seeks to encourage the study of the development of technology and its relation with society and culture. U.S. Membership: $42/year (individual); $130/year (organization); $25/year (student).

Meetings/Conferences:

Annual Meetings: Fall
2007 - Washington, DC/Oct. 18-21/350

Publications:

Newsletter. q. adv.
Technology and Culture. q. adv.

Society for the Philosophy of Sex and Love *(1977)*

Indiana University of Pennsylvania
Department of Religious Studies
Indiana, PA 15705-1087
Tel: (724)357-2310 *Fax:* (724)357-4039
E-Mail: caraway@grove.iup.edu
Members: 60 individuals
Annual Budget: under $10,000
President: Carol Caraway, Ph.D.

Historical Note

Members are academics and others. Membership: $7/year (individual); $4/year (student); $14/year (foreign).

Meetings/Conferences:

Annual Meetings: in conjunction with the American Philosophical Ass'n

Publications:

SPSL Newsletter. a.

Society for the Preservation of Oral Health *(1960)*

P.O. Box 2945
LaGrange, GA 30241
Tel: (706)845-9085 *Fax:* (706)883-8215
Members: 75 individuals
Staff: 1
Annual Budget: $10-25,000
Management Executive: Charles T. Hall, Jr.

Historical Note

Members are those who have practiced for at least five years and who concentrate on or have a strong interest in preventive dentistry. Membership: $500/year.

Meetings/Conferences:

Annual Meetings: March
2007 - Bermuda, Bermuda(Southhampton Fairmont)/March 27-Feb. 30/65

Society for the Psychological Study of Ethnic Minority Issues

Historical Note

A division of the American Psychological Association.

Society for the Psychological Study of Lesbian and Gay Issues

Historical Note

A division of the American Psychological Association.

Society for the Psychological Study of Men and Masculinity

Historical Note

A division of the American Psychological Association.

Society for the Psychological Study of Social Issues *(1936)*

208 I Street NE
Washington, DC 20002
Tel: (202)675-6956 *Fax:* (202)675-6902
E-Mail: spssi@spssi.org
Web Site: www.spssi.org
Members: 3000 individuals
Staff: 3
Annual Budget: $500-1,000,000
Executive Director: Shari Miles

Historical Note

Seeks to bring behavioral and social science theory, empirical evidence and practice into focus on human problems. Members must be college students or professionals. A division of the American Psychological Association. Membership: $25-100/year.

Meetings/Conferences:

Annual Meetings: Annual and Biennial

Publications:

Journal of Social Issues. q.
SPSSI. Sponsored Volumes.
Newsletter. 3/year.
Analysis of Social Issues and Public Policy. a.

Society for the Scientific Study of Religion *(1949)*

Alfred U -Division of Social Sciences
One Saxon Dr.
Alfred, NY 14802
Tel: (607)871-2215 *Fax:* (607)871-2085
E-Mail: sssr@alfred.edu
Web Site: www.sssrweb.org
Members: 1600 individuals
Staff: 1
Annual Budget: $100-250,000
Executive Officer: Arthur E Farnsley, III
Business Manager: Joy Sherrill

Historical Note

Founded at Harvard University in 1949 and incorporated the same year in Connecticut. Membership: $20-$100/year.

Meetings/Conferences:

Annual Meetings: Fall
2007 - Tampa, FL(Hyatt)/Nov. 2-4/500
2008 - Louisville, KY(Seelbach Hilton)/Oct. 17-19/500
2009 - Denver, CO(Westin)/Oct. 23-25/500

Publications:

Journal for the Scientific Study of Religion. q. adv.

Society for the Scientific Study of Sexuality *(1957)*

P.O. Box 416
Allentown, PA 18105
Tel: (610)530-2483 *Fax:* (610)530-2485
E-Mail: thesociety@sexscience.org
Web Site: www.sexscience.org
Members: 1000 individuals
Staff: 2
Annual Budget: $250-500,000
Executive Director: David L. Fleming, MS

Historical Note

An international professional association of researchers, clinicians and educators, who share an interest and competency in the scientific pursuit of knowledge concerning sexuality. Membership: $135/year.

Meetings/Conferences:

Annual Meetings: November

Publications:

Journal of Sex Research. q. adv.
SSSS Newsletter. q. adv.
Membership Handbook. a.
Annual Review of Sex Research. a.

Society for the Study of Amphibians and Reptiles *(1958)*
Dept. of Biological & Environmental Sciences
Western Connecticut State Univ.
Danbury, CT 06810
Tel: (203)837-8875 *Fax:* (203)837-8875
Web Site: www.ssarherps.org
Members: 2100 individuals
Annual Budget: $100-250,000
Treasurer: Theodora Pinou

Historical Note
Formerly (1967) Ohio Herpetological Society Has no paid officers or full-time staff. Membership: $40/year (individual); $70/year (organization/company); $30/year (student).

Publications:
Herpetological Review. q. adv.
Journal of Herpetology. q.

Society for the Study of Early China *(1975)*
University of California - Berkeley
Institute of East Asian Studies
Berkeley, CA 94720-2318
Tel: (510)643-6325 *Fax:* (510)643-7062
E-Mail: easia@uclink.berkeley.edu
Web Site: www.lib.chicago.edu/earlychina
Members: 350 individuals
Managing Editor: Joanne Sandstrom
E-Mail: easia@uclink.berkeley.edu

Historical Note
SSEC members are academics specializing in the study of pre-Han dynasty China. Has no paid officers or full-time staff. Membership: $30/year (individual).

Meetings/Conferences:
Annual Meetings: in conjunction with the Ass'n for Asian Studies

Publications:
Early China Journal. a. adv.

Society for the Study of Evolution *(1946)*
P.O. Box 7055
Lawrence, KS 66044
Tel: (785)843-1235 *Fax:* (785)843-1274
Toll Free: (800)627 - 0629
Web Site: http://lsvl.la.asu.edu/evolution
Members: 3100 individuals
Staff: 8
Annual Budget: $250-500,000
Contact Person: Scott Starr

Historical Note
Founded in St. Louis on March 30, 1946 as an outgrowth of the Committee on Common Problems of Genetics, Paleontology and Systematics, which was established in 1943 by the National Research Council. SSE absorbed the Society for the Study of Speciation. Promotes the study of organic evolution and the integration of the various fields of science concerned with evolution. Membership: $75/year (individual); $95/year (organization).

Meetings/Conferences:
Annual Meetings: June
2007 – Auckland, New Zealand
2008 – Minneapolis, MN
2009 – Providence, RI(Brown University)

Society for the Study of Indigenous Languages of the Americas *(1981)*
P.O. Box 555
Arcata, CA 95518-0555
Tel: (707)826-4324 *Fax:* (707)677-1676
Web Site: www.ssila.org
Members: 900 individuals
Staff: 1
Annual Budget: $10-25,000
Secretary-Treasurer: Victor Golla

Historical Note
SSILA members are academics and others in the U.S. and Canada with an interest in the languages of the native peoples of North, Central and South America. Membership: $15/year (U.S.); $25/year (Canada).

Meetings/Conferences:
Annual Meetings: With American Anthropological Ass'n or Linguistic Soc. of America

Publications:
Directory. a.
SSILA Newsletter. q.

Society for the Study of Male Psychology and Physiology *(1975)*
321 Iuka Road
Montpelier, OH 43543
Tel: (419)485-3602
Members: 180 individuals
Staff: 1
Annual Budget: under $10,000
Executive Officer: Jerry Bergman, Ph.D.

Historical Note
SSMPP members are psychiatrists, psychologists, sociologists and other professionals with an interest in the field.

Meetings/Conferences:
Annual Meetings: in conjunction with the American Psychological Ass'n

Society for the Study of Reproduction *(1967)*
1619 Monroe St.
Madison, WI 53711-2063
Tel: (608)256-2777 *Fax:* (608)256-4610
E-Mail: ssr@ssr.org
Web Site: www.ssr.org
Members: 2450 individuals
Staff: 1
Annual Budget: $1-2,000,000
Executive Director: Judith Jansen

Historical Note
Founded in 1967 at the University of Illinois, with roots that go back to the 1953 Biennial Symposia of Reproduction, SSR's members are researchers and clinicians representing many fields including physiology, immunology, molecular biology, genetic engineering, animal science, endocrinology and embryology. Membership: $25-$150/year (U.S. individual); $25-170/year (overseas individual).

Meetings/Conferences:
Annual Meetings: Summer/1,200
2007 – San Antonio, TX(Henry B. Gonzalez Convention Center)/July 22-25/1200

Publications:
Biology of Reproduction. m. adv.

Society for the Study of Social Biology *(1926)*
c/o Andrus Gerontology Center, USC
3715 McClintock Ave.
Los Angeles, CA 90089-0191
Tel: (213)740-1707 *Fax:* (213)740-0792
E-Mail: crimmin@usc.edu
Web Site: http://www-rcf.usc.edu/~crimmin/sssb
Members: 400 individuals
Annual Budget: under $10,000
Secretary-Treasurer: Dr. Eileen Crimmins

Historical Note
Founded, organized and incorporated in New York in January 1926 as the American Eugenics Society, Inc.; assumed its present name in 1973. Promotes the study of the biological and sociocultural forces affecting the structure and composition of human populations. Has no paid officers or full-time staff. Membership: $35/year.

Meetings/Conferences:
Annual Meetings: December

Publications:
Social Biology. q.

Society for the Study of Social Problems *(1951)*
901 McClung Tower
University of Tennessee
Knoxville, TN 37996-0490
Tel: (865)974-3620 *Fax:* (865)689-1534
E-Mail: sssp@utk.edu
Web Site: www.sssp1.org
Members: 1750 individuals
Staff: 3
Annual Budget: $250-500,000
Executive Officer: Thomas C. Hood, Ph.D.
Administrative Officer and Meeting Manager: Michele Smith Koontz

Historical Note
The primary objective of the Society is to promote social science research and teaching in order to bring scholarly and practical attention to the social world and its problems. Incorporated in Indiana. Membership: $20-135/year, based on income (individual); $60/year (departmental). Sustaining membership: $1,200.

Meetings/Conferences:
Annual Meetings: August/500
2007 – New York, NY(Roosevelt Hotel)/Aug. 10-12
2008 – Boston, MA(Boston Park Plaza Hotel)/July 31-Aug. 2/650

Publications:
Social Problems Forum. 3/year. adv.
Social Problems. 4/year. adv.

Society for the Study of Symbolic Interaction *(1975)*
Dept. of Sociology, Univ. of Nevada, Las Vegas
4505 Maryland Pkwy.
Las Vegas, NV 89154-5033
Tel: (702)895-0166 *Fax:* (702)895-4800
E-Mail: symbolic@unlv.nevada.edu
Web Site: http://sun.soci.niu.edu/~ssi/
Members: 650 individuals
Annual Budget: under $10,000
Editor: Simon Gottschalk

Historical Note
Members are teachers and students involved in critical theory and cultural studies, including symbolic interaction theory and research. Has no paid officers or full-time staff. Membership: dues based on level of income.

Publications:
SSSI Notes. 3/year. adv.
Symbolic Interaction. q. adv.

Society for the Teaching of Psychology

Historical Note
A division of the American Psychological Association.

Society for Theriogenology *(1973)*
P.O. Box 3007
Montgomery, AL 36109
Tel: (334)395-4666 *Fax:* (334)270-3399
E-Mail: info@therio.org
Web Site: www.therio.org
Members: 2446 individuals
Annual Budget: $25-50,000
Executive Director: Dr. Charles F. Franz

Historical Note
Formerly (1975) American Veterinary Society for the Study of Breeding Soundness. Members are veterinarians interested in animal reproduction. American College of Theriogenologists is the examination and certifying arm of SFT. Membership: $65/year.

Meetings/Conferences:
Annual Meetings: Fall with the American College of Theriogenologists

Publications:
Newsletter. bi-m.
Proceedings. a.

Society for Thermal Medicine *(1986)*
10105 Cottesmore Court
Great Falls, VA 22066-3540
Tel: (703)757-0044 *Fax:* (703)757-0454
E-Mail: admin@thermalmedicine.org
Web Site: www.thermaltherapy.org
Members: 185 individuals
Staff: 25
Account Manager: Steve Mason

Historical Note
Founded as North American Hyperthermia Society; assumed its current name in 2004. STM members are professionals from the physical, engineering, biological, chemical, and clinical and medical sciences with an interest in the field of hyperthermia.

Meetings/Conferences:
Annual Meetings: in conjunction with the Radiation Research Soc.
2007 – Washington, DC(Washington Hilton)/May 14-18/150

Publications:
Membership Directory. irreg.
NAHS Newsletter. irreg.
Internat'l Journal of Hyperthermia. bi-m.

Society for Urban Anthropology *(1979)*

Historical Note
A section of the American Anthropological Association.

Society for Uroradiology *(1974)*
4550 Post Oak Place, Suite 342
Houston, TX 77027
Tel: (713)965-0566 *Fax:* (713)960-0488
E-Mail: info@uroradiology.org
Web Site: www.uroradiology.org
Members: 300 individuals
Executive Director: Lynne K. Tiras, CMP

Historical Note
SUR members are clinical radiologists with an interest in the study of the normal and abnormal urinary tract with emphasis upon the integration of roentgenology, sonography, computed tomography, magnetic resonance imaging, interventional procedures and nuclear medicine.

Meetings/Conferences:
Annual Meetings: early Spring
2007 - Naples, FL(Hyatt Regency Resort and Spa)/Apr. 15-20

Society for Values in Higher Education *(1923)*
c/o Portland State Univ.
P.O. Box 751 - SVHE
Portland, OR 97207-0751
Tel: (503)725-2575 *Fax:* (503)725-2577
E-Mail: society@pox.edu
Web Site: www.svhe.org
Members: 1200 individuals
Staff: 1
Annual Budget: $100-250,000
Executive Director: Dr. Marvin A. Kaiser

Historical Note
Formerly (1962) National Council on Religion in Higher Education and (1976) Society for Religion in Higher Education. A network of persons in the academic world and the professions who have a special concern for the ethical and religious dimensions of their work. Membership: $80-135 (individual); $250-400/year (institution).

Meetings/Conferences:
Annual Meetings:

Publications:
Directory of Active Fellows.
SVHA Monograph Series.
SOUNDINGS, An Interdisciplinary Journal. q. adv.
Newsletter of the People of Color Caucus.

Society for Vascular Medicine and Biology
9111 Old Georgetown Road
Bethesda, MD 20814
Tel: (301)581-3464 *Fax:* (301)897-9745
Web Site: www.svmb.org
Members: 413 individuals
Staff: 1
Executive Director: Lorraine J. Bell

Historical Note
Membership: $160/year (individual).

Meetings/Conferences:
Annual Meetings: Summer

Publications:
Vasecular Medicine. m. adv.

Society for Vascular Nursing *(1982)*
7794 Grow Dr.
Pensacola, FL 32514
Tel: (850)474-6963 *Fax:* (850)484-8762
Toll Free: (888)536 - 4786
E-Mail: svn@puetzamc.com
Web Site: www.svnnet.org
Members: 800 individuals
Staff: 5
Annual Budget: $250-500,000
Nurse Consultant: Belinda E. Puetz, Ph.D., RN
E-Mail: svn@puetzamc.com

Historical Note
Formerly (1992) the Society for Peripheral Vascular Nursing. Provides national educational programs, helps development of local programs, and supports research in this specialized field. Membership: $110/year (individual US and Canada); $125/year (individual international).

Meetings/Conferences:
Annual Meetings: June
2007 - Baltimore, MD(Wyndham Baltimore Inner Harbor)/June 7-10

Publications:
SVN prn. bi-m. adv.
Journal of Vascular Nursing. q. adv.

Society for Vascular Surgery *(1945)*
633 N. St. Clair St., 24th Fl.
Chicago, IL 60611
Tel: (312)202-5600 *Fax:* (312)202-5610
Toll Free: (800)258 - 7188
Web Site: www.vascularweb.org
Members: 2100 individuals
Staff: 2
Executive Director: Rebecca Maron
Administrator: Melissa Kabadian

Historical Note
Organized in Hot Springs, VA on December 5, 1945 at a meeting of the Southern Surgical Association. Membership: $100/year.

Meetings/Conferences:
Annual Meetings: Summer
2007 - Baltimore, MD(Baltimore Convention Center)/June 7-10
2008 - San Diego, CA(San Diego Convention Center)/June 5-8
2009 - Denver, CO(Colorado Convention Center)/June 11-14

Publications:
Journal of Vascular Surgery. q. adv.

Society for Vascular Ultrasound *(1977)*
4601 Presidents Dr., Suite 260
Lanham, MD 20706-4831
Tel: (301)459-7550 *Fax:* (301)459-5651
Toll Free: (800)788 - 8346
E-Mail: svinfo@svunet.org
Web Site: www.svunet.org
Members: 3500 individuals
Staff: 4
Annual Budget: $500-1,000,000
Executive Director: Stephen R. Haracznak
Director, Membership and Meetings: Missi McLean

Historical Note
Founded and incorporated in Ohio. Formerly (1977) Society of Noninvasive Vascular Technology and then (1988) Society for Vascular Technology; assumed its curent name in 2002. Members perform diagnostic tests to determine the location of blockages in the body's circulatory system. Approximately seventy five percent of SVT members are practicing noninvasive technologists or are involved in supervision and/or education in a clinical setting. Others include physicians, researchers and other health care providers. Serves as an education and information resource in matters pertaining to noninvasive vascular technology. Membership: $110/year (professional); $135/year (foreign); $25/year (student).

Meetings/Conferences:
Annual Meetings: August

Publications:
Membership Directory (online). irreg.
e-Spectrum Newsletter (online). m. adv.
Journal for Vascular Ultrasound. q. adv.

Society for Vector Ecology *(1968)*
1966 Compton Ave.
Corona, CA 92881
Tel: (951)340-9792 *Fax:* (951)340-2515
E-Mail: sove@northwestmvcd.org
Web Site: www.sove.org
Members: 850 individuals
Annual Budget: $25-50,000
Secretary-Treasurer: Dr. Major S. Dhillon

Historical Note
A vector ecologist studies the environmental interrelationships of arthropods and other animals of public health importance (eg mosquitoes) as a basis for developing improved prevention and control measures. Members work in Mosquito Abatement Districts, Health, Agricultural and Fish and Game Departments, universities, private industry, and the Armed Forces. Formerly (1988) Society of Vector Ecologists. Membership: $50/year.

Meetings/Conferences:
Annual Meetings: October

Publications:
Journal of Vector Ecology. semi-a. adv.
Newsletter. q.

Society for Visual Anthropology *(1968)*
780 E. Fourth St., Second Floor
Brooklyn, NY 11218
Web Site: www.societyforvisualanthropology.org
Members: 525 individuals
Annual Budget: $10-25,000
Secretary: Mary Strong

Historical Note
SVA promotes a broad range of theoretical approaches to visual representation and media. Has no paid officers or full-time staff.

Meetings/Conferences:
Annual Meetings: November, with the American Anthropological Ass'n

Publications:
Visual Anthropology Review. bi-an.
Directory of Visual Anthropology.

Society of Accredited Marine Surveyors *(1986)*
4605 Cardinal Blvd.
Jacksonville, FL 32210
Tel: (904)384-1494 *Fax:* (904)388-3958
Toll Free: (800)344 - 9077
E-Mail: samshq@aol.com
Web Site: http://Marinesurvey.org
Members: 1000 individuals
Staff: 4
Annual Budget: $250-500,000
Executive Director: Mary Stahler
President: Norm LeBlanc

Historical Note
SAMS is committed to enhancing the profession of marine surveying, avoiding prejudice, conflict of interest, and maintaining professional independence. Incorporated in the State of Florida. Membership: $450/year (accredited marine surveyor).

Publications:
Subject to Survey Newsletter. q.
Membership Roster. a.

Society of Actuaries *(1949)*
475 N. Martingale Road, Suite 600
Schaumburg, IL 60173-2226
Tel: (847)706-3500 *Fax:* (847)706-3599
E-Mail: webmaster@soa.org
Web Site: www.soa.org
Members: 16800 individuals
Staff: 90
Annual Budget: $10-25,000,000
Executive Director: Sarah J. Sanford
Managing Director, Communications and Marketing: Joel Abize
Managing Director, Actuarial Practice: Cheryl Krueger
Managing Director, Continuing Education: John Riley

Historical Note
SOA was formed by a merger of the American Institute of Actuaries (1909) and the Actuarial Society of America (1889). Has an annual budget of approximately $25 million. Membership: $325/year (fellows and any member of over 4 years duration); $165/year (associate members of less than 4 years).

Meetings/Conferences:
Annual Meetings: October/1,500

Publications:
Record online.
The Future Actuary. 4/year. adv.
The Actuary. 6/year.
Monograph Series. irreg.
Transactions Reports. a.
Yearbook. a.
North American Actuarial Journal. 4/year.

Society of Air Force Clinical Surgeons *(1958)*
15 Durazno Court
Sacramento, CA 95833
Tel: (916)924-0352 *Fax:* (916)923-5987
E-Mail: christine.clark@nellis.af.mil
Web Site: www.safcs.org
Members: 750 individuals
Staff: 1

Annual Budget: $50-100,000
Executive Director: Rose Preuit Thomas

Historical Note
Chartered in the State of Texas in 1958, SAFCS promotes excellence in surgery within the Air Force, serves as a forum for presentation of scientific papers, fosters esprit de corps, and promulgates military surgical objectives.

Society of Air Force Physician Assistants

Historical Note
A chartered chapter of American Academy of Physician Assistants, which provides administrative support.

Society of Allied Weight Engineers *(1939)*
2131 Tevis Ave.
Long Beach, CA 90815
Tel: (562)596-2873 *Fax:* (562)596-2874
E-Mail: saweron@charton.net
Web Site: www.sawe.org
Members: 800 individuals
Staff: 1
Annual Budget: $50-100,000
Executive Director: Ronald L. Fox

Historical Note
Organized in Los Angeles in 1939 as the Society of Aeronautical Weight Engineers and incorporated in April 1941. The society is now international. Assumed its present name on January 1, 1973. The membership consists predominantly of engineers in aerospace, ground transportation, marine transport, and other industries concerned with mass properties or weight engineering. Membership: $45/year (individual); $450/year (company/library).

Meetings/Conferences:
Annual Meetings: Mid-May/175
2007 – Madrid, Spain(Malia Princesa)/May 26-30/150
2008 – Seattle, WA(Renaissance)/May 17-21/150

Publications:
Publication & Technical Paper Index (on-line).
Roster. a.
Conference Papers. a.
SAWE Newsletter. q. adv.
Journal of Weight Engineering. 3/year. adv.

Society of American Archivists *(1936)*
527 S. Wells St., Fifth Floor
Chicago, IL 60607
Tel: (312)922-0140 *Fax:* (312)347-1452
Web Site: www.archivists.org
Members: 4700 individuals
Staff: 10
Annual Budget: $1-2,000,000
Executive Director: Nancy Perkin Beaumont, CAE
Director, Publishing: Teresa Brinati
E-Mail: tbrinati@archivists.org

Historical Note
A professional society of individuals and institutions interested in preservation and use of archives, manuscripts and current records as well as machine-readable records, sound recordings, pictures, films and maps. Membership: $40-180/year (individual, based on salary); $225/year (organization/company).

Meetings/Conferences:
Annual Meetings: Summer/1400
2007 – Chicago, IL(Fairmont Hotel)/Aug. 27-Sept. 2/1600

Publications:
Archival Outlook. bi-m.
American Archivist. semi-a.

Society of American Business Editors and Writers *(1963)*
Missouri School of Journalism
134 Neff Annex
Columbia, MO 65211-1200
Tel: (573)882-7862 *Fax:* (573)884-1372
Web Site: www.sabew.org
Members: 3400 institutions and individuals
Staff: 2
Annual Budget: $50-100,000
Executive Director: Carrie Paden

Historical Note
Founded in 1963 as an offspring of the professional journalist society, Sigma Delta Chi. The name was originally the Society of American Business Writers and was changed to the Society of American Business and Economic Writers in April, 1976. The present name became effective in May, 1986. Members are financial, business and economic news writers and editors for print and broadcast outlets. Membership: $50/year (individual); sliding scale for institutions.

Meetings/Conferences:
Annual Meetings: April-May

Publications:
Membership Directory. a.
Business Journalist. bi-m. adv.

Society of American Fight Directors *(1977)*
1350 E. Flamingo Road, # 25
Las Vegas, NV 89119
Toll Free: (800)659 - 6579
E-Mail: secretary@safd.org
Web Site: www.safd.org
Members: 1000 individuals
Annual Budget: under $10,000
Secretary: Michael Mahaffey

Historical Note
Members are stage fight choreographers, actors and other interested individuals. SAFD trains and recognizes actor/combatants, and certifies instructors as Certified Teachers and Fight Directors. Has no paid officers or full-time staff. Membership: $35/year (domestic); $40/year (foreign).

Publications:
Fight Master. semi-a. adv.
Cutting Edge. bi-m.

Society of American Florists *(1884)*
1601 Duke St.
Alexandria, VA 22314
Tel: (703)836-8700 *Fax:* (703)836-8705
Toll Free: (800)336 - 4743
E-Mail: info@safnow.org
Web Site: www.safnow.org
Members: 12500 members
Staff: 25
Annual Budget: $5-10,000,000
Chief Executive Officer and Executive Vice President: Peter J. Moran
Director, Finance: Leonard Bowers
Director, Member Services: David Bowman
Contact: Shelley Estersohn
Chief Operating Officer: Drew N. Gruenburg
Vice President, Publishing and Communications: Kate Penn
Senior Director, Government Relations: Jeanne Little Ramsay
Senior Director, Government Relations: Lin Schmale
Director, Research and Information: Ira T. Silvergleit
Chief Information Officer: Renato Sogueco
Vice President, Consumer Marketing: Jennifer Sparks

Historical Note
Became SAF: The Center for Commercial Floriculture in 1983; resumed its original name in 1987. Society of American Florists Political Action Committee. Has an annual budget of approximately $7 million.

Meetings/Conferences:
Annual Meetings: Fall
2007 – Palm Springs, CA(La Quinta Resort and Club)/Sept. 26-29

Publications:
Floral Trend Tracker.
e-brief. w.
Week in Review. w.
Floral Management Magazine. q.
Dateline. m.

Society of American Foresters *(1900)*
5400 Grosvenor Lane
Bethesda, MD 20814-2161
Tel: (301)897-8720 *Fax:* (301)897-3690
Toll Free: (866)897 - 8720
E-Mail: safweb@safnet.org
Web Site: www.safnet.org
Members: 15000 individuals
Staff: 18
Annual Budget: $2-5,000,000
Executive Vice President and Chief Executive Officer: Michael T. Goergen, Jr.
Senior Director, Finance and Administration: Larry D. Burner, CPA
Associate Director, Forest Policy: Rita Neznek
E-Mail: neznekr@safnet.org

Historical Note
Founded by Gifford Pinchot and six other pioneer foresters. Scientific and educational association representing all segments of the forestry profession; including private and public practitioners, educators, researchers, technicians and students. Serves as the accreditation agency for professional forestry education in the U.S.

Meetings/Conferences:
Annual Meetings: Fall
2007 – Portland, OR/Oct. 24-28

Publications:
The Forestry Source. m. adv.
Forest Science. bi-m. adv.
Journal of Forestry. 8/yr. adv.
Northern Journal of Applied Forestry. q. adv.
Southern Journal of Applied Forestry. q. adv.
Western Journal of Applied Forestry. q. adv.

Society of American Gastrointestinal and Endoscopic Surgeons *(1980)*
11300 W. Olympic Blvd., Suite 600
Los Angeles, CA 90064
Tel: (310)437-0544 *Fax:* (310)437-0585
E-Mail: sagesweb@sages.org
Web Site: www.sages.org
Members: 5000 individuals
Staff: 15
Annual Budget: $2-5,000,000
Executive Director: Sallie Matthews

Historical Note
Members are surgeons performing gastrointestinal endoscopy and related minimal-access surgeries. SAGES promotes the concepts of and research in gastrointestinal endoscopy.

Meetings/Conferences:
2007 – Las Vegas, NV(Paris Las Vegas)/Apr. 19-22/1500
2008 – Philadelphia, PA(Pennsylvania Convention Center)/March 26-29/1500

Publications:
SCOPE Newsletter. bi-a. adv.
SAGES Manual.
Standards of Practice and Credentialing Guidelines. irreg.
Surgical Endoscopy Journal. m. adv.

Society of American Graphic Artists *(1915)*
32 Union Sq., Room 1214
New York, NY 10003
Tel: (212)260-5706
Web Site: www.clt.astate.edu/elind/sagamain.htm
Members: 250 individuals
Annual Budget: $10-25,000
Web Page Editor: Tom Baker
Newsletter Editor: Sandra Terry

Historical Note
Founded (1915) as the Brooklyn Society of Etchers; became the Society of American Graphic Artists in 1952 to include woodcut, lithography and other media. Any artist who has been selected twice for a SAGA exhibition in the last five years is eligible for invitation to membership. Membership enables artists to show their work in New York City through important exhibitions with substantial awards. Membership: $40/year.

Publications:
Tear Sheet. q.

Society of American Historians *(1939)*
603 Fayerweather MC 2538
Columbia University
New York, NY 10027
Tel: (212)222-4902
Members: 350 individuals
Staff: 2
Annual Budget: $25-50,000
Administrative Secretary: Ene Sirvet

Historical Note
Membership, by election, is composed of individuals who have written a scholarly historical work of literary distinction.

Meetings/Conferences:
Annual Meetings: Always in May in New York, NY

Society of American Historical Artists *(1980)*
146 Dartmouth Dr.
Oyster Bay Township, NY 11801
Tel: (516)681-8820
Members: 16 individuals
Annual Budget: under $10,000
President: John Duillo

Historical Note
A group of artists interested in preserving and portraying historical truth through art. Membership is by invitation only. Membership: $100/year.

Meetings/Conferences:
Annual Meetings: October

Society of American Indian Dentists *(1990)*
P.O. Box 9230
Surprise, AZ 85374-0137
Tel: (602)954-5160
Members: 55 individuals
Annual Budget: under $10,000
President: George Blue Spruce, Jr., D.D.S

Historical Note
Organized to support the growing number of American Indians practicing dentistry and to promote dental health in the Indian community, American Indian heritage and traditional medicine. Has no paid officers or full-time staff. Membership: $50/year (individual); $100/year (organization).

Meetings/Conferences:
Annual Meetings: July

Publications:
Membership Directory. a.

Society of American Law Teachers *(1974)*
Washington Coll. of Law, Room 446
4801 Massachusetts Ave. NW
Washington, DC 20016
Tel: (202)274-4168
E-Mail: info@saltlaw.org
Web Site: www.saltlaw.org
Members: 750 individuals
Membership Contact: David F. Chavkin

Historical Note
SALT members are law faculty. Has no paid officers or full-time staff.

Publications:
Equalizer Newsletter. q.

Society of American Magicians *(1902)*
P.O. Box 510260
St. Louis, MO 63151
Tel: (314)846-5659
Web Site: www.magicsam.com
Members: 8500 individuals
Staff: 2
Annual Budget: $100-250,000
National Administrator: Richard Blowers

Historical Note
Membership is open to professional and amateur magicians, manufacturers of magical apparatus, collectors, writers, and hobbyists. Membership: $65/year.

Meetings/Conferences:
Annual Meetings: July

Publications:
M-U-M Magazine. m. adv.

Society of American Military Engineers *(1920)*
607 Prince St.
Alexandria, VA 22314-3117
Tel: (703)549-3800 *Fax:* (703)684-0231
E-Mail: info@same.org
Web Site: www.same.org
Members: 26100 individuals
Staff: 15
Annual Budget: $1-2,000,000
Executive Director: Dr. Robert D. Wolff, P.E.
Editor in Chief/Director, Communications and Marketing: L. Eileen Erickson
Director, Membership: Melody Jordan
Director, Training and Post Operations: Steve Shephard
E-Mail: sshephard@same.org

Historical Note
Founded January 1, 1920, and incorporated in the District of Columbia in 1924. SAME's primary mission is to encourage the free exchange of ideas among military and civilian engineers. Members are professional engineers, architects, planners, designers, other related professionals, and contractors, suppliers, and manufacturers of engineering and engineering-related products. Approximately 75% of members are employed in U.S. or foreign engineering firms in the private sector; the remainder are in government (primarily military) engineering positions. Membership: $12-73/year (individual), $200-1,120/year (corporate).

Meetings/Conferences:
Annual Meetings: Spring
2007 – Philadelphia, PA

Publications:
Directory. a..
SAME's News. bi-m. adv.
The Military Engineer. bi-m. adv.
Government and Industry e-News.

Society of American Registered Architects *(1956)*
P.O. Box 280
Newport, TN 37822
Tel: (423)487-0365
Toll Free: (888)385 - 7272
Web Site: www.sara-national.org
Members: 800 individuals
Annual Budget: $100-250,000
Executive Director: Cathie Moscato

Historical Note
Established in Kansas City in 1956 by Wilfred Gregson of Atlanta. Founded as a professional society that includes the participation of all architects regardless of their roles in the architectural community. SARA follows the Golden Rule and supports the concept of profitable professionalism for its members. Membership: $225/year (individual); $65/year (associate); $225/year (industry); $15/year (student).

Meetings/Conferences:
Annual Meetings: Fall/150-200

Publications:
National Directory. a. adv.
Sarascope. bi-m. adv.

Society of American Silversmiths *(1989)*
P.O. Box 72839
Providence, RI 02907
Tel: (401)461-6840 *Fax:* (401)461-6841
E-Mail: sas@silversmithing.com
Web Site: www.silversmithing.com
Members: 220 individuals
Staff: 1
Annual Budget: under $10,000
Executive Director: Jeffrey Herman

Historical Note
SAS is dedicated to the preservation and promotion of contemporary silversmithing. Its Artisan members are silversmiths, both practicing and retired, who have been juried into SAS based on their outstanding technical skill. SAS educates the public on silversmithing and demystifies techniques through its literature and national exhibits. SAS also assists students who have a strong interest in becoming silver craftsmen. Aids students with supplier discounts and workshops. All members have access to Society's technical and marketing expertise, Artisan archives, and referral service that commissions work from its Artisans. Membership fee: $45/year (artisan); $40/year (supporting); $45/year (foreign supporting); $20/year (student).

Meetings/Conferences:
Semi-Annual Meetings:

Society of American Travel Writers *(1956)*
1500 Sunday Dr., Suite 102
Raleigh, NC 27607
Tel: (919)861-5586 *Fax:* (919)787-4916
E-Mail: satw@satw.org
Web Site: www.satw.org
Members: 1300 individuals
Staff: 3
Annual Budget: $100-250,000
Executive Director: Cathy Karr

Historical Note
Organized as the American Association of Travel Writers in Ellinor Village, FL during a convention of the National Association of Travel Organizations. Assumed its present name in 1957 and was incorporated in the District of Columbia in 1958. Membership: $120/year and $240/year.

Meetings/Conferences:
Annual Meetings: Fall

Publications:
Membership Directory. a.
The Travel Writer. 10/year.

Society of Animal Artists *(1960)*
47 Fifth Ave.
New York, NY 10003
Tel: (212)741-2880 *Fax:* (212)741-2262
E-Mail: admin@societyofanimalartists.com
Web Site: www.societyofanimalartists.com
Members: 360 individuals
Staff: 1
Administrator: Alice Price

Historical Note
SAA members are artists specializing in the portrayal of animals.

Publications:
SAA Newsletter. q.
Catalogue of Exhibition. a.

Society of Architectural Historians *(1940)*
1365 N. Astor St.
Chicago, IL 60610-2144
Tel: (312)573-1365 *Fax:* (312)573-1141
E-Mail: info@sah.org
Web Site: www.sah.org
Members: 3500 individuals
Staff: 5
Annual Budget: $1-2,000,000
Executive Director: Pauline Saliga
Manager, Meetings and Tours: Kathy Sturm

Historical Note
Provides an international forum for those interested in architecture, encourages scholarly research in the field and promotes the preservation of significant architectural monuments. A member of the American Council of Learned Societies. Membership: $115/year (individual); $250/year (institutional).

Meetings/Conferences:
Annual Meetings: Spring
2007 – Pittsburgh, PA/Apr. 11-14

Publications:
Journal. q. adv.
Newsletter. bi-m. adv.

Society of Armenian Studies *(1974)*
California State Univ., Armenian Studies Program
5245 N. Backer Ave., PB4
Fresno, CA 93740-8001
Tel: (559)278-4930 *Fax:* (559)278-2129
Web Site: http://armenianstudies.csufresno.edu/sas/AboutSAS.htm
Members: 300 individuals
Annual Budget: under $10,000
President: Barlow Der Mugrdechian

Historical Note
Founded in 1974 by a group of scholars from the University of California, Columbia University and Harvard. An affiliate of the Middle East Studies Association (Tucson, AZ), the American Historical Association (Washington, DC), and the American Association for the Advancement of Slavic Studies (Stanford, CA). SAS is dedicated to the development of Armenian Studies as an academic discipline. Has no paid officers or full-time staff. Membership fee: $40/year (individual), $15/year (student), $25/year (retired), $100/year (organization/company), $50 (donors), $100 (patrons).

Meetings/Conferences:
Annual Meetings: in conjunction with MESA annual meeting

Publications:
Journal of the SAS. a.
Newsletter. semi-a.

Roster of Members. a.
Bibliography of Articles in Armenian Studies. a.

Society of Army Physician Assistants *(1979)*
P.O. Box 07490
Ft. Myers, FL 33919
Tel: (239)482-2162
E-Mail: hal.slusher@juno.com
Web Site: www.sapa.org
Members: 1050 individuals
Staff: 1
Executive Director: Harold E. Slusher

Historical Note
An affiliate of the American Academy of Physician Assistants.

Meetings/Conferences:
Annual Meetings: Spring

Publications:
SAPA Journal. 6/year.

Society of Asian and Comparative Philosophy *(1968)*
Notre Dame University
Dept. of Gov't, International Studies
South Bend, IN 46556
Tel: (574)631-5491 *Fax:* (574)631-8209
E-Mail: fred.r.dallmayr.1@nd.edu
Web Site: www.sacpweb.org
Members: 200 individuals
Annual Budget: under $10,000
President: Fred Dallmayr

Historical Note
SACP members are academics and others with an interest in Asian philosophic systems. Membership: $20/year (student/emeritus); $35/year (individual).

Publications:
Forum Newsletter. 2/year.
SACP Directory. 5/year.
Philosophy East & West Journal. q.

Society of Atherosclerosis Imaging *(2000)*
9929 Main St., Suite C
Damascus, MD 20872
Tel: (301)253-4155 *Fax:* (301)253-5209
E-Mail: info@sai.org
Web Site: www.sai.org

Society of Automotive Analysts *(1987)*
3300 Washtenaw Ave., Suite 220
Ann Arbor, MI 48104
Tel: (734)677-3518 *Fax:* (734)677-2407
E-Mail: cybersaa@cybersaa.org
Web Site: www.cybersaa.org
Members: 500 individuals
Staff: 2
Annual Budget: $100-250,000
Executive Director: Robert E. Barba
Account Manager: Kristin Curle

Historical Note
Members are analysts involved in the automotive industry through various fields: marketing, finance, advertising, production and public relations. Membership: $125/year (individual).

Meetings/Conferences:
Annual Meetings: Winter

Publications:
Membership Directory (online).

Society of Automotive Engineers International

Historical Note
See SAE International.

Society of Behavioral Medicine *(1978)*
555 East Wells St., Suite 1100
Milwaukee, WI 53502-3832
Tel: (414)918-3156 *Fax:* (414)276-3349
E-Mail: info@sbm.org
Web Site: www.sbm.org
Members: 3000 individuals
Staff: 7
Executive Director: Susanne Burnham

Historical Note
Members are primarily physicians, psychologists, nurses and health educators concerned with the interactions of health, illness, and behavior. Membership: $230/year (associate); $230/year (full); $80/year (trainee/student).

Meetings/Conferences:
Annual Meetings: Spring/1,200
2007 – Washington, DC(Marriott Wardman Park)/March 21-24

Publications:
Behavioral Medicine Outlook. q. adv.
Annals of Behavioral Medicine. q. adv.
Directory. bien.
Proceedings. a.

Society of Biblical Literature *(1880)*
Emory Univ., The Luce Center
825 Houston Mill Road NE
Atlanta, GA 30329
Tel: (404)727-3100 *Fax:* (404)727-3101
Toll Free: (877)725 - 3334
E-Mail: sbl@sbl-site.org
Web Site: www.sbl-site.org
Members: 8000 individuals and institutions
Staff: 14
Annual Budget: $2-5,000,000
Executive Director: Kent Richards
Director, Administration and Technical Services: Missy Colee
Director, Membership Services: Theresa Lesnik

Historical Note
A member of the American Council of Learned Societies and the National Humanities Alliance, Society of Scholarly Publishing, American Association of University Press. Areas of focus include technology, research and publications. Membership: $50/year.

Meetings/Conferences:
Annual Meetings: November/8,000

Publications:
Annual Meeting Program Book. a. adv.
International Meeting Program Book. a. adv.
Multiple Monograph Series. irreg.
Journal of Biblical Literature. q. adv.
Openings; Job Opportunities for Scholars of Religion. bi-m.
Review of Biblical Literature. a. adv.
SBL Forum eMail. m. adv.

Society of Biological Psychiatry *(1945)*
c/o Mayo Clinic Jacksonville
4500 San Pablo Road, Research-Birdsall 310
Jacksonville, FL 32224
Tel: (904)953-2842 *Fax:* (904)953-7117
E-Mail: maggie@mayo.edu
Web Site: www.sobp.org
Members: 965 individuals
Staff: 1
Annual Budget: $50-100,000
Executive Director: Maggie Peterson

Historical Note
Founded in San Francisco in 1945 and incorporated in California in 1949. SOBP members are psychiatrists and research scientists form related fields. SOBP promotes the study of the biological basis of human behavior. Membership: $150/year (individual).

Meetings/Conferences:
Annual Meetings: Spring/500

Publications:
Biological Psychiatry. m. adv.

Society of Broadcast Engineers *(1964)*
9102 N. Meridian St., Suite 150
Indianapolis, IN 46260
Tel: (317)846-9000 *Fax:* (317)846-9120
E-Mail: jporay@sbe.org
Web Site: www.sbe.org
Members: 5500 individuals
Staff: 6
Annual Budget: $500-1,000,000
Executive Director: John L. Poray, CAE

Historical Note
Founded as the Institute of Broadcast Engineers. Membership includes studio and transmitter operators, announcer technicians, chief and staff engineers of large and small television and radio stations and others involved in broadcast engineering. Membership: $10/year (youth); $20/year (student); $63/year (individual); $575/year (sustaining member).

Meetings/Conferences:
Annual Meetings: Fall
2007 –

Publications:
SBE Short Circuits (online). m.
SBE Signal. bi-m. adv.
Membership Directory. a. adv.

Society of Cable Telecommunications Engineers *(1969)*
140 Philips Road
Exton, PA 19341
Tel: (610)524-1725 *Fax:* (610)363-5898
Toll Free: (800)542 - 5040
E-Mail: scte@scte.org
Web Site: www.scte.org
Members: 15000 individuals
Staff: 30
Annual Budget: $2-5,000,000
President and Chief Executive Officer: John D. Clark, Jr.
E-Mail: jclark@scte.org
Vice President, National Conferences: Lori Bower
E-Mail: lbower@scte.org
Vice President, Membership Services: Mark John
Vice President, Marketing and Business Devel.: Kimberly Maki
Vice President, Professional Devel.: Marvin Nelson
Vice President, Standards: Steve Oksala
E-Mail: soksala@scte.org
Vice President, Human Resources, Legal and Administration: Thomas R. Wilcox, III
Vice President, Finance and Administration: Patricia Zelenka
E-Mail: pzelenka@scte.org

Historical Note
The Society of Cable Telecommunications Engineers is a non-profit professional organizationth at has approx. 14,000 members in the U.S. and 70 countries worldwide, and offers a variety of programs and services for the industry's educational benefit. SCTE is an ANSI-accredited standards development organization

Meetings/Conferences:
Annual Meetings: Spring and Winter, alternating years

Publications:
Membership Directory. a. adv.
SCTE Interval. m.
SCTE Monthly. m.

Society of Carbide and Tool Engineers *(1947)*

Historical Note
A division of ASM International, which provides administrative support.

Society of Cardiovascular and Interventional Radiology

Historical Note
Became Society of Interventional Radiology in 2003.

Society of Cardiovascular Anesthesiologists *(1978)*
P.O. Box 11086
Richmond, VA 23230-1086
Tel: (804)282-0084 *Fax:* (804)282-0090
Web Site: www.scahq.org
Members: 7200 individuals
Staff: 16
Annual Budget: $1-2,000,000
Chief Staff Executive: Heather Spiess
E-Mail: heather@societyhq.com
Director, Meetings and Conventions: Kevin Johns, CAE
E-Mail: kevin@societyhq.com
Administrator: Cathryn Portillo
Membership Coordinator: Joye Stewart
Controller: David Vereen
E-Mail: david@societyhq.com

Historical Note
Membership: $175/year (individual).

Meetings/Conferences:
Annual Meetings: Spring

Publications:
Newsletter. bi-m.
Anesthesia & Analgesia. m.
Monograph. a.

Society of Certified Insurance Counselors *(1969)*
3630 N. Hills Dr.

Austin, TX 78731
Tel: (512)345-7932 *Fax:* (512)349-6194
Toll Free: (800)633 - 2165
E-Mail: alliance@scic.com
Web Site: www.scic.com
Members: 2700 individuals
Staff: 104
President: Dr. William T. Hold
Director, Marketing and Promotions: Carolyn Smith
E-Mail: csmith@scic.com

Historical Note

SCIC is the largest professional education association for insurance agents with a mandatory continuing education requirement. Membership: $85/year.

Meetings/Conferences:

Annual Meetings: MEGA Seminars

Publications:

Resources. q.

Society of Certified Kitchen and Bathroom Designers *(1967)*

Historical Note

SCKBD is the certifying arm of the National Kitchen and Bath Association, which provides administrative support.

Society of Chairmen of Academic Radiology Oncology Programs *(1966)*

Historical Note

SCAROP is a program of American Soc. for Therapeutic Radiology and Oncology, which provides administrative support

Society of Chemical Industry, American Section *(1894)*

177 Terrace Dr.
Chatham, NJ 07928
Tel: (973)635-0189 *Fax:* (973)635-0958
E-Mail: web@soci.org
Web Site: www.soci.org
Members: 800 individuals
Administrative Director: Michelle van Bleichert

Historical Note

North American office of the international organization headquartered in London, UK. Provides technical information and support to practitioners throughout the sciences and to advance applied chemistry in all its branches.

Meetings/Conferences:

Semi-annual Meetings:

Publications:

Reports on the Progress of Applied Chemistry. a.
British Polymer Journal. bi-m.
Chemistry & Industry. semi-m.
Journal of Applied Chemistry. m.
Journal of the Science of Food and Agriculture. m.

Society of Children's Book Writers and Illustrators *(1971)*

8271 Beverly Blvd.
Los Angeles, CA 90048-4515
Tel: (323)782-1010 *Fax:* (323)782-1892
E-Mail: scbwi@scbwi.org
Web Site: www.scbwi.org
Members: 19000 individuals
Staff: 3
Annual Budget: $500-1,000,000
Executive Director: Lin Oliver
Manager, Administrative Affairs: Kim Stratton
Membership/Creative Affairs/Webmaster: Lauri Veverka
Publications/Communications: Jamie Weiss

Historical Note

SCBWI acts as a network for the exchange of knowledge between children's writers, illustrators, editors, publishers and agents. Members include writers and illustrators of children's books, magazine stories and articles; writers and producers of children's television; children's book and magazine editors and publishers; agents; children's librarians, teachers and educators; bookstore owners and personnel. Membership: $50/year and $10 initiation fee.

Meetings/Conferences:

Annual Meetings: August

Publications:

SCBWI Bulletin. bi-m.

Society of Christian Ethics *(1959)*

P.O. Box 5126
St. Cloud, MN 56302-5126
Tel: (320)253-5407 *Fax:* (320)252-6984
Web Site: www.scethics.org
Members: 900 individuals
Staff: 1
Annual Budget: $50-100,000
Executive Director: Stewart W. Herman
E-Mail: sce@cord.edu

Historical Note

Formerly (1980) American Society of Christian Ethics. Promotes scholarly work in the field of Christian ethics and in the relation of Christian ethics to other traditions of ethics and to social, economic, political and cultural problems. The Society also seeks to encourage and improve the teaching of these fields in colleges, universities, and theological schools and to provide a fellowship of discourse and debate for those engaged professionally within these general fields. Associate Member of the Council of Societies for the Study of Religion. Membership: $30-160/year.

Meetings/Conferences:

Annual Meetings: mid-January/470
2007 – Dallas, TX(Hyatt Regency)/Jan. 7-7
2008 – Atlanta, GA(Hyatt Regency)/Jan. 3-6

Publications:

Journal of the Society of Christian Ethics. bien. adv.

Society of Christian Philosophers *(1978)*

Calvin College, Dept. of Philosophy
Grand Rapids, MI 49546-4388
Tel: (616)526-6421 *Fax:* (616)526-8551
Web Site: www.siu.edu/~scp/index.htm
Members: 1100 individuals
Annual Budget: $25-50,000
Secretary-Treasurer: Kelly James Clark
E-Mail: kclark@calvin.edu

Historical Note

SCP members are professors, students and others with an interest in the integration of Christianity and philosophy. Has no paid officers or full-time staff. Membership: $40/year.

Publications:

Newsletter. q.
Faith and Philosophy Journal. q.

Society of Cleaning and Restoration Technicians *(1972)*

200 Vantage Way
Franklin, TN 37067
Tel: (615)591-9610 *Fax:* (615)591-6920
Toll Free: (800)949 - 4728
E-Mail: whyscrt@scrthq.org
Web Site: www.scrthq.org
Members: 500 companies
Staff: 3
Annual Budget: $100-250,000
Administrator: Dana Rains

Historical Note

Founded as Society of Cleaning Technicians; became International Society of Cleaning Technicians in 1993, and assumed its current name in 2004. Members are professional on-site carpet and upholstery cleaners, restorers and suppliers to the industry. SCRT is a shareholder of the Institute of Inspection, Cleaning and Restoration Certification. Membership: $275/year.

Meetings/Conferences:

Annual Meetings: Summer

Publications:

The Monitor. 6/year.
Pro-Pac. 6/year.

Society of Clinical and Medical Hair Removal *(1985)*

2810 Crossroads Dr., Suite 3800
Madison, WI 53718
Tel: (608)443-2470 *Fax:* (608)443-2474
E-Mail: scmhr@reesgroupinc.com
Web Site: www.scmhr.org
Members: 350 individuals
Staff: 2
Executive Secretary: Lisa Nelson

Historical Note

Founded as Society of Clinical and Medical Electrologists by the merger of the National Electrolysis Organization and the Electrolysis Society of America. Assumed its current name in 2001. Sponsors and supports the International Commissioner for Hair Removal Certificate (same address). Membership: $155/year (individual U.S. member); $100/year (individual foreign member).

Meetings/Conferences:

Annual Meetings: Fall
2007 – Miami Beach, FL(Miami Beach Convention Center)/May 19-22/200

Publications:

Dermascope Magazine. m.
Perspectives Newsletter. q.
Directory. a.

Society of Collision Repair Specialists *(1982)*

P.O. Box 909
Prosser, WA 99350
Tel: (509)786-1214 *Fax:* (509)786-1215
Toll Free: (877)841 - 0660
E-Mail: info@scrs.com
Web Site: www.scrs.com
Members: 750 companies, 31 state affiliates
Staff: 3
Annual Budget: $250-500,000
Executive Director: Dan Risley
Executive Assistant: Linda Atkins

Historical Note

Organized in Schaumburg, IL on September 26, 1982. Members are owners and managers of auto collision repair shops, suppliers, insurance and educational associates and suppliers in the U.S., Canada, Australia, and New Zealand. SCRS distributes technical, management, marketing and sales information; works to promote professionalism within the collision repair industry; and conducts seminars and workshops on collision repair facility management and selling and marketing collision repairs. Through its director members and affiliate association, SCRS is comprised of 8,357 collision repair businesses and 58,577 specialized professionals who work with customers and insurance companies to repair collision-damaged vehicles. Membership: $300/year (individual); $350/year, minimum (association).

Meetings/Conferences:

Annual Meetings: April/100

Society of Commercial Seed Technologists *(1922)*

101 E. State St., Suite 214
Ithaca, NY 14850
Tel: (607)256-3313
E-Mail: scst@twcny.rr.com
Web Site: www.seedtechnology.net
Members: 250 individuals
Staff: 1
Annual Budget: $50-100,000
Executive Director: Anita Hall

Historical Note

Formerly (1946) Association of Commercial Seed Analysts of North America. Members are professionals involved in the testing and analysis of seeds, research on seed physiology, and seed production and handling based on the modern botanical and agricultural sciences. Membership: $250/year (Registered Seed Technologist); $75/year (research); $75/year (associate).

Meetings/Conferences:

Annual Meetings: June, with the Ass'n of Official Seed Analysts/250

Publications:

Newsletter. 3/year. adv.

Society of Competitive Intelligence Professionals *(1986)*

1700 Diagonal Road, Suite 600
Alexandria, VA 22314-2866
Tel: (703)739-0696 *Fax:* (703)739-2524
E-Mail: info@scip.org
Web Site: www.scip.org
Members: 6800 individuals

Staff: 20
Annual Budget: $2-5,000,000
Executive Director: Alexander T. Graham
Manager, Chapters and Volunteer Relations: Lisa Badolato
Director, Research and Information: Bonnie Hohhof
E-Mail: bhohhof@scip.org
Director, Business Development: Jon Lowder
E-Mail: jlowder@scip.org
Director, Marketing and Membership Development: Carolina Oliviera
Learning Director: Elizabeth Reed-Martinez
Director, Conferences: Nikki Wells
E-Mail: nwells@scip.org

Historical Note

SCIP is a international non-profit organization providing education and networking opportunities for business professionals working in the field of competitive intelligence (CI). CI is the organized process of monitoring and analyzing the competitive environment to secure and maintain competitive business advantage. SCIP members have backgrounds in market research, government intelligence, or science and technology. SCIP members enable executives to make informed decisions that keep companies responsive, well-positioned, and profitable.

Meetings/Conferences:

Annual Meetings: Spring

Publications:

Competetive Intelligence Magazine. bi-m. adv.
Journal of Competitive Intelligence and Management. q. adv.
SCIP Online. bi-w. adv.

Society of Composers *(1965)*
Old Chelsea Station, Box 450
New York, NY 10113-0450
E-Mail: secretary@societyofcomposers.org
Web Site: www.societyofcomposers.org
Members: 850 individuals
Staff: 2
Annual Budget: $25-50,000
General Manager: Gerald Warfield

Historical Note

Society of Composers, Inc. is a professional society dedicated to the promotion of composition, performance, understanding and dissemination of new and contemporary music. Members include composers and performers both in and outside of academia interested in addressing concerns for national and regional support of compositional activities.

Publications:

Journal of Music Scores. bi-a.
Newsletter. m.

Society of Composers and Lyricists *(1945)*
400 S. Beverly Dr., Suite 214
Beverly Hills, CA 90212
Tel: (310)281-2812 *Fax:* (310)284-4861
E-Mail: execdir@thescl.com
Web Site: www.thescl.com
Members: 900
Staff: 1
Executive Director and Recording Secretary: Laura Dunn

Historical Note

SCL members are professional composers and songwriters active in production and composition of music for films, television and/or multimedia.

Publications:

The Score. q.

Society of Computed Body Tomography and Magnetic Resonance *(1977)*
c/o Matrix Meetings
P.O. Box 1026
Rochester, MN 55903-1026
Tel: (507)288-5620 *Fax:* (507)288-0014
E-Mail: scbtmr@charter.net
Web Site: www.scbtmr.org
Members: 580 individuals
Executive Director: Barbara McLeod, CMP

Historical Note

SCBT/MR's primary goal is to educate practicing radiologists in the use of body CT. Continuing medical education has remained the foremost goal for the Society, which has since changed its name to reflect its emphasis and activities in cross-sectional imaging, including magnetic resonance imaging. Membership in the Society is competitive, selecting only those physicians actively involved in academic practice and research dealing with Body Computed Tomography and Magnetic Resonance Imaging.

Meetings/Conferences:

Semi-annual Meetings:

Society of Corporate Meeting Professionals *(1970)*
106 Devonshire Dr.
San Antonio, TX 78209-4206
E-Mail: info@scmp.org
Web Site: www.scmp.org
Members: 125 individuals
Staff: 3
Annual Budget: $50-100,000
Contact: Kevin M. McNally, CMP

Historical Note

Founded in Chicago in 1971; incorporated in Illinois. Formerly the Society of Company Meeting Planners; assumed its present name in 1989. Members are corporate meeting planners and convention service managers. Membership: $350/year; $50/year (student).

Meetings/Conferences:

Semi-annual Meetings: Spring Education Conference and Fall Annual Meeting

Society of Corporate Secretaries and Governance Professionals *(1946)*
521 Fifth Ave., 32nd Floor
New York, NY 10175
Tel: (212)681-2000 *Fax:* (212)681-2005
E-Mail: gloftus@governanceprofessionals.org
Web Site: www.governanceprofessionals.org
Members: 4100 individuals
Staff: 13
Annual Budget: $2-5,000,000
President: David W. Smith
E-Mail: dsmith@governanceprofessionals.org
Controller: Daniel Engel
Vice President: Geoff Loftus
Vice President: Suzanne Walker

Historical Note

Formerly American Society of Corporate Secretaries; assumed its current name on January 1, 2005. Members are principally corporate secretaries, assistant secretaries, business executives and other persons involved in duties normally associated with the corporate secretarial function. Membership: $425/year (individual); $225/year for additional members from same company.

Meetings/Conferences:

Annual Meetings: Summer/1,000

Society of Cosmetic Chemists *(1945)*
120 Wall St., Suite 2400
New York, NY 10005-4088
Tel: (212)668-1500 *Fax:* (212)668-1504
E-Mail: scc@scconline.org
Web Site: www.scconline.org
Members: 3600 individuals
Staff: 4
Annual Budget: $1-2,000,000
Executive Director: Theresa Cesario
E-Mail: tcesario@scconline.org
Membership Coordinator: Helen McCarren
E-Mail: hmccarren@scconline.org
Publications Coordinator: Doreen Scelso
E-Mail: dscelso@scconline.org

Historical Note

Founded in May 1945 and incorporated in Delaware in 1947. A member of the International Federation of Societies of Cosmetic Chemists. Membership: $100/year (individual).

Meetings/Conferences:

Semi-annual Meetings: May/various locations and December/New York, NY

Publications:

SCC Newsletter.
Journal of Cosmetic Science. bi-m. adv.

Society of Cost Estimating and Analysis *(1990)*
101 S. Whiting St., Suite 201
Alexandria, VA 22304
Tel: (703)751-8069 *Fax:* (703)461-7328
E-Mail: scea@sceaonline.net
Web Site: www.sceaonline.net
Members: 1500 individuals
Staff: 2
Annual Budget: $250-500,000
Executive Secretary: Len Cheshire

Historical Note

Formed (1990) by a merger of the National Estimating Society (1966) and the Institute of Cost Analysis (1980). SCEA members are professionals engaged primarily in the field of government contract estimating and pricing. Maintains a code of ethics to promote cooperation and good relations among members of the profession and to enhance the status of the profession. Provides certification program that supports technical and ethical standards through participation in regional workshops, involvement in professional programs, completion of accredited university courses, and successful completion of a certification examination. Membership: $55/year (individual).

Meetings/Conferences:

Annual Meetings: June

Publications:

Journal of Cost Analysis and Management. a.
The National Estimator. 2/yr. adv.

Society of Creative Designers *(1975)*
1100-H Brandywine Blvd.
P.O. Box 3388
Zanesville, OH 43702-3388
Tel: (740)452-4541 *Fax:* (740)452-2552
E-Mail: scd@offinger.com
Web Site: www.creativedesigners.org
Members: 500 individuals
Staff: 2
Annual Budget: $100-250,000
Executive Director: Mark Bennett

Historical Note

Formerly (1975) Society of Craft Designers; assumed current name in 2004. Members are designers, manufacturers, and retailers of craft items, writers for the craft industry, and other related professionals. Membership: $135/year (individual); $250/year (company).

Meetings/Conferences:

Annual: Fall/300

Publications:

Newsletter. bi-m.

Society of Critical Care Medicine *(1970)*
701 Lee St., Suite 200
Des Plaines, IL 60016
Tel: (847)827-6869 *Fax:* (847)827-6886
E-Mail: info@sccm.org
Web Site: www.sccm.org
Members: 13000 individuals
Staff: 55
Annual Budget: $10-25,000,000
Executive Vice President and Chief Executive Officer: David Julian Martin, CAE
Director, Meetings and Conventions: Pamela Dallstream
Director, Marketing: Thomas L. Joseph, M.P.S., CAE
Director, Editorial Affairs: Deborah McBride
Director, Information Technology: David W. Reid
Director, Business Affairs: Brian Schramm, CAE
Director, Program Development and Professional Affairs: Nancy Stonis, RN, BSN, MJ

Historical Note

Healthcare association for professionals involved in critical care medicine, patient care, teaching or research. Founded the American College of Critical Care Medicine in 1988 to foster excellence in the practice of multiprofessional critical care and to honor individuals whose endeavors and contributions demonstrate personal commitment to these goals. Has an annual budget of approximately $12 million. Membership: $70-325/year.

Meetings/Conferences:

2007 – Orlando, FL(Gaylord Palms Resort)/Feb. 17-21
2007 – Toronto, ON, Canada(Fairmont)/June 14-16/300
2007 – Chicago, IL(Fairmont)/Aug. 2-9
2008 – Honolulu, HI(Hawaii Convention Center)/Feb. 2-6/500

2009 – Nashville, TN(Gaylord Opryland Resort and Convention Center)/Jan. 31-Feb. 4/5000
2010 – Miami Beach, FL(Miami Beach Convention Center)/Jan. 9-13/5000
2011 – San Diego, CA(San Diego Convention Center)/Jan. 15-19/5000

Publications:
Critical Connections. bi-m. adv.
Pediatric Critical Care Medicine. bi-m. adv.
Critical Care Medicine. m. adv.

Society of Dance History Scholars *(1982)*
3416 Primm Lane
Birmingham, AL 35216
Tel: (205)978-1404 *Fax:* (205)823-2760
E-Mail: sdhs@primemanagement.net
Web Site: www.sdhs.org
Members: 450 individuals
Staff: 2
Account Manager: Jim Ranieri

Historical Note
Formerly (1983) Dance History Scholars. SDHS members are academics and teachers in the field of dance. Membership: $75/year (individual); $40/year (student); $45/year (retired); $130/year (institutional).

Meetings/Conferences:
Annual Meetings: Summer

Publications:
Studies in Dance History Monograph Series. a.
SDHS Newsletter. semi-a. adv.
SDHS Proceedings. a.

Society of Decorative Painters *(1972)*
393 N. McLean Blvd.
Wichita, KS 67203-5968
Tel: (316)269-9300 *Fax:* (316)269-9191
E-Mail: sdp@decorativepainters.org
Web Site: www.decorativepainters.org
Members: 28000 individuals
Staff: 10
Annual Budget: $2-5,000,000
Chief Financial Officer: Yvonne Banman
E-Mail: yvonne@decorativepainters.org
Editor: Cheryl Capps
E-Mail: cheryl@decorativepainters.org
Director, Teacher Services/Education: Janelle Johnson
E-Mail: janelle@decorativepainters.org

Historical Note
Founded as National Society of Tole and Decorative Painters; assumed its current name in 1993. Seeks to raise and maintain a high quality decorative art standard, to stimulate interest in and appreciation for the art of decorative painting, and to act as an information source concerning activities in the field. There are over 200 chapters. Certification in the categories of stroke or still life painting are available for Certified Decorative Artists and in the fields of floral, still life and and stroke categories for Master Decorative Artists. Absorbed Society of Decorative Painters in 1993. Membership: $40/year.

Meetings/Conferences:
Annual Meetings: Annual/5000
2007 – Anaheim, CA/May 29-June 2

Publications:
Business & Teacher Directory online.
Convention Special Catalogue. a. adv.
The Decorative Painter. bi-m. adv.

Society of Depreciation Professionals
8100-M4 Wyoming Blvd. NE
#228
Albuquerque, NM 87113
Tel: (505)867-9513 *Fax:* (505)867-0917
E-Mail: sdp@his.com
Web Site: www.depr.org
Annual Budget: $25-50,000
Executive Secretary: Rod Daniel
E-Mail: rdaniel@his.com

Historical Note
Membership: $40/year.

Publications:
SDP Journal. a. adv.
SDP Newsletter. tri-a.

Society of Diagnostic Medical Sonography *(1970)*
2745 N. Dallas Pkwy., Suite 350
Plano, TX 75093-8563
Tel: (214)473-8057 *Fax:* (214)473-8563
Toll Free: (800)229 - 9506
Web Site: www.sdms.org
Members: 13500 individuals
Staff: 12
Annual Budget: $2-5,000,000
Executive Director: Donald Haydon
E-Mail: dhaydon@sdms.org
Manager, Communications and Marketing: Craig Alcott

Historical Note
Formerly (1981) the American Society of Ultrasound Technical Specialists, SDMS was formed to promote, advance and educate its members and the medical community in the science of diasnostic medical sonography. Members are individuals employing high frequency sound for medical diagnosis. Designed to provide members with continuing education and current information on standards, trends and opportunities in the field of diagnostic medical sonography. Membership: $119/year (individual); $495/year (organization/company); $40/year (student).

Meetings/Conferences:
Annual Meetings: Fall/1,000-1,500

Publications:
Journal of Diagnostic Medical Sonography. bi-m.
SDMS News Wave. q.
Sound News. m.

Society of Economic Geologists *(1920)*
7811 Shaffer Pkwy.
Littleton, CO 80127
Tel: (720)981-7882 *Fax:* (720)981-7874
E-Mail: seg@segweb.org
Web Site: www.segweb.org
Members: 3300 individuals
Staff: 7
Annual Budget: $250-500,000
Executive Director: Brian Hoals

Historical Note
SEG advances the science of geology in relation to minerals exploration, mining and related industries. Membership includes geoscientists from 68 countries. Membership: $85/year; $10/year (students).

Meetings/Conferences:
Semi-Annual Meetings: Fall with Geological Soc. of America/Spring with Soc. for Mining, Metallurgy, and Exploration

Publications:
SEG Membership Directory. bien.
SEG Field Trip Guide Books. 1-2/year.
Economic Geology. 8/year.
SEG Newsletter. q.
Reviews in Economic Geology. irreg.
Special Publications Series. irreg.

Society of Emergency Medicine Physician Assistants *(1990)*

Historical Note
An affiliate of American Academy of Physician Assistants, which provides administrative support.

Society of Engineering Science *(1963)*
University of Arkansas, Department of Electrical Engineering
3217 Bell Engineering
Fayetteville, AR 72701
Tel: (479)575-4593
Web Site: www.sesinc.org
Members: 300 individuals
Annual Budget: under $10,000
Secretary: Vasu Varadan
E-Mail: vvvesm@engr.uark.edu

Historical Note
Multidisciplinary society of scientists and engineers concerned with research and communication between the fields of engineering and science. Membership: $25/year (individual).

Meetings/Conferences:
Annual Meetings: November at a university and biennial int'l conferences (even years)

Publications:
SES Newsletter. semi-a.
Abstracts of the Annual Meeting. a.

Society of Environmental Journalists *(1990)*
P.O. Box 2492
Jenkintown, PA 19046
Tel: (215)884-8174 *Fax:* (215)884-8175
E-Mail: sej@sej.org
Web Site: www.sej.org
Members: 1500 individuals
Staff: 5
Annual Budget: $500-1,000,000
Executive Director: Beth Parke
E-Mail: sej@sej.org

Historical Note
A nonprofit, 501 (c) (3) educational association, SEJ works toward an informed society through excellence in environmental journalism. Members are journalists and educators united to enhance the quality, accuracy and visibility of reporting on environmental issues. Membership: $40/year (individual); $30/year (student).

Meetings/Conferences:
Annual Meetings: Fall/usually in a university setting
2007 – Palo Alto, CA(Stamford)

Publications:
SEJournal. q.

Society of Environmental Toxicology and Chemistry *(1979)*
1010 N. 12th Ave.
Pensacola, FL 32501-3367
Tel: (850)469-1500 *Fax:* (850)469-9778
E-Mail: setac@setac.org
Web Site: www.setac.org
Members: 4000 individuals
Staff: 11
Annual Budget: $2-5,000,000
Co-Executive Director: Greg Schiefer

Historical Note
SETAC is a professional society established to promote the use of multidisciplinary approaches to solving problems of the impact of chemicals and technology on the environment. SETAC members are professionals in the fields of chemistry, toxicology, biology, ecology, atmospheric sciences, health sciences, earth sciences, and environmental engineering. Membership: $110/year (individual); $2,000/year (sustaining member).

Meetings/Conferences:
Annual Meetings: Fall

Publications:
SETAC Globe. bi-m. adv.
Environmental Toxicology and Chemistry. m. adv.
Integrated Environmental Assessment and Management. q. adv.

Society of Ethnobiology *(1978)*
Univ. North Carolina - CH, Anthropology Dept.
Alumni Bldg., CB 3115
Chapel Hill, NC 27599-3115
Tel: (919)962-3841 *Fax:* (919)962-1613
Web Site: www.ethnobiology.org
Members: 530individualsandinstitutions
Annual Budget: $10-25,000
Secretary-Treasurer: Margaret Searry, PhD

Historical Note
Members are individuals and institutions with an interest in the study of the interactions of plants and animals with and within the human cultural environment. Has no paid officers or full-time staff. Membership: $35/year (individual); $80/year (organization/company).

Meetings/Conferences:
Annual Meetings: Spring/200 Reno, NV(University of Nevada)

Publications:
Journal of Ethnobiology. semi-a. adv.

Society of Experimental Test Pilots *(1955)*
P.O. Box 986
Lancaster, CA 93584-0986
Tel: (661)942-9574 *Fax:* (661)940-0398
E-Mail: setp@setp.org
Web Site: www.setp.org
Members: 2000 individuals
Staff: 4

Annual Budget: $100-250,000
Executive Director: Paula S. Smith

Historical Note

Founded September 14, 1955 and incorporated in California in 1956. Sponsors the Society of Experimental Test Pilots Scholarship Foundation. Has an international membership including members from 30 countries. Membership: $110/year (member); $100/year (associate member).

Meetings/Conferences:

Annual Meetings: June in Europe and Fall in Los Angeles.

Publications:

Report to the Aerospace Profession. a.
Cockpit magazine. q.

Society of Exploration Geophysicists *(1930)*

P.O. Box 702740
Tulsa, OK 74170-2740
Tel: (918)497-5500 *Fax:* (918)497-5557
Web Site: www.seg.org
Members: 20000 individuals
Staff: 49
Annual Budget: $5-10,000,000
Executive Director: Mary L. Fleming
Director, Publications: Ted Bakamjian
Director, Finance and Operations: Nancy Carter
Director, Meetings and Marketing: Jim Lawnick
Director, Geophysics: Peter Pangman
Director: Art Schrader

Historical Note

Founded in Houston in 1930 and incorporated in Oklahoma. Has an annual budget of approximately $9 million. Membership: $75/year (individual); $1,000/year (company).

Meetings/Conferences:

Annual Meetings: Fall

Publications:

Geophysics. bi-m. adv.
The Leading Edge of Exploration. m. adv.
Yearbook. a. adv.

Society of Eye Surgeons *(1969)*

10801 Connecticut Ave.
Kensington, MD 20895
Tel: (240)290-0263 *Fax:* (240)290-0269
E-Mail: ie@iefusa.org
Web Site: www.iefusa.org/
Members: 100 individuals
Staff: 12
Annual Budget: $2-5,000,000
Executive Director: Victoria M. Sheffield
Public Affairs Officer: Calvin Baerveldt

Historical Note

An auxiliary of the International Eye Foundation (same address). The purpose of SES is to assist programs dedicated to the restoration of sight/prevention of blindness. Promotes understanding of blindness. SES annual meetings are held in conjunction with the American Academy of Ophthalmology. Membership: $50-200/year.

Publications:

Eye To Eye Newsletter. semi-a.

Society of Federal Labor and Employee Relations Professionals *(1972)*

P.O. Box 25112
Arlington, VA 22202
Tel: (703)685-4130 *Fax:* (703)685-1144
Web Site: www.sflerp.org
Members: 500 individuals
Staff: 1
Annual Budget: $50-100,000
Executive Director: Francisco J. Martinez-Alvarez
E-Mail: sflerp@sflerp.org

Historical Note

Formerly (2002) Society of Federal Labor Relations Professionals. Membership is open to representatives of unions and management and neutrals. Membership: $50/year (individual); $10/year (students).

Publications:

SFLERP Reporter Newsletter. q. adv.
Occasional Papers. irreg.

Society of Financial Examiners *(1973)*

174 Grace Blvd.
Altamonte Springs, FL 32714
Tel: (407)682-4930 *Fax:* (407)682-3175
Toll Free: (800)787 - 7633
E-Mail: info@sofe.org
Web Site: www.sofe.org
Members: 1700 individuals
Staff: 1
Annual Budget: $250-500,000
Executive Director: Paula Keyes

Historical Note

Membership: $65-250/year (individual).

Meetings/Conferences:

Annual Meetings: July/500

Publications:

The Examiner. q.
The INSIGHT. m.

Society of Financial Service Professionals *(1928)*

17 Campus Blvd., Suite 201
Newtown Square, PA 19073-3230
Tel: (610)526-2513 *Fax:* (610)527-4010
Toll Free: (800)927 - 2427 Ext: 2513
E-Mail: custserv@financialpro.org
Web Site: www.financialpro.org
Members: 19000 individuals
Staff: 43
Annual Budget: $5-10,000,000
Chief Executive Officer: Joseph E. Frack, CPA
E-Mail: jfrack@financialpro.org
Chief Financial Officer: Donna Conrad, ChFC
E-Mail: dconrad@financialpro.org
Chief Information Officer: Brian Horn
E-Mail: bhorn@financialpro.org
Managing Director, Professional Development and Corporate Services: Marshall Lipson, CLU
E-Mail: mlipson@financialpro.org
Managing Director, Computer Services and Membership: G. Ron MacDonald, CLU
E-Mail: rmacdona@financialpro.org
Director, Publications: Mary Anne Mennite
E-Mail: mmennite@financialpro.org
General Counsel: Anne M. Rigney
E-Mail: arigney@financialpro.org
Director, Public Relations: Lisa Wetherby
Vice President, Marketing and Communications: Asha Williams, Ph.D.
E-Mail: awilliams@financialpro.org

Historical Note

A multidisciplinary network of credentialed professionals working to advance education and ethical guidance for the nation's top financial advisers. Society members assist the public in their efforts to achieve personal and business-related financial goals.

Meetings/Conferences:

2007 - Tucson, AZ(Omni Tucson National Golf Resort & Spa)/Jan. 7-11
2007 - Montreal, QC, Canada(Hilton Montreal Bonaventure)/Sept. 27-29

Publications:

Newsletters for Professional Interest Sections. q.
Society Page. q.
E-Bulletin. m.
Journal of the SFSP. bi-m. adv.
Keeping Current. q.

Society of Fire Protection Engineers *(1950)*

7315 Wisconsin Ave., Suite 1225W
Bethesda, MD 20814
Tel: (301)718-2910 *Fax:* (301)718-2242
E-Mail: sfpehqtrs@sfpe.org
Web Site: www.sfpe.org
Members: 4150 individuals
Staff: 6
Annual Budget: $1-2,000,000
Executive Director: David D. Evans
Technical Director: Morgan Hurley

Historical Note

Founded October 31, 1950, as the professional section of the National Fire Protection Association. Became independent of the NFPA on Feb. 10, 1971. Membership: $185/year.

Meetings/Conferences:

Annual Meetings: With Nat'l Fire Protection Ass'n in Spring.

Publications:

SFPE Today Newsletter. bi-m.
Fire Protection Engineering Magazine. q.
Roster. a.
Proceedings. a.
Journal of Fire Protection Engineering. q.

Society of Flavor Chemists *(1959)*

3301 Rte. 66, Suite 205 Bldg. C
Neptune, NJ 07753
Tel: (732)922-3393 *Fax:* (732)922-3590
E-Mail: administrator@flavorchemist.org
Web Site: www.flavorchemist.org
Members: 500 individuals
Staff: 5
Annual Budget: $25-50,000
Administrator: Bob Bauer
E-Mail: bobbauer@afius.org

Historical Note

Sponsors symposia and related opportunities for the advancement of flavor technology.

Meetings/Conferences:

Annual Meetings: May

Publications:

Newsletter. 3/year.

Society of Flight Test Engineers *(1968)*

44814 N. Elm Ave.
Lancaster, CA 93534
Tel: (661)949-2095 *Fax:* (661)949-2096
E-Mail: sfte@sfte.org
Web Site: www.sfte.org
Members: 975 individuals
Staff: 1
Annual Budget: $50-100,000
Executive Director: Margaret Drury
E-Mail: sfte@sfte.org

Historical Note

Members are engineers whose principal professional interest is flight and ground testing of aerospace vehicles. Purpose of the Society is to improve communications in the fields of flight test operations, analysis, instrumentation and data systems. Membership: $48/year (individual); graduated scale per annual revenue (company).

Meetings/Conferences:

Annual Meetings: Fall/150
2007 - St. Louis, MO/July 30-Aug. 3

Publications:

SFTE Newsletter. m.
International Symposium Proceedings. a.
Flight Test News.

Society of Forensic Toxicologists *(1970)*

P.O. Box 5543
Mesa, AZ 85211-5543
Tel: (480)839-9106
E-Mail: info@soft-tox.org
Web Site: www.soft-tox.org
Members: 621 individuals
Annual Budget: $50-100,000
Newsletter Editor: Joseph Monforte

Historical Note

SOFT members are practicing forensic toxicologists and others with an interest in the analysis of tissue and bodily fluids for drugs and/or poisons and the interpretation of the information generated from such analyses in a judicial context. Membership: $50/year (full and associate); $15/year (student).

Meetings/Conferences:

Annual Meetings: October

Publications:

ToxTalk. q.
The Forensic Toxicology Laboratory Guidelines.
Membership Directory. a.

Society of Former Special Agents of the Federal Bureau of Investigation *(1937)*

P.O. Box 1027
Quantico, VA 22134-1027
Tel: (703)640-6469 *Fax:* (703)640-6537
E-Mail: socxfbi@socxfbi.org
Web Site: www.socxfbi.org
Members: 8000 individuals
Staff: 7
Annual Budget: $500-1,000,000

Executive Director: Scott Erskine

Historical Note

Founded and incorporated in New York in 1937. Created the Former Agents of the F.B.I. Foundation which assists needy members, deceased members' families, rehabilitation of the ill and education. Membership: $80/year.

Meetings/Conferences:

Annual Meetings: Fall

Publications:

The Grapevine Magazine. m.
Directory. a.

Society of Gastroenterology Nurses and Associates *(1973)*

401 N. Michigan Ave.
Chicago, IL 60611-4267
Tel: (312)321-5165 *Fax:* (312)527-6658
Toll Free: (800)245 - 7462
E-Mail: sgna@smithbucklin.com
Web Site: www.sgna.org
Members: 7000 individuals
Staff: 6
Annual Budget: $1-2,000,000

Historical Note

Formerly (1989) the Society of Gastrointestinal Assistants. SGNA members are nurses and other allied health care individuals working in the fields of gastroenterology/endoscopy. Membership: $105/year (individual); $90/year (affiliate).

Meetings/Conferences:

Annual Meetings: Spring/1,500

Publications:

SGNA News. m. adv.
Gastroenterology Nursing. q. adv.

Society of Gastrointestinal Radiologists *(1971)*

4550 Post Oak Place, Suite 342
Houston, TX 77027
Tel: (713)965-0566 *Fax:* (713)960-0488
E-Mail: administration@sgr.org
Web Site: www.sgr.org
Members: 319 individuals
Staff: 9
Executive Director: Lynne K. Tiras, CMP

Historical Note

SGR members are radiologists with an interest in diseases of the gastrointestinal tract.

Meetings/Conferences:

2007 – Naples, FL(Hyatt Regency Resort and Spa)/Apr. 15-20

Society of General Internal Medicine *(1978)*

2501 M St. NW
Suite 575
Washington, DC 20037
Tel: (202)887-5150 *Fax:* (202)887-5405
Toll Free: (800)822 - 3060
E-Mail: info@sgim.org
Web Site: www.sgim.org
Members: 2800 individuals
Staff: 9
Annual Budget: $1-2,000,000
Executive Director: David Karlson, Ph.D.
E-Mail: KarlsonD@sgim.org

Historical Note

Members are health professionals interested in teaching and research related to general and primary care internal medicine. Membership: $305/year (full member); $95/year (associate).

Meetings/Conferences:

Annual Meetings: Spring/1,600
2007 – Toronto, ON, Canada(Sheraton)/Apr. 25-28

Publications:

Journal of General Internal Medicine and Supplement. m. adv.
SGIM PCIM Internal Medicine.
SGIM PCIM Residency Programs Directory. bien.
SGIM Directory of General Internal Medicine Fellowship Programs. bien.
SGIM Forum newsletter. m. adv.
SGIM E-News (online). m.

Society of General Physiologists *(1946)*

P.O. Box 257
Woods Hole, MA 02543-0257
Tel: (508)540-6719 *Fax:* (508)540-0155
E-Mail: sgp@mbl.edu
Web Site: http://cellbio.emory.edu/sgp/
Members: 850 individuals
Staff: 2
Annual Budget: $10-25,000
Executive Secretary: Susan Shephard

Historical Note

Founded in 1946 at the Marine Biological Laboratory, Woods Hole, and incorporated in Massachusetts in 1966. Affiliate of the American Association for the Advancement of Science, International Union of Physiological Sciences, the National Research Council, International Union of Pure and Applied Biophysics, and the American Physiological Society Membership: $55/year.

Meetings/Conferences:

Annual Meetings: Woods Hole, MA(Marine Biological Lab.)/September/300

Publications:

Journal of General Physiology. m.

Society of Geriatric Cardiology *(1986)*

2400 N St. NW
Second Floor
Washington, DC 20036
Tel: (202)375-6199 *Fax:* (202)375-6839
E-Mail: sgcadmin@sgcard.org
Web Site: www.sgcard.org
Members: 500 individuals
Staff: 1
Annual Budget: $100-250,000
President: Richard Steingart, M.D.

Historical Note

SGC was incorporated to meet the problems resulting from cardiovascular diseases in increasing numbers of aging men and women in the United States and around the world. Membership is open to all health care professionals who have demonstrated a commitment to geriatric cardiology and who have been certified in their area of professional expertise by an appropriate agency. Membership: $95/year (physician); $50/year (associate); $50/year (trainee); $150/year (fellowship).

Meetings/Conferences:

Annual Meetings: March

Publications:

American Journal of Geriatric Cardiology. bi-m. adv.
SGC newsletter. q.

Society of Glass and Ceramic Decorators *(1963)*

47 N. Fourth St.
P.O. Box 2489
Zanesville, OH 43702
Tel: (740)588-9882 *Fax:* (740)588-0245
E-Mail: sgcd@sgcd.org
Web Site: www.sgcd.org
Members: 750 individuals
Staff: 4
Annual Budget: $500-1,000,000
Contact: Myra Smitley

Historical Note

Formerly (1984) the Society of Glass Decorators. SGCD serves members, including retailers and suppliers of commercial decorators of mugs, dinnerware, tile, glass packaging, auto window glass, and other glass and ceramic products. Membership: $250/year (individual); $1,000/year (company).

Publications:

Newsletter. adv.
SGCD Directory. adv.
Glossary of Glass & Ceramic Decorating Technology.
SGCD Seminar Program.

Society of Government Economists *(1970)*

P.O. Box 77082
Washington, DC 20013
Tel: (410)963-0134
Toll Free: (877)743 - 3266
E-Mail: sge@paintedcup.net
Web Site: www.sge-econ.org
Members: 500 individuals

Historical Note

Members are economists employed in the public sector or who are interested in the economic aspects of government policies. Has no paid officers or full-time staff. Membership: $30/year (individual); $40/year (household/supporting); $100/year (organization/company); $150/year (institutional); $10/year (student).

Publications:

SGE Bulletin. m.
Newsletter.
Membership Directory. bi-a.

Society of Government Meeting Professionals *(1980)*

908 King St., Lower Level
Alexandria, VA 22314
Tel: (703)549-0892 *Fax:* (703)549-0708
Toll Free: (800)827 - 8916
E-Mail: info@sgmp.org
Web Site: www.sgmp.org
Members: 3000 individuals
Staff: 5
Executive Director: Carl C. Thompson
E-Mail: carl.c.thompson@sgmp.org

Historical Note

Formerly (1996) Society of Government Meeting Planners. Members are persons involved in planning government meetings and individuals who supply services to government planners. Membership: $50-300/year.

Meetings/Conferences:

Annual Meetings: Spring-Summer

Publications:

Advantage Magazine. q. adv.
Newsletter. m. adv.

Society of Government Service Urologists *(1952)*

P.O. Box 681965
San Antonio, TX 78268-7202
Tel: (210)681-0587 *Fax:* (210)680-7725
E-Mail: sgsu@txdirect.net
Web Site: http://home.satx.rr.com/sgsu/
Members: 731 individuals
Staff: 2
Annual Budget: $100-250,000
Administrator: Preston Littrell

Historical Note

Membership: $50/year (individual); $800/year (organization).

Publications:

SGSU Newsletter. q.

Society of Government Travel Professionals *(1983)*

6935 Wisconsin Ave., Suite 200
Bethesda, MD 20815-6109
Tel: (301)654-8595 *Fax:* (301)654-6663
E-Mail: govtvlmkt@aol.com
Web Site: www.sgtp.org
Members: 530 organizations
Staff: 3
Annual Budget: $250-500,000
General Manager: Duncan G. Farrell, CMP

Historical Note

Formerly (2000) Society of Travel Agents in Government. SGTP was established for professional development of all organizations that provide travel services to government through mentoring and education; to promote professional standards for the procurement and operation of government travel; and to otherwise advance the interest of travel managers. SGTP members are ARC-appointed travel agents holding government travel contracts or servicing government contractors, suppliers and government or contractor travel managers. Membership: $195-450/year (by category).

Meetings/Conferences:

Semi-Annual Meetings: February and September/450

Publications:

Accessibility of Federal Government Travel Rates. a.
Membership Directory. semi-a. adv.
SGTP Report Magazine. m. adv.
SGTP 101: Principles of Government Travel Management. semi-a. adv.

State & Provincial Travel Procurement Practices & Procedures. a. adv.

Society of Gynecologic Oncologists *(1969)*
401 N. Michigan Ave.
Chicago, IL 60611
Tel: (312)321-4099 *Fax:* (312)673-6959
E-Mail: sgo@sgo.org
Web Site: www.sgo.org
Members: 1000 individuals
Staff: 7
Annual Budget: $2-5,000,000
Executive Director: Mary Eiken

Historical Note
Formerly (1994) Society of Gynecological Oncologists. Founded in 1969 by a small group of doctors interested in advancing knowledge and raising standards of practice in gynecologic oncology within the disciplines of obstetrics and gynecology. Membership: $480/year + $70 journal subscription (individual).

Meetings/Conferences:
Annual Meetings: February-March
2007 - San Diego, CA(Manchester Grand Hyatt)/March 3-7
2008 - Miami, FL(Fountainebleau Hilton Resort)/March 15-29
2009 - New Orleans, LA(Marriott)/March 7-11

Society of Hispanic Professional Engineers *(1974)*
5400 E. Olympic Blvd., Suite 210
Los Angeles, CA 90022
Tel: (323)725-3970 *Fax:* (323)725-0316
Web Site: www.shpe.org
Members: 10000 individuals
Staff: 10
National President: Diana Gomez
Executive Assistant: Lourdes Arce

Historical Note
Absorbed the Society of Hispanic Engineers in 1974. Membership: $45/year (individual); $500 lifetime (individual).

Meetings/Conferences:
Semi-Annual Meetings: February and June

Publications:
SHPE Magazine. q. adv.

Society of Illustrators *(1901)*
128 E. 63rd St.
New York, NY 10021-7303
Tel: (212)838-2560 *Fax:* (212)838-2561
Web Site: www.societyillustrators.org
Members: 900 individuals
Staff: 6
Annual Budget: $500-1,000,000
Director: Terrence Brown

Historical Note
A professional society of illustrators and art directors founded in New York in 1901 by ten of America's leading illustrators. Established a Hall of Fame in 1958 to recognize distinguished achievement in the field of illustration and a Museum of American Illustration in 1981. Most members come from the New York area. Membership: $448/year (resident artist); $272/year (non-resident); $1,500/year (corporate).

Meetings/Conferences:
Monthly Meetings:

Publications:
Annual of American Illustration. a. adv.

Society of Incentive & Travel Executives *(1973)*
401 N. Michigan Ave.
Chicago, IL 60611
Tel: (312)321-5148 *Fax:* (312)527-6783
E-Mail: hq@site-intl.org
Web Site: www.site-intl.org
Members: 1800 individuals
Staff: 10
Annual Budget: $2-5,000,000
Executive Director and Chief Executive Officer: Brenda Anderson

Historical Note
Formerly (1996) Society of Incentive Travel Executives. SITE is an individual membership society covering 70 countries. Members are: corporate users, airlines, Tourist Boards, cruise lines, destination management companies, consultants, hotels/resorts, travel agents, incentive travel houses and publications. Membership: $375/year.

Meetings/Conferences:
Annual Meetings: Summer

Publications:
Resource Directory. a. adv.
In-SITE Magazine. bi-m. adv.

Society of Independent Gasoline Marketers of America *(1958)*
11495 Sunset Hills Road, Suite 215
Reston, VA 20190
Tel: (703)709-7000 *Fax:* (703)709-7007
E-Mail: sigma@sigma.org
Web Site: www.sigma.org
Members: 270 companies, 75 associates
Staff: 10
Annual Budget: $2-5,000,000
Executive Vice President: Kenneth A. Doyle, CAE

Historical Note
Members are independent gasoline marketers. Sponsors and supports the SIGMA Political Action Committee. Absorbed the Southeast Independent Oil Marketers Association in 1988. Membership: $600-15,000/year.

Meetings/Conferences:
Semi-Annual Meetings: April and November

Publications:
Independent Gasoline Marketing. bi-m. adv.

Society of Independent Professional Earth Scientists *(1963)*
4925 Greenville Ave., Suite 1106
Dallas, TX 75206-4008
Tel: (214)363-1780 *Fax:* (214)363-8195
E-Mail: sipes@sipes.org
Web Site: www.sipes.org
Members: 1400 individuals
Staff: 2
Executive Director: Diane M. Finstrom

Historical Note
Founded in Houston, TX and chartered as a professional and scientific scoiety in 1963, SIPES is a member society of the American Geological Institute and a cooperative association with the Independent Petroleum Association of America. Members are geologists, geophysicists, engineers and other earth scientists with at least twelve years professional experience who are independent or self-employed. Sponsors and supports the SIPES Foundation, a charitable and educational foundation, chartered in Texas in 1981. Membership: $75/year.

Publications:
SIPES Newsletter. q. adv.
Membership Directory. a. adv.

Society of Independent Show Organizers *(1990)*
7000 W. Southwest Hwy.
Chicago Ridge, IL 60415
Tel: (708)361-0900 *Fax:* (708)361-6166
Toll Free: (877)937 - 7476
Web Site: www.siso.org
Members: 206 companies
Staff: 2
Annual Budget: $250-500,000
Executive Director: Mary Beth Rebedeau
E-Mail: mbrebedeau@aol.com

Historical Note
Membership: $295-$1825/year (organization/company).

Meetings/Conferences:
Annual Meetings: Spring; Summer, Executive Conference

Publications:
SISO Update. w.
VIP Directory. 2/year. adv.
News Now! (online).

Society of Industrial and Office REALTORS *(1941)*
1201 New York Ave. NW
Suite 350
Washington, DC 20005-3917
Tel: (202)449-8200 *Fax:* (202)216-9325
E-Mail: admin@sior.com
Web Site: www.sior.com
Members: 2800 individuals
Staff: 17
Annual Budget: $2-5,000,000
Executive Vice President: Richard E. Hollander
Chief Financial Officer: Tess Esposito
Vice President, Marketing: Pamela Fitzgerald
Vice President and Chief Operating Officer: Robert Hammond
E-Mail: rhammond@sior.com
Director, Communications: Linda Nasvaderani
E-Mail: lnasvaderani@sior.com

Historical Note
A professional affiliate of the National Association of Realtors, SIR was founded in Washington just prior to World War II at the instigation of the War Department to help locate specialized facilities suitable for the production of military equipment. Incorporated in the State of Illinois. Active members are brokers, consultants and appraisers. Formerly (1986) Society of Industrial Realtors. Supports the REALTORS Political Action Committee (RPAC). Membership: $935/year (active members).

Meetings/Conferences:
Semi-Annual Meetings: Spring and Fall

Publications:
Executive's Guide to Specialists in Office and Industrial Real Estate. a.
Professional Report of Industrial and Office Real Estate. q. adv.

Society of Infectious Diseases Pharmacists
823 Congress Ave.
Suite 230
Austin, TX 78701
Tel: (512)479-0425 *Fax:* (512)495-9031
E-Mail: sidp@eami.com
Web Site: www.sidp.org
Contact: Melinda Neuhauser

Historical Note
SIDP members are pharmacists actively engaged in infectious disease pharmacotherapy and research. Membership: $35/year (active or associate U.S. member); $25/year (trainee-associate).

Publications:
SIDP Newsletter. 3/year.
News Update. m.

Society of Insurance Financial Management *(1959)*
P.O. Box 9001
Mt. Vernon, NY 10552
Tel: (914)966-3180 Ext: 115 *Fax:* (914)966-3264
E-Mail: info@sifm.org
Web Site: www.sifm.org
Members: 700 individuals
Staff: 1
Annual Budget: $100-250,000
Administrative Director: Carole H. Acunto

Historical Note
Formerly (1994) Society of Insurance Accountants. Formed in 1959 by a merger of the Insurance Accountants Association and the Association of Casualty Accountants and Statisticians. Membership: $125/year (individual).

Meetings/Conferences:
Annual Meetings: Fall

Society of Insurance Research *(1970)*
691 Cross Fire Road
Marietta, GA 30064-1394
Tel: (770)426-9270 *Fax:* (770)426-9298
Web Site: www.sirnet.org
Members: 450 individuals
Staff: 3
Annual Budget: $100-250,000
Executive Director: Stanley M. Hopp
E-Mail: stanhopp@mindspring.com

Historical Note
Founded under the sponsorship of the Griffith Foundation for Insurance Education and Ohio State University to provide a communication channel and forum for the exchange of research ideas. Members are individuals actively engaged in some form of insurance research. Membership: $185/year

(individual); $2000/year (corporate or associate corporate).

Meetings/Conferences:
Annual Meetings: November

Publications:
SIR Newsletter. q. adv.

Society of Insurance Trainers and Educators *(1953)*
2120 Market St., Suite 108
San Francisco, CA 94114
Tel: (415)621-2830 *Fax:* (415)621-0889
E-Mail: ed@insurancetrainers.org
Web Site: www.insurancetrainers.org
Members: 800 individuals
Staff: 1
Annual Budget: $100-250,000
Executive Director: Lois A. Markovich, CPCU, AIM

Historical Note
Formerly (1985) Insurance Company Education Directors Society Membership composed of education and training personnel, personnel directors, and those responsible for the training function in insurance. Voting Membership: $125/year (designee); $95/year (associate); $45/year (retiree).

Meetings/Conferences:
Annual Meetings: June
2007 – Los Angeles, CA(Hollywood Renaisance)/June 22-28/250

Publications:
The Journal. a.
In-Site. bi-m.

Society of International Business Fellows
600 Peachtree St. NW
Suite 490
Atlanta, GA 30308-3621
Tel: (404)525-7423 *Fax:* (404)525-5331
E-Mail: info@sibf.org
Web Site: www.sibf.org
Members: 480 individuals
President: Astrid Pregel

Society of Interventional Radiology *(1973)*
3975 Fair Ridge Drive, Suite 400 North
Fairfax, VA 22033
Tel: (703)691-1805 *Fax:* (703)691-1855
Toll Free: (800)488 - 7284
E-Mail: info@sirweb.org
Web Site: www.sirweb.org
Members: 4800 individuals
Staff: 25
Annual Budget: $2-5,000,000
Executive Director: Peter B. Lauer
Marketing Manager: Marcia Cram
Director, Corporate Relations: Beverlee Galstan
Assistant Executive Director: Michael R. Mabry
Associate Executive Director: Tricia McClenny

Historical Note
Founded as Society of Cardiovascular and Interventional Radiology; assumed its current name in 2003. SIR is a non-profit, national scientific organization committed to improving health and the quality of life through the practice of cardiovascular and interventional radiology. The society promotes education, research, quality of care and communication in the field. Membership: $500/year (individual); $2,000/year (corporate).

Meetings/Conferences:
Annual Meetings: Spring

Publications:
Journal of Vascular & Interventional Radiology. bi-m. adv.
SCVIR News. bi-m.

Society of Invasive Cardiovascular Professionals *(1992)*
1500 Sunday Dr. Suite 102
Raleigh, NC 27607
Tel: (919)861-4546 *Fax:* (919)787-4916
E-Mail: director@sicp.com
Web Site: www.sicp.com
President: Roger Siegfried
E-Mail: director@sicp.com

Historical Note
SICP members are cardiac catheter laboratory professionals. Membership: $95/year.

Publications:
Cath-Lab Digest. irreg.

Society of Laparoendoscopic Surgeons *(1990)*
7330 S.W. 62nd Place, Suite 410
Miami, FL 33143-4825
Tel: (305)665-9959 *Fax:* (305)667-4123
Toll Free: (800)446 - 2659
E-Mail: info@sls.org
Web Site: www.sls.org
Members: 6293 individuals
Staff: 7
Annual Budget: $500-1,000,000
Chairman: Paul Alan Wetter, M.D.
Officer, Operations: Janis Chinnock
Administrator of Operations: Linda Collier
Administrator and CME Coordinator: Susan Mazzola
Director, Membership Services: Flor Tilden
E-Mail: flor@sls.org

Historical Note
SLS members are surgeons from various specialties and other health professions who are interested in advancing their expertise in the diagnostic and therapeutic uses of laparoendoscopic techniques. Membership: $199/year (individual); $1,250/year (organization/company)

Meetings/Conferences:
Annual Meetings: December/500
2007 – San Francisco, CA(Hyatt Regency)/Sept. 5-8

Publications:
Laparoscopy & SLS Report. 2/yr. adv.
Conference Registration Booklet. a. adv.
Journal of the Society of Laparoendoscopic Surgeons. q. adv.

Society of Manufacturing Engineers *(1932)*
One SME Dr.
P.O. Box 930
Dearborn, MI 48121-0930
Tel: (313)425-3000 *Fax:* (313)425-3400
Toll Free: (800)733 - 4763
Web Site: www.sme.org/
Members: 66000 individuals
Staff: 260
Annual Budget: $25-50,000,000
Executive Director and General Manager: Mark Tomlinson
Director, Communications and Marketing: Karen Manardo
Director, Expositions: Gary Mikola

Historical Note
Founded as the American Society of Tool Engineers; became the American Society of Tool and Manufacturing Engineers in 1960 and assumed its current name in 1969. SME is a professional society dedicated to advancing scientific knowledge in the field of manufacturing and to applying its resources for researching, writing, publishing and disseminating information. Supports a number of associations and technical groups, including: Association for Electronics Manufacturing, Association for Finishing Processes, Composites Manufacturing Association, Computer and Automated Systems Association, Forming Technologies Association, Machine Vision Association, Machining Technology Association, Networking and Communications in Manufacturing Group, North American Manufacturing Research Institution, Plastics Molders and Manufacturers Association, Rapid Prototyping Association, and Robotics International. Sponsors the Manufacturing Engineering Education Foundation and the Manufacturing Engineering Certification Institute, which grants the ""CMFgE'' (Certified Manufacturing Engineer), ""CMFgT'' (Certified Manufacturing Technologist), and CEI (Certified Enterprise Intergrator) designations. Has members in 70 countries and several hundred chapters around the world. Membership: $99 (one-year individual membership); $178.20 (two-year individual membership); $252.45 (three-year individual membership); plus $15 initiation fee for all new members; $156.80 (one-year reciprocal membership in SME and AME); $291.20 (two-year reciprocal membership in SME and AME); $170.24 (one-year reciprocal membership in SME and IIE).

Meetings/Conferences:
Annual Meetings: May

Publications:
Manufacturing Engineering. m. adv.

Society of Marine Consultants *(1982)*

Historical Note
Address unknown in 2006.

Society of Marine Port Engineers *(1946)*
P.O. Box 369
Eatontown, NJ 07724
Tel: (732)389-2009 *Fax:* (732)389-2264
Web Site: www.smpe.org
Members: 550 individuals
Staff: 1
Annual Budget: $50-100,000
Contact: Diane Moore
E-Mail: dmoore@smpe.org

Historical Note
Membership: $75/year.

Meetings/Conferences:
Annual Meetings: May, in New York, NY

Publications:
The De-Air-Ator. q.

Society of Maritime Arbitrators *(1963)*
30 Broad St., Seventh Floor
New York, NY 10004-2304
Tel: (212)344-2400 *Fax:* (212)344-2402
E-Mail: info@smany.org
Web Site: www.smany.org
Members: 100 individuals
Staff: 1
Annual Budget: $50-100,000
President: Klaus C.J. Mordhorst

Historical Note
Members are drawn from such fields as surveying, engineering, finance, brokerage, stevedoring, construction, repairs, sales, insurance, and terminal and vessel operations; bulk of membership is in the New York area. SMA's purpose is to help settle disputes arising from contracts for and all movements by water or involving shipbuilding and repair, and to maintain uniformity in U.S. maritime arbitration proceedings.

Publications:
The Arbitrator. q.

Society of Medical Administrators *(1914)*
D-3300 Medical Ctr. North, Vanderbilt Univ.
Nashville, TN 37232
Tel: (615)322-2156 *Fax:* (615)343-7286
Members: 100 individuals
Staff: 1
Annual Budget: under $10,000
President: Harry R. Jacobson, M.D.

Historical Note
Membership limited to 50 physicians active in administrative medicine.

Meetings/Conferences:
Annual Meetings: January/65-70

Publications:
Directory. a.
Minutes of Annual Meeting. a.

Society of Medical Consultants to the Armed Forces *(1946)*
Five Southern Way
Fredericksburg, VA 22406
Tel: (540)361-2587 *Fax:* (540)361-2589
E-Mail: smcaf@usuhs.mil
Web Site: www.smcaf.org
Members: 700 individuals
Staff: 1
Annual Budget: $10-25,000
Executive Director: Margo Cabrero

Historical Note
Organized by specialists who were consultants to the Armed Forces during World War II, SMCAF now includes individuals who have been consultants at any time to the Armed Services. Formerly Society of U.S. Medical Consultants in W.W. II.

Meetings/Conferences:
Annual Meetings: Fall, in Washington, DC

Publications:
Roster. irreg.
Newsletter. 4/year.

Society of Medical-Dental Management Consultants *(1968)*
125 Strafford Ave., Suite 300
Wayne, PA 19087
Tel: (610)687-7718 *Fax:* (610)687-7702
Toll Free: (800)826 - 2264
E-Mail: patricia01@aol.com
Web Site: www.smdmc.org
Members: 60 individuals
Staff: 2
Annual Budget: $50-100,000
Executive Secretary: Patricia Salmon

Historical Note
A professional society established in Kansas City, Missouri by 20 charter members in 1968. Membership: $450/year.

Meetings/Conferences:
Semi-Annual Meetings: Summer and Fall

Publications:
Membership Directory. irreg.
Consultant's Newsletter. m. adv.

Society of Mexican American Engineers and Scientists *(1974)*
711 W. Bay Area Blvd.
Suite 206
Webster, TX 77598
Tel: (281)557-3677 *Fax:* (281)557-3757
E-Mail: execdir@maes-natl.org
Web Site: www.maes-natl.org
Members: 6000 individuals
Staff: 3
Annual Budget: $500-1,000,000
Program Director: Keith Marrocco

Historical Note
MAES fosters cooperation among industrial, governmental, academic and professional communities to improve educational and employment opportunities for Mexican-Americans in engineering and science. Provides forums for technical presentations and runs educational assistance programs. Membership: $50/year (professional); $10/year (student); $500/year (organization/company).

Meetings/Conferences:
Annual Meetings: 1st Quarter

Publications:
MAES National Magazine. q. adv.
Annual MAES Symposium Proceedings and Career Fair. a. adv.

Society of Military Orthopaedic Surgeons *(1958)*
8610 New Braunfels Ave., Suite 705
San Antonio, TX 78217
Tel: (210)829-1239 Ext: 233 *Fax:* (210)829-5513
Toll Free: (888)329 - 1239
E-Mail: j.bennett@trueresearch.org
Web Site: www.trueresearch.org/somos
Members: 600 individuals
Staff: 1
Annual Budget: $25-50,000
Conference Director: Jennifer Bennett

Historical Note
SOMOS members are orthopedic surgeons who are on active duty or who have served in the armed forces.

Meetings/Conferences:
Annual Meetings: Fall-Winter
2007 – Vail, CO(Marriott)/Dec. 10-15

Society of Military Otolaryngologists - Head and Neck Surgeons *(1952)*
P.O. Box 923
Converse, TX 78109
Tel: (210)945-9006 *Fax:* (210)945-9024
Web Site: www.miloto.org
Members: 309 individuals
Staff: 1
Annual Budget: under $10,000
Administrative Secretary: M. Sue Pearce

Historical Note
Members are residents in training and otolaryngologists on active duty or who have served in the armed forces. Has no paid officers or full-time staff. Membership: $15/year (individual).

Meetings/Conferences:
Annual Meetings: In conjunction with the American Academy of Otolaryngology/September

Society of Mineral Analysts *(1986)*
P.O. Box 404
Lewiston, ID 83501
E-Mail: webmaster@sma-online.org
Web Site: www.sma-online.org
Members: 250 individuals
Annual Budget: $10-25,000
Managing Secretary: Patrick Braun
E-Mail: webmaster@sma-online.org

Historical Note
SMA promotes cooperation in the minerals industry. Membership: $30 initiation; $20/year.

Meetings/Conferences:
Annual Meetings: Spring/Typical Attendance: 140

Publications:
Proceedings of Annual Conference. a. adv.

Society of Motion Picture and Television Engineers *(1916)*
Three Barker Ave.
White Plains, NY 10601
Tel: (914)761-1100 *Fax:* (914)761-3115
Web Site: www.smpte.org
Members: 10000 individuals
Staff: 13
Annual Budget: $2-5,000,000
Director, Operations: Sally-Ann D'Amato

Historical Note
Founded in 1916 as the Society of Motion Picture Engineers. Incorporated in the District of Columbia. Became the Society of Motion Picture and Television Engineers in 1950. Membership: $135/year (active); $35/year (student).

Meetings/Conferences:
Semi-annual Meetings:
2007 – Brooklyn, NY(Marriott)/Oct. 24-27

Publications:
Engineering Standards. irreg.
SMPTE Journal. m. adv.

Society of Multivariate Experimental Psychology *(1960)*
University of Oklahoma, Psychology Department
Norman, OK 73019
Tel: (405)325-4511 *Fax:* (405)325-4737
E-Mail: jrodger@psy.ou.edu
Web Site: www.smep.org
Members: 65 individuals
Staff: 1
Annual Budget: under $10,000
President: Joseph Rodgers

Historical Note
SMEP members are researchers in behavioral psychology. Has no paid officers or full-time staff. Membership is limited to 65 members, and is by invitation only.

Meetings/Conferences:
Annual Meetings: October

Publications:
Multivariate Behavioral Research. q. adv.

Society of Municipal Arborists *(1964)*
P.O. Box 641
Watkinsville, GA 30677
Tel: (706)769-7412 *Fax:* (706)769-7307
E-Mail: urbanforestry@prodigy.net
Web Site: www.urban-forestry.com
Members: 900 individuals
Staff: 1
Annual Budget: $50-100,000
Executive Director: Jerri LaHaie

Historical Note
Full-time municipal arborists and companies representing products in the field. Membership: $60/year (professional); $125/year (corporate).

Meetings/Conferences:
Annual Meetings: Fall

Publications:
City Trees. bi-m. adv.
Membership List. a.

Society of National Association Publications *(1963)*
8405 Greensboro Dr., Suite 800
McLean, VA 22102
Tel: (703)506-3285 *Fax:* (703)506-3266
E-Mail: llowery@snaponline.org
Web Site: www.snaponline.org
Members: 500 individuals
Staff: 10
Annual Budget: $250-500,000
Managing Director: Lee Lowery

Historical Note
SNAP members are editors and publishers of association and professional society magazines. Associate members are suppliers of products and services to association publications. Affiliate members are publications whose primary publication is already a member of SNAP. Membership: $295-795/year, based on net ad revenue (publication); $95/year (affiliate publication); $195-495/year, based on gross revenues (associate).

Meetings/Conferences:
Annual Meetings: June in Washington, DC

Publications:
Association Publishing. bi-m. adv.

Society of Naval Architects and Marine Engineers *(1893)*
601 Pavonia Ave., Suite 400
Jersey City, NJ 07306-3881
Tel: (201)798-4800 *Fax:* (201)798-4975
Toll Free: (800)798 - 2188
E-Mail: pkimball@sname.org
Web Site: www.sname.org
Members: 9000 individuals
Staff: 18
Annual Budget: $2-5,000,000
Executive Director: Philip B. Kimball

Historical Note
Incorporated in New York, April 28, 1893. Membership: $125/year (individual).

Meetings/Conferences:
Annual Meetings: Fall

Publications:
SNAME News. q. adv.
T & R News. q.
SNAME Newsletter. semi-m. adv.

Society of Nematologists *(1961)*
P.O. Box 311
Marceline, MO 64658
Tel: (660)256-3252
E-Mail: son@direcway.com
Web Site: www.nematologists.org
Members: 600 individuals
Annual Budget: $100-250,000
Secretary: Brent S. Sipes

Historical Note
Members are individuals interested in nematodes, such as roundworms or threadworms. Member of the American Institute of Biological Sciences. Has no paid officers or full-time staff. Membership: $30/year (student member); $60/year (individual regular member); $120/year (American institution/library); $140/year (foreign or international institution/library).

Meetings/Conferences:
Annual Meetings: Summer/300

Publications:
Journal of Nematology. q.
Nematology Newsletter. q.
Membership Directory. a.

Society of Neurological Surgeons *(1920)*
600 Highland Ave.
Madison, WI 53792
Tel: (608)263-9585 *Fax:* (608)263-1728
E-Mail: dempsey@neurosurg.wisc.edu
Web Site: www.societyns.org
Members: 200 individuals
Annual Budget: $10-25,000
Secretary: Robert J. Dempsey, M.D.

Historical Note
SNS is the honorary society of neurological surgery in the United States. Has no paid officers or full-time staff.

Meetings/Conferences:
Annual Meetings: Spring/250

Society of Neurosurgical Anesthesia and Critical Care *(1973)*
520 N. Northwest Hwy.
Park Ridge, IL 60068-2573
Tel: (847)825-5586 *Fax:* (847)825-5658
E-Mail: snacc@asahq.com
Web Site: www.snacc.org
Members: 500 individuals
Staff: 3
Annual Budget: $250-500,000
Executive Director: Gary W. Hoorman

Historical Note
Formerly (1987) Society of Neurosurgical Anesthesia and Neurological Supportive Care. Members are board-certified anesthesiologists or surgeons. Provides clinical education programs and other services to members. Membership: $125/year (full member); $25/year (residency/emeritus); w/JNA subscription $254/year or $154/year.

Meetings/Conferences:
Annual Meetings: October, with the American Soc. of Anesthesiologists

Publications:
Journal of Neurosurgical Anesthesiology. 4/year.
Selected References in Neurosurgical Anesthesia/Critical Care. bien.

Society of North American Goldsmiths *(1969)*
540 Oak St.
Suite A
Eugene, OR 97401
Tel: (541)345-5689 *Fax:* (541)345-1123
E-Mail: info@snagmetalsmith.org
Web Site: www.snagmetalsmith.org
Members: 2500 individuals
Staff: 3
Annual Budget: $500-1,000,000
Executive Director: Dana Singer
E-Mail: dsinger@snagmetalsmith.org

Historical Note
Concerned with the educational, scientific, and aesthetic aspects of goldsmithing and metalsmithing. Membership: $59/year.

Meetings/Conferences:
Annual Meetings: Spring/Summer

Publications:
Metalsmith. 5/year. adv.
Newsletter. 5/year.
Membership Directory. a.

Society of Nuclear Medicine *(1954)*
1850 Samuel Morse Dr.
Reston, VA 20190-5316
Tel: (703)708-9000 *Fax:* (703)708-9015
Web Site: www.snm.org
Members: 16000 individuals
Staff: 45
Annual Budget: $5-10,000,000
Chief Executive Officer: Virginia M. Pappas, CAE
E-Mail: vpappas@snm.org
Director, Education: Lynn Barnes
Director, Public Affairs and General Counsel: Hugh Cannon
Director, Membership Services: Diana Dawkins
E-Mail: ddawkins@snm.org
Director, Meeting Services: Jane Day
E-Mail: jday@snm.org
Director, Publications: Rebecca Maxey
Director, Marketing: Joanna Spahr
E-Mail: jspahr@snm.org

Historical Note
SNM is a multi-disciplinary professional medical organization dedicated to the advancement of excellence in the education, research and clinical practice of nuclear medicine. Society membership consists of physicians, physicists, chemists, radiapharmacists, nuclear medicine technologists, and others interested in nuclear medicine and the use of radioactive isotopes in clinical practice, research and teaching. Promotes, presents and publishes research and information concerning the utilization of nuclear phenomena in the diagnosis and treatment of disease. Annual budget is approximately $7 million. Membership: $240/year (individual, full); $150/year (associate); $103/year (technologist); $175/year (affiliate).

Meetings/Conferences:
Semi-annual Meetings: June and midwinter

Publications:
Journal of Nuclear Medicine. m. adv.
NewslineOnline.
Uptake Online.
Journal of Nuclear Medicine Technology. q. adv.

Society of Otorhinolaryngology and Head/Neck Nurses *(1976)*
116 Canal St., Suite A
New Smyrna Beach, FL 32168
Tel: (386)428-1695 *Fax:* (386)423-7566
E-Mail: info@sohnnurse.com
Web Site: www.sohnnurse.com
Members: 1200 individuals
Staff: 2
Executive Director: Sandra Schwartz, RN

Historical Note
SOHN members are nurses specializing in the care of patients with ear, nose and throat disorders and head and neck cancer.

Meetings/Conferences:
Annual Meetings: Annual
2007 – Washington, DC/Sept. 14-18
2008 – Chicago, IL/Sept. 19-23

Publications:
SOHN Update Newsletter. 6/year. adv.
SOHN Journal. q. adv.

Society of Park and Recreation Educators *(1966)*
Historical Note
An affiliate of National Recreation and Park Association (same address), which provides administrative support.

Society of Pediatric Nurses *(1990)*
7794 Grow Dr.
Pensacola, FL 32514-1350
Tel: (850)494-9467 *Fax:* (850)484-8762
Toll Free: (800)723 - 2902
E-Mail: spn@puetzamc.com
Web Site: www.pedsnurses.org
Members: 2000 individuals
Staff: 3
Account Executive: Patricia Barlow

Historical Note
SPN members are nurses specializing in the nursing care of children and families. Membership: $105/year.

Meetings/Conferences:
Annual Meetings: April
2007 – Milwaukee, WI(Hyatt Regency)/Apr. 14-15/500
2008 – Denver, CO(Grand Hyatt Denver)/Apr. 4-6/500

Publications:
Journal of Pediatric Nursing. bi-m. adv.
SPN News. bi-m. adv.

Society of Pediatric Psychology
Historical Note
A section of the American Psychological Association - Clinical Psychology Division.

Society of Pelvic Reconstructive Surgeons *(1996)*
P.O. Box 52107
Atlanta, GA 30355
Tel: (404)812-1526 *Fax:* (404)812-0442
E-Mail: info@sprs.org
Web Site: http://sprs.org
Executive Director: Patricia Kovac

Historical Note
SPRS members are practicing gynecological surgeons

Society of Pelvic Surgeons *(1952)*
Univ. of Iowa Hospitals, Division of Gynecologic Oncology
4630 JCP
Iowa City, IA 52242
Tel: (319)356-2015
Members: 125 individuals
Annual Budget: under $10,000
President: Dr. Barrie Anderson

Society of Personality and Social Psychology
Historical Note
A division of the American Psychological Association.

Society of Petroleum Engineers *(1913)*
222 Palisades Creek Dr.
P.O. Box 833836
Richardson, TX 75083-3836
Tel: (972)952-9393 *Fax:* (972)952-9435
Toll Free: (800)456 - 6863
E-Mail: spedal@spe.org
Web Site: www.spe.org
Members: 69000 individuals
Staff: 120
Annual Budget: $10-25,000,000
Executive Director: Mark Rubin
Senior Manager, Meetings and Exhibits: Sally Goldesberry, CMM, CMP
Senior Manager, Marketing and Communications: Luanne Krause

Historical Note
SPE's members are technical engineers, scientists and managers engaged in the recovery of oil and gas related energy sources through wellbores. In 1913, a Standing Committee on Oil and Gas was established as part of the American Institute of Mining and Metallurgical Engineers. This became the Petroleum Division of the Institute in 1922, and the Petroleum Branch in 1949. Petroleum was added to the Institute name in 1955, and in 1957, the Society of Petroleum Engineers was formed as one of three largely autonomous societies within the AIME. In 1985, SPE incorporated separately from AIME. Has an annual budget of over $12 million. Membership: $75/year.

Meetings/Conferences:
Annual Meetings: Fall
2007 – Anaheim, CA/Nov. 11-14/8000

Publications:
SPE Projects, Facilities & Construction.
SPE Journal. q. adv.
Journal of Petroleum Technology. m. adv.
SPE Drilling & Completion. q. adv.
SPE Production & Facilities. q. adv.
SPE Reservoir Evaluation & Engineering. bi-m. adv.

Society of Petroleum Evaluation Engineers *(1962)*
1001 McKinney, Suite 801
Houston, TX 77002
Tel: (713)651-1639 *Fax:* (713)951-9659
E-Mail: bkspee@aol.com
Web Site: www.spee.org
Members: 495 individuals
Staff: 1
Executive Secretary: B.K. Buongiorno
E-Mail: bkspee@aol.com

Historical Note
SPEE members are engineers specializing in the evaluation of petroleum and natural gas properties.

Society of Petrophysicists and Well Log Analysts *(1959)*
8866 Gulf Freeway, Suite 320
Houston, TX 77017-6531
Tel: (713)947-8727 *Fax:* (713)947-7181
E-Mail: spwla@spwla.org
Web Site: www.spwla.org
Members: 3300 individuals
Staff: 2
Annual Budget: $250-500,000
Executive Director: Vicki J. King
E-Mail: spwla@spwla.org

Historical Note
Founded in Tulsa, OK in January 1959 and incorporated in Oklahoma the same year as Society of Professional Well Log Analysts; assumed its current name in 2003. Promotes the evaluation of formations, through well logging techniques, in order to locate gas, oil and other minerals. Membership: $60/year.

Meetings/Conferences:
Annual Meetings: Summer

Publications:
Petrophysics. bi-m. adv.
Transactions. a.

Society of Pharmaceutical and Biotech Trainers *(1971)*
4423 Pheasant Ridge Road, Suite 100
Roanoke, VA 24014-5300
Tel: (540)725-3859 *Fax:* (540)989-7482
E-Mail: info@spbt.org
Web Site: www.spbt.org
Members: 1000 individuals
Staff: 5
Annual Budget: $500-1,000,000
Executive Director: Brian Fagan
Director, Advertising: Jim Sullivan
Manager, Business Services: Su Taylor
Historical Note
Formerly (2000) National Society of Pharmaceutical Sales Trainers. Members are training personnel employed by pharmaceutical and biotechnologyl companies. Membership: $175/year (individual).
Meetings/Conferences:
Annual Meetings: May or June
Publications:
Focus. q. adv.

Society of Philosophers in America *(1985)*
Campus Box 148, Westfield State Coll.
Westfield, MA 01086-1630
Tel: (413)572-5362 *Fax:* (413)572-5441
Members: 120 individuals
Annual Budget: under $10,000
Treasurer: John A. Loughney
Historical Note
Dedicated to revitalizing the professional life of professors and teachers of philosophy in the U.S. Has no paid officers or full-time staff.

Society of Photographer and Artist Representatives *(1965)*
60 E. 42nd St., Suite 1166
New York, NY 10165-0006
Tel: (212)779-7464 *Fax:* (212)253-9996
E-Mail: info@spar.org
Web Site: www.spar.org
Members: 108 individuals
Staff: 1
Annual Budget: $25-50,000
Contact: Adrienne Wheeler
Historical Note
SPAR members are professionals who represent artists, photographers and stylists as well as hair and make-up artists. Membership: $150/year (general); $100/year (national); $100/year (associate).
Meetings/Conferences:
Monthly Meetings:
Publications:
SPAR Directory. a.
SPAR Do-it-yourself Kit.
SPAR Newsletter. q. adv.

Society of Physics Students *(1968)*
Historical Note
SPS is the student development affiliate of American Institute of Physics, which provides administrative support.

Society of Piping Engineers and Designers *(1980)*
One Main St., Suite N-719
Houston, TX 77002
Tel: (713)221-8224 *Fax:* (713)221-2712
E-Mail: spedweb@spedweb.org
Web Site: www.spedweb.org
Members: 750 individuals
Staff: 2
Annual Budget: $250-500,000
Executive Director and Treasurer: N.S. Nandagopal
President: Robert Sumrall
Historical Note
Members are piping professionals and technical experts interested in staying abreast of the technological advances in the field of piping and plant design. Membership: $35/year (individual); $300-500/year (company); $20/year (student).
Meetings/Conferences:
Annual Meetings: usually Houston, TX
Publications:
SPED Newsletter. q. adv.

Society of Plastics Engineers *(1942)*
14 Fairfield Dr.
Brookfield, CT 06804-0403
Tel: (203)775-0471 *Fax:* (203)775-8490
E-Mail: info@4spe.org
Web Site: www.4spe.org
Members: 23000 individuals
Staff: 32
Annual Budget: $5-10,000,000
Executive Director: Susan Oderwald
E-Mail: scoderwald@4spe.org
Managing Director, SPE Foundation: Gail R. Bristol
E-Mail: grbristol@4spe.org
Senior Manager, Training and Education Services: Tom Conklin
E-Mail: tconklin@4spe.org
Senior Manager, Events: Lesley Kyle
E-Mail: lskyle@4spe.org
Historical Note
Founded December 2, 1941 in Detroit as the Society of Plastics Sales Engineers and incorporated in Michigan in 1942. Has an annual budget of approximately $9 million. Membership: $107/year (individual member).
Meetings/Conferences:
Annual Meetings: Spring/5,000-6,000
Publications:
Plastics Engineering. m. adv.
Polymer Composites. bi-m.
Polymer Engineering and Science. m.
Plastics Engineering Europe. q.

Society of Professional Audio Recording Services *(1978)*
9 Music Sq. South, Suite 222
Nashville, TN 37203
Toll Free: (800)771 - 7727
E-Mail: spars@spars.com
Web Site: www.spars.com
Members: 250 companies
Staff: 1
Annual Budget: $100-250,000
Executive Director: Marcia Vaught-Kautz
Historical Note
Membership consists of commercial recording facilities, manufacturers, suppliers, educators, and individual professionals.
Meetings/Conferences:
Annual Meetings: Fall/AES Convention
Publications:
Time Code Primer.

Society of Professional Benefit Administrators *(1975)*
Two Wisconsin Circle, Suite 670
Chevy Chase, MD 20815
Tel: (301)718-7722 *Fax:* (301)718-9440
E-Mail: spba@erols.com
Web Site: http://users.erols.com/spba
Members: 400 companies
Staff: 5
Annual Budget: $1-2,000,000
President: Frederick D. Hunt, Jr.
Comptroller: Acacia G. Hunt
Director, Government Relations and Legal Affairs: Elizabeth Y. Leight
Vice President and Director, Federal Affairs: Anne C. Lennan
Director, Special Projects: Arlette Peterson
Director, Member Services: Kathryn Lafleur Strauss
Historical Note
Members are third-party contract administration firms (TPAs), which administer employee benefit plans for client employers and unions. Two-thirds of all U.S. workers, retirees and dependents are covered by such plans. SPBA is an active resource and reference for government policy-shapers. Of the publications put out by SPBA, the List of State TPA Statutes is available to the public at $500 per copy, and the SPBA TPA Directory for $495 per copy. Membership: $750-3,500/year (based on size).
Meetings/Conferences:
Semi-annual Meetings: Spring in Washington, DC and Fall/350
Publications:
SPBA Update (available to members only). m.
List of State TPA Statutes. a.
SPBA TPA Directory. a.

Society of Professional Investigators *(1956)*
c/o Investicorp, Inc.
705 Bedford Ave., Suite C
Bellmore, NY 11710
Tel: (516)781-5100 *Fax:* (516)783-0000
E-Mail: info@spionline.org
Web Site: www.spionline.org
Members: 375 individuals
Staff: 4
Annual Budget: $10-25,000
President: David E. Zeldin
Historical Note
SPI is dedicated to ethical principals in the field of private investigation. Membership, largely concentrated in the Connecticut, New Jersey and New York area, and consists of individuals with at least five years of experience in investigation, along with attorneys, accountants, CFE's and law enforcement officers. Membership: $50/year (individual); $25/year (student).
Meetings/Conferences:
Annual Meetings: Monthly meetings held in NYC and surrounding areas.
Publications:
SPI Newsletter. 8/year. adv.

Society of Professional Journalists *(1909)*
3909 N. Meridian St.
Indianapolis, IN 46208-4045
Tel: (317)927-8000 *Fax:* (317)920-4789
E-Mail: spj@spj.org
Web Site: www.spj.org
Members: 9500 individuals
Staff: 10
Annual Budget: $1-2,000,000
Executive Director: Terrence G. Harper, CAE
E-Mail: tharper@spj.org
Associate Executive Director: Chris Vachon
Historical Note
Founded at DePauw University in Greencastle, Indiana in 1909 as Sigma Delta Chi; became the Society of Professional Journalists, Sigma Delta Chi in 1972; assumed its present name in 1989. Membership is comprised of men and women in every field of journalism. Maintains over 300 local professional and campus chapters. Membership: $72/year (individual), $36/year (student/retired).
Meetings/Conferences:
Annual Meetings: October/1,200
2007 – Washington, DC(Hyatt Regency)/Oct. 4-7
2008 – Atlanta, GA(Hyatt Regency)
Publications:
Quill. 9/year. adv.
The Journalist. a. adv.

Society of Professional Well Log Analysts
Historical Note
Became Society of Petrophysicists and Well Log Analysts in 2003.

Society of Professors of Child and Adolescent Psychiatry *(1969)*
66 Pine Knoll Dr.
Coventry, CT 06238
Tel: (860)742-7093
E-Mail: mday7093@charter.net
Web Site: www.spcap.org
Members: 175 individuals
Staff: 1
Annual Budget: $10-25,000
Executive Administrator: Madison Day
Historical Note
Formerly (1987) Society of Professors of Child Psychiatry. A division of American Academy of Child and Adolescent Psychiatry, which provides administrative support. Membership: $150/year (individual).
Meetings/Conferences:
Annual Meetings: Spring/60
Publications:
SPCAP Directory. a.

SPCAP Newsletter. semi-a.

Society of Professors of Education *(1902)*
State Univ. of West Georgia, Dept. of Educational Leadership & FDTS
1600 Maple St.
Carrollton, GA 30118-5160
Tel: (770)836-4426 *Fax:* (770)836-4646
Web Site: www.unm.edu/~jka/spe/
Members: 400 individuals
Annual Budget: under $10,000
Secretary-Treasurer: Dr. Robert C. Morris
E-Mail: rmorris@westga.edu

Historical Note
Established as the National Society of College Teachers of Education; assumed its present name in 1969. SPE is a professional and academic association open to all individuals engaged in teacher preparation or related activities. Membership: $25/year.

Meetings/Conferences:
Annual Meetings: April, in conjunction with the American Education Research Ass'n/100

Publications:
SPE Journal - Sophist's Bane. 2/yr.
DeGarmo Lectures. a.
SPE Monograph Series. a.
SPE Newsletter - Professing Education. 4/yr.

Society of Protozoologists *(1947)*
University of Southern California, Dept. of Biological Sciences
3616 Trousdale Parkway, AHF 309
Los Angeles, CA 90089-0371
Tel: (231)740-0203
Web Site: www.uga.edu/protozoa
Members: 970 individuals
Annual Budget: $100-250,000
President: David Caron

Historical Note
Founded in 1947 as an international scientific society. An affiliate of the American Association for the Advancement of Science and member of the World Federation of Parasitologists. Members are concerned with all aspects of the study of protozoa. Membership : $70/year.

Meetings/Conferences:
Annual Meetings: Summer

Publications:
Journal of Eukaryotic Microbiology. q.
Newsletter. 3/year.

Society of Publication Designers *(1965)*
17 E. 47th St., Floor Six
New York, NY 10017-7923
Tel: (212)223-3332 *Fax:* (212)223-5880
E-Mail: mail@spd.org
Web Site: www.spd.org
Members: 1300 individuals
Staff: 1
Annual Budget: $500-1,000,000
Contact: Emily Smith

Historical Note
A professional organization which includes primarily publication art directors, editors, designers, illustrators, photographers, printers and publishers. Serves the needs of the editorial designer and art director by sponsoring annual competitions, speakers evenings, exhibitions, conferences and other activities. Membership: $195/year (individual); $495/year (corporate).

Meetings/Conferences:
Annual Meetings: No annual meeting.

Publications:
Grids. q. adv.
Publication Design Annual. a. adv.

Society of Quality Assurance *(1984)*
2365 Hunters Way
Charlottesville, VA 22911
Tel: (434)297-4772 *Fax:* (434)977-1856
E-Mail: sqa@sqa.org
Web Site: www.sqa.org
Members: 2100 individuals
Annual Budget: $250-500,000
Executive Director: Elliott Graham
E-Mail: elliot.graham@sqa.org
Manager, Educational Programs: Jennifer Alluisi
Director, Publications: Marilla Owens
Director, Programs and Meetings: Allison Travis
E-Mail: allison.travis@sqa.org

Historical Note
Founded in 1980 as Quality Assurance Roundtable; became SQA in 1984. Members are professionals in the toxicological, pharmaceutical, biological, and chemical sciences responsible for quality assurance and standards maintenance in the laboratory and workplace. Membership: $115/year (domestic); $130/year (international).

Meetings/Conferences:
Annual Meetings: April/800

Publications:
QA Newsletter. q.
QA Directory. a.
Regulatory Review Bulletin. irreg.

Society of Quantitative Analysts *(1989)*
P.O. Box 539
Webster, NY 14580-0539
Tel: (585)545-6925
E-Mail: sqa@sqa-us.org
Web Site: www.sqa-us.org
Members: 350 individuals
Staff: 1
Annual Budget: $50-100,000
Executive Director: David Carleton, CAE

Historical Note
Originally established in 1972 as the Computer Applications Symposium of the New York Society of Security Analysts before becoming (1980) the Investment Technology Association. Adopted its present name upon incorporation in 1989. SQA is concerned with the application of new and innovative techniques for finance, with particular emphasis on the use of quantitative techniques in investment management. Membership: $150/year (individual).

Meetings/Conferences:
Annual Meetings: May
2007 – New York, NY(The Helmsley Hotel)/June 18

Society of Radiologists in Ultrasound *(1976)*
44211 Slatestone Ct.
Leesburg, VA 20176
Tel: (703)858-9210 *Fax:* (703)729-4839
Web Site: www.sru.org
Members: 750 individuals
Staff: 2
Annual Budget: $100-250,000
Administrative Director: Susan Roberts

Historical Note
Founded to promote the use of diagnostic ultrasound in the field of academic radiology. Membership is open to all board-certified or board-eligible radiologists with an interest in ultrasound. Membership: $200/year.

Meetings/Conferences:
Annual Meetings: Fall

Publications:
Newsletter. q.
Membership Directory. a.
Program Book. a.

Society of Recreation Executives *(1986)*
PO Box 520
Jacks Branch Rd.
Gonzales, FL 32560
Tel: (850)937-8354 *Fax:* (850)937-8356
Toll Free: (800)281 - 9186
E-Mail: rltresource@spydee.net
Members: 3462 individuals
Staff: 3
Annual Budget: $50-100,000
National Director: K.W. Stephens

Historical Note
Members are corporate executives, business owners and institutional professionals involved in the recreation, leisure and travel industries. Membership: $100/year (individual); $250/year (corporate).

Meetings/Conferences:
Annual Meetings: August/90

Publications:
Who's Who in Recreation. a. adv.
Recreation Executive Newsletter. bi-m. adv.

Society of Reliability Engineers *(1966)*
19 Sally Lane
Madison, AL 35758
Tel: (256)876-2258
Web Site: www.sre.org
Members: 1000 individuals
Annual Budget: $10-25,000
President: Henry Cook

Meetings/Conferences:
Annual Meetings: Board of Directors' Meeting three times/year.

Publications:
Lamda Notes. q.

Society of Reproductive Surgeons *(1984)*
1209 Montgomery Hwy.
Birmingham, AL 35216-2809
Tel: (205)978-5000 *Fax:* (205)978-5005
E-Mail: cfinch@asrm.org
Web Site: www.reprodsurgery.org
Members: 500 individuals
Administrator: Cheryl Finch

Historical Note
Members are doctors specializing in gynecologic and urologic surgery. Administrative support is provided by the American Society for Reproductive Medicine. Membership: $75/year (individual).

Meetings/Conferences:
Annual Meetings: Annual meeting held with the American Soc. for Reproductive Medicine.

Society of Research Administrators International *(1967)*
1901 N. Moore St., Suite 1004
Arlington, VA 22209
Tel: (703)741-0140 *Fax:* (703)741-0142
E-Mail: info@srainternational.org
Web Site: www.srainternational.org
Members: 3200 individuals
Staff: 8
Annual Budget: $500-1,000,000
Chief Operating Officer: Tamra Hackett
E-Mail: thackett@srainternational.org

Historical Note
A professional association of individuals in industry, academia and government to improve the efficiency of research administration and the interface between the investigators and their administrative overseers. Membership: $195/year (individual).

Meetings/Conferences:
Annual Meetings: Fall/1,300
2007 – Nashville, TN(Gaylord Opryland Resort and Convention Center)/Oct. 13-17/2000

Publications:
Newsletter (electronic). m. adv.
SRA Journal. bi-m. adv.
Membership Directory. a. adv.

Society of Rheology *(1929)*
c/o American Institute of Physics
2 Huntington Quadrangle, Suite 1N01
Melville, NY 11747
Tel: (516)576-2403 *Fax:* (516)576-2223
E-Mail: rheology@aip.org
Web Site: www.rheology.org/sor
Members: 1700 individuals
Annual Budget: $10-25,000
Liason: Janis Bennett

Historical Note
Chemists, physicists, biologists, chemical engineers, and others concerned with the theory and precise measurement of the flow of matter, and the response of materials to mechanical force. Has a permanent address at the American Institute of Physics, and is one of the five founding members of that organization. Membership: $40/year (regular); $25/year (student/retired).

Publications:
Journal of Rheology. bi-m.
Rheology Bulletin. semi-a.

Society of Risk Management Consultants *(1984)*
P.O. Box 510228
Milwaukee, WI 53203
Toll Free: (800)765 - 7762

Web Site: www.srmcsociety.org
Members: 150 individuals
Annual Budget: $10-25,000
Director: Joy M. Gander
President: Jill Sherman, CPCU, ARM

Historical Note
Formed in 1984 by the consolidation of the Insurance Consultants Society and the Institute of Risk Management Consultants. Membership: $250/year.

Meetings/Conferences:
Semi-annual meetings: April and October
2007 – Minneapolis, MN
2007 – Baltimore, MD

Publications:
Membership Directory. irreg.
SRMC Journal. irreg.

Society of Roller Skating Teachers of America *(1945)*

Historical Note
An affiliate of Roller Skating Association International, which provides administrative support.

Society of Satellite Professionals International *(1983)*
NY Information and Technology Center
55 Broad St., 14th Floor
New York, NY 10004
Tel: (212)809-5199 *Fax:* (212)825-0075
E-Mail: tbond@sspi.org
Web Site: www.sspi.org
Members: 1700 individuals
Staff: 3
Annual Budget: $500-1,000,000
Executive Director: Robert Bell
E-Mail: rbell@sspi.org
Director, Development: Louis Zacharilla

Historical Note
Formerly (1988) Society of Satellite Professionals. Members are individuals in the fields of business, education, entertainment, media, science and industry who share common interests in satellite technology. Membership: $100/year (professional), $20/year (student).

Meetings/Conferences:
Annual Meeting:

Publications:
ORBITER. bi-m.
Membership Directory (online).

Society of School Librarians International *(1985)*
19 Savage St.
Charleston, SC 29401
Tel: (843)577-5351
Members: 1200 individuals
Staff: 2
Annual Budget: $100-250,000
Executive Director: Jeanne Schwartz

Historical Note
SSLI members are librarians involved with selection and utilization of technology and children's books in education. Membership: $45/year (regular member); $75/year (corporate or vendor).

Meetings/Conferences:
Annual Meetings: Winter

Publications:
SSLI Reports. bi-m. adv.

Society of Scribes *(1974)*
P.O. Box 933
New York, NY 10150
Tel: (212)452-0139
E-Mail: info@societyofscribes.org
Web Site: www.societyofscribes.org
Members: 700 individuals
Contact: Mary Ann Wolfe
E-Mail: info@societyofscribes.org

Historical Note
SOS members are calligraphers and others with an interest in book arts. Has no paid officers or full-time staff. Membership: $25/year.

Meetings/Conferences:
Annual Meetings: always last Saturday in February

Publications:
NewSOS Newsletter. 3/year. adv.

Society of Small Craft Designers *(1949)*
360 E. Randolph St., #803
Chicago, IL 60601-7332
Tel: (231)582-2924
Members: 250 individuals
Staff: 1
Annual Budget: under $10,000
President: William R. Mehaffey

Historical Note
Members are small craft designers concerned with the scientific design of yachts and small commercial vessels (up to 200 feet). Members are primarily naval architects. Membership: $20/year (individual).

Publications:
Planimeter. a.
Log Newsletter. irreg.

Society of Stage Directors and Choreographers *(1959)*
1501 Broadway, Suite 1701
New York, NY 10036-5653
Tel: (212)391-1070 *Fax:* (212)302-6195
Toll Free: (800)541 - 5204
Web Site: www.ssdc.org
Members: 2000 individuals
Staff: 12
Annual Budget: $1-2,000,000
Executive Director: Barbara Hauptman

Historical Note
SSDC is an independent labor union representing directors and choreographers in American theatre.

Meetings/Conferences:
Semi-annual Membership Meetings: May and November in New York and L.A.

Publications:
Journal of Stage Directors and Choreographers Foundation. a. adv.
SSDC Newsletter. bi-m.
SSDC Directory (online).

Society of State Directors of Health, Physical Education and Recreation *(1926)*
1900 Association Dr., Suite 100
Reston, VA 20191
Tel: (703)390-4599 *Fax:* (703)476-0988
E-Mail: smurray@aahperd.org
Web Site: www.thesociety.org
Members: 180 individuals
Staff: 4
Annual Budget: $100-250,000
Executive Director: Sharon D. Murray
HIV Program Administrator: Elizabeth Henderson
E-Mail: ehenderson@aahperd.org
Program Coordinator: Helen Leonard
Administrative Assistant: Ruth See
E-Mail: rsee@aahperd.org

Historical Note
The Society seeks to promote and improve programs of health, physical education, recreation, athletics, dance and related subjects in elementary schools, secondary schools, colleges and universities, and teacher education programs in these disciplines. Has no paid officers, 4 full-time staff. Membership: $70/year (full member); $50/year (associate).

Meetings/Conferences:
Annual Meetings: Spring, with AAHPERD/100
2007 – Baltimore, MD/March 11-12/70

Publications:
Newsletter. q.
Directory. a.

Society of Surgical Oncology *(1940)*
85 W. Algonquin Road, Suite 550
Arlington Heights, IL 60005-4425
Tel: (847)427-1400 *Fax:* (847)427-9656
Web Site: www.surgonc.org
Members: 1800 individuals
Staff: 4
Annual Budget: $1-2,000,000
Executive Director: Rick Slawny

Historical Note
Founded in 1940 as the James Ewing Society Became the Society of Surgical Oncology in 1975.

Meetings/Conferences:
Annual Meetings: March
2007 – Washington, DC(Marriott Wardman Park Hotel)/March 15-18
2008 – Chicago, IL(Sheraton Chicago)/March 13-16

Publications:
Annals of Surgical Oncology. 10/year. adv.

Society of Systematic Biologists *(1948)*
574 Widtsoe Building, Department of Zoology
Brigham Young University
Provo, UT 84602-5555
E-Mail: keith_crandall@byu.ed
Web Site: http://systbiol.org
Members: 1700 individuals
Staff: 1
Annual Budget: under $10,000
Executive Vice President: Keith Crandall

Historical Note
Formerly (1991) Society of Systematic Zoology. Founded in the District of Columbia in 1948. Affiliated with the American Association for the Advancement of Science, the American Institute of Biological Sciences, the National Research Council and the American Society of Zoologists. Promotes zoological classification. Membership: $40/year (individual); $21/year (student); $60/year (organization).

Meetings/Conferences:
2008 – Auckland, New Zealand(Allan Wilson Center)/June 18-22

Publications:
Systematic Biology. bi-m. adv.

Society of Teachers of Family Medicine *(1967)*
11400 Tomahawk Creek Pkwy.
Leawood, KS 66211
Tel: (913)906-6000 Ext: 5420 *Fax:* (913)906-6096
Toll Free: (800)274 - 2237
E-Mail: tnolte@stfm.org
Web Site: www.stfm.org
Members: 5000 individuals
Staff: 17
Annual Budget: $2-5,000,000
Executive Director: Roger A. Sherwood, CAE
E-Mail: sherwood@stfm.org
Deputy Executive Director: Stacy Brungardt
Controller: Dana Greco
Director, Communications: Traci Nolte
E-Mail: tnolte@stfm.org
Director, Meetings and Conventions: Ray Rosetta
Coordinator, Membership: Mary Ruhl
Director, Government Relations: Hope Wittenberg

Historical Note
Multidisciplinary society of health professionals concerned with family medicine education. Affiliated with the American Board of Family Practice, the American Academy of Family Physicians, and the American Academy of Family Physicians Foundation. Represents family medicine as an academic discipline on the Council of Academic Societies of the Association of American Medical Colleges.

Meetings/Conferences:
Annual Meetings: Spring/950

Publications:
Family Medicine. m. adv.
STFM Messenger (online). m. adv.

Society of Telecommunications Consultants *(1976)*
13275 State Hwy. 89
Old Station, CA 96071
Tel: (530)335-7313 *Fax:* (530)335-7360
Toll Free: (800)782 - 7670
E-Mail: stchdq@stcconsultants.org
Web Site: www.stcconsultants.org
Members: 200 consultant members
Staff: 1
Annual Budget: $250-500,000
President: Byron Battles

Historical Note
Established to meet the need for a self-regulating body in the profession. STC members are telecommunications professionals who serve clients in business, industry and government. STC represents its members in regulatory, legislative and commercial

affairs and maintains a vendor advisory council, comprised of companies offering telecommunications products and services, which supports consultant members with technical information and provides assistance in solving problems in the field. Membership: $450/year (individual); $850/year (vendor company).

Meetings/Conferences:
Semi-Annual Meetings: Spring and Fall/250

Publications:
Speakers Bureau Directory. semi-a.
Writers/Article Repository. semi-a.
STC Lines Newsletter. q.
STC Consultant Directory. irreg.
Vendor Advisory Council Membership Directory. q.

Society of the Plastics Industry *(1937)*
1667 K St. NW
Suite 1000
Washington, DC 20006
Tel: (202)974-5200 *Fax:* (202)296-7005
Web Site: www.plasticsindustry.org
Members: 1500 companies
Staff: 50
Annual Budget: $10-25,000,000
President: William R. Carteaux
Director, Federal Government Affairs: Chris Brown
Chief Financial Officer: John R. Maguire
Executive Vice President and Chief Operating Officer: Catherine A. Randazzo

Historical Note
Absorbed (1998) Plastic Drum Institute. Promotes the application and use of plastics and is the principal representative of the plastics industry. Has an annual budget of approximately $35.9 million.

Meetings/Conferences:
Annual Meetings: Fall

Publications:
SPI Link. w.
SPI Membership Directory and Buyers Guide. a.

Society of Thoracic Radiology *(1982)*
P.O. Box 1026
Rochester, MN 55903-1006
Tel: (507)288-5620 *Fax:* (507)288-0014
E-Mail: str@thoracicrad.org
Web Site: www.thoracicrad.org
Members: 500 individuals
President: Reginald Munden, DMD, MD
E-Mail: btarver@xray.indyrad.iupui.edu

Publications:
Journal of Thoracic Imagery. q.

Society of Thoracic Surgeons *(1964)*
633 N. St Clair, Suite 2320
Chicago, IL 60611-3658
Tel: (312)202-5800 *Fax:* (312)202-5801
E-Mail: sts@sts.org
Web Site: www.sts.org
Members: 4000 individuals
Staff: 20
Annual Budget: $1-2,000,000
Executive Director: Robert A. Wynbrandt
Director, Meetings and Conventions: Joyce Gambino

Historical Note
Membership: $750/year (individual).

Publications:
Annals of Thoracic Surgery. m. adv.

Society of Toxicologic Pathologists *(1971)*
1821 Michael Faraday Dr., Suite 300
Reston, VA 20190-5332
Tel: (703)438-7508 *Fax:* (703)438-3113
E-Mail: stp@toxpath.org
Web Site: www.toxpath.org
Members: 780 individuals
Annual Budget: $250-500,000
Director, Membership: Jessi Canning

Historical Note
Originally the Society of Pharmalogical and Environmental Pathlolgists. Incorporated in New Jersey in 1971; assumed its present name in 1980. Aims of STP are to advance pathology as it pertains to changes elicited by pharmacological, chemical, and environmental agents, and to encourage communication and exchange of information in this field; to evaluate criteria and requirements applied to the interpretation of pathological changes produced by drugs, chemicals, and environmental agents; to encourage the training and recognition of pathologists in these fields; and to establish registries of pathologic entities in laboratory animals. Membership: $205/year (individual); $1,500/year (organization).

Meetings/Conferences:
Annual Meetings: Summer

Publications:
Newsletter. q. adv.
Toxicologic Pathology. bi-m.

Society of Toxicology *(1961)*
1821 Michael Faraday Dr., Suite 300
Reston, VA 20190-5332
Tel: (703)438-3115 *Fax:* (703)438-3113
E-Mail: sothq@toxicology.org
Web Site: www.toxicology.org
Members: 5000 individuals
Staff: 14
Annual Budget: $2-5,000,000
Executive Director: Shawn Lamb
E-Mail: shawnl@toxicology.org
Director, Education: Betty Eidemiller
E-Mail: bettye@toxicology.org
Manager, Meetings: Heidi Prange
Deputy Director: Clarissa Russell Wilson
E-Mail: clarissa@toxicology.org
Manager, Annual Meeting Program: Nichelle Sankey
E-Mail: nichelle@toxicology.org

Historical Note
Founded and incorporated in the District of Columbia in 1961. Members are scientists concerned with the effects of chemicals on humankind and the environment. Membership: $141/year (individual); $2,500/year (organization).

Meetings/Conferences:
Annual Meetings: late Winter/5,000
2007 – Charlotte, NC(Charlotte Convention Center)/March 25-27/6000
2008 – Seattle, WA(Convention and Trade Center)/March 16-20/6000

Publications:
Toxicological Sciences. m. adv.
Communique Newsletter. bi-m. adv.
The Toxicologist. a.

Society of Trauma Nurses
1926 Waukegan Road, Suite One
Glenview, IL 60025
Web Site: www.traumanursesoc.org
Members: 1000 individuals
Staff: 5
Annual Budget: $250-500,000
Executive Director: Joyce Paschall, CAE, CMP

Historical Note
An international professional forum for nurses involved in all facets of trauma care. Membership: $100/year.

Meetings/Conferences:
Annual Meetings: Spring

Publications:
Journal of Trauma Nursing. q. adv.

Society of Tribologists and Lubrication Engineers *(1944)*
840 Busse Hwy.
Park Ridge, IL 60068-2376
Tel: (847)825-5536 *Fax:* (847)825-1456
E-Mail: information@stle.org
Web Site: www.stle.org
Members: 4000 individuals
Staff: 10
Annual Budget: $1-2,000,000
Executive Director: Edward P. Salek
E-Mail: ESalek@stle.org

Historical Note
Formerly (1987) American Society of Lubrication Engineers. Founded to advance the science of lubrication (tribology). Provides technical information and support to the industry, academia, and government. Membership: $85/year (individual); $690/year (company).

Meetings/Conferences:
Annual Meetings: Spring/1,500

Publications:
Tribology and Lubrication Engineering Magazine. m. adv.
Tribology Transactions Journal. q.

Society of United States Air Force Flight Surgeons *(1960)*
P.O. Box 35387
Brooks AFB, TX 78235-5387
Tel: (210)536-2845 *Fax:* (210)536-1779
Web Site: www.sousaffs.org
Members: 900 individuals
Annual Budget: under $10,000
Executive Director: Maj. Chris Borchardt

Historical Note
Affiliated with Aerospace Medical Association. Membership: $15/year.

Meetings/Conferences:
Annual Meetings: May/in conjunction with Aerospace Medical Ass'n.

Publications:
Soc. of USAF Flight Surgeons Newsletter.

Society of University Otolaryngologists *(1964)*
c/o USC Sch. of Medicine, Dept. of OHNS
1200 N. State St., Box 795
Los Angeles, CA 90033
Tel: (323)226-7315
Members: 525 individuals
Annual Budget: $10-25,000
Executive Officer: Donna Hoffman

Historical Note
Members are ear, nose, throat, head and neck disorder specialists working at teaching hospitals or other academic settings. Has no paid officers or full-time staff. Membership: $60/year.

Society of University Surgeons *(1938)*
1133 W. Morse Blvd., Suite 201
Winter Park, FL 32789
Tel: (407)647-7714 *Fax:* (407)629-2502
E-Mail: info@susweb.org
Web Site: www.susweb.org
Members: 1400 individuals
Staff: 3
Annual Budget: $25-50,000
Executive Director: Phil Pyster, CAE

Historical Note
Membership: $150/year.

Meetings/Conferences:
Annual Meetings: February

Publications:
Surgery. a. adv.
Program Booklet. a.

Society of University Urologists *(1967)*
1111 N. Plaza Dr., Suite 500
Schaumburg, IL 60173
Tel: (847)517-7225 *Fax:* (847)517-7229
E-Mail: info@suunet.org
Web Site: www.suunet.org
Members: 465 individuals
Staff: 1
Annual Budget: under $10,000
Executive Director: Wendy J. Weiser

Historical Note
Promotes high standards of urologic education and research. Membership: $70/year.

Meetings/Conferences:
Annual Meetings: Fall, in conjunction with the American College of Surgeons/125

Society of Urologic Nurses and Associates *(1972)*
E. Holly Ave.
P.O. Box 56
Pitman, NJ 08071-0056
Tel: (856)256-2335 *Fax:* (856)589-7463
E-Mail: suna@ajj.com
Web Site: www.suna.org
Members: 3000 individuals
Staff: 4
Annual Budget: $500-1,000,000
Executive Director: Anthony J. Jannetti

Historical Note
In 1970 the American Urological Association organized a scientific program for urological allied

health professionals; the AUAA was incorporated as a non-profit organization in 1972 and its name changed to Society of Urologic Nurses and Associates in 1995. SUNA unites urologic health care providers in promoting excellence in urologic education and professional standards for optimal care of the urologic patient. Membership: $60/year (individual); $1,500/year (company).

Meetings/Conferences:
Annual Meetings: Spring/600
2007 – Colorado Springs, CO(Broadmoor Hotel)/March 15-17/400
2007 – Phoenix, AZ(Hyatt Regency)/Oct. 12-15/600

Publications:
Urologic Nursing Journal. q. adv.
Uro-Gram Newsletter. bi-m.

Society of Vacuum Coaters *(1957)*
71 Pinon Hill Place
Albuquerque, NM 87122-1914
Tel: (505)856-7188 *Fax:* (505)856-6716
E-Mail: svcinfo@svc.org
Web Site: www.svc.org
Members: 1000 individuals
Staff: 3
Annual Budget: $500-1,000,000
Executive Director: Vivienne Harwood Mattox

Historical Note
SVC's membership is composed of individuals concerned with the use and development of vacuum coatings for large and small scale applications. Membership: $95/year (domestic individual); $95/year (foreign individual); $1,000/year (company, first year); $500/year (company after first year).

Meetings/Conferences:
Annual Meetings: Spring

Publications:
Conference Proceedings. a. adv.
SVC News Bulletin. 3/year. adv.
CD-Rom. a.

Society of Vertebrate Paleontology *(1940)*
60 Revere Dr., Suite 500
Northbrook, IL 60062
Tel: (847)480-9095 *Fax:* (847)480-9282
E-Mail: svp@vertpaleo.org
Web Site: www.vertpaleo.org
Members: 2400 individuals
Annual Budget: $500-1,000,000
Executive Director: Nancy Witty

Historical Note
SVP was established on Dec. 28, 1940. The object of the society is to advance the science of vertebrate paleontology, and to serve the common interests and facilitate the cooperation of all persons concerned with the history, evolution, comparative anatomy and taxonomy of vertebrate animals, as well as the field occurence, collection and study of fossil vertebrates and the stratigraphy of the beds in which they are found. Membership: $95/year (individual); $45/year (student).

Meetings/Conferences:
Annual Meetings: October-November/900

Publications:
Journal of Vertebrate Paleontology. q. adv.
News Bulletin. 2/year.

Society of Wine Educators *(1977)*
1212 New York Ave. NW
Suite 425
Washington, DC 20005
Tel: (202)347-5677 *Fax:* (202)347-5667
E-Mail: lairey@societyofwineeducators.org
Web Site: www.societyofwineeducators.org
Members: 1,300 individuals
Staff: 2
Annual Budget: $250-500,000
Interim Executive Director: Lisa Airey

Historical Note
SWE exists to promote accurate and professional wine education. Members include those who teach wine education classes; those who write about wine; and those associated with wine in the production, restaurant, retail and wholesale areas. Provides an annual proficiency test which includes both general wine knowledge and sensory evaluation. Membership: $500/year (industry); $250/year (nonprofit); $125/year (professional); $65/year (associate); $40/year (student).

Meetings/Conferences:
Annual Meetings: Summer/400-500

Society of Woman Geographers *(1925)*
415 E. Captiol St. SE
Washington, DC 20003-3810
Tel: (202)546-9228 *Fax:* (202)546-5232
E-Mail: swqhq@verizon.net
Web Site: www.iswg.org
Members: 600 individuals
Staff: 1
Annual Budget: $50-100,000
President: Kimberly Crews

Historical Note
Founded in New York City in 1925 and incorporated in the District of Columbia in 1937. Membership by invitation only. Officers change every three years in May. Publications distributed to members only. Membership: $40-60/year (individual).

Meetings/Conferences:
Triennial Meetings: May (2005)

Publications:
Newsletter. q.
Bulletin. a.

Society of Women Engineers *(1950)*
230 E. Ohio St., Suite 400
Chicago, IL 60611-3265
Tel: (312)596-5223 *Fax:* (312)596-5252
E-Mail: hq@swe.org
Web Site: www.swe.org
Members: 17000 individuals
Staff: 11
Annual Budget: $5-10,000,000
Executive Director: Betty Shanahan
E-Mail: executive-director@swe.org
Manager, Conferences: Jeanne Elipani
E-Mail: jeanne.elipani@swe.org

Historical Note
An educational service organization of engineering students and practicing engineers, both women and men. SWE was founded in 1949-50 when small groups of women engineers started meeting in New York, Boston, Philadelphia, and Washington. The society was incorporated in 1952. In 1976, membership was opened to men. Membership: $100/year (individual); $3,000/year (company); $20/year (student).

Meetings/Conferences:
2007 – Nashville, TN/Oct. 25-27

Publications:
SWE magazine. q. adv.

Society of Wood Science and Technology *(1958)*
One Gifford Pinchot Dr.
Madison, WI 53726-2398
Tel: (608)231-9347 *Fax:* (608)231-9592
Web Site: www.swst.org
Members: 450 individuals
Staff: 2
Annual Budget: $100-250,000
Executive Director: Vicki Herian
E-Mail: vicki@swst.org

Historical Note
Founded in June 1958 as the American Society of Wood Engineering. Became the Society of Wood Science and Technology in 1961 and incorporated in Wisconsin the same year. Membership: $75/year (individual); $25/year (student).

Meetings/Conferences:
Annual Meetings: Summer/100
2007 – Knoxville, TN(Hilton Hotel)/June 10- /150
2008 – St. Louis, MO/June 15- /150

Publications:
Wood and Fiber Science. q.

Sociological Practice Association *(1978)*
c/o SMSU, Sociology and Anthropology Dept.
901 National Ave.
Springfield, MO 65804
Tel: (614)292-3114 *Fax:* (614)292-9750
Web Site: www.socpractice.org
Members: 200 individuals
Annual Budget: under $10,000
President: Melodye G. Lehnerer

Historical Note
Members include organizational developers, program planners, community organizers, sociotherapists, counselors, gerontologists, conflict interventionists, applied social science researchers, policy planners on all levels including international practice, and many others who practice, study, teach or do research by applying sociological knowledge for positive social change. Has no paid officers or full-time staff. Membership: $80/year (individual); $150/year (organization/company).

Meetings/Conferences:
Annual Meetings: June/150

Publications:
Practicing Sociologist Newsletter. q. adv.
Directory of Members. a.
Sociological Practice: A Journal of Clinical and Applied Sociology. q. adv.

Software and Information Industry Association *(1984)*
1090 Vermont Ave., N.W., 6th Fl.
Washington, DC 20005
Tel: (202)289-7442 *Fax:* (202)289-7097
Web Site: www.siia.net
Members: 800 companies
Staff: 35
Annual Budget: $2-5,000,000
President: Kenneth A. Wasch
E-Mail: kwasch@siia.net
Vice President, Education Division: Karen Billings
E-Mail: kbillings@siia.net
Senior Vice President, Public Policy and General Counsel: Mark Bohannon
E-Mail: mbohannon@siia.net
Vice President, Marketing and Communications: Anne Griffith, M.D.
E-Mail: agriffith@siia.net
Director, Membership Services: Meg Looney
E-Mail: kwasch@siia.net
Vice President, Finance and Administration: Thomas W. Meldrum, Jr.
E-Mail: tmeldrum@siia.net

Historical Note
Members are software developers and publishers. Services include software protection, contracts reference disk, conferences, and lobbying. Has an annual budget of approximately $4 million. Membership fee based on total organizational revenues.

Publications:
Upgrade Magazine. bi-m. adv.
Newsline. m. adv.
Membership Directory. a.
Industry Daily. d.

Softwood Export Council *(1998)*
520 S.W. Sixth Ave., Suite 810
Portland, OR 97204-1514
Tel: (503)248-0406 *Fax:* (503)248-0399
E-Mail: info@softwood.org
Web Site: www.softwood.org
Members: 16 organizations
Staff: 6
President: Craig Larsen
Manager, Programs: Paul Boardman

Historical Note
SEC promotes the expansion of export markets for primary and secondary softwood products manufactured in the U.S. Members are industry associations, state export development agencies, timber grading and inspection agencies, and others involved in softwood production.

Publications:
Newsletter. bi-m.

Soil and Plant Analysis Council *(1970)*
621 Rose St.
Lincoln, NE 68502-2040
Tel: (402)437-4944 *Fax:* (402)476-7598
Web Site: www.spcouncil.com
Members: 350 individuals
Staff: 1
Annual Budget: $10-25,000

Secretary-Treasurer: Byron Vaughan
E-Mail: bvaug12345@aol.com

Historical Note

Formerly Council on Soil Testing and Plant Analysis (1994). Promotes uniform soil test and plant analysis methods, use, interpretation and terminology. Membership: $30/year.

Meetings/Conferences:

Annual Meetings: Winter

Publications:

Soil-Plant Analyst. q.

Soil and Water Conservation Society *(1945)*
945 S.W. Ankeny Road
Ankeny, IA 50023
Tel: (515)289-2331 *Fax:* (515)289-1227
E-Mail: swcs@swcs.org
Web Site: www.swcs.org
Members: 10000 individuals
Staff: 15
Annual Budget: $1-2,000,000
Executive Vice President: Craig Cox
Communications Director/Editor: Deb Hapee

Historical Note

Formerly (1987) the Soil Conservation Society of America. Incorporated in the District of Columbia in 1949. Members are researchers, consultants, and practitioners of soil and water conservation, both in the public and private sectors. SWCS promotes erosion control and water quality. Membership: $60/year (individual); $250-750/year (organization/company).

Meetings/Conferences:

Annual Meetings: Summer/1,200

Publications:

Journal of Soil and Water Conservation. bi-m. adv.
SWCS Conservogram. bi-m. adv.

Soil Science Society of America *(1936)*
677 S. Segoe Road
Madison, WI 53711
Tel: (608)273-8080 *Fax:* (608)273-2021
E-Mail: headquarters@soils.org
Members: 5946 individuals
Staff: 41
Annual Budget: $1-2,000,000
Executive Vice President: Dr. Ellen Bergfeld

Historical Note

Founded in 1936 and incorporated in Wisconsin in 1952, SSSA shares headquarters with the American Society of Agronomy and the Crop Science Society of America. SSA is dedicated to spreading knowledge and practices to sustain the world's soil resources, and

to guiding their wise use to secure an adequate, healthy food supply and a high-quality environment. Mission is to enhance sustainability of soils, the environment and society by integrating diverse scientific disciplines and principles in soil science for wide stewardship of soil and natural resources; and to advance the discovery, practice and profession of soil science through excellence in acquisition and application of knowlege to address challenges facing society, though training and professional development of scientists, and through education of and communication to the citizenry.

Meetings/Conferences:

Annual Meetings: Fall, with ASA and CSSA
2007 - New Orleans, LA(Convention Center)/Nov. 4-8

Publications:

Crop Science - Soil Science - Agronomy News. m. adv.
Vadose Zone Journal. q. adv.
Journal of Environmental Quality. bi-m. adv.
Soil Science Society of America Journal. bi-m. adv.

Solar Energy Industries Association *(1974)*
805 15th St. NW
Suite 510
Washington, DC 20005
Tel: (202)682-0556 *Fax:* (202)682-0559
E-Mail: info@seia.org
Web Site: www.seia.org
Members: 150 companies, 14 state chapters
Staff: 4
Annual Budget: $250-500,000
Executive Director: Rhone Resch

Historical Note

SEIA is the national trade association of the solar energy industry and represents concentrating solar power, photovoltaic, solar, thermal, and solar hybrid lighting industries. SEIA members are solar energy manufacturers, dealers, distributors, contractors, installers, consultants, financial institutions, law firms, and end users. Purpose is to make solar energy a mainstream and significant energy source by expanding markets, strengthening the solar industry, and educating the public on the benefits of solar energy. Supports the Solar Energy Research and Education Foundation.

Meetings/Conferences:

Annual Meetings: Winter

Solar Rating and Certification Corp. *(1980)*
1679 Clearlake Road
Cocoa, FL 32922-5703
Tel: (321)638-1537 *Fax:* (321)638-1010
Web Site: www.solar-rating.org
Members: 19 companies
Staff: 3
Annual Budget: $100-250,000
Director, Technical: Jim Huggins
E-Mail: srcc@fsec.ucf.edu

Historical Note

The SRCC is a non-profit third party certification organization whose primary purpose is the development and implementation of certification programs for solar energy equipment including solar collectors and solar water heating systems. In addition to its certification programs, the corporation also administers a laboratory accreditation program for independent test facilities evaluating solar components, subsystems and systems. Program fee: $500-2,000.

SOLE - The International Society of Logistics *(1966)*
8100 Professional Place, Suite 111
Hyattsville, MD 20785-2229
Tel: (301)459-8446 *Fax:* (301)459-1522
E-Mail: solehq@erols.com
Web Site: www.sole.org
Members: 6000 individuals
Staff: 5
Annual Budget: $1-2,000,000
Executive Director: Sarah R. James

Historical Note

Founded in 1966 as a non-profit international professional society of individuals and corporate members to promote logistics education and and technical activities. Membership: $140/year (regular); $85/year (retired); $75/year (young logistician); $40/year (student).

Meetings/Conferences:

Annual Meetings: August

Publications:

Annals. q.
Logistics Spectrum. bi-m. adv.

Solid Waste Association of North America *(1961)*

Historical Note

See under SWANA - Solid Waste Ass'n of North America.

Solid-State Circuits Society

Historical Note

A technical society of the Institute of Electrical and Electronics Engineers (IEEE). Membership in the Society, open only to IEEE members, includes subscription to a technical periodical in the field published by IEEE. All administrative support is provided by IEEE.

Solution Mining Research Institute *(1958)*
105 Apple Valley Circle
Clarks Summit, PA 18411
Tel: (570)585-8092 *Fax:* (570)585-8091
E-Mail: smri@solutionmining.org
Web Site: www.solutionmining.org
Members: 100 organizations
Staff: 4
Annual Budget: $100-250,000
Executive Director: John Voight

Historical Note

SMRI members are companies interested in the production of salt brine and solution mining of potash and soda ash, as well as production of salt caverns, used for storage of oil, gas, chemicals, compressed air, and waste. Sponsors research on behalf of the industry, monitors regulatory developments, and disseminates technical information to members and interested parties world-wide. Membership: $4,000/year (regular); $1,000-2,000/year (associate).

Meetings/Conferences:

Semi-Annual Meetings: Spring and Fall

Sommelier Society of America *(1954)*
P.O. Box 20080
New York, NY 10014-0708
Tel: (212)679-4190 *Fax:* (212)255-8959
E-Mail: info@sommeliersocietyofamerica.org
Web Site: http://sommeliersocietyofamerica.org
Members: 500 individuals
Staff: 5
Annual Budget: $25-50,000
Executive Director: Robert Moody
Administrator: Anne Woods

Historical Note

'Sommelier': French name for a wine steward. Members are wine importers and merchants, restaurant owners, caterers and others. Seeks to expand the knowledge and appreciation of fine wines and liquors. Membership: $150/year (students); $600/year (businesses or trade associations);

Meetings/Conferences:

Annual Meetings: always New York, NY/April

Songwriters Guild of America *(1931)*
1500 Harbor Blvd.
Weehawken, NJ 07087-6732
Tel: (201)867-7603 *Fax:* (201)867-7535
Web Site: www.songwritersguild.com/
Members: 4500 individuals
Staff: 20
Annual Budget: $250-500,000
Chief Operating Officer: Rundi Ream

Historical Note

Formerly Songwriters Protective Association and American Guild of Authors and Composers. Provides agreements between songwriters, composers and publishers. Maintains a Copyright Renewal Service, Royalty Collection Service, Catalog Administration Plan, songwriting workshops, collaboration service and legal activities. Membership: $84-400 (individual).

Publications:

Regional Newsletter. q. adv.
National Newsletter. a. adv.

Sorptive Minerals Institute *(1970)*
1155 15th St. NW
Suite 500
Washington, DC 20005
Tel: (202)289-2760 *Fax:* (202)530-0659
Web Site: www.sorptive.org
Members: 11 companies
Staff: 4
Annual Budget: $100-250,000
Executive Director: Lee Coogan

Historical Note

Members are companies mining, marketing and processing sorptive minerals (clays and diatomaceous earths that can absorb 75-125% of their weight in water). Membership is based on tonnage.

Meetings/Conferences:

Semi-Annual Meetings: Spring and Fall

Publications:

Memo. m.

South Asian Journalists Association *(1994)*
c/o Columbia Journalism School
2950 Broadway
New York, NY 10027
Tel: (212)854-5979 *Fax:* (212)854-7837
Web Site: www.saja.org
Members: 350 individuals
Staff: 1
Annual Budget: under $10,000

Co-Founder: Sreenath Sreenivasan
E-Mail: saja@columbia.edu

Historical Note
SAJA members are journalists of South Asian origin. Administers the SAJA Journalism Awards, given to recognize coverage of the region.

Meetings/Conferences:
Annual Meetings: early May

Publications:
SAJA-online Newsletter. irreg.
SAJA Directory.

Southern Cypress Manufacturers Association *(1905)*

Historical Note
An affiliate of Hardwood Manufacturers Association, which provides administrative support.

Souvenirs, Gifts and Novelties Trade Association *(1962)*
10 E. Athens Ave.
Ardmore, PA 19003
Tel: (610)645-6940 *Fax:* (610)645-6943
E-Mail: sgnmag@kanec.com
Web Site: www.sgnmag.com
Members: 1900 individuals
Staff: 10
Annual Budget: $500-1,000,000
President: Scott C. Borowsky

Historical Note
Association covers the resort spa and souvenir marketplace. Membership: $40/year.

Meetings/Conferences:
Annual Meetings: Winter/8,000

Publications:
EMail Reports. m. adv.
Career Center Bulletin (online, for members only). m. adv.
Souvenirs, Gifts and Novelties Magazine. 8/year. adv.

Soy Protein Council *(1971)*
1255 23rd St. NW
Washington, DC 20037-1174
Tel: (202)467-6610 *Fax:* (202)466-4949
Web Site: www.spcouncil.org
Members: 3 companies
Staff: 2
Annual Budget: $100-250,000
Executive Director and President: David A. Saunders

Historical Note
Members are processors and distributors of vegetable proteins and their products, for use and consumption in human food. Formerly (1982) the Food Protein Council.

Publications:
Soy Protein Products: Characteristics. Nutritional Aspects and Utilization.

Soyfoods Association of North America *(1978)*
1001 Connecticut Ave. NW
Suite 1120
Washington, DC 20036
Tel: (202)659-3520 *Fax:* (202)659-3522
E-Mail: info@soyfoods.org
Web Site: www.soyfoods.org
Members: 48 companies
Staff: 2
Annual Budget: $250-500,000
Executive Director: Nancy Chapman

Historical Note
Sponsors a soyfoods information center and SoyaScan bibliographic database. Membership: $500-$2,000/year, based on sales volume.

Meetings/Conferences:
Annual Meetings: Spring

Space Energy Association *(1990)*
P.O. Box 1136
Clearwater, FL 33757-1136
Tel: (727)442-3923
E-Mail: spaceenergy@earthlink.net
Members: 250 individuals
Staff: 3
Annual Budget: under $10,000
Consultant: Donald A. Kelly

Historical Note
Members are scientists and other professionals involved in study of advanced energy systems.

Publications:
Space Energy Journal. q.

Space Transportation Association *(1990)*
4305 Underwood St.
University Park, MD 20782
Web Site: www.spacetransportation.us
Members: 20 organizations
Staff: 9
Annual Budget: $100-250,000
President: Richard Coleman

Historical Note
STA represents the interests of organizations which intend to develop, build, operate and use space transportation vehicles and systems in order to provide reliable, economical, safe and routine access to space for public and private entities.

Publications:
Space Energy & Transportation Journal. q. adv.
SpaceTrans Newsletter. m.
Journal of Practical Applications in Space. q. adv.

Spain-U.S. Chamber of Commerce *(1959)*
350 Fifth Ave., Suite 2600
New York, NY 10118
Tel: (212)967-2170 Ext: 25 *Fax:* (212)564-1415
E-Mail: info@spainuscc.org
Web Site: www.spainuscc.org
Members: 400
Staff: 4
Annual Budget: $500-1,000,000
Executive Director: Lidia Del Pozo

Historical Note
Originated at a luncheon at the Biltmore Hotel February 9, 1959 and incorporated in New York April 2, 1959. Membership: $1,000/year (sustaining); $1,500/year (corporate); and $400/year (regular).

Meetings/Conferences:
Quarterly meetings:

Publications:
The Business Link. bi-a.. adv.
Trade Directory. a. adv.
Importing Food to the U.S.. a.
Visas and Work Permits for the USA. a.
Newsletter. m.. adv.

Spanish-Barb Breeders Association *(1972)*
P.O. Box 598
Anthony, FL 32617-0598
Tel: (352)622-5878
E-Mail: spbarb1@aol.com
Web Site: www.spanishbarb.com
Members: 125 individuals
Annual Budget: under $10,000
Secretary-Treasurer: Marie Martineau

Historical Note
Members are owners and breeders of Spanish-Barb horses. Has no paid officers or full-time staff. Membership: $20/year (individual); $25/year (organization/company).

Publications:
Spanish-Barb Update. semi-a.
Spanish-Barb Journal. semi-a.

Special Care Dentistry Association
401 N. Michigan Ave.
Chicago, IL 60611
Tel: (312)527-6764 *Fax:* (312)673-6663
E-Mail: scd@scdonline.org
Web Site: www.scdonline.org
Members: 1500 individuals
Staff: 3
Annual Budget: $250-500,000
Executive Director: Kristen Smith

Historical Note
Formerly (2001) Federation of Special Care Organizations. A federation of organizations in dental care. Membership: $145/year (dentist); $65/year (hygienist).

Meetings/Conferences:
Annual Meetings: Spring

Publications:
Interface Newsletter. q. adv.
Special Care in Dentistry Journal. bi-m. adv.

Special Event Sites Marketing Alliance *(2002)*
11141 Georgia Ave., Suite 503
Silver Spring, MD 20902
Tel: (301)946-6663 *Fax:* (301)946-1313
E-Mail: info@sesma.org
Web Site: www.sesma.org
Members: 100 properties and companies
Staff: 2
Executive Director: Alec Stone

Historical Note
SESMA member sites are historic or otherwise notable properties that provide meeting facilities for business and social functions.

Special Interest Group for Algorithm and Computation Theory

Historical Note
A affiliate of Ass'n for Computing Machinery, which provides administrative support.

Special Interest Group for Architecture of Computer Systems

Historical Note
An affiliate of Association for Computing Machinery, which provides administrative support.

Special Interest Group for Computer Science

Historical Note
SIGCS is administered by International Society for Technology in Education (Eugene, OR) as a service to its members.

Special Interest Group for Computer Science Education *(1970)*

Historical Note
A subsidiary of Ass'n for Computing Machinery, which provides administrative support.

Special Interest Group for Computer-Human Interaction *(1972)*

Historical Note
An affiliate of Ass'n for Computing Machinery, which provides administrative support.

Special Interest Group for Computers and Society *(1972)*
c/o Ass'n for Computing Machinery
Two Penn Plaza, Suite 701
New York, NY 10121-0701
Tel: (212)869-7440 *Fax:* (212)302-5826
E-Mail: chair_sigcas@acm.org
Web Site: www.acm.org/sigcas
Members: 800 individuals
Staff: 1
Annual Budget: $10-25,000
Program Coordinator: Irene Frawley

Historical Note
SIGCAS was created by the Association for Computing Machinery in 1969 and given permanent status in 1972. Concerned with the impact on society of computer enhancements to informational technology. Membership: $20/year (ACM member); $56/year (non-ACM).

Meetings/Conferences:
Annual Meetings: With the Association for Computing Machinery and the AFIPS Nat'l Computer Conference and Exposition.

Publications:
Computers and Society Newsletter. q.

Special Interest Group for Data Communication *(1970)*

Historical Note
An affiliate of Association for Computing Machinery, which provides administrative support.

Special Interest Group for Design of Communication *(1968)*

Historical Note
An affiliate of Association for Computing Machinery, which provides administrative support.

Special Interest Group for Information Retrieval *(1966)*

Historical Note
An affiliate of Ass'n for Computing Machinery, which provides administrative support.

Special Interest Group for Logo Educators
Historical Note
SIG/Logo is administered by International Society for Technology in Education (Eugene, OR) as a service to its members.

Special Interest Group for Measurement and Evaluation *(1971)*
Historical Note
An affiliate of Association for Computing Machinery, which provides administrative support.

Special Interest Group for Microprogramming and Microarchitecture *(1968)*
Historical Note
An affiliate of Association for Computing Machinery, which provides administrative support.

Special Interest Group for Symbolic and Algebraic Manipulation *(1967)*
Historical Note
An affiliate of Association for Computing Machinery, which provides administrative support.

Special Interest Group for Teacher Educators
Historical Note
SIGTE is administered by International Society for Technology in Education (Eugene, OR) as a service to its members.

Special Interest Group for Technology Coordinators
Historical Note
SIGTC is administered by International Society for Technology in Education (Eugene, OR) as a service to its members.

Special Interest Group for Telecommunications
Historical Note
SIG/Tel is administered by International Society for Technology in Education (Eugene, OR) as a service to its members.

Special Interest Group for University and College Computing Services *(1962)*
c/o Ass'n for Computing Machinery
Two Penn Plaza, Suite 701
New York, NY 10121-0701
Tel: (212)869-7440 *Fax:* (212)302-5826
E-Mail: infodir_SIGUCCS@acm.org
Web Site: www.acm.org/siguccs/
Members: 550 individuals
Staff: 1
Annual Budget: $100-250,000
Program Coordinator: Irene Frawley

Historical Note
SIGUCCS is a semi-autonomous subsidiary of the Association for Computing Machinery. Formerly (1984) the Special Interest Group for University Computing Centers. SIGUCCS provides a forum and support services for those involved in supplying computing and other information technology services in higher education. Members include college and university computing service professionals, administrators, consultants, technical writers, and librarians. Membership: $25/year (ACM member); $29/year (non-ACM); $7/year (student).

Meetings/Conferences:
Annual Meetings: Services Managment Symposium/Spring & Users Services Conference/Nov.

Publications:
Proceedings. a.

Special Interest Group on Accessible Computing *(1970)*
c/o Ass'n for Computing Machinery
Two Penn Plaza, Suite 701
New York, NY 10121-0701
Tel: (212)869-7440 *Fax:* (212)302-5826
Web Site: www.acm.org/sigaccess
Members: 250 individuals
Staff: 2
Annual Budget: $10-25,000
Program Coordinator: Irene Frawley

Historical Note
Formerly (1978) the Special Interest Committee for Computers and the Physically Handicapped, and then the Special Interest Group for Accessible Computing; assumed its current name in 2004. SIGACCESS is concerned with the professional interests of computing personnel with disabilities and the application of computing and information technology in solving relevant disability problems. SIGACCESS also strives to educate the public to support careers for the disabled. A program section of the Association for Computing Machinery. Membership: $15/year (ACM member); $30/year (non-ACM); $6/year (student).

Meetings/Conferences:
Annual: ACM SIGACCESS/ Fall

Publications:
Accessibility & Computing. 3/yr.

Special Interest Group on Ada Programming Language *(1981)*
Historical Note
An affiliate of Association for Computing Machinery, which provides administrative support.

Special Interest Group on APL Programming Language *(1970)*
Historical Note
An affiliate of Ass'n for Computing Machinery, which provides administrative support.

Special Interest Group on Applied Computing
Historical Note
A semi-autonomous subsidiary of Ass'n for Computing Machinery, which provides all administrative support.

Special Interest Group on Artificial Intelligence
Historical Note
An affiliate of Association for Computing Machinery, which provides administrative support.

Special Interest Group on Computer Graphics *(1968)*
Historical Note
A semi-autonomous subsidiary of the Ass'n for Computing Machinery, which provides administrative support.

Special Interest Group on Documentation *(1975)*
Historical Note
An affiliate of Association for Computing Machinery, which provides administrative support.

Special Interest Group on Hypertext/Hypermedia
Historical Note
An affiliate of Association for Computing Machinery, which provides administrative support.

Special Interest Group on Management Information Systems *(1960)*
Historical Note
An affiliate of Association for Computing Machinery, which provides administrative support.

Special Interest Group on Management of Data
Historical Note
An affiliate of Association for Computing Machinery, which provides administrative support.

Special Interest Group on Mobility of Systems, Users, Data and Computing
Historical Note
A semi-autonomous subsidiary of Ass'n for Computing Machinery, which provides all administrative support.

Special Interest Group on Multimedia *(1994)*
Historical Note
A semi-autonomous subsidiary of Ass'n for Computing Machinery, which provides all administrative support.

Special Interest Group on Operating Systems
Historical Note
An affiliate of Ass'n for Computing Machinery, which provides administrative support.

Special Interest Group on Programming Languages *(1966)*
Historical Note
A subsidiary of Ass'n for Computing Machinery, which provides administrative support.

Special Interest Group on Security, Audit, and Control *(1981)*
Historical Note
An affiliate of Association for Computing Machinery, which provides administrative support.

Special Interest Group on Software Engineering
Historical Note
An affiliate of Association for Computing Machinery, which provides administrative support.

Special Interest Group on Supporting Group Work *(1980)*
Historical Note
Formerly (1997) Special Interest Group of Office Information Systems and (1986) Special Interest Group on Office Automation. SIGGROUP is a semi-autonomous subsidiary of the Association for Computing Machinery. SIGGROUP is interested in topics related to computer-based systems that have a team or group impact in workplace settings. A strong emphasis of SIGGROUP is the integration of multiple computer-based tools and technologies and the impact on the human activities supported by those tools and technologies. Relevant issues include design, implementation, deployment, evaluation methodologies and impact that would arise when researching computer-based systems in a development environment. Membership: $28/year (ACM members); $48/year (non-ACM); $12/year (student).

Special Libraries Association *(1909)*
331 S. Patrick St.
Alexandria, VA 22314
Tel: (703)647-4900 *Fax:* (703)647-4901
E-Mail: sla@sla.org
Web Site: www.sla.org
Members: 15000 individuals
Staff: 39
Annual Budget: $5-10,000,000
Executive Director: Janice Lachance
Associate Executive Director, Membership and Leadership Services: Linda Broussard
Director, Events: Kristin Foldvik
Director, Information Center: John Latham
Director, Public Policy: Douglas Newcomb

Historical Note
A member of the Council of National Library and Information Associations, and the International Federation of Library Associations and Institutions. Incorporated in Rhode Island in 1928 and later in New York in 1959. Members are information professionals serving industry, business, research, education, news, trade and professional associations, and other institutions which use or produce specialized information. Membership: $125/year.

Meetings/Conferences:
Annual Meetings: June
2007 – Denver, CO/June 3-6
2008 – Seattle, WA/July 27-30
2009 – Washington, DC/June 14-17
2010 – New Orleans, LA/June 13-16
2011 – Philadelphia, PA/June 12-15

Publications:
Information Outlook. m. adv.

Specialized Carriers and Rigging Association *(1943)*
2750 Prosperity Ave., Suite 620
Fairfax, VA 22031-4312
Tel: (703)698-0291 *Fax:* (703)698-0297
E-Mail: info@scranet.org
Web Site: www.scranet.org
Members: 1200 individuals
Staff: 10
Annual Budget: $2-5,000,000
Executive Vice President and Chief Executive Officer: Joel Dandrea
Vice President, Transportation: Douglas Ball

Historical Note
Established as the Heavy Specialized Carriers Section-Local Cartage National Conference, it became the Heavy Specialized Carriers Conference in 1959 and assumed its present name in 1981. Members are

carriers, crane and rigging operators and millwrights engaged in the lifting and transport of heavy goods. Membership: $395-3,200/year (domestic company); $600/year (international).

Meetings/Conferences:
Annual Meetings: Spring

Publications:
Internat'l Cranes and Specialized Transport. m. adv.
News from SC&RA. w.
SC&RA Industrial Relations Bulletin. irreg.
SC&RA Newsletter. w.
SC&RA Safety Bulletin. irreg.
SC&RA Directory of Members and Equipment. a.

Specialized Information Publishers Association *(1964)*
8201 Greenboro Dr.
Suite 300
McLean, VA 22102
Tel: (703)610-0260 *Fax:* (703)610-9005
Toll Free: (800)356 - 9302
E-Mail: nepa@newsletters.org
Web Site: www.newsletters.org
Members: 700 publishers
Staff: 5
Annual Budget: $500-1,000,000
Executive Director: Patricia Wysocki
E-Mail: pwysocki@newsletters.org
Director, Membership and Meetings: Janine Lee Hergesell
Director, Meetings: Janine Lee
E-Mail: jlee@newsletters.org

Historical Note
Assumed current name in 2006. Formerly known as Newsletter & Electronic Publishers of America. Founded as the Independent Newsletter Association; it became the Newsletter Association of America in 1977 and was incorporated in the District of Columbia. Merged with the National Association of Investment Advisory Publishers in 1979. It became the Newsletter Association in 1983, the Newsletter Publishers Association in 1991, and assumed its present name in 2000. NEPA represents nearly 700 publishers producing more than 2,000 newsletters and other information services. The membership fee is based on newsletter revenue.

Meetings/Conferences:
Semi-Annual Meetings: Washington, DC/June and Fall

Publications:
Hotline. bi-w.
Directory of Members & Industry Suppliers. a.

Specialty Coffee Association of America *(1982)*
330 Golden Shore, Suite 50
Long Beach, CA 90802
Tel: (562)624-4100 *Fax:* (562)624-4101
E-Mail: coffee@scaa.org
Web Site: www.scaa.org
Members: 2500 companies
Staff: 14
Annual Budget: $2-5,000,000
Executive Director and Chief Executive Officer: Ted Lingle
Chief of Staff: Mike Ferguson
Manager, Membership Development: Wendy Jensen
Accounting Manager: David Roberson

Historical Note
Membership: $175-950/year (company).

Meetings/Conferences:
Annual Meetings: Spring
2007 – Long Beach, CA/May 4-7/8000

Publications:
Membership Directory. a. adv.
Specialty Coffee Chronicle. bi-m. adv.

Specialty Equipment Market Association *(1963)*
1575 S. Valley Vista Dr.
P.O. Box 4910
Diamond Bar, CA 91765-0910
Tel: (909)396-0289 *Fax:* (909)860-0184
E-Mail: pr@sema.org
Web Site: http://sema.org
Members: 4600 companies
Staff: 70
Annual Budget: $2-5,000,000
President and Chief Executive Officer: Christopher J. Kersting, CAE
Vice President, Marketing and Communications: Peter McGillivray
President and Chief Executive Officer: Christopher J. Kersting, CAE

Historical Note
Formerly (1966) Speed Equipment Manufacturers Association, and (1979) Specialty Equipment Manufacturers Association. Composed of companies supplying performance motor vehicle parts and accessories. Sponsors and supports the SEMA Political Network.

Meetings/Conferences:
Annual Meetings: Fall in Las Vegas, NV(Convention Center)/25,000

Publications:
SEMA e-News. w.
SEMA Fast Facts. bw.
SEMA Member Directory. a. adv.
SEMA News. m. adv.

Specialty Graphic Imaging Association *(1948)*
10015 Main St.
Fairfax, VA 22031-3489
Tel: (703)385-1335 *Fax:* (703)273-0456
Toll Free: (888)385 - 3588
Web Site: www.sgia.org
Members: 4000 companies
Staff: 38
Annual Budget: $5-10,000,000
President and Staff Chief Executive Officer: Michael Robertson
E-Mail: miker@sgia.org
Vice President, Marketing and Membership: Sondra Fry Benoudiz
E-Mail: sondra@sgia.org
Vice President, Conventions/Conferences: Sylvia Hall
Vice President, Government Affairs: Marci Kinter
E-Mail: marcik@sgia.org
Vice President, Technical Services: Johnny Shell
E-Mail: jshell@sgia.com

Historical Note
Formerly (1968) Screen Process Printing Association, (1994) Screen Printing Association International, and (2003) Screenprinting and Graphic Imaging Association International. Supports the Screen Printing Technical Foundation to conduct research, tests, studies and scientific examinations designed to provide information on screen printing, and to conduct indepth training workshops. Supports the Center for Digital Imaging. Embroidery, pad printing, digital imaging and other related graphic processes are also supported by SGIA. Membership Fee: Sliding scale based on sales volume.

Meetings/Conferences:
Annual Meetings: Fall/12,000-14,000
2007 – Orlando, FL(Convention Center)/Oct. 24-24/18000
2008 – Atlanta, GA(GA World Congress Center)/Oct. 15-18/14000
2009 – New Orleans, LA(Convention Center)/Oct. 28/14000

Publications:
Buyer's Guide (online). a. adv.
SGIA Journal. q. adv.
SGIA News. m.
Who's Who in SGIA. a.

Specialty Sleep Association *(1975)*
46639 Jones Ranch Rd.
Friant, CA 93626
Tel: (559)868-4187 *Fax:* (559)868-4185
E-Mail: tambra@netptc.net
Web Site: www.specialtysleepnet.com
Members: 80 companies
Staff: 1
Annual Budget: $50-100,000
Executive Director: Tambra Jones

Historical Note
Formed from a merger of the National Waterbed Retailers Association and the Waterbed Manufacturers Association in 1994 as the Waterbed Council, assumed its current name in 1996. SSA is a national organization of manufacturers, distributors and retailers of specialty mattresses and other sleep-related items, including foam, water, air, adjustable and other bedding products. SSA's members share the unified goal of serving the markets for specialty sleep services and related product lines.

Meetings/Conferences:
Annual Meetings: March/1,000

Publications:
Bedroom Industry. bi-m. adv.

Specialty Steel Industry of North America *(1962)*
3050 K St. NW
Suite 400
Washington, DC 20007
Tel: (202)342-8630 *Fax:* (202)342-8631
Toll Free: (800)982 - 0355
Web Site: www.ssina.com
Members: 21 companies
Annual Budget: $500-1,000,000
Secretary and Counsel: David A. Hartquist

Historical Note
Formerly (1983) Tool and Stainless Steel Industry Committee and (1994) Specialty Steel Industry of the U.S. Has no paid officers or full-time staff.

Specialty Tobacco Council *(1984)*
204 Northgate Park Dr.
Winston-Salem, NC 27106
Tel: (336)759-0391 *Fax:* (336)759-0965
Web Site: http://specialtytobacco.org
Members: 5 Companies
Staff: 2
Annual Budget: $50-100,000
Executive Director: Henry C. Roemer

Historical Note
Represents manufacturers and importers of specialty tobacco products.

Publications:
Newsletter. m.

Specialty Tool and Fastener Distributors Association *(1976)*
P.O. Box 44
Elm Grove, WI 53122
Tel: (262)784-4774 *Fax:* (262)784-5059
Toll Free: (800)352 - 2981
E-Mail: info@stafda.org
Web Site: www.stafda.org
Members: 2560 companies
Staff: 3
Annual Budget: $2-5,000,000
Executive Director: Georgia H. Foley
E-Mail: ghfoley@stafda.org
Director, Member Services: Cathy Usher

Historical Note
Members distribute or manufacture power tools, powder-actuated tools, anchors, diamond drilling equipment, fastening systems and related construction/industrial supplies. Membership: $350/year (company).

Meetings/Conferences:
Annual Meetings: November
2007 – Nashville, TN(Opryland Hotel)/Nov. 4-6
2008 – Denver, CO(Colorado Convention Center)/Nov. 9-11
2009 – New Orleans, LA(Morial Convention Center)/Nov. 9-11
2010 – Phoenix, AZ(Phoenix Civic Center)/Nov. 14-16
2011 – San Antonio, TX(Henry B. Gonzalez Convention Center)/Nov. 6-8
2012 – Orlando, FL(Orange County Convention Center)/Nov. 4-6

Publications:
Membership Directory. a.
Trade News. m.

Specialty Vehicle Institute of America *(1983)*
Two Jenner St.
Suite 150
Irvine, CA 92618-3806
Tel: (949)727-3727 *Fax:* (949)727-4216
Members: 11 companies
Staff: 40
Annual Budget: $2-5,000,000
President: Tim Buche
Vice President, Administration: Joe Di Corpo

Historical Note
A national, non-profit trade association representing manufacturers and distributors of all-terrain vehicles, SVIA's purpose is to foster and promote the safe and responsible use of specialty vehicles manufactured and/or distributed in the U.S.

Publications:
Tips and Practice for the ATV Rider.
Parents, Youngsters and ATVs.
ATV RiderCourse Handbook.

Speech and Signal Processing Acoustics Society

Historical Note
A subsidiary of the Institute of Electrical and Electronics Engineers. Membership in the Society, open only to IEEE members, includes subscription to a technical periodical in the field published by IEEE. All administrative support is provided by IEEE.

SPIE - The International Society for Optical Engineering *(1955)*

P.O. Box Ten
Bellingham, WA 98227
Tel: (360)676-3290 *Fax:* (360)647-1445
E-Mail: spie@spie.org
Web Site: www.spie.org
Members: 14000 individuals
Staff: 152
Annual Budget: $10-25,000,000
Executive Director: G. Eugene Arthurs
Director, IT and Electronic Products: Marybeth Manning
Director, Publications: Eric Pepper
Director, Events: Janice Walker

Historical Note
Members are scientists, engineers and companies interested in technology and applications of optical, electro-optical, fiber-optic, laser and photonic systems. Founded and incorporated in 1955 in California as the Society of Photographic Instrumentation Engineers; later became the Society of Photo-Optical Instrumentation Engineers and assumed its present name in 1983. A member society of the American Institute for Medical and Biological Engineering and the American Association of Engineering Socs., and an affiliate society of the American Institute of Physics. Has an annual budget of approximately $20 million. Membership: $95/year (individual); institutional dues based on annual sales volume.

Meetings/Conferences:
Annual Meetings: Winter

Publications:
OE Magazine. m. adv.
Optical Networks Magazine. bi-m. adv.
Journal of Microlithography, Microfabrication, and Microsystems. q. adv.
Journal of Biomedical Optics. q. adv.
Optical Engineering. m. adv.
Journal of Electronic Imaging. q. adv.

Spill Control Association of America *(1973)*

32500 Scenic Ln.
Franklin, MI 48025
Tel: (248)851-1936
Web Site: www.scaa-spill.org
Members: 125companiesandorganizations
Staff: 2
Annual Budget: $100-250,000
Executive Director and General Counsel: Marc K. Shaye
E-Mail: marcs@scaa-spill.org

Historical Note
Established as the Oil Spill Control Association of America, it assumed its present name in 1978. Members are companies and individuals concerned with cleaning up spills of oil and hazardous products and manufacturers of specialized products for spill control/clean-up and personnel protection. The above address is that of the law firm of Riley Roumell & Connolly, P.C. Membership: $250/year (individual); $1000/year (company).

Publications:
Spill Briefs/Newsletter. w.

Spinal Stress Research Society *(1976)*

Historical Note
Also known as Precision Chiropractic Research Society.

Sponge and Chamois Institute *(1933)*

117 Wilmot Circle
Suite Two
Scarsdale, NY 10583-6721
Tel: (914)725-4646 *Fax:* (914)725-1183
Members: 5 companies
Staff: 2
Annual Budget: $25-50,000
Executive Secretary: Jules Schwimmer

Historical Note
Members are dealers and suppliers of natural sponges and chamois leather.

Meetings/Conferences:
Annual Meetings: usually October

Sporting Arms and Ammunition Manufacturers' Institute *(1926)*

11 Mile Hill Rd.
Newtown, CT 06470
Tel: (203)426-4358
Web Site: www.saami.org
Members: 26 companies
Staff: 3
Annual Budget: $500-1,000,000
Managing Director: Rick Patterson

Historical Note
The trade association of major U.S. producers of sporting firearms, ammunition and smokeless propellants, SAAMI is active primarily in technical matters relating to voluntary industry standards and product safety.

Sporting Goods Agents Association *(1934)*

P.O. Box 998
Morton Grove, IL 60053
Tel: (847)296-3670 *Fax:* (847)827-0196
E-Mail: sgaa998@aol.com
Web Site: www.sgaaonline.org
Members: 1000 individuals
Staff: 2
Annual Budget: $100-250,000
Chief Operating Officer: Lois E. Halinton
E-Mail: sgaa998@aol.com

Historical Note
Formerly (1977) Sporting Goods Representatives Association. SGAA represents established independent manufacturers' agents in the sporting goods industry in the United States and Canada. Membership: $200/year (per head of agency); $50/year (per individual member).

Meetings/Conferences:
Annual Meetings: Winter
2007 – Las Vegas, NV(Sands Convention)/June 11-13/400

Publications:
Membership Roster. w.
Newsletter. m.

Sporting Goods Manufacturers Association *(1906)*

1150 17th St., N.W., Suite 850
Washington, DC 20036
Tel: (202)775-1762
E-Mail: info@sgma.com
Staff: 14
President and Chief Executive Officer: Tom Cove
Director, Communications: Andrea Cernich
Director, Government Relations: Bill Sells

Historical Note
Established as the Athletic Goods Manufacturers Association; became Sporting Goods Manufacturers Association in 1972, and assumed its present name in 2002. SGMA represents the interests of more than 1,000 industry-leading brands of sports products. SGMA and its member companies advocate for policies which encourage and increase public participation in sports and recreation; promote a favorable trade environment for its member companies; and establish proper safeguards and regulations for corporate responsibility, consumer product safety, and patents and trademarks.

Meetings/Conferences:
Annual Meetings: Winter
2007 – Las Vegas, NV/June 11-13

Sports Lawyers Association *(1976)*

12100 Sunset Hills Rd.
Suite 130
Reston, VA 20190
Tel: (703)437-4377 *Fax:* (703)435-4390
E-Mail: info@sportslaw.org
Web Site: www.sportslaw.org
Members: 1200 individuals
Staff: 2
Annual Budget: $250-500,000
Executive Director: Richard A. Guggolz
Deputy Executive Director: William M. Drohan, CAE

Historical Note
Members are attorneys specializing in sports law. Associate membership is available for professionals and entities having a legitimate interest in sports law. Other categories of membership are available for educators and law students. Membership: $245/year (lawyer/regular); $440/year (associate); $115/year (educator); $25/year (law student);

Meetings/Conferences:
Annual Meetings: Spring
2007 – Boston, MA(Westin Copley Plaza)/May 17-19/450
2008 – San Francisco, CA(Westin St. Francis)/May 15-17/450
2009 – Chicago, IL(Hyatt Regency)/May 14-16

Publications:
Sports Lawyers Journal. a.
Membership Directory. a.
Newsletter. m.

Sports Turf Managers Association *(1981)*

805 New Hampshire St., Suite E
Lawrence, KS 66044-2774
Tel: (760)843-2549 *Fax:* (800)366-0391
Toll Free: (800)323 - 3875
E-Mail: stmainfo@sportsturfmanager.org
Web Site: www.sportsturfmanager.org
Members: 2400 individuals
Staff: 4
Annual Budget: $1-2,000,000
Executive Director: Kim Heck

Historical Note
STMA is the professional association for sports turf managers from around the world. Members keep abreast of the latest research and technology and apply their knowledge and expertise to provide the highest quality of playing fields for athletes. Membership: $95/year (individual); $295 (corporate); $20/year (student). STMA - Experts in the Field. Partners in the Game.

Meetings/Conferences:
Annual Meetings: December
2007 – San Antonio, TX(Henry B. Gonzalez Convention Center)/Jan. 17-21
2008 – Phoenix, AZ(Phoenix Civic Plaza)/Jan. 16-20
2010 – Orlando, FL(Disney's Coronado Resort)/Jan. 13-17

Publications:
SportsTurf Magazine. m. adv.
Sports Turf Manager. bi-m. adv.
Membership Directory. a. adv.
Sports Turf Proceedings. a. adv.

Sportsplex Operators and Developers Association *(1981)*

P.O. Box 24617, Westgate Station
Rochester, NY 14624-0617
Tel: (585)426-2215 *Fax:* (585)247-3112
E-Mail: info@sportsplexoperators.com
Web Site: www.sportsplexoperators.com
Members: 1125 sports facilities
Annual Budget: $500-1,000,000
Executive Director: Don Aselin

Historical Note
Founded as Sportsplex Owners and Directors of America; assumed its current name in 1994. SODA was formed to meet the needs of the private concerns, public agencies, and other organizations that own or maintain sports complex facilities. Membership: $295/year (full member), $295/year (associate).

Meetings/Conferences:
Annual Meetings: January

Publications:
SODAsite. bi-m. adv.

SPRI, Inc. *(1982)*
77 Rumford Ave., Suite 3B
Waltham, MA 02453
Tel: (781)647-7026 *Fax:* (781)647-7222
E-Mail: info@spri.org
Web Site: www.spri.org
Members: 59 companies
Staff: 3
Annual Budget: $250-500,000
Managing Director: Linda King

Historical Note
Founded as Single-Ply Roofing Institute, SPRI members are manufacturers and marketers of sheet-applied membrane roofing materials and supplies to the industry. Membership: $1,500-7,500/year (depending on company product).

Meetings/Conferences:
Annual Meetings: January
2007 – San Diego, CA(Rancho Bernardo Inn)/Jan. 12-14

Publications:
A Professional's Guide to Specifications. a.

Spring Manufacturers Institute *(1933)*
2001 Midwest Rd.
Suite 106
Oak Brook, IL 60523-1335
Tel: (630)495-8588 *Fax:* (630)495-8595
E-Mail: info@smihq.org
Web Site: www.smihq.org
Members: 335 companies
Staff: 6
Annual Budget: $1-2,000,000
Executive Vice President: Ken Boyce, CAE
Member Services Coordinator: Kim Burd
Financial Administration Coordinator: Pashun McNulty
Manager, Communications: Rita Schauer

Historical Note
Founded as the Spring Manufacturers Association; assumed present name in 1961.

Meetings/Conferences:
Semi-Annual Meetings: Spring and Fall/300

Publications:
Springs Magazine. 6/year. adv.

Spring Research Institute *(1933)*
3034 N. Fleming Circle
Shelbyville, IN 46176
Tel: (317)398-3822
Web Site: www.springresearch.org
Members: 12 manufacturers, 6 associates
Staff: 3
Annual Budget: $100-250,000
President: John Thomson

Historical Note
Members are manufacturers of leaf springs for the automotive aftermarket.

Meetings/Conferences:
Semi-annual Meetings: Spring and Fall

SSPC: the Society for Protective Coatings *(1950)*
40 24th St., Sixth Floor
Pittsburgh, PA 15222-4656
Tel: (412)281-2331 *Fax:* (412)281-9992
Toll Free: (877)281 - 7772
E-Mail: members@sspc.org
Web Site: www.sspc.org
Members: 7500 individuals
Staff: 30
Annual Budget: $2-5,000,000
Executive Director: William L. Shoup
Controller: Barbara B. Fisher
Director, Marketing: Michael E. Kline
E-Mail: fisher@sspc.org

Historical Note
Founded as Steel Structures Painting Council; assumed its current name in 1997. Conducts research, develops standards, and disseminates information about surface preparation, application techniques, coatings, and related technology for protecting structural steel and other surfaces. Members include paint manufacturers, raw material suppliers, specifiers, applicators, government agencies, and a wide variety of end-users. Administers the Painting Contractor Certification Program. Membership: $95/year (individual); $700-5,500/year (organization).

Meetings/Conferences:
Annual Meetings: Winter/4,000
2007 – Dallas, TX(Dallas Convention Center)/Feb. 10-15
2010 – Phoenix, AZ(Phoenix Civic Plaza)/Feb. 3-10

Publications:
Journal of Protective Coatings and Linings. m. adv.
Symposium Proceedings. a.

Stable Value Investment Association *(1990)*
1025 Connecticut Ave. NW
Suite 1000
Washington, DC 20036
Tel: (202)580-7620 *Fax:* (202)580-7621
E-Mail: info@stablevalue.org
Web Site: www.stablevalue.org
President: Gina Mitchell

Historical Note
Members are firms and individuals with a professional interest in savings for retirement.

Publications:
Stable Times. q.

Stadium Managers Association *(1954)*
525 S.W. Fifth St., Suite A
Des Moines, IA 50309-4501
Tel: (515)282-8192
E-Mail: sma@assoc-mgmt.com
Web Site: www.stadiummanagers.org/
Members: 500 individuals
Staff: 3
Annual Budget: $250-500,000
Executive Director: Kerry Goodson

Historical Note
Membership: $200/year.

Meetings/Conferences:
Annual Meetings: February/350

Stained Glass Association of America *(1903)*
10009 E. 62nd St.
Raytown, MO 64133
Toll Free: (800)438 - 9581
E-Mail: headquarters@sgaaonline.com
Web Site: www.stainedglass.org
Members: 590 individuals
Staff: 3
Annual Budget: $250-500,000
Editor: Richard Gross

Historical Note
Membership is composed of stained glass studios, artists, designers, craft suppliers and others actively engaged in the craft of stained glass. Officers change annually in June. Membership: $100/year (affiliate); $100/year (related profession affiliate); $200/year (active); $50/year (student affiliate); $500/year (accredited).

Publications:
Stained Glass. q. adv.
Kaleidoscope. 3/year.

Standards Engineering Society *(1947)*
13340 S.W. 96th Ave.
Miami, FL 33176
Tel: (305)971-4798 *Fax:* (305)971-4799
Web Site: www.ses-standards.org
Members: 430 individuals
Staff: 1
Annual Budget: $50-100,000
Executive Director: Dr. H. Glenn Ziegenfuss

Historical Note
SES is professional membership society promoting the use of standards and enhancing the knowledge of standardization. Members are engineers, teachers, executives, scholars and others involved in the development and/or use of industry, government, national or international standards. Membership: $65/year (individual).

Meetings/Conferences:
Annual Meetings: Fall
2007 – San Francisco, CA/Aug. 20-21/100

Publications:
Standards Engineering. bi-m. adv.

State and Territorial Air Pollution Program Administrators *(1968)*
444 North Capitol St. NW
Suite 307
Washington, DC 20001-1512
Tel: (202)624-7864 *Fax:* (202)624-7863
E-Mail: 4clnair@sso.org
Web Site: www.cleanairworld.org
Members: 54 state & territorial agencies
Staff: 7
Annual Budget: $1-2,000,000
Executive Director: S. William Becker

Historical Note
Members are representatives from each state and territory. Shares headquarters and staff with the Association of Local Air Pollution Control Officials.

Meetings/Conferences:
Semi-annual Meetings: Spring and Fall & Air Toxics Conf. Annually

Publications:
Washington Update. w.

State Debt Management Network *(1991)*
444 N. Capital St., Suite 400
Washington, DC 20001
Tel: (202)624-8595 *Fax:* (202)624-8677
E-Mail: callen@csq.org
Web Site: www.nast.net/debtnet/index.htm
Members: 50 individuals
Staff: 2
Contact: Chris Young

Historical Note
SDMN members are state officials concerned with the issuance or management of state debt. Affiliated with the National Association of State Treasurers, serves as a professional organization for individuals responsible for the management of oversight of public debt at the state level. The purpose is to enhance debt management practices through training, development of educational materials, and data collection and dissemination. Membership: $250/year (voting/professional); $50/year (associate).

State Government Affairs Council *(1975)*
515 King St., Suite 325
Alexandria, VA 22314
Tel: (703)684-0967 *Fax:* (703)684-0968
E-Mail: stategov@sgac.org
Web Site: www.sgac.org
Members: 150 companies
Staff: 3
Annual Budget: $50-100,000
Executive Director: Elizabeth A. Loudy

Historical Note
Formed in October 1975 as an outgrowth of the National Council of State Legislatures. Members are representatives of major U.S. companies and associations that participate in the state-level public policy process. Works with the National Conference of State Legislatures, the Council of State Governments, the American Legislative Exchange Council, and various other national associations to improve state government and enhance cooperation between the business community and state government. Membership: $5,000/year.

Meetings/Conferences:
Annual Meetings: Spring
2007 – Chicago, IL(The James Chicago)/March 21-23/150

Publications:
SGAC Member Resource Handbook. a.
SGAC Bi-monthly Update. bi-m.
SGAC Annual Report. a.

State Guard Association of the United States *(1985)*
P.O. Box 1416
Fayetteville, GA 30214-1416
Tel: (770)460-1215
E-Mail: director@sgaus.org
Web Site: www.sgaus.org
Members: 2600 individuals
Staff: 2
Annual Budget: $25-50,000
Executive Director: Byers W. Coleman

Historical Note
SGAUS is the association in support of State Guards (also known as state defense forces); members are active and retired members of state defense forces. Membership: $16/year (enlisted/NCO); $25/year (officer); $25/year (unaffiliated); $30/year (general officer).

Meetings/Conferences:
Annual Meetings:

Publications:
SGAUS Journal. q.

State Higher Education Executive Officers *(1954)*
3035 Center Green Dr., Suite 100
Boulder, CO 80301-2251
Tel: (303)541-1600 *Fax:* (303)541-1639
Web Site: http://sheeo.org
Members: 50 states and provinces
Staff: 10
Annual Budget: $1-2,000,000
President: Paul E. Lingenfelter
Executive Assistant and Meetinng Planner: Gladys Kerns

Historical Note
Headquartered in Colorado, SHEEO members are the chief executive officers serving statewide coordinating boards and governing boards of postsecondary education. Members include 49 states, the District of Columbia, and the Commonwealth of Puerto Rico.

Meetings/Conferences:
Annual Meetings: Summer

State Risk and Insurance Management Association
P.O. Box 91106
1201 N. Third St., Suite G
Baton Rouge, LA 70821-9106
Tel: (225)342-8473 *Fax:* (225)342-6331
Web Site: www.strima.org
Members: 50 individuals
Annual Budget: $50-100,000
President: J.S. Bud Thompson

Historical Note
STRIMA members are state government risk and insurance managers. Membership: $200/year (organization).

States Organization for Boating Access *(1986)*
50 Water St.
Warren, RI 02885
Tel: (401)247-2224 *Fax:* (401)247-0074
E-Mail: info@sobaus.org
Web Site: www.sobaus.org
Members: 50 states and provinces
Staff: 1
Annual Budget: $500-1,000,000
Secretary: Mark Amaral

Historical Note
SOBA is devoted to the acquisition, development and administration of public recreational boating facilities around the United States and in Canada. SOBA members are states and provinces. Advisory membership is open to federal agencies, local governments, and non-profit organizations. Associate membership is available for corporations. Membership: $450 (voting); $350 (associate); $250 (advisory); $100 (individual); $25/year (affiliated) .

Meetings/Conferences:
Annual Meetings:

Publications:
Operations and Maintenance Program Guidelines for Recreational Boating Facilities.
Design Handbook for Recreational Boating and Fishing Facilities.

Station Representatives Association *(1948)*
16 W. 77th St., Suite 9-E
New York, NY 10024-5126
Tel: (212)362-8868 *Fax:* (212)362-4999
Members: 9 organizations
Staff: 1
Annual Budget: $250-500,000
Managing Director: Jerome Feniger

Historical Note
Founded (1948) as the National Association of Radio Station Representatives, Inc. Became Station Representatives Association Inc., in 1952. Broadcast sales organizations, not affiliated with a national network, who sell non-network broadcast advertising.

Meetings/Conferences:
Annual Meetings: New York City

Publications:
The Must Carry Rules.

Steel Deck Institute *(1939)*
P.O. Box 25
Fox River Grove, IL 60021-0025
Tel: (847)458-4647 *Fax:* (847)458-4648
Web Site: www.sdi.org
Members: 25 companies
Staff: 3
Annual Budget: $250-500,000
Managing Director: Steven A. Roehrig

Historical Note
Established as the Metal Roof Deck Technical Institute; assumed its present name in 1939. A non-profit association of steel deck producers and associate members furnishing products allied to steel deck use in construction. SDI provides uniform industry guidelines for the engineering, design, manufacture and field usage of steel decks.

Meetings/Conferences:
Annual Meetings: May

Publications:
Manual of Construction with Steel Deck. a.
Roof Deck Construction Handbook. a.
Composite Deck Design Handbook. a.
Diaphragm Design Manual. a.
SDI Design Manual. a.
Standard Practice Details Manual. a.

Steel Door Institute *(1954)*
30200 Detroit Rd.
Cleveland, OH 44145-1967
Tel: (440)899-0010 *Fax:* (440)892-1404
Web Site: www.steeldoor.org
Members: 11 companies
Staff: 5
Annual Budget: $50-100,000
Managing Director: J. Jeffery Wherry

Historical Note
Producers of standard steel doors and frames or commercial and industrial construction.

Meetings/Conferences:
Annual Meetings: 3/year

Steel Founders' Society of America *(1902)*
780 McArdle Dr., Unit G
Crystal Lake, IL 60014
Tel: (815)455-8240 *Fax:* (815)455-8241
Web Site: www.sfsa.org
Members: 80 corporations
Staff: 5
Annual Budget: $500-1,000,000
Executive Vice President: Raymond W. Monroe
E-Mail: monroe@sfsa.org
Planner, Meetings: Sandra Walker
E-Mail: sandra@sfsa.org

Historical Note
A technically oriented trade association serving the steel casting industry. Absorbed the Alloy Casting Institute in 1970. Has no individual membership.

Meetings/Conferences:
Annual Meetings: Fall
2007 – Girdwood, AK(Alyeska Resort)/Aug. 17-22/100

Publications:
Directory of Steel Foundries (online only). a.

Steel Joist Institute *(1928)*
3127 10th Ave., North Ext.
Myrtle Beach, SC 29577-6760
Tel: (843)626-1995 *Fax:* (843)626-5565
E-Mail: sji@steeljoist.org
Web Site: www.steeljoist.org
Members: 18 companies
Staff: 3
Technical Director: Perry Green

Historical Note
Composed of active manufacturers, the SJI cooperates with government and business agencies to establish steel joist standards.

Meetings/Conferences:
Annual Meetings: May

Publications:
Catalogue of Specifications and Load Tables.
Technical Digests.

Steel Manufacturers Association *(1988)*
1150 Connecticut Ave. NW
Suite 715
Washington, DC 20036
Tel: (202)296-1515 *Fax:* (202)296-2506
Web Site: www.steelnet.org
Members: 38 steel companies
Staff: 4
Annual Budget: $1-2,000,000
President: Thomas A. Danjczek
Manager, Mentor Services and Administration: Kristina Cushing
Manager, Public Policy and Publications: Adam Parr
Director, Environment and Energy: Eric J. Stuart

Historical Note
SMA is the largest steel trade group in North America. It is the primary association for "minimills", companies engaged in electric arc furnace/continuous caster steel production as well as hot and cold rollers of steel mill products. A growing number of integrated steel producers are also members. There are 118 associate members who are providers of materials, equipment and services to the steel industry and 6 international steel company members.

Meetings/Conferences:
Annual Meetings: Spring

Publications:
Annual Public Policy Statement. a. adv.
Annual Membership Directory. a. adv.

Steel Plate Fabricators Association Division of STI/SPFA *(1933)*
570 Oakwood Rd.
Lake Zurich, IL 60047
Tel: (847)428-8265 *Fax:* (847)438-8766
Web Site: www.spfa.org
Members: 135 companies
Staff: 3
Annual Budget: $500-1,000,000
Executive Vice President: Wayne B. Geyer

Historical Note
Formerly Steel Plate Fabricators Association; became a division of STI/SPFA and assumed its current name in 2004. Shares staff with the Steel Plate Institute Division of STI/SPFA. Membership: $750-7,000/year.

Meetings/Conferences:
Annual Meetings: Early Spring/250

Publications:
Directory of SPFA Metal Plate Fabricators. a.
Steel Plate Update. q.

Steel Recycling Institute *(1988)*
Foster Plaza Ten
680 Andersen Dr.
Pittsburgh, PA 15220-2700
Tel: (412)922-2772 *Fax:* (412)922-3213
Toll Free: (800)876 - 7274
E-Mail: sri@recycle-steel.org
Web Site: www.recycle-steel.org
Members: 60 companies
Staff: 10
Annual Budget: $500-1,000,000
President: William M. Heenan, Jr.
Administrative Assistant, Marketing and Communications: Charlene Cottrell
Vice President, Operations: Gregory L. Crawford
Manager, Public and Education Relations: James Woods

Historical Note
Promotes steel recycling and works to forge a coalition of steelmakers, can manufacturers, beverage and food companies, legislators, government officials, solid waste managers, businesses, and consumer groups. Formerly (1993) Steel Can Recycling Institute. Merged with the American Iron and Steel Institute (1999) as a department, and continues to operate under the SRI name.

Meetings/Conferences:
Annual Meetings:

Steel Shipping Container Institute *(1944)*

1101 14th St. NW
Suite S-1001
Washington, DC 20005
Tel: (202)408-1900 *Fax:* (202)408-1972
E-Mail: ssci@steelcontainers.com
Web Site: www.steelcontainers.com
Members: 57 companies
Staff: 2
Annual Budget: $500-1,000,000
Executive Director: John A. McQuaid
E-Mail: mcquaid@steelcontainers.com

Historical Note
SSCI members are makers of steel drums, barrels and pails.

Meetings/Conferences:
Semi-annual Meetings: Spring and Fall

Publications:
Packaging Vision. q.
SSCI Newsletter. q.

Steel Tank Institute Division of STI/SPFA *(1916)*

570 Oakwood Rd.
Lake Zurich, IL 60047
Tel: (847)438-8265 *Fax:* (847)438-8766
Web Site: www.steeltank.com
Members: 100 companies
Staff: 12
Annual Budget: $1-2,000,000
Executive Vice President: Wayne B. Geyer
Controller: Kevin Kroll

Historical Note
Formerly the Steel Tank Institute; became a division of STI/SPFA and assumed its current name in 2004. Conducts research and develops underground and above ground storage tank technologies and standards for the steel industry, and provides educational training and certificates. Represents its members to regulatory agencies. Absorbed (1990) Association for Composite Tanks. Shares staff with another division of STI/SPFA, the Steel Plate Fabricators Association of STI/SPFA.

Publications:
Tank Talk. q.
Membership Roster. a.
Annual Report.
Member Technology Guide. semi-a.

Steel Tube Institute of North America *(1930)*

2000 Ponce de Leon, Suite 600
Coral Gables, FL 33134
Tel: (305)421-6236 *Fax:* (305)443-1603
Web Site: www.steeltubeinstitute.org
Members: 60 companies
Staff: 4
Annual Budget: $500-1,000,000
Executive Director: William A. Wolfe
E-Mail: stina@steeltubeinstitute.org

Historical Note
Formerly (until 1960) the Formed Steel Tube Institute and (until August 1988) Welded Steel Tube Institute. Incorporated in Ohio in 1955. Members make steel tubes and pipes produced from carbon, stainless or alloy steel, for applications ranging from large structural tubing to small redrawn tubing. The Institute committees are: manufacturing/technical; standard pipe; structural tubing; mechanical tube; sprinkler/conduit; supplier relations, stainless, tubular, and hollow structural sections..

Meetings/Conferences:
Semi-Annual Meetings: Spring and Fall

Steel Window Institute *(1920)*

1300 Sumner Ave.
Cleveland, OH 44115-2851
Tel: (216)241-7333 *Fax:* (216)241-0105
E-Mail: swi@steelwindows.com
Web Site: www.steelwindows.com
Members: 7 companies
Staff: 3
Executive Secretary: John H. Addington

Historical Note
Formerly the Metal Window Institute, SWI members are United States manufacturers of windows made from hot-rolled, solid steel sections and such related products as castings, trim, mechanical operators, screens and moldings.

Meetings/Conferences:
Annual Meetings: Fall

Publications:
The Specifiers Guide to Steel Windows.

Stilbene Whitening Agents

Historical Note
An affiliate of the Synthetic Organic Chemicals Manufacturers Association which provides administrative support.

Storage Equipment Manufacturer's Association *(1972)*

Historical Note
An affiliate of Material Handling Industry of America, which provides administrative support.

Strategic Account Management Association *(1964)*

150 N. Wacker Dr., Suite 2222
Chicago, IL 60606-1607
Tel: (312)251-3131 *Fax:* (312)251-3132
E-Mail: fegley@strategicaccounts.org
Web Site: www.strategicaccounts.org
Members: 3900 individuals
Staff: 15
Annual Budget: $2-5,000,000
President and Chief Executive Officer: Lisa Napolitano
Director, Membership: Matt Fegley
Director, Meetings: Marcella Grigaliunas, CMP
E-Mail: grigalimas@strategicaccounts.org

Historical Note
Founded as National Account Marketing Association; became National Account Management Association and assumed its current name in 1999. Members are company executives concerned with sales or marketing to major national and global accounts and the special management they require. SAMA provides literature and training and conducts surveys and studies on the intricacies of large, complex account management. Incorporated in the State of Illinois. Membership: $450/year.

Meetings/Conferences:
Annual Meetings: Spring

Publications:
Velocity Magazine. q. adv.
Annual Survey of SAM Compensation. a.
Focus: Account Manager. q. adv.
Focus: Teams. q. adv.

Structural Board Association *(1976)*

25 Valleywood Dr., Unit 27
Markham, ON L3R 5-LR
Tel: (905)475-1100 *Fax:* (905)475-1101
E-Mail: info@osbguide.com
Web Site: www.osbguide.com
Members: 50 companies & institutions
Staff: 3
Annual Budget: $1-2,000,000
President and Chief Executive Officer: Mark Angelini

Historical Note
Formerly (1976) Canadian Waferboard Association and (1982) The Waferboard Association. SBA members are manufacturers and suppliers of structural panels (oriented strandboard and waferboard). Maintains a U.S. office at 1133 Connecticut Ave. NW, Washington, DC 20036.

Meetings/Conferences:
Semi-Annual Meetings: Spring and Fall
2007 – Vancouver, BC, Canada

Publications:
OSB in Wood Frame Construction. irreg.
Technical Forum Proceedings. m.
Technical Bulletin. irreg.
Newsletter. m.
News Clipping. w.

Structural Insulated Panel Association *(1990)*

P.O. Box 1699
Gig Harbor, WA 98335
Tel: (253)858-7472 *Fax:* (253)858-0272
E-Mail: billw@sips.org
Web Site: www.sips.org
Members: 200 companies and organizations
Staff: 3
Annual Budget: $250-500,000
Executive Director: William Wachtler

Historical Note
SIPA is a non-profit trade association representing manufacturers, suppliers, fabricators/distributors, design professionals, and builders committed to providing quality structural insulated panels for all segments of the construction industry.

Meetings/Conferences:
Annual Meetings:

Publications:
OnSite@SIPA. q. adv.

Structural Stability Research Council *(1944)*

301 Butler-Carlton Hall, Univ. of Missouri
Rolla, MO 65409-0030
Tel: (573)341-6610 *Fax:* (573)341-4476
E-Mail: ssrc@umr.edu
Web Site: www.stabilitycouncil.org
Members: 400 individuals
Staff: 2
Annual Budget: $100-250,000
Administrator: Christina Stratman

Historical Note
An outgrowth of the American Society of Civil Engineers Committee on Design of Structural Members, The Column Research Council was established by the Engineering Foundation in 1944. In 1976, broadened scope of its interests led to the adoption of the present name. Members are individuals, organizations or firms concerned with the investigation of stability aspects of metal and composite structures. Membership: $50/year (individual), $20-2,000 (company, organization or sponsor).

Meetings/Conferences:
Annual Meetings: Fall

Publications:
Proceedings, Annual Technical Session. a.
Annual Report & Register. a.

Stucco Manufacturers Association *(1957)*

2402 Vista Nobleza
Newport Beach, CA 92660
Tel: (949)640-9902 *Fax:* (949)640-9911
E-Mail: info@stuccomfgassoc.com
Web Site: www.stuccomfgassoc.com
Members: 30 individuals
Staff: 1
Annual Budget: $10-25,000
Executive Director: Norma S. Fox

Stuntmen's Association of Motion Pictures *(1961)*

10660 Riverside Dr., Second Floor
Suite E
Toluca Lake, CA 91602
Tel: (818)766-4334 *Fax:* (818)766-5943
E-Mail: info@stuntmen.com
Web Site: www.stuntmen.com
Members: 137 individuals
Staff: 2
Annual Budget: $50-100,000
Secretary: Harry Wowchuk

Historical Note
Members are members of the Screen Actors Guild or the American Federation of Television and Radio Artists who perform stuntwork.

Meetings/Conferences:
Monthly Meetings:

Publications:
Newsletter. m. adv.

Stuntwomen's Association of Motion Pictures *(1967)*

12457 Ventura Blvd., Suite 208
Studio City, CA 91604-2411
Tel: (818)762-0907 *Fax:* (818)762-9534
E-Mail: stuntwomen@stuntwomen.com
Web Site: www.stuntwomen.com
Members: 34 individuals
Staff: 1
Annual Budget: $10-25,000
President: Jane Austin Villanueve

Historical Note
SWAMP is an organization representing professional stuntwomen who are also full members of the Screen Actors Guild and the American Federation of Television and Radio Artists. Applicants for

membership must have been earning a living exclusively as a stuntperson for a minimum of five years.

Meetings/Conferences:
Annual Meetings: Monthly Meetings

Subcontractors Trade Association *(1966)*
570 Seventh Ave., Suite 1100
New York, NY 10018
Tel: (212)398-6220 *Fax:* (212)398-6224
E-Mail: subcontractorstrade@verizon.net
Web Site: www.stanyc.com
Members: 330 companies
Staff: 3
Annual Budget: $500-1,000,000
Executive Director: Ron Berger

Historical Note
Members are specialty and supply companies in the construction industry. Membership fee: $695/year.

Publications:
Subcontractor News. m. adv.

Submersible Wastewater Pump Association *(1976)*
1866 Sheridan Rd.
Suite 201
Highland Park, IL 60035-2545
Tel: (847)681-1868 *Fax:* (847)681-1869
E-Mail: swpaexdir@sbcglobal.net
Web Site: www.swpa.org
Members: 50 companies
Staff: 5
Annual Budget: $100-250,000
Executive Director: Charles G. Stolberg

Historical Note
The Submersible Wastewater Pump Association (SWPA) is a national trade association representing and serving the manufacturers of submersible pumps for municipal and industrial applications. Founded in 1976, SWPA's primary focus since its inception had been in three areas: Industry Guidelines, Education, and Promotion.
SWPA's Pump Manufacturers Members are manufacturers of submersible wastewater pumps for municipal and applications that can efficiently handle solids. These companies represent the bulk of shipments of solids-handling and grinder pumps in the United States.
SWPA's Component Manufacturer Members are manufacturers of component parts and accessory products for submersible pumps and pumping systems. They supply pump manufacturers and the aftermarket with access covers, alternators, basins, cords/cables, control components, control panels, electric motors, guide rail systems, phase converters, phase monitors, seals, valves, variable frequent drivers, and other components, parts, and accessories.
SWPA's Associate Members are non-manufacturers who provide services related to industry products, including distributors, rep organizations, service stations, and consulting and specifying engineering firms.

Meetings/Conferences:
Annual Meetings: Spring, Summer, Fall and Winter
2007 – Las Vegas, NV(Riviera)/March 5-6/150
2007 – San Diego, CA(The Westgate)/Oct. 13-14/85

Publications:
Membership Roster and Product Reference Guide. a. adv.

Substance Abuse Librarians and Information Specialists *(1978)*
P.O. Box 9513
Berkeley, CA 94709-0513
Tel: (510)597-3440 *Fax:* (510)985-6459
E-Mail: SALIS@ARG.ORG
Web Site: http://salis.org
Members: 150 individuals
Annual Budget: $10-25,000
Executive Director: Andrea Mitchell

Historical Note
Serves as an international network for librarians and information professionals working with material on alcohol & drugs. Membership: $50/year (associate); $30/year (institution); $100/year (full member).

Meetings/Conferences:
Annual Meetings: Spring
2007 – Boston, MA

Publications:
SALIS News. q.

Substance Abuse Program Administrators Association
12 Cottage Field Ct.
Germantown, MD 20874
Tel: (301)540-2783 *Fax:* (301)540-1756
E-Mail: exdir@sapaa.com
Web Site: www.sapaa.com
Annual Budget: $250-500,000
Executive Director: Jeff Morrison
E-Mail: exdir@sapaa.com

Historical Note
SAPAA members are individuals and companies which provide the majority of their services in the administration of workplace substance abuse prevention programs. Associate members are individuals or companies producing or manufacturing equipment or products related to drug testing services or drug testing laboratories. There is a special membership class for government entities. Membership: $550/year (regular members); $175/year (government and collection site members).

Suburban Newspapers of America *(1971)*
116 Cass St.
Traverse City, MI 49684
Toll Free: (888)486 - 2466
Web Site: www.suburban-news.org
Members: 110companies,2,000newspapers
Staff: 8
Annual Budget: $250-500,000
Executive Director: Nancy Lane

Historical Note
SNA was formed by a merger of Accredited Home Newspapers of America, the Suburban Press Foundation and the Suburban Section of the National Newspaper Association. Membership: $320-2,850/year, based on size of circulation (regular); $460/year (associate).

Meetings/Conferences:
Annual Meetings:

Publications:
SNA Membership Directory. a.
Suburban Publisher. adv.

Sugar Association *(1943)*
1101 15th St. NW
Suite 600
Washington, DC 20005
Tel: (202)785-1122 *Fax:* (202)785-5019
E-Mail: sugar@sugar.org
Web Site: www.sugar.org
Members: 16 companies
Staff: 6
Annual Budget: $5-10,000,000
President and Chief Executive Officer: Andrew C. Briscoe, III
Director, Public Relations: Melanie Miller

Historical Note
Members are processors and refiners of beet and cane sugar. Supplies science-based information on the role of sugar and carbohydrates in a healthful diet. Maintains a library of publications on the sugar industry.

Sugar Industry Technologists *(1941)*
164 N. Hall Dr.
Sugar Land, TX 77478
Tel: (281)494-2046 *Fax:* (281)494-2304
E-Mail: exedirsit@aol.com
Web Site: www.sucrose.com/sit
Members: 550 individuals
Staff: 2
Annual Budget: $50-100,000
Executive Director: Leon A. Anhaiser

Historical Note
Members are technical and administrative personnel in the cane sugar refining industry. Membership: $40/year (individual); $450/year (company).

Meetings/Conferences:
Annual Meetings: May-June
2007 – Baltimore, MD/May 6-9
2008 – Leipzig, Germany/May 25-28

Publications:
Annual Technical. a.
Proceedings. a.

Sulphur Institute, The *(1960)*
1140 Connecticut Ave. NW
Suite 612
Washington, DC 20036-4012
Tel: (202)331-9660 *Fax:* (202)293-2940
E-Mail: tsiadmin@sulphurinstitute.org
Web Site: www.sulphurinstitute.org
Members: 29 companies
Staff: 7
Annual Budget: $1-2,000,000
President: Robert J. Morris
Manager, Administration: Maia Greco
Director, Agriculture and Market Studies Programs: Donald L. Messick
Director, Industrial Programs: Harold H. Weber

Historical Note
The Sulphur Institute is an international, non-profit organization, representing the sulphur industy. The company's purpose is to promote and expand the use of sulphur in all forms throughout the world.

Publications:
Sulphur Outlook. bien.

Summer and Casual Furniture Manufacturers Association *(1959)*
P.O. Box HP-7
High Point, NC 27261
Tel: (336)884-5000 *Fax:* (336)884-5303
Web Site: www.ahfa.us
Members: 80 companies
Staff: 2
Annual Budget: $250-500,000
Executive Director: Joseph P. Logan

Historical Note
Division of American Home Furnishings Alliance. Membership: based on sales volume.

Meetings/Conferences:
Annual Meetings: Chicago, IL(Merchandise Mart)/September

Sump and Sewage Pump Manufacturers Association *(1956)*
P.O. Box 647
Northbrook, IL 60065-0647
Tel: (847)559-9233
E-Mail: hdqtrs@sspma.org
Web Site: www.sspma.org
Members: 30 companies
Staff: 2
Managing Director: Pamela W. Franzen

Historical Note
Formerly (1981) Sump Pump Manufacturers Association.

Meetings/Conferences:
Semi-annual: Typical Attendance: 15

Sunglass Association of America *(1970)*
390 N. Bridge St.
LaBelle, FL 33935
Tel: (863)612-0085 *Fax:* (863)612-0250
E-Mail: info@sunglassassociation.com
Web Site: www.sunglassassociation.com
Members: 105 companies
Staff: 2
Executive Director: Swea Nightingale

Historical Note
Members of the Association consist of firms actively engaged in the manufacture and/or importation and distribution of sunglasses, sunglass parts, components or materials, or reading glasses.

Meetings/Conferences:
Annual Meetings: Fall

Publications:
Directory. a.
Newsletter. q.

Suntanning Association for Education *(1984)*
P.O. Box 1181

Gulf Breeze, FL 32562-1181
Toll Free: (800)536 - 8255
E-Mail: suntanningedu@cox.net
Web Site: http://suntanningedu.homestead.com
Members: 500 companies
Staff: 1
Annual Budget: $250-500,000
Executive Vice President: Paul Germek
E-Mail: suntanningedu@cox.net

Historical Note
SAE is a non-profit trade association established to provide educational resources and legislative assistance to the indoor tanning industry. Membership: $115/year (salon); $350/year (distributor); $750/year (manufacturer).

Supima *(1954)*
4141 E. Broadway Rd.
Phoenix, AZ 85040-8831
Tel: (602)437-1364 *Fax:* (602)437-0143
E-Mail: info@supima.com
Web Site: www.supima.com
Members: 2400 individuals
Staff: 4
Annual Budget: $1-2,000,000
President: Jesse W. Curlee
E-Mail: jesse@supima.com
Office Manager: Nancy Boyd
E-Mail: nancy@supima.com
Executive Vice President: Marc A. Lewkowitz
E-Mail: marc@supima.com

Historical Note
Members are producers of Supima (extra-long staple) cotton. Most members are located in the Southwest. Sponsors and supports the Supima Political Action Committee (SuPac). Membership: $3/bale assessment.

Meetings/Conferences:
Annual:

Publications:
Supima News Newsletter. m.

Supply Chain Council *(1997)*
1400 I St. NW
Suite 1050
Washington, DC 20005-2209
Tel: (202)962-0440 *Fax:* (202)962-3939
E-Mail: info@supply-chain.org
Web Site: www.supply-chain.org
Members: 750 corporations
Staff: 9
Executive Director: Thomas C. Mawson
Associate Executive Director: Scott Palmer
Chief Technology Officer: Scott Stephens

Historical Note
Membership: $2,000/year (company).

Publications:
Supply Chain Letter. q.
Supply Chain Operations Reference Model. a.

Surety Association of America *(1908)*
1101 Connecticut Ave. NW
Suite 800
Washington, DC 20036
Tel: (202)463-0600 *Fax:* (202)463-0606
E-Mail: information@surety.org
Web Site: www.surety.org
Members: 650 companies
Staff: 14
Annual Budget: $2-5,000,000
President: Lynn M. Schubert
E-Mail: lschubert@surety.org
General Counsel: Edward G. Gallagher
E-Mail: egallagher@surety.org
Vice President, Public Affairs/Public Relations: Lenore Marema
Director, Regulatory Affairs, Membership and Publications: Barbara Reiff

Historical Note
Members are insurance companies underwriting fidelity, surety and forgery bonds. Absorbed the Towner Rating Bureau in 1947.

Meetings/Conferences:
Annual Meetings: *Washington DC, second Thursday in May*

Surface Design Association *(1976)*
P.O. Box 360
Sebastopol, CA 95473-0360
Tel: (707)829-3110 *Fax:* (707)829-3285
Web Site: www.surfacedesign.org
Members: 3700 individuals
Staff: 3
Annual Budget: $250-500,000
Administrator: Joy Stocksdale

Historical Note
Membership consists of individuals involved in printing, designing and dyeing art fabrics, fibers and other materials. Incorporated in the State of Missouri. Membership: $50/year (individual); $500/year (organization/company).

Meetings/Conferences:
2007 - Kansas City, MO(Art Institute)/May 31-June 3/500

Publications:
Surface Design Journal. q. adv.
SDA Newsletter. q.

Surface Engineering Coating Association *(1999)*
Univ. at Buffalo Technology Center
1576 Sweet Home Rd., Suite 102
Amherst, NY 14228
Tel: (716)791-8100 *Fax:* (716)278-8769
Web Site: www.surfaceengineering.org
Members: 18 companies
Staff: 3
Managing Director: Frederick J. Teeter

Meetings/Conferences:
Biennial: Spring and Fall/20

Surface Finishing Industry Council *(1997)*
21165 Whitfield Pl.
Suite 105
Potomac Falls, VA 20165
Tel: (703)433-2520 *Fax:* (703)433-0369
E-Mail: info@sfic.org
Web Site: www.sfic.org
Staff: 1
Annual Budget: $100-250,000
Administrator: David W. Barrack

Historical Note
SFIC is composed of three major trade associations representing the surface finishing industry.

Publications:
Surface Finishing Market Research Bureau Report. bien.
Electroplating for Automotive. a.

Surface Mount Technology Association *(1984)*
5200 Willson Rd.
Suite 215
Edina, MN 55424-1316
Tel: (952)920-7682 *Fax:* (952)926-1819
E-Mail: smta@smta.org
Web Site: www.smta.org
Members: 4100 individuals
Staff: 8
Annual Budget: $1-2,000,000
Executive Administrator: JoAnn Stromberg
Director, Chapter Relations: Gayle Jackson
Director, Communications and Information Technology: Jesse Katzman
Director, Member Services: Sis Sullivan

Historical Note
Membership: $60/year (individual); $395/year (company); $1495/year (global).

Meetings/Conferences:
Annual Meetings: Fall
2007 - Chicago, IL(Donald Stephens Convention Center)/Oct. 1-4

Publications:
SMTA News Monthly (online). m.
Membership Directory (online). w. adv.
Technical Journal & News. q.
Proceedings. a.

Surfaces in Biomaterials Foundation
1000 Westgate Dr., Suite 252
St. Paul, MN 55114
Tel: (651)290-6267 *Fax:* (651)290-2266
E-Mail: surfacesinbiomaterials@ewald.com
Web Site: www.surfaces.org
Members: 250 individuals

Historical Note
An international society of research professionals interested in the manufacture and development of new biomaterials.

Meetings/Conferences:
Annual Meetings: Fall

Surgical Infection Society *(1981)*
c/o Lena Napolitano, MD
University of Michigan Health System, 1500 E. Michigan Center Dr. - UH - 1C340
Ann Arbor, MI 48109-0033
Tel: (734)615-4775 *Fax:* (734)936-9657
Web Site: www.sisna.org
Annual Budget: $25-50,000
Secretary: Lena Napolitano, MD

Historical Note
Members are surgeons and other medical specialists with an interest in surgical infection.

Meetings/Conferences:
2007 - Toronto, ON, Canada(Westin Harbour Castle)/Apr. 18-20

Publications:
Program Book (for convention). a.

Survival and Flight Equipment Association *(1957)*

Historical Note
See the SAFE Association.

Sustainable Buildings Industry Council *(1980)*
1112 16th St. NW
Suite 240
Washington, DC 20036
Tel: (202)628-7400 *Fax:* (202)393-5043
E-Mail: sbic@sbiccouncil.org
Web Site: www.sbicouncil.org
Members: 70 companies
Staff: 8
Annual Budget: $100-250,000
Executive Director: Helen English
E-Mail: HEnglish@SBICouncil.org

Historical Note
Founded in 1980 as the Passive Solar Industries Council, assumed its present name in 1999. SBIC formed by the leading organizations in the building industry. Membership is comprised mainly of trade associations, manufacturers and suppliers interested in the construction of buildings that, by their design, use and store solar energy. Membership: $100/year (individual); $350/year (small business); $750/year (regular).

Meetings/Conferences:
Semi-annual: Spring and Fall in Washington, DC/25-50

Publications:
Buildings Inside and Out. semi-a.

SWANA - Solid Waste Association of North America *(1961)*
1100 Wayne Ave., Suite 700
P.O. Box 7219
Silver Spring, MD 20907-7219
Tel: (301)585-2898 *Fax:* (301)589-7068
Toll Free: (800)467 - 9262
E-Mail: info@swana.org
Web Site: www.swana.org
Members: 7200 individuals
Staff: 25
Annual Budget: $2-5,000,000
Executive Director/Chief Executive Officer: John H. Skinner, Ph.D.
E-Mail: jskinner@swana.org
Manager, Government Affairs: Mac Bybee
Director, Information Systems: Hugh Scott
E-Mail: hscott@swana.org
Director, Meetings and Expositions: Liesl Smith
Manager, Member and Chapter Services: Adam Tracey
Coordinator, Marketing and Communications: Evan Von Leer
E-Mail: info@swana.org
Director, Administration: Cathy Wilde
Director, Education and Marketing: MeriBeth Wojtaszek
E-Mail: info@swana.org

Historical Note
Formerly the Governmental Refuse Collection and Disposal Association (1990). SWANA members are

professionals in the private and public sectors. Membership: $165/year (public member); $325/year (private member); $225/year (private small-business member).

Meetings/Conferences:
Annual Meetings: Summer

Publications:
Electronic Newsletter. m. adv.
Municipal Solid Waste Management Magazine. m. adv.
SWANA Newsletter. m. adv.
Proceedings. a.

Swedish-American Chambers of Commerce *(1906)*
1403 King St.
Alexandria, VA 22314
Tel: (703)836-6560 *Fax:* (703)836-6561
E-Mail: admin@sacc-usa.org
Web Site: www.sacc-usa.org
Members: 2500 individuals
Staff: 10
Annual Budget: $250-500,000
President: Gunilla Girardo

Historical Note
The purposes of SACC are to advance/foster and expand harmonious commerce and trade between Sweden and the US. Membership: $150/year (individual); $3,000/year (organization).

Meetings/Conferences:
Annual Meetings: Annual Swedish-American Entrepreneural Days.

Publications:
Membership Directory. a. adv.
Newsletter. q. adv.
Subsidiary Listing. a. adv.

Swimming Pool Water Treatment Professionals *(1992)*
21939 Camille Dr.
Nuevo, CA 92567
Tel: (909)928-1050
Web Site: www.spwtp.org
Executive Director: Lyn Paymer

Historical Note
Formerly (2001) National Association of Gas Chlorinators. SPWTP provides education, research and safety training services to member swimming pool water treatment professionals. Membership: $475/year.

Publications:
NAGC Newsletter. bi-m. adv.

Swimwear Industry Manufacturers Association

Historical Note
A division of the American Apparel Manufacturers Association.

Synthetic Organic Chemical Manufacturers Association *(1921)*
1850 M St. NW
Suite 700
Washington, DC 20036-5810
Tel: (202)721-4100 *Fax:* (202)296-8120
E-Mail: info@socma.org
Web Site: www.socma.com
Members: 300 companies
Staff: 45
Annual Budget: $5-10,000,000
President: Joseph Acker
Director, Commercial Programs: Dolores Alonso
Vice President, Business and Operations: Diane McMahon

Historical Note
SOCMA represents and serves the batch, custom and small chemical industry, which produces products important to the life, health and well-being of people worldwide. SOCMA promotes innovative, safe and environmentally responsible operations that are internationally competitive and contribute to a healthy, productive economy. Achieves its mission by acclerating the potential for members' growth, working to increase the public's confidence in the chemical industry, and influencing the passage of laws and legislation that better enable members to operate in a productive manner as good corporate citizens.

Meetings/Conferences:
Annual Meetings: early Spring

Publications:
Online Membership Directory. a.
Chemical Bond Express Newsletter (online). w.
Executive Briefing. m.
Commercial Guide. a. adv.
SOCMA Newsletter. bi-w.

System Safety Society *(1962)*
P.O. Box 70
Unionville, VA 22567-0070
Tel: (540)854-8630
E-Mail: syssafe@ns.gemlink.com
Web Site: www.system-safety.org
Members: 900 individuals
Staff: 1
Annual Budget: $25-50,000
Administrator: Cathy Carter

Historical Note
Formerly (1966) the Aerospace System Safety Society. Emphasis is on methodology, development and application for hazard identification, elimination and control, through system safety engineering and management in products, systems and services. Membership: $65/year (individual); $300/year (corporate).

Meetings/Conferences:
Annual Meetings: Biennial/Odd Years

Publications:
Journal of System Safety. q. adv.

Systems, Man and Cybernetics Society

Historical Note
A technical society of the Institute of Electrical and Electronics Engineers (IEEE). Membership in the Society, open only to IEEE members, includes subscription to a technical periodical in the field published by IEEE. All administrative support is provided by IEEE.

Tag and Label Manufacturers Institute *(1933)*
40 Shuman Blvd., Suite 295
Naperville, IL 60563
Tel: (630)357-9222 *Fax:* (630)357-0192
Web Site: www.tlmi.com
Members: 320 companies
Staff: 5
Annual Budget: $1-2,000,000
President: Frank Sablone
E-Mail: fas@timi.com
Meeting Planner: Karen Jackson
E-Mail: karen@tlmi.com
Office Manager: Karen Planz
E-Mail: office@tlmi.com

Historical Note
Formally organized in Cleveland on June 15, 1933 as the Tag Manufacturers Institute. In 1962, the bylaws were revised to include converters of pressure sensitive labels, and the present name was adopted. The supplier (Associates) division was formed in 1966, and now consists of suppliers of label base stocks, presses and auxiliary equipment, plates, dies, inks, adhesvies, tag and label papers. International members accepted in 1975. Membership: $800-4,000/year (company).

Publications:
LABELEXPO Proceedings. bien..
North American Label Study. bien..
Standards Manual. irreg.
They Built An Industry. irreg.
Directory. a.
Illuminator. bi-m.
Products Guide. a.
Glossary of Pressure Sensitive Terms. irreg.

Tamworth Swine Association *(1923)*
621 N. County Rd. 850W
Greencastle, IN 46135-7769
Tel: (765)653-4913
E-Mail: tamassoc@webtv.net
Members: 150 individuals
Staff: 1
Annual Budget: under $10,000
Secretary-Treasurer: Shirley Brattain

Historical Note
Members are breeders and fanciers of Tamworth swine.

Meetings/Conferences:
Annual Meetings: September

Publications:
Tamworth News. a. adv.

TASH *(1975)*
29 W. Susquehannah Ave., Suite 210
Baltimore, MD 21204-5201
Tel: (410)828-8274 *Fax:* (410)828-6706
Web Site: www.tash.org
Members: 6000 individuals
Staff: 12
Annual Budget: $1-2,000,000
Executive Director: Nancy Weiss
E-Mail: nweiss@tash.org

Historical Note
Founded as the American Association for the Education of the Severely-Profoundly Handicapped; became (1979) the Association for the Severely Handicapped and then (1984) the Association of Persons with Severe Disabilities before assuming its current name in 1995. Members are teachers, social workers, psychologists, physical therapists, legal administrators, special education administrators, parents, self-advocates, and students. Membership: $98/year (individual); $275/year (organization/company).

Meetings/Conferences:
Annual Meetings: Fall

Publications:
JASH: Research & Practice for Persons with Severe Disabilities. q. adv.
TASH Newsletter. m. adv.

Tau Epsilon Rho Law Society *(1920)*
1951 Old Cuthbert Rd.
Suite 413
Cherry Hill, NJ 08034
Tel: (856)429-3901 *Fax:* (856)429-4846
E-Mail: director@ter-law.org
Web Site: www.ter-law.org
Members: 7500 individuals
Treasurer/Executive Director: Alan M. Tepper

Historical Note
A professional law society of judges, lawyers and law students throughout the country. Membership: $65/year (individual).

Publications:
Summons. 2-3/year.
Chancellor's Newsletter. 3-4/year.
Membership Directory. bien.

Tax Executives Institute *(1944)*
1200 G St. NW
Suite 300
Washington, DC 20005-3814
Tel: (202)638-5601 *Fax:* (202)638-5607
Web Site: www.tei.org
Members: 5400 individuals
Staff: 14
Annual Budget: $2-5,000,000
Executive Director: Timothy J. McNormally
General Counsel: Mary L. Faley
Director, Conference Planning: Deborah K. Gaffney
Director, Administration: Deborah C. Giesey
Manager, Publications: Richard Skippon
Coordinator, Membership: Da Keia Williamson

Historical Note
A professional organization of corporate tax executives. Membership is open to corporate officers and employees charged with administering their company's tax affairs. Membership: $200/year, plus $200 initiation fee.

Publications:
The Tax Executive. bi-m. adv.

Taxicab, Limousine and Paratransit Association *(1917)*
3849 Farragut Ave.
Kensington, MD 20895
Tel: (301)946-5701 *Fax:* (301)946-4641
E-Mail: info@tlpa.org
Web Site: www.tlpa.org
Members: 985 individuals
Staff: 5
Annual Budget: $1-2,000,000
Executive Vice President: Alfred B. LaGasse

Director, Research and Education: Harold E. Morgan

Historical Note

Formed as International Taxicab and Livery Association by a merger of the American Taxicabs Association, the National Association of Taxicab Owners and the Cab Research Bureau. Assumed its current name in 2000. Members are owners of taxicab, limousine, van, livery and minibus fleets. Sponsors the TLPA Political Action Committee. Membership: $18/vehicle/year; minimum $144/year, maximum $4,500.

Meetings/Conferences:

Annual Meetings: Fall/600

2007 – Denver, CO(Hyatt Regency)/Oct. 9-12

Publications:

Transportation Leader. q. adv.

Tea Association of the United States of America *(1899)*

420 Lexington Ave., Suite 825
New York, NY 10170-0002
Tel: (212)986-9415 *Fax:* (212)697-8658
E-Mail: info@teausa.org
Web Site: www.teausa.org
Members: 100 companies
Staff: 4
Annual Budget: $500-1,000,000
President: Joseph P. Simrany
E-Mail: simrany@teausa.com

Historical Note

The Tea Association is a trade association representing over 85% of the total tea business done in the U.S. There are currently over 100 firms represented by the Tea Association in the U.S. and abroad. The primary goal is to represent members' best interest on all matters of potential concern. Membership fee varies, based on revenue.

Meetings/Conferences:

Annual Meetings: October

Publications:

TeaBits. 4/year.

Tea Council of the U.S.A. *(1950)*

420 Lexington Ave., Suite 825
New York, NY 10170
Tel: (212)986-6998 *Fax:* (212)697-8658
Web Site: www.teausa.com
Members: 80 companies, 4 governments
Staff: 3
Annual Budget: $1-2,000,000
President: Joseph P. Simrany
E-Mail: simrany@teausa.org

Historical Note

Seeks to increase the consumption of hot and iced tea.

Meetings/Conferences:

Annual Meetings: with Tea Ass'n of the U.S.A.

Publications:

Tea Bits. 4/year.
Newsletter. bi-m.

Teachers of English to Speakers of Other Languages *(1966)*

700 S. Washington St., Suite 200
Alexandria, VA 22314
Tel: (703)836-0774 *Fax:* (703)836-7864
Toll Free: (888)547 - 3369
E-Mail: info@tesol.org
Web Site: www.tesol.org
Members: 13000 individuals and institutions
Staff: 26
Annual Budget: $2-5,000,000
Executive Director: Charles S. Amorosino, Jr., CAE
Director, Education Programs: John Donaldson
Director, Conference Services: Bart Ecker
Director, Communications and Marketing: Cindy Flynn
Director, Finance: Jim Trope
Director, Member Services: Pamela C. Williams

Historical Note

Promotes excellence in the teaching of the English language to speakers of other languages. Membership: $75/year.

Meetings/Conferences:

Annual Meetings: March-April

Publications:

Essential Teacher. q. adv.
TESOL Quarterly. q. adv.
TESOL Placement E-Bulletin. bi-m. adv.
TESOL Connections. bi-m. adv.

Teaching-Family Association *(1976)*

P.O. Box 2007
Midlothian, VA 23113
Tel: (804)632-0155 *Fax:* (804)639-9212
Web Site: www.teaching-family.org
Members: 400 individuals
Staff: 2
Annual Budget: $100-250,000
Executive Director: Peggy McElgunn
E-Mail: peggymcelgunn@comcast.net

Historical Note

Members are individuals providing family services to children in group home, treatment foster care and home-based service settings. Formerly (1992) the National Teaching-Family Association. Membership: $30/year (individual); $4,000/year (agency).

Meetings/Conferences:

Annual Meetings: annual

Publications:

Teaching-Family Model.
Teaching-Family Newsletter. q.
Directory of the Teaching-Family Association. a.
Standards of Ethical Conduct.

TechLaw Group *(1986)*

c/o Ackerman Public Relations
1111 Northshore Dr., Suite N-400
Knoxville, TN 37919
Tel: (865)584-0550 Ext: 105 *Fax:* (865)588-3009
Web Site: www.techlaw.org
Members: 19 firms
Staff: 2
Annual Budget: $100-250,000
Executive Director: LeAnne Slater
E-Mail: lslater@techlaw.org

Historical Note

TechLaw is an international network of law firms which serve the interests of businesses, institutions, and individuals involved with technology industries. Member firms comprise over 5,000 lawyers.

Meetings/Conferences:

Semi-Annual Meetings:

Publications:

TechLaw Update. 3-4/year.

Technical Association of the Graphic Arts *(1948)*

200 Deer Run Rd.
Sewickley, PA 15213
Tel: (412)259-1813 *Fax:* (412)741-2311
E-Mail: jallen@piagatf.org
Web Site: www.taga.org
Members: 800 individuals
Staff: 2
Annual Budget: $100-250,000
Contact: Judy Allen

Historical Note

Organized to advance the science and technology of the graphic arts. Membership: $125/year (individual); $1,000/year (organization/company).

Meetings/Conferences:

Annual Meetings: Spring/250

Publications:

TAGA Journal of Graphic Technology. 4/year.
TAGA Newsletter. 4/year.
TAGA Proceedings. a.

Technical Association of the Pulp and Paper Industry *(1915)*

15 Technology Pkwy. South
P.O. Box 105113
Atlanta, GA 30092
Tel: (770)446-1400 *Fax:* (770)446-6947
Toll Free: (800)332 - 8686
Web Site: www.tappi.org
Members: 15000 individuals
Staff: 50
Annual Budget: $5-10,000,000
Senior Vice President: Susan M. Blevins

Historical Note

Organized in 1915 as a section of the American Paper and Pulp Association. The articles of organization were revised at the first annual meeting in 1916 and the name was changed to the Technical Association of the Pulp and Paper Industry. Today, members include those professionals who work in the pulp, paper, packaging, converting, and nonwoven industries. Has an annual budget of approximately $9 million. Membership: $154/year (individual); $1,000/year (organization/company).

Meetings/Conferences:

Annual Meetings: Spring

Publications:

TAPPI Journal. m.
Solutions! For People, Processes and Paper. m. adv.

Technology and Maintenance Council of American Trucking Associations *(1954)*

2200 Mill Rd.
Alexandria, VA 22314-5388
Tel: (703)838-1763 *Fax:* (703)684-4328
E-Mail: tmc@trucking.org
Web Site: http://tmc.truckline.com
Members: 45000 companies
Staff: 9
Annual Budget: $2-5,000,000
Executive Director: Carl Kirk
Technical Director: Robert Braswell
Director, Council Development: Janet Howells-Tierney

Historical Note

Members are trucking executives, maintenance specialists, manufacturers, and suppliers interested in the improvement of trucking equipment, its maintenance, and maintenance management. Membership: 395/year (fleet member); $460/year (associate member); $75/year (technician).

Meetings/Conferences:

Triannual Meetings: Spring, Summer and Fall

Publications:

Fleet Maintenance and Technology. q. adv.
Fleet Advisor. m.
Membership Directory.
Recommended Practices Manual. a.
The Trailblazer. 3/year.

Technology Student Association *(1978)*

1914 Association Dr.
Reston, VA 20191-1540
Tel: (703)860-9000 *Fax:* (703)758-4852
Toll Free: (888)860 - 9010
E-Mail: general@tsaweb.org
Web Site: www.tsaweb.org
Members: 175000 individuals
Staff: 10
Annual Budget: $500-1,000,000
Executive Director: Dr. Rosanne T. White
Conference Manager: Donna Andrews

Historical Note

Formerly (1988) American Industrial Arts Student Association. Members are students enrolled in technology education classes. Through its national competitive program, TSA offers students a chance to make a technological contribution to society. Membership: $9/year (students); $10/year (professional/adult); $10/year (alumni).

Meetings/Conferences:

Annual Meetings: Summer

Publications:

Chapter Program Kit. a.
The School Scene. 4/year.
TSA Curricular Resource Guide. a.
TSA Directory. a.

Technology Transfer Society *(1975)*

3506 Russel Sage Lab, RPI, 110 Eighth St.
Troy, NY 12180-3590
E-Mail: sieged@rpi.edu
Web Site: www.t2society.org
Members: 200 individuals
Annual Budget: $10-25,000
President: Don Siegel

Historical Note

An international organization created to disseminate methods, knowledge and opportunities within the technology transfer community. Multidisciplinary membership is composed of professionals involved in the commercialization of technology. Membership: $125/year (individual); $600/year (corporate); $300/year (institutional and small businesses);

$35/year (student/retiree); $150/year (international).

Meetings/Conferences:
Annual Meetings: September

Publications:
T'Squared Newsletter.
Metrics Summit/Other Symposia Proceedings. a. adv.
Annual Meeting Proceedings. a. adv.
Directory. a.
Journal of Technology Transfer. q. adv.

Telecommunications Benchmarking International Group *(1996)*

4606 FM 1960 West, Suite 250
Houston, TX 77069
Tel: (281)440-5044 *Fax:* (281)440-6677
Toll Free: (888)739 - 8244
E-Mail: tbig@benchmarkingnetwork.com
Web Site: www.tbig.org
Members: 3500 individuals
Staff: 21
Annual Budget: $1-2,000,000
President: Mark T. Czarnecki

Historical Note
Members are professionals in telecommunications firms. TBIG collects data from its members on best practices in the industry.

Publications:
ebenchmarking newsletter (online). w.

Telecommunications Industry Association *(1988)*

2500 Wilson Blvd., Suite 300
Arlington, VA 22201-3834
Tel: (703)907-7700 *Fax:* (703)907-7727
E-Mail: tia@tiaonline.org
Web Site: www.tiaonline.org
Members: 600 companies
Staff: 49
Annual Budget: $10-25,000,000
Executive Vice President: Grant Seiffert
Vice President, Finance: Anna Amselle
E-Mail: aamselle@tiaonline.org
Vice President, Standards and Special Projects: Dan Bart
E-Mail: dbart@tiaonline.org
Senior Director, Engineering and Technology Policy: Bill Belt
Director, Member Services: Grace Ann Bourne
Director, Communications: Neil Gaffney
Senior Director and General Counsel of Government Affairs: Danielle Jafari
Vice President, Global Events: Andrew Janosko
Communications Manager: Jennifer Mead
Manager, Board of Directors/Events and Executive Assistant to the President: Mary Piper Waters
E-Mail: mwaters@tiaonline.org

Historical Note
Formerly (1988) the United States Telecommunications Suppliers Association. Originally a part of the United States Independent Telephone Association with which it was affiliated, TIA is a trade group of manufacturers, suppliers and support service organizations of the telecommunications industry.

Meetings/Conferences:
Annual Meetings: Summer

Publications:
Telecommunications Market Review and forecast. a.
TIA Week (electronic). w. adv.
Pulse Online Newsletter. m.

Television Bureau of Advertising *(1955)*

Three E. 54th St.
New York, NY 10022-3108
Tel: (212)486-1111 *Fax:* (212)935-5631
E-Mail: info@tvb.org
Web Site: www.tvb.org
Members: 450 television stations
Staff: 25
Annual Budget: $5-10,000,000
President: Christopher J. Rohrs
E-Mail: crohrs@tvb.org
Vice President, Communications: Gary Belis
E-Mail: gary@tvb.org
Senior Vice President, Research: Susan Cuccinello
Vice President, Member Services: Janice Garjian
E-Mail: janice@tvb.org

Historical Note
The Television Bureau of Advertising represents broadcast television stations to the advertising community. Its goal is to develop and increase advertiser dollars to U.S. Spot Television.

Telework Advisory Group for World at Work

14040 N. Northsight Blvd.
Scottsdale, AZ 85260
Toll Free: (877)951 - 9191
E-Mail: info@workingfromanywhere.org
Web Site: www.workingfromanywhere.org
Members: 50 organizations
Staff: 2
Executive Director: Amy Jantz
E-Mail: ajantz@workingfromanywhere.org

Historical Note
Founded as Telecommuting Advisory Council; assumed its current name in 2005.

Tennessee Walking Horse Breeders and Exhibitors Association *(1935)*

P.O. Box 286
Lewisburg, TN 37091
Tel: (931)359-1574 *Fax:* (931)359-7530
Toll Free: (800)359 - 1574
E-Mail: sbutt@twhbea.com
Web Site: www.twhbea.com
Members: 20000 individuals
Staff: 26
Annual Budget: $2-5,000,000
Executive Director: Charles C. Hulsey
Secretary-Treasurer: Sharon Brandon
E-Mail: sbrandon@twhbea.com
Editor, Voice Magazine: Stan Butt
E-Mail: twhbea@twhbea.com

Historical Note
Members are owners and breeders of the Tennessee Walking Horse. Formerly the Tennessee Walking Horse Breeders Association of America (1974). Membership: $60/year.

Meetings/Conferences:
Semi-annual Meetings: Usually in Lewisburg, TN/fourth Saturday in May and first Saturday in December

Publications:
Breedjournal, Voice of the Tennessee Walking Horse. m. adv.

Tennis Industry Association *(1981)*

Executive Pl., Suite 107
19 Pope Ave.
Hilton Head, SC 29938
Tel: (843)686-3036 *Fax:* (843)686-3078
E-Mail: jolyn@tennisindustry.org
Web Site: www.tennisindustry.org
Members: 50 companies and organizations
Staff: 4
Annual Budget: $1-2,000,000
Executive Director: Jolyn deBoer
E-Mail: jolyn@tennisindustry.org

Historical Note
TIA was established in 1974 as the American Tennis Industry. In 1993 the name was changed to the Tennis Industry Association to better reflect the global interests of the membership. It is a non-profit association of approximately 130 companies and organizations that provide tennis equipment, apparel, footwear, services and information. Its primary objective is to encourage recreational tennis participation. Membership: $400-8,000, based on sales volume.

Meetings/Conferences:
Annual Meetings: Semi-Annual Meetings

Publications:
TIA Today. q.
Tennis Industry Magazine. m. adv.

Teratology Society *(1960)*

1821 Michael Faraday Dr., Suite 300
Reston, VA 20190-5332
Tel: (703)438-3104 *Fax:* (703)438-3113
Web Site: www.teratology.org
Members: 750 individuals
Executive Director: Tonia Masson

Historical Note
Incorporated in the State of Ohio in 1960. The society is composed of professionals sharing a common interest in the research, prevention and treatment of birth defects.

Meetings/Conferences:
Annual Meetings: Summer
2007 – Pittsburgh, PA(Omni William Penn Hotel)/June 22-28/350
2008 – Monterey, CA(Hyatt Regency)/June 28-July 5/350
2009 – , PR(Westin Rio Mar)/June 27-July 2/350

Publications:
Teratology Primer.
Teratology Society Newsletter.
Birth Defects Research.

Test Boring Association *(1941)*

Five Mapleton Road, Suite 200
Princeton, NJ 08540
Tel: (609)514-2600 *Fax:* (609)514-2660
Members: 10 companies
Staff: 3
Annual Budget: under $10,000
Management Executive: Patrizia Zita

Historical Note
Formerly (1969) Test Boring Contractors Association.

Tetrahydrofuran Task Force *(1992)*

1850 M St. NW
Suite 700
Washington, DC 20036-5810
Tel: (202)721-4125 *Fax:* (202)296-8120
E-Mail: rossj@socma.com
Web Site: www.socma.org
Members: 6 companies
Staff: 2
Annual Budget: $50-100,000
Executive Director: Jessica Ross

Historical Note
An affiliate of the Synthetic Organic Chemical Manufacturers Association. The Tetrahydrofuran (THF) Task Force was initially organized in 1992 to conduct studies on tetrahydrofuran in response to EPA's neurotoxicity endpoint rule. The Task Force addresses state, federal, and international regulatory activities regarding THF.

Texas Longhorn Breeders Association of America *(1964)*

P.O. Box 4430
Ft. Worth, TX 76164
Tel: (817)625-6241 *Fax:* (817)625-1388
E-Mail: tlbaa@tlbaa.org
Web Site: www.tlbaa.org
Members: 4600 individuals
Staff: 10
Annual Budget: $250-500,000
President and Chief Executive Officer: Don L. King
Director, Finance: SuzAnn Spindor

Historical Note
Founded in Lawton, OK to serve as the breed registry and to preserve the Texas Longhorn through promotion, education and research. Members are breeders and fanciers of Texas Longhorn beef cattle. Member of the National Pedigree Livestock Council, National Cattlemen's Association, and U.S. Beef Breeds Council. Membership: $50/year.

Meetings/Conferences:
Annual Meetings: Fall

Publications:
Texas Longhorn Trails. m. adv.

Text and Academic Authors Association *(1987)*

P.O. Box 76477
St. Petersburg, FL 33734-6477
Tel: (727)563-0020 *Fax:* (727)230-2409
E-Mail: text@tampabay.rr.com
Web Site: www.taaonline.net
Members: 1300 individuals
Staff: 4
Annual Budget: $50-100,000
Executive Director: Richard Hull
Managing Director: Janet Tucker

Historical Note
Formerly (1987) Textbook Authors Association; assumed its current name in 1993. TAA members are creators of academic intellectual property at all levels. TAA is primarily concerned with the improvement of performance and compensation. Membership: $60/year (full member); $30/year (first-year member); $15/year (student).

Meetings/Conferences:
Annual Meetings: Summer

Publications:
The Academic Author. q. adv.

Textile Bag and Packaging Association *(1934)*
322 Davis Ave.
Drawer Eight
Dayton, OH 45401
Tel: (937)476-8272
E-Mail: tpba@aol.com
Members: 175 companies
Staff: 1
Annual Budget: $50-100,000
Secretary: Susan Spiegel

Historical Note
Formerly (1968) National Burlap Bag Dealers Association and (1984) Textile Bag Processors Association; assumed its present name in 1985. Members are manufacturers and distributors of textile bags and packaging supplies. Membership: $400/year.

Meetings/Conferences:
Semi-Annual Meetings: Spring and Winter

Publications:
The Grab Bag. semi-a. adv.
Roster. bien. adv.

Textile Bag Manufacturers Association *(1925)*
P.O. Box 386
Harrison, OH 45030
Tel: (812)637-0445
E-Mail: conron@one.net
Members: 40 companies
Staff: 2
Annual Budget: $10-25,000

Historical Note
TBMA members consist of makers of polypropylene bags, cotton bags, burlap bags and a variety of sewn products. Membership: $200-400/year.

Meetings/Conferences:
Annual Meetings:

Textile Care Allied Trades Association *(1920)*
271 Rte. 46 West, Suite D203
Fairfield, NJ 07004
Tel: (973)244-1790 *Fax:* (973)244-4455
E-Mail: info@tcata.org
Web Site: http://tcata.org
Members: 250 companies
Staff: 2
Annual Budget: $250-500,000
Chief Executive Officer: David Cotter

Historical Note
Absorbed the National Laundry Allied Trades Association and the Laundry and Dry Cleaners Machinery Manufacturers Association. Formerly (until 1982) the Laundry and Cleaners Allied Trades Association. Members are manufacturers and distributors of commercial laundry and dry cleaning machinery, equipment and supplies.

Publications:
Allied Activities. q.

Textile Converters Association *(1958)*
2001 Palmer Ave., Suite 205
Larchmont, NY 10538
Tel: (914)834-5040 *Fax:* (914)833-1350
Members: 19 companies
Staff: 1
Annual Budget: $10-25,000
Executive Director: Sidney Orenstein

Textile Distributors Association *(1938)*
980 Ave. of the Americas, Third Floor
New York, NY 10018
Tel: (212)868-2210 *Fax:* (212)868-2214
E-Mail: tda104@msn.com
Members: 85 companies
Staff: 4
Annual Budget: $250-500,000
Executive Director: Bruce F. Roberts

Historical Note
Members are converters and distributors of fabrics selling primarily to apparel manufacturers and over-the-counter trade. Formerly Textile Distributors Institute and (1965) Textile Fabric Distributors Association. Provides administrative support to the American Printed Fabrics Council, formed to promote printed fabrics.

Meetings/Conferences:
Annual Meetings: Spring, in the Poconos

Publications:
Newsletter. q.

Textile Fibers and By-Products Association *(1931)*
1531 Industrial Dr.
Griffin, GA 30224
Tel: (770)412-2325 *Fax:* (770)227-6321
E-Mail: info@TFBPA.org
Web Site: www.tfbpa.org
Members: 166 individuals
Staff: 2
Annual Budget: $25-50,000
Executive Secretary: C.E. Williams, Jr.

Historical Note
Formerly (1966) Textile Waste Association.

Meetings/Conferences:
Semi-Annual Meetings: Spring and Fall

Publications:
General Communique. 16/year.

Textile Producers and Suppliers Association
437 Madison Ave., 35th Floor
New York, NY 10022-7302
Tel: (212)907-7300 *Fax:* (212)754-0330
Members: 25 individuals
Annual Budget: $100-250,000
Counsel: Richard S. Taffet

Historical Note
TPSA was formed to address the problem of unauthorized copying of textile and decorative home furnishing designs in international markets.

Textile Rental Services Association of America *(1913)*
1800 Diagonal Rd.
Suite 200
Alexandria, VA 22314
Tel: (703)519-0029 *Fax:* (703)519-0026
Toll Free: (877)770 - 9274
E-Mail: trsa@trsa.org
Web Site: www.trsa.org
Members: 600 companies
Staff: 20
Annual Budget: $2-5,000,000
President and Chief Executive Officer: Roger Cocivera
E-Mail: rcocivera@trsa.org
Vice President, Industry Affairs: George Ferencz, Jr.
Editor: Jack Morgan
E-Mail: jmorgan@trsa.org
Director, Advertising: Debbie Smith
E-Mail: dsmith@trsa.org
Director, Government Affairs: Michael E. Wilson
E-Mail: mwilson@trsa.org

Historical Note
Members are textile rental service companies which provide uniform, linen and towel rental services to business and industry. Associate members are manufacturers, distributors and suppliers. Formerly (until 1979) known as the Linen Supply Association of America. Sponsors and supports the Textile Rental Services Association Political Action Committee.

Publications:
Profit Report. a.
TRSA Friday Fax. w.
Roster and Buyers' Guide. a. adv.
Textile Rental. m. adv.

Textured Yarn Association of America *(1971)*
P.O. Box 66
Gastonia, NC 28053
Tel: (704)824-3522 *Fax:* (704)824-0630
E-Mail: info@tyaa.org
Web Site: www.tyaa.org
Members: 300 individuals
Annual Budget: $100-250,000
Managing Director: Kim Petit

Historical Note
Members are individuals concerned with all aspects of production of man-made fibers. Membership: $60/year (individual).

Meetings/Conferences:
Semi-annual Meetings: February and July

Publications:
Newsletter. q.
Proceedings. semi-a.

Theatre Library Association *(1937)*
c/o NY Public Library for the Performing Arts
40 Lincoln Center Plaza
New York, NY 10023
Web Site: www.tla.library.unt.edu
Members: 250 individuals
Annual Budget: $10-25,000
Executive Secretary: Nancy E. Friedland

Historical Note
An affiliate of the American Library Association and the International Federation for Theatre Research. Membership: $30/year (salaried individuals); $20/year (non-salaried individuals); $30/year (institutions).

Meetings/Conferences:
Semi-Annual Meetings: Summer with ALA/100 and Fall with ASTR/200

Publications:
Performing Arts Resources. irreg.
Broadside. q.

Theatre Management Exchange

Historical Note
A focus group of the Association for Theatre in Higher Education.

Therapeutic Communities of America *(1975)*
1601 Connecticut Ave. NW
Suite 803
Washington, DC 20009
Tel: (202)296-3503 *Fax:* (202)518-5475
Web Site: www.therapeuticcommunitiesofamerica.org
Members: 500 programs
Executive Director: Linda Crawford
E-Mail: tca.office@verizon.net

Historical Note
TCA members are treatment and rehabilitation programs for substance abusers and mental illness-affected clients.

Meetings/Conferences:
Annual Meetings:

Thermal Fluids Council

Historical Note
An affiliate of the Synthetic Organic Chemicals Manufacturers Association which provides administrative support.

Thermoforming Institute

Historical Note
A division of Society of the Plastics Industry, which provides administrative support.

Theta Tau *(1904)*
815 Brazos, Suite 710
Austin, TX 78701
Tel: (512)472-1904
Toll Free: (800)264 - 1904
Web Site: www.thetatau.org
Members: 29000 individuals
Staff: 3
Annual Budget: $100-250,000
Executive Director: Michael T. Abraham
E-Mail: central@thetatau.org

Historical Note
A professional fraternity in engineering. Founded at the Univ. of Minnesota. Purpose of the fraternity is to develop and maintain a high standard of professional interest among its members, and to unite them in a strong bond of fraternal fellowship.

Meetings/Conferences:
Annual Meetings: mid-August

Publications:
Velocitas. 9/yr.
Gear of Theta Tau. semi-a. adv.

Thoroughbred Club of America *(1932)*
Box 8098
Lexington, KY 40533
Tel: (859)254-4282 *Fax:* (859)231-6131
Members: 1500 individuals
Staff: 6
Annual Budget: $50-100,000
Executive Director: Charlie Little

Historical Note
Founded as the Thoroughbred Club in 1932; name was changed to its present form the following year. Although most members live in Kentucky, the membership represents all branches of the Thoroughbred industry and comes from all parts of the U.S., Europe and Canada.

Publications:
Membership Roster. a.

Thoroughbred Owners and Breeders Association *(1961)*
P.O. Box 4367
Lexington, KY 40544-4367
Tel: (859)276-2291 *Fax:* (859)276-2462
E-Mail: info@toba.org
Web Site: www.toba.org
Members: 3000 individuals
Staff: 11
Annual Budget: $1-2,000,000
President: Daniel J. Metzger
E-Mail: metzger@toba.org
Director, Marketing and Communications: Gay Fisher
Director, Industry Relations and Development: Andrew Schweigardt

Historical Note
Members include individual owners, breeders, trainers, jockeys, veterinarians, as well as twenty state breeders' organizations. TOBA strives to keep members informed of health regulations, research developments, and legislation affecting the industry and serves as a representative for U.S. breeders at annual international meetings. Membership: $225/year.

Meetings/Conferences:
Annual Meetings: usually Saratoga Springs, NY/August

Publications:
Blood-Horse. w. adv.
TOBA Times newsletter. 3/year.

Thoroughbred Racing Associations of North America *(1942)*
420 Fair Hill Dr.
Suite One
Elkton, MD 21921-2573
Tel: (410)392-9200 *Fax:* (410)398-1366
E-Mail: info@tra-online.com
Web Site: www.tra-online.com
Members: 43 racing associations
Staff: 4
Annual Budget: $500-1,000,000
Executive Vice President: Christopher N. Scherf
Director, Service Bureau: Tony DeMarco

Historical Note
Supports the Thoroughbred Racing Protective Bureau. Formerly (1977) the Thoroughbred Racing Associations of the U.S., Inc.

Meetings/Conferences:
Annual Meetings: Spring

Publications:
TRA Directory & Record Book. a.
National Directory of Stakes Events. q. adv.

Tile Contractors' Association of America *(1903)*
Four E. 113th Terrace
Kansas City, MO 64114
Tel: (816)941-7063 *Fax:* (816)767-0194
Toll Free: (800)655 - 8453
E-Mail: tcaamerica@aol.com
Web Site: www.tcaanic.org
Members: 150 companies
Staff: 3
Annual Budget: $100-250,000
Executive Director: Patty Nolte
Past President: Vincent De Lazzero
President: Michael Maiuri

Historical Note
Members are sub-contractors engaged in installing ceramic tile. Formerly (1936) Tile and Mantle Contractors Association of America.

Meetings/Conferences:
Annual Meetings: Fall

Publications:
9300 Contractor. bi-m.

Tile Council of North America *(1945)*
100 Clemson Research Blvd.
Anderson, SC 29625
Tel: (864)646-8453 *Fax:* (864)646-2821
Web Site: www.tileusa.com
Members: 160 companies
Staff: 13
Annual Budget: $1-2,000,000
Executive Director: Eric Astrachan
E-Mail: literature@tileusa.com

Historical Note
Members are manufacturers and suppliers of ceramic wall and floor tiles. TCA's mission is to promote the use of ceramic tile.

Meetings/Conferences:
Three Annual Meetings: Spring, Fall, and Winter

Publications:
Handbook for Ceramic Tile Installation. 2/years.
ANSI A108/118. 5/year.
ANSI A137. 5/year.

Tile Roofing Institute *(1976)*
230 E. Ohio St., Suite 400
Chicago, IL 60611
Tel: (312)670-4177 *Fax:* (312)644-8557
Toll Free: (888)321 - 9236
E-Mail: info@rooftile.org
Web Site: www.tileroofing.org
Members: 91 individuals
Staff: 1
Annual Budget: $250-500,000
Managing Director: Charles A. McGrath, CAE

Historical Note
Formerly the Roof Tile Institute; founded as National Tile Roofing Manufacturers Association; assumed its current name in 2004. Manufacturers of clay and concrete roof tiles. Emphasis is on technical issues and codes that involve tile. Membership: $3,500-$100,000/year (company, depending on production output).

Meetings/Conferences:
Annual Meetings: Winter

Publications:
Newsletter. bi-m.

Tillage Equipment Council

Historical Note
A council of the Equipment Manufacturers Institute.

Tilt-up Concrete Association *(1986)*
P.O. Box 204
Mt. Vernon, IA 52314-0204
Tel: (319)895-6911 *Fax:* (319)895-8830
E-Mail: info@tilt-up.org
Web Site: www.tilt-up.org
Members: 400 companies
Staff: 4
Annual Budget: $500-1,000,000
Executive Director: J. Edward Sauter
E-Mail: esauter@tilt-up.org
Tech. Manager: Jim Baty
E-Mail: jbaty@tilt-up.org
Membership Services: Ben Saltzman

Historical Note
Incorporated in Illinois, TCA represents builders, engineers and suppliers involved with tilt-up concrete construction. Membership: $150/year (individual); $250/year (firm); $450/year (contractor); $250 or 675/year (supplier).

Meetings/Conferences:
Annual Meetings: January or February

Publications:
Tilt-Up Newsletter. q. adv.

Timber Frame Business Council *(1995)*
217 Main St., P.O. Box 1945
Hamilton, MT 59840
Tel: (406)375-0713 *Fax:* (406)375-6401
Toll Free: (888)560 - 9254
E-Mail: info@timberframe.org
Web Site: www.timberframe.org
Executive Director: Chad DeLong
E-Mail: chad@timberframe.org

Historical Note
TFBC advances the business, communications and research interests of companies engaged in the timber framing industry.

Timber Framers Guild *(1985)*
P.O. Box 60
Becket, MA 01223-0060
Tel: (413)623-9926
Toll Free: (888)453 - 0879
E-Mail: info@tfguild.org
Web Site: www.tfguild.org
Members: 1750individualsandcompanies
Staff: 5
Annual Budget: $500-1,000,000
Executive Director: Will Beemer
E-Mail: will@tfguild.org

Historical Note
Formerly (2000) Timber Framers Guild of North America. Guild members are individuals actively involved in designing and building timber frames; architects, designers and other building professionals; suppliers of tools and materials to the timber frame trade; owner-builders; timber frame owners and others with an interest in the craft. Membership: $85/year (individual).

Publications:
Timber Framing. q.
Scantlings Newsletter. 8/year.

Timber Products Manufacturers *(1916)*
951 E. Third Ave.
Spokane, WA 99202
Tel: (509)535-4646 *Fax:* (509)534-6106
E-Mail: tpm@tpmrs.com
Web Site: www.tpmrs.com
Members: 215 companies
Staff: 8
Annual Budget: $500-1,000,000
President: Charles M. Fox
E-Mail: cfox@tpmrs.com
Office Manager: Jolene K. Skjothaug
E-Mail: jskjothaug@tpmrs.com

Historical Note
Established as the Timber Products Manufacturers Association; assumed its present name in 1969. Was established to improve, promote and advance the Timber Industry; serves members throughout the Northwest and Intermountain area.

Meetings/Conferences:
Annual Meetings: No Meetings Held

Publications:
Frontline. m.
Bulletin. m.
Legal Briefing. m..

Tin Stabilizers Association *(2001)*
100 N. 20th St., Fourth Floor
Philadelphia, PA 19103
Tel: (215)564-3484 *Fax:* (215)564-2175
E-Mail: tsa@fernley.com
Web Site: www.tinstabilizers.org
Members: 5 companies
Staff: 2
Annual Budget: $50-100,000
Executive Director: John D. McGreevey

Historical Note
TSA was formed to promote the safe use of tin stabilizers, an additive used in vinyl and other plastics to improve processing characteristics.

Tire and Rim Association *(1903)*
175 Montrose West Ave.
Copley, OH 44321
Tel: (330)666-8121 *Fax:* (330)666-8340
E-Mail: tra@us-tra.org
Members: 85 companies
Staff: 3

Annual Budget: $250-500,000
Executive Vice President: J.F. Pacuit

Historical Note
The technical standardizing body for tire, rim and valve manufacturers.

Publications:
Year Book. a.
Engineering Design Information for Ground Vehicle Tires and Rims. q.

Tire Industry Association *(1957)*
1532 Pointer Ridge Pl.
Suite G
Bowie, MD 20716-1883
Tel: (301)430-7280 *Fax:* (301)430-7283
Toll Free: (800)876 - 8372
E-Mail: info@tireindustry.org
Web Site: www.tireindustry.org
Members: 3000 companies
Staff: 15
Annual Budget: $1-2,000,000
Executive Vice President: Ron Littlefield
Senior Vice President, Tech'l Education Services: Kevin Rohlwing

Historical Note
Founded as the Central States Retreaders' Association; became American Retreaders Association in 1964, and then International Tire and Rubber Association in 1996 before merging with Tire Association of North America to form current organization. Organized to provide its members with technical, marketing and management programs and continuing education. Membership: $250/year (domestic); $300/year (international).

Publications:
Today's Tire Industry.
ITRA Industry Update. bi-m.
Tire Retreading/Repair Journal. m. adv.
Commercial Tire Service Update. m. adv.

Tire Retread Information Bureau *(1974)*
900 Weldon Grove
Pacific Grove, CA 93950
Tel: (831)372-1917 *Fax:* (831)372-9210
Toll Free: (888)473 - 8732
E-Mail: info@retread.org
Web Site: www.retread.org
Members: 450 companies in 35 countries
Staff: 4
Annual Budget: $100-250,000
Managing Director: Harvey Brodsky
Associate Director: David A. Kolman

Historical Note
A non-profit organization which serves as the public relations arm of the retread industry. Gathers and disseminates information on retread passenger and truck tires to members and the general public. TRIB is not a lobbying organization. Receives logistical support from industry associations, suppliers, retreaders, and new tire manufacturers. Membership: $100/year (individual); $300/year (company).

Publications:
The Voice of Retreading. q.

Tobacco Associates *(1947)*
1725 K St. NW
Suite 512
Washington, DC 20006
Tel: (202)828-9144 *Fax:* (202)828-9149
E-Mail: taw@tobaccoassociatesinc.org
Web Site: www.tobaccoassociatesinc.org
Members: 75000 individuals
Staff: 6
Annual Budget: $1-2,000,000
President: Kirk Wayne
E-Mail: taw@tobaccoassociatesinc.org

Historical Note
Promotes export of US flue-cured tobacco.

Meetings/Conferences:
Annual Meetings: Raleigh, NC/early March

Publications:
Newsletter. q.

Tobacco Association of the U.S. *(1900)*

Historical Note
Address unknown in 2005.

Tobacco Merchants Association of the U.S.
(1915)
P.O. Box 8019
Princeton, NJ 08543-8019
Tel: (609)275-4900 *Fax:* (609)275-8379
E-Mail: tma@tma.org
Web Site: www.tma.org
Members: 167 companies
Staff: 24
Annual Budget: $1-2,000,000
President: Farrell Delman

Historical Note
Founded in 1915, the Tobacco Merchants Association was created to manage information of vital interest to the tobacco industry. The TMA continues to function as a trade association and remains dedicated to supplying fact-based information about the tobacco industry. The TMA's information is maintained through a computerized data base/website and is disseminated to a variety of interested groups, including the media. The TMA is supported by tobacco product manufacturers, industry suppliers, financial institutions, international leaf dealers, distributors and retailers all over the world. Dues: determined by type of business.

Publications:
Executive Summary. d.
Tobacco USA. bi-a.
U.S. Tobacco Weekly. w.
World Alert. w.
Leaf Bulletin. bi-w.
Tobacco Barometers. m.
Tobacco Trade Barometers(Import/Export)(6 parts). m.
Tobacco Tax Guide. q.
Executive Summary. w.
Daily Legislative Tracking.
Japan Tobacco Trade Barometer.
China Watch.
Tobacco News Network. w.

Tobacconists' Association of America *(1968)*
1211 N. Tutor Ln.
Evansville, IN 47715
Tel: (812)479-8070 *Fax:* (812)479-5939
E-Mail: taaoffice@t-a-a.com
Web Site: www.t-a-a.com/
Members: 100 companies
Staff: 1
Annual Budget: $100-250,000
Executive Director: Ted Clark

Historical Note
Members are retail tobacco dealers representing outlets throughout the U.S.

Publications:
TAA Catalog. a. adv.

Tooling Component Manufacturers Association *(1958)*

Historical Note
Address unknown in 2003.

Tortilla Industry Association *(1990)*
8201 Greensboro Dr.
Suite 300
McLean, VA 22102-9036
Tel: (703)610-0258 *Fax:* (703)610-9005
E-Mail: tortilla-info@verizon.net
Web Site: www.tortilla-info.com
Members: 180 companies
Staff: 2
Annual Budget: $500-1,000,000
Executive Director: Roberto Quinones

Historical Note
Members are manufacturers of tortillas. Affiliate members are industry suppliers. Membership: $500-2,000/year (depending on size or type).

Meetings/Conferences:
Annual Meetings: September-October/800-1,000

Publications:
Tortilla Industry News. q.

Tourist Railway Association *(1972)*
P.O. Box 1245
Chama, NM 87520-1245
Tel: (505)756-1240 *Fax:* (505)756-1238
Toll Free: (800)678 - 7246
E-Mail: train@valornet.com
Web Site: www.traininc.org
Members: 200 organizations
Staff: 2
Annual Budget: $25-50,000
Executive Director: Dan Ranger
E-Mail: train@valornet.com
Administrative Assistant: Karen Ranger
E-Mail: train@valornet.com

Historical Note
TRAIN members are railway museums, tourist railroads, product suppliers, railroad publishers, private car owners, excursion operators, and other interested persons and organizations. Its goals are to establish a professional program of standards and safety within the industry; facilitate communication among members; and provide insurance programs and governmental representation. Membership: $150-500/year (full member); $115/year (associate member).

Meetings/Conferences:
Annual Meetings: Fall
2007 – Middletown, PA(Holiday Inn Harrisburg East)
2008 – Milwaukee, WI

Publications:
Trainline. bi-m. adv.

Towing and Recovery Association of America *(1979)*
2121 Eisenhower Ave., Suite 200
Alexandria, VA 22314-4686
Tel: (703)684-7713 *Fax:* (703)684-6720
Toll Free: (800)728 - 0136
E-Mail: towserver@aol.com
Web Site: www.towserver.org
Members: 1500 companies
Staff: 6
Annual Budget: $500-1,000,000
Executive Director: Harriet Cooley

Historical Note
Members are companies operating tow-trucks and automotive recovery equipment. Subsidiary organizations include T.R.A.A. Education Foundation, and T.R.A.A. Political Action Committee. Membership: $210/year.

Meetings/Conferences:
Annual Meetings: June

Publications:
TRAA Towing News. m.
TRAA Membership Directory/Buyers Guide. a.

Towing Equipment Distributors Association

Historical Note
Part of Towing and Recovery Association of America.

Towing Equipment Manufacturers Association

Historical Note
An affiliate of the National Truck Equipment Association.

Toxicology Forum *(1975)*
1300 Eye St. NW
Suite 1010 East
Washington, DC 20005
Tel: (202)659-0030 *Fax:* (202)789-0905
E-Mail: info@toxforum.org
Web Site: www.toxforum.org
Members: 127 individuals
Staff: 4
Annual Budget: $100-250,000
President and Chief Operating Officer: David G. Longfellow

Historical Note
Forum members are individuals, corporations, universities, associations and government agencies with an interest in toxicology.

Meetings/Conferences:
2007 – Washington, DC(Westin Embassy Row)/Jan. 30-Feb. 1

Publications:
Summer Meeting Proceedings. a.
European Meeting Proceedings. a.
Winter Meeting Proceedings. a.

Toy Industry Association *(1916)*

1115 Broadway, Suite 400
New York, NY 10010-3303
Tel: (212)675-1141 *Fax:* (212)633-1429
E-Mail: info@toy-tia.org
Web Site: www.toy-tia.org
Members: 406 companies
Staff: 28
Annual Budget: $5-10,000,000
President: Carter E. Keithley

Historical Note
Founded as Toy Manufacturers of the U.S.; became Toy Manufacturers of America in 1966. Absorbed American Toy Export Association in 1992; assumed its current name in 2001. Members are major American toy manufacturers and importers. Sponsors and produces the American International Toy Fair, the largest toy trade show in America.

Meetings/Conferences:
Annual Meetings: February in New York/Toy Center & Javits Convention Center/32,000

Publications:
Toy Inventor's Guide.
American Internat'l Toy Fair Directory. a.
Toy Industry Fact Book. a.

Track Owners Association *(1991)*
417 Oak Pl.
Suite Two
Port Orange, FL 32127
Tel: (386)763-5005
E-Mail: toa@slotcar.org
Web Site: www.slotcar.org
Members: 300 individuals
Staff: 1
Annual Budget: $10-25,000,000
Secretary-Treasurer: Bob Herman
E-Mail: toa@slotcar.org

Historical Note
TOA members are owner/operators of commercial slot car racing tracks and suppliers of services and equipment. Has no paid officers or full-time staff. Membership: $60/year (operator); $100/year (manufacturer/distributor).

Meetings/Conferences:
Annual Meetings: Summer

Publications:
Creating A Business Plan. a. adv.
TOA Newsletter. m. adv.

Trade Promotion Management Association
(1989)
174 - 13771 N. Fountain Hills Blvd.
Suite 114
Fountain Hills, AZ 85268
Tel: (480)837-9704 *Fax:* (602)296-0277
E-Mail: headquarters@napaa.org
Web Site: www.napaa.org
Members: 100 individuals
Staff: 2
Annual Budget: $250-500,000
Executive Director: Deb Kuhns

Historical Note
Founded as National Association for Promotional and Advertising Allowances; assumed its current name in 2005. Members are companies and organizations that rely on cooperative advertising and promotions. Membership: $800/year (organization/company).

Meetings/Conferences:
Annual Meetings: Spring.

Publications:
NAPAA Nuggets. bi-w..
Annual Industry Survey. a.
NAPAA Newsletter. q. adv.

Trade Show Exhibitors Association *(1966)*
2301 S. Lake Shore Dr., Suite 1005
Chicago, IL 60616
Tel: (312)842-8732 *Fax:* (312)842-8744
E-Mail: tsea@tsea.org
Web Site: www.tsea.org
Members: 1500 companies
Staff: 6
Annual Budget: $1-2,000,000
President: Stephen A. Schuldenfrei
Communications Manager: Betsy Carnahan

Historical Note
Founded as the National Trade Show Exhibitors Association; became International Exhibitors Association in 1984 and assumed its present name in 1996. Awards the CME (Certified Manager of Exhibits) designation and is a member of the Center for Exhibition Industry Research. Members are companies using exhibits and events for marketing, advertising or public relations and companies that supply products and services to the exhibition and event industry. Membership: $95/year (exhibit manager); $500/year (supplier).

Meetings/Conferences:
2007 – Washington, DC(Washington D.C. Country Club)/July 30-Aug. 2

Publications:
Annual Buyers Guide (online only). a. adv.
Event Source. a. adv.
About Face: The Journal of Face to Face Marketing. q. adv.

Traffic Audit Bureau for Media Measurement
(1933)
420 Lexington Ave., Room 2520
New York, NY 10170
Tel: (212)972-8075 *Fax:* (212)972-8928
E-Mail: info@tabonline.com
Web Site: www.tabonline.com
Members: 425 companies
Staff: 6
Annual Budget: $1-2,000,000
President: Joseph C. Philport

Historical Note
Audits the circulation of the outdoor advertising media -- the 8-sheet and 30-sheet poster medium, the shelter display medium, the painted bulletin medium and others; establishes the standards for the measurement of the circulation of the outdoor advertising media.

Meetings/Conferences:
Annual Meetings: Summer

Publications:
TABBriefs Newsletter.
Planning for Out-of-Home Media. m.

Training Directors' Forum *(1985)*
P.O. Box 3867
Frederick, MD 21705
Tel: (301)696-1006 *Fax:* (301)694-5124
E-Mail: tdf@vnuexpo.com
Web Site: www.trainingdirectorsforum.com
Members: 500 individuals
Staff: 5
Marketing Manager: Michelle Davis

Meetings/Conferences:
Annual Meetings: May

Publications:
Training Directors' Forum Newsletter. m.

Training Officers Conference
2025 M St. NW
Suite 800
Washington, DC 20036
Tel: (202)973-8683 *Fax:* (202)331-0111
E-Mail: TOCinformation@aol.com
Web Site: www.trainingofficers.org
Members: 200 individuals
Annual Budget: $100-250,000

Historical Note
TOC members are federal trainers and other professionals from industry and academe who are interested in contributing to the knowledge and practice of human resources and training. Has no paid officers or full-time staff. Membership: $850/year.

Meetings/Conferences:
Annual Meetings: Spring

Publications:
TOC News. m.

Trans-Atlantic American Flag Liner Operators
(1985)
120 Wall St., Suite 2020
New York, NY 10005-4001
Tel: (212)269-2415 *Fax:* (212)269-2418
E-Mail: halevy1@attglobal.net
Web Site: www.taaflo-tpaflo.org
Members: 5 companies
Staff: 1
Annual Budget: $50-100,000
Chairman: Howard Levy

Historical Note
Formerly (1985) Atlantic and Gulf American Flag Berth Operators. Major purpose is publication of ocean freight rates on movements of military goods.

Meetings/Conferences:
Annual Meetings: Not held

Transaction Processing Performance Council
(1988)
P.O. Box 29920
San Francisco, CA 94129-0920
Tel: (415)561-6272 *Fax:* (415)561-6120
E-Mail: info@tpc.org
Web Site: www.tpc.org
Members: 31 manufacturers
Staff: 1
Annual Budget: $250-500,000
Executive Director/Administrator: Michael Majdalany

Historical Note
Members are computer and database manufacturers and individuals with an interest in transaction processing.

Meetings/Conferences:
Annual Meetings: Bimonthly; typical attendance is 50 people.

Publications:
TPC Benchmark Status Report. bi-m.

Transformer Association, The *(1974)*
P.O. Box P182
South Dartmouth, MA 02748
Tel: (508)979-5935 *Fax:* (508)979-5845
E-Mail: info@transformer-assn.org
Web Site: www.transformer-assn.org
Members: 53 companies
Staff: 2
Annual Budget: $50-100,000
Executive Director: Elizabeth B. Chambers

Historical Note
Formerly (1994) Power Conversion Products Council, International and (2000) PCPCI - The Transformer Association. Members are manufacturers and suppliers to the wall plug-in transformer/transformer charger/converter industry.

Meetings/Conferences:
Semi-annual Meetings:
2007 – Denver-Broomfield, CO(Omni Interlocken Resort)/Apr. 12-13/50

Publications:
Directory. online.
Product Index. online.

Transplantation Society *(1966)*
1111 St. Urbain St., Suite 108
Montreal, QC H2Z 1-Y6
Tel: (514)874-1717 *Fax:* (514)874-1716
E-Mail: info@transplantation-soc.org
Web Site: www.transplantation-soc.org
Members: 3000 individuals
Staff: 2
Annual Budget: $250-500,000
Executive Director: Philip A. Dombrowski
E-Mail: info@transplantation-soc.org

Historical Note
An international society of scientists dealing with all aspects of transplantation of organs and tissues. Membership: $80/year.

Meetings/Conferences:
Annual Meetings: Fall
2008 – Sydney, Australia/Aug. 9-15/3000

Publications:
Transplantation. q. adv.
Transplantation Proceedings. 8/year. adv.

Transport Workers Union of America *(1934)*
1700 Broadway, Second Floor
New York, NY 10019
Tel: (212)259-4900 *Fax:* (212)265-4537
Web Site: www.twu.org
Members: 130000 individuals
Staff: 60
Annual Budget: $5-10,000,000

Director, Communications: James Gannon
International President: James Little

Historical Note
Organized in April, 1934 in New York City as the Transport Workers Union. Chartered by the Congress of Industrial Organizations under its present title in 1937. Sponsors and supports the Transport Workers Union Political Contribution Committee.

Meetings/Conferences:
Quadrennial: Fall

Publications:
TWU Express. m.

Transportation & Logistics Council *(1974)*
120 Main St.
Huntington, NY 11743-0630
Tel: (631)549-8984 *Fax:* (631)549-8962
Web Site: www.tlcouncil.org
Members: 450 companies
Staff: 4
Annual Budget: $100-250,000
Executive Director: George C. Pezold

Historical Note
Formerly (1990) Shippers National Freight Claim Council and Transportation Claims and Prevention Council (1996). Name change was made in 1996 to indicate a broadened advocacy role on behalf of shippers/receivers. Founded as a non-profit membership association of U.S. and Canadian shippers, receivers, and carriers, TCPC is dedicated to the reduction of transit losses and the improvement of freight claim and freight charge payment procedures in domestic and international commerce. Membership: $395/year (regular); $345/year (associate).

Meetings/Conferences:
Annual Meetings: March

Publications:
Q & A. a. adv.
Trans Digest. m. adv.

Transportation Brokers Conference of America

Historical Note
A conference of Transportation Intermediaries Association.

Transportation Clubs International *(1920)*
P.O. Box 2223
Ocean Shores, WA 98569
Tel: (877)858-8627 *Fax:* (360)289-3188
E-Mail: info@transportationclubsinternational.com
Web Site: www.transportationclubsinternational.com
Members: 10000 individuals
Staff: 1
Annual Budget: $50-100,000
Executive Director: Katie deJonge

Historical Note
Members are individuals in all phases of transportation, traffic management and physical distribution.

Meetings/Conferences:
Annual Meetings: Fall

Transportation Communications International Union *(1899)*
Three Research Pl.
Rockville, MD 20850
Tel: (301)948-4910 *Fax:* (301)948-1872
Web Site: www.tcunion.org
Members: 100000 individuals
Staff: 100
International President: Robert A. Scardelletti

Historical Note
Established in Sedalia, Missouri on December 31, 1899 as the Order of Railroad Clerks of America and chartered by the American Federation of Labor the following year. Became the Brotherhood of Railway and Steamship Clerks, Freight Handlers, Express and Station Employees in 1919 and then the Brotherhood of Railway, Airline, and Steamship Clerks, Freight Handlers, Express and Station Employees (BRAC) in 1967. Assumed its present name in 1987. In 1969 it absorbed the Transportation-Communication Employees Union, the Railway Patrolmen's International Union and the Federation of Business Machine Technicians and Engineers. In 1975 it merged with the United Transport Service Employees of America (founded in 1937), and in 1978 merged with the Brotherhood of Sleeping Car Porters (founded in 1925). Absorbed the American Railway and Airway Supervisors Association in 1980; in 1986, BRAC merged with Brotherhood Railway Carmen of the United States. In addition to bargaining and representation of its members, TCU provides other services to its members, and sponsors and supports the Responsible Citizens Political League.

Meetings/Conferences:
Quadrennial Meetings: (2003)

Publications:
Interchange. 6/year.

Transportation Development Association *(1971)*
131 W. Wilson, Suite 302
Madison, WI 53703
Tel: (608)256-7044 *Fax:* (608)256-7079
Web Site: www.tdawiscon.org
Members: 400 transportation stakeholders
Staff: 2
Executive Director: Bob Cook
E-Mail: bob.cook@tdawisconsin.org

Meetings/Conferences:
Annual Meetings: Annual

Publications:
Newsletter. m.

Transportation Elevator and Grain Merchants Association *(1918)*
1300 L St. NW
Suite 1020
Washington, DC 20005-4113
Tel: (202)842-0400 *Fax:* (202)789-7223
Web Site: www.tegma.org
Members: 40 companies
Staff: 2
Annual Budget: $25-50,000
Secretary: Jula J. Kinnaird

Historical Note
Membership: $700-3250/year.

Meetings/Conferences:
Annual Meetings: February

Transportation Institute *(1968)*
5201 Auth Way
Camp Springs, MD 20746
Tel: (301)423-3335 *Fax:* (301)423-0634
E-Mail: info@trans-inst.org
Web Site: www.trans-inst.org
Members: 140 companies
Staff: 10
Annual Budget: $2-5,000,000
Chairman and President: James L. Henry

Historical Note
Members are U.S.-flag shipping, towing and dredging companies. TI is concerned with maintaining the strength of U.S. water-borne commerce.

Transportation Intermediaries Association *(1978)*
1625 Prince St., Suite 200
Alexandria, VA 23314
Tel: (703)299-5700 *Fax:* (703)836-0123
E-Mail: info@tianet.org
Web Site: www.tianet.org
Members: 800 companies
Staff: 4
Annual Budget: $500-1,000,000
President and Chief Executive Officer: Robert Voltmann
E-Mail: voltmann@tianet.org
Director, Member Services: Kelly Scott

Historical Note
Established as the Property Brokers Association of America; became the Transportation Brokers Conference of America in 1981 and assumed its present name in 1995. Absorbed American International Freight Association in 2002. Members are companies working with truckers, carriers and shippers to arrange the transport of general freight. The Logistics Conference, the Intermodal Conference, the North American Conference of Freight Forwarders, the Perishable Agricultural and Foodstuff Conference, and the Transportation Brokers Conference of America are subsidiaries of TIA. Membership: $295-995/year.

Meetings/Conferences:
Annual Meetings: Spring

Publications:
TIA LOGISTICS HOURNAL. m. adv.
TIA Membership Directory & Handbook. a. adv.

Transportation Lawyers Association *(1937)*
P.O. Box 15122
Lenexa, KS 66285-5122
Tel: (913)541-9077 *Fax:* (913)599-5340
E-Mail: snewman@goamp.com
Web Site: www.translaw.org
Members: 800 attorneys
Staff: 3
Annual Budget: $250-500,000
Executive Director: Stephanie Newman

Historical Note
Founded in Louisville, KY as the Motor Carrier Lawyers Association (MCLA); assumed its present name in 1983. Originally an international bar association for lawyers representing motor carriers before the Interstate Commerce Commission and Canadian regulatory agencies, membership is now open to attorneys representing any interstate, foreign or intrastate "transportation interest." Membership: $185/year (individual).

Meetings/Conferences:
Annual Meetings: Spring

Publications:
Transportation Lawyer. 5/year.

Transportation Research Forum *(1958)*
P.O. Box 5074
Fargo, ND 58105
Tel: (701)231-7766 *Fax:* (701)231-1945
E-Mail: info@trforum.org
Web Site: www.trforum.org
Members: 350 individuals
Staff: 11
Annual Budget: $100-250,000
Executive Director: Gene Griffith

Historical Note
An independent organization of transportation professionals, TRF's purpose is to provide an impartial meeting ground for carriers, shippers, government officials, consultants, university researchers, suppliers, and others seeking an exchange of information related to both passenger and freight transportation. Membership: $85/year.

Meetings/Conferences:
Annual Meetings: Spring
2007 – Boston, MA/March 14-17

Publications:
TRF Journal. 3/year.
Directory of Members.
Newsletter. 2/year.
Proceedings of Annual Meeting.

Transportation Safety Equipment Institute *(1962)*
Ten Laboratory Dr.
Research Triangle Park, NC 27709
Tel: (919)549-4800 *Fax:* (919)406-1306
E-Mail: tsei@mema.org
Web Site: www.tsei.org
Members: 23 companies
Staff: 2
Annual Budget: $50-100,000
Group Executive: Stephanie Brown

Historical Note
Formerly (1986) the Truck Safety Equipment Institute. Manufacturers of lighting, mirrors and emergency-vehicle products, reflectors and other devices related to motor vehicle safety.

Meetings/Conferences:
Annual Meetings: October

Publications:
TSEI Reports. irreg.

Transworld Advertising Agency Network *(1936)*
7920 Summer Lake Ct.
Ft. Myers, FL 33907
Tel: (352)753-9005
E-Mail: info@taan.org

Web Site: www.taan.org
Members: 45 agencies
Staff: 2
Annual Budget: $250-500,000
President: Gary Lessner

Historical Note

Established in 1936 as the Transamerica Advertising Agency Network, it assumed its present name in 1975. The association is an international group of medium-sized, cooperating and independent advertising agencies.

Meetings/Conferences:

Semi-annual Meetings: Winter and Summer

Publications:

Newsletter. semi-a.
Directory. a.

Trauma Care International *(1988)*
P.O. Box 4826
Baltimore, MD 21211
Tel: (410)235-7697 *Fax:* (410)235-8084
Web Site: www.itaccs.com
Members: 1000 individuals
Executive Director: Christopher M. Grande, M.D., MPH

Historical Note

Originally (1988) known as International Trauma Anesthesia and Critical Care Society before assuming its current name. ITACCS members are health care professionals with an interest in trauma/critical care anesthesiology. Membership: $100/year (individual); $1,000/year (corporate); $40/year (student).

Publications:

Trauma Care. semi-a. adv.

Travel Adventure Cinema Society *(1970)*
765 Beverly Park Pl.
Jackson, MI 49203
Toll Free: (877)279 - 7604
E-Mail: tracs_kathie@sbcglobal.net
Web Site: www.travelfilms.org
Members: 120 individuals
Staff: 1
Annual Budget: $10-25,000
Executive Secretary: Kathie Veach

Historical Note

Founded as International Motion Picture and Lecturers Association; assumed its current name in 2000. Members produce personally narrated travel films.

Meetings/Conferences:

Annual Meetings: December

Publications:

Travel Adventure Cinema Magazine. q.

Travel and Tourism Research Association *(1970)*
P.O. Box 2133
Boise, ID 83701
Tel: (208)429-9511 *Fax:* (208)429-9512
E-Mail: barb@ttra.com
Web Site: www.ttra.com
Members: 800firms,universities&agencies
Staff: 3
Annual Budget: $250-500,000
Executive Director: Patty Morgan
Manager, Account Services: Barbara Shawnee

Historical Note

Established as the Travel Research Association as the result of a merger of the Eastern and Western Councils for Travel Research on January 1, 1970. The present name was adopted in 1980. Membership: dues vary.

Meetings/Conferences:

Annual Meetings: June/500

Publications:

Directory of Travel Research Suppliers. a.
Proceedings of Annual Conference. a.
Journal of Travel Research. q. adv.
Directory of Members. a.
TTRA Members Newsletter. q. adv.

Travel Goods Association *(1938)*
Five Vaughn Dr.
Suite 105
Princeton, NJ 08540
Tel: (609)720-1200 *Fax:* (609)720-0620
Web Site: www.travel-goods.org
Members: 300 individuals
Staff: 6
Annual Budget: $2-5,000,000
President: Michele Marini Pittenger
E-Mail: MMPtga@aol.com

Historical Note

Founded as Luggage and Leather Goods Manufacturers of America; assumed its current name in 2000. TGA represents manufacturers, retailers and distributors of luggage, personal leather goods, business and computer cases, business and travel accessories, and handbags. Membership: $1,000-5,000/year (company).

Meetings/Conferences:

Annual Meetings: March/5,000
2007 – Las Vegas, NV/Feb. 27-March 1

Publications:

Travel Goods Showcase. 5/year. adv.

Travel Industry Association of America *(1941)*
1100 New York Ave. NW
Suite 450
Washington, DC 20005-3934
Tel: (202)408-8422 *Fax:* (202)408-1255
Web Site: www.tia.org
Members: 2200 organizations
Staff: 75
Annual Budget: $10-25,000,000
President and Chief Executive Officer: Roger J. Dow
E-Mail: dkoehl@tia.org
Senior Vice President, Research: Suzanne Cook, Ph.D.
E-Mail: scook@tia.org
Vice President, Technology: Jay Gray
E-Mail: dkoehl@tia.org
Senior Vice President, Finance and Administration: Frank O'Rourke
E-Mail: forourke@tia.org

Historical Note

The result of a merger of Discover America (founded in 1965) and the National Association of Travel Organizations (founded in 1941). Members are organizations such as hotels, airlines, travel agencies, etc. interested in promoting increased travel to and within the United States. Formerly (1980) known as Discover America Travel Organizations. National Councils: Destination Organizations, State Tourism Directors, Travel Attractions. Has an annual budget of approximately $15 million.

Meetings/Conferences:

Annual Meetings: Fall

Publications:

E-newsline. bi-w.

Travel Journalists Guild *(1980)*
P.O. Box 10643
Chicago, IL 60610
Tel: (312)664-9729 *Fax:* (312)664-9701
Web Site: www.tjgonline.com
Members: 75 individuals
Staff: 2
Annual Budget: $10-25,000
Executive Coordinator and Secretary: Philip D. Hoffman

Historical Note

Established in Antigua, Guatemala in 1980, TJG members are freelance authors, photographers, artists, lecturers, file makers, etc. specializing in travel with a minimum of three years experience. Membership: $150/year (individual); plus $250 initial fee.

Meetings/Conferences:

Annual Meetings: None held

Publications:

Travelwriter Marketletter. m.

Treated Wood Council *(2001)*
1111 19th St. NW
Suite 800
Washington, DC 20036
Tel: (202)463-2045 *Fax:* (202)463-2059
Web Site: www.treated-wood.org
Members: 250 organizations
Executive Director: Jeff Miller

Tree Care Industry Association *(1938)*
Three Perimeter Rd.
Unit One
Manchester, NH 03103
Tel: (603)314-5380 *Fax:* (603)314-5386
Toll Free: (800)733 - 2622
E-Mail: TCIA@treecareindustry.org
Web Site: www.treecareindustry.org
Members: 2000 tree service companies
Staff: 25
Annual Budget: $2-5,000,000
President: Cynthia Mills, CAE
E-Mail: cmills@treecareindustry.org
Vice President, Public Policy and Communications: Mark Garvin
E-Mail: garvin@treecareindustry.org
Vice President, Safety and Education: Peter Gerstenberger
E-Mail: peter@treecareindustry.org
Meeting Planner: Diane Morgan
E-Mail: garvin@treecareindustry.org

Historical Note

Formerly (1938) National Arborist Association; assumed its current name in 2003. Was formed to advance tree care companies and their interests. Membership: $339-$3,247/year (organization/company).

Meetings/Conferences:

Annual Meetings: February
2007 – Hartford, CT(Convention Center)/Nov. 9-11/3000

Publications:

Treeworker. m. adv.
Tree Care Industry Magazine. m. adv.
TCIA Reporter. m.

Tree-Ring Society *(1935)*
Univ. of Arizona
Tucson, AZ 85721
Tel: (520)621-1608 *Fax:* (520)621-8229
E-Mail: pgress@hrr.arizona.edu
Web Site: www.treeringsociety.org/index.html
Members: 350individualsandinstitutions
Staff: 1
Annual Budget: under $10,000
Administrator: Phyllis Norton-Gross

Historical Note

Membership consists of those interested in dendrochronology, the science of determining dates by matching tree-rings for archaeological, hydrological or climatological purposes. Has no paid staff. Membership: $40/year - 2 issues/year (individual member);
$20/year-2 issues/year (student); $50/year-2 issues/year (institution).

Publications:

Tree-Ring Research. semi-a.

Tributyl Phosphate Task Force *(1987)*

Historical Note

An affiliate of the Synthetic Organic Chemical Manufacturers Association, which provides administrative support.

Triological Society

Historical Note

Abbreviated name for the American Laryngological, Rhinological and Otological Society.

Truck Manufacturers Association *(1995)*
1225 New York Ave. NW
Suite 300
Washington, DC 20005
Tel: (202)638-7825 *Fax:* (202)737-3742
Web Site: www.truckmfgs.org
Members: 8 companies
Staff: 2
Annual Budget: $250-500,000
President: Robert M. Clarke

Historical Note

TMA represents the North American (including U.S. and Canadian) manufacturers of medium and heavy-duty trucks. TMA promotes the interests of the motor truck manufacturing industry by coordinating constructive dialogue, cooperative research, and technical information exchange between the truck manufacturing industry and the governmental entities that regulate the industry.

Truck Mixer Manufacturers Bureau *(1945)*

900 Spring St.
Silver Spring, MD 20910
Tel: (301)587-1400 *Fax:* (301)587-1605
Web Site: www.tmmb.org
Members: 8 companies
Staff: 2
Annual Budget: $50-100,000
Administrator: Nicole R. Maher

Historical Note

An affiliate of National Ready Mixed Concrete Association. Purpose to develop standards and guidelines for equipment production.

Publications:

Truck Mixer & Agitator Standards. irreg.

Truck Renting and Leasing Association *(1978)*
675 N. Washington St., Suite 410
Alexandria, VA 22314
Tel: (703)299-9120 *Fax:* (703)299-9115
E-Mail: ariser@trala.org
Web Site: www.trala.org
Members: 700companies,30,000locations
Staff: 6
Annual Budget: $2-5,000,000
President and Chief Executive Officer: Peter Vroom
E-Mail: pvroom@trala.org
Vice President, Government Relations: Tom James
Director, Government Relations: John Lynch
E-Mail: jlynch@trala.org
Director, Communications: Shannon Murray
Director, Events: Anne Riser
E-Mail: ariser@trala.org

Historical Note

Founded in 1978, TRALA is a non-profit trade association that serves as a unified, focused voice tor the truck renting and leasing industry. Members are firms active in full-service truck and trailer leasing, dedicated contract carriage, commercial daily truck rental, and consumer truck rental. Membership includes associate members from many industries, providing goods and services to truck lessors. Membership: $1,000-175,000year, based on power units.

Meetings/Conferences:

Annual Meetings: Spring/550
2008 – Palm Springs, CA(La Quinta Resort)/March 21-24

Publications:

Inside TRALA. bi-m.
En Route (an online business digest). bi-w.
TRALA Weekly Wire (fax). w.
TRALA Legislative Report.
TRALA Vehicle. a. adv.

Truck Trailer Manufacturers Association *(1941)*
1020 Princess St.
Alexandria, VA 22314-2289
Tel: (703)549-3010 *Fax:* (703)549-3014
Web Site: www.ttmanet.org
Members: 200 companies
Staff: 6
Annual Budget: $500-1,000,000
President: Richard P. Bowling
E-Mail: dick@ttmanet.org

Historical Note

Represents the manufacturers of truck trailers and intermodal containers; members are responsible for the manufacture of over 90% of the commercial trailers produced in the U.S.

Meetings/Conferences:

Annual Meetings: April-May/500
2007 – Aventura, FL(Turnberry Isle Resort)/May 16-20/400

Publications:

TTMA Bulletin. m.
Membership Directory. a.

Truck Writers of North America *(1988)*
4429 Back Creek Church Rd.
Charlotte, NC 28213
Tel: (704)599-0570 *Fax:* (704)509-4932
E-Mail: admin@twna.org
Web Site: www.twna.org
Members: 150 individuals
Staff: 3
Executive Director: Tom Kelley

Historical Note

Represents writers, editors, freelance journalists, and public relations and communications specialists producing information about trucks, trucking, and the trucking industry. Has no paid officers or full-time staff. Membership: for individual members, $35/year (associate-press member); $50/year (associate-nonprofit member); $100/year (associate-business); $500/year (associate-corporate member). Corporate membership is a group membership for the whole staff of an organization.

Meetings/Conferences:

Semi-Annual Meetings:

Publications:

TWNA Directory. a. adv.
TWNA Dispatch Newsletter. bi-m.

Truck-frame and Axle Repair Association *(1966)*
3741 Enterprise Dr. SW
Rochester, MN 55902
Toll Free: (800)232 - 8272
E-Mail: w.g.reich@att.net
Web Site: www.taraassociation.com
Members: 61 companies; 41 associates
Staff: 1
Annual Budget: $50-100,000
Administrator: Wayne Reich

Historical Note

Founded in Louisville, KY by 13 frame and axle repair shops. Membership is open to all companies which have been in business for two years repairing heavy-duty trucks, tractors and trailers and straightening their frames, axles and housings, as well as aligning and balancing their wheels.

Meetings/Conferences:

Semi-annual: Spring/Fall

Publications:

TARA News & Topics. m.

Trucking Management *(1963)*
499 South Capitol St. SW
Suite 502-A
Washington, DC 20003
Tel: (202)554-3060 *Fax:* (202)554-3160
Members: 8 companies
Staff: 2
Annual Budget: $2-5,000,000
President: Jim Lynch
Office Manager: Linda Barber

Historical Note

Founded as Trucking Employers; became Trucking Management in 1978, and in 1997 MFCA was formed as a successor organization. MFCA has reorganized to return to its pre-1997 structure effective October 1, 2005. The organization name has returned to Trucking Management, Inc (TMI) and TMI's primary role will be as the multii-employer bargaining association on behalf of the authorizing carriers.

Truckload Carriers Association *(1938)*
555 E. Braddock Rd.
Alexandria, VA 22314-4627
Tel: (703)838-1950 *Fax:* (703)836-6610
E-Mail: tca@truckload.org
Web Site: www.truckload.org
Members: 650 carriers, 300 affiliates
Staff: 13
Annual Budget: $2-5,000,000
President: Chris Burruss
Director, Education and Training: Virginia DeRoze
E-Mail: vderoze@truckload.org
Director, Conventions and Marketing: William Giroux, CMP
E-Mail: wgiroux@truckload.org
Director, Public Relations and Marketing: Nancy O'Liddy

Historical Note

The product of a merger in 1983 of the Common Carrier Conference-Irregular Route (founded in 1941) and the Contract Carrier Conference (founded in 1939). Formerly (1997) Interstate Truckload Carriers Conference and (1988) Interstate Carriers Conference. TCA serves as the national coordinating point, lobbying organization, and promotional arm for irregular-route common and contract truckload motor carriers. Affiliated with American Trucking Associations. Membership: $250-$6,000/year, based on gross revenues (company).

Meetings/Conferences:

Annual Meetings: March

Publications:

Convention Magazine. a. adv.
Newsletter. w.
Membership Directory. a. adv.

Truss Plate Institute *(1961)*
218 N. Lee St., Suite 312
Alexandria, VA 22314
Tel: (703)683-1010 *Fax:* (866)501-4012
E-Mail: mcassidy@tpinst.org
Web Site: www.tpinst.org
Members: 400 licensee members
Staff: 2
Annual Budget: $500-1,000,000
Executive Director: Michael A. Cassidy
E-Mail: mcassidy@tpinst.org
Director, Inspection Services: Charles B. Goehring

Historical Note

Trade association of truss plate manufacturers, allied suppliers and truss manufacturers. Incorporated in Florida. Membership: $300/year.

Tube and Pipe Association, International *(1983)*
833 Featherstone Rd.
Rockford, IL 61107-6302
Tel: (815)399-8700 *Fax:* (815)484-7700
E-Mail: info@tpatube.org
Web Site: www.tpatube.org
Members: 1800 individuals and companies
Staff: 83
President and Chief Executive Officer: Gerald M. Shankel
Manager, Member Services: Jill Klug
Director, Communications: Pat Lee
Director, Membership Services and Research: Nancy Olson

Historical Note

Formed as Tube and Pipe Fabricators Association by the merger of the Tube Fabricating Division of the Fabricators and Manufacturers Association, Internation'l and the International Pipe Association in 1990; merged with American Tube Association and assumed its current name in 1996. TPA is an educational technology association serving the metal tube and pipe producing and fabricating industries. It is an affiliate association of FMA, which provides administrative support. TPA members are eligible for FMA member benefits. Membership: $25-1850 (differing levels of membership).

Meetings/Conferences:

Annual Meetings: October

Publications:

TPJ, The Tube & Pipe Journal. 8/year. adv.

Tube Council of North America *(1957)*
1601 N. Bond St., Suite 101
Naperville, IL 60563
Tel: (630)544-5051 *Fax:* (630)544-5055
E-Mail: info@tube.org
Web Site: www.tube.org
Members: 11 companies
Staff: 2
Annual Budget: $50-100,000
Executive Director: Patrick Farrey

Historical Note

Established as the Collapsible Metal Tube Association; became the Metal Tube Packaging Council of North America in 1966 and assumed its present name in 1983. TCNA is dedicated to promoting the tube as the package of choice for dentifrice, cosmetic, pharmaceutical, household/industrial and food products. Membership fee varies, based on volume of production.

Meetings/Conferences:

Semi-Annual Meetings: Spring and Fall

Publications:

Tube Topics. q.

Tubular Exchanger Manufacturers Association *(1939)*
25 N. Broadway
Tarrytown, NY 10591
Tel: (914)332-0040 *Fax:* (914)332-1541
E-Mail: info@tema.org
Web Site: www.tema.org

Members: 18 companies
Staff: 5
Annual Budget: $100-250,000
Secretary: Richard C. Byrne

Historical Note
Sets standards for the industry, known as TEMA Standards, which are sold to the chemical processing and petroleum refining industries.

Tune-up Manufacturers Council *(1954)*
P.O. Box 13966
Research Triangle Park, NC 27709-3966
Tel: (919)549-4800 *Fax:* (919)549-4824
E-Mail: info@tune-up.org
Web Site: www.tune-up.org
Members: 8 companies
Staff: 1
Annual Budget: $25-50,000
Executive Director: Jim Lawrence

Historical Note
Founded as the Ignition Manufacturers Institute; assumed its present name in 1981. Administrative support provided by Motor and Equipment Manufacturers Association (same address).

Meetings/Conferences:
Semi-Annual Meetings: Spring and Winter

Turf and Ornamental Communicators Association *(1990)*
120 W. Main, Suite 200
Box 156
New Prague, MN 56071
Tel: (952)758-6340 *Fax:* (952)758-5813
E-Mail: tocaassociation@aol.com
Web Site: www.toca.org
Members: 175 individuals
Staff: 2
Annual Budget: $50-100,000
Executive Director: Den Gardner

Historical Note
TOCA members are individuals and companies involved in communications in the turf and ornamentals industry. Membership: $110/year (individual); $170/year (two people).

Meetings/Conferences:
Annual Meetings: Spring

Publications:
TOCA Talk. q.

Turfgrass Producers International *(1967)*
Two E. Main St.
East Dundee, IL 60118
Tel: (847)649-5555 *Fax:* (847)649-5678
Toll Free: (800)405 - 8873
E-Mail: info@turfgrasssod.org
Web Site: www.turfgrasssod.org/
Members: 1200 companies
Staff: 6
Annual Budget: $1-2,000,000
Executive Director: Kirk Hunter

Historical Note
Formerly (1994) American Sod Producers Association. TPI has continually advanced the turfgrass sod industry through the development of technical and marketing information, as well as supporting research in advancing the environmental benefits of high quality turfgrass. Membership: scale based on number of acres.

Meetings/Conferences:
Semi-Annual Meetings: Winter and Summer/600-800

Publications:
TPI Turf News. bi-m. adv.
TPI Business Management Newsletter. bi-m.

Turkish Studies Association *(1971)*
Dept. of History, Princeton University
129 Dickinson Hall
Princeton, NJ 08544
Tel: (609)258-1802
E-Mail: turk@princeton.edu
Web Site: www.h-net.org/~thetsa/
Members: 500 individuals
Annual Budget: under $10,000
Secretary-Treasurer: Molly Greene
E-Mail: turk@princeton.edu

Historical Note
TSA membership consists of academics, institutions and professional organizations with an interest in Turkish culture, history and language. Sponsors several awards in recognition of achievement in Turkish/Ottoman scholarship, language, and education. Has no paid officers or full-time staff.

Meetings/Conferences:
Annual Meetings: in conjunction with the Middle East Studies Ass'n of North America.

Publications:
The Turkish Studies Association Journal. semi-a..
TSA Bulletin. semi-a. adv.
Membership Roster. irreg.

Turnaround Management Association *(1988)*
100 South Wacker Dr., Suite 850
Chicago, IL 60606
Tel: (312)578-6900 *Fax:* (312)578-8336
E-Mail: info@turnaround.org
Web Site: www.turnaround.org
Members: 7300 individuals
Staff: 12
Annual Budget: $2-5,000,000
Executive Director: Linda M. Delgadillo, CAE
Director, Public Relations: Cecilia Green
Director, Fund Development: Joseph R. Karel

Historical Note
TMA members are in the corporate renewal industry, comprised of financial advisers, operational consultants, crisis managers, interim executives, attorneys, accountants, appraisers, commercial lenders, venture capitalists and other service providers who have an interest in the revitalization of financially distressed businesses and the representation of stakeholders in these entities. Membership is also available for individuals in academia or government. TMA provides opportunities for professional development, networking, certification and reference/research services for its members. Membership: $275/year (individual member); $115/year (individual student/academic/government member); $65/year (student).

Meetings/Conferences:
Semi-annual Meetings: Spring/Fall
2007 – Dallas, TX(Four Seasons)/March 28-31
2007 – Boston, MA(Marriott Copley Place)/Oct. 16-19

Publications:
Annual Report. a.
Journal of Corporate Renewal. 10/year. adv.
Directory of Members & Services. a. adv.

Twentieth-Century Spanish Association of America *(1976)*
Univ. of CO, Dept. of Spanish/Portuguese
McKenna Language Bldg., 278 UCB
Boulder, CO 80309-0278
Tel: (303)492-5900 *Fax:* (303)492-3699
E-Mail: sssas@colorado.edu
Members: 1000 individuals
Staff: 3
Executive Secretary: Luis T. Gonzalez del Valle
Senior Publications Assistant: Marilyn G. Ratclift Mensing

Historical Note
Formerly (2000) Society of Spanish and Spanish-American Studies. Members are academics and others with an interest in contemporary Spanish and Spanish-American art, literature and culture.

Publications:
Anales de la Literatura Espanola Contemporanea. 3/year. adv.
Siglo XX/20th Century Journal. irreg.

Type Directors Club *(1947)*
127 W. 25th St., Eighth Floor
New York, NY 10001
Tel: (212)633-8943 *Fax:* (212)633-8944
E-Mail: director@tdc.org
Web Site: www.tdc.org
Members: 725 individuals
Staff: 1
Annual Budget: $100-250,000
Executive Director: Carol Wahler

Historical Note
Members are professionals involved in typography. Membership is international. Membership: $125/year (individual); $300/year (corporate).

Meetings/Conferences:
Annual Meetings:

Publications:
Letterspace Newsletter. semi-a.
Typography Annual. a.

U.S. - Taiwan Business Council *(1976)*
1700 N. Moore St., Suite 1703
Arlington, VA 22209
Tel: (703)465-2930 *Fax:* (703)465-2937
E-Mail: council@us-taiwan.org
Web Site: www.us-taiwan.org
Members: 300 organizations
Staff: 6
Annual Budget: $250-500,000
President: Rupert Hammond-Chambers
E-Mail: rupertjhe@us-taiwan.org
Vice President: Lotta Danielson-Murphy
E-Mail: lottadm@us-taiwan.org

Historical Note
Council members are organizations with an interest in promoting economic ties between the two countries.

Publications:
Taiwan Business Bulletin. w.
Sector Specific Business Bulletins. w.
Defense Security Report. q.
Semiconductor Report. q.
Membership List. a.

U.S. Apple Association *(1970)*
8233 Old Courthouse Rd.
Suite 200
Vienna, VA 22182-3816
Tel: (703)442-8850 *Fax:* (703)790-0845
Toll Free: (800)781 - 4443
E-Mail: sschaffer@usapple.org
Web Site: www.usapple.org
Members: 450 companies
Staff: 8
Annual Budget: $1-2,000,000
President and Chief Executive Officer: Nancy E. Foster
Manager, Membership/Communications: Shannon Schaffer

Historical Note
Formed by the merger of the International Apple Association (1895) and the National Apple Institute (1935) as International Apple Institute; assumed its current name in 1996. Members are U.S. and foreign firms, other than retailers, which handle apples. Membership: $100-2,000/year (based on volume of apples grown, packed, processed, and/or sold annually).

Meetings/Conferences:
Annual Meetings: August

Publications:
Apple News. m.
Market News. m.
An Apple a Day - online. q.

U.S. Grains Council *(1960)*
1400 K St. NW
Suite 1200
Washington, DC 20005
Tel: (202)789-0789 *Fax:* (202)898-0522
E-Mail: grains@grains.org
Web Site: www.grains.org
Members: 90 producer groups & companies
Staff: 50
Annual Budget: $10-25,000,000
President and Chief Executive Officer: Kenneth Hobbie

Historical Note
Formerly (1998) U.S. Feed Grains Council. Founded by representatives of the agricultural community to promote the export of U.S. feed grain products (e.g., sorghum, barley, corn). USGC works under contract with the Foreign Agricultural Service of the U.S. Department of Agriculture to increase dollar sales abroad of U.S. feed grains.

Meetings/Conferences:
Semi-annual Meetings: Winter and Summer/300
2007 – Toronto, ON, Canada(Marriott)/July 21-25

Publications:
Global Update newsletter. w.
Annual Report. a.
Membership Directory. a.
Meeting Program. semi-a.

U.S. Internet Industry Association *(1994)*
5810 Kingstowne Center Dr., Suite 120, PMB 212
Alexandria, VA 22315-5711
Tel: (703)924-0006 *Fax:* (703)924-4203
Web Site: www.usiia.org
Members: 400 companies
Staff: 3
Annual Budget: $250-500,000
President and Chief Executive Officer: David P. McClure
E-Mail: dmcclure@usiia.org

Historical Note
Founded as Association of Online Professionals; assumed its present name in 1999. Membership: $150/year (individual); $1000-$25,000/year (company/organization).

Meetings/Conferences:
Annual Meetings: Fall

Publications:
USIIA Bulletin. w.

U.S. Lacrosse *(1998)*
113 W. University Pkwy.
Baltimore, MD 21210
Tel: (410)235-6882 Ext: 102 *Fax:* (410)366-6735
E-Mail: info@uslacrosse.org
Web Site: www.uslacrosse.org
Members: 200000 individuals
Staff: 40
Annual Budget: $5-10,000,000
Executive Director: Steve Stenersen
E-Mail: npatrick@uslacrosse.org
Women's Division Director: Ann Carpenetti
Managing Director, Programs and Services: Josh Christian
Men's Division Director: Jody Martin
E-Mail: tcantabene@uslacrosse.org
Controller and Director, Finance: Cara Morris
E-Mail: cmorris@uslacrosse.org
Managing Director, Membership: Art Zito

Historical Note
The national governing body of lacrosse.

Meetings/Conferences:
Annual Meetings: Winter
2007 – Philadelphia, PA(Convention Center)/Jan. 11-14

Publications:
Lacrosse Magazine. 8/year. adv.

U.S. Metric Association *(1916)*
10245 Andasol Ave.
Northridge, CA 91325-1504
Tel: (818)363-5606
E-Mail: hillger@cira.colostate.edu
Web Site: http://lamar.colostate.edu/~hillger/
Members: 1500 individuals
Staff: 1
Annual Budget: $25-50,000
Executive Director: Valerie Antoine

Historical Note
USMA is dedicated to the promotion of U.S. conversion to the use of the metric system as its only measurement system and assists the public in using the system correctly. Members are companies, government agencies, libraries, educators, industry personnel and other individuals with an interest in the metric system. Presents private sector information at government metric transition meetings and furnishes information on the modernized metric system Systeme International (SI). Membership: $30/year (individual); $150/year (corporate); $500/one-time payment (lifetime).

Publications:
Metric Today. bi-m. adv.
Guide to the Use of the Metric System (SI Version). irreg.

U.S. Pan Asian American Chamber of Commerce *(1984)*
1329 18th St. NW
Washington, DC 20036
Tel: (202)296-5221 *Fax:* (202)296-5225
Web Site: www.uspaacc.com
Members: 8000 individuals and companies
Staff: 6
Annual Budget: $100-250,000
President and Chief Executive Officer: Susan Au Allen
E-Mail: susanallen@uspaacc.com

Historical Note
USPAACC is a national non-profit organization representing Asian and non-Asian businesses and professionals. Primary objective is to help members achieve their economic growth through a wide variety of educational and advocacy programs. USPAACC's corporate members are furniture companies. Membership: $250/year (individual); $5,000-10,000/year (company).

Meetings/Conferences:
Annual Meetings: Spring

Publications:
East-West Report. q. adv.
Directory of Asian-American Organizations. a. adv.
E-News (online). bi-m. adv.

U.S. Poultry and Egg Association *(1947)*
1530 Cooledge Rd.
Tucker, GA 30084-7303
Tel: (770)493-9401 *Fax:* (770)493-9257
Web Site: www.poultryegg.org/
Members: 600 companies
Staff: 20
President: Don Dalton
Executive Vice President: Dr. Charles Olentine
Vice President, Educational Programs: Larry Brown
President: Don Dalton
Exhibit Manager: Lauren Kosko-Patty
E-Mail: lkosko@poultryegg.com
Vice President, Communications: Sylvia Small
Vice President, Environmental Programs: John Starkey

Historical Note
Founded as Southeastern Poultry and Egg Association to promote the poultry and egg industries. Members are producers of broiler, eggs, or turkeys, and firms that provide products and services to the poultry industry. Membership: $300/year.

Meetings/Conferences:
Annual Meetings: Winter

Publications:
The Communicator. 2/year.
IPE Feather News. a.
Expo Flash. m.
News & Views. m.

U.S. Psychiatric Rehabiliation Association
601 N. Hammonds Ferry Rd.
Suite A
Linthicum, MD 21090
Tel: (410)789-7054 *Fax:* (410)789-7675
E-Mail: info@uspra.org
Web Site: www.uspra.org
Members: 999 individuals
Staff: 6
Annual Budget: $500-1,000,000
Chief Executive Officer: Marcic Granahan

Historical Note
Purpose of USPRA is to help advance the role, scope and quality of services designed to facilitate the community readjustment of people with psychiatric disabilities. Formerly International Association of Psychsocial Rehabilitation Services; assumed its current name in 2004. Membership: $90/year (individual member); $30/year (associate individual member); $170-4,000/year (organization; varies according to budget).

Publications:
PSR Journal. q. adv.
Psychosocial Rehabilitation Journal.

U.S. Rice Producers Group
Historical Note
A division of USA Rice Federation, which provides administrative support.

U.S. Wheat Associates *(1980)*
1620 I St. NW
Suite 801
Washington, DC 20006
Tel: (202)463-0999 *Fax:* (202)785-1052
E-Mail: info@uswheat.org
Web Site: www.uswheat.org
Members: 18 state organizations
Staff: 85
Annual Budget: $10-25,000,000
President: Alan Tracy
Director, Communications: Dawn Forsythe
Director, Information Services: Terry Herman

Historical Note
U.S. Wheat associates is the export market development organization representing the U.S. wheat industry. Market development activities include trade servicing, technical assistance, market analysis, and consumer promotion.

Publications:
USW Wheat Letter. bi-w.

U.S.-ASEAN Business Council *(1983)*
1101 17th St. NW
Suite 411
Washington, DC 20036-4720
Tel: (202)289-1911 *Fax:* (202)289-0519
E-Mail: mail@usasean.org
Web Site: www.us-asean.org
Members: 600 companies
Staff: 16
Annual Budget: $2-5,000,000
President: Matthew Daley
Executive Vice President: Virginia Foote

Historical Note
Formerly (1997) U.S.-ASEAN Council for Business and Technology, The Council strives to expand trade and investment ties between the U.S. and ASEAN (Association of Southeast Asian Nations, including Brunei Darussalam, Indonesia, Malaysia, Philippines, Singapore Thailand and Vietnam) by implementing programs which assist companies to identify and compete for opportunities. The Council also supports government policies that foster the expansion of commercial ties.

Meetings/Conferences:
Annual Meetings: always Washington, DC

U.S.-Russia Business Council *(1993)*
1701 Pennsylvania Ave. NW
Suite 520
Washington, DC 20006
Tel: (202)739-9180 *Fax:* (202)659-5920
E-Mail: info@usrbc.org
Web Site: www.usrbc.org
Members: 240 corporations
Staff: 12
Annual Budget: $1-2,000,000
President: Eugene K. Lawson
Director, Communications and External Affairs: Svetlana Minjack

Historical Note
Membership: $1,250-10,000/year (organization) according to annual sales.

Meetings/Conferences:
Semi-annual Meetings: Fall/Spring

Publications:
Russian Economic Survey. m.
Russia Business Watch (RBW). q. adv.

U.S.A. Dry Pea and Lentil Council *(1949)*
2780 W. Pullman Rd.
Moscow, ID 83843
Tel: (208)882-3023 *Fax:* (208)882-6406
Web Site: www.pea-lentil.com
Members: 2000-4000 individuals
Staff: 7
Annual Budget: $500-1,000,000
President and Chief Executive Officer: Tim McGreevy
E-Mail: pulse@pea-lentil.com

Historical Note
Merged with the American Dry Pea and Lentil Association in 1994. USADPLC members are concerned with growing, warehousing, processing and merchandising peas, lentils and chickpeas.

Publications:
Pulse Pipeline. w. adv.

U.S.A. Rice Council
Historical Note
A division of USA Rice Federation, which provides administrative support.

U.S.A. Rice Federation *(1994)*
4301 N. Fairfax Dr., Suite 425
Arlington, VA 22203-1627
Tel: (703)236-2300 *Fax:* (703)351-8162
E-Mail: riceinfo@usarice.com
Web Site: www.usarice.com
Members: 3 organizations
Staff: 33
Annual Budget: $10-25,000,000
President: Stuart E. Proctor, Jr.
Vice President, Member Services: Patricia Alderson
Historical Note
Founded as The Rice Industry. Became the Rice Council for Market Development in 1960, and assumed its present name in 1990. The USA Rice Federation is an umbrella organization representing three associations: U.S. Rice Producers Group, Rice Millers Association, and U.S.A. Rice Council. It supports the U.S.'s rice producers, millers, marketers and others in allied industries. Has an annual budget of approximately $5.6 million.
Publications:
USA Rice Weekly. w.
USA Rice Quarterly. q.

U.S.A. Toy Library Association *(1984)*
1326 Wilmette Ave.
Wilmette, IL 60091-2566
Tel: (847)920-9030 *Fax:* (847)920-9032
Web Site: http://usatla.deltacollege.org
Members: 200 individuals
Staff: 2
Annual Budget: $10-25,000
Executive Director: Judith Q. Iacuzzi
E-Mail: usatla@aol.com
Historical Note
Built on the idea that play and toys are an important part of a child's healthy growth and development; receives about ten inquiries per week from individuals interested in establishing a toy library or bettering an existing one. Membership: $55/year (basic), $165/year (organization).
Publications:
Child's Play Newsletter. q. adv.
Toy Library Operators Manual. a.

UFCW Textile Council *(1901)*
Historical Note
An affiliate of United Food and Commercial Workers, which provides administrative support.

Ultrasonic Industry Association *(1956)*
P.O. Box 2307
Dayton, OH 45401-2307
Tel: (937)586-3725 *Fax:* (937)586-3699
E-Mail: uia@ultrasonics.org
Web Site: www.ultrasonics.org
Members: 106 companies
Staff: 1
Annual Budget: $50-100,000
Executive Director: Francine W. Rickenbach, C.A.E.
Historical Note
UIA members are united in changing the world of medicine and industry through ultrasonics by providing access to educators, researchers, engineers, users, products and applications leading to the advancement of ultrasonic technology. Membership:$15/year (student); $105/year (individual); $275/year (foreign); $675/year (corporate); 575/year (sustaining).
Meetings/Conferences:
2007 – London, United Kingdom(Nat Physical Lab)/March 19-21/150
Publications:
Vibrations Newsletter. q. adv.
Membership Directory. a.

Ultrasonics, Ferroelectrics and Frequency Control Society
Historical Note
A technical society of the Institute of Electrical and Electronics Engineers (IEEE). Membership in the Society, open only to IEEE members, includes subscription to a technical periodical in the field published by IEEE. All administrative support is provided by IEEE.

Underground Equipment Council
Historical Note
A council of the Equipment Manufacturers Institute.

Undersea and Hyperbaric Medical Society *(1967)*
P.O. Box 1020
Dunkirk, MD 20754
Tel: (410)257-6606 *Fax:* (410)257-6617
E-Mail: uhms@uhms.org
Web Site: www.uhms.org
Members: 2000 individuals
Staff: 4
Annual Budget: $500-1,000,000
Executive Director: Don Chandler
E-Mail: execdir@uhms.org
Managing Editor: Ann McMillan
E-Mail: ann@uhms.org
Office Manager: Lisa Wasdin
E-Mail: lisa@uhms.org
Historical Note
Formerly (1986) Undersea Medical Society. Membership: $225/year (individual); $750/year (organization).
Meetings/Conferences:
Annual Meetings: Summer
Publications:
Undersea & Hyperbaric Medicine Journal. q. adv.
Pressure newsletter (on CD). bi-m. adv.

Unfinished Furniture Association *(1990)*
15000 Commerce Pkwy.
Suite C
Mt. Laurel, NJ 08054
Tel: (856)439-0500 *Fax:* (856)439-0525
Toll Free: (800)487 - 8321
E-Mail: ufa@ahint.com
Web Site: www.unfinishedfurniture.org
Members: 700 companies
Staff: 7
Annual Budget: $500-1,000,000
Executive Director: Michele Biordi
Historical Note
Membership: fees based on sales by type of company (associate, manufacturer, retailer and sales rep).
Meetings/Conferences:
2007 – Columbus, OH/June 23-26
Publications:
Unfinished Business News. bi-m. adv.

Uni-Bell PVC Pipe Association *(1971)*
2655 Villa Creek Dr., Suite 155
Dallas, TX 75234
Tel: (972)243-3902 *Fax:* (972)243-3907
E-Mail: info@uni-bell.org
Web Site: www.uni-bell.org
Members: 56 companies
Staff: 7
Annual Budget: $1-2,000,000
Executive Director: Robert Walker
Historical Note
A non-profit technical, educational and research oriented organization. Association members are producers of gasketed PVC pipe used in buried water, sewer and irrigation lines.
Meetings/Conferences:
Annual Meetings: Spring
Publications:
Uni-Bell PVC Pipe News. q.

Unified Abrasives Manufacturers Association *(1999)*
30200 Detroit Rd.
Cleveland, OH 44145-1967
Tel: (440)899-0010 *Fax:* (440)892-1404
Web Site: www.uama.org
Members: 37 companies
Staff: 5
Annual Budget: $100-250,000
Managing Director: J. Jeffery Wherry
E-Mail: jjw@wherryassoc.com
Historical Note
Founded as the Grinding Wheel Manufacturers Association; became (1948) the Grinding Wheel Institute and assumed its current name in 1999. In 2002, the divisions of the former UAMA reorganized as Unified Abrasives Manufacturers Association.
Meetings/Conferences:
Semi-Annual Meetings: Spring/Fall
Publications:
Vision. semi-a. adv.

Uniform and Textile Service Association *(1933)*
1300 N. 17th St., Suite 750
Arlington, VA 22209-3801
Tel: (703)247-2600 *Fax:* (703)841-4750
Toll Free: (800)486 - 6745
E-Mail: info@utsa.com
Web Site: www.utsa.com
Members: 120 companies
Staff: 9
Annual Budget: $2-5,000,000
President and Chief Executive Officer: David F. Hobson
Director, Finance, Administration, Meetings and Membership: Deborah Hodges
Director, Communications and Information Services: Kenneth E. Koepper
Director, Environmental Affairs and Government: Tony Wagner
Historical Note
Formerly (1993) the Institute of Industrial Launderers. Members are companies that rent reusable textile products (e.g., shop towels, uniforms), and provide laundering services to commercial and industrial customers.
Meetings/Conferences:
Annual Meetings: Fall
Publications:
UTSA Scoop. w.
Inside Textile Service. a. adv.
Industrial Launderer. m. adv.

Uniformed Services Academy of Family Physicians *(1973)*
2301 N. Parham Rd.
Suite Four
Richmond, VA 23229
Tel: (804)968-4436 *Fax:* (804)968-4418
Web Site: www.usafp.org
Members: 2000 individuals
Staff: 2
Annual Budget: $250-500,000
Executive Director: Terrence Schulte, CAE
Meetings/Conferences:
Annual Meetings: Spring
Publications:
Newsletter. q. adv.

UniForum Association *(1980)*
P.O. Box 3177
Annapolis, MD 21403
Tel: (410)715-9500 *Fax:* (240)465-0207
Toll Free: (800)333 - 8649
Web Site: www.uniforum.org
Members: 5000 individuals
President: Alan Fedder
E-Mail: afedder@uniforum.org
Historical Note
Founded as International Association of Open Systems; assumed its current name in 1997. UniForum members are computer hardware and software developers, vendors and users working in an open systems environment. Membership: $95/year.
Publications:
Journal of Open Computing. q.

Union for Radical Political Economics *(1968)*
418 N. Pleasant St.
Amherst, MA 01002
Tel: (413)577-0806 *Fax:* (413)577-0261
E-Mail: urpe@labornet.org
Web Site: www.urpe.org
Members: 1100 individuals
Staff: 2
Annual Budget: $100-250,000
Administrator: Germai Mehenie
E-Mail: urpe@labornet.org
Historical Note
An interdisciplinary association devoted to the study, development, and application of political economic analysis to social problems. A member of the Allied

Social Science Associations. Membership: $20/year ($30-55/year with subscription).

Meetings/Conferences:
Semi-annual Meetings: Summer Conference in August and with Allied Social Science Ass'ns in December

Publications:
Review of Radical Political Economics. q.
URPE Newsletter. q.

Union for Reform Judaism *(1873)*
633 Third Ave.
New York, NY 10017-6778
Tel: (212)650-4000 *Fax:* (212)650-4159
E-Mail: urj@urj.org
Web Site: http://urj.org
Members: 910 congregations
Staff: 300
Annual Budget: $10-25,000,000
President: Rabbi Eric H. Yoffie
Director, Communications: Emily Grotta
Director, Meetings and Conventions: Robin Hirsh
Chief Administrative Officer: Michael Kimmel
Chief Financial Officer: Les Pitner
Senior Vice President: Rabbi Lennard Thal
Chief Information Officer: Peter Weinrobe

Historical Note
URJ is the parent body of Reform synagogues of the U.S. and Canada. It provides programs and services for every aspect of synagogue life such as worship, adult and child education, management, and religious action. Has a budget of approximately $20 million.

Meetings/Conferences:
Biennial Meetings: Odd years/3,500-5,000

Publications:
Reform Judaism. q. adv.
RJ Magazine.

Union of American Hebrew Congregations

Historical Note
Became Union for Reform Judaism in 2003.

Union of American Physicians and Dentists *(1972)*
1330 Broadway, Suite 730
Oakland, CA 94612-2506
Tel: (510)839-0193 *Fax:* (510)763-8756
Toll Free: (800)622 - 0909
E-Mail: uapd@uapd.com
Web Site: www.uapd.com
Members: 10000 individuals
Staff: 12
Annual Budget: $2-5,000,000
Executive Director: Gary Robinson

Historical Note
A labor union representing physicians and dentists in fourteen states who bargain with government entities, hospitals and employers. Membership: $440/year.

Meetings/Conferences:
Triennial meetings:

Publications:
UAPD Report. m.

UNITE-HERE *(1900)*
275 Seventh Ave.
New York, NY 10001-6708
Tel: (212)265-7000
Web Site: www.uniteunion.org
Members: 200000 individuals
Staff: 1000
Annual Budget: $10-25,000,000
General President: Bruce Raynor
Press Secretary: Amanda Cooper

Historical Note
Organized as International Ladies Garment Workers Union and chartered by the American Federation of Labor in 1900; merged (1995) with Amalgamated Clothing and Textile Workers Union to become Union of Needletrades, Industrial and Textile Employees; assumed the name UNITE in 2003. Merged with Hotel Employees and Restaurant Employees International Union and assumed its current name in 2004.

Meetings/Conferences:
Triennial Meetings: (2006)

Publications:
United magazine. q.

United Abrasives Manufacturers Association, Coated Division *(1933)*

Historical Note
See Unified Abrasives Manufacturers Ass'n.

United American Nurses, AFL-CIO *(2000)*
8515 Georgia Ave., Suite 400
Silver Spring, MD 20910-3492
Tel: (301)628-5118 *Fax:* (301)628-5347
E-Mail: uaninfo@uannurse.org
Web Site: www.uannurse.org
Members: 100,000 individuals
National. Executive Director: Susan Bianchi-Sand
E-Mail: uaninfo@uannurse.org

Historical Note
A labor union affiliated with the American Nurses Association (same address) and the AFL-CIO. UAN represents registered nurses in the federal, public, and private sectors.

United Applications Standards Group *(2000)*
P.O. Box 1435
Des Moines, IA 50305-1435
Tel: (515)289-4467 *Fax:* (515)289-4468
Web Site: www.uasg.org
Members: 43 companies
Staff: 2
Annual Budget: $50-100,000
President: Ward Schneider

Historical Note
Members are graphics installation contractors, screen printers, designers and others involved in the commercial graphics industry.

Publications:
Newsletter. q.

United Association for Labor Education *(1959)*
P.O. Box 390401
Cambridge, MA 02139
Tel: (617)287-7352 *Fax:* (617)287-7404
Web Site: www.uale.org
Members: 480 individuals
Treasurer: Tess Ewing

Historical Note
Founded as University and College Labor Education Association; absorbed Workers Education Union Local 189 and assumed its current name in 2000. Members are institutions with labor education programs and individuals with an interest in labor education. Has no paid officers or full-time staff.

Publications:
Labor Studies Journal. q.
Abstracts. a.
Membership Directory. a.
Research Resource Directory. a.

United Association of Equipment Leasing *(1974)*
78120 Calle Estado
Suite 201
La Quinta, CA 92253
Tel: (760)564-2227 *Fax:* (760)564-2206
Web Site: www.uael.org
Members: 400 companies
Staff: 4
Annual Budget: $500-1,000,000
Executive Director: Joe Woodley
E-Mail: jwoodley@uael.org

Historical Note
Founded as Western Association of Equipment Lessors; became UAEL: a National Equipment Leasing Association in 1993, and assumed its current name in 1995.

Meetings/Conferences:
Semi-Annual Meeitngs:: Spring and Fall

Publications:
Newsline - online. q. adv.
Membership Directory - online. a. adv.

United Association of Journeymen and Apprentices of the Plumbing and Pipe Fitting Industry of U.S. and Canada *(1889)*
901 Massachusetts Ave. NW
Washington, DC 20001
Tel: (202)628-5823 *Fax:* (202)628-5024
Web Site: www.ua.org
Members: 320000 individuals
Staff: 150
Annual Budget: $5-10,000,000
General President: William P. Hite

Historical Note
Organized in Washington, DC on October 7, 1889 as the United Association of Journeymen, Plumbers, Gas Fitters, Steam Fitters and Steam Fitters Helpers of the United States and Canada. Affiliated with the American Federation of Labor in 1897 and adopted its present name in 1947. Has a budget of about $23 million. Sponsors and supports the U.A. Political Education Committee.

Meetings/Conferences:
Quinquennial Meetings:: Summer (2006)

Publications:
General Officers Report. w.

United Braford Breeders *(1969)*
422 E. Main St.
Suite 218
Nacogdoches, TX 75961-5214
Tel: (936)569-8200 *Fax:* (936)569-9556
Web Site: www.brafords.org
Members: 500 individuals
Staff: 4
Annual Budget: $100-250,000
Executive Director: Rodney L. Roberson
E-Mail: roberson@brafords.org

Historical Note
Formerly (1994) International Braford Association. Members are breeders of Braford cattle. Maintains breed registry. Membership: $50/year.

Publications:
Braford News. q. adv.

United Brotherhood of Carpenters and Joiners of America *(1881)*
5701 Silver Hill Rd.
Forestville, MD 20747
Tel: (301)736-6660 *Fax:* (301)420-3023
Web Site: www.carpenters.org
Members: 520000 individuals
Staff: 150
Annual Budget: $50-100,000,000
President: Douglas J. McCarron
Vice President: Douglas Banes
Secretary-Treasurer: Andy Silins

Historical Note
Established August 8, 1881 in Chicago as the Brotherhood of Carpenters and Joiners. Merged in 1888 with the United Order of Carpenters to form the present organization. Absorbed the Wood, Wire and Metal Lathers International Union in 1979. Absorbed the Tile, Marble, Terrazzo, Finishers, Shopworkers & Granite Cutters International Union in 1988. A charter member of the American Federation of Labor, the Brotherhood today has an annual budget of approximately $66.5 million.

Meetings/Conferences:
Quinquennial Meetings:: (2006)

Publications:
Carpenter Magazine. bi-m. adv.

United Developers Council

Historical Note
An affiliate of the National Association of Real Estate Brokers.

United Egg Producers *(1982)*
1720 Windward Concourse, Suite 230
Alpharetta, GA 30005
Tel: (770)360-9220 *Fax:* (770)360-7058
E-Mail: info@unitedegg.com
Web Site: www.unitedegg.com
Members: 220 manufacturers
Staff: 10
President and Chief Executive Officer: Albert E. Pope
Senior Vice President: Gene Gregory

Historical Note
Trade association of egg producers and manufacturers of egg products (liquid, dry and frozen) for use in further processed products.

Publications:
United Voices. bi-m.

United Electrical, Radio and Machine Workers of America *(1936)*
One Gateway Center, Suite 1400
Pittsburgh, PA 15222-1416
Tel: (412)471-8919 *Fax:* (412)471-8999
Web Site: www.ranknfile-ue.org
Members: 35000 individuals
Staff: 90
Annual Budget: $2-5,000,000
President: John H. Hovis, Jr.
Office Manager: Edward C. Huot
Secretary-Treasurer: Bruce Klipple
Historical Note
Established in Buffalo in March, 1936, and chartered by the Congress of Industrial Organizations the same year. Withheld per capita payments from the CIO in 1948 and later expelled. It is now an independent union.
Meetings/Conferences:
Annual Meetings: Summer
Publications:
UE News. m.

United Engineering Foundation *(1904)*
P.O. Box 70
Mount Vernon, VA 22121-0070
Tel: (973)244-2328 *Fax:* (973)882-5155
E-Mail: engfnd@aol.com
Web Site: www.uefoundation.org
Members: 5 engineering organizations
Staff: 2
Annual Budget: $500-1,000,000
Executive Director: David L. Belden, Ph.D., PE
E-Mail: engfnd@aol.com
Historical Note
Founded in New York, NY as the United Engineering Society; became Engineering Foundation, Inc. in 1930, then United Engineering Trustees in 1931 and assumed its current name in 1999. UET's member engineering societies represent a collective membership of over 750,000 people. UET operates an annual grants program that provides grants to further the engineering profession.
Meetings/Conferences:
Annual Meetings: Fourth Thursday in January in New York, NY (by invitation only).

United Farm Workers of America *(1962)*
P.O. Box 62
Keene, CA 93531
Tel: (213)368-0688 Ext: 269 *Fax:* (213)368-0699
E-Mail: execoffice@ufwmail.com
Web Site: www.ufw.org
Members: 26000 individuals
Staff: 125
Annual Budget: $2-5,000,000
Contact: Jocelyn Sherman
Historical Note
Organized in 1962 by Cesar E. Chavez as the National Farm Workers Association. In 1966 the National Farm Workers Association and the Agricultural Workers Organizing Committee merged to become the United Farm Workers of America affiliated with the AFL-CIO. Sponsors and supports the National United Farm Workers Volunteer Political Action Committee. Membership: 2% of what each member earns
while they earn while they work.
Meetings/Conferences:
Biennial meetings: even years

United Federation of Police & Security Officers *(1980)*
540 N. State Rd., Box 76
Briarcliff Manor, NY 10510-0076
Tel: (914)941-4103 *Fax:* (914)941-4472
Toll Free: (800)227 - 4291
Members: 200 individuals
Staff: 2
Annual Budget: $100-250,000
President: Ralph M. Purdy
Historical Note
Promotes the welfare of its members, aids them in their need for mutual benefits, protection and improvement of their social and financial conditions. Membership: $7.50/week.
Meetings/Conferences:
Annual Meetings: September
Publications:
Federation of Police Security News. 5/year. adv.

United Food and Commercial Workers International Union *(1979)*
1775 K St. NW
Washington, DC 20006
Tel: (202)223-3111 *Fax:* (202)466-1562
E-Mail: press@ufcw.org
Web Site: www.ufcw.org
Members: 1.4 million individuals
Annual Budget: $5-10,000,000
International President: Joseph P. Hansen
Director, Human Resources: Bette Mercer
Secretary-Treasurer: Anthony Perrone
Legislative/Political Affairs Director: Michael J. Wilson
Historical Note
Formed (1979) by a merger of the Retail Clerks International Union (founded in 1888) and Amalgamated Meat Cutters and Butcher Workmen of North America (founded in 1897). Absorbed Affiliated Barbers, Beauticians, and Allied Industries International Association in 1980; United Retail Workers in 1981; Insurance Workers International Union in 1983; Canadian Brewery and Distillery Workers in 1986; International Union of Life Insurance Agents in 1992; United Garment Workers of America in 1994; Distillery, Wine and Allied Workers' International Union in 1996 and International Chemical Workers Union in 1997. Represents workers in the retail, meat packing, food processing, hair care, insurance, health care, footwear and fur industry.
Publications:
Working America. semi-m.

United Fresh Fruit and Vegetable Association *(1904)*
1901 Pennsylvania Ave. NW
Suite 1100
Washington, DC 20006
Tel: (202)303-3400 *Fax:* (202)303-3433
E-Mail: united@uffva.org
Web Site: www.uffva.org
Members: 1000 companies
Staff: 12
Annual Budget: $2-5,000,000
President and Chief Executive Officer: Thomas E. Stenzel, CAE
Director, Legislative Affairs: Keira Franz
Vice President, Public Policy: Robert Guenther
Historical Note
The United Fresh Fruit and Vegetable Association is an international trade association representing the fresh produce industry. Member firms supply the majority of fresh produce grown and sold in the United States, and include grower/shippers, brokers, truckers and other transportation specialists, wholesalers, foodservice distributors and operators, retailers and allied suppliers.
Meetings/Conferences:
Annual Meetings: February/8,000

United Fresh Produce Association *(1987)*
1901 Pennsylvania Ave. NW
Suite 1100
Washington, DC 20006
Tel: (202)303-3400 *Fax:* (202)303-3433
Web Site: www.fresh-cuts.org
Members: 1000 companies
Staff: 24
Annual Budget: $2-5,000,000
Executive Vice President, New Business Development: Jerry Welcome
Historical Note
Formerly the International Fresh-Cut Produce Association; assumed its current name in 2006. Members are companies involved in the processing of fresh fruits and vegetables for commercial distribution. Membership: $700-1500/year (organization/company); $140/year (government/university/individual).
Meetings/Conferences:
Annual Meetings: Spring
2007 – Palm Springs, CA/Apr. 26-28

United Infants and Childrens Wear Association *(1933)*
1430 Broadway, Room 1603
New York, NY 10018-3308
Tel: (212)244-2953 *Fax:* (212)221-3540
Members: 4 companies
Staff: 1
Annual Budget: $100-250,000
Director/ Counsel: Alex J. Glauberman
Historical Note
Represents independent clothing manufacturers. Membership concentrated in the northeastern U.S. Associated Corset and Brassiere Manufacturers and Industrial Association of Juvenile Apparel Manufacturers are affiliates of UICWA.
Meetings/Conferences:
Annual Meetings: Not held

United Jewish Communities *(1932)*
P.O. Box 30, Old Chelsea Station
New York, NY 10113
Tel: (212)284-6500 *Fax:* (212)284-6835
E-Mail: info@ujc.org
Web Site: www.ujc.org
Members: 155 organizations
Staff: 80
President and Chief Executive Officer: Howard Rieger
Historical Note
Founded as Council of Jewish Federations; assumed current name in 2000.

United Lightning Protection Association *(1936)*
426 North Ave.
Libertyville, IL 60048
Toll Free: (800)668 - 8572
E-Mail: info@ulpa.org
Web Site: www.ulpa.org
Members: 95 individuals
Staff: 1
Annual Budget: $10-25,000
President: Tom Weir
E-Mail: info@ulpa.org
Historical Note
ULPA members are manufacturers, distributors, field engineers and installers of lightning protection or supression equipment. Membership: $200/year (full member); $50/year (associate).
Meetings/Conferences:
Annual Meetings: Spring
Publications:
More Static. q. adv.

United Methodist Association of Health and Welfare Ministries *(1940)*
407 Corporate Center Dr., Suite B
Vandalia, OH 45377
Tel: (937)415-3624 *Fax:* (937)222-7364
Toll Free: (800)441 - 4901
E-Mail: uma@umassociation.org
Web Site: www.umassociation.org
Members: 75 individuals
Staff: 5
Annual Budget: $500-1,000,000
President: Rev. Dr. Mearle L. Griffith
Coordinator, Member Services: Kristen Cress
Coordinator, Programs: E. Ronelle Hill
Vice President: Teresa A. Trost
E-Mail: ttrost@umassociation.org
Historical Note
Organized in 1940 as the National Association of Methodist Hospitals and Homes. Became the National Association of Health and Welfare Ministries, United Methodist Church in 1969 and assumed its present name in 1983. Is now independent of The United Methodist Church. Acts as a network for the various long-term care, retirement, family and children's service and community organizations related to the UMC. Membership: $75/year (individual); $650-$4,540/year (institution, based on budget).
Meetings/Conferences:
Annual Meetings: Spring/500
Publications:
Connextion. q.
Member News. w. adv.

United Mine Workers of America International Union *(1890)*
8315 Lee Hwy.
Fairfax, VA 22031
Tel: (703)208-7200 *Fax:* (703)208-7227
Web Site: www.umwa.org
Members: 120000 individuals
Staff: 100
Annual Budget: $50-100,000,000
President: Cecil E. Roberts
Secretary Treasurer: Daniel J. Kane

Historical Note
Formed January 25, 1890, in Columbus, Ohio, by the merger of the Knights of Labor and the National Progressive Union of Miners and Mine Laborers. Chartered as an industrial union by the American Federation of Labor, it left the AFL to form the Congress of Industrial Organizations (CIO) in 1938. The union affiliated with the AFL-CIO in 1989. Has an annual budget of approximately $62.4 million. Sponsors and supports the Coal Miners Political Action Committee (COMPAC).

Meetings/Conferences:
Quadrennial Meetings: (2006)

Publications:
UMW Journal. bi-m.

United Motorcoach Association *(1971)*
113 S. West St., Fourth Floor
Alexandria, VA 22314
Tel: (703)838-2929 *Fax:* (703)838-2950
Toll Free: (800)424 - 8262
E-Mail: info@uma.org
Web Site: www.uma.org
Members: 1000 companies
Staff: 6
Annual Budget: $2-5,000,000
President and Chief Executive Officer: Victor Parra

Historical Note
Formerly (1995) United Bus Owners of America. UMA serves the intercity bus industry, with particular emphasis on charter and tour transportation companies.

Publications:
Bus and Motorcoach News. bi-m.
Membership Directory. a.
The Docket. bi-m.

United Nations Staff Union *(1946)*
United Nations Plaza, Room S-525
New York, NY 10017
Tel: (212)963-7076 *Fax:* (212)963-3367
E-Mail: SUnion-User1@un.org
Web Site: www.unstaffunion.org
Members: 12000 individuals
Staff: 3
Annual Budget: $1-2,000,000
President: Rosemarie Waters
E-Mail: SUnion-User1@un.org
Second Vice President: Guy Candusso

Historical Note
Open to all staff of the United Nations Secretariat. Membership: monthly dues based on earnings.

Meetings/Conferences:
Annual Meetings: March

Publications:
What's New. m.
UN Staff Report. bi-m.
Staff Committee Bulletins (SCB's). irreg.

United Ostomy Association *(1962)*

Historical Note
Incorporated in New York, UOA is a not-for-profit mutual aid organization. Members are individuals who have undergone ostomy surgery, their families, and members of the medical, enterostomal therapy and nursing professions. Membership: $25/year.

United Producers *(1962)*
5909 Cleveland Ave.
P.O. Box 29800
Columbus, OH 43229
Tel: (614)890-6666 *Fax:* (614)890-4776
Web Site: www.uproducers.com
Members: 36000 individuals
Staff: 315
Annual Budget: $2-5,000,000
President and Chief Executive Officer: Dennis Bolling

Historical Note
Formerly (2000) Interstate Producers Livestock Association. Absorbed the Producers Livestock Marketing Association in 1968. A cooperative marketing organization owned by farmers and ranchers in the United States' corn belt, Midwest and Southeast.

Meetings/Conferences:
Annual Meetings:

United Product Formulators and Distributors Association *(1968)*
2034 Beaver Ruin Rd.
Norcross, GA 30071
Tel: (770)417-1418 *Fax:* (770)417-1419
Web Site: www.pestworld.org/upfda/
Members: 100 companies
Staff: 1
Annual Budget: $50-100,000
Executive Director: Valera B. Jessee
E-Mail: vjupfda@aol.com

Historical Note
Formerly (1988) United Pesticide Formulators and Distributors Association. Members are firms which are directly involved in formulating and distributing products or equipment to the pest control industry. Seeks to upgrade the pest control industry by promoting cooperation between customer and supplier and cooperating with government authorities for proper liaison and communication. Membership: $300/year (company).

Meetings/Conferences:
Annual Meetings:

Publications:
Update. q.

United Professional Horsemen's Association *(1968)*
4059 Iron Works Pkwy., Suite Two
Lexington, KY 40511
Tel: (859)231-5070 *Fax:* (859)255-2774
Web Site: www.uphaonline.com
Members: 1300 individuals
Staff: 1
Annual Budget: $50-100,000
Executive Secretary: Karen G. Richardson
E-Mail: uphakgr@aol.com

Historical Note
Founded in 1968 to give professional trainers of American Saddlebreds, Morgan and Hackney ponies a united voice in the show horse industry. Membership: $50/year.

Meetings/Conferences:
Annual Meetings: January/400-500

Publications:
UPHA Directory. a. adv.
UPHAppenings. 3/year.

United Scenic Artists *(1918)*
29 W. 38th St., 15th Floor
New York, NY 10018
Tel: (212)581-0300 *Fax:* (212)977-2011
E-Mail: usa829@ad.com
Web Site: www.usa829.org
Members: 4500 individuals
Staff: 15
Annual Budget: $1-2,000,000
National Business Manager: Michael McBride

Historical Note
Founded as American Society of Scenic Painters; later chartered as Local 38 of National Alliance of Theatrical Stage Employees. Reconstituted as an independent union, United Scenic Artists Association in 1912, and became affiliated with the Brotherhood of Painters as Local 829 in 1918. USA Local 829 members are scenic artists, set designers, art directors, costume designers, lighting designers, and mural artists for Broadway, television, film, and commercial and regional theatre.

Meetings/Conferences:
Annual Meetings: New York, Chicago, Los Angeles and Miami

Publications:
Newsletter. m.

United Shoe Retailers Association *(1978)*
P.O. Box 847
La Verne, CA 91750
Tel: (909)593-9188 *Fax:* (909)593-9189
Web Site: www.usraonline.org
Members: 1000 store locations
Staff: 2
Executive Director: Joni Percoski
E-Mail: joni@usraonline.org

Historical Note
USRA represents shoe retailers nationwide. Membership: $95/year.

Meetings/Conferences:
Annual Meetings: Spring/250

Publications:
Newsletter. 4/year. adv.

United Soybean Board *(1990)*
16640 Chesterfield Grove, Suite 130
Chesterfield, MO 63005-1422
Tel: (636)530-1777 *Fax:* (636)530-1560
Toll Free: (800)989 - 8721
Web Site: www.unitedsoybean.org
Staff: 2
Annual Budget: $25-50,000,000
Chief Executive Officer: John Becherer
E-Mail: jbecherer@unitedsoybean.com

Historical Note
Organized to manage the National Soybean Checkoff, USB provides promotion, marketing, and research activities to create increased profitability for U.S. soybean farmers.

Meetings/Conferences:
Annual Meetings: Winter

United States Advanced Ceramics Association *(1985)*
1800 M St. NW, Suite 300
Washington, DC 20036-5802
Tel: (202)293-6253 *Fax:* (202)223-5537
E-Mail: usaca@ttcorp.com
Web Site: www.advancedceramics.org
Members: 16 companies
Staff: 3
Executive Director: Jeff Serfass
Deputy Director: Brian Schorr

Historical Note
USACA represents the advanced ceramics materials industry. Members include raw material suppliers, parts manufacturers and parts users with U.S. facilities.

Meetings/Conferences:
Semi-annual Meetings: Spring and Fall

United States and Canadian Academy of Pathology *(1906)*
3643 Walton Way Extension
Augusta, GA 30909-4507
Tel: (706)733-7550 *Fax:* (706)733-8033
Web Site: www.uscap.org
Members: 9300 individuals
Staff: 5
Annual Budget: $1-2,000,000
Executive Director: Fred G. Silva
E-Mail: fsilva@uscap.org

Historical Note
Formerly International Association of Medical Museums and (1987) International Academy of Pathology. USCAP seeks to advance Pathology teaching, practice and research. Seeks to provide its members with new information both at the investigative and applied practice levels and to reinforce and update their knowledge in their area of interest and expertise. Membership: $125/year (individual).

Meetings/Conferences:
Annual Meetings: Febraury-March
2007 – San Diego, CA(Hyatt)/March 24-30/3000
2008 – Atlanta, GA(Hyatt)/March 8-14/3000

Publications:
Laboratory Investigation. m. adv.
Modern Pathology. m. adv.

United States Animal Health Association *(1896)*
P.O. Box K 227

Richmond, VA 23288
Tel: (804)285-3210 *Fax:* (804)285-3367
E-Mail: usaha@usaha.org
Web Site: www.usaha.org
Members: 1400 individuals
Staff: 2
Annual Budget: $50-100,000
President: Dr. Rick Willer
Administrative Secretary: Linda Ragland

Historical Note
Formed in 1896 as the National Association of State Livestock Sanitary Boards to combat one disease affecting cattle, it became the United States Livestock Sanitary Association in 1911 and assumed its present name in 1968. Absorbed the National Assembly of Chief Livestock Health Officials in 1973. Seeks to prevent, control and eliminate livestock diseases. Membership: $60/year (individual); $300/year (organization/company).

Meetings/Conferences:
Annual Meetings: October/900

Publications:
Foreign Animal Disease Handbook. irreg.
Newsletter. q.
Proceedings. a.
Johne's Booklets and CDs. irreg.

United States Aquaculture Suppliers Association *(1989)*
c/o AREA, P.O. Box 901303
Homestead, FL 33090
Tel: (305)248-4205 *Fax:* (305)248-1756
E-Mail: info@aquaculturesuppliers.com
Web Site: www.aquaculturesuppliers.com
Members: 60 businesses
Secretary: Jason Mulvihill
E-Mail: jason@areainc.com

Historical Note
USASA members are companies producing feed, equipment, and other materials for use in aquaculture. Has no paid officers or full-time staff. Membership: $125/year.

Meetings/Conferences:
Annual Meetings: February

Publications:
Directory. a.

United States Army Warrant Officers Association *(1972)*
462 Herndon Pkwy., Suite 207
Herndon, VA 20170-5235
Tel: (703)742-7727 *Fax:* (703)742-7728
Toll Free: (800)587 - 2962
E-Mail: usawoa@cavtel.net
Web Site: www.usawoa.org
Members: 6000 individuals
Staff: 2
Annual Budget: $250-500,000
Office Manager: Herb Rundgren

Historical Note
USAWOA is a professional organization dedicated to the improvement of the Warrant Officer Corps through the dissemination of professional information. Membership is open to Army warrant officers regardless of component or status (active, reserve or retired). Membership: $30/year (retired warrant officers); $45/year (all others).

Meetings/Conferences:
Annual Meetings: Generally on a military installation, in the fall

Publications:
Newsliner. m. adv.

United States Association for Computational Mechanics *(1988)*
Scientific Computation Research Center
7011 CIL Building, 110 Eighth St.
Troy, NY 12180-3590
Tel: (518)276-3590 *Fax:* (518)276-4886
E-Mail: office@scorec.rpi.edu
Web Site: www.usacm.org
Members: 500 individuals and institutions
Staff: 1
Annual Budget: $50-100,000
Contact: Marge Verville
E-Mail: office@scorec.rpi.edu

Historical Note
Members are individuals and institutions concerned with computational mechanics. Membership: $25/year.

Meetings/Conferences:
Biennial Meetings: (2003)

Publications:
Newsletter. bi-m.

United States Association for Energy Economics *(1992)*
28790 Chagrin Blvd., Suite 350
Cleveland, OH 44122
Tel: (216)464-2785 *Fax:* (216)464-2768
E-Mail: usaee@usaee.org
Web Site: www.usaee.org
Members: 1000 individuals
Staff: 2
Annual Budget: $100-250,000
Executive Director: David L. Williams

Historical Note
An affiliate of the International Association for Energy Economics (same address); USAEE members are automatically members of IAEE as well. USAEE provides a forum for the exchange of ideas, experience and issues among professionals interested in energy economics and to provide enhanced services to its membership. Members include economists, corporate planners, engineers, geologists, environmentalists, consultants, journalists, researchers from private industry and government and faculty from colleges and universities. Membership: $60/year (individual); $1,000/year (company).

Meetings/Conferences:
Annual Meetings: Fall

Publications:
USAEE Dialogue. 3/year. adv.
IAEE/USAEE Membership Directory. a. adv.
IAEE Newsletter. q. adv.
The Energy Journal. q. adv.

United States Association of Importers of Textiles and Apparel *(1989)*
13 E. 16th St., Sixth Floor
New York, NY 10003-1114
Tel: (212)463-0089 *Fax:* (212)463-0583
E-Mail: quota@aol.com
Web Site: www.usaita.com
Members: 200 companies
Staff: 3
Annual Budget: $500-1,000,000
Executive Director: Laura E. Jones
Director, Membership: Deborah Ward

Historical Note
USA-ITA, formed by nine founding company members in January 1989, represents members' interests to the government and within the industry. Membership: $1,000-16,500/year (corporate).

Meetings/Conferences:
Annual Meetings: Fall

Publications:
Electronic Bulletin Board for Textile & Apparel Information.
Attn: Apparel Trade and Transportation Newsletter. m.
Customs Overview. m.
USA-ITA Membership Directory. bien.

United States Association of Independent Gymnastic Clubs *(1972)*
450 N. End Ave.
Suite 20F
New York, NY 10282
Tel: (212)227-9792 *Fax:* (212)227-9793
Toll Free: (800)480 - 0201
E-Mail: usaigcpsny2@aol.com
Web Site: www.usaigc.com
Members: 300 clubs
Staff: 3
Annual Budget: $100-250,000
Vice President: Paul Spadaro
E-Mail: usaigcpsny2@aol.com

Historical Note
Members are not-for-profit clubs. Membership: $100/year.

Publications:
Trends. q.

United States Basketball Writers Association *(1956)*
1818 Chouteau Avenue
St. Louis, MO 63103
Tel: (314)421-0339
E-Mail: webmaster@sportswriters.net
Web Site: www.sportswriters.net/usbwa
Members: 1000 individuals
Staff: 1
Annual Budget: under $10,000
Executive Director: Joe Mitch

Historical Note
Membership: $35/year.

Meetings/Conferences:
Annual Meetings: In conjunction with finals of NCAA tournament

Publications:
The Tip-Off. 7/year.

United States Beef Breeds Council *(1952)*
3003 S. Loop West, Suite 140
Houston, TX 77054
Tel: (713)349-0854
Members: 22 associations
Annual Budget: $10-25,000
President: Jim B. Reeves

Historical Note
Members are the chief executive officers of national purebred cattle organizations.

Meetings/Conferences:
Semi-annual Conferences:

United States Beet Sugar Association *(1911)*
1156 15th St. NW
Suite 1019
Washington, DC 20005
Tel: (202)296-4820 *Fax:* (202)331-2065
E-Mail: usba@beetsugar.org
Web Site: www.beetsugar.org
Members: 8 companies
Staff: 4
Annual Budget: $1-2,000,000
President: James Johnson
Vice President, Public Affairs: Elin Peltz

Historical Note
Established as the United States Beet Sugar Industry; became the United States Sugar Manufacturers Association in 1914 and assumed its present name in 1926. Sponsors the Beet Sugar Political Action Committee.

Meetings/Conferences:
Annual Meetings: February

Publications:
American Beet Sugar Companies. a.

United States Bowling Congress *(1943)*
5301 South 76th St.
Greendale, WI 53129-1127
Tel: (414)423-3332 *Fax:* (414)421-8560
Toll Free: (800)514 - 2695
E-Mail: bowlinfo@bowl.com
Web Site: www.bowl.com
Members: 32 organizations
Annual Budget: $1-2,000,000
Chief Executive Officer: Roger Dalkin
General Counsel: Kevin Dornberger
Chief Operating Officer: Jack Mordini
Chief Information Officer: Tim Payne

Historical Note
Formerly (1995) National Bowling Council and then Bowling Inc.; assumed its current name in 2005. Serves as an umbrella organization for all facets of the sport of bowling: equipment manufacturers, bowling centers, and players' associations. Its purpose is to promote the sport of bowling. Membership: $5,000/year (organization/company).

Meetings/Conferences:
Annual Meetings:

United States Bowling Instructors Association *(1984)*
P.O. Box 564
Palatine, IL 60078
Tel: (847)359-0682

Members: 450 individuals
Staff: 2
Annual Budget: under $10,000
Executive Director: Thomas C. Kouros

United States Business and Industry Council *(1933)*
910 16th St. NW
Suite 300
Washington, DC 20006
Tel: (202)728-1980 *Fax:* (202)728-1981
Toll Free: (800)767 - 2267
E-Mail: council@usbusiness.org
Web Site: www.usbusiness.org
Members: 1500 companies
Staff: 7
Annual Budget: $500-1,000,000
President: Kevin L. Kearns
Vice President: Stephen V. Heller

Historical Note
Formerly United States Business and Industrial Council (1998). Established as the Southern States Industrial Council; became (1973) the United States Industrial Council and assumed its current name in 1998. USBIC members come from family-owned and closely held domestic companies; USBIC represents their interests in trade, taxation, regulation and other matters relevant to domestic businesses.

Meetings/Conferences:
Annual Meetings: June/Ritz Carlton/Arlington, VA

Publications:
Business Voice Monographs.
Legislative Action Report. w.

United States Canola Association *(1989)*
600 Pennsylvania Ave. SE
Suite 320
Washington, DC 20003-4316
Tel: (202)969-8113 *Fax:* (202)969-7036
Members: 50 producers and processors
Staff: 4
Executive Director: John D. Gordley

Historical Note
USCA members are producers and processors of canola and rapeseed. Membership: $25-50/year (individual); $500-2,500/year (organization/company).

United States Chamber of Commerce *(1912)*
1615 H St. NW
Washington, DC 20062-2000
Tel: (202)659-6000
Toll Free: (800)638 - 6582
Web Site: www.uschamber.com
Members: 18392 businesses and organizations
Staff: 1100
Annual Budget: $50-100,000,000
President and Chief Executive Officer: Thomas J. Donohue
Executive Vice President and Chief Legal Officer: Stanton Anderson
Executive Vice President and Chief Operating Officer: Suzanne Clark
Senior Vice President, Congressional and Public Affairs: Rolf Lundberg
Vice President, Communications: Linda Rozett

Historical Note
Organized at a conference called by President Taft on April 22, 1912 in Washington, DC. The Chamber was formed on the recommendation of President Taft, who saw the need for a "central organization" to give Congress the benefit of the thinking of the business community on national problems and issues affecting the economy. Now, it is generally regarded as the spokesgroup for U.S. business. It is the world's largest business federation, composed of more than 215,000 companies, plus 3,000 local and state chambers of commerce and 1,200 trade and professional associations. Sponsors and supports the National Chamber Alliance for Politics. Has an annual budget of approximately $65.8 million.

Publications:
Nation's Business. m. adv.
The Business Advocate. bi-m. adv.

United States Committee on Irrigation and Drainage *(1951)*
1616 17th St., Suite 483
Denver, CO 80202
Tel: (303)628-5430 *Fax:* (303)628-5431
Web Site: www.uscid.org
Members: 500 individuals
Staff: 1
Annual Budget: $50-100,000
Executive Vice President: Larry D. Stephens

Historical Note
Incorporated in Colorado. Formerly (1967) United States National Committee, International Commission on Irrigation and Drainage and (1984) United States Committee on Irrigation, Drainage and Flood Control. USCID, a not-for-profit professional organization, is the U.S. national committee of the International Commission on Irrigation and Drainage. USCID provides a forum for multidisciplinary discussion of issues related to irrigation, drainage and flood control. Membership: $50/year (individual); $90/year (library); $300/year (water districts and institutions); $600/year (corporate).

Meetings/Conferences:
Semi-Annual Meetings: Spring/Fall

Publications:
USCID Newsletter. trien. adv.
USCID Membership Directory. a. adv.

United States Conference of Catholic Bishops *(1966)*
3211 Fourth St. NE
Washington, DC 20017-1194
Tel: (202)541-3000 *Fax:* (202)541-3166
Web Site: www.usccb.org
Members: 400 individuals
Staff: 350
Annual Budget: $25-50,000,000
General Secretary: Rev. Msgr. William P. Fay

Historical Note
Formed (2001) by the merger of the National Conference of Catholic Bishops and the United States Catholic Conference. Founded in 1917 as the National Catholic War Council. Has an annual budget of approximately $41 million.

Meetings/Conferences:
Annual Meetings: November/ Washington, DC

Publications:
NCCB/USCC Report. m.

United States Conference of City Human Services Officials *(1980)*
1620 I St. NW, Fourth Floor
Washington, DC 20006
Tel: (202)293-7330 *Fax:* (202)293-2352
Members: 500 individuals
Staff: 1
Assistant Executive Director: Crystal Swann
E-Mail: cswann@usmayors.org

Historical Note
Members are municipal employees responsible for human services issues. An affiliate of U.S. Conference of Mayors.

Meetings/Conferences:
Annual Meetings:

United States Conference of Mayors *(1932)*
1620 I St. NW
Washington, DC 20006
Tel: (202)293-7330 *Fax:* (202)293-2352
E-Mail: info@usmayors.org
Web Site: www.usmayors.org
Members: 1183 individuals
Staff: 45
Annual Budget: $5-10,000,000
Executive Director: J. Thomas Cochran
Director, Meetings: Carol Edwards

Historical Note
An organization of city governments. Membership limited to the 1,183 U.S. cities with more than 30,000 population. Affiliated with the United States Conference of Local Health Officers and the U.S. Conference of Human Services Officers. Has an annual budget of $7.6 million.

Publications:
U.S. Mayor Newspaper. bi-w.
The Mayors of America's Principal Cities Directory. semi-a.
Resolutions Adopted - Annual Conference of Mayors. a.
AIDS Information Exchange. bi-m.
CORRE Newsletter. m.
Labor Management Relations Service. bi-m.
Local Health Officers News. bi-m.

United States Contract Tower Association *(1995)*

Historical Note
A division of American Ass'n of Airport Executives, which provides administrative support.

United States Council for International Business *(1945)*
1212 Ave. of the Americas, 21st Floor
New York, NY 10036-1689
Tel: (212)354-4480 *Fax:* (212)575-0327
E-Mail: info@uscib.org
Web Site: www.uscib.org
Members: 300 companies and organizations
Staff: 45
Annual Budget: $5-10,000,000
President and Chief Executive Officer: Peter M. Robinson
Vice President, Investment Policy: Stephen J. Canner
Vice President and Chief Financial Officer: Paul Cronin
Senior Vice President, Washington: Timothy E. Deal
Senior Vice President, Carnet Operations: Cynthia Duncan
Executive Vice President and Senior Policy Officer: Ronnie L. Goldberg
Vice President, Communications: Jonathan A. Huneke
Vice President, Administration: Rasma Mednis

Historical Note
U.S. affiliate of the following international organizations having consultative status with intergovernmental agencies: the International Chamber of Commerce (ICC), the International Organization of Employers (IOE) and the Business and Industry Advisory Committee (BIAC) to the Organization for Economic Cooperation and Development (OECD). As the U.S. representative of each of these associations, the Council ensures that their views are those endorsed by the American business community and endeavors to similarly influence U.S. government policy. Also serves as the official issuing and guaranteeing authority for ATA Carnets (customs documents allowing temporary, duty-free import and export of goods destined for eventual export). Maintains a Washington, DC office. Has an annual budget of approximately $7 million.

Meetings/Conferences:
Annual Dinner: November-December

Publications:
Business & Environment Report. irreg.
Focus on Issues. irreg.
International Labor Affairs Report. irreg.
Annual Report. a.
Council Newsletter. bi-m.
IGO Report. m.

United States Court Reporters Association *(1946)*
4731 N. Western Ave.
Chicago, IL 60625-2012
Toll Free: (800)628 - 2730
E-Mail: uscra@uscra.org
Web Site: www.uscra.org
Members: 400 individuals
Annual Budget: $50-100,000
President: JoAnn Bachellor
E-Mail: uscra@uscra.org

Historical Note
USCRA members are the official reporters in the United States District Courts. Has no paid officers or full-time staff. Membership: $150/year (regular); $50/year (associate); $75/year (job-share); $50/year (supporting); $35/year (student).

Publications:
The Circuit Rider. q. adv.

United States Cross Country Coaches Association
5327 Newport Dr.
Lisle, IL 60532
Tel: (630)960-3049 *Fax:* (630)960-3218
E-Mail: xcpoll@aol.com

Web Site: www.uscccа.org
Members: 300 individuals
Annual Budget: under $10,000
Public Relations Director: Dan Kopriva

Historical Note
Formerly National Collegiate Cross Country Coaches Association. Membership drawn from NCAA-accredited men's track programs. Has no paid officers or full-time staff. Membership: $225/year (individual).

Meetings/Conferences:
Annual Meetings: *With Nat'l College Athletic Ass'n, in conjunction with the National Cross Country Meet.*

Publications:
USCCCA Newsletter. a. adv.

United States Cutting Tool Institute *(1988)*
1300 Sumner Ave.
Cleveland, OH 44115-2851
Tel: (216)241-7333 *Fax:* (216)241-0105
E-Mail: uscti@taol.com
Web Site: www.uscti.com
Members: 100 companies
Staff: 2
Annual Budget: $100-250,000
Secretary-Treasurer: Charles M. Stockinger

Historical Note
USCTI was formed in 1988 by the merger of the Metal Cutting Tool Institute and the Cutting Tool Manufacturers of America. USTCI represents more than two-thirds of the domestic cutting tool market.

Publications:
Informer. semi-a.

United States Durum Growers Association *(1957)*
4023 State St.
Bismarck, ND 58503
Tel: (701)222-2204 *Fax:* (701)223-0018
E-Mail: agdakota@btnet.net
Web Site: www.durumgrowers.com
Members: 1000 individuals
Staff: 3
Annual Budget: $25-50,000
Executive Director: Dan Wogsland

Historical Note
Formed (1957) as the Durum Growers Association of the United States; assumed its current name in 1981.

Publications:
Durum Kernel. q.

United States Energy Association *(1930)*
1300 Pennsylvania Ave. NW
Suite 550, Mailbox 142
Washington, DC 20004-3022
Tel: (202)312-1230 *Fax:* (202)682-1682
Web Site: www.usea.org
Members: 160 businesses and individuals
Staff: 36
Annual Budget: $5-10,000,000
Executive Director: Barry K. Worthington
Financial Manager: Brian D. Kearns

Historical Note
Supports the objectives of the World Energy Council and serves as the U.S. Member Committee. Has annual budget of $6 million. Membership: $5,000/year (company).

Meetings/Conferences:
Annual Meetings: *May*

Publications:
USEA Today. m.
World Energy Council Journal. bien.
Annual Report. a.

United States Equestrian Federation *(1917)*
4047 Iron Works Pkwy.
Lexington, KY 40511
Tel: (859)258-2472 *Fax:* (859)231-6662
Web Site: www.equestrian.org
Members: 71000 individuals
Staff: 97
Annual Budget: $5-10,000,000
Chief Executive Officer: John R. Long
President: David O'Connor

Historical Note
Founded as American Horse Shows Association; became Equestrian USA in 2002, before merging (2004) with the United States Equestrian team to form the present organization. Dedicated to equestrianism at all levels of proficiency. Has an annual budget of approximately $6 million. Membership: $35/year (junior); $40-85/year (senior); $125-$800/year (organization/competition).

Meetings/Conferences:
Annual Meetings: *Winter*

Publications:
Equestrian Magazine. 10/year. adv.
Rule Book. a.

United States Federation for Culture Collections *(1970)*
Bionomics International
3023 Kramer St.
Wheaton, MD 20902
Tel: (301)942-6316 *Fax:* (603)308-5656
Web Site: http://usfcc.us
Members: 150organizationsandindividuals
Annual Budget: under $10,000
Vice President: Micha Krichevsky

Historical Note
Members are individuals and organizations concerned with maintaining culture collections and running taxonomic studies on micro-organisms. Has no paid staff. Leadership changes annually. Membership: $20/year (individual); $150/year (company).

Meetings/Conferences:
Semi-Annual: May/100

Publications:
USFCC Newsletter. q. adv.
Advances in Culture Collections. irreg.
Perspectives in Culture Collections. irreg.

United States Federation of Scholars and Scientists *(1938)*
c/o Physics Dept.
California State University
Fullerton, CA 92834-6866
Tel: (714)278-3421 *Fax:* (714)278-5810
E-Mail: rdittman@fullerton.edu
Members: 200 individuals
Staff: 2
Annual Budget: under $10,000
President: Roger Dittmann
E-Mail: rdittman@fullerton.edu

Historical Note
Formerly (1988) American Association of Scientific Workers, the U.S. affiliate of the World Federation of Scientific Workers. Primarily concerned with the impact of science upon society, especially on a global/international scale. Also affiliated with the American Association for the Advancement of Science. Other affiliates include: Concerned Philosophers for Peace, Southern California Federation of Scientists, and the California Peace Academy. Membership: $25/year (individual); $2.50 per capita/year (organization).

Meetings/Conferences:
Annual Meetings: *Held in conjunction with international conference.*

Publications:
Proceedings.
Concerned Scholar. bi-m.

United States Fencing Coaches Association *(1941)*
138 E. Racine Pl.
Mundelein, IL 60060
Tel: (847)444-7811
Toll Free: (888)927 - 6687
Web Site: www.usfca.org
Members: 400 individuals
Annual Budget: under $10,000
Secretary: Don Badowski

Historical Note
Established in 1941 as the National Fencing Coaches Association of America; assumed its present name in 1982. Member of the National Collegiate Athletic Association and the International Academy of Arms. Affiliated with the U.S. Fencing Association. Members are fencing teachers who conduct clinics and workshops to train fencing instructors. The association accredits Fencing Masters in various grades. Membership: $50/year.

Meetings/Conferences:
Annual Meetings: *Summer*

Publications:
Directory. a.
Swordmaster. q. adv.

United States Golf Association *(1894)*
P.O. Box 708
Far Hills, NJ 07931-0708
Tel: (908)234-2300 *Fax:* (908)234-9687
E-Mail: usga@usga.org
Web Site: www.usga.org
Members: 750000 individuals
Staff: 200
Annual Budget: $25-50,000,000
Executive Director: David B. Fay
E-Mail: usga@usga.org

Historical Note
An association of member clubs and courses formed on December 22, 1894. Conducts the U.S. Open, Senior Open and Women's Open Championships, the Walker and Curtis Cup matches and ten national amateur championships. The governing body of golf in the United States. Has an annual budget of over $30 million. Street address is Liberty Corner Road, Far Hills, NJ. Membership: $100/year.

Meetings/Conferences:
Annual Meetings: *Winter*

Publications:
Golf Journal. 10/year.
Green Section Record. bi-m.

United States Harness Writers' Association *(1947)*
Box 1314
Mechanicsburg, PA 17055
Tel: (717)379-5125
E-Mail: ushwa@paonline.com
Web Site: www.ushwa.org
Members: 250 individuals
Staff: 1
Annual Budget: $50-100,000
Secretary: Jerry Connors
E-Mail: ushwa@paonline.com

Historical Note
Members are journalists who cover harness racing. Has no paid staff or permanent headquarters. Membership: $40/year.

Meetings/Conferences:
Annual Meetings: *February*
2007 – Atlantic City, NJ(Borgata)/Feb. 24-25

Publications:
Newsletter. q.

United States Hide, Skin and Leather Association *(1980)*

Historical Note
A division of American Meat Institute, which provides administrative support

United States Hispanic Chamber of Commerce *(1979)*
2175 K St. NW
Suite 100
Washington, DC 20037
Tel: (202)842-1212 *Fax:* (202)842-3221
E-Mail: ushcc@ushcc.com
Web Site: www.ushcc.com
Members: 1000000 individuals
Staff: 20
Annual Budget: $1-2,000,000
President and Chief Executive Officer: Michael Barrera
Chief Operating Officer: Allen Gutierrez
Vice President, Communications: Guillermo Meneses

Historical Note
USHCC is a national trade association of local Hispanic chambers of commerce, business associations and individuals advocating Hispanic domestic and international economic interests. Membership: $150/year (individual); $300/year (organization/company).

Meetings/Conferences:
Annual Meetings: *Fall*

Publications:
Networking Newsletter. bi-m. adv.
Convention Magazine. a. adv.

United States Industrial Fabrics Institute

Historical Note
A division of Industrial Fabrics Association International.

United States Institute for Theatre Technology *(1960)*

6443 Ridings Rd.
Syracuse, NY 13206
Tel: (315)463-6463 *Fax:* (315)463-6525
Toll Free: (800)938 - 7488
Web Site: www.usitt.org
Members: 4000 individuals
Staff: 6
Annual Budget: $500-1,000,000
Manager, Public Relations and Marketing: Barbara E.R. Lucas

Historical Note
USITT members are design, production and technology professionals in the performing arts and entertainment industry. USITT promotes the advancement of knowledge and skills of its members by promoting innovation and creativity; by sponsoring projects, programs, research and symposia; by recognizing excellence and significant contributions to the industry; and by producing its Annual Conference and Stage Expo. Membership: $95-150/year (individual); $180-1000/year (organization/company).

Meetings/Conferences:
Annual Meetings: Spring
2007 – Phoenix, AZ/March 14-17

Publications:
Sightlines. m. adv.
Theatre Design and Technology. q. adv.
USITT Membership Directory. a. adv.

United States Internet Service Provider Association *(1991)*

1330 Connecticut Ave. NW
Washington, DC 20036
Tel: (202)862-3816 *Fax:* (202)261-0604
Web Site: www.usispa.org
Members: 7 corporations
Staff: 5
Annual Budget: $1-2,000,000
Contact: Kate Dean
E-Mail: kdean@steptoe.com

Historical Note
Founded as Commercial Internet Exchange Association; assumed its current name in 2002. USISPA members are companies that offer TCP/IP or OSI data internetworking to the general public.

United States Junior Chamber of Commerce *(1920)*

P.O. Box Seven
Tulsa, OK 74102-0007
Tel: (918)584-2481 *Fax:* (918)584-4422
Toll Free: (800)529 - 2337
E-Mail: directorcommunication@usjaycees.org
Web Site: www.usjaycees.org
Members: 107000 individuals
Staff: 25
Annual Budget: $2-5,000,000
Executive Vice President: John K.S. Shiroma, CAE

Historical Note
Also known as the U.S. Jaycees. Acts as a service training and advocacy organization for individuals between ages 21 and 39, providing leadership training through participation in community programs.

Meetings/Conferences:
Annual Meetings: June

Publications:
Jaycees Magazine. q. adv.

United States Lifesaving Association *(1964)*

P.O. Box 322
Avon-By-the-Sea, NJ 07717
Tel: (714)968-9360
Toll Free: (866)367 - 8752
Web Site: www.usla.org
Members: 6000 individuals
Staff: 1
Annual Budget: $50-100,000
Membership Liaison: Charles Hartl
E-Mail: guard4life@aol.com

Historical Note
Founded as the National Surf Life Saving Association of America, it assumed its present name in 1979. A professional and educational organization of open water lifeguards and rescue personnel, it supports the annual National Lifeguard Championships. Membership: $25/year.

Meetings/Conferences:
Semi-Annual Meetings:

Publications:
American Lifeguard. q. adv.

United States Marine Safety Association *(1987)*

5050 Industrial Rd.
Farmingdale, NJ 07727
Tel: (732)751-0102 *Fax:* (732)751-0508
Web Site: www.usmsa.org
Members: 145 companies
Staff: 2
Annual Budget: $50-100,000
Executive Director: Tom Thompson
E-Mail: usmsa@usmsa.org

Historical Note
Formerly U.S. Lifesaving Manufacturing Association, USMSA was reorganized and incorporated in Philadelphia, PA in 1987. Members are manufacturers of and service organizations, including trainers, for all types of marine safety equipment. Promotes safety and survival for all who earn a living at sea and serves as a forum for the effective use of marine safety equipment. Membership: $100-800/year.

Publications:
Marine Safety Newsletter. q.
Membership Directory. a.

United States Meat Export Federation *(1976)*

1050 17th St., Suite 2200
Denver, CO 80265
Tel: (303)623-6328 *Fax:* (303)623-0297
Web Site: www.usmef.org
Members: 150 organizations
Staff: 50
Annual Budget: $10-25,000,000
President and Chief Executive Officer: Philip M. Seng
Chief Financial Officer: Ruth Brown
Senior Vice President, Export Services: Paul Clayton
Vice President, Administration: Janel Domurat
Vice President, Trade Development: Richard Fritz
Vice President, Information Services: Lynn R. Heize
Vice President, International Programs: Thomas Lipetzky
Senior Vice President, Policy, Planning and Research: Thad Lively

Historical Note
Trade association of livestock producers and feeders, packers, purveyors and exporters, agribusiness, agriservice interests, farm organizations, and other promotional groups united in their interest in developing international markets for U.S. beef, pork, and lamb. Has an annual budget of approximately $20 million. Membership: $2,500-6,000/year, incremental (organization).

Meetings/Conferences:
Semi-annual Meetings: May and November

Publications:
MEF Action. irreg.
Export Reports. irreg.
Exporter Directory. irreg.
Export Newsline. w.
Beef Letter. m.
Pork Letter. m.

United States National Committee of the International Dairy Federation *(1980)*

P.O. Box 930398
Verona, WI 53593
Tel: (608)663-1250 Ext: 112 *Fax:* (608)848-7675
Web Site: www.usnac.org
Members: 57 companies
Staff: 1
Annual Budget: $100-250,000
National Secretary: Debra Wendorf-Boyke
E-Mail: usnacsec@usnac.org

Historical Note
Members are milk producers, dairy product manufacturers and suppliers, dairy scientists and educators, associations and other representatives of the U.S. dairy industry. US-IDF is a member of the International Dairy Federation, which is headquartered are in Brussels, Belgium. Membership: $150-750/year (individual); $1,260-6,000/year (company).

Meetings/Conferences:
Semi-Annual Meetings: Spring and Fall (Chicago, IL area)

Publications:
Proceedings of IDF Seminars and Meetings. q.
Technical Bulletins. 10-15/yr.
Technical Standards. irreg.

United States Parachute Association *(1946)*

5401 Southpoint Centre Blvd.
Fredericksburg, VA 22407
Tel: (540)604-9740 *Fax:* (540)604-9741
Toll Free: (800)371 - 8772
E-Mail: uspa@uspa.org
Web Site: www.uspa.org
Members: 35000 individuals
Staff: 13
Annual Budget: $2-5,000,000
Executive Director: Christopher J. Needels
E-Mail: cneedels@uspa.org
President: Glenn Bangs
Director, Safety and Training: Jim Crouch
E-Mail: jcrouch@uspa.org
Director, Membership: Michelle Garvin
E-Mail: mgarvin@uspa.org
Director, Government Relations and Group Membership: Edward M. Scott
E-Mail: escott@uspa.org
Director, Communications: Shonda Smith
E-Mail: ssmith@uspa.org

Historical Note
USPA is a non-profit association dedicated to the promotion of safe skydiving and the support of those who enjoy it as well as drop zones and other organizations. Sponsors Instructor Rating Program to train and certify instructors and examiners. Membership: $51.00/year (new member); $49.00/year (renewal).

Meetings/Conferences:
Semi-Annual Meetings: Winter, usually in Alexandria, VA, and Summer

Publications:
Parachutist Magazine. m. adv.

United States Pharmacopeia *(1820)*

12601 Twinbrook Pkwy.
Rockville, MD 20852-1790
Tel: (301)881-0666 *Fax:* (301)816-8236
Toll Free: (800)881 - 0666
E-Mail: info@usp.org
Web Site: www.usp.org
Members: 400 orgs., institutions & agencies
Staff: 290
Annual Budget: $50-100,000,000
Executive Vice President and Chief Executive Officer: Roger L. Williams, M.D.
Senior Vice President and General Counsel: Susan de Mars
Chief Business Officer: John T. Fowler

Historical Note
Established in 1820, USP sets public standards for drugs, dietary supplements, and other health care technologies. Composed of representatives of medical and pharmaceutical organizations, colleges and the Federal Government. Publishes the official compendia for drugs in the United States and some foreign countries.

Meetings/Conferences:
Quinquennial Meetings:
2010 –

Publications:
USP-NF. a.
Pharmacopial Forum. bi-m.
USP Dictionary of Drug Names. a.

United States Professional Tennis Association *(1927)*

3535 Briarpark Dr., Suite One
Houston, TX 77042

Tel: (713)978-7782 *Fax:* (713)978-7780
Toll Free: (800)877 - 8248
E-Mail: uspta@uspta.org
Web Site: www.uspta.org
Members: 13000 individuals
Staff: 27
Annual Budget: $5-10,000,000
Chief Executive Officer: Tim Heckler
Director, Operations: Rich Fanning
E-Mail: rich.fanning@uspta.org
Director, Communications: Shawna Riley
E-Mail: shawna.riley@uspta.org

Historical Note
USPTA is the non-profit trade association for professional tennis teachers. It was created to raise the standards of tennis teaching as a profession and increase interest in and awareness of the sport. Membership: $210/year.

Meetings/Conferences:
Annual Meetings: September

Publications:
Addvantage Magazine. m. adv.
Convention Commemorative Program. a. adv.
Directory. a. adv.

United States Racquet Stringers Association *(1975)*
330 Main St.
Vista, CA 92084
Tel: (760)536-1177 *Fax:* (760)536-1171
E-Mail: usrsa@racquettech.com
Web Site: www.racquettech.com
Members: 7000 individuals
Staff: 10
Annual Budget: $500-1,000,000
Executive Director: David Bone

Historical Note
USRSA provides information necessary for professional racquet stringing. Membership: $95/year.

Publications:
Racquet Tech Magazine. m. adv.
Stringer's Digest. a. adv.

United States Rowing Association
Two Wall St.
Princeton, NJ 08540
Tel: (609)751-0070 *Fax:* (609)924-1578
Toll Free: (800)314 - 4769
Web Site: www.usrowing.org
Members: 15000 individuals
Staff: 20
Annual Budget: $2-5,000,000
Executive Director: Glenn Merry
E-Mail: glenn@usrowing.org
Director, Communications: Brett Johnson
E-Mail: brett@usrowing.org
Manager, Member Services and Merchandise: Kelly McGlynn
Comptroller: Alix Robertson
E-Mail: alix@usrowing.org

Historical Note
A nonprofit membership organization, recognized by the U.S. Olympic Committee as the national governing body for the sport of rowing in the United States. Formed in 1982 by the merger of the National Association of Amateur Oarsmen (est. 1872) and the National Women's Rowing Association (est. in the early 1960s). USRowing selects, trains and manages the teams that represent the U.S. in international competition, including in the Olympics, World Championships and Pan American Games. It also registers hundreds of regattas across the U.S. each year, ensuring that they are run under specific safety guidelines; provides programs to educate rowing judge-referees and coaches; stages three national championship regattas annually; and conducts regional championships and national team selection events.

Publications:
USRowing. 6/year. adv.

United States Ski Association *(1977)*
1500 Kearns Blvd., Box 100
Park City, UT 84060
Tel: (435)649-9090 *Fax:* (435)649-3613
Web Site: www.ussa.org
Members: 3000 individuals
Staff: 3
Annual Budget: $250-500,000
President and Chief Executive Officer: Bill Marolt
E-Mail: dmccann@ussa.org
Vice President, Marketing and Communications: Tom Kelly
E-Mail: dmccann@ussa.org

Historical Note
USSA is the national governing body for Olympic skiing in the U.S. Membership: $80/year.

Meetings/Conferences:
Annual Meetings:

Publications:
American Ski Coach. 4/year. adv.

United States Soccer Federation *(1913)*
1801 S. Prairie Ave.
Chicago, IL 60616
Tel: (312)808-1300 *Fax:* (312)808-1301
Web Site: www.ussoccer.com
Members: 3000000 individuals
Staff: 100
Annual Budget: $25-50,000,000
Executive Vice President: Sunil Gulati
President: Dr. Bob Contiguglia
Chief Executive Officer: Daniel T. Flynn

Historical Note
A federation of amateur and youth soccer associations, formerly United States Football Association. U.S. Soccer is the governing body for the sport in the U.S. and manages eleven national teams. Has an annual budget of approximately $30 million.

Meetings/Conferences:
Annual Meetings: Mid-summer

Publications:
Media Guide. a.

United States Society on Dams *(1928)*
1616 17th St., Suite 483
Denver, CO 80202
Tel: (303)628-5430 *Fax:* (303)628-5431
Web Site: www.ussdams.org
Members: 1150 individuals and companies
Staff: 1
Annual Budget: $50-100,000
Executive Director: Larry D. Stephens

Historical Note
Founded as United States Committee on Large Dams; assumed its current name in 2000. USSD is part of the International Commission on Large Dams. USSD members are individuals and organizations involved in the design, construction, and maintenance of large dams. Membership: $85/year (individual); $650/year (organization); $2,800 (sustaining).

Meetings/Conferences:
Annual Meetings: Spring

Publications:
Newsletter. trien. adv.
Membership Directory. a. adv.
Proceedings of Annual Meetings. a.

United States Swim School Association *(1988)*
P.O. Box 17208
Fountain Hills, AZ 85269
Tel: (480)837-5525 *Fax:* (480)836-8277
E-Mail: info@usswimschools.org
Web Site: www.usswimschools.org
Members: 250 swim schools
Staff: 1
Annual Budget: $250-500,000
Executive Director: Sue Mackie
E-Mail: office@usswimschools.org

Historical Note
Membership: $300-520/year (organization/company).

Publications:
Swimformation. q. adv.
eNews. m.

United States Targhee Sheep Association *(1951)*
P.O. Box 427
Chinook, MT 59523
Tel: (406)357-3337
Members: 270 individuals
Staff: 1
Annual Budget: $25-50,000
Secretary-Treasurer: Cheryl M. Schuldt

Historical Note
A member of the National Pedigreed Livestock Council. Membership: $25/life (individual).

Meetings/Conferences:
Annual Meetings: Summer

Publications:
Targhee Talk.
Directory. a. adv.

United States Telecom Association *(1897)*
607 14th St. NW
Suite 400
Washington, DC 20005
Tel: (202)326-7300 *Fax:* (202)326-7333
Web Site: www.usta.org
Members: 1200 telephone companies
Staff: 73
Annual Budget: $5-10,000,000
President and Chief Executive Officer: Walter B. McCormick, Jr.
Senior Vice President, Membership, Marketing and Business Development: John Abel
Senior Vice President, Strategic Communications: Thomas S. Amontree
Executive Vice President: Regina Hopper

Historical Note
Formerly Independent Telephone Association of America and National Independent Telephone, it became United States Telephone Association in 1983 and assumed its present name in 2000. Originally formed to represent domestic non-Bell System companies in the telephone industry, USTA now accepts membership from companies previously affiliated with AT&T. Sponsors and supports the USTA Political Action Committee. Has an annual budget of approximately $12.4 million. Membership: fees based on company size, measured by telephone access lines.

Meetings/Conferences:
Annual Meetings: October

Publications:
USTA Industry Directory.
Emergency Preparedness Planning.
Phone Facts 2003.

United States Tennis Association *(1881)*
70 W. Red Oak Ln.
White Plains, NY 10604-3602
Tel: (914)696-7000 *Fax:* (914)696-7167
Web Site: www.usta.com
Members: 500000 individuals
Staff: 150
Annual Budget: Over $100,000,000
Executive Director: Lee Hamilton
Senior Director, Membership: Barrie Markowitz
Managing Director, Marketing and Communications: David Newman

Historical Note
An association of organizations and individuals interested in the promotion of tennis. Formerly (1975) United States Lawn Tennis Association. Sponsors the U.S. teams for the Fed, Davis Cup, and Olympic competitions. Runs the U.S. Open Tennis Championships, held annually at Flushing, NY. Also runs the national championships for juniors, seniors and amateurs, as well as thousands of tournaments at the local level. Membership: $25/year (adult); $25-95/year (organization).

Meetings/Conferences:
Annual Meetings: Spring

Publications:
Tennis USTA. m. adv.
Yearbook and Tennis Guide. a. adv.

United States Tour Operators Association *(1972)*
275 Madison Ave., Suite 2014
New York, NY 10016
Tel: (212)599-6599 *Fax:* (212)599-6744
E-Mail: information@ustoa.com
Web Site: www.ustoa.com
Members: 61 individuals
Staff: 4
Annual Budget: $1-2,000,000
President: Robert E. Whitley
E-Mail: information@ustoa.com

Historical Note
Organized in California but expanded to national membership in 1975. Members are wholesale tour operators and suppliers to the tour industry.

Meetings/Conferences:
Annual Meetings: Winter

Publications:
Membership Directory. a.

United States Trademark Association *(1878)*

Historical Note
See International Trademark Association.

United States Trotting Association *(1938)*
750 Michigan Ave.
Columbus, OH 43215-1191
Toll Free: (877)800 - 8782
Web Site: www.ustrotting.com
Members: 25000 individuals
Staff: 70
Annual Budget: $5-10,000,000
Executive Vice President: Eric Sharbaugh
E-Mail: ems@ustrotting.com
Director, Public Relations: John Pawlak
E-Mail: jpawlak@ustrotting.com

Historical Note
USTA members include officials, breeders, owners, trainers and drivers of standardbred trotting horses. USTA licenses drivers/officials and maintains a registry of horses. Has an annual budget of approximately $7.8 million. Membership: $66/year (new members); $50/year (renewal).

Meetings/Conferences:
Annual Meetings: usually in Columbus, OH/March

Publications:
Hoof Beats. m. adv.
Trotting & Pacing Guide. a.
Sires & Dams Book. a.
Membership List. a.

United States Trout Farmers Association *(1954)*
111 W. Washington St.
Suite One
Charles Town, WV 25414-1529
Tel: (304)728-2189 *Fax:* (304)728-2196
E-Mail: ustfa@frontiernet.net
Web Site: www.ustfa.org
Members: 300 individuals
Staff: 1
Annual Budget: $50-100,000
Executive Administrator: Mary Lee
E-Mail: ustfa@frontiernet.net

Historical Note
USTFA members are trout farmers, academics, equipment suppliers and others with an interest in raising trout commercially.

Meetings/Conferences:
Annual Meetings: Winter

Publications:
Trout Talk. q. adv.

United States Tuna Foundation *(1977)*
1101 17th St. NW
Suite 609
Washington, DC 20036
Tel: (202)857-0610 *Fax:* (202)331-9686
E-Mail: info@tunafacts.com
Web Site: www.tunafacts.com
Members: 3 companies, plus boats supplying tuna for domestic processing
Staff: 5
Annual Budget: $250-500,000
Executive Director: David Barney

Historical Note
Trade association representing the tuna industry.

United States-Austrian Chamber of Commerce *(1949)*
165 W. 46th St., Suite 1112
New York, NY 10036
Tel: (212)819-0117 *Fax:* (212)819-0345
Web Site: www.usatchamber.com
Members: 120 companies
Staff: 1
Annual Budget: $50-100,000
Executive Director: Elizabeth Shumau

Historical Note
Founded to promote trade between the United States and Austria through seminars and luncheon meetings. Membership: $200/year (small housing); $500/year (organization/company); $1,500/year (flagship).

Meetings/Conferences:
Annual Meetings: New York, NY, last week in May

United States-China Business Council *(1973)*
1818 N St. NW, Suite 200
Washington, DC 20036
Tel: (202)429-0340 *Fax:* (202)775-2476
E-Mail: info@uschina.org
Web Site: www.uschina.org
Members: 250 companies
Staff: 25
Annual Budget: $2-5,000,000
President: John Frisbie
Director, Membership Services: E. Palmer Golson

Historical Note
Founded in 1973, the USCBC is a not-for-profit, member-supported organization of American companies engaged in business relations with the People's Republic of China. Membership is limited to companies incorporated in the United States. Individuals, non-profit organization, and government and academic institutions are not eligible for membership.

Meetings/Conferences:
Annual Meetings: Holds four conferences a year, in Winter/Spring/Summer/Fall. Two of these yearly conferences are held in Washington, DC; the other two in China.

Publications:
The China Business Review. bi-m. adv.

United States-Mexico Chamber of Commerce *(1973)*
1300 Pennsylvania Ave. NW
Suite g-003
Washington, DC 20004
Tel: (202)312-1520 *Fax:* (202)312-1530
Toll Free: (888)876 - 2621
E-Mail: news-hq@usmcoc.org
Web Site: www.usmcoc.org
Members: 1500 companies
Staff: 12
Annual Budget: $500-1,000,000
President and Chief Executive Officer: Albert Zapanta
Director, Communications: Gerardo Funes

Historical Note
Maintains U.S. offices in Chicago, Dallas, Houston, Los Angeles, Miami, Milwaukee, Monterrey, New York and Seattle, and Mexican offices in Aguascalientes, Guadalajara and Mexico City. Membership: $200-7,500/year.

Meetings/Conferences:
Monthly Meetings: Regional

Publications:
Alliance Magazine. bi-m. adv.
Chamber News. irreg. adv.
Directory. a. adv.
Inline Newsletter. m. adv.
Special Reports. irreg.

United States-New Zealand Council *(1986)*
1801 F St. NW
Washington, DC 20006
Tel: (202)842-0772 *Fax:* (202)842-0749
E-Mail: info@usnzcouncil.org
Web Site: www.usnzcouncil.org
Members: 400 individuals
Staff: 2
President: John E. Mullen
Director, Operations: Jeremy Quinn
E-Mail: info@usnzcouncil.org

Historical Note
USNZC members are individuals and organizations with an interest in fostering good relations and improved economic ties between New Zealand and the United States. Membership: $100/year (individual); $3,000-$10,000/year (corporate).

United Steel, Paper and Forestry, Rubber, Manufacturing, Energy, Allied Industrial and Service Workers International Union *(2005)*
Five Gateway Center
Pittsburgh, PA 15222
Tel: (412)562-2400 *Fax:* (615)731-6362
E-Mail: johill@steelworkers-usw.org
Web Site: www.steelworkers-usw.org
Members: 250,000
Staff: 250
Annual Budget: $50-100,000
Vice President, Administration: Jim Pannell
Director, Communications: Lynne Baker
Director, Research and Education: Joan Hill

Historical Note
Formed (2005) by a merger of two unions: the United Steel Workers (USW) and the Paper, Allied-Industrial, Chemical and Energy Workers International Union (PACE).

United Steelworkers of America *(1942)*
President: Leo W. Gerard

Historical Note
Established as the Steel Workers Organizing Committee (SWOC) in 1936 to coordinate the massive drive to organize the North American steel industry, the organization grew in just six years to become the United Steelworkers in 1942. The USW is 1.2 million working and retired members throughout the United States and Canada, working together to improve jobs; to build a better future for our families; and to promote fairness, justice and equality both on the job and in society.

Publications:
Steelabor. m.

United Suffolk Sheep Association *(1935)*
P.O. Box 256
Newton, UT 84327-0256
Tel: (435)563-6105 *Fax:* (435)563-9356
E-Mail: unitedsuffolk@comcast.net
Web Site: www.u-s-s-a.org
Members: 2500 individuals
Staff: 4
Annual Budget: $100-250,000
Breed Secretary: Annette Benson
E-Mail: unitedsuffolk@comcast.net

Historical Note
Maintains pedigree registry and promotes the Suffolk breed. Merged with American Suffolk Sheep Association in 1998. Member of the National Pedigree Livestock Council. NSSA also oversees the National Junior Suffolk Sheep Association. Membership: $20/year (individual).

Meetings/Conferences:
Annual Meetings: November

Publications:
Suffolk News. q. adv.

United Synagogue of Conservative Judaism *(1913)*
155 Fifth Ave.
New York, NY 10010-6802
Tel: (212)533-7800 *Fax:* (212)353-9439
E-Mail: info@uscj.org
Web Site: www.uscj.org
Members: 760 congregations
Staff: 150
Annual Budget: $10-25,000,000
Executive Vice President: Rabbi Jerome M. Epstein
E-Mail: epstein@uscj.org
Director, Public Affairs: Joanne Palmer
E-Mail: palmer@uscj.org

Historical Note
Member congregations are conservative U.S. and Canadian congregations. Associated with the Federation of Jewish Men's Clubs, the Women's League for Conservative Judaism, the Jewish Theological Seminary of America and the Rabbinical Assembly.

Meetings/Conferences:
Biennial Meetings: odd years

Publications:
Kadima. 3/yr.
The Next Step. 4/yr.
United Synagogue Review. 2/yr. adv.
Your Child. 3/yr.
Achshav. bi-m.
Program Bank. q.
eNews. m.

United Telecom Council *(1948)*
1901 Pennsylvania Ave. NW, Fifth Floor
Washington, DC 20006
Tel: (202)872-0030 *Fax:* (202)872-1331
Toll Free: (800)900 - 4882
E-Mail: marketing@utc.org
Web Site: www.utc.org
Members: 900 companies
Staff: 16
Annual Budget: $2-5,000,000
President and Chief Executive Officer: William R. Moroney
E-Mail: marketing@utc.org
Vice President, Operations: Kathleen Fitzpatrick
Vice President and General Counsel: Jill Lyon
E-Mail: jill.lyon@utc.org
Vice President, Member Services: Karnel Thomas
Manager, Marketing Communications: Kristy Weinshel

Historical Note
The United Telecom Council (UTC) is a global trade association that produces a business, regulatory, and technological environment for companies that own, manage, or provide critical telecommunications systems in support of their core businesses. Founded in 1948, UTC represents electric, gas, and water utilities; natural gas pipelines; other critical infrastructure entities and industry stakeholders.

Meetings/Conferences:
Annual Meetings: *May/1,400*

Publications:
UTC Journal. q. adv.
UTC Alert. bi-w. adv.
UTC Industry Intelligence. bi-w. adv.
Broadband Powerline. Q. adv.

United Transportation Union *(1969)*
14600 Detroit Ave.
Cleveland, OH 44107-4250
Tel: (216)228-9400 *Fax:* (216)228-5755
E-Mail: utunews@utu.org
Web Site: www.utu.org
Members: 82000 individuals
Staff: 100
Annual Budget: $2-5,000,000
International President: Paul C. Thompson
E-Mail: president@utu.org
General Secretary and Treasurer: Dan E. Johnson
E-Mail: utunews@utu.org

Historical Note
Product of a merger of the Brotherhood of Locomotive Firemen and Enginemen (1873); Brotherhood of Railroad Trainmen (1883); Order of Railway Conductors and Brakemen (1868); and Switchmen's Union of North America (1894). Absorbed (1972) Federated Council of the International Association of Railway Employees and merged (1985) with Railroad Yardmasters of America. Sponsors and supports the Transportation Political Education League.

Publications:
UTU News. m.

United Union of Roofers, Waterproofers and Allied Workers *(1919)*
1660 L St. NW
Suite 800
Washington, DC 20036-5646
Tel: (202)463-7663 *Fax:* (202)463-6906
E-Mail: roofers@unionroofers.com
Web Site: www.unionroofers.com
Members: 22000 individuals
Staff: 30
Annual Budget: $2-5,000,000
International President: John C. Martini
E-Mail: roofers@unionroofers.com

Historical Note
The result of a merger in Pittsburgh, Pennsylvania, September 8, 1919 of the International Slate and Tile Roofers Union of America (founded in 1902) and the International Brotherhood of Composition Roofers, Damp and Waterproof Workers of the United States and Canada (founded in 1905). Chartered by the American Federation of Labor in 1919. Known as the United Slate, Tile and Composition Roofers, Damp and Waterproof Workers Association until 1978.

Meetings/Conferences:
Quinquennial Meetings: *(2003)*

Publications:
United Union of Roofers, Waterproofers and Allied Workers Journal. q.

United Weighers Association
543 Fourth Ave.
Brooklyn, NY 11215
Tel: (718)499-3640
President and Business Agent: Michael Gorry

Historical Note
Members are weighers of raw material imported in to the United States by ship.

Universities Council on Water Resources *(1962)*
1000 Farner Dr.
Room 4535
Carbondale, IL 62901-4526
Tel: (618)536-7571 *Fax:* (618)453-2671
E-Mail: ucowr@siu.edu
Web Site: http://ucowr.siu.edu/
Members: 86 institutions; 3 foreign affil.
Staff: 2
Annual Budget: $50-100,000
Executive Director: Christopher L. Lant, Ph.D.

Historical Note
Founded as the Universities Council on Hydrology in 1962; assumed its present name in 1964. A voluntary organization of universities engaged in education, research, public service, international activities, and legislative pursuits relevant to all aspects of water resources. Membership: $350/year (domestic institution); $75/year (foreign affiliate); $70/year (individual).

Meetings/Conferences:
Annual Meetings: *Summer*

Publications:
Water Resources Update. q.
Proceedings of Annual Meetings. a.

Universities Research Association *(1965)*
1111 19th St. NW
Suite 400
Washington, DC 20036
Tel: (202)293-1382 *Fax:* (202)293-5012
E-Mail: info@ura.nw.dc.us
Web Site: www.ura-hq.org
Members: 90 institutions
Staff: 8
Annual Budget: Over $100,000,000
President: Frederick H. Bernthal
Vice President and Secretary: Ezra Heitowit
General Counsel: William Schmidt
Chief Financial Officer: Benjamin G. Strauss

Historical Note
URA is a consortium of universities whose purpose is to manage the Fermi National Laboratory in Chicago, IL. Has an annual budget of approximately $300 million. Initial membership cost: $10,000; no annual dues.

Meetings/Conferences:
January or February: always in Washington, DC

Publications:
URA Brochure. a.

Universities Space Research Association *(1969)*
10211 Wincopin Circle, Suite 500
Columbia, MD 21044-3432
Tel: (410)730-2656 *Fax:* (410)730-3496
E-Mail: info@usra.edu
Web Site: www.usra.edu
Members: 97 institutions
Staff: 18
Annual Budget: $250-500,000
President and Chief Executive Officer: Dr. David C. Black
E-Mail: info@usra.edu

Historical Note
A consortium of universities that manage research institutes and programs, primarily for NASA.

Meetings/Conferences:
Annual Meetings: *Washington, DC/March*

Publications:
Lunar and Planetary Information Bulletin. q.
USRA Newsletter. q.

University and College Designers Association *(1971)*
199 West Enon Springs Rd., Suite 300
Smyrna, TN 37167
Tel: (615)459-4559 *Fax:* (615)459-5229
E-Mail: info@ucda.com
Web Site: www.ucda.com
Members: 1000 individuals
Staff: 2
Annual Budget: $250-500,000
Executive Director: Tadson Bussey
E-Mail: tadson@ucda.com

Historical Note
Members are individuals involved in visual communication design for colleges and universities. Membership: $145/year.

Meetings/Conferences:
Annual Meetings: *September-October*
2007 - Toronto, ON, Canada(Hilton)/September

Publications:
Designer magazine. q.
Membership Directory. a.
Home Page Newsletter. m.

University Aviation Association *(1947)*
3410 Skyway Dr.
Auburn, AL 36830-6444
Tel: (334)844-2434 *Fax:* (334)844-2432
Web Site: http://uaa.auburn.edu
Members: 450 individuals
Staff: 5
Annual Budget: $250-500,000
Executive Director: Carolyn Williamson, CAE
E-Mail: uaa@auburn.edu

Historical Note
Members are individuals, institutions, and corporations concerned with aviation education at the university level. Membership: $45/year (individual); $20/year (student); $350/year (organization/company).

Meetings/Conferences:
Annual Meetings: *Fall*

Publications:
Collegiate Aviation Guide. bien.
Collegiate Aviation News. q. adv.
UAA Scholarship Directory. a.

University Continuing Education Association *(1915)*
One Dupont Circle NW
Suite 615
Washington, DC 20036-1168
Tel: (202)659-3130 *Fax:* (202)785-0374
E-Mail: postmaster@ucea.edu
Web Site: www.ucea.edu
Members: 2000 individuals
Staff: 8
Annual Budget: $500-1,000,000
Executive Director: Dr. Kay Kohl
Director, Administration: John Hager
Director, Membership and International Affairs: Cyrus Homayounpour
Director, Programs: Tracy Klein
Director, Conferences: Liz Lear

Historical Note
Formerly (1980) known as the National University Extension Association and then (1996) National University Continuing Education Association. Members are accredited colleges and universities with continuing higher education programs and professional staff.

Meetings/Conferences:
Annual Meetings: *April/May*

Publications:
Steal These Ideas Please. trien.
In Focus: A Newsletter of UCEA. 10/yr. adv.
Independent Study Catalog. bien.
Innovations in Continuing Education. a.
Continuing Higher Education Review (CHER) Journal. a.
UCEA Membership Directory. a.
Lifelong Learning Trends. bien.

University Council for Educational Administration *(1957)*
One University Stn. - D5400
Austin, TX 78712
Tel: (512)475-8592 *Fax:* (512)471-5975

E-Mail: plinglee@mail.utexas.edu
Web Site: www.ucea.org
Members: 74 universities
Staff: 7
Annual Budget: $250-500,000
Executive Director: Michelle D. Young
E-Mail: execucea@missouri.edu

Historical Note

A private, non-profit corporation consisting of major universities of the United States and Canada. Established to improve the professional preparation of educational administrators. Proposed in 1954 and established at Columbia Univ. in 1957, the central office was moved to Ohio State and UCEA began operations with a full-time staff and 34 charter members in 1959. Membership: $2,000/year.

Meetings/Conferences:

Annual Meetings: Fall

Publications:

UCEA Review. 3/year. adv.
Educational Administration Quarterly. 5/year. adv.
Journal of Cases in Educational Administration. 4/year.
Journal of Research on Leadership Education. 3/yr.

University Film and Video Association *(1947)*
Univ. of Illinois Press, UFVA Membership Office
1325 S. Oak St.
Champaign, IL 61820
Tel: (217)244-0626 *Fax:* (217)244-9910
Toll Free: (866)244 - 0626
Web Site: www.ufva.org
Members: 800 individuals
Contact: Cheryl Jestis

Historical Note

Members are instructors and film makers concerned with the production and study of film. Originally the University Film Producers Association, it became the University Film Association in 1968 and assumed its present name in 1982. Membership: $50/year (individual); $100/year (institution); $25/year (student); $250/year (sustaining member).

Meetings/Conferences:

Annual Meetings: August

Publications:

Journal of Film and Video. q.
UFVA Digest. bi-m.
Membership Directory. a.

University Photographers Association of America *(1961)*
SUNY Brockport
350 New Campus Dr.
Brockport, NY 14420-2931
Tel: (585)395-2133 *Fax:* (585)395-2723
Web Site: www.upaa.org
Members: 300 individuals
Annual Budget: $10-25,000
President: Jim Dusen
E-Mail: jdusen@brockport.edu

Historical Note

Members are college and university photographers who are concerned with the application and practice of photography. Has no paid staff or permanent address; officers change annually. Membership: $25/year (individual); $100/year (organization).

Publications:

Contact Sheet Journal. 3-4/year. adv.
University Photographer Magazine. a.

University Risk Management and Insurance Association *(1966)*
P.O. Box 1027
Bloomington, IN 47402
Tel: (812)855-6833 *Fax:* (812)856-3149
E-Mail: urmia@urmia.org
Web Site: www.urmia.org
Members: 300 colleges/universities
Staff: 1
Annual Budget: $100-250,000
Associate Executive Director: Jenny Whittington

Historical Note

Members are colleges and universities with insurance or risk management offices.

Meetings/Conferences:

Annual Meetings: September-October

Publications:

Newsletter. 5/year. adv.
Membership Directory. 1/year.
URMIA Journal. 1/year. adv.

University/Resident Theatre Association *(1969)*
1560 Broadway, Suite 712
New York, NY 10036-1518
Tel: (212)221-1130 *Fax:* (212)869-2752
E-Mail: info@urta.com
Web Site: www.urta.com
Members: 48 graduate schools and theaters
Staff: 4
Annual Budget: $500-1,000,000
Executive Director: Scott L. Steele
Office Manager: Johana Castro
Director, Member Services: Sara Falconer

Historical Note

U/RTA acts as a liaison between graduate educational training and professional theater in the U.S. Programs include the National Unified Auditions, Contract Management Program, U/RTA Panelist Bureau, and the U/RTA-Equity Contract, each of which help provide continuity among preprofessional and professional theater. Membership: $2082/year (organization).

Meetings/Conferences:

Three Meetings Annually: New York, NY/January; San Francisco, CA/February

Publications:

U/RTA Update Newsletter. 2/year. adv.
U/RTA Dir. of Member Training. adv.

Upholstered Furniture Action Council *(1975)*
Box 2436
High Point, NC 27261
Tel: (336)885-5065 *Fax:* (336)885-5072
Members: 6 associations
Annual Budget: $500-1,000,000
Executive Director: Joseph Ziolkowski
Legal Counsel: Mary M. McNamara

Historical Note

UFAC is an association of upholstered furniture manufacturers, retailers and suppliers organized to conduct research into more fire resistant upholstering methods and to encourage voluntary compliance throughout the industry.

Meetings/Conferences:

Annual Meetings: Not held.

Urban Affairs Association *(1969)*
University of Delaware
Newark, DE 19716
Tel: (302)831-1681 *Fax:* (302)831-4225
E-Mail: uaa@udel.edu
Web Site: www.udel.edu/uaa
Members: 550 individuals
Staff: 3
Annual Budget: $100-250,000
Executive Director: Margaret Wilder
E-Mail: uaa@udel.edu

Historical Note

Members are urban specialists from private or public universities who are involved in teaching, research or public service. Promotes more effective policies and procedures relating to the study of urban affairs and urbanization. Formerly (1981) Council of University Institutes for Urban Affairs. Membership: $45-60/year (individual); $30/year (student); $295/year (institution).

Meetings/Conferences:

Annual Meetings: Spring

Publications:

Urban Affairs Newsletter. bien.
Journal of Urban Affairs. q.

Urban and Regional Information Systems Association *(1963)*
1460 Renaissance Dr., Suite 305
Park Ridge, IL 60068
Tel: (847)824-6300 *Fax:* (847)824-6363
E-Mail: info@urisa.org
Web Site: www.urisa.org
Members: 3600 individuals
Staff: 9
Annual Budget: $1-2,000,000
Executive Director: Wendy Francis
E-Mail: wfrancis@urisa.org
Chief Operating Officer and Director, Conferences and Meetings: Christine Dionne
E-Mail: cdionne@urisa.org

Historical Note

URISA is the educational/professional association for users and providers of information systems and geographic information systems (GIS) in the public and private sector. Membership: $150/year.

Meetings/Conferences:

Annual Meetings: Summer/Fall

Publications:

URISA News. bi-m. adv.
URISA Journal. m. adv.

Urban Financial Services Coalition *(1975)*
1300 L St. NW
Suite 825
Washington, DC 20005
Tel: (202)289-8335 *Fax:* (202)842-0567
E-Mail: ufsc@ufscnet.org
Web Site: www.ufscnet.org/
Members: 2000 individuals
Staff: 2
Annual Budget: $250-500,000
Director, Member Services: Machelle Maner
E-Mail: ufsc@ufscnet.org

Historical Note

Formerly (2000) National Association of Urban Bankers. Members, primarily from large institutions in major metropolitan areas, are minority professionals in the banking industry and related fields. Membership: annual dues vary by chapter (individual); $5,000-10,000/year, varies by assets (corporate).

Meetings/Conferences:

Annual Meetings: June

Publications:

Monthly News. m.
Conference Journal. a.
Urban Banker Newsletter. q.
Profiles and Perspectives. semi-a.

Urban History Association *(1988)*
Department of History, University of Dayton
300 College Park
Dayton, OH 45469-1540
Tel: (937)229-2824 *Fax:* (937)229-4400
Web Site: http://uha.udayton.edu
Members: 425 individuals
Annual Budget: $10-25,000
Executive Secretary: Janet R. Bednarek
E-Mail: janet.bednarek@notes.udayton.edu

Historical Note

Members are historians and professors of history interested in the development of cities. Recognizes excellence in the field through an annual awards competition. Has no paid officers or full-time staff.

Meetings/Conferences:

Biennial Meetings: (2004)

Publications:

Newslatter. Semi-a.

Urban Land Institute *(1936)*
1025 Thomas Jefferson St. NW
Suite 500 West
Washington, DC 20007-5201
Tel: (202)624-7000 *Fax:* (202)624-7140
Toll Free: (800)321 - 5011
Web Site: www.uli.org
Members: 26700 individuals
Staff: 120
Annual Budget: $25-50,000,000
President: Richard M. Rosan
E-Mail: hbroadus@uli.org
Director, Media Relations: Marge Fahey
Senior Vice President, Strategic Development: Ann Oliveri, CAE
E-Mail: hbroadus@uli.org
Managing Director, Communications: Trisha Riggs
E-Mail: priggs@uli.org

Historical Note
Conducts research in various fields of real estate including identifying and interpreting land use trends in relation to the changing needs of its users. Consists of developers, architects, public officials and others concerned with land planning and development. Official name is ULI - the Urban Land Institute. Has an annual budget of approximately $13 million. Full Membership: $850/year (private-sector); $285/year (government official or academician). Associate Membership: $265/year (private sector); $165/year (public sector). International Membership: $330/year (individual); $185/year (public); $1,000/year (corporate); $65/year (student).

Meetings/Conferences:
Semi-Annual Meetings: Fall and Spring

Publications:
Land Use Digest. m.
Project Reference File. q.
Urban Land. m. adv.
ULI in the Future. a.
ULI News Roundup. w.

Urban Libraries Council *(1971)*
1603 Orrington Ave., Suite 1080
Evanston, IL 60201
Tel: (847)866-9999 *Fax:* (847)866-9989
Web Site: www.urbanlibraries.org
Members: 133 libraries, 16 corporations
Staff: 6
Annual Budget: $1-2,000,000
President: Martin J. Gomez

Historical Note
Formerly (1975) Urban Libraries Trustees Council. Members are public libraries of cities with a population above 50,000. Membership: $1,000-10,000/year.

Meetings/Conferences:
Annual Meetings: in conjunction with the American Libraries Ass'n.

Publications:
ULC Exchange. 11/yr.

Urology Society of America *(2000)*
305 Second Ave., Suite 200
Waltham, MA 02451
Tel: (781)895-9078 *Fax:* (781)895-9088
Web Site: www.urologysocietyofamerica.org
Members: 1900 individuals
Staff: 5
Annual Budget: $500-1,000,000
Executive Director: Wesley E. Harrington, CAE

Historical Note
Membership: $325/year.

Meetings/Conferences:
Annual Meetings: Spring
2007 – Orlando, FL(Dolphin Hotel)/March 15-18/650

Publications:
Practice Management News. m. adv.

US Composting Council *(1991)*
4250 Veteran's Memorial Hwy., Suite 275
Holbrook, NY 11741
Tel: (631)737-4931 *Fax:* (631)737-4939
E-Mail: uscc@compostingcouncil.org
Web Site: www.compostingcouncil.org
Members: 500 businesses
Staff: 5
Annual Budget: $250-500,000
Executive Director: Dr. Stuart Buckner

Historical Note
Established in 1990, the USCC works to develop, expand, and promote the composting industry through encouraging, supporting, and performing research, improving management practices, establishing standards, educating professionals and the public about the benefits of composting and compost utilization, enhancing compost product quality, and developing training materials for composters, and markets for compost products. USCC members include compost producers, marketers, equipment manufacturers, product suppliers, academic institutions, public agencies, nonprofit groups and consulting/engineering firms.

Meetings/Conferences:
Annual Meetings: November

Publications:
Compost Communicator (online newsletter). q.

USA Poultry and Egg Export Council *(1984)*
2300 W. Park Place Blvd., Suite 100
Stone Mountain, GA 30087
Tel: (770)413-0006 *Fax:* (770)413-0007
E-Mail: usapeec@usapeec.org
Web Site: www.usapeec.org
Members: 200 companies
Staff: 40
Annual Budget: $25-50,000,000
President: James H. Sumner
Vice President, Communications: Toby Moore

Historical Note
Members are poultry and egg producers, processors, and traders interested in developing export markets. Membership: dues based on export volume. Has an annual budget of approximately $10 million.

Publications:
Monday Line. w.

USA Taekwonda
One Olympic Plaza, Suite 104C
Colorado Springs, CO 80909-5746
Tel: (719)866-4632 *Fax:* (719)866-4642
Web Site: www.usa-taekwondo.org
Members: 15000
Staff: 13
Director, Events: Monica Paul

Meetings/Conferences:
Annual Meetings: November

Usability Professionals' Association *(1991)*
140 N. Bloomingdale Rd.
Bloomingdale, IL 60108-1017
Tel: (630)980-4997 *Fax:* (630)351-8490
E-Mail: office@upassoc.org
Web Site: www.upassoc.org
Members: 2400 individuals
Staff: 3
Annual Budget: $500-1,000,000
Executive Director: John E. Kasper, Ph.D., CAE

Historical Note
UPA is a professional organization established to aid in the creation of more usable products and services. Membership: $85/year (professional); $20/year (student).

Meetings/Conferences:
Annual Meetings: Summer

Publications:
UPA Voice Newsletter. bi-m.
User Experience. 3/year. adv.

Used Oil Management Association *(1981)*
Patton Boggs LLP
2550 M St. NW
Washington, DC 20037-1350
Tel: (202)457-6420 *Fax:* (202)457-6315
Web Site: www.uoma.com
Members: 5 companies
Associate Director, Marketing and Membership: Mary Beth Bosco

Historical Note
Formerly the Waste Oil Heating Manufacturers Association (1996). Members are manufacturers of heaters designed to burn used oil.

Meetings/Conferences:
Annual Meetings: November

Used Truck Association *(1988)*
P.O. Box 603
Indianapolis, IN 46206
Tel: (817)439-3900
Toll Free: (877)438 - 7882
Web Site: www.uta.org
Members: 286 individuals
Staff: 13
Annual Budget: $50-100,000
President: H.E. "Eddie" Walker

Historical Note
Founded as Used Truck Sales Network; became National Used Truck Association in 1994 and assumed its current name in 1995. UTA's mission is to serve those companies, organizations and individuals involved in the used truck industry in support of their primary business activities, and to be a leader in promoting professionalism in the used truck industry. Membership: $25/year (individual); $350/year (company).

Publications:
UTA Industry Watch. m. adv.
Membership Directory. 2/year. adv.

Utility Arborist Association *(1970)*
P.O. Box 3129
Champaign, IL 61826-3129
Tel: (217)355-9411 Ext: 234 *Fax:* (217)355-9516
Web Site: www.isa-arbor.com/uaa
Members: 1700 individuals
Staff: 2
Annual Budget: $100-250,000
Executive Director: Derek Vannice
E-Mail: dvannice@isa-arbor.com

Historical Note
An affiliate of International Society of Arboriculture, which provides administrative support. UAA members are utility line clearance arborists and others involved in line clearance operations. Membership: $25/year (individual).

Meetings/Conferences:
Annual Meetings: always August
2007 – Honolulu, HI(Convention Center)/July 28-Aug. 1/500
2008 – St. Louis, MO(Convention Center)/July 26-30/500

Publications:
Utility Arborist Membership Directory. a. adv.
Utility Arborist Newsletter. q. adv.

Utility Communicators International *(1922)*
229 E. Ridgewood Rd.
Georgetown, TX 78628
Tel: (512)869-1313 *Fax:* (512)864-7203
Web Site: www.uci-online.com
Members: 400 individuals
Staff: 1
Annual Budget: $50-100,000
Executive Director: Elliot Boardman

Historical Note
Members are advertising, public relations and communications directors of public utilities, their agencies and trade allies. Formerly (1977) Public Utilities Advertising Association; then became the Public Utilities Communicators Association before adopting its present name in 1989. Membership: $350/year (individual); $550/year (organization/company).

Meetings/Conferences:
Annual Meetings: June

Publications:
Newsletter. bi-m.

Utility Workers Union of America *(1945)*
815 16th St. NW
Washington, DC 20006
Tel: (202)974-8200 *Fax:* (202)974-8201
Web Site: www.uwua.org
Members: 50000 individuals
Staff: 24
Annual Budget: $2-5,000,000
President: Donald E. Wightman
Secretary-Treasurer: Gary M. Ruffner

Historical Note
Founded in 1945 through the merger of the Utility Workers Organizing Committee (which had been set up by the CIO in 1938) and the Brotherhood of Consolidated Edison Employees; chartered by the Congress of Industrial Organizations the same year. Affiliated with AFL-CIO. Sponsors and supports the Committee on Political Action as well as the Utility Workers Union of America Political Contributions Committee.

Meetings/Conferences:
Annual Meetings: Summer

Publications:
Light. q.

Vacation Rental Managers Association *(1985)*
P.O. Box 1202
Santa Cruz, CA 95061-1202
Tel: (831)426-8762 *Fax:* (831)458-3637
E-Mail: info@vrma.com

Web Site: www.vrma.com
Members: 600 companies
Staff: 3
Annual Budget: $500-1,000,000
Executive Director: Michael Sarka, CMP
E-Mail: info@vrma.com

Historical Note
VRMA members are companies that manage short-term rental/vacation properties; associate members are companies that provide services to the rental industry. Membership: $370/year; $485/year (associate/supplier).

Meetings/Conferences:
Annual Meetings: *September, October, or November Alternate East (odd numbered years) and West (even numbered years)*

Publications:
VRMA Membership Roster. a. adv.
VRMA Review. q. adv.

Vacuum Cleaner Manufacturers Association *(1913)*

Historical Note
Absorbed by Association of Home Appliance Manufacturers in 2004.

Vacuum Dealers Trade Association *(1981)*

2724 Second Ave.
Des Moines, IA 50313-4933
Tel: (515)282-9101 *Fax:* (515)282-4483
Toll Free: (800)367 - 5651
E-Mail: mail@vdta.com
Web Site: www.vdta.com
Members: 2200 individuals
Staff: 12
Annual Budget: $250-500,000
President: Judy Patterson
E-Mail: mail@vdta.com

Historical Note
Vacuum cleaner retailers, sewing machine retailers, manufacturers and distributors. Membership: $75/year (individual); $500/year (corporate).

Publications:
VDTA Floor Care & Sewing Professional. adv.
VDTA News Central Vac Professional. m. adv.
Sewing & Embroidery Professional. m. adv.
Quilting Professional. q. adv.

Valve Manufacturers Association of America *(1938)*

1050 17th St. NW
Suite 280
Washington, DC 20036-5503
Tel: (202)331-8105 *Fax:* (202)296-0378
E-Mail: vma@vma.org
Web Site: www.vma.org
Members: 100 companies
Staff: 4
Annual Budget: $1-2,000,000
President: William S. Sandler, CAE
Manager, Meetings and Exhibits: Ryda Ruth Cusack

Historical Note
Founded as the Valve Manufacturers Association in 1938; added "of America" in 1985. Membership: $3,000/year, minimum (corporate).

Meetings/Conferences:
Annual Meetings: *Fall*
2007 – Amelia Island, FL(Ritz-Carlton)/Oct. 11-14/150
2008 – Tucson, AZ(Lowes Ventura Canyon)/Oct. 23-26/150

Publications:
VMA Quick Read. w.
Valve Magazine. q. adv.

Valve Repair Council *(1989)*

1050 17th St. NW
Suite 280
Washington, DC 20036-5503
Tel: (202)331-0104 *Fax:* (202)296-0378
E-Mail: mpasternak@vma.org
Members: 30 companies
Staff: 1
Annual Budget: $50-100,000
Executive Director: Marc Pasternak
E-Mail: mpasternak@vma.org

Historical Note
Formerly (1994) Valve Remanufacturers Council. Affiliated with the Valve Manufacturers Association of America, VRC promotes the OEM approach in valve and actuator repair. VRC membership is open to all VMA members who have either in-house service operations or out-of-plant service facilities, as well as their authorized independent facilities. Membership: $2,000/year (single location); $2,500/year (multiple locations).

Publications:
VRC Review. q.

Van Alen Institute *(1894)*

30 W. 22nd St., Sixth Floor
New York, NY 10010
Tel: (212)924-7000 *Fax:* (212)366-5836
E-Mail: vanalen@vanalen.org
Web Site: www.vanalen.org
Members: 600 individuals
Staff: 5
Annual Budget: $500-1,000,000
Associate Director, Research and Development: Katherine Romero
E-Mail: vanalen@vanalen.org
Office Administrator: Marcus Woollen
E-Mail: vanalen@vanalen.org

Historical Note
Established as the Society of Beaux-Arts Architects; became (1916) the Beaux-Arts Institute of Design and then (1956) National Institute for Architectural Education before assuming its current name in 1996. VAI is devoted to promoting excellece in architectural education and bridging the gap between the academic and professional sectors. VAI's New York headquarters is an active center for exhibitions, lectures, and other events of interest to the architectural community. Membership: $25/year (students); $50/year (Members); $100/year (Contributors); $500/year (Benefactors); $1,000/year (Sustaining Benefactors); $2,500/year (Patrons).

Meetings/Conferences:
Annual Meetings: *Always in October at the Institute's headquarters*

Publications:
Van Alen Report. a.

Van Body Manufacturers Division

Historical Note
A division of the National Truck Equipment Association.

Variable Electronic Components Institute *(1960)*

P.O. Box 1070
Vista, CA 92085-1070
Tel: (760)631-0178 *Fax:* (760)631-7827
E-Mail: veci2@cox.net
Web Site: www.veci-vrci.com
Members: 35 companies
Staff: 2
Annual Budget: $25-50,000
Executive Director: Stanley Kukawka

Historical Note
Formerly (1964) Precision Potentiometer Manufacturers Association and then (1997) Variable Resistive Components Institute before assuming its current name. VECI maintains and publishes potentionometer and encoder standards, as well as market statistics for potentionmeters and encoders. Membership: $250-2,000/year .

Meetings/Conferences:
Annual Meetings:

Vehicular Technology Society

Historical Note
A technical society of the Institute of Electrical and Electronics Engineers (IEEE). Membership in the Society, open only to IEEE members, includes subscription to a technical periodical in the field published by IEEE. All administrative support is provided by IEEE.

Venezuelan American Association of the U.S. *(1936)*

30 Vesey St., Suite 506
New York, NY 10007
Tel: (212)233-7776 *Fax:* (212)233-7779
E-Mail: andean@nyct.net
Web Site: www.venezuelanamerican.org
Members: 50 individuals
Staff: 3
Annual Budget: $25-50,000
Executive Secretary: Linda Calvet
E-Mail: andean@nyct.net

Historical Note
Promotes the expansion of trade relations between the U.S. and Venezuela. Membership: $200/year (individual); $500/year (corporate); and $2,000/year (supporting).

Meetings/Conferences:
Monthly Luncheons:

Veterinary Botanical Medical Association *(2000)*

1785 Poplar Dr.
Kennesaw, GA 30144
E-Mail: office@vbma.org
Web Site: www.vbma.org
Members: 130 individuals
Staff: 1
Executive Director: Jasmine C. Lyon

Historical Note
VBMA members are veterinarians and herbalists dedicated to developing responsible herbal practice.

Veterinary Cancer Society

P.O. Box 1763
Spring Valley, CA 91979
Tel: (619)474-8929 *Fax:* (619)474-8947
E-Mail: vcs@cox.net
Web Site: www.vetcancersociety.org
Members: 750 individuals
Staff: 1
Annual Budget: $100-250,000
Executive Director: Barbara J. McGehee
E-Mail: vcs@cox.net

Historical Note
Membership: $30/year (individual); $10/year (interns/students).

Meetings/Conferences:
Annual Meetings: *Fall*

Publications:
Membership Directory (online).
Proceedings of Annual Meeting. a.
Veterinary Cancer Society Newsletter. q.

Veterinary Hospital Managers Association *(1981)*

48 Howard St.
Albany, NY 12207-1715
Tel: (518)433-8911 *Fax:* (518)463-8656
E-Mail: admin@vhma.org
Web Site: www.vhma.org
Members: 1000 individuals
Staff: 4
Annual Budget: $100-250,000
Executive Director: Christine Quinn Shupe, CAE
E-Mail: admin@vhma.org

Historical Note
Formed to provide individuals who are actively involved in Veterinary Practice Management with a means of effective communication and interaction. Members include veterinarians, hospital administrators, practice managers and office managers. Membership: $95/year (individual).

Meetings/Conferences:
Annual Meetings: *November*

Publications:
Practice Pulse Newsletter. m.

Veterinary Orthopedic Society *(1972)*

P.O. Box 705
Okemos, MI 48805-0705
Tel: (517)381-2468 *Fax:* (517)381-2468
E-Mail: vosdvmsecretary@sbcglobal.net
Web Site: www.vosdvm.org
Members: 650 individuals
Annual Budget: under $10,000
Executive Secretary: Maralyn R. Probst
E-Mail: vosdvmsecretary@sbcglobal.net

Historical Note
VOS members are veterinarians with an interest in orthopedic surgery. Membership: $100/year (individual).

Meetings/Conferences:
Annual Meetings: *Winter*

Publications:
VOS Newsletter.
Veterinary and Comparative Orthopedics and Traumatology journal.
Membership List. irreg.

Viatical and Life Settlement Association of America *(1994)*
1504 E. Concord St.
Orlando, FL 32803
Tel: (407)894-3797 *Fax:* (407)897-1325
E-Mail: support@vlsaa.com
Web Site: www.vlsaa.com
Members: 28 companies
Staff: 2
Annual Budget: $100-250,000
Executive Director: Doug Head
E-Mail: support@vlsaa.com
Historical Note
Founded as Viatical Association of America; assumed its current name in 2000. Members are companies who purchase life insurance policies from people with terminal illnesses. Works to establish reasonable regulation for the industry. Membership: $5,000/year.

Vibration Institute *(1972)*
6262 S. Kingery Hwy.
Suite 212
Willowbrook, IL 60527
Tel: (630)654-2254 *Fax:* (630)654-2271
E-Mail: vibinst@anet.com
Web Site: www.vibinst.com
Members: 3000 individuals
Staff: 6
Annual Budget: $500-1,000,000
Director: Ronald L. Eshleman, Ph.D.
E-Mail: vibinst@anet.com
Historical Note
Founded as the Vibration Foundation, it reorganized in 1973 under its present name. Members are companies and individuals concerned with measuring and analyzing machinery vibration. Membership: $60/year (US); $75/year (foreign); $500/year (corporate).
Meetings/Conferences:
Annual Meetings: June
2007 - San Antonio, TX(Menger Hotel)/June 19-22
Publications:
Vibrations Magazine. q. adv.
Proceedings. a.

Victorian Society in America *(1966)*
205 S. Camac St.
Philadelphia, PA 19107-5402
Tel: (215)545-8340 *Fax:* (215)545-8379
E-Mail: info@victoriansociety.org
Web Site: www.victoriansociety.org
Members: 3000 individuals
Staff: 1
Annual Budget: $100-250,000
Business Manager: John Cooper
E-Mail: info@victoriansociety.org
Historical Note
Members are historians, preservationists and others with an interest in the study of nineteenth century America. Membership: $45/year (individual).
Publications:
Nineteenth Century. semi-a. adv.
Victorian. q. adv.

Video Electronics Standards Association *(1989)*
860 Hillview Ct.
Suite 150
Milpitas, CA 95035-4558
Tel: (408)957-9270 *Fax:* (408)957-9277
Web Site: www.vesa.org
Members: 125 companies
Staff: 2
Executive Director: Bill Lempesis
E-Mail: bill@vesa.org
Manager, Member Services: Joan White
E-Mail: joan@vesa.org
Historical Note
Based in Milpitas, CA, VESA is an international trade association serving the video display market.

Video Software Dealers Association *(1981)*
16530 Ventura Blvd., Suite 400
Encino, CA 91436-4551
Tel: (818)385-1500 *Fax:* (818)385-0567
Web Site: www.vsda.org
Members: 1,500 companies
Staff: 16
Annual Budget: $2-5,000,000
President: Crossan R. Andersen
E-Mail: vsda@vsda.org
Vice President, Public Affairs: Sean Devlin Bersell
E-Mail: sbersell@vsda.org
Vice President, Marketing and Industry Relations: Carrie Dieterich
E-Mail: cdieterich@vsda.org
Vice President, Membership and Strategic Initiatives: Mark Fisher
E-Mail: mfisher@vsda.org
Historical Note
Regular members are retailers and distributors of pre-recorded video products (VHS, DVD and console video games); associate members are manufacturers and suppliers of products to the industry. Has annual budget of approximately $4 million. Membership fee varies with number of retail stores and volume, and depends upon type of membership (associate or regular).
Meetings/Conferences:
Annual Meetings: July/Las Vegas, NV
Publications:
VSDA Annual Report. a.
VSDA Voice - Online. m. adv.

Vinegar Institute *(1967)*
5775 Peachtree-Dunwoody Rd., Bldg. G
Suite 500
Atlanta, GA 30342-1558
Tel: (404)252-3663 *Fax:* (404)252-0774
E-Mail: vi@kellencompany.com
Web Site: www.versatilevinegar.org
Members: 42 companies
Staff: 4
Annual Budget: $100-250,000
Executive Director: Pamela A. Chumley
Historical Note
Membership composed of makers and bottlers of vinegar, as well as suppliers to the industry. Membership: dues vary by sales (company).
Meetings/Conferences:
Annual Meetings: February-March
Publications:
Basic Reference Manual.
Technically Speaking About Vinegar.

Vinifera Wine Growers Association *(1973)*
P.O. Box 10045
Alexandria, VA 22310
Tel: (703)922-7049 *Fax:* (703)922-0617
E-Mail: thewinexchange@aol.com
Members: 350 individuals
Staff: 2
Annual Budget: $25-50,000
President: Gordon Murchie
E-Mail: thewinexchange@aol.com
Secretary and Editor: Anita Murchie
Historical Note
Originally founded to support the growth of Vinifera variety wine grapes in the eastern U.S., VWGA now suports the whole spectrum of the U.S. wine industry, including limited lobbying. Disseminates information on the history and current developments of interest to the domestic wine industry, and supports the production and marketing of quality U.S. wines. Membership: $25/year (domestic); $35/year (foreign).
Meetings/Conferences:
Annual Meetings: usually in conjunction with the Virginia Wine Festival/late September
Publications:
Wine Exchange. q. adv.

Vinyl Acetate Council *(1995)*
1250 Connecticut Ave. NW
Suite 700
Washington, DC 20036
Tel: (202)419-1500 *Fax:* (202)659-8037
E-Mail: rfensterheim@regnet.com
Web Site: www.vinylacetate.org
Members: 6 companies
Staff: 2
Annual Budget: $100-250,000
Executive Director: Robert J. Fensterheim
Historical Note
Formerly (1995) Vinyl Acetate Toxicology Group. VAC sponsors and monitors research to evaluate the health effects of vinyl acetate, and makes these evaluations available to the various regulatory agencies with an interest in health and safety.

Vinyl Institute *(1982)*
1300 Wilson Blvd., Suite 800
Arlington, VA 22209
Tel: (703)741-5670 *Fax:* (703)741-5672
Web Site: www.vinylinfo.org
Members: 32 companies
Staff: 4
Annual Budget: $2-5,000,000
President: Tim Burns
Historical Note
A division of the Society of the Plastics Industry, The Vinyl Institute is a trade association representing the leading U.S. manufacturers of vinyl, vinyl chloride monomer and vinyl additives and modifiers as well as film and sheet producers. The Institute's principal activities are education and advocacy, and include the sponsorship of extensive scientific research.
Meetings/Conferences:
Annual Meetings: May
Publications:
Vinyl Today and Tomorrow - online.

Vinyl Siding Institute *(1976)*
1201 15th St. NW
Suite 220
Washington, DC 20005
Tel: (202)587-5100 *Fax:* (202)587-5127
Toll Free: (888)367 - 8741
E-Mail: vsi@vinylsiding.org
Web Site: www.vinylsiding.org
Members: 450 individuals
Staff: 8
Annual Budget: $1-2,000,000
President: Jery Y. Huntley
Historical Note
A business unit of the Society of the Plastics Industry, VSI promotes the growth of the vinyl siding industry, acting as advocate and central communications resource for its membership, sponsors certification program, works with code and regulatory bodies and provides a forum for the exchange of information on technology and issues important to the industry. Compiles statistics. Membership: cost varies in accordance with sales.
Publications:
Vinyl Siding Installation: A How-To Guide.
Vinyl Siding Installation: A How-To Video.
Certified Products List.
Vinyl Siding Cleaning and Maintenance Guide.

Viola da Gamba Society of America *(1962)*
4440 Trieste Dr.
Carlsbad, CA 92008
Tel: (760)729-6679
Web Site: www.vdgsa.org
Members: 700 individuals
Staff: 1
Executive Secretary: Alice Renken
E-Mail: arenken@sandwich.net
Historical Note
VdGSA members are professional musicians, music teachers and amateur players of the viola da gamba, a bass instrument related to the cello. Sponsors workshops, competitions, and other activities. Membership: $25/year (individual).
Meetings/Conferences:
Annual Meetings: late July-early August
Publications:
Journal of the VdGSA. a.
VdGSA Newsletter. q. adv.
Membership List. a.

Violin Society of America *(1973)*
48 Academy St.

Poughkeepsie, NY 12601
Tel: (845)542-7557 *Fax:* (845)452-7618
E-Mail: info@vsa.to
Web Site: www.vsa.to
Members: 1800 individuals
Staff: 1
Executive Director: Robert Martinez

Historical Note
VSA Members are makers/restorers, dealers, players, teachers, and collectors of instruments and bows of the violin family.

Meetings/Conferences:
Annual Meetings: November

Publications:
VSA Journal. irreg. adv.
Newsletter. 3/year. adv.
Papers. semi-a.

Vision Council of America *(1985)*
1700 Diagonal Road, Suite 500
Alexandria, VA 22314
Tel: (703)548-4560 *Fax:* (703)548-4580
E-Mail: vca@visionsite.org
Web Site: www.visionsite.org
Members: 700 companies
Staff: 27
Annual Budget: $5-10,000,000
Chief Executive Officer: William C. Thomas
Vice President, Communications: Joe La Mountain
Vice President, Member Operations: Deborah Malakoff
E-Mail: dmalakoff@visionsite.org

Historical Note
Formerly (1989) Vision Industry Council of America. Absorbed OMA: the Optical Industry Association in 2000. Promotes eyecare and eyewear in the United States through public relations programs, trade shows and practice-building programs for eyecare professionals.

Publications:
Check Yearly See Clearly.
Ideas That Work. q.

Visiting Nurse Associations of America *(1983)*
99 Summer St., Suite 1700
Boston, MA 02110
Tel: (617)737-3200 *Fax:* (617)737-1144
Toll Free: (888)866 - 8773
E-Mail: vnaa@vnaa.org
Web Site: www.vnaa.org
Members: 415 organizations
Staff: 15
Annual Budget: $2-5,000,000
President and Chief Executive Officer: Carolyn Markey
E-Mail: cmarkey@vnaa.org
Vice President, Finance and Human Resources: Patricia Bernard
E-Mail: pbernard@vnaa.org
Vice President, Legislative and Public Affairs: Kathy Thompson
E-Mail: kthompson@vnaa.org

Historical Note
Superseded the American Affiliation of Visiting Nurse Associations and Services in 1986. Members are non-profit, community-based home and community health care providers. VNAA provides membership programs, educational events, business development, managed care marketing and contracting, communications, national imaging and group purchasing services for its members.

Meetings/Conferences:
Annual Meetings: Spring/500

Publications:
Nursing Procedure Manual.
VNA Membership Guide. a.
All VNA's Directory. a.

Visitor Studies Association *(1991)*
8175-A Sheridan Blvd., Suite 362
Arvada, CO 80003-1928
Tel: (303)467-2200 *Fax:* (303)467-0064
E-Mail: info@visitorstudies.org
Web Site: www.visitorstudies.org
Members: 365 individuals
Annual Budget: $100-250,000
President: Mary Ellen Munley
E-Mail: info@visitorstudies.org

Historical Note
Members are professionals at various institutions interested in studying audience experiences at museums, zoos, parks, etc. Promotes research in visitor participation and applications of such research to programming and policy. Membership: Basic-$60, Full-$100, Supporting-$250, Sustaining-$500, Patron-$1000, Institutional-$300, Student-$30.

Meetings/Conferences:
Annual Meetings: Summer

Publications:
Annual Conference Abstracts. a.
Visitor Studies Today. 3/year.
Membership Directory. a.

Visual Resources Association *(1982)*
4201 Wilson Blvd.
110-331
Arlington, VA 22203
Tel: (202)422-4876
E-Mail: join@vraweb.org
Web Site: www.vraweb.org
Members: 800 individuals
Annual Budget: $100-250,000
Membership Services Coordinator: Liz Hernandez

Historical Note
VRA is a professional association devoted to the study of visual materials. Members include slide and photograph curators, electronic media professionals, film and video librarians, photo archivists, slide/microfilm/digital image producers, rights and reproduction officials, photographers, art historians, and others concerned with visual materials. Membership: varies (individual); $145/year (institution); $25/year (student/retired).

Meetings/Conferences:
Annual Meetings: Spring
2007 – Kansas City, MO/March 27-Apr. 1

Publications:
Online Directory.
VRA Bulletin Journal. q. adv.

Visually Impaired Data Processors International *(1970)*

Historical Note
An affiliate of American Council of the Blind, which provides administrative support.

Vocational Evaluation and Career Assesement Professionals *(1967)*
P.O. Box 26273
Colorado Springs, CO 80936
Tel: (719)638-4787 *Fax:* (719)638-6153
E-Mail: vecap@ctam-der.com
Web Site: www.vecap.org
Members: 300 individuals
Staff: 2
Annual Budget: $25-50,000
President: Joseph Ashley
E-Mail: joe.ashley@drs.virginia.gov

Historical Note
Formerly (1967) Vocational Evaluation and Work Adjustment Association; assumed its current name in 2003. VECAP represents the interests of professionals in vocational evaluation. Membership: $70/year.

Meetings/Conferences:
Semi-Annual: National Forum

Publications:
VECAP Journal. 2/yr.

Voice and Speech Trainer's Association

Historical Note
A focus group of the Association for Theatre in Higher Education.

Voices for America's Children *(1984)*
1522 K St. NW
Suite 600
Washington, DC 20005-1202
Tel: (202)289-0777 *Fax:* (202)289-0776
E-Mail: voices@voicesforamericaschildren.org
Web Site: www.voicesforamericaschildren.org
Members: 64 organizations
Staff: 14
Annual Budget: $1-2,000,000
President: Tamara Lucas Copeland
Vice President, Finance and Administration: Daniel Hooks
Director, Member Services: Lisa Macey
Director, Federal Policy and Advocacy: Debbie Stein
Director, Communications: Monica Zimmer

Historical Note
Formerly (1984) National Association of Child Advocates; assumed its current name in 2003. Works to increase the capabilities and effectiveness of state and local child advocacy organizations. Membership: $500/year minumum, based on budget.

Meetings/Conferences:
Annual Meetings: January

Publications:
Issue Briefs. irreg.
Fact Sheets. irreg.

Voluntary Protection Programs Participants Association
7600-E Leesburg Pike, Suite 440
Falls Church, VA 22043-2004
Tel: (703)761-1146 *Fax:* (703)761-1148
E-Mail: administration@vpppa.org
Web Site: www.vpppa.org
Members: 1200 Worksites
Staff: 10
Annual Budget: $1-2,000,000
Manager, Communications and Outreach: Sanna Razza
Manager, Government Affairs: Michele Myers

Historical Note
Members are companies and sites which participate in voluntary protection programs coordinated by OSHA or the Dept. of Energy. Membership: $125-2,500/year.

Meetings/Conferences:
Annual Meetings: Fall/1,900
2007 – Washington, DC(Marriott Wardman Park)/Aug. 26-30
2008 – Anaheim, CA(Anaheim Marriott Hotel)/Aug. 24-28
2009 – San Antonio, TX(San Antonio Marriott Rivercenter and Riverwalk)/Aug. 23-27
2010 – Orlando, FL(Orlando World Center Marriott)/Aug. 22-26
2011 – New Orleans, LA(New Orleans Marriott)/Aug. 28-Sept. 2
2012 – Anaheim, CA(Anaheim Marriott Hotel)/Aug. 19-23

Publications:
The Leader. q.

WACRA - World Association for Case Method Research and Application *(1984)*
23 Mackintosh Ave.
Needham, MA 02492-1218
Tel: (781)444-8982 *Fax:* (781)444-1548
E-Mail: wacra@rcn.com
Web Site: www.wacra.org
Members: 2000 individuals
Executive Director: Dr. Hans E. Klein
E-Mail: wacra@rcn.com

Historical Note
WACRA members are professionals and academicians with an interest in the use of the case method and other interactive methods in teaching, training and planning. Membership: $75/year (individual); $60/year (student); $390/year (organization).

Meetings/Conferences:
2007 – Lucca, Italy/Jan. 3-6
2007 – Guadalajara, Mexico/July 1-4

Publications:
IJCRA - The Interactive Journal of Case Method Research and Application. q.
Interactive Teaching and Learning In A Global Context.
Interactive Teaching and Learning Across Disciplines.
Interactive Teaching & Learning.
Interactive Teaching and the Multimedia Revolution.
Collection of International Case Studies.
Interactive Journal For Case Method Application. a.
Case Method Research and Application. a. adv.
WACRA NEWSletter. semi-a. adv.
Interactive Teaching & Emerging Technologies.
Teaching & Interactive Methods.

The Art of Interactive Teaching.
Innovation Through Cooperation.

Walking Horse Owners Association of America *(1976)*
Tennessee Miller Coliseum
304-A West Thompson Lane
Murfreesboro, TN 37129
Tel: (615)494-8822 *Fax:* (615)494-8825
E-Mail: whoa@walkinghorseowners.com
Web Site: www.walkinghorseowners.com
Members: 8000 individuals
Staff: 5
Annual Budget: $250-500,000
Executive Director: Tommy Hall
E-Mail: whoa@walkinghorseowners.com

Historical Note
Members own and exhibit Tennessee Walking horses. Sponsors the International Grand Championship Walking Horse Show held in Murfreesboro, TN. Membership: $50/year.

Meetings/Conferences:
Annual Meetings: February

Walking Horse Trainers Association *(1968)*
P.O. Box 61
Shelbyville, TN 37162
Tel: (931)684-5866 *Fax:* (931)684-5895
E-Mail: walkinghorsetrai@bellsouth.net
Web Site: www.walkinghorsetrainers.com
Members: 700 individuals
Staff: 2
Annual Budget: $25-50,000
President: David Landrum
Executive Secretary and Office Manager: Marcia M. Allison

Historical Note
Trainers of Tennessee Walking Horses. Works for unity in the horse industry and sponsors continuing research. Membership: $100/year.

Meetings/Conferences:
Annual Meetings: Winter

Publications:
From the Horse's Mouth. q.

Wallcoverings Association *(1992)*
401 N. Michigan Ave.
Chicago, IL 60611-4267
Tel: (312)644-6610 *Fax:* (312)527-6705
E-Mail: rpietrzak@smithbucklin.org
Web Site: www.wallcoverings.org
Members: 100 companies
Staff: 3
Annual Budget: $500-1,000,000
Executive Director: Ron Pietrzak
Convention Manager: Marisa Vallaba

Historical Note
The product of a merger in 1992 of the Wallcovering Manufacturers Association and the Wallcovering Distributors Association in 1992. Membership: dues based on annual wallcovering sales volume.

Meetings/Conferences:
2007 - Orlando, FL/Feb. 9-13/350
2008 - Marco Island, FL/Feb. 7-11/300

Publications:
Regulatory Report. m.
Newsletter. q.

Walnut Council *(1970)*
1011 N. 725 West
West Lafayette, IN 47906
Tel: (765)583-3501 *Fax:* (765)583-3512
E-Mail: walnutcouncil@walnutcouncil.org
Web Site: www.walnutcouncil.org
Members: 960 individuals
Staff: 1
Annual Budget: $25-50,000
Director: Liz Jackson
E-Mail: jackson@purdue.edu

Historical Note
WC is an international association representing woodland owners, foresters, forest scientists and wood-producing industry representatives in over 45 states and seven foreign countries. Membership: $25/year (individual).

Meetings/Conferences:
2007 - Dubuque, IA(Grand River Ctr.)/300
2008 - Columbia, MD(Holiday Inn Select)/Aug. 3-6

Publications:
Walnut Council Bulletin. 3/year.

Warehousing Education and Research Council *(1977)*
1100 Jorie Blvd., Suite 170
Oak Brook, IL 60523-4413
Tel: (630)990-0001 *Fax:* (630)990-0256
E-Mail: operations@werc.org
Web Site: www.werc.org
Members: 3500 individuals
Staff: 8
Annual Budget: $2-5,000,000
Executive Director: Robert L. Shaunnessey
Deputy Executive Director: Rita Coleman
E-Mail: rcoleman@werc.org
Director, Marketing and Membership: Susan Levand
Director, Conference and Chapter Relations: Michael Mikitka
E-Mail: mmikitka@werc.org
Director, Operations: Mike Moss
E-Mail: mmoss@werc.org

Historical Note
A professional society for warehousing executives and managers. Works to improve warehousing through education and research. Membership: $265/year.

Meetings/Conferences:
Annual Meetings: Spring
2007 - Nashville, TN(Gaylord Opryland)/Apr. 22-25/1200

Publications:
WERC Watch Report. 3/year.
WERCSHEET. m.
Membership Directory. a.

Waste Equipment Technology Association *(1972)*
4301 Connecticut Ave. NW
Suite 300
Washington, DC 20008-2403
Tel: (202)244-4700 *Fax:* (202)966-4824
Toll Free: (800)424 - 2869
E-Mail: membership@envasns.org
Web Site: www.wastec.org
Members: 225 companies
Staff: 3
Annual Budget: $500-1,000,000
Executive Vice President: Gary T. Satterfield
E-Mail: garys@envasns.org
Director, Member Services: Christine Henderson

Historical Note
A constituent group of Environmental Industry Associations, WASTEC represents designers, manufacturers, distributors and consultants of technology and systems for the management of wastes and recycling. Membership: annual dues vary, based on revenue.

Meetings/Conferences:
Semi-annual Meetings: with the Environmental Industry Ass'ns

Publications:
WASTEC's Equipment Technology News. bi-m.
WASTEC Business Management Series. irreg.
Directory of Member Products and Services. a. adv.
Listing of WASTEC Rated Stationary Compactors. trien.
ANSI Z245 Series Standards. irreg.
WASTEC Recommended Practices Series. irreg.

Water and Sewer Distributors of America *(1979)*
100 N. 20th St.
Fourth Floor
Philadelphia, PA 19103
Tel: (215)564-3484 *Fax:* (215)963-9785
E-Mail: wasda@fernley.com
Web Site: www.wasda.org
Members: 125 companies
Staff: 2
Annual Budget: $100-250,000
Executive Director: Lindsay Groff

Historical Note
Members are distributors and manufacturers of products to the contractor, municipal water and sewer markets. Membership: $300-5,000/year (company).

Publications:
Directory. a. adv.
Connections Newsletter. q.

Water and Wastewater Equipment Manufacturers Association *(1908)*
Box 17402
Washington, DC 20041
Tel: (703)444-1777 *Fax:* (703)444-1779
Web Site: www.wwema.org
Members: 60 companies
Staff: 3
Annual Budget: $250-500,000
President: Dawn C. Kristof

Historical Note
Formerly Water and Sewage Works Manufacturers Association. Membership: $2,500-17,000/year (company).

Meetings/Conferences:
Annual Meetings: Fall

Publications:
WWEMA Washington Analysis. bi-m.

Water Environment Federation *(1928)*
601 Wythe St.
Alexandria, VA 22314-1994
Tel: (703)684-2400 *Fax:* (703)684-2492
Toll Free: (800)666 - 0206
E-Mail: csc@wef.org
Web Site: www.wef.org
Members: 36000 individuals
Staff: 87
Annual Budget: $10-25,000,000
Executive Director: William J. Bertera
Deputy Executive Director, Marketing and Business Development: Jack Benson
E-Mail: jbenson@wef.org
Director, Public Information: Lori Burkhammer
E-Mail: lburkhammer@wef.org
Director, Governance and Affiliate Development: Phyllis Eastman
E-Mail: peastman@wef.org
Program Director, Conferences: Pam Henry
Program Director, Conference Programs: Susan Merther
E-Mail: smerther@wef.org
Chief Financial Officer: Mike Nutter
E-Mail: mnutter@wef.org
Deputy Director, Administration: Timothy Ricker
E-Mail: tricker@wef.org
Program Director, Journals and Books: Berinda Ross
E-Mail: bross@wef.org
Program Director, Exhibitions: Nanette Tucker
E-Mail: ntucker@wef.org
Director, Government Affairs: Timothy S. Williams
E-Mail: twilliams@wef.org

Historical Note
The Water Environment Federation is a not-for-profit technical and educational organization that was founded in 1928. Its mission is to preserve and enhance the global water environment. Federation members are water quality specialists from around the world, including environmental, civil and chemical engineers, biologists, chemists, government officials, treatment plant managers and operators, laboratory technicians, college professors, researchers, students and equipment manufacturers and distributors. WEF has an annual budget of approximately $20 million. Has a second web site at http://www.weftec.org

Meetings/Conferences:
Annual Meetings: Fall/14,000
2007 - San Diego, CA(Convention Center)/Oct. 13-17

Publications:
Industrial Wastewater. bi-m. adv.
Water Environment Laboratory Solutions. bi-m.
Water Environment Regulation Watch. m.
Water Environment Research. bi-m. adv.
Utility Executive. bi-m.
Watershed and Wet Weather Technical Bulletin. q.

Biosolids Technical Bulletin. bi-m.
Water Environment & Technology. m. adv.
Federation Highlights. m.

Water Equipment Wholesalers and Suppliers Association *(1960)*

Historical Note
A division of the National Ground Water Association.

Water Quality Association *(1974)*
4151 Naperville Road
Lisle, IL 60532
Tel: (630)505-0160 *Fax:* (630)505-9637
E-Mail: info@wqa.org
Web Site: www.wqa.org
Members: 2500 companies
Staff: 31
Annual Budget: $2-5,000,000
Executive Director: Peter Censky
Senior Meeting Planner: Jeannine Collins, CMP
Communications Manager and Executive Editor: John Ferguson
Director, Membership and Marketing: Margit Fotre
Controller: Wayne H. Jorgensen, CPA

Historical Note
Merger of the Water Conditioning Association International (1945) and the Water Conditioning Foundation (1948). A not-for-profit international trade association representing firms and individuals engaged in the design, manufacture, production, distribution, and sale of equipment, products, supplies and services for providing quality water for specific uses in residential, commercial, industrial and institutional establishments. Membership is voluntary. The Water Quality Research Foundation, formerly (1971) the Water Conditioning Research Council, is its research and educational arm.

Meetings/Conferences:
Annual Meetings: March

Publications:
WQA Newsletter. bi-m.

Water Sports Industry Association *(1977)*
P.O. Box 568512
Orlando, FL 32856-8512
Tel: (407)251-9039
E-Mail: wsiaheadquarters@earthlink.net
Web Site: www.watersportsindustry.com
Members: 200 companies
Staff: 2
Annual Budget: $100-250,000
Executive Director: Larry Meddock
E-Mail: wsiaheadquarters@earthlink.net

Historical Note
Founded as Water Ski Industry Association. WSIA members are leading manufacturers, dealers and sales representatives of water sports. Works to promote the sport through activities such as International Novice Water Ski Tour sponsor (grassroots fun tournaments), national public relations programs promoting water sports and water recreation through print media, radio and television, publications, awards, market research and Census of Sales Reports, and other sports education and warning announcements. Incorporated in the State of Florida.

Meetings/Conferences:
Annual Meetings: September, at WaterSki/Wakeboard Expo
2007 – Park City, UT(The Lodge at Mountainside--David Holland's)/Feb. 25-27/200

Publications:
Water Sports Retailer. 8/yr. adv.

Water Systems Council *(1932)*
1101 30th St. NW
Suite 500
Washington, DC 20007
Tel: (202)625-4387 *Fax:* (202)625-4363
Toll Free: (888)395 - 1033
E-Mail: wsc@watersystemscouncil.org
Web Site: www.watersystemscouncil.org
Members: 61 companies
Staff: 2
Annual Budget: $250-500,000
Executive Director: Kathleen Stanley
Director, Member Services: Kathryn Auth
Coordinator, Publications and Training Events: Lauri Rice

Historical Note
Formerly the National Association of Domestic and Farm Pump Manufacturers. Members are manufacturers and distributors of pumps, component products and accessories for private water systems (wells) for residential and agricultural applications. Membership: $350/year (distributors); membership dues for manufacturers based on sales volume.

Meetings/Conferences:
Semi-annual Meetings: Spring and Fall

Publications:
Well Connected Newsletter. q.

WaterJet Technology Association *(1983)*
906 Olive St., Suite 1200
St. Louis, MO 63101-1434
Tel: (314)241-1445 *Fax:* (314)241-1449
E-Mail: wjta@wjta.org
Web Site: www.wjta.org
Members: 850 individuals
Annual Budget: $100-250,000
Manager: Mark S. Birenbaum, Ph.D.

Historical Note
Created in 1983 by members of the water jetting industry acting in concert with university faculty and government officials to provide a means of service, communication, and education within the rapidly developing industry of water jet technology. Members include leading researchers, manufacturers, and users of water jet technology. Membership: $60/year (individual); $400/year (company).

Meetings/Conferences:
Biennial Meetings: Summer
2007 – Houston, TX(Marriott Westchase)/Aug. 19-21

Publications:
Jet News. bi-m. adv.
Proceedings of the American Water Jet Conference. bien.

Waterproofing Contractors Association *(1971)*
8608 Timberwind Dr.
Raleigh, NC 27615
Tel: (919)870-6923
E-Mail: mail@thewaterproofers.org
Web Site: www.thewaterproofers.org
Members: 60 firms
Staff: 1
Annual Budget: $25-50,000
Executive Director: Kelly Andrews

Historical Note
Founded as a regional association, WCA now provides representation and other benefits to member contractors around the country. Membership: $175/year (organization)

Meetings/Conferences:
Annual Meetings: September

Publications:
Membership Directory. a. adv.
Newsletter. q. adv.

Weather Modification Association *(1951)*
P.O. Box 26926
Fresno, CA 93729-6926
Tel: (559)434-3486
Web Site: www.weathermodification.org
Members: 200 individuals
Staff: 1
Annual Budget: under $10,000
Executive Secretary: Hilda Duckering

Historical Note
Formerly (1967) Weather Control Research Association.

Meetings/Conferences:
Annual Meetings: Spring

Publications:
Journal of Weather Modification. a.

Web Printing Association *(1978)*

Historical Note
An affiliate of Printing Industries of America, which provides administtrative support.

Web Sling and Tiedown Association *(1973)*
2105 Laurel Bush Road, Suite 200
Bel Air, MD 21015
Tel: (443)640-1070 *Fax:* (443)640-1031
E-Mail: wstda@ksgroup.org
Web Site: www.wstda.com
Members: 90 companies
Staff: 3
Annual Budget: $100-250,000
Executive Director: Fred C. Stringfellow

Historical Note
Members are manufacturers of web slings which are used as hoists in various industrial lifting operations and web tiedowns used in cargo control trucking operations. Formerly (1988) the Web Sling Association. Membership: $500-2,200/year.

Meetings/Conferences:
Annual Meetings: Spring
2007 – Scottsdale, AZ(Doubletree Paradise Valley)/May 6-9/80

Publications:
Uplifting News. semi-a. adv.

WEB: Worldwide Employee Benefits Network *(1982)*
1700 Pennsylvania Ave. NW
Suite 400
Washington, DC 20006
Toll Free: (888)795 - 6862
E-Mail: info@webnetwork.org
Web Site: www.webnetwork.org
Members: 1900 individuals
Staff: 3
Annual Budget: $250-500,000
Administrator: Sherlynn Hendershot

Historical Note
WEB members are benefits professionals including human resource managers, plan administrators, attorneys, consultants and actuaries. WEB provides education and networking opportunities. Membership: $125/year.

Meetings/Conferences:
Quarterly Meetings:

Publications:
WEB Network. 10/year.
JobBank. m.
Membership Directory. a.

Wedding and Event Videographers Association International *(1994)*
8499 S. Tamiami Trail #208
Sarasota, FL 34238
Tel: (941)923-5334 *Fax:* (941)921-3836
E-Mail: info@weva.com
Web Site: www.weva.com
Chairman: Roy Chapman
E-Mail: rc@weva.com

Historical Note
WEVA members are professional wedding and event videogaphers.

Publications:
Wedding & Event Videograpy. q. adv.

Wedding and Portrait Photographers International *(1974)*
1312 Lincoln Blvd.
P.O. Box 2003
Santa Monica, CA 90406
Tel: (310)451-0090 *Fax:* (310)395-9058
E-Mail: bhurter@rfpublishing.com
Web Site: www.wppinow.com
Members: 3500 individuals
Staff: 17
Annual Budget: $250-500,000
Chief Executive Officer: Steve Sheanin
E-Mail: ssheanin@rfpublishing.com
President: Skip Cohen
Contact: Bill Hurter
E-Mail: bhurter@rfpublishing.com

Historical Note
Formerly Wedding Photographers of America and Wedding Photographers International, WPPI assumed its present name in 1995. Promotes high artistic and technical standards; serves as a forum for the exchange of knowledge and experience; and offers instruction in techniques, advertising, sales, promotion, marketing, public relations, accounting, management and tax planning. Membership: $75/year.

Meetings/Conferences:
Annual Meetings: February-March
Publications:
WPPI Photography Monthly Newsletter. m.
Rangefinder. m. adv.

Weed Science Society of America *(1953)*
P.O. Box 7050
Lawrence, KS 66044
Tel: (785)843-1235 *Fax:* (785)843-1274
Toll Free: (800)627 - 0629
E-Mail: wssa@allenpress.com
Web Site: www.wssa.net
Members: 2000 individuals
Annual Budget: $500-1,000,000
Executive Secretary: Joyce Lancaster
E-Mail: wssa@allenpress.com
Historical Note
Founded as the Weed Society of America, it absorbed the Association of Regional Weed Control Conferences in 1956 and assumed its present name in 1963. Has members from the U.S., Mexico, overseas, and Canada. Membership: $75/year (individual); $139/year (organization/company).
Meetings/Conferences:
Annual Meetings: February
Publications:
Weed Science. bi-m.
Weed Technology. q. adv.

Welding Research Council *(1935)*
P.O. Box 1942
New York, NY 10156
Tel: (216)658-3847 *Fax:* (216)658-3854
E-Mail: wrc@forengineers.org
Web Site: www.forengineers.org/wrc/
Members: 300 organizations
Staff: 4
Annual Budget: $2-5,000,000
Executive Director: Martin Prager, Ph.D.
Historical Note
Established by the Engineering Foundation to conduct and coordinate welding research. Membership: $1,250/year (domestic); $1,320/year (international).
Meetings/Conferences:
Annual Meetings: Not held
Publications:
Reports of Progress. bi-m.
WRC Bulletin. 10/year.
Welding Research Abroad. 10/year.
Welding Research News. q.
Welding Research Supplement. m.

Wellness Councils of America *(1985)*
9802 Nicholas St., Suite 315
Omaha, NE 68114-2106
Tel: (402)827-3590 *Fax:* (402)827-3594
E-Mail: wellworkplace@welcoa.org
Web Site: www.welcoa.org
Members: 3000 individuals
Staff: 5
President: Dr. David M. Hunnicutt
Historical Note
WELCOA is dedicated to promoting healthier lifestyles for all Americans, especially through health promotion activities at the workplace. Membership: varies depending on local membership status.
Meetings/Conferences:
Annual Meetings: Fall
Publications:
Well Workplace Newsletter. m.

Welsh Pony and Cob Society of America *(1906)*
P.O. Box 2977
Winchester, VA 22604
Tel: (540)667-6195 *Fax:* (540)667-3766
E-Mail: wpcsa@crosslink.net
Web Site: www.welshpony.org
Members: 1800 individuals
Staff: 5
Annual Budget: $100-250,000
Executive Secretary-Treasurer: Lisa L. Landis
E-Mail: wpcsa@crosslink.net
Historical Note
Founded as the Welsh Pony and Cob Society of America in Illinois in 1906; reinstituted after a period of inactivity in Indiana in 1946 as Welsh Pony Society of America; reassumed its original name in 1986. Membership: $30/year (individual); $40/year (organization/company).
Publications:
Member-Breeder Directory. irreg.
Welsh Pony Review. q. adv.
Welsh Pony Studbook. irreg.
Nat'l Welsh Pony Yearbook. a. adv.

Western Association for Art Conservation *(1975)*
c/o Balboa Art Conservation Center
P.O. Box 3755
San Diego, CA 92163-1755
Tel: (619)239-9702 *Fax:* (619)236-0141
E-Mail: lxs2002@hotmail.com
Web Site: http://palimpsest.stanford.edu/waac/
Members: 500 individuals
Annual Budget: $25-50,000
Secretary: Alexis Miller
Historical Note
WAAC members are art conservators, restorers and related professionals. Formerly (1977) Western Association of Art Conservators. Membership: $30/year (individual); $35/year (U.S. institution).
Meetings/Conferences:
Annual Meetings: Fall
Publications:
Membership Directory. a.
WAAC Newsletter. 3/yr.

Western Dredging Association *(1979)*
P.O. Box 5797
Vancouver, WA 98668-5797
Tel: (360)750-0209 *Fax:* (360)750-1445
E-Mail: weda@comcast.net
Web Site: www.westerndredging.org
Members: 3000 individuals
Annual Budget: $50-100,000
Executive Director: Lawrence M. Patella
E-Mail: weda@comcast.net
Historical Note
A non-profit organization encouraging growth and education in the fields of dredging, navigation and marine engineering. WEDA is a regional organization covering North, Central and South America and, in addition to the Central Dredging Association (CEDA) and the Eastern Dredging Association (EADA), constitutes the World Organization of Dredging Associations (WODA). World Dredging Conferences (WODCONs) with representatives from WEDA, CEDA, and EADA are held every three years in addition to the annual WEDA general meetings. Has no paid staff. Membership fee: $50/year (regular); $15/year (student); $250/year (organization).
Meetings/Conferences:
Annual Meetings: May/150
Publications:
Directory. a.
Newsletter. q.
Proceedings of Technical Papers. a.

Western Economic Association International *(1922)*
7400 Center Ave., Suite 109
Huntington Beach, CA 92647-3039
Tel: (714)898-3222 *Fax:* (714)891-6715
E-Mail: info@weainternational.org
Web Site: www.weainternational.org
Members: 1800 individuals
Staff: 3
Annual Budget: $250-500,000
Executive Vice President: Anil K. Puri
E-Mail: anil.puri@weainternational.org
Historical Note
WEAI is a non-profit educational organization which seeks to promote mutually beneficial exchange of ideas between economists in academia and those working in government and business. WEAI strives to communicate economic knowledge outside the profession. Members are individuals, corporations, universities, and other organizations. Membership: $60/year.
Meetings/Conferences:
Annual Meetings: Summer
Publications:
Contemporary Economic Policy. q. adv.
Economic Inquiry. q. adv.
Conference Program. a. adv.

Western History Association *(1961)*
MSC06 3370
One University of New Mexico
Albuquerque, NM 87131-0001
Tel: (505)277-5234 *Fax:* (505)277-5275
E-Mail: wha@unm.edu
Web Site: www.unm.edu/~wha
Members: 1900 individuals
Staff: 2
Annual Budget: $250-500,000
Executive Director: Paul Andrew Hutton
E-Mail: wha@unm.edu
Historical Note
WHA members are academic historians and others with an interest in the history of the American West. Membership: $55/year (individual); $150/year (institution); $20/year (student).
Meetings/Conferences:
Annual Meetings: October
Publications:
Montana, The Magazine of Western History. q.
Western Historical Quarterly Journal. q. adv.
WHA Newsletter. semi-a. adv.

Western Literature Association *(1966)*
3200 Old Main Hill
Utah State Univ.
Logan, UT 84322-3200
Tel: (435)797-1603 *Fax:* (435)797-4099
E-Mail: wal@cc.usu.edu
Web Site: www.usu.edu/westlit/
Members: 600 individuals
Staff: 3
Annual Budget: $25-50,000
Editor: Melody Graulich
Historical Note
WLA members are scholars and others with an interest in western regional literary genre. Membership: $30/year (individual).
Meetings/Conferences:
Annual Meetings: Fall
2007 – Tacoma, WA
2008 – Boulder, CO
Publications:
Western American Literature. q. adv.

Western Music Association *(1988)*
3342 Cedarhill Dr.
San Angelo, TX 76904
Toll Free: (877)588 - 3747
E-Mail: rogerbanks@cox.net
Web Site: www.westernmusic.org
Members: 1000 individuals
Staff: 1
Annual Budget: $50-100,000
Executive Director: Roger Banks
E-Mail: rogerbanks@cox.net
Director, Events: Rick Huff
Historical Note
WMA is dedicated to preserving and advancing the history, literature and performance of western music. Members are western music afficionados and performers. Membership: $50-1000/year.
Publications:
The Western Way. q. adv.

Western Red Cedar Pole Association *(2000)*
2405 61st Ave. SE
Mercer Island, WA 98040
Toll Free: (800)410 - 1917
E-Mail: info@wrcpa.org
Web Site: www.wrcpa.org
Members: 7 companies
Staff: 1
Annual Budget: under $10,000
Publisher: Dean Matthews
E-Mail: info@wrcpa.org
Meetings/Conferences:
Annual Meetings: June
Publications:
Cedar Pole News. 2/year.

Western Red Cedar Lumber Association *(1954)*

1501-700 West Pender St.
Pender Place One, Business Building
Vancouver, BC V6C 1-GB
Tel: (604)684-0266 *Fax:* (604)687-4930
Toll Free: (877)852 - 3757
E-Mail: lang@wrcla.org
Web Site: www.wrcla.org
Members: 19 companies
Staff: 5
Annual Budget: $1-2,000,000
General Manager: Peter Lang
E-Mail: lang@wrcla.org

Meetings/Conferences:
Annual Meetings: Summer

Publications:
Cedar Scene. q.
Buyer's Guide. a.

Western Writers of America *(1953)*
1012 Fair St.
Franklin, TN 37064
Tel: (615)791-1444
Web Site: www.westernwriters.org
Members: 630 individuals
Staff: 2
Annual Budget: $50-100,000,000
Executive Director: James A. Crutchfield

Historical Note
WWA is an organization of professional writers devoted to the literature, history, and culture of the American West. Bestows the Spur Award for achievement in the field.

Meetings/Conferences:
Annual Meetings: Summer
2007 - Scottsdale, AZ/June
2008 - Taos, NM/June

Publications:
Roundup Magazine. 6/year. adv.

Western-English Trade Association *(1963)*
451 E. 58th Ave., Suite 4323
Denver, CO 80216-8468
Tel: (303)295-2001 *Fax:* (303)295-6108
E-Mail: weta@netway.net
Web Site: www.wetaonline.com
Members: 148 companies
Staff: 1
Annual Budget: $100-250,000
Executive Director: Glenda Chipps
E-Mail: weta@netway.net

Historical Note
Founded as Western and English Apparel and Equipment Manufacturers Association; became Western and English Manufacturers Association in 1976 and assumed its current name in 2002. Members are manufacturers and retailers of Western and English style riding equipment and clothes.

Meetings/Conferences:
Annual Meetings: Summer/125

Publications:
WAEMA Watch. q.

Wheat Quality Council *(1938)*
PO Box 966
Pierre, SD 57501-0966
Tel: (605)224-5187 *Fax:* (605)224-0517
Web Site: www.wheatqualitycouncil.org
Members: 125 organizations
Staff: 2
Annual Budget: $250-500,000
Executive Vice President: Ben Handcock

Historical Note
Established as the Kansas Wheat Improvemnt Association; assumed its present name in 1980. A not-for-profit organization of agri-business groups that invest in continuing wheat quality improvement. Membership: $100-12,000/year.

Meetings/Conferences:
Annual Meetings: Winter
2007 - Kansas City, MO(Embassy Suites)/Feb. 20-22/150

White House Correspondents Association *(1914)*
1920 N St. NW
Suite 300
Washington, DC 20036
Tel: (202)452-4836
Web Site: www.whca.net
Members: 600 individuals
Annual Budget: $100-250,000
Executive Director: Julie Whiston

Historical Note
Established in February, 1914. Members are media reporters assigned to coverage of Presidential political news. Has no paid officers or full-time staff.

Meetings/Conferences:
Annual Meetings: Washington, DC/Spring

White House News Photographers Association *(1921)*
P.O. Box 7119, Ben Franklin Stn.
Washington, DC 20044-7119
Tel: (202)785-5230
E-Mail: info@whnpa.org
Web Site: www.whnpa.org
Members: 525 individuals
Staff: 11
Annual Budget: $250-500,000
President: Susan Walsh
E-Mail: info@whnpa.org

Historical Note
Founded in June 1921 with 24 charter members, membership is limited to photojournalists who regularly cover the White House and Washington Metropolitan area for local and network TV and local and national newspapers and magazines. Annual events include a Photo Contest, professional seminars, worldwide Photo Exhibit, high school seminar, and an awards dinner honoring the President of the United States. Membership: $75/year (individual).

Meetings/Conferences:
Annual Meetings: Dinner in Washington, DC.

Publications:
The White House News Photographer Awards Book. a. adv.
Photo-Op. 4-6/year. adv.

Wholesale Beer Association Executives of America *(1946)*
1101 Livingston Ave.
Charleston, WV 25302-1030
Tel: (304)343-8514 *Fax:* (304)342-3983
Members: 43 individuals
Treasurer: Armilda Perry

Historical Note
Formerly (1946) National Association of State Beer Association Secretaries, (1977) State Beer Association of Executives of America. Members are executives of state beer distributor associations. Has no paid officers or full-time staff; officers change annually. Membership: $125/year (individual).

Meetings/Conferences:
Annual Meetings: Fall

Publications:
WBAE Directory. bi-a.

Wholesale Florist and Florist Supplier Association *(1926)*
147 Old Solomons Island Road, Suite 302
Annapolis, MD 21401
Tel: (410)573-0400 *Fax:* (410)573-5001
Toll Free: (888)289 - 3372
E-Mail: info@wffsa.org
Web Site: www.wffsa.org
Members: 700 companies
Staff: 6
Executive Vice President and Chief Executive Officer: James Wanko
E-Mail: jwanko@wffsa.org
Director, Education and Meetings: Tina Brown
E-Mail: tbrown@wffsa.org
Director, Membership Services: Ken Hess
E-Mail: khess@wffsa.org

Historical Note
Until 1961 known as the Wholesale Commission Florists of America. Membership: $495-995/year (company).

Meetings/Conferences:
Annual Meetings: Spring/450
2007 - Phoenix, AZ(Hyatt Regency)/Feb. 21-24
2008 - Tampa, FL(Marriott Waterside)/March 5-8/900

Publications:
Membership Directory. a. adv.

WIFS - Women in Insurance and Financial Services *(1939)*
6748 Wauconda Dr.
Larkspur, CO 80118
Tel: (303)681-9777 *Fax:* (303)681-3221
Toll Free: (866)264 - 9437
E-Mail: wifsmanagement@aol.com
Web Site: www.w-wifs.org
Members: 500 individuals
Staff: 2
Annual Budget: $100-250,000
Executive Director: Judi Chase
E-Mail: wifsmanagement@aol.com

Historical Note
Formerly (1987) Women Life Underwriters Conference and (2000) WLUC - Women in Insurance and Financial Services. Membership: $100/year (individual); $2,500-$25,000/year (company).

Meetings/Conferences:
Annual Meetings: Fall/150

Publications:
Newsletter. a. adv.
Directory. a. adv.

Wild Bird Feeding Institute *(1984)*
1305 N. Tahoe Trail
Sioux Falls, SD 57110
Toll Free: (888)839 - 1237
E-Mail: info@wbfi.org
Web Site: www.wbfi.org
Members: 157 companies
Staff: 3
Annual Budget: $50-100,000
Executive Director: Susan Hays
E-Mail: info@wbfi.org

Historical Note
Members are bird feeder manufacturing, seed packing, and processing companies and related brokers, distributors, retailers and suppliers. Organized primarily to promote the sales of bird feeding products.

Meetings/Conferences:
Semi-Annual Meetings: *Summer and Fall*

Publications:
WBFI Newsline. q.

Wild Blueberry Association of North America *(1981)*
P.O. Box 1130
Kennebunkport, ME 04046-1130
Tel: (207)967-5024 *Fax:* (207)967-5023
Toll Free: (800)233 - 9453
E-Mail: wildblueberries@gwi.net
Web Site: www.wildblueberries.com
Members: 75 individuals
Staff: 3
Annual Budget: $1-2,000,000
Executive Director: John M. Sauve
E-Mail: wildblueberries@gwi.net

Historical Note
An international trade/promotion association of producers and processors of wild blueberries from Maine and eastern Canada. Membership fee varies, based on production.

Meetings/Conferences:
Annual Meetings: Spring

Publications:
The Wild Times. q.

Wilderness Education Association *(1978)*
900 E. Seventh St.
Bloomington, IN 47405
Tel: (812)855-4095 *Fax:* (812)855-8697
E-Mail: wea@indiana.edu
Web Site: www.weainfo.org
Members: 350 individuals, 50 affilates
Staff: 3
Annual Budget: $50-100,000

Historical Note
WEA promotes wilderness safety through its standardized curriculum for wilderness interpreters,

park employees and other interested professionals. Membership: $75/year (individual); $250/year (organization/company); $35/year (student); $1000 (life-time)

Meetings/Conferences:
Annual Meetings: February

Publications:
Journal of the Wilderness Education Association. 3/yr. adv.
TABS (Trustees & Affiliates Briefing System). bi-m.
Proceedings of the Annual National Conference. a. adv.

Wilderness Medical Society *(1983)*
810 E. 10th St.
P.O. Box 1897
Lawrence, KS 66044
Toll Free: (800)627 - 0629
E-Mail: wms@wms.org
Web Site: www.wms.org
Members: 3800 individuals
Staff: 4
Annual Budget: $500-1,000,000
Executive Director: Joyce Lancaster
E-Mail: jlancaster@wms.org

Historical Note
Members are physicians, allied health specialists and other qualified individuals with an interest in wilderness medicine and the practice of the health sciences in wilderness environments. Membership: 150/year (individual).

Publications:
Wilderness and Environmental Medicine Journal. q. adv.
Wilderness Medicine Letter magazine. q. adv.

Wildlife Disease Association *(1951)*
P.O. Box 1897
Lawrence, KS 66044-8897
Tel: (785)843-1221 *Fax:* (785)843-1274
Toll Free: (800)627 - 0629
E-Mail: wda@allenpress.com
Web Site: www.wildlifedisease.org/
Members: 1000 individuals
Staff: 1
Annual Budget: $25-50,000
Business Manager: Scott Starr
E-Mail: wda@allenpress.com

Historical Note
Formed in March 1951 in Milwaukee, WI at the North American Wildlife Conference. Originally the Committee on Wildlife Diseases, the name was changed to the Wildlife Disease Association in 1952 and the association was incorporated in Illinois in 1964. Membership: $55/year (individual); $95/year (organization); $27.50/year (student).

Meetings/Conferences:
Annual Meetings: August

Publications:
Journal of Wildlife Diseases. q.
Newsletter. q.

Wildlife Management Institute *(1911)*
1146 19th St. NW
Suite 700
Washington, DC 20036
Tel: (202)371-1808
Web Site: www.wildlifemanagementinstitute.org
Members: 700 individuals
Staff: 15
Annual Budget: $1-2,000,000
President: Steven A. Williams
Executive Vice President: Richard E. McCabe

Historical Note
Incorporated as WMI in New York in 1946; the programs of the Institute have been in existence under various names since 1911. Sponsors the annual North American Wildlife and Natural Resources Conference. Membership: $35/year (individual); variable (organization).

Meetings/Conferences:
Annual Meetings: Spring
2007 - Portland, OR(Portland Hilton and Towers)/March 20-24

Publications:
Outdoor News Bulletin. m.
Conference Transactions. a.

Wildlife Society, The *(1937)*
5410 Grosvenor Ln.
Suite 200
Bethesda, MD 20814-2144
Tel: (301)897-9770 *Fax:* (301)530-2471
E-Mail: tws@wildlife.org
Web Site: www.wildlife.org
Members: 9000 individuals
Staff: 12
Annual Budget: $1-2,000,000
Executive Director: Michael Hutchins, PhD
Program Director: Sandra Staples-Bortner

Historical Note
Originated in the District of Columbia in 1936 during the North American Wildlife Conference. Originally the Society of Wildlife Specialists, it became The Wildlife Society in 1937 and was incorporated in the District of Columbia in 1948. Member society of the Renewable Natural Resources Foundation. Membership: $64/year.

Meetings/Conferences:
Annual Meetings: September/October/1,500-2,200
2007 - Tucson, AZ(Tucson Convention Center)/Sept. 22-26/1500

Publications:
Wildlife Society Bulletin. q. adv.
Journal of Wildlife Management. q.
The Wildlifer. bi-m.

Window and Door Manufacturers Association *(1926)*
1400 E. Touhy Ave., Suite 470
Des Plaines, IL 60018-3305
Tel: (847)299-5200 *Fax:* (847)299-1286
Toll Free: (800)223 - 2301
E-Mail: admin@wdma.com
Web Site: www.wdma.com
Members: 150 companies
Staff: 10
Annual Budget: $2-5,000,000
President: Joel Hoiland

Historical Note
Founded as the National Door Manufacturers Association; became the National Woodwork Manufacturers Association, Inc. in 1950. In 1985 it became the National Wood Window and Door Association; assumed its current name in 1998. Absorbed the Ponderosa Pine Woodwork Association in 1975. Members are makers of standard building products such as doors, windows, and frames.

Meetings/Conferences:
Annual Meetings: Febraury/250
2007 - , HI(Fairmont Orchard)/Feb. 24-28

Publications:
WDMA Newsletter. m.
Membership Directory. a.

Window Council *(1958)*
2850 S. Ocean Blvd., Suite 114
Palm Beach, FL 33480-6205
Tel: (561)533-0991 *Fax:* (561)533-7466
Web Site: http://franksfitzgerald.com/
Members: 5 companies
Staff: 1
Annual Budget: under $10,000
President: Frank S. Fitzgerald, CAE, DABFE, FACFE

Historical Note
Organized to develop window safety programs for children.

Window Covering Safety Council *(1994)*
355 Lexington Ave., 17th Floor
New York, NY 10017-6603
Tel: (212)297-2122 *Fax:* (212)370-9047
Toll Free: (800)506 - 4636
Web Site: www.windowcoverings.org
Executive Director: Peter S. Rush

Window Coverings Association of America *(1987)*
2646 Hwy. 109, Suite 205
Grover, MO 63040
Tel: (636)273-4090 *Fax:* (636)273-4439
Toll Free: (888)298 - 9222
E-Mail: info@wcaa.org
Web Site: www.wcaa.org
Members: 1400 companies
Staff: 1
Annual Budget: $250-500,000
Executive Director: Mark Nortman
E-Mail: info@wcaa.org

Historical Note
Members are window covering retailers. WCAA was established to make available educational and motivational seminars, improve the decorating industry and encourage a code of ethics for fair business practices. Membership: $125/year (company).

Publications:
WCAA Cover Story Newsletter. bi-m. adv.
WCAA Membership Directory. a. adv.

Window Coverings Manufacturers Association *(1985)*
355 Lexington Ave., 17th Floor
New York, NY 10017-6603
Tel: (212)297-2122 *Fax:* (212)370-9047
Web Site: www.wcmanet.org
Members: 11 companies
Staff: 4
Executive Director: Carolynn Jennings

Historical Note
Originally the Venetian Blind Institute (1942); later became the Venetian Blind Association (1977); the United States Venetian Blind Association (1985); and then the American Window Coverings Manufacturers Association (1995). Represents manufacturers of hard window coverings.

Meetings/Conferences:
Annual Meetings: Spring

Publications:
American Nat'l Standard for Safety of Corded Window Products.

Wine and Spirits Shippers Association *(1976)*
11800 Sunrise Valley Dr., Suite 332
Reston, VA 20191-5396
Tel: (703)860-2300 *Fax:* (703)860-2422
E-Mail: info@wssa.com
Web Site: www.wssa.com
Members: 500 companies
Staff: 12
Annual Budget: $1-2,000,000
Managing Director: Geoffrey N. Giovanetti
E-Mail: ggiovanetti@wssa.com

Historical Note
WSSA is a non-profit shippers association composed of importers and exporters of beverages and allied products. The Association negotiates for preferential ocean freight rates for members and currently has contracts with 30 steamship lines. WSSA also arranges for transportation and cargo insurance for products shipped internationally. Membership: $100/year (company).

Publications:
WSSA Grapevine. q.

Wine and Spirits Wholesalers of America *(1943)*
805 15th St. NW, Suite 430
Washington, DC 20005-2203
Tel: (202)371-9792 *Fax:* (202)789-2405
Web Site: www.wswa.org
Members: 350 establishments
Staff: 17
Annual Budget: $5-10,000,000
President and Chief Executive Officer: Craig Wolf
Senior Vice President, Public Affairs and Communications: Karen G. Elliott
Senior Vice President, Government Affairs: James Rowland

Historical Note
WSWA members handle 90% of all wine and spirits sold in free market states. Sponsors and supports the Wine and Spirits Wholesalers of America Political Action Committee. Membership: $1,150-36,000/year (company).

Meetings/Conferences:
Annual Meetings: Spring/2,500
2007 - Orlando, FL(Swan & Dolphin Hotel)/Apr. 28-May 2

Publications:
Last Call (email).

WSWA Membership Roster and Industry Directory. a. adv.

WineAmerica *(1978)*
1212 New York Ave. NW
Suite 425
Washington, DC 20005
Tel: (202)783-2756 *Fax:* (202)347-6341
Toll Free: (800)879 - 4537
E-Mail: info@wineamerica.org
Web Site: www.wineamerica.org
Members: 824 wineries
Staff: 5
Director, Communications/Membership Services: Jenny Mattingley
E-Mail: info@wineamerica.org
President: Bill Nelson

Historical Note
Founded as Association of American Vintners; became American Vintners Association in 1992 and assumed its current name in 2002. Members are wine producers.

Meetings/Conferences:
Annual Meetings: 35-75

Publications:
Newsletter. m.

Wire and Cable Industry Suppliers Association *(1918)*
1867 W. Market St.
Akron, OH 44313
Tel: (330)864-2122 *Fax:* (330)864-5298
E-Mail: info@wcisa.org
Web Site: www.wcisa.org
Members: 100 companies
Staff: 1
Annual Budget: $25-50,000
Executive Director: Michael McNulty
E-Mail: info@wcisa.org

Historical Note
Founded as Wire Machinery Builders Association; became Wire Industry Suppliers Association in 1987, and assumed its current name in 2002. Membership: $350-750/year (company).

Meetings/Conferences:
Annual Meetings: Spring

Publications:
Exec. Newsletter. a.

Wire Association International *(1930)*
1570 Boston Post Rd., Box 578
Guilford, CT 06437-0578
Tel: (203)453-2777 *Fax:* (203)453-8384
E-Mail: sfetteroll@wirenet.org
Web Site: www.wirenet.org
Members: 2400
Staff: 16
Annual Budget: $5-10,000,000
Executive Director: Steven J. Fetteroll
E-Mail: sfetteroll@wirenet.org

Historical Note
Formerly (1977) the Wire Association Inc. Members are individuals involved in wire manufacturing, wire forming and fabricating and supplying the wire and cable industry. Membership: $95/year.

Meetings/Conferences:
Annual Meetings: Spring
2007 – Cleveland, OH(Cleveland I-X Center)/May 5-10/5000

Publications:
Wire Journal International. m. adv.
Wire Journal International Reference Guide. a. adv.

Wire Fabricators Association *(1976)*
710 E. Ogden Ave., Suite 600
Naperville, IL 60563-8614
Tel: (630)579-3278 *Fax:* (630)369-2488
Members: 45 companies
Staff: 5
Executive Director: Amy Hannon

Historical Note
Members are manufacturers of items composed principally of low carbon steel wire. Membership: $300-500/year (company, based on number of employees).

Meetings/Conferences:
Annual Meetings: Winter

Wire Reinforcement Institute *(1930)*
942 Main St., Suite 300
Hartford, CT 06103
Toll Free: (800)552 - 4974
E-Mail: admin@wirereinforcementinstitute.org
Web Site: www.wirereinforcementinstitute.org
Members: 22 companies
Staff: 1
Annual Budget: $100-250,000
Marketing Consultant: Terri Albert
E-Mail: admin@wirereinforcementinstitute.org

Historical Note
Members produce welded wire reinforcement for reinformed concrete and construction precast components according to the standards and specification of the American Society for Testing and Materials, and the American Concrete Institute.

Meetings/Conferences:
Semi-Annual Meetings: Spring and Fall

Publications:
Membership Listing.
Best Sellers Publications Listing.

Wire Rope Technical Board *(1959)*
801 N. Fairfax St., Suite 211
Alexandria, VA 22314-1757
Tel: (703)299-8550 *Fax:* (703)299-9233
E-Mail: wrtb@usa.net
Web Site: www.domesticwirerope.com/wrtb
Members: 8 companies
Staff: 2
Annual Budget: $50-100,000
Executive Director: Kimberly A. Korbel

Meetings/Conferences:
Annual Meetings: June/November

Wire Service Guild *(1958)*
1501 Broadway, Suite 708
New York, NY 10036
Tel: (212)869-9290 *Fax:* (212)840-0687
E-Mail: union@newsmediaguild.org
Web Site: www.wsg.org
Members: 1000 individuals
Staff: 3
Administrator: Kevin Keane
E-Mail: union@newsmediaguild.org

Historical Note
Labor union representing editorial and commercial department employees of two wire services, Associated Press and United Press International. An affiliate of the Newspaper Guild.

Publications:
WiReport Newsletter. m.

Wirebound Box Manufacturers Association *(1907)*
P.O. Box 531335
Mountain Brook, IN 35253-1335
Tel: (205)823-3448 *Fax:* (205)823-3449
E-Mail: hrushing@usit.net
Web Site: www.wireboundbox.com
Members: 8 companies
Staff: 1
Annual Budget: $100-250,000
Executive Vice President: Hugh J. Rushing

Historical Note
Manufacturers of wirebound boxes and crates designed to ship meat, poultry, fruit and vegetables. Dissolved in 2004.

Meetings/Conferences:
Semi-annual Meetings: Spring and Fall

Publications:
Directory of the Wirebound Box Industry. a.

Wireless Communications Association International *(1988)*
1333 H St. NW
Suite 700W
Washington, DC 20005
Tel: (202)452-7823 *Fax:* (202)452-0041
Web Site: www.wcai.com
Members: 250 companies
Staff: 7
Annual Budget: $2-5,000,000
President and Chief Executive Officer: Andrew T. Kreig
E-Mail: president@wcai.com
Events and Programs Coordinator: Meredith Cicerchia
Controller: Rose DiMartino
E-Mail: rose@wcai.com
Office Manager: Soraya Fuentes
Director, International Affairs: Horacio A Oyhanarte
Communications Director: Susan Polyakova
Director, Web and IT Services: Angela Wagner

Historical Note
Founded in 1988, the WCA is the world's principal non-profit trade association representing the wireless broadband industry. The WCA's mission is to foster the growth of such services, including voice, data, Internet, e-commerce and video applications. WCA's membership of 250 companies is comprised of the industry's leading carriers, vendors and consultants from six continents.

Meetings/Conferences:
2007 – San Jose, CA(Fairmont Hotel)/Jan. 14-19/1900
2007 – Washington, DC(Omni Sheraton Hotel)/June 11-14/1800

Publications:
Weekly Member Bulletin. w. adv.

Wireless Dealers Association *(1986)*
9746 Tappenbeck Dr.
Houston, TX 77055
Tel: (713)467-0077
Toll Free: (800)624 - 6918
E-Mail: contact@wirelessindustry.com
Web Site: www.wirelessindustry.com
Members: 2500 locations
Staff: 36
Annual Budget: $500-1,000,000
President: Bob Hutchinson
E-Mail: contact@wirelessindustry.com

Historical Note
Founded as National Association of Cellular Agents; assumed its current name in 1996. Business association made up of cellular and wireless communications agents, dealers, resellers, carriers, manufacturers, distributors and importers. Membership: $395-$15,000/year (company).

Meetings/Conferences:
Annual Meetings: October/November

Publications:
Wireless Review.
Wireless Week.
Twice Magazine.
Cellular & Mobile International.
Interactive Weekly.
Mobile Radio Technology.
RCR Magazine.
RF Design.

Wiring Harness Manufacturers Association *(1993)*
7500 Flying Cloud Dr., Suite 900
Eden Prairie, MN 55344
Tel: (952)253-6225 *Fax:* (952)835-4774
E-Mail: whma@whma.org
Web Site: www.whma.org
Members: 200 companies
Staff: 3
Executive Director: Jim Manke, CAE

Historical Note
WHMA represents the interests and concerns of over 100 U.S. and Canadian manufacturers of electronic cable assemblies, cord sets and wiring harnesses, and over 50 suppliers to this industry.

Meetings/Conferences:
Semi-Annual Meetings: Spring and Fall

Publications:
Wiring Harness News. bi-m.

Women Band Directors International *(1969)*
345 Overlook Dr.
West Lafayette, IN 47906
Tel: (765)463-1738
Web Site: www.WomenBandDirectors.org
Members: 355 individuals
Staff: 1
Annual Budget: under $10,000
Executive Secretary: Gladys Stone Wright

E-Mail: agwright@gte.net

Historical Note

Chartered in 1969 as Women Band Directors National Association; assumed current name in 1997. WBDI's active members are women engaged in directing bands and women who have been directors but are not presently so engaged. Membership: $25/year (individual); $50/year (company).

Publications:

Band World Magazine. 5/year. adv.
Woman Conductor Journal. 3/year. adv.
Women and Music: A Journal of Gender and Culture.
Newsletter. q.
WBDNA Directory. a.

Women Chefs and Restaurateurs *(1993)*

304 W. Liberty St., Suite 201
Louisville, KY 40202-3011
Tel: (502)581-0300 *Fax:* (502)589-3602
Toll Free: (877)927 - 7787
E-Mail: wcr@hqtrs.com
Web Site: www.womenchefs.org
Members: 2000 individuals
Staff: 3
Annual Budget: $250-500,000
Executive Director: Lieann O'Brien

Historical Note

Founded as International Association of Women Chefs and Restaurateurs; assumed its current name in 1997. WCR is a trade association for women employed in the restaurant industry. Its mission is to promote the education and advancement of women in the restaurant industry. Membership: $175/year (executive); $85/year (professional); $50/year (student); $250/year (small business); $1,500/year (coprorate).

Meetings/Conferences:

Annual Meetings: always New York, NY/Spring/300

Publications:

Entrez Newsletter. q.

Women Construction Owners and Executives, USA *(1984)*

4401A Connecticut Ave. NW
Washington, DC 20008
Toll Free: (800)788 - 3548
E-Mail: wcoeusa@aol.com
Web Site: www.wcoeusa.org
Members: 100 individuals
Staff: 1
Annual Budget: $50-100,000
National President: Ida Brooker

Historical Note

Members are women who seek to promote the role of women business enterprises in the construction industry. WCOE also seeks to provide resources for members to enhance their professional development, to create a legislative network to monitor and pursue legislation advantageous to the business community. Membership: $200-250/year, plus chapter dues.

Meetings/Conferences:

Semi-annual Meetings: Spring and Fall

Publications:

The Turning Point. m. adv.

Women Executives in Public Relations *(1946)*

P.O. Box 7657, FDR Stn.
New York, NY 10150-7657
Tel: (212)859-7375
E-Mail: info@wepr.org
Web Site: www.wepr.org
Members: 125 individuals
Annual Budget: $25-50,000
Administrator: Barbara Coen

Historical Note

WEPR members are women and men senior executives with an interest in the professional advancement of women in the public relations field. Membership: $150/year (individual).

Meetings/Conferences:

Monthly Meetings: September to June in New York City

Publications:

Network Newsletter. q.

Women Executives in State Government *(1983)*

167 W. Main St., Suite 600
Lexington, KY 40507
Tel: (859)514-9150 *Fax:* (859)514-9166
E-Mail: wesg@wesg.org
Web Site: www.wesg.org
Members: 280 individuals
Staff: 4
Annual Budget: $500-1,000,000
Executive Director: Tracy Tucker

Historical Note

Members are women serving in the statewide elected or cabinet-level appointed positions in the executive branch of state government. Membership: $495/year (full members); $295/year (associate); $95/year (alumnae).

Meetings/Conferences:

Annual Meetings: July-September

Publications:

Magazine. q.
WESG Membership Directory. a.
Annual Report. a.

Women in Aerospace *(1984)*

2200 Wilson Blvd.
Suite 102-248
Arlington, VA 22201
Tel: (703)522-7745 *Fax:* (703)522-4226
E-Mail: info@womeninaerospace.org
Web Site: www.womeninaerospace.org
Members: 300 individuals
Annual Budget: under $10,000
Contact Person: Mary Kelly
E-Mail: info@womeninaerospace.org

Historical Note

WIA, a professional society providing a formal network for women working in the aerospace field, is dedicated to expanding women's opportunities for career advancement and increasing their visibility as aerospace professionals. Members include journalists, industry executives, government officials and congressional staff. Membership: $35/year (individual); $500/year (organization/company).

Publications:

WIA Newsletter. m. adv.

Women in Agribusiness

P.O. Box 986
Kearney, MO 64060-0986
Tel: (816)898-0870 *Fax:* (816)459-8382
E-Mail: icevinlandusa@sbcglobal.net
Members: 150 individuals
Staff: 1
Annual Budget: under $10,000
President: Dolores Hamelin
E-Mail: icevinlandusa@sbcglobal.net

Historical Note

WIA was established to organize women in agribusiness and to provide a forum on subjects concerning the industry. Has no paid officers or full-time staff. Membership: $15/year (U.S.); $20/year (foreign).

Publications:

Women in Agribusiness Bulletin. q. adv.

Women in Aviation International *(1994)*

Morning Star Airport
3647 State Route 503 South
West Alexandria, OH 45387
Tel: (937)893-4647 *Fax:* (937)839-4645
Web Site: www.wai.org
Members: 6800 individuals
Staff: 6
Annual Budget: $1-2,000,000
President: Peggy Baty-Chabrian, Ph.D.
Contact: Sue Coon

Historical Note

WAI members include pilots, air traffic controllers, airport managers, engineers, flight attendants, and others with an internest in encouraging women to seek professional opportunites in aviation. Membership: $39/year (individual); $29/year (student); $400/year (corporate).

Meetings/Conferences:

Annual Meetings: March

Publications:

Aviation for Women Magazine. bi-m. adv.
Annual Conference Program. a. adv.

Women in Cable and Telecommunications *(1979)*

14555 Avlon Pkwy., Suite 250
Chantilly, VA 20151
Tel: (703)234-9810 *Fax:* (703)817-1595
E-Mail: information@wict.org
Web Site: www.wict.org
Members: 5300 individuals
Staff: 13
Annual Budget: $2-5,000,000
President and Chief Executive Officer: Benita Fitzgerald Mosley
E-Mail: information@wict.org
Vice President, Strategic Initiatives: Parthavi Das
E-Mail: pdas@wict.org
Vice President, Business Development: Robin Pearson
E-Mail: rpearson@wict.org
Director, Marketing and Communications: Tom Quash
E-Mail: tquash@wict.org
Associate Director, Membership and Chapter Relations: Robin Burke Zahory
E-Mail: rzahory@wict.org

Historical Note

Founded in 1979. Formerly (1994) Women in Cable. By educating women with professional goals, WICT provides opportunities for leadership, networking, and advocacy in the industry. Membership: $125/year; $200/year (executive); $50/year (entry).

Meetings/Conferences:

Annual Meetings: Annual

Publications:

Membership Directory. a. adv.
Insight Newsletter. q.
The Source. bi-m.

Women in Cell Biology *(1972)*

Historical Note

A committee of American Society for Cell Biology, which provides administrative support.

Women in Endocrinology *(1975)*

Division Pharm-Tox, A1915 Univ. of Texas
Austin, TX 78712
Tel: (512)471-3669 *Fax:* (512)471-5002
Web Site: www.women-in-endo.org/we.html
Members: 400 individuals
Secretary-Treasurer: Andrea C. Gore

Historical Note

Founded to help increase the visibility and participation by women in the acitvities of the Endocrine Society, and by extension the field of endocrinology. Provides travel grants and other services to members. Has no paid officers or full-time staff. Membership: $30/year (professional); $10/year (resident/post-doctoral).

Meetings/Conferences:

Annual Meetings: June/200

Publications:

Women in Endocrinology Newsletter. 3/year.

Women in Energy *(1978)*

P.O. Box 105252
Jefferson City, MO 65110-5252
Tel: (573)635-6448
Members: 50 individuals
Annual Budget: under $10,000
President: Judy Gustafson

Historical Note

Members are persons employed in energy and related energy businesses working in areas such as science, engineering, finance, consumer education, communications, home economics, etc. Membership: $50/year.

Meetings/Conferences:

Annual Meetings: September

Publications:

Women in Energy Newsletter. q. adv.

Women in Film *(1973)*

8857 W. Olympic Blvd., Suite 201
Beverly Hills, CA 90211
Tel: (310)657-5144 *Fax:* (310)657-5154
E-Mail: info@wif.org
Web Site: www.wif.org

Members: 2300 individuals
Staff: 5
Annual Budget: $250-500,000
Executive Director: Gayle Nachlis

Historical Note
WIF is a professional organization in the communications industry with the commitment to recognize, develop and actively promote the visions of women. General members of WIF must have a minimum of three years of professional experience in the executive, guild or craft areas of the industry. Membership: $100/year (individual).

Meetings/Conferences:
Semi-Annual Meetings: June and September

Publications:
Reel News Newsletter. bi-m. adv.

Women in Film and Video *(1979)*
1233 20th St. NW
Suite 401
Washington, DC 20036
Tel: (202)429-9438 *Fax:* (202)429-9440
E-Mail: membersip@wifv.org
Web Site: www.wifv.org
Members: 1,300 Members (D.C. Chapter)
Staff: 2
Annual Budget: $100-250,000
Executive Director: Melissa Houghton

Historical Note
WIFV members are women employed in film, television, video and electronic multi-media production. Comprises an international network of 40 chapters, representing over 10,000 individuals. Membership: $100/year (professional); $175/year (executive); $40/year (student).

Publications:
Membership Directory. a. adv.
Gala Program Book. a. adv.
Newsletter. m.

Women in Government *(1988)*
2600 Virginia Ave. NW
Suite 709
Washington, DC 20037-1905
Tel: (202)333-0825 *Fax:* (202)333-0875
E-Mail: wig@womeningovernment.org
Web Site: www.womeningovernment.org
Members: 136 individuals
Staff: 15
Annual Budget: $1-2,000,000
Executive Director and President: Susan Crosby
E-Mail: wig@womeningovernment.org

Historical Note
WIG members are women holding elected offices at the state levels.

Meetings/Conferences:
Regional Meetings: Various locations, Summer and Fall

Publications:
Newsletter. q.
Membership Directory. a.

Women in Government Relations *(1975)*
801 N. Fairfax St., Suite 211
Alexandria, VA 22314-1757
Tel: (703)299-8546 *Fax:* (703)299-9233
E-Mail: info@wgr.org
Web Site: www.wgr.org
Members: 600 individuals
Staff: 3
Annual Budget: $250-500,000
Senior Advisor: Kimberly A. Korbel
Executive Director: Emily M. Bardach
Membership and Events Coordinator: Andrea Korbel

Historical Note
An association of professionals in government relations dedicated to the professional and educational development of women in the field of government relations. Membership: $45-195/year (individual).

Meetings/Conferences:
Annual Meetings: Washington, DC in March or April

Publications:
WGR This Week. w.

Women in International Security *(1987)*
c/o Center for Peace and Security Studies, Georgetown Univ.
3600 N St. NW
Washington, DC 20007
Tel: (202)687-3366 *Fax:* (202)687-3233
E-Mail: wiisinfo@georgetown.edu
Web Site: http://wiis.georgetown.edu
Members: 1200 individuals
Staff: 4
Annual Budget: $500-1,000,000
Executive Director: Meaghan Keeler-Pettigrew

Historical Note
WIIS is dedicated to increasing the influence of women in the field of foreign and defense affairs and enhancing the dialogue on international security. Offers comprehensive programs designed to foster and promote women in government, business, think tanks, academia and the media. WIIS is a non-profit, nonpartisan, educational program. Membership: $30-1,000/year (individual); $250/year (non-profit institution); $5,000/year (corporate).

Publications:
WIIS Words. q.
Jobs Hotline. bi-m.

Women in Management *(1978)*
P.O. Box 1032
Dundee, IL 60118-7032
Tel: (847)946-6285 *Fax:* (847)683-3751
Toll Free: (877)946 - 6285
E-Mail: nationalwim@aol.com
Web Site: www.wimonline.org
Members: 850 individuals
Staff: 3
Annual Budget: $50-100,000
Administrator: Nancy Haines
E-Mail: nationalwim@aol.com

Historical Note
Members are professionals in corporate, academic, not-for-profit, government, or entrepreneurial sectors of management or are licensed, degreed professionals.

Publications:
National Directory. a. adv.
Memorandum. q. adv.

Women in Mining National *(1972)*
P.O. Box 260246
Lakewood, CO 80226-0246
Tel: (303)298-1535
E-Mail: wim@womeninmining.org
Web Site: www.womeninmining.org
Members: 600 individuals
Annual Budget: $10-25,000
Director, Membership: Karen Jass

Historical Note
WIM is a nationwide organization composed of individuals employed by, associated with, or interested in the mining industry. Membership: $30/year (individual).

Meetings/Conferences:
Annual Meetings: April

Publications:
Women in Mining - Nat'l Quarterly. q.
WIM-Membership Directory. a.

Women in Municipal Government *(1974)*

Historical Note
An affiliate of National League of Cities, which provides administrative support.

Women in Packaging *(1993)*
4290 Bells Ferry Rd.
Suite 106-17
Kennesaw, GA 30144-1300
Tel: (678)594-6872 *Fax:* (770)928-2338
E-Mail: wpstaff@womeninpackaging.org
Web Site: www.womeninpackaging.org
Members: 800 individuals
Chief People Packager: JoAnn R. Hines
Business Development Specialist: Gina Urgena

Historical Note
WP members are professionals employed at all levels in the packaging industry. Membership: $100/year (mentor); $80/year (individual); $35/year (student); $100-500/year, varies by annual sales and/or purchasing (corporate).

Publications:
Packaging Horizons. q.
Update Newsletter. bi-m.
Career Hotline. m.

Women In Production

Historical Note
Became Partnership in Print Production in 2003.

Women in Scholarly Publishing *(1979)*
c/o Coughlin Indexing Services, Inc.
1106 West St.
Annapolis, MD 21401
Tel: (410)269-0978
E-Mail: information@womeninscholarlypublishing.org
Web Site: www.womeninscholarlypublishing.org/
Members: 525 individuals
Annual Budget: under $10,000
President: Maria Coughlin
E-Mail: mariac@indexing.com

Historical Note
WISP is a non-profit feminist organization devoted to the education and professional advancement of its members. Supports the principles and goals of equity for women on all levels and in all areas of scholarly publishing. Has no paid officers or full-time staff. Membership: $10-40/year.

Meetings/Conferences:
Annual Meetings: Held in conjunction with the Ass'n of American University Presses

Publications:
Membership Directory. a.
Newsletter. a.

Women in Technology International
13351-D Riverside Dr., Suite 441
Sherman Oaks, CA 91423
Tel: (818)788-9484 *Fax:* (818)788-9410
Toll Free: (800)334 - 9484
E-Mail: info@witi.org
Web Site: www.witi.org
Members: 4000 individuals
Staff: 15
Annual Budget: $500-1,000,000
President and Chief Executive Officer: David Leighton

Historical Note
WITI is a professional association of women working in private and public technology corporations. Seeks to support and expand the number of women working in managerial capacities in the technology industry. Sponsors several conferences and networking opportunities for its members. Membership: $125/year.

Meetings/Conferences:
Annual Meetings: June

Publications:
WITI Magazine. 5/year.

Women in the Fire Service *(1983)*
P.O. Box 5446
Madison, WI 53705
Tel: (608)233-4768 *Fax:* (608)233-4879
E-Mail: info@wfsi.org
Web Site: www.wfsi.org
Members: 820 individuals
Staff: 3
Annual Budget: $50-100,000
Executive Director: Terese M. Floren

Historical Note
Formerly (1989) Women in Fire Suppression. WFS is a network of and for women firefighters and other fire service women. Membership: $40/year (individual); $50/year (company).

Meetings/Conferences:
Annual Meetings: May

Publications:
Firework Newsletter. bi-m..
WFS Quarterly Journal. q.

Women of the Motion Picture Industry, International *(1953)*
Twentieth Century Fox
P.O. Box 900
Beverly Hills, CA 90213

Tel: (310)369-4083 *Fax:* (310)369-8903
Web Site: www.wompi.org
Members: 600 individuals
Staff: 1
Annual Budget: $10-25,000
Contact: Lili Beaudin
E-Mail: president@wompi.org

Historical Note

WOMPI exists to promote professionalism in the motion picture industry and to contribute to the community through service projects. Membership: $35/year.

Meetings/Conferences:

Annual Meetings: September

Women's Basketball Coaches Association *(1981)*

4646 Lawrenceville Hwy.
Lilburn, GA 30047-3620
Tel: (770)279-8027 *Fax:* (770)279-8473
E-Mail: wbca@wbca.org
Web Site: www.wbca.org
Members: 4200 individuals
Staff: 14
Annual Budget: $1-2,000,000
Chief Executive Officer: Beth Bass
Chief Operating Officer: Shannon Reynolds
Director, Membership and Convention Services: Dorinda Schremmer

Historical Note

WBCA members include coaches, athletic directors, officials and others with an interest in women's basketball. Membership: $75/year (individual); $150/year (organization/company).

Meetings/Conferences:

2007 – Cleveland, OH/March 31-Apr. 3
2008 – Tampa, FL/Apr. 5-8
2009 – St. Louis, MO/Apr. 4-7
2010 – San Antonio, TX/Apr. 3-6
2011 – Indianapolis, IN

Publications:

At the Buzzer. bi-m. adv.
Fast Break Alert. bi-m. adv.
Coaching Women's Basketball. m. adv.
Net.News.

Women's Caucus for Art *(1972)*

P.O. Box 1498
Canal Street Stn.
New York, NY 10013
Tel: (212)634-0007
E-Mail: info@nationalwca.org
Web Site: www.nationalwca.org
Members: 1500 individuals
Staff: 1
Annual Budget: $50-100,000
President: Jennifer Colby

Historical Note

WCA members are women artists and educators, art historians and critics, gallery and museum professionals and collectors. Membership: $30/year (individual); $75/year (organization).

Meetings/Conferences:

Annual Meetings: February/300-800
2007 – New York, NY(Hilton)/Feb. 17-19

Publications:

Member News. 3/yr.
Honors Catalogue. 1/yr.

Women's Caucus for Political Science *(1969)*

San Diego State Univ., Dept. of Political Science
San Diego, CA 92182
Tel: (619)594-5208 *Fax:* (619)594-7302
Web Site: www.slu.edu/colleges/AS/WS/docs/staff/caucus/main.html
Members: 900 individuals
Treasurer: Ronee Schreiber, Ph.D.

Historical Note

WCPS is a non-profit organization that works to improve the status of women educators in the profession of political science by promoting equal opportunity for women political scientists in employment, promotion and tenure decisions, and in graduate school admissions and financial aid. Membership: $30/year (faculty members and other professionals); $30/year (institutions); free for students.

Meetings/Conferences:

Annual Meetings: in conjunction with the American Political Science Ass'n

Publications:

WCPS Quarterly Newsletter. q. adv.

Women's Caucus for the Modern Languages *(1970)*

Dept. of Modern Languages
Ohio Northern University
Ada, OH 45810
Web Site: www.umass.edu/wcml/
Members: 650 individuals
Annual Budget: under $10,000
Secretary-Treasurer: Roseanna Dufault

Historical Note

Members are women with a professional interest in the teaching and study of modern languages. Has no paid staff. Membership: $5-25/year, varies with salary (individual).

Meetings/Conferences:

Annual Meetings: With the Modern Language Ass'n/Dec. 27-30

Publications:

Concerns. 3/year.

Women's Classical Caucus *(1972)*

Department of Classics, U. of Illinois, 4080 FLB
707 S. Mathews Ave
Urbana, IL 61801
Tel: (217)333-7327
Members: 600 individuals
Secretary-Treasurer: Maryline Parca

Historical Note

WCC members are academics working in the fields of ancient history, art history, archaeology, and classical languages with an interest in gender issues. Membership: $150/year (lifetime membership); $15/year (regular member); $5/year (retiree); $3/year (student, after first year); first year students free.

Meetings/Conferences:

Annual Meetings: Winter
2007 – San Diego, CA/Jan. 4-7

Publications:

Cloelia newsletter. semi-a. adv.

Women's College Coalition *(1972)*

125 Michigan Ave. NE
Suite 340
Washington, DC 20017
Tel: (202)234-0443 *Fax:* (202)234-0445
E-Mail: msm@trinitydc.edu
Web Site: www.womenscolleges.org
Members: 59 institutions
Staff: 2
Annual Budget: $100-250,000
Executive Director: Susan Lennon
E-Mail: msm@trinitydc.edu

Historical Note

Founded in 1972 WCC is a national organization of women's two-year and four-year colleges, including both public and private, independent and church-related institutions. The Coalition's purpose is to communicate the contributions of both women's colleges and their graduates to their communities and the nation at large to initiate and support research dealing with women and higher education and through programming advocate for enhancing opportunities for women students.

Meetings/Conferences:

Annual Meetings: Fall

Publications:

Membership Directory. bien.

Women's Council of REALTORS *(1938)*

430 N. Michigan Ave.
Chicago, IL 60611-4093
Toll Free: (800)245 - 8512
E-Mail: ads@wcr.org
Web Site: www.wcr.org
Members: 17000 individuals
Staff: 9
Annual Budget: $1-2,000,000
Director, Marketing and Publications: Dianna Dearen

Historical Note

A professional development group for women in real estate. Provides a referral network and referral, relocation training, leadership training, and chapter programs on the local, state, and national levels. Membership: varies, according to chapter membership.

Meetings/Conferences:

Annual Meetings: Fall/with the Nat'l Ass'n of Realtors/1,000

Publications:

Connections Magazine. 6/year. adv.
Referral Roster (Membership Directory). a. adv.

Women's Foodservice Forum *(1989)*

101 N. Wacker Dr., Suite 606
Chicago, IL 60606
Toll Free: (866)368 - 8008
Web Site: www.womensfoodserviceforum.com
Members: 2100 individuals
Staff: 6
Annual Budget: $2-5,000,000
Executive Director: Patricia Venetucci

Historical Note

WFF members are men and women executives in the food service and hospitality industries. Membership: $225/year (individual); $150/year (educator).

Meetings/Conferences:

Annual Meetings: Spring

Publications:

WFF Magazine. semi-a.
Newsletter. bi-m.

Women's International Bowling Congress

5301 S. 76th St.
Greendale, WI 53129-1117
Tel: (414)421-9000 *Fax:* (414)421-4420
E-Mail: wibcexec@bowlinginc.com
Staff: 3
Executive Director: Roseann Kuhn

Historical Note

An affiliate of Bowling Inc. (same address).

Meetings/Conferences:

Annual Meetings: Spring

Women's International Network of Utility Professionals *(1923)*

P.O. Box 335
Whites Creek, TN 37189
E-Mail: winup@comcast.net
Web Site: www.winup.org
Members: 350 individuals
Staff: 1
Annual Budget: $50-100,000
President: Rita Simpson
E-Mail: winup@comcast.net

Historical Note

Founded as Electrical Women's Round Table; incorporated in New York in 1927. Assumed its current name in 1988. Members hold consumer-related positions in public relations, advertising, editing, and education, either at utilities or companies connected to the energy industry. Membership: $66/year, plus local chapter dues.

Meetings/Conferences:

Annual Meetings: Fall

Publications:

Membership Directory. a.
Newsletter. q.

Women's Jewelry Association *(1981)*

373 Route 46 West, Bldg. E, Suite 215
Fairfield, NJ 07004
Tel: (973)575-7190 *Fax:* (973)575-1445
E-Mail: info@womensjewelry.org
Web Site: www.womensjewelry.org
Members: 1000 individuals
Staff: 20
Annual Budget: $250-500,000
President: Anna Martin
E-Mail: info@womensjewelry.org

Historical Note

WJA seeks to provide a network for women in the jewelry industry. Members are jewelry industry professionals. Membership: $150/year (new member); $125/year (renewing member).

Meetings/Conferences:
Semi-annual Meetings:

Publications:
Newletter. 2/year.
Directory. a. adv.

Women's National Book Association *(1917)*
42 Maplewood St.
Larchmont, NY 10538-1633
Tel: (212)208-4629
E-Mail: publicity@bookbuzz.com
Web Site: www.wnba-books.org
Members: 1200 individuals
Annual Budget: $10-25,000
Public Relations Contact: Susannah Greenberg

Historical Note
Founded in 1917 as an organization of women and men in all occupations allied to the book publishing industry. Members include publishers, authors, librarians, literary agents, editors, illustrators and booksellers. Has no paid staff. Membership: $15/year, minimum (individual); $200-$600/year (organization).

Publications:
The Bookwoman. q.
Chapter Newsletters. m.

Women's Professional Rodeo Association *(1948)*
1235 Lake Plaza Dr., Suite 127
Colorado Springs, CO 80906
Tel: (719)576-0900 *Fax:* (719)576-1386
Web Site: www.wpra.com
Members: 2300 individuals
Staff: 4
Annual Budget: $250-500,000
Executive Secretary: Eva Jean Smith

Historical Note
WPRA was originally organized to replace trick riding in the rodeos. Modern purpose is to provide professional-level competitions and prize money for women athletes in the rodeo arena. Members are competitors in professional girl rodeos and in barrel races in rodeos sanctioned by the Rodeo Cowboys Association. Formerly (1980) the Girls' Rodeo Association and (1981) the Professional Women's Rodeo Association. Membership: $300/year.

Meetings/Conferences:
Annual Meetings: December, in conjunction with the Nat'l Finals

Publications:
Women's Pro Rodeo News. m. adv.
Rule Book & Reference Guide. a.

Women's Regional Publications of America *(1986)*
P.O. Box 300302
St. Louis, MO 63130
Tel: (314)997-6262 *Fax:* (314)567-7849
E-Mail: stlwyp@wypstlouis.com
Web Site: www.womensregionalpublications.org
Members: 20 publishers
Staff: 1
Annual Budget: $10-25,000
Executive Director: Jan Scott
E-Mail: stlwyp@wypstlouis.com

Historical Note
Formerly (2002) National Association of Women's Yellow Pages. WRPA members are publishers of women's business directories and women's magazines. Membership is limited to one member per specified geographic region.

Meetings/Conferences:
2007 – Santa Fe, NM/June/30

Women's Transportation Seminar *(1977)*
1701 K St. NW
Suite 800
Washington, DC 20006
Tel: (202)955-5085 *Fax:* (202)955-5088
E-Mail: wts@wtsinternational.org
Web Site: www.wtsnational.org
Members: 4000 individuals
Staff: 2
Annual Budget: $500-1,000,000
Executive Director: Diane James, CAE

Historical Note
Members are male and female transportation professionals, and public and private suppliers of transportation services. Founded in Washington, DC to enhance personal advancement and professional recognition for members. Membership: $75-165/year (individual); corporate membership varies.

Meetings/Conferences:
Annual Meetings: May
2007 – San Diego, CA(Wydham)/May 2-4/400

Publications:
Transcript newsletter. q.
WTS Nat'l Membership Directory. a.
W/M DBE Directory. a.

Wood Component Manufacturers Association *(1929)*
741 Butlers Gate
Suite 100
Marietta, GA 30068
Tel: (770)565-6660 *Fax:* (770)565-6663
Web Site: www.woodcomponents.org
Members: 150 companies
Staff: 3
Annual Budget: $100-250,000
Executive Director: Steven V. Lawser, CAE

Historical Note
Formerly (1984) Hardwood Dimension Manufacturers Association and (1996) National Dimension Manufacturers Association. Members are manufacturers of wood component products for the furniture and kitchen cabinet industries as well as other wood parts users.

Meetings/Conferences:
Annual Meetings: Spring/200
2007 – St. Petersburg, FL(Renaissance)/Apr. 25-28

Wood Machinery Manufacturers of America *(1899)*
100 N. 20th St., Fourth Floor
Philadelphia, PA 19103-1443
Tel: (215)564-3484 *Fax:* (215)963-9785
E-Mail: wmma@fernley.com
Web Site: www.wmma.org
Members: 225 companies
Staff: 5
Annual Budget: $1-2,000,000
Executive Vice President: Kenneth R. Hutton

Historical Note
a trade association of U.S. manufacturers of woodworking equipment, cutting tools accessories, with associate distributers, suppliers, consultants, publications and service provider members.

Meetings/Conferences:
Annual Meetings: Spring/300
2007 – St. Petersburg, FL(Vinoy)/Apr. 25-28

Publications:
Product Guide. bien.
The Cutting Edge. m.

Wood Moulding and Millwork Producers Association *(1963)*
507 First St.
Woodland, CA 95695-4025
Tel: (530)661-9591 *Fax:* (530)661-9586
Toll Free: (800)550 - 7889
E-Mail: info@wmmpa.com
Web Site: http://wmmpa.com
Members: 120 companies
Staff: 3
Annual Budget: $500-1,000,000
Executive Vice President: Kellie Schroeder
E-Mail: kelli@wmmpa.com
Director, Programs and Finance: Kimberly Lister
Technical Consultant: Robert "Bob" Weiglein

Historical Note
Established as the Western Wood Moulding Producers; became the Western Wood Moulding and Millwork Producers in 1968 and assumed its present name in 1978. Membership: $83-1,100/mo., based on board footage production.

Meetings/Conferences:
Semi-annual Meetings: February and August

Publications:
Case 'n Base News. m.
Directory of Members, Products, & Services. a.

Wood Products Manufacturers Association *(1929)*
175 State Road East
Westminster, MA 01473-1208
Tel: (978)874-5445 *Fax:* (978)874-9946
E-Mail: woodprod@wpma.org
Web Site: www.wpma.org
Members: 702 companies
Staff: 5
Executive Director: Phillip A. Bibeau
E-Mail: woodprod@wpma.org
Director, Association Services: Albert J. Bibeau
E-Mail: woodprod@wpma.org

Historical Note
Formerly Wood Turners Service Bureau and Wood Turners and Shapers Association (1978). Incorporated in Massachusetts in 1967, WPMA members represent all facets of the wood industry. Purpose is to promote friendly business relations by providing a forum through which information can be disseminated and shared among members Membership: $470-1,050/year, based on company size.

Meetings/Conferences:
Semi-Annual Meetings: Spring and Fall

Publications:
Newsletter. m. adv.
Membership Directory. a. adv.

Wood Truss Council of America *(1983)*
6300 Enterprise Lane
Madison, WI 53719
Tel: (608)274-4849 *Fax:* (608)274-3329
E-Mail: wtca@sbcindustry.com
Web Site: www.sbcindustry.com
Members: 1100 companies
Staff: 35
Annual Budget: $1-2,000,000
Executive Director: Kirk Grundahl, P.E.

Historical Note
WTCA is an international not-for-profit trade association. Members are companies that manufacture metal plate-connected wood trusses and related components. Includes nearly 800 manufacturers, 280 suppliers and related services companies, and 32 chapters. Purpose is to provide services to its member companies to help expand market share by promoting the common interests of its members, and to help ensure growth, continuity and increased professionalism in the industry. Membership: varies based on sales volume (manufacturers); $648/year (associates); $125/year (professional members).

Meetings/Conferences:
Annual Meetings: Fall
2007 – Columbus, OH(Convention Center)/Oct. 3-5/3000

Publications:
Structural Building Components Magazine. 9/year. adv.

Woodworking Machinery Industry Association *(1978)*
5024-R Campbell Blvd.
Baltimore, MD 21236-5974
Tel: (410)931-8100 *Fax:* (410)931-8111
E-Mail: info@wmia.org
Web Site: www.wmia.org
Members: 163 companies
Staff: 3
Annual Budget: $250-500,000
Executive Director: Bill Miller, CAE
E-Mail: info@wmia.org

Historical Note
Formerly (1997) Woodworking Machinery Importers Association of America. WMIA members are chief executives of woodworking machinery importing and distributing companies primarily concerned with the import of woodworking machinery. Membership: $600/year (company).

Meetings/Conferences:
Annual Meetings:

Publications:
Newsletter (online). 6/yr.
Directory. bien.

Wool Manufacturers Council *(1956)*

Historical Note
A council of the Northern Textile Association.

Workgroup for Electronic Data Interchange *(1991)*

12020 Sunrise Valley Dr., Suite 100
Reston, VA 20191
Tel: (703)391-2716 *Fax:* (703)391-2759
Web Site: www.wedi.org
Members: 300 companies/individuals
Staff: 5
Annual Budget: $500-1,000,000
Executive Vice President: James A. Schuping, CAE
Director, SNIP: Kristin Becker
E-Mail: kbecker@wedi.org
Director, Administrative and Member Services: Lisa Berretta
E-Mail: lberretta@wedi.org
Director, Regional Education and Operations: Ann Marie Railing
E-Mail: lrailing@wedi.org

Historical Note
WEDI represents companies and organizations active in the healthcare industry. The Workgroup was created to help streamline the practice of healthcare administration by standardizing electronic communications and increasing members' knowledge of EDI (electronic data interchange) technology and electronic commerce. Membership: $300/year (individual); $1000-$5000/year (organization).

Meetings/Conferences:
Annual Meetings: Spring

WorkPlace Furnishings *(1963)*

3574 E. Kemper Rd.
Cincinnati, OH 45241
Tel: (513)563-0048 *Fax:* (513)563-1822
E-Mail: info@workplacefun.com
Web Site: www.workplacefurn.com
Members: 90 independent dealers
Staff: 5
Annual Budget: $1-2,000,000
President and Chief Executive Officer: G.E. Russell
E-Mail: gerussell@workplacefun.com
Vice President, Marketing: Victor Maffe
E-Mail: vmaffe@workpacefurn.com

Historical Note
Incorporated in Ohio as MIV (More in Value) Inc.; later became National Association of Office Furniture Dealers, and assumed its current name in 1999. WPF is a marketing group providing advertising, catalogues and related services to its member dealers. Membership: $1,200-2,400/year.

Meetings/Conferences:
Annual Meetings: first Quarter

Publications:
The Informer. q.

World Affairs Councils of America *(1964)*

1800 K St. NW
Suite 1014
Washington, DC 20006
Tel: (202)833-4557 *Fax:* (202)833-4555
E-Mail: waca@worldaffairscouncils.org
Web Site: www.worldaffairscouncils.org
Members: 86 organizations
Staff: 4
Annual Budget: $500-1,000,000
President: Jerry W. Leach
Program Director: Ljiljana Komnenic
Director, Communications: Cheryl Stronczer

Historical Note
Formerly (1982) National Council of Community World Affairs Organizations. Became National Council of World Affairs Organizations. Changed name to World Affairs Councils of America in 1997. NCWAO members are world affairs councils and similar organizations. Membership: $100-$900/year (organization).

Meetings/Conferences:
Annual Meetings: Winter

Publications:
Directory of WCA. 2/year.
Study Tour Reports. 5/year.
Speakers Newsletter: May We Suggest. m.
Operations Papers. q.
World Affairs Newsletter. m.

World Airline Entertainment Association *(1979)*

8201 Greensboro Dr., Suite 300
McLean, VA 22102
Tel: (703)610-9021 *Fax:* (703)610-9005
E-Mail: info@waea.org
Web Site: www.waea.org
Members: 400 companies
Staff: 9
Annual Budget: $2-5,000,000
Executive Director: John L. Fiegel
E-Mail: info@waea.org

Historical Note
WAEA members are companies involved in all aspects of the inflight entertainment and cabin management industry including airlines, equipment manufacturers, distributors and producers of short subject feature length films, audio and video program producers, advertising representatives and magazine publishers.

Meetings/Conferences:
Annual Meetings: Fall
2007 – Toronto, Canada(Convention Center)/Sept. 17-20/1300
2008 – Long Beach, CA(Convention Center)/Sept. 8-11/1600
2009 – Kuala Lumpur, Malaysia(Convention Center)/Oct. 19-22/1100

Publications:
Avion Magazine. q. adv.

World Allergy Organization - IACCI *(1951)*

555 E. Wells St. 11th Floor
Milwaukee, WI 53202
Tel: (414)276-1791 *Fax:* (414)276-3349
E-Mail: info@worldallergy.org
Web Site: www.worldallergy.org
Members: 74 regional and national societies
Staff: 4
Annual Budget: $500-1,000,000
Executive Director: Stanley Mandarich
E-Mail: info@worldallergy.org

Historical Note
Founded (1951) as International Association of Allergology and Clinical Immunology at the First International Congress of Allergology in Zurich, Switzerland; assumed current name in 2000. Mission is to be a global resource and advocate in the field of allergy, advancing excellence in clinical care, education, research and training through an international alliance of allergy and clinical immunology societies.

Meetings/Conferences:
Biennial Meetings: late Summer-early Fall
2007 – Bangkok, Thailand/Dec. 2-6/4000

Publications:
Directory.
ACII - Journal of the World Allergy Organization. 6/year. adv.
Internat'l Archives of Allergy and Immunology. m.

World Aquaculture Society *(1970)*

143 J.M. Parker Coliseum
Louisiana State University
Baton Rouge, LA 70806
Tel: (225)578-3137 *Fax:* (225)578-3493
E-Mail: wasmas@aol.com
Web Site: www.was.org
Members: 4000 individuals
Staff: 4
Annual Budget: $100-250,000
Director, Home Office: Juliette L. Massey
E-Mail: wasmas@aol.com

Historical Note
Formerly (1986) the World Mariculture Society Members are individuals and companies interested in the cultivation of aquatic plants and animals for food purposes. Membership: $60/year (individual); $250/year (corporation); $40/year (student); $100/year (sustaining).

Meetings/Conferences:
Annual Meetings: Spring

Publications:
Journal of the World Aquaculture Society. q.
World Aquaculture Magazine. q.

World Association for Infant Mental Health *(1992)*

University Outreach & Engagement
Kellogg Center, Garden Level, #24, MI State University
East Lansing, MI 48824
Tel: (517)432-3793 *Fax:* (517)432-3694
E-Mail: waimh@msu.edu
Web Site: www.waimh.org
Members: 1200 individuals
Staff: 1
Annual Budget: $2-5,000,000
Executive Director: Hiram E. Fitzgerald, Ph.D.
E-Mail: waimh@msu.edu

Historical Note
Formed (1992) by the merger of the World Association for Infant Psychiatry and Allied Disciplines and the International Association for Infant Mental Health. Members are child psychiatrists, child psychologists, nurses, social workers, and other professionals with an interest in mental development and disorders in children under 3 years of age and in families of small children. Membership: $70/year.

Meetings/Conferences:
Biennial Meetings:

Publications:
Infant Mental Health Journal. bi-m. adv.
Signal Newsletter. q. adv.

World Association of Alcohol Beverage Industries *(1944)*

P.O. Box 4027
Frankfort, KY 40604
Tel: (502)352-2715 *Fax:* (866)631-9325
Toll Free: (800)466 - 6920
E-Mail: sewhite@fewpb.net
Web Site: www.waabi.org
Members: 12 chapters
Staff: 1
Annual Budget: $25-50,000
Executive Director: Sheila White

Historical Note
Formerly known as the National Women's Association of Allied Beverage Industries. Administrative support provided by Distilled Spirits Council of the U.S. Membership: $35/year (individual); $25/year (company).

Meetings/Conferences:
Annual Meetings: Summer/200

Publications:
Industry World. q.

World Association of Veterinary Anatomists *(1957)*

Virginia Tech
VA-MD Reg'l College of Veterinary Medicine
Blacksburg, VA 24060
President: Larry Freeman
E-Mail: lfreeman@vt.edu

Historical Note
American Chapter of the international organization, headquartered in Bern Switzerland. Encourages the study of anatomy in the field of taxonomy.

World Floor Covering Association *(1960)*

2211 E. Howell Ave.
Anaheim, CA 92806-6009
Tel: (714)978-6440 *Fax:* (714)978-6066
Toll Free: (800)624 - 6880
E-Mail: wfca@wfca.org
Web Site: www.wfca.org
Members: 2800 companies
Staff: 10
Annual Budget: $5-10,000,000
Chief Executive Officer: D. Christopher Davis
Director, Operations: Terry Hearne
Director, Technical Services: Jon Namba
E-Mail: jnamba@wfca.org
Membership Projects Manager: Jenny Ostad
E-Mail: jostad@wfca.org
Director, Finance and Administration: Cammie Weitzel

Historical Note
WFCA is the largest advocacy association representing floor covering retailers and allied service providers. Product of a merger of the Western Floor Covering Association and the American Floorcovering Association in 1994. Membership: $225/year (regular); $800/year (associate).

Publications:
From the First Floor Newsletter. q.

World Future Society *(1966)*
7910 Woodmont Ave., Suite 450
Bethesda, MD 20814-3032
Tel: (301)656-8274 *Fax:* (301)951-0394
Toll Free: (800)989 - 8274
E-Mail: info@wfs.org
Web Site: www.wfs.org
Members: 25000 individuals
Staff: 11
Annual Budget: $1-2,000,000
President: Timothy C. Mack
E-Mail: info@wfs.org
Vice President, Membership and Conference Operations: Susan Echard
E-Mail: info@wfs.org

Historical Note
An association of scientists, educators, government officials and others interested in social and technological developments of the future. Membership: $49/year.

Meetings/Conferences:
Annual Meetings: Summer

Publications:
The Futurist. bi-m. adv.
Future Survey. m.
Futures Research Quarterly. q.

World Gold Council *(1987)*
444 Madison Ave., Suite 301
New York, NY 10022
Tel: (212)317-3800 *Fax:* (212)688-0410
E-Mail: info@gold.org
Web Site: www.gold.org
Members: 11 individuals
Staff: 11
Annual Budget: $5-10,000,000
Managing Director: John Colnan
E-Mail: info@gold.org

Historical Note
The United States and regional office (covering North and South America) of the global organization headquartered in London, United Kingdom. WGC promotes the uses of gold and gold products to consumers, investors, manufacturers, and the public sector.

World History Association *(1982)*
Univ. of Hawai at Manoa
2530 Dole St., Sakamaki Hall A203
Honolulu, HI 96822
Tel: (808)956-7688 *Fax:* (808)956-9600
E-Mail: thewha@hawaii.edu
Web Site: www.thewha.org
Members: 1400 individuals
Staff: 2
Annual Budget: $25-50,000
Executive Director: Rob White
E-Mail: thewha@hawaii.edu

Historical Note
Members are teachers, academics and others with an interest in the teaching of and research in world and cross-cultural history. Membership: $60/year (individuals); $30/year (students/retirees); $45/year (new professionals).

Meetings/Conferences:
Annual Meetings: in conjunction with AHA annual meeting

Publications:
Journal of World History. q.. adv.
World History Bulletin. semi-a. adv.

World International Nail and Beauty Association *(1981)*
1221 N. Lake View
Anaheim, CA 92807
Tel: (714)779-9883 *Fax:* (714)779-9972
Toll Free: (800)624 - 5777
Members: 6000 buyers
Staff: 4
Annual Budget: $250-500,000
President: Jim George

Historical Note
Formerly (1984) the National Association of Nail Artists and (1987) the National Aesthetician and Nail Artist Association. Members are manicurists, pedicurists and aestheticians as well as manufacturers and suppliers of beauty products. Primarily functions as a buyer's club for its members. Membership: $40/year (individual).

Meetings/Conferences:
Annual Meetings: none held

World Media Association
3600 New York Ave NE, Third Floor
Washington, DC 20002
Tel: (202)636-3124 *Fax:* (202)635-9227
E-Mail: wma@wmassociation.com
Web Site: www.wmassociation.com
Members: 6000 individuals
Staff: 3
Annual Budget: $100-250,000
General Manager: Tomiko Duggan

Historical Note
WMA promotes freedom of the press in places and encourages the responsible use of that freedom.

World Research Foundation *(1977)*
41 Bell Rock Plaza
Sedona, AZ 86351
Tel: (928)284-3300 *Fax:* (928)284-3530
E-Mail: info@wrf.org
Web Site: www.wrf.org
Members: 41000 individuals
Staff: 15
Annual Budget: $1-2,000,000
Founder: LaVerne Boeckman
E-Mail: laverne@wrf.org

Historical Note
Membership fee varies; $20/year minimum.

Publications:
World Research News. q.
Bulletins. q.

World Shoe Association *(1942)*
15821 Ventura Blvd., Suite 415
Encino, CA 91436
Tel: (818)379-9400 *Fax:* (818)379-9410
Web Site: www.wsashow.com
Members: 4500 individuals
Staff: 18
Annual Budget: $5-10,000,000
Chief Operating Officer: Diane Stone

Historical Note
Founded as Western Shoe Associates, WSA organizes international buying markets. Represents the USA and 73 foreign countries. Membership: $70year (regular).

Meetings/Conferences:
Buying Markets: February and August

Publications:
Manufacturers-WSA Members Directory. bien. adv.
Show Guide. bien.
Buyers Guide. q. adv.
WSA Newsletter. q.
WSA Today. bi-a. adv.

World Sign Associates *(1947)*
9035 Wadsworth Pkwy., Suite 2250
Westminster, CO 80021
Tel: (303)427-7252 *Fax:* (303)427-7090
Web Site: www.wsanetwork.org
Members: 185 companies
Staff: 3
Annual Budget: $250-500,000
Executive Vice President: Jerry L. Righthouse

Historical Note
WSA members are companies involved in the design, manufacture, installation and maintenance of electrical signs, and suppliers to the industry. Membership: $780/year (company).

Meetings/Conferences:
Annual Meetings: August-September/200

Publications:
Newsletter. q. adv.

World Teleport Association *(1985)*
NY Information and Technology Center
55 Broad St., 14th Floor
New York, NY 10004
Tel: (212)825-0218
E-Mail: chinablue@worldteleport.org
Web Site: www.worldteleport.org
Members: 650 individuals/130 companies
Staff: 4
Annual Budget: $250-500,000
Executive Director: Robert Bell
E-Mail: rbell@worldteleport.org
Director, Member Services: China Blue
E-Mail: chinablue@worldteleport.org
Director, Development: Louis Zacharilla
E-Mail: lzacharilla@worldteleport.org

Historical Note
Mission is to promote the understanding, development and use of teleports as a means to achieve economic, political and social progress locally, regionally and worldwide. Membership: $650-$16,500/year (organization/company).

Publications:
Uplink. q.

World Trade Centers Association *(1970)*
60 E. 42nd St., Suite 1901
New York, NY 10165
Tel: (212)432-2626 *Fax:* (212)488-0064
Toll Free: (800)937 - 8886
E-Mail: wtca@wtca.org
Web Site: www.wtca.org
Members: 277 organizations
President and Chief Executive Officer: Guy F. Tozzoli
E-Mail: gtozzoli@wtca.org

Historical Note
WTCA develops programs and services that foster international trade. Members are trade centers, enterprise zones, and other organizations that exist to promote free and fair trade globally.

World Umpires Association *(1969)*
P.O. Box 394
Neenah, WI 54957
Tel: (321)633-7018
E-Mail: questions@worldumpires.com
Web Site: www.worldumpires.com
Members: 56 individuals
Staff: 3
Annual Budget: $10-25,000
President: John Hirschbeck
E-Mail: questions@worldumpires.com

Historical Note
Supersedes Major League Umpires Association. Acts as bargaining agent in negotiations with Major League Baseball.

Publications:
WUA Newsletter. m.

World War Two Studies Association *(1967)*
208 Eisenhower Hall, Kansas State Univ.
Manhattan, KS 66506-1002
Tel: (785)532-0374 *Fax:* (785)532-7004
Web Site: http://h-net.msu.edu/~war/wwtsa/
Members: 350 individuals
Secretary-Treasurer and Editor: Mark Parillo

Historical Note
Members are academics and others with an interest in the study of the World War II period. Membership: $15/year (individual); $5/year (student).

Meetings/Conferences:
Annual Meetings: in conjunction with AHA annual meeting

Publications:
Newsletter. semi-a.

World Waterpark Association *(1980)*
8826 Santa Fe Dr., Suite 310
Overland Park, KS 66212
Tel: (913)599-0300 *Fax:* (913)599-0520
E-Mail: gkellogg@waterparks.org
Web Site: www.waterparks.org
Members: 900 parks; 450 suppliers
Staff: 5

Annual Budget: $500-1,000,000
President and Chief Executive Officer: Rick Root
Director, Communications: Gina B. Kellogg
E-Mail: gkellogg@waterparks.org
Director, Trade Shows and Supplier Relations: Patty Miller
E-Mail: gkellogg@waterparks.org

Historical Note
WWA members are owners and operators of water leisure facilities. Membership: $295-495/year.

Meetings/Conferences:
Annual Meetings: Fall

Publications:
World Waterpark Magazine. 10/year. adv.
Buyer's Guide. a. adv.
Developers Reference. a. adv.

World Watusi Association *(1984)*
P.O. Box 14
Crawford, NE 69339
Tel: (308)665-3919 *Fax:* (308)665-1931
E-Mail: mail@watusicattle.com
Web Site: www.watusicattle.com
Members: 300 individuals
Staff: 1
Annual Budget: $10-25,000
Registrar: Maureen Neidhardt

Historical Note
Members are owners, breeders and others interested in the Watusi cattle breed. Membership: $25/year.

Meetings/Conferences:
Annual Meetings: Fall

Publications:
Rare Breeds Journal. bi-m. adv.

World Wide Pet Industry Association *(1951)*
406 S. First Ave.
Arcadia, CA 91006-3829
Tel: (626)447-2222 *Fax:* (626)447-8350
Toll Free: (800)999 - 7295
E-Mail: info@wwpia.org
Web Site: www.wwpia.org
Members: 520 companies
Staff: 9
Annual Budget: $1-2,000,000
Executive Vice President: Douglas L. Poindexter, CAE
E-Mail: info@wwpia.org

Historical Note
Formerly (1994) Western World Pet Supply Association. WWPIA represents and promotes the interests of pet industry manufacturers, importers, product distributors, breeder/livestock distributors and manufacturers' representatives and retailers. Membership: $550/year (company).

Meetings/Conferences:
Annual Trade Shows: September

World's Poultry Science Association, U.S.A. Branch *(1965)*
20 Eastwood Roads
Storrs, CT 06268
Tel: (860)429-3053 *Fax:* (860)487-0572
Web Site: www.wpsa.com
Members: 450 individuals
Staff: 1
Annual Budget: $10-25,000
Secretary-Treasurer: Dr. P. Aho

Historical Note
U.S. members of the World's Poultry Science Association. Promotes U.S. participation in World's Poultry Congresses, held every 4 years. Membership: $35/year (individual); $48/year (organization); $10/year (student).

Meetings/Conferences:
Annual Meetings: With Poultry Science Ass'n at Land Grant colleges.

Publications:
World's Poultry Science Journal. 3/year.

WorldatWork *(1955)*
14040 N. Northsight Blvd.
Scottsdale, AZ 85260-3627
Tel: (480)951-9191 *Fax:* (480)483-8352
E-Mail: customerrelations@worldatwork.org
Web Site: www.worldatwork.org
Members: 26000 individuals
Staff: 135
Annual Budget: $10-25,000,000
President: Anne C. Ruddy
Director, Strategy and Marketing: Don Griffith
Director, Public Affairs: Ryan Johnson
Director, Professional Development: Bonnie Kabin
Director, Human Resources: Kip Kipley
Director, Finance and Information Technology: Greg Nelson
Manager, Media Relations: Marcia Rhodes
Director, Business Development: Betty Scharfman

Historical Note
WorldatWork was formerly known as American Compensation Association and assumed its current name in 2000. Members are HR professionals responsible for implementing total rewards - compensation, benefits, work-life, performance and recognition, development and career opportunities. Has an annual budget of $25 million. Membership: $325/year for new members; $225/year for renewing members (individual). As of 2006, WorldatWork had 30,000 members in 30 countries.

Meetings/Conferences:
Annual Meetings: May/1100-1300

Publications:
The Alliance. m. adv.
workspan. m. adv.
WorldatWork Journal. q.

Wound, Ostomy and Continence Nurses Society *(1968)*
15000 Commerce Pkwy., Suite C
Mt. Laurel, NJ 08054
Tel: (856)439-0500 *Fax:* (856)439-0525
Toll Free: (888)224 - 9626 Ext:
E-Mail: info@wocn.org
Web Site: www.wocn.org
Members: 4000 individuals
Staff: 15
Annual Budget: $1-2,000,000
Executive Director: Deborah Unger, MSOLQ

Historical Note
Formerly (1992) International Association for Enterostomal Therapy, WOCN is a professional, international nursing society representing WOC(ET) nurses and other nurse professionals who provide acute and rehabilitative care to people with select disorders of the gastrointestinal, genitourinary, and integumentary systems. Membership: $65-$110/year (individual), $600/year (industry).

Meetings/Conferences:
Annual Meetings: June

Publications:
Guidelines for Management. irreg.
Journal of Wound, Ostomy and Continence Nursing. bi-m. adv.
WOCN News. q. adv.
Membership Directory. a.

Woven Wire Products Association *(1942)*
c/o Newark Wire Works
1059 King George Post Road
Edison, NJ 08837
Tel: (732)661-2001
E-Mail: jps@newarkwireworks.com
Web Site: www.wovenwire.org
Members: 18 companies
Staff: 1
Annual Budget: $25-50,000
President: J. P. Spellman
E-Mail: jps@newarkwireworks.com

Historical Note
Promotes the use of wire mesh products.

Publications:
Newsletter. m.

Writers Guild of America, East *(1954)*
555 W. 57th St., Suite 1230
New York, NY 10019
Tel: (212)767-7800 *Fax:* (212)582-1909
E-Mail: info@wgaeast.org
Web Site: www.wgaeast.org
Members: 4100 individuals
Staff: 21
Annual Budget: $2-5,000,000
Executive Director: Mona Mangan
E-Mail: info@wgaeast.org

Historical Note
Founded in New York City in 1954 as an independent labor union representing writers in motion pictures, television and radio. Affiliated with the Writers Guild of America, West.

Publications:
On Writing. 3/year.
Writers Guild East Newsletter. bi-m. adv.

Writers Guild of America, West *(1933)*
7000 W. Third St.
Los Angeles, CA 90048-4329
Tel: (323)951-4000 *Fax:* (323)782-4800
Toll Free: (800)548 - 4532
Web Site: www.wga.org
Members: 8500 individuals
Staff: 120
Annual Budget: $10-25,000,000
President: Patric Verrone
Vice President: David N. Weiss

Historical Note
Founded in Los Angeles, CA in 1933 as an independent labor union representing writers in the motion picture, broadcast, cable and new technologies industries. Membership: 1.5% of income.

Meetings/Conferences:
Annual Meetings: Annual Membership Meeting in September in Los Angeles, Awards Show in February, also in Los Angeles

Publications:
"Written By". 9/year. adv.
Now Playing (e-newsletter).
The Craft of Writing for Film and Television Magazine.

Writing Instrument Manufacturers Association *(1943)*
15000 Commerce Pkwy., Suite C
Mt. Laurel, NJ 08054
Tel: (856)638-0426 *Fax:* (856)439-0525
E-Mail: wima@ahint.com
Web Site: www.wima.org
Members: 40 companies
Staff: 2
Annual Budget: $100-250,000
Executive Director: Robert Waller, Jr., CAE

Historical Note
Founded as the Fountain Pen and Mechanical Pencil Manufacturers Association, it assumed its present name in 1963. Merged with Pencil Makers Association in 1994.

Publications:
Writing Instrument Industry Online Directory. adv.

WTA Tour *(1973)*
One Progress Plaza, Suite 1500
St. Petersburg, FL 33701
Tel: (727)895-5000 *Fax:* (727)894-1982
Web Site: www.wtatour.com
Members: 1600 individuals
Staff: 32
Annual Budget: $2-5,000,000
Chief Executive Officer: Larry Scott

Historical Note
Originally Women's Tennis Association; became (1986) Women's International Tennis Association; reverted to its original name in 1990. Absorbed WTA Tour Players Association in 1995 and assumed the name WTA Tour. Members are professional women tennis players. Sponsors tournaments in 28 countries worldwide. Full membership: $1000/year.

Publications:
Notes and Notecards (in season). w.

Xi Psi Phi *(1889)*
160 S. Bellwood Dr.
Suite Z
Alton, IL 62024
Tel: (618)307-5433
Members: 20000 individuals
Supreme Secretary-Treasurer: Dr. Keith W. Dickey

Historical Note
An international professional dental fraternity. Organized February 8, 1889 at the University of Michigan. Affiliated with the American Dental Interfraternity Council.

Meetings/Conferences:

Annual Meetings: Spring

Publications:

Xi Psi Phi Quarterly. q. adv.

Xplor International *(1981)*

24238 Hawthorne Blvd.

Torrance, CA 90505-6505

Tel: (310)373-3633 *Fax:* (310)375-4240

Toll Free: (800)669 - 7567

E-Mail: info@xplor.org

Web Site: www.xplor.org

Members: 5000 individuals

Staff: 45

Annual Budget: $2-5,000,000

President and Chief Executive Officer: Harold "Skip" Henk

Global Conference Curriculum and Speakers: Stephanie Donlou

Historical Note

Formerly known as Electronic Document Systems Association. Also known as Xplor International/Electronics Documents Systems Association. Provides programs, forums, and related services which enhance the use of electronic document systems to achieve organizational goals. Membership: $125/year (individual); $450/year (organization/company).

Publications:

Product and Services Reference Guide. a. adv.

The Xplorer. m.

Xploration. semi-a.

Yacht Brokers Association of America *(1920)*

105 Eastern Ave., Suite 104

Annapolis, MD 21403-3300

Tel: (410)263-1014 *Fax:* (410)263-1659

Web Site: www.ybaa.com

Members: 1500 individuals

Staff: 9

Annual Budget: $100-250,000

Executive Director: Joseph M. Thompson, Jr.

Accounting Manager: Diana J. Crompton, CPA

Program Development Manager: Robb Fish

Certification Program Manager: Mary L. Hollan

Membership Development Manager: Amy Luckado

Conference Manager: Aimee Murphy

Director, Communications and Conferences: Kristin B. Thompson

Historical Note

Founded as Yacht Architects and Brokers Association and assumed its present name in 1999. YBAA promotes the interests of professional yacht brokers through its Code of Ethics, legislative and regulatory involvement and certification program, as well as conducting education and dissemination of pertinent information. Membership: $325-800/year (corporate); $450/year (affiliate).

Meetings/Conferences:

Annual Meetings: January

Publications:

YBAA Annual Directory. a. adv.

Yacht Broker News. q. adv.

Yellow Pages Association *(1988)*

Two Connell Dr., First Floor

Berkeley Heights, NJ 07922-2747

Tel: (908)286-2380 *Fax:* (908)286-0620

Web Site: www.ypassociation.org

Members: 400 companies

Staff: 36

Annual Budget: $10-25,000,000

President: Negley Norton

Director, Communications: Christopher G. Bacey

E-Mail: christopher.bacey@ypassociation.org

Chief Financial Officer: Donna Borowicz

Historical Note

Formed as Yellow Pages Publishers Association; the result of the merger of American Association of Yellow Pages Publishers and National Yellow Pages Service Association. Became Yellow Pages Integrated Media Association in 2001 before reassuming orgininal name in 2004. Members are companies publishing yellow pages and other specialty directories. Suppliers to the industry are associate members. Has an annual budget of approximately $12 million.

Publications:

Rates & Data Publication. m. adv.

Young Entrepreneurs Organization *(1987)*

1199 N. Fairfax St., Suite 200

Alexandria, VA 22314

Tel: (703)519-6700 *Fax:* (703)519-1864

E-Mail: info@yeo.org

Web Site: www.yeo.org

Members: 5000 individuals

Staff: 40

Vice President, Communications and Marketing: Karen R. Seidman

E-Mail: kseidman@yeo.org

Historical Note

YEO provides education and professional support to businesspeople who are founders or controlling shareholders of their businesses. Membership, by invitation only, is restricted to executives under the age of 39 whose companies have gross annual sales of $1 million or more.

Meetings/Conferences:

Semi-Annual Meetings: Summer and Winter

Young Menswear Association *(1937)*

47 W. 34th St., Suite 534

New York, NY 10001

Tel: (212)594-6422 *Fax:* (212)594-9349

E-Mail: the-yma@att.net

Web Site: www.the-yma.com

Members: 350 individuals

Staff: 1

Annual Budget: $100-250,000

Secretary-Treasurer: Joe Rivers

Historical Note

Represents the textile and apparel industries. Scholarships and financial funding to students interested in the industry promote leadership and role models.

Meetings/Conferences:

Annual Meetings: January/400

Publications:

Newsletter. q.

Young Presidents' Organization *(1950)*

600 E. Las Colinas Blvd., Suite 1000

Irving, TX 75039

Tel: (972)587-1500

Toll Free: (800)773 - 7976

E-Mail: askypo@ypo.org

Web Site: www.ypo.org

Members: 9500 individuals

Staff: 90

Annual Budget: $10-25,000,000

Chief Executive Officer: Lee Ward

E-Mail: askypo@ypo.org

Historical Note

Members are company presidents under age 50 whose companies employ at least 50 individuals and have either $7 million in annual sales or $140 million in total assets. Has an annual budget of approximately $22 million.

Meetings/Conferences:

Quarterly Meetings:

Publications:

YPO Worldwide. q.

Youth Symphony Orchestras

Historical Note

A division of the American Symphony Orchestra League.

Zonta International *(1919)*

557 W. Randolph

Chicago, IL 60661-2206

Tel: (312)930-5848 *Fax:* (312)930-0951

E-Mail: zontaintl@zonta.org

Web Site: www.zonta.org

Members: 32000 individuals

Staff: 16

Annual Budget: $1-2,000,000

Executive Director: Janet Halstead

E-Mail: zontaintl@zonta.org

Historical Note

Classified service organization of executives and professionals working to advance the status of women worldwide through service and advocacy.

Meetings/Conferences:

Biennial Meetings: June-July in even years

2008 – Rotterdam, Netherlands

2010 – Bangkok, Thailand

Publications:

The Zontian. q.

2007 National Trade and Professional Associations

Subject Index

Every active organization listed in NTPA has been indexed in one or more subject headings, which reflect the products or professions the organization in question represents. For example, the American Association of Nurse Anesthetists is listed under ANESTHESIOLOGY, MEDICINE, and NURSING.

Association of Directory Marketing(194)
Association of Free Community Papers(198)
Association of Hispanic Advertising Agencies(200)
Association of Independent Commercial Producers(200)
Association of National Advertisers(205)
Audit Bureau of Circulations(222)
Automotive Communication Council(223)
BPA Worldwide(232)
Business Marketing Association(235)
Cabletelevision Advertising Bureau(236)
Direct Marketing Association(285)
Eight Sheet Outdoor Advertising Association(290)
Freestanding Insert Council of North America(312)
Healthcare Marketing and Communications Council(324)
ICOM, International Communications Agency Network(330)
Inflatable Advertising Dealers Association(338)
Insurance Marketing Communications Association(345)
Interactive Advertising Bureau(346)
Intermarket Agency Network(347)
International Advertising Association(348)
International Newspaper Marketing Association(381)
International Sign Association(386)
Mailing & Fulfillment Service Association(410)
Marketing Agencies Association Worldwide(412)
Marketing and Advertising Global Network(412)
Media Credit Association(415)
Media Research Directors Association(416)
National Association of Publishers' Representatives(467)
National Potato Promotion Board(533)
Outdoor Advertising Association of America(569)
POPAI The Global Association for Marketing at Retail(580)
PROMAX International(590)
Promotion Marketing Association(590)
Promotional Products Association International(591)
Publishers Publicity Association(593)
Radio Advertising Bureau(594)
Retail Advertising and Marketing Association International(601)
Station Representatives Association(653)
Television Bureau of Advertising(659)
Trade Promotion Management Association(663)
Traffic Audit Bureau for Media Measurement(663)
Transworld Advertising Agency Network(664)
Utility Communicators International(681)

AEROSPACE

Aerospace Department Chairmen's Association(10)
Aerospace Industries Association of America(10)
Aerospace Medical Association(10)
Air Traffic Control Association(13)
Air Transport Association of America(13)
Aircraft Builders Council(14)
Airports Council International/North America(15)
American Association of Airport Executives(38)
American Astronautical Society(54)
American Institute of Aeronautics and Astronautics(94)
Association for Unmanned Vehicle Systems International(181)
Cargo Airline Association(238)
Council of Defense and Space Industry Associations(271)
General Aviation Manufacturers Association(315)
Institute of Navigation(343)
International Association of Machinists and Aerospace Workers(359)
International Union, United Automobile, Aerospace and Agricultural Implement Workers of America(396)
National Aeronautic Association(427)
National Air Carrier Association(428)
National Air Traffic Controllers Association(428)
National Association of Air Traffic Specialists(438)
National Training Systems Association(547)
Society for the Advancement of Material and Process Engineering(626)
Society of Allied Weight Engineers(630)
Society of Cost Estimating and Analysis(634)
Society of Flight Test Engineers(636)
Women in Aerospace(691)

AESTHETICS

Aestheticians International Association(10)
American Academy of Esthetic Dentistry(22)
American Society for Aesthetic Plastic Surgery(126)
American Society for Aesthetics(126)
American Society for Dental Aesthetics(128)
Indoor Tanning Association(336)

AGING

American Academy of Anti-Aging Medicine(20)
American Aging Association(30)
American Association for Geriatric Psychiatry(35)
American Association of Homes and Services for the Aging(43)
American Association of Retired Persons(50)
American Association of Retirement Communities(50)
American College of Health Care Administrators(66)
American Federation for Aging Research(82)
American Geriatrics Society(87)
American Seniors Housing Association(124)
American Society on Aging(147)
Assisted Living Federation of America(164)
Association for Gerontology in Higher Education(173)
Association of Jewish Aging Services(202)
Gerontological Society of America(316)
National Academy of Elder Law Attorneys(426)
National Adult Day Services Association(427)
National Association for the Support of Long-Term Care(437)
National Association of Activity Professionals(437)
National Association of Area Agencies on Aging(439)
National Association of Nutrition and Aging Services Programs(463)
National Association of Professional Geriatric Care Managers(466)
National Association of State Units on Aging(476)
National Council on the Aging(503)
National Hospice and Palliative Care Organization(517)
Pharmaceutical Care Management Association(575)

AGRICULTURE

Agribusiness Council(12)
Agricultural and Industrial Manufacturers' Representatives Association(12)
Agricultural History Society(12)
Agricultural Retailers Association(12)
Agriculture Council of America(12)
Alpha Gamma Rho(17)
American Agricultural Economics Association(30)
American Agricultural Editors Association(30)
American Agricultural Law Association(30)
American Agriculture Movement(30)
American Association for Agricultural Education(33)
American Association of Crop Insurers(41)
American Association of Grain Inspection and Weighing Agencies(43)
American Corn Growers Association(74)
American Farm Bureau Federation(81)
American Forage and Grassland Council(84)
American Herbalists Guild(90)
American Oilseed Coalition(110)
American Peanut Research and Education Society(113)
American Polypay Sheep Association(116)
American Seed Trade Association(124)
American Sheep Industry Association(125)
American Society for Plasticulture(131)
American Society of Agricultural Appraisers(133)
American Society of Agricultural Consultants(133)
American Society of Agronomy(133)
American Society of Animal Science(134)
American Society of Farm Managers and Rural Appraisers(137)
American Sugar Alliance(150)
Animal Transportation Association(157)
AOAC International(158)
Aquacultural Engineering Society(159)
Aquatic Plant Management Society(159)
ASABE - the Society for Engineering in Agricultural, Food and Biological Systems(162)
Association for Communication Excellence(169)
Association for International Agricultural and Extension Education(175)
Association for International Agriculture and Rural Development(175)
Association for Living History, Farm and Agricultural Museums(176)
Association of American Feed Control Officials(184)
Association of American Plant Food Control Officials(185)
Association of Official Seed Analysts(206)
Association of Official Seed Certifying Agencies(206)
Braunvieh Association of America(232)
Chemical Producers and Distributors Association(243)
Council for Agricultural Science and Technology(268)
Cranberry Institute(278)
Crop Insurance Research Bureau(279)
Crop Science Society of America(279)
CropLife America(279)
Epsilon Sigma Phi(297)
Farm Equipment Manufacturers Association(301)
Farmers Educational and Co-operative Union of America(301)
Fertilizer Institute(305)
Fresh Produce and Floral Council(312)
Fresh Produce Association of the Americas(312)
Futures Industry Association(313)
Hop Growers of America(328)
Hydroponic Merchants Association(330)
Hydroponic Society of America(330)
International Herb Association(375)
International Maple Syrup Institute(379)
International Silo Association(386)
International Union, United Automobile, Aerospace and Agricultural Implement Workers of America(396)
International Weed Science Society(397)
Irrigation Association(400)
Kamut Association of North America(403)
Land Improvement Contractors of America(405)
National Agri-Marketing Association(428)
National Agricultural Aviation Association(428)
National Alfalfa Alliance(429)
National Alliance of Independent Crop Consultants(429)
National Association of Agricultural Educators(438)
National Association of Agricultural Fair Agencies(438)
National Association of Agriculture Employees(438)
National Association of County Agricultural Agents(447)

National Association of Extension 4-H Agents(451)
National Association of FSA County Office Employees(454)
National Association of State Departments of Agriculture(474)
National Association of Wheat Growers(481)
National Block and Bridle Club(485)
National Cattlemen's Beef Association(488)
National Cooperative Business Association(496)
National Council for Agricultural Education(497)
National Council of Agricultural Employers(498)
National Council of Commercial Plant Breeders(498)
National Crop Insurance Services(504)
National Dairy Herd Improvement Association(504)
National Extension Association of Family and Consumer Sciences(508)
National Farmers Organization(508)
National FFA Organization(510)
National Grange(514)
National Grape Cooperative Association(515)
National Hay Association(516)
National Institute for Farm Safety(520)
National Onion Association(529)
National Plant Board(533)
National Postsecondary Agriculture Student Organization(533)
National Potato Council(533)
National Potato Promotion Board(533)
National Sunflower Association(545)
New York Mercantile Exchange(552)
North America Colleges and Teachers of Agriculture(553)
North American Agricultural Marketing Officials(554)
North American Maple Syrup Council(558)
Organic Crop Improvement Association International(566)
Organic Trade Association(566)
Organization of Professional Employees of the U.S. Department of Agriculture(567)
Potash & Phosphate Institute(581)
Scottish Blackface Sheep Breeders Association(606)
Society of Commercial Seed Technologists(633)
Soil and Water Conservation Society(647)
Soil Science Society of America(647)
Turf and Ornamental Communicators Association(667)
Turfgrass Producers International(667)
U.S. Poultry and Egg Association(668)
U.S.A. Dry Pea and Lentil Council(668)
United Fresh Fruit and Vegetable Association(671)
United States Aquaculture Suppliers Association(673)
United States Canola Association(674)
United States Committee on Irrigation and Drainage(674)
Weed Science Society of America(687)
Wheat Quality Council(688)
Wild Blueberry Association of North America(688)
Women in Agribusiness(691)

AGRONOMY
American Society of Agronomy(133)
Association of Women Soil Scientists(220)
Crop Science Society of America(279)
Soil and Plant Analysis Council(646)
Soil Science Society of America(647)
Weed Science Society of America(687)

AIR CONDITIONING
Air Conditioning Contractors of America(13)
Air Diffusion Council(13)
Air Distributing Institute(13)
Air Movement and Control Association International(13)
AirConditioning and Refrigeration Institute(14)
American Society of Heating, Refrigerating and Air-Conditioning Engineers(139)
Associated Air Balance Council(164)
Associated Specialty Contractors(166)
Association of Industry Manufacturers' Representatives(201)
Cooling Technology Institute(265)
HARDI - Heating, Airconditioning, and Refrigeration Distributors International(321)
International Association of Heat and Frost Insulators and Asbestos Workers(357)
International District Energy Association(369)
International Ground Source Heat Pump Association(374)
Mechanical Service Contractors of America(415)
Mobile Air Conditioning Society Worldwide(420)
National Air Duct Cleaners Association(428)
National Air Filtration Association(428)
National Association of Power Engineers(465)
Partnership for Air-Conditioning, Heating Refrigeration Accreditation(571)
Plumbing-Heating-Cooling Contractors - National Association(579)
Refrigerating Engineers and Technicians Association(597)
Sheet Metal and Air Conditioning Contractors' National Association(610)
Solar Energy Industries Association(647)

AIR POLLUTION see also POLLUTION
Air and Waste Management Association(12)
American Association for Aerosol Research(33)
Association of Local Air Pollution Control Officials(203)
Emissions Markets Association(293)
Institute of Clean Air Companies(340)
Manufacturers of Emission Controls Association(411)
National Air Duct Cleaners Association(428)
National Council for Air and Stream Improvement(497)
State and Territorial Air Pollution Program Administrators(652)

AIRPLANES
Aeronautical Repair Station Association(10)
Airborne Law Enforcement Association(14)
Aircraft Electronics Association(14)
Aircraft Locknut Manufacturers Association(14)
Aircraft Owners and Pilots Association(14)
Airlines Electronic Engineering Committee(14)
Aviation Distributors and Manufacturers Association International(224)
Aviation Maintenance Foundation International(225)
Aviation Suppliers Association(225)
Express Delivery & Logistics Association(300)
General Aviation Manufacturers Association(315)
Helicopter Association International(325)
The International Air Cargo Association(348)
Light Aircraft Manufacturers Association(408)
National Aircraft Finance Association(428)
National Aircraft Resale Association(428)
National Association of Aircraft and Communication Suppliers(438)
Organization of Black Airline Pilots(567)
Professional Aviation Maintenance Association(586)
Professional Women Controllers(590)
Seaplane Pilots Association(607)
Soaring Society of America(612)
United States Parachute Association(676)

AIRPORTS
Aeronautical Repair Station Association(10)
Airport Consultants Council(14)
Airport Ground Transportation Association(15)
Airports Council International/North America(15)
American Association of Airport Executives(38)
International Association of Airport Duty Free Stores(352)
National Air Traffic Controllers Association(428)

ALLERGY
American Academy of Allergy, Asthma, and Immunology(20)
American Association of Certified Allergists(39)
American College of Allergy, Asthma and Immunology(64)
Joint Council of Allergy, Asthma, and Immunology(402)
Society for Investigative Dermatology(620)
Society for Leukocyte Biology(621)
World Allergy Organization - IACCI(695)

ALUMINUM
Aluminum Association(18)
Aluminum Extruders Council(18)
Aluminum Foil Container Manufacturers Association(18)
American Architectural Manufacturers Association(32)
Cookware Manufacturers Association(265)
Non-Ferrous Founders' Society(553)
Tube Council of North America(666)

AMBULANCES
American Ambulance Association(30)
National Association of Emergency Medical Technicians(450)

ANATOMY
American Association of Anatomists(38)

ANESTHESIOLOGY
American Academy of Anesthesiologist Assistants(20)
American Association of Nurse Anesthetists(46)
American Dental Society of Anesthesiology(79)
American Osteopathic College of Anesthesiologists(111)
American Society for the Advancement of Sedation and Anesthesia in Dentistry(132)
American Society of Anesthesia Technologists and Technicians(134)
American Society of Anesthesiologists(134)
American Society of PeriAnesthesia Nurses(144)
American Society of Regional Anesthesia and Pain Medicine(145)
Association of University Anesthesiologists(219)
International Anesthesia Research Society(349)
International Federation of Nurse Anesthetists(371)
Society for Education in Anesthesia(616)
Society for Obstetric Anesthesia and Perinatology(622)
Society for Pediatric Anesthesia(623)
Society of Cardiovascular Anesthesiologists(632)
Society of Neurosurgical Anesthesia and Critical Care(641)

ANTHROPOLOGY
African Studies Association(11)
American Anthropological Association(31)
American Association of Physical Anthropologists(48)
American Folklore Society(84)
American Institute for Maghrib Studies(94)
American Quaternary Association(121)
American Society for Ethnohistory(129)
Archaeological Institute of America(160)
Association for Social Anthropology in Oceania(178)
Association for the Study of Classical African Civilizations(180)
Association for the Study of Play(181)
Independent Scholars of Asia(335)
International Society for the Comparative Studies of Civilizations(389)
Social Science Research Council(613)
Society for Applied Anthropology(613)
Society for Cross-Cultural Research(616)

Society for Economic Anthropology(616)
Society for Human Ecology(619)
Society for the Anthropology of Food and Nutrition(627)
Society for Visual Anthropology(629)
Society of Ethnobiology(635)

ANTIQUES

Antiquarian Booksellers Association of America(157)
Art and Antique Dealers League of America(161)
Industry Council for Tangible Assets(337)
National Antique and Art Dealers Association of America(430)

APPAREL

American Apparel & Footwear Association(31)
American Apparel Producers Network(32)
American Cloak and Suit Manufacturers Association(63)
Apparel Graphics Institute(159)
Association of Bridal Consultants(188)
Belt Association(227)
Cashmere and Camel Hair Manufacturers Institute(238)
Chamber of Commerce of the Apparel Industry(243)
Clothing Manufacturers Association of the U.S.A.(248)
Costume Society of America(267)
Council of Fashion Designers of America(272)
Custom Tailors and Designers Association of America(280)
Embroidery Council of America(292)
Embroidery Trade Association(292)
Fashion Accessories Shippers Association(301)
Fashion Group International(301)
Greater Blouse, Skirt and Undergarment Association(320)
Headwear Information Bureau(322)
Home Sewing Association(327)
Hosiery Association, The(328)
International Association of Clothing Designers and Executives(355)
International Formalwear Association(373)
International Textile and Apparel Association(394)
The Knitting Guild Association(404)
National Association of Resale & Thrift Shops(469)
National Association of Uniform Manufacturers and Distributors(480)
National Costumers Association(496)
Neckwear Association of America(551)
Pleaters, Stitchers and Embroiderers Association(579)
Professional Apparel Association(585)
Professional Association of Custom Clothiers(585)
SGMA(651)
Sunglass Association of America(655)
UNITE-HERE(670)
United Infants and Childrens Wear Association(671)
Western-English Trade Association(688)
Young Menswear Association(698)

APPLIANCES

Appliance Parts Distributors Association(159)
Association of Home Appliance Manufacturers(200)
Association of Progressive Rental Organizations(210)
Gas Appliance Manufacturers Association(314)
National Appliance Parts Suppliers Association(430)
National Appliance Service Association(430)
North American Retail Dealers Association(559)

APPRAISERS

American Academy of State Certified Appraisers(29)
American Society of Agricultural Appraisers(133)
American Society of Appraisers(134)
American Society of Farm Managers and Rural Appraisers(137)
Appraisal Institute(159)
Appraisers Association of America(159)
Association of Average Adjusters of the U.S.(187)
Association of Machinery and Equipment Appraisers(203)
Collector Car Appraisers International(250)
Counselors of Real Estate(277)
ECRI(288)
Independent Automotive Damage Appraisers Association(333)
Institute of Business Appraisers(340)
International Association of Assessing Officers(353)
International Society of Appraisers(390)
Mortgage Bankers Association(421)
National Association of Fire Investigators(452)
National Association of Independent Fee Appraisers(457)
National Association of Independent Insurance Adjusters(457)
National Association of Jewelry Appraisers(459)
National Association of Master Appraisers(461)
National Association of Public Insurance Adjusters(467)
National Association of Real Estate Appraisers(468)
National Association of REALTORS(468)
National Association of Review Appraisers and Mortgage Underwriters(469)
Professional Women's Appraisal Association(590)
Property Loss Research Bureau(591)

ARABIC

American Association of Teachers of Arabic(52)
American Mideast Business Associates(106)
Middle East Studies Association of North America(418)

ARBITRATION

American Arbitration Association(32)
National Academy of Arbitrators(426)
Society of Maritime Arbitrators(639)

ARCHAEOLOGY

American Numismatic Society(109)
American Schools of Oriental Research(124)
American Society of Papyrologists(143)
Archaeological Institute of America(160)
Early Sites Research Society(288)
Institute of Nautical Archaeology(343)
National Association of State Archaeologists(473)
National Conference of State Historic Preservation Officers(494)
Register of Professional Archeologists(598)
Society for American Archaeology(613)
Society for Archaeological Sciences(614)
Society for Historical Archaeology(618)
Society for Industrial Archeology(620)
Tree-Ring Society(665)

ARCHERY

Archery Range and Retailers Organization(160)
Archery Trade Association(160)

ARCHITECTURE

American College of Healthcare Architects(66)
American Council of Engineering Companies(75)
American Cultural Resources Association(77)
American Institute of Architects(94)
American Institute of Architecture Students(94)
American Institute of Building Design(95)
American Society of Architectural Illustrators(134)
American Society of Golf Course Architects(138)
American Society of Landscape Architects(140)
Architectural Engineering Institute(160)
Architectural Precast Association(160)
Association for Bridge Construction and Design(168)
Association of Collegiate Schools of Architecture(191)
Association of University Architects(219)
Council of Educational Facility Planners, International(271)
Council of Landscape Architectural Registration Boards(273)
Design-Build Institute of America(283)
National Alliance of Preservation Commissions(430)
National Association of Architectural Metal Manufacturers(438)
National Council of Architectural Registration Boards(498)
Professional Services Management Association(589)
Residential Space Planners International(600)
Society for Marketing Professional Services(621)
Society of American Registered Architects(631)
Society of Architectural Historians(631)
Society of Naval Architects and Marine Engineers(640)
Sustainable Buildings Industry Council(656)
Urban Land Institute(680)
Van Alen Institute(682)

ARCHIVISTS

Academy of Certified Archivists(2)
Association of Catholic Diocesan Archivists(189)
Association of Moving Image Archivists(205)
Council of Archives and Research Libraries in Jewish Studies(270)
National Association of Government Archives and Records Administrators(454)
Society of American Archivists(630)

ARTS, THE

Alliance of Artists Communities(16)
Alliance of Professional Tattooists(17)
Allied Artists of America(17)
American Abstract Artists(19)
American Academy of Arts & Sciences(20)
American Art Therapy Association(32)
American Artists Professional League(32)
American Arts Alliance(32)
American Council for Southern Asian Art(75)
American Craft Council(77)
American Hungarian Educators Association(92)
American Institute for Conservation of Historic and Artistic Works(93)
American Institute of Graphic Arts(96)
American Medallic Sculpture Association(104)
American Society for Aesthetics(126)
American Society for Hispanic Art Historical Studies(130)
American Society of Artists(134)
American Society of Marine Artists(141)
American Theatre Critics Association(151)
Americans for the Arts(156)
Art and Antique Dealers League of America(161)
The Art and Creative Materials Institute(161)
Art Dealers Association of America(161)
Art Directors Guild/Scenic, Title and Graphic Artists(161)
Art Libraries Society of North America(161)
Art Therapy Credentials Board(162)
Artist-Blacksmiths' Association of North America(162)
Association for Textual Scholarship in Art History(179)
Association for the Calligraphic Arts(180)
Association of Art Museum Directors(186)
Association of Arts Administration Educators(186)
Association of Hispanic Arts(200)
Association of International Photography Art Dealers(202)
Association of Medical Illustrators(204)
Association of Performing Arts Presenters(207)
Association of Talent Agents(216)
Black Theatre Network(231)

Catalogue Raisonne Scholars Association(239)
College Art Association(251)
Congress on Research in Dance(261)
Copyright Society of the U.S.A.(266)
Cottage Industry Miniaturists Trade Association(267)
Council of Colleges of Arts and Sciences(271)
Council on Fine Art Photography(276)
Council on Technology Teacher Education(277)
Craft Retailers Association for Tomorrow(278)
Dramatists Guild of America(287)
Federation of Modern Painters and Sculptors(304)
Glass Art Society(317)
Handweavers Guild of America(321)
Historians of Islamic Art(326)
Historians of Netherlandish Art(326)
Indian Arts and Crafts Association(336)
International Association of Art Critics(353)
International Conference of Symphony and Opera Musicians(367)
International Council of Fine Arts Deans(367)
International Documentary Association(369)
International Society for the Performing Arts(389)
International Society of Copier Artists(391)
Museum Computer Network(423)
National Alliance for Musical Theatre(429)
National Antique and Art Dealers Association of America(430)
National Art Education Association(431)
National Art Materials Trade Association(431)
National Assembly of State Arts Agencies(431)
National Association of Artists' Organizations(439)
National Association of Schools of Art and Design(470)
National Association of Schools of Dance(470)
National Association of Schools of Music(470)
National Association of Schools of Theatre(471)
National Association of Women Artists(481)
National Cartoonists Society(487)
National Council of Art Administrators(498)
National Guild of Community Schools of the Arts(515)
National Institute of American Doll Artists(520)
National Sculpture Society(539)
National Society of Mural Painters(542)
National Society of Painters in Casein and Acrylic(542)
National Watercolor Society(549)
North American Performing Arts Managers and Agents(559)
OPERA America(565)
Print Council of America(583)
Private Art Dealers Association(584)
Professional Women Singers Association(590)
Renaissance Society of America(599)
Sculptors Guild(607)
Smocking Arts Guild of America(612)
Society of American Graphic Artists(630)
Society of American Historical Artists(631)
Society of Animal Artists(631)
Society of Decorative Painters(635)
Society of Illustrators(638)
Society of Photographer and Artist Representatives(642)
Society of Publication Designers(643)
Society of Scribes(644)
Surface Design Association(656)
United States Institute for Theatre Technology(676)
University/Resident Theatre Association(680)
Van Alen Institute(682)
Visual Resources Association(684)
Western Association for Art Conservation(687)
Women's Caucus for Art(693)

ASBESTOS

Asbestos Cement Product Producers Association(162)
Asbestos Information Association/North America(162)
Environmental Information Association(296)
Fluid Sealing Association(308)
Independent Sealing Distributors(335)
International Association of Heat and Frost Insulators and Asbestos Workers(357)
Resilient Floor Covering Institute(600)

ASPHALT

Asphalt Emulsion Manufacturers Association(163)
Asphalt Institute(163)
Asphalt Recycling and Reclaiming Association(163)
Asphalt Roofing Manufacturers Association(163)
Association of Asphalt Paving Technologists(186)
National Asphalt Pavement Association(431)
Resilient Floor Covering Institute(600)

ASTROLOGY

American Federation of Astrologers, Inc.(82)

ASTRONOMY

American Association of Variable Star Observers(53)
American Astronomical Society(54)
Association of Universities for Research in Astronomy(219)
International Planetarium Society(383)
Universities Space Research Association(679)

AUCTIONS

Burley Auction Warehouse Association(235)
National Auctioneers Association(482)
National Auto Auction Association(482)

AUDIO-VISUAL

American Association for Vocational Instructional Materials(37)
American Society for Photogrammetry and Remote Sensing(131)
Association for Educational Communications and Technology(172)
Association for Recorded Sound Collections(177)
Association of Biomedical Communications Directors(187)
Association of Cinema and Video Laboratories(190)
Association of Moving Image Archivists(205)
Audio Engineering Society(222)
Communications Media Management Association(255)
Independent Professional Representatives Organization(335)
InfoCom International(338)
Interactive Audio Special Interest Group(346)
International Association of Audio Visual Communicators(353)
International Documentary Association(369)
International Recording Media Association(384)
International Society for Performance Improvement(388)
International Society of Communication Specialists(391)
MIDI Manufacturers Association(418)
National Academy of Recording Arts and Sciences(427)
National Association of Media and Technology Centers(461)
National Association of Recording Merchandisers(468)
National Association of Self-Instructional Language Programs(471)
National Systems Contractors Association(545)
Online Audiovisual Catalogers(565)
Recording Industry Association of America(596)
Society for Cinema and Media Studies(615)
Society of Professional Audio Recording Services(642)
United States Institute for Theatre Technology(676)
Video Software Dealers Association(683)

AUDITORIUM MANAGERS

International Association of Assembly Managers(353)

AUTHORS see also PRESS, WRITERS

American Society of Composers, Authors and Publishers(136)
American Society of Journalists and Authors(140)
Association of Authors' Representatives(186)
Authors Guild(222)
Authors League of America(222)
Children's Literature Association(244)
Council of Literary Magazines and Presses(273)
Dramatists Guild of America(287)
Intellectual Property Owners Association(345)
International Food, Wine and Travel Writers Association(372)
National Association of Home and Workshop Writers(456)
Romance Writers of America(603)
Society of American Business Editors and Writers(630)
Songwriters Guild of America(647)
Text and Academic Authors Association(659)

AUTOMOBILES see also MOTOR VEHICLES

Alternatives Fuel Vehicle Network(18)
American International Automobile Dealers Association(98)
American Salvage Pool Association(124)
American Society of Body Engineers(135)
Association of Automotive Aftermarket Distributors(186)
Association of Finance and Insurance Professionals(196)
Association of International Automobile Manufacturers(201)
Automotive Communication Council(223)
Automotive Industry Action Group(223)
Automotive Maintenance Repair Association(223)
Automotive Public Relations Council(224)
Automotive Service Association(224)
Automotive Training Managers Council(224)
Collector Car Appraisers International(250)
Driving School Association of America(287)
Gasoline and Automotive Service Dealers Association(314)
Heavy Duty Brake Manufacturers Council(325)
Inter-Industry Conference on Auto Collision Repair(346)
International Association of Auto Theft Investigators(353)
Japan Automobile Manufacturers Association(400)
Liability Insurance Research Bureau(407)
National Association of Fleet Resale Dealers(453)
National Association of Minority Automobile Dealers(462)
National Automobile Dealers Association(482)
National Independent Automobile Dealers Association(518)
National Limousine Association(525)
National Mobility Equipment Dealers Association(527)
National Motorsports Press Association(528)
National Vehicle Leasing Association(548)
Original Equipment Suppliers Association(568)
Performance Warehouse Association(573)
QVM/CMC Vehicle Manufacturers Association(594)
Society of Automotive Analysts(632)
Spring Research Institute(652)
Tire and Rim Association(661)
Truck Manufacturers Association(665)

AUTOMOTIVE INDUSTRY see GARAGES, MOTOR VEHICLES

Alternatives Fuel Vehicle Network(18)

AVIATION

Air Force Association(13)
Air Line Pilots Association, International(13)
Air Traffic Control Association(13)
Air Transport Association of America(13)
Aircraft Builders Council(14)
Airline Industrial Relations Conference(14)

International Society of Beverage Technologists(390)
National Alcohol Beverage Control Association(429)
National Association of Beverage Importers-Wine-Spirits-Beer(439)
National Coffee Association of the U.S.A.(490)
National United Merchants Beverage Association(548)
Specialty Coffee Association of America(650)
Tea Association of the United States of America(658)
Tea Council of the U.S.A.(658)
World Association of Alcohol Beverage Industries(695)

BIBLE
American Academy of Religion(28)
American Schools of Oriental Research(124)
Catholic Biblical Association of America(239)
Christian Stewardship Association(246)
Society of Biblical Literature(632)

BICYCLES
Bicycle Product Suppliers Association(228)
Bicycle Shippers Association(228)
National Bicycle Dealers Association(484)

BILLIARDS
Billiard Congress of America(228)

BIOLOGY
American Association of Stratigraphic Palynologists(51)
American Biological Safety Association(57)
The American Electrophoresis Society(80)
American Institute for Medical and Biological Engineering(94)
American Institute of Biological Sciences(94)
American Institute of Fishery Research Biologists(96)
American Microscopical Society(106)
American Society for Biochemistry and Molecular Biology(126)
American Society for Cell Biology(127)
American Society for Cytotechnology(128)
American Society for Photobiology(131)
American Society for Reproductive Medicine(132)
American Society of Cytopathology(137)
American Society of Limnology and Oceanography(140)
American Society of Naturalists(142)
American Society of Plant Biologists(144)
Association for Biology Laboratory Education(168)
Association for Gnotobiotics(173)
Association for Tropical Biology and Conservation(181)
Association of Ecosystem Research Centers(194)
Beta Beta Beta(228)
BioCommunications Association(229)
Bioelectromagnetics Society(229)
Biological Stain Commission(229)
Biomedical Engineering Society(229)
Biophysical Society(229)
Biotechnology Industry Organization(229)
Council of Science Editors(274)
Ecological Society of America(288)
Endocrine Society(294)
Engineering in Medicine and Biology Society(295)
Environmental Mutagen Society(296)
Federation of American Socs. for Experimental Biology(303)
Herpetologists' League(325)
Histochemical Society(326)
Human Biology Association(329)
International Society for Analytical Cytology(386)
International Society for Chronobiology(386)
International Society for Developmental Psychobiology(387)
International Society for Magnetic Resonance in Medicine(387)
International Society for Plastination(388)
Lepidoptera Research Foundation(407)
National Association of Biology Teachers(440)
Natural Science Collections Alliance(551)
North American Benthological Society(555)
North American Lake Management Society(557)
Paleontological Society(570)
Phycological Society of America(577)
The Protein Society(591)
RNA Society(602)
Society for Biomaterials(614)
Society for Chaos Theory in Psychology and Life Sciences(615)
Society for Conservation Biology(615)
Society for Cryobiology(616)
Society for Developmental Biology(616)
Society for Epidemiologic Research(617)
Society for Experimental Biology and Medicine(617)
Society for In Vitro Biology(619)
Society for Leukocyte Biology(621)
Society for Mathematical Biology(621)
Society for Physical Regulation in Biology and Medicine(624)
Society for the Study of Amphibians and Reptiles(628)
Society for the Study of Evolution(628)
Society for the Study of Reproduction(628)
Society for the Study of Social Biology(628)
Society for Vascular Medicine and Biology(629)
Society of Biological Psychiatry(632)
Society of Rheology(643)
Transplantation Society(663)
United States Federation for Culture Collections(675)

BIRDS
American Ornithologists' Union(110)
Association of Avian Veterinarians(187)
Association of Field Ornithologists(196)
Wild Bird Feeding Institute(688)

BLACKS see also MINORITIES
African-American Library and Information Science Association(11)
African-American Women's Clergy Association(11)
American Association of Blacks in Energy(38)
American Health and Beauty Aids Institute(89)
Association for the Study of African American Life and History(180)
Association of African American Museums(183)
Association of Black Cardiologists(187)
Association of Black Foundation Executives(187)
Association of Black Psychologists(187)
Association of Black Sociologists(187)
BCA(226)
Black Americans in Publishing(230)
Black Broadcasters Alliance(230)
Black Caucus of the American Library Association(230)
Black Coaches Association(230)
Black Entertainment and Sports Lawyers Association(230)
Black Filmmaker Foundation(230)
Black Retail Action Group(230)
Black Theatre Network(231)
Coalition of Black Trade Unionists(249)
Consortium for Graduate Study and Management(262)
Inter-America Travel Agents Society(346)
National Alliance of Black School Educators(429)
National Alliance of Postal and Federal Employees(429)
National Association for Equal Opportunity in Higher Education(433)
National Association of Black Accountants(440)
National Association of Black Journalists(440)
National Association of Black Social Workers(440)
National Association of Black Women Entrepreneurs(440)
National Association of Black-Owned Broadcasters(440)
National Association of Blacks in Criminal Justice(440)
National Association of Colored Women's Clubs(445)
National Association of Investment Companies(459)
National Association of Minority Contractors(462)
National Association of Negro Business and Professional Women's Clubs(462)
National Association of Real Estate Brokers(468)
National Bankers Association(483)
National Bar Association(483)
National Beauty Culturists' League(484)
National Black Caucus of State Legislators(484)
National Black MBA Association(484)
National Black Nurses Association(484)
National Black Police Association(484)
National Black Public Relations Society(485)
National Coalition of Black Meeting Planners(490)
National Conference of Black Lawyers(492)
National Conference of Black Mayors(492)
National Council of Black Engineers and Scientists(498)
National Dental Association(505)
National Economic Association(505)
National Forum for Black Public Administrators(512)
National Insurance Association(521)
National Medical Association(526)
National Minority Business Council(527)
National Newspaper Publishers Association(529)
National Organization for the Professional Advancement of Black Chemists and Chemical Engineers(530)
Organization of Black Airline Pilots(567)
Urban Financial Services Coalition(680)

BLIND
Access Technology Association(6)
American Council of the Blind(76)
American Medical Rehabilitation Providers Association(104)
Association for Education and Rehabilitation of the Blind and Visually Impaired(172)
International Association of Audio Information Services(353)
National Council of State Agencies for the Blind(500)
National Industries for the Blind(519)
Prevent Blindness America(583)

BLUEPRINTS
International Reprographic Association(385)

BOATING
American Boat and Yacht Council(58)
American Boat Builders and Repairers Association(58)
American Society of Marine Artists(141)
Boating Writers International(231)
International Marina Institute(379)
Marine Retailers Association of America(412)
National Association of Charterboat Operators(442)
National Association of Marine Services(461)
National Association of State Boating Law Administrators(473)
National Marine Bankers Association(525)
National Marine Manufacturers Association(526)
National Marine Representatives Association(526)
Personal Watercraft Industry Association(574)
Society of Accredited Marine Surveyors(629)
Society of Small Craft Designers(644)
States Organization for Boating Access(653)
United States Rowing Association(677)
Yacht Brokers Association of America(698)

BOILERS
American Boiler Manufacturers Association(58)
Council of Industrial Boiler Owners(272)
Hydronics Institute Division of GAMA(330)
Pressure Vessel Manufacturers Association(583)

BOOKS see also LIBRARIES
American Association for Vocational Instructional Materials(37)
American Book Producers Association(58)
American Booksellers Association(58)
American Wholesale Booksellers Association(154)
Antiquarian Booksellers Association of America(157)
Association of Booksellers for Children(188)
Binding Industries Association(228)
Book Industry Study Group, Inc.(231)
Book Manufacturers' Institute(231)
CBA(240)
Children's Book Council(244)
Children's Literature Association(244)
Guild of Book Workers(321)
International Society of Copier Artists(391)
Jewish Book Council(401)
Library Binding Institute(407)
Manuscript Society(412)
Miniature Book Society(420)
National Association of College Stores(444)
National Association of State Textbook Administrators(476)
Periodical and Book Association of America(573)
Society of Children's Book Writers and Illustrators(633)
Society of Scribes(644)
Women's National Book Association(694)

BOTANY
American Bryological and Lichenological Society(59)
American Fern Society(83)
American Phytopathological Society(115)
American Society of Pharmacognosy(144)
American Society of Plant Taxonomists(144)
Botanical Society of America(231)
Council on Botanical and Horticultural Libraries(275)
Genetics Society of America(315)
International Society for Molecular Plant Microbe Interactions(387)
Mycological Society of America(424)
National Association of Plant Patent Owners(465)
National Council of Commercial Plant Breeders(498)
Natural Science Collections Alliance(551)
Organization for Tropical Studies(567)
Phycological Society of America(577)
Society for Economic Botany(616)
Society of Commercial Seed Technologists(633)
Veterinary Botanical Medical Association(682)

BOTTLES see also BEVERAGE INDUSTRY
Glass, Molders, Pottery, Plastics and Allied Workers International Union(317)

BOWLING
Bowling Proprietors Association of America(231)
Bowling Writers Association of America(232)
NAIR -- the International Association of Bowling Lane Specialists(425)
Professional Bowlers Association of America(586)
United States Bowling Congress(673)
United States Bowling Instructors Association(673)

BOXES see also BAGS, CONTAINERS
Fibre Box Association(305)
National Paperbox Association(531)
Retail Packaging Manufacturers Association(601)
Wirebound Box Manufacturers Association(690)

BRASS
Brass and Bronze Ingot Industry(232)
Copper and Brass Fabricators Council(266)
Copper and Brass Servicenter Association(266)
Plumbing Manufacturers Institute(579)

BREWERS
American Malting Barley Association(102)
American Society of Brewing Chemists(135)
Beer Institute(227)
Brewers Association(232)
Brewers' Association of America(232)
Hop Growers of America(328)
Master Brewers Association of the Americas(413)
National Beer Wholesalers Association(484)

BRIQUETS
Institute for Briquetting and Agglomeration(339)

BROADCASTERS see RADIO-TV
Organization of State Broadcasting Executives(568)

BRONZE
Brass and Bronze Ingot Industry(232)

BROOMS & BRUSHES
American Brush Manufacturers Association(59)

BUSINESS
AACSB - the Association to Advance Collegiate Schools of Business(1)
Academy of International Business(3)
Academy of Legal Studies in Business(4)
Agribusiness Council(12)
Alliance of Area Business Publications(16)
Alpha Kappa Psi(18)
American Association of Minority Businesses(45)
American Benefits Council(56)
American Business Conference(60)
American Business Media(60)
American Business Women's Association(60)
American Independent Business Alliance(93)
American Society of Business Publication Editors(135)
APICS - The Association for Operations Management(158)
Associated Business Writers of America(164)
Association for Business Communication(168)
Association for Business Simulation and Experiential Learning(168)
Association for Corporate Growth(171)
Association for University Business and Economic Research(181)
Association of Corporate Counsel(193)
Association of Management/International Association of Management(203)
Association of Master of Business Administration Executives(204)
Association of School Business Officials International(212)
BPA Worldwide(232)
BritishAmerican Business Inc.(233)
Business and Professional Women/USA(235)
Business Council(235)
Business Forms Management Association(235)
Business Higher Education Forum(235)
Business History Conference(235)
Business Professionals of America(236)
Career College Association(237)
Coalition of Service Industries(249)
College Athletic Business Management Association(251)
Colombian American Association(252)
Committee of 200(254)
Consortium for Graduate Study and Management(262)
Council for Ethics in Economics(268)
Council of Better Business Bureaus(271)
Delta Pi Epsilon(282)
Delta Sigma Pi(283)
Ecuadorean American Association(288)
Ethics Officer Association(298)
Export Institute of the United States(300)
Family Firm Institute(300)
Financial Management Association International(306)
Foundation for Russian-American Economic Cooperation(311)
Futures Industry Association(313)
Industrial Asset Management Council(336)
Industrial Foundation of America(337)
Information Technology Industry Council(338)
Institute of Business Appraisers(340)
Institute of Certified Business Counselors(340)
Institute of Certified Healthcare Business Consultants(340)
International Alliance for Women(348)
International Association for Business and Society(349)
International Association of Business Communicators(354)
International Association of Used Equipment Dealers(361)
International Business Brokers Association(364)
International Business Music Association(364)
International Contract Center Benchmarking Consortium(367)
International Function Point Users Group(373)
International Network of Merger and Acquisition Partners(380)
International Reciprocal Trade Association(384)
International Swaps and Derivatives Association(393)
Latin Business Association(405)
National AMBUCS(430)
National Association for the Self-Employed(436)
National Association of Blacks in Criminal Justice(440)
National Association of Business Consultants(441)
National Association for Business Economics(441)
National Association of Business Political Action Committees(441)
National Association of Church Business Administration(443)
National Association of College and University Business Officers(444)
National Association of Corporate Directors(446)
National Association of Manufacturers(460)
National Association of Negro Business and Professional Women's Clubs(462)
National Association of Women Business Owners(481)
National Black MBA Association(484)
National Bureau of Certified Consultants(485)
National Business Association(486)
National Business Education Association(486)
National Business Owners Association(486)
National Cooperative Business Association(496)
National Family Business Council(508)
National Federation of Independent Business(509)
National Hispanic Corporate Council(517)
National Mail Order Association(525)
National Minority Business Council(527)
National Minority Supplier Development Council(527)
National Society of Hispanic MBAs(541)
Nine to Five, National Association of Working Women(553)
North American Case Research Association(555)
Organization Development Institute(566)
Organization Development Network(566)
Organizational Systems Research Association(568)
Outdoor Amusement Business Association(569)
Phi Chi Theta(575)
Phi Gamma Nu(576)

Product Development and Management Association(585)
Small Business Exporters Association of the United States(611)
SOCAP International(612)
Society of American Business Editors and Writers(630)
Society of Competitive Intelligence Professionals(633)
Society of Corporate Secretaries and Governance Professionals(634)
Society of International Business Fellows(639)
State Government Affairs Council(652)
Supply Chain Council(656)
Telecommunications Benchmarking International Group(659)
U.S. - Taiwan Business Council(667)
U.S. Pan Asian American Chamber of Commerce(668)
United Applications Standards Group(670)
United States Business and Industry Council(674)
United States Chamber of Commerce(674)
United States Junior Chamber of Commerce(676)
Venezuelan American Association of the U.S.(682)
WACRA - World Association for Case Method Research and Application(684)
World Trade Centers Association(696)
Young Entrepreneurs Organization(698)
Young Presidents' Organization(698)
Zonta International(698)

CAMPING
American Camp Association(60)
National Association of RV Parks and Campgrounds(470)
National Forest Recreation Association(512)
Recreation Vehicle Dealers Association of North America(596)
Recreation Vehicle Industry Association(596)

CANCER
American Association for Cancer Education(33)
American Association for Cancer Research(34)
American Cancer Society(60)
American College of Mohs Micrographic Surgery and Cutaneous Oncology(67)
American Radium Society(121)
American Society for Cytotechnology(128)
American Society for Therapeutic Radiology and Oncology(133)
American Society of Clinical Oncology(136)
American Society of Pediatric Hematology/Oncology(143)
American Society of Preventive Oncology(145)
Association of Community Cancer Centers(192)
Association of Pediatric Hematology/Oncology Nurses(207)
Association of Pediatric Oncology Social Workers(207)
National Association for Proton Therapy(435)
National Cancer Registrars Association(486)
Oncology Nursing Society(564)
Society for Leukocyte Biology(621)
Society for Radiation Oncology Administrators(624)
Society of Surgical Oncology(644)
Veterinary Cancer Society(682)

CANS
Can Manufacturers Institute(237)
Composite Can and Tube Institute(256)

CARDIOLOGY
Alliance of Cardiovascular Professionals(16)
American College of Angiology(64)
American College of Cardiology(64)
American College of Cardiovascular Administrators(64)
American Heart Association(90)
American Society of Echocardiography(137)
American Society of Nuclear Cardiology(142)
Association of Black Cardiologists(187)
Association of Professors of Cardiology(209)
Heart Rhythm Society(324)
Society for Cardiovascular Angiography and Interventions(614)
Society for Cardiovascular Magnetic Resonance(614)
Society of Cardiovascular Anesthesiologists(632)
Society of Geriatric Cardiology(637)
Society of Invasive Cardiovascular Professionals(639)

CARPETS see also RUGS
American Floorcovering Alliance(84)
Association of Specialists in Cleaning and Restoration International(214)
Carpet and Rug Institute(238)
Carpet Cushion Council(238)
Oriental Rug Importers Association of America(568)
Oriental Rug Retailers of America(568)

CARWASH
Carwash Owner's and Supplier's Association(238)
International Carwash Association(364)

CATHOLIC
American Catholic Correctional Chaplains Association(61)
American Catholic Historical Association(61)
American Catholic Philosophical Association(61)
Association for Social Economics(178)
Association for the Sociology of Religion(180)
Association of Catholic Colleges and Universities(188)
Association of Catholic TV and Radio Syndicators(189)
Association of Jesuit Colleges and Universities(202)
Augustinian Educational Association(222)
Catholic Academy for Communication Arts Professionals(239)
Catholic Biblical Association of America(239)
Catholic Book Publishers Association(239)
Catholic Campus Ministry Association(239)
Catholic Charities USA(239)
Catholic Health Association of the United States(240)
Catholic Library Association(240)
Catholic Medical Association(240)
Catholic Press Association(240)
Catholic Theological Society of America(240)
Conference of Major Superiors of Men, U.S.A.(259)
Jesuit Secondary Education Association(401)
National Association of Catholic Chaplains(442)
National Association of Catholic School Teachers(442)
National Association of Diocesan Ecumenical Officers(449)
National Association of Pastoral Musicians(464)
National Association of State Catholic Conference Directors(474)
National Catholic Band Association(487)
National Catholic Cemetery Conference(487)
National Catholic Development Conference(487)
National Catholic Educational Association(487)
National Catholic Educational Exhibitors(487)
National Catholic Pharmacists Guild of the United States(488)
National Conference of Catechetical Leadership(493)
National Conference of Diocesan Vocation Directors(493)
National Council of Catholic Women(498)
National Federation of Priests' Councils(510)
North American Academy of Ecumenists(554)
United States Conference of Catholic Bishops(674)

CATS
American Association of Feline Practitioners(43)
American Boarding Kennels Association(58)
International Professional Groomers(383)

CATTLE
American Angus Association(31)
American Association of Bovine Practitioners(39)
American Beefalo World Registry(56)
American Blonde D'Aquitaine Association(57)
American Brahman Breeders Association(59)
American Brahmousin Council(59)
American Bralers Association(59)
American British White Park Association(59)
American Chianina Association(62)
American Dexter Cattle Association(79)
American Galloway Breeders Association(86)
American Gelbvieh Association(86)
American Genetic Association(86)
American Guernsey Association(87)
American Hereford Association(90)
American Highland Cattle Association(90)
American International Charolais Association(98)
American International Marchigiana Society(98)
American Jersey Cattle Association(99)
American Maine-Anjou Association(102)
American Milking Devon Association(106)
American Milking Shorthorn Society(106)
American Murray Grey Association(107)
American National CattleWomen(108)
American Pinzgauer Association(115)
American Red Brangus Association(122)
American Red Poll Association(122)
American Romagnola Association(123)
American Salers Association(123)
American Shorthorn Association(125)
American Simmental Association(125)
American Tarentaise Association(150)
Amerifax Cattle Association(156)
Ankole Watusi International Registry(157)
Ayrshire Breeders' Association(225)
Barzona Breeders Association of America(226)
Beef Improvement Federation(227)
Beefmaster Breeders United(227)
Belted Galloway Society(227)
Brown Swiss Cattle Breeders Association of the U.S.A.(234)
Devon Cattle Association(284)
Gelbray International(315)
Holstein Association USA(327)
International Brangus Breeders Association(363)
International Miniature Cattle Breeders Society(380)
Irish Blacks Cattle Society(399)
National Association of Animal Breeders(438)
National Bison Association(484)
National Cattlemen's Beef Association(488)
National Mastitis Council(526)
North American Limousin Foundation(558)
North American South Devon Association(561)
Parthenais Cattle Breeders Association of America(571)
Piedmontese Association of the United States(577)
Purebred Dairy Cattle Association(593)
Purebred Dexter Cattle Association of North America(593)
Red and White Dairy Cattle Association(597)
Red Angus Association of America(597)
Santa Gertrudis Breeders International(605)
Texas Longhorn Breeders Association of America(659)
United Braford Breeders(670)
United States Beef Breeds Council(673)
World Watusi Association(697)

CEMETERIES see also FUNERALS
Accredited Pet Cemetery Society(7)
American Institute of Commemorative Art(95)
Funeral Consumers Alliance(312)

International Association of Pet Cemeteries(360)
International Cemetery and Funeral Association(364)
International Memorialization Supply Association(379)
Monument Builders of North America(421)
National Catholic Cemetery Conference(487)
National Concrete Burial Vault Association(492)

CERAMICS see also CHINA

American Ceramic Society(61)
Art Glass Association(161)
Associated Glass and Pottery Manufacturers(165)
Ceramic Manufacturers Association(241)
Ceramic Tile Distributors Association(241)
Gift and Collectibles Guild(316)
International Ceramic Association(364)
Keramos Fraternity(403)
Materials and Methods Standards Association(414)
National Council on Education for the Ceramic Arts(502)
National Institute of Ceramic Engineers(520)
Refractory Ceramic Fibers Coalition(597)
Tile Contractors' Association of America(661)
United States Advanced Ceramics Association(672)

CHAINS

American Chain Association(61)
Chain Link Fence Manufacturers Institute(242)
National Association of Chain Manufacturers(442)

CHAMBER OF COMMERCE

ACCRA - Ass'n of Applied Community Researchers(6)
American Chamber of Commerce Executives(61)
American Indonesian Chamber of Commerce(93)
American Mideast Business Associates(106)
American-Israel Chamber of Commerce and Industry(156)
American-Uzbekistan Chamber of Commerce(156)
Argentina-American Chamber of Commerce(160)
Association of American Chambers of Commerce in Latin America(184)
Belgian American Chamber of Commerce in the United States(227)
Brazilian American Chamber of Commerce(232)
BritishAmerican Business Inc.(233)
Chamber of Commerce of the Apparel Industry(243)
Colombian American Association(252)
Council of Better Business Bureaus(271)
Council of State Chambers of Commerce(274)
Danish-American Chamber of Commerce (USA)(281)
Ecuadorean American Association(288)
European-American Business Council(298)
Finnish American Chamber of Commerce(307)
French-American Chamber of Commerce(312)
German American Chamber of Commerce(316)
Greater Washington Board of Trade(320)
Hellenic-American Chamber of Commerce(325)
Icelandic American Chamber of Commerce(330)
International Downtown Association(369)
Ireland Chamber of Commerce in the U.S.(399)
Italy-America Chamber of Commerce(400)
Latin Chamber of Commerce of U.S.A.(405)
National Black Chamber of Commerce(484)
National U.S.-Arab Chamber of Commerce(548)
Netherlands Chamber of Commerce in the United States(551)
North American-Chilean Chamber of Commerce(562)
Norwegian-American Chamber of Commerce(562)
Philippine-American Chamber of Commerce(576)
Portugal-United States Chamber of Commerce(581)
Romanian-American Chamber of Commerce(603)
Spain-U.S. Chamber of Commerce(648)
Swedish-American Chambers of Commerce(657)
United States Chamber of Commerce(674)
United States Council for International Business(674)
United States Hispanic Chamber of Commerce(675)
United States Junior Chamber of Commerce(676)
United States-Austrian Chamber of Commerce(678)
United States-Mexico Chamber of Commerce(678)
United States-New Zealand Council(678)
Venezuelan American Association of the U.S.(682)

CHAPLAINS

American Catholic Correctional Chaplains Association(61)
Assembly of Episcopal Healthcare Chaplains(164)
Association of Professional Chaplains(208)
Catholic Campus Ministry Association(239)
JWB Jewish Chaplains Council(403)
Military Chaplains Association of the U.S.(419)
National Association of Catholic Chaplains(442)
National Federation of Temple Brotherhoods(510)
National Institute of Business and Industrial Chaplaincy(520)
Network on Ministry in Specialized Settings(552)

CHEMICALS & CHEMICAL INDUSTRY

AACC International(1)
Acrylonitrile Group(8)
Agricultural Retailers Association(12)
Alkylphenols and Ethoxylates Research Council(15)
Alliance for Responsible Atmospheric Policy(16)
Alpha Chi Sigma(17)
American Association for Clinical Chemistry(34)
American Association of Textile Chemists and Colorists(53)
American Chemical Society(62)
American Chemical Society - Rubber Division(62)
American Chemistry Council(62)
American Coke and Coal Chemicals Institute(63)
American College of Toxicology(71)
American Fiber Manufacturers Association(83)
American Fire Safety Council(84)
American Institute of Chemical Engineers(95)
American Institute of Chemists(95)
American Leather Chemists Association(101)
American Microchemical Society(106)
American Oil Chemists' Society(110)
American Society for Biochemistry and Molecular Biology(126)
American Society for Mass Spectrometry(130)
American Society for Neurochemistry(130)
American Society of Brewing Chemists(135)
Aniline Association(157)
AOAC International(158)
Aspirin Foundation of America(164)
Association of Consulting Chemists and Chemical Engineers(192)
Association of Defensive Spray Manufacturers(193)
Association of Official Racing Chemists(206)
Basic Acrylic Monomer Manufacturers(226)
Chemical Coaters Association International(243)
Chemical Fabrics and Film Association(243)
Chemical Heritage Foundation(243)
Chemical Industry Data Exchange(243)
Chemical Producers and Distributors Association(243)
Chemical Sources Association(243)
Chlorinated Paraffins Industry Association(245)
Chlorine Chemistry Council(245)
Chlorine Institute(245)
CIIT Centers for Health Research(247)
Color Pigments Manufacturers Association(253)
Combustion Institute(253)
Consumer Specialty Products Association(263)
Council for Chemical Research(268)
CropLife America(279)
Dibasic Esters Group(284)
Drug, Chemical and Associated Technologies Association(287)
Electrochemical Society(291)
Emulsion Polymers Council(294)
ETAD North America(298)
Ethylene Oxide Sterilization Association(298)
Federation of Analytical Chemistry and Spectroscopy Societies(303)
Federation of Socs. for Coatings Technology(304)
Fertilizer Institute(305)
Geochemical Society(315)
Halogenated Solvents Industry Alliance(321)
Halon Alternatives Research Corp.(321)
Histochemical Society(326)
Independent Liquid Terminals Association(334)
Industrial Chemical Research Association(336)
Institute for Polyacrylate Absorbents(339)
International Chemical Workers Union Council/UFCW(365)
International Isotope Society(377)
International Ozone Association-Pan American Group Branch(382)
Materials Marketing Associates(414)
Materials Technology Institute(414)
Methacrylate Producers Association(418)
Methanol Institute(418)
National Aerosol Association(428)
National Association of Chemical Distributors(442)
National Chemical Credit Association(488)
National Organization for the Professional Advancement of Black Chemists and Chemical Engineers(530)
National Pest Management Association(532)
North American Catalysis Society(555)
North American Polyelectrolyte Producers Association(559)
Organic Reactions Catalysis Society(566)
Photo Chemical Machining Institute(576)
Pine Chemicals Association(578)
Polyisocyanurate Insulation Manufacturers Association(580)
Polyurethane Foam Association(580)
Powder Coating Institute(582)
Process Equipment Manufacturers' Association(584)
Professional Landscape Network(588)
Sales Association of the Chemical Industry(604)
SB Latex Council(605)
Silicones Environmental, Health and Safety Council of North America(610)
Society for Environmental Geochemistry and Health(617)
Society of Chemical Industry, American Section(633)
Society of Cosmetic Chemists(634)
Society of Environmental Toxicology and Chemistry(635)
Society of Flavor Chemists(636)
Society of Mineral Analysts(640)
Society of Toxicology(645)
Soil and Plant Analysis Council(646)
Solution Mining Research Institute(647)
Spill Control Association of America(651)
Swimming Pool Water Treatment Professionals(657)
Synthetic Organic Chemical Manufacturers Association(657)
Test Boring Association(659)
Tetrahydrofuran Task Force(659)

Tubular Exchanger Manufacturers Association(666)
Vinyl Acetate Council(683)

CHILDREN
American Academy of Pediatric Dentistry(26)
American Association of Children's Residential Centers(39)
American Association of Early Childhood Educators(42)
American Professional Society on the Abuse of Children(117)
American Society of Pediatric Nephrology(143)
Association for Child Psychoanalysis(169)
Association for Childhood Education International(169)
Association for Library Service to Children(175)
Association of Children's Museums(189)
Association of Jewish Family and Children's Agencies(202)
Child Neurology Society(244)
Child Welfare League of America(244)
Children's Book Council(244)
Children's Literature Association(244)
Choristers Guild(245)
Council for Exceptional Children(268)
Council for Professional Recognition(269)
CWLA - Child Mental Health Division(280)
Early Childhood Education Institute(288)
Foster Family-Based Treatment Association(311)
International Academy for Child Brain Development(347)
International Nanny Association(380)
International Society of Psychiatric-Mental Health Nurses(392)
Jewish Social Service Professionals Association(402)
National Association for Family Child Care(433)
National Association for the Education of Young Children(436)
National Association of Child Care Professionals(443)
National Association of Child Care Resource and Referral Agencies(443)
National Association of Children's Hospitals(443)
National Association of Counsel for Children(446)
National Association of Private Special Education Centers(465)
National Association of Public Child Welfare Administrators(467)
National Child Care Association(489)
National Fellowship of Child Care Executives(510)
National Guardianship Association(515)
National Student Assistance Association(544)
Parenting Publications of America(571)
Society for Adolescent Medicine(613)
Society for Research in Child Development(624)
Society for Research on Adolescence(624)
Society of Children's Book Writers and Illustrators(633)
Teaching-Family Association(658)
U.S.A. Toy Library Association(669)
Voices for America's Children(684)
World Association for Infant Mental Health(695)

CHINA see also CERAMICS
Gift Associates Interchange Network(317)

CHINESE
American Association for Chinese Studies(34)
Association for Asian Studies(167)
Chinese Language Teachers Association(245)
Chinese-American Librarians Association(245)
United States-China Business Council(678)

CHIROPRACTORS
American Chiropractic Association(62)
American Chiropractic Registry of Radiologic Technologists(62)
American College of Chiropractic Orthopedists(64)
Association of Chiropractic Colleges(189)
Chiropractic Council on Physiological Therapeutics and Rehabilitation(245)
Congress of Chiropractic State Associations(261)
Council on Chiropractic Education(275)
Council on Chiropractic Orthopedics(275)
Council on Diagnostic Imaging to the A.C.A.(275)
Federation of Straight Chiropractors and Organizations(304)
International Chiropractors Association(365)

CHOCOLATE
American Cocoa Research Institute(63)
Chocolate Manufacturers Association(245)
Cocoa Merchants' Association of America(250)

CIRCULATION
International Newspaper Marketing Association(381)

CLAY
American Ceramic Society(61)
Brick Industry Association(232)
Clay Minerals Society(247)
Expanded Shale, Clay and Slate Institute(299)
National Clay Pipe Institute(490)
National Clay Pottery Association(490)
Refractories Institute(597)
Sorptive Minerals Institute(647)
Stucco Manufacturers Association(654)
Tile Council of North America(661)

CLEANERS
Association of Specialists in Cleaning and Restoration International(214)
Building Service Contractors Association International(234)
Cleaning Equipment Trade Association(247)
Cleaning Management Institute(247)
Coin Laundry Association(250)
International Fabricare Institute(371)
International Kitchen Exhaust Cleaning Association(377)
International Maintenance Institute(379)
International Window Cleaning Association(397)
Laundry and Dry Cleaning International Union(405)
Multi-Housing Laundry Association(422)
National Association of Diaper Services(449)
National Association of Institutional Linen Management(458)
National Chimney Sweep Guild(489)
National Cleaners Association(490)
Power Washers of North America(582)
Secondary Materials and Recycled Textiles Association(607)
Soap and Detergent Association(612)
Society of Cleaning and Restoration Technicians(633)
Textile Care Allied Trades Association(660)
Textile Rental Services Association of America(660)
Uniform and Textile Service Association(669)

CLUBS see also FRATERNAL ORGANIZATIONS
Alpha Chi Sigma(17)
Alpha Kappa Psi(18)
Alpha Omega International Dental Fraternity(18)
Alpha Zeta Omega(18)
American Community Cultural Center Association(72)
American Dental Interfraternity Council(79)
Association of College Honor Societies(191)
Beta Alpha Psi(228)
Beta Phi Mu(228)
Business and Professional Women/USA(235)
Club Managers Association of America(249)
College Fraternity Editors Association(251)
Continental Dorset Club(264)
Delta Pi Epsilon(282)
Delta Sigma Delta(282)
Delta Sigma Pi(283)
Delta Theta Phi(283)
Distributive Education Clubs of America(286)
Fraternity Executives Association(311)
Gamma Iota Sigma(313)
General Federation of Women's Clubs(315)
Girls Incorporated(317)
International Health, Racquet and Sportsclub Association(374)
International League of Professional Baseball Clubs(378)
International Legal Fraternity of Phi Delta Phi(378)
International Military Community Executives Association(379)
Iota Tau Tau(399)
Keramos Fraternity(403)
Mu Phi Epsilon(422)
National AMBUCS(430)
National Association of Colored Women's Clubs(445)
National Association of Litho Clubs(460)
National Association of Negro Business and Professional Women's Clubs(462)
National Block and Bridle Club(485)
National Club Association(490)
National Federation of Music Clubs(509)
National Garden Clubs(513)
National Pan-Hellenic Council(531)
National Panhellenic Conference(531)
National Writers Association(550)
North American Interfraternity Conference(557)
Omega Tau Sigma(564)
Omicron Kappa Upsilon(564)
Overseas Press Club of America(570)
Phi Alpha Delta(575)
Pi Lambda Theta(577)
Professional Fraternity Association(587)
Psi Omega(591)
Skills USA(611)
United States Association of Independent Gymnastic Clubs(673)
Xi Psi Phi(697)

COACHES
American Baseball Coaches Association(56)
American Football Coaches Association(84)
American Hockey Coaches Association(91)
American Swimming Coaches Association(150)
American Volleyball Coaches Association(153)
Black Coaches Association(230)
College Swimming Coaches Association of America(252)
Golf Coaches Association of America(318)
ICAAAA Coaches Association(330)
Intercollegiate Tennis Association(346)
International Coach Federation(365)
International Shooting Coaches Association(386)
National Alliance for Youth Sports(429)
National Association for Girls and Women in Sport(433)
National Association of Academic Advisors for Athletes(437)
National Association of Basketball Coaches(439)
National Athletic Trainers' Association(482)
National High School Athletic Coaches Association(517)
National Interscholastic Swimming Coaches Association(522)
National Soccer Coaches Association of America(540)
National Strength and Conditioning Association(543)
Professional Ski Instructors of America(589)
U.S. Lacrosse(668)
United States Cross Country Coaches Association(674)
United States Ski Association(677)
Women's Basketball Coaches Association(693)

COAL
American Coal Ash Association(63)
American Coke and Coal Chemicals Institute(63)

American Concrete Pipe Association(73)
American Concrete Pressure Pipe Association(73)
American Concrete Pumping Association(73)
American Society of Concrete Contractors(136)
Architectural Precast Association(160)
Asbestos Cement Product Producers Association(162)
Autoclaved Aerated Concrete Products Association(222)
Cement Employers Association(241)
Cement Kiln Recycling Coalition(241)
Concrete Foundations Association(258)
Concrete Plant Manufacturers Bureau(258)
Concrete Reinforcing Steel Institute(259)
Concrete Sawing and Drilling Association(259)
Expanded Shale, Clay and Slate Institute(299)
Foundation for Pavement Preservation(311)
Insulating Concrete Form Association(344)
Interlocking Concrete Pavement Institute(347)
International Concrete Repair Institute(366)
International Grooving and Grinding Association(374)
Masonry Heater Association of North America(413)
Masonry Society, The(413)
National Concrete Burial Vault Association(492)
National Concrete Masonry Association(492)
National Lime Association(525)
National Precast Concrete Association(534)
National Ready Mixed Concrete Association(535)
Operative Plasterers' and Cement Masons' International Association of the United States and Canada(565)
Ornamental Concrete Producers Association(568)
Portland Cement Association(581)
Post-Tensioning Institute(581)
Precast/Prestressed Concrete Institute(582)
Tilt-up Concrete Association(661)
Truck Mixer Manufacturers Bureau(665)

CONFECTIONERS

American Wholesale Marketers Association(155)
Bakery, Confectionery, Tobacco Workers and Grain Millers International Union(225)
Chocolate Manufacturers Association(245)
National Confectioners Association of the United States(492)
National Confectionery Sales Association(492)
Retail Confectioners International(601)

CONSERVATION

Air and Waste Management Association(12)
American College of Toxicology(71)
American Fisheries Society(84)
American Forests(85)
American Institute for Conservation of Historic and Artistic Works(93)
American Littoral Society(102)
American Nature Study Society(108)
American Ornithologists' Union(110)
American Water Resources Association(154)
Association for Conservation Information(170)
Association for Preservation Technology International(177)
Association of Conservation Engineers(192)
Association of Energy Engineers(195)
Association of Fish and Wildlife Agencies(197)
Association of Moving Image Archivists(205)
Association of State and Interstate Water Pollution Control Administrators(214)
Association of State Floodplain Managers(216)
Association of State Wetland Managers(216)
Conservation and Preservation Charities of America(261)
Delta Waterfowl Foundation(283)
Ecological Society of America(288)
Energy and Environmental Building Association(294)
Federal Water Quality Association(302)
Forest History Society(310)
Forestry Conservation Communications Association(310)
Groundwater Management Districts Association(320)
International Association of Natural Resource Pilots(359)
International Ecotourism Society(370)
International Erosion Control Association(371)
Land Improvement Contractors of America(405)
Land Trust Alliance(405)
Mining and Metallurgical Society of America(420)
National Association for Interpretation(434)
National Association of Conservation Districts(445)
National Association of Environmental Professionals(451)
National Association of Flood and Stormwater Management Agencies(453)
National Association of Recreation Resource Planners(468)
National Association of Service and Conservation Corps(471)
National Association of State Archaeologists(473)
National Association of State Land Reclamationists(475)
National Association of University Fisheries and Wildlife Programs(480)
National Conference of State Historic Preservation Officers(494)
National Institute for Animal Agriculture(520)
National Parks Conservation Association(532)
National Recreation and Parks Association(535)
National Shellfisheries Association(539)
National Speleological Society(542)
National Water Resources Association(548)
National Wildlife Rehabilitators Association(549)
North American Gamebird Association(557)
Organization of Wildlife Planners(568)
Outdoor Writers Association of America(569)
Society for Range Management(624)
Soil and Water Conservation Society(647)
Water Environment Federation(685)
Wildlife Disease Association(689)
Wildlife Management Institute(689)
Wildlife Society, The(689)

CONSTRUCTION

Air Distributing Institute(13)
Aluminum Anodizers Council(18)
American Architectural Manufacturers Association(32)
American College of Construction Lawyers(65)
American Concrete Institute(72)
American Concrete Pumping Association(73)
American Construction Inspectors Association(74)
American Council for Construction Education(75)
American Fence Association(83)
American Institute of Building Design(95)
American Institute of Constructors(95)
American Institute of Inspectors(96)
American Institute of Steel Construction(97)
American Institute of Timber Construction(98)
American Pipe Fittings Association(115)
American Road and Transportation Builders Association(123)
American Seniors Housing Association(124)
American Society of Concrete Contractors(136)
American Society of Home Inspectors(139)
American Society of Professional Estimators(145)
American Sports Builders Association(148)
American Subcontractors Association(149)
American Underground-Construction Association(152)
Architectural Woodwork Institute(160)
ASFE/The Best People on Earth(162)
Associated Air Balance Council(164)
Associated Builders and Contractors(164)
Associated Construction Distributors International(165)
Associated Construction Publications(165)
Associated Equipment Distributors(165)
Associated General Contractors of America(165)
Associated Owners and Developers(165)
Associated Schools of Construction(166)
Associated Specialty Contractors(166)
Association for Bridge Construction and Design(168)
Association of Asphalt Paving Technologists(186)
Association of Construction Inspectors(192)
Association of Diving Contractors International(194)
Association of Equipment Management Professionals(195)
Association of Equipment Manufacturers(195)
Association of Major City and County Building Officials(203)
Association of Millwork Distributors(205)
Association of Professional Model Makers(209)
Association of the Wall and Ceiling Industries-International(218)
Barre Granite Association(226)
Brick Industry Association(232)
Bridge Grid Flooring Manufacturers Association(232)
Builders Hardware Manufacturers Association(234)
Building Owners and Managers Association International(234)
Building Owners and Managers Institute International(234)
Cast Stone Institute(238)
Cedar Shake and Shingle Bureau(240)
Ceilings and Interior Systems Construction Association(241)
Ceramic Tile Institute of America(242)
Certified Contractors NetWork(242)
Chain Link Fence Manufacturers Institute(242)
Cold Formed Parts and Machine Institute(250)
Community Associations Institute(255)
Concrete Reinforcing Steel Institute(259)
Construction Financial Management Association(262)
Construction Innovation Forum(262)
Construction Management Association of America(262)
Construction Marketing Research Council(262)
Construction Owners Association of America(263)
Construction Specifications Institute(263)
Construction Writers Association(263)
Council for Affordable and Rural Housing(268)
CPA Construction Industry Association(278)
Deep Foundations Institute(282)
Design-Build Institute of America(283)
Directional Crossing Contractors Association(285)
Distribution Business Management Association(286)
Distribution Contractors Association(286)
Door and Access Systems Manufacturers' Association, International(286)
Door and Hardware Institute(287)
Dredging Contractors of America(287)
Energy and Environmental Building Association(294)
EPDM Roofing Association(297)
EPS Molders Association(297)
Expanded Shale, Clay and Slate Institute(299)
Federal Facilities Council(302)
Finishing Contractors Association(306)
Golf Course Builders Association of America(318)
Hand Tools Institute(321)
Housing Education and Research Association(329)
Independent Distributors Association(333)
Independent Electrical Contractors(334)
Indiana Limestone Institute of America(336)
Industrial Foundation of America(337)
Interlocking Concrete Pavement Institute(347)
International Builders Exchange Executives(363)

International Code Council(365)
International Institute for Lath and Plaster(376)
International Slurry Surfacing Association(386)
International Society for Pharmaceutical Engineering(388)
International Window Film Association(397)
Laborers' International Union of North America(404)
Log Home Builders Association of North America(409)
Manufactured Housing Association for Regulatory Reform(410)
Mason Contractors Association of America(413)
Masonry Society, The(413)
Mechanical Contractors Association of America(415)
Mechanical Service Contractors of America(415)
Metal Building Contractors and Erectors Association(417)
Metal Building Manufacturers Association(417)
Metal Construction Association(417)
National Academy of Building Inspection Engineers(426)
National Asphalt Pavement Association(431)
National Association of Architectural Metal Manufacturers(438)
National Association of Business Consultants(441)
National Association of Elevator Contractors(450)
National Association of Home Builders(456)
National Association of Home Inspectors(456)
National Association of Miscellaneous, Ornamental and Architectural Products Contractors(462)
National Association of the Remodeling Industry(479)
National Association of Women in Construction(481)
National Building Granite Quarries Association(485)
National Concrete Masonry Association(492)
National Conference of States on Building Codes and Standards(494)
National Council of Erectors, Fabricators and Riggers(498)
National Demolition Association(505)
National Environmental Balancing Bureau(507)
National Frame Builders Association(512)
National Guild of Professional Paperhangers(515)
National Housing and Rehabilitation Association(518)
National Housing Conference(518)
National Institute of Building Sciences(520)
National Institute of Steel Detailing(521)
National Lime Association(525)
National Lumber and Building Material Dealers Association(525)
National Multi Housing Council(528)
National Plasterers Council(533)
National Precast Concrete Association(534)
National Quartz Producers Council(534)
National Railroad Construction and Maintenance Association(534)
National Ready Mixed Concrete Association(535)
National Roofing Contractors Association(537)
National Slag Association(540)
National Stone, Sand and Gravel Association(543)
National Terrazzo and Mosaic Association(546)
National Tile Contractors Association(546)
National Utility Contractors Association(548)
NEA - the Association of Union Constructors(551)
North American Contractors Association(556)
North American Society for Trenchless Technology(561)
Operative Plasterers' and Cement Masons' International Association of the United States and Canada(565)
Outdoor Power Equipment and Engine Service Association(569)
Painting and Decorating Contractors of America(570)
Perlite Institute(573)
Pile Driving Contractors Association(577)
Pipe Fabrication Institute(578)
Portable Sanitation Association International(581)
Post-Tensioning Institute(581)
Power and Communication Contractors Association(582)
Precast/Prestressed Concrete Institute(582)
Professional Construction Estimators Association of America(586)
Professional Women in Construction(590)
Rubber Pavements Association(603)
Safety Glazing Certification Council(604)
Scaffold Industry Association(605)
Scaffolding, Shoring and Forming Institute(605)
Sheet Metal Workers' International Association(610)
Specialty Tool and Fastener Distributors Association(650)
SPRI, Inc.(652)
Steel Joist Institute(653)
Structural Insulated Panel Association(654)
Structural Stability Research Council(654)
Stucco Manufacturers Association(654)
Subcontractors Trade Association(655)
Sustainable Buildings Industry Council(656)
Tile Contractors' Association of America(661)
Tilt-up Concrete Association(661)
Timber Frame Business Council(661)
Timber Framers Guild(661)
Truck Mixer Manufacturers Bureau(665)
Truss Plate Institute(666)
United Brotherhood of Carpenters and Joiners of America(670)
United Union of Roofers, Waterproofers and Allied Workers(679)
Vinyl Siding Institute(683)
Window and Door Manufacturers Association(689)
Women Construction Owners and Executives, USA(691)
Wood Truss Council of America(694)

CONSULTANTS

Airport Consultants Council(14)
American Association of Dental Consultants(41)
American Association of Healthcare Consultants(43)
American Association of Legal Nurse Consultants(44)
American Association of Political Consultants(49)
American Consultants League(74)
American Council of Engineering Companies(75)
American Society of Agricultural Consultants(133)
American Society of Consultant Pharmacists(136)
American Society of Consulting Arborists(136)
American Society of Trial Consultants(147)
American Society of Wedding Professionals(147)
Association for Wedding Professionals International(182)
Association of Bridal Consultants(188)
Association of Career Firms International(188)
Association of Consulting Chemists and Chemical Engineers(192)
Association of Consulting Foresters of America(192)
Association of Executive Search Consultants(196)
Association of Federal Communications Consulting Engineers(196)
Association of Internal Management Consultants(201)
Association of Management Consulting Firms(203)
Association of Productivity Specialists(208)
Association of Professional Communication Consultants(208)
Association of Professional Investment Consultants(209)
CPA Auto Dealer Consultants Association(278)
ECRI(288)
Foodservice Consultants Society International(309)
Freight Transportation Consultants Association(312)
Independent Computer Consultants Association(333)
Institute of Certified Healthcare Business Consultants(340)
Institute of Management Consultants USA(342)
International Association of Career Consulting Firms(354)
International Association of Professional Security Consultants(360)
International Network of Merger and Acquisition Partners(380)
IT Financial Management Association(400)
National Alliance of Independent Crop Consultants(429)
National Association of Export Companies(451)
National Association of Independent Public Finance Advisors(457)
National Association of Personal Financial Advisors(464)
National Association of Vision Professionals(480)
National Bureau of Certified Consultants(485)
National Council of Acoustical Consultants(498)
North American Association of Educational Negotiators(554)
Parliamentary Associates(571)
Professional and Technical Consultants Association(585)
Professional Services Council(589)
Project Management Institute(590)
Public Relations Society of America(593)
Society of Medical Consultants to the Armed Forces(639)
Society of Medical-Dental Management Consultants(640)
Society of Risk Management Consultants(643)

CONSUMERS

American Council on Consumer Interests(76)
American Financial Services Association(83)
Association for Consumer Research(171)
Consumer Credit Insurance Association(263)
Consumer Federation of America(263)
Electricity Consumers Resource Council(291)
Insurance Consumer Affairs Exchange(345)
National Association of Consumer Advocates(446)
National Association of Consumer Agency Administrators(446)
National Association of State Utility Consumer Advocates(477)
National Consumers League(495)
Ombudsman Association, The(564)
SOCAP International(612)

CONTAINERS see also BAGS, BOXES, CANS

Aluminum Foil Container Manufacturers Association(18)
Association of Independent Corrugated Converters(200)
Closure Manufacturers Association(248)
Compressed Gas Association(257)
Containerization and Intermodal Institute(264)
Fibre Box Association(305)
Flexible Intermediate Bulk Container Association(307)
Foodservice and Packaging Institute(309)
Glass Packaging Institute(317)
National Association of Container Distributors(446)
National Wooden Pallet and Container Association(550)

Paper Shipping Sack Manufacturers Association(571)
Paperboard Packaging Council(571)
Plastic Shipping Container Institute(578)
Pressure Vessel Manufacturers Association(583)
Research and Development Associates for Military Food and Packaging Systems(599)
Reusable Industrial Packaging Association(601)
Steel Shipping Container Institute(653)

CONTRACTORS

ADSC: The International Association of Foundation Drilling(8)
Air Conditioning Contractors of America(13)
American Subcontractors Association(149)
Associated Builders and Contractors(164)
Associated General Contractors of America(165)
Associated Specialty Contractors(166)
Association of Bituminous Contractors(187)
Association of the Wall and Ceiling Industries-International(218)
Building Service Contractors Association International(234)
Ceilings and Interior Systems Construction Association(241)
Certified Contractors NetWork(242)
Concrete Foundations Association(258)
Contract Services Association of America(264)
Directional Crossing Contractors Association(285)
Exhibition Services and Contractors Association(299)
Floor Covering Installation Contractors Association(308)
Independent Electrical Contractors(334)
Independent Professional Painting Contractors Association of America(335)
Insulation Contractors Association of America(345)
International Association for Cold Storage Construction(349)
International Association of Geophysical Contractors(357)
International Association of Lighting Management Companies(359)
International Concrete Repair Institute(366)
International Council of Employers of Bricklayers and Allied Craftworkers(367)
International Institute for Lath and Plaster(376)
Land Improvement Contractors of America(405)
Mason Contractors Association of America(413)
Mechanical Contractors Association of America(415)
Mechanical Service Contractors of America(415)
National Association of Minority Contractors(462)
National Association of Miscellaneous, Ornamental and Architectural Products Contractors(462)
National Association of Reinforcing Steel Contractors(469)
National Association of Solar Contractors(472)
National Association of Waterproofing and Structural Repair Contractors(481)
National Certified Pipe Welding Bureau(488)
National Contract Management Association(495)
National Council of Erectors, Fabricators and Riggers(498)
National Demolition Association(505)
National Drilling Association(505)
National Electrical Contractors Association(506)
National Environmental Balancing Bureau(507)
National Insulation Association(521)
National Property Management Association(534)
National Roof Deck Contractors Association(537)
National Roofing Contractors Association(537)
National School Transportation Association(538)
National Tile Contractors Association(546)
North American Contractors Association(556)
Painting and Decorating Contractors of America(570)
Pile Driving Contractors Association(577)
Pipe Line Contractors Association(578)
Plumbing-Heating-Cooling Contractors - National Association(579)
Scaffold Industry Association(605)
Sealant, Waterproofing and Restoration Institute(607)
Sheet Metal and Air Conditioning Contractors' National Association(610)
Subcontractors Trade Association(655)
Tile Contractors' Association of America(661)
United Association of Equipment Leasing(670)
Waterproofing Contractors Association(686)

CONVENTIONS see also EXHIBITS

American Federation of Astrologers, Inc.(82)
Association for Convention Marketing Executives(171)
Association for Convention Operations Management(171)
Association of Collegiate Conference and Events Directors International(191)
Association of Destination Management Executives(193)
Association of Meeting Professionals(204)
Center for Exhibition Industry Research(241)
Connected International Meeting Professionals Association(261)
Convention Industry Council(265)
Council of Protocol Executives(274)
Destination Marketing Association International(283)
Electronic Distribution Show Corporation(291)
Exhibition Services and Contractors Association(299)
Financial and Insurance Conference Planners(305)
Foundation for International Meetings(311)
International Association for Modular Exhibitry(351)
International Association of Assembly Managers(353)
International Association of Conference Center Administrators(355)
International Association of Conference Centers(355)
International Special Events Society(393)
Meeting Professionals International(416)
National Association of Reunion Managers(469)
National Coalition of Black Meeting Planners(490)
North American Farm Show Council(557)
Professional Convention Management Association(587)
Professional Show Managers Association(589)
Religious Conference Management Association(599)
Society of Corporate Meeting Professionals(634)
Society of Independent Show Organizers(638)

COOKING

American Culinary Federation(77)
International Association of Culinary Professionals(355)
International Food Service Executives' Association(372)
National Association of Catering Executives(442)
National Barbecue Association(483)
Research Chefs Association(600)
Women Chefs and Restaurateurs(691)

COOPERATIVES

ACL - Association for Consortium Leadership(7)
Association of Cooperative Educators(192)
Burley Tobacco Growers Cooperative Association(235)
Cooperative Education and Internship Association(265)
Farm Credit Council(301)
Farmers Educational and Co-operative Union of America(301)
Flue-Cured Tobacco Cooperative Stabilization Corporation(308)
Funeral Consumers Alliance(312)
National Association of Housing Cooperatives(456)
National Cooperative Business Association(496)
National Council of Farmer Cooperatives(499)
National Farmers Organization(508)
National Rural Electric Cooperative Association(537)
National Society of Accountants for Cooperatives(541)
National Telecommunications Cooperative Association(546)
Profit Sharing/401(k) Council of America(590)
Quality Bakers of America Cooperative(594)
United Producers(672)

COPPER

American Bureau of Metal Statistics(59)
American Copper Council(74)
Copper and Brass Fabricators Council(266)
Copper and Brass Servicenter Association(266)
Copper Development Association(266)
International Copper Association(367)
Non-Ferrous Founders' Society(553)
Society of Mineral Analysts(640)

CORN

American Corn Growers Association(74)
Corn Refiners Association(266)
Home Baking Association(327)
National Corn Growers Association(496)
National Futures Association(513)

CORRECTION see also LAW, POLICE, SECURITY

American Association for Correctional and Forensic Psychology(34)
American Association of Mental Health Professionals in Corrections(45)
American Catholic Correctional Chaplains Association(61)
American Correctional Association(74)
American Correctional Chaplains Association(74)
American Correctional Health Services Association(74)
American Criminal Justice Association/Lambda Alpha Epsilon(77)
American Jail Association(99)
American Jewish Correctional Chaplains Association(99)
American Probation and Parole Association(117)
American Society of Criminology(137)
Association Correctional Food Service Affiliates(166)
Association of State Correctional Administrators(215)
Association on Programs for Female Offenders(221)
Correctional Education Association(266)
Correctional Vendors Association(267)
Federal Probation and Pre-trial Officers Association(302)
International Association of Addictions and Offender Counselors(352)
International Association of Correctional Officers(355)
International Community Corrections Association(366)
International Conference of Police Chaplains(366)
National Association of Juvenile Correctional Agencies(459)
National Correctional Industries Association(496)
National Council on Crime and Delinquency(502)

National Juvenile Detention Association(523)
North American Association of Wardens and Superintendents(555)
Osborne Association(569)
United Federation of Police & Security Officers(671)

COSMETICS & COSMETOLOGY
Aestheticians International Association(10)
American Association of Cosmetology Schools(41)
American Electrology Association(80)
American Hair Loss Council(88)
American Health and Beauty Aids Institute(89)
American Society of Hair Restoration Surgery(138)
American Society of Perfumers(143)
Association of Cosmetologists and Hairdressers(193)
Cosmetic Executive Women(267)
Cosmetic Industry Buyers and Suppliers(267)
Cosmetic, Toiletry and Fragrance Association(267)
Drug, Chemical and Associated Technologies Association(287)
Fragrance Foundation(311)
Independent Cosmetic Manufacturers and Distributors(333)
Intercoiffure America/Canada(346)
International Aloe Science Council(349)
International Association of Color Manufacturers(355)
International Chain Salon Association(365)
National Beauty Culturists' League(484)
National Cosmetology Association(496)
National Interstate Council of State Boards of Cosmetology(522)
Professional Beauty Association(586)
Regulatory Affairs Professionals Society(598)
Salon Association, The(605)
Society of Clinical and Medical Hair Removal(633)
Society of Cosmetic Chemists(634)
World International Nail and Beauty Association(696)

COTTON
American Cotton Shippers Association(74)
Cotton Council International(267)
Cotton Warehouse Association of America(267)
Industrial Fabrics Association International(336)
National Cotton Batting Institute(496)
National Cotton Council of America(496)
National Cotton Ginners' Association(496)
New York Board of Trade(552)
Supima(656)

COTTONSEED
American Oil Chemists' Society(110)
National Cottonseed Products Association(496)

COUNSEL
American College of Trust and Estate Counsel(71)
Association for Financial Counseling and Planning Education(173)
Federation of Defense and Corporate Counsel(303)
Giving Institute(317)
International Association of Marriage and Family Counselors(359)
Investment Adviser Association(398)
North American Canon Law Society(555)

COUNSELING see also VOCATIONAL GUIDANCE
American Association for Marriage and Family Therapy(36)
American Association of Pastoral Counselors(47)
American Association of Sexuality Educators, Counselors and Therapists(51)
American Counseling Association(76)
American Family Therapy Academy(81)
American Mental Health Counselors Association(105)
American School Counselor Association(124)
Association for University and College Counseling Center Directors(181)
International Association of Addictions and Offender Counselors(352)
International Association of Counseling Services(355)
International Association of Counselors and Therapists(355)
NAADAC -- the Association for Addiction Professionals(424)
National Association for College Admission Counseling(432)
National Career Development Association(487)
National Rehabilitation Counseling Association(535)

COUNTY
American Federation of State, County and Municipal Employees(82)
County Executives of America(277)
International Association of Clerks, Recorders, Election Officials and Treasurers(354)
National Association of Counties(447)
National Association of County Agricultural Agents(447)
National Association of County and City Health Officials(447)
National Association of County Engineers(447)
National Association of County Intergovernmental Relations Officials(447)
National Association of County Recorders, Election Officials and Clerks(447)

CREDIT see also FINANCE
ACA International, The Association of Credit and Collection Professionals(2)
Advertising Media Credit Executives Association, International(9)
Affordable Housing Tax Credit Coalition(10)
Allied Finance Adjusters Conference(17)
American Association of Credit Union Leagues(41)
American Bankruptcy Institute(55)
American Finance Association(83)
American Financial Services Association(83)
American Recovery Association(122)
Broadcast Cable Credit Association(233)
Capital Markets Credit Analysts Society(237)
Coalition of Higher Education Assistance Organizations(249)
Commercial Finance Association(253)
Commercial Mortgage Securities Association(253)
Consumer Bankers Association(263)
Consumer Credit Insurance Association(263)
Consumer Data Industry Association(263)
Credit Professionals International(279)
Credit Research Foundation(279)
Credit Union Executives Society(279)
Credit Union National Association(279)
Defense Credit Union Council(282)
Education Credit Union Council(289)
Electronic Transactions Association(292)
Farm Credit Council(301)
FCIB-NACM Corp.(301)
Information Technologies Credit Union Association(338)
International Association of Financial Crimes Investigators(357)
International Energy Credit Association(370)
Jewelers Board of Trade(401)
MasterCard International(413)
Media Credit Association(415)
Motion Picture and Television Credit Association(421)
National Association of Consumer Credit Administrators(446)
National Association of Credit Management(448)
National Association of Credit Union Chairmen(448)
National Association of Credit Union Service Organizations(448)
National Association of Federal Credit Unions(452)
National Association of Mortgage Brokers(462)
National Association of State Credit Union Supervisors(474)
National Chemical Credit Association(488)
National Council of Postal Credit Unions(500)
National Credit Reporting Association(503)
National Credit Union Management Association(503)
National Federation of Community Development Credit Unions(509)
National Foundation for Credit Counseling(512)
RMA - The Risk Management Association(602)
Smart Card Alliance(611)

CRIMINOLOGY
Academy of Criminal Justice Sciences(3)
American Criminal Justice Association/Lambda Alpha Epsilon(77)
American Polygraph Association(116)
American Society of Criminology(137)
American Society of Questioned Document Examiners(145)
Association of Certified Fraud Examiners(189)
Council of International Investigators(273)
Independent Association of Questioned Document Examiners(333)
International Association for Identification(350)
International Association for the Study of Organized Crime(351)
International Society of Crime Prevention Practitioners(391)
Justice Research and Statistics Association(403)
National Association of Investigative Specialists(459)
National Criminal Justice Association(503)
Society of Professional Investigators(642)

CRYOGENICS
American Association of Tissue Banks(53)
Compressed Gas Association(257)
Society for Cryobiology(616)

CUSTOMS
Customs and International Trade Bar Association(280)
National Customs Brokers and Forwarders Association of America(504)
National Treasury Employees Union(547)

CYBERNETICS
Society for Computer Simulation(615)

CYTOLOGY
American Society for Cytotechnology(128)
American Society of Cytopathology(137)
Society for In Vitro Biology(619)

DAIRY INDUSTRY
American Butter Institute(60)
American Dairy Products Institute(78)
American Dairy Science Association(78)
Certified Milk Producers Association of America(242)
Dairy Management(281)
International Association of Food Industry Suppliers(357)
International Association of Ice Cream Vendors(358)
International Dairy Foods Association(368)
International Dairy-Deli-Bakery Association(369)
International Ice Cream Association(375)
National Cheese Institute(488)
National Dairy Herd Improvement Association(504)
National Ice Cream Mix Association(518)
National Ice Cream Retailers Association(518)
National Mastitis Council(526)
National Milk Producers Federation(527)
National Yogurt Association(550)
New York Mercantile Exchange(552)

United States National Committee of the International Dairy Federation(676)

DANCE

American Alliance for Health, Physical Education, Recreation and Dance(30)
American Dance Guild(78)
American Dance Therapy Association(78)
American Guild of Musical Artists(88)
Callerlab-International Association of Square Dance Callers(236)
Congress on Research in Dance(261)
Council of Dance Administrators(271)
Dance Critics Association(281)
Dance Educators of America(281)
Dance Masters of America(281)
Dance/USA(281)
IDEA, The Health and Fitness Association(330)
International Association of Round Dance Teachers(361)
National Association of Schools of Dance(470)
National Ballroom and Entertainment Association(483)
National Dance Association(504)
National Dance Council of America(504)
National Sports and Fitness Association(543)
North American Folk Music and Dance Alliance(557)
Society of Dance History Scholars(635)

DATA PROCESSING

AeA - Advancing the Business of Technology(9)
AFSM International(11)
American Council for Technology(75)
American Medical Informatics Association(104)
American Payroll Association(113)
American Society for Information Science and Technology(130)
Ass'n of Learning Providers(164)
Association for Computational Linguistics(170)
Association for Computers and the Humanities(170)
Association for Computing Machinery(170)
Association for Federal Information Resources Management(173)
Association for Financial Technology(173)
Association for Women in Computing(182)
Association for Work Process Improvement(183)
Association of Information and Dissemination Centers(201)
Association of Information Technology Professionals(201)
Association of Management/International Association of Management(203)
Association of Public Data Users(210)
Association of Rehabilitation Programs in Computer Technology(211)
Association of Service and Computer Dealers International(213)
Association of Shareware Professionals(214)
Black Data Processing Associates(230)
Business Software Alliance(236)
Classification Society of North America(247)
Computer and Communications Industry Association(257)
Computer Assisted Language Instruction Consortium(257)
Computer Law Association(258)
Computer Measurement Group(258)
Computerized Medical Imaging Society(258)
Computing Technology Industry Association(258)
Council for Electronic Revenue Communication Advancement(268)
Data Interchange Standards Association(281)
Data Management Association International(282)
EDUCAUSE(290)
Electronic Funds Transfer Association(292)
Equipment Leasing Association of America(297)
Geoscience Information Society(316)
Geospatial Information Technology Association(316)
Government Management Information Sciences(318)
IEEE Computer Society(331)
Independent Computer Consultants Association(333)
Information Storage Industry Consortium(338)
Information Systems Audit and Control Association(338)
Information Technology Association of America(338)
Information Technology Industry Council(338)
Institute for Certification of Computing Professionals(339)
International Association for Human Resource Information Management(350)
International Recording Media Association(384)
International Society for Technology in Education(389)
Internet Alliance(397)
IT Financial Management Association(400)
MEMA Information Services Council(416)
NaSPA: the Network and System Professionals Association(425)
National Association of Computerized Tax Processors(445)
National Association of Health Data Organizations(455)
National Association of State Chief Information Officers(474)
National Federation of Abstracting and Information Services(508)
National Training Systems Association(547)
North American Fuzzy Information Processing Society(557)
Online Audiovisual Catalogers(565)
Society for Applied Learning Technology(614)
Society for Information Display(620)
Society for Information Management(620)
Software and Information Industry Association(646)
Special Interest Group for Computers and Society(648)
Special Interest Group for University and College Computing Services(649)
Special Interest Group on Accessible Computing(649)
Technology Transfer Society(658)
United States Internet Service Provider Association(676)
Urban and Regional Information Systems Association(680)
Workgroup for Electronic Data Interchange(695)
Xplor International(698)

DEAF see also HEARING

Access Technology Association(6)
ADARA(8)
Alexander Graham Bell Association for the Deaf and Hard of Hearing(15)
American Academy of Audiology(20)
American Association of Eye and Ear Hospitals(42)
American Auditory Society(55)
American Neurotology Society(109)
American Speech-Language-Hearing Association(148)
American Tinnitus Association(151)
Conference of Educational Administrators of Schools and Programs for the Deaf(259)
Council of American Instructors of the Deaf(270)
Council on Education of the Deaf(276)
International Hearing Society(375)
International Visual Literacy Association(396)
National Hearing Conservation Association(516)
National Student Speech Language Hearing Association(544)
Registry of Interpreters for the Deaf(598)

DECORATORS

Residential Space Planners International(600)
Society of Glass and Ceramic Decorators(637)

DEHYDRATORS

AFIA-Alfalfa Processors Council(11)
American Dehydrated Onion and Garlic Association(78)

DENTISTRY

Academy of Dental Materials(3)
Academy of Dentistry for Persons with Disabilities(3)
Academy of Dentistry International(3)
Academy of General Dentistry(3)
Academy of Laser Dentistry(3)
Academy of Operative Dentistry(4)
Academy of Oral Dynamics(4)
Academy of Osseointegration(5)
Academy of Prosthodontics(5)
Alpha Omega International Dental Fraternity(18)
American Academy of Cosmetic Dentistry(21)
American Academy of Craniofacial Pain(21)
American Academy of Dental Group Practice(21)
American Academy of Dental Practice Administration(21)
American Academy of Dental Sleep Medicine(21)
American Academy of Esthetic Dentistry(22)
American Academy of Fixed Prosthodontics(23)
American Academy of Gnathologic Orthopedics(23)
American Academy of Gold Foil Operators(23)
American Academy of Implant Dentistry(23)
American Academy of Maxillofacial Prosthetics(24)
American Academy of Oral and Maxillofacial Pathology(25)
American Academy of Oral and Maxillofacial Radiology(25)
American Academy of Oral Medicine(25)
American Academy of Orofacial Pain(26)
American Academy of Orthotists and Prosthetists(26)
American Academy of Pediatric Dentistry(26)
American Academy of Periodontology(27)
American Academy of Restorative Dentistry(28)
American Academy of the History of Dentistry(29)
American Association for Dental Research(34)
American Association for Functional Orthodontics(35)
American Association of Dental Consultants(41)
American Association of Dental Editors(41)
American Association of Dental Examiners(42)
American Association of Endodontists(42)
American Association of Hospital Dentists(44)
American Association of Oral and Maxillofacial Surgeons(47)
American Association of Orthodontists(47)
American Association of Public Health Dentistry(50)
American Association of Women Dentists(54)
American Cleft Palate-Craniofacial Association(63)
American College of Dentists(65)
American College of Oral and Maxillofacial Surgeons(68)
American College of Prosthodontists(70)
American Dental Assistants Association(78)
American Dental Association(78)
American Dental Education Association(78)
American Dental Hygienists' Association(78)
American Dental Interfraternity Council(79)
American Dental Society of Anesthesiology(79)
American Endodontic Society(81)
American Equilibration Society(81)
American Institute of Oral Biology(97)
American Prosthodontic Society(117)
American Society for Dental Aesthetics(128)
American Society for Geriatric Dentistry(129)
American Society for the Advancement of Sedation and Anesthesia in Dentistry(132)
American Society for the Study of Orthodontics(132)
American Society of Forensic Odontology(138)

American Society of Master Dental Technologists(141)
American Student Dental Association(149)
American Veterinary Dental Society(153)
Association of Managed Care Dentists(203)
Association of State and Territorial Dental Directors(215)
Christian Medical & Dental Associations(246)
College of Diplomates of the American Board of Orthodontics(251)
Delta Dental Plans Association(282)
Delta Sigma Delta(282)
Dental Dealers of America(283)
Dental Group Management Association(283)
Dental Trade Alliance(283)
Hispanic Dental Association(326)
Holistic Dental Association(327)
Indian Dental Association (USA)(336)
International Academy of Gnathology - American Section(348)
International Academy of Oral Medicine and Toxicology(348)
International Analgesia Society(349)
International Association for Orthodontics(351)
International College of Cranio-Mandibular Orthopedics(365)
International College of Dentists, U.S.A. Section(366)
International Congress of Oral Implantologists(367)
International Union of Industrial Service Transport Health Employees(395)
Medical-Dental-Hospital Business Associates(416)
National Association of Dental Assistants(448)
National Association of Dental Laboratories(448)
National Association of Dental Plans(449)
National Association of Seventh-Day Adventist Dentists(472)
National Dental Association(505)
National Dental Hygienists' Association(505)
Omicron Kappa Upsilon(564)
Organization of Teachers of Oral Diagnosis(568)
Pierre Fauchard Academy(577)
Psi Omega(591)
Sigma Epsilon Delta Dental Fraternity(610)
Society for the Preservation of Oral Health(627)
Society of American Indian Dentists(631)
Society of Medical-Dental Management Consultants(640)
Special Care Dentistry Association(648)
Union of American Physicians and Dentists(670)
Xi Psi Phi(697)

DERMATOLOGY

American Academy of Dermatology(21)
American College of Mohs Micrographic Surgery and Cutaneous Oncology(67)
American Osteopathic College of Dermatology(112)
American Skin Association(126)
American Society for Dermatologic Surgery(128)
American Society of Dermatological Retailers(137)
American Society of Dermatology(137)
American Society of Dermatopathology(137)
Dermatology Nurses' Association(283)
Medical Mycological Society of the Americas(416)
North American Clinical Dermatological Society(556)
Society for Investigative Dermatology(620)
Society for Pediatric Dermatology(623)

DESIGN

American Council of Engineering Companies(75)
American Craft Council(77)
American Design Drafting Association(79)
American Institute of Building Design(95)
American Society of Furniture Designers(138)
American Society of Interior Designers(140)
Association of Professional Design Firms(208)
Association of University Interior Designers(219)
Bridge Grid Flooring Manufacturers Association(232)
Broadcast Designers' Association(233)
Construction Management Association of America(262)
Council of Fashion Designers of America(272)
Design Management Institute(283)
Design-Build Institute of America(283)
Environmental Design Research Association(296)
Exhibit Designers and Producers Association(299)
Foodservice Consultants Society International(309)
Graphic Artists Guild(319)
Industrial Designers Society of America(336)
Interior Design Educators Council(347)
Interior Design Society(347)
International Association of Clothing Designers and Executives(355)
International Association of Lighting Designers(358)
International Interior Design Association(377)
National Association of Schools of Art and Design(470)
National Kitchen and Bath Association(523)
National Technical Services Association(546)
Organization of Black Designers(567)
Professional Services Management Association(589)
SAE International(604)
Society for Environmental Graphic Design(617)
Society for Marketing Professional Services(621)
Society for News Design(622)
Society of Creative Designers(634)
Society of Piping Engineers and Designers(642)
Society of Publication Designers(643)
Society of Small Craft Designers(644)
Surface Design Association(656)
United Scenic Artists(672)
University and College Designers Association(679)

DIAMONDS

Diamond Council of America(284)
Diamond Manufacturers and Importers Association of America(284)
Industrial Diamond Association of America(336)
National Association of Jewelry Appraisers(459)

DIETARY FOODS

American Dietetic Association(79)
Dietary Managers Association(284)
National Nutritional Foods Association(529)

DOCTORS see DENTISTRY, MEDICINE, OSTEOPATHY, SURGERY

Society of Army Physician Assistants(632)

DOGS

American Boarding Kennels Association(58)
American Canine Sports Medicine Association(61)
American Kennel Club(100)
International Professional Groomers(383)
National Association of Dog Obedience Instructors(450)
Professional Handlers Association(587)

DOORS

American Association of Automatic Door Manufacturers(38)
Association of Millwork Distributors(205)
Door and Access Systems Manufacturers' Association, International(286)
International Door Association(369)
Steel Door Institute(653)
Window and Door Manufacturers Association(689)

DRAFTING

American Design Drafting Association(79)
National Institute of Steel Detailing(521)

DRUGS see also PHARMACEUTICAL INDUSTRY

American Academy of Addiction Psychiatry(20)
American Academy of Clinical Toxicology(21)
American Academy of Veterinary and Comparative Toxicology(29)
American Clinical Laboratory Association(63)
American College of Apothecaries(64)
Aspirin Foundation of America(164)
Association of Food and Drug Officials(197)
Association of Medical Education and Research in Substance Abuse(204)
Association of Official Racing Chemists(206)
Chain Drug Marketing Association(242)
Consumer Healthcare Products Association(263)
Council for Responsible Nutrition(270)
Drug Information Association(287)
Drug, Chemical and Associated Technologies Association(287)
Food and Drug Law Institute(309)
Generic Pharmaceutical Association(315)
Healthcare Distribution Management Association(323)
International Association of Color Manufacturers(355)
International Society for Pharmacoeconomics and Outcomes Research(388)
NAADAC -- the Association for Addiction Professionals(424)
NAGMR Consumer Product Brokers(425)
National Association of Chain Drug Stores(442)
National Association of State Alcohol and Drug Abuse Directors(473)
National Association of Substance Abuse Trainers and Educators(478)
National Community Pharmacists Association(491)
PDA - an International Association for Pharmaceutical Science and Technology(572)
Society of Forensic Toxicologists(636)
Society of Toxicology(645)
Substance Abuse Program Administrators Association(655)
United States Pharmacopeia(676)

DYES

ETAD North America(298)

ECONOMICS

AACE International(1)
American Agricultural Economics Association(30)
American Association of Family and Consumer Sciences(43)
American Economic Association(80)
American Real Estate and Urban Economics Association(121)
Association for Comparative Economic Studies(170)
Association for Evolutionary Economics(172)
Association for Management Information in Financial Services(176)
Association for Social Economics(178)
Association for University Business and Economic Research(181)
Association of Environmental and Resource Economists(195)
Association of Private Enterprise Education(208)
Association of Third World Studies(218)
Conference of Business Economists(259)
Econometric Society(288)
Economic History Association(288)
Financial Management Association International(306)
History of Economics Society(326)
Institute of Management Accountants(342)
International Economic Development Council(370)

International Society for Ecological Economics(387)
International Society for Pharmacoeconomics and Outcomes Research(388)
International Society of Parametric Analysts(392)
Mineral Economics and Management Society(419)
National Association for Business Economics(441)
National Association of Forensic Economics(453)
National Economic Association(505)
National Extension Association of Family and Consumer Sciences(508)
Social Science History Association(612)
Social Science Research Council(613)
Society for Economic Anthropology(616)
Society for Economic Botany(616)
Society for the Advancement of Economic Theory(626)
Society for the Advancement of Socio-Economics(626)
Society of American Business Editors and Writers(630)
Society of Automotive Analysts(632)
Society of Government Economists(637)
Union for Radical Political Economics(669)
United States Association for Energy Economics(673)
Western Economic Association International(687)

EDUCATION

AACSB - the Association to Advance Collegiate Schools of Business(1)
Academic Language Therapy Association(2)
Academy of Criminal Justice Sciences(3)
Academy of Homiletics(3)
Academy of International Business(3)
Academy of Management(4)
Academy of Security Educators and Trainers(5)
Accreditation Council for Pharmacy Education(6)
Accrediting Bureau of Health Education Schools(7)
Accrediting Council for Continuing Education and Training(7)
Accrediting Council for Independent Colleges and Schools(7)
Accrediting Council on Education in Journalism and Mass Communications(7)
ACL - Association for Consortium Leadership(7)
ACPA - College Student Educators Association(7)
ADED - the Association for Driver Rehabilitation Specialists(8)
Aerospace Department Chairmen's Association(10)
AFT - Public Employees(11)
Alliance for Continuing Medical Education(15)
Alliance of Associations of Teachers of Japanese(16)
American Academy of Advertising(20)
American Academy of Religion(28)
American Academy of Teachers of Singing(29)
American Accounting Association(29)
American Alliance for Theatre and Education(30)
American Association for Adult and Continuing Education(33)
American Association for Agricultural Education(33)
American Association for Cancer Education(33)
American Association for Career Education(34)
American Association for Chinese Studies(34)
American Association for Employment in Education(34)
American Association for Health Education(35)
American Association for the Advancement of Slavic Studies(36)
American Association for Vocational Instructional Materials(37)
American Association for Women in Community Colleges(37)
American Association of Chairmen of Departments of Psychiatry(39)
American Association of Christian Schools(39)
American Association of Classified School Employees(39)
American Association of Colleges for Teacher Education(40)
American Association of Colleges of Osteopathic Medicine(40)
American Association of Colleges of Pharmacy(40)
American Association of Colleges of Podiatric Medicine(40)
American Association of Collegiate Registrars and Admissions Officers(40)
American Association of Community Colleges(41)
American Association of Cosmetology Schools(41)
American Association of Diabetes Educators(42)
American Association of Early Childhood Educators(42)
American Association of Family and Consumer Sciences(43)
American Association of Philosophy Teachers(48)
American Association of Physics Teachers(48)
American Association of Presidents of Independent Colleges and Universities(49)
American Association of School Administrators(50)
American Association of School Librarians(50)
American Association of School Personnel Administrators(51)
American Association of Sexuality Educators, Counselors and Therapists(51)
American Association of State Colleges and Universities(51)
American Association of Teachers of Arabic(52)
American Association of Teachers of French(52)
American Association of Teachers of German(52)
American Association of Teachers of Italian(52)
American Association of Teachers of Spanish and Portuguese(52)
American Association of University Administrators(53)
American Association of University Professors(53)
American Association on Mental Retardation(54)
American Board of Medical Specialties(57)
American Bridge Teachers' Association(59)
American Classical League(63)
American College of Counselors(65)
American College of Dentists(65)
American College of Medical Quality(67)
American College of Musicians(67)
American Collegiate Retailing Association(72)
American Comparative Literature Association(72)
American Conference of Academic Deans(73)
American Council of Learned Societies(75)
American Council on Education(76)
American Council on the Teaching of Foreign Languages(76)
American Councils for International Education(76)
American Dental Education Association(78)
American Driver and Traffic Safety Education Association(79)
American Education Finance Association(80)
American Educational Research Association(80)
American Educational Studies Association(80)
American Federation of School Administrators(82)
American Federation of Teachers(82)
American Humanist Association(92)
American Humor Studies Association(92)
American Hungarian Educators Association(92)
American Institute of Indian Studies(96)
American Management Association(102)
American Mathematical Association of Two Year Colleges(103)
American Meat Science Association(104)
American Medical Rehabilitation Providers Association(104)
American Montessori Society(106)
American Nature Study Society(108)
American Peanut Research and Education Society(113)
American Philosophical Association(114)
American School Counselor Association(124)
American Schools Association(124)
American Schools of Oriental Research(124)
American Society for Bioethics and Humanities(127)
American Society for Engineering Education(128)
American String Teachers Association(149)
American Technical Education Association(150)
American Vocational Education Personnel Development Association(153)
Associated Collegiate Press, National Scholastic Press Association(165)
Associated Schools of Construction(166)
Association for Applied Interactive Multimedia(167)
Association for Asian American Studies(167)
Association for Biblical Higher Education(168)
Association for Biology Laboratory Education(168)
Association for Borderlands Studies(168)
Association for Business Communication(168)
Association for Business Simulation and Experiential Learning(168)
Association for Canadian Studies in the United States(168)
Association for Career and Technical Education(169)
Association for Career and Technical Education Research(169)
Association for Childhood Education International(169)
Association for Clinical Pastoral Education(169)
Association for College and University Religious Affairs(169)
Association for Communication Excellence(169)
Association for Computers and the Humanities(170)
Association for Continuing Higher Education(171)
Association for Direct Instruction(171)
Association for Documentary Editing(171)
Association for Education and Rehabilitation of the Blind and Visually Impaired(172)
Association for Education in Journalism and Mass Communication(172)
Association for Educational Communications and Technology(172)
Association for Experiential Education(172)
Association for Financial Counseling and Planning Education(173)
Association for General and Liberal Studies(173)
Association for Gerontology in Higher Education(173)
Association for Graphic Arts Training(173)
Association for Hospital Medical Education(174)
Association for Informal Logic and Critical Thinking(174)
Association for Information Media and Equipment(174)
Association for Information Systems(175)
Association for Institutional Research(175)
Association for Integrative Studies(175)
Association for International Agricultural and Extension Education(175)
Association for International Agriculture and Rural Development(175)
Association for Jewish Studies(175)

Association for Library and Information Science Education(175)
Association for Science Teacher Education(178)
Association for Supervision and Curriculum Development(178)
Association for Surgical Education(178)
Association for Technology in Music Instruction(178)
Association for the Advancement of Baltic Studies(179)
Association for the Advancement of Computing in Education(179)
Association for the Advancement of International Education(179)
Association for the Study of Higher Education(181)
Association for the Study of Play(181)
Association for Theatre in Higher Education(181)
Association for University Business and Economic Research(181)
Association of Academic Chairmen of Plastic Surgery(183)
Association of Advanced Rabbinical and Talmudic Schools(183)
Association of African Studies Programs(183)
Association of American Colleges and Universities(184)
Association of American Educators(184)
Association of American Law Schools(184)
Association of American Medical Colleges(184)
Association of American Universities(185)
Association of American Veterinary Medical Colleges(186)
Association of Arts Administration Educators(186)
Association of Biomedical Communications Directors(187)
Association of Black Nursing Faculty in Higher Education(187)
Association of Boarding Schools, The(188)
Association of Catholic Colleges and Universities(188)
Association of Chairmen of Departments of Mechanics(189)
Association of Christian Schools International(190)
Association of Christian Teachers(190)
Association of College Administration Professionals(190)
Association of College and University Auditors(190)
Association of College and University Housing Officers-International(191)
Association of College and University Telecommunications Administrators(191)
Association of College Unions International(191)
Association of Collegiate Business Schools and Programs(191)
Association of Collegiate Schools of Architecture(191)
Association of Collegiate Schools of Planning(191)
Association of Community College Trustees(192)
Association of Community Health Nursing Educators(192)
Association of Community Tribal Schools(192)
Association of Cooperative Educators(192)
Association of Departments of English(193)
Association of Departments of Foreign Languages(193)
Association of Educational Publishers(194)
Association of Educational Service Agencies(194)
Association of Educational Therapists(194)
Association of Educators in Imaging and Radiologic Sciences(194)
Association of Episcopal Colleges(195)
Association of Governing Boards of Universities and Colleges(199)
Association of Graduate Liberal Studies Programs(199)
Association of Higher Education Facilities Officers(199)
Association of International Education Administrators(201)
Association of Jesuit Colleges and Universities(202)
Association of Leadership Educators(203)
Association of Lutheran Secondary Schools(203)
Association of Management/International Association of Management(203)
Association of Military Colleges and Schools of the U.S.(205)
Association of Muslim Social Scientists(205)
Association of Natural Resource Enforcement Trainers(205)
Association of Performing Arts Presenters(207)
Association of Postgraduate Physician Assistant Programs(208)
Association of Presbyterian Colleges and Universities(208)
Association of Professional Schools of International Affairs(209)
Association of Professors of Cardiology(209)
Association of Professors of Medicine(209)
Association of Professors of Mission(210)
Association of Program Directors in Internal Medicine(210)
Association of School Business Officials International(212)
Association of Schools and Colleges of Optometry(213)
Association of Schools of Allied Health Professions(213)
Association of Schools of Journalism and Mass Communication(213)
Association of Schools of Public Health(213)
Association of Small Business Development Centers(214)
Association of Specialized and Professional Accreditors(214)
Association of State Supervisors of Mathematics(216)
Association of Supervisory and Administrative School Personnel(216)
Association of Teacher Educators(217)
Association of Teachers of Latin American Studies(217)
Association of Teachers of Maternal and Child Health(217)
Association of Teachers of Preventive Medicine(217)
Association of Teachers of Technical Writing(217)
Association of Theological Schools in the United States and Canada(218)
Association of University Architects(219)
Association of University Professors of Ophthalmology(219)
Association of University Programs in Health Administration(219)
Association of Writers and Writing Programs(221)
Association on Higher Education and Disability(221)
Augustinian Educational Association(222)
Aviation Technician Education Council(225)
Bibliographical Society of America(228)
Brazilian Studies Association(232)
Broadcast Education Association(233)
Business Higher Education Forum(235)
Business Professionals of America(236)
Campus Safety, Health and Environmental Management Association(237)
Career College Association(237)
Career Planning and Adult Development Network(238)
Chinese Language Teachers Association(245)
Christian College Consortium(245)
Christian Educators Association International(246)
Christian Schools International(246)
Classroom Publishers Association(247)
Coalition of Essential Schools(249)
Coalition of Higher Education Assistance Organizations(249)
College and University Professional Association for Human Resources(250)
College Art Association(251)
College Band Directors National Association(251)
College English Association(251)
College Media Advisers(251)
College Music Society(251)
College Reading and Learning Association(252)
College Theology Society(252)
Commission on Accreditation of Allied Health Education Programs(254)
Committee on History in the Classroom(254)
Community College Business Officers(255)
Community College Journalism Association(256)
Community Colleges Humanities Association(256)
Comparative and International Education Society(256)
Computer Assisted Language Instruction Consortium(257)
Conference of Educational Administrators of Schools and Programs for the Deaf(259)
Conference on College Composition and Communication(260)
Conference on English Education(260)
Conference on English Leadership(260)
Conference on Jewish Social Studies(261)
Conference on Latin American History(261)
Consortium for Graduate Study and Management(262)
Consortium for School Networking(262)
Consortium of College and University Media Centers(262)
Consortium of Social Science Associations(262)
Cooperative Education and Internship Association(265)
Cooperative Work Experience Education Association(265)
Correctional Education Association(266)
Council for Adult and Experiential Learning(267)
Council for Advancement and Support of Education(267)
Council for American Private Education(268)
Council for Art Education(268)
Council for Christian Colleges and Universities(268)
Council for Elementary Science International(268)
Council for Ethics in Economics(268)
Council for European Studies(268)
Council for Exceptional Children(268)
Council for Higher Education Accreditation(269)
Council for Jewish Education(269)
Council for Learning Disabilities(269)
Council for Opportunity in Education(269)
Council for Professional Recognition(269)
Council for Resource Development(269)
Council for Spiritual and Ethical Education(270)
Council for the Advancement of Standards in Higher Education(270)
Council of Administrators of Special Education(270)
Council of American Instructors of the Deaf(270)
Council of Chief State School Officers(271)
Council of Colleges of Acupuncture and Oriental Medicine(271)
Council of Colleges of Arts and Sciences(271)
Council of Educational Facility Planners, International(271)
Council of Graduate Schools(272)
Council of Independent Colleges(272)
Council of the Great City Schools(275)
Council on Chiropractic Education(275)
Council on Education of the Deaf(276)
Council on Governmental Relations(276)
Council on Library-Media Technicians(276)
Council on Occupational Education(276)
Council on Social Work Education(277)

Council on Technology Teacher Education(277)
Creative Education Foundation(278)
Dance Educators of America(281)
Dance Masters of America(281)
Decision Sciences Institute(282)
Delta Pi Epsilon(282)
Delta Society(283)
Distance Education and Training Council(285)
Distributive Education Clubs of America(286)
Early Childhood Education Institute(288)
Education Industry Association(289)
Education Law Association(289)
Education Writers Association(289)
Educational Paperback Association(289)
Educational Theatre Association(289)
EDUCAUSE(290)
Electrical and Computer Engineering Department Heads Association(290)
Evangelical Training Association(298)
Family and Consumer Sciençes Education Association(300)
Family, Career, and Community Leaders of America(300)
Federal Education Association(302)
Federation of State Humanities Councils(304)
Foundation for Independent Higher Education(311)
Future Business Leaders of America-Phi Beta Lambda(313)
Graduate Management Admission Council(319)
Health Care Education Association(322)
Hispanic Association of Colleges and Universities(325)
History of Economics Society(326)
History of Education Society(327)
Housing Education and Research Association(329)
Independent Educational Consultants Association(334)
Independent Research Libraries Association(335)
Independent Scholars of Asia(335)
Indian Educators Federation(336)
InSight(339)
Institute of Behavioral and Applied Management(340)
Instructional Telecommunications Council(344)
Insulated Cable Engineers Association(344)
Intercollegiate Broadcasting System(346)
Interior Design Educators Council(347)
International Association for Computer Information Systems(349)
International Association for Continuing Education and Training(349)
International Association for Jazz Education(351)
International Association for Language Learning Technology(351)
International Association for the Study of Cooperation in Education(351)
International Association for Truancy and Dropout Prevention(352)
International Association of Baptist Colleges and Universities(353)
International Association of Campus Law Enforcement Administrators(354)
International Association of School Librarianship(361)
International Childbirth Education Association(365)
International Council of Fine Arts Deans(367)
International Council on Education for Teaching(368)
International Council on Hotel, Restaurant and Institutional Education(368)
International Double Reed Society(369)
International Dyslexia Association(370)
International Engineering Consortium(370)
International Graphic Arts Education Association(374)
International Listening Association(378)
International Reading Association(384)
International Society for Educational Planning(387)
International Society for Performance Improvement(388)
International Society for Technology in Education(389)
International Society of Certified Employee Benefit Specialists(390)
International Society of Fire Service Instructors(391)
International Society of Travel and Tourism Educators(392)
International Technology Education Association(393)
International Visual Literacy Association(396)
International Writing Centers Association(397)
Jean Piaget Society(400)
Jesuit Secondary Education Association(401)
Jewish Education Service of North America(401)
Jewish Educators Assembly(402)
Journalism Education Association(402)
Kappa Delta Epsilon(403)
Kappa Delta Pi(403)
Kappa Kappa Iota(403)
Latin American Studies Association(405)
League for Innovation in the Community College(406)
Lutheran Education Association(409)
Lutheran Educational Conference of North America(409)
Marketing Education Association(413)
Mathematical Association of America(414)
MENC: The National Association for Music Education(417)
Military Impacted Schools Association(419)
Modern Language Association of America(420)
Music and Entertainment Industry Educators Association(423)
Music Teachers National Association(423)
NAFSA: Association of International Educators(424)
National Academic Advising Association(426)
National Academy of Education(426)
National Academy of Opticianry(427)
National Adult Education Professional Development Consortium(427)
National Alliance of Black School Educators(429)
National Art Education Association(431)
National Association for Bilingual Education(431)
National Association for Campus Activities(432)
National Association for Chicana and Chicano Studies(432)
National Association for College Admission Counseling(432)
National Association for Developmental Education(432)
National Association for Equal Opportunity in Higher Education(433)
National Association for Family and Community Education(433)
National Association for Humanities Education(434)
National Association for Kinesiology and Physical Education in Higher Education(434)
National Association for Practical Nurse Education and Service(435)
National Association for Pupil Transportation(435)
National Association for Research in Science Teaching(435)
National Association for the Education of Young Children(436)
National Association for Trade and Industrial Education(437)
National Association for Year-Round Education(437)
National Association of African American Studies(438)
National Association of Agricultural Educators(438)
National Association of Agricultural Fair Agencies(438)
National Association of Biology Teachers(440)
National Association of Catholic School Teachers(442)
National Association of College and University Attorneys(444)
National Association of College and University Business Officers(444)
National Association of College and University Food Services(444)
National Association of College Auxiliary Services(444)
National Association of College Wind and Percussion Instructors(444)
National Association of Colleges and Employers(444)
National Association of Collegiate Directors of Athletics(444)
National Association of Credential Evaluation Services, Inc.(447)
National Association of Educational Buyers(450)
National Association of Educational Office Professionals(450)
National Association of Elementary School Principals(450)
National Association of Episcopal Schools(451)
National Association of Family Development Centers(452)
National Association of Federal Education Program Administrators(452)
National Association of Federally Impacted Schools(452)
National Association of Flight Instructors(453)
National Association of Forensic Economics(453)
National Association of Geoscience Teachers(454)
National Association of Graduate Admissions Professionals(454)
National Association of Independent Colleges and Universities(457)
National Association of Independent Schools(457)
National Association of Industrial and Technical Teacher Educators(458)
National Association of Industrial Technology(458)
National Association of Juvenile Correctional Agencies(459)
National Association of Media and Technology Centers(461)
National Association of Medical Minority Educators(461)
National Association of Parliamentarians(463)
National Association of Principals of Schools for Girls(465)
National Association of Private Special Education Centers(465)
National Association of Private, Nontraditional Schools and Colleges with Accrediting Commission for Higher Education(465)
National Association of Professors of Hebrew in American Institutions of Higher Learning(466)
National Association of Pupil Services Administrators(467)
National Association of School Music Dealers(470)
National Association of School Nurses(470)
National Association of Schools of Art and Design(470)
National Association of Schools of Dance(470)
National Association of Schools of Music(470)
National Association of Schools of Public Affairs and Administration(470)
National Association of Schools of Theatre(471)
National Association of Secondary School Principals(471)
National Association of Self-Instructional Language Programs(471)
National Association of Special Needs State Administrators(472)
National Association of State Administrators and Supervisors of Private Schools(473)

National Association of State Boards of Education(473)
National Association of State Directors of Career Technical Education Consortium(474)
National Association of State Directors of Migrant Education(474)
National Association of State Directors of Special Education(475)
National Association of State Directors of Teacher Education and Certification(475)
National Association of State Supervisors of Trade and Industrial Education(476)
National Association of State Textbook Administrators(476)
National Association of State Universities and Land Grant Colleges(477)
National Association of Student Affairs Professionals(477)
National Association of Student Financial Aid Administrators(477)
National Association of Student Personnel Administrators(478)
National Association of Substance Abuse Trainers and Educators(478)
National Association of Supervisors for Business Education(478)
National Association of Teacher Educators for Family Consumer Sciences(478)
National Association of Teachers of Singing(478)
National Association of Teachers' Agencies(478)
National Association of Temple Educators(479)
National Association of Test Directors(479)
National Association of Underwater Instructors(480)
National Association of Veterans Program Administrators(480)
National Association of Workforce Development Professionals(482)
National Business Education Association(486)
National Catholic Educational Association(487)
National Catholic Educational Exhibitors(487)
National Coalition of Alternative Community Schools(490)
National Coalition of Girls Schools(490)
National Collegiate Athletic Association(491)
National Collegiate Honors Council(491)
National Community Education Association(491)
National Conference of Yeshiva Principals(495)
National Council for Agricultural Education(497)
National Council for Geographic Education(497)
National Council for Marketing and Public Relations(497)
National Council for the Social Studies(497)
National Council for Workforce Education(497)
National Council of Administrative Women in Education(498)
National Council of Art Administrators(498)
National Council of Higher Education Loan Programs(499)
National Council of State Supervisors for Languages(501)
National Council of Supervisors of Mathematics(501)
National Council of Teachers of English(501)
National Council of Teachers of Mathematics(501)
National Council of Writing Program Administrators(502)
National Council on Education for the Ceramic Arts(502)
National Council on Rehabilitation Education(503)
National Council on Student Development(503)
National Council on Teacher Retirement(503)
National Dance Association(504)
National Earth Science Teachers Association(505)
National Education Association(506)
National Education Knowledge Industry Association(506)
National Educational Telecommunications Association(506)
National Extension Association of Family and Consumer Sciences(508)
National Federation Coaches Association(508)
National Federation of Modern Language Teachers Associations(509)
National Federation of Nonpublic School State Accrediting Associations(510)
National Federation of State High School Associations(510)
National Guild of Community Schools of the Arts(515)
National Guild of Piano Teachers(515)
National Head Start Association(516)
National Humanities Alliance(518)
National Indian Education Association(519)
National Marine Educators Association(526)
National Middle School Association(527)
National Music Council(528)
National Organization for Human Service Education(530)
National Organization of Nurse Practitioner Faculties(530)
National Orientation Directors Association(530)
National Postsecondary Agriculture Student Organization(533)
National Reading Conference(535)
National Rural Education Association(537)
National School Boards Association(538)
National School Public Relations Association(538)
National School Supply and Equipment Association(538)
National School Transportation Association(538)
National Science Education Leadership Association(538)
National Science Teachers Association(539)
National Society for Experiential Education(540)
National Society for Hebrew Day Schools(541)
National Society for the Study of Education(541)
National Staff Development Council(543)
National Student Assistance Association(544)
National Student Employment Association(544)
National Tutoring Association(548)
NFHS Music Association(553)
North America Colleges and Teachers of Agriculture(553)
North American Academy of Ecumenists(554)
North American Association for Environmental Education(554)
North American Association of Educational Negotiators(554)
North American Association of Professors of Christian Education(554)
North American Association of Summer Sessions(555)
North American Council of Automotive Teachers(556)
North American Professional Driver Education Association(559)
North American Simulation and Gaming Association(560)
North American Small Business International Trade Educators(560)
Organization for Tropical Studies(567)
Organization of American Kodaly Educators(567)
Organization of Teachers of Oral Diagnosis(568)
Organizational Behavior Teaching Society(568)
Organizational Systems Research Association(568)
Phi Delta Kappa(575)
Philosophy of Education Society(576)
Pi Lambda Theta(577)
Presbyterian Health, Education and Welfare Association(583)
Professional and Organizational Development Network in Higher Education(585)
Professional Association for Childhood Education(585)
Professional Association of Christian Educators(585)
Professional Association of Diving Instructors(585)
Real Estate Educators Association(595)
Religious Education Association(599)
Research Association of Minority Professors(600)
Rhetoric Society of America(601)
School Management Study Group(606)
School Science and Mathematics Association(606)
Skills USA(611)
Society for Academic Emergency Medicine(613)
Society for Applied Learning Technology(614)
Society for Cinema and Media Studies(615)
Society for College and University Planning(615)
Society for Education in Anesthesia(616)
Society for French Historical Studies(617)
Society for Historians of American Foreign Relations(618)
Society for History Education(618)
Society for Intercultural Education, Training and Research - USA(620)
Society for Iranian Studies(620)
Society for Maternal Fetal Medicine(621)
Society for Nutrition Education(622)
Society for Photographic Education(623)
Society for Public Health Education(624)
Society for Textual Scholarship(626)
Society for the Advancement of Education(626)
Society for the Advancement of Scandinavian Study(626)
Society for Values in Higher Education(629)
Society of Armenian Studies(631)
Society of Certified Insurance Counselors(632)
Society of Insurance Trainers and Educators(639)
Society of Philosophers in America(642)
Society of Professors of Child and Adolescent Psychiatry(642)
Society of Professors of Education(643)
Society of Teachers of Family Medicine(644)
Society of Wine Educators(646)
Special Interest Group for University and College Computing Services(649)
State Debt Management Network(652)
State Higher Education Executive Officers(653)
Teachers of English to Speakers of Other Languages(658)
Technology Student Association(658)
Text and Academic Authors Association(659)
United Association for Labor Education(670)
United States Swim School Association(677)
Universities Council on Water Resources(679)
Universities Research Association(679)
University and College Designers Association(679)
University Aviation Association(679)
University Continuing Education Association(679)
University Council for Educational Administration(679)
University Film and Video Association(680)
University Photographers Association of America(680)
University/Resident Theatre Association(680)
Urban Affairs Association(680)
Van Alen Institute(682)
WACRA - World Association for Case Method Research and Application(684)
Western History Association(687)
Women's College Coalition(693)
World Future Society(696)
World History Association(696)

ELECTRICITY & ELECTRONICS

AeA - Advancing the Business of Technology(9)
Aircraft Electronics Association(14)
Airlines Electronic Engineering Committee(14)
ALMA - the International Loudspeaker Association(17)

American Association for Crystal Growth(34)
American Metal Detector Manufacturers Association(105)
American Public Power Association(120)
AOC(158)
Armed Forces Communications and Electronics Association(161)
Association for Electronic Health Care Transactions(172)
Association for Work Process Improvement(183)
Association of Edison Illuminating Companies(194)
Association of United States Night Vision Manufacturers(219)
Audio Engineering Society(222)
Bioelectromagnetics Society(229)
Central Station Alarm Association(241)
Consumer Electronics Association(263)
Contract Services Association of America(264)
Custom Electronic Design and Installation Association(280)
Edison Electric Institute(289)
Edison Welding Institute(289)
Electric Drive Transportation Association(290)
Electric Power Research Institute(290)
Electrical Apparatus Service Association(290)
Electrical Equipment Representatives Association(291)
Electrical Generating Systems Association(291)
Electrical Insulation Conference(291)
Electrical Manufacturing and Coil Winding Association(291)
Electrical Overstress/Electrostatic Discharge Association(291)
Electricity Consumers Resource Council(291)
Electrochemical Society(291)
Electronic Commerce Code Management Association(291)
Electronic Distribution Show Corporation(291)
Electronic Industries Alliance(292)
Electronics Representatives Association(292)
Electronics Technicians Association International(292)
Energy Telecommunications and Electrical Association(294)
EUCG(298)
IEEE Communications Society(330)
IEEE Instrumentation and Measurement Society(331)
IEEE Magnetics Society(331)
IEEE Microwave Theory and Techniques Society(331)
IEEE Power Electronics Society(331)
IEEE Signal Processing Society(331)
Independent Distributors of Electronics Association(334)
Independent Electrical Contractors(334)
Infrared Data Association(338)
Institute of Electrical and Electronics Engineers(341)
Institute of Nuclear Power Operations(343)
International Association of Electrical Inspectors(356)
International Association of Electronics Recyclers(356)
International Brotherhood of Electrical Workers(363)
International Electrical Testing Association(370)
International Engineering Consortium(370)
International Institute of Connector and Interconnection Technology(376)
International League of Electrical Associations(378)
International Magnetics Association(378)
International Microelectronics and Packaging Society(379)
International Microwave Power Institute(379)
International Sign Association(386)
International Society of Certified Electronics Technicians(390)
International Union of Electronic, Electrical, Salaried, Machine, and Furniture Workers-CWA(395)
IPC - Association Connecting Electronics Industries(399)
IPC - Surface Mount Equipment Manufacturers Association(399)
Joint Electron Device Engineering Council(402)
Laser and Electro-Optics Manufacturers' Association(405)
Laser Institute of America(405)
Lightning Protection Institute(408)
Microbeam Analysis Society(418)
National Association of Electrical Distributors(450)
National Association of State Utility Consumer Advocates(477)
National Electrical Contractors Association(506)
National Electrical Manufacturers Association(506)
National Electrical Manufacturers Representatives Association(506)
National Electronic Distributors Association(506)
National Electronic Service Dealers Association(506)
National Food and Energy Council(511)
National Hydropower Association(518)
National Marine Electronics Association(526)
National Rural Electric Cooperative Association(537)
North American Electric Reliability Council(556)
Nuclear Energy Institute(563)
Power and Communication Contractors Association(582)
Power Sources Manufacturers Association(582)
Professional Service Association(589)
Semiconductor Environmental Safety and Health Association(608)
Semiconductor Equipment and Materials International(608)
Semiconductor Industry Association(608)
Surface Mount Technology Association(656)
Transformer Association, The(663)
United Electrical, Radio and Machine Workers of America(671)
Variable Electronic Components Institute(682)
Video Electronics Standards Association(683)
Women's International Network of Utility Professionals(693)
World Research Foundation(696)

ELEVATORS

Elevator Industries Association(292)
International Union of Elevator Constructors(395)
National Association of Elevator Contractors(450)
National Association of Elevator Safety Authorities International(450)
National Association of Vertical Transportation Professionals(480)
National Elevator Industry(506)

EMPLOYEES & EMPLOYMENT

AFT - Public Employees(11)
Alliance of National Staffing and Employment Resources(17)
American Association for Employment in Education(34)
American Congress of Community Supports and Employment Services(73)
American Counseling Association(76)
American Payroll Association(113)
American Staffing Association(149)
Association of Career Firms International(188)
Association of Career Professionals International(188)
Association of Executive Search Consultants(196)
Association of Farmworker Opportunity Programs(196)
Association of Talent Agents(216)
Career Planning and Adult Development Network(238)
Cement Employers Association(241)
Cooperative Work Experience Education Association(265)
Correctional Vendors Association(267)
Customer Relations Institute(280)
Drug and Alcohol Testing Industry Association(287)
Employee Assistance Professionals Association(293)
Employee Assistance Society of North America(293)
Employee Benefit Research Institute(293)
Employee Involvement Association(293)
Employee Relocation Council/Worldwide ERC(293)
Employers Council on Flexible Compensation(293)
ERISA Industry Committee(297)
ESOP Association(297)
Human Resource Planning Society(329)
International Association of Counseling Services(355)
International Association of Jewish Vocational Services(358)
International Association of Workforce Professionals(362)
International Foundation of Employee Benefit Plans(373)
International Society of Certified Employee Benefit Specialists(390)
National Association for Health Care Recruitment(433)
National Association for Law Placement(434)
National Association of Executive Recruiters(451)
National Association of Personnel Services(464)
National Association of State Workforce Agencies(477)
National Association of Teachers' Agencies(478)
National Association of Workforce Boards(482)
National Association of Workforce Development Professionals(482)
National Conference on Public Employee Retirement Systems(495)
National Credit Reporting Association(503)
National Employment Lawyers Association(507)
National Public Employer Labor Relations Association(534)
North American Transportation Employee Relations Association(562)
Office and Professional Employees International Union(564)
Service Employees International Union(609)
Society of Federal Labor and Employee Relations Professionals(636)
United Association for Labor Education(670)
WEB: Worldwide Employee Benefits Network(686)

ENERGY

American Association of Blacks in Energy(38)
American Hydrogen Association(92)
American Solar Energy Society(147)
American Wind Energy Association(155)
Association of Energy Engineers(195)
Association of Energy Services Professionals, International(195)
Association of Professional Energy Managers(209)
Electric Power Supply Association(290)
Energy Bar Association(294)
Energy Frontiers International(294)
Energy Telecommunications and Electrical Association(294)
Federal Network for Sustainability(302)
Fuel Cell Power Association(312)
Fusion Power Associates(313)
Geothermal Energy Association(316)
Geothermal Resources Council(316)
Integrated Waste Services Association(345)
International Association for Hydrogen Energy(350)
International Private Infrastructure Association(383)

Lignite Energy Council(408)
Municipal Waste Management Association(422)
National Association of Energy Service Companies(451)
National Association of Solar Contractors(472)
National Association of State Energy Officials(475)
National Energy Assistance Directors Association(507)
National Food and Energy Council(511)
National Hydrogen Association(518)
National Hydropower Association(518)
Pellet Fuels Institute(573)
Power Sources Manufacturers Association(582)
Solar Energy Industries Association(647)
Solar Rating and Certification Corp.(647)
Space Energy Association(648)
Sustainable Buildings Industry Council(656)
United States Association for Energy Economics(673)
United States Energy Association(675)
Voluntary Protection Programs Participants Association(684)
Women in Energy(691)

ENGINEERING

AACE International(1)
Academy of Applied Science(2)
Airlines Electronic Engineering Committee(14)
Alpha Chi Sigma(17)
American Academy of Environmental Engineers(22)
American Academy of Mechanics(24)
American Association of Engineering Societies(42)
American Automatic Control Council(55)
American Ceramic Society(61)
American Chain Association(61)
American Concrete Institute(72)
American Council of Engineering Companies(75)
American Engineering Association(81)
American Filtration and Separations Society(83)
American Helicopter Society International(90)
American Indian Science and Engineering Society(93)
American Institute for Medical and Biological Engineering(94)
American Institute of Chemical Engineers(95)
American Institute of Engineers(95)
American Institute of Mining, Metallurgical, and Petroleum Engineers(96)
American Public Works Association(120)
American Society for Engineering Education(128)
American Society for Engineering Management(128)
American Society for Healthcare Engineering(129)
American Society for Precision Engineering(132)
American Society for Quality(132)
American Society of Baking(134)
American Society of Body Engineers(135)
American Society of Certified Engineering Technicians(135)
American Society of Civil Engineers(135)
American Society of Gas Engineers(138)
American Society of Heating, Refrigerating and Air-Conditioning Engineers(139)
American Society of Highway Engineers(139)
American Society of Mechanical Engineers(141)
American Society of Naval Engineers(142)
American Society of Plumbing Engineers(144)
American Society of Safety Engineers(146)
American Society of Sanitary Engineering(146)
American Society of Test Engineers(146)
American Underground-Construction Association(152)
American Water Resources Association(154)
American Water Works Association(154)
American Welding Society(154)
Architectural Engineering Institute(160)
ASABE - the Society for Engineering in Agricultural, Food and Biological Systems(162)
ASFE/The Best People on Earth(162)
ASM International(163)
Associated Builders and Contractors(164)
Association for Bridge Construction and Design(168)
Association for Computing Machinery(170)
Association for Facilities Engineering(172)
Association for Iron and Steel Technology(175)
Association of Asphalt Paving Technologists(186)
Association of Chairmen of Departments of Mechanics(189)
Association of Conservation Engineers(192)
Association of Consulting Chemists and Chemical Engineers(192)
Association of Diesel Specialists(194)
Association of Energy Engineers(195)
Association of Environmental and Engineering Geologists(195)
Association of Environmental Engineering and Science Professors(195)
Association of Federal Communications Consulting Engineers(196)
Association of Muslim Scientists and Engineers(205)
ASTM International(221)
Audio Engineering Society(222)
Biomedical Engineering Society(229)
Brotherhood of Locomotive Engineers and Trainmen(233)
Combustion Institute(253)
Commission on Professionals in Science and Technology(254)
Construction Management Association of America(262)
Construction Specifications Institute(263)
Council of Engineering and Scientific Society Executives(271)
Council on Forest Engineering(276)
Cryogenic Engineering Conference(280)
Cryogenic Society of America(280)
Deep Foundations Institute(282)
Design-Build Institute of America(283)
Electrical and Computer Engineering Department Heads Association(290)
Electrochemical Society(291)
Engineering in Medicine and Biology Society(295)
Federation of Materials Socs.(304)
Fluid Power Society(308)
Geoscience and Remote Sensing Society(316)
Human Factors and Ergonomics Society(329)
IEEE Signal Processing Society(331)
IEEE Society on Social Implications of Technology(332)
Illuminating Engineering Society of North America(332)
Institute of Electrical and Electronics Engineers(341)
Institute of Environmental Sciences and Technology(341)
Institute of Hazardous Materials Management(341)
Institute of Industrial Engineers(341)
Institute of Noise Control Engineering(343)
Institute of Transportation Engineers(344)
Insulated Cable Engineers Association(344)
Insurance Loss Control Association(345)
International Council on Systems Engineering(368)
International Engineering Consortium(370)
International Federation of Professional and Technical Engineers(371)
International Reprographic Association(385)
International Society for Pharmaceutical Engineering(388)
International Test and Evaluation Association(394)
International Union of Operating Engineers(395)
ISA(400)
Joint Electron Device Engineering Council(402)
Keramos Fraternity(403)
Marine Technology Society(412)
Materials Properties Council(414)
MTM Association for Standards and Research(422)
NACE International(424)
NARTE(425)
National Academy of Engineering of the United States of America(426)
National Association of County Engineers(447)
National Association of Minority Engineering Program Administrators(462)
National Association of Power Engineers(465)
National Board of Boiler and Pressure Vessel Inspectors(485)
National Conference of Regulatory Utility Commission Engineers(494)
National Council of Black Engineers and Scientists(498)
National Council of Examiners for Engineering and Surveying(499)
National Institute of Building Sciences(520)
National Institute of Ceramic Engineers(520)
National Institute of Packaging, Handling and Logistics Engineers(521)
National Institute of Steel Detailing(521)
National Society of Professional Engineers(542)
National Technical Services Association(546)
North American Contractors Association(556)
North American Die Casting Association(556)
North American Manufacturing Research Institution of SME(558)
North American Membrane Society(558)
Professional Engineers in Private Practice(587)
Professional Services Management Association(589)
Railway Engineering-Maintenance Suppliers Association(595)
Refrigerating Engineers and Technicians Association(597)
Refrigeration Service Engineers Society(597)
Rehabilitation Engineering and Assistive Technology Society of North America(598)
Research and Engineering Council of the NAPL(600)
Research Council on Structural Connections(600)
Robotic Industries Association(602)
SAE International(604)
SAVE International(605)
Sigma Phi Delta(610)
Society for Experimental Mechanics(617)
Society for Imaging Science & Technology(619)
Society for Maintenance Reliability Professionals(621)
Society for Mining, Metallurgy, and Exploration(622)
Society for the Advancement of Material and Process Engineering(626)
Society for the History of Technology(627)
Society of Allied Weight Engineers(630)
Society of American Military Engineers(631)
Society of Broadcast Engineers(632)
Society of Cable Telecommunications Engineers(632)
Society of Engineering Science(635)
Society of Fire Protection Engineers(636)
Society of Flight Test Engineers(636)
Society of Hispanic Professional Engineers(638)
Society of Independent Professional Earth Scientists(638)
Society of Manufacturing Engineers(639)
Society of Marine Port Engineers(639)
Society of Mexican American Engineers and Scientists(640)
Society of Motion Picture and Television Engineers(640)
Society of Naval Architects and Marine Engineers(640)
Society of Petroleum Engineers(641)
Society of Petroleum Evaluation Engineers(641)
Society of Piping Engineers and Designers(642)
Society of Plastics Engineers(642)
Society of Reliability Engineers(643)
Society of Rheology(643)

Society of Tribologists and Lubrication Engineers(645)
Society of Women Engineers(646)
SOLE - The International Society of Logistics(647)
SPIE - The International Society for Optical Engineering(651)
Standards Engineering Society(652)
Structural Stability Research Council(654)
Surface Engineering Coating Association(656)
Surface Mount Technology Association(656)
System Safety Society(657)
Theta Tau(660)
United Engineering Foundation(671)
Water Environment Federation(685)
Western Dredging Association(687)

ENGINES

AERA - Engine Rebuilders Association(9)
ASME International Gas Turbine Institute(163)
Contractors Pump Bureau(264)
Electrical Generating Systems Association(291)
Engine Manufacturers Association(295)
Filter Manufacturers Council(305)
SMMA - The Motor and Motion Association(612)

ENGLISH

American Comparative Literature Association(72)
American Humor Studies Association(92)
Association for Documentary Editing(171)
Association for Informal Logic and Critical Thinking(174)
Association of Departments of English(193)
Association of Literary Scholars and Critics(203)
College English Association(251)
Conference on College Composition and Communication(260)
Conference on English Education(260)
Conference on English Leadership(260)
International Society for General Semantics(387)
National Conference on Research in Language and Literacy(495)
National Council of Teachers of English(501)
National Council of Writing Program Administrators(502)
Pharmaceutical Printed Literature Association(575)
Renaissance Society of America(599)
Rhetoric Society of America(601)
Society for New Language Study(622)
Teachers of English to Speakers of Other Languages(658)
Western Literature Association(687)

ENTERTAINMENT

American Amusement Machine Association(31)
American Disc Jockey Association(79)
Amusement and Music Operators Association(156)
Association of Talent Agents(216)
Black Entertainment and Sports Lawyers Association(230)
Clowns of America, International(248)
Entertainment Services and Technology Association(295)
Entertainment Software Association(295)
International Association of Speakers Bureaus(361)
International Entertainment Buyers Association(370)
International Game Developers Association(374)
National Alliance for Musical Theatre(429)
National Association for Campus Activities(432)
National Association of Ticket Brokers(479)
National Ballroom and Entertainment Association(483)
National Conference of Personal Managers(494)
National Society of Film Critics(541)
Outdoor Amusement Business Association(569)
Production Equipment Rental Association(585)
Showmen's League of America(610)

ENTOMOLOGY

American Entomological Society(81)
American Phytopathological Society(115)
Association of Applied IPM Ecologists(186)
Coleopterists Society(250)
Entomological Society of America(295)
National Association for Interpretation(434)
National Pest Management Association(532)
Society for Vector Ecology(629)

ENVIRONMENT

Acrylonitrile Group(8)
Air Conditioning Contractors of America(13)
American Association for Aerosol Research(33)
American Council on Science and Health(76)
American Institute of Hydrology(96)
American Society for Environmental History(128)
American Society of Mining and Reclamation(141)
Aspirin Foundation of America(164)
Association for the Environmental Health of Soils(180)
Association of Ecosystem Research Centers(194)
Association of Environmental and Resource Economists(195)
Association of Environmental Engineering and Science Professors(195)
Conservation and Preservation Charities of America(261)
Council on Certification of Health, Environmental and Safety Technologists(275)
Environmental Assessment Association(296)
Environmental Bankers Association(296)
Environmental Business Association, The(296)
Environmental Design Research Association(296)
Environmental Information Association(296)
Environmental Mutagen Society(296)
ETAD North America(298)
Federation of Environmental Technologists(303)
Institute for Polyacrylate Absorbents(339)
Institute of Environmental Sciences and Technology(341)
International Association of Wildland Fire(361)
International Ecotourism Society(370)
International Lead Zinc Research Organization(377)
International Society for Ecological Economics(387)
International Society for Ecological Modelling-North American Chapter(387)
National Association for Environmental Management(433)
National Association of Environmental Professionals(451)
National Association of Local Government Environmental Professionals(460)
National Association of Noise Control Officials(463)
National Conference of Local Environmental Health Administrators(493)
National Environmental Balancing Bureau(507)
National Environmental Health Association(507)
National Environmental, Safety and Health Training Association(507)
National Institutes for Water Resources(521)
National Registry of Environmental Professionals(535)
NORA: An Association of Responsible Recyclers(553)
North American Association for Environmental Education(554)
Plant Growth Regulators Society of America(578)
Renewable Natural Resources Foundation(599)
Silicones Environmental, Health and Safety Council of North America(610)
Society for Ecological Restoration(616)
Society for Environmental Geochemistry and Health(617)
Society for Human Ecology(619)
Society for Occupational and Environmental Health(622)
Society of Environmental Journalists(635)
Society of Environmental Toxicology and Chemistry(635)
Steel Recycling Institute(653)
Surfaces in Biomaterials Foundation(656)
Synthetic Organic Chemical Manufacturers Association(657)
Test Boring Association(659)
World Research Foundation(696)

EXAMINERS

American Society of Home Inspectors(139)
Association of Regulatory Boards of Optometry(211)
National Association of Disability Examiners(449)
National Association of Document Examiners(449)
National Conference of Bar Examiners(492)
National Council of Examiners for Engineering and Surveying(499)

EXECUTIVES

Advertising Media Credit Executives Association, International(9)
American Association of Airport Executives(38)
American Association of Credit Union Leagues(41)
American Association of Medical Society Executives(45)
American Chamber of Commerce Executives(61)
American College of Cardiovascular Administrators(64)
American College of Physician Executives(69)
American Society of Association Executives & Center for Association Leadership(134)
Association of Executive and Administrative Professionals(196)
Association of Executive Search Consultants(196)
Association of Fundraising Professionals(198)
Association of Master of Business Administration Executives(204)
Association of Membership and Marketing Executives(204)
Association of Travel Marketing Executives(218)
Automotive Trade Association Executives(224)
Chief Executives Organization(244)
Community Action Partnership(255)
Congress of Chiropractic State Associations(261)
Cosmetic Executive Women(267)
Council of Engineering and Scientific Society Executives(271)
Council of State Association Presidents(274)
County Executives of America(277)
Credit Union Executives Society(279)
Executive Women International(299)
Financial Executives International(305)
Food Industry Association Executives(309)
Fraternity Executives Association(311)
Incentive Marketing Association(332)
International Association of Golf Administrators(357)
International Builders Exchange Executives(363)
International Downtown Association(369)
International Food Service Executives' Association(372)
International Military Community Executives Association(379)
International Society of Facilities Executives(391)
International Society of Hotel Association Executives(391)
International Society of Restaurant Association Executives(392)
Licensing Executives Society(407)

National Association of Catering Executives(442)
National Association of Corporate Treasurers(446)
National Association of Credit Union Chairmen(448)
National Association of Television Program Executives(478)
National Council of State Pharmacy Association Executives(501)
Newspaper Association Managers(552)
Nursery and Landscape Association Executives of North America(563)
Police Executive Research Forum(580)
Professional Society for Sales and Marketing Training(589)
Sales and Marketing Executives International(604)
Senior Executives Association(609)
Society of Corporate Secretaries and Governance Professionals(634)
Society of Incentive & Travel Executives(638)
Tax Executives Institute(657)
Zonta International(698)

EXHIBITS see also CONVENTIONS

American Academy of Equine Art(22)
Center for Exhibition Industry Research(241)
Convention Industry Council(265)
Display Distributors Association(285)
Exhibit Designers and Producers Association(299)
Exhibition Services and Contractors Association(299)
Healthcare Convention and Exhibitors Association(323)
International Association for Exhibition Management(350)
International Association of Assembly Managers(353)
International Association of Fairs and Expositions(356)
International Festivals and Events Association(371)
International Laser Display Association(377)
International Special Events Society(393)
Meeting Professionals International(416)
National Association of Agricultural Fair Agencies(438)
National Association of Consumer Shows(446)
National Catholic Educational Exhibitors(487)
North American Farm Show Council(557)
Religious Conference Management Association(599)
Society of Independent Show Organizers(638)
Trade Show Exhibitors Association(663)
Visitor Studies Association(684)

EXPLOSIVES

American Pyrotechnics Association(120)
Institute of Makers of Explosives(342)
International Association of Bomb Technicians and Investigators(354)
International Society of Explosives Engineers(391)

EXPORTS

American Association of Exporters and Importers(42)
American Hardwood Export Council(89)
Association of Dark Leaf Tobacco Dealers and Exporters(193)
Association of Foreign Trade Representatives(197)
California Dried Fruit Export Association(236)
FCIB-NACM Corp.(301)
Independent Distributors Association(333)
Leaf Tobacco Exporters Association(406)
National Association of Export Companies(451)
National Council on International Trade Development(502)
North American Export Grain Association(557)
Northwest Fruit Exporters(562)
Organization of Women in International Trade(568)
Overseas Automotive Council(570)
Small Business Exporters Association of the United States(611)
U.S. Grains Council(667)
United States Meat Export Federation(676)

FARMS

American Farm Bureau Federation(81)
American Forage and Grassland Council(84)
Association of Farmworker Opportunity Programs(196)
Farm Credit Council(301)
Farm Equipment Manufacturers Association(301)
Farm Equipment Wholesalers Association(301)
Farmers Educational and Co-operative Union of America(301)
Herb Growing & Marketing Network(325)
National Association of Farm Broadcasting(452)
National Council of Agricultural Employers(498)
National Council of Farmer Cooperatives(499)
National Farmers Organization(508)
National FFA Organization(510)
National Food and Energy Council(511)
North American Equipment Dealers Association(556)
REALTORS Land Institute(596)
United Farm Workers of America(671)

FASTENERS

Cold Formed Parts and Machine Institute(250)
Gasket Fabricators Association(314)
Industrial Fasteners Institute(337)
International Staple, Nail and Tool Association(393)
National Fastener Distributors Association(508)
Specialty Tool and Fastener Distributors Association(650)

FATS & OILS

American Oil Chemists' Society(110)
Drug, Chemical and Associated Technologies Association(287)
Independent Liquid Terminals Association(334)
Institute of Shortening and Edible Oils(344)
International Castor Oil Association(364)
International Oil Mill Superintendents Association(381)
National Candle Association(487)
National Cottonseed Products Association(496)
National Institute of Oilseed Products(521)
National Oilseed Processors Association(529)
National Renderers Association(536)
National Sunflower Association(545)

FEED & GRAIN

AFIA-Alfalfa Processors Council(11)
American Feed Industry Association(83)
Association of American Feed Control Officials(184)
Distilled Spirits Council of the U.S.(286)
Distillers Grains Technology Council(286)
Grain Elevator and Processing Society(319)
International Association of Operative Millers(359)
National Corn Growers Association(496)
National Grain and Feed Association(514)
National Grain Trade Council(514)
U.S. Grains Council(667)
United States Durum Growers Association(675)

FERTILIZERS

Agricultural Retailers Association(12)
Association of American Plant Food Control Officials(185)
Fertilizer Institute(305)
International Union of Petroleum and Industrial Workers(396)
Lawn Institute(406)
Potash & Phosphate Institute(581)

FILMS

Academy of Motion Picture Arts and Sciences(4)
Alliance of Motion Picture and Television Producers(17)
American Association for Vocational Instructional Materials(37)
American Cinema Editors(62)
American Federation of Musicians of the United States and Canada(82)
American Federation of Television and Radio Artists(83)
American Society of Cinematographers(135)
Art Directors Guild/Scenic, Title and Graphic Artists(161)
Association for Information Media and Equipment(174)
Association of Cinema and Video Laboratories(190)
Association of Film Commissioners International(196)
Association of Independent Commercial Producers(200)
Association of Moving Image Archivists(205)
Black Filmmaker Foundation(230)
Consortium of College and University Media Centers(262)
Directors Guild of America(285)
Free Speech Coalition(312)
Historians Film Committee/Film & History(326)
Independent Feature Project(334)
Independent Film and Television Alliance(334)
International Animated Film Society, ASIFA-Hollywood(349)
International Association of Audio Visual Communicators(353)
International Theatre Equipment Association(394)
International Ticketing Association(394)
Motion Picture and Television Credit Association(421)
Motion Picture Association of America(421)
National Alliance for Media Arts and Culture(429)
National Association of Theatre Owners(479)
National Association of Video Distributors(480)
Producer's Guild of America(584)
Screen Actors Guild(606)
Society for Cinema and Media Studies(615)
Society for Visual Anthropology(629)
Society of Composers and Lyricists(634)
Society of Motion Picture and Television Engineers(640)
Stuntmen's Association of Motion Pictures(654)
Stuntwomen's Association of Motion Pictures(654)
Travel Adventure Cinema Society(665)
United Scenic Artists(672)
University Film and Video Association(680)
Wedding and Event Videographers Association International(686)
Women in Film(691)
Women in Film and Video(692)
Women of the Motion Picture Industry, International(692)
Writers Guild of America, East(697)
Writers Guild of America, West(697)

FINANCE see also CREDIT

AACE International(1)
ACA International, The Association of Credit and Collection Professionals(2)
American Association of Healthcare Administrative Management(43)
American Association of Individual Investors(44)
American Association of Residential Mortgage Regulators(50)
American Bankruptcy Institute(55)
American Cash Flow Association(61)
American Education Finance Association(80)
American Finance Association(83)
American Financial Services Association(83)
American Society of Military Comptrollers(141)
Association for Financial Counseling and Planning Education(173)
Association for Financial Professionals(173)

FIRE

FIREARMS

FISH AND FISHING

FLOORING

FOOD INDUSTRY

Chemical Sources Association(243)
Chinese American Food Society(245)
Corn Refiners Association(266)
Flavor and Extract Manufacturers Association of the United States(307)
Food and Drug Law Institute(309)
Food Distribution Research Society(309)
Food Industry Suppliers Association(309)
Foodservice Equipment Distributors Association(310)
The Foodservice Group, Inc.(310)
Fresh Produce and Floral Council(312)
Glutamate Association (United States)(318)
Greek Food and Wine Institute(320)
Herb Growing & Marketing Network(325)
Home Baking Association(327)
Institute of Food Technologists(341)
International Association for Food Protection(350)
International Association of Color Manufacturers(355)
International Dairy-Deli-Bakery Association(369)
International Food Additives Council(372)
International Food Information Council(372)
International Foodservice Editorial Council(372)
International Formula Council(373)
International Frozen Food Association(373)
International Institute of Ammonia Refrigeration(376)
International Maple Syrup Institute(379)
International Technical Caramel Association(393)
Juice Products Association(402)
Leafy Greens Council(406)
National Association for the Specialty Food Trade(436)
National Association of Convenience Stores(446)
National Association of Flavors and Food-Ingredient Systems(453)
National Association of Pizza Operators(464)
National Association of Produce Market Managers(465)
National Barbecue Association(483)
National Confectioners Association of the United States(492)
National Corn Growers Association(496)
National Food and Energy Council(511)
National Frozen and Refrigerated Foods Association(513)
National Frozen Dessert and Fast Food Association(513)
National Honey Packers and Dealers Association(517)
National Onion Association(529)
National Pasta Association(532)
National Potato Council(533)
National Potato Promotion Board(533)
National Seasoning Manufacturers Association(539)
National Sugar Brokers Association(544)
Network of Ingredient Marketing Specialists(551)
North American Meat Processors Association(558)
North American Natural Casing Association(558)
Organic Trade Association(566)
Peanut and Tree Nut Processors Association(572)
Pet Food Institute(574)
Pickle Packers International(577)
Popcorn Institute(580)
Potato Association of America(581)
Produce Marketing Association(584)
Refrigerated Foods Association(597)
Research and Development Associates for Military Food and Packaging Systems(599)
Snack Food Association(612)
Society of Flavor Chemists(636)
Soy Protein Council(648)
Soyfoods Association of North America(648)
Sugar Association(655)
U.S. Apple Association(667)
United Food and Commercial Workers International Union(671)
United States Beet Sugar Association(673)
Vinegar Institute(683)
Wild Blueberry Association of North America(688)

FOOD PROCESSORS

American Cheese Society(61)
American Dehydrated Onion and Garlic Association(78)
American Frozen Food Institute(85)
American Peanut Product Manufacturers(113)
American Shrimp Processors Association(125)
Apple Processors Association(159)
Apple Products Research and Education Council(159)
Association of Smoked Fish Processors(214)
Biscuit and Cracker Manufacturers' Association(229)
Calorie Control Council(237)
Commercial Food Equipment Service Association(253)
Concord Grape Association(258)
Food Processing Machinery and Supplies Association(309)
Food Products Association(309)
Frozen Potato Products Institute(312)
Grocery Manufacturers Association(320)
Institute of Food Technologists(341)
International Association of Food Industry Suppliers(357)
International Association of Operative Millers(359)
International Dairy-Deli-Bakery Association(369)
International Foodservice Manufacturers Association(372)
International Formula Council(373)
International Hydrolized Protein Council(375)
International Jelly and Preserve Association(377)
International Natural Sausage Casing Association(380)
Juice Products Association(402)
National Association of Margarine Manufacturers(461)
National Chicken Council(489)
National Frozen and Refrigerated Foods Association(513)
National Frozen Pizza Institute(513)
National Meat Canners Association(526)
National Oilseed Processors Association(529)
National Pecan Shellers Association(532)
National Shrimp Industry Association(539)
North American Millers Association(558)
Process Equipment Manufacturers' Association(584)
Rice Millers' Association(602)
Tortilla Industry Association(662)
United Egg Producers(670)
United Fresh Produce Association(671)
United States Durum Growers Association(675)

FOOD SERVICES

American Association of Meat Processors(45)
American Society for Healthcare Food Service Administrators(129)
Association Correctional Food Service Affiliates(166)
BCA(226)
BMC - A Foodservice Sales and Marketing Council(231)
Commercial Food Equipment Service Association(253)
Dietary Managers Association(284)
Food Industry Association Executives(309)
Food Marketing Institute(309)
Food Shippers of America(309)
Foodservice Consultants Society International(309)
The Foodservice Group, Inc.(310)
Hospitality Institute of Technology and Management(328)
International Council on Hotel, Restaurant and Institutional Education(368)
International Food Service Executives' Association(372)
International Foodservice Distributors Association(372)
International Foodservice Manufacturers Association(372)
International Inflight Food Service Association(376)
Manufacturers' Agents Association for the Foodservice Industry(411)
Meals On Wheels Association of America(414)
Mobile Industrial Caterers' Association International(420)
National Association for the Specialty Food Trade(436)
National Association of Church Food Service(443)
National Association of College and University Food Services(444)
National Association of Concessionaires(445)
National Association of Flour Distributors(453)
National Association of Pizza Operators(464)
National Automatic Merchandising Association(482)
National Council of Chain Restaurants(498)
National Frozen Dessert and Fast Food Association(513)
National Park Hospitality Association(531)
National Poultry and Food Distributors Association(533)
National Restaurant Association(536)
National Society for Healthcare Foodservice Management(540)
North American Association of Food Equipment Manufacturers(554)
North American Meat Processors Association(558)
School Nutrition Association(606)
Society for Foodservice Management(617)
UNITE-HERE(670)
Women's Foodservice Forum(693)

FOOTBALL

American Football Coaches Association(84)
Football Writers Association of America(310)
National Football League(511)
National Football League Players Association(511)
Professional Football Athletic Trainers Society(587)
Professional Football Writers of America(587)

FOREIGN SERVICE

American Foreign Service Association(85)
American Foreign Service Protective Association(85)
Diplomatic and Consular Officers, Retired(284)

FOREIGN TRADE see also EXPORTS, IMPORTS, WEBB-POMERENE ACT

American Association of Exporters and Importers(42)
American Indonesian Chamber of Commerce(93)
American-Israel Chamber of Commerce and Industry(156)
American-Uzbekistan Chamber of Commerce(156)
Association of Foreign Trade Representatives(197)
Bankers' Association for Finance and Trade(226)
Brazilian American Chamber of Commerce(232)
BritishAmerican Business Inc.(233)
Canadian-American Business Council(237)
Colombian American Association(252)
Council of the Americas(275)
Danish-American Chamber of Commerce (USA)(281)
Ecuadorean American Association(288)
EMTA - Trade Association for the Emerging Markets(294)
European-American Business Council(298)
Export Institute of the United States(300)

International Interior Design Association(377)
International Sleep Products Association(386)
Juvenile Products Manufacturers Association(403)
NASFM(425)
National Association of Resale & Thrift Shops(469)
National Cotton Batting Institute(496)
National Home Furnishings Association(517)
National Independent Nursery Furniture Retailers Association(519)
Quarters Furniture Manufacturers Association(594)
Scientific Equipment and Furniture Association(606)
Specialty Sleep Association(650)
Summer and Casual Furniture Manufacturers Association(655)
Unfinished Furniture Association(669)
Upholstered Furniture Action Council(680)
Wood Component Manufacturers Association(694)
WorkPlace Furnishings(695)

FURS

American Karakul Sheep Registry(100)
American Legend Cooperative(101)
Fur Commission USA(312)
Fur Information Council of America(313)
National Trappers Association(547)

GARAGES

Automotive Lift Institute, Inc.(223)
Automotive Maintenance Repair Association(223)
Automotive Service Association(224)
Door and Access Systems Manufacturers' Association, International(286)
International Door Association(369)
Society of Collision Repair Specialists(633)

GARDENING

American Horticultural Society(91)
American Seed Trade Association(124)
American Society of Consulting Arborists(136)
Association for Hose and Accessories Distribution(174)
Garden Writers Association(314)
International Waterlily and Water Gardening Society(397)
Lawn and Garden Dealers' Association(406)
Lawn and Garden Marketing and Distribution Association(406)
Lawn Institute(406)
Mulch and Soil Council(422)
National Garden Clubs(513)
North American Horticultural Supply Association(557)
North American Plant Preservation Council(559)
Professional Grounds Management Society(587)
Professional Landscape Network(588)

GAS

American Association for Aerosol Research(33)
American Gas Association(86)
American Hydrogen Association(92)
American Public Gas Association(119)
American Society of Gas Engineers(138)
Compressed Air and Gas Institute(257)
Compressed Gas Association(257)
Distribution Contractors Association(286)
Domestic Petroleum Council(286)
Gas Appliance Manufacturers Association(314)
Gas Processors Association(314)
Gas Processors Suppliers Association(314)
Gas Technology Institute(314)
Gas Turbine Association(314)
Gasification Technologies Council(314)
Interstate Natural Gas Association of America(398)
Liaison Committee of Cooperating Oil and Gas Associations(407)
National Association of Division Order Analysts(449)
National Association of Royalty Owners(469)
National Energy Services Association(507)
National Ocean Industries Association(529)
National Propane Gas Association(534)
Natural Gas Supply Association(550)
Natural Gas Vehicle Coalition(551)
Pipe Line Contractors Association(578)
Pressure Vessel Manufacturers Association(583)
Society of Petrophysicists and Well Log Analysts(641)

GASOLINE

American Truck Stop Operators Association(152)
Gasoline and Automotive Service Dealers Association(314)
Renewable Fuels Association(599)
Service Station Dealers of America and Allied Trades(609)
Society of Independent Gasoline Marketers of America(638)

GASTROENTEROLOGY

American College of Gastroenterology(66)
American Gastroenterological Association(86)
American Lithotripsy Society(102)
American Motility Society(107)
American Society for Parenteral and Enteral Nutrition(131)
Gastroenterology Research Group(315)
North American Society for Pediatric Gastroenterology, Hepatology and Nutrition(561)
Society of American Gastrointestinal and Endoscopic Surgeons(630)
Society of Gastroenterology Nurses and Associates(637)

GEARS

American Gear Manufacturers Association(86)

GENEALOGY

Association of Professional Genealogists(209)
National Genealogical Society(513)

GENETICS

American College of Medical Genetics(67)
The American Electrophoresis Society(80)
American Genetic Association(86)
American Society of Gene Therapy(138)
American Society of Human Genetics(139)
Behavior Genetics Association(227)
Environmental Mutagen Society(296)
Genetics Society of America(315)
International Embryo Transfer Society(370)
National Society of Genetic Counselors(541)
National Tay-Sachs and Allied Diseases Association(545)
Society for the Study of Evolution(628)
Society for Theriogenology(628)

GEOGRAPHY

American Geographical Society(87)
American Institute of Bangladesh Studies(94)
American Institute of Indian Studies(96)
American Society of Geolinguistics(138)
Association for Arid Lands Studies(167)
Association of American Geographers(184)
Association of Third World Studies(218)
Geospatial Information Technology Association(316)
National Council for Geographic Education(497)
Organization for Tropical Studies(567)
Society for the History of Discoveries(627)
Society of Woman Geographers(646)

GEOLOGY

American Association of Petroleum Geologists(47)
American Association of Stratigraphic Palynologists(51)
American Geological Institute(87)
American Geophysical Union(87)
American Institute of Professional Geologists(97)
American Rock Mechanics Association(123)
ASFE/The Best People on Earth(162)
Association for Women Geoscientists(182)
Association of American State Geologists(185)
Association of Earth Science Editors(194)
Association of Environmental and Engineering Geologists(195)
Clay Minerals Society(247)
Computer Oriented Geological Society(258)
Earthquake Engineering Research Institute(288)
Geochemical Society(315)
Geological Society of America(315)
Geoscience Information Society(316)
History of Earth Sciences Society(326)
International Association for Mathematical Geology(351)
International Association of Hydrogeologists(358)
National Association for Black Geologists and Geophysicists(432)
National Association of Geoscience Teachers(454)
National Association of State Boards of Geology(473)
Paleontological Society(570)
Seismological Society of America(608)
Society for Mining, Metallurgy, and Exploration(622)
Society for Organic Petrology(623)
Society of Economic Geologists(635)
Society of Exploration Geophysicists(636)
Society of Independent Professional Earth Scientists(638)
Society of Petrophysicists and Well Log Analysts(641)

GERMAN

American Association of Teachers of German(52)
German American Chamber of Commerce(316)

GERONTOLOGY

American Aging Association(30)
American Association for Geriatric Psychiatry(35)
American Federation for Aging Research(82)
American Geriatrics Society(87)
American Society on Aging(147)
Association for Gerontology in Higher Education(173)
Gerontological Society of America(316)
International Psychogeriatric Association(383)
National Association of Area Agencies on Aging(439)
National Certification Council for Activity Professionals(488)
National Council on the Aging(503)
National Gerontological Nursing Association(513)
Society of Geriatric Cardiology(637)

GLASS see also BOTTLES

American Ceramic Society(61)
American Scientific Glassblowers Society(124)
Associated Glass and Pottery Manufacturers(165)
Gift Associates Interchange Network(317)
Glass Art Society(317)
Glass Association of North America(317)
Glass Packaging Institute(317)
Glass, Molders, Pottery, Plastics and Allied Workers International Union(317)
Glazing Industry Code Committee(317)
National Association of Container Distributors(446)
National Glass Association(513)
National Industrial Sand Association(519)
National Sunroom Association(545)
Society of Glass and Ceramic Decorators(637)
Stained Glass Association of America(652)

GLOVES

International Glove Association(374)

GOATS

American Angora Goat Breeder's Association(31)
American Association of Small Ruminant Practitioners(51)
American Dairy Goat Association(77)
American Goat Society(87)
International Nubian Breeders Association(381)
Mohair Council of America(421)

GOLD

International Precious Metals Institute(383)
Manufacturing Jewelers and Suppliers of America(411)
Society of Mineral Analysts(640)
Society of North American Goldsmiths(641)
World Gold Council(696)

GOLF

American Society of Golf Course Architects(138)
Association of Golf Merchandisers(199)
Golf Coaches Association of America(318)
Golf Course Builders Association of America(318)
Golf Course Superintendents Association of America(318)
Golf Range Association of America(318)
Golf Writers Association of America(318)
International Association of Amusement Parks and Attractions(352)
International Association of Golf Administrators(357)
Ladies Professional Golf Association(404)
National Association of Golf Tournament Directors(454)
National Golf Car Manufacturers Association(514)
National Golf Course Owners Association(514)
National Golf Foundation(514)
PGA TOUR Tournaments Association(575)
Professional Golfers Association of America(587)
Professional Putters Association(588)
United States Golf Association(675)

GOVERNMENT see also MILITARY

AFT - Public Employees(11)
Air Traffic Control Association(13)
Airports Council International/North America(15)
American Academy of Diplomacy(22)
American Association for Budget and Program Analysis(33)
American Association of Motor Vehicle Administrators(45)
American Association of Police Polygraphists(49)
American Association of Port Authorities(49)
American Association of Public Health Dentistry(50)
American Association of State Climatologists(51)
American Association of State Highway and Transportation Officials(51)
American Conference of Governmental Industrial Hygienists(73)
American Correctional Association(74)
American Correctional Chaplains Association(74)
American Council of State Savings Supervisors(75)
American Federation of Government Employees(82)
American Federation of School Administrators(82)
American Federation of State, County and Municipal Employees(82)
American Foreign Service Association(85)
American Judges Association(99)
American League of Lobbyists(101)
American Legislative Exchange Council(101)
American National Standards Institute(108)
American Public Works Association(120)
American Society for Public Administration(132)
American Society of Access Professionals(133)
AOAC International(158)
Apiary Inspectors of America(158)
Ass'n of Procurement Technical Assistance Centers(164)
Association Correctional Food Service Affiliates(166)
Association for Federal Information Resources Management(173)
Association of Administrative Law Judges(183)
Association of American Feed Control Officials(184)
Association of American Pesticide Control Officials(185)
Association of American Plant Food Control Officials(185)
Association of American Seed Control Officials(185)
Association of American State Geologists(185)
Association of Boards of Certification(188)
Association of Conservation Engineers(192)
Association of Film Commissioners International(196)
Association of Fish and Wildlife Agencies(197)
Association of Food and Drug Officials(197)
Association of Former Agents of the U.S. Secret Service(197)
Association of Former Intelligence Officers(198)
Association of Former OSI Special Agents(198)
Association of Government Accountants(199)
Association of Labor Relations Agencies(202)
Association of Local Air Pollution Control Officials(203)
Association of Major City and County Building Officials(203)
Association of Maternal and Child Health Programs(204)
Association of Official Seed Analysts(206)
Association of Official Seed Certifying Agencies(206)
Association of Paroling Authorities, International(207)
Association of Public Health Laboratories(210)
Association of Public Treasurers of the United States and Canada(211)
Association of Public-Safety Communications Officers- International(211)
Association of Racing Commissioners International(211)
Association of Real Estate License Law Officials(211)
Association of State and Interstate Water Pollution Control Administrators(214)
Association of State and Territorial Dental Directors(215)
Association of State and Territorial Directors of Nursing(215)
Association of State and Territorial Health Officials(215)
Association of State and Territorial Public Health Nutrition Directors(215)
Association of State and Territorial Solid Waste Management Officials(215)
Association of State Correctional Administrators(215)
Association of Technical and Supervisory Professionals(217)
Association of University Technology Managers(219)
Chief Officers of State Library Agencies(244)
Coalition for Government Procurement(249)
Coalition for Juvenile Justice(249)
College Savings Plans Network(252)
Commercial Vehicle Safety Alliance(254)
Commissioned Officers Association of the United States Public Health Service(254)
Community Leadership Association(256)
Conference of State Bank Supervisors(260)
Conference of State Court Adminstrators(260)
Council of Large Public Housing Authorities(273)
Council of State Administrators of Vocational Rehabilitation(274)
Council of State and Territorial Epidemiologists(274)
Council of State Community Development Agencies(274)
Council of State Governments(275)
Council on Governmental Ethics Laws(276)
Council on Licensure, Enforcement and Regulation(276)
Council On State Taxation(277)
County Executives of America(277)
Delta Phi Epsilon(282)
Diplomatic and Consular Officers, Retired(284)
Directors of Health Promotion and Public Health Education(285)
DRI International(287)
Energy Bar Association(294)
Epsilon Sigma Phi(297)
Federal Administrative Law Judges Conference(301)
Federal and Armed Forces Librarians Roundtable(301)
Federal Bar Association(302)
Federal Facilities Council(302)
Federal Judges Association(302)
Federal Law Enforcement Officers Association(302)
Federal Managers Association(302)
Federal Network for Sustainability(302)
Federal Physicians Association(302)
Federal Probation and Pre-trial Officers Association(302)
Federal Water Quality Association(302)
Federally Employed Women(302)
Federation of Associations of Regulatory Boards(303)
Federation of State Medical Boards of the United States(304)
Federation of Tax Administrators(304)
Government Finance Officers Association of the United States and Canada(318)
Government Management Information Sciences(318)
Governors Highway Safety Association(319)
Groundwater Management Districts Association(320)
Hispanic Elected Local Officials(326)
Homeland Security Industries Association(328)
International Association of Assessing Officers(353)
International Association of Bedding and Furniture Law Officials(354)
International Association of Chiefs of Police(354)
International Association of Clerks, Recorders, Election Officials and Treasurers(354)
International Association of Correctional Officers(355)
International Association of Electrical Inspectors(356)
International Association of Emergency Managers(356)
International Association of Fire Chiefs(357)
International Association of Industrial Accident Boards and Commissions(358)
International Association of Milk Control Agencies(359)
International Association of Official Human Rights Agencies(359)
International Association of Plumbing and Mechanical Officials(360)
International Bridge, Tunnel and Turnpike Association(363)
International City/County Management Association(365)
International Conference of Funeral Service Examining Boards(366)
International Fire Marshals Association(372)
International Institute of Municipal Clerks(376)
International Municipal Lawyers Association(380)
International Municipal Signal Association(380)
Interstate Council on Water Policy(398)
Interstate Oil and Gas Commission(398)
Justice Research and Statistics Association(403)
Mine Safety Institute of America(419)

NASTD - Technology Professionals Serving State Government(426)
National Active and Retired Federal Employees Association(427)
National Affordable Housing Management Association(428)
National Alcohol Beverage Control Association(429)
National Alliance of Postal and Federal Employees(429)
National Alliance of Preservation Commissions(430)
National Alliance of State and Territorial AIDS Directors(430)
National American Indian Housing Council(430)
National Assembly of State Arts Agencies(431)
National Association for County Community and Economic Development(432)
National Association for Government Training and Development(433)
National Association for Health and Fitness(433)
National Association for Search and Rescue(436)
National Association for State Community Services Programs(436)
National Association of Agricultural Fair Agencies(438)
National Association of Agriculture Employees(438)
National Association of Air Traffic Specialists(438)
National Association of Assistant United States Attorneys(439)
National Association of Attorneys General(439)
National Association of Barber Boards(439)
National Association of Blacks In Government(440)
National Association of Chiefs of Police(443)
National Association of Clean Water Agencies(443)
National Association of Conservation Districts(445)
National Association of Consumer Credit Administrators(446)
National Association of Councils on Developmental Disabilities(446)
National Association of Counties(447)
National Association of County Agricultural Agents(447)
National Association of County and City Health Officials(447)
National Association of County Engineers(447)
National Association of County Health Facility Administrators(447)
National Association of County Intergovernmental Relations Officials(447)
National Association of County Recorders, Election Officials and Clerks(447)
National Association of Crime Victim Compensation Boards(448)
National Association of Development Companies(449)
National Association of Development Organizations(449)
National Association of Federal Credit Unions(452)
National Association of Federal Education Program Administrators(452)
National Association of Federal Veterinarians(452)
National Association of Flood and Stormwater Management Agencies(453)
National Association of Government Archives and Records Administrators(454)
National Association of Government Communicators(454)
National Association of Government Defined Contribution Administrators(454)
National Association of Government Labor Officials(454)
National Association of Hispanic Federal Executives(455)
National Association of Housing and Redevelopment Officials(456)
National Association of Housing Information Managers(457)
National Association of Insurance Commissioners(458)
National Association of Juvenile Correctional Agencies(459)
National Association of Local Boards of Health(460)
National Association of Local Government Auditors(460)
National Association of Local Housing Finance Agencies(460)
National Association of Media and Technology Centers(461)
National Association of Medicaid Directors(461)
National Association of Noise Control Officials(463)
National Association of Postmasters of the United States(465)
National Association of Public Child Welfare Administrators(467)
National Association of Public Sector Equal Opportunity Officers(467)
National Association of Pupil Services Administrators(467)
National Association of Regional Councils(469)
National Association of Regulatory Utility Commissioners(469)
National Association of Secretaries of State(471)
National Association of Special Needs State Administrators(472)
National Association of State Administrators and Supervisors of Private Schools(473)
National Association of State Agencies for Surplus Property(473)
National Association of State Alcohol and Drug Abuse Directors(473)
National Association of State Archaeologists(473)
National Association of State Auditors, Comptrollers and Treasurers(473)
National Association of State Aviation Officials(473)
National Association of State Boards of Accountancy(473)
National Association of State Boards of Education(473)
National Association of State Boating Law Administrators(473)
National Association of State Budget Officers(473)
National Association of State Charity Officials(474)
National Association of State Chief Administrators(474)
National Association of State Chief Information Officers(474)
National Association of State Controlled Substances Authorities(474)
National Association of State Credit Union Supervisors(474)
National Association of State Departments of Agriculture(474)
National Association of State Development Agencies(474)
National Association of State Directors of Developmental Disability Services(474)
National Association of State Directors of Special Education(475)
National Association of State Directors of Teacher Education and Certification(475)
National Association of State Directors of Veterans Affairs(475)
National Association of State Election Directors(475)
National Association of State Emergency Medical Services Officials(475)
National Association of State Energy Officials(475)
National Association of State Facilities Administrators(475)
National Association of State Fire Marshals(475)
National Association of State Foresters(475)
National Association of State Land Reclamationists(475)
National Association of State Mental Health Program Directors(476)
National Association of State Outdoor Recreation Liaison Officers(476)
National Association of State Park Directors(476)
National Association of State Personnel Executives(476)
National Association of State Procurement Officials(476)
National Association of State Retirement Administrators(476)
National Association of State Supervisors of Trade and Industrial Education(476)
National Association of State Textbook Administrators(476)
National Association of State Treasurers(476)
National Association of State Units on Aging(476)
National Association of State Utility Consumer Advocates(477)
National Association of State Workforce Agencies(477)
National Association of Towns and Townships(479)
National Association of Unclaimed Property Administrators(479)
National Black Caucus of State Legislators(484)
National Board of Boiler and Pressure Vessel Inspectors(485)
National Border Patrol Council(485)
National Child Support Enforcement Association(489)
National Community Development Association(491)
National Conference of Bankruptcy Judges(492)
National Conference of Black Mayors(492)
National Conference of Commissioners on Uniform State Laws(493)
National Conference of Insurance Legislators(493)
National Conference of Local Environmental Health Administrators(493)
National Conference of Regulatory Utility Commission Engineers(494)
National Conference of State Fleet Administrators(494)
National Conference of State Historic Preservation Officers(494)
National Conference of State Legislatures(494)
National Conference of State Liquor Administrators(494)
National Conference of State Social Security Administrators(494)
National Conference of States on Building Codes and Standards(494)
National Conference on Public Employee Retirement Systems(495)
National Conference on Weights and Measures(495)
National Council of Legislators from Gaming States(499)
National Council of Local Human Service Administrators(499)
National Council of State Agencies for the Blind(500)
National Council of State Emergency Medical Services Training Coordinators(500)
National Council of State Housing Agencies(500)
National Council of State Supervisors for Languages(501)
National Criminal Justice Association(503)
National District Attorneys Association(505)
National Emergency Management Association(507)
National Federation of Federal Employees(509)
National Federation of Municipal Analysts(509)
National Forum for Black Public Administrators(512)

National Foundation for Women Legislators(512)
National Government Publishing Association(514)
National Governors Association(514)
National Grants Management Association(514)
National Institute of Governmental Purchasing(520)
National Juvenile Detention Association(523)
National League of Cities(524)
National League of Postmasters of the U.S.(524)
National Lieutenant Governors Association(524)
National Plant Board(533)
National Public Employer Labor Relations Association(534)
National Society of Compliance Professionals(541)
National Treasury Employees Union(547)
National Weather Service Employees Organization(549)
National WIC Association(549)
North American Agricultural Marketing Officials(554)
North American Gaming Regulators Association(557)
North American Securities Administrators Association(560)
Nurses Organization of Veterans Affairs(563)
Organization of Professional Employees of the U.S. Department of Agriculture(567)
Organization of State Broadcasting Executives(568)
Organization of Wildlife Planners(568)
Patent and Trademark Office Society(572)
Professional Managers Association(588)
Public Agency Risk Managers Association(592)
Public Employees Roundtable(592)
Public Housing Authorities Directors Association(592)
Public Risk Management Association(593)
Senior Executives Association(609)
Society for History in the Federal Government(618)
Society of Cost Estimating and Analysis(634)
Society of Federal Labor and Employee Relations Professionals(636)
Society of Former Special Agents of the Federal Bureau of Investigation(636)
Society of Government Economists(637)
Society of Government Meeting Professionals(637)
Society of Government Travel Professionals(637)
Society of State Directors of Health, Physical Education and Recreation(644)
State and Territorial Air Pollution Program Administrators(652)
State Debt Management Network(652)
State Government Affairs Council(652)
State Higher Education Executive Officers(653)
State Risk and Insurance Management Association(653)
States Organization for Boating Access(653)
SWANA -- Solid Waste Association of North America(656)
United States Animal Health Association(672)
United States Conference of City Human Services Officials(674)
United States Conference of Mayors(674)
Urban and Regional Information Systems Association(680)
Voluntary Protection Programs Participants Association(684)
Women Executives in State Government(691)
Women in Government(692)
Women in Government Relations(692)
World Affairs Councils of America(695)

GRAIN see also FEED & GRAIN

AACC International(1)
American Association of Grain Inspection and Weighing Agencies(43)
American Malting Barley Association(102)
International Wild Rice Association(397)
National Futures Association(513)
National Grain and Feed Association(514)
National Grain Sorghum Producers(514)
National Grain Trade Council(514)
New York Mercantile Exchange(552)
North American Export Grain Association(557)
Renewable Fuels Association(599)
Transportation Elevator and Grain Merchants Association(664)
U.S. Grains Council(667)
Wheat Quality Council(688)

GRAPHIC ARTS

American Academy of Equine Art(22)
American Institute of Graphic Arts(96)
Association for Graphic Arts Training(173)
Association of Professional Design Firms(208)
Business Forms Management Association(235)
Graphic Artists Guild(319)
Graphic Arts Marketing Information Service(319)
Graphic Arts Sales Foundation(319)
Graphic Arts Technical Foundation(319)
Graphic Communications Conference, IBT(319)
Guild of Book Workers(321)
Guild of Natural Science Illustrators(321)
In-Plant Printing and Mailing Association(332)
International Graphic Arts Education Association(374)
National Association for Printing Leadership(435)
National Association of Limited Edition Dealers(460)
NPES, The Association for Suppliers of Printing, Publishing and Converting Technologies(563)
Printing Brokerage/Buyers Association International(584)
Research and Engineering Council of the NAPL(600)
Society for Technical Communication(626)
Society of American Graphic Artists(630)
Specialty Graphic Imaging Association(650)
Technical Association of the Graphic Arts(658)
Type Directors Club(667)

GROCERS

Association of Coupon Professionals(193)
CIES, The Food Business Forum(246)
Food Marketing Institute(309)
Fresh Produce Association of the Americas(312)
Grocery Manufacturers Association(320)
Mexican-American Grocers Association(418)
National Grocers Association(515)

GYNECOLOGY

AAGL -- Advancing Minimally Invasive Gynecology Worldwide(1)
American Academy of Fertility Care Professionals(23)
American College of Obstetricians and Gynecologists(68)
American College of Osteopathic Obstetricians and Gynecologists(69)
American Society for Colposcopy and Cervical Pathology(127)
American Urogynecologic Society(153)
Association of Maternal and Child Health Programs(204)
Association of Professors of Gynecology and Obstetrics(209)
Association of Women's Health, Obstetric and Neonatal Nurses(220)
Gynecologic Oncology Group(321)
Gynecologic Surgery Society(321)
International Childbirth Education Association(365)
National Abortion Federation(426)
National Family Planning and Reproductive Health Association(508)
Society for Gynecologic Investigation(618)
Society of Gynecologic Oncologists(638)

HANDICAPPED see also BLIND, DEAF

Academy of Dentistry for Persons with Disabilities(3)
Access Technology Association(6)
Association on Higher Education and Disability(221)
National AMBUCS(430)
National Association of State Directors of Developmental Disability Services(474)
National Independent Living Association(519)
Society for Disability Studies(616)

HANDWRITING

American College of Forensic Examiners(66)
American Handwriting Analysis Foundation(88)
Council of Graphological Socs.(272)
National Association of Document Examiners(449)
National Society for Graphology(540)

HARDWARE

American Hardware Manufacturers Association(88)
American Rolling Door Institute(123)
Association for Hose and Accessories Distribution(174)
Builders Hardware Manufacturers Association(234)
Building Material Dealers Association(234)
Door and Hardware Institute(287)
National Marine Distributors Association(526)
North American Retail Hardware Association(559)
Service Specialists Association(609)
Window Covering Safety Council(689)

HEALTH CARE

Academy of Clinical Laboratory Physicians and Scientists(2)
Academy of Dispensing Audiologists(3)
Academy of Managed Care Providers(4)
AcademyHealth(6)
Accreditation Association for Ambulatory Health Care(6)
Accrediting Bureau of Health Education Schools(7)
Advanced Medical Technology Association(8)
Alliance of Cardiovascular Professionals(16)
America's Blood Centers(19)
America's Health Insurance Plans(19)
American Academy of Health Care Providers-Addictive Disorders(23)
American Academy of Hospice and Palliative Medicine(23)
American Academy of Nurse Practitioners(25)
American Academy of Pain Management(26)
American Academy of Professional Coders(27)
American Academy of Somnology(28)
American Association for Continuity of Care(34)
American Association for Health Education(35)
American Association for Health Freedom(35)
American Association for Homecare(35)
American Association for Medical Transcription(36)
American Association of Birth Centers(38)
American Association of Eye and Ear Hospitals(42)
American Association of Healthcare Administrative Management(43)
American Association of Homes and Services for the Aging(43)
American Association of Integrated Healthcare Delivery Systems(44)
American Association of Preferred Provider Organizations(49)
American Association of Spinal Cord Injury Nurses(51)
American Association of Surgical Physician Assistants(52)
American Baptist Homes and Hospitals Association(55)
American Board of Quality Assurance and Utilization Review Physicians(58)
American Clinical Laboratory Association(63)
American College Health Association(63)
American College of Health Care Administrators(66)

American College of Healthcare Information Administrators(66)
American College of Medical Practice Executives(67)
American College of Physician Executives(69)
American Correctional Health Services Association(74)
American Council on Science and Health(76)
American Health Care Association(89)
American Health Lawyers Association(89)
American Health Planning Association(89)
American Health Quality Association(89)
American Herbal Products Association(90)
American Holistic Medical Association(91)
American Managed Behavioral Healthcare Association(102)
American Massage Therapy Association(103)
American Medical Directors Association(104)
American Medical Group Association(104)
American Medical Informatics Association(104)
American Naprapathic Association(108)
American Neurotology Society(109)
American Obesity Association(109)
American Organization for Bodywork Therapies of Asia(110)
American Psychiatric Nurses Association(118)
American Registry of Medical Assistants(122)
American School Health Association(124)
American Society for Bioethics and Humanities(127)
American Society of Addiction Medicine(133)
American Society of Cataract and Refractive Surgery(135)
American Trauma Society(152)
Animal Health Institute(157)
Assisted Living Federation of America(164)
Assistive Technology Industry Association(164)
Association for Death Education and Counseling(171)
Association for Electronic Health Care Transactions(172)
Association for Research in Otolaryngology(177)
Association of Academic Health Centers(183)
Association of Academic Health Sciences Library Directors(183)
Association of Air Medical Services(183)
Association of Asian-Pacific Community Health Organizations(186)
Association of Family Medicine Residency Directors(196)
Association of Healthcare Internal Auditors(199)
Association of Maternal and Child Health Programs(204)
Association of Medical Education and Research in Substance Abuse(204)
Association of Occupational and Environmental Clinics(206)
Association of Occupational Health Professionals in Healthcare(206)
Association of Oncology Social Work(206)
Association of Pediatric Oncology Social Workers(207)
Association of Public Health Laboratories(210)
Association of Rheumatology Health Professionals(212)
Association of SIDS and Infant Mortality Programs(214)
Association of State and Territorial Public Health Nutrition Directors(215)
Association of Teachers of Maternal and Child Health(217)
Billings Ovulation Method Association of the United States(228)
Catholic Health Association of the United States(240)
Chronic Disease Directors(246)
Collaborative Family Healthcare Association(250)
College of Healthcare Information Management Executives(251)
Commission on Accreditation of Allied Health Education Programs(254)
Council of Colleges of Acupuncture and Oriental Medicine(271)
Council on Certification of Health, Environmental and Safety Technologists(275)
Directors of Health Promotion and Public Health Education(285)
Disease Management Association of America(285)
Drug and Alcohol Testing Industry Association(287)
Emergency Department Practice Management Association(292)
Federation of American Hospitals(303)
Global Health Council(317)
Health & Sciences Communications Association(322)
Health Care Compliance Association(322)
Health Care Education Association(322)
Health Forum(323)
Health Industry Business Communications Council(323)
Health Industry Group Purchasing Association(323)
Health Industry Representatives Association(323)
Health Ministries Association(323)
Healthcare Billing and Management Association(323)
Healthcare Compliance Packaging Council(323)
Healthcare Convention and Exhibitors Association(323)
Healthcare Financial Management Association(324)
Hospice Association of America(328)
Hospital Presidents Association(328)
International Academy for Child Brain Development(347)
International Academy of Behavioral Medicine, Counseling and Psychotherapy(347)
International Academy of Health Care Professionals(348)
International Association Colon Hydro Therapy(349)
International Association of Eating Disorders Professionals(356)
International Association of Healthcare Central Service Materiel Management(357)
International College of Applied Kinesiology(365)
International Federation for Artificial Organs(371)
International Iridology Practitioners Association(377)
International Lactation Consultant Association(377)
International Listening Association(378)
International Phototherapy Association(383)
International Society for Prosthetics and Orthotics - United States(388)
Jewish Social Service Professionals Association(402)
Medical Records Institute(416)
Midwives Alliance of North America(419)
National Academies of Practice(426)
National Academy of Clinical Biochemistry(426)
National Adult Day Services Association(427)
National Alliance for Hispanic Health(429)
National Alliance of State and Territorial AIDS Directors(430)
National Association for Health Care Recruitment(433)
National Association for Healthcare Quality(433)
National Association for Home Care(434)
National Association for Medical Direction of Respiratory Care(434)
National Association for the Support of Long-Term Care(437)
National Association Medical Staff Services(437)
National Association of Addiction Treatment Providers(438)
National Association of Boards of Examiners of Long Term Care Administrators(440)
National Association of Community Health Centers(445)
National Association of County and City Health Officials(447)
National Association of County Health Facility Administrators(447)
National Association of First Responders(452)
National Association of Health Data Organizations(455)
National Association of Health Services Executives(455)
National Association of Health Underwriters(455)
National Association of Health Unit Coordinators(455)
National Association of Healthcare Consultants(455)
National Association of Hospital Hospitality Houses(456)
National Association of Local Boards of Health(460)
National Association of Managed Care Physicians(460)
National Association of Medicaid Directors(461)
National Association of Professional Geriatric Care Managers(466)
National Association of Public Hospitals and Health Systems(467)
National Association of Rehabilitation Providers and Agencies(469)
National Association of School Nurses(470)
National Association of Social Workers(472)
National Association of State Alcohol and Drug Abuse Directors(473)
National Association of State Veterans Homes(477)
National Certification Council for Activity Professionals(488)
National Committee for Quality Assurance(491)
National Council for Prescription Drug Programs(497)
National Council of State Emergency Medical Services Training Coordinators(500)
National CPA Health Care Advisors Association(503)
National Family Caregivers Association(508)
National Health Association(516)
National Health Care Anti-Fraud Association(516)
National Health Council(516)
National Hospice and Palliative Care Organization(517)
National Organization for Associate Degree Nursing(529)
National Organization for Competency Assurance(530)
National Organization of Nurse Practitioner Faculties(530)
National Perinatal Association(532)
National Prison Hospice Association(534)
National Register of Health Service Providers in Psychology(535)
National Society for Healthcare Foodservice Management(540)
National Society of Genetic Counselors(541)
National Spinal Cord Injury Association(542)
National Sports and Fitness Association(543)
National Stroke Association(544)
National Subacute and Postacute Care Association(544)
National Tay-Sachs and Allied Diseases Association(545)
National Wellness Institute(549)
Neurodevelopmental Treatment Association(552)
Plasma Protein Therapeutics Association(578)
Presbyterian Health, Education and Welfare Association(583)
Preventive Cardiovascular Nurses Association(583)

Professional Association of Health Care Office Management(586)
Regulatory Affairs Professionals Society(598)
Rolf Institute(602)
Society for Imaging Informatics in Medicine(619)
Society for Medical Decision Making(621)
Society for Occupational and Environmental Health(622)
Society for Public Health Education(624)
Society for the Advancement of Women's Health Research(626)
Society of Atherosclerosis Imaging(632)
Society of Professional Benefit Administrators(642)
Society of State Directors of Health, Physical Education and Recreation(644)
Therapeutic Communities of America(660)
Visiting Nurse Associations of America(684)
Wellness Councils of America(687)
Workgroup for Electronic Data Interchange(695)
World Research Foundation(696)

HEARING see also DEAF

Academy of Dispensing Audiologists(3)
Academy of Rehabilitative Audiology(5)
American Academy of Audiology(20)
American Academy of Otolaryngology-Head and Neck Surgery(26)
American Osteopathic Colleges of Ophthalmology and Otolaryngology - Head and Neck Surgery(112)
Better Hearing Institute(228)
Hearing Industries Association(324)
National Black Association for Speech, Language and Hearing(484)

HEATING

Air Conditioning Contractors of America(13)
Air Movement and Control Association International(13)
AirConditioning and Refrigeration Institute(14)
American Society of Heating, Refrigerating and Air-Conditioning Engineers(139)
American Solar Energy Society(147)
American Supply Association(150)
Associated Air Balance Council(164)
Association of Home Appliance Manufacturers(200)
Association of Industry Manufacturers' Representatives(201)
Gas Appliance Manufacturers Association(314)
HARDI - Heating, Airconditioning, and Refrigeration Distributors International(321)
Hearth Patio & Barbecue Association(324)
Heat Exchange Institute(324)
Hydronics Institute Division of GAMA(330)
Industrial Heating Equipment Association(337)
International District Energy Association(369)
International Ground Source Heat Pump Association(374)
Masonry Heater Association of North America(413)
Mechanical Service Contractors of America(415)
National Association of Oil Heating Service Managers(463)
National Association of Power Engineers(465)
National Electrical Contractors Association(506)
National Electrical Manufacturers Association(506)
National Kerosene Heater Association(523)
Plumbing-Heating-Cooling Contractors - National Association(579)
Radiant Panel Association(594)
Solar Energy Industries Association(647)
Sustainable Buildings Industry Council(656)
Used Oil Management Association(681)

HELICOPTERS

American Helicopter Society International(90)
Army Aviation Association of America(161)
Association of Air Medical Services(183)
Helicopter Association International(325)

HERPETOLOGY

American Society of Ichthyologists and Herpetologists(139)
Herpetologists' League(325)
Society for the Study of Amphibians and Reptiles(628)

HISTORY

Academy of Accounting Historians(2)
Agricultural History Society(12)
American Academy of Research Historians of Medieval Spain(28)
American Academy of the History of Dentistry(29)
American Antiquarian Society(31)
American Association for State and Local History(36)
American Association for the History of Medicine(37)
American Association for the History of Nursing(37)
American Association for the Study of Hungarian History(37)
American Catholic Historical Association(61)
American College of Health Care Administrators(66)
American Conference for Irish Studies(73)
American Cultural Resources Association(77)
American Folklore Society(84)
American Historical Association(91)
American Hungarian Educators Association(92)
American Institute for Conservation of Historic and Artistic Works(93)
American Institute for Patristic and Byzantine Studies(94)
American Institute of Bangladesh Studies(94)
American Institute of the History of Pharmacy(97)
American Italian Historical Association(99)
American Jewish Historical Society(99)
American Journalism Historians Association(99)
American Men's Studies Association(105)
American Musicological Society(107)
American Numismatic Society(109)
American Oriental Society(110)
American Printing History Association(117)
American Society for Environmental History(128)
American Society for Ethnohistory(129)
American Society for Legal History(130)
American Society of Church History(135)
American Society of Papyrologists(143)
American Studies Association(149)
Archaeological Institute of America(160)
Archivists and Librarians in the History of the Health Sciences(160)
Association for Asian Studies(167)
Association for Documentary Editing(171)
Association for Living History, Farm and Agricultural Museums(176)
Association for the Bibliography of History(180)
Association for the Study of African American Life and History(180)
Association for the Study of Nationalities(181)
Association of Ancient Historians(186)
Association of Caribbean Studies(188)
Business History Conference(235)
Charles Homer Haskins Society(243)
Cheiron: The International Society for the History of Behavioral and Social Sciences(243)
Committee on History in the Classroom(254)
Committee on Lesbian and Gay History(254)
Conference for the Study of Political Thought(259)
Conference of Historical Journals(259)
Conference on Asian History(260)
Conference on Faith and History(261)
Conference on Latin American History(261)
Conservation and Preservation Charities of America(261)
Coordinating Council for Women in History(265)
Costume Society of America(267)
Council for European Studies(268)
Czechoslovak History Conference(281)
Economic History Association(288)
Federation of State Humanities Councils(304)
Forest History Society(310)
Group for the Use of Psychology in History(320)
Historians Film Committee/Film & History(326)
Historians of American Communism(326)
History of Earth Sciences Society(326)
History of Economics Society(326)
History of Education Society(327)
History of Science Society(327)
Immigration and Ethnic History Society(332)
Independent Scholars of Asia(335)
International Psychohistorical Association(383)
Latin American Studies Association(405)
Medieval Academy of America(416)
Middle East Studies Association of North America(418)
Modern Greek Studies Association(420)
National Alliance of Preservation Commissions(430)
National Alliance of Statewide Preservation Organizations(430)
National Association for Armenian Studies and Research(431)
National Association for Ethnic Studies(433)
National Association for Interpretation(434)
National Conference of State Historic Preservation Officers(494)
National Council on Public History(502)
National Genealogical Society(513)
North American Conference on British Studies(556)
North American Society for Sport History(561)
Oral History Association(566)
Organization of American Historians(567)
Phi Alpha Theta(575)
Renaissance Society of America(599)
Romanian Studies Association of America(603)
Social Science History Association(612)
Social Science Research Council(613)
Society for Ancient Greek Philosophy(613)
Society for French Historical Studies(617)
Society for German-American Studies(617)
Society for Historians of American Foreign Relations(618)
Society for Historians of the Early American Republic(618)
Society for Historians of the Gilded Age and Progressive Era(618)
Society for Historical Archaeology(618)
Society for History Education(618)
Society for History in the Federal Government(618)
Society for Industrial Archeology(620)
Society for Italian Historical Studies(621)
Society for Military History(622)
Society for Reformation Research(624)
Society for Romanian Studies(625)
Society for Spanish and Portuguese Historical Studies(625)
Society for the History of Authorship, Reading and Publishing(627)
Society for the History of Discoveries(627)
Society for the History of Technology(627)
Society for the Study of Early China(628)
Society of American Historians(630)
Society of American Historical Artists(631)
Society of Architectural Historians(631)
Society of Armenian Studies(631)
Turkish Studies Association(667)
Urban History Association(680)
Victorian Society in America(683)
Western History Association(687)
Western Music Association(687)
World History Association(696)
World War Two Studies Association(696)

HOCKEY

American Hockey Coaches Association(91)
American Hockey League(91)

National Hockey League(517)
National Hockey League Players' Association(517)

HOME FURNISHINGS

American Craft Council(77)
American Lighting Association(101)
Home Fashion Products Association(327)
Home Furnishings International Association(327)
International Furnishings and Design Association(373)
International Home Furnishings Representatives Association(375)
Kitchen Cabinet Manufacturers Association(403)
National Association of Decorative Fabric Distributors(448)
National Association of Floor Covering Distributors(453)
National Home Furnishings Association(517)
National Kitchen and Bath Association(523)
Paint and Decorating Retailers Association(570)
Window Coverings Manufacturers Association(689)

HONEY

American Beekeeping Federation(56)
Apiary Inspectors of America(158)
National Honey Packers and Dealers Association(517)

HORSES

American Association of Equine Practitioners(42)
American Association of Owners and Breeders of Peruvian Paso Horses(47)
American Bashkir Curly Registry(56)
American Buckskin Registry Association(59)
American Connemara Pony Society(74)
American Cream Draft Horse Association(77)
American Crossbred Pony Registry(77)
American Donkey and Mule Society(79)
American Farrier's Association(82)
American Hackney Horse Society(88)
American Hanoverian Society(88)
American Horse Council(91)
American Horse Publications Association(91)
American Miniature Horse Association(106)
American Morgan Horse Association(106)
American Mustang Association(107)
American Paint Horse Association(112)
American Paso Fino Horse Association(113)
American Quarter Horse Association(120)
American Saddlebred Horse Association(123)
American Shetland Pony Club/American Miniature Horse Registry(125)
American Shire Horse Association(125)
American Suffolk Horse Association(150)
American Trakehner Association(152)
American Warmblood Registry(154)
American Welara Pony Society(154)
American White/American Creme Horse Registry(154)
Appaloosa Horse Club(159)
Arabian Horse Association(160)
Association for Equine Sports Medicine(172)
Association of Official Racing Chemists(206)
Belgian Draft Horse Corp. of America(227)
CHA - Certified Horsemanship Association(242)
Cleveland Bay Horse Society of North America(248)
Clydesdale Breeders of the United States(249)
Colorado Ranger Horse Association(253)
Dude Ranchers' Association(288)
Galiceno Horse Breeders Association(313)
Harness Horsemen International(322)
International Andalusian and Lusitano Horse Association(349)
International Buckskin Horse Association(363)
International Union of Journeymen Horseshoers and Allied Trades(395)
Jockey Club(402)
KWPN of North America(404)
Lipizzan Association of North America(408)
Missouri Fox Trotting Horse Breed Association(420)
National Barrel Horse Association(483)
National Cutting Horse Association(504)
National Horsemen's Benevolent and Protective Association(517)
National Reining Horse Association(535)
National Show Horse Registry(539)
National Spotted Saddle Horse Association(543)
National Turf Writers Association(547)
Palomino Horse Association(570)
Palomino Horse Breeders of America(570)
Paso Fino Horse Association(572)
Percheron Horse Association of America(573)
Peruvian Paso Horse Registry of North America(574)
Pinto Horse Association of America(578)
Pony of the Americas Club(580)
Purebred Hanoverian Association of America Breeders and Owners(593)
Purebred Morab Horse Association(593)
Racking Horse Breeders Association of America(594)
Spanish-Barb Breeders Association(648)
Tennessee Walking Horse Breeders and Exhibitors Association(659)
Thoroughbred Club of America(661)
Thoroughbred Owners and Breeders Association(661)
Thoroughbred Racing Associations of North America(661)
United Professional Horsemen's Association(672)
United States Equestrian Federation(675)
United States Harness Writers' Association(675)
Walking Horse Owners Association of America(685)
Walking Horse Trainers Association(685)
Welsh Pony and Cob Society of America(687)
Women's Professional Rodeo Association(694)

HORTICULTURE

All-America Rose Selections(15)
American Herbalists Guild(90)
American Horticultural Society(91)
American Horticultural Therapy Association(92)
American Institute of Floral Designers(96)
American Nursery and Landscape Association(109)
American Pomological Society(117)
American Public Gardens Association(119)
American Seed Trade Association(124)
American Society for Horticultural Science(130)
American Society of Consulting Arborists(136)
American Society of Landscape Architects(140)
American Society of Plant Biologists(144)
American Society of Plant Taxonomists(144)
Association of Professional Landscape Designers(209)
Association of Specialty Cut Flower Growers(214)
Botanical Society of America(231)
Council on Botanical and Horticultural Libraries(275)
Extra Touch Florists Association(300)
Horticultural Research Institute(328)
Hydroponic Society of America(330)
Independent Turf and Ornamental Distributors Association(336)
International Cut Flower Growers Association(368)
International Fruit Tree Association(373)
International Plant Propagators Society(383)
International Society of Arboriculture(390)
International Turfgrass Society(395)
International Waterlily and Water Gardening Society(397)
Lawn and Garden Dealers' Association(406)
Lawn Institute(406)
Mulch and Soil Council(422)
National Association of Plant Patent Owners(465)
National Council of Commercial Plant Breeders(498)
National Garden Clubs(513)
National Greenhouse Manufacturers Association(515)
National Peach Council(532)
National Plant Board(533)
National Roadside Vegetation Management Association(537)
North American Flowerbulb Wholesalers Association(557)
North American Horticultural Supply Association(557)
Perennial Plant Association(573)
Plant Growth Regulators Society of America(578)
Society of American Florists(630)
Society of Municipal Arborists(640)
Soil and Plant Analysis Council(646)
Tree Care Industry Association(665)
Utility Arborist Association(681)
Wholesale Florist and Florist Supplier Association(688)

HOSPITALS

Acute Long Term Hospital Association(8)
American Academy of Medical Administrators(24)
American Animal Hospital Association(31)
American Association of Colleges of Nursing(40)
American Association of Eye and Ear Hospitals(42)
American Association of Healthcare Consultants(43)
American Association of Hospital Dentists(44)
American Association of Integrated Healthcare Delivery Systems(44)
American Association of Physicists in Medicine(48)
American Association of Psychiatric Administrators(49)
American Baptist Homes and Hospitals Association(55)
American College of Healthcare Executives(66)
American College of Managed Care Administrators(67)
American Healthcare Radiology Administrators(90)
American Hospital Association(92)
American Network of Community Options and Resources(108)
American Society for Healthcare Central Service Professionals(129)
American Society for Healthcare Engineering(129)
American Society for Healthcare Environmental Services(129)
American Society for Healthcare Food Service Administrators(129)
American Society for Healthcare Human Resources Administration(129)
American Society for Healthcare Risk Management(129)
American Society of Directors of Volunteer Services(137)
American Society of Health-System Pharmacists(139)
Assembly of Episcopal Healthcare Chaplains(164)
Association for Ambulatory Behavorial Healthcare(167)
Association for Healthcare Philanthropy(173)
Association for Healthcare Resource and Materials Management(174)
Association for Hospital Medical Education(174)
Association of Air Medical Services(183)
Association of Community Cancer Centers(192)
Association of Professional Chaplains(208)
Association of Program Directors in Internal Medicine(210)
Association of University Programs in Health Administration(219)

Catholic Health Association of the United States(240)
Clinical and Laboratory Standards Institute(248)
Dietary Managers Association(284)
ECRI(288)
Emergency Medicine Residents' Association(292)
Emergency Nurses Association(293)
Federation of American Hospitals(303)
Health Forum(323)
Healthcare Financial Management Association(324)
Healthcare Information and Management Systems Society(324)
Hospital Presidents Association(328)
International Association for Healthcare Security and Safety(350)
International Association of Healthcare Central Service Materiel Management(357)
International Executive Housekeepers Association(371)
Medical-Dental-Hospital Business Associates(416)
National Association Medical Staff Services(437)
National Association of Addiction Treatment Providers(438)
National Association of Children's Hospitals(443)
National Association of Healthcare Access Management(455)
National Association of Hospital Hospitality Houses(456)
National Association of Psychiatric Health Systems(467)
National Association of Public Hospitals and Health Systems(467)
National Association of Urban Hospitals(480)
National Council of Health Facilities Finance Authorities(499)
National Hospice and Palliative Care Organization(517)
North American Association For Ambulatory Care(554)
Society for Academic Emergency Medicine(613)
Society for Healthcare Consumer Advocacy(618)
Society for Healthcare Strategy and Market Development(618)
Society for Social Work Leadership in Health Care(625)
United Methodist Association of Health and Welfare Ministries(671)
Veterinary Hospital Managers Association(682)

HOTELS
American Culinary Federation(77)
American Hotel & Lodging Association(92)
Associated Luxury Hotels(165)
BMC - A Foodservice Sales and Marketing Council(231)
Council of Hotel and Restaurant Trainers(272)
Green Hotels Association(320)
Hospitality Financial and Technology Professionals(328)
Hospitality Sales and Marketing Association International(329)
Hotel Brokers International(329)
Hotel Electronic Distribution Network Association(329)
International Council on Hotel, Restaurant and Institutional Education(368)
International Executive Housekeepers Association(371)
International Society of Hospitality Consultants(391)
International Society of Hotel Association Executives(391)
National Bed and Breakfast Association(484)
National Council of Chain Restaurants(498)
Network of Executive Women in Hospitality(551)
Professional Association of Innkeepers International(586)
Select Registry/Distinguished Inns of North America(608)
Small Luxury Hotels of the World(611)
Travel and Tourism Research Association(665)
Travel Industry Association of America(665)
UNITE-HERE(670)

HOUSEWARES
American Edged Products Manufacturers Association(80)
Associated Glass and Pottery Manufacturers(165)
Association of Home Appliance Manufacturers(200)
Cookware Manufacturers Association(265)
International Guild of Candle Artisans(374)
International Housewares Association(375)
National Association of Resale & Thrift Shops(469)
Sponge and Chamois Institute(651)

HYDRAULICS
Fluid Controls Institute(308)
Fluid Power Distributors Association(308)
Fluid Power Society(308)
National Fluid Power Association(511)
Western Dredging Association(687)

HYGIENE
American Board of Industrial Hygiene(57)
American Conference of Governmental Industrial Hygienists(73)
American Industrial Hygiene Association(93)
International Association of Hygienic Physicians(358)
National Health Association(516)

HYPNOSIS
American Academy of Medical Hypnoanalysts(24)
American Association of Professional Hypnotherapists(49)
American Council of Hypnotist Examiners(75)
American Guild of Hypnotherapists(88)
American Hypnosis Association(92)
American Society of Clinical Hypnosis(135)
National Board for Certified Clinical Hypnotherapists(485)
National Society of Hypnotherapists(542)
Society for Clinical and Experimental Hypnosis(615)

ICE
International Association of Ice Cream Vendors(358)
International Packaged Ice Association(382)

IMMUNOLOGY
Academy of Veterinary Allergy and Clinical Immunology(6)
American Association of Immunologists(44)
American Association of Veterinary Immunologists(53)
American Society for Histocompatability and Immunogenetics(130)
Clinical Immunology Society(248)
Joint Council of Allergy, Asthma, and Immunology(402)
Society for Mucosal Immunology(622)
Transplantation Society(663)
World Allergy Organization - IACCI(695)

IMPORTS
American Association of Exporters and Importers(42)
American Import Shippers Association(93)
American Importers and Exporters Meat Products Group(93)
American Importers Association(93)
American Institute for International Steel(94)
American International Automobile Dealers Association(98)
Association of Food Industries(197)
Association of Foreign Trade Representatives(197)
Association of International Automobile Manufacturers(201)
Bicycle Shippers Association(228)
Diamond Manufacturers and Importers Association of America(284)
Greek Food and Wine Institute(320)
Independent Distributors Association(333)
International Wood Products Association(397)
Meat Importers' Council of America(415)
National Association for the Specialty Food Trade(436)
National Association of Beverage Importers-Wine-Spirits-Beer(439)
National Council on International Trade Development(502)
Organization of Women in International Trade(568)
Oriental Rug Importers Association of America(568)
Overseas Automotive Council(570)
Professional Picture Framers Association(588)
United States Association of Importers of Textiles and Apparel(673)
Woodworking Machinery Industry Association(694)

INDUSTRIAL PLANTS
American Board of Industrial Hygiene(57)
CoreNet Global(266)
International Safety Equipment Association(385)
National Association of Industrial and Office Properties(458)
National Association of Manufacturers(460)

INDUSTRIAL RELATIONS
Airline Industrial Relations Conference(14)
Elevator Industries Association(292)
Industrial Foundation of America(337)
Industry Coalition on Technology Transfer(337)
Labor and Employment Relations Association(404)
National Association of Industrial Technology(458)
National Industrial Council - Employer Association Group(519)
National Industrial Council - State Associations Group(519)
North American Technician Excellence(562)
Society for Human Resource Management(619)

INFORMATION PROCESSING see DATA PROCESSING
College of Healthcare Information Management Executives(251)
Federal Network for Sustainability(302)
International Alliance of Technology Integrators(348)

INSTRUMENTS
Analytical and Life Science Systems Association(157)
Instrumentation Testing Association(344)
International Horn Society(375)
International Trumpet Guild(395)
International Tuba-Euphonium Association(395)
ISA(400)
National Association of Professional Band Instrument Repair Technicians(465)
Optical Imaging Association(565)
SPIE - The International Society for Optical Engineering(651)

INSULATION
Alliance for the Polyurethane Industry(16)
American Architectural Manufacturers Association(32)
EIFS Industry Members Association(290)
Insulation Contractors Association of America(345)
International Association for Cold Storage Construction(349)
National Insulation Association(521)
North American Building Material Distribution Association(555)

North American Insulation Manufacturers Association(557)
Perlite Institute(573)

INSURANCE INDUSTRY

Alliance of Claims Assistance Professionals(16)
Alliance of Insurance Agents and Brokers(17)
America's Health Insurance Plans(19)
American Academy of Actuaries(19)
American Academy of Insurance Medicine(24)
American Agents Association(30)
American Association of Crop Insurers(41)
American Association of Dental Consultants(41)
American Association of Insurance Management Consultants(44)
American Association of Managing General Agents(45)
American Bail Coalition(55)
American Benefits Council(56)
American Council of Life Insurers(75)
American Institute for CPCU - Insurance Institute of America(93)
American Institute of Marine Underwriters(96)
American Insurance Association(98)
American Insurance Marketing and Sales Society(98)
American Nuclear Insurers(109)
American Prepaid Legal Services Institute(117)
American Risk and Insurance Association(123)
American Society for Healthcare Risk Management(129)
American Society of Law, Medicine and Ethics(140)
American Society of Pension Professionals and Actuaries(143)
American Society of Safety Engineers(146)
Americas Association of Cooperative/Mutual Insurance Socs.(156)
Appraisers Association of America(159)
Associated Risk Managers(166)
Association for Advanced Life Underwriting(167)
Association of Average Adjusters of the U.S.(187)
Association of Defense Trial Attorneys(193)
Association of Finance and Insurance Professionals(196)
Association of Financial Guaranty Insurors(197)
Association of Health Insurance Advisors(199)
Association of Home Office Life Underwriters(200)
Association of Insurance Compliance Professionals(201)
Association of Life Insurance Counsel(203)
Aviation Insurance Association(225)
Blue Cross and Blue Shield Association(231)
Captive Insurance Companies Association(237)
Casualty Actuarial Society(239)
Committee of Annuity Insurers(254)
Conference of Consulting Actuaries(259)
Consumer Credit Insurance Association(263)
Council of Insurance Agents and Brokers(272)
Council on Employee Benefits(276)
CPCU Society(278)
Crop Insurance Research Bureau(279)
Direct Marketing Insurance and Financial Services Council(285)
Employee Benefit Research Institute(293)
Federation of Defense and Corporate Counsel(303)
Financial and Insurance Conference Planners(305)
Fraternal Field Managers Association(311)
GAMA International(313)
Gamma Iota Sigma(313)
Independent Automotive Damage Appraisers Association(333)
Independent Insurance Agents and Brokers of America(334)
Inland Marine Underwriters Association(339)
Institute for Business & Home Safety(339)
Insurance Accounting and Systems Association(345)
Insurance Consumer Affairs Exchange(345)
Insurance Information Institute(345)
Insurance Institute for Highway Safety(345)
Insurance Loss Control Association(345)
Insurance Marketing Communications Association(345)
Inter-Industry Conference on Auto Collision Repair(346)
Intermediaries and Reinsurance Underwriters Association(347)
International Association for Insurance Law - United States Chapter(350)
International Association of Accident Reconstruction Specialists(352)
International Association of Arson Investigators(353)
International Association of Defense Counsel(356)
International Association of Industrial Accident Boards and Commissions(358)
International Association of Insurance Receivers(358)
International Claim Association(365)
International Foundation of Employee Benefit Plans(373)
International Insurance Society(376)
Intersure, Ltd.(398)
Liability Insurance Research Bureau(407)
Life Insurers Council(407)
Lightning Protection Institute(408)
LIMRA International(408)
LOMA(409)
Mass Marketing Insurance Institute(413)
Million Dollar Round Table(419)
Mortgage Insurance Companies of America(421)
National Association of Catastrophe Adjusters(442)
National Association of Dental Plans(449)
National Association of Disability Evaluating Professionals(449)
National Association of Fire Investigators(452)
National Association of Fraternal Insurance Counsellors(454)
National Association of Health Underwriters(455)
National Association of Independent Fee Appraisers(457)
National Association of Independent Insurance Adjusters(457)
National Association of Independent Insurance Auditors and Engineers(457)
National Association of Independent Life Brokerage Agencies(457)
National Association of Insurance and Financial Advisors(458)
National Association of Insurance Commissioners(458)
National Association of Insurance Women(458)
National Association of Mutual Insurance Companies(462)
National Association of Professional Insurance Agents(466)
National Association of Professional Surplus Lines Offices(466)
National Association of Public Insurance Adjusters(467)
National Association of Surety Bond Producers(478)
National Cargo Bureau(487)
National Committee for Quality Assurance(491)
National Conference of Insurance Legislators(493)
National Council of Self-Insurers(500)
National Council on Compensation Insurance(502)
National Crop Insurance Services(504)
National Fraternal Congress of America(512)
National Health Care Anti-Fraud Association(516)
National Insurance Association(521)
National Insurance Crime Bureau(522)
National Organization of Life and Health Insurance Guaranty Associations(530)
National Risk Retention Association(537)
National Society of Insurance Premium Auditors(542)
National Structured Settlements Trade Association(544)
National Truck and Heavy Equipment Claims Council(547)
North American Bar-Related Title Insurers(555)
Organization of Flying Adjusters(567)
Physician Insurers Association of America(577)
Professional Insurance Communicators of America(587)
Professional Insurance Marketing Association(588)
Professional Liability Agents Network(588)
Professional Liability Underwriting Society(588)
Property Casualty Conferences(591)
Property Casualty Insurers Association of America(591)
Property Loss Research Bureau(591)
Public Agency Risk Managers Association(592)
Public Risk Management Association(593)
Reinsurance Association of America(598)
Risk and Insurance Management Society(602)
Safety and Loss Prevention Management Council(604)
Self Insurance Institute of America, Inc.(608)
Shipowners Claims Bureau(610)
Society for Risk Analysis(625)
Society of Actuaries(629)
Society of Certified Insurance Counselors(632)
Society of Financial Service Professionals(636)
Society of Insurance Financial Management(638)
Society of Insurance Research(638)
Society of Insurance Trainers and Educators(639)
Society of Professional Benefit Administrators(642)
Society of Risk Management Consultants(643)
State Risk and Insurance Management Association(653)
Surety Association of America(656)
Transportation & Logistics Council(664)
University Risk Management and Insurance Association(680)
Viatical and Life Settlement Association of America(683)
WIFS - Women in Insurance and Financial Services(688)

INVENTORS

National Congress of Inventor Organizations(495)

INVESTMENTS see also FINANCE, SECURITIES INDUSTRY

American Association of Individual Investors(44)
Association for Enterprise Opportunity(172)
Association of Investment Management Sales Executives(202)
CFA Institute(242)
College Savings Foundation(252)
Colombian American Association(252)
Council of Institutional Investors(272)
Ecuadorean American Association(288)
EMTA - Trade Association for the Emerging Markets(294)
Fixed Income Analysts Society(307)
Forum for Investor Advice(311)
Global Association of Risk Professionals(317)
Independent Investors Protective League(334)
Investment Adviser Association(398)
Investment Company Institute(398)
Investment Management Consultants Association(399)
Investment Program Association(399)
Investment Recovery Association(399)
National Association of Investment Professionals(459)
National Association of Personal Financial Advisors(464)
National Association of Real Estate Investment Managers(468)

National Association of Real Estate Investment Trusts(468)
National Association of Securities Dealers(471)
National Association of Small Business Investment Companies(472)
National Association of Stock Plan Professionals(477)
National Council of Real Estate Investment Fiduciaries(500)
National Investment Banking Association(522)
National Investor Relations Institute(522)
National Venture Capital Association(548)
Organization for International Investment(567)
Pension Real Estate Association(573)
Portfolio Management Institute(581)
Society of Quantitative Analysts(643)
Venezuelan American Association of the U.S.(682)

IRON & STEEL INDUSTRY

American Foundry Society(85)
American Institute for International Steel(94)
American Institute of Steel Construction(97)
American Iron and Steel Institute(98)
American Iron Ore Association(99)
Association for Iron and Steel Technology(175)
Association of Steel Distributors(216)
Bridge Grid Flooring Manufacturers Association(232)
Cast Iron Soil Pipe Institute(238)
Cold Finished Steel Bar Institute(250)
Concrete Reinforcing Steel Institute(259)
Cooling Technology Institute(265)
Ductile Iron Pipe Research Association(287)
Ductile Iron Society(288)
Institute of Scrap Recycling Industries(343)
International Association of Bridge, Structural, Ornamental and Reinforcing Iron Workers(354)
International Brotherhood of Boilermakers, Iron Ship Builders, Blacksmiths, Forgers and Helpers(363)
Iron Casting Research Institute(399)
Metal Service Center Institute(417)
National Association of Reinforcing Steel Contractors(469)
National Association of Steel Pipe Distributors(477)
National Blacksmiths and Weldors Association(485)
National Corrugated Steel Pipe Association(496)
National Council of Erectors, Fabricators and Riggers(498)
National Institute of Steel Detailing(521)
National Slag Association(540)
NEA - the Association of Union Constructors(551)
Reusable Industrial Packaging Association(601)
Scaffolding, Shoring and Forming Institute(605)
Specialty Steel Industry of North America(650)
SSPC: the Society for Protective Coatings(652)
Steel Deck Institute(653)
Steel Door Institute(653)
Steel Founders' Society of America(653)
Steel Joist Institute(653)
Steel Manufacturers Association(653)
Steel Plate Fabricators Association Division of STI/SPFA(653)
Steel Recycling Institute(653)
Steel Shipping Container Institute(653)
Steel Tank Institute Division of STI/SPFA(654)
Steel Tube Institute of North America(654)
Steel Window Institute(654)
Truss Plate Institute(666)

ITALIAN

American Association of Teachers of Italian(52)
Society for Italian Historical Studies(621)

JEWELRY & GEMS

Accredited Gemologists Association(6)
American Gem Society(86)
American Gem Trade Association(86)
Diamond Council of America(284)
Diamond Manufacturers and Importers Association of America(284)
Gemological Institute of America(315)
Gift Association of America(317)
Indian Arts and Crafts Association(336)
Jewelers Board of Trade(401)
Jewelers of America(401)
Jewelers Shipping Association(401)
Jewelers Vigilance Committee(401)
Jewelers' Security Alliance of the U.S.(401)
Jewelry Information Center(401)
Leading Jewelers Guild(406)
Manufacturing Jewelers and Suppliers of America(411)
Metal Findings Manufacturers Association(417)
National Association of Jewelry Appraisers(459)
Silver Users Association(611)
Society of North American Goldsmiths(641)
Women's Jewelry Association(693)

JEWISH

American Conference of Cantors(73)
American Jewish Correctional Chaplains Association(99)
American Jewish Historical Society(99)
American Jewish Press Association(99)
American Society of Sephardic Studies(146)
Association for Jewish Studies(175)
Association of Advanced Rabbinical and Talmudic Schools(183)
Association of Jewish Aging Services(202)
Association of Jewish Center Professionals(202)
Association of Jewish Family and Children's Agencies(202)
Association of Jewish Libraries(202)
Cantors Assembly(237)
Central Conference of American Rabbis(241)
Church and Synagogue Library Association(246)
Council for Jewish Education(269)
Council of American Jewish Museums(270)
Council of Archives and Research Libraries in Jewish Studies(270)
International Association of Jewish Vocational Services(358)
Jewish Book Council(401)
Jewish Community Centers Association of North America(401)
Jewish Education Service of North America(401)
Jewish Educators Assembly(402)
Jewish Social Service Professionals Association(402)
JWB Jewish Chaplains Council(403)
National Association of Family Development Centers(452)
National Association of Temple Administrators(479)
National Association of Temple Educators(479)
National Conference of Yeshiva Principals(495)
National Society for Hebrew Day Schools(541)
National Tay-Sachs and Allied Diseases Association(545)
Rabbinical Assembly(594)
Society for Humanistic Judaism(619)
Union for Reform Judaism(670)
United Jewish Communities(671)
United Synagogue of Conservative Judaism(678)

JOURNALISM

Accrediting Council on Education in Journalism and Mass Communications(7)
American Journalism Historians Association(99)
American Society of Journalists and Authors(140)
Asian American Journalists Association(162)
Associated Collegiate Press, National Scholastic Press Association(165)
Association for Education in Journalism and Mass Communication(172)
Association for Women in Communications(182)
Association for Women Journalists(182)
Association of Earth Science Editors(194)
Association of Food Journalists(197)
Association of Schools of Journalism and Mass Communication(213)
Boating Writers International(231)
Community College Journalism Association(256)
Investigative Reporters and Editors(398)
Journalism Education Association(402)
National Academy of Television Journalists(427)
National Association of Black Journalists(440)
National Association of Hispanic Journalists(455)
National Lesbian and Gay Journalists Association(524)
Native American Journalists Association(550)
Society of Environmental Journalists(635)
Society of Professional Journalists(642)
South Asian Journalists Association(647)
Travel Journalists Guild(665)
Truck Writers of North America(666)
White House Correspondents Association(688)

JUDGES

American Judges Association(99)
American Judicature Society(99)
Association of Administrative Law Judges(183)
Conference of Chief Justices(259)
Federal Administrative Law Judges Conference(301)
Judge Advocates Association(402)
National Association of Women Judges(481)
National Conference of Bankruptcy Judges(492)
National Council of Juvenile and Family Court Judges(499)
National Gymnastics Judges Association(516)
National Judges Association(522)

LABOR UNIONS

Actors' Equity Association(8)
AFT Healthcare(11)
Air Line Pilots Association, International(13)
Amalgamated Transit Union(18)
American Association of Classified School Employees(39)
American Association of University Professors(53)
American Federation of Government Employees(82)
American Federation of Labor and Congress of Industrial Organizations(82)
American Federation of Musicians of the United States and Canada(82)
American Federation of School Administrators(82)
American Federation of State, County and Municipal Employees(82)
American Federation of Teachers(82)
American Federation of Television and Radio Artists(83)
American Foreign Service Association(85)
American Guild of Musical Artists(88)
American Guild of Variety Artists(88)
American Nurses Association(109)
American Postal Workers Union(117)
American Train Dispatchers Association(152)
Art Directors Guild/Scenic, Title and Graphic Artists(161)
Associated Actors and Artistes of America(164)
Association of American Educators(184)
Association of Civilian Technicians(190)
Association of Flight Attendants - CWA(197)
Association of Labor Relations Agencies(202)
Association of Theatrical Press Agents and Managers(218)
Association of Volleyball Professionals(220)
Atlantic Independent Union(221)
Bakery, Confectionery, Tobacco Workers and Grain Millers International Union(225)
Brotherhood of Locomotive Engineers and Trainmen(233)
Brotherhood of Maintenance of Way Employees(233)
Brotherhood of Railroad Signalmen(233)
Brotherhood Railway Carmen/TCU(233)

Christian Labor Association of the United States of America(246)
Coalition of Black Trade Unionists(249)
Coalition of Labor Union Women(249)
Communications Workers of America(255)
Congress of Independent Unions(261)
Directors Guild of America(285)
Federal Education Association(302)
Glass, Molders, Pottery, Plastics and Allied Workers International Union(317)
Graphic Artists Guild(319)
Graphic Communications Conference, IBT(319)
Guild of Italian American Actors(321)
Hebrew Actors Union(325)
International Alliance of Theatrical Stage Employees and Moving Picture Technicians of the U.S., Its Territories and Canada(348)
International Allied Printing Trades Association(349)
International Association of Bridge, Structural, Ornamental and Reinforcing Iron Workers(354)
International Association of Fire Fighters(357)
International Association of Heat and Frost Insulators and Asbestos Workers(357)
International Association of Machinists and Aerospace Workers(359)
International Association of Tool Craftsmen(361)
International Brotherhood of Boilermakers, Iron Ship Builders, Blacksmiths, Forgers and Helpers(363)
International Brotherhood of Electrical Workers(363)
International Brotherhood of Teamsters, AFL-CIO(363)
International Chemical Workers Union Council/UFCW(365)
International Council of Employers of Bricklayers and Allied Craftworkers(367)
International Federation of Professional and Technical Engineers(371)
International Guards Union of America(374)
International Labor Communications Association(377)
International Longshore and Warehouse Union(378)
International Longshoremen's Association, AFL-CIO(378)
International Masonry Institute(379)
International Plate Printers', Die Stampers' and Engravers' Union of North America(383)
International Security Officers, Police, and Guards Union(386)
International Union of Bricklayers and Allied Craftsworkers(395)
International Union of Electronic, Electrical, Salaried, Machine, and Furniture Workers-CWA(395)
International Union of Elevator Constructors(395)
International Union of Industrial Service Transport Health Employees(395)
International Union of Journeymen Horseshoers and Allied Trades(395)
International Union of Operating Engineers(395)
International Union of Painters and Allied Trades(396)
International Union of Petroleum and Industrial Workers(396)
International Union of Police Associations, AFL-CIO(396)
International Union Security, Police and Fire Professionals of America(396)
International Union, United Automobile, Aerospace and Agricultural Implement Workers of America(396)
Laborers' International Union of North America(404)
Laundry and Dry Cleaning International Union(405)
Machine Printers and Engravers Association of the United States(409)
Major League Baseball Players Association(410)
Marine Engineers Beneficial Association(412)
National Air Traffic Controllers Association(428)
National Alliance of Postal and Federal Employees(429)
National Association of Air Traffic Specialists(438)
National Association of Broadcast Employees and Technicians - Communications Workers of America(441)
National Association of FSA County Office Employees(454)
National Association of Government Employees(454)
National Association of Government Labor Officials(454)
National Association of Letter Carriers(460)
National Association of Postal Supervisors(465)
National Basketball Players Association(483)
National Basketball Referees Association(483)
National Border Patrol Council(485)
National Conference of Brewery and Soft Drink Workers - United States and Canada(493)
National Conference of Firemen and Oilers, SEIU(493)
National Education Association(506)
National Federation of Federal Employees(509)
National Federation of Independent Unions(509)
National Federation of Licensed Practical Nurses(509)
National Football League Players Association(511)
National Fraternal Order of Police(512)
National Hockey League Players' Association(517)
National Labor Relations Board Professional Association(523)
National Organization of Industrial Trade Unions(530)
National Organization of Legal Services Workers(530)
National Postal Mail Handlers Union(533)
National Rural Letter Carriers' Association(537)
National Treasury Employees Union(547)
National Weather Service Employees Organization(549)
National Writers Union(550)
Newspaper Guild - CWA(552)
Office and Professional Employees International Union(564)
Operative Plasterers' and Cement Masons' International Association of the United States and Canada(565)
Patent and Trademark Office Society(572)
Patent Office Professional Association(572)
Retail, Wholesale and Department Store Union(601)
Rubber and Plastics Industry Conference of the United Steelworkers of America(603)
Screen Actors Guild(606)
Seafarers' International Union(607)
Service Employees International Union(609)
Sheet Metal Workers' International Association(610)
Society of Stage Directors and Choreographers(644)
Transport Workers Union of America(663)
Transportation Communications International Union(664)
Union of American Physicians and Dentists(670)
UNITE-HERE(670)
United American Nurses, AFL-CIO(670)
United Association of Journeymen and Apprentices of the Plumbing and Pipe Fitting Industry of U.S. and Canada(670)
United Brotherhood of Carpenters and Joiners of America(670)
United Electrical, Radio and Machine Workers of America(671)
United Farm Workers of America(671)
United Federation of Police & Security Officers(671)
United Food and Commercial Workers International Union(671)
United Mine Workers of America International Union(672)
United Nations Staff Union(672)
United Scenic Artists(672)
United Transportation Union(679)
United Union of Roofers, Waterproofers and Allied Workers(679)
Utility Workers Union of America(681)
Wire Service Guild(690)
Writers Guild of America, East(697)
Writers Guild of America, West(697)

LABORATORIES

American Association for Laboratory Accreditation(35)
American Association of Bioanalysts(38)
American Association of Veterinary Laboratory Diagnosticians(53)
American Clinical Laboratory Association(63)
American College of Laboratory Animal Medicine(66)
American Council of Independent Laboratories(75)
American Society for Clinical Laboratory Science(127)
American Society of Laboratory Animal Practitioners(140)
Analytical Laboratory Managers Association(157)
Association for Assessment and Accreditation of Laboratory Animal Care International(168)
Association for Gnotobiotics(173)
Association of Cinema and Video Laboratories(190)
Association of Clinical Scientists(190)
Association of Public Health Laboratories(210)
Clinical and Laboratory Standards Institute(248)
Clinical Laboratory Management Association(248)
Clinical Ligand Assay Society(248)
COLA(250)
Independent Laboratory Distributors Association(334)
Laboratory Animal Management Association(404)
Laboratory Products Association(404)
National Association for Biomedical Research(431)
National Association of Dental Laboratories(448)
National Association of Scientific Materials Managers(471)
National Phlebotomy Association(533)
National Society for Histotechnology(541)
NCSL International(551)
Optical Laboratories Association(566)
SAMA Group of Associations(605)
Scientific Equipment and Furniture Association(606)

LACE

Schiffli Lace and Embroidery Manufacturers Association(606)

LADDERS

American Ladder Institute(100)

LANDSCAPING

American Cultural Resources Association(77)
American Nursery and Landscape Association(109)
American Society of Landscape Architects(140)
Association of Professional Landscape Designers(209)
Council of Landscape Architectural Registration Boards(273)
International Erosion Control Association(371)
Lawn and Garden Dealers' Association(406)
Lawn Institute(406)

National Institute on Park and Grounds Management(521)
Professional Grounds Management Society(587)
Professional Landscape Network(588)
Turfgrass Producers International(667)

LANGUAGE

Alliance of Associations of Teachers of Japanese(16)
American Association of Language Specialists(44)
American Association of Teachers of Esperanto(52)
American Association of Teachers of Italian(52)
American Association of Teachers of Slavic and East European Languages(52)
American Association of Teachers of Turkic Languages(53)
American Classical League(63)
American Conference for Irish Studies(73)
American Council on the Teaching of Foreign Languages(76)
American Councils for International Education(76)
American Dialect Society(79)
American Hungarian Educators Association(92)
American Philological Association(114)
American Society of Geolinguistics(138)
Association of Departments of Foreign Languages(193)
Chinese Language Teachers Association(245)
Computer Assisted Language Instruction Consortium(257)
Independent Scholars of Asia(335)
International Association for Language Learning Technology(351)
Linguistic Association of Canada and the United States(408)
Modern Language Association of America(420)
National Association for Bilingual Education(431)
National Association of Professors of Hebrew in American Institutions of Higher Learning(466)
National Association of Self-Instructional Language Programs(471)
National Black Association for Speech, Language and Hearing(484)
National Council of State Supervisors for Languages(501)
National Council of Teachers of English(501)
National Federation of Modern Language Teachers Associations(509)
National Student Speech Language Hearing Association(544)
Romanian Studies Association of America(603)
Semiotic Society of America(608)
Slovak Studies Association(611)
Society for New Language Study(622)
Society for the Study of Indigenous Languages of the Americas(628)
Teachers of English to Speakers of Other Languages(658)
Women's Caucus for the Modern Languages(693)

LARYNGOLOGY

American Academy of Otolaryngology-Head and Neck Surgery(26)
American Head and Neck Society(89)
American Laryngological Association(100)
American Laryngological, Rhinological and Otological Society(100)
American Osteopathic Colleges of Ophthalmology and Otolaryngology - Head and Neck Surgery(112)
Association of Otolaryngology Administrators(207)
Society of University Otolaryngologists(645)

LAW

Academy of Legal Studies in Business(4)
Adjutants General Association of the United States(8)
American Academy of Appellate Lawyers(20)
American Academy of Estate Planning Attorneys(22)
American Academy of Forensic Sciences(23)
American Academy of Matrimonial Lawyers(24)
American Academy of Psychiatry and the Law(28)
American Agricultural Law Association(30)
American Association for Paralegal Education(36)
American Association of Attorney-Certified Public Accountants(38)
American Association of Code Enforcement(40)
American Association of Law Libraries(44)
American Association of Legal Nurse Consultants(44)
American Association of Nurse Attorneys, The(46)
American Bar Association(56)
American Board of Forensic Psychology(57)
American College of Bankruptcy(64)
American College of Construction Lawyers(65)
American College of Legal Medicine(66)
American College of Mortgage Attorneys(67)
American College of Real Estate Lawyers(70)
American College of Tax Counsel(71)
American College of Trial Lawyers(71)
American College of Trust and Estate Counsel(71)
American Criminal Justice Association/Lambda Alpha Epsilon(77)
American Foreign Law Association(85)
American Health Lawyers Association(89)
American Immigration Lawyers Association(92)
American Institute of Parliamentarians(97)
American Intellectual Property Law Association(98)
American Judges Association(99)
American Judicature Society(99)
American Land Title Association(100)
American Law Institute(100)
American Prepaid Legal Services Institute(117)
American Psychology-Law Society(119)
American Society for Legal History(130)
American Society of Access Professionals(133)
American Society of Comparative Law(136)
American Society of Criminology(137)
American Society of International Law(140)
American Society of Law, Medicine and Ethics(140)
American Society of Notaries(142)
American Society of Questioned Document Examiners(145)
American Society of Trial Consultants(147)
American Tort Reform Association(152)
Association for Continuing Legal Education(171)
Association of Administrative Law Judges(183)
Association of American Law Schools(184)
Association of Attorney-Mediators(186)
Association of Commercial Finance Attorneys(192)
Association of Corporate Counsel(193)
Association of Defense Trial Attorneys(193)
Association of Eminent Domain Professionals(195)
Association of Family and Conciliation Courts(196)
Association of Legal Administrators(203)
Association of Life Insurance Counsel(203)
Association of Paroling Authorities, International(207)
Association of Real Estate License Law Officials(211)
Association of Reporters of Judicial Decisions(212)
Association of Transportation Professionals(218)
Association of Trial Lawyers of America(218)
Black Entertainment and Sports Lawyers Association(230)
Canon Law Society of America(237)
Christian Legal Society(246)
Coalition for Juvenile Justice(249)
Commercial Law League of America(253)
Computer Law Association(258)
Conference of Chief Justices(259)
Conference of State Court Adminstrators(260)
Conference on Consumer Finance Law(260)
Copyright Society of the U.S.A.(266)
Customs and International Trade Bar Association(280)
Defense Research Institute(282)
Delta Theta Phi(283)
Education Law Association(289)
Energy Bar Association(294)
Federal Administrative Law Judges Conference(301)
Federal Bar Association(302)
Federal Communications Bar Association(302)
Federal Judges Association(302)
Federation of Defense and Corporate Counsel(303)
Food and Drug Law Institute(309)
Giving Institute(317)
Hispanic National Bar Association(326)
Independent Association of Questioned Document Examiners(333)
Institute of Judicial Administration(342)
Inter-American Bar Association(346)
International Academy of Trial Lawyers(348)
International Association for Insurance Law - United States Chapter(350)
International Association for Philosophy of Law and Social Philosophy - American Section(351)
International Association of Attorneys and Executives in Corporate Real Estate(353)
International Association of Bedding and Furniture Law Officials(354)
International Association of Defense Counsel(356)
International Association of Law Enforcement Firearms Instructors(358)
International Association of Privacy Professionals(360)
International Intellectual Property Alliance(377)
International Legal Fraternity of Phi Delta Phi(378)
International Municipal Lawyers Association(380)
International Paralegal Management Association(382)
International Society of Barristers(390)
International Trade Commission Trial Lawyers Association(394)
Iota Tau Tau(399)
Judge Advocates Association(402)
Law and Society Association(406)
Legal Marketing Association(407)
Maritime Law Association of the U.S.(412)
NALS(425)
National Academy of Arbitrators(426)
National Academy of Elder Law Attorneys(426)
National American Indian Court Judges Association(430)
National Association for Court Management(432)
National Association for Law Placement(434)
National Association of Assistant United States Attorneys(439)
National Association of Attorneys General(439)
National Association of Bond Lawyers(441)
National Association of College and University Attorneys(444)
National Association of Consumer Advocates(446)
National Association of Criminal Defense Lawyers(448)
National Association of Forensic Economics(453)
National Association of Judiciary Interpreters and Translators(459)
National Association of Latino Elected and Appointed Officials(459)
National Association of Legal Assistants(459)
National Association of Legal Investigators(459)
National Association of Legal Search Consultants(460)

National Association of Professional Process Servers(466)
National Association of Railroad Trial Counsel(467)
National Association of Retail Collection Attorneys(469)
National Association of Shareholder and Consumer Attorneys(472)
National Association of State Boating Law Administrators(473)
National Association of Women Judges(481)
National Association of Women Lawyers(482)
National Bar Association(483)
National Black Caucus of State Legislators(484)
National Conference of Appellate Court Clerks(492)
National Conference of Bankruptcy Judges(492)
National Conference of Bar Examiners(492)
National Conference of Black Lawyers(492)
National Conference of Commissioners on Uniform State Laws(493)
National Conference of Insurance Legislators(493)
National Conference of State Legislatures(494)
National Conference of Women's Bar Associations(494)
National Council of Juvenile and Family Court Judges(499)
National Court Reporters Association(503)
National Criminal Justice Association(503)
National Defender Investigator Association(504)
National Disability Rights Network(505)
National District Attorneys Association(505)
National Employment Lawyers Association(507)
National Federation of Paralegal Associations(510)
National Foundation for Women Legislators(512)
National Judges Association(522)
National Juvenile Court Services Association(523)
National Labor Relations Board Professional Association(523)
National Lawyers Guild(523)
National Legal Aid and Defender Association(524)
National Lesbian and Gay Law Association(524)
National Litigation Support Services Association(525)
National Network of Estate Planning Attorneys(528)
National Organization of Social Security Claimants' Representatives(530)
National Paralegal Association(531)
National Verbatim Reporters Association(548)
North American Bar-Related Title Insurers(555)
Patent and Trademark Office Society(572)
Patent Office Professional Association(572)
Phi Alpha Delta(575)
Practising Law Institute(582)
Professional Bail Agents of the United States(586)
Scribes(607)
Society of American Law Teachers(631)
Sports Lawyers Association(651)
Tau Epsilon Rho Law Society(657)
TechLaw Group(658)
Transportation Lawyers Association(664)
United States Court Reporters Association(674)

LAW ENFORCEMENT see POLICE

International Association of Accident Reconstruction Specialists(352)

LEAD

American Bureau of Metal Statistics(59)
International Lead Zinc Research Organization(377)
National Lead Burning Association(523)

LEATHER GOODS see also SHOES

American Leather Chemists Association(101)
Belt Association(227)
Fluid Sealing Association(308)
International Glove Association(374)
Leather Apparel Association(406)
Leather Industries of America(407)
National Fashion Accessories Association(508)
National Luggage Dealers Association(525)
NIBA - The Belting Association(553)
Saddle, Harness, and Allied Trade Association(604)
Sponge and Chamois Institute(651)
Travel Goods Association(665)
Western-English Trade Association(688)

LECTURES

Society of Armenian Studies(631)
Travel Adventure Cinema Society(665)

LIBRARIES

African-American Library and Information Science Association(11)
American Association of Law Libraries(44)
American Association of School Librarians(50)
American Library Association(101)
American Society for Information Science and Technology(130)
American Society of Indexers(139)
American Theological Library Association(151)
Archivists and Librarians in the History of the Health Sciences(160)
Art Libraries Society of North America(161)
Asian/Pacific American Librarians Association(163)
Association for Information Media and Equipment(174)
Association for Library and Information Science Education(175)
Association for Library Collections and Technical Services(175)
Association for Library Service to Children(175)
Association for Library Trustees and Advocates(176)
Association for Population/Family Planning Libraries and Information Centers, International(176)
Association for Recorded Sound Collections(177)
Association for the Bibliography of History(180)
Association of Academic Health Sciences Library Directors(183)
Association of Christian Librarians(189)
Association of College and Research Libraries(190)
Association of Jewish Libraries(202)
Association of Mental Health Librarians(204)
Association of Research Libraries(212)
Association of Seventh-Day Adventist Librarians(213)
Association of Specialized and Cooperative Library Agencies(214)
Association of Vision Science Librarians(220)
Beta Phi Mu(228)
Bibliographical Society of America(228)
Black Caucus of the American Library Association(230)
Book Industry Study Group, Inc.(231)
Catholic Library Association(240)
Chief Officers of State Library Agencies(244)
Chinese-American Librarians Association(245)
Church and Synagogue Library Association(246)
Council of Archives and Research Libraries in Jewish Studies(270)
Council on Botanical and Horticultural Libraries(275)
Council on Library-Media Technicians(276)
Evangelical Church Library Association(298)
Federal and Armed Forces Librarians Roundtable(301)
Geoscience Information Society(316)
Independent Research Libraries Association(335)
International Association of Aquatic and Marine Science Libraries and Information Centers(352)
International Association of Music Libraries, United States Branch(359)
International Association of School Librarianship(361)
Library Administration and Management Association(407)
Library and Information Technology Association(407)
Library Binding Institute(407)
Medical Library Association(416)
Middle East Librarians' Association(418)
Music Library Association(423)
National Church Library Association(489)
Online Audiovisual Catalogers(565)
Public Library Association(592)
Society of American Archivists(630)
Society of School Librarians International(644)
Special Libraries Association(649)
Substance Abuse Librarians and Information Specialists(655)
Theatre Library Association(660)
U.S.A. Toy Library Association(669)
Urban Libraries Council(681)

LIGHTING

American Lighting Association(101)
Illuminating Engineering Society of North America(332)
International Association of Lighting Designers(358)
International Association of Lighting Management Companies(359)
National Association of Independent Lighting Distributors(457)
National Council on Qualifications for the Lighting Professions(502)
National Electrical Contractors Association(506)

LINGUISTICS

Alliance of Associations of Teachers of Japanese(16)
American Association for Applied Linguistics(33)
American Association of Phonetic Sciences(48)
American Councils for International Education(76)
American Name Society(107)
American Society of Geolinguistics(138)
Association for Computational Linguistics(170)
Linguistic Association of Canada and the United States(408)
Linguistic Society of America(408)

LIQUOR

American Beverage Licensees(57)
Distilled Spirits Council of the U.S.(286)
Distillers Grains Technology Council(286)
National Alcohol Beverage Control Association(429)
National Association of Beverage Importers-Wine-Spirits-Beer(439)
National Conference of State Liquor Administrators(494)
Wine and Spirits Shippers Association(689)
Wine and Spirits Wholesalers of America(689)

LIVESTOCK

Alpines International(18)
American and Delaine-Merino Record Association(31)
American Angora Goat Breeder's Association(31)
American Angus Association(31)
American Berkshire Association(56)
American Brahman Breeders Association(59)
American British White Park Association(59)
American Chianina Association(62)
American Dairy Goat Association(77)
American Embryo Transfer Association(81)
American Feed Industry Association(83)
American Galloway Breeders Association(86)
American Gelbvieh Association(86)
American Genetic Association(86)
American Guernsey Association(87)
American Hampshire Sheep Association(88)
American Hereford Association(90)
American Highland Cattle Association(90)

American International Charolais Association(98)
American Jersey Cattle Association(99)
American Maine-Anjou Association(102)
American Milking Shorthorn Society(106)
American Murray Grey Association(107)
American Rambouillet Sheep Breeders Association(121)
American Red Poll Association(122)
American Romney Breeders Association(123)
American Shorthorn Association(125)
American Shropshire Registry Association(125)
American Simmental Association(125)
American Society of Animal Science(134)
American Tarentaise Association(150)
Amerifax Cattle Association(156)
Animal Transportation Association(157)
Ayrshire Breeders' Association(225)
Barzona Breeders Association of America(226)
Beefmaster Breeders United(227)
Braunvieh Association of America(232)
Brown Swiss Cattle Breeders Association of the U.S.A.(234)
Exotic Wildlife Association(299)
Holstein Association USA(327)
International Nubian Breeders Association(381)
Livestock Marketing Association(409)
Livestock Publications Council(409)
National Association of Animal Breeders(438)
National Block and Bridle Club(485)
National Cattlemen's Beef Association(488)
National Congress of Animal Trainers and Breeders(495)
National Hereford Hog Record Association(517)
National Institute for Animal Agriculture(520)
National Lincoln Sheep Breeders Association(525)
National Livestock Producers Association(525)
National Miniature Donkey Association(527)
National Swine Improvement Federation(545)
North American Clun Forest Association(556)
North American Corriente Association(556)
North American Deer Farmers Association(556)
North American Elk Breeders Association(556)
Poland China Record Association(579)
Purebred Dairy Cattle Association(593)
Santa Gertrudis Breeders International(605)
Society for Range Management(624)
United Producers(672)
United Suffolk Sheep Association(678)

LOCKS

Associated Locksmiths of America(165)
International Association of Home Safety and Security Professionals(358)
Safe and Vault Technicians Association(604)
Security Hardware Distributors Association(607)

LUBRICANTS

Automotive Oil Change Association(224)
Independent Lubricant Manufacturers Association(335)
International Castor Oil Association(364)
National Lubricating Grease Institute(525)
Society of Tribologists and Lubrication Engineers(645)

MACHINE TOOL INDUSTRY

American Machine Tool Distributors Association(102)
AMT - The Association For Manufacturing Technology(156)
Cemented Carbide Producers Association(241)
Equipment Service Association(297)
Fluid Power Distributors Association(308)
Fluid Power Society(308)
Hand Tools Institute(321)
International Association of Tool Craftsmen(361)
Machine Knife Association(409)
Machinery Dealers National Association(409)
National Tooling and Machining Association(546)
North American Sawing Association(560)
Power Tool Institute(582)
Society of Manufacturing Engineers(639)
United States Cutting Tool Institute(675)

MACHINERY

Agricultural and Industrial Manufacturers' Representatives Association(12)
American Gear Manufacturers Association(86)
American Textile Machinery Association(151)
Associated Equipment Distributors(165)
Association of Equipment Manufacturers(195)
Association of Machinery and Equipment Appraisers(203)
Association of Suppliers to the Paper Industry(216)
BEMA - The Baking Industry Suppliers Association(227)
Cleaning Equipment Trade Association(247)
Compressed Air and Gas Institute(257)
Contractors Pump Bureau(264)
Conveyor Equipment Manufacturers Association(265)
Crane Certification Association of America(278)
Fabricators and Manufacturers Association, International(300)
Farm Equipment Manufacturers Association(301)
Farm Equipment Wholesalers Association(301)
Fire Equipment Manufacturers' Association(307)
Fluid Power Society(308)
Food Processing Machinery and Supplies Association(309)
Heat Exchange Institute(324)
International Association of Diecutting and Diemaking(356)
International Association of Food Industry Suppliers(357)
International Association of Machinists and Aerospace Workers(359)
Manufacturers Alliance/MAPI(411)
Mechanical Power Transmission Association(415)
National Emergency Equipment Dealers Association(506)
National Fluid Power Association(511)
National Troubleshooting Association(547)
North American Equipment Dealers Association(556)
Outdoor Power Equipment Aftermarket Association(569)
Outdoor Power Equipment and Engine Service Association(569)
Outdoor Power Equipment Institute(569)
Packaging Machinery Manufacturers Institute(570)
Power Transmission Distributors Association(582)
Power-Motion Technology Representatives Association(582)
Precision Machined Products Association(583)
Service Dealers Association(609)
Spring Manufacturers Institute(652)
Textile Care Allied Trades Association(660)
Vibration Institute(683)
Wood Machinery Manufacturers of America(694)
Woodworking Machinery Industry Association(694)

MAGIC

International Brotherhood of Magicians(363)
Magic Dealers Association(410)
Society of American Magicians(631)

MAIL

Alliance of Nonprofit Mailers(17)
Association for Postal Commerce(177)
Direct Marketing Association(285)
Direct Selling Association(285)
Mail Systems Management Association(410)
Mailing & Fulfillment Service Association(410)
National Mail Order Association(525)
National Postal Mail Handlers Union(533)
National Star Route Mail Contractors Association(543)
Nationwide Alternate Delivery Alliance(550)
Parcel Shippers Association(571)
Periodical Publications Association(573)
Pharmaceutical Care Management Association(575)

MAMMALOGY

American Society of Mammalogists(141)
American Society of Primatologists(145)

MANAGEMENT

Academy of Management(4)
AFCOM(10)
AFSM International(11)
Alliance for Nonprofit Management(15)
American Academy of Ambulatory Care Nursing(20)
American Association of Managing General Agents(45)
American College of Healthcare Executives(66)
American Healthcare Radiology Administrators(90)
American Management Association(102)
American Society for Engineering Management(128)
American Society for Public Administration(132)
Analytical Laboratory Managers Association(157)
APICS - The Association for Operations Management(158)
ARMA International(160)
Association Chief Executive Council(166)
Association for Information and Image Management International(174)
Association for Public Policy Analysis and Management(177)
Association for Women in Management(182)
Association of Information Technology Professionals(201)
Association of Internal Management Consultants(201)
Association of Management Consulting Firms(203)
Association of Productivity Specialists(208)
Association of Professional Energy Managers(209)
Association of Proposal Management Professionals(210)
Association of Sales Administration Managers(212)
Association of School Business Officials International(212)
Association of University Research Parks(219)
Athletic Equipment Managers Association(221)
Automotive Trade Association Executives(224)
Biotech Medical Management Association(229)
Building Owners and Managers Association International(234)
Building Owners and Managers Institute International(234)
Business Forms Management Association(235)
Christian Management Association(246)
Clinical Laboratory Management Association(248)
Club Managers Association of America(249)
College Athletic Business Management Association(251)
Communications Media Management Association(255)
Construction Financial Management Association(262)
Construction Management Association of America(262)
Council of Supply Chain Management Professionals(275)
Decision Sciences Institute(282)
Environmental Industry Associations(296)
Federal Managers Association(302)
Financial Management Association International(306)
Fraternal Field Managers Association(311)
Fulfillment Management Association(312)
GAMA International(313)
Golf Course Superintendents Association of America(318)

Groundwater Management Districts Association(320)
Healthcare Financial Management Association(324)
Healthcare Information and Management Systems Society(324)
Hospitality Sales and Marketing Association International(329)
In-Plant Printing and Mailing Association(332)
Independent Association of Accredited Registrars(333)
Institute for Supply Management(340)
Institute of Behavioral and Applied Management(340)
Institute of Career Certification International(340)
Institute of Certified Professional Managers(340)
Institute of Certified Records Managers(340)
Institute of Management Consultants USA(342)
Institute of Real Estate Management(343)
International Association for Exhibition Management(350)
International Association of Assembly Managers(353)
International Association of Association Management Companies(353)
International Association of Healthcare Central Service Materiel Management(357)
International City/County Management Association(365)
International Council for Small Business(367)
International Customer Service Association(368)
International Facility Management Association(371)
International Public Management Association for Human Resources(384)
International Society for Performance Improvement(388)
International Society for the Performing Arts(389)
International Society of Facilities Executives(391)
International Ticketing Association(394)
LOMA(409)
Medical Group Management Association(416)
Mineral Economics and Management Society(419)
National Association of Case Management(441)
National Association of Credit Management(448)
National Association of Flood and Stormwater Management Agencies(453)
National Association of Postal Supervisors(465)
National Association of Professional Organizers(466)
National Association of Scientific Materials Managers(471)
National Association of Service Managers(472)
National Classification Management Society(490)
National Contract Management Association(495)
National Council of Agricultural Employers(498)
National Council of Social Security Management Associations(500)
National Credit Union Management Association(503)
National Grants Management Association(514)
National Institute of Management Counsellors(521)
National Institute of Packaging, Handling and Logistics Engineers(521)
National Institute on Park and Grounds Management(521)
National Management Association(525)
National Property Management Association(534)
National Safety Management Society(538)
Newspaper Association Managers(552)
Newspaper Purchasing Management Association(553)
North American Performing Arts Managers and Agents(559)
Object Management Group(563)
Paper Industry Management Association(571)
Product Development and Management Association(585)
Professional Association of Health Care Office Management(586)
Professional Convention Management Association(587)
Professional Managers Association(588)
Professional Services Management Association(589)
Project Management Institute(590)
Radiology Business Management Association(595)
Religious Conference Management Association(599)
Restaurant Facility Management Association(600)
School Management Study Group(606)
Society for Advancement of Management(613)
Society for Foodservice Management(617)
Society for Information Management(620)
Society of Medical-Dental Management Consultants(640)
Sports Turf Managers Association(651)
State Risk and Insurance Management Association(653)
Turnaround Management Association(667)
University Council for Educational Administration(679)
Veterinary Hospital Managers Association(682)
Women in Management(692)
WorldatWork(697)
Young Presidents' Organization(698)

MANUFACTURERS

Adhesive and Sealant Council(8)
Advanced Medical Technology Association(8)
AeA - Advancing the Business of Technology(9)
AERA - Engine Rebuilders Association(9)
Aerospace Industries Association of America(10)
Agricultural and Industrial Manufacturers' Representatives Association(12)
Agricultural Retailers Association(12)
AIM Global(12)
Air Diffusion Council(13)
Air Distributing Institute(13)
AirConditioning and Refrigeration Institute(14)
Alliance of Automobile Manufacturers(16)
ALMA - the International Loudspeaker Association(17)
Aluminum Anodizers Council(18)
Aluminum Association(18)
Aluminum Extruders Council(18)
Aluminum Foil Container Manufacturers Association(18)
American Amusement Machine Association(31)
American Apparel & Footwear Association(31)
American Architectural Manufacturers Association(32)
American Association of Automatic Door Manufacturers(38)
American Bearing Manufacturing Association(56)
American Beverage Association(56)
American Boiler Manufacturers Association(58)
American Brush Manufacturers Association(59)
American Chain Association(61)
American Chemistry Council(62)
American Cloak and Suit Manufacturers Association(63)
American Coke and Coal Chemicals Institute(63)
American Composites Manufacturers Association(72)
American Concrete Institute(72)
American Concrete Pavement Association(72)
American Concrete Pipe Association(73)
American Concrete Pressure Pipe Association(73)
American Edged Products Manufacturers Association(80)
American Electroplaters and Surface Finishers Society(80)
American Feed Industry Association(83)
American Fence Association(83)
American Fiber Manufacturers Association(83)
American Fire Safety Council(84)
American Fire Sprinkler Association(84)
American Flock Association(84)
American Floorcovering Alliance(84)
American Foundry Society(85)
American Galvanizers Association(86)
American Gear Manufacturers Association(86)
American Hardware Manufacturers Association(88)
American Herbal Products Association(90)
American Home Furnishings Alliance(91)
American Incense Manufacturers Association(93)
American Innerspring Manufacturers(93)
American Institute of Aeronautics and Astronautics(94)
American Institute of Steel Construction(97)
American Institute of Timber Construction(98)
American Iron and Steel Institute(98)
American Ladder Institute(100)
American Lighting Association(101)
American Measuring Tool Manufacturers Association(103)
American Mold Builders Association(106)
American Orthotic and Prosthetic Association(111)
American Peanut Council(113)
American Pet Products Manufacturers Association(114)
American Petroleum Institute(114)
American Pharmacists Association(114)
American Pipe Fittings Association(115)
American Pyrotechnics Association(120)
American Road and Transportation Builders Association(123)
American Society for Quality(132)
American Solar Energy Society(147)
American Textile Machinery Association(151)
American Watch Association(154)
American Welding Society(154)
American Wire Cloth Institute(155)
American Wire Producers Association(155)
AMT - The Association For Manufacturing Technology(156)
Amusement Industry Manufacturers and Suppliers International(156)
APA - The Engineered Wood Association(158)
APICS - The Association for Operations Management(158)
APMI International(158)
Appalachian Hardwood Manufacturers(158)
Apple Products Research and Education Council(159)
Archery Trade Association(160)
Architectural Precast Association(160)
Architectural Woodwork Institute(160)
The Art and Creative Materials Institute(161)
Asia America MultiTechnology Association(162)
Asphalt Emulsion Manufacturers Association(163)
Asphalt Institute(163)
Asphalt Recycling and Reclaiming Association(163)
Asphalt Roofing Manufacturers Association(163)
Associated Builders and Contractors(164)
Associated Cooperage Industries of America(165)
Associated Glass and Pottery Manufacturers(165)
Associated Pipe Organ Builders of America(166)
Associated Wire Rope Fabricators(166)
Association for Manufacturing Excellence(176)
Association for Unmanned Vehicle Systems International(181)
Association of Energy Service Companies(195)
Association of Equipment Manufacturers(195)

Association of Home Appliance Manufacturers(200)
Association of Independent Corrugated Converters(200)
Association of Industrial Metallizers, Coaters and Laminators(201)
Association of Medical Diagnostic Manufacturers(204)
Association of Oil Pipe Lines(206)
Association of Pool and Spa Professionals(208)
Association of Rotational Molders, International(212)
Association of Steel Distributors(216)
Association of the Wall and Ceiling Industries-International(218)
Association of United States Night Vision Manufacturers(219)
Association of Vacuum Equipment Manufacturers International(220)
Automatic Transmission Rebuilders Association(223)
Automotive Aftermarket Industry Association(223)
Automotive Lift Institute, Inc.(223)
Automotive Occupant Restraints Council(224)
Automotive Parts Remanufacturers Association(224)
Automotive Recyclers Association(224)
Aviation Distributors and Manufacturers Association International(224)
Awards and Recognition Association(225)
Basic Acrylic Monomer Manufacturers(226)
Battery Council International(226)
Beer Institute(227)
Belt Association(227)
BEMA - The Baking Industry Suppliers Association(227)
Book Manufacturers' Institute(231)
Brake Manufacturers Council(232)
Brick Industry Association(232)
Builders Hardware Manufacturers Association(234)
Business and Institutional Furniture Manufacturers Association International(235)
Calorie Control Council(237)
Can Manufacturers Institute(237)
Carpet and Rug Institute(238)
Carpet Cushion Council(238)
Casket and Funeral Supply Association of America(238)
Cast Iron Soil Pipe Institute(238)
Casting Industry Suppliers Association(239)
Cedar Shake and Shingle Bureau(240)
Cemented Carbide Producers Association(241)
Ceramic Manufacturers Association(241)
Ceramic Tile Institute of America(242)
Chain Link Fence Manufacturers Institute(242)
Chemical Fabrics and Film Association(243)
Chemical Producers and Distributors Association(243)
Chlorinated Paraffins Industry Association(245)
Chlorine Institute(245)
Chocolate Manufacturers Association(245)
Cigar Association of America(247)
Cleaning Equipment Trade Association(247)
Clothing Manufacturers Association of the U.S.A.(248)
Coin Laundry Association(250)
Cold Finished Steel Bar Institute(250)
Color Pigments Manufacturers Association(253)
Composite Can and Tube Institute(256)
Composite Panel Association(257)
Compressed Air and Gas Institute(257)
Computer and Communications Industry Association(257)
Concrete Anchor Manufacturers Association(258)
Concrete Plant Manufacturers Bureau(258)
Concrete Reinforcing Steel Institute(259)
Consortium for Advanced Manufacturing International(262)
Consumer Electronics Association(263)
Consumer Healthcare Products Association(263)
Consumer Specialty Products Association(263)
Contact Lens Manufacturers Association(264)
Converting Equipment Manufacturers Association(265)
Conveyor Equipment Manufacturers Association(265)
Cookware Manufacturers Association(265)
Cooling Technology Institute(265)
Copper and Brass Fabricators Council(266)
Copper and Brass Servicenter Association(266)
Cordage Institute(266)
Corn Refiners Association(266)
Cosmetic, Toiletry and Fragrance Association(267)
Cotton Council International(267)
Council of Defense and Space Industry Associations(271)
Council of Manufacturing Associations(273)
CPA Manufacturing Services Association(278)
Craft & Hobby Association(278)
Dental Trade Alliance(283)
Diamond Manufacturers and Importers Association of America(284)
Distilled Spirits Council of the U.S.(286)
Distribution Business Management Association(286)
Diving Equipment and Marketing Association(286)
Door and Access Systems Manufacturers' Association, International(286)
Door and Hardware Institute(287)
Ductile Iron Society(288)
EIFS Industry Members Association(290)
Electrical Generating Systems Association(291)
Electrical Manufacturing and Coil Winding Association(291)
Electrocoat Association(291)
Electronic Distribution Show Corporation(291)
Electronic Industries Alliance(292)
Embroidery Council of America(292)
Energy Frontiers International(294)
Engine Manufacturers Association(295)
Envelope Manufacturers Association(296)
EPS Molders Association(297)
Equipment and Tool Institute(297)
Equipment Service Association(297)
Exhibit Designers and Producers Association(299)
Expansion Joint Manufacturers Association(299)
Fabricators and Manufacturers Association, International(300)
Farm Equipment Manufacturers Association(301)
Fertilizer Institute(305)
Fibre Box Association(305)
Film and Bag Federation(305)
Filter Manufacturers Council(305)
Financial and Security Products Association(305)
Fire and Emergency Manufacturers and Services Association(307)
Fire Equipment Manufacturers' Association(307)
Flavor and Extract Manufacturers Association of the United States(307)
Flexible Packaging Association(307)
Fluid Controls Institute(308)
Fluid Sealing Association(308)
Food Processing Machinery and Supplies Association(309)
Foodservice and Packaging Institute(309)
Forest Resources Association(310)
Forging Industry Association(310)
Friction Materials Standards Institute(312)
Frozen Potato Products Institute(312)
Game Manufacturers Association(313)
Gas Appliance Manufacturers Association(314)
Gas Processors Association(314)
General Aviation Manufacturers Association(315)
Gift Associates Interchange Network(317)
Glass Packaging Institute(317)
Grocery Manufacturers Association(320)
Guitar and Accessories Marketing Association(321)
Gypsum Association(321)
Hand Tools Institute(321)
Hardwood Manufacturers Association(322)
Hardwood Plywood and Veneer Association(322)
Hearing Industries Association(324)
Heat Exchange Institute(324)
Heavy Duty Manufacturers Association(325)
Home Improvement Research Institute(327)
Hosiery Association, The(328)
Hydraulic Institute(329)
Incentive Manufacturers and Representatives Association(332)
INDA, Association of the Nonwoven Fabrics Industry(333)
Independent Cosmetic Manufacturers and Distributors(333)
Independent Distributors Association(333)
Independent Lubricant Manufacturers Association(335)
Independent Office Products and Furniture Dealers Association(335)
Industrial Diamond Association of America(336)
Industrial Fabrics Association International(336)
Industrial Fasteners Institute(337)
Industrial Heating Equipment Association(337)
Industrial Perforators Association(337)
Industrial Truck Association(337)
Industry Council for Tangible Assets(337)
InfoCom International(338)
Information Technology Industry Council(338)
Institute for Briquetting and Agglomeration(339)
Institute of Clean Air Companies(340)
Institute of Makers of Explosives(342)
Institute of Paper Science and Technology(343)
Institute of Scrap Recycling Industries(343)
Institute of Shortening and Edible Oils(344)
Inter-Industry Conference on Auto Collision Repair(346)
Interactive Audio Special Interest Group(346)
International Association of Diecutting and Diemaking(356)
International Association of Electronic Keyboard Manufacturers(356)
International Association of Food Industry Suppliers(357)
International Cadmium Association(364)
International Card Manufacturers Association(364)
International Cast Polymer Association(364)
International Compressor Remanufacturers Association(366)
International Disk Drive Equipment and Materials Association(369)
International Door Association(369)
International Electronic Article Surveillance Manufacturers Association(370)
International Engraved Graphics Association(370)
International Food Additives Council(372)
International Formula Council(373)
International Furniture Transportation and Logistics Council(373)
International Glove Association(374)
International Housewares Association(375)
International Ice Cream Association(375)
International Imaging Industry Association(376)
International Institute for Lath and Plaster(376)
International Institute of Ammonia Refrigeration(376)
International Institute of Synthetic Rubber Producers(376)
International Jelly and Preserve Association(377)
International Magnesium Association(378)
International Magnetics Association(378)
International Marking and Identification Association(379)

International Oxygen Manufacturers Association(382)
International Ozone Association-Pan American Group Branch(382)
International Packaged Ice Association(382)
International Recording Media Association(384)
International Safety Equipment Association(385)
International Sign Association(386)
International Silk Association(386)
International Sleep Products Association(386)
International Snowmobile Manufacturers Association(386)
International Society for Respiratory Protection(389)
International Staple, Nail and Tool Association(393)
International Theatre Equipment Association(394)
International Wood Products Association(397)
Investment Casting Institute(398)
IPA - The Association of Graphic Solutions Providers(399)
IPC - Association Connecting Electronics Industries(399)
Irrigation Association(400)
ISA(400)
ISSA(400)
Joint Electron Device Engineering Council(402)
Juice Products Association(402)
Juvenile Products Manufacturers Association(403)
Kitchen Cabinet Manufacturers Association(403)
Laboratory Products Association(404)
Leather Industries of America(407)
Light Aircraft Manufacturers Association(408)
Lightning Protection Institute(408)
Machine Knife Association(409)
Manufactured Housing Association for Regulatory Reform(410)
Manufactured Housing Institute(411)
Manufacturers Alliance/MAPI(411)
Manufacturers Representatives of America(411)
Manufacturers Standardization Society of the Valve and Fittings Industry(411)
Manufacturers' Agents National Association(411)
Manufacturing Jewelers and Suppliers of America(411)
Maple Flooring Manufacturers Association(412)
Marine Fabricators Association(412)
Mass Finishing Job Shops Association(413)
Material Handling Industry of America(414)
Mechanical Power Transmission Association(415)
Medical Device Manufacturers Association(416)
Metal Building Manufacturers Association(417)
Metal Findings Manufacturers Association(417)
Metal Framing Manufacturers Association(417)
Metal Powder Industries Federation(417)
Metal Treating Institute(417)
Methacrylate Producers Association(418)
MIDI Manufacturers Association(418)
Mobile Air Conditioning Society Worldwide(420)
Monument Builders of North America(421)
Motor and Equipment Manufacturers Association(421)
Motorcycle Industry Council(421)
Mulch and Soil Council(422)
NABIM - the International Band and Orchestral Products Association(424)
NAGMR Consumer Product Brokers(425)
NASFM(425)
National Asphalt Pavement Association(431)
National Association for Information Destruction(434)
National Association of Architectural Metal Manufacturers(438)
National Association of Chain Manufacturers(442)
National Association of Display Industries(449)
National Association of Fundraising Ticket Manufacturers(454)
National Association of Graphic and Product Identification Manufacturers(455)
National Association of Manufacturers(460)
National Association of Margarine Manufacturers(461)
National Association of Metal Finishers(461)
National Association of Pipe Fabricators(464)
National Association of Printing Ink Manufacturers(465)
National Association of Trailer Manufacturers(479)
National Association of Uniform Manufacturers and Distributors(480)
National Automatic Merchandising Association(482)
National Burglar and Fire Alarm Association(486)
National Candle Association(487)
National Cheese Institute(488)
National Church Goods Association(489)
National Clay Pipe Institute(490)
National Clay Pottery Association(490)
National Coil Coating Association(490)
National Concrete Burial Vault Association(492)
National Concrete Masonry Association(492)
National Confectioners Association of the United States(492)
National Corrugated Steel Pipe Association(496)
National Cotton Batting Institute(496)
National Cottonseed Products Association(496)
National Council for Advanced Manufacturing(496)
National Electrical Manufacturers Association(506)
National Electrical Manufacturers Representatives Association(506)
National Elevator Industry(506)
National Fashion Accessories Association(508)
National Fire Sprinkler Association(511)
National Fluid Power Association(511)
National Frame Builders Association(512)
National Frozen and Refrigerated Foods Association(513)
National Golf Car Manufacturers Association(514)
National Greenhouse Manufacturers Association(515)
National Hardwood Lumber Association(516)
National Industrial Council - Employer Association Group(519)
National Industrial Council - State Associations Group(519)
National Kerosene Heater Association(523)
National Kitchen and Bath Association(523)
National Lead Burning Association(523)
National Lime Association(525)
National Lubricating Grease Institute(525)
National Marine Manufacturers Association(526)
The National NeedleArts Association(528)
National Ornamental and Miscellaneous Metals Association(531)
National Paint and Coatings Association(531)
National Paperbox Association(531)
National Pasta Association(532)
National Pharmaceutical Council(533)
National Precast Concrete Association(534)
National Propane Gas Association(534)
National Quartz Producers Council(534)
National Reloading Manufacturers Association(536)
National Renderers Association(536)
National School Supply and Equipment Association(538)
National Seasoning Manufacturers Association(539)
National Slag Association(540)
National Sporting Goods Association(543)
National Terrazzo and Mosaic Association(546)
National Textile Association(546)
National Tooling and Machining Association(546)
National Wooden Pallet and Container Association(550)
Neckwear Association of America(551)
NIBA - The Belting Association(553)
NOFMA: the Wood Flooring Manufacturers Association(553)
North American Association of Food Equipment Manufacturers(554)
North American Insulation Manufacturers Association(557)
North American Punch Manufacturers Association(559)
North American Retail Hardware Association(559)
North American Sawing Association(560)
NPES, The Association for Suppliers of Printing, Publishing and Converting Technologies(563)
Nuclear Energy Institute(563)
Optical Laboratories Association(566)
Optical Society of America(566)
Orthopedic Surgical Manufacturers Association(569)
Outdoor Power Equipment Institute(569)
Packaging Machinery Manufacturers Institute(570)
Paint and Decorating Retailers Association(570)
Paper Machine Clothing Council(571)
Paper Shipping Sack Manufacturers Association(571)
Paperboard Packaging Council(571)
Peanut and Tree Nut Processors Association(572)
Pedorthic Footwear Association(572)
Personal Watercraft Industry Association(574)
Pet Food Institute(574)
Petroleum Equipment Institute(574)
Pharmaceutical Research and Manufacturers of America(575)
Photoimaging Manufacturers and Distributors Association(576)
Piano Manufacturers Association International(577)
Pine Chemicals Association(578)
Pipe Fabrication Institute(578)
Plastic Pipe and Fittings Association(578)
Plastic Shipping Container Institute(578)
Plastic Soft Materials Manufacturers Association(578)
Plastics Pipe Institute(579)
Plumbing and Drainage Institute(579)
Polyisocyanurate Insulation Manufacturers Association(580)
Polyurethane Manufacturers Association(580)
Porcelain Enamel Institute(580)
Portable Sanitation Association International(581)
Portland Cement Association(581)
Post-Print Manufacturers Association(581)
Potash & Phosphate Institute(581)
Powder Actuated Tool Manufacturers Institute(582)
Power Sources Manufacturers Association(582)
Power Tool Institute(582)
Power Transmission Distributors Association(582)
Precision Machined Products Association(583)
Precision Metalforming Association(583)
Pressure Sensitive Tape Council(583)
Pressure Vessel Manufacturers Association(583)
Pressure Washer Manufacturers Association(583)
Private Label Manufacturers Association(584)
Production and Operations Management Society(585)
Production Engine Remanufacturers Association(585)
Professional Picture Framers Association(588)
QVM/CMC Vehicle Manufacturers Association(594)
Railway Engineering-Maintenance Suppliers Association(595)
Railway Tie Association(595)
Recording Industry Association of America(596)

Recreation Vehicle Industry Association(596)
Refractories Institute(597)
Refractory Ceramic Fibers Coalition(597)
Remanufacturing Institute, The(599)
Resistance Welder Manufacturers' Association(600)
Robotic Industries Association(602)
Roof Coatings Manufacturers Association(603)
Rubber Manufacturers Association(603)
Safe and Vault Technicians Association(604)
SAMA Group of Associations(605)
Scaffold Industry Association(605)
Scaffolding, Shoring and Forming Institute(605)
Scale Manufacturers Association(605)
Schiffli Lace and Embroidery Manufacturers Association(606)
School, Home and Office Products Association(606)
Scientific Equipment and Furniture Association(606)
Screen Manufacturers Association(607)
Secondary Materials and Recycled Textiles Association(607)
Security Industry Association(607)
Semiconductor Equipment and Materials International(608)
Semiconductor Industry Association(608)
SGMA(651)
Silver Institute(611)
SMMA - The Motor and Motion Association(612)
Snack Food Association(612)
Soap and Detergent Association(612)
Society for Imaging Informatics in Medicine(619)
Society of Manufacturing Engineers(639)
Society of the Plastics Industry(645)
Solar Energy Industries Association(647)
Space Transportation Association(648)
Specialty Equipment Market Association(650)
Sporting Arms and Ammunition Manufacturers' Institute(651)
SPRI, Inc.(652)
Spring Manufacturers Institute(652)
Steel Deck Institute(653)
Steel Door Institute(653)
Steel Founders' Society of America(653)
Steel Joist Institute(653)
Steel Manufacturers Association(653)
Steel Plate Fabricators Association Division of STI/SPFA(653)
Steel Shipping Container Institute(653)
Steel Tank Institute Division of STI/SPFA(654)
Steel Tube Institute of North America(654)
Steel Window Institute(654)
Stucco Manufacturers Association(654)
Submersible Wastewater Pump Association(655)
Summer and Casual Furniture Manufacturers Association(655)
Sump and Sewage Pump Manufacturers Association(655)
Sunglass Association of America(655)
Synthetic Organic Chemical Manufacturers Association(657)
Tag and Label Manufacturers Institute(657)
Tennis Industry Association(659)
Textile Bag Manufacturers Association(660)
Textile Care Allied Trades Association(660)
Textile Fibers and By-Products Association(660)
Tile Council of North America(661)
Tile Roofing Institute(661)
Timber Products Manufacturers(661)
Tire Industry Association(662)
Toy Industry Association(662)
Transformer Association, The(663)
Transportation Safety Equipment Institute(664)
Travel Goods Association(665)
Truck Mixer Manufacturers Bureau(665)
Truck Trailer Manufacturers Association(666)
Tube and Pipe Association, International(666)
Tube Council of North America(666)
Tubular Exchanger Manufacturers Association(666)
Tune-up Manufacturers Council(667)
Ultrasonic Industry Association(669)
Unified Abrasives Manufacturers Association(669)
United Infants and Childrens Wear Association(671)
United Product Formulators and Distributors Association(672)
United States Beet Sugar Association(673)
United States Cutting Tool Institute(675)
United States Marine Safety Association(676)
Usability Professionals' Association(681)
Valve Manufacturers Association of America(682)
Valve Repair Council(682)
Variable Electronic Components Institute(682)
Vinegar Institute(683)
Water Quality Association(686)
Water Systems Council(686)
Web Sling and Tiedown Association(686)
Western-English Trade Association(688)
Window and Door Manufacturers Association(689)
Window Coverings Manufacturers Association(689)
Wire Reinforcement Institute(690)
Wire Rope Technical Board(690)
Wirebound Box Manufacturers Association(690)
Wiring Harness Manufacturers Association(690)
Wood Component Manufacturers Association(694)
Wood Machinery Manufacturers of America(694)
Wood Moulding and Millwork Producers Association(694)
Wood Products Manufacturers Association(694)
Woven Wire Products Association(697)
Writing Instrument Manufacturers Association(697)

MAPS

American Congress on Surveying and Mapping(73)
Geospatial Information Technology Association(316)
International Map Trade Association(379)
North American Cartographic Information Society(555)

MARKET RESEARCH

American Association for Public Opinion Research(36)
Association of Independent Information Professionals(200)
Council of American Survey Research Organizations(270)
Marketing Research Association(413)
National Golf Foundation(514)

MARKETING

ABA Marketing Network(1)
Academy of Marketing Science(4)
Advertising and Marketing International Network(9)
Advertising Research Foundation(9)
American Floorcovering Alliance(84)
American Marketing Association(103)
American Railway Development Association(121)
Association for Accounting Marketing(167)
Association of Investment Management Sales Executives(202)
Association of Retail Marketing Services(212)
Association of Travel Marketing Executives(218)
Biomedical Marketing Association(229)
Chain Drug Marketing Association(242)
Cherry Marketing Institute(243)
Color Marketing Group(252)
Communications Marketing Association(255)
Construction Marketing Research Council(262)
Copper Development Association(266)
Council for Marketing and Opinion Research(269)
Direct Marketing Association(285)
Direct Marketing Insurance and Financial Services Council(285)
Direct Selling Association(285)
Distributive Education Clubs of America(286)
Electrical Generating Systems Association(291)
Electronic Retailing Association(292)
Freestanding Insert Council of North America(312)
Fulfillment Management Association(312)
Glass Association of North America(317)
Graphic Arts Marketing Information Service(319)
Incentive Federation(332)
Incentive Marketing Association(332)
Independent Film and Television Alliance(334)
Insurance Marketing Communications Association(345)
International Society for Quality-of-Life Studies(388)
Legal Marketing Association(407)
LIMRA International(408)
Livestock Marketing Association(409)
Manufacturers' Agents National Association(411)
Marketing Agencies Association Worldwide(412)
Marketing Education Association(413)
Marketing Research Association(413)
Mass Marketing Insurance Institute(413)
Materials Marketing Associates(414)
Medical Marketing Association(416)
Multi-Level Marketing International Association(422)
National Agri-Marketing Association(428)
National Association for Campus Activities(432)
National Association of Collegiate Marketing Administrators(445)
National Association of Display Industries(449)
National Association of Export Companies(451)
National Council of Exchangors(499)
National Potato Promotion Board(533)
North American Agricultural Marketing Officials(554)
Petroleum Marketers Association of America(574)
Photo Marketing Association-International(576)
Private Label Manufacturers Association(584)
Produce Marketing Association(584)
Product Development and Management Association(585)
Professional Insurance Marketing Association(588)
Promotion Marketing Association(590)
Sales and Marketing Executives International(604)
Society for Marketing Professional Services(621)
Society of Independent Gasoline Marketers of America(638)
Specialty Equipment Market Association(650)
Strategic Account Management Association(654)
Trade Show Exhibitors Association(663)
United Producers(672)

MATERIAL HANDLING

AIM Global(12)
Conveyor Equipment Manufacturers Association(265)
Dangerous Goods Advisory Council(281)
Distribution Business Management Association(286)
Industrial Truck Association(337)
Institute of Hazardous Materials Management(341)
Institutional and Service Textile Distributors Association(344)
Material Handling Equipment Distributors Association(414)
Material Handling Industry of America(414)
National Wooden Pallet and Container Association(550)
Scale Manufacturers Association(605)

Web Sling and Tiedown Association(686)

MATHEMATICS

American Academy of Actuaries(19)
American Mathematical Association of Two Year Colleges(103)
American Mathematical Society(103)
American Statistical Association(149)
Association for Computing Machinery(170)
Association for Symbolic Logic(178)
Association for Women in Mathematics(182)
Association of State Supervisors of Mathematics(216)
Casualty Actuarial Society(239)
Conference Board of the Mathematical Sciences(259)
Econometric Society(288)
Institute for Operations Research and the Management Sciences(339)
Institute of Mathematical Statistics(342)
International Association for Mathematical Geology(351)
International Biometric Society(362)
International Society for Ecological Modelling-North American Chapter(387)
Mathematical Association of America(414)
National Council of Supervisors of Mathematics(501)
National Council of Teachers of Mathematics(501)
North American Fuzzy Information Processing Society(557)
Psychometric Society(592)
School Science and Mathematics Association(606)
Society for Industrial and Applied Mathematics(619)
Society for Mathematical Biology(621)
Society for Natural Philosophy(622)
Society of Actuaries(629)
Society of Multivariate Experimental Psychology(640)
United States Association for Computational Mechanics(673)

MEASUREMENT

American National Metric Council(108)
American National Standards Institute(108)
American Society for Precision Engineering(132)
Benchmarking Network Association(227)
Cold Formed Parts and Machine Institute(250)
International Function Point Users Group(373)
Mathematical Association of America(414)
Measurement, Control and Automation Association(415)
National Conference on Weights and Measures(495)
National Council of Teachers of Mathematics(501)
U.S. Metric Association(668)
United Weighers Association(679)

MEAT

American Association of Meat Processors(45)
American Importers and Exporters Meat Products Group(93)
American Meat Institute(103)
American Meat Science Association(104)
American National CattleWomen(108)
Association of Technical and Supervisory Professionals(217)
Beef Improvement Federation(227)
Meat Importers' Council of America(415)
Meat Industry Suppliers Alliance(415)
National Meat Association(526)
National Meat Canners Association(526)
National Pork Producers Council(533)
National Renderers Association(536)
National Seasoning Manufacturers Association(539)
New York Mercantile Exchange(552)
North American Meat Processors Association(558)
United States Meat Export Federation(676)

MEDICINE

AABB(1)
AAGL -- Advancing Minimally Invasive Gynecology Worldwide(1)
Academy of Ambulatory Foot and Ankle Surgery(2)
Academy of Aphasia(2)
Academy of Behavioral Medicine Research(2)
Academy of Clinical Laboratory Physicians and Scientists(2)
Academy of Medical-Surgical Nurses(4)
Academy of Psychosomatic Medicine(5)
Acute Long Term Hospital Association(8)
Aerospace Medical Association(10)
Air Medical Physician Association(13)
Alliance for Continuing Medical Education(15)
Alliance of Cardiovascular Professionals(16)
Ambulatory Pediatric Association(19)
America's Blood Centers(19)
American Academy for Cerebral Palsy and Developmental Medicine(19)
American Academy of Allergy, Asthma, and Immunology(20)
American Academy of Anti-Aging Medicine(20)
American Academy of Clinical Neurophysiology(21)
American Academy of Cosmetic Surgery(21)
American Academy of Dermatology(21)
American Academy of Disability Evaluating Physicians(22)
American Academy of Emergency Medicine(22)
American Academy of Environmental Medicine(22)
American Academy of Facial Plastic and Reconstructive Surgery(22)
American Academy of Family Physicians(22)
American Academy of Fertility Care Professionals(23)
American Academy of Gnathologic Orthopedics(23)
American Academy of Health Care Providers-Addictive Disorders(23)
American Academy of Health Physics(23)
American Academy of Home Care Physicians(23)
American Academy of Hospice and Palliative Medicine(23)
American Academy of Implant Dentistry(23)
American Academy of Insurance Medicine(24)
American Academy of Medical Acupuncture(24)
American Academy of Medical Administrators(24)
American Academy of Medical Management(24)
American Academy of Neurological and Orthopaedic Surgeons(24)
American Academy of Neurology(25)
American Academy of Ophthalmology(25)
American Academy of Oral and Maxillofacial Radiology(25)
American Academy of Oral Medicine(25)
American Academy of Orofacial Pain(26)
American Academy of Orthopaedic Surgeons(26)
American Academy of Orthotists and Prosthetists(26)
American Academy of Osteopathy(26)
American Academy of Otolaryngology-Head and Neck Surgery(26)
American Academy of Pain Medicine(26)
American Academy of Pediatrics(27)
American Academy of Physical Medicine and Rehabilitation(27)
American Academy of Physician Assistants(27)
American Academy of Podiatric Sports Medicine(27)
American Academy of Somnology(28)
American Academy of Sports Physicians(29)
American Academy of Thermology(29)
American Academy of Wound Management(29)
American Academy on Communication in Healthcare(29)
American Acupuncture Association(29)
American Aging Association(30)
American Ambulance Association(30)
American Anaplastology Association(31)
American Ass'n of Ambulatory Surgery Centers(32)
American Association for Accreditation of Ambulatory Surgery Facilities(33)
American Association for Cancer Education(33)
American Association for Cancer Research(34)
American Association for Functional Orthodontics(35)
American Association for Geriatric Psychiatry(35)
American Association for Hand Surgery(35)
American Association for Homecare(35)
American Association for Medical Transcription(36)
American Association for Pediatric Ophthalmology and Strabismus(36)
American Association for Respiratory Care(36)
American Association for the History of Medicine(37)
American Association for the Study of Liver Diseases(37)
American Association for the Surgery of Trauma(37)
American Association for Therapeutic Humor(37)
American Association for Thoracic Surgery(37)
American Association for Women Podiatrists(37)
American Association of Anatomists(38)
American Association of Bioanalysts(38)
American Association of Certified Allergists(39)
American Association of Certified Orthoptists(39)
American Association of Chairmen of Departments of Psychiatry(39)
American Association of Clinical Endocrinologists(39)
American Association of Clinical Urologists(40)
American Association of Colleges of Osteopathic Medicine(40)
American Association of Colleges of Podiatric Medicine(40)
American Association of Diabetes Educators(42)
American Association of Genitourinary Surgeons(43)
American Association of Hip and Knee Surgeons(43)
American Association of Immunologists(44)
American Association of Medical Assistants(45)
American Association of Medical Milk Commissions(45)
American Association of Medical Society Executives(45)
American Association of Naturopathic Physicians(46)
American Association of Neurological Surgeons(46)
American Association of Neuromuscular & Electrodiagnostic Medicine(46)
American Association of Neuropathologists(46)
American Association of Neuroscience Nurses(46)
American Association of Nurse Anesthetists(46)
American Association of Oral and Maxillofacial Surgeons(47)
American Association of Oriental Medicine(47)
American Association of Orthopaedic Medicine(47)
American Association of Osteopathic Women Physicians(47)
American Association of Pathologists' Assistants(47)
American Association of Physician Specialists(48)
American Association of Physicians and Health Care Professionals(48)
American Association of Physicists in Medicine(48)
American Association of Plastic Surgeons(48)

American Society of Tropical Medicine and Hygiene(147)
American Spinal Injury Association(148)
American Sports Medicine Association(148)
American Surgical Association(150)
American Telemedicine Association(151)
American Thoracic Society(151)
American Thyroid Association(151)
American Tinnitus Association(151)
American Trauma Society(152)
American Urological Association(153)
American Venous Forum(153)
American Veterinary Society of Animal Behavior(153)
Anxiety Disorders Association of America(157)
Applied Research Ethics National Association(159)
Associated Professional Sleep Socs.(166)
Association for Academic Surgery(166)
Association for Ambulatory Behavorial Healthcare(167)
Association for Chemoreception Sciences(169)
Association for Gerontology in Higher Education(173)
Association for Hospital Medical Education(174)
Association for Professionals in Infection Control and Epidemiology(177)
Association for Psychoanalytic Medicine(177)
Association for Research in Nervous and Mental Disease(177)
Association for Research in Vision and Ophthalmology(178)
Association for the Advancement of Automotive Medicine(179)
Association for the Advancement of Medical Instrumentation(179)
Association for the Advancement of Wound Care(180)
Association for the Behavioral Sciences and Medical Education(180)
Association for the Treatment of Sexual Abusers(181)
Association of Academic Chairmen of Plastic Surgery(183)
Association of Academic Physiatrists(183)
Association of American Indian Physicians(184)
Association of American Medical Colleges(184)
Association of American Physicians(185)
Association of American Physicians and Surgeons(185)
Association of Biomedical Communications Directors(187)
Association of Bone and Joint Surgeons(188)
Association of Children's Prosthetic-Orthotic Clinics(189)
Association of Clinical Scientists(190)
Association of Educators in Imaging and Radiologic Sciences(194)
Association of Family Medicine Administration(196)
Association of Family Medicine Residency Directors(196)
Association of Freestanding Radiation Oncology Centers(198)
Association of Genetic Technologists(198)
Association of Medical Education and Research in Substance Abuse(204)
Association of Medical Illustrators(204)
Association of Medical School Pediatric Department Chairs(204)
Association of Military Surgeons of the U.S.(205)
Association of Neurosurgical Physician Assistants(205)
Association of Organ Procurement Organizations(206)
Association of Osteopathic State Executive Directors(206)
Association of Otolaryngology Administrators(207)
Association of Pathology Chairs(207)
Association of Pediatric Hematology/Oncology Nurses(207)
Association of Physician Assistants in Cardiovascular Surgery(207)
Association of Physician Assistants in Obstetrics and Gynecology(208)
Association of Plastic Surgery Assistants(208)
Association of Polysomnographic Technologists(208)
Association of Postgraduate Physician Assistant Programs(208)
Association of Professors of Cardiology(209)
Association of Professors of Gynecology and Obstetrics(209)
Association of Professors of Medicine(209)
Association of Program Directors in Internal Medicine(210)
Association of Program Directors in Radiology(210)
Association of Program Directors in Surgery(210)
Association of Reproductive Health Professionals(212)
Association of Rheumatology Health Professionals(212)
Association of SIDS and Infant Mortality Programs(214)
Association of Subspecialty Professors(216)
Association of Surgical Technologists(216)
Association of Teachers of Preventive Medicine(217)
Association of Telehealth Service Providers(217)
Association of University Anesthesiologists(219)
Association of University Radiologists(219)
Association of Vascular and Interventional Radiographers(220)
Association of Women Surgeons(220)
Association of Women's Health, Obstetric and Neonatal Nurses(220)
Behavior Genetics Association(227)
BioCommunications Association(229)
Biomedical Engineering Society(229)
Biomedical Marketing Association(229)
Biotech Medical Management Association(229)
Black Psychiatrists of America(230)
Case Management Society of America(238)
Catecholamine Club(239)
Catholic Medical Association(240)
Certification Board for Urologic Nurses and Associates(242)
Cervical Spine Research Society(242)
Child Neurology Society(244)
Chinese American Medical Society(245)
Christian Medical & Dental Associations(246)
Civil Aviation Medical Association(247)
Clerkship Directors in Internal Medicine(248)
Clinical and Laboratory Standards Institute(248)
Clinical Immunology Society(248)
Clinical Ligand Assay Society(248)
Clinical Orthopaedic Society(248)
College of American Pathologists(251)
Computerized Medical Imaging Society(258)
Congress of Lung Association Staffs(261)
Congress of Neurological Surgeons(261)
Conservative Orthopaedics International Association(261)
Council of Medical Specialty Socs.(273)
Council of Musculoskeletal Specialty Socs.(273)
Council of State and Territorial Epidemiologists(274)
Council on Diagnostic Imaging to the A.C.A.(275)
Council on Resident Education in Obstetrics and Gynecology(277)
Cranial Academy(278)
Cystic Fibrosis Foundation(281)
Delta Society(283)
Drug and Alcohol Testing Industry Association(287)
Drug Information Association(287)
EEG and Clinical Neuroscience Society(290)
Emergency Medicine Residents' Association(292)
Endocrine Fellows Foundation(294)
Endocrine Society(294)
Engineering in Medicine and Biology Society(295)
Eye Bank Association of America(300)
Federal Physicians Association(302)
Federated Ambulatory Surgery Association(303)
Federation of State Medical Boards of the United States(304)
Fleischner Society(307)
Foundation for Advances in Medicine and Science(311)
Gastroenterology Research Group(315)
Genetics Society of America(315)
Gerontological Society of America(316)
Glove Shippers Association(318)
Gynecologic Oncology Group(321)
Gynecologic Surgery Society(321)
Harvey Society(322)
Health & Sciences Communications Association(322)
Health Industry Distributors Association(323)
Health Physics Society(323)
Healthcare Convention and Exhibitors Association(323)
Healthcare Leadership Council(324)
Heart Rhythm Society(324)
Histochemical Society(326)
Human Biology Association(329)
Independent Medical Distributors Association(335)
Infectious Diseases Society of America(338)
International Academy of Behavioral Medicine, Counseling and Psychotherapy(347)
International Academy of Oral Medicine and Toxicology(348)
International Analgesia Society(349)
International Anesthesia Research Society(349)
International Association for Continuing Education and Training(349)
International Association for the Study of Pain(352)
International Association of Eating Disorders Professionals(356)
International Association of Physicians in AIDS Care(360)
International Atherosclerosis Society(362)
International Childbirth Education Association(365)
International College of Surgeons(366)
International Embryo Transfer Society(370)
International Federation for Artificial Organs(371)
International Liver Transplantation Society(378)
International Oceanic Society(381)
International Pediatric Nephrology Association(382)
International Research Council of Neuromuscular Disorders(385)
International Society for Antiviral Research(386)
International Society for Experimental Hematology(387)
International Society for Heart and Lung Transplantation(387)
International Society for Infectious Diseases(387)
International Society for Magnetic Resonance in Medicine(387)
International Society for Pharmacoeconomics and Outcomes Research(388)
International Society for Preventive Oncology(388)
International Society for the Study of Subtle Energies and Energy Medicine(389)
International Society for Traumatic Stress Studies(389)
International Stress Management Association - U.S. Branch(393)
International Union of Industrial Service Transport Health Employees(395)
Intersocietal Accreditation Commission(398)
Islamic Medical Association of North America(400)
Joint Council of Allergy, Asthma, and Immunology(402)

Lamaze International(404)
Medical Device Manufacturers Association(416)
Medical Group Management Association(416)
Medical Library Association(416)
Medical Marketing Association(416)
Medical Mycological Society of the Americas(416)
Medical Records Institute(416)
Medical-Dental-Hospital Business Associates(416)
Midwives Alliance of North America(419)
Movement Disorder Society(422)
Musculoskeletal Tumor Society(422)
NATCO - The Organization for Transplant Professionals(426)
National Academy of Clinical Biochemistry(426)
National Academy of Neuropsychology(426)
National Association for Medical Direction of Respiratory Care(434)
National Association for Proton Therapy(435)
National Association Medical Staff Services(437)
National Association of Children's Hospitals(443)
National Association of Emergency Medical Technicians(450)
National Association of EMS Physicians(451)
National Association of First Responders(452)
National Association of Managed Care Physicians(460)
National Association of Medical Examiners(461)
National Association of Nephrology Technologists and Technicians(462)
National Association of Orthopaedic Technologists(463)
National Association of Physician Recruiters(464)
National Association of Professional Geriatric Care Managers(466)
National Association of State Emergency Medical Services Officials(475)
National Association of VA Physicians and Dentists(480)
National Association of Veterans' Research and Education Foundations(480)
National Center for Homeopathy(488)
National Coalition of Abortion Providers(490)
National Committee for Quality Assurance(491)
National Council on Radiation Protection and Measurements(502)
National Hemophilia Foundation(516)
National Hispanic Medical Association(517)
National Institute for Electromedical Information(520)
National Kidney Foundation(523)
National Marrow Donor Program(526)
National Medical Association(526)
National Organization for Associate Degree Nursing(529)
National Renal Administrators Association(536)
National Rural Health Association(537)
National Stroke Association(544)
National Student Osteopathic Medical Association(544)
National Surgical Assistant Association(545)
Neurosurgical Society of America(552)
North American Association For Ambulatory Care(554)
North American Clinical Dermatological Society(556)
North American Menopause Society(558)
North American Skull Base Society(560)
North American Society for Cardiac Imaging(560)
North American Society for Dialysis and Transplantation(560)
North American Society for Pediatric Gastroenterology, Hepatology and Nutrition(561)
North American Spine Society(561)
Orthopaedic Research Society(568)
Orthopaedic Trauma Association(569)
Phi Rho Sigma Medical Society(576)
Phlebology Society of America(576)
Plasma Protein Therapeutics Association(578)
Plastic Surgery Admininstrative Association(578)
Plastic Surgery Research Council(579)
Professional Association of Health Care Office Management(586)
Radiation Research Society(594)
Radiological Society of North America(594)
Renal Physicians Association(599)
Research Society on Alcoholism(600)
Ruth Jackson Orthopaedic Society(603)
Scoliosis Research Society(606)
Shock Society(610)
Society for Academic Emergency Medicine(613)
Society for Adolescent Medicine(613)
Society for Assisted Reproductive Technology(614)
Society for Biomaterials(614)
Society for Cardiovascular Angiography and Interventions(614)
Society for Cardiovascular Magnetic Resonance(614)
Society for Clinical Trials(615)
Society for Clinical Vascular Surgery(615)
Society for Developmental and Behavioral Pediatrics(616)
Society for Ear, Nose and Throat Advances in Children(616)
Society for Education in Anesthesia(616)
Society for Epidemiologic Research(617)
Society for Experimental Biology and Medicine(617)
Society for Gynecologic Investigation(618)
Society for Healthcare Epidemiology of America(618)
Society for Hematopathology(618)
Society for In Vitro Biology(619)
Society for Investigative Dermatology(620)
Society for Leukocyte Biology(621)
Society for Menstrual Cycle Research(621)
Society for Neuroscience(622)
Society for Obstetric Anesthesia and Perinatology(622)
Society for Pediatric Pathology(623)
Society for Pediatric Radiology(623)
Society for Pediatric Research(623)
Society for Pediatric Urology(623)
Society for Physical Regulation in Biology and Medicine(624)
Society for Radiation Oncology Administrators(624)
Society for Reproductive Endocrinology and Infertility(624)
Society for Sex Therapy and Research(625)
Society for Surgery of the Alimentary Tract(625)
Society for the Study of Male Psychology and Physiology(628)
Society for Thermal Medicine(628)
Society for Vascular Medicine and Biology(629)
Society for Vascular Surgery(629)
Society for Vascular Ultrasound(629)
Society of American Gastrointestinal and Endoscopic Surgeons(630)
Society of Behavioral Medicine(632)
Society of Biological Psychiatry(632)
Society of Cardiovascular Anesthesiologists(632)
Society of Computed Body Tomography and Magnetic Resonance(634)
Society of Critical Care Medicine(634)
Society of Diagnostic Medical Sonography(635)
Society of Eye Surgeons(636)
Society of Forensic Toxicologists(636)
Society of Gastroenterology Nurses and Associates(637)
Society of Gastrointestinal Radiologists(637)
Society of General Internal Medicine(637)
Society of Geriatric Cardiology(637)
Society of Gynecologic Oncologists(638)
Society of Interventional Radiology(639)
Society of Laparoendoscopic Surgeons(639)
Society of Medical Administrators(639)
Society of Medical Consultants to the Armed Forces(639)
Society of Medical-Dental Management Consultants(640)
Society of Military Otolaryngologists - Head and Neck Surgeons(640)
Society of Neurological Surgeons(640)
Society of Nuclear Medicine(641)
Society of Reproductive Surgeons(643)
Society of Surgical Oncology(644)
Society of Teachers of Family Medicine(644)
Society of Thoracic Surgeons(645)
Society of United States Air Force Flight Surgeons(645)
Society of University Otolaryngologists(645)
Society of University Surgeons(645)
Society of University Urologists(645)
Surgical Infection Society(656)
Transplantation Society(663)
Trauma Care International(665)
Undersea and Hyperbaric Medical Society(669)
Uniformed Services Academy of Family Physicians(669)
Union of American Physicians and Dentists(670)
United States and Canadian Academy of Pathology(672)
United States Pharmacopeia(676)
Veterinary Botanical Medical Association(682)
Wilderness Medical Society(689)
Women in Endocrinology(691)
World Allergy Organization - IACCI(695)
Wound, Ostomy and Continence Nurses Society(697)

MENTAL HEALTH

American Academy of Medical Hypnoanalysts(24)
American Association of Behavioral Therapists(38)
American Association of Chairmen of Departments of Psychiatry(39)
American Association of Children's Residential Centers(39)
American Association of Mental Health Professionals in Corrections(45)
American Association of Pastoral Counselors(47)
American Association of Psychiatric Technicians(50)
American College of Mental Health Administration(67)
American Group Psychotherapy Association(87)
American Managed Behavioral Healthcare Association(102)
American Mental Health Counselors Association(105)
American Music Therapy Association(107)
American Network of Community Options and Resources(108)
American Orthopsychiatric Association(111)
American Psychological Association(118)
American Society of Addiction Medicine(133)
Association for Applied Psychophysiology and Biofeedback(167)
Association for Comprehensive Energy Psychology(170)
Association for the Advancement of Psychology(179)
Association of Mental Health Librarians(204)
Association of Professional Chaplains(208)
Employee Assistance Professionals Association(293)
NADD: Association for Persons with Developmental Disabilities and Mental Health Needs(424)
National Alliance for Hispanic Health(429)
National Association for Rural Mental Health(436)
National Association for the Advancement of Psychoanalysis(436)
National Association of Addiction Treatment Providers(438)
National Association of Councils on Developmental Disabilities(446)

Certified Milk Producers Association of America(242)
Dairy Management(281)
International Association for Food Protection(350)
International Association of Milk Control Agencies(359)
International Dairy-Deli-Bakery Association(369)
Milk Industry Foundation(419)
National Dairy Herd Improvement Association(504)
National Frozen Pizza Institute(513)
National Mastitis Council(526)
National Milk Producers Federation(527)
National Yogurt Association(550)

MILLERS see also FEED & GRAIN, GRAIN, WHEAT

AACC International(1)
International Association of Operative Millers(359)
North American Millers Association(558)
Rice Millers' Association(602)

MILLINERY

American Society for Eighteenth-Century Studies(128)

MINERALOGY

American Crystallographic Association(77)
Geochemical Society(315)
Mineralogical Society of America(419)
SEPM - Society for Sedimentary Geology(609)

MINERALS

American Iron Ore Association(99)
American-European Soda Ash Shipping Association(156)
Asbestos Information Association/North America(162)
Association of the Wall and Ceiling Industries-International(218)
Clay Minerals Society(247)
Coal Technology Association(249)
Gypsum Association(321)
Mineral Economics and Management Society(419)
National Association of Royalty Owners(469)
National Mining Association(527)
National Slag Association(540)
North American Insulation Manufacturers Association(557)
Salt Institute(605)
Sulphur Institute, The(655)
World Gold Council(696)

MINING INDUSTRY

American Institute of Mining, Metallurgical, and Petroleum Engineers(96)
American Society of Mining and Reclamation(141)
Asbestos Information Association/North America(162)
Association of Bituminous Contractors(187)
China Clay Producers Association(244)
Mine Safety Institute of America(419)
Mineral Economics and Management Society(419)
Mining and Metallurgical Society of America(420)
National Association of State Land Reclamationists(475)
National Mining Association(527)
National Ready Mixed Concrete Association(535)
National Stone, Sand and Gravel Association(543)
Perlite Institute(573)
Silver Institute(611)
Society for Mining, Metallurgy, and Exploration(622)
Society of Economic Geologists(635)
Society of Exploration Geophysicists(636)
Society of Mineral Analysts(640)
Solution Mining Research Institute(647)
Sorptive Minerals Institute(647)
United Mine Workers of America International Union(672)
Women in Mining National(692)
World Gold Council(696)

MINORITIES see also BLACKS

American Association of Blacks in Energy(38)
American Association of Minority Businesses(45)
Asian American Certified Public Accountants(162)
Asian American Journalists Association(162)
Black Coaches Association(230)
Chinese American Medical Society(245)
Community Action Partnership(255)
Conference of Minority Transportation Officials(259)
Consortium for Graduate Study and Management(262)
Hispanic Association of Colleges and Universities(325)
Hispanic Elected Local Officials(326)
Hispanic National Bar Association(326)
Indian Educators Federation(336)
Latin Business Association(405)
Mexican-American Grocers Association(418)
National Alliance for Hispanic Health(429)
National Association for Bilingual Education(431)
National Association for Ethnic Studies(433)
National Association of Black Journalists(440)
National Association of Black Professors(440)
National Association of Blacks In Government(440)
National Association of Hispanic Federal Executives(455)
National Association of Investment Companies(459)
National Association of Latino Elected and Appointed Officials(459)
National Association of Medical Minority Educators(461)
National Association of Minority Automobile Dealers(462)
National Association of Minority Contractors(462)
National Association of Minority Engineering Program Administrators(462)
National Association of Minority Media Executives(462)
National Association of Securities Professionals(471)
National Federation of Hispanic Owned Newspapers(509)
National Forum for Black Public Administrators(512)
National Hispanic Medical Association(517)
National Indian Education Association(519)
National Minority Supplier Development Council(527)
National Optometric Association(529)
National Society of Hispanic MBAs(541)
Organization of Black Airline Pilots(567)
Society of Mexican American Engineers and Scientists(640)
United States Hispanic Chamber of Commerce(675)
Women in Management(692)

MOTOR VEHICLES see also AUTOMOBILES

AERA - Engine Rebuilders Association(9)
Alliance for the Polyurethane Industry(16)
Alliance of Automobile Manufacturers(16)
American Association of Motor Vehicle Administrators(45)
American Automotive Leasing Association(55)
American Bus Association(60)
American Highway Users Alliance(90)
American International Automobile Dealers Association(98)
American Society of Body Engineers(135)
American Truck Dealers(152)
American Trucking Associations(152)
Association for Commuter Transportation(169)
Association for the Advancement of Automotive Medicine(179)
Association of Equipment Management Professionals(195)
Association of International Automobile Manufacturers(201)
Automatic Transmission Rebuilders Association(223)
Automotive Aftermarket Industry Association(223)
Automotive Body Parts Association(223)
Automotive Fleet and Leasing Association(223)
Automotive Industry Action Group(223)
Automotive Lift Institute, Inc.(223)
Automotive Maintenance Repair Association(223)
Automotive Market Research Council(223)
Automotive Occupant Restraints Council(224)
Automotive Parts Remanufactuers Association(224)
Automotive Public Relations Council(224)
Automotive Recyclers Association(224)
Automotive Service Association(224)
Automotive Trade Association Executives(224)
Bearing Specialist Association(226)
Brake Manufacturers Council(232)
Buses International Association(235)
Car Care Council(237)
Commercial Vehicle Safety Alliance(254)
Coordinating Research Council(265)
Equipment and Tool Institute(297)
Filter Manufacturers Council(305)
Friction Materials Standards Institute(312)
Heavy Duty Representatives Association(325)
Independent Armored Car Operators Association(333)
Independent Automotive Damage Appraisers Association(333)
Intelligent Transportation Society of America(345)
Inter-Industry Conference on Auto Collision Repair(346)
Intermodal Association of North America(347)
International Motor Press Association(380)
International Union, United Automobile, Aerospace and Agricultural Implement Workers of America(396)
Manufactured Housing Institute(411)
Manufacturers of Emission Controls Association(411)
MEMA Information Services Council(416)
Mobile Air Conditioning Society Worldwide(420)
Motor and Equipment Manufacturers Association(421)
Motorcycle Industry Council(421)
Motorcycle Safety Foundation(422)
National Association for Stock Car Auto Racing(436)
National Association of Fleet Administrators(453)
National Auto Auction Association(482)
National Automobile Dealers Association(482)
National Automotive Radiator Service Association(483)
National Conference of State Fleet Administrators(494)
National Independent Automobile Dealers Association(518)
National Mobility Equipment Dealers Association(527)
National Tractor Parts Dealer Association(546)
National Truck Equipment Association(547)
National Truck Leasing System(547)
National Wheel and Rim Association(549)
North American Council of Automotive Teachers(556)
North American Professional Driver Education Association(559)
Overseas Automotive Council(570)
Power-Motion Technology Representatives Association(582)
Production Engine Remanufacturers Association(585)

Recreation Vehicle Dealers Association of North America(596)
Recreational Vehicle Aftermarket Association(596)
SAE International(604)
Society of Automotive Analysts(632)
Society of Collision Repair Specialists(633)
Specialty Equipment Market Association(650)
Taxicab, Limousine and Paratransit Association(657)
Tire Industry Association(662)
Tire Retread Information Bureau(662)
Towing and Recovery Association of America(662)
Transportation Safety Equipment Institute(664)
Truck-frame and Axle Repair Association(666)
Tune-up Manufacturers Council(667)
United Motorcoach Association(672)
Used Truck Association(681)

MOTORCYCLES

American Motorcyclist Association(107)
Motorcycle Industry Council(421)
Motorcycle Safety Foundation(422)

MUSEUMS

American Association of Museums(45)
Association for Living History, Farm and Agricultural Museums(176)
Association of African American Museums(183)
Association of Art Museum Directors(186)
Association of Children's Museums(189)
Association of College and University Museums and Galleries(191)
Association of Railway Museums(211)
Association of Science Museum Directors(213)
Association of Science-Technology Centers(213)
Council of American Jewish Museums(270)
Council of American Maritime Museums(270)
International Museum Theater Alliance(380)
International Sports Heritage Association(393)
Museum Computer Network(423)
Museum Education Roundtable(423)
Museum Store Association(423)
Museum Trustee Association(423)
Natural Science Collections Alliance(551)
Visitor Studies Association(684)

MUSHROOMS

American Mushroom Institute(107)
North American Mycological Association(558)

MUSIC see also BANDS

Academy of Country Music(3)
Accordion Federation of North America(6)
Accordionists and Teachers Guild International(6)
American Accordionists Association(29)
American Bandmasters Association(55)
American Choral Directors Association(62)
American College of Musicians(67)
American Composers Alliance(72)
American Federation of Musicians of the United States and Canada(82)
American Federation of Violin and Bow Makers(83)
American Guild of Music(88)
American Guild of Musical Artists(88)
American Guild of Organists(88)
American Harp Society(89)
American Hungarian Educators Association(92)
American Music Conference(107)
American Music Therapy Association(107)
American Musicians Union(107)
American Musicological Society(107)
American School Band Directors' Association(124)
American Society of Music Arrangers and Composers(142)
American String Teachers Association(149)
American Symphony Orchestra League(150)
American Viola Society(153)
Amusement and Music Operators Association(156)
Associated Pipe Organ Builders of America(166)
Association for Technology in Music Instruction(178)
Association of Concert Bands(192)
Cantors Assembly(237)
Chamber Music America(242)
Choristers Guild(245)
Chorus America(245)
Church Music Publishers Association(246)
College Band Directors National Association(251)
College Music Society(251)
Conductors Guild(259)
Country Music Association(277)
Country Radio Broadcasters, Inc.(277)
Delta Omicron(282)
Fellowship of United Methodists in Music and Worship Arts(305)
Gospel Music Association(318)
Guild of American Luthiers(321)
Guitar and Accessories Marketing Association(321)
Intercollegiate Men's Choruses, an International Association of Male Choruses(346)
International Association for Jazz Education(351)
International Association of Electronic Keyboard Manufacturers(356)
International Association of Music Libraries, United States Branch(359)
International Bluegrass Music Association(362)
International Business Music Association(364)
International Clarinet Association(365)
International Computer Music Association(366)
International Conference of Symphony and Opera Musicians(367)
International Double Reed Society(369)
International Federation for Choral Music(371)
International Guild of Symphony, Opera and Ballet Musicians(374)
International Horn Society(375)
International Society for the Performing Arts(389)
International Society of Bassists(390)
International Tuba-Euphonium Association(395)
MENC: The National Association for Music Education(417)
Mu Phi Epsilon(422)
Music and Entertainment Industry Educators Association(423)
Music Critics Association of North America(423)
Music Distributors Association(423)
Music Library Association(423)
Music Publishers' Association of the United States(423)
Music Teachers National Association(423)
NABIM - the International Band and Orchestral Products Association(424)
NAMM - the International Music Products Association(425)
National Association of College Wind and Percussion Instructors(444)
National Association of Pastoral Musicians(464)
National Association of Professional Band Instrument Repair Technicians(465)
National Association of School Music Dealers(470)
National Association of Schools of Music(470)
National Ballroom and Entertainment Association(483)
National Band Association(483)
National Catholic Band Association(487)
National Federation of Music Clubs(509)
National Flute Association(511)
National Guild of Piano Teachers(515)
National Music Council(528)
National Music Publishers' Association(528)
National Opera Association(529)
NFHS Music Association(553)
North American Folk Music and Dance Alliance(557)
North American Saxophone Alliance(560)
Organization of American Kodaly Educators(567)
Percussion Marketing Council(573)
Percussive Arts Society(573)
Phi Mu Alpha Sinfonia(576)
Piano Manufacturers Association International(577)
Piano Technicians Guild(577)
Retail Print Music Dealers Association(601)
Society for Asian Music(614)
Society for Ethnomusicology(617)
Society of Composers(634)
Society of Composers and Lyricists(634)
Society of Professional Audio Recording Services(642)
Songwriters Guild of America(647)
Viola da Gamba Society of America(683)
Violin Society of America(683)
Western Music Association(687)
Women Band Directors International(690)
Women's Classical Caucus(693)

NATURALISTS

American Association of Wildlife Veterinarians(54)
American Society of Naturalists(142)
Association of Natural Resource Enforcement Trainers(205)
Conservation and Preservation Charities of America(261)
Guild of Natural Science Illustrators(321)
National Association for Interpretation(434)

NECKWEAR

Neckwear Association of America(551)

NEUROLOGY

Academy of Aphasia(2)
American Academy for Cerebral Palsy and Developmental Medicine(19)
American Academy of Neurological and Orthopaedic Surgeons(24)
American Academy of Neurology(25)
American Association of Neurological Surgeons(46)
American Association of Neuromuscular & Electrodiagnostic Medicine(46)
American Association of Neuropathologists(46)
American Association of Neuroscience Nurses(46)
American Clinical Neurophysiology Society(63)
American College of Neuropsychopharmacology(68)
American Epilepsy Society(81)
American Headache Society(89)
American Neurological Association(108)
American Society for Experimental NeuroTherapeutics(129)
American Society for Neurochemistry(130)
American Society for Pediatric Neurosurgery(131)
American Society for Stereotactic and Functional Neurosurgery(132)
American Society of Electroneurodiagnostic Technologists(137)
American Society of Neuroimaging(142)
American Society of Neuroradiology(142)
American Society of Neurorehabilitation(142)
Association for Research in Nervous and Mental Disease(177)
Child Neurology Society(244)
Congress of Neurological Surgeons(261)
EEG and Clinical Neuroscience Society(290)
International Neural Network Society(381)
National Multiple Sclerosis Society(528)
National Tay-Sachs and Allied Diseases Association(545)
Neurosurgical Society of America(552)
North American Neuro-Ophthalmology Society(559)
Society for Neuroscience(622)
Society of Neurological Surgeons(640)
Society of Neurosurgical Anesthesia and Critical Care(641)

NEWSPAPERS

Alliance of Area Business Publications(16)
American Association of Sunday and Feature Editors(52)
American Court and Commercial Newspapers(77)
American Jewish Press Association(99)
American Society of Newspaper Editors(142)
Associated Press Managing Editors(166)
Association of Alternative Newsweeklies(184)
Association of Food Journalists(197)
Audit Bureau of Circulations(222)
Foreign Press Association(310)
Independent Free Papers of America(334)
Inter American Press Association(345)
International Digital Enterprise Alliance(369)
International Newspaper Financial Executives(381)
International Newspaper Group(381)
International Newspaper Marketing Association(381)
International Society of Weekly Newspaper Editors(392)
Investigative Reporters and Editors(398)
National Association of Hispanic Publications(456)
National Association of Minority Media Executives(462)
National Conference of Editorial Writers(493)
National Federation of Hispanic Owned Newspapers(509)
National Newspaper Association(528)
National Newspaper Publishers Association(529)
National Society of Newspaper Columnists(542)
Newspaper Association Managers(552)
Newspaper Association of America(552)
Newspaper Guild - CWA(552)
Newspaper Purchasing Management Association(553)
Organization of News Ombudsmen(567)
Red Tag News Publications Association(597)
Society for News Design(622)
Suburban Newspapers of America(655)
Wire Service Guild(690)

NONPROFIT

Alliance for Nonprofit Management(15)
Alliance of Nonprofit Mailers(17)
International Housewares Representatives Association(375)
International Society for Third-Sector Research(389)
National Council of Nonprofit Associations(500)
Not-for-Profit Services Association(562)

NOTIONS

Craft & Hobby Association(278)
Gift Association of America(317)
Home Sewing Association(327)
Society of Creative Designers(634)
Souvenirs, Gifts and Novelties Trade Association(648)

NUCLEAR ENERGY

American Association of Physicists in Medicine(48)
American College of Nuclear Medicine(68)
American Nuclear Insurers(109)
American Nuclear Society(109)
Council on the Safe Transportation of Hazardous Articles(277)
Health Physics Society(323)
Institute of Nuclear Materials Management(343)
Institute of Nuclear Power Operations(343)
International Association for Hydrogen Energy(350)
National Council on Radiation Protection and Measurements(502)
National Lead Burning Association(523)
Nuclear Energy Institute(563)
Nuclear Information and Records Management Association(563)
Nuclear Suppliers Association(563)
Professional Reactor Operator Society(589)
Radiation Research Society(594)
Society of Nuclear Medicine(641)
Universities Research Association(679)

NUMISMATICS

American Numismatic Society(109)
Industry Council for Tangible Assets(337)
Professional Currency Dealers Association(587)
Professional Numismatists Guild(588)

NURSERIES

All-America Rose Selections(15)
American Nursery and Landscape Association(109)
Horticultural Research Institute(328)
National Association of Plant Patent Owners(465)
Nursery and Landscape Association Executives of North America(563)

NURSING

Academy of Medical-Surgical Nurses(4)
AFT Healthcare(11)
Air & Surface Transport Nurses Association(12)
Alpha Tau Delta(18)
American Academy of Ambulatory Care Nursing(20)
American Academy of Nurse Practitioners(25)
American Academy of Nursing(25)
American Assembly for Men in Nursing(33)
American Association for the History of Nursing(37)
American Association of Colleges of Nursing(40)
American Association of Critical-Care Nurses(41)
American Association of Diabetes Educators(42)
American Association of Legal Nurse Consultants(44)
American Association of Managed Care Nurses(44)
American Association of Neuroscience Nurses(46)
American Association of Nurse Anesthetists(46)
American Association of Nurse Attorneys, The(46)
American Association of Occupational Health Nurses(47)
American Association of Spinal Cord Injury Nurses(51)
American Board of Nursing Specialties(57)
American College of Health Care Administrators(66)
American College of Nurse Practitioners(68)
American College of Nurse-Midwives(68)
American Holistic Nurses Association(91)
American Licensed Practical Nurses Association(101)
American Nephrology Nurses Association(108)
American Nurses Association(109)
American Organization of Nurse Executives(110)
American Psychiatric Nurses Association(118)
American Radiological Nurses Association(121)
American School Health Association(124)
American Society of Ophthalmic Registered Nurses(143)
American Society of Pain Management Nurses(143)
American Society of PeriAnesthesia Nurses(144)
American Society of Plastic Surgical Nurses(144)
American Society of Podiatric Medical Assistants(144)
AORN(158)
Association of Black Nursing Faculty in Higher Education(187)
Association of Camp Nurses(188)
Association of Community Health Nursing Educators(192)
Association of Nurses in AIDS Care(206)
Association of Pediatric Hematology/Oncology Nurses(207)
Association of Rehabilitation Nurses(211)
Association of State and Territorial Directors of Nursing(215)
Association of Women's Health, Obstetric and Neonatal Nurses(220)
Chi Eta Phi Sorority(244)
Consortium of Behavioral Health Nurses and Associates(262)
Dermatology Nurses' Association(283)
Developmental Disabilities Nurses Association(284)
Emergency Nurses Association(293)
Home Healthcare Nurses Association(327)
Hospice and Palliative Nurses Association(328)
Infusion Nurses Society(338)
International Association of Forensic Nurses(357)
International Federation of Nurse Anesthetists(371)
International Nurses Society on Addictions(381)
International Society of Psychiatric Consultation Liaison Nurses(392)
International Society of Psychiatric-Mental Health Nurses(392)
International Transplant Nurses Society(394)
NANDA International(425)
National Alliance of Nurse Practitioners(429)
National Association for Health Care Recruitment(433)
National Association for Home Care(434)
National Association for Practical Nurse Education and Service(435)
National Association of Clinical Nurse Specialists(443)
National Association of Directors of Nursing Administration in Long Term Care(449)
National Association of Hispanic Nurses(456)
National Association of Neonatal Nurses(462)
National Association of Nurse Massage Therapists(463)
National Association of Nurse Practitioners in Women's Health(463)
National Association of Orthopaedic Nurses(463)
National Association of Pediatric Nurse Practitioners(464)
National Association of Physician Nurses(464)
National Association of School Nurses(470)
National Black Nurses Association(484)
National Council of State Boards of Nursing(500)
National Federation of Licensed Practical Nurses(509)
National Gerontological Nursing Association(513)
National League for Nursing(523)
National Nursing Staff Development Organization(529)
National Organization for Associate Degree Nursing(529)
National Organization of Nurse Practitioner Faculties(530)
National Perinatal Association(532)
National Rural Health Association(537)
National Student Nurses Association(544)
Nurse Healers - Professional Associates International(563)
Nurses Organization of Veterans Affairs(563)
Oncology Nursing Society(564)
Preventive Cardiovascular Nurses Association(583)
Respiratory Nursing Society(600)
Society for Vascular Nursing(629)
Society of Gastroenterology Nurses and Associates(637)
Society of Otorhinolaryngology and Head/Neck Nurses(641)
Society of Pediatric Nurses(641)
Society of Trauma Nurses(645)

Society of Urologic Nurses and Associates(645)
United American Nurses, AFL-CIO(670)
Visiting Nurse Associations of America(684)
Wound, Ostomy and Continence Nurses Society(697)

NUTRITION
American Academy of Nutrition(25)
American Academy of Pediatrics(27)
American Association of Nutritional Consultants(46)
American College of Nutrition(68)
American College of Veterinary Nutrition(71)
American Council on Science and Health(76)
American Dietetic Association(79)
American Society for Nutrition(131)
American Society for Parenteral and Enteral Nutrition(131)
American Society of Animal Science(134)
Association of State and Territorial Public Health Nutrition Directors(215)
Consultant Dietitians in Health Care Facilities(263)
Council for Responsible Nutrition(270)
Institute of Food Technologists(341)
International and American Associations of Clinical Nutritionists(349)
International Formula Council(373)
National Association of Nutrition and Aging Services Programs(463)
National Nutritional Foods Association(529)
Society for Nutrition Education(622)

NUTS
American Peanut Council(113)
American Peanut Research and Education Society(113)
American Peanut Shellers Association(113)
National Pecan Shellers Association(532)
Northern Nut Growers Association(562)
Peanut and Tree Nut Processors Association(572)
Walnut Council(685)

OBSTETRICS
American Academy of Thermology(29)
American Association of Birth Centers(38)
American College of Obstetricians and Gynecologists(68)
American College of Osteopathic Obstetricians and Gynecologists(69)
Association for Birth Psychology(168)
Association of Maternal and Child Health Programs(204)
Association of Professors of Gynecology and Obstetrics(209)
Association of Women's Health, Obstetric and Neonatal Nurses(220)
Lamaze International(404)
Midwives Alliance of North America(419)
National Family Planning and Reproductive Health Association(508)
National Perinatal Association(532)
Society for Obstetric Anesthesia and Perinatology(622)

OCEANOGRAPHY
American Meteorological Society(105)
American Society of Limnology and Oceanography(140)
Diving Equipment and Marketing Association(286)
Estuarine Research Federation(297)
Institute of Diving(341)
Marine Technology Society(412)
Maritime Law Association of the U.S.(412)
National Association of Marine Surveyors(461)
National Marine Educators Association(526)
National Ocean Industries Association(529)
North American Society for Oceanic History(560)
Oceanography Society(564)
World Aquaculture Society(695)

OFFICE EQUIPMENT
Association for Federal Information Resources Management(173)
Business and Institutional Furniture Manufacturers Association International(235)
Business Products Credit Association(235)
Business Technology Association(236)
Copier Dealers Association(266)
Independent Office Products and Furniture Dealers Association(335)
Information Technology Industry Council(338)
ISDA - The Office Systems Cooperative(400)
Modular Building Institute(420)
National Association of State Catholic Conference Directors(474)
Office Furniture Distribution Association(564)
Retail Solutions Providers Association(601)
WorkPlace Furnishings(695)

OILS
American Oilseed Coalition(110)
Drilling Engineering Association(287)
Fragrance Materials Association of the United States(311)
Gasification Technologies Council(314)
North American Olive Oil Association(559)

OPHTHALMOLOGY
American Academy of Ophthalmology(25)
American Association for Pediatric Ophthalmology and Strabismus(36)
American Association of Certified Orthoptists(39)
American College of Eye Surgeons(65)
American College of Veterinary Ophthalmologists(71)
American Ophthalmological Society(110)
American Osteopathic Colleges of Ophthalmology and Otolaryngology - Head and Neck Surgery(112)
American Society of Contemporary Ophthalmology(136)
American Society of Ophthalmic Plastic and Reconstructive Surgery(143)
American Society of Ophthalmic Registered Nurses(143)
American Society of Veterinary Ophthalmology(147)
Association for Research in Vision and Ophthalmology(178)
Association of Technical Personnel in Ophthalmology(217)
Association of University Professors of Ophthalmology(219)
Contact Lens Association of Ophthalmologists(264)
Eye Bank Association of America(300)
International Association of Ocular Surgeons(359)
International Perimetric Society(382)
International Society of Refractive Surgery of the American Academy of Ophthalmology(392)
North American Neuro-Ophthalmology Society(559)
Ophthalmic Photographers' Society(565)
Outpatient Ophthalmic Surgery Society(569)
Society of Eye Surgeons(636)

OPTICAL
American Society for Precision Engineering(132)
American Society of Cataract and Refractive Surgery(135)
American Society of Ocularists(143)
American Society of Retina Specialists(145)
Association of United States Night Vision Manufacturers(219)
Contact Lens Council(264)
Contact Lens Manufacturers Association(264)
Contact Lens Society of America(264)
Inter-Society Color Council(346)
National Academy of Opticianry(427)
National Association of Vision Professionals(480)
Optical Imaging Association(565)
Optical Laboratories Association(566)
Optical Society of America(566)
Opticians Association of America(566)
SPIE - The International Society for Optical Engineering(651)
Vision Council of America(684)

OPTOMETRY
American Academy of Optometry(25)
American Optometric Association(110)
American Optometric Student Association(110)
American Society of Retina Specialists(145)
Armed Forces Optometric Society(161)
Association of Regulatory Boards of Optometry(211)
Association of Schools and Colleges of Optometry(213)
Association of Vision Science Librarians(220)
College of Optometrists in Vision Development(252)
Contact Lens Manufacturers Association(264)
Contact Lens Society of America(264)
National Association of Optometrists and Opticians(463)
National Contact Lens Examiners(495)
National Optometric Association(529)
Society for Excellence in Eyecare(617)

ORGANS
American Guild of Organists(88)
American Institute of Organbuilders(97)
Associated Pipe Organ Builders of America(166)
International Association of Electronic Keyboard Manufacturers(356)

ORIENTAL
American Schools of Oriental Research(124)
Association for Asian Studies(167)
Oriental Rug Importers Association of America(568)
Society of Asian and Comparative Philosophy(632)

ORTHODONTICS
American Academy of Gnathologic Orthopedics(23)
American Academy of Orthotists and Prosthetists(26)
American Association of Orthodontists(47)
American Society for the Study of Orthodontics(132)
International Association for Orthodontics(351)

ORTHOPEDICS
Academy of Osseointegration(5)
American Academy of Gnathologic Orthopedics(23)
American Academy of Neurological and Orthopaedic Surgeons(24)
American Academy of Orthopaedic Surgeons(26)
American Association of Orthopaedic Medicine(47)
American Board of Podiatric Orthopedics and Primary Podiatric Medicine(57)
American College of Foot and Ankle Orthopedics and Medicine(65)
American College of Foot and Ankle Surgeons(66)
American Orthopaedic Association(110)
American Orthopaedic Foot and Ankle Society(111)
American Orthopaedic Society for Sports Medicine(111)
American Osteopathic Academy of Orthopedics(111)
American Society for Surgery of the Hand(132)
American Spinal Injury Association(148)
Arthroscopy Association of North America(162)
Association of Bone and Joint Surgeons(188)
Association of Children's Prosthetic-Orthotic Clinics(189)
Clinical Orthopaedic Society(248)

Conservative Orthopaedics International Association(261)
International Society of Arthroscopy, Knee Surgery and Orthopaedic Sports Medicine(390)
National Association of Orthopaedic Nurses(463)
National Association of Orthopaedic Technologists(463)
National Student Osteopathic Medical Association(544)
Orthopaedic Research Society(568)
Orthopaedic Section - American Physical Therapy Association(568)
Orthopaedic Trauma Association(569)
Orthopedic Surgical Manufacturers Association(569)
Pediatric Orthopedic Society of North America(572)
Pedorthic Footwear Association(572)
Ruth Jackson Orthopaedic Society(603)
Society of Military Orthopaedic Surgeons(640)

OSTEOPATHY
American Academy of Osteopathy(26)
American Association of Colleges of Osteopathic Medicine(40)
American College of Neuropsychiatrists(68)
American College of Osteopathic Emergency Physicians(69)
American College of Osteopathic Family Physicians(69)
American College of Osteopathic Internists(69)
American College of Osteopathic Obstetricians and Gynecologists(69)
American College of Osteopathic Pain Management and Sclerotherapy(69)
American College of Osteopathic Pediatricians(69)
American College of Osteopathic Surgeons(69)
American Osteopathic Academy for Sports Medicine(111)
American Osteopathic Academy of Orthopedics(111)
American Osteopathic Association(111)
American Osteopathic Board of Physical Medicine and Rehabilitation(111)
American Osteopathic College of Allergy and Immunology(111)
American Osteopathic College of Anesthesiologists(111)
American Osteopathic College of Dermatology(112)
American Osteopathic College of Occupational and Preventive Medicine(112)
American Osteopathic College of Pathologists(112)
American Osteopathic College of Proctology(112)
American Osteopathic College of Radiology(112)
American Osteopathic College of Rheumatology(112)
American Osteopathic Colleges of Ophthalmology and Otolaryngology - Head and Neck Surgery(112)
Association of Osteopathic State Executive Directors(206)
Cranial Academy(278)
National Association of Osteopathic Foundations(463)
Osteoarthritis Research Society International(569)

OXYGEN
International Oxygen Manufacturers Association(382)
International Ozone Association-Pan American Group Branch(382)
Society for Free Radical Biology and Medicine(617)

PACKAGING
Alliance of Foam Packaging Recyclers(16)
Aluminum Foil Container Manufacturers Association(18)
American Family Therapy Academy(81)
American Flock Association(84)
Aseptic Packaging Council(162)
Composite Can and Tube Institute(256)
Contract Packaging Association(264)
Express Carriers Association(300)
Fibre Box Association(305)
Flexible Packaging Association(307)
Foodservice and Packaging Institute(309)
Glass Packaging Institute(317)
Healthcare Compliance Packaging Council(323)
Institute of Packaging Professionals(343)
International Beverage Packaging Association(362)
International Corrugated Packaging Foundation(367)
International Safe Transit Association(385)
Label Packaging Suppliers Council(404)
Meat Industry Suppliers Alliance(415)
National Institute of Packaging, Handling and Logistics Engineers(521)
National Paperbox Association(531)
Packaging Machinery Manufacturers Institute(570)
Paper Shipping Sack Manufacturers Association(571)
Paperboard Packaging Council(571)
Polystyrene Packaging Council(580)
Produce Marketing Association(584)
Recycled Paperboard Technical Association(597)
Research and Development Associates for Military Food and Packaging Systems(599)
Retail Packaging Manufacturers Association(601)
Reusable Industrial Packaging Association(601)
Tube Council of North America(666)
Wirebound Box Manufacturers Association(690)
Women in Packaging(692)

PAINT AND PAINTING
American Academy of Equine Art(22)
Chemical Coaters Association International(243)
Federation of Socs. for Coatings Technology(304)
Finishing Contractors Association(306)
Independent Professional Painting Contractors Association of America(335)
International Cadmium Association(364)
International Union of Painters and Allied Trades(396)
National Paint and Coatings Association(531)
Paint and Decorating Retailers Association(570)
Painting and Decorating Contractors of America(570)
Powder Coating Institute(582)
SSPC: the Society for Protective Coatings(652)

PALEONTOLOGY
Paleontological Research Institution(570)
SEPM - Society for Sedimentary Geology(609)
Society of Vertebrate Paleontology(646)

PAPER INDUSTRY see also PULP
American Forest and Paper Association(85)
American Society of Papyrologists(143)
Association of Independent Corrugated Converters(200)
Association of Suppliers to the Paper Industry(216)
Book Industry Study Group, Inc.(231)
Foodservice and Packaging Institute(309)
Forest Resources Association(310)
INDA, Association of the Nonwoven Fabrics Industry(333)
Institute of Paper Science and Technology(343)
International Corrugated Packaging Foundation(367)
Manufacturers Representatives of America(411)
National Council for Air and Stream Improvement(497)
National Paperbox Association(531)
NPTA Alliance(563)
Paper and Plastic Representatives Management Council(571)
Paper Distribution Council(571)
Paper Industry Management Association(571)
Paper Machine Clothing Council(571)
Paper Shipping Sack Manufacturers Association(571)
Paperboard Packaging Council(571)
Pulp and Paper Safety Association(593)
Sales Association of the Paper Industry(604)
Sanitary Supply Wholesaling Association(605)
Society of Scribes(644)
Technical Association of the Pulp and Paper Industry(658)
Wallcoverings Association(685)

PARASITOLOGY
American Association of Veterinary Parasitologists(54)
American Society of Parasitologists(143)
Society of Nematologists(640)
Society of Protozoologists(643)

PARKING
International Parking Institute(382)
National Parking Association(531)

PARKS
American Land Rights Association(100)
American Public Gardens Association(119)
Association of Partners for Public Lands(207)
International Association of Amusement Parks and Attractions(352)
International Ecotourism Society(370)
National Association of Industrial and Office Properties(458)
National Association of State Park Directors(476)
National Institute on Park and Grounds Management(521)
National Park Hospitality Association(531)
National Parks Conservation Association(532)
National Recreation and Parks Association(535)
Recreational Park Trailer Industry Association(596)
Society of Municipal Arborists(640)
Visitor Studies Association(684)
World Waterpark Association(696)

PATENTS
American Intellectual Property Law Association(98)
Association of University Technology Managers(219)
Intellectual Property Owners Association(345)
International Intellectual Property Alliance(377)
Licensing Executives Society(407)
National Association of Plant Patent Owners(465)
Patent and Trademark Office Society(572)
Patent Office Professional Association(572)

PATHOLOGY
American Association of Avian Pathologists(38)
American Association of Pathologists' Assistants(47)
American College of Veterinary Pathologists(72)
American Pathology Foundation(113)
American Society for Investigative Pathology(130)
Association for Molecular Pathology(176)
Association of Pathology Chairs(207)
College of American Pathologists(251)
Intersociety Council For Pathology Information(398)
National Society for Histotechnology(541)
Society for Invertebrate Pathology(620)
Society of Toxicologic Pathologists(645)
United States and Canadian Academy of Pathology(672)

PATTERNS
Home Sewing Association(327)

PEDIATRICS

Academy of Breastfeeding Medicine(2)
Ambulatory Pediatric Association(19)
American Academy of Pediatrics(27)
American Association for Pediatric Ophthalmology and Strabismus(36)
American College of Osteopathic Pediatricians(69)
American Pediatric Society(113)
American Pediatric Surgical Association(113)
American Society for Pediatric Neurosurgery(131)
American Society of Pediatric Hematology/Oncology(143)
American Society of Pediatric Nephrology(143)
Association of Children's Prosthetic-Orthotic Clinics(189)
Association of Medical School Pediatric Department Chairs(204)
Association of Pediatric Hematology/Oncology Nurses(207)
Association of Pediatric Program Directors(207)
International Association of Infant Massage(358)
International Pediatric Nephrology Association(382)
International Pediatric Transplant Association(382)
National Association of Pediatric Nurse Practitioners(464)
North American Society for Pediatric Gastroenterology, Hepatology and Nutrition(561)
Pediatric Orthopedic Society of North America(572)
Society for Developmental and Behavioral Pediatrics(616)
Society for Pediatric Anesthesia(623)
Society for Pediatric Dermatology(623)
Society for Pediatric Psychology(623)
Society for Pediatric Radiology(623)
Society for Pediatric Research(623)
Society for Pediatric Urology(623)
Society of Pediatric Nurses(641)

PENCILS AND PENS

Writing Instrument Manufacturers Association(697)

PERSONNEL

ACPA - College Student Educators Association(7)
American Association for Employment in Education(34)
American Association of School Personnel Administrators(51)
American Counseling Association(76)
American Society for Healthcare Central Service Professionals(129)
American Society for Healthcare Human Resources Administration(129)
Cable and Telecommunications Human Resources Association(236)
Cement Employers Association(241)
College and University Professional Association for Human Resources(250)
Employee Assistance Professionals Association(293)
Employee Relocation Council/Worldwide ERC(293)
Human Resource Planning Society(329)
International Association for Human Resource Information Management(350)
International Association for Truancy and Dropout Prevention(352)
International Association of Corporate and Professional Recruitment(355)
International Association of Correctional Training Personnel(355)
International Association of Counseling Services(355)
International Association of Workforce Professionals(362)
International Public Management Association for Human Resources(384)
Jesuit Association of Student Personnel Administrators(401)
National Association for Health Care Recruitment(433)
National Association for Law Placement(434)
National Association of Church Personnel Administrators(443)
National Association of Educational Office Professionals(450)
National Association of Legal Search Consultants(460)
National Association of Personnel Services(464)
National Association of Professional Employer Organizations(466)
National Association of State Personnel Executives(476)
National Association of Student Personnel Administrators(478)
National Human Resources Association(518)
SHRM Global Forum(610)
Society for Human Resource Management(619)

PEST CONTROL

Aquatic Plant Management Society(159)
Association of American Pesticide Control Officials(185)
Association of Applied IPM Ecologists(186)
Chemical Producers and Distributors Association(243)
CropLife America(279)
National Animal Control Association(430)
National Pest Management Association(532)
United Product Formulators and Distributors Association(672)

PETROLEUM INDUSTRY

ADSC: The International Association of Foundation Drilling(8)
American Association of Petroleum Geologists(47)
American Association of Professional Landmen(49)
American Institute of Mining, Metallurgical, and Petroleum Engineers(96)
American Petroleum Institute(114)
Association of Diving Contractors International(194)
Association of Energy Service Companies(195)
Association of Oil Pipe Lines(206)
Coordinating Research Council(265)
Council of Petroleum Accountants Socs.(273)
Domestic Petroleum Council(286)
Drilling Engineering Association(287)
Energy Security Council(294)
Energy Telecommunications and Electrical Association(294)
Energy Traffic Association(294)
Fiberglass Tank and Pipe Institute(305)
Gas Machinery Research Council(314)
Independent Liquid Terminals Association(334)
Independent Lubricant Manufacturers Association(335)
Independent Petroleum Association of America(335)
Independent Terminal Operators Association(336)
International Association of Drilling Contractors(356)
International Association of Geophysical Contractors(357)
International Energy Credit Association(370)
International Oil Scouts Association(381)
International Slurry Surfacing Association(386)
International Union of Petroleum and Industrial Workers(396)
Interstate Natural Gas Association of America(398)
Interstate Oil and Gas Commission(398)
Liaison Committee of Cooperating Oil and Gas Associations(407)
National Association of Division Order Analysts(449)
National Association of Oil Heating Service Managers(463)
National Association of Royalty Owners(469)
National Drilling Association(505)
National Lubricating Grease Institute(525)
National Ocean Industries Association(529)
National Petrochemical & Refiners Association(532)
National Petroleum Council(532)
National Propane Gas Association(534)
Natural Gas Supply Association(550)
NORA: An Association of Responsible Recyclers(553)
Petroleum Equipment Institute(574)
Petroleum Equipment Suppliers Association(574)
Petroleum Investor Relations Association(574)
Petroleum Marketers Association of America(574)
Petroleum Technology Transfer Council(574)
Pipeline Research Council International(578)
Service Station Dealers of America and Allied Trades(609)
Society of Exploration Geophysicists(636)
Society of Independent Gasoline Marketers of America(638)
Society of Petroleum Engineers(641)
Society of Petroleum Evaluation Engineers(641)
Society of Petrophysicists and Well Log Analysts(641)
Solution Mining Research Institute(647)
Spill Control Association of America(651)
Tubular Exchanger Manufacturers Association(666)

PETS see also SPECIFIC ANIMAL

Accredited Pet Cemetery Society(7)
American Animal Hospital Association(31)
American Association of Feline Practitioners(43)
American Boarding Kennels Association(58)
American Pet Boarding Association(114)
American Pet Products Manufacturers Association(114)
Association of Pet Dog Trainers(207)
Independent Pet and Animal Transportation Association International(335)
International Association of Pet Cemeteries(360)
International Professional Groomers(383)
National Association for Biomedical Research(431)
National Association of Professional Pet Sitters(466)
National Dog Groomers Association of America(505)
National Taxidermists Association(545)
Pet Food Institute(574)
Pet Industry Distributors Association(574)
Pet Industry Joint Advisory Council(574)
Pet Sitters International(574)
World Wide Pet Industry Association(697)

PHARMACEUTICAL INDUSTRY see also DRUGS

Academy of Managed Care Pharmacy(4)
Accreditation Council for Pharmacy Education(6)
Alpha Zeta Omega(18)
American Association of Colleges of Pharmacy(40)
American Association of Pharmaceutical Scientists(48)
American Clinical Laboratory Association(63)
American Pharmacists Association(114)
American Society for Automation in Pharmacy(126)
Chain Drug Marketing Association(242)
Consumer Healthcare Products Association(263)
Controlled Release Society(265)
Generic Pharmaceutical Association(315)
Healthcare Compliance Packaging Council(323)
Healthcare Distribution Management Association(323)
Healthcare Marketing and Communications Council(324)
Inter-Society Color Council(346)

International Academy of Compounding Pharmacists(347)
International Federation of Pharmaceutical Wholesalers(371)
International Pharmaceutical Excipients Council of the Americas(382)
International Society for Pharmaceutical Engineering(388)
International Society for Pharmacoepidemiology(388)
Kappa Psi Pharmaceutical Fraternity(403)
National Association of Chain Drug Stores(442)
National Community Pharmacists Association(491)
National Council for Prescription Drug Programs(497)
National Council of State Pharmacy Association Executives(501)
National Pharmaceutical Council(533)
PDA - an International Association for Pharmaceutical Science and Technology(572)
Pharmaceutical Care Management Association(575)
Pharmaceutical Printed Literature Association(575)
Pharmaceutical Research and Manufacturers of America(575)
Regulatory Affairs Professionals Society(598)
Society for Biomolecular Sciences(614)
Society for Clinical Data Management(615)
Society of Pharmaceutical and Biotech Trainers(642)

PHARMACOLOGY

Academy of Student Pharmacists(5)
Accreditation Council for Pharmacy Education(6)
American Academy of Clinical Toxicology(21)
American Academy of Veterinary and Comparative Toxicology(29)
American Academy of Veterinary Pharmacology and Therapeutics(29)
American Association of Colleges of Pharmacy(40)
American College of Apothecaries(64)
American College of Clinical Pharmacology(64)
American College of Clinical Pharmacy(65)
American College of Neuropsychopharmacology(68)
American Institute of the History of Pharmacy(97)
American Society for Clinical Pharmacology and Therapeutics(127)
American Society for Pharmacology and Experimental Therapeutics(131)
American Society of Clinical Psychopharmacology(136)
American Society of Consultant Pharmacists(136)
American Society of Health-System Pharmacists(139)
American Society of Pharmacognosy(144)
Association of Clinical Research Professionals(190)
Biomedical Engineering Society(229)
Federation of American Socs. for Experimental Biology(303)
International Society for Pharmacoeconomics and Outcomes Research(388)
Lambda Kappa Sigma(405)
National Association of Boards of Pharmacy(440)
National Catholic Pharmacists Guild of the United States(488)
Society of Infectious Diseases Pharmacists(638)
United States Pharmacopeia(676)

PHILANTHROPY

Awards & Recognition Industry Educational Foundation(225)
Giving USA Foundation(317)
Independent Sector(336)
National Network of Grantmakers(528)
Philanthropy Roundtable(576)

PHILATELY

American Philatelic Society - Writers Unit #30(114)
American Stamp Dealers' Association(149)

PHILOLOGY

American Philological Association(114)
American Society of Papyrologists(143)

PHILOSOPHY

American Association of Philosophy Teachers(48)
American Catholic Philosophical Association(61)
American Philosophical Association(114)
American Philosophical Society(114)
American Society for Political and Legal Philosophy(131)
Association for Informal Logic and Critical Thinking(174)
Association for Philosophy of the Unconscious(176)
Association for Practical and Professional Ethics(177)
Association for Symbolic Logic(178)
Association of Muslim Social Scientists(205)
Association of Philosophy Journal Editors(207)
Conference of Philosophical Socs.(260)
Federation of State Humanities Councils(304)
International Association for Philosophy and Literature(351)
International Association for Philosophy of Law and Social Philosophy - American Section(351)
Jean Piaget Society(400)
Metaphysical Society of America(418)
North American Society for Social Philosophy(561)
Philosophy of Education Society(576)
Philosophy of Science Association(576)
Semiotic Society of America(608)
Society for Ancient Greek Philosophy(613)
Society for Business Ethics(614)
Society for Medieval and Renaissance Philosophy(621)
Society for Natural Philosophy(622)
Society for New Language Study(622)
Society for Philosophy and Technology(623)
Society for Philosophy of Religion(623)
Society for the Advancement of American Philosophy(626)
Society for the Philosophy of Sex and Love(627)
Society for the Study of Symbolic Interaction(628)
Society of Asian and Comparative Philosophy(632)
Society of Christian Philosophers(633)
Society of Philosophers in America(642)

PHONOGRAPHS

American Society for Photogrammetry and Remote Sensing(131)
Amusement and Music Operators Association(156)
Music and Entertainment Industry Educators Association(423)
National Academy of Recording Arts and Sciences(427)
National Association of Recording Merchandisers(468)
Recording Industry Association of America(596)

PHOTOGRAPHY

Advertising Photographers of America(9)
American Society for Photobiology(131)
American Society of Media Photographers(141)
American Society of Photographers(144)
American Society of Picture Professionals(144)
Antique and Amusement Photographers International(157)
Association of Bridal Consultants(188)
Association of International Photography Art Dealers(202)
BioCommunications Association(229)
Council on Fine Art Photography(276)
Evidence Photographers International Council(299)
Independent Photo Imagers(335)
International Fire Photographers Association(372)
International Graphic Arts Education Association(374)
International Imaging Industry Association(376)
International Reprographic Association(385)
National Association of Photo Equipment Technicians(464)
National Press Photographers Association(534)
North American Nature Photography Association(558)
Photo Chemical Machining Institute(576)
Photo Marketing Association-International(576)
Photoimaging Manufacturers and Distributors Association(576)
Picture Agency Council of America(577)
PrintImage International(584)
Professional Photographers of America(588)
Professional Women Photographers(590)
Silver Users Association(611)
Society for Imaging Science & Technology(619)
Society for Photographic Education(623)
Society of Photographer and Artist Representatives(642)
SPIE - The International Society for Optical Engineering(651)
University Photographers Association of America(680)
Wedding and Portrait Photographers International(686)
White House News Photographers Association(688)

PHYSICAL EDUCATION

American Alliance for Health, Physical Education, Recreation and Dance(30)
Association for the Advancement of Applied Sport Psychology(179)
IDEA, The Health and Fitness Association(330)
International Physical Fitness Association(383)
National Association for Girls and Women in Sport(433)
National Association for Sport and Physical Education(436)
National Association of Collegiate Women Athletic Administrators(445)
Phi Epsilon Kappa(576)
Society of State Directors of Health, Physical Education and Recreation(644)

PHYSICS

Acoustical Society of America(7)
American Academy of Thermology(29)
American Association for Crystal Growth(34)
American Association of Physicists in Medicine(48)
American Association of Physics Teachers(48)
American Astronomical Society(54)
American College of Medical Physics(67)
American Crystallographic Association(77)
American Geophysical Union(87)
American Institute of Physics(97)
American Nuclear Society(109)
American Physical Society(115)
American Society for Laser Medicine and Surgery(130)
American Solar Energy Society(147)
ASM International(163)
AVS Science and Technology Society(225)
Biophysical Society(229)
Calorimetry Conference(237)
Coblentz Society(250)
Combustion Institute(253)
Cryogenic Engineering Conference(280)
Fusion Power Associates(313)
Health Physics Society(323)
International Association for Hydrogen Energy(350)
Microscopy Society of America(418)
National Society of Black Physicists(541)

Society for Applied Spectroscopy(614)
Society of Rheology(643)

PHYSIOLOGY
American Association for Aerosol Research(33)
American Clinical Neurophysiology Society(63)
American Physiological Society(115)
American Society of Plant Biologists(144)
EEG and Clinical Neuroscience Society(290)
Federation of American Socs. for Experimental Biology(303)
National Association for Medical Direction of Respiratory Care(434)
Optical Society of America(566)
Society of General Physiologists(637)

PHYTOPATHOLOGY
American Phytopathological Society(115)
Society of Nematologists(640)

PILOTS
Air Line Pilots Association, International(13)
Aircraft Owners and Pilots Association(14)
American Pilots' Association(115)
International Association of Natural Resource Pilots(359)
International Organization of Masters, Mates and Pilots(382)
Organization of Black Airline Pilots(567)
Society of Experimental Test Pilots(635)

PIPES
Air Distributing Institute(13)
American Concrete Pipe Association(73)
American Concrete Pressure Pipe Association(73)
American Pipe Fittings Association(115)
Asbestos Cement Product Producers Association(162)
Association of Oil Pipe Lines(206)
Cast Iron Soil Pipe Institute(238)
Coal Technology Association(249)
Directional Crossing Contractors Association(285)
Distribution Contractors Association(286)
Ductile Iron Pipe Research Association(287)
Expansion Joint Manufacturers Association(299)
Fiberglass Tank and Pipe Institute(305)
International Slurry Surfacing Association(386)
National Association of Pipe Coating Applicators(464)
National Association of Steel Pipe Distributors(477)
National Certified Pipe Welding Bureau(488)
National Clay Pipe Institute(490)
National Corrugated Steel Pipe Association(496)
Pipe Fabrication Institute(578)
Pipe Line Contractors Association(578)
Plastic Pipe and Fittings Association(578)
Plastics Pipe Institute(579)
Society of Piping Engineers and Designers(642)
Tube and Pipe Association, International(666)
Uni-Bell PVC Pipe Association(669)
United Association of Journeymen and Apprentices of the Plumbing and Pipe Fitting Industry of U.S. and Canada(670)

PLANNING
American College of Contingency Planners(65)
American Health Planning Association(89)
American Institute of Certified Planners(95)
American Planning Association(116)
Association of Collegiate Schools of Planning(191)
CoreNet Global(266)
Council of Educational Facility Planners, International(271)
DRI International(287)
Financial and Insurance Conference Planners(305)
Financial Planning Association(306)
International Association for Impact Assessment(350)
International Society of Meeting Planners(391)
International Society of Parametric Analysts(392)
Meeting Professionals International(416)
National Alliance of Preservation Commissions(430)
National Association of Development Organizations(449)
National Association of Environmental Professionals(451)
National Association of Housing and Redevelopment Officials(456)
National Association of Recreation Resource Planners(468)
National Association of Regional Councils(469)
National Association of State Development Agencies(474)
National Criminal Justice Association(503)
National Emergency Management Association(507)
Project Management Institute(590)
Society for College and University Planning(615)
Society of Competitive Intelligence Professionals(633)
Society of Government Meeting Professionals(637)
Urban Land Institute(680)

PLASTICS INDUSTRY
Academy of Dental Materials(3)
Adhesive and Sealant Council(8)
Alliance for the Polyurethane Industry(16)
Alliance of Foam Packaging Recyclers(16)
American Composites Manufacturers Association(72)
American Plastics Council(116)
American Society for Plasticulture(131)
Association of Rotational Molders, International(212)
Chemical Fabrics and Film Association(243)
Closure Manufacturers Association(248)
Film and Bag Federation(305)
Foil Stamping and Embossing Association(308)
Glove Shippers Association(318)
INDA, Association of the Nonwoven Fabrics Industry(333)
Independent Sealing Distributors(335)
International Association of Plastics Distributors(360)
International Card Manufacturers Association(364)
International Cast Polymer Association(364)
International Society for Plastination(388)
Manufacturers Representatives of America(411)
National Association for PET Container Resources(435)
Paper and Plastic Representatives Management Council(571)
Plastic Shipping Container Institute(578)
Plastic Soft Materials Manufacturers Association(578)
Plastics Pipe Institute(579)
Polyurethane Manufacturers Association(580)
Roof Coatings Manufacturers Association(603)
Rubber and Plastics Industry Conference of the United Steelworkers of America(603)
Society of Plastics Engineers(642)
Society of the Plastics Industry(645)
Vinyl Institute(683)
Vinyl Siding Institute(683)

PLUMBING
American Society of Plumbing Engineers(144)
American Society of Sanitary Engineering(146)
American Supply Association(150)
Associated Specialty Contractors(166)
Association of Industry Manufacturers' Representatives(201)
Cast Iron Soil Pipe Institute(238)
International Association of Plumbing and Mechanical Officials(360)
Manufacturers Standardization Society of the Valve and Fittings Industry(411)
Plastic Pipe and Fittings Association(578)
Plumbing and Drainage Institute(579)
Plumbing Contractors of America(579)
Plumbing Manufacturers Institute(579)
Plumbing-Heating-Cooling Contractors - National Association(579)
Porcelain Enamel Institute(580)
United Association of Journeymen and Apprentices of the Plumbing and Pipe Fitting Industry of U.S. and Canada(670)
Valve Manufacturers Association of America(682)

PLYWOOD
APA - The Engineered Wood Association(158)
Hardwood Plywood and Veneer Association(322)

PODIATRY
Academy of Ambulatory Foot and Ankle Surgery(2)
American Academy of Podiatric Practice Management(27)
American Academy of Podiatric Sports Medicine(27)
American Association for Women Podiatrists(37)
American Association of Colleges of Podiatric Medicine(40)
American Association of Hospital and Healthcare Podiatrists(43)
American Board of Podiatric Orthopedics and Primary Podiatric Medicine(57)
American College of Foot and Ankle Orthopedics and Medicine(65)
American College of Foot and Ankle Surgeons(66)
American College of Podiatric Radiologists(70)
American Podiatric Circulatory Society(116)
American Podiatric Medical Association(116)
American Podiatric Medical Students' Association(116)
American Podiatric Medical Writers Association(116)
American Society of Podiatric Medical Assistants(144)
American Society of Podiatric Medicine(145)
American Society of Podiatry Executives(145)
Federation of Podiatric Medical Boards(304)
National College of Foot Surgeons(490)

POETRY
National Association for Poetry Therapy(435)
Poetry Society of America(579)

POLICE
Airborne Law Enforcement Association(14)
American Academy of Forensic Sciences(23)
American Association of Motor Vehicle Administrators(45)
American Association of Police Polygraphists(49)
American Criminal Justice Association/Lambda Alpha Epsilon(77)
American Federation of Police and Concerned Citizens(82)
American Jail Association(99)
American Polygraph Association(116)
American Society of Criminology(137)
American Society of Forensic Odontology(138)
Association of Firearm and Toolmark Examiners(197)
Association of Former Agents of the U.S. Secret Service(197)
Association of Public-Safety Communications Officers- International(211)
Central Station Alarm Association(241)
Commission on Accreditation for Law Enforcement Agencies(254)
Evidence Photographers International Council(299)
Federal Bureau of Investigation Agents Association(302)
Federal Law Enforcement Officers Association(302)
High Technology Crime Investigation Association(325)
International Association for Identification(350)

Binding Industries Association(228)
Business Forms Management Association(235)
Calendar Marketing Association(236)
Check Payment Systems Association(243)
Digital Printing and Imaging Association(284)
Federation of Socs. for Coatings Technology(304)
Flexographic Prepress Platemakers Association(308)
Flexographic Technical Association(308)
Foil Stamping and Embossing Association(308)
Graphic Arts Marketing Information Service(319)
Graphic Communications Conference, IBT(319)
Gravure Association of America(320)
Imaging Supplies Coalition for International Intellectual Property Protection(332)
In-Plant Printing and Mailing Association(332)
International Allied Printing Trades Association(349)
International Association of Printing House Craftsmen(360)
International Digital Enterprise Alliance(369)
International Metal Decorators Association(379)
International Plate Printers', Die Stampers' and Engravers' Union of North America(383)
International Society of Copier Artists(391)
IPA - The Association of Graphic Solutions Providers(399)
Machine Printers and Engravers Association of the United States(409)
Master Printers of America(413)
National Association for Printing Leadership(435)
National Association of Litho Clubs(460)
National Association of Printing Ink Manufacturers(465)
National Government Publishing Association(514)
NPES, The Association for Suppliers of Printing, Publishing and Converting Technologies(563)
Partnership in Print Production(572)
Post-Print Manufacturers Association(581)
PrintImage International(584)
Printing Brokerage/Buyers Association International(584)
Printing Industries of America(584)
Printing Industry Credit Executives(584)
Reprographic Services Association(599)
Society of Scribes(644)
Specialty Graphic Imaging Association(650)
Tag and Label Manufacturers Institute(657)

PRISONS see CORRECTION

Correctional Vendors Association(267)

PROCTOLOGY

American Osteopathic College of Proctology(112)
American Society of Colon and Rectal Surgeons(136)

PSYCHOLOGY & PSYCHIATRY

Academy for Eating Disorders(2)
Academy of Aphasia(2)
Academy of Organizational and Occupational Psychiatry(4)
American Academy of Addiction Psychiatry(20)
American Academy of Child and Adolescent Psychiatry(20)
American Academy of Clinical Psychiatrists(21)
American Academy of Psychiatry and the Law(28)
American Academy of Psychoanalysis and Dynamic Psychiatry(28)
American Academy of Psychotherapists(28)
American Academy of Sleep Medicine(28)
American Association for Correctional and Forensic Psychology(34)
American Association for Geriatric Psychiatry(35)
American Association for Marriage and Family Therapy(36)
American Association of Chairmen of Departments of Psychiatry(39)
American Association of Children's Residential Centers(39)
American Association of Community Psychiatrists(41)
American Association of Directors of Psychiatric Residency Training(42)
American Association of Mental Health Professionals in Corrections(45)
American Association of Professional Hypnotherapists(49)
American Association of Psychiatric Administrators(49)
American Association of Psychiatric Technicians(50)
American Association of Spinal Cord Injury Psychologists and Social Workers(51)
American Association of Suicidology(52)
American Association on Mental Retardation(54)
American Board of Forensic Psychology(57)
American Board of Professional Psychology(58)
American College of Forensic Psychiatry(66)
American College of Neuropsychiatrists(68)
American College of Neuropsychopharmacology(68)
American College of Psychiatrists(70)
American College of Psychoanalysts(70)
American Family Therapy Academy(81)
American Group Psychotherapy Association(87)
American Mental Health Counselors Association(105)
American Neuropsychiatric Association(108)
American Orthopsychiatric Association(111)
American Pain Society(112)
American Psychiatric Association(117)
American Psychiatric Nurses Association(118)
American Psychoanalytic Association(118)
American Psychological Association(118)
American Psychological Association - Division of Psychoanalysis(118)
American Psychological Association - Division of Psychotherapy(118)
American Psychological Association - Society of Clinical Psychology(119)
American Psychological Society(119)
American Psychology-Law Society(119)
American Psychopathological Association(119)
American Psychosomatic Society(119)
American Psychotherapy Association(119)
American Society for Adolescent Psychiatry(126)
American Society of Addiction Medicine(133)
American Society of Clinical Psychopharmacology(136)
American Society of Electroneurodiagnostic Technologists(137)
American Society of Group Psychotherapy and Psychodrama(138)
American Society of Psychoanalytic Physicians(145)
American Society of Psychopathology of Expression(145)
American Society of Trial Consultants(147)
Asian American Psychological Association(163)
Association for Advancement of Behavior Therapy(167)
Association for Applied Psychophysiology and Biofeedback(167)
Association for Behavior Analysis(168)
Association for Birth Psychology(168)
Association for Child Psychoanalysis(169)
Association for Comprehensive Energy Psychology(170)
Association for Conflict Resolution(170)
Association for Humanistic Psychology(174)
Association for Psychoanalytic Medicine(177)
Association for Research in Nervous and Mental Disease(177)
Association for the Advancement of Applied Sport Psychology(179)
Association for the Advancement of Psychology(179)
Association for the Advancement of Psychotherapy(179)
Association for the Study of Dreams(180)
Association for Transpersonal Psychology(181)
Association for Women in Psychology(182)
Association of Aviation Psychologists(187)
Association of Black Psychologists(187)
Association of Gay and Lesbian Psychiatrists(198)
Association of Psychology Postdoctoral and Internship Centers(210)
Association of State and Provincial Psychology Boards(215)
Association of Traumatic Stress Specialists(218)
Attention Deficit Disorder Association(222)
Black Psychiatrists of America(230)
Cheiron: The International Society for the History of Behavioral and Social Sciences(243)
CWLA - Child Mental Health Division(280)
Federation of Behavioral, Psychological and Cognitive Sciences(303)
Group for the Use of Psychology in History(320)
Human Factors and Ergonomics Society(329)
International Academy for Child Brain Development(347)
International Academy of Behavioral Medicine, Counseling and Psychotherapy(347)
International Association for Near Death Studies(351)
International Association of Counselors and Therapists(355)
International Communication Association(366)
International Council of Psychologists(368)
International Dyslexia Association(370)
International Graphoanalysis Society(374)
International Neuropsychological Society(381)
International Psychogeriatric Association(383)
International Psychohistorical Association(383)
International Society for Adolescent Psychiatry & Psychology(386)
International Society for Developmental Psychobiology(387)
International Society for Quality-of-Life Studies(388)
International Society for Research on Aggression(388)
International Society for the Study of Dissociation(389)
International Society of Political Psychology(392)
International Society of Psychiatric Consultation Liaison Nurses(392)
International Society of Psychiatric-Mental Health Nurses(392)
International Stress Management Association - U.S. Branch(393)
International Transactional Analysis Association(394)
Jean Piaget Society(400)
MTM Association for Standards and Research(422)
National Academy of Neuropsychology(426)
National Association for Research and Therapy of Homosexuality(435)
National Association for Rural Mental Health(436)
National Association for the Advancement of Psychoanalysis(436)
National Association for the Education of Young Children(436)
National Association of Psychiatric Health Systems(467)
National Association of School Psychologists(470)
National Mental Health Association(527)
National Psychological Association for Psychoanalysis(534)
National Register of Health Service Providers in Psychology(535)
North American Society for the Psychology of Sport and Physical Activity(561)
North American Society of Adlerian Psychology(561)

Organization Development Institute(566)
Organizational Behavior Teaching Society(568)
Parapsychological Association(571)
Psychology Society(592)
Psychometric Society(592)
Psychonomic Society(592)
Sleep Research Society(611)
Society for Adolescent Medicine(613)
Society for Chaos Theory in Psychology and Life Sciences(615)
Society for Computers in Psychology(615)
Society for Cross-Cultural Research(616)
Society for Industrial and Organizational Psychology(620)
Society for Pediatric Psychology(623)
Society for Personality Assessment(623)
Society for Psychophysiological Research(624)
Society for Research in Child Development(624)
Society for Research on Adolescence(624)
Society for the Exploration of Psychotherapy Integration(627)
Society for the Psychological Study of Social Issues(627)
Society for the Scientific Study of Sexuality(627)
Society for the Study of Male Psychology and Physiology(628)
Society for the Study of Symbolic Interaction(628)
Society of Behavioral Medicine(632)
Society of Biological Psychiatry(632)
Society of Multivariate Experimental Psychology(640)
Society of Professors of Child and Adolescent Psychiatry(642)
World Association for Infant Mental Health(695)

PUBLIC HEALTH

AABB(1)
American Academy of Environmental Medicine(22)
American Academy of Sanitarians(28)
American Association of Medical Milk Commissions(45)
American Association of Poison Control Centers(48)
American Association of Public Health Dentistry(50)
American Association of Public Health Physicians(50)
American Institute of Stress(97)
American Mosquito Control Association(106)
American Public Health Association(119)
American School Health Association(124)
American Sexually Transmitted Diseases Association(125)
American Society of Tropical Medicine and Hygiene(147)
Association for Professionals in Infection Control and Epidemiology(177)
Association of Schools of Allied Health Professions(213)
Association of Schools of Public Health(213)
Association of State and Territorial Health Officials(215)
Association of Teachers of Preventive Medicine(217)
Commissioned Officers Association of the United States Public Health Service(254)
Infectious Diseases Society of America(338)
International Association of Milk Control Agencies(359)
International Cadmium Association(364)
National Association for Public Health Statistics and Information Systems(435)
National Association of Advisors for the Health Professions(438)
National Association of County and City Health Officials(447)
National Association of Disability Examiners(449)
National Association of Public Hospitals and Health Systems(467)
National Association of State Alcohol and Drug Abuse Directors(473)
National Conference of Local Environmental Health Administrators(493)
National Council on Radiation Protection and Measurements(502)
National Family Planning and Reproductive Health Association(508)
National Health Council(516)
National Human Services Assembly(518)
National Rehabilitation Association(535)
National Rehabilitation Counseling Association(535)
National Rural Health Association(537)
Society for Environmental Geochemistry and Health(617)
Society for Epidemiologic Research(617)
Society for Nutrition Education(622)
Society for Public Health Education(624)
Society for Vector Ecology(629)
Society of Forensic Toxicologists(636)
Vocational Evaluation and Career Assessement Professionals(684)

PUBLIC RELATIONS

Agriculture Council of America(12)
American Association for Affirmative Action(33)
American League of Lobbyists(101)
Association for Conservation Information(170)
Association of Celebrity Personal Assistants(189)
Association of Image Consultants International(200)
Automotive Public Relations Council(224)
Baptist Communicators Association(226)
Council for Advancement and Support of Education(267)
Council of Communication Management(271)
Customer Relations Institute(280)
International Association of Business Communicators(354)
International Public Relations Association - U.S. Section(384)
National Association of Consumer Advocates(446)
National Black Public Relations Society(485)
National Conference of Personal Managers(494)
National Council for Marketing and Public Relations(497)
National Council on Public Polls(502)
National Golf Foundation(514)
National Investor Relations Institute(522)
National School Public Relations Association(538)
PROMAX International(590)
Public Affairs Council(592)
Public Relations Society of America(593)
Religion Communicators Council(598)
Society for Healthcare Strategy and Market Development(618)
Women Executives in Public Relations(691)
Women in Government Relations(692)

PUBLIC WORKS

American Public Works Association(120)
American Tort Reform Association(152)
National Congress for Community Economic Development(495)

PUBLISHING

American Book Producers Association(58)
American Horse Publications Association(91)
American Medical Publishers' Association(104)
American Society of Composers, Authors and Publishers(136)
American Society of Indexers(139)
Associated Construction Publications(165)
Association of American Publishers(185)
Association of American University Presses(185)
Association of Art Editors(186)
Association of Directory Publishers(194)
Association of Free Community Papers(198)
Association of Test Publishers(217)
Audio Publishers Association(222)
Audit Bureau of Circulations(222)
Black Americans in Publishing(230)
Book Industry Study Group, Inc.(231)
BPA Worldwide(232)
Calendar Marketing Association(236)
Catholic Book Publishers Association(239)
CBA(240)
Church Music Publishers Association(246)
City and Regional Magazine Association(247)
Classroom Publishers Association(247)
Comics Magazine Association of America(253)
Copyright Society of the U.S.A.(266)
Council of Literary Magazines and Presses(273)
Educational Paperback Association(289)
Evangelical Christian Publishers Association(298)
Independent Free Papers of America(334)
Inter American Press Association(345)
International Digital Enterprise Alliance(369)
International Regional Magazine Association(385)
Livestock Publications Council(409)
Magazine Publishers of America(409)
Music Publishers' Association of the United States(423)
National Association of Hispanic Publications(456)
National Association of Independent Publishers(457)
National Association of Independent Publishers Representatives(457)
National Association of Publishers' Representatives(467)
National Directory Publishing Association(505)
National Music Publishers' Association(528)
National Newspaper Publishers Association(529)
National Trade Circulation Foundation(547)
Parenting Publications of America(571)
Periodical and Book Association of America(573)
PMA, the Independent Book Publishers Association(579)
Protestant Church-Owned Publishers Association(591)
Publishers Publicity Association(593)
Small Publishers Association of North America(611)
Society for Scholarly Publishing(625)
Society for Technical Communication(626)
Society of National Association Publications(640)
Society of Publication Designers(643)
Software and Information Industry Association(646)
Specialized Information Publishers Association(650)
Women in Scholarly Publishing(692)
Women's Regional Publications of America(694)
Yellow Pages Association(698)

PULP see also PAPER INDUSTRY

American Forest and Paper Association(85)
Association of Suppliers to the Paper Industry(216)
Forest Resources Association(310)
Lignin Institute(408)
Pine Chemicals Association(578)
Technical Association of the Pulp and Paper Industry(658)

PUMPS

American Concrete Pumping Association(73)
Contractors Pump Bureau(264)
Hydraulic Institute(329)
Submersible Wastewater Pump Association(655)
Sump and Sewage Pump Manufacturers Association(655)
Water Systems Council(686)
Western Dredging Association(687)

PURCHASING

American Purchasing Society(120)
Association for Healthcare Resource and Materials Management(174)

Coalition for Government Procurement(249)
Electronic Commerce Code Management Association(291)
Institute for Supply Management(340)
National Association of Educational Buyers(450)
National Association of State Procurement Officials(476)
National Institute of Governmental Purchasing(520)
National Purchasing Institute(534)
Printing Brokerage/Buyers Association International(584)

RABBITS

American Rabbit Breeders Association(121)

RACING

American Greyhound Track Operators Association(87)
Association of Official Racing Chemists(206)
Association of Racing Commissioners International(211)
Harness Tracks of America(322)
International Hot Rod Association(375)
Jockey Club(402)
Jockeys' Guild(402)
National Association for Stock Car Auto Racing(436)
National Association of Off-Track Betting(463)
Thoroughbred Racing Associations of North America(661)
United States Harness Writers' Association(675)
United States Trotting Association(678)

RADIO-TV

Alliance for Community Media(15)
Alliance of Motion Picture and Television Producers(17)
American Auto Racing Writers and Broadcasters Association(55)
American Disc Jockey Association(79)
American Federation of Musicians of the United States and Canada(82)
American Federation of Television and Radio Artists(83)
American Radio Relay League(121)
American Sportscasters Association(148)
American Women in Radio and Television(155)
Antenna Measurement Techniques Association(157)
Art Directors Guild/Scenic, Title and Graphic Artists(161)
Association for Educational Communications and Technology(172)
Association for Maximum Service Television(176)
Association of Catholic TV and Radio Syndicators(189)
Association of College and University Telecommunications Administrators(191)
Association of Federal Communications Consulting Engineers(196)
Association of Independent Commercial Producers(200)
Association of Public Television Stations(210)
Association of Public-Safety Communications Officers- International(211)
Black Broadcasters Alliance(230)
Broadcast Cable Credit Association(233)
Broadcast Cable Financial Management Association(233)
Broadcast Designers' Association(233)
Broadcast Education Association(233)
Cable & Telecommunications Association for Marketing(236)
Cabletelevision Advertising Bureau(236)
Catholic Academy for Communication Arts Professionals(239)
Caucus for Television Producers, Writers & Directors(240)
Community Broadcasters Association(255)
Country Radio Broadcasters, Inc.(277)
Directors Guild of America(285)
Electronic Industries Alliance(292)
Enterprise Wireless Alliance(295)
Health & Sciences Communications Association(322)
Intercollegiate Broadcasting System(346)
International Association of Audio Information Services(353)
International Association of Broadcast Monitors(354)
International Documentary Association(369)
International Radio and Television Society(384)
International Union of Electronic, Electrical, Salaried, Machine, and Furniture Workers-CWA(395)
Internet Alliance(397)
Land Mobile Communications Council(405)
Media Rating Council(415)
Motion Picture and Television Credit Association(421)
Music and Entertainment Industry Educators Association(423)
NARTE(425)
National Academy of Television Arts and Sciences(427)
National Association of Black-Owned Broadcasters(440)
National Association of Broadcast Employees and Technicians - Communications Workers of America(441)
National Association of Broadcasters(441)
National Association of Farm Broadcasting(452)
National Association of Media Brokers(461)
National Association of Minority Media Executives(462)
National Association of State Radio Networks(476)
National Association of Telecommunications Officers and Advisors(478)
National Association of Television Program Executives(478)
National Broadcast Association for Community Affairs(485)
National Cable & Telecommunications Association(486)
National Educational Telecommunications Association(506)
National Federation of Community Broadcasters(509)
National Religious Broadcasters(536)
National Sportscasters and Sportswriters Association(543)
National Translator Association(547)
North American Retail Dealers Association(559)
Organization of News Ombudsmen(567)
PCIA - the Wireless Industry Association(572)
PROMAX International(590)
Public Broadcasting Management Association(592)
Public Radio News Directors(592)
Public Radio Program Directors Association(592)
Radio Advertising Bureau(594)
Radio and Television Correspondents Association(594)
Radio-Television News Directors Association(594)
Satellite Broadcasting and Communications Association(605)
Screen Actors Guild(606)
Society for Cinema and Media Studies(615)
Society of Broadcast Engineers(632)
Society of Cable Telecommunications Engineers(632)
Society of Motion Picture and Television Engineers(640)
Station Representatives Association(653)
Television Bureau of Advertising(659)
United Electrical, Radio and Machine Workers of America(671)
Video Software Dealers Association(683)
Women in Cable and Telecommunications(691)
Writers Guild of America, East(697)
Writers Guild of America, West(697)

RADIOLOGY

Academy of Radiology Research(5)
American Academy of Oral and Maxillofacial Radiology(25)
American Academy of Thermology(29)
American Association for Women Radiologists(37)
American Chiropractic Registry of Radiologic Technologists(62)
American College of Nuclear Physicians(68)
American College of Podiatric Radiologists(70)
American College of Radiation Oncology(70)
American College of Radiology(70)
American College of Veterinary Radiology(72)
American Healthcare Radiology Administrators(90)
American Institute of Ultrasound in Medicine(98)
American Osteopathic College of Radiology(112)
American Radiological Nurses Association(121)
American Radium Society(121)
American Registry of Radiologic Technologists(122)
American Roentgen Ray Society(123)
American Society for Therapeutic Radiology and Oncology(133)
American Society of Electroneurodiagnostic Technologists(137)
American Society of Emergency Radiology(137)
American Society of Head and Neck Radiology(138)
American Society of Neuroimaging(142)
American Society of Neuroradiology(142)
American Society of Radiologic Technologists(145)
Association of Educators in Imaging and Radiologic Sciences(194)
Association of Program Directors in Radiology(210)
Association of Residents in Radiation Oncology(212)
Association of University Radiologists(219)
Association of Vascular and Interventional Radiographers(220)
Clinical Ligand Assay Society(248)
Computerized Medical Imaging Society(258)
Conference of Radiation Control Program Directors(260)
Council on Diagnostic Imaging to the A.C.A.(275)
Fleischner Society(307)
Microbeam Analysis Society(418)
National Association for Proton Therapy(435)
National Council on Radiation Protection and Measurements(502)
North American Society for Cardiac Imaging(560)
Radiation Research Society(594)
Radiological Society of North America(594)
Radiology Business Management Association(595)
Society for Cardiovascular Magnetic Resonance(614)
Society for Imaging Informatics in Medicine(619)
Society for Pediatric Radiology(623)
Society for Radiation Oncology Administrators(624)
Society for Uroradiology(629)
Society of Computed Body Tomography and Magnetic Resonance(634)
Society of Gastrointestinal Radiologists(637)
Society of Interventional Radiology(639)
Society of Radiologists in Ultrasound(643)
Society of Thoracic Radiology(645)

RAILROADS

American Association of Railroad Superintendents(50)
American Institute for Shippers Associations(94)
American Railway Development Association(121)

American Railway Engineering and Maintenance of Way Association(121)
American Short Line and Regional Railroad Association(125)
American Train Dispatchers Association(152)
Association of American Railroads(185)
Association of Railway Museums(211)
Association of Transportation Professionals(218)
Brotherhood of Locomotive Engineers and Trainmen(233)
Brotherhood of Maintenance of Way Employees(233)
Brotherhood of Railroad Signalmen(233)
Brotherhood Railway Carmen/TCU(233)
Intermodal Association of North America(347)
International Association of Railway Operating Officers(360)
International Cargo Security Council(364)
Mechanical Association Railcar Technical Services(415)
National Association of Property Tax Representatives - Transportation, Energy, Communications(467)
National Association of Railroad Trial Counsel(467)
National Association of Regulatory Utility Commissioners(469)
National Conference of Firemen and Oilers, SEIU(493)
National Railroad Construction and Maintenance Association(534)
North American Rail Shippers Association(559)
Railway Engineering-Maintenance Suppliers Association(595)
Railway Industrial Clearance Association of North America(595)
Railway Supply Institute(595)
Railway Systems Suppliers(595)
Railway Tie Association(595)
Steel Manufacturers Association(653)
Tourist Railway Association(662)
Transportation Communications International Union(664)
United Transportation Union(679)

READING

College Reading and Learning Association(252)
International Dyslexia Association(370)
International Reading Association(384)
International Visual Literacy Association(396)
National Reading Conference(535)

REAL ESTATE

AIR Commercial Real Estate Association(12)
American Association of Residential Mortgage Regulators(50)
American College of Real Estate Lawyers(70)
American Land Title Association(100)
American Real Estate and Urban Economics Association(121)
American Real Estate Society(121)
American Resort Development Association(122)
American Society of Appraisers(134)
American Society of Farm Managers and Rural Appraisers(137)
American Society of Roommate Services(145)
Appraisal Institute(159)
Association of Foreign Investors in Real Estate(197)
Association of Real Estate License Law Officials(211)
Association of Real Estate Women(211)
Building Owners and Managers Association International(234)
Building Owners and Managers Institute International(234)
CCIM Institute(240)
Commercial Real Estate Women Network(253)
Community Associations Institute(255)
CoreNet Global(266)
Corporate Facility Advisors(266)
Council of Multiple Listing Service(273)
Council of Real Estate Brokerage Managers(274)
Council of Residential Specialists(274)
Counselors of Real Estate(277)
Hotel Brokers International(329)
Institute of Real Estate Management(343)
International Association of Attorneys and Executives in Corporate Real Estate(353)
International Council of Shopping Centers(368)
International Real Estate Federation - American Chapter(384)
International Real Estate Institute(384)
International Right of Way Association(385)
Land Trust Alliance(405)
Mortgage Bankers Association(421)
Mortgage Insurance Companies of America(421)
National Affordable Housing Management Association(428)
National Apartment Association(430)
National Association of Home Builders(456)
National Association of Housing and Redevelopment Officials(456)
National Association of Housing Cooperatives(456)
National Association of Independent Fee Appraisers(457)
National Association of Installation Developers(458)
National Association of Master Appraisers(461)
National Association of Mortgage Brokers(462)
National Association of Real Estate Appraisers(468)
National Association of Real Estate Brokers(468)
National Association of Real Estate Companies(468)
National Association of Real Estate Editors(468)
National Association of Real Estate Investment Managers(468)
National Association of Real Estate Investment Trusts(468)
National Association of REALTORS(468)
National Association of Review Appraisers and Mortgage Underwriters(469)
National Business Incubation Association(486)
National Council of Exchangors(499)
National Federation of Housing Counselors(509)
National Housing and Rehabilitation Association(518)
National Institute of Building Sciences(520)
National Multi Housing Council(528)
National Real Estate Investors Association(535)
Professional Housing Management Association(587)
Property Owners Association(591)
Real Estate Buyers Agent Council(595)
Real Estate Educators Association(595)
Real Estate Information Professionals Association(596)
Real Estate Round Table(596)
REALTORS Land Institute(596)
Society of Industrial and Office REALTORS(638)
Urban Land Institute(680)
Women's Council of REALTORS(693)

RECORDS MANAGEMENT

American Health Information Management Association(89)
ARMA International(160)
Institute of Certified Records Managers(340)
International Association of Clerks, Recorders, Election Officials and Treasurers(354)
Medical Records Institute(416)
Nuclear Information and Records Management Association(563)
Professional Records and Information Services Management International(589)
Property Records Industry Association(591)

RECREATION

Academy of Leisure Sciences(4)
Aerobics and Fitness Association of America(10)
America Outdoors(19)
American Alliance for Health, Physical Education, Recreation and Dance(30)
American Council on Exercise(76)
American Gaming Association(86)
American Recreation Coalition(122)
American Spa and Health Resort Association(148)
American Sportfishing Association(148)
American Therapeutic Recreation Association(151)
Amusement Industry Manufacturers and Suppliers International(156)
Aquatic Exercise Association(159)
The Art and Creative Materials Institute(161)
Callerlab-International Association of Square Dance Callers(236)
Dude Ranchers' Association(288)
Employee Services Management Association(293)
Exercise-Safety Association(299)
Hobby Manufacturers Association(327)
International Association for the Leisure and Entertainment Industry(351)
International Association of Amusement Parks and Attractions(352)
International Family Recreation Association(371)
International Spa Association(392)
International Sport Show Producers Association(393)
Marine Retailers Association of America(412)
National Association of Casino and Theme Party Operators(441)
National Association of Off-Track Betting(463)
National Association of Recreation Resource Planners(468)
National Association of State Outdoor Recreation Liaison Officers(476)
National Bed and Breakfast Association(484)
National Council for Therapeutic Recreation Certification(497)
National Exercise Trainers Association(508)
National Forest Recreation Association(512)
National Health Club Association(516)
National Indian Gaming Association(519)
National Party Boat Owners Alliance(532)
National Recreation and Parks Association(535)
National Ski and Snowboard Retailers Association(539)
National Sporting Goods Association(543)
National Sports and Fitness Association(543)
National Tractor Pullers Association(546)
North American Society for Sport History(561)
Professional Paddlesports Association(588)
Professional Tattoo Artists Guild(589)
Pyrotechnics Guild International(593)
Recreation Vehicle Dealers Association of North America(596)
Recreation Vehicle Industry Association(596)
Recreational Park Trailer Industry Association(596)
Recreational Vehicle Manufacturer's Clubs Association(597)
Resort and Commercial Recreation Association(600)
Society of Recreation Executives(643)
Society of State Directors of Health, Physical Education and Recreation(644)
Specialty Vehicle Institute of America(650)
Stadium Managers Association(652)
Suntanning Association for Education(655)
Track Owners Association(663)
United States Parachute Association(676)
Wilderness Education Association(688)
World Waterpark Association(696)
Yacht Brokers Association of America(698)

REFRACTORIES

Brick Industry Association(232)
Casting Industry Suppliers Association(239)
Refractories Institute(597)

REFRIGERATION

AirConditioning and Refrigeration Institute(14)

American Society of Heating, Refrigerating and Air-Conditioning Engineers(139)
Cryogenic Society of America(280)
Frozen Potato Products Institute(312)
HARDI - Heating, Airconditioning, and Refrigeration Distributors International(321)
International Association for Cold Storage Construction(349)
International Association of Refrigerated Warehouses(360)
International Institute of Ammonia Refrigeration(376)
National Frozen Pizza Institute(513)
Refrigerating Engineers and Technicians Association(597)
Refrigeration Service Engineers Society(597)

REHABILITATION

Access Technology Association(6)
ADARA(8)
American Academy of Physical Medicine and Rehabilitation(27)
American Association of Cardiovascular and Pulmonary Rehabilitation(39)
American Association of Spinal Cord Injury Nurses(51)
American Congress of Rehabilitation Medicine(73)
American Medical Rehabilitation Providers Association(104)
American Occupational Therapy Association(109)
American Osteopathic Board of Physical Medicine and Rehabilitation(111)
American Physical Therapy Association(115)
Association of Academic Physiatrists(183)
Association of Halfway House Alcoholism Programs of North America(199)
Association of Rehabilitation Nurses(211)
Association of Rehabilitation Programs in Computer Technology(211)
Association of Rheumatology Health Professionals(212)
Association of Specialized and Cooperative Library Agencies(214)
Council of State Administrators of Vocational Rehabilitation(274)
International Association of Rehabilitation Professionals(360)
International Community Corrections Association(366)
International Society for Prosthetics and Orthotics - United States(388)
National Association for Rehabilitation Leadership(435)
National Association of Rehabilitation Providers and Agencies(469)
National Council on Rehabilitation Education(503)
National Rehabilitation Association(535)
National Rehabilitation Counseling Association(535)
National Subacute and Postacute Care Association(544)
Rehabilitation Engineering and Assistive Technology Society of North America(598)
TASH(657)
U.S. Psychiatric Rehabiliation Association(668)

RELIGION see also CATHOLIC, JEWISH

Academy of Homiletics(3)
Academy of Parish Clergy(5)
African-American Women's Clergy Association(11)
American Academy of Ministry(24)
American Academy of Religion(28)
American Association of Pastoral Counselors(47)
American Conference of Cantors(73)
American Correctional Chaplains Association(74)
American Humanist Association(92)
American Jewish Correctional Chaplains Association(99)
American Society of Church History(135)
American Society of Missiology(141)
American Theological Library Association(151)
Associated Church Press(164)
Association for Biblical Higher Education(168)
Association for Clinical Pastoral Education(169)
Association for the Development of Religious Information Systems(180)
Association for the Sociology of Religion(180)
Association of Christian Librarians(189)
Association of Christian Schools International(190)
Association of Christian Therapists(190)
Association of Episcopal Colleges(195)
Association of Gospel Rescue Missions(199)
Association of North American Missions(205)
Association of Professors of Mission(210)
Association of Statisticians of American Religious Bodies(216)
Association of Theological Schools in the United States and Canada(218)
Canon Law Society of America(237)
Cantors Assembly(237)
Catholic Biblical Association of America(239)
Catholic Book Publishers Association(239)
Catholic Theological Society of America(240)
CBA(240)
Central Conference of American Rabbis(241)
Choristers Guild(245)
Christian College Consortium(245)
Christian Labor Association of the United States of America(246)
Christian Legal Society(246)
Christian Management Association(246)
Christian Medical & Dental Associations(246)
Christian Schools International(246)
Christian Stewardship Association(246)
Church and Synagogue Library Association(246)
College Theology Society(252)
Conference of Major Superiors of Men, U.S.A.(259)
Council for Christian Colleges and Universities(268)
Council for Jewish Education(269)
Council for Spiritual and Ethical Education(270)
Council of Societies for the Study of Religion(274)
Evangelical Christian Publishers Association(298)
Evangelical Church Library Association(298)
Evangelical Council for Financial Accountability(298)
Evangelical Press Association(298)
Evangelical Training Association(298)
Federation of Diocesan Liturgical Commissions(303)
Fellowship of United Methodists in Music and Worship Arts(305)
Institute on Religion in an Age of Science(344)
International Association of Baptist Colleges and Universities(353)
International Association of Women Ministers(361)
International Conference of Police Chaplains(366)
Lutheran Education Association(409)
Lutheran Educational Conference of North America(409)
National Association for Treasurers of Religious Institutes(437)
National Association of Baptist Professors of Religion(439)
National Association of Church Business Administration(443)
National Association of Church Food Service(443)
National Association of Church Personnel Administrators(443)
National Association of Ecumenical and Interreligious Staff(450)
National Association of Episcopal Schools(451)
National Association of Evangelicals(451)
National Association of Pastoral Musicians(464)
National Association of Seventh-Day Adventist Dentists(472)
National Association of Temple Administrators(479)
National Association of Temple Educators(479)
National Campus Ministries Association(486)
National Church Goods Association(489)
National Church Library Association(489)
National Conference of Catechetical Leadership(493)
National Conference of Yeshiva Principals(495)
National Council of the Churches of Christ in the U.S.A.(501)
National Federation of Priests' Councils(510)
National Religious Broadcasters(536)
North American Academy of Ecumenists(554)
North American Academy of Liturgy(554)
North American Association for the Study of Religion(554)
North American Association of Christians in Social Work(554)
North American Association of Professors of Christian Education(554)
North American Canon Law Society(555)
Orthodox Theological Society in America(568)
Presbyterian Health, Education and Welfare Association(583)
Professional Association of Christian Educators(585)
Protestant Church-Owned Publishers Association(591)
Rabbinical Assembly(594)
Religion Communicators Council(598)
Religion Newswriters Association(598)
Religious Communication Association(598)
Religious Conference Management Association(599)
Religious Education Association(599)
Religious Research Association(599)
Society for Philosophy of Religion(623)
Society for the Scientific Study of Religion(627)
Society for Values in Higher Education(629)
Society of Biblical Literature(632)
Society of Christian Ethics(633)
Union for Reform Judaism(670)
United States Conference of Catholic Bishops(674)
United Synagogue of Conservative Judaism(678)

RENTALS

American Automotive Leasing Association(55)
American Rental Association(122)
Association of Progressive Rental Organizations(210)
Automotive Fleet and Leasing Association(223)
Consortium of College and University Media Centers(262)
Corporate Housing Providers Association(266)
Equipment Leasing Association of America(297)
Institute of International Container Lessors(342)
National Association of Diaper Services(449)
National Association of Equipment Leasing Brokers(451)
National Leased Housing Association(524)
National Multi Housing Council(528)
National Truck Leasing System(547)
North American Retail Dealers Association(559)
Office Business Center Association International(564)
Production Equipment Rental Association(585)
Textile Rental Services Association of America(660)
Truck Renting and Leasing Association(666)
Uniform and Textile Service Association(669)
United Association of Equipment Leasing(670)
Vacation Rental Managers Association(681)

RESEARCH

Academy of Dental Materials(3)
Academy of Radiology Research(5)
Academy of Surgical Research(5)
ACCRA - Ass'n of Applied Community Researchers(6)

Advanced Transit Association(9)
Advertising Research Foundation(9)
American Academy of Sleep Medicine(28)
American Association for Cancer Research(34)
American Association for Dental Research(34)
American Association for Public Opinion Research(36)
American Cocoa Research Institute(63)
American Educational Research Association(80)
American Evaluation Association(81)
American Federation for Medical Research(82)
American Federation of Astrologers, Inc.(82)
American Heartworm Society(90)
American Institute of Fishery Research Biologists(96)
American Pain Society(112)
American Peanut Research and Education Society(113)
American Sleep Apnea Association(126)
American Society for Bone and Mineral Research(127)
American Society for Precision Engineering(132)
American Society for Theatre Research(132)
American Society of Gene Therapy(138)
American Society of Human Genetics(139)
American Society of Preventive Oncology(145)
Association for Applied Psychophysiology and Biofeedback(167)
Association for Assessment and Accreditation of Laboratory Animal Care International(168)
Association for Career and Technical Education Research(169)
Association for Consumer Research(171)
Association for Institutional Research(175)
Association for Molecular Pathology(176)
Association for Research in Nervous and Mental Disease(177)
Association for Research in Vision and Ophthalmology(178)
Association for University Business and Economic Research(181)
Association of College and Research Libraries(190)
Association of Ecosystem Research Centers(194)
Association of Independent Information Professionals(200)
Association of Independent Research Institutes(200)
Association of Research Directors(212)
Association of Research Libraries(212)
Association of Universities for Research in Astronomy(219)
Association of University Research Parks(219)
Association of University Technology Managers(219)
Community Financial Services Association of America(256)
Computer Oriented Geological Society(258)
Conference of Research Workers in Animal Diseases(260)
Congress on Research in Dance(261)
Consortium for Advanced Manufacturing International(262)
Consortium of Social Science Associations(262)
Coordinating Research Council(265)
CoreNet Global(266)
Council for Chemical Research(268)
Council of American Overseas Research Centers(270)
Council of American Survey Research Organizations(270)
Crop Insurance Research Bureau(279)
Cystic Fibrosis Foundation(281)
Defense Research Institute(282)
Delta Society(283)
Distillers Grains Technology Council(286)
Ductile Iron Pipe Research Association(287)
ECRI(288)
Electric Power Research Institute(290)
Environmental Design Research Association(296)
Estuarine Research Federation(297)
Federation of Behavioral, Psychological and Cognitive Sciences(303)
Food Distribution Research Society(309)
Gastroenterology Research Group(315)
Governmental Research Association(319)
Horticultural Research Institute(328)
Industrial Chemical Research Association(336)
Industrial Research Institute(337)
Institute for Operations Research and the Management Sciences(339)
Institute of Medicine(343)
Insurance Institute for Highway Safety(345)
International Academy for Child Brain Development(347)
International Anesthesia Research Society(349)
International Association for Impact Assessment(350)
International Coordinating Committee on Solid State Sensors and Actuators Research(367)
International Copper Association(367)
International Institute of Forecasters(376)
International Lead Zinc Research Organization(377)
International Microelectronics and Packaging Society(379)
International Society for Quality-of-Life Studies(388)
International Society of Exposure Analysis(391)
Labor and Employment Relations Association(404)
Latin American Studies Association(405)
LIMRA International(408)
Materials Research Society(414)
Military Operations Research Society(419)
MTM Association for Standards and Research(422)
National Association for Armenian Studies and Research(431)
National Association for Biomedical Research(431)
National Association for Research and Therapy of Homosexuality(435)
National Association for Research in Science Teaching(435)
National Association of Addiction Treatment Providers(438)
National Association of Forensic Economics(453)
National Association of Veterans' Research and Education Foundations(480)
National Conference on Research in Language and Literacy(495)
National Council of University Research Administrators(501)
National Education Knowledge Industry Association(506)
National Hydrogen Association(518)
National Institutes for Water Resources(521)
National Spinal Cord Injury Association(542)
North American Case Research Association(555)
North American Manufacturing Research Institution of SME(558)
Optical Society of America(566)
Organizational Systems Research Association(568)
Orthopaedic Research Society(568)
Osteoarthritis Research Society International(569)
Paleontological Research Institution(570)
Plastic Surgery Research Council(579)
Police Executive Research Forum(580)
Product Development and Management Association(585)
Project Management Institute(590)
Property Loss Research Bureau(591)
Psychonomic Society(592)
Qualitative Research Consultants Association(593)
Radiation Research Society(594)
Recycled Paperboard Technical Association(597)
Research and Development Associates for Military Food and Packaging Systems(599)
Research and Engineering Council of the NAPL(600)
Research Association of Minority Professors(600)
Research Chefs Association(600)
Research Council on Structural Connections(600)
Social Science Research Council(613)
Society for Cross-Cultural Research(616)
Society for Economic Botany(616)
Society for Epidemiologic Research(617)
Society for Gynecologic Investigation(618)
Society for Intercultural Education, Training and Research - USA(620)
Society for Pediatric Research(623)
Society for Research in Child Development(624)
Society for the Advancement of Women's Health Research(626)
Society for the Study of Male Psychology and Physiology(628)
Society of Armenian Studies(631)
Society of Atherosclerosis Imaging(632)
Society of Insurance Research(638)
Society of Quality Assurance(643)
Society of Research Administrators International(643)
Transportation Research Forum(664)
Travel and Tourism Research Association(665)
Universities Council on Water Resources(679)
Universities Research Association(679)
Universities Space Research Association(679)
Welding Research Council(687)
Wheat Quality Council(688)

RESTAURANTS

American Culinary Federation(77)
American Truck Stop Operators Association(152)
BMC - A Foodservice Sales and Marketing Council(231)
Council of Hotel and Restaurant Trainers(272)
Council of Independent Restaurants of America(272)
International Council on Hotel, Restaurant and Institutional Education(368)
International Food Service Executives' Association(372)
International Society of Restaurant Association Executives(392)
Mexican Restaurant and Cantina Association(418)
Mobile Industrial Caterers' Association International(420)
National Council of Chain Restaurants(498)
National Restaurant Association(536)
Restaurant Facility Management Association(600)
Women Chefs and Restaurateurs(691)

RETAILERS see also MERCHANDISING

American Association of Franchisees and Dealers(43)
American Association of Meat Processors(45)
American Booksellers Association(58)
American Collegiate Retailing Association(72)
Association for Retail Technology Standards(178)
Association of Booksellers for Children(188)
Association of Coupon Professionals(193)
Association of Retail Travel Agents(212)
Black Retail Action Group(230)
Building Material Dealers Association(234)
Casual Furniture Retailers(239)
CBA(240)
CIES, The Food Business Forum(246)
Computing Technology Industry Association(258)
Food Marketing Institute(309)
Home Improvement Research Institute(327)
International Council of Shopping Centers(368)
International Crystal Federation(368)
International Electronic Article Surveillance Manufacturers Association(370)

International Map Trade Association(379)
Jewelers of America(401)
Leading Jewelers Guild(406)
Marine Retailers Association of America(412)
Mystery Shopping Providers Association(424)
NAMM - the International Music Products Association(425)
National Antique and Art Dealers Association of America(430)
National Association for Retail Marketing Services(436)
National Association of College Stores(444)
National Association of Convenience Stores(446)
National Association of Resale & Thrift Shops(469)
National Catalog Managers Association(487)
National Community Pharmacists Association(491)
National Grocers Association(515)
National Home Furnishings Association(517)
National Ice Cream Retailers Association(518)
National Independent Flag Dealers Association(519)
National Luggage Dealers Association(525)
National Retail Federation(536)
National Retail Hobby Stores Association(536)
National Shoe Retailers Association(539)
National Ski and Snowboard Retailers Association(539)
National Sporting Goods Association(543)
North American Retail Dealers Association(559)
North American Retail Hardware Association(559)
Oriental Rug Retailers of America(568)
Professional Picture Framers Association(588)
Professional Retail Store Maintenance Association(589)
Retail Advertising and Marketing Association International(601)
Retail Confectioners International(601)
Retail Industry Leaders Association(601)
Retail Packaging Manufacturers Association(601)
Retail Tobacco Dealers of America(601)
Retail, Wholesale and Department Store Union(601)
Retailer's Bakery Association(601)
Vacuum Dealers Trade Association(682)
WorkPlace Furnishings(695)

RICE
International Wild Rice Association(397)
Rice Millers' Association(602)
U.S.A. Rice Federation(669)

ROADWAYS
American Association of State Highway and Transportation Officials(51)
American Highway Users Alliance(90)
American Road and Transportation Builders Association(123)
Associated Equipment Distributors(165)
Association of Asphalt Paving Technologists(186)
International Bridge, Tunnel and Turnpike Association(363)
International Grooving and Grinding Association(374)
International Road Federation(385)
National Asphalt Pavement Association(431)
National Association of Women Highway Safety Leaders(481)

ROBOTICS
American Automatic Control Council(55)
American Society of Mechanical Engineers(141)
Association for Unmanned Vehicle Systems International(181)
Automated Imaging Association(222)
Consortium for Advanced Manufacturing International(262)
Robotic Industries Association(602)
Society of Manufacturing Engineers(639)

ROLLERSKATING
Roller Skating Association International(602)

ROOFING
Asphalt Roofing Manufacturers Association(163)
EPDM Roofing Association(297)
National Roof Deck Contractors Association(537)
National Roofing Contractors Association(537)
Perlite Institute(573)
RCI, Inc.(595)
Roof Coatings Manufacturers Association(603)
Sealant, Waterproofing and Restoration Institute(607)
SPRI, Inc.(652)
Steel Deck Institute(653)
Tile Roofing Institute(661)
United Union of Roofers, Waterproofers and Allied Workers(679)

RUBBER & RUBBER PRODUCTS
American Chemical Society - Rubber Division(62)
Carpet Cushion Council(238)
Fluid Sealing Association(308)
Independent Sealing Distributors(335)
International Institute of Synthetic Rubber Producers(376)
Rubber and Plastics Industry Conference of the United Steelworkers of America(603)
Rubber Manufacturers Association(603)
Rubber Trade Association of North America(603)
Society of the Plastics Industry(645)
Tire and Rim Association(661)
Tire Industry Association(662)
Tire Retread Information Bureau(662)

SAFETY
American Academy of Safety Education(28)
American Biological Safety Association(57)
American College of Contingency Planners(65)
American Driver and Traffic Safety Education Association(79)
American Highway Users Alliance(90)
American Society of Mechanical Engineers(141)
American Society of Safety Engineers(146)
American Traffic Safety Services Association(152)
Association for the Advancement of Automotive Medicine(179)
Association of State Dam Safety Officials(215)
ASTM International(221)
Automatic Fire Alarm Association(222)
Automotive Occupant Restraints Council(224)
Board of Certified Safety Professionals(231)
Campus Safety, Health and Environmental Management Association(237)
Commercial Vehicle Safety Alliance(254)
Council on Certification of Health, Environmental and Safety Technologists(275)
Crane Certification Association of America(278)
Defense Fire Protection Association(282)
Disaster Preparedness and Emergency Response Association(285)
Fire Suppression Systems Association(307)
Flight Safety Foundation(308)
Governors Highway Safety Association(319)
Human Factors and Ergonomics Society(329)
Institute of Nuclear Materials Management(343)
Institute of Nuclear Power Operations(343)
Insurance Institute for Highway Safety(345)
International Association of Dive Rescue Specialists(356)
International Association of Electrical Inspectors(356)
International Association of Home Safety and Security Professionals(358)
International Federation of Inspection Agencies - Americas Committee(371)
International Safety Equipment Association(385)
International Society of Air Safety Investigators(389)
Lightning Protection Institute(408)
Mine Safety Institute of America(419)
Motorcycle Safety Foundation(422)
Mountain Rescue Association(422)
National Association of Elevator Safety Authorities International(450)
National Association of State Boating Law Administrators(473)
National Association of Women Highway Safety Leaders(481)
National EMS Pilots Association(507)
National Fire Protection Association(510)
National Independent Fire Alarm Distributors(519)
National Safety Council(538)
National Safety Management Society(538)
SAFE Association(604)
Safety Equipment Distributors Association(604)
System Safety Society(657)
Transportation Safety Equipment Institute(664)
United States Lifesaving Association(676)
United States Marine Safety Association(676)
United States Parachute Association(676)
Voluntary Protection Programs Participants Association(684)
Window Council(689)

SALESMEN
Agricultural and Industrial Manufacturers' Representatives Association(12)
Allied Trades of the Baking Industry(17)
American Association of Professional Sales Engineers(49)
Association of Industry Manufacturers' Representatives(201)
Association of Sales Administration Managers(212)
Electrical Equipment Representatives Association(291)
Electronics Representatives Association(292)
Health Industry Representatives Association(323)
Heavy Duty Representatives Association(325)
Independent Professional Representatives Organization(335)
International Home Furnishings Representatives Association(375)
Manufacturers' Agents Association for the Foodservice Industry(411)
Manufacturers' Agents National Association(411)
Materials Marketing Associates(414)
Multi-Level Marketing International Association(422)
NAGMR Consumer Product Brokers(425)
National Association of Flour Distributors(453)
National Association of Health Underwriters(455)
National Association of Independent Publishers Representatives(457)
National Confectionery Sales Association(492)
National Electrical Manufacturers Representatives Association(506)
National Field Selling Association(510)
National Marine Representatives Association(526)
Power-Motion Technology Representatives Association(582)
Professional Society for Sales and Marketing Training(589)
Radio Advertising Bureau(594)
Sales and Marketing Executives International(604)
Sales Association of the Chemical Industry(604)
Sales Association of the Paper Industry(604)
School, Home and Office Products Association(606)
Specialty Tool and Fastener Distributors Association(650)
Sporting Goods Agents Association(651)

SALVAGE
American Salvage Pool Association(124)

Association of Diving Contractors International(194)

SAND

National Industrial Sand Association(519)
National Stone, Sand and Gravel Association(543)

SANITATION

American Academy of Sanitarians(28)
American Society of Sanitary Engineering(146)
Association of Environmental Engineering and Science Professors(195)
Association of State and Territorial Solid Waste Management Officials(215)
Baking Industry Sanitation Standards Committee(225)
International Association for Food Protection(350)
ISSA(400)
National Association of Clean Water Agencies(443)
National Environmental Health Association(507)
Portable Sanitation Association International(581)
SWANA - Solid Waste Association of North America(656)

SAVINGS & LOAN see also BANKING

America's Community Bankers(19)
American Council of State Savings Supervisors(75)
Financial Managers Society(306)

SAWS

Concrete Sawing and Drilling Association(259)
North American Sawing Association(560)

SCALES

International Society of Weighing and Measurement(392)
Scale Manufacturers Association(605)

SCIENCE

Academy of Applied Science(2)
American Academy of Arts & Sciences(20)
American Academy of Forensic Sciences(23)
American Association for Artificial Intelligence(33)
American Association for the Advancement of Science(36)
American Association of Phonetic Sciences(48)
American Board of Bioanalysis(57)
American Council on Science and Health(76)
American Dairy Science Association(78)
The American Electrophoresis Society(80)
American Filtration and Separations Society(83)
American Heartworm Society(90)
American Indian Science and Engineering Society(93)
American Institute of Biological Sciences(94)
American Meat Science Association(104)
American Pain Society(112)
American Peptide Society(113)
American Society for Bone and Mineral Research(127)
American Society for Clinical Laboratory Science(127)
American Society for Horticultural Science(130)
American Society of Animal Science(134)
AOC(158)
Association for Library and Information Science Education(175)
Association for Molecular Pathology(176)
Association for Politics and the Life Sciences(176)
Association for Science Teacher Education(178)
Association for Women Geoscientists(182)
Association for Women in Science(182)
Association of Biomolecular Resource Facilities(187)
Association of Science Museum Directors(213)
Association of Science-Technology Centers(213)
Chemical Sources Association(243)
Computer Oriented Geological Society(258)
Conference Board of the Mathematical Sciences(259)
Council for Agricultural Science and Technology(268)
Council for Near-Infrared Spectroscopy(269)
Council of Colleges of Arts and Sciences(271)
Crop Science Society of America(279)
Decision Sciences Institute(282)
Disease Management Association of America(285)
Environmental and Engineering Geophysical Society(296)
Fusion Power Associates(313)
Guild of Natural Science Illustrators(321)
History of Science Society(327)
Hydroponic Society of America(330)
Institute of Environmental Sciences and Technology(341)
Institute on Religion in an Age of Science(344)
International Association for Near Death Studies(351)
International Coordinating Committee on Solid State Sensors and Actuators Research(367)
International Foundation for Telemetering(373)
International Hydrofoil Society(375)
International Isotope Society(377)
International Research Council of Neuromuscular Disorders(385)
International Society for Clinical Densitometry(386)
International Society for Research on Aggression(388)
International Society of Chemical Ecology(390)
Movement Disorder Society(422)
National Academy of Clinical Biochemistry(426)
National Academy of Recording Arts and Sciences(427)
National Academy of Sciences(427)
National Academy of Television Arts and Sciences(427)
National Association for Research in Science Teaching(435)
National Association of Academies of Science(437)
National Association of Science Writers(471)
National Council of Black Engineers and Scientists(498)
National Institute of Building Sciences(520)
National Lipid Association(525)
National Science Education Leadership Association(538)
National Science Teachers Association(539)
New York Academy of Sciences(552)
North American Neuromodulation Society(559)
Philosophy of Science Association(576)
Poultry Science Association(581)
RNA Society(602)
School Science and Mathematics Association(606)
Society for Applied Anthropology(613)
Society for Environmental Geochemistry and Health(617)
Society for Social Studies of Science(625)
Society of Commercial Seed Technologists(633)
Society of Ethnobiology(635)
Society of Hispanic Professional Engineers(638)
Society of Protozoologists(643)
Society of Quality Assurance(643)
Society of Wood Science and Technology(646)
Soil Science Society of America(647)
Space Transportation Association(648)
Teratology Society(659)
Tree-Ring Society(665)
Weed Science Society of America(687)

SCIENTIFIC

American Academy of Somnology(28)
The American Electrophoresis Society(80)
American Glovebox Society(87)
American Peptide Society(113)
American Rock Mechanics Association(123)
American Scientific Glassblowers Society(124)
Commission on Professionals in Science and Technology(254)
Controlled Release Society(265)
Council of Scientific Society Presidents(274)
International Microelectronics and Packaging Society(379)
Measurement, Control and Automation Association(415)
New York Academy of Sciences(552)
SAMA Group of Associations(605)
Scientific Equipment and Furniture Association(606)
Society for Biomolecular Sciences(614)
Society for Chaos Theory in Psychology and Life Sciences(615)
Society for Cross-Cultural Research(616)
Society for Free Radical Biology and Medicine(617)
United States Federation of Scholars and Scientists(675)

SCIENTISTS

Academy of Applied Science(2)
American Association of Pharmaceutical Scientists(48)
American Association of Radon Scientists and Technologists(50)
Association for Molecular Pathology(176)
Association of Clinical Scientists(190)
Association of Management/International Association of Management(203)
Association of Muslim Scientists and Engineers(205)
Calorimetry Conference(237)
Commission on Professionals in Science and Technology(254)
Electrochemical Society(291)
Federation of American Scientists(303)
National Technical Association(545)
New York Academy of Sciences(552)
Society for Imaging Science & Technology(619)
Society of Engineering Science(635)
Space Energy Association(648)
World Future Society(696)

SCULPTURE

American Academy of Equine Art(22)
American Medallic Sculpture Association(104)
Sculptors Guild(607)

SECRETARIES

American Association of Medical Assistants(45)
Association of Certified Professional Secretaries(189)
Association of Executive and Administrative Professionals(196)
Executive Women International(299)
International Association of Administrative Professionals(352)
NALS(425)
National Court Reporters Association(503)

SECURITIES INDUSTRY see also BANKING, FINANCE, INVESTMENTS

American Association of Individual Investors(44)
American Stock Exchange(149)
Commercial Mortgage Securities Association(253)
Consolidated Tape Association(262)
ESOP Association(297)
Fixed Income Analysts Society(307)
Forum for Investor Advice(311)
Independent Investors Protective League(334)
Investment Program Association(399)
Mutual Fund Education Alliance(423)
National Association for Variable Annuities(437)
National Association of Bond Lawyers(441)
National Association of Securities Dealers(471)
National Association of Securities Professionals(471)
National Investor Relations Institute(522)
New York Stock Exchange(552)

North American Securities Administrators Association(560)
NYSE Arca(563)
Securities Transfer Association(607)
Security Traders Association(608)
Shareholder Services Association(609)
Society of Quantitative Analysts(643)

SECURITY

Academy of Security Educators and Trainers(5)
American Society for Amusement Park Security and Safety(126)
ASIS International(163)
Central Station Alarm Association(241)
Computer Security Institute(258)
Energy Security Council(294)
Espionage Research Institute(297)
Financial and Security Products Association(305)
Independent Armored Car Operators Association(333)
Information Systems Audit and Control Association(338)
Information Systems Security Association(338)
Institute of Nuclear Materials Management(343)
International Association for Computer Systems Security(349)
International Association for Healthcare Security and Safety(350)
International Association for Identification(350)
International Association of Bomb Technicians and Investigators(354)
International Association of Campus Law Enforcement Administrators(354)
International Association of Home Safety and Security Professionals(358)
International Association of Personal Protection Agents(360)
International Association of Professional Security Consultants(360)
International Association of Special Investigation Units(361)
International Association of Workforce Professionals(362)
International Guards Union of America(374)
International Security Management Association(385)
International Security Officers, Police, and Guards Union(386)
International Union Security, Police and Fire Professionals of America(396)
Jewelers' Security Alliance of the U.S.(401)
National Alarm Association of America(429)
National Armored Car Association(431)
National Association of Chiefs of Police(443)
National Association of Security Companies(471)
National Burglar and Fire Alarm Association(486)
National Classification Management Society(490)
National Council of Investigation and Security Services(499)
National Defense Industrial Association(504)
North American Association of Wardens and Superintendents(555)
Operations Security Professionals Society(565)
Security Industry Association(607)
Women in International Security(692)

SEEDS

American Seed Trade Association(124)
Association of American Seed Control Officials(185)
Association of Official Seed Analysts(206)
Society of Commercial Seed Technologists(633)

SEWING

Home Sewing Association(327)
Sewn Products Equipment and Suppliers of the Americas(609)

SEX

American Association of Sexuality Educators, Counselors and Therapists(51)
American Society of Andrology(133)
Association for the Treatment of Sexual Abusers(181)
Society for the Philosophy of Sex and Love(627)
Society for the Scientific Study of Sexuality(627)

SHEEP see also WOOL

American and Delaine-Merino Record Association(31)
American Association of Small Ruminant Practitioners(51)
American Border Leicester Association(58)
American Cheviot Sheep Society(62)
American Cotswold Record Association(74)
American Hampshire Sheep Association(88)
American Karakul Sheep Registry(100)
American North Country Cheviot Sheep Association(109)
American Polypay Sheep Association(116)
American Rambouillet Sheep Breeders Association(121)
American Romney Breeders Association(123)
American Sheep Industry Association(125)
American Shropshire Registry Association(125)
American Southdown Breeders Association(148)
Columbia Sheep Breeders Association of America(253)
Continental Dorset Club(264)
Finnsheep Breeders Association(307)
Montadale Sheep Breeders Association(421)
National Lamb Feeders Association(523)
National Lincoln Sheep Breeders Association(525)
National Tunis Sheep Registry(547)
Natural Colored Wool Growers Association(550)
North American Clun Forest Association(556)
North American Wensleydale Sheep Association(562)
Scottish Blackface Sheep Breeders Association(606)
United States Targhee Sheep Association(677)
United Suffolk Sheep Association(678)

SHIPPING INDUSTRY

Airforwarders Association(14)
American Association of Port Authorities(49)
American Bureau of Shipping(59)
American Import Shippers Association(93)
American Institute of Marine Underwriters(96)
American Maritime Association(103)
American Maritime Congress(103)
American Pilots' Association(115)
American Shipbuilding Association(125)
American Society of Naval Engineers(142)
Association of Average Adjusters of the U.S.(187)
Association of Ship Brokers and Agents (U.S.A.)(214)
Bulk Carrier Conference(235)
Chamber of Shipping of America(243)
Committee for Private Offshore Rescue and Towing (C-PORT)(254)
Council of American Maritime Museums(270)
Council of American Master Mariners(270)
Cruise Lines International Association(280)
Fashion Accessories Shippers Association(301)
Inland Marine Underwriters Association(339)
Institute of International Container Lessors(342)
Institute of Navigation(343)
Interferry(347)
International Brotherhood of Boilermakers, Iron Ship Builders, Blacksmiths, Forgers and Helpers(363)
International Cargo Gear Bureau(364)
International Longshore and Warehouse Union(378)
International Longshoremen's Association, AFL-CIO(378)
International Vessel Operators Hazardous Materials Association(396)
Jewelers Shipping Association(401)
Lake Carriers' Association(404)
Marine Engineers Beneficial Association(412)
Marine Technology Society(412)
Maritime Law Association of the U.S.(412)
Messenger Courier Association of the Americas(417)
National Association of Marine Services(461)
National Association of Marine Surveyors(461)
National Association of Waterfront Employers(481)
National Cargo Bureau(487)
National Council on International Trade Development(502)
National Marine Distributors Association(526)
National Maritime Alliance(526)
Offshore Marine Service Association(564)
Plastic Shipping Container Institute(578)
Propeller Club of the United States(591)
Seafarers' International Union(607)
Shipbuilders Council of America(610)
Shipowners Claims Bureau(610)
Society of Marine Port Engineers(639)
Society of Maritime Arbitrators(639)
Society of Naval Architects and Marine Engineers(640)
Trans-Atlantic American Flag Liner Operators(663)
Transportation & Logistics Council(664)
Transportation Institute(664)

SHOES see also LEATHER GOODS

Footwear Distributors and Retailers of America(310)
Metal Findings Manufacturers Association(417)
National Shoe Retailers Association(539)
Pedorthic Footwear Association(572)
United Shoe Retailers Association(672)
World Shoe Association(696)

SIGNALS

International Municipal Signal Association(380)
Railway Systems Suppliers(595)

SIGNS

International Marking and Identification Association(379)
International Sign Association(386)
National Association of Sign Supply Distributors(472)
Outdoor Advertising Association of America(569)
POPAI The Global Association for Marketing at Retail(580)
Society for Environmental Graphic Design(617)
World Sign Associates(696)

SILK

International Silk Association(386)

SILVER

International Precious Metals Institute(383)
Manufacturing Jewelers and Suppliers of America(411)
Silver Institute(611)
Silver Users Association(611)
Society of American Silversmiths(631)

SINGING

American Academy of Teachers of Singing(29)
American Choral Directors Association(62)
Cantors Assembly(237)
Chorus America(245)
National Association of Teachers of Singing(478)
National Opera Association(529)
OPERA America(565)

SKIING

Cross Country Ski Areas Association(279)
National Ski and Snowboard Retailers Association(539)
National Ski Areas Association(540)
National Ski Patrol System(540)
North American Snowsports Journalists Association(560)
Professional Ski Instructors of America(589)
SnowSports Industries America(612)
United States Ski Association(677)

Water Sports Industry Association(686)

SLATE
Expanded Shale, Clay and Slate Institute(299)

SLAVIC
American Association for the Advancement of Slavic Studies(36)
American Councils for International Education(76)
Society for Romanian Studies(625)
Society for Slovene Studies(625)

SMALL BUSINESS
American Association of Individual Investors(44)
American Small Businesses Association(126)
Association of Small Business Development Centers(214)
Future Business Leaders of America-Phi Beta Lambda(313)
International Association of Airport Duty Free Stores(352)
International Council for Small Business(367)
International Reciprocal Trade Association(384)
The Knitting Guild Association(404)
National Association of Black Women Entrepreneurs(440)
National Association of Development Companies(449)
National Association of Investment Companies(459)
National Association of Small Business Investment Companies(472)
National Business Incubation Association(486)
National Federation of Independent Business(509)
National Small Business Association(540)
North American Small Business International Trade Educators(560)
Small Business Council of America(611)
Small Business Legislative Council(611)
Small Publishers Association of North America(611)
Souvenirs, Gifts and Novelties Trade Association(648)

SOCCER
Major Indoor Soccer League(410)
Major League Soccer(410)
National Intercollegiate Soccer Officials Association(522)
National Soccer Coaches Association of America(540)
Soccer Industry Council of America(612)
United States Soccer Federation(677)

SOCIAL WORKERS
Alliance for Children and Families(15)
Alliance of Information and Referral Systems(17)
American Association of Spinal Cord Injury Psychologists and Social Workers(51)
American Association of Suicidology(52)
American Orthopsychiatric Association(111)
Association of Christian Therapists(190)
Association of Family and Conciliation Courts(196)
Association of Jewish Family and Children's Agencies(202)
Association of Junior Leagues International(202)
Association of Oncology Social Work(206)
Association of Pediatric Oncology Social Workers(207)
Association of Social Work Boards(214)
Association of YMCA Professionals(221)
Catholic Charities USA(239)
Clinical Social Work Federation(248)
Community Action Partnership(255)
Council on Social Work Education(277)
International Association for Truancy and Dropout Prevention(352)
International Community Corrections Association(366)
Jewish Social Service Professionals Association(402)
National Association for Community Mediation(432)
National Association for Home Care(434)
National Association for Rural Mental Health(436)
National Association of Area Agencies on Aging(439)
National Association of Black Social Workers(440)
National Association of Foster Grandparent Program Directors(453)
National Association of Puerto Rican/Hispanic Social Workers(467)
National Association of Social Workers(472)
National Human Services Assembly(518)
National Network for Social Work Managers(528)
National Organization of Social Security Claimants' Representatives(530)
National Student Assistance Association(544)
North American Association of Christians in Social Work(554)
Society for Social Work Leadership in Health Care(625)
TASH(657)
World Association for Infant Mental Health(695)

SOCIOLOGY
African Studies Association(11)
American Association of Suicidology(52)
American Association on Mental Retardation(54)
American Men's Studies Association(105)
American Real Estate and Urban Economics Association(121)
American Society of Geolinguistics(138)
American Sociological Association(147)
Association for Applied and Clinical Sociology(167)
Association for Humanist Sociology(174)
Association for the Sociology of Religion(180)
Association for the Study of Classical African Civilizations(180)
Association of Black Sociologists(187)
Cheiron: The International Society for the History of Behavioral and Social Sciences(243)
Community Development Society(256)
Human Behavior and Evolution Society(329)
International Association for Business and Society(349)
International Rural Sociology Association(385)
International Society for Quality-of-Life Studies(388)
International Society for the Comparative Studies of Civilizations(389)
International Studies Association(393)
International Transactional Analysis Association(394)
Law and Society Association(406)
National Association of Neighborhoods(462)
National Council on Family Relations(502)
North American Society for the Sociology of Sport(561)
Population Association of America(580)
Rural Sociological Society(603)
Social Science History Association(612)
Society for Disability Studies(616)
Society for Social Studies of Science(625)
Society for the Advancement of Socio-Economics(626)
Society for the Psychological Study of Social Issues(627)
Society for the Scientific Study of Religion(627)
Society for the Study of Social Problems(628)
Society for the Study of Symbolic Interaction(628)
Sociological Practice Association(646)

SOYBEANS
American Oilseed Coalition(110)
American Soybean Association(148)
National Oilseed Processors Association(529)
United Soybean Board(672)

SPANISH
American Association of Teachers of Spanish and Portuguese(52)
Association of Hispanic Arts(200)
National Alliance for Hispanic Health(429)
Society for Spanish and Portuguese Historical Studies(625)
Twentieth-Century Spanish Association of America(667)

SPEAKERS
American Institute of Parliamentarians(97)
American Seminar Leaders Association(124)
International Association of Speakers Bureaus(361)
National Association of Parliamentarians(463)
National Forensic Association(512)
National Speakers Association(542)

SPECTROSCOPY
American Society for Mass Spectrometry(130)
Coblentz Society(250)
Federation of Analytical Chemistry and Spectroscopy Societies(303)
Society for Applied Spectroscopy(614)

SPEECH
Academy of Aphasia(2)
Alexander Graham Bell Association for the Deaf and Hard of Hearing(15)
American Cleft Palate-Craniofacial Association(63)
American Forensic Association(85)
American Neurotology Society(109)
American Speech-Language-Hearing Association(148)
International Dyslexia Association(370)
National Black Association for Speech, Language and Hearing(484)
National Communication Association(491)
National Forensic Association(512)
National Student Speech Language Hearing Association(544)
NFHS Speech Debate and Theatre Association(553)
Religious Communication Association(598)

SPELEOLOGY
National Caves Association(488)
National Speleological Society(542)

SPORTING GOODS
Archery Trade Association(160)
Association of Surfing Professionals - North America(216)
Awards and Recognition Association(225)
Diving Equipment and Marketing Association(286)
International Association of Skateboard Companies(361)
International Snowmobile Manufacturers Association(386)
International Sport Show Producers Association(393)
National Association of Sporting Goods Wholesalers(472)
National Reloading Manufacturers Association(536)
National Ski and Snowboard Retailers Association(539)
National Sporting Goods Association(543)
National Taxidermists Association(545)
SGMA(651)
SnowSports Industries America(612)
Soccer Industry Council of America(612)
Sporting Arms and Ammunition Manufacturers' Institute(651)
Sporting Goods Agents Association(651)
United States Racquet Stringers Association(677)
Western-English Trade Association(688)

SPORTS see also SPECIFIC SPORT

American Academy of Podiatric Sports Medicine(27)
American Academy of Sports Physicians(29)
American Bridge Teachers' Association(59)
American Canine Sports Medicine Association(61)
American College of Sports Medicine(70)
American Orthopaedic Society for Sports Medicine(111)
American Osteopathic Academy for Sports Medicine(111)
American Society of Golf Course Architects(138)
American Sports Medicine Association(148)
American Volleyball Coaches Association(153)
Archery Range and Retailers Organization(160)
Association for the Advancement of Applied Sport Psychology(179)
Association for the Study of Play(181)
Association for Women in Sports Media(182)
Association of Talent Agents(216)
Association of Volleyball Professionals(220)
Association of YMCA Professionals(221)
Athletic Equipment Managers Association(221)
ATP(221)
Billiard Congress of America(228)
Black Entertainment and Sports Lawyers Association(230)
Bowling Proprietors Association of America(231)
College Athletic Business Management Association(251)
College Gymnastics Association(251)
College Sports Information Directors of America(252)
Collegiate Commissioners Association(252)
Football Writers Association of America(310)
Game Manufacturers Association(313)
Golf Coaches Association of America(318)
Harness Tracks of America(322)
ICAAAA Coaches Association(330)
Ice Skating Institute(330)
IDEA, The Health and Fitness Association(330)
Institute of Diving(341)
International Association of Golf Administrators(357)
International Professional Rodeo Association(383)
International Sport Show Producers Association(393)
International Sports Heritage Association(393)
Ladies Professional Golf Association(404)
Major League Soccer(410)
National Aeronautic Association(427)
National Alliance for Youth Sports(429)
National Association for Girls and Women in Sport(433)
National Association for Kinesiology and Physical Education in Higher Education(434)
National Association for Sport and Physical Education(436)
National Association of Academic Advisors for Athletes(437)
National Association of Athletic Development Directors(439)
National Association of Collegiate Directors of Athletics(444)
National Association of Collegiate Marketing Administrators(445)
National Association of Golf Tournament Directors(454)
National Association of Intercollegiate Athletics(458)
National Association of Jai Alai Frontons(459)
National Association of Professional Baseball Leagues(466)
National Association of Sports Officials(472)
National Athletic Trainers' Association(482)
National Basketball Athletic Trainers Association(483)
National Christian College Athletic Association(489)
National Collegiate Athletic Association(491)
National Collegiate Wrestling Association(491)
National Cutting Horse Association(504)
National Federation Coaches Association(508)
National Federation of Officials Association(510)
National Federation of State High School Associations(510)
National Football League Players Association(511)
National Golf Foundation(514)
National Gymnastics Judges Association(516)
National High School Athletic Coaches Association(517)
National Hockey League(517)
National Hockey League Players' Association(517)
National Intercollegiate Soccer Officials Association(522)
National Interscholastic Athletic Administrators Association(522)
National Intramural-Recreational Sports Association(522)
National Junior College Athletic Association(523)
National Reining Horse Association(535)
National Rifle Association of America(536)
National Shooting Sports Foundation(539)
National Show Horse Registry(539)
National Soccer Coaches Association of America(540)
National Sportscasters and Sportswriters Association(543)
National Strength and Conditioning Association(543)
North American Gamebird Association(557)
North American Society for Sport History(561)
North American Society for Sport Management(561)
North American Society for the Psychology of Sport and Physical Activity(561)
Professional Association of Diving Instructors(585)
Professional Association of Volleyball Officials(586)
Professional Baseball Athletic Trainers Society(586)
Professional Bowlers Association of America(586)
Professional Football Athletic Trainers Society(587)
Professional Golfers Association of America(587)
Professional Hockey Writers' Association(587)
Professional Putters Association(588)
Professional Rodeo Cowboys Association(589)
Professional Skaters Association(589)
Professional Ski Instructors of America(589)
Resort and Commercial Recreation Association(600)
Roller Skating Association International(602)
Specialty Vehicle Institute of America(650)
Sports Lawyers Association(651)
Sports Turf Managers Association(651)
Sportsplex Operators and Developers Association(651)
Thoroughbred Owners and Breeders Association(661)
United States Association of Independent Gymnastic Clubs(673)
United States Fencing Coaches Association(675)
USA Taekwonda(681)
Women's Basketball Coaches Association(693)
Women's International Bowling Congress(693)
World Umpires Association(696)

STANDARDS

Alliance for Telecommunications Industry Solutions(16)
American Association for Laboratory Accreditation(35)
American Association of Medical Milk Commissions(45)
American Boat and Yacht Council(58)
American College of Medical Quality(67)
American National Metric Council(108)
American National Standards Institute(108)
American Society for Quality(132)
American Society of Mechanical Engineers(141)
Association of Machinery and Equipment Appraisers(203)
ASTM International(221)
Automatic Meter Reading Association(223)
Automotive Industry Action Group(223)
Baking Industry Sanitation Standards Committee(225)
Clinical and Laboratory Standards Institute(248)
Cold Formed Parts and Machine Institute(250)
Construction Specifications Institute(263)
Controlled Environment Testing Association(264)
Friction Materials Standards Institute(312)
International Code Council(365)
Manufactured Housing Institute(411)
Manufacturers Standardization Society of the Valve and Fittings Industry(411)
Materials and Methods Standards Association(414)
Media Rating Council(415)
MTM Association for Standards and Research(422)
National Certification Commission(488)
National Conference of States on Building Codes and Standards(494)
National Conference on Weights and Measures(495)
National Council for Therapeutic Recreation Certification(497)
National Environmental Balancing Bureau(507)
National Fire Protection Association(510)
National Information Standards Organization(520)
NCSL International(551)
Solar Rating and Certification Corp.(647)
Standards Engineering Society(652)
Tire and Rim Association(661)
Transformer Association, The(663)
Tubular Exchanger Manufacturers Association(666)
U.S. Metric Association(668)

STATIONERY

Business Products Credit Association(235)
Document Management Industries Association(286)
Envelope Manufacturers Association(296)
Greeting Card Association(320)
Independent Office Products and Furniture Dealers Association(335)
International Engraved Graphics Association(370)
Office Products Wholesalers Association(564)
Postcard and Souvenir Distributors Association(581)
Tag and Label Manufacturers Institute(657)
Writing Instrument Manufacturers Association(697)

STATISTICS

American Academy of Actuaries(19)
American Agricultural Economics Association(30)
American Association for Public Opinion Research(36)
American Bureau of Metal Statistics(59)
American Economic Association(80)
American Financial Services Association(83)
American Public Health Association(119)
American Sociological Association(147)
American Statistical Association(149)
Association for Federal Information Resources Management(173)
Association of Public Data Users(210)
Association of Statisticians of American Religious Bodies(216)
Casualty Actuarial Society(239)
Caucus for Women in Statistics(240)
Conference of Consulting Actuaries(259)

Council of Professional Associations on Federal Statistics(273)
Econometric Society(288)
Institute of Mathematical Statistics(342)
Insurance Accounting and Systems Association(345)
International Biometric Society(362)
International Society of Exposure Analysis(391)
Justice Research and Statistics Association(403)
National Association for Public Health Statistics and Information Systems(435)
National Association for Business Economics(441)
National Cancer Registrars Association(486)
National Council on Compensation Insurance(502)
National Crop Insurance Services(504)
Population Association of America(580)
Society of Actuaries(629)
Society of Automotive Analysts(632)

STONE

American Institute of Commemorative Art(95)
Barre Granite Association(226)
Cast Stone Institute(238)
Indiana Limestone Institute of America(336)
International Cast Polymer Association(364)
Marble Institute of America(412)
National Building Granite Quarries Association(485)
National Quartz Producers Council(534)

STORAGE

Independent Liquid Terminals Association(334)
International Association for Cold Storage Construction(349)
Professional Records and Information Services Management International(589)

STORES

American Beverage Licensees(57)
International Council of Shopping Centers(368)
NASFM(425)
National Association of Chain Drug Stores(442)
National Association of College Stores(444)
National Association of Convenience Stores(446)
National Grocers Association(515)
North American Retail Hardware Association(559)
Retail, Wholesale and Department Store Union(601)

SUGAR

American Association of Candy Technologists(39)
American Society of Sugar Beet Technologists(146)
American Sugar Alliance(150)
American Sugar Cane League of the U.S.A.(150)
American Sugarbeet Growers Association(150)
Beet Sugar Development Foundation(227)
National Confectioners Association of the United States(492)
National Sugar Brokers Association(544)
Sugar Association(655)
Sugar Industry Technologists(655)
United States Beet Sugar Association(673)

SURGERY

Academy of Ambulatory Foot and Ankle Surgery(2)
Academy of Medical-Surgical Nurses(4)
Academy of Osseointegration(5)
Academy of Surgical Research(5)
American Academy of Facial Plastic and Reconstructive Surgery(22)
American Academy of Implant Dentistry(23)
American Academy of Neurological and Orthopaedic Surgeons(24)
American Academy of Orthopaedic Surgeons(26)
American Academy of Orthotists and Prosthetists(26)
American Academy of Otolaryngology-Head and Neck Surgery(26)
American Ass'n of Ambulatory Surgery Centers(32)
American Association for Hand Surgery(35)
American Association for the Surgery of Trauma(37)
American Association for Thoracic Surgery(37)
American Association of Genitourinary Surgeons(43)
American Association of Neurological Surgeons(46)
American Association of Oral and Maxillofacial Surgeons(47)
American Association of Physician Specialists(48)
American Association of Plastic Surgeons(48)
American Association of Surgical Physician Assistants(52)
American Association of Tissue Banks(53)
American Broncho-Esophagological Association(59)
American Burn Association(60)
American College for Advancement in Medicine(63)
American College of Angiology(64)
American College of Chest Physicians(64)
American College of Eye Surgeons(65)
American College of Foot and Ankle Surgeons(66)
American College of International Physicians(66)
American College of Mohs Micrographic Surgery and Cutaneous Oncology(67)
American College of Oral and Maxillofacial Surgeons(68)
American College of Osteopathic Surgeons(69)
American College of Surgeons(71)
American College of Veterinary Surgeons(72)
American Head and Neck Society(89)
American Shoulder and Elbow Surgeons(125)
American Society for Aesthetic Plastic Surgery(126)
American Society for Artificial Internal Organs(126)
American Society for Dermatologic Surgery(128)
American Society for Laser Medicine and Surgery(130)
American Society for Pediatric Neurosurgery(131)
American Society for Reconstructive Microsurgery(132)
American Society for Stereotactic and Functional Neurosurgery(132)
American Society for Surgery of the Hand(132)
American Society of Abdominal Surgeons(133)
American Society of Cataract and Refractive Surgery(135)
American Society of Colon and Rectal Surgeons(136)
American Society of General Surgeons(138)
American Society of Hair Restoration Surgery(138)
American Society of Lipo-Suction Surgery(140)
American Society of Maxillofacial Surgeons(141)
American Society of Plastic Surgeons(144)
American Society of Plastic Surgical Nurses(144)
American Society of Transplant Surgeons(146)
American Surgical Association(150)
Arthroscopy Association of North America(162)
Association for Academic Surgery(166)
Association for Surgical Education(178)
Association of American Physicians and Surgeons(185)
Association of Bone and Joint Surgeons(188)
Association of Military Surgeons of the U.S.(205)
Association of Surgical Technologists(216)
Association of Women Surgeons(220)
Clinical Orthopaedic Society(248)
Congress of Neurological Surgeons(261)
Federated Ambulatory Surgery Association(303)
Health Industry Distributors Association(323)
Heart Rhythm Society(324)
International Association of Ocular Surgeons(359)
International College of Surgeons(366)
International Pediatric Transplant Association(382)
International Society for Heart and Lung Transplantation(387)
International Society for Minimally-Invasive Cardiac Surgery(387)
International Society of Arthroscopy, Knee Surgery and Orthopaedic Sports Medicine(390)
International Society of Hair Restoration Surgery(391)
Neurosurgical Society of America(552)
Orthopedic Surgical Manufacturers Association(569)
Plastic Surgery Research Council(579)
Shock Society(610)
Society for Biomaterials(614)
Society for Clinical Vascular Surgery(615)
Society for Surgery of the Alimentary Tract(625)
Society for Vascular Surgery(629)
Society of Air Force Clinical Surgeons(629)
Society of American Gastrointestinal and Endoscopic Surgeons(630)
Society of Eye Surgeons(636)
Society of Laparoendoscopic Surgeons(639)
Society of Neurological Surgeons(640)
Society of Neurosurgical Anesthesia and Critical Care(641)
Society of Pelvic Surgeons(641)
Society of Reproductive Surgeons(643)
Society of Thoracic Surgeons(645)
Society of United States Air Force Flight Surgeons(645)
Society of University Surgeons(645)
Surgical Infection Society(656)
Transplantation Society(663)

SURPLUS

Institute of Scrap Recycling Industries(343)
Machinery Dealers National Association(409)

SURVEYORS

American Congress on Surveying and Mapping(73)
Management Association for Private Photogrammetric Surveyors(410)
National Association of Marine Surveyors(461)
National Society of Professional Surveyors(542)
Society of Accredited Marine Surveyors(629)

SWIMMING

American Swimming Coaches Association(150)
Association of Pool and Spa Professionals(208)
College Swimming Coaches Association of America(252)
Diving Equipment and Marketing Association(286)
International Association of Dive Rescue Specialists(356)
National Association of Underwater Instructors(480)
United States Lifesaving Association(676)
United States Swim School Association(677)

SWINE

American Association of Swine Veterinarians(52)
American Berkshire Association(56)
Chester White Swine Record Association(244)
National Association of Swine Records(478)
National Hereford Hog Record Association(517)
National Pork Producers Council(533)
National Spotted Swine Record(543)
National Swine Improvement Federation(545)
National Swine Registry(545)
Poland China Record Association(579)
Tamworth Swine Association(657)

TAXES

Affordable Housing Tax Credit Coalition(10)
American Payroll Association(113)
American Property Tax Counsel(117)
American Society of Tax Professionals(146)

Council for International Tax Education(269)
Council On State Taxation(277)
Federation of Tax Administrators(304)
Institute for Professionals in Taxation(339)
International Association of Assessing Officers(353)
International Tax Institute(393)
National Association of Computerized Tax Processors(445)
National Association of Enrolled Agents(451)
National Association of Property Tax Representatives - Transportation, Energy, Communications(467)
National Association of Royalty Owners(469)
National Association of Tax Professionals(478)
National Tax Association(545)
National Tax Lien Association(545)
National Treasury Employees Union(547)
Society of Depreciation Professionals(635)
Tax Executives Institute(657)

TAXONOMY
American Society of Plant Taxonomists(144)
Society of Systematic Biologists(644)

TEACHERS see EDUCATION
National Association of Black Professors(440)

TELEPHONES
Alliance for Telecommunications Industry Solutions(16)
American Public Communications Council(119)
American Teleservices Association(151)
Association of TeleServices International(217)
Cable and Telecommunications Human Resources Association(236)
Communications Supply Service Association(255)
COMPTEL(257)
International Right of Way Association(385)
National ALEC Association/ Prepaid Communications Association(429)
National Emergency Number Association(507)
National Exchange Carrier Association(507)
National Telecommunications Cooperative Association(546)
North-American Association of Telecommunications Dealers(562)
Organization for the Promotion and Advancement of Small Telecommunications Companies(567)
PCIA - the Wireless Industry Association(572)
Society of Telecommunications Consultants(644)
Telecommunications Industry Association(659)
United States Telecom Association(677)
Wireless Dealers Association(690)
Yellow Pages Association(698)

TELEVISION see RADIO-TV
Alliance of Black Telecommunications Employees(16)

TENNIS
American Sports Builders Association(148)
ATP(221)
Intercollegiate Tennis Association(346)
International Health, Racquet and Sportsclub Association(374)
Professional Tennis Registry(589)
Tennis Industry Association(659)
United States Professional Tennis Association(676)
United States Racquet Stringers Association(677)
United States Tennis Association(677)
WTA Tour(697)

TESTING
American Association for Laboratory Accreditation(35)
American Association of Textile Chemists and Colorists(53)
American Council of Independent Laboratories(75)
American Society for Histocompatability and Immunogenetics(130)
American Society for Nondestructive Testing(131)
American Society for Quality(132)
Association of Test Publishers(217)
ASTM International(221)
Cardiovascular Credentialing International(237)
Controlled Environment Testing Association(264)
International Electrical Testing Association(370)
International Test and Evaluation Association(394)
Society for Clinical Trials(615)
Society of Experimental Test Pilots(635)
Society of Flight Test Engineers(636)

TEXTILES
American Association of Textile Chemists and Colorists(53)
American Fiber Manufacturers Association(83)
American Flock Association(84)
American Reusable Textile Association(122)
American Textile Machinery Association(151)
Carpet and Rug Institute(238)
Color Association of the United States(252)
Cordage Institute(266)
Cotton Council International(267)
Fiber Society(305)
Handweavers Guild of America(321)
Home Fashion Products Association(327)
INDA, Association of the Nonwoven Fabrics Industry(333)
Industrial Fabrics Association International(336)
Institutional and Service Textile Distributors Association(344)
International Sleep Products Association(386)
International Textile and Apparel Association(394)
The Knitting Guild Association(404)
Mohair Council of America(421)
National Association of Decorative Fabric Distributors(448)
National Council of Textile Organizations(501)
National Textile Association(546)
Pine Chemicals Association(578)
Schiffli Lace and Embroidery Manufacturers Association(606)
Shippers of Recycled Textiles(610)
Surface Design Association(656)
Textile Bag and Packaging Association(660)
Textile Bag Manufacturers Association(660)
Textile Care Allied Trades Association(660)
Textile Converters Association(660)
Textile Distributors Association(660)
Textile Fibers and By-Products Association(660)
Textile Producers and Suppliers Association(660)
Textile Rental Services Association of America(660)
United States Association of Importers of Textiles and Apparel(673)
Young Menswear Association(698)

THEATRE
American Alliance for Theatre and Education(30)
American Association of Community Theatre(41)
American Dance Guild(78)
American Society for Theatre Research(132)
American Society of Group Psychotherapy and Psychodrama(138)
American Society of Theatre Consultants(146)
American Theatre Critics Association(151)
Association for Theatre in Higher Education(181)
Association of Theatre Movement Educators(218)
Association of Theatrical Press Agents and Managers(218)
Black Theatre Network(231)
Dramatists Guild of America(287)
Educational Theatre Association(289)
International Museum Theater Alliance(380)
International Theatre Equipment Association(394)
International Ticketing Association(394)
League of American Theatres and Producers(406)
League of Historic American Theatres(406)
League of Resident Theatres(406)
Literary Managers and Dramaturgs of the Americas(408)
National Alliance for Musical Theatre(429)
National Association for Drama Therapy(432)
National Association of Schools of Theatre(471)
National Association of Theatre Owners(479)
National Costumers Association(496)
NFHS Speech Debate and Theatre Association(553)
Society of American Fight Directors(630)
Society of Stage Directors and Choreographers(644)
Theatre Library Association(660)
United Scenic Artists(672)
United States Institute for Theatre Technology(676)
University/Resident Theatre Association(680)

THERAPEUTICS
American Art Therapy Association(32)
American Association for Marriage and Family Therapy(36)
American Association for Respiratory Care(36)
American Association of Behavioral Therapists(38)
American Association of Professional Hypnotherapists(49)
American Dance Therapy Association(78)
American Family Therapy Academy(81)
American Group Psychotherapy Association(87)
American Horticultural Therapy Association(92)
American Kinesiotherapy Association(100)
American Massage Therapy Association(103)
American Music Therapy Association(107)
American Occupational Therapy Association(109)
American Organization for Bodywork Therapies of Asia(110)
American Physical Therapy Association(115)
American Physical Therapy Association - Private Practice Section(115)
American Polarity Therapy Association(116)
American Psychological Association - Division of Psychotherapy(118)
American Society for Clinical Pharmacology and Therapeutics(127)
American Society for Experimental NeuroTherapeutics(129)
American Society for Pharmacology and Experimental Therapeutics(131)
American Society for Therapeutic Radiology and Oncology(133)
American Society of Group Psychotherapy and Psychodrama(138)
American Society of Hand Therapists(138)
American Society for the Alexander Technique(146)
American Therapeutic Recreation Association(151)
Associated Bodywork and Massage Professionals(164)
Association for Play Therapy(176)
Federation of American Socs. for Experimental Biology(303)
Federation of State Boards of Physical Therapy(304)
Infusion Nurses Society(338)
International Association of Infant Massage(358)
National Association for Drama Therapy(432)
National Association for Holistic Aromatherapy(434)
National Association of Substance Abuse Trainers and Educators(478)

National Coalition of Creative Arts Therapies Associations(490)
National Council for Therapeutic Recreation Certification(497)
National Remotivation Therapy Organization(536)
Society for Light Treatment and Biological Rhythms(621)

TILES

Ceramic Tile Distributors Association(241)
Ceramic Tile Institute of America(242)
Materials and Methods Standards Association(414)
National Terrazzo and Mosaic Association(546)
National Tile Contractors Association(546)
Resilient Floor Covering Institute(600)
Tile Contractors' Association of America(661)
Tile Council of North America(661)
Tile Roofing Institute(661)

TIMBER

American Forest Resource Council(85)
National Woodland Owners Association(550)
Timber Products Manufacturers(661)
Western Red Cedar Pole Association(687)

TIN

American Tin Trade Association(151)
Tin Stabilizers Association(661)

TOBACCO INDUSTRY

Association of Dark Leaf Tobacco Dealers and Exporters(193)
Bakery, Confectionery, Tobacco Workers and Grain Millers International Union(225)
Bright Belt Warehouse Association(232)
Burley Auction Warehouse Association(235)
Burley Tobacco Growers Cooperative Association(235)
Cigar Association of America(247)
Flue-Cured Tobacco Cooperative Stabilization Corporation(308)
Leaf Tobacco Exporters Association(406)
Pipe Tobacco Council(578)
Retail Tobacco Dealers of America(601)
Society for Research on Nicotine and Tobacco(625)
Specialty Tobacco Council(650)
Tobacco Associates(662)
Tobacco Merchants Association of the U.S.(662)
Tobacconists' Association of America(662)

TOOLS

American Knife and Tool Institute(100)
American Measuring Tool Manufacturers Association(103)
Equipment and Tool Institute(297)
Equipment Service Association(297)
Hand Tools Institute(321)
International Association of Tool Craftsmen(361)
International Saw and Knife Association(385)
International Staple, Nail and Tool Association(393)
National Tooling and Machining Association(546)
North American Punch Manufacturers Association(559)
Powder Actuated Tool Manufacturers Institute(582)
Power Tool Institute(582)
Specialty Steel Industry of North America(650)
Specialty Tool and Fastener Distributors Association(650)
United States Cutting Tool Institute(675)

TOXICOLOGY

American Academy of Clinical Toxicology(21)
American Academy of Veterinary and Comparative Toxicology(29)
American College of Medical Toxicology(67)
American College of Toxicology(71)
Association of American Pesticide Control Officials(185)
International Academy of Oral Medicine and Toxicology(348)
International Association of Forensic Toxicologists(357)
Society of Toxicology(645)
Toxicology Forum(662)

TOYS

American Specialty Toy Retailing Association(148)
Association for the Study of Play(181)
Cottage Industry Miniaturists Trade Association(267)
Hobby Manufacturers Association(327)
Kite Trade Association International(403)
Toy Industry Association(662)
U.S.A. Toy Library Association(669)

TRACK AND FIELD

American Sports Builders Association(148)

TRADEMARKS

Intellectual Property Owners Association(345)
International Licensing Industry Merchandisers' Association(378)
International Trademark Association(394)
Licensing Executives Society(407)

TRAFFIC

Advanced Transit Association(9)
American Association of Motor Vehicle Administrators(45)
American Society of Transportation and Logisitcs(146)
American Traffic Safety Services Association(152)
Institute of Transportation Engineers(344)
National Association of Traffic Accident Reconstructionists and Investigators(479)
The National Industrial Transportation League(519)

TRAILERS

Manufactured Housing Institute(411)
Modular Building Institute(420)
National Trailer Dealers Association(547)
Recreation Vehicle Industry Association(596)
Recreational Park Trailer Industry Association(596)
Truck Trailer Manufacturers Association(666)

TRAINING

Academy of Security Educators and Trainers(5)
Accrediting Council for Continuing Education and Training(7)
American Society for Training and Development(133)
American Technical Education Association(150)
Association for Career and Technical Education(169)
Association for Information Media and Equipment(174)
Automotive Training Managers Council(224)
Driving School Association of America(287)
Evangelical Training Association(298)
International Association of Correctional Training Personnel(355)
International Association of Culinary Professionals(355)
International Association of Round Dance Teachers(361)
International Society for Performance Improvement(388)
International Society of Fire Service Instructors(391)
National Association of Workforce Boards(482)
National Association of Workforce Development Professionals(482)
National Basketball Athletic Trainers Association(483)
National Business Incubation Association(486)
National Environmental, Safety and Health Training Association(507)
National Training Systems Association(547)
North American Transportation Management Institute(562)
Professional Baseball Athletic Trainers Society(586)
Professional Football Athletic Trainers Society(587)
Professional Society for Sales and Marketing Training(589)
Professional Tennis Registry(589)
Society for Intercultural Education, Training and Research - USA(620)
Society of Insurance Trainers and Educators(639)
Training Directors' Forum(663)
Training Officers Conference(663)
United Professional Horsemen's Association(672)
United States Fencing Coaches Association(675)
Walking Horse Trainers Association(685)

TRANSLATORS

American Literary Translators Association(101)
American Translators Association(152)
National Association of Judiciary Interpreters and Translators(459)

TRANSPORTATION

Advanced Transit Association(9)
Agricultural and Food Transporters Conference(12)
Air Transport Association of America(13)
Airport Ground Transportation Association(15)
Amalgamated Transit Union(18)
American Association of Private Railroad Car Owners(49)
American Association of State Highway and Transportation Officials(51)
American Bus Association(60)
American Coal Ash Association(63)
American Public Transportation Association(120)
American Society of Transportation and Logisitcs(146)
American Waterways Operators(154)
Animal Transportation Association(157)
Association for Commuter Transportation(169)
Association of Air Medical Services(183)
Association of Oil Pipe Lines(206)
Association of Ship Brokers and Agents (U.S.A.)(214)
Association of Transportation Professionals(218)
Automotive Fleet and Leasing Association(223)
Bulk Carrier Conference(235)
Buses International Association(235)
Certified Claims Professional Accreditation Council(242)
Committee for Private Offshore Rescue and Towing (C-PORT)(254)
Community Transportation Association of America(256)
Conference of Minority Transportation Officials(259)
Council on the Safe Transportation of Hazardous Articles(277)
Dangerous Goods Advisory Council(281)
Delta Nu Alpha Transportation Fraternity(282)
Electric Drive Transportation Association(290)
Energy Traffic Association(294)
Expediting Management Association(299)
Express Delivery & Logistics Association(300)
Extra Touch Florists Association(300)
Freight Transportation Consultants Association(312)
Governors Highway Safety Association(319)
Household Goods Forwarders Association of America(329)
Independent Pet and Animal Transportation Association International(335)
Institute of Nuclear Materials Management(343)
Institute of Transportation Engineers(344)
Intelligent Transportation Society of America(345)
Interferry(347)

TRAVEL

TREES

TRUCKING INDUSTRY

ULTRASONICS

UNIFORMS

UPHOLSTERY

UROLOGY

UTILITIES

National Submetering and Utility Allocation Association(544)
National Utility Contractors Association(548)
United Telecom Council(679)
Utility Arborist Association(681)
Utility Communicators International(681)
Utility Workers Union of America(681)

VACUUM

Association of Industrial Metallizers, Coaters and Laminators(201)
Association of Vacuum Equipment Manufacturers International(220)
AVS Science and Technology Society(225)
Society of Vacuum Coaters(646)
Vacuum Dealers Trade Association(682)

VALVES

Fluid Controls Institute(308)
Manufacturers Standardization Society of the Valve and Fittings Industry(411)
Valve Manufacturers Association of America(682)
Valve Repair Council(682)

VENDING

Amusement and Music Operators Association(156)
Correctional Vendors Association(267)
International Association of Ice Cream Vendors(358)
Multi-Housing Laundry Association(422)
National Automatic Merchandising Association(482)
National Bulk Vendors Association(485)

VENTILATORS

Air Movement and Control Association International(13)
Associated Air Balance Council(164)

VETERINARY

Academy of Veterinary Allergy and Clinical Immunology(6)
Academy of Veterinary Homeopathy(6)
American Academy of Veterinary and Comparative Toxicology(29)
American Academy of Veterinary Pharmacology and Therapeutics(29)
American Animal Hospital Association(31)
American Association for Laboratory Animal Science(35)
American Association of Avian Pathologists(38)
American Association of Bovine Practitioners(39)
American Association of Equine Practitioners(42)
American Association of Feline Practitioners(43)
American Association of Industrial Veterinarians(44)
American Association of Small Ruminant Practitioners(51)
American Association of Swine Veterinarians(52)
American Association of Veterinary Clinicians(53)
American Association of Veterinary Immunologists(53)
American Association of Veterinary Laboratory Diagnosticians(53)
American Association of Veterinary Parasitologists(54)
American Association of Veterinary State Boards(54)
American Association of Wildlife Veterinarians(54)
American Association of Zoo Keepers(54)
American Association of Zoo Veterinarians(54)
American Board of Veterinary Practitioners(58)
American College of Laboratory Animal Medicine(66)
American College of Veterinary Anesthesiologists(71)
American College of Veterinary Dermatology(71)
American College of Veterinary Internal Medicine(71)
American College of Veterinary Nutrition(71)
American College of Veterinary Ophthalmologists(71)
American College of Veterinary Pathologists(72)
American College of Veterinary Radiology(72)
American College of Veterinary Surgeons(72)
American Embryo Transfer Association(81)
American Heartworm Society(90)
American Holistic Veterinary Medical Association(91)
American Society of Laboratory Animal Practitioners(140)
American Society of Veterinary Ophthalmology(147)
American Veterinary Dental Society(153)
American Veterinary Distributors Association(153)
American Veterinary Medical Association(153)
American Veterinary Society of Animal Behavior(153)
Animal Health Institute(157)
Association for Equine Sports Medicine(172)
Association for Gnotobiotics(173)
Association for Women Veterinarians(182)
Association of American Veterinary Medical Colleges(186)
Association of Avian Veterinarians(187)
Conference of Research Workers in Animal Diseases(260)
Delta Society(283)
International Association of Equine Dentistry(356)
International Embryo Transfer Society(370)
National Association of Federal Veterinarians(452)
National Mastitis Council(526)
National Wildlife Rehabilitators Association(549)
Omega Tau Sigma(564)
Society for Theriogenology(628)
United States Animal Health Association(672)
Veterinary Botanical Medical Association(682)
Veterinary Cancer Society(682)
Veterinary Hospital Managers Association(682)
Veterinary Orthopedic Society(682)
Wildlife Disease Association(689)
Women in Agribusiness(691)
World Association of Veterinary Anatomists(695)

VITAMINS

Council for Responsible Nutrition(270)

VOCATIONAL GUIDANCE

American Association for Career Education(34)
American Association for Employment in Education(34)
American Counseling Association(76)
American Medical Rehabilitation Providers Association(104)
American Technical Education Association(150)
American Vocational Education Personnel Development Association(153)
Association for Career and Technical Education(169)
Association for Career and Technical Education Research(169)
Business Professionals of America(236)
Career Planning and Adult Development Network(238)
Commission on Certification of Work Adjustment and Vocational Evaluation Specialists(254)
Council of State Administrators of Vocational Rehabilitation(274)
Distributive Education Clubs of America(286)
Family, Career, and Community Leaders of America(300)
Future Business Leaders of America-Phi Beta Lambda(313)
Independent Educational Consultants Association(334)
International Association of Counseling Services(355)
International Association of Jewish Vocational Services(358)
National Academic Advising Association(426)
National Association for Trade and Industrial Education(437)
National Association of Advisors for the Health Professions(438)
National Association of Agricultural Educators(438)
National Association of Industrial and Technical Teacher Educators(458)
National Association of Pupil Services Administrators(467)
National Association of State Supervisors of Trade and Industrial Education(476)
National Career Development Association(487)
National Conference of Diocesan Vocation Directors(493)
National FFA Organization(510)
National Postsecondary Agriculture Student Organization(533)
Skills USA(611)
Technology Student Association(658)
Vocational Evaluation and Career Assessement Professionals(684)

VOLUNTEER

American Society of Directors of Volunteer Services(137)
Independent Sector(336)
International Society for Third-Sector Research(389)
National Association of Foster Grandparent Program Directors(453)
National Association of Retired Senior Volunteer Program Directors(469)
National Volunteer Fire Council(548)

WAREHOUSES

Affiliated Warehouse Companies(10)
American Chain of Warehouses(61)
Bright Belt Warehouse Association(232)
Burley Auction Warehouse Association(235)
Cotton Warehouse Association of America(267)
Council of Supply Chain Management Professionals(275)
Distribution Business Management Association(286)
International Association of Refrigerated Warehouses(360)
International Warehouse Logistics Association(396)
Performance Warehouse Association(573)
Recreational Vehicle Aftermarket Association(596)
Self Storage Association(608)
Warehousing Education and Research Council(685)

WASTE

Asphalt Recycling and Reclaiming Association(163)
Association of State and Territorial Solid Waste Management Officials(215)
Automotive Recyclers Association(224)
Center for Waste Reduction Technologies(241)
Environmental Business Association, The(296)
Environmental Industry Associations(296)
Environmental Technology Council(297)
Ground Water Protection Council(320)
Integrated Waste Services Association(345)
Investment Recovery Association(399)
Municipal Waste Management Association(422)
National Association of Sewer Service Companies(472)
National Association of Wastewater Transporters(480)
National Onsite Wastewater Recycling Association(529)
National Solid Wastes Management Association(542)
Plumbing and Drainage Institute(579)

Submersible Wastewater Pump Association(655)
SWANA - Solid Waste Association of North America(656)
US Composting Council(681)
Waste Equipment Technology Association(685)
Water and Wastewater Equipment Manufacturers Association(685)

WATCHES

American Watch Association(154)
American Watchmakers-Clockmakers Institute(154)
Jewelry Industry Distributors Association(401)
National Time Equipment Association(546)

WATER

American Filtration and Separations Society(83)
American Institute of Hydrology(96)
American Membrane Technology Association(105)
American Society of Irrigation Consultants(140)
American Society of Limnology and Oceanography(140)
American Water Resources Association(154)
American Water Works Association(154)
Association of Boards of Certification(188)
Association of Metropolitan Water Agencies(204)
Association of State and Interstate Water Pollution Control Administrators(214)
Association of State Dam Safety Officials(215)
Association of State Drinking Water Administrators(215)
Association of Water Technologies(220)
Evaporative Cooling Institute(299)
Federal Water Quality Association(302)
Ground Water Protection Council(320)
Groundwater Management Districts Association(320)
International Bottled Water Association(362)
International Desalination Association(369)
International Ozone Association-Pan American Group Branch(382)
International Water Resources Association(396)
Interstate Council on Water Policy(398)
Irrigation Association(400)
National Association of Clean Water Agencies(443)
National Association of Flood and Stormwater Management Agencies(453)
National Association of Water Companies(480)
National Drilling Association(505)
National Ground Water Association(515)
National Hydropower Association(518)
National Institutes for Water Resources(521)
National Marine Electronics Association(526)
National Onsite Wastewater Recycling Association(529)
National Rural Water Association(538)
National Utility Contractors Association(548)
National Water Resources Association(548)
North American Lake Management Society(557)
Process Equipment Manufacturers' Association(584)
River Management Society(602)
Soil and Water Conservation Society(647)
Sump and Sewage Pump Manufacturers Association(655)
United States Committee on Irrigation and Drainage(674)
United States Society on Dams(677)
Universities Council on Water Resources(679)
Water and Sewer Distributors of America(685)
Water and Wastewater Equipment Manufacturers Association(685)
Water Environment Federation(685)
Water Quality Association(686)
Water Sports Industry Association(686)
Water Systems Council(686)
WaterJet Technology Association(686)
World Waterpark Association(696)

WATERPROOFERS

Asphalt Roofing Manufacturers Association(163)
Sealant, Waterproofing and Restoration Institute(607)

WATERWAYS

American Waterways Operators(154)
Committee for Private Offshore Rescue and Towing (C-PORT)(254)
Dredging Contractors of America(287)
Estuarine Research Federation(297)
Independent Terminal Operators Association(336)
Lake Carriers' Association(404)
National Waterways Conference(549)
Professional Paddlesports Association(588)
River Management Society(602)
Shipbuilders Council of America(610)
Western Dredging Association(687)

WEBB-POMERENE ACT

American Cotton Shippers Association(74)
American Natural Soda Ash Corporation(108)
American Poultry International(117)
American-European Soda Ash Shipping Association(156)
California Dried Fruit Export Association(236)
Motion Picture Association(421)
Northwest Fruit Exporters(562)

WELFARE

American Benefits Council(56)
American Public Human Services Association(120)
Association of Jewish Family and Children's Agencies(202)
Child Welfare League of America(244)
Community Action Partnership(255)
National Association of Public Child Welfare Administrators(467)
National Association of State Retirement Administrators(476)
National Conference of State Social Security Administrators(494)
National Council of Local Human Service Administrators(499)
National Organization of Social Security Claimants' Representatives(530)
National WIC Association(549)
Presbyterian Health, Education and Welfare Association(583)
Voices for America's Children(684)

WHEAT

Home Baking Association(327)
National Association of Wheat Growers(481)
National Futures Association(513)
U.S. Wheat Associates(668)
United States Durum Growers Association(675)
Wheat Quality Council(688)

WHOLESALERS

American Association of Meat Processors(45)
American Machine Tool Distributors Association(102)
American Nursery and Landscape Association(109)
American Supply Association(150)
American Traffic Safety Services Association(152)
American Wholesale Booksellers Association(154)
American Wholesale Marketers Association(155)
Appliance Parts Distributors Association(159)
Associated Equipment Distributors(165)
Association for High Technology Distribution(174)
Association for Hose and Accessories Distribution(174)
Association of Food Industries(197)
Association of Pool and Spa Professionals(208)
Association of Steel Distributors(216)
Aviation Distributors and Manufacturers Association International(224)
Bearing Specialist Association(226)
Bicycle Product Suppliers Association(228)
Biscuit and Cracker Manufacturers' Association(229)
Board of Trade of the Wholesale Seafood Merchants(231)
Copper and Brass Servicenter Association(266)
Craft & Hobby Association(278)
Dental Dealers of America(283)
Display Distributors Association(285)
Document Management Industries Association(286)
Door and Hardware Institute(287)
Farm Equipment Wholesalers Association(301)
Financial and Security Products Association(305)
Fluid Power Distributors Association(308)
Food Industry Suppliers Association(309)
Food Marketing Institute(309)
Foodservice Equipment Distributors Association(310)
Gases and Welding Distributors Association(314)
General Merchandise Distributors Council(315)
HARDI - Heating, Airconditioning, and Refrigeration Distributors International(321)
Health Industry Distributors Association(323)
Healthcare Distribution Management Association(323)
Independent Laboratory Distributors Association(334)
Independent Medical Distributors Association(335)
Independent Office Products and Furniture Dealers Association(335)
InfoCom International(338)
Institutional and Service Textile Distributors Association(344)
International Association of Plastics Distributors(360)
International Federation of Pharmaceutical Wholesalers(371)
International Furniture Suppliers Association(373)
ISSA(400)
Jewelry Industry Distributors Association(401)
Lawn and Garden Marketing and Distribution Association(406)
Machinery Dealers National Association(409)
Material Handling Equipment Distributors Association(414)
Metal Service Center Institute(417)
Monument Builders of North America(421)
Music Distributors Association(423)
National Appliance Parts Suppliers Association(430)
National Association of Chemical Distributors(442)
National Association of Container Distributors(446)
National Association of Decorative Fabric Distributors(448)
National Association of Electrical Distributors(450)
National Association of Fire Equipment Distributors(452)
National Association of Floor Covering Distributors(453)
National Association of Flour Distributors(453)
National Association of Marine Services(461)
National Association of Recording Merchandisers(468)
National Association of Sporting Goods Wholesalers(472)
National Association of Steel Pipe Distributors(477)
National Association of Video Distributors(480)
National Association of Wholesaler-Distributors(481)
National Beer Wholesalers Association(484)
National Candle Association(487)
National Electronic Distributors Association(506)
National Fastener Distributors Association(508)

National Frozen and Refrigerated Foods Association(513)
National Grocers Association(515)
National Kitchen and Bath Association(523)
National Marine Distributors Association(526)
National Poultry and Food Distributors Association(533)
National School Supply and Equipment Association(538)
National Truck Equipment Association(547)
National Wheel and Rim Association(549)
North American Building Material Distribution Association(555)
North American Meat Processors Association(558)
North American Wholesale Lumber Association(562)
North-American Association of Telecommunications Dealers(562)
NPTA Alliance(563)
Office Products Wholesalers Association(564)
Optical Laboratories Association(566)
Outdoor Power Equipment and Engine Service Association(569)
Pet Industry Distributors Association(574)
Petroleum Equipment Institute(574)
Petroleum Equipment Suppliers Association(574)
Pharmaceutical Research and Manufacturers of America(575)
Power Transmission Distributors Association(582)
Professional Beauty Association(586)
Professional Picture Framers Association(588)
Quality Bakers of America Cooperative(594)
Recreational Vehicle Aftermarket Association(596)
Retail, Wholesale and Department Store Union(601)
Safety Equipment Distributors Association(604)
Sanitary Supply Wholesaling Association(605)
Security Hardware Distributors Association(607)
United Product Formulators and Distributors Association(672)
Wallcoverings Association(685)
Wholesale Florist and Florist Supplier Association(688)
Wine and Spirits Wholesalers of America(689)

WINDOWS

Association of Millwork Distributors(205)
International Window Film Association(397)
Safety Glazing Certification Council(604)
Screen Manufacturers Association(607)
Steel Window Institute(654)
Window Council(689)
Window Coverings Association of America(689)
Window Coverings Manufacturers Association(689)

WINE

American Society for Enology and Viticulture(128)
American Wine Society(155)
Association of Winery Suppliers(220)
Concord Grape Association(258)
Greek Food and Wine Institute(320)
Home Wine and Beer Trade Association(328)
Society of Wine Educators(646)
Sommelier Society of America(647)
Vinifera Wine Growers Association(683)
Wine and Spirits Shippers Association(689)
Wine and Spirits Wholesalers of America(689)
WineAmerica(690)

WIRE

American Wire Cloth Institute(155)
American Wire Producers Association(155)
Associated Wire Rope Fabricators(166)
Insulated Cable Engineers Association(344)
Paper Machine Clothing Council(571)
Wire Association International(690)
Wire Fabricators Association(690)
Wire Reinforcement Institute(690)
Wire Rope Technical Board(690)
Woven Wire Products Association(697)

WOMEN

African-American Women's Clergy Association(11)
American Association for Women in Community Colleges(37)
American Association for Women Podiatrists(37)
American Association for Women Radiologists(37)
American Association of Family and Consumer Sciences(43)
American Association of Occupational Health Nurses(47)
American Association of Women Dentists(54)
American Business Women's Association(60)
American Medical Women's Association(105)
American National CattleWomen(108)
American Society of Women Accountants(147)
American Woman's Society of Certified Public Accountants(155)
American Women in Radio and Television(155)
Association for Women Geoscientists(182)
Association for Women in Communications(182)
Association for Women in Computing(182)
Association for Women in Management(182)
Association for Women in Mathematics(182)
Association for Women in Psychology(182)
Association for Women in Science(182)
Association for Women in Sports Media(182)
Association for Women Veterinarians(182)
Association for Women's Rights in Development(183)
Association of Girl Scout Executive Staff(198)
Association of Junior Leagues International(202)
Association of Real Estate Women(211)
Association of Women Soil Scientists(220)
Association of Women Surgeons(220)
Black Americans in Publishing(230)
Business and Professional Women/USA(235)
Caucus for Women in Statistics(240)
Coalition of Labor Union Women(249)
Commercial Real Estate Women Network(253)
Committee of 200(254)
Coordinating Council for Women in History(265)
Cosmetic Executive Women(267)
Credit Professionals International(279)
Executive Women International(299)
Fashion Group International(301)
Federally Employed Women(302)
Financial Women International(306)
General Federation of Women's Clubs(315)
Girls Incorporated(317)
Intercoiffure America/Canada(346)
International Alliance for Women(348)
International Alliance for Women in Music(348)
International Association of Women Ministers(361)
International Association of Women Police(362)
International Aviation Womens Association(362)
International Council of Psychologists(368)
International Furnishings and Design Association(373)
Iota Tau Tau(399)
Ladies Professional Golf Association(404)
Midwives Alliance of North America(419)
NALS(425)
National Association for Girls and Women in Sport(433)
National Association for Practical Nurse Education and Service(435)
National Association of Black Women Entrepreneurs(440)
National Association of Collegiate Women Athletic Administrators(445)
National Association of Colored Women's Clubs(445)
National Association of Commissions for Women(445)
National Association of Insurance Women(458)
National Association of Negro Business and Professional Women's Clubs(462)
National Association of Professional Mortgage Women(466)
National Association of Women Artists(481)
National Association of Women Business Owners(481)
National Association of Women Highway Safety Leaders(481)
National Association of Women in Construction(481)
National Association of Women Judges(481)
National Association of Women Lawyers(482)
National Conference of Women's Bar Associations(494)
National Council of Administrative Women in Education(498)
National Council of Catholic Women(498)
National Family Planning and Reproductive Health Association(508)
National Federation of Press Women(510)
National Foundation for Women Legislators(512)
National Human Resources Association(518)
National League of American Pen Women(524)
National Women's Studies Association(549)
Nine to Five, National Association of Working Women(553)
Organization of Women in International Trade(568)
Partnership in Print Production(572)
Pi Lambda Theta(577)
Professional Association of Volleyball Officials(586)
Professional Women Controllers(590)
Professional Women in Construction(590)
Ruth Jackson Orthopaedic Society(603)
Society of Woman Geographers(646)
Society of Women Engineers(646)
Stuntwomen's Association of Motion Pictures(654)
WEB: Worldwide Employee Benefits Network(686)
WIFS - Women in Insurance and Financial Services(688)
Women Band Directors International(690)
Women Chefs and Restaurateurs(691)
Women Construction Owners and Executives, USA(691)
Women Executives in Public Relations(691)
Women Executives in State Government(691)
Women in Aerospace(691)
Women in Agribusiness(691)
Women in Cable and Telecommunications(691)
Women in Endocrinology(691)
Women in Energy(691)
Women in Film(691)
Women in Film and Video(692)
Women in Government(692)
Women in Government Relations(692)
Women in International Security(692)
Women in Management(692)
Women in Mining National(692)
Women in Packaging(692)
Women in Scholarly Publishing(692)
Women in Technology International(692)
Women in the Fire Service(692)
Women of the Motion Picture Industry, International(692)
Women's Caucus for Art(693)
Women's Caucus for the Modern Languages(693)
Women's College Coalition(693)
Women's Council of REALTORS(693)
Women's Foodservice Forum(693)
Women's International Network of Utility Professionals(693)
Women's Jewelry Association(693)
Women's National Book Association(694)
Women's Professional Rodeo Association(694)
Women's Regional Publications of America(694)
Women's Transportation Seminar(694)
World Association of Alcohol Beverage Industries(695)

WTA Tour(697)
Zonta International(698)

WOOD & WOOD PRODUCTS

American Federation of Violin and Bow Makers(83)
American Fiberboard Association(83)
American Forest and Paper Association(85)
American Forest Resource Council(85)
American Forests(85)
American Hardwood Export Council(89)
American Home Furnishings Alliance(91)
American Institute of Timber Construction(98)
American Walnut Manufacturers Association(153)
American Wood Preservers Institute(155)
American Wood-Preservers' Association(155)
APA - The Engineered Wood Association(158)
Appalachian Hardwood Manufacturers(158)
Architectural Woodwork Institute(160)
Association of Millwork Distributors(205)
Association of Woodworking-Furnishings Suppliers(221)
California Redwood Association(236)
Cedar Shake and Shingle Bureau(240)
Cellulose Insulation Manufacturers Association(241)
Composite Panel Association(257)
Forest Industries Telecommunications(310)
Forest Products Society(310)
Forest Resources Association(310)
Hardwood Manufacturers Association(322)
Hardwood Plywood and Veneer Association(322)
Hearth Patio & Barbecue Association(324)
International Concatenated Order of Hoo-Hoo(366)
International Wood Products Association(397)
Log Home Builders Association of North America(409)
Maple Flooring Manufacturers Association(412)
Mulch and Soil Council(422)
National Christmas Tree Association(489)
National Frame Builders Association(512)
National Hardwood Lumber Association(516)
National Lumber and Building Material Dealers Association(525)
National Wood Flooring Association(550)
National Wood Tank Institute(550)
National Wooden Pallet and Container Association(550)
NOFMA: the Wood Flooring Manufacturers Association(553)
North American Building Material Distribution Association(555)
North American Wholesale Lumber Association(562)
Railway Tie Association(595)
Society of Wood Science and Technology(646)
Softwood Export Council(646)
Structural Board Association(654)
Surface Finishing Industry Council(656)
Timber Frame Business Council(661)
Timber Framers Guild(661)
Timber Products Manufacturers(661)
Treated Wood Council(665)
Truss Plate Institute(666)
Western Red Cedar Pole Association(687)
Western Red Cedar Lumber Association(687)
Window and Door Manufacturers Association(689)
Wood Component Manufacturers Association(694)
Wood Machinery Manufacturers of America(694)
Wood Moulding and Millwork Producers Association(694)
Wood Products Manufacturers Association(694)
Wood Truss Council of America(694)
Woodworking Machinery Industry Association(694)

WOOL see also SHEEP

American Sheep Industry Association(125)
Natural Colored Wool Growers Association(550)
Scottish Blackface Sheep Breeders Association(606)

WRITERS see also AUTHORS, PRESS

American Auto Racing Writers and Broadcasters Association(55)
American Medical Writers Association(105)
American Podiatric Medical Writers Association(116)
American Society of Journalists and Authors(140)
Associated Business Writers of America(164)
Association for Communication Excellence(169)
Association for Women in Sports Media(182)
Association of Food Journalists(197)
Association of Literary Scholars and Critics(203)
Association of Professional Communication Consultants(208)
Association of Writers and Writing Programs(221)
Bowling Writers Association of America(232)
Children's Literature Association(244)
Construction Writers Association(263)
Council of Literary Magazines and Presses(273)
Dance Critics Association(281)
Dog Writers' Association of America(286)
Editorial Freelancers Association(289)
Education Writers Association(289)
Football Writers Association of America(310)
Garden Writers Association(314)
Golf Writers Association of America(318)
International Food, Wine and Travel Writers Association(372)
International Motor Press Association(380)
International Travel Writers and Editors Association(395)
International Women's Writing Guild(397)
International Writing Centers Association(397)
Mystery Writers of America(424)
National Association of Hispanic Journalists(455)
National Association of Science Writers(471)
National Book Critics Circle(485)
National Conference of Editorial Writers(493)
National Council of Writing Program Administrators(502)
National League of American Pen Women(524)
National Sportscasters and Sportswriters Association(543)
National Turf Writers Association(547)
National Writers Association(550)
National Writers Union(550)
North American Snowsports Journalists Association(560)
Outdoor Writers Association of America(569)
Professional Association of Resume Writers and Career Coaches(586)
Professional Basketball Writers' Association(586)
Professional Football Writers of America(587)
Professional Hockey Writers' Association(587)
Religion Newswriters Association(598)
Romance Writers of America(603)
Science Fiction and Fantasy Writers of America(606)
Scribes(607)
Society for Technical Communication(626)
Society for Technological Advancement of Reporting(626)
Society of American Business Editors and Writers(630)
Society of American Travel Writers(631)
Society of Children's Book Writers and Illustrators(633)
South Asian Journalists Association(647)
Travel Journalists Guild(665)
United States Basketball Writers Association(673)
United States Harness Writers' Association(675)
Western Writers of America(688)
Writers Guild of America, East(697)
Writers Guild of America, West(697)

YARN

The National NeedleArts Association(528)
Textured Yarn Association of America(660)

ZINC

American Bureau of Metal Statistics(59)
American Zinc Association(156)
International Lead Zinc Research Organization(377)

ZOOLOGY

American Association of Zoo Keepers(54)
American Association of Zoo Veterinarians(54)
American Society of Ichthyologists and Herpetologists(139)
American Society of Limnology and Oceanography(140)
American Society of Naturalists(142)
American Zoo and Aquarium Association(156)
Animal Behavior Society(157)
Entomological Society of America(295)
Genetics Society of America(315)
Natural Science Collections Alliance(551)
Organization for Tropical Studies(567)
Paleontological Society(570)
Society for Integrative and Comparative Biology(620)
Society for Invertebrate Pathology(620)
Society for the Study of Amphibians and Reptiles(628)
Society of Nematologists(640)
Society of Protozoologists(643)
Society of Systematic Biologists(644)

2007 National Trade and Professional Associations

Geographic Index

All active organizations in NTPA can be found here under the city and state where they are headquartered.

ALABAMA

Anniston

National Association of Federal Education Program Administrators(452)

Auburn

American Association of Bovine Practitioners(39)
American Collegiate Retailing Association(72)
University Aviation Association(679)

Birmingham

Alliance for Continuing Medical Education(15)
American Assembly for Men in Nursing(33)
American Association for Applied Linguistics(33)
American Society for Reproductive Medicine(132)
American Wood-Preservers' Association(155)
Association of Edison Illuminating Companies(194)
Collegiate Commissioners Association(252)
Ductile Iron Pipe Research Association(287)
Governmental Research Association(319)
International Analgesia Society(349)
International Andalusian and Lusitano Horse Association(349)
Society for Assisted Reproductive Technology(614)
Society for Reproductive Endocrinology and Infertility(624)
Society of Dance History Scholars(635)
Society of Reproductive Surgeons(643)

Decatur

Racking Horse Breeders Association of America(594)

Florence

Beta Beta Beta(228)
College Sports Information Directors of America(252)

Hueytown

National Roadside Vegetation Management Association(537)

Huntsville

Metaphysical Society of America(418)
National Speleological Society(542)

Jacksonville

American Association of Retirement Communities(50)
National Council for Geographic Education(497)

Madison

Society of Reliability Engineers(643)

Mobile

International Public Relations Association - U.S. Section(384)

Montgomery

Association of Real Estate License Law Officials(211)
Association of State and Provincial Psychology Boards(215)
Society for Theriogenology(628)

Mountain Brook

Cookware Manufacturers Association(265)

Orange Beach

National Association of Charterboat Operators(442)
National Association of First Responders(452)

Spanish Fort

Education Credit Union Council(289)

Tuscaloosa

Association of Ecosystem Research Centers(194)
North American Association for the Study of Religion(554)

ARIZONA

Avondale

American Society of Architectural Illustrators(134)

Cabot

International Association of Railway Operating Officers(360)

Chandler

IMAGE Society(332)
International Society of Parametric Analysts(392)

Flagstaff

American Holistic Nurses Association(91)

Fountain Hills

Trade Promotion Management Association(663)
United States Swim School Association(677)

Glendale

American Disc Jockey Association(79)
EUCG(298)

Goodyear

Casting Industry Suppliers Association(239)

Harrison

American British White Park Association(59)

Litchfield Park

National Conference of State Fleet Administrators(494)

Mesa

American Hydrogen Association(92)
American Psychological Association - Division of Psychotherapy(118)
Association of Halfway House Alcoholism Programs of North America(199)
Society of Forensic Toxicologists(636)

Nogales

Fresh Produce Association of the Americas(312)

Phoenix

American Academy of Dental Group Practice(21)
Asian American Psychological Association(163)
Association of Golf Merchandisers(199)
Communications Fraud Control Association(255)
Dental Group Management Association(283)
Health Industry Business Communications Council(323)
League for Innovation in the Community College(406)
National Association for Information Destruction(434)
National Association of Elevator Safety Authorities International(450)
National Association of Railroad Trial Counsel(467)
National Association of Solar Contractors(472)
National Association of State Administrators and Supervisors of Private Schools(473)

National Environmental, Safety and Health Training Association(507)
Post-Tensioning Institute(581)
Scaffold Industry Association(605)
Supima(656)

Prescott

National Council of Exchangors(499)
National Renal Administrators Association(536)

Scottsdale

American Association of Cosmetology Schools(41)
American Osteopathic College of Allergy and Immunology(111)
Association of Retail Travel Agents(212)
College Swimming Coaches Association of America(252)
Council of Educational Facility Planners, International(271)
Council on Chiropractic Education(275)
International Ozone Association-Pan American Group Branch(382)
National Association of Sales Professionals(470)
National Council for Prescription Drug Programs(497)
Professional Beauty Association(586)
Residential Space Planners International(600)
Salon Association, The(605)
Society for Menstrual Cycle Research(621)
Telework Advisory Group for World at Work(659)
WorldatWork(697)

Sedona

World Research Foundation(696)

Surprise

Society of American Indian Dentists(631)

Tempe

American Federation of Astrologers, Inc.(82)
American Orthopsychiatric Association(111)
Association for Comparative Economic Studies(170)
Association of College and University Printers(191)
Construction Marketing Research Council(262)
Evangelical Christian Publishers Association(298)
Institute for Supply Management(340)
Manuscript Society(412)
Marketing Education Association(413)
National Speakers Association(542)
Rubber Pavements Association(603)

Tucson

American Institute for Maghrib Studies(94)
American Society for Apheresis(126)
Association of American Physicians and Surgeons(185)
Association of Certified Professional Secretaries(189)
Council of Independent Restaurants of America(272)
Harness Tracks of America(322)
International Studies Association(393)
Middle East Studies Association of North America(418)
National Academy of Elder Law Attorneys(426)
National Association of Professional Geriatric Care Managers(466)
National Association of Self-Instructional Language Programs(471)
National Federation of Modern Language Teachers Associations(509)
National Guardianship Association(515)
Society for Ecological Restoration(616)
Tree-Ring Society(665)

Yuma

American Incense Manufacturers Association(93)

ARKANSAS

Arkadelphia

National Association of Barber Boards(439)

Eureka Springs

Antique and Amusement Photographers International(157)

Fayetteville

Conference of Historical Journals(259)
International Conference of Funeral Service Examining Boards(366)
Society of Engineering Science(635)

Gurdon

International Concatenated Order of Hoo-Hoo(366)

Hot Springs Village

Aluminum Foil Container Manufacturers Association(18)

Little Rock

Agricultural History Society(12)
Apiary Inspectors of America(158)
Case Management Society of America(238)
Communications Supply Service Association(255)
Delta Pi Epsilon(282)
National Federation of Nonpublic School State Accrediting Associations(510)
National Interstate Council of State Boards of Cosmetology(522)

Searcy

Cooperative Work Experience Education Association(265)

CALIFORNIA

Alameda

Association for Humanistic Psychology(174)

Aliso Viejo

American Association of Critical-Care Nurses(41)
American Institute of Inspectors(96)
Council of Communication Management(271)
National Purchasing Institute(534)

Alta Loma

National Aerosol Association(428)

Anaheim

World Floor Covering Association(695)
World International Nail and Beauty Association(696)

Arcadia

American Sports Medicine Association(148)
World Wide Pet Industry Association(697)

Arcata

Society for the Study of Indigenous Languages of the Americas(628)

Balboa Island

American College of Forensic Psychiatry(66)

Berkeley

American Association of Teachers of Slavic and East European Languages(52)
American Finance Association(83)
Association for the Study of Dreams(180)
Independent Scholars of Asia(335)
International Coordinating Committee on Solid State Sensors and Actuators Research(367)
International Society for Magnetic Resonance in Medicine(387)
Society for the Study of Early China(628)
Substance Abuse Librarians and Information Specialists(655)

Beverly Hills

Academy of Motion Picture Arts and Sciences(4)
International Association of Corporate and Professional Recruitment(355)
Lepidoptera Research Foundation(407)
Producer's Guild of America(584)
Society of Composers and Lyricists(634)
Women in Film(691)
Women of the Motion Picture Industry, International(692)

Bodega Bay

American Academy of Fixed Prosthodontics(23)
American Electrology Association(80)

Borrego Springs

Society for History Education(618)

Buena Park

Independent Distributors of Electronics Association(334)

Burbank

Academy of Country Music(3)
American Auto Racing Writers and Broadcasters Association(55)
Association of Educational Therapists(194)
Association of Professional Energy Managers(209)
Caucus for Television Producers, Writers & Directors(240)
International Animated Film Society, ASIFA-Hollywood(349)
Motion Picture and Television Credit Association(421)

Campo

National Border Patrol Council(485)

Canoga Park

Free Speech Coalition(312)

Carlsbad

American Music Conference(107)
Gemological Institute of America(315)
NAMM - the International Music Products Association(425)
Viola da Gamba Society of America(683)

Chico

American Society of Retina Specialists(145)

China

Certified Milk Producers Association of America(242)

Citrus Heights

American Anaplastology Association(31)
American Association of Industrial Veterinarians(44)

Claremont

Association for Women Veterinarians(182)
Conference for the Study of Political Thought(259)

Commerce

Association of Woodworking-Furnishings Suppliers(221)

Concord

National Association of Stock Plan Professionals(477)

Corona

Society for Vector Ecology(629)

Coronado

Fur Commission USA(312)

Corte Madera

Conservation and Preservation Charities of America(261)

Costa Mesa

National Bicycle Dealers Association(484)

Covina

Society for the Advancement of Material and Process Engineering(626)

Culver City

Ceramic Tile Institute of America(242)

Cypress

AAGL -- Advancing Minimally Invasive Gynecology Worldwide(1)

Dana Point

Association of Proposal Management Professionals(210)

Davis

American Association of Veterinary Laboratory Diagnosticians(53)
American Association of Wildlife Veterinarians(54)
American Society for Enology and Viticulture(128)
Catecholamine Club(239)
Conference on Latin American History(261)
Geothermal Resources Council(316)
International Weed Science Society(397)

Del Mar

Information Technologies Credit Union Association(338)
National Association of Credit Union Chairmen(448)
National Association of Credit Union Supervisory and Auditing Committees(448)
National Council of Postal Credit Unions(500)

Diamond Bar

International Food, Wine and Travel Writers Association(372)
Specialty Equipment Market Association(650)

Dunwoody

Kappa Delta Epsilon(403)

El Centro

American College of Chiropractic Orthopedists(64)

El Cerrito

Hydroponic Society of America(330)
Seismological Society of America(608)

El Dorado Hills

International Association of Financial Crimes Investigators(357)

El Segundo

Petroleum Investor Relations Association(574)

El Sobrante

American Institute of Engineers(95)

Encino

Alliance of Motion Picture and Television Producers(17)
American Academy of Sports Physicians(29)
American Apitherapy Society(31)
American Society of Music Arrangers and Composers(142)
National Association for Research and Therapy of Homosexuality(435)
National College of Foot Surgeons(490)
Video Software Dealers Association(683)
World Shoe Association(696)

Fallbrook

Professional Numismatists Guild(588)

Folsom

North American Blueberry Council(555)

Fresno

Association for Play Therapy(176)
Mu Phi Epsilon(422)
Society of Armenian Studies(631)
Weather Modification Association(686)

Friant

Futon Association International(313)
Specialty Sleep Association(650)

Fullerton

Accordion Federation of North America(6)
United States Federation of Scholars and Scientists(675)

Gilroy

Bicycle Shippers Association(228)

Glendale

American Council of Hypnotist Examiners(75)

Hermosa Beach

American Association for Career Education(34)
International Map Trade Association(379)

Hollywood

American Society of Cinematographers(135)
Association of Cinema and Video Laboratories(190)
Association of Moving Image Archivists(205)

Huntington Beach

Association of Surfing Professionals - North America(216)
Western Economic Association International(687)

Imperial Beach

Electrical Manufacturing and Coil Winding Association(291)

Irvine

American College of Trial Lawyers(71)
American Society of Gas Engineers(138)
Chinese-American Librarians Association(245)
Motorcycle Industry Council(421)
Motorcycle Safety Foundation(422)
North American Conference on British Studies(556)
Radiology Business Management Association(595)
Specialty Vehicle Institute of America(650)

Keene

United Farm Workers of America(671)

La Habra

Interactive Audio Special Interest Group(346)
MIDI Manufacturers Association(418)

La Mirada

Fresh Produce and Floral Council(312)

La Quinta

United Association of Equipment Leasing(670)

La Verne

Alliance of Insurance Agents and Brokers(17)
United Shoe Retailers Association(672)

Lafayette

International Institute for Lath and Plaster(376)

Laguna Beach

American Pathology Foundation(113)
Healthcare Billing and Management Association(323)
Neurodevelopmental Treatment Association(552)

Laguna Hills

American College for Advancement in Medicine(63)

Lake Forest

Association of Industry Manufacturers' Representatives(201)
Manufacturers' Agents National Association(411)
Power-Motion Technology Representatives Association(582)

Lakeside

National Council of Administrative Women in Education(498)

Lancaster

Independent Armored Car Operators Association(333)
Society of Experimental Test Pilots(635)
Society of Flight Test Engineers(636)

Loma Linda

American Institute of Oral Biology(97)
National Association of Seventh-Day Adventist Dentists(472)

Loma Rica

North American Wensleydale Sheep Association(562)

Long Beach

Academy of Managed Care Providers(4)
American Association of Philosophy Teachers(48)
American Society of Questioned Document Examiners(145)
National Sports and Fitness Association(543)
Society of Allied Weight Engineers(630)
Specialty Coffee Association of America(650)

Longmont

Disaster Preparedness and Emergency Response Association(285)

Los Alamitos

American Society for Aesthetic Plastic Surgery(126)

Los Angeles

Advertising Photographers of America(9)
African-American Library and Information Science Association(11)
AIR Commercial Real Estate Association(12)
Alliance of Area Business Publications(16)
American Academy of Medical Acupuncture(24)
American Academy of Research Historians of Medieval Spain(28)
American Association of Medical Milk Commissions(45)
American College of Trust and Estate Counsel(71)
American Harp Society(89)
American Head and Neck Society(89)

Association for Academic Surgery(166)
Association for the Study of Classical African Civilizations(180)
Association for Women in Psychology(182)
Association of Celebrity Personal Assistants(189)
Association of Latino Professionals in Accounting and Finance(203)
Association of Talent Agents(216)
Association of Volleyball Professionals(220)
Broadcast Designers' Association(233)
City and Regional Magazine Association(247)
Directors Guild of America(285)
Endocrine Fellows Foundation(294)
IEEE Industry Applications Society(331)
IEEE Instrumentation and Measurement Society(331)
IEEE Power Electronics Society(331)
Independent Film and Television Alliance(334)
International Documentary Association(369)
International Pediatric Nephrology Association(382)
Latin Business Association(405)
Leading Jewelers Guild(406)
Mexican-American Grocers Association(418)
National Association of Business Travel Agents(441)
National Association of Composers, USA(445)
National Association of Latino Elected and Appointed Officials(459)
National Association of Real Estate Investment Managers(468)
National Association of Television Program Executives(478)
National Black Public Relations Society(485)
National Congress of Inventor Organizations(495)
Parenting Publications of America(571)
PROMAX International(590)
Screen Actors Guild(606)
Society for the Study of Social Biology(628)
Society of American Gastrointestinal and Endoscopic Surgeons(630)
Society of Children's Book Writers and Illustrators(633)
Society of Hispanic Professional Engineers(638)
Society of Protozoologists(643)
Society of University Otolaryngologists(645)
Writers Guild of America, West(697)

Manhattan Beach

PMA, the Independent Book Publishers Association(579)

Menlo Park

American Association for Artificial Intelligence(33)
Asia America MultiTechnology Association(162)

Milpitas

Video Electronics Standards Association(683)

Mission Viejo

Association of American Educators(184)

Modesto

American Association for Medical Transcription(36)

Monrovia

Jockeys' Guild(402)

Monterey

Professional Liability Agents Network(588)

Monterey Park

Driving School Association of America(287)

Napa

National Association of Geoscience Teachers(454)

Newport Beach

American Society of Dermatological Retailers(137)
National Association of Credit Union Service Organizations(448)
Stucco Manufacturers Association(654)

North Hollywood

International Association of Golf Administrators(357)

Northridge

Society for Economic Anthropology(616)
U.S. Metric Association(668)

Novato

California Redwood Association(236)
Mining and Metallurgical Society of America(420)

Nuevo

Swimming Pool Water Treatment Professionals(657)

Oakland

Association of Asian-Pacific Community Health Organizations(186)
Black Psychiatrists of America(230)
Coalition of Essential Schools(249)
Earthquake Engineering Research Institute(288)
National Council on Crime and Delinquency(502)
National Federation of Community Broadcasters(509)
National Institute of Steel Detailing(521)
National Meat Association(526)
Union of American Physicians and Dentists(670)

Oceanside

National Public Employer Labor Relations Association(534)

Ocotillo

International Association of Audio Visual Communicators(353)

Old Station

Society of Telecommunications Consultants(644)

Ontario

International Association of Plumbing and Mechanical Officials(360)

Orange

AFCOM(10)
Association of Professional Ball Players of America(208)

Oxnard

Association of Applied IPM Ecologists(186)
Automatic Transmission Rebuilders Association(223)

Pacific Grove

Tire Retread Information Bureau(662)

Pacifica

Career Planning and Adult Development Network(238)
Laser and Electro-Optics Manufacturers' Association(405)
National Association for Humanities Education(434)
Professional and Technical Consultants Association(585)

Palm Desert

Performance Warehouse Association(573)

Palo Alto

American Association of Professional Hypnotherapists(49)
Association for Transpersonal Psychology(181)
Electric Power Research Institute(290)

Paramount

International Union of Petroleum and Industrial Workers(396)
Magic Dealers Association(410)

Pasadena

American Seminar Leaders Association(124)
Christian Educators Association International(246)
International Webmasters Association(397)

Pismo Beach

American Association for Correctional and Forensic Psychology(34)

Pleasanton

International Transactional Analysis Association(394)
Light Aircraft Manufacturers Association(408)

Pomona

Association for Equine Sports Medicine(172)

Rancho Cucamonga

International Institute of Municipal Clerks(376)

Rancho Santa Margarita

International Association of Skateboard Companies(361)
Professional Association of Diving Instructors(585)

Redding

American Buckskin Registry Association(59)

Redondo Beach

National Council of Black Engineers and Scientists(498)

Rohnert Park

Society for Philosophy and Technology(623)

Roseville

High Technology Crime Investigation Association(325)

Sacramento

American Association of Mental Health Professionals in Corrections(45)
American Association of Oriental Medicine(47)
American Association of Psychiatric Technicians(50)
American Criminal Justice Association/Lambda Alpha Epsilon(77)
American Dehydrated Onion and Garlic Association(78)
American Society of Dermatology(137)
Association for Wedding Professionals International(182)
Association of Membership and Marketing Executives(204)
California Dried Fruit Export Association(236)
National Council on Teacher Retirement(503)
Society of Air Force Clinical Surgeons(629)

Salinas

Refrigerating Engineers and Technicians Association(597)

San Anselmo

Academy of Homiletics(3)

San Carlos

German American Business Association(316)

San Clemente
Christian Management Association(246)

San Diego
Accredited Gemologists Association(6)
American Academy of Estate Planning Attorneys(22)
American Association of Behavioral Therapists(38)
American Association of Franchisees and Dealers(43)
American College of Veterinary Dermatology(71)
American Council on Exercise(76)
American Peptide Society(113)
Association for Comprehensive Energy Psychology(170)
Association for Social Anthropology in Oceania(178)
Customer Relations Institute(280)
Diving Equipment and Marketing Association(286)
Holistic Dental Association(327)
IDEA, The Health and Fitness Association(330)
Information Storage Industry Consortium(338)
International Academy of Gnathology - American Section(348)
Mountain Rescue Association(422)
Multi-Level Marketing International Association(422)
National Association for Year-Round Education(437)
National Bureau of Certified Consultants(485)
Organization of News Ombudsmen(567)
Service Industry Association(609)
Society for Computer Simulation(615)
Society for Software Quality(625)
Western Association for Art Conservation(687)
Women's Caucus for Political Science(693)

San Francisco
All-America Rose Selections(15)
American Academy of Ophthalmology(25)
American Association for Pediatric Ophthalmology and Strabismus(36)
American Ophthalmological Society(110)
American Society of Ophthalmic Registered Nurses(143)
American Society on Aging(147)
Asian American Certified Public Accountants(162)
Asian American Journalists Association(162)
Association for Women in Computing(182)
Association of University Professors of Ophthalmology(219)
Computer Security Institute(258)
Display Distributors Association(285)
Fibre Channel Industry Association(305)
International Association of Business Communicators(354)
International Computer Music Association(366)
International Game Developers Association(374)
International Longshore and Warehouse Union(378)
International Society of Refractive Surgery of the American Academy of Ophthalmology(392)
Medical Marketing Association(416)
National Alliance for Media Arts and Culture(429)
National Employment Lawyers Association(507)
National Society of Newspaper Columnists(542)
Open Group(565)
Professional Association for Childhood Education(585)
SCSI Trade Association(607)
Society of Insurance Trainers and Educators(639)
Transaction Processing Performance Council(663)

San Jose
American Handwriting Analysis Foundation(88)
American Voice Input/Output Society(153)
EDA Consortium(288)
National Association for Chicana and Chicano Studies(432)
Personal Computer Memory Card International Association(573)
Public Agency Risk Managers Association(592)
Semiconductor Equipment and Materials International(608)
Semiconductor Industry Association(608)
Society for Information Display(620)

San Juan Capistrano
Glove Shippers Association(318)

San Marcos
Extra Touch Florists Association(300)

San Pedro
National Watercolor Society(549)

San Ramon
International Multimedia Telecommunications Consortium(380)
International Society of Arthroscopy, Knee Surgery and Orthopaedic Sports Medicine(390)

Santa Ana
National Nutritional Foods Association(529)

Santa Barbara
American Association of Teachers of Esperanto(52)
IT Financial Management Association(400)

Santa Clara
AeA - Advancing the Business of Technology(9)
Economic History Association(288)

Santa Clarita
National Flute Association(511)

Santa Cruz
International Association of Rehabilitation Professionals(360)
Vacation Rental Managers Association(681)

Santa Monica
Association of Managed Care Dentists(203)
Human Factors and Ergonomics Society(329)
National Academy of Recording Arts and Sciences(427)
National Association of Retired Senior Volunteer Program Directors(469)
Wedding and Portrait Photographers International(686)

Santa Rosa
American Association of Owners and Breeders of Peruvian Paso Horses(47)
American Glovebox Society(87)
Peruvian Paso Horse Registry of North America(574)

Sebastopol
Surface Design Association(656)

Sherman Oaks
Aerobics and Fitness Association of America(10)
Production Equipment Rental Association(585)
Women in Technology International(692)

Sonoma
American Society of Baking(134)
National Association for PET Container Resources(435)

Sonora
American Academy of Pain Management(26)

Spring Valley
Veterinary Cancer Society(682)

Stanford
American Broncho-Esophagological Association(59)
American Conference for Irish Studies(73)
Conference on Jewish Social Studies(261)

Studio City
Art Directors Guild/Scenic, Title and Graphic Artists(161)
Stuntwomen's Association of Motion Pictures(654)

Sun City
Armed Forces Broadcasters Association(161)

Sunnyvale
International Disk Drive Equipment and Materials Association(369)

Tarzana
American Hypnosis Association(92)

Thousand Oaks
Community College Journalism Association(256)

Toluca Lake
Alpha Tau Delta(18)
Stuntmen's Association of Motion Pictures(654)

Torrance
American Board of Podiatric Orthopedics and Primary Podiatric Medicine(57)
International Right of Way Association(385)
Xplor International(698)

Tujunga
Association of Railway Museums(211)

Universal City
American Cinema Editors(62)

Venice
Public Radio Program Directors Association(592)

Ventura
International Association of Infant Massage(358)

Vista
United States Racquet Stringers Association(677)
Variable Electronic Components Institute(682)

Walnut Creek
American Academy of Gnathologic Orthopedics(23)
Cooperative Education and Internship Association(265)
Infrared Data Association(338)
National Safety Management Society(538)

West Hollywood
Fur Information Council of America(313)

Whittier
National Broadcast Association for Community Affairs(485)

Woodlake
National Forest Recreation Association(512)

Woodland

Wood Moulding and Millwork Producers Association(694)

Woodland Hills

International Foundation for Telemetering(373)

Yucaipa

American Construction Inspectors Association(74)
American Mustang Association(107)

Yucca Valley

American Welara Pony Society(154)

COLORADO

Arvada

International Society for the Study of Subtle Energies and Energy Medicine(389)
National Translator Association(547)
Visitor Studies Association(684)

Aurora

AGN International - North America(11)
American Coal Ash Association(63)
American Society of Bariatric Physicians(134)
Arabian Horse Association(160)
Geospatial Information Technology Association(316)
Outpatient Ophthalmic Surgery Society(569)

Boulder

Alliance of Associations of Teachers of Japanese(16)
American Homebrewers Association(91)
American Society for Theatre Research(132)
American Solar Energy Society(147)
Association for Experiential Education(172)
Association for Theatre in Higher Education(181)
Association for University Business and Economic Research(181)
Behavior Genetics Association(227)
Brewers Association(232)
Brewers' Association of America(232)
Geological Society of America(315)
Masonry Society, The(413)
National Prison Hospice Association(534)
NCSL International(551)
Rolf Institute(602)
Society for Mathematical Biology(621)
State Higher Education Executive Officers(653)
Twentieth-Century Spanish Association of America(667)

Broomfield

American Academy of Medical Hypnoanalysts(24)
International Titanium Association(394)

Centennial

American Galvanizers Association(86)
American Institute of Timber Construction(98)
National Cattlemen's Beef Association(488)

Colorado Springs

American Academy of Forensic Sciences(23)
American Boarding Kennels Association(58)
Association for the Advancement of Psychology(179)
Association of Christian Schools International(190)
Billiard Congress of America(228)
CBA(240)
General Merchandise Distributors Council(315)
Help Desk Institute(325)
International Academy of Behavioral Medicine, Counseling and Psychotherapy(347)
National Association of Marine Services(461)
National Junior College Athletic Association(523)
National Livestock Producers Association(525)
National Strength and Conditioning Association(543)
Professional Rodeo Cowboys Association(589)
Small Publishers Association of North America(611)
USA Taekwonda(681)
Vocational Evaluation and Career Assessement Professionals(684)
Women's Professional Rodeo Association(694)

Denver

American Highland Cattle Association(90)
American Horticultural Therapy Association(92)
American Society of Agricultural Consultants(133)
American Society of Farm Managers and Rural Appraisers(137)
American Society of Sugar Beet Technologists(146)
American Water Works Association(154)
AORN(158)
Association of Environmental and Engineering Geologists(195)
Association of Professional Schools of International Affairs(209)
Beet Sugar Development Foundation(227)
Communications Marketing Association(255)
Computer Oriented Geological Society(258)
Council of American Jewish Museums(270)
Council of Petroleum Accountants Socs.(273)
Environmental and Engineering Geophysical Society(296)
Financial Planning Association(306)
Health Industry Representatives Association(323)
International Sport Show Producers Association(393)
International Tuba-Euphonium Association(395)
Museum Store Association(423)
National Academy of Neuropsychology(426)
National Association of Counsel for Children(446)
National Association of Legal Investigators(459)
National Civic League(489)
National Conference of Local Environmental Health Administrators(493)
National Conference of State Legislatures(494)
National Conference of State Social Security Administrators(494)
National Environmental Health Association(507)
National Potato Promotion Board(533)
North American Transportation Management Institute(562)
Portfolio Management Institute(581)
United States Committee on Irrigation and Drainage(674)
United States Meat Export Federation(676)
United States Society on Dams(677)
Western-English Trade Association(688)

Englewood

American College of Medical Practice Executives(67)
American Hernia Society(90)
American National CattleWomen(108)
American Sheep Industry Association(125)
American Society of General Surgeons(138)
Association of Physician Assistants in Cardiovascular Surgery(207)
Medical Group Management Association(416)
National Stroke Association(544)
North American Limousin Foundation(558)

Erie

National Council on Education for the Ceramic Arts(502)

Evergreen

American Education Finance Association(80)
Associated Bodywork and Massage Professionals(164)

Fairplay

Independent Laboratory Distributors Association(334)

Ft. Collins

Associated Schools of Construction(166)
Association for University and College Counseling Center Directors(181)
Association of Collegiate Conference and Events Directors International(191)
Conference of Research Workers in Animal Diseases(260)
International Association of Dive Rescue Specialists(356)
National Association for Interpretation(434)
Organization of Wildlife Planners(568)

Glenwood Springs

Association of Equipment Management Professionals(195)

Grand Junction

National Association of Private, Nontraditional Schools and Colleges with Accrediting Commission for Higher Education(465)

Greeley

American Association for Women in Community Colleges(37)
National Council for Marketing and Public Relations(497)
National Onion Association(529)

Greenwood Village

Air & Surface Transport Nurses Association(12)
Farmers Educational and Co-operative Union of America(301)
Investment Management Consultants Association(399)
National Hearing Conservation Association(516)

Highlands Ranch

National Health Club Association(516)

Idaho Springs

Association of Free Community Papers(198)

Johnstown

Irish Blacks Cattle Society(399)

Lakewood

American Animal Hospital Association(31)
American College of Veterinary Internal Medicine(71)
National Council of Supervisors of Mathematics(501)
National Ski Areas Association(540)
National Ski Patrol System(540)
Professional Ski Instructors of America(589)
Women in Mining National(692)

Larkspur

American Warmblood Registry(154)
WIFS - Women in Insurance and Financial Services(688)

Littleton

American Institute of Mining, Metallurgical, and Petroleum Engineers(96)
Association of Surgical Technologists(216)
Society for Mining, Metallurgy, and Exploration(622)
Society of Economic Geologists(635)

Loveland

Radiant Panel Association(594)

Lyons
International Clarinet Association(365)

Monument
International Textile and Apparel Association(394)

Morrison
International Electrical Testing Association(370)

Nederland
Professional and Organizational Development Network in Higher Education(585)

Niwot
American Psychological Association - Society of Clinical Psychology(119)

Parker
American Salers Association(123)
Associated Business Writers of America(164)
National Writers Association(550)
North American South Devon Association(561)

Poncha Springs
History of Earth Sciences Society(326)

Rollinsville
ICOM, International Communications Agency Network(330)

Silt
Alpines International(18)

Steamboat Springs
International Erosion Control Association(371)

Westminster
American Gelbvieh Association(86)
American Institute of Professional Geologists(97)
Association of Professional Genealogists(209)
National Bison Association(484)
Reprographic Services Association(599)
World Sign Associates(696)

Wheat Ridge
American Society of Indexers(139)
Association for Applied Psychophysiology and Biofeedback(167)
Association of Community Health Nursing Educators(192)
National Quartz Producers Council(534)
North American Nature Photography Association(558)
Society for Range Management(624)
Society for Scholarly Publishing(625)

Woodland Park
American Association of Orthopaedic Medicine(47)

CONNECTICUT

Bethel
Society for Experimental Mechanics(617)

Bloomfield
American Academy of Psychiatry and the Law(28)
American Academy of Psychoanalysis and Dynamic Psychiatry(28)
American Clinical Neurophysiology Society(63)
Professional Show Managers Association(589)

Botsford
North American Association of Christians in Social Work(554)

Branford
Association of Master of Business Administration Executives(204)

Brookfield
Society of Plastics Engineers(642)

Cheshire
American Herbalists Guild(90)

Colchester
Society for Cross-Cultural Research(616)

Cornwall Bridge
National Society of Compliance Professionals(541)

Coventry
Society of Professors of Child and Adolescent Psychiatry(642)

Danbury
Coblentz Society(250)
International Union of Journeymen Horseshoers and Allied Trades(395)
Society for Biomolecular Sciences(614)
Society for the Study of Amphibians and Reptiles(628)

East Windsor Hill
International Association for Near Death Studies(351)

Essex
National Marine Distributors Association(526)
Outdoor Power Equipment and Engine Service Association(569)

Fairfield
National Association of Teachers' Agencies(478)

Glastonbury
American Academy of Clinical Psychiatrists(21)
American Nuclear Insurers(109)
Council for Marketing and Opinion Research(269)
Marketing Research Association(413)

Greenwich
American Pet Products Manufacturers Association(114)

Groton
National Party Boat Owners Alliance(532)

Guilford
Wire Association International(690)

Hamden
American National Metric Council(108)

Hartford
American Association for Continuity of Care(34)
Pension Real Estate Association(573)
Wire Reinforcement Institute(690)

Jewett City
Health & Sciences Communications Association(322)

Madison
Friction Materials Standards Institute(312)

Middletown
Association of State Correctional Administrators(215)
National Defender Investigator Association(504)

Monroe
Army Aviation Association of America(161)

New Canaan
Golf Range Association of America(318)

New Haven
American Society of Church History(135)
Neurosurgical Society of America(552)

New Milford
Association of Bridal Consultants(188)

Newington
American Radio Relay League(121)

Newtown
National Shooting Sports Foundation(539)
Sporting Arms and Ammunition Manufacturers' Institute(651)

Norwalk
Association of Postgraduate Physician Assistant Programs(208)
National Bed and Breakfast Association(484)

Shelton
BPA Worldwide(232)

Simsbury
National Defined Contribution Council(505)

Stamford
Marketing Agencies Association Worldwide(412)

Storrs
World's Poultry Science Association, U.S.A. Branch(697)

Stratford
American Institute of Building Design(95)

Suffield
ISDA - The Office Systems Cooperative(400)

Washington
Historians of American Communism(326)

West Hartford
American Epilepsy Society(81)
Association of College and University Auditors(190)
International Association of Campus Law Enforcement Administrators(354)
International Society for Clinical Densitometry(386)

Westport
American Natural Soda Ash Corporation(108)
Major Indoor Soccer League(410)

Windsor
LIMRA International(408)

DELAWARE

Middletown
American College of Osteopathic Pain Management and Sclerotherapy(69)

Newark
American Philosophical Association(114)
Association of Theatre Movement Educators(218)
International Reading Association(384)
Produce Marketing Association(584)
Urban Affairs Association(680)

Wilmington

Academy of Veterinary Homeopathy(6)
American Academy of Veterinary Pharmacology and Therapeutics(29)
American Institute of Parliamentarians(97)
American Public Gardens Association(119)
American Society of Cytopathology(137)
Business History Conference(235)
International Association of Used Equipment Dealers(361)
North American Catalysis Society(555)
Small Business Council of America(611)

DISTRICT OF COLUMBIA

Washington

AABC Commissioning Group(1)
ABA Marketing Network(1)
Academy of Radiology Research(5)
Academy of Student Pharmacists(5)
AcademyHealth(6)
Accrediting Council for Continuing Education and Training(7)
Accrediting Council for Independent Colleges and Schools(7)
ACPA - College Student Educators Association(7)
Acrylonitrile Group(8)
Advanced Medical Technology Association(8)
Affordable Housing Tax Credit Coalition(10)
African-American Women's Clergy Association(11)
AFT - Public Employees(11)
AFT Healthcare(11)
Agribusiness Council(12)
Agricultural Retailers Association(12)
Air Line Pilots Association, International(13)
Air Transport Association of America(13)
Airforwarders Association(14)
Airline Industrial Relations Conference(14)
Airports Council International/North America(15)
Alexander Graham Bell Association for the Deaf and Hard of Hearing(15)
Alkylphenols and Ethoxylates Research Council(15)
Alliance for Community Media(15)
Alliance for Nonprofit Management(15)
Alliance for Telecommunications Industry Solutions(16)
Alliance of Automobile Manufacturers(16)
Alliance of Nonprofit Mailers(17)
Amalgamated Transit Union(18)
America's Blood Centers(19)
America's Community Bankers(19)
America's Health Insurance Plans(19)
American Academy of Actuaries(19)
American Academy of Addiction Psychiatry(20)
American Academy of Child and Adolescent Psychiatry(20)
American Academy of Diplomacy(22)
American Academy of Wound Management(29)
American Advertising Federation(29)
American Arts Alliance(32)
American Association for Affirmative Action(33)
American Association for Clinical Chemistry(34)
American Association for the Advancement of Science(36)
American Association of Blacks in Energy(38)
American Association of Colleges for Teacher Education(40)
American Association of Colleges of Nursing(40)
American Association of Collegiate Registrars and Admissions Officers(40)
American Association of Community Colleges(41)
American Association of Credit Union Leagues(41)
American Association of Crop Insurers(41)
American Association of Engineering Societies(42)
American Association of Exporters and Importers(42)
American Association of Homes and Services for the Aging(43)
American Association of Language Specialists(44)
American Association of Museums(45)
American Association of Naturopathic Physicians(46)
American Association of Poison Control Centers(48)
American Association of Political Consultants(49)
American Association of Private Railroad Car Owners(49)
American Association of Public Health Physicians(50)
American Association of Residential Mortgage Regulators(50)
American Association of Retired Persons(50)
American Association of State Colleges and Universities(51)
American Association of State Highway and Transportation Officials(51)
American Association of Suicidology(52)
American Association of University Professors(53)
American Association on Mental Retardation(54)
American Astronomical Society(54)
American Bail Coalition(55)
American Bakers Association(55)
American Bankers Association(55)
American Bearing Manufacturing Association(56)
American Benefits Council(56)
American Beverage Association(56)
American Beverage Institute(56)
American Bus Association(60)
American Business Conference(60)
American Catholic Historical Association(61)
American Chemical Society(62)
American Clinical Laboratory Association(63)
American Coke and Coal Chemicals Institute(63)
American College of Cardiology(64)
American College of Nurse Practitioners(68)
American College of Obstetricians and Gynecologists(68)
American College of Preventive Medicine(70)
American College of Tax Counsel(71)
American Concrete Pavement Association(72)
American Conference of Academic Deans(73)
American Congress of Community Supports and Employment Services(73)
American Corn Growers Association(74)
American Council of Engineering Companies(75)
American Council of Independent Laboratories(75)
American Council of Life Insurers(75)
American Council of the Blind(76)
American Council on Education(76)
American Councils for International Education(76)
American Dental Education Association(78)
American Educational Research Association(80)
American Electroplaters and Surface Finishers Society(80)
American Family Therapy Academy(81)
American Farm Bureau Federation(81)
American Federation of Government Employees(82)
American Federation of Labor and Congress of Industrial Organizations(82)
American Federation of School Administrators(82)
American Federation of State, County and Municipal Employees(82)
American Federation of Teachers(82)
American Financial Services Association(83)
American Fire Safety Council(84)
American Foreign Service Association(85)
American Foreign Service Protective Association(85)
American Forest and Paper Association(85)
American Forests(85)
American Gaming Association(86)
American Gas Association(86)
American Geophysical Union(87)
American Hardwood Export Council(89)
American Health Care Association(89)
American Health Lawyers Association(89)
American Health Quality Association(89)
American Highway Users Alliance(90)
American Historical Association(91)
American Horse Council(91)
American Hotel & Lodging Association(92)
American Humanist Association(92)
American Immigration Lawyers Association(92)
American Institute for Conservation of Historic and Artistic Works(93)
American Institute for International Steel(94)
American Institute for Medical and Biological Engineering(94)
American Institute for Shippers Associations(94)
American Institute of Architects(94)
American Institute of Architecture Students(94)
American Institute of Biological Sciences(94)
American Institute of Certified Planners(95)
American Insurance Association(98)
American Iron and Steel Institute(98)
American Jewish Press Association(99)
American Land Title Association(100)
American Legislative Exchange Council(101)
American Licensed Practical Nurses Association(101)
American Logistics Association(102)
American Managed Behavioral Healthcare Association(102)
American Maritime Congress(103)
American Meat Institute(103)
American Medical Rehabilitation Providers Association(104)
American Mushroom Institute(107)
American National Standards Institute(108)
American Nursery and Landscape Association(109)
American Obesity Association(109)
American Oilseed Coalition(110)
American Organization of Nurse Executives(110)
American Peanut Product Manufacturers(113)
American Petroleum Institute(114)
American Pharmacists Association(114)
American Pilots' Association(115)
American Political Science Association(116)
American Postal Workers Union(117)
American Psychological Association(118)
American Psychological Society(119)
American Public Gas Association(119)
American Public Health Association(119)
American Public Human Services Association(120)
American Public Power Association(120)
American Public Transportation Association(120)
American Recreation Coalition(122)
American Resort Development Association(122)
American Road and Transportation Builders Association(123)
American Seniors Housing Association(124)
American Shipbuilding Association(125)
American Short Line and Regional Railroad Association(125)
American Sleep Apnea Association(126)
American Society for Bone and Mineral Research(127)
American Society for Engineering Education(128)
American Society for Microbiology(130)
American Society for Public Administration(132)
American Society of Access Professionals(133)
American Society of Association Executives & Center for Association Leadership(134)
American Society of Hematology(139)

American Society of Interior Designers(140)
American Society of International Law(140)
American Society of Landscape Architects(140)
American Society of Nephrology(142)
American Sociological Association(147)
American Spice Trade Association(148)
American Studies Association(149)
American Sugarbeet Growers Association(150)
American Telemedicine Association(151)
American Tort Reform Association(152)
American Urogynecologic Society(153)
American Watch Association(154)
American Wind Energy Association(155)
American Zinc Association(156)
American-Uzbekistan Chamber of Commerce(156)
Americans for the Arts(156)
Animal Health Institute(157)
Apple Processors Association(159)
Aseptic Packaging Council(162)
Asphalt Roofing Manufacturers Association(163)
Aspirin Foundation of America(164)
Associated Air Balance Council(164)
Associated Luxury Hotels(165)
Association for Canadian Studies in the United States(168)
Association for Conflict Resolution(170)
Association for Convention Marketing Executives(171)
Association for Electronic Health Care Transactions(172)
Association for Federal Information Resources Management(173)
Association for Gerontology in Higher Education(173)
Association for Maximum Service Television(176)
Association for Philosophy of the Unconscious(176)
Association for Professionals in Infection Control and Epidemiology(177)
Association for Public Policy Analysis and Management(177)
Association for Retail Technology Standards(178)
Association for the Study of African American Life and History(180)
Association for Tropical Biology and Conservation(181)
Association for Women in Management(182)
Association for Women in Science(182)
Association of Academic Health Centers(183)
Association of Alternative Newsweeklies(184)
Association of American Chambers of Commerce in Latin America(184)
Association of American Colleges and Universities(184)
Association of American Geographers(184)
Association of American Law Schools(184)
Association of American Medical Colleges(184)
Association of American Railroads(185)
Association of American Universities(185)
Association of American Veterinary Medical Colleges(186)
Association of Bituminous Contractors(187)
Association of Black Psychologists(187)
Association of Black Sociologists(187)
Association of Boarding Schools, The(188)
Association of Career Firms International(188)
Association of Career Professionals International(188)
Association of Catholic Colleges and Universities(188)
Association of Children's Museums(189)
Association of Collegiate Schools of Architecture(191)
Association of Community College Trustees(192)
Association of Corporate Counsel(193)
Association of Direct Response Fundraising Counsel(194)
Association of Environmental and Resource Economists(195)
Association of Farmworker Opportunity Programs(196)
Association of Federal Communications Consulting Engineers(196)
Association of Fish and Wildlife Agencies(197)
Association of Flight Attendants - CWA(197)
Association of Foreign Investors in Real Estate(197)
Association of Freestanding Radiation Oncology Centers(198)
Association of Governing Boards of Universities and Colleges(199)
Association of Home Appliance Manufacturers(200)
Association of Independent Research Institutes(200)
Association of International Photography Art Dealers(202)
Association of Investment Management Sales Executives(202)
Association of Jesuit Colleges and Universities(202)
Association of Jewish Aging Services(202)
Association of Local Air Pollution Control Officials(203)
Association of Maternal and Child Health Programs(204)
Association of Medical Diagnostic Manufacturers(204)
Association of Meeting Professionals(204)
Association of Metropolitan Water Agencies(204)
Association of Occupational and Environmental Clinics(206)
Association of Oil Pipe Lines(206)
Association of Performing Arts Presenters(207)
Association of Professional Investment Consultants(209)
Association of Professors of Medicine(209)
Association of Program Directors in Internal Medicine(210)
Association of Psychology Postdoctoral and Internship Centers(210)
Association of Public Television Stations(210)
Association of Reproductive Health Professionals(212)
Association of Research Libraries(212)
Association of Schools of Allied Health Professions(213)
Association of Schools of Public Health(213)
Association of Science-Technology Centers(213)
Association of State and Interstate Water Pollution Control Administrators(214)
Association of State and Territorial Directors of Nursing(215)
Association of State and Territorial Health Officials(215)
Association of State and Territorial Solid Waste Management Officials(215)
Association of State Drinking Water Administrators(215)
Association of Subspecialty Professors(216)
Association of Teachers of Maternal and Child Health(217)
Association of Teachers of Preventive Medicine(217)
Association of Test Publishers(217)
Association of Trial Lawyers of America(218)
Association of Universities for Research in Astronomy(219)
Association of Women's Health, Obstetric and Neonatal Nurses(220)
Aviation Suppliers Association(225)
Bankers' Association for Finance and Trade(226)
Beer Institute(227)
Biotechnology Industry Organization(229)
Bituminous Coal Operators Association(229)
Broadcast Education Association(233)
Building Owners and Managers Association International(234)
Business and Professional Women/USA(235)
Business Council(235)
Business Higher Education Forum(235)
Business Software Alliance(236)
Can Manufacturers Institute(237)
Canadian-American Business Council(237)
Career College Association(237)
Cargo Airline Association(238)
Catholic Biblical Association of America(239)
Cement Kiln Recycling Coalition(241)
Chamber of Shipping of America(243)
Check Payment Systems Association(243)
Chi Eta Phi Sorority(244)
Chief Warrant and Warrant Officers Association, United States Coast Guard(244)
Child Welfare League of America(244)
Chlorinated Paraffins Industry Association(245)
Chorus America(245)
Cigar Association of America(247)
Clerkship Directors in Internal Medicine(248)
Coalition for Government Procurement(249)
Coalition for Juvenile Justice(249)
Coalition of Black Trade Unionists(249)
Coalition of Higher Education Assistance Organizations(249)
Coalition of Labor Union Women(249)
Coalition of Publicly Traded Partnerships(249)
Coalition of Service Industries(249)
College Savings Foundation(252)
Commercial Vehicle Safety Alliance(254)
Commission on Professionals in Science and Technology(254)
Committee of Annuity Insurers(254)
Communications Workers of America(255)
Community Action Partnership(255)
Community Transportation Association of America(256)
COMPTEL(257)
Computer and Communications Industry Association(257)
Computer Ethics Institute(257)
Computerized Medical Imaging Society(258)
Computing Research Association(258)
Conference Board of the Mathematical Sciences(259)
Conference of Minority Transportation Officials(259)
Conference of State Bank Supervisors(260)
Congress of Lung Association Staffs(261)
Consortium for School Networking(262)
Consortium of Social Science Associations(262)
Consumer Data Industry Association(263)
Consumer Federation of America(263)
Consumer Healthcare Products Association(263)
Consumer Specialty Products Association(263)
Contact Lens Manufacturers Association(264)
Copper and Brass Fabricators Council(266)
Corn Refiners Association(266)
Correctional Vendors Association(267)
Cosmetic, Toiletry and Fragrance Association(267)
Cotton Council International(267)
Cotton Warehouse Association of America(267)
Council for Advancement and Support of Education(267)
Council for Chemical Research(268)
Council for Christian Colleges and Universities(268)
Council for Higher Education Accreditation(269)
Council for Opportunity in Education(269)
Council for Professional Recognition(269)
Council for Resource Development(269)
Council for Responsible Nutrition(270)
Council for the Advancement of Standards in Higher Education(270)
Council of American Overseas Research Centers(270)
Council of Chief State School Officers(271)
Council of Graduate Schools(272)
Council of Independent Colleges(272)
Council of Infrastructure Financing Authorities(272)
Council of Institutional Investors(272)
Council of Insurance Agents and Brokers(272)

Council of Large Public Housing Authorities(273)
Council of Manufacturing Associations(273)
Council of Scientific Society Presidents(274)
Council of State Community Development Agencies(274)
Council of the Great City Schools(275)
Council on Education of the Deaf(276)
Council on Foundations(276)
Council on Governmental Relations(276)
Council on Resident Education in Obstetrics and Gynecology(277)
Council On State Taxation(277)
County Executives of America(277)
CropLife America(279)
CTIA - The Wireless Association(280)
Customs and International Trade Bar Association(280)
CWLA - Child Mental Health Division(280)
Dance/USA(281)
Dangerous Goods Advisory Council(281)
Defense Credit Union Council(282)
Delta Phi Epsilon(282)
Design-Build Institute of America(283)
Destination Marketing Association International(283)
Dibasic Esters Group(284)
Digital Media Association(284)
Diplomatic and Consular Officers, Retired(284)
Direct Selling Association(285)
Directors of Health Promotion and Public Health Education(285)
Disease Management Association of America(285)
Distance Education and Training Council(285)
Distilled Spirits Council of the U.S.(286)
Domestic Petroleum Council(286)
Dredging Contractors of America(287)
DRI International(287)
Driver Employer Council of America(287)
Drug and Alcohol Testing Industry Association(287)
Early Childhood Education Institute(288)
Ecological Society of America(288)
Edison Electric Institute(289)
Education Writers Association(289)
EDUCAUSE(290)
Electric Drive Transportation Association(290)
Electric Power Supply Association(290)
Electricity Consumers Resource Council(291)
Electronic Transactions Association(292)
Emissions Markets Association(293)
Employee Benefit Research Institute(293)
Employee Relocation Council/Worldwide ERC(293)
Employers Council on Flexible Compensation(293)
Emulsion Polymers Council(294)
Energy Bar Association(294)
Entertainment Software Association(295)
Environmental Business Association, The(296)
Environmental Industry Associations(296)
Environmental Technology Council(297)
ERISA Industry Committee(297)
ESOP Association(297)
ETAD North America(298)
European-American Business Council(298)
Eye Bank Association of America(300)
Farm Credit Council(301)
Federal Administrative Law Judges Conference(301)
Federal and Armed Forces Librarians Roundtable(301)
Federal Bar Association(302)
Federal Communications Bar Association(302)
Federal Education Association(302)
Federal Facilities Council(302)
Federal Network for Sustainability(302)
Federal Physicians Association(302)
Federal Water Quality Association(302)
Federally Employed Women(302)
Federation of American Hospitals(303)
Federation of American Scientists(303)
Federation of Behavioral, Psychological and Cognitive Sciences(303)
Federation of Diocesan Liturgical Commissions(303)
Federation of Materials Socs.(304)
Federation of Tax Administrators(304)
Fertilizer Institute(305)
Film and Bag Federation(305)
Financial Services Roundtable(306)
Flavor and Extract Manufacturers Association of the United States(307)
Food and Drug Law Institute(309)
Food Marketing Institute(309)
Food Products Association(309)
Footwear Distributors and Retailers of America(310)
Foundation for Independent Higher Education(311)
Fragrance Materials Association of the United States(311)
Futures Industry Association(313)
General Aviation Manufacturers Association(315)
General Federation of Women's Clubs(315)
Geothermal Energy Association(316)
Gerontological Society of America(316)
Global Health Council(317)
Global Offset and Countertrade Association(317)
Glutamate Association (United States)(318)
Governors Highway Safety Association(319)
Graphic Communications Conference, IBT(319)
Greater Washington Board of Trade(320)
Greeting Card Association(320)
Grocery Manufacturers Association(320)
Guild of Natural Science Illustrators(321)
Gynecologic Surgery Society(321)
Gypsum Association(321)
Healthcare Leadership Council(324)
Heart Rhythm Society(324)
Hispanic Elected Local Officials(326)
Hispanic National Bar Association(326)
Home Healthcare Nurses Association(327)
Homeland Security Industries Association(328)
Horticultural Research Institute(328)
Hospice Association of America(328)
ICAAAA Coaches Association(330)
IEEE Computer Society(331)
IEEE Magnetics Society(331)
Independent Bakers Association(333)
Independent Community Bankers of America(333)
Independent Liquid Terminals Association(334)
Independent Petroleum Association of America(335)
Independent Sector(336)
Independent Terminal Operators Association(336)
Indoor Tanning Association(336)
Industrial Minerals Association - North America(337)
Industrial Truck Association(337)
Industry Coalition on Technology Transfer(337)
Information Technology Industry Council(338)
Institute for Polyacrylate Absorbents(339)
Institute for Responsible Housing Preservation(339)
Institute of Career Certification International(340)
Institute of Clean Air Companies(340)
Institute of International Finance(342)
Institute of Makers of Explosives(342)
Institute of Management Consultants USA(342)
Institute of Medicine(343)
Institute of Scrap Recycling Industries(343)
Institute of Shortening and Edible Oils(344)
Institute of Transportation Engineers(344)
Institutional and Service Textile Distributors Association(344)
Instructional Telecommunications Council(344)
Integrated Waste Services Association(345)
Intellectual Property Owners Association(345)
Intelligent Transportation Society of America(345)
Inter-American Bar Association(346)
Interlocking Concrete Pavement Institute(347)
International Allied Printing Trades Association(349)
International Association for Continuing Education and Training(349)
International Association for the Study of Organized Crime(351)
International Association of Airport Duty Free Stores(352)
International Association of Bridge, Structural, Ornamental and Reinforcing Iron Workers(354)
International Association of Color Manufacturers(355)
International Association of Fire Fighters(357)
International Association of Official Human Rights Agencies(359)
International Banana Association(362)
International Biometric Society(362)
International Bridge, Tunnel and Turnpike Association(363)
International Brotherhood of Electrical Workers(363)
International Brotherhood of Teamsters, AFL-CIO(363)
International Cargo Security Council(364)
International City/County Management Association(365)
International Claim Association(365)
International Communication Association(366)
International Community Corrections Association(366)
International Council for Small Business(367)
International Council of Employers of Bricklayers and Allied Craftworkers(367)
International Crystal Federation(368)
International Dairy Foods Association(368)
International Downtown Association(369)
International Economic Development Council(370)
International Ecotourism Society(370)
International Electronic Article Surveillance Manufacturers Association(370)
International Food Information Council(372)
International Franchise Association(373)
International Hydrolized Protein Council(375)
International Ice Cream Association(375)
International Intellectual Property Alliance(377)
International Labor Communications Association(377)
International Legal Fraternity of Phi Delta Phi(378)
International Marina Institute(379)
International Microelectronics and Packaging Society(379)
International Municipal Lawyers Association(380)
International Oxygen Manufacturers Association(382)
International Society for Antiviral Research(386)
International Society for Experimental Hematology(387)
International Technical Caramel Association(393)
International Trade Commission Trial Lawyers Association(394)
International Union of Bricklayers and Allied Craftsworkers(395)
International Union of Electronic, Electrical, Salaried, Machine, and Furniture Workers-CWA(395)
International Union of Operating Engineers(395)
International Union of Painters and Allied Trades(396)
Internet Alliance(397)
Interstate Natural Gas Association of America(398)
Investment Adviser Association(398)
Investment Company Institute(398)
Investment Program Association(399)
IPC - Surface Mount Equipment Manufacturers Association(399)
Japan Automobile Manufacturers Association(400)

Jesuit Secondary Education Association(401)
Judge Advocates Association(402)
Juice Products Association(402)
Justice Research and Statistics Association(403)
Laborers' International Union of North America(404)
Lamaze International(404)
Land Trust Alliance(405)
Leather Industries of America(407)
Lighter Association(408)
Linguistic Society of America(408)
Managed Funds Association(410)
Manufactured Housing Association for Regulatory Reform(410)
Manufacturers of Emission Controls Association(411)
Marine Engineers Beneficial Association(412)
Mathematical Association of America(414)
Medical Device Manufacturers Association(416)
Messenger Courier Association of the Americas(417)
Metal Finishing Suppliers Association(417)
Milk Industry Foundation(419)
Mortgage Bankers Association(421)
Mortgage Insurance Companies of America(421)
Motion Picture Association(421)
Motion Picture Association of America(421)
Municipal Waste Management Association(422)
Museum Education Roundtable(423)
Museum Trustee Association(423)
NAFSA: Association of International Educators(424)
National Abortion Federation(426)
National Academy of Clinical Biochemistry(426)
National Academy of Education(426)
National Academy of Engineering of the United States of America(426)
National Academy of Sciences(427)
National Adult Day Services Association(427)
National Adult Education Professional Development Consortium(427)
National Agricultural Aviation Association(428)
National Air Duct Cleaners Association(428)
National Air Traffic Controllers Association(428)
National ALEC Association/ Prepaid Communications Association(429)
National Alliance for Hispanic Health(429)
National Alliance of Black School Educators(429)
National Alliance of Nurse Practitioners(429)
National Alliance of Postal and Federal Employees(429)
National Alliance of State and Territorial AIDS Directors(430)
National American Indian Housing Council(430)
National Assembly of State Arts Agencies(431)
National Association for Bilingual Education(431)
National Association for Biomedical Research(431)
National Association for Community Mediation(432)
National Association for County Community and Economic Development(432)
National Association for Environmental Management(433)
National Association for Home Care(434)
National Association for Law Placement(434)
National Association for State Community Services Programs(436)
National Association for the Education of Young Children(436)
National Association for the Self-Employed(436)
National Association Medical Staff Services(437)
National Association of Affordable Housing Lenders(438)
National Association of Aircraft and Communication Suppliers(438)
National Association of Area Agencies on Aging(439)
National Association of Attorneys General(439)
National Association of Black Social Workers(440)
National Association of Black-Owned Broadcasters(440)
National Association of Blacks In Government(440)
National Association of Boards of Examiners of Long Term Care Administrators(440)
National Association of Broadcast Employees and Technicians - Communications Workers of America(441)
National Association of Broadcasters(441)
National Association for Business Economics(441)
National Association of Business Political Action Committees(441)
National Association of Clean Water Agencies(443)
National Association of College and University Attorneys(444)
National Association of College and University Business Officers(444)
National Association of Colored Women's Clubs(445)
National Association of Conservation Districts(445)
National Association of Consumer Advocates(446)
National Association of Corporate Directors(446)
National Association of Counties(447)
National Association of County and City Health Officials(447)
National Association of County Engineers(447)
National Association of County Intergovernmental Relations Officials(447)
National Association of Criminal Defense Lawyers(448)
National Association of Development Organizations(449)
National Association of Energy Service Companies(451)
National Association of Enrolled Agents(451)
National Association of Evangelicals(451)
National Association of Federal Veterinarians(452)
National Association of Federally Impacted Schools(452)
National Association of Flood and Stormwater Management Agencies(453)
National Association of Foreign-Trade Zones(453)
National Association of Government Labor Officials(454)
National Association of Healthcare Access Management(455)
National Association of Healthcare Consultants(455)
National Association of Hispanic Journalists(455)
National Association of Hispanic Nurses(456)
National Association of Hispanic Publications(456)
National Association of Home Builders(456)
National Association of Housing and Redevelopment Officials(456)
National Association of Housing Cooperatives(456)
National Association of Independent Colleges and Universities(457)
National Association of Independent Schools(457)
National Association of Installation Developers(458)
National Association of Investment Companies(459)
National Association of Letter Carriers(460)
National Association of Local Government Environmental Professionals(460)
National Association of Local Housing Finance Agencies(460)
National Association of Manufacturers(460)
National Association of Margarine Manufacturers(461)
National Association of Media Brokers(461)
National Association of Medicaid Directors(461)
National Association of Metal Finishers(461)
National Association of Minority Contractors(462)
National Association of Negro Business and Professional Women's Clubs(462)
National Association of Neighborhoods(462)
National Association of Nurse Practitioners in Women's Health(463)
National Association of Nutrition and Aging Services Programs(463)
National Association of Plant Patent Owners(465)
National Association of Police Organizations(465)
National Association of Private Special Education Centers(465)
National Association of Psychiatric Health Systems(467)
National Association of Public Child Welfare Administrators(467)
National Association of Public Hospitals and Health Systems(467)
National Association of Real Estate Investment Trusts(468)
National Association of Regional Councils(469)
National Association of Regulatory Utility Commissioners(469)
National Association of Retail Collection Attorneys(469)
National Association of Schools of Public Affairs and Administration(470)
National Association of Secretaries of State(471)
National Association of Securities Dealers(471)
National Association of Securities Professionals(471)
National Association of Service and Conservation Corps(471)
National Association of Shareholder and Consumer Attorneys(472)
National Association of Small Business Investment Companies(472)
National Association of Social Workers(472)
National Association of State Alcohol and Drug Abuse Directors(473)
National Association of State Budget Officers(473)
National Association of State Catholic Conference Directors(474)
National Association of State Departments of Agriculture(474)
National Association of State Development Agencies(474)
National Association of State Directors of Career Technical Education Consortium(474)
National Association of State Directors of Migrant Education(474)
National Association of State Fire Marshals(475)
National Association of State Foresters(475)
National Association of State Units on Aging(476)
National Association of State Universities and Land Grant Colleges(477)
National Association of State Workforce Agencies(477)
National Association of Student Financial Aid Administrators(477)
National Association of Student Personnel Administrators(478)
National Association of Surety Bond Producers(478)
National Association of Theatre Owners(479)
National Association of Towns and Townships(479)
National Association of Veterans Program Administrators(480)
National Association of Vision Professionals(480)

National Association of Water Companies(480)
National Association of Waterfront Employers(481)
National Association of Wheat Growers(481)
National Association of Wholesaler-Distributors(481)
National Association of Women Judges(481)
National Association of Workforce Boards(482)
National Association of Workforce Development Professionals(482)
National Bankers Association(483)
National Bar Association(483)
National Basketball Referees Association(483)
National Beauty Culturists' League(484)
National Black Caucus of State Legislators(484)
National Black Chamber of Commerce(484)
National Black Police Association(484)
National Building Granite Quarries Association(485)
National Business Aviation Association(486)
National Cable & Telecommunications Association(486)
National Candle Association(487)
National Catholic Educational Association(487)
National Cheese Institute(488)
National Chicken Council(489)
National Child Care Association(489)
National Child Support Enforcement Association(489)
National Club Association(490)
National Coalition of Abortion Providers(490)
National Committee for Quality Assurance(491)
National Communication Association(491)
National Community Development Association(491)
National Conference of Brewery and Soft Drink Workers - United States and Canada(493)
National Conference of Catechetical Leadership(493)
National Conference of Firemen and Oilers, SEIU(493)
National Conference of Regulatory Utility Commission Engineers(494)
National Conference of State Historic Preservation Officers(494)
National Conference on Public Employee Retirement Systems(495)
National Congress for Community Economic Development(495)
National Consumers League(495)
National Cooperative Business Association(496)
National Council for Advanced Manufacturing(496)
National Council of Agricultural Employers(498)
National Council of Architectural Registration Boards(498)
National Council of Chain Restaurants(498)
National Council of Farmer Cooperatives(499)
National Council of Higher Education Loan Programs(499)
National Council of Local Human Service Administrators(499)
National Council of Nonprofit Associations(500)
National Council of Social Security Management Associations(500)
National Council of State Housing Agencies(500)
National Council of Textile Organizations(501)
National Council of University Research Administrators(501)
National Council on International Trade Development(502)
National Council on the Aging(503)
National Criminal Justice Association(503)
National Customs Brokers and Forwarders Association of America(504)
National Dental Association(505)
National Dental Hygienists' Association(505)
National Disability Rights Network(505)
National Education Association(506)
National Education Knowledge Industry Association(506)
National Energy Assistance Directors Association(507)
National Family Planning and Reproductive Health Association(508)
National Federation of Federal Employees(509)
National Federation of Independent Business(509)
National Football League Players Association(511)
National Foreign Trade Council(511)
National Forum for Black Public Administrators(512)
National Foundation for Women Legislators(512)
National Governors Association(514)
National Grain and Feed Association(514)
National Grain Trade Council(514)
National Grange(514)
National Grape Cooperative Association(515)
National Guard Association of the U.S.(515)
National Health Care Anti-Fraud Association(516)
National Health Council(516)
National Hispanic Medical Association(517)
National Home Equity Mortgage Association(517)
National Housing and Rehabilitation Association(518)
National Housing Conference(518)
National Human Services Assembly(518)
National Humanities Alliance(518)
National Hydrogen Association(518)
National Hydropower Association(518)
National Indian Education Association(519)
National Indian Gaming Association(519)
National Industrial Council - Employer Association Group(519)
National Industrial Council - State Associations Group(519)
National Industrial Sand Association(519)
National Institute of Building Sciences(520)
National Institute of Oilseed Products(521)
National Labor Relations Board Professional Association(523)
National League of American Pen Women(524)
National League of Cities(524)
National Leased Housing Association(524)
National Legal Aid and Defender Association(524)
National Lesbian and Gay Journalists Association(524)
National Lesbian and Gay Law Association(524)
National Lumber and Building Material Dealers Association(525)
National Meat Canners Association(526)
National Medical Association(526)
National Mining Association(527)
National Multi Housing Council(528)
National Music Publishers' Association(528)
National Newspaper Publishers Association(529)
National Ocean Industries Association(529)
National Oilseed Processors Association(529)
National Organization for Competency Assurance(530)
National Organization for the Professional Advancement of Black Chemists and Chemical Engineers(530)
National Organization of Nurse Practitioner Faculties(530)
National Paint and Coatings Association(531)
National Parking Association(531)
National Parks Conservation Association(532)
National Pasta Association(532)
National Petrochemical & Refiners Association(532)
National Petroleum Council(532)
National Postal Mail Handlers Union(533)
National Potato Council(533)
National Propane Gas Association(534)
National Railroad Construction and Maintenance Association(534)
National Register of Health Service Providers in Psychology(535)
National Restaurant Association(536)
National Retail Federation(536)
National Reverse Mortgage Lenders Association(536)
National Small Business Association(540)
National Solid Wastes Management Association(542)
National Star Route Mail Contractors Association(543)
National Structured Settlements Trade Association(544)
National Student Assistance Association(544)
National Subacute and Postacute Care Association(544)
National Tax Association(545)
National Treasury Employees Union(547)
National Turkey Federation(548)
National U.S.-Arab Chamber of Commerce(548)
National Volunteer Fire Council(548)
National Weather Service Employees Organization(549)
National WIC Association(549)
Nationwide Alternate Delivery Alliance(550)
Natural Gas Supply Association(550)
Natural Gas Vehicle Coalition(551)
Natural Science Collections Alliance(551)
Newspaper Guild - CWA(552)
North American Association for Environmental Education(554)
North American Export Grain Association(557)
North American Millers Association(558)
North American Polyelectrolyte Producers Association(559)
North American Securities Administrators Association(560)
North American Society for Oceanic History(560)
North American Transportation Employee Relations Association(562)
Nuclear Energy Institute(563)
Nurses Organization of Veterans Affairs(563)
Optical Society of America(566)
Organization for International Investment(567)
Organization for the Promotion and Advancement of Small Telecommunications Companies(567)
Organization of Black Designers(567)
Organization of Professional Employees of the U.S. Department of Agriculture(567)
Organization of Women in International Trade(568)
Outdoor Advertising Association of America(569)
Outdoor Power Equipment Aftermarket Association(569)
Paper Machine Clothing Council(571)
Parcel Shippers Association(571)
Personal Watercraft Industry Association(574)
Pet Food Institute(574)
Pet Industry Joint Advisory Council(574)
Pharmaceutical Care Management Association(575)
Pharmaceutical Research and Manufacturers of America(575)
Philanthropy Roundtable(576)
Pickle Packers International(577)
Pipe Tobacco Council(578)
Plastic Shipping Container Institute(578)
Police Executive Research Forum(580)
POPAI The Global Association for Marketing at Retail(580)
Professional Bail Agents of the United States(586)
Professional Managers Association(588)
Public Affairs Council(592)
Public Employees Roundtable(592)
Public Housing Authorities Directors Association(592)
Radio and Television Correspondents Association(594)
Radio-Television News Directors Association(594)
Railway Supply Institute(595)

FLORIDA

Alachua

Altamonte Springs

Anthony

Bay Harbor

Belle Glade

Boca Raton

Bonita Springs

Boynton Beach

Bradenton

Champions Gate

Clearwater

Cocoa

Coral Gables

Coral Springs

Dania

Davie

Daytona Beach

Delray Beach
American Consultants League(74)
Association of Service and Computer Dealers International(213)
North-American Association of Telecommunications Dealers(562)

Destin
International Conference of Police Chaplains(366)

Dunedin
National Property Management Association(534)

Ft. Lauderdale
American Swimming Coaches Association(150)
Copier Dealers Association(266)
Independent Investors Protective League(334)
National Association of Federally Licensed Firearms Dealers(452)
National Association of Forensic Accountants(453)

Ft. Myers
AFSM International(11)
American Bridge Teachers' Association(59)
American Canine Sports Medicine Association(61)
Architectural Precast Association(160)
Resort and Commercial Recreation Association(600)
Society of Army Physician Assistants(632)
Transworld Advertising Agency Network(664)

Ft. Pierce
International Association of Aquatic and Marine Science Libraries and Information Centers(352)

Gainesville
Academy of Operative Dentistry(4)
American Association of Phonetic Sciences(48)
Association for Communication Excellence(169)
Association for International Agricultural and Extension Education(175)
Epsilon Sigma Phi(297)
Food Distribution Research Society(309)
History of Science Society(327)
International Newspaper Group(381)
Society for Spanish and Portuguese Historical Studies(625)

Gonzales
International Family Recreation Association(371)
Society of Recreation Executives(643)

Gulf Breeze
Suntanning Association for Education(655)

Haines City
Autoclaved Aerated Concrete Products Association(222)

Highland City
National Association of Independent Publishers(457)

Hollywood
NASFM(425)
National Association of Display Industries(449)

Homestead
United States Aquaculture Suppliers Association(673)

Homosassa
International Society of Beverage Technologists(390)

Hudson
National Association of Business Consultants(441)

Indian Rocks Beach
Preferred Funeral Directors International(583)

Jacksonville
American Association of Clinical Endocrinologists(39)
Council on Governmental Ethics Laws(276)
International Herb Association(375)
National Association of Teachers of Singing(478)
National Council of Industrial Naval Air Stations(499)
National Independent Living Association(519)
National Lipid Association(525)
National Wheel and Rim Association(549)
Society of Accredited Marine Surveyors(629)
Society of Biological Psychiatry(632)

Jacksonville Beach
Metal Treating Institute(417)

Jensen Beach
American Association of Surgical Physician Assistants(52)
Association of Neurosurgical Physician Assistants(205)

Jupiter
American Real Estate Society(121)
Library Binding Institute(407)
National Golf Foundation(514)

LaBelle
Sunglass Association of America(655)

Lake Mary
Automatic Fire Alarm Association(222)

Lakeland
National Tutoring Association(548)
Seaplane Pilots Association(607)

Longwood
National Concrete Burial Vault Association(492)
National Intercollegiate Soccer Officials Association(522)

Maitland
Alliance of Professional Tattooists(17)

Marco Island
Association of Internal Management Consultants(201)

Melbourne
American Greyhound Track Operators Association(87)
International Association of Conference Center Administrators(355)

Miami
American Welding Society(154)
Comparative and International Education Society(256)
Independent Affiliation of Independent Accounting Firms(333)
Inter American Press Association(345)
The International Air Cargo Association(348)
International Association for Hydrogen Energy(350)
International Association of Black Professional Fire Fighters(354)
Latin Chamber of Commerce of U.S.A.(405)
Phi Delta Epsilon Medical Fraternity(575)
Production and Operations Management Society(585)
Resistance Welder Manufacturers' Association(600)
Society of Laparoendoscopic Surgeons(639)
Standards Engineering Society(652)

Mulberry
American Reusable Textile Association(122)

Naples
American Chain Association(61)
Conveyor Equipment Manufacturers Association(265)
Incentive Federation(332)
Mechanical Power Transmission Association(415)
North American Punch Manufacturers Association(559)
Scale Manufacturers Association(605)

New Port Richey
American Board of Quality Assurance and Utilization Review Physicians(58)
Association of Millwork Distributors(205)

New Smyrna Beach
Society of Otorhinolaryngology and Head/Neck Nurses(641)

North Miami
American Society of Ichthyologists and Herpetologists(139)

Orange Park
Pile Driving Contractors Association(577)

Orlando
American Cash Flow Association(61)
Association for Biblical Higher Education(168)
Exercise-Safety Association(299)
International Accounts Payable Professionals(348)
Laser Institute of America(405)
National Association for Health Care Recruitment(433)
Scribes(607)
Viatical and Life Settlement Association of America(683)
Water Sports Industry Association(686)

Palm Beach
Printing Brokerage/Buyers Association International(584)
Screen Manufacturers Association(607)
Window Council(689)

Palm Beach Gardens
Professional Golfers Association of America(587)

Palm Coast
Book Manufacturers' Institute(231)
National Campus Ministries Association(486)

Palm Harbor
American College of Eye Surgeons(65)
Society for Excellence in Eyecare(617)

Panama City Beach
Institute of Diving(341)

Pensacola
American Radiological Nurses Association(121)
American Society of Plastic Surgical Nurses(144)
International Precious Metals Institute(383)
National Association of Recreation Resource Planners(468)
National Gerontological Nursing Association(513)
National Nursing Staff Development Organization(529)

National Organization for Associate Degree Nursing(529)
National Tax Lien Association(545)
Professional Association of Health Care Office Management(586)
Society for Vascular Nursing(629)
Society of Environmental Toxicology and Chemistry(635)
Society of Pediatric Nurses(641)

Plant City

National Watermelon Association(549)
Paso Fino Horse Association(572)

Plantation

Institute of Business Appraisers(340)

Ponte Vedra Beach

ATP(221)
International Sports Heritage Association(393)
PGA TOUR Tournaments Association(575)

Port Charlotte

National Plasterers Council(533)

Port Orange

Track Owners Association(663)

Port St. Lucie

Amusement Industry Manufacturers and Suppliers International(156)
National Association of Sporting Goods Wholesalers(472)

Safety Harbor

American Importers Association(93)

Sarasota

Academy of Parish Clergy(5)
American Accounting Association(29)
International Society for the Comparative Studies of Civilizations(389)
National Association of Fire Investigators(452)
Wedding and Event Videographers Association International(686)

South Daytona

American Horse Publications Association(91)

South Miami

National Association of Cruise Oriented Agencies(448)

St. Augustine

American Culinary Federation(77)
Conference of Educational Administrators of Schools and Programs for the Deaf(259)

St. Petersburg

Concrete Sawing and Drilling Association(259)
National Association of Professional Baseball Leagues(466)
National Drilling Association(505)
Professional Association of Resume Writers and Career Coaches(586)
Text and Academic Authors Association(659)
WTA Tour(697)

Stuart

American Membrane Technology Association(105)

Tallahassee

American Academy of Anesthesiologist Assistants(20)
American Association of Physicians and Health Care Professionals(48)
American Society of Naturalists(142)
American Society of Notaries(142)
American Society of Podiatry Executives(145)
Association for Institutional Research(175)
Association of Collegiate Schools of Planning(191)
Association of Osteopathic State Executive Directors(206)
Beta Phi Mu(228)
National Association of Dental Laboratories(448)
National Association of Public Sector Equal Opportunity Officers(467)

Tampa

AACSB - the Association to Advance Collegiate Schools of Business(1)
Alpha Zeta Omega(18)
American College of Physician Executives(69)
Association of Battery Recyclers(187)
Association of Mental Health Librarians(204)
BICSI(228)
Federation of Defense and Corporate Counsel(303)
Financial Management Association International(306)
Home Improvement Research Institute(327)
Institute for Business & Home Safety(339)
International Packaged Ice Association(382)
International Society for Pharmaceutical Engineering(388)
National Association of Underwater Instructors(480)
National Health Association(516)
National Mobility Equipment Dealers Association(527)
North American Academy of Ecumenists(554)
Phi Alpha Theta(575)

Titusville

American Federation of Police and Concerned Citizens(82)
National Association of Chiefs of Police(443)

Treasure Island

National Hay Association(516)

Valrico

Home Wine and Beer Trade Association(328)
North American Association For Ambulatory Care(554)

West Palm Beach

Association of Eminent Domain Professionals(195)
National Alliance for Youth Sports(429)

Weston

National Association of Legal Search Consultants(460)

Windermere

American Society for Neurochemistry(130)

Winter Park

International Alliance for Women in Music(348)
National Association of Minority Engineering Program Administrators(462)
National Cartoonists Society(487)
Outdoor Amusement Business Association(569)
Society of University Surgeons(645)

Yulee

American Association of Zoo Veterinarians(54)

GEORGIA

Albany

American Peanut Shellers Association(113)
National Association of Student Affairs Professionals(477)

Alpharetta

American Correctional Health Services Association(74)
Coordinating Research Council(265)
National Electronic Distributors Association(506)
United Egg Producers(670)

Americus

Association of Third World Studies(218)

Athens

American Association of Avian Pathologists(38)
Coleopterists Society(250)
Community Leadership Association(256)
Council for Spiritual and Ethical Education(270)
Fiduciary and Risk Management Association(305)
National Alliance of Preservation Commissions(430)
National Investment Banking Association(522)
Society for Philosophy of Religion(623)

Atlanta

American Academy of Religion(28)
American Apparel Producers Network(32)
American Association of Occupational Health Nurses(47)
American Association of Physician Specialists(48)
American Cancer Society(60)
American College of Rheumatology(70)
American Society of Heating, Refrigerating and Air-Conditioning Engineers(139)
American Spinal Injury Association(148)
Apple Products Research and Education Council(159)
ASME International Gas Turbine Institute(163)
Association for Commuter Transportation(169)
Association for Dressings and Sauces(171)
Association for Information Systems(175)
Association for Management Information in Financial Services(176)
Association of Black Cardiologists(187)
Association of Energy Engineers(195)
Association of Fund-Raising Distributors and Suppliers(198)
Association of Home Office Life Underwriters(200)
Association of Rheumatology Health Professionals(212)
Calorie Control Council(237)
Chronic Disease Directors(246)
Concord Grape Association(258)
Construction Owners Association of America(263)
CoreNet Global(266)
Council of State and Territorial Epidemiologists(274)
Council on Occupational Education(276)
Decision Sciences Institute(282)
Exhibit Designers and Producers Association(299)
Healthcare Convention and Exhibitors Association(323)
Institute for Professionals in Taxation(339)
Institute of Nuclear Power Operations(343)
Institute of Paper Science and Technology(343)
International Food Additives Council(372)
International Formula Council(373)
International Inflight Food Service Association(376)
International Jelly and Preserve Association(377)
International Military Community Executives Association(379)
Life Insurers Council(407)
Lignin Institute(408)
LOMA(409)
Manufacturers' Agents Association for the Foodservice Industry(411)
National Association for Kinesiology and Physical Education in Higher Education(434)
National Association of Church Food Service(443)
National Association of Medical Examiners(461)

National Basketball Athletic Trainers Association(483)
National Credit Union Management Association(503)
National Golf Car Manufacturers Association(514)
National Institute of American Doll Artists(520)
National Pecan Shellers Association(532)
Pine Chemicals Association(578)
Portable Rechargeable Battery Association(581)
Professional Baseball Athletic Trainers Society(586)
Professional Football Athletic Trainers Society(587)
Professional Photographers of America(588)
Refrigerated Foods Association(597)
Research Chefs Association(600)
Society for Cryobiology(616)
Society for Pediatric Psychology(623)
Society of Biblical Literature(632)
Society of International Business Fellows(639)
Society of Pelvic Reconstructive Surgeons(641)
Technical Association of the Pulp and Paper Industry(658)
Vinegar Institute(683)

Augusta
International Society for Research on Aggression(388)
National Barrel Horse Association(483)
Society for Hematopathology(618)
Society for Pediatric Pathology(623)
United States and Canadian Academy of Pathology(672)

Avondale Estates
International Paralegal Management Association(382)

Bainbridge
Herpetologists' League(325)

Bremen
National Association of Limited Edition Dealers(460)

Carrollton
Insulated Cable Engineers Association(344)
Society of Professors of Education(643)

College Park
Association of Aviation Psychologists(187)

Columbus
Independent Automotive Damage Appraisers Association(333)
Retail Tobacco Dealers of America(601)
Shareholder Services Association(609)

Conyers
National Association of Elevator Contractors(450)

Dalton
American Floorcovering Alliance(84)
Carpet and Rug Institute(238)

Decatur
Association for Clinical Pastoral Education(169)
Association for Humanist Sociology(174)
National American Legion Press Association(430)
National Funeral Directors and Morticians Association(513)

Douglasville
Council for Near-Infrared Spectroscopy(269)

Duluth
IGAF Worldwide(332)
PKF North American Network(578)

East Point
National Conference of Black Mayors(492)

Evans
American Academy of Oral and Maxillofacial Radiology(25)

Farmington
Artist-Blacksmiths' Association of North America(162)

Fayetteville
Railway Tie Association(595)
State Guard Association of the United States(652)

Ft. Valley
Council of Administrators of Special Education(270)

Gainesville
National Poultry and Food Distributors Association(533)

Griffin
Textile Fibers and By-Products Association(660)

Jesup
American Beekeeping Federation(56)

Kennesaw
Veterinary Botanical Medical Association(682)
Women in Packaging(692)

LaGrange
Plant Growth Regulators Society of America(578)
Society for the Preservation of Oral Health(627)

Lawrenceville
American Academy of Sanitarians(28)

Lilburn
Midwives Alliance of North America(419)
Women's Basketball Coaches Association(693)

Macon
China Clay Producers Association(244)

Marietta
American Salvage Pool Association(124)
Community Broadcasters Association(255)
The Foodservice Group, Inc.(310)
International Society of Communication Specialists(391)
Open Applications Group(565)
Society of Insurance Research(638)
Wood Component Manufacturers Association(694)

McDonough
National Ornamental and Miscellaneous Metals Association(531)

Morrow
EIFS Industry Members Association(290)

Newnan
Recreational Park Trailer Industry Association(596)

Norcross
Associated Construction Publications(165)
Industrial Asset Management Council(336)
Institute of Industrial Engineers(341)
National Association of Professional Organizers(466)
Porcelain Enamel Institute(580)
Potash & Phosphate Institute(581)

United Product Formulators and Distributors Association(672)

Roswell
American Academy of Medical Management(24)
American Educational Studies Association(80)
Health Ministries Association(323)

Savannah
American Board of Forensic Psychology(57)
American Board of Professional Psychology(58)
National Federation of Housing Counselors(509)

Smyrna
American Institute of Hydrology(96)

Stone Mountain
American Cultural Resources Association(77)
USA Poultry and Egg Export Council(681)

Suwanee
Handweavers Guild of America(321)

Tucker
Poultry Breeders of America(581)
U.S. Poultry and Egg Association(668)

Watkinsville
Society of Municipal Arborists(640)

Winterville
American Association for Vocational Instructional Materials(37)

HAWAII

Honolulu
Chinese Language Teachers Association(245)
International Association for Philosophy of Law and Social Philosophy - American Section(351)
Society for Economic Botany(616)
World History Association(696)

Lanai City
International Horn Society(375)

IDAHO

Boise
International Association of Round Dance Teachers(361)
International Festivals and Events Association(371)
National Association of State Outdoor Recreation Liaison Officers(476)
Travel and Tourism Research Association(665)

Lewiston
Society of Mineral Analysts(640)

Meridian
American College of Veterinary Ophthalmologists(71)

Moscow
Appaloosa Horse Club(159)
U.S.A. Dry Pea and Lentil Council(668)

Pocatello
School Management Study Group(606)

Rupert
North America Colleges and Teachers of Agriculture(553)

Twin Falls
American Society of Agricultural Appraisers(133)

ILLINOIS

Alsip

NAIR -- the International Association of Bowling Lane Specialists(425)

Alton

American Dental Interfraternity Council(79)
Congress of Independent Unions(261)
Xi Psi Phi(697)

Arlington Heights

Academy of Osseointegration(5)
Air Movement and Control Association International(13)
American Association of Certified Allergists(39)
American College of Allergy, Asthma and Immunology(64)
American College of Osteopathic Family Physicians(69)
American Society for Blood and Marrow Transplantation(127)
American Society of Colon and Rectal Surgeons(136)
American Society of Maxillofacial Surgeons(141)
American Society of Plastic Surgeons(144)
Association for Manufacturing Excellence(176)
Association of Academic Chairmen of Plastic Surgery(183)
Fulfillment Services Association of America(312)
National Association of Personal Financial Advisors(464)
Society of Surgical Oncology(644)

Aurora

American Brush Manufacturers Association(59)
American Purchasing Society(120)
International Chain Salon Association(365)

Bannockburn

IPC - Association Connecting Electronics Industries(399)

Barrington

Association for the Advancement of Automotive Medicine(179)

Batavia

American Heartworm Society(90)
Cryogenic Engineering Conference(280)

Beecher

American Chain of Warehouses(61)

Bloomingdale

American Society of Clinical Hypnosis(135)
National Credit Reporting Association(503)
Usability Professionals' Association(681)

Bloomington

American Rabbit Breeders Association(121)

Buffalo Grove

AERA - Engine Rebuilders Association(9)
Construction Writers Association(263)

Byron

Professional Reactor Operator Society(589)

Carbondale

American Association of Teachers of French(52)
International Water Resources Association(396)
National Association of State Land Reclamationists(475)
National Council on Rehabilitation Education(503)
Philosophy of Education Society(576)
Society for the Advancement of American Philosophy(626)
Universities Council on Water Resources(679)

Champaign

American Society for Hispanic Art Historical Studies(130)
Association of Environmental Engineering and Science Professors(195)
International Society of Arboriculture(390)
Labor and Employment Relations Association(404)
National Association of Advisors for the Health Professions(438)
National Council on Student Development(503)
National Gymnastics Judges Association(516)
Society for the Advancement of Economic Theory(626)
University Film and Video Association(680)
Utility Arborist Association(681)

Charleston

Institute of Behavioral and Applied Management(340)

Chicago

Academy of Dentistry for Persons with Disabilities(3)
Academy of Dispensing Audiologists(3)
Academy of General Dentistry(3)
Accreditation Council for Pharmacy Education(6)
African American Contractors Association(11)
African-American Natural Foods Association(11)
Allied Finance Adjusters Conference(17)
American Academy of Anti-Aging Medicine(20)
American Academy of Cosmetic Surgery(21)
American Academy of Disability Evaluating Physicians(22)
American Academy of Esthetic Dentistry(22)
American Academy of Implant Dentistry(23)
American Academy of Matrimonial Lawyers(24)
American Academy of Pediatric Dentistry(26)
American Academy of Periodontology(27)
American Academy of Physical Medicine and Rehabilitation(27)
American Association for Hand Surgery(35)
American Association of Cardiovascular and Pulmonary Rehabilitation(39)
American Association of Dental Examiners(42)
American Association of Diabetes Educators(42)
American Association of Endodontists(42)
American Association of Healthcare Consultants(43)
American Association of Hospital Dentists(44)
American Association of Individual Investors(44)
American Association of Law Libraries(44)
American Association of Legal Nurse Consultants(44)
American Association of Medical Assistants(45)
American Association of Osteopathic Women Physicians(47)
American Association of School Librarians(50)
American Association of Women Dentists(54)
American Bar Association(56)
American Board of Preventive Medicine(57)
American Burn Association(60)
American College of Foot and Ankle Surgeons(66)
American College of Healthcare Executives(66)
American College of Osteopathic Emergency Physicians(69)
American College of Prosthodontists(70)
American College of Psychiatrists(70)
American College of Surgeons(71)
American Conference of Cantors(73)
American Dental Assistants Association(78)
American Dental Association(78)
American Dental Society of Anesthesiology(79)
American Dietetic Association(79)
American Health and Beauty Aids Institute(89)
American Health Information Management Association(89)
American Hospital Association(92)
American Institute of Indian Studies(96)
American Institute of Steel Construction(97)
American Ladder Institute(100)
American Library Association(101)
American Marketing Association(103)
American Medical Association(104)
American Osteopathic Association(111)
American Osteopathic Board of Physical Medicine and Rehabilitation(111)
American Osteopathic College of Pathologists(112)
American Planning Association(116)
American Prepaid Legal Services Institute(117)
American Property Tax Counsel(117)
American Radium Society(121)
American Schools Association(124)
American Society for Clinical Pathology(127)
American Society for Geriatric Dentistry(129)
American Society for Healthcare Central Service Professionals(129)
American Society for Healthcare Engineering(129)
American Society for Healthcare Environmental Services(129)
American Society for Healthcare Human Resources Administration(129)
American Society for Healthcare Risk Management(129)
American Society for Political and Legal Philosophy(131)
American Society for Reconstructive Microsurgery(132)
American Society of Directors of Volunteer Services(137)
American Society of Hair Restoration Surgery(138)
American Society of Hand Therapists(138)
American Society of Lipo-Suction Surgery(140)
American Society of Pediatric Nephrology(143)
American Society of Plumbing Engineers(144)
American Specialty Toy Retailing Association(148)
American Student Dental Association(149)
American Supply Association(150)
American Theological Library Association(151)
Appraisal Institute(159)
Assistive Technology Industry Association(164)
Association for Healthcare Resource and Materials Management(174)
Association for Library Collections and Technical Services(175)
Association for Library Service to Children(175)
Association for Library Trustees and Advocates(176)
Association of Catholic Diocesan Archivists(189)
Association of College and Research Libraries(190)
Association of Independent Trust Companies(200)
Association of Information Technology Professionals(201)
Association of Professional Researchers for Advancement(209)
Association of Specialized and Cooperative Library Agencies(214)
Association of Specialized and Professional Accreditors(214)
Association of Steel Distributors(216)
Bank Administration Institute(225)
Battery Council International(226)
Blue Cross and Blue Shield Association(231)
Brass and Bronze Ingot Industry(232)
Business Marketing Association(235)
CCIM Institute(240)
Center for Exhibition Industry Research(241)
Chemical Industry Data Exchange(243)
Classification Society of North America(247)
Commercial Law League of America(253)
Committee of 200(254)
Consumer Credit Insurance Association(263)

Council for Adult and Experiential Learning(267)
Council of Real Estate Brokerage Managers(274)
Council of Residential Specialists(274)
Counselors of Real Estate(277)
Cremation Association of North America(279)
Defense Research Institute(282)
Electrical and Computer Engineering Department Heads Association(290)
Electronic Distribution Show Corporation(291)
Electronics Representatives Association(292)
Engine Manufacturers Association(295)
Federal Judges Association(302)
Financial and Insurance Conference Planners(305)
Financial Managers Society(306)
Financial Services Technology Network(306)
Gift and Collectibles Guild(316)
Government Finance Officers Association of the United States and Canada(318)
Health Forum(323)
Healthcare Information and Management Systems Society(324)
InSight(339)
Institute of Certified Healthcare Business Consultants(340)
Institute of Food Technologists(341)
Institute of Real Estate Management(343)
International Association of Defense Counsel(356)
International Association of Healthcare Central Service Materiel Management(357)
International Association of Lighting Designers(358)
International Association of Physicians in AIDS Care(360)
International Business Brokers Association(364)
International Carwash Association(364)
International College of Surgeons(366)
International Customer Service Association(368)
International Engineering Consortium(370)
International Federation for Choral Music(371)
International Foodservice Manufacturers Association(372)
International Formalwear Association(373)
International Housewares Representatives Association(375)
International Interior Design Association(377)
International Magnetics Association(378)
International Reprographic Association(385)
International Special Events Society(393)
Library Administration and Management Association(407)
Library and Information Technology Association(407)
Medical Library Association(416)
Metal Framing Manufacturers Association(417)
Microscopy Society of America(418)
Monument Builders of North America(421)
National Association of Architectural Metal Manufacturers(438)
National Association of Bond Lawyers(441)
National Association of Concessionaires(445)
National Association of Fire Equipment Distributors(452)
National Association of Floor Covering Distributors(453)
National Association of Independent Fee Appraisers(457)
National Association of Orthopaedic Nurses(463)
National Association of Real Estate Companies(468)
National Association of REALTORS(468)
National Association of Women Highway Safety Leaders(481)
National Association of Women Lawyers(482)
National Automatic Merchandising Association(482)
National Black MBA Association(484)
National Bulk Vendors Association(485)
National Catholic Band Association(487)
National Conference of Commissioners on Uniform State Laws(493)
National Cosmetology Association(496)
National Council of Real Estate Investment Fiduciaries(500)
National Council of State Boards of Nursing(500)
National Fastener Distributors Association(508)
National Federation of Priests' Councils(510)
National Futures Association(513)
National Institute of Pension Administrators(521)
National Marine Bankers Association(525)
National Marine Manufacturers Association(526)
National Network for Social Work Managers(528)
National Society for the Study of Education(541)
National Society of Genetic Counselors(541)
National Student Osteopathic Medical Association(544)
North American Association of Food Equipment Manufacturers(554)
North American Building Material Distribution Association(555)
NYSE Arca(563)
Popcorn Institute(580)
Power Transmission Distributors Association(582)
Precast/Prestressed Concrete Institute(582)
Pressure Vessel Manufacturers Association(583)
Prevent Blindness America(583)
Professional Convention Management Association(587)
Profit Sharing/401(k) Council of America(590)
Public Library Association(592)
Railway Industrial Clearance Association of North America(595)
Real Estate Buyers Agent Council(595)
REALTORS Land Institute(596)
Red Tag News Publications Association(597)
Showmen's League of America(610)
Society for Disability Studies(616)
Society for Healthcare Consumer Advocacy(618)
Society for Healthcare Strategy and Market Development(618)
Society for Information Management(620)
Society for Iranian Studies(620)
Society for Vascular Surgery(629)
Society of American Archivists(630)
Society of Architectural Historians(631)
Society of Gastroenterology Nurses and Associates(637)
Society of Gynecologic Oncologists(638)
Society of Incentive & Travel Executives(638)
Society of Small Craft Designers(644)
Society of Thoracic Surgeons(645)
Society of Women Engineers(646)
Special Care Dentistry Association(648)
Strategic Account Management Association(654)
Tile Roofing Institute(661)
Trade Show Exhibitors Association(663)
Travel Journalists Guild(665)
Turnaround Management Association(667)
United States Court Reporters Association(674)
United States Soccer Federation(677)
Wallcoverings Association(685)
Women's Council of REALTORS(693)
Women's Foodservice Forum(693)
Zonta International(698)

Chicago Ridge

Society of Independent Show Organizers(638)

Cicero

American Society of Podiatric Medical Assistants(144)

Crystal Lake

International Association of Diecutting and Diemaking(356)
Steel Founders' Society of America(653)

Decatur

National Association of County Agricultural Agents(447)

Deerfield

Selected Independent Funeral Homes(539)

DeKalb

Association for Career and Technical Education Research(169)
Society for Computers in Psychology(615)

Des Plaines

American Academy of Medical Administrators(24)
American College of Cardiovascular Administrators(64)
American College of Contingency Planners(65)
American College of Healthcare Information Administrators(66)
American College of Managed Care Administrators(67)
American Society of Home Inspectors(139)
American Society of Safety Engineers(146)
Association of Coupon Professionals(193)
Emergency Nurses Association(293)
Gas Technology Institute(314)
Institute for Certification of Computing Professionals(339)
International Concrete Repair Institute(366)
International Warehouse Logistics Association(396)
MTM Association for Standards and Research(422)
National Association of the Remodeling Industry(479)
National Catholic Cemetery Conference(487)
National Insurance Crime Bureau(522)
North American Bar-Related Title Insurers(555)
PrintImage International(584)
Property Casualty Insurers Association of America(591)
Refrigeration Service Engineers Society(597)
Society of Critical Care Medicine(634)
Window and Door Manufacturers Association(689)

Downers Grove

Association of Women Surgeons(220)
Coin Laundry Association(250)
Independent Medical Distributors Association(335)
Liability Insurance Research Bureau(407)
Property Loss Research Bureau(591)

Dundee

Women in Management(692)

East Dundee

Lawn Institute(406)
Turfgrass Producers International(667)

East Moline

Mass Finishing Job Shops Association(413)

Effingham

Omega Tau Sigma(564)

Elgin

American Naprapathic Association(108)
Council of Fleet Specialists(272)
Foodservice Equipment Distributors Association(310)
Recycled Paperboard Technical Association(597)

Elk Grove Village

American Academy of Pediatrics(27)
American Amusement Machine Association(31)
American College of Occupational and Environmental Medicine(68)
Fibre Box Association(305)
International Professional Groomers(383)
National Ice Cream Retailers Association(518)

Elmhurst

American Dairy Products Institute(78)
Employee Services Management Association(293)

Evanston

American Board of Medical Specialties(57)
American Massage Therapy Association(103)
Association for College and University Religious Affairs(169)
Federation of Associations of Regulatory Boards(303)
Urban Libraries Council(681)

Fox River Grove

Steel Deck Institute(653)

Frankfort

International Association of Attorneys and Executives in Corporate Real Estate(353)

Galva

Association for the Sociology of Religion(180)
Religious Research Association(599)

Geneva

International Society of Hair Restoration Surgery(391)
National Association of Independent Insurance Adjusters(457)

Glen Ellyn

American Endodontic Society(81)
American Fence Association(83)
Bearing Specialist Association(226)
Ceramic Tile Distributors Association(241)
Evangelical Church Library Association(298)
National Church Goods Association(489)
Plastic Pipe and Fittings Association(578)

Glendale Heights

International Association for Healthcare Security and Safety(350)

Glenview

Academy of Veterinary Allergy and Clinical Immunology(6)
American Academy of Hospice and Palliative Medicine(23)
American Academy of Pain Medicine(26)
American Association of Neuroscience Nurses(46)
American Pain Society(112)
American Society for Bioethics and Humanities(127)
American Society of Pediatric Hematology/Oncology(143)
Appliance Parts Distributors Association(159)
Association for Corporate Growth(171)
Association of Pediatric Hematology/Oncology Nurses(207)
Association of Rehabilitation Nurses(211)
Awards and Recognition Association(225)
Awards & Recognition Industry Educational Foundation(225)
Christian Stewardship Association(246)
Freestanding Insert Council of North America(312)
Giving Institute(317)
Giving USA Foundation(317)
Insulating Concrete Form Association(344)
Legal Marketing Association(407)
Metal Construction Association(417)
National Association for Healthcare Quality(433)
National Association of Neonatal Nurses(462)
National Luggage Dealers Association(525)
National Registry of Environmental Professionals(535)
North American Benthological Society(555)
North American Neuromodulation Society(559)
North American Professional Driver Education Association(559)
North American Retail Dealers Association(559)
Paper Industry Management Association(571)
Retail Confectioners International(601)
Society of Trauma Nurses(645)

Grayslake

National Congress of Animal Trainers and Breeders(495)

Gurnee

American Association for Accreditation of Ambulatory Surgery Facilities(33)
National Marine Representatives Association(526)

Hampshire

American College of Psychoanalysts(70)

Harvard

American Shropshire Registry Association(125)

Highland Park

National Shrimp Industry Association(539)
National Submetering and Utility Allocation Association(544)
Submersible Wastewater Pump Association(655)

Hillside

Air Distributing Institute(13)

Hines

American Kinesiotherapy Association(100)

Hoffman Estates

Association of Forensic Document Examiners(197)
Inter-Industry Conference on Auto Collision Repair(346)

Homewood

National Association of State Radio Networks(476)

Itasca

Associated Risk Managers(166)
Campus Safety, Health and Environmental Management Association(237)
National Safety Council(538)

Jacksonville

American Dialect Society(79)

La Grange

International Staple, Nail and Tool Association(393)
North American Spine Society(561)

La Grange Park

American Nuclear Society(109)

Lake Bluff

Casket and Funeral Supply Association of America(238)
Council of Medical Specialty Socs.(273)
Post-Print Manufacturers Association(581)

Lake Forest

American Spa and Health Resort Association(148)
International Marking and Identification Association(379)
National Family Business Council(508)

Lake Zurich

Insurance Consumer Affairs Exchange(345)
Steel Plate Fabricators Association Division of STI/SPFA(653)
Steel Tank Institute Division of STI/SPFA(654)

Lemont

Council on Library-Media Technicians(276)

Libertyville

United Lightning Protection Association(671)

Lincolnshire

Association of Legal Administrators(203)

Lincolnwood

American Society of Contemporary Ophthalmology(136)
ISSA(400)

Lisle

Association for Preservation Technology International(177)
Association of Black Nursing Faculty in Higher Education(187)
Land Improvement Contractors of America(405)
United States Cross Country Coaches Association(674)
Water Quality Association(686)

Lombard

Islamic Medical Association of North America(400)

Long Grove

Conference of Consulting Actuaries(259)

Mahomet

American College of Veterinary Anesthesiologists(71)

Moline

American Rental Association(122)
Association of Official Seed Certifying Agencies(206)

Montgomery

National Association of Independent Public Finance Advisors(457)

Morton

American Shetland Pony Club/American Miniature Horse Registry(125)

Morton Grove

American Equilibration Society(81)
Sporting Goods Agents Association(651)

Mt. Prospect

National Association of Boards of Pharmacy(440)
National Ski and Snowboard Retailers Association(539)
National Sporting Goods Association(543)

Mundelein

American Art Therapy Association(32)
American Biological Safety Association(57)
United States Fencing Coaches Association(675)

Naperville

Association of Girl Scout Executive Staff(198)
Cable and Telecommunications Human Resources Association(236)
Contract Packaging Association(264)

Incentive Manufacturers and Representatives Association(332)
Incentive Marketing Association(332)
Institute of Packaging Professionals(343)
National Association of Container Distributors(446)
Tag and Label Manufacturers Institute(657)
Tube Council of North America(666)
Wire Fabricators Association(690)

Normal

Council on Technology Teacher Education(277)
National Association of Industrial and Technical Teacher Educators(458)
National Association of Professional Band Instrument Repair Technicians(465)

Northbrook

Academy for Eating Disorders(2)
American College of Chest Physicians(64)
American Pediatric Surgical Association(113)
American Society of Dermatopathology(137)
American Society of Pharmacognosy(144)
American Society of Tropical Medicine and Hygiene(147)
Association for Death Education and Counseling(171)
Association of University Technology Managers(219)
Automatic Meter Reading Association(223)
Institute of Nuclear Materials Management(343)
International Society for Analytical Cytology(386)
International Society for Traumatic Stress Studies(389)
Maple Flooring Manufacturers Association(412)
Pressure Sensitive Tape Council(583)
Society of Vertebrate Paleontology(646)
Sump and Sewage Pump Manufacturers Association(655)

Northfield

Broadcast Cable Credit Association(233)
Broadcast Cable Financial Management Association(233)
College of American Pathologists(251)
International Psychogeriatric Association(383)

Oak Brook

American Society for Gastrointestinal Endoscopy(129)
American Society of Head and Neck Radiology(138)
American Society of Neuroradiology(142)
Associated Equipment Distributors(165)
Association of Program Directors in Radiology(210)
Association of Rotational Molders, International(212)
Association of University Radiologists(219)
Council of Supply Chain Management Professionals(275)
Delta Dental Plans Association(282)
National Fraternal Congress of America(512)
Radiological Society of North America(594)
Spring Manufacturers Institute(652)
Warehousing Education and Research Council(685)

Oak Park

Cryogenic Society of America(280)
Marine Retailers Association of America(412)

Oakbrook Terrace

Computing Technology Industry Association(258)
National Truck Leasing System(547)

Palatine

American Academy of Dental Practice Administration(21)
American Chiropractic Registry of Radiologic Technologists(62)
American Fiberboard Association(83)
American Society of Artists(134)
Independent Cosmetic Manufacturers and Distributors(333)
Joint Council of Allergy, Asthma, and Immunology(402)
United States Bowling Instructors Association(673)

Park Ridge

American Association of Nurse Anesthetists(46)
American Egg Board(80)
American Medical Technologists(105)
American Society of Anesthesiologists(134)
American Society of Regional Anesthesia and Pain Medicine(145)
Association of University Anesthesiologists(219)
Million Dollar Round Table(419)
Non-Ferrous Founders' Society(553)
Society for Education in Anesthesia(616)
Society of Neurosurgical Anesthesia and Critical Care(641)
Society of Tribologists and Lubrication Engineers(645)
Urban and Regional Information Systems Association(680)

Pecatonica

Clydesdale Breeders of the United States(249)

Pekin

International Association of Eating Disorders Professionals(356)

Peoria

Association of Defense Trial Attorneys(193)
Chester White Swine Record Association(244)
National Spotted Swine Record(543)
Poland China Record Association(579)

Plainfield

Association of Technical and Supervisory Professionals(217)

Prairie View

American Pet Boarding Association(114)

River Forest

Lutheran Education Association(409)

Riverside

Mail Systems Management Association(410)

Rockford

Catholic Book Publishers Association(239)
Fabricators and Manufacturers Association, International(300)
National Association of Health Unit Coordinators(455)
Tube and Pipe Association, International(666)

Rolling Meadows

American Association of Neurological Surgeons(46)
American Society for Dermatologic Surgery(128)
Commission on Certification of Work Adjustment and Vocational Evaluation Specialists(254)
Information Systems Audit and Control Association(338)
Institute of Environmental Sciences and Technology(341)
Metal Service Center Institute(417)
North American Wholesale Lumber Association(562)

Roselle

American Mold Builders Association(106)

Rosemont

American Academy for Cerebral Palsy and Developmental Medicine(19)
American Academy of Orthopaedic Surgeons(26)
American Association of Hip and Knee Surgeons(43)
American Association of Oral and Maxillofacial Surgeons(47)
American Orthopaedic Association(110)
American Orthopaedic Foot and Ankle Society(111)
American Orthopaedic Society for Sports Medicine(111)
American Shoulder and Elbow Surgeons(125)
American Society for Surgery of the Hand(132)
American Society of Orthopaedic Physician's Assistants(143)
Arthroscopy Association of North America(162)
Association of Bone and Joint Surgeons(188)
Association of Children's Prosthetic-Orthotic Clinics(189)
Cervical Spine Research Society(242)
Council of Musculoskeletal Specialty Socs.(273)
Dairy Management(281)
International Housewares Association(375)
National Roofing Contractors Association(537)
Orthopaedic Research Society(568)
Orthopaedic Trauma Association(569)
Pediatric Orthopedic Society of North America(572)
Ruth Jackson Orthopaedic Society(603)

Savoy

American Dairy Science Association(78)
American Embryo Transfer Association(81)
American Meat Science Association(104)
American Society of Animal Science(134)
Board of Certified Safety Professionals(231)
Council on Certification of Health, Environmental and Safety Technologists(275)
International Embryo Transfer Society(370)
Poultry Science Association(581)

Schaumburg

Air Diffusion Council(13)
American Academy of Dermatology(21)
American Architectural Manufacturers Association(32)
American Association of Clinical Urologists(40)
American College of Legal Medicine(66)
American Foundry Society(85)
American Hardware Manufacturers Association(88)
American Society of Andrology(133)
American Veterinary Medical Association(153)
Association of Professional Chaplains(208)
Audit Bureau of Circulations(222)
Concrete Reinforcing Steel Institute(259)
Congress of Neurological Surgeons(261)
Mason Contractors Association of America(413)
National Association of Executive Recruiters(451)
Plumbing Manufacturers Institute(579)
Society of Actuaries(629)
Society of University Urologists(645)

Skokie

International Association of Ocular Surgeons(359)
Portland Cement Association(581)

South Barrington

Amusement and Music Operators Association(156)

Springfield

American Association of Public Health Dentistry(50)
American Neurotology Society(109)
American Otological Society(112)
American Quaternary Association(121)
Association for Surgical Education(178)
Association of Science Museum Directors(213)
Hispanic Dental Association(326)
National Association of Special Needs State Administrators(472)

St. Charles

Ceilings and Interior Systems Construction Association(241)
Dietary Managers Association(284)

Sugar Grove

International Visual Literacy Association(396)

Tinley Park

American Association of Railroad Superintendents(50)

Urbana

American Oil Chemists' Society(110)
Conference on College Composition and Communication(260)
Conference on English Education(260)
Conference on English Leadership(260)
National Council of Teachers of English(501)
Rhetoric Society of America(601)
Women's Classical Caucus(693)

Vernon Hills

Material Handling Equipment Distributors Association(414)

Wauconda

Aluminum Anodizers Council(18)
Aluminum Extruders Council(18)
International Magnesium Association(378)

West Chicago

Alliance of Claims Assistance Professionals(16)

Westchester

American Academy of Dental Sleep Medicine(21)
American Academy of Sleep Medicine(28)
Associated Professional Sleep Socs.(166)
Association of Polysomnographic Technologists(208)
Healthcare Financial Management Association(324)
Professional Currency Dealers Association(587)
Sleep Research Society(611)

Wheaton

American Academy of Oral and Maxillofacial Pathology(25)
American Society of Business Publication Editors(135)
Calendar Marketing Association(236)
Casual Furniture Retailers(239)
EEG and Clinical Neuroscience Society(290)
Evangelical Training Association(298)
National Association of Ticket Brokers(479)
National Independent Flag Dealers Association(519)
National Retail Hobby Stores Association(536)

Wheeling

International Council on Education for Teaching(368)
North American Die Casting Association(556)

Willowbrook

Vibration Institute(683)

Wilmette

Accreditation Association for Ambulatory Health Care(6)
Boating Writers International(231)
U.S.A. Toy Library Association(669)

INDIANA

Anderson

Lipizzan Association of North America(408)

Bedford

Indiana Limestone Institute of America(336)
National Trappers Association(547)

Bloomington

Animal Behavior Society(157)
Association for Educational Communications and Technology(172)
Association for Practical and Professional Ethics(177)
Association of College Unions International(191)
Conference on Asian History(260)
National Pan-Hellenic Council(531)
Organization of American Historians(567)
Phi Delta Kappa(575)
Pi Lambda Theta(577)
Society for Ethnomusicology(617)
University Risk Management and Insurance Association(680)
Wilderness Education Association(688)

Carmel

Association of Fraternity Advisors(198)

East Chicago

National Optometric Association(529)

Elkhart

American Association of Professional Sales Engineers(49)

Evansville

Phi Mu Alpha Sinfonia(576)
Tobacconists' Association of America(662)

Franklin

American Safe Deposit Association(123)

Greencastle

Electronics Technicians Association International(292)
Tamworth Swine Association(657)

Greenville

American Association of Dental Consultants(41)

Huntington

Conference on Faith and History(261)
Society for Romanian Studies(625)

Indianapolis

Alpha Chi Sigma(17)
Alpha Kappa Psi(18)
American Academy of Maxillofacial Prosthetics(24)
American Academy of Osteopathy(26)
American College of Counselors(65)
American College of Sports Medicine(70)
American Congress of Rehabilitation Medicine(73)
American Teleservices Association(151)
Association of Natural Resource Enforcement Trainers(205)
Biomedical Marketing Association(229)
Black Coaches Association(230)
Corporate Housing Providers Association(266)
Cranial Academy(278)
Custom Electronic Design and Installation Association(280)
Interior Design Educators Council(347)
International Association of Speakers Bureaus(361)
Kappa Delta Pi(403)
National Alliance of Statewide Preservation Organizations(430)
National Association of Mutual Insurance Companies(462)
National Association of Orthopaedic Technologists(463)
National Association of State Agencies for Surplus Property(473)
National Collegiate Athletic Association(491)
National Committee on Planned Giving(491)
National Costumers Association(496)
National Council of Acoustical Consultants(498)
National Council on Public History(502)
National Federation Coaches Association(508)
National Federation of Music Clubs(509)
National Federation of Officials Association(510)
National Federation of State High School Associations(510)
National FFA Organization(510)
National Interscholastic Athletic Administrators Association(522)
National Panhellenic Conference(531)
National Postsecondary Agriculture Student Organization(533)
National Precast Concrete Association(534)
NFHS Music Association(553)
NFHS Speech Debate and Theatre Association(553)
North American Interfraternity Conference(557)
North American Retail Hardware Association(559)
Phi Epsilon Kappa(576)
Phi Rho Sigma Medical Society(576)
Pony of the Americas Club(580)
Professional Insurance Communicators of America(587)
Property Casualty Conferences(591)
Religious Conference Management Association(599)
Roller Skating Association International(602)
Society for Free Radical Biology and Medicine(617)
Society for Nutrition Education(622)
Society for Pediatric Dermatology(623)
Society of Broadcast Engineers(632)
Society of Professional Journalists(642)
Used Truck Association(681)

Kokomo

National Appliance Service Association(430)

Martinsville

American Camp Association(60)
Association of Shareware Professionals(214)

Mountain Brook

Wirebound Box Manufacturers Association(690)

Muncie

Association for General and Liberal Studies(173)
Charles Homer Haskins Society(243)

Plainfield

Association of Muslim Scientists and Engineers(205)
National Chimney Sweep Guild(489)

Portage

Pulp and Paper Safety Association(593)

Shelby

International Buckskin Horse Association(363)

Shelbyville

Spring Research Institute(652)

South Bend

American Wholesale Booksellers Association(154)
IEEE Society on Social Implications of Technology(332)
Society of Asian and Comparative Philosophy(632)

St. John

International Energy Credit Association(370)

Valparaiso

Natural Colored Wool Growers Association(550)

Vincennes

National Association of Juvenile Correctional Agencies(459)

Wabash

Belgian Draft Horse Corp. of America(227)

Wakarusa

Recreational Vehicle Manufacturer's Clubs Association(597)

Walkerton

American North Country Cheviot Sheep Association(109)

Warsaw

American Association of Nutritional Consultants(46)

West Lafayette

Aerospace Department Chairmen's Association(10)
American Berkshire Association(56)
Association of American Feed Control Officials(184)
Association of University Interior Designers(219)
Committee on History in the Classroom(254)
National Association of Swine Records(478)
National Swine Registry(545)
Walnut Council(685)
Women Band Directors International(690)

Zionsville

American Walnut Manufacturers Association(153)

IOWA

Ames

American Agricultural Economics Association(30)
American Association of Veterinary Immunologists(53)
American Council on Consumer Interests(76)
Association for Gnotobiotics(173)
Association of Boards of Certification(188)
Consortium of College and University Media Centers(262)
Council for Agricultural Science and Technology(268)
Institute of Noise Control Engineering(343)
National Farmers Organization(508)
National Swine Improvement Federation(545)
North American Society for the Psychology of Sport and Physical Activity(561)
Society for the History of Technology(627)

Ankeny

Associated Construction Distributors International(165)
Soil and Water Conservation Society(647)

Bettendorf

National Association of Osteopathic Foundations(463)
Society for German-American Studies(617)

Buffalo

International Security Management Association(385)

Cedar Rapids

Association for Information Media and Equipment(174)
National Association of Media and Technology Centers(461)
National Systems Contractors Association(545)

Decorah

National Ballroom and Entertainment Association(483)

Des Moines

Alliance of National Staffing and Employment Resources(17)
American Judicature Society(99)
Association of Former Agents of the U.S. Secret Service(197)
Association of Image Consultants International(200)
Federal Probation and Pre-trial Officers Association(302)
International Association for Food Protection(350)
International Association of Lighting Management Companies(359)
International Association of Professional Security Consultants(360)
International Network of Merger and Acquisition Partners(380)
National Association for Poetry Therapy(435)
National Rural Economic Developers Association(537)
Stadium Managers Association(652)
United Applications Standards Group(670)
Vacuum Dealers Trade Association(682)

Guttenberg

American School Band Directors' Association(124)

Iowa City

American Association of Certified Orthoptists(39)
Farm Equipment Wholesalers Association(301)
International Business Music Association(364)
International Perimetric Society(382)
North American Saxophone Alliance(560)
Society of Pelvic Surgeons(641)

Milo

American Hampshire Sheep Association(88)
American Polypay Sheep Association(116)
National Lincoln Sheep Breeders Association(525)

Mt. Vernon

Concrete Foundations Association(258)
Tilt-up Concrete Association(661)

Perry

American Association of Swine Veterinarians(52)

Red Oak

Independent Association of Questioned Document Examiners(333)

Sioux City

American Association of Grain Inspection and Weighing Agencies(43)

Urbandale

National Pork Producers Council(533)

Waterloo

Consultant Dietitians in Health Care Facilities(263)

West Des Moines

National Independent Fire Alarm Distributors(519)

KANSAS

Baldwin City

Association for Informal Logic and Critical Thinking(174)

Colby

Groundwater Management Districts Association(320)

Kansas City

International Brotherhood of Boilermakers, Iron Ship Builders, Blacksmiths, Forgers and Helpers(363)
Piano Technicians Guild(577)

Lawrence

Accrediting Council on Education in Journalism and Mass Communications(7)
American Society for Photobiology(131)
Association of Medical Illustrators(204)
Commercial Real Estate Women Network(253)
Golf Course Superintendents Association of America(318)
Mycological Society of America(424)
National Frame Builders Association(512)
Paleontological Society(570)
Print Council of America(583)
Radiation Research Society(594)
Society for the Study of Evolution(628)
Sports Turf Managers Association(651)
Weed Science Society of America(687)
Wilderness Medical Society(689)
Wildlife Disease Association(689)

Leavenworth

Society for Military History(622)

Leawood

American Academy of Family Physicians(22)
Association of Family Medicine Administration(196)
Association of Family Medicine Residency Directors(196)
International Association of Operative Millers(359)
International Association of Plastics Distributors(360)
Society of Teachers of Family Medicine(644)

Lenexa

American Association for Public Opinion Research(36)
American College of Healthcare Architects(66)
American Society of Pain Management Nurses(143)
ARMA International(160)
Association of Genetic Technologists(198)
NATCO - The Organization for Transplant Professionals(426)
National Association of EMS Physicians(451)
National Association of Graduate Admissions Professionals(454)
Transportation Lawyers Association(664)

Manhattan

Baking Industry Sanitation Standards Committee(225)
Beef Improvement Federation(227)
Intercollegiate Men's Choruses, an International Association of Male Choruses(346)
International Association for Jazz Education(351)
Journalism Education Association(402)
National Academic Advising Association(426)
World War Two Studies Association(696)

Mission

National Soccer Coaches Association of America(540)

Mission Woods

Allied Trades of the Baking Industry(17)

Olathe

American Association of School Personnel Administrators(51)
Devon Cattle Association(284)
National Association of Intercollegiate Athletics(458)
National Interscholastic Swimming Coaches Association(522)

Overland Park

Agriculture Council of America(12)
American Medical Society for Sports Medicine(105)
Association of Collegiate Business Schools and Programs(191)
BEMA - The Baking Industry Suppliers Association(227)
Council for Learning Disabilities(269)
Crop Insurance Research Bureau(279)
National Agri-Marketing Association(428)
National Auctioneers Association(482)
National Crop Insurance Services(504)
World Waterpark Association(696)

Oxford

Professional Association of Volleyball Officials(586)

Shawnee Mission

International College of Applied Kinesiology(365)
Metal Building Contractors and Erectors Association(417)

Spring Hill

Ankole Watusi International Registry(157)

Topeka

American Association of Zoo Keepers(54)
Foil Stamping and Embossing Association(308)
Glass Association of North America(317)
Glazing Industry Code Committee(317)
Home Baking Association(327)
National Association of Trailer Manufacturers(479)
National Sunroom Association(545)

Walton

American International Marchigiana Society(98)

Wichita

Advertising and Marketing International Network(9)
American Academy of Environmental Medicine(22)
National Association of Educational Office Professionals(450)
Society of Decorative Painters(635)

KENTUCKY

Bowling Green

American Association of Small Ruminant Practitioners(51)
National Institute for Animal Agriculture(520)

Covington

National Real Estate Investors Association(535)
Retail Packaging Manufacturers Association(601)

Florence

National Association for Family and Community Education(433)
National Lieutenant Governors Association(524)

Frankfort

Conference of Radiation Control Program Directors(260)
International Association of Workforce Professionals(362)
National Association of State Directors of Veterans Affairs(475)
National Turf Writers Association(547)
World Association of Alcohol Beverage Industries(695)

Henderson

National Association of Video Distributors(480)

Hodgenville

Purebred Morab Horse Association(593)

Lexington

American Academy of Equine Art(22)
American Association of Equine Practitioners(42)
American Farrier's Association(82)
American Hackney Horse Society(88)
American Hanoverian Society(88)
American Probation and Parole Association(117)
American Saddlebred Horse Association(123)
American Society of Mining and Reclamation(141)
American Volleyball Coaches Association(153)
Asphalt Institute(163)
Association of Caribbean Studies(188)
Association of College and University Telecommunications Administrators(191)
Association of Racing Commissioners International(211)
Association of State Dam Safety Officials(215)
Automotive Occupant Restraints Council(224)
Burley Auction Warehouse Association(235)
Burley Tobacco Growers Cooperative Association(235)
Chief Officers of State Library Agencies(244)
College Savings Plans Network(252)
Council of State Governments(275)
Council on Licensure, Enforcement and Regulation(276)
International Coach Federation(365)
International Spa Association(392)
NASTD - Technology Professionals Serving State Government(426)
National Association of Agricultural Educators(438)
National Association of Government Defined Contribution Administrators(454)
National Association of Local Government Auditors(460)
National Association of State Auditors, Comptrollers and Treasurers(473)
National Association of State Boating Law Administrators(473)
National Association of State Chief Administrators(474)
National Association of State Chief Information Officers(474)
National Association of State Facilities Administrators(475)
National Association of State Personnel Executives(476)
National Association of State Procurement Officials(476)
National Association of State Treasurers(476)
National Association of Unclaimed Property Administrators(479)
National Emergency Management Association(507)
National Horsemen's Benevolent and Protective Association(517)
National Tour Association(546)
Society for French Historical Studies(617)
Thoroughbred Club of America(661)
Thoroughbred Owners and Breeders Association(661)
United Professional Horsemen's Association(672)
United States Equestrian Federation(675)
Women Executives in State Government(691)

Louisville

American Association of Preferred Provider Organizations(49)
American Cheese Society(61)
American Society for Healthcare Food Service Administrators(129)
Associated Cooperage Industries of America(165)
Association of Presbyterian Colleges and Universities(208)
Association of Statisticians of American Religious Bodies(216)
Distillers Grains Technology Council(286)
Foodservice Consultants Society International(309)
International Association of Culinary Professionals(355)
Mexican Restaurant and Cantina Association(418)
Mobile Industrial Caterers' Association International(420)
National Association of Equipment Leasing Brokers(451)
National Association of Pizza Operators(464)
National Council of Art Administrators(498)
National Show Horse Registry(539)
Network of Ingredient Marketing Specialists(551)
North American Association of Professors of Christian Education(554)
Presbyterian Health, Education and Welfare Association(583)
Railway Systems Suppliers(595)
Society for Foodservice Management(617)
Women Chefs and Restaurateurs(691)

Middletown

American Institute of Commemorative Art(95)

Morehead

Organizational Systems Research Association(568)

Park City

National Caves Association(488)

Richmond

National Association of Institutional Linen Management(458)
National Juvenile Detention Association(523)

LOUISIANA

Alexandria

Religious Education Association(599)

Baton Rouge

Association of Independent Information Professionals(200)
National Association of State Archaeologists(473)
National Association of State Retirement Administrators(476)
Society for Social Studies of Science(625)
State Risk and Insurance Management Association(653)
World Aquaculture Society(695)

Gonzales

National Conference of State Liquor Administrators(494)

Harahan

Offshore Marine Service Association(564)

Kenner

American Guild of Hypnotherapists(88)

New Orleans

American Shrimp Processors Association(125)
American Society of Primatologists(145)
International Fire Photographers Association(372)
National Association of Substance Abuse Trainers and Educators(478)

Ruston

ADED - the Association for Driver Rehabilitation Specialists(8)

Shreveport

National Association of Pipe Coating Applicators(464)

Slidell

National Taxidermists Association(545)

Thibodaux

American Sugar Cane League of the U.S.A.(150)

MAINE

Augusta

National Council of State Supervisors for Languages(501)

Bar Harbor

Society for Human Ecology(619)

Kennebunkport

Wild Blueberry Association of North America(688)

Orono

Potato Association of America(581)

Phillips

Association of Traumatic Stress Specialists(218)

Portland

Coordinating Council for Women in History(265)

Readfield

International Association for the Study of Cooperation in Education(351)

Scarborough

National Association of African American Studies(438)
National Association of School Nurses(470)

Windham

Association of Winery Suppliers(220)

York

International Association of Privacy Professionals(360)

MARYLAND

Adamstown

American Society of Laboratory Animal Practitioners(140)

Adelphi

National Association of Black Journalists(440)

Annapolis

Airlines Electronic Engineering Committee(14)
American Academy of Environmental Engineers(22)
American Boat and Yacht Council(58)
Asphalt Emulsion Manufacturers Association(163)
Asphalt Recycling and Reclaiming Association(163)
Association for Hose and Accessories Distribution(174)
Association for Recorded Sound Collections(177)
Association of Transportation Professionals(218)
Committee for Private Offshore Rescue and Towing (C-PORT)(254)
Independent Sealing Distributors(335)
International Masonry Institute(379)
International Slurry Surfacing Association(386)
Plasma Protein Therapeutics Association(578)
UniForum Association(669)
Wholesale Florist and Florist Supplier Association(688)
Women in Scholarly Publishing(692)
Yacht Brokers Association of America(698)

Arnold

Building Owners and Managers Institute International(234)

Ashton

Chinese American Food Society(245)

Baltimore

Accountants for the Public Interest(6)
American Catholic Correctional Chaplains Association(61)
American College Health Association(63)
American Institute of Floral Designers(96)
Association of Academic Physiatrists(183)
Black Broadcasters Alliance(230)
Council of American Master Mariners(270)
Fire Suppression Systems Association(307)
International Association of Forensic Toxicologists(357)
International Association of Special Investigation Units(361)
International Beverage Dispensing Equipment Association(362)
International Dyslexia Association(370)
International Society for Third-Sector Research(389)
International Society of Restaurant Association Executives(392)
League of Historic American Theatres(406)
Music Critics Association of North America(423)
National Association of Educational Buyers(450)
National Association of Sewer Service Companies(472)
National Association of Sign Supply Distributors(472)
National Association of Waterproofing and Structural Repair Contractors(481)
National Conference of Diocesan Vocation Directors(493)
National Correctional Industries Association(496)
National Council of Investigation and Security Services(499)
National Economic Association(505)
National Finance Adjusters(510)
National Sugar Brokers Association(544)
Office Products Wholesalers Association(564)
Phi Alpha Delta(575)
Professional Basketball Writers' Association(586)
Professional Fraternity Association(587)
Professional Grounds Management Society(587)
Register of Professional Archeologists(598)
Society for Clinical Trials(615)
Society for the Advancement of Socio-Economics(626)
TASH(657)
Trauma Care International(665)
U.S. Lacrosse(668)
Woodworking Machinery Industry Association(694)

Bel Air

American Holistic Veterinary Medical Association(91)
American Veterinary Distributors Association(153)
Flexographic Prepress Platemakers Association(308)
Lawn and Garden Marketing and Distribution Association(406)
Pet Industry Distributors Association(574)
Postcard and Souvenir Distributors Association(581)
Safety Equipment Distributors Association(604)
Web Sling and Tiedown Association(686)

Bethesda

AABB(1)
Academy of Psychosomatic Medicine(5)
Adhesive and Sealant Council(8)
American Alliance for Theatre and Education(30)
American Association for Geriatric Psychiatry(35)
American Association of Anatomists(38)
American Association of Bank Directors(38)
American Association of Immunologists(44)
American Beverage Licensees(57)
American College of Foot and Ankle Orthopedics and Medicine(65)
American College of Gastroenterology(66)
American College of Medical Genetics(67)
American College of Medical Quality(67)
American College of Osteopathic Internists(69)
American College of Radiation Oncology(70)
American College of Toxicology(71)
American Fisheries Society(84)
American Gastroenterological Association(86)
American Medical Informatics Association(104)
American Occupational Therapy Association(109)
American Physiological Society(115)
American Podiatric Medical Association(116)
American Podiatric Medical Students' Association(116)
American Pyrotechnics Association(120)
American Society for Biochemistry and Molecular Biology(126)
American Society for Cell Biology(127)
American Society for Clinical Laboratory Science(127)
American Society for Investigative Pathology(130)
American Society for Nutrition(131)
American Society for Pharmacology and Experimental Therapeutics(131)
American Society for Photogrammetry and Remote Sensing(131)
American Society of Health-System Pharmacists(139)
American Society of Human Genetics(139)
American Society of Nuclear Cardiology(142)
Associated Specialty Contractors(166)
Association for Financial Professionals(173)
Association for Molecular Pathology(176)
Association of Chiropractic Colleges(189)
Association of Military Surgeons of the U.S.(205)
Association of Pathology Chairs(207)
Association of Professors of Cardiology(209)
Association of Program Directors in Surgery(210)
Association of Small Foundations(214)
Automotive Aftermarket Industry Association(223)
Automotive Communication Council(223)
Automotive Maintenance Repair Association(223)
Biophysical Society(229)
Car Care Council(237)
Chief Executives Organization(244)
Council of State Administrators of Vocational Rehabilitation(274)
Council on Employee Benefits(276)
Cystic Fibrosis Foundation(281)

Federation of American Socs. for Experimental Biology(303)
Gastroenterology Research Group(315)
Genetics Society of America(315)
International Society for Pharmacoepidemiology(388)
International Truck Parts Association(395)
Intersociety Council For Pathology Information(398)
National Association of Community Health Centers(445)
National Association of School Psychologists(470)
National Catalog Managers Association(487)
National Council of State Agencies for the Blind(500)
National Council on Radiation Protection and Measurements(502)
National Directory Publishing Association(505)
National Electrical Contractors Association(506)
National Information Standards Organization(520)
National Spinal Cord Injury Association(542)
PDA - an International Association for Pharmaceutical Science and Technology(572)
The Protein Society(591)
Renewable Natural Resources Foundation(599)
RNA Society(602)
Secondary Materials and Recycled Textiles Association(607)
Shippers of Recycled Textiles(610)
Society for Developmental Biology(616)
Society for Leukocyte Biology(621)
Society for Mucosal Immunology(622)
Society for Vascular Medicine and Biology(629)
Society of American Foresters(630)
Society of Fire Protection Engineers(636)
Society of Government Travel Professionals(637)
Wildlife Society, The(689)
World Future Society(696)

Bowie

American Association for Adult and Continuing Education(33)
National Society for Histotechnology(541)
Service Station Dealers of America and Allied Trades(609)
Tire Industry Association(662)

Buckeystown

American Genetic Association(86)

Burtonsville

Council of Colleges of Acupuncture and Oriental Medicine(271)

Cabin John

International Hydrofoil Society(375)

Calverton

Intermodal Association of North America(347)

Camp Springs

Seafarers' International Union(607)
Transportation Institute(664)

Chestertown

Science Fiction and Fantasy Writers of America(606)

Chevy Chase

American Association of Colleges of Osteopathic Medicine(40)
American Hungarian Educators Association(92)
American Society of Addiction Medicine(133)
Endocrine Society(294)
Environmental Information Association(296)
International Private Infrastructure Association(383)
National Association of Veterans' Research and Education Foundations(480)
National Certification Commission(488)
Romanian-American Chamber of Commerce(603)
Society of Professional Benefit Administrators(642)

College Park

American Association of Physicists in Medicine(48)
American Association of Physics Teachers(48)
American Association of Sunday and Feature Editors(52)
American Institute of Physics(97)
American Physical Society(115)
National Women's Studies Association(549)

Columbia

Advertising Media Credit Executives Association, International(9)
American Dance Therapy Association(78)
American Medical Directors Association(104)
Association of Specialists in Cleaning and Restoration International(214)
Chain Link Fence Manufacturers Institute(242)
COLA(250)
Credit Research Foundation(279)
FCIB-NACM Corp.(301)
International Union of Elevator Constructors(395)
Intersocietal Accreditation Commission(398)
Marine Technology Society(412)
National Association of Catering Executives(442)
National Association of Credit Management(448)
National Shoe Retailers Association(539)
Pedorthic Footwear Association(572)
Universities Space Research Association(679)

Crisfield

National Association of Black Professors(440)

Crofton

Alliance of Foam Packaging Recyclers(16)
Association of Professors of Gynecology and Obstetrics(209)
EPS Molders Association(297)

Damascus

Society of Atherosclerosis Imaging(632)

Darnestown

Association for the Advancement of Baltic Studies(179)

Dunkirk

Undersea and Hyperbaric Medical Society(669)

Earleville

Costume Society of America(267)

Easton

Bulk Carrier Conference(235)

Edgewater

International Aviation Womens Association(362)
National Aircraft Finance Association(428)
National Onsite Wastewater Recycling Association(529)

Edgewood

American Academy of Home Care Physicians(23)
National Academies of Practice(426)

Elkridge

Correctional Education Association(266)

Elkton

Thoroughbred Racing Associations of North America(661)

Ellicott City

American Sports Builders Association(148)
Professional Association of Custom Clothiers(585)

Finksburg

International Double Reed Society(369)

Forestville

United Brotherhood of Carpenters and Joiners of America(670)

Frederick

Aircraft Owners and Pilots Association(14)
American Association for Laboratory Accreditation(35)
Bioelectromagnetics Society(229)
National Auto Auction Association(482)
Quarters Furniture Manufacturers Association(594)
Society for Applied Spectroscopy(614)
Society for Physical Regulation in Biology and Medicine(624)
Training Directors' Forum(663)

Ft. Washington

Black Entertainment and Sports Lawyers Association(230)
Certified Claims Professional Accreditation Council(242)
Espionage Research Institute(297)
National Tooling and Machining Association(546)

Gaithersburg

American College of Dentists(65)
American Congress on Surveying and Mapping(73)
AOAC International(158)
Coal Technology Association(249)
Composite Panel Association(257)
Fusion Power Associates(313)
National Environmental Balancing Bureau(507)
National Society of Professional Surveyors(542)

Germantown

American Society of Psychoanalytic Physicians(145)
Council for American Private Education(268)
International Association of Approved Basketball Officials(352)
Substance Abuse Program Administrators Association(655)

Greenbelt

Academy of Criminal Justice Sciences(3)
Black Data Processing Associates(230)
National Association of Black Accountants(440)

Hagerstown

American Jail Association(99)
American Society for Colposcopy and Cervical Pathology(127)

Hanover

Institute for Operations Research and the Management Sciences(339)

Hyattsville

SOLE - The International Society of Logistics(647)

Kensington

Bakery, Confectionery, Tobacco Workers and Grain Millers International Union(225)
National Family Caregivers Association(508)
Society of Eye Surgeons(636)

Taxicab, Limousine and Paratransit Association(657)

Landover

American Railway Engineering and Maintenance of Way Association(121)
Association of Firearm and Toolmark Examiners(197)
Biomedical Engineering Society(229)
Commissioned Officers Association of the United States Public Health Service(254)
Contact Lens Council(264)
National Academy of Opticianry(427)
National Phlebotomy Association(533)
Reusable Industrial Packaging Association(601)

Landover Hills

National Association of Air Traffic Specialists(438)

Lanham

Entomological Society of America(295)
International Association of Heat and Frost Insulators and Asbestos Workers(357)
National Asphalt Pavement Association(431)
National Association of Minority Automobile Dealers(462)
National Association of Real Estate Brokers(468)
Society for Vascular Ultrasound(629)

Largo

Association of Supervisory and Administrative School Personnel(216)

Laurel

American Institute of Ultrasound in Medicine(98)
Executive Women in Government(299)
International Fabricare Institute(371)
Operative Plasterers' and Cement Masons' International Association of the United States and Canada(565)

Linthicum

American Urological Association(153)
Flexible Packaging Association(307)
National Automotive Finance Association(483)
U.S. Psychiatric Rehabiliation Association(668)

Linthicum Heights

International Organization of Masters, Mates and Pilots(382)

Mt. Airy

American Federation of Violin and Bow Makers(83)

Myersville

ADARA(8)

Ocean Pines

Apparel Graphics Institute(159)

Olney

Association for Childhood Education International(169)
Professional Handlers Association(587)

Owings Mills

Association of Commercial Finance Attorneys(192)

Pasadena

American Board of Periodontology(57)

Port Republic

Estuarine Research Federation(297)

Potomac

Association of Military Colleges and Schools of the U.S.(205)
Education Industry Association(289)
National Seasoning Manufacturers Association(539)
Peanut and Tree Nut Processors Association(572)

Princess Anne

Association of Research Directors(212)

Rockville

American Academy of Appellate Lawyers(20)
American Academy of Optometry(25)
American Association of Colleges of Podiatric Medicine(40)
American College of Mortgage Attorneys(67)
American College of Real Estate Lawyers(70)
American College of Veterinary Surgeons(72)
American Institute of Professional Bookkeepers(97)
American Machine Tool Distributors Association(102)
American Medical Writers Association(105)
American Registry of Diagnostic Medical Sonographers(122)
American Society of Consulting Arborists(136)
American Society of Plant Biologists(144)
American Speech-Language-Hearing Association(148)
Association for Assessment and Accreditation of Laboratory Animal Care International(168)
Association for Research in Vision and Ophthalmology(178)
Association of Community Cancer Centers(192)
Association of Schools and Colleges of Optometry(213)
Brotherhood Railway Carmen/TCU(233)
Caucus for Women in Statistics(240)
Forest Resources Association(310)
Institute of Hazardous Materials Management(341)
International College of Dentists, U.S.A. Section(366)
International Kitchen Exhaust Cleaning Association(377)
International Natural Sausage Casing Association(380)
International Society of Weighing and Measurement(392)
Interstate Council on Water Policy(398)
Mechanical Contractors Association of America(415)
Mechanical Service Contractors of America(415)
National Association of Beverage Importers-Wine-Spirits-Beer(439)
National Association of Commissions for Women(445)
National Certified Pipe Welding Bureau(488)
National Conference on Weights and Measures(495)
National Council for Community Behavioral Healthcare(497)
National School Public Relations Association(538)
National Student Speech Language Hearing Association(544)
Oceanography Society(564)
Periodical Publications Association(573)
Physician Insurers Association of America(577)
Plumbing Contractors of America(579)
Regulatory Affairs Professionals Society(598)
Renal Physicians Association(599)
Resilient Floor Covering Institute(600)
Society for Historical Archaeology(618)
Transportation Communications International Union(664)
United States Pharmacopeia(676)

Salisbury

Czechoslovak History Conference(281)
National Academy of Television Journalists(427)

Severna Park

Industry Council for Tangible Assets(337)
International Society for Ecological Modelling-North American Chapter(387)
Iota Tau Tau(399)
National Marine Electronics Association(526)

Silver Spring

American College of Nurse-Midwives(68)
American Herbal Products Association(90)
American Music Therapy Association(107)
American Nurses Association(109)
American Society for Information Science and Technology(130)
American Society for Parenteral and Enteral Nutrition(131)
American Zoo and Aquarium Association(156)
Anxiety Disorders Association of America(157)
ASFE/The Best People on Earth(162)
Association for Information and Image Management International(174)
Association of Public Health Laboratories(210)
Association of Public Treasurers of the United States and Canada(211)
Biscuit and Cracker Manufacturers' Association(229)
CIES, The Food Business Forum(246)
Concrete Plant Manufacturers Bureau(258)
Conference of Major Superiors of Men, U.S.A.(259)
International Federation of Professional and Technical Engineers(371)
International Society for Performance Improvement(388)
National Association for Equal Opportunity in Higher Education(433)
National Association for Proton Therapy(435)
National Association for Public Health Statistics and Information Systems(435)
National Association for Treasurers of Religious Institutes(437)
National Association of Health Services Executives(455)
National Association of Pastoral Musicians(464)
National Association of State Aviation Officials(473)
National Association of State Utility Consumer Advocates(477)
National Black Nurses Association(484)
National Board for Certified Clinical Hypnotherapists(485)
National Coalition of Black Meeting Planners(490)
National Coalition of Creative Arts Therapies Associations(490)
National Conference of Executives of The ARC(493)
National Council for the Social Studies(497)
National Foundation for Credit Counseling(512)
National Ready Mixed Concrete Association(535)
National School Supply and Equipment Association(538)
Organization of Black Airline Pilots(567)
Population Association of America(580)
Society for the Exploration of Psychotherapy Integration(627)
Special Event Sites Marketing Alliance(648)
SWANA - Solid Waste Association of North America(656)
Truck Mixer Manufacturers Bureau(665)
United American Nurses, AFL-CIO(670)

Stevenson

NAGMR Consumer Product Brokers(425)

Suitland

Air Force Sergeants Association(13)

Takoma Park

Association of Seventh-Day Adventist Librarians(213)

Thurmont

National Ornamental Goldfish Growers Association(531)

Timonium

American Society of Trial Consultants(147)
International Metal Decorators Association(379)

University Park

Space Transportation Association(648)

Upper Marlboro

American Trauma Society(152)
International Association of Machinists and Aerospace Workers(359)

Walkersville

American Academy of Podiatric Sports Medicine(27)

West Bethesda

Council on Fine Art Photography(276)

Wheaton

Association of Partners for Public Lands(207)
United States Federation for Culture Collections(675)

MASSACHUSETTS

Agawam

American Society for Amusement Park Security and Safety(126)

Amherst

Association for the Environmental Health of Soils(180)
Law and Society Association(406)
Union for Radical Political Economics(669)

Athol

Office Furniture Distribution Association(564)

Becket

Timber Framers Guild(661)

Bedford

IEEE Microwave Theory and Techniques Society(331)

Belmont

National Association for Armenian Studies and Research(431)

Beverly

American Association for Thoracic Surgery(37)
American Association of Plastic Surgeons(48)
American Federation for Medical Research(82)
American Surgical Association(150)
International Society for Minimally-Invasive Cardiac Surgery(387)
Society for Clinical Vascular Surgery(615)
Society for Pediatric Urology(623)
Society for Surgery of the Alimentary Tract(625)

Boston

Advanced Transit Association(9)
American Flock Association(84)
American Meteorological Society(105)
American Schools of Oriental Research(124)
American Society of Law, Medicine and Ethics(140)
Applied Research Ethics National Association(159)
Archaeological Institute of America(160)
Association for Textual Scholarship in Art History(179)
Association for Work Process Improvement(183)
Association of Literary Scholars and Critics(203)
Cashmere and Camel Hair Manufacturers Institute(238)
Design Management Institute(283)
Family Firm Institute(300)
International Health, Racquet and Sportsclub Association(374)
International Society for Infectious Diseases(387)
International Society of Exposure Analysis(391)
Medical Records Institute(416)
National Textile Association(546)
Society for Clinical and Experimental Hypnosis(615)
Visiting Nurse Associations of America(684)

Brighton

National Tay-Sachs and Allied Diseases Association(545)

Brookline

American Academy of the History of Dentistry(29)
American Society of Psychopathology of Expression(145)
Orthodox Theological Society in America(568)

Burlington

American Association of Genitourinary Surgeons(43)
International Association for Human Resource Information Management(350)

Cambridge

American Academy of Arts & Sciences(20)
American Association for the Advancement of Slavic Studies(36)
American Association of Variable Star Observers(53)
Jean Piaget Society(400)
Medieval Academy of America(416)
United Association for Labor Education(670)

Canton

Association of Smoked Fish Processors(214)
Research Council on Structural Connections(600)

Chestnut Hill

Society for Italian Historical Studies(621)

Chicopee

National Association of Power Engineers(465)

Concord

Hospital Presidents Association(328)
International Association of Music Libraries, United States Branch(359)
National Coalition of Girls Schools(490)

Devens

Organic Reactions Catalysis Society(566)

East Dennis

Photo Chemical Machining Institute(576)

East Wareham

Cranberry Institute(278)

Everett

Association for Documentary Editing(171)

Fairhaven

American Evaluation Association(81)

Florence

American Society for the Alexander Technique(146)

Gardner

International Furniture Transportation and Logistics Council(373)

Gloucester

American Hockey Coaches Association(91)

Greenfield

Organic Trade Association(566)

Hadley

Creative Education Foundation(278)

Hanson

The Art and Creative Materials Institute(161)
Council for Art Education(268)

Lexington

International Isotope Society(377)

Ludlow

National Tunis Sheep Registry(547)

Lunenburg

Electrical Insulation Conference(291)

Lynn

Jewish Funeral Directors of America(402)

Lynnfield

Fire and Emergency Manufacturers and Services Association(307)
Fire Apparatus Manufacturers' Association(307)

Malden

National Association of Environmental Professionals(451)
Phycological Society of America(577)

Marlborough

National Investment Company Service Association(522)

Medford

International Institute of Forecasters(376)

Medway

NARTE(425)

Melrose

American Society of Abdominal Surgeons(133)

Middleton

American Academy of Podiatric Practice Management(27)

Needham

Catholic Medical Association(240)
College Gymnastics Association(251)
Object Management Group(563)
WACRA - World Association for Case Method Research and Application(684)

North Andover

Plumbing and Drainage Institute(579)

Northampton

American Men's Studies Association(105)

Norwood

Infusion Nurses Society(338)

Nutting Lake

American Society of Test Engineers(146)

Peabody
International Society of Facilities Executives(391)

Pelham
National Institutes for Water Resources(521)

Pittsfield
Catholic Library Association(240)

Plympton
American Cotswold Record Association(74)

Quincy
International Fire Marshals Association(372)
National Association of Government Employees(454)
National Association of State Controlled Substances Authorities(474)
National Fire Protection Association(510)

Raynham
Orthopedic Surgical Manufacturers Association(569)

Rochester
American Society of Irrigation Consultants(140)

Salem
American Venous Forum(153)
Newspaper Association Managers(552)
North American Society for Cardiac Imaging(560)

South Dartmouth
SMMA - The Motor and Motion Association(612)
Transformer Association, The(663)

Springfield
American Hockey League(91)

Sudbury
American Healthcare Radiology Administrators(90)

Topsfield
International Desalination Association(369)

Wakefield
Computer Law Association(258)

Waltham
American Lithotripsy Society(102)
Ethics Officer Association(298)
SPRI, Inc.(652)
Urology Society of America(681)

Wellesley
Institute of Certified Travel Agents(340)

Westborough
International District Energy Association(369)

Westfield
American Registry of Medical Assistants(122)
International Trumpet Guild(395)
Society of Philosophers in America(642)

Westford
International Firestop Council(372)
National Roof Deck Contractors Association(537)

Westminster
Wood Products Manufacturers Association(694)

Whitinsville
National Association of State Directors of Teacher Education and Certification(475)

Williamstown
Catalogue Raisonne Scholars Association(239)

Wilmington
International Association for Modular Exhibitry(351)

Woburn
National Lead Burning Association(523)

Woods Hole
Society of General Physiologists(637)

Worcester
American Antiquarian Society(31)
International Society for Preventive Oncology(388)

MICHIGAN

Alto
Music Distributors Association(423)

Ann Arbor
American Oriental Society(110)
American Society for Clinical Investigation(127)
Association for Asian Studies(167)
Athletic Equipment Managers Association(221)
Automated Imaging Association(222)
College of Healthcare Information Management Executives(251)
International Society of Barristers(390)
National Association of Industrial Technology(458)
National Coalition of Alternative Community Schools(490)
Organization of Teachers of Oral Diagnosis(568)
Robotic Industries Association(602)
Social Science History Association(612)
Society for College and University Planning(615)
Society for Research in Child Development(624)
Society for Research on Adolescence(624)
Society for Textual Scholarship(626)
Society of Automotive Analysts(632)
Surgical Infection Society(656)

Battle Creek
Children's Literature Association(244)

Belleville
American Motility Society(107)
Association of American Physicians(185)

Big Rapids
National Council for Workforce Education(497)

Bloomfield Hills
Construction Innovation Forum(262)

Burton
Association for the Behavioral Sciences and Medical Education(180)

Crystal Falls
National Association of County Health Facility Administrators(447)

Dearborn
Association of Cosmetologists and Hairdressers(193)
North American Manufacturing Research Institution of SME(558)
Society of Manufacturing Engineers(639)

Detroit
Association for Business Simulation and Experiential Learning(168)
International Union, United Automobile, Aerospace and Agricultural Implement Workers of America(396)
National Association of Black Women Entrepreneurs(440)

East Lansing
Academy of International Business(3)
Association for the Study of Higher Education(181)
Association of College Honor Societies(191)
Institute of Public Utilities(343)
International Safe Transit Association(385)
National Association of College and University Food Services(444)
World Association for Infant Mental Health(695)

Farmington
National Trailer Dealers Association(547)

Farmington Hills
American College of Neuropsychiatrists(68)
American Concrete Institute(72)
Independent Professional Representatives Organization(335)
National Truck Equipment Association(547)
Society for Humanistic Judaism(619)

Flint
Association of Women Soil Scientists(220)
International Physical Fitness Association(383)
National Orientation Directors Association(530)

Flushing
Smocking Arts Guild of America(612)

Franklin
Spill Control Association of America(651)

Grand Ledge
International Association of Accident Reconstruction Specialists(352)

Grand Rapids
Business and Institutional Furniture Manufacturers Association International(235)
Christian Schools International(246)
Protestant Church-Owned Publishers Association(591)
Society of Christian Philosophers(633)

Haslett
International Cut Flower Growers Association(368)
International Snowmobile Manufacturers Association(386)

Holland
Society for Reformation Research(624)

Houghton
Society for Industrial Archeology(620)

Jackson
National Association of Photo Equipment Technicians(464)
Photo Marketing Association-International(576)
Professional Picture Framers Association(588)
Travel Adventure Cinema Society(665)

Kalamazoo
Association for Behavior Analysis(168)
Association of Rehabilitation Programs in Computer Technology(211)
Association of University Architects(219)

Lansing
American Board of Industrial Hygiene(57)
Cherry Marketing Institute(243)

National Association of Agricultural Fair Agencies(438)
National Association of Disability Examiners(449)
National Plant Board(533)
Society for Academic Emergency Medicine(613)

Livonia

International Hearing Society(375)

Marshall

Select Registry/Distinguished Inns of North America(608)

Mt. Pleasant

American Baseball Coaches Association(56)

Nokomis

Aquatic Exercise Association(159)

Novi

Chain Drug Marketing Association(242)

Okemos

Veterinary Orthopedic Society(682)

Roseville

International Union Security, Police and Fire Professionals of America(396)

Saline

North American Case Research Association(555)

Southfield

Association of Public Data Users(210)
Automotive Industry Action Group(223)
Brotherhood of Maintenance of Way Employees(233)

St. Clair Shores

International Society of Travel and Tourism Educators(392)
National Association of Resale & Thrift Shops(469)

St. Joseph

ASABE - the Society for Engineering in Agricultural, Food and Biological Systems(162)

Sterling Heights

American Society of Body Engineers(135)

Traverse City

Association of Directory Publishers(194)
Suburban Newspapers of America(655)

Troy

Original Equipment Suppliers Association(568)

Walled Lake

Associated Wire Rope Fabricators(166)

Warren

American Guild of Music(88)

Wayne

Clinical Ligand Assay Society(248)

West Bloomfield

Academy of Prosthodontics(5)
Conservative Orthopaedics International Association(261)
Floor Covering Installation Contractors Association(308)
Industrial Chemical Research Association(336)

Willis

National Association of Agriculture Employees(438)

Ypsilanti

Association for Applied and Clinical Sociology(167)

Zeeland

Christian Labor Association of the United States of America(246)

MINNESOTA

Alexandria

Association of Construction Inspectors(192)
Environmental Assessment Association(296)
International Real Estate Institute(384)
International Society of Meeting Planners(391)
International Travel Writers and Editors Association(395)
National Association of Real Estate Appraisers(468)
National Association of Review Appraisers and Mortgage Underwriters(469)
Professional Women's Appraisal Association(590)

Bemidji

Association of Camp Nurses(188)
Ornamental Concrete Producers Association(568)

Bloomington

Energy and Environmental Building Association(294)
Portable Sanitation Association International(581)

Cottage Grove

Association of American Seed Control Officials(185)

Duluth

American Academy of Health Care Providers-Addictive Disorders(23)
Association for Consumer Research(171)
North American Canon Law Society(555)

Eden Prairie

Academy of Surgical Research(5)
Agricultural and Industrial Manufacturers' Representatives Association(12)
American Railway Development Association(121)
Laboratory Animal Management Association(404)
Wiring Harness Manufacturers Association(690)

Edina

IPA - The Association of Graphic Solutions Providers(399)
Surface Mount Technology Association(656)

Forest Lake

Cleaning Equipment Trade Association(247)

Houston

North American Clun Forest Association(556)

Lake City

North American Deer Farmers Association(556)

Mankato

National Forensic Association(512)

Mendota Heights

International Association for Identification(350)

Minneapolis

ACA International, The Association of Credit and Collection Professionals(2)
Academy of Aphasia(2)
Aircraft Builders Council(14)
American Neurological Association(108)
American Society of Neuroimaging(142)
American Society of Neurorehabilitation(142)
American Underground-Construction Association(152)
Associated Collegiate Press, National Scholastic Press Association(165)
Association Correctional Food Service Affiliates(166)
Association for Chemoreception Sciences(169)
Captive Insurance Companies Association(237)
Controlled Release Society(265)
Employee Assistance Society of North America(293)
Evangelical Press Association(298)
Export Institute of the United States(300)
Flexible Intermediate Bulk Container Association(307)
Grain Elevator and Processing Society(319)
Health Care Compliance Association(322)
International Academy of Trial Lawyers(348)
International Association of Printing House Craftsmen(360)
International Childbirth Education Association(365)
National Association of Home Inspectors(456)
National Council on Family Relations(502)
National Exercise Trainers Association(508)
National Mail Order Association(525)
National Marrow Donor Program(526)
National Network of Grantmakers(528)
National Risk Retention Association(537)
North American Neuro-Ophthalmology Society(559)
Plastic Surgery Admininstrative Association(578)
Professional Liability Underwriting Society(588)

Moorhead

International Association for Language Learning Technology(351)
Organization of American Kodaly Educators(567)

New Prague

American Agricultural Editors Association(30)
Turf and Ornamental Communicators Association(667)

New Richland

American Cheviot Sheep Society(62)

Northfield

International Alliance of Technology Integrators(348)

Outing

International Wild Rice Association(397)

Prior Lake

International Ceramic Association(364)

Richfield

American Filtration and Separations Society(83)

Rochester

American Association of Neuromuscular & Electrodiagnostic Medicine(46)
Professional Skaters Association(589)
Society of Computed Body Tomography and Magnetic Resonance(634)
Society of Thoracic Radiology(645)
Truck-frame and Axle Repair Association(666)

Roseville

American Association of Pathologists' Assistants(47)

Financial Women International(306)
Industrial Fabrics Association International(336)

St. Cloud

Billings Ovulation Method Association of the United States(228)
National Association for Rural Mental Health(436)
National Wildlife Rehabilitators Association(549)
Society of Christian Ethics(633)

St. Joseph

Society for Business Ethics(614)

St. Louis Park

Association of Art Editors(186)

St. Paul

AACC International(1)
American Academy of Neurology(25)
American Phytopathological Society(115)
American Registry of Radiologic Technologists(122)
American Society of Brewing Chemists(135)
American Theatre Critics Association(151)
Association of Asphalt Paving Technologists(186)
Association of Cooperative Educators(192)
Association of Technical Personnel in Ophthalmology(217)
Automotive Fleet and Leasing Association(223)
Child Neurology Society(244)
Contact Lens Association of Ophthalmologists(264)
Council of Engineering and Scientific Society Executives(271)
Hospitality Institute of Technology and Management(328)
International Society for Molecular Plant Microbe Interactions(387)
Leafy Greens Council(406)
Marine Fabricators Association(412)
Master Brewers Association of the Americas(413)
National Association of Fundraising Ticket Manufacturers(454)
National Association of Investment Professionals(459)
National Association of School Resource Officers(470)
National Association of State Supervisors of Trade and Industrial Education(476)
North American Gaming Regulators Association(557)
Qualitative Research Consultants Association(593)
Surfaces in Biomaterials Foundation(656)

Stillwater

National Church Library Association(489)

Waconia

National Small Shipments Traffic Conference(540)

Watertown

American Dexter Cattle Association(79)

MISSISSIPPI

Booneville

Institute on Religion in an Age of Science(344)

Clinton

National Association of Emergency Medical Technicians(450)

Hattiesburg

National Band Association(483)
National Government Publishing Association(514)
National Verbatim Reporters Association(548)

Indianola

Catfish Farmers of America(239)
Catfish Institute(239)

Itta Bena

National Conference of Black Political Scientists(492)

Jackson

American Poultry International(117)
National Association of Medical Minority Educators(461)
National Association of Supervisors for Business Education(478)
National Tile Contractors Association(546)

Mississippi State

Association for International Agriculture and Rural Development(175)

Ocean Springs

National Marine Educators Association(526)

Southaven

National Cotton Batting Institute(496)

Vicksburg

Aquatic Plant Management Society(159)

Wesson

American Society of Certified Engineering Technicians(135)

MISSOURI

Ava

Missouri Fox Trotting Horse Breed Association(420)

Bethany

American Pinzgauer Association(115)
American Red Poll Association(122)

Bloomfield

National Association of FSA County Office Employees(454)

Blue Springs

Society for Adolescent Medicine(613)

Boonville

American Karakul Sheep Registry(100)

Bridgeton

International Association of Arson Investigators(353)

California

Association of Paroling Authorities, International(207)

Chesterfield

American Academy on Communication in Healthcare(29)
American Pancreatic Association(112)
National Christmas Tree Association(489)
National Corn Growers Association(496)
National Wood Flooring Association(550)
United Soybean Board(672)

Columbia

Association of American Plant Food Control Officials(185)
Investigative Reporters and Editors(398)
Microbeam Analysis Society(418)
National Association for Research in Science Teaching(435)
National Association of Animal Breeders(438)
National Newspaper Association(528)
Rural Sociological Society(603)
Society of American Business Editors and Writers(630)

Elsberry

Piedmontese Association of the United States(577)

Fenton

North American Equipment Dealers Association(556)
Paint and Decorating Retailers Association(570)

Grain Valley

Owner-Operator Independent Drivers Association(570)

Grandview

International Association of Personal Protection Agents(360)

Grover

Window Coverings Association of America(689)

Independence

Aircraft Electronics Association(14)
Early Sites Research Society(288)
National Association of Parliamentarians(463)
Parliamentary Associates(571)

Jackson

National Clay Pottery Association(490)

Jefferson City

Association of Conservation Engineers(192)
International Association of Correctional Training Personnel(355)
Women in Energy(691)

Joplin

International Society of Weekly Newspaper Editors(392)

Kansas City

Accredited Pet Cemetery Society(7)
Alpha Gamma Rho(17)
American Association of Veterinary State Boards(54)
American Business Women's Association(60)
American College of Clinical Pharmacy(65)
American Hereford Association(90)
American International Charolais Association(98)
American Osteopathic College of Anesthesiologists(111)
American Public Works Association(120)
American Society of Electroneurodiagnostic Technologists(137)
Association for Accounting Marketing(167)
Association of Gospel Rescue Missions(199)
Aviation Insurance Association(225)
Business Technology Association(236)
Distribution and LTL Carriers Association(286)
Electrical Equipment Representatives Association(291)
Hotel Brokers International(329)
International Association of Administrative Professionals(352)
International Association of Assessing Officers(353)
International Window Cleaning Association(397)
Investment Recovery Association(399)
Livestock Marketing Association(409)
Mass Marketing Insurance Institute(413)
Mutual Fund Education Alliance(423)
National Animal Control Association(430)
National Association of Basketball Coaches(439)
National Association of Foster Grandparent Program Directors(453)
National Association of Insurance Commissioners(458)

National Association of Professional Surplus Lines Offices(466)
National Lubricating Grease Institute(525)
National Rural Health Association(537)
Philosophy of Science Association(576)
Sealant, Waterproofing and Restoration Institute(607)
Tile Contractors' Association of America(661)

Kearney

In-Plant Printing and Mailing Association(332)
Women in Agribusiness(691)

Kirksville

American Osteopathic College of Dermatology(112)
National Association of College Wind and Percussion Instructors(444)

Marceline

Society of Nematologists(640)

Maryland Heights

Professional Football Writers of America(587)

Maryville

Lightning Protection Institute(408)

Milan

American Osteopathic College of Radiology(112)

Nelson

Palomino Horse Association(570)

Nixa

Ophthalmic Photographers' Society(565)

North Kansas City

American Tarentaise Association(150)
North American Corriente Association(556)

O'Fallon

Business Products Credit Association(235)

Platte City

American Chianina Association(62)
American Maine-Anjou Association(102)
National Association of Farm Broadcasting(452)
North American Elk Breeders Association(556)

Prairie Home

Purebred Dexter Cattle Association of North America(593)

Raytown

Stained Glass Association of America(652)

Rolla

American Society for Engineering Management(128)
Structural Stability Research Council(654)

Springfield

American College of Forensic Examiners(66)
American Psychotherapy Association(119)
International Association of Fairs and Expositions(356)
Society for Environmental Geochemistry and Health(617)
Sociological Practice Association(646)

St. Charles

College of Diplomates of the American Board of Orthodontics(251)
Concrete Anchor Manufacturers Association(258)
Powder Actuated Tool Manufacturers Institute(582)

St. Joseph

American Angus Association(31)
American Association of Veterinary Parasitologists(54)

St. Louis

Airport Ground Transportation Association(15)
American Academy of Fertility Care Professionals(23)
American Association of Bioanalysts(38)
American Association of Orthodontists(47)
American Board of Bioanalysis(57)
American Fern Society(83)
American Humor Studies Association(92)
American Optometric Association(110)
American Optometric Student Association(110)
American Society of Comparative Law(136)
American Society of Concrete Contractors(136)
American Society of Theatre Consultants(146)
American Soybean Association(148)
Association of Defensive Spray Manufacturers(193)
Association of Regulatory Boards of Optometry(211)
Black Theatre Network(231)
Botanical Society of America(231)
Catholic Health Association of the United States(240)
Consortium for Graduate Study and Management(262)
Credit Professionals International(279)
Electrical Apparatus Service Association(290)
Farm Equipment Manufacturers Association(301)
Geochemical Society(315)
Independent Computer Consultants Association(333)
International Association of Conference Centers(355)
International Brotherhood of Magicians(363)
International Order of the Golden Rule(381)
Materials Technology Institute(414)
National Association of Electrical Distributors(450)
National Catholic Pharmacists Guild of the United States(488)
National Garden Clubs(513)
National Troubleshooting Association(547)
Painting and Decorating Contractors of America(570)
Society of American Magicians(631)
United States Basketball Writers Association(673)
WaterJet Technology Association(686)
Women's Regional Publications of America(694)

Warrensburg

American Academy of Safety Education(28)
Associated Pipe Organ Builders of America(166)

Willow Springs

Scottish Blackface Sheep Breeders Association(606)

MONTANA

Bozeman

American Independent Business Alliance(93)
American Simmental Association(125)
Housing Education and Research Association(329)

Butte

Association of American State Geologists(185)

Chinook

United States Targhee Sheep Association(677)

Eureka

American Society of Forensic Odontology(138)

Great Falls

Armed Forces Optometric Society(161)
Kamut Association of North America(403)

Hamilton

Timber Frame Business Council(661)

Helena

Association of Film Commissioners International(196)

Missoula

American Galloway Breeders Association(86)
Association for Technology in Music Instruction(178)
College Music Society(251)
Outdoor Writers Association of America(569)
River Management Society(602)

NEBRASKA

Arnold

National Blacksmiths and Weldors Association(485)

Beatrice

Assembly of Episcopal Healthcare Chaplains(164)

Bellevue

Military Impacted Schools Association(419)

Crawford

World Watusi Association(697)

Fremont

International Guild of Candle Artisans(374)

Hastings

Amerifax Cattle Association(156)
College Reading and Learning Association(252)

Lincoln

Adjutants General Association of the United States(8)
American Psychology-Law Society(119)
American Romagnola Association(123)
American Society of Parasitologists(143)
Association for Women Geoscientists(182)
Braunvieh Association of America(232)
Golf Course Builders Association of America(318)
Human Behavior and Evolution Society(329)
International Association of Correctional Officers(355)
National Association of Housing Information Managers(457)
National Collegiate Honors Council(491)
Organic Crop Improvement Association International(566)
Soil and Plant Analysis Council(646)

Naper

American White/American Creme Horse Registry(154)

Omaha

American Laryngological, Rhinological and Otological Society(100)
American Shorthorn Association(125)
Community Banking Advisors Network(255)
CPA Auto Dealer Consultants Association(278)
CPA Construction Industry Association(278)
CPA Manufacturing Services Association(278)
International League of Electrical Associations(378)
National CPA Health Care Advisors Association(503)
National Network of Estate Planning Attorneys(528)
Not-for-Profit Services Association(562)
Wellness Councils of America(687)

NEVADA

Baker
National Association of Home and Workshop Writers(456)

Ely
American Bashkir Curly Registry(56)

Henderson
Exhibition Services and Contractors Association(299)
Instrumentation Testing Association(344)
International Beverage Packaging Association(362)
National Conference of Personal Managers(494)

Las Vegas
American Academy of Neurological and Orthopaedic Surgeons(24)
American Academy of Somnology(28)
American Gem Society(86)
Association of Plastic Surgery Assistants(208)
Freight Transportation Consultants Association(312)
International Food Service Executives' Association(372)
National Society of Hypnotherapists(542)
Pierre Fauchard Academy(577)
Society for the Study of Symbolic Interaction(628)
Society of American Fight Directors(630)

Reno
American Murray Grey Association(107)
Council for Elementary Science International(268)
National Council of Juvenile and Family Court Judges(499)
National Juvenile Court Services Association(523)

NEW HAMPSHIRE

Atkinson
Association of TeleServices International(217)

Chester
American College of Laboratory Animal Medicine(66)

Concord
Academy of Applied Science(2)

Dover
North American Association of Summer Sessions(555)

Dunbarton
Christian College Consortium(245)

Durham
History of Economics Society(326)

Etna
American Academy of Gold Foil Operators(23)

Gilford
International Association of Law Enforcement Firearms Instructors(358)

Goshen
Cleveland Bay Horse Society of North America(248)

Hanover
Association of African Studies Programs(183)
Plastic Surgery Research Council(579)

Manchester
Tree Care Industry Association(665)

Nashua
American Community Cultural Center Association(72)
National Human Resources Association(518)

New Durham
American Milking Devon Association(106)

Plainfield
International Association of Broadcast Monitors(354)

Winchester
Cross Country Ski Areas Association(279)

Windham
Nuclear Information and Records Management Association(563)

NEW JERSEY

Avalon
Imaging Supplies Coalition for International Intellectual Property Protection(332)

Avon-by-the-Sea
United States Lifesaving Association(676)

Bayville
Association for Women in Sports Media(182)
Government Management Information Sciences(318)

Berkeley Heights
Yellow Pages Association(698)

Bound Brook
American Society for the Advancement of Sedation and Anesthesia in Dentistry(132)

Branchburg
Intermediaries and Reinsurance Underwriters Association(347)

Butler
Coalition of Visionary Resources(250)
Hobby Manufacturers Association(327)

Chatham
American Bureau of Metal Statistics(59)
Society of Chemical Industry, American Section(633)

Cherry Hill
American Association of Insurance Management Consultants(44)
American Association of Teachers of German(52)
American Society of PeriAnesthesia Nurses(144)
Fluid Power Distributors Association(308)
Fluid Power Society(308)
National Association of Pediatric Nurse Practitioners(464)
Tau Epsilon Rho Law Society(657)

Cinnaminson
International Castor Oil Association(364)

Dumont
American Musicians Union(107)

East Brunswick
Association of Jewish Family and Children's Agencies(202)
Jewish Social Service Professionals Association(402)

East Rutherford
International Silk Association(386)

Eatontown
Society of Marine Port Engineers(639)

Edison
American Osteopathic College of Rheumatology(112)
National Technical Services Association(546)
Woven Wire Products Association(697)

Elizabeth
American Importers and Exporters Meat Products Group(93)

Elmwood Park
American Institute of Food Distribution(96)
Craft & Hobby Association(278)

Englewood Cliffs
Association of Ship Brokers and Agents (U.S.A.)(214)
National Organization of Social Security Claimants' Representatives(530)

Fairfield
Textile Care Allied Trades Association(660)
Women's Jewelry Association(693)

Fairview
Embroidery Council of America(292)
Schiffli Lace and Embroidery Manufacturers Association(606)

Far Hills
United States Golf Association(675)

Farmingdale
United States Marine Safety Association(676)

Flemington
Food Industry Association Executives(309)

Florham Park
Financial Executives International(305)

Franklin Lakes
American Society of Anesthesia Technologists and Technicians(134)

Ft. Lee
Media Research Directors Association(416)

Glen Rock
American Association of Candy Technologists(39)

Hackensack
American Prosthodontic Society(117)
Foster Family-Based Treatment Association(311)

Hackettstown
National Kitchen and Bath Association(523)

Hadden Heights
Professional Association of Innkeepers International(586)

Harrington Park
International Motor Press Association(380)

Hawthorne
Deep Foundations Institute(282)

Hazlet
Affiliated Warehouse Companies(10)
Securities Transfer Association(607)

Highland Park
Historians of Netherlandish Art(326)

Hillsborough
American Association of Feline Practitioners(43)
Ombudsman Association, The(564)

Holmdel
Containerization and Intermodal Institute(264)

Howell
Property Owners Association(591)

Iselin
National Association of Fleet Administrators(453)

Jersey City
Global Association of Risk Professionals(317)
Society of Naval Architects and Marine Engineers(640)

Kearny
American Accordionists Association(29)

Lanoka Harbor
American Association for the History of Nursing(37)

Laurence Harbor
Association of Sales Administration Managers(212)

Lawrenceville
International Society for Pharmacoeconomics and Outcomes Research(388)

Livingston
Association of Average Adjusters of the U.S.(187)

Logan Township
Association of Educational Publishers(194)

Lyndhurst
Chemical Sources Association(243)

Mahwah
Foundation for Advances in Medicine and Science(311)

Manalapan
Harness Horsemen International(322)

Marlton
National Association of Recording Merchandisers(468)
National Limousine Association(525)

Maywood
Society for Experimental Biology and Medicine(617)

Mendham
Power Sources Manufacturers Association(582)

Merceville
Forum for Investor Advice(311)

Middlesex
American Microchemical Society(106)

Montvale
Institute of Management Accountants(342)
Investment Casting Institute(398)

Montville
National Association of Flour Distributors(453)

Moorestown
International Hard Anondizing Association(374)

Mt. Laurel
American Association for Aerosol Research(33)
American Mosquito Control Association(106)
American Society for Histocompatability and Immunogenetics(130)
American Society of Transplantation(146)
Attention Deficit Disorder Association(222)
International Liver Transplantation Society(378)
International Pediatric Transplant Association(382)
Juvenile Products Manufacturers Association(403)
National Association of Professional Pet Sitters(466)
National Automotive Radiator Service Association(483)
Office Business Center Association International(564)
Osteoarthritis Research Society International(569)
Product Development and Management Association(585)
Receptive Services Association of America(596)
Society for Biomaterials(614)
Society for Developmental and Behavioral Pediatrics(616)
Unfinished Furniture Association(669)
Wound, Ostomy and Continence Nurses Society(697)
Writing Instrument Manufacturers Association(697)

Mt. Royal
American Academy of Orofacial Pain(26)
American Association for Paralegal Education(36)
American Headache Society(89)
Association for Research in Otolaryngology(177)
Custom Tailors and Designers Association of America(280)
Real Estate Educators Association(595)
Society for Cardiovascular Magnetic Resonance(614)

Neptune
Association of Food Industries(197)
National Association of Flavors and Food-Ingredient Systems(453)
National Honey Packers and Dealers Association(517)
North American Olive Oil Association(559)
Society of Flavor Chemists(636)

New Brunswick
African Studies Association(11)

New Providence
Ireland Chamber of Commerce in the U.S.(399)
National Council of Self-Insurers(500)

Newark
Community Colleges Humanities Association(256)
Omicron Kappa Upsilon(564)

Newton
American Crossbred Pony Registry(77)

Old Bridge
Photoimaging Manufacturers and Distributors Association(576)

Palmyra
Atlantic Independent Union(221)

Paramus
National Association for Printing Leadership(435)

Parlin
Financial Markets Association - USA(306)

Parsippany
Hydraulic Institute(329)
International Financial Services Association(372)
Quality Bakers of America Cooperative(594)

Pennington
Electrochemical Society(291)

Piscataway
American Association of State Climatologists(51)
Engineering in Medicine and Biology Society(295)
IEEE Signal Processing Society(331)

Pitman
Academy of Medical-Surgical Nurses(4)
Accordionists and Teachers Guild International(6)
American Academy of Ambulatory Care Nursing(20)
American Nephrology Nurses Association(108)
Certification Board for Urologic Nurses and Associates(242)
Dermatology Nurses' Association(283)
International Association of Forensic Nurses(357)
Society of Urologic Nurses and Associates(645)

Princeton
American Association of Teachers of Turkic Languages(53)
American Society of Group Psychotherapy and Psychodrama(138)
APMI International(158)
Construction Financial Management Association(262)
International Recording Media Association(384)
Metal Powder Industries Federation(417)
National Association of Document Examiners(449)
North American Electric Reliability Council(556)
Test Boring Association(659)
Tobacco Merchants Association of the U.S.(662)
Travel Goods Association(665)
Turkish Studies Association(667)
United States Rowing Association(677)

Princeton Junction
ALMA - the International Loudspeaker Association(17)
Alpha Omega International Dental Fraternity(18)
Association for Convention Operations Management(171)
International Card Manufacturers Association(364)
International Function Point Users Group(373)
International Furnishings and Design Association(373)
Smart Card Alliance(611)

Ramsey
Association for Child Psychoanalysis(169)

Red Bank
Association of Retail Marketing Services(212)

Ridgefield Park
Academy of Organizational and Occupational Psychiatry(4)

Rio Grande
Independent Free Papers of America(334)

River Edge
American Society of Wedding Professionals(147)

Robbinsville
Drug, Chemical and Associated Technologies Association(287)

Rocky Hill
Purebred Hanoverian Association of America Breeders and Owners(593)

Rutherford
CPA Associates International(277)

Sandy Hook Highlands
American Littoral Society(102)

Secaucus
International Oceanic Society(381)
Oriental Rug Importers Association of America(568)

Skillman
Intercollegiate Tennis Association(346)

Somerset
Alliance of Black Telecommunications Employees(16)

Somerville
American Association for Crystal Growth(34)

South Orange
Organization Development Network(566)

South Plainfield
National Police and Security Officers Association of America(533)

Sparta
Association of Consulting Chemists and Chemical Engineers(192)

Springfield
Sales Association of the Chemical Industry(604)

Toms River
Sigma Phi Delta(610)

Trenton
American Association for Therapeutic Humor(37)
Association for Conservation Information(170)
Association of Labor Relations Agencies(202)

Tuckerton
American Mideast Business Associates(106)

Turnersville
Computer Measurement Group(258)

Upper Montclair
International Congress of Oral Implantologists(367)
National Music Council(528)

Vincentown
Power Washers of North America(582)

Voorhees
American Organization for Bodywork Therapies of Asia(110)

Weehawken
Songwriters Guild of America(647)

West Caldwell
American Society of Perfumers(143)

West Orange
Professional Hockey Writers' Association(587)

West Windsor
National Association of Noise Control Officials(463)

Westfield
Council of Hotel and Restaurant Trainers(272)

Whippany
National Exchange Carrier Association(507)

Woodbridge
National Association of Printing Ink Manufacturers(465)

Wyckhoff
International Psychohistorical Association(383)

NEW MEXICO

Albuquerque
Alternatives Fuel Vehicle Network(18)
American Indian Science and Engineering Society(93)
American Luggage Dealers Association(102)
American Society of Radiologic Technologists(145)
Association of Educators in Imaging and Radiologic Sciences(194)
Association of Vacuum Equipment Manufacturers International(220)
Financial and Security Products Association(305)
Indian Arts and Crafts Association(336)
Indian Educators Federation(336)
National Conference on Research in Language and Literacy(495)
Society for Radiation Oncology Administrators(624)
Society of Depreciation Professionals(635)
Society of Vacuum Coaters(646)
Western History Association(687)

Chama
Tourist Railway Association(662)

Hobbs
Soaring Society of America(612)

Las Cruces
Association for Borderlands Studies(168)
Association of Official Seed Analysts(206)
Evaporative Cooling Institute(299)

Santa Fe
American Society for Mass Spectrometry(130)
Analytical Laboratory Managers Association(157)
Association of Biomolecular Resource Facilities(187)
Federation of Analytical Chemistry and Spectroscopy Societies(303)

Socorro
Association of Earth Science Editors(194)

NEW YORK

Albany
Academy of Certified Archivists(2)
Association of Life Insurance Counsel(203)
Continental Basketball Association(264)
International Association of Electronics Recyclers(356)
International Association of Milk Control Agencies(359)
International Narcotic Enforcement Officers Association(380)
National Association for Pupil Transportation(435)
National Association of Government Archives and Records Administrators(454)
North American Association of Wardens and Superintendents(555)
Veterinary Hospital Managers Association(682)

Alfred
Society for the Scientific Study of Religion(627)

Amherst
Surface Engineering Coating Association(656)

Batavia
National Association of Off-Track Betting(463)

Bay Terrace
National Institute for Electromedical Information(520)

Bayside
American Cloak and Suit Manufacturers Association(63)
Baseball Writers Association of America(226)
Dance Masters of America(281)

Bellmore
Society of Professional Investigators(642)

Berne
Association of State Wetland Managers(216)

Binghamton
American Name Society(107)
Society for Ancient Greek Philosophy(613)

Brentwood
National Association of Puerto Rican/Hispanic Social Workers(467)

Briarcliff Manor
Academy of Management(4)
Institute of International Container Lessors(342)
United Federation of Police & Security Officers(671)

Brockport
Congress on Research in Dance(261)
University Photographers Association of America(680)

Bronx
American Institute of Fishery Research Biologists(96)
American Laryngological Association(100)
Association for the Advancement of Psychotherapy(179)
Harvey Society(322)
International Society for Adolescent Psychiatry & Pyschology(386)

Brooklyn
American Abstract Artists(19)
American Association of Hospital and Healthcare Podiatrists(43)
American Podiatric Circulatory Society(116)
Historians of Islamic Art(326)
International Society of Copier Artists(391)
National Association of Family Development Centers(452)
National Student Nurses Association(544)
Society for Visual Anthropology(629)
United Weighers Association(679)

Buffalo
American Crystallographic Association(77)
Association for the Bibliography of History(180)
Collector Car Appraisers International(250)

Conference of Philosophical Socs.(260)
Gift Associates Interchange Network(317)
International Society for Educational Planning(387)
National Association for Health and Fitness(433)
National Association of Independent Lighting Distributors(457)
National Chemical Credit Association(488)
Owner Operators of America(570)

Cedarhurst
Jewish Educators Assembly(402)

Chatham
Picture Agency Council of America(577)

Clinton
International Association of Auto Theft Investigators(353)

Cohoes
Professional Service Association(589)

Corona
Black Caucus of the American Library Association(230)

Cortland
Automotive Lift Institute, Inc.(223)
National Academy of Arbitrators(426)

Dix Hills
International Association for Computer Systems Security(349)

East Hampton
Educational Paperback Association(289)

Ellenburg Depot
International Association of Pet Cemeteries(360)

Farmingdale
NPTA Alliance(563)
Paper Distribution Council(571)
Sales Association of the Paper Industry(604)
Society for the Advancement of Education(626)

Flushing
American Acupuncture Association(29)

Forest Hills
American Podiatric Medical Writers Association(116)

Galway
American College of Oral and Maxillofacial Surgeons(68)

Garden City
Scientific Equipment and Furniture Association(606)

Geneseo
National Counter Intelligence Corps Association(503)

Glen Cove
American Stamp Dealers' Association(149)

Glen Oaks
American Society of Clinical Psychopharmacology(136)

Great Neck
National Institute of Management Counsellors(521)
Sigma Epsilon Delta Dental Fraternity(610)

Hamburg
College English Association(251)

Hamilton
Association of Professional Model Makers(209)

Hempstead
National Catholic Development Conference(487)

Henderson Harbor
Safety Glazing Certification Council(604)

Holbrook
US Composting Council(681)

Huntington
American Society for the Study of Orthodontics(132)
Independent Professional Painting Contractors Association of America(335)
National Association of Publishers' Representatives(467)
Transportation & Logistics Council(664)

Hyde Park
International Foodservice Editorial Council(372)

Inwood
Gasoline and Automotive Service Dealers Association(314)

Ithaca
Association for Asian American Studies(167)
Online Audiovisual Catalogers(565)
Paleontological Research Institution(570)
Society for Asian Music(614)
Society for Natural Philosophy(622)
Society of Commercial Seed Technologists(633)

Jackson Heights
American Association of Spinal Cord Injury Nurses(51)
American Association of Spinal Cord Injury Psychologists and Social Workers(51)
American Paraplegia Society(113)

Jamaica
American Association for the Study of Hungarian History(37)
Indian Dental Association (USA)(336)
National Organization of Industrial Trade Unions(530)

Kingston
American Institute for Patristic and Byzantine Studies(94)
NADD: Association for Persons with Developmental Disabilities and Mental Health Needs(424)

Larchmont
Textile Converters Association(660)
Women's National Book Association(694)

Latham
Cleaning Management Institute(247)
Respiratory Nursing Society(600)

Little Neck
Association of Teachers of Latin American Studies(217)

Liverpool
National Earth Science Teachers Association(505)

Long Island City
Greek Food and Wine Institute(320)
Osborne Association(569)

Mamaroneck
American Jewish Correctional Chaplains Association(99)

Manhasset
Shock Society(610)

Maryknoll
Association of Catholic TV and Radio Syndicators(189)

Melville
Acoustical Society of America(7)
International Association of Electronic Keyboard Manufacturers(356)
Society of Rheology(643)

Middletown
Chamber of Commerce of the Apparel Industry(243)

Millbrook
National Frozen Dessert and Fast Food Association(513)

Mineola
National Conference of CPA Practitioners(493)

Monsey
Council for Jewish Education(269)

Mt. Vernon
International Association for Insurance Law - United States Chapter(350)
Professional Tattoo Artists Guild(589)
Society of Insurance Financial Management(638)

Nesconset
Phlebology Society of America(576)

New City
National Council for Therapeutic Recreation Certification(497)

New Hampton
North American Serials Interest Group(560)

New Hartford
American College of Clinical Pharmacology(64)

New Hyde Park
Cosmetic Industry Buyers and Suppliers(267)

New Rochelle
Academy of Breastfeeding Medicine(2)
American Import Shippers Association(93)
College Theology Society(252)
Federal Bureau of Investigation Agents Association(302)

New Windsor
Intercollegiate Broadcasting System(346)

New York
Academy of Political Science(5)
Actors' Equity Association(8)
Advertising Council(9)
Advertising Research Foundation(9)
Africa Travel Association(11)
Allied Artists of America(17)
American Academy of Teachers of Singing(29)
American Arbitration Association(32)
American Artists Professional League(32)
American Association for Chinese Studies(34)
American Association of Advertising Agencies(37)
American Book Producers Association(58)
American Business Media(60)
American Catholic Philosophical Association(61)

American College of Podiatric Radiologists(70)
American Composers Alliance(72)
American Copper Council(74)
American Council for Southern Asian Art(75)
American Council of Learned Societies(75)
American Council on Science and Health(76)
American Craft Council(77)
American Dance Guild(78)
American Federation for Aging Research(82)
American Federation of Musicians of the United States and Canada(82)
American Federation of Television and Radio Artists(83)
American Foreign Law Association(85)
American Geographical Society(87)
American Geriatrics Society(87)
American Group Psychotherapy Association(87)
American Guild of Musical Artists(88)
American Guild of Organists(88)
American Guild of Variety Artists(88)
American Indonesian Chamber of Commerce(93)
American Institute of Certified Public Accountants(95)
American Institute of Chemical Engineers(95)
American Institute of Graphic Arts(96)
American Institute of Marine Underwriters(96)
American Jewish Historical Society(99)
American Kennel Club(100)
American Lung Association(102)
American Management Association(102)
American Medical Publishers' Association(104)
American Montessori Society(106)
American Numismatic Society(109)
American Printing History Association(117)
American Psychoanalytic Association(118)
American Psychopathological Association(119)
American Skin Association(126)
American Society for Dental Aesthetics(128)
American Society for Legal History(130)
American Society of Composers, Authors and Publishers(136)
American Society of Geolinguistics(138)
American Society of Hypertension(139)
American Society of Journalists and Authors(140)
American Society of Magazine Editors(141)
American Society of Mechanical Engineers(141)
American Society of Roommate Services(145)
American Sportscasters Association(148)
American Stock Exchange(149)
American Symphony Orchestra League(150)
American Thoracic Society(151)
American-European Soda Ash Shipping Association(156)
American-Israel Chamber of Commerce and Industry(156)
Antiquarian Booksellers Association of America(157)
Appraisers Association of America(159)
Archivists and Librarians in the History of the Health Sciences(160)
Argentina-American Chamber of Commerce(160)
Art and Antique Dealers League of America(161)
Art Dealers Association of America(161)
Associated Actors and Artistes of America(164)
Associated Press Managing Editors(166)
Association for Advancement of Behavior Therapy(167)
Association for Birth Psychology(168)
Association for Business Communication(168)
Association for Computing Machinery(170)
Association for Jewish Studies(175)
Association for Psychoanalytic Medicine(177)
Association for Research in Nervous and Mental Disease(177)
Association for the Study of Food and Society(181)
Association for the Study of Nationalities(181)
Association of Advanced Rabbinical and Talmudic Schools(183)
Association of American Publishers(185)
Association of American University Presses(185)
Association of Art Museum Directors(186)
Association of Authors' Representatives(186)
Association of Black Foundation Executives(187)
Association of Chartered Accountants in the United States(189)
Association of Departments of English(193)
Association of Departments of Foreign Languages(193)
Association of Episcopal Colleges(195)
Association of Executive Search Consultants(196)
Association of Financial Guaranty Insurors(197)
Association of Foreign Trade Representatives(197)
Association of Hispanic Arts(200)
Association of Independent Commercial Producers(200)
Association of Jewish Center Professionals(202)
Association of Jewish Libraries(202)
Association of Junior Leagues International(202)
Association of Management Consulting Firms(203)
Association of National Advertisers(205)
Association of Pediatric Oncology Social Workers(207)
Association of Philosophy Journal Editors(207)
Association of Productivity Specialists(208)
Association of Real Estate Women(211)
Association of Theatrical Press Agents and Managers(218)
Association of Travel Marketing Executives(218)
Association of Vision Science Librarians(220)
Audio Engineering Society(222)
Authors Guild(222)
Authors League of America(222)
AVS Science and Technology Society(225)
BCA(226)
Belgian American Chamber of Commerce in the United States(227)
Belt Association(227)
Beta Alpha Psi(228)
Bibliographical Society of America(228)
BKR International(229)
Black Americans in Publishing(230)
Black Filmmaker Foundation(230)
Black Retail Action Group(230)
Board of Trade of the Wholesale Seafood Merchants(231)
Book Industry Study Group, Inc.(231)
Brazilian American Chamber of Commerce(232)
BritishAmerican Business Inc.(233)
Builders Hardware Manufacturers Association(234)
Cabletelevision Advertising Bureau(236)
Cantors Assembly(237)
Center for Waste Reduction Technologies(241)
Central Conference of American Rabbis(241)
Chamber Music America(242)
Children's Book Council(244)
Chinese American Medical Society(245)
Clothing Manufacturers Association of the U.S.A.(248)
Cocoa Merchants' Association of America(250)
College Art Association(251)
Colombian American Association(252)
Color Association of the United States(252)
Comics Magazine Association of America(253)
Commercial Finance Association(253)
Commercial Mortgage Securities Association(253)
Community Development Venture Capital Alliance(256)
Consolidated Tape Association(262)
Copper Development Association(266)
Copyright Society of the U.S.A.(266)
Cosmetic Executive Women(267)
Council for European Studies(268)
Council of Archives and Research Libraries in Jewish Studies(270)
Council of Fashion Designers of America(272)
Council of Literary Magazines and Presses(273)
Council of Protocol Executives(274)
Council of the Americas(275)
Cruise Lines International Association(280)
Dance Critics Association(281)
Danish-American Chamber of Commerce (USA)(281)
Diamond Manufacturers and Importers Association of America(284)
Direct Marketing Association(285)
Direct Marketing Insurance and Financial Services Council(285)
Dramatists Guild of America(287)
Econometric Society(288)
Ecuadorean American Association(288)
Editorial Freelancers Association(289)
EMTA - Trade Association for the Emerging Markets(294)
Entertainment Services and Technology Association(295)
Fashion Accessories Shippers Association(301)
Fashion Group International(301)
Federation of Modern Painters and Sculptors(304)
Financial Services Technology Consortium(306)
Finnish American Chamber of Commerce(307)
Fixed Income Analysts Society(307)
Foreign Press Association(310)
Fragrance Foundation(311)
French-American Chamber of Commerce(312)
Fulfillment Management Association(312)
German American Chamber of Commerce(316)
Girls Incorporated(317)
Graphic Artists Guild(319)
Greater Blouse, Skirt and Undergarment Association(320)
Group for the Use of Psychology in History(320)
Guild of Book Workers(321)
Guild of Italian American Actors(321)
Guitar and Accessories Marketing Association(321)
Headwear Information Bureau(322)
Hebrew Actors Union(325)
Hellenic-American Chamber of Commerce(325)
Hispanic Organization of Latin Actors(326)
Home Fashion Products Association(327)
Human Resource Planning Society(329)
Icelandic American Chamber of Commerce(330)
IEEE Communications Society(330)
Illuminating Engineering Society of North America(332)
Independent Feature Project(334)
Inland Marine Underwriters Association(339)
Institute of Electrical and Electronics Engineers(341)
Institute of International Bankers(342)
Institute of Judicial Administration(342)
Insurance Information Institute(345)
Interactive Advertising Bureau(346)
International Advertising Association(348)
International Alliance of Theatrical Stage Employees and Moving Picture Technicians of the U.S., Its Territories and Canada(348)
International Association of Art Critics(353)
International Association of Clothing Designers and Executives(355)
International Cargo Gear Bureau(364)
International Copper Association(367)
International Council of Shopping Centers(368)
International Insurance Society(376)
International Licensing Industry Merchandisers' Association(378)
International Longshoremen's Association, AFL-CIO(378)
International Museum Theater Alliance(380)
International Radio and Television Society(384)
International Swaps and Derivatives Association(393)
International Tax Institute(393)
International Theatre Equipment Association(394)
International Ticketing Association(394)
International Trademark Association(394)

International Union of Industrial Service Transport Health Employees(395)
International Women's Writing Guild(397)
Italy-America Chamber of Commerce(400)
Jewelers of America(401)
Jewelers Vigilance Committee(401)
Jewelers' Security Alliance of the U.S.(401)
Jewelry Information Center(401)
Jewish Book Council(401)
Jewish Community Centers Association of North America(401)
Jewish Education Service of North America(401)
Jockey Club(402)
JWB Jewish Chaplains Council(403)
League of American Theatres and Producers(406)
League of Resident Theatres(406)
Leather Apparel Association(406)
Literary Managers and Dramaturgs of the Americas(408)
Magazine Publishers of America(409)
Major League Baseball - Office of the Commissioner(410)
Major League Baseball Players Association(410)
Major League Soccer(410)
Maritime Law Association of the U.S.(412)
Materials Properties Council(414)
Media Credit Association(415)
Media Rating Council(415)
Modern Language Association of America(420)
Music Publishers' Association of the United States(423)
Mystery Writers of America(424)
NABIM - the International Band and Orchestral Products Association(424)
National Academy of Television Arts and Sciences(427)
National Alliance for Musical Theatre(429)
National Antique and Art Dealers Association of America(430)
National Association for Multi-Ethnicity in Communications(434)
National Association for the Advancement of Psychoanalysis(436)
National Association for the Specialty Food Trade(436)
National Association of Episcopal Schools(451)
National Association of Export Companies(451)
National Association of Independent Publishers Representatives(457)
National Association of State Charity Officials(474)
National Association of Temple Educators(479)
National Association of Uniform Manufacturers and Distributors(480)
National Association of Women Artists(481)
National Basketball Association(483)
National Basketball Players Association(483)
National Book Critics Circle(485)
National Cargo Bureau(487)
National Cleaners Association(490)
National Coffee Association of the U.S.A.(490)
National Conference of Black Lawyers(492)
National Conference of Yeshiva Principals(495)
National Council of the Churches of Christ in the U.S.A.(501)
National Fashion Accessories Association(508)
National Federation of Community Development Credit Unions(509)
National Federation of Temple Brotherhoods(510)
National Football League(511)
National Guild of Community Schools of the Arts(515)
National Hemophilia Foundation(516)
National Hockey League(517)
National Kidney Foundation(523)
National Lawyers Guild(523)
National League for Nursing(523)
National Minority Business Council(527)
National Minority Supplier Development Council(527)
National Multiple Sclerosis Society(528)
National Organization of Legal Services Workers(530)
National Psychological Association for Psychoanalysis(534)
National Sculpture Society(539)
National Society for Graphology(540)
National Society for Healthcare Foodservice Management(540)
National Society for Hebrew Day Schools(541)
National Society of Film Critics(541)
National Society of Mural Painters(542)
National Trade Circulation Foundation(547)
National Writers Union(550)
Neckwear Association of America(551)
Netherlands Chamber of Commerce in the United States(551)
New York Academy of Sciences(552)
New York Board of Trade(552)
New York Mercantile Exchange(552)
New York Stock Exchange(552)
North American Fuzzy Information Processing Society(557)
North American Natural Casing Association(558)
North American Performing Arts Managers and Agents(559)
North American-Chilean Chamber of Commerce(562)
Norwegian-American Chamber of Commerce(562)
Office and Professional Employees International Union(564)
OPERA America(565)
Overseas Press Club of America(570)
Partnership in Print Production(572)
Periodical and Book Association of America(573)
Philippine-American Chamber of Commerce(576)
Pipe Fabrication Institute(578)
Plastic Soft Materials Manufacturers Association(578)
Pleaters, Stitchers and Embroiderers Association(579)
Poetry Society of America(579)
Portugal-United States Chamber of Commerce(581)
Practising Law Institute(582)
Printing Industry Credit Executives(584)
Private Art Dealers Association(584)
Private Label Manufacturers Association(584)
Professional Women in Construction(590)
Professional Women Photographers(590)
Professional Women Singers Association(590)
Promotion Marketing Association(590)
Psychology Society(592)
Public Relations Society of America(593)
Publishers Publicity Association(593)
Rabbinical Assembly(594)
Radio Advertising Bureau(594)
Religion Communicators Council(598)
Renaissance Society of America(599)
Retail, Wholesale and Department Store Union(601)
Risk and Insurance Management Society(602)
Sculptors Guild(607)
Security Traders Association(608)
Shipowners Claims Bureau(610)
Small Luxury Hotels of the World(611)
Social Science Research Council(613)
Society of American Graphic Artists(630)
Society of American Historians(630)
Society of Animal Artists(631)
Society of Composers(634)
Society of Corporate Secretaries and Governance Professionals(634)
Society of Cosmetic Chemists(634)
Society of Illustrators(638)
Society of Maritime Arbitrators(639)
Society of Photographer and Artist Representatives(642)
Society of Publication Designers(643)
Society of Satellite Professionals International(644)
Society of Scribes(644)
Society of Stage Directors and Choreographers(644)
Sommelier Society of America(647)
South Asian Journalists Association(647)
Spain-U.S. Chamber of Commerce(648)
Special Interest Group for Computers and Society(648)
Special Interest Group for University and College Computing Services(649)
Special Interest Group on Accessible Computing(649)
Station Representatives Association(653)
Subcontractors Trade Association(655)
Tea Association of the United States of America(658)
Tea Council of the U.S.A.(658)
Television Bureau of Advertising(659)
Textile Distributors Association(660)
Textile Producers and Suppliers Association(660)
Theatre Library Association(660)
Toy Industry Association(662)
Traffic Audit Bureau for Media Measurement(663)
Trans-Atlantic American Flag Liner Operators(663)
Transport Workers Union of America(663)
Type Directors Club(667)
Union for Reform Judaism(670)
UNITE-HERE(670)
United Infants and Childrens Wear Association(671)
United Jewish Communities(671)
United Nations Staff Union(672)
United Scenic Artists(672)
United States Association of Importers of Textiles and Apparel(673)
United States Association of Independent Gymnastic Clubs(673)
United States Council for International Business(674)
United States Tour Operators Association(677)
United States-Austrian Chamber of Commerce(678)
United Synagogue of Conservative Judaism(678)
University/Resident Theatre Association(680)
Van Alen Institute(682)
Venezuelan American Association of the U.S.(682)
Welding Research Council(687)
Window Covering Safety Council(689)
Window Coverings Manufacturers Association(689)
Wire Service Guild(690)
Women Executives in Public Relations(691)
Women's Caucus for Art(693)
World Gold Council(696)
World Teleport Association(696)
World Trade Centers Association(696)
Writers Guild of America, East(697)
Young Menswear Association(698)

Newark

International Municipal Signal Association(380)

Newburgh

Organizational Behavior Teaching Society(568)

Northport

Elevator Industries Association(292)

Old Brookville

International Academy of Health Care Professionals(348)

Oneonta

American Association of Physical Anthropologists(48)

Oyster Bay Township

Society of American Historical Artists(631)

Patterson
National Fire Sprinkler Association(511)

Pelham
Dance Educators of America(281)

Pittsford
National Association for Drama Therapy(432)
National Association of Pupil Services Administrators(467)

Port Jefferson
Council of American Survey Research Organizations(270)

Poughkeepsie
Association for Symbolic Logic(178)
National Council on Public Polls(502)
Violin Society of America(683)

Purchase
MasterCard International(413)

Queensbury
International Vessel Operators Hazardous Materials Association(396)

Rego Park
National Association of Jewelry Appraisers(459)

Rochester
American Association of Teachers of Italian(52)
American Wine Society(155)
Biological Stain Commission(229)
Collaborative Family Healthcare Association(250)
Gravure Association of America(320)
International Reciprocal Trade Association(384)
Sportsplex Operators and Developers Association(651)

Rockville Center
Rubber Trade Association of North America(603)

Rome
Electrical Overstress/Electrostatic Discharge Association(291)
National Miniature Donkey Association(527)

Ronkonkoma
Catholic Press Association(240)
Flexographic Technical Association(308)

Rye
International Society for the Performing Arts(389)

Salem
National Elevator Industry(506)

Scarsdale
Sponge and Chamois Institute(651)

Sowego
National Association of School Safety and Law Enforcement Officers(470)

Staten Island
American Italian Historical Association(99)

Stony Brook
Association of Biomedical Communications Directors(187)
Association of SIDS and Infant Mortality Programs(214)
International Association for Philosophy and Literature(351)

Syosset
Interactive Multimedia and Collaborative Communications Association(346)

Syracuse
Institute of Certified Records Managers(340)
International Society of Political Psychology(392)
United States Institute for Theatre Technology(676)

Tarrytown
American Booksellers Association(58)
American Wire Cloth Institute(155)
Capital Markets Credit Analysts Society(237)
Cold Formed Parts and Machine Institute(250)
Expansion Joint Manufacturers Association(299)
Hand Tools Institute(321)
Institute of Store Planners(344)
National Electrical Manufacturers Representatives Association(506)
Tubular Exchanger Manufacturers Association(666)

Ticonderoga
National Real Estate Forum(535)

Troy
National Conference of Insurance Legislators(493)
National Council of Legislators from Gaming States(499)
Technology Transfer Society(658)
United States Association for Computational Mechanics(673)

Warnerville
Nurse Healers - Professional Associates International(563)

Warwick
American Rhinologic Society(123)

Webster
Society of Quantitative Analysts(643)

West Coxsackie
International Grooving and Grinding Association(374)

West Hempstead
International Security Officers, Police, and Guards Union(386)

White Plains
American Maritime Association(103)
Council for International Tax Education(269)
International Imaging Industry Association(376)
Society of Motion Picture and Television Engineers(640)
United States Tennis Association(677)

Whitestone
American Society of Master Dental Technologists(141)

Wykagyl
American Society of Sephardic Studies(146)

Yonkers
American Institute of Stress(97)

NORTH CAROLINA

Apex
Equipment and Tool Institute(297)

Asheville
National Association of Hospital Hospitality Houses(456)

Banner Elk
National Association of Personnel Services(464)

Cary
INDA, Association of the Nonwoven Fabrics Industry(333)
Parapsychological Association(571)

Chapel Hill
American Association for Women Podiatrists(37)
American Cleft Palate-Craniofacial Association(63)
Association of Medical School Pediatric Department Chairs(204)
Professional Putters Association(588)
Society of Ethnobiology(635)

Charlotte
American Association of Minority Businesses(45)
Hosiery Association, The(328)
Insurance Marketing Communications Association(345)
Material Handling Industry of America(414)
National Association of Extension 4-H Agents(451)
Professional Construction Estimators Association of America(586)
Retail Solutions Providers Association(601)
Truck Writers of North America(666)

Durham
Association for Biology Laboratory Education(168)
Association of Graduate Liberal Studies Programs(199)
Association of International Education Administrators(201)
Council of Multiple Listing Service(273)
Forest History Society(310)
Insurance Accounting and Systems Association(345)
National Association of Blacks in Criminal Justice(440)
National Association of County Recorders, Election Officials and Clerks(447)
National Association of Professional Background Screeners(465)
National Insurance Association(521)
National Press Photographers Association(534)
Organization for Tropical Studies(567)
Property Records Industry Association(591)
Real Estate Information Professionals Association(596)

Fayetteville
Slovak Studies Association(611)

Franklin
National Association of Computerized Tax Processors(445)

Garner
American Society of Crime Laboratory Directors(137)
National Federation of Licensed Practical Nurses(509)

Gastonia
Textured Yarn Association of America(660)

Greensboro
American Polarity Therapy Association(116)
Art Therapy Credentials Board(162)
Commercial Food Equipment Service Association(253)
Food Industry Suppliers Association(309)

National Board for Certified Counselors(485)
North American Contractors Association(556)
Psychometric Society(592)

Greenville

American Association for the History of Medicine(37)
International Planetarium Society(383)
National Association of Teacher Educators for Family Consumer Sciences(478)
National Maritime Alliance(526)

High Point

American Home Furnishings Alliance(91)
Appalachian Hardwood Manufacturers(158)
Interior Design Society(347)
International Furniture Suppliers Association(373)
International Home Furnishings Market Authority(375)
International Home Furnishings Representatives Association(375)
National AMBUCS(430)
National Home Furnishings Association(517)
Summer and Casual Furniture Manufacturers Association(655)
Upholstered Furniture Action Council(680)

Hillsborough

BioCommunications Association(229)

Huntersville

Association on Higher Education and Disability(221)
National Art Materials Trade Association(431)

King

Pet Sitters International(574)

Madison

American Scientific Glassblowers Society(124)

New Bern

Association of State and Territorial Dental Directors(215)

New London

American Society of Furniture Designers(138)

Ocean Isle Beach

National Association of Litho Clubs(460)

Raleigh

American College of Epidemiology(65)
American Society for Cytotechnology(128)
American Society for Precision Engineering(132)
American Society of Echocardiography(137)
Bright Belt Warehouse Association(232)
Cardiovascular Credentialing International(237)
Controlled Environment Testing Association(264)
Council of State Chambers of Commerce(274)
Fiber Society(305)
Flue-Cured Tobacco Cooperative Stabilization Corporation(308)
International Lactation Consultant Association(377)
International Nurses Society on Addictions(381)
Leaf Tobacco Exporters Association(406)
Multi-Housing Laundry Association(422)
National Association for Government Training and Development(433)
National Association of State Park Directors(476)
National Block and Bridle Club(485)
National Science Education Leadership Association(538)
North American Gamebird Association(557)
Nursery and Landscape Association Executives of North America(563)
RCI, Inc.(595)
Sewn Products Equipment and Suppliers of the Americas(609)
Society for In Vitro Biology(619)
Society of American Travel Writers(631)
Society of Invasive Cardiovascular Professionals(639)
Waterproofing Contractors Association(686)

Research Triangle Park

American Association of Textile Chemists and Colorists(53)
American Sexually Transmitted Diseases Association(125)
Association of Diesel Specialists(194)
Automotive Market Research Council(223)
Automotive Public Relations Council(224)
Brake Manufacturers Council(232)
CIIT Centers for Health Research(247)
Filter Manufacturers Council(305)
Heavy Duty Brake Manufacturers Council(325)
Heavy Duty Business Forum(325)
Heavy Duty Manufacturers Association(325)
International Lead Zinc Research Organization(377)
ISA(400)
MEMA Information Services Council(416)
Motor and Equipment Manufacturers Association(421)
National Council for Air and Stream Improvement(497)
Overseas Automotive Council(570)
Transportation Safety Equipment Institute(664)
Tune-up Manufacturers Council(667)

Salisbury

National Sportscasters and Sportswriters Association(543)

Spindale

American Dairy Goat Association(77)

Wake Forest

Council on Diagnostic Imaging to the A.C.A.(275)

West Garner

Professional Records and Information Services Management International(589)

Wilmington

National Association of Collegiate Women Athletic Administrators(445)
Society for the History of Authorship, Reading and Publishing(627)

Winston-Salem

American Psychological Association - Division of Psychoanalysis(118)
American Society for Eighteenth-Century Studies(128)
American Truck Stop Operators Association(152)
International Federation of Nurse Anesthetists(371)
National Surgical Assistant Association(545)
Specialty Tobacco Council(650)

NORTH DAKOTA

Bismarck

Delta Waterfowl Foundation(283)
Lignite Energy Council(408)
National Sunflower Association(545)
United States Durum Growers Association(675)

Dickinson

National Association for Rehabilitation Leadership(435)

Fargo

American Academy of Veterinary and Comparative Toxicology(29)
American Bryological and Lichenological Society(59)
International Association for Impact Assessment(350)
International Society of Chemical Ecology(390)
Montadale Sheep Breeders Association(421)
National High School Athletic Coaches Association(517)
Transportation Research Forum(664)

Grand Forks

Public Radio News Directors(592)

Wahpeton

American Technical Education Association(150)

OHIO

Ada

Women's Caucus for the Modern Languages(693)

Akron

American Chemical Society - Rubber Division(62)
Association of Nurses in AIDS Care(206)
International Chemical Workers Union Council/UFCW(365)

Athens

Human Biology Association(329)
National Business Incubation Association(486)

Aurora

American Board of Nursing Specialties(57)
College of Optometrists in Vision Development(252)

Beachwood

Institute of Mathematical Statistics(342)

Bowling Green

National Association of Local Boards of Health(460)
North American Society for the Sociology of Sport(561)
Society for Industrial and Organizational Psychology(620)

Brecksville

Precision Machined Products Association(583)

Cedarville

Association of Christian Librarians(189)

Chesterland

Organization Development Institute(566)

Cincinnati

American Clinical and Climatological Association(63)
American Conference of Governmental Industrial Hygienists(73)
American Society of Papyrologists(143)
Association for Facilities Engineering(172)
Catholic Campus Ministry Association(239)
Chemical Coaters Association International(243)
Educational Theatre Association(289)
Electrocoat Association(291)
Geoscience Information Society(316)
Industrial Heating Equipment Association(337)
Music Teachers National Association(423)
National Association of Church Personnel Administrators(443)
National Association of Directors of Nursing Administration in Long Term Care(449)
National Association of Vertical Transportation Professionals(480)
Society for Ear, Nose and Throat Advances in Children(616)
WorkPlace Furnishings(695)

Cleveland
Academy of Accounting Historians(2)
American Association of Automatic Door Manufacturers(38)
American Association of Neuropathologists(46)
American Iron Ore Association(99)
American Measuring Tool Manufacturers Association(103)
American Society for Stereotactic and Functional Neurosurgery(132)
American Train Dispatchers Association(152)
Association of Personal Computer User Groups(207)
Brotherhood of Locomotive Engineers and Trainmen(233)
Cemented Carbide Producers Association(241)
Chemical Fabrics and Film Association(243)
College Athletic Business Management Association(251)
Compressed Air and Gas Institute(257)
Conference of Business Economists(259)
Council of Development Finance Agencies(271)
Door and Access Systems Manufacturers' Association, International(286)
Fire Equipment Manufacturers' Association(307)
Fluid Controls Institute(308)
Forging Industry Association(310)
Heat Exchange Institute(324)
Industrial Fasteners Institute(337)
International Anesthesia Research Society(349)
International Society of Explosives Engineers(391)
Lake Carriers' Association(404)
Machine Knife Association(409)
Marble Institute of America(412)
Metal Building Manufacturers Association(417)
National Association of Athletic Development Directors(439)
National Association of Collegiate Directors of Athletics(444)
National Association of Collegiate Marketing Administrators(445)
National Coil Coating Association(490)
National Confectionery Sales Association(492)
National Technical Association(545)
North American Menopause Society(558)
North American Sawing Association(560)
Percussion Marketing Council(573)
Power Tool Institute(582)
Pressure Washer Manufacturers Association(583)
Scaffolding, Shoring and Forming Institute(605)
Society for American Baseball Research(613)
Society for Investigative Dermatology(620)
Society for Obstetric Anesthesia and Perinatology(622)
Steel Door Institute(653)
Steel Window Institute(654)
Unified Abrasives Manufacturers Association(669)
United States Association for Energy Economics(673)
United States Cutting Tool Institute(675)
United Transportation Union(679)

Columbus
American Association for Employment in Education(34)
American Association of Code Enforcement(40)
American Association of Nurse Attorneys, The(46)
American Association of Veterinary Clinicians(53)
American Folklore Society(84)
American Neuropsychiatric Association(108)
American Society for Nondestructive Testing(131)
American Society of Criminology(137)
Association for Financial Counseling and Planning Education(173)
Association of College and University Housing Officers-International(191)
Association of Credit Union Internal Auditors(193)
Association of Leadership Educators(203)
Ayrshire Breeders' Association(225)
Business Professionals of America(236)
Classroom Publishers Association(247)
Community Development Society(256)
Council for Ethics in Economics(268)
Council of Graphological Socs.(272)
Edison Welding Institute(289)
Game Manufacturers Association(313)
Gamma Iota Sigma(313)
HARDI - Heating, Airconditioning, and Refrigeration Distributors International(321)
Industrial Diamond Association of America(336)
Insurance Loss Control Association(345)
Intercoiffure America/Canada(346)
International Neuropsychological Society(381)
International Rural Sociology Association(385)
Iron Casting Research Institute(399)
National Association of Consumer Credit Administrators(446)
National Board of Boiler and Pressure Vessel Inspectors(485)
National Society of Insurance Premium Auditors(542)
National Tractor Pullers Association(546)
Network Professional Association(552)
Society for Historians of American Foreign Relations(618)
United Producers(672)
United States Trotting Association(678)

Copley
Tire and Rim Association(661)

Dayton
American Automatic Control Council(55)
American Osteopathic Colleges of Ophthalmology and Otolaryngology - Head and Neck Surgery(112)
American Woman's Society of Certified Public Accountants(155)
Association for Accounting Administration(166)
Association of Destination Management Executives(193)
Catholic Academy for Communication Arts Professionals(239)
Cellulose Insulation Manufacturers Association(241)
Education Law Association(289)
Employee Involvement Association(293)
Inflatable Advertising Dealers Association(338)
Materials Marketing Associates(414)
National Alarm Association of America(429)
National Associated CPA Firms(431)
National Association of Nephrology Technologists and Technicians(462)
National Catholic Educational Exhibitors(487)
National Guild of Professional Paperhangers(515)
National Management Association(525)
National Society of Accountants for Cooperatives(541)
SAVE International(605)
School, Home and Office Products Association(606)
Textile Bag and Packaging Association(660)
Ultrasonic Industry Association(669)
Urban History Association(680)

Delaware
Miniature Book Society(420)

Dublin
International League of Professional Baseball Clubs(378)
International Society for Prosthetics and Orthotics - United States(388)

Elyria
Delta Theta Phi(283)

Findlay
National Association for Developmental Education(432)

Fredericktown
Percheron Horse Association of America(573)

Fremont
Society for Historians of the Gilded Age and Progressive Era(618)

Granville
Liaison Committee of Cooperating Oil and Gas Associations(407)

Grove City
Food Shippers of America(309)

Harrison
American Watchmakers-Clockmakers Institute(154)
Jewelry Industry Distributors Association(401)
Textile Bag Manufacturers Association(660)

Hicksville
Academy of Dentistry International(3)

Hilliard
Perennial Plant Association(573)

Huber Heights
National Association of Nurse Massage Therapists(463)

Independence
Association of Concert Bands(192)
Precision Metalforming Association(583)

Jacobsburg
American and Delaine-Merino Record Association(31)

Kent
American School Health Association(124)
Modern Greek Studies Association(420)

Lancaster
International Research Council of Neuromuscular Disorders(385)

Lewis Center
American Concrete Pumping Association(73)

Marblehead
National Association of Optometrists and Opticians(463)

Materials Park
ASM International(163)

Medina
Heavy Duty Representatives Association(325)
Service Specialists Association(609)

Mentor
National Association of Trade Exchanges(479)

Montpelier
Society for the Study of Male Psychology and Physiology(628)

Nevada
Columbia Sheep Breeders Association of America(253)

New Albany
Association for Financial Technology(173)

Newark
American Trakehner Association(152)

North Bloomfield

Association for Living History, Farm and Agricultural Museums(176)

North Olmstead

Ductile Iron Society(288)

Norwalk

International Hot Rod Association(375)

Oberlin

Association of Specialty Cut Flower Growers(214)
National Association of College Stores(444)

Oxford

Academy of Legal Studies in Business(4)
American Classical League(63)
American Society of Plant Taxonomists(144)
Association for Integrative Studies(175)
College Fraternity Editors Association(251)
Delta Sigma Pi(283)
National Council of Writing Program Administrators(502)
National Staff Development Council(543)
Society for Photographic Education(623)

Painesville

International Federation for Artificial Organs(371)

Pickerington

American Motorcyclist Association(107)

Reynoldsburg

American Guernsey Association(87)
American Jersey Cattle Association(99)

Seven Hills

Phi Gamma Nu(576)

Sunbury

North American Farm Show Council(557)

Swanton

Sanitary Supply Wholesaling Association(605)

Toledo

American Society for Virology(133)
North American Membrane Society(558)

University Heights

Catholic Theological Society of America(240)

Vandalia

United Methodist Association of Health and Welfare Ministries(671)

Waynesville

American Association of Police Polygraphists(49)

West Alexandria

Women in Aviation International(691)

West Milton

American Rolling Door Institute(123)
International Door Association(369)

Westerville

American Ceramic Society(61)
International Executive Housekeepers Association(371)
National Ground Water Association(515)
National Middle School Association(527)
Religion Newswriters Association(598)

Westlake

American Society of Sanitary Engineering(146)

Wilberforce

Association of African American Museums(183)

Willoughby

Phi Beta(575)

Willoughby Hills

North American Association of State and Provincial Lotteries(554)

Wilmington

National Food and Energy Council(511)

Youngstown

International Association of Hygienic Physicians(358)

Zanesville

Art Glass Association(161)
Ceramic Manufacturers Association(241)
The Knitting Guild Association(404)
The National NeedleArts Association(528)
Society of Creative Designers(634)
Society of Glass and Ceramic Decorators(637)

OKLAHOMA

Ardmore

Gelbray International(315)

Bethany

Pinto Horse Association of America(578)

Broken Arrow

American Academy of Restorative Dentistry(28)
National Career Development Association(487)

Cleveland

Historians Film Committee/Film & History(326)

Duncan

National Rural Water Association(538)

Edmond

Environmental Design Research Association(296)
National Association of Pipe Fabricators(464)

Hominy

Finnsheep Breeders Association(307)

Lawton

Percussive Arts Society(573)

Maud

National Judges Association(522)

McCurtain

Barzona Breeders Association of America(226)

Norman

Golf Coaches Association of America(318)
National Rural Education Association(537)
Society for Cinema and Media Studies(615)
Society of Multivariate Experimental Psychology(640)

Oklahoma City

American Choral Directors Association(62)
Association of Alternate Postal Systems(184)
Association of American Indian Physicians(184)
Civil Aviation Medical Association(247)
Conference on Consumer Finance Law(260)
Ground Water Protection Council(320)
International Professional Rodeo Association(383)
Interstate Oil and Gas Commission(398)
National Association of Royalty Owners(469)
National Reining Horse Association(535)
Professional Women Controllers(590)
Society for Applied Anthropology(613)

Shawnee

American Journalism Historians Association(99)

Stillwater

American Peanut Research and Education Society(113)
American Society of Mammalogists(141)
American Society of Veterinary Ophthalmology(147)
International Association for Computer Information Systems(349)
International Ground Source Heat Pump Association(374)

Tulsa

Airborne Law Enforcement Association(14)
American Association of Petroleum Geologists(47)
Association of Professional Communication Consultants(208)
Augustinian Educational Association(222)
Gas Processors Association(314)
Gas Processors Suppliers Association(314)
Kappa Kappa Iota(403)
Lawn and Garden Dealers' Association(406)
NALS(425)
National Association of Insurance Women(458)
National Association of Legal Assistants(459)
Palomino Horse Breeders of America(570)
Petroleum Equipment Institute(574)
SEPM - Society for Sedimentary Geology(609)
Society of Exploration Geophysicists(636)
United States Junior Chamber of Commerce(676)

Weatherford

Kappa Psi Pharmaceutical Fraternity(403)

OREGON

Astoria

Council of American Maritime Museums(270)

Beaverton

Association for the Treatment of Sexual Abusers(181)
International Shooting Coaches Association(386)

Canby

American Border Leicester Association(58)

Corvallis

Council on Forest Engineering(276)
International Institute of Fisheries Economics and Trade(376)
National Intramural-Recreational Sports Association(522)

Creswell

SAFE Association(604)

Eugene

American Agricultural Law Association(30)
Association for Direct Instruction(171)
Forest Industries Telecommunications(310)
International Society for Technology in Education(389)
National Student Employment Association(544)
Society of North American Goldsmiths(641)

Gladstone

North American Mycological Association(558)

Grants Pass

American Romney Breeders Association(123)

Hood River

National Cherry Growers and Industries Foundation(489)

Portable Computer and Communications Association(580)

Irrigon
International Nubian Breeders Association(381)

Lake Oswego
Academy of Dental Materials(3)
National Reloading Manufacturers Association(536)

Medford
Association of Insolvency and Restructuring Advisors(201)

Otis
Kite Trade Association International(403)

Portland
American Academy of Psychotherapists(28)
American Forest Resource Council(85)
American Tinnitus Association(151)
Association of Administrative Law Judges(183)
Association of Telehealth Service Providers(217)
Building Commissioning Association(234)
Business Forms Management Association(235)
Church and Synagogue Library Association(246)
International Laser Display Association(377)
International Society of Hotel Association Executives(391)
National Association of Consumer Shows(446)
National Association of Professional Process Servers(466)
National Conference of Women's Bar Associations(494)
North American Academy of Liturgy(554)
Society for Intercultural Education, Training and Research - USA(620)
Society for Values in Higher Education(629)
Softwood Export Council(646)

Salem
Motorist Information and Services Association(422)
National Association of State Textbook Administrators(476)
National Lamb Feeders Association(523)
North American Association of Educational Negotiators(554)

Sublimity
American Association of Classified School Employees(39)

Sutherlin
KWPN of North America(404)

Tigard
Building Material Dealers Association(234)

West Linn
Institute of Certified Business Counselors(340)

PENNSYLVANIA

Allentown
Express Carriers Association(300)
Society for the Scientific Study of Sexuality(627)

Ambler
American Society of Marine Artists(141)
National Association of Wastewater Transporters(480)

Ardmore
Certified Contractors NetWork(242)
Souvenirs, Gifts and Novelties Trade Association(648)

Bendersville
Belted Galloway Society(227)

Bethel Park
International Society for Respiratory Protection(389)

Bethlehem
Cement Employers Association(241)
Electronic Commerce Code Management Association(291)
Healthcare Marketing and Communications Council(324)
National Association of Colleges and Employers(444)

Blue Bell
American Society for Automation in Pharmacy(126)
Federation of Socs. for Coatings Technology(304)

Brookville
International Glove Association(374)

Bryn Mawr
American Microscopical Society(106)
Carpet Cushion Council(238)

Burgettestown
American Poultry Association(117)

Butler
Abrasive Engineering Society(2)

Camp Hill
Recreational Vehicle Aftermarket Association(596)

Carlisle
Equipment Service Association(297)
Oral History Association(566)

Carnegie
National Association of Diocesan Ecumenical Officers(449)

Clark
National Dog Groomers Association of America(505)

Clarks Summit
Solution Mining Research Institute(647)

Coatesville
Dog Writers' Association of America(286)

Collegeville
Association of College and University Museums and Galleries(191)

Coopersburg
Paper Shipping Sack Manufacturers Association(571)

Crystal Spring
Red and White Dairy Cattle Association(597)

Dingmans Ferry
American Nature Study Society(108)

Doylestown
International Plate Printers', Die Stampers' and Engravers' Union of North America(383)
National Demolition Association(505)

East Petersburg
National Association of Oil Heating Service Managers(463)

East Stroudsburg
Association for Computational Linguistics(170)

Elizabethtown
American Association of Meat Processors(45)

Elkins Park
Academy of Oral Dynamics(4)
International Council of Psychologists(368)

Ephrata
American Academy of State Certified Appraisers(29)

Erie
Association of Ancient Historians(186)
International Association of Home Safety and Security Professionals(358)
International Association of School Librarianship(361)

Etters
Northern Nut Growers Association(562)

Export
International Memorialization Supply Association(379)

Exton
American Association of Teachers of Spanish and Portuguese(52)
National Freight Transportation Association(512)
Society of Cable Telecommunications Engineers(632)

Flourtown
North American Society for Pediatric Gastroenterology, Hepatology and Nutrition(561)

Gettysburg
Forestry Conservation Communications Association(310)

Glen Mills
American Veterinary Society of Animal Behavior(153)

Greensburg
Associated Glass and Pottery Manufacturers(165)

Harrisburg
American Academy of Clinical Toxicology(21)
American College of Veterinary Radiology(72)
Association of American Editorial Cartoonists(184)
Association of Professional Landscape Designers(209)
Aviation Technician Education Council(225)
International Association of Bedding and Furniture Law Officials(354)
National Association of Clinical Nurse Specialists(443)
National Conference of Editorial Writers(493)
National Frozen and Refrigerated Foods Association(513)
National Greenhouse Manufacturers Association(515)
National Perinatal Association(532)
Perlite Institute(573)

Hazleton
American College of Nuclear Medicine(68)

Hellertown
Federation of Straight Chiropractors and Organizations(304)

Hershey
International Association for the Leisure and Entertainment Industry(351)

North American Society of Adlerian Psychology(561)

Homestead

National United Merchants Beverage Association(548)

Honesdale

Evidence Photographers International Council(299)

Horsham

Drug Information Association(287)

Hunker

Mine Safety Institute of America(419)

Indiana

American Driver and Traffic Safety Education Association(79)
Society for the Philosophy of Sex and Love(627)

Irwin

Association for Hospital Medical Education(174)

Jenkintown

Society of Environmental Journalists(635)

Johnstown

Association of State and Territorial Public Health Nutrition Directors(215)
Gift Association of America(317)

Kennett Square

Mineral Economics and Management Society(419)

King of Prussia

American Association of Managing General Agents(45)

Laceyville

International Association of Counselors and Therapists(355)

Lancaster

Distribution Business Management Association(286)
National Association of Addiction Treatment Providers(438)
Society for Archaeological Sciences(614)

Lansdale

Mobile Air Conditioning Society Worldwide(420)

Lebanon

American Association of Chairmen of Departments of Psychiatry(39)
American Association of Directors of Psychiatric Residency Training(42)
American Association of Radon Scientists and Technologists(50)
Cast Stone Institute(238)
National Association of Independent Insurance Auditors and Engineers(457)

Lehigh Valley

National Association of Chain Manufacturers(442)

Lemont

North American Society for Sport History(561)

Levittown

National Constables Association(495)

Lewisberry

Federal Law Enforcement Officers Association(302)

Lewisburg

Association for Evolutionary Economics(172)
National Institute of Packaging, Handling and Logistics Engineers(521)

Malvern

American Institute for CPCU - Insurance Institute of America(93)
American Risk and Insurance Association(123)
Association for the Advancement of Wound Care(180)
Chiropractic Council on Physiological Therapeutics and Rehabilitation(245)
CPCU Society(278)

Maple Glen

Association of Information and Dissemination Centers(201)

McKeesport

National Fellowship of Child Care Executives(510)

Mechanicsburg

United States Harness Writers' Association(675)

Media

American Aging Association(30)
American College of Veterinary Nutrition(71)
Glass, Molders, Pottery, Plastics and Allied Workers International Union(317)

Monroeville

Home Sewing Association(327)

Montgomeryville

Bicycle Product Suppliers Association(228)

Moon Township

Association of Directory Marketing(194)

Mount Union

National Association of Forensic Economics(453)

New Kensington

International Graphoanalysis Society(374)

New Tripoli

National Remotivation Therapy Organization(536)

Newtown

American Institute of Biomedical Climatology(95)

Newtown Square

Project Management Institute(590)
Society of Financial Service Professionals(636)

Perkiomenville

American Association of Birth Centers(38)

Philadelphia

Academy of Ambulatory Foot and Ankle Surgery(2)
American Academy of Political and Social Science(27)
American Association for Cancer Research(34)
American College of Physicians(69)
American Entomological Society(81)
American Institute of Bangladesh Studies(94)
American Institute of Chemists(95)
American Law Institute(100)
American Musicological Society(107)
American Philological Association(114)
American Philosophical Society(114)
American Society of Media Photographers(141)
Association for High Technology Distribution(174)
Association for Population/Family Planning Libraries and Information Centers, International(176)
Association of Gay and Lesbian Psychiatrists(198)
Association of Oncology Social Work(206)
Aviation Distributors and Manufacturers Association International(224)
Chemical Heritage Foundation(243)
Craft Retailers Association for Tomorrow(278)
Dental Dealers of America(283)
Gases and Welding Distributors Association(314)
Gynecologic Oncology Group(321)
Inter-America Travel Agents Society(346)
International Association of Association Management Companies(353)
International Association of Ice Cream Vendors(358)
International Association of Jewish Vocational Services(358)
Jesuit Association of Student Personnel Administrators(401)
Middle East Librarians' Association(418)
NANDA International(425)
National Association of Artists' Organizations(439)
National Association of Catholic School Teachers(442)
National Federation of Abstracting and Information Services(508)
National Federation of Independent Unions(509)
National Field Selling Association(510)
National Vehicle Leasing Association(548)
National Wood Tank Institute(550)
North American Horticultural Supply Association(557)
Opportunity Finance Network(565)
Radiation Therapy Oncology Group(594)
RMA - The Risk Management Association(602)
Security Hardware Distributors Association(607)
Society for Historians of the Early American Republic(618)
Society for Industrial and Applied Mathematics(619)
Society for Medical Decision Making(621)
Society for Social Work Leadership in Health Care(625)
Tin Stabilizers Association(661)
Victorian Society in America(683)
Water and Sewer Distributors of America(685)
Wood Machinery Manufacturers of America(694)

Pittsburgh

Air and Waste Management Association(12)
American Association for the Surgery of Trauma(37)
American College of Mental Health Administration(67)
American Hair Loss Council(88)
American Paso Fino Horse Association(113)
Association for Bridge Construction and Design(168)
Association for Science Teacher Education(178)
Association of Otolaryngology Administrators(207)
Association of Theological Schools in the United States and Canada(218)
Combustion Institute(253)
Council of State Association Presidents(274)
Council on Botanical and Horticultural Libraries(275)
Hardwood Manufacturers Association(322)
Hospice and Palliative Nurses Association(328)
International Association for Business and Society(349)
International Association of Career Consulting Firms(354)
International Transplant Nurses Society(394)
Latin American Studies Association(405)
Laundry and Dry Cleaning International Union(405)

Marketing and Advertising Global Network(412)
National Black Association for Speech, Language and Hearing(484)
National Federation of Municipal Analysts(509)
Oncology Nursing Society(564)
Refractories Institute(597)
Rubber and Plastics Industry Conference of the United Steelworkers of America(603)
SSPC: the Society for Protective Coatings(652)
Steel Recycling Institute(653)
United Electrical, Radio and Machine Workers of America(671)
United Steel, Paper and Forestry, Rubber, Manufacturing, Energy, Allied Industrial and Service Workers International Union(678)

Plymouth Meeting

ECRI(288)

Richboro

American Tin Trade Association(151)

Richeyville

Clowns of America, International(248)

Sewickley

Graphic Arts Technical Foundation(319)
Printing Industries of America(584)
Technical Association of the Graphic Arts(658)

Silver Spring

Herb Growing & Marketing Network(325)

Slippery Rock

History of Education Society(327)
North American Society for Sport Management(561)

Solebury

National Paralegal Association(531)

State College

American Society for Plasticulture(131)
Independent Turf and Ornamental Distributors Association(336)
North American Strawberry Growers Association(562)

Stroudsburg

International Association of Women Ministers(361)

Titusville

Pyrotechnics Guild International(593)

Uniontown

American Society of Highway Engineers(139)

University Park

American Pomological Society(117)
International Council of Fine Arts Deans(367)
International Writing Centers Association(397)

Valley Forge

American Baptist Homes and Hospitals Association(55)

Wampum

Colorado Ranger Horse Association(253)

Warrendale

AIM Global(12)
Association for Iron and Steel Technology(175)
Materials Research Society(414)
Minerals, Metals and Materials Society, The(420)
SAE International(604)

Wayne

Aircraft Locknut Manufacturers Association(14)
Bank Insurance and Securities Association(226)
Clinical and Laboratory Standards Institute(248)
Clinical Laboratory Management Association(248)
Copper and Brass Servicenter Association(266)
Cordage Institute(266)
Fluid Sealing Association(308)
Gasket Fabricators Association(314)
National Association of Diaper Services(449)
National Classification Management Society(490)
Professional Apparel Association(585)
Society of Medical-Dental Management Consultants(640)

West Chester

Graphic Arts Sales Foundation(319)

West Conshohocken

ASTM International(221)

West Lawn

National Slag Association(540)

West Mifflin

Bridge Grid Flooring Manufacturers Association(232)

West Point

Calorimetry Conference(237)

Westchester

National Association of Traffic Accident Reconstructionists and Investigators(479)

Wexford

Association of Occupational Health Professionals in Healthcare(206)
Biotech Medical Management Association(229)

Whitehall

National Society of Painters in Casein and Acrylic(542)

Wyndmoor

International Academy for Child Brain Development(347)

York

Association of Food and Drug Officials(197)

RHODE ISLAND

Cranston

Jewelers Shipping Association(401)

Narragansett

National Shellfisheries Association(539)

North Kingstown

Society for News Design(622)

North Scituate

Continental Dorset Club(264)

Providence

Alliance of Artists Communities(16)
American Association of University Administrators(53)
American Mathematical Society(103)
Association of Medical Education and Research in Substance Abuse(204)
Committee on Lesbian and Gay History(254)
Machine Printers and Engravers Association of the United States(409)
Manufacturing Jewelers and Suppliers of America(411)
Metal Findings Manufacturers Association(417)
Society of American Silversmiths(631)

Warren

American Boat Builders and Repairers Association(58)
States Organization for Boating Access(653)

Warwick

Jewelers Board of Trade(401)

Westerly

Association of YMCA Professionals(221)

SOUTH CAROLINA

Anderson

National Association of Baptist Professors of Religion(439)
Tile Council of North America(661)

Blythewood

National Association of Produce Market Managers(465)

Charleston

American Professional Society on the Abuse of Children(117)
Association for Applied Interactive Multimedia(167)
Association for Continuing Higher Education(171)
National Golf Course Owners Association(514)
North American Council of Automotive Teachers(556)
Psi Omega(591)
Society of School Librarians International(644)

Clemson

National Association of University Fisheries and Wildlife Programs(480)
National Council of Examiners for Engineering and Surveying(499)

Columbia

American Bandmasters Association(55)
Association for Education in Journalism and Mass Communication(172)
Association of Schools of Journalism and Mass Communication(213)
Association on Programs for Female Offenders(221)
National Association for Campus Activities(432)
National Association of Bankruptcy Trustees(439)
National Association of Chapter 13 Trustees(442)
National Association of Decorative Fabric Distributors(448)
National Association of State Boards of Geology(473)
National Educational Telecommunications Association(506)
National Peach Council(532)
Organization of State Broadcasting Executives(568)
Public Broadcasting Management Association(592)
Society for Medieval and Renaissance Philosophy(621)

Darlington

National Motorsports Press Association(528)

Effingham

American Shire Horse Association(125)

Ft. Mill

Association of Industrial Metallizers, Coaters and Laminators(201)
Converting Equipment Manufacturers Association(265)

Greenville
Association of Pet Dog Trainers(207)
National Christian College Athletic Association(489)

Greenwood
North American Flowerbulb Wholesalers Association(557)

Hilton Head
American Agents Association(30)
Professional Tennis Registry(589)
Tennis Industry Association(659)

Johns Island
Master Printers of America(413)

Lexington
Congress of Chiropractic State Associations(261)
International Association of Structural Movers(361)
National Conference of Bankruptcy Judges(492)

Myrtle Beach
Steel Joist Institute(653)

North Charleston
American Metalcasting Consortium(105)

Salem
National Association of Case Management(441)

Simpsonville
International Society of Crime Prevention Practitioners(391)
National Association of Graphic and Product Identification Manufacturers(455)
Self Insurance Institute of America, Inc.(608)

SOUTH DAKOTA

Flandreau
National Hereford Hog Record Association(517)

Hot Springs
International Association of Wildland Fire(361)

Pierre
National Council of Health Facilities Finance Authorities(499)
Wheat Quality Council(688)

Rapid City
National American Indian Court Judges Association(430)

Sioux Falls
Lutheran Educational Conference of North America(409)
Wild Bird Feeding Institute(688)

Sisseton
Association of Community Tribal Schools(192)

Vermillion
Native American Journalists Association(550)

TENNESSEE

Bartlett
American College of Apothecaries(64)

Brentwood
National Association of Consumer Agency Administrators(446)

Bristol
Christian Medical & Dental Associations(246)

Chattanooga
American Association of Christian Schools(39)
American Polygraph Association(116)
Association of Private Enterprise Education(208)
Cast Iron Soil Pipe Institute(238)

Cleveland
Cookie and Snack Bakers Association(265)

Collierville
National Alliance of Independent Crop Consultants(429)

Cordova
National Cottonseed Products Association(496)

Franklin
American Academy of Ministry(24)
National Kerosene Heater Association(523)
Society of Cleaning and Restoration Technicians(633)
Western Writers of America(688)

Gallatin
Association of Dark Leaf Tobacco Dealers and Exporters(193)

Jefferson City
American Ass'n of Ambulatory Surgery Centers(32)
Delta Omicron(282)

Johnson City
Association for the Study of Play(181)
International Stress Management Association - U.S. Branch(393)

Kingsport
Associated Funeral Directors International(165)

Knoxsville
International Society for Plastination(388)

Knoxville
America Outdoors(19)
American Academy of Nutrition(25)
College and University Professional Association for Human Resources(250)
International Association for Truancy and Dropout Prevention(352)
Polyurethane Foam Association(580)
Society for Invertebrate Pathology(620)
Society for Maintenance Reliability Professionals(621)
Society for the Study of Social Problems(628)
TechLaw Group(658)

Lewisburg
Tennessee Walking Horse Breeders and Exhibitors Association(659)

Memphis
American Association for Laboratory Animal Science(35)
American Cotton Shippers Association(74)
American Innerspring Manufacturers(93)
American Mathematical Association of Two Year Colleges(103)
American Society for Pediatric Neurosurgery(131)
Association of Automotive Aftermarket Distributors(186)
College Media Advisers(251)
Fraternity Executives Association(311)
National Cotton Council of America(496)
National Cotton Ginners' Association(496)
National Hardwood Lumber Association(516)
National Time Equipment Association(546)
NOFMA: the Wood Flooring Manufacturers Association(553)
North American Folk Music and Dance Alliance(557)
Omega Delta(564)

Murfreesboro
Baptist Communicators Association(226)
National Spotted Saddle Horse Association(543)
Walking Horse Owners Association of America(685)

Nashville
American Association for State and Local History(36)
American Board of Veterinary Practitioners(58)
American College of Neuropsychopharmacology(68)
American Economic Association(80)
American Society of Professional Estimators(145)
American Veterinary Dental Society(153)
Association for the Development of Religious Information Systems(180)
Brazilian Studies Association(232)
Church Music Publishers Association(246)
Country Music Association(277)
Country Radio Broadcasters, Inc.(277)
Delta Nu Alpha Transportation Fraternity(282)
Diamond Council of America(284)
Fellowship of United Methodists in Music and Worship Arts(305)
Gospel Music Association(318)
International Association of Baptist Colleges and Universities(353)
International Bluegrass Music Association(362)
International Conference of Symphony and Opera Musicians(367)
International Engraved Graphics Association(370)
International Entertainment Buyers Association(370)
Musculoskeletal Tumor Society(422)
Music and Entertainment Industry Educators Association(423)
National Association of State Boards of Accountancy(473)
National Fraternal Order of Police(512)
Society of Medical Administrators(639)
Society of Professional Audio Recording Services(642)

Newburn
American Design Drafting Association(79)

Newport
Society of American Registered Architects(631)

Oak Ridge
Association for Library and Information Science Education(175)

Pleasant View
International Society of Fire Service Instructors(391)

Sevierville
National Association of Activity Professionals(437)

Shelbyville
Walking Horse Trainers Association(685)

Smyrna
National Association of Fleet Resale Dealers(453)
University and College Designers Association(679)

Whites Creek
Women's International Network of Utility Professionals(693)

TEXAS

Addison

International and American Associations of Clinical Nutritionists(349)
International Society for Heart and Lung Transplantation(387)
Professional Retail Store Maintenance Association(589)

Alvarado

American Miniature Horse Association(106)

Amarillo

American Quarter Horse Association(120)
Health Care Education Association(322)
International Guards Union of America(374)

Arlington

BMC - A Foodservice Sales and Marketing Council(231)
Bowling Proprietors Association of America(231)
Manufacturers Representatives of America(411)
National Association of Division Order Analysts(449)
National Independent Automobile Dealers Association(518)
Paper and Plastic Representatives Management Council(571)
Society for the History of Discoveries(627)

Arp

Parthenais Cattle Breeders Association of America(571)

Austin

Amalgamated Printers' Association(18)
American Academy of Nurse Practitioners(25)
American College of Construction Lawyers(65)
American College of Musicians(67)
American Comparative Literature Association(72)
American Society of Missiology(141)
Association for Continuing Legal Education(171)
Association for Social Economics(178)
Association of Certified Fraud Examiners(189)
Association of Professors of Mission(210)
Association of Progressive Rental Organizations(210)
College Band Directors National Association(251)
Foundation for Pavement Preservation(311)
Hospitality Financial and Technology Professionals(328)
International Association of Hydrogeologists(358)
National Association of Child Care Professionals(443)
National Association of Investigative Specialists(459)
National Barbecue Association(483)
National Council on Qualifications for the Lighting Professions(502)
National Guard Executive Directors Association(515)
National Guild of Piano Teachers(515)
National Organization for Human Service Education(530)
Psychonomic Society(592)
Research Society on Alcoholism(600)
Service Dealers Association(609)
Society of Certified Insurance Counselors(632)
Society of Infectious Diseases Pharmacists(638)
Theta Tau(660)
University Council for Educational Administration(679)
Women in Endocrinology(691)

Bedford

Automotive Service Association(224)
Council of American Instructors of the Deaf(270)

Boerne

Industrial Foundation of America(337)

Brooks AFB

Society of United States Air Force Flight Surgeons(645)

Burleson

Consortium for Advanced Manufacturing International(262)

Burton

American Bralers Association(59)

Caldwell

American Society of Photographers(144)

Canyon

National Opera Association(529)

Carrollton

Phi Chi Theta(575)

College Station

American Association for Agricultural Education(33)
Institute of Nautical Archaeology(343)
National Association of Academic Advisors for Athletes(437)

Colleyville

Association of Finance and Insurance Professionals(196)

Converse

Society of Military Otolaryngologists - Head and Neck Surgeons(640)

Coppell

International Association of Assembly Managers(353)

Corpus Christi

International Association of Marriage and Family Counselors(359)
International Compressor Remanufacturers Association(366)
National Chief Petty Officers' Association(489)
Society for Advancement of Management(613)

Crowley

International Oil Mill Superintendents Association(381)

Dallas

Academic Language Therapy Association(2)
ADSC: The International Association of Foundation Drilling(8)
American Association of Community Psychiatrists(41)
American Association of Psychiatric Administrators(49)
American Fire Sprinkler Association(84)
American Gem Trade Association(86)
American Heart Association(90)
American Lighting Association(101)
American Society for Adolescent Psychiatry(126)
American Society of Breast Disease(135)
American Viola Society(153)
Associated Locksmiths of America(165)
Association of Attorney-Mediators(186)
Automotive Oil Change Association(224)
Directional Crossing Contractors Association(285)
Embroidery Trade Association(292)
Federation of State Medical Boards of the United States(304)
Football Writers Association of America(310)
Gas Machinery Research Council(314)
Home Furnishings International Association(327)
Ice Skating Institute(330)
Independent Distributors Association(333)
International Association for Exhibition Management(350)
International Newspaper Marketing Association(381)
International Society of Bassists(390)
Meeting Professionals International(416)
Mystery Shopping Providers Association(424)
National Association of Dental Plans(449)
National Association of School Music Dealers(470)
National Athletic Trainers' Association(482)
National Business Association(486)
National Collegiate Wrestling Association(491)
National Corrugated Steel Pipe Association(496)
Pipe Line Contractors Association(578)
Professional Association of Christian Educators(585)
Retail Print Music Dealers Association(601)
Safe and Vault Technicians Association(604)
Society of Independent Professional Earth Scientists(638)
Uni-Bell PVC Pipe Association(669)

Denton

Asian/Pacific American Librarians Association(163)
Association of Teachers of Technical Writing(217)
International Association of Equine Dentistry(356)
Red Angus Association of America(597)

DeSoto

Academy of Rehabilitative Audiology(5)

Dripping Springs

American Red Brangus Association(122)

Fredonia

American Southdown Breeders Association(148)

Ft. Worth

American Association of Professional Landmen(49)
American College of Osteopathic Obstetricians and Gynecologists(69)
American Paint Horse Association(112)
Association for Women Journalists(182)
International Society for General Semantics(387)
International Society of Certified Electronics Technicians(390)
Livestock Publications Council(409)
National Association of Women in Construction(481)
National Cutting Horse Association(504)
National Electronic Service Dealers Association(506)
Professional Insurance Marketing Association(588)
Texas Longhorn Breeders Association of America(659)

Gainesville

National Tractor Parts Dealer Association(546)

Galveston

International Society for Chronobiology(386)

Garland

American Metal Detector Manufacturers Association(105)
Choristers Guild(245)

Georgetown

American Forage and Grassland Council(84)

Association of Christian Teachers(190)
Association of Energy Services Professionals, International(195)
International Regional Magazine Association(385)
Utility Communicators International(681)

Godley

Galiceno Horse Breeders Association(313)

Grand Prairie

American Engineering Association(81)

Grand Saline

American Blonde D'Aquitaine Association(57)

Grapevine

American Small Businesses Association(126)

Holly Lake Ranch

Independent Pet and Animal Transportation Association International(335)

Houston

American Association for Women Radiologists(37)
American Association of Stratigraphic Palynologists(51)
American Brahman Breeders Association(59)
American Bureau of Shipping(59)
American Institute of Organbuilders(97)
American Society of Emergency Radiology(137)
Animal Transportation Association(157)
Association of Diving Contractors International(194)
Association of Energy Service Companies(195)
Association of Visual Merchandise Representatives(220)
Auto Suppliers Benchmarking Association(222)
Automotive Body Parts Association(223)
Benchmarking Network Association(227)
Cooling Technology Institute(265)
Council of Societies for the Study of Religion(274)
Drilling Engineering Association(287)
Energy Security Council(294)
Energy Traffic Association(294)
Fiberglass Tank and Pipe Institute(305)
Fleischner Society(307)
Golf Writers Association of America(318)
Green Hotels Association(320)
International Association of Clerks, Recorders, Election Officials and Treasurers(354)
International Association of Drilling Contractors(356)
International Association of Geophysical Contractors(357)
International Atherosclerosis Society(362)
International Contract Center Benchmarking Consortium(367)
International Facility Management Association(371)
International Institute of Synthetic Rubber Producers(376)
International Maintenance Institute(379)
International Nanny Association(380)
International Oil Scouts Association(381)
Linguistic Association of Canada and the United States(408)
Materials and Methods Standards Association(414)
NACE International(424)
National Association for Black Geologists and Geophysicists(432)
National Association of Scientific Materials Managers(471)
National Association of State Election Directors(475)
National Energy Services Association(507)
National Federation of Hispanic Owned Newspapers(509)
National Institute of Business and Industrial Chaplaincy(520)
Petroleum Equipment Suppliers Association(574)
Petroleum Technology Transfer Council(574)
Retirement Industry Trust Association(601)
Semiotic Society of America(608)
Society for Pediatric Radiology(623)
Society for Uroradiology(629)
Society of Gastrointestinal Radiologists(637)
Society of Petroleum Evaluation Engineers(641)
Society of Petrophysicists and Well Log Analysts(641)
Society of Piping Engineers and Designers(642)
Telecommunications Benchmarking International Group(659)
United States Beef Breeds Council(673)
United States Professional Tennis Association(676)
Wireless Dealers Association(690)

Hurst

American Academy of Craniofacial Pain(21)
National Association of Dog Obedience Instructors(450)

Ingram

Exotic Wildlife Association(299)

Irving

American Association for Respiratory Care(36)
American College of Emergency Physicians(65)
American Concrete Pipe Association(73)
American Recovery Association(122)
Emergency Medicine Residents' Association(292)
Energy Telecommunications and Electrical Association(294)
International Aloe Science Council(349)
National Burglar and Fire Alarm Association(486)
National Society of Hispanic MBAs(541)
Plastics Pipe Institute(579)
Promotional Products Association International(591)
Young Presidents' Organization(698)

Kingsville

Santa Gertrudis Breeders International(605)

Lago Vista

American Association of Community Theatre(41)

Ledbetter

American Suffolk Horse Association(150)

Levelland

American Rambouillet Sheep Breeders Association(121)

Lewisville

American Donkey and Mule Society(79)

Longview

Association of North American Missions(205)
National Appliance Parts Suppliers Association(430)

Lubbock

American Academy of Advertising(20)
American Leather Chemists Association(101)
Association for Arid Lands Studies(167)
National Grain Sorghum Producers(514)
North American Small Business International Trade Educators(560)
School Science and Mathematics Association(606)

Mico

Medical Mycological Society of the Americas(416)

Nacogdoches

United Braford Breeders(670)

North Richland Hills

National Association of Catastrophe Adjusters(442)

Orange

Ass'n of Procurement Technical Assistance Centers(164)

Panhandle

American Agriculture Movement(30)

Pearland

North American Society for Dialysis and Transplantation(560)

Pinehurst

International Iridology Practitioners Association(377)

Pipe Creek

American Goat Society(87)

Plano

Piano Manufacturers Association International(577)
Restaurant Facility Management Association(600)
Society of Diagnostic Medical Sonography(635)

Prairie View

Research Association of Minority Professors(600)

Ranger

American Ostrich Association(112)

Richardson

American Literary Translators Association(101)
Distribution Contractors Association(286)
International Association of Electrical Inspectors(356)
National Association of Church Business Administration(443)
North American Rail Shippers Association(559)
Society of Petroleum Engineers(641)

Roanoke

National Pawnbrokers Association(532)

Rocksprings

American Angora Goat Breeder's Association(31)

Round Rock

Computer Event Marketing Association(257)
Organization of Flying Adjusters(567)

San Angelo

American Emu Association(81)
Mohair Council of America(421)
Western Music Association(687)

San Antonio

American Council for Construction Education(75)
American Payroll Association(113)
Beefmaster Breeders United(227)
Hispanic Association of Colleges and Universities(325)
International Association Colon Hydro Therapy(349)
International Brangus Breeders Association(363)
International Builders Exchange Executives(363)
National Association of Master Appraisers(461)

National Association of Property Tax Representatives - Transportation, Energy, Communications(467)
National Independent Nursery Furniture Retailers Association(519)
Research and Development Associates for Military Food and Packaging Systems(599)
Society of Corporate Meeting Professionals(634)
Society of Government Service Urologists(637)
Society of Military Orthopaedic Surgeons(640)

San Marcos

Computer Assisted Language Instruction Consortium(257)
International Society of Applied Intelligence(390)
Romanian Studies Association of America(603)

Spring

Romance Writers of America(603)

Sugar Land

International Academy of Compounding Pharmacists(347)
Sugar Industry Technologists(655)

Sunnyvale

Aestheticians International Association(10)

Temple

Fraternal Field Managers Association(311)

The Woodlands

American Pediatric Society(113)
Society for Pediatric Research(623)

Tyler

CHA - Certified Horsemanship Association(242)
Religious Communication Association(598)

Victoria

National Association of Steel Pipe Distributors(477)

Waco

American Football Coaches Association(84)
American Society of Limnology and Oceanography(140)

Webster

Society of Mexican American Engineers and Scientists(640)

Whitesboro

American Brahmousin Council(59)

UTAH

Clearfield

Society for Epidemiologic Research(617)

Dammeron Valley

American Auditory Society(55)

Logan

Association for Politics and the Life Sciences(176)
Western Literature Association(687)

Newton

United Suffolk Sheep Association(678)

Park City

United States Ski Association(677)

Provo

American Association of Presidents of Independent Colleges and Universities(49)
Society for the Advancement of Scandinavian Study(626)
Society of Systematic Biologists(644)

Salt Lake City

Academy of Clinical Laboratory Physicians and Scientists(2)
Academy of Leisure Sciences(4)
Air Medical Physician Association(13)
American Academy of Professional Coders(27)
Archery Trade Association(160)
Executive Women International(299)
Expanded Shale, Clay and Slate Institute(299)
National Academy of Building Inspection Engineers(426)
National Association for Family Child Care(433)
National Association of Certified Valuation Analysts(442)
National Association of Health Data Organizations(455)

Spanish Fork

Association for Graphic Arts Training(173)

VERMONT

Barre

Barre Granite Association(226)

Bennington

American Cream Draft Horse Association(77)

Brattleboro

Holstein Association USA(327)

Concord

Society for New Language Study(622)

Ferrisburg

International Maple Syrup Institute(379)

Hardwick

Association of American Pesticide Control Officials(185)

Middlebury

Association of Clinical Scientists(190)

Randolph

Masonry Heater Association of North America(413)

Shelburne

American Morgan Horse Association(106)

South Burlington

Funeral Consumers Alliance(312)

Woodstock

Carbonated Beverage Institute(237)

VIRGINIA

Alexandria

Academy of Managed Care Pharmacy(4)
Acute Long Term Hospital Association(8)
Aeronautical Repair Station Association(10)
Aerospace Medical Association(10)
Agricultural and Food Transporters Conference(12)
Air Traffic Control Association(13)
Airport Consultants Council(14)
American Academy of Facial Plastic and Reconstructive Surgery(22)
American Academy of Orthotists and Prosthetists(26)
American Academy of Otolaryngology-Head and Neck Surgery(26)
American Academy of Physician Assistants(27)
American Association for Dental Research(34)
American Association for Homecare(35)
American Association for Marriage and Family Therapy(36)
American Association for the Study of Liver Diseases(37)
American Association of Airport Executives(38)
American Association of Colleges of Pharmacy(40)
American Association of Family and Consumer Sciences(43)
American Association of Port Authorities(49)
American Automotive Leasing Association(55)
American Bankruptcy Institute(55)
American Chamber of Commerce Executives(61)
American College of Health Care Administrators(66)
American College of Osteopathic Surgeons(69)
American Correctional Association(74)
American Council on the Teaching of Foreign Languages(76)
American Counseling Association(76)
American Diabetes Association(79)
American Gear Manufacturers Association(86)
American Geological Institute(87)
American Helicopter Society International(90)
American Horticultural Society(91)
American Institute of Constructors(95)
American Institute of Homeopathy(96)
American International Automobile Dealers Association(98)
American League of Lobbyists(101)
American Medical Group Association(104)
American Medical Women's Association(105)
American Mental Health Counselors Association(105)
American Moving and Storage Association(107)
American Network of Community Options and Resources(108)
American Orthotic and Prosthetic Association(111)
American Osteopathic College of Proctology(112)
American Peanut Council(113)
American Physical Therapy Association(115)
American Physical Therapy Association - Private Practice Section(115)
American Public Communications Council(119)
American Rock Mechanics Association(123)
American School Counselor Association(124)
American Seed Trade Association(124)
American Society for Clinical Pharmacology and Therapeutics(127)
American Society for Horticultural Science(130)
American Society for Training and Development(133)
American Society of Clinical Oncology(136)
American Society of Consultant Pharmacists(136)
American Society of Military Comptrollers(141)
American Society of Naval Engineers(142)
American Society of Picture Professionals(144)
American Society of Transplant Surgeons(146)
American Society of Travel Agents(146)
American Sportfishing Association(148)
American Staffing Association(149)
American Statistical Association(149)
American Subcontractors Association(149)
American Therapeutic Recreation Association(151)
American Translators Association(152)
American Trucking Associations(152)
American Wire Producers Association(155)
Analytical and Life Science Systems Association(157)
AOC(158)
APICS - The Association for Operations Management(158)
ASIS International(163)
Assisted Living Federation of America(164)
Association for Career and Technical Education(169)
Association for Education and Rehabilitation of the Blind and Visually Impaired(172)
Association for Supervision and Curriculum Development(178)

Association for Women in Communications(182)
Association of Air Medical Services(183)
Association of Clinical Research Professionals(190)
Association of Consulting Foresters of America(192)
Association of Corporate Travel Executives(193)
Association of Fundraising Professionals(198)
Association of Government Accountants(199)
Association of Higher Education Facilities Officers(199)
Association of Independent Corrugated Converters(200)
Association of Machinery and Equipment Appraisers(203)
Association of Naval Aviation(205)
Association of Pool and Spa Professionals(208)
Association of Women in the Metal Industries(220)
Better Hearing Institute(228)
Binding Industries Association(228)
Cable & Telecommunications Association for Marketing(236)
Canon Law Society of America(237)
Catholic Charities USA(239)
Chemical Producers and Distributors Association(243)
Club Managers Association of America(249)
Color Marketing Group(252)
Color Pigments Manufacturers Association(253)
Community Associations Institute(255)
Community Financial Services Association of America(256)
Composite Can and Tube Institute(256)
Construction Specifications Institute(263)
Council for Affordable and Rural Housing(268)
Council for Electronic Revenue Communication Advancement(268)
Council of Professional Associations on Federal Statistics(273)
Council on Social Work Education(277)
Dental Trade Alliance(283)
Document Management Industries Association(286)
Enlisted Association of the National Guard of the United States(295)
Envelope Manufacturers Association(296)
Environmental Bankers Association(296)
EPDM Roofing Association(297)
Federal Managers Association(302)
Federated Ambulatory Surgery Association(303)
Federation of State Boards of Physical Therapy(304)
Fleet Reserve Association(307)
Flight Safety Foundation(308)
Food Processing Machinery and Supplies Association(309)
Glass Packaging Institute(317)
Graphic Arts Marketing Information Service(319)
Health Industry Distributors Association(323)
Hearing Industries Association(324)
Helicopter Association International(325)
Household Goods Forwarders Association of America(329)
Independent Electrical Contractors(334)
Independent Insurance Agents and Brokers of America(334)
Independent Lubricant Manufacturers Association(335)
Independent Office Products and Furniture Dealers Association(335)
Infectious Diseases Society of America(338)
Insulation Contractors Association of America(345)
International Association for Cold Storage Construction(349)
International Association of Addictions and Offender Counselors(352)
International Association of Amusement Parks and Attractions(352)
International Association of Chiefs of Police(354)
International Association of Counseling Services(355)
International Association of Refrigerated Warehouses(360)
International Bottled Water Association(362)
International Corrugated Packaging Foundation(367)
International Digital Enterprise Alliance(369)
International Public Management Association for Human Resources(384)
International Refrigerated Transportation Association(384)
International Road Federation(385)
International Sign Association(386)
International Sleep Products Association(386)
International Society of Hospitality Consultants(391)
International Union of Police Associations, AFL-CIO(396)
International Wood Products Association(397)
Laboratory Products Association(404)
Licensing Executives Society(407)
Machinery Dealers National Association(409)
Mailing & Fulfillment Service Association(410)
Meals On Wheels Association of America(414)
Meat Industry Suppliers Alliance(415)
Military Officers Association of America(419)
Military Operations Research Society(419)
NAADAC -- the Association for Addiction Professionals(424)
National Accounting and Finance Council(427)
National Active and Retired Federal Employees Association(427)
National Aeronautic Association(427)
National Affordable Housing Management Association(428)
National Air Transportation Association(428)
National Aircraft Resale Association(428)
National Alcohol Beverage Control Association(429)
National Apartment Association(430)
National Association for College Admission Counseling(432)
National Association for Practical Nurse Education and Service(435)
National Association for the Support of Long-Term Care(437)
National Association of Chain Drug Stores(442)
National Association of Children's Hospitals(443)
National Association of Computer Consultant Businesses(445)
National Association of Convenience Stores(446)
National Association of Councils on Developmental Disabilities(446)
National Association of Crime Victim Compensation Boards(448)
National Association of Elementary School Principals(450)
National Association of Golf Tournament Directors(454)
National Association of Postal Supervisors(465)
National Association of Postmasters of the United States(465)
National Association of Professional Employer Organizations(466)
National Association of Professional Insurance Agents(466)
National Association of Security Companies(471)
National Association of State Boards of Education(473)
National Association of State Directors of Developmental Disability Services(474)
National Association of State Directors of Special Education(475)
National Association of State Energy Officials(475)
National Association of State Mental Health Program Directors(476)
National Association of Telecommunications Officers and Advisors(478)
National Association of VA Physicians and Dentists(480)
National Beer Wholesalers Association(484)
National Business Travel Association(486)
National Cancer Registrars Association(486)
National Center for Homeopathy(488)
National Community Pharmacists Association(491)
National Council for Agricultural Education(497)
National Council of Commercial Plant Breeders(498)
National Defense Transportation Association(504)
National District Attorneys Association(505)
National EMS Pilots Association(507)
National Head Start Association(516)
National Hospice and Palliative Care Organization(517)
National Industries for the Blind(519)
National Insulation Association(521)
National League of Postmasters of the U.S.(524)
National Mental Health Association(527)
National Motor Freight Traffic Association(527)
National Naval Officers Association(528)
National Organization of Black Law Enforcement Executives(530)
National Paperbox Association(531)
National Private Truck Council(534)
National Rehabilitation Association(535)
National Renderers Association(536)
National Rural Letter Carriers' Association(537)
National School Boards Association(538)
National School Transportation Association(538)
National Sheriffs' Association(539)
National Society for Experiential Education(540)
National Society of Accountants(541)
National Society of Professional Engineers(542)
National Stone, Sand and Gravel Association(543)
National Tank Truck Carriers Conference(545)
National Wooden Pallet and Container Association(550)
NATSO, Representing America's Travel Plazas and Truckstops(550)
Naval Reserve Association(551)
Non Commissioned Officers Association of the U.S.A.(553)
North American Insulation Manufacturers Association(557)
Optical Imaging Association(565)
Outdoor Power Equipment Institute(569)
Paperboard Packaging Council(571)
Passenger Vessel Association(572)
PCIA - the Wireless Industry Association(572)
Polyisocyanurate Insulation Manufacturers Association(580)
Powder Coating Institute(582)
Power and Communication Contractors Association(582)
Professional Aviation Maintenance Association(586)
Professional Engineers in Private Practice(587)
Professional Services Management Association(589)
Public Risk Management Association(593)
Registry of Interpreters for the Deaf(598)
Safety and Loss Prevention Management Council(604)
Salt Institute(605)
SAMA Group of Associations(605)
School Nutrition Association(606)
Security Industry Association(607)
Self Storage Association(608)
SHRM Global Forum(610)
Snack Food Association(612)
SOCAP International(612)
Society for Healthcare Epidemiology of America(618)
Society for Human Resource Management(619)
Society for Marketing Professional Services(621)
Society of American Florists(630)
Society of American Military Engineers(631)

Society of Competitive Intelligence Professionals(633)
Society of Cost Estimating and Analysis(634)
Society of Government Meeting Professionals(637)
Special Libraries Association(649)
State Government Affairs Council(652)
Swedish-American Chambers of Commerce(657)
Teachers of English to Speakers of Other Languages(658)
Technology and Maintenance Council of American Trucking Associations(658)
Textile Rental Services Association of America(660)
Towing and Recovery Association of America(662)
Transportation Intermediaries Association(664)
Truck Renting and Leasing Association(666)
Truck Trailer Manufacturers Association(666)
Truckload Carriers Association(666)
Truss Plate Institute(666)
U.S. Internet Industry Association(668)
United Motorcoach Association(672)
Vinifera Wine Growers Association(683)
Vision Council of America(684)
Water Environment Federation(685)
Wire Rope Technical Board(690)
Women in Government Relations(692)
Young Entrepreneurs Organization(698)

Annandale

Association Chief Executive Council(166)
National Association of Academies of Science(437)
National Emergency Equipment Dealers Association(506)

Arlington

ACCRA - Ass'n of Applied Community Researchers(6)
Accrediting Commission for Career Schools and Colleges of Technology(7)
Aerospace Industries Association of America(10)
AFIA-Alfalfa Processors Council(11)
Air Conditioning Contractors of America(13)
Air Force Association(13)
AirConditioning and Refrigeration Institute(14)
Alliance for Responsible Atmospheric Policy(16)
Alliance for the Polyurethane Industry(16)
Aluminum Association(18)
American Anthropological Association(31)
American Apparel & Footwear Association(31)
American Association for Health Freedom(35)
American Association of Eye and Ear Hospitals(42)
American Association of Motor Vehicle Administrators(45)
American Association of Pharmaceutical Scientists(48)
American Association of School Administrators(50)
American Butter Institute(60)
American Chemistry Council(62)
American Chiropractic Association(62)
American Composites Manufacturers Association(72)
American Court and Commercial Newspapers(77)
American Feed Industry Association(83)
American Fiber Manufacturers Association(83)
American Intellectual Property Law Association(98)
American Plastics Council(116)
American Psychiatric Association(117)
American Psychiatric Nurses Association(118)
American Society of Pension Professionals and Actuaries(143)
American Society of Transportation and Logisitcs(146)
American Sugar Alliance(150)
American Waterways Operators(154)
Asbestos Cement Product Producers Association(162)
Asbestos Information Association/North America(162)
Associated Builders and Contractors(164)
Associated General Contractors of America(165)
Association for Enterprise Opportunity(172)
Association for Postal Commerce(177)
Association for the Advancement of Medical Instrumentation(179)
Association for Unmanned Vehicle Systems International(181)
Association of Educational Service Agencies(194)
Association of International Automobile Manufacturers(201)
Association of the United States Army(218)
Association of University Programs in Health Administration(219)
Casualty Actuarial Society(239)
Chlorine Chemistry Council(245)
Clinical Social Work Federation(248)
Consumer Bankers Association(263)
Consumer Electronics Association(263)
Contract Services Association of America(264)
Corporate Facility Advisors(266)
Council for Exceptional Children(268)
Council of Better Business Bureaus(271)
Council of Defense and Space Industry Associations(271)
Electronic Industries Alliance(292)
Electronic Retailing Association(292)
Employee Assistance Professionals Association(293)
Energy Frontiers International(294)
Equipment Leasing Association of America(297)
Federation of State Humanities Councils(304)
Foundation for International Meetings(311)
Gas Appliance Manufacturers Association(314)
Gasification Technologies Council(314)
Generic Pharmaceutical Association(315)
Geoscience and Remote Sensing Society(316)
Halogenated Solvents Industry Alliance(321)
Halon Alternatives Research Corp.(321)
Health Industry Group Purchasing Association(323)
Healthcare Distribution Management Association(323)
Hearth Patio & Barbecue Association(324)
Hydronics Institute Division of GAMA(330)
Independent Association of Accredited Registrars(333)
Industrial Research Institute(337)
Information Technology Association of America(338)
Insurance Institute for Highway Safety(345)
International Cast Polymer Association(364)
International Chiropractors Association(365)
International Council of Cruise Lines(367)
International Federation of Inspection Agencies - Americas Committee(371)
International Institute of Ammonia Refrigeration(376)
International Pharmaceutical Excipients Council of the Americas(382)
International Real Estate Federation - American Chapter(384)
International Safety Equipment Association(385)
Joint Electron Device Engineering Council(402)
Manufactured Housing Institute(411)
Manufacturers Alliance/MAPI(411)
Meat Importers' Council of America(415)
Methanol Institute(418)
Military Chaplains Association of the U.S.(419)
National Air Carrier Association(428)
National Association of Chemical Distributors(442)
National Association of Child Care Resource and Referral Agencies(443)
National Association of Federal Credit Unions(452)
National Association of Health Underwriters(455)
National Association of State Credit Union Supervisors(474)
National Council of Catholic Women(498)
National Defense Industrial Association(504)
National Emergency Number Association(507)
National Federation of Press Women(510)
National Genealogical Society(513)
National Grocers Association(515)
National Hispanic Corporate Council(517)
National Ice Cream Mix Association(518)
National Lime Association(525)
National Milk Producers Federation(527)
National Rural Electric Cooperative Association(537)
National Science Teachers Association(539)
National Society of Black Physicists(541)
National Telecommunications Cooperative Association(546)
National Training Systems Association(547)
National Utility Contractors Association(548)
National Venture Capital Association(548)
National Water Resources Association(548)
National Waterways Conference(549)
NEA - the Association of Union Constructors(551)
North American Society for Trenchless Technology(561)
North American Technician Excellence(562)
Packaging Machinery Manufacturers Institute(570)
Partnership for Air-Conditioning, Heating Refrigeration Accreditation(571)
Patent and Trademark Office Society(572)
Patent Office Professional Association(572)
Pellet Fuels Institute(573)
Petroleum Marketers Association of America(574)
Pipeline Research Council International(578)
Polystyrene Packaging Council(580)
Professional Services Council(589)
Rehabilitation Engineering and Assistive Technology Society of North America(598)
Retail Industry Leaders Association(601)
Rice Millers' Association(602)
Society for Conservation Biology(615)
Society for Technical Communication(626)
Society of Federal Labor and Employee Relations Professionals(636)
Society of Research Administrators International(643)
Telecommunications Industry Association(659)
The National Industrial Transportation League(519)
U.S. - Taiwan Business Council(667)
U.S.A. Rice Federation(669)
Uniform and Textile Service Association(669)
Vinyl Institute(683)
Visual Resources Association(684)
Women in Aerospace(691)

Ashburn

National Recreation and Parks Association(535)

Ashland

American Association of Sexuality Educators, Counselors and Therapists(51)

Berryville

Academy of Security Educators and Trainers(5)

Blacksburg

Adhesion Society(8)
American Academy of Mechanics(24)
Association of Chairmen of Departments of Mechanics(189)
International Society for Quality-of-Life Studies(388)
National Institute of Ceramic Engineers(520)
World Association of Veterinary Anatomists(695)

Burke

Association of Small Business Development Centers(214)

Council of Industrial Boiler Owners(272)

Chantilly

Automotive Parts Remanufactuers Association(224)
Clay Minerals Society(247)
Compressed Gas Association(257)
Door and Hardware Institute(287)
Mineralogical Society of America(419)
National Association for Search and Rescue(436)
Production Engine Remanufacturers Association(585)
Remanufacturing Institute, The(599)
Sheet Metal and Air Conditioning Contractors' National Association(610)
Women in Cable and Telecommunications(691)

Charlottesville

CFA Institute(242)
Community College Business Officers(255)
Modular Building Institute(420)
National Association of College Auxiliary Services(444)
National Weather Association(549)
Society of Quality Assurance(643)

Chatham

American Vocational Education Personnel Development Association(153)

Chesapeake

Association for the Advancement of Computing in Education(179)
National Association of Marine Surveyors(461)

Chincoteague

Society for Light Treatment and Biological Rhythms(621)

Culpeper

Association of Social Work Boards(214)

Dulles

Industrial Designers Society of America(336)

Earlysville

American Society of Ocularists(143)

Fairfax

Alliance of Information and Referral Systems(17)
American Association of Attorney-Certified Public Accountants(38)
American Association of Healthcare Administrative Management(43)
American Association of Pastoral Counselors(47)
American College of Bankruptcy(64)
American College of Medical Toxicology(67)
American Council for Technology(75)
American Industrial Hygiene Association(93)
American Society for Therapeutic Radiology and Oncology(133)
American Society of Cataract and Refractive Surgery(135)
American Society of Ophthalmic Administrators(143)
American String Teachers Association(149)
American Wholesale Marketers Association(155)
American Wood Preservers Institute(155)
Armed Forces Communications and Electronics Association(161)
Association for Ambulatory Behavorial Healthcare(167)
Association for Women in Mathematics(182)
Association of Residents in Radiation Oncology(212)
Association of Writers and Writing Programs(221)
Automotive Recyclers Association(224)
Building Service Contractors Association International(234)
Commission on Accreditation for Law Enforcement Agencies(254)
Connected International Meeting Professionals Association(261)
Digital Printing and Imaging Association(284)
Electronic Funds Transfer Association(292)
Independent Educational Consultants Association(334)
InfoCom International(338)
Institute of Navigation(343)
International Association of Fire Chiefs(357)
International Society of Transport Aircraft Trading(392)
International Test and Evaluation Association(394)
National Armored Car Association(431)
National Association of Government Communicators(454)
National Association of Independent Life Brokerage Agencies(457)
National Association of Miscellaneous, Ornamental and Architectural Products Contractors(462)
National Association of Reinforcing Steel Contractors(469)
National Community Education Association(491)
National Council of Erectors, Fabricators and Riggers(498)
National Pest Management Association(532)
National Rifle Association of America(536)
Optical Laboratories Association(566)
Propeller Club of the United States(591)
Recreation Vehicle Dealers Association of North America(596)
Silver Users Association(611)
Society for Industrial Microbiology(620)
Society of Interventional Radiology(639)
Specialized Carriers and Rigging Association(649)
Specialty Graphic Imaging Association(650)
United Mine Workers of America International Union(672)

Fairfax Station

Council on the Safe Transportation of Hazardous Articles(277)

Falls Church

Access Technology Association(6)
Accrediting Bureau of Health Education Schools(7)
American Association for Budget and Program Analysis(33)
American Association of Early Childhood Educators(42)
American Health Planning Association(89)
American Pipe Fittings Association(115)
American Textile Machinery Association(151)
American Thyroid Association(151)
Association for Advanced Life Underwriting(167)
Association for Healthcare Philanthropy(173)
Association of Executive and Administrative Professionals(196)
Association of Health Insurance Advisors(199)
Association of Healthcare Internal Auditors(199)
Association of Suppliers to the Paper Industry(216)
Association of the Wall and Ceiling Industries-International(218)
Cold Finished Steel Bar Institute(250)
Data Interchange Standards Association(281)
Defense Fire Protection Association(282)
Express Delivery & Logistics Association(300)
Financial Markets Association(306)
Foodservice and Packaging Institute(309)
GAMA International(313)
Healthcare Compliance Packaging Council(323)
Hotel Electronic Distribution Network Association(329)
International Association of Emergency Managers(356)
International Aviation Ground Support Association(362)
International Code Council(365)
International Foodservice Distributors Association(372)
Irrigation Association(400)
National Association of Dental Assistants(448)
National Association of Insurance and Financial Advisors(458)
National Association of Physician Nurses(464)
National Association of RV Parks and Campgrounds(470)
National Association of State Emergency Medical Services Officials(475)
National Council of State Emergency Medical Services Training Coordinators(500)
Naval Enlisted Reserve Association(551)
Pharmaceutical Printed Literature Association(575)
Plumbing-Heating-Cooling Contractors - National Association(579)
Process Equipment Manufacturers' Association(584)
Railway Engineering-Maintenance Suppliers Association(595)
Society for Personality Assessment(623)
Voluntary Protection Programs Participants Association(684)

Fredericksburg

American Traffic Safety Services Association(152)
International Parking Institute(382)
Society of Medical Consultants to the Armed Forces(639)
United States Parachute Association(676)

Front Royal

Brotherhood of Railroad Signalmen(233)

Glen Allen

American Association of Integrated Healthcare Delivery Systems(44)
American Association of Managed Care Nurses(44)
American College of Managed Care Medicine(67)
National Association of Managed Care Physicians(460)

Goldvein

International Association of Bomb Technicians and Investigators(354)

Great Falls

Fuel Cell Power Association(312)
Gas Turbine Association(314)
International Cadmium Association(364)
Society for Thermal Medicine(628)

Hamilton

Basic Acrylic Monomer Manufacturers(226)
Methacrylate Producers Association(418)
National Military Intelligence Association(527)
Operations Security Professionals Society(565)

Harrisonburg

Institute of Certified Professional Managers(340)
Saddle, Harness, and Allied Trade Association(604)

Haymarket

NORA: An Association of Responsible Recyclers(553)

Herndon

American Society of Appraisers(134)
American Society of Extra-Corporeal Technology(137)

Association of Major City and County Building Officials(203)
Association of Muslim Social Scientists(205)
Contact Lens Society of America(264)
NACHA - The Electronic Payments Association(424)
National Association of Hispanic Federal Executives(455)
National Association of Industrial and Office Properties(458)
National Concrete Masonry Association(492)
National Conference of States on Building Codes and Standards(494)
National Institute of Governmental Purchasing(520)
National Organization of Life and Health Insurance Guaranty Associations(530)
Opticians Association of America(566)
Professional Landscape Network(588)
Silicones Environmental, Health and Safety Council of North America(610)
United States Army Warrant Officers Association(673)

Kilmarnock

Closure Manufacturers Association(248)

Lake Ridge

Aniline Association(157)
Ass'n of Learning Providers(164)
Ethylene Oxide Sterilization Association(298)
National Association of Assistant United States Attorneys(439)

Leesburg

American Council of State Savings Supervisors(75)
American Osteopathic College of Occupational and Preventive Medicine(112)
American Roentgen Ray Society(123)
Automotive Training Managers Council(224)
International Council of Air Shows(367)
National Association for Trade and Industrial Education(437)
Professional Housing Management Association(587)
Skills USA(611)
Society for Imaging Informatics in Medicine(619)
Society of Radiologists in Ultrasound(643)

Manassas

Association of Teacher Educators(217)
Garden Writers Association(314)
Hydroponic Merchants Association(330)
International Federation of Pharmaceutical Wholesalers(371)
Mulch and Soil Council(422)
National Rehabilitation Counseling Association(535)
National Religious Broadcasters(536)

Martinsville

International Window Film Association(397)

McLean

Ambulatory Pediatric Association(19)
American Academy of Health Physics(23)
American Ambulance Association(30)
American Association of Tissue Banks(53)
American Frozen Food Institute(85)
American Ornithologists' Union(110)
American Psychosomatic Society(119)
American Society of Women Accountants(147)
American Truck Dealers(152)
Americas Association of Cooperative/Mutual Insurance Socs.(156)
AMT - The Association For Manufacturing Technology(156)
Associated Owners and Developers(165)
Association of Christian Therapists(190)
Association of Former Intelligence Officers(198)
Association of Hispanic Advertising Agencies(200)
Association of Organ Procurement Organizations(206)
Association of Pediatric Program Directors(207)
Association of Water Technologies(220)
Audio Publishers Association(222)
Automotive Trade Association Executives(224)
Construction Management Association of America(262)
Convention Industry Council(265)
Emergency Department Practice Management Association(292)
Enterprise Wireless Alliance(295)
Frozen Potato Products Institute(312)
Graduate Management Admission Council(319)
Health Physics Society(323)
Hospitality Sales and Marketing Association International(329)
International Alliance for Women(348)
International Association of Food Industry Suppliers(357)
International Frozen Food Association(373)
International Society for Quality of Life Research(388)
International Society for the Study of Dissociation(389)
Land Mobile Communications Council(405)
Medical-Dental-Hospital Business Associates(416)
National Association of Development Companies(449)
National Association of Minority Media Executives(462)
National Association of Mortgage Brokers(462)
National Association of Women Business Owners(481)
National Automobile Dealers Association(482)
National Contract Management Association(495)
National Fisheries Institute(511)
National Frozen Pizza Institute(513)
National Glass Association(513)
National Yogurt Association(550)
Retailer's Bakery Association(601)
Semiconductor Environmental Safety and Health Association(608)
SnowSports Industries America(612)
Society for Integrative and Comparative Biology(620)
Society for Occupational and Environmental Health(622)
Society for Risk Analysis(625)
Society of National Association Publications(640)
Specialized Information Publishers Association(650)
Tortilla Industry Association(662)
World Airline Entertainment Association(695)

Mechanicsville

International Microwave Power Institute(379)

Middlebrook

American Connemara Pony Society(74)

Middleburg

American Water Resources Association(154)

Middleton

Alliance of Cardiovascular Professionals(16)

Midlothian

National Association of Disability Evaluating Professionals(449)
Teaching-Family Association(658)

Mount Vernon

United Engineering Foundation(671)

Norfolk

ACL - Association for Consortium Leadership(7)
Newspaper Purchasing Management Association(553)

Poquosou

Network on Ministry in Specialized Settings(552)

Potomac Falls

American Edged Products Manufacturers Association(80)
National Association of Public Insurance Adjusters(467)
Surface Finishing Industry Council(656)

Purcellville

National Terrazzo and Mosaic Association(546)

Quantico

Society of Former Special Agents of the Federal Bureau of Investigation(636)

Reston

American Academy of Audiology(20)
American Alliance for Health, Physical Education, Recreation and Dance(30)
American Association for Health Education(35)
American Brachytherapy Society(59)
American College of Medical Physics(67)
American College of Nuclear Physicians(68)
American College of Radiology(70)
American Concrete Pressure Pipe Association(73)
American Institute of Aeronautics and Astronautics(94)
American Medical Student Association(105)
American Society of Civil Engineers(135)
American Society of Newspaper Editors(142)
Architectural Engineering Institute(160)
Architectural Woodwork Institute(160)
Association of Insurance Compliance Professionals(201)
Association of School Business Officials International(212)
Association of University Research Parks(219)
Association of Vascular and Interventional Radiographers(220)
Brick Industry Association(232)
Council of Science Editors(274)
Distributive Education Clubs of America(286)
Environmental Mutagen Society(296)
Family, Career, and Community Leaders of America(300)
Federation of International Trade Associations(304)
Future Business Leaders of America-Phi Beta Lambda(313)
Hardwood Plywood and Veneer Association(322)
Inter-Society Color Council(346)
International Graphic Arts Education Association(374)
International Technology Education Association(393)
Internet Society(398)
Kitchen Cabinet Manufacturers Association(403)
Management Association for Private Photogrammetric Surveyors(410)
MENC: The National Association for Music Education(417)
National Art Education Association(431)
National Association for Girls and Women in Sport(433)
National Association for Sport and Physical Education(436)
National Association for Variable Annuities(437)
National Association of Biology Teachers(440)
National Association of Corporate Treasurers(446)
National Association of Rehabilitation Providers and Agencies(469)
National Association of Schools of Art and Design(470)

National Association of Schools of Dance(470)
National Association of Schools of Music(470)
National Association of Schools of Theatre(471)
National Association of Secondary School Principals(471)
National Business Education Association(486)
National Council of Teachers of Mathematics(501)
National Dance Association(504)
National Grants Management Association(514)
National Pharmaceutical Council(533)
North American Meat Processors Association(558)
North American Skull Base Society(560)
NPES, The Association for Suppliers of Printing, Publishing and Converting Technologies(563)
Recreation Vehicle Industry Association(596)
Society for Organic Petrology(623)
Society of Independent Gasoline Marketers of America(638)
Society of Nuclear Medicine(641)
Society of State Directors of Health, Physical Education and Recreation(644)
Society of Toxicologic Pathologists(645)
Society of Toxicology(645)
Sports Lawyers Association(651)
Technology Student Association(658)
Teratology Society(659)
Wine and Spirits Shippers Association(689)
Workgroup for Electronic Data Interchange(695)

Richmond

American College of Osteopathic Pediatricians(69)
American Insurance Marketing and Sales Society(98)
American Real Estate and Urban Economics Association(121)
Association of State Supervisors of Mathematics(216)
Clinical Orthopaedic Society(248)
Conductors Guild(259)
Council of Dance Administrators(271)
Independent Research Libraries Association(335)
International Association of Law Enforcement Intelligence Analysts(358)
International Council on Hotel, Restaurant and Institutional Education(368)
National Council of State Pharmacy Association Executives(501)
Oriental Rug Retailers of America(568)
Society for Pediatric Anesthesia(623)
Society of Cardiovascular Anesthesiologists(632)
Uniformed Services Academy of Family Physicians(669)
United States Animal Health Association(672)

Roanoke

Association of United States Night Vision Manufacturers(219)
Mechanical Association Railcar Technical Services(415)
Society of Pharmaceutical and Biotech Trainers(642)

Rosslyn

Chlorine Institute(245)
National Electrical Manufacturers Association(506)

Springfield

American Astronautical Society(54)
Association of Former OSI Special Agents(198)
Chief Petty Officers Association(244)
Christian Legal Society(246)
Label Packaging Suppliers Council(404)
National Association for Uniformed Services and Society of Military Widows(437)
National Contact Lens Examiners(495)
Nuclear Suppliers Association(563)
Professional Paddlesports Association(588)
Senior Army Reserve Commanders Association(609)
Society for Imaging Science & Technology(619)

Staunton

Association of College Administration Professionals(190)

Sterling

International Cemetery and Funeral Association(364)
International Newspaper Financial Executives(381)
International Society of Air Safety Investigators(389)
National Association of Urban Hospitals(480)

Stuart

National Business Owners Association(486)

Triangle

American College of International Physicians(66)

Unionville

System Safety Society(657)

Vienna

American Boiler Manufacturers Association(58)
American Cocoa Research Institute(63)
American Philatelic Society - Writers Unit #30(114)
American Women in Radio and Television(155)
Central Station Alarm Association(241)
Chocolate Manufacturers Association(245)
Council of Landscape Architectural Registration Boards(273)
Finishing Contractors Association(306)
Manufacturers Standardization Society of the Valve and Fittings Industry(411)
National Association for Medical Direction of Respiratory Care(434)
National Confectioners Association of the United States(492)
National Court Reporters Association(503)
National Investor Relations Institute(522)
National Park Hospitality Association(531)
National Woodland Owners Association(550)
Newspaper Association of America(552)
U.S. Apple Association(667)

Virginia Beach

Association of Management/International Association of Management(203)
Marine Corps Reserve Association(412)
National Air Filtration Association(428)
National Certification Council for Activity Professionals(488)

Warrenton

Association of Military Banks of America(205)
Intersure, Ltd.(398)
QVM/CMC Vehicle Manufacturers Association(594)
Society for Applied Learning Technology(614)

White Stone

Research and Engineering Council of the NAPL(600)

Williamsburg

American Association of Teachers of Arabic(52)
American Judges Association(99)
Conference of Chief Justices(259)
Conference of State Court Adminstrators(260)
Council of Colleges of Arts and Sciences(271)
International Society for Developmental Psychobiology(387)
Measurement, Control and Automation Association(415)
National Association for Court Management(432)
National Conference of Appellate Court Clerks(492)

Winchester

American Association for Functional Orthodontics(35)
Evangelical Council for Financial Accountability(298)
National Extension Association of Family and Consumer Sciences(508)
Welsh Pony and Cob Society of America(687)

Woodbridge

Association of Civilian Technicians(190)

WASHINGTON

Bainbridge Island

Association of Field Ornithologists(196)

Battle Ground

American Land Rights Association(100)

Bellevue

Association of Professional Design Firms(208)
Data Management Association International(282)
Delta Society(283)
International Saw and Knife Association(385)

Bellingham

Cottage Industry Miniaturists Trade Association(267)
National Association for Ethnic Studies(433)
SPIE - The International Society for Optical Engineering(651)

Blaine

Consortium of Behavioral Health Nurses and Associates(262)
Developmental Disabilities Nurses Association(284)

Bothell

National Truck and Heavy Equipment Claims Council(547)

Bremerton

Eight Sheet Outdoor Advertising Association(290)

Covington

International Miniature Cattle Breeders Society(380)

Edmonds

American Academy of Oral Medicine(25)
American Holistic Medical Association(91)
American Medallic Sculpture Association(104)
National Association of Professional Mortgage Women(466)
National Federation of Paralegal Associations(510)

Ellensburg

Family and Consumer Sciences Education Association(300)

Everett

National Association of Test Directors(479)

Gig Harbor

Structural Insulated Panel Association(654)

Kennewick

National Alfalfa Alliance(429)

Kent

National Association of Casino and Theme Party Operators(441)

Lynnwood
American Society of Tax Professionals(146)

Mercer Island
Western Red Cedar Pole Association(687)

Monroe
Log Home Builders Association of North America(409)

Ocean Shores
Transportation Clubs International(664)

Olympia
Association of Reporters of Judicial Decisions(212)

Otis Orchards
National Association of Air Medical Communication Specialists(438)

Prosser
Society of Collision Repair Specialists(633)

Puyallup
North American Clinical Dermatological Society(556)

Renton
International Society of Appraisers(390)
National Association of Reunion Managers(469)

Richland
Keramos Fraternity(403)

Ridgefield
National Association of Temple Administrators(479)

Sammamish
Antenna Measurement Techniques Association(157)

Seattle
Adventure Travel Trade Association(9)
American Dental Hygienists' Association(78)
American Legend Cooperative(101)
American Society for Environmental History(128)
Association of Academic Health Sciences Library Directors(183)
At-sea Processors Association(221)
Council of International Investigators(273)
Foundation for Russian-American Economic Cooperation(311)
Glass Art Society(317)
Histochemical Society(326)
International Association for the Study of Pain(352)
International Association of Tour Managers - North American Region(361)
International College of Cranio-Mandibular Orthopedics(365)
International Council on Systems Engineering(368)
International Guild of Symphony, Opera and Ballet Musicians(374)
International Plant Propagators Society(383)
National Association of Judiciary Interpreters and Translators(459)
Professional Bowlers Association of America(586)
Society for Slovene Studies(625)

Spokane
Buses International Association(235)
National Association for Holistic Aromatherapy(434)
Timber Products Manufacturers(661)

Sumas
Cedar Shake and Shingle Bureau(240)
Sales and Marketing Executives International(604)

Tacoma
APA - The Engineered Wood Association(158)
Guild of American Luthiers(321)
National Association of Ecumenical and Interreligious Staff(450)

Vancouver
Crane Certification Association of America(278)
Institute of Inspection Cleaning and Restoration Certification(341)
Western Dredging Association(687)

Wenatchee
International Fruit Tree Association(373)

Yakima
Hop Growers of America(328)
Northwest Fruit Exporters(562)

Zillah
American Beefalo World Registry(56)

WEST VIRGINIA

Charles Town
National Institute for Farm Safety(520)
United States Trout Farmers Association(678)

Charleston
Independent Photo Imagers(335)
National Council of Coal Lessors(498)
Wholesale Beer Association Executives of America(688)

Hedgesville
National Association of Science Writers(471)

Morgantown
AACE International(1)

Renick
North American Plant Preservation Council(559)

Shepherdstown
Aquacultural Engineering Society(159)

Wheeling
American Academy of Thermology(29)

WISCONSIN

Appleton
National Association of Tax Professionals(478)

Beloit
American Milking Shorthorn Society(106)
Brown Swiss Cattle Breeders Association of the U.S.A.(234)

Brookfield
American Society of Golf Course Architects(138)
International Foundation of Employee Benefit Plans(373)
International Society of Certified Employee Benefit Specialists(390)
National Funeral Directors Association(513)

De Pere
National Institute on Park and Grounds Management(521)

Elm Grove
Specialty Tool and Fastener Distributors Association(650)

Fox Point
Bowling Writers Association of America(232)

Greendale
United States Bowling Congress(673)
Women's International Bowling Congress(693)

Hales Corners
Intermarket Agency Network(347)

Hudson
American Academy of Clinical Neurophysiology(21)

La Crosse
Orthopaedic Section - American Physical Therapy Association(568)

Lake Geneva
National Clay Pipe Institute(490)

Luxemburg
International Silo Association(386)

Madison
American Academy of Cosmetic Dentistry(21)
American Association for Cancer Education(33)
American College of Veterinary Pathologists(72)
The American Electrophoresis Society(80)
American Institute of the History of Pharmacy(97)
American Osteopathic Academy for Sports Medicine(111)
American Society of Agronomy(133)
American Society of Preventive Oncology(145)
Association for the Advancement of Applied Sport Psychology(179)
Association of Arts Administration Educators(186)
Association of Family and Conciliation Courts(196)
Association of Physician Assistants in Obstetrics and Gynecology(208)
Association of State Floodplain Managers(216)
Credit Union Executives Society(279)
Credit Union National Association(279)
Crop Science Society of America(279)
Forest Products Society(310)
International Association of Industrial Accident Boards and Commissions(358)
International Dairy-Deli-Bakery Association(369)
International Neural Network Society(381)
International Society of Psychiatric Consultation Liaison Nurses(392)
International Society of Psychiatric-Mental Health Nurses(392)
Media Communications Association International(415)
National Association of Professors of Hebrew in American Institutions of Higher Learning(466)
National Conference of Bar Examiners(492)
National Mastitis Council(526)
North American Lake Management Society(557)
Preventive Cardiovascular Nurses Association(583)
Purebred Dairy Cattle Association(593)
Society for Psychophysiological Research(624)
Society for Research on Nicotine and Tobacco(625)
Society for the Study of Reproduction(628)
Society of Clinical and Medical Hair Removal(633)
Society of Neurological Surgeons(640)
Society of Wood Science and Technology(646)
Soil Science Society of America(647)
Transportation Development Association(664)
Women in the Fire Service(692)
Wood Truss Council of America(694)

Manitowish Waters
Institute for Briquetting and Agglomeration(339)

Mequon
Association of Lutheran Secondary Schools(203)

Merrill
North American Maple Syrup Council(558)

Middleton
Association of Booksellers for Children(188)
Music Library Association(423)

Milwaukee
Alliance for Children and Families(15)
American Academy of Allergy, Asthma, and Immunology(20)
American Academy of Emergency Medicine(22)
American Academy of Nursing(25)
American Association of Children's Residential Centers(39)
American Association of Dental Editors(41)
American Association of Medical Society Executives(45)
American College of Mohs Micrographic Surgery and Cutaneous Oncology(67)
American Malting Barley Association(102)
American Society for Aesthetics(126)
American Society for Experimental NeuroTherapeutics(129)
American Society for Quality(132)
American Society of Gene Therapy(138)
Association of Equipment Manufacturers(195)
Clinical Immunology Society(248)
Contractors Pump Bureau(264)
Federation of Environmental Technologists(303)
International Association for Orthodontics(351)
Movement Disorder Society(422)
National Association of Catholic Chaplains(442)
National Association of Credential Evaluation Services, Inc.(447)
National Association of Service Managers(472)
National Fluid Power Association(511)
Nine to Five, National Association of Working Women(553)
North American Cartographic Information Society(555)
Polyurethane Manufacturers Association(580)
Scoliosis Research Society(606)
Society for Clinical Data Management(615)
Society of Behavioral Medicine(632)
Society of Risk Management Consultants(643)
World Allergy Organization - IACCI(695)

Muskego
Lambda Kappa Sigma(405)

Neenah
World Umpires Association(696)

Nekoosa
Delta Sigma Delta(282)

Oak Creek
Information Systems Security Association(338)
NaSPA: the Network and System Professionals Association(425)
National Reading Conference(535)

Oconomowoc
Association of Food Journalists(197)

Onalaska
Council on Chiropractic Orthopedics(275)

Oregon
Archery Range and Retailers Organization(160)

Oshkosh
National Association of Flight Instructors(453)

Pewaukee
Society for Chaos Theory in Psychology and Life Sciences(615)

Plover
National Association for Retail Marketing Services(436)

Racine
Carwash Owner's and Supplier's Association(238)
International Association of Tool Craftsmen(361)
National Association of Sports Officials(472)

River Falls
American Forensic Association(85)
Immigration and Ethnic History Society(332)
International Listening Association(378)

Shawano
Network of Executive Women in Hospitality(551)

Spooner
International Association of Natural Resource Pilots(359)

Stevens Point
National Wellness Institute(549)

Stoughton
Associated Church Press(164)

Verona
National Dairy Herd Improvement Association(504)
United States National Committee of the International Dairy Federation(676)

Waterloo
National Association of Fraternal Insurance Counsellors(454)

Waukesha
NIBA - The Belting Association(553)

Waupun
American Correctional Chaplains Association(74)

Wausau
American Society for Laser Medicine and Surgery(130)

West Allis
International Society for Ecological Economics(387)

WYOMING

Basin
Aviation Maintenance Foundation International(225)

Buffalo
National Association of State Veterans Homes(477)

Cheyenne
North American Agricultural Marketing Officials(554)

Cody
American Custom Gunmakers Guild(77)
American Knife and Tool Institute(100)
Dude Ranchers' Association(288)

Sheridan
Association for the Advancement of International Education(179)

2007 National Trade and Professional Associations

Budget Index

Every organization that has provided annual budget data will be found in one of the fourteen categories below, from Under $10,000 to Over $100 Million.

Over $100,000,000

American Association of Retired Persons(50)
American Bar Association(56)
American Bureau of Shipping(59)
American Cancer Society(60)
American Chemical Society(62)
American Diabetes Association(79)
American Heart Association(90)
American Institute of Certified Public Accountants(95)
American Medical Association(104)
American Society of Composers, Authors and Publishers(136)
Association of Pet Dog Trainers(207)
Blue Cross and Blue Shield Association(231)
College of American Pathologists(251)
Coordinating Research Council(265)
Gas Technology Institute(314)
Institute of Electrical and Electronics Engineers(341)
International Association of Machinists and Aerospace Workers(359)
International Union, United Automobile, Aerospace and Agricultural Implement Workers of America(396)
MasterCard International(413)
National Academy of Sciences(427)
National Association of Mutual Insurance Companies(462)
National Association of Securities Dealers(471)
National Collegiate Athletic Association(491)
National Council of the Churches of Christ in the U.S.A.(501)
National Council on Compensation Insurance(502)
National Education Association(506)
National Marrow Donor Program(526)
National Rifle Association of America(536)
National Rural Electric Cooperative Association(537)
Service Employees International Union(609)
United States Tennis Association(677)
Universities Research Association(679)

$50-100,000,000

Air Line Pilots Association, International(13)
American Academy of Family Physicians(22)
American Academy of Pediatrics(27)
American Arbitration Association(32)
American Bankers Association(55)
American Councils for International Education(76)
American Dental Association(78)
American Federation of Teachers(82)
American Hospital Association(92)
American Institute of Architects(94)
American Institute of Physics(97)
American Petroleum Institute(114)
American Psychological Association(118)
American Society of Mechanical Engineers(141)
Association of American Medical Colleges(184)
Association of Real Estate License Law Officials(211)
ATP(221)
Cast Stone Institute(238)
CFA Institute(242)
Communications Workers of America(255)
Computing Technology Industry Association(258)
Cookie and Snack Bakers Association(265)
Edison Electric Institute(289)
Graduate Management Admission Council(319)
Institute of Nuclear Power Operations(343)
International Brotherhood of Teamsters, AFL-CIO(363)
Laborers' International Union of North America(404)
National Association of Insurance Commissioners(458)
National Association of Letter Carriers(460)
National Association of REALTORS(468)
National Cattlemen's Beef Association(488)
National Federation of Independent Business(509)
National Fire Protection Association(510)
National Multiple Sclerosis Society(528)
New York Board of Trade(552)
Project Management Institute(590)
SAE International(604)
Society for Human Resource Management(619)
United Brotherhood of Carpenters and Joiners of America(670)
United States Chamber of Commerce(674)
United States Pharmacopeia(676)
Western Writers of America(688)

$25-50,000,000

Academy of Motion Picture Arts and Sciences(4)
Aircraft Owners and Pilots Association(14)
American Academy of Orthopaedic Surgeons(26)
American Association for Cancer Research(34)
American Association of Motor Vehicle Administrators(45)
American Chemistry Council(62)
American College of Cardiology(64)
American College of Obstetricians and Gynecologists(68)
American College of Physicians(69)
American College of Surgeons(71)
American Council of Life Insurers(75)
American Council on Education(76)
American Dietetic Association(79)
American Federation of Television and Radio Artists(83)
American Forest and Paper Association(85)
American Gas Association(86)
American Iron and Steel Institute(98)
American Library Association(101)
American Lung Association(102)
American Metalcasting Consortium(105)
American Physical Society(115)
American Plastics Council(116)
American Psychiatric Association(117)
American Quarter Horse Association(120)
American Society for Microbiology(130)
American Society for Quality(132)
American Society of Civil Engineers(135)
American Society of Health-System Pharmacists(139)
American Soybean Association(148)
American Speech-Language-Hearing Association(148)
American Trucking Associations(152)
APICS - The Association for Operations Management(158)
Association for Computing Machinery(170)
Association for Supervision and Curriculum Development(178)
Association of American Railroads(185)
ASTM International(221)
Biotechnology Industry Organization(229)
Credit Union National Association(279)
Direct Marketing Association(285)
ECRI(288)
Electronic Industries Alliance(292)
Food Marketing Institute(309)
IEEE Computer Society(331)
International Brotherhood of Boilermakers, Iron Ship Builders, Blacksmiths, Forgers and Helpers(363)
International Council of Shopping Centers(368)
International Masonry Institute(379)
Investment Company Institute(398)
Ladies Professional Golf Association(404)
LIMRA International(408)
Mortgage Bankers Association(421)
National Association of Broadcasters(441)
National Association of Chain Drug Stores(442)
National Association of Convenience Stores(446)
National Association of Home Builders(456)
National Cable & Telecommunications Association(486)
National Council on the Aging(503)
National Futures Association(513)
National Insurance Crime Bureau(522)

National Kidney Foundation(523)
National Marine Manufacturers Association(526)
National Pork Producers Council(533)
National Restaurant Association(536)
National Safety Council(538)
Newspaper Association of America(552)
Nuclear Energy Institute(563)
Portland Cement Association(581)
Professional Association of Diving Instructors(585)
Professional Rodeo Cowboys Association(589)
Radiological Society of North America(594)
Screen Actors Guild(606)
Semiconductor Equipment and Materials International(608)
Society of Manufacturing Engineers(639)
United Soybean Board(672)
United States Conference of Catholic Bishops(674)
United States Golf Association(675)
United States Soccer Federation(677)
Urban Land Institute(680)
USA Poultry and Egg Export Council(681)

$10-25,000,000

AABB(1)
Academy of General Dentistry(3)
Actors' Equity Association(8)
Advanced Medical Technology Association(8)
AeA - Advancing the Business of Technology(9)
Air Force Association(13)
Air Transport Association of America(13)
Alliance for Telecommunications Industry Solutions(16)
Alliance of Automobile Manufacturers(16)
America's Community Bankers(19)
America's Health Insurance Plans(19)
American Academy of Allergy, Asthma, and Immunology(20)
American Academy of Dermatology(21)
American Academy of Neurology(25)
American Academy of Ophthalmology(25)
American Academy of Otolaryngology-Head and Neck Surgery(26)
American Academy of Physician Assistants(27)
American Association for Clinical Chemistry(34)
American Association of Advertising Agencies(37)
American Association of Critical-Care Nurses(41)
American Association of Homes and Services for the Aging(43)
American Association of Individual Investors(44)
American Association of Neurological Surgeons(46)
American Association of Oral and Maxillofacial Surgeons(47)
American Association of Orthodontists(47)
American Association of Petroleum Geologists(47)
American Association of Pharmaceutical Scientists(48)
American Association of School Administrators(50)
American College of Chest Physicians(64)
American College of Emergency Physicians(65)
American College of Healthcare Executives(66)
American College of Radiology(70)
American Council of Engineering Companies(75)
American Egg Board(80)
American Farm Bureau Federation(81)
American Federation of State, County and Municipal Employees(82)
American Gastroenterological Association(86)
American Geophysical Union(87)
American Health Care Association(89)
American Health Information Management Association(89)
American Hotel & Lodging Association(92)
American Industrial Hygiene Association(93)
American Institute for CPCU - Insurance Institute of America(93)
American Institute of Aeronautics and Astronautics(94)
American Institute of Chemical Engineers(95)
American Insurance Association(98)
American Kennel Club(100)
American Marketing Association(103)
American Massage Therapy Association(103)
American Mathematical Society(103)
American National Standards Institute(108)
American Nurses Association(109)
American Occupational Therapy Association(109)
American Optometric Association(110)
American Osteopathic Association(111)
American Paint Horse Association(112)
American Payroll Association(113)
American Physical Therapy Association(115)
American Physiological Society(115)
American Planning Association(116)
American Podiatric Medical Association(116)
American Postal Workers Union(117)
American Public Health Association(119)
American Public Transportation Association(120)
American Society for Biochemistry and Molecular Biology(126)
American Society for Clinical Pathology(127)
American Society for Engineering Education(128)
American Society for Training and Development(133)
American Society of Anesthesiologists(134)
American Society of Association Executives & Center for Association Leadership(134)
American Society of Cataract and Refractive Surgery(135)
American Society of Clinical Oncology(136)
American Society of Heating, Refrigerating and Air-Conditioning Engineers(139)
American Society of Hematology(139)
American Society of Interior Designers(140)
American Society of Radiologic Technologists(145)
American Society of Travel Agents(146)
American Thoracic Society(151)
American Urological Association(153)
American Veterinary Medical Association(153)
American Water Works Association(154)
American Welding Society(154)
Americans for the Arts(156)
AMT - The Association For Manufacturing Technology(156)
AORN(158)
APA - The Engineered Wood Association(158)
Appraisal Institute(159)
Arabian Horse Association(160)
ASM International(163)
Associated Builders and Contractors(164)
Associated General Contractors of America(165)
Association for Financial Professionals(173)
Association for Information and Image Management International(174)
Association of Christian Schools International(190)
Association of Flight Attendants - CWA(197)
Association of the United States Army(218)
Association of Trial Lawyers of America(218)
Audit Bureau of Circulations(222)
Automotive Industry Action Group(223)
BICSI(228)
BPA Worldwide(232)
Brotherhood of Locomotive Engineers and Trainmen(233)
Can Manufacturers Institute(237)
Catholic Health Association of the United States(240)
CCIM Institute(240)
Chemical Heritage Foundation(243)
Child Welfare League of America(244)
CIIT Centers for Health Research(247)
Copper Development Association(266)
Cosmetic, Toiletry and Fragrance Association(267)
Cotton Council International(267)
Council for Adult and Experiential Learning(267)
Council for Advancement and Support of Education(267)
Council of Better Business Bureaus(271)
Council of Chief State School Officers(271)
Council of Insurance Agents and Brokers(272)
Council of State Governments(275)
Council on Foundations(276)
Credit Union Executives Society(279)
CTIA - The Wireless Association(280)
Distilled Spirits Council of the U.S.(286)
Edison Welding Institute(289)
EDUCAUSE(290)
Employee Relocation Council/Worldwide ERC(293)
Endocrine Society(294)
Federation of American Socs. for Experimental Biology(303)
Federation of State Medical Boards of the United States(304)
Financial Planning Association(306)
Food Products Association(309)
Gemological Institute of America(315)
Golf Course Superintendents Association of America(318)
Healthcare Financial Management Association(324)
Healthcare Information and Management Systems Society(324)
Holstein Association USA(327)
IEEE Communications Society(330)
Independent Community Bankers of America(333)
Independent Insurance Agents and Brokers of America(334)
InfoCom International(338)
Information Systems Audit and Control Association(338)
Institute for Supply Management(340)
Institute of Food Technologists(341)
Institute of Internal Auditors(342)
Institute of International Finance(342)
Institute of Management Accountants(342)
Institute of Medicine(343)
Institute of Paper Science and Technology(343)
Institute of Real Estate Management(343)
Insurance Institute for Highway Safety(345)
International Alliance of Technology Integrators(348)
International Association of Amusement Parks and Attractions(352)
International Association of Bridge, Structural, Ornamental and Reinforcing Iron Workers(354)
International Association of Fire Fighters(357)
International Association of Plumbing and Mechanical Officials(360)
International City/County Management Association(365)
International Copper Association(367)
International Foundation of Employee Benefit Plans(373)
International Reading Association(384)
International Union of Electronic, Electrical, Salaried, Machine, and Furniture Workers-CWA(395)
International Union of Operating Engineers(395)
International Union of Painters and Allied Trades(396)
IPC - Association Connecting Electronics Industries(399)
ISA(400)
Livestock Marketing Association(409)
LOMA(409)
Material Handling Industry of America(414)
Medical Group Management Association(416)
Meeting Professionals International(416)
Military Officers Association of America(419)
Mortgage Insurance Companies of America(421)

$5-10,000,000

Broadcast Designers' Association(233)
Brotherhood of Maintenance of Way Employees(233)
Building Owners and Managers Association International(234)
Cable & Telecommunications Association for Marketing(236)
CBA(240)
Chlorine Chemistry Council(245)
Christian Medical & Dental Associations(246)
Communications Supply Service Association(255)
Community Transportation Association of America(256)
Construction Specifications Institute(263)
Consumer Bankers Association(263)
Consumer Data Industry Association(263)
Consumer Healthcare Products Association(263)
CoreNet Global(266)
Council for Christian Colleges and Universities(268)
Council for Exceptional Children(268)
Council of Residential Specialists(274)
Council of Supply Chain Management Professionals(275)
CPCU Society(278)
Craft & Hobby Association(278)
CropLife America(279)
Cruise Lines International Association(280)
Custom Electronic Design and Installation Association(280)
Data Interchange Standards Association(281)
Defense Research Institute(282)
Delta Dental Plans Association(282)
Direct Selling Association(285)
Document Management Industries Association(286)
Door and Hardware Institute(287)
Emergency Nurses Association(293)
Engine Manufacturers Association(295)
Environmental Industry Associations(296)
Equipment Leasing Association of America(297)
Fabricators and Manufacturers Association, International(300)
Federation of American Hospitals(303)
Federation of State Boards of Physical Therapy(304)
Financial Executives International(305)
Financial Services Roundtable(306)
Gas Appliance Manufacturers Association(314)
General Merchandise Distributors Council(315)
Geological Society of America(315)
Girls Incorporated(317)
Glass, Molders, Pottery, Plastics and Allied Workers International Union(317)
Global Health Council(317)
Government Finance Officers Association of the United States and Canada(318)
Graphic Arts Technical Foundation(319)
Greater Washington Board of Trade(320)
Grocery Manufacturers Association(320)
Health Forum(323)
Health Industry Distributors Association(323)
Healthcare Distribution Management Association(323)
Heart Rhythm Society(324)
Helicopter Association International(325)
IEEE Signal Processing Society(331)
Independent Film and Television Alliance(334)
Independent Sector(336)
Industrial Fabrics Association International(336)
Infectious Diseases Society of America(338)
Information Technology Association of America(338)
Institute for Operations Research and the Management Sciences(339)
Institute of Industrial Engineers(341)
Institute of Scrap Recycling Industries(343)
Institute of Transportation Engineers(344)
Insurance Information Institute(345)
Intelligent Transportation Society of America(345)
Inter-Industry Conference on Auto Collision Repair(346)
International Association of Chiefs of Police(354)
International Brotherhood of Electrical Workers(363)
International Facility Management Association(371)
International Food Information Council(372)
International Foodservice Manufacturers Association(372)
International Franchise Association(373)
International Health, Racquet and Sportsclub Association(374)
International Housewares Association(375)
International Lead Zinc Research Organization(377)
International Longshoremen's Association, AFL-CIO(378)
International Sleep Products Association(386)
International Society for Technology in Education(389)
International Trademark Association(394)
International Union of Bricklayers and Allied Craftsworkers(395)
Interstate Natural Gas Association of America(398)
Investment Management Consultants Association(399)
ISSA(400)
Magazine Publishers of America(409)
Manufacturers Alliance/MAPI(411)
Marine Engineers Beneficial Association(412)
Mechanical Contractors Association of America(415)
Metal Service Center Institute(417)
Modern Language Association of America(420)
Motion Picture Association(421)
Motion Picture Association of America(421)
Motorcycle Safety Foundation(422)
NACHA - The Electronic Payments Association(424)
NAFSA: Association of International Educators(424)
National Active and Retired Federal Employees Association(427)
National American Indian Housing Council(430)
National Apartment Association(430)
National Association for College Admission Counseling(432)
National Association for Printing Leadership(435)
National Association for the Education of Young Children(436)
National Association of Broadcast Employees and Technicians - Communications Workers of America(441)
National Association of Business Consultants(441)
National Association of Children's Hospitals(443)
National Association of College and University Business Officers(444)
National Association of County and City Health Officials(447)
National Association of Electrical Distributors(450)
National Association of Federal Credit Unions(452)
National Association of Health Underwriters(455)
National Association of Housing and Redevelopment Officials(456)
National Association of Industrial and Office Properties(458)
National Association of Real Estate Investment Trusts(468)
National Association of Regulatory Utility Commissioners(469)
National Association of Tax Professionals(478)
National Association of Wholesaler-Distributors(481)
National Athletic Trainers' Association(482)
National Basketball Association(483)
National Beer Wholesalers Association(484)
National Black MBA Association(484)
National Board of Boiler and Pressure Vessel Inspectors(485)
National Catholic Educational Association(487)
National Community Pharmacists Association(491)
National Conference of Bar Examiners(492)
National Cooperative Business Association(496)
National Cotton Council of America(496)
National Council on Crime and Delinquency(502)
National Court Reporters Association(503)
National Football League(511)
National Foundation for Credit Counseling(512)
National Funeral Directors Association(513)
National Glass Association(513)
National Ground Water Association(515)
National Head Start Association(516)
National Hemophilia Foundation(516)
National Hockey League(517)
National Industries for the Blind(519)
National Institute of Building Sciences(520)
National Kitchen and Bath Association(523)
National League for Nursing(523)
National Medical Association(526)
National Mental Health Association(527)
National Paint and Coatings Association(531)
National Potato Promotion Board(533)
National Precast Concrete Association(534)
National Propane Gas Association(534)
National Ready Mixed Concrete Association(535)
National Recreation and Parks Association(535)
National Retail Federation(536)
National Society of Professional Engineers(542)
National Stone, Sand and Gravel Association(543)
National Tour Association(546)
New York Stock Exchange(552)
North American Die Casting Association(556)
Opportunity Finance Network(565)
Organization for Tropical Studies(567)
Osborne Association(569)
PCIA - the Wireless Industry Association(572)
Pharmaceutical Care Management Association(575)
Photo Marketing Association-International(576)
POPAI The Global Association for Marketing at Retail(580)
Potash & Phosphate Institute(581)
Precast/Prestressed Concrete Institute(582)
Precision Metalforming Association(583)
Private Label Manufacturers Association(584)
Professional Bowlers Association of America(586)
Professional Photographers of America(588)
Property Loss Research Bureau(591)
Public Relations Society of America(593)
Radio Advertising Bureau(594)
Recreation Vehicle Industry Association(596)
Retail Industry Leaders Association(601)
Retail, Wholesale and Department Store Union(601)
Risk and Insurance Management Society(602)
Satellite Broadcasting and Communications Association(605)
School Nutrition Association(606)
School, Home and Office Products Association(606)
Semiconductor Industry Association(608)
Sheet Metal and Air Conditioning Contractors' National Association(610)
Sheet Metal Workers' International Association(610)
Society for Applied Learning Technology(614)
Society for Environmental Graphic Design(617)
Society for Industrial and Applied Mathematics(619)
Society for Neuroscience(622)
Society of American Florists(630)
Society of Exploration Geophysicists(636)
Society of Financial Service Professionals(636)

Society of Nuclear Medicine(641)
Society of Plastics Engineers(642)
Society of Women Engineers(646)
Special Libraries Association(649)
Specialty Graphic Imaging Association(650)
Sugar Association(655)
Synthetic Organic Chemical Manufacturers Association(657)
Television Bureau of Advertising(659)
Toy Industry Association(662)
Transport Workers Union of America(663)
U.S. Lacrosse(668)
United Association of Journeymen and Apprentices of the Plumbing and Pipe Fitting Industry of U.S. and Canada(670)
United Food and Commercial Workers International Union(671)
United Mine Workers of America International Union(672)
United States Conference of Mayors(674)
United States Council for International Business(674)
United States Energy Association(675)
United States Equestrian Federation(675)
United States Professional Tennis Association(676)
United States Telecom Association(677)
United States Trotting Association(678)
Vision Council of America(684)
Wine and Spirits Wholesalers of America(689)
Wire Association International(690)
World Floor Covering Association(695)
World Gold Council(696)
World Shoe Association(696)

$2-5,000,000

AACC International(1)
AACSB - the Association to Advance Collegiate Schools of Business(1)
ACA International, The Association of Credit and Collection Professionals(2)
Academy of Managed Care Pharmacy(4)
Academy of Osseointegration(5)
Accreditation Association for Ambulatory Health Care(6)
Accrediting Council for Independent Colleges and Schools(7)
Acoustical Society of America(7)
ACPA - College Student Educators Association(7)
Advertising Council(9)
Advertising Research Foundation(9)
AFCOM(10)
AFSM International(11)
AFT Healthcare(11)
Air and Waste Management Association(12)
AIR Commercial Real Estate Association(12)
Air Force Sergeants Association(13)
Air Movement and Control Association International(13)
Air Traffic Control Association(13)
Aircraft Electronics Association(14)
Airports Council International/North America(15)
Alexander Graham Bell Association for the Deaf and Hard of Hearing(15)
Alliance for Children and Families(15)
America's Blood Centers(19)
American Academy of Arts & Sciences(20)
American Academy of Audiology(20)
American Academy of Child and Adolescent Psychiatry(20)
American Academy of Cosmetic Surgery(21)
American Academy of Forensic Sciences(23)
American Academy of Nurse Practitioners(25)
American Academy of Optometry(25)
American Academy of Pain Management(26)
American Academy of Physical Medicine and Rehabilitation(27)
American Accounting Association(29)
American Advertising Federation(29)
American Alliance for Health, Physical Education, Recreation and Dance(30)
American Angus Association(31)
American Antiquarian Society(31)
American Apparel & Footwear Association(31)
American Association for Artificial Intelligence(33)
American Association for Geriatric Psychiatry(35)
American Association for Homecare(35)
American Association for Laboratory Animal Science(35)
American Association for Marriage and Family Therapy(36)
American Association for Medical Transcription(36)
American Association of Airport Executives(38)
American Association of Colleges for Teacher Education(40)
American Association of Colleges of Osteopathic Medicine(40)
American Association of Colleges of Pharmacy(40)
American Association of Collegiate Registrars and Admissions Officers(40)
American Association of Endodontists(42)
American Association of Equine Practitioners(42)
American Association of Family and Consumer Sciences(43)
American Association of Law Libraries(44)
American Association of Occupational Health Nurses(47)
American Association of Physician Specialists(48)
American Association of Physics Teachers(48)
American Association of Professional Landmen(49)
American Association of Textile Chemists and Colorists(53)
American Association of University Professors(53)
American Association on Mental Retardation(54)
American Bakers Association(55)
American Benefits Council(56)
American Board of Medical Specialties(57)
American Business Media(60)
American Business Women's Association(60)
American Camp Association(60)
American Chamber of Commerce Executives(61)
American Choral Directors Association(62)
American College Health Association(63)
American College of Clinical Pharmacy(65)
American College of Foot and Ankle Surgeons(66)
American College of Nurse-Midwives(68)
American College of Occupational and Environmental Medicine(68)
American College of Osteopathic Family Physicians(69)
American College of Physician Executives(69)
American College of Prosthodontists(70)
American College of Trial Lawyers(71)
American College of Veterinary Internal Medicine(71)
American Composites Manufacturers Association(72)
American Conference of Governmental Industrial Hygienists(73)
American Council of Learned Societies(75)
American Council on the Teaching of Foreign Languages(76)
American Craft Council(77)
American Culinary Federation(77)
American Economic Association(80)
American Educational Research Association(80)
American Federation for Medical Research(82)
American Federation of Government Employees(82)
American Federation of Police and Concerned Citizens(82)
American Fence Association(83)
American Financial Services Association(83)
American Fisheries Society(84)
American Foreign Service Association(85)
American Frozen Food Institute(85)
American Gear Manufacturers Association(86)
American Gem Society(86)
American Gem Trade Association(86)
American Geriatrics Society(87)
American Guild of Musical Artists(88)
American Guild of Organists(88)
American Hardwood Export Council(89)
American Headache Society(89)
American Health Quality Association(89)
American Healthcare Radiology Administrators(90)
American Highway Users Alliance(90)
American Historical Association(91)
American Hockey League(91)
American Home Furnishings Alliance(91)
American Horticultural Society(91)
American Indian Science and Engineering Society(93)
American Institute of Biological Sciences(94)
American Institute of Food Distribution(96)
American Institute of Graphic Arts(96)
American Institute of Steel Construction(97)
American Institute of Ultrasound in Medicine(98)
American Intellectual Property Law Association(98)
American International Automobile Dealers Association(98)
American Jersey Cattle Association(99)
American Land Title Association(100)
American Logistics Association(102)
American Luggage Dealers Association(102)
American Machine Tool Distributors Association(102)
American Medical Directors Association(104)
American Medical Group Association(104)
American Medical Informatics Association(104)
American Medical Technologists(105)
American Medical Women's Association(105)
American Miniature Horse Association(106)
American Montessori Society(106)
American Morgan Horse Association(106)
American Moving and Storage Association(107)
American Nephrology Nurses Association(108)
American Neurological Association(108)
American Nursery and Landscape Association(109)
American Organization of Nurse Executives(110)
American Orthotic and Prosthetic Association(111)
American Pain Society(112)
American Peanut Council(113)
American Peanut Shellers Association(113)
American Pet Products Manufacturers Association(114)
American Phytopathological Society(115)
American Pilots' Association(115)
American Political Science Association(116)
American Probation and Parole Association(117)
American Psychiatric Nurses Association(118)
American Public Communications Council(119)
American Public Gas Association(119)
American Public Human Services Association(120)
American Registry of Diagnostic Medical Sonographers(122)
American School Counselor Association(124)
American Sheep Industry Association(125)
American Simmental Association(125)
American Society for Aesthetic Plastic Surgery(126)
American Society for Bone and Mineral Research(127)
American Society for Cell Biology(127)
American Society for Clinical Investigation(127)
American Society for Clinical Pharmacology and Therapeutics(127)
American Society for Horticultural Science(130)
American Society for Investigative Pathology(130)
American Society for Parenteral and Enteral Nutrition(131)

American Society for Photogrammetry and Remote Sensing(131)
American Society of Addiction Medicine(133)
American Society of Appraisers(134)
American Society of Echocardiography(137)
American Society of Home Inspectors(139)
American Society of Lipo-Suction Surgery(140)
American Society of Military Comptrollers(141)
American Society of Nuclear Cardiology(142)
American Society of Transplant Surgeons(146)
American Society of Transplantation(146)
American Society on Aging(147)
American Sociological Association(147)
American Sportfishing Association(148)
American Subcontractors Association(149)
American Sugar Cane League of the U.S.A.(150)
American Theological Library Association(151)
American Tort Reform Association(152)
American Translators Association(152)
American Waterways Operators(154)
American Wholesale Marketers Association(155)
American Wind Energy Association(155)
American Zoo and Aquarium Association(156)
Animal Health Institute(157)
AOAC International(158)
AOC(158)
Arthroscopy Association of North America(162)
ASABE - the Society for Engineering in Agricultural, Food and Biological Systems(162)
ASME International Gas Turbine Institute(163)
Asphalt Institute(163)
Associated Construction Publications(165)
Associated Equipment Distributors(165)
Association for Career and Technical Education(169)
Association for Corporate Growth(171)
Association for Enterprise Opportunity(172)
Association for Healthcare Philanthropy(173)
Association for Iron and Steel Technology(175)
Association for Manufacturing Excellence(176)
Association of Academic Health Centers(183)
Association of Air Medical Services(183)
Association of American Educators(184)
Association of American Geographers(184)
Association of American Law Schools(184)
Association of American Universities(185)
Association of Black Cardiologists(187)
Association of College and Research Libraries(190)
Association of College and University Housing Officers-International(191)
Association of Community College Trustees(192)
Association of Corporate Counsel(193)
Association of Cosmetologists and Hairdressers(193)
Association of Executive Search Consultants(196)
Association of Fish and Wildlife Agencies(197)
Association of Free Community Papers(198)
Association of Governing Boards of Universities and Colleges(199)
Association of Government Accountants(199)
Association of Higher Education Facilities Officers(199)
Association of Home Appliance Manufacturers(200)
Association of International Automobile Manufacturers(201)
Association of Millwork Distributors(205)
Association of National Advertisers(205)
Association of Occupational and Environmental Clinics(206)
Association of Oil Pipe Lines(206)
Association of Performing Arts Presenters(207)
Association of Progressive Rental Organizations(210)
Association of Public Health Laboratories(210)
Association of Public Television Stations(210)
Association of Public-Safety Communications Officers- International(211)
Association of Reproductive Health Professionals(212)
Association of Research Libraries(212)
Association of School Business Officials International(212)
Association of Science-Technology Centers(213)
Association of Social Work Boards(214)
Association of State and Provincial Psychology Boards(215)
Association of State and Territorial Health Officials(215)
Association of Surgical Technologists(216)
Association of the Wall and Ceiling Industries-International(218)
Association of Theological Schools in the United States and Canada(218)
Association of Universities for Research in Astronomy(219)
Association of University Technology Managers(219)
Association of Woodworking-Furnishings Suppliers(221)
Audio Engineering Society(222)
Automotive Recyclers Association(224)
AVS Science and Technology Society(225)
Awards and Recognition Association(225)
Beer Institute(227)
Billiard Congress of America(228)
Biophysical Society(229)
Bituminous Coal Operators Association(229)
Bowling Proprietors Association of America(231)
Brick Industry Association(232)
Building Owners and Managers Institute International(234)
Building Service Contractors Association International(234)
Business Technology Association(236)
Cabletelevision Advertising Bureau(236)
Career College Association(237)
Carpet and Rug Institute(238)
Case Management Society of America(238)
Casualty Actuarial Society(239)
Chain Drug Marketing Association(242)
Chamber Music America(242)
Chief Executives Organization(244)
Chlorine Institute(245)
Christian Legal Society(246)
Christian Schools International(246)
Chronic Disease Directors(246)
Cigar Association of America(247)
Clinical and Laboratory Standards Institute(248)
Clinical Laboratory Management Association(248)
Club Managers Association of America(249)
College and University Professional Association for Human Resources(250)
College Art Association(251)
Commercial Finance Association(253)
Commercial Real Estate Women Network(253)
Commission on Accreditation for Law Enforcement Agencies(254)
Committee of 200(254)
Community Associations Institute(255)
Community Financial Services Association of America(256)
Composite Panel Association(257)
Compressed Gas Association(257)
COMPTEL(257)
Computer Measurement Group(258)
Computing Research Association(258)
Concrete Reinforcing Steel Institute(259)
Conference of State Bank Supervisors(260)
Connected International Meeting Professionals Association(261)
Conservative Orthopaedics International Association(261)
Construction Financial Management Association(262)
Consumer Federation of America(263)
Consumer Specialty Products Association(263)
Council for Opportunity in Education(269)
Council for Professional Recognition(269)
Council for Responsible Nutrition(270)
Council of Graduate Schools(272)
Council of Independent Colleges(272)
Council of Institutional Investors(272)
Council of Real Estate Brokerage Managers(274)
Council of State and Territorial Epidemiologists(274)
Council of the Great City Schools(275)
Council on Social Work Education(277)
Council On State Taxation(277)
Delta Waterfowl Foundation(283)
Design-Build Institute of America(283)
Destination Marketing Association International(283)
Disease Management Association of America(285)
Distributive Education Clubs of America(286)
DRI International(287)
Ecological Society of America(288)
Educational Theatre Association(289)
Electric Power Supply Association(290)
Electrical Apparatus Service Association(290)
Electrochemical Society(291)
Electronic Retailing Association(292)
Electronic Transactions Association(292)
Employee Assistance Professionals Association(293)
Employee Benefit Research Institute(293)
EMTA - Trade Association for the Emerging Markets(294)
Enterprise Wireless Alliance(295)
Entomological Society of America(295)
ESOP Association(297)
Extra Touch Florists Association(300)
Family, Career, and Community Leaders of America(300)
Farm Credit Council(301)
Farmers Educational and Co-operative Union of America(301)
Federal Law Enforcement Officers Association(302)
Federated Ambulatory Surgery Association(303)
Federation of American Scientists(303)
Federation of Socs. for Coatings Technology(304)
Fertilizer Institute(305)
Fibre Box Association(305)
Financial and Insurance Conference Planners(305)
Financial Managers Society(306)
Flavor and Extract Manufacturers Association of the United States(307)
Fleet Reserve Association(307)
Flexible Packaging Association(307)
Flexographic Technical Association(308)
Flight Safety Foundation(308)
Food and Drug Law Institute(309)
Foundation for Russian-American Economic Cooperation(311)
French-American Chamber of Commerce(312)
Future Business Leaders of America-Phi Beta Lambda(313)
Futures Industry Association(313)
GAMA International(313)
Gases and Welding Distributors Association(314)
General Aviation Manufacturers Association(315)
Generic Pharmaceutical Association(315)
Geospatial Information Technology Association(316)
German American Chamber of Commerce(316)
Gerontological Society of America(316)
Graphic Communications Conference, IBT(319)
Health Care Compliance Association(322)
Hearth Patio & Barbecue Association(324)
Heavy Duty Manufacturers Association(325)
Hispanic Association of Colleges and Universities(325)
Home Furnishings International Association(327)
Hospitality Sales and Marketing Association International(329)
Household Goods Forwarders Association of America(329)
Ice Skating Institute(330)

National Contract Management Association(495)
National Corn Growers Association(496)
National Cosmetology Association(496)
National Council for Community Behavioral Healthcare(497)
National Council for Prescription Drug Programs(497)
National Council for the Social Studies(497)
National Council of Farmer Cooperatives(499)
National Council of State Housing Agencies(500)
National Council of Teachers of English(501)
National Crop Insurance Services(504)
National Cutting Horse Association(504)
National District Attorneys Association(505)
National Environmental Health Association(507)
National Federation of Federal Employees(509)
National Federation of State High School Associations(510)
National FFA Organization(510)
National Fire Sprinkler Association(511)
National Fisheries Institute(511)
National Foreign Trade Council(511)
National Frozen and Refrigerated Foods Association(513)
National Grain and Feed Association(514)
National Grocers Association(515)
National Guard Association of the U.S.(515)
National Hardwood Lumber Association(516)
National Hockey League Players' Association(517)
National Home Equity Mortgage Association(517)
National Home Furnishings Association(517)
National Hospice and Palliative Care Organization(517)
National Housing Conference(518)
National Independent Automobile Dealers Association(518)
National Institute of Governmental Purchasing(520)
National Intramural-Recreational Sports Association(522)
National League of Postmasters of the U.S.(524)
National Management Association(525)
National Milk Producers Federation(527)
National Motor Freight Traffic Association(527)
National Multi Housing Council(528)
National Nutritional Foods Association(529)
National Organization of Life and Health Insurance Guaranty Associations(530)
National Pest Management Association(532)
National Pharmaceutical Council(533)
National Private Truck Council(534)
National Reining Horse Association(535)
National Renderers Association(536)
National Rural Health Association(537)
National Sheriffs' Association(539)
National Soccer Coaches Association of America(540)
National Society of Accountants(541)
National Society of Hispanic MBAs(541)
National Speakers Association(542)
National Sporting Goods Association(543)
National Staff Development Council(543)
National Strength and Conditioning Association(543)
National Stroke Association(544)
National Student Nurses Association(544)
National Systems Contractors Association(545)
National Tank Truck Carriers Conference(545)
National Tooling and Machining Association(546)
National Truck Equipment Association(547)
National Utility Contractors Association(548)
National Venture Capital Association(548)
National Wood Flooring Association(550)
NATSO, Representing America's Travel Plazas and Truckstops(550)
Natural Gas Supply Association(550)
Newspaper Guild - CWA(552)
North American Association of Food Equipment Manufacturers(554)
North American Insulation Manufacturers Association(557)
North American Menopause Society(558)
North American Retail Dealers Association(559)
North American Securities Administrators Association(560)
North American Spine Society(561)
North American Technician Excellence(562)
NPES, The Association for Suppliers of Printing, Publishing and Converting Technologies(563)
NPTA Alliance(563)
Office and Professional Employees International Union(564)
Open Group(565)
OPERA America(565)
Operative Plasterers' and Cement Masons' International Association of the United States and Canada(565)
Organization of American Historians(567)
Original Equipment Suppliers Association(568)
Outdoor Advertising Association of America(569)
Outdoor Power Equipment Institute(569)
Owner-Operator Independent Drivers Association(570)
Packaging Machinery Manufacturers Institute(570)
Paint and Decorating Retailers Association(570)
Painting and Decorating Contractors of America(570)
PDA - an International Association for Pharmaceutical Science and Technology(572)
Pension Real Estate Association(573)
Petroleum Equipment Institute(574)
Petroleum Marketers Association of America(574)
Petroleum Technology Transfer Council(574)
Phi Delta Kappa(575)
Physician Insurers Association of America(577)
Plumbing Contractors of America(579)
Plumbing-Heating-Cooling Contractors - National Association(579)
PMA, the Independent Book Publishers Association(579)
Police Executive Research Forum(580)
Prevent Blindness America(583)
Producer's Guild of America(584)
Professional Beauty Association(586)
Professional Golfers Association of America(587)
Professional Liability Underwriting Society(588)
Professional Skaters Association(589)
Promotion Marketing Association(590)
Public Affairs Council(592)
Public Risk Management Association(593)
Radio-Television News Directors Association(594)
RCI, Inc.(595)
Real Estate Round Table(596)
Recreation Vehicle Dealers Association of North America(596)
Regulatory Affairs Professionals Society(598)
Reserve Officers Association of the U.S.(600)
Retail Tobacco Dealers of America(601)
Rubber Manufacturers Association(603)
Salon Association, The(605)
Seafarers' International Union(607)
Security Industry Association(607)
Security Traders Association(608)
Self Insurance Institute of America, Inc.(608)
Self Storage Association(608)
Silicones Environmental, Health and Safety Council of North America(610)
Skills USA(611)
Snack Food Association(612)
SnowSports Industries America(612)
Soap and Detergent Association(612)
SOCAP International(612)
Society for Biomolecular Sciences(614)
Society for College and University Planning(615)
Society for Conservation Biology(615)
Society for Imaging Informatics in Medicine(619)
Society for Information Display(620)
Society for Investigative Dermatology(620)
Society for Marketing Professional Services(621)
Society for Mining, Metallurgy, and Exploration(622)
Society for Research in Child Development(624)
Society for Technical Communication(626)
Society of American Foresters(630)
Society of American Gastrointestinal and Endoscopic Surgeons(630)
Society of Biblical Literature(632)
Society of Cable Telecommunications Engineers(632)
Society of Competitive Intelligence Professionals(633)
Society of Corporate Secretaries and Governance Professionals(634)
Society of Decorative Painters(635)
Society of Diagnostic Medical Sonography(635)
Society of Environmental Toxicology and Chemistry(635)
Society of Eye Surgeons(636)
Society of Gynecologic Oncologists(638)
Society of Incentive & Travel Executives(638)
Society of Independent Gasoline Marketers of America(638)
Society of Industrial and Office REALTORS(638)
Society of Interventional Radiology(639)
Society of Motion Picture and Television Engineers(640)
Society of Naval Architects and Marine Engineers(640)
Society of Teachers of Family Medicine(644)
Society of Toxicology(645)
Software and Information Industry Association(646)
Specialized Carriers and Rigging Association(649)
Specialty Coffee Association of America(650)
Specialty Equipment Market Association(650)
Specialty Tool and Fastener Distributors Association(650)
Specialty Vehicle Institute of America(650)
SSPC: the Society for Protective Coatings(652)
Strategic Account Management Association(654)
Surety Association of America(656)
SWANA - Solid Waste Association of North America(656)
Tax Executives Institute(657)
Teachers of English to Speakers of Other Languages(658)
Technology and Maintenance Council of American Trucking Associations(658)
Tennessee Walking Horse Breeders and Exhibitors Association(659)
Textile Rental Services Association of America(660)
The National Industrial Transportation League(519)
Transportation Institute(664)
Travel Goods Association(665)
Tree Care Industry Association(665)
Truck Renting and Leasing Association(666)
Trucking Management(666)
Truckload Carriers Association(666)
Turnaround Management Association(667)
U.S.-ASEAN Business Council(668)
Uniform and Textile Service Association(669)
Union of American Physicians and Dentists(670)
United Electrical, Radio and Machine Workers of America(671)
United Farm Workers of America(671)
United Fresh Fruit and Vegetable Association(671)
United Fresh Produce Association(671)
United Motorcoach Association(672)
United Producers(672)
United States Junior Chamber of Commerce(676)
United States Parachute Association(676)

United States Rowing Association(677)
United States-China Business Council(678)
United Telecom Council(679)
United Transportation Union(679)
United Union of Roofers, Waterproofers and Allied Workers(679)
Utility Workers Union of America(681)
Video Software Dealers Association(683)
Vinyl Institute(683)
Visiting Nurse Associations of America(684)
Warehousing Education and Research Council(685)
Water Quality Association(686)
Welding Research Council(687)
Window and Door Manufacturers Association(689)
Wireless Communications Association International(690)
Women in Cable and Telecommunications(691)
Women's Foodservice Forum(693)
World Airline Entertainment Association(695)
World Association for Infant Mental Health(695)
Writers Guild of America, East(697)
WTA Tour(697)
Xplor International(698)

$1-2,000,000

AACE International(1)
Academy of Management(4)
AcademyHealth(6)
Accrediting Council for Continuing Education and Training(7)
Adhesive and Sealant Council(8)
ADSC: The International Association of Foundation Drilling(8)
AERA - Engine Rebuilders Association(9)
AGN International - North America(11)
Agricultural Retailers Association(12)
Alliance for Continuing Medical Education(15)
Alliance for Nonprofit Management(15)
Alpha Gamma Rho(17)
Aluminum Extruders Council(18)
Ambulatory Pediatric Association(19)
American Academy of Disability Evaluating Physicians(22)
American Academy of Emergency Medicine(22)
American Academy of Facial Plastic and Reconstructive Surgery(22)
American Academy of Implant Dentistry(23)
American Academy of Medical Administrators(24)
American Academy of Orthotists and Prosthetists(26)
American Academy of Pain Medicine(26)
American Academy of Religion(28)
American Academy of Sleep Medicine(28)
American Agricultural Economics Association(30)
American Ambulance Association(30)
American Architectural Manufacturers Association(32)
American Association for Dental Research(34)
American Association for State and Local History(36)
American Association of Cardiovascular and Pulmonary Rehabilitation(39)
American Association of Christian Schools(39)
American Association of Colleges of Nursing(40)
American Association of Cosmetology Schools(41)
American Association of Engineering Societies(42)
American Association of Exporters and Importers(42)
American Association of Managing General Agents(45)
American Association of Medical Assistants(45)
American Association of Neuromuscular & Electrodiagnostic Medicine(46)
American Association of Port Authorities(49)
American Association of Preferred Provider Organizations(49)
American Association of Teachers of German(52)
American Association of Veterinary State Boards(54)
American Boarding Kennels Association(58)
American Boat and Yacht Council(58)
American Burn Association(60)
American Business Conference(60)
American Chemical Society - Rubber Division(62)
American Cocoa Research Institute(63)
American College for Advancement in Medicine(63)
American College of Cardiovascular Administrators(64)
American College of Contingency Planners(65)
American College of Forensic Examiners(66)
American College of Gastroenterology(66)
American College of Managed Care Administrators(67)
American College of Medical Genetics(67)
American College of Medical Practice Executives(67)
American College of Musicians(67)
American College of Osteopathic Emergency Physicians(69)
American College of Osteopathic Internists(69)
American College of Osteopathic Surgeons(69)
American College of Preventive Medicine(70)
American College of Psychiatrists(70)
American College of Radiation Oncology(70)
American College of Veterinary Surgeons(72)
American Concrete Pipe Association(73)
American Council of Independent Laboratories(75)
American Council of the Blind(76)
American Council on Science and Health(76)
American Dairy Goat Association(77)
American Dairy Science Association(78)
American Dental Assistants Association(78)
American Electroplaters and Surface Finishers Society(80)
American Epilepsy Society(81)
American Fiber Manufacturers Association(83)
American Fire Sprinkler Association(84)
American Forest Resource Council(85)
American Gelbvieh Association(86)
American Greyhound Track Operators Association(87)
American Helicopter Society International(90)
American Historical Association(91)
American International Charolais Association(98)
American Jail Association(99)
American Jewish Historical Society(99)
American Judicature Society(99)
American Laryngological, Rhinological and Otological Society(100)
American Legend Cooperative(101)
American Lighting Association(101)
American Maine-Anjou Association(102)
American Medical Rehabilitation Providers Association(104)
American Medical Student Association(105)
American Medical Writers Association(105)
American Mental Health Counselors Association(105)
American Network of Community Options and Resources(108)
American Numismatic Society(109)
American Orthopaedic Association(110)
American Orthopaedic Foot and Ankle Society(111)
American Orthopaedic Society for Sports Medicine(111)
American Physical Therapy Association - Private Practice Section(115)
American Psychoanalytic Association(118)
American Psychological Society(119)
American Railway Engineering and Maintenance of Way Association(121)
American Recovery Association(122)
American Saddlebred Horse Association(123)
American School Health Association(124)
American Seed Trade Association(124)
American Shetland Pony Club/American Miniature Horse Registry(125)
American Short Line and Regional Railroad Association(125)
American Society for Blood and Marrow Transplantation(127)
American Society for Clinical Laboratory Science(127)
American Society for Colposcopy and Cervical Pathology(127)
American Society for Enology and Viticulture(128)
American Society for Healthcare Human Resources Administration(129)
American Society for Healthcare Risk Management(129)
American Society for Histocompatability and Immunogenetics(130)
American Society for Mass Spectrometry(130)
American Society for Nutrition(131)
American Society for Public Administration(132)
American Society of Animal Science(134)
American Society of Cinematographers(135)
American Society of Colon and Rectal Surgeons(136)
American Society of Concrete Contractors(136)
American Society of Farm Managers and Rural Appraisers(137)
American Society of Human Genetics(139)
American Society of International Law(140)
American Society of Media Photographers(141)
American Society of Naval Engineers(142)
American Society of Newspaper Editors(142)
American Society of PeriAnesthesia Nurses(144)
American Society of Plumbing Engineers(144)
American Society of Regional Anesthesia and Pain Medicine(145)
American Society of Tropical Medicine and Hygiene(147)
American Solar Energy Society(147)
American Swimming Coaches Association(150)
American Teleservices Association(151)
American Thyroid Association(151)
American Tinnitus Association(151)
American Train Dispatchers Association(152)
American Trauma Society(152)
American Urogynecologic Society(153)
American Volleyball Coaches Association(153)
American Water Resources Association(154)
American Wood Preservers Institute(155)
Amusement and Music Operators Association(156)
Anxiety Disorders Association of America(157)
Aquatic Exercise Association(159)
Architectural Woodwork Institute(160)
ASFE/The Best People on Earth(162)
Asian American Journalists Association(162)
Asphalt Roofing Manufacturers Association(163)
Aspirin Foundation of America(164)
Associated Locksmiths of America(165)
Associated Professional Sleep Socs.(166)
Association for Advancement of Behavior Therapy(167)
Association for Asian Studies(167)
Association for Assessment and Accreditation of Laboratory Animal Care International(168)
Association for Childhood Education International(169)
Association for Conflict Resolution(170)
Association for Educational Communications and Technology(172)
Association for Facilities Engineering(172)
Association for Healthcare Resource and Materials Management(174)
Association for Information Systems(175)
Association for Institutional Research(175)
Association for Maximum Service Television(176)
Association for Postal Commerce(177)
Association for Work Process Improvement(183)

Association of Alternative Newsweeklies(184)
Association of American University Presses(185)
Association of American Veterinary Medical Colleges(186)
Association of Children's Museums(189)
Association of Civilian Technicians(190)
Association of College and University Telecommunications Administrators(191)
Association of College Unions International(191)
Association of Collegiate Business Schools and Programs(191)
Association of Collegiate Schools of Architecture(191)
Association of Construction Inspectors(192)
Association of Energy Engineers(195)
Association of Energy Service Companies(195)
Association of Farmworker Opportunity Programs(196)
Association of Financial Guaranty Insurors(197)
Association of Foreign Investors in Real Estate(197)
Association of Gospel Rescue Missions(199)
Association of Health Insurance Advisors(199)
Association of Hispanic Advertising Agencies(200)
Association of Independent Corrugated Converters(200)
Association of Industrial Metallizers, Coaters and Laminators(201)
Association of Information Technology Professionals(201)
Association of Local Air Pollution Control Officials(203)
Association of Management Consulting Firms(203)
Association of Management/International Association of Management(203)
Association of Maternal and Child Health Programs(204)
Association of Military Surgeons of the U.S.(205)
Association of Nurses in AIDS Care(206)
Association of Organ Procurement Organizations(206)
Association of Professional Chaplains(208)
Association of Racing Commissioners International(211)
Association of Rehabilitation Nurses(211)
Association of Rotational Molders, International(212)
Association of Small Business Development Centers(214)
Association of Specialists in Cleaning and Restoration International(214)
Association of State and Territorial Solid Waste Management Officials(215)
Association of Theatrical Press Agents and Managers(218)
Association of University Programs in Health Administration(219)
At-sea Processors Association(221)
Auto Suppliers Benchmarking Association(222)
Automated Imaging Association(222)
Automatic Meter Reading Association(223)
Automatic Transmission Rebuilders Association(223)
Automotive Oil Change Association(224)
Automotive Parts Remanufactuers Association(224)
Bankers' Association for Finance and Trade(226)
Battery Council International(226)
Beefmaster Breeders United(227)
Benchmarking Network Association(227)
Beta Alpha Psi(228)
Black Coaches Association(230)
Black Data Processing Associates(230)
Board of Certified Safety Professionals(231)
Broadcast Cable Credit Association(233)
Broadcast Cable Financial Management Association(233)
Brotherhood of Railroad Signalmen(233)
Burley Tobacco Growers Cooperative Association(235)
Business and Professional Women/USA(235)
Business Marketing Association(235)
Business Professionals of America(236)
California Redwood Association(236)
Catholic Charities USA(239)
Cedar Shake and Shingle Bureau(240)
Cement Kiln Recycling Coalition(241)
Center for Exhibition Industry Research(241)
Central Conference of American Rabbis(241)
Central Station Alarm Association(241)
Children's Book Council(244)
Choristers Guild(245)
Christian Management Association(246)
CIES, The Food Business Forum(246)
Coin Laundry Association(250)
College Music Society(251)
Color Marketing Group(252)
Commercial Law League of America(253)
Commercial Vehicle Safety Alliance(254)
Community Action Partnership(255)
Community Development Venture Capital Alliance(256)
Computer and Communications Industry Association(257)
Computer Security Institute(258)
Conference of Consulting Actuaries(259)
Consortium for Advanced Manufacturing International(262)
Consortium for School Networking(262)
Construction Management Association of America(262)
Consumer Credit Insurance Association(263)
Continental Basketball Association(264)
Contract Services Association of America(264)
Convention Industry Council(265)
Corn Refiners Association(266)
Council for Higher Education Accreditation(269)
Council for International Tax Education(269)
Council of American Survey Research Organizations(270)
Council of Educational Facility Planners, International(271)
Council of the Americas(275)
Council on Occupational Education(276)
Counselors of Real Estate(277)
Country Music Association(277)
Country Radio Broadcasters, Inc.(277)
CPAmerica International(278)
Crop Science Society of America(279)
Dairy Management(281)
Dance/USA(281)
Dangerous Goods Advisory Council(281)
Deep Foundations Institute(282)
Delta Sigma Pi(283)
Delta Society(283)
Dental Trade Alliance(283)
Design Management Institute(283)
Dietary Managers Association(284)
Digital Printing and Imaging Association(284)
Distance Education and Training Council(285)
Distribution Business Management Association(286)
Diving Equipment and Marketing Association(286)
Drug Information Association(287)
Drug, Chemical and Associated Technologies Association(287)
Earthquake Engineering Research Institute(288)
EIFS Industry Members Association(290)
Electrical Manufacturing and Coil Winding Association(291)
Electrical Overstress/Electrostatic Discharge Association(291)
Electricity Consumers Resource Council(291)
Electronics Representatives Association(292)
Employers Council on Flexible Compensation(293)
Energy and Environmental Building Association(294)
Enlisted Association of the National Guard of the United States(295)
Entertainment Services and Technology Association(295)
Envelope Manufacturers Association(296)
Environmental Assessment Association(296)
Environmental Technology Council(297)
Evangelical Council for Financial Accountability(298)
Eye Bank Association of America(300)
Family Firm Institute(300)
Fashion Group International(301)
FCIB-NACM Corp.(301)
Federal Bar Association(302)
Federal Managers Association(302)
Finishing Contractors Association(306)
Flue-Cured Tobacco Cooperative Stabilization Corporation(308)
Foodservice Consultants Society International(309)
Forest Products Society(310)
Forest Resources Association(310)
Forging Industry Association(310)
Forum for Investor Advice(311)
Foundation for Independent Higher Education(311)
Fragrance Foundation(311)
Freestanding Insert Council of North America(312)
Game Manufacturers Association(313)
Gas Machinery Research Council(314)
General Federation of Women's Clubs(315)
Genetics Society of America(315)
Glass Packaging Institute(317)
Gospel Music Association(318)
Grain Elevator and Processing Society(319)
Gravure Association of America(320)
Ground Water Protection Council(320)
Gypsum Association(321)
HARDI - Heating, Airconditioning, and Refrigeration Distributors International(321)
Hardwood Plywood and Veneer Association(322)
Health Physics Society(323)
Hearing Industries Association(324)
Home Sewing Association(327)
Hosiery Association, The(328)
Hospitality Financial and Technology Professionals(328)
Human Factors and Ergonomics Society(329)
Human Resource Planning Society(329)
Hydraulic Institute(329)
IGAF Worldwide(332)
Independent Affiliation of Independent Accounting Firms(333)
Independent Automotive Damage Appraisers Association(333)
Independent Educational Consultants Association(334)
Independent Feature Project(334)
Independent Liquid Terminals Association(334)
Independent Lubricant Manufacturers Association(335)
Industrial Designers Society of America(336)
Industrial Fasteners Institute(337)
Industrial Truck Association(337)
Institute of Business Appraisers(340)
Institute of Inspection Cleaning and Restoration Certification(341)
Institute of Makers of Explosives(342)
Institute of Navigation(343)
Institute of Packaging Professionals(343)
Integrated Waste Services Association(345)
Intellectual Property Owners Association(345)
Inter American Press Association(345)
International Academy of Trial Lawyers(348)
International Advertising Association(348)
International Association for Continuing Education and Training(349)
International Association for Exhibition Management(350)
International Association for Jazz Education(351)
International Association for the Study of Pain(352)

National Electrical Manufacturers Representatives Association(506)
National Electronic Distributors Association(506)
National Employment Lawyers Association(507)
National Energy Services Association(507)
National Environmental Balancing Bureau(507)
National Family Business Council(508)
National Family Planning and Reproductive Health Association(508)
National Federation of Community Development Credit Unions(509)
National Fluid Power Association(511)
National Football League Players Association(511)
National Forum for Black Public Administrators(512)
National Fraternal Congress of America(512)
National Genealogical Society(513)
National Golf Course Owners Association(514)
National Golf Foundation(514)
National Guild of Piano Teachers(515)
National Health Care Anti-Fraud Association(516)
National Health Council(516)
National Hispanic Medical Association(517)
National Human Services Assembly(518)
National Indian Gaming Association(519)
National Institute of Pension Administrators(521)
National Insulation Association(521)
National Interscholastic Athletic Administrators Association(522)
National Investment Company Service Association(522)
National Investor Relations Institute(522)
National Junior College Athletic Association(523)
National Legal Aid and Defender Association(524)
National Lesbian and Gay Journalists Association(524)
National Lumber and Building Material Dealers Association(525)
National Marine Electronics Association(526)
National Middle School Association(527)
National Music Publishers' Association(528)
National Network of Estate Planning Attorneys(528)
National Newspaper Association(528)
National Ocean Industries Association(529)
National Oilseed Processors Association(529)
National Organization of Black Law Enforcement Executives(530)
National Organization of Industrial Trade Unions(530)
National Parking Association(531)
National Pawnbrokers Association(532)
National Petrochemical & Refiners Association(532)
National Petroleum Council(532)
National Press Photographers Association(534)
National Register of Health Service Providers in Psychology(535)
National Rehabilitation Association(535)
National School Public Relations Association(538)
National School Supply and Equipment Association(538)
National Ski Areas Association(540)
National Society of Compliance Professionals(541)
National Structured Settlements Trade Association(544)
National Subacute and Postacute Care Association(544)
National Swine Registry(545)
National Technical Services Association(546)
National Tile Contractors Association(546)
National Training Systems Association(547)
National Truck Leasing System(547)
National Turkey Federation(548)
National U.S.-Arab Chamber of Commerce(548)
National Wooden Pallet and Container Association(550)
Natural Gas Vehicle Coalition(551)
Naval Reserve Association(551)
NEA - the Association of Union Constructors(551)
Nine to Five, National Association of Working Women(553)
NOFMA: the Wood Flooring Manufacturers Association(553)
North American Building Material Distribution Association(555)
North American Limousin Foundation(558)
North American Millers Association(558)
North American Wholesale Lumber Association(562)
Optical Laboratories Association(566)
Opticians Association of America(566)
Organic Crop Improvement Association International(566)
Organic Trade Association(566)
Organization for International Investment(567)
Organization for the Promotion and Advancement of Small Telecommunications Companies(567)
Orthopaedic Section - American Physical Therapy Association(568)
Paperboard Packaging Council(571)
Paso Fino Horse Association(572)
Pedorthic Footwear Association(572)
Percussive Arts Society(573)
Personal Watercraft Industry Association(574)
Pet Food Institute(574)
Pet Industry Joint Advisory Council(574)
Petroleum Equipment Suppliers Association(574)
Phi Alpha Delta(575)
Piano Technicians Guild(577)
Pinto Horse Association of America(578)
PKF North American Network(578)
Plasma Protein Therapeutics Association(578)
Plastics Pipe Institute(579)
Portable Rechargeable Battery Association(581)
Post-Tensioning Institute(581)
Powder Coating Institute(582)
Power Transmission Distributors Association(582)
Precision Machined Products Association(583)
PrintImage International(584)
Printing Brokerage/Buyers Association International(584)
Professional Engineers in Private Practice(587)
Professional Housing Management Association(587)
Professional Landscape Network(588)
Professional Picture Framers Association(588)
Professional Services Council(589)
Professional Tennis Registry(589)
PROMAX International(590)
The Protein Society(591)
Qualitative Research Consultants Association(593)
Quality Bakers of America Cooperative(594)
Rabbinical Assembly(594)
Radiology Business Management Association(595)
Red Angus Association of America(597)
Regional Airline Association(597)
Renal Physicians Association(599)
Renewable Fuels Association(599)
Renewable Natural Resources Foundation(599)
Retailer's Bakery Association(601)
Robotic Industries Association(602)
Rolf Institute(602)
Roller Skating Association International(602)
Romance Writers of America(603)
Safety and Loss Prevention Management Council(604)
Sales and Marketing Executives International(604)
Salt Institute(605)
SAMA Group of Associations(605)
Scaffold Industry Association(605)
Select Registry/Distinguished Inns of North America(608)
SEPM - Society for Sedimentary Geology(609)
SHRM Global Forum(610)
Soaring Society of America(612)
Society for Academic Emergency Medicine(613)
Society for American Archaeology(613)
Society for Biomaterials(614)
Society for Computer Simulation(615)
Society for Healthcare Strategy and Market Development(618)
Society for Imaging Science & Technology(619)
Society for Industrial and Organizational Psychology(620)
Society for Information Management(620)
Society for the Advancement of Material and Process Engineering(626)
Society for the Study of Reproduction(628)
Society of American Archivists(630)
Society of American Military Engineers(631)
Society of Architectural Historians(631)
Society of Cardiovascular Anesthesiologists(632)
Society of Cosmetic Chemists(634)
Society of Fire Protection Engineers(636)
Society of Gastroenterology Nurses and Associates(637)
Society of General Internal Medicine(637)
Society of Professional Benefit Administrators(642)
Society of Professional Journalists(642)
Society of Stage Directors and Choreographers(644)
Society of Surgical Oncology(644)
Society of Thoracic Surgeons(645)
Society of Tribologists and Lubrication Engineers(645)
Soil and Water Conservation Society(647)
Soil Science Society of America(647)
SOLE - The International Society of Logistics(647)
Sports Turf Managers Association(651)
Spring Manufacturers Institute(652)
State and Territorial Air Pollution Program Administrators(652)
State Higher Education Executive Officers(653)
Steel Manufacturers Association(653)
Steel Tank Institute Division of STI/SPFA(654)
Structural Board Association(654)
Sulphur Institute, The(655)
Supima(656)
Surface Mount Technology Association(656)
Tag and Label Manufacturers Institute(657)
TASH(657)
Taxicab, Limousine and Paratransit Association(657)
Tea Council of the U.S.A.(658)
Telecommunications Benchmarking International Group(659)
Tennis Industry Association(659)
Thoroughbred Owners and Breeders Association(661)
Tile Council of North America(661)
Tire Industry Association(662)
Tobacco Associates(662)
Tobacco Merchants Association of the U.S.(662)
Trade Show Exhibitors Association(663)
Traffic Audit Bureau for Media Measurement(663)
Turfgrass Producers International(667)
U.S. Apple Association(667)
U.S.-Russia Business Council(668)
Uni-Bell PVC Pipe Association(669)
United Nations Staff Union(672)
United Scenic Artists(672)
United States and Canadian Academy of Pathology(672)
United States Beet Sugar Association(673)
United States Bowling Congress(673)
United States Hispanic Chamber of Commerce(675)
United States Internet Service Provider Association(676)
United States Tour Operators Association(677)
Urban and Regional Information Systems Association(680)
Urban Libraries Council(681)

Valve Manufacturers Association of America(682)
Vinyl Siding Institute(683)
Voices for America's Children(684)
Voluntary Protection Programs Participants Association(684)
Western Red Cedar Lumber Association(687)
Wild Blueberry Association of North America(688)
Wildlife Management Institute(689)
Wildlife Society, The(689)
Wine and Spirits Shippers Association(689)
Women in Aviation International(691)
Women in Government(692)
Women's Basketball Coaches Association(693)
Women's Council of REALTORS(693)
Wood Machinery Manufacturers of America(694)
Wood Truss Council of America(694)
WorkPlace Furnishings(695)
World Future Society(696)
World Research Foundation(696)
World Wide Pet Industry Association(697)
Wound, Ostomy and Continence Nurses Society(697)
Zonta International(698)

$500-1,000,000

AAGL -- Advancing Minimally Invasive Gynecology Worldwide(1)
Academy of Criminal Justice Sciences(3)
Academy of International Business(3)
Academy of Political Science(5)
Academy of Student Pharmacists(5)
Aeronautical Repair Station Association(10)
Aerospace Medical Association(10)
African Studies Association(11)
Airport Consultants Council(14)
Alliance of Information and Referral Systems(17)
Alliance of Motion Picture and Television Producers(17)
Alliance of Nonprofit Mailers(17)
Alpha Kappa Psi(18)
Alpha Omega International Dental Fraternity(18)
America Outdoors(19)
American Academy of Addiction Psychiatry(20)
American Academy of Advertising(20)
American Academy of Dental Group Practice(21)
American Academy of Hospice and Palliative Medicine(23)
American Academy of Medical Acupuncture(24)
American Academy of Osteopathy(26)
American Amusement Machine Association(31)
American Association for Accreditation of Ambulatory Surgery Facilities(33)
American Association for Adult and Continuing Education(33)
American Association for Hand Surgery(35)
American Association for the Advancement of Slavic Studies(36)
American Association for the Surgery of Trauma(37)
American Association of Anatomists(38)
American Association of Bioanalysts(38)
American Association of Blacks in Energy(38)
American Association of Bovine Practitioners(39)
American Association of Colleges of Podiatric Medicine(40)
American Association of Franchisees and Dealers(43)
American Association of Healthcare Administrative Management(43)
American Association of Immunologists(44)
American Association of Integrated Healthcare Delivery Systems(44)
American Association of Meat Processors(45)
American Association of Medical Society Executives(45)
American Association of Naturopathic Physicians(46)
American Association of Neuroscience Nurses(46)
American Association of Oriental Medicine(47)
American Association of Pastoral Counselors(47)
American Association of School Librarians(50)
American Association of Sexuality Educators, Counselors and Therapists(51)
American Association of Spinal Cord Injury Nurses(51)
American Association of Swine Veterinarians(52)
American Association of Teachers of French(52)
American Baseball Coaches Association(56)
American Board of Industrial Hygiene(57)
American Board of Podiatric Orthopedics and Primary Podiatric Medicine(57)
American Boiler Manufacturers Association(58)
American Brahman Breeders Association(59)
American Bureau of Metal Statistics(59)
American Cleft Palate-Craniofacial Association(63)
American Coal Ash Association(63)
American Coke and Coal Chemicals Institute(63)
American College of Apothecaries(64)
American College of Clinical Pharmacology(64)
American College of Dentists(65)
American College of Mohs Micrographic Surgery and Cutaneous Oncology(67)
American College of Oral and Maxillofacial Surgeons(68)
American College of Real Estate Lawyers(70)
American College of Trust and Estate Counsel(71)
American College of Veterinary Pathologists(72)
American Congress of Rehabilitation Medicine(73)
American Congress on Surveying and Mapping(73)
American Corn Growers Association(74)
American Council for Technology(75)
American Dairy Products Institute(78)
American Equilibration Society(81)
American Evaluation Association(81)
American Farrier's Association(82)
American Federation of Astrologers, Inc.(82)
American Federation of School Administrators(82)
American Galvanizers Association(86)
American Geographical Society(87)
American Group Psychotherapy Association(87)
American Guernsey Association(87)
American Herbal Products Association(90)
American Horse Council(91)
American Humanist Association(92)
American Institute for Conservation of Historic and Artistic Works(93)
American Institute of Architecture Students(94)
American Institute of Floral Designers(96)
American Institute of Marine Underwriters(96)
American Institute of Professional Geologists(97)
American Institute of Timber Construction(98)
American Lithotripsy Society(102)
American Malting Barley Association(102)
American Mideast Business Associates(106)
American Mold Builders Association(106)
American Music Therapy Association(107)
American Orthopsychiatric Association(111)
American Ostrich Association(112)
American Pediatric Surgical Association(113)
American Philological Association(114)
American Philosophical Association(114)
American Professional Society on the Abuse of Children(117)
American Purchasing Society(120)
American Pyrotechnics Association(120)
American Rabbit Breeders Association(121)
American Recreation Coalition(122)
American Salers Association(123)
American Schools of Oriental Research(124)
American Seminar Leaders Association(124)
American Seniors Housing Association(124)
American Shipbuilding Association(125)
American Shorthorn Association(125)
American Skin Association(126)
American Society for Dermatologic Surgery(128)
American Society for Healthcare Environmental Services(129)
American Society for Information Science and Technology(130)
American Society of Agricultural Appraisers(133)
American Society of Bariatric Physicians(134)
American Society of Clinical Hypnosis(135)
American Society of Cytopathology(137)
American Society of Electroneurodiagnostic Technologists(137)
American Society of Extra-Corporeal Technology(137)
American Society of Hand Therapists(138)
American Society of Law, Medicine and Ethics(140)
American Society of Limnology and Oceanography(140)
American Society of Ophthalmic Administrators(143)
American Society of Pediatric Hematology/Oncology(143)
American Society of Picture Professionals(144)
American Society of Sanitary Engineering(146)
American Spice Trade Association(148)
American Stamp Dealers' Association(149)
American String Teachers Association(149)
American Student Dental Association(149)
American Studies Association(149)
American Sugarbeet Growers Association(150)
American Textile Machinery Association(151)
American Therapeutic Recreation Association(151)
American Truck Stop Operators Association(152)
American Watchmakers-Clockmakers Institute(154)
Analytical and Life Science Systems Association(157)
APMI International(158)
Army Aviation Association of America(161)
The Art and Creative Materials Institute(161)
Ass'n of Learning Providers(164)
Associated Air Balance Council(164)
Associated Risk Managers(166)
Association Correctional Food Service Affiliates(166)
Association for Clinical Pastoral Education(169)
Association for Education and Rehabilitation of the Blind and Visually Impaired(172)
Association for Education in Journalism and Mass Communication(172)
Association for Experiential Education(172)
Association for Financial Counseling and Planning Education(173)
Association for Gerontology in Higher Education(173)
Association for Hose and Accessories Distribution(174)
Association for Library Collections and Technical Services(175)
Association for Library Service to Children(175)
Association for Molecular Pathology(176)
Association for Play Therapy(176)
Association for Public Policy Analysis and Management(177)
Association for Research in Nervous and Mental Disease(177)
Association for Research in Vision and Ophthalmology(178)
Association for the Treatment of Sexual Abusers(181)
Association for Unmanned Vehicle Systems International(181)
Association of Academic Physiatrists(183)

Association of American Physicians and Surgeons(185)
Association of Boarding Schools, The(188)
Association of Bridal Consultants(188)
Association of Catholic Colleges and Universities(188)
Association of Chiropractic Colleges(189)
Association of Community Cancer Centers(192)
Association of Diesel Specialists(194)
Association of Directory Marketing(194)
Association of Directory Publishers(194)
Association of Diving Contractors International(194)
Association of Educational Publishers(194)
Association of Educational Service Agencies(194)
Association of Energy Services Professionals, International(195)
Association of Environmental and Engineering Geologists(195)
Association of Film Commissioners International(196)
Association of Finance and Insurance Professionals(196)
Association of Food Industries(197)
Association of Fraternity Advisors(198)
Association of Hispanic Arts(200)
Association of International Photography Art Dealers(202)
Association of Investment Management Sales Executives(202)
Association of Jesuit Colleges and Universities(202)
Association of Jewish Aging Services(202)
Association of Jewish Family and Children's Agencies(202)
Association of Latino Professionals in Accounting and Finance(203)
Association of Partners for Public Lands(207)
Association of Professional Investment Consultants(209)
Association of Professional Researchers for Advancement(209)
Association of Professors of Gynecology and Obstetrics(209)
Association of Regulatory Boards of Optometry(211)
Association of Rheumatology Health Professionals(212)
Association of Schools and Colleges of Optometry(213)
Association of Schools of Allied Health Professions(213)
Association of Schools of Public Health(213)
Association of State and Interstate Water Pollution Control Administrators(214)
Association of State Dam Safety Officials(215)
Association of State Drinking Water Administrators(215)
Association of State Floodplain Managers(216)
Association of Surfing Professionals - North America(216)
Association of TeleServices International(217)
Association of Test Publishers(217)
Association of University Radiologists(219)
Association of Water Technologies(220)
Association of Writers and Writing Programs(221)
Association of YMCA Professionals(221)
Association on Higher Education and Disability(221)
Authors Guild(222)
Automatic Fire Alarm Association(222)
Automotive Maintenance Repair Association(223)
Aviation Maintenance Foundation International(225)
Aviation Suppliers Association(225)
Barre Granite Association(226)
Basic Acrylic Monomer Manufacturers(226)
Bearing Specialist Association(226)
BEMA - The Baking Industry Suppliers Association(227)
Better Hearing Institute(228)
Biomedical Engineering Society(229)
Biscuit and Cracker Manufacturers' Association(229)
BKR International(229)
Brazilian American Chamber of Commerce(232)
BritishAmerican Business Inc.(233)
Brown Swiss Cattle Breeders Association of the U.S.A.(234)
Business and Institutional Furniture Manufacturers Association International(235)
Business Council(235)
Business Higher Education Forum(235)
Business Products Credit Association(235)
Calorie Control Council(237)
Car Care Council(237)
Cast Iron Soil Pipe Institute(238)
Catholic Campus Ministry Association(239)
Catholic Press Association(240)
Center for Waste Reduction Technologies(241)
Ceramic Tile Distributors Association(241)
Certified Contractors NetWork(242)
Chamber of Shipping of America(243)
Chemical Producers and Distributors Association(243)
Cherry Marketing Institute(243)
Chorus America(245)
City and Regional Magazine Association(247)
Cleaning Equipment Trade Association(247)
Coalition for Juvenile Justice(249)
Coalition of Service Industries(249)
Color Pigments Manufacturers Association(253)
Commission on Accreditation of Allied Health Education Programs(254)
Commissioned Officers Association of the United States Public Health Service(254)
Community Leadership Association(256)
Concrete Foundations Association(258)
Concrete Sawing and Drilling Association(259)
Conference of Minority Transportation Officials(259)
Conference of Radiation Control Program Directors(260)
Congress of Neurological Surgeons(261)
Contact Lens Council(264)
Contact Lens Manufacturers Association(264)
Contact Lens Society of America(264)
Cooling Technology Institute(265)
Copper and Brass Fabricators Council(266)
Council for Agricultural Science and Technology(268)
Council for Chemical Research(268)
Council for Marketing and Opinion Research(269)
Council for Spiritual and Ethical Education(270)
Council of American Overseas Research Centers(270)
Council of Independent Restaurants of America(272)
Council of Industrial Boiler Owners(272)
Council of Landscape Architectural Registration Boards(273)
Council of Large Public Housing Authorities(273)
Council of Literary Magazines and Presses(273)
Council of State Administrators of Vocational Rehabilitation(274)
Council on Chiropractic Education(275)
Council on Employee Benefits(276)
Council on Licensure, Enforcement and Regulation(276)
Council on Resident Education in Obstetrics and Gynecology(277)
CPA Associates International(277)
Credit Research Foundation(279)
Cremation Association of North America(279)
Customer Relations Institute(280)
Decision Sciences Institute(282)
Dermatology Nurses' Association(283)
Directors of Health Promotion and Public Health Education(285)
Distribution Contractors Association(286)
Dramatists Guild of America(287)
Dredging Contractors of America(287)
Drug and Alcohol Testing Industry Association(287)
EDA Consortium(288)
Education Writers Association(289)
Electronic Commerce Code Management Association(291)
Electronic Distribution Show Corporation(291)
Electronic Funds Transfer Association(292)
Electronics Technicians Association International(292)
Emergency Department Practice Management Association(292)
Employee Services Management Association(293)
Endocrine Fellows Foundation(294)
Energy Bar Association(294)
Energy Telecommunications and Electrical Association(294)
Equipment and Tool Institute(297)
European-American Business Council(298)
Evangelical Christian Publishers Association(298)
Evangelical Training Association(298)
Executive Women International(299)
Export Institute of the United States(300)
Farm Equipment Manufacturers Association(301)
Federal Communications Bar Association(302)
Federal Education Association(302)
Federal Facilities Council(302)
Federally Employed Women(302)
Federation of Defense and Corporate Counsel(303)
Federation of State Humanities Councils(304)
Federation of Tax Administrators(304)
Financial Management Association International(306)
Financial Women International(306)
Fluid Power Distributors Association(308)
Fluid Power Society(308)
Foil Stamping and Embossing Association(308)
Foodservice and Packaging Institute(309)
Footwear Distributors and Retailers of America(310)
Forest History Society(310)
Forest Industries Telecommunications(310)
Fragrance Materials Association of the United States(311)
Fresh Produce and Floral Council(312)
Fresh Produce Association of the Americas(312)
Fur Information Council of America(313)
Gas Processors Association(314)
Geothermal Resources Council(316)
Giving Institute(317)
Glass Art Society(317)
Glass Association of North America(317)
Golf Coaches Association of America(318)
Governors Highway Safety Association(319)
Graphic Artists Guild(319)
Graphic Arts Marketing Information Service(319)
Greater Blouse, Skirt and Undergarment Association(320)
Greeting Card Association(320)
Gynecologic Oncology Group(321)
Halogenated Solvents Industry Alliance(321)
Hardwood Manufacturers Association(322)
Harness Tracks of America(322)
Health Industry Business Communications Council(323)
Healthcare Billing and Management Association(323)
Healthcare Marketing and Communications Council(324)
Home Improvement Research Institute(327)
Hospice and Palliative Nurses Association(328)
Hotel Brokers International(329)
Hydronics Institute Division of GAMA(330)
IEEE Industry Applications Society(331)
IEEE Instrumentation and Measurement Society(331)
IEEE Magnetics Society(331)
In-Plant Printing and Mailing Association(332)
Independent Cosmetic Manufacturers and Distributors(333)
Industrial Asset Management Council(336)
Industrial Foundation of America(337)

Information Systems Security Association(338)
Inland Marine Underwriters Association(339)
Institute for Certification of Computing Professionals(339)
Institute of Environmental Sciences and Technology(341)
Institute of Hazardous Materials Management(341)
Institute of International Container Lessors(342)
Institute of Judicial Administration(342)
Institute of Management Consultants USA(342)
Institute of Mathematical Statistics(342)
Institute of Nautical Archaeology(343)
Insurance Accounting and Systems Association(345)
Intercollegiate Tennis Association(346)
Interior Design Society(347)
International Association for Identification(350)
International Association for Impact Assessment(350)
International Association for Orthodontics(351)
International Association for the Leisure and Entertainment Industry(351)
International Association of Arson Investigators(353)
International Association of Audio Visual Communicators(353)
International Association of Clerks, Recorders, Election Officials and Treasurers(354)
International Association of Culinary Professionals(355)
International Association of Diecutting and Diemaking(356)
International Association of Emergency Managers(356)
International Association of Healthcare Central Service Materiel Management(357)
International Association of Jewish Vocational Services(358)
International Association of Law Enforcement Firearms Instructors(358)
International Association of Lighting Designers(358)
International Association of Rehabilitation Professionals(360)
International Association of Tour Managers - North American Region(361)
International Association of Workforce Professionals(362)
International Banana Association(362)
International Biometric Society(362)
International Brangus Breeders Association(363)
International Card Manufacturers Association(364)
International Cast Polymer Association(364)
International Code Council(365)
International College of Dentists, U.S.A. Section(366)
International College of Surgeons(366)
International Communication Association(366)
International Concrete Repair Institute(366)
International Council on Hotel, Restaurant and Institutional Education(368)
International Documentary Association(369)
International Downtown Association(369)
International Function Point Users Group(373)
International Ground Source Heat Pump Association(374)
International Imaging Industry Association(376)
International Inflight Food Service Association(376)
International Legal Fraternity of Phi Delta Phi(378)
International Liver Transplantation Society(378)
International Magnesium Association(378)
International Marina Institute(379)
International Newspaper Financial Executives(381)
International Newspaper Marketing Association(381)
International Pediatric Nephrology Association(382)
International Pharmaceutical Excipients Council of the Americas(382)
International Precious Metals Institute(383)
International Public Relations Association - U.S. Section(384)
International Security Management Association(385)
International Snowmobile Manufacturers Association(386)
International Society for Analytical Cytology(386)
International Society for Experimental Hematology(387)
International Society for Pharmacoepidemiology(388)
International Society for Traumatic Stress Studies(389)
International Society of Appraisers(390)
International Society of Hospitality Consultants(391)
International Society of Transport Aircraft Trading(392)
International Studies Association(393)
International Test and Evaluation Association(394)
International Transactional Analysis Association(394)
International Travel Writers and Editors Association(395)
Internet Alliance(397)
Investment Casting Institute(398)
Investment Program Association(399)
Ireland Chamber of Commerce in the U.S.(399)
ISDA - The Office Systems Cooperative(400)
Jewelers Vigilance Committee(401)
Jewelry Information Center(401)
Jewish Social Service Professionals Association(402)
Kitchen Cabinet Manufacturers Association(403)
The Knitting Guild Association(404)
Laboratory Products Association(404)
Lake Carriers' Association(404)
Lamaze International(404)
Land Improvement Contractors of America(405)
Latin Chamber of Commerce of U.S.A.(405)
Lawn and Garden Dealers' Association(406)
League for Innovation in the Community College(406)
Liability Insurance Research Bureau(407)
Log Home Builders Association of North America(409)
Manufacturers' Agents Association for the Foodservice Industry(411)
Marine Retailers Association of America(412)
Marine Technology Society(412)
Master Printers of America(413)
Materials Properties Council(414)
Materials Technology Institute(414)
Meals On Wheels Association of America(414)
Mechanical Service Contractors of America(415)
Medieval Academy of America(416)
Metal Construction Association(417)
Metal Treating Institute(417)
Microscopy Society of America(418)
Military Operations Research Society(419)
Mineralogical Society of America(419)
Monument Builders of North America(421)
Multi-Housing Laundry Association(422)
Mycological Society of America(424)
NADD: Association for Persons with Developmental Disabilities and Mental Health Needs(424)
NALS(425)
NASTD - Technology Professionals Serving State Government(426)
NATCO - The Organization for Transplant Professionals(426)
National Academy of Opticianry(427)
National Aeronautic Association(427)
National Air Carrier Association(428)
National AMBUCS(430)
National Association for Biomedical Research(431)
National Association for Community Mediation(432)
National Association for Court Management(432)
National Association for Family and Community Education(433)
National Association for Health Care Recruitment(433)
National Association for Pupil Transportation(435)
National Association for the Support of Long-Term Care(437)
National Association for Treasurers of Religious Institutes(437)
National Association for Year-Round Education(437)
National Association of Addiction Treatment Providers(438)
National Association of Agricultural Educators(438)
National Association of Air Traffic Specialists(438)
National Association of Basketball Coaches(439)
National Association of Black Social Workers(440)
National Association of Black-Owned Broadcasters(440)
National Association for Business Economics(441)
National Association of Chiefs of Police(443)
National Association of Church Business Administration(443)
National Association of Church Personnel Administrators(443)
National Association of Collegiate Women Athletic Administrators(445)
National Association of Concessionaires(445)
National Association of Councils on Developmental Disabilities(446)
National Association of Counsel for Children(446)
National Association of Credit Union Service Organizations(448)
National Association of Development Companies(449)
National Association of Elevator Contractors(450)
National Association of Environmental Professionals(451)
National Association of Episcopal Schools(451)
National Association of Extension 4-H Agents(451)
National Association of Farm Broadcasting(452)
National Association of Federally Impacted Schools(452)
National Association of Floor Covering Distributors(453)
National Association of Foreign-Trade Zones(453)
National Association of Fundraising Ticket Manufacturers(454)
National Association of Government Defined Contribution Administrators(454)
National Association of Graduate Admissions Professionals(454)
National Association of Home Inspectors(456)
National Association of Housing Cooperatives(456)
National Association of Institutional Linen Management(458)
National Association of Local Boards of Health(460)
National Association of Local Housing Finance Agencies(460)
National Association of Managed Care Physicians(460)
National Association of Master Appraisers(461)
National Association of Nurse Practitioners in Women's Health(463)
National Association of Pizza Operators(464)

National Association of Private Special Education Centers(465)
National Association of Professional Organizers(466)
National Association of Real Estate Investment Managers(468)
National Association of School Resource Officers(470)
National Association of Schools of Public Affairs and Administration(470)
National Association of Securities Professionals(471)
National Association of Sewer Service Companies(472)
National Association of State Boating Law Administrators(473)
National Association of State Budget Officers(473)
National Association of State Development Agencies(474)
National Association of State Emergency Medical Services Officials(475)
National Association of State Retirement Administrators(476)
National Association of State Treasurers(476)
National Association of Teachers of Singing(478)
National Association of Telecommunications Officers and Advisors(478)
National Association of Towns and Townships(479)
National Association of Uniform Manufacturers and Distributors(480)
National Association of Women in Construction(481)
National Association of Women Judges(481)
National Association of Workforce Development Professionals(482)
National Auctioneers Association(482)
National Bankers Association(483)
National Bison Association(484)
National Black Caucus of State Legislators(484)
National Black Nurses Association(484)
National Border Patrol Council(485)
National Cancer Registrars Association(486)
National Candle Association(487)
National Career Development Association(487)
National Catholic Cemetery Conference(487)
National Catholic Development Conference(487)
National Child Support Enforcement Association(489)
National Christian College Athletic Association(489)
National Christmas Tree Association(489)
National Collegiate Honors Council(491)
National Community Education Association(491)
National Conference of Black Mayors(492)
National Conference on Weights and Measures(495)
National Corrugated Steel Pipe Association(496)
National Cottonseed Products Association(496)
National Council of Catholic Women(498)
National Council of Higher Education Loan Programs(499)
National Council of Nonprofit Associations(500)
National Council of Real Estate Investment Fiduciaries(500)
National Council on Education for the Ceramic Arts(502)
National Dental Association(505)
National Electronic Service Dealers Association(506)
National Elevator Industry(506)
National Environmental, Safety and Health Training Association(507)
National Federation Coaches Association(508)
National Federation of Community Broadcasters(509)
National Federation of Officials Association(510)
National Federation of Paralegal Associations(510)
National Finance Adjusters(510)
National Foundation for Women Legislators(512)
National Fraternal Order of Police(512)
National Guild of Community Schools of the Arts(515)
National High School Athletic Coaches Association(517)
National Hydropower Association(518)
National Indian Education Association(519)
National Industrial Sand Association(519)
National Information Standards Organization(520)
National Interstate Council of State Boards of Cosmetology(522)
National Lawyers Guild(523)
National Lime Association(525)
National Limousine Association(525)
National Luggage Dealers Association(525)
National Meat Association(526)
National Mobility Equipment Dealers Association(527)
The National NeedleArts Association(528)
National Network of Grantmakers(528)
National Newspaper Publishers Association(529)
National Ornamental and Miscellaneous Metals Association(531)
National Paperbox Association(531)
National Potato Council(533)
National Property Management Association(534)
National Registry of Environmental Professionals(535)
National Renal Administrators Association(536)
National Sculpture Society(539)
Selected Independent Funeral Homes(539)
National Shoe Retailers Association(539)
National Show Horse Registry(539)
National Ski Patrol System(540)
National Small Shipments Traffic Conference(540)
National Society for Hebrew Day Schools(541)
National Society for Histotechnology(541)
National Society of Genetic Counselors(541)
National Speleological Society(542)
National Star Route Mail Contractors Association(543)
National Student Speech Language Hearing Association(544)
National Tractor Pullers Association(546)
National Volunteer Fire Council(548)
National Water Resources Association(548)
National WIC Association(549)
National Writers Union(550)
National Yogurt Association(550)
NCSL International(551)
NIBA - The Belting Association(553)
Non-Ferrous Founders' Society(553)
North American Association For Ambulatory Care(554)
North American Association for Environmental Education(554)
North American Association of State and Provincial Lotteries(554)
North American Export Grain Association(557)
North American Folk Music and Dance Alliance(557)
North American Interfraternity Conference(557)
North American Meat Processors Association(558)
North American Nature Photography Association(558)
North American Society for Trenchless Technology(561)
Office Products Wholesalers Association(564)
Offshore Marine Service Association(564)
Organization Development Network(566)
Outdoor Amusement Business Association(569)
Paper Industry Management Association(571)
Passenger Vessel Association(572)
Personal Computer Memory Card International Association(573)
Pet Industry Distributors Association(574)
Pet Sitters International(574)
PGA TOUR Tournaments Association(575)
Phi Alpha Theta(575)
Pi Lambda Theta(577)
Pickle Packers International(577)
Plastic Pipe and Fittings Association(578)
Plumbing Manufacturers Institute(579)
Polyisocyanurate Insulation Manufacturers Association(580)
Polystyrene Packaging Council(580)
Population Association of America(580)
Porcelain Enamel Institute(580)
Poultry Science Association(581)
Power and Communication Contractors Association(582)
Pressure Sensitive Tape Council(583)
Preventive Cardiovascular Nurses Association(583)
Product Development and Management Association(585)
Professional Association of Health Care Office Management(586)
Professional Association of Innkeepers International(586)
Professional Aviation Maintenance Association(586)
Professional Insurance Marketing Association(588)
Professional Records and Information Services Management International(589)
Professional Ski Instructors of America(589)
Profit Sharing/401(k) Council of America(590)
Public Employees Roundtable(592)
Public Housing Authorities Directors Association(592)
Public Library Association(592)
Racking Horse Breeders Association of America(594)
Radiant Panel Association(594)
Railway Supply Institute(595)
Recreational Park Trailer Industry Association(596)
Red and White Dairy Cattle Association(597)
Refractories Institute(597)
Registry of Interpreters for the Deaf(598)
Religious Conference Management Association(599)
Research and Development Associates for Military Food and Packaging Systems(599)
Research and Engineering Council of the NAPL(600)
Resilient Floor Covering Institute(600)
Retail Advertising and Marketing Association International(601)
Retail Confectioners International(601)
Retail Packaging Manufacturers Association(601)
Reusable Industrial Packaging Association(601)
Santa Gertrudis Breeders International(605)
Scoliosis Research Society(606)
Seismological Society of America(608)
Senior Executives Association(609)
Silver Institute(611)
Society for Applied Spectroscopy(614)
Society for Assisted Reproductive Technology(614)
Society for Cardiovascular Angiography and Interventions(614)
Society for Cardiovascular Magnetic Resonance(614)
Society for Experimental Mechanics(617)
Society for Gynecologic Investigation(618)
Society for Healthcare Epidemiology of America(618)
Society for In Vitro Biology(619)
Society for Integrative and Comparative Biology(620)
Society for Maintenance Reliability Professionals(621)
Society for News Design(622)
Society for Nutrition Education(622)
Society for Public Health Education(624)
Society for Range Management(624)
Society for the Advancement of Education(626)

Society for the Psychological Study of Social Issues(627)
Society for Vascular Ultrasound(629)
Society of Broadcast Engineers(632)
Society of Children's Book Writers and Illustrators(633)
Society of Environmental Journalists(635)
Society of Former Special Agents of the Federal Bureau of Investigation(636)
Society of Glass and Ceramic Decorators(637)
Society of Illustrators(638)
Society of Laparoendoscopic Surgeons(639)
Society of Mexican American Engineers and Scientists(640)
Society of North American Goldsmiths(641)
Society of Pharmaceutical and Biotech Trainers(642)
Society of Publication Designers(643)
Society of Research Administrators International(643)
Society of Satellite Professionals International(644)
Society of Urologic Nurses and Associates(645)
Society of Vacuum Coaters(646)
Society of Vertebrate Paleontology(646)
Souvenirs, Gifts and Novelties Trade Association(648)
Spain-U.S. Chamber of Commerce(648)
Specialized Information Publishers Association(650)
Specialty Steel Industry of North America(650)
Sporting Arms and Ammunition Manufacturers' Institute(651)
Sportsplex Operators and Developers Association(651)
States Organization for Boating Access(653)
Steel Founders' Society of America(653)
Steel Plate Fabricators Association Division of STI/SPFA(653)
Steel Recycling Institute(653)
Steel Shipping Container Institute(653)
Steel Tube Institute of North America(654)
Subcontractors Trade Association(655)
Tea Association of the United States of America(658)
Technology Student Association(658)
Thoroughbred Racing Associations of North America(661)
Tilt-up Concrete Association(661)
Timber Framers Guild(661)
Timber Products Manufacturers(661)
Tortilla Industry Association(662)
Towing and Recovery Association of America(662)
Transportation Intermediaries Association(664)
Truck Trailer Manufacturers Association(666)
Truss Plate Institute(666)
U.S. Psychiatric Rehabiliation Association(668)
U.S.A. Dry Pea and Lentil Council(668)
Undersea and Hyperbaric Medical Society(669)
Unfinished Furniture Association(669)
United Association of Equipment Leasing(670)
United Engineering Foundation(671)
United Methodist Association of Health and Welfare Ministries(671)
United States Association of Importers of Textiles and Apparel(673)
United States Business and Industry Council(674)
United States Institute for Theatre Technology(676)
United States Racquet Stringers Association(677)
United States-Mexico Chamber of Commerce(678)
University Continuing Education Association(679)
University/Resident Theatre Association(680)
Upholstered Furniture Action Council(680)
Urology Society of America(681)
Usability Professionals' Association(681)
Vacation Rental Managers Association(681)
Van Alen Institute(682)
Vibration Institute(683)
Wallcoverings Association(685)
Waste Equipment Technology Association(685)
Weed Science Society of America(687)
Wilderness Medical Society(689)
Wireless Dealers Association(690)
Women Executives in State Government(691)
Women in International Security(692)
Women in Technology International(692)
Women's Transportation Seminar(694)
Wood Moulding and Millwork Producers Association(694)
Workgroup for Electronic Data Interchange(695)
World Affairs Councils of America(695)
World Allergy Organization - IACCI(695)
World Waterpark Association(696)

$250-500,000

Academy of Ambulatory Foot and Ankle Surgery(2)
Academy of Dentistry for Persons with Disabilities(3)
Academy of Psychosomatic Medicine(5)
Academy of Radiology Research(5)
ACCRA - Ass'n of Applied Community Researchers(6)
Acrylonitrile Group(8)
Adventure Travel Trade Association(9)
Advertising and Marketing International Network(9)
Affiliated Warehouse Companies(10)
Agricultural and Food Transporters Conference(12)
Agriculture Council of America(12)
Airline Industrial Relations Conference(14)
All-America Rose Selections(15)
Alliance for Community Media(15)
Alliance for Responsible Atmospheric Policy(16)
Alliance of Artists Communities(16)
Alliance of Cardiovascular Professionals(16)
Allied Finance Adjusters Conference(17)
American Academy for Cerebral Palsy and Developmental Medicine(19)
American Academy of Dental Sleep Medicine(21)
American Academy of Environmental Medicine(22)
American Academy of Esthetic Dentistry(22)
American Academy of Fixed Prosthodontics(23)
American Academy of Matrimonial Lawyers(24)
American Academy of Orofacial Pain(26)
American Academy of Psychiatry and the Law(28)
American Academy of Psychoanalysis and Dynamic Psychiatry(28)
American Academy of Wound Management(29)
American Agriculture Movement(30)
American Art Therapy Association(32)
American Arts Alliance(32)
American Association for Aerosol Research(33)
American Association for Employment in Education(34)
American Association for Functional Orthodontics(35)
American Association for Health Education(35)
American Association for Health Freedom(35)
American Association for Paralegal Education(36)
American Association for Vocational Instructional Materials(37)
American Association of Attorney-Certified Public Accountants(38)
American Association of Birth Centers(38)
American Association of Classified School Employees(39)
American Association of Clinical Urologists(40)
American Association of Credit Union Leagues(41)
American Association of Crop Insurers(41)
American Association of Hospital Dentists(44)
American Association of Legal Nurse Consultants(44)
American Association of Minority Businesses(45)
American Association of Neuropathologists(46)
American Association of Public Health Dentistry(50)
American Association of School Personnel Administrators(51)
American Association of Spinal Cord Injury Psychologists and Social Workers(51)
American Association of Suicidology(52)
American Association of Teachers of Spanish and Portuguese(52)
American Association of Variable Star Observers(53)
American Association of Veterinary Laboratory Diagnosticians(53)
American Association of Zoo Veterinarians(54)
American Astronautical Society(54)
American Automatic Control Council(55)
American Automotive Leasing Association(55)
American Bearing Manufacturing Association(56)
American Beekeeping Federation(56)
American Beverage Licensees(57)
American Board of Periodontology(57)
American Board of Professional Psychology(58)
American Board of Veterinary Practitioners(58)
American Brachytherapy Society(59)
American Brush Manufacturers Association(59)
American Chianina Association(62)
American Clinical Laboratory Association(63)
American College of Foot and Ankle Orthopedics and Medicine(65)
American College of Legal Medicine(66)
American College of Medical Quality(67)
American College of Neuropsychopharmacology(68)
American College of Nuclear Physicians(68)
American College of Nurse Practitioners(68)
American College of Nutrition(68)
American College of Osteopathic Obstetricians and Gynecologists(69)
American College of Veterinary Ophthalmologists(71)
American Concrete Pavement Association(72)
American Concrete Pressure Pipe Association(73)
American Concrete Pumping Association(73)
American Conference of Cantors(73)
American Construction Inspectors Association(74)
American Copper Council(74)
American Crystallographic Association(77)
American Dental Society of Anesthesiology(79)
American Driver and Traffic Safety Education Association(79)
American Education Finance Association(80)
American Family Therapy Academy(81)
American Filtration and Separations Society(83)
American Finance Association(83)
American Fire Safety Council(84)
American Folklore Society(84)
American Forests(85)
American Guild of Variety Artists(88)
American Hanoverian Society(88)
American Health and Beauty Aids Institute(89)
American Holistic Medical Association(91)
American Holistic Nurses Association(91)
American Institute for Medical and Biological Engineering(94)
American Institute of Building Design(95)
American Institute of Constructors(95)
American Institute of Mining, Metallurgical, and Petroleum Engineers(96)
American Land Rights Association(100)
American Licensed Practical Nurses Association(101)
American Managed Behavioral Healthcare Association(102)
American Mathematical Association of Two Year Colleges(103)
American Mosquito Control Association(106)
American Mushroom Institute(107)
American Music Conference(107)
American Paraplegia Society(113)
American Polarity Therapy Association(116)

American Prepaid Legal Services Institute(117)
American Psychological Association - Division of Psychoanalysis(118)
American Psychological Association - Society of Clinical Psychology(119)
American Public Gardens Association(119)
American Real Estate Society(121)
American Red Brangus Association(122)
American Salvage Pool Association(124)
American Sightseeing International(125)
American Sleep Apnea Association(126)
American Society for Adolescent Psychiatry(126)
American Society for Artificial Internal Organs(126)
American Society for Bioethics and Humanities(127)
American Society for Eighteenth-Century Studies(128)
American Society for Geriatric Dentistry(129)
American Society for Healthcare Central Service Professionals(129)
American Society for Healthcare Food Service Administrators(129)
American Society for Laser Medicine and Surgery(130)
American Society for Photobiology(131)
American Society for Precision Engineering(132)
American Society of Abdominal Surgeons(133)
American Society of Access Professionals(133)
American Society of Andrology(133)
American Society of Baking(134)
American Society of Clinical Psychopharmacology(136)
American Society of Consulting Arborists(136)
American Society of Criminology(137)
American Society of Dermatopathology(137)
American Society of Directors of Volunteer Services(137)
American Society of General Surgeons(138)
American Society of Head and Neck Radiology(138)
American Society of Hypertension(139)
American Society of Journalists and Authors(140)
American Society of Neuroimaging(142)
American Society of Notaries(142)
American Society of Parasitologists(143)
American Society of Pharmacognosy(144)
American Society of Plastic Surgical Nurses(144)
American Society of Professional Estimators(145)
American Society of Women Accountants(147)
American Specialty Toy Retailing Association(148)
American Spinal Injury Association(148)
American Sports Builders Association(148)
American Warmblood Registry(154)
American Watch Association(154)
American Wine Society(155)
American Wire Producers Association(155)
American Woman's Society of Certified Public Accountants(155)
American Women in Radio and Television(155)
American Zinc Association(156)
Americas Association of Cooperative/Mutual Insurance Socs.(156)
Animal Behavior Society(157)
Antiquarian Booksellers Association of America(157)
Appraisers Association of America(159)
Art Therapy Credentials Board(162)
Artist-Blacksmiths' Association of North America(162)
Asphalt Emulsion Manufacturers Association(163)
Associated Collegiate Press, National Scholastic Press Association(165)
Association for Academic Surgery(166)
Association for Applied Psychophysiology and Biofeedback(167)
Association for Biblical Higher Education(168)
Association for Child Psychoanalysis(169)
Association for Commuter Transportation(169)
Association for Consumer Research(171)
Association for Continuing Legal Education(171)
Association for Convention Operations Management(171)
Association for Death Education and Counseling(171)
Association for High Technology Distribution(174)
Association for Management Information in Financial Services(176)
Association for Research in Otolaryngology(177)
Association for Symbolic Logic(178)
Association for the Advancement of Automotive Medicine(179)
Association for the Advancement of International Education(179)
Association for the Advancement of Psychology(179)
Association for the Environmental Health of Soils(180)
Association for the Study of African American Life and History(180)
Association for the Study of Nationalities(181)
Association for Women in Communications(182)
Association for Women in Mathematics(182)
Association for Women in Science(182)
Association for Women's Rights in Development(183)
Association of Advanced Rabbinical and Talmudic Schools(183)
Association of Avian Veterinarians(187)
Association of Black Psychologists(187)
Association of Booksellers for Children(188)
Association of College Administration Professionals(190)
Association of College and University Auditors(190)
Association of Collegiate Conference and Events Directors International(191)
Association of Credit Union Internal Auditors(193)
Association of Destination Management Executives(193)
Association of Edison Illuminating Companies(194)
Association of Equipment Management Professionals(195)
Association of Family and Conciliation Courts(196)
Association of Federal Communications Consulting Engineers(196)
Association of Fund-Raising Distributors and Suppliers(198)
Association of Genetic Technologists(198)
Association of Golf Merchandisers(199)
Association of Healthcare Internal Auditors(199)
Association of Home Office Life Underwriters(200)
Association of Insurance Compliance Professionals(201)
Association of Medical Illustrators(204)
Association of Metropolitan Water Agencies(204)
Association of Naval Aviation(205)
Association of Occupational Health Professionals in Healthcare(206)
Association of Pathology Chairs(207)
Association of Pediatric Hematology/Oncology Nurses(207)
Association of Polysomnographic Technologists(208)
Association of Professional Ball Players of America(208)
Association of Professional Design Firms(208)
Association of Program Directors in Internal Medicine(210)
Association of Proposal Management Professionals(210)
Association of Psychology Postdoctoral and Internship Centers(210)
Association of Public Treasurers of the United States and Canada(211)
Association of Retail Marketing Services(212)
Association of Retail Travel Agents(212)
Association of Service and Computer Dealers International(213)
Association of Specialized and Professional Accreditors(214)
Association of State and Territorial Dental Directors(215)
Association of State and Territorial Public Health Nutrition Directors(215)
Association of Steel Distributors(216)
Association of Supervisory and Administrative School Personnel(216)
Association of Talent Agents(216)
Association of Teacher Educators(217)
Association of Teachers of Preventive Medicine(217)
Association of University Research Parks(219)
Association of Vacuum Equipment Manufacturers International(220)
Association of Women in the Metal Industries(220)
Association of Women Surgeons(220)
Audio Publishers Association(222)
Automotive Body Parts Association(223)
Automotive Occupant Restraints Council(224)
Aviation Insurance Association(225)
Beet Sugar Development Foundation(227)
Belgian Draft Horse Corp. of America(227)
Binding Industries Association(228)
BioCommunications Association(229)
Bioelectromagnetics Society(229)
Biomedical Marketing Association(229)
Black Filmmaker Foundation(230)
Book Manufacturers' Institute(231)
Botanical Society of America(231)
Braunvieh Association of America(232)
Broadcast Education Association(233)
Builders Hardware Manufacturers Association(234)
Business Forms Management Association(235)
Callerlab-International Association of Square Dance Callers(236)
Canon Law Society of America(237)
Cantors Assembly(237)
Captive Insurance Companies Association(237)
Casket and Funeral Supply Association of America(238)
Casting Industry Suppliers Association(239)
Catfish Farmers of America(239)
Catholic Biblical Association of America(239)
Cellulose Insulation Manufacturers Association(241)
Cement Employers Association(241)
Ceramic Tile Institute of America(242)
CHA - Certified Horsemanship Association(242)
Check Payment Systems Association(243)
Chester White Swine Record Association(244)
China Clay Producers Association(244)
Christian Labor Association of the United States of America(246)
Clay Minerals Society(247)
Cleaning Management Institute(247)
Clinical Immunology Society(248)
Clinical Ligand Assay Society(248)
Closure Manufacturers Association(248)
Cocoa Merchants' Association of America(250)
College of Optometrists in Vision Development(252)
Color Association of the United States(252)
Commercial Food Equipment Service Association(253)
Commission on Professionals in Science and Technology(254)
Communications Fraud Control Association(255)
Composite Can and Tube Institute(256)
Compressed Air and Gas Institute(257)
Conference of Major Superiors of Men, U.S.A.(259)
Conference on College Composition and Communication(260)
Congress of Independent Unions(261)

Lawn and Garden Marketing and Distribution Association(406)
League of Historic American Theatres(406)
Leather Apparel Association(406)
Library Administration and Management Association(407)
Library and Information Technology Association(407)
Linguistic Society of America(408)
Lutheran Education Association(409)
Lutheran Educational Conference of North America(409)
Machinery Dealers National Association(409)
Management Association for Private Photogrammetric Surveyors(410)
Manufactured Housing Association for Regulatory Reform(410)
Manufacturers Standardization Society of the Valve and Fittings Industry(411)
Maple Flooring Manufacturers Association(412)
Marine Corps Reserve Association(412)
Marketing Agencies Association Worldwide(412)
Marketing and Advertising Global Network(412)
Masonry Society, The(413)
Mass Marketing Insurance Institute(413)
Measurement, Control and Automation Association(415)
Meat Importers' Council of America(415)
Media Rating Council(415)
Medical Device Manufacturers Association(416)
Medical Marketing Association(416)
Messenger Courier Association of the Americas(417)
Metal Building Contractors and Erectors Association(417)
Metal Finishing Suppliers Association(417)
Methacrylate Producers Association(418)
Middle East Studies Association of North America(418)
Modular Building Institute(420)
Multi-Level Marketing International Association(422)
Museum Trustee Association(423)
Music Library Association(423)
Mystery Shopping Providers Association(424)
NARTE(425)
National Accounting and Finance Council(427)
National Air Filtration Association(428)
National Alliance for Media Arts and Culture(429)
National Alliance of Independent Crop Consultants(429)
National Association for Environmental Management(433)
National Association for Family Child Care(433)
National Association for Girls and Women in Sport(433)
National Association for Health and Fitness(433)
National Association for Practical Nurse Education and Service(435)
National Association of Activity Professionals(437)
National Association of Architectural Metal Manufacturers(438)
National Association of Beverage Importers-Wine-Spirits-Beer(439)
National Association of Blacks in Criminal Justice(440)
National Association of Business Political Action Committees(441)
National Association of Child Care Professionals(443)
National Association of Corporate Treasurers(446)
National Association of County Agricultural Agents(447)
National Association of County Engineers(447)
National Association of Cruise Oriented Agencies(448)
National Association of Disability Evaluating Professionals(449)
National Association of Educational Office Professionals(450)
National Association of Elevator Safety Authorities International(450)
National Association of Emergency Medical Technicians(450)
National Association of Energy Service Companies(451)
National Association of Evangelicals(451)
National Association of First Responders(452)
National Association of Golf Tournament Directors(454)
National Association of Health Data Organizations(455)
National Association of Health Services Executives(455)
National Association of Healthcare Access Management(455)
National Association of Healthcare Consultants(455)
National Association of Hispanic Publications(456)
National Association of Industrial Technology(458)
National Association of Installation Developers(458)
National Association of Investment Companies(459)
National Association of Medicaid Directors(461)
National Association of Medical Examiners(461)
National Association of Minority Contractors(462)
National Association of Minority Engineering Program Administrators(462)
National Association of Neighborhoods(462)
National Association of Nephrology Technologists and Technicians(462)
National Association of Nutrition and Aging Services Programs(463)
National Association of Oil Heating Service Managers(463)
National Association of Parliamentarians(463)
National Association of Physician Recruiters(464)
National Association of Pipe Coating Applicators(464)
National Association of Power Engineers(465)
National Association of Professional Geriatric Care Managers(466)
National Association of Professional Mortgage Women(466)
National Association of Professional Pet Sitters(466)
National Association of Professional Process Servers(466)
National Association of Public Child Welfare Administrators(467)
National Association of Railroad Trial Counsel(467)
National Association of Real Estate Brokers(468)
National Association of Resale & Thrift Shops(469)
National Association of Secretaries of State(471)
National Association of Sporting Goods Wholesalers(472)
National Association of State Aviation Officials(473)
National Association of State Directors of Career Technical Education Consortium(474)
National Association of State Directors of Migrant Education(474)
National Association of State Directors of Teacher Education and Certification(475)
National Association of State Radio Networks(476)
National Association of VA Physicians and Dentists(480)
National Association of Veterans' Research and Education Foundations(480)
National Association of Video Distributors(480)
National Association of Waterfront Employers(481)
National Association of Workforce Boards(482)
National Automotive Finance Association(483)
National Bulk Vendors Association(485)
National Bureau of Certified Consultants(485)
National Center for Homeopathy(488)
National Certified Pipe Welding Bureau(488)
National Chemical Credit Association(488)
National Chimney Sweep Guild(489)
National Conference of Catechetical Leadership(493)
National Conference of CPA Practitioners(493)
National Conference of State Historic Preservation Officers(494)
National Conference of States on Building Codes and Standards(494)
National Conference on Public Employee Retirement Systems(495)
National Contact Lens Examiners(495)
National Costumers Association(496)
National Council for Geographic Education(497)
National Council of Agricultural Employers(498)
National Council of Chain Restaurants(498)
National Council of University Research Administrators(501)
National Council on Qualifications for the Lighting Professions(502)
National Credit Reporting Association(503)
National Credit Union Management Association(503)
National Dairy Herd Improvement Association(504)
National Defined Contribution Council(505)
National Education Knowledge Industry Association(506)
National Extension Association of Family and Consumer Sciences(508)
National Fastener Distributors Association(508)
National Federation of Abstracting and Information Services(508)
National Federation of Licensed Practical Nurses(509)
National Federation of Priests' Councils(510)
National Frame Builders Association(512)
National Funeral Directors and Morticians Association(513)
National Grain Sorghum Producers(514)
National Grain Trade Council(514)
National Grants Management Association(514)
National Guild of Professional Paperhangers(515)
National Housing and Rehabilitation Association(518)
National Hydrogen Association(518)
National Institute for Animal Agriculture(520)
National Kerosene Heater Association(523)
National Leased Housing Association(524)
National Livestock Producers Association(525)
National Lubricating Grease Institute(525)
National Marine Distributors Association(526)
National Minority Business Council(527)
National Nursing Staff Development Organization(529)
National Onion Association(529)
National Onsite Wastewater Recycling Association(529)
National Organization for Associate Degree Nursing(529)
National Organization for Competency Assurance(530)
National Organization for the Professional Advancement of Black Chemists and Chemical Engineers(530)
National Organization of Nurse Practitioner Faculties(530)
National Park Hospitality Association(531)
National Perinatal Association(532)
National Phlebotomy Association(533)
National Public Employer Labor Relations Association(534)
National Railroad Construction and Maintenance Association(534)

National Reverse Mortgage Lenders Association(536)
National School Transportation Association(538)
National Society for Experiential Education(540)
National Society for Healthcare Foodservice Management(540)
National Society of Accountants for Cooperatives(541)
National Society of Professional Surveyors(542)
National Solid Wastes Management Association(542)
National Spinal Cord Injury Association(542)
National Sunflower Association(545)
National Tax Association(545)
National Tay-Sachs and Allied Diseases Association(545)
National Terrazzo and Mosaic Association(546)
National Textile Association(546)
National Trappers Association(547)
National Vehicle Leasing Association(548)
National Watermelon Association(549)
National Waterways Conference(549)
National Weather Service Employees Organization(549)
National Wellness Institute(549)
National Wheel and Rim Association(549)
National Wildlife Rehabilitators Association(549)
Native American Journalists Association(550)
Naval Enlisted Reserve Association(551)
NORA: An Association of Responsible Recyclers(553)
North American Contractors Association(556)
North American Equipment Dealers Association(556)
North American Neuro-Ophthalmology Society(559)
North American Skull Base Society(560)
North American Society for Pediatric Gastroenterology, Hepatology and Nutrition(561)
North American Transportation Management Institute(562)
Northwest Fruit Exporters(562)
Nurses Organization of Veterans Affairs(563)
Office Business Center Association International(564)
Organization of American Kodaly Educators(567)
Organization of Black Airline Pilots(567)
Organization of Black Designers(567)
Oriental Rug Retailers of America(568)
Ornamental Concrete Producers Association(568)
Orthopaedic Research Society(568)
Outdoor Power Equipment Aftermarket Association(569)
Outdoor Writers Association of America(569)
Paleontological Research Institution(570)
Paleontological Society(570)
Paper Shipping Sack Manufacturers Association(571)
Pediatric Orthopedic Society of North America(572)
Perennial Plant Association(573)
Performance Warehouse Association(573)
Phi Mu Alpha Sinfonia(576)
Photoimaging Manufacturers and Distributors Association(576)
Phycological Society of America(577)
Piano Manufacturers Association International(577)
Picture Agency Council of America(577)
Pine Chemicals Association(578)
Poetry Society of America(579)
Polyurethane Foam Association(580)
Polyurethane Manufacturers Association(580)
Pony of the Americas Club(580)
Portable Sanitation Association International(581)
Portfolio Management Institute(581)
Power Washers of North America(582)
Production Engine Remanufacturers Association(585)
Professional Apparel Association(585)
Professional Association of Resume Writers and Career Coaches(586)
Professional Association of Volleyball Officials(586)
Professional Grounds Management Society(587)
Professional Numismatists Guild(588)
Professional Society for Sales and Marketing Training(589)
Professional Women in Construction(590)
Propeller Club of the United States(591)
Psychology Society(592)
Public Agency Risk Managers Association(592)
Railway Engineering-Maintenance Suppliers Association(595)
Railway Systems Suppliers(595)
Railway Tie Association(595)
Real Estate Educators Association(595)
REALTORS Land Institute(596)
Receptive Services Association of America(596)
Recycled Paperboard Technical Association(597)
Rubber Pavements Association(603)
Safety Equipment Distributors Association(604)
Safety Glazing Certification Council(604)
Sales Association of the Paper Industry(604)
Sealant, Waterproofing and Restoration Institute(607)
Seaplane Pilots Association(607)
Secondary Materials and Recycled Textiles Association(607)
Securities Transfer Association(607)
Semiconductor Environmental Safety and Health Association(608)
Shipbuilders Council of America(610)
Showmen's League of America(610)
Sleep Research Society(611)
Smocking Arts Guild of America(612)
Society for American Baseball Research(613)
Society for Applied Anthropology(613)
Society for Developmental Biology(616)
Society for Excellence in Eyecare(617)
Society for Experimental Biology and Medicine(617)
Society for Foodservice Management(617)
Society for Free Radical Biology and Medicine(617)
Society for Healthcare Consumer Advocacy(618)
Society for Historical Archaeology(618)
Society for Leukocyte Biology(621)
Society for Medical Decision Making(621)
Society for Obstetric Anesthesia and Perinatology(622)
Society for Pediatric Anesthesia(623)
Society for Pediatric Dermatology(623)
Society for Pediatric Radiology(623)
Society for Pediatric Research(623)
Society for Personality Assessment(623)
Society for Research on Nicotine and Tobacco(625)
Society for Risk Analysis(625)
Society for Social Work Leadership in Health Care(625)
Society for the Scientific Study of Sexuality(627)
Society for the Study of Evolution(628)
Society for the Study of Social Problems(628)
Society for Vascular Nursing(629)
Society of Accredited Marine Surveyors(629)
Society of Collision Repair Specialists(633)
Society of Cost Estimating and Analysis(634)
Society of Economic Geologists(635)
Society of Financial Examiners(636)
Society of Government Travel Professionals(637)
Society of Independent Show Organizers(638)
Society of National Association Publications(640)
Society of Neurosurgical Anesthesia and Critical Care(641)
Society of Petrophysicists and Well Log Analysts(641)
Society of Piping Engineers and Designers(642)
Society of Quality Assurance(643)
Society of Telecommunications Consultants(644)
Society of Toxicologic Pathologists(645)
Society of Trauma Nurses(645)
Society of Wine Educators(646)
Solar Energy Industries Association(647)
Songwriters Guild of America(647)
Soyfoods Association of North America(648)
Special Care Dentistry Association(648)
Sports Lawyers Association(651)
SPRI, Inc.(652)
Stadium Managers Association(652)
Stained Glass Association of America(652)
Station Representatives Association(653)
Steel Deck Institute(653)
Structural Insulated Panel Association(654)
Substance Abuse Program Administrators Association(655)
Suburban Newspapers of America(655)
Summer and Casual Furniture Manufacturers Association(655)
Suntanning Association for Education(655)
Surface Design Association(656)
Swedish-American Chambers of Commerce(657)
Texas Longhorn Breeders Association of America(659)
Textile Care Allied Trades Association(660)
Textile Distributors Association(660)
Tile Roofing Institute(661)
Tire and Rim Association(661)
Trade Promotion Management Association(663)
Transaction Processing Performance Council(663)
Transplantation Society(663)
Transportation Lawyers Association(664)
Transworld Advertising Agency Network(664)
Travel and Tourism Research Association(665)
Truck Manufacturers Association(665)
U.S. - Taiwan Business Council(667)
U.S. Internet Industry Association(668)
Uniformed Services Academy of Family Physicians(669)
United States Army Warrant Officers Association(673)
United States Ski Association(677)
United States Swim School Association(677)
United States Tuna Foundation(678)
Universities Space Research Association(679)
University and College Designers Association(679)
University Aviation Association(679)
University Council for Educational Administration(679)
Urban Financial Services Coalition(680)
US Composting Council(681)
Vacuum Dealers Trade Association(682)
Walking Horse Owners Association of America(685)
Water and Wastewater Equipment Manufacturers Association(685)
Water Systems Council(686)
WEB: Worldwide Employee Benefits Network(686)
Wedding and Portrait Photographers International(686)
Western Economic Association International(687)
Western History Association(687)
Wheat Quality Council(688)
White House News Photographers Association(688)
Window Coverings Association of America(689)
Women Chefs and Restaurateurs(691)
Women in Film(691)
Women in Government Relations(692)
Women's Jewelry Association(693)
Women's Professional Rodeo Association(694)
Woodworking Machinery Industry Association(694)
World International Nail and Beauty Association(696)
World Sign Associates(696)

World Teleport Association(696)

$100-250,000

Academy of Dentistry International(3)
Academy of Legal Studies in Business(4)
Academy of Medical-Surgical Nurses(4)
Academy of Operative Dentistry(4)
Access Technology Association(6)
Accountants for the Public Interest(6)
Accrediting Council on Education in Journalism and Mass Communications(7)
ADED - the Association for Driver Rehabilitation Specialists(8)
Affordable Housing Tax Credit Coalition(10)
Agricultural and Industrial Manufacturers' Representatives Association(12)
Air & Surface Transport Nurses Association(12)
Airborne Law Enforcement Association(14)
Airport Ground Transportation Association(15)
Alliance of Area Business Publications(16)
Alliance of Foam Packaging Recyclers(16)
Alpha Chi Sigma(17)
Aluminum Anodizers Council(18)
American Academy of Ambulatory Care Nursing(20)
American Academy of Clinical Psychiatrists(21)
American Academy of Clinical Toxicology(21)
American Academy of Dental Practice Administration(21)
American Academy of Nursing(25)
American Academy of Oral and Maxillofacial Pathology(25)
American Academy of Oral Medicine(25)
American Academy of Podiatric Practice Management(27)
American Academy of Podiatric Sports Medicine(27)
American Academy of State Certified Appraisers(29)
American Aging Association(30)
American Agricultural Editors Association(30)
American Alliance for Theatre and Education(30)
American Apparel Producers Network(32)
American Ass'n of Ambulatory Surgery Centers(32)
American Association for Applied Linguistics(33)
American Association for Continuity of Care(34)
American Association for Pediatric Ophthalmology and Strabismus(36)
American Association for Public Opinion Research(36)
American Association for Women in Community Colleges(37)
American Association of Avian Pathologists(38)
American Association of Code Enforcement(40)
American Association of Community Theatre(41)
American Association of Dental Consultants(41)
American Association of Dental Examiners(42)
American Association of Healthcare Consultants(43)
American Association of Managed Care Nurses(44)
American Association of Orthopaedic Medicine(47)
American Association of Owners and Breeders of Peruvian Paso Horses(47)
American Association of Plastic Surgeons(48)
American Association of Political Consultants(49)
American Association of Private Railroad Car Owners(49)
American Association of Radon Scientists and Technologists(50)
American Association of Women Dentists(54)
American Association of Zoo Keepers(54)
American Auditory Society(55)
American Berkshire Association(56)
American Board of Forensic Psychology(57)
American Boat Builders and Repairers Association(58)
American Chain of Warehouses(61)
American Cheese Society(61)
American Cinema Editors(62)
American Clinical Neurophysiology Society(63)
American College of Angiology(64)
American College of Bankruptcy(64)
American College of Construction Lawyers(65)
American College of International Physicians(66)
American College of Laboratory Animal Medicine(66)
American College of Medical Physics(67)
American College of Neuropsychiatrists(68)
American College of Osteopathic Pediatricians(69)
American College of Tax Counsel(71)
American Composers Alliance(72)
American Conference of Academic Deans(73)
American Consultants League(74)
American Correctional Health Services Association(74)
American Council for Construction Education(75)
American Council of Hypnotist Examiners(75)
American Council of State Savings Supervisors(75)
American Council on Consumer Interests(76)
American Criminal Justice Association/Lambda Alpha Epsilon(77)
American Dance Guild(78)
American Dance Therapy Association(78)
American Dehydrated Onion and Garlic Association(78)
American Design Drafting Association(79)
American Electrology Association(80)
American Endodontic Society(81)
American Flock Association(84)
American Hackney Horse Society(88)
American Hampshire Sheep Association(88)
American Harp Society(89)
American Herbalists Guild(90)
American Hernia Society(90)
American Highland Cattle Association(90)
American Hockey Coaches Association(91)
American Holistic Veterinary Medical Association(91)
American Horticultural Therapy Association(92)
American Independent Business Alliance(93)
American Indonesian Chamber of Commerce(93)
American Innerspring Manufacturers(93)
American Institute for Maghrib Studies(94)
American Institute of Chemists(95)
American Institute of Hydrology(96)
American Institute of the History of Pharmacy(97)
American Insurance Marketing and Sales Society(98)
American Ladder Institute(100)
American League of Lobbyists(101)
American Leather Chemists Association(101)
American Littoral Society(102)
American Maritime Association(103)
American Milking Shorthorn Society(106)
American Musicological Society(107)
American Oilseed Coalition(110)
American Ornithologists' Union(110)
American Osteopathic College of Anesthesiologists(111)
American Osteopathic College of Dermatology(112)
American Osteopathic Colleges of Ophthalmology and Otolaryngology - Head and Neck Surgery(112)
American Peanut Product Manufacturers(113)
American Pediatric Society(113)
American Pipe Fittings Association(115)
American Polygraph Association(116)
American Property Tax Counsel(117)
American Prosthodontic Society(117)
American Psychotherapy Association(119)
American Radiological Nurses Association(121)
American Radium Society(121)
American Registry of Medical Assistants(122)
American Risk and Insurance Association(123)
American Safe Deposit Association(123)
American Schools Association(124)
American Scientific Glassblowers Society(124)
American Society for Aesthetics(126)
American Society for Dental Aesthetics(128)
American Society for Engineering Management(128)
American Society for Experimental NeuroTherapeutics(129)
American Society of Agricultural Consultants(133)
American Society of Anesthesia Technologists and Technicians(134)
American Society of Brewing Chemists(135)
American Society of Business Publication Editors(135)
American Society of Group Psychotherapy and Psychodrama(138)
American Society of Ichthyologists and Herpetologists(139)
American Society of Indexers(139)
American Society of Mammalogists(141)
American Society of Maxillofacial Surgeons(141)
American Society of Mining and Reclamation(141)
American Society of Neurorehabilitation(142)
American Society of Ophthalmic Registered Nurses(143)
American Society of Pain Management Nurses(143)
American Society of Perfumers(143)
American Society of Plant Taxonomists(144)
American Society of Preventive Oncology(145)
American Society of Transportation and Logisitcs(146)
American Society of Trial Consultants(147)
American Sportscasters Association(148)
American Technical Education Association(150)
American Telemedicine Association(151)
American Trakehner Association(152)
American Underground-Construction Association(152)
American Veterinary Dental Society(153)
American Veterinary Distributors Association(153)
American Wood-Preservers' Association(155)
American-Israel Chamber of Commerce and Industry(156)
Appalachian Hardwood Manufacturers(158)
Apple Processors Association(159)
Apple Products Research and Education Council(159)
Appliance Parts Distributors Association(159)
Archery Trade Association(160)
Architectural Engineering Institute(160)
Architectural Precast Association(160)
Argentina-American Chamber of Commerce(160)
Art Glass Association(161)
Art Libraries Society of North America(161)
Asia America MultiTechnology Association(162)
Asphalt Recycling and Reclaiming Association(163)
Associated Owners and Developers(165)
Associated Press Managing Editors(166)
Associated Wire Rope Fabricators(166)
Association for Accounting Administration(166)
Association for Accounting Marketing(167)
Association for Ambulatory Behavorial Healthcare(167)
Association for Business Communication(168)
Association for Canadian Studies in the United States(168)
Association for Comprehensive Energy Psychology(170)
Association for Computational Linguistics(170)
Association for Continuing Higher Education(171)
Association for Financial Technology(173)
Association for Hospital Medical Education(174)
Association for Humanistic Psychology(174)

Association for Library and Information Science Education(175)
Association for Library Trustees and Advocates(176)
Association for Practical and Professional Ethics(177)
Association for Preservation Technology International(177)
Association for Surgical Education(178)
Association for the Advancement of Applied Sport Psychology(179)
Association for the Advancement of Baltic Studies(179)
Association for the Advancement of Psychotherapy(179)
Association for the Advancement of Wound Care(180)
Association for the Sociology of Religion(180)
Association for the Study of Higher Education(181)
Association for Theatre in Higher Education(181)
Association for Transpersonal Psychology(181)
Association of Administrative Law Judges(183)
Association of Alternate Postal Systems(184)
Association of Art Museum Directors(186)
Association of Asphalt Paving Technologists(186)
Association of Battery Recyclers(187)
Association of Bituminous Contractors(187)
Association of Black Sociologists(187)
Association of Christian Therapists(190)
Association of Clinical Scientists(190)
Association of Collegiate Schools of Planning(191)
Association of Consulting Foresters of America(192)
Association of Coupon Professionals(193)
Association of Direct Response Fundraising Counsel(194)
Association of Episcopal Colleges(195)
Association of Executive and Administrative Professionals(196)
Association of Food and Drug Officials(197)
Association of Former Intelligence Officers(198)
Association of Freestanding Radiation Oncology Centers(198)
Association of Girl Scout Executive Staff(198)
Association of Image Consultants International(200)
Association of Industry Manufacturers' Representatives(201)
Association of Insolvency and Restructuring Advisors(201)
Association of International Education Administrators(201)
Association of Jewish Center Professionals(202)
Association of Literary Scholars and Critics(203)
Association of Meeting Professionals(204)
Association of Military Banks of America(205)
Association of Official Seed Analysts(206)
Association of Official Seed Certifying Agencies(206)
Association of Otolaryngology Administrators(207)
Association of Presbyterian Colleges and Universities(208)
Association of Professional Genealogists(209)
Association of Professional Schools of International Affairs(209)
Association of Professors of Medicine(209)
Association of Real Estate Women(211)
Association of State Correctional Administrators(215)
Association of State Wetland Managers(216)
Association of Suppliers to the Paper Industry(216)
Association of Technical Personnel in Ophthalmology(217)
Association of Transportation Professionals(218)
Association of Traumatic Stress Specialists(218)
Automotive Trade Association Executives(224)
Aviation Distributors and Manufacturers Association International(224)
Ayrshire Breeders' Association(225)
Baking Industry Sanitation Standards Committee(225)
BCA(226)
Belgian American Chamber of Commerce in the United States(227)
Bibliographical Society of America(228)
Biological Stain Commission(229)
Book Industry Study Group, Inc.(231)
Brewers' Association of America(232)
Bridge Grid Flooring Manufacturers Association(232)
Bulk Carrier Conference(235)
Campus Safety, Health and Environmental Management Association(237)
Career Planning and Adult Development Network(238)
Cargo Airline Association(238)
Carpet Cushion Council(238)
Casual Furniture Retailers(239)
Catholic Academy for Communication Arts Professionals(239)
Catholic Library Association(240)
Chain Link Fence Manufacturers Institute(242)
Chemical Coaters Association International(243)
Chi Eta Phi Sorority(244)
Chief Petty Officers Association(244)
Child Neurology Society(244)
Children's Literature Association(244)
Chocolate Manufacturers Association(245)
Christian College Consortium(245)
Clinical Orthopaedic Society(248)
Clinical Social Work Federation(248)
Clothing Manufacturers Association of the U.S.A.(248)
Clydesdale Breeders of the United States(249)
Coal Technology Association(249)
Coalition for Government Procurement(249)
Coalition of Higher Education Assistance Organizations(249)
Coalition of Labor Union Women(249)
Coalition of Publicly Traded Partnerships(249)
Cold Finished Steel Bar Institute(250)
College Swimming Coaches Association of America(252)
Communications Media Management Association(255)
Community College Business Officers(255)
Computer Event Marketing Association(257)
Conductors Guild(259)
Congress of Chiropractic State Associations(261)
Congress of Lung Association Staffs(261)
Consortium of Behavioral Health Nurses and Associates(262)
Consortium of College and University Media Centers(262)
Consultant Dietitians in Health Care Facilities(263)
Cookware Manufacturers Association(265)
Copyright Society of the U.S.A.(266)
Corporate Facility Advisors(266)
Costume Society of America(267)
Cotton Warehouse Association of America(267)
Council for American Private Education(268)
Council for Learning Disabilities(269)
Council of American Jewish Museums(270)
Council of Communication Management(271)
Council of Engineering and Scientific Society Executives(271)
Council of Professional Associations on Federal Statistics(273)
Council of Societies for the Study of Religion(274)
Council on Diagnostic Imaging to the A.C.A.(275)
Council on Governmental Ethics Laws(276)
Cranberry Institute(278)
Cross Country Ski Areas Association(279)
Cryogenic Engineering Conference(280)
Custom Tailors and Designers Association of America(280)
Dance Educators of America(281)
Delta Pi Epsilon(282)
Delta Theta Phi(283)
Direct Marketing Insurance and Financial Services Council(285)
Door and Access Systems Manufacturers' Association, International(286)
Ductile Iron Society(288)
Dude Ranchers' Association(288)
Econometric Society(288)
Economic History Association(288)
Editorial Freelancers Association(289)
Education Industry Association(289)
EEG and Clinical Neuroscience Society(290)
Eight Sheet Outdoor Advertising Association(290)
Electrical Equipment Representatives Association(291)
Employee Assistance Society of North America(293)
Energy Security Council(294)
Environmental Bankers Association(296)
Environmental Design Research Association(296)
Epsilon Sigma Phi(297)
Estuarine Research Federation(297)
Ethylene Oxide Sterilization Association(298)
Evangelical Press Association(298)
Exhibition Services and Contractors Association(299)
Express Carriers Association(300)
Farm Equipment Wholesalers Association(301)
Federation of Analytical Chemistry and Spectroscopy Societies(303)
Federation of Behavioral, Psychological and Cognitive Sciences(303)
Federation of Environmental Technologists(303)
Federation of Straight Chiropractors and Organizations(304)
Fellowship of United Methodists in Music and Worship Arts(305)
Film and Bag Federation(305)
Filter Manufacturers Council(305)
Financial and Security Products Association(305)
Financial Markets Association(306)
Fire Equipment Manufacturers' Association(307)
Fire Suppression Systems Association(307)
Flexographic Prepress Platemakers Association(308)
Floor Covering Installation Contractors Association(308)
Food Industry Association Executives(309)
Foodservice Equipment Distributors Association(310)
Forestry Conservation Communications Association(310)
Fraternity Executives Association(311)
Friction Materials Standards Institute(312)
Fulfillment Services Association of America(312)
Futon Association International(313)
Gas Processors Suppliers Association(314)
Gas Turbine Association(314)
Gasket Fabricators Association(314)
Geochemical Society(315)
German American Business Association(316)
Glove Shippers Association(318)
Greek Food and Wine Institute(320)
Guild of American Luthiers(321)
Gynecologic Surgery Society(321)
Halon Alternatives Research Corp.(321)
Health & Sciences Communications Association(322)
Health Industry Representatives Association(323)
Herb Growing & Marketing Network(325)
Herpetologists' League(325)
Hispanic National Bar Association(326)
Hobby Manufacturers Association(327)
Home Baking Association(327)
Home Healthcare Nurses Association(327)
Hop Growers of America(328)

Imaging Supplies Coalition for International Intellectual Property Protection(332)
Incentive Federation(332)
Independent Armored Car Operators Association(333)
Independent Distributors Association(333)
Independent Pet and Animal Transportation Association International(335)
Indian Educators Federation(336)
Indiana Limestone Institute of America(336)
Industrial Diamond Association of America(336)
Industrial Heating Equipment Association(337)
Industry Council for Tangible Assets(337)
Information Technologies Credit Union Association(338)
Institute for Responsible Housing Preservation(339)
Institute of Certified Records Managers(340)
Institute of Diving(341)
Institute of Noise Control Engineering(343)
Institute of Store Planners(344)
Instructional Telecommunications Council(344)
Instrumentation Testing Association(344)
Insurance Marketing Communications Association(345)
Inter-American Bar Association(346)
Interactive Multimedia and Collaborative Communications Association(346)
Intercoiffure America/Canada(346)
Intercollegiate Broadcasting System(346)
Interferry(347)
International Academy of Oral Medicine and Toxicology(348)
International Alliance for Women(348)
International Association Colon Hydro Therapy(349)
International Association for Cold Storage Construction(349)
International Association for Computer Systems Security(349)
International Association for Hydrogen Energy(350)
International Association for Modular Exhibitry(351)
International Association of Attorneys and Executives in Corporate Real Estate(353)
International Association of Baptist Colleges and Universities(353)
International Association of Black Professional Fire Fighters(354)
International Association of Counseling Services(355)
International Association of Geophysical Contractors(357)
International Association of Ice Cream Vendors(358)
International Association of Official Human Rights Agencies(359)
International Association of Round Dance Teachers(361)
International Association of Skateboard Companies(361)
International Association of Speakers Bureaus(361)
International Association of Used Equipment Dealers(361)
International Association of Women Police(362)
International Atherosclerosis Society(362)
International Brotherhood of Magicians(363)
International Buckskin Horse Association(363)
International Builders Exchange Executives(363)
International Concatenated Order of Hoo-Hoo(366)
International Corrugated Packaging Foundation(367)
International Embryo Transfer Society(370)
International Entertainment Buyers Association(370)
International Family Recreation Association(371)
International Federation for Artificial Organs(371)
International Food Additives Council(372)
International Food, Wine and Travel Writers Association(372)
International Foodservice Editorial Council(372)
International Fruit Tree Association(373)
International Furniture Suppliers Association(373)
International Glove Association(374)
International Grooving and Grinding Association(374)
International Horn Society(375)
International Institute of Forecasters(376)
International Jelly and Preserve Association(377)
International Kitchen Exhaust Cleaning Association(377)
International Labor Communications Association(377)
International Maintenance Institute(379)
International Marking and Identification Association(379)
International Microwave Power Institute(379)
International Nanny Association(380)
International Neural Network Society(381)
International Nurses Society on Addictions(381)
International Oceanic Society(381)
International Pediatric Transplant Association(382)
International Plant Propagators Society(383)
International Real Estate Federation - American Chapter(384)
International Reciprocal Trade Association(384)
International Research Council of Neuromuscular Disorders(385)
International Society for Ecological Economics(387)
International Society for General Semantics(387)
International Society for Preventive Oncology(388)
International Society of Air Safety Investigators(389)
International Society of Arthroscopy, Knee Surgery and Orthopaedic Sports Medicine(390)
International Society of Barristers(390)
International Society of Certified Electronics Technicians(390)
International Society of Communication Specialists(391)
International Society of Crime Prevention Practitioners(391)
International Society of Facilities Executives(391)
International Society of Parametric Analysts(392)
International Society of Political Psychology(392)
International Society of Psychiatric-Mental Health Nurses(392)
International Society of Restaurant Association Executives(392)
International Society of Travel and Tourism Educators(392)
International Textile and Apparel Association(394)
International Waterlily and Water Gardening Society(397)
International Webmasters Association(397)
International Women's Writing Guild(397)
Intersociety Council For Pathology Information(398)
Investment Recovery Association(399)
Islamic Medical Association of North America(400)
IT Financial Management Association(400)
Jesuit Secondary Education Association(401)
Jewish Educators Assembly(402)
Kappa Kappa Iota(403)
Kappa Psi Pharmaceutical Fraternity(403)
Kite Trade Association International(403)
Lambda Kappa Sigma(405)
Laser and Electro-Optics Manufacturers' Association(405)
Latin American Studies Association(405)
Leaf Tobacco Exporters Association(406)
Library Binding Institute(407)
Life Insurers Council(407)
Lighter Association(408)
Lignin Institute(408)
Livestock Publications Council(409)
Manufacturers Representatives of America(411)
Meat Industry Suppliers Alliance(415)
Media Credit Association(415)
Military Impacted Schools Association(419)
Mobile Industrial Caterers' Association International(420)
Mu Phi Epsilon(422)
Mulch and Soil Council(422)
Musculoskeletal Tumor Society(422)
Museum Computer Network(423)
Mystery Writers of America(424)
National Academies of Practice(426)
National Academy of Arbitrators(426)
National Academy of Neuropsychology(426)
National Adult Education Professional Development Consortium(427)
National Alfalfa Alliance(429)
National Animal Control Association(430)
National Appliance Parts Suppliers Association(430)
National Association for Armenian Studies and Research(431)
National Association for Developmental Education(432)
National Association for Medical Direction of Respiratory Care(434)
National Association for Research in Science Teaching(435)
National Association for Rural Mental Health(436)
National Association for Sport and Physical Education(436)
National Association for the Advancement of Psychoanalysis(436)
National Association of African American Studies(438)
National Association of Agriculture Employees(438)
National Association of Assistant United States Attorneys(439)
National Association of Black Women Entrepreneurs(440)
National Association of Charterboat Operators(442)
National Association of Computer Consultant Businesses(445)
National Association of Consumer Advocates(446)
National Association of Consumer Agency Administrators(446)
National Association of Consumer Shows(446)
National Association of County Recorders, Election Officials and Clerks(447)
National Association of Credit Union Chairmen(448)
National Association of Credit Union Supervisory and Auditing Committees(448)
National Association of Decorative Fabric Distributors(448)
National Association of Division Order Analysts(449)
National Association of Equipment Leasing Brokers(451)
National Association of Federal Education Program Administrators(452)
National Association of Federal Veterinarians(452)
National Association of Fleet Resale Dealers(453)
National Association of Flight Instructors(453)
National Association of Flood and Stormwater Management Agencies(453)
National Association of FSA County Office Employees(454)
National Association of Geoscience Teachers(454)
National Association of Government Communicators(454)

National Association of Graphic and Product Identification Manufacturers(455)
National Association of Health Unit Coordinators(455)
National Association of Hospital Hospitality Houses(456)
National Association of Independent Insurance Adjusters(457)
National Association of Independent Lighting Distributors(457)
National Association of Investigative Specialists(459)
National Association of Jewelry Appraisers(459)
National Association of Judiciary Interpreters and Translators(459)
National Association of Legal Search Consultants(460)
National Association of Margarine Manufacturers(461)
National Association of Marine Services(461)
National Association of Minority Media Executives(462)
National Association of Miscellaneous, Ornamental and Architectural Products Contractors(462)
National Association of Negro Business and Professional Women's Clubs(462)
National Association of Optometrists and Opticians(463)
National Association of Orthopaedic Technologists(463)
National Association of Physician Nurses(464)
National Association of Pipe Fabricators(464)
National Association of Principals of Schools for Girls(465)
National Association of Private, Nontraditional Schools and Colleges with Accrediting Commission for Higher Education(465)
National Association of Public Insurance Adjusters(467)
National Association of Pupil Services Administrators(467)
National Association of Real Estate Editors(468)
National Association of Rehabilitation Providers and Agencies(469)
National Association of Reinforcing Steel Contractors(469)
National Association of Retired Senior Volunteer Program Directors(469)
National Association of Royalty Owners(469)
National Association of Sales Professionals(470)
National Association of Science Writers(471)
National Association of Scientific Materials Managers(471)
National Association of Security Companies(471)
National Association of Sign Supply Distributors(472)
National Association of State Facilities Administrators(475)
National Association of State Foresters(475)
National Association of State Procurement Officials(476)
National Association of State Utility Consumer Advocates(477)
National Association of State Veterans Homes(477)
National Association of Steel Pipe Distributors(477)
National Association of Swine Records(478)
National Association of Temple Administrators(479)
National Association of Temple Educators(479)
National Association of Ticket Brokers(479)
National Association of Trade Exchanges(479)
National Association of Unclaimed Property Administrators(479)
National Association of Women Highway Safety Leaders(481)
National Barbecue Association(483)
National Black Police Association(484)
National Block and Bridle Club(485)
National Board for Certified Clinical Hypnotherapists(485)
National Certification Commission(488)
National Certification Council for Activity Professionals(488)
National Cherry Growers and Industries Foundation(489)
National Church Goods Association(489)
National Classification Management Society(490)
National Clay Pipe Institute(490)
National Coalition of Abortion Providers(490)
National Coalition of Black Meeting Planners(490)
National Coalition of Girls Schools(490)
National Collegiate Wrestling Association(491)
National Conference of Black Lawyers(492)
National Conference of Editorial Writers(493)
National Conference of Executives of The ARC(493)
National Conference of State Fleet Administrators(494)
National Cotton Ginners' Association(496)
National Council for Marketing and Public Relations(497)
National Council for Workforce Education(497)
National Council of Black Engineers and Scientists(498)
National Council of Health Facilities Finance Authorities(499)
National Council of Postal Credit Unions(500)
National Council of Social Security Management Associations(500)
National Council of Supervisors of Mathematics(501)
National Council on Rehabilitation Education(503)
National Dance Association(504)
National Dog Groomers Association of America(505)
National Drilling Association(505)
National Emergency Management Association(507)
National EMS Pilots Association(507)
National Family Caregivers Association(508)
National Fashion Accessories Association(508)
National Federation of Modern Language Teachers Associations(509)
National Federation of Music Clubs(509)
National Federation of Press Women(510)
National Field Selling Association(510)
National Flute Association(511)
National Food and Energy Council(511)
National Freight Transportation Association(512)
National Greenhouse Manufacturers Association(515)
National Hay Association(516)
National Hearing Conservation Association(516)
National Horsemen's Benevolent and Protective Association(517)
National Human Resources Association(518)
National Humanities Alliance(518)
National Ice Cream Retailers Association(518)
National Independent Flag Dealers Association(519)
National Industrial Council - Employer Association Group(519)
National Industrial Council - State Associations Group(519)
National Institute for Electromedical Information(520)
National Institute of Oilseed Products(521)
National Institute of Steel Detailing(521)
National Institutes for Water Resources(521)
National Intercollegiate Soccer Officials Association(522)
National Juvenile Detention Association(523)
National League of American Pen Women(524)
National Lesbian and Gay Law Association(524)
National Lieutenant Governors Association(524)
National Mail Order Association(525)
National Maritime Alliance(526)
National Mastitis Council(526)
National Military Intelligence Association(527)
National Optometric Association(529)
National Pasta Association(532)
National Postsecondary Agriculture Student Organization(533)
National Poultry and Food Distributors Association(533)
National Purchasing Institute(534)
National Reading Conference(535)
National Rehabilitation Counseling Association(535)
National Retail Hobby Stores Association(536)
National Risk Retention Association(537)
National Rural Education Association(537)
National Slag Association(540)
National Society for the Study of Education(541)
National Society of Insurance Premium Auditors(542)
National Spotted Saddle Horse Association(543)
National Spotted Swine Record(543)
National Student Assistance Association(544)
National Submetering and Utility Allocation Association(544)
National Surgical Assistant Association(545)
National Taxidermists Association(545)
National Translator Association(547)
National Weather Association(549)
National Women's Studies Association(549)
National Woodland Owners Association(550)
Natural Science Collections Alliance(551)
Neckwear Association of America(551)
Neurodevelopmental Treatment Association(552)
North American Association of Christians in Social Work(554)
North American Benthological Society(555)
North American Clinical Dermatological Society(556)
North American Corriente Association(556)
North American Deer Farmers Association(556)
North American Gaming Regulators Association(557)
North American Natural Casing Association(558)
North American Serials Interest Group(560)
North American Society of Adlerian Psychology(561)
North American South Devon Association(561)
North-American Association of Telecommunications Dealers(562)
Ombudsman Association, The(564)
Operations Security Professionals Society(565)
Organization of Professional Employees of the U.S. Department of Agriculture(567)
Organizational Behavior Teaching Society(568)
Outdoor Power Equipment and Engine Service Association(569)
Overseas Automotive Council(570)
Parcel Shippers Association(571)
Parenting Publications of America(571)
Partnership in Print Production(572)
Patent Office Professional Association(572)
Peanut and Tree Nut Processors Association(572)
Pellet Fuels Institute(573)
Periodical and Book Association of America(573)
Peruvian Paso Horse Registry of North America(574)
Pharmaceutical Printed Literature Association(575)
Philippine-American Chamber of Commerce(576)
Phlebology Society of America(576)
Photo Chemical Machining Institute(576)
Pierre Fauchard Academy(577)
Pile Driving Contractors Association(577)
Pipe Tobacco Council(578)
Plastic Shipping Container Institute(578)
Postcard and Souvenir Distributors Association(581)
Power Sources Manufacturers Association(582)

Power-Motion Technology Representatives Association(582)
Preferred Funeral Directors International(583)
Printing Industry Credit Executives(584)
Process Equipment Manufacturers' Association(584)
Production and Operations Management Society(585)
Professional and Organizational Development Network in Higher Education(585)
Professional and Technical Consultants Association(585)
Professional Association for Childhood Education(585)
Professional Association of Christian Educators(585)
Professional Association of Custom Clothiers(585)
Professional Bail Agents of the United States(586)
Professional Construction Estimators Association of America(586)
Professional Managers Association(588)
Professional Paddlesports Association(588)
Professional Putters Association(588)
Professional Services Management Association(589)
Professional Women's Appraisal Association(590)
Property Casualty Conferences(591)
Property Owners Association(591)
Psi Omega(591)
Psychonomic Society(592)
Public Broadcasting Management Association(592)
Public Radio Program Directors Association(592)
Real Estate Information Professionals Association(596)
Recreational Vehicle Aftermarket Association(596)
Refrigerated Foods Association(597)
Refrigerating Engineers and Technicians Association(597)
Religion Communicators Council(598)
Religion Newswriters Association(598)
Religious Education Association(599)
Renaissance Society of America(599)
Resistance Welder Manufacturers' Association(600)
Roof Coatings Manufacturers Association(603)
Rural Sociological Society(603)
SAFE Association(604)
Sales Association of the Chemical Industry(604)
SAVE International(605)
SB Latex Council(605)
Scale Manufacturers Association(605)
School Management Study Group(606)
School Science and Mathematics Association(606)
Scientific Equipment and Furniture Association(606)
Security Hardware Distributors Association(607)
Senior Army Reserve Commanders Association(609)
Service Dealers Association(609)
Service Industry Association(609)
Service Specialists Association(609)
Service Station Dealers of America and Allied Trades(609)
Sewn Products Equipment and Suppliers of the Americas(609)
Shock Society(610)
Silver Users Association(611)
Small Business Legislative Council(611)
Small Publishers Association of North America(611)
Smart Card Alliance(611)
SMMA - The Motor and Motion Association(612)
Soccer Industry Council of America(612)
Society for Advancement of Management(613)
Society for Clinical and Experimental Hypnosis(615)
Society for Clinical Data Management(615)
Society for Clinical Vascular Surgery(615)
Society for Developmental and Behavioral Pediatrics(616)
Society for Humanistic Judaism(619)
Society for Intercultural Education, Training and Research - USA(620)
Society for Pediatric Pathology(623)
Society for Pediatric Psychology(623)
Society for Photographic Education(623)
Society for Radiation Oncology Administrators(624)
Society for Scholarly Publishing(625)
Society for the Scientific Study of Religion(627)
Society for the Study of Amphibians and Reptiles(628)
Society for Values in Higher Education(629)
Society of American Magicians(631)
Society of American Registered Architects(631)
Society of American Travel Writers(631)
Society of Automotive Analysts(632)
Society of Cleaning and Restoration Technicians(633)
Society of Creative Designers(634)
Society of Experimental Test Pilots(635)
Society of Geriatric Cardiology(637)
Society of Government Service Urologists(637)
Society of Insurance Financial Management(638)
Society of Insurance Research(638)
Society of Insurance Trainers and Educators(639)
Society of Nematologists(640)
Society of Professional Audio Recording Services(642)
Society of Protozoologists(643)
Society of Radiologists in Ultrasound(643)
Society of School Librarians International(644)
Society of State Directors of Health, Physical Education and Recreation(644)
Society of Wood Science and Technology(646)
Solar Rating and Certification Corp.(647)
Solution Mining Research Institute(647)
Sorptive Minerals Institute(647)
Soy Protein Council(648)
Space Transportation Association(648)
Special Interest Group for University and College Computing Services(649)
Spill Control Association of America(651)
Sporting Goods Agents Association(651)
Spring Research Institute(652)
Structural Stability Research Council(654)
Submersible Wastewater Pump Association(655)
Surface Finishing Industry Council(656)
Sustainable Buildings Industry Council(656)
Teaching-Family Association(658)
TechLaw Group(658)
Technical Association of the Graphic Arts(658)
Textile Producers and Suppliers Association(660)
Textured Yarn Association of America(660)
Theta Tau(660)
Tile Contractors' Association of America(661)
Tire Retread Information Bureau(662)
Tobacconists' Association of America(662)
Toxicology Forum(662)
Training Officers Conference(663)
Transportation & Logistics Council(664)
Transportation Research Forum(664)
Tubular Exchanger Manufacturers Association(666)
Type Directors Club(667)
U.S. Pan Asian American Chamber of Commerce(668)
Unified Abrasives Manufacturers Association(669)
Union for Radical Political Economics(669)
United Braford Breeders(670)
United Federation of Police & Security Officers(671)
United Infants and Childrens Wear Association(671)
United States Association for Energy Economics(673)
United States Association of Independent Gymnastic Clubs(673)
United States Cutting Tool Institute(675)
United States National Committee of the International Dairy Federation(676)
United Suffolk Sheep Association(678)
University Risk Management and Insurance Association(680)
Urban Affairs Association(680)
Utility Arborist Association(681)
Veterinary Cancer Society(682)
Veterinary Hospital Managers Association(682)
Viatical and Life Settlement Association of America(683)
Victorian Society in America(683)
Vinegar Institute(683)
Vinyl Acetate Council(683)
Visitor Studies Association(684)
Visual Resources Association(684)
Water and Sewer Distributors of America(685)
Water Sports Industry Association(686)
WaterJet Technology Association(686)
Web Sling and Tiedown Association(686)
Welsh Pony and Cob Society of America(687)
Western-English Trade Association(688)
White House Correspondents Association(688)
WIFS - Women in Insurance and Financial Services(688)
Wire Reinforcement Institute(690)
Wirebound Box Manufacturers Association(690)
Women in Film and Video(692)
Women's College Coalition(693)
Wood Component Manufacturers Association(694)
World Aquaculture Society(695)
World Media Association(696)
Writing Instrument Manufacturers Association(697)
Yacht Brokers Association of America(698)
Young Menswear Association(698)

$50-100,000

Academy of Aphasia(2)
Academy of Dental Materials(3)
Academy of Dispensing Audiologists(3)
ADARA(8)
Advertising Media Credit Executives Association, International(9)
AFIA-Alfalfa Processors Council(11)
Africa Travel Association(11)
Air Diffusion Council(13)
Air Medical Physician Association(13)
Alliance of Associations of Teachers of Japanese(16)
ALMA - the International Loudspeaker Association(17)
Aluminum Foil Container Manufacturers Association(18)
American Academy of Appellate Lawyers(20)
American Academy of Diplomacy(22)
American Academy of Environmental Engineers(22)
American Academy of Equine Art(22)
American Academy of Gnathologic Orthopedics(23)
American Academy of Home Care Physicians(23)
American Academy of Insurance Medicine(24)
American Academy of Maxillofacial Prosthetics(24)
American Academy of Oral and Maxillofacial Radiology(25)
American Academy of Thermology(29)
American Agricultural Law Association(30)
American Artists Professional League(32)
American Association for Crystal Growth(34)
American Association for the History of Medicine(37)
American Association of Automatic Door Manufacturers(38)
American Association of Grain Inspection and Weighing Agencies(43)
American Association of Nurse Attorneys, The(46)

American Association of Physicians and Health Care Professionals(48)
American Association of Presidents of Independent Colleges and Universities(49)
American Association of Railroad Superintendents(50)
American Association of Stratigraphic Palynologists(51)
American Association of Sunday and Feature Editors(52)
American Association of Surgical Physician Assistants(52)
American Association of Teachers of Slavic and East European Languages(52)
American Association of University Administrators(53)
American Association of Veterinary Clinicians(53)
American Bashkir Curly Registry(56)
American Butter Institute(60)
American Catholic Philosophical Association(61)
American Chain Association(61)
American Chiropractic Registry of Radiologic Technologists(62)
American College of Chiropractic Orthopedists(64)
American College of Mental Health Administration(67)
American College of Nuclear Medicine(68)
American College of Veterinary Radiology(72)
American Court and Commercial Newspapers(77)
American Cultural Resources Association(77)
American Dexter Cattle Association(79)
American Donkey and Mule Society(79)
American Edged Products Manufacturers Association(80)
American Federation of Violin and Bow Makers(83)
American Fiberboard Association(83)
American Floorcovering Alliance(84)
American Forage and Grassland Council(84)
American Forensic Association(85)
American Guild of Music(88)
American Head and Neck Society(89)
American Health Planning Association(89)
American Horse Publications Association(91)
American Hydrogen Association(92)
American Institute for Shippers Associations(94)
American Institute of Commemorative Art(95)
American Institute of Engineers(95)
American Institute of Homeopathy(96)
American Institute of Parliamentarians(97)
American Institute of Stress(97)
American Iron Ore Association(99)
American Jewish Press Association(99)
American Judges Association(99)
American Medical Publishers' Association(104)
American National Metric Council(108)
American Neuropsychiatric Association(108)
American Ophthalmological Society(110)
American Oriental Society(110)
American Osteopathic Academy for Sports Medicine(111)
American Osteopathic College of Rheumatology(112)
American Peanut Research and Education Society(113)
American Railway Development Association(121)
American Rambouillet Sheep Breeders Association(121)
American Rhinologic Society(123)
American Romagnola Association(123)
American Society for Apheresis(126)
American Society for Automation in Pharmacy(126)
American Society for Cytotechnology(128)
American Society for Ethnohistory(129)
American Society for Neurochemistry(130)
American Society of Artists(134)
American Society of Certified Engineering Technicians(135)
American Society of Church History(135)
American Society of Comparative Law(136)
American Society of Missiology(141)
American Society of Photographers(144)
American Society of Primatologists(145)
American Society of Wedding Professionals(147)
American Tarentaise Association(150)
American-Uzbekistan Chamber of Commerce(156)
Amusement Industry Manufacturers and Suppliers International(156)
Aniline Association(157)
Animal Transportation Association(157)
Antenna Measurement Techniques Association(157)
Antique and Amusement Photographers International(157)
Archery Range and Retailers Organization(160)
Asbestos Information Association/North America(162)
Associated Actors and Artistes of America(164)
Associated Church Press(164)
Associated Construction Distributors International(165)
Associated Funeral Directors International(165)
Associated Schools of Construction(166)
Association for Communication Excellence(169)
Association for Convention Marketing Executives(171)
Association for Equine Sports Medicine(172)
Association for Evolutionary Economics(172)
Association for Living History, Farm and Agricultural Museums(176)
Association for Science Teacher Education(178)
Association for Tropical Biology and Conservation(181)
Association for Women Geoscientists(182)
Association for Women in Psychology(182)
Association of Academic Health Sciences Library Directors(183)
Association of American Editorial Cartoonists(184)
Association of Bone and Joint Surgeons(188)
Association of Career Firms International(188)
Association of Chartered Accountants in the United States(189)
Association of Christian Librarians(189)
Association of Cinema and Video Laboratories(190)
Association of Community Health Nursing Educators(192)
Association of Cooperative Educators(192)
Association of Departments of Foreign Languages(193)
Association of Family Medicine Residency Directors(196)
Association of Gay and Lesbian Psychiatrists(198)
Association of Independent Information Professionals(200)
Association of Internal Management Consultants(201)
Association of Labor Relations Agencies(202)
Association of Life Insurance Counsel(203)
Association of Machinery and Equipment Appraisers(203)
Association of Medical Diagnostic Manufacturers(204)
Association of Medical Education and Research in Substance Abuse(204)
Association of Medical School Pediatric Department Chairs(204)
Association of Moving Image Archivists(205)
Association of Oncology Social Work(206)
Association of Paroling Authorities, International(207)
Association of Physician Assistants in Cardiovascular Surgery(207)
Association of Professional Model Makers(209)
Association of Public Data Users(210)
Association of Residents in Radiation Oncology(212)
Association of Specialized and Cooperative Library Agencies(214)
Association of Teachers of Latin American Studies(217)
Association of Travel Marketing Executives(218)
Association of University Professors of Ophthalmology(219)
Automotive Fleet and Leasing Association(223)
Automotive Market Research Council(223)
Automotive Training Managers Council(224)
Aviation Technician Education Council(225)
Belt Association(227)
Belted Galloway Society(227)
Beta Beta Beta(228)
Bicycle Product Suppliers Association(228)
Black Caucus of the American Library Association(230)
Black Entertainment and Sports Lawyers Association(230)
Black Retail Action Group(230)
BMC - A Foodservice Sales and Marketing Council(231)
Brake Manufacturers Council(232)
Bright Belt Warehouse Association(232)
Burley Auction Warehouse Association(235)
Catholic Book Publishers Association(239)
Catholic Medical Association(240)
Caucus for Television Producers, Writers & Directors(240)
Cemented Carbide Producers Association(241)
Chief Officers of State Library Agencies(244)
Chief Warrant and Warrant Officers Association, United States Coast Guard(244)
Chinese Language Teachers Association(245)
Church and Synagogue Library Association(246)
Civil Aviation Medical Association(247)
Classroom Publishers Association(247)
Clowns of America, International(248)
College Media Advisers(251)
College of Diplomates of the American Board of Orthodontics(251)
College Reading and Learning Association(252)
Collegiate Commissioners Association(252)
Columbia Sheep Breeders Association of America(253)
Comics Magazine Association of America(253)
Commission on Certification of Work Adjustment and Vocational Evaluation Specialists(254)
Committee for Private Offshore Rescue and Towing (C-PORT)(254)
Communications Marketing Association(255)
Community Colleges Humanities Association(256)
Community Development Society(256)
Computer Assisted Language Instruction Consortium(257)
Computer Law Association(258)
Concrete Anchor Manufacturers Association(258)
Concrete Plant Manufacturers Bureau(258)
Conference of Educational Administrators of Schools and Programs for the Deaf(259)
Conference on English Leadership(260)
Construction Writers Association(263)
Continental Dorset Club(264)
Converting Equipment Manufacturers Association(265)
Cottage Industry Miniaturists Trade Association(267)
Council of American Instructors of the Deaf(270)
Council of Defense and Space Industry Associations(271)
Council of State Chambers of Commerce(274)
Credit Professionals International(279)
Cryogenic Society of America(280)
Danish-American Chamber of Commerce (USA)(281)
Display Distributors Association(285)
Distillers Grains Technology Council(286)
Driver Employer Council of America(287)
Environmental Business Association, The(296)

Equipment Service Association(297)
Evidence Photographers International Council(299)
Family and Consumer Sciences Education Association(300)
Federation of Associations of Regulatory Boards(303)
Federation of Materials Socs.(304)
Finnish American Chamber of Commerce(307)
Fire and Emergency Manufacturers and Services Association(307)
Fire Apparatus Manufacturers' Association(307)
Fixed Income Analysts Society(307)
Fleischner Society(307)
Flexible Intermediate Bulk Container Association(307)
Food Industry Suppliers Association(309)
The Foodservice Group, Inc.(310)
Foundation for International Meetings(311)
Frozen Potato Products Institute(312)
Fulfillment Management Association(312)
Funeral Consumers Alliance(312)
Gamma Iota Sigma(313)
Gift Association of America(317)
Global Offset and Countertrade Association(317)
Heat Exchange Institute(324)
Heavy Duty Business Forum(325)
High Technology Crime Investigation Association(325)
Hispanic Organization of Latin Actors(326)
Histochemical Society(326)
History of Education Society(327)
Home Fashion Products Association(327)
Home Wine and Beer Trade Association(328)
Hydroponic Merchants Association(330)
Hydroponic Society of America(330)
Independent Association of Accredited Registrars(333)
Independent Laboratory Distributors Association(334)
Independent Turf and Ornamental Distributors Association(336)
Industrial Perforators Association(337)
Institute for Briquetting and Agglomeration(339)
Institutional and Service Textile Distributors Association(344)
Insulated Cable Engineers Association(344)
Inter-Society Color Council(346)
International Academy of Behavioral Medicine, Counseling and Psychotherapy(347)
International Association for Computer Information Systems(349)
International Association for Insurance Law - United States Chapter(350)
International Association for Mathematical Geology(351)
International Association of Auto Theft Investigators(353)
International Association of Conference Center Administrators(355)
International Association of Counselors and Therapists(355)
International Association of Golf Administrators(357)
International Association of Insurance Receivers(358)
International Association of Law Enforcement Intelligence Analysts(358)
International Association of Marriage and Family Counselors(359)
International Association of Ocular Surgeons(359)
International Association of Pet Cemeteries(360)
International Association of Professional Security Consultants(360)
International Association of Wildland Fire(361)
International Beverage Packaging Association(362)
International Chain Salon Association(365)
International Council for Small Business(367)
International Council of Fine Arts Deans(367)
International Council of Psychologists(368)
International Double Reed Society(369)
International Engraved Graphics Association(370)
International Federation of Inspection Agencies - Americas Committee(371)
International Firestop Council(372)
International Furniture Transportation and Logistics Council(373)
International Listening Association(378)
International Magnetics Association(378)
International Motor Press Association(380)
International Network of Merger and Acquisition Partners(380)
International Newspaper Group(381)
International Ozone Association-Pan American Group Branch(382)
International Planetarium Society(383)
International Refrigerated Transportation Association(384)
International Regional Magazine Association(385)
International Security Officers, Police, and Guards Union(386)
International Society of Applied Intelligence(390)
International Society of Bassists(390)
International Society of Chemical Ecology(390)
International Society of Hotel Association Executives(391)
International Tax Institute(393)
International Technical Caramel Association(393)
International Tuba-Euphonium Association(395)
International Water Resources Association(396)
Interstate Council on Water Policy(398)
Intersure, Ltd.(398)
IPC - Surface Mount Equipment Manufacturers Association(399)
Kappa Delta Epsilon(403)
Mail Systems Management Association(410)
Manuscript Society(412)
Marine Fabricators Association(412)
Marketing Education Association(413)
Materials Marketing Associates(414)
Medical-Dental-Hospital Business Associates(416)
Military Chaplains Association of the U.S.(419)
Motion Picture and Television Credit Association(421)
Mountain Rescue Association(422)
Municipal Waste Management Association(422)
Museum Education Roundtable(423)
Music Distributors Association(423)
National Academy of Clinical Biochemistry(426)
National Aerosol Association(428)
National Alliance of Preservation Commissions(430)
National Appliance Service Association(430)
National Armored Car Association(431)
National Association for Holistic Aromatherapy(434)
National Association for Proton Therapy(435)
National Association of Academies of Science(437)
National Association of Bankruptcy Trustees(439)
National Association of Barber Boards(439)
National Association of Colored Women's Clubs(445)
National Association of Container Distributors(446)
National Association of Crime Victim Compensation Boards(448)
National Association of Dental Assistants(448)
National Association of Disability Examiners(449)
National Association of Display Industries(449)
National Association of Ecumenical and Interreligious Staff(450)
National Association of Export Companies(451)
National Association of Fire Investigators(452)
National Association of Flour Distributors(453)
National Association of Government Archives and Records Administrators(454)
National Association of Hispanic Federal Executives(455)
National Association of Independent Publishers Representatives(457)
National Association of Legal Investigators(459)
National Association of Limited Edition Dealers(460)
National Association of Litho Clubs(460)
National Association of Marine Surveyors(461)
National Association of Media Brokers(461)
National Association of Medical Minority Educators(461)
National Association of Nurse Massage Therapists(463)
National Association of Publishers' Representatives(467)
National Association of Recreation Resource Planners(468)
National Association of Solar Contractors(472)
National Association of State Agencies for Surplus Property(473)
National Association of State Chief Administrators(474)
National Association of State Park Directors(476)
National Association of State Personnel Executives(476)
National Association of Vertical Transportation Professionals(480)
National Association of Wastewater Transporters(480)
National Association of Waterproofing and Structural Repair Contractors(481)
National Association of Women Artists(481)
National Band Association(483)
National Basketball Athletic Trainers Association(483)
National Black Association for Speech, Language and Hearing(484)
National Broadcast Association for Community Affairs(485)
National Catalog Managers Association(487)
National Church Library Association(489)
National Coalition of Alternative Community Schools(490)
National Concrete Burial Vault Association(492)
National Conference of Insurance Legislators(493)
National Conference of State Liquor Administrators(494)
National Constables Association(495)
National Correctional Industries Association(496)
National Council of Erectors, Fabricators and Riggers(498)
National Council of Exchangors(499)
National Council of Investigation and Security Services(499)
National Council of Local Human Service Administrators(499)
National Council of Self-Insurers(500)
National Council of State Agencies for the Blind(500)
National Council of State Emergency Medical Services Training Coordinators(500)
National Council on International Trade Development(502)
National Council on Public History(502)
National Federation of Hispanic Owned Newspapers(509)
National Federation of Housing Counselors(509)
National Forest Recreation Association(512)
National Gerontological Nursing Association(513)
National Government Publishing Association(514)
National Honey Packers and Dealers Association(517)
National Institute of Ceramic Engineers(520)

National Institute on Park and Grounds Management(521)
National Insurance Association(521)
National Lamb Feeders Association(523)
National Marine Representatives Association(526)
National Network for Social Work Managers(528)
National Opera Association(529)
National Organization of Social Security Claimants' Representatives(530)
National Orientation Directors Association(530)
National Pan-Hellenic Council(531)
National Panhellenic Conference(531)
National Peach Council(532)
National Pecan Shellers Association(532)
National Police and Security Officers Association of America(533)
National Roof Deck Contractors Association(537)
National Shellfisheries Association(539)
National Sports and Fitness Association(543)
National Sportscasters and Sportswriters Association(543)
National Student Employment Association(544)
National Student Osteopathic Medical Association(544)
National Time Equipment Association(546)
National Trailer Dealers Association(547)
National Tutoring Association(548)
National Watercolor Society(549)
National Writers Association(550)
Network of Ingredient Marketing Specialists(551)
Neurosurgical Society of America(552)
North American Association of Educational Negotiators(554)
North American Association of Summer Sessions(555)
North American Blueberry Council(555)
North American Gamebird Association(557)
North American Horticultural Supply Association(557)
North American Membrane Society(558)
North American Professional Driver Education Association(559)
North American Rail Shippers Association(559)
North American Retail Hardware Association(559)
North American Small Business International Trade Educators(560)
North American Society for Cardiac Imaging(560)
North American Strawberry Growers Association(562)
Norwegian-American Chamber of Commerce(562)
Nuclear Information and Records Management Association(563)
Ophthalmic Photographers' Society(565)
Optical Imaging Association(565)
Oral History Association(566)
Organic Reactions Catalysis Society(566)
Orthopedic Surgical Manufacturers Association(569)
Owner Operators of America(570)
Paper Machine Clothing Council(571)
Percheron Horse Association of America(573)
Phi Chi Theta(575)
Phi Epsilon Kappa(576)
Phi Rho Sigma Medical Society(576)
Philosophy of Science Association(576)
Piedmontese Association of the United States(577)
Pipe Fabrication Institute(578)
Plastic Soft Materials Manufacturers Association(578)
Plastic Surgery Admininstrative Association(578)
Plastic Surgery Research Council(579)
Portable Computer and Communications Association(580)
Potato Association of America(581)
Powder Actuated Tool Manufacturers Institute(582)
Presbyterian Health, Education and Welfare Association(583)
Pressure Vessel Manufacturers Association(583)
Pressure Washer Manufacturers Association(583)
Production Equipment Rental Association(585)
Professional Baseball Athletic Trainers Society(586)
Professional Football Athletic Trainers Society(587)
Professional Service Association(589)
Protestant Church-Owned Publishers Association(591)
Psychometric Society(592)
Public Radio News Directors(592)
Pulp and Paper Safety Association(593)
Pyrotechnics Guild International(593)
Quarters Furniture Manufacturers Association(594)
Red Tag News Publications Association(597)
Religious Research Association(599)
Remanufacturing Institute, The(599)
Research Society on Alcoholism(600)
Resort and Commercial Recreation Association(600)
Retail Print Music Dealers Association(601)
River Management Society(602)
Romanian-American Chamber of Commerce(603)
Sanitary Supply Wholesaling Association(605)
Schiffli Lace and Embroidery Manufacturers Association(606)
Science Fiction and Fantasy Writers of America(606)
Screen Manufacturers Association(607)
Shareholder Services Association(609)
Social Science History Association(612)
Society for Clinical Trials(615)
Society for Cryobiology(616)
Society for Economic Botany(616)
Society for Epidemiologic Research(617)
Society for Ethnomusicology(617)
Society for History Education(618)
Society for Industrial Archeology(620)
Society for Industrial Microbiology(620)
Society for Military History(622)
Society for Occupational and Environmental Health(622)
Society for Software Quality(625)
Society for the Advancement of Socio-Economics(626)
Society of Air Force Clinical Surgeons(629)
Society of Allied Weight Engineers(630)
Society of American Business Editors and Writers(630)
Society of Biological Psychiatry(632)
Society of Christian Ethics(633)
Society of Commercial Seed Technologists(633)
Society of Corporate Meeting Professionals(634)
Society of Federal Labor and Employee Relations Professionals(636)
Society of Flight Test Engineers(636)
Society of Forensic Toxicologists(636)
Society of Marine Port Engineers(639)
Society of Maritime Arbitrators(639)
Society of Medical-Dental Management Consultants(640)
Society of Municipal Arborists(640)
Society of Quantitative Analysts(643)
Society of Recreation Executives(643)
Society of Woman Geographers(646)
Specialty Sleep Association(650)
Specialty Tobacco Council(650)
Standards Engineering Society(652)
State Government Affairs Council(652)
State Risk and Insurance Management Association(653)
Steel Door Institute(653)
Stuntmen's Association of Motion Pictures(654)
Sugar Industry Technologists(655)
Tetrahydrofuran Task Force(659)
Text and Academic Authors Association(659)
Textile Bag and Packaging Association(660)
Thoroughbred Club of America(661)
Tin Stabilizers Association(661)
Trans-Atlantic American Flag Liner Operators(663)
Transformer Association, The(663)
Transportation Clubs International(664)
Transportation Safety Equipment Institute(664)
Truck Mixer Manufacturers Bureau(665)
Truck-frame and Axle Repair Association(666)
Tube Council of North America(666)
Turf and Ornamental Communicators Association(667)
Ultrasonic Industry Association(669)
United Applications Standards Group(670)
United Product Formulators and Distributors Association(672)
United Professional Horsemen's Association(672)
United States Animal Health Association(672)
United States Association for Computational Mechanics(673)
United States Committee on Irrigation and Drainage(674)
United States Court Reporters Association(674)
United States Harness Writers' Association(675)
United States Lifesaving Association(676)
United States Marine Safety Association(676)
United States Society on Dams(677)
United States Trout Farmers Association(678)
United States-Austrian Chamber of Commerce(678)
United Steel, Paper and Forestry, Rubber, Manufacturing, Energy, Allied Industrial and Service Workers International Union(678)
Universities Council on Water Resources(679)
Used Truck Association(681)
Utility Communicators International(681)
Valve Repair Council(682)
Western Dredging Association(687)
Western Music Association(687)
Wild Bird Feeding Institute(688)
Wilderness Education Association(688)
Wire Rope Technical Board(690)
Women Construction Owners and Executives, USA(691)
Women in Management(692)
Women in the Fire Service(692)
Women's Caucus for Art(693)
Women's International Network of Utility Professionals(693)

$25-50,000

Abrasive Engineering Society(2)
Academic Language Therapy Association(2)
Academy of Clinical Laboratory Physicians and Scientists(2)
Academy of Veterinary Allergy and Clinical Immunology(6)
Accredited Gemologists Association(6)
ACL - Association for Consortium Leadership(7)
Aestheticians International Association(10)
Air Distributing Institute(13)
Aircraft Locknut Manufacturers Association(14)
Alpha Tau Delta(18)
Alpha Zeta Omega(18)
American Academy of Fertility Care Professionals(23)
American Academy of Gold Foil Operators(23)
American Academy of Mechanics(24)
American Academy of Ministry(24)
American Academy of Restorative Dentistry(28)
American Accordionists Association(29)
American Assembly for Men in Nursing(33)
American Association for Agricultural Education(33)
American Association for Budget and Program Analysis(33)
American Association for Cancer Education(33)
American Association for Correctional and Forensic Psychology(34)
American Association for the History of Nursing(37)

American Association for Women Podiatrists(37)
American Association for Women Radiologists(37)
American Association of Behavioral Therapists(38)
American Association of Certified Orthoptists(39)
American Association of Dental Editors(41)
American Association of Hospital and Healthcare Podiatrists(43)
American Association of Industrial Veterinarians(44)
American Association of Mental Health Professionals in Corrections(45)
American Association of Physical Anthropologists(48)
American Association of Police Polygraphists(49)
American Association of Small Ruminant Practitioners(51)
American Association of Teachers of Italian(52)
American Association of Veterinary Parasitologists(54)
American Blonde D'Aquitaine Association(57)
American Book Producers Association(58)
American Bralers Association(59)
American Bridge Teachers' Association(59)
American Bryological and Lichenological Society(59)
American Buckskin Registry Association(59)
American Catholic Historical Association(61)
American Classical League(63)
American Clinical and Climatological Association(63)
American Cloak and Suit Manufacturers Association(63)
American College of Counselors(65)
American College of Osteopathic Pain Management and Sclerotherapy(69)
American Comparative Literature Association(72)
American Connemara Pony Society(74)
American Embryo Transfer Association(81)
American Hypnosis Association(92)
American Institute of Inspectors(96)
American Institute of Oral Biology(97)
American Institute of Organbuilders(97)
American Laryngological Association(100)
American Literary Translators Association(101)
American Membrane Technology Association(105)
American Murray Grey Association(107)
American Organization for Bodywork Therapies of Asia(110)
American Osteopathic College of Occupational and Preventive Medicine(112)
American Osteopathic College of Pathologists(112)
American Otological Society(112)
American Pharmacists Association(114)
American Pinzgauer Association(115)
American Polypay Sheep Association(116)
American Poultry Association(117)
American Printing History Association(117)
American Reusable Textile Association(122)
American Rock Mechanics Association(123)
American School Band Directors' Association(124)
American Sexually Transmitted Diseases Association(125)
American Shire Horse Association(125)
American Shrimp Processors Association(125)
American Society for Legal History(130)
American Society for Plasticulture(131)
American Society for Theatre Research(132)
American Society of Body Engineers(135)
American Society of Breast Disease(135)
American Society of Dermatological Retailers(137)
American Society of Furniture Designers(138)
American Society of Golf Course Architects(138)
American Society of Irrigation Consultants(140)
American Society of Naturalists(142)
American Society of Papyrologists(143)
American Society of Podiatric Medical Assistants(144)
American Society of Questioned Document Examiners(145)
American Viola Society(153)
Amerifax Cattle Association(156)
Aquatic Plant Management Society(159)
Asbestos Cement Product Producers Association(162)
Associated Cooperage Industries of America(165)
Associated Pipe Organ Builders of America(166)
Associated Specialty Contractors(166)
Association for Applied and Clinical Sociology(167)
Association for Business Simulation and Experiential Learning(168)
Association for Comparative Economic Studies(170)
Association for Federal Information Resources Management(173)
Association for Information Media and Equipment(174)
Association for Politics and the Life Sciences(176)
Association for Recorded Sound Collections(177)
Association for Social Economics(178)
Association for the Behavioral Sciences and Medical Education(180)
Association for the Calligraphic Arts(180)
Association for the Study of Dreams(180)
Association for University and College Counseling Center Directors(181)
Association of African American Museums(183)
Association of Applied IPM Ecologists(186)
Association of Average Adjusters of the U.S.(187)
Association of Black Nursing Faculty in Higher Education(187)
Association of Career Professionals International(188)
Association of Celebrity Personal Assistants(189)
Association of Children's Prosthetic-Orthotic Clinics(189)
Association of Community Tribal Schools(192)
Association of Concert Bands(192)
Association of Consulting Chemists and Chemical Engineers(192)
Association of Defense Trial Attorneys(193)
Association of Environmental and Resource Economists(195)
Association of Environmental Engineering and Science Professors(195)
Association of Former Agents of the U.S. Secret Service(197)
Association of Independent Trust Companies(200)
Association of Jewish Libraries(202)
Association of Military Colleges and Schools of the U.S.(205)
Association of North American Missions(205)
Association of Official Racing Chemists(206)
Association of Pediatric Oncology Social Workers(207)
Association of Professors of Cardiology(209)
Association of Program Directors in Radiology(210)
Association of Third World Studies(218)
Barzona Breeders Association of America(226)
Beef Improvement Federation(227)
Black Psychiatrists of America(230)
Board of Trade of the Wholesale Seafood Merchants(231)
Boating Writers International(231)
California Dried Fruit Export Association(236)
Ceramic Manufacturers Association(241)
Chemical Sources Association(243)
Cold Formed Parts and Machine Institute(250)
Coleopterists Society(250)
Collector Car Appraisers International(250)
College Band Directors National Association(251)
College English Association(251)
College Sports Information Directors of America(252)
College Theology Society(252)
Colombian American Association(252)
Comparative and International Education Society(256)
Concord Grape Association(258)
Conference Board of the Mathematical Sciences(259)
Conference of Research Workers in Animal Diseases(260)
Conference on Consumer Finance Law(260)
Congress on Research in Dance(261)
Copier Dealers Association(266)
Cosmetic Industry Buyers and Suppliers(267)
Council for Art Education(268)
Council for Jewish Education(269)
Council of American Master Mariners(270)
Council of Hotel and Restaurant Trainers(272)
Council of International Investigators(273)
Council of State Association Presidents(274)
Council on Education of the Deaf(276)
Customs and International Trade Bar Association(280)
Dance Critics Association(281)
Data Management Association International(282)
Delta Omicron(282)
Dental Dealers of America(283)
Disaster Preparedness and Emergency Response Association(285)
Early Sites Research Society(288)
Ecuadorean American Association(288)
Energy Traffic Association(294)
Federal Physicians Association(302)
Fiber Society(305)
Fluid Controls Institute(308)
Food Distribution Research Society(309)
Foreign Press Association(310)
Gift and Collectibles Guild(316)
Golf Writers Association of America(318)
Guild of Natural Science Illustrators(321)
Guitar and Accessories Marketing Association(321)
Harvey Society(322)
Heavy Duty Representatives Association(325)
Holistic Dental Association(327)
Hospital Presidents Association(328)
Human Biology Association(329)
Icelandic American Chamber of Commerce(330)
Independent Investors Protective League(334)
Independent Professional Representatives Organization(335)
Industry Coalition on Technology Transfer(337)
Institute of Certified Business Counselors(340)
Institute on Religion in an Age of Science(344)
Intermarket Agency Network(347)
International Association of Career Consulting Firms(354)
International Association of Correctional Officers(355)
International Association of Milk Control Agencies(359)
International Association of School Librarianship(361)
International Castor Oil Association(364)
International Clarinet Association(365)
International Graphic Arts Education Association(374)
International Guild of Candle Artisans(374)
International Institute for Lath and Plaster(376)
International Laser Display Association(377)
International Oil Mill Superintendents Association(381)
International Perimetric Society(382)
International Rural Sociology Association(385)
International Silo Association(386)
International Society for Quality-of-Life Studies(388)
International Society of Psychiatric Consultation Liaison Nurses(392)
International Sports Heritage Association(393)

Judge Advocates Association(402)
Kamut Association of North America(403)
Label Packaging Suppliers Council(404)
Leafy Greens Council(406)
Lightning Protection Institute(408)
Lipizzan Association of North America(408)
Literary Managers and Dramaturgs of the Americas(408)
Machine Printers and Engravers Association of the United States(409)
Masonry Heater Association of North America(413)
Mechanical Power Transmission Association(415)
Media Research Directors Association(416)
Mining and Metallurgical Society of America(420)
Modern Greek Studies Association(420)
NABIM - the International Band and Orchestral Products Association(424)
NAGMR Consumer Product Brokers(425)
National Association for Drama Therapy(432)
National Association for Government Training and Development(433)
National Association for Kinesiology and Physical Education in Higher Education(434)
National Association of Catastrophe Adjusters(442)
National Association of Consumer Credit Administrators(446)
National Association of Document Examiners(449)
National Association of Executive Recruiters(451)
National Association of Forensic Economics(453)
National Association of Government Labor Officials(454)
National Association of Independent Public Finance Advisors(457)
National Association of Jai Alai Frontons(459)
National Association of Media and Technology Centers(461)
National Association of Reunion Managers(469)
National Association of School Music Dealers(470)
National Association of School Safety and Law Enforcement Officers(470)
National Association of Service Managers(472)
National Association of Seventh-Day Adventist Dentists(472)
National Association of State Outdoor Recreation Liaison Officers(476)
National Association of Traffic Accident Reconstructionists and Investigators(479)
National Association of University Fisheries and Wildlife Programs(480)
National Association of Veterans Program Administrators(480)
National Association of Vision Professionals(480)
National Catholic Educational Exhibitors(487)
National Caves Association(488)
National Conference of Firemen and Oilers, SEIU(493)
National Conference of Yeshiva Principals(495)
National Conference on Research in Language and Literacy(495)
National Council of Commercial Plant Breeders(498)
National Federation of Independent Unions(509)
National Fellowship of Child Care Executives(510)
National Frozen Dessert and Fast Food Association(513)
National Guard Executive Directors Association(515)
National Gymnastics Judges Association(516)
National Institute of American Doll Artists(520)
National Marine Bankers Association(525)
National Marine Educators Association(526)
National Meat Canners Association(526)
National Music Council(528)
National Organization for Human Service Education(530)
National Prison Hospice Association(534)
National Roadside Vegetation Management Association(537)
National Rural Water Association(538)
National Safety Management Society(538)
National Science Education Leadership Association(538)
National Society of Hypnotherapists(542)
National Society of Newspaper Columnists(542)
National Trade Circulation Foundation(547)
National Verbatim Reporters Association(548)
Newspaper Association Managers(552)
Newspaper Purchasing Management Association(553)
North America Colleges and Teachers of Agriculture(553)
North American Association of Professors of Christian Education(554)
North American Bar-Related Title Insurers(555)
North American Council of Automotive Teachers(556)
North American Farm Show Council(557)
North American Flowerbulb Wholesalers Association(557)
North American Manufacturing Research Institution of SME(558)
North American Mycological Association(558)
North American Performing Arts Managers and Agents(559)
North American Plant Preservation Council(559)
North American Snowsports Journalists Association(560)
North American Society for Sport History(561)
North American Transportation Employee Relations Association(562)
Northern Nut Growers Association(562)
Nuclear Suppliers Association(563)
Nurse Healers - Professional Associates International(563)
Omicron Kappa Upsilon(564)
Organization Development Institute(566)
Paper and Plastic Representatives Management Council(571)
Partnership for Air-Conditioning, Heating Refrigeration Accreditation(571)
Philosophy of Education Society(576)
Plant Growth Regulators Society of America(578)
Portugal-United States Chamber of Commerce(581)
Professional Currency Dealers Association(587)
Professional Fraternity Association(587)
Professional Reactor Operator Society(589)
Professional Women Photographers(590)
Purebred Dexter Cattle Association of North America(593)
QVM/CMC Vehicle Manufacturers Association(594)
Register of Professional Archeologists(598)
Respiratory Nursing Society(600)
Rhetoric Society of America(601)
Scaffolding, Shoring and Forming Institute(605)
Sigma Epsilon Delta Dental Fraternity(610)
Society for Business Ethics(614)
Society for Disability Studies(616)
Society for Ear, Nose and Throat Advances in Children(616)
Society for Education in Anesthesia(616)
Society for Light Treatment and Biological Rhythms(621)
Society for Physical Regulation in Biology and Medicine(624)
Society for Psychophysiological Research(624)
Society for Sex Therapy and Research(625)
Society for Social Studies of Science(625)
Society for the Advancement of Scandinavian Study(626)
Society for Theriogenology(628)
Society for Vector Ecology(629)
Society of American Historians(630)
Society of Christian Philosophers(633)
Society of Composers(634)
Society of Depreciation Professionals(635)
Society of Flavor Chemists(636)
Society of Military Orthopaedic Surgeons(640)
Society of Photographer and Artist Representatives(642)
Society of University Surgeons(645)
Sommelier Society of America(647)
Sponge and Chamois Institute(651)
State Guard Association of the United States(652)
Surgical Infection Society(656)
System Safety Society(657)
Textile Fibers and By-Products Association(660)
Tourist Railway Association(662)
Transportation Elevator and Grain Merchants Association(664)
Tune-up Manufacturers Council(667)
U.S. Metric Association(668)
United States Durum Growers Association(675)
United States Targhee Sheep Association(677)
Variable Electronic Components Institute(682)
Venezuelan American Association of the U.S.(682)
Vinifera Wine Growers Association(683)
Vocational Evaluation and Career Assessement Professionals(684)
Walking Horse Trainers Association(685)
Walnut Council(685)
Waterproofing Contractors Association(686)
Western Association for Art Conservation(687)
Western Literature Association(687)
Wildlife Disease Association(689)
Women Executives in Public Relations(691)
World Association of Alcohol Beverage Industries(695)
World History Association(696)
Woven Wire Products Association(697)

$10-25,000

Academy of Oral Dynamics(4)
Academy of Parish Clergy(5)
Academy of Rehabilitative Audiology(5)
Academy of Security Educators and Trainers(5)
Accordion Federation of North America(6)
Accordionists and Teachers Guild International(6)
Advanced Transit Association(9)
Agricultural History Society(12)
Allied Artists of America(17)
Allied Trades of the Baking Industry(17)
American Academy of Medical Hypnoanalysts(24)
American Academy of Sports Physicians(29)
American Academy of the History of Dentistry(29)
American Academy of Veterinary and Comparative Toxicology(29)
American Academy of Veterinary Pharmacology and Therapeutics(29)
American Agents Association(30)
American Apitherapy Society(31)
American Association for Therapeutic Humor(37)
American Association of Certified Allergists(39)
American Association of Chairmen of Departments of Psychiatry(39)
American Association of Early Childhood Educators(42)
American Association of Feline Practitioners(43)
American Association of Philosophy Teachers(48)
American Association of Psychiatric Administrators(49)
American Association of Teachers of Arabic(52)
American Bandmasters Association(55)
American British White Park Association(59)
American Cheviot Sheep Society(62)
American College of Psychoanalysts(70)
American College of Veterinary Dermatology(71)
American College of Veterinary Nutrition(71)
American Conference for Irish Studies(73)
American Cotton Shippers Association(74)

American Dialect Society(79)
American Educational Studies Association(80)
The American Electrophoresis Society(80)
American Entomological Society(81)
American Fern Society(83)
American Foreign Law Association(85)
American Goat Society(87)
American Handwriting Analysis Foundation(88)
American Institute of Bangladesh Studies(94)
American Institute of Fishery Research Biologists(96)
American Journalism Historians Association(99)
American Microscopical Society(106)
American Name Society(107)
American Naprapathic Association(108)
American Osteopathic Board of Physical Medicine and Rehabilitation(111)
American Pet Boarding Association(114)
American Podiatric Medical Writers Association(116)
American Pomological Society(117)
American Quaternary Association(121)
American Real Estate and Urban Economics Association(121)
American Romney Breeders Association(123)
American Shropshire Registry Association(125)
American Society for the Study of Orthodontics(132)
American Society of Forensic Odontology(138)
American Society of Gas Engineers(138)
American Society of Laboratory Animal Practitioners(140)
American Society of Music Arrangers and Composers(142)
American Society of Sugar Beet Technologists(146)
American Society of Tax Professionals(146)
American Society of Theatre Consultants(146)
American Southdown Breeders Association(148)
American Sports Medicine Association(148)
American Theatre Critics Association(151)
American Tin Trade Association(151)
American Veterinary Society of Animal Behavior(153)
American Walnut Manufacturers Association(153)
American Welara Pony Society(154)
American Wholesale Booksellers Association(154)
Ankole Watusi International Registry(157)
Art and Antique Dealers League of America(161)
Assembly of Episcopal Healthcare Chaplains(164)
Associated Business Writers of America(164)
Association Chief Executive Council(166)
Association for Biology Laboratory Education(168)
Association for Bridge Construction and Design(168)
Association for Conservation Information(170)
Association for Humanist Sociology(174)
Association for Integrative Studies(175)
Association for the Study of Food and Society(181)
Association for University Business and Economic Research(181)
Association for Women in Computing(182)
Association for Women in Sports Media(182)
Association of American Pesticide Control Officials(185)
Association of American Physicians(185)
Association of American Plant Food Control Officials(185)
Association of Arts Administration Educators(186)
Association of Authors' Representatives(186)
Association of Biomedical Communications Directors(187)
Association of Camp Nurses(188)
Association of Catholic Diocesan Archivists(189)
Association of Certified Professional Secretaries(189)
Association of College and University Museums and Galleries(191)
Association of College and University Printers(191)
Association of College Honor Societies(191)
Association of Conservation Engineers(192)
Association of Earth Science Editors(194)
Association of Information and Dissemination Centers(201)
Association of Muslim Scientists and Engineers(205)
Association of Osteopathic State Executive Directors(206)
Association of Productivity Specialists(208)
Association of Railway Museums(211)
Association of Rehabilitation Programs in Computer Technology(211)
Association of State and Territorial Directors of Nursing(215)
Association of Teachers of Maternal and Child Health(217)
Association of United States Night Vision Manufacturers(219)
Association of University Architects(219)
Association of University Interior Designers(219)
Athletic Equipment Managers Association(221)
Automotive Aftermarket Industry Association(223)
Automotive Communication Council(223)
Baptist Communicators Association(226)
Behavior Genetics Association(227)
Black Theatre Network(231)
Bowling Writers Association of America(232)
Brass and Bronze Ingot Industry(232)
Brazilian Studies Association(232)
Calorimetry Conference(237)
Carwash Owner's and Supplier's Association(238)
Catecholamine Club(239)
Catholic Theological Society of America(240)
Certified Claims Professional Accreditation Council(242)
Chinese American Medical Society(245)
Chinese-American Librarians Association(245)
Church Music Publishers Association(246)
Classification Society of North America(247)
College Athletic Business Management Association(251)
College Fraternity Editors Association(251)
Conference on Faith and History(261)
Construction Marketing Research Council(262)
Coordinating Council for Women in History(265)
Council for Elementary Science International(268)
Council on Chiropractic Orthopedics(275)
Council on Technology Teacher Education(277)
Dental Group Management Association(283)
Devon Cattle Association(284)
Diamond Manufacturers and Importers Association of America(284)
Driving School Association of America(287)
Evangelical Church Library Association(298)
Expansion Joint Manufacturers Association(299)
Expediting Management Association(299)
Federal Administrative Law Judges Conference(301)
Federal Probation and Pre-trial Officers Association(302)
Finnsheep Breeders Association(307)
Fraternal Field Managers Association(311)
Freight Transportation Consultants Association(312)
Gastroenterology Research Group(315)
Geoscience Information Society(316)
Guild of Book Workers(321)
Guild of Italian American Actors(321)
Headwear Information Bureau(322)
Hebrew Actors Union(325)
Historians of Netherlandish Art(326)
History of Earth Sciences Society(326)
History of Economics Society(326)
Housing Education and Research Association(329)
Independent Terminal Operators Association(336)
Institute of Behavioral and Applied Management(340)
Institute of Career Certification International(340)
Inter-America Travel Agents Society(346)
International Association for Language Learning Technology(351)
International Association for Philosophy and Literature(351)
International Association for Truancy and Dropout Prevention(352)
International Association of Audio Information Services(353)
International Association of Dive Rescue Specialists(356)
International Association of Hygienic Physicians(358)
International Association of Personal Protection Agents(360)
International Association of Railway Operating Officers(360)
International Association of Tool Craftsmen(361)
International Association of Women Ministers(361)
International Aviation Womens Association(362)
International Business Music Association(364)
International Ceramic Association(364)
International Compressor Remanufacturers Association(366)
International Frozen Food Association(373)
International Guards Union of America(374)
International Hard Anondizing Association(374)
International Herb Association(375)
International Iridology Practitioners Association(377)
International League of Electrical Associations(378)
International Memorialization Supply Association(379)
International Physical Fitness Association(383)
International Plate Printers', Die Stampers' and Engravers' Union of North America(383)
International Psychohistorical Association(383)
International Saw and Knife Association(385)
International Silk Association(386)
International Society for Adolescent Psychiatry & Psychology(386)
International Society for Chronobiology(386)
International Society for Developmental Psychobiology(387)
International Society for Prosthetics and Orthotics - United States(388)
International Society for the Comparative Studies of Civilizations(389)
International Society of Weekly Newspaper Editors(392)
International Truck Parts Association(395)
International Union of Journeymen Horseshoers and Allied Trades(395)
International Wild Rice Association(397)
Iota Tau Tau(399)
Jean Piaget Society(400)
Land Mobile Communications Council(405)
Light Aircraft Manufacturers Association(408)
Materials and Methods Standards Association(414)
Mechanical Association Railcar Technical Services(415)
MEMA Information Services Council(416)
Metal Framing Manufacturers Association(417)
Microbeam Analysis Society(418)
Midwives Alliance of North America(419)
Mineral Economics and Management Society(419)
Motorist Information and Services Association(422)

under $10,000

American Association of Candy Technologists(39)
American Association of Genitourinary Surgeons(43)
American Association of Insurance Management Consultants(44)
American Association of Language Specialists(44)
American Association of Medical Milk Commissions(45)
American Association of Phonetic Sciences(48)
American Association of Professional Hypnotherapists(49)
American Association of Public Health Physicians(50)
American Association of State Climatologists(51)
American Association of Teachers of Esperanto(52)
American Association of Teachers of Turkic Languages(53)
American Association of Veterinary Immunologists(53)
American Association of Wildlife Veterinarians(54)
American Auto Racing Writers and Broadcasters Association(55)
American Beefalo World Registry(56)
American Border Leicester Association(58)
American Broncho-Esophagological Association(59)
American Catholic Correctional Chaplains Association(61)
American College of Podiatric Radiologists(70)
American Collegiate Retailing Association(72)
American Correctional Chaplains Association(74)
American Cotswold Record Association(74)
American Cream Draft Horse Association(77)
American Crossbred Pony Registry(77)
American Dental Interfraternity Council(79)
American Emu Association(81)
American Galloway Breeders Association(86)
American Guild of Hypnotherapists(88)
American Humor Studies Association(92)
American Hungarian Educators Association(92)
American Incense Manufacturers Association(93)
American Institute for Patristic and Byzantine Studies(94)
American Institute of Biomedical Climatology(95)
American International Marchigiana Society(98)
American Italian Historical Association(99)
American Jewish Correctional Chaplains Association(99)
American Karakul Sheep Registry(100)
American Medallic Sculpture Association(104)
American Metal Detector Manufacturers Association(105)
American Microchemical Society(106)
American Milking Devon Association(106)
American Musicians Union(107)
American Mustang Association(107)
American Nature Study Society(108)
American Neurotology Society(109)
American North Country Cheviot Sheep Association(109)
American Obesity Association(109)
American Osteopathic College of Allergy and Immunology(111)
American Osteopathic College of Proctology(112)
American Pancreatic Association(112)
American Philatelic Society - Writers Unit #30(114)
American Psychology-Law Society(119)
American Psychopathological Association(119)
American Society for Amusement Park Security and Safety(126)
American Society for Environmental History(128)
American Society for Pediatric Neurosurgery(131)
American Society for Stereotactic and Functional Neurosurgery(132)
American Society for the Advancement of Sedation and Anesthesia in Dentistry(132)
American Society of Crime Laboratory Directors(137)
American Society of Geolinguistics(138)
American Society of Marine Artists(141)
American Society of Master Dental Technologists(141)
American Society of Podiatric Medicine(145)
American Society of Podiatry Executives(145)
American Society of Psychoanalytic Physicians(145)
American Society of Psychopathology of Expression(145)
American Society of Sephardic Studies(146)
American Society of Veterinary Ophthalmology(147)
American Spa and Health Resort Association(148)
American Suffolk Horse Association(150)
American Vocational Education Personnel Development Association(153)
American White/American Creme Horse Registry(154)
Analytical Laboratory Managers Association(157)
Apiary Inspectors of America(158)
Applied Research Ethics National Association(159)
Aquacultural Engineering Society(159)
Archivists and Librarians in the History of the Health Sciences(160)
Armed Forces Broadcasters Association(161)
Asian American Psychological Association(163)
Asian/Pacific American Librarians Association(163)
Associated Glass and Pottery Manufacturers(165)
Association for Birth Psychology(168)
Association for Borderlands Studies(168)
Association for Career and Technical Education Research(169)
Association for College and University Religious Affairs(169)
Association for Computers and the Humanities(170)
Association for General and Liberal Studies(173)
Association for Gnotobiotics(173)
Association for Informal Logic and Critical Thinking(174)
Association for International Agricultural and Extension Education(175)
Association for International Agriculture and Rural Development(175)
Association for Philosophy of the Unconscious(176)
Association for Population/Family Planning Libraries and Information Centers, International(176)
Association for Psychoanalytic Medicine(177)
Association for Social Anthropology in Oceania(178)
Association for Technology in Music Instruction(178)
Association for Textual Scholarship in Art History(179)
Association for the Bibliography of History(180)
Association for the Development of Religious Information Systems(180)
Association for the Study of Play(181)
Association for Women Veterinarians(182)
Association of African Studies Programs(183)
Association of American Seed Control Officials(185)
Association of American State Geologists(185)
Association of Ancient Historians(186)
Association of Aviation Psychologists(187)
Association of Caribbean Studies(188)
Association of Catholic TV and Radio Syndicators(189)
Association of Chairmen of Departments of Mechanics(189)
Association of Dark Leaf Tobacco Dealers and Exporters(193)
Association of Defensive Spray Manufacturers(193)
Association of Ecosystem Research Centers(194)
Association of Firearm and Toolmark Examiners(197)
Association of Foreign Trade Representatives(197)
Association of Forensic Document Examiners(197)
Association of Leadership Educators(203)
Association of Major City and County Building Officials(203)
Association of Membership and Marketing Executives(204)
Association of Mental Health Librarians(204)
Association of Muslim Social Scientists(205)
Association of Neurosurgical Physician Assistants(205)
Association of Philosophy Journal Editors(207)
Association of Physician Assistants in Obstetrics and Gynecology(208)
Association of Professional Communication Consultants(208)
Association of Professors of Mission(210)
Association of Sales Administration Managers(212)
Association of Science Museum Directors(213)
Association of Seventh-Day Adventist Librarians(213)
Association of State Supervisors of Mathematics(216)
Association of Statisticians of American Religious Bodies(216)
Association of Technical and Supervisory Professionals(217)
Association of University Anesthesiologists(219)
Association of Vision Science Librarians(220)
Association of Visual Merchandise Representatives(220)
Association of Women Soil Scientists(220)
Association on Programs for Female Offenders(221)
Augustinian Educational Association(222)
Automotive Public Relations Council(224)
Baseball Writers Association of America(226)
Black Americans in Publishing(230)
Buses International Association(235)
Business History Conference(235)
Caucus for Women in Statistics(240)
Certified Milk Producers Association of America(242)
Cheiron: The International Society for the History of Behavioral and Social Sciences(243)
Chinese American Food Society(245)
Chiropractic Council on Physiological Therapeutics and Rehabilitation(245)
Cleveland Bay Horse Society of North America(248)
Coblentz Society(250)
College Gymnastics Association(251)
Colorado Ranger Horse Association(253)
Committee on Lesbian and Gay History(254)
Community College Journalism Association(256)
Computerized Medical Imaging Society(258)
Conference for the Study of Political Thought(259)
Conference of Philosophical Socs.(260)
Conference on English Education(260)
Conference on Latin American History(261)
Consolidated Tape Association(262)
Containerization and Intermodal Institute(264)
Contractors Pump Bureau(264)
Cooperative Work Experience Education Association(265)
Council of American Maritime Museums(270)
Council of Archives and Research Libraries in Jewish Studies(270)

Council of Graphological Socs.(272)
Council on Botanical and Horticultural Libraries(275)
Council on Library-Media Technicians(276)
Czechoslovak History Conference(281)
Dog Writers' Association of America(286)
Evaporative Cooling Institute(299)
Federal and Armed Forces Librarians Roundtable(301)
Federal Water Quality Association(302)
Federation of Modern Painters and Sculptors(304)
Galiceno Horse Breeders Association(313)
Gelbray International(315)
Governmental Research Association(319)
Groundwater Management Districts Association(320)
Hispanic Elected Local Officials(326)
Historians of American Communism(326)
ICAAAA Coaches Association(330)
Immigration and Ethnic History Society(332)
Independent Professional Painting Contractors Association of America(335)
Independent Research Libraries Association(335)
Independent Scholars of Asia(335)
Indian Dental Association (USA)(336)
Insurance Loss Control Association(345)
Intercollegiate Men's Choruses, an International Association of Male Choruses(346)
International Academy for Child Brain Development(347)
International Academy of Health Care Professionals(348)
International Alliance for Women in Music(348)
International Association for Philosophy of Law and Social Philosophy - American Section(351)
International Association for the Study of Cooperation in Education(351)
International Association for the Study of Organized Crime(351)
International Association of Aquatic and Marine Science Libraries and Information Centers(352)
International Association of Bedding and Furniture Law Officials(354)
International Association of Correctional Training Personnel(355)
International Association of Electronic Keyboard Manufacturers(356)
International Association of Hydrogeologists(358)
International Association of Music Libraries, United States Branch(359)
International Fire Photographers Association(372)
International Hydrofoil Society(375)
International Museum Theater Alliance(380)
International Nubian Breeders Association(381)
International Oil Scouts Association(381)
International Professional Groomers(383)
International Society for Ecological Modelling-North American Chapter(387)
International Society for Educational Planning(387)
International Society for Research on Aggression(388)
International Society of Copier Artists(391)
International Sport Show Producers Association(393)
International Stress Management Association - U.S. Branch(393)
International Trade Commission Trial Lawyers Association(394)
International Visual Literacy Association(396)
International Writing Centers Association(397)
Irish Blacks Cattle Society(399)
Jesuit Association of Student Personnel Administrators(401)
JWB Jewish Chaplains Council(403)
Keramos Fraternity(403)
Laboratory Animal Management Association(404)
Liaison Committee of Cooperating Oil and Gas Associations(407)
Linguistic Association of Canada and the United States(408)
Magic Dealers Association(410)
Mass Finishing Job Shops Association(413)
Metal Findings Manufacturers Association(417)
Metaphysical Society of America(418)
Middle East Librarians' Association(418)
Mine Safety Institute of America(419)
Montadale Sheep Breeders Association(421)
National American Legion Press Association(430)
National Association for Humanities Education(434)
National Association for Poetry Therapy(435)
National Association of Agricultural Fair Agencies(438)
National Association of Casino and Theme Party Operators(441)
National Association of Chain Manufacturers(442)
National Association of Composers, USA(445)
National Association of County Health Facility Administrators(447)
National Association of County Intergovernmental Relations Officials(447)
National Association of Credential Evaluation Services, Inc.(447)
National Association of Home and Workshop Writers(456)
National Association of Investment Professionals(459)
National Association of Professors of Hebrew in American Institutions of Higher Learning(466)
National Association of Property Tax Representatives - Transportation, Energy, Communications(467)
National Association of Special Needs State Administrators(472)
National Association of State Administrators and Supervisors of Private Schools(473)
National Association of State Archaeologists(473)
National Association of State Catholic Conference Directors(474)
National Association of State Charity Officials(474)
National Association of State Directors of Veterans Affairs(475)
National Association of State Land Reclamationists(475)
National Association of State Supervisors of Trade and Industrial Education(476)
National Association of State Textbook Administrators(476)
National Association of Substance Abuse Trainers and Educators(478)
National Association of Supervisors for Business Education(478)
National Association of Teachers' Agencies(478)
National Association of Test Directors(479)
National Black Public Relations Society(485)
National Blacksmiths and Weldors Association(485)
National Catholic Band Association(487)
National Catholic Pharmacists Guild of the United States(488)
National Clay Pottery Association(490)
National Confectionery Sales Association(492)
National Conference of Appellate Court Clerks(492)
National Conference of Local Environmental Health Administrators(493)
National Council of State Supervisors for Languages(501)
National Council on Public Polls(502)
National Directory Publishing Association(505)
National Economic Association(505)
National Federation of Nonpublic School State Accrediting Associations(510)
National Hereford Hog Record Association(517)
National Independent Nursery Furniture Retailers Association(519)
National Lead Burning Association(523)
National Lincoln Sheep Breeders Association(525)
National Ornamental Goldfish Growers Association(531)
National Party Boat Owners Alliance(532)
National Quartz Producers Council(534)
National Society for Graphology(540)
National Society of Black Physicists(541)
National Society of Film Critics(541)
National Society of Mural Painters(542)
National Swine Improvement Federation(545)
National Troubleshooting Association(547)
National Tunis Sheep Registry(547)
National Wood Tank Institute(550)
NFHS Music Association(553)
NFHS Speech Debate and Theatre Association(553)
North American Academy of Ecumenists(554)
North American Canon Law Society(555)
North American Cartographic Information Society(555)
North American Clun Forest Association(556)
North American Fuzzy Information Processing Society(557)
North American Maple Syrup Council(558)
North American Simulation and Gaming Association(560)
Omega Delta(564)
Omega Tau Sigma(564)
Online Audiovisual Catalogers(565)
Organization of Teachers of Oral Diagnosis(568)
Orthodox Theological Society in America(568)
Palomino Horse Association(570)
Paper Distribution Council(571)
Patent and Trademark Office Society(572)
Poland China Record Association(579)
Poultry Breeders of America(581)
Print Council of America(583)
Professional Basketball Writers' Association(586)
Professional Hockey Writers' Association(587)
Professional Insurance Communicators of America(587)
Professional Women Singers Association(590)
Purebred Morab Horse Association(593)
Recreational Vehicle Manufacturer's Clubs Association(597)
Religious Communication Association(598)
Romanian Studies Association of America(603)
Ruth Jackson Orthopaedic Society(603)
Saddle, Harness, and Allied Trade Association(604)
Scottish Blackface Sheep Breeders Association(606)
Slovak Studies Association(611)
Society for Ancient Greek Philosophy(613)
Society for Chaos Theory in Psychology and Life Sciences(615)
Society for Cross-Cultural Research(616)
Society for Environmental Geochemistry and Health(617)
Society for French Historical Studies(617)
Society for Historians of the Gilded Age and Progressive Era(618)
Society for History in the Federal Government(618)
Society for Human Ecology(619)
Society for Italian Historical Studies(621)
Society for Medieval and Renaissance Philosophy(621)
Society for Menstrual Cycle Research(621)
Society for Natural Philosophy(622)
Society for New Language Study(622)
Society for Pediatric Urology(623)
Society for Philosophy of Religion(623)
Society for Reformation Research(624)
Society for Romanian Studies(625)
Society for Slovene Studies(625)
Society for Textual Scholarship(626)
Society for the Philosophy of Sex and Love(627)

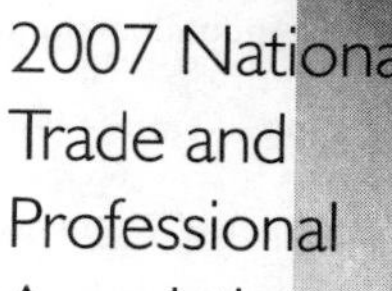

2007 National Trade and Professional Associations

Executive Index

All Individuals appearing in the Association Index appear here, in alphabetical order.

Aaronson, M.D., Donald W.
Joint Council of Allergy, Asthma, and Immunology(402)
Abbarno, G. John M.
Conference of Philosophical Socs.(260)
Abbott, Barbara
American Society of Human Genetics(139)
Abbott, Mark
Major League Soccer(410)
Abbott, Martha
American Council on the Teaching of Foreign Languages(76)
Abbott, Steve
International Society for Technology in Education(389)
Abboud, Jeffrey S.
Fuel Cell Power Association(312)
Gas Turbine Association(314)
Abby, Dean R.
Society for Clinical and Experimental Hypnosis(615)
Abdelsamad, Dr. Moustafa H.
Society for Advancement of Management(613)
Abdullah, Najah
International Ecotourism Society(370)
Abel, John
United States Telecom Association(677)
Abel, Joseph
Healthcare Financial Management Association(324)
Abel, Marilyn
Educational Paperback Association(289)
Abernathy, Wayne
American Bankers Association(55)
Abize, Joel
Society of Actuaries(629)
Ablondi, Jay
International Health, Racquet and Sportsclub Association(374)
Abounader, John
International Association of Auto Theft Investigators(353)
Abousleman, Fred
National Association of Regional Councils(469)
Abraham, Michael T.
Theta Tau(660)
Abrams, Fran
IPC - Association Connecting Electronics Industries(399)
Abramson, Bob
Information Systems Audit and Control Association(338)
Abrate, Jayne
American Association of Teachers of French(52)
Accardo, Paul
Council of Supply Chain Management Professionals(275)
Acerra, Erika
National Association for Community Mediation(432)
Aceves, John B.
National Association of Postal Supervisors(465)
Achenbach, Robert
American Agricultural Law Association(30)
Acker, Joseph
Synthetic Organic Chemical Manufacturers Association(657)
Ackerman, Jennifer Hart
Security Industry Association(607)
Ackerman, Judy E.
American Mathematical Association of Two Year Colleges(103)
Ackerman, Lucy
American College of Veterinary Internal Medicine(71)
Ackerman, Terry A.
Psychometric Society(592)
Ackley, Steve
American Council on the Teaching of Foreign Languages(76)
Acott, Mike
National Asphalt Pavement Association(431)
Acquard, Charles A.
National Association of State Utility Consumer Advocates(477)
Acunto, Carole H.
Society of Insurance Financial Management(638)
Acunto, Stephen C.
International Association for Insurance Law - United States Chapter(350)
Adamczyk, Joan
Association of Master of Business Administration Executives(204)
Adamonis, Richard C.
New York Stock Exchange(552)
Adams, Barry K.
National Council of Industrial Naval Air Stations(499)
Adams, Beverly
American Council of Independent Laboratories(75)
Adams, Dr. Gary
National Cotton Council of America(496)
Adams, Gary W.
American Academy of Podiatric Practice Management(27)
Adams, Joan
National Student Employment Association(544)
Adams, Kerry
American Institute for Maghrib Studies(94)
Adams, Linda
Aircraft Electronics Association(14)
Adams, Mark
American Association of Oral and Maxillofacial Surgeons(47)
Adams, Patricia L.
National Pharmaceutical Council(533)
Adams, Suzanne
Foreign Press Association(310)
Adams, CAE, Thomas L.
Association of Clinical Research Professionals(190)
Adams, Victoria J.
International Franchise Association(373)
Adams-Taylor, Sharon
American Association of School Administrators(50)
Adamson, Audrey
National Pork Producers Council(533)
Adamson, J. Douglas
ABA Marketing Network(1)
Adcock, Carol
American Leather Chemists Association(101)
Addington, John H.
American Association of Automatic Door Manufacturers(38)
Compressed Air and Gas Institute(257)
Door and Access Systems Manufacturers' Association, International(286)
Fire Equipment Manufacturers' Association(307)
Fluid Controls Institute(308)
Heat Exchange Institute(324)
National Coil Coating Association(490)

Pressure Washer Manufacturers Association(583)
Scaffolding, Shoring and Forming Institute(605)
Steel Window Institute(654)

Addison, Ieda
BCA(226)

Addy, Leslie
International Association of Printing House Craftsmen(360)

Adelizzi, Michael
Mason Contractors Association of America(413)

Adelson, Robin
Children's Book Council(244)

Adey, John
American Boat and Yacht Council(58)

Adkins, Darlene
National Consumers League(495)

Adkins, Dinah
National Business Incubation Association(486)

Adkins, Jonathan
Governors Highway Safety Association(319)

Adkins, JD, Shirlyn A.
American Association of Neuromuscular & Electrodiagnostic Medicine(46)

Adler, Gary
National Association of Ticket Brokers(479)

Admundson, Jan
National Association of Manufacturers(460)

Afes, Sandy
American Association of Motor Vehicle Administrators(45)

Agan, Colleen
National Community Pharmacists Association(491)

Agbayani, Nina
Association of Asian-Pacific Community Health Organizations(186)

Agee, Bob R.
International Association of Baptist Colleges and Universities(353)

Ahearn, Cheryl
American Society of Travel Agents(146)

Ahearn, Jennifer
American Association of Colleges of Nursing(40)

Ahern, Jennie G.
International Isotope Society(377)

Ahlers, Sr., Glen-Peter
Scribes(607)

Aho, Dr. P.
World's Poultry Science Association, U.S.A. Branch(697)

Ahuja, Kelley
Institute of Food Technologists(341)

Aiken, Paul
Authors Guild(222)
Authors League of America(222)

Aiken, Peter
Data Management Association International(282)

Aiken-O'Neill, Patricia
Eye Bank Association of America(300)

Airey, Lisa
Society of Wine Educators(646)

Aitken, Herve H.
North American Transportation Employee Relations Association(562)

Aitken, Paul D.
American Association on Mental Retardation(54)

Aizenberq, CEM, Stuart
National Automatic Merchandising Association(482)

Akbari, Hamid
Society for Iranian Studies(620)

Ake, Tiffany
American Society of Hematology(139)

Al Kire, JoAnne
National Marrow Donor Program(526)

Alampi, Richard J.
Sales Association of the Chemical Industry(604)

Albanese, Jay
International Association for the Study of Organized Crime(351)

Albaugh, Bill
Association for Iron and Steel Technology(175)

Albers, Donald J.
Mathematical Association of America(414)

Albers, D.V.M., John W.
American Animal Hospital Association(31)

Albert, Beverly
American Association of Endodontists(42)

Albert, Holly
Arthroscopy Association of North America(162)

Albert, Ida
American Guernsey Association(87)

Albert, Stephen C.
Community Associations Institute(255)

Albert, Terri
Wire Reinforcement Institute(690)

Alberti, Jane Marie
National Funeral Directors Association(513)

Albertson, Mila
Greeting Card Association(320)

Albrecht, Eric
Ladies Professional Golf Association(404)

Alcott, Craig
Society of Diagnostic Medical Sonography(635)

Alden, M.D., FAAP, Errol
American Academy of Pediatrics(27)

Alden, James
Shareholder Services Association(609)

Alderman, Jerry
National Home Furnishings Association(517)

Alderson, Patricia
U.S.A. Rice Federation(669)

Alderson, Sandy
Major League Baseball - Office of the Commissioner(410)

Aldrich, SPHR, Gail
Society for Human Resource Management(619)

Aldrich, Rob
Land Trust Alliance(405)

Aldrich, Soo
Association of Foreign Investors in Real Estate(197)

Aldridge, Richard
National Council of Teachers of Mathematics(501)

Aleshire, Ph.D., Rev. Daniel O.
Association of Theological Schools in the United States and Canada(218)

Alevy, Susan
National Independent Living Association(519)

Alexander, Aundreia
American Baptist Homes and Hospitals Association(55)

Alexander, Cheryl
Parapsychological Association(571)

Alexander, Joe
National Association of Real Estate Appraisers(468)

Alexander, Linda
International Right of Way Association(385)

Alexander, CRNI, Mary
Infusion Nurses Society(338)

Alexander, Nick
International Food Information Council(372)

Alexander, William
Latin Chamber of Commerce of U.S.A.(405)

Alfano, Sr., M.D., Louis F.
American Society of Abdominal Surgeons(133)

Alfaro, Manuel
Hispanic Organization of Latin Actors(326)

Alford, Harry
National Black Chamber of Commerce(484)

Alger, Aurelie M.
American Association of Plastic Surgeons(48)
American Federation for Medical Research(82)
International Society for Minimally-Invasive Cardiac Surgery(387)
Society for Pediatric Urology(623)

Ali, Ph.D., Moonis
International Society of Applied Intelligence(390)

Alin, Michael
American Society of Interior Designers(140)

Allan, Brian B.
National Automatic Merchandising Association(482)

Allard, Dave
Lignite Energy Council(408)

Allegretti, Thomas A.
American Waterways Operators(154)

Allen, Ben
National Head Start Association(516)

Allen, Ph.D, Dan J.
American Association of Behavioral Therapists(38)

Allen, Dianne
North American Retail Hardware Association(559)

Allen, Eric
Healthcare Convention and Exhibitors Association(323)

Allen, Geoff
International Institute of Forecasters(376)

Allen, MD, MPH, James R.
American Sexually Transmitted Diseases Association(125)

Allen, Jessica L.
National Affordable Housing Management Association(428)

Allen, Judy
Technical Association of the Graphic Arts(658)

Allen, Kenneth
American Council for Technology(75)

Allen, Larry
Coalition for Government Procurement(249)

Allen, Linda
American Physiological Society(115)

Allen, Maria
BritishAmerican Business Inc.(233)

Allen, Mark S.
International Foodservice Distributors Association(372)

Allen, Mark B.
International Order of the Golden Rule(381)

Allen, Mary
Shipbuilders Council of America(610)

Allen, Van
Radio Advertising Bureau(594)

Alles, Peter
National Fluid Power Association(511)

Alley, Jennifer
National Association of Collegiate Women Athletic Administrators(445)

Allison, Linda S.
National Association of Independent Colleges and Universities(457)

Allison, Marcia M.
Walking Horse Trainers Association(685)
Allison, Richard
American College of Musicians(67)
National Guild of Piano Teachers(515)
Allman, Amy
National Association for Health Care Recruitment(433)
Allman, Cathy
National Association for Health Care Recruitment(433)
Allmon, Dr. Warren D.
Paleontological Research Institution(570)
Allmond, Bill
National Association of Chemical Distributors(442)
Alluisi, Jennifer
Society of Quality Assurance(643)
Almgren, Kenneth D.
National Association of Broadcasters(441)
Almond, Nicole
American Academy of Dental Group Practice(21)
Almond, Tonya
Defense Research Institute(282)
Almy, David
National Air Transportation Association(428)
Alongi, Deene
American Planning Association(116)
Alonso, Dolores
Synthetic Organic Chemical Manufacturers Association(657)
Alonzo, Anne
National Foreign Trade Council(511)
Alsmeyer, Dr. Richard H.
National Seasoning Manufacturers Association(539)
Alston, Denise
Governors Highway Safety Association(319)
Alt, Curt
Hardwood Plywood and Veneer Association(322)
Altenbaugh, Richard J.
History of Education Society(327)
Alter, Steven
American Symphony Orchestra League(150)
Alterman, Marcia
Professional Association of Volleyball Officials(586)
Alterman, Stephen A.
Cargo Airline Association(238)
Altesman, Albert
Board of Trade of the Wholesale Seafood Merchants(231)
Altimier, Paul V.
International Beverage Packaging Association(362)
Altman, CAE, E.T. "Bill"
Hardwood Plywood and Veneer Association(322)
Altruda, Carol
American College of Angiology(64)
Altschul, Michael F.
CTIA - The Wireless Association(280)
Alvar, Marcia
Public Radio Program Directors Association(592)
Alvarado, Audrey
National Council of Nonprofit Associations(500)
Alvarez, Ph.D., Alvin N.
Asian American Psychological Association(163)
Alvarez, Chris
American Association of Critical-Care Nurses(41)
Amand, VMD, Wilbur B.
American College of Veterinary Nutrition(71)
Amaral, Mark
American Boat Builders and Repairers Association(58)
States Organization for Boating Access(653)
Ambers, CPIA, CIC, CPSR, Kitty
American Insurance Marketing and Sales Society(98)
Ames, Steven
Community College Journalism Association(256)
Ammon, Dr. Rob
North American Society for Sport Management(561)
Amontree, Thomas S.
United States Telecom Association(677)
Amorosino, Jr., CAE, Charles S.
Teachers of English to Speakers of Other Languages(658)
Ams, John G.
National Society of Accountants(541)
Amselle, Anna
Telecommunications Industry Association(659)
Anagnos, Christine
Association of Art Museum Directors(186)
Anagnostelis, Debbie
Society for Pediatric Research(623)
Anapol, Michele
National Housing Conference(518)
Anchors, Kathy
National Credit Union Management Association(503)
Anciu, Jessica
Academy of Student Pharmacists(5)
Anders, Kenneth E.
Intercoiffure America/Canada(346)
Andersen, Crossan R.
Video Software Dealers Association(683)
Andersen, CAE, Gerald
Neckwear Association of America(551)
Andersen, Dr. Kent
North American Limousin Foundation(558)
Andersen, Ph.D., Melvin E.
CIIT Centers for Health Research(247)
Anderson, Dr. Barrie
Society of Pelvic Surgeons(641)
Anderson, Brenda
Society of Incentive & Travel Executives(638)
Anderson, Byron
American Hydrogen Association(92)
Anderson, Cle
American Association for Adult and Continuing Education(33)
Anderson, Dale L.
Certified Claims Professional Accreditation Council(242)
Anderson, Jr., Daniel S.
National Conference of Firemen and Oilers, SEIU(493)
Anderson, Darrell D.
National Swine Registry(545)
Anderson, Denise
Building Service Contractors Association International(234)
Anderson, Gary A.
International Association of Operative Millers(359)
Anderson, Glen R.
Pressure Sensitive Tape Council(583)
Anderson, DPM, Jane
American Association for Women Podiatrists(37)
Anderson, Joanne B.
American Academy of Actuaries(19)
Anderson, John A.
Electricity Consumers Resource Council(291)
Anderson, Jon R.
Baking Industry Sanitation Standards Committee(225)
Anderson, Keri
National Council of Examiners for Engineering and Surveying(499)
Anderson, Linda S.
Attention Deficit Disorder Association(222)
Anderson, Lori J.
Association for Chemoreception Sciences(169)
North American Neuro-Ophthalmology Society(559)
Anderson, Lori M.
International Sign Association(386)
Anderson, M. Kent
International Institute of Ammonia Refrigeration(376)
Anderson, Mallory C.
National Association of Home Inspectors(456)
Anderson, CAE, Mark
American Society for Surgery of the Hand(132)
Anderson, Mary Ann
National Association of Theatre Owners(479)
Anderson, Dr. Michael J.
International Federation for Choral Music(371)
Anderson, CPA, Nancy L.
American Academy of Medical Administrators(24)
American College of Cardiovascular Administrators(64)
Anderson, Norman B.
American Psychological Association(118)
Anderson, Phyllis
North American Spine Society(561)
Anderson, Richard
National School Boards Association(538)
Anderson, Rozanne
ACA International, The Association of Credit and Collection Professionals(2)
Anderson, CAE, Shaine
American Composites Manufacturers Association(72)
Anderson, Shelley
Association of Celebrity Personal Assistants(189)
Anderson, Stanton
United States Chamber of Commerce(674)
Anderson, Steve
Forest History Society(310)
Anderson, CAE, Steven C.
National Restaurant Association(536)
Anderson, William
Independent Film and Television Alliance(334)
Anderson, William R.
CBA(240)
Anderton, Phil
ATP(221)
Andrade, Alec
National Association of Hispanic Publications(456)
Andrea, Dave
Original Equipment Suppliers Association(568)
Andreas, Mike
National Association of Real Estate Appraisers(468)
Andrejeski, Mark
American College of Rheumatology(70)

Andresen, Randi V.
American Association of Oral and Maxillofacial Surgeons(47)

Andrew, Stephanie
National Institute of Steel Detailing(521)

Andrews, David A.
American Hockey League(91)

Andrews, Donna
Technology Student Association(658)

Andrews, John
American Natural Soda Ash Corporation(108)

Andrews, Kelly
Waterproofing Contractors Association(686)

Andrews, Margaret
National Environmental Balancing Bureau(507)

Angebranndt, Jennifer M.
National Multi Housing Council(528)

Angelini, Mark
Structural Board Association(654)

Angelo, Julie
American Association of Community Theatre(41)

Angle, Casey
Intercollegiate Tennis Association(346)

Angle, Joanne G.
Association for Research in Vision and Ophthalmology(178)

Angove, R. Lawrence
Association of Directory Publishers(194)

Anhaiser, Leon A.
Sugar Industry Technologists(655)

Anis, Patricia A.
International Food, Wine and Travel Writers Association(372)

Ankus, Joseph
National Association of Legal Search Consultants(460)

Annotti, Joseph
Property Casualty Insurers Association of America(591)

Answorth, Susan
American College Health Association(63)

Antes, Tina
Alpines International(18)

Anthony, Sc.D., Donald B.
Council for Chemical Research(268)

Anthony, Edwin R.
Edison Electric Institute(289)

Anthony, Virginia Q.
American Academy of Child and Adolescent Psychiatry(20)

Antoine, Valerie
U.S. Metric Association(668)

Antolick, Steven G.
International Association of Airport Duty Free Stores(352)

Antonelos, Christina
Reserve Officers Association of the U.S.(600)

Apkarian, Dr. Albert
National College of Foot Surgeons(490)

Apodaca, CAE, Armando
International Right of Way Association(385)

Apostolik, Richard
Global Association of Risk Professionals(317)

Apostolos, Paul
National Roofing Contractors Association(537)

Appel, Robert
National Community Pharmacists Association(491)

Appel, Sherry Conway
National League of Cities(524)

Appelgren, Bruce
American Association on Mental Retardation(54)

Apple, MS, RN, Kathy
National Council of State Boards of Nursing(500)

Apple, Ph.D., Martin A.
Council of Scientific Society Presidents(274)

Applebaum, Steward
Retail, Wholesale and Department Store Union(601)

Appleby, James
American Pharmacists Association(114)

Appleyard, George
National Association of Diocesan Ecumenical Officers(449)

Apted, Michael
Directors Guild of America(285)

Aranda, Peter
Consortium for Graduate Study and Management(262)

Araujo, Claudio
National Association of Hispanic Journalists(455)

Arbeit, Roy M.
American Arbitration Association(32)

Arbury, Jim
National Multi Housing Council(528)

Arce, Lourdes
Society of Hispanic Professional Engineers(638)

Arceneaux, Michael
Association of Metropolitan Water Agencies(204)

Archambeault, Paul R.
Air Transport Association of America(13)

Archer, Dennis
Board of Certified Safety Professionals(231)

Archer, Jim
Northwest Fruit Exporters(562)

Archer, Patrick
American Peanut Council(113)

Archey, William T.
AeA - Advancing the Business of Technology(9)

Archibald, David
Association for Canadian Studies in the United States(168)

Ardalan, Rick
National Concrete Masonry Association(492)

Ardans, Dr. Alex
American Association of Veterinary Laboratory Diagnosticians(53)

Ardis, Mike
National Association of Professional Surplus Lines Offices(466)

Arend, Tom
American College of Cardiology(64)

Arendt, Lucie
International Dairy-Deli-Bakery Association(369)

Areno, CAE, Patricia M.
Building Owners and Managers Association International(234)

Arger, Marcia
Associated Equipment Distributors(165)

Argow, Keith A.
National Woodland Owners Association(550)

Armato, Leonard
Association of Volleyball Professionals(220)

Armistead, H. Ellis
National Association of Legal Investigators(459)

Armitage, Katie
Associated Bodywork and Massage Professionals(164)

Armour, Becky
National Orientation Directors Association(530)

Armour, Henry O.
National Association of Convenience Stores(446)

Arms, Anneli
Federation of Modern Painters and Sculptors(304)

Armstrong, Carol
National Panhellenic Conference(531)

Armstrong, Cheryl
National Association of College Auxiliary Services(444)

Armstrong, Daniel
American Public Works Association(120)

Armstrong, CAE, Elizabeth B.
International Association of Emergency Managers(356)
National Association of State Emergency Medical Services Officials(475)

Armstrong, J. Alan
Association of Clinical Research Professionals(190)

Armstrong, Robert G.
American Academy of Estate Planning Attorneys(22)

Arnatt, Julie
National Association of College Auxiliary Services(444)

Arndt, Judy
American Cash Flow Association(61)

Arnett, John E.
Copper and Brass Fabricators Council(266)

Arnold, Elizabeth
Oriental Rug Retailers of America(568)

Arnold, Jeff
North American Transportation Management Institute(562)

Arnold, Jeffrey
Association of Rotational Molders, International(212)

Arnold, Mary
Credit Union Executives Society(279)

Arnold, Peter D.
Council of Fashion Designers of America(272)

Arnold, MA, MHPE, Roberta E.
Radiological Society of North America(594)

Arnold, Thomas P.
Insulated Cable Engineers Association(344)

Arnold, W. Ray
Copper Development Association(266)

Arocho, Antonio
Hispanic National Bar Association(326)

Aron, Jeff M.
Federation of American Scientists(303)

Aronson, Richard
College Gymnastics Association(251)

Arrendondo, Donna Fiedler
Hispanic Association of Colleges and Universities(325)

Arsdale, Linda
NATSO, Representing America's Travel Plazas and Truckstops(550)

Arteaga, Roland
Defense Credit Union Council(282)

Artemakis, Angelo
American Society of Neuroradiology(142)

Arthur, E. Vaughn
Dangerous Goods Advisory Council(281)

Arthur, Steve
Grocery Manufacturers Association(320)

Arthurs, G. Eugene
SPIE - The International Society for Optical Engineering(651)

Artman, Scott
Information Systems Audit and Control Association(338)
Arture, Nicholas
Association of Hispanic Arts(200)
Arvo, Sue
National Catholic Educational Association(487)
Arzt, Leonard
National Association for Proton Therapy(435)
Asbury, Donna L.
Association of Partners for Public Lands(207)
Asdal, Robert K.
Hydraulic Institute(329)
Aselin, Don
Sportsplex Operators and Developers Association(651)
Ashburn, Ronald E.
Association for Iron and Steel Technology(175)
Ashby, L. DeWitt
National Association of State Departments of Agriculture(474)
Ashby, C.P.A., Lucius
National Association of Securities Professionals(471)
Ashely, Brandon
National Indian Education Association(519)
Ashley, Jennifer
International Association of Fire Chiefs(357)
Ashley, Joseph
Vocational Evaluation and Career Assessement Professionals(684)
Ashley, Stefanie
International Spa Association(392)
Ashton, Germaine
National Association of Black Journalists(440)
Asken, Evie
Association of University Architects(219)
Askew, Alex
BCA(226)
Aslan, Barbara
National Association of Concessionaires(445)
Aspinall, Judy
Chain Drug Marketing Association(242)
Asplen, Laure
International Union of Electronic, Electrical, Salaried, Machine, and Furniture Workers-CWA(395)
Assey, Elizabeth
Consumer Healthcare Products Association(263)
Astner, Janet L.
American Sociological Association(147)
Astrachan, Eric
Tile Council of North America(661)
Astudillo, Rene
Asian American Journalists Association(162)
Atherton, Dale
Craft & Hobby Association(278)
Atienza, Jaime
Association of Farmworker Opportunity Programs(196)
Atkin, Brett
North American Simulation and Gaming Association(560)
Atkins, Hilary
Air Conditioning Contractors of America(13)
Atkins, Kristin
Ass'n of Learning Providers(164)
Atkins, Linda
Society of Collision Repair Specialists(633)
Atkins, Louis M.
National Association of Postal Supervisors(465)
Atkinson, Baxter
American Federation of School Administrators(82)
Atkinson, Dale
Federation of Associations of Regulatory Boards(303)
Atkinson, Sandi
American Football Coaches Association(84)
Attaway, Fritz E.
Motion Picture Association of America(421)
Atterbury, M.P.A., R.D., L.A.N., Cynthia
Association of State and Territorial Public Health Nutrition Directors(215)
Atwood, Jerolyn
National Association of Advisors for the Health Professions(438)
Atwood, Tyler
American Morgan Horse Association(106)
Au Allen, Susan
U.S. Pan Asian American Chamber of Commerce(668)
Auer, Albert
Food and Drug Law Institute(309)
Auer, Ken
Farm Credit Council(301)
Auglis, Linda
National Beer Wholesalers Association(484)
Augustine, Megan
American College of Forensic Examiners(66)
Augustine, Nancy B.
Association of Directory Marketing(194)
Augustyn, John
Metal Findings Manufacturers Association(417)
Auld, MPH, CHES, Elaine
Society for Public Health Education(624)
Aulerich, Sylvia
Council on Forest Engineering(276)
Austell, Mike
Hosiery Association, The(328)
Austin, Dale L.
Federation of State Medical Boards of the United States(304)
Austin, Erik W.
Social Science History Association(612)
Austin, Kenneth W.
Association of Black Foundation Executives(187)
Austin, Michael
Paint and Decorating Retailers Association(570)
Auth, Kathryn
Water Systems Council(686)
Avery, Susan E.
International Association of Plastics Distributors(360)
Aviv, Diana
Independent Sector(336)
Axelrod, Felice
Council of Protocol Executives(274)
Ayaz, Sandi
National Tutoring Association(548)
Ayers, Carolyn S.
Animal Health Institute(157)
Ayers, Gail S.
Commercial Real Estate Women Network(253)
Ayers, Laraine
Recreational Park Trailer Industry Association(596)
Ayers, Rebecca
National Ski Patrol System(540)
Ayllon, Gina
Professional Association for Childhood Education(585)
Ayres, Debbie
Document Management Industries Association(286)
Baase, Charlie
American Academy of Cosmetic Surgery(21)
American Society of Lipo-Suction Surgery(140)
Baber, Patti Jo
American League of Lobbyists(101)
Bacak, Jr., Walter W.
American Translators Association(152)
Baccante, Richard
American Institute of Physics(97)
Baccari, Carmella
National Association for Bilingual Education(431)
Bacey, Christopher G.
Yellow Pages Association(698)
Bach, Karen
National Intramural-Recreational Sports Association(522)
Bachellor, JoAnn
United States Court Reporters Association(674)
Bachner, John P.
ASFE/The Best People on Earth(162)
Backus, Susan
National Meat Canners Association(526)
Badillo, Kelly C.
Automotive Recyclers Association(224)
Badolato, Lisa
Society of Competitive Intelligence Professionals(633)
Badowski, Don
United States Fencing Coaches Association(675)
Badsing, John
National Catholic Band Association(487)
Baerenklau, Laura
American Association of Neuroscience Nurses(46)
Baerveldt, Calvin
Society of Eye Surgeons(636)
Baeta, Augusto
Institute of Internal Auditors(342)
Bagin, APR, Richard
National School Public Relations Association(538)
Baglivi, Anthony
American Guild of Organists(88)
Bagot, Nancy
Electric Power Supply Association(290)
Bahr, Jennifer Luitjens
Farmers Educational and Co-operative Union of America(301)
Bailes, M.D., Joseph M.
American Society of Clinical Oncology(136)
Bailey, Brent K.
Coordinating Research Council(265)
Bailey, Clare
American Academy of Professional Coders(27)
Bailey, Debra L.
American Osteopathic Colleges of Ophthalmology and Otolaryngology - Head and Neck Surgery(112)
Bailey, Edjuan
Meeting Professionals International(416)
Bailey, Linda
National Fire Protection Association(510)
Bailey, Pamela G.
Cosmetic, Toiletry and Fragrance Association(267)
Bailey, Pamela R.
National Association of Certified Valuation Analysts(442)

Bailey, Richard
American College of Obstetricians and Gynecologists(68)

Bailey, Stephen
National Management Association(525)

Bailey, Traci
Broadcast Education Association(233)

Baime, David
American Association of Community Colleges(41)

Bainwol, Mitch
Recording Industry Association of America(596)

Bair, James
North American Millers Association(558)

Baird, Robert W.
Independent Electrical Contractors(334)

Bakamjian, Ted
Society of Exploration Geophysicists(636)

Baker, Ann Meier
Chorus America(245)

Baker, Carolyn
International Association of Addictions and Offender Counselors(352)

Baker, Chuck
National Railroad Construction and Maintenance Association(534)

Baker, David H.
Lighter Association(408)
Plastic Shipping Container Institute(578)

Baker, Donna M.
Gemological Institute of America(315)

Baker, Jr., Joe
International Cargo Security Council(364)

Baker, Judy
Select Registry/Distinguished Inns of North America(608)

Baker, Lynne
United Steel, Paper and Forestry, Rubber, Manufacturing, Energy, Allied Industrial and Service Workers International Union(678)

Baker, Mike
National Bicycle Dealers Association(484)

Baker, Pam
North American Wholesale Lumber Association(562)

Baker, Peter M.
Laser Institute of America(405)

Baker, Rachel
National Association of Secretaries of State(471)

Baker, Sally
American Association of Equine Practitioners(42)

Baker, Tom
Society of American Graphic Artists(630)

Baker, Wayne
National Junior College Athletic Association(523)

Bakowski, Nancy
Association for Women in Science(182)

Baksa, Barbara
National Association of Stock Plan Professionals(477)

Balakgie, CAE, Carla
Electronic Transactions Association(292)

Balasa, JD,CAE, Donald A.
American Association of Medical Assistants(45)

Balch, Alan F.
American Saddlebred Horse Association(123)

Baldovin, Lynnette
Association of Defense Trial Attorneys(193)

Baldwin, Leah
National Emergency Management Association(507)

Baldwin, Michael
American Society of Plastic Surgeons(144)

Baldwin, CAE, Rand A.
Aluminum Extruders Council(18)

Balek, William C.
ISSA(400)

Balestrero, Gregory
Project Management Institute(590)

Balija, CAE, James J.
International Association for Healthcare Security and Safety(350)

Balin, M.D., Ph.D., FACP, Arthur K.
American Aging Association(30)

Balint, Annette
INDA, Association of the Nonwoven Fabrics Industry(333)

Balk, Dr. Melvin
American College of Laboratory Animal Medicine(66)

Balko, Gregg B.
Society for the Advancement of Material and Process Engineering(626)

Balko, Ron
International Association for Language Learning Technology(351)

Ball, Douglas
Specialized Carriers and Rigging Association(649)

Ball, M.D., JD, John R.
American Society for Clinical Pathology(127)

Ball, Susan
College Art Association(251)

Ballance, CAE, John B.
Materials Research Society(414)

Ballen, Debra T.
American Insurance Association(98)

Ballman, DVM, Mark
Omega Tau Sigma(564)

Ballon, Layla
Oncology Nursing Society(564)

Ballou, Ph.D., Stephen W.
Association of Boards of Certification(188)

Balmer, Thomas M.
National Ice Cream Mix Association(518)
National Milk Producers Federation(527)

Baloh, Diane L.
American Concrete Institute(72)

Balough, Mike
National Council of Higher Education Loan Programs(499)

Balzer, Howard
Professional Football Writers of America(587)

Bancroft, Elizabeth
Association of Former Intelligence Officers(198)

Banes, Douglas
United Brotherhood of Carpenters and Joiners of America(670)

Bangs, Glenn
United States Parachute Association(676)

Bank, Ben
American Academy of Ophthalmology(25)

Banks, Glen P.
International Organization of Masters, Mates and Pilots(382)

Banks, Roger
Western Music Association(687)

Banks, Thomas
American Society of Interior Designers(140)

Banman, Yvonne
Society of Decorative Painters(635)

Bannister, James R.
Association for Financial Technology(173)

Bannwarth, Mandie
International Window Cleaning Association(397)

Baran, Leo J.
North American Die Casting Association(556)

Baranski, Jim
National Stroke Association(544)

Barba, Robert E.
Society of Automotive Analysts(632)

Barbaro, Dr. Nicholas M.
Neurosurgical Society of America(552)

Barbell, Kathy
Child Welfare League of America(244)

Barber, Al
National Association of Minority Contractors(462)

Barber, Linda
Trucking Management(666)

Barbour, Charlene B.
National Federation of Licensed Practical Nurses(509)

Barclay, AAE, Charles M.
American Association of Airport Executives(38)

Barcroft, Ann R.
Bank Administration Institute(225)

Bardach, Emily M.
American Wire Producers Association(155)
Women in Government Relations(692)

Barden, Doug
National Federation of Temple Brotherhoods(510)

Bardos, Gordon
Association for the Study of Nationalities(181)

Barenie, Mark
Institute of Food Technologists(341)

Barford, Mark A.
Appalachian Hardwood Manufacturers(158)

Barimo, Basil J.
Air Transport Association of America(13)

Baris, David
American Association of Bank Directors(38)

Barker, Dr. Robert H.
American Fiber Manufacturers Association(83)

Barker, Russell E.
Peanut and Tree Nut Processors Association(572)

Barker, Ph.D., M.D., Steven J.
Association of University Anesthesiologists(219)

Barkley, Nelda
International Accounts Payable Professionals(348)

Barlow, Patricia
National Nursing Staff Development Organization(529)
National Organization for Associate Degree Nursing(529)
Society of Pediatric Nurses(641)

Barnes, Bill
National League of Cities(524)

Barnes, Cindy
International Institute of Connector and Interconnection Technology(376)

Barnes, James G.
National Medical Association(526)

Barnes, Janet
Estuarine Research Federation(297)

Barnes, Jerry G.
General Merchandise Distributors Council(315)

Barnes, Joseph L.
Fleet Reserve Association(307)

Barnes, Krista
National Council of Teachers of Mathematics(501)
Barnes, Luke
American College of Physician Executives(69)
Barnes, Lynn
Society of Nuclear Medicine(641)
Barnes, Reginald D.
Directors Guild of America(285)
Barnes, Sheila
Appraisal Institute(159)
Barnett, Kim
Assistive Technology Industry Association(164)
Barnett, Lauren A.
Society for Healthcare Strategy and Market Development(618)
Barnett, Lynn
American Association of Community Colleges(41)
Barnett, Marcia
Home Healthcare Nurses Association(327)
Barnett, Ronald
Autoclaved Aerated Concrete Products Association(222)
Barnette, Diane
National Council of Juvenile and Family Court Judges(499)
Barney, David
United States Tuna Foundation(678)
Barney, George B.
Portland Cement Association(581)
Barney, Michael J.
National Bureau of Certified Consultants(485)
Barngrover, Joan A.
National Fraternal Congress of America(512)
Barnhart, Jeffrey E.
International Card Manufacturers Association(364)
Barnhart, Dr. Stephen R.
International Association of Personal Protection Agents(360)
Barnhisel, Richard I.
American Society of Mining and Reclamation(141)
Barnhurst, Kevin
Air Line Pilots Association, International(13)
Barocci, Robert
Advertising Research Foundation(9)
Baron, Jim
American Traffic Safety Services Association(152)
Baron, Linda
National Association for Community Mediation(432)
Barondess, Linda Hiddemen
American Geriatrics Society(87)
Barone, Dr. Joseph
North American Fuzzy Information Processing Society(557)
Baroody, Michael E.
National Association of Manufacturers(460)
Baroody, CAE, Monica
American Physical Therapy Association - Private Practice Section(115)
Barr, Frankie Jean
National Ski Patrol System(540)
Barr, Karen
Investment Adviser Association(398)
Barrack, David W.
American Edged Products Manufacturers Association(80)
Surface Finishing Industry Council(656)
Barratt, CMP, Michael E.
Automotive Aftermarket Industry Association(223)
Barre, David
Association of Corporate Counsel(193)
Barrera, Michael
United States Hispanic Chamber of Commerce(675)
Barrett, M.D., David M.
American Association of Genitourinary Surgeons(43)
Barrett, G. Jaia
Association of Research Libraries(212)
Barrett, Jerome A.
American Academy of Sleep Medicine(28)
Associated Professional Sleep Socs.(166)
Barrett, Wayne
Society for the Advancement of Education(626)
Barrientos, June
American Institute of Oral Biology(97)
Barron, Laurence
American Hotel & Lodging Association(92)
Barron, Margaret R.
Council on Library-Media Technicians(276)
Barrows, Suzanne
Association of Pool and Spa Professionals(208)
Barry, Michael
American College of Preventive Medicine(70)
Barry, Patricia
International Financial Services Association(372)
Barsa, Bonnie J.
National Marine Electronics Association(526)
Barsdate, Kelly J.
National Assembly of State Arts Agencies(431)
Barsook, Beverly
Museum Store Association(423)
Barstow, Bob
Association of Automotive Aftermarket Distributors(186)
Barstow, Scott
American Counseling Association(76)
Bart, Dan
Telecommunications Industry Association(659)
Bartelmay, Janet L.
Association of American Railroads(185)
Barth, Judith
Snack Food Association(612)
Bartholomew, Jean M.
Association of Medical School Pediatric Department Chairs(204)
Bartholomew, Joy A.
Estuarine Research Federation(297)
Bartholomew, Lori
Physician Insurers Association of America(577)
Bartkowski, Molly
Association of Meeting Professionals(204)
Bartlett, Megan Riccardi
National Association for Search and Rescue(436)
Bartlett, Norman F.
American Society of Irrigation Consultants(140)
Bartlett, Steve
Financial Services Roundtable(306)
Baruth, Ed
American Water Works Association(154)
Baruth, Monia Joda
American Water Works Association(154)
Barwacz, Rick
American Society of Anesthesiologists(134)
Barzin, Mariam
International Society for Magnetic Resonance in Medicine(387)
Basa, Eniko Molnar
American Hungarian Educators Association(92)
Basak, Chandrim
International Downtown Association(369)
Baskerville, J.D., Lezli
National Association for Equal Opportunity in Higher Education(433)
Baskette, Michael
American Culinary Federation(77)
Bass, Beth
Women's Basketball Coaches Association(693)
Bass, Janet
AFT Healthcare(11)
Bass, CAE, Marie
American Association of Cardiovascular and Pulmonary Rehabilitation(39)
Bass, Steve
New York Board of Trade(552)
Bassan, Ronny
American-Israel Chamber of Commerce and Industry(156)
Bassett, Patrick F.
National Association of Independent Schools(457)
Basso, Jack
American Association of State Highway and Transportation Officials(51)
Bastas, Thomas G.
Association of Civilian Technicians(190)
Bataria, Rob
International Association of Fire Chiefs(357)
Bates, USA (Ret.), Maj. Gen. Barry
National Defense Industrial Association(504)
Bates, Cassandra
Advertising Research Foundation(9)
Bates, Chris
Independent Office Products and Furniture Dealers Association(335)
Bateson, Dan
American Association of Engineering Societies(42)
Batra, Romesh
American Academy of Mechanics(24)
Batra, Subhash K.
Fiber Society(305)
Batson, Ruth
American Gem Society(86)
Battaglia, CAE, Richard D.
International Society for Performance Improvement(388)
Battles, Byron
Society of Telecommunications Consultants(644)
Battrell, Ann
American Dental Hygienists' Association(78)
Baty, Jim
Concrete Foundations Association(258)
Tilt-up Concrete Association(661)
Baty-Chabrian, Ph.D., Peggy
Women in Aviation International(691)
Baudrau, Donna
American Physical Society(115)
Bauer, Anita
National Association of Electrical Distributors(450)
Bauer, Anne Watson
Association for Childhood Education International(169)
Bauer, Bob
Association of Food Industries(197)
National Association of Flavors and Food-Ingredient Systems(453)

National Honey Packers and Dealers Association(517)
North American Olive Oil Association(559)
Society of Flavor Chemists(636)

Bauer, David
American Road and Transportation Builders Association(123)

Bauer, Kate
American Association of Birth Centers(38)

Bauerle-Berg, Kathie
Professional Bail Agents of the United States(586)

Baugh, Jerry R.
Consumer Bankers Association(263)

Baulig, Laurie
Rubber Manufacturers Association(603)

Baum, Dan
Building Owners and Managers Institute International(234)

Baum, Hadassah
Beta Alpha Psi(228)

Bauman, Christopher
American Society for Quality(132)

Bauman, Dawn
Community Associations Institute(255)

Baumann, James
Association of College and University Housing Officers-International(191)

Baur, Michael
American Catholic Philosophical Association(61)

Bavaria, Susan
Arabian Horse Association(160)

Baxter, Margaret
Original Equipment Suppliers Association(568)

Baxter-Bellamy, Amy L.
Society for Historians of the Early American Republic(618)

Bayer, Amy
Media Communications Association International(415)

Baylor, Robert
National Propane Gas Association(534)

Bayne, Neil F.
National Academy of Television Journalists(427)

Beach, Kelly
National Auto Auction Association(482)

Beach, Thomas
Patent and Trademark Office Society(572)

Beachum, Jeff
Interior Design Educators Council(347)

Beacom, David
National Science Teachers Association(539)

Beady, Charles H.
Foundation for Independent Higher Education(311)

Beales, Char
Cable & Telecommunications Association for Marketing(236)

Beales, Glenn
National Association of Corporate Treasurers(446)

Beall, Ph.D., Bret S.
Association for Death Education and Counseling(171)

Beall, Ph.D., Robert J.
Cystic Fibrosis Foundation(281)

Beals, CAE, Kimberly
International Pharmaceutical Excipients Council of the Americas(382)

Beam, Dr. David
National Society of Black Physicists(541)

Bean, David
National League of Cities(524)

Beane, Deanna
Association of Science-Technology Centers(213)

Beard, Allison E.
American College of Nurse Practitioners(68)

Beard, Jeff
American Council of Engineering Companies(75)

Bearer, Donna
American Association of Owners and Breeders of Peruvian Paso Horses(47)

Beaston, Lon
America's Blood Centers(19)

Beatty, Barbara Fitzgerald
American Society of Ophthalmic Plastic and Reconstructive Surgery(143)

Beaty, Libby
National Association of Telecommunications Officers and Advisors(478)

Beaty, Lisa
Institute of Navigation(343)

Beauchamp, L.G.
International Brotherhood of Boilermakers, Iron Ship Builders, Blacksmiths, Forgers and Helpers(363)

Beaudin, Lili
Women of the Motion Picture Industry, International(692)

Beaulieu, Jackie
Healthcare Convention and Exhibitors Association(323)

Beaumont, Jr., Guy D.
American College of Osteopathic Surgeons(69)

Beaumont, CAE, Nancy Perkin
Society of American Archivists(630)

Beavers, Leslie
National Association of State Directors of Veterans Affairs(475)

Becherer, John
United Soybean Board(672)

Beck, Allison
International Association of Machinists and Aerospace Workers(359)

Beck, Deborah
Nurses Organization of Veterans Affairs(563)

Beck, Ph.D., Edward
National Registry of Environmental Professionals(535)

Beck, Judy
American Association of Colleges for Teacher Education(40)

Beck, Margaret
Motor and Equipment Manufacturers Association(421)

Becker, Christine
National League of Cities(524)

Becker, Fred
National Association of Federal Credit Unions(452)

Becker, Jeanine
American Society for Quality(132)

Becker, Jeffrey G.
Beer Institute(227)

Becker, Kim
American Medical Student Association(105)

Becker, Kristin
Workgroup for Electronic Data Interchange(695)

Becker, Leslie
Guild of Natural Science Illustrators(321)

Becker, Mila
American Society of Hematology(139)

Becker, S. William
Association of Local Air Pollution Control Officials(203)
State and Territorial Air Pollution Program Administrators(652)

Becker, Sandra L.
International Society of Certified Employee Benefit Specialists(390)

Becker, Scott J.
Association of Public Health Laboratories(210)

Becker-Doyle, CAE, Eve
National Athletic Trainers' Association(482)

Beckner, Gary
Association of American Educators(184)

Beckwith, Lyle
National Association of Convenience Stores(446)

Bectel, Robin M.
North American Insulation Manufacturers Association(557)

Bedford, Frank
American Osteopathic Association(111)

Beditz, Dr. Joseph
National Golf Foundation(514)

Bedlin, Howard
National Council on the Aging(503)

Bednarek, Janet R.
Urban History Association(680)

Bednarski, Karen
International Sports Heritage Association(393)
Professional Society for Sales and Marketing Training(589)

Bednash, Geraldine
American Association of Colleges of Nursing(40)

Beemer, Will
Timber Framers Guild(661)

Beene, Keith
Baptist Communicators Association(226)

Beery, Sharon
Golf Coaches Association of America(318)

Beggan, Blair
Association of Air Medical Services(183)

Begley, Janet
International Association of Conference Center Administrators(355)

Behr, Ken
Evangelical Council for Financial Accountability(298)

Behrens, Ellen
National Association of College and University Food Services(444)

Beilfuss, Rudolf
PKF North American Network(578)

Beilman, Mark
Reprographic Services Association(599)

Belar, Cynthia
American Psychological Association(118)

Belden, Ph.D., PE, David L.
United Engineering Foundation(671)

Belefski, Mary
Federal Water Quality Association(302)

Belew, Joe
Consumer Bankers Association(263)

Belfiore, Maddalena
American Accordionists Association(29)

Belford, Kevin B.
American Gas Association(86)

Belis, Gary
Television Bureau of Advertising(659)

Belkin, Kristin Lohse
Historians of Netherlandish Art(326)

Bell, David E.
American Iron and Steel Institute(98)

Bell, Derrick
National Wellness Institute(549)
Bell, Lorraine J.
North American Society for Cardiac Imaging(560)
Society for Vascular Medicine and Biology(629)
Bell, Peter H.
National Housing and Rehabilitation Association(518)
National Reverse Mortgage Lenders Association(536)
Bell, Richard
American Pancreatic Association(112)
Bell, Robert
Society of Satellite Professionals International(644)
World Teleport Association(696)
Bell, Tamara
International Society for Magnetic Resonance in Medicine(387)
Bellamy, Eric
Association for Supervision and Curriculum Development(178)
Bellande, Ph.D., Bruce
Alliance for Continuing Medical Education(15)
Bellantone, Paul
Promotional Products Association International(591)
Beller, Ph.D., Ron
American Society of Clinical Oncology(136)
Bellis-Jones, Hugh
American Hanoverian Society(88)
Bellizzi, John J.
International Narcotic Enforcement Officers Association(380)
Bellocq, Remi
National Horsemen's Benevolent and Protective Association(517)
Bellows, M.D., Randall T.
American Society of Contemporary Ophthalmology(136)
International Association of Ocular Surgeons(359)
Belmont, CAE, Barbara
School Nutrition Association(606)
Belt, Bill
Telecommunications Industry Association(659)
Beltz, George R.
International Union of Petroleum and Industrial Workers(396)
Benard, D.P.M., Marc A.
American Board of Podiatric Orthopedics and Primary Podiatric Medicine(57)
Benavent, Ana Elisa
International Association of Amusement Parks and Attractions(352)
Benbow, Ann
American Geological Institute(87)
Bendel, Julianne
American Academy of Esthetic Dentistry(22)
American Association of Legal Nurse Consultants(44)
Bender, Neal
IPC - Association Connecting Electronics Industries(399)
Benish, Susan
National Church Library Association(489)
Benjamin, Daniel
Display Distributors Association(285)
Benjamin, David A
Intercollegiate Tennis Association(346)
Benjamin, M.D., FACP, Georges
American Public Health Association(119)
Benjamin, CAE, Maynard H.
Envelope Manufacturers Association(296)
Benne, Susan
Antiquarian Booksellers Association of America(157)
Bennett, Janis
Society of Rheology(643)
Bennett, Jennifer
Society of Military Orthopaedic Surgeons(640)
Bennett, Malissa R.
American Orthotic and Prosthetic Association(111)
Bennett, Mark
Society of Creative Designers(634)
Bennett, Robbie S.
American Polygraph Association(116)
Bennett, Thomas P.
Corporate Facility Advisors(266)
Bennett, Vaneeda
American Diabetes Association(79)
Bennett, CAE, SPHR, Yvonne C.
American Agricultural Economics Association(30)
Benoit, Mike
Cement Kiln Recycling Coalition(241)
Benoudiz, Sondra Fry
Specialty Graphic Imaging Association(650)
Benshoff, Sharon
National Council on Rehabilitation Education(503)
Bensky, Carol
American Prosthodontic Society(117)
Benson, Annette
United Suffolk Sheep Association(678)
Benson, Bruce
Fibre Box Association(305)
Benson, Jr., Edwin W.
Country Music Association(277)
Benson, Jack
Water Environment Federation(685)
Benson, DDS, James M.
International Academy of Gnathology - American Section(348)
Benson, Dr. John
American College of Veterinary Anesthesiologists(71)
Benson, Laura
American Zoo and Aquarium Association(156)
Benson, Peter R.
Electronic Commerce Code Management Association(291)
Benson, Robert
Associated Bodywork and Massage Professionals(164)
Benson, T.C.
Americans for the Arts(156)
Bentley, Beth
American Lighting Association(101)
Benton, Jeani
SAFE Association(604)
Bentsen, Kenneth E.
Equipment Leasing Association of America(297)
Bentz, Ingo
German American Chamber of Commerce(316)
Berchem, Steve
American Staffing Association(149)
Berckmeyer, Jack
National Middle School Association(527)
Berdeaux, Susan
National Caves Association(488)
Berens, Michael
American Society of Interior Designers(140)
Berg, Amanda
Jewelry Information Center(401)
Berg, Cathy
ACA International, The Association of Credit and Collection Professionals(2)
Berg, David A.
Air Transport Association of America(13)
Berg, Jennifer
Association for the Study of Food and Society(181)
Bergen, Joseph
American Lung Association(102)
Berger, Janice
Independent Educational Consultants Association(334)
Berger, Ron
Subcontractors Trade Association(655)
Berger, Steve
Craft & Hobby Association(278)
Bergeron, Rob
National Society of Professional Engineers(542)
Bergeson, Ph.D., David J.
Awards and Recognition Association(225)
Bergfeld, Dr. Ellen
American Society of Agronomy(133)
Crop Science Society of America(279)
Soil Science Society of America(647)
Berggren, Jerry
National Association of Dental Plans(449)
Berggren, Todd
Geological Society of America(315)
Bergland, Betty A.
Immigration and Ethnic History Society(332)
Bergman, CAE, David W.
IPC - Association Connecting Electronics Industries(399)
Bergman, Ph.D., Jerry
Society for the Study of Male Psychology and Physiology(628)
Bergman, Marilyn
American Society of Composers, Authors and Publishers(136)
Bergman, CAE, William S.
Outdoor Power Equipment Aftermarket Association(569)
Bergquist, Gloria
Alliance of Automobile Manufacturers(16)
Bergson, Henry P.
National Electrical Manufacturers Representatives Association(506)
Bergstein, Stanley F.
Harness Tracks of America(322)
Berito, William M.
National Association of Foreign-Trade Zones(453)
Berk, Kenneth
Object Management Group(563)
Berkeley, Michael J.
American Medical Association(104)
Berkland, Eric
Council of Residential Specialists(274)
Berkman, Ph.D., Harold W.
Academy of Marketing Science(4)
Berkowitz, Eric
American Alliance for Health, Physical Education, Recreation and Dance(30)
Berkowitz, Lee
Printing Industry Credit Executives(584)
Berkowitz, Nancy
Oncology Nursing Society(564)
Berlin, Robert H.
Society for Military History(622)
Berlin, Sandra
American Anthropological Association(31)
Berlowitz, Leslie Cohen
American Academy of Arts & Sciences(20)

Berman, Dr. Alan L.
American Association of Suicidology(52)
Berman, Mira
Africa Travel Association(11)
Berman, Patricia L.
American Land Title Association(100)
Berman, Richard B.
American Beverage Institute(56)
Bermont, Hubert
American Consultants League(74)
Bernabei, Raymond
National Intercollegiate Soccer Officials Association(522)
Bernaido, Meg
Association of Surfing Professionals - North America(216)
Bernarads, John
International Association of Skateboard Companies(361)
Bernard, Jo
American Cheviot Sheep Society(62)
Bernard, Patricia
Visiting Nurse Associations of America(684)
Bernard, Richard P.
New York Stock Exchange(552)
Bernat, Andrew
Computing Research Association(258)
Bernhards, John
Alliance for Telecommunications Industry Solutions(16)
Bernstein, Brian A.
American Chemical Society(62)
Bernstein, Edward
Industrial Research Institute(337)
Bernstein, James
American Society for Pharmacology and Experimental Therapeutics(131)
Bernstein, Marc
Institute of Food Technologists(341)
Bernthal, Frederick H.
Universities Research Association(679)
Berretta, Lisa
Workgroup for Electronic Data Interchange(695)
Berrington, Craig A.
American Insurance Association(98)
Berry, David A.
Community Colleges Humanities Association(256)
Berry, Kathie
Associated Builders and Contractors(164)
Berry, Jr., Ph.D., Lemuel
National Association of African American Studies(438)
Berry, CAE, MBA, M. Suzanne C.
American Epilepsy Society(81)
International Society for Clinical Densitometry(386)
Berry, Michael
National Ski Areas Association(540)
Berry, CAE, Peter J.
International Association of Campus Law Enforcement Administrators(354)
Bersahi, Maribeth
Assisted Living Federation of America(164)
Bersell, Sean Devlin
Video Software Dealers Association(683)
Berson, Ginny Z.
National Federation of Community Broadcasters(509)
Berta, John A.
Slovak Studies Association(611)
Bertagna, Joe
American Hockey Coaches Association(91)
Bertalmio, Genny
Popcorn Institute(580)
Bertera, William J.
Water Environment Federation(685)
Berthelsen, Richard
National Football League Players Association(511)
Bertke, Laura
International Spa Association(392)
Berzan, Jane
National Association of Convenience Stores(446)
Besesparis, Jr., Ted
National Association of Professional Insurance Agents(466)
Besore, Celia
Central Station Alarm Association(241)
Bess, Kindra
International Society for Pharmaceutical Engineering(388)
Bess, Pamela L.
BMC - A Foodservice Sales and Marketing Council(231)
Manufacturers Representatives of America(411)
Paper and Plastic Representatives Management Council(571)
Power-Motion Technology Representatives Association(582)
Bessette, Robert D.
Council of Industrial Boiler Owners(272)
Best, Glenna
National Defined Contribution Council(505)
Best, Robert
International Society for Pharmaceutical Engineering(388)
Betit, Eileen
International Union of Bricklayers and Allied Craftsworkers(395)
Bettiga, Bart A.
National Tile Contractors Association(546)
Bettin, MA, Christopher
American Association of Nurse Anesthetists(46)
Bettman, Gary B.
National Hockey League(517)
Betts, Lisa R.
ESOP Association(297)
Betz, Robert B.
American Association of Eye and Ear Hospitals(42)
Health Industry Group Purchasing Association(323)
Betzner, Claudia J.
Service Industry Association(609)
Beutler, CRNA, MS, Jeffery M.
American Association of Nurse Anesthetists(46)
Bevard, Jill
National Pest Management Association(532)
Bevel, Michael
International Recording Media Association(384)
Beverage, Richard
Association of Professional Ball Players of America(208)
Beyda, DPH, Vivian
American Association of Spinal Cord Injury Nurses(51)
American Association of Spinal Cord Injury Psychologists and Social Workers(51)
American Paraplegia Society(113)
Bez, D.O., Bert M.
American Osteopathic College of Anesthesiologists(111)
Bezner, PT, Janet
American Physical Therapy Association(115)
Bhatia, S. Joseph
American National Standards Institute(108)
Biacchi, Tony
American Risk and Insurance Association(123)
Bianca, Zulma
Association for Enterprise Opportunity(172)
Bianchi, Maria
American Ambulance Association(30)
Bianchi-Sand, Susan
United American Nurses, AFL-CIO(670)
Bianchini, Lori
National Council of Teachers of English(501)
Bianco, Celso
America's Blood Centers(19)
Bianucci, Deborah L.
Bank Administration Institute(225)
Biasi, Gwen
National Association of the Remodeling Industry(479)
Bibbs-Sanders, Angelia
National Academy of Recording Arts and Sciences(427)
Bibby, Douglas M.
National Multi Housing Council(528)
Bibeau, Albert J.
Wood Products Manufacturers Association(694)
Bibeau, Phillip A.
Wood Products Manufacturers Association(694)
Biddle, Harry
American Academy of Otolaryngology-Head and Neck Surgery(26)
Biderman, David
Environmental Industry Associations(296)
Biegel, Douglas A.
COLA(250)
Bien, Amos
International Ecotourism Society(370)
Bier, Marilyn
ARMA International(160)
Biggs, Sondra
American Academy of Family Physicians(22)
Bikel, Theodore
Associated Actors and Artistes of America(164)
Bilak, CMP, Karen
Building Service Contractors Association International(234)
Bilchik, Shay
Child Welfare League of America(244)
CWLA - Child Mental Health Division(280)
Biles, Paula
International Waterlily and Water Gardening Society(397)
Bilke, Darrell
Pinto Horse Association of America(578)
Billeb, Jan
American Custom Gunmakers Guild(77)
American Knife and Tool Institute(100)
Billey, Scott A.
Professional Liability Underwriting Society(588)
Billings, Doralee
Professional Association of Custom Clothiers(585)
Billings, Karen
Software and Information Industry Association(646)
Billingsley, William
Association of African American Museums(183)
Billington, Van
Retail Confectioners International(601)
Billups, Jr., Clinton Ford
National Conference of Personal Managers(494)

Binder, APC, Paul J.
Academy of Parish Clergy(5)
Binfa, Patricia
International College of Surgeons(366)
Bing, Richard
National Association of Criminal Defense Lawyers(448)
Bingham, Anthony
American Society for Training and Development(133)
Bingham, Suzanne A.
American College of Bankruptcy(64)
Binns, Polly
Council for Resource Development(269)
Binzel, William
National Foundation for Credit Counseling(512)
Biondi, Brien
Chief Executives Organization(244)
Biordi, Michele
Unfinished Furniture Association(669)
Bird, Bill
Art Glass Association(161)
Bird, Graham
Open Group(565)
Bird, Mary Lynne
American Geographical Society(87)
Bird, Wesley
American Camp Association(60)
Birdsong, James R.
RCI, Inc.(595)
Birenbaum, Ph.D., Mark S.
American Association of Bioanalysts(38)
American Board of Bioanalysis(57)
Association of Defensive Spray Manufacturers(193)
WaterJet Technology Association(686)
Birkofer, Julie
Plasma Protein Therapeutics Association(578)
Birks, Heather
Broadcast Education Association(233)
Birne, Howard
Chamber of Commerce of the Apparel Industry(243)
Birschel, Dee
International Foundation of Employee Benefit Plans(373)
Bisacquino, Thomas J.
National Association of Industrial and Office Properties(458)
Bischoff, Martin
French-American Chamber of Commerce(312)
Bishop, Dana
Refractory Ceramic Fibers Coalition(597)
Bishop, John R.
National Association of College and University Attorneys(444)
Bishop, Sandy
American Academy of Audiology(20)
Bishop, Shirley
Association of Academic Health Sciences Library Directors(183)
Council of International Investigators(273)
International Council on Systems Engineering(368)
Bishop, Tara
National Council of University Research Administrators(501)
Bishop, Toby J.F.
Association of Certified Fraud Examiners(189)
Bitting, Christina
American Association of State Colleges and Universities(51)
Bittman, Ann W.
American Forest and Paper Association(85)
Bix, Amy
Society for the History of Technology(627)
Bizzozero, Peter
American Traffic Safety Services Association(152)
Bjalobok, M.S., Frances
American Hackney Horse Society(88)
Bjerkness, Michelle
American Phytopathological Society(115)
Black, Dr. David C.
Universities Space Research Association(679)
Black, Edward J.
Computer and Communications Industry Association(257)
Black, James
National Association of State Workforce Agencies(477)
Black, MBA, CPA, CVA, Parnell
National Association of Certified Valuation Analysts(442)
Black, Peter D.
BPA Worldwide(232)
Black, Robert
American Society for Engineering Education(128)
Blackburn, D.V.M., Dale E.
American Shropshire Registry Association(125)
Blackstone, Jon
Society for Surgery of the Alimentary Tract(625)
Blackwell, Carl
National Marine Manufacturers Association(526)
Blades, Heather
American Psychotherapy Association(119)
Blair, Paul
Council of Supply Chain Management Professionals(275)
Blair, Phil
American Association for the Advancement of Science(36)
Blais, Patrick
National Alliance of State and Territorial AIDS Directors(430)
Blake, Brenda
Rubber and Plastics Industry Conference of the United Steelworkers of America(603)
Blake, Jamie G.
National Association of Small Business Investment Companies(472)
Blake, Patricia
American Society for Gastrointestinal Endoscopy(129)
Blake, Peggy
INDA, Association of the Nonwoven Fabrics Industry(333)
Blakely, Mack
International Society of Certified Electronics Technicians(390)
National Electronic Service Dealers Association(506)
Blakeslee, Michael
MENC: The National Association for Music Education(417)
Blanchard, Sharon
National Association of Towns and Townships(479)
Bland, Jacqueline M.
Graphic Arts Marketing Information Service(319)
Blaney, Desane
Association of Golf Merchandisers(199)
Blankenship, Jim
American Association of Petroleum Geologists(47)
Blankenship, Peggy
Community Development Society(256)
Blankstein, Lois
International Trademark Association(394)
Blasdell, Jennifer
National Abortion Federation(426)
Blatman, Judy
Council for Responsible Nutrition(270)
Blatt, Jennifer
Semiconductor Equipment and Materials International(608)
Blatzer, Bruce T.
Iron Casting Research Institute(399)
Blazar, Betsy
American Society for Nondestructive Testing(131)
Blazauskas, Roman G.
Consumer Healthcare Products Association(263)
Blazevic, Angela
International Association of Assessing Officers(353)
Blessing, Peter H.
International Tax Institute(393)
Blevins, Susan M.
Technical Association of the Pulp and Paper Industry(658)
Blicker, Stacey
International Titanium Association(394)
Bliss, Deborah
Association of State Supervisors of Mathematics(216)
Blistein, Adam D.
American Philological Association(114)
Blixrud, Julia
Association of Research Libraries(212)
Bloch, Dr. Milton
American Society for the Study of Orthodontics(132)
Block, Dr. Barry
American Podiatric Medical Writers Association(116)
Block, Fred B.
American Incense Manufacturers Association(93)
Block, CAE, CFRE, Marsha S.
American Group Psychotherapy Association(87)
Blom, Deborah
Association of Collegiate Conference and Events Directors International(191)
Blom, Don
National School Boards Association(538)
Blondes, Chellie
American Academy of Orthotists and Prosthetists(26)
Bloom, Dr. Darrell
International Council on Education for Teaching(368)
Bloom, Lauren M.
American Academy of Actuaries(19)
Bloom, Rochelle R.
Fragrance Foundation(311)
Bloomfield, Shirley
National Telecommunications Cooperative Association(546)
Bloomhuff, Amy
American Conference of Governmental Industrial Hygienists(73)
Blough, Kathryn
Association of American Publishers(185)
Blovin, Kathleen
National Business Aviation Association(486)

Blowers, Richard
Society of American Magicians(631)
Blue, China
World Teleport Association(696)
Blue Spruce, Jr., D.D.S, George
Society of American Indian Dentists(631)
Bluhm, Chris
American Occupational Therapy Association(109)
Blum, Jared O.
Polyisocyanurate Insulation Manufacturers Association(580)
Blumenthal, Heidi
Associated General Contractors of America(165)
Blumenthal, Kent J.
National Intramural-Recreational Sports Association(522)
Blust, Steven
Institute of International Container Lessors(342)
Blyth, Debby
Kamut Association of North America(403)
Boa, J. Michael
Casualty Actuarial Society(239)
Boardman, Elliot
Association of Energy Services Professionals, International(195)
Utility Communicators International(681)
Boardman, Paul
Softwood Export Council(646)
Bobowski, CPA, Robert
International Sleep Products Association(386)
Bobrow, CAE, CMP, Maryanne
American Anaplastology Association(31)
American Association of Industrial Veterinarians(44)
Boca, Kim
Native American Journalists Association(550)
Bocchi, Gregory J.
Powder Coating Institute(582)
Bockel, USAR (Ret.), Maj. Gen. David R.
Reserve Officers Association of the U.S.(600)
Boddicker, John A.
American Maine-Anjou Association(102)
Bode, Brooke
International Newspaper Marketing Association(381)
Bode, William H.
Environmental Business Association, The(296)
Independent Terminal Operators Association(336)
Boden, Barbara
Institute of Certified Healthcare Business Consultants(340)
Boden, Natalie
Radiological Society of North America(594)
Bodley, Alice
American Nurses Association(109)
Boeckman, LaVerne
World Research Foundation(696)
Boehme, Karen
National Fluid Power Association(511)
Boeke, Elinore
Personal Watercraft Industry Association(574)
Boel, Bridget
National Head Start Association(516)
Boese, Albert B.
Post-Print Manufacturers Association(581)
Boettcher, Bonna
Music Library Association(423)
Bogel, Barbara A.
American Academy of Physical Medicine and Rehabilitation(27)
Bogenrief, Jennifer
Health Industry Distributors Association(323)
Boggs, George R.
American Association of Community Colleges(41)
Boggs, M.B.A., Pamela
North American Menopause Society(558)
Boghosian, Heidi
National Lawyers Guild(523)
Bogren, Scott
Community Transportation Association of America(256)
Bohannon, Mark
Software and Information Industry Association(646)
Bohle, Suzanne
PGA TOUR Tournaments Association(575)
Bohm, John
National Association of Housing and Redevelopment Officials(456)
Bohman, Jr., Raynard F.
International Furniture Transportation and Logistics Council(373)
Bohnert, Craig
National Soccer Coaches Association of America(540)
Boland, Jean
American Federation of State, County and Municipal Employees(82)
Boland, Mary
American Copper Council(74)
Bolen, Edward M.
National Business Aviation Association(486)
Boles, Margaret
COMPTEL(257)
Boling, Jeanne
Case Management Society of America(238)
Bolinger, Chrysta
Catholic Campus Ministry Association(239)
Bollig, Jeff
Golf Course Superintendents Association of America(318)
Bolling, Dennis
United Producers(672)
Bollinger, Jr., Paul P.
Air Traffic Control Association(13)
Bollt, Anita
National Association for College Admission Counseling(432)
Bolman, CAE, Thomas E.
International Association of Conference Centers(355)
Bolze, Ron
American Shorthorn Association(125)
Bombardiere, Ralph
Gasoline and Automotive Service Dealers Association(314)
Bomberger, Irvin
American Orthopaedic Society for Sports Medicine(111)
Bomgardner, Paul M.
Commercial Vehicle Safety Alliance(254)
Bonaparte, Sueli
Brazilian American Chamber of Commerce(232)
Bond, Doug
Association of Dark Leaf Tobacco Dealers and Exporters(193)
Bonds, Roger G.
American Academy of Medical Management(24)
Bone, David
United States Racquet Stringers Association(677)
Bone, David L.
Fellowship of United Methodists in Music and Worship Arts(305)
Boney, Maurice W.
Irish Blacks Cattle Society(399)
BonGiorni, Emily
Investment Program Association(399)
Bonner, Bill
American Society of Body Engineers(135)
Bonner, John
Council for Agricultural Science and Technology(268)
Bonner, Laura A.
American Association for Crystal Growth(34)
Bonner, Linda Hanifin
National Onsite Wastewater Recycling Association(529)
Bonner, T.J.
National Border Patrol Council(485)
Bonoff, Steve
IPA - The Association of Graphic Solutions Providers(399)
Bonosaro, Carol A.
Senior Executives Association(609)
Bonsaint, Rebecca R.
American Association of Plastic Surgeons(48)
Booberg, Carl
American Thoracic Society(151)
Booher, C. William
National Association of VA Physicians and Dentists(480)
Boone, Jonnie
North American Elk Breeders Association(556)
Boone, Tamea A.
National Association for Uniformed Services and Society of Military Widows(437)
Boop, M.D., Frederick A.
American Society for Pediatric Neurosurgery(131)
Booth, James
Professional Records and Information Services Management International(589)
Bopp, Andrew
Glass Packaging Institute(317)
Hearing Industries Association(324)
Borawski, CAE, Paul
American Society for Quality(132)
Borchardt, Maj. Chris
Society of United States Air Force Flight Surgeons(645)
Borchardt, Robert O.
America's Health Insurance Plans(19)
Borchers, James A.
Concrete Anchor Manufacturers Association(258)
Powder Actuated Tool Manufacturers Institute(582)
Borck, Noel C.
NEA - the Association of Union Constructors(551)
Bordeaux, Dr. Roger
Association of Community Tribal Schools(192)
Borden, Enid A.
Meals On Wheels Association of America(414)
Borden, Mike
Real Estate Information Professionals Association(596)
Borer, David
Association of Flight Attendants - CWA(197)
Borgsiewicz, Shelly
Catholic Charities USA(239)
Borgstrom, Ph.D., Karl F.
Construction Specifications Institute(263)

Borich, Alexis
American College of Veterinary Dermatology(71)
Boris, Stan
National Truck Leasing System(547)
Borland, D.O., Joe S.
American Sports Medicine Association(148)
Bornstein, Ph.D., Robert
International Neuropsychological Society(381)
Bornstein, Sandra
American Neuropsychiatric Association(108)
Borowicz, Donna
Yellow Pages Association(698)
Borowski, CAE, Patricia A.
National Association of Professional Insurance Agents(466)
Borowsky, Scott C.
Souvenirs, Gifts and Novelties Trade Association(648)
Borschke, CAE, Daniel C.
National Association for Retail Marketing Services(436)
Boruff, Chet
Association of Official Seed Certifying Agencies(206)
Borut, Donald J.
National League of Cities(524)
Bosak, Kathy
National Association of Counties(447)
Bosarge, Johnette
National Marine Educators Association(526)
Bosco, Mary Beth
Used Oil Management Association(681)
Bose, James
International Ground Source Heat Pump Association(374)
Boskey, Craig
National Marine Manufacturers Association(526)
Bosland, Neil
AACSB - the Association to Advance Collegiate Schools of Business(1)
Bosley, Lowell
International Magnetics Association(378)
Bosley, Scott
American Society of Newspaper Editors(142)
Boss, Cedric
Public Relations Society of America(593)
Boss, Terry D.
Interstate Natural Gas Association of America(398)
Bossert, Wayne
Groundwater Management Districts Association(320)
Bossey, Robert D.
International Association of Law Enforcement Firearms Instructors(358)
Bostian, Larry
National Consumers League(495)
Bostick-Dobbs, Sheila
National Council of Catholic Women(498)
Bostley, SSJ, Jean R.
Catholic Library Association(240)
Boswell, Pamela L.
American Public Transportation Association(120)
Bouchard, Pam
National Hospice and Palliative Care Organization(517)
Bouchard, Steve
Association of Trial Lawyers of America(218)
Bougae, Cyd
Club Managers Association of America(249)
Boughman, Dr. Joann A.
American Society of Human Genetics(139)
Bouhan, Richard M.
National Association of Professional Surplus Lines Offices(466)
Boulter, Spencer
International Society for the Study of Dissociation(389)
Boulton, Lyndie McHenry
American Society for Enology and Viticulture(128)
Bourdeau, Judy
Employee Assistance Society of North America(293)
Bourdon, Cathleen
Association of Specialized and Cooperative Library Agencies(214)
Bourdreaux, Gary
Energy Security Council(294)
Bourdrez, Michiel M.
National Council of Architectural Registration Boards(498)
Bourgholtzer, Tony
Foundation for Advances in Medicine and Science(311)
Bouris, Greg
Major League Baseball Players Association(410)
Bourke, Michelle
National Contract Management Association(495)
Bourne, Grace Ann
Telecommunications Industry Association(659)
Bourseau, Sandy
American Society of Home Inspectors(139)
Boutin, Marc
National Health Council(516)
Bova, CAE, Steve
Financial and Insurance Conference Planners(305)
International Reprographic Association(385)
Bowen, Christopher
New York Mercantile Exchange(552)
Bowen, Deborah
American College of Healthcare Executives(66)
Bowen, Roger A.
American Association of University Professors(53)
Bower, Lori
Society of Cable Telecommunications Engineers(632)
Bower, Tim
Society for Medical Decision Making(621)
Society for Social Work Leadership in Health Care(625)
Bowers, Diane K.
Council of American Survey Research Organizations(270)
Bowers, Ellen
Council of Graphological Socs.(272)
Bowers, D.D.S., Gerald M.
American Academy of Periodontology(27)
American Board of Periodontology(57)
Bowers, Ph.D., Dr. Jan
Family and Consumer Sciences Education Association(300)
Bowers, CAE, John
International Longshoremen's Association, AFL-CIO(378)
Bowers, Leonard
Society of American Florists(630)
Bowers, Michael
American Association for Marriage and Family Therapy(36)
Bowers, Rita
ACPA - College Student Educators Association(7)
Bowie, Mary
American Association of Museums(45)
Bowles, Sandra
Handweavers Guild of America(321)
Bowling, Pat
American Home Furnishings Alliance(91)
Bowling, Richard P.
Truck Trailer Manufacturers Association(666)
Bowman, ARM, Alison
Council of Insurance Agents and Brokers(272)
Bowman, Bobbi
American Society of Newspaper Editors(142)
Bowman, CMP, Danielle
National Precast Concrete Association(534)
Bowman, David
Society of American Florists(630)
Bowman, Frank
Nuclear Energy Institute(563)
Bowman, Gloria
Counselors of Real Estate(277)
Bowman, Jerry
American Society of Indexers(139)
Bowman, Kellie
Association of College and University Telecommunications Administrators(191)
Bowman, Kenneth R.
Sealant, Waterproofing and Restoration Institute(607)
Bowman, Lisa S.
Society for Marketing Professional Services(621)
Bowman, P.
Brass and Bronze Ingot Industry(232)
Bowser, Kathleen
Professional Handlers Association(587)
Bowyer, Brent
Independent Photo Imagers(335)
Box, Allison
American Rental Association(122)
Box, Doug
American Society of Photographers(144)
Box, Wana Dee
National Association of Royalty Owners(469)
Boyce, Brad
American Rabbit Breeders Association(121)
Boyce, CAE, Ken
Spring Manufacturers Institute(652)
Boyce, Rusty
Association of State and Territorial Health Officials(215)
Boyd, Ben
Service Employees International Union(609)
Boyd, Dennis W.
National Association of Assistant United States Attorneys(439)
Boyd, Lisa
Human Resource Planning Society(329)
Boyd, Nancy
Supima(656)
Boyer, CAE, Kaye Kittle
Costume Society of America(267)
Boyer, Phil
Aircraft Owners and Pilots Association(14)
Boylan, Jennifer K.
Society for Pediatric Radiology(623)
Boyle, Diane
Association of Health Insurance Advisors(199)
Association of Healthcare Internal Auditors(199)

Boyle, J. Patrick
American Meat Institute(103)

Boyle, Jonathan
National Association of Professional Geriatric Care Managers(466)

Boyle, Joseph M.
National Association of Federal Credit Unions(452)

Boyle, Paul
Newspaper Association of America(552)

Boyle, Terence
Delta Phi Epsilon(282)

Boyles, Deron
American Educational Studies Association(80)

Boyles, Paula
DRI International(287)

Boyne, Gil
American Council of Hypnotist Examiners(75)

Boynes, Shawn
Association for Professionals in Infection Control and Epidemiology(177)

Boynton, Rex P.
North American Technician Excellence(562)

Bozans, Gloria
Prevent Blindness America(583)

Brabec, Todd
American Society of Composers, Authors and Publishers(136)

Brachman, Sarah
Independent Educational Consultants Association(334)

Bracken, Anne
Association of Corporate Counsel(193)

Brackett, Lyn
Self Storage Association(608)

Brada, Josef C.
Association for Comparative Economic Studies(170)

Braddom, Ed.D., Carolyn L.
Association of Academic Physiatrists(183)

Braden, Joseph
NANDA International(425)

Bradford, Ph.D., Dr. E. James
AOAC International(158)

Bradford, Hazel
International Masonry Institute(379)

Bradley, Beverly
Medical Library Association(416)

Bradley, Christopher L.
Black Coaches Association(230)

Bradley, Harry
American Nuclear Society(109)

Bradley, CSP, Janice Comer
International Safety Equipment Association(385)

Bradley, Jeanette
American Mold Builders Association(106)

Bradley, Pam
National Association of Public Hospitals and Health Systems(467)

Bradley, Tom
Council of American Master Mariners(270)

Bradley, William
American Gear Manufacturers Association(86)

Bradshaw, Brett
Coalition of Essential Schools(249)

Bradshaw, Cindy
National Certification Council for Activity Professionals(488)

Bradshaw, Jacquelyn
Packaging Machinery Manufacturers Institute(570)

Brady, David J.
International Facility Management Association(371)

Brady, Janine
Hydronics Institute Division of GAMA(330)

Brady, Phillip D.
National Automobile Dealers Association(482)

Brady, DMD, Robert E.
International College of Dentists, U.S.A. Section(366)

Braen, Beth
National Association of Television Program Executives(478)

Braendel, Eric
American Bus Association(60)

Bragaw, Richard
Academy of Osseointegration(5)

Bragg, Debra
National Council on Student Development(503)

Bragg, Lynn Munroe
American Cocoa Research Institute(63)
Chocolate Manufacturers Association(245)

Brahms, Thomas W.
Institute of Transportation Engineers(344)

Brakey, Jacqueline
Society for Epidemiologic Research(617)

Bram, Jim
National Association of Underwater Instructors(480)

Bramlage, MBA, MPH, SPHR, CCP, Rusty
CIIT Centers for Health Research(247)

Bramson, DDS, James B.
American Dental Association(78)

Branagan, Carmine
American Craft Council(77)

Branch, L. Maurice
American Logistics Association(102)

Branch, Rodney
Business Marketing Association(235)

Branch, Steve
Society for Computer Simulation(615)

Brand, Maya
Professional Beauty Association(586)

Brand, Myles
National Collegiate Athletic Association(491)

Brandel, Norma "Dusty"
American Auto Racing Writers and Broadcasters Association(55)

Brandenberger, Joel
National Turkey Federation(548)

Brandl, Philip J.
International Housewares Association(375)

Brandon, Carolyn
CTIA - The Wireless Association(280)

Brandon, Sharon
Tennessee Walking Horse Breeders and Exhibitors Association(659)

Brandt, Bill
International Association of Accident Reconstruction Specialists(352)

Brandt, Deborah
American Academy of Optometry(25)

Brandt, Rebecca
American Academy of Allergy, Asthma, and Immunology(20)

Brann, Esther
Adhesion Society(8)

Brannon, Barbara A.
Society for the History of Authorship, Reading and Publishing(627)

Branscum, Dale
International Brotherhood of Boilermakers, Iron Ship Builders, Blacksmiths, Forgers and Helpers(363)

Branson, Craig
American Society of Newspaper Editors(142)

Branson, Dana
National Cherry Growers and Industries Foundation(489)

Branter, Noreen
National Association of Professional Baseball Leagues(466)

Brantigan, Kathleen Aylsworth
International Tuba-Euphonium Association(395)

Brantley, Andy
College and University Professional Association for Human Resources(250)

Branton, Janet
Real Estate Buyers Agent Council(595)

Brashears, Sandy
Devon Cattle Association(284)

Brasse, Denise
National Retail Federation(536)

Braswell, C.A.E., Ricki
National Association of Dental Laboratories(448)

Braswell, Robert
Technology and Maintenance Council of American Trucking Associations(658)

Bratcher, Kristin
National Juvenile Detention Association(523)

Brattain, Shirley
Tamworth Swine Association(657)

Brauer, Ph.D., CSP, CPE, Roger L.
Board of Certified Safety Professionals(231)
Council on Certification of Health, Environmental and Safety Technologists(275)

Braun, Bill
Air and Waste Management Association(12)

Braun, Patrick
Society of Mineral Analysts(640)

Braun, Theresa C.
American Institute of Physics(97)

Braun, Werner
Carpet and Rug Institute(238)

Bravo, Ellen
Nine to Five, National Association of Working Women(553)

Bray, Charlie
International Association of Amusement Parks and Attractions(352)

Bray, Janet B.
Association for Career and Technical Education(169)

Brazell, CAE, CMP, Torryn
National Grants Management Association(514)

Brazil-Nichols, Laura
North American Society for Dialysis and Transplantation(560)

Brebner, Nancy
Insurance Consumer Affairs Exchange(345)

Breckenridge, Gwynn
American Association for Dental Research(34)

Breden, CAE, CMP, Cathy
International Association for Exhibition Management(350)

Breeden, Christine
Association of Social Work Boards(214)

Breedlove, Adrienne
Mechanical Contractors Association of America(415)

Breitback, Kim
Society for Clinical Data Management(615)

Brenen, Edward
American Legend Cooperative(101)

Brennan, Maria E.
American Women in Radio and Television(155)
Brennan, Michael
Certification Board for Urologic Nurses and Associates(242)
Brennan, Paul D.
National Board of Boiler and Pressure Vessel Inspectors(485)
Brennan Lisak, Cate
National Athletic Trainers' Association(482)
Brenner, Daniel
National Cable & Telecommunications Association(486)
Brenner, Mary Beth
Association of Rehabilitation Nurses(211)
Brenner, AIA, William
National Institute of Building Sciences(520)
Breslow, Brooke
American Society of Breast Disease(135)
Bresnahan, Tom
Computer Oriented Geological Society(258)
Bresolin, Ph.D., Linda
Radiological Society of North America(594)
Bretcko, Kathi
Independent Laboratory Distributors Association(334)
Bretthauer, CAE, Donald
International Association of Administrative Professionals(352)
Brevik, Leonard C.
National Association of Professional Insurance Agents(466)
Brevitz, Karl
National Association of College and University Attorneys(444)
Brewer, Bill
American Quarter Horse Association(120)
Brewer, John B.
American Moving and Storage Association(107)
Brewer, Lynn M.
American Bus Association(60)
Brewster, Scott
International Warehouse Logistics Association(396)
Brey, Megan
American Medical Directors Association(104)
Brey, Mike
Inter-Industry Conference on Auto Collision Repair(346)
Brice, Steve
National Industries for the Blind(519)
Briceland-Betts, Tim
Child Welfare League of America(244)
Bridge, Debbie
American College of Emergency Physicians(65)
Bridgeman, Pete
Association of Technical and Supervisory Professionals(217)
Bridgman, Elizabeth
Association for the Advancement of Medical Instrumentation(179)
Brier, M. William
Edison Electric Institute(289)
Briese, CAE, Garry
International Association of Fire Chiefs(357)
Brigham, Dana A.
International Union of Elevator Constructors(395)
Brighindi, Nancy
American Society of Addiction Medicine(133)
Bright, Danielle
American Dental Hygienists' Association(78)
Bright, David
International Sleep Products Association(386)
Brightup, Craig
National Roofing Contractors Association(537)
Brill, Bernard D.
Secondary Materials and Recycled Textiles Association(607)
Shippers of Recycled Textiles(610)
Brill, Laurie
Lutheran Educational Conference of North America(409)
Brimsek, CAE, Tobi A.
Society for American Archaeology(613)
Brinati, Teresa
Society of American Archivists(630)
Brinegar, Pamela
Council on Licensure, Enforcement and Regulation(276)
Brinegar, Richard S.
International Webmasters Association(397)
Brink, Cheryl
National Business Incubation Association(486)
Brinkmann, Robert
National League of Postmasters of the U.S.(524)
Brintnall, Michael A.
American Political Science Association(116)
Briscoe, III, Andrew C.
Sugar Association(655)
Briscoe, Causby
National Association of Insurance Women(458)
Bristol, Gail R.
Society of Plastics Engineers(642)
Britton, Karen
NASTD - Technology Professionals Serving State Government(426)
Brobeck, Stephen
Consumer Federation of America(263)
Brocker, Jerold
Piedmontese Association of the United States(577)
Brodendel, Jane E.
National Association of Letter Carriers(460)
Broderick, D.O., Paul
American Osteopathic College of Proctology(112)
Brodie, Bridget
American College of Medical Quality(67)
Brodin, Robert A.
Airline Industrial Relations Conference(14)
Brodsky, Harvey
Tire Retread Information Bureau(662)
Brodsky, Marc H.
American Institute of Physics(97)
Broff, Nancy
Career College Association(237)
Broman, Bruce
Precision Metalforming Association(583)
Bronston, D.C., Leo
Council on Chiropractic Orthopedics(275)
Brooker, Ida
Women Construction Owners and Executives, USA(691)
Brookhart, Sarah
American Psychological Society(119)
Brookhouser, MD, Patrick
American Laryngological, Rhinological and Otological Society(100)
Brookover, Patrick
American Council of Engineering Companies(75)
Brooks, Becky
International Spa Association(392)
Brooks, Ph.D., Gene
American Choral Directors Association(62)
Brooks, Mitch
National Plasterers Council(533)
Broom, Joe
Mobile Industrial Caterers' Association International(420)
Brosche, Marcus
American Bralers Association(59)
Brosky, Robert E.
National Association of State Boards of Accountancy(473)
Broussard, Linda
Special Libraries Association(649)
Brown, Allen
Open Group(565)
Brown, Allison
International Society of Parametric Analysts(392)
Brown, Amy
Community Broadcasters Association(255)
Brown, Andrea
American Association of Meat Processors(45)
Brown, Antonio
National Association of Real Estate Brokers(468)
Brown, Betty Berndt
Photo Chemical Machining Institute(576)
Brown, Bob
National Tile Contractors Association(546)
Brown, Carol
International Association of Women Ministers(361)
Brown, Carolyn W.
Family, Career, and Community Leaders of America(300)
Brown, Chris
Society of the Plastics Industry(645)
Brown, Chris
Juvenile Products Manufacturers Association(403)
Brown, Chris
National Association of Broadcasters(441)
Brown, Christopher
Association for Borderlands Studies(168)
Brown, Craig
National Cotton Council of America(496)
Brown, Cynthia
American College of Surgeons(71)
Brown, Cynthia L.
American Shipbuilding Association(125)
Brown, Danny C.
National Association of Industrial and Technical Teacher Educators(458)
Brown, David L.
America Outdoors(19)
Brown, CAE, Dennis
Equipment Leasing Association of America(297)
Brown, Dennis
Association for the Study of Higher Education(181)
Brown, Diane Alicia
Association of State Floodplain Managers(216)
Brown, Donna
National Association of County and City Health Officials(447)
Brown, Elsa P.
American College of Obstetricians and Gynecologists(68)
Brown, F. Elizabeth
National Council of Examiners for Engineering and Surveying(499)
Brown, Frank
National Hockey League(517)

Brown, Fred
National Association of Elementary School Principals(450)
Brown, Gwendolyn
National Truck Equipment Association(547)
Brown, J. Noah
Association of Community College Trustees(192)
Brown, James
Council of State Governments(275)
Brown, Jr., James P.
Paperboard Packaging Council(571)
Brown, Janet E.
Equipment Service Association(297)
Brown, Jessamy
Association for Women Journalists(182)
Brown, Karen H.
Food Marketing Institute(309)
Brown, Kerwin
BEMA - The Baking Industry Suppliers Association(227)
Brown, Kevin
American Sociological Association(147)
Brown, Larry
U.S. Poultry and Egg Association(668)
Brown, Lisa
American Society of Ophthalmic Registered Nurses(143)
Association of University Professors of Ophthalmology(219)
Brown, Manson
National Naval Officers Association(528)
Brown, Mary Ellen
Association for Advancement of Behavior Therapy(167)
Brown, Nancy A.
American Heart Association(90)
Brown, Patricia S.
Architectural Engineering Institute(160)
Brown, Peter D.
ACPA - College Student Educators Association(7)
Brown, Jr., R. Franklin
Copper and Brass Servicenter Association(266)
Brown, Ragen
Offshore Marine Service Association(564)
Brown, Richard W.
National Petrochemical & Refiners Association(532)
Brown, Richard G.
National Federation of Federal Employees(509)
Brown, Rick
Associated General Contractors of America(165)
Brown, Robin
America Outdoors(19)
Brown, Robin O.
Roller Skating Association International(602)
Brown, Ronald
Infrared Data Association(338)
Brown, Ruth
United States Meat Export Federation(676)
Brown, Stephanie
Transportation Safety Equipment Institute(664)
Brown, Sylvia
Computerized Medical Imaging Society(258)
Brown, Terrence
Society of Illustrators(638)
Brown, Tim
National Association of Dental Plans(449)
Brown, Capt. Timothy A.
International Organization of Masters, Mates and Pilots(382)
Brown, Tina
Wholesale Florist and Florist Supplier Association(688)
Brown, Vercilla A.
Black Data Processing Associates(230)
Brown, Jr., Ph.D., William S.
American Association of Phonetic Sciences(48)
Brown II, M. Christopher
American Association of Colleges for Teacher Education(40)
Brown-Collier, Elba K.
Association for Social Economics(178)
Browne, Bill
Organization of Black Designers(567)
Browne, USN (Ret.), V.Adm. Herbert A.
Armed Forces Communications and Electronics Association(161)
Browne, Joe
National Football League(511)
Brownell, Larry
Marketing Research Association(413)
Browning, Joann
Association of Theatre Movement Educators(218)
Browning, Roger K.
American Pharmacists Association(114)
Browning, MPH, Susan M.
American Burn Association(60)
Brownstein, Joanne
Association of Authors' Representatives(186)
Broyles, Jimmy
Smocking Arts Guild of America(612)
Bruce, Tammy
American Hampshire Sheep Association(88)
Brueggeman, Robert
Professional Numismatists Guild(588)
Brugge, Parker
American Wood Preservers Institute(155)
Brumm, Loren
Instructional Telecommunications Council(344)
Brune, Christine W.
American Horse Publications Association(91)
Bruner, Ronald G.
Gas Processors Association(314)
Brungardt, Stacy
Society of Teachers of Family Medicine(644)
Brunke, Erika
Computer Event Marketing Association(257)
Brunner, CAE, Michael E.
National Telecommunications Cooperative Association(546)
Bruno, Nicole
American Orthopsychiatric Association(111)
Bruns, Andrea
PCIA - the Wireless Industry Association(572)
Bruns, Ronald A.
American Society of Anesthesiologists(134)
Brunson, Melanie
American Council of the Blind(76)
Brunton, Melissa K.
Direct Selling Association(285)
Bruss, Joanne
International Society of Travel and Tourism Educators(392)
Brust, Haley J.
National Society for Experiential Education(540)
Bryan, Jr., Charles F.
Independent Research Libraries Association(335)
Bryan, Gordon C.
National Marrow Donor Program(526)
Bryant, Adena
Regulatory Affairs Professionals Society(598)
Bryant, Ed.D., CAE, Anne L.
National School Boards Association(538)
Bryant, B.J.
American Association for Employment in Education(34)
Bryant, Dr. Cedric X.
American Council on Exercise(76)
Bryant, Kathy
Federated Ambulatory Surgery Association(303)
Bryant, Laurie
Meat Importers' Council of America(415)
Bryant, Robert M.
National Insurance Crime Bureau(522)
Bryant, M.D., J.D., Thomas E.
Aspirin Foundation of America(164)
Bryson, Randy
Consortium of Behavioral Health Nurses and Associates(262)
Developmental Disabilities Nurses Association(284)
Buchanan, D.O., Steve P.
American College of Osteopathic Obstetricians and Gynecologists(69)
Buche, Tim
Motorcycle Industry Council(421)
Motorcycle Safety Foundation(422)
Specialty Vehicle Institute of America(650)
Bucholz, Tim
POPAI The Global Association for Marketing at Retail(580)
Buck, Helen M.
Jewelers' Security Alliance of the U.S.(401)
Buckingham, Ray
Golf Course Superintendents Association of America(318)
Buckley, Ellen R.
National Field Selling Association(510)
Buckley, Jean M.
Future Business Leaders of America-Phi Beta Lambda(313)
Buckley, Mary
American Art Therapy Association(32)
Buckley, Maurice A.
Ireland Chamber of Commerce in the U.S.(399)
Buckley, Mona
Professional Insurance Marketing Association(588)
Buckley, Pamela K.
Kappa Delta Pi(403)
Bucklin, Audra
International Association of Broadcast Monitors(354)
Buckner, Dr. Stuart
US Composting Council(681)
Buczak, Darelene J.
American College of Chest Physicians(64)
Budd, Cheryl
National Council on Compensation Insurance(502)
Budetti, Maureen
National Association of Independent Colleges and Universities(457)
Budway, Robert B.
Can Manufacturers Institute(237)
Budzinski, Joseph W.
International Cemetery and Funeral Association(364)
Budzinski, Linda
International Cemetery and Funeral Association(364)
Buehner, Jackie
American National CattleWomen(108)

Buffenbarger, R. Thomas
International Association of Machinists and Aerospace Workers(359)

Buffington, Cynthia
Mechanical Contractors Association of America(415)

Buis, Tom
Farmers Educational and Co-operative Union of America(301)

Bulak, Debra
American Culinary Federation(77)

Bulter, PhD, Francine
North American Nature Photography Association(558)

Bumanis, Al
American Music Therapy Association(107)

Bumpass, Robin
Filter Manufacturers Council(305)

Bunce, Peter J.
General Aviation Manufacturers Association(315)

Bunch, Michelle
North American Insulation Manufacturers Association(557)

Bundy, Ken
Association of Personal Computer User Groups(207)

Bunn, J.T.
Leaf Tobacco Exporters Association(406)

bunnell, diana
American Society of Radiologic Technologists(145)

Bunse, Dr. Ben W.
German American Chamber of Commerce(316)

Buongiorno, B.K.
Society of Petroleum Evaluation Engineers(641)

Bura, Keith
Academy of General Dentistry(3)

Burak, Rob
Interlocking Concrete Pavement Institute(347)

Burandt, Gary
ICOM, International Communications Agency Network(330)

Burch, Christine
National Association of Public Hospitals and Health Systems(467)

Burcham, Frank
Alternatives Fuel Vehicle Network(18)

Burd, Kim
Spring Manufacturers Institute(652)

Burden, Kathleen
Golf Course Superintendents Association of America(318)

Burdette, Alan
Society for Ethnomusicology(617)

Burdge, Carol
International Glove Association(374)

Burdon, Conigsby
COLA(250)

Bureau, Amanda
Association of Fraternity Advisors(198)

Burfeind, III, William F.
Consumer Credit Insurance Association(263)

Burgart, Patti
International Entertainment Buyers Association(370)

Burger, Anna
Service Employees International Union(609)

Burger, Kathryn
American Theatre Critics Association(151)

Burger, Rev. Stephen E.
Association of Gospel Rescue Missions(199)

Burger, Tom
Professional Managers Association(588)

Burgeson, Charlene
National Association for Sport and Physical Education(436)

Burgess, Becky
National Association of Electrical Distributors(450)

Burin, James M.
Flight Safety Foundation(308)

Burk, Brett J.
Semiconductor Environmental Safety and Health Association(608)
Society for Integrative and Comparative Biology(620)

Burk, Jr., Richard J.
American Academy of Health Physics(23)
American Ornithologists' Union(110)
Health Physics Society(323)
Society for Risk Analysis(625)

Burkard, Joyce
Independent Computer Consultants Association(333)

Burke, April
Association of Independent Research Institutes(200)

Burke, Ph.D., John E.
Accreditation Association for Ambulatory Health Care(6)

Burke, John R.
Foodservice and Packaging Institute(309)

Burke, Kevin
American Apparel & Footwear Association(31)

Burke, Lawrence P.
Light Aircraft Manufacturers Association(408)

Burke, Patricia A.
International Desalination Association(369)

Burkert, Paula
American College of Sports Medicine(70)

Burkgren, D.V.M., MBA, Thomas J.
American Association of Swine Veterinarians(52)

Burkhammer, Lori
Water Environment Federation(685)

Burkhard, C.
Guild of Book Workers(321)

Burkhart, Ph.D., Diane
American Osteopathic Association(111)

Burkholder, Rebecca
National Consumers League(495)

Burks, Patrick
American Geological Institute(87)

Burner, CPA, Larry D.
Society of American Foresters(630)

Burnett, Jefferson
National Association of Independent Schools(457)

Burney, LouAnn
American Resort Development Association(122)

Burnham, Karen H.
Fire and Emergency Manufacturers and Services Association(307)
Fire Apparatus Manufacturers' Association(307)

Burnham, Susanne
Society of Behavioral Medicine(632)

Burns, Bobby
National Association of Federal Education Program Administrators(452)

Burns, CHR, Elaine M.
International Home Furnishings Representatives Association(375)

Burns, Kristine
Oncology Nursing Society(564)

Burns, Krystina
Appaloosa Horse Club(159)

Burns, Lillian
MTM Association for Standards and Research(422)

Burns, Mary Ann
Futures Industry Association(313)

Burns, Ph.D, Sharon
Association for Financial Counseling and Planning Education(173)

Burns, Tim
Vinyl Institute(683)

Burns, CAE, William M.
Association for Play Therapy(176)

Burnstein, Jeffrey A.
Automated Imaging Association(222)

Burr, Tracy
National Reading Conference(535)

Burrell, Cassie
American Welding Society(154)

Burrell, Lizabeth L.
Maritime Law Association of the U.S.(412)

Burroughs, Elise S.
Society for News Design(622)

Burrows, Robert
Institute of Environmental Sciences and Technology(341)

Burrus, William
American Postal Workers Union(117)

Burruss, Chris
Truckload Carriers Association(666)

Bursjek, Brian
Flavor and Extract Manufacturers Association of the United States(307)
Fragrance Materials Association of the United States(311)
International Association of Color Manufacturers(355)
Pickle Packers International(577)

Burt, Christine
Leather Industries of America(407)

Burt, David
Alternatives Fuel Vehicle Network(18)

Burton, Alan K.
Mining and Metallurgical Society of America(420)

Burton, Bill
National Association of Video Distributors(480)

Burton, CAE, Susan
American College of Health Care Administrators(66)

Busby, Dan
Evangelical Council for Financial Accountability(298)

Bush, Casey
Headwear Information Bureau(322)

Bush, J.D., CAE, Milton M.
Independent Association of Accredited Registrars(333)
International Federation of Inspection Agencies - Americas Committee(371)

Bush, Patricia
Coalition of Visionary Resources(250)

Bushaw, William
Phi Delta Kappa(575)

Buska, Daniel
Academy of General Dentistry(3)

Busley, Marc R.
National Quartz Producers Council(534)

Bussard, William K.
Retail Solutions Providers Association(601)

Bussey, Tadson
University and College Designers Association(679)

Butcher, Deena
Hospice and Palliative Nurses Association(328)

Butcher, Kathy
National Ground Water Association(515)
Butcher, Steven
Rubber Manufacturers Association(603)
Butera, Jessica
Million Dollar Round Table(419)
Butler, Ph.D., Francine
Association for Applied Psychophysiology and Biofeedback(167)
Butler, Ph.D., CAE, Francine
Association of Community Health Nursing Educators(192)
Butler, Ph.D., CAE, Francine
Society for Scholarly Publishing(625)
Butler, Kathleen M.
American Society of Notaries(142)
Butler, Sarina
American Bar Association(56)
Butler, Staci
Association for Unmanned Vehicle Systems International(181)
Butler, Stan
Institute of Food Technologists(341)
Butler, CAE, Susan R.
National School Boards Association(538)
Butt, Stan
Tennessee Walking Horse Breeders and Exhibitors Association(659)
Butterfield, Jeanne A.
American Immigration Lawyers Association(92)
Buttner Fiordi, Heidi
American Academy of Child and Adolescent Psychiatry(20)
Buzby, Barry
National Industrial Council - State Associations Group(519)
Buzynski, Dawn
American Judicature Society(99)
Buzzerd, Jr. CAE, Harry W.
Process Equipment Manufacturers' Association(584)
Buzzerd, Judith O.
Process Equipment Manufacturers' Association(584)
Bybee, Mac
SWANA - Solid Waste Association of North America(656)
Byer, Eric
National Air Transportation Association(428)
Byer, Dr. Glenn CJ
North American Academy of Liturgy(554)
Byers, Laurie
National Head Start Association(516)
Byers, CAE, Michele
Emergency Medicine Residents' Association(292)
Bynum, Evita
Association of Black Sociologists(187)
Bynum, Laura
Paperboard Packaging Council(571)
Byrd, Alicia
National Council of State Boards of Nursing(500)
Byrd, John
AMT - The Association For Manufacturing Technology(156)
Byrd, Michelle
Independent Feature Project(334)
Byrd, Phillip W.
American Importers Association(93)
Byrd, Ricardo
National Association of Neighborhoods(462)
Byrne, Richard C.
American Wire Cloth Institute(155)
Cold Formed Parts and Machine Institute(250)
Expansion Joint Manufacturers Association(299)
Hand Tools Institute(321)
Tubular Exchanger Manufacturers Association(666)
Bystedt, Maarit
Finnish American Chamber of Commerce(307)
Caballero, Jeffrey B.
Association of Asian-Pacific Community Health Organizations(186)
Cabral, Sam A.
International Union of Police Associations, AFL-CIO(396)
Cabrera, Vanessa
American Amusement Machine Association(31)
Cabrero, Margo
Society of Medical Consultants to the Armed Forces(639)
Cady, Cindy
National Association of Community Health Centers(445)
Caesar, Fred
Catholic Health Association of the United States(240)
Caffarelli, Patrick
National Automatic Merchandising Association(482)
Cafruny, Madalyn
American Public Power Association(120)
Cahill, Irene
National Court Reporters Association(503)
Cahill, Judith A.
Academy of Managed Care Pharmacy(4)
Cahill, Leslie
American Seed Trade Association(124)
Cahill McDonald, Dorothy
American Podiatric Medical Students' Association(116)
Cain, Lisa
Association of Maternal and Child Health Programs(204)
Cairns, Ann
Geological Society of America(315)
Calabrese, David
Association of Home Appliance Manufacturers(200)
Calabrese, Denise
Association of Professional Landscape Designers(209)
Perlite Institute(573)
Calabrese, Katie
Career College Association(237)
Calambokidis, Joan B.
International Masonry Institute(379)
Calderon, Inge
American Supply Association(150)
Caldwell, Alan
International Association of Fire Chiefs(357)
Caldwell, Brett
International Brotherhood of Teamsters, AFL-CIO(363)
Caldwell, Corey
Association of Flight Attendants - CWA(197)
Caldwell, Heather
National Utility Contractors Association(548)
Caldwell, May
International Society of Fire Service Instructors(391)
Caldwell, R. Michael
American Institute of Timber Construction(98)
Caldwell, Susan M.
Information Systems Audit and Control Association(338)
Cale-Roberts, Catherine
National Business Association(486)
Calegari, Dorothy
American Glovebox Society(87)
Calhoun, A. Cedric
Regulatory Affairs Professionals Society(598)
Calhoun, Craig
Social Science Research Council(613)
Calhoun, Terry
Society for College and University Planning(615)
Call, Jerry
American Foundry Society(85)
Callahan, CCE, CRF, William Terrence "Terry"
Credit Research Foundation(279)
Callavaro, Rick
American Foundry Society(85)
Callender, Mary
National Intramural-Recreational Sports Association(522)
Callery, T. Grant
National Association of Securities Dealers(471)
Calvet, Linda
Colombian American Association(252)
Venezuelan American Association of the U.S.(682)
Calvin, Mike
American Association of Motor Vehicle Administrators(45)
Calvo, CAE, Roque J.
Electrochemical Society(291)
Cameron, Jill
National Association of Police Organizations(465)
Cammarata, Ken
American Society of Head and Neck Radiology(138)
Camp, Camille G.
Association of State Correctional Administrators(215)
Camp, George M.
Association of State Correctional Administrators(215)
Campagna, Shannon
Retail Industry Leaders Association(601)
Campana, Kevin
National Association of School Resource Officers(470)
Campbell, B. H.
Council for Near-Infrared Spectroscopy(269)
Campbell, Debbie
American Association of Colleges of Nursing(40)
Campbell, DuVonne
American Society of Radiologic Technologists(145)
Campbell, Jason
Society for Range Management(624)
Campbell, Jeannie
National Council for Community Behavioral Healthcare(497)
Campbell, Jennifer
International Association of Infant Massage(358)
Campbell, Ph.D., Karen L.
American Society of Nephrology(142)
Campbell, Karen K.
American Criminal Justice Association/Lambda Alpha Epsilon(77)
Campbell, CFEE, Kaye
International Festivals and Events Association(371)
Campbell, Leslie
Commercial Law League of America(253)

Campbell, CMP, CAE, Linda
American Association of Healthcare Consultants(43)
Campbell, Madelyn
Oral History Association(566)
Campbell, Mike
National Association of Intercollegiate Athletics(458)
Campbell, Rachel E.
National Automatic Merchandising Association(482)
Campbell, Renee
International Association of Lighting Designers(358)
Campbell, Stephen F.
Commercial Vehicle Safety Alliance(254)
Campbell, Steve
Association for the Advancement of Medical Instrumentation(179)
Campbell, Susan
International Association of Infant Massage(358)
Campbell, Terry
Bright Belt Warehouse Association(232)
Campobenedetto, Judi
Precision Metalforming Association(583)
Campoy, Robert
American Water Works Association(154)
Candelaria, Teri
National Association of State Administrators and Supervisors of Private Schools(473)
Candusso, Guy
United Nations Staff Union(672)
Canfield, Pat
National Society of Professional Surveyors(542)
Canner, Stephen J.
United States Council for International Business(674)
Canning, Jessi
Society of Toxicologic Pathologists(645)
Cannon, Gail
Professional Insurance Marketing Association(588)
Cannon, Hugh
Society of Nuclear Medicine(641)
Cannon, Ph.D., Hugh M.
Association for Business Simulation and Experiential Learning(168)
Cannon, Kathy
American Pediatric Society(113)
Cantriel, Don
National Rural Letter Carriers' Association(537)
Cantwell, Jeff
National Federation of Independent Business(509)
Cappella, Elena A.
American Law Institute(100)
Cappitell, MBA, CAE, Susan B.
American Roentgen Ray Society(123)
Capps, Cheryl
Society of Decorative Painters(635)
Caraley, Demetrios
Academy of Political Science(5)
Caraway, Ph.D., Carol
Society for the Philosophy of Sex and Love(627)
Carbone, William J.
American Association of Physician Specialists(48)
Card, Noel
American Academy of Actuaries(19)
Carden, Jacalyn
Association of State and Territorial Health Officials(215)
Cardenas, Lilly A.
Hispanic Association of Colleges and Universities(325)
Cardez, Anthony
Overseas Automotive Council(570)
Cardona, Jeanne L.
Association of Ship Brokers and Agents (U.S.A.)(214)
Cardwell, Gail Davis
Mortgage Bankers Association(421)
Cardwell, Nancy
International Bluegrass Music Association(362)
Carey, Joseph
Society for Neuroscience(622)
Carey, Steve
National Trailer Dealers Association(547)
National Truck Equipment Association(547)
Cargill, Mary
Dance Critics Association(281)
Carl, Carlton
Association of Trial Lawyers of America(218)
Carleton, CAE, David
Society of Quantitative Analysts(643)
Carley, Wayne W.
National Association of Biology Teachers(440)
Carli, Lorraine
National Fire Protection Association(510)
Carlitti, Rocco
CTIA - The Wireless Association(280)
Carlson, Brenda S.
American Dairy Science Association(78)
Carlson, Carol
National Association of Agricultural Fair Agencies(438)
Carlson, Donna J. D.
Rubber Pavements Association(603)
Carlson, Douglas
Rubber Pavements Association(603)
Carlson, Ginger Macchi
Congress on Research in Dance(261)
Carlson, Marla
Consultant Dietitians in Health Care Facilities(263)
Carlson, Robert
Council of the Great City Schools(275)
Carlson, Sherry
North American Wensleydale Sheep Association(562)
Carmichael, Michael
American Bail Coalition(55)
Carmichael, Neil
American Arbitration Association(32)
Carmigiano, Christie
Precision Metalforming Association(583)
Carnahan, Betsy
Trade Show Exhibitors Association(663)
Carnes, Bruce
National Cable & Telecommunications Association(486)
Carnes, Mary
Armed Forces Broadcasters Association(161)
Carnes, Woneta
American Construction Inspectors Association(74)
Carnevale, VMD, Richard A.
Animal Health Institute(157)
Carney, James D.
National Truck Equipment Association(547)
Carolla, CAE, Adrianne
Air and Waste Management Association(12)
Caron, David
Society of Protozoologists(643)
Caron, Louise Q.
International Licensing Industry Merchandisers' Association(378)
Caron, Ron
International Ozone Association-Pan American Group Branch(382)
Carow, III, L. Jack
American Society of General Surgeons(138)
Carpenetti, Ann
U.S. Lacrosse(668)
Carpenter, Dave
International Iridology Practitioners Association(377)
Carpenter, Diane
American Sportfishing Association(148)
Carpenter, Ellen
National Cotton Council of America(496)
Carpenter, Isaac
American Dental Hygienists' Association(78)
Carpenter, James W.
International Association of Electrical Inspectors(356)
Carpenter, Joan
Red and White Dairy Cattle Association(597)
Carpenter, Jot
CTIA - The Wireless Association(280)
Carpenter, Katherine "Sue"
Institute of Public Utilities(343)
Carr, Chuck
Institute of Scrap Recycling Industries(343)
Carr, James
National Association of Intercollegiate Athletics(458)
Carr, CMD, Kelly
Safe and Vault Technicians Association(604)
Carr, Patrick
Indian Educators Federation(336)
Carrera, Irina
National Association of Self-Instructional Language Programs(471)
Carreras, Lisa
International Association of Attorneys and Executives in Corporate Real Estate(353)
Carrico, Ph.D., Christine K.
American Society for Pharmacology and Experimental Therapeutics(131)
Carrillo, Joseph
National Association of Hispanic Publications(456)
Carrington, Bel
Household Goods Forwarders Association of America(329)
Carroll, Jr., Charles T.
National Association of Waterfront Employers(481)
Carroll, David
Gas Technology Institute(314)
Carroll, William F.
Portable Sanitation Association International(581)
Carroll, Ph.D., William J.
American Reusable Textile Association(122)
Carson, Susan
Alpha Tau Delta(18)
Carstensen, Russell V.
NARTE(425)
Cartagena, Jonathan
National Association of Private Special Education Centers(465)
Carteaux, William R.
Society of the Plastics Industry(645)
Carter, Barbara
Society for Human Ecology(619)

Carter, Cathy
System Safety Society(657)
Carter, Curtis L.
American Society for Aesthetics(126)
Carter, Dave
National Bison Association(484)
Carter, Gene R.
Association for Supervision and Curriculum Development(178)
Carter, Gennice T.
AcademyHealth(6)
Carter, Gloria
Aerospace Medical Association(10)
Carter, Jerry
National Council of Examiners for Engineering and Surveying(499)
Carter, Katherine French
Laboratory Products Association(404)
Carter, Nancy
Society of Exploration Geophysicists(636)
Carter, Steve
American Society of Nuclear Cardiology(142)
Carter, FAIA, Virgil R.
American Society of Mechanical Engineers(141)
Cartier, CAE, Brian
National Association of College Stores(444)
Cartwright, Betty
American Association for Laboratory Animal Science(35)
Cartwright, Ted
Institute of Food Technologists(341)
Carvalho, Barbara
National Council on Public Polls(502)
Cascio, Pat
International Nanny Association(380)
Case, David R.
Environmental Technology Council(297)
Case, Kathleen
American Association for Cancer Research(34)
Case, Ed.D., Larry D.
National FFA Organization(510)
Casey, Brian
International Home Furnishings Market Authority(375)
Casey, Dwight L.
Plumbing-Heating-Cooling Contractors - National Association(579)
Casey, Joanne F. "Joni"
Intermodal Association of North America(347)
Casey, Joseph G.
National Association of Pediatric Nurse Practitioners(464)
Casey, Samuel B.
Christian Legal Society(246)
Casey-Landry, Diane M.
America's Community Bankers(19)
Caspe, Lynda
Federation of Modern Painters and Sculptors(304)
Caspers, Karen Dunn
American Dental Hygienists' Association(78)
Cassaday, Barbara
Piano Technicians Guild(577)
Cassedy, CAE, Joan Walsh
American Council of Independent Laboratories(75)
Casserly, Michael
Council of the Great City Schools(275)
Cassidy, Daniel J.
Cable & Telecommunications Association for Marketing(236)
Cassidy, Kathleen M.
American Short Line and Regional Railroad Association(125)
Cassidy, Michael A.
Truss Plate Institute(666)
Cassidy, Philip E.
Business Council(235)
Castaldo, John
Barre Granite Association(226)
Casterta, Daniele
International Association of Association Management Companies(353)
Castignoli, Doreen
BPA Worldwide(232)
Castner, Harvey
Edison Welding Institute(289)
Castner, Stephen
American Galloway Breeders Association(86)
Castor, Harold
Industrial Chemical Research Association(336)
Castor, Dr. Stephen R.
Conservative Orthopaedics International Association(261)
Castro, Johana
University/Resident Theatre Association(680)
Caswell, Don
International Brotherhood of Boilermakers, Iron Ship Builders, Blacksmiths, Forgers and Helpers(363)
Catalon, Dr. Katie B.
National Beauty Culturists' League(484)
Caterisano, Katerina
Association of Chartered Accountants in the United States(189)
Partnership in Print Production(572)
Cates-Wessel, Kathryn
American Academy of Addiction Psychiatry(20)
Cathcart, D. Christopher
Consumer Specialty Products Association(263)
Cathcart, Sherrie
American Association for the Study of Liver Diseases(37)
Catizone, Carmen A.
National Association of Boards of Pharmacy(440)
Cattanach, Julie
International Association for Food Protection(350)
Cattaneo, Joseph J.
Glass Packaging Institute(317)
Cauble, CPA, Eric
Medical Group Management Association(416)
Cavallo, Jaye
Major Indoor Soccer League(410)
Cavanagh, Michael
Council for Electronic Revenue Communication Advancement(268)
Cavanaugh, Gloria
American Society on Aging(147)
Cavaney, CAE, Red
American Petroleum Institute(114)
Cavazos, Oscar
Service Dealers Association(609)
Cavdill, Brian
National Propane Gas Association(534)
Ceballos, Jose
National Air Traffic Controllers Association(428)
Cecchine, Melissa
American Staffing Association(149)
Cedarquist, Scott
ASABE - the Society for Engineering in Agricultural, Food and Biological Systems(162)
Ceh, Victoria
International Society of Hair Restoration Surgery(391)
Cely, Antonette
National Institute of American Doll Artists(520)
Censky, Peter
Water Quality Association(686)
Censky, Steve
American Soybean Association(148)
Centra, Cathy
Hearth Patio & Barbecue Association(324)
Cepriano, Cherilyn
Emergency Department Practice Management Association(292)
Cernich, Andrea
SGMA(651)
Certner, David
American Association of Retired Persons(50)
Certo, Jane
American Society of PeriAnesthesia Nurses(144)
Cervarich, Margaret
National Asphalt Pavement Association(431)
Cesario, Theresa
Society of Cosmetic Chemists(634)
Chabin, James
PROMAX International(590)
Chabin, Jim
Broadcast Designers' Association(233)
Chace, Richard
Security Industry Association(607)
Chaffee, Clarence L.
Council of Landscape Architectural Registration Boards(273)
Chaimovich, Jason
American Hockey League(91)
Chamberlain, CAE, Henry
Building Owners and Managers Association International(234)
Chamberlin, Michael M.
EMTA - Trade Association for the Emerging Markets(294)
Chambers, Bill H.
SMMA - The Motor and Motion Association(612)
Chambers, Elizabeth B.
SMMA - The Motor and Motion Association(612)
Transformer Association, The(663)
Chambers, Glenda
National Association of State Retirement Administrators(476)
Chambers, Michele
American Academy of Fertility Care Professionals(23)
Chambers, Ray
National Railroad Construction and Maintenance Association(534)
Chambers, Shannon
National Aeronautic Association(427)
Chambers, Tom
National Association of Criminal Defense Lawyers(448)
Chambers, Walton
American Gaming Association(86)
Chambliss, Amanda
Association for Communication Excellence(169)
Chamiec-Case, Rick
North American Association of Christians in Social Work(554)
Chamness, Charles M.
National Association of Mutual Insurance Companies(462)

Champagne, Jennifer
National Association of State Credit Union Supervisors(474)
Chan, Kim
Association of Performing Arts Presenters(207)
Chan, Susan D.
American Association of Zoo Keepers(54)
Chanda, David
Association for Conservation Information(170)
Chandick, Marie
Association of SIDS and Infant Mortality Programs(214)
Chandler, Don
Undersea and Hyperbaric Medical Society(669)
Chandler, Gary R.
National Civic League(489)
Chandler, Michelle
National Association of Securities Professionals(471)
Chandler, Sylvia E.
Association for the Advancement of Medical Instrumentation(179)
Chandler, Terry
Diamond Council of America(284)
Chaney, G.P. Russ
International Association of Plumbing and Mechanical Officials(360)
Chaney, W. Calvin
American College of Emergency Physicians(65)
Chang, Amy L.
American Society for Microbiology(130)
Chang, Eleanor
American Booksellers Association(58)
Chanin, Robert
National Education Association(506)
Chao, Tom
Destination Marketing Association International(283)
Chapman, Cindy
Commission on Certification of Work Adjustment and Vocational Evaluation Specialists(254)
Chapman, Deb
International Sleep Products Association(386)
Chapman, Eric
Continental Basketball Association(264)
Chapman, James
National Association of Federal Credit Unions(452)
Chapman, Jr., James H.
International Union of Elevator Constructors(395)
Chapman, Nancy
Soyfoods Association of North America(648)
Chapman, Roy
Wedding and Event Videographers Association International(686)
Chappell, Jeffrey
National Association of Certified Valuation Analysts(442)
Chappell, Dr. Rebecca
Music and Entertainment Industry Educators Association(423)
Charland, Tom
North American Association For Ambulatory Care(554)
Charletta, Janice
American Architectural Manufacturers Association(32)
Charlton, R. Knight
American Dental Society of Anesthesiology(79)
Charmas, Daniel
American Stock Exchange(149)
Charness, Myron
National Association of Publishers' Representatives(467)
Charron, Thomas J.
National District Attorneys Association(505)
Chase, Judi
WIFS - Women in Insurance and Financial Services(688)
Chase, Matthew
National Association of Development Organizations(449)
Chase, Oscar
Institute of Judicial Administration(342)
Chase, Paul
Financial Executives International(305)
Chase, Sue
National Fluid Power Association(511)
Chastain, Jr., Merritt B.
National Association of Pipe Coating Applicators(464)
Chauvin, William
American Shrimp Processors Association(125)
Chavez-Thompson, Linda
American Federation of Labor and Congress of Industrial Organizations(82)
Chavkin, David F.
Society of American Law Teachers(631)
Chaw, Terisa E.
National Employment Lawyers Association(507)
Chawszczewski, Susanne
National Association of Catholic Chaplains(442)
Cheatham, Craig
Association of Real Estate License Law Officials(211)
Cheek, Felicia
American Apparel & Footwear Association(31)
Chelena, Kay
National Association of Extension 4-H Agents(451)
Chelf, Lauren
Biophysical Society(229)
Chell, MD, Jeffrey W.
National Marrow Donor Program(526)
Chen, Lilly Lee
Linguistic Association of Canada and the United States(408)
Cheney, Liana
Association for Textual Scholarship in Art History(179)
Cheney, Rev. Peter G.
National Association of Episcopal Schools(451)
Cheng, Kipp
American Association of Advertising Agencies(37)
Chernin, D.M.D., David A.
American Academy of the History of Dentistry(29)
Cheshire, Len
Society of Cost Estimating and Analysis(634)
Cheshire, Lisa
Association of College and University Telecommunications Administrators(191)
Chesser, Michael
ASABE - the Society for Engineering in Agricultural, Food and Biological Systems(162)
Chestang, Nicole M.
Graduate Management Admission Council(319)
Chetelat, Caroline
COLA(250)
Chevalier, Greg
National Reloading Manufacturers Association(536)
Chezem, Amy
Juvenile Products Manufacturers Association(403)
Chianchiano, Dolph
National Kidney Foundation(523)
Chiappardi, F.J.
National Federation of Independent Unions(509)
Chilcott, Susan
American Association of State Colleges and Universities(51)
Childers, Jana
Academy of Homiletics(3)
Childers, Patricia
Incentive Marketing Association(332)
Childress, James M.
Gasification Technologies Council(314)
Childress, Mary
American Wind Energy Association(155)
Childs, John
Optical Society of America(566)
Childs, Matt
American Concrete Pipe Association(73)
Chill, Nancy
Endocrine Society(294)
Chilson, Sue
American Bashkir Curly Registry(56)
Chilton, Cindy
Palomino Horse Breeders of America(570)
Chinnock, Janis
Society of Laparoendoscopic Surgeons(639)
Chipps, Glenda
Western-English Trade Association(688)
Chivari, Laurel
Computing Technology Industry Association(258)
Chizmadia, Richard
American Guild of Music(88)
Choate, Lisa
American Councils for International Education(76)
Choi, Chong-Hie
Association of Higher Education Facilities Officers(199)
Chopard, Kay
National Criminal Justice Association(503)
Chorbajian, Dr. Torcom
Society for Mathematical Biology(621)
Chow, Christine
Color Association of the United States(252)
Chow, Ph.D., Ida
Society for Developmental Biology(616)
Chow, Peter
American Association for Chinese Studies(34)
Choyke, Barbara
American College of Occupational and Environmental Medicine(68)
Christantiello, Gerri
National Association of Export Companies(451)
Christensen, Bekah
American Association of Oriental Medicine(47)
Christensen, Lynne
Cedar Shake and Shingle Bureau(240)
Christensen, Rod
National Alfalfa Alliance(429)
Christensen, Todd
National Human Services Assembly(518)
Christensen, Valerie
Association of Educators in Imaging and Radiologic Sciences(194)

Christian, Alex T.
Percheron Horse Association of America(573)
Christian, Josh
U.S. Lacrosse(668)
Christiano, Sam
National Association of State Boards of Geology(473)
Christianson, Bill
Orthopedic Surgical Manufacturers Association(569)
Christie, Dolores
Catholic Theological Society of America(240)
Christie, Jeanne
Association of State Wetland Managers(216)
Christie, Lorna
Produce Marketing Association(584)
Christie, CAE, Stephen M.
Automotive Oil Change Association(224)
Christie, Susan
American Public Human Services Association(120)
Christie, Tracy
National Asphalt Pavement Association(431)
Christina, D.P.M., James
American Podiatric Medical Association(116)
Christison, Carol L.
International Dairy-Deli-Bakery Association(369)
Christman, Yvette
National Futures Association(513)
Christmas, Rob
American Greyhound Track Operators Association(87)
Christner, Windy K.
American Pharmacists Association(114)
Chubb, Michael
Association of Smoked Fish Processors(214)
Chumley, Pamela A.
Concord Grape Association(258)
International Inflight Food Service Association(376)
International Jelly and Preserve Association(377)
Vinegar Institute(683)
Chung, Ph.D., CSHM, Jeffrey
National Safety Management Society(538)
Church, Edward
International Safe Transit Association(385)
Church, CAE, Jerilyn
Bearing Specialist Association(226)
Church, Richard
Ceramic Tile Distributors Association(241)
Plastic Pipe and Fittings Association(578)
Church, Rick
National Church Goods Association(489)
Churchill, Ron
AFSM International(11)
Chvotkin, Alan L.
Professional Services Council(589)
Cialone, Dr. Henry J.
Edison Welding Institute(289)
Ciccone, John
American Society of Cataract and Refractive Surgery(135)
Cicerchia, Meredith
Wireless Communications Association International(690)
Cicerone, Ralph J.
National Academy of Sciences(427)
Ciocci, Linda Church
National Hydropower Association(518)
Cioffari, Nancy C.
American Association of Colleges of Osteopathic Medicine(40)
Cioni, Karen
International Warehouse Logistics Association(396)
Cipriani, Jack
National Conference of Brewery and Soft Drink Workers - United States and Canada(493)
Cirner, Randall
National Conference of Diocesan Vocation Directors(493)
Cisternino, Mark
Flexographic Technical Association(308)
Ciukaj, Mary Beth
Council of Residential Specialists(274)
Cizik, Dr. Richard
National Association of Evangelicals(451)
Claghorn, Karey
American Polypay Sheep Association(116)
Clancy, Mary K.
Intermediaries and Reinsurance Underwriters Association(347)
Clare, Edwin S.
Production Equipment Rental Association(585)
Clark, Ph.D., Betsy
Ladies Professional Golf Association(404)
Clark, Bill
American Institute for Shippers Associations(94)
Clark, CPA, Carol
Association of Public Health Laboratories(210)
Clark, Cheryl
Meat Industry Suppliers Alliance(415)
Clark, Deana
National Association of Health Data Organizations(455)
Clark, Donna
International Society for Pharmaceutical Engineering(388)
Clark, Donna
American Traffic Safety Services Association(152)
Clark, Douglas R.
American Schools of Oriental Research(124)
Clark, Elizabeth
Art Libraries Society of North America(161)
Clark, Elizabeth J.
National Association of Social Workers(472)
Clark, J.R.
Association of Private Enterprise Education(208)
Clark, James D.
International Union of Electronic, Electrical, Salaried, Machine, and Furniture Workers-CWA(395)
Clark, Jr., John D.
Society of Cable Telecommunications Engineers(632)
Clark, John S.
National Association of Broadcast Employees and Technicians - Communications Workers of America(441)
Clark, Julia A.
International Federation of Professional and Technical Engineers(371)
Clark, Katherine E.
Information Technologies Credit Union Association(338)
National Association of Credit Union Supervisory and Auditing Committees(448)
Clark, Kelly James
Society of Christian Philosophers(633)
Clark, Mary Ann
Council of Societies for the Study of Religion(274)
Clark, Matthew
PDA - an International Association for Pharmaceutical Science and Technology(572)
Clark, Niki M.
National Association of Home Builders(456)
Clark, Pat
American Academy of Child and Adolescent Psychiatry(20)
Clark, Jr., Ray L.
Leafy Greens Council(406)
Clark, Ruth M.
Mailing & Fulfillment Service Association(410)
Clark, Stan
Association of College Administration Professionals(190)
Clark, Susan
Associated Press Managing Editors(166)
Clark, Suzanne
United States Chamber of Commerce(674)
Clark, Ted
Tobacconists' Association of America(662)
Clark-Jones, Sue
Association of Film Commissioners International(196)
Clarke, Boyd
Certified Milk Producers Association of America(242)
Clarke, George
Selected Independent Funeral Homes(539)
Clarke, James L.
American Society of Association Executives & Center for Association Leadership(134)
Clarke, FHFMA, Richard L.
Healthcare Financial Management Association(324)
Clarke, Robert M.
Truck Manufacturers Association(665)
Claudy, Lynn
National Association of Broadcasters(441)
Claver, Amy
American Society for Bioethics and Humanities(127)
Clawson, Thomas
National Board for Certified Counselors(485)
Claymore, Paul
Auto Suppliers Benchmarking Association(222)
International Contract Center Benchmarking Consortium(367)
Clayton, Carolyn B.
National Association of Church Food Service(443)
Clayton, Charles P.
Association of Program Directors in Internal Medicine(210)
Clayton, John
American Society of Music Arrangers and Composers(142)
Clayton, Paul
United States Meat Export Federation(676)
Cleary, Michael J.
National Association of Collegiate Directors of Athletics(444)
Cleary, Patrick
National Association of Manufacturers(460)
Cleary, Susan
Independent Film and Television Alliance(334)
Cleave, Paula
American Bar Association(56)
Cleaver, Sha'Dana
American Academy of Child and Adolescent Psychiatry(20)
Cleaver, Walter J.
Human Resource Planning Society(329)

Clegg, Suzanne Thulin
Manufactured Housing Institute(411)
Clemans, Terry W.
National Credit Reporting Association(503)
Clements, Fred
National Bicycle Dealers Association(484)
Clements, John
National Active and Retired Federal Employees Association(427)
Clements, Rosemary A.
ESOP Association(297)
Clemons, CAE, CMP, Calvin K.
National Association of Sign Supply Distributors(472)
Office Products Wholesalers Association(564)
Clemons, CAE, Calvin K.
Register of Professional Archeologists(598)
Clemons, Claudia J.
National Association of Waterproofing and Structural Repair Contractors(481)
Clendenin, CAE, Peter C.
National Association for the Support of Long-Term Care(437)
Clendenning, Bonnie R.
Archaeological Institute of America(160)
Clendenning, Rick
International Metal Decorators Association(379)
Cleveland, Ken
American Academy of Orofacial Pain(26)
Cleveland, Kenneth
Society for Healthcare Epidemiology of America(618)
Cline, Jason
Roller Skating Association International(602)
Cline, MSG Michael P.
Enlisted Association of the National Guard of the United States(295)
Clingman, Ed
National Electronic Service Dealers Association(506)
Clore, Sarah
National Association of Agriculture Employees(438)
Clothier, Carol A.
Federation of State Medical Boards of the United States(304)
Clowers, Lisa
Healthcare Distribution Management Association(323)
Clutter, Ted J.
Geothermal Resources Council(316)
Clyde, Allan
Council on Foundations(276)
Coane, RADM Casey
Naval Reserve Association(551)
Coates, Monica L.
Organization for International Investment(567)
Coates, Vivian H.
ECRI(288)
Cobuluis, Karen
National Emergency Management Association(507)
Cochran, Barbara
Radio-Television News Directors Association(594)
Cochran, J. Thomas
United States Conference of Mayors(674)
Cochran, Jill E.
American Association of Endodontists(42)
Cochran, CAE, CMP, Kathleen D.
National Association of Health Underwriters(455)
Cocivera, Roger
Textile Rental Services Association of America(660)
Codding, Fred H.
National Association of Miscellaneous, Ornamental and Architectural Products Contractors(462)
National Association of Reinforcing Steel Contractors(469)
National Council of Erectors, Fabricators and Riggers(498)
Coduri, John B.
Association of YMCA Professionals(221)
Cody, Alison
Manufacturers' Agents Association for the Foodservice Industry(411)
Coe, CMP, Janet
American Society of Appraisers(134)
Coe, Wendy
American College of Veterinary Pathologists(72)
Coen, Barbara
Women Executives in Public Relations(691)
Coen, Joseph
Association of Catholic Diocesan Archivists(189)
Coffey, Katharine
National Art Materials Trade Association(431)
Coffey, Matthew B.
National Tooling and Machining Association(546)
Cogbill, Cindy
North American Folk Music and Dance Alliance(557)
Cohen, Beth
Laser Institute of America(405)
Cohen, Bob
Information Technology Association of America(338)
Cohen, Dan
National Association of Installation Developers(458)
Cohen, Dasha
American Medical Informatics Association(104)
Cohen, Genie
International Association of Jewish Vocational Services(358)
Cohen, Gregory M.
American Highway Users Alliance(90)
Cohen, Helene
American Law Institute(100)
Cohen, Jeffrey
American Financial Services Association(83)
Cohen, CAE, Jonathan
Air Line Pilots Association, International(13)
Cohen, Larry
Communications Workers of America(255)
Cohen, Lewis
Coalition of Essential Schools(249)
Cohen, Marsha A.
Reinsurance Association of America(598)
Cohen, Megan
International Dyslexia Association(370)
Cohen, Pat
Lignin Institute(408)
Cohen, Skip
Wedding and Portrait Photographers International(686)
Cohner, Cynthia
American Health Lawyers Association(89)
Colaianni, CAE, Peter L.
Document Management Industries Association(286)
Colarulli, Dana R.
Intellectual Property Owners Association(345)
Colbert, Adeena
American Society for Aesthetic Plastic Surgery(126)
Colbert, Robert
Catholic Charities USA(239)
Colbert, Scott
American Conference of Cantors(73)
Colbourne, William J.
Blue Cross and Blue Shield Association(231)
Colby, Gerald
National Writers Union(550)
Colby, Jennifer
Women's Caucus for Art(693)
Cole, Dan
Consumer Electronics Association(263)
Cole, RODC, Dr. Donald W.
Organization Development Institute(566)
Cole, Donna Lee
National Association of Manufacturers(460)
Cole, Jeff
American Pinzgauer Association(115)
Cole, CAE, CMP, Joanne J.
American Association of Feline Practitioners(43)
Cole, Kenneth
National Guild of Community Schools of the Arts(515)
Cole, Lisa A.
Physician Insurers Association of America(577)
Cole, Melissa
Foster Family-Based Treatment Association(311)
Cole, Steven J.
Council of Better Business Bureaus(271)
Colee, Missy
Society of Biblical Literature(632)
Coleman, Byers W.
State Guard Association of the United States(652)
Coleman, Carolyn
National League of Cities(524)
Coleman, Dorothy
National Association of Manufacturers(460)
Coleman, Frank
Distilled Spirits Council of the U.S.(286)
Coleman, CAE, Jacquelyn T.
American Academy of Psychiatry and the Law(28)
American Academy of Psychoanalysis and Dynamic Psychiatry(28)
American Clinical Neurophysiology Society(63)
Coleman, James E.
National Association of Printing Ink Manufacturers(465)
Coleman, Jennifer
International Licensing Industry Merchandisers' Association(378)
Coleman, Pamela
National Association of Real Estate Investment Trusts(468)
Coleman, Richard
Space Transportation Association(648)
Coleman, Rita
Warehousing Education and Research Council(685)
Colitz, Judy
International Housewares Association(375)
Collado, III, Emilio G.
American Watch Association(154)
Collatz, Mark
Adhesive and Sealant Council(8)

Colletti, John
Public Relations Society of America(593)
Collicott, MD, FACS, Paul E.
American College of Surgeons(71)
Collie, III,CAE, H. Cris
Employee Relocation Council/Worldwide ERC(293)
Collier, Arlene
Joint Electron Device Engineering Council(402)
Collier, Linda
Society of Laparoendoscopic Surgeons(639)
Collier, Trish
National Association of College and University Food Services(444)
Colligan, Caitlin
National Telecommunications Cooperative Association(546)
Collins, Andre
National Football League Players Association(511)
Collins, Brad
American Solar Energy Society(147)
Collins, Bridget
American Kinesiotherapy Association(100)
Collins, Christie
American Concrete Pumping Association(73)
Collins, Doris D.
National Multi Housing Council(528)
Collins, James
National Rural Electric Cooperative Association(537)
Collins, CMP, Jeannine
Water Quality Association(686)
Collins, John H.
American Welara Pony Society(154)
Collins, Mary
Broadcast Cable Credit Association(233)
Broadcast Cable Financial Management Association(233)
Collins, Mimi
National Association of Colleges and Employers(444)
Collins, Patricia
Farm Equipment Wholesalers Association(301)
Collins, Polly P.
National Society of Professional Engineers(542)
Collins, Richard
American College of Clinical Pharmacy(65)
Collins, Sharon
International Inflight Food Service Association(376)
Collinson, Kelly
Association of Professors of Gynecology and Obstetrics(209)
Collishaw, Karen J.
American College of Cardiology(64)
Colnan, John
World Gold Council(696)
Colquhoun, Marcia
American Crystallographic Association(77)
Colucci, Marlene
American Hotel & Lodging Association(92)
Colville, Mary
National Chicken Council(489)
Comeau, Melissa
Association for Work Process Improvement(183)
Comer, Dr. Charles
National Optometric Association(529)
Comer, Edward H.
Edison Electric Institute(289)
Comlin, William
National Association of Traffic Accident Reconstructionists and Investigators(479)
Commons, Larry
National Athletic Trainers' Association(482)
Comparato, Fred
Association of College and University Housing Officers-International(191)
Comstock, Earl
COMPTEL(257)
Comstock, Heather
Correctional Education Association(266)
Comstock, W. Stephen
American Society of Heating, Refrigerating and Air-Conditioning Engineers(139)
Concio, Jose
Periodical and Book Association of America(573)
Conder, Dean
National Conference of State Social Security Administrators(494)
Conery, Ph.D., Leslie
International Society for Technology in Education(389)
Conklin, Tom
Society of Plastics Engineers(642)
Conkling, Ph.D., John A.
American Pyrotechnics Association(120)
Conley, John
National Tank Truck Carriers Conference(545)
Conley, Ph.D., Stephen
American Association of Sexuality Educators, Counselors and Therapists(51)
Conlin, Sue
Nurse Healers - Professional Associates International(563)
Conlon, Peggy
Advertising Council(9)
Connell, Maura
American Diabetes Association(79)
Connell, Stephanie
Academy of Veterinary Homeopathy(6)
Connelly, David
Open Applications Group(565)
Connelly, John P.
National Fisheries Institute(511)
Conner, Len
Association of Gospel Rescue Missions(199)
Conner, P.E., Terence D.
American Society of Highway Engineers(139)
Connolly, Una
National Asphalt Pavement Association(431)
Connor, Paul
National Association of Local Government Environmental Professionals(460)
Connor, Tina
National Alliance of Statewide Preservation Organizations(430)
Connors, CTC, Bill
National Business Travel Association(486)
Connors, Jerry
United States Harness Writers' Association(675)
Connors, Jerry C.
Data Interchange Standards Association(281)
Conrad, ChFC, Donna
Society of Financial Service Professionals(636)
Conrad, Shawn
National Lumber and Building Material Dealers Association(525)
Conrardy, Chris
Edison Welding Institute(289)
Constable, Tina
Publishers Publicity Association(593)
Conticelli, Peter
American Cloak and Suit Manufacturers Association(63)
Contiguglia, Dr. Bob
United States Soccer Federation(677)
Contreras, Mercy
Communications Marketing Association(255)
Conyers, Debbie
National Electronic Distributors Association(506)
Coogan, Lee
Sorptive Minerals Institute(647)
Cook, Barbara H.
National Ornamental and Miscellaneous Metals Association(531)
Cook, Bill
Advertising Research Foundation(9)
Cook, Billy D.
Institute for Professionals in Taxation(339)
Cook, Bob
Transportation Development Association(664)
Cook, Darel
Promotional Products Association International(591)
Cook, Deborah
Association of Ecosystem Research Centers(194)
Cook, Gail
American Canine Sports Medicine Association(61)
Cook, Gloria
American Oil Chemists' Society(110)
Cook, Henry
Society of Reliability Engineers(643)
Cook, Hope
Association Correctional Food Service Affiliates(166)
Cook, Jill
American School Counselor Association(124)
Cook, Ken
National Association of Service Managers(472)
Cook, Kristina C.
National Affordable Housing Management Association(428)
Cook, Linda D.
Epsilon Sigma Phi(297)
Cook, Nancy K.
Pet Food Institute(574)
Cook, Perry
International Computer Music Association(366)
Cook, Peter L.
National Association of Water Companies(480)
Cook, Ph.D., Suzanne
Travel Industry Association of America(665)
Cook, Timothy
Independent Community Bankers of America(333)
Cook, Tom
National Renderers Association(536)
Cooke, Joan F.
ISSA(400)
Cooke, Stephanie
Refrigerated Foods Association(597)
Cooley, Cheryl
American Society of Farm Managers and Rural Appraisers(137)
Cooley, Harriet
Towing and Recovery Association of America(662)
Coon, Richard A.
Recreation Vehicle Industry Association(596)
Coon, Sue
Women in Aviation International(691)
Cooney, Brian
Manufactured Housing Institute(411)

Coons, Nancy
Retail Packaging Manufacturers Association(601)
Cooper, Amanda
UNITE-HERE(670)
Cooper, Benjamin
Association of Oil Pipe Lines(206)
Cooper, Christina
National Council of Farmer Cooperatives(499)
Cooper, Donna
American Real Estate Society(121)
Cooper, John
Victorian Society in America(683)
Cooper, Margaret J.
National Association of Colored Women's Clubs(445)
Cooper, Nancy
National Association of Decorative Fabric Distributors(448)
Cooper, Robert W.
American Federation of Astrologers, Inc.(82)
Cooper, Roger B.
American Gas Association(86)
Cooper, Sara
National Consumers League(495)
Cooper, CAE, Valerie
Greeting Card Association(320)
Cooper, CAE, Valerie B.
National Candle Association(487)
Copan, Jay
American Gas Association(86)
Copeland, J. Joseph
National AMBUCS(430)
Copeland, Tamara Lucas
Voices for America's Children(684)
Copen, Nancy
Association for Research in Vision and Ophthalmology(178)
Coppock, Daren
National Association of Wheat Growers(481)
Corbin, Lauren
National Association of Federal Credit Unions(452)
Corcoran, Jim
National Confectioners Association of the United States(492)
Corcoran, Kate E.
Medical Library Association(416)
Corcoran, CAE, Kevin
American Chiropractic Association(62)
Corcoran, Shannon
American Society of Sanitary Engineering(146)
Corcoran, Thomas
American Association of Diabetes Educators(42)
Cordes, Anne M.
American Academy of Hospice and Palliative Medicine(23)
Cordier, Pamela J.
Pulp and Paper Safety Association(593)
Cordova, Cathy
International Association of Physicians in AIDS Care(360)
Core, David L.
Association of Independent Corrugated Converters(200)
Core, Sherri
National Association of Government Communicators(454)
Coren, Pat
American Littoral Society(102)
Corkern, Tricia
American Recovery Association(122)
Cormany, Dennis
Promotional Products Association International(591)
Corn, Missy
Pony of the Americas Club(580)
Cornelious, Melvin
National United Merchants Beverage Association(548)
Correa, Dr. A.C.
Association for Arid Lands Studies(167)
Correll, Pamela
American Shire Horse Association(125)
Correll, Rich A.
College of Healthcare Information Management Executives(251)
Corrie, David
Radiation Therapy Oncology Group(594)
Corrigan, Kathy
American Association of Exporters and Importers(42)
Cortese, Antonia
American Federation of Teachers(82)
Cortina, Tom
Halon Alternatives Research Corp.(321)
Corts, Dr. Paul R.
Council for Christian Colleges and Universities(268)
Coscetta, Holly
National Conference of CPA Practitioners(493)
Costello, David A.
National Association of State Boards of Accountancy(473)
Costello, Megan
Association of Corporate Travel Executives(193)
Costello, Patti
American Society for Healthcare Environmental Services(129)
Cote, Andre
Enterprise Wireless Alliance(295)
Cote, Arthur E.
National Fire Protection Association(510)
Cote, Charles
Pharmaceutical Care Management Association(575)
Cothron-Searles, Stephanie
National Speleological Society(542)
Cotteleer, Lynn A.
American Association of Law Libraries(44)
Cotter, Christine
American Society of Psychoanalytic Physicians(145)
Cotter, David
Textile Care Allied Trades Association(660)
Cottone, Donna
Motion Picture and Television Credit Association(421)
Cottrell, Charlene
Steel Recycling Institute(653)
Cottrell, Nina
Council of Residential Specialists(274)
Coughlin, Maria
Women in Scholarly Publishing(692)
Coughlin, Michele
Business Marketing Association(235)
Coulson, Lake A.
Plumbing-Heating-Cooling Contractors - National Association(579)
Coulter, Kathryn
Coalition for Government Procurement(249)
Counter, III, Nicholas
Alliance of Motion Picture and Television Producers(17)
Counts, Andy S.
American Home Furnishings Alliance(91)
Cournoyer, David
Society for Cross-Cultural Research(616)
Cousens, M. Bonnie
Society for Humanistic Judaism(619)
Cousin, James L.
AORN(158)
Cousins, Yvonne
Society for Sex Therapy and Research(625)
Cout, Jennifer
Defense Research Institute(282)
Couture, Neal J.
National Contract Management Association(495)
Covall, Mark J.
National Association of Psychiatric Health Systems(467)
Cove, Brian
Commercial Finance Association(253)
Cove, Tom
SGMA(651)
Soccer Industry Council of America(612)
Covington, Tammy
International Home Furnishings Market Authority(375)
Cowan, Ann E.
Cable & Telecommunications Association for Marketing(236)
Cowan, CAE, Robert
Professional Convention Management Association(587)
Cowan, Tor
AFT Healthcare(11)
Cowan, Wendy B.
American Society of Civil Engineers(135)
Cowden, Joseph L.
National Automobile Dealers Association(482)
Cowsert, David
Association of Automotive Aftermarket Distributors(186)
Cox, CAE, Ann R.
American Association of Occupational Health Nurses(47)
Cox, Craig
Soil and Water Conservation Society(647)
Cox, David R.
American Board of Professional Psychology(58)
Cox, Hank
National Association of Manufacturers(460)
Cox, Jim
American Association of Cosmetology Schools(41)
Cox, Joseph J.
Chamber of Shipping of America(243)
Cox, Phyllis
National Tractor Parts Dealer Association(546)
Cox, Sharon
Flexographic Technical Association(308)
Cox, Stephen R.
National Association of State Departments of Agriculture(474)
Cox, Virginia
Consumer Healthcare Products Association(263)
Coyne, James K.
National Air Transportation Association(428)
Crabtree, Sissy
American Association of Clinical Endocrinologists(39)
Craft, M.D., George S.
Phi Delta Epsilon Medical Fraternity(575)
Craig, James M.
American Institute of Marine Underwriters(96)
Craig, Jim
American Petroleum Institute(114)

Craig, Kathleen T.
American Association of Neurological Surgeons(46)
Craig, Maureen
Crane Certification Association of America(278)
Craig, Rick
Owner-Operator Independent Drivers Association(570)
Craig, Stuart
AACC International(1)
Crain, Greg
National Taxidermists Association(545)
Cram, Marcia
Society of Interventional Radiology(639)
Cramer, Connie
National Home Furnishings Association(517)
Crandall, Chydie
North American Transportation Management Institute(562)
Crandall, Derrick A.
American Recreation Coalition(122)
Crandall, Keith
Society of Systematic Biologists(644)
Crane, Angus
North American Insulation Manufacturers Association(557)
Crane, Stephen C.
American Academy of Physician Assistants(27)
Cranmer, RCDD, David C.
BICSI(228)
Crassweller, Robert
American Pomological Society(117)
Craven, David
Federation of American Socs. for Experimental Biology(303)
Craven, Laura Merkel
Association of Women Soil Scientists(220)
Craven, Robert
Council of State Association Presidents(274)
Crawford, Carol
National Conference of Black Mayors(492)
Crawford, Christopher L.
National Association of Development Companies(449)
Crawford, Debra
American Society for Quality(132)
Crawford, Diane C.
National Phlebotomy Association(533)
Crawford, Gregory L.
Steel Recycling Institute(653)
Crawford, James
National Association for Bilingual Education(431)
Crawford, Linda
Therapeutic Communities of America(660)
Crawford, Mel H.
Consumer Federation of America(263)
Crawford, Tom
Photo Marketing Association-International(576)
Crayton, Luanne
American Staffing Association(149)
Creagan, Jane
American Music Therapy Association(107)
Cree, Sandra
International Association of Bedding and Furniture Law Officials(354)
Creech, Denise
American Chemical Society(62)
Creeden, W.M.
International Brotherhood of Boilermakers, Iron Ship Builders, Blacksmiths, Forgers and Helpers(363)
Creely, Kathy
Association for Social Anthropology in Oceania(178)
Cregan, James
Magazine Publishers of America(409)
Crerar, Ken A.
Council of Insurance Agents and Brokers(272)
Crespo, Mario
National Exercise Trainers Association(508)
Cress, Kristen
United Methodist Association of Health and Welfare Ministries(671)
Cressy, Peter H.
Distilled Spirits Council of the U.S.(286)
Crews, Kimberly
Society of Woman Geographers(646)
Crews, Mary Ann
National Association of Decorative Fabric Distributors(448)
Crider, Joyce
National Conference of Catechetical Leadership(493)
Crimmins, Dr. Eileen
Society for the Study of Social Biology(628)
Crimmins, James
Society for Pediatric Pathology(623)
Crispin, Cheryl
Mortgage Bankers Association(421)
Crissman, Joan
National Association of Student Financial Aid Administrators(477)
Crist, Katrina
American Society of Transplant Surgeons(146)
Cristol, Richard E.
Association for Dressings and Sauces(171)
National Association of Margarine Manufacturers(461)
National Institute of Oilseed Products(521)
National Pasta Association(532)
Critchlow, Charles H.
American-European Soda Ash Shipping Association(156)
Crites, Sonia
National Association of Electrical Distributors(450)
Croce, Ginger D.
American Bus Association(60)
Croce, Nick
American Psychiatric Nurses Association(118)
Crocker, Chris
National Association for the Specialty Food Trade(436)
Crolius, Robert W.
Refractories Institute(597)
Crompton, CPA, Diana J.
Association for Hose and Accessories Distribution(174)
Independent Sealing Distributors(335)
Yacht Brokers Association of America(698)
Cronin, Brian P.
Professional Association of Diving Instructors(585)
Cronin, Edward J.
American Healthcare Radiology Administrators(90)
Cronin, Jim
International Radio and Television Society(384)
Cronin, Kevin
American Academy of Actuaries(19)
Cronin, Paul
United States Council for International Business(674)
Crook, Stephen
American Printing History Association(117)
Cropper, Cabell C.
National Criminal Justice Association(503)
Crosby, John
American Osteopathic Association(111)
Crosby, Joseph
Council On State Taxation(277)
Crosby, Kim
Health Care Education Association(322)
Crosby, Mark F.
Enterprise Wireless Alliance(295)
Crosby, Miriam
American Peanut Shellers Association(113)
Crosby, Susan
Women in Government(692)
Croser, M. Doreen
American Association on Mental Retardation(54)
Croson, Matt
Packaging Machinery Manufacturers Institute(570)
Cross, Louis
North American Cartographic Information Society(555)
Cross, Susan
National Association of Concessionaires(445)
Crossley, Mark
ASABE - the Society for Engineering in Agricultural, Food and Biological Systems(162)
Crossman, Paul
National Fire Protection Association(510)
Crouch, Jim
United States Parachute Association(676)
Crouch, John R.
American Angus Association(31)
Crouch, Lori
Education Writers Association(289)
Crouch, Madeleine
American Viola Society(153)
International Society of Bassists(390)
National Association of School Music Dealers(470)
Retail Print Music Dealers Association(601)
Crouse, Cynthia C.
International Association of Diecutting and Diemaking(356)
Crouse, Jeff
NAADAC -- the Association for Addiction Professionals(424)
Crow, Eileen M.
Healthcare Financial Management Association(324)
Crowder, Richard T.
American Seed Trade Association(124)
Crowe, Alan H.
National Association of Professional Process Servers(466)
Crowe, M.D., Mark A.
North American Clinical Dermatological Society(556)
Crowe, Mary DiFiore
Association for Women in Computing(182)
Crowley, James M.
Society for Industrial and Applied Mathematics(619)
Crowley, Mark
Independent Electrical Contractors(334)
Crowley, Sheila
Association for Convention Marketing Executives(171)
Crowne, James
American Intellectual Property Law Association(98)

Crowner, Robert
North American Case Research Association(555)
Crowther, David T.
Council for Elementary Science International(268)
Cruea, Renee
Academy of Radiology Research(5)
Cruel, Doris J.
National Association of State Boards of Education(473)
Crum, Kevin
Association of Racing Commissioners International(211)
Crump, CMP, CAE, John L.
National Bar Association(483)
Cruse, Angela M.
Metal Building Contractors and Erectors Association(417)
Crutcher, Dr. Cheryl B.
American Association for Women in Community Colleges(37)
Crutchfield, James A.
Western Writers of America(688)
Cryan, Teresa V.
Institute for Operations Research and the Management Sciences(339)
Crye, J. Michael
International Council of Cruise Lines(367)
Crystal, D.D.S., David
American Society for the Advancement of Sedation and Anesthesia in Dentistry(132)
Csiszar, Ernie
Property Casualty Insurers Association of America(591)
Cubbage, Brian
American Subcontractors Association(149)
Cuccinello, Susan
Television Bureau of Advertising(659)
Cudworth, Carol
Society for Mining, Metallurgy, and Exploration(622)
Cueroni, Nancy
National Marine Distributors Association(526)
Outdoor Power Equipment and Engine Service Association(569)
Culhane, Bridget
Oncology Nursing Society(564)
Culkin, CAE, Douglas S.
National Apartment Association(430)
Cullen, Genevieve
Electric Drive Transportation Association(290)
Cullen, Kay
National Child Support Enforcement Association(489)
Cumbragh, Lee
American Fence Association(83)
Cummings, Karen
Master Brewers Association of the Americas(413)
Cummings, Lauren
National Association of State Budget Officers(473)
Cummings, Tonya
National Tour Association(546)
Cummings-Gaghan, Deborah
National Lime Association(525)
Cummins, Bob
American Brahmousin Council(59)
Cummins, Joan
American Council for Southern Asian Art(75)
Cummiskey, Melissa
Geological Society of America(315)
Cuneo, Jr., John F.
National Congress of Animal Trainers and Breeders(495)
Cunix, Nadine
American Association of Diabetes Educators(42)
Cunningham, Bob
National Association of Manufacturers(460)
Cunningham, Brenda
American Association of Petroleum Geologists(47)
Cunningham, Colleen S.
Financial Executives International(305)
Cunningham, Dottie
Commercial Mortgage Securities Association(253)
Cunningham, Glinda
American Ostrich Association(112)
Cunningham, Julie A.
Conference of Minority Transportation Officials(259)
Cunningham, Mike
American Nephrology Nurses Association(108)
Cunningham, Sean
Cabletelevision Advertising Bureau(236)
Cunningham, Virginia
American Academy of Ophthalmology(25)
Cupit, Teresa
National Association of Manufacturers(460)
Curle, Kristin
Society of Automotive Analysts(632)
Curlee, Jesse W.
Supima(656)
Curley, Ian
National Juvenile Court Services Association(523)
Curran, Sullivan D.
Fiberglass Tank and Pipe Institute(305)
Currey, CMP, Mary E.
Child Neurology Society(244)
Currie, S.J., Charles L.
Association of Jesuit Colleges and Universities(202)
Currie, Lara Mehr
Council on the Safe Transportation of Hazardous Articles(277)
International Vessel Operators Hazardous Materials Association(396)
Currie, Tyler
National Hockey League Players' Association(517)
Curris, Ph.D., Constantine
American Association of State Colleges and Universities(51)
Curry, George E.
National Newspaper Publishers Association(529)
Curry Rodriguez, Ph.D., Julia
National Association for Chicana and Chicano Studies(432)
Curtin, M.D., Tom
National Association of Community Health Centers(445)
Curtis, Brandon
Chain Drug Marketing Association(242)
Curtis, Chester
Air Force Association(13)
Curtis, Ed.D, Martha
Council of Dance Administrators(271)
Curtis, Millie
Intersure, Ltd.(398)
Curtis, Terrill
American Academy of Professional Coders(27)
Curtis, Tom
American Water Works Association(154)
Cusack, Ryda Ruth
Valve Manufacturers Association of America(682)
Cushing, Kristina
Steel Manufacturers Association(653)
Cushman, Charles S.
American Land Rights Association(100)
Cushman, Margaret J.
National Association for Home Care(434)
Custer, Susan
Society for Research in Child Development(624)
Cuthbertson, Bruce
Flexible Intermediate Bulk Container Association(307)
Cutshall, Harriet
American Society of Appraisers(134)
Cutting, Vickie
American Society for Eighteenth-Century Studies(128)
Cyphers, Frank
International Chemical Workers Union Council/UFCW(365)
Cyphers, Gary
American Public Human Services Association(120)
National Council of Local Human Service Administrators(499)
Cyr, Dale R.
American Registry of Diagnostic Medical Sonographers(122)
Cyrus-Albritton, Sylvia Y.
Association for the Study of African American Life and History(180)
Czarnecki, Mark T.
Benchmarking Network Association(227)
Telecommunications Benchmarking International Group(659)
Czopek, Edwin C.
Healthcare Financial Management Association(324)
D'Agostino, Bellinda
American Association for Geriatric Psychiatry(35)
D'Agostino, Bruce
Construction Management Association of America(262)
D'Alesandro, Janet
International Association of Forensic Nurses(357)
D'Amato, Sally-Ann
Society of Motion Picture and Television Engineers(640)
D'Amore, Ph.D., Michael
North American Catalysis Society(555)
D'Angelo, Cynthia
National Association of College Stores(444)
D'Aniello, Charles A.
Association for the Bibliography of History(180)
D'Souza, Henry J.
Helicopter Association International(325)
D'Uva, Matthew
National Association of Insurance and Financial Advisors(458)
Dacus, Corie
Council of Engineering and Scientific Society Executives(271)
Daenzer, David
American Scientific Glassblowers Society(124)
Daggett, Chuck
American Dexter Cattle Association(79)
Daggett Manner, Sharon
National Association of Educational Office Professionals(450)

Daghlian, Lara
Global Association of Risk Professionals(317)
Dahl, Gary
Distribution and LTL Carriers Association(286)
Dahl, Tom
American Association of Grain Inspection and Weighing Agencies(43)
Dahl, William
Botanical Society of America(231)
Dahlin, Joan
Organization of American Kodaly Educators(567)
Dailey, Cheryl
National Council of Juvenile and Family Court Judges(499)
Dailing, Clifford D.
National Rural Letter Carriers' Association(537)
Dakin, Rebecca
Association of Collegiate Conference and Events Directors International(191)
DalBello, Richard
Satellite Broadcasting and Communications Association(605)
Dale, James R.
Metal Powder Industries Federation(417)
Dale, Terry L.
Cruise Lines International Association(280)
Daley, Matthew
U.S.-ASEAN Business Council(668)
Dalious, Sandra
National Association of Colleges and Employers(444)
Dalkin, Roger
United States Bowling Congress(673)
Dallahan, Frank
Manufacturing Jewelers and Suppliers of America(411)
Dallara, Charles H.
Institute of International Finance(342)
Dallas, Judy
Association of College and University Housing Officers-International(191)
Dallmayr, Fred
Society of Asian and Comparative Philosophy(632)
Dallstream, Pamela
Society of Critical Care Medicine(634)
Dalsing, Michael D.
American Venous Forum(153)
Dalton, Don
Poultry Breeders of America(581)
U.S. Poultry and Egg Association(668)
Daly, William
National Hockey League(517)
Damey, Annette
International Association of Food Industry Suppliers(357)
Damgard, John M.
Futures Industry Association(313)
Dammrich, Thomas J.
National Marine Manufacturers Association(526)
Damon, Christopher A.
American Medical Technologists(105)
Dana, Charles
Farm Credit Council(301)
Dana, Nazie
Society for Environmental Graphic Design(617)
Danback, Gary
Institute of International Container Lessors(342)
Dancy, Beth
National Shrimp Industry Association(539)
Dancy, David
American Public Works Association(120)
Dandrea, Joel
Specialized Carriers and Rigging Association(649)
Dandridge-Charles, Vivian
National Association of Independent Schools(457)
Daniel, J. Todd
National Ornamental and Miscellaneous Metals Association(531)
Daniel, Linda M.
National Association of Independent Lighting Distributors(457)
Daniel, Rod
Society of Depreciation Professionals(635)
Daniel, Stacee
American College of Veterinary Ophthalmologists(71)
Daniels, Ann
American Public Works Association(120)
Daniels, Janet
American Horticultural Society(91)
Daniels, John Y.
American Association of Textile Chemists and Colorists(53)
Daniels, Lisa
International Association of Assessing Officers(353)
Daniels, Marcia C.
Precision Metalforming Association(583)
Daniels, Margery Berg
International Society for Third-Sector Research(389)
Daniels, Russell
American Society of Home Inspectors(139)
Danielson-Murphy, Lotta
U.S. - Taiwan Business Council(667)
Danish, Susan
Association of Junior Leagues International(202)
Danjczek, Thomas A.
Steel Manufacturers Association(653)
Dankmeyer, Todd
National Community Pharmacists Association(491)
Dannenfeldt, Paula
National Association of Clean Water Agencies(443)
Danner, Dan
National Federation of Independent Business(509)
Dannheim, Karen
Academy of Rehabilitative Audiology(5)
Darby, Stephanie O.
Biomedical Engineering Society(229)
Darcy, Keith T.
Ethics Officer Association(298)
Darling, Jr., Albert
Business Technology Association(236)
Darling, Cynthia
Computer Ethics Institute(257)
Darmohraj, CAE, Andrew
American Pet Products Manufacturers Association(114)
Darnell, Lucas
American Frozen Food Institute(85)
Darr, Linda Bauer
American Bus Association(60)
Darraugh, Barbara
National Parking Association(531)
Darrow, Alan
National Air Transportation Association(428)
Darrow, Joan Arnold
Accordionists and Teachers Guild International(6)
Das, Parthavi
Women in Cable and Telecommunications(691)
Dashiell, Judy
National Fisheries Institute(511)
Dathorne, Ph.D., O.R.
Association of Caribbean Studies(188)
Daugherty, Carley
American White/American Creme Horse Registry(154)
Daughtry, Ph.D., Lillian H.
American Vocational Education Personnel Development Association(153)
Daughtry, Jr., Sylvester
Commission on Accreditation for Law Enforcement Agencies(254)
Daulaire, Nils
Global Health Council(317)
Daum, Helen
International Ceramic Association(364)
Dauscher, Ph.D., CPCU, Kenneth R.
American Institute for CPCU - Insurance Institute of America(93)
Davenport, Bonnie
Association for Humanistic Psychology(174)
Davenport, Cynthia A.
Association of Specialized and Professional Accreditors(214)
Daves, Marsha
Skills USA(611)
Davey, Tara
Council of Hotel and Restaurant Trainers(272)
David, Lenny
American Association for Therapeutic Humor(37)
Davidek, Cheryl
National Council of Juvenile and Family Court Judges(499)
Davidge, Cammy
American Land Title Association(100)
Davidshofer, Charles
Association for University and College Counseling Center Directors(181)
Davidson, Beverly
American Academy of Clinical Psychiatrists(21)
National Defender Investigator Association(504)
Davidson, Ph.D., Dan E.
American Councils for International Education(76)
Davidson, Daryl
Association for Unmanned Vehicle Systems International(181)
Davidson, Joel P.
Hospital Presidents Association(328)
Davidson, June
American Seminar Leaders Association(124)
Davidson, Richard J.
American Hospital Association(92)
Davidson, Wendy
American Institute of Professional Geologists(97)
Davie, Cassie
NACE International(424)
Davies, Christy
American Indian Science and Engineering Society(93)
Davies, Marshall
Public Risk Management Association(593)
Davies, CPA, P. Stratton
American College of Chest Physicians(64)

Davis, Alan
National Association for Campus Activities(432)
Davis, JD, MPH, Amy L.
Applied Research Ethics National Association(159)
Davis, Ann
American Academy of Physician Assistants(27)
Davis, Betsy
APICS - The Association for Operations Management(158)
Davis, Bill
American Anthropological Association(31)
Davis, Bruce
Academy of Motion Picture Arts and Sciences(4)
Davis, D. Christopher
World Floor Covering Association(695)
Davis, Deb
Operations Security Professionals Society(565)
Davis, Donald
National Council on the Aging(503)
Davis, Doreen
College Art Association(251)
Davis, Ph.D., Edward L.
Distributive Education Clubs of America(286)
Davis, Dr. Gary S.
North American Gamebird Association(557)
Davis, Gene
School Management Study Group(606)
Davis, Jeffrey
Association of Public Television Stations(210)
Davis, Jim
American Federation of Government Employees(82)
Davis, John
National Kidney Foundation(523)
Davis, Jolanta
American Association for the Advancement of Slavic Studies(36)
Davis, Kellie
American Society for Engineering Management(128)
Davis, Ken
Association of Professional Communication Consultants(208)
Davis, Marleine
National U.S.-Arab Chamber of Commerce(548)
Davis, Mary Ellen
Association of College and Research Libraries(190)
Davis, Michael
National Association of Convenience Stores(446)
Davis, Michael G.
American Alliance for Health, Physical Education, Recreation and Dance(30)
Davis, Michael P.
American Malting Barley Association(102)
Davis, Michelle
Training Directors' Forum(663)
Davis, Peter
IDEA, The Health and Fitness Association(330)
Davis, R. Richard
Congress of Independent Unions(261)
Davis, M.D., Ramona
Black Psychiatrists of America(230)
Davis, Randall P.
International Association of Amusement Parks and Attractions(352)
Davis, Robert
America's Community Bankers(19)
Davis, Rod
Marketing Education Association(413)
Davis, Ron
Marine Engineers Beneficial Association(412)
Davis, Scott
International Alliance of Technology Integrators(348)
Davis, Seth
Geochemical Society(315)
Davis, CAE, Steven
American Industrial Hygiene Association(93)
Davis, Sydney
American Academy of Audiology(20)
Davis, Tara
Society for Mining, Metallurgy, and Exploration(622)
Davis, Terry
American Association for State and Local History(36)
Daw, Ann
National Association for the Specialty Food Trade(436)
Dawkins, Diana
Society of Nuclear Medicine(641)
Dawson, Janene
American Society of Pain Management Nurses(143)
Dawson, Rhett B.
Information Technology Industry Council(338)
Day, Ph.D., Carol Brunson
Council for Professional Recognition(269)
Day, Christine
Association for Experiential Education(172)
Day, Jane
Society of Nuclear Medicine(641)
Day, Josephine
Project Management Institute(590)
Day, Madison
Society of Professors of Child and Adolescent Psychiatry(642)
Day, Robert D.
Renewable Natural Resources Foundation(599)
Dayak, Meena
National Council for Community Behavioral Healthcare(497)
Dayton, Sandy
Justice Research and Statistics Association(403)
De Angelis, Franco
Italy-America Chamber of Commerce(400)
De Bock, Veronique
French-American Chamber of Commerce(312)
De Korne, James
Christian Schools International(246)
De La Paz, Katie
International Technology Education Association(393)
De La Riva, Patricia
Inter-American Bar Association(346)
De Lazzero, Vincent
Tile Contractors' Association of America(661)
de Leon, Eleanor
Licensing Executives Society(407)
de los Santos, Gerardo E.
League for Innovation in the Community College(406)
de Mars, Susan
United States Pharmacopeia(676)
De Sousa, Christian
International Society for Pharmaceutical Engineering(388)
de Sousa, Mary
National Council of Architectural Registration Boards(498)
Dea, Francesca
National Association of Insurance and Financial Advisors(458)
DeAcetis, Judy
American Society of Tropical Medicine and Hygiene(147)
Deal, Edmond
Association of American State Geologists(185)
Deal, Timothy E.
United States Council for International Business(674)
Dean, Carol A.
Building Service Contractors Association International(234)
Dean, Colleen
National Dance Association(504)
Dean, CAE, Jeffrey L.
International Society of Explosives Engineers(391)
Dean, Karol
Association for Women in Psychology(182)
Dean, Kate
United States Internet Service Provider Association(676)
Dean, Kathleen
Casualty Actuarial Society(239)
Dean, Richard
Air Force Sergeants Association(13)
Dean, Ph.D., Stephen O.
Fusion Power Associates(313)
Dean, Virginia
American Bankers Association(55)
Deane, Deborah J.
National Association of Master Appraisers(461)
DeAngelis, MD, MPH, Catherine D.
American Medical Association(104)
DeAngelis, Donna
Association of Social Work Boards(214)
Deardorff, Darla
Association of International Education Administrators(201)
Dearen, Dianna
Women's Council of REALTORS(693)
Debatin, Gloria
Mu Phi Epsilon(422)
DeBaugh, Mark
ABA Marketing Network(1)
DeBoer, Jeffrey D.
Real Estate Round Table(596)
deBoer, Jolyn
Tennis Industry Association(659)
DeBoer, Kathy
American Volleyball Coaches Association(153)
Debus, Tim
International Banana Association(362)
DeCaprio, Robert L.
Messenger Courier Association of the Americas(417)
DeCelle, Arthur
Beer Institute(227)
Deck, Litsa
American Correctional Association(74)
Decker, Curtis L.
National Disability Rights Network(505)
Decker, Erin
ISDA - The Office Systems Cooperative(400)
DeConcini, Barbara
American Academy of Religion(28)
DeCrappeo, Anthony
Council on Governmental Relations(276)
Decyk, Betsy Newell
American Association of Philosophy Teachers(48)
Dee, Ph.D., Norbert
National Petrochemical & Refiners Association(532)

Deegan, John
Military Impacted Schools Association(419)
Deely, John
Semiotic Society of America(608)
Deem, Cheryl A.
American Spice Trade Association(148)
Deering, Anne-Lise
American Medallic Sculpture Association(104)
DeFaveri, Amy
American Society of Plastic Surgical Nurses(144)
DeFeo, Philip D.
NYSE Arca(563)
DeFlorian, Terri A.
Orthopaedic Section - American Physical Therapy Association(568)
Degen, Linda
Respiratory Nursing Society(600)
Degli-Angeli, Helen
Manufacturers' Agents National Association(411)
Degnon, CAE, George K.
American Psychosomatic Society(119)
Association of Christian Therapists(190)
Society for Occupational and Environmental Health(622)
Degnon, Laura E.
Association of Pediatric Program Directors(207)
Degnon, Marge
Ambulatory Pediatric Association(19)
DeGraaf, Rita K.
Conference of Consulting Actuaries(259)
DeHaan, Steve
National Home Furnishings Association(517)
deJonge, Katie
Transportation Clubs International(664)
DeKoker, Neil
Original Equipment Suppliers Association(568)
Del Polito, Ph.D., Gene A.
Association for Postal Commerce(177)
Del Pozo, Lidia
Spain-U.S. Chamber of Commerce(648)
Del Valle, Casilda
National Minority Supplier Development Council(527)
Del Valle, M.D., John
Gastroenterology Research Group(315)
dela Pewa, Fred
American Import Shippers Association(93)
Delacruz, Charles
National Grain and Feed Association(514)
Delahanty, James L.
Omicron Kappa Upsilon(564)
DeLauro, Danielle
Cabletelevision Advertising Bureau(236)
DeLemos, Anne
International Society for Magnetic Resonance in Medicine(387)
Delgadillo, CAE, Linda M.
Turnaround Management Association(667)
Delgado, Ph.D., Jane L.
National Alliance for Hispanic Health(429)
Delgado, Jeffrey
American Thoracic Society(151)
Delk, Wade
Check Payment Systems Association(243)
National Organization for Competency Assurance(530)
Dellert, Ed
American College of Chest Physicians(64)
Delman, Farrell
Tobacco Merchants Association of the U.S.(662)
DeLoach, Roy
National Association of Mortgage Brokers(462)
Delollis, Kathy M.
Precision Metalforming Association(583)
DeLoney, Jim
National Association of Recreation Resource Planners(468)
DeLong, Anne H.
Catholic Medical Association(240)
DeLong, Chad
Timber Frame Business Council(661)
DeLuca, Peter
Minerals, Metals and Materials Society, The(420)
DeLuca, Russell
National Association of Independent Insurance Auditors and Engineers(457)
DeLucia, Robert J.
Airline Industrial Relations Conference(14)
Demangone, Anthony
National Association of Federal Credit Unions(452)
DeMarco, Kathleen A.
Fluid Power Distributors Association(308)
DeMarco, Tony
Thoroughbred Racing Associations of North America(661)
DeMarines, Jane
National American Indian Housing Council(430)
DeMasters, Carol
Association of Food Journalists(197)
DeMattos, Rebecca Dopkin
National Association of Mortgage Brokers(462)
Demchuk, Dr. Thomas D.
American Association of Stratigraphic Palynologists(51)
DeMers, Ed.d., Stephen T.
Association of State and Provincial Psychology Boards(215)
DeMichiel, Helen
National Alliance for Media Arts and Culture(429)
Dempsey, Donna
Film and Bag Federation(305)
Dempsey, M.D., Robert J.
Society of Neurological Surgeons(640)
Dempster, Dr. Judith S.
American Academy of Nurse Practitioners(25)
Dencker, Tim
National Association of Electrical Distributors(450)
Denham, Laurie
American Society of Transportation and Logisitcs(146)
Denis, Ingrid
Association of Occupational and Environmental Clinics(206)
Denis, Maurice
National Association of Community Health Centers(445)
Denison, Carletta
Petroleum Equipment Institute(574)
Denne, Eileen E.
American Society of Travel Agents(146)
Dennett, Diana
America's Health Insurance Plans(19)
Dennett, Paul W.
American Benefits Council(56)
Dennis, Bethany
Association of Professional Landscape Designers(209)
Denny, Beth
American Society for Cytotechnology(128)
Denny, Catherine
American Prepaid Legal Services Institute(117)
Denston, Sue
Process Equipment Manufacturers' Association(584)
Denston, Susan A.
National Association of State Emergency Medical Services Officials(475)
Dent, Jr., William H.
North American Association for Environmental Education(554)
Deomano, Ph.D., Edgar
National Wooden Pallet and Container Association(550)
DePoy, Sandra
American Resort Development Association(122)
DePriest, Darryl L.
American Bar Association(56)
Der Mugrdechian, Barlow
Society of Armenian Studies(631)
Derks, Paula
Aircraft Electronics Association(14)
Dermer, Alicia
Academy of Breastfeeding Medicine(2)
Dern, Adrienne
National Association of Area Agencies on Aging(439)
DeRose, Joe
American Academy of Religion(28)
Derouin, Cherie
Independent Pet and Animal Transportation Association International(335)
DeRoze, Virginia
Truckload Carriers Association(666)
Dersheid, Sue
American Soybean Association(148)
Dershowitz, Toby
American Jewish Press Association(99)
DeRupo, Joe
National Coffee Association of the U.S.A.(490)
Des Roches, Debbie Brown
SnowSports Industries America(612)
DeSarno, Judith M.
National Family Planning and Reproductive Health Association(508)
DeSimone, Jim
Safe and Vault Technicians Association(604)
DesJardins, Joe
Society for Business Ethics(614)
Desmarais, CAE, Maurice A.
Battery Council International(226)
International Business Brokers Association(364)
National Association of Floor Covering Distributors(453)
Desmond, Ed
Entertainment Software Association(295)
Detlefsen, Clay
International Dairy Foods Association(368)
Detmer, M.D., Don E.
American Medical Informatics Association(104)
Deutsch-Layne, Erika
American Society for Precision Engineering(132)
DeVaul, Chuck
Owner Operators of America(570)
Develen, Carolyn
North American Menopause Society(558)
Devereux, Erik
Association for Public Policy Analysis and Management(177)
Devine, James R.
Chain Drug Marketing Association(242)

DeVoll, Jody
Association of Public Health Laboratories(210)
DeVries, Christine M.
American Association for Geriatric Psychiatry(35)
DeVries, Harold L.
Independent Community Bankers of America(333)
DeVroomen, Jack
North American Flowerbulb Wholesalers Association(557)
Dewalt, Jeff
Oncology Nursing Society(564)
Dewey, W. Dennis
National Assembly of State Arts Agencies(431)
DeWyngaert, Brian
American Federation of Government Employees(82)
Dexter, David
Snack Food Association(612)
Dey, Sharon
National Petrochemical & Refiners Association(532)
DeYoung, Jean
American College of Surgeons(71)
Dhariwal, Kewal
Institute for Certification of Computing Professionals(339)
Dhillon, Dr. Major S.
Society for Vector Ecology(629)
Di Bella, Anna
National League of American Pen Women(524)
Di Corpo, Joe
Specialty Vehicle Institute of America(650)
Di Iorio, Matt
Associated Equipment Distributors(165)
Di Leonardo, Melissa
Association of Jesuit Colleges and Universities(202)
Di Polvere, Edward J.
National Association of Noise Control Officials(463)
Diamond, Al
American Association of Insurance Management Consultants(44)
Diamond, Carrie
National Society for Histotechnology(541)
Diamond, Paula
Council of Colleges of Acupuncture and Oriental Medicine(271)
Diana, Cathy
American Institute of Chemical Engineers(95)
Dibblee, Robert
National Association of Real Estate Investment Trusts(468)
DiBenedetto, Mike
Resort and Commercial Recreation Association(600)
DiBlasi, Joan M.
Shareholder Services Association(609)
DiCampli, Edward
Helicopter Association International(325)
DiCarlo, Sam J.
International Dairy Foods Association(368)
Dichirico, Jimmy
Latin Business Association(405)
Dichtl, John
Organization of American Historians(567)
Dickerson, Dawn D.
National Student Speech Language Hearing Association(544)
Dickey, Christa
American College of Sports Medicine(70)
Dickey, Jessie
American Literary Translators Association(101)
Dickey, Dr. Keith W.
American Dental Interfraternity Council(79)
Xi Psi Phi(697)
Dickman, Robert S.
American Institute of Aeronautics and Astronautics(94)
Dicks, Pete
Exhibit Designers and Producers Association(299)
Lignin Institute(408)
Dickson, Fran
Professional Women Photographers(590)
Dickson, Mary P.
National Association of Broadcasters(441)
Dickstein, Michele
Aviation Suppliers Association(225)
DiCostanzo, Steven J.
Golf Range Association of America(318)
Dicus, Todd C.
American Academy of Family Physicians(22)
Diehl, Gary M.
Skills USA(611)
Dierks, Neil
National Pork Producers Council(533)
Diermeir, CFA, Jeffrey J.
CFA Institute(242)
Diers, Christine Paige
Public Radio News Directors(592)
Dierson, Thomas E.
Portugal-United States Chamber of Commerce(581)
Dieterich, Carrie
Video Software Dealers Association(683)
Dietrich, Becca
DRI International(287)
Dietz, Sheila
Alliance of National Staffing and Employment Resources(17)
National Association for Poetry Therapy(435)
Dietz, Tim
Self Storage Association(608)
DiFanis, Anita M.
Association of Art Museum Directors(186)
DiGiovanni, Carvin
Association of Pool and Spa Professionals(208)
Dill, Kevin
American Society of PeriAnesthesia Nurses(144)
Dill, Lisa
American Psychotherapy Association(119)
Dillehay, Charles B.
Health Ministries Association(323)
Dillingham, Anna
Association of Public Health Laboratories(210)
Dillingham, Tim
American Littoral Society(102)
Dillon, Bill
National Association of College and University Business Officers(444)
Dillon, Donald W.
Piano Manufacturers Association International(577)
Dillon, Ph.D., Kathleen E.
American Association of Teachers of Slavic and East European Languages(52)
Dillon, JCD, Rev. Thomas
North American Canon Law Society(555)
Dillon, Tracy
NASFM(425)
Dilworth, Leslie Gallery
Society for Environmental Graphic Design(617)
DiMartino, Rose
Wireless Communications Association International(690)
Dimatteo, Katherine
Organic Trade Association(566)
Dimond, Steve
NAGMR Consumer Product Brokers(425)
Dinegar, Chris
Association for the Advancement of Medical Instrumentation(179)
Dingee, Joe
Academy of General Dentistry(3)
Dingeldey, Carol
American Academy of Periodontology(27)
Dingley, David P.
International Castor Oil Association(364)
Dinneen, Robert
Renewable Fuels Association(599)
Dionne, Christine
Urban and Regional Information Systems Association(680)
DiPaola, Steve
Actors' Equity Association(8)
DiPrimo, Laura
Hydraulic Institute(329)
Dispensa, Paul C.
Liability Insurance Research Bureau(407)
Distelhorst, CAE, Garis F.
Marble Institute of America(412)
Distelhorst, Helen
Marble Institute of America(412)
Distelhorst, Michael
Council for Ethics in Economics(268)
Dittmann, Roger
United States Federation of Scholars and Scientists(675)
Divine, Dennis
Association of Public-Safety Communications Officers- International(211)
Divver, Barbara
National Golf Foundation(514)
Dixon, Georganne
American College of Mohs Micrographic Surgery and Cutaneous Oncology(67)
Dixon, Melanie
National Court Reporters Association(503)
Dixon-Terry, Eleanor
Society for Public Health Education(624)
Doak, Ph.D., Gordon A.
National Association of Animal Breeders(438)
Doak, Jennifer
Financial Managers Society(306)
Doan, Violet S.
IEEE Computer Society(331)
Doane, E. David
Independent Liquid Terminals Association(334)
Dobrez, Tom
National Association of State Radio Networks(476)
Dobrowolski, Mary Ellen
Air Force Association(13)
Dobson, Darla
Association for Research in Otolaryngology(177)
Dobson, Sharon
American Institute of Chemists(95)
Dockery, Robert
Disaster Preparedness and Emergency Response Association(285)
Dodd, Donna
Association of Collegiate Schools of Planning(191)

Dodds, Deborah
Cooperative Education and Internship Association(265)
Dodds, Edward W.
Association for the Development of Religious Information Systems(180)
Dodge, Sarah
Petroleum Marketers Association of America(574)
Dodson, Kathleen A.
American Orthotic and Prosthetic Association(111)
Doell, Paul H.
National Air Carrier Association(428)
Doescher, Vickey
American Association of Franchisees and Dealers(43)
Doggett, Enid
American Federation of Government Employees(82)
Doherty, CAE, Mark G.
Institute for Operations Research and the Management Sciences(339)
Doherty, Mary
National Rural Letter Carriers' Association(537)
Doherty, Robert
American College of Physicians(69)
Doi, David
Coalition for Juvenile Justice(249)
Dolan, Gregory A.
Methanol Institute(418)
Dolan, Jack
American Council of Life Insurers(75)
Dolan, Ph.D., FACHE, CAE, Thomas C.
American College of Healthcare Executives(66)
Dolibois, CAE, Robert J.
American Nursery and Landscape Association(109)
Dolim, Barbara A.
Mechanical Service Contractors of America(415)
Dolim, Michael P.
National Environmental Balancing Bureau(507)
Dolling, Dave
Aerospace Department Chairmen's Association(10)
Doluak, Chris
National Shooting Sports Foundation(539)
Doman, Janet
International Academy for Child Brain Development(347)
Dombrowski, Philip A.
Transplantation Society(663)
Domnitz, Avin Mark
American Booksellers Association(58)
Domurat, Janel
United States Meat Export Federation(676)
Donadio, Brian J.
American College of Osteopathic Internists(69)
Donahey, PE, Rex C.
American Concrete Institute(72)
Donahue, George M.
Association of Flight Attendants - CWA(197)
Donahue, Marla
Flexible Packaging Association(307)
Donahue, Michael D.
American Association of Advertising Agencies(37)
Donald, Samuel L.
Association of Research Directors(212)
Donaldson, Danielle
National Association for Home Care(434)
Donaldson, Edward
Small Luxury Hotels of the World(611)
Donaldson, John
Teachers of English to Speakers of Other Languages(658)
Donaldson, Marcy
Investment Management Consultants Association(399)
Donaldson, FLMI, CLU, Thomas P.
LOMA(409)
Donegan, Susan
Computer Law Association(258)
Donegan, Jr., Thomas J.
Cosmetic, Toiletry and Fragrance Association(267)
Donio, Jim
National Association of Recording Merchandisers(468)
Donlou, Stephanie
Xplor International(698)
Donnally, CPA, Bianca
American Public Power Association(120)
Donneberger, T. Karl
International Turfgrass Society(395)
Donnelly, PhD, Maureen A.
American Society of Ichthyologists and Herpetologists(139)
Donnelly, Patrick
CropLife America(279)
Donnelly, Thomas F.
National Water Resources Association(548)
Donner, Martin
International Newspaper Group(381)
Donoghue, CPCA, Edward A.
National Elevator Industry(506)
Donoho, Patrick
International Bottled Water Association(362)
Donohoe, Susan
National Association of Computer Consultant Businesses(445)
Donohue, Sharon King
National Committee for Quality Assurance(491)
Donohue, Thomas J.
United States Chamber of Commerce(674)
Donovan, David L.
Association for Maximum Service Television(176)
Donovan, Lois
Ass'n of Learning Providers(164)
Donovan, Susan
Jesuit Association of Student Personnel Administrators(401)
Doodeman, Karen
NASFM(425)
Dooley, Cal
Food Products Association(309)
Dooley, Connie
Petroleum Equipment Institute(574)
Dooley, CAE, Elizabeth
American Society of Gene Therapy(138)
Doolittle, Susan
National Association for Business Economics(441)
Dopp, Mark
American Meat Institute(103)
Doria, Guy
Club Managers Association of America(249)
Dorman, DVM., Ph.D., David
CIIT Centers for Health Research(247)
Dornberger, Kevin
United States Bowling Congress(673)
Dorsey, Pamela
Aluminum Association(18)
Doss, Joseph K.
International Bottled Water Association(362)
Doster, Travis
Foodservice Consultants Society International(309)
Dotolo, Ph.D., Lawrence G.
ACL - Association for Consortium Leadership(7)
Doubet, Sherry
American Salers Association(123)
North American South Devon Association(561)
Doucette, Robert M.
National Association of Conservation Districts(445)
Doucette, Vic
National Federation of Priests' Councils(510)
Doug, Allen
National Football League Players Association(511)
Dougherty, John J.
Operative Plasterers' and Cement Masons' International Association of the United States and Canada(565)
Dougherty, Meredith
International Safe Transit Association(385)
Dougherty, CMP, Terry
Refrigerated Foods Association(597)
Douglas, James S.
American Society for Investigative Pathology(130)
Association of Pathology Chairs(207)
Douglas, Kevin
AFSM International(11)
Douglass, John W.
Aerospace Industries Association of America(10)
Douglass, Laurie
American Chiropractic Association(62)
Dove, Susan
Outdoor Power Equipment Aftermarket Association(569)
Dover, CAE, Marge
National Association of Legal Assistants(459)
Dovi, Daniel
Association of Medical Diagnostic Manufacturers(204)
Dow, Roger J.
Travel Industry Association of America(665)
Dowden, C. James
Alliance of Area Business Publications(16)
American Academy of Medical Acupuncture(24)
City and Regional Magazine Association(247)
Parenting Publications of America(571)
Dowling, Jennifer
National Venture Capital Association(548)
Downey, J. Thomas
Casualty Actuarial Society(239)
Downey, Morgan
American Obesity Association(109)
Downey, Myrna
Hardwood Plywood and Veneer Association(322)
Downey, Tim
National Cattlemen's Beef Association(488)
Downham, Max C.
International College of Surgeons(366)
Downing, Denise
International Hard Anondizing Association(374)
Downing, G. Dan
ECRI(288)
Downing, Jere
Cranberry Institute(278)
Downs, Christian
Association of Community Cancer Centers(192)

Downs, Maureen E.
American Association of Pharmaceutical Scientists(48)
Doyle, Ed
Aluminum Foil Container Manufacturers Association(18)
Doyle, Elizabeth
Meals On Wheels Association of America(414)
Doyle, Frank
NAFSA: Association of International Educators(424)
Doyle, J. Andrew
National Paint and Coatings Association(531)
Doyle, John
American Beverage Institute(56)
Doyle, CAE, Kenneth A.
Society of Independent Gasoline Marketers of America(638)
Doyle, CAE, Laura Fleming
American Academy of Audiology(20)
Doyle, Richard M.
International Sleep Products Association(386)
Doyle, Stephen P.
Central Station Alarm Association(241)
Doyle, Thomas B.
National Ski and Snowboard Retailers Association(539)
National Sporting Goods Association(543)
Doyle-Kimball, Mary
National Association of Real Estate Editors(468)
Dragon, Kay
Geological Society of America(315)
Dragon, Margaret
Health Care Compliance Association(322)
Drain, David L.
Foodservice Consultants Society International(309)
Drake, Chris
Employee Assistance Professionals Association(293)
Drake, Lawrence
Radiant Panel Association(594)
Drake, Lisa C.
American Association for Laboratory Accreditation(35)
Drake, O. Burtch
American Association of Advertising Agencies(37)
Dreger, Marianne
American College of Occupational and Environmental Medicine(68)
Drennan, Andrew
International Association of Food Industry Suppliers(357)
Drennen, Nancy
Community Banking Advisors Network(255)
CPA Auto Dealer Consultants Association(278)
CPA Construction Industry Association(278)
CPA Manufacturing Services Association(278)
National CPA Health Care Advisors Association(503)
Not-for-Profit Services Association(562)
Drescher, Howard S.
LIMRA International(408)
Dreskin, Joan
Interstate Natural Gas Association of America(398)
Dressen, Tim
ACA International, The Association of Credit and Collection Professionals(2)
Dressler, Barbara
Purebred Hanoverian Association of America Breeders and Owners(593)
Dressler, CCAP, Susan A.
Alliance of Claims Assistance Professionals(16)
Drevna, Charles
National Petrochemical & Refiners Association(532)
Drew, Steve
Radiological Society of North America(594)
Drewsen, Alan C.
International Trademark Association(394)
Dreyer, Johnny
Gas Processors Association(314)
Dreyfus, Susan
Alliance for Children and Families(15)
Driggs, Kathi
Club Managers Association of America(249)
Drinan, James M.
American Association of Endodontists(42)
Driscoll, Daniel A.
National Futures Association(513)
Driscoll, Hope
Association of Farmworker Opportunity Programs(196)
Dristas, Victor
National Association of Real Estate Investment Trusts(468)
Driver, Michael C.
Materials Research Society(414)
Droeger, Michael
Semiconductor Equipment and Materials International(608)
Drohan, CAE, William M.
Sports Lawyers Association(651)
Dropkin, Keith
National Investment Company Service Association(522)
Drown, Stephen
International Association of Pet Cemeteries(360)
Droz, Fred
American Institute of Inspectors(96)
Council of Communication Management(271)
National Purchasing Institute(534)
Drozda, Thomas
SAE International(604)
Drury, Margaret
Society of Flight Test Engineers(636)
Dube, Bob
Allied Finance Adjusters Conference(17)
Dubin, Alvin
American Osteopathic Colleges of Ophthalmology and Otolaryngology - Head and Neck Surgery(112)
Dubnicka, Thomas J.
Bank Administration Institute(225)
Dubro, Alec
International Labor Communications Association(377)
Dubroff, Rich
Professional Basketball Writers' Association(586)
Ducat, Howard C.
American Society of Appraisers(134)
Ducate, CEM, CMP, Douglas
Center for Exhibition Industry Research(241)
Duckering, Hilda
Weather Modification Association(686)
Duckworth, Tara
Motion Picture Association(421)
Motion Picture Association of America(421)
Dudley, Bobette
Country Music Association(277)
Dudley, Hubert T.
International Firestop Council(372)
National Roof Deck Contractors Association(537)
Dudley, Lynn D.
American Benefits Council(56)
Dudley, Regina A.
Power Washers of North America(582)
Dudley, Stephanie D.
Population Association of America(580)
Duduit, Michael
American Academy of Ministry(24)
Duensing, Lenore
American Academy of Pain Management(26)
Duensino, Tiffany
Arthroscopy Association of North America(162)
Duesterberg, Dr. Thomas J.
Manufacturers Alliance/MAPI(411)
Duesterhaus, Rich
National Association of Conservation Districts(445)
Dufane, Amy
Optical Society of America(566)
Dufault, Roseanna
Women's Caucus for the Modern Languages(693)
Duff, Daniel
American Public Transportation Association(120)
Duff, Michael J.
Analytical and Life Science Systems Association(157)
Duffee, Nicole
American Association for Laboratory Animal Science(35)
Duffin, Michael B.
Precision Machined Products Association(583)
Duffy, Debra
National Wildlife Rehabilitators Association(549)
Duffy, Kevin C.
At-sea Processors Association(221)
Duffy, Stephen
American Academy of Facial Plastic and Reconstructive Surgery(22)
Duffy, Susan
International Council for Small Business(367)
Duffy, William J.
AORN(158)
Duffy, William R.
Imaging Supplies Coalition for International Intellectual Property Protection(332)
Duffy, William T.
National School Supply and Equipment Association(538)
Dugan, Michael
Gas Technology Institute(314)
Dugard, Dr. Paul
Halogenated Solvents Industry Alliance(321)
Duggan, Tomiko
World Media Association(696)
Duillo, John
Society of American Historical Artists(631)
Dukes, Diane
Professional Liability Underwriting Society(588)
Duley, Nancy
Barzona Breeders Association of America(226)
Dulicai, Dianne
National Coalition of Creative Arts Therapies Associations(490)
Dullinger, Thomas G.
American Natural Soda Ash Corporation(108)
Dumaresq, Ph.D., R.
Aviation Technician Education Council(225)
DuMelle, Fran
American Lung Association(102)

DuMouchelle, GG, Joseph
Accredited Gemologists Association(6)
Dunbar, Michael
Associated Builders and Contractors(164)
Dunbar, Paul
National Exchange Carrier Association(507)
Duncan, Bonnie N.
National Electrical Contractors Association(506)
Duncan, Cynthia
United States Council for International Business(674)
Duncan, Ph.D., Douglas G.
Mortgage Bankers Association(421)
Duncan, Harley
Federation of Tax Administrators(304)
Duncan, Mallory B.
National Retail Federation(536)
Dundas, Bill
International Sign Association(386)
Dungan, Arthur
Chlorine Institute(245)
Dungy, Gwendolyn Jordan
National Association of Student Personnel Administrators(478)
Dunkel, Dr. Alexander
National Association of Self-Instructional Language Programs(471)
Dunkin, Ellen
Risk and Insurance Management Society(602)
Dunlap, Brian
National Propane Gas Association(534)
Dunlap, Dennis
American Marketing Association(103)
Dunlap, Earl
National Juvenile Detention Association(523)
Dunlap, Ellen S.
American Antiquarian Society(31)
Dunlavey, Barbara
Biomedical Engineering Society(229)
Dunman, ReNee S.
American Association for Affirmative Action(33)
Dunn, Alexandra
National Association of Clean Water Agencies(443)
Dunn, Laura
Society of Composers and Lyricists(634)
Dunn, Richard S.
American Philosophical Society(114)
Dunn, Rob
American Resort Development Association(122)
Dunn, Sidney N.
Cranial Academy(278)
DuPuy, Bob
Major League Baseball - Office of the Commissioner(410)
Duran, Catherine
American Institute of Professional Geologists(97)
Durcksak, Connie
PCIA - the Wireless Industry Association(572)
Durgin, Gloria
National Association of School Nurses(470)
Durham, CAE, Judith B.
Architectural Woodwork Institute(160)
Durham, CAE, L. Leon
National Association of Housing and Redevelopment Officials(456)
Durkin, Helen A.
International Health, Racquet and Sportsclub Association(374)
Durkin, Tom
International Health, Racquet and Sportsclub Association(374)
Durrani, Usman R.
Islamic Medical Association of North America(400)
Durst, Cheryl
International Interior Design Association(377)
Durst, Richard
International Council of Fine Arts Deans(367)
Durston, Deryck
Association for Clinical Pastoral Education(169)
Dusen, Jim
University Photographers Association of America(680)
Dussor, William
International Health, Racquet and Sportsclub Association(374)
Dustman, Karl
Percussion Marketing Council(573)
Dutra, Geri
American Classical League(63)
Duttlinger, Don
Petroleum Technology Transfer Council(574)
Duty, Kimberly D.
National Multi Housing Council(528)
Duval, Jeanne-Marie
American Councils for International Education(76)
Duvall, Henry
Council of the Great City Schools(275)
Duvic, Philip
Architectural Woodwork Institute(160)
Dwyer, John W.
Lignite Energy Council(408)
Dwyer, Michael R.
National Automotive Radiator Service Association(483)
Dye, Carl M.
American Schools Association(124)
Dye, Jane
Society for Cinema and Media Studies(615)
Dye, Leon
American Poultry International(117)
Dyekman, Larry
National Futures Association(513)
Dyer, Christopher
Congress of Lung Association Staffs(261)
Dyer, Michael J.
American Association of Colleges of Osteopathic Medicine(40)
Dyer, CAE, Randy
Early Childhood Education Institute(288)
International Electronic Article Surveillance Manufacturers Association(370)
National Structured Settlements Trade Association(544)
Dykema, CAE, Sue
American Society for Aesthetic Plastic Surgery(126)
Dykstra, Gregg
National Association of Mutual Insurance Companies(462)
Dyson, Peter
American Society of Media Photographers(141)
Dziegielewski, Ben
International Water Resources Association(396)
Dziuban, CAE, Robert L.
Optical Laboratories Association(566)
Dziura, Stephen
Business Professionals of America(236)
Eagle, Blake
National Council of Real Estate Investment Fiduciaries(500)
Eakin, Ph.D., Marshall C.
Brazilian Studies Association(232)
Earl, Sharon
International Municipal Signal Association(380)
Early, Carole A.
National Association of Colored Women's Clubs(445)
Earnest, Garee W.
Association of Leadership Educators(203)
Earnest, Steve
American Society for Training and Development(133)
Earp, Wendy
Motor and Equipment Manufacturers Association(421)
Eason, Tracee
Education Writers Association(289)
East, Bill
National Association of State Directors of Special Education(475)
East, Kenneth
American Planning Association(116)
East, Stephany
American Forest and Paper Association(85)
Eastlake, Jon
Delta Society(283)
Eastman, Mary
Association of Schools and Colleges of Optometry(213)
Eastman, Phyllis
Water Environment Federation(685)
Easton, Jr., John J.
Edison Electric Institute(289)
Eaton, CAE, Duane
Produce Marketing Association(584)
Eaton, Judith
Council for Higher Education Accreditation(269)
Eaton, Terry R.
Association of Firearm and Toolmark Examiners(197)
Eberle, Diane
American Institute of Ultrasound in Medicine(98)
Ebersole, Sheryl
American Jail Association(99)
Eberspacher, Jack E.
Agricultural Retailers Association(12)
Ebert, Ph.D., Andrew G.
Apple Products Research and Education Council(159)
International Food Additives Council(372)
Lignin Institute(408)
Echard, Susan
World Future Society(696)
Ecker, Bart
Teachers of English to Speakers of Other Languages(658)
Ecker, Robert H.
Aircraft Locknut Manufacturers Association(14)
Cordage Institute(266)
Fluid Sealing Association(308)
Gasket Fabricators Association(314)
Eckhaus, Leonard
AFCOM(10)
Eddy, Dan McLeod
National Association of Crime Victim Compensation Boards(448)
Eddy, Kathryn
American Boarding Kennels Association(58)
Edelman, Sheldon M.
Belt Association(227)
Plastic Soft Materials Manufacturers Association(578)

Pleaters, Stitchers and Embroiderers Association(579)
Edelson, Gilbert S.
Art Dealers Association of America(161)
Edelstein, Edward
Jewish Educators Assembly(402)
Eder, Debra
American Psychoanalytic Association(118)
Edgar, Rev.Dr. Robert
National Council of the Churches of Christ in the U.S.A.(501)
Edmunds, Lori B.
American Association of Endodontists(42)
Edmunds, William A.
International Order of the Golden Rule(381)
Edwards, Carol
United States Conference of Mayors(674)
Edwards, PE, Dan
National Corrugated Steel Pipe Association(496)
Edwards, Dave
American Society of Health-System Pharmacists(139)
Edwards, Deborah L.
AcademyHealth(6)
Edwards, Jill
National Association of Insurance and Financial Advisors(458)
Edwards, Karen Gray
American Sociological Association(147)
Edwards, Lisa
International Society for Heart and Lung Transplantation(387)
Edwards, III, Martin E.
Interstate Natural Gas Association of America(398)
Edwards, Maury
National Council of State Housing Agencies(500)
Edwards, Peggy
Professional Tennis Registry(589)
Edwards, Tony M.
National Association of Real Estate Investment Trusts(468)
Edwards Sr., Eddie
Black Broadcasters Alliance(230)
Eelman, Peter
AMT - The Association For Manufacturing Technology(156)
Egan, Conrad E.
National Housing Conference(518)
Egan, Robert S.
American Bryological and Lichenological Society(59)
Eget, Susan M.
American Association of Neurological Surgeons(46)
Egger, Kenneth
American Arbitration Association(32)
Ehlinger, Betty Gorsegner
Association for Information Media and Equipment(174)
National Association of Media and Technology Centers(461)
Eichmiller, Linda
Association of State and Interstate Water Pollution Control Administrators(214)
Eid, Tony
Aerobics and Fitness Association of America(10)
Eidemiller, Betty
Society of Toxicology(645)
Eidenmuller, Michael
Religious Communication Association(598)
Eiken, Mary
Society of Gynecologic Oncologists(638)
Eils, Larry M.
National Automatic Merchandising Association(482)
Eimer, CAE, Mary Jane
Association for Advancement of Behavior Therapy(167)
Einreinhofer, Roy
National Association of State Directors of Teacher Education and Certification(475)
Eisele, John C.
American Association of Teachers of Arabic(52)
Eiseman, Maria
American Society for Investigative Pathology(130)
Eisenberg, Barry S.
American College of Occupational and Environmental Medicine(68)
Eisenberg, Emily
Farmers Educational and Co-operative Union of America(301)
Eisenburg, Lea D.
International Foodservice Manufacturers Association(372)
Eisner, Bill
Intermarket Agency Network(347)
Ek, Sue
Billings Ovulation Method Association of the United States(228)
Ekdahl, Dale
Association of Construction Inspectors(192)
Environmental Assessment Association(296)
Ekdahl, Jon N.
American Medical Association(104)
Ekman, Richard
Council of Independent Colleges(272)
Elbin, Kelly
Professional Golfers Association of America(587)
Elcock, Lorelle
National Association for Treasurers of Religious Institutes(437)
Elder, Nancy L.
American Society for Microbiology(130)
Elderkin, Ann
American Society for Bone and Mineral Research(127)
Eldredge, Nancy
National Association of Forensic Economics(453)
Eldridge, Kathy
National Association of Catholic Chaplains(442)
Eldridge, Roger
National Milk Producers Federation(527)
Elfand, Julie
Interlocking Concrete Pavement Institute(347)
Eliades, CAE, George K.
Automotive Recyclers Association(224)
Elipani, Jeanne
Society of Women Engineers(646)
Elkins, Angie
American Music Therapy Association(107)
Ellashek, CAE, Daniel E.
Precision Metalforming Association(583)
Ellenbogen, MD, FACS, Richard E.
Congress of Neurological Surgeons(261)
Eller, Gerry
Foundation for Pavement Preservation(311)
Ellerman, Troy
Professional Rodeo Cowboys Association(589)
Elliot, Joanne P.
North American Bar-Related Title Insurers(555)
Elliott, Diane
American Association of Private Railroad Car Owners(49)
Elliott, Jere
Association of Christian Schools International(190)
Elliott, Joanne
Naval Enlisted Reserve Association(551)
Elliott, Joel
Association of Administrative Law Judges(183)
Elliott, Karen G.
Wine and Spirits Wholesalers of America(689)
Elliott, Rachel
American Association for Hand Surgery(35)
Elliott, S. Richard
International Union of Journeymen Horseshoers and Allied Trades(395)
Elliott, Teri
NACE International(424)
Elliott, Troy
Association of Social Work Boards(214)
Elliott, RPh, MBA, CAE, Victoria E.
Osteoarthritis Research Society International(569)
Society for Biomaterials(614)
Ellis, Aaron
American Association of Port Authorities(49)
Ellis, Brook
Gemological Institute of America(315)
Ellis, David J.
American Horticultural Society(91)
Ellis, Dr. Gary D.
Academy of Leisure Sciences(4)
Ellis, Kim
Professional Construction Estimators Association of America(586)
Ellis, Marietta Wheaton
Society for In Vitro Biology(619)
Ellis, Marilyn
ADSC: The International Association of Foundation Drilling(8)
Ellis, Mark G.
Industrial Minerals Association - North America(337)
Ellis, Dr. Robert P.
Conference of Research Workers in Animal Diseases(260)
Ellis, Steve
Homeland Security Industries Association(328)
Ellis, CAE, Tony
National Association of College Stores(444)
Ellis, Wanda
American Floorcovering Alliance(84)
Ellsworth, DeWelle F. "Skip"
Log Home Builders Association of North America(409)
Elman, Carolyn Bufton
American Business Women's Association(60)
Elman, Janet Rice
Association of Children's Museums(189)
Elmendorf, Edward M.
American Association of State Colleges and Universities(51)
Elmendorf, Fritz
Consumer Bankers Association(263)
Elsbree, Amy
National League of Cities(524)
Elwood, Thomas W.
Association of Schools of Allied Health Professions(213)
Ely, CAE, Karl
American Society of Association Executives & Center for Association Leadership(134)

Emamali, Bernadeen
National Association of Beverage Importers-Wine-Spirits-Beer(439)
Emard, Esther
National Committee for Quality Assurance(491)
Emely, Ph.D., Charles
American Railway Engineering and Maintenance of Way Association(121)
Emely, CAE, Mary Ann
American Council of Engineering Companies(75)
Emery, Mark
Project Management Institute(590)
Emmerson, Richard K.
Medieval Academy of America(416)
Emmert, Jr., John C.
American Arbitration Association(32)
Ence, Ronald K.
Independent Community Bankers of America(333)
Endean, John
American Business Conference(60)
Eng, Ann
International Trademark Association(394)
Engel, Daniel
Society of Corporate Secretaries and Governance Professionals(634)
Engelbreit, Ronald W.
American Association of Neurological Surgeons(46)
Engelhardt, James F.
Manufacturers Alliance/MAPI(411)
Engelman, Liz
Literary Managers and Dramaturgs of the Americas(408)
Engh, Fred C.
National Alliance for Youth Sports(429)
England, Norm
Portable Rechargeable Battery Association(581)
Engle, CMP, CAE, Jeffrey W.
American Academy of Pain Medicine(26)
Engle, Mark
Freestanding Insert Council of North America(312)
Metal Construction Association(417)
Engle, William
Association of Telehealth Service Providers(217)
Englebrecht, Kaye
National Association of Orthopaedic Nurses(463)
Engler, Brian
Military Operations Research Society(419)
Engler, John M.
National Association of Manufacturers(460)
English, Glenn L.
National Rural Electric Cooperative Association(537)
English, Helen
Sustainable Buildings Industry Council(656)
Englund, Thomas H.
Christian College Consortium(245)
Engman, John
Project Management Institute(590)
Ennis, Lori
American Motility Society(107)
Association of American Physicians(185)
Ensign, Thomas
Million Dollar Round Table(419)
Ensinger, Robert
National Foundation for Credit Counseling(512)
Epperson, CAE, Gary L.
Alpha Kappa Psi(18)
Epstein, Gary C.
American Medical Association(104)
Epstein, Rabbi Jerome M.
United Synagogue of Conservative Judaism(678)
Epstein, Sc.D., Mark
International Society for Pharmacoepidemiology(388)
Society for Mucosal Immunology(622)
Erbe, Gary T.
Allied Artists of America(17)
Erceg, Linda Ebner
Association of Camp Nurses(188)
Ericksen, Jack
Blue Cross and Blue Shield Association(231)
Erickson, Audrea
Corn Refiners Association(266)
Erickson, L. Eileen
Society of American Military Engineers(631)
Erickson, Nancy
American Society for Theatre Research(132)
Association for Theatre in Higher Education(181)
Erlewine, Meredith
National Business Incubation Association(486)
Ernst, Charles
College English Association(251)
Ernst, Margaret
National Chicken Council(489)
Erskine, Scott
Society of Former Special Agents of the Federal Bureau of Investigation(636)
Erstling, Mark
Association of Public Television Stations(210)
Ervin, Ph.D., Gerard L.
National Federation of Modern Language Teachers Associations(509)
Ervin, Jeannie
Composite Panel Association(257)
Esau, Jr., Richard H.
Marine Corps Reserve Association(412)
Escamilla, Marie
Building Material Dealers Association(234)
Esheley, Don
National Association for Trade and Industrial Education(437)
Esher, Cynthia A.
Measurement, Control and Automation Association(415)
Eshkenazi, CPA, CHE, CAE, Abe
APICS - The Association for Operations Management(158)
Eshleman, Ph.D., Ronald L.
Vibration Institute(683)
Espelage, Arthur J.
Canon Law Society of America(237)
Esposito, Donna
National Association of Cruise Oriented Agencies(448)
Esposito, Tess
Society of Industrial and Office REALTORS(638)
Essandoh, Robin
National Congress for Community Economic Development(495)
Esser, Jeffrey L.
Government Finance Officers Association of the United States and Canada(318)
Esslinger, Jonathan
American Society of Civil Engineers(135)
Esslinger, Theodore L.
American Bryological and Lichenological Society(59)
Estabrook, Randy
Architectural Woodwork Institute(160)
Estal, Holly
American Academy of Medical Administrators(24)
Estel, Holly
American College of Cardiovascular Administrators(64)
Estersohn, Shelley
Society of American Florists(630)
Estes, Marilyn
National Association for Research in Science Teaching(435)
Estes, Nancy
Independent Distributors Association(333)
Esti, Jeanne
Association of Trial Lawyers of America(218)
Estrada, Larry
National Association for Ethnic Studies(433)
Estreicher, Samuel
Institute of Judicial Administration(342)
Etheridge, Heather
Healthcare Financial Management Association(324)
Ethier, CAE, Donald
Equipment Leasing Association of America(297)
Ethridge, Winifred E.
National Frozen and Refrigerated Foods Association(513)
Etkin, CAE, Steven A.
Association of the Wall and Ceiling Industries-International(218)
Etshied, Karl J.
Recreational Vehicle Aftermarket Association(596)
Eubanks, Susan H.
National Board for Certified Counselors(485)
Eubanks, Thomas
National Association of State Archaeologists(473)
Evans, Christine
American Society of Furniture Designers(138)
Evans, Constance
Advertising Photographers of America(9)
Evans, David D.
Society of Fire Protection Engineers(636)
Evans, F. Lamar
National Government Publishing Association(514)
Evans, Gregory
Chamber Music America(242)
Evans, Jerry L.
Federal Probation and Pre-trial Officers Association(302)
Evans, Jim
Professional Putters Association(588)
Evans, Karen V.
Air Transport Association of America(13)
Evans, Kathy
National Alliance for Musical Theatre(429)
Evans, Kelly
National Verbatim Reporters Association(548)
Evans, Mary
Association of Technical Personnel in Ophthalmology(217)
Evans, Nicholas
Intellectual Property Owners Association(345)
Evans, Penny
American Osteopathic College of Pathologists(112)
Evans, Valerie
American Association of Physics Teachers(48)
Evans-Doyle, Deb
NACHA - The Electronic Payments Association(424)

Even, Matthew
Federation of State Humanities Councils(304)
Evenbaas, Robert
American College of Clinical Pharmacy(65)
Everett, Brian
National Small Shipments Traffic Conference(540)
Everett, Donna R.
Organizational Systems Research Association(568)
Everett, Michelle
Education Writers Association(289)
Everett, Teresa
International Association of Black Professional Fire Fighters(354)
Everhart, Lori
Association of Collegiate Conference and Events Directors International(191)
Everly, Ronald
National Association for Home Care(434)
Evey, Walker Lee
Design-Build Institute of America(283)
Ewald, Dave
Automotive Fleet and Leasing Association(223)
Ewald, Eric
North American Gaming Regulators Association(557)
Ewing, John H.
American Mathematical Society(103)
Ewing, Kathleen
Association of International Photography Art Dealers(202)
Institutional and Service Textile Distributors Association(344)
Ewing, Tess
United Association for Labor Education(670)
Eyles, Marynell
American Connemara Pony Society(74)
Ezer, David
Chamber Music America(242)
Faber, JoAnn
American College of Allergy, Asthma and Immunology(64)
Faber, Stuart J.
National Association of Business Travel Agents(441)
Fabian, Lawrence
Advanced Transit Association(9)
Fabian, Nelson E.
National Conference of Local Environmental Health Administrators(493)
National Environmental Health Association(507)
Faga, Betsy
North American Millers Association(558)
Fagan, Brian
Society of Pharmaceutical and Biotech Trainers(642)
Fagan, James F.
Research and Development Associates for Military Food and Packaging Systems(599)
Fahey, Kevin
Society for American Archaeology(613)
Fahey, Marge
Urban Land Institute(680)
Fahrenkopf, Jr., Frank J.
American Gaming Association(86)
Fahrenkrog, Steve
Project Management Institute(590)
Fahy, Barbara
Mail Systems Management Association(410)
Fails, Angela
Association of Energy Service Companies(195)
Fair, Pamm
Screen Actors Guild(606)
Fajnor, Paul J.
Audit Bureau of Circulations(222)
Falardeau, John
American Chiropractic Association(62)
Falconer, Sara
University/Resident Theatre Association(680)
Faley, Mary L.
Tax Executives Institute(657)
Falk, Charles H.
New York Board of Trade(552)
Falk, Jon
Athletic Equipment Managers Association(221)
Falkenstein, Donald
Council for Advancement and Support of Education(267)
Fallis, Charles L.
National Active and Retired Federal Employees Association(427)
Fallon, MHSA, Marie M.
National Association of Local Boards of Health(460)
Faltinek, Ph.D., CAE, James L.
National Sporting Goods Association(543)
Falzarano, CAE, Andrea
American Council of State Savings Supervisors(75)
Council for Learning Disabilities(269)
Fanella, Kelly
American Society of Safety Engineers(146)
Fanning, Betsy
Association for Information and Image Management International(174)
Fanning, CAE, Deborah M.
The Art and Creative Materials Institute(161)
Council for Art Education(268)
Fanning, Rich
United States Professional Tennis Association(676)
Fantaci, Kim
American Woman's Society of Certified Public Accountants(155)
Association for Accounting Administration(166)
Inflatable Advertising Dealers Association(338)
Materials Marketing Associates(414)
National Associated CPA Firms(431)
National Guild of Professional Paperhangers(515)
National Society of Accountants for Cooperatives(541)
SAVE International(605)
Faoro, Daniel
National Association of Chain Drug Stores(442)
Farabi, Dianne
International Society for Prosthetics and Orthotics - United States(388)
Farberman, Rhea K.
American Psychological Association(118)
Farbman, Ed.D., Andrea H.
American Music Therapy Association(107)
Fardy, Ian
Health Industry Distributors Association(323)
Fargo, Timothy J.
Design-Build Institute of America(283)
Farley, Donald
Forging Industry Association(310)
Farley, James
National Association of Government Employees(454)
Farmer, Gary
American Association for Vocational Instructional Materials(37)
Farmer, Paul
American Institute of Certified Planners(95)
American Planning Association(116)
Farnsley, III, Arthur E
Society for the Scientific Study of Religion(627)
Farnsworth, Jan E.
Portland Cement Association(581)
Farr, Carl
National Association of Wholesaler-Distributors(481)
Farr, James
National Association of Produce Market Managers(465)
Farrell, CMP, Duncan G.
Society of Government Travel Professionals(637)
Farrell, Gerard M.
Commissioned Officers Association of the United States Public Health Service(254)
Farrell, USAF (Ret.), Lt. Gen. Lawrence P.
National Defense Industrial Association(504)
Farrell, Meggan
American Society of Civil Engineers(135)
Farrell, Richard T.
Council of Infrastructure Financing Authorities(272)
Farrell, Scott
American Association of Oral and Maxillofacial Surgeons(47)
Farrell, Tim
American Hardware Manufacturers Association(88)
Farrey, Patrick
Tube Council of North America(666)
Farris, Melinda
International Association of Operative Millers(359)
Farrow, Scott
International Association for Continuing Education and Training(349)
Farstrup, Alan E.
International Reading Association(384)
Fasco, Bobbi
American Institute of Building Design(95)
Fassold, Jim
American Society of Perfumers(143)
Fast, Ken
Association of Gospel Rescue Missions(199)
Fathie, Ph.D., M.D., Kazem
American Academy of Neurological and Orthopaedic Surgeons(24)
Fathy, Moira
National Science Teachers Association(539)
Faught, Shellie
Association of Progressive Rental Organizations(210)
Faul, Colin
Mason Contractors Association of America(413)
Faust, Thomas N.
National Sheriffs' Association(539)
Fausti, John J.
National Association of Aircraft and Communication Suppliers(438)
Fay, David B.
United States Golf Association(675)
Fay, Rev. Msgr. William P.
United States Conference of Catholic Bishops(674)
Fazio, Damon
American Polarity Therapy Association(116)
Feal, Rosemary G.
Modern Language Association of America(420)
Fearis, Dave
Golf Course Superintendents Association of America(318)

Feather, Ph.D., CAE, John
American Society of Consultant Pharmacists(136)
Feather Clancy, Felicity
American Chiropractic Association(62)
Featheringham, Robert R.
Sigma Phi Delta(610)
Featherston, Phyllis
National Bed and Breakfast Association(484)
Fedder, Alan
UniForum Association(669)
Fee, Patricia
Packaging Machinery Manufacturers Institute(570)
Feehan, David M.
International Downtown Association(369)
Feehery, John
Motion Picture Association(421)
Feeney, Patti
Ice Skating Institute(330)
Fegley, Matt
Strategic Account Management Association(654)
Feher, Ph.D., Leslie
Association for Birth Psychology(168)
Fehr, Donald
Major League Baseball Players Association(410)
Feil, Karen
Gift and Collectibles Guild(316)
Feild, David
Multi-Housing Laundry Association(422)
Feinberg, Ted
National Association of School Psychologists(470)
Feld, CAE, Frances
Communications Fraud Control Association(255)
Felder, Monica J.
National Rural Letter Carriers' Association(537)
Feldkamp, Thomas
Institute for Briquetting and Agglomeration(339)
Feldman, MPA, Brad L.
Association of Credit Union Internal Auditors(193)
National Society of Insurance Premium Auditors(542)
Feldman, Rick
National Association of Television Program Executives(478)
Feldman, Susan
Salt Institute(605)
Felix, Peter
Association of Executive Search Consultants(196)
Fellers, CAE, Dave
Radiological Society of North America(594)
Fellin, Jr., Eileen M.
Association of Average Adjusters of the U.S.(187)
Fellman, Glenn
International Kitchen Exhaust Cleaning Association(377)
Fells, Robert M.
International Cemetery and Funeral Association(364)
Felsher, Jennifer
American Health Quality Association(89)
Fendrick, Craig
North American Farm Show Council(557)
Feniger, Jerome
Station Representatives Association(653)
Fenner, Mike
Council of Residential Specialists(274)
Fenner, Ph.D., Susan
International Association of Administrative Professionals(352)
Fennimore, Laura
Oncology Nursing Society(564)
Fenno, Phyllis
National Council of Examiners for Engineering and Surveying(499)
Fensterheim, Robert J.
Acrylonitrile Group(8)
Alkylphenols and Ethoxylates Research Council(15)
Chlorinated Paraffins Industry Association(245)
Emulsion Polymers Council(294)
North American Polyelectrolyte Producers Association(559)
SB Latex Council(605)
Vinyl Acetate Council(683)
Fenstermaker, Charles
Clinical Laboratory Management Association(248)
Fenza, D.W.
Association of Writers and Writing Programs(221)
Ference, Gregory C.
Czechoslovak History Conference(281)
Ferencz, Jr., George
Textile Rental Services Association of America(660)
Fergus, Tom
National Truck and Heavy Equipment Claims Council(547)
Ferguson, Cindy
Association of Progressive Rental Organizations(210)
Ferguson, Gregory
National Association for College Admission Counseling(432)
Ferguson, John
Water Quality Association(686)
Ferguson, Mike
Specialty Coffee Association of America(650)
Ferguson, Mike W.
Self Insurance Institute of America, Inc.(608)
Ferguson, Monique
National School Supply and Equipment Association(538)
Fernandes, John J.
AACSB - the Association to Advance Collegiate Schools of Business(1)
Fernandes, Sameira
Public Affairs Council(592)
Fernandez, Daniel C.
The International Air Cargo Association(348)
Fernandez, Elia
Information Systems Audit and Control Association(338)
Fernlund, Steve
Freight Transportation Consultants Association(312)
Feroz, Ray
National Association for Rehabilitation Leadership(435)
Ferrandino, Dr. Vincent L.
National Association of Elementary School Principals(450)
Ferrante, Anne
American Pet Products Manufacturers Association(114)
Ferrante, Maria
Packaging Machinery Manufacturers Institute(570)
Ferrara, Gregory B.
National Grocers Association(515)
Ferraris, Laura
Audit Bureau of Circulations(222)
Ferrell, Yvonne
National Association of State Outdoor Recreation Liaison Officers(476)
Ferrero, Tom
National Association of Wastewater Transporters(480)
Ferri, Annette
International Wood Products Association(397)
Ferris, M.D., Daron
American Society for Colposcopy and Cervical Pathology(127)
Ferrone, Chris
Picture Agency Council of America(577)
Ferruggio, Geri
Shock Society(610)
Fertel, Marvin
Nuclear Energy Institute(563)
Fetgatter, CPA, James A.
Association of Foreign Investors in Real Estate(197)
Fetsko, Bonnie
Association of Professors of Gynecology and Obstetrics(209)
Fetteroll, Steven J.
Wire Association International(690)
Fetzner, Joanne
Association of Environmental Engineering and Science Professors(195)
Fickeissen, Janet L.
American Association for the History of Nursing(37)
Ficker, John B.
The National Industrial Transportation League(519)
Fidoruk, Liz
Mason Contractors Association of America(413)
Fiegel, John L.
World Airline Entertainment Association(695)
Field, Alexander J.
Economic History Association(288)
Fields, Carl M.
Electrical Apparatus Service Association(290)
Fields, Cheryl
National Association of State Universities and Land Grant Colleges(477)
Fields, Jennifer
Aestheticians International Association(10)
Fields, Tim
International Association of Baptist Colleges and Universities(353)
Fiels, Keith M.
American Library Association(101)
Fier, DDS, Marvin A.
American Society for Dental Aesthetics(128)
Figoten, Jeremy
National Apartment Association(430)
File, Jayma
Environmental and Engineering Geophysical Society(296)
Filipiak, Nadine M.
American Society for Clinical Pathology(127)
Filipovich, Christine C.
National Association of Clinical Nurse Specialists(443)
Filler, Marshall
Aeronautical Repair Station Association(10)
Filling, Constance
College of American Pathologists(251)
Finch, Cheryl
Society of Reproductive Surgeons(643)
Fine, Camden R.
Independent Community Bankers of America(333)

Fine, Frank
American Luggage Dealers Association(102)
Fine, MS, MBA, Glen
Clinical and Laboratory Standards Institute(248)
Fine, Steven
Materials and Methods Standards Association(414)
Fineran, Larry
National Association of Manufacturers(460)
Finigian, Terry
American Academy of Pain Management(26)
Finke, Ph.D., Wayne H.
American Society of Geolinguistics(138)
Finkelstein, Allan
Jewish Community Centers Association of North America(401)
Finkelstein, Jim B.
American Beverage Association(56)
Finkle, Jeffrey A.
International Economic Development Council(370)
National Association of Installation Developers(458)
Finkle, Jillian
International Museum Theater Alliance(380)
Finley, Fred B.
Rubber Trade Association of North America(603)
Finley, Guy
International Recording Media Association(384)
Finley, Saundra
Phi Chi Theta(575)
Finnegan, Brian
Professional Aviation Maintenance Association(586)
Finnegan, Jr., Joseph P.
Conference of Educational Administrators of Schools and Programs for the Deaf(259)
Finnerty, John
Fixed Income Analysts Society(307)
Finney, Adam
National Nutritional Foods Association(529)
Finney, Sally
Academy for Eating Disorders(2)
American Society of Tropical Medicine and Hygiene(147)
Finstrom, Diane M.
Society of Independent Professional Earth Scientists(638)
Finucane, John
National Association of College Stores(444)
Fiore, Maria
National Housing Conference(518)
Fiore, Paul
Service Station Dealers of America and Allied Trades(609)
Firman, James
National Council on the Aging(503)
Firtu, Dianna
North American Export Grain Association(557)
Fisch, Sanford M.
American Academy of Estate Planning Attorneys(22)
Fischer, Albert J.
International Weed Science Society(397)
Fischer, Christine
International Council of Cruise Lines(367)
Fischer, Kurt W.
Jean Piaget Society(400)
Fischetti, Tom
International Association of Amusement Parks and Attractions(352)
Fish, Kathleen
Association of Management Consulting Firms(203)
Fish, Robb
Association for Hose and Accessories Distribution(174)
Yacht Brokers Association of America(698)
Fishburn, Ellen
Association of Railway Museums(211)
Fisher, Barbara B.
SSPC: the Society for Protective Coatings(652)
Fisher, Colleen M.
Council for Affordable and Rural Housing(268)
Fisher, Ph.D., CAE, Donald W.
American Medical Group Association(104)
Fisher, Gay
Thoroughbred Owners and Breeders Association(661)
Fisher, Kim
Construction Owners Association of America(263)
Fisher, Larry
American Nurses Association(109)
Fisher, Linda
Laborers' International Union of North America(404)
Fisher, Mark
Video Software Dealers Association(683)
Fisher, Michael
National Association of Consumer Shows(446)
Fisher, Ron
Defense Fire Protection Association(282)
Fisher, Sharon
American College Health Association(63)
Fisher, Timothy
National Association for Printing Leadership(435)
Fisher, William E.
International Fabricare Institute(371)
Fishman, Rabbi Joshua
National Society for Hebrew Day Schools(541)
Fishman, Marilyn
Endocrine Fellows Foundation(294)
Fitch, Carolyn
Association of Major City and County Building Officials(203)
National Conference of States on Building Codes and Standards(494)
Fitch, Laura Macary
Employee Relocation Council/Worldwide ERC(293)
Fitch, Michael T.N.
PCIA - the Wireless Industry Association(572)
Fithian, John
National Association of Theatre Owners(479)
Fitzgerald, Brian
Business Higher Education Forum(235)
Fitzgerald, CAE, DABFE, FACFE, Frank S.
Screen Manufacturers Association(607)
Window Council(689)
Fitzgerald, Ph.D., Hiram E.
World Association for Infant Mental Health(695)
Fitzgerald, Judy
National Insurance Crime Bureau(522)
Fitzgerald, Marilyn H.
American Academy of Physician Assistants(27)
Fitzgerald, Michael
American Osteopathic Association(111)
Fitzgerald, Pamela
Society of Industrial and Office REALTORS(638)
Fitzgerald Mosley, Benita
Women in Cable and Telecommunications(691)
Fitzpatrick, James
American Agents Association(30)
Fitzpatrick, Kathleen
United Telecom Council(679)
Fitzpatrick, Michael
International Association of Bridge, Structural, Ornamental and Reinforcing Iron Workers(354)
Flaherty, Richard G.
American Association for Clinical Chemistry(34)
Flaherty, Roberta D.
National Academic Advising Association(426)
Flanagan, Anne
American Association of Poison Control Centers(48)
Flanagan, Ed
Bridge Grid Flooring Manufacturers Association(232)
Flanagan, CAE, Michael
American Association for Public Opinion Research(36)
Flanagan, CAE, Michael P.
National Association of Graduate Admissions Professionals(454)
Flanagan, Sarah A.
National Association of Independent Colleges and Universities(457)
Flanigan, Jim
American Veterinary Medical Association(153)
Flannery, Tim
National Federation Coaches Association(508)
National Federation of Officials Association(510)
Flater, M.E. "Rhett"
American Helicopter Society International(90)
Flatten, Amy
American Physical Society(115)
Flax, Margery L.
Mystery Writers of America(424)
Fleck, Maelu
American Association of Orthopaedic Medicine(47)
Fleharty, Rosemary
Purebred Dexter Cattle Association of North America(593)
Fleischmann, Mary Walker
Counselors of Real Estate(277)
Fleishell, Sherri
ADARA(8)
Fleiss, M.D., Paul M.
American Association of Medical Milk Commissions(45)
Fleming, Arthur
Opportunity Finance Network(565)
Fleming, MS, David L.
Society for the Scientific Study of Sexuality(627)
Fleming, Gayla
Ceramic Manufacturers Association(241)
Fleming, Mary L.
Society of Exploration Geophysicists(636)
Fleming, Mick
American Chamber of Commerce Executives(61)
Flemming-Hunter, Sheila Y.
Association for the Study of African American Life and History(180)
Fletcher, Donna
National Spotted Saddle Horse Association(543)
Fletcher, Ken
International Association of Equine Dentistry(356)

Fletcher, Nancy J.
Outdoor Advertising Association of America(569)
Fletcher, D.S.W., Robert
NADD: Association for Persons with Developmental Disabilities and Mental Health Needs(424)
Fletcher, Suzanne
National Business Travel Association(486)
Fletcher, Zach
ASFE/The Best People on Earth(162)
Flint, Alex
Nuclear Energy Institute(563)
Flippo, Karen
National Association of Councils on Developmental Disabilities(446)
Flora, Scott
Small Publishers Association of North America(611)
Floren, Roger
National District Attorneys Association(505)
Floren, Terese M.
Women in the Fire Service(692)
Flores, Ph.D., Antonio R.
Hispanic Association of Colleges and Universities(325)
Flores, Rose
National Council on International Trade Development(502)
Flory, Kelly
National Marine Representatives Association(526)
Flory, Mary
American Mustang Association(107)
Flower, Nancy
Compressed Gas Association(257)
Floyd, Richard
College Band Directors National Association(251)
Fluegel, Pat
Kappa Kappa Iota(403)
Flynn, Cindy
Teachers of English to Speakers of Other Languages(658)
Flynn, Daniel T.
United States Soccer Federation(677)
Flynn, Deirdre
North American Association of Food Equipment Manufacturers(554)
Flynn, James F.
CPA Associates International(277)
Flynn, John J.
International Union of Bricklayers and Allied Craftsworkers(395)
Flynn, William J.
National Postal Mail Handlers Union(533)
Fochs, Patricia
Purebred Morab Horse Association(593)
Foerter, Dave
Institute of Clean Air Companies(340)
Fogel, Henry
American Symphony Orchestra League(150)
Fogelgren, Bob
Dance/USA(281)
Fogelson, Megan
American Association of Neuromuscular & Electrodiagnostic Medicine(46)
Fogleman, Ken
International Transactional Analysis Association(394)
Foldvik, Kristin
Special Libraries Association(649)
Foley, David
American Association of Equine Practitioners(42)
Foley, Georgia H.
Specialty Tool and Fastener Distributors Association(650)
Foley, Linda K.
Newspaper Guild - CWA(552)
Foley, Michelle
National Postsecondary Agriculture Student Organization(533)
Foley, Patricia T.
American Bureau of Metal Statistics(59)
Foley, Paul
Golf Course Builders Association of America(318)
Foley, Sue
Illuminating Engineering Society of North America(332)
Foley, Tom
Academy of General Dentistry(3)
Foley, Walter "Chip"
American Iron and Steel Institute(98)
Folio, Sam
American Federation of Musicians of the United States and Canada(82)
Folz, Christina E.
AcademyHealth(6)
Folz, Diane
National Institute of Ceramic Engineers(520)
Fontaine, Monita
National Marine Manufacturers Association(526)
Fonza, Ph.D., Marjorie A.
Association of Black Nursing Faculty in Higher Education(187)
Foote, Virginia
U.S.-ASEAN Business Council(668)
Forbes, Gordon
Association of Theatrical Press Agents and Managers(218)
Forbragd, Roxanna D.
Association of Certified Professional Secretaries(189)
Forburger, Melissa T.
American College of Medical Genetics(67)
Force, Marie S.
Association of Government Accountants(199)
Ford, Bernard
National League of Cities(524)
Ford, Betty
AACC International(1)
American Phytopathological Society(115)
Ford, Jim
American Petroleum Institute(114)
Ford, Karla A.
American Poultry International(117)
Forde, Kevin M.
Federal Judges Association(302)
Fordjour, Isaac
National Marrow Donor Program(526)
Fore, Gary
National Asphalt Pavement Association(431)
Fore, Jr., Troy H.
American Beekeeping Federation(56)
Forester, Annika
Association of Applied IPM Ecologists(186)
Forgeron, Sandrine
American Law Institute(100)
Forkenbrock, John B.
National Association of Federally Impacted Schools(452)
Formwalt, Lee W.
Organization of American Historians(567)
Forrest, Wayne
American Indonesian Chamber of Commerce(93)
Forrester, CAE, Larry L.
Property Casualty Conferences(591)
Forrey, Patrick
National Air Traffic Controllers Association(428)
Forssberg, Larry
North American Retail Dealers Association(559)
Forster, Amanda
Healthcare Distribution Management Association(323)
Forsythe, Dawn
U.S. Wheat Associates(668)
Forsythe, Sandra
American Collegiate Retailing Association(72)
Forte, Robin
American Association of Professional Landmen(49)
Fortin, Andrew
National Club Association(490)
Fortin, Guy
Pipe Fabrication Institute(578)
Fortman, Jr., Fred
American Society of Safety Engineers(146)
Fortney, Mary Martha
National Association of State Credit Union Supervisors(474)
Foscue, Amy
Gypsum Association(321)
Foshee, Emily
National Investment Banking Association(522)
Foss, Catherine B.
Plastic Surgery Research Council(579)
Foss, Richard A.
National Association of Surety Bond Producers(478)
Foss, Vanessa O.
American Society for Information Science and Technology(130)
Foster, Allison J.
Association of Schools of Public Health(213)
Foster, Dawn O'Day
International Society of Transport Aircraft Trading(392)
Foster, Nancy E.
U.S. Apple Association(667)
Foster, Richard M.
New York Board of Trade(552)
Foster, Robert
Evaporative Cooling Institute(299)
Foster, Stephen P.
International Society of Chemical Ecology(390)
Fothergill, Annette
Medical Mycological Society of the Americas(416)
Foti, Ph.D., M.D., Margaret
American Association for Cancer Research(34)
Fotre, Margit
Water Quality Association(686)
Foulkes, Tim
National Restaurant Association(536)
Fournier, Christine
American Sightseeing International(125)
Fouse, David
American Public Health Association(119)
Fowler, John T.
United States Pharmacopeia(676)
Fox, Abbey
Independent Community Bankers of America(333)

Fox, Charles M.
Timber Products Manufacturers(661)
Fox, D.M.D., MP, Christopher
American Association for Dental Research(34)
Fox, Frank X.
Professional Association of Resume Writers and Career Coaches(586)
Fox, Gary C.
Medical Group Management Association(416)
Fox, Gretchen
North American Building Material Distribution Association(555)
Fox, John G.
Society for Applied Learning Technology(614)
Fox, Ken
Endocrine Society(294)
Fox, Norma S.
Stucco Manufacturers Association(654)
Fox, Ronald L.
Society of Allied Weight Engineers(630)
Fox, CAE, Susan E.
American Association of Law Libraries(44)
Fox, Ted
National Association of Photo Equipment Technicians(464)
Photo Marketing Association-International(576)
Professional Picture Framers Association(588)
Foy, Kim
Exercise-Safety Association(299)
Frack, CPA, Joseph E.
Society of Financial Service Professionals(636)
Frado, Chris
Cross Country Ski Areas Association(279)
Frame, James W.
National Exchange Carrier Association(507)
Francen, Merry
Printing Brokerage/Buyers Association International(584)
Francis, Carl
National Football League Players Association(511)
Francis, J. Bruce
Association for Humanistic Psychology(174)
Francis, Wendy
Urban and Regional Information Systems Association(680)
Francisco, Jr., George G.
National Conference of Firemen and Oilers, SEIU(493)
Frank, Abe
National Collegiate Athletic Association(491)
Frank, Dean
National Precast Concrete Association(534)
Frank, Ph.D., Elizabeth L.
Academy of Clinical Laboratory Physicians and Scientists(2)
Frank, Ph.D., Martin
American Physiological Society(115)
Frank, Matthew
Biological Stain Commission(229)
Frank, Paul D.
Information Storage Industry Consortium(338)
Frank, Peter C.
Screen Actors Guild(606)
Franke, Roger
National Association of Fundraising Ticket Manufacturers(454)
Frankel, James
Art and Antique Dealers League of America(161)
Frankel, Lee
Fresh Produce Association of the Americas(312)
Frankfort, Faye
American Podiatric Medical Association(116)
Franklin, Bobby
CTIA - The Wireless Association(280)
Franklin, Fatina
National Conference of Regulatory Utility Commission Engineers(494)
Franklin, Jim
Red Tag News Publications Association(597)
Franklin, Jr., CAE, Joe T.
American Gear Manufacturers Association(86)
Franklin, Michele Grassley
National Extension Association of Family and Consumer Sciences(508)
Franklin, Sherry
National Association of Supervisors for Business Education(478)
Frantz, David
Paper Machine Clothing Council(571)
Franz, Dr. Charles F.
Society for Theriogenology(628)
Franz, Jana
Society for Ecological Restoration(616)
Franz, Ph.D., Judy R.
American Physical Society(115)
Franz, Keira
United Fresh Fruit and Vegetable Association(671)
Franzen, Pamela W.
Sump and Sewage Pump Manufacturers Association(655)
Franzon, Nancy
Orthopaedic Trauma Association(569)
Frascella, Albert
National Council for the Social Studies(497)
Fraschillo, Thomas V.
National Band Association(483)
Frawley, Irene
Special Interest Group for Computers and Society(648)
Special Interest Group for University and College Computing Services(649)
Special Interest Group on Accessible Computing(649)
Frazier, Alice
National School Supply and Equipment Association(538)
Frazier, Kendal
National Cattlemen's Beef Association(488)
Frazier, Steven
National Association of Criminal Defense Lawyers(448)
Frede, Candace
American Council of Learned Societies(75)
Frederick, Jim
Institute of Paper Science and Technology(343)
Frederickson, David J.
Farmers Educational and Co-operative Union of America(301)
Fredrickson, Sheila
National Electronic Service Dealers Association(506)
Freedenberg, Paul
AMT - The Association For Manufacturing Technology(156)
Freedenberg, Sam
National Association of Small Business Investment Companies(472)
Freedman, CAE, Adina Rae
Association of Avian Veterinarians(187)
Freedman, Randy
American Road and Transportation Builders Association(123)
Freeman, Jason
American Society for Amusement Park Security and Safety(126)
Freeman, ABC, APR, Julie A.
International Association of Business Communicators(354)
Freeman, Larry
World Association of Veterinary Anatomists(695)
Freeman, Lori
Association for the Advancement of Medical Instrumentation(179)
International Test and Evaluation Association(394)
Freeman, Michael V.
Healthcare Leadership Council(324)
Freese, Malissa
Silver Institute(611)
Fregin, Nancy J.
American Society of Artists(134)
Freher-Lyons, Donna
American Peptide Society(113)
Frehill, Lisa M.
Commission on Professionals in Science and Technology(254)
Freihaut, Carol
American Optometric Student Association(110)
Freitas, Stephen
Outdoor Advertising Association of America(569)
French, David
International Franchise Association(373)
French, Margie
Cosmetic Executive Women(267)
Frendak, Diane K.
Association of Science-Technology Centers(213)
Frendberg, Donald
HARDI - Heating, Airconditioning, and Refrigeration Distributors International(321)
Frendt, Donna
Sanitary Supply Wholesaling Association(605)
Frenette, Alexandre
French-American Chamber of Commerce(312)
Frentz, Peter W.
Institute of Transportation Engineers(344)
Freridge, Michelle L.
Free Speech Coalition(312)
Freshman, Phil
Association of Art Editors(186)
Frett, Deborah L.
Business and Professional Women/USA(235)
Frey, James S.
National Association of Credential Evaluation Services, Inc.(447)
Frey, Jane
American Association of Meat Processors(45)
Frey, Kelly
American School Counselor Association(124)
Frey, CST, MS, Kevin
Association of Surgical Technologists(216)
Freysinger, Carol
Juice Products Association(402)
National Institute of Oilseed Products(521)
Frick, Jill
International Economic Development Council(370)
Frick, Ph.D., CHMM, John H.
Institute of Hazardous Materials Management(341)
Frick, MS, Neil
National Hemophilia Foundation(516)

Fricke, Karen
Association for Asian Studies(167)
Fried, Brandon
Airforwarders Association(14)
Fried, M.D., Marvin P.
American Laryngological Association(100)
Friedberg, Jeremy
Association of Commercial Finance Attorneys(192)
Friederich, M.D., Mary Anna
Society for Menstrual Cycle Research(621)
Friedland, Nancy E.
Theatre Library Association(660)
Friedman, Barbara S.
Association of American Medical Colleges(184)
Friedman, David
National Petrochemical & Refiners Association(532)
Friedman, Jerry W.
American Public Human Services Association(120)
National Association of Public Child Welfare Administrators(467)
Friedman, Miles
National Association of State Development Agencies(474)
Friedman, Ronald J.
Diamond Manufacturers and Importers Association of America(284)
Friend, Patricia A.
Association of Flight Attendants - CWA(197)
Frink, Diane
National Association of Student Affairs Professionals(477)
Frinzi, Dominic H.
Harness Horsemen International(322)
Frisbie, John
United States-China Business Council(678)
Fritz, Richard
United States Meat Export Federation(676)
Fritz, Richard D.
American Association of Petroleum Geologists(47)
Fritzlen, Susan
Association of Government Accountants(199)
Froelich, F.E.
National Association of Waterfront Employers(481)
Froelich, Warren
American Association for Cancer Research(34)
Froeschl, Carol
Society for the Advancement of Economic Theory(626)
Frohlich, William H.
NPTA Alliance(563)
Paper Distribution Council(571)
Fromberg, Rob
Healthcare Financial Management Association(324)
Fromyer, Mary O.
National Council on International Trade Development(502)
Froom, Aimee
Historians of Islamic Art(326)
Fry, Sonya K.
Overseas Press Club of America(570)
Fry, III, Thomas A.
National Ocean Industries Association(529)
Frye, Cary
International Dairy Foods Association(368)
Frye, CMM, Jim
International Marina Institute(379)
Frye, D.O., Joyce
American Institute of Homeopathy(96)
Frye, Larry R.
American Walnut Manufacturers Association(153)
Frye, Mary
Home Furnishings International Association(327)
Fryshman, Ph.D., Bernard
Association of Advanced Rabbinical and Talmudic Schools(183)
Fuchs, Penny Bender
American Association of Sunday and Feature Editors(52)
Fuentes, Soraya
Wireless Communications Association International(690)
Fugolo, Rev. Joseph
American Italian Historical Association(99)
Fuleki, Lucy
American Watchmakers-Clockmakers Institute(154)
Fullem, Rita
Food and Drug Law Institute(309)
Fuller, CAE, Erin M.
National Association of Women Business Owners(481)
Fuller, Ivonne
National Medical Association(526)
Fuller, Lee
Independent Petroleum Association of America(335)
Fuller, Mark G.
Biotech Medical Management Association(229)
Fuller, Truman S.
Association of Reporters of Judicial Decisions(212)
Fullerton, John
National Frame Builders Association(512)
Fullerton, Madeline
Central Station Alarm Association(241)
Fulmer, Rise
The National NeedleArts Association(528)
Fulmer, Sherry
National Barrel Horse Association(483)
Fulton, Kenneth R.
National Academy of Sciences(427)
Funes, Gerardo
United States-Mexico Chamber of Commerce(678)
Funk, Carla J.
Medical Library Association(416)
Funk, Pat
Association of Retail Travel Agents(212)
Furman, Nelly
Association of Departments of Foreign Languages(193)
Furness, Roger K.
Audio Engineering Society(222)
Fursland, Richard
BritishAmerican Business Inc.(233)
Fussell, Sue Kraft
Association of Fraternity Advisors(198)
Fussell, Susan
National Confectioners Association of the United States(492)
Futrell, Cathy
Association for Healthcare Resource and Materials Management(174)
Gabay, Jeannette
Laser Institute of America(405)
Gabbert, Bill
International Association of Wildland Fire(361)
Gable, CAE, Ty E.
National Precast Concrete Association(534)
Gabri, CAE, David
Associated Luxury Hotels(165)
Gaddis, Evan R.
National Electrical Manufacturers Association(506)
Gaede, Mark
National Association of Wheat Growers(481)
Gaer, Samuel
New York Mercantile Exchange(552)
Gaffney, Carol
Securities Transfer Association(607)
Gaffney, Deborah K.
Tax Executives Institute(657)
Gaffney, Neil
Telecommunications Industry Association(659)
Gage, John
American Federation of Government Employees(82)
Gage, Larry S.
National Association of Public Hospitals and Health Systems(467)
Gager, William C.
Automotive Parts Remanufactuers Association(224)
Production Engine Remanufacturers Association(585)
Remanufacturing Institute, The(599)
Gagnon, David
Organic Trade Association(566)
Gaidry, James
AFSM International(11)
Gaine, John G.
Managed Funds Association(410)
Gaines, Ann
Seaplane Pilots Association(607)
Gainey, Linda K.
American Pharmacists Association(114)
Galant, Frank
National Rural Electric Cooperative Association(537)
Galanty, Jr., Walter E.
National Association of Golf Tournament Directors(454)
Galaska, Jason
National Association of Athletic Development Directors(439)
National Association of Collegiate Directors of Athletics(444)
Galatis, Jon
Oncology Nursing Society(564)
Galbraith, Bruce W.
National Association of Principals of Schools for Girls(465)
Galbraith, Suellen
American Network of Community Options and Resources(108)
Gale, David B.
North American Association of State and Provincial Lotteries(554)
Gale, Ph.D., George D.
Philosophy of Science Association(576)
Galindo, Joanne
National Association for Community Mediation(432)
Gallacher, Heidi S.
Hotel Electronic Distribution Network Association(329)
Gallagher, Edward G.
Surety Association of America(656)
Gallagher, Indrani Kowlessar
American Society for the Alexander Technique(146)
Gallagher, Janne
Council on Foundations(276)

Gallagher, Kelly
Evangelical Christian Publishers Association(298)
Gallagher, Patricia E.
Archivists and Librarians in the History of the Health Sciences(160)
Gallagher, Thomas P.
Dairy Management(281)
Gallanis, Peter G.
National Organization of Life and Health Insurance Guaranty Associations(530)
Gallant, Claudia
National Association of Independent Schools(457)
Gallant, Ph.D., Lewis E.
National Association of State Alcohol and Drug Abuse Directors(473)
Gallela, Anthony
Game Manufacturers Association(313)
Galler, Jerry
American College of Medical Toxicology(67)
Galler, CMP, Sharon
American Association of Healthcare Administrative Management(43)
Galligan-Stierle, Michael
Association of Catholic Colleges and Universities(188)
Galloway, Libba
Ladies Professional Golf Association(404)
Galloway, Philip
ATP(221)
Gallt, Jack
National Association of State Procurement Officials(476)
Galstan, Beverlee
Society of Interventional Radiology(639)
Gamadia, Pradeep
American Theological Library Association(151)
Gambaro, Patrick L.
New York Board of Trade(552)
Gambino, Joyce
Society of Thoracic Surgeons(645)
Gamble, Lois
National Association of Child Care Professionals(443)
Games, MBA, Louise
Clinical and Laboratory Standards Institute(248)
Gammonley, Kevin
North American Building Material Distribution Association(555)
Gander, Joy M.
Society of Risk Management Consultants(643)
Gandorf, CAE, James D.
Mathematical Association of America(414)
Gangloff, Deborah
American Forests(85)
Ganley, Melissa
Association of Professors of Gynecology and Obstetrics(209)
Gannon, Gail
Mechanical Contractors Association of America(415)
Gannon, James
Transport Workers Union of America(663)
Gannon, Ph.D., John L.
American Association for Correctional and Forensic Psychology(34)
Gannon, Nancy
Coalition for Juvenile Justice(249)
Ganoe, CAE, John H.
Association of Water Technologies(220)
Gans, Pharm.D., John A.
American Pharmacists Association(114)
Gantenberg, CHE, James B.
American Society of Neuroradiology(142)
Ganter, Lissa
Law and Society Association(406)
Gantz, Henry
Catfish Institute(239)
Gara, Nicole
American Academy of Physician Assistants(27)
Garber, Bill
Appraisal Institute(159)
Garber, Don
Major League Soccer(410)
Garber, Judy
National Association of Oil Heating Service Managers(463)
Garber, Paula J.
Society for Personality Assessment(623)
Garbini, Robert
National Ready Mixed Concrete Association(535)
Garbini, Robert A.
Concrete Plant Manufacturers Bureau(258)
Garcia, Amy
National Association of School Nurses(470)
Garcia, Claudia
International Webmasters Association(397)
Garcia, Eduardo
American Society of Group Psychotherapy and Psychodrama(138)
Garcia, Kristin
National Council of State Boards of Nursing(500)
Garcia, CAE, Louis
SOCAP International(612)
Garcia, Rick
Association of Hispanic Advertising Agencies(200)
Garcia, Thomas
National Tooling and Machining Association(546)
Gardiner, Stephen L.
American Microscopical Society(106)
Gardner, Benton W.
Sewn Products Equipment and Suppliers of the Americas(609)
Gardner, Cecilia L.
Jewelers Vigilance Committee(401)
Gardner, Chris
MEMA Information Services Council(416)
Motor and Equipment Manufacturers Association(421)
Gardner, Den
American Agricultural Editors Association(30)
Turf and Ornamental Communicators Association(667)
Gardner, Gary
American Gas Association(86)
Gardner, Marilyn B.
Association for Childhood Education International(169)
Gardner, Michael
Gypsum Association(321)
Garfield, Robert
National Frozen Pizza Institute(513)
Garfinkel, Jennifer
AABB(1)
Garfinkel, John P.
ISSA(400)
Garjian, Janice
Television Bureau of Advertising(659)
Garland, Kristine J.
Composite Can and Tube Institute(256)
Garman, Cathy
Contract Services Association of America(264)
Garnant, Bev
American Society of Concrete Contractors(136)
Garneau, Greg
National Press Photographers Association(534)
Garner, Perry
National Farmers Organization(508)
Garner, William
National Football League Players Association(511)
Garnett, Mary
Printing Industries of America(584)
Garpow, William R.
Recreational Park Trailer Industry Association(596)
Garrett, Charles
American Metal Detector Manufacturers Association(105)
Garrett, Daniel D.
Prevent Blindness America(583)
Garrett, CMP, Marlene
American Fire Sprinkler Association(84)
Garrison, Dr. Howard H.
Federation of American Socs. for Experimental Biology(303)
Garrison, Julie
International Association of Lighting Management Companies(359)
Garrison, Kenneth
FCIB-NACM Corp.(301)
Garrison, Laurie
National Association of Collegiate Directors of Athletics(444)
Garry, Joe
American Musicians Union(107)
Garth, Russell Y.
Council of Independent Colleges(272)
Garvin, Mark
Tree Care Industry Association(665)
Garvin, Michelle
United States Parachute Association(676)
Gascon, Sharon L.
National Association of Water Companies(480)
Gaskin, CAE, William E.
Precision Metalforming Association(583)
Gasmin, Sharon
MasterCard International(413)
Gastwirth, D.P.M., Glenn B.
American Podiatric Medical Association(116)
Gates, Cathleen C.
American College of Cardiology(64)
Gates, Christopher T.
National Civic League(489)
Gates, Derek
Paleontological Society(570)
Gathro, Dr. Richard L.
Council for Christian Colleges and Universities(268)
Gattari, Lynn
National Miniature Donkey Association(527)
Gatza, Paul
American Homebrewers Association(91)
Brewers Association(232)
Gaudieri, Millicent Hall
Association of Art Museum Directors(186)
Gauigan, Katrine
Cleaning Management Institute(247)
Gault, Roger T.
Engine Manufacturers Association(295)
Gauntt, Jim
Railway Tie Association(595)
Gautschy, Sharon
American Medical Technologists(105)

Gavel, Jennifer
International Embryo Transfer Society(370)
Gavilan, Horacio
Association of Hispanic Advertising Agencies(200)
Gavin, Carol D.
Food and Drug Law Institute(309)
Gawell, Karl
Geothermal Energy Association(316)
Gaynes, Elizabeth
Osborne Association(569)
Gaynor, Charlene F.
Association of Educational Publishers(194)
Gear, Jon H.
Council of Petroleum Accountants Socs.(273)
Gearhart, Eric V.
Skills USA(611)
Geary, CAE, Michael
American Institute of Architecture Students(94)
Geary, Susan
National Association of Home and Workshop Writers(456)
Gebhart, Kathleen
Association of Biomedical Communications Directors(187)
Gedansky, Lewis
Project Management Institute(590)
Gee, Sharon
National Assembly of State Arts Agencies(431)
Gee, Talbot M.
Association for High Technology Distribution(174)
Aviation Distributors and Manufacturers Association International(224)
Security Hardware Distributors Association(607)
Geehr, Shelley Wilks
Chemical Heritage Foundation(243)
Geenen, Mark
International Disk Drive Equipment and Materials Association(369)
Geerdes, Richard M.
National Automatic Merchandising Association(482)
Gehl, Elisabeth
Business and Professional Women/USA(235)
Gehrisch, Michael D.
Destination Marketing Association International(283)
Geib, Ruthann
American Sugarbeet Growers Association(150)
Geigle, Linda
National Association for Family Child Care(433)
Gelardi, Laury A.
National Guardianship Association(515)
Gelfand, Jane
Commercial Mortgage Securities Association(253)
Gelinskey, Jennifer
Polyurethane Manufacturers Association(580)
Gell, Sheila
Association of Freestanding Radiation Oncology Centers(198)
Geller, Perry
Brotherhood of Maintenance of Way Employees(233)
Gellert, George
American Importers and Exporters Meat Products Group(93)
Gelvin, CMP, Beverly
Nursery and Landscape Association Executives of North America(563)
Gemora, Irvin
National Association of Sewer Service Companies(472)
Genco, Peter
International Association of School Librarianship(361)
Gennardo, Ann
International Ticketing Association(394)
Genovese, Tammy
Country Music Association(277)
Gentilcore, Diana
Alliance of Foam Packaging Recyclers(16)
Gentille, John R.
Mechanical Contractors Association of America(415)
George, Connie
Society for History Education(618)
George, Janet
National Time Equipment Association(546)
George, Jim
World International Nail and Beauty Association(696)
George, Leslie
National Systems Contractors Association(545)
George, Warren S.
Amalgamated Transit Union(18)
Gerard, Jack N.
American Chemistry Council(62)
Gerbasi, CRNA, Ph.D., Francis
American Association of Nurse Anesthetists(46)
Gerber, Phyllis
Columbia Sheep Breeders Association of America(253)
Gerdano, Samuel J.
American Bankruptcy Institute(55)
Gerente, Mary Gordon
Hispanic Elected Local Officials(326)
Gergeley, Susan
Society for Healthcare Strategy and Market Development(618)
Gerkin, Daniel R.
National Mining Association(527)
Germain, Christopher
American Federation of Violin and Bow Makers(83)
Germek, Paul
Suntanning Association for Education(655)
Gerow, John
American Murray Grey Association(107)
Gerrasimides, Pam
National Association of State Workforce Agencies(477)
Gerrshkowitz, Jayne C.
National Tay-Sachs and Allied Diseases Association(545)
Gerry, Janelle
Association for Women Geoscientists(182)
Gershenfeld, Dr. Matti
International Council of Psychologists(368)
Gerspacher, Julie
American Association of Police Polygraphists(49)
Gerstenberger, Peter
Tree Care Industry Association(665)
Gervais, Glynne
National Network for Social Work Managers(528)
Gettelfinger, Ron
International Union, United Automobile, Aerospace and Agricultural Implement Workers of America(396)
Gettemy, James
International Association for Identification(350)
Gettings, Robert M.
National Association of State Directors of Developmental Disability Services(474)
Geyer, Wayne B.
Steel Plate Fabricators Association Division of STI/SPFA(653)
Steel Tank Institute Division of STI/SPFA(654)
Geylin, Mike
International Motor Press Association(380)
Ghezzi, Sandy
Craft & Hobby Association(278)
Ghorbani, Danny D.
Manufactured Housing Association for Regulatory Reform(410)
Ghossoub, Joseph
International Advertising Association(348)
Giaimo, Eileen
American Society of Ophthalmic Administrators(143)
Giampaoli, Mychalene
Museum Education Roundtable(423)
Giancola, P.E., Anthony R.
National Association of County Engineers(447)
Giannakos, Carrie
National Appliance Service Association(430)
Giano, Sheila
National Association of College Stores(444)
Gibbons, James
National Industries for the Blind(519)
Gibbs, Dr. Janis
Society for Reformation Research(624)
Giblin, Vincent
International Union of Operating Engineers(395)
Gibney, Cathy
American Correctional Association(74)
Gibson, Jr., CAE, Charles W.
Associated Locksmiths of America(165)
Safe and Vault Technicians Association(604)
Gibson, Claudia G.
National Association of Community Health Centers(445)
Gibson, Jennifer
National Association of Chemical Distributors(442)
Regulatory Affairs Professionals Society(598)
Gibson, Jenny
Color Marketing Group(252)
Gibson, John
National Cotton Council of America(496)
Gibson, Larry
National Grocers Association(515)
Gibson, Sandra
Association of Performing Arts Presenters(207)
Gibson, CMP, Sheree
National Association of Collegiate Women Athletic Administrators(445)
Gidley, Debbie
American Association of Women Dentists(54)
Giebner, Cara R.
Heavy Duty Representatives Association(325)
Service Specialists Association(609)
Giertz, J. Fred
National Tax Association(545)
Giese, Harold
Hispanic Association of Colleges and Universities(325)
Giese, James H.
Institute of Food Technologists(341)
Giese, Theodore L.
Abrasive Engineering Society(2)
Giesea, John C.
Security Traders Association(608)

Giesey, Deborah C.
Tax Executives Institute(657)
Giesler, Linda
National Association of Case Management(441)
Giganti, Ed
Catholic Health Association of the United States(240)
Giglio, Mary
Renewable Fuels Association(599)
Gikas, Stamatis
Hellenic-American Chamber of Commerce(325)
Gil, Lisa
Professional Bowlers Association of America(586)
Gilanshah, Ellie
The National Industrial Transportation League(519)
Gilbert, Jeffrey
Associated Wire Rope Fabricators(166)
Gilbert, CHME, CHA, Robert
Hospitality Sales and Marketing Association International(329)
Gilbertson, Lynne
National Council for Prescription Drug Programs(497)
Gilden, Lisa
Catholic Health Association of the United States(240)
Gildersleeve, Sterling
Association of Halfway House Alcoholism Programs of North America(199)
Giles, Chris
Galiceno Horse Breeders Association(313)
Gill, Brian
Master Printers of America(413)
Gill, Gordon C.
International Association of Geophysical Contractors(357)
Gill, Michael
Frozen Potato Products Institute(312)
Gill, Ralph M.
Professional Insurance Marketing Association(588)
Gilland, Dean R.
National Automatic Merchandising Association(482)
Gilland, Eloise
Earthquake Engineering Research Institute(288)
Gillen, Neal P.
American Cotton Shippers Association(74)
Gillespie, PharmD, Jeann Lee
National Pharmaceutical Council(533)
Gilligan, Daniel
Petroleum Marketers Association of America(574)
Gilligan, Tom
Association for Electronic Health Care Transactions(172)
Gillin, Donna
Council for Marketing and Opinion Research(269)
Gillmeister, Jim
Association of Rehabilitation Nurses(211)
Gilman, Ada
National Society for Graphology(540)
Gilmore, Chandra T.
American Association of Colleges of Pharmacy(40)
Gilmore, James L.
At-sea Processors Association(221)
Gilmore, Kelli
American Astronomical Society(54)
Gilpin, Susan
Committee of 200(254)
Gilson, Ph.D., Erika H.
American Association of Teachers of Turkic Languages(53)
Gilson, Susan
National Association of Flood and Stormwater Management Agencies(453)
Ginsberg, Ellen
Nuclear Energy Institute(563)
Ginsberg, Mark
National Association for the Education of Young Children(436)
Gioffre, Patrick
National Rural Electric Cooperative Association(537)
Giordano, Christine
Society for Biomolecular Sciences(614)
Giordano, Sam P.
American Association for Respiratory Care(36)
Giovanetti, Geoffrey N.
Wine and Spirits Shippers Association(689)
Girardo, Gunilla
Swedish-American Chambers of Commerce(657)
Giroux, CMP, William
Truckload Carriers Association(666)
Gish-Panjada, Dede
National Association of EMS Physicians(451)
Githens, William F.
RMA - The Risk Management Association(602)
Giuffrida, Michael
Institute of Career Certification International(340)
Giunta, Jim
National Collegiate Wrestling Association(491)
Givens, Holly
Organic Trade Association(566)
Givler, Peter J.
Association of American University Presses(185)
Glade, Brian J.
SHRM Global Forum(610)
Glajar, Dr. Valentina
Romanian Studies Association of America(603)
Glakas, Nick
Career College Association(237)
Glann, Alex
International Warehouse Logistics Association(396)
Glanz, Susan
American Association for the Study of Hungarian History(37)
Glas, Bradley J.
National Party Boat Owners Alliance(532)
Glascock, John L.
American Real Estate and Urban Economics Association(121)
Glass, Caitlin
Alliance of Artists Communities(16)
Glass, Dick
Electronics Technicians Association International(292)
Glass, CHE, Maureen
American College of Healthcare Executives(66)
Glass, Vicki
National Association of Development Organizations(449)
Glasscock, Kimberly W.
National Association of Fleet Resale Dealers(453)
Glassmann, Laura
Belted Galloway Society(227)
Glauberman, Alex J.
United Infants and Childrens Wear Association(671)
Glavin, Kristin
American Orthopaedic Association(110)
Glawe, Laura Porfilio
National Funeral Directors Association(513)
Glazer, Melinda
National Association of Government Labor Officials(454)
Glazier, Mitch
Recording Industry Association of America(596)
Glazner, Steve
Association of Higher Education Facilities Officers(199)
Gleason, Alan
Soaring Society of America(612)
Gleason, Diane
National Air Transportation Association(428)
Gleason, Jr., John P.
Portland Cement Association(581)
Gleason, Kathryn
National Pharmaceutical Council(533)
Gleason, Ruth
Association for Applied Psychophysiology and Biofeedback(167)
Society for Scholarly Publishing(625)
Glenn, Kimberly
American Society for Histocompatability and Immunogenetics(130)
Glenn, Phyllis
International Society for Heart and Lung Transplantation(387)
Glick, Barry
North American Plant Preservation Council(559)
Glickman, Dan R.
Motion Picture Association(421)
Motion Picture Association of America(421)
Glisson, Jo Anne
American Clinical Laboratory Association(63)
Glover, Ph.D., Robert W.
National Association of State Mental Health Program Directors(476)
Gloyd, D.V.M, Joe
American Academy of Veterinary Pharmacology and Therapeutics(29)
Glucksman, Daniel I.
International Safety Equipment Association(385)
Glumac, Ed
National Association of Scientific Materials Managers(471)
Gmiter, Cheri D.
Marketing and Advertising Global Network(412)
Gnass, Stephen Paul
National Congress of Inventor Organizations(495)
Goble, Tanya
Pile Driving Contractors Association(577)
Goddard, Carol A.
Association of Physician Assistants in Cardiovascular Surgery(207)
Goddard, Richard B.
Beer Institute(227)
Goddard, Stephen
Print Council of America(583)
Godfrey, Ph.D., Paul Joseph
National Institutes for Water Resources(521)
Godwin, Jean C.
American Association of Port Authorities(49)
Goedhard, Bart A.
Propeller Club of the United States(591)
Goehring, Charles B.
Truss Plate Institute(666)

Goergen, Jr., Michael T.
Society of American Foresters(630)

Goessel, CAE, Arthur D.
Independent Affiliation of Independent Accounting Firms(333)

Goetz, Christopher
International Federation of Pharmaceutical Wholesalers(371)

Goetz, Tom
Associated Construction Distributors International(165)

Goetz, William
International Federation of Pharmaceutical Wholesalers(371)

Goetze, David
Association for Politics and the Life Sciences(176)

Goff, Ron
American Institute of Timber Construction(98)

Goheen, John
National Guard Association of the U.S.(515)

Gojak, Linda
National Council of Supervisors of Mathematics(501)

Gold, Debra
Committee of 200(254)

Gold, Jody
American Medical Society for Sports Medicine(105)

Gold, Ryan Gates
National Catholic Development Conference(487)

Goldberg, Bert J.
Association of Jewish Family and Children's Agencies(202)
Jewish Social Service Professionals Association(402)

Goldberg, Geoffrey
Association for Bridge Construction and Design(168)

Goldberg, Joan R.
American Society for Cell Biology(127)

Goldberg, Jodi
National Society of Accountants(541)

Goldberg, Linda
NACE International(424)

Goldberg, Ph.D., Michael I.
American Society for Microbiology(130)

Goldberg, Peter
Alliance for Children and Families(15)

Goldberg, Robert C.
Business Technology Association(236)

Goldberg, Ronnie L.
United States Council for International Business(674)

Goldberg, Sharon C.
Pediatric Orthopedic Society of North America(572)

Golden, Kathie S.
National Conference of Black Political Scientists(492)

Golden, CAE, Mark J.
National Court Reporters Association(503)

Golden, Steve
Institute of Certified Records Managers(340)

Goldesberry, CMM, CMP, Sally
Society of Petroleum Engineers(641)

Golding, Lloyd L.
American Truck Stop Operators Association(152)

Goldman, Jack
Hearth Patio & Barbecue Association(324)

Goldman, Patricia B.
American Association of Colleges for Teacher Education(40)

Goldman, Senta
Society for Reproductive Endocrinology and Infertility(624)

Goldman, D.P.M, Steven
American College of Podiatric Radiologists(70)

Goldschmidt, CAE, Andrew
National Association of Counties(447)

Goldsmith, Helene
Parliamentary Associates(571)

Goldsmith, Jerry
American Association for Clinical Chemistry(34)

Goldsmith, Rae
Council for Advancement and Support of Education(267)

Goldstein, Robert
International Society for Magnetic Resonance in Medicine(387)

Goldstein, Dr. Stanley
American Podiatric Circulatory Society(116)

Golike, Jacki
National Roofing Contractors Association(537)

Golla, Victor
Society for the Study of Indigenous Languages of the Americas(628)

Golodner, Linda F.
National Consumers League(495)

Golson, E. Palmer
United States-China Business Council(678)

Gomez, Diana
Society of Hispanic Professional Engineers(638)

Gomez, Martin J.
Urban Libraries Council(681)

Gondles, Jr., CAE, James A.
American Correctional Association(74)

Gonzales, Magda
Hispanic Association of Colleges and Universities(325)

Gonzales Smith, Esther
National Society of Hispanic MBAs(541)

Gonzalez, Alma R.
National Bureau of Certified Consultants(485)

Gonzalez, CPA, Juan G.
Flight Safety Foundation(308)

Gonzalez, Rene
Hispanic Association of Colleges and Universities(325)

Gonzalez del Valle, Luis T.
Twentieth-Century Spanish Association of America(667)

Gonze, Robert
Associated Glass and Pottery Manufacturers(165)

Good, Carl
National Roofing Contractors Association(537)

Good, Lisa S.
National Federation of Municipal Analysts(509)

Good, CAE, William
National Roofing Contractors Association(537)

Goodard, Carol
American Hernia Society(90)

Goode, Sandra
American Association of Clinical Endocrinologists(39)

Goode, Tracy
American College of Chest Physicians(64)

Goodell, Roger
National Football League(511)

Gooden, Angela
Geoscience Information Society(316)

Goodermuth, Annlouise
Association for Research in Nervous and Mental Disease(177)

Goodman, Gillian
International Association of Fire Chiefs(357)

Goodman, John
AERA - Engine Rebuilders Association(9)

Goodman, Lenn
Metaphysical Society of America(418)

Goodnight, Julie
CHA - Certified Horsemanship Association(242)

Goodnight, Lisa
National Association of Black Journalists(440)

Goodrich, Kristina
Industrial Designers Society of America(336)

Goodson, Kerry
Stadium Managers Association(652)

Goodwin, Eric
American Orthopaedic Society for Sports Medicine(111)

Goodwin, Frank
International Lead Zinc Research Organization(377)

Goodwin, Katherine
Society for the History of Discoveries(627)

Goodwin, Michael
Office and Professional Employees International Union(564)

Gordan, D.V.M., John
Omega Tau Sigma(564)

Gordis, Deborah
American College of Nurse-Midwives(68)

Gordley, John D.
United States Canola Association(674)

Gordon, Alan S.
American Guild of Musical Artists(88)

Gordon, Dr. Andrew G.
National Cotton Council of America(496)

Gordon, Art
Federal Law Enforcement Officers Association(302)

Gordon, Barbara
American Society for Biochemistry and Molecular Biology(126)

Gordon, Herbert D.
Association of Directory Marketing(194)

Gordon, Ph.D., Julie P.
Econometric Society(288)

Gordon, Shannon
Electric Power Supply Association(290)

Gore, Andrea C.
Women in Endocrinology(691)

Gore, Dorothy
CBA(240)

Gorelick, Richard
Graphic Arts Sales Foundation(319)

Gorenburg, PhD, Dmitry P.
American Association for the Advancement of Slavic Studies(36)

Gorg, Brian
DRI International(287)

Gorham, Millicent
National Black Nurses Association(484)

Gorin, CAE, Susan
National Association of School Psychologists(470)

Gorman, John
Conference of State Bank Supervisors(260)

Gorman, John A.
International Organization of Masters, Mates and Pilots(382)

Gorman, Kim
American Board of Quality Assurance and Utilization Review Physicians(58)

Gorman, Mark
Distilled Spirits Council of the U.S.(286)

Gorman, Mary
National Association of Children's Hospitals(443)

Gorry, Michael
United Weighers Association(679)

Gorski, CAE, Thomas A.
Rehabilitation Engineering and Assistive Technology Society of North America(598)

Gorski, Walter
American Association for Homecare(35)

Gort, Wilfredo (Willy)
Latin Chamber of Commerce of U.S.A.(405)

Gosnell, Chestine
Evangelical Christian Publishers Association(298)

Goss, David C.
American Coal Ash Association(63)

Goss, Edward
Arthroscopy Association of North America(162)

Goss, Katie
American Academy of Periodontology(27)

Goss, Kenneth A.
Air Force Association(13)

Gossard, Shirley
American Neurotology Society(109)

Gossett, Bruce
American Society of Civil Engineers(135)

Gottschalk, Simon
Society for the Study of Symbolic Interaction(628)

Gottwald, Michele
American Institute of Mining, Metallurgical, and Petroleum Engineers(96)

Gottwald, Rich
Plastics Pipe Institute(579)

Goudeseune, Scott
American Council on Exercise(76)

Gould, Glenn
Preferred Funeral Directors International(583)

Gould, Mark
American Library Association(101)

Goulding, Tressa
Scoliosis Research Society(606)

Govin-Hart, Michael
Association of Literary Scholars and Critics(203)

Govindan M.D., Srini
American Academy of Thermology(29)

Goyer, Anne
Chemical Coaters Association International(243)
Industrial Heating Equipment Association(337)

Goza, Joel S.
ESOP Association(297)

Gradera, Betty
Latin Chamber of Commerce of U.S.A.(405)

Gradwohl, Dick
International Miniature Cattle Breeders Society(380)

Grady, John
Association of the United States Army(218)

Graeff, Catherine
National Council for Prescription Drug Programs(497)

Graff, Brian H.
American Society of Pension Professionals and Actuaries(143)

Graham, Alexander T.
Society of Competitive Intelligence Professionals(633)

Graham, Daniel W.
International Foundation of Employee Benefit Plans(373)
International Society of Certified Employee Benefit Specialists(390)

Graham, Diane
American Association of Motor Vehicle Administrators(45)

Graham, Elliott
Society of Quality Assurance(643)

Graham, IV, John H.
American Society of Association Executives & Center for Association Leadership(134)

Graham, Lawrence T.
National Confectioners Association of the United States(492)

Graham, Mark
National Roofing Contractors Association(537)

Graham, Scott
CBA(240)

Graham Poole, Kathleen
American Society for Colposcopy and Cervical Pathology(127)

Grainger, John
National Truck Leasing System(547)

Gramm, Stefanie
Foundation for International Meetings(311)

Granahan, Marcic
U.S. Psychiatric Rehabiliation Association(668)

Grande, M.D., MPH, Christopher M.
Trauma Care International(665)

Grandi, Edward
American Sleep Apnea Association(126)

Grandin, Steve
Academy of Certified Archivists(2)
National Association of Government Archives and Records Administrators(454)

Grannis, Renee
Association of Bridal Consultants(188)

Grant, Abigail
Clinical Social Work Federation(248)

Grant, Allen
Precision Metalforming Association(583)

Grass, Peter T.
Asphalt Institute(163)

Gration, CAE, Laurence
National Council of State Emergency Medical Services Training Coordinators(500)

Grau, John M.
National Electrical Contractors Association(506)

Graulich, Melody
Western Literature Association(687)

Gravatt, Nancy
American Iron and Steel Institute(98)

Graves, Bill
American Trucking Associations(152)

Graves, Dick
National Association of State Agencies for Surplus Property(473)

Graves, Donna C.
Burley Auction Warehouse Association(235)

Graves, Thomas J.
National Paint and Coatings Association(531)

Graves, Wayne S.
Association for Computing Machinery(170)

Gray, CAE, Albert C.
National Society of Professional Engineers(542)

Gray, Charles D.
National Association of Regulatory Utility Commissioners(469)

Gray, Gerald
American Forests(85)

Gray, Jay
Travel Industry Association of America(665)

Gray, John M.
Healthcare Distribution Management Association(323)

Gray, Mary Ann
Institute of Certified Business Counselors(340)

Gray, Neil
International Bridge, Tunnel and Turnpike Association(363)

Gray, Paula
National Council of Black Engineers and Scientists(498)

Gray, Philip H.
Association of American Pesticide Control Officials(185)

Gray, Jr., Robin B.
National Electronic Distributors Association(506)

Gray, Shandra R.
Delta Sigma Pi(283)

Gray, Tom
American Wind Energy Association(155)

Grealey, Mary
Healthcare Leadership Council(324)

Grear, Sandra B.
College of American Pathologists(251)

Greasley, Corrinne
International Swaps and Derivatives Association(393)

Greco, Dana
Society of Teachers of Family Medicine(644)

Greco, Greg
International Graphoanalysis Society(374)

Greco, Krista A.
American Society for Reconstructive Microsurgery(132)

Greco, Maia
Sulphur Institute, The(655)

Greeley, Erica
National Council of Nonprofit Associations(500)

Green, Cecilia
Turnaround Management Association(667)

Green, Chris
Producer's Guild of America(584)

Green, Judy L.
Family Firm Institute(300)

Green, Kimberly A.
National Association of State Directors of Career Technical Education Consortium(474)

Green, Marcia
National Association for Humanities Education(434)

Green, CFC, CPSS, Marj
Document Management Industries Association(286)

Green, Mark
Jewelers Shipping Association(401)

Green, Paul
Mortgage Bankers Association(421)

Green, Perry
Steel Joist Institute(653)

Green, Ruth
American College of Veterinary Internal Medicine(71)

Green, William H.
Council for International Tax Education(269)

Green, Yanecia
National Sheriffs' Association(539)

Greenagel, John
Semiconductor Industry Association(608)
Greenaway, Douglas A.
National WIC Association(549)
Greenbaum, Amy
Jewelers Vigilance Committee(401)
Greenbaum, Edna Fine
Council of Protocol Executives(274)
Greenberg, Janice
Automatic Meter Reading Association(223)
Greenberg, Jay
National Council on the Aging(503)
Greenberg, M.P.P., Pamela
American Managed Behavioral Healthcare Association(102)
Greenberg, Robert
American Gastroenterological Association(86)
Greenberg, Susannah
Women's National Book Association(694)
Greenberger, Phyllis M.
Society for the Advancement of Women's Health Research(626)
Greene, Holly M.
Association for Equine Sports Medicine(172)
Greene, Liz
National Association of Industrial and Office Properties(458)
Greene, Molly
Turkish Studies Association(667)
Greene, Richard
Laser Institute of America(405)
Greene, Robert
National Association of Investment Companies(459)
Greene, Sarah M.
National Head Start Association(516)
Greenlee, Ph.D., William F.
CIIT Centers for Health Research(247)
Greenrose, Karen
American Association of Preferred Provider Organizations(49)
Greenstein, Judi
Editorial Freelancers Association(289)
Greenwald, Jeffrey
National Concrete Masonry Association(492)
Greenwalt, Patricia
American Society for Engineering Education(128)
Greenway, CMP, Julia
Futures Industry Association(313)
Greenwood, James C.
Biotechnology Industry Organization(229)
Greenwood, Karen E.
American Medical Informatics Association(104)
Greenwood, Scotty
Canadian-American Business Council(237)
Greer, Dr. Chris L.
RNA Society(602)
Grefe, Richard
American Institute of Graphic Arts(96)
Gregg, Seth
Club Managers Association of America(249)
Gregoire, Larry V.
International Chemical Workers Union Council/UFCW(365)
Gregory, Doug
American Association of Clinical Endocrinologists(39)
Gregory, Gene
United Egg Producers(670)
Gregory, Janice
ERISA Industry Committee(297)
Gregory, Michele
American Association of Neurological Surgeons(46)
Gregory, Dr. Richard O.
American Society for Laser Medicine and Surgery(130)
Gregory, MPH, Susanne
Association of State and Territorial Public Health Nutrition Directors(215)
Gremer, Carrie A.
American Association of Endodontists(42)
Gretsuk, Steven
American Federation of State, County and Municipal Employees(82)
Grever, Kimberly
National Association of Computer Consultant Businesses(445)
Gribskov, Cheryl
Motorist Information and Services Association(422)
Grider, Jody
Master Brewers Association of the Americas(413)
Griesing, Dennis C.
Soap and Detergent Association(612)
Griffenhagen, George
American Philatelic Society - Writers Unit #30(114)
Griffin, Jenn
International Association for Business and Society(349)
Griffin, Michael G.
County Executives of America(277)
Griffin, Patricia
Green Hotels Association(320)
Griffin, Susan
National Council for the Social Studies(497)
Griffith, M.D., Anne
Software and Information Industry Association(646)
Griffith, Carlsen
National League of Cities(524)
Griffith, David
National Association of State Boards of Education(473)
Griffith, Don
WorldatWork(697)
Griffith, Gene
Transportation Research Forum(664)
Griffith, Joan
National Paperbox Association(531)
Griffith, Rev. Dr. Mearle L.
United Methodist Association of Health and Welfare Ministries(671)
Griffiths, Gene
International Marking and Identification Association(379)
Griffiths, Harley M.
American Association of Advertising Agencies(37)
Grigaliunas, CMP, Marcella
Strategic Account Management Association(654)
Grigg, Bill
American Dehydrated Onion and Garlic Association(78)
Griggs, Harris B.
International Engraved Graphics Association(370)
Griggs, Karen C.
National Aircraft Finance Association(428)
Griggs, Megan
Intellectual Property Owners Association(345)
Grilliot, D.C., James R.
International Research Council of Neuromuscular Disorders(385)
Grimes, Joanna
American Association for Clinical Chemistry(34)
Grimes, Joe
International Public Management Association for Human Resources(384)
Grimes, Richard P.
Assisted Living Federation of America(164)
Grimison, Matt
Aerospace Industries Association of America(10)
Grimm, Rick
National Institute of Governmental Purchasing(520)
Grinnan, Suzanne E.
Society for Imaging Science & Technology(619)
Grisamore, Judith S.
American Association for Laboratory Animal Science(35)
Griscom, Dan
Association of College and University Housing Officers-International(191)
Grisso, PhD, Thomas
American Board of Forensic Psychology(57)
Grochala, Ann
Independent Community Bankers of America(333)
Groeneveld, CCIM, CAE, Susan J.
CCIM Institute(240)
Groff, Lindsay
Water and Sewer Distributors of America(685)
Grogan, James A.
International Association of Heat and Frost Insulators and Asbestos Workers(357)
Groner, Sheldon M.
National Association of Real Estate Investment Trusts(468)
Gross, Debbie
Council of Large Public Housing Authorities(273)
Gross, Gail C.
National Association of Elementary School Principals(450)
Gross, Lauren
American Association of Immunologists(44)
Gross, Renita
Independent Liquid Terminals Association(334)
Gross, Richard
Stained Glass Association of America(652)
Grosse, Larry
Associated Schools of Construction(166)
Grossfeld, Robin
Association of Corporate Counsel(193)
Grossgart, Chris
International Association of Business Communicators(354)
Grossman, M.D., John H.
Society for Gynecologic Investigation(618)
Grossman, Mary
Society for the Advancement of Socio-Economics(626)
Grost, Gregg
Golf Coaches Association of America(318)
Groth, Donald
National Association of Off-Track Betting(463)
Groton, Jeffrey
National Association of Women Judges(481)
Grotta, Emily
Union for Reform Judaism(670)
Groundwater, John
Passenger Vessel Association(572)

Grover, Christopher
California Redwood Association(236)
Groves, Betty J.
Clydesdale Breeders of the United States(249)
Grubb, Sloane
Campus Safety, Health and Environmental Management Association(237)
Grubbe, Frederick H.
National Fraternal Congress of America(512)
Grube, Ed
Lutheran Education Association(409)
Gruber, John
Association for the Treatment of Sexual Abusers(181)
Grudnik, Lynn
National Health Association(516)
Gruebnau, Pam
Associated Equipment Distributors(165)
Gruenburg, Drew N.
Society of American Florists(630)
Grummon, Phyllis
Society for College and University Planning(615)
Grundahl, P.E., Kirk
Wood Truss Council of America(694)
Grunewald, Ralph E.
National Association of Criminal Defense Lawyers(448)
Grupe, Michael
National Association of Real Estate Investment Trusts(468)
Grutzkuhn, Bill
National Association of Enrolled Agents(451)
Grymala, Lorraine D.
American Academy of Health Care Providers-Addictive Disorders(23)
Guare, Kathryn
Global Health Council(317)
Guccione, Ph.D., Andrew
American Physical Therapy Association(115)
Guenther, Robert
United Fresh Fruit and Vegetable Association(671)
Guerra, Alfredo
National Council on Compensation Insurance(502)
Guffey, C.J. "Cliff"
American Postal Workers Union(117)
Guggolz, Richard A.
American Brachytherapy Society(59)
Association of Insurance Compliance Professionals(201)
Sports Lawyers Association(651)
Guibor, M.D., Pierre
International Oceanic Society(381)
Guidera, Kathleen
Energy and Environmental Building Association(294)
Guilbeau, Merlin J.
National Burglar and Fire Alarm Association(486)
Guilliard, Michelle D.
Foundation for Independent Higher Education(311)
Gulati, Sunil
United States Soccer Federation(677)
Gulick, Kelly
American Trakehner Association(152)
Gulka, Craig
NCSL International(551)
Gump, Jr., Richard A.
Directional Crossing Contractors Association(285)
Gunderson, Steven
Council on Foundations(276)
Gundling, Richard
Healthcare Financial Management Association(324)
Gunkel, Robert
Aquatic Plant Management Society(159)
Gunn, Gil
Association of Automotive Aftermarket Distributors(186)
Gunstream, Robby D.
College Music Society(251)
Gupta, Ph.D., Sushil K.
Production and Operations Management Society(585)
Gurley, Susan
Association of Corporate Travel Executives(193)
Gurthet, H. Louis
American Institute of Steel Construction(97)
Gusdorf, CAE, Lori
Association of Fundraising Professionals(198)
Gustafson, Deborah S.
The Art and Creative Materials Institute(161)
Gustafson, Elyse R.
Institute of Mathematical Statistics(342)
Gustafson, Judy
Women in Energy(691)
Gustavson, Mary Agnes
Leather Industries of America(407)
Guston, Sheila
American Society of Anesthesia Technologists and Technicians(134)
Guthrie, Lee
Healthcare Financial Management Association(324)
Guthrie, Susan
National Multi Housing Council(528)
Gutierrez, Allen
United States Hispanic Chamber of Commerce(675)
Gutt, CAE, Phillip A.
American Society for Apheresis(126)
Guy-Dyer, Karen
American Healthcare Radiology Administrators(90)
Guzman, Vivianna
American Management Association(102)
Gwiazdowski, Amy
ESOP Association(297)
Gwyn, Mike
American Metalcasting Consortium(105)
Gyouai, Norma
American Moving and Storage Association(107)
Haag, David
Association of Rheumatology Health Professionals(212)
Haas, Bill
Automotive Service Association(224)
Haase, Ken
National Futures Association(513)
Haber, Jon
Association of Trial Lawyers of America(218)
Haber, Ph.D., Pierre C.
Psychology Society(592)
Haberstro, Philip
National Association for Health and Fitness(433)
Habingreither, William
American College of Physicians(69)
Hacke, Kevin
Cremation Association of North America(279)
International Special Events Society(393)
Hacker, CAE, Steven G.
International Association for Exhibition Management(350)
Hackett, Carol
Delta Nu Alpha Transportation Fraternity(282)
Hackett, Emily
Internet Alliance(397)
Hackett, Frank
National Auto Auction Association(482)
Hackett, Jeremiah
Society for Medieval and Renaissance Philosophy(621)
Hackett, FACHE, CAE, Karen L.
American Academy of Orthopaedic Surgeons(26)
Hackett, Susan
Association of Corporate Counsel(193)
Hackett, Tamra
Society of Research Administrators International(643)
Hackler, Cullen L.
Porcelain Enamel Institute(580)
Hadley, Jr., Joseph E.
Aniline Association(157)
Hadley, Josie
American Association of Professional Hypnotherapists(49)
Hadley, C.A.E., Sherry W.
Airborne Law Enforcement Association(14)
Haer, Amie
American Podiatric Medical Association(116)
Haffner, Terri
American Agricultural Economics Association(30)
American Council on Consumer Interests(76)
Hafkemeyer, Inge
International Association of Administrative Professionals(352)
Hagan, Martha
Society for Pediatric Psychology(623)
Hageman, Charles H.
Forging Industry Association(310)
Hager, John
University Continuing Education Association(679)
Hager, Worth
National Waterways Conference(549)
Hagerty, Denise
American Medical Association(104)
Haggard, Ted
National Association of Evangelicals(451)
Haggarty, James
Animal Transportation Association(157)
Hahn, FACHE, Cynthia
American College of Healthcare Executives(66)
Hahn, Hannelore
International Women's Writing Guild(397)
Hahn, Martin J.
Glutamate Association (United States)(318)
International Hydrolized Protein Council(375)
Hahn, Patricia A.
Airports Council International/North America(15)
Hahn, Peter
Society for Historians of American Foreign Relations(618)
Hahs, Don M.
Brotherhood of Locomotive Engineers and Trainmen(233)
Hailey, CAE, Tammy
NALS(425)
Haines, G. William
Carpet Cushion Council(238)

Haines, Nancy
Women in Management(692)
Hajji, Jackie
American Society of Consultant Pharmacists(136)
Halal, CAE, Anne
American Meat Institute(103)
Halamandaris, Val J.
National Association for Home Care(434)
Halbert, Stacy L.
AcademyHealth(6)
Halbun, Bernie
Alliance for Continuing Medical Education(15)
Hale, D. Brett
American Gaming Association(86)
Hale, Donna Sizemore
American String Teachers Association(149)
Hale, Gene
International Aloe Science Council(349)
Hale, Glen
International Council of Shopping Centers(368)
Hale, Mark
Automotive Service Association(224)
Hale, M.D., Ralph W.
American College of Obstetricians and Gynecologists(68)
Hale, Robert F.
American Society of Military Comptrollers(141)
Haley, Jeff
Radio Advertising Bureau(594)
Haley, Michael L.
International Communication Association(366)
Halinton, Lois E.
Sporting Goods Agents Association(651)
Hall, Adam
Chorus America(245)
Hall, Anita
Society of Commercial Seed Technologists(633)
Hall, Bruce
National Earth Science Teachers Association(505)
Hall, Jr., Charles T.
Plant Growth Regulators Society of America(578)
Society for the Preservation of Oral Health(627)
Hall, Dave
International Society for Pharmaceutical Engineering(388)
Hall, Deborah
Association for Supervision and Curriculum Development(178)
Hall, Dorothy
National Council of Juvenile and Family Court Judges(499)
Hall, E. Thomas
Skills USA(611)
Hall, Fletcher R.
Agricultural and Food Transporters Conference(12)
Hall, Gloria
International Society for Pharmaceutical Engineering(388)
Hall, Jan
ADSC: The International Association of Foundation Drilling(8)
Hall, Jason Y.
American Association of Museums(45)
Hall, John V.
Ductile Iron Society(288)
Hall, Ph.D., Judy E.
National Register of Health Service Providers in Psychology(535)
Hall, Lance
American Society for Training and Development(133)
Hall, Mary Ann
National Association of Chemical Distributors(442)
Hall, Nancy
Association for Child Psychoanalysis(169)
Hall, Nick
Mobile Industrial Caterers' Association International(420)
Society for Foodservice Management(617)
Hall, Raymond J.
Electronics Representatives Association(292)
Hall, Reggie R.
Newspaper Association of America(552)
Hall, C.A.E., Robert
American Academy of Cosmetic Dentistry(21)
Hall, Sarah M.
American Society of Criminology(137)
Hall, Steven
American Council of Engineering Companies(75)
Hall, Sylvia
Digital Printing and Imaging Association(284)
Specialty Graphic Imaging Association(650)
Hall, Tommy
Walking Horse Owners Association of America(685)
Haller, Andrea
American Massage Therapy Association(103)
Haller, Ralph
Forestry Conservation Communications Association(310)
Land Mobile Communications Council(405)
Halligan, Jo
Association of Traumatic Stress Specialists(218)
Hallisay, Paul L.
Air Line Pilots Association, International(13)
Hallman, Linda D.
American Medical Women's Association(105)
Halperin, Fredric
National Association of Real Estate Investment Managers(468)
Halperin, Jerome
Food and Drug Law Institute(309)
Halpern, Ilisa
Oncology Nursing Society(564)
Halstead, Janet
Zonta International(698)
Hamberger, Edward R.
Association of American Railroads(185)
Hamblin, Jane
American Dental Education Association(78)
Hamby, Zhi
National Military Intelligence Association(527)
Hamel, Ph.D., Dr. Willem A.
Association of Management/International Association of Management(203)
Hamelin, Dolores
Women in Agribusiness(691)
Hamilton, C. Todd
American Volleyball Coaches Association(153)
Hamilton, Carol M.
American Association for Artificial Intelligence(33)
Hamilton, Ph.D., Donny L.
Institute of Nautical Archaeology(343)
Hamilton, Dorothy
Project Management Institute(590)
Hamilton, Ph.D., J. Ogden
Pi Lambda Theta(577)
Hamilton, Jenifer
American Society of Hematology(139)
Hamilton, Lee
United States Tennis Association(677)
Hamilton, Philip W.
American Society of Mechanical Engineers(141)
Hamilton, Rae
National Electrical Manufacturers Association(506)
Hamilton, W. Mark
American Mental Health Counselors Association(105)
Hamlin, CAE, Deborah M.
Irrigation Association(400)
Hamlin, Tina
Independent Petroleum Association of America(335)
Hamm, L. Arnold
Flue-Cured Tobacco Cooperative Stabilization Corporation(308)
Hamm, Rita
International Association for Impact Assessment(350)
Hamm, Dr. William E.
Foundation for Independent Higher Education(311)
Hammel, Ph.D., Joy
Society for Disability Studies(616)
Hammer, Thomas A.
American Oilseed Coalition(110)
National Oilseed Processors Association(529)
Hammerberg, Tom
Automatic Fire Alarm Association(222)
Hammond, John
North American Retail Hardware Association(559)
Hammond, Robert
Society of Industrial and Office REALTORS(638)
Hammond-Chambers, Rupert
U.S. - Taiwan Business Council(667)
Hammonds, Timothy
Food Marketing Institute(309)
Hammontree, Hannah
Farm Equipment Manufacturers Association(301)
Hamod, David
National U.S.-Arab Chamber of Commerce(548)
Hamor, Kathy
College Savings Foundation(252)
Hampshire, Frank
Automotive Market Research Council(223)
Hampton, Beth T.
Optical Society of America(566)
Hampton, Ronald E.
National Black Police Association(484)
Hamric, DMD, Robert E.
International Analgesia Society(349)
Hamwright, Jr., W. Albert
International Foundation of Employee Benefit Plans(373)
Hanagan, Nancy E.
Healthcare Distribution Management Association(323)
Hancock, Christopher
Design Management Institute(283)
Hancock, Ph.D., Don
International Association of Assembly Managers(353)
Handcock, Ben
Wheat Quality Council(688)
Hanen, Laura
National Alliance of State and Territorial AIDS Directors(430)
Haney, James A.
National Association of Basketball Coaches(439)

Haney, Rick
Showmen's League of America(610)
Hankin, Ph.D., Robert A.
American Academy of Dental Group Practice(21)
Dental Group Management Association(283)
Health Industry Business Communications Council(323)
Hankins, Miriam
National Propane Gas Association(534)
Hanle, John
American Bar Association(56)
Hanley, Christopher
International Union of Operating Engineers(395)
Hanley, CAE, William H.
Illuminating Engineering Society of North America(332)
Hanline, Gail
Air Traffic Control Association(13)
Hanlon, Mike
International Interior Design Association(377)
Hanna, Betty
International Association of Healthcare Central Service Materiel Management(357)
Hanna, Craig
American Academy of Actuaries(19)
Hanna, Dennis L.
American School Band Directors' Association(124)
Hanna, Gerri
Alexander Graham Bell Association for the Deaf and Hard of Hearing(15)
Hannah, Becky
Business Professionals of America(236)
Hanneman, Richard L.
Salt Institute(605)
Hanni, Jr., CAE, M. John
American Society of Dermatology(137)
Hannon, Amy
Wire Fabricators Association(690)
Hannon, Cecelia
National Association of Criminal Defense Lawyers(448)
Hannum, Jane
Nuclear Information and Records Management Association(563)
Hans, Heather
Executive Women International(299)
Hansalik, Konrad
American Artists Professional League(32)
Hansen, Christine
Interstate Oil and Gas Commission(398)
Hansen, Ed
American Association of Zoo Keepers(54)
Hansen, Glenn
BPA Worldwide(232)
Hansen, Jay
National Asphalt Pavement Association(431)
Hansen, Joseph P.
United Food and Commercial Workers International Union(671)
Hansen, Mike
Calendar Marketing Association(236)
Hansen, Robert
National Opera Association(529)
Hansen, Shelly D.
American Association of Neuromuscular & Electrodiagnostic Medicine(46)
Hanson, Ardis
Association of Mental Health Librarians(204)
Hanson, David O.
International Rural Sociology Association(385)
Hanson, USNR, Capt. Marshall A.
Reserve Officers Association of the U.S.(600)
Hapee, Deb
Soil and Water Conservation Society(647)
Happ, Pamela R.
Society for Obstetric Anesthesia and Perinatology(622)
Haptas, Maggie
National Association of Independent Fee Appraisers(457)
Haracznak, Stephen R.
Society for Vascular Ultrasound(629)
Haralson, III, M.D., Robert
American Academy of Orthopaedic Surgeons(26)
Haraseth, Ron
Association of Public-Safety Communications Officers- International(211)
Harb, Kim
National Ocean Industries Association(529)
Harbel, Jennifer
National Air Duct Cleaners Association(428)
Hard, Frank
Carpet and Rug Institute(238)
Harden, Krysta
National Association of Conservation Districts(445)
Hardesty, Constance
American Animal Hospital Association(31)
Hardiman, Nancy
American Society of Agricultural Consultants(133)
Hardiman, CAE, Tom
Modular Building Institute(420)
Hardin, Charles M.
Conference of Radiation Control Program Directors(260)
Harding, Juliet
National Active and Retired Federal Employees Association(427)
Hardman, Dennis J.
APA - The Engineered Wood Association(158)
Hardwick, Linda
American Society for Photobiology(131)
Hardy, Bethany
Institute of Medicine(343)
Hardy, Connie
ARMA International(160)
Hardy, George D.
National Terrazzo and Mosaic Association(546)
Hardy, Jr., M.D., George E.
Association of State and Territorial Health Officials(215)
Hardy, Rick
National Barrel Horse Association(483)
Harke, APR, Jerry R.
National Concrete Masonry Association(492)
Harker, Roy
Association of Gay and Lesbian Psychiatrists(198)
Harkin, Bonnie
International Association of Eating Disorders Professionals(356)
Harkins, Richard W.
Lake Carriers' Association(404)
Harlan, Mimi
Cast Stone Institute(238)
Harley, William G.
Outdoor Power Equipment Institute(569)
Harman, Donna
American Forest and Paper Association(85)
Harman, Jennifer
National Association of Telecommunications Officers and Advisors(478)
Harmon, Jocelyn
National Council of Nonprofit Associations(500)
Harmon, MPH, Linda L.
Lamaze International(404)
Harnett, Craig
National Hockey League(517)
Haroz, Sam
American Society for Gastrointestinal Endoscopy(129)
Harper, Carol
American Academy of Pain Management(26)
Harper, Claudia
Central Station Alarm Association(241)
Harper, Howard
SEPM - Society for Sedimentary Geology(609)
Harper, Monica
National Association of Equipment Leasing Brokers(451)
Harper, Sharon
National Association of Limited Edition Dealers(460)
Harper, CAE, Terrence G.
Society of Professional Journalists(642)
Harralson, Heidi H.
American Handwriting Analysis Foundation(88)
Harrell, Alvin C.
Conference on Consumer Finance Law(260)
Harrell, Sherry
National Appliance Parts Suppliers Association(430)
Harrell, Tylene
National Association of Negro Business and Professional Women's Clubs(462)
Harrington, Anna
National Association of State Land Reclamationists(475)
Harrington, Patricia A.
American Bridge Teachers' Association(59)
Harrington, CAE, Wesley E.
American Lithotripsy Society(102)
Urology Society of America(681)
Harrington-Carlisle, Judy
Aircraft Builders Council(14)
Harris, Allen
National Council of State Agencies for the Blind(500)
Harris, Ann
Society for Range Management(624)
Harris, Audrey
American Society of Directors of Volunteer Services(137)
Harris, Bill
National Association for the Education of Young Children(436)
Harris, C. Coleman
National Council for Agricultural Education(497)
Harris, Curt
National Association of State Workforce Agencies(477)
Harris, Dalen
National Association of County Intergovernmental Relations Officials(447)
Harris, Danny
National Association of Fire Equipment Distributors(452)
Harris, Darcy
International Graphic Arts Education Association(374)
Harris, FAIA, David A.
National Institute of Building Sciences(520)

Harris, Edward J.
American Antiquarian Society(31)
Harris, M.Ed., James L.
Civil Aviation Medical Association(247)
Harris, Judy
National Tunis Sheep Registry(547)
Harris, Laura
American College of Tax Counsel(71)
Harris, USAF(Ret.), Col. Marvin J.
Military Officers Association of America(419)
Harris, CAE, Mary Busey
National Association of the Remodeling Industry(479)
Harris, CAE, Nicole
National Glass Association(513)
Harris, Dr. Phillip
Association for Educational Communications and Technology(172)
Harris, Robert
Air Movement and Control Association International(13)
Harris, Robert J.
Industrial Fasteners Institute(337)
Harris, Russell
Association for Computing Machinery(170)
Harris, Dr. William G.
Association of Test Publishers(217)
Harris, Jr., William R.
Army Aviation Association of America(161)
Harris Blinton, Kimberly
Direct Selling Association(285)
Harrison, Debra
OPERA America(565)
Harrison, III, Frank R.
Society for Philosophy of Religion(623)
Harrison, Joseph M.
American Moving and Storage Association(107)
Harrison, Joy
American Horticultural Therapy Association(92)
Harrison, Lisa
American Chemistry Council(62)
Harrison, CAE, Sheilah J.
American Financial Services Association(83)
Harrold, Rita
Illuminating Engineering Society of North America(332)
Harrow, Fran
Leather Apparel Association(406)
Harrow, Richard
Leather Apparel Association(406)
Harsha, Barbara L.
Governors Highway Safety Association(319)
Harsha, Peter
Computing Research Association(258)
Hart, Jr., Clyde
American Bus Association(60)
Hart, Dan
International Business Music Association(364)
Hart, David A.
Association for Conflict Resolution(170)
Hart, Norma A.
National Bankers Association(483)
Hartigan, II, Maurice H.
RMA - The Risk Management Association(602)
Hartl, Charles
United States Lifesaving Association(676)
Hartle, Jill
American Academy of Ophthalmology(25)
International Society of Refractive Surgery of the American Academy of Ophthalmology(392)
Hartle, Terry W.
American Council on Education(76)
Hartley, Angela
National Industries for the Blind(519)
Hartley, Steve
National Association Medical Staff Services(437)
Hartlove, Michelle D.
National Association of Vision Professionals(480)
Hartman, Stanley I.
American Institute of Professional Bookkeepers(97)
Hartquist, David A.
Specialty Steel Industry of North America(650)
Hartranft, Scott
National Committee for Quality Assurance(491)
Hartwell, David
Association for Public Policy Analysis and Management(177)
Hartwick, Ken
Police Executive Research Forum(580)
Hartwig, Matt
Renewable Fuels Association(599)
Hartzman, Matthew
College of American Pathologists(251)
Harvell, Rick
National Association of School Safety and Law Enforcement Officers(470)
Harvey, Brett
American Society of Journalists and Authors(140)
Harward, Richard J.
Scottish Blackface Sheep Breeders Association(606)
Harwell, Ken
American Red Poll Association(122)
Harwick, Dennis P.
Captive Insurance Companies Association(237)
Harwood Mattox, Vivienne
Association of Vacuum Equipment Manufacturers International(220)
Society of Vacuum Coaters(646)
Haselbusch, Jewetta
Industrial Fasteners Institute(337)
Haskin, Kris
North American Neuromodulation Society(559)
Hassassian, Sima
International Public Management Association for Human Resources(384)
Hasselmo, Ph.D., Nils
Association of American Universities(185)
Hasslinger, Donna
Council for Advancement and Support of Education(267)
Hassmiller, Dr. Bob
Community College Business Officers(255)
National Association of College Auxiliary Services(444)
Hasson, Karen R.
American Society for Bone and Mineral Research(127)
Hastings, Andy
International Guild of Candle Artisans(374)
Hastings, Patricia A.
Materials Research Society(414)
Hatch, Laura Wayland-Smith
Gravure Association of America(320)
Hatch, Marty
Society for Asian Music(614)
Hatcher, Dr. Donald L.
Association for Informal Logic and Critical Thinking(174)
Hatfield, Dr. Thomas A.
National Art Education Association(431)
Hatfield-Goldman, Jan
Employee Relocation Council/Worldwide ERC(293)
Hathaway, Kris
National Association of Dental Plans(449)
Hatherill, William
Federation of State Boards of Physical Therapy(304)
Hattaway, Davin E.
American Institute of Constructors(95)
Hatton, Rev. Phyllicia M.
Black Entertainment and Sports Lawyers Association(230)
Hatzer, Dawn
National Child Care Association(489)
Haug, Dr. Steven P.
American Academy of Maxillofacial Prosthetics(24)
Haugen, Barbara
Council of Insurance Agents and Brokers(272)
Hauptman, Barbara
Society of Stage Directors and Choreographers(644)
Hauser, Melanie
Golf Writers Association of America(318)
Haverkamp, Jim
National Press Photographers Association(534)
Hawbaker, Scott
National Association of County Agricultural Agents(447)
Hawbecker, Mary
National Association of Community Health Centers(445)
Hawes, Jean
Outdoor Power Equipment Institute(569)
Hawhee, D.
Rhetoric Society of America(601)
Hawkins, Alicia
National Volunteer Fire Council(548)
Hawkins, Brian L.
EDUCAUSE(290)
Hawkins, III, CAE, Charles E.
National Stone, Sand and Gravel Association(543)
Hawkins, Jr., Daniel R.
National Association of Community Health Centers(445)
Hawkins, David
National Association for College Admission Counseling(432)
Hawkins, Donald T.
Association of Information and Dissemination Centers(201)
Hawkins, Elizabeth
Association of Women in the Metal Industries(220)
Hearing Industries Association(324)
International Society of Hospitality Consultants(391)
Hawkins, Dr. Frank T.
Research Association of Minority Professors(600)
Hawkins, John
National Association of Independent Schools(457)
Hawkins, Julie
American Soybean Association(148)
Hawkinson, Brian P.
Public Affairs Council(592)
Hawks, APR, John K.
Association of Retail Travel Agents(212)

Hawley, John
American Society for Clinical Investigation(127)
Hawrysz, David
National Futures Association(513)
Hawthorne, Paul
Aeronautical Repair Station Association(10)
Haydon, Donald
Society of Diagnostic Medical Sonography(635)
Hayes, Margaret
Fashion Group International(301)
Hayes, Phillip
American Sugar Alliance(150)
Hayes, Robin
American Counseling Association(76)
Hayes, Roger A.
Casting Industry Suppliers Association(239)
Hayes, Tim
AIR Commercial Real Estate Association(12)
Haymes, Raymond
Human Behavior and Evolution Society(329)
Haynes, Douglas
North American Conference on British Studies(556)
Haynes, Gail C.
Pension Real Estate Association(573)
Haynes, Kimberly
Architectural Woodwork Institute(160)
Hays, Dan
International Bluegrass Music Association(362)
Hays, Marjorie L.
National Chief Petty Officers' Association(489)
Hays, Susan
Wild Bird Feeding Institute(688)
Haywood, Lauren E.
National Rural Electric Cooperative Association(537)
Hazard, Barbara
Computer Measurement Group(258)
Hazelett, Brent
Brake Manufacturers Council(232)
Hazeltine, CAE, Derek
Professional Liability Underwriting Society(588)
Hazen, Paul
National Cooperative Business Association(496)
Hazle, Jeff
National Petrochemical & Refiners Association(532)
Heaberlin, Sandra
Lipizzan Association of North America(408)
Head, Doug
Viatical and Life Settlement Association of America(683)
Head, Terry
Household Goods Forwarders Association of America(329)
Healey, Maureen
Personal Watercraft Industry Association(574)
Healey, Patrick T.
Friction Materials Standards Institute(312)
Healey, Tim
Society for Natural Philosophy(622)
Healy, James
HARDI - Heating, Airconditioning, and Refrigeration Distributors International(321)
Healy, CAE, John J.
American Machine Tool Distributors Association(102)
Healy, Michael
Book Industry Study Group, Inc.(231)
Healy, Suzanne
Association of Higher Education Facilities Officers(199)
Heard, Robert
American College of Emergency Physicians(65)
Hearn, Keith
American Association of Psychiatric Technicians(50)
Hearne, Terry
World Floor Covering Association(695)
Heath, Susan
International Interior Design Association(377)
Heberlein, John R.
Optical Society of America(566)
Hebert, David E.
American Health Care Association(89)
Heck, Kim
Sports Turf Managers Association(651)
Hecker, Larry
Automotive Maintenance Repair Association(223)
Hecker, Sarah
Prevent Blindness America(583)
Heckler, Tim
United States Professional Tennis Association(676)
Heckman, Julie
American Pyrotechnics Association(120)
Hedgecock, Joan
American Medical Student Association(105)
Hedgeman, Dr. Betty
National Rehabilitation Counseling Association(535)
Hedgpeth, Kim
American Federation of Television and Radio Artists(83)
Hedland, Amy K.
North American Spine Society(561)
Hedland, Kathleen L.
Council of Supply Chain Management Professionals(275)
Hedlund, Julie
NACHA - The Electronic Payments Association(424)
Hedrick, Janet
American Foreign Service Association(85)
Heenan, Jr., William M.
Steel Recycling Institute(653)
Heesen, Mark
National Venture Capital Association(548)
Heeter, Judy
Major League Baseball Players Association(410)
Heffernan, Richard
International Economic Development Council(370)
Heftman, Mary P.
National Restaurant Association(536)
Hegmann, Bill
National Exchange Carrier Association(507)
Heide, Ross J.
Association of Federal Communications Consulting Engineers(196)
Heider, Claret M.
National Institute of Building Sciences(520)
Heider, Lawrence E.
Association of American Veterinary Medical Colleges(186)
Heiman, Gary
American Psychopathological Association(119)
Heimlich, John P.
Air Transport Association of America(13)
Heimowitz, Mike
American Fire Safety Council(84)
Heimpel, Carol
American Association of Physics Teachers(48)
Heinze, Bernd
American Association of Managing General Agents(45)
Heinze, Ph.D., Ruth-Inge
Independent Scholars of Asia(335)
Heisler, William
National Association of Seventh-Day Adventist Dentists(472)
Heissenbuttel, Anne E.
National Association of State Foresters(475)
Heitmann, Sandie
Association of Plastic Surgery Assistants(208)
Heitowit, Ezra
Universities Research Association(679)
Heize, Lynn R.
United States Meat Export Federation(676)
Heldorf, Barbara
Home Baking Association(327)
Helein, Ruth
American Psychological Association - Division of Psychoanalysis(118)
National Surgical Assistant Association(545)
Hellenbrand, Carmen
Preventive Cardiovascular Nurses Association(583)
Heller, Christian
AACE International(1)
Heller, Stephen V.
United States Business and Industry Council(674)
Hellman, Ralph
Information Technology Industry Council(338)
Hellquist, Kristin
National Council of State Boards of Nursing(500)
Hellwig, Kirstin
American Society of Interior Designers(140)
Helmes, Dr. C. Tucker
ETAD North America(298)
Helms, Cindy
International Hearing Society(375)
Helms, W. David
AcademyHealth(6)
Helmsing, Pam
National Christmas Tree Association(489)
Helsing, Karen
Association of Schools of Public Health(213)
Helton, Mike
National Association for Stock Car Auto Racing(436)
Helwig, Debra
IGAF Worldwide(332)
Helwig, H. Kurt
Electronic Funds Transfer Association(292)
Hemphill, John
North American Society for Trenchless Technology(561)
Hemphill, Linda
American Association for Dental Research(34)
Hemsley, Mike
Irrigation Association(400)
Henden, Arne
American Association of Variable Star Observers(53)
Hendershot, Marcia
American College of Radiology(70)
Hendershot, Sherlynn
WEB: Worldwide Employee Benefits Network(686)
Henderson, Betty
Associated Locksmiths of America(165)

Henderson, Christine
Waste Equipment Technology Association(685)
Henderson, Elizabeth
Society of State Directors of Health, Physical Education and Recreation(644)
Henderson, Harold
National Football League(511)
Henderson, John
American Councils for International Education(76)
Henderson, Julie
National Frozen and Refrigerated Foods Association(513)
Henderson, Kevin
National Association of Basketball Coaches(439)
Henderson, Lavette
National Dental Association(505)
Henderson, Linda
National Association of College and University Attorneys(444)
Hendricks, Donald
Organization of Flying Adjusters(567)
Hendrickson, Mary Lynn
Associated Church Press(164)
Hendrickson, Ronald M.
International Chiropractors Association(365)
Henebry, Martha
American Association of Collegiate Registrars and Admissions Officers(40)
Heney, Daniel
Maple Flooring Manufacturers Association(412)
Heng, Betty
Physician Insurers Association of America(577)
Hengesbaugh, Bernard L.
American Medical Association(104)
Henk, Harold "Skip"
Xplor International(698)
Henke, Mike
ACA International, The Association of Credit and Collection Professionals(2)
Henley, M.D., Douglas
American Academy of Family Physicians(22)
Hennage, Ph.D., David W.
IEEE Computer Society(331)
Hennessy, Darlene
Association of Forensic Document Examiners(197)
Hennessy, Mary
Industrial Fabrics Association International(336)
Henning, Glenda L.
Investment Adviser Association(398)
Henning, William H.
National Conference of Commissioners on Uniform State Laws(493)
Henrichs, CAE, Ronald A.
American Academy of Dermatology(21)
Henriksen, CAE, Melissa
American Composites Manufacturers Association(72)
Henriquez, Santa
American College of Nutrition(68)
Henry, CAE, Howard C.
Incentive Federation(332)
Henry, James L.
Transportation Institute(664)
Henry, Mina
International Association of Clothing Designers and Executives(355)
Henry, Pam
Water Environment Federation(685)
Henry, DVM, Roger
International Society for Plastination(388)
Henry, Winna C.
International and American Associations of Clinical Nutritionists(349)
Hensel, Bob
Mobile Air Conditioning Society Worldwide(420)
Hensel, George R.
Driving School Association of America(287)
Hensely, Sue
National Restaurant Association(536)
Hensley, Julie
Delta Omicron(282)
Hepp, Ronnie
Recreation Vehicle Dealers Association of North America(596)
Heppenheimer, Susan
American Society of Master Dental Technologists(141)
Heppes, CAE, Jerry
Door and Hardware Institute(287)
Herbst, Peter R.
Society for Technical Communication(626)
Hercey, M.P.A., Connie
Association of Psychology Postdoctoral and Internship Centers(210)
Herd, Michael
NACHA - The Electronic Payments Association(424)
Heredia, Priscilla
Society for the Advancement of Material and Process Engineering(626)
Hergesell, Janine Lee
Specialized Information Publishers Association(650)
Herian, Vicki
Society of Wood Science and Technology(646)
Herman, Bob
Track Owners Association(663)
Herman, Jeffrey
Society of American Silversmiths(631)
Herman, Jonathan
National Guild of Community Schools of the Arts(515)
Herman, Nate
American Apparel & Footwear Association(31)
Herman, Stewart W.
Society of Christian Ethics(633)
Herman, Terry
U.S. Wheat Associates(668)
Herman-Betzen, Marsha
Association of College Unions International(191)
Hermann, CAE, Peter R.
ARMA International(160)
Hernandez, Debra
Alliance of Information and Referral Systems(17)
Hernandez, Liz
Visual Resources Association(684)
Hernandez, Montserrat
Ecuadorean American Association(288)
Hernick, Mark
American Land Title Association(100)
Herren, Leslie
The International Air Cargo Association(348)
Herrera, Manuel
Hispanic Organization of Latin Actors(326)
Herrera, CMP, Maricel M.
Association for Molecular Pathology(176)
Herrick, Ned
Graphic Arts Technical Foundation(319)
Herrick, II, CAE, Raymond W.
Foodservice Equipment Distributors Association(310)
Herrin, Deborah C.
Optical Society of America(566)
Herring, K. Lee
American Sociological Association(147)
Herron, Dr. Daniel J.
Academy of Legal Studies in Business(4)
Hershey, David
National Accounting and Finance Council(427)
Hershman, Jerome
Guitar and Accessories Marketing Association(321)
Hertzberg, Liza
National Consumers League(495)
Heru, Nzinga Ratibisha
Association for the Study of Classical African Civilizations(180)
Hervey, Marcie
American National CattleWomen(108)
Herzau, Irene
Association for the Advancement of Automotive Medicine(179)
Herzog, Frederick J.
Fulfillment Services Association of America(312)
Hess, Annette
American Academy of Nursing(25)
Hess, John W.
Geological Society of America(315)
Hess, Ken
Wholesale Florist and Florist Supplier Association(688)
Hessel, Carolyn
Jewish Book Council(401)
Hetzel, Glen
National Institute for Farm Safety(520)
Heuer, Greg
Architectural Woodwork Institute(160)
Heun, Ph.D., Linda
American Association of Colleges of Osteopathic Medicine(40)
Heuser, Patricia E.
American Society for Plasticulture(131)
Independent Turf and Ornamental Distributors Association(336)
North American Strawberry Growers Association(562)
Heusser, Ed.D., H. Earl
National Association of Private, Nontraditional Schools and Colleges with Accrediting Commission for Higher Education(465)
Heusser, Psy.D., Irene Dolly
National Association of Private, Nontraditional Schools and Colleges with Accrediting Commission for Higher Education(465)
Hewitt, Sherry
Building Owners and Managers Institute International(234)
Hewlett, Marcy
Association of TeleServices International(217)
Hewry, Holly
Renewable Fuels Association(599)
Heyedahl, Elisabeth
American Wood Preservers Institute(155)
Heyman, Annette H.
American Registry of Medical Assistants(122)
Hiatt, Richard S.
National Food and Energy Council(511)
Hickey, Carolyn
Health Industry Group Purchasing Association(323)
Hickey, David
International Sign Association(386)

Hickey, David L.
International Union Security, Police and Fire Professionals of America(396)
Hickey, Jr., James J.
American Horse Council(91)
Hickman, Del
Multi-Level Marketing International Association(422)
Hickman, CAE, Sabeena
American Composites Manufacturers Association(72)
International Cast Polymer Association(364)
Hicks, Cari
Airport Consultants Council(14)
Hicks, Gary
Aviation Insurance Association(225)
Mass Marketing Insurance Institute(413)
Hicks, Matthew
Council for Spiritual and Ethical Education(270)
Hicks, Wayne
Black Data Processing Associates(230)
Hieb, James
Marble Institute of America(412)
Hiernu, C. Penny
International Society for the Study of Subtle Energies and Energy Medicine(389)
Higby, Dr. Gregory J.
American Institute of the History of Pharmacy(97)
Higgenbotham, Francine
International Technical Caramel Association(393)
Higginbotham, Patricia
Air Transport Association of America(13)
Higgins, Barbara C.
Plumbing Manufacturers Institute(579)
Higgins, Dr. William
American Osteopathic College of Allergy and Immunology(111)
Higgs, Christopher
Ladies Professional Golf Association(404)
Hightower, Leigh
Materials and Methods Standards Association(414)
Hileman, Tony
American Humanist Association(92)
Hilgers, Ken
ISA(400)
Hill, Ann
Flight Safety Foundation(308)
Hill, Sr., Bill
American Small Businesses Association(126)
Hill, Brenna
American Association for Health Freedom(35)
Hill, Candy
Catholic Charities USA(239)
Hill, Cece
International Association of Correctional Officers(355)
Hill, Debbie
National Association of Professional Surplus Lines Offices(466)
Hill, E. Ronelle
United Methodist Association of Health and Welfare Ministries(671)
Hill, Edwin D.
International Brotherhood of Electrical Workers(363)
Hill, Joan
United Steel, Paper and Forestry, Rubber, Manufacturing, Energy, Allied Industrial and Service Workers International Union(678)
Hill, Laurie
Association of Progressive Rental Organizations(210)
Hill, Lee H.
American Waterways Operators(154)
Hill, Linda
International Map Trade Association(379)
Hill, Richard B.
American Society for Information Science and Technology(130)
Hill, Robert L.
American Association of Blacks in Energy(38)
Hill, Sandy
International Map Trade Association(379)
Hill, Terry
International Franchise Association(373)
Hill, Thomas S.
American Association of Professional Sales Engineers(49)
Hill, Tom
Institute of Inspection Cleaning and Restoration Certification(341)
Hill, Tucker
Northern Nut Growers Association(562)
Hilla, Elizabeth B.
Health Industry Distributors Association(323)
Hillman, Bill
National Utility Contractors Association(548)
Hillman, Renee
Federation of Straight Chiropractors and Organizations(304)
Hillsman, Sally T.
American Sociological Association(147)
Hilson, Amy C.
Association of State and Provincial Psychology Boards(215)
Hilton, Kevin J.
NEA - the Association of Union Constructors(551)
Hilton, Thomas
Academy of Dental Materials(3)
Hilton, Troy
National Association of Basketball Coaches(439)
Hilvers, Anthony
IPC - Association Connecting Electronics Industries(399)
Himpler, William
American Financial Services Association(83)
Hinchman, Joan
National Society of Compliance Professionals(541)
Hinckley, Kathleen W.
Association of Professional Genealogists(209)
Hinckley, CMP, Stewart A.
American College of Osteopathic Pediatricians(69)
American Society of Extra-Corporeal Technology(137)
Clinical Orthopaedic Society(248)
Society for Pediatric Anesthesia(623)
Hinde, John
Amusement Industry Manufacturers and Suppliers International(156)
Hinen, CAE, Karen
Association of College and University Auditors(190)
Hines, JoAnn R.
Women in Packaging(692)
Hines, Linda L.
Association of Military Surgeons of the U.S.(205)
Hingoraney, Rishi
American Court and Commercial Newspapers(77)
National Federation of Press Women(510)
Hinton, Skip
Organization of State Broadcasting Executives(568)
Hinton, Wilbur H. "Skip"
National Educational Telecommunications Association(506)
Hirsch, Ric
Entertainment Software Association(295)
Hirschbeck, John
World Umpires Association(696)
Hirschhorn, Eric L.
Industry Coalition on Technology Transfer(337)
Hirsh, Robin
Union for Reform Judaism(670)
Hitchcock, Chuck
National Lubricating Grease Institute(525)
Hitchcock, Reed
Asphalt Roofing Manufacturers Association(163)
Roof Coatings Manufacturers Association(603)
Hite, William P.
United Association of Journeymen and Apprentices of the Plumbing and Pipe Fitting Industry of U.S. and Canada(670)
Hitz, C. Breck
Laser and Electro-Optics Manufacturers' Association(405)
Hixon, Thomas E.
National Electrical Manufacturers Association(506)
Hlavacek, Roy
Institute of Food Technologists(341)
Hlibka, Nadia
Middle East Studies Association of North America(418)
Hnatiuk, EdD, RN, CAE, Cynthia
Academy of Medical-Surgical Nurses(4)
American Academy of Ambulatory Care Nursing(20)
Dermatology Nurses' Association(283)
Hoaglan, Larry
Communications Supply Service Association(255)
Hoagland, Michael P.
American Forest and Paper Association(85)
Hoals, Brian
Society of Economic Geologists(635)
Hoarle, Kimberly
American Academy of Dermatology(21)
Hoban, Roseanne M.
National Association of Independent Public Finance Advisors(457)
Hobart, Mary
American Radio Relay League(121)
Hobbie, Kenneth
U.S. Grains Council(667)
Hobbie, Richard A.
National Association of State Workforce Agencies(477)
Hobbs, Dale
Association of Automotive Aftermarket Distributors(186)
Hobby, Ellen
Council on Foundations(276)
Hobby, Greg
Society for Foodservice Management(617)
Hoboy, Lance K.
PDA - an International Association for Pharmaceutical Science and Technology(572)
Hobrock, Carole
National Intramural-Recreational Sports Association(522)

Hobson, David F.
Uniform and Textile Service Association(669)
Hobson, Joseph
Asphalt Roofing Manufacturers Association(163)
Hobut, Eileen
International Magnesium Association(378)
Hochstetler, Paula
Airport Consultants Council(14)
Hock, RN, Cindy N.
American Medical Directors Association(104)
Hockel, Jack L.
American Academy of Gnathologic Orthopedics(23)
Hodapp, Ted
American Physical Society(115)
Hodes, Carol
National Institute of Governmental Purchasing(520)
Hodges, Christy
Home Furnishings International Association(327)
Hodges, Deborah
Uniform and Textile Service Association(669)
Hodges, James H.
National Meat Canners Association(526)
Hodges, Jeff
College Sports Information Directors of America(252)
Hodson, Colleen
Dude Ranchers' Association(288)
Hoelter, Matt
The American Electrophoresis Society(80)
Hoenninger, Ph.D., A.R.
International Association Colon Hydro Therapy(349)
Hoerle, Heather
National Association of Independent Schools(457)
Hofacre, Dr. Charles L.
American Association of Avian Pathologists(38)
Hoffa, James P.
International Brotherhood of Teamsters, AFL-CIO(363)
Hoffacker, Claudia
Health Care Compliance Association(322)
Hoffbuhr, Jack W.
American Water Works Association(154)
Hoffman, Ann Marie
National Rehabilitation Association(535)
Hoffman, Bill
Object Management Group(563)
Hoffman, Carrie
National Association of Metal Finishers(461)
Hoffman, Donna
Society of University Otolaryngologists(645)
Hoffman, Jennifer
Association of Social Work Boards(214)
Hoffman, Kathleen
Association of Social Work Boards(214)
Hoffman, Kenneth W.
Consumer Healthcare Products Association(263)
Hoffman, Philip D.
Travel Journalists Guild(665)
Hoffmann, Heinz K.
Independent Professional Painting Contractors Association of America(335)
Hoffpauir, Elvis L.
Mobile Air Conditioning Society Worldwide(420)
Hofman, Steven
American Association of School Librarians(50)
Hogan, CAE, Carol T.
American Sports Builders Association(148)
Hogan, David
National Retail Federation(536)
Hogan, Ph.D., M. Michelle
American Association of Immunologists(44)
Hogan, Mark
National Concrete Masonry Association(492)
Hogan, Matt
Association of Fish and Wildlife Agencies(197)
Hoggard, CAE, PAHM, Kerry B.
American Health Lawyers Association(89)
Hogle, Maureen
Association of State Dam Safety Officials(215)
Hohhof, Bonnie
Society of Competitive Intelligence Professionals(633)
Hohimer, Colette Iocca
Association of Bone and Joint Surgeons(188)
Hoiland, Joel
International Warehouse Logistics Association(396)
Window and Door Manufacturers Association(689)
Holaday, Gerald W.
American Poultry International(117)
Holbus, Ed
Carwash Owner's and Supplier's Association(238)
Hold, Dr. William T.
Society of Certified Insurance Counselors(632)
Holden, Fran
League of Historic American Theatres(406)
Holderby, Marla
Musculoskeletal Tumor Society(422)
Holdgreve, Christopher
National Grain and Feed Association(514)
Holdsworth, Thomas W.
Skills USA(611)
Holehan, Lt. Col. William
Reserve Officers Association of the U.S.(600)
Holeman, Scott
National Association of Insurance Commissioners(458)
Hollan, II, James F.
National Shoe Retailers Association(539)
Hollan, Mary L.
Yacht Brokers Association of America(698)
Holland, Dorothy
American Association of Teachers of Esperanto(52)
Holland, Kimberly
Professional Liability Underwriting Society(588)
Holland, Lisa
Community Action Partnership(255)
Holland, Michael M.
American Council for Construction Education(75)
Holland, Peter
CoreNet Global(266)
Holland, AAP, Priscilla
NACHA - The Electronic Payments Association(424)
Hollander, Ellie
American Association of Retired Persons(50)
Hollander, Richard E.
Society of Industrial and Office REALTORS(638)
Hollenbeck, Sonya
Earthquake Engineering Research Institute(288)
Holler, Richard
Association of Shareware Professionals(214)
Holleyman, II, Robert W.
Business Software Alliance(236)
Hollfelder, Jack
American Marketing Association(103)
Holliday, Peggy W.
National Science Education Leadership Association(538)
Holliday, Tom
Retail Advertising and Marketing Association International(601)
Holliday, Wayne
American Society for Nondestructive Testing(131)
Holliday, Wendy
National Association of College Stores(444)
Hollingsworth, Tracy
Manufacturers Alliance/MAPI(411)
Hollins, Cheryl J.
American Highway Users Alliance(90)
Hollis, Nicholas E.
Agribusiness Council(12)
Holloman, Bridget
National Motorsports Press Association(528)
Holloway, Tom
Conference on Latin American History(261)
Holman, James E.
National Blacksmiths and Weldors Association(485)
Holmberg, Laura
NARTE(425)
Holmes, June T.
Property Casualty Insurers Association of America(591)
Holmes, Karen Tucker
Association of Women's Health, Obstetric and Neonatal Nurses(220)
Holmes, Rory
INDA, Association of the Nonwoven Fabrics Industry(333)
Holmgren, Hoag
Professional and Organizational Development Network in Higher Education(585)
Holoviak, Judy
American Geophysical Union(87)
Holst, CFP, Eugene R.
National Association of Osteopathic Foundations(463)
Holt, Brad
Document Management Industries Association(286)
Holt, Brenda
Power Transmission Distributors Association(582)
Holt, Elizabeth
American Gem Trade Association(86)
Holt, Jean
National District Attorneys Association(505)
Holt, Lawrence J.
National Council of Self-Insurers(500)
Holt, Tim
National School Supply and Equipment Association(538)
Holt, Tracy
National Association of Workforce Development Professionals(482)
Holton, Ann
American Academy of Facial Plastic and Reconstructive Surgery(22)
Holway, David
National Association of Government Employees(454)
Holzinger, Albert
Institute of Internal Auditors(342)
Holzman, CMP, Ellyn
American Academy of Insurance Medicine(24)

Homanick, Thomas
National Association of Colleges and Employers(444)
Homayounpour, Cyrus
University Continuing Education Association(679)
Homer, Jennifer
American Society for Training and Development(133)
Honaker, L. Michael
American Psychological Association(118)
Hone, Karen A.
Health Industry Representatives Association(323)
Honey, Martha
International Ecotourism Society(370)
Honeycutt, Gina
National Correctional Industries Association(496)
Honeycutt, Michael
Air Conditioning Contractors of America(13)
Honeycutt, CAE, Nancy R.
American Student Dental Association(149)
Honley, Steve
American Foreign Service Association(85)
Hood, Rita J.
AGN International - North America(11)
Hood, Ph.D., Thomas C.
Society for the Study of Social Problems(628)
Hoog, Adam
American College of Sports Medicine(70)
Hooks, Daniel
Voices for America's Children(684)
Hooks, Norma
International Double Reed Society(369)
Hooper, Jeff
National Cutting Horse Association(504)
Hoorman, Gary W.
American Society of Regional Anesthesia and Pain Medicine(145)
Society for Education in Anesthesia(616)
Society of Neurosurgical Anesthesia and Critical Care(641)
Hooten, George W.
National American Legion Press Association(430)
Hoover, Anne H.
American Health Lawyers Association(89)
Hoover, Carrie
International Public Management Association for Human Resources(384)
Hoover, MD, Eddie
National Medical Association(526)
Hope, Amy
AACC International(1)
International Society for Molecular Plant Microbe Interactions(387)
Hope, Amy
Master Brewers Association of the Americas(413)
Hope, Jan
REALTORS Land Institute(596)
Hope, Robert
Radiological Society of North America(594)
Hope, Samuel
National Association of Schools of Art and Design(470)
National Association of Schools of Dance(470)
National Association of Schools of Music(470)
National Association of Schools of Theatre(471)
Hoper, Mark
Fabricators and Manufacturers Association, International(300)
Hopkins, Debra
Continental Dorset Club(264)
Hopkins, Gerri
Association of Retail Marketing Services(212)
Hopp, Stanley M.
Society of Insurance Research(638)
Hopper, Ph.D., David L.
American Academy of Somnology(28)
Hopper, CAE, J. Alexander
Professional Photographers of America(588)
Hopper, Regina
United States Telecom Association(677)
Hoppert, Donald
American Public Health Association(119)
Horch, Tammy
American Society of Architectural Illustrators(134)
Horel, Paul L.
Crop Insurance Research Bureau(279)
Horen, Ph.D., Ian
Painting and Decorating Contractors of America(570)
Horiguchi, Yusuke
Institute of International Finance(342)
Horn, Ashley
American Association of Clinical Endocrinologists(39)
Horn, Betty B.
Label Packaging Suppliers Council(404)
Horn, Brian
Society of Financial Service Professionals(636)
Horn, Esther
Computer Assisted Language Instruction Consortium(257)
Horn, Lisa
Promotional Products Association International(591)
Horn, Lucille Dinon
American Anthropological Association(31)
Horne, Scott
Institute of Scrap Recycling Industries(343)
Horner, Michael J.
National Association of Water Companies(480)
Horner, Mickey
Art Therapy Credentials Board(162)
Horning, Brian
College Athletic Business Management Association(251)
National Association of Collegiate Directors of Athletics(444)
Horowitz, Roger
Business History Conference(235)
Horsley, John C.
American Association of State Highway and Transportation Officials(51)
Horton, Raquel
Self Insurance Institute of America, Inc.(608)
Horvath, Eve
National Litigation Support Services Association(525)
Horvath, R. Skip
Natural Gas Supply Association(550)
Horwich, Ann
Physician Insurers Association of America(577)
Horzepa, Joseph
Power Sources Manufacturers Association(582)
Hoskie, Joni
American Academy of Optometry(25)
Hoskins, Angela
National Association of Pizza Operators(464)
Hoskins, Jr., M.D., H. Dunbar
American Academy of Ophthalmology(25)
Hoskins, Kathy
Council of Science Editors(274)
National Association of Corporate Treasurers(446)
Hossack, Diana
OPERA America(565)
Hostetler, Jim
National Association of Health Underwriters(455)
Hoting, Hilarie
Grocery Manufacturers Association(320)
Hotz, Jane L.
Farm Equipment Wholesalers Association(301)
Hou, Paul
National Electrical Manufacturers Association(506)
Hough, Douglas R.
Institute of Diving(341)
Hough, Harry E.
American Purchasing Society(120)
Hough, Robert
Red Angus Association of America(597)
Houghland, Jr., CAE, Paul
National Hardwood Lumber Association(516)
Houghton, Melissa
Women in Film and Video(692)
Houngbedji, Brigitte
Illuminating Engineering Society of North America(332)
Hourahan, P.E., Glenn
Air Conditioning Contractors of America(13)
House, Chuck
Grain Elevator and Processing Society(319)
Houston, Betsy
Federation of Materials Socs.(304)
Houston, Brant
Investigative Reporters and Editors(398)
Houston, Ph.D., K. Todd
Alexander Graham Bell Association for the Deaf and Hard of Hearing(15)
Houston, Katherine
Global Offset and Countertrade Association(317)
Houston, Paul D.
American Association of School Administrators(50)
Hovanky, Thoai
National Association of Independent Schools(457)
Hovey, Lisa K.
International Association for Food Protection(350)
Hovis, Jr., John H.
United Electrical, Radio and Machine Workers of America(671)
Howard, Angelina
Nuclear Energy Institute(563)
Howard, Ann
American Association for Homecare(35)
Howard, III, Eli
Sheet Metal and Air Conditioning Contractors' National Association(610)
Howard, Fred
Case Management Society of America(238)
Howard, Jerry
National Association of Home Builders(456)
Howard, Karen
American Association of Naturopathic Physicians(46)
Howard, Keith
American Society for Healthcare Food Service Administrators(129)
Howard, Laura
National Association of Nutrition and Aging Services Programs(463)
Howard, Marvin
International Beverage Dispensing Equipment Association(362)

Howard, Vern
National Christian College Athletic Association(489)
Howarth, Randall S.
Association of Ancient Historians(186)
Howe, Jr., Edwin A.
National Real Estate Forum(535)
Howe, William H.
Association of Bituminous Contractors(187)
Howell, Dita
National Association of Graphic and Product Identification Manufacturers(455)
Howell, Jack
IEEE Communications Society(330)
Howell, Mary
American Apparel & Footwear Association(31)
Howell, Steve
American Institute of Aeronautics and Astronautics(94)
Howells-Tierney, Janet
Technology and Maintenance Council of American Trucking Associations(658)
Howlett, Jr., Clifford T.
Chlorine Chemistry Council(245)
Hoyer, Maggie
Organization Development Network(566)
Hoyle, Robin
American Venous Forum(153)
Hoyt, Donald
Carbonated Beverage Institute(237)
Hrzic, Diyana
AMT - The Association For Manufacturing Technology(156)
Hsu, Pi-Lan
CPCU Society(278)
Hsu, Stephanie
Association for Asian American Studies(167)
Huband, Dr. Frank L.
American Society for Engineering Education(128)
Hubbard, Dan
National Business Aviation Association(486)
Huber, R. James
National Association of Chain Drug Stores(442)
Huberman, Mark A.
International Association of Hygienic Physicians(358)
Hucker, Douglas K.
American Gem Trade Association(86)
Hudgins, Chris
Association of Home Appliance Manufacturers(200)
Hudlin, Warrington
Black Filmmaker Foundation(230)
Hudson, Glen
National Sportscasters and Sportswriters Association(543)
Hudson, J. William
International Association for Cold Storage Construction(349)
International Association of Refrigerated Warehouses(360)
International Refrigerated Transportation Association(384)
Hudson, Lesley M.
American Spinal Injury Association(148)
Huestis, Marilyn A.
International Association of Forensic Toxicologists(357)
Huff, Charlie
International Association of Milk Control Agencies(359)
Huff, Rick
Western Music Association(687)
Huffhines, Craig
American Hereford Association(90)
Huffman, Jr., Dr. D.C.
American College of Apothecaries(64)
Huffman, Ph.D., Randall
American Meat Institute(103)
Huffman, Robert
Association of Edison Illuminating Companies(194)
Huget, Laurie
Cryogenic Society of America(280)
Huggins, Jim
Solar Rating and Certification Corp.(647)
Huggins, P.E., Roland
American Fire Sprinkler Association(84)
Hughes, Cathy
NAMM - the International Music Products Association(425)
Hughes, Dede
National Association of Women in Construction(481)
Hughes, Dyanne
American Association of School Administrators(50)
Hughes, Gail D.
Association of Paroling Authorities, International(207)
Hughes, II, Gordon T.
American Business Media(60)
Hughes, J. Trevor
International Association of Privacy Professionals(360)
Hughes, Jeff
GAMA International(313)
Hughes, John P.
Electricity Consumers Resource Council(291)
Hughes, Joseph E.M.
Shipowners Claims Bureau(610)
Hughes, Kathleen M.
Public Library Association(592)
Hughes, Kathy
National Certification Council for Activity Professionals(488)
Hughes, Ken
American Rental Association(122)
Hughes, Melanie K.
National Greenhouse Manufacturers Association(515)
Hughes, Mike
National Golf Course Owners Association(514)
Hughes, Nancy
American Academy of Physician Assistants(27)
Hughes, Robert
National Association for the Self-Employed(436)
Hughes, CAE, Sharon M.
National Council of Agricultural Employers(498)
Huidston, Pat
Catholic Charities USA(239)
Hull, Donna M.
ASABE - the Society for Engineering in Agricultural, Food and Biological Systems(162)
Hull, Patricia
National Association of Professional Mortgage Women(466)
Hull, Richard
Text and Academic Authors Association(659)
Hull, Sharon
American Catholic Correctional Chaplains Association(61)
Hull, W.N.
International Association of Railway Operating Officers(360)
Hull, Warren R.
American Paso Fino Horse Association(113)
Hulsey, Charles C.
Tennessee Walking Horse Breeders and Exhibitors Association(659)
Hult, G. Tomas M.
Academy of International Business(3)
Hultquist, Nancy
Pedorthic Footwear Association(572)
Hultz, Gloria
North American Association of Wardens and Superintendents(555)
Hume-Pratuch, Jeffery E.
National Association of Independent Colleges and Universities(457)
Humes, Paul
National Ground Water Association(515)
Humphrey, Carol Sue
American Journalism Historians Association(99)
Humphrey, Missy
Art Directors Guild/Scenic, Title and Graphic Artists(161)
Humphreys, Adell
National Air Traffic Controllers Association(428)
Humphreys, Debra
Association of American Colleges and Universities(184)
Huneke, Jonathan A.
United States Council for International Business(674)
Hung, Dr. David P.J.
American Acupuncture Association(29)
Hungiville, Beth L.
Marine Fabricators Association(412)
Hunkler, Chris
Professional Golfers Association of America(587)
Hunn, Bruce
American Society of Heating, Refrigerating and Air-Conditioning Engineers(139)
Hunnam, Joan
Reusable Industrial Packaging Association(601)
Hunnicutt, Dr. David M.
Wellness Councils of America(687)
Hunsicker, Dr. Ronald J.
National Association of Addiction Treatment Providers(438)
Hunt, Jr., A. Lee
International Association of Drilling Contractors(356)
Hunt, Acacia G.
Society of Professional Benefit Administrators(642)
Hunt, Chris
Infusion Nurses Society(338)
Hunt, David
Family, Career, and Community Leaders of America(300)
Hunt, Elizabeth K.
Basic Acrylic Monomer Manufacturers(226)
Methacrylate Producers Association(418)
Hunt, Jr., Frederick D.
Society of Professional Benefit Administrators(642)
Hunt, Jayne Ellen
Consumer Bankers Association(263)
Hunt, Joseph
International Association of Bridge, Structural, Ornamental and Reinforcing Iron Workers(354)

Hunt, Nancy R.
American Academy of Psychotherapists(28)
Hunt, Pamela S.
International Society for Developmental Psychobiology(387)
Hunt, Scott
Endocrine Society(294)
Hunter, Bruce
American Association of School Administrators(50)
Hunter, Cecilia
American Association of Physicists in Medicine(48)
Hunter, Chris
College Savings Plans Network(252)
Hunter, Claudia
National Precast Concrete Association(534)
Hunter, G. William
National Basketball Players Association(483)
Hunter, Karen
American Concrete Pipe Association(73)
Hunter, Kirk
Turfgrass Producers International(667)
Hunter, Lesley E.
Association of Water Technologies(220)
Hunter, Michael
American Council of Life Insurers(75)
Hunter, Shelley
American Academy of Equine Art(22)
Hunter, T. Kirk
Lawn Institute(406)
Huntley, Jery Y.
Vinyl Siding Institute(683)
Huot, Edward C.
United Electrical, Radio and Machine Workers of America(671)
Hurley, Gerald C.
National Industrial Sand Association(519)
Hurley, Karen A.
National Fastener Distributors Association(508)
Hurley, Karin S.
International Formalwear Association(373)
Hurley, Morgan
Society of Fire Protection Engineers(636)
Hurley, Patrick
American Association of Candy Technologists(39)
Hurson, John
Cosmetic, Toiletry and Fragrance Association(267)
Hurst, Julia
National Lieutenant Governors Association(524)
Hurt, Frank
Bakery, Confectionery, Tobacco Workers and Grain Millers International Union(225)
Hurt, Symone
COLA(250)
Hurter, Bill
Wedding and Portrait Photographers International(686)
Hurtgen, Nancy
BioCommunications Association(229)
Hurula, Barbara
Federation of Environmental Technologists(303)
Huse, Brian
Robotic Industries Association(602)
Hussey, Patricia
Consolidated Tape Association(262)
Huston, CTRS, Ann D.
American Therapeutic Recreation Association(151)
Huston, Sandy
Christian Management Association(246)
Hutchcraft, Sid
Pony of the Americas Club(580)
Hutchcraft, Tom
American Council of Independent Laboratories(75)
Hutcherson, Carolyn
American College of Nurse Practitioners(68)
Hutcherson, Victor
Society for Applied Spectroscopy(614)
Hutchings, Carol
High Technology Crime Investigation Association(325)
Hutchins, PhD, Michael
Wildlife Society, The(689)
Hutchinson, Bob
Wireless Dealers Association(690)
Hutchinson, Edward "Ted"
American Society of Law, Medicine and Ethics(140)
Hutchinson, Suzanne C.
Mortgage Insurance Companies of America(421)
Hutchison, Karen
International Society of Weighing and Measurement(392)
Society for Historical Archaeology(618)
Hutchison, Russell E.
Contractors Pump Bureau(264)
Hutton, Kenneth R.
National Vehicle Leasing Association(548)
Wood Machinery Manufacturers of America(694)
Hutton, Paul Andrew
Western History Association(687)
Hutton, Sandra
International Textile and Apparel Association(394)
Hutton, Steve
All-America Rose Selections(15)
Huxel, Robert
National Fraternal Congress of America(512)
Huynh, Thuan
Association of School Business Officials International(212)
Hyatt, David F.
National Automobile Dealers Association(482)
Hyde, Barbara
American Society for Microbiology(130)
Hyde, Jay
National Governors Association(514)
Hyman, Andrew
National Association of State Mental Health Program Directors(476)
Hyps, Brian M.
American Society of Plant Biologists(144)
Hytten, Kathy
Philosophy of Education Society(576)
Iacuzzi, Judith Q.
U.S.A. Toy Library Association(669)
Ian, Jennifer
Public Relations Society of America(593)
Iasiello, Camille S.
National Association of Chemical Distributors(442)
Ibitz, Brenda
National Precast Concrete Association(534)
Ibrahim, Tod
Association of Professors of Medicine(209)
Association of Subspecialty Professors(216)
Clerkship Directors in Internal Medicine(248)
Ice, Gillian H.
Human Biology Association(329)
Iciek, James E.
National Academy of Opticianry(427)
Ide, Ruby
American Beefalo World Registry(56)
Ignagni, CAE, Karen M.
America's Health Insurance Plans(19)
Igoe, Kim
American Association of Museums(45)
Iliff, Heather
Alliance for Nonprofit Management(15)
Ilon, Lynn
Comparative and International Education Society(256)
Inchauteguiz, Peter
American Association of Pharmaceutical Scientists(48)
Ingemie, David J.
SnowSports Industries America(612)
Ingersoll, Cheryl
Fashion Group International(301)
Ingle, Gary
Music Teachers National Association(423)
Ingley, Kathryn P.
International Association of Electrical Inspectors(356)
Ingoglia, Charles
National Council for Community Behavioral Healthcare(497)
Ingraham, Peggy
Meals On Wheels Association of America(414)
Ingram, Charles
National Association of State Departments of Agriculture(474)
Ingram, Tom
Diving Equipment and Marketing Association(286)
Ingrassia, Phil
Recreation Vehicle Dealers Association of North America(596)
Inman, Harry A.
Inter-American Bar Association(346)
Inman, Pam Hewlett
American Hotel & Lodging Association(92)
Intorre, Ben
American Musicians Union(107)
Ireland, CAE, Evelyn F.
National Association of Dental Plans(449)
Ireland, Michael
Association for Facilities Engineering(172)
Irick, Nicole
Omega Delta(564)
Irish, Anne
Association of Booksellers for Children(188)
Irmiter, Charles
American Symphony Orchestra League(150)
Irons, Jessica Jones
National Humanities Alliance(518)
Irvin, David
American Association for Cancer Research(34)
Irvine, M. Susie
American Financial Services Association(83)
Isaacs, Ph.D., Harold
Association of Third World Studies(218)
Isbell, Elizabeth A.
Council of Landscape Architectural Registration Boards(273)
Isler, Merle
Alliance of Black Telecommunications Employees(16)
Israel, Lillian
Association for Computing Machinery(170)
Israelite, David
National Music Publishers' Association(528)

Itarralde, Elsie
National Association of the Remodeling Industry(479)

Iversen, Eric
American Society for Engineering Education(128)

Ives, Ralph
Advanced Medical Technology Association(8)

Ivie, George
Media Rating Council(415)

Ivory, Megan
Advanced Medical Technology Association(8)

Ivory, Shanda T.
National Association for College Admission Counseling(432)

Ivy, Joanne C.
American Egg Board(80)

Ivy, Lloyd M.
American Fire Sprinkler Association(84)

Jachnicki, Robert J.
National Insurance Crime Bureau(522)

Jackman, Diane
Association for Career and Technical Education Research(169)

Jackman, Ph.D., Wm. Jay
National Association of Agricultural Educators(438)

Jackobson, Carlotta
Cosmetic Executive Women(267)

Jackson, Andrew P.
Black Caucus of the American Library Association(230)

Jackson, Carolyn
American Association of Family and Consumer Sciences(43)

Jackson, Deb
Fulfillment Management Association(312)

Jackson, Dorothy
American Gaming Association(86)

Jackson, Gayle
Surface Mount Technology Association(656)

Jackson, Greg
Associated Locksmiths of America(165)

Jackson, Judith
National Association of Black Social Workers(440)

Jackson, Karen
Tag and Label Manufacturers Institute(657)

Jackson, Kim E.
International Parking Institute(382)

Jackson, Liz
Walnut Council(685)

Jackson, Ph.D., Marcia
American College of Cardiology(64)

Jackson, Megan
National Family Planning and Reproductive Health Association(508)

Jackson, Robin
International Corrugated Packaging Foundation(367)

Jacob, Maryann
Poetry Society of America(579)

Jacober, Steven L.
School, Home and Office Products Association(606)

Jacobs, Christine
Association of Military Banks of America(205)

Jacobs, David
Eight Sheet Outdoor Advertising Association(290)

Jacobs, Gabriella
Association for Facilities Engineering(172)

Jacobs, Jane
North American Meat Processors Association(558)

Jacobs, Jeff P.
American Society for Clinical Pathology(127)

Jacobs, Jerald A.
American Society of Association Executives & Center for Association Leadership(134)

Jacobs, Karl
American Teleservices Association(151)

Jacobs, Madeleine
American Chemical Society(62)

Jacobshagen, CAE, Rosemary
Appliance Parts Distributors Association(159)
North American Retail Dealers Association(559)

Jacobsohn, Alice
Environmental Industry Associations(296)

Jacobson, CAE, Eric
American Lighting Association(101)

Jacobson, Gretchen
NACE International(424)

Jacobson, M.D., Harry R.
Society of Medical Administrators(639)

Jacobson, Jon
American Benefits Council(56)

Jacobson, Mark
National Intramural-Recreational Sports Association(522)

Jacobson, Shirley
American Institute of Aeronautics and Astronautics(94)

Jacobson, Terry
Endocrine Society(294)

Jacques, Kimberley
Physician Insurers Association of America(577)

Jaeger, Art
National Cooperative Business Association(496)

Jaeger, Kathleen D.
Generic Pharmaceutical Association(315)

Jaeger, Stefan
National Society of Professional Engineers(542)

Jafari, Danielle
Telecommunications Industry Association(659)

Jaffeson, AICP, ACA, Richard C.
National Certification Commission(488)

Jagoe, John R.
Export Institute of the United States(300)

Jagtiani, Patricia W.
Natural Gas Supply Association(550)

Jahn, Christopher L.
Contract Services Association of America(264)

Jaimes, Doris
National Investment Company Service Association(522)

Jakab, M.D., Irene
American Society of Psychopathology of Expression(145)

Jakusz, Heather
International Interior Design Association(377)

Jamall, Cheryl
American Boiler Manufacturers Association(58)

James, CAE, Diane
Women's Transportation Seminar(694)

James, Lawrence P.
International Foundation for Telemetering(373)

James, CAE, Philip J.
National Glass Association(513)

James, CPA, Richard J.
American Institute of Architects(94)

James, Sarah R.
SOLE - The International Society of Logistics(647)

James, Steve
Bowling Writers Association of America(232)

James, Tom
Truck Renting and Leasing Association(666)

Jamison, Dixie
National Alcohol Beverage Control Association(429)

Janela, Joseph
Endocrine Society(294)

Janik, Laurene K.
National Association of REALTORS(468)

Janis, Lenore
Professional Women in Construction(590)

Jannetti, Anthony J.
Society of Urologic Nurses and Associates(645)

Janny, June
America's Community Bankers(19)

Janosko, Andrew
Telecommunications Industry Association(659)

Janovy, Dr. John
American Society of Parasitologists(143)

Janowiak, Robert M.
Electrical and Computer Engineering Department Heads Association(290)

Jansen, Judith
Society for the Study of Reproduction(628)

Janssen, Nancy
Food Processing Machinery and Supplies Association(309)

Jansto, Bob
Association of Trial Lawyers of America(218)

Jantsch, CAE, APR, Dawn
American Culinary Federation(77)

Jantz, Amy
Telework Advisory Group for World at Work(659)

Janz, Milli
American Community Cultural Center Association(72)

Janzen, Judith M.
Church and Synagogue Library Association(246)

Jarboe, Ed
National Association of Professional Organizers(466)

Jardine, Ellen
Association for Experiential Education(172)

Jarvis, Gigi
Industrial Designers Society of America(336)

Jarvis, Susan
Municipal Waste Management Association(422)

Jaspram, Elaine
Meeting Professionals International(416)

Jass, Karen
Women in Mining National(692)

Jaworowski, Michelle
National Association of Electrical Distributors(450)

Jaworski, Janet L.
American Membrane Technology Association(105)

Jeager, J.
Embroidery Council of America(292)

Jeanneret, Matt
American Road and Transportation Builders Association(123)

Jeffries, Craig
American Ass'n of Ambulatory Surgery Centers(32)

Jeffries, Dottie
American Psychoanalytic Association(118)

Jelinek, Laura
American Association of Oral and Maxillofacial Surgeons(47)
Jeng, Ling Hwey
Asian/Pacific American Librarians Association(163)
Jenkins, Annie
Association for the Advancement of International Education(179)
Jenkins, Missy
Pharmaceutical Care Management Association(575)
Jenkins, CMP, Ozzie
National Association of Health Services Executives(455)
Jenkins, Ozzie
National Coalition of Black Meeting Planners(490)
Jenkins, Tonja
National Burglar and Fire Alarm Association(486)
Jennings, Carolynn
Home Fashion Products Association(327)
National Society for Healthcare Foodservice Management(540)
Window Coverings Manufacturers Association(689)
Jennings, Gary
American Southdown Breeders Association(148)
Jennings, Patricia T.
American Moving and Storage Association(107)
Jennings, Robert
Evidence Photographers International Council(299)
Jennison, Richard
Brick Industry Association(232)
Jenny, Louis J.
National Association of Water Companies(480)
Jensen, O.S.B., Joseph
Catholic Biblical Association of America(239)
Jensen, Wendy
Specialty Coffee Association of America(650)
Jeon, Jorri
American Hotel & Lodging Association(92)
Jeppesen, Rebecca
Hispanic Dental Association(326)
Jepson, Frank
American Logistics Association(102)
Jernigan, Bryan
National Association of Federally Impacted Schools(452)
Jerome, Michele
Community Associations Institute(255)
Jesse, William
Million Dollar Round Table(419)
Jessee, Valera B.
United Product Formulators and Distributors Association(672)
Jessee, M.D., FACMPE, William F.
American College of Medical Practice Executives(67)
Medical Group Management Association(416)
Jessup, Dave
American Association of Wildlife Veterinarians(54)
Jester, Jennifer Coffman
American Arbitration Association(32)
Jestis, Cheryl
University Film and Video Association(680)
Jesuele, Neil J.
Health Forum(323)
Jett, Brenda
National Show Horse Registry(539)
Jetton, Shellie
Association of Talent Agents(216)
Jeune, Victoria
American Association of Clinical Endocrinologists(39)
Jewart, Sheilah
American Society for Neurochemistry(130)
Jewell, Jane
Science Fiction and Fantasy Writers of America(606)
Jilly, Julie
Professional Tennis Registry(589)
Jockers, Matthew
American Conference for Irish Studies(73)
Jodon, Teresa
Horticultural Research Institute(328)
Joffe, Joan
National Association of Broadcasters(441)
Joffe, Judy
National Council on Compensation Insurance(502)
Johanns, Patrick
Alpha Chi Sigma(17)
Johanson, RN, MN, Wanda L.
American Association of Critical-Care Nurses(41)
Johanssen, Pamela
Association of Professors of Gynecology and Obstetrics(209)
Johansson, Daniel
Healthcare Financial Management Association(324)
John, Mark
Society of Cable Telecommunications Engineers(632)
Johns, Jacqueline
Institute for Operations Research and the Management Sciences(339)
Johns, Joe
Radio and Television Correspondents Association(594)
Johns, CAE, Kevin
Society of Cardiovascular Anesthesiologists(632)
Johns, Robert
National Dental Association(505)
National Dental Hygienists' Association(505)
Johnson, Dr. Alice L.
National Turkey Federation(548)
Johnson, Angela
National Association of Investment Companies(459)
Johnson, Anna
American Association of Medical Assistants(45)
Johnson, Dr. Bradley R.
Keramos Fraternity(403)
Johnson, Brett
United States Rowing Association(677)
Johnson, Bruce
Audit Bureau of Circulations(222)
Johnson, Cass
National Council of Textile Organizations(501)
Johnson, Catherine
COLA(250)
Johnson, Chelli
American Society of Hand Therapists(138)
Johnson, Cindy
International Association of Printing House Craftsmen(360)
Johnson, Cliff
NACE International(424)
Johnson, Clifford
National League of Cities(524)
Johnson, D. Wanda
National Indian Education Association(519)
Johnson, Dan E.
United Transportation Union(679)
Johnson, APR, Deanna
American Benefits Council(56)
Johnson, Debbie
American Diabetes Association(79)
Johnson, Deborah S.
Professional Women's Appraisal Association(590)
Johnson, Diane E.
Livestock Publications Council(409)
Johnson, Donald
Hearth Patio & Barbecue Association(324)
Johnson, Fred
Credit Union Executives Society(279)
Johnson, Fred
National Cotton Council of America(496)
Johnson, Gary
Association for Direct Instruction(171)
Johnson, Gay
National Association of Nurse Practitioners in Women's Health(463)
Johnson, Holly
North American Deer Farmers Association(556)
Johnson, Holly LaCroix
Institute for Supply Management(340)
Johnson, Jalmer M.
Air Line Pilots Association, International(13)
Johnson, James
United States Beet Sugar Association(673)
Johnson, Janelle
Society of Decorative Painters(635)
Johnson, Jennifer
American Society for Engineering Education(128)
Johnson, Jennifer J.
Council on Social Work Education(277)
Johnson, John
National Association of State Boating Law Administrators(473)
Johnson, Kathy
Organization of Black Designers(567)
Johnson, Kathy A.
National Association for Multi-Ethnicity in Communications(434)
Johnson, Katie Kenney
American Society of Law, Medicine and Ethics(140)
Johnson, Kelly M.
American Institute of Steel Construction(97)
Johnson, Ken
Pharmaceutical Research and Manufacturers of America(575)
Johnson, Kent
Classroom Publishers Association(247)
Johnson, Kim
Racking Horse Breeders Association of America(594)
Johnson, Laura
American Music Conference(107)
Johnson, Lee
National Association of Pupil Services Administrators(467)
Johnson, Mac
National Potato Promotion Board(533)
Johnson, Marlene M.
NAFSA: Association of International Educators(424)
Johnson, Michele
International Society of Arthroscopy, Knee Surgery and Orthopaedic Sports Medicine(390)

Johnson, Penelope
Council of Musculoskeletal Specialty Socs.(273)
Johnson, R. Craig
International Congress of Oral Implantologists(367)
Johnson, Rashod
Mason Contractors Association of America(413)
Johnson, Richard A.
Brotherhood Railway Carmen/TCU(233)
Johnson, Rob
Billiard Congress of America(228)
Johnson, Robert
Log Home Builders Association of North America(409)
Johnson, Robert G.
Association of Construction Inspectors(192)
Environmental Assessment Association(296)
International Real Estate Institute(384)
International Society of Meeting Planners(391)
International Travel Writers and Editors Association(395)
National Association of Real Estate Appraisers(468)
National Association of Review Appraisers and Mortgage Underwriters(469)
Johnson, Robert J.
National Association for Information Destruction(434)
Johnson, Robert K.
National Rural Water Association(538)
Johnson, Robert W.
Outdoor Amusement Business Association(569)
Johnson, Ryan
WorldatWork(697)
Johnson, Seth
American Guernsey Association(87)
Johnson, Sheryl
National Home Furnishings Association(517)
Johnson, Sonjya
American College of Osteopathic Surgeons(69)
Johnson, Steven D.
PrintImage International(584)
Johnson, Suzanne N.
International Brangus Breeders Association(363)
Johnson, CAE, Tanya Howe
National Committee on Planned Giving(491)
Johnson, Tom
National Directory Publishing Association(505)
Johnson, Vera
National Technical Services Association(546)
Johnson, Vic
NAFSA: Association of International Educators(424)
Johnson, Wanda
Endocrine Society(294)
Johnson, William
National Association of Police Organizations(465)
Johnson, William A.
American Society of Papyrologists(143)
Johnston, James J.
Owner-Operator Independent Drivers Association(570)
Johnston, Richard
Home Improvement Research Institute(327)
Johnston, Robert A.
American Academy of Physician Assistants(27)
Jolly, Robb
American Concrete Pavement Association(72)
Jones, Aislinn
American Academy of Religion(28)
Jones, Allison
National Alliance of Independent Crop Consultants(429)
Jones, Arnita A.
American Historical Association(91)
Jones, Arun W.
American Society of Missiology(141)
Jones, Brien K.
National Association of Certified Valuation Analysts(442)
Jones, Bruce H.
Commercial Finance Association(253)
Jones, David C.
International Trumpet Guild(395)
Jones, DeEtta
Association of Research Libraries(212)
Jones, Denise M.
American Society of Anesthesiologists(134)
Jones, Dolores C.
National Association of Pediatric Nurse Practitioners(464)
Jones, Donald C.
American Association of Clinical Endocrinologists(39)
Jones, Donald R.
American College of Chest Physicians(64)
Jones, Emily
American Shoulder and Elbow Surgeons(125)
Jones, Enid-Mai
Association of Schools and Colleges of Optometry(213)
Jones, Georgi
American Buckskin Registry Association(59)
Jones, Geri Duncan
American Health and Beauty Aids Institute(89)
Jones, Judith
National Association for Family and Community Education(433)
Jones, Laura E.
United States Association of Importers of Textiles and Apparel(673)
Jones, Dr. Linda
American Institute of Fishery Research Biologists(96)
Jones, Louisa E.
International Association for the Study of Pain(352)
Jones, Lynda
American Society of Ophthalmic Administrators(143)
Jones, Lynda
American Society of Addiction Medicine(133)
Jones, Michael
American Optometric Association(110)
Jones, Michael A.
National Juvenile Detention Association(523)
Jones, CMP, Michele M.
National Insulation Association(521)
Jones, Michelle
National Association of Independent Life Brokerage Agencies(457)
Jones, Newton B.
International Brotherhood of Boilermakers, Iron Ship Builders, Blacksmiths, Forgers and Helpers(363)
Jones, Patrick
International Bridge, Tunnel and Turnpike Association(363)
Jones, Penelope
National Academy of Clinical Biochemistry(426)
Jones, Penni
Independent Cosmetic Manufacturers and Distributors(333)
Jones, Randall T.
National Council of Farmer Cooperatives(499)
Jones, Jr., Ed.D., Robert P.
American Association for Thoracic Surgery(37)
American Surgical Association(150)
Society for Surgery of the Alimentary Tract(625)
Jones, Stella
Food Industry Suppliers Association(309)
Jones, Tambra
Futon Association International(313)
Specialty Sleep Association(650)
Jones, Tom
National School Public Relations Association(538)
Jones, Walter L.
Pine Chemicals Association(578)
Jordan, Cheryl
Healthcare Distribution Management Association(323)
Jordan, CAE, Janet
Congress of Chiropractic State Associations(261)
Jordan, Melody
Society of American Military Engineers(631)
Jordan, USAF(Ret.), Col. Michael
Military Officers Association of America(419)
Jorgensen, CPA, Wayne H.
Water Quality Association(686)
Jorpeland, Marshall S.
National Court Reporters Association(503)
Jorss, Ann
American Seed Trade Association(124)
National Council of Commercial Plant Breeders(498)
Joseph, Jeff
Consumer Electronics Association(263)
Joseph, M.P.S., CAE, Thomas L.
Society of Critical Care Medicine(634)
Joseph-Biddle, Jacqui
National Council of Teachers of English(501)
Josephson, Philip
Alpha Gamma Rho(17)
Joslin, Randy
Electrical Apparatus Service Association(290)
Jost, Mary
International Foundation of Employee Benefit Plans(373)
Jourdain, Charles
California Redwood Association(236)
Joy, Michele
Association of Oil Pipe Lines(206)
Joyce, Sherman "Tiger"
American Tort Reform Association(152)
Joyner, Nelson T.
Federation of International Trade Associations(304)
Joynes, Ed
National Association of Wholesaler-Distributors(481)
Juberts, Anita
Association for the Advancement of Baltic Studies(179)
Judd, Robert
American Musicological Society(107)
Judd, William
National Association of Power Engineers(465)
Judson, CMP, Bennett
National Roofing Contractors Association(537)
Jugenheimer, Donald
American Academy of Advertising(20)
Juhl, Jan
AERA - Engine Rebuilders Association(9)
Julia, Thomas A.
Composite Panel Association(257)

Julian, Carla
Associated General Contractors of America(165)
Juliano, Rich
American Road and Transportation Builders Association(123)
Juncan, Nicole
American Lighting Association(101)
Juneman, Gregory J.
International Federation of Professional and Technical Engineers(371)
Jurgonis, Charlie
American Federation of State, County and Municipal Employees(82)
Jurigian, Sandra L.
National Association for Armenian Studies and Research(431)
Jurkash, John
Government Finance Officers Association of the United States and Canada(318)
Jursnick, Robert
National Strength and Conditioning Association(543)
Jurus, William L.
American Chain of Warehouses(61)
Just, Marilee
Extra Touch Florists Association(300)
Justis, Ralph
Consumer Electronics Association(263)
Kaatz, Ervin
Santa Gertrudis Breeders International(605)
Kabadian, Melissa
Society for Vascular Surgery(629)
Kabin, Bonnie
WorldatWork(697)
Kachelski, CAE, Barbara
Credit Union Executives Society(279)
Kadrich, Lee
Automotive Aftermarket Industry Association(223)
Kagan, Eve Gamzu
American College of Toxicology(71)
Kahan, Alan
Entomological Society of America(295)
Kahan, Marlene
American Society of Magazine Editors(141)
Kahn, III, Charles N.
Federation of American Hospitals(303)
Kahn, Jerry
International Physical Fitness Association(383)
Kahn, CAE, Lynn
American Society of Plastic Surgeons(144)
Kahn, Ph.D., Richard
American Diabetes Association(79)
Kaiser, Don
Pellet Fuels Institute(573)
Kaiser, Dr. Marvin A.
Society for Values in Higher Education(629)
Kaiser, Timothy G.
Public Housing Authorities Directors Association(592)
Kaitz, James
Association for Financial Professionals(173)
Kajiwara, Karen
Natural Science Collections Alliance(551)
Kalert, Jane
AAGL -- Advancing Minimally Invasive Gynecology Worldwide(1)
Kalinich, Dr. Lila J.
Association for Psychoanalytic Medicine(177)
Kalisch, Bert
American Public Gas Association(119)
Kalish, Susan
Hearth Patio & Barbecue Association(324)
Kalkwarf, Jonathan
Metal Service Center Institute(417)
Kaller, Richard
Certified Contractors NetWork(242)
Kalteis, Natasha
General Federation of Women's Clubs(315)
Kam, Karl
International Advertising Association(348)
Kamann, Kris
Continental Basketball Association(264)
Kamenicky, Jean
American Romney Breeders Association(123)
Kamin, Jamie
Association of State and Interstate Water Pollution Control Administrators(214)
Kaminsky, Harry
American Arbitration Association(32)
Kampman, Rosalba
Biophysical Society(229)
Kanaby, Robert F.
National Federation of State High School Associations(510)
Kanagy, David L.
Society for Mining, Metallurgy, and Exploration(622)
Kane, Anthony
American Association of State Highway and Transportation Officials(51)
Kane, Daniel J.
United Mine Workers of America International Union(672)
Kane, Dennis
American Egg Board(80)
Kane, Francis J.
International Copper Association(367)
Kane, Gerry
Association for Iron and Steel Technology(175)
Kane, Terry M.
Industrial Diamond Association of America(336)
Kania, John
IPC - Association Connecting Electronics Industries(399)
IPC - Surface Mount Equipment Manufacturers Association(399)
Kaniewski, Donald J.
Laborers' International Union of North America(404)
Kaniss, Phyllis
American Academy of Political and Social Science(27)
Kanitra, Paul
Associated Locksmiths of America(165)
Kankam-Boadu, Yvonne
American Council on Education(76)
Kanon, Carolyn
American Bankruptcy Institute(55)
Kantor, Jane
American Holistic Medical Association(91)
Kanwit, Stephanie
America's Health Insurance Plans(19)
Kaplan, Alex
Organization for International Investment(567)
Kaplan, Dr. Alfred Schnell
National Association of Family Development Centers(452)
Kaplan, Dan
Automotive Aftermarket Industry Association(223)
Kaplan, Joe
Professional Tattoo Artists Guild(589)
Kaplan, Keith
Fur Information Council of America(313)
Kaplan, Marianne G.
American Spinal Injury Association(148)
Kaplan, Robert A.
Clothing Manufacturers Association of the U.S.A.(248)
Kaplan, Stephanie
Power Transmission Distributors Association(582)
Kappas, George
American Hypnosis Association(92)
Kappel, Dawn
National Council of State Boards of Nursing(500)
Karasu, M.D., T. Byram
Association for the Advancement of Psychotherapy(179)
Karch, Cathy
CPCU Society(278)
Karcher, David A.
American Society of Cataract and Refractive Surgery(135)
Karel, Joseph R.
Turnaround Management Association(667)
Karen, Jay
National Golf Course Owners Association(514)
Karlson, Ph.D., David
Society of General Internal Medicine(637)
Karlsson, Jens
Society for Cryobiology(616)
Karney, R. J.
American Farm Bureau Federation(81)
Karol, Robin
Product Development and Management Association(585)
Karpel, Richard
Association of Alternative Newsweeklies(184)
Karpers-Burke, Mary
Society for Clinical Trials(615)
Karpick, Carey
Association of Health Insurance Advisors(199)
Karr, Cathy
Society of American Travel Writers(631)
Karson, Jennifer
Dietary Managers Association(284)
Kasabian, Robert J.
International Newspaper Financial Executives(381)
Kasper, Joan
National Association for Printing Leadership(435)
Kasper, Ph.D., CAE, John E.
American Society of Clinical Hypnosis(135)
Usability Professionals' Association(681)
Kasperian, Seta
Motion Picture and Television Credit Association(421)
Kass, Fritz
Intercollegiate Broadcasting System(346)
Kass, Jim
National Golf Foundation(514)
Kassalen, Beth A.
International Transplant Nurses Society(394)
Kassouf, Kass
Consumer Healthcare Products Association(263)
Kastner, Michael E.
National Truck Equipment Association(547)
Kasunich, Cheryl
American Academy of Physician Assistants(27)
Katanick, CAE, Sandra
Intersocietal Accreditation Commission(398)

Katos, Demetrios
Orthodox Theological Society in America(568)
Katsoris, Elaine
Refrigeration Service Engineers Society(597)
Katterman, William
International Silk Association(386)
Katz, David
American Book Producers Association(58)
Katz, Eliza
Association of Children's Museums(189)
Katz, Irv
National Human Services Assembly(518)
Katz, Jonathan
National Assembly of State Arts Agencies(431)
Katz, Kyle
Producer's Guild of America(584)
Katzman, Jesse
Surface Mount Technology Association(656)
Kaufman, Herb
SAE International(604)
Kausar, M.D., Rehana
Islamic Medical Association of North America(400)
Kautter, CAE, Tina
Society for Technological Advancement of Reporting(626)
Kautter, CAE, Willard S.
National Association of Physician Recruiters(464)
Kauvar, Joanne
Council of American Jewish Museums(270)
Kavanaugh, Larry
American Iron and Steel Institute(98)
Kaveny, Don
American College of Osteopathic Surgeons(69)
Kay, Maggie
American Podiatric Medical Association(116)
Kay, Malvina
Independent Sector(336)
Kay, Sally
Hosiery Association, The(328)
Kay, Stephen R.
International Bottled Water Association(362)
Kaylor, Debbie
National Cattlemen's Beef Association(488)
Kays, B. Thomas
Psi Omega(591)
Kealing, Susan
National Foundation for Credit Counseling(512)
Kean, Richard I.
Business Marketing Association(235)
Keane, Christopher M.
American Geological Institute(87)
Keane, Kevin
Wire Service Guild(690)
Keane, Kevin P.
International Association of Printing House Craftsmen(360)
Keane, Kevin W.
American Beverage Association(56)
Keane, Lawrence
National Shooting Sports Foundation(539)
Keane, CAE, Tony
NACE International(424)
Kearns, Brian D.
United States Energy Association(675)
Kearns, Cathleen B.
American Association of Colleges of Osteopathic Medicine(40)
Kearns, Kevin L.
United States Business and Industry Council(674)
Kearns, Michael
National Ocean Industries Association(529)
Keating, Frank
American Council of Life Insurers(75)
Keating, Patricia H.
Air Distributing Institute(13)
Keating, Ted
National Association of Postal Supervisors(465)
Keating, Rev. Ted
Conference of Major Superiors of Men, U.S.A.(259)
Keck, Daniel E.
Healthcare Financial Management Association(324)
Keck, Layne C.
National Society of Hypnotherapists(542)
Keebler, Barbara A.
National Catholic Educational Association(487)
Keefe, Marilyn
National Family Planning and Reproductive Health Association(508)
Keegel, C. Thomas
International Brotherhood of Teamsters, AFL-CIO(363)
Keehan, DC, Sr. Carol
Catholic Health Association of the United States(240)
Keel, Judith K.
Association of Women Surgeons(220)
Independent Medical Distributors Association(335)
Keeler, Kelley
Associated General Contractors of America(165)
Keeler-Pettigrew, Meaghan
Women in International Security(692)
Keeling, CAE, J. Michael
ESOP Association(297)
Keeling, John R.
National Potato Council(533)
Keen, Mary Lou
American Gem Trade Association(86)
Keenan, CAE, Barbara Byrd
Institute of Food Technologists(341)
Keenan, Ed.D., Derek
Association of Christian Schools International(190)
Keenan, Mary
American Nuclear Society(109)
Keene, Robert C.
American Academy of Gold Foil Operators(23)
Keene, Steve
Disaster Preparedness and Emergency Response Association(285)
Keeney, Tyler T.
Mailing & Fulfillment Service Association(410)
Keenum, John M.
American Antiquarian Society(31)
Keese, Bill
Association of Progressive Rental Organizations(210)
Keeter, Phil
Marine Retailers Association of America(412)
Kehlbeck, Keith
Select Registry/Distinguished Inns of North America(608)
Keightly, John
Catholic Charities USA(239)
Keilitz, Dave
American Baseball Coaches Association(56)
Keillor, Cynthia L.
Microscopy Society of America(418)
Keippel, Judy
National Association of Women Highway Safety Leaders(481)
Keiser, Lauren
Music Publishers' Association of the United States(423)
Keith, David
National Religious Broadcasters(536)
Keith, Floyd
Black Coaches Association(230)
Keith, Kendell W.
National Grain and Feed Association(514)
Keithley, Carter E.
Toy Industry Association(662)
Kell, Brian
American Thoracic Society(151)
Kelleher, Jack
Amusement and Music Operators Association(156)
Kelleher, Linda
National Investor Relations Institute(522)
Kelleher, Rita
Association of Schools of Public Health(213)
Keller, Billilynne
Custom Electronic Design and Installation Association(280)
Keller, Jennifer
National Federation of Music Clubs(509)
Keller, Kevin
Association for Financial Professionals(173)
Keller, Michael
Commercial Finance Association(253)
Keller, Michael E.
American Society of Test Engineers(146)
Keller, Robin
Business Technology Association(236)
Kelley, Allison
Romance Writers of America(603)
Kelley, Charles M.
Dance Educators of America(281)
Kelley, Colleen M.
National Treasury Employees Union(547)
Kelley, Kara
Electronic Retailing Association(292)
Kelley, Lisa
Career College Association(237)
Kelley, Tom
Truck Writers of North America(666)
Kelliher, Bruce M.
National Automobile Dealers Association(482)
Kellmeyer, Amy
Hospice and Palliative Nurses Association(328)
Kellner, John R.
Gynecologic Oncology Group(321)
Kellner, Stephen S.
Consumer Specialty Products Association(263)
Kellogg, Gina B.
World Waterpark Association(696)
Kellough, Jalane
Electrical Generating Systems Association(291)
Kelly, Andrea
International Association of Infant Massage(358)
Kelly, Charles L.
American Association of Minority Businesses(45)
Kelly, Donald A.
Space Energy Association(648)
Kelly, Glenn
Federal Bureau of Investigation Agents Association(302)
Kelly, Henry
Federation of American Scientists(303)

Kelly, Herman
International Regional Magazine Association(385)
Kelly, Mary
Women in Aerospace(691)
Kelly, Michael
Association of Philosophy Journal Editors(207)
Kelly, Michael
National Kitchen and Bath Association(523)
Kelly, Natalie Strawn
Military Operations Research Society(419)
Kelly, Patrick
Aluminum Association(18)
Kelly, Paul T.
Retail Industry Leaders Association(601)
Kelly, Rhonda L.
National Association of Chain Drug Stores(442)
Kelly, Sharon
Association of Suppliers to the Paper Industry(216)
Kelly, Suzanne
National Academy of Arbitrators(426)
Kelly, Thomas J.
New York Academy of Sciences(552)
Kelly, Tom
United States Ski Association(677)
Kelly Carpenter, Jennifer A.
American Waterways Operators(154)
Kelly Thomas, Karen
National Association of Pediatric Nurse Practitioners(464)
Kemmis, Barbara
American Theological Library Association(151)
Kemnitz, D'Arcy
National Lesbian and Gay Law Association(524)
Kemp, Steve
National Association of Healthcare Access Management(455)
Kemp, CAE, Steven C.
American Urogynecologic Society(153)
Kemp, Todd E.
National Grain and Feed Association(514)
Kemper, Coletta I.
Council of Insurance Agents and Brokers(272)
Kempner, Jonathan L.
Mortgage Bankers Association(421)
Kendall, AnnaMaria
Material Handling Equipment Distributors Association(414)
Kendall, David J.
Brown Swiss Cattle Breeders Association of the U.S.A.(234)
Kendall, David J.
American Milking Shorthorn Society(106)
Kenderdine, Melanie
Gas Technology Institute(314)
Kendrick, Julie
Institute of Environmental Sciences and Technology(341)
Kennedy, Dennis J.
Distribution Contractors Association(286)
Kennedy, CSP, George
National Utility Contractors Association(548)
Kennedy, Jr., Gerald J.
Plumbing-Heating-Cooling Contractors - National Association(579)
Kennedy, Heather
National Association of Fire Investigators(452)
Kennedy, Jane E.
National Federation of Paralegal Associations(510)
Kennedy, John
National Association of Fire Investigators(452)
Kennedy, John J.
Jewelers' Security Alliance of the U.S.(401)
Kennedy, Judith A.
National Association of Affordable Housing Lenders(438)
Kennedy, IACPR, Kay
International Association of Corporate and Professional Recruitment(355)
Kennedy, Kevin
National Association of State Election Directors(475)
Kennedy, Lisa
American Berkshire Association(56)
Kennedy, Maureen
Institute of Certified Travel Agents(340)
Kennedy, Michael E.
Associated General Contractors of America(165)
Kennedy, Miki
Professional Association of Volleyball Officials(586)
Kennedy, Sandra
Retail Industry Leaders Association(601)
Kennedy, Thomas J.
Association of State and Territorial Solid Waste Management Officials(215)
Kennett, Earle
National Institute of Building Sciences(520)
Kenny, Patrick W.
International Insurance Society(376)
Kent, David L.
Amalgamated Printers' Association(18)
Kent, Geoffrey
Opportunity Finance Network(565)
Kent, John G.
Safety Glazing Certification Council(604)
Kent, Lorna D.
American Society for Microbiology(130)
Kent, Nicholas
North American Wholesale Lumber Association(562)
Kent, Norma G.
American Association of Community Colleges(41)
Kenyon, Dione D.
Jewelers Board of Trade(401)
Kenyon, Lowell Anson
Council on Fine Art Photography(276)
Kenyon, Michael
Percussive Arts Society(573)
Keough, Katherine
National Association of State Controlled Substances Authorities(474)
Kepler, Robert
America's Blood Centers(19)
Kepner, Susan
Association for Surgical Education(178)
Keramidas, Ph.D., CAE, Sherry
Regulatory Affairs Professionals Society(598)
Kerchval, Michael P.
International Council of Shopping Centers(368)
Kerins, Arlene
International Advertising Association(348)
Kerkhoven, Paul
Natural Gas Vehicle Coalition(551)
Kernelli, Kirn
National Meat Association(526)
Kerns, Gladys
State Higher Education Executive Officers(653)
Kerns, Samuel
American Public Transportation Association(120)
Kerr, Doris
American Seniors Housing Association(124)
Kerr, Jill K.
Physician Insurers Association of America(577)
Kerr, Joanna
Association for Women's Rights in Development(183)
Kerr, John W.
Atlantic Independent Union(221)
Kerr, Robert
National Association of Enrolled Agents(451)
Kerrick, Sharon
American Nuclear Society(109)
Kershow, Michael R.
International Crystal Federation(368)
Kersting, CAE, Christopher J.
Specialty Equipment Market Association(650)
Kerzner, Robert A.
LIMRA International(408)
Kessler, Dr. James W.
Poultry Science Association(581)
Ketch, Todd
American Health Quality Association(89)
Kettering, Carolyn K.
American Society of Heating, Refrigerating and Air-Conditioning Engineers(139)
Kettering, Susan
American Hair Loss Council(88)
Keyes, Liz
American Pharmacists Association(114)
Keyes, Paula
International Association of Insurance Receivers(358)
Society of Financial Examiners(636)
Keyser, Alden
Association for Work Process Improvement(183)
Keyser, Angela R.
American Association of Physicists in Medicine(48)
Khoury, Dr. Bernard V.
American Association of Physics Teachers(48)
Kianka, Kim
American Association for Homecare(35)
Kiefer, Randy
Institute for Operations Research and the Management Sciences(339)
Kieffer, Donald
National Hay Association(516)
Kiener, Robert C.
Precision Machined Products Association(583)
Kiera, JCB, MDiv, Rev. Timothy A.
North American Canon Law Society(555)
Kiernan, Thomas C.
National Parks Conservation Association(532)
Kiessling, Kathryn
Children's Literature Association(244)
Kight, Kimberly
Mailing & Fulfillment Service Association(410)
Kikta, Katie
General Federation of Women's Clubs(315)
Kildahl, Debra
ACA International, The Association of Credit and Collection Professionals(2)
Kilfeather, Stephanie
Association of American Railroads(185)
Killalea, Mike
Drilling Engineering Association(287)
Killan, Linda
American Medical Student Association(105)
Killgore, Lucille
American Association of Clinical Endocrinologists(39)

Kilmer, Marc
American Congress of Community Supports and Employment Services(73)
Kilmer, Pat
Geological Society of America(315)
Kim, Charles
American Council of Engineering Companies(75)
Kim, Hank H.
National Conference on Public Employee Retirement Systems(495)
Kim, Helen
National Propane Gas Association(534)
Kim, Luenna H.
National Society of Newspaper Columnists(542)
Kimball, John
Newspaper Association of America(552)
Kimball, Philip B.
Society of Naval Architects and Marine Engineers(640)
Kimble, Mark
Association of Performing Arts Presenters(207)
Kimble, Viveca
Society for Investigative Dermatology(620)
Kimmel, Brian
National Association of Convenience Stores(446)
Kimmel, Kathryn
Gemological Institute of America(315)
Kimmel, Michael
Union for Reform Judaism(670)
Kimmich, Allison
National Women's Studies Association(549)
Kimura-Fay, Ayuko
American Society of Hematology(139)
Kinateder, Fred
International Council of Employers of Bricklayers and Allied Craftworkers(367)
Kinder, James A.
National Association of Graphic and Product Identification Manufacturers(455)
Self Insurance Institute of America, Inc.(608)
Kindinger, Paul E.
North American Equipment Dealers Association(556)
King, Byran
International Brotherhood of Boilermakers, Iron Ship Builders, Blacksmiths, Forgers and Helpers(363)
King, Connie M.
American and Delaine-Merino Record Association(31)
King, Dan
American Association of University Administrators(53)
King, CFE, Dexter G.
International Association of Assembly Managers(353)
King, Don L.
Texas Longhorn Breeders Association of America(659)
King, Eileen N.
Outdoor Writers Association of America(569)
King, George W.K.
American Institute of Biomedical Climatology(95)
King, Jamie
National Association for Interpretation(434)
King, Karen
American Society for Nutrition(131)
King, Kathy
Miniature Book Society(420)
King, Kristina
International Society for Magnetic Resonance in Medicine(387)
King, L.D.
International Academy of Compounding Pharmacists(347)
King, Linda
SPRI, Inc.(652)
King, Marilen
Assisted Living Federation of America(164)
King, Mark
National Association of Teachers' Agencies(478)
King, Robin R.
Aluminum Association(18)
King, Roland
National Association of Independent Colleges and Universities(457)
King, Sheril
American Academy for Cerebral Palsy and Developmental Medicine(19)
Association of Children's Prosthetic-Orthotic Clinics(189)
King, Sherry
National Association of Broadcast Employees and Technicians - Communications Workers of America(441)
King, Steve
American College of Foot and Ankle Surgeons(66)
King, CAE, Steven T.
Lawn and Garden Marketing and Distribution Association(406)
Pet Industry Distributors Association(574)
Postcard and Souvenir Distributors Association(581)
King, Tekoa
American College of Nurse-Midwives(68)
King, Tom
American Association of Veterinary Clinicians(53)
King, Vicki J.
Society of Petrophysicists and Well Log Analysts(641)
Kinnaird, Jula J.
National Grain Trade Council(514)
Transportation Elevator and Grain Merchants Association(664)
Kinnaird, Chaplain Will
Network on Ministry in Specialized Settings(552)
Kinnecome, Linda
National Utility Contractors Association(548)
Kinney, Alison
Institute of Judicial Administration(342)
Kinnunen, Nadine
American Society of Gene Therapy(138)
Kinter, Kathy
Biscuit and Cracker Manufacturers' Association(229)
Kinter, Marci
Digital Printing and Imaging Association(284)
Specialty Graphic Imaging Association(650)
Kipley, Kip
WorldatWork(697)
Kipnis, Ken
International Association for Philosophy of Law and Social Philosophy - American Section(351)
Kirby, George W.
National Catholic Educational Association(487)
Kirby, Patsy
American Electrology Association(80)
Kirch, Darrell G.
Association of American Medical Colleges(184)
Kirchhoff, Richard W.
National Association of State Departments of Agriculture(474)
Kirchner, Douglas
National Association of Certified Valuation Analysts(442)
Kirchner, Gerald
Magic Dealers Association(410)
Kirchner, Paul G.
American Pilots' Association(115)
Kirchoff, Mary
American Chemical Society(62)
Kireta, Sr., Andrew G.
Copper Development Association(266)
Kirk, Carl
Technology and Maintenance Council of American Trucking Associations(658)
Kirk, CAE, Ken
National Association of Clean Water Agencies(443)
Kirk, Linda D.
Institute for Responsible Housing Preservation(339)
Kirk, Michael K.
American Intellectual Property Law Association(98)
Kirk, Jr., Phillip J.
Council of State Chambers of Commerce(274)
Kirk, Sharon
National Petrochemical & Refiners Association(532)
Kirkconnell, Ellenor A.
Alliance of Nonprofit Mailers(17)
Kirkland, Katherine H.
Association of Occupational and Environmental Clinics(206)
Kirkpatrick, Charles
National Association of Barber Boards(439)
Kirkpatrick, James R.
American Astronautical Society(54)
Kirkwood, John
American Lung Association(102)
Kirson, Amy
International Society for Antiviral Research(386)
Kishbaugh, Connie
International Childbirth Education Association(365)
Kisner, Ken
National Council of Exchangors(499)
Kissel, Kimberly
Roller Skating Association International(602)
Kistler, Susan
American Evaluation Association(81)
Kita, Mary L.
Beer Institute(227)
Kitterman, Dennis
National Council for Prescription Drug Programs(497)
Kitts, Tracy
National Business Incubation Association(486)
Kiyak, Tunga
Academy of International Business(3)
Kizart, Vanessa
American Society for Gastrointestinal Endoscopy(129)
Kjellberg, Kevin
EEG and Clinical Neuroscience Society(290)
Klabunde, Dave
National Confectioners Association of the United States(492)
Klamke, Stephan E.
EIFS Industry Members Association(290)

Klapthor, James
Institute of Food Technologists(341)
Klatt, Gabriella Daley
American Correctional Association(74)
Klatz, MD, DO, Ronald
American Academy of Anti-Aging Medicine(20)
Klayman, Wanda
International Bridge, Tunnel and Turnpike Association(363)
Kleczka, Caley A.
Movement Disorder Society(422)
Klegon, Ph.D., Douglas
American College of Healthcare Executives(66)
Klein, Bill
Alliance for Telecommunications Industry Solutions(16)
Klein, Dr. Hans E.
WACRA - World Association for Case Method Research and Application(684)
Klein, James A.
American Benefits Council(56)
Klein, Ken
Outdoor Advertising Association of America(569)
Klein, Kim
National Association of Real Estate Companies(468)
Klein, Kolleen
Radiological Society of North America(594)
Klein, Lisa
Cosmetic Executive Women(267)
Klein, Rick
National Association of Manufacturers(460)
Klein, MCS, NBCCH, Ron
National Board for Certified Clinical Hypnotherapists(485)
Klein, Susan Humphreys
International Society for Pharmaceutical Engineering(388)
Klein, Tracy
University Continuing Education Association(679)
Kleine, CAE, Douglas M.
National Association of Housing Cooperatives(456)
Kleingartner, Larry
National Sunflower Association(545)
Kleinman, Melodye
National Association of Retired Senior Volunteer Program Directors(469)
Kleinz, Karen
National School Public Relations Association(538)
Kleppick, Margie
Association for Hospital Medical Education(174)
Klim, Edward J.
International Snowmobile Manufacturers Association(386)
Klimp, Jack W.
Gas Appliance Manufacturers Association(314)
Kline, Michael E.
SSPC: the Society for Protective Coatings(652)
Kline, Richard
Glass, Molders, Pottery, Plastics and Allied Workers International Union(317)
Klingel, Stephen J.
National Council on Compensation Insurance(502)
Klinger, Earl
Society for Marketing Professional Services(621)
Klinger, Raymond W.
National Ornamental Goldfish Growers Association(531)
Klinke, Michelle
American Society of Hematology(139)
Klippenstein, Glen
American Chianina Association(62)
Klipping, Beth
Society for Research on Nicotine and Tobacco(625)
Klipple, Bruce
United Electrical, Radio and Machine Workers of America(671)
Klipstein, Richard
National Organization of Life and Health Insurance Guaranty Associations(530)
Kloese, Barbara
Natural Colored Wool Growers Association(550)
Klos, Bernie
IPC - Surface Mount Equipment Manufacturers Association(399)
Klos, Diana Mitsu
American Society of Newspaper Editors(142)
Kloss, RRA, Linda L.
American Health Information Management Association(89)
Klug, Jill
Tube and Pipe Association, International(666)
Kmak, James
Academy of Osseointegration(5)
Knapp, CAE, Jolene
Society for College and University Planning(615)
Knapp, Karna
Rolf Institute(602)
Knapp, Ph.D., Richard M.
Association of American Medical Colleges(184)
Knell, Margaret
Inter-Industry Conference on Auto Collision Repair(346)
Knettler, Tim R.
Federation of State Medical Boards of the United States(304)
Knezovich, CAE, Jeffrey P.
American Academy of Cosmetic Surgery(21)
American Society of Hair Restoration Surgery(138)
American Society of Lipo-Suction Surgery(140)
Knight, Adam
League of Resident Theatres(406)
Knight, Brian D.
National Association of State Credit Union Supervisors(474)
Knight, Curtis
RMA - The Risk Management Association(602)
Knight, Margaret
Association of American Indian Physicians(184)
Knight, Ph.D., Prentice
CoreNet Global(266)
Knight, Tom
National Frame Builders Association(512)
Knizner, Peggy
National Agricultural Aviation Association(428)
Knopes, Andy
Air and Waste Management Association(12)
Knopp, Linda
National Business Incubation Association(486)
Knott, Mary
Residential Space Planners International(600)
Knott, Vicki
Belgian Draft Horse Corp. of America(227)
Knowdell, Richard L.
Career Planning and Adult Development Network(238)
Knowles, Janet K.
American Fire Sprinkler Association(84)
Knox, Stephanie
National Hydropower Association(518)
Kobaly, Sheila
National Investment Company Service Association(522)
Kobetz, Dr. Richard W.
Academy of Security Educators and Trainers(5)
Koblenz, Andrew
National Automobile Dealers Association(482)
Kochkin, Ph.D., Sergei
Better Hearing Institute(228)
Kociolek, Bob
American Society of Home Inspectors(139)
Kocmieroski, Matthew
International Guild of Symphony, Opera and Ballet Musicians(374)
Koepke, Richard
International Society for Analytical Cytology(386)
International Society for Traumatic Stress Studies(389)
Koepke, Rick
Association for Death Education and Counseling(171)
Koepke-Williams, Sherry
American Moving and Storage Association(107)
Koepper, Kenneth E.
Uniform and Textile Service Association(669)
Koetje, David
Christian Schools International(246)
Kogel, J.M. Elzea
Clay Minerals Society(247)
Kohl, Dr. Kay
University Continuing Education Association(679)
Kohlhepp, Todd
American International Automobile Dealers Association(98)
Kohlmoos, James W.
National Education Knowledge Industry Association(506)
Kohut, Carleen C.
National Retail Federation(536)
Kokrda, Kevin
Engine Manufacturers Association(295)
Kolar, CAE, Mary Jane
National Council on Qualifications for the Lighting Professions(502)
Kolb, Jim
American Road and Transportation Builders Association(123)
Kolbe, Linda
Conference Board of the Mathematical Sciences(259)
Kolbe, Sherry L.
National Association of Private Special Education Centers(465)
Kolbe, Stanley
Sheet Metal and Air Conditioning Contractors' National Association(610)
Koleda, Michael
Energy Frontiers International(294)
Kolman, David A.
Tire Retread Information Bureau(662)
Kolodziej, Richard R.
Natural Gas Vehicle Coalition(551)
Kolojeski, Tracy
National Association of Sporting Goods Wholesalers(472)

Kolstad, James L.
National Association of Chemical Distributors(442)
Koltai, Peter
American Broncho-Esophagological Association(59)
Kolus, Cheryl
Organization of Wildlife Planners(568)
Komnenic, Ljiljana
World Affairs Councils of America(695)
Kong, Ph.D., J.D, B. Waine
Association of Black Cardiologists(187)
Kong, Cindy
Association of Science-Technology Centers(213)
Kono, Kathleen
ASTM International(221)
Koob, MPA, Susan
Preventive Cardiovascular Nurses Association(583)
Koontz, Michele Smith
Society for the Study of Social Problems(628)
Kopcinski, Ray
Million Dollar Round Table(419)
Kopenhaver, Janet
American Wire Producers Association(155)
Koper, Stephen
National Guard Association of the U.S.(515)
Kopernick, James
International Plate Printers', Die Stampers' and Engravers' Union of North America(383)
Kopriva, Dan
United States Cross Country Coaches Association(674)
Kopycki, William J.
Middle East Librarians' Association(418)
Korb, Thomas
Association for Advanced Life Underwriting(167)
Korbel, Andrea
Women in Government Relations(692)
Korbel, Kimberly A.
American Wire Producers Association(155)
Wire Rope Technical Board(690)
Women in Government Relations(692)
Korczak, CAE, Edward S.
National Wood Flooring Association(550)
Korfmacher, CMP, Krista
Credit Union Executives Society(279)
Kormondy, Karen
National Grape Cooperative Association(515)
Kornbluh, Harvey
Associated Owners and Developers(165)
Kornhauser, Ph.D., Dr. Stanley H.
National Institute for Electromedical Information(520)
Korson, II, Philip J.
Cherry Marketing Institute(243)
Korson, Teri
Distribution Contractors Association(286)
Kosesan, Richard
National Lamb Feeders Association(523)
Kosior, Laurel
Colorado Ranger Horse Association(253)
Kosko-Patty, Lauren
U.S. Poultry and Egg Association(668)
Koslowe, Rabbi Irving
American Jewish Correctional Chaplains Association(99)
Koss, Pamela
Glass Art Society(317)
Kost, Richard S.
Aviation Maintenance Foundation International(225)
Kostecki, Ph.D., Paul T.
Association for the Environmental Health of Soils(180)
Kotler, Greta
American Society of Association Executives & Center for Association Leadership(134)
Kotrba, Linda
American Association of Surgical Physician Assistants(52)
Association of Neurosurgical Physician Assistants(205)
Kotula, Kathryn
National Association of Medicaid Directors(461)
Kouneski, Anthony M.
American Public Transportation Association(120)
Kouris, John R.
Defense Research Institute(282)
Kouros, Thomas C.
United States Bowling Instructors Association(673)
Kovac, Patricia
Society of Pelvic Reconstructive Surgeons(641)
Kovacs, Elizabeth A.
Association of Management Consulting Firms(203)
Kovalesky, Pat
EUCG(298)
Kovalsky, Debbie
American Astronomical Society(54)
Kovins, Mike
International Association of Electronic Keyboard Manufacturers(356)
Kowalczyk, Mercy
IEEE Signal Processing Society(331)
Kowalik, Amy
American Goat Society(87)
Kowalski, Gloria
Portable Computer and Communications Association(580)
Kowalski, CAE, Michael J.
American Water Resources Association(154)
Kozak, Jerome J.
American Butter Institute(60)
National Milk Producers Federation(527)
Kozal, Dr. Richard A.
Pierre Fauchard Academy(577)
Koziol, Patricia S.
Hobby Manufacturers Association(327)
Koziol, Patrick
Million Dollar Round Table(419)
Krack, CKO, CAE, James J.
American Boarding Kennels Association(58)
Kraemer, CCCE, Carol
American Society of Tax Professionals(146)
Kraemer, Mike
North American Equipment Dealers Association(556)
Kraft, Andrew
Interactive Advertising Bureau(346)
Kraich, Norbert
Association of Investment Management Sales Executives(202)
Krajczar, Richard
Association for the Advancement of International Education(179)
Kralka, Peter
American College of Epidemiology(65)
Controlled Environment Testing Association(264)
Kramer, Tony
Council on Governmental Ethics Laws(276)
Kranek, Robert E.
American Bureau of Shipping(59)
Kranz, Steve
Council On State Taxation(277)
Krapp, Christian
American Nuclear Society(109)
Kraus, Maribeth T.
Modern Language Association of America(420)
Kraus, Timothy R.
Heavy Duty Brake Manufacturers Council(325)
Heavy Duty Business Forum(325)
Heavy Duty Manufacturers Association(325)
Krause, Dennis
International Interior Design Association(377)
Krause, Luanne
Society of Petroleum Engineers(641)
Krause, Maureen K.
National Shellfisheries Association(539)
Kraushaar, Kevin J.
Consumer Healthcare Products Association(263)
Kraut, Alan G.
American Psychological Society(119)
Krauthamer, Judith
Marine Technology Society(412)
Kravitz, Roberta
International Society for Magnetic Resonance in Medicine(387)
Krebs, Frederick J.
Association of Corporate Counsel(193)
Krebs, Rob
American Plastics Council(116)
Kreger, Bertram
Academy of Oral Dynamics(4)
Krehbiel, Ken
National Council of Teachers of Mathematics(501)
Kreig, Andrew T.
Wireless Communications Association International(690)
Kreimer, Stephen H.
Professional Bail Agents of the United States(586)
Kreizman, Janet B.
Endocrine Society(294)
Kresci, David
Grain Elevator and Processing Society(319)
Kress, W. John
Association for Tropical Biology and Conservation(181)
Krichbaum, JD, John
American Burn Association(60)
Krichevsky, Micha
United States Federation for Culture Collections(675)
Kriegel, CAE, Robin
American Society for Parenteral and Enteral Nutrition(131)
Kriem-Miller, Mima
General Federation of Women's Clubs(315)
Krisberg, Ph.D., Barry
National Council on Crime and Delinquency(502)
Krisfalusi, Marisa
General Federation of Women's Clubs(315)
Krissoff, Michael R.
Asphalt Emulsion Manufacturers Association(163)
Asphalt Recycling and Reclaiming Association(163)
International Slurry Surfacing Association(386)

Kristof, Dawn C.
Water and Wastewater Equipment Manufacturers Association(685)
Krodell, Helena
Jewelry Information Center(401)
Kroh, Lerrene
National Sunflower Association(545)
Krohm, Greg
International Association of Industrial Accident Boards and Commissions(358)
Kroll, Kevin
Steel Tank Institute Division of STI/SPFA(654)
Kroll, William
America's Community Bankers(19)
Krolman, Walter
ICAAAA Coaches Association(330)
Krom, Cynthia L.
Organizational Behavior Teaching Society(568)
Krone, Barbara
National Parking Association(531)
Krone, David
National Cable & Telecommunications Association(486)
Krueger, Cheryl
Society of Actuaries(629)
Krueger, Dawn
National Fluid Power Association(511)
Krueger, Keith
Consortium for School Networking(262)
Kruger, Fred
International Association of Natural Resource Pilots(359)
Kruger, Robert M.
Business Software Alliance(236)
Krugman, Scott
National Retail Federation(536)
Krump, Betty
American Technical Education Association(150)
Kruse, USN (Ret.), Capt. Dennis K.
American Society of Naval Engineers(142)
Krut, Stephen F.
American Association of Meat Processors(45)
Krzywicki, John
American Galvanizers Association(86)
Ku, Charlotte
American Society of International Law(140)
Kubarth, Michael
International Association of Tool Craftsmen(361)
Kube, Thomas
Council of Educational Facility Planners, International(271)
Kuberry, Frank
Pyrotechnics Guild International(593)
Kubis, Dianne K.
American College of Allergy, Asthma and Immunology(64)
American Society of Colon and Rectal Surgeons(136)
Kudart, Cindy
Committee of 200(254)
Kuehn, Jan
National Wood Flooring Association(550)
Kugler, Ellen J.
National Association of Urban Hospitals(480)
Kugler, Phil
AFT Healthcare(11)
Kuhn, Kathryn
National Community Pharmacists Association(491)
Kuhn, Linda
International Longshore and Warehouse Union(378)
Kuhn, Roseann
Women's International Bowling Congress(693)
Kuhn, CAE, Thomas R.
Edison Electric Institute(289)
Kuhns, Deb
Trade Promotion Management Association(663)
Kuk, Thomas J.
American Society of Baking(134)
Kukawka, Stanley
Variable Electronic Components Institute(682)
Kukoda, Steve
International Copper Association(367)
Kulick, Jeffrey
National School Transportation Association(538)
Kull, Ted
Society for Industrial and Applied Mathematics(619)
Kundu, Jai
Safety and Loss Prevention Management Council(604)
Kurkian, Scott
Professional Photographers of America(588)
Kurkul, Doug
National Association of Manufacturers(460)
Kurokawa, Ken
Computer and Communications Industry Association(257)
Kurpiel, Judy
International Professional Groomers(383)
Kurtis, Dean
International Housewares Association(375)
Kurtz, John
International Staple, Nail and Tool Association(393)
Kurylko, Natalie
Association for Experiential Education(172)
Kurzak, Mary Beth
International Association of Defense Counsel(356)
Kurzeja, Richard E.
International Buckskin Horse Association(363)
Kushnier, Gary
American National Standards Institute(108)
Kusiak, Joe
American Society of Home Inspectors(139)
Kutschke, Pamela
American Association of Certified Orthoptists(39)
Kutska, Helen
National Petrochemical & Refiners Association(532)
Kutt, Patricia
American Public Works Association(120)
Kuvin, Brad F.
Precision Metalforming Association(583)
Kuyper, Mark
Evangelical Christian Publishers Association(298)
Kvaal, Ann
Financial Women International(306)
Kwart, Michael
Insulation Contractors Association of America(345)
Kyes, Danielle
Society for the Advancement of Women's Health Research(626)
Kyger, Jim
Printing Industries of America(584)
Kyle, Lesley
Society of Plastics Engineers(642)
Kyle, Linda
Rubber Pavements Association(603)
Kysilko, David
National Association of State Boards of Education(473)
L'Ecuyer, Susan
National Association of Recording Merchandisers(468)
La Mountain, Joe
Vision Council of America(684)
Laabs, Jonathan
Lutheran Education Association(409)
Laatsch, Shawn
International Planetarium Society(383)
Labarr, Paul
National Business Owners Association(486)
LaBella, Gary
Recreation Vehicle Industry Association(596)
LaBella, Jeanne
American Public Power Association(120)
LaBure, Chris
National Association of Marine Surveyors(461)
Lacagnina, Mark
Flight Safety Foundation(308)
LaCava, Patricia K.
National Alcohol Beverage Control Association(429)
Lacey, Catherine
American Resort Development Association(122)
Lacey, Robert
International Allied Printing Trades Association(349)
Lachance, Janice
Special Libraries Association(649)
Lacivita, Brendan I.
ERISA Industry Committee(297)
Lackman, Susan Cohn
International Alliance for Women in Music(348)
LaCorte, Jean
National Association of Flour Distributors(453)
Lacovara, Bob
American Composites Manufacturers Association(72)
Lacquaniti, Mary
Healthcare Marketing and Communications Council(324)
LaCroix, Nicki
National Association for Healthcare Quality(433)
Lacy, Shari
International Bluegrass Music Association(362)
Lacy, USA(Ret.), Col. Warren
Military Officers Association of America(419)
Lada, Cathy
American Chamber of Commerce Executives(61)
Laddbush, Kathleen
Association of Catholic Colleges and Universities(188)
Ladner, Marian
Organization of Women in International Trade(568)
Ladner, Susan
National Sugar Brokers Association(544)
LaFevre, Sandra L.
Reinsurance Association of America(598)
Laffarque, Amy
Pension Real Estate Association(573)
LaFlair, Erin
American Academy of Otolaryngology-Head and Neck Surgery(26)
LaFortune, Gray
Ceramic Tile Institute of America(242)
LaFountain, Becky
North American Society of Adlerian Psychology(561)

Lagana, Brian
Pedorthic Footwear Association(572)
LaGasse, Alfred B.
Taxicab, Limousine and Paratransit Association(657)
LaGasse, CAE, Robert C.
Garden Writers Association(314)
Hydroponic Merchants Association(330)
Mulch and Soil Council(422)
Lage, David
National Alliance of Postal and Federal Employees(429)
Lagershausen, Jack L.
Air Diffusion Council(13)
LaHaie, Jerri
Society of Municipal Arborists(640)
Lai, Teddy
Greater Blouse, Skirt and Undergarment Association(320)
Laible, Myron
Outdoor Advertising Association of America(569)
Laingen, Bruce
American Academy of Diplomacy(22)
Lakatos, Jackie
Council on Library-Media Technicians(276)
Lally, Carol
International Foodservice Editorial Council(372)
Lally, Sue
Coin Laundry Association(250)
Lamar, Stephen
American Apparel & Footwear Association(31)
Lamb, Shawn
Society of Toxicology(645)
Lambe, Maureen
National Apartment Association(430)
Lamber, Wendy
American Concrete Pipe Association(73)
Lambert, Michael P.
Distance Education and Training Council(285)
Lambert, Mike
Association of Automotive Aftermarket Distributors(186)
Lambert, Susan
National Cattlemen's Beef Association(488)
Lambert, Susan J.
Iron Casting Research Institute(399)
Lambert, Theresa
National Association of State Units on Aging(476)
Lamm, Thomas
Information Systems Audit and Control Association(338)
Lamond, Joe
NAMM - the International Music Products Association(425)
Lamonte, Jill
Association of Independent Information Professionals(200)
Lampe, Betsy
National Association of Independent Publishers(457)
LaMura, Rene
Polyisocyanurate Insulation Manufacturers Association(580)
Lamy, Jonathan
Recording Industry Association of America(596)
Lancaster, Joyce
Weed Science Society of America(687)
Wilderness Medical Society(689)
Lanctot, Suzanne
National Environmental, Safety and Health Training Association(507)
Landacre, Jessica K.
Intellectual Property Owners Association(345)
Landers, Roger
Professional Association of Health Care Office Management(586)
Landers, Valerie
Illuminating Engineering Society of North America(332)
Landfare, Jeremy
Healthcare Information and Management Systems Society(324)
Landis, Lisa L.
Welsh Pony and Cob Society of America(687)
Landmesser, Leora
National Council of the Churches of Christ in the U.S.A.(501)
Landon, Edwin O.
Institute of Packaging Professionals(343)
Landrum, David
Walking Horse Trainers Association(685)
Landry, Lori
Community Development Society(256)
Network Professional Association(552)
Landsberg, Bruce
Aircraft Owners and Pilots Association(14)
Landwehr, Christy
CHA - Certified Horsemanship Association(242)
Landy, Rosalie
International Society for Adolescent Psychiatry & Psychology(386)
Lane, Bob
Association of College and University Printers(191)
Lane, Carol Ann
Lake Carriers' Association(404)
Lane, Carolyn
Society for Hematopathology(618)
Lane, Mary Ellen
Council of American Overseas Research Centers(270)
Lane, Nancy
Suburban Newspapers of America(655)
Lang, Heather Monroe
Institute of Food Technologists(341)
Lang, Peter
Western Red Cedar Lumber Association(687)
Lang, AAP, Scott
NACHA - The Electronic Payments Association(424)
Lang, Will
American Association of Colleges of Pharmacy(40)
Lange, David
American Association of Petroleum Geologists(47)
Lange, Dr. Mark D.
National Cotton Council of America(496)
Langer, Gary
National Association of State Supervisors of Trade and Industrial Education(476)
Langfeld, Patricia
National Parking Association(531)
Langham, Anna
National League of Cities(524)
Langill, Ph.D., Thomas J.
American Galvanizers Association(86)
Langley, Catherine
Opticians Association of America(566)
Langley, Mark
Project Management Institute(590)
Langman, Mary
Medical Library Association(416)
Langstraat, Laura A.
National Crop Insurance Services(504)
Lanigan, Diane
National Organization of Legal Services Workers(530)
Lanka, Daniel
American College of Oral and Maxillofacial Surgeons(68)
Lanke, CAE, Eric
American Academy of Allergy, Asthma, and Immunology(20)
Lankford, Terri
American Association of Exporters and Importers(42)
Lanning, Karen
National Council of Higher Education Loan Programs(499)
Lant, Ph.D., Christopher L.
Universities Council on Water Resources(679)
Lao, Mitu
American Traffic Safety Services Association(152)
Lapetina, Susan
American Apparel & Footwear Association(31)
LaPiana, William P.
American Society for Legal History(130)
LaPierre, Jr., Wayne R.
National Rifle Association of America(536)
LaPorte, Erin
PGA TOUR Tournaments Association(575)
Lapp, Rabbi David
JWB Jewish Chaplains Council(403)
Lapsansky, Mary Ellen
Fragrance Foundation(311)
Lara, Rebecca
American Holistic Nurses Association(91)
Largent, Steve
CTIA - The Wireless Association(280)
Larimer, Gail Pierce
Antique and Amusement Photographers International(157)
Larimer, Jane
NACHA - The Electronic Payments Association(424)
Larimer, Ted
Antique and Amusement Photographers International(157)
Larkin, Daphne
Country Music Association(277)
Larkin, J. Stephen
Aluminum Association(18)
Larkins, Cassandra
Society for Sex Therapy and Research(625)
Larkins, Jerry F.
American Society of Appraisers(134)
Larmett, Kathleen M.
National Council of University Research Administrators(501)
Larris, Jeffrey
International Ticketing Association(394)
Larry, Damon
National Organization for the Professional Advancement of Black Chemists and Chemical Engineers(530)
Larsen, Craig
Softwood Export Council(646)
Larsen, Dana B.
International Studies Association(393)
Larsen, David
American College of Chest Physicians(64)
Larsen, CPA, Erick
Association for Financial Professionals(173)
Larson, Anita
Association of State Floodplain Managers(216)
Larson, Larry A.
Association of State Floodplain Managers(216)

Larson, Robert
Independent Association of Questioned Document Examiners(333)
Larson, Terry
Mass Finishing Job Shops Association(413)
Laskey, Linda
American Water Works Association(154)
Lasky, Daniel
National Organization of Industrial Trade Unions(530)
Latham, John
Special Libraries Association(649)
Latham, Tim
American Society of Certified Engineering Technicians(135)
Lathrop, Cara
Kappa Delta Pi(403)
Latta, Carol J.
Decision Sciences Institute(282)
Lattimer, Cheri
Case Management Society of America(238)
Lattimore, Burk
American Rambouillet Sheep Breeders Association(121)
Lau, Leilynne
Asia America MultiTechnology Association(162)
Lauber, M.D., Jeffrey
American Society of Dermatological Retailers(137)
Lauck, Larry
American Lighting Association(101)
Lauer, Peter B.
Society of Interventional Radiology(639)
Lauerman, David P.
National Exchange Carrier Association(507)
Laufer, Lucille J.
Oriental Rug Importers Association of America(568)
Launchbaugh, Cynthia
ARMA International(160)
Laurence, David
Association of Departments of English(193)
Laurie, Joyce A.
Automotive Oil Change Association(224)
Laursen, Finn
Christian Educators Association International(246)
Laury, Tanya
American Society of Professional Estimators(145)
Laushman, Judy M.
Association of Specialty Cut Flower Growers(214)
Lauth, Rosemary S.
American Association of State Colleges and Universities(51)
LaValley, CAE, Alison
National Roofing Contractors Association(537)
Laven, Frances
Academy of Aphasia(2)
Laverty, Faye
Interior Design Society(347)
Lavery, Michael J.
Audit Bureau of Circulations(222)
Lavigne, Patrick
National Rural Electric Cooperative Association(537)
Lavin, J. Kevin
National Weather Association(549)
Law, Richard
Association of Former OSI Special Agents(198)
Lawler, Bette
American Institute of Chemical Engineers(95)
Lawler, Bonnie
National Federation of Abstracting and Information Services(508)
Lawler, CAE, Colleen
American Academy of Family Physicians(22)
Lawler, CMP, Nancy
National Asphalt Pavement Association(431)
Lawlor, Anita Horne
International Health, Racquet and Sportsclub Association(374)
Lawnick, Jim
Society of Exploration Geophysicists(636)
Lawniczak, Jon
AcademyHealth(6)
Lawrence, Brian D.
American Society of Wedding Professionals(147)
Lawrence, Fred
Independent Petroleum Association of America(335)
Lawrence, Jim
Tune-up Manufacturers Council(667)
Lawrence, Kathie S.
Association of Certified Fraud Examiners(189)
Lawrence, Marilyn E.
International Municipal Signal Association(380)
Lawrence, Timothy W.
Skills USA(611)
Laws, Tracey
Reinsurance Association of America(598)
Lawser, CAE, Steven V.
Wood Component Manufacturers Association(694)
Lawson, Christine
American Association for Budget and Program Analysis(33)
Lawson, Eugene K.
U.S.-Russia Business Council(668)
Lawson, John
Association of Public Television Stations(210)
Lawson, Dr. Michael S.
Professional Association of Christian Educators(585)
Lawson, Quentin
National Alliance of Black School Educators(429)
Lawson, Richard
American Association of Pharmaceutical Scientists(48)
Lawson, Richard
Council of Residential Specialists(274)
Lawton, Henry W.
International Psychohistorical Association(383)
Lax, Brenda
National Association of Foster Grandparent Program Directors(453)
Laxton, Christopher E.
American Association of Diabetes Educators(42)
Layne, George
Forging Industry Association(310)
Lazier, CAE, CMP, Carol L.
American Society of Plastic Surgeons(144)
Lea, Daniel
Cellulose Insulation Manufacturers Association(241)
Leab, Daniel
Historians of American Communism(326)
Leach, Jerry W.
World Affairs Councils of America(695)
Leahigh, Alan K.
American Society for Blood and Marrow Transplantation(127)
Leahy, Betteanne
Hearth Patio & Barbecue Association(324)
Leahy, Patricia
National Rehabilitation Association(535)
Lear, Liz
University Continuing Education Association(679)
Leary, Lou Ann
American Nephrology Nurses Association(108)
Leary, Susan
National Academy of Recording Arts and Sciences(427)
Leary, MALA, Thomas A.
Healthcare Information and Management Systems Society(324)
Leasure, Mark
Infectious Diseases Society of America(338)
Leavens, Donald
National Electrical Manufacturers Association(506)
Leavens, John
National Association of Intercollegiate Athletics(458)
Lebby, CMP, Kathryn
Association for Play Therapy(176)
LeBlanc, Michelle
Association for Women Veterinarians(182)
LeBlanc, Norm
Society of Accredited Marine Surveyors(629)
LeBlanc, Virginia
National Pan-Hellenic Council(531)
LeClerc, Anthony
Captive Insurance Companies Association(237)
Lederer, Jr., Robert F
National Pest Management Association(532)
Lederman, Stephanie
American Federation for Aging Research(82)
Ledoux, Amy
American Society of Association Executives & Center for Association Leadership(134)
LeDoux, Diana
National Potato Promotion Board(533)
Lee, Andrea
Accreditation Association for Ambulatory Health Care(6)
Lee, April C.T.
Association for Maximum Service Television(176)
Lee, Brad
National Mail Order Association(525)
Lee, Dale
ISA(400)
Lee, David
International Association of Amusement Parks and Attractions(352)
Lee, David C.
National Truck Equipment Association(547)
Lee, Dr. Grayce
American Guild of Hypnotherapists(88)
Lee, Janine
Specialized Information Publishers Association(650)
Lee, Jr., Jessie
National Organization of Black Law Enforcement Executives(530)
Lee, Mary
United States Trout Farmers Association(678)
Lee, Maureen Elgersman
Coordinating Council for Women in History(265)
Lee, Pat
Fabricators and Manufacturers Association, International(300)
Tube and Pipe Association, International(666)

Lee, T.S. (Chip)
ISA(400)
Lee, Thomas F.
American Federation of Musicians of the United States and Canada(82)
Lee, Tony
Craft & Hobby Association(278)
Lee, Vicki
International Association of Fire Chiefs(357)
Leeds, Robert X.
American Pet Boarding Association(114)
Leedy, Lynda M.
American Academy of Physical Medicine and Rehabilitation(27)
Leemaster, Alesha
Interstate Oil and Gas Commission(398)
Leeper, Gary E.
Portfolio Management Institute(581)
Leeper, CAE, Laura Downes
American Association for Hand Surgery(35)
Lefcourt, Hal
National Constables Association(495)
LeFevour, Mary Kay C.
Society for Ecological Restoration(616)
Leffel, Chris
Composite Panel Association(257)
Leftwich, Bruce
Career College Association(237)
Legaspi, Angie
American Society for Surgery of the Hand(132)
Legon, Richard D.
Association of Governing Boards of Universities and Colleges(199)
LeGrand, CMP, Crista
Fire Suppression Systems Association(307)
International Society of Restaurant Association Executives(392)
Lehmann, Aleya
Appraisers Association of America(159)
Lehmuth, Georgette
National Catholic Development Conference(487)
Lehner, Cyndee
Association for the Behavioral Sciences and Medical Education(180)
Lehnerer, Melodye G.
Sociological Practice Association(646)
LeHouillier, Brian
American Society for Quality(132)
Lehr, Scott
International Franchise Association(373)
Leibold, Peter
American Health Lawyers Association(89)
Leight, Elizabeth Y.
Society of Professional Benefit Administrators(642)
Leighton, David
Women in Technology International(692)
Leighton, Ron
American Society of Landscape Architects(140)
Leighty, Carol
National Council of Administrative Women in Education(498)
Leimbach, Jill
National Association of Credit Management(448)
Leininger, Robert
Music Critics Association of North America(423)
Leipold, James
National Association for Law Placement(434)
LeMar, Tina R.
American Entomological Society(81)
LeMaster, Lynn H.
Edison Electric Institute(289)
Lemay, Helen Schneider
American Society of Limnology and Oceanography(140)
Lembesis, Felicia
National Association of Professional Pet Sitters(466)
Lemieux, Russell A.
Association of Fund-Raising Distributors and Suppliers(198)
Lemire, Carol C.
American College of Toxicology(71)
Lemke, Denise
Clinical Immunology Society(248)
Lemke, George W.
Casket and Funeral Supply Association of America(238)
Lemke, Lee R.
China Clay Producers Association(244)
Lemke, Randal
InfoCom International(338)
Lemons, Jack
National Association for Government Training and Development(433)
Lemos, Mara
Council of the Americas(275)
Lempesis, Bill
Video Electronics Standards Association(683)
Lempke, Maj. Gen. Roger P.
Adjutants General Association of the United States(8)
LeMunyan, Laura
Emissions Markets Association(293)
Lenard, Jeff
National Association of Convenience Stores(446)
Lenard, Liz
American Academy of Oral and Maxillofacial Pathology(25)
Lenaway, Robert
Association of Rehabilitation Programs in Computer Technology(211)
Leng, Janet E.
National Association of Ecumenical and Interreligious Staff(450)
Lenhard, Mary Nell
Blue Cross and Blue Shield Association(231)
Lennan, Anne C.
Society of Professional Benefit Administrators(642)
Lennard, Ian
National Cargo Bureau(487)
Lennon, Susan
Women's College Coalition(693)
Lennox, Christi
American Academy of Periodontology(27)
Lentz, Judy
Hospice and Palliative Nurses Association(328)
Lenz, Edward A.
American Staffing Association(149)
Leo, Sue
National Association for Drama Therapy(432)
Leonard, Dan
America's Health Insurance Plans(19)
Leonard, Helen
Society of State Directors of Health, Physical Education and Recreation(644)
Leonard, John
American Swimming Coaches Association(150)
Leonard, Kate
Correctional Vendors Association(267)
Leonardo, Arthur A.
North American Association of Wardens and Superintendents(555)
Leone, Rosalie
Association of Millwork Distributors(205)
Leongini, Mary Beth
Rehabilitation Engineering and Assistive Technology Society of North America(598)
Lependorf, Jeffrey
Council of Literary Magazines and Presses(273)
Lereah, David
National Association of REALTORS(468)
Lerman, Richard J.
National Association of Uniform Manufacturers and Distributors(480)
Lerner, Ph.D., Jeffrey C.
ECRI(288)
Lescar, Eric
Institute of International Finance(342)
Leshner, Alan I.
American Association for the Advancement of Science(36)
Lesieur, Michelle P.
American Registry of Medical Assistants(122)
Leslie, James
International Association of Machinists and Aerospace Workers(359)
Leslie, Melissa
Distribution Contractors Association(286)
Lesnik, Theresa
Society of Biblical Literature(632)
Lessister, Fay
National Association of Blacks in Criminal Justice(440)
Lessner, Gary
Transworld Advertising Agency Network(664)
Lester, Rosalyn
Costume Society of America(267)
Leto, Lt. Col. Louis
Reserve Officers Association of the U.S.(600)
Letow, Jan
Mechanical Contractors Association of America(415)
Lettice, Paula G.
Entomological Society of America(295)
Lettieri, Trish
American Physical Society(115)
Letwat, JD, MPH, Julie K.
American College of Foot and Ankle Surgeons(66)
LeVan, William H.
Cast Iron Soil Pipe Institute(238)
Levand, Susan
Warehousing Education and Research Council(685)
LeVasseur, Michal
National Council for Geographic Education(497)
Lever, Alvin
American College of Chest Physicians(64)
Levi, Bob
National Association of Postmasters of the United States(465)
Levi, Ed
Apiary Inspectors of America(158)
Levin, Barbara
Forum for Investor Advice(311)
Levin, Mark
Chain Link Fence Manufacturers Institute(242)
Levin-Reisman, Rika
Jewish Education Service of North America(401)

Levine, Felice J.
American Educational Research Association(80)
Levine, Gail B.
National Association of Jewelry Appraisers(459)
Levine, Melissa
American Society of Hypertension(139)
Levitan, Ph.D., Thomas
American Association of Colleges of Osteopathic Medicine(40)
Levitas, Howard
Enterprise Wireless Alliance(295)
Levrio, Ph.D., Jay
American Podiatric Medical Association(116)
Levy, CAE, Beverly I.
American College of Mortgage Attorneys(67)
Levy, Eileen
Land Improvement Contractors of America(405)
Levy, Howard
Trans-Atlantic American Flag Liner Operators(663)
Levy, Prof. Jacob
American Society for Political and Legal Philosophy(131)
Levy, Jill
American Federation of School Administrators(82)
Levy, Michael
Polystyrene Packaging Council(580)
Levy, Michele
Council of the Americas(275)
Lew, Margaret A.
Footwear Distributors and Retailers of America(310)
Lewelling, Joe
Association for the Advancement of Medical Instrumentation(179)
Lewis, Allison L.
Association of Teachers of Preventive Medicine(217)
Lewis, Carol
Forest Products Society(310)
Lewis, Carolyn
Billiard Congress of America(228)
Lewis, Ph.D., CPCU, Christine L.
American Institute for CPCU - Insurance Institute of America(93)
Lewis, Faith
Footwear Distributors and Retailers of America(310)
Lewis, Flint H.
American Chemical Society(62)
Lewis, Frederick L.
National Training Systems Association(547)
Lewis, Gary
Geological Society of America(315)
Lewis, Jacqueline
National Association of Schools of Public Affairs and Administration(470)
Lewis, Jennifer
Association for Women in Mathematics(182)
Lewis, John
American Architectural Manufacturers Association(32)
Lewis, Karen
Forging Industry Association(310)
Lewis, Pat
Council of Large Public Housing Authorities(273)
Lewis, Renee J.
American Concrete Institute(72)
Lewis, CAE, Richard
Forest Resources Association(310)
Lewis, Sylvia
American Planning Association(116)
Lewis, Toni F.
National Association of Minority Media Executives(462)
Lewis-Pickett, Linda R.
American Association of Motor Vehicle Administrators(45)
Lewkowitz, Marc A.
Supima(656)
Leyden, Christine G.
American Association for Continuity of Care(34)
Libbey, Patrick
National Association of County and City Health Officials(447)
Liberatore, Arlette
Society for Industrial and Applied Mathematics(619)
Licata, Lisa
National Alliance for Youth Sports(429)
Licata, Michael J
International Foodservice Manufacturers Association(372)
Licciardi, Lillie
Offshore Marine Service Association(564)
Lichtenberger, Mark
Radiological Society of North America(594)
Lichtenstein, Jack D.P.
ASIS International(163)
Lieber, H. Stephen
Healthcare Information and Management Systems Society(324)
Liebman, Dan
National Turf Writers Association(547)
Liebman, Lance
American Law Institute(100)
Lief, Brett E.
National Council of Higher Education Loan Programs(499)
Lief, Dr. Thomas
National Association of Substance Abuse Trainers and Educators(478)
Liggett, Howard C.
National Tax Lien Association(545)
Liggett, Martha L.
American Society of Hematology(139)
Ligon, Lois
American Academy of Dental Sleep Medicine(21)
Ligon, Tamika
North American Association of State and Provincial Lotteries(554)
Liimatta, Rev. Michael
Association of Gospel Rescue Missions(199)
Lily, Cindi
Federation of Analytical Chemistry and Spectroscopy Societies(303)
Lim, Maribel
American Thoracic Society(151)
Lindeman, CMP, Kent A.
National Association of Orthopaedic Technologists(463)
Society for Free Radical Biology and Medicine(617)
Lindemann, Todd V.
Industrial Fabrics Association International(336)
Linder, Ronald G.
American Association of Colleges of Pharmacy(40)
Lindholm, Douglas L.
Council On State Taxation(277)
Lindley, Ray
National Association of State Textbook Administrators(476)
Lindner, Kathy
Direct Selling Association(285)
Lindner, CAE, Randy L.
National Association of Boards of Examiners of Long Term Care Administrators(440)
Lindsay, Bruce D.
Heart Rhythm Society(324)
Lindsay, David
Society for American Archaeology(613)
Lindsay, Lisa
National Association of Emergency Medical Technicians(450)
Lindsay, Mike
International Saw and Knife Association(385)
Lindstrom, Bill
Association of Film Commissioners International(196)
Lingenfelter, Paul E.
State Higher Education Executive Officers(653)
Lingle, Ted
Specialty Coffee Association of America(650)
Link, Kevin
Association for Management Information in Financial Services(176)
Link, Nina B.
Magazine Publishers of America(409)
Linkous, Jonathan D.
American Telemedicine Association(151)
Linn, Michael R.
National Independent Automobile Dealers Association(518)
Linsky, Norm
Society for Cardiovascular Angiography and Interventions(614)
Linville, Jeff
American Institute of Timber Construction(98)
Liodice, Robert D.
Association of National Advertisers(205)
Lioi, Margaret M.
Chamber Music America(242)
Lipetzky, Thomas
United States Meat Export Federation(676)
Lippin, Linda
Society for Information Display(620)
Lippincott, John
Council for Advancement and Support of Education(267)
Lipscomb, Scott
Association for Technology in Music Instruction(178)
Lipsey, Dawn
International Association of Special Investigation Units(361)
Lipsey, Ph.D., Jerry
American Simmental Association(125)
Lipson, CLU, Marshall
Society of Financial Service Professionals(636)
Lipton, Don
American Farm Bureau Federation(81)
Lipton, Karen Shoos
AABB(1)
Lisack, Jr., CAE, John
American Association of Pharmaceutical Scientists(48)
List, Barry
Institute for Operations Research and the Management Sciences(339)
Lister, Kimberly
Wood Moulding and Millwork Producers Association(694)

Litch, Scott
American Academy of Pediatric Dentistry(26)
Litke, S. Scot
ADSC: The International Association of Foundation Drilling(8)
Little, Barbara Vines
National Genealogical Society(513)
Little, Beth A.
American Society of Bariatric Physicians(134)
Little, Dr. Bruce W.
American Veterinary Medical Association(153)
Little, Charlie
Thoroughbred Club of America(661)
Little, James
Transport Workers Union of America(663)
Littlefield, Cyndy
Association of Jesuit Colleges and Universities(202)
Littlefield, Darcy
National Conference of Executives of The ARC(493)
Littlefield, Ron
Tire Industry Association(662)
Littler, Norm
American Bus Association(60)
Littleton, Jeff
American Society of Heating, Refrigerating and Air-Conditioning Engineers(139)
Littrell, Preston
Society of Government Service Urologists(637)
Livalldais, Pierre
American Blonde D'Aquitaine Association(57)
Lively, Jr., H. Randolph
American Financial Services Association(83)
Lively, Nancy H.
American Cream Draft Horse Association(77)
Lively, Thad
United States Meat Export Federation(676)
Livingston, Ph.D., Jefferis H.
National Association of Business Consultants(441)
Llevellyn, Melissa
American Society for Clinical Pharmacology and Therapeutics(127)
Lloyd, John
National Institute of Building Sciences(520)
Lloyd, Timothy
American Folklore Society(84)
Loar, Granville
Association for Accounting Marketing(167)
Lobb, Richard
National Chicken Council(489)
Loberret, John
Property Casualty Insurers Association of America(591)
Lobring, Dan
Legal Marketing Association(407)
Lochiatto, Carla
American Society of Association Executives & Center for Association Leadership(134)
Locke, Timm
NOFMA: the Wood Flooring Manufacturers Association(553)
Locker, Debra
International Spa Association(392)
Lockert, Barbara
National Sportscasters and Sportswriters Association(543)
Lockridge, Jack D.
Federal Bar Association(302)
Lockwood, Bill
American Society for Automation in Pharmacy(126)
Lockwood, Martha
American Association of Political Consultants(49)
Lodge, Stephen G.
National Confectioners Association of the United States(492)
Loew, Ed.M., Ann T.
American College of Veterinary Surgeons(72)
Loffer, M.D., Franklin
AAGL -- Advancing Minimally Invasive Gynecology Worldwide(1)
Lofgren, Lousanne (Zan)
American Orthopaedic Foot and Ankle Society(111)
LoFrumento, John
American Society of Composers, Authors and Publishers(136)
Loftus, Geoff
Society of Corporate Secretaries and Governance Professionals(634)
Loftus, Jerome C.
QVM/CMC Vehicle Manufacturers Association(594)
Loftus, Thomas
American Osteopathic College of Occupational and Preventive Medicine(112)
Logan, Joseph P.
Summer and Casual Furniture Manufacturers Association(655)
Logsdon, Peggy
American Association of Small Ruminant Practitioners(51)
Loh, Leon
International Institute of Synthetic Rubber Producers(376)
Lohmiller, Sheila
Network of Executive Women in Hospitality(551)
Lohrentz, Greg
Meeting Professionals International(416)
Lohrentz, PMAC, Sandra
American Society of Podiatric Medical Assistants(144)
Loise, Vicki
Association of University Technology Managers(219)
Lombardi, Sioban
Committee of 200(254)
Lonbardini, Carol
Alliance of Motion Picture and Television Producers(17)
Long, Christopher S.
International Door Association(369)
Long, Claire M.
National Register of Health Service Providers in Psychology(535)
Long, Jennie
Association of College and University Housing Officers-International(191)
Long, John R.
United States Equestrian Federation(675)
Long, Kristi
National Business Travel Association(486)
Long, Rosita S.
American Rolling Door Institute(123)
Long, Dr. Scott
Kappa Psi Pharmaceutical Fraternity(403)
Long, Shirley
Clowns of America, International(248)
Longfellow, David G.
Toxicology Forum(662)
Longie, Joanne
National Council for Prescription Drug Programs(497)
Longstreth, Leland B.
American Institute of Commemorative Art(95)
Longsworth, Phillip
Aerobics and Fitness Association of America(10)
Looney, Meg
Software and Information Industry Association(646)
Lopez, Linda
American Political Science Association(116)
Lopez, Lisa
Association of Latino Professionals in Accounting and Finance(203)
Lopez, CAE, Molly
International Association of Lighting Management Companies(359)
National Rural Economic Developers Association(537)
Lopez, Ramon
Association for Unmanned Vehicle Systems International(181)
Lopinsky, Lisa
Public Risk Management Association(593)
Lorch, Robert
Psychonomic Society(592)
Lorenzi, Larry
Distributive Education Clubs of America(286)
Lorrain, Dr. Charles R.
International Conference of Police Chaplains(366)
Lospaluto, Dawn A.
National Association for Printing Leadership(435)
Lotz, David
Actors' Equity Association(8)
Lou, Elvie
International Electronic Article Surveillance Manufacturers Association(370)
Loube, Paul J.
International Association of Approved Basketball Officials(352)
Loudenslager, Doug
National FFA Organization(510)
Loudy, Elizabeth A.
State Government Affairs Council(652)
Lough, Leah
Association for the Advancement of Medical Instrumentation(179)
Loughney, John A.
Society of Philosophers in America(642)
Loughney, Kerry
National Community Education Association(491)
Loughney, Maura
Society for Industrial Microbiology(620)
Loughry, Kevin
Object Management Group(563)
Louie, Arthur
Asian American Certified Public Accountants(162)
Loussedes, Kelly
National Association of Health Underwriters(455)
Lovan, Wanda
Botanical Society of America(231)
Lovato, Helen
Council of American Instructors of the Deaf(270)
Love, Denise
National Association of Health Data Organizations(455)
Love, Felisa
Conference on English Leadership(260)

Lovejoy, Bret D.
American Council on the Teaching of Foreign Languages(76)
Lovell, Deanna
INDA, Association of the Nonwoven Fabrics Industry(333)
Lowden, Joan
American Association of Airport Executives(38)
Lowder, Jon
Society of Competitive Intelligence Professionals(633)
Lowder, Mark J.
Middle East Studies Association of North America(418)
Lowe, Aaron
Automotive Aftermarket Industry Association(223)
Lowe, Christine
Society for Industrial Microbiology(620)
Lowe, M. Dawn
New York Mercantile Exchange(552)
Lowe, Stan
American Society of Health-System Pharmacists(139)
Lowell, CML, CMS, David
Associated Locksmiths of America(165)
Lowenfish, Sonja K.
American Warmblood Registry(154)
Lowenstein, Douglas S.
Entertainment Software Association(295)
Lowery, Lee
Society of National Association Publications(640)
Lowery, Martin
National Rural Electric Cooperative Association(537)
Lowman, Rodney W.
American Plastics Council(116)
Lubell, Michael
American Physical Society(115)
Lubic, James E.
American Watchmakers-Clockmakers Institute(154)
Lubic, Jim
Jewelry Industry Distributors Association(401)
Lubkeman, Dan
Hydroponic Society of America(330)
Lubold, Jenny
American Academy of Otolaryngology-Head and Neck Surgery(26)
Lubragge, Diana M.
Copper and Brass Servicenter Association(266)
Lubrano, Gina
Organization of News Ombudsmen(567)
Lucas, Barbara E.R.
United States Institute for Theatre Technology(676)
Lucas, Elizabeth M.
American Massage Therapy Association(103)
Lucas, James K.
Disaster Preparedness and Emergency Response Association(285)
Lucas, Michele
Farm Credit Council(301)
Lucas, Paula
Commercial Law League of America(253)
Lucero, Morgan
National Association of College and University Food Services(444)
Lucey, FAIA, Lenore M.
National Council of Architectural Registration Boards(498)
Luck, Bonny
Ceilings and Interior Systems Construction Association(241)
Luckado, Amy
Association for Hose and Accessories Distribution(174)
Independent Sealing Distributors(335)
Yacht Brokers Association of America(698)
Luckett, Scott
National Catalog Managers Association(487)
Luckman, Bettie
National Electrical Contractors Association(506)
Luczyk, Sarah
National Child Care Association(489)
Ludeman, Ruth
Association of Executive and Administrative Professionals(196)
National Association of Dental Assistants(448)
Ludena, Chris
National Investment Company Service Association(522)
Ludwig, Jeff
Personal Watercraft Industry Association(574)
Ludwig, Karen
Association of Surgical Technologists(216)
Ludwig, Kristin
American Society of Clinical Oncology(136)
Luedeka, Robert J.
Polyurethane Foam Association(580)
Luedeke, Katherine A.
American Horse Council(91)
Luehrsen, Mary
NAMM - the International Music Products Association(425)
Luhr, Gary W.
Association of Presbyterian Colleges and Universities(208)
Luisi, Jim
Society for Information Management(620)
Lukasik, Kathleen
Association of Independent Trust Companies(200)
Financial Services Technology Network(306)
Luke, M.D., Robert G.
American Clinical and Climatological Association(63)
Luke, William A.
Buses International Association(235)
Lukens, David R.
Associated General Contractors of America(165)
Luker, Mark A.
EDUCAUSE(290)
Lulloff, Alan
Association of State Floodplain Managers(216)
Lulofs, Neal
Audit Bureau of Circulations(222)
Lund, Brad
Healthcare Billing and Management Association(323)
Neurodevelopmental Treatment Association(552)
Lund, Christine
American Society of Radiologic Technologists(145)
Lund, Jackie
National Association for Kinesiology and Physical Education in Higher Education(434)
Lundberg, Rolf
United States Chamber of Commerce(674)
Lundebjerg, Nancy
American Geriatrics Society(87)
Lundgren, Dr. Elizabeth
Ankole Watusi International Registry(157)
Lung, Tina
Employee Relocation Council/Worldwide ERC(293)
Lunzer, Bernard J.
Newspaper Guild - CWA(552)
Luper, Brenda
American Chamber of Commerce Executives(61)
Luria, Don
Council of Independent Restaurants of America(272)
Lusignan, Heather
International Association of Audio Information Services(353)
Lusk, Michelle
Cement Kiln Recycling Coalition(241)
Lust, Tim
National Grain Sorghum Producers(514)
Lustig, Edgar L.
American Society of Theatre Consultants(146)
Luther, Dr. Charles A.
Geoscience and Remote Sensing Society(316)
Luurs, CAE, Kenneth J.
National Association of Bond Lawyers(441)
Luz, Amy McKenna
Association for Enterprise Opportunity(172)
Luzier, Kelly
International Union of Painters and Allied Trades(396)
Lyle, Judy
Association of Occupational Health Professionals in Healthcare(206)
Lyman, Bob
Naval Reserve Association(551)
Lyman, Joseph E.
Insulating Concrete Form Association(344)
Lyman, Mary
Coalition of Publicly Traded Partnerships(249)
Lymn, Nadine
Ecological Society of America(288)
Lynch, Annette
National Association of Collegiate Women Athletic Administrators(445)
Lynch, Connie
National Association of Surety Bond Producers(478)
Lynch, Jean
Academy of Osseointegration(5)
Lynch, Jennifer English
American Immigration Lawyers Association(92)
Medical-Dental-Hospital Business Associates(416)
Lynch, Jim
Trucking Management(666)
Lynch, John
Truck Renting and Leasing Association(666)
Lynch, John H.
North American Securities Administrators Association(560)
Lynch, Kevin
National Industries for the Blind(519)
Lynch, Marvin
American Association of Motor Vehicle Administrators(45)
Lynch, Robert L.
Americans for the Arts(156)
Lynch, Scott
National Association of Local Housing Finance Agencies(460)
Lynch, Tom
National Tank Truck Carriers Conference(545)

Lyndane, Patricia
Environmental Industry Associations(296)
Lynn, John E.
Methanol Institute(418)
Lynn, Randi
North American Folk Music and Dance Alliance(557)
Lyon, Chris
Fibre Channel Industry Association(305)
Lyon, Herb
ISDA - The Office Systems Cooperative(400)
Lyon, Jasmine C.
Veterinary Botanical Medical Association(682)
Lyon, Jill
United Telecom Council(679)
Lyon, M.D., M.P., Joseph L.
Society for Epidemiologic Research(617)
Lyon, Mary Sue
Power Transmission Distributors Association(582)
Lyons, Catherine
International Sleep Products Association(386)
Lyons, Chris
American Association for Laboratory Animal Science(35)
Lyons, Clinton
National Legal Aid and Defender Association(524)
Lyons, Coley
Society for Industrial and Applied Mathematics(619)
Lyons, John
American Kennel Club(100)
Lyons, Marsha
Christian Management Association(246)
Lyons, Pamela
International Association for Mathematical Geology(351)
Lyons, Rachel
American Arts Alliance(32)
Lytle, David
International Laser Display Association(377)
Mable, Phyllis
Council for the Advancement of Standards in Higher Education(270)
Mabry, Michael R.
Society of Interventional Radiology(639)
Mabry, Vickie
National Pecan Shellers Association(532)
Macalino, Tonya
Business Forms Management Association(235)
MacCarthy, Timothy
Association of International Automobile Manufacturers(201)
MacDonald, CLU, G. Ron
Society of Financial Service Professionals(636)
MacDonald, Linda
North American Agricultural Marketing Officials(554)
MacDonald, Mary Lehman
AFT Healthcare(11)
Macey, Lisa
Voices for America's Children(684)
Macfarlane, Ann
National Association of Judiciary Interpreters and Translators(459)
Macgregor, Ian
National Association of Geoscience Teachers(454)
Mach, Ray
Partnership for Air-Conditioning, Heating Refrigeration Accreditation(571)
MacIlwaine, Paula
American Water Works Association(154)
Mack, Timothy C.
World Future Society(696)
Mack, Toby
Associated Equipment Distributors(165)
Mackay, Connie
Association of Christian Therapists(190)
Mackenzie, Joan
National Association for Research and Therapy of Homosexuality(435)
Mackes, Ph.D., Marilyn F.
National Association of Colleges and Employers(444)
Mackey, Mark
Livestock Marketing Association(409)
Mackey, Mark J.
National Association for Variable Annuities(437)
Mackey, Michelle
International Association for Exhibition Management(350)
MacKie, II, Robb S.
American Bakers Association(55)
Mackie, Sue
United States Swim School Association(677)
Mackin, Robert E.
Association of Financial Guaranty Insurors(197)
MacKinnon, Douglas
Hop Growers of America(328)
MacKinnon, Gail
National Cable & Telecommunications Association(486)
Mackintosh, Esther
Federation of State Humanities Councils(304)
MacLeod, Alistair
North American Society for Social Philosophy(561)
MacLeod, Sarah
Aeronautical Repair Station Association(10)
Macnab, Alistair
Animal Transportation Association(157)
Macoy, Ian
NACHA - The Electronic Payments Association(424)
MacPherson, Jim
America's Blood Centers(19)
Madden, Dennis
Automatic Transmission Rebuilders Association(223)
Madden, Patrick
Association of Performing Arts Presenters(207)
Maddox, Lyn
American Society of Tropical Medicine and Hygiene(147)
Maddux, Daniel J.
American Payroll Association(113)
Maddux, Michael S.
American College of Clinical Pharmacy(65)
Mader, Richard E.
Association for Retail Technology Standards(178)
Madsen, Kristen
National Academy of Recording Arts and Sciences(427)
Maehara, CFRE, CAE, Paulette V.
Association of Fundraising Professionals(198)
Maenner, Anna
National Association of Fraternal Insurance Counsellors(454)
Maffe, Victor
WorkPlace Furnishings(695)
Maffei, Trish
Fashion Group International(301)
Mafrica, Leonard
Oncology Nursing Society(564)
Magathan, Jeanie
Automotive Parts Remanufactuers Association(224)
Magee, Kellee
American Nursery and Landscape Association(109)
Maggi, CAE, Dennis J.
American College of Trial Lawyers(71)
Maggiore, Anne F.
International Anesthesia Research Society(349)
Maghraoui, Lisa
National Automobile Dealers Association(482)
Magid, Donni
Metal Powder Industries Federation(417)
Magnan, Patrick
National Court Reporters Association(503)
Magness, Rita Chua
American Academy of Facial Plastic and Reconstructive Surgery(22)
Magnuson, Mary
National Association of Fundraising Ticket Manufacturers(454)
Magnuson, Norman
Consumer Data Industry Association(263)
Magnuson, Peter
Association for Career and Technical Education(169)
Magone, Carla
Independent Lubricant Manufacturers Association(335)
Magrogan, Mary
Institute for Operations Research and the Management Sciences(339)
Magruder, Lora
Organization for the Promotion and Advancement of Small Telecommunications Companies(567)
Maguire, D.D.S., John J.
Association of Managed Care Dentists(203)
Maguire, John R.
Society of the Plastics Industry(645)
Mahaffey, CAE, J.C. (Chris)
American College of Foot and Ankle Surgeons(66)
Mahaffey, Michael
Society of American Fight Directors(630)
Mahan, Megan
American Ceramic Society(61)
Mahan, L.P.N., Patrick
National Association for Practical Nurse Education and Service(435)
Maher, James R.
American Land Title Association(100)
Maher, Kevin
American Hotel & Lodging Association(92)
Maher, Nicole R.
Truck Mixer Manufacturers Bureau(665)
Maher, Patrick
Personal Computer Memory Card International Association(573)
Mahler, Cyndi
National Association for Search and Rescue(436)
Mahlmann, John J.
MENC: The National Association for Music Education(417)
Mahurin, Dr. Ronald P.
Council for Christian Colleges and Universities(268)
Maibach, Michael
European-American Business Council(298)

Maiman, Janice
American Institute of Certified Public Accountants(95)
Maine, Lucinda L.
American Association of Colleges of Pharmacy(40)
Mairena, Sue
American Association for Homecare(35)
Mais, Holly
American Institute of Timber Construction(98)
Maiuri, Michael
Tile Contractors' Association of America(661)
Maixner, Betsy
National Association of State Departments of Agriculture(474)
Majdalany, Michael
Transaction Processing Performance Council(663)
Majewski, Priscilla
American Association of Hip and Knee Surgeons(43)
Maki, Kimberly
Society of Cable Telecommunications Engineers(632)
Maki, Reid
Association of Farmworker Opportunity Programs(196)
Makin, Michael
Graphic Arts Technical Foundation(319)
Printing Industries of America(584)
Makino, Seiichi
Alliance of Associations of Teachers of Japanese(16)
Makowski, Ann
Society for Environmental Graphic Design(617)
Makowski, Robert
Minerals, Metals and Materials Society, The(420)
Malakoff, Deborah
Vision Council of America(684)
Malan, Todd M.
Organization for International Investment(567)
Malara, Toby J.
National Technical Services Association(546)
Malarkey, Faye A.
Regional Airline Association(597)
Malbin, Irene L.
Cosmetic, Toiletry and Fragrance Association(267)
Malchesky, D.Eng., Paul S.
International Federation for Artificial Organs(371)
Male, CAE, Jane
Electrical Equipment Representatives Association(291)
Investment Recovery Association(399)
Malek, Tarah
Paso Fino Horse Association(572)
Males, Eric
National Lime Association(525)
Malet, D.O., Sidney
American Osteopathic College of Rheumatology(112)
Maline, Karen F.
Justice Research and Statistics Association(403)
Mallernee, II, Rollin E.
National Basketball Athletic Trainers Association(483)
Professional Baseball Athletic Trainers Society(586)
Professional Football Athletic Trainers Society(587)
Mallett, Jetaun
National Black MBA Association(484)
Mallia, Robert A.
International Council of Shopping Centers(368)
Mallie, Michael
American Osteopathic Association(111)
Mallin, Thomas W.
Property Loss Research Bureau(591)
Mallon, Francis J.
American Physical Therapy Association(115)
Mallory, Gail
Oncology Nursing Society(564)
Mallory, CAE, James L.
Non-Ferrous Founders' Society(553)
Malloy, Cheryl Patton
Mortgage Bankers Association(421)
Malloy, Maureen
Society for American Archaeology(613)
Malloy, Michelle
National Association of Regulatory Utility Commissioners(469)
Malloy, Thomas J.
Intermodal Association of North America(347)
Malme, Jerry
National Counter Intelligence Corps Association(503)
Malone, Beverly
National League for Nursing(523)
Malone, Karen
Healthcare Information and Management Systems Society(324)
Malone, Robert J.
History of Science Society(327)
Maloney, Sally A.
Equipment Leasing Association of America(297)
Maloney, Shirley
National Association of Industrial and Office Properties(458)
Maloney, William A.
American Society of Travel Agents(146)
Maloney Jr., CAE, James D.
Community Leadership Association(256)
Malott, Ph.D., Maria E.
Association for Behavior Analysis(168)
Manak, Pat
National Association of Athletic Development Directors(439)
National Association of Collegiate Directors of Athletics(444)
Manardo, Karen
Society of Manufacturing Engineers(639)
Manasse, Dr. Henri R.
American Society of Health-System Pharmacists(139)
Mancini, Jr., Frank W.
International Security Officers, Police, and Guards Union(386)
Mancini, John F.
Association for Information and Image Management International(174)
Mancino, Ed.D., RN, CAE, Diane J.
National Student Nurses Association(544)
Mancuso, CAE, Dawn M.
Association of Air Medical Services(183)
Mandarich, Stanley
World Allergy Organization - IACCI(695)
Mandel, Jed R.
Engine Manufacturers Association(295)
Mandelbaum, Mark
Association for Computing Machinery(170)
Mandrier, Brian J.
National Association of Healthcare Consultants(455)
Maner, Machelle
Urban Financial Services Coalition(680)
Manes, Stone
National Clay Pottery Association(490)
Mangan, Mona
Writers Guild of America, East(697)
Manger, Donald
Association of Specialists in Cleaning and Restoration International(214)
Mangiaracina, Gina
Anxiety Disorders Association of America(157)
Manginelli, Dina
American Society for Artificial Internal Organs(126)
Mangione, Peter T.
Footwear Distributors and Retailers of America(310)
Mangual, J.A. "Yogi"
National Industries for the Blind(519)
Mangum, Judy
American College of Osteopathic Surgeons(69)
Manke, CAE, Jim
Academy of Surgical Research(5)
Agricultural and Industrial Manufacturers' Representatives Association(12)
Laboratory Animal Management Association(404)
Wiring Harness Manufacturers Association(690)
Manley, Edward
International Food Service Executives' Association(372)
Manley, Jillian
American Academy of Pain Management(26)
Manley, Larry
NAMM - the International Music Products Association(425)
Manlove, Beverly
General Federation of Women's Clubs(315)
Mann, Barton
American Orthopaedic Society for Sports Medicine(111)
Mann, Robert
Dance Masters of America(281)
Mann, Robyn
American Society of Pediatric Nephrology(143)
Mann, Wendy
National Telecommunications Cooperative Association(546)
Mann, William
American Philosophical Association(114)
Manning, Leecia
Magazine Publishers of America(409)
Manning, Marybeth
SPIE - The International Society for Optical Engineering(651)
Mano, Barry
National Association of Sports Officials(472)
Manoni, Marietta
Society for Biomolecular Sciences(614)
Manoogian, Antran
International Animated Film Society, ASIFA-Hollywood(349)
Manser, Virginia A.
Cooling Technology Institute(265)
Mansfield, Rebecca A.
American Osteopathic College of Dermatology(112)
Mansfield, Rodger
National Corn Growers Association(496)
Manspeaker, Barbara
American Association of Zoo Keepers(54)
Mansur, Bernadette
National Hockey League(517)
Mantler, Francis
National Garden Clubs(513)

Manziek, Dr. Larry
International Precious Metals Institute(383)
Manzione, Ph.D., G. Thomas
Rolf Institute(602)
Maola, David
Drug Information Association(287)
Mapa, Charles W.
National League of Postmasters of the U.S.(524)
Maple, Howard
American Institute of Organbuilders(97)
Maples Dunn, Ph.D., Mary
American Philosophical Society(114)
Maraney, John V. "Skip"
National Star Route Mail Contractors Association(543)
Marans, Jerrold
Sheet Metal and Air Conditioning Contractors' National Association(610)
Marcello, Jr., C.J.
Paso Fino Horse Association(572)
Marchese, Anthony J.
International Foodservice Manufacturers Association(372)
Marchiondo, Dr. Alan
American Association of Veterinary Parasitologists(54)
Marchionna, Susan
National Council on Crime and Delinquency(502)
Marchyshyn, Jim
International Hot Rod Association(375)
Marcum, Jr., John P.
Association of Statisticians of American Religious Bodies(216)
Marcum, Larry
National Environmental Health Association(507)
Marcus, Lynne G.
American College of Chest Physicians(64)
Marcus, Shel
American Equilibration Society(81)
Marcy, Charles
National Head Start Association(516)
Mardock, APR, CAE, Marsha
National Speakers Association(542)
Mare, Doris
National Psychological Association for Psychoanalysis(534)
Marema, Lenore
Surety Association of America(656)
Maresch, Wayne
Land Improvement Contractors of America(405)
Margaritis, John
Independent Armored Car Operators Association(333)
Margolis, Wendy
Association of Science-Technology Centers(213)
Marguilies, Beth
National Electrical Contractors Association(506)
Marhevko, Tom
National Marine Manufacturers Association(526)
Mariano, Joseph N.
Direct Selling Association(285)
Maric, Tara
Council of Real Estate Brokerage Managers(274)
Marion, Joseph
Association of Service and Computer Dealers International(213)
North-American Association of Telecommunications Dealers(562)
Markel, Richard
Association for Wedding Professionals International(182)
Markels, Gail
Entertainment Software Association(295)
Markese, John
American Association of Individual Investors(44)
Markey, Carolyn
Visiting Nurse Associations of America(684)
Markham, Diane
Reserve Officers Association of the U.S.(600)
Markkanen, Jennifer
American Academy of Sleep Medicine(28)
Associated Professional Sleep Socs.(166)
Markovchick, Kathryn
International Association for the Study of Cooperation in Education(351)
Markovich, CPCU, AIM, Lois A.
Society of Insurance Trainers and Educators(639)
Markowitz, Barrie
United States Tennis Association(677)
Markowitz, Jan
National Association for Public Health Statistics and Information Systems(435)
Markowski, Paul
American Academy of Otolaryngology-Head and Neck Surgery(26)
Marks, Gary H.
Association for the Advancement of Computing in Education(179)
Marks, CAE, James R.
CPCU Society(278)
Markwart, Luther A.
American Sugarbeet Growers Association(150)
Markwood, Priscilla
Association of Pathology Chairs(207)
Markwood, Sandra
National Association of Area Agencies on Aging(439)
Marlette, C. Alan
Automotive Trade Association Executives(224)
Marlow, M.D., John
Gynecologic Surgery Society(321)
Marmon, Christina
American Political Science Association(116)
Marois, Beverly J.
Masonry Heater Association of North America(413)
Marolt, Bill
United States Ski Association(677)
Maron, Rebecca
Society for Vascular Surgery(629)
Marovec, FMP, Lisa L.
Council of Hotel and Restaurant Trainers(272)
Marrero, Kimberly
International Association of Forensic Nurses(357)
Marrocco, Keith
Society of Mexican American Engineers and Scientists(640)
Marshall, Danielle
Case Management Society of America(238)
Marshall, Louise
International Swaps and Derivatives Association(393)
Marshall, Marian
Mason Contractors Association of America(413)
Marshall, Martha
National Association of Disability Examiners(449)
Marshall, Stephanie
American Council on Education(76)
Marshall, Terry
International Community Corrections Association(366)
Marshall, Thomas A.
American Association of Neurological Surgeons(46)
Marshall, Wade
National Catholic Educational Association(487)
Marsico, Dale J.
Community Transportation Association of America(256)
Marston, Steve
National Association of Certified Valuation Analysts(442)
Marston, Twig
Beef Improvement Federation(227)
Mart, Warren
International Association of Machinists and Aerospace Workers(359)
Martell, Peter
Ice Skating Institute(330)
Marti, Ph.D., Judith E.
Society for Economic Anthropology(616)
Martin, Ph.D., A. Dallas
National Association of Student Financial Aid Administrators(477)
Martin, Anna
Women's Jewelry Association(693)
Martin, Beverly
National Community Pharmacists Association(491)
Martin, Bill
Gravure Association of America(320)
Martin, Bob
Career College Association(237)
Martin, Bridget D.
International Brotherhood of Boilermakers, Iron Ship Builders, Blacksmiths, Forgers and Helpers(363)
Martin, Ph.D., Carol L.
African Studies Association(11)
Martin, CAE, Charles "Chuck"
American Physical Therapy Association(115)
Martin, Chris
National Council of Higher Education Loan Programs(499)
Martin, Danny
American Society of Naval Engineers(142)
Martin, CAE, David Julian
Society of Critical Care Medicine(634)
Martin, Edward J.
Association of Racing Commissioners International(211)
Martin, Gary C.
North American Export Grain Association(557)
Martin, Jody
U.S. Lacrosse(668)
Martin, Kelly
American International Automobile Dealers Association(98)
Martin, Mary
National Intramural-Recreational Sports Association(522)
Martin, Michael J.
National Association for Pupil Transportation(435)
Martin, Pam
RMA - The Risk Management Association(602)
Martin, Patricia
International Sleep Products Association(386)
Martin, Patrick
Society for Industrial Archeology(620)

Martin, Dr. Paul
Lawn and Garden Dealers' Association(406)
Martin, Renee C.
National Association of Document Examiners(449)
Martin, Robert L.
National Emergency Number Association(507)
Martin, Ronald T.
American Association of Orthodontists(47)
Martin, CNE, CCNA, Sherry
APICS - The Association for Operations Management(158)
Martin, Suzanne
American Society of Newspaper Editors(142)
Martin, Teri
Association of American Geographers(184)
Martin, Tracey
American Psychological Association - Division of Psychotherapy(118)
Martin, Vance G.
Conservation and Preservation Charities of America(261)
Martine, Brian
Metaphysical Society of America(418)
Martineau, Marie
Spanish-Barb Breeders Association(648)
Martinez, Anne R.
American Podiatric Medical Association(116)
Martinez, Deb
National Shoe Retailers Association(539)
Martinez, Emmy
National Alliance for Youth Sports(429)
Martinez, Lina
National Federation of Hispanic Owned Newspapers(509)
Martinez, Mark
Association of Professional Energy Managers(209)
Martinez, Michele
American Academy of Allergy, Asthma, and Immunology(20)
Martinez, Nubia
International Advertising Association(348)
Martinez, Robert
Violin Society of America(683)
Martinez, Samanthi
Association of Professional Model Makers(209)
Martinez-Alvarez, Francisco J.
Society of Federal Labor and Employee Relations Professionals(636)
Martini, John C.
United Union of Roofers, Waterproofers and Allied Workers(679)
Martino, Salvatore
American Society of Radiologic Technologists(145)
Martinson, Gregory
Independent Community Bankers of America(333)
Martori, CAE, Joanne
Association of Coupon Professionals(193)
Martucci, Jr., James C.
American Association of Advertising Agencies(37)
Marvelle, Kevin
American Academy of Physician Assistants(27)
Marx, Daniel
Digital Printing and Imaging Association(284)
Marx, Eric C.
National Labor Relations Board Professional Association(523)
Marzelli, Alan G.
Jockey Club(402)
Maslyn, Mark
American Farm Bureau Federation(81)
Mason, Angela
American Association for Women Radiologists(37)
Mason, Anna Marie
Society for Imaging Informatics in Medicine(619)
Mason, CMP, Cathy
American Academy of Physical Medicine and Rehabilitation(27)
Mason, Cordelia
American Academy of Craniofacial Pain(21)
Mason, Dave
American Physical Therapy Association(115)
Mason, Debra L.
Religion Newswriters Association(598)
Mason, Juliet
American Council on the Teaching of Foreign Languages(76)
Mason, Mike
Farm Credit Council(301)
Mason, Robert
National Insurance Crime Bureau(522)
Mason, Steve
Society for Thermal Medicine(628)
Massare, Ph.D., John S.
Contact Lens Association of Ophthalmologists(264)
Massello, DBA, Carolyn S.
International Stress Management Association - U.S. Branch(393)
Massey, Dr. Joseph M.
International Brangus Breeders Association(363)
Massey, Juliette L.
World Aquaculture Society(695)
Massoff, Mrs. Nathan
Sigma Epsilon Delta Dental Fraternity(610)
Masson, Tonia
Environmental Mutagen Society(296)
Teratology Society(659)
Mast, Hale
Fiduciary and Risk Management Association(305)
Matako, Nancy
American Association of Meat Processors(45)
Mather, Tom
Self Insurance Institute of America, Inc.(608)
Mathers, Kathy O.
Fertilizer Institute(305)
Mathes, Karen
American Academy of Family Physicians(22)
Mathews, Alexander S.
Animal Health Institute(157)
Mathews, Bill
National Association of Professional Band Instrument Repair Technicians(465)
Mathews, Dan
National Automatic Merchandising Association(482)
Mathews, Nancy Mowll
Catalogue Raisonne Scholars Association(239)
Mathis, Michael
International Brotherhood of Teamsters, AFL-CIO(363)
Maticic, Marilyn A.
Association for Advanced Life Underwriting(167)
Matikonis, Kathleen
Society for Light Treatment and Biological Rhythms(621)
Matilick, Sam
National Association of Enrolled Agents(451)
Matlon, Ph.D., Ronald J.
American Society of Trial Consultants(147)
Mattai, P. Rudy
International Society for Educational Planning(387)
Matte, Christa
Can Manufacturers Institute(237)
Matteozzi, Soledad
Argentina-American Chamber of Commerce(160)
Matter, John
National Ballroom and Entertainment Association(483)
Matternas, John J.
American Academy of State Certified Appraisers(29)
Matthews, Bill
Conference of State Bank Supervisors(260)
Matthews, Cheryl
National Paint and Coatings Association(531)
Matthews, Sr., Darryl R.
National Association of Black Accountants(440)
Matthews, Dean
Western Red Cedar Pole Association(687)
Matthews, John
Federation of State Humanities Councils(304)
Matthews, Kelly
Reserve Officers Association of the U.S.(600)
Matthews, Sallie
Society of American Gastrointestinal and Endoscopic Surgeons(630)
Matthews, Stuart
Flight Safety Foundation(308)
Matthews, Tammi
American Society of Baking(134)
Matthews, Tracy
American Public Gardens Association(119)
Mattingley, Jenny
WineAmerica(690)
Mattingly, Joseph M.
Gas Appliance Manufacturers Association(314)
Mattison, Jay
National Dairy Herd Improvement Association(504)
Mattoni, Rudolf H.T.
Lepidoptera Research Foundation(407)
Mattson, Kristina
Credit Union Executives Society(279)
Matulionis, MSPH, Rose Marie
Directors of Health Promotion and Public Health Education(285)
Matura, Donna L.
Association of Productivity Specialists(208)
Matyas, PhD, Marsha Lakes
American Physiological Society(115)
Matz, Marshall
School Nutrition Association(606)
Matz, Jr, USA (Ret.), MG William M.
National Association for Uniformed Services and Society of Military Widows(437)
Mauck, Kathy
American Society for Clinical Pathology(127)
Maue, Carolyn
American College of Mental Health Administration(67)
Mauer, Michael
American Association of University Professors(53)
Mauldin, Deborah
American Dance Guild(78)
Maurer, D.O., Robert S.
American Osteopathic College of Rheumatology(112)

Mauriello, David
International Society for Ecological Modelling-North American Chapter(387)
Maves, MD, MBA, Michael D.
American Medical Association(104)
Mawson, Thomas C.
Supply Chain Council(656)
Maxey, Rebecca
Society of Nuclear Medicine(641)
Maxey, Tim
Regulatory Affairs Professionals Society(598)
Maxwell, James
American Mathematical Society(103)
Maxwell, Robert J.
National Association of Beverage Importers-Wine-Spirits-Beer(439)
Maxwell, Susan
National Association of Advisors for the Health Professions(438)
May, Christian
Federal Network for Sustainability(302)
May, J. Thomas
Society for Applied Anthropology(613)
May, James N.
National Association of School Psychologists(470)
May, James C.
Air Transport Association of America(13)
May, Jill
International Association of Diecutting and Diemaking(356)
May, Lynn
American Society of Radiologic Technologists(145)
May, Mary
Associated Locksmiths of America(165)
May, Mike
Soccer Industry Council of America(612)
May, Robert
North American Punch Manufacturers Association(559)
May, Simeon
National Association of Church Business Administration(443)
May, Stacy
American Association of Pharmaceutical Scientists(48)
May, III, Virgil Robert
National Association of Disability Evaluating Professionals(449)
Mayberry, Peter C.
INDA, Association of the Nonwoven Fabrics Industry(333)
Mayberry, Peter G.
Healthcare Compliance Packaging Council(323)
Pharmaceutical Printed Literature Association(575)
Maycock, Ellen
American Mathematical Society(103)
Mayer, Cathy
Marble Institute of America(412)
Mayer, Joseph L.
Copper and Brass Fabricators Council(266)
Mayes, Brenda J.
American Academy of Periodontology(27)
Mayes, Sara
Fashion Accessories Shippers Association(301)
Mayfield, CMP, Karin
National Home Furnishings Association(517)
Mayfield, Sarah
Association of State Dam Safety Officials(215)
Maynard, Ph.D., John
Employee Assistance Professionals Association(293)
Mayo, Rhenda
American Welding Society(154)
Mays, John
National Animal Control Association(430)
Mayuga, Stacy
Agricultural Retailers Association(12)
Maze, Ilana
National Association of Health Underwriters(455)
Mazur, Melva E.
American Association for Homecare(35)
Mazur, Jr., Michael J.
International Paralegal Management Association(382)
Mazza, Lorraine
International Council of Shopping Centers(368)
Mazzola, Susan
Society of Laparoendoscopic Surgeons(639)
McAdoo, Doug
American Society of Consultant Pharmacists(136)
McAlister, Roy E.
American Hydrogen Association(92)
McAllister, Patricia
Council of Graduate Schools(272)
McAndrews, Lawrence A.
National Association of Children's Hospitals(443)
McAninch, Jay
Archery Trade Association(160)
McArdle, Bernice
National Marine Bankers Association(525)
McArthur, Lisa
International Ground Source Heat Pump Association(374)
McAuliffe, Jack
American Symphony Orchestra League(150)
McAuliffe, Sherry
American Osteopathic Association(111)
McBride, Deborah
Society of Critical Care Medicine(634)
McBride, Gene
Fraternal Field Managers Association(311)
McBride, III, James
Affiliated Warehouse Companies(10)
McBride, John J.
Livestock Marketing Association(409)
McBride, Marsha J.
National Association of Broadcasters(441)
McBride, CAE, Maurice H.
National Petrochemical & Refiners Association(532)
McBride, Michael
United Scenic Artists(672)
McBride, Neil
Business Software Alliance(236)
McCabe, John M.
National Conference of Commissioners on Uniform State Laws(493)
McCabe, John J.
Association of Foreign Trade Representatives(197)
McCabe, Ph.D., Philip
Academy of Behavioral Medicine Research(2)
McCabe, Richard E.
Wildlife Management Institute(689)
McCafferty, Teresa
Independent Petroleum Association of America(335)
McCain, Byron
American Assembly for Men in Nursing(33)
McCall, Dr. John W.
American Heartworm Society(90)
McCall, Linda
Association of American University Presses(185)
McCallen, Tiffany
Religion Newswriters Association(598)
McCalley, Barbara
Ophthalmic Photographers' Society(565)
McCandless, Jerri
American Network of Community Options and Resources(108)
McCann, Daisy S.
Clinical Ligand Assay Society(248)
McCann, RN, DNS.c, Kathleen
National Association of Psychiatric Health Systems(467)
McCann, Nancy Kaplan
American Society of Cataract and Refractive Surgery(135)
McCarren, Helen
Society of Cosmetic Chemists(634)
McCarroll, Ollie
American Osteopathic Association(111)
McCarron, Douglas J.
United Brotherhood of Carpenters and Joiners of America(670)
McCarron, Sheila
National Council of Catholic Women(498)
McCartan, Patrick
Aerospace Industries Association of America(10)
McCarter, Katherine
Ecological Society of America(288)
McCarthy, Brian A.
Computing Technology Industry Association(258)
McCarthy, Chris
Fragrance Materials Association of the United States(311)
McCarthy, (Ret.), Lt. Gen. Dennis
Reserve Officers Association of the U.S.(600)
McCarthy, James A.
Snack Food Association(612)
McCarthy, Richard
American Land Title Association(100)
McCartney, Marion
American College of Nurse-Midwives(68)
McCarty, James K.
Manufacturing Jewelers and Suppliers of America(411)
McCarty, Kathy
International Council on Hotel, Restaurant and Institutional Education(368)
McCashion, Linda
National Potato Promotion Board(533)
McCaskill, Charlotte
American Institute of Certified Planners(95)
McCauley, Gail R.
Building Service Contractors Association International(234)
McCauley, Lisa
Association of Retail Marketing Services(212)
McClay, Allen
CIES, The Food Business Forum(246)
McCleary, Deitra
American Emu Association(81)
McClelland, John
American Rental Association(122)
McClelland, Rita K.
Association of Home Appliance Manufacturers(200)
McClendon, CAE, Brent
International Wood Products Association(397)
McClenny, Tricia
Society of Interventional Radiology(639)

McClure, David P.
U.S. Internet Industry Association(668)
McClure, Kent D.
Animal Health Institute(157)
McClure, Orla
Plastic Surgery Admininstrative Association(578)
McConnell, Ann
General Merchandise Distributors Council(315)
McConnell, Barbara
Food Industry Association Executives(309)
McConnell, Chuck
Public Broadcasting Management Association(592)
McConnell, David T.
General Merchandise Distributors Council(315)
McConnell, Robert
National Association of State Foresters(475)
McConnell, Dr. Sally N.
National Association of Elementary School Principals(450)
McConnon, Pat
Council of State and Territorial Epidemiologists(274)
McCorkle, Michele
Oncology Nursing Society(564)
McCormack, Jeanne
American Composites Manufacturers Association(72)
McCormick, Jennifer
American Cinema Editors(62)
McCormick, Jr., Walter B.
United States Telecom Association(677)
McCourt, James P. "Bud"
International Association of Heat and Frost Insulators and Asbestos Workers(357)
McCown, Colin
American Wood-Preservers' Association(155)
McCoy, Keith
National Association of Manufacturers(460)
McCoy, Laura
Council of Independent Colleges(272)
McCracken, Keith
Marketing Agencies Association Worldwide(412)
McCracken, Todd O.
National Small Business Association(540)
McCrackin, Leah
American Society of Dermatopathology(137)
Institute of Nuclear Materials Management(343)
McCray, Kevin
National Ground Water Association(515)
McCrensky, Jay
International Private Infrastructure Association(383)
Romanian-American Chamber of Commerce(603)
McCullough, Carol
Association of Clinical Research Professionals(190)
McCullough, CAE, Don R.
National Barbecue Association(483)
McCullough, Kristen
National Association of Fire Equipment Distributors(452)
McCullough, Lynn
ALMA - the International Loudspeaker Association(17)
Association for Convention Operations Management(171)
International Furnishings and Design Association(373)
McCurdy, David
Electronic Industries Alliance(292)
McCutchan, Valerie
National Intramural-Recreational Sports Association(522)
McCutcheon, Russell T.
North American Association for the Study of Religion(554)
McDermott, Shane
American Thoracic Society(151)
McDonald, PBVM, Sr. Dale
National Catholic Educational Association(487)
Mcdonald, Helene
Museum Computer Network(423)
McDonald, John
Central Station Alarm Association(241)
McDonald, Mary
American Philosophical Society(114)
McDonald, Nancy
American Board of Professional Psychology(58)
McDonald, M.D., F.A., Walter J.
Council of Medical Specialty Socs.(273)
McDonnell, Lori
Association of Aviation Psychologists(187)
McDonnell, Mary
Social Science Research Council(613)
McDonough, Doug
American Dental Assistants Association(78)
McDonough, Timothy
American Council on Education(76)
McDougal, Claudia A.
Outpatient Ophthalmic Surgery Society(569)
McDougall, Carol
American Bakers Association(55)
McDowell, Ella
National Council for the Social Studies(497)
McDowell, Thomas H.
National Association of Trade Exchanges(479)
McElgunn, Peggy
Alliance of Cardiovascular Professionals(16)
Teaching-Family Association(658)
McElroy, Arvel
National Interscholastic Swimming Coaches Association(522)
McElroy, Deborah C.
Regional Airline Association(597)
McElroy, Edward J.
AFT - Public Employees(11)
American Federation of Teachers(82)
McEntee, Christine W.
American Institute of Architects(94)
McEntee, Elliott C.
NACHA - The Electronic Payments Association(424)
McEntee, Gerald W.
American Federation of State, County and Municipal Employees(82)
McEwen, Darryl D.
International Association of Used Equipment Dealers(361)
McEwen, Jane W.
International Packaged Ice Association(382)
McFadden, Lisa
American Association of Immunologists(44)
McFadden, Luke
American Subcontractors Association(149)
McFarland, Debra A.
Aircraft Electronics Association(14)
McFarland, Laurel
National Association of Schools of Public Affairs and Administration(470)
McFarland, Robert
National Religious Broadcasters(536)
McFarlin, Bill
International Association for Jazz Education(351)
McGarry, Dennis
Document Management Industries Association(286)
Mcgary, Patrick
American Society for Parenteral and Enteral Nutrition(131)
McGavin, Dianne
Biophysical Society(229)
McGeary, MT (ASCP), MSHA, Jennifer K.
Clinical and Laboratory Standards Institute(248)
McGee, Fred L.
Architectural Precast Association(160)
McGee, Gerald J.
International Copper Association(367)
McGee, James M.
National Alliance of Postal and Federal Employees(429)
McGee, Jr., Thomas C.
Inter-Industry Conference on Auto Collision Repair(346)
McGeehan, Donna
International Castor Oil Association(364)
McGeehan, James D.
Project Management Institute(590)
McGehee, Barbara J.
Veterinary Cancer Society(682)
McGehee, Elton
Cement Employers Association(241)
McGill, Jennifer H.
Association for Education in Journalism and Mass Communication(172)
Association of Schools of Journalism and Mass Communication(213)
McGill, Sharon
American Osteopathic Association(111)
McGillicuddy, Linda K.
American Headache Society(89)
McGillivray, Peter
Specialty Equipment Market Association(650)
McGinly, Ph.D., CAE, William C.
Association for Healthcare Philanthropy(173)
McGinnis, Cheryl
American Tinnitus Association(151)
McGlynn, Kelly
United States Rowing Association(677)
McGoff, Dr. Michael F.
American Name Society(107)
Mcgonegle, Pat
National Pork Producers Council(533)
McGough, Michael
National Investor Relations Institute(522)
McGrane, Mary
International Trademark Association(394)
McGrath, C. Peter
National Association of State Universities and Land Grant Colleges(477)
McGrath, CAE, Charles A.
Interlocking Concrete Pavement Institute(347)
Tile Roofing Institute(661)
McGrath, JD, Eileen
American Society of Addiction Medicine(133)
McGrath, Julie
AORN(158)
McGraw, James L.
International Institute of Synthetic Rubber Producers(376)
McGraw, Scott
International Association of Tour Managers - North American Region(361)

McGreevey, III, James A.
American Beverage Association(56)
McGreevey, John D.
Tin Stabilizers Association(661)
McGreevy, Lisa
Financial Services Roundtable(306)
McGreevy, Tim
U.S.A. Dry Pea and Lentil Council(668)
McGuckin, Tim
International Bridge, Tunnel and Turnpike Association(363)
McGuffin, Michael
American Herbal Products Association(90)
McGuinness, Nargis
Danish-American Chamber of Commerce (USA)(281)
McGuire, Jim
BPA Worldwide(232)
McGuire, Joseph M.
Association of Home Appliance Manufacturers(200)
McGuire, Leigh A.
Security Industry Association(607)
McGuire, Paul
Independent Community Bankers of America(333)
McGuire, Sean
Plumbing Contractors of America(579)
McGuirk, Dennis P.
IPC - Association Connecting Electronics Industries(399)
McGurgan, Diane
National Association of Science Writers(471)
McHugh, Kathleen
American Specialty Toy Retailing Association(148)
McInerney, USAF (Ret.), Maj. Gen. Jim
National Defense Industrial Association(504)
McInerney, Joseph A.
American Hotel & Lodging Association(92)
McInerney, Marianne
American International Automobile Dealers Association(98)
McIntire-Strasburg, Janice
American Humor Studies Association(92)
McIntosh, Bruce D.
Portland Cement Association(581)
McIntosh, Maxine
Biophysical Society(229)
McInturff, Doug
International Wild Rice Association(397)
McIntyre, Jeanne
American Academy of Otolaryngology-Head and Neck Surgery(26)
McIntyre, John
Community Financial Services Association of America(256)
McIntyre, Marcia
American Pancreatic Association(112)
McIntyre, Maria A.
Council of Supply Chain Management Professionals(275)
McIver, Krystyna
AOAC International(158)
McKay, Carol
National Consumers League(495)
McKay, Charles
American Psychological Association(118)
McKay, Michael W.
American Craft Council(77)
McKee, David
American Traffic Safety Services Association(152)
McKee, Pamela
National Congress for Community Economic Development(495)
McKee, Richard
Diplomatic and Consular Officers, Retired(284)
McKeel, Chava
Golf Course Superintendents Association of America(318)
McKeever, III, Joseph F.
Committee of Annuity Insurers(254)
McKelvy, Dorothy
Project Management Institute(590)
McKelway, Zan
National Rural Electric Cooperative Association(537)
McKenna, Robert
Motor and Equipment Manufacturers Association(421)
McKenney, James
American Association of Community Colleges(41)
McKenney, Patrice
International Society for Experimental Hematology(387)
McKenzie, Gary
National Pest Management Association(532)
McKenzie, Ken
National Association for Retail Marketing Services(436)
McKenzie, Shirley C.
American Dairy Goat Association(77)
McKernan, Dennis
Irrigation Association(400)
McKew, Robert E.
American Financial Services Association(83)
McKiernan, Patricia
Graphic Artists Guild(319)
McKinley, Ron
National Network of Grantmakers(528)
McKinney, Danny
Burley Tobacco Growers Cooperative Association(235)
McKinney, Darren
American Tort Reform Association(152)
McKinney, Larry
Association for Biblical Higher Education(168)
McKinney, Sarah
Academy of General Dentistry(3)
McKinnis, Marilyn F.
Helicopter Association International(325)
McKinnon, Russell
National Rural Electric Cooperative Association(537)
McKittrick, Tom
Purebred Dairy Cattle Association(593)
McKnelly, Philip K.
National Association of State Park Directors(476)
McKuen, Rod
American Guild of Variety Artists(88)
McLaughlin, Julie
National Insulation Association(521)
McLaughlin, Linda
Medical Records Institute(416)
McLaughlin, Sharon
American Music Conference(107)
McLean, Ephraim R.
Association for Information Systems(175)
McLean, Missi
Society for Vascular Ultrasound(629)
McLean, Rebecca
National Real Estate Investors Association(535)
McLellan, Sharon K.
Association of Official Racing Chemists(206)
McLendon, Dr. Lennox L.
National Adult Education Professional Development Consortium(427)
McLennon, Nancy
Organization for International Investment(567)
McLeod, CMP, Barbara
Society of Computed Body Tomography and Magnetic Resonance(634)
McLeod, Beverly
Council of State and Territorial Epidemiologists(274)
McLeod, Elizabeth
International Society of Beverage Technologists(390)
McLeod, Michael R.
American Association of Crop Insurers(41)
McLin, Joyce A.
American Safe Deposit Association(123)
McMahon, Colleen
Council of Residential Specialists(274)
McMahon, Diane
Synthetic Organic Chemical Manufacturers Association(657)
McMahon, J. Michael
National Association of Pastoral Musicians(464)
McMahon, Jim
Construction Marketing Research Council(262)
McManus, James
Seaplane Pilots Association(607)
McMillan, Alan
National Safety Council(538)
McMillan, Ann
Undersea and Hyperbaric Medical Society(669)
McMillan, Donna
Association of Science-Technology Centers(213)
McMillan, Kurt C.
Contract Services Association of America(264)
McMillan, Reed
American Craft Council(77)
McMonigal, Dennice
International Electrical Testing Association(370)
McMorris, Lamell J.
National Basketball Referees Association(483)
McMullen, Karen
Association for Unmanned Vehicle Systems International(181)
McMullin, Craig
Association of Free Community Papers(198)
McMurrey, Nancy
American Academy of Nurse Practitioners(25)
McNally, Denise
National Association of Medical Examiners(461)
McNally, CMP, Kevin M.
Society of Corporate Meeting Professionals(634)
McNamara, Captain James J.
National Cargo Bureau(487)
McNamara, K. Brian
International Sign Association(386)
McNamara, Mary M.
Upholstered Furniture Action Council(680)
McNamara, Patrick J.
Chemical Sources Association(243)
McNamara, Sean A.
ACCRA - Ass'n of Applied Community Researchers(6)
McNeal, Joan
American Apparel & Footwear Association(31)

McNees, Lynne Walker
International Spa Association(392)
McNeil, Ira
Integrated Waste Services Association(345)
McNeil, C.O.O, James M.
Bank Administration Institute(225)
McNeil, Regina
National Exchange Carrier Association(507)
McNerney, John
Mechanical Contractors Association of America(415)
McNormally, Timothy J.
Tax Executives Institute(657)
McNulty, Pashun
Spring Manufacturers Institute(652)
McQuaid, John A.
Steel Shipping Container Institute(653)
McSlarrow, Kyle E.
National Cable & Telecommunications Association(486)
McSpadden, Gail
National Association of Federally Impacted Schools(452)
McSweeney, Mark
National Chimney Sweep Guild(489)
McTighe, Joseph W.
Council for American Private Education(268)
McWhorter, Kristin
National Poultry and Food Distributors Association(533)
McWilliams, Evelyn
Material Handling Equipment Distributors Association(414)
Mead, Chris
American Chamber of Commerce Executives(61)
Mead, Jennifer
Telecommunications Industry Association(659)
Mead, Kevin
IGAF Worldwide(332)
Mead, Leslie
Association of Cooperative Educators(192)
Mead, Renee
National Association of Reunion Managers(469)
Meade, Elizabeth W.
Helicopter Association International(325)
Meade, Jeanne
Aviation Suppliers Association(225)
Meade, Robert E.
American Arbitration Association(32)
Meals, Torian
National ALEC Association/ Prepaid Communications Association(429)
Mealy, Lynne
International Association for Human Resource Information Management(350)
Mecklenborg, Mark
American Ceramic Society(61)
Meddock, Larry
Water Sports Industry Association(686)
Medert, Kurt
American Gear Manufacturers Association(86)
Medick, CPA, CAE, Susan
Automotive Aftermarket Industry Association(223)
Medlin, CAE, E. Lander
Association of Higher Education Facilities Officers(199)
Mednis, Rasma
United States Council for International Business(674)
Meegan, Jo
Evangelical Christian Publishers Association(298)
Meehan, APR, Joan
American Nurses Association(109)
Meehan, Peggy
National Council of State Housing Agencies(500)
Meek, Gary
Association of Gospel Rescue Missions(199)
Meenan, John M.
Air Transport Association of America(13)
Megivern, Kathleen
Commission on Accreditation of Allied Health Education Programs(254)
Mehaffey, William R.
Society of Small Craft Designers(644)
Mehaffy, George
American Association of State Colleges and Universities(51)
Mehenie, Germai
Union for Radical Political Economics(669)
Mehren, David F.
National Association of Independent Insurance Adjusters(457)
Meinecke, Dana
National Pawnbrokers Association(532)
Meinsler, Lucille F.
American Association of Chairmen of Departments of Psychiatry(39)
American Association of Directors of Psychiatric Residency Training(42)
Meisel, William
American Voice Input/Output Society(153)
Meiselman, Heather
Academy of Laser Dentistry(3)
Meisinger, SPHR, Susan R.
Society for Human Resource Management(619)
Melancon, Barry C.
American Institute of Certified Public Accountants(95)
Melaniphy, Margie
International Chain Salon Association(365)
Meldrum, Jr., Thomas W.
Software and Information Industry Association(646)
Mell, Kandi
Juvenile Products Manufacturers Association(403)
Mella, Jeanne L.
Association of American Medical Colleges(184)
Melnicove, Susan A.
ASIS International(163)
Melnykovich, Ph.D., George O.
Meat Industry Suppliers Alliance(415)
Melstrand, Graham
American Council on Exercise(76)
Melton, Diane
IEEE Magnetics Society(331)
Melton, Gary L.
American Train Dispatchers Association(152)
Melton, Joetta
American Academy of Family Physicians(22)
Melveger, Alvin
American Microchemical Society(106)
Melville, Scott
Healthcare Distribution Management Association(323)
Menashes, Matt
Professional Paddlesports Association(588)
Mendelson, Jordana
American Society for Hispanic Art Historical Studies(130)
Mendenhall, Wendy
BritishAmerican Business Inc.(233)
Mendes, David
American Subcontractors Association(149)
Mendez, C. Paul
National Association of Workforce Development Professionals(482)
Mendez, Garry
Association of Public-Safety Communications Officers- International(211)
Mendez, Kenneth
Advanced Medical Technology Association(8)
Mendicino, Jr., Joseph A.
American Law Institute(100)
Meneses, Guillermo
United States Hispanic Chamber of Commerce(675)
Menick, John
College Art Association(251)
Menitoff, Rabbi Paul J.
Central Conference of American Rabbis(241)
Menning, Reo
Silicones Environmental, Health and Safety Council of North America(610)
Mennis, Liam
Screen Actors Guild(606)
Mennite, Mary Anne
Society of Financial Service Professionals(636)
Mentaberry, Mary
National Council of Juvenile and Family Court Judges(499)
Mentzer, Kenneth D.
North American Insulation Manufacturers Association(557)
Menyo, Laurie
ECRI(288)
Mercado, Christine
Licensing Executives Society(407)
Mercado, Georgette
National Society of Compliance Professionals(541)
Mercer, Bette
United Food and Commercial Workers International Union(671)
Mercer, Lee W.
National Association of Small Business Investment Companies(472)
Mercill, Alan
International Pharmaceutical Excipients Council of the Americas(382)
Mericle, II, Richard E.
Alliance for the Polyurethane Industry(16)
Mericsko, John
National Association of County and City Health Officials(447)
Merrell, Joan
Association for the Calligraphic Arts(180)
Merrill, Clarence
Christian Labor Association of the United States of America(246)
Merrill, Nancy
Association of Theological Schools in the United States and Canada(218)
Merrill, Rick
Promotional Products Association International(591)
Merriman, Klein S.
NASFM(425)
National Association of Display Industries(449)
Merriman, Tim
National Association for Interpretation(434)
Merritt, Mark
Pharmaceutical Care Management Association(575)
Merry, Glenn
United States Rowing Association(677)
Merry, Jack
APA - The Engineered Wood Association(158)

Merry, Jr., Peter
American Disc Jockey Association(79)
Merry, Susan
National School Boards Association(538)
Merther, Susan
Water Environment Federation(685)
Mertz, Alan
American Clinical Laboratory Association(63)
Merydith, Chuck
Precast/Prestressed Concrete Institute(582)
Mesiano, Vincent
Embroidery Council of America(292)
Mesirow, Robert
CTIA - The Wireless Association(280)
Messervey, John E.
National Family Business Council(508)
Messick, Donald L.
Sulphur Institute, The(655)
Metalitz, Steven
International Intellectual Property Alliance(377)
Metaxas, Amy
Intermediaries and Reinsurance Underwriters Association(347)
Metcalf, Allan
American Dialect Society(79)
Metcalf, Cindy
American Academy of Restorative Dentistry(28)
Metcalf, Kathy J.
Chamber of Shipping of America(243)
Metcalfe, Sandy
American Society of Addiction Medicine(133)
Meteyer, Marc J.
Compressed Gas Association(257)
Metter, Kristine
AcademyHealth(6)
Metts, SJ, Ralph
Jesuit Secondary Education Association(401)
Metzger, Daniel J.
Thoroughbred Owners and Breeders Association(661)
Metzger, Jeanne
National Venture Capital Association(548)
Metzger, Kristen L.
International Association of Aquatic and Marine Science Libraries and Information Centers(352)
Metzler, Christina
American Occupational Therapy Association(109)
Meyer, Adele R.
National Association of Resale & Thrift Shops(469)
Meyer, Brian
American Society of Health-System Pharmacists(139)
Meyer, Linn
American College of Surgeons(71)
Meyer, Michelle
National Electronic Distributors Association(506)
Meyer, Rev. Russell L.
North American Academy of Ecumenists(554)
Meyer, Terry
American Water Resources Association(154)
Meyerhoeffer, J.A.
Railway Engineering-Maintenance Suppliers Association(595)
Meyers, Rabbi Joel H.
Rabbinical Assembly(594)
Meyers, Louis J.
North American Folk Music and Dance Alliance(557)
Meyers, Mary
American College of Foot and Ankle Surgeons(66)
Meyers, N. Marshall
Pet Industry Joint Advisory Council(574)
Meyners, Ginger
National Association of Child Care Professionals(443)
Mica, Daniel A.
Credit Union National Association(279)
Michael, Janetta
Peruvian Paso Horse Registry of North America(574)
Michael, Scott
American Moving and Storage Association(107)
Michael, MS, Stephen
Association for Ambulatory Behavorial Healthcare(167)
Michaels, Bob
Association of Trial Lawyers of America(218)
Michaels, Ted
Integrated Waste Services Association(345)
Michalevich, Greg
Association of Conservation Engineers(192)
Michalik, John J.
Association of Legal Administrators(203)
Michalski, Lauren
Association of Transportation Professionals(218)
Michalski, Richard P.
International Association of Machinists and Aerospace Workers(359)
Michel, Harriet R.
National Minority Supplier Development Council(527)
Michels, Linda
AAGL -- Advancing Minimally Invasive Gynecology Worldwide(1)
Michels, Nicola
German American Chamber of Commerce(316)
Michelson, Paul
Conference on Faith and History(261)
Society for Romanian Studies(625)
Micich, Mitchell
Independent Feature Project(334)
Mickal, Chris E.
International Fire Photographers Association(372)
Middlebrook, Melanie
ARMA International(160)
Middleton, Fred
National Cotton Batting Institute(496)
Midwood, Barry
CPCU Society(278)
Miedema, Amy
National Contract Management Association(495)
Mighetto, Lisa
American Society for Environmental History(128)
Mihalik, Lisa
Environmental Information Association(296)
Mihills, Ronald
Research and Engineering Council of the NAPL(600)
Mikal, Lindsey
Senior Executives Association(609)
Mikitka, Michael
Warehousing Education and Research Council(685)
Mikola, Gary
Society of Manufacturing Engineers(639)
Milac, Dr. Metod M.
Society for Slovene Studies(625)
Milby, David D.
National Association of Unclaimed Property Administrators(479)
Milchen, Jeff
American Independent Business Alliance(93)
Miles, Barbro
American Family Therapy Academy(81)
Miles, CMP, Kimberly
American Hotel & Lodging Association(92)
Miles, Mark
American Society of Landscape Architects(140)
Miles, Marlene
Fresh Produce Association of the Americas(312)
Miles, Michele G.
Institute of Business Appraisers(340)
Miles, Raymond C.
Institute of Business Appraisers(340)
Miles, Shari
Society for the Psychological Study of Social Issues(627)
Miles, Willma
American Correctional Health Services Association(74)
Milkey, Dr. Robert W.
American Astronomical Society(54)
Millar, Lynn
National Industries for the Blind(519)
Millar, William W.
American Public Transportation Association(120)
Miller, Alexis
Western Association for Art Conservation(687)
Miller, Allen
Information Technology Association of America(338)
Miller, Ph.D., Anne W.
Association of School Business Officials International(212)
Miller, CAE, Bill
Woodworking Machinery Industry Association(694)
Miller, Caroline
Association for Postal Commerce(177)
Miller, Charla
AACE International(1)
Miller, Cordie
American Society of Retina Specialists(145)
Miller, Della
AVS Science and Technology Society(225)
Miller, Derek
International Housewares Association(375)
Miller, Diane
Institute of Real Estate Management(343)
Miller, Ed
American Chianina Association(62)
Miller, Ed
American College of Forensic Psychiatry(66)
Miller, Edward
American Land Title Association(100)
Miller, Edward L.
American Chemical Society - Rubber Division(62)
Miller, Fred
Home Improvement Research Institute(327)
Miller, Galen
National Hospice and Palliative Care Organization(517)
Miller, Gordon
National Cosmetology Association(496)
Miller, Heidi
Council of Graduate Schools(272)
Miller, Jeff
Treated Wood Council(665)

Miller, Joe
Association of Industry Manufacturers' Representatives(201)

Miller, DVM, John G.
Association for Assessment and Accreditation of Laboratory Animal Care International(168)

Miller, Judy
Entomological Society of America(295)

Miller, Judy M.
Graphic Arts Sales Foundation(319)

Miller, Julie
Society for Maternal Fetal Medicine(621)

Miller, Kenneth E.
Office Furniture Distribution Association(564)

Miller, Kenneth W.
American Association of Colleges of Pharmacy(40)

Miller, Lauren
Association for Hose and Accessories Distribution(174)
Independent Sealing Distributors(335)

Miller, Lenne
Endocrine Society(294)

Miller, Leslie
National Staff Development Council(543)

Miller, Louise S.
Association of Pediatric Hematology/Oncology Nurses(207)

Miller, JD, CAE, M. Lance
Metal Treating Institute(417)

Miller, Maggie
Intermodal Association of North America(347)

Miller, Matt
Association of Independent Commercial Producers(200)

Miller, Melanie
Sugar Association(655)

Miller, Michael J.
College of American Pathologists(251)

Miller, JD, Michael J.
Association for the Advancement of Medical Instrumentation(179)

Miller, Michelle
National Association for Holistic Aromatherapy(434)

Miller, Miriam
National Association of College and University Attorneys(444)

Miller, Patty
World Waterpark Association(696)

Miller, Paul A.
Silver Users Association(611)

Miller, Pete
Society for Software Quality(625)

Miller, Peter L.
American Institute for CPCU - Insurance Institute of America(93)

Miller, Rebecca
National Book Critics Circle(485)

Miller, FAIA, Robert L.
National Institute of Building Sciences(520)

Miller, Scott
National Paperbox Association(531)

Miller, O.D., Stephen C.
College of Optometrists in Vision Development(252)

Miller, MPH, M.D., Stephen H.
American Board of Medical Specialties(57)

Miller, Susan
Alliance for Telecommunications Industry Solutions(16)

Miller, Tim
Allied Trades of the Baking Industry(17)

Miller, Wayne
American Health Lawyers Association(89)

Miller Thorpe, Michelle
National Association of Railroad Trial Counsel(467)

Millican, William
ARMA International(160)

Mills, CAE, Cynthia
Tree Care Industry Association(665)

Mills, Diana
National Federation of Licensed Practical Nurses(509)

Mills, Gayla
American Society of Radiologic Technologists(145)

Mills, Kathreja
Jesuit Secondary Education Association(401)

Mills, Lorraine Herzing
Copper Development Association(266)

Mills, Stephanie
National Certified Pipe Welding Bureau(488)
Plumbing Contractors of America(579)

Milner, CAE, Neil
Conference of State Bank Supervisors(260)

Milon, Patricia
America's Community Bankers(19)

Milz, Michael A.
National Association of Catholic School Teachers(442)

Mims, JoAnne
Associated Locksmiths of America(165)

Miner, Anuja
American Butter Institute(60)

Miner, Stephen
American Wind Energy Association(155)

Mininger, Wayne
National Onion Association(529)

Minjack, Svetlana
U.S.-Russia Business Council(668)

Minkema, Kenneth P.
American Society of Church History(135)

Minkley-Sims, Lea
American Association for Medical Transcription(36)

Minnis, James
National Automobile Dealers Association(482)

Minnix, Jr., D. Min., William L.
American Association of Homes and Services for the Aging(43)

Minor, Deborah
American Academy of Religion(28)

Minter, Karl
Organization of Black Airline Pilots(567)

Minton, Eric
Reserve Officers Association of the U.S.(600)

Minton, Reggie
National Association of Basketball Coaches(439)

Mintz, Suzanne
National Family Caregivers Association(508)

Miretzky, Debra
National Society for the Study of Education(541)

Mirick, USAF, MSC (Ret.), Col. Steven C.
Association of Military Surgeons of the U.S.(205)

Mirmelstein, Ross F.
National Sheriffs' Association(539)

Mirrnezam, Al
American Council on Exercise(76)

Mishra, Anita
AOAC International(158)

Misra, Pradeep
American Automatic Control Council(55)

Mister, CAE, Steven M.
Council for Responsible Nutrition(270)

Mitas, M.D., FACP, John A.
American College of Physicians(69)

Mitch, Joe
United States Basketball Writers Association(673)

Mitchell, Andrea
Substance Abuse Librarians and Information Specialists(655)

Mitchell, Brad
American Association of Equine Practitioners(42)

Mitchell, Brenda G.
National Council of the Churches of Christ in the U.S.A.(501)

Mitchell, Gina
Stable Value Investment Association(652)

Mitchell, Janice
Media Credit Association(415)

Mitchell, Jenny
American Frozen Food Institute(85)

Mitchell, Larry
American Corn Growers Association(74)

Mitchell, LeeAnn
Artist-Blacksmiths' Association of North America(162)

Mitchell, Mark
National Association of Independent Schools(457)

Mitchell, Peter
International Union of Electronic, Electrical, Salaried, Machine, and Furniture Workers-CWA(395)

Mitchell, Dr. Robert B.
Delta Pi Epsilon(282)

Mitchell, Ruth
American Supply Association(150)

Mitchell, Stevan
Entertainment Software Association(295)

Mitchem, Ph.D., Arnold L.
Council for Opportunity in Education(269)

Mitstifer, Dorothy I.
Association of College Honor Societies(191)

Mittelstadt, Eric
National Council for Advanced Manufacturing(496)

Mittelsteadt, Tina
National Sunflower Association(545)

Mobley, Randy
International League of Professional Baseball Clubs(378)

Mochnal, George
Forging Industry Association(310)

Moen, Ronald S.
American Dietetic Association(79)

Moeser, Erica
National Conference of Bar Examiners(492)

Moffett, CMP, Janis
International Association of Financial Crimes Investigators(357)

Moghul, Alan
National Association of State Alcohol and Drug Abuse Directors(473)

Mohan, Barry
American Meteorological Society(105)

Mohay, Mark
Automotive Recyclers Association(224)

Mohelnitzky, Kathy
Association of Physician Assistants in Obstetrics and Gynecology(208)

Moisand, CFP, Daniel B.
Financial Planning Association(306)
Molchan, Andrew
National Association of Federally Licensed Firearms Dealers(452)
Molick, Christine J.
National Conference of Bankruptcy Judges(492)
Molina, David S.
Association for Transpersonal Psychology(181)
Molino, John
American Logistics Association(102)
Molino, CAE, Michael A.
Recreation Vehicle Dealers Association of North America(596)
Molitar, Peggy
International Association of Diecutting and Diemaking(356)
Moll, Barbara M.
National Automatic Merchandising Association(482)
Moll, Gary
American Forests(85)
Moll, Nancy
Child Welfare League of America(244)
Mollison, Char
Council on Foundations(276)
Molpus, C. Manly
Grocery Manufacturers Association(320)
Molstad, Renee
American Society of Neurorehabilitation(142)
Mona, CAE, Stephen F.
Golf Course Superintendents Association of America(318)
Monahan, Frank
National Association of State Catholic Conference Directors(474)
Monahan, CAE, Thomas A.
National Concrete Burial Vault Association(492)
Monas, Silvia
KWPN of North America(404)
Moneymaker, Carol
Accrediting Bureau of Health Education Schools(7)
Monfasani, John
Renaissance Society of America(599)
Monforte, Joseph
Society of Forensic Toxicologists(636)
Monk, Carl C.
Association of American Law Schools(184)
Monroe, Ph.D, Eric G.
IMAGE Society(332)
Monroe, Raymond W.
Steel Founders' Society of America(653)
Monroe, Terry
COMPTEL(257)
Montagnolo, Anthony J.
ECRI(288)
Montague, Patti
School Nutrition Association(606)
Montes, Alicia
International Society for Pharmaceutical Engineering(388)
Monteverde, Susan
American Association of Port Authorities(49)
Montfort, Emily
Bankers' Association for Finance and Trade(226)
Montfort, Linda
AMT - The Association For Manufacturing Technology(156)
Montgomery, Dean
American Health Planning Association(89)
Montgomery, Lauraeyn
American Academy of Cosmetic Surgery(21)
American Society of Lipo-Suction Surgery(140)
Montgomery, Nevin B.
National Frozen and Refrigerated Foods Association(513)
Monti, Ph.D., Michael
Association of Collegiate Schools of Architecture(191)
Montoya, Carol
Professional Aviation Maintenance Association(586)
Montoya, CAE, James D.
International Association of Speakers Bureaus(361)
Montoya, Ken
National Air Traffic Controllers Association(428)
Montplaisir, Ronald J.
National Troubleshooting Association(547)
Montwieler, William J.
Industrial Truck Association(337)
Moody, John P.
Government Management Information Sciences(318)
Moody, Michelle
American Society of Hematology(139)
Moody, Randall
National Education Association(506)
Moody, Robert
Sommelier Society of America(647)
Moody, Dr. William J.
American Bandmasters Association(55)
Moon, Kathleen
American Harp Society(89)
Mooneyham, Bob
National Rural Education Association(537)
Mooneyham, Scott
International Lead Zinc Research Organization(377)
Moore, Allison
Fresh Produce Association of the Americas(312)
Moore, Andrew D.
National Agricultural Aviation Association(428)
Moore, Bob
Institute of Food Technologists(341)
Moore, Cameron
National Association of Regional Councils(469)
Moore, Detlef B.
American Association of Dental Editors(41)
International Association for Orthodontics(351)
Moore, Diane
Society of Marine Port Engineers(639)
Moore, Edie
Society for Adolescent Medicine(613)
Moore, Dr. Jeannette A.
National Block and Bridle Club(485)
Moore, Jerry
American Society of Gas Engineers(138)
Moore, Joe
International Health, Racquet and Sportsclub Association(374)
Moore, Jon
Professional Housing Management Association(587)
Moore, M. Melissa
ASABE - the Society for Engineering in Agricultural, Food and Biological Systems(162)
Moore, Mike
National Association of Professional Baseball Leagues(466)
Moore, Mike
ADSC: The International Association of Foundation Drilling(8)
Moore, Mildred E.
Montadale Sheep Breeders Association(421)
Moore, Mindy
Ladies Professional Golf Association(404)
Moore, Nicole Casal
National Conference of State Legislatures(494)
Moore, Pam
NACHA - The Electronic Payments Association(424)
Moore, Pamela C.
Healthcare Distribution Management Association(323)
Moore, R.N., Pearl
Oncology Nursing Society(564)
Moore, Ryan J.
Non-Ferrous Founders' Society(553)
Moore, Sabrina
North American Meat Processors Association(558)
Moore, Terry
Association of Pediatric Oncology Social Workers(207)
Moore, Toby
USA Poultry and Egg Export Council(681)
Moore, Virginia
American Mental Health Counselors Association(105)
Moorhead, Tracey
Disease Management Association of America(285)
Mooring, John E.
National Association of Housing Information Managers(457)
Mopsik, Eugene
American Society of Media Photographers(141)
Morahg, Gilead
National Association of Professors of Hebrew in American Institutions of Higher Learning(466)
Morales, Alex
National Precast Concrete Association(534)
Morales, Joyce
Association of Battery Recyclers(187)
Moran, Frank
Association for Work Process Improvement(183)
Moran, Ph.D., Mary Jo
National Association of Church Personnel Administrators(443)
Moran, Patti
Pet Sitters International(574)
Moran, Peter J.
Society of American Florists(630)
Moran, Saly
International Society for Magnetic Resonance in Medicine(387)
Morano, Linda
American Mental Health Counselors Association(105)
Morano, Tom
American Financial Services Association(83)
Mordente, Jack
National Association of Veterans Program Administrators(480)
Mordhorst, Klaus C.J.
Society of Maritime Arbitrators(639)
Mordini, Jack
United States Bowling Congress(673)
Moret, Phyllis
American Society of Consultant Pharmacists(136)

Morgan, Alan
National Rural Health Association(537)
Morgan, Ben
National Cottonseed Products Association(496)
Morgan, Cheryl
Pine Chemicals Association(578)
Morgan, Diane
Tree Care Industry Association(665)
Morgan, Harold E.
Taxicab, Limousine and Paratransit Association(657)
Morgan, Jack
Textile Rental Services Association of America(660)
Morgan, Jeff
Futures Industry Association(313)
Morgan, Patty
Travel and Tourism Research Association(665)
Morgan, MBA, Richard D.
American Congress of Rehabilitation Medicine(73)
Morgan, Suzanne
International Wood Products Association(397)
Morin, Don
American Academy of Periodontology(27)
Mork, Grodon R.
Committee on History in the Classroom(254)
Morland, Joe
International Brotherhood of Boilermakers, Iron Ship Builders, Blacksmiths, Forgers and Helpers(363)
Morley, Jr., James E.
National Association of College and University Business Officers(444)
Moroney, William R.
United Telecom Council(679)
Morris, Cara
U.S. Lacrosse(668)
Morris, Dana
Object Management Group(563)
Morris, Deborah W.
National Concrete Masonry Association(492)
Morris, Delores
Industrial Perforators Association(337)
Morris, Griff
National Academy of Recording Arts and Sciences(427)
Morris, Jay
National Association of Federal Credit Unions(452)
Morris, Jennifer
North American Performing Arts Managers and Agents(559)
Morris, D.O., Morton
American Osteopathic Academy of Orthopedics(111)
Morris, R. E. "Skip"
International League of Electrical Associations(378)
Morris, Raymond A.
SAE International(604)
Morris, Dr. Robert C.
Society of Professors of Education(643)
Morris, Robert J.
Sulphur Institute, The(655)
Morris, Valerie
RMA - The Risk Management Association(602)
Morrison, Ph.D., CAE, Barbara L.
Air Movement and Control Association International(13)
Morrison, James
Small Business Exporters Association of the United States(611)
Morrison, Jeff
Substance Abuse Program Administrators Association(655)
Morrison, Martha M.
Self Storage Association(608)
Morrison, Marvin
International Council of Shopping Centers(368)
Morrison, Robert
National Association of State Alcohol and Drug Abuse Directors(473)
Morrison, Seth
Cable & Telecommunications Association for Marketing(236)
Morrison, Steve
National Association of FSA County Office Employees(454)
Morrison, Tom
Metal Treating Institute(417)
Morriss, Robyn L.
Reinsurance Association of America(598)
Morrissette, Michael
Dangerous Goods Advisory Council(281)
Morrissey, Bob
National Watermelon Association(549)
Morrow, Hugh
International Cadmium Association(364)
Morter, Rebecca
Bankers' Association for Finance and Trade(226)
Morton, Sara
National Tour Association(546)
Moscato, Cathie
Society of American Registered Architects(631)
Mosedale, Susan
International Association of Amusement Parks and Attractions(352)
Moser, Charlie
National Association of Postmasters of the United States(465)
Moser, Jeff
Farmers Educational and Co-operative Union of America(301)
Moses, Ginnah
American Highland Cattle Association(90)
Moses, Kim
Envelope Manufacturers Association(296)
Moses, Timothy
American Academy of Dermatology(21)
Moshlak, Kim
Association of American Universities(185)
Moskal, Melissa
Committee for Private Offshore Rescue and Towing (C-PORT)(254)
Drug and Alcohol Testing Industry Association(287)
Moskal, Patt L.
American College of Osteopathic Family Physicians(69)
Mosley, Carolyn
Chi Eta Phi Sorority(244)
Mosley, Kimberly
American College of Healthcare Executives(66)
Mosman, Jim
National Council on Teacher Retirement(503)
Moss, Debra A.
International Franchise Association(373)
Moss, Mike
Warehousing Education and Research Council(685)
Mostellar, Donna
Gift Associates Interchange Network(317)
Mostrom, Dr. Michelle S.
American Academy of Veterinary and Comparative Toxicology(29)
Motelet, Cie
NIBA - The Belting Association(553)
Motion, Joanna
Council for Advancement and Support of Education(267)
Motley, John
Food Marketing Institute(309)
Motten, Alexander F.
Association for Biology Laboratory Education(168)
Moulos, Paulette
National Safety Council(538)
Moulton, JD, MPH, Benjamin
American Society of Law, Medicine and Ethics(140)
Moulton, Meg
National Coalition of Girls Schools(490)
Mountford, Mardi K.
International Formula Council(373)
Research Chefs Association(600)
Mountjoy, E. Leo
North American Rail Shippers Association(559)
Mounts, Keith
American Society for Engineering Education(128)
Mourad, Teresa
North American Association for Environmental Education(554)
Mouttet, Nate
Council for Christian Colleges and Universities(268)
Moyer, Brian R.
National Association of Environmental Professionals(451)
Moyer, Sara
American Angus Association(31)
Moyer, William
Independent Petroleum Association of America(335)
Moynihan, Sian
Professional Convention Management Association(587)
Mrosko, Cathryn A.
Security Industry Association(607)
Much, Morrie
National Bulk Vendors Association(485)
Mucklow, Rosemary M.
National Meat Association(526)
Mudie, Georgianne
Profit Sharing/401(k) Council of America(590)
Muehlbauer, Charles
Marble Institute of America(412)
Muehlbauer, CAE, Eric J.
North American Spine Society(561)
Mueller, Rhonda
Catholic Health Association of the United States(240)
Muench, Timothy
Association of American University Presses(185)
Muenchmeyer, Gerry
National Association of Sewer Service Companies(472)
Mugan, Daniel J.
Association of Teachers of Latin American Studies(217)
Muha, Denise
National Leased Housing Association(524)
Mulder, Gary
Protestant Church-Owned Publishers Association(591)
Muldoon, John
National Association of Children's Hospitals(443)

Mulholland, Jill P.
Automotive Occupant Restraints Council(224)
Mullaly, Cynthia
National Shoe Retailers Association(539)
Pedorthic Footwear Association(572)
Mullaney, Helen M.
National Finance Adjusters(510)
Mullen, Dan
AIM Global(12)
Mullen, John E.
United States-New Zealand Council(678)
Muller, Gail
International Recording Media Association(384)
Muller, Richard S.
International Coordinating Committee on Solid State Sensors and Actuators Research(367)
Mulligan, Clark
American Association of Attorney-Certified Public Accountants(38)
Mulligan-Fairfield, Diane
National Stroke Association(544)
Mullin, Tracy
National Retail Federation(536)
Mullings, Lisa
NATSO, Representing America's Travel Plazas and Truckstops(550)
Mullins, Lawrence W.
Independent Electrical Contractors(334)
Mullins, Molly Alton
Electronic Retailing Association(292)
Mullis, Connie
Profit Sharing/401(k) Council of America(590)
Mulvey, Faye
Cleveland Bay Horse Society of North America(248)
Mulvihill, Jason
United States Aquaculture Suppliers Association(673)
Munari, CAE, Donna
American Medical Writers Association(105)
Muncy, CAE, Steve A.
American Fire Sprinkler Association(84)
Mundell, George
National Private Truck Council(534)
Munden, DMD, MD, Reginald
Society of Thoracic Radiology(645)
Mundschenk, Chris
North American Building Material Distribution Association(555)
Mundy, Ray
Airport Ground Transportation Association(15)
Munford, Sue
Distribution Business Management Association(286)
Munksgaard, Larry
National Interscholastic Athletic Administrators Association(522)
Munley, Mary Ellen
Visitor Studies Association(684)
Munoz, Ph.D, Julio E.
Inter American Press Association(345)
Munro, Malcolm
Contract Services Association of America(264)
Muns, Ron
Help Desk Institute(325)
Munson, Angie
Bicycle Shippers Association(228)
Munter-Koenig, Holly J.
Comics Magazine Association of America(253)
Murchie, Anita
Vinifera Wine Growers Association(683)
Murchie, Gordon
Vinifera Wine Growers Association(683)
Murdoch-Kinch, Ph.D., Carol Anne
Organization of Teachers of Oral Diagnosis(568)
Murdock, Tom
National Dance Council of America(504)
Murner, Doreen
National Association of Educational Buyers(450)
Murphy, Aimee
Association for Hose and Accessories Distribution(174)
Independent Sealing Distributors(335)
Yacht Brokers Association of America(698)
Murphy, Christopher M.
International Claim Association(365)
Murphy, Cynthia Miller
Oncology Nursing Society(564)
Murphy, Gretchen
American Academy of Dermatology(21)
Murphy, Heather
Board of Certified Safety Professionals(231)
Murphy, James A.
Glove Shippers Association(318)
Murphy, CPA, Jennifer
National Association of Health Underwriters(455)
Murphy, John
Association of American Chambers of Commerce in Latin America(184)
Murphy, John
Food Shippers of America(309)
Murphy, John C.
National Association for County Community and Economic Development(432)
National Association of Local Housing Finance Agencies(460)
Murphy, Lisa I.
Rubber Manufacturers Association(603)
Murphy, Ph.D., Maureen
Federation of American Socs. for Experimental Biology(303)
Murphy, Pat
North American Technician Excellence(562)
Murphy, Patricia
Expediting Management Association(299)
Murphy, Patrick
Partnership for Air-Conditioning, Heating Refrigeration Accreditation(571)
Murphy, Scott
ASTM International(221)
Murphy, Sue
National Human Resources Association(518)
Murphy, Dr. Timothy J.
American Association for Agricultural Education(33)
Murphy, Zell
Association of Independent Corrugated Converters(200)
Murrah, Wendy
National Contract Management Association(495)
Murray, Candance
International Association for Identification(350)
Murray, Heather
Anxiety Disorders Association of America(157)
Murray, John
Pharmaceutical Care Management Association(575)
Murray, John F. "Jack"
Institute for Polyacrylate Absorbents(339)
Murray, Marrilyn
National Luggage Dealers Association(525)
Murray, Rick
Country Music Association(277)
Murray, Shannon
Truck Renting and Leasing Association(666)
Murray, Sharon D.
Society of State Directors of Health, Physical Education and Recreation(644)
Murrey, Patricia
Petroleum Marketers Association of America(574)
Murtaugh, Pat
National Association of Fleet Administrators(453)
Musacchio, Robert A.
American Medical Association(104)
Muscanelli, Peter R.
International Association of Electronics Recyclers(356)
Muse, CAE, Tonya
Envelope Manufacturers Association(296)
Musick, Marjorie
National Association of Public Insurance Adjusters(467)
Muskin, Alies
Anxiety Disorders Association of America(157)
Mustard, Todd
NEA - the Association of Union Constructors(551)
Muth, Kate
Association for Postal Commerce(177)
Mutnik, Gail E.
American Association for Clinical Chemistry(34)
Mutter, Reginald
Bulk Carrier Conference(235)
Myara, Norma
Motion Picture and Television Credit Association(421)
Mycka, Mary
International Network of Merger and Acquisition Partners(380)
Myer, John M.
Holstein Association USA(327)
Myers, Barbra
Association of Public-Safety Communications Officers- International(211)
Myers, Christy A.
American Society of Cytopathology(137)
Myers, Laura
American Alliance for Health, Physical Education, Recreation and Dance(30)
Myers, Dr. Linda
American Association for Women in Community Colleges(37)
Myers, Marilyn
Independent Electrical Contractors(334)
Myers, Melanie
American Traffic Safety Services Association(152)
Myers, Melinda
Independent Office Products and Furniture Dealers Association(335)
Myers, Michele
Voluntary Protection Programs Participants Association(684)
Myers, Molly M.
National Venture Capital Association(548)
Myers, Pierce
Parcel Shippers Association(571)
Myers, Richard
PDA - an International Association for Pharmaceutical Science and Technology(572)

Myers, Richard
Nuclear Energy Institute(563)
Myers, Robert
Edison Welding Institute(289)
Myers, Robert
IEEE Industry Applications Society(331)
IEEE Instrumentation and Measurement Society(331)
IEEE Power Electronics Society(331)
Myers, Robert J.
Association for Business Communication(168)
Myers, Stephen
College of American Pathologists(251)
Myers, Tina
Society for Marketing Professional Services(621)
Myers, Vickie R.
American Sugar Alliance(150)
Myers, Vincent
American Foreign Service Protective Association(85)
Myerson, Adam
Philanthropy Roundtable(576)
Mynatt, Danny
National Association of Baptist Professors of Religion(439)
Myott, Larry
International Maple Syrup Institute(379)
N. Priddy, Ronald
National Air Carrier Association(428)
Naake, Larry E.
National Association of Counties(447)
Naasz, Kraig
National Mining Association(527)
Naber, Tom
National Association of Electrical Distributors(450)
Nabors, Lyn O'Brien
Calorie Control Council(237)
Nachlis, Gayle
Women in Film(691)
Nadler, Molly
American Association of Dental Examiners(42)
Naegele, Ray
Medical Library Association(416)
Nagle, Kurt J.
American Association of Port Authorities(49)
Nagle, Tom
International Dairy Foods Association(368)
Nagorsky, Edward
National Kitchen and Bath Association(523)
Nagy, Edward C.
Academy of Radiology Research(5)
Naimark, Richard
American Arbitration Association(32)
Namba, Jon
World Floor Covering Association(695)
Nandagopal, N.S.
Society of Piping Engineers and Designers(642)
Naor, Gal
Association of College and University Housing Officers-International(191)
Napier, CAE, Bennett E.
National Association of Dental Laboratories(448)
Napolitano, MD, Lena
Surgical Infection Society(656)
Napolitano, Lisa
Strategic Account Management Association(654)
Nappier, Sherry
American Association of Orthodontists(47)
Narcisso, Deborah
Council of Graduate Schools(272)
Nardone, Angel E.
American Wine Society(155)
Nardone, Natalie
American Salvage Pool Association(124)
Narotsky, Evan
Association for Experiential Education(172)
Nash, Pamela
American Association for Clinical Chemistry(34)
Nason, Karen
Association of Rehabilitation Nurses(211)
Nasri, Fred
International Right of Way Association(385)
Nassiri, Jane
Radio-Television News Directors Association(594)
Nasvaderani, Linda
Society of Industrial and Office REALTORS(638)
Natale, PE, FNSPE, Patrick J.
American Society of Civil Engineers(135)
Nathan, Jan
PMA, the Independent Book Publishers Association(579)
Nathan, Terry
PMA, the Independent Book Publishers Association(579)
Nation, Larry M.
American Association of Petroleum Geologists(47)
Navis, CAE, Sheila R.
American Society of Electroneurodiagnostic Technologists(137)
Nawn, John
Professional Convention Management Association(587)
Nazareth, Maria
American College of Nurse-Midwives(68)
Neaderland, Louise
International Society of Copier Artists(391)
Neal Ballard, Wanda
PDA - an International Association for Pharmaceutical Science and Technology(572)
Nealis, Nora
National Cleaners Association(490)
Nee, Frances
International Association of Golf Administrators(357)
Needels, Christopher J.
United States Parachute Association(676)
Needham, Jenny
Society for Information Display(620)
Neely, Susan
American Beverage Association(56)
Neer, Mark
National Defender Investigator Association(504)
Neff, Michael W.
American Society for Horticultural Science(130)
Neff, Theodore L.
Post-Tensioning Institute(581)
Negron, Barbara
North American Natural Casing Association(558)
Negron, Jr., Francisco
National School Boards Association(538)
Nehemiah, Gloria
American Academy of Optometry(25)
Nehra, DeAnne
Council on Resident Education in Obstetrics and Gynecology(277)
Neibch, Julie
Association of Girl Scout Executive Staff(198)
Neiburgs, M.D., Herbert E.
International Society for Preventive Oncology(388)
Neidhardt, Maureen
World Watusi Association(697)
Neigh, Janet E.
Hospice Association of America(328)
Neill, Kim
American Association of Clinical Endocrinologists(39)
Neiman, Harvey L.
American College of Radiology(70)
Neirkirk, John
Society for American Archaeology(613)
Nekvasil, Glen
Lake Carriers' Association(404)
Nelson, Bill
WineAmerica(690)
Nelson, Dr. Charles Thomas
American Heartworm Society(90)
Nelson, Dan
General Merchandise Distributors Council(315)
Nelson, Deborah
Geological Society of America(315)
Nelson, Diane
Information Systems Audit and Control Association(338)
Nelson, Douglas T.
CropLife America(279)
Nelson, E. Colette
American Subcontractors Association(149)
Nelson, Greg
WorldatWork(697)
Nelson, Jim
RMA - The Risk Management Association(602)
Nelson, Joyce
National Multiple Sclerosis Society(528)
Nelson, Lisa
Society of Clinical and Medical Hair Removal(633)
Nelson, Marvin
Society of Cable Telecommunications Engineers(632)
Nelson, Maura
Council of Insurance Agents and Brokers(272)
Nelson, Michael U.
North American Association of Summer Sessions(555)
Nelson, Robert F.
National Coffee Association of the U.S.A.(490)
Nelson, Shirley
Middle East Studies Association of North America(418)
Nelson, Stephanie
American Romagnola Association(123)
Braunvieh Association of America(232)
Nelson, CMP, Steven C.
AACC International(1)
American Phytopathological Society(115)
Master Brewers Association of the Americas(413)
Nelson, Stuart
International Conference of Police Chaplains(366)
Nelson, Susan J.
American Society of Transplantation(146)
Nelson, Susan R.
American Underground-Construction Association(152)
Nelson, Thomas
American Association of Retired Persons(50)

Nelson, William B.
NACHA - The Electronic Payments Association(424)
Nelson-Rowe, Laurel
American Society for Quality(132)
Nemchek, Chris
National Association for the Specialty Food Trade(436)
Nemec, Debra
International Window Cleaning Association(397)
Sealant, Waterproofing and Restoration Institute(607)
Nepi, Lisa
National Society of Compliance Professionals(541)
Neri, Miko
National Association of Regional Councils(469)
Nershi, Dave
Society for Industrial and Organizational Psychology(620)
Nesbitt, Charlotte A.
National Association of Juvenile Correctional Agencies(459)
Nesbitt, Fred
National Conference on Public Employee Retirement Systems(495)
Nesbitt, Paul
National Property Management Association(534)
Ness, Harvey
Lignite Energy Council(408)
Nettles, Clay
Registry of Interpreters for the Deaf(598)
Neubert, Thomas
German American Business Association(316)
Neuburger, Rebecca
Police Executive Research Forum(580)
Neufeld, Jay
Cantors Assembly(237)
Neuhauser, Melinda
Society of Infectious Diseases Pharmacists(638)
Neuman, Mary Ann
Association of Cosmetologists and Hairdressers(193)
Neuman, Nicole
International Bridge, Tunnel and Turnpike Association(363)
Neuman, Pamela
National Petrochemical & Refiners Association(532)
Neumann, Madeline
National Flute Association(511)
Neuvelt, Carol Singer
National Association for Environmental Management(433)
Nevius, Anna
Caucus for Women in Statistics(240)
Newborn, Tangie
Alliance for Nonprofit Management(15)
National Association of Black Journalists(440)
Newcomb, Dave
National Asphalt Pavement Association(431)
Newcomb, Douglas
Special Libraries Association(649)
Newell, CAE, CPC, Janine
Association of Educational Therapists(194)
Newell, William H.
Association for Integrative Studies(175)
Newhall, Amy W.
Middle East Studies Association of North America(418)
Newhouse, Teri
American Public Works Association(120)
Newman, Bill
NAFSA: Association of International Educators(424)
Newman, David
United States Tennis Association(677)
Newman, Edward
American Society for Cell Biology(127)
Newman, Jeffrey
American Oil Chemists' Society(110)
Newman, Joel
AFIA-Alfalfa Processors Council(11)
American Feed Industry Association(83)
Newman, Robert
Independent Film and Television Alliance(334)
Newman, Stephanie
Association of Genetic Technologists(198)
Transportation Lawyers Association(664)
Newman, Sue
Institute of International Finance(342)
Newman, Susan
National Retail Federation(536)
Newman, Susan B.
Seismological Society of America(608)
Newman, Susan S.
International Real Estate Federation - American Chapter(384)
Newpher, Richard
American Farm Bureau Federation(81)
Newsome, James E.
New York Mercantile Exchange(552)
Newsome, Rosetta
Institute of Food Technologists(341)
Newton, Allison L.
National Council for Geographic Education(497)
Newton, Grant
Association of Insolvency and Restructuring Advisors(201)
Newton, Susan
American Association of Credit Union Leagues(41)
Newton, Vicki
Oncology Nursing Society(564)
Nexon, David
Advanced Medical Technology Association(8)
Neznek, Rita
Society of American Foresters(630)
Nguyen, H.T.
Federal Education Association(302)
Nicholas, Lynn B.
American Diabetes Association(79)
Nicholas, Ralph W.
American Institute of Indian Studies(96)
Nichols, Barb
National Association of Nurse Massage Therapists(463)
Nichols, Jim
Professional Rodeo Cowboys Association(589)
Nichols, Marshall W.
National Petroleum Council(532)
Nichols, Willard R.
American Public Communications Council(119)
Nichols-Franco, Wilma J.
National Association of Blacks in Criminal Justice(440)
Nicholson, Pamela Ly
National Conference of Women's Bar Associations(494)
Nicholson, Richard S.
American Association for the Advancement of Science(36)
Nicholson, Wanda R.
Association of American Editorial Cartoonists(184)
Nickel-Snowiss, Sharon
Conference for the Study of Political Thought(259)
Nickens, Nathan
Assisted Living Federation of America(164)
Nickerson, Amy
Copyright Society of the U.S.A.(266)
Nickless, Tracy L.
Center for Exhibition Industry Research(241)
Nicoletto, Kathy
American Rental Association(122)
Nicolici, Florence
American Architectural Manufacturers Association(32)
Niebuhr, Bonnie
American Board of Nursing Specialties(57)
Niebuhr, Mary
Linguistic Society of America(408)
Nied, Erin
Sealant, Waterproofing and Restoration Institute(607)
Niedenberger, Ray
National Fellowship of Child Care Executives(510)
Nieft, Sarah
National Association of Parliamentarians(463)
Nielsen, M.D., David
American Academy of Otolaryngology-Head and Neck Surgery(26)
Nielsen, Dori
National Council on Education for the Ceramic Arts(502)
Nielson Price, Deon
National Association of Composers, USA(445)
Niespodziewanski, Felix
American College of Surgeons(71)
Nightingale, Swea
Sunglass Association of America(655)
Nigohosian, Ken
Alliance of Insurance Agents and Brokers(17)
Nigro, Joseph J.
Sheet Metal Workers' International Association(610)
Niman, Neil
History of Economics Society(326)
Niner, Maryann
American Chamber of Commerce Executives(61)
Ning, Cynthia
Chinese Language Teachers Association(245)
Nipper, Joe
American Public Power Association(120)
Nisankarao, Raj
National Business Association(486)
Nissalke, Alan
American Logistics Association(102)
Nivet, MS, Marc A.
National Association of Medical Minority Educators(461)
Niwa, Rose
American Apitherapy Society(31)
Noakes, Pamela
National Association for Girls and Women in Sport(433)
Noe, A. Allen
CropLife America(279)
Noel, Dr. Rodney
Association of American Feed Control Officials(184)
Noel, Yvonne
Health Industry Distributors Association(323)
Nofsinger, John B.
Material Handling Industry of America(414)

Nolan, Debra
Library Binding Institute(407)
Nolan, Pat
General Federation of Women's Clubs(315)
Nolan, Susan F.
National Conference of Insurance Legislators(493)
National Council of Legislators from Gaming States(499)
Noll, Betsy
National Conference on Research in Language and Literacy(495)
Nolte, Patty
Tile Contractors' Association of America(661)
Nolte, Traci
Society of Teachers of Family Medicine(644)
Noonan, Gary P.
American Academy of Sanitarians(28)
Noone, Kelley
Association of Public Treasurers of the United States and Canada(211)
Noone, CAE, Stephen J.
American Academy of Osteopathy(26)
Nord, Dr. G. Daryl
International Association for Computer Information Systems(349)
Norlin, Dennis
American Theological Library Association(151)
Norlin, Kersten
American Arbitration Association(32)
Norman, D.Engr., Bill M.
National Cotton Ginners' Association(496)
Norman, Patricia
National Medical Association(526)
Normandy, Joseph
National Association of Independent Life Brokerage Agencies(457)
Norrell, Randy
American Historical Association(91)
Norrils, Renee
North American Membrane Society(558)
Norris, Ann
Dance/USA(281)
Norris, Joanne
National Association of Local Government Auditors(460)
Norris, Nicki
College of American Pathologists(251)
Norris, Nina
National Council of Examiners for Engineering and Surveying(499)
North, Moraith G.
American Association of Colleges of Podiatric Medicine(40)
Northcott, Hallock
American Association of Exporters and Importers(42)
Northcutt, Ben
International Erosion Control Association(371)
Northrop, Clyde
Nationwide Alternate Delivery Alliance(550)
Nortman, Mark
Window Coverings Association of America(689)
Norton, Debra
National Interstate Council of State Boards of Cosmetology(522)
Norton, JoAnne
Chemical Industry Data Exchange(243)
Norton, Karin L.
Enterprise Wireless Alliance(295)
Norton, Leanne
Bowling Proprietors Association of America(231)
Norton, Negley
Yellow Pages Association(698)
Norton-Gross, Phyllis
Tree-Ring Society(665)
Norvell, Lawrence J.
Delta Society(283)
Nosal, Judi
North American Building Material Distribution Association(555)
Notini, Jill A.
Association of Home Appliance Manufacturers(200)
Novak, CPM, Paul
Institute for Supply Management(340)
Novak, Richard
Association of Governing Boards of Universities and Colleges(199)
Novelli, William
American Association of Retired Persons(50)
Novy, Richard W.
California Dried Fruit Export Association(236)
Nowak, Vincent
Livestock Marketing Association(409)
Nowling, LeeAnn
ISSA(400)
Noyes, Elizabeth J.
American Academy of Pediatrics(27)
Nuernberg, Toni
ACA International, The Association of Credit and Collection Professionals(2)
Nuhn, Peter
National Weather Service Employees Organization(549)
Nuland, Chris L.
American Association of Clinical Endocrinologists(39)
Nunes, Frank
International Institute for Lath and Plaster(376)
Nunez, Damaris
American Society of Orthopaedic Physician's Assistants(143)
Nunn, Mark
Manufactured Housing Institute(411)
Nunn, Robert H.
Photoimaging Manufacturers and Distributors Association(576)
Nunn, Steve
Open Group(565)
Nunnally-Olsen, Timothy M.
Council of Defense and Space Industry Associations(271)
Nunnery, Ronald L.
American Meat Institute(103)
Nusbaum, Howard C.
American Resort Development Association(122)
Nusser, Sarah
National Association for County Community and Economic Development(432)
Nussman, Mike
American Sportfishing Association(148)
Nusz, Dr. LaWayne T.
Association for Gnotobiotics(173)
Nuti, Paul
American Anthropological Association(31)
Nutt, Charlie
National Academic Advising Association(426)
Nutter, Franklin W.
Reinsurance Association of America(598)
Nutter, Mike
Water Environment Federation(685)
Nuzzaco, Mark J.
NPES, The Association for Suppliers of Printing, Publishing and Converting Technologies(563)
O' Beirne, Kim
National Customs Brokers and Forwarders Association of America(504)
O'Block, Ph.D., Robert L.
American College of Forensic Examiners(66)
O'Brien, Joyce
Association of Fundraising Professionals(198)
O'Brien, Lieann
International Association of Culinary Professionals(355)
Women Chefs and Restaurateurs(691)
O'Brien, Martin J.
National Association of Service and Conservation Corps(471)
O'Brien, Mary
Laundry and Dry Cleaning International Union(405)
O'Brien, Meghan G.
Committee of 200(254)
O'Brien, CAE, Michael
Manufactured Housing Institute(411)
O'Brien, Patrick
America's Community Bankers(19)
O'Brien, Patrick A.
Concrete Sawing and Drilling Association(259)
National Drilling Association(505)
O'Bryon, CAE, David S.
Association of Chiropractic Colleges(189)
O'Carroll, Peggy
American Society of Maxillofacial Surgeons(141)
Association of Academic Chairmen of Plastic Surgery(183)
O'Connell, Edward L.
American Association of Port Authorities(49)
O'Connell, Jack
Baseball Writers Association of America(226)
O'Conner, Pat
National Association of Professional Baseball Leagues(466)
O'Connor, Barbara
International Bridge, Tunnel and Turnpike Association(363)
O'Connor, David
United States Equestrian Federation(675)
O'Connor, Martha S.
Council on Chiropractic Education(275)
O'Connor, Mary
American Nephrology Nurses Association(108)
O'Connor, Mary
National Association of College and University Food Services(444)
O'Connor, Mary Kay
International Dairy-Deli-Bakery Association(369)
O'Connor, Timothy
National Potato Promotion Board(533)
O'Day, Paul T.
American Fiber Manufacturers Association(83)
O'Donnell, Kathleen
International Ticketing Association(394)
O'Donnell, CIH, Lynn
American Board of Industrial Hygiene(57)
O'Donoghue, Michael
International Microelectronics and Packaging Society(379)
O'Dowd, Kyle
National Association of Criminal Defense Lawyers(448)
O'Gilvie, Shanna
National Association of Academic Advisors for Athletes(437)
O'Gorman, R.W. "Bob"
Automotive Lift Institute, Inc.(223)

O'Gorman, Robert
Religious Education Association(599)
O'Grady, Felice
Society for Experimental Biology and Medicine(617)
O'Grady, Ph.D., Richard T.
American Institute of Biological Sciences(94)
O'Halloran, Kathleen
National Investment Company Service Association(522)
O'Kane, Margaret E.
National Committee for Quality Assurance(491)
O'Keefe, Amy E.
Committee of 200(254)
O'Keefe, Tom
National Association of Investment Professionals(459)
O'Liddy, Nancy
Truckload Carriers Association(666)
O'Malley, Cari
American Tort Reform Association(152)
O'Malley, Jim
American Institute of Certified Public Accountants(95)
O'Neil, Janet
Antenna Measurement Techniques Association(157)
O'Neil, CAE, Peter J.
American Industrial Hygiene Association(93)
O'Neil, Tim
Society for Mining, Metallurgy, and Exploration(622)
O'Neill, Bill
National Association of Farm Broadcasting(452)
O'Neill, Bob
International City/County Management Association(365)
O'Neill, Brian
Insurance Institute for Highway Safety(345)
O'Neill, Jennifer
National Federation of Abstracting and Information Services(508)
O'Neill, Joe
National Conference of State Fleet Administrators(494)
O'Neill, Joseph
New York Board of Trade(552)
O'Neill, Robert
Manufacturers Standardization Society of the Valve and Fittings Industry(411)
O'Rourke, Frank
Travel Industry Association of America(665)
O'Rourke, Patricia
Association of Schools and Colleges of Optometry(213)
O'Rourke, Richard J.
Magazine Publishers of America(409)
O'Shea, Carol
National Association for Developmental Education(432)
O'Sullivan, Annie
National Organization of Nurse Practitioner Faculties(530)
O'Sullivan, Sue
American College of Legal Medicine(66)
O'Sullivan, Susan
Concrete Reinforcing Steel Institute(259)
O'Sullivan, Terence M.
Laborers' International Union of North America(404)
O'Sullivan, William P.
National Organization of Life and Health Insurance Guaranty Associations(530)
O'Toole, Pam
National Association of Trailer Manufacturers(479)
O'Toole, Peter
Association of Catholic Diocesan Archivists(189)
O'Toole, Timothy
Mason Contractors Association of America(413)
Oakley, Bill
National Association of Pizza Operators(464)
Oakley, Janet
American Association of State Highway and Transportation Officials(51)
Oare, Gail A.
Materials Research Society(414)
Obalil, Deborah
Alliance of Artists Communities(16)
Obey, Craig
National Parks Conservation Association(532)
Ochs, Michael
Independent Office Products and Furniture Dealers Association(335)
Odell, Andrew L.
American Foreign Law Association(85)
Oderkirk, Kimberly
Floor Covering Installation Contractors Association(308)
Oderwald, Susan
Society of Plastics Engineers(642)
Odland, Gerald C.
Association for Childhood Education International(169)
Odom, Joy
Association for International Agriculture and Rural Development(175)
Oetjen, Mary E.
American College of Counselors(65)
Oettinger, Edward C.
Manuscript Society(412)
Offen, CAE, Neil H.
Direct Selling Association(285)
Offringa, Kate
North American Insulation Manufacturers Association(557)
Ofuani, Sharon
National Association of Public Sector Equal Opportunity Officers(467)
Ogden, B.J.
Council of Industrial Boiler Owners(272)
Oglesby Cook, Jacqueline
American Health Quality Association(89)
Ogrodzinski, Henry M.
National Association of State Aviation Officials(473)
Oie, Gretchen A.
Electronic Distribution Show Corporation(291)
Oishi, Roy T.
Airlines Electronic Engineering Committee(14)
Okada, Daryn
American Society of Cinematographers(135)
Oksala, Steve
Society of Cable Telecommunications Engineers(632)
Older, Nicole
Cleaning Management Institute(247)
Olek, Meggan
American Academy of Audiology(20)
Olentine, Dr. Charles
U.S. Poultry and Egg Association(668)
Oliveira, Horacio
American Association of Colleges of Nursing(40)
Oliver, Lin
Society of Children's Book Writers and Illustrators(633)
Oliverez, Manuel
National Association of Hispanic Federal Executives(455)
Oliveri, CAE, Ann
Urban Land Institute(680)
Oliveto, Betsy
Anxiety Disorders Association of America(157)
Oliviera, Carolina
Society of Competitive Intelligence Professionals(633)
Olley, Lorraine
Library Administration and Management Association(407)
Olsen, Jon
Geological Society of America(315)
Olsen, Timothy L.
Guild of American Luthiers(321)
Olson, Beth
Soap and Detergent Association(612)
Olson, Jeff
American Forests(85)
Olson, Jennifer
International Society for Magnetic Resonance in Medicine(387)
Olson, Jon
International Writing Centers Association(397)
Olson, Julie
American International Charolais Association(98)
Olson, Nancy
Fabricators and Manufacturers Association, International(300)
Tube and Pipe Association, International(666)
Olson, Nancy J.
Association of Christian Librarians(189)
Olson, Rebecca
National Council for Marketing and Public Relations(497)
Olson, Rob
Delta Waterfowl Foundation(283)
Olson, Sydney
American Osteopathic Association(111)
Omansky, Michelle
North American Building Material Distribution Association(555)
Omlie, Lynne J.
Distilled Spirits Council of the U.S.(286)
Ongaro, Frank
American Iron Ore Association(99)
Onieal, Marie-Eileen
National Alliance of Nurse Practitioners(429)
Onstott, Mark P.
National Interscholastic Swimming Coaches Association(522)
Onuszko, Rhonda
National Sporting Goods Association(543)
Opatick, CAE, Richard E.
American Bearing Manufacturing Association(56)
Ophof, Tucker
American Association for Homecare(35)
Oppenheim, Ellen
Magazine Publishers of America(409)
Orange, Stephanie
Risk and Insurance Management Society(602)
Orantes, Sobeida
Mechanical Service Contractors of America(415)
Orchowsky, Ph.D., Stan
Justice Research and Statistics Association(403)

Orem, Donna
National Association of Independent Schools(457)
Orenstein, Sidney
Textile Converters Association(660)
Orfanopoulos, Nick
National Association of Television Program Executives(478)
Oribabor, Cheryl
International Function Point Users Group(373)
Orient, M.D., Jane M.
Association of American Physicians and Surgeons(185)
Orlando, Angela
American Society of Home Inspectors(139)
Orms, CAE, R. Norris
Healthcare Information and Management Systems Society(324)
Orr, CAE, Stan
Association of Equipment Management Professionals(195)
Orrico, JD, Katie
American Association of Neurological Surgeons(46)
Orth, Inge
German American Chamber of Commerce(316)
Orth, J. Neil
American International Charolais Association(98)
Ortiz, Miquela
Analytical Laboratory Managers Association(157)
Ortiz-Ramos, Natalie
American Society for Parenteral and Enteral Nutrition(131)
Orvik, Gelaine
National High School Athletic Coaches Association(517)
Orwick, Peter
American Sheep Industry Association(125)
Osborn, Judy
ASME International Gas Turbine Institute(163)
Osborn, Nancy
National Association of Minority Media Executives(462)
Osborne, Camille
Satellite Broadcasting and Communications Association(605)
Osborne, Catherine M.
Iota Tau Tau(399)
Osborne, Michelle
International Nubian Breeders Association(381)
Osburn, Janice
Association of Official Seed Analysts(206)
Osgood, Barbara
National Association of Government Employees(454)
Oskarsson, Petur
Icelandic American Chamber of Commerce(330)
Osmanski, CMP, Rick
Radio-Television News Directors Association(594)
Ospina, John
American Welding Society(154)
Ostad, Jenny
World Floor Covering Association(695)
Oster, CAE, Susan M.
International Psychogeriatric Association(383)
Ostermiller, Jerry
Council of American Maritime Museums(270)
Ostrum, Gus
American Nephrology Nurses Association(108)
Ott, Jim
American College of Physicians(69)
Ott, Melanie
National Council of Teachers of Mathematics(501)
Ott-Chiappetta, Tina
International Public Management Association for Human Resources(384)
Ottley, Elaine
American Traffic Safety Services Association(152)
Otto, Robert
International Association of Counselors and Therapists(355)
Ouellette, CRNA, MEd, FAAN, Sandra M.
International Federation of Nurse Anesthetists(371)
Over, Stephen M.
Professional Ski Instructors of America(589)
Overstreet, John
Indoor Tanning Association(336)
Overturf, Dwight
RMA - The Risk Management Association(602)
Owen, Elizabeth
National Association of Consumer Agency Administrators(446)
Owen, Kaymie T.
American Veterinary Distributors Association(153)
Safety Equipment Distributors Association(604)
Owen, Richard D.
National Institute of Packaging, Handling and Logistics Engineers(521)
Owens, Barbara
National Committee on Planned Giving(491)
Owens, David K.
Edison Electric Institute(289)
Owens, Jim
Indiana Limestone Institute of America(336)
Owens, Marilla
Society of Quality Assurance(643)
Owens, Tom
Professional Liability Agents Network(588)
Oxer, Bethany
American Society for Clinical Pharmacology and Therapeutics(127)
Oyhanarte, Horacio A
Wireless Communications Association International(690)
Ozburn, Jr., K. Grant
American Short Line and Regional Railroad Association(125)
Pace, Jill H.
American College of Real Estate Lawyers(70)
Pace, John
ASTM International(221)
Pace, Robert S.
American-Uzbekistan Chamber of Commerce(156)
Pacella, Mark
National Association of State Charity Officials(474)
Pachavis, Robert H.
Materials Research Society(414)
Pacuit, J.F.
Tire and Rim Association(661)
Paden, Carrie
Society of American Business Editors and Writers(630)
Padgett, Ph.D., Kathryn A.
American Academy of Pain Management(26)
Padilla, John
American Society of Radiologic Technologists(145)
Paganessi, Jason
Academy of General Dentistry(3)
Page, Debbie
National Association of Basketball Coaches(439)
Page, Jim
American Dairy Products Institute(78)
Page, Kelly
International Concrete Repair Institute(366)
Page, Rebecca
Association of Vascular and Interventional Radiographers(220)
Paget, Michael
National Renal Administrators Association(536)
Paine, Elizabeth
Federation of State Humanities Councils(304)
Paine, Glen
International Organization of Masters, Mates and Pilots(382)
Painter, Doug
National Shooting Sports Foundation(539)
Palacio-Grottola, Sonia
National Association of Puerto Rican/Hispanic Social Workers(467)
Palantino, Susan A.
Society for Industrial and Applied Mathematics(619)
Palatiello, John M.
Management Association for Private Photogrammetric Surveyors(410)
Palatka, CAE, Andrew
Business Forms Management Association(235)
Palazzolo, Joseph A.
Cosmetic Industry Buyers and Suppliers(267)
Palcher, Jennifer
Healthcare Convention and Exhibitors Association(323)
Pales, Cathy
National Association of College Auxiliary Services(444)
Pallari, Amy
Building Commissioning Association(234)
Pallozola, Chris
American Academy on Communication in Healthcare(29)
Palmer, Brett
National Association of Insurance Commissioners(458)
Palmer, Jeff
Powder Coating Institute(582)
Palmer, Joanne
United Synagogue of Conservative Judaism(678)
Palmer, Mark
North American Wholesale Lumber Association(562)
Palmer, Paull
Association of Christian Teachers(190)
Palmer, Sara
Middle East Studies Association of North America(418)
Palmer, Scott
Supply Chain Council(656)
Palmer, Tony M.
Instrumentation Testing Association(344)
Palmieri, Lisa
International Association of Law Enforcement Intelligence Analysts(358)
Palumbo, Guy
Guild of Italian American Actors(321)
Palys, CAE, Beth W.
American Academy of Appellate Lawyers(20)
American Society of Consulting Arborists(136)
National Conference on Weights and Measures(495)

Pangman, Peter
Society of Exploration Geophysicists(636)
Panjada, Dede Gish
NATCO - The Organization for Transplant Professionals(426)
Pannell, Jim
United Steel, Paper and Forestry, Rubber, Manufacturing, Energy, Allied Industrial and Service Workers International Union(678)
Pannone, Barbara
Graphic Artists Guild(319)
Pantea, Victor
National Association of Credit Union Service Organizations(448)
Pantos, George J.
Self Insurance Institute of America, Inc.(608)
Pantuso, Erica
Healthcare Information and Management Systems Society(324)
Pantuso, Peter J.
American Bus Association(60)
Paolino, John
National Federation of Federal Employees(509)
Papacosma, S. Victor
Modern Greek Studies Association(420)
Paparozzi, Andrew
National Association for Printing Leadership(435)
Papazian, Charles
Brewers' Association of America(232)
Papineau, Vicki
College Reading and Learning Association(252)
Papp, Sharon
American Foreign Service Association(85)
Pappas, CAE, Virginia M.
American College of Nuclear Physicians(68)
Society of Nuclear Medicine(641)
Paque, CAE, Mike
Ground Water Protection Council(320)
Para, Pamela J.
American Society for Healthcare Risk Management(129)
Paradis, Roland
Association of Home Office Life Underwriters(200)
Parca, Maryline
Women's Classical Caucus(693)
Parent, Neil
National Conference of Catechetical Leadership(493)
Parillo, Mark
World War Two Studies Association(696)
Park, Judy
National Active and Retired Federal Employees Association(427)
Park, Kimberly
Federation of International Trade Associations(304)
Park, Peter S.
College Music Society(251)
Parke, Beth
Society of Environmental Journalists(635)
Parker, Brad
North American Limousin Foundation(558)
Parker, Bruce J.
Environmental Industry Associations(296)
National Solid Wastes Management Association(542)
Parker, Carol
CHA - Certified Horsemanship Association(242)
Parker, CAE, David N.
American Gas Association(86)
Parker, Erich
Aseptic Packaging Council(162)
Parker, Jennifer
Association of Regulatory Boards of Optometry(211)
Parker, Rick
North America Colleges and Teachers of Agriculture(553)
Parker, Sally
National Foundation for Credit Counseling(512)
Parker, Scott D.
NORA: An Association of Responsible Recyclers(553)
Parker, Thomas Warren
Gas Appliance Manufacturers Association(314)
Parkerson, Robert W.
National Crop Insurance Services(504)
Parkin, Scott L.
National Council on the Aging(503)
Parks, Dawn
National Environmental Health Association(507)
Parks, Elizabeth
American Society for Clinical Pathology(127)
Parks, Kathy
International Home Furnishings Representatives Association(375)
Parks, Sherry
American British White Park Association(59)
Parlow, Pamela
International Union of Petroleum and Industrial Workers(396)
Parman, CPA, Sherri
CoreNet Global(266)
Parmelee, Ken
National Rural Letter Carriers' Association(537)
Parr, Adam
Steel Manufacturers Association(653)
Parr, David
American Brush Manufacturers Association(59)
Parra, Victor
United Motorcoach Association(672)
Parris, Ph.D., George
American Wood Preservers Institute(155)
Parris, Ken
Offshore Marine Service Association(564)
Parrish, Craig
Cookie and Snack Bakers Association(265)
Parrish, Pamela
EDA Consortium(288)
National Association of Division Order Analysts(449)
Parrish, Patty
The National NeedleArts Association(528)
Parrish, Robin
International Association of Administrative Professionals(352)
Parrish, Sue
American Society of Professional Estimators(145)
Parry, Hugh
Prevent Blindness America(583)
Parsley, Gloria
Bioelectromagnetics Society(229)
Society for Physical Regulation in Biology and Medicine(624)
Parsley, DPM, Nancy
American Podiatric Medical Association(116)
Parson, Steve
National Community Education Association(491)
Parsons, Joan
Society for Radiation Oncology Administrators(624)
Parsons, Rachel
Recreation Vehicle Industry Association(596)
Partin, Tom
American Forest Resource Council(85)
Partland, J.P.
Editorial Freelancers Association(289)
Partridge, Chuck
American Occupational Therapy Association(109)
Paschal, Jeanette D.
National Association of Small Business Investment Companies(472)
Paschal, Michael
Association for Asian Studies(167)
Paschall, CAE, CMP, Joyce
Society of Trauma Nurses(645)
Pasco, Richard
American Peanut Product Manufacturers(113)
Pashby, Michael
Magazine Publishers of America(409)
Pasquale, Kim
Club Managers Association of America(249)
Pasqualone, Traci
National Association of RV Parks and Campgrounds(470)
Pass, Constance W.
American Mathematical Society(103)
Pass, Martina L.
National Association of State Workforce Agencies(477)
Passi, CAE, Mary Ann
Corporate Housing Providers Association(266)
Society for Nutrition Education(622)
Passiment, EdM, Elissa
American Society for Clinical Laboratory Science(127)
Passons, Donna
American College of Construction Lawyers(65)
Association for Continuing Legal Education(171)
Pasternak, Marc
Valve Repair Council(682)
Patek, Frank
Phi Alpha Delta(575)
Patel, Nilesh
Indian Dental Association (USA)(336)
Patella, Lawrence M.
Western Dredging Association(687)
Paterkiewicz, CAE, Robert J.
American Society of Home Inspectors(139)
Paterson, Penny
American Wholesale Marketers Association(155)
Patrick, Trishonda
National Home Furnishings Association(517)
Patterson, Helaine
American Educational Research Association(80)
Patterson, Judy
Vacuum Dealers Trade Association(682)
Patterson, Judy
American Gaming Association(86)
Patterson, Rick
Sporting Arms and Ammunition Manufacturers' Institute(651)
Pattie, Kenton
Association Chief Executive Council(166)
National Emergency Equipment Dealers Association(506)
Pattillo, Wesley M. "Pat"
National Council of the Churches of Christ in the U.S.A.(501)

Pattison, Scott
National Association of State Budget Officers(473)
Patton, David
American Councils for International Education(76)
Patton, Jane-Ann
Association for Bridge Construction and Design(168)
Patton, Leah
American Donkey and Mule Society(79)
Patty, Birgit
American Association of Textile Chemists and Colorists(53)
Patzer, Greg
International Magnesium Association(378)
Paukert, Linda
International Oil Mill Superintendents Association(381)
Paul, Joel M.
Federal Administrative Law Judges Conference(301)
Paul, Mike
National Association of Swine Records(478)
Paul, R. Kevin
Conductors Guild(259)
Paul, Raymond
Association of Oil Pipe Lines(206)
Paulet, Jean Pierre
Belgian American Chamber of Commerce in the United States(227)
Pauline, Janice
National League of Cities(524)
Paull, Dalene
International Conference of Funeral Service Examining Boards(366)
Paulos, Gregory
American Society for Gastrointestinal Endoscopy(129)
Pavina, Linda J.
American College of Osteopathic Pain Management and Sclerotherapy(69)
Pavlik, John M.
Academy of Motion Picture Arts and Sciences(4)
Pawlak, John
United States Trotting Association(678)
Pawliger, Caryn
Public Affairs Council(592)
Pawlson, Greg
National Committee for Quality Assurance(491)
Paymer, Lyn
Swimming Pool Water Treatment Professionals(657)
Payne, Becky
Ayrshire Breeders' Association(225)
Payne, Michael L.
International Association of Airport Duty Free Stores(352)
Payne, Stephen
Pet Food Institute(574)
Payne, Tim
United States Bowling Congress(673)
Peach, Philip
International Society of Hotel Association Executives(391)
Peacy, Kelly
Professional Convention Management Association(587)
Pearce, Dorcas
Financial Markets Association(306)
Pearce, M. Sue
Society of Military Otolaryngologists - Head and Neck Surgeons(640)
Pearcy, Jeff
American Association for Accreditation of Ambulatory Surgery Facilities(33)
Pearl, Wendy
Country Music Association(277)
Pearson, John
Christian Management Association(246)
Pearson, Robin
Women in Cable and Telecommunications(691)
Pechman, Jr., Robert D.
American College of Veterinary Radiology(72)
Peck, Ernie
Council of Colleges of Arts and Sciences(271)
Pecoulas, Margo
American Academy of Periodontology(27)
Pedersen, Marsha
American College of Foot and Ankle Surgeons(66)
Pedersen, Wes
Public Affairs Council(592)
Pederson, Clay
Farmers Educational and Co-operative Union of America(301)
Pederson, Debbie
Association for Death Education and Counseling(171)
Pederson, Linda
National Association of Women Artists(481)
Peeler, Suzanne
American Society of Ophthalmic Administrators(143)
Peeno, Dr. Larry N.
National Art Education Association(431)
Peitz, Michael
Educational Theatre Association(289)
Peitzman, M.D., Andrew
American Association for the Surgery of Trauma(37)
Pelletier, Brian
Computing Technology Industry Association(258)
Peloso, Amy
International Radio and Television Society(384)
Peltier, Jean-Mari
National Council of Farmer Cooperatives(499)
Peltz, Elin
United States Beet Sugar Association(673)
Peluso, Rick
American Society of Interior Designers(140)
Pemberton, Phyllis
National Flute Association(511)
Pembroke Callihan, Le'ann
American Association of Professional Landmen(49)
Pence, Randall G.
National Concrete Masonry Association(492)
Pendleton, Andrea
American Association of Anatomists(38)
Penhale, Laurel
American Advertising Federation(29)
Penn, David
American Public Power Association(120)
Penn, Deborah
American Public Power Association(120)
Penn, Kate
Society of American Florists(630)
Penna, Dick
Aluminum Extruders Council(18)
Pennington, Deneen
National Career Development Association(487)
Pennington, Martha
National Ornamental and Miscellaneous Metals Association(531)
Penoyar, Melanie
Hospitality Sales and Marketing Association International(329)
Penrod, James T.
Council of Landscape Architectural Registration Boards(273)
Peppe, Ron
Association of Corporate Counsel(193)
Pepper, Eric
SPIE - The International Society for Optical Engineering(651)
Pepper, Samuel J.
National Association for Year-Round Education(437)
Pepper, Vincent
National Association of Media Brokers(461)
Percoski, Joni
United Shoe Retailers Association(672)
Perdue, Jeffery
National Association of College Auxiliary Services(444)
Perera, Rey
American Karakul Sheep Registry(100)
Perez, Nykia N.
Association for Population/Family Planning Libraries and Information Centers, International(176)
Perez, Wendi
American Rhinologic Society(123)
Perhac, Joyce
Home Sewing Association(327)
Perham, Charlotte
Plumbing-Heating-Cooling Contractors - National Association(579)
Perkins, Anne
PCIA - the Wireless Industry Association(572)
Perkins, DDS, M. Dean
Association of State and Territorial Dental Directors(215)
Perla, Jill
American Association for the Advancement of Science(36)
Perlman, Eva
Association of Public Health Laboratories(210)
Perlman, Jeffry
American Advertising Federation(29)
Perlman, Victor
American Society of Media Photographers(141)
Perone, Marie
National Student Osteopathic Medical Association(544)
Perren, Pat
Inter-Industry Conference on Auto Collision Repair(346)
Perrin, Dan
North American Council of Automotive Teachers(556)
Perrin, Nancy
American College of Clinical Pharmacy(65)
Perrone, Anthony
United Food and Commercial Workers International Union(671)
Perry, Armilda
Wholesale Beer Association Executives of America(688)
Perry, George
American Association of Neuropathologists(46)
Perry, John
NACE International(424)
Perry, Michael
Investment Casting Institute(398)
Perry, Steven M.
International Association of Food Industry Suppliers(357)

Perry, Susan
International Technology Education Association(393)
Perry, Tracy
American Association of Nutritional Consultants(46)
Perry, William
International Union of Industrial Service Transport Health Employees(395)
Persaud, Dev
National Student Nurses Association(544)
Persinger, Gary S.
National Pharmaceutical Council(533)
Perusich, Karl
IEEE Society on Social Implications of Technology(332)
Pesce, CAE, Irene K.
National Catholic Cemetery Conference(487)
Peters, Don
National Chemical Credit Association(488)
Peters, Eugene F.
Electric Power Supply Association(290)
Petersen, Joe
Society for Maintenance Reliability Professionals(621)
Petersen, Pat
Air Medical Physician Association(13)
Petersen, Rolf
American Foundry Society(85)
Peterson, Arlette
Society of Professional Benefit Administrators(642)
Peterson, Carolyn
Association of Metropolitan Water Agencies(204)
Peterson, Cyndi
DRI International(287)
Peterson, Donald L.
Air Force Association(13)
Peterson, Jeff
Foil Stamping and Embossing Association(308)
Peterson, Lauren I.
Black Coaches Association(230)
Peterson, Lynn
American Psychological Association - Society of Clinical Psychology(119)
Peterson, Lynn
American Psychology-Law Society(119)
Peterson, Maggie
Society of Biological Psychiatry(632)
Peterson, Mark G.
American Institute of Certified Public Accountants(95)
Peterson, Maureen
American Occupational Therapy Association(109)
Peterson, Scott
Nuclear Energy Institute(563)
Peterson, Stacy
Recreational Vehicle Manufacturer's Clubs Association(597)
Peterson, Theodore L.
Consumer Healthcare Products Association(263)
Petit, Kim
Textured Yarn Association of America(660)
Petrick, Camille
American Orthopaedic Society for Sports Medicine(111)
Petrowski, Mary Jane
Association of College and Research Libraries(190)
Pettit, Amy
Lamaze International(404)
Pettit, C.L.
Reusable Industrial Packaging Association(601)
Petty, Ph.D., CAE, Gary Frank
National Private Truck Council(534)
Peveiler, Fran
Healthcare Information and Management Systems Society(324)
Pezold, George C.
Transportation & Logistics Council(664)
Pfaff, Gary
American College of Radiology(70)
Pfarr Thompson, Shannon
Qualitative Research Consultants Association(593)
Pfeffer, RN, Linda D.
Aerobics and Fitness Association of America(10)
Pfeiffer, Ph.D., Stephen M.
Association for the Advancement of Psychology(179)
Pfister, Steve
National Retail Federation(536)
Pflanz, Steve
Academy of Organizational and Occupational Psychiatry(4)
Pflugfelder, Angela
American Organization for Bodywork Therapies of Asia(110)
Pfotenhauer, Kurt P.
Mortgage Bankers Association(421)
Phair, Linda
Graduate Management Admission Council(319)
Pheasant, Susan
International Fruit Tree Association(373)
Phelleps, Moya
National Mining Association(527)
Phelps, David
American Institute for International Steel(94)
Phelps, George R.
North American Insulation Manufacturers Association(557)
Phelps, Greg
National Ground Water Association(515)
Phelps, Laura
American Mushroom Institute(107)
Phelps, Stacey
Preventive Cardiovascular Nurses Association(583)
Phelus, Dean
American Association of Museums(45)
Philbin, Tamara
American Chamber of Commerce Executives(61)
Philiph-Patel, Bharat
Board of Certified Safety Professionals(231)
Philipp, Will
NAFSA: Association of International Educators(424)
Philips, Chris Ann
American Association of Neurological Surgeons(46)
Phillips, Bill
International Association of Home Safety and Security Professionals(358)
Phillips, Donna
National Council on the Aging(503)
Phillips, Elizabeth T.
Foodservice and Packaging Institute(309)
Phillips, Jackie
National Association of Certified Valuation Analysts(442)
Phillips, John
National Association of Insurance and Financial Advisors(458)
Phillips, Larisa K.
Appraisal Institute(159)
Phillips, Laurelle
Association for the Study of Play(181)
Phillips, Ronald B.
Animal Health Institute(157)
Phillips-Turner, Julie
Professional Paddlesports Association(588)
Philport, Joseph C.
Traffic Audit Bureau for Media Measurement(663)
Philpott, Martina
International Andalusian and Lusitano Horse Association(349)
Piccione, Lisa
National Business Aviation Association(486)
Pichon, Sharon R.
American Association of Pharmaceutical Scientists(48)
Pickard, Mary J.
National Association of Teacher Educators for Family Consumer Sciences(478)
Pickel, Robert
International Swaps and Derivatives Association(393)
Pickens, Mary Alice
Association for Unmanned Vehicle Systems International(181)
Pickerel, CAE, M. Kirk
Associated Builders and Contractors(164)
Pickett, Jenny
National Agri-Marketing Association(428)
Pickett, Peggy J.
American Association of Textile Chemists and Colorists(53)
Pickett, W.D.
Brotherhood of Railroad Signalmen(233)
Piening, Robert
Professional Services Council(589)
Pier, Gwen
National Sculpture Society(539)
Pierce, Jacquelyn
General Federation of Women's Clubs(315)
Pierce, Mike
International Furniture Suppliers Association(373)
National Home Furnishings Association(517)
Pierre-Louis, Stanley
Recording Industry Association of America(596)
Pierson, Carol
National Federation of Community Broadcasters(509)
Pietrangelo, Anthony
Nuclear Energy Institute(563)
Pietrangelo, Renee
American Network of Community Options and Resources(108)
Pietranton, Ph.D., Arlene
American Speech-Language-Hearing Association(148)
Pietrzak, Ron
American Ladder Institute(100)
Association of Steel Distributors(216)
Wallcoverings Association(685)
Pigg, Bob J.
Asbestos Cement Product Producers Association(162)
Asbestos Information Association/North America(162)
Pigg, Edie
Rural Sociological Society(603)
Pigg, Kenneth E.
Rural Sociological Society(603)

Pignato, Robert
American Wholesale Marketers Association(155)
Pihos, Diana
American Association of Diabetes Educators(42)
Pike, Mary L.
National Association of Housing and Redevelopment Officials(456)
Pike, Walter
National Association of Air Traffic Specialists(438)
Pilgrim, Judy
American Feed Industry Association(83)
Pilliod, Cason
Distribution Contractors Association(286)
Pimpinella, Lisa
Electrical Overstress/Electrostatic Discharge Association(291)
Pincus, David
Society for Chaos Theory in Psychology and Life Sciences(615)
Pincus, Shirley
Inter-Industry Conference on Auto Collision Repair(346)
Pine, Mel
American Wood Preservers Institute(155)
Pine, Sue
International Association of Association Management Companies(353)
Pines, Steve
Education Industry Association(289)
Pinkerton, Sharon L.
Air Transport Association of America(13)
Pinkham, Douglas G.
Public Affairs Council(592)
Pinnock, Sharon
American Federation of Government Employees(82)
Pinou, Theodora
Society for the Study of Amphibians and Reptiles(628)
Pinsky, Mark
Opportunity Finance Network(565)
Pintarelli, Chester
National Association of County Health Facility Administrators(447)
Pintozzi, Bonnie
Association of Directory Publishers(194)
Piper, Morley
Newspaper Association Managers(552)
Piper, Nancy
Accredited Pet Cemetery Society(7)
Piper, Robert
Associated Builders and Contractors(164)
Piper, Scott
International Inflight Food Service Association(376)
Pipkin, Ronald M.
Law and Society Association(406)
Pisano, Susan
America's Health Insurance Plans(19)
Pitner, Les
Union for Reform Judaism(670)
Pitt, Sarah
Council of State Governments(275)
Pitt, Stephen R.
National Automobile Dealers Association(482)
Pittas, Jim
Packaging Machinery Manufacturers Institute(570)
Pittenger, Michele Marini
Travel Goods Association(665)
Pittman, Lyn
Society for Ethnomusicology(617)
Pitts, Donnie
National Rural Letter Carriers' Association(537)
Pitts, Francis M.
American College of Healthcare Architects(66)
Pixler, Joe
American Society for Healthcare Risk Management(129)
Pizzica, Dr. Albert
National Perinatal Association(532)
Pizzo, Lori
International Downtown Association(369)
Place, Ph.D., Nick T.
Association for International Agricultural and Extension Education(175)
Plack, Janice L.
American Society of Anesthesiologists(134)
Planz, Karen
Tag and Label Manufacturers Institute(657)
Plasker, James R.
American Society for Photogrammetry and Remote Sensing(131)
Plassa, Stephanie
Electrochemical Society(291)
Platt, Teresa
Fur Commission USA(312)
Pless, Dana M.
SAE International(604)
Plummer, Glenda
Music Distributors Association(423)
Plummer, Roger
International Engineering Consortium(370)
Pochelski, Louise A.
Council of Supply Chain Management Professionals(275)
Pociask, Martin
Helicopter Association International(325)
Podgorski, Dennis
Government Finance Officers Association of the United States and Canada(318)
Podruchny, Carolyn
American Society for Ethnohistory(129)
Pogaceanu, Alina
American Seminar Leaders Association(124)
Pohlmann, Susan
International Security Management Association(385)
Poindexter, CAE, Douglas L.
World Wide Pet Industry Association(697)
Poitras, Albert A.
Machine Printers and Engravers Association of the United States(409)
Polak, Joe
North American Maple Syrup Council(558)
Polancic, Joan
American Society for Clinical Laboratory Science(127)
Polansky, Sara
Health Industry Business Communications Council(323)
Polburn, Aaron
International Hot Rod Association(375)
Polich, Gerald
Intercollegiate Men's Choruses, an International Association of Male Choruses(346)
Polivka, Melissa
Mason Contractors Association of America(413)
Polizotto, Jim
International Multimedia Telecommunications Consortium(380)
Pollack, Richard
American Hospital Association(92)
Polley, Cathy
National Association of Chain Drug Stores(442)
Pollitt, Gary R.
Military Chaplains Association of the U.S.(419)
Pollock, Wendy
Association of Science-Technology Centers(213)
Polls, Irwin
North American Benthological Society(555)
Polly, Kris D.
National Water Resources Association(548)
Polski, Joseph P.
International Association for Identification(350)
Polskin, Howard
Magazine Publishers of America(409)
Polvinale, CMP, Bonnie
American Physical Therapy Association(115)
Polyakova, Susan
Wireless Communications Association International(690)
Pomerantz, CAE, Paul
American Society of Plastic Surgeons(144)
Pomilia, Joseph
Insurance Accounting and Systems Association(345)
Pons, Ted E.
American Arbitration Association(32)
Poole, Kitt
American Councils for International Education(76)
Pooley, June
American College of Veterinary Internal Medicine(71)
Pope, Albert E.
United Egg Producers(670)
Pope, Sally
National Association of State Development Agencies(474)
Pope, Stuart
Catholic Charities USA(239)
Popkin, Jeremy
Society for French Historical Studies(617)
Popkin, Karol J.
American Public Transportation Association(120)
Popovich, Luke
National Mining Association(527)
Poppler, Meredith
International Health, Racquet and Sportsclub Association(374)
Poray, CAE, John L.
Society of Broadcast Engineers(632)
Porinchak, Laura M.
Association of the Wall and Ceiling Industries-International(218)
Porr, Susannah F.
National Association of Steel Pipe Distributors(477)
Porte, Phillip
National Association for Medical Direction of Respiratory Care(434)
Porter, Cynthia S.
American Society of Pediatric Hematology/Oncology(143)
Porter, Dennis
Credit Union Executives Society(279)
Porter, Gregg
National Head Start Association(516)
Porter, Ph.D., Leah C.
American Cocoa Research Institute(63)
Porter, CME, Melissa
Association of Air Medical Services(183)

National EMS Pilots Association(507)
Portillo, Bruce
Bankers' Association for Finance and Trade(226)
Portillo, Cathryn
Society of Cardiovascular Anesthesiologists(632)
Portner, Courtney
National Air Traffic Controllers Association(428)
Porzio, Stephen
American Statistical Association(149)
Posen, Marion J.
Mobile Air Conditioning Society Worldwide(420)
Possick, Rabbi A. Moshe
National Conference of Yeshiva Principals(495)
Post, Patrick
National Small Business Association(540)
Posten, Ramsey
National Association for Stock Car Auto Racing(436)
Potter, Carol
Professional Association of Health Care Office Management(586)
Potter, Edward
Americas Association of Cooperative/Mutual Insurance Socs.(156)
Potter, Jan
American Gear Manufacturers Association(86)
Potter, Jennifer
Society for Imaging Science & Technology(619)
Potter, Jonathan
Digital Media Association(284)
Potter, Mary
American Society for Nondestructive Testing(131)
Potter, Steve
International Foodservice Distributors Association(372)
Potts, Daniel L.
American National Metric Council(108)
Potts, Julie A.
American Farm Bureau Federation(81)
Poulianos, Kaliope
National Association for Home Care(434)
Pound, William T.
National Conference of State Legislatures(494)
Poux, Danielle
National Association of County and City Health Officials(447)
Powars, Laura
International Economic Development Council(370)
Powell, Beth
American Mental Health Counselors Association(105)
Powell, Devon
American Herbal Products Association(90)
Powell, CMP, Diane
American Medical Technologists(105)
Powell, Earl N.
Design Management Institute(283)
Powell, John T.
American Peanut Shellers Association(113)
Powell, CM, Lynn S.
Institute of Certified Professional Managers(340)
Powell, Marge
International Herb Association(375)
Powell, Melissa
American Miniature Horse Association(106)
Powell, Penny
National Association of Real Estate Investment Managers(468)
Powell, Robert
American College of Nuclear Medicine(68)
Powell, Russell
Energy Traffic Association(294)
Powell, Thomas
American Meat Science Association(104)
Power, CAE, Mary
Convention Industry Council(265)
Power, Stacie
American Association of Franchisees and Dealers(43)
Powers, Bill
American Nurses Association(109)
Powers, CAE, Celeste M.
Independent Lubricant Manufacturers Association(335)
Powers, Charley
Japan Automobile Manufacturers Association(400)
Powers, Christy
North American Nature Photography Association(558)
Powers, John
Institute of Industrial Engineers(341)
Powers, Kate
National Ski Areas Association(540)
Powers, Kevin
American Society of Radiologic Technologists(145)
Powers, Stephanie J.
National Association of Workforce Boards(482)
Powers, Sukana
American College Health Association(63)
Powills, Suzanne
National Safety Council(538)
Poynter, Kinney
National Association of State Auditors, Comptrollers and Treasurers(473)
Praeger, Amy E.
American Shipbuilding Association(125)
Prager, Ph.D., Martin
Materials Properties Council(414)
Welding Research Council(687)
Pramstaller, CFC,CAE, Michael E.
Document Management Industries Association(286)
Prange, Heidi
Society of Toxicology(645)
Prass, Paul
Fluid Power Society(308)
Prast, CAE, LLIF, John J.
Million Dollar Round Table(419)
Prather, Catherine
National Tour Association(546)
Prats, CAE, Lisa M.
Building Owners and Managers Association International(234)
Pratt, James W.
American Forensic Association(85)
International Listening Association(378)
Pratt, Stuart K.
Consumer Data Industry Association(263)
Precourt, CAE, Ronald D.
National Telecommunications Cooperative Association(546)
Preede, Ken
American Seniors Housing Association(124)
Pregel, Astrid
Society of International Business Fellows(639)
Prentice, William
American Dental Association(78)
Presley, Pamela
NASFM(425)
Presser, Arthur
American Academy of Nutrition(25)
Pressly, Jr., David L.
National Association of Home Builders(456)
Pressman, CAE, Florence
Jewish Funeral Directors of America(402)
Presti, Sue
Express Delivery & Logistics Association(300)
Preston, Daniel S.
Saddle, Harness, and Allied Trade Association(604)
Prestwood-Hanisko, Tricia
Exhibition Services and Contractors Association(299)
Pretanik, Stephen
National Chicken Council(489)
Preus, Anthony
Society for Ancient Greek Philosophy(613)
Preuss, Del R.
Ornamental Concrete Producers Association(568)
Prewitt, Jean M.
Independent Film and Television Alliance(334)
Prey, D.D.S., John H.
Delta Sigma Delta(282)
Preziosi, Ph.D., CAE, Peter
American Association for Medical Transcription(36)
Prible, John
Independent Insurance Agents and Brokers of America(334)
Pribyl, Katie
General Aviation Manufacturers Association(315)
Price, Alice
Society of Animal Artists(631)
Price, CST, BS, Ben
Association of Surgical Technologists(216)
Price, Bonny F.
American Society of Appraisers(134)
Price, Carole A.
American Ostrich Association(112)
Price, Elizabeth
Building Service Contractors Association International(234)
Price, Gary W.
Dental Trade Alliance(283)
Price, Heather
Commercial Food Equipment Service Association(253)
Price, Jennifer
American Academy of Estate Planning Attorneys(22)
Price, Karen
National School Supply and Equipment Association(538)
Price, Lari
International Technology Education Association(393)
Price, Larry
ABA Marketing Network(1)
Price, Peter
National Academy of Television Arts and Sciences(427)
Price, Robert
American Physiological Society(115)
Price-Baugh, Ricki
Council of the Great City Schools(275)
Price-Shehan, Julie
National Association of Computer Consultant Businesses(445)

Priddy, Dana
American Public Works Association(120)
Prillaman, Hunter
National Lime Association(525)
Primiano, Amy
Precision Metalforming Association(583)
Prince, Paul M.
National Sporting Goods Association(543)
Prince, Sue Ann
American Philosophical Society(114)
Principato, Gregory O.
Airports Council International/North America(15)
Prior, Sylvia
Accordion Federation of North America(6)
Prober, Josh
American Osteopathic Association(111)
Probst, Maralyn R.
Veterinary Orthopedic Society(682)
Procter-Rogers, Cheryl
Public Relations Society of America(593)
Proctor, Angie
Aquatic Exercise Association(159)
Proctor, CMP, Karen A.
American Association of Advertising Agencies(37)
Proctor, Jr., Stuart E.
Rice Millers' Association(602)
U.S.A. Rice Federation(669)
Profaizer, Linda
National Association of RV Parks and Campgrounds(470)
Prokuski, B.
National Defense Industrial Association(504)
Prolario-Foley, Elena
College Theology Society(252)
Proost, Jay
American Society of Agricultural Appraisers(133)
Proscal, Dana
Clinical Laboratory Management Association(248)
Prosser, David
American Concrete Pressure Pipe Association(73)
Proteau, Gregory
Boating Writers International(231)
Protzel, Janet J.
International Order of the Golden Rule(381)
Proulx, Thomas
Society for Experimental Mechanics(617)
Prouty, Sally T.
National Association of Service and Conservation Corps(471)
Prue, Penny L.
American Health Care Association(89)
Pruett, Greg
American Gas Association(86)
Pruitt, Alison
Association of Eminent Domain Professionals(195)
Prunty, Kathy
Greeting Card Association(320)
National Candle Association(487)
Prusik, Gregory C.
National Futures Association(513)
Ptakowski, Kristin Krueger
American Academy of Child and Adolescent Psychiatry(20)
Puccinelli, Mary Beth
Conference of State Bank Supervisors(260)
Puckett, Dr. Gary
Council on Occupational Education(276)
Puetz, Ph.D., RN, Belinda E.
American Radiological Nurses Association(121)
National Gerontological Nursing Association(513)
Society for Vascular Nursing(629)
Pugh, Ruth C.
National Rural Letter Carriers' Association(537)
Pugh, William W.
National Motor Freight Traffic Association(527)
Pugliese, Brian
Automatic Meter Reading Association(223)
Pugliese, MBA, MS, Lola R.
Clinical and Laboratory Standards Institute(248)
Pulliam, Mel
American Football Coaches Association(84)
Puntney, Linda S.
Journalism Education Association(402)
Purcell, Frank
American Association of Nurse Anesthetists(46)
Purcell, Luann
Council of Administrators of Special Education(270)
Purdy, Ph.D., Dean
North American Society for the Sociology of Sport(561)
Purdy, Ralph M.
United Federation of Police & Security Officers(671)
Puri, Anil K.
Western Economic Association International(687)
Puri, Ishwar K.
Association of Chairmen of Departments of Mechanics(189)
Purser, CAE, Craig
National Beer Wholesalers Association(484)
Purvin, Jr., Robert L.
American Association of Franchisees and Dealers(43)
Pusch, Margaret D. "Peggy"
Society for Intercultural Education, Training and Research - USA(620)
Pusey, Leigh Ann
American Insurance Association(98)
Putnam, Rob
International Lead Zinc Research Organization(377)
Puzon, CAPT Ike
Naval Reserve Association(551)
Pyeatt, Dale M.
National Guard Executive Directors Association(515)
Pyle, David
American Finance Association(83)
Pyle, Nicholas A.
Independent Bakers Association(333)
National Grape Cooperative Association(515)
Pyle, Ron
Automotive Service Association(224)
Pyle, Taryn
Association of Independent Corrugated Converters(200)
Pysarchuk, Jocelyn
International Interior Design Association(377)
Pyster, Phil
National Association of Minority Engineering Program Administrators(462)
Pyster, CAE, Phil
Society of University Surgeons(645)
Pyzik, DC, Lawrence
American Chiropractic Registry of Radiologic Technologists(62)
Quackenbush, Ph.D., Margery
National Association for the Advancement of Psychoanalysis(436)
Qualls, Ph.D., Constance Dean
National Black Association for Speech, Language and Hearing(484)
Quarles, Otelia
National Potato Council(533)
Quarles, Susan D.
American Immigration Lawyers Association(92)
Quash, Tom
Women in Cable and Telecommunications(691)
Queen, Pam
International Professional Rodeo Association(383)
Quek, Lay
American Massage Therapy Association(103)
Quick, Deborah L.
American College of Psychoanalysts(70)
Quijano, Ellison M.
Philippine-American Chamber of Commerce(576)
Quimby, Michael
Associated Pipe Organ Builders of America(166)
Quinlan, Terence A.
IT Financial Management Association(400)
Quinn, Alice
Poetry Society of America(579)
Quinn, Brendan
National Business Owners Association(486)
Quinn, Jr., Harold P.
National Mining Association(527)
Quinn, Jeremy
United States-New Zealand Council(678)
Quinn, C.P.A., C.A.E., Lynn Grossman
APICS - The Association for Operations Management(158)
Quinn, Warren A.
American Nursery and Landscape Association(109)
Quinones, Roberto
Tortilla Industry Association(662)
Quinsey, Bryan
American Farrier's Association(82)
Quint, Jeff
National Systems Contractors Association(545)
Quirk, John
Amerifax Cattle Association(156)
Ra'anan, Alice
American Physiological Society(115)
Raab, David
Computing Technology Industry Association(258)
Raabe, Carol
Council of Residential Specialists(274)
Raber, Roger W.
National Association of Corporate Directors(446)
Rachuig, Brenda
Association of Attorney-Mediators(186)
Racicot, Marc F.
American Insurance Association(98)
Raczka, Laurel
National Association of Artists' Organizations(439)
Raczynski, Michelle
National Society of Hispanic MBAs(541)
Radack, James
National Mental Health Association(527)
Rader, Robert S.
American Association of Public Health Physicians(50)

Rader, Russ
Insurance Institute for Highway Safety(345)
Rado, Russ
American Association of Managing General Agents(45)
Radonjic, Jasna
American Composers Alliance(72)
Radosta, DVM, Lisa
American Veterinary Society of Animal Behavior(153)
Radoszewski, Tony
Plastics Pipe Institute(579)
Radulovic, Jon
National Hospice and Palliative Care Organization(517)
Raffaelli, Reba
National Association of Industrial and Office Properties(458)
Raffel, CAE, Louis B.
American Egg Board(80)
Ragaisis, Karen
International Society of Psychiatric Consultation Liaison Nurses(392)
Ragan, Lorri Lee
American Land Title Association(100)
Ragas, Aisha
National Association for Black Geologists and Geophysicists(432)
Ragland, Linda
United States Animal Health Association(672)
Raguse, Tom
Association of Visual Merchandise Representatives(220)
Rahman, Lynn
IPC - Association Connecting Electronics Industries(399)
Rahrig, Philip G.
American Galvanizers Association(86)
Raichle, CCE, Robert
International Energy Credit Association(370)
Railing, Ann Marie
Workgroup for Electronic Data Interchange(695)
Raiman, Gail A.
Associated Builders and Contractors(164)
Rainer, Peter
National Society of Film Critics(541)
Rainey, Terence J.
Association for Healthcare Philanthropy(173)
Rains, Jr., Alan T.
Family, Career, and Community Leaders of America(300)
Rains, Dana
Society of Cleaning and Restoration Technicians(633)
Raitor, Mark
Independent Community Bankers of America(333)
Rajsky, Gregory T.
Aluminum Anodizers Council(18)
Aluminum Extruders Council(18)
Rajwany, Nur
National Council of State Boards of Nursing(500)
Raker, Jacky Sher
American Association of Airport Executives(38)
Rakow, Randall E.
NIBA - The Belting Association(553)
Raley, Nancy
National Association of Independent Schools(457)
Raley-King, Jackwelyn
American Veterinary Distributors Association(153)
Safety Equipment Distributors Association(604)
Ralls, D.D.S., Stephen A.
American College of Dentists(65)
Ramarui, Jenny
Oceanography Society(564)
Ramati, Becca
Association of Reproductive Health Professionals(212)
Ramey, Drucilla S.
National Association of Women Judges(481)
Ramey, Steve
Animal Behavior Society(157)
Ramiah, Kalpana
Association of Teachers of Maternal and Child Health(217)
Ramirez, Bruce
Council for Exceptional Children(268)
Ramirez, Jr., Saul N.
National Association of Housing and Redevelopment Officials(456)
Ramlow, Sharon
International Hot Rod Association(375)
Ramminger, Scott S.
American Wholesale Marketers Association(155)
Rampersad, Mia
International Housewares Association(375)
Ramsay, James Bradford
National Association of Regulatory Utility Commissioners(469)
Ramsay, Jeanne Little
Society of American Florists(630)
Ramsay, Katherine
Society for Experimental Mechanics(617)
Ramsey, Cindy
American Gem Society(86)
Ramsey, John
National Association for Court Management(432)
National Conference of Appellate Court Clerks(492)
Ramsey, Judith
American Boat and Yacht Council(58)
Ramsey, Kathryn J.
National Committee on Planned Giving(491)
Ramsey, Teresa
National Association of Nurse Massage Therapists(463)
Ramsier, Mary Bamer
American School Health Association(124)
Ramus, Dr. Robert L.
Academy of Dentistry International(3)
Rancilio, Charlotte
Credit Professionals International(279)
Rancourt, Linda M.
National Parks Conservation Association(532)
Randall, Gregg
National Tractor Pullers Association(546)
Randall, Michele E.
Bibliographical Society of America(228)
Randall, Richard
National Network of Estate Planning Attorneys(528)
Randall, Susan
American Milking Devon Association(106)
Randazzo, Catherine A.
Society of the Plastics Industry(645)
Randol, USA (Ret.), Col. Doyle
American College Health Association(63)
Raney, Jennifer
National Corrugated Steel Pipe Association(496)
Ranger, Dan
Tourist Railway Association(662)
Ranger, Karen
Tourist Railway Association(662)
Ranieri, Jim
Society of Dance History Scholars(635)
Ranieri, Paul
Association for General and Liberal Studies(173)
Ranieri, Robert
American Association for Applied Linguistics(33)
Rankin, Matt
American Society for Public Administration(132)
Rankin, Paul W.
Reusable Industrial Packaging Association(601)
Ransome, Whitney
National Coalition of Girls Schools(490)
Rappa, Lindsay
International Society for Minimally-Invasive Cardiac Surgery(387)
Rappaport, Theresa
Deep Foundations Institute(282)
Rappel, James F.
Portland Cement Association(581)
Rascon, Martha
Fresh Produce Association of the Americas(312)
Rasmussen, Mark
Professional Reactor Operator Society(589)
Rasmussen, Priscilla
Association for Computational Linguistics(170)
Rasor, Robert
American Motorcyclist Association(107)
Rassam, Gus
American Fisheries Society(84)
Rasul, Christine
AMT - The Association For Manufacturing Technology(156)
Ratcliffe, Dolores
National Association of Black Women Entrepreneurs(440)
Ratclift Mensing, Marilyn G.
Twentieth-Century Spanish Association of America(667)
Rathbun, Todd
National Council on the Aging(503)
Ratley, James D.
Association of Certified Fraud Examiners(189)
Rauch, Carolyn
Entertainment Software Association(295)
Rauglas, Dirk
MTM Association for Standards and Research(422)
Raulin, Wendy
Endocrine Society(294)
Raulston, Carol
National Mining Association(527)
Rausch, Jim
Dredging Contractors of America(287)
Rauscher, Ken
National Plant Board(533)
Rawdon, Lyn
Health Industry Distributors Association(323)
Rawson, W. Randall
American Boiler Manufacturers Association(58)
Ray, Melissa
National Rural Letter Carriers' Association(537)
Ray, P. Joanne
American Society for Gastrointestinal Endoscopy(129)

Ray, Ron
Inter-Industry Conference on Auto Collision Repair(346)

Raybuck, Bob
National Truck Equipment Association(547)

Rayman, Dr. Russell B.
Aerospace Medical Association(10)

Raymond, David A.
American Council of Engineering Companies(75)

Raymond, Leo
Mailing & Fulfillment Service Association(410)

Raymond, Michael J.
American Wholesale Booksellers Association(154)

Raymond, Rosalind
Sheet Metal and Air Conditioning Contractors' National Association(610)

Raynaud, Caroline
German American Business Association(316)

Raynes, CAE, Jeffry W.
Institute of Electrical and Electronics Engineers(341)

Raynes, CAE, Linda J.
Electrical Apparatus Service Association(290)

Raynor, Bruce
UNITE-HERE(670)

Razza, Sanna
Voluntary Protection Programs Participants Association(684)

Read, Doug
American Society of Heating, Refrigerating and Air-Conditioning Engineers(139)

Read, Mary Margaret
American Suffolk Horse Association(150)

Read, Patricia
Independent Sector(336)

Read, Robin
National Foundation for Women Legislators(512)

Reading, Reid
Latin American Studies Association(405)

Reagan, Donna
National Association of Sales Professionals(470)

Ream, Rundi
Songwriters Guild of America(647)

Reardon, Susan
American Foreign Service Association(85)

Reardon, Thomas
Business and Institutional Furniture Manufacturers Association International(235)

Rebar, M.D., Robert W.
American Society for Reproductive Medicine(132)

Rebedeau, Mary Beth
Society of Independent Show Organizers(638)

Rebel, Nick
American Academy of Neurological and Orthopaedic Surgeons(24)

Rebuck, Patricia
Palomino Horse Association(570)

Rector, Esq., John M.
National Community Pharmacists Association(491)

Redd, Eileen
International Test and Evaluation Association(394)

Redden, Marlene
National Frozen and Refrigerated Foods Association(513)

Reddy, Neil
National Council for Advanced Manufacturing(496)

Reder, Nancy
National Association of State Directors of Special Education(475)

Redman, Michael
American Beverage Association(56)

Redmon, Patricia
Council of Large Public Housing Authorities(273)

Reed, Billy E.
American Engineering Association(81)

Reed, Doris A.
Association of Supervisory and Administrative School Personnel(216)

Reed, Jerry
Callerlab-International Association of Square Dance Callers(236)

Reed, John W.
International Society of Barristers(390)

Reed, Joy
Association of State and Territorial Directors of Nursing(215)

Reed, Kim
American Red Brangus Association(122)

Reed, Lydia M.
Association of University Programs in Health Administration(219)

Reed, Sloane
American College of Managed Care Medicine(67)

Reed, Thomas M.
American School Health Association(124)

Reed-Martinez, Elizabeth
Society of Competitive Intelligence Professionals(633)

Reeder, Robin
NACHA - The Electronic Payments Association(424)

Reedy, Elizabeth
North American Clun Forest Association(556)

Reedy, John
International Oil Scouts Association(381)

Rees, Michael
Sculptors Guild(607)

Rees, Susan
Media Communications Association International(415)

Rees, Susan M.
American Osteopathic Academy for Sports Medicine(111)
International Neural Network Society(381)
Society for Psychophysiological Research(624)

Reese, Marily
National Forest Recreation Association(512)

Reeves, Amanda
Society for Foodservice Management(617)

Reeves, Jim B.
United States Beef Breeds Council(673)

Reeves, Maria
International Compressor Remanufacturers Association(366)

Reeves, Robert M.
Institute of Shortening and Edible Oils(344)

Reeves, Shelly
National Association of Women in Construction(481)

Regan, Susan
Hardwood Manufacturers Association(322)

Regelbrugge, Craig J.
American Nursery and Landscape Association(109)
National Association of Plant Patent Owners(465)

Rehr, Ph.D., David K.
National Association of Broadcasters(441)

Rehrig, Norita H.
National Association of Colleges and Employers(444)

Reich, Margaret
American Physiological Society(115)

Reich, Wayne
Truck-frame and Axle Repair Association(666)

Reichbart, CMP, Susan
College and University Professional Association for Human Resources(250)

Reichelt-Pepper, CAE, Christine
National Funeral Directors Association(513)

Reichenberg, CAE, Neil E.
International Public Management Association for Human Resources(384)

Reichle, Donna
National Association of Home Builders(456)

Reicks, Laura
National Association for Treasurers of Religious Institutes(437)

Reid, C.J.
American Association of School Administrators(50)

Reid, David W.
Society of Critical Care Medicine(634)

Reid, Ph.D., Jerry B.
American Registry of Radiologic Technologists(122)

Reid, Karen A.
Employee Relocation Council/Worldwide ERC(293)

Reid, CAE, Kenneth D.
American Water Resources Association(154)

Reid, Michelle M.
Real Estate Round Table(596)

Reid, Pamlea J.
Association of Machinery and Equipment Appraisers(203)

Reid, CM, Robert
Institute of Certified Professional Managers(340)

Reid, Valerie
Hydraulic Institute(329)

Reif, Susan
National Association for Printing Leadership(435)

Reiff, Barbara
Surety Association of America(656)

Reighart, CMP, CMM, CAE, Glenn M.
National Community Pharmacists Association(491)

Reihl, Kathy
Association of Nurses in AIDS Care(206)

Reilly, Barbara
National Customs Brokers and Forwarders Association of America(504)

Reilly, Deborah Sykes
National Association of Independent Colleges and Universities(457)

Reilly, Edward T.
American Management Association(102)

Reilly, Jr., Matthew B.
American Short Line and Regional Railroad Association(125)

Reilly, Peter
Council of the Americas(275)

Reilly, Vanessa
Association of Medical Illustrators(204)

Reimer, Chris
National Ground Water Association(515)

Reinecke, Ralph
American Apparel & Footwear Association(31)

Reinemer, Michael
American Association for Homecare(35)

Reiner, D.D.S., Abraham
American Academy of Oral Medicine(25)

Reinerman, Alan J.
Society for Italian Historical Studies(621)

Reinfried, Robert A.
American Chain Association(61)
Conveyor Equipment Manufacturers Association(265)
Mechanical Power Transmission Association(415)
Scale Manufacturers Association(605)

Reinsch, William
National Foreign Trade Council(511)

Reinshuttle, Bob
American Society of Extra-Corporeal Technology(137)

Reisinger, Brenda
Public Agency Risk Managers Association(592)

Reisinger, Jan
American Academy of Clinical Toxicology(21)

Reiter, Ph.D, Henry H.
International Academy of Health Care Professionals(348)

Relethford, John H.
American Association of Physical Anthropologists(48)

Remaley, Donald F.
Railway Systems Suppliers(595)

Remington, Edward M.
National Association of Industrial and Office Properties(458)

Renfrow, Rachel
American Psychotherapy Association(119)

Renicks, Philip M.
Association of Christian Schools International(190)

Renk, CAE, Karen
Association of Girl Scout Executive Staff(198)
Incentive Marketing Association(332)

Renk, CAE, CMP, Thomas F.
Incentive Manufacturers and Representatives Association(332)

Renken, Alice
Viola da Gamba Society of America(683)

Renkes, Robert N.
Petroleum Equipment Institute(574)

Renkey, Mahala
Project Management Institute(590)

Renna, Steve
Real Estate Round Table(596)

Renner, Dennis W.
Association of American Colleges and Universities(184)

Renner, Megan
Institute of Management Consultants USA(342)
Museum Trustee Association(423)

Renner, Robert
ISA(400)

Rentz, DO, FACN, Louis E.
American College of Neuropsychiatrists(68)

Renzelman, Leslie
Golf Course Superintendents Association of America(318)

Renzetti, Kathy
Association for Healthcare Philanthropy(173)

Renzi, Dave
American Helicopter Society International(90)

Repsold, Brad
North American Spine Society(561)

Resch, Rhone
Solar Energy Industries Association(647)

Resnick, Michael
National School Boards Association(538)

Rettie, Tracy
American Staffing Association(149)

Reuland, Fred
Library Administration and Management Association(407)

Reusze, Kurt
National Committee on Planned Giving(491)

Reutershan, Donald
National Council of State Supervisors for Languages(501)

Rewey, Frederic
American Cash Flow Association(61)

Reynolds, Bernard D.
Retailer's Bakery Association(601)

Reynolds, Jeffrey L.
National Dog Groomers Association of America(505)

Reynolds, CAE, John R.
National Roadside Vegetation Management Association(537)

Reynolds, Kenneth W.
The Foodservice Group, Inc.(310)

Reynolds, Leslie
National Association of Secretaries of State(471)

Reynolds, Margaret
Linguistic Society of America(408)

Reynolds, Perry
International Housewares Association(375)

Reynolds, Shannon
Women's Basketball Coaches Association(693)

Rezai, Ali R.
American Society for Stereotactic and Functional Neurosurgery(132)

Rhame, USA(Ret.), Lt.Gen. Thomas
Association of the United States Army(218)

Rhee, So
International Clarinet Association(365)

Rheingold, Ira
National Association of Consumer Advocates(446)

Rhett, Candace R.
International Federation of Professional and Technical Engineers(371)

Rhinehart, Robert S.
American Association of Business Valuation Specialists(39)
American Association of Physicians and Health Care Professionals(48)

Rhoades, Kevin
Outdoor Writers Association of America(569)

Rhoads, Shelia
Ass'n of Procurement Technical Assistance Centers(164)

Rhoden, Joyce
International Maintenance Institute(379)

Rhodes, Andrew
American Society of Magazine Editors(141)

Rhodes, Marcia
WorldatWork(697)

Rhodes, Michael D.
Association of Federal Communications Consulting Engineers(196)

Riba, Ronald
Information Systems Audit and Control Association(338)

Riccetti, Rose
National Fraternal Congress of America(512)

Ricci, Joseph
National Association of Security Companies(471)

Rice, Jr., George S.
Association of Public-Safety Communications Officers- International(211)

Rice, Lauri
Water Systems Council(686)

Rice, LuAnn
National Association for Rural Mental Health(436)

Rice, Patricia
National Association of Health Unit Coordinators(455)

Rice, Philip L.
Organization for International Investment(567)

Rice, Sallyanne
Professional Women Controllers(590)

Rice, Teresa
National Energy Services Association(507)

Rice, Wayne
NEA - the Association of Union Constructors(551)

Rich, Phyllis
Nuclear Energy Institute(563)

Richard, Erica
American Morgan Horse Association(106)

Richards, Chris
Association of Independent Corrugated Converters(200)

Richards, Dave A.
Institute of Internal Auditors(342)

Richards, Kent
Society of Biblical Literature(632)

Richards, Liz
Material Handling Equipment Distributors Association(414)

Richards, III, Marty
Business Professionals of America(236)

Richards, Ray
American Staffing Association(149)

Richardson, Alan H.
American Public Power Association(120)

Richardson, Bonnie
Motion Picture Association of America(421)

Richardson, MS, RD, LD, Cecilia
National WIC Association(549)

Richardson, Charles L.
National Environmental, Safety and Health Training Association(507)

Richardson, Deborah S.
International Society for Research on Aggression(388)

Richardson, Douglas B.
Association of American Geographers(184)

Richardson, Karen G.
United Professional Horsemen's Association(672)

Richardson, Steve
Football Writers Association of America(310)

Richardt, CMP, Deborah
American Thoracic Society(151)

Richert, Dr. John
National Multiple Sclerosis Society(528)

Riches, Robert
National Health Club Association(516)

Richetti, Donald N.
AOC(158)

Richey, Benjamin
National Institute for Animal Agriculture(520)

Richison, Sindie
International Brotherhood of Magicians(363)

Richmond-Garza, E.
American Comparative Literature Association(72)

Rickenbach, C.A.E., Francine W.
Association of Destination Management Executives(193)
Employee Involvement Association(293)
National Association of Nephrology Technologists and Technicians(462)
Ultrasonic Industry Association(669)

Ricker, Timothy
Water Environment Federation(685)

Ricketts, Mimi
National Corn Growers Association(496)

Rickles, M.D., Frederick R.
Federation of American Socs. for Experimental Biology(303)

Rickwalder, Janay
International Sign Association(386)

Riddell, M. Gatz
American Association of Bovine Practitioners(39)

Riddell, Mary
International Association of Workforce Professionals(362)

Riddick, Blenda
Council of Large Public Housing Authorities(273)

Riddle, Anthony
Alliance for Community Media(15)

Riddlebaugh, Gene D.
National Alarm Association of America(429)

Rideout, Tonya S.
EPDM Roofing Association(297)

Ridge, M.D., John
American Head and Neck Society(89)

Ridgely, Janet
American Chiropractic Association(62)

Rieger, Howard
United Jewish Communities(671)

Rieger, Penny S.
Caucus for Television Producers, Writers & Directors(240)

Riegle, Nancy
National Association of Chain Drug Stores(442)

Rieman, Garth
National Council of State Housing Agencies(500)

Rienhardt, Jim
American Nature Study Society(108)

Rienzo, Michael D.
Silver Institute(611)

Ries, P.E., John P.
Expanded Shale, Clay and Slate Institute(299)

Riesett, Kathleen Kelley
Organization for the Promotion and Advancement of Small Telecommunications Companies(567)

Riessman, Janet
Association of Reproductive Health Professionals(212)

Rigel, Vicki
American Cotswold Record Association(74)

Riggott, Brenda
American Association of Neuromuscular & Electrodiagnostic Medicine(46)

Riggs, Carol
Select Registry/Distinguished Inns of North America(608)

Riggs, Ed
National Association of Litho Clubs(460)

Riggs, Trisha
Urban Land Institute(680)

Righthouse, Jerry L.
World Sign Associates(696)

Rigney, Anne M.
Society of Financial Service Professionals(636)

Rigney, Robert
American Association of Tissue Banks(53)

Rile, Jr., Howard C.
American Society of Questioned Document Examiners(145)

Riley, Ph.D., Bob
National Council for Therapeutic Recreation Certification(497)

Riley, Brian
General Aviation Manufacturers Association(315)

Riley, Janet
American Meat Institute(103)

Riley, John
Society of Actuaries(629)

Riley, Margaret
Association of College and University Telecommunications Administrators(191)

Riley, Rachele M.
American Association for Functional Orthodontics(35)

Riley, Shawna
United States Professional Tennis Association(676)

Rimmerman, Ph.D., Harlan
National Auctioneers Association(482)

Rinaldi, Dr. Bob
American Association of Oral and Maxillofacial Surgeons(47)

Rinaldi, DPM, Frank
American Association of Hospital and Healthcare Podiatrists(43)

Rinaldi, Joan
Silver Institute(611)

Rinaldi, Paul
National Air Traffic Controllers Association(428)

Rindelaub, Jim
Choristers Guild(245)

Rines, Robert
Academy of Applied Science(2)

Ringo, Lori
National Association of Catastrophe Adjusters(442)

Rinkenberger, Kathy
International Association of Professional Security Consultants(360)

Rinn, Miriam
JWB Jewish Chaplains Council(403)

Rios, Dr. Elena V.
National Hispanic Medical Association(517)

Rios, Jason
National Council of Agricultural Employers(498)

Riotto, Charles
International Licensing Industry Merchandisers' Association(378)

Ripley, Barrett F.
American Flock Association(84)

Ripley, Heather
Public Risk Management Association(593)

Rippen, Harrison W.
National Wood Tank Institute(550)

Rippentrop, CAE, Gary D.
ACA International, The Association of Credit and Collection Professionals(2)

Ripper, Jessica
Alexander Graham Bell Association for the Deaf and Hard of Hearing(15)

Ripperton, Ryan T.
Phi Mu Alpha Sinfonia(576)

Riser, Anne
Truck Renting and Leasing Association(666)

Risinger, Beth B.
International Executive Housekeepers Association(371)

Risley, Dan
Society of Collision Repair Specialists(633)

Riso, Guy
Federation of American Socs. for Experimental Biology(303)

Risotto, Stephen P.
Halogenated Solvents Industry Alliance(321)

Ristau, Ed.D., Karen
National Catholic Educational Association(487)

Ritchey, Ph.D., CAE, David A.
Association of Teacher Educators(217)

Ritt, Mary Jo
Aluminum Extruders Council(18)

Ritterbusch, Chad
American Society of Golf Course Architects(138)

Rittner, Toby
Council of Development Finance Agencies(271)

Ritzi, Cheryl
American Academy of Physical Medicine and Rehabilitation(27)

Rivard, Karen
Association for the Advancement of Psychology(179)

Rivera, Ivette
National Automobile Dealers Association(482)

Rivera, Margaret
American Association of Community Colleges(41)

Rivera, Sharon
Association of Latino Professionals in Accounting and Finance(203)

Rivera, Susan K.
American Society of Forensic Odontology(138)

Rivers, James A.
Psi Omega(591)

Rivers, Joe
Young Menswear Association(698)

Rizzuto, A. Anthony
American Conference of Governmental Industrial Hygienists(73)

Roach, Robert
Sheet Metal and Air Conditioning Contractors' National Association(610)

Roark, Carrol
American College of Eye Surgeons(65)

Roark, Trent
Society for Excellence in Eyecare(617)

Roba, William
Society for German-American Studies(617)

Robbins, Beth
Business and Professional Women/USA(235)

Robbins, Darlene
National Association of Conservation Districts(445)

Robbins, Mark
Career College Association(237)

Roberson, David
Specialty Coffee Association of America(650)

Roberson, Dee
Home Wine and Beer Trade Association(328)

Roberson, Kara
National Association of Women in Construction(481)

Roberson, Rodney L.
United Braford Breeders(670)

Roberts, Alan I.
Dangerous Goods Advisory Council(281)

Roberts, Bruce F.
Textile Distributors Association(660)

Roberts, Bruce T.
National Community Pharmacists Association(491)
Roberts, Cassandra
National Council for the Social Studies(497)
Roberts, Cecil E.
United Mine Workers of America International Union(672)
Roberts, David
Healthcare Information and Management Systems Society(324)
Roberts, David E.
National Frozen Dessert and Fast Food Association(513)
Roberts, Dustin
Golf Coaches Association of America(318)
Roberts, Elizabeth
Geospatial Information Technology Association(316)
Roberts, Ed.S., Gregory
ACPA - College Student Educators Association(7)
Roberts, Jennifer
Government Finance Officers Association of the United States and Canada(318)
Roberts, John H.
International Grooving and Grinding Association(374)
Roberts, Julian
American Association of Preferred Provider Organizations(49)
Roberts, Karen
American Society of Travel Agents(146)
Roberts, Kimberly
NATSO, Representing America's Travel Plazas and Truckstops(550)
Roberts, Mark
National Association of Computer Consultant Businesses(445)
Roberts, Mark C.
Mineral Economics and Management Society(419)
Roberts, Michael
American Gastroenterological Association(86)
Roberts, Radell
International Society of Political Psychology(392)
Roberts, Roger
American Association of State Highway and Transportation Officials(51)
Roberts, Susan
Society of Radiologists in Ultrasound(643)
Roberts, Terry L.
Potash & Phosphate Institute(581)
Robertson, Alix
United States Rowing Association(677)
Robertson, Carolyn
National Association of Underwater Instructors(480)
Robertson, Chuck
National American Indian Court Judges Association(430)
Robertson, D. Mark
American College of Sports Medicine(70)
Robertson, David N.
Association of Finance and Insurance Professionals(196)
Robertson, Gordon
American Sportfishing Association(148)
Robertson, John
Mechanical Association Railcar Technical Services(415)
Robertson, Maria
School Nutrition Association(606)
Robertson, Michael
Specialty Graphic Imaging Association(650)
Robertson, Mike
Digital Printing and Imaging Association(284)
Robertson, Ric
Academy of Motion Picture Arts and Sciences(4)
Robertson, Scott
NAMM - the International Music Products Association(425)
Robertson, Susan
American Society of Association Executives & Center for Association Leadership(134)
Robey, Michael H.
National Contact Lens Examiners(495)
Robin, Karen
American Herbal Products Association(90)
Robin, Lisa A.
Federation of State Medical Boards of the United States(304)
Robinson, Ph.D., Allen
American Driver and Traffic Safety Education Association(79)
Robinson, Amy
Direct Selling Association(285)
Robinson, Billie
Soap and Detergent Association(612)
Robinson, Blades
International Association of Dive Rescue Specialists(356)
Robinson, Camille
National Association of Dog Obedience Instructors(450)
Robinson, Charles L.
Electronic Industries Alliance(292)
Robinson, Colleen
Snack Food Association(612)
Robinson, Dave
American Association of State Climatologists(51)
Robinson, Dorothy
Eye Bank Association of America(300)
Robinson, Gary
Union of American Physicians and Dentists(670)
Robinson, CAE, J. Lawrence
Color Pigments Manufacturers Association(253)
Robinson, John D.
Public Relations Society of America(593)
Robinson, John F.
National Minority Business Council(527)
Robinson, Katie
National Conference of Commissioners on Uniform State Laws(493)
Robinson, Lynn P.
American Gastroenterological Association(86)
Robinson, Mark
Machinery Dealers National Association(409)
Robinson, Mike
Council of State Governments(275)
Robinson, Nancy J.
Livestock Marketing Association(409)
Robinson, Peter M.
United States Council for International Business(674)
Robinson, Roxanne M.
American Association for Laboratory Accreditation(35)
Robinson, Sharon P.
American Association of Colleges for Teacher Education(40)
Robinson, Wil
Association of Fundraising Professionals(198)
Robinson, William L.
National Association of Marine Services(461)
Robischon, Rose
North American Serials Interest Group(560)
Robison, Lee H.
Association of Field Ornithologists(196)
Robison, Steve
American Foundry Society(85)
Rocca, Elizabeth
OPERA America(565)
Rocca, Jason Della
International Game Developers Association(374)
Roche, David
Jewelers Shipping Association(401)
Roche, Joyce M.
Girls Incorporated(317)
Roche, Robyn
International Association of Food Industry Suppliers(357)
Rochell, Judy
American College of Physician Executives(69)
Rochman, Julie
American Insurance Association(98)
Rock, Frederick M.
American Society of Laboratory Animal Practitioners(140)
Rock, Rebecca
International Association of Lighting Designers(358)
Rocker, Regina
New York Board of Trade(552)
Rockers, Dr. Michael M.
National Federation of Nonpublic School State Accrediting Associations(510)
Rockey, Sherry
Independent Sector(336)
Rockne, Jennifer
American Independent Business Alliance(93)
Rockwell, Shelley
American Judges Association(99)
Conference of State Court Adminstrators(260)
Rodan, CPM, Lance
National Association of Dental Laboratories(448)
Rodden, Joseph M.
Association of Reproductive Health Professionals(212)
Rodeffer, Maggie
National Guardianship Association(515)
Rodenberg, Harriet
Phi Rho Sigma Medical Society(576)
Rodgers, Alexis L.
American Board of Medical Specialties(57)
Rodgers, Jr., Clifton E.
Real Estate Round Table(596)
Rodgers, De
American Academy of Environmental Medicine(22)
Rodgers, Jonathan
American Oriental Society(110)
Rodgers, Joseph
Society of Multivariate Experimental Psychology(640)
Rodgers, Paul
American Sheep Industry Association(125)
Rodgers, Tykia
National Pan-Hellenic Council(531)
Rodman, Stanley A.
Automotive Body Parts Association(223)
Rodnan, Nancy
American Society for Biochemistry and Molecular Biology(126)

Rodrigues, John
National Association of Independent Schools(457)
Rodriguez, Bob
Automotive Training Managers Council(224)
Rodzwicz, Edward
Brotherhood of Locomotive Engineers and Trainmen(233)
Roeder, Henry J.
National Business Travel Association(486)
Roehrig, Steven A.
Steel Deck Institute(653)
Roeling, Dana L.
National Mobility Equipment Dealers Association(527)
Roemer, Henry C.
Specialty Tobacco Council(650)
Roenigk, William P.
National Chicken Council(489)
Roesslein, Corrie
Institute of Environmental Sciences and Technology(341)
Rogala, CAE, Joan
Lambda Kappa Sigma(405)
Rogan, Elizabeth
Optical Society of America(566)
Roger, Judy
North American Mycological Association(558)
Rogers, Carol S.
AACE International(1)
Rogers, Ed
History of Earth Sciences Society(326)
Rogers, Jan
International Association of Food Industry Suppliers(357)
Rogers, Joseph E.L.
Center for Waste Reduction Technologies(241)
Rogers, Maureen
Herb Growing & Marketing Network(325)
Rogers, Paul
American Correctional Chaplains Association(74)
Rogers, Susan K.
Society for College and University Planning(615)
Rogers, Tim
National Association of Manufacturers(460)
Rogers, Todd P.
Casualty Actuarial Society(239)
Rogin, Carole M.
Association of Women in the Metal Industries(220)
Hearing Industries Association(324)
International Society of Hospitality Consultants(391)
National Society for Experiential Education(540)
Rohlwing, Kevin
Tire Industry Association(662)
Rohrs, Christopher J.
Television Bureau of Advertising(659)
Roland, Becky
Association of Environmental and Engineering Geologists(195)
Rolater, Rick
American Institute of Mining, Metallurgical, and Petroleum Engineers(96)
Rolden, Richard R.
National Propane Gas Association(534)
Rolland, Sean
Association of State and Interstate Water Pollution Control Administrators(214)
Roller, Debbie
American Society of Andrology(133)
Rollin, Miriam
National Association of Counsel for Children(446)
Rollins, Morag
American Arbitration Association(32)
Rollins, Peter C.
Historians Film Committee/Film & History(326)
Rollins, Wendy
American Lighting Association(101)
Rolnicki, Tom E.
Associated Collegiate Press, National Scholastic Press Association(165)
Rolofson, George
CropLife America(279)
Roman, Ivan
National Association of Hispanic Journalists(455)
Roman, Lori
American Legislative Exchange Council(101)
Romanick, Sara J.
National Association of Federal Credit Unions(452)
Romano, Brenda
Construction Innovation Forum(262)
Romano, Bud
American College of Occupational and Environmental Medicine(68)
Romano, Kathy
National Association of Directors of Nursing Administration in Long Term Care(449)
Romano, Rosina
Rehabilitation Engineering and Assistive Technology Society of North America(598)
Romeo, Bob
Academy of Country Music(3)
Romeo, Kelly
American Land Title Association(100)
Romer, Kirsten
Semiconductor Industry Association(608)
Romero, Katherine
Van Alen Institute(682)
Romm, Tracy
American Herbalists Guild(90)
Romo, Kathy
Associated Locksmiths of America(165)
Safe and Vault Technicians Association(604)
Ronan, Charlotte P.
American Association of Veterinary State Boards(54)
Ronay, J. Christopher
Institute of Makers of Explosives(342)
Roncketti, Nancy E.
International Association of Counseling Services(355)
Roney, Jack
American Sugar Alliance(150)
Ronsheim, Douglas M.
American Association of Pastoral Counselors(47)
Rood, David
National Association of College Auxiliary Services(444)
Rook, Kathy
Recreational Park Trailer Industry Association(596)
Rooney, Denise C.
Association of Food and Drug Officials(197)
Rooney, Francis P.
Biscuit and Cracker Manufacturers' Association(229)
Root, Rick
World Waterpark Association(696)
Ropelewski, CPCU, AU, ARM, CPIW, Deb
Professional Liability Underwriting Society(588)
Rosado, Edwin
National Association of Counties(447)
Rosales, Henry
Geospatial Information Technology Association(316)
Rosan, Richard M.
Urban Land Institute(680)
Rosch, M.D., Paul J.
American Institute of Stress(97)
Roscoe, Timothy
Clinical and Laboratory Standards Institute(248)
Rose, Bernice
American College of Obstetricians and Gynecologists(68)
Rose, Christine
American College of Foot and Ankle Surgeons(66)
Rose, John N.
Organization for the Promotion and Advancement of Small Telecommunications Companies(567)
Rose, Judy
Law and Society Association(406)
Rose, Kay
Mycological Society of America(424)
Rose, Melane
National Confectioners Association of the United States(492)
Rose, Stephen
American Council on Education(76)
Rosen, APR, Jody B.
Communications Media Management Association(255)
Rosen, Myra
Private Label Manufacturers Association(584)
Rosen, Roslyn
Council on Education of the Deaf(276)
Rosenbaum, Ron
Club Managers Association of America(249)
Rosenberg, Ernie
Soap and Detergent Association(612)
Rosenberg, Linda
National Council for Community Behavioral Healthcare(497)
Rosenberg, Robert
National Pest Management Association(532)
Rosenblat, Arney
National Multiple Sclerosis Society(528)
Rosenblatt, Carol
Coalition of Labor Union Women(249)
Rosenblatt, Daniel N.
International Association of Chiefs of Police(354)
Rosenblatt, Sherrie
National Turkey Federation(548)
Rosenbrook, Olga
Computer Event Marketing Association(257)
Rosencrance, CMP, Debra
American Academy of Ophthalmology(25)
Rosenstein, Peter
American Academy of Orthotists and Prosthetists(26)
Rosenthal, Clifford N.
National Federation of Community Development Credit Unions(509)
Rosenthal, Gwenn E.
ESOP Association(297)
Rosenthal, Lisa
International Organization of Masters, Mates and Pilots(382)
Rosenthal, Roger
National Association of State Directors of Migrant Education(474)

Rosenzweig, CAE, Claire
Promotion Marketing Association(590)
Rosenzweig, Harvey
Association of Jewish Center Professionals(202)
Rosetta, Ray
Society of Teachers of Family Medicine(644)
Rosier, Ronald C.
Conference Board of the Mathematical Sciences(259)
Rosner, Patrice
National Council of the Churches of Christ in the U.S.A.(501)
Roso, Yvette
Cargo Airline Association(238)
Rosprim, Richard
American Association of Professional Landmen(49)
Rosquist, Elaine
Destination Marketing Association International(283)
Ross, Berinda
Water Environment Federation(685)
Ross, Diedre Irwin
American Library Association(101)
Ross, Emily
National Association of Nutrition and Aging Services Programs(463)
Ross, Farren
National Association of Health Underwriters(455)
Ross, Gilbert
American Council on Science and Health(76)
Ross, Jerilyn
Anxiety Disorders Association of America(157)
Ross, Jessica
Dibasic Esters Group(284)
Tetrahydrofuran Task Force(659)
Ross, John
Appraisal Institute(159)
Ross, Joy
Outdoor Power Equipment Aftermarket Association(569)
Ross, Laura
International Conference of Symphony and Opera Musicians(367)
Ross, Lou
Microbeam Analysis Society(418)
Ross, Lynne M.
National Association of Attorneys General(439)
Ross, Natasha
Association of Air Medical Services(183)
Ross, Paul
Associated Risk Managers(166)
Ross, Tara
Executive Women International(299)
Rossell, Kathleen M.
Association of Legal Administrators(203)
Rossen, Leslie E.
National Labor Relations Board Professional Association(523)
Rosseter, Robert
American Association of Colleges of Nursing(40)
Rossi, Frank
American Arbitration Association(32)
Rossignol, Denise
Phlebology Society of America(576)
Rossman, D.V.M., Richard
Academy of Veterinary Allergy and Clinical Immunology(6)
Roszman, Beth
National Association of State Chief Information Officers(474)
Rotblatt, CAE, Martin
International Society for Clinical Densitometry(386)
Roth, Daniel J.
National Futures Association(513)
Roth, Jay D.
Directors Guild of America(285)
Roth, PE, Jerry
International Society for Pharmaceutical Engineering(388)
Roth, Larry
American Society of Civil Engineers(135)
Roth, Marcie
National Spinal Cord Injury Association(542)
Roth, Mark
American Federation of Government Employees(82)
Roth, Mary
Risk and Insurance Management Society(602)
Roth, Mitch
National Academy of Recording Arts and Sciences(427)
Roth, Scott
Art Directors Guild/Scenic, Title and Graphic Artists(161)
Rothaermel, Diane
Forging Industry Association(310)
Rothbart, Cheryl
American Society of Consultant Pharmacists(136)
Rothholz, Mitchel C.
American Pharmacists Association(114)
Rothman, Eric
American Road and Transportation Builders Association(123)
Rothstein, Bob
American Moving and Storage Association(107)
Roton, Frances
American Association of Community Psychiatrists(41)
American Association of Psychiatric Administrators(49)
American Society for Adolescent Psychiatry(126)
Rotstein, Margaret
Society for Invertebrate Pathology(620)
Roueche, Len
Interferry(347)
Rougvie, Carol
International Society of Exposure Analysis(391)
Rourke, Kelly
OPERA America(565)
Rouse, Geri
American Seminar Leaders Association(124)
Roush, Kathy
Beta Beta Beta(228)
Rouzie, Patricia
National Beer Wholesalers Association(484)
Row, FACHE, Constance F.
American Academy of Home Care Physicians(23)
Rowan, Matthew J.
Health Industry Distributors Association(323)
Rowe, Amanda W.
International Society for Heart and Lung Transplantation(387)
Rowe, Jeanine
American Association for Geriatric Psychiatry(35)
Rowe, Joe
Retail Tobacco Dealers of America(601)
Rowe, Robert
Independent Community Bankers of America(333)
Rowello, Trudie
North American Horticultural Supply Association(557)
Rowland, James
Wine and Spirits Wholesalers of America(689)
Rowland, Laureen
American College of Medical Physics(67)
Rowson, Sharon
National Aerosol Association(428)
Roy, Keely
American Embryo Transfer Association(81)
Royal, Valerie
NAFSA: Association of International Educators(424)
Roybal, Joseph A.
International Guards Union of America(374)
Royer, Kyle H.
Council for Christian Colleges and Universities(268)
Rozak, Frank
National Association of Optometrists and Opticians(463)
Rozett, Linda
United States Chamber of Commerce(674)
Ruane, CAE, T. Peter
American Road and Transportation Builders Association(123)
Rubillo, James M.
National Council of Teachers of Mathematics(501)
Rubin, Burton J.
American Society of Travel Agents(146)
Rubin, Ph.D., Elaine R.
Association of Academic Health Centers(183)
Rubin, Linda
International Association of Correctional Training Personnel(355)
Rubin, Ph.D, MHP, Marcia
American School Health Association(124)
Rubin, Mark
Society of Petroleum Engineers(641)
Rubin, Ph.D., Norma H.
International Society for Chronobiology(386)
Rubin, Susan
National Association of Social Workers(472)
Rubino, Victor J.
Practising Law Institute(582)
Rubinstein, Ellis
New York Academy of Sciences(552)
Rubinstein, Lori
Entertainment Services and Technology Association(295)
Rubseman, John
National Child Care Association(489)
Ruby, David G.
Recycled Paperboard Technical Association(597)
Ruch, Sandra J.
International Documentary Association(369)
Ruck, Sean
National Kitchen and Bath Association(523)
Ruckman, Cynthia E.
National Association of College Stores(444)
Rudd, M.D., Gene
Christian Medical & Dental Associations(246)
Ruddy, Anne C.
WorldatWork(697)
Ruden, Paul
American Society of Travel Agents(146)
Rudowicz, Michael
American Amusement Machine Association(31)

Rudy, Gary
Independent Free Papers of America(334)
Rudzinski, Laura J.
National Association of Independent Fee Appraisers(457)
National Institute of Pension Administrators(521)
Ruehle, Melanie
American Spa and Health Resort Association(148)
Ruffin, Thomas
National Conference of Black Lawyers(492)
Ruffner, Gary M.
Utility Workers Union of America(681)
Ruhl, Mary
Society of Teachers of Family Medicine(644)
Ruiz, Teofilo F.
American Academy of Research Historians of Medieval Spain(28)
Ruland, Susan E.
International Dairy Foods Association(368)
Rumpf, Morgan
Directors Guild of America(285)
Rumsfield, Charles
North American Professional Driver Education Association(559)
Runci, Matthew A.
Jewelers of America(401)
Rundgren, Herb
United States Army Warrant Officers Association(673)
Rundquist, Kristina
American Society of Travel Agents(146)
Runge, Jon
American Water Works Association(154)
Runyon, Rex A.
American Feed Industry Association(83)
Ruppert, Chris
Association for Applied Psychophysiology and Biofeedback(167)
Rusboldt, Robert
Independent Insurance Agents and Brokers of America(334)
Rush, CAE, Iris
Regulatory Affairs Professionals Society(598)
Rush, Lee
National Student Assistance Association(544)
Rush, Peter S.
Builders Hardware Manufacturers Association(234)
Window Covering Safety Council(689)
Rushing, Anne
American Society for Experimental NeuroTherapeutics(129)
Rushing, Hugh J.
Cookware Manufacturers Association(265)
Wirebound Box Manufacturers Association(690)
Rusnak, Andy
American Composites Manufacturers Association(72)
International Cast Polymer Association(364)
Russell, Barry
Independent Petroleum Association of America(335)
Russell, CPA, Denis
American Podiatric Medical Association(116)
Russell, G.E.
WorkPlace Furnishings(695)
Russell, Dr. John
Academy of Managed Care Providers(4)
National Sports and Fitness Association(543)
Russell, Ph.D., Terrence R.
Association for Institutional Research(175)
Russell, Thomas R.
American College of Surgeons(71)
Russell Wilson, Clarissa
Society of Toxicology(645)
Russo, Jennifer
American Society of Clinical Psychopharmacology(136)
Russo, Michael L.
Gift Association of America(317)
Russo, Phillip E.
National Association of Fleet Administrators(453)
Rust, Marti
American Apparel & Footwear Association(31)
Rustigan, Janet E.
International Foodservice Manufacturers Association(372)
Rutherford, Tamra
Association for Comprehensive Energy Psychology(170)
Rutkauskas, D.D.S., John S.
American Academy of Pediatric Dentistry(26)
Rutledge, Penny
American College of Obstetricians and Gynecologists(68)
Rutt, Kelly
Environmental Information Association(296)
Ruyak, Doreen Kelly
National Association of Corporate Directors(446)
Ruzicka, Steven D.
Association of Boarding Schools, The(188)
Ryan, Elaine
American Public Human Services Association(120)
Ryan, George H.
Graphic Arts Technical Foundation(319)
Ryan, Joel
National Head Start Association(516)
Ryan, John
Conference of State Bank Supervisors(260)
Ryan, John P.
Glass, Molders, Pottery, Plastics and Allied Workers International Union(317)
Ryan, USN(Ret.), VADM Norbert R.
Military Officers Association of America(419)
Ryan, Stephen M.
Major Indoor Soccer League(410)
Ryan, Tim
Association of Public-Safety Communications Officers- International(211)
Ryan, William
Optical Society of America(566)
Rychard, Gary
American Association of Classified School Employees(39)
Rydell, Catherine
American Academy of Neurology(25)
Ryder, CPA, Harry
National Roofing Contractors Association(537)
Rydman, Phil
Association of Gospel Rescue Missions(199)
Ryland, Harvey G.
Institute for Business & Home Safety(339)
Ryndak, Heather
International Association of Lighting Designers(358)
Rytting, Robyn
Expanded Shale, Clay and Slate Institute(299)
Rzepka, Laura
American Conference of Academic Deans(73)
Sabbath, Larry
National Armored Car Association(431)
Sablone, Frank
Tag and Label Manufacturers Institute(657)
Sacco, Michael
Seafarers' International Union(607)
Saccoccio, Lou
National Health Care Anti-Fraud Association(516)
Sacerdote, John
National Association of Personnel Services(464)
Sachs, Cathy D.P.
American Society of Picture Professionals(144)
Sachs, Harold
Fashion Accessories Shippers Association(301)
National Fashion Accessories Association(508)
Sachs, Lorraine P.
National Association of State Boards of Accountancy(473)
Sachs, Rusty
National Association of Flight Instructors(453)
Sacks, Irving
International Association for Modular Exhibitry(351)
Sadat, Leila
American Society of Comparative Law(136)
Saeman, Anne
National Mastitis Council(526)
Safi, Dr. Louay M.
Association of Muslim Social Scientists(205)
Sagan, Andrew
Professional Fraternity Association(587)
Saggese, Marty
Society for Neuroscience(622)
Sahel, Heidi A.
American Association for Cancer Education(33)
American Society of Preventive Oncology(145)
Sahler, Stephen
American Institute of Professional Bookkeepers(97)
Sakkestad, Barbara A.
Coal Technology Association(249)
Salamon, Ed
Country Radio Broadcasters, Inc.(277)
Salario, Pamela D.
National Conference of State Liquor Administrators(494)
Salberg, Kay
American Tin Trade Association(151)
Saldana, Patricia
Organic Crop Improvement Association International(566)
Sale, David M.
Council of Colleges of Acupuncture and Oriental Medicine(271)
Salek, Edward P.
Society of Tribologists and Lubrication Engineers(645)
Salem, MA, Peter
Association of Family and Conciliation Courts(196)
Saliga, Pauline
Society of Architectural Historians(631)
Salisbury, Dallas L.
Employee Benefit Research Institute(293)
Salisbury, Judith K.
American Association of Dental Consultants(41)
Salmon, Patricia
Society of Medical-Dental Management Consultants(640)
Saltzman, Ben
Tilt-up Concrete Association(661)
Salusky, Isidro B.
International Pediatric Nephrology Association(382)

Salzman, Fred
Dental Dealers of America(283)
Salzman, Russell C.
Institute of Real Estate Management(343)
Samblanet, Phillip
Masonry Society, The(413)
Samborski, Robert
Geospatial Information Technology Association(316)
Samian, Pat
American Men's Studies Association(105)
Sample, Janet
American Philosophical Association(114)
Sampson, Sherri
Graduate Management Admission Council(319)
Samuel, Antoinette
American Society for Public Administration(132)
Sanabria, Susan
National Multiple Sclerosis Society(528)
Sanchez, Debra
Association of Public Television Stations(210)
SandBakken, John
National Sunflower Association(545)
Sanders, Barbara
American Tinnitus Association(151)
Sanders, Charles
National Music Publishers' Association(528)
Sanders, Ph.D., David
National Music Council(528)
Sanders, Lee
American Bakers Association(55)
Sandford, Juliet
National Writers Union(550)
Sandherr, Stephen E.
Associated General Contractors of America(165)
Sandler, CAE, William S.
Valve Manufacturers Association of America(682)
Sandoro, James T.
Collector Car Appraisers International(250)
Sandoval, Dennis
American Academy of Estate Planning Attorneys(22)
Sands, Merrill
Independent Investors Protective League(334)
Sandstrom, Joanne
Society for the Study of Early China(628)
Sandusky, Vincent R.
Finishing Contractors Association(306)
Sanford, USN (Ret.), RAdm. Frederic G.
Association of Military Surgeons of the U.S.(205)
Sanford, Sarah J.
Society of Actuaries(629)
Sankey, C. Patrick
International Road Federation(385)
Sankey, Greg
Collegiate Commissioners Association(252)
Sankey, Nichelle
Society of Toxicology(645)
Sanner, Ed
International Society of Communication Specialists(391)
Sansolo, Michael
Food Marketing Institute(309)
Sansone, CAE, David C.
Precision Metalforming Association(583)
Sansone, Torry Mark
American Society of Hypertension(139)
Sansoni, Brian
Soap and Detergent Association(612)
Sant, Brad
American Road and Transportation Builders Association(123)
Santa, Jr., Donald F.
Interstate Natural Gas Association of America(398)
Santana, Elizabeth
International Engineering Consortium(370)
Santantonio, Wendy
National Insulation Association(521)
Santi, Pat
Dog Writers' Association of America(286)
Santomauro, Michael
American Society of Roommate Services(145)
Santora, Kathleen Curry
National Association of College and University Attorneys(444)
Santore, Richard A.
Associated Funeral Directors International(165)
Santoro, Carlo
Italy-America Chamber of Commerce(400)
Santorum, Daniel
Professional Tennis Registry(589)
Santos, Antonio
Manufacturers of Emission Controls Association(411)
Saporta, Vicki
National Abortion Federation(426)
Sapp, Charles L.
International Embryo Transfer Society(370)
Saran, Chitaranjan
American Academy of Safety Education(28)
Sarasin, CAE, Leslie G.
American Frozen Food Institute(85)
International Frozen Food Association(373)
National Yogurt Association(550)
Sarfati, Susan
American Society of Association Executives & Center for Association Leadership(134)
Sarka, CMP, Michael
Vacation Rental Managers Association(681)
Sarris, Tracy
International Association for the Leisure and Entertainment Industry(351)
Sasala, Raymond J.
National Association of Consumer Credit Administrators(446)
Saskin, Ted
National Hockey League Players' Association(517)
Satagaj, John
Small Business Legislative Council(611)
Satagaj Orrock, Regina
International Health, Racquet and Sportsclub Association(374)
Satterfield, Gary T.
Waste Equipment Technology Association(685)
Sauer, Bernard
Hebrew Actors Union(325)
Saunders, David A.
American Association of Residential Mortgage Regulators(50)
American Coke and Coal Chemicals Institute(63)
International Oxygen Manufacturers Association(382)
Soy Protein Council(648)
Saunders, Jim
Professional and Technical Consultants Association(585)
Saunders, III, John E.
National Forum for Black Public Administrators(512)
Saunders, Laurie M.
American Society of Appraisers(134)
Saunders, Sherry
Business and Professional Women/USA(235)
Sauter, J. Edward
Concrete Foundations Association(258)
Tilt-up Concrete Association(661)
Sauve, John M.
Wild Blueberry Association of North America(688)
Savage, CAE, Bruce A.
Manufactured Housing Institute(411)
Savage, Drew
Association of Membership and Marketing Executives(204)
Savarese, Joseph B.
American Stamp Dealers' Association(149)
Savey, Michelle
At-sea Processors Association(221)
Savitt, Ph.D., Todd L.
American Association for the History of Medicine(37)
Sawicki, Dorothea L.
American Society for Virology(133)
Sawyer, Chris
American College of Sports Medicine(70)
Sawyer, Gina
American Association for State and Local History(36)
Sawyer, Ron
Professional Service Association(589)
Sawyer, Steven F.
International Fire Marshals Association(372)
Saxon, Ph.D., Ross
Association of Diving Contractors International(194)
Sayadian, Helga
Information Technology Industry Council(338)
Sayenga, Donald
National Association of Chain Manufacturers(442)
Sayers, Maria J.
National Housing Conference(518)
Saylor, Bonnie
Society for Applied Spectroscopy(614)
Scafidi, Frank G.
National Insurance Crime Bureau(522)
Scales, Aileen
Consortium of College and University Media Centers(262)
Scalise, George
Semiconductor Industry Association(608)
Scangarello, June
American Society of Mechanical Engineers(141)
Scanlan, Frank
Society for Human Resource Management(619)
Scanlan, Joanne
Council on Foundations(276)
Scanlan, Mark
Independent Community Bankers of America(333)
Scanlin, Marge
American Camp Association(60)
Scanlon, Elise
Accrediting Commission for Career Schools and Colleges of Technology(7)
Scanlon, Jennifer
Coordinating Council for Women in History(265)
Scanlon, Jr., Mike
Self Storage Association(608)
Scaramastro, Thomas R.
Chief Petty Officers Association(244)
Scarano, Philip
National Trade Circulation Foundation(547)

Scarborough, Jim
International Nurses Society on Addictions(381)
Scarborough, William
Project Management Institute(590)
Scardelletti, Robert A.
Transportation Communications International Union(664)
Scarratt, Kenneth
American Gem Trade Association(86)
Scawney, Mike
Academy of Osseointegration(5)
Scelso, Doreen
Society of Cosmetic Chemists(634)
Schaefer, Miriam Fisher
Chemical Heritage Foundation(243)
Schafer, Heather
National Volunteer Fire Council(548)
Schafer, Larry
Renewable Fuels Association(599)
Schaffer, Shannon
U.S. Apple Association(667)
Schaitberger, Harold A.
International Association of Fire Fighters(357)
Schamu, Nancy
National Conference of State Historic Preservation Officers(494)
Schapiro, Mary L.
National Association of Securities Dealers(471)
Scharf, CAE, Eric G.
Association of Professional Investment Consultants(209)
Scharfman, Betty
WorldatWork(697)
Schatz, Curt
American Society of Radiologic Technologists(145)
Schauer, David A.
National Council on Radiation Protection and Measurements(502)
Schauer, Rita
Spring Manufacturers Institute(652)
Schaus, Susan
American Academy of Periodontology(27)
Schauseil, CMP, Robin
National Association of Credit Management(448)
Schecter, Suzanne
American Entomological Society(81)
Schedler, Michael F.
National Association for PET Container Resources(435)
Schein, Edward A.
National Association of Solar Contractors(472)
Schell, Gordon
National Association for Campus Activities(432)
Schellinger, Carol
National Registry of Environmental Professionals(535)
Schenke, Roger
American College of Physician Executives(69)
Scheppach, Ph.D., Raymond C.
National Governors Association(514)
Scher, Linda
American Neurological Association(108)
Scherer, Allison
American Academy of Dermatology(21)
Scherf, Christopher N.
Thoroughbred Racing Associations of North America(661)
Schewbly, Brian
American Guernsey Association(87)
Schiappa, Cheryl
Cosmetic, Toiletry and Fragrance Association(267)
Schicker, R.J.E., Rabbi Stanley
National Association of Temple Educators(479)
Schieber, Vicki A.
Council on Employee Benefits(276)
Schiefer, Greg
Society of Environmental Toxicology and Chemistry(635)
Schieren, Ph.D., George A.
National Association of Forensic Economics(453)
Schiering, Dr. David
Coblentz Society(250)
Schiffer, Noelle
Original Equipment Suppliers Association(568)
Schild, David
Foster Family-Based Treatment Association(311)
Schild, Melanie
Fraternity Executives Association(311)
Schiller, Carole
Institute of Packaging Professionals(343)
Schilling, III, Edward L.
Contact Lens Council(264)
Schilling, William C.
Delta Sigma Pi(283)
Schinkel, MBA, CPA, Helen N.
CIIT Centers for Health Research(247)
Schiumo, Frank
Cocoa Merchants' Association of America(250)
Schlegel, Stephen C.
International Association of Food Industry Suppliers(357)
Schleicher, CAE, Renee S.
American Academy of Medical Administrators(24)
American College of Cardiovascular Administrators(64)
American College of Contingency Planners(65)
American College of Healthcare Information Administrators(66)
American College of Managed Care Administrators(67)
Schless, David S.
American Seniors Housing Association(124)
Schleyer, C.M.P., Lynae
National Automatic Merchandising Association(482)
Schlichenmayer, Ed
National Association of College Stores(444)
Schlict, Jim
American Diabetes Association(79)
Schloss, Marcel
Direct Marketing Association(285)
Schlosser, Kara
Council of Chief State School Officers(271)
Schmader, CFEE, Steve Wood
International Festivals and Events Association(371)
Schmahl, David
InSight(339)
Schmale, Lin
Society of American Florists(630)
Schmatz, Kathleen
Automotive Aftermarket Industry Association(223)
Schmelzer, CAE, Peter L.
American College of Osteopathic Family Physicians(69)
Schmermund, Robert F.
America's Community Bankers(19)
Schmid, Ph.D., Charles
Acoustical Society of America(7)
Schmidt, Charlie
National Association of College Stores(444)
Schmidt, David B.
International Food Information Council(372)
Schmidt, Jennifer
American Society for Clinical Pathology(127)
Schmidt, Prof. Klaus M.
Council on Technology Teacher Education(277)
Schmidt, DA, Lois
Clinical and Laboratory Standards Institute(248)
Schmidt, Mary Ann
Association of Earth Science Editors(194)
Schmidt, Pamela J.
Ass'n of Learning Providers(164)
Schmidt, Susan
Alliance of Associations of Teachers of Japanese(16)
Schmidt, Vernon F.
Farm Equipment Manufacturers Association(301)
Schmidt, William
Universities Research Association(679)
Schmitt, Chris
American Society of Newspaper Editors(142)
Schmittling, Gordon
American Academy of Family Physicians(22)
Schmucker, C. David
Business Products Credit Association(235)
Schmucker, Debbie
Business Products Credit Association(235)
Schnabel, David J.
National Association of Episcopal Schools(451)
Schneider, Carol G.
Association of American Colleges and Universities(184)
Schneider, Paula
American Society of Cataract and Refractive Surgery(135)
American Society of Ophthalmic Administrators(143)
Schneider, Richard
Non Commissioned Officers Association of the U.S.A.(553)
Schneider, Sari Jill
International Military Community Executives Association(379)
Schneider, Tina
Associated Builders and Contractors(164)
Schneider, Ward
United Applications Standards Group(670)
Schneider, Zona J.
American Shetland Pony Club/American Miniature Horse Registry(125)
Schneiders, Karl F.
Judge Advocates Association(402)
Schnell, Robert K.
Farm Equipment Manufacturers Association(301)
Schoen, Kurt
National Association of College Stores(444)
Schoenbrun, CAE, FAAO, Lois
American Academy of Optometry(25)
Schoenfelder, Lynn
American Academy of Physician Assistants(27)
Schoenwald, John
AFSM International(11)
Scholnick, Bruce N.
National Wooden Pallet and Container Association(550)
Scholten, Mieka
Self Insurance Institute of America, Inc.(608)

Schomer, P.D.
Institute of Noise Control Engineering(343)
Schonauer, Janis
Ombudsman Association, The(564)
Schoneboom, Kathy
International Association of Administrative Professionals(352)
Schoolcraft, Steven
Board of Certified Safety Professionals(231)
Schoor, Larry
National Forensic Association(512)
Schoppmann, Kenneth
Licensing Executives Society(407)
Schorle, Tracy
National Association of Independent Fee Appraisers(457)
Schorr, Brian
United States Advanced Ceramics Association(672)
Schott, Tina M.
Contact Lens Society of America(264)
Schrader, Art
Society of Exploration Geophysicists(636)
Schrader, CAE, Josephine N.
Association of Professional Chaplains(208)
Schrag, Brian
Association for Practical and Professional Ethics(177)
Schramm, CAE, Brian
Society of Critical Care Medicine(634)
Schrank, Mandy Bingaman
Education Law Association(289)
Schrecengost, Ruby
National Hereford Hog Record Association(517)
Schreiber, Ph.D., Ronee
Women's Caucus for Political Science(693)
Schreibman, CAE, Ron
National Association of Wholesaler-Distributors(481)
Schremmer, Dorinda
Women's Basketball Coaches Association(693)
Schreyer, Fred
Professional Bowlers Association of America(586)
Schroder, Bernie
IDEA, The Health and Fitness Association(330)
Schroeder, Kellie
Wood Moulding and Millwork Producers Association(694)
Schroeder, Lori
Commission on Accreditation of Allied Health Education Programs(254)
Schroeder, Patricia
Association of American Publishers(185)
Schroer, Mary S.
Associated Builders and Contractors(164)
Schroeter, Joe
American Shetland Pony Club/American Miniature Horse Registry(125)
Schronk, Wendell E.
Beefmaster Breeders United(227)
Schropp, Mary Ann
Society for Academic Emergency Medicine(613)
Schryver, Dave
American Public Gas Association(119)
Schubert, Lynn M.
Surety Association of America(656)
Schuchart, Cathy
School Nutrition Association(606)
Schueneman, Martha
Editorial Freelancers Association(289)
Schuldenfrei, Stephen A.
Trade Show Exhibitors Association(663)
Schuldt, Cheryl M.
United States Targhee Sheep Association(677)
Schull, Ann
International Society of Air Safety Investigators(389)
Schulte, Cindy
National Mail Order Association(525)
Schulte, John
National Mail Order Association(525)
Schulte, John
National Air Duct Cleaners Association(428)
Schulte, DBA, FACHE, Margaret F.
Healthcare Information and Management Systems Society(324)
Schulte, Rainer
American Literary Translators Association(101)
Schulte, CAE, Terrence
Uniformed Services Academy of Family Physicians(669)
Schultz, CAPT Art
Naval Reserve Association(551)
Schultz, Betty
ASTM International(221)
Schultz, Eric
American Correctional Association(74)
Schultz, James
American Iron and Steel Institute(98)
Schultz, Michele
Society for In Vitro Biology(619)
Schultz, Dr. V.A.
American Society of Veterinary Ophthalmology(147)
Schulz, Monika
Association for Healthcare Philanthropy(173)
Schulz, T. J.
Airport Consultants Council(14)
Schulze, James
Council of Supply Chain Management Professionals(275)
Schumacher, J. Donald
National Hospice and Palliative Care Organization(517)
Schuman, Ph.D., Nancy
Phi Beta(575)
Schuping, CAE, James A.
Workgroup for Electronic Data Interchange(695)
Schur, Larry
National Independent Nursery Furniture Retailers Association(519)
Schust, Diane
National Education Association(506)
Schust, Sunny Mays
American Association of State Highway and Transportation Officials(51)
Schuster, Neil D.
Intelligent Transportation Society of America(345)
Schute, Diane
Chemical Producers and Distributors Association(243)
Schutz, Carol A.
Gerontological Society of America(316)
Schwab, Paul M.
Association of Organ Procurement Organizations(206)
Schwab, William M.
Construction Financial Management Association(262)
Schwartz, Alec M.
American Prepaid Legal Services Institute(117)
Schwartz, Jeanne
Society of School Librarians International(644)
Schwartz, Kathleen A.
American Rental Association(122)
Schwartz, Laura
Renaissance Society of America(599)
Schwartz, Louis O.
American Sportscasters Association(148)
Schwartz, Maureen M.
BKR International(229)
Schwartz, Michael
American Society of Podiatry Executives(145)
Schwartz, Rick
IDEA, The Health and Fitness Association(330)
Schwartz, Rita C.
National Association of Catholic School Teachers(442)
Schwartz, RN, Sandra
Society of Otorhinolaryngology and Head/Neck Nurses(641)
Schwartz, Sharon
Society for Mining, Metallurgy, and Exploration(622)
Schwartz, Shirley
Council of the Great City Schools(275)
Schwartz, CEM, Susan L.
Exhibition Services and Contractors Association(299)
Schwartz, Thomas K.
American Society of Sugar Beet Technologists(146)
Beet Sugar Development Foundation(227)
Schwartz, Tina
American Amusement Machine Association(31)
Schwechter, Melvin S.
Customs and International Trade Bar Association(280)
Schweigardt, Andrew
Thoroughbred Owners and Breeders Association(661)
Schweitzer, John
American Composites Manufacturers Association(72)
Schweitzer, Lisa T.
National Telecommunications Cooperative Association(546)
Schwimmer, Jules
Sponge and Chamois Institute(651)
Sciamanna, John
Child Welfare League of America(244)
Sciana, Rev. Bernard
Augustinian Educational Association(222)
Scibelli, Gabriele
Federal Bureau of Investigation Agents Association(302)
Sciotto, Nancy J.
National Electrical Manufacturers Representatives Association(506)
Sciuto, Bernie
American Academy of Home Care Physicians(23)
Sclove, Ph.D., Stanley L.
Classification Society of North America(247)
Scofield, Julie M.
National Alliance of State and Territorial AIDS Directors(430)
Scollo, Janet
International Association for Near Death Studies(351)
Scorca, Marc A.
OPERA America(565)
Scott, Alexander R.
Minerals, Metals and Materials Society, The(420)

Scott, Alicia
Clinical Ligand Assay Society(248)
Scott, Brigette Settles
National Association of Public Hospitals and Health Systems(467)
Scott, Devon
North American Meat Processors Association(558)
Scott, Donald A.
Associated General Contractors of America(165)
Scott, Edward M.
United States Parachute Association(676)
Scott, Hugh
SWANA - Solid Waste Association of North America(656)
Scott, Jan
Women's Regional Publications of America(694)
Scott, John H.
College of American Pathologists(251)
Scott, John A.
American Academy of Medical Hypnoanalysts(24)
Scott, Kelly
Transportation Intermediaries Association(664)
Scott, Kimberly
Periodical Publications Association(573)
Scott, Larry
WTA Tour(697)
Scott, Leslie
National Association of State Personnel Executives(476)
Scott, Lisa
Periodical and Book Association of America(573)
Scott, Lorraine A.
Phi Gamma Nu(576)
Scott, Malvise A.
National Association of Community Health Centers(445)
Scott, Pat
Association of College and University Telecommunications Administrators(191)
Scott, Phillip
National Council for Prescription Drug Programs(497)
Scott, Reginald
Federal and Armed Forces Librarians Roundtable(301)
Scott, Sally R.
Society for Ear, Nose and Throat Advances in Children(616)
Scott, Sherry L.
National Juvenile Detention Association(523)
Scott, Theresa L.
SEPM - Society for Sedimentary Geology(609)
Scott, Thomas A.
Association of Christian Schools International(190)
Scott, William E.
Society for Marketing Professional Services(621)
Scott-Pinkney, Pamela
American Historical Association(91)
Scotti, Marie J.
International Advertising Association(348)
Scribner, Jean
Assembly of Episcopal Healthcare Chaplains(164)
Scully, Jr., Jay
American Psychiatric Association(117)
Scully, John
Automotive Service Association(224)
Seabaugh, Steve
National Wood Flooring Association(550)
Seabrook, Tracy
National Association of County Recorders, Election Officials and Clerks(447)
Seaburn, Cathryn
American Institute of Hydrology(96)
Seale, Charly
Exotic Wildlife Association(299)
Searcy, Tim
American Teleservices Association(151)
Searry, PhD, Margaret
Society of Ethnobiology(635)
Sears, Mary
American Association of Diabetes Educators(42)
Seay, Jared A.
Association for Applied Interactive Multimedia(167)
Seay, Sharon L.
National Funeral Directors and Morticians Association(513)
Sederholm, Pamela
American Automotive Leasing Association(55)
Sedlack, Richard I.
Soap and Detergent Association(612)
See, Jeff
Organic Crop Improvement Association International(566)
See, Ruth
Society of State Directors of Health, Physical Education and Recreation(644)
Seeden, Tim
Association for Preservation Technology International(177)
Seeger, Arline
National Lime Association(525)
Seeger, Kristin
American Forest and Paper Association(85)
Seegers, Gina
Academy of Osseointegration(5)
Seelinger, Helena
NACE International(424)
Seffrin, Ph.D., John R.
American Cancer Society(60)
Segal, Susan
Council of the Americas(275)
Seibert, September
Insurance Marketing Communications Association(345)
Seidl, Lawrence
National Association of Catholic Chaplains(442)
Seidman, Karen R.
Young Entrepreneurs Organization(698)
Seiffert, Grant
Telecommunications Industry Association(659)
Seiler, Karen
College of Diplomates of the American Board of Orthodontics(251)
Seim, M.D., M.P.H., FASBP, Harold C.
American Society of Bariatric Physicians(134)
Seitter, Keith L.
American Meteorological Society(105)
Selan, Janisse
American Orthopaedic Society for Sports Medicine(111)
Selby, Dedra
Automotive Aftermarket Industry Association(223)
Selig, Bud
Major League Baseball - Office of the Commissioner(410)
Selig, Eliza
Hospitality Financial and Technology Professionals(328)
Sells, Bill
SGMA(651)
Sells, William H.
Environmental Industry Associations(296)
Seltz, Judy
Association for Supervision and Curriculum Development(178)
Selverling, Joseph
Reinsurance Association of America(598)
Sem, O.D., Steven R.
Armed Forces Optometric Society(161)
Semer, CAE, Jeri A.
Association of College and University Telecommunications Administrators(191)
Semones, Michelle
National Beer Wholesalers Association(484)
Senes, Meridyth M.
American Association for Paralegal Education(36)
Custom Tailors and Designers Association of America(280)
Real Estate Educators Association(595)
Seng, Philip M.
United States Meat Export Federation(676)
Senior, M.D., Brent
American Rhinologic Society(123)
Senior, Charles
American College of Physicians(69)
Senior, Jane
American College of Sports Medicine(70)
Senter, David L.
American Corn Growers Association(74)
Senzee, Katherine
Public Housing Authorities Directors Association(592)
Sepin, Lawrence
American Dental Assistants Association(78)
Serels, Ph.D., M. Mitchell
American Society of Sephardic Studies(146)
Serena, Thomas J.
American Gastroenterological Association(86)
Serfass, Jeff
United States Advanced Ceramics Association(672)
Sergel, Richard P.
North American Electric Reliability Council(556)
Serota, Scott P.
Blue Cross and Blue Shield Association(231)
Settlemire, Mary Ann
American Association of Community Colleges(41)
Setuff, Denise
American Association for Dental Research(34)
Sever, Jorge
International Society of Appraisers(390)
Sevush, Ralph
Dramatists Guild of America(287)
Seward, Skip
American Meat Institute(103)
Seward, William
American Society of Plastic Surgeons(144)
Sexton, Dawn
Association of Family Medicine Administration(196)
Sexton, CAE, Deborah
Professional Convention Management Association(587)
Sexton, III, Thomas W.
National Futures Association(513)

Seyler, Ruth
National Technical Services Association(546)

Seymour, Christopher R.
National Lipid Association(525)

Seymour, Dianne
International Sport Show Producers Association(393)

Sfikas, Peter M.
American Dental Association(78)

Sforza, Wayne V.
American Association of State Colleges and Universities(51)

Sgrignoli, David
American College of Physicians(69)

Sgueo, James M.
National Alcohol Beverage Control Association(429)

Shaddix, Pat
American Association of Retirement Communities(50)

Shadrick, Dorothy
National Academy of Neuropsychology(426)

Shaevel, Evelyn
Medical Library Association(416)

Shaffer, Joan
American College of Angiology(64)

Shaffer, Mark A.
National Antique and Art Dealers Association of America(430)

Shaffer, Patricia
Institute for Operations Research and the Management Sciences(339)

Shafranski-Campobello, Nancy
Printing Industries of America(584)

Shagoury, Antoine
American Stock Exchange(149)

Shaham, Lauren
National Adult Day Services Association(427)

Shaikh, Ph.D., Rashid
New York Academy of Sciences(552)

Shakntana, Hend
American Public Works Association(120)

Shalby, Chris
International Institute of Municipal Clerks(376)

Shambarger, Peter
Association for Recorded Sound Collections(177)

Shamdosky, Gerry
National Association for the Specialty Food Trade(436)

Shanahan, Betty
Society of Women Engineers(646)

Shanahan, CAE, Thomas
National Roofing Contractors Association(537)

Shandley, Carey
ACA International, The Association of Credit and Collection Professionals(2)

Shane, Francis J.
National Limousine Association(525)

Shane, Larry I.
Federation of Podiatric Medical Boards(304)

Shaner, CAE, Thomas C.
Professional Grounds Management Society(587)

Shaner, Thomas C.
American Institute of Floral Designers(96)

Shank, Fred
Institute of Food Technologists(341)

Shankel, Gerald M.
Fabricators and Manufacturers Association, International(300)
Tube and Pipe Association, International(666)

Shanklin, Patty C.
American Angora Goat Breeder's Association(31)

Shanley, Claire
American Society of Access Professionals(133)
International Biometric Society(362)

Shanley, Peter J.
Small Business Council of America(611)

Shannon, James M.
National Fire Protection Association(510)

Shannon, Kevin
Association for Commuter Transportation(169)

Shapiro, Gary
Consumer Electronics Association(263)

Shapiro, Nancy
National Academy of Recording Arts and Sciences(427)

Sharafinski, Todd
Engine Manufacturers Association(295)

Sharak, Robert L.
Cruise Lines International Association(280)

Sharbaugh, Eric
United States Trotting Association(678)

Shareef, Omar S.
African American Contractors Association(11)

Shark, Nancy
International Sleep Products Association(386)

Sharma, Dan
American Composites Manufacturers Association(72)

Sharman, Craig
National Volunteer Fire Council(548)

Sharman, Paul
Institute of Management Accountants(342)

Sharoff, Brian
Private Label Manufacturers Association(584)

Sharp, Debra
Research Society on Alcoholism(600)

Sharp, Jack
International Association of Hydrogeologists(358)

Sharp, DC, DACRB, Jan
Chiropractic Council on Physiological Therapeutics and Rehabilitation(245)

Sharp, Norman F.
Cigar Association of America(247)
Pipe Tobacco Council(578)

Sharpe, Patrick
National Association of Sports Officials(472)

Shaub, Beth
American Podiatric Medical Association(116)

Shaud, John
Air Force Association(13)

Shaumyan, Galina
American Association for the Advancement of Slavic Studies(36)

Shaunnessey, Robert L.
Warehousing Education and Research Council(685)

Shavalay, Peter
American College of Radiology(70)

Shaw, Al
International Association of Round Dance Teachers(361)

Shaw, AAP, Deborah
NACHA - The Electronic Payments Association(424)

Shaw, Diane
Clinical Ligand Assay Society(248)

Shaw, H.V. "Skip"
National Frozen and Refrigerated Foods Association(513)

Shaw, Marie
American Association of Diabetes Educators(42)

Shaw, Susanne
Accrediting Council on Education in Journalism and Mass Communications(7)

Shawnee, Barbara
Travel and Tourism Research Association(665)

Shay, Matt
International Franchise Association(373)

Shay, Robert
National Council of Art Administrators(498)

Shay, Russell
Land Trust Alliance(405)

Shaye, Marc K.
Spill Control Association of America(651)

Shayka, David
National Council of Teachers of Mathematics(501)

Shea, Diane
National Association of State Energy Officials(475)

Shea, CAE, Donald B.
Rubber Manufacturers Association(603)

Shea, Helene
Organic Reactions Catalysis Society(566)

Shea, Ph.D., Timothy J.
American Academy of Environmental Engineers(22)

Sheanin, Steve
Wedding and Portrait Photographers International(686)

Sheehan, Denise
National Glass Association(513)

Sheer, Vickie
Dance Educators of America(281)

Sheets, Susan L.
National Aircraft Resale Association(428)

Sheets, Trina Hembree
National Emergency Management Association(507)

Shefchik, Joe
International Silo Association(386)

Sheffield, Constance M.
Intermodal Association of North America(347)

Sheffield, Victoria M.
Society of Eye Surgeons(636)

Sheketoff, Emily
American Library Association(101)

Shelby, Richard D.
American Gas Association(86)

Sheldon, Jeanna
Hosiery Association, The(328)

Sheldon, Jim
National Soccer Coaches Association of America(540)

Sheldrick, Ph.D., Reg
American Guild of Hypnotherapists(88)

Shelk, John E.
Electric Power Supply Association(290)

Shell, Johnny
Specialty Graphic Imaging Association(650)

Shelley, Barry J.
American Radio Relay League(121)

Shelton, M.D., Clough
American Otological Society(112)

Shelton, Ed.D, Jody
American Association of School Personnel Administrators(51)

Shepard, Dr. R.S.
Holistic Dental Association(327)

Shephard, Steve
Society of American Military Engineers(631)

Shephard, Susan
Society of General Physiologists(637)
Shepherd, Donna M.
American Federation of Police and Concerned Citizens(82)
National Association of Chiefs of Police(443)
Sheppard, Craig
Association of Industrial Metallizers, Coaters and Laminators(201)
Converting Equipment Manufacturers Association(265)
Sheppard, Jeffrey
National Association of Student Financial Aid Administrators(477)
Sheppard, Mike
American Urological Association(153)
Sheramy, Ph.D., Rona
Association for Jewish Studies(175)
Sherer, Scott P.
NaSPA: the Network and System Professionals Association(425)
Sheridan, Cynthia
Plumbing-Heating-Cooling Contractors - National Association(579)
Sheridan, Judith
Association for Living History, Farm and Agricultural Museums(176)
Sheridan, Rosemary
American Public Transportation Association(120)
Sheridan, Thomas
Gas Technology Institute(314)
Sherman, Amy
Council for Adult and Experiential Learning(267)
Sherman, Ph.D., Brian S.
Association for Humanist Sociology(174)
Sherman, Cary
Recording Industry Association of America(596)
Sherman, Gail
PDA - an International Association for Pharmaceutical Science and Technology(572)
Sherman, CPCU, ARM, Jill
Society of Risk Management Consultants(643)
Sherman, Jocelyn
United Farm Workers of America(671)
Sherman, Kathy
Coin Laundry Association(250)
Sherrill, Joy
Society for the Scientific Study of Religion(627)
Sherry, Karen
American Society of Composers, Authors and Publishers(136)
Sherwood, CAE, Roger A.
Society of Teachers of Family Medicine(644)
Sherwood, Scott
Real Estate Round Table(596)
Sheward, APR, Michael
National Association of Government Communicators(454)
Shiarappa, Kathy
Food Industry Association Executives(309)
Shick, Maureen
American College of Psychiatrists(70)
Shields, Deborah
National Emergency Number Association(507)
Shields, Jeff
National Association of College and University Business Officers(444)
Shields, Wayne C.
Association of Reproductive Health Professionals(212)
Shields, William
American College of Radiology(70)
Shiffert, CAE, John A.
National Association of Diaper Services(449)
Shih, Peter W.
American Advertising Federation(29)
Shils, Ph.D., Edward B.
Dental Dealers of America(283)
Shimpi, Arun
National Industries for the Blind(519)
Shinn, Michele
Association for Continuing Higher Education(171)
Shipe, Ginny
Council of Real Estate Brokerage Managers(274)
Shipp, Daniel K.
International Safety Equipment Association(385)
Shipp, Michael K.
ADED - the Association for Driver Rehabilitation Specialists(8)
Shipp, W. Jeffrey
Farm Credit Council(301)
Shirley, Bryan
Manufacturers' Agents National Association(411)
Shirley, Teresa M.
National Association of Elevator Contractors(450)
Shiroma, CAE, John K.S.
United States Junior Chamber of Commerce(676)
Shirras, Peter
Independent Sector(336)
Shively, Robert A.
National Auctioneers Association(482)
Shivers, Chris
American Brahman Breeders Association(59)
Shoaf, Jeff
Associated General Contractors of America(165)
Shockley, Floyd
Coleopterists Society(250)
Sholar, Ph.D., J. Ronald
American Peanut Research and Education Society(113)
Sholars, Kent
Contract Services Association of America(264)
Sholl, Shelly
National Association of Air Medical Communication Specialists(438)
Shomers, Suzanne
Door and Hardware Institute(287)
Shomett, Louis E.
American Psychological Society(119)
Shonerd, Rene
National Apartment Association(430)
Shook, Ray
American Welding Society(154)
Resistance Welder Manufacturers' Association(600)
Shor, Nancy G.
National Organization of Social Security Claimants' Representatives(530)
Shore, Katherine Harrison
International Council of Cruise Lines(367)
Short, Marsha
Gas Machinery Research Council(314)
Short, Thomas
International Alliance of Theatrical Stage Employees and Moving Picture Technicians of the U.S., Its Territories and Canada(348)
Shott, Christine
American Mathematical Association of Two Year Colleges(103)
Shoup, William L.
SSPC: the Society for Protective Coatings(652)
Shriver, Ann L.
International Institute of Fisheries Economics and Trade(376)
Shrout, Dr. Michael K.
American Academy of Oral and Maxillofacial Radiology(25)
Shrum, Wesley
Society for Social Studies of Science(625)
Shuck, J. Vincent
American Academy of Implant Dentistry(23)
Shulke, David
American Health Quality Association(89)
Shulman, Carole K.
Professional Skaters Association(589)
Shulman, Joni
American Association of Neurological Surgeons(46)
Shulman, Stephanie
American Horticultural Therapy Association(92)
Shuman, Alan
National Association of State Fire Marshals(475)
Shumate, John P.
American Foreign Service Protective Association(85)
Shumau, Elizabeth
United States-Austrian Chamber of Commerce(678)
Shupe, CAE, Christine Quinn
Veterinary Hospital Managers Association(682)
Shuter, Dale
Electrical Apparatus Service Association(290)
Shutley, Michael
National Restaurant Association(536)
Sibert, Steve
Grocery Manufacturers Association(320)
Sidiropoulos, Anthony
Independent Community Bankers of America(333)
Siebenthaler, Alan
National Precast Concrete Association(534)
Sieber, Heather
National Investor Relations Institute(522)
Siegal, Nancy L.
National Association of Service and Conservation Corps(471)
Siegel, Don
Technology Transfer Society(658)
Siegel, Elisa K.
Association of American Medical Colleges(184)
Siegel, Gail A.
National Association of Resale & Thrift Shops(469)
Siegel, Richard A.
Council of Archives and Research Libraries in Jewish Studies(270)
Siegfried, John
American Economic Association(80)
Siegfried, Roger
Society of Invasive Cardiovascular Professionals(639)
Sieli, Shiel V.
American Institute of Timber Construction(98)
Siemietkowski, Susan
American Frozen Food Institute(85)
Sigler, Ph.D., Andrea
Connected International Meeting Professionals Association(261)

Sigmon, CAE, Joyce
American Academy of Implant Dentistry(23)
Sikes, Britt
Copier Dealers Association(266)
Sikkila, Dorothy A.
National Association of Collegiate Directors of Athletics(444)
Sikora, Lisa
Mine Safety Institute of America(419)
Silas, Pamala
American Indian Science and Engineering Society(93)
Silbermann, CAE, Bryan E.
Produce Marketing Association(584)
Silcox, Clark R.
National Electrical Manufacturers Association(506)
Silins, Andy
United Brotherhood of Carpenters and Joiners of America(670)
Silliman, Matthew
North American Society for Social Philosophy(561)
Silva, Fred G.
United States and Canadian Academy of Pathology(672)
Silva, Mike
Jewelers Shipping Association(401)
Silver, Howard J.
Consortium of Social Science Associations(262)
Silver, Martha
Organization for the Promotion and Advancement of Small Telecommunications Companies(567)
Silver, Mary
Hydraulic Institute(329)
Silver, Pamela
Academic Language Therapy Association(2)
Silvergleit, Ira T.
Society of American Florists(630)
Silverio, Craig
Packaging Machinery Manufacturers Institute(570)
Silverman, CAE, SPHR, Dale K.
Association of Woodworking-Furnishings Suppliers(221)
Silverman, Hope
Professional Apparel Association(585)
Silverman, Prof. Hugh J.
International Association for Philosophy and Literature(351)
Silverman, Mark
Golf Range Association of America(318)
Silverman, Nancy
Association of Children's Museums(189)
Silvers, Faith
National Consumers League(495)
Simek, James A.
Professional Currency Dealers Association(587)
Simering, Jeff
Council of the Great City Schools(275)
Siminovsky, Gail
Academy of Laser Dentistry(3)
Simmon, Christine
Generic Pharmaceutical Association(315)
Simmonds, Dr. Warren L.
American Society of Podiatric Medicine(145)
Simmons, Barbara
American Association of Neuroscience Nurses(46)
Simmons, Cathy
American Cash Flow Association(61)
Simmons, Cindy
American Society of Heating, Refrigerating and Air-Conditioning Engineers(139)
Simmons, MPA, Diane
American Association of Neuroscience Nurses(46)
National Association for Healthcare Quality(433)
National Association of Neonatal Nurses(462)
Simmons, Katie
International Society for Magnetic Resonance in Medicine(387)
Simmons, Mike
Log Home Builders Association of North America(409)
Simms, Cheryl
African-American Natural Foods Association(11)
Simon, Jim
American Sugar Cane League of the U.S.A.(150)
Simon, Lisa
International Coach Federation(365)
Simon, William
International Academy of Behavioral Medicine, Counseling and Psychotherapy(347)
Simoneau, Bob
National Association of State Workforce Agencies(477)
Simoneaux, Mimi
Pharmaceutical Research and Manufacturers of America(575)
Simpson, Alan
National Association for the Education of Young Children(436)
Simpson, Cindy
American Moving and Storage Association(107)
Simpson, Freddie N.
Brotherhood of Maintenance of Way Employees(233)
Simpson, Janice
Association of Moving Image Archivists(205)
Simpson, Jennifer
International Titanium Association(394)
Simpson, Judy
American Music Therapy Association(107)
Simpson, Lisa
American Staffing Association(149)
Simpson, Michael
National Council for the Social Studies(497)
Simpson, Rita
Women's International Network of Utility Professionals(693)
Simpson, Sheila
Hosiery Association, The(328)
Simpson, Thomas D.
Railway Supply Institute(595)
Simrany, Joseph P.
Tea Association of the United States of America(658)
Tea Council of the U.S.A.(658)
Sims, Brenda
Association of Teachers of Technical Writing(217)
Sims, Helena
NACHA - The Electronic Payments Association(424)
Sinclair, Laura
National Institute on Park and Grounds Management(521)
Sinclair, Stefan
Association for Computers and the Humanities(170)
Sinclair, Steve
National Institute on Park and Grounds Management(521)
Sinesou, Megan
American Society of Naval Engineers(142)
Sing, Michael J.
Amalgamated Transit Union(18)
Singer, MHA, Dale
Renal Physicians Association(599)
Singer, Dana
Society of North American Goldsmiths(641)
Singer, Janet
Environmental Design Research Association(296)
Singer, Richard
National Golf Foundation(514)
Singer, Dr. Robert H.
Harvey Society(322)
Singer, Terry E.
National Association of Energy Service Companies(451)
Singerling, CCM,CEC, James B.
Club Managers Association of America(249)
Singh, Conchita
Fresh Produce Association of the Americas(312)
Singhal, Ram
Flexible Packaging Association(307)
Singleton, John
International Organization of Masters, Mates and Pilots(382)
Sink, Vaughn
Advertising and Marketing International Network(9)
Siok, William J.
American Institute of Professional Geologists(97)
Sipes, Brent S.
Society of Nematologists(640)
Sipes, Marsha
International Association of Arson Investigators(353)
Sirex, Debbie
American Association of Meat Processors(45)
Sirgy, M. Joseph
International Society for Quality-of-Life Studies(388)
Sirvello, III, Tony
International Association of Clerks, Recorders, Election Officials and Treasurers(354)
Sirvet, Ene
Society of American Historians(630)
Sisco, August L.
National Association of Architectural Metal Manufacturers(438)
Pressure Vessel Manufacturers Association(583)
Siske, Blaine
Energy Telecommunications and Electrical Association(294)
Sitler, Penny
The Knitting Guild Association(404)
Sizemore, Ray
College and University Professional Association for Human Resources(250)
Sjoberg, Judith
American Society for Mass Spectrometry(130)
Sjolander, Ray
International Association for the Leisure and Entertainment Industry(351)
Skarich, Maggie
American Association of Children's Residential Centers(39)
Skarstedt, Jennifer
National Costumers Association(496)

Skelton, Robert
American Society of Association Executives & Center for Association Leadership(134)

Skiados, Don P.
Air Line Pilots Association, International(13)

Skiba, Tom
Community Associations Institute(255)

Skiera, Jim
International Society of Arboriculture(390)

Skinner, Ph.D., John H.
SWANA - Solid Waste Association of North America(656)

Skinner, Ronald A.
Association of School Business Officials International(212)

Skippon, Richard
Tax Executives Institute(657)

Skjothaug, Jolene K.
Timber Products Manufacturers(661)

Sklarow, Mark H.
Independent Educational Consultants Association(334)

Skomal, Susan
American Anthropological Association(31)

Slack, Glenn N.
National Institute for Animal Agriculture(520)

Slagle, CAE, G. Stephen
Promotional Products Association International(591)

Slakie, Marcia
Door and Hardware Institute(287)

Slate, II, William K.
American Arbitration Association(32)

Slater, John
Sleep Research Society(611)

Slater, Joseph
Association of American Plant Food Control Officials(185)

Slater, LeAnne
TechLaw Group(658)

Slatkin, Ph.D., David J.
American Society of Pharmacognosy(144)

Slaughter, Bob
National Petrochemical & Refiners Association(532)

Slawny, James R.
American College of Allergy, Asthma and Immunology(64)
American Society of Colon and Rectal Surgeons(136)

Slawny, Rick
American Association of Certified Allergists(39)
Society of Surgical Oncology(644)

Sleeper, Steve
Professional Beauty Association(586)
Salon Association, The(605)

Sleigh, Stephen R.
International Association of Machinists and Aerospace Workers(359)

Slesinger, Phyllis K.
Mortgage Bankers Association(421)

Slesinger, Scott L.
Environmental Technology Council(297)

Sliwa, James
American Society for Microbiology(130)

Sloan, Katrina Smith
American Association of Homes and Services for the Aging(43)

Sloan, Lawrence D.
Adhesive and Sealant Council(8)

Sloan, Richard S.
International Association of Machinists and Aerospace Workers(359)

Sloane, Heywood
Bank Insurance and Securities Association(226)

Slocum, Joshua
Funeral Consumers Alliance(312)

Slocumb, Dennis J.
International Union of Police Associations, AFL-CIO(396)

Slusher, Harold E.
Society of Army Physician Assistants(632)

Slutsky, Bernice
American Seed Trade Association(124)

Small, Barbara
Future Business Leaders of America-Phi Beta Lambda(313)

Small, Glenda
National Insurance Association(521)

Small, Katherine
National Association of Temple Administrators(479)

Small, Sylvia
U.S. Poultry and Egg Association(668)

Smallbrook, Linda
American Philosophical Association(114)

Smarr, Lawrence E.
Physician Insurers Association of America(577)

Smart, Amy
Country Music Association(277)

Smeallie, Peter
American Rock Mechanics Association(123)

Smiley-Oyen, Ann L.
North American Society for the Psychology of Sport and Physical Activity(561)

Smith, GBA, Barbara
American Thoracic Society(151)

Smith, CAE, Barbara R.
American Thyroid Association(151)

Smith, Ph.D., Becky J.
American Association for Health Education(35)

Smith, Bergitta
American Society of Plastic Surgeons(144)

Smith, Bruce W.
Book Manufacturers' Institute(231)

Smith, Carl
North American Technician Excellence(562)

Smith, Carol E.
American Association of Colleges for Teacher Education(40)

Smith, Carolyn
Society of Certified Insurance Counselors(632)

Smith, Catherine K.
Delta Theta Phi(283)

Smith, Cynthia
American College of Osteopathic Surgeons(69)

Smith, Cynthia
Finnsheep Breeders Association(307)

Smith, Darrell
International Window Film Association(397)

Smith, Captain David R.
Council of American Master Mariners(270)

Smith, David R.
Interlocking Concrete Pavement Institute(347)

Smith, David W.
Society of Corporate Secretaries and Governance Professionals(634)

Smith, Debbie
Textile Rental Services Association of America(660)

Smith, Diann
Council On State Taxation(277)

Smith, Doug
International Foodservice Manufacturers Association(372)

Smith, Ed
Conference of State Bank Supervisors(260)

Smith, Eileen
ASIS International(163)

Smith, Emily
Society of Publication Designers(643)

Smith, Eric H.
International Intellectual Property Alliance(377)

Smith, Eva Jean
Women's Professional Rodeo Association(694)

Smith, Frances
American Association of Physics Teachers(48)

Smith, DDS, Gregory E.
Academy of Operative Dentistry(4)

Smith, J. Thomas
National Kerosene Heater Association(523)

Smith, Jason
Hospitality Sales and Marketing Association International(329)

Smith, Jim
International Lactation Consultant Association(377)

Smith, Jodi L.
National Association of College and University Food Services(444)

Smith, Joyce E.
National Association for College Admission Counseling(432)

Smith, Kathryn J.
American Association of Neuromuscular & Electrodiagnostic Medicine(46)

Smith, Kevin
Academy of Osseointegration(5)

Smith, Kim
International Academy of Oral Medicine and Toxicology(348)

Smith, Kristen
Academy of Dentistry for Persons with Disabilities(3)
American Association of Hospital Dentists(44)
American Society for Geriatric Dentistry(129)
National Society of Genetic Counselors(541)
Special Care Dentistry Association(648)

Smith, Liesl
SWANA - Solid Waste Association of North America(656)

Smith, Linda
National Association of Child Care Resource and Referral Agencies(443)

Smith, Dr. Lora
Herpetologists' League(325)

Smith, Luke E.
National Academy of Television Arts and Sciences(427)

Smith, Lynn
National Family Business Council(508)

Smith, Lynn
Association of Fundraising Professionals(198)

Smith, Marci
American Society of Brewing Chemists(135)

Smith, Ph.D., Marilyn Dix
International Society for Pharmacoeconomics and Outcomes Research(388)

Smith, Michelle
Mutual Fund Education Alliance(423)

Smith, Neal
American Jersey Cattle Association(99)

Smith, Ollie
National Association of Child Care Resource and Referral Agencies(443)

Smith, Pamela A.
American Osteopathic College of Radiology(112)

Smith, Patsy
American Society of Professional Estimators(145)

Smith, Paula S.
Society of Experimental Test Pilots(635)

Smith, Peg L.
American Camp Association(60)

Smith, Philip
American Association for Laboratory Accreditation(35)

Smith, Ph.D., Robert L.
International Association of Marriage and Family Counselors(359)

Smith, Ronald
American Dietetic Association(79)

Smith, Ronald A.
North American Society for Sport History(561)

Smith, CPA, Sam
National Contract Management Association(495)

Smith, Sandra L.
National Association of College and University Food Services(444)

Smith, Shonda
United States Parachute Association(676)

Smith, Stanley L.
Glass Association of North America(317)
Glazing Industry Code Committee(317)
National Sunroom Association(545)

Smith, Stephan
Association on Higher Education and Disability(221)

Smith, Stephanie
Security Industry Association(607)

Smith, MS, CAE, Steve
American Academy of Physical Medicine and Rehabilitation(27)

Smith, Steven M.
Association of Residents in Radiation Oncology(212)

Smith, Susan Snyder
National Confectioners Association of the United States(492)

Smith, Sylvia
Society for the Advancement of Material and Process Engineering(626)

Smith, Jr., Taylor
Association of Christian Schools International(190)

Smith, CAE, Ted M.
ACA International, The Association of Credit and Collection Professionals(2)

Smith, Theresa E.
National Consumers League(495)

Smith, Thomas W.
North American Retail Hardware Association(559)

Smith, Valerie
American College of Osteopathic Obstetricians and Gynecologists(69)

Smith, Wayne
National Association of Sporting Goods Wholesalers(472)

Smith, Ph.D., William B.
American Statistical Association(149)

Smith, Jr, William C.
Industrial Foundation of America(337)

Smith, William S.
Association of Universities for Research in Astronomy(219)

Smith-Ingley, Gwyn
American Jail Association(99)

Smith-Wright, Terry
Association of University Interior Designers(219)

Smitherman, Dr. Ken
Association of Christian Schools International(190)

Smitley, Myra
Society of Glass and Ceramic Decorators(637)

Smitter, Roger
National Communication Association(491)

Smolinski, Katherine
Association of Oncology Social Work(206)

Smoot, Cassandra
National Conference on Public Employee Retirement Systems(495)

Smrz, Perry
International Association of Physicians in AIDS Care(360)

Smurthwaite, Lex
American Paint Horse Association(112)

Smythe, Nancy
American Cleft Palate-Craniofacial Association(63)

Smythe, William K.
NPES, The Association for Suppliers of Printing, Publishing and Converting Technologies(563)

Snead, Rebecca P.
National Council of State Pharmacy Association Executives(501)

Snell, Roy
Health Care Compliance Association(322)

Snethen, Tara
American Society for Investigative Pathology(130)

Snider, Jill
International Bluegrass Music Association(362)

Snipes, Jason
Council of the Great City Schools(275)

Snodgress, Faye
Kappa Delta Pi(403)

Snorton, Dr. Teresa
Association for Clinical Pastoral Education(169)

Snow, Michael S.
American Hardwood Export Council(89)

Snowden, K. Dane
CTIA - The Wireless Association(280)

Snyder, Andrea
Dance/USA(281)

Snyder, Anthony
American Society of Home Inspectors(139)

Snyder, PE, CEng, Joel
American Institute of Engineers(95)

Snyder, Karol B.
National Association of State Directors of Developmental Disability Services(474)

Snyder, Rev. Larry
Catholic Charities USA(239)

Snyder, Lee D.
International Society for the Comparative Studies of Civilizations(389)

Snyder, Marie
National Football League Players Association(511)

Snyder, Jr., Ph.D., Oscar P.
Hospitality Institute of Technology and Management(328)

Snyder, Russell K.
Asphalt Roofing Manufacturers Association(163)

Snyder, Stephen F.
National Association of Jai Alai Frontons(459)

Snyder, Wallace S.
American Advertising Federation(29)

Sobel, Allan D.
American Judicature Society(99)

Sobel, MD, Ph.D, Mark E.
American Society for Investigative Pathology(130)
Association for Molecular Pathology(176)
Association of Pathology Chairs(207)
Intersociety Council For Pathology Information(398)

Socknat, Matt
National Sheriffs' Association(539)

Sofer, Ph.D., Stephen
American Association of Spinal Cord Injury Nurses(51)
American Association of Spinal Cord Injury Psychologists and Social Workers(51)
American Paraplegia Society(113)

Sofranko, Ph.D., John A.
American Institute of Chemical Engineers(95)

Sogueco, Renato
Society of American Florists(630)

Sok, Michelle
American Association of Pathologists' Assistants(47)

Sokolowski, Ron
Health & Sciences Communications Association(322)

Solarz, Barry
American Iron and Steel Institute(98)

Solem, Michael
Association of American Geographers(184)

Soler, Eileen
Association of Asphalt Paving Technologists(186)

Soles, Thomas J.
Sheet Metal and Air Conditioning Contractors' National Association(610)

Soley, Dr. Richard
Object Management Group(563)

Solfermoser, Connie
Society for Mining, Metallurgy, and Exploration(622)

Solie, Candice
Association of Public-Safety Communications Officers- International(211)

Sollman, David
National Trappers Association(547)

Solomon, David
American Jewish Historical Society(99)

Solomon, Ronni P.
ECRI(288)

Soloway, Stan Z.
Professional Services Council(589)

Soltesz, Betty
Society for Biomolecular Sciences(614)

Somers, Fred
American Occupational Therapy Association(109)

Somers, Jr., Fred L.
National Golf Car Manufacturers Association(514)

Somers, Rebecca
National Association of Federal Credit Unions(452)

Somerville, Nancy
American Society of Landscape Architects(140)

Somerville, Robert D.
American Bureau of Shipping(59)

Somes-Schloesser, Jayne
Mortgage Bankers Association(421)

Sondrup, Steven P.
Society for the Advancement of Scandinavian Study(626)

Soppelsa, Betty
NAFSA: Association of International Educators(424)

Sorensen, CAE, C. Mitchell
Professional Show Managers Association(589)
Sorensen, Heidi
Alliance for Nonprofit Management(15)
Sorian, Richard
National Committee for Quality Assurance(491)
Sorley, Dr. Lewis
Association of Military Colleges and Schools of the U.S.(205)
Sorrell, Susan
Association of State Dam Safety Officials(215)
Soto, Carlos
National Hispanic Corporate Council(517)
Soto, Ron
American Association of Franchisees and Dealers(43)
Soto, Steven A.
Mexican-American Grocers Association(418)
Soto-Clarke, Trina
International Downtown Association(369)
Soule, Jeff
American Planning Association(116)
Soutar, Sammi
American Association of Code Enforcement(40)
Southard, Greta
Public Library Association(592)
Southworth, Howie
DRI International(287)
Souza, Caryn
Community Transportation Association of America(256)
Sovinski, David
International Masonry Institute(379)
Sower, Suzanne
American Filtration and Separations Society(83)
Sox, M.D., MACP, Harold C.
American College of Physicians(69)
Soyster, Karen
National Association of Industrial and Office Properties(458)
Spadaro, Paul
United States Association of Independent Gymnastic Clubs(673)
Spaeder, Shannon
National Association of Independent Schools(457)
Spagnudo, John
Insurance Information Institute(345)
Spahr, CAE, Frederick T.
American Society for Nutrition(131)
Spahr, Joanna
Society of Nuclear Medicine(641)
Spain, Cathy
National League of Cities(524)
Spalding, Kristie
American Council on Exercise(76)
Span, Derrick Len
Community Action Partnership(255)
Spangler, David C.
Consumer Healthcare Products Association(263)
Spanier, Robert
American College of Physicians(69)
Spar, Edward J.
Council of Professional Associations on Federal Statistics(273)
Sparkman, David
American Moving and Storage Association(107)
Sparks, Ph.D., Dennis
National Staff Development Council(543)
Sparks, Jennifer
Society of American Florists(630)
Sparks, Lillian
National Indian Education Association(519)
Sparks, Richard A.
IEEE Microwave Theory and Techniques Society(331)
Spaulding, Karen
National Academy of Engineering of the United States of America(426)
Spaulding, Kenneth
International Hydrofoil Society(375)
Spawn, James A.
American Tarentaise Association(150)
North American Corriente Association(556)
Spears, Jimmie
Cabletelevision Advertising Bureau(236)
Spears, Linda
Child Welfare League of America(244)
Spears, Linda
CWLA - Child Mental Health Division(280)
Spears, Tracy
National Association of the Remodeling Industry(479)
Specker, Steven R.
Electric Power Research Institute(290)
Speckhardt, Roy
American Humanist Association(92)
Spector, Nancy
National Council of State Boards of Nursing(500)
Speelmon, Patricia A.
National Collegiate Honors Council(491)
Speer, Ph.D., J. Alexander
Mineralogical Society of America(419)
Speer, Wilbur
National Active and Retired Federal Employees Association(427)
Speight, Emily
Marine Technology Society(412)
Spellman, J. P.
Woven Wire Products Association(697)
Spencer, David
North American-Chilean Chamber of Commerce(562)
Spencer, Dr. Harrison C.
Association of Schools of Public Health(213)
Spencer, Lisa
American Oil Chemists' Society(110)
Spencer, Michelle
American Society of Women Accountants(147)
Audio Publishers Association(222)
Spencer, Todd
Owner-Operator Independent Drivers Association(570)
Spencer, William B.
Associated Builders and Contractors(164)
Spiegel, Susan
Textile Bag and Packaging Association(660)
Spielberger, Ronald
College Media Advisers(251)
Spielman, Victoria E.
Affordable Housing Tax Credit Coalition(10)
Spiess, Heather
Society of Cardiovascular Anesthesiologists(632)
Spilhaus, Fred
American Geophysical Union(87)
Spilhaus, Karl H.
Cashmere and Camel Hair Manufacturers Institute(238)
National Textile Association(546)
Spiliotopolous, Kathy
Greek Food and Wine Institute(320)
Spilman, Aneta
FCIB-NACM Corp.(301)
Spina, Ph.D., CAE, Joseph H.
National Association of College and University Food Services(444)
Spindler, Robert P.
National Council of Postal Credit Unions(500)
Spindor, SuzAnn
Texas Longhorn Breeders Association of America(659)
Spinelli, Emily
American Association of Teachers of Spanish and Portuguese(52)
Spinosa, James
International Longshore and Warehouse Union(378)
Spitzer, Ben
Red Angus Association of America(597)
Splittstoesser, Robin
American Association of Neuromuscular & Electrodiagnostic Medicine(46)
Spragens, Lori
Association of State Dam Safety Officials(215)
Sprague, Daniel M.
Council of State Governments(275)
Sprei, Douglas
NPES, The Association for Suppliers of Printing, Publishing and Converting Technologies(563)
Sprindzunas, Deborah
Association for Healthcare Resource and Materials Management(174)
Springer, Jack M.
Metal Framing Manufacturers Association(417)
Springer, Michael
American Academy of Family Physicians(22)
Sprinkel, Elizabeth A.
American Institute for CPCU - Insurance Institute of America(93)
Sprung, Dennis B.
American Kennel Club(100)
Sprung, Lowrie
National Watercolor Society(549)
Spurlock, Lisa
Entomological Society of America(295)
Squair, Philip
National Propane Gas Association(534)
Squiccimari, Larry
Schiffli Lace and Embroidery Manufacturers Association(606)
Sreenivasan, Sreenath
South Asian Journalists Association(647)
Sroka, John W.
Sheet Metal and Air Conditioning Contractors' National Association(610)
Sroufe, Ph.D, Gerald E.
American Educational Research Association(80)
St. Amour, Lynn
Internet Society(398)
St. Clair, Byron
National Translator Association(547)
St. Clair, Kathie
Association of University Research Parks(219)
St. John, CAE, William S.
Dietary Managers Association(284)
St. Martin, Charlotte
League of American Theatres and Producers(406)
St. Pierre, Mary
National Association for Home Care(434)
Staab, Ph.D., Wayne J.
American Auditory Society(55)
Stables, Carolyn
Academy of Managed Care Pharmacy(4)

Stableski, Bob
NAFSA: Association of International Educators(424)
Stachelski, Kaydene
Audit Bureau of Circulations(222)
Stack, Michael J.
ASIS International(163)
Stacy, Sarah
National Technical Services Association(546)
Stacy, Susan B.
American College of Osteopathic Internists(69)
Staff, Charlie
Distillers Grains Technology Council(286)
Staffanou, DDS, MS, Dr. Robert S.
American Academy of Fixed Prosthodontics(23)
Stahl, Ph.D., William
Histochemical Society(326)
Stahler, Mary
Society of Accredited Marine Surveyors(629)
Stahr, Patricia D.
Society for Maternal Fetal Medicine(621)
Stalder, Ph.D., Ken
National Swine Improvement Federation(545)
Staley, Kelly
Institute of Packaging Professionals(343)
Stalknecht, Paul T.
Air Conditioning Contractors of America(13)
Stallings, Erin
Alliance of Professional Tattooists(17)
Stallings, Margaret
North American Society for Pediatric Gastroenterology, Hepatology and Nutrition(561)
Stallings, Mike
Behavior Genetics Association(227)
Stallman, Robert
American Farm Bureau Federation(81)
Stallone, Steve
International Longshore and Warehouse Union(378)
Stallworth, Shauna D.
Organization of Black Designers(567)
Stanard, Mina
National Parks Conservation Association(532)
Stanek, Kathy
National Association of Tax Professionals(478)
Stanfield, Leslie
National Business Education Association(486)
Stankiewicz, Carrie
American Association for Geriatric Psychiatry(35)
Stanlaske, Dotty
National Association of Elevator Safety Authorities International(450)
Stanley, Dan
American Trucking Associations(152)
Stanley, Kathleen
Water Systems Council(686)
Stanley, Lynda
Federal Facilities Council(302)
Stano, Phillip E.
Association of Life Insurance Counsel(203)
Stanton, Melanie
American Pediatric Surgical Association(113)
Stanton, Michael
Alliance of Automobile Manufacturers(16)
Stanton, Robert G.
American Society for Aesthetic Plastic Surgery(126)
Staples-Bortner, Sandra
Wildlife Society, The(689)
Stapleton, Terry R.
American Postal Workers Union(117)
Stark, Dan
American Public Gardens Association(119)
Starkey, John
U.S. Poultry and Egg Association(668)
Starkey, Keith
Professional Women's Appraisal Association(590)
Starkweather, Kendall N.
International Technology Education Association(393)
Starner, Ronald
Industrial Asset Management Council(336)
Starr, Jay
International Council of Shopping Centers(368)
Starr, Scott
Society for the Study of Evolution(628)
Wildlife Disease Association(689)
Starr, Sharon
IPC - Association Connecting Electronics Industries(399)
Statham, Stu
Association of Former Agents of the U.S. Secret Service(197)
Staton, Susan
Association of American Universities(185)
Stawarz, Jay
International Cut Flower Growers Association(368)
Stebbins, Dr. Chad D.
International Society of Weekly Newspaper Editors(392)
Steede, Neil
Early Sites Research Society(288)
Steel, William
National Grange(514)
Steele, Lu Ann
Mechanical Contractors Association of America(415)
Steele, Scott L.
University/Resident Theatre Association(680)
Stefanou, Harry
Project Management Institute(590)
Steffens, Brian
National Newspaper Association(528)
Steffes, Peter
National Defense Industrial Association(504)
Steger, Bill
Collaborative Family Healthcare Association(250)
Steighner, Dan
Minerals, Metals and Materials Society, The(420)
Stein, Dean K.
American Psychoanalytic Association(118)
Stein, Debbie
Voices for America's Children(684)
Stein, Martin L.
National Parking Association(531)
Stein, Norman R.
International Society for Infectious Diseases(387)
Stein, Pete
National Association of Health Underwriters(455)
Steinbach, John W.
International Foundation of Employee Benefit Plans(373)
Steinbecher, Ed
American Education Finance Association(80)
Steiner, Betsy
Alliance of Foam Packaging Recyclers(16)
EPS Molders Association(297)
Steiner, Gina
American Society of Anesthesiologists(134)
Steingart, M.D., Richard
Society of Geriatric Cardiology(637)
Steinhardt, David
International Digital Enterprise Alliance(369)
Steinmetz, Bob
Newspaper Purchasing Management Association(553)
Steirer, Terry
National Association of Collegiate Directors of Athletics(444)
Stellar, Charles
America's Health Insurance Plans(19)
Stellato, Tana
American Society of Health-System Pharmacists(139)
Stelzig, Chris
Entomological Society of America(295)
Stember, Lee Ann C.
National Council for Prescription Drug Programs(497)
Stemme, Fred O.
National Corn Growers Association(496)
Stemper-Johnson, CAE, CMP, Linda
Credit Union Executives Society(279)
Stenersen, Steve
U.S. Lacrosse(668)
Stengel, Angela
Oncology Nursing Society(564)
Stengel, Ginny
Self Storage Association(608)
Stenzel, CAE, Thomas E.
United Fresh Fruit and Vegetable Association(671)
Stephens, CAE, Angela Moore
American Group Psychotherapy Association(87)
Stephens, Jaime
Color Marketing Group(252)
Stephens, Jay A.
American Institute of Architects(94)
Stephens, Ph.D., John F.
American Studies Association(149)
Stephens, K.W.
International Family Recreation Association(371)
Society of Recreation Executives(643)
Stephens, Larry D.
United States Committee on Irrigation and Drainage(674)
United States Society on Dams(677)
Stephens, Scott
Supply Chain Council(656)
Stephens, Sherry A.
Petroleum Equipment Suppliers Association(574)
Stephens Jackson, Ann
International Atherosclerosis Society(362)
Stepp, Derek D.
Association for Gerontology in Higher Education(173)
Stepuszek, Mark
Advertising Media Credit Executives Association, International(9)
Steranka, Joe
Professional Golfers Association of America(587)
Sterling, Kim
IPC - Association Connecting Electronics Industries(399)
Sterling, Lesley
Equipment Leasing Association of America(297)
Sterling, Scott
Greater Washington Board of Trade(320)

Stern, Andrew L.
Service Employees International Union(609)
Stern, David
National Basketball Association(483)
Stern, Ronald J.
Patent Office Professional Association(572)
Sternberg, Rob
Society for Archaeological Sciences(614)
Stertz, Marc H.
National Automobile Dealers Association(482)
Stertzer, David
Association for Advanced Life Underwriting(167)
Steurer, Stephen J.
Correctional Education Association(266)
Steve, Jaime
American Wind Energy Association(155)
Stevener, Sarah
Farm Equipment Manufacturers Association(301)
Stevens, Bart
National Council of Higher Education Loan Programs(499)
Stevens, M.D., David
Christian Medical & Dental Associations(246)
Stevens, James T.
American Kennel Club(100)
Stevens, Joe
AirConditioning and Refrigeration Institute(14)
Stevens, Kent R.
International Trade Commission Trial Lawyers Association(394)
Stevens, Michael
Conference of State Bank Supervisors(260)
Stevens, Patricia
National Information Standards Organization(520)
Stevens, Paul Schott
Investment Company Institute(398)
Stevens, Ph.D., Timothy S.
Association for College and University Religious Affairs(169)
Stevenson, David
American Society of Naval Engineers(142)
Stevenson, Sharon
National Center for Homeopathy(488)
Stevenson, Terry
National Association of Ticket Brokers(479)
National Independent Flag Dealers Association(519)
Stevenson, Vans
Motion Picture Association of America(421)
Steward, Joye
American Society of Extra-Corporeal Technology(137)
Steward, Lisa
Nuclear Energy Institute(563)
Stewart, Butch
International Professional Rodeo Association(383)
Stewart, Debra
Council of Graduate Schools(272)
Stewart, Ernest
Monument Builders of North America(421)
Stewart, Gordon
Insurance Information Institute(345)
Stewart, Bishop Imagene B.
African-American Women's Clergy Association(11)
Stewart, Joye
Society of Cardiovascular Anesthesiologists(632)
Stewart, Karen J.
International Visual Literacy Association(396)
Stewart, Laura
Petroleum Marketers Association of America(574)
Stewart, Mike
American Association for Cancer Research(34)
Stewart, Regina
National Society of Mural Painters(542)
Stewart, Richard J.
American Academy of Orthopaedic Surgeons(26)
Stewart, Scott
National Livestock Producers Association(525)
Stewart, Thomas E.
Liaison Committee of Cooperating Oil and Gas Associations(407)
Stibelman, Maria
National Flute Association(511)
Stickle, Ph.D., Warren E.
Chemical Producers and Distributors Association(243)
Stidinger, Stephen
AFSM International(11)
Stier, Jeff
American Council on Science and Health(76)
Stierle, Linda J.
American Nurses Association(109)
Stikkers, Dr. Kenneth W.
Society for the Advancement of American Philosophy(626)
Stiklestad, Lynn
Archery Range and Retailers Organization(160)
Stiles, Jamie
National Association of Computerized Tax Processors(445)
Stiles, Nancy
American Society of Marine Artists(141)
Still, Ph.D., Steven M.
Perennial Plant Association(573)
Stillman, Bradley C.
American College of Gastroenterology(66)
Association of Program Directors in Surgery(210)
Stimson, Kay
National Association of Secretaries of State(471)
Stine, Linda
Fresh Produce and Floral Council(312)
Stine, Sandra
National Cottonseed Products Association(496)
Stine, Vince
American Association for Clinical Chemistry(34)
Stinebert, Chris S.
Manufactured Housing Institute(411)
Stinson, Patrick B.
Employee Services Management Association(293)
Stinton, CAE, Dale A.
National Association of REALTORS(468)
Stirpe, David
Alliance for Responsible Atmospheric Policy(16)
Stith, James H.
American Institute of Physics(97)
Stivers, Donna
Intersociety Council For Pathology Information(398)
Stobridge, USAF (Ret.), Col. Steven P.
Military Officers Association of America(419)
Stock, CAE, Arlene
Association of Real Estate Women(211)
Stockdale, Steve
International Society for General Semantics(387)
Stocker, Frederick T.
Manufacturers Alliance/MAPI(411)
Stockinger, Charles M.
American Measuring Tool Manufacturers Association(103)
Chemical Fabrics and Film Association(243)
Metal Building Manufacturers Association(417)
North American Sawing Association(560)
Power Tool Institute(582)
United States Cutting Tool Institute(675)
Stockman, Brian
American Society of Farm Managers and Rural Appraisers(137)
Stocksdale, Joy
Surface Design Association(656)
Stoddard, Rob
National Cable & Telecommunications Association(486)
Stodhill, Paige
International Association of Workforce Professionals(362)
Stohlton, John B.
American Association of Presidents of Independent Colleges and Universities(49)
Stoiber, Susanne
Institute of Medicine(343)
Stokes, Lillian
Chi Eta Phi Sorority(244)
Stokes, Terry
National Cattlemen's Beef Association(488)
Stolberg, Charles G.
National Submetering and Utility Allocation Association(544)
Submersible Wastewater Pump Association(655)
Stolzer, Ernie
Quality Bakers of America Cooperative(594)
Stone, Alec
Special Event Sites Marketing Alliance(648)
Stone, Bill
Institute on Religion in an Age of Science(344)
Stone, Denise
Irrigation Association(400)
Stone, Diane
World Shoe Association(696)
Stone, Don
Organization for Tropical Studies(567)
Stone, Marcia
National Association of State Chief Administrators(474)
National Association of State Facilities Administrators(475)
Stone, Reese J.
National Medical Association(526)
Stone, Richard
International Society of Air Safety Investigators(389)
Stone-Wachtel, Svetlana
New York Academy of Sciences(552)
Stoner, Dena
National Rural Electric Cooperative Association(537)
Stoner, Floyd
American Bankers Association(55)
Stong, Pamela A.
Association of Legal Administrators(203)
Stonis, RN, BSN, MJ, Nancy
Society of Critical Care Medicine(634)
Storat, Richard
Paper Shipping Sack Manufacturers Association(571)
Stork, Dennis
International Right of Way Association(385)

Stottlemyer, Todd
National Federation of Independent Business(509)
Stotts, Michael
National Academy of Building Inspection Engineers(426)
Stoupa, Steve
American Chiropractic Association(62)
Stowe, James L.
International Association of Official Human Rights Agencies(359)
Stowell, Shannon
Adventure Travel Trade Association(9)
Stowell Corder, Susan
Association of Public-Safety Communications Officers- International(211)
Strackbein, William C.
Laboratory Products Association(404)
Optical Imaging Association(565)
SAMA Group of Associations(605)
Straley, Tina H.
Mathematical Association of America(414)
Strand, Sheila
American College of Cardiology(64)
Strang, Lynne
American Financial Services Association(83)
Strass, Elaine
American Society of Human Genetics(139)
Genetics Society of America(315)
Stratigos, Nicholas G.
Printing Industries of America(584)
Stratman, Christina
Structural Stability Research Council(654)
Stratton, Kim
Society of Children's Book Writers and Illustrators(633)
Stratton, Mark
North American Manufacturing Research Institution of SME(558)
Stratulat, Mihaela-Daniela
Geothermal Energy Association(316)
Straughan, Joe
Mexican Restaurant and Cantina Association(418)
Strauss, Benjamin G.
Universities Research Association(679)
Strauss, David
Association of Farmworker Opportunity Programs(196)
Strauss, Kathryn Lafleur
Society of Professional Benefit Administrators(642)
Strauss, Michael S.
National Association of Academies of Science(437)
Stravino, Laura
Organic Trade Association(566)
Streckfuss, Diane
Advertising Research Foundation(9)
Streeper, Martha J.
Federation of Defense and Corporate Counsel(303)
Street, Rene
American Business Women's Association(60)
Streeter, Teresa
National Association of State Universities and Land Grant Colleges(477)
Streight, David
Council for Spiritual and Ethical Education(270)
Strell, Bruce
Alpha Zeta Omega(18)
Stretch, Dr. George
American Naprapathic Association(108)
Stricker, Ph.D., George
Society for the Exploration of Psychotherapy Integration(627)
Strickland, Carla
Commercial Food Equipment Service Association(253)
Strickland, Sue
American Apparel Producers Network(32)
Strickland, Tom
International Professional Rodeo Association(383)
Stringfellow, Fred C.
Flexographic Prepress Platemakers Association(308)
Web Sling and Tiedown Association(686)
Strittmatter, Aimee
Association for Library Service to Children(175)
Strom, David J.
AFT Healthcare(11)
Stromberg, JoAnn
Surface Mount Technology Association(656)
Stromberg, Roger
Conference of State Bank Supervisors(260)
Stromoski, Rick
National Cartoonists Society(487)
Stronczer, Cheryl
World Affairs Councils of America(695)
Strong, Maria
International Intellectual Property Alliance(377)
Strong, Mary
Society for Visual Anthropology(629)
Strong, Dr. Stacie I.
National Association of Women Lawyers(482)
Strother, Lynn
Human Factors and Ergonomics Society(329)
Strother, CAE, Pamela
National Lesbian and Gay Journalists Association(524)
Stroud, Pamela
International Institute of Forecasters(376)
Stroud, Rick
International Association of Administrative Professionals(352)
Stroud, Troy F.
Ductile Iron Pipe Research Association(287)
Stroup, Jr., USA(R, Lt.Gen. Theodore G.
Association of the United States Army(218)
Strozier, Charles B.
Group for the Use of Psychology in History(320)
Struchen, Shirley
Religion Communicators Council(598)
Strunk, Albert
American College of Obstetricians and Gynecologists(68)
Stuart, Eric J.
Steel Manufacturers Association(653)
Stuart, Greg
Interactive Advertising Bureau(346)
Stuart, Karen
Association of Talent Agents(216)
Stuart, Mark
National Industrial Council - Employer Association Group(519)
Stubblebine, Hollee
National Potato Council(533)
Stuck, Janine M.
Council of Supply Chain Management Professionals(275)
Stucky, Stacie
American Association of Neuromuscular & Electrodiagnostic Medicine(46)
Studebaker, Kim
National Council of Juvenile and Family Court Judges(499)
Studnicki, Susan
Independent Educational Consultants Association(334)
Stueber, Ross E.
Association of Lutheran Secondary Schools(203)
Stuenzi, Dan
National Network of Estate Planning Attorneys(528)
Stull, Scott
American Cultural Resources Association(77)
Stultz, Mark
Natural Gas Supply Association(550)
Stumpf, Dominique
National Pest Management Association(532)
Stuntz, Franki K.
National Ocean Industries Association(529)
Sturdevant, Kenton E.
Forest Industries Telecommunications(310)
Sturke, Cynthia
Inter-Society Color Council(346)
Sturm, John F.
Newspaper Association of America(552)
Sturm, Kathy
Society of Architectural Historians(631)
Stygar, Jr., Edward J.
American Art Therapy Association(32)
American Biological Safety Association(57)
American Pathology Foundation(113)
Styles, Dr. Bonnie W.
American Quaternary Association(121)
Association of Science Museum Directors(213)
Styles, Scott
America's Health Insurance Plans(19)
Styll, John
Gospel Music Association(318)
Subrin, Berton
Senior Executives Association(609)
Suchecki, Joseph L.
Engine Manufacturers Association(295)
Suda-Blake, Kimberly
American Academy of Periodontology(27)
Sufka, Kenneth M.
Associated Air Balance Council(164)
Sukenik, John
Health Forum(323)
Sulen, Frank
National Association of College Stores(444)
Sulkow, Rob
NABIM - the International Band and Orchestral Products Association(424)
Sullins, John
Society for Philosophy and Technology(623)
Sullivan, (Ret.), Gen. Gordon R.
Association of the United States Army(218)
Sullivan, Isabel "Mimi"
National Wooden Pallet and Container Association(550)
Sullivan, Jerome
American Association of Collegiate Registrars and Admissions Officers(40)
Sullivan, Jim
Society of Pharmaceutical and Biotech Trainers(642)
Sullivan, Kaye
American Public Works Association(120)
Sullivan, Lisa R.
American Association of Physicists in Medicine(48)
Sullivan, Marcia Z.
Consumer Bankers Association(263)
Sullivan, Michael J.
Sheet Metal Workers' International Association(610)

Sullivan, Patricia
Association for Death Education and Counseling(171)

Sullivan, Sis
Surface Mount Technology Association(656)

Sullivan, Stephen M.
American Short Line and Regional Railroad Association(125)

Sultan, Sally
Academy of Marketing Science(4)

Summer, Morton
Council for Jewish Education(269)

Summers, Annette L.
Association of Career Firms International(188)
Association of Career Professionals International(188)

Summers, Joyce
National Association of Catering Executives(442)

Summers, Kent
NFHS Music Association(553)
NFHS Speech Debate and Theatre Association(553)

Summy, Elizabeth
American Society for Healthcare Risk Management(129)

Sumner, Curt W.
American Congress on Surveying and Mapping(73)

Sumner, David
American Radio Relay League(121)

Sumner, James H.
USA Poultry and Egg Export Council(681)

Sumner, Sandra
American Alliance for Health, Physical Education, Recreation and Dance(30)

Sumpter, Darrell
American Apparel & Footwear Association(31)

Sumrall, Robert
Society of Piping Engineers and Designers(642)

Sunderland, Janice
Association for Hose and Accessories Distribution(174)

Sunderman, Jr., M.D., F. William
Association of Clinical Scientists(190)

Sunshine, Robert
International Theatre Equipment Association(394)

Suppan, Michael D.
National Public Employer Labor Relations Association(534)

Suppe, Frederick
Charles Homer Haskins Society(243)

Surak, Christopher
American Wood Preservers Institute(155)

Surian, Barbara
American Seed Trade Association(124)

Suritz, Chuck
National Sporting Goods Association(543)

Surprenant, Nancy
NAIR -- the International Association of Bowling Lane Specialists(425)

Susman, Elizabeth
Society for Research on Adolescence(624)

Susser, Peter A.
Driver Employer Council of America(287)

Sussman, Ira
Cabletelevision Advertising Bureau(236)

Sutermaster, Dena Jean
Hospice and Palliative Nurses Association(328)

Sutherland, Mittie D.
Academy of Criminal Justice Sciences(3)

Sutherland, Shelly
Foundation for Russian-American Economic Cooperation(311)

Sutherland, Tracey E.
American Accounting Association(29)

Sutter, Julie
Association of Professional Researchers for Advancement(209)
Center for Exhibition Industry Research(241)
International Customer Service Association(368)

Sutton, Beth
American Dairy Products Institute(78)

Sutton, Claudia Mansfield
American Association of School Administrators(50)

Sutton, David J.
Scientific Equipment and Furniture Association(606)

Sutton, Debi
International Sleep Products Association(386)

Sutton, Mark
Gas Processors Association(314)
Gas Processors Suppliers Association(314)

Sutton, William G.
AirConditioning and Refrigeration Institute(14)

Suydam, Linda A.
Consumer Healthcare Products Association(263)

Svazas, Janet
American Academy of Oral and Maxillofacial Pathology(25)
American Society of Business Publication Editors(135)
Casual Furniture Retailers(239)
National Retail Hobby Stores Association(536)

Svedman, Katherine J.
American Society for Dermatologic Surgery(128)

Svendsen, Pam
Association of Investment Management Sales Executives(202)

Svinicki, CAE, Jane A.
Polyurethane Manufacturers Association(580)

Swaim, Sue
National Middle School Association(527)

Swain, Lori
National Cancer Registrars Association(486)

Swan, Sharon J.
American Society for Clinical Pharmacology and Therapeutics(127)

Swanda, Ron
General Aviation Manufacturers Association(315)

Swaney, Julie
National Foundation for Women Legislators(512)

Swann, Amy M.
Association of Reproductive Health Professionals(212)

Swann, Crystal
United States Conference of City Human Services Officials(674)

Swanson, Lise
Association of University Radiologists(219)

Swartwout, Jim
American Osteopathic Association(111)

Swatos, Jr., Ph.D., William H.
Religious Research Association(599)

Swatos, Jr., Ph.D, William H.
Association for the Sociology of Religion(180)

Sweeney, Barbara J.
National Association of Securities Dealers(471)

Sweeney, Chuck
Graphic Arts Technical Foundation(319)

Sweeney, John R.
National Association of University Fisheries and Wildlife Programs(480)

Sweeney, John J.
American Federation of Labor and Congress of Industrial Organizations(82)

Sweeney, Kate
Cosmetic Executive Women(267)

Sweeney, Les
Associated Bodywork and Massage Professionals(164)

Swenson, Diane
National Association of Federal Credit Unions(452)

Swenson, Kurt
National Building Granite Quarries Association(485)

Swiacki, Eve C.
American College of Physicians(69)

Swientek, Bob
Institute of Food Technologists(341)

Swift, Ed
Chief Warrant and Warrant Officers Association, United States Coast Guard(244)

Swinburn, CAE, John S.
Embroidery Trade Association(292)
Mystery Shopping Providers Association(424)

Swindle, Geri
Federation of American Socs. for Experimental Biology(303)

Swisher, Kent
American Seed Trade Association(124)

Swisher, Randall S.
American Wind Energy Association(155)

Sybinsky, Peter
Association of Maternal and Child Health Programs(204)

Syers, Tekla
Institute of Food Technologists(341)

Sylvan, Dr. Donald A.
Jewish Education Service of North America(401)

Sylvestri, Virginia
American Society for Healthcare Central Service Professionals(129)
Society for Healthcare Consumer Advocacy(618)

Szabat, Ronald
American Society of Anesthesiologists(134)

Szanjkovics, Sandor
American Massage Therapy Association(103)

Szpak, Carole
National Association of Psychiatric Health Systems(467)

Szrom, Ed
Institute of Scrap Recycling Industries(343)

Szufnar, Elizabeth A.
National Conference of State Historic Preservation Officers(494)

Szurgot, Karyn
American Osteopathic Association(111)

Szymanski, Pat
International Brotherhood of Teamsters, AFL-CIO(363)

Taddei, Dan
National Association of the Remodeling Industry(479)

Taffet, Richard S.
Textile Producers and Suppliers Association(660)

Taft, James
Association of State Drinking Water Administrators(215)

Tahar, Joanna
American Geophysical Union(87)
Tahirkheli, Sharon N.
American Geological Institute(87)
Talbott, Brian
Association of Educational Service Agencies(194)
Talbott, Scott
Financial Services Roundtable(306)
Tallaksen, Inger M.
Norwegian-American Chamber of Commerce(562)
Talley, Robbie
Automotive Service Association(224)
Talley, Sandi
Destination Marketing Association International(283)
Talone, Ph.D., Patricia A.
Catholic Health Association of the United States(240)
Tan, Caroline
River Management Society(602)
Tancin, Charlotte
Council on Botanical and Horticultural Libraries(275)
Tannahill, Sharon K.
National Classification Management Society(490)
Tannehill, CMP, Lora
American Society of Neuroradiology(142)
Tanner, Donald E.
National Board of Boiler and Pressure Vessel Inspectors(485)
Tanner, Ronald
National Association for the Specialty Food Trade(436)
Tanz, Jayne
International Electrical Testing Association(370)
Tanzi, CPCM, Vito A.
National Bureau of Certified Consultants(485)
Tanzman, Howard
American College of Surgeons(71)
Tapscott, Eleanor
American Society of Hematology(139)
Tarallo, Mary Jo
SnowSports Industries America(612)
Tarantino, Christie
Academy of General Dentistry(3)
Tarantino, Teresa
National Confectionery Sales Association(492)
Tarbert, Jeffrey
American Public Power Association(120)
Tarker, Lisa A.
Federation of Diocesan Liturgical Commissions(303)
Tarnove, Lorraine
American Medical Directors Association(104)
Tarnowski, Ray
Automotive Recyclers Association(224)
Tarter, John (Jack) R.
National Association of State Veterans Homes(477)
Tassoni, John Paul
National Council of Writing Program Administrators(502)
Tate, Lisa M.
National Association of Children's Hospitals(443)
Tate, Pamela
Council for Adult and Experiential Learning(267)
Tatu, Marian
American Society for Engineering Education(128)
Taute, Lisa
American Society of Radiologic Technologists(145)
Tauzin, W.J. "Billy"
Pharmaceutical Research and Manufacturers of America(575)
Taylor, Andrew
Association of Arts Administration Educators(186)
Taylor, Bob
National Air Traffic Controllers Association(428)
Taylor, Carrie
American Hampshire Sheep Association(88)
Taylor, Charlene
Academy of Osseointegration(5)
Taylor, Charles
RMA - The Risk Management Association(602)
Taylor, Charles T.
National Association of Activity Professionals(437)
Taylor, Christy M.
American Alliance for Theatre and Education(30)
Taylor, CPC, CTS, Conrad
National Association of Personnel Services(464)
Taylor, Crispin
American Society of Plant Biologists(144)
Taylor, Dan
International Financial Services Association(372)
Taylor, Dianne E.
Council of State Community Development Agencies(274)
Taylor, Gary J.
Association of Fish and Wildlife Agencies(197)
Taylor, Gray
National Association of Convenience Stores(446)
Taylor, Sr., John S.
National Venture Capital Association(548)
Taylor, Kimberly
National Medical Association(526)
Taylor, L. David
National Association of Community Health Centers(445)
Taylor, Leona
Association of Pool and Spa Professionals(208)
Taylor, Mary C.
Library and Information Technology Association(407)
Taylor, Mary Lou
Sheet Metal and Air Conditioning Contractors' National Association(610)
Taylor, Melissa
Racking Horse Breeders Association of America(594)
Taylor, CAE, Michael R.
National Demolition Association(505)
Taylor, Pamela
National Association of State Treasurers(476)
Taylor, Peter
National Association of Federal Credit Unions(452)
Taylor, Phyllis M.
Consumer Healthcare Products Association(263)
Taylor, Richard
Motion Picture Association of America(421)
Taylor, Steve
Appaloosa Horse Club(159)
Taylor, Su
Society of Pharmaceutical and Biotech Trainers(642)
Tayman, Ava Ann
Society for Gynecologic Investigation(618)
Teaff, Grant
American Football Coaches Association(84)
Teates, Melissa
Paperboard Packaging Council(571)
Tedeschi, George
Graphic Communications Conference, IBT(319)
Teeter, Frederick J.
Surface Engineering Coating Association(656)
Teicher, Oren
American Booksellers Association(58)
Teisler, CAE, David
Association for Advancement of Behavior Therapy(167)
Telego, D.J.
Environmental Bankers Association(296)
Telego, T.C.
Environmental Bankers Association(296)
Tella, Edie
Institute of Store Planners(344)
Tellmann, Ron
National Committee on Planned Giving(491)
Temple, CAE, Linda
Regulatory Affairs Professionals Society(598)
Templeton, Don A.
National Council of Health Facilities Finance Authorities(499)
Tena-Perez, Dr. Lydia
National Council for Workforce Education(497)
Tendler, Elaine
National Association of Waterfront Employers(481)
Tendler, Paul M.
American Licensed Practical Nurses Association(101)
TenEyck, Martie
American International Marchigiana Society(98)
Tenley, Jr., George W.
Pipeline Research Council International(578)
Tennant, Christopher J.
Coordinating Research Council(265)
Teplitz, Janice
American Association of Oral and Maxillofacial Surgeons(47)
Tepper, Alan M.
Tau Epsilon Rho Law Society(657)
Terault, Michael
National Sheriffs' Association(539)
Terhaar, Allen
Cotton Council International(267)
Terova, Marie
Council of Chief State School Officers(271)
Terpack, Sue Steiner
Combustion Institute(253)
Terrell, Maria E.
International Newspaper Marketing Association(381)
Terry, Carolyn
National Association of Minority Media Executives(462)
Terry, Charles
American Hydrogen Association(92)
Terry, Michelle "Mikki" Lambert
Association for Supervision and Curriculum Development(178)
Terry, Sandra
Society of American Graphic Artists(630)

Terry-Sharp, Kathleen
American Anthropological Association(31)
Tesdell, Kerwin
Community Development Venture Capital Alliance(256)
Teske, David
Association of College Unions International(191)
Teter, Harry
American Trauma Society(152)
Tetschner, CAE, Stacy
National Speakers Association(542)
Tettambel, D.O., Melicien A.
American Association of Osteopathic Women Physicians(47)
Teutsch, William J.
Association of Surgical Technologists(216)
Thacker, Dr. Eileen
American Association of Veterinary Immunologists(53)
Thacker, Jim
National Association of Institutional Linen Management(458)
Thacker, Jimmie
International Association for Truancy and Dropout Prevention(352)
Thackray, Arnold
Chemical Heritage Foundation(243)
Thackston, Chris
American Bankruptcy Institute(55)
Thain, John A.
New York Stock Exchange(552)
Thal, Rabbi Lennard
Union for Reform Judaism(670)
Thaler, Bradford
National Association of Federal Credit Unions(452)
Thanangaden, Thomas
Academy of Motion Picture Arts and Sciences(4)
Tharp, David W.
International Association for Food Protection(350)
Thayer, Jay
Nuclear Energy Institute(563)
Thayer, Susan C.
Association of Professors of Cardiology(209)
Theall, Dwight
American Association of Family and Consumer Sciences(43)
Theil, Brian
AOAC International(158)
Theilacker, Jay
Cryogenic Engineering Conference(280)
Theobald, Stanley C.
ASM International(163)
Theriaque, CAP, Tia
National Health Care Anti-Fraud Association(516)
Theroit, Diane
National Academy of Recording Arts and Sciences(427)
Thevenot, Laura
American Society for Therapeutic Radiology and Oncology(133)
Thies, Kimberly D.
International Microwave Power Institute(379)
Thigpen, Yvonne E.
Evangelical Training Association(298)
Thill, Janet
International Association of Plastics Distributors(360)
Thoele, Regina G.
National Futures Association(513)
Thom, Kathy
Council on Diagnostic Imaging to the A.C.A.(275)
Thomas, Barbara L.
National Black MBA Association(484)
Thomas, Beth A.
International Concatenated Order of Hoo-Hoo(366)
Thomas, Beverly V.
National Independent Fire Alarm Distributors(519)
Thomas, Bret
National Catholic Educational Exhibitors(487)
Thomas, Dawn
National Association for Campus Activities(432)
Thomas, Greg
American Academy of Physician Assistants(27)
Thomas, J.J.
Black Retail Action Group(230)
Thomas, James A.
ASTM International(221)
Thomas, Karen
Independent Community Bankers of America(333)
Thomas, Karnel
United Telecom Council(679)
Thomas, Kathryn J.
International Order of the Golden Rule(381)
Thomas, Michael B.
Society for Economic Botany(616)
Thomas, Nancy
Consortium for Advanced Manufacturing International(262)
Thomas, Ralph D.
National Association of Investigative Specialists(459)
Thomas, Richard
American Anthropological Association(31)
Thomas, Robert
American Association of Clinical Endocrinologists(39)
Thomas, Robert D.
National Concrete Masonry Association(492)
Thomas, Rose Preuit
Society of Air Force Clinical Surgeons(629)
Thomas, Sandy
American Association of Textile Chemists and Colorists(53)
Thomas, Sandy
American North Country Cheviot Sheep Association(109)
Thomas, Shawna
National Meat Association(526)
Thomas, Sheri
Medical Marketing Association(416)
Thomas, Susan
Audit Bureau of Circulations(222)
Thomas, Tina
Association for the Advancement of Wound Care(180)
Thomas, William C.
Vision Council of America(684)
Thomasell, Jim
Association of Clinical Research Professionals(190)
Thomashower, James E.
American Guild of Organists(88)
Thomason, Robert T.
National Campus Ministries Association(486)
Thompson, Barbara J.
National Council of State Housing Agencies(500)
Thompson, Carl C.
Society of Government Meeting Professionals(637)
Thompson, Cheryl
National Head Start Association(516)
Thompson, Chris
Council for Advancement and Support of Education(267)
Thompson, Chuck
Cabletelevision Advertising Bureau(236)
Thompson, Cici
Employee Relocation Council/Worldwide ERC(293)
Thompson, Rev. Dr. Don
Association of Episcopal Colleges(195)
Thompson, Jr., Douglas H.
CPAmerica International(278)
Thompson, J.S. Bud
State Risk and Insurance Management Association(653)
Thompson, M.D., James N.
Federation of State Medical Boards of the United States(304)
Thompson, Jr., Joseph M.
Association for Hose and Accessories Distribution(174)
Independent Sealing Distributors(335)
Yacht Brokers Association of America(698)
Thompson, Judy
National Chimney Sweep Guild(489)
Thompson, Karen
International Association of Emergency Managers(356)
Thompson, Ph.D., Karen C.
Calorimetry Conference(237)
Thompson, Kathy
Visiting Nurse Associations of America(684)
Thompson, Kristin B.
Association for Hose and Accessories Distribution(174)
Independent Sealing Distributors(335)
Yacht Brokers Association of America(698)
Thompson, Lonna
Association of Public Television Stations(210)
Thompson, Jr., Louis M.
National Investor Relations Institute(522)
Thompson, Michael
Cosmetic, Toiletry and Fragrance Association(267)
Thompson, Nanice
American Society for Clinical Pathology(127)
Thompson, Otis N.
Organization of Professional Employees of the U.S. Department of Agriculture(567)
Thompson, Pamela
American Organization of Nurse Executives(110)
Thompson, Paul C.
United Transportation Union(679)
Thompson, Roger
Association of the United States Army(218)
Thompson, Ronda
Controlled Release Society(265)
Thompson, Thomas E.
International Council of Cruise Lines(367)
Thompson, Tom
United States Marine Safety Association(676)
Thomson, John
Spring Research Institute(652)
Thorn, Amy Z.
Distribution Business Management Association(286)
Thorner, John
National Recreation and Parks Association(535)

Thornhill, Alan
Society for Conservation Biology(615)
Thornton, Rob
International District Energy Association(369)
Thornton, CPCU, Ronald G.
Inland Marine Underwriters Association(339)
Thorsby, Lise
Association of Program Directors in Radiology(210)
Thorsby, Mark O.
International Carwash Association(364)
Thorson, Ingrid
Roller Skating Association International(602)
Thrasher, Fred
National Association for Law Placement(434)
Threndyle, Steve
North American Snowsports Journalists Association(560)
Thrift, Jim
Agricultural Retailers Association(12)
Thuermer, Kitty
National Association of Independent Schools(457)
Thumann, Albert
Association of Energy Engineers(195)
Thuriot, Nolty J.
National Ocean Industries Association(529)
Thurman, Charles E.
Electrical Manufacturing and Coil Winding Association(291)
Thurman, F. Anthony
American Guild of Organists(88)
Thurman, Kevin
Direct Marketing Insurance and Financial Services Council(285)
Tibbs, Drita
Biophysical Society(229)
Tibor, Marie
Greater Washington Board of Trade(320)
Tiekert, D.V.M., Carvel G.
American Holistic Veterinary Medical Association(91)
Tielborg, J. Patrick
Pipe Line Contractors Association(578)
Tiglio, Mike
National Association of Broadcast Employees and Technicians - Communications Workers of America(441)
Tigner, Robert
Association of Direct Response Fundraising Counsel(194)
Tilden, Flor
Society of Laparoendoscopic Surgeons(639)
Tiller, Michael
Compressed Gas Association(257)
Tilley, Linda
National Athletic Trainers' Association(482)
Tilli, Marcella
Car Care Council(237)
Tillipman, Harvey
Association of Jewish Aging Services(202)
Tillman, Bob
ARMA International(160)
Tillman, Wallace F.
National Rural Electric Cooperative Association(537)
Timmons, Debbie
Association of Clinical Research Professionals(190)
Timmons, Jay
National Association of Manufacturers(460)
Timmons, Richard F.
American Short Line and Regional Railroad Association(125)
Timmons, Tim
National Home Furnishings Association(517)
Timony, Margaret M.
Drug, Chemical and Associated Technologies Association(287)
Tinch, Jennifer
National Academy of Education(426)
Tingley, Staci
National Committee on Planned Giving(491)
Tinkle, Theresa
Society for Textual Scholarship(626)
Tinkleman, Alan
American Podiatric Medical Association(116)
Tipping, Jeff
National Soccer Coaches Association of America(540)
Tipton, Constance E.
International Dairy Foods Association(368)
International Ice Cream Association(375)
Milk Industry Foundation(419)
National Cheese Institute(488)
Tiras, CMP, Lynne K.
Society for Uroradiology(629)
Society of Gastrointestinal Radiologists(637)
Tirozzi, Gerald N.
National Association of Secondary School Principals(471)
Tischendorf, Todd J.
American Board of Medical Specialties(57)
Tittsworth, David G.
Investment Adviser Association(398)
Titus, C. Richard
Kitchen Cabinet Manufacturers Association(403)
Titus, Janet
Kitchen Cabinet Manufacturers Association(403)
Tjornechoj, Dan
American Academy of Clinical Neurophysiology(21)
Toaspern, John
National Potato Promotion Board(533)
Tobias, Karen
National Management Association(525)
Tobin, John
Design Management Institute(283)
Tobin, Lori
American College of Sports Medicine(70)
Tobin, Victoria
National Association of Professional Geriatric Care Managers(466)
Tobin, Ph.D., William J.
Access Technology Association(6)
American Association of Early Childhood Educators(42)
Todd, Brian L.
American Institute of Food Distribution(96)
Todd, Terri
North American Millers Association(558)
Toiv, Barry
Association of American Universities(185)
Tolbert, Terry
National Federation of Housing Counselors(509)
Tollerton, Kathy
American Society for Engineering Education(128)
Tolley, William R.
American Concrete Institute(72)
Tollison, Jr., Alfred C.
Institute of Nuclear Power Operations(343)
Tolman, S. Richard
National Corn Growers Association(496)
Tolpegin, Tanya
Professional Landscape Network(588)
Tolson, CAE, Pamela
American Association of Public Health Dentistry(50)
Tomlinson, Mark
Society of Manufacturing Engineers(639)
Tommone, Nanci Ann
Motion Picture and Television Credit Association(421)
Tomson, Tracy
Restaurant Facility Management Association(600)
Toner, H. Patrick
International Cast Polymer Association(364)
Toohey, Bill
American Road and Transportation Builders Association(123)
Tooker, M.D., MBA, FACP, John
American College of Physicians(69)
Topp, William
National Association of Sports Officials(472)
Torma, Carolyn
American Planning Association(116)
Torres, Alicia
American Institute of Physics(97)
Torres, Darlene R.
Association of Catholic TV and Radio Syndicators(189)
Torres, Joseph
National Association of Hispanic Journalists(455)
Torrey, Julia Krauss
Cargo Airline Association(238)
Toscas, James G.
Precast/Prestressed Concrete Institute(582)
Tosi, Gloria Cataneo
American Maritime Congress(103)
Toso, Octavia
Council of Residential Specialists(274)
Totenbier, Sally
American Dance Therapy Association(78)
Toth, Michael
Professional Beauty Association(586)
Touloumes, Kenneth
Association for Federal Information Resources Management(173)
Towers, Margaret
Association of Financial Guaranty Insurors(197)
Towle, John M.
Performance Warehouse Association(573)
Townley, John
National Defender Investigator Association(504)
Townsend, Leon
National Association of Neighborhoods(462)
Townsend, Linda
Association of Consulting Chemists and Chemical Engineers(192)
Towse, Yvonne
AVS Science and Technology Society(225)
Tozzi, Federico
Italy-America Chamber of Commerce(400)
Tozzoli, Guy F.
World Trade Centers Association(696)
Tracey, Adam
SWANA - Solid Waste Association of North America(656)
Tracey, CAE, Jack
National Automotive Finance Association(483)
Tracy, Alan
U.S. Wheat Associates(668)

Tracy, CMP, Cara
National Speakers Association(542)
Tracy, Karen K.
American Pharmacists Association(114)
Trainer, Ryan
International Sleep Products Association(386)
Tran, Carina
American Academy of Nursing(25)
Tran, Jennifer
International College of Surgeons(366)
Tranvankha, Paul
International Natural Sausage Casing Association(380)
Trautwein, Janet
National Association of Health Underwriters(455)
Travis, Allison
Society of Quality Assurance(643)
Travis, Dr. Joseph
American Society of Naturalists(142)
Travis, R.
Nuclear Suppliers Association(563)
Travis, Sheila
National Association of Certified Valuation Analysts(442)
Traweek, Lori S.
American Gas Association(86)
Traxler, Sallie
Association of College and University Housing Officers-International(191)
Traylor, Julie
National Association of College Stores(444)
Trebach, Susan
Council for Opportunity in Education(269)
Treichel, Janet M.
National Business Education Association(486)
Tremper Hanover, Lisa
Association of College and University Museums and Galleries(191)
Trenti, Nancy
National Association of Psychiatric Health Systems(467)
Trey, Liza
American Land Title Association(100)
Trinh, Didier-Kim Q.
Federal Managers Association(302)
Trinidad, Helen
National Hispanic Corporate Council(517)
Tripp, Jr., Raymond P.
Society for New Language Study(622)
Trisco, Rev. Robert
American Catholic Historical Association(61)
Trombino, CAE, C. James
APMI International(158)
Metal Powder Industries Federation(417)
Tromly, Karen
National Potato Promotion Board(533)
Troop, Michael
National Propane Gas Association(534)
Trope, Jim
Teachers of English to Speakers of Other Languages(658)
Trost, Teresa A.
United Methodist Association of Health and Welfare Ministries(671)
Trotz, Sheryl
American Society of Emergency Radiology(137)
Troup, Emile W.J.
Research Council on Structural Connections(600)
Trouten, Doug
Evangelical Press Association(298)
Troutman, Sandra
National Association of State Credit Union Supervisors(474)
Troy, Rev. Nancy K.
Presbyterian Health, Education and Welfare Association(583)
Trsar, Terence
Information Systems Audit and Control Association(338)
Truitt, Dr. Gordon E.
National Association of Pastoral Musicians(464)
Truitt, Jay
National Cattlemen's Beef Association(488)
Trujillo, Kayley
Mountain Rescue Association(422)
Trull, Frankie L.
National Association for Biomedical Research(431)
Trumbold, Carol
American Academy of Dermatology(21)
Trumbull, Melissa
National Association of State Emergency Medical Services Officials(475)
Trumka, Richard L.
American Federation of Labor and Congress of Industrial Organizations(82)
Truncale, CAE, Joseph P.
National Association for Printing Leadership(435)
Truncellito, Gene
American Arbitration Association(32)
Trust, David
Professional Photographers of America(588)
Truswell, Hallie
International College of Cranio-Mandibular Orthopedics(365)
Tryon, Sharon L.
Mathematical Association of America(414)
Tse, Kenneth
North American Saxophone Alliance(560)
Tseng, Sally C.
Chinese-American Librarians Association(245)
Tsirpanlis, Dr. Constantine N.
American Institute for Patristic and Byzantine Studies(94)
Tsuchiya, Paul
National Academy of Recording Arts and Sciences(427)
Tubbesing, Susan K.
Earthquake Engineering Research Institute(288)
Tuchman, Eric
American Arbitration Association(32)
Tuchman, Phyllis
International Association of Art Critics(353)
Tucker, Colleen McKenna
International Insurance Society(376)
Tucker, Dana
American Forage and Grassland Council(84)
Tucker, Deborah
National Association for Variable Annuities(437)
Tucker, Janet
Text and Academic Authors Association(659)
Tucker, Jim
International Association of Fairs and Expositions(356)
Tucker, Nanette
Water Environment Federation(685)
Tucker, Sonya
Reinsurance Association of America(598)
Tucker, Tracy
Chief Officers of State Library Agencies(244)
National Association of Government Defined Contribution Administrators(454)
Women Executives in State Government(691)
Tudryn, Joyce M.
International Radio and Television Society(384)
Tuff, Suzanne
International Association of Administrative Professionals(352)
Tuggle, Nora
American Society of Radiologic Technologists(145)
Tulipane, Barbara
Electronic Retailing Association(292)
Tulipane, CMP, Jean
Cosmetic, Toiletry and Fragrance Association(267)
Tull, Erin
National Fluid Power Association(511)
Tulloch, Thomas C.
North American Association of State and Provincial Lotteries(554)
Tully, Brian
Food Marketing Institute(309)
Tum-Suden, Robert J.
Financial Markets Association - USA(306)
Tumin, Zachary
Financial Services Technology Consortium(306)
Tuminello, Holly
Petroleum Marketers Association of America(574)
Tunis, Harry
National Council of Teachers of Mathematics(501)
Tunstall, Jr., Graydon A.
Phi Alpha Theta(575)
Tuohy, NCAC II, CCDC III, Cynthia Moreno
NAADAC -- the Association for Addiction Professionals(424)
Turek, Judi
Evangelical Church Library Association(298)
Turf, Ellen
National Association of Personal Financial Advisors(464)
Turner, Ph.D., CAE, Ann T.
American Association for Laboratory Animal Science(35)
Turner, Archie
National Academy of Sciences(427)
Turner, Barbara
American College of Physicians(69)
Turner, George
National Freight Transportation Association(512)
Turner, George D.
American Nuclear Insurers(109)
Turner, Julie A.
Plumbing-Heating-Cooling Contractors - National Association(579)
Turner, Kathleen
Association of American Medical Colleges(184)
Turner, Dr. Mark D.
National Economic Association(505)
Turner, CAE, Marsha L.
International Association of Lighting Designers(358)
Turner, Robin M.
National Association of Rehabilitation Providers and Agencies(469)
Turner, Seth
Association for Career and Technical Education(169)
Turner, CSE, Willis
Sales and Marketing Executives International(604)

Tutka, Richard
Electrical Apparatus Service Association(290)
Tuttle, Jr, CAE, Marvin W.
Financial Planning Association(306)
Tuuri, Rick
Inter-Industry Conference on Auto Collision Repair(346)
Twarog, Daniel
North American Die Casting Association(556)
Tweten, Linda
Scaffold Industry Association(605)
Twitty, Moira
American Academy of Cosmetic Surgery(21)
American Society of Lipo-Suction Surgery(140)
Twombly, Sean
American Political Science Association(116)
Tyckoson, Jr., E. Gilbert
American Railway Development Association(121)
Tyeryar, CAE, Clay D.
American Pipe Fittings Association(115)
American Textile Machinery Association(151)
Association of Suppliers to the Paper Industry(216)
Cold Finished Steel Bar Institute(250)
International Aviation Ground Support Association(362)
Tyle, Mark
American Massage Therapy Association(103)
Tyler, Humphrey S.
Cleaning Management Institute(247)
Tyler, MA, RN, Judith
National Student Nurses Association(544)
Tyme, Nadia
Association for Public Policy Analysis and Management(177)
Tyree, Ketti
Hardwood Plywood and Veneer Association(322)
Tyron, Barbara
Electric Power Research Institute(290)
Uackel, Robert
Association of Labor Relations Agencies(202)
Uarmecky, Stacy
Association for Iron and Steel Technology(175)
Ubl, Stephen J.
Advanced Medical Technology Association(8)
Uebel, Kathleen
American Academy of Dental Practice Administration(21)
Ugoretz, Mark J.
ERISA Industry Committee(297)
Uhlick, Lawrence R.
Institute of International Bankers(342)
Uhlig, Marylouise
Executive Women in Government(299)
Ullman, Eloise
Industry Council for Tangible Assets(337)
Ulrich, R.Ph., Susan
American College of Clinical Pharmacology(64)
Uncapher, Mark
Information Technology Association of America(338)
Underhill, Jr., Henry W.
International Municipal Lawyers Association(380)
Underwood, Cathy
American Pain Society(112)
Underwood, Karen
National Maritime Alliance(526)
Underwood, Terry Kay
International College of Applied Kinesiology(365)
Underwood, Tom
American Horticultural Society(91)
Unger, MSOLQ, Deborah
Wound, Ostomy and Continence Nurses Society(697)
Unger, Peter S.
American Association for Laboratory Accreditation(35)
Ungerer, Richard A.
American Montessori Society(106)
Unus, Iqbal
Association of Muslim Scientists and Engineers(205)
Upshaw, Gene
National Football League Players Association(511)
Upton, Richard D.
American Lighting Association(101)
Urbanowicz, Nancy
Academy of Management(4)
Urbaytis, Cindy
Institute for Supply Management(340)
Urch, Sharon
American College for Advancement in Medicine(63)
Urgena, Gina
Women in Packaging(692)
Usher, Cathy
Specialty Tool and Fastener Distributors Association(650)
Ussery, Joanne
Inter-America Travel Agents Society(346)
Utian, M.D., Ph.D, Wulf H.
North American Menopause Society(558)
Utterback, Lynda
National Ice Cream Retailers Association(518)
Vaccaro, Jack A.
Sales Association of the Paper Industry(604)
Vachon, Chris
Society of Professional Journalists(642)
Vaden-Williams, Sheila
National Association of Minority Automobile Dealers(462)
Vaeth, Dean
American Massage Therapy Association(103)
Vaidyanathan, Rajiv
Association for Consumer Research(171)
Valachovic, D.M.D., M.P.H, Richard W.
American Dental Education Association(78)
ValeCruz, Teresita T.
Council of the Great City Schools(275)
Valenta, Judy
Religious Conference Management Association(599)
Valente, Ph.D., CAE, Carmine M.
American Institute of Ultrasound in Medicine(98)
Valentine, H. Jeffrey
National Paralegal Association(531)
Valentine, Harold A.
Cooperative Work Experience Education Association(265)
Valentine, Heather
Council for Opportunity in Education(269)
Valenzuela, CAE, Pamela
Association for Women in Communications(182)
Valenzuela, Rudy
National Association of Hispanic Nurses(456)
Valeri, Gina
American Pet Products Manufacturers Association(114)
Valerio, Marcie
Automatic Meter Reading Association(223)
Valero, Rob
National Association of Real Estate Investment Trusts(468)
Vallaba, Marisa
Wallcoverings Association(685)
Valponi, Donna
American Academy of Family Physicians(22)
Valusek, Bill
American College of Chiropractic Orthopedists(64)
Valverde, Remal E.
International Weed Science Society(397)
Van Aken, Eddie
American Council of Independent Laboratories(75)
Van Alstyne, Stacy
International Foundation of Employee Benefit Plans(373)
Van Amborg, Kent
Gases and Welding Distributors Association(314)
Society for Cardiovascular Magnetic Resonance(614)
van Bleichert, Michelle
Society of Chemical Industry, American Section(633)
Van Coverden, Thomas
National Association of Community Health Centers(445)
Van Daniker, Relmond P.
Association of Government Accountants(199)
Van de Water, Jerome
Paperboard Packaging Council(571)
Van Den Berghe, Randall
Case Management Society of America(238)
Van Den Bussche, Ronald A.
American Society of Mammalogists(141)
Van Denmark, Kelly
Hearth Patio & Barbecue Association(324)
Van DeVelde, Gerry
Council of Insurance Agents and Brokers(272)
Van Dongen, Dirk
National Association of Wholesaler-Distributors(481)
Van Eaton, Susan
American Forest and Paper Association(85)
Van Heche, R.
Netherlands Chamber of Commerce in the United States(551)
Van Horn, Catherine
National Association of Pediatric Nurse Practitioners(464)
Van Horn, Charles
International Recording Media Association(384)
Van Loo, Bill
Marine Engineers Beneficial Association(412)
Van Meter, Elizabeth
National Association of State Chief Information Officers(474)
Van Norman, Mark
National Indian Gaming Association(519)
Van Ostrand, Andrew
Health Industry Distributors Association(323)
Van Petten, Vance
Producer's Guild of America(584)
Van Sickle, Bud
Lightning Protection Institute(408)
Van Zeeland, David
International Foundation of Employee Benefit Plans(373)
Vance, Audi
International Executive Housekeepers Association(371)

Vance, Beverly
American Mathematical Association of Two Year Colleges(103)
Vance, Buddy
American Agriculture Movement(30)
Vance, Jacqueline
American Medical Directors Association(104)
Vance, Melinda
Gamma Iota Sigma(313)
Vancko, Ellen P.
North American Electric Reliability Council(556)
VanDe Hei, Diane
Association of Metropolitan Water Agencies(204)
Vande Hey, J. Todd
American Medical Association(104)
Vandel, Robert H.
Flight Safety Foundation(308)
VandenBos, Gary R.
American Psychological Association(118)
Vanderbilt, Marjorie W.
American Association for Geriatric Psychiatry(35)
Vanderbilt, William
Computing Technology Industry Association(258)
Vanderhoof, Randy
Smart Card Alliance(611)
Vanderploeg, MD, MPH, James
American Board of Preventive Medicine(57)
Vanderstel, David G.
National Council on Public History(502)
Vanderwert, Wayne
American Gelbvieh Association(86)
VanderZalm, Jeannie
National Council of Examiners for Engineering and Surveying(499)
Vandeyar, David J.
National Fire Sprinkler Association(511)
VanDine, Michael
National Clay Pipe Institute(490)
VanDorn, Bonnie
Association of Science-Technology Centers(213)
Vanghel, James E.
National Association of Credit Management(448)
Vannice, Derek
Utility Arborist Association(681)
VanWert, Karen
Smocking Arts Guild of America(612)
Varadan, Vasu
Society of Engineering Science(635)
Varchione, Bob
National Association of Collegiate Marketing Administrators(445)
Vardabash, Krista
International Reciprocal Trade Association(384)
Vargas, Arturo
National Association of Latino Elected and Appointed Officials(459)
Vargas, Christina
PrintImage International(584)
Vargo, Franklin
National Association of Manufacturers(460)
Varner, Sarah C.
APICS - The Association for Operations Management(158)
Varroney, Daniel
Association for Corporate Growth(171)
Vary, George F.
American Zinc Association(156)
Vasek, Donald J.
Enterprise Wireless Alliance(295)
Vasquez, Sara
International Society for Magnetic Resonance in Medicine(387)
Vassallo, Barbara
National Apartment Association(430)
Vassilikos, Margaret
Newspaper Association of America(552)
Vastine, Jr., J. Robert
Coalition of Service Industries(249)
Vaughan, Byron
Soil and Plant Analysis Council(646)
Vaughan-Pratner, Judith
National Association of Commissions for Women(445)
Vaught-Kautz, Marcia
Society of Professional Audio Recording Services(642)
Vausht, Brian
American Soybean Association(148)
Veach, Kathie
Travel Adventure Cinema Society(665)
Veal, Steve
National Soccer Coaches Association of America(540)
Veale, Paula
Advertising Council(9)
Vecchione, Bob
National Association of Collegiate Directors of Athletics(444)
Veech, Barbara
National League of Postmasters of the U.S.(524)
Veeck, CAFS, Alan C.
National Air Filtration Association(428)
Veeck, Lisa
ISSA(400)
Velasco, Lynette
Black Americans in Publishing(230)
Venator, John A.
Computing Technology Industry Association(258)
Vencl, Nada
Association of Concert Bands(192)
Venetucci, Patricia
Women's Foodservice Forum(693)
Venit, Mark L.
Apparel Graphics Institute(159)
Ventrell, Marvin R.
National Association of Counsel for Children(446)
Ver Eecke, Wilfried
Association for Philosophy of the Unconscious(176)
Verberg, Kelly
American Staffing Association(149)
Verdegaal, Mary
International Licensing Industry Merchandisers' Association(378)
Vereen, David
Society of Cardiovascular Anesthesiologists(632)
Verhey, Karen
Society for College and University Planning(615)
Verhs, Kristin L.
American Zoo and Aquarium Association(156)
Vernazza, Gail
Association of African Studies Programs(183)
Vernon, Larry
Association for Educational Communications and Technology(172)
Verrone, Patric
Writers Guild of America, West(697)
Verville, Marge
United States Association for Computational Mechanics(673)
Vessely, Ed.D., Jeffery
Phi Epsilon Kappa(576)
Vetere, Bob
American Pet Products Manufacturers Association(114)
Veverka, Lauri
Society of Children's Book Writers and Illustrators(633)
Veziroglu, Ph.D., T. Nejat
International Association for Hydrogen Energy(350)
Viands, Michael
Organization for the Promotion and Advancement of Small Telecommunications Companies(567)
Vickers, Mary Susan
National Association of State Workforce Agencies(477)
Vickery, Antigone
Association of Schools of Public Health(213)
Victorson, USA (Ret.), Col. Mark
National Defense Transportation Association(504)
Viehland, Doug
Association of Collegiate Business Schools and Programs(191)
Vieiera, Isabel
Association of Medical Education and Research in Substance Abuse(204)
Vigilante, Richard
Association of Jesuit Colleges and Universities(202)
Vigilante, Theresa
Professional Women in Construction(590)
Villani, Joseph
National School Boards Association(538)
Villanueve, Jane Austin
Stuntwomen's Association of Motion Pictures(654)
Villata, Mark
North American Blueberry Council(555)
Vincent, CAE, Donald A.
Robotic Industries Association(602)
Vincent, Ph.D., Michael A.
American Society of Plant Taxonomists(144)
Vincerti, Dominique
Institute of Internal Auditors(342)
Vinci, Brian J.
Aquacultural Engineering Society(159)
Viniello, John A.
National Fire Sprinkler Association(511)
Vinson, Scott
National Council of Chain Restaurants(498)
Vipperman, Carol
Foundation for Russian-American Economic Cooperation(311)
Virnig, Sherid
National Conference of Editorial Writers(493)
Vis, Dr. Morgan L.
Phycological Society of America(577)
Visbal, Mark A.
Security Industry Association(607)
Visconti, Charles G.
International Cargo Gear Bureau(364)
Vise-Brown, Michele
National Institute for Animal Agriculture(520)
Vitti-Alexander, Maria Rosaria
American Association of Teachers of Italian(52)
Vittoria, Andy
AOC(158)

Vlasses, Peter H.
Accreditation Council for Pharmacy Education(6)
Vogel, Heidi
International Horn Society(375)
Vogel, Mark
Association for the Behavioral Sciences and Medical Education(180)
Vogel, Michael
Housing Education and Research Association(329)
Vogel, Toney
American Society of Human Genetics(139)
Vogt, Anna
Appraisal Institute(159)
Vogt, Gerry
American College of Trust and Estate Counsel(71)
Vohs, CAE, Maggie
Kite Trade Association International(403)
Voicheck, Kelly
Property Owners Association(591)
Voight, Gerald F.
American Concrete Pavement Association(72)
Voight, John
Solution Mining Research Institute(647)
Voigt, Marilyn
Association of Environmental and Resource Economists(195)
Voisine, Don
American Abstract Artists(19)
Volgy, Thomas J.
International Studies Association(393)
Volk, Kim E.
Delta Dental Plans Association(282)
Vollstadt, Theresa
International Society of Psychiatric-Mental Health Nurses(392)
Volpe, Angelo
National Wheel and Rim Association(549)
Voltmann, Robert
Transportation Intermediaries Association(664)
Von Leer, Evan
SWANA - Solid Waste Association of North America(656)
Von Wald, Dr. Kristin
Association for Experiential Education(172)
Voorhees, Heidi
Institute of Food Technologists(341)
Vorck, Fred
National Society of Compliance Professionals(541)
Vossburg, Don
National Association of the Remodeling Industry(479)
Votaw, Carmen Delgado
Alliance for Children and Families(15)
Vrabec, John M.
Financial and Security Products Association(305)
Vranas, CAE, Chris P.
American Association of Orthodontists(47)
Vroom, Jay J.
CropLife America(279)
Vroom, Peter
Truck Renting and Leasing Association(666)
Vroomen, Dr. Harry
Fertilizer Institute(305)
Vu, Kathie
Ladies Professional Golf Association(404)
Vukovljak, Lana
American Association of Diabetes Educators(42)
Vulliet, Ph.D., Richard
Catecholamine Club(239)
Waaser, Carol
Actors' Equity Association(8)
Wacht, Pete
National Court Reporters Association(503)
Wachter, Donna
Association of Professors of Gynecology and Obstetrics(209)
Wachtler, Janice
American College of Osteopathic Emergency Physicians(69)
Wachtler, William
Structural Insulated Panel Association(654)
Waddington, Maureen
Bicycle Product Suppliers Association(228)
Wade, Richard H.
American Hospital Association(92)
Wade, Sam
National Rural Water Association(538)
Wade, Stewart H.
American Bureau of Shipping(59)
Wade, Yvonne
Film and Bag Federation(305)
Wadham, Dana
National Association of Child Care Professionals(443)
Wadsworth, Harrison
Coalition of Higher Education Assistance Organizations(249)
Waegemann, C. Peter
Medical Records Institute(416)
Waff, William D.R.
Senior Army Reserve Commanders Association(609)
Wagaman, Terry R.
National Slag Association(540)
Wagner, Angela
Wireless Communications Association International(690)
Wagner, Elizabeth
National Association of Bond Lawyers(441)
Wagner, Ernie
Automotive Training Managers Council(224)
Wagner, Dr. Eugene
Association for Science Teacher Education(178)
Wagner, Louis E.
American Fiberboard Association(83)
Wagner, Peggy
Radiology Business Management Association(595)
Wagner, Polly
Associated Cooperage Industries of America(165)
Wagner, Rhonda
NACE International(424)
Wagner, Robin
Association of Otolaryngology Administrators(207)
Wagner, Tim
Power and Communication Contractors Association(582)
Wagner, Tony
Uniform and Textile Service Association(669)
Wagoner, Ralph
Lutheran Educational Conference of North America(409)
Wagus, Carl
American Architectural Manufacturers Association(32)
Wahler, Carol
Type Directors Club(667)
Wahler, Tracy
Futures Industry Association(313)
Wahlquist, Richard
American Staffing Association(149)
Waibel, Di
American Border Leicester Association(58)
Walch, Margaret
Color Association of the United States(252)
Waldron, Deanna
American Society of Interior Designers(140)
Waldron, Dillian
Human Resource Planning Society(329)
Walker, Bobbi
National Association of Charterboat Operators(442)
Walker, Dr. Charles
American Association of Christian Schools(39)
Walker, Charles
National Peach Council(532)
Walker, Daisy
Private Art Dealers Association(584)
Walker, Dana
National Board for Certified Counselors(485)
Walker, CAE, Dee Ann
American Board of Veterinary Practitioners(58)
American Veterinary Dental Society(153)
Walker, H.E. "Eddie"
Used Truck Association(681)
Walker, Jacki
American Counseling Association(76)
Walker, Janice
SPIE - The International Society for Optical Engineering(651)
Walker, Joseph L.
International Safety Equipment Association(385)
Walker, Julie A.
American Association of School Librarians(50)
Walker, LaKimba D.S.
National Black Caucus of State Legislators(484)
Walker, Lisa A.
International Imaging Industry Association(376)
Walker, Lisa J.
Education Writers Association(289)
Walker, Margaret
Council of Fleet Specialists(272)
Walker, Marjory
American Innerspring Manufacturers(93)
Walker, Norma
Council for Advancement and Support of Education(267)
Walker, Richard G.
American Architectural Manufacturers Association(32)
Walker, Robert
American Music Conference(107)
Walker, Robert
Uni-Bell PVC Pipe Association(669)
Walker, Sandra
Steel Founders' Society of America(653)
Walker, Sharon
Electrical Insulation Conference(291)
Walker, Suzanne
Society of Corporate Secretaries and Governance Professionals(634)
Walker, Tony
Corn Refiners Association(266)
Walker, Wendy
American Association for the Advancement of Slavic Studies(36)
Wall, Amanda
Council for Agricultural Science and Technology(268)

Wall, Dan
National Reining Horse Association(535)
Wall, Jack
Chester White Swine Record Association(244)
National Spotted Swine Record(543)
Poland China Record Association(579)
Wall, CAE, Martin A.
Association of Schools and Colleges of Optometry(213)
Wall, M.D., Michael
International Perimetric Society(382)
Wall Bush, Karen
Association for Women in Sports Media(182)
Wall-Becker, Leslie
International Society of Appraisers(390)
Wallace, Brian
Coin Laundry Association(250)
Wallace, Chuck
National Council of Examiners for Engineering and Surveying(499)
Wallace, Jr., Donald L.
Cotton Warehouse Association of America(267)
Wallace, Ellen N.
National Organization of Legal Services Workers(530)
Wallach, Louise
Air and Waste Management Association(12)
Waller, Jr., CAE, Robert
Juvenile Products Manufacturers Association(403)
Writing Instrument Manufacturers Association(697)
Wallington, Alta
American Society for Investigative Pathology(130)
Wallis, Ph.D., Norman E.
Academy of Psychosomatic Medicine(5)
American College of Foot and Ankle Orthopedics and Medicine(65)
American College of Radiation Oncology(70)
Walls, John
CTIA - The Wireless Association(280)
Walmer, Caren
American Association of Radon Scientists and Technologists(50)
Waloff, Harriet
Academy of Ambulatory Foot and Ankle Surgery(2)
Walpert, William C.
Brotherhood of Locomotive Engineers and Trainmen(233)
Walsh, Darin
American Association for Dental Research(34)
Walsh, Edward
American Society of Professional Estimators(145)
Walsh, Jack
National Alliance for Media Arts and Culture(429)
Walsh, Patricia
American Wholesale Booksellers Association(154)
Walsh, Susan
White House News Photographers Association(688)
Walter, Daniel G.
Associated Specialty Contractors(166)
National Electrical Contractors Association(506)
Walter, Diane
Financial Managers Society(306)
Walter, Judy
American Society of Health-System Pharmacists(139)
Walter, Muriel J.
Engine Manufacturers Association(295)
Walter, Tim
Association of Small Foundations(214)
Walter, Velva
National District Attorneys Association(505)
Walters, Darlene A.
American Institute of Physics(97)
Walters, Jon F.
International Brotherhood of Electrical Workers(363)
Walters, William
Acute Long Term Hospital Association(8)
Walz, Renee
Lignite Energy Council(408)
Wamsley, Herbert C.
Intellectual Property Owners Association(345)
Wanchisen, Ph.D., Barbara
Federation of Behavioral, Psychological and Cognitive Sciences(303)
Wanda, John
American Chiropractic Association(62)
Wang, M.D., H.H.
Chinese American Medical Society(245)
Wangman, CAE, Carl A.
Legal Marketing Association(407)
Wangman, Janice H.
Association for Corporate Growth(171)
Wanko, James
Wholesale Florist and Florist Supplier Association(688)
Warchot, Louis P.
Association of American Railroads(185)
Ward, Amelia
Association of Ecosystem Research Centers(194)
Ward, Carolyn
National Council of Investigation and Security Services(499)
Ward, David
American Council on Education(76)
Ward, Deborah
United States Association of Importers of Textiles and Apparel(673)
Ward, Jeff
National Middle School Association(527)
Ward, Kerry
Association for Library Trustees and Advocates(176)
Ward, Lee
Young Presidents' Organization(698)
Ward, Malene
Eye Bank Association of America(300)
Ward, Michael F.
Biomedical Marketing Association(229)
Ward, Sandy
National Athletic Trainers' Association(482)
Wardell, Dwight
American Society for Engineering Education(128)
Warden-Saunders, RN, Joan C.
National Association of Directors of Nursing Administration in Long Term Care(449)
Ware, Bill
National Association of Property Tax Representatives - Transportation, Energy, Communications(467)
Ware, Viveca
Independent Community Bankers of America(333)
Warfield, Gerald
Society of Composers(634)
Warfield, Timothy R.
National Association for State Community Services Programs(436)
Waring, Christopher
Association of Polysomnographic Technologists(208)
Warkentine, Dr. Barbara
American Institute of Fishery Research Biologists(96)
Warner, Ann Iona
American Institute of Parliamentarians(97)
Warner, Dave
National Pork Producers Council(533)
Warner, John
Association of Winery Suppliers(220)
Warner, Katy Moss
American Horticultural Society(91)
Warner, Michael
American Association of Diabetes Educators(42)
Warner, CAE, Stephen M.
Industrial Fabrics Association International(336)
Warren, Anne
American Academy of Forensic Sciences(23)
Warren, David L.
National Association of Independent Colleges and Universities(457)
Warren, III, Hugh
Catfish Farmers of America(239)
Warren, Jim
Fabricators and Manufacturers Association, International(300)
Warren, Willard
National Institute of Management Counsellors(521)
Warsinskey, Rick
National Council of Social Security Management Associations(500)
Wartenberg Kagan, Ph.D., Ute
American Numismatic Society(109)
Wartman, M.D., Ph.D, Steven A.
Association of Academic Health Centers(183)
Warwick, Peter D.
Society for Organic Petrology(623)
Warye, Kathy
Association for Professionals in Infection Control and Epidemiology(177)
Wasch, Kenneth A.
Software and Information Industry Association(646)
Wasdin, Lisa
Undersea and Hyperbaric Medical Society(669)
Washington, Jeff
American Correctional Association(74)
Washington, Lisa
Design-Build Institute of America(283)
Wasieleski, Carol
Cleaning Equipment Trade Association(247)
Waslawski, Pam
Fleischner Society(307)
Wasser, Daniel
International Ticketing Association(394)
Waszak, Angel
American College of Psychiatrists(70)
Watchinski, Robert I.
American Academy of Family Physicians(22)
Waters, Eva M.
Association of Racing Commissioners International(211)
Waters, Mary Piper
Telecommunications Industry Association(659)
Waters, Richard
American College of Chest Physicians(64)

Waters, Ron
Association of Progressive Rental Organizations(210)
Waters, Rosemarie
United Nations Staff Union(672)
Watkins, Julia M.
Council on Social Work Education(277)
Watkins, Lynn
National Association of Federally Impacted Schools(452)
Watkins, Roger
National Lincoln Sheep Breeders Association(525)
Watkins, Ruth
Fusion Power Associates(313)
Watland, Alice J.
American Telemedicine Association(151)
Watsey, Anna
National Association of Local Housing Finance Agencies(460)
Watson, Charlotte
American Society for Engineering Education(128)
Watson, David R.
Commercial Law League of America(253)
Watson, Donna
Missouri Fox Trotting Horse Breed Association(420)
Watson, Mark
Radiological Society of North America(594)
Watson, Mary Ellen
American Urogynecologic Society(153)
Watson, Michael S.
American College of Medical Genetics(67)
Watson, Susan
International Association of Dive Rescue Specialists(356)
Watts, Adrienne
National School Supply and Equipment Association(538)
Watts, George B.
National Chicken Council(489)
Waugh, Jan M.
Association of Legal Administrators(203)
Waxman, John R.
Maple Flooring Manufacturers Association(412)
Way, Ralph
International Association of Bomb Technicians and Investigators(354)
Wayne, Kirk
Tobacco Associates(662)
Weakley, James H. I.
Lake Carriers' Association(404)
Weatherford, Catherine J.
National Association of Insurance Commissioners(458)
Weatherhead, John
Associated Construction Publications(165)
Weaver, CMP, Brenda L.
American Geophysical Union(87)
Weaver, Brian L.
American Psychological Society(119)
Weaver, David A.
Mailing & Fulfillment Service Association(410)
Weaver, Jerrod A.
Non-Ferrous Founders' Society(553)
Weaver, Peggy
National Council of Teachers of English(501)
Webb, Dr. Adele
Association of Nurses in AIDS Care(206)
Webb, C. Edwin
American College of Clinical Pharmacy(65)
Webb, Christine
International Association of Career Consulting Firms(354)
Webb, Eddie
Black Theatre Network(231)
Webb, Glenda
Hotel Brokers International(329)
Webb, Jr., William H.
National Sporting Goods Association(543)
Webber, Deborah
Institute for Supply Management(340)
Webber, Frederick L.
Alliance of Automobile Manufacturers(16)
Weber, Bill
Association of Pool and Spa Professionals(208)
Weber, M.A., Cynthia W.
Association of Family Medicine Residency Directors(196)
Weber, Harold H.
Sulphur Institute, The(655)
Webster, Carol H.
National Association of Chapter 13 Trustees(442)
Webster, Duane
Association of Research Libraries(212)
Webster, Hugh
Packaging Machinery Manufacturers Institute(570)
Wechsler, Steven A.
National Association of Real Estate Investment Trusts(468)
Wedemeyer, Cara
Contract Services Association of America(264)
Weeks, David W.
Institute of Nuclear Power Operations(343)
Weerts, Richard
National Association of College Wind and Percussion Instructors(444)
Weglewski, ICPS, Donna
International Society of Crime Prevention Practitioners(391)
Wegmeyer, Harriet
Fertilizer Institute(305)
Wegrzyn, Susanne R.
National Club Association(490)
Wehner, Joan O'Hara
National Association of State Foresters(475)
Wehrman, Christine
American Rental Association(122)
Weickert, Brent
National Nutritional Foods Association(529)
Weidenheimer, Kimberlee
American Institute of Constructors(95)
Weidler, Joyce
American Skin Association(126)
Weidlich, Barbara V.
National Investment Company Service Association(522)
Weidner, III, M. Robert
Metal Service Center Institute(417)
Weiglein, Robert "Bob"
Wood Moulding and Millwork Producers Association(694)
Weil, Ph.D., FACHE, Peter
American College of Healthcare Executives(66)
Weiler, Paul
National Association of Federal Credit Unions(452)
Weimer, Jerry
Church Music Publishers Association(246)
Weinberg, CAE, Myrl
National Health Council(516)
Weindruch, Larry
National Sporting Goods Association(543)
Weiner, William
International Housewares Representatives Association(375)
Weingarten, Rick
American Library Association(101)
Weinraub, Ellen
National Investment Company Service Association(522)
Weinrobe, Peter
Union for Reform Judaism(670)
Weinshel, Kristy
United Telecom Council(679)
Weinstein, Ph.D., Debra
Society for Leukocyte Biology(621)
Weir, Jr., Henry S.
National Association of First Responders(452)
Weir, James M.
Giving Institute(317)
Paper Industry Management Association(571)
Weir, Tom
United Lightning Protection Association(671)
Weirs, Christopher
American Society of Addiction Medicine(133)
Weisenbach, Phil
Edison Welding Institute(289)
Weiser, Judy
International Phototherapy Association(383)
Weiser, Wendy J.
American Association of Clinical Urologists(40)
American College of Legal Medicine(66)
Society of University Urologists(645)
Weisman, Avril
Community Action Partnership(255)
Weiss, David N.
Writers Guild of America, West(697)
Weiss, Elissa
Professional Women Singers Association(590)
Weiss, Gerard
COLA(250)
Weiss, Jamie
Society of Children's Book Writers and Illustrators(633)
Weiss, Joan C.
Justice Research and Statistics Association(403)
Weiss, Karl E.
National Lead Burning Association(523)
Weiss, Nancy
TASH(657)
Weiss, Paul
National Foundation for Credit Counseling(512)
Weiss, Richard H.
National Grange(514)
Weiss, Suzanne M.
American Association of Homes and Services for the Aging(43)
Weissmann, Pat
American Association of Railroad Superintendents(50)
Weitzel, Cammie
World Floor Covering Association(695)
Weitzenfeld, JoAnn
Association for Manufacturing Excellence(176)
Welbon, Ph.D, Guy
American Institute of Bangladesh Studies(94)
Welborn, Brenda
Orthopaedic Research Society(568)
Welburn, Brenda L.
National Association of State Boards of Education(473)

Welch, Shannon
Employee Assistance Professionals Association(293)
Welch, Stephen J.
American College of Chest Physicians(64)
Welch, Teresa Foster
National Athletic Trainers' Association(482)
Welch, Thomas F.
National Insurance Crime Bureau(522)
Welch, Tiffany
Academy of Accounting Historians(2)
Welcome, Jerry
United Fresh Produce Association(671)
Weldon, Julie
Metal Construction Association(417)
Wellard, Charles
American Bakers Association(55)
Welle, Noreen
Radio-Television News Directors Association(594)
Weller, Jr., Paul S.
Apple Processors Association(159)
Wells, Byron R.
American Society for Eighteenth-Century Studies(128)
Wells, Earl
American Society of Crime Laboratory Directors(137)
Wells, Elaine
Association of Vision Science Librarians(220)
Wells, Elizabeth
Snack Food Association(612)
Wells, Elizabeth C.
International Downtown Association(369)
Wells, Janell
Council of Educational Facility Planners, International(271)
Wells, Ken
Offshore Marine Service Association(564)
Wells, Kennedy
Black Coaches Association(230)
Wells, Nikki
Society of Competitive Intelligence Professionals(633)
Wells, Paula D.
Labor and Employment Relations Association(404)
Welsh, Angela
Society for Investigative Dermatology(620)
Welsh, Tim
Associated Builders and Contractors(164)
Welte, RN, Kathy
National Marrow Donor Program(526)
Wendel, Jennifer
Roller Skating Association International(602)
Wenderski, Susan L.
National Sporting Goods Association(543)
Wendorf-Boyke, Debra
United States National Committee of the International Dairy Federation(676)
Wenger, Lisa
Association for Childhood Education International(169)
Wenhold, Dave
National Court Reporters Association(503)
Wenning, Thomas F.
National Grocers Association(515)
Wenther, Jay B.
American Association of Meat Processors(45)
Wentworth, Eryl
American Institute for Conservation of Historic and Artistic Works(93)
Wentworth, Liza
National Society of Compliance Professionals(541)
Wentworth, Randolph N.
Land Trust Alliance(405)
Wentz, Roger
American Traffic Safety Services Association(152)
Werlinich, Marci
Outdoor Advertising Association of America(569)
Werlinich, Tom
American College of Emergency Physicians(65)
Werner, Aviva
EMTA - Trade Association for the Emerging Markets(294)
Werts, D.D.S., Ramon
American Endodontic Society(81)
Wertz, Sheila
Construction Writers Association(263)
Wessel, Robert A.
Gypsum Association(321)
Wessels, Terry
Catholic Book Publishers Association(239)
West, Annie
Association of Occupational Health Professionals in Healthcare(206)
West, Barbara F.
National Association of Veterans' Research and Education Foundations(480)
West, Ford B.
Fertilizer Institute(305)
West, Jade
National Association of Wholesaler-Distributors(481)
West, James
Leading Jewelers Guild(406)
West, Lorraine J.
American Academy of Matrimonial Lawyers(24)
West, Sue
Catholic Academy for Communication Arts Professionals(239)
West-Evans, Kathy
Council of State Administrators of Vocational Rehabilitation(274)
Westaway, Maxine
International Alliance for Women(348)
Westbrook, Jerry
American Society for Engineering Management(128)
Wester, Suzanne
American Academy of Pediatric Dentistry(26)
Westerfield, Mary Lou
Actors' Equity Association(8)
Western, Chandra
National Community Development Association(491)
Western, Linda
National Fluid Power Association(511)
Westlake, James H.
American Truck Dealers(152)
Westman, David
Emergency Nurses Association(293)
Weston, Stacey
American Symphony Orchestra League(150)
Wetherby, Lisa
Society of Financial Service Professionals(636)
Wetter, M.D., Paul Alan
Society of Laparoendoscopic Surgeons(639)
Wetzel, Florence J.
RMA - The Risk Management Association(602)
Wexler, Chuck
Police Executive Research Forum(580)
Whalen, MBA, CAE, Kay A.
American Academy of Allergy, Asthma, and Immunology(20)
American Academy of Emergency Medicine(22)
Whalen, Matt
National Defender Investigator Association(504)
Whaley, Audra
Producer's Guild of America(584)
Wharton, Dennis
National Association of Broadcasters(441)
Whatley, John
Alliance of Automobile Manufacturers(16)
Whayne, Jeannie M.
Conference of Historical Journals(259)
Wheat, Tim
International Legal Fraternity of Phi Delta Phi(378)
Whedener, Jennifer
Design-Build Institute of America(283)
Wheeler, Adrienne
Society of Photographer and Artist Representatives(642)
Wheeler, Alonzo
National Federation of Independent Unions(509)
Wheeler, Bruce
International Society of Psychiatric-Mental Health Nurses(392)
Wheeler, Dave
Automotive Communication Council(223)
Wheeler, Eric L.
Association of Naval Aviation(205)
Wheeler, Ph.D., Gerald F.
National Science Teachers Association(539)
Wheeler, Leslie G.
Hearth Patio & Barbecue Association(324)
Wheeler, M. Cass
American Heart Association(90)
Wheeler, Richard M.
Elevator Industries Association(292)
Wheeler, Terri
National Coalition of Alternative Community Schools(490)
Wheeler, Victoria
Material Handling Industry of America(414)
Whelan, Daniel J.
Association of Professional Schools of International Affairs(209)
Whelan, Dr. Elizabeth
American Council on Science and Health(76)
Whelan, June M.
National Petrochemical & Refiners Association(532)
Whelchel, Sandy
Associated Business Writers of America(164)
National Writers Association(550)
Wherry, Gretchen
Association for Unmanned Vehicle Systems International(181)
Wherry, J. Jeffery
Cemented Carbide Producers Association(241)
Machine Knife Association(409)
Steel Door Institute(653)
Unified Abrasives Manufacturers Association(669)
Whidden, Glenn H.
Espionage Research Institute(297)
Whiston, Julie
White House Correspondents Association(688)
Whitaker, Betty
American Nurses Association(109)
Whitaker, Peggy
Country Music Association(277)

Whitby, Twyla N.
National Association of Negro Business and Professional Women's Clubs(462)

White, Andrew
North American Association of State and Provincial Lotteries(554)

White, Arthur L.
School Science and Mathematics Association(606)

White, JD, CAE, Cynthia
National Association of Retail Collection Attorneys(469)

White, Denny
ASIS International(163)

White, Eldon
Agriculture Council of America(12)
National Agri-Marketing Association(428)

White, Gregory
National Academy of Education(426)

White, Jr., Henry F.
American Bar Association(56)

White, Jerry L.
International Association of Conference Centers(355)

White, Joan
Video Electronics Standards Association(683)

White, John
Association for Computing Machinery(170)

White, John S.
Association of Alternate Postal Systems(184)

White, Johnny
Assisted Living Federation of America(164)

White, Kim
North American Equipment Dealers Association(556)

White, Leland
National Society of Professional Engineers(542)

White, Mary
Conference of State Bank Supervisors(260)

White, Patrick
Association of American Universities(185)

White, Richard
Automotive Aftermarket Industry Association(223)
Car Care Council(237)

White, Rob
World History Association(696)

White, Robert
National Electrical Contractors Association(506)

White, Jr., Robert C.
American Academy of Teachers of Singing(29)

White, Dr. Rosanne T.
Technology Student Association(658)

White, Sheila
World Association of Alcohol Beverage Industries(695)

White, Stephen
Delta Dental Plans Association(282)

White, Tim
National Ski Areas Association(540)

White, Tom
Interactive Audio Special Interest Group(346)
MIDI Manufacturers Association(418)

White Wu, Pamela
International Society of Certified Employee Benefit Specialists(390)

Whitebread, Alan
North American Small Business International Trade Educators(560)

Whitefield, Barbara
American Society of Radiologic Technologists(145)

Whitehead, Bruce
National Interscholastic Athletic Administrators Association(522)

Whitehead, Diane
National Head Start Association(516)

Whitehead, James R.
American College of Sports Medicine(70)

Whitehead, William C.
Plumbing and Drainage Institute(579)

Whitfield, Susan
National Council of Examiners for Engineering and Surveying(499)

Whiting, Richard M.
Financial Services Roundtable(306)

Whitley, Robert E.
United States Tour Operators Association(677)

Whitman, James A.
National Association of Chain Drug Stores(442)

Whitmer, Pattye
American Society of Cataract and Refractive Surgery(135)

Whitmore, Bob
National Precast Concrete Association(534)

Whitney, Fran
Association for Symbolic Logic(178)

Whitney, Hannah
American Association of State Highway and Transportation Officials(51)

Whitney, Melinda
Independent Liquid Terminals Association(334)

Whitsitt, William F.
Domestic Petroleum Council(286)

Whittemore, Ilsa
Hospitality Sales and Marketing Association International(329)

Whitten, Phil
College Swimming Coaches Association of America(252)

Whittington, Jenny
University Risk Management and Insurance Association(680)

Whitworth, Maria
Mobile Air Conditioning Society Worldwide(420)

Whyms, Robyn
National Council of Juvenile and Family Court Judges(499)

Whyte, CAE, CFCI, Bonnie B.
Association for Women in Management(182)
Employers Council on Flexible Compensation(293)

Wible, Robert C.
National Conference of States on Building Codes and Standards(494)

Wible, Tori Jo
American Prepaid Legal Services Institute(117)

Wickham, Kate
American Society for Healthcare Engineering(129)

Wicklund, Carl
American Probation and Parole Association(117)

Wickman, Bryan
Association for Direct Instruction(171)

Wicks, Stephanie J.
American School Counselor Association(124)

Wickwire, Ph.D., Pat Nellor
American Association for Career Education(34)

Widing, Jessica
Association of Oncology Social Work(206)

Widmer, Janet M.
Congress of Lung Association Staffs(261)

Wiegand, Douglas
Resilient Floor Covering Institute(600)

Wiegand, Wayne
Beta Phi Mu(228)

Wiegerink, Robin
American Society of Echocardiography(137)

Wiemer-Hastings, Katja
Society for Computers in Psychology(615)

Wiener, Robin K.
Institute of Scrap Recycling Industries(343)

Wiens, Dr. Jonathan
Academy of Prosthodontics(5)

Wiermanski, David
Healthcare Leadership Council(324)

Wierzynski, Barbara
Futures Industry Association(313)

Wiesenmaier, Hubert
American Import Shippers Association(93)

Wieting, Mark W.
American Academy of Orthopaedic Surgeons(26)

Wightman, Donald E.
Utility Workers Union of America(681)

Wiitala, Janice
Healthcare Financial Management Association(324)

Wilber, Kathryn
American Benefits Council(56)

Wilcox, Alison
American Society of Newspaper Editors(142)

Wilcox, Jenifer
American Society of Interior Designers(140)

Wilcox, Kevin
American Society of Newspaper Editors(142)

Wilcox, III, Thomas R.
Society of Cable Telecommunications Engineers(632)

Wilde, Cathy
SWANA - Solid Waste Association of North America(656)

Wilder, Margaret
Urban Affairs Association(680)

Wilding, Holly L.
National Organization of Life and Health Insurance Guaranty Associations(530)

Wiles, Harry
American Beverage Licensees(57)

Wiley, Birne
Association of North American Missions(205)

Wiley, Douglas S.
National Association of Broadcasters(441)

Wilhilde, Peggy
Association of American Railroads(185)

Wilhout, Gene
Council of Chief State School Officers(271)

Wilk, P.Eng, CSSP, Robert J.
International Association for Computer Systems Security(349)

Wilkerson, Dean
American College of Emergency Physicians(65)

Wilkerson, Linda
International Academy of Trial Lawyers(348)

Wilkerson, Richard
Association for the Study of Dreams(180)

Wilkes, Ann
Snack Food Association(612)

Wilkins, Ronnie
American College of Neuropsychopharmacology(68)

Wilkinson, M.D., Charles P.
American Ophthalmological Society(110)

Wilkinson, Drane
National Alliance of Preservation Commissions(430)

Wilkinson, Earl
International Newspaper Marketing Association(381)

Wilkinson, Stephen
International Lead Zinc Research Organization(377)

Willard, Zane
Mohair Council of America(421)

Willburn, Jerry
International Brotherhood of Boilermakers, Iron Ship Builders, Blacksmiths, Forgers and Helpers(363)

Willer, Dr. Rick
United States Animal Health Association(672)

Willett, Teresa G.
American Association of Language Specialists(44)

Williams, Amy
American Association for Aerosol Research(33)
International Pediatric Transplant Association(382)

Williams, Ph.D., Asha
Society of Financial Service Professionals(636)

Williams, Ashley
Self Insurance Institute of America, Inc.(608)

Williams, Bob
National Collegiate Athletic Association(491)

Williams, Brenda A.
Conference of Chief Justices(259)

Williams, C. Fred
Agricultural History Society(12)

Williams, Jr., C.E.
Textile Fibers and By-Products Association(660)

Williams, Carol A.
Aluminum Association(18)

Williams, Ph.D., CAE, Cathlene
Association of Fundraising Professionals(198)

Williams, David L.
Conference of Business Economists(259)
United States Association for Energy Economics(673)

Williams, Deanne
American College of Nurse-Midwives(68)

Williams, Ph.D., Dennis E.
North American Association of Professors of Christian Education(554)

Williams, Don
International Shooting Coaches Association(386)

Williams, Fred
Association for Education in Journalism and Mass Communication(172)

Williams, Jackie
National Council of Acoustical Consultants(498)

Williams, James A.
International Union of Painters and Allied Trades(396)

Williams, Jr., James W.
Governmental Research Association(319)

Williams, Jennifer
Passenger Vessel Association(572)

Williams, Jimmy C.
Parthenais Cattle Breeders Association of America(571)

Williams, John
Independent Automotive Damage Appraisers Association(333)

Williams, Joseph
American Arbitration Association(32)

Williams, Karen
Professional Association of Health Care Office Management(586)

Williams, Karen
National Pharmaceutical Council(533)

Williams, Kelly
Community Development Venture Capital Alliance(256)

Williams, Kenneth
Printing Industries of America(584)

Williams, Kimberly
American College of Nurse Practitioners(68)

Williams, Laura
Council of State Governments(275)

Williams, Len
American Logistics Association(102)

Williams, Linda
American Society of Consultant Pharmacists(136)

Williams, Lyle
National Subacute and Postacute Care Association(544)

Williams, MT, Mary
Association for Molecular Pathology(176)

Williams, Michael
Recording Industry Association of America(596)

Williams, Michael
Coalition of Black Trade Unionists(249)

Williams, Michael C.
North American Equipment Dealers Association(556)

Williams, Nancy
National Association of Boards of Examiners of Long Term Care Administrators(440)

Williams, CAE, Pamela
Cable and Telecommunications Human Resources Association(236)

Williams, Pamela C.
Teachers of English to Speakers of Other Languages(658)

Williams, Paul
Assisted Living Federation of America(164)

Williams, Paul C.
National Association of Independent Publishers Representatives(457)

Williams, Robert G.
Association of United States Night Vision Manufacturers(219)

Williams, Rodney
International Association of Assembly Managers(353)

Williams, Roger J.
Accrediting Council for Continuing Education and Training(7)

Williams, M.D., Roger L.
United States Pharmacopeia(676)

Williams, Ryan
National Association of Black Journalists(440)

Williams, M.D., Sterling
American College of Obstetricians and Gynecologists(68)

Williams, Steven A.
Wildlife Management Institute(689)

Williams, Susan
National Utility Contractors Association(548)

Williams, Timothy S.
Water Environment Federation(685)

Williams, Vanessa R.
National Conference of Black Mayors(492)

Williams, III, M.D., William C.
American Association of Integrated Healthcare Delivery Systems(44)
American Association of Managed Care Nurses(44)
American College of Managed Care Medicine(67)
National Association of Managed Care Physicians(460)

Williams, Willie B.
National Technical Association(545)

Williams, Willie S.
Association of Black Psychologists(187)

Williamson, CAE, Carolyn
University Aviation Association(679)

Williamson, Cheryle
Express Carriers Association(300)

Williamson, Da Keia
Tax Executives Institute(657)

Williamson, Darla
Closure Manufacturers Association(248)

Williamson, Jeffrey
American Medical Informatics Association(104)

Williamson, CAE, John
North American Interfraternity Conference(557)

Williamson, Kent D.
Conference on College Composition and Communication(260)
Conference on English Education(260)
Conference on English Leadership(260)
National Council of Teachers of English(501)

Williamson, Sandy
National Soccer Coaches Association of America(540)

Willingham, Christal
National Family Caregivers Association(508)

Willis, Anita
ARMA International(160)

Willis, Max
International Association of Fairs and Expositions(356)

Willis, Tom
National Council for Community Behavioral Healthcare(497)

Wills, Jean M.
American Oil Chemists' Society(110)

Willson, Danae Loran
Association of Professional Design Firms(208)

Willson, Peters D.
National Association of Children's Hospitals(443)

Wilson, Angie
Automotive Service Association(224)

Wilson, Bascombe J.
Disaster Preparedness and Emergency Response Association(285)

Wilson, Brie
National Turkey Federation(548)

Wilson, Bruce A.
Physician Insurers Association of America(577)

Wilson, Carolyn
National Asphalt Pavement Association(431)

Wilson, Catherine
National Council of Farmer Cooperatives(499)

Wilson, Charles J.
Industrial Fasteners Institute(337)

Wilson, Christine
Employee Relocation Council/Worldwide ERC(293)

Wilson, Chuck
National Systems Contractors Association(545)

Wilson, Connie
Ladies Professional Golf Association(404)

Wilson, Dana
Child Welfare League of America(244)

Wilson, David A.
Graduate Management Admission Council(319)

Wilson, Denise DeLosada
American Association for Pediatric Ophthalmology and Strabismus(36)

Wilson, Don
Association of Small Business Development Centers(214)

Wilson, Erin
National Association for Campus Activities(432)
Wilson, George M.
Conference on Asian History(260)
Wilson, Glenda K.
Black Coaches Association(230)
Wilson, James
National Association of Blacks In Government(440)
Wilson, Janet
American Academy of Emergency Medicine(22)
Wilson, Jennifer
National Medical Association(526)
Wilson, Jennifer Joy
National Stone, Sand and Gravel Association(543)
Wilson, John I.
National Education Association(506)
Wilson, Julie
International Spa Association(392)
Wilson, Ken
NAMM - the International Music Products Association(425)
Wilson, Kerry
National Association of Flood and Stormwater Management Agencies(453)
Wilson, Kevin
American Society for Cell Biology(127)
Wilson, LeAnn
Association for Career and Technical Education(169)
Wilson, LeeAnne
National Association of Manufacturers(460)
Wilson, Linda
American Association of Family and Consumer Sciences(43)
Wilson, Lorna Johnston
Energy Bar Association(294)
Wilson, Lorraine
National Education Association(506)
Wilson, Lynn C.
Association of Consulting Foresters of America(192)
Wilson, Marci
American Cheese Society(61)
Wilson, Michael
International Foundation of Employee Benefit Plans(373)
Wilson, Michael E.
Textile Rental Services Association of America(660)
Wilson, Michael J.
United Food and Commercial Workers International Union(671)
Wilson, MD, MHP, Modena H.
American Medical Association(104)
Wilson, Pamela
International Society for Minimally-Invasive Cardiac Surgery(387)
Society for Clinical Vascular Surgery(615)
Wilson, Roger G.
Blue Cross and Blue Shield Association(231)
Wilson, Ron
North American Association of Educational Negotiators(554)
Wilson, Tyler J.
American Orthotic and Prosthetic Association(111)
Wilson, Wendy
International Association of Women Police(362)
Wilt, Charles
Association for Library Collections and Technical Services(175)
Wilton, Frank S.
Advanced Medical Technology Association(8)
Wiltraut, Douglas
National Society of Painters in Casein and Acrylic(542)
Wiltshire, Sara
National Air Duct Cleaners Association(428)
Winans, Charles A.
National Association of Concessionaires(445)
Winch, Jesse
American Society for Photogrammetry and Remote Sensing(131)
Winchester, Nancy
American Society of Plant Biologists(144)
Winckler, Susan C.
American Pharmacists Association(114)
Windecker, Geri
National Association of Casino and Theme Party Operators(441)
Windsor, Dave
Association of Natural Resource Enforcement Trainers(205)
Wing, Lori
Potato Association of America(581)
Wingate-Bey, Sandra
American Society for Engineering Education(128)
Winge, Carol
North American Lake Management Society(557)
Winkelmann, John Paul
National Catholic Pharmacists Guild of the United States(488)
Winn, CMP, Michelle
Association of Osteopathic State Executive Directors(206)
Winslow, Bill
International Sign Association(386)
Winston, Andrew
Cheiron: The International Society for the History of Behavioral and Social Sciences(243)
Winston, James
National Association of Black-Owned Broadcasters(440)
Winter, Cynthia
National Council on Family Relations(502)
Winter, Delorise A.
Cotton Council International(267)
Winter, Eleanor
National Cable & Telecommunications Association(486)
Winterbottom, Michael
General Merchandise Distributors Council(315)
Winters, Pat
Society for Maintenance Reliability Professionals(621)
Winters, CAE, Patrick E.
National Risk Retention Association(537)
Winters, Ted
North American Elk Breeders Association(556)
Winton, David L.
Association of Proposal Management Professionals(210)
Winton, Peggy
Association for Information and Image Management International(174)
Wirth, Lawrence R.
American Council of Learned Societies(75)
Wirth, Leon C.
CBA(240)
Wise, Susan L.
National Council of Architectural Registration Boards(498)
Wisel, Lee Marie
Association of Seventh-Day Adventist Librarians(213)
Wiseman, Gail
Institute of Food Technologists(341)
Wisniewski, Joe
Clinical Laboratory Management Association(248)
Witham, Pamela B.
Contact Lens Manufacturers Association(264)
Withers, Barbara
National Association of Institutional Linen Management(458)
Witkowski, Corrina Ross
Military Operations Research Society(419)
Witt, James Lee
International Code Council(365)
Wittenberg, Hope
Society of Teachers of Family Medicine(644)
Wittenborn, John
Leather Industries of America(407)
Wittich, Karin
American Association of Oral and Maxillofacial Surgeons(47)
Wittner, Ann M.
American Osteopathic Association(111)
Witty, Nancy
Society of Vertebrate Paleontology(646)
Wixson, Bobby
Society for Environmental Geochemistry and Health(617)
Wlazlowski, Tiffany
American Trucking Associations(152)
Wlezien, Peggy
Cervical Spine Research Society(242)
Wnuk, Steve R.
American Society for Quality(132)
Wobbekind, Richard
Association for University Business and Economic Research(181)
Woelfer, Jr., Justin
National Tile Contractors Association(546)
Woerth, Capt. Duane E.
Air Line Pilots Association, International(13)
Wogsland, Dan
United States Durum Growers Association(675)
Wojdyla, Karen
Air & Surface Transport Nurses Association(12)
National Hearing Conservation Association(516)
Wojtaszek, MeriBeth
SWANA - Solid Waste Association of North America(656)
Wojtkiclo, Tina
Manufacturing Jewelers and Suppliers of America(411)
Wold, Ben
National Marine Manufacturers Association(526)
Wolf, Christina
North American Spine Society(561)
Wolf, Craig
Wine and Spirits Wholesalers of America(689)
Wolf, Jonathan
Independent Film and Television Alliance(334)
Wolf, Laura J.
Engineering in Medicine and Biology Society(295)
Wolf, Sandra DeVincent
Materials Research Society(414)
Wolfe, CAE, Frank I.
Hospitality Financial and Technology Professionals(328)

Wolfe, Mark
National Energy Assistance Directors Association(507)
Wolfe, Mary Ann
Society of Scribes(644)
Wolfe, Patricia
Federally Employed Women(302)
Wolfe, Sheemon
International Association of Audio Visual Communicators(353)
Wolfe, Steve
National Coffee Association of the U.S.A.(490)
Wolfe, William A.
Steel Tube Institute of North America(654)
Wolff, P.E., Dr. Robert D.
Society of American Military Engineers(631)
Wolfsohn, Tom
American Association of Motor Vehicle Administrators(45)
Wolfsohn, Venlo J.
International Truck Parts Association(395)
Wolfson, Stanley M.
American Society of Plumbing Engineers(144)
Wolk, Sue
National Court Reporters Association(503)
Wolkoff, Neal L.
American Stock Exchange(149)
Wollan, PhD, PHR, Melody
Institute of Behavioral and Applied Management(340)
Wolley, Iris
Online Audiovisual Catalogers(565)
Wolters, John
Christian Schools International(246)
Womack, Dr. James E.
American Genetic Association(86)
Wommack, Jaime
American Psychotherapy Association(119)
Wong, Cindy
International Ticketing Association(394)
Wong, Eddie
Council on Social Work Education(277)
Wong, Richard
American School Counselor Association(124)
Wong, BS, CAE, Susan
National Student Nurses Association(544)
Wood, Beverly
Association of Cinema and Video Laboratories(190)
Wood, Britt
Retail Industry Leaders Association(601)
Wood, CMD, Cindy
American Association of Nurse Anesthetists(46)
Wood, Dan
National Christian College Athletic Association(489)
Wood, Doris
Multi-Level Marketing International Association(422)
Wood, D.O., Ph.D, Douglas L.
American Association of Colleges of Osteopathic Medicine(40)
Wood, Henry
Association for Experiential Education(172)
Wood, James
International Alliance of Theatrical Stage Employees and Moving Picture Technicians of the U.S., Its Territories and Canada(348)
Wood, Janet
National Electronic Distributors Association(506)
Wood, Joel
Council of Insurance Agents and Brokers(272)
Wood, Kelly
National Christian College Athletic Association(489)
Wood, Lauren
American Student Dental Association(149)
Wood, Trinlie
Midwives Alliance of North America(419)
Wood, Virginia Steele
North American Society for Oceanic History(560)
Woodbury, David
American Society of Naval Engineers(142)
Wooden, CHFM, SASHE, Dale
American Society for Healthcare Engineering(129)
Woodley, Joe
United Association of Equipment Leasing(670)
Woodring, D.Div., DeWayne S.
Religious Conference Management Association(599)
Woodring, Donna
Religious Conference Management Association(599)
Woods, Anne
Sommelier Society of America(647)
Woods, Dana
American Association of Critical-Care Nurses(41)
Woods, David F.
National Association of Insurance and Financial Advisors(458)
Woods, James
Steel Recycling Institute(653)
Woods, Michele
SEPM - Society for Sedimentary Geology(609)
Woods, Ph.D., S. Miles
National Association of Black Professors(440)
Woods, T.L.
Accountants for the Public Interest(6)
Woodward, Barbara
Building Service Contractors Association International(234)
Woodward, Michael
American Association of Physicists in Medicine(48)
Woodward, Risa
American Association for State and Local History(36)
Wooley, Ph.D., CHES, Susan
American School Health Association(124)
Woollen, Marcus
Van Alen Institute(682)
Woolley, Leslie
Conference of State Bank Supervisors(260)
Wooten, Kawania
American Chamber of Commerce Executives(61)
Wooten, Ken
Ladies Professional Golf Association(404)
Workman, James
Graphic Arts Technical Foundation(319)
Workman, Mark E.
National Council of Teachers of Mathematics(501)
Workman, Sherry
National Association of Child Care Professionals(443)
Worth, Brian
Independent Electrical Contractors(334)
Worth, FSMPS, Ronald
Professional Services Management Association(589)
Society for Marketing Professional Services(621)
Worthington, Barry K.
United States Energy Association(675)
Worthington, Carol
American Academy of Facial Plastic and Reconstructive Surgery(22)
Wott, John A.
International Plant Propagators Society(383)
Wowchuk, Harry
Stuntmen's Association of Motion Pictures(654)
Wray, David L.
Profit Sharing/401(k) Council of America(590)
Wright, Daphne
American Professional Society on the Abuse of Children(117)
Wright, David
Aircraft Owners and Pilots Association(14)
Wright, Dennis
Soaring Society of America(612)
Wright, Don K.
International Public Relations Association - U.S. Section(384)
Wright, Dr. Frank
National Religious Broadcasters(536)
Wright, Gladys Stone
Women Band Directors International(690)
Wright, Gretchen
Association of Women's Health, Obstetric and Neonatal Nurses(220)
Wright, Janet
Professional Insurance Communicators of America(587)
Wright, Jo Elyn Wakefield
National Opera Association(529)
Wright, Karen
Financial Management Association International(306)
Wright, Mark
National Association of Boards of Examiners of Long Term Care Administrators(440)
Wright, Paul R.
American Medical Student Association(105)
Wright, Raymond
Independent Professional Representatives Organization(335)
Wright, Robert E.
Petroleum Investor Relations Association(574)
Wright, Rosa
National Small Business Association(540)
Wright, Ted
National Association of Pipe Fabricators(464)
Wright, Victoria
National Indian Gaming Association(519)
Wroblewski, Carolyn R.
Electrochemical Society(291)
Wuertz, Karen
National Futures Association(513)
Wulf, Ph.D., William A.
National Academy of Engineering of the United States of America(426)
Wulster-Radcliffe, Meghan C.
American Society of Animal Science(134)
Wyche, Chris
National Soccer Coaches Association of America(540)
Wykle, USA (Ret.), Lt. Gen. Kenneth R.
National Defense Transportation Association(504)
Wylie, USN(Ret.), Capt. Peter C.
Military Officers Association of America(419)
Wyman, Eben
National Utility Contractors Association(548)

Wynbrandt, Robert A.
Society of Thoracic Surgeons(645)
Wynn, Geoff
American Association of Clinical Endocrinologists(39)
Wynne, Brian
Electric Drive Transportation Association(290)
Wysocki, Allen
Food Distribution Research Society(309)
Wysocki, Patricia
Specialized Information Publishers Association(650)
Wysocki, Susan
National Association of Nurse Practitioners in Women's Health(463)
Wyss, Dianne
National Indian Gaming Association(519)
Yablonski, Cynthia A.
The Protein Society(591)
Yacker, Marc
Electricity Consumers Resource Council(291)
Yadao, M.D., Alex P.
American College of International Physicians(66)
Yager, Milan P.
National Association of Professional Employer Organizations(466)
Yamashiro, Jennifer
Society for Photographic Education(623)
Yandle, Oliver
International Association of Defense Counsel(356)
Yanes, Richard P.
Clinical Social Work Federation(248)
Yang, Felix
Advertising Research Foundation(9)
Yanikoski, Richard
Association of Catholic Colleges and Universities(188)
Yankus, Bill
International Association for Insurance Law - United States Chapter(350)
Yannelis, Nicholas
Society for the Advancement of Economic Theory(626)
Yanson, Matt
Quarters Furniture Manufacturers Association(594)
Yarwood, Bruce
American Health Care Association(89)
Yates, Dan
Ground Water Protection Council(320)
Yates, Rita J.
American Academy of Podiatric Sports Medicine(27)
Yatskievych, Dr. George
American Fern Society(83)
Yeager, Barbara
National Committee on Planned Giving(491)
Yeager, Don M.
Gelbray International(315)
Yearout, Dottie
National Association of Basketball Coaches(439)
Yearsley, David
International Memorialization Supply Association(379)
Yearwood, Patricia
American Society for Public Administration(132)
Yeaton, Dr. George
American Crossbred Pony Registry(77)
Yeh, Christine
Life Insurers Council(407)
Yeninas, Barbara Spector
Containerization and Intermodal Institute(264)
Yeo, CPA, BBA, William E.
American Association of Nurse Anesthetists(46)
Yep, Richard
American Counseling Association(76)
Yerger, Ann
Council of Institutional Investors(272)
Yeske, Ph.D., Ronald
National Council for Air and Stream Improvement(497)
Yess, Mary E.
Electrochemical Society(291)
Yetzer, Von
American Academy of Medical Administrators(24)
American College of Cardiovascular Administrators(64)
Yilmaz, CPA, MBA, Ece
American College of Nutrition(68)
Yingling, Edward L.
American Bankers Association(55)
Yingst, Richard A.
Financial Managers Society(306)
Yoder, Susan E.
American Association of Neuromuscular & Electrodiagnostic Medicine(46)
Yoes, Patrick
National Fraternal Order of Police(512)
Yoffie, Rabbi Eric H.
Union for Reform Judaism(670)
York, Deborah
Association for Library and Information Science Education(175)
Yoshikane, Pauleen
Fresh Produce and Floral Council(312)
Yost, MBA, Sandra L.
American Academy of Disability Evaluating Physicians(22)
Young, Charlene E.
American Water Resources Association(154)
Young, Chris
National Registry of Environmental Professionals(535)
State Debt Management Network(652)
Young, Dave
National Defender Investigator Association(504)
Young, David
Bituminous Coal Operators Association(229)
Young, Donald A.
International Facility Management Association(371)
Young, Joanne W.
International Aviation Womens Association(362)
Young, Mark
ATP(221)
Young, Michelle D.
University Council for Educational Administration(679)
Young, Penny L.
Plumbing-Heating-Cooling Contractors - National Association(579)
Young, Ph.D., Richard A.
National Registry of Environmental Professionals(535)
Young, S.
National Association of Physician Nurses(464)
Young, Steven
Association of Independent Corrugated Converters(200)
Young, Susan
Association of Executive and Administrative Professionals(196)
Young, Taiia Smart
Girls Incorporated(317)
Young, William H.
National Association of Letter Carriers(460)
Youngberg, Phyllis
National Association of Hospital Hospitality Houses(456)
Youngblood, James H.
Heart Rhythm Society(324)
Ysais, David
National Broadcast Association for Community Affairs(485)
Yu, Pauline
American Council of Learned Societies(75)
Yungmann, George
National Association of Real Estate Investment Trusts(468)
Yunich, Rob
National Small Business Association(540)
Yusif, CAE, I.F.
American Mideast Business Associates(106)
Yuska, Charles D.
Packaging Machinery Manufacturers Institute(570)
Zaborowski, Robert
Flexible Packaging Association(307)
Zacharias, Ken
National Paint and Coatings Association(531)
Zacharilla, Louis
Society of Satellite Professionals International(644)
World Teleport Association(696)
Zack, Jeff
International Association of Fire Fighters(357)
Zaczek, Judy
Association of Physician Assistants in Obstetrics and Gynecology(208)
Zaglanicszny, Larry
National Association of Student Financial Aid Administrators(477)
Zaharatos, Julie
American Geriatrics Society(87)
Zahory, Robin Burke
Women in Cable and Telecommunications(691)
Zahra, Robert
National Association of Executive Recruiters(451)
Zajc, John
Society for American Baseball Research(613)
Zando, Kate
Adhesive and Sealant Council(8)
Zapanta, Albert
United States-Mexico Chamber of Commerce(678)
Zapf, Donna
Association of Graduate Liberal Studies Programs(199)
Zappala, Fern
American Society of Health-System Pharmacists(139)
Zappone, Toni
American Society of Ocularists(143)
Zaro, PhD, Joan
Endocrine Society(294)
Zarski, Mike
American Osteopathic Association(111)
Zaterman, Sunia
Council of Large Public Housing Authorities(273)
Zauber, USAF(Ret.), Col. Glenn R.
Military Officers Association of America(419)

Zaucha, Thomas K.
National Grocers Association(515)

Zeitz, Joyce G.
Society for Assisted Reproductive Technology(614)

Zeldin, David E.
Society of Professional Investigators(642)

Zelenka, Patricia
Society of Cable Telecommunications Engineers(632)

Zelesnick, Stan
Contract Packaging Association(264)

Zelkin, Carol
Interactive Multimedia and Collaborative Communications Association(346)

Zeller, Ralph J.
National Judges Association(522)

Zellmer, M.P.H., William
American Society of Health-System Pharmacists(139)

Zeltzer, Jeffrey L.
National Home Equity Mortgage Association(517)

Zenger, Pepper L.
American Osteopathic Board of Physical Medicine and Rehabilitation(111)

Zenker, Wendy
National Council on the Aging(503)

Zenor, Stanley D.
Federal Communications Bar Association(302)

Zepke, Todd
North American Contractors Association(556)

Zepp, James
Justice Research and Statistics Association(403)

Zerfas, Lorraine B.
Education Credit Union Council(289)

Zern, Kristin
Association of Travel Marketing Executives(218)

Zetwick, Mary B.
Reinsurance Association of America(598)

Zhuang, Ziqing
International Society for Respiratory Protection(389)

Zick, Greg
Alexander Graham Bell Association for the Deaf and Hard of Hearing(15)

Ziebart, Geoff
National Association of Business Political Action Committees(441)

Ziegenfuss, Dr. H. Glenn
Standards Engineering Society(652)

Ziegler, CPCU, AAI, AAE, Cynthia
Casualty Actuarial Society(239)

Ziegler, Deborah
Council for Exceptional Children(268)

Ziegler, Robert F.
Federation of Socs. for Coatings Technology(304)

Zielke, Mark D.
ASABE - the Society for Engineering in Agricultural, Food and Biological Systems(162)

Zier, Ed
National Recreation and Parks Association(535)

Zietsman, Johann
International Society for the Performing Arts(389)

Zietz, Lew
National Air Traffic Controllers Association(428)

Zil, M.D., J.D., J.S.
American Association of Mental Health Professionals in Corrections(45)

Zimmer, Janie
American Academy of Sports Physicians(29)

Zimmer, Monica
Voices for America's Children(684)

Zimmer-Loew, Helene
American Association of Teachers of German(52)

Zimmerman, Bill
American Dental Association(78)

Zimmerman, Lee
Investment Management Consultants Association(399)

Zimmerman, Mark
Actors' Equity Association(8)

Zimmerman, Troy
National Kidney Foundation(523)

Zimmermann, Glenn
International Association of Rehabilitation Professionals(360)

Zinberg, Stanley
American College of Obstetricians and Gynecologists(68)

Ziolkowski, Joseph
Upholstered Furniture Action Council(680)

Zipperstein, Steven J.
Conference on Jewish Social Studies(261)

Zipser, Andrew
Newspaper Guild - CWA(552)

Zipser, Neal
Automotive Public Relations Council(224)

Zita, Patrizia
Test Boring Association(659)

Zito, Art
U.S. Lacrosse(668)

Zitowski, Marcia
Healthcare Information and Management Systems Society(324)

Zizis, Margaret
NaSPA: the Network and System Professionals Association(425)

Zlockie, MBA, John J.
Clinical and Laboratory Standards Institute(248)

Zmiewski, Mark
RMA - The Risk Management Association(602)

Zoks, Liza
Drug Information Association(287)

Zollar, Carolyn C.
American Medical Rehabilitation Providers Association(104)

Zotto, Frank T.
American Arbitration Association(32)

Zouboff, Tamara
Belgian American Chamber of Commerce in the United States(227)

Zuber, CAE, Susan
National Association of Enrolled Agents(451)

Zuccaro, Matthew
Helicopter Association International(325)

Zucker, Evan
American Society of Primatologists(145)

Zulu, Itibari M.
African-American Library and Information Science Association(11)

Zunich, Butch
National Gymnastics Judges Association(516)

Zuniga, Jose M.
International Association of Physicians in AIDS Care(360)

Zuraski, Theresa
Association for the Advancement of Medical Instrumentation(179)

Zyla, Paul
National Marrow Donor Program(526)

2007 National Trade and Professional Associations

Acronym Index

All the organizations that have supplied an acronym are listed here in alphabetical order by acronym.

4As Associated Actors and Artistes of America(164)
9to5 Nine to Five, National Association of Working Women(553)
A&WMA Air and Waste Management Association(12)
A2LA American Association for Laboratory Accreditation(35)
A4M American Academy of Anti-Aging Medicine(20)
AA Academy of Aphasia(2)
Aniline Association(157)
AAA Alliance of Insurance Agents and Brokers(17)
Allied Artists of America(17)
American Abstract Artists(19)
American Academy of Actuaries(19)
American Academy of Audiology(20)
American Accordionists Association(29)
American Accounting Association(29)
American Acupuncture Association(29)
American Agents Association(30)
American Ambulance Association(30)
American Anaplastology Association(31)
American Angus Association(31)
American Anthropological Association(31)
American Arbitration Association(32)
American Arts Alliance(32)
American Association of Anatomists(38)
Appraisers Association of America(159)
Association for Accounting Administration(166)
Association of Average Adjusters of the U.S.(187)
AAA, 3As American Academy of Advertising(20)
AAA-CPA American Association of Attorney-Certified Public Accountants(38)
AAAA American Academy of Anesthesiologist Assistants(20)
American Association for Affirmative Action(33)
American Association of Advertising Agencies(37)
Antique Appraisal Association of America(157)
Army Aviation Association of America(161)
AAAAI American Academy of Allergy, Asthma, and Immunology(20)
AAAASF American Association for Accreditation of Ambulatory Surgery Facilities(33)
AAACE American Association for Adult and Continuing Education(33)
AAACN American Academy of Ambulatory Care Nursing(20)
AAAD Association of Automotive Aftermarket Distributors(186)
AAADM American Association of Automatic Door Manufacturers(38)
AAAE American Association for Agricultural Education(33)
American Association of Airport Executives(38)
Association of Arts Administration Educators(186)
AAAHC Accreditation Association for Ambulatory Health Care(6)
AAAI American Association for Artificial Intelligence(33)
AAAL American Academy of Appellate Lawyers(20)
American Association for Applied Linguistics(33)
AAALAC Association for Assessment and Accreditation of Laboratory Animal Care International(168)
AAAM Alliance of Automobile Manufacturers(16)
Association for the Advancement of Automotive Medicine(179)
Association of African American Museums(183)
AAAP American Academy of Addiction Psychiatry(20)
American Association of Avian Pathologists(38)
AAAR American Association for Aerosol Research(33)
AAAS American Academy of Arts & Sciences(20)
American Association for the Advancement of Science(36)
Association for Asian American Studies(167)
AAASC American Ass'n of Ambulatory Surgery Centers(32)
AAASP Association for the Advancement of Applied Sport Psychology(179)
AAASS American Association for the Advancement of Slavic Studies(36)
AAB American Association of Bioanalysts(38)
AABB AABB(1)
AABC American Association of Birth Centers(38)
Associated Air Balance Council(164)
AABD American Association of Bank Directors(38)
AABE American Association of Blacks in Energy(38)
AABH Association for Ambulatory Behavorial Healthcare(167)
AABP Alliance of Area Business Publications(16)
American Association of Bovine Practitioners(39)
AABPA American Association for Budget and Program Analysis(33)
AABS Association for the Advancement of Baltic Studies(179)
AABT American Association of Behavioral Therapists(38)
Association for Advancement of Behavior Therapy(167)
AABVS American Association of Business Valuation Specialists(39)
AAC Alliance of Artists Communities(16)
Aluminum Anodizers Council(18)
AAC&U Association of American Colleges and Universities(184)
AAC/MIS Americas Association of Cooperative/Mutual Insurance Socs.(156)
AACA American Association of Certified Allergists(39)
AACAP American Academy of Child and Adolescent Psychiatry(20)
AACC American Association for Clinical Chemistry(34)
American Association for Continuity of Care(34)
American Association of Community Colleges(41)
American Automatic Control Council(55)
Argentina-American Chamber of Commerce(160)
AACCLA Association of American Chambers of Commerce in Latin America(184)
AACD American Academy of Cosmetic Dentistry(21)
AACDP American Association of Chairmen of Departments of Psychiatry(39)
AACE AACE International(1)
American Association for Cancer Education(33)

American Association for Career Education(34)
American Association of Clinical Endocrinologists(39)
American Association of Code Enforcement(40)
Association for the Advancement of Computing in Education(179)
AACFP American Association for Correctional and Forensic Psychology(34)
AACG American Association for Crystal Growth(34)
AACH American Academy on Communication in Healthcare(29)
AACI American Association of Crop Insurers(41)
AACN American Academy of Clinical Neurophysiology(21)
American Association of Colleges of Nursing(40)
American Association of Critical-Care Nurses(41)
AACO American Association of Certified Orthoptists(39)
AACOM American Association of Colleges of Osteopathic Medicine(40)
AACP American Academy of Clinical Psychiatrists(21)
American Academy of Craniofacial Pain(21)
American Association of Colleges of Pharmacy(40)
American Association of Community Psychiatrists(41)
AACPA Asian American Certified Public Accountants(162)
Autoclaved Aerated Concrete Products Association(222)
AACPDM American Academy for Cerebral Palsy and Developmental Medicine(19)
AACPM American Association of Colleges of Podiatric Medicine(40)
AACPS Association of Academic Chairmen of Plastic Surgery(183)
AACR American Association for Cancer Research(34)
AACRAO American Association of Collegiate Registrars and Admissions Officers(40)
AACRC American Association of Children's Residential Centers(39)
AACS American Academy of Cosmetic Surgery(21)
American Association for Chinese Studies(34)
American Association of Christian Schools(39)
American Association of Cosmetology Schools(41)
AACSB AACSB - the Association to Advance Collegiate Schools of Business(1)
AACSE American Association of Classified School Employees(39)
AACT American Academy of Clinical Toxicology(21)
American Association of Candy Technologists(39)
American Association of Community Theatre(41)
AACTE American Association of Colleges for Teacher Education(40)
AACU American Association of Clinical Urologists(40)
AACUL American Association of Credit Union Leagues(41)
AACVPR American Association of Cardiovascular and Pulmonary Rehabilitation(39)
AAD American Academy of Dermatology(21)
American Academy of Diplomacy(22)
AADC American Association of Dental Consultants(41)
AADE American Association of Dental Editors(41)
American Association of Dental Examiners(42)
American Association of Diabetes Educators(42)
AADEP American Academy of Disability Evaluating Physicians(22)
AADGP American Academy of Dental Group Practice(21)
AADLA Art and Antique Dealers League of America(161)
AADPA American Academy of Dental Practice Administration(21)
AADPRT American Association of Directors of Psychiatric Residency Training(42)
AADR American Association for Dental Research(34)
AADSM American Academy of Dental Sleep Medicine(21)
AAE American Association of Endodontists(42)
Association of American Educators(184)
Association of Art Editors(186)
AAEA American Academy of Equine Art(22)
American Agricultural Economics Association(30)
American Agricultural Editors Association(30)
AAEC Association of American Editorial Cartoonists(184)
AAECE American Association of Early Childhood Educators(42)
AAED American Academy of Esthetic Dentistry(22)
AAEE American Academy of Environmental Engineers(22)
American Association for Employment in Education(34)
AAEEH American Association of Eye and Ear Hospitals(42)
AAEI American Association of Exporters and Importers(42)
AAEM American Academy of Emergency Medicine(22)
American Academy of Environmental Medicine(22)
AAEP American Association of Equine Practitioners(42)
AAEPA American Academy of Estate Planning Attorneys(22)
AAES American Association of Engineering Societies(42)
AAF American Advertising Federation(29)
AAFA American Apparel & Footwear Association(31)
AAFAS Academy of Ambulatory Foot and Ankle Surgery(2)
AAFCO Association of American Feed Control Officials(184)
AAFCP American Academy of Fertility Care Professionals(23)
AAFCS American Association of Family and Consumer Sciences(43)
AAFD American Association of Franchisees and Dealers(43)
AAFO American Association for Functional Orthodontics(35)
AAFP American Academy of Family Physicians(22)
American Academy of Fixed Prosthodontics(23)
American Association of Feline Practitioners(43)
AAfPE American Association for Paralegal Education(36)
AAFPRS American Academy of Facial Plastic and Reconstructive Surgery(22)
AAFRC Giving Institute(317)
AAFS American Academy of Forensic Sciences(23)
AAG Association of American Geographers(184)
AAGBA American Angora Goat Breeder's Association(31)
AAGFO American Academy of Gold Foil Operators(23)
AAGIWA American Association of Grain Inspection and Weighing Agencies(43)
AAGL AAGL -- Advancing Minimally Invasive Gynecology Worldwide(1)
AAGO American Academy of Gnathologic Orthopedics(23)
AAGP American Association for Geriatric Psychiatry(35)
AAGUS American Association of Genitourinary Surgeons(43)
AAH Academy of Accounting Historians(2)
Association of Ancient Historians(186)
AAHA American Animal Hospital Association(31)
American Association of Handwriting Analysts(43)
AAHAM American Association of Healthcare Administrative Management(43)
AAHC American Association of Healthcare Consultants(43)
AAHCP American Academy of Home Care Physicians(23)
AAHCPAD American Academy of Health Care Providers-Addictive Disorders(23)
AAHD American Academy of the History of Dentistry(29)
American Association of Hospital Dentists(44)
AAHE American Association for Health Education(35)
AAHF American Association for Health Freedom(35)
AAHKS American Association of Hip and Knee Surgeons(43)
AAHM American Association for the History of Medicine(37)
AAHN American Association for the History of Nursing(37)
AAHomecare American Association for Homecare(35)
AAHP America's Health Insurance Plans(19)
American Academy of Health Physics(23)
American Association of Hospital and Healthcare Podiatrists(43)
AAHPERD American Alliance for Health, Physical Education, Recreation and Dance(30)
AAHPM American Academy of Hospice and Palliative Medicine(23)
AAHS American Association for Hand Surgery(35)
AAHSA American Association of Homes and Services for the Aging(43)
AAHSLD Association of Academic Health Sciences Library Directors(183)
AAI Aluminum Association(18)
American Association of Immunologists(44)
AAIA Automotive Aftermarket Industry Association(223)
AAID American Academy of Implant Dentistry(23)
AAIE Association for the Advancement of International Education(179)
Association of Applied IPM Ecologists(186)

AAIHDS American Association of Integrated Healthcare Delivery Systems(44)
AAII American Association of Individual Investors(44)
AAIM American Academy of Insurance Medicine(24)
Association for Applied Interactive Multimedia(167)
AAIMCO American Association of Insurance Management Consultants(44)
AAIP American Academy of Implant Prosthodontics(24)
Association of American Indian Physicians(184)
AAIV American Association of Industrial Veterinarians(44)
AAJA Asian American Journalists Association(162)
AALA American Agricultural Law Association(30)
American Automotive Leasing Association(55)
AALAS American Association for Laboratory Animal Science(35)
AALISA African-American Library and Information Science Association(11)
AALJ Association of Administrative Law Judges(183)
AALL American Association of Law Libraries(44)
AALNC American Association of Legal Nurse Consultants(44)
AALS Association for Arid Lands Studies(167)
Association of American Law Schools(184)
AALU Association for Advanced Life Underwriting(167)
AAM American Academy of Mechanics(24)
American Academy of Ministry(24)
American Agriculture Movement(30)
American Association of Museums(45)
Association for Accounting Marketing(167)
Association of Attorney-Mediators(186)
AAMA American Academy of Medical Acupuncture(24)
American Academy of Medical Administrators(24)
American Amusement Machine Association(31)
American Architectural Manufacturers Association(32)
American Association of Medical Assistants(45)
Asia America MultiTechnology Association(162)
AAMB American Association of Minority Businesses(45)
AAMC Association of American Medical Colleges(184)
AAMCN American Association of Managed Care Nurses(44)
AAMD Association of Art Museum Directors(186)
AAMFT American Association for Marriage and Family Therapy(36)
AAMGA American Association of Managing General Agents(45)
AAMH American Academy of Medical Hypnoanalysts(24)
AAMHPC American Association of Mental Health Professionals in Corrections(45)
AAMI Association for the Advancement of Medical Instrumentation(179)
AAML American Academy of Matrimonial Lawyers(24)
AAMM American Academy of Medical Management(24)
AAMMC American Association of Medical Milk Commissions(45)
AAMN American Assembly for Men in Nursing(33)
AAMP American Academy of Maxillofacial Prosthetics(24)
American Association of Meat Processors(45)
AAMR American Association on Mental Retardation(54)
AAMS Association of Air Medical Services(183)
AAMSE American Association of Medical Society Executives(45)
AAMT American Association for Medical Transcription(36)
AAMVA American Association of Motor Vehicle Administrators(45)
AAN American Academy of Neurology(25)
American Academy of Nursing(25)
Association of Alternative Newsweeklies(184)
AANA American Association of Nurse Anesthetists(46)
Arthroscopy Association of North America(162)
AANC American Association of Nutritional Consultants(46)
AANEM American Association of Neuromuscular & Electrodiagnostic Medicine(46)
AANFA African-American Natural Foods Association(11)
AANN American Association of Neuroscience Nurses(46)
AANOS American Academy of Neurological and Orthopaedic Surgeons(24)
AANP American Academy of Nurse Practitioners(25)
American Association of Naturopathic Physicians(46)
American Association of Neuropathologists(46)
AANS American Association of Neurological Surgeons(46)
AAO American Academy of Ophthalmology(25)
American Academy of Optometry(25)
American Academy of Osteopathy(26)
American Association of Orthodontists(47)
AAO-HNS American Academy of Otolaryngology-Head and Neck Surgery(26)
AAOBPPH American Association of Owners and Breeders of Peruvian Paso Horses(47)
AAOHN American Association of Occupational Health Nurses(47)
AAOM American Academy of Oral Medicine(25)
American Association of Oriental Medicine(47)
American Association of Orthopaedic Medicine(47)
AAOMP American Academy of Oral and Maxillofacial Pathology(25)
AAOMR American Academy of Oral and Maxillofacial Radiology(25)
AAOMS American Association of Oral and Maxillofacial Surgeons(47)
AAOP American Academy of Orofacial Pain(26)
American Academy of Orthotists and Prosthetists(26)
AAOS American Academy of Orthopaedic Surgeons(26)
AAOWP American Association of Osteopathic Women Physicians(47)
AAP American Academy of Pediatrics(27)
American Academy of Periodontology(27)
American Academy of Psychoanalysis and Dynamic Psychiatry(28)
American Academy of Psychotherapists(28)
Association for the Advancement of Psychology(179)
Association for the Advancement of Psychotherapy(179)
Association of Academic Physiatrists(183)
Association of American Physicians(185)
Association of American Publishers(185)
Association of Aviation Psychologists(187)
AAPA American Academy of Physician Assistants(27)
American Association of Pathologists' Assistants(47)
American Association of Physical Anthropologists(48)
American Association of Port Authorities(49)
American Association of Psychiatric Administrators(49)
Asian American Psychological Association(163)
AAPA-APAC AFIA-Alfalfa Processors Council(11)
AAPB Association for Applied Psychophysiology and Biofeedback(167)
AAPC American Academy of Professional Coders(27)
American Association of Pastoral Counselors(47)
American Association of Political Consultants(49)
AAPCC American Association of Poison Control Centers(48)
AAPCHO Association of Asian-Pacific Community Health Organizations(186)
AAPCO Association of American Pesticide Control Officials(185)
AAPD American Academy of Pediatric Dentistry(26)
AAPFCO Association of American Plant Food Control Officials(185)
AAPG American Association of Petroleum Geologists(47)
AAPH American Association of Professional Hypnotherapists(49)
AAPHD American Association of Public Health Dentistry(50)
AAPHP American Association of Public Health Physicians(50)
AAPI Antique and Amusement Photographers International(157)
AAPICU American Association of Presidents of Independent Colleges and Universities(49)
AAPL American Academy of Psychiatry and the Law(28)
American Artists Professional League(32)
American Association of Professional Landmen(49)
AAPM American Academy of Pain Management(26)
American Academy of Pain Medicine(26)
American Association of Physicists in Medicine(48)
AAPM&R American Academy of Physical Medicine and Rehabilitation(27)
AAPN American Apparel Producers Network(32)
AAPOR American Association for Public Opinion Research(36)

AAPOS American Association for Pediatric Ophthalmology and Strabismus(36)
AAPP American Association of Police Polygraphists(49)
AAPPM American Academy of Podiatric Practice Management(27)
AAPPO American Association of Preferred Provider Organizations(49)
AAPRCO American Association of Private Railroad Car Owners(49)
AAPS American Association of Pharmaceutical Scientists(48)
American Association of Phonetic Sciences(48)
American Association of Physician Specialists(48)
American Association of Plastic Surgeons(48)
Association of Alternate Postal Systems(184)
Association of American Physicians and Surgeons(185)
AAPSE American Association of Professional Sales Engineers(49)
AAPSM American Academy of Podiatric Sports Medicine(27)
AAPSS American Academy of Political and Social Science(27)
AAPT American Association of Philosophy Teachers(48)
American Association of Physics Teachers(48)
American Association of Psychiatric Technicians(50)
Association of Asphalt Paving Technologists(186)
AAR American Academy of Religion(28)
Association of American Railroads(185)
Association of Authors' Representatives(186)
AARC American Association for Respiratory Care(36)
American Association of Retirement Communities(50)
AARD American Academy of Restorative Dentistry(28)
AARHMS American Academy of Research Historians of Medieval Spain(28)
AARMR American Association of Residential Mortgage Regulators(50)
AARP American Association of Retired Persons(50)
AARS All-America Rose Selections(15)
American Association of Railroad Superintendents(50)
AARST American Association of Radon Scientists and Technologists(50)
AARTS Association of Advanced Rabbinical and Talmudic Schools(183)
AARWBA American Auto Racing Writers and Broadcasters Association(55)
AAS Academy of Applied Science(2)
American Academy of Sanitarians(28)
American Academy of Somnology(28)
American Antiquarian Society(31)
American Apitherapy Society(31)
American Association of Suicidology(52)
American Astronautical Society(54)
American Astronomical Society(54)
American Auditory Society(55)
Association for Academic Surgery(166)
Association for Asian Studies(167)
AASA American Association of School Administrators(50)
AASC American Association of State Climatologists(51)
AASCIN American Association of Spinal Cord Injury Nurses(51)
AASCIPSW American Association of Spinal Cord Injury Psychologists and Social Workers(51)
AASCO Association of American Seed Control Officials(185)
AASCU American Association of State Colleges and Universities(51)
AASE American Academy of Safety Education(28)
AASECT American Association of Sexuality Educators, Counselors and Therapists(51)
AASFE American Association of Sunday and Feature Editors(52)
AASG Association of American State Geologists(185)
AASHH American Association for the Study of Hungarian History(37)
AASHTO American Association of State Highway and Transportation Officials(51)
AASL American Association of School Librarians(50)
AASLD American Association for the Study of Liver Diseases(37)
AASLH American Association for State and Local History(36)
AASM American Academy of Sleep Medicine(28)
AASP American Academy of Sports Physicians(29)
American Association of Stratigraphic Palynologists(51)
Association of African Studies Programs(183)
AASPA American Association of School Personnel Administrators(51)
American Association of Surgical Physician Assistants(52)
AASRP American Association of Small Ruminant Practitioners(51)
AAST American Association for the Surgery of Trauma(37)
AASV American Association of Swine Veterinarians(52)
AAT American Academy of Thermology(29)
AATA American Art Therapy Association(32)
American Association of Teachers of Arabic(52)
AATB American Association of Tissue Banks(53)
AATCC American Association of Textile Chemists and Colorists(53)
AATE American Alliance for Theatre and Education(30)
American Association of Teachers of Esperanto(52)
AATF American Association of Teachers of French(52)
AATG American Association of Teachers of German(52)
AATH American Association for Therapeutic Humor(37)
AATI American Association of Teachers of Italian(52)
AATJ Alliance of Associations of Teachers of Japanese(16)
AATS American Academy of Teachers of Singing(29)
American Association for Thoracic Surgery(37)
AATSEEL American Association of Teachers of Slavic and East European Languages(52)
AATSP American Association of Teachers of Spanish and Portuguese(52)
AATT American Association of Teachers of Turkic Languages(53)
AAU Association of American Universities(185)
AAUA American Association of University Administrators(53)
AAUP American Association of University Professors(53)
Association of American University Presses(185)
AAV Association of Avian Veterinarians(187)
AAVC American Association of Veterinary Clinicians(53)
AAVCT American Academy of Veterinary and Comparative Toxicology(29)
AAVI American Association of Veterinary Immunologists(53)
AAVIM American Association for Vocational Instructional Materials(37)
AAVLD American Association of Veterinary Laboratory Diagnosticians(53)
AAVMC Association of American Veterinary Medical Colleges(186)
AAVP American Association of Veterinary Parasitologists(54)
AAVPT American Academy of Veterinary Pharmacology and Therapeutics(29)
AAVSB American Association of Veterinary State Boards(54)
AAVSO American Association of Variable Star Observers(53)
AAWC Association for the Advancement of Wound Care(180)
AAWCA African-American Women's Clergy Association(11)
AAWCC American Association for Women in Community Colleges(37)
AAWD American Association of Women Dentists(54)
AAWM American Academy of Wound Management(29)
AAWP American Association for Women Podiatrists(37)
AAWR American Association for Women Radiologists(37)
AAWV American Association of Wildlife Veterinarians(54)
AAZK American Association of Zoo Keepers(54)
AAZV American Association of Zoo Veterinarians(54)
ABA Air Brake Association(12)
American Bakers Association(55)
American Bandmasters Association(55)
American Bankers Association(55)
American Bar Association(56)
American Berkshire Association(56)
American Beverage Association(56)
American Booksellers Association(58)
American Bralers Association(59)
American Breed Association(59)
American Burn Association(60)
American Bus Association(60)
Association for Behavior Analysis(168)
Ayrshire Breeders' Association(225)
ABAA American Blonde D'Aquitaine Association(57)
Antiquarian Booksellers Association of America(157)
ABANA Artist-Blacksmiths' Association of North America(162)
ABB American Board of Bioanalysis(57)
ABBA American Brahman Breeders Association(59)
ABBRA American Boat Builders and Repairers Association(58)
ABC Agribusiness Council(12)
Aircraft Builders Council(14)
America's Blood Centers(19)
American Bail Coalition(55)

American Benefits Council(56)
American Brahmousin Council(59)
American Business Conference(60)
Associated Builders and Contractors(164)
Association for Business Communication(168)
Association of Bituminous Contractors(187)
Association of Black Cardiologists(187)
Association of Boards of Certification(188)
Association of Booksellers for Children(188)
Association of Bridal Consultants(188)
Audit Bureau of Circulations(222)
Automated Builders Consortium(222)
ABCA American Baseball Coaches Association(56)
ABCD Association for Bridge Construction and Design(168)
Association of Biomedical Communications Directors(187)
ABCR American Bashkir Curly Registry(56)
ABEA American Broncho-Esophagological Association(59)
ABF American Beekeeping Federation(56)
ABFE Association of Black Foundation Executives(187)
ABFP American Board of Forensic Psychology(57)
ABH Association for the Bibliography of History(180)
ABHE Association for Biblical Higher Education(168)
ABHES Accrediting Bureau of Health Education Schools(7)
ABHHA American Baptist Homes and Hospitals Association(55)
ABI American Bankruptcy Institute(55)
American Beverage Institute(56)
American Butter Institute(60)
ABIH American Board of Industrial Hygiene(57)
ABJS Association of Bone and Joint Surgeons(188)
ABKA American Boarding Kennels Association(58)
ABL American Beverage Licensees(57)
ABLA American Border Leicester Association(58)
ABLE Association for Biology Laboratory Education(168)
ABLS American Bryological and Lichenological Society(59)
ABM Academy of Breastfeeding Medicine(2)
American Business Media(60)
ABMA American Bearing Manufacturing Association(56)
American Boiler Manufacturers Association(58)
American Brush Manufacturers Association(59)
ABMP Associated Bodywork and Massage Professionals(164)
ABMR Academy of Behavioral Medicine Research(2)
ABMS American Board of Medical Specialties(57)
American Bureau of Metal Statistics(59)
ABNF Association of Black Nursing Faculty in Higher Education(187)
ABNS American Board of Nursing Specialties(57)
ABP American Board of Periodontology(57)
Association for Birth Psychology(168)
ABPA American Book Producers Association(58)
Automotive Body Parts Association(223)
ABPM American Board of Preventive Medicine(57)
ABPOPPM American Board of Podiatric Orthopedics and Primary Podiatric Medicine(57)
ABPP American Board of Professional Psychology(58)
ABPsi Association of Black Psychologists(187)
ABQAURP American Board of Quality Assurance and Utilization Review Physicians(58)
ABR Association of Battery Recyclers(187)
ABRA American Buckskin Registry Association(59)
ABRF Association of Biomolecular Resource Facilities(187)
ABS American Brachytherapy Society(59)
American Bureau of Shipping(59)
Animal Behavior Society(157)
Association for Borderlands Studies(168)
Association of Black Sociologists(187)
ABSA American Biological Safety Association(57)
ABSAME Association for the Behavioral Sciences and Medical Education(180)
ABSEL Association for Business Simulation and Experiential Learning(168)
ABTA American Bridge Teachers' Association(59)
ABTE Alliance of Black Telecommunications Employees(16)
ABVP American Board of Veterinary Practitioners(58)
ABWA American Business Women's Association(60)
Associated Business Writers of America(164)
ABWPA American British White Park Association(59)
ABWR American Beefalo World Registry(56)
ABYC American Boat and Yacht Council(58)
AC National Alfalfa Alliance(429)
ACA ACA International, The Association of Credit and Collection Professionals(2)
Academy of Certified Archivists(2)
Agriculture Council of America(12)
American Camp Association(60)
American Chain Association(61)
American Chianina Association(62)
American Chiropractic Association(62)
American College of Angiology(64)
American College of Apothecaries(64)
American Composers Alliance(72)
American Correctional Association(74)
American Counseling Association(76)
American Crystallographic Association(77)
Amerifax Cattle Association(156)
Association for Communication Administration(169)
Association for the Calligraphic Arts(180)
ACAA American Coal Ash Association(63)
ACAAI American College of Allergy, Asthma and Immunology(64)
ACAD American Conference of Academic Deans(73)
ACAM American College for Advancement in Medicine(63)
ACAP Alliance of Claims Assistance Professionals(16)
Association of College Administration Professionals(190)
ACAUS Association of Chartered Accountants in the United States(189)
ACB America's Community Bankers(19)
American College of Bankruptcy(64)
American Council of the Blind(76)
Association of Concert Bands(192)
ACBMA Associated Corset and Brassiere Manufacturers Association(165)
ACBSP Association of Collegiate Business Schools and Programs(191)
ACC Airport Consultants Council(14)
American Chemistry Council(62)
American College of Cardiology(64)
American College of Counselors(65)
American Conference of Cantors(73)
American Copper Council(74)
Association of Chiropractic Colleges(189)
Automotive Communication Council(223)
ACC America Association of Corporate Counsel(193)
ACC&CE Association of Consulting Chemists and Chemical Engineers(192)
ACCA Air Conditioning Contractors of America(13)
American Clinical and Climatological Association(63)
American College of Cardiovascular Administrators(64)
American Correctional Chaplains Association(74)
Express Delivery & Logistics Association(300)
ACCC Association of Community Cancer Centers(192)
ACCCA American Catholic Correctional Chaplains Association(61)
American Community Cultural Center Association(72)
ACCCI American Coke and Coal Chemicals Institute(63)
ACCE American Chamber of Commerce Executives(61)
American Council for Construction Education(75)
ACCED-I Association of Collegiate Conference and Events Directors International(191)
ACCET Accrediting Council for Continuing Education and Training(7)
ACCI American Council on Consumer Interests(76)
ACCL American College of Construction Lawyers(65)
ACCN American Court and Commercial Newspapers(77)
ACCO American College of Chiropractic Orthopedists(64)
ACCP American College of Chest Physicians(64)
American College of Clinical Pharmacology(64)
American College of Clinical Pharmacy(65)
American College of Contingency Planners(65)
ACCRA ACCRA - Ass'n of Applied Community Researchers(6)
ACCSCT Accrediting Commission for Career Schools and Colleges of Technology(7)
ACCSES American Congress of Community Supports and Employment Services(73)
ACCT Association of Community College Trustees(192)
ACCU Association of Catholic Colleges and Universities(188)
ACD American College of Dentists(65)

Associated Construction Distributors International(165)
ACDA American Choral Directors Association(62)
Association of Catholic Diocesan Archivists(189)
ACDHA American Cream Draft Horse Association(77)
ACDM Association of Chairmen of Departments of Mechanics(189)
ACE American Cinema Editors(62)
American College of Epidemiology(65)
American Council on Education(76)
American Council on Exercise(76)
Association for Communication Excellence(169)
Association of Conservation Engineers(192)
Association of Cooperative Educators(192)
ACEC American Council of Engineering Companies(75)
Association Chief Executive Council(166)
ACEI Association for Childhood Education International(169)
ACEJMC Accrediting Council on Education in Journalism and Mass Communications(7)
ACEP American College of Emergency Physicians(65)
Association for Comprehensive Energy Psychology(170)
ACerS American Ceramic Society(61)
ACES American College of Eye Surgeons(65)
Association for Comparative Economic Studies(170)
ACF American Culinary Federation(77)
Association of Consulting Foresters of America(192)
ACFA American Cash Flow Association(61)
Association of Commercial Finance Attorneys(192)
ACFAOM American College of Foot and Ankle Orthopedics and Medicine(65)
ACFAS American College of Foot and Ankle Surgeons(66)
ACFE American College of Forensic Examiners(66)
Association of Certified Fraud Examiners(189)
ACFP American College of Forensic Psychiatry(66)
ACFSA Association Correctional Food Service Affiliates(166)
ACG American College of Gastroenterology(66)
Association for Corporate Growth(171)
ACGA American Corn Growers Association(74)
ACGG American Custom Gunmakers Guild(77)
ACGIH American Conference of Governmental Industrial Hygienists(73)
ACH Association for Computers and the Humanities(170)
Association of Cosmetologists and Hairdressers(193)
ACHA American Catholic Historical Association(61)
American College Health Association(63)
American College of Healthcare Architects(66)
ACHCA American College of Health Care Administrators(66)
ACHE American College of Healthcare Executives(66)
American Council of Hypnotist Examiners(75)
Association for Continuing Higher Education(171)
AChemS Association for Chemoreception Sciences(169)
ACHIA American College of Healthcare Information Administrators(66)
ACHNE Association of Community Health Nursing Educators(192)
ACHS Association of College Honor Societies(191)
ACHSA American Correctional Health Services Association(74)
ACI American Concrete Institute(72)
Association for Conservation Information(170)
Association of Construction Inspectors(192)
ACI-NA Airports Council International/North America(15)
ACIA American Construction Inspectors Association(74)
Associated Cooperage Industries of America(165)
ACICS Accrediting Council for Independent Colleges and Schools(7)
ACIL American Council of Independent Laboratories(75)
ACIP American College of International Physicians(66)
ACIS American Conference for Irish Studies(73)
ACJA/LAE American Criminal Justice Association/Lambda Alpha Epsilon(77)
ACJS Academy of Criminal Justice Sciences(3)
ACL ACL - Association for Consortium Leadership(7)
American Classical League(63)
American Consultants League(74)
Association for Computational Linguistics(170)
Association of Christian Librarians(189)
ACLA American Clinical Laboratory Association(63)
American Comparative Literature Association(72)
ACLAM American College of Laboratory Animal Medicine(66)
ACLEA Association for Continuing Legal Education(171)
ACLI American Council of Life Insurers(75)
ACLM American College of Legal Medicine(66)
ACLPS Academy of Clinical Laboratory Physicians and Scientists(2)
ACLS American Council of Learned Societies(75)
ACM Academy of Country Music(3)
Alliance for Community Media(15)
American College of Musicians(67)
Association for Computing Machinery(170)
Association of Children's Museums(189)
ACMA American College of Mortgage Attorneys(67)
American Composites Manufacturers Association(72)
ACMCA American College of Managed Care Administrators(67)
ACMCFI Association of Career Firms International(188)
ACMCM American College of Managed Care Medicine(67)
ACME Alliance for Continuing Medical Education(15)
Association for Convention Marketing Executives(171)
ACMG American College of Medical Genetics(67)
ACMHA American College of Mental Health Administration(67)
ACMI The Art and Creative Materials Institute(161)
ACMMSCO American College of Mohs Micrographic Surgery and Cutaneous Oncology(67)
ACMP American College of Medical Physics(67)
ACMPE American College of Medical Practice Executives(67)
ACMQ American College of Medical Quality(67)
ACMT American College of Medical Toxicology(67)
ACN American College of Neuropsychiatrists(68)
American College of Nutrition(68)
Association of Camp Nurses(188)
ACNM American College of Nuclear Medicine(68)
American College of Nurse-Midwives(68)
ACNP American College of Neuropsychopharmacology(68)
American College of Nuclear Physicians(68)
American College of Nurse Practitioners(68)
ACNS American Clinical Neurophysiology Society(63)
ACOEM American College of Occupational and Environmental Medicine(68)
ACOEP American College of Osteopathic Emergency Physicians(69)
ACOFP American College of Osteopathic Family Physicians(69)
ACOG American College of Obstetricians and Gynecologists(68)
ACOI American College of Osteopathic Internists(69)
ACOM Association for Convention Operations Management(171)
ACOMS American College of Oral and Maxillofacial Surgeons(68)
ACOOG American College of Osteopathic Obstetricians and Gynecologists(69)
ACOP American College of Osteopathic Pediatricians(69)
ACOPMS American College of Osteopathic Pain Management and Sclerotherapy(69)
ACOS American College of Osteopathic Surgeons(69)
ACP American College of Physicians(69)
American College of Prosthodontists(70)
American College of Psychiatrists(70)
Associated Church Press(164)
Associated Construction Publications(165)
Association for Child Psychoanalysis(169)
Association of Coupon Professionals(193)
ACP/NSPA Associated Collegiate Press, National Scholastic Press Association(165)
ACPA ACPA - College Student Educators Association(7)
Affiliated Conference of Practicing Accountants International(10)
American Catholic Philosophical Association(61)
American Cleft Palate-Craniofacial Association(63)
American Concrete Pavement Association(72)
American Concrete Pipe Association(73)

American Concrete Pumping Association(73)
Association of Celebrity Personal Assistants(189)
ACPE Accreditation Council for Pharmacy Education(6)
American College of Physician Executives(69)
Association for Clinical Pastoral Education(169)
ACPM American College of Preventive Medicine(70)
ACPOC Association of Children's Prosthetic-Orthotic Clinics(189)
ACPPA American Concrete Pressure Pipe Association(73)
Asbestos Cement Product Producers Association(162)
ACPR American College of Podiatric Radiologists(70)
American Crossbred Pony Registry(77)
ACPS American Connemara Pony Society(74)
Association of Certified Professional Secretaries(189)
ACPsa American College of Psychoanalysts(70)
ACR American College of Radiology(70)
American College of Rheumatology(70)
Association for Conflict Resolution(170)
Association for Consumer Research(171)
ACRA American Collegiate Retailing Association(72)
American Cotswold Record Association(74)
American Cultural Resources Association(77)
ACREL American College of Real Estate Lawyers(70)
ACRI American Cocoa Research Institute(63)
ACRL Association of College and Research Libraries(190)
ACRM American Congress of Rehabilitation Medicine(73)
ACRO American College of Radiation Oncology(70)
ACRP Association of Clinical Research Professionals(190)
ACRRT American Chiropractic Registry of Radiologic Technologists(62)
ACS American Cancer Society(60)
American Cheese Society(61)
American Chemical Society(62)
American College of Surgeons(71)
Association of Caribbean Studies(188)
ACSA American Cotton Shippers Association(74)
Association of Collegiate Schools of Architecture(191)
ACSAA American Council for Southern Asian Art(75)
ACSH American Council on Science and Health(76)
ACSI Association of Christian Schools International(190)
ACSM American College of Sports Medicine(70)
American Congress on Surveying and Mapping(73)
ACSMA American Canine Sports Medicine Association(61)
American Cloak and Suit Manufacturers Association(63)
ACSP Association of Collegiate Schools of Planning(191)
ACSS American Cheviot Sheep Society(62)
ACSSS American Council of State Savings Supervisors(75)
ACSUS Association for Canadian Studies in the United States(168)
ACT American College of Toxicology(71)
American Council for Technology(75)
Association for Commuter Transportation(169)
Association of Christian Teachers(190)
Association of Christian Therapists(190)
Association of Civilian Technicians(190)
ACTC American College of Tax Counsel(71)
ACTE Association for Career and Technical Education(169)
Association of Corporate Travel Executives(193)
ACTEC American College of Trust and Estate Counsel(71)
ACTER Association for Career and Technical Education Research(169)
ACTFL American Council on the Teaching of Foreign Languages(76)
ACTL American College of Trial Lawyers(71)
ACTR/ACCELS American Councils for International Education(76)
ACTRA American Car and Truck Rental Association(61)
ACTRS Association of Catholic TV and Radio Syndicators(189)
ACTS Association of Community Tribal Schools(192)
ACUA Association of College and University Auditors(190)
ACUHO-I Association of College and University Housing Officers-International(191)
ACUI Association of College Unions International(191)
ACUIA Association of Credit Union Internal Auditors(193)
ACUMG Association of College and University Museums and Galleries(191)
ACUP Association of College and University Printers(191)
ACURA Association for College and University Religious Affairs(169)
ACUTA Association of College and University Telecommunications Administrators(191)
ACVA American College of Veterinary Anesthesiologists(71)
ACVD American College of Veterinary Dermatology(71)
ACVIM American College of Veterinary Internal Medicine(71)
ACVL Association of Cinema and Video Laboratories(190)
ACVN American College of Veterinary Nutrition(71)
ACVO American College of Veterinary Ophthalmologists(71)
ACVP Alliance of Cardiovascular Professionals(16)
American College of Veterinary Pathologists(72)
ACVR American College of Veterinary Radiology(72)
ACVS American College of Veterinary Surgeons(72)
ACW American Chain of Warehouses(61)
AD Council Advertising Council(9)
ADA Academy of Dispensing Audiologists(3)
American Dental Association(78)
American Diabetes Association(79)
American Dietetic Association(79)
ADAA American Dental Assistants Association(78)
Anxiety Disorders Association of America(157)
Art Dealers Association of America(161)
ADARA ADARA(8)
ADC Air Diffusion Council(13)
ADCA Aerospace Department Chairmen's Association(10)
American Dexter Cattle Association(79)
ADCI Association of Diving Contractors International(194)
ADDA American Design Drafting Association(79)
ADE Association for Documentary Editing(171)
Association of Departments of English(193)
ADEA American Dental Education Association(78)
ADEC Association for Death Education and Counseling(171)
ADED ADED - the Association for Driver Rehabilitation Specialists(8)
ADFL Association of Departments of Foreign Languages(193)
ADG American Dance Guild(78)
Art Directors Guild/Scenic, Title and Graphic Artists(161)
ADGA American Dairy Goat Association(77)
ADHA American Dental Hygienists' Association(78)
ADI Academy of Dentistry International(3)
Air Distributing Institute(13)
Association for Direct Instruction(171)
ADIC American Dental Interfraternity Council(79)
ADJA American Disc Jockey Association(79)
ADLTDE Association of Dark Leaf Tobacco Dealers and Exporters(193)
ADM Academy of Dental Materials(3)
Association of Directory Marketing(194)
ADMA Aviation Distributors and Manufacturers Association International(224)
ADME Association of Destination Management Executives(193)
ADMRA American and Delaine-Merino Record Association(31)
ADMS American Donkey and Mule Society(79)
ADOGA American Dehydrated Onion and Garlic Association(78)
ADP Association of Directory Publishers(194)
ADPD Academy of Dentistry for Persons with Disabilities(3)
ADPI American Dairy Products Institute(78)
ADRFCO Association of Direct Response Fundraising Counsel(194)
ADRIS Association for the Development of Religious Information Systems(180)
ADS American Dialect Society(79)
Association for Dressings and Sauces(171)
Association of Diesel Specialists(194)
ADSA American Dairy Science Association(78)
American Dental Society of Anesthesiology(79)
ADSC ADSC: The International Association of Foundation Drilling(8)
ADSM Association of Defensive Spray Manufacturers(193)
ADTA American Dance Therapy Association(78)

Association of Defense Trial Attorneys(193)
ADTSEA American Driver and Traffic Safety Education Association(79)
AdvaMed Advanced Medical Technology Association(8)
AEA Actors' Equity Association(8)
AeA - Advancing the Business of Technology(9)
Aircraft Electronics Association(14)
American Economic Association(80)
American Electrology Association(80)
American Emu Association(81)
American Engineering Association(81)
American Evaluation Association(81)
Aquatic Exercise Association(159)
Augustinian Educational Association(222)
AEAP Association of Executive and Administrative Professionals(196)
AEB American Egg Board(80)
AEC Aluminum Extruders Council(18)
Association of Episcopal Colleges(195)
AECRE International Association of Attorneys and Executives in Corporate Real Estate(353)
AECT Association for Educational Communications and Technology(172)
AED Academy for Eating Disorders(2)
Associated Equipment Distributors(165)
AEDP Association of Eminent Domain Professionals(195)
AEE Association for Experiential Education(172)
Association of Energy Engineers(195)
AEEC Airlines Electronic Engineering Committee(14)
AEESP Association of Environmental Engineering and Science Professors(195)
AEFA American Education Finance Association(80)
AEG Association of Environmental and Engineering Geologists(195)
AEHC Assembly of Episcopal Healthcare Chaplains(164)
AEHS Association for the Environmental Health of Soils(180)
AEI Architectural Engineering Institute(160)
AEIC Association of Edison Illuminating Companies(194)
AEJMC Association for Education in Journalism and Mass Communication(172)
AEM Association of Equipment Manufacturers(195)
AEMA Asphalt Emulsion Manufacturers Association(163)
Athletic Equipment Managers Association(221)
AEO Association for Enterprise Opportunity(172)
AEP Association of Educational Publishers(194)
AEPMA American Edged Products Manufacturers Association(80)
AEPP Education Industry Association(289)
AER Association for Education and Rehabilitation of the Blind and Visually Impaired(172)
AERA AERA - Engine Rebuilders Association(9)
American Educational Research Association(80)
AERC Association of Ecosystem Research Centers(194)
AERE Association of Environmental and Resource Economists(195)
AERS Association of Educators in Imaging and Radiologic Sciences(194)
AES Abrasive Engineering Society(2)
The American Electrophoresis Society(80)
American Endodontic Society(81)
American Entomological Society(81)
American Epilepsy Society(81)
American Equilibration Society(81)
Aquacultural Engineering Society(159)
Audio Engineering Society(222)
AESA American Educational Studies Association(80)
Association of Educational Service Agencies(194)
AESC Association of Energy Service Companies(195)
Association of Executive Search Consultants(196)
AESE Association of Earth Science Editors(194)
AESF American Electroplaters and Surface Finishers Society(80)
AESM Association for Equine Sports Medicine(172)
AESP Association of Energy Services Professionals, International(195)
AESSA American-European Soda Ash Shipping Association(156)
AET Association of Educational Therapists(194)
AETA American Embryo Transfer Association(81)
AETS Association for Science Teacher Education(178)
AF American Forests(85)
AF&PA American Forest and Paper Association(85)
AfA Air Force Association(13)
Airforwarders Association(14)
American Farrier's Association(82)
American Fence Association(83)
American Fiberboard Association(83)
American Finance Association(83)
American Flock Association(84)
American Floorcovering Alliance(84)
American Forensic Association(85)
Aspirin Foundation of America(164)
Association of Flight Attendants - CWA(197)
Association of Fraternity Advisors(198)
AFA, INC American Federation of Astrologers, Inc.(82)
AFAA Aerobics and Fitness Association of America(10)
Automatic Fire Alarm Association(222)
AFAC Allied Finance Adjusters Conference(17)
AFAR American Federation for Aging Research(82)
AFAUSSS Association of Former Agents of the U.S. Secret Service(197)
AFBA Armed Forces Broadcasters Association(161)
AFBF American Farm Bureau Federation(81)
AFCA American Football Coaches Association(84)
AFCC Association of Family and Conciliation Courts(196)
AFCCE Association of Federal Communications Consulting Engineers(196)
AFCEA Armed Forces Communications and Electronics Association(161)
AFCI Association of Film Commissioners International(196)
AFCMA Aluminum Foil Container Manufacturers Association(18)
AFCOM AFCOM(10)
AFCP Association of Free Community Papers(198)
AFCPE Association for Financial Counseling and Planning Education(173)
AFDE Association of Forensic Document Examiners(197)
AFDI Associated Funeral Directors International(165)
AFDO Association of Food and Drug Officials(197)
AFE Association for Facilities Engineering(172)
AFEE Association for Evolutionary Economics(172)
AFEHCT Association for Electronic Health Care Transactions(172)
AFFI American Frozen Food Institute(85)
AFFIRM Association for Federal Information Resources Management(173)
AFGC American Forage and Grassland Council(84)
AFGE American Federation of Government Employees(82)
AFGI Association of Financial Guaranty Insurors(197)
AFI Association of Food Industries(197)
AFIA American Feed Industry Association(83)
AFIO Association of Former Intelligence Officers(198)
AFIP Association of Finance and Insurance Professionals(196)
AFIRE Association of Foreign Investors in Real Estate(197)
AFJ Association of Food Journalists(197)
AFL-CIO American Federation of Labor and Congress of Industrial Organizations(82)
AFLA American Foreign Law Association(85)
Automotive Fleet and Leasing Association(223)
AFM American Federation of Musicians of the United States and Canada(82)
AFMA American Fiber Manufacturers Association(83)
Association of Family Medicine Administration(196)
AFMR American Federation for Medical Research(82)
AFNA Accordion Federation of North America(6)
AFO Association of Field Ornithologists(196)
AFOP Association of Farmworker Opportunity Programs(196)
AFOS Armed Forces Optometric Society(161)
AFOSISA Association of Former OSI Special Agents(198)
AFP Association for Financial Professionals(173)
Association of Fundraising Professionals(198)
AFP&CC American Federation of Police and Concerned Citizens(82)
AFPR Alliance of Foam Packaging Recyclers(16)
AFPRD Association of Family Medicine Residency Directors(196)
AFRC American Forest Resource Council(85)
AFRDS Association of Fund-Raising Distributors and Suppliers(198)
AFROC Association of Freestanding Radiation Oncology Centers(198)
AFS American Fern Society(83)

American Filtration and Separations Society(83)
American Fisheries Society(84)
American Folklore Society(84)
American Foundry Society(85)
AFSA Air Force Sergeants Association(13)
American Federation of School Administrators(82)
American Financial Services Association(83)
American Fire Sprinkler Association(84)
American Foreign Service Association(85)
AFSCME American Federation of State, County and Municipal Employees(82)
AFSMI AFSM International(11)
AFSPA American Foreign Service Protective Association(85)
AFT American Federation of Teachers(82)
Association for Financial Technology(173)
AFTA American Family Therapy Academy(81)
AFTE Association of Firearm and Toolmark Examiners(197)
AFTHC AFT Healthcare(11)
AFTR Association of Foreign Trade Representatives(197)
AFTRA American Federation of Television and Radio Artists(83)
AFVBM American Federation of Violin and Bow Makers(83)
AFWPI Association for Wedding Professionals International(182)
AG Association for Gnotobiotics(173)
Authors Guild(222)
AGA Accredited Gemologists Association(6)
American Galvanizers Association(86)
American Gaming Association(86)
American Gas Association(86)
American Gastroenterological Association(86)
American Gelbvieh Association(86)
American Genetic Association(86)
American Guernsey Association(87)
Art Glass Association(161)
Association of Government Accountants(199)
AGAT Association for Graphic Arts Training(173)
AGAUS Adjutants General Association of the United States(8)
AGB Association of Governing Boards of Universities and Colleges(199)
AGBA American Galloway Breeders Association(86)
AGBELL Alexander Graham Bell Association for the Deaf and Hard of Hearing(15)
AGCA Associated General Contractors of America(165)
AGD Academy of General Dentistry(3)
AGE American Aging Association(30)
AGH American Guild of Hypnotherapists(88)
AGHE Association for Gerontology in Higher Education(173)
AGI American Geological Institute(87)
Apparel Graphics Institute(159)
AGLP Association of Gay and Lesbian Psychiatrists(198)
AGLS Association for General and Liberal Studies(173)
AGLSP Association of Graduate Liberal Studies Programs(199)
AGM American Guild of Music(88)
Association of Golf Merchandisers(199)
AGMA American Gear Manufacturers Association(86)
American Guild of Musical Artists(88)
AGN-NA AGN International - North America(11)
AGO American Guild of Organists(88)
AGPA American Group Psychotherapy Association(87)
AGPM Associated Glass and Pottery Manufacturers(165)
AGR Alpha Gamma Rho(17)
AGRM Association of Gospel Rescue Missions(199)
AGS American Gem Society(86)
American Geographical Society(87)
American Geriatrics Society(87)
American Glovebox Society(87)
American Goat Society(87)
AGSES Association of Girl Scout Executive Staff(198)
AGT Association of Genetic Technologists(198)
AGTA Airport Ground Transportation Association(15)
American Gem Trade Association(86)
AGTOA American Greyhound Track Operators Association(87)
AGU American Geophysical Union(87)
AGVA American Guild of Variety Artists(88)
AH Academy of Homiletics(3)
AH&LA American Hotel & Lodging Association(92)
AHA American Heart Association(90)
American Hereford Association(90)
American Historical Association(91)
American Homebrewers Association(91)
American Hospital Association(92)
American Humanist Association(92)
American Hydrogen Association(92)
American Hypnosis Association(92)
Arabian Horse Association(160)
Association of Hispanic Arts(200)
AHAA Association of Hispanic Advertising Agencies(200)
AHAF American Handwriting Analysis Foundation(88)
AHAM Association of Home Appliance Manufacturers(200)
AHBAI American Health and Beauty Aids Institute(89)
AHC American Horse Council(91)
Association of Academic Health Centers(183)
AHCA American Health Care Association(89)
American Highland Cattle Association(90)
American Hockey Coaches Association(91)
AHEA American Hungarian Educators Association(92)
AHEAD Association on Higher Education and Disability(221)
AHEC American Hardwood Export Council(89)
AHFA American Home Furnishings Alliance(91)
AHG American Herbalists Guild(90)
AHHAP Association of Halfway House Alcoholism Programs of North America(199)
AHHS American Hackney Horse Society(88)
AHI Animal Health Institute(157)
AHIA Association of Health Insurance Advisors(199)
Association of Healthcare Internal Auditors(199)
AHIMA American Health Information Management Association(89)
AHL American Hockey League(91)
AHLA American Health Lawyers Association(89)
AHLC American Hair Loss Council(88)
AHMA American Hardware Manufacturers Association(88)
American Holistic Medical Association(91)
AHME Association for Hospital Medical Education(174)
AHMI Appalachian Hardwood Manufacturers(158)
AHNA American Holistic Nurses Association(91)
AHNS American Head and Neck Society(89)
AHOU Association of Home Office Life Underwriters(200)
AHP American Horse Publications Association(91)
Association for Healthcare Philanthropy(173)
Association for Humanistic Psychology(174)
AHPA American Health Planning Association(89)
American Herbal Products Association(90)
AHQA American Health Quality Association(89)
AHRA American Healthcare Radiology Administrators(90)
AHRMM Association for Healthcare Resource and Materials Management(174)
AHS Agricultural History Society(12)
American Hanoverian Society(88)
American Harp Society(89)
American Headache Society(89)
American Heartworm Society(90)
American Helicopter Society International(90)
American Hernia Society(90)
American Horticultural Society(91)
Association for Humanist Sociology(174)
AHSA American Hampshire Sheep Association(88)
American Humor Studies Association(92)
AHTA American Horticultural Therapy Association(92)
AHTCC Affordable Housing Tax Credit Coalition(10)
AHTD Association for High Technology Distribution(174)
AHVMA American Holistic Veterinary Medical Association(91)
AI Alpines International(18)
Asphalt Institute(163)
AIA Aerospace Industries Association of America(10)
Aestheticians International Association(10)
American Institute of Architects(94)
American Insurance Association(98)
Apiary Inspectors of America(158)
Archaeological Institute of America(160)
Automated Imaging Association(222)
Aviation Insurance Association(225)
AIA/NA Asbestos Information Association/North America(162)
AIAA American Institute of Aeronautics and Astronautics(94)
AIADA American International Automobile Dealers Association(98)
AIAEE Association for International Agricultural and Extension Education(175)
AIAG Automotive Industry Action Group(223)
AIAM Association of International Automobile Manufacturers(201)

AIARD Association for International Agriculture and Rural Development(175)
AIAS American Institute of Architecture Students(94)
AIAUS American Importers Association(93)
AIB Academy of International Business(3)
AIBC American Institute of Biomedical Climatology(95)
AIBD American Institute of Building Design(95)
AIBS American Institute of Biological Sciences(94)
AIC American Institute for Conservation of Historic and Artistic Works(93)
American Institute of Chemists(95)
American Institute of Constructors(95)
AICA American Institute of Commemorative Art(95)
American International Charolais Association(98)
AICA/US International Association of Art Critics(353)
AICAE American Indian Council of Architects and Engineers(93)
AICC American Indonesian Chamber of Commerce(93)
Association of Independent Corrugated Converters(200)
AICCI American-Israel Chamber of Commerce and Industry(156)
AIChE American Institute of Chemical Engineers(95)
AICI Association of Image Consultants International(200)
AICP American Institute of Certified Planners(95)
Association of Independent Commercial Producers(200)
Association of Insurance Compliance Professionals(201)
AICPA American Institute of Certified Public Accountants(95)
AICPCU/IIA American Institute for CPCU - Insurance Institute of America(93)
AIDA-US International Association for Insurance Law - United States Chapter(350)
AIE American Institute of Engineers(95)
AIEA Association of International Education Administrators(201)
AIEMPG American Importers and Exporters Meat Products Group(93)
AIFD American Institute of Floral Designers(96)
American Institute of Food Distribution(96)
AIFRB American Institute of Fishery Research Biologists(96)
AIGA American Institute of Graphic Arts(96)
AIH American Institute of Homeopathy(96)
American Institute of Hydrology(96)
AIHA American Industrial Hygiene Association(93)
American Italian Historical Association(99)
AIHP American Institute of the History of Pharmacy(97)
AII American Institute of Inspectors(96)
AIIM Association for Information and Image Management International(174)
AIIP Association of Independent Information Professionals(200)
AIIS American Institute for International Steel(94)
American Institute of Indian Studies(96)
AILA American Immigration Lawyers Association(92)
AILACT Association for Informal Logic and Critical Thinking(174)
AIM AIM Global(12)
American Innerspring Manufacturers(93)
AIM/R Association of Industry Manufacturers' Representatives(201)
AIMA American Incense Manufacturers Association(93)
AIMBE American Institute for Medical and Biological Engineering(94)
AIMC Association of Internal Management Consultants(201)
AIMCAL Association of Industrial Metallizers, Coaters and Laminators(201)
AIME American Institute of Mining, Metallurgical, and Petroleum Engineers(96)
Association for Information Media and Equipment(174)
AIMR CFA Institute(242)
AIMRA Agricultural and Industrial Manufacturers' Representatives Association(12)
AIMS American Institute for Maghrib Studies(94)
American Insurance Marketing and Sales Society(98)
American International Marchigiana Society(98)
Amusement Industry Manufacturers and Suppliers International(156)
AIMSE Association of Investment Management Sales Executives(202)
AIMU American Institute of Marine Underwriters(96)
AIO American Institute of Organbuilders(97)
AIOA American Iron Ore Association(99)
AIOB American Institute of Oral Biology(97)
AIP American Institute of Parliamentarians(97)
American Institute of Physics(97)
AIPAD Association of International Photography Art Dealers(202)
AIPB American Institute of Professional Bookkeepers(97)
AIPBS American Institute for Patristic and Byzantine Studies(94)
AIPG American Institute of Professional Geologists(97)
AIPLA American Intellectual Property Law Association(98)
AIR AIR Commercial Real Estate Association(12)
Association for Institutional Research(175)
AIRA Association of Insolvency and Restructuring Advisors(201)
AIRCON Airline Industrial Relations Conference(14)
AIREB Association of Industrial Real Estate Brokers(201)
AIRI Association of Independent Research Institutes(200)
AIRS Alliance of Information and Referral Systems(17)
AIS American Institute of Stress(97)
Association for Information Systems(175)
Association for Integrative Studies(175)
AISA American Institute for Shippers Associations(94)
AISC American Institute of Steel Construction(97)
AISES American Indian Science and Engineering Society(93)
AISI American Iron and Steel Institute(98)
AIST Association for Iron and Steel Technology(175)
AITC American Institute of Timber Construction(98)
AITCO Association of Independent Trust Companies(200)
AITP Association of Information Technology Professionals(201)
AIU Atlantic Independent Union(221)
AIUM American Institute of Ultrasound in Medicine(98)
AIVF Association of Independent Video and Filmmakers(201)
AJA American Jail Association(99)
American Judges Association(99)
AJAS Association of Jewish Aging Services(202)
AJCA American Jersey Cattle Association(99)
AJCCA American Jewish Correctional Chaplains Association(99)
AJCP Association of Jewish Center Professionals(202)
AJCU Association of Jesuit Colleges and Universities(202)
AJFCA Association of Jewish Family and Children's Agencies(202)
AJHA American Journalism Historians Association(99)
AJHS American Jewish Historical Society(99)
AJL Association of Jewish Libraries(202)
AJLI Association of Junior Leagues International(202)
AJPA American Jewish Press Association(99)
AJS American Judicature Society(99)
Association for Jewish Studies(175)
AKC American Kennel Club(100)
AKPsi Alpha Kappa Psi(18)
AKSR American Karakul Sheep Registry(100)
AKTA American Kinesiotherapy Association(100)
AKTI American Knife and Tool Institute(100)
ALA American Laryngological Association(100)
American Library Association(101)
American Lighting Association(101)
American Logistics Association(102)
American Lung Association(102)
Association of Legal Administrators(203)
Authors League of America(222)
ALAPCO Association of Local Air Pollution Control Officials(203)
ALC American Legend Cooperative(101)
ALCA American Leather Chemists Association(101)
ALCTS Association for Library Collections and Technical Services(175)
ALD Academy of Laser Dentistry(3)
ALDA American Luggage Dealers Association(102)
ALE Association of Leadership Educators(203)
ALEA Airborne Law Enforcement Association(14)
ALEC American Legislative Exchange Council(101)
ALFA Assisted Living Federation of America(164)
ALHFAM Association for Living History, Farm and Agricultural Museums(176)
ALHHS Archivists and Librarians in the History of the Health Sciences(160)
ALHI Associated Luxury Hotels(165)
ALI American Ladder Institute(100)
American Law Institute(100)

Automotive Lift Institute, Inc.(223)
ALIC Association of Life Insurance Counsel(203)
ALISE Association for Library and Information Science Education(175)
ALL American League of Lobbyists(101)
ALMA Aircraft Locknut Manufacturers Association(14)
ALMA - the International Loudspeaker Association(17)
Analytical Laboratory Managers Association(157)
ALOA Associated Locksmiths of America(165)
ALPA Air Line Pilots Association, International(13)
ALPFA Association of Latino Professionals in Accounting and Finance(203)
ALPNA American Licensed Practical Nurses Association(101)
ALRA American Land Rights Association(100)
Association of Labor Relations Agencies(202)
ALROS American Laryngological, Rhinological and Otological Society(100)
ALS Academy of Leisure Sciences(4)
American Lithotripsy Society(102)
American Littoral Society(102)
ALSB Academy of Legal Studies in Business(4)
ALSC Association for Library Service to Children(175)
Association of Literary Scholars and Critics(203)
ALSS Association of Lutheran Secondary Schools(203)
ALSSA Analytical and Life Science Systems Association(157)
ALTA Academic Language Therapy Association(2)
American Land Title Association(100)
American Literary Translators Association(101)
Association for Library Trustees and Advocates(176)
ALTHA Acute Long Term Hospital Association(8)
AMA American Management Association(102)
American Maritime Association(103)
American Marketing Association(103)
American Medical Association(104)
American Monument Association(106)
American Motorcyclist Association(107)
American Mustang Association(107)
AMAA American Maine-Anjou Association(102)
AMATYC American Mathematical Association of Two Year Colleges(103)
AMBA American Malting Barley Association(102)
American Mideast Business Associates(106)
American Mold Builders Association(106)
Association of Master of Business Administration Executives(204)
Association of Military Banks of America(205)
AMBHA American Managed Behavioral Healthcare Association(102)
AMC American Maritime Congress(103)
American Metalcasting Consortium(105)
American Music Conference(107)
AMCA Air Movement and Control Association International(13)
American Mosquito Control Association(106)
AMCBO Association of Major City and County Building Officials(203)
AMCD Association of Managed Care Dentists(203)
AMCEA Advertising Media Credit Executives Association, International(9)
AMCF Association of Management Consulting Firms(203)
AMCHP Association of Maternal and Child Health Programs(204)
AMCP Academy of Managed Care Pharmacy(4)
Academy of Managed Care Providers(4)
AMCSUS Association of Military Colleges and Schools of the U.S.(205)
AMD Association of Millwork Distributors(205)
AMDA American Medical Directors Association(104)
American Milking Devon Association(106)
AMDM Association of Medical Diagnostic Manufacturers(204)
AMDMA American Metal Detector Manufacturers Association(105)
AME Association for Manufacturing Excellence(176)
AMEA Association of Machinery and Equipment Appraisers(203)
AMERSA Association of Medical Education and Research in Substance Abuse(204)
AMFI Aviation Maintenance Foundation International(225)
AMGA American Medical Group Association(104)
American Murray Grey Association(107)
AMHA American Miniature Horse Association(106)
American Morgan Horse Association(106)
AMHCA American Mental Health Counselors Association(105)
AMHL Association of Mental Health Librarians(204)
AMI American Meat Institute(103)
American Mushroom Institute(107)
Association of Medical Illustrators(204)
AMIA American Medical Informatics Association(104)
Association of Moving Image Archivists(205)
AMIBA American Independent Business Alliance(93)
AMIFS Association for Management Information in Financial Services(176)
AMIN Advertising and Marketing International Network(9)
AMINTAPHIL International Association for Philosophy of Law and Social Philosophy - American Section(351)
AMME Association of Membership and Marketing Executives(204)
AMOA Amusement and Music Operators Association(156)
AMP Association for Molecular Pathology(176)
AMPA Air Medical Physician Association(13)
American Medical Publishers' Association(104)
AMPAS Academy of Motion Picture Arts and Sciences(4)
AmPepSoc American Peptide Society(113)
AMPs Association of Meeting Professionals(204)
AMPTP Alliance of Motion Picture and Television Producers(17)
AMQUA American Quaternary Association(121)
AMRA Automatic Meter Reading Association(223)
Automotive Maintenance Repair Association(223)
AMRC Automotive Market Research Council(223)
AMRPA American Medical Rehabilitation Providers Association(104)
AMS Academy of Marketing Science(4)
American Mathematical Society(103)
American Meteorological Society(105)
American Microchemical Society(106)
American Microscopical Society(106)
American Montessori Society(106)
American Motility Society(107)
American Musicological Society(107)
AMSA American Meat Science Association(104)
American Medallic Sculpture Association(104)
American Medical Student Association(105)
American Men's Studies Association(105)
American Moving and Storage Association(107)
AmSAT American Society for the Alexander Technique(146)
AMSE Association of Muslim Scientists and Engineers(205)
AmSECT American Society of Extra-Corporeal Technology(137)
AMSN Academy of Medical-Surgical Nurses(4)
AMSPDC Association of Medical School Pediatric Department Chairs(204)
AMSS American Milking Shorthorn Society(106)
Association of Muslim Social Scientists(205)
AMSSM American Medical Society for Sports Medicine(105)
AMSUS Association of Military Surgeons of the U.S.(205)
AMT American Medical Technologists(105)
AMT - The Association For Manufacturing Technology(156)
AMTA American Massage Therapy Association(103)
American Membrane Technology Association(105)
American Mobile Telecommunications Association(106)
American Music Therapy Association(107)
Antenna Measurement Techniques Association(157)
AMTDA American Machine Tool Distributors Association(102)
AMTMA American Measuring Tool Manufacturers Association(103)
AMU American Musicians Union(107)
AMWA American Medical Women's Association(105)
American Medical Writers Association(105)
Association of Metropolitan Water Agencies(204)
ANA American Naprapathic Association(108)
American Neurological Association(108)
American Nurses Association(109)
Association of National Advertisers(205)
Association of Naval Aviation(205)

ANAC Association of Nurses in AIDS Care(206)
ANAM Association of North American Missions(205)
ANBA American Nurses in Business Association(109)
ANCCSA American North Country Cheviot Sheep Association(109)
ANCOR American Network of Community Options and Resources(108)
ANCW American National CattleWomen(108)
ANG Acrylonitrile Group(8)
ANI American Nuclear Insurers(109)
ANLA American Nursery and Landscape Association(109)
ANM Alliance of Nonprofit Mailers(17)
ANMC American National Metric Council(108)
ANNA American Nephrology Nurses Association(108)
ANPA American Neuropsychiatric Association(108)
ANRET Association of Natural Resource Enforcement Trainers(205)
ANS American Name Society(107)
American Neurotology Society(109)
American Nuclear Society(109)
American Numismatic Society(109)
North American Neuromodulation Society(559)
ANSAC American Natural Soda Ash Corporation(108)
ANSERTeam Alliance of National Staffing and Employment Resources(17)
ANSI American National Standards Institute(108)
ANSPA Association of Neurosurgical Physician Assistants(205)
ANSS American Nature Study Society(108)
ANVM Association of United States Night Vision Manufacturers(219)
AO Academy of Osseointegration(5)
Alpha Omega International Dental Fraternity(18)
America Outdoors(19)
AOA American Obesity Association(109)
American Optometric Association(110)
American Orthopaedic Association(110)
American Osteopathic Association(111)
American Ostrich Association(112)
Association of Otolaryngology Administrators(207)
AOAAM American Osteopathic Academy of Addiction Medicine(111)
AOAC AOAC International(158)
AOAO American Osteopathic Academy of Orthopedics(111)
AOASM American Osteopathic Academy for Sports Medicine(111)
AOBPMR American Osteopathic Board of Physical Medicine and Rehabilitation(111)
AOBTA American Organization for Bodywork Therapies of Asia(110)
AOC American Oilseed Coalition(110)
AOC(158)
AOCA American Osteopathic College of Anesthesiologists(111)
Automotive Oil Change Association(224)
AOCAI American Osteopathic College of Allergy and Immunology(111)
AOCD American Osteopathic College of Dermatology(112)
AOCOO-HNS American Osteopathic Colleges of Ophthalmology and Otolaryngology - Head and Neck Surgery(112)
AOCP American Osteopathic College of Pathologists(112)
AOCPM American Osteopathic College of Occupational and Preventive Medicine(112)
AOCPr American Osteopathic College of Proctology(112)
AOCR American Osteopathic College of Radiology(112)
AOCS American Oil Chemists' Society(110)
AOD Academy of Operative Dentistry(4)
Academy of Oral Dynamics(4)
Associated Owners and Developers(165)
AOEC Association of Occupational and Environmental Clinics(206)
AOFAS American Orthopaedic Foot and Ankle Society(111)
AOHP Association of Occupational Health Professionals in Healthcare(206)
AOM Academy of Management(4)
AoM/IAoM Association of Management/International Association of Management(203)
AONE American Organization of Nurse Executives(110)
AOOP Academy of Organizational and Occupational Psychiatry(4)
AOPA Aircraft Owners and Pilots Association(14)
American Orthotic and Prosthetic Association(111)
AOPL Association of Oil Pipe Lines(206)
AOPO Association of Organ Procurement Organizations(206)
AORC Association of Official Racing Chemists(206)
Automotive Occupant Restraints Council(224)
AORN AORN(158)
AOS American Ophthalmological Society(110)
American Oriental Society(110)
American Otological Society(112)
AOSA American Optometric Student Association(110)
Association of Official Seed Analysts(206)
AOSCA Association of Official Seed Certifying Agencies(206)
AOSED Association of Osteopathic State Executive Directors(206)
AOSSM American Orthopaedic Society for Sports Medicine(111)
AOSW Association of Oncology Social Work(206)
AOTA American Occupational Therapy Association(109)
AOU American Ornithologists' Union(110)
AP Academy of Prosthodontics(5)
AP-LS American Psychology-Law Society(119)
APA Amalgamated Printers' Association(18)
Ambulatory Pediatric Association(19)
American Pancreatic Association(112)
American Payroll Association(113)
American Philological Association(114)
American Philosophical Association(114)
American Pilots' Association(115)
American Pinzgauer Association(115)
American Planning Association(116)
American Polygraph Association(116)
American Poultry Association(117)
American Psychiatric Association(117)
American Psychological Association(118)
American Psychotherapy Association(119)
American Pyrotechnics Association(120)
APA - The Engineered Wood Association(158)
Apple Processors Association(159)
Architectural Precast Association(160)
At-sea Processors Association(221)
Audio Publishers Association(222)
APA-DP American Psychological Association - Division of Psychotherapy(118)
APA/CP American Psychological Association - Society of Clinical Psychology(119)
APACVS Association of Physician Assistants in Cardiovascular Surgery(207)
APAI Association of Paroling Authorities, International(207)
APALA Asian/Pacific American Librarians Association(163)
APAN Advertising Photographers of America(9)
APAOG Association of Physician Assistants in Obstetrics and Gynecology(208)
APBA American Pet Boarding Association(114)
APBPA Association of Professional Ball Players of America(208)
APC Academy of Parish Clergy(5)
American Peanut Council(113)
American Plastics Council(116)
Aseptic Packaging Council(162)
Association of Pathology Chairs(207)
Association of Professional Chaplains(208)
Association of Professors of Cardiology(209)
APCC American Public Communications Council(119)
Association of Professional Communication Consultants(208)
APCS Accredited Pet Cemetery Society(7)
American Podiatric Circulatory Society(116)
APCU Association of Presbyterian Colleges and Universities(208)
APCUG Association of Personal Computer User Groups(207)
APDA Appliance Parts Distributors Association(159)
APDF Association of Professional Design Firms(208)
APDIM Association of Program Directors in Internal Medicine(210)
APDR Association of Program Directors in Radiology(210)
APDS Association of Program Directors in Surgery(210)
APDT Association of Pet Dog Trainers(207)
APDU Association of Public Data Users(210)
APEM Association of Professional Energy Managers(209)
APERC Alkylphenols and Ethoxylates Research Council(15)
APF American Pathology Foundation(113)
APFA American Pipe Fittings Association(115)
APFHA American Paso Fino Horse Association(113)
APFO Association on Programs for Female Offenders(221)
APG Association of Professional Genealogists(209)
APGA American Public Gardens Association(119)
American Public Gas Association(119)
APGO Association of Professors of Gynecology and Obstetrics(209)
APHA American Paint Horse Association(112)
American Pharmacists Association(114)

American Printing History Association(117)
American Public Health Association(119)
APhA-ASP Academy of Student Pharmacists(5)
ApHC Appaloosa Horse Club(159)
APHL Association of Public Health Laboratories(210)
APHSA American Public Human Services Association(120)
API Accountants for the Public Interest(6)
Alliance for the Polyurethane Industry(16)
American Petroleum Institute(114)
American Poultry International(117)
APIC Association for Professionals in Infection Control and Epidemiology(177)
Association of Professional Investment Consultants(209)
APICS APICS - The Association for Operations Management(158)
APJE Association of Philosophy Journal Editors(207)
APLD Association of Professional Landscape Designers(209)
APLIC-I Association for Population/Family Planning Libraries and Information Centers, International(176)
APLS Association for Politics and the Life Sciences(176)
APM Academy of Psychosomatic Medicine(5)
Association for Psychoanalytic Medicine(177)
Association of Professors of Medicine(209)
Association of Professors of Mission(210)
APMA American Podiatric Medical Association(116)
APME Associated Press Managing Editors(166)
APMI APMI International(158)
APMM Association of Professional Model Makers(209)
APMP Association of Proposal Management Professionals(210)
APMS Aquatic Plant Management Society(159)
APMSA American Podiatric Medical Students' Association(116)
APMWA American Podiatric Medical Writers Association(116)
APNA American Psychiatric Nurses Association(118)
APOBA Associated Pipe Organ Builders of America(166)
APON Association of Pediatric Hematology/Oncology Nurses(207)
APOSW Association of Pediatric Oncology Social Workers(207)
APPA American Probation and Parole Association(117)
American Psychopathological Association(119)
American Public Power Association(120)
APPAM Association for Public Policy Analysis and Management(177)
APPAP Association of Postgraduate Physician Assistant Programs(208)
APPD Association of Pediatric Program Directors(207)
APPE Association for Practical and Professional Ethics(177)
Association of Private Enterprise Education(208)
APPIC Association of Psychology Postdoctoral and Internship Centers(210)
APPL Association of Partners for Public Lands(207)
APPMA American Pet Products Manufacturers Association(114)
APPMI American Peanut Product Manufacturers(113)
APRA Association of Professional Researchers for Advancement(209)
Automotive Parts Remanufacturers Association(224)
APRC Automotive Public Relations Council(224)
APRES American Peanut Research and Education Society(113)
APRO Association of Progressive Rental Organizations(210)
APS Academy of Political Science(5)
American Pain Society(112)
American Paraplegia Society(113)
American Pediatric Society(113)
American Philosophical Society(114)
American Physiological Society(115)
American Phytopathological Society(115)
American Pomological Society(117)
American Prosthodontic Society(117)
American Psychological Society(119)
American Psychosomatic Society(119)
American Purchasing Society(120)
Association of Productivity Specialists(208)
APS Physics American Physical Society(115)
APSA American Peanut Shellers Association(113)
American Pediatric Surgical Association(113)
American Political Science Association(116)
American Polypay Sheep Association(116)
Association of Plastic Surgery Assistants(208)
APsaA American Psychoanalytic Association(118)
APSAC American Professional Society on the Abuse of Children(117)
APSIA Association of Professional Schools of International Affairs(209)
APSP Association of Pool and Spa Professionals(208)
APSS Associated Professional Sleep Socs.(166)
APSWU American Philatelic Society - Writers Unit #30(114)
APT Alliance of Professional Tattooists(17)
Association for Play Therapy(176)
Association for Psychological Type(177)
Association of Polysomnographic Technologists(208)
APT Int'l Association for Preservation Technology International(177)
APTA American Physical Therapy Association(115)
American Polarity Therapy Association(116)
American Public Transportation Association(120)
APTAC Ass'n of Procurement Technical Assistance Centers(164)
APTC American Property Tax Counsel(117)
APTS Association of Public Television Stations(210)
APU Association for Philosophy of the Unconscious(176)
APWA American Public Works Association(120)
APWU American Postal Workers Union(117)
AQHA American Quarter Horse Association(120)
ARA Academy of Rehabilitative Audiology(5)
Agricultural Retailers Association(12)
American Recovery Association(122)
American Rental Association(122)
American Romagnola Association(123)
Automotive Recyclers Association(224)
Awards and Recognition Association(225)
ARBA American Rabbit Breeders Association(121)
American Red Brangus Association(122)
American Romney Breeders Association(123)
ARBO Association of Regulatory Boards of Optometry(211)
ARC American Recreation Coalition(122)
ARCI Association of Racing Commissioners International(211)
ARD Association of Research Directors(212)
ARDA American Railway Development Association(121)
American Resort Development Association(122)
ARDI American Rolling Door Institute(123)
ARDMS American Registry of Diagnostic Medical Sonographers(122)
ARELLO Association of Real Estate License Law Officials(211)
AREMA American Railway Engineering and Maintenance of Way Association(121)
ARENA Applied Research Ethics National Association(159)
ARES American Real Estate Society(121)
AREUEA American Real Estate and Urban Economics Association(121)
AREW Association of Real Estate Women(211)
ARHP Association of Reproductive Health Professionals(212)
Association of Rheumatology Health Professionals(212)
ARI AirConditioning and Refrigeration Institute(14)
ARIA American Risk and Insurance Association(123)
ARJD Association of Reporters of Judicial Decisions(212)
ARL Association of Research Libraries(212)
ARLIS/NA Art Libraries Society of North America(161)
ARM Associated Risk Managers(166)
Association of Railway Museums(211)
ARMA American Registry of Medical Assistants(122)
American Rock Mechanics Association(123)
Asphalt Roofing Manufacturers Association(163)
ARMA Int'l ARMA International(160)
ARMI Association of Rotational Molders, International(212)
ARMS Association of Retail Marketing Services(212)
ARN Association of Rehabilitation Nurses(211)
ARNA American Radiological Nurses Association(121)
ARNMD Association for Research in Nervous and Mental Disease(177)
ARO Association for Research in Otolaryngology(177)
ARPCT Association of Rehabilitation Programs in Computer Technology(211)
ARR Academy of Radiology Research(5)
ARRA Asphalt Recycling and Reclaiming Association(163)

ARRL American Radio Relay League(121)
ARRO Archery Range and Retailers Organization(160)
Association of Residents in Radiation Oncology(212)
ARRS American Roentgen Ray Society(123)
ARRT American Registry of Radiologic Technologists(122)
ARS American Radium Society(121)
American Rhinologic Society(123)
ARSA Aeronautical Repair Station Association(10)
ARSBA American Rambouillet Sheep Breeders Association(121)
ARSC Association for Recorded Sound Collections(177)
ARTA American Reusable Textile Association(122)
Association of Retail Travel Agents(212)
ARTBA American Road and Transportation Builders Association(123)
ARTS Association for Retail Technology Standards(178)
ARVC National Association of RV Parks and Campgrounds(470)
ARVO Association for Research in Vision and Ophthalmology(178)
AS Adhesion Society(8)
ASA Acoustical Society of America(7)
African Studies Association(11)
American Salers Association(123)
American Schools Association(124)
American Shipbuilding Association(125)
American Shorthorn Association(125)
American Simmental Association(125)
American Skin Association(126)
American Society for Aesthetics(126)
American Society of Agronomy(133)
American Society of Anesthesiologists(134)
American Society of Appraisers(134)
American Society of Artists(134)
American Society on Aging(147)
American Sociological Association(147)
American Soybean Association(148)
American Sportfishing Association(148)
American Sportscasters Association(148)
American Staffing Association(149)
American Statistical Association(149)
American Studies Association(149)
American Subcontractors Association(149)
American Sugar Alliance(150)
American Supply Association(150)
American Surgical Association(150)
Automotive Service Association(224)
Aviation Suppliers Association(225)
ASAA American Sleep Apnea Association(126)
American Society of Agricultural Appraisers(133)
ASAAD American Society for the Advancement of Sedation and Anesthesia in Dentistry(132)
ASABE ASABE - the Society for Engineering in Agricultural, Food and Biological Systems(162)
ASAC American Society of Agricultural Consultants(133)
ASAE American Society of Association Executives & Center for Association Leadership(134)
ASAHP Association of Schools of Allied Health Professions(213)
ASAI American Society of Architectural Illustrators(134)
ASAIO American Society for Artificial Internal Organs(126)
ASALH Association for the Study of African American Life and History(180)
ASAM American Society of Addiction Medicine(133)
Association of Sales Administration Managers(212)
ASAO Association for Social Anthropology in Oceania(178)
ASAP American Society for Adolescent Psychiatry(126)
American Society for Automation in Pharmacy(126)
American Society of Access Professionals(133)
ASAPS American Society for Aesthetic Plastic Surgery(126)
ASAPSS American Society for Amusement Park Security and Safety(126)
ASARB Association of Statisticians of American Religious Bodies(216)
ASAS American Society of Abdominal Surgeons(133)
American Society of Animal Science(134)
ASASP Association of Supervisory and Administrative School Personnel(216)
ASATT American Society of Anesthesia Technologists and Technicians(134)
ASB American Society of Baking(134)
ASBA American Southdown Breeders Association(148)
American Sports Builders Association(148)
Association of Ship Brokers and Agents (U.S.A.)(214)
Auto Suppliers Benchmarking Association(222)
ASBC American Society of Brewing Chemists(135)
ASBD American Society of Breast Disease(135)
ASBDA American School Band Directors' Association(124)
ASBDC Association of Small Business Development Centers(214)
ASBE American Society of Body Engineers(135)
ASBH American Society for Bioethics and Humanities(127)
ASBMB American Society for Biochemistry and Molecular Biology(126)
ASBMR American Society for Bone and Mineral Research(127)
ASBMT American Society for Blood and Marrow Transplantation(127)
ASBO Association of School Business Officials International(212)
ASBP American Society of Bariatric Physicians(134)
ASBPE American Society of Business Publication Editors(135)
ASC Adhesive and Sealant Council(8)
American Society of Cinematographers(135)
American Society of Criminology(137)
American Society of Cytopathology(137)
Associated Schools of Construction(166)
Associated Specialty Contractors(166)
ASCA American School Counselor Association(124)
American Society of Consulting Arborists(136)
American Swimming Coaches Association(150)
Association of State Correctional Administrators(215)
ASCAC Association for the Study of Classical African Civilizations(180)
ASCAP American Society of Composers, Authors and Publishers(136)
ASCB American Society for Cell Biology(127)
ASCC American Society of Concrete Contractors(136)
ASCCP American Society for Colposcopy and Cervical Pathology(127)
ASCD Association for Supervision and Curriculum Development(178)
ASCDI Association of Service and Computer Dealers International(213)
ASCE American Society of Civil Engineers(135)
ASCET American Society of Certified Engineering Technicians(135)
ASCFG Association of Specialty Cut Flower Growers(214)
ASCH American Society of Church History(135)
American Society of Clinical Hypnosis(135)
ASCI American Society for Clinical Investigation(127)
ASCL American Society of Comparative Law(136)
American Sugar Cane League of the U.S.A.(150)
ASCLA Association of Specialized and Cooperative Library Agencies(214)
ASCLD American Society of Crime Laboratory Directors(137)
ASCLS American Society for Clinical Laboratory Science(127)
ASCO American Society of Clinical Oncology(136)
American Society of Contemporary Ophthalmology(136)
Association of Schools and Colleges of Optometry(213)
ASCP American Society for Clinical Pathology(127)
American Society of Clinical Psychopharmacology(136)
American Society of Consultant Pharmacists(136)
American Society of Consulting Planners(136)
ASCPT American Society for Clinical Pharmacology and Therapeutics(127)
ASCR Association of Specialists in Cleaning and Restoration International(214)
ASCRS American Society of Cataract and Refractive Surgery(135)
American Society of Colon and Rectal Surgeons(136)
ASCT American Society for Cytotechnology(128)
ASD American Society of Dermatology(137)
Association for the Study of Dreams(180)
Association of Steel Distributors(216)
ASDA American Society for Dental Aesthetics(128)
American Stamp Dealers' Association(149)
American Student Dental Association(149)
ASDAL Association of Seventh-Day Adventist Librarians(213)
ASDP American Society of Dermatopathology(137)
ASDR American Society of Dermatological Retailers(137)
ASDS American Society for Dermatologic Surgery(128)

ASDSO Association of State Dam Safety Officials(215)
ASDVS American Society of Directors of Volunteer Services(137)
ASDWA Association of State Drinking Water Administrators(215)
ASE American Society for Ethnohistory(129)
American Society of Echocardiography(137)
American Stock Exchange(149)
Association for Social Economics(178)
Association for Surgical Education(178)
ASECS American Society for Eighteenth-Century Studies(128)
ASEE American Society for Engineering Education(128)
ASEH American Society for Environmental History(128)
ASEM American Society for Engineering Management(128)
ASENT American Society for Experimental NeuroTherapeutics(129)
ASER American Society of Emergency Radiology(137)
ASES American Shoulder and Elbow Surgeons(125)
American Solar Energy Society(147)
ASET Academy of Security Educators and Trainers(5)
American Society of Electroneurodiagnostic Technologists(137)
ASEV American Society for Enology and Viticulture(128)
ASF Association of Small Foundations(214)
ASFA American Society for Apheresis(126)
ASFD American Society of Furniture Designers(138)
ASFE ASFE/The Best People on Earth(162)
ASFMRA American Society of Farm Managers and Rural Appraisers(137)
ASFO American Society of Forensic Odontology(138)
ASFP Association of Smoked Fish Processors(214)
ASFPM Association of State Floodplain Managers(216)
ASFS Association for the Study of Food and Society(181)
ASG American Society of Geolinguistics(138)
ASGA American Sugarbeet Growers Association(150)
ASGCA American Society of Golf Course Architects(138)
ASGD American Society for Geriatric Dentistry(129)
ASGE American Society for Gastrointestinal Endoscopy(129)
American Society of Gas Engineers(138)
ASGPP American Society of Group Psychotherapy and Psychodrama(138)
ASGS American Scientific Glassblowers Society(124)
American Society of General Surgeons(138)
ASGT American Society of Gene Therapy(138)
ASH Academy of Scientific Hypnotherapy(5)
American Society of Hematology(139)
American Society of Hypertension(139)
ASHA American Saddlebred Horse Association(123)
American School Health Association(124)
American Seniors Housing Association(124)
American Shire Horse Association(125)
American Speech-Language-Hearing Association(148)
American Suffolk Horse Association(150)
ASHAHS American Society for Hispanic Art Historical Studies(130)
ASHCSP American Society for Healthcare Central Service Professionals(129)
ASHE American Society for Healthcare Engineering(129)
American Society of Highway Engineers(139)
Association for the Study of Higher Education(181)
ASHES American Society for Healthcare Environmental Services(129)
ASHFSA American Society for Healthcare Food Service Administrators(129)
ASHG American Society of Human Genetics(139)
ASHHRA American Society for Healthcare Human Resources Administration(129)
ASHI American Society for Histocompatability and Immunogenetics(130)
American Society of Home Inspectors(139)
ASHNR American Society of Head and Neck Radiology(138)
ASHP American Society of Health-System Pharmacists(139)
ASHRA American Spa and Health Resort Association(148)
ASHRAE American Society of Heating, Refrigerating and Air-Conditioning Engineers(139)
ASHRM American Society for Healthcare Risk Management(129)
ASHRS American Society of Hair Restoration Surgery(138)
ASHS American Society for Horticultural Science(130)
ASHT American Society of Hand Therapists(138)
ASI Allied Stone Industries(17)
American Sheep Industry Association(125)
American Sightseeing International(125)
American Society of Indexers(139)
Aviation Safety Institute(225)
ASIA American Spinal Injury Association(148)
ASIC American Society of Irrigation Consultants(140)
ASID American Society of Interior Designers(140)
ASIDIC Association of Information and Dissemination Centers(201)
ASIFA-Hollywood International Animated Film Society, ASIFA-Hollywood(349)
ASIH American Society of Ichthyologists and Herpetologists(139)
ASIL American Society of International Law(140)
ASIP American Society for Investigative Pathology(130)
Association of SIDS and Infant Mortality Programs(214)
ASIS American Society for Information Science and Technology(130)
ASIS International(163)
ASIWPCA Association of State and Interstate Water Pollution Control Administrators(214)
ASJA American Society of Journalists and Authors(140)
ASJMC Association of Schools of Journalism and Mass Communication(213)
ASL Association for Symbolic Logic(178)
ASLA American Seminar Leaders Association(124)
American Society of Landscape Architects(140)
ASLAP American Society of Laboratory Animal Practitioners(140)
ASLET American Society of Law Enforcement Trainers(140)
ASLH American Society for Legal History(130)
ASLME American Society of Law, Medicine and Ethics(140)
ASLMS American Society for Laser Medicine and Surgery(130)
ASLO American Society of Limnology and Oceanography(140)
ASLRA American Short Line and Regional Railroad Association(125)
ASLSS American Society of Lipo-Suction Surgery(140)
ASM American Society for Microbiology(130)
American Society of Mammalogists(141)
American Society of Missiology(141)
ASMA Aerospace Medical Association(10)
American Society of Marine Artists(141)
American Sports Medicine Association(148)
ASMAC American Society of Music Arrangers and Composers(142)
ASMC American Society of Military Comptrollers(141)
ASMD Association of Science Museum Directors(213)
ASMDT American Society of Master Dental Technologists(141)
ASME American Society of Magazine Editors(141)
American Society of Mechanical Engineers(141)
ASMEIGTI ASME International Gas Turbine Institute(163)
ASMP American Society of Media Photographers(141)
ASMR American Society of Mining and Reclamation(141)
ASMS American Society for Mass Spectrometry(130)
American Society of Maxillofacial Surgeons(141)
ASN American Society for Neurochemistry(130)
American Society for Nutrition(131)
American Society of Naturalists(142)
American Society of Nephrology(142)
American Society of Neuroimaging(142)
American Society of Notaries(142)
Association for the Study of Nationalities(181)
ASNC American Society of Nuclear Cardiology(142)
ASNE American Society of Naval Engineers(142)
American Society of Newspaper Editors(142)
ASNR American Society of Neuroradiology(142)
American Society of Neurorehabilitation(142)
ASNT American Society for Nondestructive Testing(131)
ASO American Society of Ocularists(143)

ASOA American Society of Ophthalmic Administrators(143)
ASOL American Symphony Orchestra League(150)
ASOPA American Society of Orthopaedic Physician's Assistants(143)
ASOPRS American Society of Ophthalmic Plastic and Reconstructive Surgery(143)
ASOR American Schools of Oriental Research(124)
ASORN American Society of Ophthalmic Registered Nurses(143)
ASOSS American Society of Sephardic Studies(146)
ASP American Society for Photobiology(131)
American Society for Plasticulture(131)
American Society of Papyrologists(143)
American Society of Parasitologists(143)
American Society of Perfumers(143)
American Society of Pharmacognosy(144)
American Society of Photographers(144)
American Society of Primatologists(145)
Association of Shareware Professionals(214)
Association of Subspecialty Professors(216)
ASPA American Salvage Pool Association(124)
American Shrimp Processors Association(125)
American Society for Public Administration(132)
American Society of Pension Professionals and Actuaries(143)
Association of Specialized and Professional Accreditors(214)
ASPAN American Society of PeriAnesthesia Nurses(144)
ASPB American Society of Plant Biologists(144)
ASPC/AMHR American Shetland Pony Club/American Miniature Horse Registry(125)
ASPE American Society for Precision Engineering(132)
American Society of Plumbing Engineers(144)
American Society of Podiatry Executives(145)
American Society of Professional Estimators(145)
American Society of Psychopathology of Expression(145)
ASPEN American Society for Parenteral and Enteral Nutrition(131)
ASPET American Society for Pharmacology and Experimental Therapeutics(131)
ASPH Association of Schools of Public Health(213)
ASPHO American Society of Pediatric Hematology/Oncology(143)
ASPI Association of Suppliers to the Paper Industry(216)
ASPLP American Society for Political and Legal Philosophy(131)
ASPM American Society of Podiatric Medicine(145)
ASPMA American Society of Podiatric Medical Assistants(144)
ASPMN American Society of Pain Management Nurses(143)
ASPN American Society for Pediatric Neurosurgery(131)
American Society of Pediatric Nephrology(143)
ASPNA Association of Surfing Professionals - North America(216)
ASPO American Society of Preventive Oncology(145)
ASPP American Society of Picture Professionals(144)
American Society of Psychoanalytic Physicians(145)
ASPPB Association of State and Provincial Psychology Boards(215)
ASPRS American Society for Photogrammetry and Remote Sensing(131)
ASPRSN American Society of Plastic Surgical Nurses(144)
ASPS American Society of Plastic Surgeons(144)
ASPT American Society of Plant Taxonomists(144)
ASQ American Society for Quality(132)
ASQDE American Society of Questioned Document Examiners(145)
ASR Academy of Surgical Research(5)
Association for the Sociology of Religion(180)
ASRA American Shropshire Registry Association(125)
American Society of Regional Anesthesia and Pain Medicine(145)
ASRM American Society for Reconstructive Microsurgery(132)
American Society for Reproductive Medicine(132)
ASRS American Society of Retina Specialists(145)
American Society of Roommate Services(145)
ASRT American Society of Radiologic Technologists(145)
Ass.Clin.Sci Association of Clinical Scientists(190)
ASSBT American Society of Sugar Beet Technologists(146)
ASSE American Society of Safety Engineers(146)
American Society of Sanitary Engineering(146)
ASSFN American Society for Stereotactic and Functional Neurosurgery(132)
ASSH American Society for Surgery of the Hand(132)
ASSM Association of State Supervisors of Mathematics(216)
ASSO American Society for the Study of Orthodontics(132)
AST American Society of Transplantation(146)
Association of Surgical Technologists(216)
ASTA American Seed Trade Association(124)
American Society of Travel Agents(146)
American Spice Trade Association(148)
American String Teachers Association(149)
ASTC American Society of Theatre Consultants(146)
American Society of Trial Consultants(147)
Association of Science-Technology Centers(213)
ASTCDPD Chronic Disease Directors(246)
ASTD American Society for Training and Development(133)
ASTDA American Sexually Transmitted Diseases Association(125)
ASTDD Association of State and Territorial Dental Directors(215)
ASTDN Association of State and Territorial Directors of Nursing(215)
ASTE American Society of Test Engineers(146)
ASTHO Association of State and Territorial Health Officials(215)
ASTL American Society of Transportation and Logisitcs(146)
ASTM ASTM International(221)
ASTMH American Society of Tropical Medicine and Hygiene(147)
ASTNA Air & Surface Transport Nurses Association(12)
ASTP American Society of Tax Professionals(146)
ASTPHND Association of State and Territorial Public Health Nutrition Directors(215)
ASTR American Society for Theatre Research(132)
ASTRA American Specialty Toy Retailing Association(148)
ASTRO American Society for Therapeutic Radiology and Oncology(133)
ASTS American Society of Transplant Surgeons(146)
ASTSWMO Association of State and Territorial Solid Waste Management Officials(215)
ASV American Society for Virology(133)
ASVO American Society of Veterinary Ophthalmology(147)
ASWA American Society of Women Accountants(147)
ASWB Association of Social Work Boards(214)
ASWLS Scribes(607)
ASWM Association of State Wetland Managers(216)
ASWP American Society of Wedding Professionals(147)
ATA Access Technology Association(6)
Africa Travel Association(11)
Air Transport Association of America(13)
American Tarentaise Association(150)
American Telemedicine Association(151)
American Teleservices Association(151)
American Thyroid Association(151)
American Tinnitus Association(151)
American Trakehner Association(152)
American Translators Association(152)
American Trucking Associations(152)
American Tunaboat Association(152)
Animal Transportation Association(157)
Archery Trade Association(160)
Association of Talent Agents(216)
ATAE Automotive Trade Association Executives(224)
ATBC Association for Tropical Biology and Conservation(181)
ATBI Allied Trades of the Baking Industry(17)
ATC Agricultural and Food Transporters Conference(12)
ATCA Air Traffic Control Association(13)
American Theatre Critics Association(151)
ATCB Art Therapy Credentials Board(162)
ATD Alpha Tau Delta(18)
American Truck Dealers(152)
ATDD-BLE American Train Dispatchers Association(152)
ATE Association of Teacher Educators(217)
ATEA American Technical Education Association(150)

ATEC Aviation Technician Education Council(225)
ATG Accordionists and Teachers Guild International(6)
ATHE Association for Theatre in Higher Education(181)
ATIA Assistive Technology Industry Association(164)
ATIS Alliance for Telecommunications Industry Solutions(16)
ATLA American Theological Library Association(151)
Association of Trial Lawyers of America(218)
ATLAS Association of Teachers of Latin American Studies(217)
ATLLP Association of Transportation Professionals(218)
ATMA American Textile Machinery Association(151)
ATMC Automotive Training Managers Council(224)
ATMCH Association of Teachers of Maternal and Child Health(217)
ATME Association of Theatre Movement Educators(218)
Association of Travel Marketing Executives(218)
ATMI Association for Technology in Music Instruction(178)
ATP Association for Transpersonal Psychology(181)
Association of Test Publishers(217)
ATPAM Association of Theatrical Press Agents and Managers(218)
ATPM Association of Teachers of Preventive Medicine(217)
ATPO Association of Technical Personnel in Ophthalmology(217)
ATRA Advanced Transit Association(9)
American Therapeutic Recreation Association(151)
American Tort Reform Association(152)
Automatic Transmission Rebuilders Association(223)
ATS American Thoracic Society(151)
American Trauma Society(152)
Association of Theological Schools in the United States and Canada(218)
ATSA Association for the Treatment of Sexual Abusers(181)
ATSAH Association for Textual Scholarship in Art History(179)
ATSI Association of TeleServices International(217)
ATSOA American Truck Stop Operators Association(152)
ATSP Association of Technical and Supervisory Professionals(217)
Association of Telehealth Service Providers(217)
ATSS Association of Traumatic Stress Specialists(218)
ATSSA American Traffic Safety Services Association(152)
ATTA Adventure Travel Trade Association(9)
American Tin Trade Association(151)
ATTW Association of Teachers of Technical Writing(217)
ATU Amalgamated Transit Union(18)
ATWS Association of Third World Studies(218)
AUA American Underground-Construction Association(152)
American Urological Association(153)
Association of University Anesthesiologists(219)
Association of University Architects(219)
AUBER Association for University Business and Economic Research(181)
AUCC American-Uzbekistan Chamber of Commerce(156)
AUCCCD Association for University and College Counseling Center Directors(181)
AUGS American Urogynecologic Society(153)
AUID Association of University Interior Designers(219)
AUPHA Association of University Programs in Health Administration(219)
AUPO Association of University Professors of Ophthalmology(219)
AUR Association of University Radiologists(219)
AURA Association of Universities for Research in Astronomy(219)
AURP Association of University Research Parks(219)
AUSA Association of the United States Army(218)
AUTM Association of University Technology Managers(219)
AUVSI Association for Unmanned Vehicle Systems International(181)
AVACI Academy of Veterinary Allergy and Clinical Immunology(6)
AVCA American Volleyball Coaches Association(153)
AVDA American Veterinary Distributors Association(153)
AVDS American Veterinary Dental Society(153)
AVEM Association of Vacuum Equipment Manufacturers International(220)
AVEPDA American Vocational Education Personnel Development Association(153)
AVF American Venous Forum(153)
AVH Academy of Veterinary Homeopathy(6)
AVIOS American Voice Input/Output Society(153)
AVIR Association of Vascular and Interventional Radiographers(220)
AVMA American Veterinary Medical Association(153)
AVMR Association of Visual Merchandise Representatives(220)
AVP Association of Volleyball Professionals(220)
AVS American Viola Society(153)
AVS Science and Technology Society(225)
AVSAB American Veterinary Society of Animal Behavior(153)
AVSL Association of Vision Science Librarians(220)
AWA American Watch Association(154)
AWACHR American White/American Creme Horse Registry(154)
AWBA American Wholesale Booksellers Association(154)
AWC Affiliated Warehouse Companies(10)
Association for Women in Communications(182)
Association for Women in Computing(182)
AWCI American Watchmakers-Clockmakers Institute(154)
American Wire Cloth Institute(155)
Association of the Wall and Ceiling Industries-International(218)
AWEA American Wind Energy Association(155)
AWFS Association of Woodworking-Furnishings Suppliers(221)
AWG Association for Women Geoscientists(182)
AWHONN Association of Women's Health, Obstetric and Neonatal Nurses(220)
AWI Architectural Woodwork Institute(160)
AWID Association for Women's Rights in Development(183)
AWIR Ankole Watusi International Registry(157)
AWIS Association for Women in Science(182)
AWJ Association for Women Journalists(182)
AWM Association for Women in Mathematics(182)
AWMA American Walnut Manufacturers Association(153)
American Wholesale Marketers Association(155)
AWMI Association of Women in the Metal Industries(220)
AWO American Waterways Operators(154)
AWP Association for Women in Psychology(182)
Association of Writers and Writing Programs(221)
AWPA American Wire Producers Association(155)
American Wood-Preservers' Association(155)
AWPI American Wood Preservers Institute(155)
AWPS American Welara Pony Society(154)
AWR American Warmblood Registry(154)
AWRA American Water Resources Association(154)
AWRF Associated Wire Rope Fabricators(166)
AWRT American Women in Radio and Television(155)
AWS American Welding Society(154)
American Wine Society(155)
Association of Winery Suppliers(220)
Association of Women Surgeons(220)
AWSCPA American Woman's Society of Certified Public Accountants(155)
AWSM Association for Women in Sports Media(182)
AWSS Association of Women Soil Scientists(220)
AWT Association of Water Technologies(220)
AWV Association for Women Veterinarians(182)
AWWA American Water Works Association(154)
AYP Association of YMCA Professionals(221)
AZA American Zinc Association(156)
American Zoo and Aquarium Association(156)
AZO Alpha Zeta Omega(18)
BA Belt Association(227)
BAA Braunvieh Association of America(232)
Brewers' Association of America(232)
BABi BritishAmerican Business Inc.(233)
BAC International Union of Bricklayers and Allied Craftsworkers(395)
BACC Belgian American Chamber of Commerce in the United States(227)
Brazilian American Chamber of Commerce(232)
BAEB Bituminous and Aggregate Equipment Bureau(229)
BAFT Bankers' Association for Finance and Trade(226)
BAI Bank Administration Institute(225)

BAMM Basic Acrylic Monomer Manufacturers(226)
BAP Beta Alpha Psi(228)
BAWA Burley Auction Warehouse Association(235)
BBA Black Broadcasters Alliance(230)
BBAA Barzona Breeders Association of America(226)
BBII Brass and Bronze Ingot Industry(232)
BBU Beefmaster Breeders United(227)
BBWA Bright Belt Warehouse Association(232)
BBWAA Baseball Writers Association of America(226)
BC Business Council(235)
BCA Baptist Communicators Association(226)
BCA(226)
Billiard Congress of America(228)
BioCommunications Association(229)
Black Coaches Association(230)
Building Commissioning Association(234)
BCALA Black Caucus of the American Library Association(230)
BCBSA Blue Cross and Blue Shield Association(231)
BCC Bulk Carrier Conference(235)
BCCA Broadcast Cable Credit Association(233)
BCFM Broadcast Cable Financial Management Association(233)
BCI Battery Council International(226)
BCMA Biscuit and Cracker Manufacturers' Association(229)
BCOA Bituminous Coal Operators Association(229)
BCSP Board of Certified Safety Professionals(231)
BCTGM Bakery, Confectionery, Tobacco Workers and Grain Millers International Union(225)
BDA Broadcast Designers' Association(233)
BDHCA Belgian Draft Horse Corp. of America(227)
BDPA Black Data Processing Associates(230)
BEA Broadcast Education Association(233)
BEMA BEMA - The Baking Industry Suppliers Association(227)
BEMS Bioelectromagnetics Society(229)
BESLA Black Entertainment and Sports Lawyers Association(230)
BFF Black Filmmaker Foundation(230)
BFMA Business Forms Management Association(235)
BGA Barre Granite Association(226)
Behavior Genetics Association(227)
BGFMA Bridge Grid Flooring Manufacturers Association(232)
BGS Belted Galloway Society(227)
BHC Business History Conference(235)
BHEF Business Higher Education Forum(235)
BHI Better Hearing Institute(228)
BHMA Builders Hardware Manufacturers Association(234)
BI Beer Institute(227)
BIA Binding Industries Association(228)
Brick Industry Association(232)
Buses International Association(235)
BICSI BICSI(228)
BIF Beef Improvement Federation(227)
BIFMA Internat'l Business and Institutional Furniture Manufacturers Association International(235)
BIO Biotechnology Industry Organization(229)
BISA Bank Insurance and Securities Association(226)
BISG Book Industry Study Group, Inc.(231)
BISSC Baking Industry Sanitation Standards Committee(225)
BKR BKR International(229)
BLE Brotherhood of Locomotive Engineers and Trainmen(233)
BMA Biomedical Marketing Association(229)
Business Marketing Association(235)
BMC BMC - A Foodservice Sales and Marketing Council(231)
Brake Manufacturers Council(232)
BMDA Building Material Dealers Association(234)
BMES Biomedical Engineering Society(229)
BMI Book Manufacturers' Institute(231)
BMMA Biotech Medical Management Association(229)
BMWED Brotherhood of Maintenance of Way Employees(233)
BNA Benchmarking Network Association(227)
BOMA Building Owners and Managers Association International(234)
BOMA-USA Billings Ovulation Method Association of the United States(228)
BOMI Building Owners and Managers Institute International(234)
BPA Black Psychiatrists of America(230)
BPA Worldwide(232)
Business Professionals of America(236)
BPAA Bowling Proprietors Association of America(231)
BPCA Business Products Credit Association(235)
BPS Biophysical Society(229)
BPSA Bicycle Product Suppliers Association(228)
BPW/USA Business and Professional Women/USA(235)
BRAG Black Retail Action Group(230)
BRASA Brazilian Studies Association(232)
BRC/TCU Brotherhood Railway Carmen/TCU(233)
BRS Brotherhood of Railroad Signalmen(233)
BSA Bearing Specialist Association(226)
Bibliographical Society of America(228)
Bicycle Shippers Association(228)
Botanical Society of America(231)
Business Software Alliance(236)
BSC Biological Stain Commission(229)
BSC/NAHB Building Systems Councils of the National Association of Home Builders(234)
BSCAI Building Service Contractors Association International(234)
BSCBA Brown Swiss Cattle Breeders Association of the U.S.A.(234)
BSDF Beet Sugar Development Foundation(227)
BSWC National Conference of Brewery and Soft Drink Workers - United States and Canada(493)
BTA Business Technology Association(236)
BTGCA Burley Tobacco Growers Cooperative Association(235)
BTN Black Theatre Network(231)
BTWSM Board of Trade of the Wholesale Seafood Merchants(231)
BWAA Bowling Writers Association of America(232)
BWI Boating Writers International(231)
BWIP Black Americans in Publishing(230)
C-PORT Committee for Private Offshore Rescue and Towing (C-PORT)(254)
C200 Committee of 200(254)
CA Cantors Assembly(237)
Cranial Academy(278)
CAA Cargo Airline Association(238)
Cigar Association of America(247)
College Art Association(251)
Colombian American Association(252)
CAAHEP Commission on Accreditation of Allied Health Education Programs(254)
CAAP Committee of American Axle Producers(254)
CAB Cabletelevision Advertising Bureau(236)
CABC Canadian-American Business Council(237)
CABMA College Athletic Business Management Association(251)
CADCA CPA Auto Dealer Consultants Association(278)
CAEL Council for Adult and Experiential Learning(267)
CAFS Chinese American Food Society(245)
CAGI Compressed Air and Gas Institute(257)
CAH Conference on Asian History(260)
CAI Committee of Annuity Insurers(254)
Community Associations Institute(255)
CAID Council of American Instructors of the Deaf(270)
CAJM Council of American Jewish Museums(270)
CALA Chinese-American Librarians Association(245)
CALEA Commission on Accreditation for Law Enforcement Agencies(254)
CALICO Computer Assisted Language Instruction Consortium(257)
CALLERLAB Callerlab-International Association of Square Dance Callers(236)
CAM-I Consortium for Advanced Manufacturing International(262)
CAMA Civil Aviation Medical Association(247)
Concrete Anchor Manufacturers Association(258)
CAMACOL Latin Chamber of Commerce of U.S.A.(405)
CAMM Council of American Maritime Museums(270)
Council of American Master Mariners(270)
CAMS Chinese American Medical Society(245)
CANA Cremation Association of North America(279)
CAORC Council of American Overseas Research Centers(270)
CAP College of American Pathologists(251)
Community Action Partnership(255)
CAPE Council for American Private Education(268)
CARH Council for Affordable and Rural Housing(268)
CARLJS Council of Archives and Research Libraries in Jewish Studies(270)
CAS Casualty Actuarial Society(239)
Council for the Advancement of Standards in Higher Education(270)
CASBA Cookie and Snack Bakers Association(265)
CASE Council for Advancement and Support of Education(267)
Council of Administrators of Special Education(270)
CASRO Council of American Survey Research Organizations(270)
CAST Council for Agricultural Science and Technology(268)

CAUS Color Association of the United States(252)
CBA Catholic Biblical Association of America(239)
CBA(240)
Community Broadcasters Association(255)
Consumer Bankers Association(263)
Continental Basketball Association(264)
CBAN Community Banking Advisors Network(255)
CBBB Council of Better Business Bureaus(271)
CBC Children's Book Council(244)
CBDNA College Band Directors National Association(251)
CBE Conference of Business Economists(259)
CBFC Copper and Brass Fabricators Council(266)
CBHL Council on Botanical and Horticultural Libraries(275)
CBHNA Consortium of Behavioral Health Nurses and Associates(262)
CBHSNA Cleveland Bay Horse Society of North America(248)
CBI Carbonated Beverage Institute(237)
CBMS Conference Board of the Mathematical Sciences(259)
CBPA Catholic Book Publishers Association(239)
CBSA Copper and Brass Servicenter Association(266)
CBTU Coalition of Black Trade Unionists(249)
CBUNA Certification Board for Urologic Nurses and Associates(242)
CBUS Clydesdale Breeders of the United States(249)
CC Calorimetry Conference(237)
Catecholamine Club(239)
Controllers Council(265)
US Composting Council(681)
CCA Career College Association(237)
Collegiate Commissioners Association(252)
Copywriter's Council of America(266)
CCAA Crane Certification Association of America(278)
CCAI Chamber of Commerce of the Apparel Industry(243)
Chemical Coaters Association International(243)
Collector Car Appraisers International(250)
CCAIT Community College Association for Instruction and Technology(255)
CCAOM Council of Colleges of Acupuncture and Oriental Medicine(271)
CCAR Central Conference of American Rabbis(241)
CCAS Council of Colleges of Arts and Sciences(271)
CCBO Community College Business Officers(255)
CCC Calorie Control Council(237)
Car Care Council(237)
Carpet Cushion Council(238)
Chlorine Chemistry Council(245)
Christian College Consortium(245)
CCCC Conference on College Composition and Communication(260)
CCCU Council for Christian Colleges and Universities(268)
CCE Council on Chiropractic Education(275)
CCFL Conference on Consumer Finance Law(260)
CCG Gift and Collectibles Guild(316)
CCHA Community Colleges Humanities Association(256)
CCI Cotton Council International(267)
CCIA Computer and Communications Industry Association(257)
Consumer Credit Insurance Association(263)
CPA Construction Industry Association(278)
CCIC Property Casualty Conferences(591)
CCIM CCIM Institute(240)
CCJ Conference of Chief Justices(259)
CCJA Community College Journalism Association(256)
CCM Council of Communication Management(271)
CCMA Catholic Campus Ministry Association(239)
CCMI Cashmere and Camel Hair Manufacturers Institute(238)
CCN Certified Contractors NetWork(242)
CCO Council on Chiropractic Orthopedics(275)
CCPA Cemented Carbide Producers Association(241)
China Clay Producers Association(244)
CCPAC Certified Claims Professional Accreditation Council(242)
CCPTR Chiropractic Council on Physiological Therapeutics and Rehabilitation(245)
CCR Council for Chemical Research(268)
CCSA Congress of Chiropractic State Associations(261)
CCSAA Cross Country Ski Areas Association(279)
CCSSO Council of Chief State School Officers(271)
CCTI Composite Can and Tube Institute(256)
CCTMA Closed Circuit Television Manufacturers Association(248)
CCUMC Consortium of College and University Media Centers(262)
CCWAVES Commission on Certification of Work Adjustment and Vocational Evaluation Specialists(254)
CCWH Coordinating Council for Women in History(265)
CDA Copier Dealers Association(266)
Copper Development Association(266)
CDABO College of Diplomates of the American Board of Orthodontics(251)
CDC Continental Dorset Club(264)
CDFA Council of Development Finance Agencies(271)
CDFEA California Dried Fruit Export Association(236)
CDHCF Consultant Dietitians in Health Care Facilities(263)
CDI Council on Diagnostic Imaging to the A.C.A.(275)
CDIA Consumer Data Industry Association(263)
CDIM Clerkship Directors in Internal Medicine(248)
CDMA Chain Drug Marketing Association(242)
CDS Community Development Society(256)
CDVCA Community Development Venture Capital Alliance(256)
CEA Cement Employers Association(241)
College English Association(251)
Consumer Electronics Association(263)
Cooperative Education and Internship Association(265)
Correctional Education Association(266)
County Executives of America(277)
CEAI Christian Educators Association International(246)
CEASD Conference of Educational Administrators of Schools and Programs for the Deaf(259)
CEB Council on Employee Benefits(276)
CEC Council for Exceptional Children(268)
Cryogenic Engineering Conference(280)
CECPR Council for Professional Recognition(269)
CED Council on Education of the Deaf(276)
CEDIA Custom Electronic Design and Installation Association(280)
CEE Conference on English Education(260)
Council for Ethics in Economics(268)
CEF Creative Education Foundation(278)
CEFPI Council of Educational Facility Planners, International(271)
CEI Computer Ethics Institute(257)
CEIR Center for Exhibition Industry Research(241)
CEL Conference on English Leadership(260)
CEMA Computer Event Marketing Association(257)
Converting Equipment Manufacturers Association(265)
Conveyor Equipment Manufacturers Association(265)
CEO Chief Executives Organization(244)
CERCA Council for Electronic Revenue Communication Advancement(268)
CerMA Ceramic Manufacturers Association(241)
CES Coalition of Essential Schools(249)
Council for European Studies(268)
CESI Council for Elementary Science International(268)
CESSE Council of Engineering and Scientific Society Executives(271)
CETA Cleaning Equipment Trade Association(247)
Controlled Environment Testing Association(264)
CEW Cosmetic Executive Women(267)
CFA Catfish Farmers of America(239)
Commercial Finance Association(253)
Concrete Foundations Association(258)
Consumer Federation of America(263)
CFAE Council for Art Education(268)
CFAP Council on Fine Art Photography(276)
CFCA Communications Fraud Control Association(255)
CFDA Council of Fashion Designers of America(272)
CFEA College Fraternity Editors Association(251)
CFESA Commercial Food Equipment Service Association(253)
CFF Cystic Fibrosis Foundation(281)
CFFA Chemical Fabrics and Film Association(243)
CFH Conference on Faith and History(261)
CFHA Collaborative Family Healthcare Association(250)
CFMA Construction Financial Management Association(262)
CFPMI Cold Formed Parts and Machine Institute(250)
CFR Casual Furniture Retailers(239)
CFS Council of Fleet Specialists(272)
CFSA Casket and Funeral Supply Association of America(238)
Community Financial Services Association of America(256)

CFSBI Cold Finished Steel Bar Institute(250)
CFSEB International Conference of Funeral Service Examining Boards(366)
CG Choristers Guild(245)
Conductors Guild(259)
CGA College Gymnastics Association(251)
Compressed Gas Association(257)
Concord Grape Association(258)
CGCS Council of the Great City Schools(275)
CGP Coalition for Government Procurement(249)
CGS Council of Graduate Schools(272)
CGSM Consortium for Graduate Study and Management(262)
CHA CHA - Certified Horsemanship Association(242)
CHA-US Catholic Health Association of the United States(240)
CHART Council of Hotel and Restaurant Trainers(272)
CHC Committee on History in the Classroom(254)
Czechoslovak History Conference(281)
CHEA Council for Higher Education Accreditation(269)
CHF Chemical Heritage Foundation(243)
CHIME College of Healthcare Information Management Executives(251)
CHJ Conference of Historical Journals(259)
ChLA Children's Literature Association(244)
CHPA Consumer Healthcare Products Association(263)
Corporate Housing Providers Association(266)
CI Catfish Institute(239)
Chlorine Institute(245)
Combustion Institute(253)
Cordage Institute(266)
Cranberry Institute(278)
CIAB Council of Insurance Agents and Brokers(272)
CIBO Council of Industrial Boiler Owners(272)
CIBS Cosmetic Industry Buyers and Suppliers(267)
CIC Convention Industry Council(265)
Council of Independent Colleges(272)
CICA Captive Insurance Companies Association(237)
CICE Council of Insurance Company Executives(273)
CIDX Chemical Industry Data Exchange(243)
CIES CIES, The Food Business Forum(246)
Comparative and International Education Society(256)
CIF Construction Innovation Forum(262)
CIFA Council of Infrastructure Financing Authorities(272)
CII Containerization and Intermodal Institute(264)
Council of Institutional Investors(272)
Council of International Investigators(273)
CIIT CIIT Centers for Health Research(247)
CIMA Cellulose Insulation Manufacturers Association(241)
CIMPA Connected International Meeting Professionals Association(261)
CIMTA Cottage Industry Miniaturists Trade Association(267)
CIRA Council of Independent Restaurants of America(272)
CIRB Crop Insurance Research Bureau(279)
CIS Clinical Immunology Society(248)
CISA Casting Industry Suppliers Association(239)
CISCA Ceilings and Interior Systems Construction Association(241)
CISPI Cast Iron Soil Pipe Institute(238)
CITBA Customs and International Trade Bar Association(280)
CITE Council for International Tax Education(269)
CIU Congress of Independent Unions(261)
CJE Council for Jewish Education(269)
CJJ Coalition for Juvenile Justice(249)
CJSS Conference on Jewish Social Studies(261)
CKRC Cement Kiln Recycling Coalition(241)
CLA Catholic Library Association(240)
Coin Laundry Association(250)
Community Leadership Association(256)
Computer Law Association(258)
CLA-USA Christian Labor Association of the United States of America(246)
CLAH Conference on Latin American History(261)
CLAO Contact Lens Association of Ophthalmologists(264)
CLARB Council of Landscape Architectural Registration Boards(273)
CLAS Clinical Ligand Assay Society(248)
Congress of Lung Association Staffs(261)
CLC Contact Lens Council(264)
CLD Council for Learning Disabilities(269)
CLEAR Council on Licensure, Enforcement and Regulation(276)
CLFMI Chain Link Fence Manufacturers Institute(242)
CLGH Committee on Lesbian and Gay History(254)
CLIA Cruise Lines International Association(280)
CLLA Commercial Law League of America(253)
CLMA Clinical Laboratory Management Association(248)
Contact Lens Manufacturers Association(264)
CLMP Council of Literary Magazines and Presses(273)
CLPHA Council of Large Public Housing Authorities(273)
CLS Christian Legal Society(246)
CLSA Canon Law Society of America(237)
Contact Lens Society of America(264)
CLSI Clinical and Laboratory Standards Institute(248)
CLTA Chinese Language Teachers Association(245)
CLUW Coalition of Labor Union Women(249)
CMA Calendar Marketing Association(236)
Catholic Medical Association(240)
Chamber Music America(242)
Chocolate Manufacturers Association(245)
Christian Management Association(246)
Closure Manufacturers Association(248)
College Media Advisers(251)
Communications Marketing Association(255)
Cookware Manufacturers Association(265)
Council of Manufacturing Associations(273)
Country Music Association(277)
CMA-USA Clothing Manufacturers Association of the U.S.A.(248)
CMAA Club Managers Association of America(249)
Cocoa Merchants' Association of America(250)
Comics Magazine Association of America(253)
Construction Management Association of America(262)
CMCAS Capital Markets Credit Analysts Society(237)
CMDA Christian Medical & Dental Associations(246)
CMG Color Marketing Group(252)
Computer Measurement Group(258)
CMI Can Manufacturers Institute(237)
Cherry Marketing Institute(243)
Cleaning Management Institute(247)
CMIS Computerized Medical Imaging Society(258)
CMMA Communications Media Management Association(255)
CMOR Council for Marketing and Opinion Research(269)
CMPA Church Music Publishers Association(246)
CMPAA Certified Milk Producers Association of America(242)
CMRC Construction Marketing Research Council(262)
CMS Clay Minerals Society(247)
College Music Society(251)
CMSA Case Management Society of America(238)
Commercial Mortgage Securities Association(253)
CMSM Conference of Major Superiors of Men, U.S.A.(259)
CMSS Council of Medical Specialty Socs.(273)
CNIRS Council for Near-Infrared Spectroscopy(269)
CNS Child Neurology Society(244)
Congress of Neurological Surgeons(261)
COA Commissioned Officers Association of the United States Public Health Service(254)
Council of the Americas(275)
COAA Construction Owners Association of America(263)
COAI Clowns of America, International(248)
CODA Council of Dance Administrators(271)
CODSIA Council of Defense and Space Industry Associations(271)
COE Council for Opportunity in Education(269)
Council on Occupational Education(276)
COF Council on Foundations(276)
COFE Council on Forest Engineering(276)
COGEL Council on Governmental Ethics Laws(276)
COGR Council on Governmental Relations(276)
COGS Computer Oriented Geological Society(258)
COHEAO Coalition of Higher Education Assistance Organizations(249)
COIA Conservative Orthopaedics International Association(261)
COLA COLA(250)
COLT Council on Library-Media Technicians(276)
COMPA Conference of Minority Public Administrators(259)
COMPTEL COMPTEL(257)
CompTIA Computing Technology Industry Association(258)
COMSOC IEEE Communications Society(330)
COMSS Council of Musculoskeletal Specialty Socs.(273)
COMTO Conference of Minority Transportation Officials(259)
COPAFS Council of Professional Associations on Federal Statistics(273)

COPAS Council of Petroleum Accountants Socs.(273)
COPE Council of Protocol Executives(274)
COPS Conference of Philosophical Socs.(260)
CoPTP Coalition of Publicly Traded Partnerships(249)
CORD Congress on Research in Dance(261)
COS Clinical Orthopaedic Society(248)
COSA Carwash Owner's and Supplier's Association(238)
COSC Council of State Chambers of Commerce(274)
COSCA Conference of State Court Adminstrators(260)
COSCDA Council of State Community Development Agencies(274)
CoSIDA College Sports Information Directors of America(252)
COSLA Chief Officers of State Library Agencies(244)
CoSN Consortium for School Networking(262)
COSSA Consortium of Social Science Associations(262)
COST Council On State Taxation(277)
COSTHA Council on the Safe Transportation of Hazardous Articles(277)
COVA Council of Vehicle Associations(275)
COVD College of Optometrists in Vision Development(252)
COVR Coalition of Visionary Resources(250)
CPA Catholic Press Association(240)
Chlorobenzene Producers Association(245)
Classroom Publishers Association(247)
Composite Panel Association(257)
Contract Packaging Association(264)
CPAAI CPA Associates International(277)
CPADN Career Planning and Adult Development Network(238)
CPAI CPAmerica International(278)
CPB Contractors Pump Bureau(264)
CPCU CPCU Society(278)
CPDA Chemical Producers and Distributors Association(243)
CPI Credit Professionals International(279)
CPIA Chlorinated Paraffins Industry Association(245)
CPMA Color Pigments Manufacturers Association(253)
CPMB Concrete Plant Manufacturers Bureau(258)
CPOA Chief Petty Officers Association(244)
CPPA Corrugated Polyethylene Pipe Association(267)
CPSA Check Payment Systems Association(243)
CPST Commission on Professionals in Science and Technology(254)
CRA California Redwood Association(236)
Computing Research Association(258)
Corn Refiners Association(266)
CRAFT Craft Retailers Association for Tomorrow(278)
CRB Council of Real Estate Brokerage Managers(274)
Country Radio Broadcasters, Inc.(277)
CRC Coordinating Research Council(265)
CRCPD Conference of Radiation Control Program Directors(260)
CRD Council for Resource Development(269)
CRE Counselors of Real Estate(277)
CREOG Council on Resident Education in Obstetrics and Gynecology(277)
CRF Credit Research Foundation(279)
CRHA Colorado Ranger Horse Association(253)
CRI Carpet and Rug Institute(238)
Customer Relations Institute(280)
CRLA College Reading and Learning Association(252)
CRM Commercial Refrigerator Manufacturers Division - ARI(254)
CRMA City and Regional Magazine Association(247)
CRN Council for Responsible Nutrition(270)
CRS Controlled Release Society(265)
Council of Residential Specialists(274)
CRSA Catalogue Raisonne Scholars Association(239)
CRSI Concrete Reinforcing Steel Institute(259)
CRWAD Conference of Research Workers in Animal Diseases(260)
CS Coblentz Society(250)
CSA Chamber of Shipping of America(243)
Chemical Sources Association(243)
Contract Services Association of America(264)
Costume Society of America(267)
Cryogenic Society of America(280)
CSAA Central Station Alarm Association(241)
CSAP Council of State Association Presidents(274)
CSAVR Council of State Administrators of Vocational Rehabilitation(274)
CSBA Columbia Sheep Breeders Association of America(253)
CSBS Conference of State Bank Supervisors(260)
CSCAA College Swimming Coaches Association of America(252)
CSCMP Council of Supply Chain Management Professionals(275)
CSDA Concrete Sawing and Drilling Association(259)
CSE Council of Science Editors(274)
CSEE Council for Spiritual and Ethical Education(270)
CSF College Savings Foundation(252)
CSG Council of State Governments(275)
CSHEMA Campus Safety, Health and Environmental Management Association(237)
CSI Cast Stone Institute(238)
Christian Schools International(246)
Coalition of Service Industries(249)
Computer Security Institute(258)
Construction Specifications Institute(263)
CSLA Church and Synagogue Library Association(246)
CSNA Classification Society of North America(247)
CSPA Consumer Specialty Products Association(263)
CSPN College Savings Plans Network(252)
CSPT Conference for the Study of Political Thought(259)
CSRS Cervical Spine Research Society(242)
CSSA Communications Supply Service Association(255)
Crop Science Society of America(279)
CSSB Cedar Shake and Shingle Bureau(240)
CSSP Council of Scientific Society Presidents(274)
CSSR Council of Societies for the Study of Religion(274)
CSTE Council of State and Territorial Epidemiologists(274)
CSUSA Copyright Society of the U.S.A.(266)
CSWE Council on Social Work Education(277)
CSWF Clinical Social Work Federation(248)
CTA Coal Technology Association(249)
Consolidated Tape Association(262)
CTAA Community Transportation Association of America(256)
CTAM Cable & Telecommunications Association for Marketing(236)
CTDA Ceramic Tile Distributors Association(241)
Custom Tailors and Designers Association of America(280)
CTFA Cosmetic, Toiletry and Fragrance Association(267)
CTHRA Cable and Telecommunications Human Resources Association(236)
CTI Cooling Technology Institute(265)
CTIA CTIA - The Wireless Association(280)
CTIOA Ceramic Tile Institute of America(242)
CTPWD Caucus for Television Producers, Writers & Directors(240)
CTS College Theology Society(252)
CTSA Catholic Theological Society of America(240)
CTTE Council on Technology Teacher Education(277)
CUES Credit Union Executives Society(279)
CUNA Credit Union National Association(279)
CUPA-HR College and University Professional Association for Human Resources(250)
CVA Correctional Vendors Association(267)
CVSA Commercial Vehicle Safety Alliance(254)
CWA Communications Workers of America(255)
Construction Writers Association(263)
CWAA Cotton Warehouse Association of America(267)
CWEEA Cooperative Work Experience Education Association(265)
CWLA Child Welfare League of America(244)
CWLA/AAPSC CWLA - Child Mental Health Division(280)
CWOA Chief Warrant and Warrant Officers Association, United States Coast Guard(244)
CWRT Center for Waste Reduction Technologies(241)
CWS Caucus for Women in Statistics(240)
CWSRA Chester White Swine Record Association(244)
DACC Danish-American Chamber of Commerce (USA)(281)
DACOR Diplomatic and Consular Officers, Retired(284)
DAMA Data Management Association International(282)
DASMA Door and Access Systems Manufacturers' Association, International(286)
DATIA Drug and Alcohol Testing Industry Association(287)
DBE Dibasic Esters Group(284)
DBIA Design-Build Institute of America(283)
DBM Distribution Business Management Association(286)
DCA Dance Critics Association(281)
Devon Cattle Association(284)
Diamond Council of America(284)
Distribution Contractors Association(286)
Dredging Contractors of America(287)
DCAT Drug, Chemical and Associated Technologies Association(287)
DCCA Directional Crossing Contractors Association(285)
DCUC Defense Credit Union Council(282)

DDA Dental Dealers of America(283)
Display Distributors Association(285)
DDNA Developmental Disabilities Nurses Association(284)
DDPA Delta Dental Plans Association(282)
DEA Dance Educators of America(281)
Drilling Engineering Association(287)
DECA Distributive Education Clubs of America(286)
Driver Employer Council of America(287)
DEMA Diving Equipment and Marketing Association(286)
DERA Disaster Preparedness and Emergency Response Association(285)
DETC Distance Education and Training Council(285)
DFI Deep Foundations Institute(282)
DFPA Defense Fire Protection Association(282)
DG Dramatists Guild of America(287)
DGA Directors Guild of America(285)
DGAC Dangerous Goods Advisory Council(281)
DGMA Dental Group Management Association(283)
DGTC Distillers Grains Technology Council(286)
DHI Door and Hardware Institute(287)
DHPE Directors of Health Promotion and Public Health Education(285)
DIA Drug Information Association(287)
DINA Select Registry/Distinguished Inns of North America(608)
DIPRA Ductile Iron Pipe Research Association(287)
DIS Ductile Iron Society(288)
DISA Data Interchange Standards Association(281)
DISCUS Distilled Spirits Council of the U.S.(286)
DLCA Distribution and LTL Carriers Association(286)
DMA Dance Masters of America(281)
Dietary Managers Association(284)
Digital Media Association(284)
Direct Marketing Association(285)
DMAA Disease Management Association of America(285)
DMAC Direct Marketing Agency Council(285)
DMI Dairy Management(281)
Design Management Institute(283)
DMIA Diamond Manufacturers and Importers Association of America(284)
Document Management Industries Association(286)
DMIFSC Direct Marketing Insurance and Financial Services Council(285)
DNA Delta Nu Alpha Transportation Fraternity(282)
Dermatology Nurses' Association(283)
DO Delta Omicron(282)
DPA Design Professionals Association(283)
DPC Domestic Petroleum Council(286)
DPE Delta Pi Epsilon(282)
DPI Digital Printing and Imaging Association(284)
DRA Dude Ranchers' Association(288)
DRI Defense Research Institute(282)
DRII DRI International(287)
DSA Direct Selling Association(285)
DSAA Driving School Association of America(287)
DSD Delta Sigma Delta(282)
DSI Decision Sciences Institute(282)
DSP Delta Sigma Pi(283)
DTA Dental Trade Alliance(283)
DTP Delta Theta Phi(283)
DWAA Dog Writers' Association of America(286)
DWF Delta Waterfowl Foundation(283)
EAA Ecuadorean American Association(288)
Environmental Assessment Association(296)
EABC European-American Business Council(298)
EANGUS Enlisted Association of the National Guard of the United States(295)
EAPA Employee Assistance Professionals Association(293)
EASA Electrical Apparatus Service Association(290)
EASNA Employee Assistance Society of North America(293)
EBA Energy Bar Association(294)
Environmental Bankers Association(296)
EBAA Eye Bank Association of America(300)
EBRI Employee Benefit Research Institute(293)
ECA Electrocoat Association(291)
Embroidery Council of America(292)
Express Carriers Association(300)
ECCMA Electronic Commerce Code Management Association(291)
ECEDHA Electrical and Computer Engineering Department Heads Association(290)
ECEI Early Childhood Education Institute(288)
ECFA Evangelical Council for Financial Accountability(298)
ECFC Employers Council on Flexible Compensation(293)
ECI Evaporative Cooling Institute(299)
ECLA Evangelical Church Library Association(298)
ECNS EEG and Clinical Neuroscience Society(290)
ECPA Evangelical Christian Publishers Association(298)
ECRI ECRI(288)
ECS Electrochemical Society(291)
ECUC Education Credit Union Council(289)
EDAC EDA Consortium(288)
EDPA Exhibit Designers and Producers Association(299)
EDPMA Emergency Department Practice Management Association(292)
EDRA Environmental Design Research Association(296)
EDS Electronic Distribution Show Corporation(291)
EDTA Educational Theatre Association(289)
Electric Drive Transportation Association(290)
EDUCAUSE EDUCAUSE(290)
EEBA Energy and Environmental Building Association(294)
EEGS Environmental and Engineering Geophysical Society(296)
EEI Edison Electric Institute(289)
EERA Electrical Equipment Representatives Association(291)
EERI Earthquake Engineering Research Institute(288)
EFA Editorial Freelancers Association(289)
EFF Endocrine Fellows Foundation(294)
EFI Energy Frontiers International(294)
EFTA Electronic Funds Transfer Association(292)
EGSA Electrical Generating Systems Association(291)
EHA Economic History Association(288)
EIA Electronic Industries Alliance(292)
Elevator Industries Association(292)
Employee Involvement Association(293)
Environmental Industry Associations(296)
Environmental Information Association(296)
EIC Electrical Insulation Conference(291)
EIMA EIFS Industry Members Association(290)
EJMA Expansion Joint Manufacturers Association(299)
ELA Education Law Association(289)
Equipment Leasing Association of America(297)
ELCON Electricity Consumers Resource Council(291)
EMA Emissions Markets Association(293)
Engine Manufacturers Association(295)
Envelope Manufacturers Association(296)
Expediting Management Association(299)
EMBS Engineering in Medicine and Biology Society(295)
EMC Association of Equipment Management Professionals(195)
EMCWA Electrical Manufacturing and Coil Winding Association(291)
EMRA Emergency Medicine Residents' Association(292)
EMS Environmental Mutagen Society(296)
EMTA EMTA - Trade Association for the Emerging Markets(294)
ENA Emergency Nurses Association(293)
ENTELEC Energy Telecommunications and Electrical Association(294)
EOA Ethics Officer Association(298)
EOS/ESD Electrical Overstress/Electrostatic Discharge Association(291)
EOSA Ethylene Oxide Sterilization Association(298)
EPA Educational Paperback Association(289)
Evangelical Press Association(298)
EPC Emulsion Polymers Council(294)
EPIC Evidence Photographers International Council(299)
EPRI Electric Power Research Institute(290)
EPSA Electric Power Supply Association(290)
EPSMA EPS Molders Association(297)
ERA Electronic Retailing Association(292)
Electronics Representatives Association(292)
EPDM Roofing Association(297)
ERC Employee Relocation Council/Worldwide ERC(293)
ERF Estuarine Research Federation(297)
ERI Espionage Research Institute(297)
ERIC ERISA Industry Committee(297)
ES Econometric Society(288)
Endocrine Society(294)
ESA Ecological Society of America(288)
Entertainment Software Association(295)
Entomological Society of America(295)
Equipment Service Association(297)
Exercise-Safety Association(299)
ESC Energy Security Council(294)
ESCA Exhibition Services and Contractors Association(299)
ESCSI Expanded Shale, Clay and Slate Institute(299)
ESM Employee Services Management Association(293)
ESOAA Eight Sheet Outdoor Advertising Association(290)
ESP Epsilon Sigma Phi(297)

ESRS Early Sites Research Society(288)
ESTA Entertainment Services and Technology Association(295)
ETA Electronic Transactions Association(292)
Embroidery Trade Association(292)
Energy Traffic Association(294)
Evangelical Training Association(298)
ETA-I Electronics Technicians Association International(292)
ETAD ETAD North America(298)
ETC Environmental Technology Council(297)
ETI Equipment and Tool Institute(297)
EUCG EUCG(298)
EWA Education Writers Association(289)
Exotic Wildlife Association(299)
EWG Executive Women in Government(299)
EWI Edison Welding Institute(289)
Executive Women International(299)
FACC Finnish American Chamber of Commerce(307)
French-American Chamber of Commerce(312)
FACSS Federation of Analytical Chemistry and Spectroscopy Societies(303)
FAFLRT Federal and Armed Forces Librarians Roundtable(301)
FAH Federation of American Hospitals(303)
FALJC Federal Administrative Law Judges Conference(301)
FAMA Fire Apparatus Manufacturers' Association(307)
FAMS Foundation for Advances in Medicine and Science(311)
FARB Federation of Associations of Regulatory Boards(303)
FAS Federation of American Scientists(303)
FASA Fashion Accessories Shippers Association(301)
Federated Ambulatory Surgery Association(303)
FASEB Federation of American Socs. for Experimental Biology(303)
FBA Federal Bar Association(302)
Fibre Box Association(305)
Finnsheep Breeders Association(307)
FBF Film and Bag Federation(305)
FBIAA Federal Bureau of Investigation Agents Association(302)
FBLA-PBL Future Business Leaders of America-Phi Beta Lambda(313)
FBPCS Federation of Behavioral, Psychological and Cognitive Sciences(303)
FCA Finishing Contractors Association(306)
Funeral Consumers Alliance(312)
FCBA Federal Communications Bar Association(302)
FCC Farm Credit Council(301)
FCCA Forestry Conservation Communications Association(310)
FCCLA Family, Career, and Community Leaders of America(300)
FCE National Association for Family and Community Education(433)
FCI Fluid Controls Institute(308)
FCIA Fibre Channel Industry Association(305)
FCICA Floor Covering Installation Contractors Association(308)
FCSEA Family and Consumer Sciences Education Association(300)
FCSI Foodservice Consultants Society International(309)
FCTCSC Flue-Cured Tobacco Cooperative Stabilization Corporation(308)
FCUSA Fur Commission USA(312)
FDCC Federation of Defense and Corporate Counsel(303)
FDLC Federation of Diocesan Liturgical Commissions(303)
FDLI Food and Drug Law Institute(309)
FDRA Footwear Distributors and Retailers of America(310)
FDRS Food Distribution Research Society(309)
FEA Federal Education Association(302)
Fraternity Executives Association(311)
FEDA Foodservice Equipment Distributors Association(310)
FEI Financial Executives International(305)
FEMA Farm Equipment Manufacturers Association(301)
Fire Equipment Manufacturers' Association(307)
Flavor and Extract Manufacturers Association of the United States(307)
FEMSA Fire and Emergency Manufacturers and Services Association(307)
FET Federation of Environmental Technologists(303)
FEW Federally Employed Women(302)
FEWA Farm Equipment Wholesalers Association(301)
FFA National FFA Organization(510)
FFC Federal Facilities Council(302)
FFC/SME Forming and Fabricating Community of SME(311)
FFI Family Firm Institute(300)
FFMA Fraternal Field Managers Association(311)
FFTA Foster Family-Based Treatment Association(311)
FGI Fashion Group International(301)
FHS Forest History Society(310)
FIA Forging Industry Association(310)
Forum for Investor Advice(311)
Futures Industry Association(313)
FIAE Food Industry Association Executives(309)
FIASI Fixed Income Analysts Society(307)
FIBCA Flexible Intermediate Bulk Container Association(307)
FICA Fur Information Council of America(313)
FIHE Foundation for Independent Higher Education(311)
FIM Foundation for International Meetings(311)
FIRMA Fiduciary and Risk Management Association(305)
FISA Food Industry Suppliers Association(309)
FIT Forest Industries Telecommunications(310)
FITA Federation of International Trade Associations(304)
FJA Federal Judges Association(302)
FLEOA Federal Law Enforcement Officers Association(302)
FMA Fabricators and Manufacturers Association, International(300)
Federal Managers Association(302)
Financial Management Association International(306)
Financial Markets Association(306)
Fragrance Materials Association of the United States(311)
Fulfillment Management Association(312)
FMC Filter Manufacturers Council(305)
FMI Food Marketing Institute(309)
FMPS Federation of Modern Painters and Sculptors(304)
FMS Federation of Materials Socs.(304)
Financial Managers Society(306)
FMSI Friction Materials Standards Institute(312)
FNS Federal Network for Sustainability(302)
FPA Federal Physicians Association(302)
Financial Planning Association(306)
Flexible Packaging Association(307)
Food Products Association(309)
Foreign Press Association(310)
Fusion Power Associates(313)
FPAA Fresh Produce Association of the Americas(312)
FPDA Fluid Power Distributors Association(308)
FPFC Fresh Produce and Floral Council(312)
FPI Foodservice and Packaging Institute(309)
FPMA Food Processing Machinery and Supplies Association(309)
FPMB Federation of Podiatric Medical Boards(304)
FPP Foundation for Pavement Preservation(311)
FPPA Flexographic Prepress Platemakers Association(308)
FPPI Frozen Potato Products Institute(312)
FPPOA Federal Probation and Pre-trial Officers Association(302)
FPS Fluid Power Society(308)
Forest Products Society(310)
FRA Fleet Reserve Association(307)
Forest Resources Association(310)
FRAEC Foundation for Russian-American Economic Cooperation(311)
FRCA American Fire Safety Council(84)
FS Fiber Society(305)
Fleischner Society(307)
FSA Fluid Sealing Association(308)
Food Shippers of America(309)
FSAA Fulfillment Services Association of America(312)
FSC Free Speech Coalition(312)
FSCO Federation of Straight Chiropractors and Organizations(304)
FSCT Federation of Socs. for Coatings Technology(304)
FSEA Foil Stamping and Embossing Association(308)
FSF Flight Safety Foundation(308)
FSG The Foodservice Group, Inc.(310)
FSHC Federation of State Humanities Councils(304)
FSIC Freestanding Insert Council of North America(312)
FSMB Federation of State Medical Boards of the United States(304)
FSP Society of Financial Service Professionals(636)
FSR Financial Services Roundtable(306)
FSSA Fire Suppression Systems Association(307)
FSTC Financial Services Technology Consortium(306)
FSTN Financial Services Technology Network(306)
FTA Federation of Tax Administrators(304)
Flexographic Technical Association(308)
FTCA Freight Transportation Consultants Association(312)
FTPI Fiberglass Tank and Pipe Institute(305)
FUMMWA Fellowship of United Methodists in Music and Worship Arts(305)
FWAA Football Writers Association of America(310)

FWI Financial Women International(306)
FWQA Federal Water Quality Association(302)
GA Gypsum Association(321)
GAA Gift Association of America(317)
Gravure Association of America(320)
GABA German American Business Association(316)
GACC German American Chamber of Commerce(316)
GAGN Graphic Artists Guild(319)
GAIN Gift Associates Interchange Network(317)
GAL Guild of American Luthiers(321)
GAMA Game Manufacturers Association(313)
Gas Appliance Manufacturers Association(314)
General Aviation Manufacturers Association(315)
Guitar and Accessories Marketing Association(321)
GAMA Internat'l GAMA International(313)
GAMIS Graphic Arts Marketing Information Service(319)
GANA Glass Association of North America(317)
GARP Global Association of Risk Professionals(317)
GAS Glass Art Society(317)
GASDA Gasoline and Automotive Service Dealers Association(314)
GASF Graphic Arts Sales Foundation(319)
GATF Graphic Arts Technical Foundation(319)
GAWDA Gases and Welding Distributors Association(314)
GBSUA Greater Blouse, Skirt and Undergarment Association(320)
GBW Guild of Book Workers(321)
GCA Greeting Card Association(320)
GCAA Golf Coaches Association of America(318)
GCBAA Golf Course Builders Association of America(318)
GCC/IBT Graphic Communications Conference, IBT(319)
GCM National Association of Professional Geriatric Care Managers(466)
GCSAA Golf Course Superintendents Association of America(318)
GEA Geothermal Energy Association(316)
GEAPS Grain Elevator and Processing Society(319)
GFA Gasket Fabricators Association(314)
GFOA Government Finance Officers Association of the United States and Canada(318)
GFWC General Federation of Women's Clubs(315)
GFWI Greek Food and Wine Institute(320)
GHBA Galiceno Horse Breeders Association(313)
GHC Global Health Council(317)
GHSA Governors Highway Safety Association(319)
GI Gelbray International(315)
GIA Gemological Institute of America(315)
GIAA Guild of Italian American Actors(321)
GICC Glazing Industry Code Committee(317)
GIS Gamma Iota Sigma(313)
Geoscience Information Society(316)
GITA Geospatial Information Technology Association(316)
GMA Gospel Music Association(318)
Grocery Manufacturers Association(320)
GMAC Graduate Management Admission Council(319)
GMDA Groundwater Management Districts Association(320)
GMDC General Merchandise Distributors Council(315)
GMIS Government Management Information Sciences(318)
GMP Glass, Molders, Pottery, Plastics and Allied Workers International Union(317)
GMRC Gas Machinery Research Council(314)
GNSI Guild of Natural Science Illustrators(321)
GOCA Global Offset and Countertrade Association(317)
GOG Gynecologic Oncology Group(321)
GPA Gas Processors Association(314)
GPhA Generic Pharmaceutical Association(315)
GPI Glass Packaging Institute(317)
National Association of Graphic and Product Identification Manufacturers(455)
GPSA Gas Processors Suppliers Association(314)
GRA Governmental Research Association(319)
GRAA Golf Range Association of America(318)
GRC Geothermal Resources Council(316)
GRG Gastroenterology Research Group(315)
GRSS Geoscience and Remote Sensing Society(316)
GS Geochemical Society(315)
GSA Genetics Society of America(315)
Geological Society of America(315)
Gerontological Society of America(316)
Glove Shippers Association(318)
GSS Gynecologic Surgery Society(321)
GTA Gas Turbine Association(314)
GTC Gasification Technologies Council(314)
GTI Gas Technology Institute(314)
GUPH Group for the Use of Psychology in History(320)
GWA Garden Writers Association(314)
GWAA Golf Writers Association of America(318)
GWBOT Greater Washington Board of Trade(320)
GWPC Ground Water Protection Council(320)
HAA Hospice Association of America(328)
HACC Hellenic-American Chamber of Commerce(325)
HACU Hispanic Association of Colleges and Universities(325)
HAI Helicopter Association International(325)
HARC Halon Alternatives Research Corp.(321)
HARDI HARDI - Heating, Airconditioning, and Refrigeration Distributors International(321)
HAU Hebrew Actors Union(325)
HBA Home Baking Association(327)
Human Biology Association(329)
HBES Human Behavior and Evolution Society(329)
HBI Hotel Brokers International(329)
HBMA Healthcare Billing and Management Association(323)
HBPA National Horsemen's Benevolent and Protective Association(517)
HCAA National CPA Health Care Advisors Association(503)
HCCA Health Care Compliance Association(322)
HCEA Health Care Education Association(322)
Healthcare Convention and Exhibitors Association(323)
HCPC Healthcare Compliance Packaging Council(323)
HCS Histochemical Society(326)
HDA Hispanic Dental Association(326)
Holistic Dental Association(327)
HDBF Heavy Duty Business Forum(325)
HDBMC Heavy Duty Brake Manufacturers Council(325)
HDI Help Desk Institute(325)
HDMA Healthcare Distribution Management Association(323)
Heavy Duty Manufacturers Association(325)
HDRA Heavy Duty Representatives Association(325)
HEDNA Hotel Electronic Distribution Network Association(329)
HEI Heat Exchange Institute(324)
HELO Hispanic Elected Local Officials(326)
HERA Housing Education and Research Association(329)
HES History of Economics Society(326)
History of Education Society(327)
HeSCA Health & Sciences Communications Association(322)
HESS History of Earth Sciences Society(326)
HFC Historians Film Committee/Film & History(326)
HFES Human Factors and Ergonomics Society(329)
HFIA Home Furnishings International Association(327)
HFM National Society for Healthcare Foodservice Management(540)
HFMA Healthcare Financial Management Association(324)
HFPA Home Fashion Products Association(327)
HFTP Hospitality Financial and Technology Professionals(328)
HGA Handweavers Guild of America(321)
Hop Growers of America(328)
HGMN Herb Growing & Marketing Network(325)
HHGFAA Household Goods Forwarders Association of America(329)
HHI Harness Horsemen International(322)
HHNA Home Healthcare Nurses Association(327)
HI Hydraulic Institute(329)
Hydronics Institute Division of GAMA(330)
HIA Craft & Hobby Association(278)
Hearing Industries Association(324)
Historians of Islamic Art(326)
HIB Headwear Information Bureau(322)
HIBCC Health Industry Business Communications Council(323)
HIDA Health Industry Distributors Association(323)
HIGPA Health Industry Group Purchasing Association(323)
HIMSS Healthcare Information and Management Systems Society(324)
HIRA Health Industry Representatives Association(323)
HIRI Home Improvement Research Institute(327)
HITM Hospitality Institute of Technology and Management(328)
HL Herpetologists' League(325)
HLC Healthcare Leadership Council(324)
HMA Hardwood Manufacturers Association(322)
Health Ministries Association(323)

Hobby Manufacturers Association(327)
Hydroponic Merchants Association(330)
HMCC Healthcare Marketing and Communications Council(324)
HNA Historians of Netherlandish Art(326)
HNBA Hispanic National Bar Association(326)
HOAC Historians of American Communism(326)
HOLA Hispanic Organization of Latin Actors(326)
HPA Hospital Presidents Association(328)
HPBA Hearth Patio & Barbecue Association(324)
HPNA Hospice and Palliative Nurses Association(328)
HPS Health Physics Society(323)
HPVA Hardwood Plywood and Veneer Association(322)
HRI Horticultural Research Institute(328)
HRPS Human Resource Planning Society(329)
HS Harvey Society(322)
HSA Home Sewing Association(327)
Hydroponic Society of America(330)
HSGTA High Speed Ground Transportation Association(325)
HSIA Halogenated Solvents Industry Alliance(321)
Homeland Security Industries Association(328)
HSMAI Hospitality Sales and Marketing Association International(329)
HSS History of Science Society(327)
HTA Harness Tracks of America(322)
HTCIA High Technology Crime Investigation Association(325)
HTI Hand Tools Institute(321)
HWBTA Home Wine and Beer Trade Association(328)
I-ACT International Association Colon Hydro Therapy(349)
I-CAR Inter-Industry Conference on Auto Collision Repair(346)
I-CHRIE International Council on Hotel, Restaurant and Institutional Education(368)
I-PRO Independent Professional Representatives Organization(335)
I3A International Imaging Industry Association(376)
IA Internet Alliance(397)
Irrigation Association(400)
IA-SIG Interactive Audio Special Interest Group(346)
IAA International Advertising Association(348)
Investment Adviser Association(398)
IAABO International Association of Approved Basketball Officials(352)
IAACN International and American Associations of Clinical Nutritionists(349)
IAADFS International Association of Airport Duty Free Stores(352)
IAAI International Association of Arson Investigators(353)
IAAIS International Association of Audio Information Services(353)
IAAM International Association of Assembly Managers(353)
IAAMC International Association of Association Management Companies(353)
IAAO International Association of Assessing Officers(353)
IAAOC International Association of Addictions and Offender Counselors(352)
IAAP International Association of Administrative Professionals(352)
IAAPA International Association of Amusement Parks and Attractions(352)
IAAR Independent Association of Accredited Registrars(333)
IAARS International Association of Accident Reconstruction Specialists(352)
IAATI International Association of Auto Theft Investigators(353)
IAAVC International Association of Audio Visual Communicators(353)
IAB Interactive Advertising Bureau(346)
IABA Inter-American Bar Association(346)
IABC International Association of Business Communicators(354)
IABCU International Association of Baptist Colleges and Universities(353)
IABFLO International Association of Bedding and Furniture Law Officials(354)
IABM International Association of Broadcast Monitors(354)
IABMCP International Academy of Behavioral Medicine, Counseling and Psychotherapy(347)
IABPFF International Association of Black Professional Fire Fighters(354)
IABS International Association for Business and Society(349)
IABSORIW International Association of Bridge, Structural, Ornamental and Reinforcing Iron Workers(354)
IABTI International Association of Bomb Technicians and Investigators(354)
IACA Indian Arts and Crafts Association(336)
IACBD International Academy for Child Brain Development(347)
IACC Icelandic American Chamber of Commerce(330)
International Association of Conference Centers(355)
Italy-America Chamber of Commerce(400)
IACCA International Association of Conference Center Administrators(355)
IACCF International Association of Career Consulting Firms(354)
IACDE International Association of Clothing Designers and Executives(355)
IACET International Association for Continuing Education and Training(349)
IACIS International Association for Computer Information Systems(349)
IACLEA International Association of Campus Law Enforcement Administrators(354)
IACM International Association of Color Manufacturers(355)
IACMP Association of Career Professionals International(188)
IACO International Association of Correctional Officers(355)
IACOA Independent Armored Car Operators Association(333)
IACP International Academy of Compounding Pharmacists(347)
International Association of Chiefs of Police(354)
International Association of Culinary Professionals(355)
IACPR International Association of Corporate and Professional Recruitment(355)
IACREOT International Association of Clerks, Recorders, Election Officials and Treasurers(354)
IACS International Association of Counseling Services(355)
IACSC International Association for Cold Storage Construction(349)
IACSS International Association for Computer Systems Security(349)
IACT International Association of Counselors and Therapists(355)
IACTP International Association of Correctional Training Personnel(355)
IADA Independent Automotive Damage Appraisers Association(333)
Inflatable Advertising Dealers Association(338)
IADC International Association of Defense Counsel(356)
International Association of Drilling Contractors(356)
IADD International Association of Diecutting and Diemaking(356)
IADRS International Association of Dive Rescue Specialists(356)
IAED International Association of Equine Dentistry(356)
IAEDP International Association of Eating Disorders Professionals(356)
IAEI International Association of Electrical Inspectors(356)
IAEKM International Association of Electronic Keyboard Manufacturers(356)
IAEM International Association for Exhibition Management(350)
International Association of Emergency Managers(356)
IAER International Association of Electronics Recyclers(356)
IAFC International Association of Fire Chiefs(357)
IAFCI International Association of Financial Crimes Investigators(357)
IAFE International Association of Fairs and Expositions(356)
IAFF International Association of Fire Fighters(357)
IAFIS International Association of Food Industry Suppliers(357)
IAFN International Association of Forensic Nurses(357)
IAFP International Association for Food Protection(350)
IAFWA Association of Fish and Wildlife Agencies(197)
IAG International Academy of Gnathology - American Section(348)
IAGA International Association of Golf Administrators(357)
IAGC International Association of Geophysical Contractors(357)
IAGSA International Aviation Ground Support Association(362)
IAH International Association of Hydrogeologists(358)
IAHCP International Academy of Health Care Professionals(348)
IAHCSMM International Association of Healthcare Central Service Materiel Management(357)
IAHE International Association for Hydrogen Energy(350)
IAHFIAW International Association of Heat and Frost Insulators and Asbestos Workers(357)
IAHP International Association of Hygienic Physicians(358)
IAHSS International Association for Healthcare Security and Safety(350)

IAHSSP International Association of Home Safety and Security Professionals(358)
IAI Independent Affiliation of Independent Accounting Firms(333)
International Association for Identification(350)
IAIA International Association for Impact Assessment(350)
IAIABC International Association of Industrial Accident Boards and Commissions(358)
IAICV International Association of Ice Cream Vendors(358)
IAIM International Association of Infant Massage(358)
IAIR International Association of Insurance Receivers(358)
IAJAM Industrial Association of Juvenile Apparel Manufacturers(336)
IAJE International Association for Jazz Education(351)
IAJVS International Association of Jewish Vocational Services(358)
IALD International Association of Lighting Designers(358)
IALEFI International Association of Law Enforcement Firearms Instructors(358)
IALEI International Association for the Leisure and Entertainment Industry(351)
IALEIA International Association of Law Enforcement Intelligence Analysts(358)
IALHA International Andalusian and Lusitano Horse Association(349)
IALLT International Association for Language Learning Technology(351)
IAMAW International Association of Machinists and Aerospace Workers(359)
IAMC Industrial Asset Management Council(336)
IAMCA International Association of Milk Control Agencies(359)
IAME International Association for Modular Exhibitry(351)
IAMFC International Association of Marriage and Family Counselors(359)
IAMG International Association for Mathematical Geology(351)
IAML-US International Association of Music Libraries, United States Branch(359)
IAMSLIC International Association of Aquatic and Marine Science Libraries and Information Centers(352)
IAN Intermarket Agency Network(347)
IANA Intermodal Association of North America(347)
IANDS International Association for Near Death Studies(351)
IANRP International Association of Natural Resource Pilots(359)
IAO International Association for Orthodontics(351)
IAOHRA International Association of Official Human Rights Agencies(359)
IAOM International Association of Operative Millers(359)
IAOMT International Academy of Oral Medicine and Toxicology(348)
IAOPC International Association of Pet Cemeteries(360)
IAOS International Association of Ocular Surgeons(359)
IAPA/SIP Inter American Press Association(345)
IAPAC International Association of Physicians in AIDS Care(360)
IAPD International Association of Plastics Distributors(360)
IAPHC International Association of Printing House Craftsmen(360)
IAPL International Association for Philosophy and Literature(351)
IAPMO International Association of Plumbing and Mechanical Officials(360)
IAPP International Accounts Payable Professionals(348)
International Association of Privacy Professionals(360)
IAPPA International Association of Personal Protection Agents(360)
IAPSC International Association of Professional Security Consultants(360)
IAPTA International Allied Printing Trades Association(349)
IAQDE Independent Association of Questioned Document Examiners(333)
IAROO International Association of Railway Operating Officers(360)
IARS International Anesthesia Research Society(349)
IARW International Association of Refrigerated Warehouses(360)
IAS International Analgesia Society(349)
International Atherosclerosis Society(362)
IASA Insurance Accounting and Systems Association(345)
IASB International Association of Speakers Bureaus(361)
IASC International Aloe Science Council(349)
International Association of Skateboard Companies(361)
IASCE International Association for the Study of Cooperation in Education(351)
IASIU International Association of Special Investigation Units(361)
IASL International Association of School Librarianship(361)
IASM International Association of Structural Movers(361)
IASOC International Association for the Study of Organized Crime(351)
IASP International Association for the Study of Pain(352)
IATC International Association of Tool Craftsmen(361)
IATDP International Association for Truancy and Dropout Prevention(352)
IATI International Alliance of Technology Integrators(348)
IATL International Academy of Trial Lawyers(348)
IATM International Association of Tour Managers - North American Region(361)
IATSE International Alliance of Theatrical Stage Employees and Moving Picture Technicians of the U.S., Its Territories and Canada(348)
IAUED International Association of Used Equipment Dealers(361)
IAWA International Aviation Womens Association(362)
IAWF International Association of Wildland Fire(361)
IAWM International Alliance for Women in Music(348)
International Association of Women Ministers(361)
IAWP International Association of Women Police(362)
International Association of Workforce Professionals(362)
IB Irish Blacks Cattle Society(399)
IBA Independent Bakers Association(333)
Institute for Briquetting and Agglomeration(339)
Institute of Business Appraisers(340)
International Banana Association(362)
IBAM Institute of Behavioral and Applied Management(340)
IBB International Brotherhood of Boilermakers, Iron Ship Builders, Blacksmiths, Forgers and Helpers(363)
IBBA International Brangus Breeders Association(363)
International Business Brokers Association(364)
IBCMC Institute of Career Certification International(340)
IBDEA International Beverage Dispensing Equipment Association(362)
IBEE International Builders Exchange Executives(363)
IBEW International Brotherhood of Electrical Workers(363)
IBHA International Buckskin Horse Association(363)
IBHS Institute for Business & Home Safety(339)
IBM International Brotherhood of Magicians(363)
IBMA International Bluegrass Music Association(362)
International Business Music Association(364)
IBPA International Beverage Packaging Association(362)
IBPAT International Union of Painters and Allied Trades(396)
IBS Brewers Association(232)
Intercollegiate Broadcasting System(346)
International Biometric Society(362)
IBT International Brotherhood of Teamsters, AFL-CIO(363)
IBTTA International Bridge, Tunnel and Turnpike Association(363)
IBWA International Bottled Water Association(362)
IC4A ICAAAA Coaches Association(330)
ICA Intercoiffure America/Canada(346)
International Carwash Association(364)
International Ceramic Association(364)
International Chiropractors Association(365)
International Claim Association(365)
International Clarinet Association(365)
International Communication Association(366)
International Copper Association(367)
ICAA Insulation Contractors Association of America(345)
ICAC Institute of Clean Air Companies(340)
ICAE Insurance Consumer Affairs Exchange(345)
ICAK International College of Applied Kinesiology(365)
ICAS International Council of Air Shows(367)
ICAVL Intersocietal Accreditation Commission(398)
ICBA Independent Community Bankers of America(333)
ICBC Institute of Certified Business Counselors(340)
ICC International Code Council(365)

ICCA Independent Computer Consultants Association(333)
International Community Corrections Association(366)
ICCBC International Contract Center Benchmarking Consortium(367)
ICCL International Council of Cruise Lines(367)
ICCMO International College of Cranio-Mandibular Orthopedics(365)
ICCP Institute for Certification of Computing Professionals(339)
ICCSSSAR International Coordinating Committee on Solid State Sensors and Actuators Research(367)
ICCUSA Ireland Chamber of Commerce in the U.S.(399)
ICD-USA International College of Dentists, U.S.A. Section(366)
ICdA International Cadmium Association(364)
ICE International Council of Employers of Bricklayers and Allied Craftworkers(367)
ICEA Insulated Cable Engineers Association(344)
International Childbirth Education Association(365)
ICET International Council on Education for Teaching(368)
ICF International Coach Federation(365)
International Crystal Federation(368)
ICFA Insulating Concrete Form Association(344)
International Cemetery and Funeral Association(364)
ICFAD International Council of Fine Arts Deans(367)
ICFGA International Cut Flower Growers Association(368)
ICGB International Cargo Gear Bureau(364)
ICHBC Institute of Certified Healthcare Business Consultants(340)
ICI Investment Casting Institute(398)
Investment Company Institute(398)
ICMA International Card Manufacturers Association(364)
International City/County Management Association(365)
International Computer Music Association(366)
ICMAD Independent Cosmetic Manufacturers and Distributors(333)
ICOA International Castor Oil Association(364)
ICOHH International Concatenated Order of Hoo-Hoo(366)
ICOI International Congress of Oral Implantologists(367)
ICOM ICOM, International Communications Agency Network(330)
ICOTT Industry Coalition on Technology Transfer(337)
ICP International Council of Psychologists(368)
ICPA Financial and Insurance Conference Planners(305)
International Cast Polymer Association(364)
ICPC International Conference of Police Chaplains(366)
ICPF International Corrugated Packaging Foundation(367)
ICPI Interlocking Concrete Pavement Institute(347)
Intersociety Council For Pathology Information(398)
ICPM Institute of Certified Professional Managers(340)
ICRA Industrial Chemical Research Association(336)
International Compressor Remanufacturers Association(366)
ICRI International Concrete Repair Institute(366)
Iron Casting Research Institute(399)
ICRM Institute of Certified Records Managers(340)
ICS International College of Surgeons(366)
ICSA International Chain Salon Association(365)
International Customer Service Association(368)
ICSB International Council for Small Business(367)
ICSC International Cargo Security Council(364)
International Council of Shopping Centers(368)
ICSOM International Conference of Symphony and Opera Musicians(367)
ICTA Industry Council for Tangible Assets(337)
Institute of Certified Travel Agents(340)
ICWP Interstate Council on Water Policy(398)
ICWUC/UFCW International Chemical Workers Union Council/UFCW(365)
IDA Independent Distributors Association(333)
Industrial Diamond Association of America(336)
International Desalination Association(369)
International Documentary Association(369)
International Door Association(369)
International Downtown Association(369)
International Dyslexia Association(370)
IDA(USA) Indian Dental Association (USA)(336)
IDDBA International Dairy-Deli-Bakery Association(369)
IDEA IDEA, The Health and Fitness Association(330)
Independent Distributors of Electronics Association(334)
International District Energy Association(369)
IDEAlliance International Digital Enterprise Alliance(369)
IDEC Interior Design Educators Council(347)
IDEMA International Disk Drive Equipment and Materials Association(369)
IDFA International Dairy Foods Association(368)
IDRS International Double Reed Society(369)
IDS Interior Design Society(347)
IDSA Industrial Designers Society of America(336)
Infectious Diseases Society of America(338)
IEASMA International Electronic Article Surveillance Manufacturers Association(370)
IEBA International Entertainment Buyers Association(370)
IEC Independent Electrical Contractors(334)
International Engineering Consortium(370)
IECA Independent Educational Consultants Association(334)
International Erosion Control Association(371)
IEDC International Economic Development Council(370)
IEEE Institute of Electrical and Electronics Engineers(341)
IEEE - I & M IEEE Instrumentation and Measurement Society(331)
IEEE-IAS IEEE Industry Applications Society(331)
IEEE-PELS IEEE Power Electronics Society(331)
IEEE-SSIT IEEE Society on Social Implications of Technology(332)
IEEE/CS IEEE Computer Society(331)
IEEE/MTT-S IEEE Microwave Theory and Techniques Society(331)
IEF Indian Educators Federation(336)
IEGA International Engraved Graphics Association(370)
IEHA International Executive Housekeepers Association(371)
IEHS Immigration and Ethnic History Society(332)
IESNA Illuminating Engineering Society of North America(332)
IEST Institute of Environmental Sciences and Technology(341)
IETS International Embryo Transfer Society(370)
IFA Industrial Foundation of America(337)
International Formalwear Association(373)
International Franchise Association(373)
IFAC International Food Additives Council(372)
IFAI Industrial Fabrics Association International(336)
IFAO International Federation for Artificial Organs(371)
IFC International Firestop Council(372)
International Formula Council(373)
IFCM International Federation for Choral Music(371)
IFDA International Foodservice Distributors Association(372)
International Furnishings and Design Association(373)
IFEA International Festivals and Events Association(371)
IFEBP International Foundation of Employee Benefit Plans(373)
IFEC International Foodservice Editorial Council(372)
IFFA International Frozen Food Association(373)
IFI Incentive Federation(332)
Industrial Fasteners Institute(337)
International Fabricare Institute(371)
IFIA-AC International Federation of Inspection Agencies - Americas Committee(371)
IFIC International Food Information Council(372)
IFMA International Facility Management Association(371)
International Fire Marshals Association(372)
International Foodservice Manufacturers Association(372)
IFNA International Federation of Nurse Anesthetists(371)
IFP Independent Feature Project(334)
IFPA Independent Free Papers of America(334)
International Fire Photographers Association(372)
IFPTE International Federation of Professional and Technical Engineers(371)
IFPUG International Function Point Users Group(373)

IFPW International Federation of Pharmaceutical Wholesalers(371)
IFRA International Family Recreation Association(371)
International Furniture Rental Association(373)
IFSA International Financial Services Association(372)
International Furniture Suppliers Association(373)
International Inflight Food Service Association(376)
IFSEA International Food Service Executives' Association(372)
IFT Institute of Food Technologists(341)
International Foundation for Telemetering(373)
IFTA Independent Film and Television Alliance(334)
International Fruit Tree Association(373)
IFTLC International Furniture Transportation and Logistics Council(373)
IFWTWA International Food, Wine and Travel Writers Association(372)
IGA International Glove Association(374)
IGAEA International Graphic Arts Education Association(374)
IGAF IGAF Worldwide(332)
IGAS International Graphoanalysis Society(374)
IGCA International Guild of Candle Artisans(374)
IGDA International Game Developers Association(374)
IGGA International Grooving and Grinding Association(374)
IGPE International Guild of Professional Electrologists(374)
IGSHPA International Ground Source Heat Pump Association(374)
IGSOBM International Guild of Symphony, Opera and Ballet Musicians(374)
IGUA International Guards Union of America(374)
IHA International Herb Association(375)
International Housewares Association(375)
IHAA International Hard Anondizing Association(374)
IHEA Industrial Heating Equipment Association(337)
International Health Evaluation Association(374)
IHFMA International Home Furnishings Market Authority(375)
IHFRA International Home Furnishings Representatives Association(375)
IHMM Institute of Hazardous Materials Management(341)
IHPC International Hydrolized Protein Council(375)
IHRA International Hot Rod Association(375)
International Housewares Representatives Association(375)
IHRIM International Association for Human Resource Information Management(350)
IHRSA International Health, Racquet and Sportsclub Association(374)
IHS International Hearing Society(375)
International Horn Society(375)
International Hydrofoil Society(375)
IIA Institute of Internal Auditors(342)
IIABA Independent Insurance Agents and Brokers of America(334)
IIAR International Institute of Ammonia Refrigeration(376)
IICA International Ice Cream Association(375)
IICIT International Institute of Connector and Interconnection Technology(376)
IICL Institute of International Container Lessors(342)
IICRC Institute of Inspection Cleaning and Restoration Certification(341)
IIDA International Interior Design Association(377)
IIE Institute of Industrial Engineers(341)
IIF Institute of International Finance(342)
International Institute of Forecasters(376)
IIFET International Institute of Fisheries Economics and Trade(376)
IIHS Insurance Institute for Highway Safety(345)
III Insurance Information Institute(345)
IILP International Institute for Lath and Plaster(376)
IIMC International Institute of Municipal Clerks(376)
IIPA International Intellectual Property Alliance(377)
International Iridology Practitioners Association(377)
IIPL Independent Investors Protective League(334)
IIS International Insurance Society(376)
International Isotope Society(377)
IISRP International Institute of Synthetic Rubber Producers(376)
IJA Institute of Judicial Administration(342)
IJMA Infant and Juvenile Manufacturers Association(337)
IJPA International Jelly and Preserve Association(377)
IKECA International Kitchen Exhaust Cleaning Association(377)
ILA International Listening Association(378)
International Longshoremen's Association, AFL-CIO(378)
ILCA Insurance Loss Control Association(345)
International Labor Communications Association(377)
International Lactation Consultant Association(377)
ILDA Independent Laboratory Distributors Association(334)
International Laser Display Association(377)
ILEA International League of Electrical Associations(378)
ILIA Indiana Limestone Institute of America(336)
ILMA Independent Lubricant Manufacturers Association(335)
ILPBC International League of Professional Baseball Clubs(378)
ILTA Independent Liquid Terminals Association(334)
ILTS International Liver Transplantation Society(378)
ILWU International Longshore and Warehouse Union(378)
ILZRO International Lead Zinc Research Organization(377)
IMA Incentive Marketing Association(332)
Institute of Management Accountants(342)
International Magnesium Association(378)
International Magnetics Association(378)
IMA-NA Industrial Minerals Association - North America(337)
IMAGE IMAGE Society(332)
IMANA Islamic Medical Association of North America(400)
IMAP International Network of Merger and Acquisition Partners(380)
IMAPS International Microelectronics and Packaging Society(379)
IMC Institute of Management Consultants USA(342)
Intercollegiate Men's Choruses, an International Association of Male Choruses(346)
IMCA Insurance Marketing Communications Association(345)
Investment Management Consultants Association(399)
IMCEA International Military Community Executives Association(379)
IMDA Independent Medical Distributors Association(335)
IME Institute of Makers of Explosives(342)
IMI International Maintenance Institute(379)
International Marina Institute(379)
International Masonry Institute(379)
IMIA International Marking and Identification Association(379)
IMLA International Municipal Lawyers Association(380)
IMPA International Motor Press Association(380)
IMPI International Microwave Power Institute(379)
IMRA Incentive Manufacturers and Representatives Association(332)
International Manufacturers Representatives Association(379)
Retail Industry Leaders Association(601)
IMS Institute of Mathematical Statistics(342)
IMSA International Memorialization Supply Association(379)
International Municipal Signal Association(380)
IMSI International Maple Syrup Institute(379)
IMTA International Map Trade Association(379)
IMTAL International Museum Theater Alliance(380)
IMTC International Multimedia Telecommunications Consortium(380)
IMUA Inland Marine Underwriters Association(339)
INA Institute of Nautical Archaeology(343)
International Nanny Association(380)
INBA International Nubian Breeders Association(381)
INCE Institute of Noise Control Engineering(343)
INCOSE International Council on Systems Engineering(368)
INDA INDA, Association of the Nonwoven Fabrics Industry(333)
INEOA International Narcotic Enforcement Officers Association(380)
INFE International Newspaper Financial Executives(381)
INFORMS Institute for Operations Research and the Management Sciences(339)
ING International Newspaper Group(381)
INGAA Interstate Natural Gas Association of America(398)
INMA International Newspaper Marketing Association(381)
INMM Institute of Nuclear Materials Management(343)
INNS International Neural Network Society(381)

INPO Institute of Nuclear Power Operations(343)
INS Infusion Nurses Society(338)
International Neuropsychological Society(381)
INSCA International Natural Sausage Casing Association(380)
INSIC Information Storage Industry Consortium(338)
INTA International Trademark Association(394)
INTIX International Ticketing Association(394)
IntNSA International Nurses Society on Addictions(381)
IOA-PAGB International Ozone Association-Pan American Group Branch(382)
IOCV International Organization of Citrus Virologists(382)
IOD Institute of Diving(341)
IOGC Interstate Oil and Gas Commission(398)
IOM Institute of Medicine(343)
IOMA International Oxygen Manufacturers Association(382)
IOMSA International Oil Mill Superintendents Association(381)
ION Institute of Navigation(343)
IOPFDA Independent Office Products and Furniture Dealers Association(335)
IoPP Institute of Packaging Professionals(343)
IOS International Oceanic Society(381)
IOSA International Oil Scouts Association(381)
IPA Industrial Perforators Association(337)
Institute for Polyacrylate Absorbents(339)
International Phototherapy Association(383)
International Platform Association(383)
International Psychogeriatric Association(383)
International Psychohistorical Association(383)
Investment Program Association(399)
IPA - The Association of Graphic Solutions Providers(399)
IPAA Independent Petroleum Association of America(335)
IPATA Independent Pet and Animal Transportation Association International(335)
IPC IPC - Association Connecting Electronics Industries(399)
IPCA International Energy Credit Association(370)
IPEC-Americas International Pharmaceutical Excipients Council of the Americas(382)
IPFA International Physical Fitness Association(383)
IPG International Professional Groomers(383)
IPI Independent Photo Imagers(335)
International Parking Institute(382)
IPIA International Packaged Ice Association(382)
International Private Infrastructure Association(383)
IPMA In-Plant Printing and Mailing Association(332)
International Paralegal Management Association(382)
IPMA-HR International Public Management Association for Human Resources(384)
IPMI International Precious Metals Institute(383)
IPNA International Pediatric Nephrology Association(382)
IPO Intellectual Property Owners Association(345)
IPPA Independent Professional Painting Contractors Association of America(335)
IPPDSEU-NA International Plate Printers', Die Stampers' and Engravers' Union of North America(383)
IPPS International Plant Propagators Society(383)
IPRA International Professional Rodeo Association(383)
International Public Relations Association - U.S. Section(384)
IPS International Perimetric Society(382)
International Planetarium Society(383)
IPST Institute of Paper Science and Technology(343)
IPT Institute for Professionals in Taxation(339)
IPTA International Pediatric Transplant Association(382)
IPU Institute of Public Utilities(343)
IRA International Reading Association(384)
IRAS Institute on Religion in an Age of Science(344)
IRCND International Research Council of Neuromuscular Disorders(385)
IrDA Infrared Data Association(338)
IRE Investigative Reporters and Editors(398)
IREF International Real Estate Federation - American Chapter(384)
IREI International Real Estate Institute(384)
IREM Institute of Real Estate Management(343)
IRF International Road Federation(385)
IRgA International Reprographic Association(385)
IRHP Institute for Responsible Housing Preservation(339)
IRI Industrial Research Institute(337)
IRLA Independent Research Libraries Association(335)
IRMA International Recording Media Association(384)
International Regional Magazine Association(385)
IRSA International Rural Sociology Association(385)
IRTA International Reciprocal Trade Association(384)
International Refrigerated Transportation Association(384)
IRTS International Radio and Television Society(384)
IRUA Intermediaries and Reinsurance Underwriters Association(347)
IRWA International Right of Way Association(385)
IS Independent Sector(336)
IS&T Society for Imaging Science & Technology(619)
IS-SS International Society of Statistical Science(392)
ISA Ass'n of Learning Providers(164)
Independent Scholars of Asia(335)
International Sign Association(386)
International Silk Association(386)
International Silo Association(386)
International Society of Appraisers(390)
International Society of Arboriculture(390)
International Studies Association(393)
ISA(400)
ISAC International Society for Analytical Cytology(386)
ISACA Information Systems Audit and Control Association(338)
ISAI International Society of Applied Intelligence(390)
ISAKOS International Society of Arthroscopy, Knee Surgery and Orthopaedic Sports Medicine(390)
ISANTA International Staple, Nail and Tool Association(393)
ISAPP International Society for Adolescent Psychiatry & Pyschology(386)
ISAR International Society for Antiviral Research(386)
ISASI International Society of Air Safety Investigators(389)
ISB International Society of Bassists(390)
ISBT International Society of Beverage Technologists(390)
ISC Imaging Supplies Coalition for International Intellectual Property Protection(332)
International Society for Chronobiology(386)
ISCA International Shooting Coaches Association(386)
International Society of Copier Artists(391)
ISCC Inter-Society Color Council(346)
ISCD International Society for Clinical Densitometry(386)
ISCE International Society of Chemical Ecology(390)
ISCEBS International Society of Certified Employee Benefit Specialists(390)
ISCET International Society of Certified Electronics Technicians(390)
ISCPP International Society of Crime Prevention Practitioners(391)
ISCS International Society of Communication Specialists(391)
ISCSC International Society for the Comparative Studies of Civilizations(389)
ISD Independent Sealing Distributors(335)
ISDA International Swaps and Derivatives Association(393)
ISDA - The Office Systems Cooperative(400)
ISDP International Society for Developmental Psychobiology(387)
ISEA International Safety Equipment Association(385)
International Society of Exposure Analysis(391)
ISEE International Society for Ecological Economics(387)
International Society of Explosives Engineers(391)
ISEH International Society for Experimental Hematology(387)
ISEM International Society for Ecological Modelling-North American Chapter(387)
ISEO Institute of Shortening and Edible Oils(344)
ISEP International Society for Educational Planning(387)
ISES International Special Events Society(393)
ISFE International Society of Facilities Executives(391)
ISFSI International Society of Fire Service Instructors(391)
ISGS International Society for General Semantics(387)
ISHA International Sports Heritage Association(393)
ISHAE International Society of Hotel Association Executives(391)

ISHBSS Cheiron: The International Society for the History of Behavioral and Social Sciences(243)
ISHC International Society of Hospitality Consultants(391)
ISHLT International Society for Heart and Lung Transplantation(387)
ISHRS International Society of Hair Restoration Surgery(391)
ISI Ice Skating Institute(330)
ISID International Society for Infectious Diseases(387)
ISKA International Saw and Knife Association(385)
ISM Institute for Supply Management(340)
ISMA International Security Management Association(385)
International Snowmobile Manufacturers Association(386)
International Stress Management Association - U.S. Branch(393)
ISMICS International Society for Minimally-Invasive Cardiac Surgery(387)
ISMP International Society of Meeting Planners(391)
ISMPMI International Society for Molecular Plant Microbe Interactions(387)
ISMRM International Society for Magnetic Resonance in Medicine(387)
ISOB International Society of Barristers(390)
ISOC Internet Society(398)
ISOPGU International Security Officers, Police, and Guards Union(386)
ISP Institute of Store Planners(344)
ISPA International Sleep Products Association(386)
International Society for the Performing Arts(389)
International Society of Parametric Analysts(392)
International Spa Association(392)
ISPCLN International Society of Psychiatric Consultation Liaison Nurses(392)
ISPE International Society for Pharmaceutical Engineering(388)
International Society for Pharmacoepidemiology(388)
ISPI International Society for Performance Improvement(388)
ISPN International Society of Psychiatric-Mental Health Nurses(392)
ISPO International Society for Preventive Oncology(388)
International Society for Prosthetics and Orthotics - United States(388)
ISPOR International Society for Pharmacoeconomics and Outcomes Research(388)
ISP International Society for Plastination(388)
ISPP International Society of Political Psychology(392)
ISQOLS International Society for Quality-of-Life Studies(388)
ISRA International Society for Research on Aggression(388)
ISRAE International Society of Restaurant Association Executives(392)
ISRI Institute of Scrap Recycling Industries(343)
ISRP International Society for Respiratory Protection(389)
ISRS/AAO International Society of Refractive Surgery of the American Academy of Ophthalmology(392)
ISSA Information Systems Security Association(338)
International Slurry Surfacing Association(386)
ISSA(400)
ISSD International Society for the Study of Dissociation(389)
ISSPA International Sport Show Producers Association(393)
ISSSEEM International Society for the Study of Subtle Energies and Energy Medicine(389)
ISTA International Safe Transit Association(385)
ISTAT International Society of Transport Aircraft Trading(392)
ISTDA Institutional and Service Textile Distributors Association(344)
ISTE International Society for Technology in Education(389)
ISTR International Society for Third-Sector Research(389)
ISTSS International Society for Traumatic Stress Studies(389)
ISTTE International Society of Travel and Tourism Educators(392)
ISWM International Society of Weighing and Measurement(392)
ISWNE International Society of Weekly Newspaper Editors(392)
ITA Enterprise Wireless Alliance(295)
Indoor Tanning Association(336)
Industrial Truck Association(337)
Instrumentation Testing Association(344)
Intercollegiate Tennis Association(346)
International Titanium Association(394)
ITAA Information Technology Association of America(338)
International Textile and Apparel Association(394)
International Transactional Analysis Association(394)
ITAC Telework Advisory Group for World at Work(659)
ITACCS Trauma Care International(665)
ITAS Inter-America Travel Agents Society(346)
ITC Instructional Telecommunications Council(344)
ITCA Interactive Multimedia and Collaborative Communications Association(346)
International Technical Caramel Association(393)
ITCTLA International Trade Commission Trial Lawyers Association(394)
ITCUA Information Technologies Credit Union Association(338)
ITE Institute of Transportation Engineers(344)
ITEA International Technology Education Association(393)
International Test and Evaluation Association(394)
International Theatre Equipment Association(394)
International Tuba-Euphonium Association(395)
ITG International Trumpet Guild(395)
ITI International Tax Institute(393)
ITIC Information Technology Industry Council(338)
ITMFA IT Financial Management Association(400)
ITNS International Transplant Nurses Society(394)
ITOA Independent Terminal Operators Association(336)
ITODA Independent Turf and Ornamental Distributors Association(336)
ITPA International Truck Parts Association(395)
ITRA Tire Industry Association(662)
ITS International Turfgrass Society(395)
ITS America Intelligent Transportation Society of America(345)
ITT Iota Tau Tau(399)
ITWEA International Travel Writers and Editors Association(395)
IUE-CWA International Union of Electronic, Electrical, Salaried, Machine, and Furniture Workers-CWA(395)
IUEC International Union of Elevator Constructors(395)
IUISTHE International Union of Industrial Service Transport Health Employees(395)
IUJAT International Union of Journeymen Horseshoers and Allied Trades(395)
IUOE International Union of Operating Engineers(395)
IUPA International Union of Police Associations, AFL-CIO(396)
IUPIW International Union of Petroleum and Industrial Workers(396)
IVLA International Visual Literacy Association(396)
IWA International Webmasters Association(397)
IWCA International Window Cleaning Association(397)
International Writing Centers Association(397)
IWFA International Window Film Association(397)
IWGS International Waterlily and Water Gardening Society(397)
IWLA International Warehouse Logistics Association(396)
IWPA International Wood Products Association(397)
IWRA International Water Resources Association(396)
International Wild Rice Association(397)
IWSA Integrated Waste Services Association(345)
IWSS International Weed Science Society(397)
IWWG International Women's Writing Guild(397)
JA Jewelers of America(401)
JAA Judge Advocates Association(402)
JAMA Japan Automobile Manufacturers Association(400)
JASPA Jesuit Association of Student Personnel Administrators(401)
JBC Jewish Book Council(401)
JBT Jewelers Board of Trade(401)
JCAAI Joint Council of Allergy, Asthma, and Immunology(402)
JCCA Jewish Community Centers Association of North America(401)
JEA Jewish Educators Assembly(402)
Journalism Education Association(402)
JEDEC Joint Electron Device Engineering Council(402)
JESNA Jewish Education Service of North America(401)
JFDA Jewish Funeral Directors of America(402)
JG Jockeys' Guild(402)
JIC Jewelry Information Center(401)
JIDA Jewelry Industry Distributors Association(401)
JPA Juice Products Association(402)
JPMA Juvenile Products Manufacturers Association(403)
JPS Jean Piaget Society(400)
JRSA Justice Research and Statistics Association(403)
JSA Jewelers Shipping Association(401)

JSA-US	Jewelers' Security Alliance of the U.S.(401)
JSEA	Jesuit Secondary Education Association(401)
JSSPA	Jewish Social Service Professionals Association(402)
JVC	Jewelers Vigilance Committee(401)
JWBJCC	JWB Jewish Chaplains Council(403)
KANA	Kamut Association of North America(403)
KCMA	Kitchen Cabinet Manufacturers Association(403)
KDE	Kappa Delta Epsilon(403)
KDP	Kappa Delta Pi(403)
KF	Keramos Fraternity(403)
KKI	Kappa Kappa Iota(403)
KTAI	Kite Trade Association International(403)
KWPN-NA	KWPN of North America(404)
LA	Lighter Association(408)
LAA	Leather Apparel Association(406)
LACUS	Linguistic Association of Canada and the United States(408)
LAMA	Laboratory Animal Management Association(404)
	Latin American Management Association(405)
	Library Administration and Management Association(407)
	Light Aircraft Manufacturers Association(408)
LANA	Lipizzan Association of North America(408)
LASA	Latin American Studies Association(405)
LBA	Latin Business Association(405)
LBI	Library Binding Institute(407)
LCA	Lake Carriers' Association(404)
LDCIU	Laundry and Dry Cleaning International Union(405)
LEA	Lutheran Education Association(409)
LEC	Lignite Energy Council(408)
LECNA	Lutheran Educational Conference of North America(409)
LEOMA	Laser and Electro-Optics Manufacturers' Association(405)
LERA	Labor and Employment Relations Association(404)
LES	Licensing Executives Society(407)
LGC	Leafy Greens Council(406)
LGDA	Lawn and Garden Dealers' Association(406)
LGMDA	Lawn and Garden Marketing and Distribution Association(406)
LHAT	League of Historic American Theatres(406)
LHBANA	Log Home Builders Association of North America(409)
LI	Lawn Institute(406)
	Lignin Institute(408)
LIA	Laser Institute of America(405)
	Leather Industries of America(407)
LIAISON	Liaison Committee of Cooperating Oil and Gas Associations(407)
LIC	Life Insurers Council(407)
LICA	Land Improvement Contractors of America(405)
LIMA	International Licensing Industry Merchandisers' Association(378)
LIMRA	LIMRA International(408)
LIRB	Liability Insurance Research Bureau(407)
LITA	Library and Information Technology Association(407)
LIUNA	Laborers' International Union of North America(404)
LJG	Leading Jewelers Guild(406)
LKS	Lambda Kappa Sigma(405)
LMA	Legal Marketing Association(407)
	Livestock Marketing Association(409)
LMCC	Land Mobile Communications Council(405)
LMDA	Literary Managers and Dramaturgs of the Americas(408)
LMOA	Locomotive Maintenance Officers' Association(409)
LMPS	Lift Manufacturers Product Section - Material Handling Institute(408)
LOMA	LOMA(409)
LORT	League of Resident Theatres(406)
LPA	Laboratory Products Association(404)
LPC	Livestock Publications Council(409)
LPGA	Ladies Professional Golf Association(404)
LPI	Lightning Protection Institute(408)
LPSC	Label Packaging Suppliers Council(404)
LRF	Lepidoptera Research Foundation(407)
LSA	Law and Society Association(406)
	Linguistic Society of America(408)
LTA	Land Trust Alliance(405)
LTEA	Leaf Tobacco Exporters Association(406)
MAA	Mathematical Association of America(414)
	Medieval Academy of America(416)
MAAW	Marketing Agencies Association Worldwide(412)
MACS	Mobile Air Conditioning Society Worldwide(420)
MAES	Society of Mexican American Engineers and Scientists(640)
MAFSI	Manufacturers' Agents Association for the Foodservice Industry(411)
MAGA	Mexican-American Grocers Association(418)
MAGNET	Marketing and Advertising Global Network(412)
MANA	Manufacturers' Agents National Association(411)
	Midwives Alliance of North America(419)
MAPI	Manufacturers Alliance/MAPI(411)
MAPPS	Management Association for Private Photogrammetric Surveyors(410)
MARTS	Mechanical Association Railcar Technical Services(415)
MAS	Microbeam Analysis Society(418)
MBA	Mortgage Bankers Association(421)
MBAA	Master Brewers Association of the Americas(413)
MBCEA	Metal Building Contractors and Erectors Association(417)
MBI	Modular Building Institute(420)
MBMA	Metal Building Manufacturers Association(417)
MBNA	Monument Builders of North America(421)
MBS	Miniature Book Society(420)
MC	MasterCard International(413)
MCA	Media Credit Association(415)
	Metal Construction Association(417)
	Military Chaplains Association of the U.S.(419)
	Mohair Council of America(421)
MCAA	Mason Contractors Association of America(413)
	Measurement, Control and Automation Association(415)
	Mechanical Contractors Association of America(415)
	Messenger Courier Association of the Americas(417)
MCAI	Media Communications Association International(415)
MCANA	Music Critics Association of North America(423)
MCBR	International Miniature Cattle Breeders Society(380)
MCN	Museum Computer Network(423)
MCRA	Marine Corps Reserve Association(412)
MDA	Magic Dealers Association(410)
	Music Distributors Association(423)
MDHBA	Medical-Dental-Hospital Business Associates(416)
MDMA	Medical Device Manufacturers Association(416)
MDNA	Machinery Dealers National Association(409)
MDRT	Million Dollar Round Table(419)
MDS	Movement Disorder Society(422)
MEA	Marketing Education Association(413)
MEBA	Marine Engineers Beneficial Association(412)
MECA	Manufacturers of Emission Controls Association(411)
MEIEA	Music and Entertainment Industry Educators Association(423)
MELA	Middle East Librarians' Association(418)
MEMA	Motor and Equipment Manufacturers Association(421)
MEMS	Mineral Economics and Management Society(419)
MENC	MENC: The National Association for Music Education(417)
MER	Museum Education Roundtable(423)
MESA	Middle East Studies Association of North America(418)
MFA	Managed Funds Association(410)
	Marine Fabricators Association(412)
MFEA	Mutual Fund Education Alliance(423)
MFJSA	Mass Finishing Job Shops Association(413)
MFMA	Maple Flooring Manufacturers Association(412)
	Metal Findings Manufacturers Association(417)
	Metal Framing Manufacturers Association(417)
MFSA	Mailing & Fulfillment Service Association(410)
	Metal Finishing Suppliers Association(417)
MFTHBA	Missouri Fox Trotting Horse Breed Association(420)
MGMA	Medical Group Management Association(416)
MGSA	Modern Greek Studies Association(420)
MHA	Masonry Heater Association of North America(413)
MHARR	Manufactured Housing Association for Regulatory Reform(410)
MHEDA	Material Handling Equipment Distributors Association(414)
MHI	Manufactured Housing Institute(411)
MHIA	Material Handling Industry of America(414)
MI	Methanol Institute(418)
MI2	Mass Marketing Insurance Institute(413)
MIA	Marble Institute of America(412)
MIC	Motorcycle Industry Council(421)
	Music Industry Conference(423)
MICA	Meat Importers' Council of America(415)
	Mobile Industrial Caterers' Association International(420)
	Mortgage Insurance Companies of America(421)
MIF	Milk Industry Foundation(419)
MISA	Meat Industry Suppliers Alliance(415)
	Military Impacted Schools Association(419)

Motorist Information and Services Association(422)
MISC MEMA Information Services Council(416)
MISL Major Indoor Soccer League(410)
MJSA Manufacturing Jewelers and Suppliers of America(411)
MKA Machine Knife Association(409)
MLA Maritime Law Association of the U.S.(412)
Medical Library Association(416)
Modern Language Association of America(420)
Multi-Housing Laundry Association(422)
Music Library Association(423)
MLB Major League Baseball - Office of the Commissioner(410)
MLBPA Major League Baseball Players Association(410)
MLMIA Multi-Level Marketing International Association(422)
MLS Major League Soccer(410)
MLUA World Umpires Association(696)
MMA Materials Marketing Associates(414)
Medical Marketing Association(416)
MIDI Manufacturers Association(418)
MMP International Organization of Masters, Mates and Pilots(382)
MMSA Materials and Methods Standards Association(414)
Medical Mycological Society of the Americas(416)
Mining and Metallurgical Society of America(420)
MOAA Military Officers Association of America(419)
MOE Mu Phi Epsilon(422)
MORS Military Operations Research Society(419)
MOWAA Meals On Wheels Association of America(414)
MPA Magazine Publishers of America(409)
Master Printers of America(413)
Methacrylate Producers Association(418)
Motion Picture Association(421)
Music Publishers' Association of the United States(423)
MPAA Motion Picture Association of America(421)
MPC Materials Properties Council(414)
MPEA Machine Printers and Engravers Association of the United States(409)
MPI Meeting Professionals International(416)
MPIF Metal Powder Industries Federation(417)
MPTA Mechanical Power Transmission Association(415)
MPTCA Motion Picture and Television Credit Association(421)
MR&CA Mexican Restaurant and Cantina Association(418)
MRA Manufacturers Representatives of America(411)
Marketing Research Association(413)
Mountain Rescue Association(422)
MRAA Marine Retailers Association of America(412)
MRC Media Rating Council(415)
MRDA Media Research Directors Association(416)
MRI Medical Records Institute(416)
MRS Materials Research Society(414)
MS IEEE Magnetics Society(331)
Manuscript Society(412)
MSA CPA Manufacturing Services Association(278)
Metaphysical Society of America(418)
Microscopy Society of America(418)
Mineralogical Society of America(419)
Museum Store Association(423)
Mycological Society of America(424)
MSBA Montadale Sheep Breeders Association(421)
MSC Mulch and Soil Council(422)
MSCA Mechanical Service Contractors of America(415)
MSCI Metal Service Center Institute(417)
MSF Motorcycle Safety Foundation(422)
MSIA Mine Safety Institute of America(419)
MSMA Mail Systems Management Association(410)
MSS Manufacturers Standardization Society of the Valve and Fittings Industry(411)
MSTS Musculoskeletal Tumor Society(422)
MSTV Association for Maximum Service Television(176)
MTA Museum Trustee Association(423)
MTA US&C Association of Public Treasurers of the United States and Canada(211)
MTI Materials Technology Institute(414)
Metal Treating Institute(417)
MTMA MTM Association for Standards and Research(422)
MTNA Music Teachers National Association(423)
MTS Marine Technology Society(412)
MWA Mystery Writers of America(424)
MWMA Municipal Waste Management Association(422)
N-OADN National Organization for Associate Degree Nursing(529)
N4A National Association of Academic Advisors for Athletes(437)
National Association of Area Agencies on Aging(439)
NAA National Academy of Arbitrators(426)
National Aeronautic Association(427)
National Aerosol Association(428)
National Apartment Association(430)
National Auctioneers Association(482)
Neckwear Association of America(551)
Newspaper Association of America(552)
NAAA National Agricultural Aviation Association(428)
National Alarm Association of America(429)
National Auto Auction Association(482)
NAAAS National Association of African American Studies(438)
NAAB National Association of Animal Breeders(438)
NAACS National Association of Air Medical Communication Specialists(438)
National Association of Aircraft and Communication Suppliers(438)
NAADAA National Antique and Art Dealers Association of America(430)
NAADAC NAADAC -- the Association for Addiction Professionals(424)
NAADD National Association of Athletic Development Directors(439)
NAAE National Association of Agricultural Educators(438)
National Association of Agriculture Employees(438)
North American Academy of Ecumenists(554)
NAAEE North American Association for Environmental Education(554)
NAAFA National Association of Agricultural Fair Agencies(438)
NAAG National Association of Attorneys General(439)
NAAHL National Association of Affordable Housing Lenders(438)
NAAHP National Association of Advisors for the Health Professions(438)
NAAL North American Academy of Liturgy(554)
NAAMM National Association of Architectural Metal Manufacturers(438)
NAAMO North American Agricultural Marketing Officials(554)
NAAO National Association of Artists' Organizations(439)
NAAP National Association for the Advancement of Psychoanalysis(436)
National Association of Activity Professionals(437)
NAAS National Association of Academies of Science(437)
NAASR National Association for Armenian Studies and Research(431)
North American Association for the Study of Religion(554)
NAASS North American Association of Summer Sessions(555)
NAATP National Association of Addiction Treatment Providers(438)
NAATS National Association of Air Traffic Specialists(438)
NAAUSA National Association of Assistant United States Attorneys(439)
NAAWS North American Association of Wardens and Superintendents(555)
NAB National Association of Boards of Examiners of Long Term Care Administrators(440)
National Association of Broadcasters(441)
NABA National Association of Black Accountants(440)
NABB National Association of Barber Boards(439)
NABC National Association of Basketball Coaches(439)
National Association of Business Consultants(441)
North American Blueberry Council(555)
NABCA National Alcohol Beverage Control Association(429)
NABCCCE National Association of Boards, Commissions, and Councils of Catholic Education(441)
NABCJ National Association of Blacks in Criminal Justice(440)
NABCO National Association of Black County Officials(440)
NABE National Association for Bilingual Education(431)
National Association of Bar Executives(439)
National Association for Business Economics(441)
NABET-CWA National Association of Broadcast Employees and Technicians - Communications Workers of America(441)
NABG National Association of Blacks In Government(440)
NABGG National Association for Black Geologists and Geophysicists(432)
NABI National Association of Beverage Importers-Wine-Spirits-Beer(439)
NABIE National Academy of Building Inspection Engineers(426)
NABIM NABIM - the International Band and Orchestral Products Association(424)
NABJ National Association of Black Journalists(440)
NABL National Association of Bond Lawyers(441)

NABOB National Association of Black-Owned Broadcasters(440)
NABP National Association of Black Professors(440)
National Association of Boards of Pharmacy(440)
NABPAC National Association of Business Political Action Committees(441)
NABPR National Association of Baptist Professors of Religion(439)
NABPS National Association of Professional Background Screeners(465)
NABR National Association for Biomedical Research(431)
NABRTI North American Bar-Related Title Insurers(555)
NABS North American Benthological Society(555)
NABSE National Alliance of Black School Educators(429)
NABSW National Association of Black Social Workers(440)
NABT National Association of Bankruptcy Trustees(439)
National Association of Biology Teachers(440)
NABTA National Association of Business Travel Agents(441)
NABWE National Association of Black Women Entrepreneurs(440)
NAC National Association of Concessionaires(445)
NACA National Air Carrier Association(428)
National Animal Control Association(430)
National Armored Car Association(431)
National Association for Campus Activities(432)
National Association of Catastrophe Adjusters(442)
National Association of Consumer Advocates(446)
North American Contractors Association(556)
North American Corriente Association(556)
NACAA National Association of Consumer Agency Administrators(446)
National Association of County Agricultural Agents(447)
NACAC National Association for College Admission Counseling(432)
NACADA National Academic Advising Association(426)
NACAS National Association of College Auxiliary Services(444)
NACAT North American Council of Automotive Teachers(556)
NACB National Academy of Clinical Biochemistry(426)
NACBA National Association of Church Business Administration(443)
NACBS North American Conference on British Studies(556)
NACC National Association of Catholic Chaplains(442)
National Association of Counsel for Children(446)
Norwegian-American Chamber of Commerce(562)
NACCA National Association of Consumer Credit Administrators(446)
NACCB National Association of Computer Consultant Businesses(445)
NACCC North American-Chilean Chamber of Commerce(562)
NACCED National Association for County Community and Economic Development(432)
NACCHO National Association of County and City Health Officials(447)
NACCP National Association of Child Care Professionals(443)
NACCRRA National Association of Child Care Resource and Referral Agencies(443)
NACCS National Association for Chicana and Chicano Studies(432)
NACD National Association of Chemical Distributors(442)
National Association of Conservation Districts(445)
National Association of Container Distributors(446)
National Association of Corporate Directors(446)
NACDA National Association of Collegiate Directors of Athletics(444)
NACDD National Association of Councils on Developmental Disabilities(446)
NACDL National Association of Criminal Defense Lawyers(448)
NACDS National Association of Chain Drug Stores(442)
North American Clinical Dermatological Society(556)
NACE NACE International(424)
National Association of Catering Executives(442)
National Association of Colleges and Employers(444)
National Association of County Engineers(447)
NACES National Association of Credential Evaluation Services, Inc.(447)
NACFA North American Clun Forest Association(556)
NACFAM National Council for Advanced Manufacturing(496)
NACFS National Association of Church Food Service(443)
NACHA NACHA - The Electronic Payments Association(424)
NACHC National Association of Community Health Centers(445)
NACHFA National Association of County Health Facility Administrators(447)
NACHRI National Association of Children's Hospitals(443)
NACIRO National Association of County Intergovernmental Relations Officials(447)
NACIS North American Cartographic Information Society(555)
NACLS North American Canon Law Society(555)
NACM National Association for Court Management(432)
National Association of Case Management(441)
National Association of Chain Manufacturers(442)
National Association of Credit Management(448)
NACMA National Association of Collegiate Marketing Administrators(445)
NACNS National Association of Clinical Nurse Specialists(443)
NACO National Association of Charterboat Operators(442)
National Association of Counties(447)
NACOA National Association of Cruise Oriented Agencies(448)
NACOP National Association of Chiefs of Police(443)
NACPA National Association of Church Personnel Administrators(443)
NACPAF National Associated CPA Firms(431)
NACPO National Association of Casino and Theme Party Operators(441)
NACRA North American Case Research Association(555)
NACRC National Association of County Recorders, Election Officials and Clerks(447)
NACS National Association for Check Safekeeping(432)
National Association of College Stores(444)
National Association of Consumer Shows(446)
National Association of Convenience Stores(446)
North American Catalysis Society(555)
NACST National Association of Catholic School Teachers(442)
NACSW North American Association of Christians in Social Work(554)
NACT National Association of Corporate Treasurers(446)
NACTA North America Colleges and Teachers of Agriculture(553)
NACTP National Association of Computerized Tax Processors(445)
NACTT National Association of Chapter 13 Trustees(442)
NACUA National Association of College and University Attorneys(444)
NACUBO National Association of College and University Business Officers(444)
NACUC National Association of Credit Union Chairmen(448)
NACUFS National Association of College and University Food Services(444)
NACUSA National Association of Composers, USA(445)
NACUSAC National Association of Credit Union Supervisory and Auditing Committees(448)
NACUSO National Association of Credit Union Service Organizations(448)
NACVA National Association of Certified Valuation Analysts(442)
NACVCB National Association of Crime Victim Compensation Boards(448)
NACW National Association of Commissions for Women(445)
NACWA National Association of Clean Water Agencies(443)
NACWAA National Association of Collegiate Women Athletic Administrators(445)
NACWC National Association of Colored Women's Clubs(445)
NACWPI National Association of College Wind and Percussion Instructors(444)
NADA National Association of Dental Assistants(448)
National Automobile Dealers Association(482)
Nationwide Alternate Delivery Alliance(550)
NADCA National Air Duct Cleaners Association(428)
North American Die Casting Association(556)
NADCO National Association of Development Companies(449)
NADD NADD: Association for Persons with Developmental Disabilities and Mental Health Needs(424)
NADE National Association for Developmental Education(432)
National Association of Disability Examiners(449)
National Association of Document Examiners(449)
NADeFA North American Deer Farmers Association(556)
NADEO National Association of Diocesan Ecumenical Officers(449)

NADEP National Association of Disability Evaluating Professionals(449)
NADFD National Association of Decorative Fabric Distributors(448)
NADI National Association of Display Industries(449)
NADL National Association of Dental Laboratories(448)
NADO National Association of Development Organizations(449)
NADOA National Association of Division Order Analysts(449)
NADOI National Association of Dog Obedience Instructors(450)
NADONA/LTC National Association of Directors of Nursing Administration in Long Term Care(449)
NADP National Association of Dental Plans(449)
NADS National Association of Diaper Services(449)
NADSA National Adult Day Services Association(427)
NADT National Association for Drama Therapy(432)
NAE National Academy of Engineering of the United States of America(426)
National Association of Evangelicals(451)
Nursery and Landscape Association Executives of North America(563)
NAE4-HA National Association of Extension 4-H Agents(451)
NAEA National Art Education Association(431)
National Association of Enrolled Agents(451)
NAEB National Association of Educational Buyers(450)
NAEBA North American Elk Breeders Association(556)
NAEC National Association of Elevator Contractors(450)
NAED National Academy of Education(426)
National Association of Electrical Distributors(450)
NAEDA North American Equipment Dealers Association(556)
NAEGA North American Export Grain Association(557)
NAEIS National Association of Ecumenical and Interreligious Staff(450)
NAELA National Academy of Elder Law Attorneys(426)
NAELB National Association of Equipment Leasing Brokers(451)
NAEM National Association for Environmental Management(433)
NAEMSP National Association of EMS Physicians(451)
NAEMT National Association of Emergency Medical Technicians(450)
NAEN North American Association of Educational Negotiators(554)
NAEOP National Association of Educational Office Professionals(450)
NAEP National Association of Environmental Professionals(451)
NAEPDC National Adult Education Professional Development Consortium(427)
NAER National Association of Executive Recruiters(451)
NAES National Association for Ethnic Studies(433)
National Association of Episcopal Schools(451)
NAESA National Association of Elevator Safety Authorities International(450)
NAESCO National Association of Energy Service Companies(451)
NAESP National Association of Elementary School Principals(450)
NAEYC National Association for the Education of Young Children(436)
NAF National Abortion Federation(426)
National Automotive Finance Association(483)
NAFA National Air Filtration Association(428)
National Aircraft Finance Association(428)
National Association of Fleet Administrators(453)
National Association of Forensic Accountants(453)
NAFAC North American Association For Ambulatory Care(554)
NAFB National Association of Farm Broadcasting(452)
NAFC National Accounting and Finance Council(427)
NAFCC National Association for Family Child Care(433)
NAFCD National Association of Floor Covering Distributors(453)
NAFCM National Association for Community Mediation(432)
NAFCU National Association of Federal Credit Unions(452)
NAFD National Association of Flour Distributors(453)
NAFE National Association of Forensic Economics(453)
NAFED National Association of Fire Equipment Distributors(452)
NAFEM North American Association of Food Equipment Manufacturers(554)
NAFEO National Association for Equal Opportunity in Higher Education(433)
NAFEPA National Association of Federal Education Program Administrators(452)
NAFFS National Association of Flavors and Food-Ingredient Systems(453)
NAFGPD National Association of Foster Grandparent Program Directors(453)
NAFI National Association of Fire Investigators(452)
National Association of Flight Instructors(453)
NAFIC National Association of Fraternal Insurance Counsellors(454)
NAFIPS North American Fuzzy Information Processing Society(557)
NAFIS National Association of Federally Impacted Schools(452)
NAFLFD National Association of Federally Licensed Firearms Dealers(452)
NAFR National Association of First Responders(452)
NAFRD National Association of Fleet Resale Dealers(453)
NAFSA NAFSA: Association of International Educators(424)
NAFSC North American Farm Show Council(557)
NAFSMA National Association of Flood and Stormwater Management Agencies(453)
NAFTM National Association of Fundraising Ticket Manufacturers(454)
NAFTZ National Association of Foreign-Trade Zones(453)
NAFV National Association of Federal Veterinarians(452)
NAFWA North American Flowerbulb Wholesalers Association(557)
NAGA North American Gamebird Association(557)
NAGAP National Association of Graduate Admissions Professionals(454)
NAGARA National Association of Government Archives and Records Administrators(454)
NAGC National Association of Government Communicators(454)
NAGDCA National Association of Government Defined Contribution Administrators(454)
NAGE National Association of Government Employees(454)
NAGGL National Association of Government Guaranteed Lenders(454)
NAGLO National Association of Government Labor Officials(454)
NAGMR NAGMR Consumer Product Brokers(425)
NAGRA North American Gaming Regulators Association(557)
NAGT National Association of Geoscience Teachers(454)
NAGTAD National Association for Government Training and Development(433)
NAGTD National Association of Golf Tournament Directors(454)
NAGWS National Association for Girls and Women in Sport(433)
NAHA National Association for Holistic Aromatherapy(434)
NAHAD Association for Hose and Accessories Distribution(174)
NAHAM National Association of Healthcare Access Management(455)
NAHB National Association of Home Builders(456)
NAHC National Association for Home Care(434)
National Association of Healthcare Consultants(455)
National Association of Housing Cooperatives(456)
NAHCO National Association of Hispanic County Officials(455)
NAHCR National Association for Health Care Recruitment(433)
NAHDO National Association of Health Data Organizations(455)
NAHDSA National Association of Family Development Centers(452)
NAHE National Association for Humanities Education(434)
NAHF National Association for Health and Fitness(433)
NAHFE National Association of Hispanic Federal Executives(455)
NAHH National Alliance for Hispanic Health(429)
NAHHH National Association of Hospital Hospitality Houses(456)
NAHI National Association of Home Inspectors(456)
NAHIM National Association of Housing Information Managers(457)
NAHJ National Association of Hispanic Journalists(455)
NAHMA National Affordable Housing Management Association(428)
NAHN National Association of Hispanic Nurses(456)
NAHP National Association of Hispanic Publications(456)
NAHQ National Association for Healthcare Quality(433)
NAHRO National Association of Housing and Redevelopment Officials(456)
NAHSA North American Horticultural Supply Association(557)
NAHSE National Association of Health Services Executives(455)

NAHU National Association of Health Underwriters(455)
NAHUC National Association of Health Unit Coordinators(455)
NAHWW National Association of Home and Workshop Writers(456)
NAI National Association for Interpretation(434)
National Association of Independent Insurance Auditors and Engineers(457)
NAIA National Association of Intercollegiate Athletics(458)
NAIC National Association of Insurance Commissioners(458)
National Association of Investment Companies(459)
NAICC National Alliance of Independent Crop Consultants(429)
NAICJA National American Indian Court Judges Association(430)
NAICU National Association of Independent Colleges and Universities(457)
NAID National Association for Information Destruction(434)
National Association of Installation Developers(458)
NAIFA National Association of Independent Fee Appraisers(457)
National Association of Insurance and Financial Advisors(458)
NAIHC National American Indian Housing Council(430)
NAIIA National Association of Independent Insurance Adjusters(457)
NAILBA National Association of Independent Life Brokerage Agencies(457)
NAILD National Association of Independent Lighting Distributors(457)
NAILM National Association of Institutional Linen Management(458)
NAIMA North American Insulation Manufacturers Association(557)
NAIOP National Association of Industrial and Office Properties(458)
NAIP National Association of Independent Publishers(457)
National Association of Investment Professionals(459)
NAIPFA National Association of Independent Public Finance Advisors(457)
NAIPR National Association of Independent Publishers Representatives(457)
NAIR NAIR -- the International Association of Bowling Lane Specialists(425)
NAIS National Association of Independent Schools(457)
National Association of Investigative Specialists(459)
NAIT National Association of Industrial Technology(458)
NAITTE National Association of Industrial and Technical Teacher Educators(458)
NAIW National Association of Insurance Women(458)
NAJA National Association of Jewelry Appraisers(459)
Native American Journalists Association(550)
NAJAF National Association of Jai Alai Frontons(459)
NAJCA National Association of Juvenile Correctional Agencies(459)
NAJIT National Association of Judiciary Interpreters and Translators(459)
NAKPEHE National Association for Kinesiology and Physical Education in Higher Education(434)
NALA National Association of Legal Assistants(459)
NALA/PCA National ALEC Association/ Prepaid Communications Association(429)
NALBOH National Association of Local Boards of Health(460)
NALC National Association of Letter Carriers(460)
National Association of Litho Clubs(460)
NALED National Association of Limited Edition Dealers(460)
NALEO National Association of Latino Elected and Appointed Officials(459)
NALF North American Limousin Foundation(558)
NALGA National Association of Local Government Auditors(460)
NALGEP National Association of Local Government Environmental Professionals(460)
NALHFA National Association of Local Housing Finance Agencies(460)
NALI National Association of Legal Investigators(459)
NALMCO International Association of Lighting Management Companies(359)
NALMS North American Lake Management Society(557)
NALP National Association for Law Placement(434)
NALPA National American Legion Press Association(430)
NALS NALS(425)
NALSC National Association of Legal Search Consultants(460)
NAM National Association of Manufacturers(460)
Newspaper Association Managers(552)
NAMA National Agri-Marketing Association(428)
National Association of Master Appraisers(461)
National Automatic Merchandising Association(482)
North American Millers Association(558)
North American Mycological Association(558)
NAMAC National Alliance for Media Arts and Culture(429)
NAMAD National Association of Minority Automobile Dealers(462)
NAMB National Association of Media Brokers(461)
National Association of Mortgage Brokers(462)
NAMBUCS National AMBUCS(430)
NAMC National Association of Minority Contractors(462)
NAMCP National Association of Managed Care Physicians(460)
NAMDRC National Association for Medical Direction of Respiratory Care(434)
NAME National Association of Medical Examiners(461)
NAMEPA National Association of Minority Engineering Program Administrators(462)
NAMF National Association of Metal Finishers(461)
NAMIC National Association for Multi-Ethnicity in Communications(434)
National Association of Mutual Insurance Companies(462)
NAMM NAMM - the International Music Products Association(425)
National Association of Margarine Manufacturers(461)
NAMME National Association of Medical Minority Educators(461)
National Association of Minority Media Executives(462)
NAMOA National Association of Miscellaneous, Ornamental and Architectural Products Contractors(462)
NAMP North American Meat Processors Association(558)
NAMRI/SME North American Manufacturing Research Institution of SME(558)
NAMS National Association of Marine Services(461)
National Association of Marine Surveyors(461)
North American Membrane Society(558)
North American Menopause Society(558)
NAMSB National Association of Men's Sportswear Buyers(461)
NAMSC North American Maple Syrup Council(558)
NAMSS National Association Medical Staff Services(437)
NAMT National Alliance for Musical Theatre(429)
NAMTA National Art Materials Trade Association(431)
NAMTC National Association of Media and Technology Centers(461)
NAN National Academy of Neuropsychology(426)
National Association of Neighborhoods(462)
NANASP National Association of Nutrition and Aging Services Programs(463)
NANBPWC National Association of Negro Business and Professional Women's Clubs(462)
NANCA North American Natural Casing Association(558)
NANCO National Association of Noise Control Officials(463)
NANDA NANDA International(425)
NANMT National Association of Nurse Massage Therapists(463)
NANN National Association of Neonatal Nurses(462)
NANOS North American Neuro-Ophthalmology Society(559)
NANP National Alliance of Nurse Practitioners(429)
NANPA North American Nature Photography Association(558)
NANT National Association of Nephrology Technologists and Technicians(462)
NAO National Academy of Opticianry(427)
NAOF National Association of Osteopathic Foundations(463)
NAOHSM National Association of Oil Heating Service Managers(463)
NAON National Association of Orthopaedic Nurses(463)
NAOO National Association of Optometrists and Opticians(463)
NAOOA North American Olive Oil Association(559)
NAOSMM National Association of Scientific Materials Managers(471)
NAOT National Association of Orthopaedic Technologists(463)
NAOTB National Association of Off-Track Betting(463)
NAP National Academies of Practice(426)
National Association of Parliamentarians(463)
NAPA National Asphalt Pavement Association(431)

NAPAA Trade Promotion Management Association(663)
NAPAMA North American Performing Arts Managers and Agents(559)
NAPBIRT National Association of Professional Band Instrument Repair Technicians(465)
NAPBL National Association of Professional Baseball Leagues(466)
NAPC National Alliance of Preservation Commissions(430)
NAPCA National Association of Pipe Coating Applicators(464)
NAPCE North American Association of Professors of Christian Education(554)
NAPCOR National Association for PET Container Resources(435)
NAPCWA National Association of Public Child Welfare Administrators(467)
NAPDEA North American Professional Driver Education Association(559)
NAPE National Association of Power Engineers(465)
NAPEO National Association of Professional Employer Organizations(466)
NAPET National Association of Photo Equipment Technicians(464)
NAPF National Association of Pipe Fabricators(464)
NAPFA National Association of Personal Financial Advisors(464)
NAPFE National Alliance of Postal and Federal Employees(429)
NAPH National Association of Professors of Hebrew in American Institutions of Higher Learning(466)
National Association of Public Hospitals and Health Systems(467)
NAPHS National Association of Psychiatric Health Systems(467)
NAPHSIS National Association for Public Health Statistics and Information Systems(435)
NAPIA National Association of Public Insurance Adjusters(467)
NAPIM National Association of Printing Ink Manufacturers(465)
NAPL National Association for Printing Leadership(435)
NAPMA North American Punch Manufacturers Association(559)
NAPMM National Association of Produce Market Managers(465)
NAPMW National Association of Professional Mortgage Women(466)
NAPN National Association of Physician Nurses(464)
NAPNAP National Association of Pediatric Nurse Practitioners(464)
NAPNES National Association for Practical Nurse Education and Service(435)
NAPNSC National Association of Private, Nontraditional Schools and Colleges with Accrediting Commission for Higher Education(465)
NAPO National Association of Pizza Operators(464)
National Association of Police Organizations(465)
National Association of Professional Organizers(466)
NAPPA North American Polyelectrolyte Producers Association(559)
NAPPC North American Plant Preservation Council(559)
NAPPO National Association of Plant Patent Owners(465)
NAPPS National Association of Professional Pet Sitters(466)
National Association of Professional Process Servers(466)
NAPR National Association of Physician Recruiters(464)
National Association of Publishers' Representatives(467)
NAPRHSW National Association of Puerto Rican/Hispanic Social Workers(467)
NAPS National Association of Personnel Services(464)
National Association of Postal Supervisors(465)
NAPSA National Appliance Parts Suppliers Association(430)
National Association of Pupil Services Administrators(467)
NAPSEC National Association of Private Special Education Centers(465)
NAPSEO National Association of Public Sector Equal Opportunity Officers(467)
NAPSG National Association of Principals of Schools for Girls(465)
NAPSLO National Association of Professional Surplus Lines Offices(466)
NAPT National Association for Poetry Therapy(435)
National Association for Proton Therapy(435)
National Association for Pupil Transportation(435)
NAPTR-TEC National Association of Property Tax Representatives - Transportation, Energy, Communications(467)
NAPUS National Association of Postmasters of the United States(465)
NAR National Association of REALTORS(468)
NARA National Aircraft Resale Association(428)
National Association of Rehabilitation Providers and Agencies(469)
NARAMU National Association of Review Appraisers and Mortgage Underwriters(469)
NARAS National Academy of Recording Arts and Sciences(427)
NARC National Association of Regional Councils(469)
NARCA National Association of Retail Collection Attorneys(469)
NARDA North American Retail Dealers Association(559)
NAREA National Association of Real Estate Appraisers(468)
NAREB National Association of Real Estate Brokers(468)
NAREC National Association of Real Estate Companies(468)
NAREE National Association of Real Estate Editors(468)
NaREIA National Real Estate Investors Association(535)
NAREIM National Association of Real Estate Investment Managers(468)
NAREIT National Association of Real Estate Investment Trusts(468)
NARFE National Active and Retired Federal Employees Association(427)
NARI National Association of Rehabilitation Instructors(469)
National Association of the Remodeling Industry(479)
NARM National Association of Recording Merchandisers(468)
National Association of Reunion Managers(469)
NARMH National Association for Rural Mental Health(436)
NARMS National Association for Retail Marketing Services(436)
NARO National Association of Royalty Owners(469)
NARPPS International Association of Rehabilitation Professionals(360)
NARRP National Association of Recreation Resource Planners(468)
NARS National Association of Rehabilitation Secretaries(469)
North American Rail Shippers Association(559)
NARSA National Automotive Radiator Service Association(483)
NARSC National Association of Reinforcing Steel Contractors(469)
NARST National Association for Research in Science Teaching(435)
NARSVPD National Association of Retired Senior Volunteer Program Directors(469)
NARTC National Association of Railroad Trial Counsel(467)
NARTE NARTE(425)
NARTH National Association for Research and Therapy of Homosexuality(435)
NARTS National Association of Resale & Thrift Shops(469)
NARUC National Association of Regulatory Utility Commissioners(469)
NAS National Academy of Sciences(427)
NASA National Appliance Service Association(430)
National Association of State Archaeologists(473)
North American Sawing Association(560)
North American Saxophone Alliance(560)
NASAA National Assembly of State Arts Agencies(431)
North American Securities Administrators Association(560)
NASACT National Association of State Auditors, Comptrollers and Treasurers(473)
NASAD National Association of Schools of Art and Design(470)
NASADAD National Association of State Alcohol and Drug Abuse Directors(473)
NASAGA North American Simulation and Gaming Association(560)
NASAO National Association of State Aviation Officials(473)
NASAP National Association of Student Affairs Professionals(477)
North American Society of Adlerian Psychology(561)
NASAR National Association for Search and Rescue(436)
NASASP National Association of State Agencies for Surplus Property(473)
NASASPS National Association of State Administrators and Supervisors of Private Schools(473)
NASATE National Association of Substance Abuse Trainers and Educators(478)
NASBA National Association of State Boards of Accountancy(473)
NASBE National Association of State Boards of Education(473)
National Association of Supervisors for Business Education(478)
NASBG National Association of State Boards of Geology(473)
NASBIC National Association of Small Business Investment Companies(472)
NASBITE North American Small Business International Trade Educators(560)
NASBLA National Association of State Boating Law Administrators(473)

NASBO National Association of State Budget Officers(473)
NASBP National Association of Surety Bond Producers(478)
NASBS North American Skull Base Society(560)
NASC National Association of Solar Contractors(472)
NASCA National Association of State Chief Administrators(474)
NASCAR National Association for Stock Car Auto Racing(436)
NASCAT National Association of Shareholder and Consumer Attorneys(472)
NASCC National Association of Service and Conservation Corps(471)
NASCCD National Association of State Catholic Conference Directors(474)
NASCI North American Society for Cardiac Imaging(560)
NASCIO National Association of State Chief Information Officers(474)
NASCO National Association of Security Companies(471)
National Association of State Charity Officials(474)
NASCOE National Association of FSA County Office Employees(454)
NASCSA National Association of State Controlled Substances Authorities(474)
NASCSP National Association for State Community Services Programs(436)
NASCUS National Association of State Credit Union Supervisors(474)
NASD National Association of Schools of Dance(470)
National Association of Securities Dealers(471)
NASDA National Association of State Departments of Agriculture(474)
National Association of State Development Agencies(474)
North American South Devon Association(561)
NASDAD National Association of Seventh-Day Adventist Dentists(472)
NASDCTEC National Association of State Directors of Career Technical Education Consortium(474)
NASDDDS National Association of State Directors of Developmental Disability Services(474)
NASDME National Association of State Directors of Migrant Education(474)
NASDSE National Association of State Directors of Special Education(475)
NASDT North American Society for Dialysis and Transplantation(560)
NASDTEC National Association of State Directors of Teacher Education and Certification(475)
NASDVA National Association of State Directors of Veterans Affairs(475)
NASE National Association for the Self-Employed(436)
NASED National Association of State Election Directors(475)
NASEMSO National Association of State Emergency Medical Services Officials(475)
NASEO National Association of State Energy Officials(475)
NASF National Association of State Foresters(475)
NASFA National Association of State Facilities Administrators(475)
NASFAA National Association of Student Financial Aid Administrators(477)
NASFM NASFM(425)
National Association of State Fire Marshals(475)
NASFT National Association for the Specialty Food Trade(436)
NASGA North American Strawberry Growers Association(562)
NASGW National Association of Sporting Goods Wholesalers(472)
NASIG North American Serials Interest Group(560)
NASILP National Association of Self-Instructional Language Programs(471)
NASJA North American Snowsports Journalists Association(560)
NASL National Association for the Support of Long-Term Care(437)
NASLR National Association of State Land Reclamationists(475)
NASM National Association of Schools of Music(470)
National Association of Service Managers(472)
NASMD National Association of Medicaid Directors(461)
National Association of School Music Dealers(470)
NASMHPD National Association of State Mental Health Program Directors(476)
NASN National Association of School Nurses(470)
NASNSA National Association of Special Needs State Administrators(472)
NASO National Association of Sports Officials(472)
NASOH North American Society for Oceanic History(560)
NASORLO National Association of State Outdoor Recreation Liaison Officers(476)
NASP National Association of Sales Professionals(470)
National Association of School Psychologists(470)
National Association of Securities Professionals(471)
NaSPA NaSPA: the Network and System Professionals Association(425)
National Association of Student Personnel Administrators(478)
NASPAA National Association of Schools of Public Affairs and Administration(470)
NASPAC National Subacute and Postacute Care Association(544)
NASPD National Association of State Park Directors(476)
National Association of Steel Pipe Distributors(477)
NASPE Heart Rhythm Society(324)
National Association for Sport and Physical Education(436)
National Association of State Personnel Executives(476)
NASPGHAN North American Society for Pediatric Gastroenterology, Hepatology and Nutrition(561)
NASPL North American Association of State and Provincial Lotteries(554)
NASPO National Alliance of Statewide Preservation Organizations(430)
National Association of State Procurement Officials(476)
NASPP National Association of Stock Plan Professionals(477)
NASPPR National Association of Service Providers in Private Rehabilitation(472)
NASPSPA North American Society for the Psychology of Sport and Physical Activity(561)
NASR National Association of Swine Records(478)
NASRA National Association of State Retirement Administrators(476)
NASRO National Association of School Resource Officers(470)
NASS National Association of Secretaries of State(471)
North American Spine Society(561)
NASSCO National Association of Sewer Service Companies(472)
NASSD National Association of Sign Supply Distributors(472)
NASSH North American Society for Sport History(561)
NASSLEO National Association of School Safety and Law Enforcement Officers(470)
NASSM National Association of State Supervisors of Music(476)
North American Society for Sport Management(561)
NASSP National Association of Secondary School Principals(471)
North American Society for Social Philosophy(561)
North American Society of Scaffold Professionals(561)
NASSS North American Society for the Sociology of Sport(561)
NASSTIE National Association of State Supervisors of Trade and Industrial Education(476)
NASSTRAC National Small Shipments Traffic Conference(540)
NAST National Association of Schools of Theatre(471)
National Association of State Treasurers(476)
NASTA National Association of State Textbook Administrators(476)
NASTAD National Alliance of State and Territorial AIDS Directors(430)
NASTD NASTD - Technology Professionals Serving State Government(426)
NASTT North American Society for Trenchless Technology(561)
NASUA National Association of State Units on Aging(476)
NASUCA National Association of State Utility Consumer Advocates(477)
NASULGC National Association of State Universities and Land Grant Colleges(477)
NASVH National Association of State Veterans Homes(477)
NASW National Association of Science Writers(471)
National Association of Social Workers(472)
NASWA National Association of State Workforce Agencies(477)
NATA National Air Transportation Association(428)
National Association of Teachers' Agencies(478)
National Association of Temple Administrators(479)
National Athletic Trainers' Association(482)
NATARI National Association of Traffic Accident Reconstructionists and Investigators(479)
NATAS National Academy of Television Arts and Sciences(427)
NATaT National Association of Towns and Townships(479)
NATB National Association of Ticket Brokers(479)
NATCA National Air Traffic Controllers Association(428)

NATCO NATCO - The Organization for Transplant Professionals(426)
NATCP National Association of Tribal Court Personnel(479)
NATD National Association of Test Directors(479)
North-American Association of Telecommunications Dealers(562)
NATE National Association of Temple Educators(479)
National Association of Trade Exchanges(479)
North American Technician Excellence(562)
NATEFACS National Association of Teacher Educators for Family Consumer Sciences(478)
NATIE National Association for Trade and Industrial Education(437)
NATIRA North American Transportation Employee Relations Association(562)
NATJ National Academy of Television Journalists(427)
NATM National Association of Trailer Manufacturers(479)
NATMI North American Transportation Management Institute(562)
NATO National Association of Theatre Owners(479)
NATOA National Association of Telecommunications Officers and Advisors(478)
NATP National Association of Tax Professionals(478)
NATPE National Association of Television Program Executives(478)
NATRI National Association for Treasurers of Religious Institutes(437)
NATS National Association of Teachers of Singing(478)
NATSO NATSO, Representing America's Travel Plazas and Truckstops(550)
NAUFWP National Association of University Fisheries and Wildlife Programs(480)
NAUH National Association of Urban Hospitals(480)
NAUI National Association of Underwater Instructors(480)
NAUMD National Association of Uniform Manufacturers and Distributors(480)
NAUPA National Association of Unclaimed Property Administrators(479)
NAUS/SMW National Association for Uniformed Services and Society of Military Widows(437)
NAVA National Association for Variable Annuities(437)
NAVAPD National Association of VA Physicians and Dentists(480)
NAVD National Association of Video Distributors(480)
NAVP National Association of Vision Professionals(480)
NAVPA National Association of Veterans Program Administrators(480)
NAVREF National Association of Veterans' Research and Education Foundations(480)
NAVTP National Association of Vertical Transportation Professionals(480)
NAW National Association of Wholesaler-Distributors(481)
NAWA National Association of Women Artists(481)
NAWB National Association of Workforce Boards(482)
NAWBO National Association of Women Business Owners(481)
NAWC National Association of Water Companies(480)
NAWDP National Association of Workforce Development Professionals(482)
NAWE National Association of Waterfront Employers(481)
NAWG National Association of Wheat Growers(481)
NAWHSL National Association of Women Highway Safety Leaders(481)
NAWIC National Association of Women in Construction(481)
NAWJ National Association of Women Judges(481)
NAWL National Association of Women Lawyers(482)
NAWLA North American Wholesale Lumber Association(562)
NAWSA North American Wensleydale Sheep Association(562)
NAWSRC National Association of Waterproofing and Structural Repair Contractors(481)
NAWT National Association of Wastewater Transporters(480)
NAYRE National Association for Year-Round Education(437)
NAYS National Alliance for Youth Sports(429)
NBA National Band Association(483)
National Bankers Association(483)
National Bar Association(483)
National Basketball Association(483)
National Bison Association(484)
National Business Association(486)
NBAA National Business Aviation Association(486)
NBACA National Broadcast Association for Community Affairs(485)
NBASLH National Black Association for Speech, Language and Hearing(484)
NBATA National Basketball Athletic Trainers Association(483)
NBBA National Bed and Breakfast Association(484)
NBBC National Block and Bridle Club(485)
NBBI National Board of Boiler and Pressure Vessel Inspectors(485)
NBBQA National Barbecue Association(483)
NBCC National Black Chamber of Commerce(484)
National Book Critics Circle(485)
National Bureau of Certified Consultants(485)
NBCCH National Board for Certified Clinical Hypnotherapists(485)
NBCFAE National Black Coalition of Federal Aviation Employees(484)
NBCL National Beauty Culturists' League(484)
NBCLEO National Black Caucus of Local Elected Officials(484)
NBCSL National Black Caucus of State Legislators(484)
NBDA National Bicycle Dealers Association(484)
NBEA National Ballroom and Entertainment Association(483)
National Business Education Association(486)
NBFAA National Burglar and Fire Alarm Association(486)
NBGQA National Building Granite Quarries Association(485)
NBHA National Barrel Horse Association(483)
NBIA National Business Incubation Association(486)
NBMBAA National Black MBA Association(484)
NBMDA North American Building Material Distribution Association(555)
NBNA National Black Nurses Association(484)
NBOA National Business Owners Association(486)
NBPA National Basketball Players Association(483)
National Black Police Association(484)
NBPC National Border Patrol Council(485)
NBPRS National Black Public Relations Society(485)
NBRA National Basketball Referees Association(483)
NBTA National Business Travel Association(486)
NBVA National Bulk Vendors Association(485)
NBWA National Beer Wholesalers Association(484)
National Blacksmiths and Weldors Association(485)
NCA National Candle Association(487)
National Caves Association(488)
National Cleaners Association(490)
National Club Association(490)
National Coffee Association of the U.S.A.(490)
National Communication Association(491)
National Confectioners Association of the United States(492)
National Constables Association(495)
National Cosmetology Association(496)
National Costumers Association(496)
NCAA National Collegiate Athletic Association(491)
National Council of Art Administrators(498)
NCAC National Council of Acoustical Consultants(498)
NCACC National Conference of Appellate Court Clerks(492)
NCACS National Coalition of Alternative Community Schools(490)
NCAE National Council for Agricultural Education(497)
National Council of Agricultural Employers(498)
NCAP National Coalition of Abortion Providers(490)
NCARB National Council of Architectural Registration Boards(498)
NCASI National Council for Air and Stream Improvement(497)
NCATB National Congress of Animal Trainers and Breeders(495)
NCAWE National Council of Administrative Women in Education(498)
NCB National Cargo Bureau(487)
NCBA National Catholic Band Association(487)
National Cattlemen's Beef Association(488)
National Cooperative Business Association(496)
NCBE National Conference of Bar Examiners(492)
NCBES National Council of Black Engineers and Scientists(498)
NCBF National Conference of Bar Foundations(492)
NCBFAA National Customs Brokers and Forwarders Association of America(504)
NCBI National Cotton Batting Institute(496)
NCBJ National Conference of Bankruptcy Judges(492)
NCBL National Conference of Black Lawyers(492)
NCBM National Conference of Black Mayors(492)

NCBMP National Coalition of Black Meeting Planners(490)
NCBVA National Concrete Burial Vault Association(492)
NCC National Certification Commission(488)
National Chicken Council(489)
National Cotton Council of America(496)
National Council of the Churches of Christ in the U.S.A.(501)
NCCA National Chemical Credit Association(488)
National Child Care Association(489)
National Coil Coating Association(490)
NCCAA National Christian College Athletic Association(489)
NCCAP National Certification Council for Activity Professionals(488)
NCCATA National Coalition of Creative Arts Therapies Associations(490)
NCCBH National Council for Community Behavioral Healthcare(497)
NCCC National Catholic Cemetery Conference(487)
NCCD National Council on Crime and Delinquency(502)
NCCED National Congress for Community Economic Development(495)
NCCI National Council on Compensation Insurance(502)
NCCL National Conference of Catechetical Leadership(493)
National Council of Coal Lessors(498)
NCCPAP National Conference of CPA Practitioners(493)
NCCPB National Council of Commercial Plant Breeders(498)
NCCR National Council of Chain Restaurants(498)
NCCUSL National Conference of Commissioners on Uniform State Laws(493)
NCCW National Council of Catholic Women(498)
NCDA National Career Development Association(487)
National Community Development Association(491)
NCDC National Catholic Development Conference(487)
NCDVD National Conference of Diocesan Vocation Directors(493)
NCE National Conference of Executives of The ARC(493)
National Council of Exchangors(499)
NCEA National Catholic Educational Association(487)
National Community Education Association(491)
NCECA National Council on Education for the Ceramic Arts(502)
NCEE National Catholic Educational Exhibitors(487)
NCEES National Council of Examiners for Engineering and Surveying(499)
NCEFR National Council of Erectors, Fabricators and Riggers(498)
NCEW National Conference of Editorial Writers(493)
NCFC National Council of Farmer Cooperatives(499)
NCFO National Conference of Firemen and Oilers, SEIU(493)
NCFR National Council on Family Relations(502)
NCFTJ National Conference of Federal Trial Judges(493)
NCGA National Church Goods Association(489)
National Corn Growers Association(496)
National Cotton Ginners' Association(496)
NCGE National Council for Geographic Education(497)
NCGIF National Cherry Growers and Industries Foundation(489)
NCGS National Coalition of Girls Schools(490)
NCH National Center for Homeopathy(488)
NCHA National Cutting Horse Association(504)
NCHC National Collegiate Honors Council(491)
NCHELP National Council of Higher Education Loan Programs(499)
NCHFFA National Council of Health Facilities Finance Authorities(499)
NCI National Cheese Institute(488)
NCIA National Correctional Industries Association(496)
NCICA National Counter Intelligence Corps Association(503)
NCINAS National Council of Industrial Naval Air Stations(499)
NCIO National Congress of Inventor Organizations(495)
NCIS National Crop Insurance Services(504)
NCISS National Council of Investigation and Security Services(499)
NCITD National Council on International Trade Development(502)
NCJA National Criminal Justice Association(503)
NCJFCJ National Council of Juvenile and Family Court Judges(499)
NCL National Civic League(489)
National Consumers League(495)
NCLA National Church Library Association(489)
NCLE National Contact Lens Examiners(495)
NCLEHA National Conference of Local Environmental Health Administrators(493)
NCLGS National Council of Legislators from Gaming States(499)
NCLSHSA National Council of Local Human Service Administrators(499)
NCMA National Campus Ministries Association(486)
National Catalog Managers Association(487)
National Concrete Masonry Association(492)
National Contract Management Association(495)
NCME National Council on Measurement in Education(502)
NCMIE National Council of Music Importers and Exporters(500)
NCMPR National Council for Marketing and Public Relations(497)
NCMS National Classification Management Society(490)
NCNA National Council of Nonprofit Associations(500)
NCOA National Council on the Aging(503)
Non Commissioned Officers Association of the U.S.A.(553)
NCOBPS National Conference of Black Political Scientists(492)
NCOIL National Conference of Insurance Legislators(493)
NCOPM National Conference of Personal Managers(494)
NCPA National Community Pharmacists Association(491)
National Cottonseed Products Association(496)
NCPCU National Council of Postal Credit Unions(500)
NCPDP National Council for Prescription Drug Programs(497)
NCPERS National Conference on Public Employee Retirement Systems(495)
NCPG National Catholic Pharmacists Guild of the United States(488)
National Committee on Planned Giving(491)
NCPH National Council on Public History(502)
NCPI National Clay Pipe Institute(490)
NCPMA National Clay Pottery Association(490)
NCPOA National Chief Petty Officers' Association(489)
NCPP National Council on Public Polls(502)
NCPWB National Certified Pipe Welding Bureau(488)
NCQA National Committee for Quality Assurance(491)
NCQLP National Council on Qualifications for the Lighting Professions(502)
NCRA National Cancer Registrars Association(486)
National Court Reporters Association(503)
National Credit Reporting Association(503)
NCRE National Council on Rehabilitation Education(503)
NCREIF National Council of Real Estate Investment Fiduciaries(500)
NCRLL National Conference on Research in Language and Literacy(495)
NCRP National Council on Radiation Protection and Measurements(502)
NCRUCE National Conference of Regulatory Utility Commission Engineers(494)
NCS National Cartoonists Society(487)
NCSA National Confectionery Sales Association(492)
NCSAB National Council of State Agencies for the Blind(500)
NCSBCS National Conference of States on Building Codes and Standards(494)
NCSBN National Council of State Boards of Nursing(500)
NCSCJ National Conference of Specialized Court Judges(494)
NCSD National Council on Student Development(503)
NCSDCJC National Council of State Directors of Community Colleges(500)
NCSEA National Child Support Enforcement Association(489)
NCSEMSTC National Council of State Emergency Medical Services Training Coordinators(500)
NCSFA National Conference of State Fleet Administrators(494)
NCSG National Chimney Sweep Guild(489)
NCSGC National Garden Clubs(513)
NCSHA National Council of State Housing Agencies(500)
NCSHPO National Conference of State Historic Preservation Officers(494)
NCSI National Council of Self-Insurers(500)
NCSL National Conference of State Legislatures(494)
NCSLA National Conference of State Liquor Administrators(494)
NCSLI NCSL International(551)
NCSM National Council of Supervisors of Mathematics(501)
NCSPA National Corrugated Steel Pipe Association(496)

NCSPAE National Council of State Pharmacy Association Executives(501)
NCSS National Council for the Social Studies(497)
NCSSFL National Council of State Supervisors for Languages(501)
NCSSMA National Council of Social Security Management Associations(500)
NCSSSA National Conference of State Social Security Administrators(494)
NCTA National Cable & Telecommunications Association(486)
National Christmas Tree Association(489)
National Council of Textile Organizations(501)
NCTE National Council of Teachers of English(501)
NCTM National Council of Teachers of Mathematics(501)
NCTR National Council on Teacher Retirement(503)
NCTRC National Council for Therapeutic Recreation Certification(497)
NCUMA National Credit Union Management Association(503)
NCURA National Council of University Research Administrators(501)
NCWA National Collegiate Wrestling Association(491)
NCWBA National Conference of Women's Bar Associations(494)
NCWE National Council for Workforce Education(497)
NCWGA Natural Colored Wool Growers Association(550)
NCWM National Conference on Weights and Measures(495)
NCYP National Conference of Yeshiva Principals(495)
NDA National Dance Association(504)
National Dental Association(505)
National Drilling Association(505)
NDAA National District Attorneys Association(505)
NDBC National Dry Bean Council(505)
NDCA National Dance Council of America(504)
NDCC National Defined Contribution Council(505)
NDGAA National Dog Groomers Association of America(505)
NDHA National Dental Hygienists' Association(505)
NDHIA National Dairy Herd Improvement Association(504)
NDIA National Defender Investigator Association(504)
National Defense Industrial Association(504)
NDPA National Directory Publishing Association(505)
NDRN National Disability Rights Network(505)
NDTA National Defense Transportation Association(504)
Neurodevelopmental Treatment Association(552)
NEA National Economic Association(505)
National Education Association(506)
NEA - the Association of Union Constructors(551)
NEADA National Energy Assistance Directors Association(507)
NEAFCS National Extension Association of Family and Consumer Sciences(508)
NEBB National Environmental Balancing Bureau(507)
NECA National Electrical Contractors Association(506)
National Exchange Carrier Association(507)
NEDA National Electronic Distributors Association(506)
NEEDA National Emergency Equipment Dealers Association(506)
NEHA National Environmental Health Association(507)
NEI Nuclear Energy Institute(563)
NEII National Elevator Industry(506)
NEKIA National Education Knowledge Industry Association(506)
NELA National Employment Lawyers Association(507)
NEMA National Electrical Manufacturers Association(506)
National Emergency Management Association(507)
NEMRA National Electrical Manufacturers Representatives Association(506)
NEMSPA National EMS Pilots Association(507)
NENA National Emergency Number Association(507)
NERA Naval Enlisted Reserve Association(551)
NERC North American Electric Reliability Council(556)
NESA National Energy Services Association(507)
NESDA National Electronic Service Dealers Association(506)
NESHTA National Environmental, Safety and Health Training Association(507)
NESTA National Earth Science Teachers Association(505)
NETA International Electrical Testing Association(370)
National Educational Telecommunications Association(506)
National Exercise Trainers Association(508)
NETL National Export Traffic League(508)
NEWH Network of Executive Women in Hospitality(551)
NEXCO National Association of Export Companies(451)
NFA National Finance Adjusters(510)
National Flute Association(511)
National Forensic Association(512)
National Futures Association(513)
NFAA National Fashion Accessories Association(508)
NFAIS National Federation of Abstracting and Information Services(508)
NFBA National Frame Builders Association(512)
NFBC National Family Business Council(508)
NFBPA National Forum for Black Public Administrators(512)
NFCA National Family Caregivers Association(508)
National Federation Coaches Association(508)
National Fraternal Congress of America(512)
NFCB National Federation of Community Broadcasters(509)
NFCC National Foundation for Credit Counseling(512)
NFCCE National Fellowship of Child Care Executives(510)
NFCDCU National Federation of Community Development Credit Unions(509)
NFD&FFA National Frozen Dessert and Fast Food Association(513)
NFDA National Fastener Distributors Association(508)
National Funeral Directors Association(513)
NFDMA National Funeral Directors and Morticians Association(513)
NFE Northwest Fruit Exporters(562)
NFEC National Food and Energy Council(511)
NFFE National Federation of Federal Employees(509)
NFFS Non-Ferrous Founders' Society(553)
NFHC National Federation of Housing Counselors(509)
NFHON National Federation of Hispanic Owned Newspapers(509)
NFHSMA NFHS Music Association(553)
NFHSSDTA NFHS Speech Debate and Theatre Association(553)
NFI National Fisheries Institute(511)
NFIB National Federation of Independent Business(509)
NFIU National Federation of Independent Unions(509)
NFL National Football League(511)
NFLPA National Football League Players Association(511)
NFLPN National Federation of Licensed Practical Nurses(509)
NFMA National Federation of Municipal Analysts(509)
NFMC National Federation of Music Clubs(509)
NFMLTA National Federation of Modern Language Teachers Associations(509)
NFNSSAA National Federation of Nonpublic School State Accrediting Associations(510)
NFO National Farmers Organization(508)
NFOA National Federation of Officials Association(510)
NFOP National Fraternal Order of Police(512)
NFPA National Federation of Paralegal Associations(510)
National Fire Protection Association(510)
National Fluid Power Association(511)
NFPC National Federation of Priests' Councils(510)
NFPI National Frozen Pizza Institute(513)
NFPRHA National Family Planning and Reproductive Health Association(508)
NFPW National Federation of Press Women(510)
NFRA National Forest Recreation Association(512)
National Frozen and Refrigerated Foods Association(513)
NFSA National Field Selling Association(510)
National Fire Sprinkler Association(511)
NFSHSA National Federation of State High School Associations(510)
NFTA National Freight Transportation Association(512)
NFTB National Federation of Temple Brotherhoods(510)
NFTC National Foreign Trade Council(511)
NFU Farmers Educational and Co-operative Union of America(301)
NFWL National Foundation for Women Legislators(512)
NGA National Glass Association(513)
National Governors Association(514)
National Grocers Association(515)
National Guardianship Association(515)
NGAUS National Guard Association of the U.S.(515)
NGC National Goose Council(514)

NGCA National Grape Cooperative Association(515)
NGCMA National Golf Car Manufacturers Association(514)
NGCOA National Golf Course Owners Association(514)
NGCSA National Guild of Community Schools of the Arts(515)
NGEDA National Guard Executive Directors Association(515)
NGF National Golf Foundation(514)
NGFA National Grain and Feed Association(514)
NGJA National Gymnastics Judges Association(516)
NGMA National Grants Management Association(514)
National Greenhouse Manufacturers Association(515)
NGNA National Gerontological Nursing Association(513)
NGPA National Government Publishing Association(514)
NGPP National Guild of Professional Paperhangers(515)
NGPT National Guild of Piano Teachers(515)
NGS National Genealogical Society(513)
NGSA Natural Gas Supply Association(550)
NGSP National Grain Sorghum Producers(514)
NGTC National Grain Trade Council(514)
NGVC Natural Gas Vehicle Coalition(551)
NGWA National Ground Water Association(515)
NH&RA National Housing and Rehabilitation Association(518)
NH-PAI Nurse Healers - Professional Associates International(563)
NHA National Hay Association(516)
National Health Association(516)
National Humanities Alliance(518)
National Hydrogen Association(518)
National Hydropower Association(518)
NHC National Health Council(516)
National Housing Conference(518)
NHCA National Health Club Association(516)
National Hearing Conservation Association(516)
NHCAA National Health Care Anti-Fraud Association(516)
NHCC National Hispanic Corporate Council(517)
NHEMA National Home Equity Mortgage Association(517)
NHF National Hemophilia Foundation(516)
NHFA National Home Furnishings Association(517)
NHHRA National Hereford Hog Record Association(517)
NHL National Hockey League(517)
NHLA National Hardwood Lumber Association(516)
NHLPA National Hockey League Players' Association(517)
NHMA National Hispanic Medical Association(517)
NHPCO National Hospice and Palliative Care Organization(517)
NHPDA National Honey Packers and Dealers Association(517)
NHRA National Human Resources Association(518)
NHSA National Head Start Association(516)
NHSACA National High School Athletic Coaches Association(517)
NIA National Insulation Association(521)
National Insurance Association(521)
NIAA National Institute for Animal Agriculture(520)
NIAAA National Interscholastic Athletic Administrators Association(522)
NIADA National Independent Automobile Dealers Association(518)
National Institute of American Doll Artists(520)
NIB National Industries for the Blind(519)
NIBA National Investment Banking Association(522)
NIBA - The Belting Association(553)
NIBESA Financial and Security Products Association(305)
NIBIC National Institute of Business and Industrial Chaplaincy(520)
NIBS National Institute of Building Sciences(520)
NIC National Industrial Council - Employer Association Group(519)
National Industrial Council - State Associations Group(519)
North American Interfraternity Conference(557)
NICB National Insurance Crime Bureau(522)
NICE National Institute of Ceramic Engineers(520)
NICMA National Ice Cream Mix Association(518)
NICRA National Ice Cream Retailers Association(518)
NICSA National Investment Company Service Association(522)
NICSBC National Interstate Council of State Boards of Cosmetology(522)
NIEA National Indian Education Association(519)
NIEI National Institute for Electromedical Information(520)
NIFAD National Independent Fire Alarm Distributors(519)
NIFDA National Independent Flag Dealers Association(519)
NIFS National Institute for Farm Safety(520)
NIGA National Indian Gaming Association(519)
NIGP National Institute of Governmental Purchasing(520)
NILA National Independent Living Association(519)
NIMC National Institute of Management Counsellors(521)
NIMS Network of Ingredient Marketing Specialists(551)
NINFRA National Independent Nursery Furniture Retailers Association(519)
NIOP National Institute of Oilseed Products(521)
NIPA National Institute of Pension Administrators(521)
NIPGM National Institute on Park and Grounds Management(521)
NIPHLE National Institute of Packaging, Handling and Logistics Engineers(521)
NIRI National Investor Relations Institute(522)
NIRMA Nuclear Information and Records Management Association(563)
NIRSA National Intramural-Recreational Sports Association(522)
NISA National Industrial Sand Association(519)
NISCA National Interscholastic Swimming Coaches Association(522)
NISD National Institute of Steel Detailing(521)
NISO National Information Standards Organization(520)
NISOA National Intercollegiate Soccer Officials Association(522)
NITL The National Industrial Transportation League(519)
NIWR National Institutes for Water Resources(521)
NJA National Judges Association(522)
NJCAA National Junior College Athletic Association(523)
NJCSA National Juvenile Court Services Association(523)
NJDA National Juvenile Detention Association(523)
NKBA National Kitchen and Bath Association(523)
NKF National Kidney Foundation(523)
NKHA National Kerosene Heater Association(523)
NLA National Lime Association(525)
National Limousine Association(525)
National Lipid Association(525)
NLADA National Legal Aid and Defender Association(524)
NLAPW National League of American Pen Women(524)
NLBA National Lead Burning Association(523)
NLBMDA National Lumber and Building Material Dealers Association(525)
NLC National League of Cities(524)
NLCOC Netherlands Chamber of Commerce in the United States(551)
NLDA National Luggage Dealers Association(525)
NLFA National Lamb Feeders Association(523)
NLG National Lawyers Guild(523)
NLGA National Lieutenant Governors Association(524)
NLGI National Lubricating Grease Institute(525)
NLGJA National Lesbian and Gay Journalists Association(524)
NLGLA National Lesbian and Gay Law Association(524)
NLHA National Leased Housing Association(524)
NLN National League for Nursing(523)
NLPA National Livestock Producers Association(525)
NLPM National League of Postmasters of the U.S.(524)
NLRBPA National Labor Relations Board Professional Association(523)
NLSBA National Lincoln Sheep Breeders Association(525)
NLSSA National Litigation Support Services Association(525)
NMA National Management Association(525)
National Maritime Alliance(526)
National Meat Association(526)
National Medical Association(526)
National Mining Association(527)
NMBA National Marine Bankers Association(525)
NMBC National Minority Business Council(527)
NMC National Mastitis Council(526)
National Music Council(528)
NMCA National Meat Canners Association(526)
NMDA International Metal Decorators Association(379)
National Marine Distributors Association(526)
National Miniature Donkey Association(527)
NMDP National Marrow Donor Program(526)

NMEA National Marine Educators Association(526)
National Marine Electronics Association(526)
NMEDA National Mobility Equipment Dealers Association(527)
NMFTA National Motor Freight Traffic Association(527)
NMHA National Mental Health Association(527)
NMHC National Multi Housing Council(528)
NMIA National Military Intelligence Association(527)
NMMA National Marine Manufacturers Association(526)
NMOA National Mail Order Association(525)
NMPA National Motorsports Press Association(528)
National Music Publishers' Association(528)
NMPF National Milk Producers Federation(527)
NMRA National Marine Representatives Association(526)
NMSA National Middle School Association(527)
NMSDC National Minority Supplier Development Council(527)
NMSS National Multiple Sclerosis Society(528)
NNA National Newspaper Association(528)
NNEPA National Network of Estate Planning Attorneys(528)
NNFA National Nutritional Foods Association(529)
NNG National Network of Grantmakers(528)
NNGA Northern Nut Growers Association(562)
NNOA National Naval Officers Association(528)
NNPA National Newspaper Publishers Association(529)
NNSDO National Nursing Staff Development Organization(529)
NNSWM National Network for Social Work Managers(528)
NOA National Onion Association(529)
National Opera Association(529)
National Optometric Association(529)
NOBC National Organization of Bar Counsel(530)
NOBCChE National Organization for the Professional Advancement of Black Chemists and Chemical Engineers(530)
NOBCO National Organization of Black County Officials(530)
NOBLE National Organization of Black Law Enforcement Executives(530)
NOCA National Organization for Competency Assurance(530)
NODA National Orientation Directors Association(530)
NOFMA NOFMA: the Wood Flooring Manufacturers Association(553)
NOGGA National Ornamental Goldfish Growers Association(531)
NOHSE National Organization for Human Service Education(530)
NOIA National Ocean Industries Association(529)
NOITU National Organization of Industrial Trade Unions(530)
NOLHGA National Organization of Life and Health Insurance Guaranty Associations(530)
NOLSW National Organization of Legal Services Workers(530)
NOMMA National Ornamental and Miscellaneous Metals Association(531)
NONPF National Organization of Nurse Practitioner Faculties(530)
NOPA National Oilseed Processors Association(529)
NORA NORA: An Association of Responsible Recyclers(553)
NOSSCR National Organization of Social Security Claimants' Representatives(530)
NOVA Nurses Organization of Veterans Affairs(563)
NOWRA National Onsite Wastewater Recycling Association(529)
NPA National Paperbox Association(531)
National Paralegal Association(531)
National Parking Association(531)
National Pasta Association(532)
National Pawnbrokers Association(532)
National Perinatal Association(532)
National Phlebotomy Association(533)
Network Professional Association(552)
NPAP National Psychological Association for Psychoanalysis(534)
NPB National Plant Board(533)
NPBOA National Party Boat Owners Alliance(532)
NPC National Panhellenic Conference(531)
National Peach Council(532)
National Petroleum Council(532)
National Pharmaceutical Council(533)
National Plasterers Council(533)
National Potato Council(533)
NPCA National Paint and Coatings Association(531)
National Parks Conservation Association(532)
National Precast Concrete Association(534)
NPELRA National Public Employer Labor Relations Association(534)
NPES NPES, The Association for Suppliers of Printing, Publishing and Converting Technologies(563)
NPFDA National Poultry and Food Distributors Association(533)
NPGA National Propane Gas Association(534)
NPHA National Park Hospitality Association(531)
National Prison Hospice Association(534)
NPHC National Pan-Hellenic Council(531)
NPI National Purchasing Institute(534)
NPM National Association of Pastoral Musicians(464)
NPMA National Pest Management Association(532)
National Property Management Association(534)
Newspaper Purchasing Management Association(553)
NPMHU National Postal Mail Handlers Union(533)
NPPA National Press Photographers Association(534)
NPPB National Potato Promotion Board(533)
NPPC National Pork Producers Council(533)
NPRA National Petrochemical & Refiners Association(532)
NPSA National Pecan Shellers Association(532)
NPSOAA National Police and Security Officers Association of America(533)
NPTA NPTA Alliance(563)
NPTC National Private Truck Council(534)
NPWH National Association of Nurse Practitioners in Women's Health(463)
NQPC National Quartz Producers Council(534)
NRA National Rehabilitation Association(535)
National Renderers Association(536)
National Restaurant Association(536)
National Rifle Association of America(536)
Naval Reserve Association(551)
NRAA National Association for Rehabilitation Leadership(435)
National Renal Administrators Association(536)
NRB National Religious Broadcasters(536)
NRC National Railroad Construction and Maintenance Association(534)
National Reading Conference(535)
NRCA National Rehabilitation Counseling Association(535)
National Roofing Contractors Association(537)
NRDCA National Roof Deck Contractors Association(537)
NREA National Rural Education Association(537)
NRECA National Rural Electric Cooperative Association(537)
NREDA National Rural Economic Developers Association(537)
NREF National Real Estate Forum(535)
NREP National Registry of Environmental Professionals(535)
NRF National Retail Federation(536)
NRHA National Reining Horse Association(535)
National Rural Health Association(537)
North American Retail Hardware Association(559)
NRHSA National Retail Hobby Stores Association(536)
NRHSPP National Register of Health Service Providers in Psychology(535)
NRLCA National Rural Letter Carriers' Association(537)
NRMA National Reloading Manufacturers Association(536)
NRMCA National Ready Mixed Concrete Association(535)
NRMLA National Reverse Mortgage Lenders Association(536)
NRPA National Recreation and Parks Association(535)
NRRA National Risk Retention Association(537)
NRTO National Remotivation Therapy Organization(536)
NRVMA National Roadside Vegetation Management Association(537)
NRWA National Rural Water Association(538)
NSA National Shellfisheries Association(539)
National Sheriffs' Association(539)
National Slag Association(540)
National Society of Accountants(541)
National Speakers Association(542)
National Stroke Association(544)
National Sunflower Association(545)
National Sunroom Association(545)
Neurosurgical Society of America(552)
Not-for-Profit Services Association(562)
Nuclear Suppliers Association(563)
NSAA National Ski Areas Association(540)
National Student Assistance Association(544)

OESA Original Equipment Suppliers Association(568)
OFA Organization of Flying Adjusters(567)
OFDA Office Furniture Distribution Association(564)
OFII Organization for International Investment(567)
OFN Opportunity Finance Network(565)
OGR International Order of the Golden Rule(381)
OHA Oral History Association(566)
OKU Omicron Kappa Upsilon(564)
OLA Optical Laboratories Association(566)
OLAC Online Audiovisual Catalogers(565)
OMG Object Management Group(563)
OMSA Offshore Marine Service Association(564)
ONO Organization of News Ombudsmen(567)
ONS Oncology Nursing Society(564)
OOA Owner Operators of America(570)
OOIDA Owner-Operator Independent Drivers Association(570)
OOSS Outpatient Ophthalmic Surgery Society(569)
OPASTCO Organization for the Promotion and Advancement of Small Telecommunications Companies(567)
OPC Overseas Press Club of America(570)
OPCMIA Operative Plasterers' and Cement Masons' International Association of the United States and Canada(565)
OPEAA Outdoor Power Equipment Aftermarket Association(569)
OPEDA Organization of Professional Employees of the U.S. Department of Agriculture(567)
OPEESA Outdoor Power Equipment and Engine Service Association(569)
OPEI Outdoor Power Equipment Institute(569)
OPEIU Office and Professional Employees International Union(564)
OPIA Optical Imaging Association(565)
OPS Operations Security Professionals Society(565)
Ophthalmic Photographers' Society(565)
OPWA Office Products Wholesalers Association(564)
ORCS Organic Reactions Catalysis Society(566)
ORIA Oriental Rug Importers Association of America(568)
ORRA Oriental Rug Retailers of America(568)
ORS Orthopaedic Research Society(568)
ORTHO American Orthopsychiatric Association(111)
OSA Optical Society of America(566)
OSBE Organization of State Broadcasting Executives(568)
OSMA Orthopedic Surgical Manufacturers Association(569)
OSRA Organizational Systems Research Association(568)
OTA Organic Trade Association(566)
Orthopaedic Trauma Association(569)
OTOD Organization of Teachers of Oral Diagnosis(568)
OTS Omega Tau Sigma(564)
Organization for Tropical Studies(567)
OTSA Orthodox Theological Society in America(568)
OWAA Outdoor Writers Association of America(569)
OWP Organization of Wildlife Planners(568)
P3 Partnership in Print Production(572)
PA Parapsychological Association(571)
Parliamentary Associates(571)
PAA Population Association of America(580)
Potato Association of America(581)
Professional Apparel Association(585)
PAC Public Affairs Council(592)
PACA Picture Agency Council of America(577)
PACC Professional Association of Custom Clothiers(585)
PACE Professional Association for Childhood Education(585)
Professional Association of Christian Educators(585)
PAD Phi Alpha Delta(575)
PADA Private Art Dealers Association(584)
PADI Professional Association of Diving Instructors(585)
PAHCOM Professional Association of Health Care Office Management(586)
PAHRA Partnership for Air-Conditioning, Heating Refrigeration Accreditation(571)
PAI Apple Products Research and Education Council(159)
PAII Professional Association of Innkeepers International(586)
PAMA Professional Aviation Maintenance Association(586)
PARMA Public Agency Risk Managers Association(592)
PARW/CC Professional Association of Resume Writers and Career Coaches(586)
PAS National Postsecondary Agriculture Student Organization(533)
Percussive Arts Society(573)
PAT Phi Alpha Theta(575)
PATCA Professional and Technical Consultants Association(585)
PATMI Powder Actuated Tool Manufacturers Institute(582)
PAUS Piedmontese Association of the United States(577)
PAVO Professional Association of Volleyball Officials(586)
PBA Poultry Breeders of America(581)
Professional Beauty Association(586)
Professional Bowlers Association of America(586)
PBAA Periodical and Book Association of America(573)
PBATS Professional Baseball Athletic Trainers Society(586)
PBBAI Printing Brokerage/Buyers Association International(584)
PBMA Public Broadcasting Management Association(592)
PBNPA Peanut and Tree Nut Processors Association(572)
PBUS Professional Bail Agents of the United States(586)
PBWA Professional Basketball Writers' Association(586)
PCA Pine Chemicals Association(578)
Plumbing Contractors of America(579)
Portland Cement Association(581)
Print Council of America(583)
PCBAA Parthenais Cattle Breeders Association of America(571)
PCCA Portable Computer and Communications Association(580)
Power and Communication Contractors Association(582)
PCDA Professional Currency Dealers Association(587)
PCEA Professional Construction Estimators Association of America(586)
PCI Powder Coating Institute(582)
Precast/Prestressed Concrete Institute(582)
Property Casualty Insurers Association of America(591)
PCIA PCIA - the Wireless Industry Association(572)
PCMA Pharmaceutical Care Management Association(575)
Professional Convention Management Association(587)
PCMCIA Personal Computer Memory Card International Association(573)
PCMI Photo Chemical Machining Institute(576)
PCNA Preventive Cardiovascular Nurses Association(583)
PCPA Protestant Church-Owned Publishers Association(591)
PCRA Poland China Record Association(579)
PCSDA Postcard and Souvenir Distributors Association(581)
PCUS Propeller Club of the United States(591)
PDA PDA - an International Association for Pharmaceutical Science and Technology(572)
PDC Paper Distribution Council(571)
PDCA Painting and Decorating Contractors of America(570)
Pile Driving Contractors Association(577)
Purebred Dairy Cattle Association(593)
Purebred Dexter Cattle Association of North America(593)
PDI Plumbing and Drainage Institute(579)
PDK Phi Delta Kappa(575)
PDMA Product Development and Management Association(585)
PDP International Legal Fraternity of Phi Delta Phi(378)
PDRA Paint and Decorating Retailers Association(570)
PEI Petroleum Equipment Institute(574)
Porcelain Enamel Institute(580)
PEMA Process Equipment Manufacturers' Association(584)
PEPP Professional Engineers in Private Practice(587)
PER Public Employees Roundtable(592)
PERA Production Engine Remanufacturers Association(585)
Production Equipment Rental Association(585)
PERF Police Executive Research Forum(580)
PES Philosophy of Education Society(576)
PESA Petroleum Equipment Suppliers Association(574)
PFA Pedorthic Footwear Association(572)
Pierre Fauchard Academy(577)
Polyurethane Foam Association(580)
Professional Fraternity Association(587)
PFATS Professional Football Athletic Trainers Society(587)
PFDI Preferred Funeral Directors International(583)
PFHA Paso Fino Horse Association(572)
PFI Pellet Fuels Institute(573)
Pet Food Institute(574)
Pipe Fabrication Institute(578)
PFWA Professional Football Writers of America(587)
PGA Producer's Guild of America(584)
Professional Golfers Association of America(587)
PGATTA PGA TOUR Tournaments Association(575)
PGI Pyrotechnics Guild International(593)
PGMS Professional Grounds Management Society(587)

PGRSA Plant Growth Regulators Society of America(578)
PHA Palomino Horse Association(570)
Percheron Horse Association of America(573)
Professional Handlers Association(587)
PHAABO Purebred Hanoverian Association of America Breeders and Owners(593)
PHADA Public Housing Authorities Directors Association(592)
PHBA Palomino Horse Breeders of America(570)
PHCC Plumbing-Heating-Cooling Contractors - National Association(579)
PHEWA Presbyterian Health, Education and Welfare Association(583)
PhiDE Phi Delta Epsilon Medical Fraternity(575)
PHILAMCHAM Philippine-American Chamber of Commerce(576)
PHMA Professional Housing Management Association(587)
PhRMA Pharmaceutical Research and Manufacturers of America(575)
PHWA Professional Hockey Writers' Association(587)
PI Popcorn Institute(580)
PrintImage International(584)
PIA National Association of Professional Insurance Agents(466)
Printing Industries of America(584)
PIAA Physician Insurers Association of America(577)
PICA Professional Insurance Communicators of America(587)
PICE Printing Industry Credit Executives(584)
PIDA Pet Industry Distributors Association(574)
PIJAC Pet Industry Joint Advisory Council(574)
PIMA Paper Industry Management Association(571)
Polyisocyanurate Insulation Manufacturers Association(580)
Professional Insurance Marketing Association(588)
PIRA Petroleum Investor Relations Association(574)
PLA Public Library Association(592)
PLAN Professional Liability Agents Network(588)
PLANET Professional Landscape Network(585)
Professional Landscape Network(588)
PLCA Pipe Line Contractors Association(578)
PLI Practising Law Institute(582)
PLMA Private Label Manufacturers Association(584)
PLRB Property Loss Research Bureau(591)
PLT Pi Lambda Theta(577)
PLUS Professional Liability Underwriting Society(588)
PMA PMA, the Independent Book Publishers Association(579)
Polyurethane Manufacturers Association(580)
Precision Metalforming Association(583)
Produce Marketing Association(584)
Professional Managers Association(588)
Promotion Marketing Association(590)
PMA-I Photo Marketing Association-International(576)
PMAA Petroleum Marketers Association of America(574)
PMAI Piano Manufacturers Association International(577)
PMC Percussion Marketing Council(573)
PMCC Paper Machine Clothing Council(571)
PMDA Photoimaging Manufacturers and Distributors Association(576)
PMHA Purebred Morab Horse Association(593)
PMI Plumbing Manufacturers Institute(579)
Portfolio Management Institute(581)
Project Management Institute(590)
PMMI Packaging Machinery Manufacturers Institute(570)
PMPA Precision Machined Products Association(583)
PMSA Professional Show Managers Association(589)
PNG Professional Numismatists Guild(588)
PoA Pony of the Americas Club(580)
Property Owners Association(591)
POD Network Professional and Organizational Development Network in Higher Education(585)
POMS Production and Operations Management Society(585)
POPA Patent Office Professional Association(572)
POPAI POPAI The Global Association for Marketing at Retail(580)
POSNA Pediatric Orthopedic Society of North America(572)
POSTCOM Association for Postal Commerce(177)
PPA Parenting Publications of America(571)
Perennial Plant Association(573)
Periodical Publications Association(573)
Professional Paddlesports Association(588)
Professional Photographers of America(588)
Professional Putters Association(588)
Publishers Publicity Association(593)
PPAI Promotional Products Association International(591)
PPC Paperboard Packaging Council(571)
PPFA Plastic Pipe and Fittings Association(578)
Professional Picture Framers Association(588)
PPHRNA Peruvian Paso Horse Registry of North America(574)
PPI Pickle Packers International(577)
Plastics Pipe Institute(579)
Potash & Phosphate Institute(581)
PPLA Pharmaceutical Printed Literature Association(575)
PPMA Political Products Manufacturers Association(580)
Post-Print Manufacturers Association(581)
PPRMC Paper and Plastic Representatives Management Council(571)
PPS American Physical Therapy Association - Private Practice Section(115)
PPSA Pulp and Paper Safety Association(593)
PPTA Plasma Protein Therapeutics Association(578)
PRBA Portable Rechargeable Battery Association(581)
PRC Internat'l Pipeline Research Council International(578)
PRCA Professional Rodeo Cowboys Association(589)
PREA Pension Real Estate Association(573)
PRI Paleontological Research Institution(570)
PRIA Property Records Industry Association(591)
PRIMA Public Risk Management Association(593)
PRISM Internatl Professional Records and Information Services Management International(589)
PRNDI Public Radio News Directors(592)
PROS Professional Reactor Operator Society(589)
PRPD Public Radio Program Directors Association(592)
PRS Pattern Recognition Society(572)
PRSA Public Relations Society of America(593)
PRSM Professional Retail Store Maintenance Association(589)
PS Paleontological Society(570)
Psychology Society(592)
Psychometric Society(592)
Psychonomic Society(592)
PSA Parcel Shippers Association(571)
Philosophy of Science Association(576)
Phycological Society of America(577)
Poetry Society of America(579)
Poultry Science Association(581)
Professional Service Association(589)
Professional Skaters Association(589)
PSAA Plastic Surgery Admininstrative Association(578)
PSAI Portable Sanitation Association International(581)
PSC Professional Services Council(589)
PSCA Profit Sharing/401(k) Council of America(590)
PSCI Plastic Shipping Container Institute(578)
PSEA Pleaters, Stitchers and Embroiderers Association(579)
PSI Pet Sitters International(574)
PSIA Professional Ski Instructors of America(589)
PSMA Power Sources Manufacturers Association(582)
Professional Services Management Association(589)
PSMMA Plastic Soft Materials Manufacturers Association(578)
PSPC Polystyrene Packaging Council(580)
PSRC Plastic Surgery Research Council(579)
PSSMA Paper Shipping Sack Manufacturers Association(571)
PSTC Pressure Sensitive Tape Council(583)
PTAG Professional Tattoo Artists Guild(589)
PTC Pipe Tobacco Council(578)
PTDA Power Transmission Distributors Association(582)
PTG Piano Technicians Guild(577)
PtHA Pinto Horse Association of America(578)
PTI Post-Tensioning Institute(581)
Power Tool Institute(582)
PTOS Patent and Trademark Office Society(572)
PTR Professional Tennis Registry(589)
PTRA Power-Motion Technology Representatives Association(582)
PTTC Petroleum Technology Transfer Council(574)
PUSCC Portugal-United States Chamber of Commerce(581)
PVA Passenger Vessel Association(572)
PVMA Pressure Vessel Manufacturers Association(583)
PWA Performance Warehouse Association(573)
PWAA Professional Women's Appraisal Association(590)
PWC Professional Women Controllers(590)

Professional Women in Construction(590)
PWIA Personal Watercraft Industry Association(574)
PWMA Pressure Washer Manufacturers Association(583)
PWNA Power Washers of North America(582)
PWP Professional Women Photographers(590)
PWSA Professional Women Singers Association(590)
QBA Quality Bakers of America Cooperative(594)
QFMA Quarters Furniture Manufacturers Association(594)
QRCA Qualitative Research Consultants Association(593)
QVMCMCVMA QVM/CMC Vehicle Manufacturers Association(594)
R&DA Research and Development Associates for Military Food and Packaging Systems(599)
R&E COUNCIL Research and Engineering Council of the NAPL(600)
RA Rabbinical Assembly(594)
RAA Regional Airline Association(597)
Reinsurance Association of America(598)
RAAA Red Angus Association of America(597)
RAB Radio Advertising Bureau(594)
RACC Romanian-American Chamber of Commerce(603)
RAMA Retail Advertising and Marketing Association International(601)
RAMP Research Association of Minority Professors(600)
RAPS Regulatory Affairs Professionals Society(598)
RBA Retailer's Bakery Association(601)
RBMA Radiology Business Management Association(595)
RCA Religious Communication Association(598)
Research Chefs Association(600)
RCC Religion Communicators Council(598)
RCFC Refractory Ceramic Fibers Coalition(597)
RCI RCI, Inc.(595)
Retail Confectioners International(601)
RCMA Religious Conference Management Association(599)
Roof Coatings Manufacturers Association(603)
RCRA Resort and Commercial Recreation Association(600)
RCSC Research Council on Structural Connections(600)
REA Religious Education Association(599)
REBAC Real Estate Buyers Agent Council(595)
REEA Real Estate Educators Association(595)
REIPA Real Estate Information Professionals Association(596)
REMSA Railway Engineering-Maintenance Suppliers Association(595)
RER Real Estate Round Table(596)
RESNA Rehabilitation Engineering and Assistive Technology Society of North America(598)
RETA Refrigerating Engineers and Technicians Association(597)
RFA Refrigerated Foods Association(597)
Renewable Fuels Association(599)
RFCI Resilient Floor Covering Institute(600)
RFMA Restaurant Facility Management Association(600)
RHBAA Racking Horse Breeders Association of America(594)
RI Rolf Institute(602)
RIA Robotic Industries Association(602)
RIAA Recording Industry Association of America(596)
RICA Railway Industrial Clearance Association of North America(595)
RID Registry of Interpreters for the Deaf(598)
RIMS Risk and Insurance Management Society(602)
RIPA Reusable Industrial Packaging Association(601)
RITA Retirement Industry Trust Association(601)
RJOS Ruth Jackson Orthopaedic Society(603)
RLI REALTORS Land Institute(596)
RMA Rice Millers' Association(602)
RMA - The Risk Management Association(602)
Rubber Manufacturers Association(603)
RMS River Management Society(602)
RNA Religion Newswriters Association(598)
RNA Society(602)
RNRF Renewable Natural Resources Foundation(599)
RNS Respiratory Nursing Society(600)
ROA Reserve Officers Association of the U.S.(600)
ROUNDALAB International Association of Round Dance Teachers(361)
RPA Radiant Panel Association(594)
Register of Professional Archeologists(598)
Renal Physicians Association(599)
Rubber Pavements Association(603)
RPIC Rubber and Plastics Industry Conference of the United Steelworkers of America(603)
RPMA Retail Packaging Manufacturers Association(601)
RPMDA Retail Print Music Dealers Association(601)
RPTA Recycled Paperboard Technical Association(597)
RPTIA Recreational Park Trailer Industry Association(596)
RRA Religious Research Association(599)
RRS Radiation Research Society(594)
RSA Railway Supply Institute(595)
Receptive Services Association of America(596)
Renaissance Society of America(599)
Reprographic Services Association(599)
Research Society on Alcoholism(600)
Rhetoric Society of America(601)
Roller Skating Association International(602)
RSAA Romanian Studies Association of America(603)
RSES Refrigeration Service Engineers Society(597)
RSNA Radiological Society of North America(594)
RSPA Retail Solutions Providers Association(601)
RSPI Residential Space Planners International(600)
RSS Rural Sociological Society(603)
RSSI Railway Systems Suppliers(595)
RTA Railway Tie Association(595)
Rubber Trade Association of North America(603)
RTAM/SME Rapid Technologies & Additive Manufacturing Community of SME(595)
RTCA Radio and Television Correspondents Association(594)
RTDA Retail Tobacco Dealers of America(601)
RTNDA Radio-Television News Directors Association(594)
RTNPA Red Tag News Publications Association(597)
RTOG Radiation Therapy Oncology Group(594)
RVAA Recreational Vehicle Aftermarket Association(596)
RVDA Recreation Vehicle Dealers Association of North America(596)
RVIA Recreation Vehicle Industry Association(596)
RVMCA Recreational Vehicle Manufacturer's Clubs Association(597)
RWA Romance Writers of America(603)
RWDCA Red and White Dairy Cattle Association(597)
RWDSU Retail, Wholesale and Department Store Union(601)
RWMA Resistance Welder Manufacturers' Association(600)
S&LPMC Safety and Loss Prevention Management Council(604)
SA Sugar Association(655)
SAA Society for American Archaeology(613)
Society of American Archivists(630)
Society of Animal Artists(631)
Society of Automotive Analysts(632)
Sunglass Association of America(655)
Surety Association of America(656)
SAAMI Sporting Arms and Ammunition Manufacturers' Institute(651)
SAAP Society for the Advancement of American Philosophy(626)
SABEW Society of American Business Editors and Writers(630)
SABR Society for American Baseball Research(613)
SACC-USA Swedish-American Chambers of Commerce(657)
SACI Sales Association of the Chemical Industry(604)
SACP Society of Asian and Comparative Philosophy(632)
SAE SAE International(604)
Society for the Advancement of Education(626)
Suntanning Association for Education(655)
SAEM Society for Academic Emergency Medicine(613)
SAET Society for the Advancement of Economic Theory(626)
SAF Society of American Florists(630)
Society of American Foresters(630)
SAFCS Society of Air Force Clinical Surgeons(629)
SAFD Society of American Fight Directors(630)
SAFE SAFE Association(604)
SAFN Society for the Anthropology of Food and Nutrition(627)
SAG Screen Actors Guild(606)
SAGA Smocking Arts Guild of America(612)
Society of American Graphic Artists(630)
SAGES Society of American Gastrointestinal and Endoscopic Surgeons(630)
SAGP Society for Ancient Greek Philosophy(613)
SAH Society of American Historians(630)
Society of Architectural Historians(631)
SAHA Society of American Historical Artists(631)

SAI Society of Atherosclerosis Imaging(632)
SAID Society of American Indian Dentists(631)
SAJA South Asian Journalists Association(647)
SALIS Substance Abuse Librarians and Information Specialists(655)
SALT Society for Applied Learning Technology(614)
Society of American Law Teachers(631)
SAM Society for Adolescent Medicine(613)
Society for Advancement of Management(613)
Society for Asian Music(614)
Society of American Magicians(631)
SAMA SAMA Group of Associations(605)
Strategic Account Management Association(654)
SAME Society of American Military Engineers(631)
SAMP Stuntmen's Association of Motion Pictures(654)
SAMPE Society for the Advancement of Material and Process Engineering(626)
SAMS Society of Accredited Marine Surveyors(629)
SANA Soyfoods Association of North America(648)
SANTA Souvenirs, Gifts and Novelties Trade Association(648)
SAPA Society of Army Physician Assistants(632)
SAPAA Substance Abuse Program Administrators Association(655)
SAPI Sales Association of the Paper Industry(604)
SARA Society of American Registered Architects(631)
SARCA Senior Army Reserve Commanders Association(609)
SART Society for Assisted Reproductive Technology(614)
SAS Association for Applied and Clinical Sociology(167)
Society for Applied Spectroscopy(614)
Society for Archaeological Sciences(614)
Society of American Silversmiths(631)
Society of Armenian Studies(631)
SASE Society for the Advancement of Socio-Economics(626)
SASS Society for the Advancement of Scandinavian Study(626)
SATW Society of American Travel Writers(631)
SAVE SAVE International(605)
SAVTA Safe and Vault Technicians Association(604)
SAWE Society of Allied Weight Engineers(630)
SBA Structural Board Association(654)
SBBA Spanish-Barb Breeders Association(648)
SBCA Satellite Broadcasting and Communications Association(605)
Small Business Council of America(611)
SBCS Society for Buddhist-Christian Studies(614)
SBE Society for Business Ethics(614)
Society of Broadcast Engineers(632)
SBEA Small Business Exporters Association of the United States(611)
SBIC Sustainable Buildings Industry Council(656)
SBL Society of Biblical Literature(632)
SBLC SB Latex Council(605)
Small Business Legislative Council(611)
SBM Society of Behavioral Medicine(632)
SBS Society for Biomolecular Sciences(614)
SBSBA Scottish Blackface Sheep Breeders Association(606)
SC Sculptors Guild(607)
Society for Cryobiology(616)
SC&RA Specialized Carriers and Rigging Association(649)
SCA Shipbuilders Council of America(610)
Smart Card Alliance(611)
Society of Cardiovascular Anesthesiologists(632)
SCAA Specialty Coffee Association of America(650)
Spill Control Association of America(651)
SCAI Society for Cardiovascular Angiography and Interventions(614)
SCB Shipowners Claims Bureau(610)
Society for Conservation Biology(615)
SCBT/MR Society of Computed Body Tomography and Magnetic Resonance(634)
SCBWI Society of Children's Book Writers and Illustrators(633)
SCC Society of Cosmetic Chemists(634)
Supply Chain Council(656)
SCCM Society of Critical Care Medicine(634)
SCCR Society for Cross-Cultural Research(616)
SCD Society of Creative Designers(634)
Special Care Dentistry Association(648)
SCDM Society for Clinical Data Management(615)
SCE Society of Christian Ethics(633)
SCEA Society of Cost Estimating and Analysis(634)
SCEH Society for Clinical and Experimental Hypnosis(615)
SCFMA Summer and Casual Furniture Manufacturers Association(655)
SCI Society of Composers(634)
Sponge and Chamois Institute(651)
SCIAS Society of Chemical Industry, American Section(633)
SCIC Society of Certified Insurance Counselors(632)
SCiP Society for Computers in Psychology(615)
Society of Competitive Intelligence Professionals(633)
SCL Society of Composers and Lyricists(634)
SCMA Southern Cypress Manufacturers Association(648)
SCMHR Society of Clinical and Medical Hair Removal(633)
SCMP Society of Corporate Meeting Professionals(634)
SCMR Society for Cardiovascular Magnetic Resonance(614)
SCMS Society for Cinema and Media Studies(615)
SCP Society of Christian Philosophers(633)
SCRS Society of Collision Repair Specialists(633)
SCRT Society of Cleaning and Restoration Technicians(633)
SCS Society for Computer Simulation(615)
SCSITA SCSI Trade Association(607)
SCST Society of Commercial Seed Technologists(633)
SCT Society for Clinical Trials(615)
SCTE Society of Cable Telecommunications Engineers(632)
Society of Carbide and Tool Engineers(632)
SCTPLS Society for Chaos Theory in Psychology and Life Sciences(615)
SCUP Society for College and University Planning(615)
SCVIR Society of Interventional Radiology(639)
SCVS Society for Clinical Vascular Surgery(615)
SDA Soap and Detergent Association(612)
Surface Design Association(656)
SDB Society for Developmental Biology(616)
SDBP Society for Developmental and Behavioral Pediatrics(616)
SDHS Society of Dance History Scholars(635)
SDI Steel Deck Institute(653)
Steel Door Institute(653)
SDMN State Debt Management Network(652)
SDMS Society of Diagnostic Medical Sonography(635)
SDP Society of Decorative Painters(635)
Society of Depreciation Professionals(635)
SDS Society for Disability Studies(616)
SEA Senior Executives Association(609)
Society for Economic Anthropology(616)
Society for Education in Anesthesia(616)
Space Energy Association(648)
SEB Society for Economic Botany(616)
SEBM Society for Experimental Biology and Medicine(617)
SEC Softwood Export Council(646)
SECA Surface Engineering Coating Association(656)
SEDA Safety Equipment Distributors Association(604)
SEE Society for Excellence in Eyecare(617)
SEFA Scientific Equipment and Furniture Association(606)
SEG Society of Economic Geologists(635)
Society of Exploration Geophysicists(636)
SEGD Society for Environmental Graphic Design(617)
SEGH Society for Environmental Geochemistry and Health(617)
SEHSC Silicones Environmental, Health and Safety Council of North America(610)
SEIA Solar Energy Industries Association(647)
SEIU Service Employees International Union(609)
SEJ Society of Environmental Journalists(635)
SEM Society for Ethnomusicology(617)
Society for Experimental Mechanics(617)
SEMA Specialty Equipment Market Association(650)
SEMI Semiconductor Equipment and Materials International(608)
SENTAC Society for Ear, Nose and Throat Advances in Children(616)
SEPI Society for the Exploration of Psychotherapy Integration(627)
SEPM SEPM - Society for Sedimentary Geology(609)
SER Society for Ecological Restoration(616)
Society for Epidemiologic Research(617)
SES Society of Engineering Science(635)
Society of Eye Surgeons(636)
Standards Engineering Society(652)

SESMA Special Event Sites Marketing Alliance(648)
SETAC Society of Environmental Toxicology and Chemistry(635)
SETP Society of Experimental Test Pilots(635)
SFA Snack Food Association(612)
SfAA Society for Applied Anthropology(613)
SFB Society for Biomaterials(614)
SFC Society of Flavor Chemists(636)
SFHS Society for French Historical Studies(617)
SFIC Surface Finishing Industry Council(656)
SFLERP Society of Federal Labor and Employee Relations Professionals(636)
SFM Society for Foodservice Management(617)
SFN Society for Neuroscience(622)
SFPE Society of Fire Protection Engineers(636)
SFRBM Society for Free Radical Biology and Medicine(617)
SFSA Steel Founders' Society of America(653)
SFSAFBI Society of Former Special Agents of the Federal Bureau of Investigation(636)
SFT Society for Theriogenology(628)
SFTE Society of Flight Test Engineers(636)
SFWA Science Fiction and Fantasy Writers of America(606)
SGA Songwriters Guild of America(647)
SGAA Sporting Goods Agents Association(651)
Stained Glass Association of America(652)
SGAC State Government Affairs Council(652)
SGAS Society for German-American Studies(617)
SGAUS State Guard Association of the United States(652)
SGBI Santa Gertrudis Breeders International(605)
SGC Society of Geriatric Cardiology(637)
SGCC Safety Glazing Certification Council(604)
SGCD Society of Glass and Ceramic Decorators(637)
SGE Society of Government Economists(637)
SGI Society for Gynecologic Investigation(618)
SGIA Specialty Graphic Imaging Association(650)
SGIM Society of General Internal Medicine(637)
SGMA SGMA(651)
SGMP Society of Government Meeting Professionals(637)
SGNA Society of Gastroenterology Nurses and Associates(637)
SGO Society of Gynecologic Oncologists(638)
SGP Society of General Physiologists(637)
SGR Society of Gastrointestinal Radiologists(637)
SGSU Society of Government Service Urologists(637)
SGTP Society of Government Travel Professionals(637)
SH Society for Hematopathology(618)
SHA Society for Historical Archaeology(618)
SHAFR Society for Historians of American Foreign Relations(618)
SHARP Society for the History of Authorship, Reading and Publishing(627)
SHATA Saddle, Harness, and Allied Trade Association(604)
SHCA Society for Healthcare Consumer Advocacy(618)
SHD Society for the History of Discoveries(627)
SHDA Security Hardware Distributors Association(607)
SHE Society for History Education(618)
Society for Human Ecology(619)
SHEA Society for Healthcare Epidemiology of America(618)
SHEAR Society for Historians of the Early American Republic(618)
SHEEO State Higher Education Executive Officers(653)
SHFG Society for History in the Federal Government(618)
SHGAPE Society for Historians of the Gilded Age and Progressive Era(618)
SHJ Society for Humanistic Judaism(619)
SHOPA School, Home and Office Products Association(606)
SHOT Society for the History of Technology(627)
SHPE Society of Hispanic Professional Engineers(638)
SHRM Society for Human Resource Management(619)
SHRMGF SHRM Global Forum(610)
SHSMD Society for Healthcare Strategy and Market Development(618)
SI Salt Institute(605)
Silver Institute(611)
Society of Illustrators(638)
SIA Scaffold Industry Association(605)
Security Industry Association(607)
Semiconductor Industry Association(608)
Service Industry Association(609)
SnowSports Industries America(612)
Society for Industrial Archeology(620)
SIAM Society for Industrial and Applied Mathematics(619)
SICA Soccer Industry Council of America(612)
SICB Society for Integrative and Comparative Biology(620)
SICP Society of Invasive Cardiovascular Professionals(639)
SID Society for Information Display(620)
Society for Investigative Dermatology(620)
SIDEKA Sigma Delta Kappa(610)
SIDP Society of Infectious Diseases Pharmacists(638)
SIETAR-USA Society for Intercultural Education, Training and Research - USA(620)
SIFM Society of Insurance Financial Management(638)
SIGACCESS Special Interest Group on Accessible Computing(649)
SIGCAS Special Interest Group for Computers and Society(648)
SIGMA Society of Independent Gasoline Marketers of America(638)
SIGUCCS Special Interest Group for University and College Computing Services(649)
SIHS Society for Italian Historical Studies(621)
SIIA Self Insurance Institute of America, Inc.(608)
Software and Information Industry Association(646)
SIIM Society for Imaging Informatics in Medicine(619)
SIM Society for Industrial Microbiology(620)
Society for Information Management(620)
SIOP Society for Industrial and Organizational Psychology(620)
SIOR Society of Industrial and Office REALTORS(638)
SIP Society for Invertebrate Pathology(620)
SIPA Specialized Information Publishers Association(650)
Structural Insulated Panel Association(654)
SIPES Society of Independent Professional Earth Scientists(638)
SIR Society of Insurance Research(638)
SIS Society for Iranian Studies(620)
Surgical Infection Society(656)
SISO Society of Independent Show Organizers(638)
SIT Sugar Industry Technologists(655)
SITE Society of Incentive & Travel Executives(638)
Society of Insurance Trainers and Educators(639)
SIU Seafarers' International Union(607)
SIVB Society for In Vitro Biology(619)
SJI Steel Joist Institute(653)
SLA Showmen's League of America(610)
Special Libraries Association(649)
Sports Lawyers Association(651)
SLB Society for Leukocyte Biology(621)
SLEMA Schiffli Lace and Embroidery Manufacturers Association(606)
SLH Small Luxury Hotels of the World(611)
SLS Society of Laparoendoscopic Surgeons(639)
SLTBR Society for Light Treatment and Biological Rhythms(621)
SMA Scale Manufacturers Association(605)
Screen Manufacturers Association(607)
Society of Maritime Arbitrators(639)
Society of Mineral Analysts(640)
Society of Municipal Arborists(640)
Stadium Managers Association(652)
Steel Manufacturers Association(653)
Stucco Manufacturers Association(654)
SMACNA Sheet Metal and Air Conditioning Contractors' National Association(610)
SMART Secondary Materials and Recycled Textiles Association(607)
SMB Society for Mathematical Biology(621)
SMCAF Society of Medical Consultants to the Armed Forces(639)
SMCR Society for Menstrual Cycle Research(621)
SMD Society of Medical-Dental Management Consultants(640)
SMDM Society for Medical Decision Making(621)
SME Society for Mining, Metallurgy, and Exploration(622)
Society of Manufacturing Engineers(639)
SMEI Sales and Marketing Executives International(604)
SMEMA IPC - Surface Mount Equipment Manufacturers Association(399)
SMEP Society of Multivariate Experimental Psychology(640)
SMFM Society for Maternal Fetal Medicine(621)
SMH Society for Military History(622)
SMI Society for Mucosal Immunology(622)
Sorptive Minerals Institute(647)
Spring Manufacturers Institute(652)

SMMA SMMA - The Motor and Motion Association(612)
SMPE Society of Marine Port Engineers(639)
SMPS Society for Marketing Professional Services(621)
SMPTE Society of Motion Picture and Television Engineers(640)
SMRI Solution Mining Research Institute(647)
SMRP Society for Maintenance Reliability Professionals(621)
Society for Medieval and Renaissance Philosophy(621)
SMSG School Management Study Group(606)
SMT Professional Society for Sales and Marketing Training(589)
SMTA Surface Mount Technology Association(656)
SMWIA Sheet Metal Workers' International Association(610)
SNA School Nutrition Association(606)
Suburban Newspapers of America(655)
SNACC Society of Neurosurgical Anesthesia and Critical Care(641)
SNAG Society of North American Goldsmiths(641)
SNAME Society of Naval Architects and Marine Engineers(640)
SNAP Society of National Association Publications(640)
SND Society for News Design(622)
SNE Society for Nutrition Education(622)
SNLS Society for New Language Study(622)
SNM Society of Nuclear Medicine(641)
SNP Society for Natural Philosophy(622)
SNS Society of Neurological Surgeons(640)
SOA Society of Actuaries(629)
SOAP Society for Obstetric Anesthesia and Perinatology(622)
SOBA States Organization for Boating Access(653)
SOBP Society of Biological Psychiatry(632)
SOCAP SOCAP International(612)
SOCISAFFS Society of United States Air Force Flight Surgeons(645)
SOCMA Synthetic Organic Chemical Manufacturers Association(657)
SODA Sportsplex Operators and Developers Association(651)
SOEH Society for Occupational and Environmental Health(622)
SOFE Society of Financial Examiners(636)
SOFT Society of Forensic Toxicologists(636)
SOHN Society of Otorhinolaryngology and Head/Neck Nurses(641)
SOLE SOLE - The International Society of Logistics(647)
SOMA National Student Osteopathic Medical Association(544)
Society of Medical Administrators(639)
SOMOS Society of Military Orthopaedic Surgeons(640)
SON Society of Nematologists(640)
SOP Society of Protozoologists(643)
SOPHE Society for Public Health Education(624)
SOPHIA Society of Philosophers in America(642)
SOR Society of Rheology(643)
SORT Shippers of Recycled Textiles(610)
SOS Society of Scribes(644)
SOT Society of Toxicology(645)
SOVE Society for Vector Ecology(629)
SPA Seaplane Pilots Association(607)
Society for Pediatric Anesthesia(623)
Society for Personality Assessment(623)
Sociological Practice Association(646)
SPAC Soil and Plant Analysis Council(646)
SPAN Small Publishers Association of North America(611)
SPAR Society of Photographer and Artist Representatives(642)
SPARS Society of Professional Audio Recording Services(642)
SPBA Society of Professional Benefit Administrators(642)
SPBT Society of Pharmaceutical and Biotech Trainers(642)
SPC Soy Protein Council(648)
SPCAP Society of Professors of Child and Adolescent Psychiatry(642)
SPD Society for Pediatric Dermatology(623)
Society of Publication Designers(643)
SPE Society for Photographic Education(623)
Society of Petroleum Engineers(641)
Society of Plastics Engineers(642)
Society of Professors of Education(643)
SPED Society of Piping Engineers and Designers(642)
SPEE Society of Petroleum Evaluation Engineers(641)
SPESA Sewn Products Equipment and Suppliers of the Americas(609)
SPFA Steel Plate Fabricators Association Division of STI/SPFA(653)
SPFPA International Union Security, Police and Fire Professionals of America(396)
SPI Society of Professional Investigators(642)
Society of the Plastics Industry(645)
SPIE SPIE - The International Society for Optical Engineering(651)
SPJ Society of Professional Journalists(642)
SPN Society of Pediatric Nurses(641)
SPOH Society for the Preservation of Oral Health(627)
SPP Society for Pediatric Pathology(623)
Society for Pediatric Psychology(623)
SPR Society for Pediatric Radiology(623)
Society for Pediatric Research(623)
Society for Philosophy of Religion(623)
Society for Psychophysiological Research(624)
SPRBM Society for Physical Regulation in Biology and Medicine(624)
SPRE Society of Park and Recreation Educators(641)
SPRI SPRI, Inc.(652)
SPRS Society of Pelvic Reconstructive Surgeons(641)
SPS IEEE Signal Processing Society(331)
Society of Pelvic Surgeons(641)
Society of Physics Students(642)
SPSL Society for the Philosophy of Sex and Love(627)
SPSSI Society for the Psychological Study of Social Issues(627)
SPT Society for Philosophy and Technology(623)
SPU Society for Pediatric Urology(623)
SPWLA Society of Petrophysicists and Well Log Analysts(641)
SPWTP Swimming Pool Water Treatment Professionals(657)
SQA Society of Quality Assurance(643)
Society of Quantitative Analysts(643)
SRA Society for Research on Adolescence(624)
Society for Risk Analysis(625)
Society of Research Administrators International(643)
Station Representatives Association(653)
SRCC Solar Rating and Certification Corp.(647)
SRCD Society for Research in Child Development(624)
SRE Society of Recreation Executives(643)
Society of Reliability Engineers(643)
SREI Society for Reproductive Endocrinology and Infertility(624)
SRI Spring Research Institute(652)
Steel Recycling Institute(653)
SRM Society for Range Management(624)
SRMC Society of Risk Management Consultants(643)
SRNT Society for Research on Nicotine and Tobacco(625)
SROA Society for Radiation Oncology Administrators(624)
SRR Society for Reformation Research(624)
SRS Scoliosis Research Society(606)
Sleep Research Society(611)
Society for Romanian Studies(625)
Society of Reproductive Surgeons(643)
SRSTA Society of Roller Skating Teachers of America(644)
SRU Society of Radiologists in Ultrasound(643)
SS Shock Society(610)
SSA Seismological Society of America(608)
Self Storage Association(608)
Semiconductor Environmental Safety and Health Association(608)
Semiotic Society of America(608)
Service Specialists Association(609)
Shareholder Services Association(609)
Slovak Studies Association(611)
Soaring Society of America(612)
Sommelier Society of America(647)
Specialty Sleep Association(650)
SSAR Society for the Study of Amphibians and Reptiles(628)
SSAT Society for Surgery of the Alimentary Tract(625)
SSB Society of Systematic Biologists(644)
SSCD Society of Small Craft Designers(644)
SSCI Steel Shipping Container Institute(653)
SSDA-AT Service Station Dealers of America and Allied Trades(609)
SSDC Society of Stage Directors and Choreographers(644)
SSDHPER Society of State Directors of Health, Physical Education and Recreation(644)
SSE Society for the Study of Evolution(628)
SSEC Society for the Study of Early China(628)
SSFI Scaffolding, Shoring and Forming Institute(605)
SSHA Social Science History Association(612)
SSILA Society for the Study of Indigenous Languages of the Americas(628)
SSINA Specialty Steel Industry of North America(650)
SSLI Society of School Librarians International(644)
SSMA School Science and Mathematics Association(606)
SSMPP Society for the Study of Male Psychology and Physiology(628)
SSO Society of Surgical Oncology(644)
SSP Society for Scholarly Publishing(625)
SSPC SSPC: the Society for Protective Coatings(652)
SSPHS Society for Spanish and Portuguese Historical Studies(625)

SSPI Society of Satellite Professionals International(644)
SSPMA Sump and Sewage Pump Manufacturers Association(655)
SSQ Society for Software Quality(625)
SSR Society for the Study of Reproduction(628)
SSRC Social Science Research Council(613)
Structural Stability Research Council(654)
SSS Society for Slovene Studies(625)
System Safety Society(657)
SSSA Soil Science Society of America(647)
SSSB Society for the Study of Social Biology(628)
SSSI Society for the Study of Symbolic Interaction(628)
SSSP Society for the Study of Social Problems(628)
SSSR Society for the Scientific Study of Religion(627)
SSSS Society for Social Studies of Science(625)
Society for the Scientific Study of Sexuality(627)
SSTAR Society for Sex Therapy and Research(625)
SSWA Sanitary Supply Wholesaling Association(605)
SSWLHC Society for Social Work Leadership in Health Care(625)
STA Securities Transfer Association(607)
Security Traders Association(608)
Space Transportation Association(648)
Subcontractors Trade Association(655)
STAFDA Specialty Tool and Fastener Distributors Association(650)
STAPPA State and Territorial Air Pollution Program Administrators(652)
STAR Society for Technological Advancement of Reporting(626)
STATENETS Radio National Association of State Radio Networks(476)
STC Society for Technical Communication(626)
Society of Telecommunications Consultants(644)
Specialty Tobacco Council(650)
STFM Society of Teachers of Family Medicine(644)
STI Steel Tank Institute Division of STI/SPFA(654)
Steel Tube Institute of North America(654)
STLE Society of Tribologists and Lubrication Engineers(645)
STM Society for Thermal Medicine(628)
STMA Sports Turf Managers Association(651)
STN Society of Trauma Nurses(645)
STP Society of Toxicologic Pathologists(645)
STR Society of Thoracic Radiology(645)
STRIMA State Risk and Insurance Management Association(653)
STS Society for Textual Scholarship(626)
Society of Thoracic Surgeons(645)
SUA Silver Users Association(611)
SUNA Society of Urologic Nurses and Associates(645)
SUO Society of University Otolaryngologists(645)
SUR Society for Uroradiology(629)
SUS Society of University Surgeons(645)
SUU Society of University Urologists(645)
SVA Society for Visual Anthropology(629)
SVC Society of Vacuum Coaters(646)
SVHE Society for Values in Higher Education(629)
SVIA Specialty Vehicle Institute of America(650)
Stable Value Investment Association(652)
SVMB Society for Vascular Medicine and Biology(629)
SVN Society for Vascular Nursing(629)
SVP Society of Vertebrate Paleontology(646)
SVS Society for Vascular Surgery(629)
SVU Society for Vascular Ultrasound(629)
SWAMP Stuntwomen's Association of Motion Pictures(654)
SWANA SWANA - Solid Waste Association of North America(656)
SWCS Soil and Water Conservation Society(647)
SWE Society of Wine Educators(646)
Society of Women Engineers(646)
SWG Society of Woman Geographers(646)
SWHR Society for the Advancement of Women's Health Research(626)
SWI Steel Window Institute(654)
SWPA Section for Women in Public Administration(607)
Submersible Wastewater Pump Association(655)
SWRI Sealant, Waterproofing and Restoration Institute(607)
SWST Society of Wood Science and Technology(646)
T2S Technology Transfer Society(658)
TA Tea Association of the United States of America(658)
Tobacco Associates(662)
TAA Text and Academic Authors Association(659)
Tobacconists' Association of America(662)
TAAFLO Trans-Atlantic American Flag Liner Operators(663)
TAALS American Association of Language Specialists(44)
TAAN Transworld Advertising Agency Network(664)
TAANA American Association of Nurse Attorneys, The(46)
TAB Traffic Audit Bureau for Media Measurement(663)
TABS Association of Boarding Schools, The(188)
TAGA Technical Association of the Graphic Arts(658)
TAPPI Technical Association of the Pulp and Paper Industry(658)
TARA Truck-frame and Axle Repair Association(666)
TASDA American Safe Deposit Association(123)
TASH TASH(657)
TASP Association for the Study of Play(181)
TAUS Tobacco Association of the U.S.(662)
TAWPI Association for Work Process Improvement(183)
TBA Test Boring Association(659)
TBIG Telecommunications Benchmarking International Group(659)
TBMA Bond Market Association(231)
Textile Bag Manufacturers Association(660)
TBP Tributyl Phosphate Task Force(665)
TBPA Textile Bag and Packaging Association(660)
TC Tea Council of the U.S.A.(658)
TCA Textile Converters Association(660)
Therapeutic Communities of America(660)
Thoroughbred Club of America(661)
Tile Council of North America(661)
Tilt-up Concrete Association(661)
Truckload Carriers Association(666)
TCAA Tile Contractors' Association of America(661)
TCATA Textile Care Allied Trades Association(660)
TCI Transportation Clubs International(664)
TCIA Tree Care Industry Association(665)
TCMA Tooling Component Manufacturers Association(662)
TCNA Tube Council of North America(666)
TCSAA Twentieth-Century Spanish Association of America(667)
TCU Transportation Communications International Union(664)
TDA Textile Distributors Association(660)
Transportation Development Association(664)
TDC Type Directors Club(667)
TEBA Environmental Business Association, The(296)
TEGMA Transportation Elevator and Grain Merchants Association(664)
TEI Tax Executives Institute(657)
TEMA Tubular Exchanger Manufacturers Association(666)
TER Tau Epsilon Rho Law Society(657)
TESOL Teachers of English to Speakers of Other Languages(658)
TF Toxicology Forum(662)
TFA Teaching-Family Association(658)
TFBC Timber Frame Business Council(661)
TFBPA Textile Fibers and By-Products Association(660)
TFF Fragrance Foundation(311)
TFG Timber Framers Guild(661)
TFI Fertilizer Institute(305)
TGA Travel Goods Association(665)
TGA-US Glutamate Association (United States)(318)
THA Hosiery Association, The(328)
The ARF Advertising Research Foundation(9)
THF Health Forum(323)
TI Thermoforming Institute(660)
Transportation Institute(664)
TIA Telecommunications Industry Association(659)
Tennis Industry Association(659)
Tortilla Industry Association(662)
Toy Industry Association(662)
Transportation Intermediaries Association(664)
Travel Industry Association of America(665)
TIACA The International Air Cargo Association(348)
TIAFT International Association of Forensic Toxicologists(357)
TIAW International Alliance for Women(348)
TIES International Ecotourism Society(370)
TJC Jockey Club(402)
TJG Travel Journalists Guild(665)
TKGA The Knitting Guild Association(404)
TLA Theatre Library Association(660)
Transportation Lawyers Association(664)
TLBAA Texas Longhorn Breeders Association of America(659)
TLC Transportation & Logistics Council(664)
TLMI Tag and Label Manufacturers Institute(657)
TLPA Taxicab, Limousine and Paratransit Association(657)
TMA Tobacco Merchants Association of the U.S.(662)
Truck Manufacturers Association(665)

USCIB United States Council for International Business(674)
USCID United States Committee on Irrigation and Drainage(674)
USCJ United Synagogue of Conservative Judaism(678)
USCM United States Conference of Mayors(674)
USCRA United States Court Reporters Association(674)
USCTI United States Cutting Tool Institute(675)
USDGA United States Durum Growers Association(675)
USEA United States Energy Association(675)
USEF United States Equestrian Federation(675)
USFCA United States Fencing Coaches Association(675)
USFCC United States Federation for Culture Collections(675)
USFSS United States Federation of Scholars and Scientists(675)
USGA United States Golf Association(675)
USGC U.S. Grains Council(667)
USHCC United States Hispanic Chamber of Commerce(675)
USHWA United States Harness Writers' Association(675)
USIIA U.S. Internet Industry Association(668)
USISPA United States Internet Service Provider Association(676)
USITT United States Institute for Theatre Technology(676)
USJCC United States Junior Chamber of Commerce(676)
USLA United States Lifesaving Association(676)
USMA U.S. Metric Association(668)
USMCOC United States-Mexico Chamber of Commerce(678)
USMEF United States Meat Export Federation(676)
USMSA United States Marine Safety Association(676)
USNZC United States-New Zealand Council(678)
USP United States Pharmacopeia(676)
USPA United States Parachute Association(676)
USPAACC U.S. Pan Asian American Chamber of Commerce(668)
USPOULTRY U.S. Poultry and Egg Association(668)
USPRA U.S. Psychiatric Rehabiliation Association(668)
USPTA United States Professional Tennis Association(676)
USRA United Shoe Retailers Association(672)
Universities Space Research Association(679)
USRBC U.S.-Russia Business Council(668)
USRSA United States Racquet Stringers Association(677)
USSA United States Ski Association(677)
United Suffolk Sheep Association(678)
USSD United States Society on Dams(677)
USTA United States Telecom Association(677)
United States Tennis Association(677)
United States Trotting Association(678)
USTF United States Tuna Foundation(678)
USTFA United States Trout Farmers Association(678)
USTOA United States Tour Operators Association(677)
USTSA United States Targhee Sheep Association(677)
USW U.S. Wheat Associates(668)
United Steel, Paper and Forestry, Rubber, Manufacturing, Energy, Allied Industrial and Service Workers International Union(678)
UTA Used Truck Association(681)
UTC United Telecom Council(679)
UTSA Uniform and Textile Service Association(669)
UTU United Transportation Union(679)
UURWAW United Union of Roofers, Waterproofers and Allied Workers(679)
UWA United Weighers Association(679)
UWUA Utility Workers Union of America(681)
VAAUS Venezuelan American Association of the U.S.(682)
VAC Vinyl Acetate Council(683)
VAI Van Alen Institute(682)
VBMA Veterinary Botanical Medical Association(682)
VCA Vision Council of America(684)
VCS Veterinary Cancer Society(682)
VdGSA Viola da Gamba Society of America(683)
VDTA Vacuum Dealers Trade Association(682)
VECAP Vocational Evaluation and Career Assessement Professionals(684)
VECI Variable Electronic Components Institute(682)
VESA Video Electronics Standards Association(683)
VHMA Veterinary Hospital Managers Association(682)
VI Vibration Institute(683)
Vinegar Institute(683)
Vinyl Institute(683)
VLSAA Viatical and Life Settlement Association of America(683)
VMA Valve Manufacturers Association of America(682)
VNAA Visiting Nurse Associations of America(684)
VOHMA International Vessel Operators Hazardous Materials Association(396)
VOS Veterinary Orthopedic Society(682)
VPPPA Voluntary Protection Programs Participants Association(684)
VRA Visual Resources Association(684)
VRC Valve Repair Council(682)
VRMA Vacation Rental Managers Association(681)
VSA Victorian Society in America(683)
Violin Society of America(683)
Visitor Studies Association(684)
VSDA Video Software Dealers Association(683)
VSI Vinyl Siding Institute(683)
VWGA Vinifera Wine Growers Association(683)
WA Wallcoverings Association(685)
WAABI World Association of Alcohol Beverage Industries(695)
WAAC Western Association for Art Conservation(687)
WACA World Affairs Councils of America(695)
WACRA WACRA - World Association for Case Method Research and Application(684)
WAEA World Airline Entertainment Association(695)
WAI Wire Association International(690)
Women in Aviation International(691)
WAIMH World Association for Infant Mental Health(695)
WAO World Allergy Organization - IACCI(695)
WAS World Aquaculture Society(695)
WASDA Water and Sewer Distributors of America(685)
WASTEC Waste Equipment Technology Association(685)
WAVA World Association of Veterinary Anatomists(695)
WAW WorldatWork(697)
WBAE Wholesale Beer Association Executives of America(688)
WBANA Wild Blueberry Association of North America(688)
WBCA Women's Basketball Coaches Association(693)
WBDNA Women Band Directors International(690)
WBFI Wild Bird Feeding Institute(688)
WBMA Wirebound Box Manufacturers Association(690)
WC Walnut Council(685)
WCA Waterproofing Contractors Association(686)
Wellness Councils of America(687)
Wireless Communications Association International(690)
Women's Caucus for Art(693)
WCAA Window Coverings Association of America(689)
WCC Women's Classical Caucus(693)
Women's College Coalition(693)
WCISA Wire & Cable Industry Suppliers Association(690)
WCMA Window Coverings Manufacturers Association(689)
Wood Component Manufacturers Association(694)
WCML Women's Caucus for the Modern Languages(693)
WCOE/USA Women Construction Owners and Executives, USA(691)
WCPS Women's Caucus for Political Science(693)
WCR Women Chefs and Restaurateurs(691)
Women's Council of REALTORS(693)
WCSC Window Covering Safety Council(689)
WDA Wildlife Disease Association(689)
Wireless Dealers Association(690)
WDMA Window and Door Manufacturers Association(689)
WE Women in Endocrinology(691)
Women in Energy(691)
WEA Wilderness Education Association(688)
WEAI Western Economic Association International(687)
WEB WEB: Worldwide Employee Benefits Network(686)
WEDA Western Dredging Association(687)
WEDI Workgroup for Electronic Data Interchange(695)
WEF Water Environment Federation(685)
WEPR Women Executives in Public Relations(691)
WERC Warehousing Education and Research Council(685)
WESG Women Executives in State Government(691)
WETA Western-English Trade Association(688)
WEVA Int'l Wedding and Event Videographers Association International(686)
WF&FSA Wholesale Florist and Florist Supplier Association(688)
WFA Wire Fabricators Association(690)
WFCA World Floor Covering Association(695)
WFF Women's Foodservice Forum(693)
WFS Women in the Fire Service(692)

World Future Society(696)
WGAE Writers Guild of America, East(697)
WGAw Writers Guild of America, West(697)
WGC World Gold Council(696)
WGR Women in Government Relations(692)
WHA Western History Association(687)
World History Association(696)
WHCA White House Correspondents Association(688)
WHMA Wiring Harness Manufacturers Association(690)
WHNPA White House News Photographers Association(688)
WHOA Walking Horse Owners Association of America(685)
WHTA Walking Horse Trainers Association(685)
WIA Women in Aerospace(691)
Women in Agribusiness(691)
WIBC Women's International Bowling Congress(693)
WICT Women in Cable and Telecommunications(691)
WIF Women in Film(691)
WIFS WIFS - Women in Insurance and Financial Services(688)
WIFV Women in Film and Video(692)
WIG Women in Government(692)
WIIS Women in International Security(692)
WIIT Organization of Women in International Trade(568)
WIM Women in Management(692)
Women in Mining National(692)
WIMA Writing Instrument Manufacturers Association(697)
WINBA World International Nail and Beauty Association(696)
WINUP Women's International Network of Utility Professionals(693)
WISP Women in Scholarly Publishing(692)
WITI Women in Technology International(692)
WJA Women's Jewelry Association(693)
WJTA WaterJet Technology Association(686)
WLA Western Literature Association(687)
WMA Weather Modification Association(686)
Western Music Association(687)
World Media Association(696)
WMI Wildlife Management Institute(689)
WMIA Woodworking Machinery Industry Association(694)
WMMA Wood Machinery Manufacturers of America(694)
WMMPA Wood Moulding and Millwork Producers Association(694)
WMS Wilderness Medical Society(689)
WNBA Women's National Book Association(694)
WOCN Wound, Ostomy and Continence Nurses Society(697)
WOMPI Women of the Motion Picture Industry, International(692)
WP Women in Packaging(692)
WPA National Council of Writing Program Administrators(502)
WPCSA Welsh Pony and Cob Society of America(687)
WPF WorkPlace Furnishings(695)
WPMA Wood Products Manufacturers Association(694)
WPPI Wedding and Portrait Photographers International(686)
WPRA Women's Professional Rodeo Association(694)
WPSA World's Poultry Science Association, U.S.A. Branch(697)
WQA Water Quality Association(686)
WQC Wheat Quality Council(688)
WRC Welding Research Council(687)
WRCLA Western Red Cedar Lumber Association(687)
WRCPA Western Red Cedar Pole Association(687)
WRF World Research Foundation(696)
WRI Wire Reinforcement Institute(690)
WRPA Women's Regional Publications of America(694)
WRTB Wire Rope Technical Board(690)
WSA World Shoe Association(696)
World Sign Associates(696)
WSC Water Systems Council(686)
WSG Wire Service Guild(690)
WSIA Water Sports Industry Association(686)
WSSA Weed Science Society of America(687)
Wine and Spirits Shippers Association(689)
WSTDA Web Sling and Tiedown Association(686)
WSWA Wine and Spirits Wholesalers of America(689)
WTA World Teleport Association(696)
WTA Tour WTA Tour(697)
WTCA Wood Truss Council of America(694)
World Trade Centers Association(696)
WTS Women's Transportation Seminar(694)
WWA Western Writers of America(688)
World Waterpark Association(696)
World Watusi Association(697)
WWEMA Water and Wastewater Equipment Manufacturers Association(685)
WWPA Woven Wire Products Association(697)
WWPIA World Wide Pet Industry Association(697)
WWTSA World War Two Studies Association(696)
XI Xplor International(698)
YBAA Yacht Brokers Association of America(698)
YEO Young Entrepreneurs Organization(698)
YMA Young Menswear Association(698)
YPA Yellow Pages Association(698)
YPO Young Presidents' Organization(698)
ZI Zonta International(698)

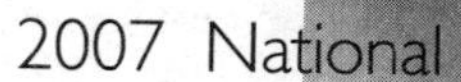

2007 National Trade and Professional Associations

Meetings Index

Meetings scheduled for 2007 are listed below, organized by meeting location.

ALABAMA

Birmingham

American Peanut Research and Education Society — Wynfrey Hotel/July 10-14

ALASKA

Anchorage

Adjutants General Association of the United States — June 3-7

American Association of Birth Centers — Marriott/Oct. 3-8/200

Girdwood

Steel Founders' Society of America — Alyeska Resort/Aug. 17-22/100

ARIZONA

Chandler

Advanced Medical Technology Association — Sheraton Wild Horse Pass/March 7-9

Flagstaff

Associated Schools of Construction — Northern Arizona University/Apr. 1- /150

Glendale

Football Writers Association of America — Jan. 5-9

Litchfield Park

American Chain Association — Wigwam/Apr. 1-4/6

Mechanical Power Transmission Association — Wigwam/Apr. 1-4/45

Phoenix

Air Movement and Control Association International — J.W. Marriott/Oct. 12-15

Alliance for Continuing Medical Education — JW Marriott/Jan. 17-20/1500

American Academy of Cosmetic Surgery — Biltmore Resort/Jan. 25-28

American Association of Neuromuscular & Electrodiagnostic Medicine — J.W. Marriott/Desert Ridge/Oct. 17-20/1000

American College of Osteopathic Emergency Physicians — Wild Horse Pass Resort/Apr. 10-14

American College of Prosthodontists — Westin Kierland/Oct. 31-Nov. 3/1000

American Fire Sprinkler Association — Marriott Desert Ridge/Sept. 26-30

American Indian Science and Engineering Society — Nov. 1-3/2200

American Society for Parenteral and Enteral Nutrition — Jan. 28-31

American Society of Hair Restoration Surgery — Biltmore Resort/Jan. 25-28/800

American Society of Hand Therapists — Oct. 4-7

Closure Manufacturers Association — Pointe South Mountain/Feb. 3-March 5

Commercial Finance Association — J.W. Marriott Desert Ridge Resort and Spa/Nov. 7-9

Construction Financial Management Association — Marriott's Desert Ridge/May 19-23

Copper and Brass Servicenter Association — Sheraton Wild Horse(Dates TBA)/230

Council of Industrial Boiler Owners — South Points Mountain Resort/Oct. 17-19

Electrical Equipment Representatives Association — Marriott Desert Ridge/April

International Association of Refrigerated Warehouses — Sheraton Wild Horse Pass/Apr. 21-26

International Economic Development Council — West Kierland Resort/Sept. 16-19

International Paralegal Management Association — Westin Kirkland/Oct. 10-13

International Refrigerated Transportation Association — Sheraton Wild Horse Pass/Apr. 21-26

Investigative Reporters and Editors — Arizona Biltmore Resort and Spa/June 7-10

Lamaze International — Sheraton Wild Horse Pass/Sept. 8-10

Materials Marketing Associates — February/40

Mobile Air Conditioning Society Worldwide — Phoenix Hyatt/Feb. 1-3/2500

National Association of Clinical Nurse Specialists — Hyatt Regency/Feb. 28-March 3/400

National Association of Nurse Massage Therapists — Hilton Garden Inn/June 7-9/100

National Forum for Black Public Administrators — Phoenix Civic Plaza/Apr. 21-25/1100

National School Public Relations Association — South Point Resort/July/750

Performance Warehouse Association — Pointe South Mountain/Sept. 24-26

Society of Urologic Nurses and Associates — Hyatt Regency/Oct. 12-15/600

United States Institute for Theatre Technology — March 14-17

Wholesale Florist and Florist Supplier Association — Hyatt Regency/Feb. 21-24

Scottsdale

Aircraft Builders Council — Fairmont Scottsdale Princess/Sept. 23-25

American Academy of Dental Practice Administration — Hyatt Gainey Ranch/Feb. 28-March 4/600

American Auditory Society — Embassy Suites/Nov. 4-6/350

American Medical Group Association — Westin Kierland/Feb. 28-March 3

American Society for Horticultural Science — Westin/July 16-19
Council on the Safe Transportation of Hazardous Articles — Apr. 22-25
Federation of Defense and Corporate Counsel — Fairmont Scottsdale Princess/Feb. 25-March 4
Financial and Insurance Conference Planners — Scottsdale Princess Fairmont/Nov. 11-15/650
Flexographic Prepress Platemakers Association — Doubletree Paradise Valley Resort/Feb. 18-20/100
General Merchandise Distributors Council — J.W. Marriott Desert Ridge Resort and Spa/June 1-5
Healthcare Billing and Management Association — Hilton/March 8-10
Investment Recovery Association — Doubletree/May 7-9
Metal Construction Association — Marriott/Jan. 12-15
National Association of State Chief Information Officers — Camelback Marriott/Sept. 30-Oct. 3
National Council on Teacher Retirement — Westin/Oct. 7-11
National Lubricating Grease Institute — Fairmont Scottsdale Princess/June 10-12/300
Web Sling and Tiedown Association — Doubletree Paradise Valley/May 6-9/80
Western Writers of America — June

Tempe

American Society for Legal History — Oct. 25-28

Tucson

American College of Physician Executives — Westin La Paloma/Nov. 11-16
Council of Hotel and Restaurant Trainers — July
Cranial Academy — Marriott University Park/June 21-24/150
Distance Education and Training Council — Omni Tucson/Apr. 15-17
Institute of Nuclear Materials Management — Marriott/July 15-19
International Academy of Oral Medicine and Toxicology — Marriott/March 15-17/200
International Association of Structural Movers — Feb. 14-18
National Association of Jewelry Appraisers — Tuscon Convention Center/Jan. 29-30/80
Process Equipment Manufacturers' Association — Loews/Feb. 28-March 4/90
Research and Development Associates for Military Food and Packaging Systems — Ventana Canyon Resort(Dates TBA)/260
Society of Financial Service Professionals — Omni Tucson National Golf Resort & Spa/Jan. 7-11
Wildlife Society, The — Tucson Convention Center/Sept. 22-26/1500
National Association of Principals of Schools for Girls — Ventana Canyon/Feb. 25-28/200

ARKANSAS

Little Rock

International Association of Conference Center Administrators — C.A. Vines Arkansas 4-H Center/Nov. 5-9

CALIFORNIA

Anaheim

AABB — Oct. 20-23
American Association for Public Opinion Research — Hyatt Regency Orange County/May 16-20/900
American Urological Association — May 19-24
AOAC International — Hyatt Regency Orange County/Sept. 16-20
Association for Supervision and Curriculum Development — Anaheim Convention Center/March 17-19
Club Managers Association of America — Anaheim Marriott/Feb. 23-27
Electrical Overstress/Electrostatic Discharge Association — Disneyland Hotel/Sept. 16-21
Family, Career, and Community Leaders of America — July 7-13
Government Finance Officers Association of the United States and Canada — June 10-13
International Foundation of Employee Benefit Plans — Nov. 4-7/6000
National Association for Health and Fitness — Apr. 29-30
National Association of Elementary School Principals — Apr. 13-17
National Association of State Utility Consumer Advocates — Nov. 11-14
National Student Nurses Association — Convention Center/Apr. 11-15/3000
Piano Manufacturers Association International — Convention Center/Jan. 18-21
Power Sources Manufacturers Association — Disneyland Hotel/Feb. 25-March 1
Society of Decorative Painters — May 29-June 2
Society of Petroleum Engineers — Nov. 11-14/8000

Carlsbad

Association of Steel Distributors — La Costa Resort/March 16-20/100

Dana Point

American Apparel & Footwear Association — St. Regis/Feb. 28-March 2/250
American College of Construction Lawyers — Ritz Carlton/Feb. 22-25
Ceramic Tile Distributors Association — Laguna Cliffs Marriott/Nov. 7-11
Pet Industry Distributors Association — St. Regis Monarch Beach/Jan. 31-Feb. 3/225

Fresno

National Onion Association — July 18-21

Half Moon Bay

College of Diplomates of the American Board of Orthodontics — Ritz Carlton/July 15-19

Hollywood

American Society of Appraisers — Renaissance/July 22-25
Association for Play Therapy — (Dates TBA)

Huntington Beach

American Architectural Manufacturers Association — Hyatt Regency/June 10-13
Forging Industry Association — Hyatt Regency/May 4-8/200

Indian Wells

Association of University Professors of Ophthalmology — Renaissance Esmeralda/Feb. 1-3/300
Christian College Consortium — The Miramonte Resort/March 21-24
National Association of Government Defined Contribution Administrators — Hyatt Grand Champions Resort and Spa/Sept. 15-19
National Association of Pipe Coating Applicators — Renaissance/Apr. 11-15/240
Plastic Pipe and Fittings Association — Renaissance Esmeralda/March 3-7

La Jolla

Society for Technological Advancement of Reporting — Hilton Torrey Pines/Apr. 26-28

La Quinta

National Alcohol Beverage Control Association — La Quinta Resort/May 16-20/850

Laguna Beach

NASFM — St. Regis/Nov. 5-7/250

Lake Tahoe

American Association of Attorney-Certified Public Accountants — Squaw Valley Resort/June 23-29
National Association of State Facilities Administrators — Montbleu/June 10-14/150

Long Beach

American Association of Petroleum Geologists — Apr. 1-4
Controlled Release Society — July 7-11
North American Council of Automotive Teachers — (Dates TBA)
Specialty Coffee Association of America — May 4-7/8000

Los Angeles

Association of Environmental and Engineering Geologists — Sheraton, Universal Studios/Sept. 24-28/800
Association of Science-Technology Centers — California Science Center/Nov. 3-6

Biomedical Engineering Society — Wilshire Grand(Dates TBA)/2500
Cantors Assembly — May 6-10
Independent Educational Consultants Association — Hollywood Renaissance/Nov. 6-10/1200
International Textile and Apparel Association — Omni/Nov. 5-10
IPC - Association Connecting Electronics Industries — Feb. 20-22
IPC - Surface Mount Equipment Manufacturers Association — Convention Center/Feb. 20-27
National Parking Association — Renaissance Hollywood/Oct. 22-25/1000
Society for Investigative Dermatology — Century Plaza Hotel/May 9-12
Society for Radiation Oncology Administrators — Oct. 27-Nov. 1
Society of Insurance Trainers and Educators — Hollywood Renaisance/June 22-28/250

Malibu

Organizational Behavior Teaching Society — Pepperdine University/June 1-

Monarch Beach

Juice Products Association — St. Regis Resort/Apr. 15-18/350

Monterey

American Academy of Veterinary Pharmacology and Therapeutics — Asilomar Conference Center/May 24-28
Fire and Emergency Manufacturers and Services Association — Oct. 3-7
Fire Apparatus Manufacturers' Association — Oct. 3-6
Foundation for Advances in Medicine and Science — Portola Plaza/Apr. 10-12/400
Golf Course Builders Association of America — Hyatt/Aug. 1-4
Information Storage Industry Consortium — Portola Plaza Hotel/July 15-18
National Association for Medical Direction of Respiratory Care — Monterey Plaza/March 22-24
National Association of Real Estate Companies — June

Napa Valley

American Sugar Alliance — Silverado Resort and Spa/Aug. 4-8

Palm Desert

Conveyor Equipment Manufacturers Association — Marriott/March 9-13
General Merchandise Distributors Council — J.W. Marriott Desert Springs Resort and Spa/Sept. 7-10
Power Transmission Distributors Association — Marriott Desert Springs Resort & Spa/Oct. 18-20/800

Palm Springs

American Bakers Association — La Quinta Resort/March 18-21/200
American Institute of Oral Biology — Hilton/Oct. 19-22/125
American Moving and Storage Association — La Quinta Resort/Apr. 23-26
Association of Test Publishers — Westin Mission Hills/Feb. 5-7
Association of Women in the Metal Industries — Esmerelda/November
Farm Credit Council — Marriott/Jan. 14-16
International Society for Antiviral Research — Westin Mission Hills/Apr. 29-May 3
National Institute of Oilseed Products — Marriott Rancho Las Palmas Resort & Spa/March 21-25
Society of American Florists — La Quinta Resort and Club/Sept. 26-29
United Fresh Produce Association — Apr. 26-28

Palo Alto

Plastic Surgery Research Council — Stanford Park/June 18-23
Society of Environmental Journalists — Stamford(Dates TBA)

Pasadena

Association of Professional Landscape Designers — Hilton/March 4/200

Pomona

Music and Entertainment Industry Educators Association — California State Polytechnic University(Dates TBA)

Rancho Mirage

Association of Destination Management Executives — Westin Mission Hills/Feb. 7-11/160
Industrial Research Institute — Rancho Las Palmas Resort/May 6-9

Sacramento

American Boarding Kennels Association — Hyatt/Oct. 17-20/400
American Chamber of Commerce Executives — Aug. 1-4
Career Planning and Adult Development Network — Hyatt Regency/Nov. 7-11/800
Environmental Design Research Association — Sheraton Grand Hotel/May 30-June 3
International Right of Way Association — June 17-20

San Diego

Academy of Clinical Laboratory Physicians and Scientists — UC San Diego/June 7-9/150
Academy of General Dentistry — San Diego Convention Center/June 27-July 1/6000
American Academy of Allergy, Asthma, and Immunology — Feb. 23-27
American Academy of Orthopaedic Surgeons — Feb. 14-18
American Academy of Religion — Nov. 17-20
American Association for Clinical Chemistry — July 15-19
American Association of Pharmaceutical Scientists — Convention Center/Nov. 12-16
American Burn Association — Manchester Grand Hyatt/March 20-23
American College of Neuropsychiatrists — Sept. 30-Oct. 4
American College of Obstetricians and Gynecologists — May 5-9
American College of Physicians — Apr. 19-21
American College of Radiation Oncology — Hotel del Coronado/Feb. 22-24
American Philological Association — Marriott/Jan. 4-7
American Phytopathological Society — July 28-Aug. 1
American Psychiatric Association — May 19-24
American Schools of Oriental Research — (Dates TBA)
American Society for Clinical Laboratory Science — July 17-21
American Society of Cataract and Refractive Surgery — Apr. 28-May 2/7000
American Society of Human Genetics — Oct. 23-27
American Society of Lipo-Suction Surgery — Manchester Grand Hyatt/Jan. 25-28
American Society of Ophthalmic Administrators — Marriott San Diego Marina and Yacht Club/Apr. 1- /2000
American Truck Dealers — Convention Center/Apr. 14-16/2500
Association for Behavior Analysis — Hyatt/May 25-29
Association for Healthcare Resource and Materials Management — Marriott/Aug. 12-15
Association of College Administration Professionals — March 10-13
Association of Community College Trustees — Hyatt(Dates TBA)
Association of Public Treasurers of the United States and Canada — (Dates TBA)
Association of Teacher Educators — Manchester Grand Hyatt/Feb. 17-21/2000
BEMA - The Baking Industry Suppliers Association — Del Coronado/June 24-26
Catholic Campus Ministry Association — Town and Country/Jan. 4-7/350
Civil Aviation Medical Association — Marriott Mission Valley/Oct. 10-14/150
Community Action Partnership — Manchester Grand Hyatt/Aug. 28-31
Congress of Neurological Surgeons — Sept. 15-20
Consumer Bankers Association — Manchester Grand Hyatt/Sept. 23-26
Dietary Managers Association — Hyatt Regency/July 1-5
Education Law Association — Catamaran/Nov. 14-17/500
Entomological Society of America — Town and Country Hotel/Dec. 10-13
International Association for Identification — Town and Country Convention Center/July 22-27
International Association of Plumbing and Mechanical Officials — Doubletree San Diego/Sept. 23-27
International Card Manufacturers Association — (Dates TBA)
International Society for Quality-of-Life Studies — San Diego Marriott/Dec. 6-9
International Wood Products Association — Loews Coronado Bay/March 28-30/350

Irrigation Association — Convention Center/Dec. 9-11/7000
National Academy of Clinical Biochemistry — July 15-19
National Association of Public Insurance Adjusters — Hotel del Coronado/June 20-24
National Cherry Growers and Industries Foundation — Jan. 25
National Council for the Social Studies — (Dates TBA)
National Council on Rehabilitation Education — Marriott Mission Valley/Feb. 22-25/325
National Guild of Professional Paperhangers — Sheraton/Sept. 4-7
National Lesbian and Gay Journalists Association — Westin Horton Plaza/Aug. 30-Sept. 2/650
North American Association of Educational Negotiators — Catamaran Resort/March 11-14
North American Fuzzy Information Processing Society — June 24-27
Sealant, Waterproofing and Restoration Institute — Rancho Bernardo Inn/Oct. 14-16/200
SMMA - The Motor and Motion Association — Rancho Bernardo Inn/May 9-11/80
Society for Neuroscience — Nov. 3-7
Society for Pediatric Pathology — Hyatt/March 24-25/225
Society of Gynecologic Oncologists — Manchester Grand Hyatt/March 3-7
SPRI, Inc. — Rancho Bernardo Inn/Jan. 12-14
Submersible Wastewater Pump Association — The Westgate/Oct. 13-14/85
United States and Canadian Academy of Pathology — Hyatt/March 24-30/3000
Water Environment Federation — Convention Center/Oct. 13-17
Women's Classical Caucus — Jan. 4-7
Women's Transportation Seminar — Wydham/May 2-4/400

San Francisco

American Academy of Orthotists and Prosthetists — Marriott/March 21-24/2000
American Academy of the History of Dentistry — (Dates TBA)
American Association for the Advancement of Science — Feb. 15-19
American Bar Association — Aug. 9-15
American Board of Professional Psychology — Moscone Center/Aug. 17-20
American College of Clinical Pharmacology — The Palace Hotel/Sept. 9-11/300
American College of Dentists — Sept. 26-27
American College of Osteopathic Surgeons — Marriott/Oct. 18-21/1000
American Dental Association — Sept. 27-30
American Fisheries Society — Marriott/Sept. 2-6
American Geophysical Union — Dec. 10-14/13000
American Institute of Fishery Research Biologists — Marriott Downtown/Sept. 2-7/1500
American Law Institute — May 14-16
American Osteopathic College of Proctology — San Francisco Marriott/Oct. 18-21/40
American Psychological Association — Aug. 16-19
American Society of Anesthesiologists — Convention Center/Oct. 13-17
American Society of Interior Designers — March 15-18
American Society of Landscape Architects — Convention Center/Oct. 5-9
American Society of Nephrology — Oct. 31-Nov. 5
American Society of Transplant Surgeons — Convention Center/May 5-9/5000
American Society of Transplantation — Convention Center/May 5-9
American Sociological Association — Hilton/Aug. 4-7
American Translators Association — Hyatt Regency/Oct. 31-Nov. 3/1500
Arthroscopy Association of North America — Apr. 26-29
Association of University Technology Managers — San Francisco Marriott/March 8-10/2000
Cervical Spine Research Society — Palace Hotel/Nov. 29-Dec. 1
Council on Social Work Education — Nov. 27-30
Cremation Association of North America — Fairmont Hotel/Aug. 15-18/500
Delta Sigma Delta — Sept. 27-30
Floor Covering Installation Contractors Association — Argonaut/March 14-17/150
Gerontological Society of America — San Francisco Hilton/Nov. 16-20/3500
Independent Pet and Animal Transportation Association International — (Dates TBA)
International Communication Association — Hilton/May 24-28/2000
Laser Institute of America — Marriott/March 19-22
Materials Research Society — Moscone West/Apr. 9-13
Medical Marketing Association — (Dates TBA)/300
National Asphalt Pavement Association — San Francisco Marriott/Feb. 18-21
National Association for Humanities Education — (Dates TBA)
National Association of Boards of Examiners of Long Term Care Administrators — Hotel Nikko/June 13-15/80
National Association of Women Lawyers — Aug. 8-
National Exchange Carrier Association — Hyatt Regency/Sept. 23-27
National Grain and Feed Association — Westin St. Francis/March 18-20
National Stone, Sand and Gravel Association — The Westin St. Francis Hotel/Feb. 28-March 2
Reserve Officers Association of the U.S. — Marriott/June 27-30/1000
Scaffold Industry Association — July
Society for Healthcare Strategy and Market Development — San Francisco Marriott/Sept. 17-21/1200
Society for Pediatric Psychology — Aug. 17-20
Society of Laparoendoscopic Surgeons — Hyatt Regency/Sept. 5-8
Standards Engineering Society — Aug. 20-21/100

San Jose

Association for Professionals in Infection Control and Epidemiology — June 24-28
North American Association of Professors of Christian Education — Marriott/Oct. 18-20
Wireless Communications Association International — Fairmont Hotel/Jan. 14-19/1900

Santa Barbara

National Association for Printing Leadership — Four Season/March 7-11/275

Sunnyvale

National Costumers Association — July 6-12

Ventura

Association for Wedding Professionals International — Crowne Plaza/Apr. 22-25

COLORADO

Boulder

American Society of Questioned Document Examiners — Harvest Millennium/Aug. 11-16/130
International Society for the Study of Subtle Energies and Energy Medicine — Millenium/June 21-27

Colorado Springs

American Academy of Osteopathy — Broadmoor/March 21-25/1000
American Surgical Association — The Broadmoor/Apr. 26-28
Association of Pathology Chairs — Cheyenne Mountain Springs/July 18-21/250
Automatic Fire Alarm Association — Broadmoor/Apr. 18-20
Callerlab-International Association of Square Dance Callers — Sheraton/Apr. 2-4
Commission on Accreditation for Law Enforcement Agencies — (Dates TBA)
Deep Foundations Institute — The Broadmoor/Oct. 11-13/350
Evangelical Press Association — Doubletree/May/400
Independent Sealing Distributors — Oct. 31-Nov. 2
International Association of Dive Rescue Specialists — Sheraton/Sept. 26-29
North American Building Material Distribution Association — The Broadmoor/Nov. 3-4
Society of Urologic Nurses and Associates — Broadmoor Hotel/March 15-17/400

Copper

Association for the Behavioral Sciences and Medical Education — Copper Convention Center/Oct. 17-21/150

Denver

Alliance of Area Business Publications — Grahd Hyatt Denver/June 21-23
American Academy of Audiology — Apr. 18-21/6000

American Animal Hospital Association — Colorado Convention Center/March 17-21
American Association of Public Health Dentistry — Marriott Tech Center/Apr. 30-May 2
American Cleft Palate-Craniofacial Association — Omni Interlocken/Apr. 23-28/550
American Psychoanalytic Association — June 20-24
APMI International — May 13-6/1200
Association of Genetic Technologists — Marriott Tech Center/May 31-June 3
Association of Millwork Distributors — Nov. 1-6
Association of Program Directors in Radiology — Hyatt Denver Convention Center/Apr. 25-28
Association of University Radiologists — Hyatt Denver Convention Center/Apr. 25-28
Case Management Society of America — Hyatt Regency/June 19-23
City and Regional Magazine Association — Grand Hyatt Denver/May 5-7/500
Commercial Real Estate Women Network — Hyatt Regency/Oct. 3-6
Edison Electric Institute — Hyatt Regency Convention Center/June 17-20/100
EUCG — City Center Marriot/Sept. 30-30
Geological Society of America — Oct. 28-31
Library and Information Technology Association — Marriott/Oct. 4-7
Metal Powder Industries Federation — Denver Covention Center/May 13-16/1500
Million Dollar Round Table — June 10-13
Mineralogical Society of America — (Dates TBA)
National Association of Sports Officials — July 29-31
National Collegiate Honors Council — Hyatt/Oct. 29-Nov. 5/1800
National Council of Architectural Registration Boards — (Dates TBA)
National Society for Histotechnology — Oct. 26-31
National Wood Flooring Association — Denver Convention Center/Apr. 11-14/4000
North American Limousin Foundation — Doubletree Hotel/Jan. 8
Society for Adolescent Medicine — Marriott/March 28-31/700
Society for Industrial Microbiology — Denver Hyatt Regency/July 29-Aug. 2/650
Society for Mining, Metallurgy, and Exploration — Convention Center/Feb. 25-28/4500
Special Libraries Association — June 3-6
Taxicab, Limousine and Paratransit Association — Hyatt Regency/Oct. 9-12

Denver-Broomfield

Transformer Association, The — Omni Interlocken Resort/Apr. 12-13/50

Keystone

American Society for Blood and Marrow Transplantation — Keystone Resort/Feb. 8-12/1750
Metal Treating Institute — Keystone Resort/July 10-15/150
National Association for Law Placement — Keystone Resort/Apr. 25-28
National Association of Counsel for Children — Keystone Resort/Aug. 15-18/500

Vail

Society of Military Orthopaedic Surgeons — Marriott/Dec. 10-15

CONNECTICUT

Hartford

Federation of Diocesan Liturgical Commissions — Bradley Airport Sheraton/Oct. 9-13
National Institute of Governmental Purchasing — Aug. 4-8
Tree Care Industry Association — Convention Center/Nov. 9-11/3000

DISTRICT OF COLUMBIA

Washington

AAGL -- Advancing Minimally Invasive Gynecology Worldwide — Marriott Wardman Park/November
Academy of Aphasia — (Dates TBA)
Air Force Association — Marriott Wardman Park/Sept. 24-26
American Academy of Clinical Psychiatrists — Wyndham Hotel/March 30-Apr. 1
American Academy of Otolaryngology-Head and Neck Surgery — Sept. 16-19
American Academy of Periodontology — Oct. 27-30
American Academy of Political and Social Science — Reagan Hill Trade Center/Apr. 29/50
American Association of Colleges of Nursing — The Fairmont/March 17-20/400
American Association of Colleges of Nursing — The Fairmont/Oct. 20-23/600
American Association of Industrial Veterinarians — July 14-18
American Association of Neurological Surgeons — Convention Center/Apr. 14-19
American Association of University Professors — Omni Shoreham/June 7-10/400
American Association of Veterinary Parasitologists — July 14-18
American Bankruptcy Institute — JW Marriott/Apr. 12-15
American College of Radiology — Hilton Washington/May 19-24
American Council of Life Insurers — Omni Shoreham Hotel/Oct. 21-23
American Horse Council — L'Enfant Plaza Hotel/June 17-19
American Horticultural Therapy Association — Oct. 26-27
American Leather Chemists Association — Marriott/June 20-24
American Medical Student Association — Hyatt Regency Crystal City/March 7-11
American Neurological Association — Marriott Wardman Park/Oct. 7-10
American Public Gardens Association — Hyatt Regency/June 26-30
American Public Health Association — Nov. 3-7
American Rhinologic Society — Sept. 15-17/300
American Society for Biochemistry and Molecular Biology — Convention Center/Apr. 28-March 2
American Society for Cell Biology — Convention Center/Dec. 1-5
American Society for Investigative Pathology — Convention Center/Apr. 28-May 2/13000
American Society for Nutrition — Apr. 28-May 2
American Society for Pharmacology and Experimental Therapeutics — Convention Center/Apr. 28-May 2
American Society for Public Administration — Omni Shoreham/March 23-27/1200
American Society of Newspaper Editors — JW Marriott/March 27-30
American Walnut Manufacturers Association — Sept. 12-15/1200
Association for Library Collections and Technical Services — June 21-27
Association for Public Policy Analysis and Management — Washington Marriott/Nov. 8-10/1400
Association of American Editorial Cartoonists — Mayflower Hotel/July 4-7
Association of American Law Schools — Jan. 2-6
Association of American Veterinary Medical Colleges — Marriott Wardman Park/March 3-5
Association of Catholic Colleges and Universities — Washington Court Hotel/Feb. 3-5/250
Association of Civilian Technicians — September
Association of Direct Response Fundraising Counsel — Williard Intercontinental/February/41
Association of Freestanding Radiation Oncology Centers — Grand Hyatt/May 14-15
Association of Health Insurance Advisors — Sept. 8-12
Association of Occupational and Environmental Clinics — Nov. 4-8
Association of Public Television Stations — Ritz Carlton/Feb. 12-14
Association of Rehabilitation Nurses — Hilton Washington/Oct. 3-6/1000
Association of Research Libraries — Oct. 16-19
Chinese-American Librarians Association — June 21-27
College Media Advisers — Hilton/Oct. 25-28
Community College Journalism Association — Aug. 9-12
Community College Journalism Association — Oct. 25-28
Construction Writers Association — May
Council for Higher Education Accreditation — Omni Shoreham/Jan. 29-31
Council of the Great City Schools — Marriott/March 16-20/300
CWLA - Child Mental Health Division — Feb. 26-28
ESOP Association — May 15-16

Federation of American Hospitals — Marriott Wardman Park/March 4-7
Federation of American Socs. for Experimental Biology — Washington Convention Center/Apr. 28-May 2
Independent Insurance Agents and Brokers of America — Marriott Wardman Park/Apr. 25-29
Joint Council of Allergy, Asthma, and Immunology — (Dates TBA)
Manufacturers Alliance/MAPI — June 14-15
National Association for State Community Services Programs — Washington Marriott/Feb. 12-16
National Association of Certified Valuation Analysts — Omni Shoreham/June 6-9
National Association of Electrical Distributors — Marriott Wardman Park/May 5-9
National Association of Insurance and Financial Advisors — Sept. 8-12
National Association of Minority Media Executives — Ritz Carlton/July 10-12/200
National Association of Professional Process Servers — Capitol Marriott/May 17-21/215
National Association of Psychiatric Health Systems — May 5-9
National Association of Secretaries of State — Feb. 9-12
National Association of Security Companies — May 15-16/100
National Grants Management Association — Reagan International Center/Apr. 24-26/450
National Hardwood Lumber Association — Washington Hilton/Sept. 12-15/1100
National Hospice and Palliative Care Organization — Omni Shoreham/Apr. 19-21
National Lawyers Guild — October
National Lieutenant Governors Association — Westin Embassy Row/March 14-16
National Lumber and Building Material Dealers Association — Ritz Carlton/Apr. 14-16
National Park Hospitality Association — Madison Hotel/March 4-6
National Risk Retention Association — Sept. 26-28
National Society of Compliance Professionals — J. W. Marriott/Oct. 17-19
National WIC Association — The Sofitel/March 10-14/150
Natural Science Collections Alliance — Capital Hilton/May 14-15
Naval Reserve Association — Sheraton Crystal City/Apr. 26-28
Professional Liability Underwriting Society — Nov. 7-9
Professional Services Management Association — Grand Hyatt/Aug. 22-25/900
Psychology Society — The Willard/November/300
Society for Assisted Reproductive Technology — Oct. 13-17
Society for Experimental Biology and Medicine — Apr. 28-May 2
Society for Free Radical Biology and Medicine — Renaissance Hotel/Nov. 14-18/650
Society for Healthcare Strategy and Market Development — Marriott Wardman Park/Oct. 3-6/1200
Society for Marketing Professional Services — Grand Hyatt/Aug. 22-25/1000
Society for Public Health Education — Oct. 31-Nov. 2
Society for Reproductive Endocrinology and Infertility — October
Society for Surgery of the Alimentary Tract — May 19-23
Society for the History of Technology — Oct. 18-21/350
Society for Thermal Medicine — Washington Hilton/May 14-18/150
Society of Behavioral Medicine — Marriott Wardman Park/March 21-24
Society of Otorhinolaryngology and Head/Neck Nurses — Sept. 14-18
Society of Professional Journalists — Hyatt Regency/Oct. 4-7
Society of Surgical Oncology — Marriott Wardman Park Hotel/March 15-18
Toxicology Forum — Westin Embassy Row/Jan. 30-Feb. 1
Trade Show Exhibitors Association — Washington D.C. Country Club/July 30-Aug. 2
Voluntary Protection Programs Participants Association — Marriott Wardman Park/Aug. 26-30
Wireless Communications Association International — Omni Sheraton Hotel/June 11-14/1800

FLORIDA

Marco Island

National Coil Coating Association — Marco Island Marriott/Apr. 14-17

Amelia Island

Academy of Psychosomatic Medicine — Amelia Island Plantation/Nov. 14-18
American College of Physician Executives — Ritz Carlton/Jan. 20-25
Fluid Controls Institute — Amelia Island Plantation/March 30-Apr. 3
Valve Manufacturers Association of America — Ritz-Carlton/Oct. 11-14/150

Aventura

Flexible Packaging Association — Fairmont Turnberry/Feb. 28-March 2
Pipe Line Contractors Association — Turnberry/February
Truck Trailer Manufacturers Association — Turnberry Isle Resort/May 16-20/400

Boca Raton

American College of Neuropsychopharmacology — Boca Raton Resort/Dec. 9-13

Bonita Springs

National Sporting Goods Association — Hyatt Regency Coconut Pointe Resort and Spa/May 20-23/400

Coral Gables

Academy of Marketing Science — Biltmore/May 23-26/250

Daytona Beach

National Mobility Equipment Dealers Association — Hilton/Feb. 7-10

Destin

Consumer Credit Insurance Association — Hilton Sandestin/Apr. 28-March 1/180

Duck Key

National Council of Legislators from Gaming States — Hawk's Cay Resort/Jan. 12-14/110

Ft. Lauderdale

Compressed Gas Association — Harbor Beach Marriott/March 16-18/250
International Association of Airport Duty Free Stores — Broward County Convention Center/Apr. 22-26
National Optometric Association — Harbor Beach Marriott/July 8-13
National Organization of Black Law Enforcement Executives — (Dates TBA)
Office Furniture Distribution Association — Lago Mar/May 2-4

Gainesville

Association for Symbolic Logic — March 10-13
Consortium of College and University Media Centers — Oct. 18-22/200

Hollywood

American Hernia Society — Diplomat Resort & Spa/March 8-11/400
American Medical Directors Association — Diplomat Hotel/March 29-Apr. 1/2000
Association of College and University Telecommunications Administrators — Westin Diplomat Resort and Spa/July 29-Aug. 2
Bank Insurance and Securities Association — March 10-14/600
Pediatric Orthopedic Society of North America — Diplomat/May 23-26

Jacksonville

National Correctional Industries Association — Hyatt Regency/March 25-28/600

Key Biscayne

Managed Funds Association — Ritz Carlton/Feb. 11-13

Key Largo

Hearing Industries Association — Ocean Reef Club/Feb. 14-17

Key West

Affordable Housing Tax Credit Coalition — Jan. 29-30

Fire Apparatus Manufacturers' Association — March 23-27

Kissimmee

International Claim Association — Gaylord Palms/Sept. 30-Oct. 2
International Spa Association — Gaylord Palms Resort and Convention Center/Nov. 12-15
National Pest Management Association — Gaylord Palms Resort/Oct. 17-20

Lake Buena Vista

International Association for Food Protection — Disney Contemporary Resort/July 8-11/1600

Marco Island

American Architectural Manufacturers Association — Marriott/Feb. 11-14
American Gear Manufacturers Association — Marco Island Marriott/March 15-17
Bearing Specialist Association — Marriott/May 5-8
Compressed Air and Gas Institute — Marco Island Marriott/May 4-7
Exhibit Designers and Producers Association — Marco Island Marriott Resort/Nov. 28-30
Fluid Sealing Association — Marriott Resort/Apr. 25-27/120
Manufacturers Standardization Society of the Valve and Fittings Industry — Marco Island beach Resort/May 7-10/160

Miami

American Association of Political Consultants — Eden Roc Hotel/Feb. 21-23
American Bar Association — Feb. 7-13
American College of Medical Quality — InterContinental Hotel/Feb. 22-24
Black Coaches Association — Doral Golf Resort/May 30-June 2/300
College Savings Foundation — Miami Beach Resort and Spa/Feb. 7-9
Council of Development Finance Agencies — May 22-24
Family Firm Institute — Fairmont Turnderry Isle Resort/Oct. 17-20
International Precious Metals Institute — Doral/June 9-12
National Association of Housing Cooperatives — Sept. 26-29/600
National Renderers Association — Ritz Carlton/Oct. 23-26/400
Renaissance Society of America — March 22-24
Society for Photographic Education — Radisson/March 15-18

Miami Beach

American Public Communications Council — Loews/June 27-29/600
National Fire Protection Association — Miami Beach Convention Center/July 24-26
Society for Spanish and Portuguese Historical Studies — Apr. 19-22
Society of Clinical and Medical Hair Removal — Miami Beach Convention Center/May 19-22/200

Naples

American College of Mohs Micrographic Surgery and Cutaneous Oncology — Registry Resort/May 4-6
Consumer Healthcare Products Association — Ritz-Carlton Golf Resort/March 15-17
National Oilseed Processors Association — Ritz Golf Resort/Feb. 4-8/200
Plastic Pipe and Fittings Association — Ritz Carlton Golf Resort/Oct. 6-10
Society for Uroradiology — Hyatt Regency Resort and Spa/Apr. 15-20
Society of Gastrointestinal Radiologists — Hyatt Regency Resort and Spa/Apr. 15-20

Orlando

ACPA - College Student Educators Association — Gaylord & Marriott/March 31-4/6500
ADSC: The International Association of Foundation Drilling — Buena Vista Palace Resort/Jan. 31-Feb. 3/1500
Air Conditioning Contractors of America — March 5-8
Airborne Law Enforcement Association — July 18-21
American Architectural Manufacturers Association — Marriott Grand Lakes/Oct. 14-17
American Association of Bioanalysts — Rosen Centre Hotel/May 17-19
American Association of Colleges of Pharmacy — Disney Yacht and Beach Club Resort/July 14-18
American Association of Individual Investors — Hilton/Nov. 8-10
American Association of Neuroscience Nurses — Gaylord Palms Resort/Apr. 29-May 2/1000
American Association of Spinal Cord Injury Nurses — Gaylord Palms/Aug. 27-29
American Association of Spinal Cord Injury Psychologists and Social Workers — Gaylord Palms/Aug. 27-29
American Association of Swine Veterinarians — March 3-6/900
American Baseball Coaches Association — Orlando World Center/Jan. 4-7
American College of Nutrition — Hilton Resort/Sept. 19-23/400
American College of Physician Executives — Hyatt Grand Cypress/May 5-10
American Culinary Federation — Orlando World Marriott Resort/July 20-23
American Edged Products Manufacturers Association — Villas of Grand Cypress/May 2-5
American Fence Association — Orange County Convention Center/Jan. 31-Feb. 2
American Healthcare Radiology Administrators — Gaylord Palms Hotel/July 8-12
American Immigration Lawyers Association — Orlando World Center Marriott Resort/June 13-17
American Lithotripsy Society — Dolphin Hotels/March 15-18/650
American Medical Technologists — Swan and Dolphin Resort/July 9-14/300
American Paraplegia Society — Gaylord Palms/Aug. 27-29
American Pediatric Surgical Association — J.W. Marriott/May 23-27/650
American Society of Electroneurodiagnostic Technologists — July 18-21/500
American Woman's Society of Certified Public Accountants — Coronado Springs/Oct. 24-27
AORN — March 11-15
Association of Collegiate Business Schools and Programs — Wyndham Plaza/June 29-July 2
Association of Nurses in AIDS Care — Swan/Nov. 8-11/1000
Association of University Programs in Health Administration — May 31-June 3
Association of Women's Health, Obstetric and Neonatal Nurses — June 23-27/2200
Brick Industry Association — Gaylord Palms/March 29-31/700
Ceilings and Interior Systems Construction Association — Walt Disney World/Apr. 4-8/1000
Christian Medical & Dental Associations — The Buena Vista Palace/June 20-24/600
Commission on Accreditation of Allied Health Education Programs — Rosen Center/Apr. 13-14/90
Digital Printing and Imaging Association — Orange County Convention Center/Oct. 24-27
Distributive Education Clubs of America — Apr. 28-May 1
Express Carriers Association — Portofino/May 14-17/400
Financial Management Association International — Caribe Royale Resort/Oct. 17-20
Foster Family-Based Treatment Association — Disney's Coronado Springs Resort/July 29-Aug. 1/700
HARDI - Heating, Airconditioning, and Refrigeration Distributors International — Orlando World Center Marriott Resort/Oct. 6-9
IEEE Power Electronics Society — (Dates TBA)
Independent Automotive Damage Appraisers Association — Omni Resort/June 14-15/120
Infusion Nurses Society — June 2-7/1500
Interlocking Concrete Pavement Institute — Feb. 22-24/200
International Anesthesia Research Society — Wyndham Palace/March 23-27/1000
International Foodservice Manufacturers Association — J.W. Marriott Orlando, Grande Lakes/March 4-7
International Safe Transit Association — Coronado Springs/March 27-30/350
International Titanium Association — Rosen Shingle Creek/Oct. 7-9
Investment Recovery Association — Rosen/Sept. 14-17
Juvenile Products Manufacturers Association — Apr. 23-5
Messenger Courier Association of the Americas — Portofino Bay/May 14-20
National Air Transportation Association — March 20-

National Association of Collegiate Directors of Athletics — June 7-10
National Association of Graduate Admissions Professionals — Apr. 25-28/900
National Association of Trailer Manufacturers — Coronado Springs Resort/Jan. 29-Feb. 2
National Association of Women in Construction — Caribe Royale/Sept. 5-8/600
National Child Support Enforcement Association — Marriot Orlando World Center Resort/Aug. 5-9
National Collegiate Athletic Association — Jan. 5-9
National Conference of Bankruptcy Judges — Oct. 10-13
National Council on Compensation Insurance — Portofino Bay Hotel/May 10-11/650
National Gerontological Nursing Association — Doubletree Hotel at Entrance to Universal Orlando/Oct. 19-21
National Kidney Foundation — Dolphin Resort/Apr. 10-14/2000
National Organization for the Professional Advancement of Black Chemists and Chemical Engineers — JW Marriott Grande Lakes Resort/Apr. 1-7
National Paperbox Association — Marriott Grande Lake/Apr. 18-21/200
National Religious Broadcasters — Rosen Hotel & Convention Center/Feb. 16-21
National Shooting Sports Foundation — Orange County Convention Center/Jan. 11-14
National Telecommunications Cooperative Association — Swan and Dolphin/Feb. 4-7
North American Retail Hardware Association — Hyatt Grand Cypress/June 11-13/350
RCI, Inc. — Rosen Shingle Creek Resort/March 1-6
Society for Applied Learning Technology — Int'l Plaza Resort and Spa/Jan. 31-Feb. 2
Society for Cardiovascular Angiography and Interventions — March 9-12
Society of Critical Care Medicine — Gaylord Palms Resort/Feb. 17-21
Specialty Graphic Imaging Association — Convention Center/Oct. 24-24/18000
Urology Society of America — Dolphin Hotel/March 15-18/650
Wallcoverings Association — Feb. 9-13/350
Wine and Spirits Wholesalers of America — Swan & Dolphin Hotel/Apr. 28-May 2

Palm Beach Gardens

Electric Power Supply Association — PGA Resort/Jan. 25-28/120
North American Horticultural Supply Association — PGA National Resort/June 3-6

Panama City

National Association of Industrial Technology — Edgewater Resort/Oct. 24-27

Pensacola

Association of Concert Bands — Feb. 28-March 4

Pointe Vedra Beach

Education Credit Union Council — Marriott/Feb. 17-20

Sarasota

National Elevator Industry — March 28/45

St. Augustine

American Association of Railroad Superintendents — Renaissance Hotel World Golf Village/Feb. 25-27/170

St. Pete Beach

American College of Neuropsychiatrists — Tradewinds/May 2-5

St. Petersburg

Accrediting Council on Education in Journalism and Mass Communications — Westin/March 24-24/75
American Brush Manufacturers Association — Renaissance/March 14-17
Compressed Gas Association — Renaissance Vinoy/March 18-21
Gas Appliance Manufacturers Association — Renaissance Vinoy Resort/May 5-8
Wood Component Manufacturers Association — Renaissance/Apr. 25-28
Wood Machinery Manufacturers of America — Vinoy/Apr. 25-28

Tampa

AIM Global — Feb. 26-27
American Association for Women in Community Colleges — Tampa Convention Center/Apr. 14-17
American Association of Community Colleges — Tampa Convention Center/Apr. 14-17
American Society for Photogrammetry and Remote Sensing — Marriott Tampa/May 7-11
American Soybean Association — March 1-3
Association for Childhood Education International — Hyatt Regency/May 2-5
Association for the Advancement of Wound Care — Convention Center/Apr. 28-May 1
International Association of Administrative Professionals — Convention Center/July 29-Apr. 1
International Parking Institute — Tampa Convention Center/May 20-23
International Society for Clinical Densitometry — Marriott Waterside/March 14-17
National Association of Health Unit Coordinators — Sheraton Suite Airport/Aug. 8-11/200
National Corn Growers Association — (Dates TBA)
National Federation of Paralegal Associations — Hyatt Regency/Oct. 18-21/250
National Federation of Priests' Councils — Hyatt Regency/Apr. 23-26
North American Association of Christians in Social Work — (Dates TBA)
Radiation Therapy Oncology Group — Marriott Waterside/Feb. 1-4
Religious Research Association — Hyatt Regency/Nov. 2-4
Society for Applied Anthropology — Hyatt Downtown/March 27-31
Society for the Scientific Study of Religion — Hyatt/Nov. 2-4/500

GEORGIA

Atlanta

Alliance for Nonprofit Management — July/500
American Academy of Cosmetic Dentistry — May 15-20
American Association for State and Local History — Omni Hotel/Sept. 5-8
American Catholic Historical Association — Hilton, Marriott, Hyatt/Jan. 4-7
American Concrete Institute — Hilton/Apr. 22-26
American Council of Independent Laboratories — Inter-Continental Buckhead/Oct. 13-16
American Historical Association — Hilton Marriot/Jan. 4-7/6000
American Institute of the History of Pharmacy — March 16-19
American Morgan Horse Association — Renaissance Waverly/Feb. 15-17
American Pharmacists Association — March 16-20
American Probation and Parole Association — Sheraton Atlanta/Feb. 11-14
American Society of Farm Managers and Rural Appraisers — Hyatt/Feb. 14-17
American Society of Golf Course Architects — Westin Buckhead/Apr. 28-May 2
American Society of Hematology — Dec. 8-11
American Society of Transportation and Logisitcs — Convention Center/Nov. 11-
Art Libraries Society of North America — Sheraton Midtown/Apr. 26-May 1
Association of College and University Auditors — Omni/Sept. 28-Oct. 3
Association of Gospel Rescue Missions — Hilton/May 15-19/1000
Association of State Supervisors of Mathematics — March 17-20
CBA — Georgia World Congress Center/July 8-12
Coordinating Council for Women in History — Jan. 4-7
Correctional Education Association — Marriott Marquis/July 8-11
Council on Licensure, Enforcement and Regulation — Westin Peachtree Plaza/Sept. 6-8
Environmental Mutagen Society — Hyatt Regency/Oct. 21-24/500
Foundation for Independent Higher Education — Ritz-Carlton(Dates TBA)/50
International Association of Healthcare Central Service Materiel Management — Omni/Apr. 29-May 2

International Festivals and Events Association — Omni Hotel/Sept. 17-21
International Society for Technology in Education — June 24-27
National Association of Convenience Stores — Georgia World Congressional Center/Nov. 6-9/25000
National Association of Extension 4-H Agents — Oct. 21-25
National Association of Nephrology Technologists and Technicians — Sheraton Downtown/March 9-11/400
National Association of Uniform Manufacturers and Distributors — Hilton/Apr. 13-17
National Council of Teachers of Mathematics — March 21-24
National Dental Association — Marriott/July 27-Aug. 1/2000
National Nursing Staff Development Organization — Sheraton Atlanta/July 26-29
National School Supply and Equipment Association — Georgia World Congress Center/March 1-3
National Strength and Conditioning Association — Hilton Hotel/July 11-14

Savannah

Adhesive and Sealant Council — Hyatt Regency/Apr. 15-18
Associated Air Balance Council — Westin Savannah/Oct. 18-21
Association of Occupational Health Professionals in Healthcare — Marriott Riverfront/Sept. 26-29/300
Educational Paperback Association — Hyatt Regency/Jan. 31-Feb. 3
EUCG — Hyatt Riverfront/March 25-25
Kappa Kappa Iota — Hilton DeSoto/June 30-July 3/350
National Catalog Managers Association — Hyatt Regency/May 5-8
National Council for Workforce Education — Marriott/Oct. 27-30/450
National Hearing Conservation Association — Hyatt Regency/Feb. 15-17/250

HAWAII

Honolulu

American Association of Oral and Maxillofacial Surgeons — Hawaii Convention Center/Oct. 10-13/5000
American Society for Engineering Education — June 24-27
Association of Science Museum Directors — Bishop Museum/Feb. 21-26
CPCU Society — Hawaiian Convention Center/Sept. 8-11/5000
International Society of Arboriculture — July 28-Aug. 1
National Medical Association — Aug. 3-9
Utility Arborist Association — Convention Center/July 28-Aug. 1/500

Kona

American College of Veterinary Ophthalmologists — Oct. 21-27/700

Maui

Concrete Sawing and Drilling Association — Westin/Feb. 23-27
North American Association of Summer Sessions — Sheraton Maui/Nov. 11-14/185
Sealant, Waterproofing and Restoration Institute — Hyatt Regency Maui/Feb. 25-28

Oahu

IEEE Signal Processing Society — May 15-19

Wailea

National Onion Association — Nov. 28-Dec. 2

IDAHO

Boise

National Association for State Community Services Programs — Red Lion Hotel/Sept. 18-21

Coeur D'Alene

Conference of State Bank Supervisors — Coeur d'Alene Resort/May 30-Jan. 1/350
Independent Medical Distributors Association — Coeur d'Alene Resort/June 2-May 5
Select Registry/Distinguished Inns of North America — Coeur D'Alene Resort/May 6-9

Sun Valley

Federation of Defense and Corporate Counsel — Sun Valley Resort/July 22-29

ILLINOIS

Aledo

National Hereford Hog Record Association — Aug. 25- /50

Bloomingdale

National Field Selling Association — Indian Lake/June

Champaign

Classification Society of North America — University of Illinois/June 7-10/150

Chicago

ACA International, The Association of Credit and Collection Professionals — Hyatt Regency/July 25-26/1200
Academy of Accounting Historians — Aug. 5-8
Academy of Organizational and Occupational Psychiatry — University Club/Apr. 14-15
Accrediting Council on Education in Journalism and Mass Communications — Westin/March 24- /75
Accrediting Council on Education in Journalism and Mass Communications — Sheraton/Aug. 31- /75
Aluminum Anodizers Council — Marriott Lincolnshire/Oct. 8-11/120
American Academy of Fixed Prosthodontics — Marriott Downtown/Feb. 23-24/800
American Academy of Oral and Maxillofacial Radiology — Knickerbocker/Nov. 28-Dec. 2/125
American Academy of Restorative Dentistry — Drake Hotel/Feb. 24-25
American Accounting Association — Aug. 5-8
American Association of Museums — May 13-17
American Association of Railroad Superintendents — Indian Lakes/July 29-30/200
American Brachytherapy Society — Sheraton/Apr. 29-May 1
American College for Advancement in Medicine — May 5-11
American College of Veterinary Surgeons — Sheraton Hotel & Towers/Oct. 18-20
American Economic Association — Jan. 5-7
American Harp Society — Roosevelt University/June 18-21
American Land Title Association — Hilton/Oct. 10-14
American Medical Association — June 23-27
American Pancreatic Association — Wyndham/Nov. 1-3/200
American Prosthodontic Society — Westin River North/Feb. 22-23/350
American Purchasing Society — Sept. 1- /25
American Society for Clinical Investigation — Fairmont Hotel/Apr. 13-15
American Society of Neuroradiology — Hyatt Regency Chicago/June 9-15
American Society of Plant Biologists — July 7-11
American Society of Plant Taxonomists — July 7-11
American Welding Society — McCormick Place/Nov. 11-14/20000
The Art and Creative Materials Institute — Navy Pier(Dates TBA)
Association of Black Nursing Faculty in Higher Education — Marriott/June 13-17/100
Association of Children's Museums — Westin, Michigan Ave./May 10-11
Association of College and University Museums and Galleries — Northwestern University(Dates TBA)/100
Association of Hispanic Advertising Agencies — Drake/Apr. 25-27
Association of Insolvency and Restructuring Advisors — Westin Chicago River North/June 6-9
Association of North American Missions — Awana Hotel/Apr. 18-20
Association of Professional Researchers for Advancement — July 25-28
Association of University Anesthesiologists — Sheraton/Apr. 26-28
Automotive Maintenance Repair Association — May 2- /75
Building Service Contractors Association International — McCormick Place Hyatt/Apr. 13-17/1000
Catholic Health Association of the United States — Marriott Downtown/June 17-19
Commercial Law League of America — Westin - Michigan Ave./Apr. 19-22
Construction Writers Association — October

Conveyor Equipment Manufacturers Association — Hilton/Sept. 20-21/60
Council for Advancement and Support of Education — Chicago Marriott Downtown/July 8-10
Dance/USA — June 14-16/400
Food Marketing Institute — May 5-8
Future Business Leaders of America-Phi Beta Lambda — June 23-July 1/7000
Institute of Food Technologists — McCormick Place/July 28-Aug. 1
International Academy of Trial Lawyers — Four Seasons/Apr. 10-15/300
International Association of Culinary Professionals — Chicago Hilton Hotel/Apr. 11-14
International Public Management Association for Human Resources — Marriott Downtown/Sept. 29-Oct. 3
International Stress Management Association - U.S. Branch — July
International Trademark Association — Apr. 28-May 2
Leafy Greens Council — (Dates TBA)
Managed Funds Association — Fairmont/June 11-13
National Art Materials Trade Association — Navy Pier/Apr. 19-21/3500
National Association of Bond Lawyers — Sheraton Chicago Hotel and Towers/Sept. 26-28
National Association of Personal Financial Advisors — Sheraton/May 2-5
National Association of Printing Ink Manufacturers — Eaglewood/Sept. 5-8/200
National Association of Recording Merchandisers — Chicago Hilton/Apr. 29-May 1
National Auto Auction Association — Hilton Chicago/Sept. 17-22/1400
National Council of State Boards of Nursing — Chicago Marriott/Aug. 7-10
National Lesbian and Gay Law Association — Chicago Hilton/Sept. 6-8
National Network for Social Work Managers — University of Illinois, Chicago/Apr. 13-14/100
National Wildlife Rehabilitators Association — Indian Lakes Resort/March 13-17/500
Naval Reserve Association — Oak Brook Marriott Hotel/Oct. 4-6
NPES, The Association for Suppliers of Printing, Publishing and Converting Technologies — Fairmont Hotel Chicago/March 27-28
Organization of American Kodaly Educators — The Palmer House Hilton/March 20-25/1200
Radiological Society of North America — McCormick Place/Nov. 25-30
Research Society on Alcoholism — Hyatt Regency/July 7-13/1500
School Nutrition Association — Convention Center/July 15-18/65000
Social Science History Association — Nov. 15-19
Society for Academic Emergency Medicine — Sheraton/May 16-19/1800
Society for Clinical Data Management — Hyatt Regency/Sept. 16-19
Society for College and University Planning — Sherton Hotel & Towers/July 7-11/1800
Society for Economic Botany — June 4-7
Society for Pediatric Dermatology — Westin Chicago/July 12-15/300
Society of American Archivists — Fairmont Hotel/Aug. 27-Sept. 2/1600
Society of Critical Care Medicine — Fairmont/Aug. 2-9
State Government Affairs Council — The James Chicago/March 21-23/150
Surface Mount Technology Association — Donald Stephens Convention Center/Oct. 1-4

INDIANA

Indianapolis

Academy of International Business — June
American Academy of Nurse Practitioners — Convention Center/June 20-24
American Society for Mass Spectrometry — June 3-7
Association for Iron and Steel Technology — Indiana Convention Center/May 7-10
Black Coaches Association — Hyatt Regency(Dates TBA)/400
CBA — Indiana Convention Center/Jan. 29-Feb. 2
International Association of Counseling Services — (Dates TBA)
National Association of Pastoral Musicians — Indiana Convention Center/July 9-13
National Private Truck Council — Indiana Convention Center/Apr. 29-May 1/900
National Truck Equipment Association — March 6-9
NFHS Music Association — Nov. 9-10
NFHS Speech Debate and Theatre Association — October
Optical Laboratories Association — Convention Center/Nov. 15-17/1500
Society for In Vitro Biology — Westin/June 9-13/600

IOWA

Dubuque

Walnut Council — Grand River Ctr.(Dates TBA)/300

KANSAS

Dodge City

Red Angus Association of America — Sept. 25-29

Overland Park

International Association of Operative Millers — Sheraton and Overland Park Convetion Center/May 5-9/1000

KENTUCKY

Lexington

Association for Biology Laboratory Education — University of Kentucky/June 5-9
Association of Bone and Joint Surgeons — Radisson Plaza/Apr. 11-15
National Association of State Budget Officers — Hyatt Regency/July 16-19/250
Palomino Horse Breeders of America — March 15-17/250

Louisville

American Association of Medical Assistants — Downtown Marriott/Sept. 7-11
Association for the Advancement of Applied Sport Psychology — (Dates TBA)
Association for the Study of Higher Education — Marriott/Nov. 7-10
Council for Exceptional Children — Apr. 18-21
International Municipal Signal Association — Louisville Marriott Downtown/Aug. 15-22
Kappa Delta Pi — Marriott/Nov. 1-3/1500
National Taxidermists Association — Clarion Hotel and Conference Center/July 18-21
North American Association of State and Provincial Lotteries — Louisville Marriott/Oct. 3-6
Religion Communicators Council — Marriott Downtown/Apr. 26-28
Religious Conference Management Association — Convention Center/Jan. 30-Feb. 2/1390
SMMA - The Motor and Motion Association — October/80

LOUISIANA

Baton Rouge

American Society for Environmental History — Sheraton/March 1-4/400
National Association of African American Studies — Marriott/Feb. 12-17

New Orleans

Aerospace Medical Association — Sheraton and Marriott/May 13-17
American Association for the Advancement of Slavic Studies — Marriott/Nov. 15-18
American Association of Pathologists' Assistants — Fairmont/Sept. 8-14/350
American Association of School Administrators — March 1-4
American College of Healthcare Executives — Marriott-Sheraton/March 19-22/4500
American College of Occupational and Environmental Medicine — New Orleans Marriott/May 4-9
American College of Surgeons — Oct. 7-11
American Conference of Academic Deans — Jan. 24-27

American Dental Hygienists' Association — Sheraton/June 20-27
American Health Quality Association — New Orleans Marriott/Feb. 13-15
American Mathematical Society — Marriott/Sheraton/Jan. 4-7
American Polygraph Association — Hilton/July 19-24
American Rental Association — Feb. 12-15
American Society for Healthcare Engineering — Convention Center/July 8-11/3000
American Society of Agronomy — Convention Center/Nov. 4-8
American Society of Andrology — Hyatt Regency/Apr. 18-24/300
American Society of Ophthalmic Registered Nurses — Nov. 9-12
Association for Women in Mathematics — (Dates TBA)
Association of Jewish Aging Services — Hilton New Orleans Riverside/March 10-13/300
Association of Women Soil Scientists — Nov. 4-8
Crop Science Society of America — Convention Center/Nov. 4-8/4000
Czechoslovak History Conference — Marriott/Nov. 15-16
Farm Equipment Wholesalers Association — Sheraton/Oct. 24-27
Healthcare Information and Management Systems Society — Feb. 25-March 1
International Association of Chiefs of Police — Oct. 13-17
International Fabricare Institute — May 17-20
International Facility Management Association — Oct. 24-26/6000
Interstate Oil and Gas Commission — Omni Royal/Sept. 23-25
National Association of College and University Business Officers — July 21-24
National Council on Education for the Ceramic Arts — Hyatt/March 28-31
National Federation of Community Broadcasters — Sheraton/Apr. 11-14/500
National League of Cities — Nov. 13-17/6000
Paso Fino Horse Association — Jan. 19-21
Public Radio News Directors — Royal Sonesta/July 19-June 21
Risk and Insurance Management Society — Apr. 29-May 3
Soil Science Society of America — Convention Center/Nov. 4-8

MAINE

Portland

American Society of Pharmacognosy — Holiday Inn/July 14-18/500
International Association of Milk Control Agencies — Sheraton/Aug. 4-8

MARYLAND

Adelphi

American Astronautical Society — Marriott/March 20-21/400
Home Improvement Research Institute — Marriott/Apr. 25- /125

Baltimore

Academy for Eating Disorders — Baltimore Marriott Waterfront/May 2-5/750
American Academy of Medical Acupuncture — Baltimore Marriott Waterfront/Apr. 27-29
American Association for Health Education — Convention Center/March 13-17/5000
American Education Finance Association — Sheraton Inner Harbor/March 22-24/325
American Evaluation Association — Wyndham Inner Harbor/Nov. 5-10
Association of College and Research Libraries — March 29-Apr. 1
Association of Collegiate Conference and Events Directors International — Renaissance/March 25-28/450
Association of Public-Safety Communications Officers-International — Baltimore Convention Center/Aug. 5-9
Biophysical Society — Convention Center/March 3-7
Catholic Library Association — Apr. 10-13
College and University Professional Association for Human Resources — Baltimore Marriott Waterfront/Nov. 8-11
Construction Specifications Institute — (Dates TBA)
Human Factors and Ergonomics Society — Baltimore Waterfront Marriott/Oct. 1-5
International Marking and Identification Association — July 12-14/500
National Academic Advising Association — Convention Center/Oct. 18-21
National Catholic Educational Exhibitors — Apr. 10-13
National Conference of Diocesan Vocation Directors — Tremont/Sept. 22-27
National Organization of Social Security Claimants' Representatives — Baltimore Marriott Waterfront/Apr. 18-21
NIBA - The Belting Association — Marriott Waterfront/Sept. 19-22/500
Society for Healthcare Epidemiology of America — Marriott/Apr. 14-17/1000
Society for the Advancement of Material and Process Engineering — Baltimore Convention Center/June 4-8
Society for Vascular Nursing — Wyndham Baltimore Inner Harbor/June 7-10
Society for Vascular Surgery — Baltimore Convention Center/June 7-10
Society of Risk Management Consultants — (Dates TBA)
Society of State Directors of Health, Physical Education and Recreation — March 11-12/70
Sugar Industry Technologists — May 6-9

Bowie

Chief Warrant and Warrant Officers Association, United States Coast Guard — Comfort Inn/Apr. 11-14/50

Branson

International Truck Parts Association — Chateau on the Lake/Apr. 6-8/75

College Park

Society for History in the Federal Government — National Archives/March 8-8

Frederick

Society for Military History — Apr. 19-22/500

MASSACHUSETTS

Boston

American Academy of Appellate Lawyers — Fairmont Copley Plaza/Sept. 27-29
American Academy of Child and Adolescent Psychiatry — Sheraton Boston Hotel/Oct. 23-28
American Academy of Neurology — Apr. 28-May 5
American Academy of Physical Medicine and Rehabilitation — Hynes Convention Center/Sept. 27-30
American Association of Suicidology — Park Plaza/Apr. 16-19/700
American College of Osteopathic Internists — Marriott Copley Place/Oct. 10-14
American Health Care Association — Oct. 7-10
American Speech-Language-Hearing Association — Nov. 15-17
Association for Asian Studies — Marriott/March 22-25
Association for the Advancement of Medical Instrumentation — June 16-18
Campus Safety, Health and Environmental Management Association — Seaport Boston/July 21-25
Independent Educational Consultants Association — Westin Copley Place/Apr. 25-28/1300
International Association for Healthcare Security and Safety — July 24-27
International Fire Marshals Association — June 3-7
League of Historic American Theatres — Boston Park Plaza/July 25-28/250
Materials Research Society — Hynes Convention Center/Nov. 26-30
National Association for Healthcare Quality — Sept. 9-12
National Association for Variable Annuities — The Westin Copley Place/Sept. 9-11
National Association of Child Care Professionals — Seaport/Apr. 25-28/500
National Association of Public Hospitals and Health Systems — Westin Hotel/June/225
National Association of State Administrators and Supervisors of Private Schools — Hyatt Harborside/Apr. 22-25
National Fire Protection Association — Boston Convention & Exhibition Center/June 3-7

National Society of Black Physicists — Sheraton/Feb. 21-25
Orthopaedic Trauma Association — Sheraton/Oct. 18-20
The Protein Society — July 21-25
Public Risk Management Association — Hynes Convention Center/June 10-13/2000
Society for Research in Child Development — March 29-Apr. 1
Sports Lawyers Association — Westin Copley Plaza/May 17-19/450
Substance Abuse Librarians and Information Specialists — (Dates TBA)
Transportation Research Forum — March 14-17
Turnaround Management Association — Marriott Copley Place/Oct. 16-19

Cambridge

American Academy of Political and Social Science — Harvard University/September
Photo Chemical Machining Institute — Massachusetts Institute of Technology/Apr. 23-25

MICHIGAN

Ann Arbor

North American Manufacturing Research Institution of SME — University of Michigan/May 22-25

Dearborn

American School Band Directors' Association — Hyatt Regency/June 27-30

Detroit

American Counseling Association — March 21-25
American Gear Manufacturers Association — Cobo Center/Oct. 7-10/3000
American String Teachers Association — Detroit Marriott Renaissance Hotel/March 7-10
Association for Iron and Steel Technology — Sept. 17-20
International Association of Addictions and Offender Counselors — Convention Center/March 21-25/300
National Pan-Hellenic Council — Hyatt Dearborn/Oct. 17-21

Grand Rapids

American Rabbit Breeders Association — Oct. 14-18
Association of American Pesticide Control Officials — July 27-29
Community Leadership Association — Amway Grand Rapids/May 3-6/700
International Conference of Police Chaplains — June 25-29
National Rural Letter Carriers' Association — (Dates TBA)

Harbor Springs

Christian Schools International — Boyne Highlands Resort/July 25-28/500

Mackinac Island

Conference of State Court Adminstrators — Grand Hotel(Dates TBA)

Traverse City

American Institute of Professional Geologists — Park Place Hotel/Oct. 7-11

MINNESOTA

Medora

National Sunflower Association — Medora Community Center/Jan. 27-28/150

Minneapolis

Alliance for Community Media — (Dates TBA)
American Academy of Dental Sleep Medicine — Hilton/June 8-10
American Academy of Sleep Medicine — Minneapolis Convention Center/June 9-14/5000
American Association of Physicists in Medicine — July 22-26
American Society for Histocompatability and Immunogenetics — Hyatt/Oct. 8-12/900
American Veterinary Dental Society — Hyatt Regency/Oct. 19-21
ASABE - the Society for Engineering in Agricultural, Food and Biological Systems — June 17-20
Associated Professional Sleep Socs. — June 9-14/5000
Electrical Apparatus Service Association — Convention Center/June 24-27/3000
International Conference of Symphony and Opera Musicians — (Dates TBA)
NAFSA: Association of International Educators — May 27-June 1/7000
National Associated CPA Firms — Radisson/July 18-22/100
National Association of State Emergency Medical Services Officials — Hyatt/October/220
National Intramural-Recreational Sports Association — Conventin Center/Apr. 18-21/2000
National Society of Accountants for Cooperatives — Marriott/Aug. 8-10
Organization of American Historians — Hilton/March 29-Apr. 1
Public Radio Program Directors Association — Marriott City Center/Sept. 26-29
Society for Technical Communication — May 13-16
Society of Risk Management Consultants — (Dates TBA)

MISSOURI

Kansas City

Adhesive and Sealant Council — Hyatt Regency/Oct. 7-10
American Academy of Oral and Maxillofacial Pathology — May 4-9
American Association of School Personnel Administrators — Oct. 17-20
Association for Enterprise Opportunity — Hyatt Regency/May 15-18
International Food Service Executives' Association — Marriott Hotel/Apr. 6-9/1000
National Association of Farm Broadcasting — Nov. 14-16
National Association of Intercollegiate Athletics — Marriott/March 17-20
National Conference of Editorial Writers — Fairmont Hotel/Sept. 26-29
National Tour Association — Nov. 2-6
Piano Technicians Guild — Hyatt Crown Center/June 20-24
Skills USA — Bartle Hall/June 24-29/14000
Surface Design Association — Art Institute/May 31-June 3/500
Visual Resources Association — March 27-Apr. 1
Wheat Quality Council — Embassy Suites/Feb. 20-22/150

Springfield

Livestock Marketing Association — June 14-17

St. Louis

American Society for Healthcare Environmental Services — America's Center/Sept. 30-Oct. 4/1000
American Society of Colon and Rectal Surgeons — (Dates TBA)
American Wood-Preservers' Association — Hyatt Union Station/May 6-8
Association of Research Libraries — May 22-25
Business Forms Management Association — Hilton/May 6-10/350
Masonry Society, The — June 1-3
Musculoskeletal Tumor Society — Ritz Carlton/May 10-12/250
NALS — Sheraton Westport/Oct. 9-14
National Association of Animal Breeders — The Westin/Aug. 23-23/30
National Association of Church Personnel Administrators — Hyatt Regency/Apr. 22-26
National Association of Orthopaedic Nurses — America's Center/May 19-23
National Organization of Social Security Claimants' Representatives — Hyatt Regency Union Station/Oct. 17-21
Ombudsman Association, The — Apr. 11-14
Printing Industry Credit Executives — Sept. 18-20
Real Estate Educators Association — Hyatt Regency/June 10-13
Society for American Baseball Research — Adams Mark/July 26-29
Society of Flight Test Engineers — July 30-Aug. 3

MONTANA

Grand Rapids

Association of American Plant Food Control Officials — Amway Grand Hotel/July 29-31

NEVADA

Incline Village

ADSC: The International Association of Foundation Drilling — Hyatt Regency Lake Tahoe Resort/July 25-28/200

Lake Tahoe

National Poultry and Food Distributors Association — Hyatt Lake Tahoe/July 15-18/240

Las Vegas

Academy of Medical-Surgical Nurses — (Dates TBA)
American Academy of Ambulatory Care Nursing — Sheraton/March 29-Apr. 2
American Academy of Emergency Medicine — Caesar's Palace/March 12-14
American Academy of Neurological and Orthopaedic Surgeons — (Dates TBA)
American Academy of Pain Management — Red Rock Resort/Sept. 26-30/1200
American Ambulance Association — Hilton/Nov. 28-Dec. 3
American Association of Nutritional Consultants — Renaissance Las Vegas Hotel/Nov. 15-18
American College of Surgeons — Apr. 22-25
American Council on Exercise — Rio Hotel/September/500
American Gaming Association — Convention Center/Nov. 13-15
American Miniature Horse Association — Imperial Palace/Feb. 22-25/350
American Payroll Association — May 22-26
American Society of Gas Engineers — Red Rock/June 14-16/100
American Wholesale Marketers Association — Hilton/Feb. 21-23
Antique and Amusement Photographers International — Gold Coast Hotel/Feb. 6-8
ASIS International — Sept. 24-27
Associated Equipment Distributors — Convention Center/Jan. 16-18
Association of Fund-Raising Distributors and Suppliers — Paris Las Vegas/Jan. 7-11
Association of Legal Administrators — Mandalay Bay Resort/Apr. 30-May 3
Association of Woodworking-Furnishings Suppliers — Las Vegas Convention Center/July 18-21
Automotive Parts Remanufactuers Association — Rivera Hotel/Oct. 27-29
Awards and Recognition Association — Las Vegas Convention Center/Feb. 20-25
Billiard Congress of America — Sands Convention Center/Apr. 12-14/6000
Bowling Writers Association of America — June 24-29/100
Broadcast Cable Credit Association — Rio Suites/May 22-24
Broadcast Cable Financial Management Association — Rio Suites Hotel/May 22-24
Broadcast Education Association — Convention Center/Apr. 18-21/1800
Contact Lens Association of Ophthalmologists — Caesars Palace/Oct. 5-6
Custom Tailors and Designers Association of America — Feb. 12-14
Dance Educators of America — June 16-21
Document Management Industries Association — (Dates TBA)
Electronics Technicians Association International — Flamingo Hotel/Feb. 25-27/250
Home Sewing Association — Rio Hotel/Sept. 18-20/1500
Hotel Brokers International — Harrah's/Jan. 30-Feb. 1/75
Institute for Supply Management — Bally's Convention Center/May 6-9/3000
International Association of Special Investigation Units — Caesar's Palace/Sept. 9-12
International Cemetery and Funeral Association — Mandalay Bay/March 20-23
International Council of Shopping Centers — Convention Center/May 20-23
International Society for Pharmaceutical Engineering — Caesar's Palace/Nov. 4-7
IT Financial Management Association — Mirage Resort/June 25-29/250
Marble Institute of America — (Dates TBA)
National Apartment Association — Mandalay Bay/June 28-30
National Association of College Auxiliary Services — MGM Grand/Oct. 28-31
National Association of Dental Laboratories — Bellagio/Jan. 28-30/250
National Association of Display Industries — (Dates TBA)
National Association of Home Inspectors — The Riveria/Feb. 18-21/400
National Association of Pizza Operators — March 20-22/5000
National Association of Secondary School Principals — Feb. 23-25
National Association of Tax Professionals — Caesar's/July 23-26/1000
National Association of Television Program Executives — Mandalay Bay/Jan. 16-18
National Association of Ticket Brokers — (Dates TBA)
National Automobile Dealers Association — Feb. 9-12
National Bulk Vendors Association — Caesar's Palace/Apr. 19-22/700
National Conference of Insurance Legislators — Renaissance Las Vegas Hotel/Nov. 15-18
National Council for Community Behavioral Healthcare — MGM Grand/March 26-27/1300
National Demolition Association — Mirage/Apr. 1-4/1700
National Fire Sprinkler Association — Red Rock Resort/May 3-6/1200
National Limousine Association — Venetian Resort and Casino/Jan. 28-30
National Lumber and Building Material Dealers Association — JW Marriot and Spa/Oct. 4-6
National Organization for Associate Degree Nursing — Flamingo/Nov. 5-12/300
National Retail Hobby Stores Association — Hilton/May 29-June 2
National Shoe Retailers Association — (Dates TBA)
National Ski and Snowboard Retailers Association — Convention Center/Jan. 23- /50
National Tank Truck Carriers Conference — Mandalay Bay/May 7-9/550
National Utility Contractors Association — Caesar's Palace/Feb. 11-14
Polyurethane Manufacturers Association — Apr. 22-24
Promotional Products Association International — Mandalay Bay/Jan. 3-6
Retailer's Bakery Association — Mandalay Bay Resort and Casino/Sept. 8-10
Roller Skating Association International — Riviera/Aug. 27-30
SGMA — June 11-13
Sheet Metal and Air Conditioning Contractors' National Association — Mandaly Bay/Oct. 21-25
Society for Advancement of Management — Harrah's Hotel/March 25-28/500
Society of American Gastrointestinal and Endoscopic Surgeons — Paris Las Vegas/Apr. 19-22/1500
Sporting Goods Agents Association — Sands Convention/June 11-13/400
Submersible Wastewater Pump Association — Riviera/March 5-6/150
Travel Goods Association — Feb. 27-March 1

Reno

American Association of School Librarians — Oct. 25-28
American Custom Gunmakers Guild — Silver Legacy/Jan. 26-28
American Society for Enology and Viticulture — Grand Sierra Resort/June 20-22/2000
Athletic Equipment Managers Association — John Ascuaga's Nugget/June 6-9
Government Management Information Sciences — John Ascuaga's Nugget Casino Resort/June 24-27/580
International Association of Emergency Managers — Silver Legacy Resort/Nov. 11-15
International Brotherhood of Magicians — (Dates TBA)
National Association of Workforce Development Professionals — Nuggett/May 20-23

NEW HAMPSHIRE

West Lebanon

American Milking Shorthorn Society — June 27-30

NEW JERSEY

Atlantic City

Dance Educators of America — June 25-29
National Association of Pizza Operators — Sept. 12-13/850
National Conference of Local Environmental Health Administrators — (Dates TBA)/100
National Environmental Health Association — (Dates TBA)/1500
National Environmental, Safety and Health Training Association — June/1200
United States Harness Writers' Association — Borgata/Feb. 24-25

New Brunswick

International Association of Conference Centers — The Heldrich/Apr. 19-22

Princeton Junction

Academy of Parish Clergy — Princeton University/Apr. 24-26/90

Secaucus

National Cleaners Association — Meadowlands Exposition Center/September

NEW MEXICO

Albuquerque

Alternatives Fuel Vehicle Network — Marriott/October/70
American Farrier's Association — Convention Center/Feb. 26-March 3
American Horse Publications Association — Albuquerque Marriot Pyramid North/June 21-23/150
Association of Educators in Imaging and Radiologic Sciences — Hyatt/June
Indian Arts and Crafts Association — March 30-31
National Association of Postmasters of the United States — Sept. 8-13

Santa Fe

Association for Living History, Farm and Agricultural Museums — El Rancho de los Golordrinas/June 2-6/125
Clay Minerals Society — June 2-7
Women's Regional Publications of America — June/30

NEW YORK

Bront Brook

National Association of Puerto Rican/Hispanic Social Workers — SUNY- Stony Brook/June 9- /400

Brooklyn

Society of Motion Picture and Television Engineers — Marriott/Oct. 24-27

Ithaca

International Double Reed Society — Ithaca College/June 12-16

Kerhonkson

American Conference of Cantors — Hudson Valley Resort and Spa/June 24-28

New York

American Association of Colleges for Teacher Education — Hilton/Feb. 24-27
American Hungarian Educators Association — St. Johns College/April/100
American Montessori Society — Marriott Marquis/March 1-4/3500
American Psychoanalytic Association — June 17-21
American Society for Aesthetic Plastic Surgery — (Dates TBA)
American Society of Business Publication Editors — Roosevelt Hotel/July 31-Aug. 2
American Thyroid Association — Sheraton New York/Oct. 4-7
Association for the Sociology of Religion — Marriott Marquis/Aug. 13-15
Association of Jewish Family and Children's Agencies — Roosevelt(Dates TBA)/500
Association of Real Estate License Law Officials — Hyatt/Sept. 14-17/350
Association of Ship Brokers and Agents (U.S.A.) — February/100
Broadcast Designers' Association — Hilton/June 12-14
Building Owners and Managers Association International — Javitz Center/July 21-24/5000
Children's Book Council — (Dates TBA)
College Art Association — Feb. 14-17
College Media Advisers — Roosevelt Hotel/March 15-17
Conference on College Composition and Communication — Hilton/March 21-24
Conference on English Leadership — Nov. 21-23/150
Expanded Shale, Clay and Slate Institute — September/30
Fulfillment Management Association — The Princeton Club(Dates TBA)/200
International Association for Jazz Education — Hilton and Sheraton(Dates TBA)
International Documentary Association — Sept. 1- /20
International Downtown Association — Marriott Marquis/Sept. 15-18
International Institute of Forecasters — Marriott Marquis/June 24-27
International Society for the Performing Arts — Jan. 16-18
National Art Education Association — March 14-18
National Association Medical Staff Services — (Dates TBA)
National Association of School Psychologists — Hilton New York/March 27-31
National Business Education Association — Marriott/Apr. 4-7/1500
PMA, the Independent Book Publishers Association — May 29-31
Population Association of America — Marriott Marquis/March 28-31/1700
Society for Industrial and Organizational Psychology — Marriott Marquis/Apr. 27-29
Society for the Study of Social Problems — Roosevelt Hotel/Aug. 10-12
Society of Quantitative Analysts — The Helmsley Hotel/June 18
Women's Caucus for Art — Hilton/Feb. 17-19

Oneonta

National Intercollegiate Soccer Officials Association — July 13-16

Rochester

International Graphic Arts Education Association — Rochester Institute of Technology(Dates TBA)

NORTH CAROLINA

Asheville

National Watermelon Association — Grove Park Inn/Feb. 21-25/400

Charlotte

American Association for Laboratory Animal Science — Convention Center/Oct. 14-18/4000
Association on Higher Education and Disability — July 17-21
Environmental Information Association — Charlotte Marriott City Center/March 17-21/300
National Association of Orthopaedic Technologists — Hilton City Center/Aug. 1-4/300
Society of Toxicology — Charlotte Convention Center/March 25-27/6000

Greensboro

Commission on Accreditation for Law Enforcement Agencies — (Dates TBA)

Raleigh

National Barbecue Association — Hilton North/Feb. 14-17/1500

Research Triangle Park

International Society of Exposure Analysis — Oct. 14-18

NORTH DAKOTA

Bismarck

Lignite Energy Council — Civic Center/Oct. 24-25/400

OHIO

Cincinnati

American Academy of Advertising — (Dates TBA)

American Coal Ash Association — N. Kentucky Convention Center/May/600
American Hackney Horse Society — Westin/January
American Massage Therapy Association — Hilton/Sept. 26-29/1000
Association for Practical and Professional Ethics — Hilton Cincinnati Netherland Plaza/Feb. 23-25
Monument Builders of North America — Hyatt/Jan. 19-22
Society for the Advancement of Material and Process Engineering — Hilton Cincinnati Netherland Plaza/Oct. 29-Nov. 1

Cleveland

Wire Association International — Cleveland I-X Center/May 5-10/5000
Women's Basketball Coaches Association — March 31-Apr. 3

Columbus

National Association of Activity Professionals — Apr. 15-21
National Certification Council for Activity Professionals — April
National Conference of Catechetical Leadership — Hyatt/Apr. 8-12
Percussive Arts Society — Columbus Convention Center/Oct. 31-Nov. 3/7000
Society for Ethnomusicology — Hyatt Capital Square/Oct. 24-28
Unfinished Furniture Association — June 23-26
Wood Truss Council of America — Convention Center/Oct. 3-5/3000

OKLAHOMA

Oklahoma City

Amalgamated Printers' Association — (Dates TBA)
Enlisted Association of the National Guard of the United States — Westin Hotel/Aug. 12-15/2000
National Rural Education Association — October

Tulsa

Arabian Horse Association — November/600
NALS — Doubletree Warren Place/March 6-10

OREGON

Corvallis

American Society for Virology — Oregon State University/July 14-18/1500

Portland

American Agricultural Economics Association — July 29-Aug. 1/1400
Association of Insurance Compliance Professionals — Hilton/Oct. 28-31/650
Governors Highway Safety Association — Portland Hilton Hotel/Sept. 23-26
International Society of Political Psychology — (Dates TBA)
National Association of Boards of Pharmacy — Hilton Hotel and Executive Tower/May 19-22/425
National Association of State Textbook Administrators — Doubletree Lloyd Center/July 21-24
Pulp and Paper Safety Association — Jantzen Beach/June 10-13
Society of American Foresters — Oct. 24-28
Wildlife Management Institute — Portland Hilton and Towers/March 20-24

PENNSYLVANIA

Hershey

Association of Clinical Scientists — Hershey Lodge/May 16-20

Middletown

Tourist Railway Association — Holiday Inn Harrisburg East(Dates TBA)

Philadelphia

American Academy of Physician Assistants — May 26-31
American Academy of Podiatric Sports Medicine — (Dates TBA)
American Association of Endodontists — Philadelphia Convention Center/Apr. 25-28
American Association of Physical Anthropologists — March 27-Apr. 3
American College of Medical Practice Executives — Philadelphia Convention Center/Oct. 28-31
American Epilepsy Society — Nov. 30-Dec. 4
American Health Information Management Association — Oct. 6-11
American Industrial Hygiene Association — June 1-7
American Legislative Exchange Council — Downtown Marriott/July 25-29
American Podiatric Medical Writers Association — Marriott/Aug. 16-19/100
American Probation and Parole Association — Marriott Downtown/July 8-11
American Society of Tropical Medicine and Hygiene — Nov. 4-8/1500
American Theological Library Association — June 13-16
Association for College and University Religious Affairs — University of Pennsylvania(Dates TBA)
Association for Continuing Legal Education — Loews Philadelphia/July 28-31
Association for Healthcare Philanthropy — Oct. 3-7
Color Pigments Manufacturers Association — June 13-14/50
Craft Retailers Association for Tomorrow — (Dates TBA)
General Federation of Women's Clubs — Marriott/June
Graduate Management Admission Council — Marriott/June 14-16/600
Healthcare Convention and Exhibitors Association — Pennsylvania Convention Center/June 9-12/700
Medical Group Management Association — Oct. 7-10
Medical Library Association — May 18-23
National Association of Black Accountants — Philadelphia Downtown Marriott/June 19-23
National Council of Examiners for Engineering and Surveying — Aug. 22-25
National Federation of Abstracting and Information Services — Ritz Carlton/Feb. 25-27
Society of American Military Engineers — (Dates TBA)
U.S. Lacrosse — Convention Center/Jan. 11-14

Pittsburgh

Destination Marketing Association International — July 18-21/900
Institute of Transportation Engineers — David L. Lawrence Convention Center/Aug. 5-8
International Association of Music Libraries, United States Branch — Hilton Pittsburgh/Feb. 26-March 3
Masonry Society, The — Nov. 8-13/100
Music Library Association — Feb. 28-March 4
National Council on Family Relations — Hilton/Nov. 5-10
National Federation of Paralegal Associations — Omni William Penn/July 19-20/300
National Fraternal Congress of America — Sept. 6-8
National WIC Association — The David Lawrence Convention Center/Apr. 27-May 2/1304
North American Society for the Sociology of Sport — Marriott/Nov. 2-8
Society of Architectural Historians — Apr. 11-14
Teratology Society — Omni William Penn Hotel/June 22-28/350

Valley Forge

Church and Synagogue Library Association — Hilton/July 15-17/200

Washington

Association of Railway Museums — Pennsylvania Trolley Museum(Dates TBA)

PUERTO RICO

Puerto Rico

American Concrete Institute — Wyndham El Conquistador/Oct. 14-18

Rio Grande

American Society for Reconstructive Microsurgery — Westin Rio Mar/Jan. 13-16

San Juan

Financial Women International — Sept. 30-Oct. 2
National Employment Lawyers Association — Westin Rio Mar Resort and Golf Club/June 27-30
National Guard Association of the U.S. — Aug. 25-27

RHODE ISLAND

Providence

Estuarine Research Federation — Convention Center/Nov. 4-8
Society for Imaging Informatics in Medicine — Rhode Island Convention Center/June 7-10

SOUTH CAROLINA

Charleston

Cigar Association of America — Charleston Place/Oct. 11-14/180
Council of Hotel and Restaurant Trainers — February
Epsilon Sigma Phi — Francis Marion Hotel/Sept. 8-14
Inland Marine Underwriters Association — Wild Dunes/Apr. 15-18/150
Outdoor Power Equipment Aftermarket Association — Feb. 22-25
Sanitary Supply Wholesaling Association — Charleston Place/June 25-28/70

Columbia

North American Benthological Society — Columbia Metropolitan Convention Center/June 3-7/800

Hilton Head

Hardwood Plywood and Veneer Association — Westin Resort Hilton Head Island/March 24-26
Scale Manufacturers Association — Crowne Plaza/Apr. 17-19/35
Shareholder Services Association — (Dates TBA)

Myrtle Beach

National Defender Investigator Association — Apr. 18-20
National Institute of Steel Detailing — Hilton/March 15-17/100
Postcard and Souvenir Distributors Association — Myrtle Beaceh Sheraton/Sept. 25-29/250

SOUTH DAKOTA

Rapid City

American Association of Motor Vehicle Administrators — Best Western Ramkota Hotel/Aug. 21-23/500

TENNESSEE

Chattanooga

Cryogenic Engineering Conference — Convention Center/July 17-20

Knoxville

Dance Educators of America — June 24-29/400
Holstein Association USA — June 23-26
Society of Wood Science and Technology — Hilton Hotel/June 10- /150

Memphis

American College of Clinical Pharmacy — Memphis Convention Center/Apr. 22-25
Association of Graduate Liberal Studies Programs — October
Federation of Analytical Chemistry and Spectroscopy Societies — Cook Convention Center/Oct. 12-18
National Association of First Responders — Airport Marriott/Sept. 2-5/1500
Pickle Packers International — The Peabody Hotel/Oct. 2-4/250
Regional Airline Association — Memphis Convention Center/May 21-24/1400
Rhetoric Society of America — Peabody Hotel/May 26-29/600

Nashville

AACE International — July 15-18/700
American Biological Safety Association — (Dates TBA)
American College of Medical Genetics — Renaissance Convention Center/March 22-25/1500
American Jail Association — May 20-24
American National CattleWomen — Jan. 31-Feb. 3
Associated Builders and Contractors — Gaylord Opryland/March 21-25
Association for Continuing Legal Education — Loews Vanderbilt/Jan. 27-30
Association of Credit Union Internal Auditors — Sheraton Downtown/June 5-8
Chlorine Institute — Loew's Vanderbilt/Sept. 30-Oct. 3/200
Country Radio Broadcasters, Inc. — Nashville Convention Center/Feb. 28-March 2
Door and Hardware Institute — Opryland/Oct. 15-20
Electrical Manufacturing and Coil Winding Association — Opryland Convention Center/Sept. 24-26
Employee Involvement Association — Hilton/Sept. 19-21/200
International Bluegrass Music Association — Oct. 1-7
International Municipal Lawyers Association — Oct. 28-31
International Window Cleaning Association — Opryland Hotel/Jan. 30-Feb. 3
IT Financial Management Association — Gaylord Opryland Hotel/March 26-30/125
Lutheran Education Association — Gaylord Opryland/March 15-17/400
Master Brewers Association of the Americas — Gaylord Opryland Hotel/Oct. 26-28
Metaphysical Society of America — Vanderbilt University/March 11-12
NACE International — Convention Center/Apr. 22-26
National Association for Campus Activities — Gaylord Opryland/Feb. 17-21/2500
National Association of Equipment Leasing Brokers — Gaylord Opryland Hotel/May 17-19
National Association of School Nurses — Gaylord's Opryland Hotel/June 28-July 1/1400
National Association of Wastewater Transporters — Opryland/Feb. 7-10
National Cattlemen's Beef Association — Jan. 31-Feb. 3
National Coil Coating Association — Gaylord Opryland Resort/Sept. 25-28
National Interscholastic Athletic Administrators Association — Opryland/Dec. 14-18/2500
Society of Research Administrators International — Gaylord Opryland Resort and Convention Center/Oct. 13-17/2000
Society of Women Engineers — Oct. 25-27
Specialty Tool and Fastener Distributors Association — Opryland Hotel/Nov. 4-6
Warehousing Education and Research Council — Gaylord Opryland/Apr. 22-25/1200

TEXAS

Austin

American Group Psychotherapy Association — Hilton Austin/March 5-10
American Sports Builders Association — Hyatt Regency/Dec. 1-5/275
Association of State Dam Safety Officials — Hilton/Sept. 9-13/850
Council of Science Editors — Hilton Austin/May 18-22
Health Industry Distributors Association — Hyatt Regency Lost Pines Resort and Spa/Feb. 27-March 2
Interior Design Educators Council — March 4-11
International Foodservice Editorial Council — Omni/Oct. 23-26/185
KWPN of North America — March 1-4
NAMM - the International Music Products Association — July 27-31
National Alliance for Media Arts and Culture — Oct. 17-20
National Association for College Admission Counseling — Austin Convention Center/Sept. 27-29
National Association of State Textbook Administrators — Crowne Plaza/Feb. 13-15
National Association of the Remodeling Industry — Marriott Austin at The Capital/March 21-24
National Cotton Ginners' Association — Hilton Austin/Feb. 1-5/100
North American Spine Society — Austin Convention Center/Oct. 23-27/6250
Society for American Archaeology — Apr. 25-29

Dallas

ADED - the Association for Driver Rehabilitation Specialists — Hyatt Regency/July 27-31/300
American Association of Hip and Knee Surgeons — Conference Center/Nov. 2-4/700
American College of Allergy, Asthma and Immunology — Gaylord Texan/Nov. 9-14/4000
American Dental Education Association — March 29-Apr. 2

American Nephrology Nurses Association — Wyndham Anatole/Apr. 22-25
American Society of Heating, Refrigerating and Air-Conditioning Engineers — Jan. 29-31
Assisted Living Federation of America — May 14-17
Association for Women in Sports Media — (Dates TBA)
Automotive Oil Change Association — Dallas Convention Center/Apr. 28-May 2/3200
Gas Machinery Research Council — Hyatt Reunion/Oct. 1-3/700
International Association of Plastics Distributors — Hyatt Regency Dallas at Reunion/Oct. 4-7
International Dyslexia Association — Adam's Mark Hotel/Nov. 14-17/3500
International Reprographic Association — Gaylord Texan/May 9-11
Lawn and Garden Marketing and Distribution Association — Westin Centre Park/Jan. 17-19/125
Measurement, Control and Automation Association — Hilton/May 20-22/130
National Collegiate Wrestling Association — Renaissance/March 8-11/600
National Registry of Environmental Professionals — Marriott/Oct. 16-19
National Staff Development Council — Dec. 1-5
North American Menopause Society — Gaylord Texan/Oct. 3-7
Radio Advertising Bureau — Feb. 8-11
Romance Writers of America — Hyatt Regency/July 11-14/2100
Society for Clinical and Experimental Hypnosis — Adam's Mark Hotel/Jan. 19-23/250
Society of Christian Ethics — Hyatt Regency/Jan. 7-7
SSPC: the Society for Protective Coatings — Dallas Convention Center/Feb. 10-15
Turnaround Management Association — Four Seasons/March 28-31

Ft. Worth

International Association of Speakers Bureaus — Apr. 26-28
National Emergency Number Association — June 9-14

Galveston

International Association of Drilling Contractors — Moody Gardens Hotel/Oct. 31-Nov. 2

Grapevine

American Bus Association — Jan. 27-31/3000
American Society for Laser Medicine and Surgery — Gaylord Texan Resort/Apr. 11-15/2100
Expanded Shale, Clay and Slate Institute — Gaylord Texan/May 8-10/50
Financial Managers Society — Gaylord Opryland Texas/June 24-26
Grain Elevator and Processing Society — Opryland Convention Center/March 3-6/1800
National Association of Church Business Administration — Gaylord Texan/July 11-15
National Association of Mutual Insurance Companies — Gaylord Texan/Sept. 16-19
National Board of Boiler and Pressure Vessel Inspectors — Gaylord Texan Resort/May 14-18
National Committee on Planned Giving — Gaylord Texan on Lake Grapvine/Oct. 10-13

Houston

American Foundry Society — Hilton Americas(Dates TBA)
American Society of Cytopathology — Hilton/Nov. 2-7/900
American Society of Preventive Oncology — Marriott/March 15-18
Chlorine Institute — JW Marriott/March 18-21
Energy Telecommunications and Electrical Association — Hilton Americas/Apr. 11-13/1750
National Association of Catering Executives — Houston Marriott/July 15-18
National Association of Fleet Administrators — Houston Americas/May 7-10/3000
National Association of Professional Pet Sitters — Hyatt Regency/Jan. 26-28/200
North American Catalysis Society — June 17-21
Produce Marketing Association — Oct. 12-15
SAVE International — Westin/May 1-
WaterJet Technology Association — Marriott Westchase/Aug. 19-21

Lubbock

North American Society for Sport History — Texas Technical University/May 25-27

San Antonio

AACC International — San Antonio Convention Center/Oct. 7-10
Academy of Osseointegration — San Antonio Convention Center/March 8-10/3200
American Academy of Forensic Sciences — Convention Center/Feb. 19-24
American Academy of Medical Hypnoanalysts — (Dates TBA)
American Aging Association — (Dates TBA)
American College Health Association — Marriott Rivercenter and Riverwalk/May 29-June 2
American Football Coaches Association — Convention Center/Jan. 7-10/7300
American Institute of Architects — May 3-5
American Meteorological Society — Jan. 14-18
American Public Works Association — Henry B. Gonzales Covention Center/Sept. 9-12
American Society of Animal Science — July 8-12
American Traffic Safety Services Association — Convention Center/Jan. 28-30
Association for the Advancement of Computing in Education — March 26-30
Association of Medical School Pediatric Department Chairs — Westin La Cantera/March 7-12/300
Cement Employers Association — The Hotel Contessa/February/40
Chinese Language Teachers Association — Nov. 16-18
Community Colleges Humanities Association — St. Anthony Hotel/Oct. 25-27/400
Conference of Consulting Actuaries — Westin La Cantera/Oct. 21-24
Gas Processors Association — March 12-14
Geospatial Information Technology Association — Convention Center/March 4-7/3000
Health Ministries Association — Hyatt Riverwalk/June 21-24/500
International Technology Education Association — Convention Center/March 15-17/2000
National Association of Industrial and Technical Teacher Educators — (Dates TBA)
National Association of Resale & Thrift Shops — Sheraton Gunter Hotel/June 22-25/300
National Frozen and Refrigerated Foods Association — Marriott/Oct. 13-16/1100
National Ice Cream Retailers Association — Crowne Plaza/Nov. 7-10
National Truck and Heavy Equipment Claims Council — Hyatt Regency/Oct. 4-7
Poultry Science Association — July 8-12
Professional Photographers of America — Convention Center/Jan. 14-16
Religion Newswriters Association — Sept. 27-30/250
Society for the Study of Reproduction — Henry B. Gonzalez Convention Center/July 22-25/1200
Sports Turf Managers Association — Henry B. Gonzalez Convention Center/Jan. 17-21
Vibration Institute — Menger Hotel/June 19-22

San Marcos

Computer Assisted Language Instruction Consortium — Texas State University/May 22-26/400

UTAH

Park City

Water Sports Industry Association — The Lodge at Mountainside--David Holland's/Feb. 25-27/200

Salt Lake City

American Association for Crystal Growth — Aug. 12-17
American Association of Cardiovascular and Pulmonary Rehabilitation — Oct. 18-21
American Society of Sugar Beet Technologists — Little America/Feb. 28-March 3
American Statistical Association — Convention Center/July 29-Aug. 2
Association for Technology in Music Instruction — Little America/Nov. 15-18/400
Association of Professors of Gynecology and Obstetrics — Grand American/March 7-11/900

College Music Society — Little America/Nov. 15-18/400
Council on Resident Education in Obstetrics and Gynecology — Grand America Hotel/March 7-10
Emergency Nurses Association — Sept. 26-29
Hardwood Plywood and Veneer Association — Salt Lake City Marriott Downtown/Sept. 9-11
Hospice and Palliative Nurses Association — Salt Palace Convention Center/Feb. 14-17/2000

Weber County

Mountain Rescue Association — (Dates TBA)

VERMONT

Burlington

American Academy of Advertising — Sheraton/Apr. 12-15
National Association of State Boating Law Administrators — Wyndham/Sept. 4-11/300

VIRGINIA

Arlington

American Society of Naval Engineers — Hyatt Regency Crystal City/June 18-20
Society for Personality Assessment — Sheraton National/March 7-11/400

Berryville

Academy of Security Educators and Trainers — Highlands Lodge/Apr. 12-14

Charlottesville

Association for Social Anthropology in Oceania — Omni Hotel/Feb. 21-24

Crystal City

International Society for Pharmacoeconomics and Outcomes Research — Marriott/May 19-23/1500

Newport News

Children's Literature Association — Christopher Newport University/June 14-16/250

Norfolk

American Association of Port Authorities — (Dates TBA)
Credit Professionals International — Renaissance Hotel/June 21-24

Richmond

National Association of Counties — July 13-17
National Association of County Recorders, Election Officials and Clerks — July 12-16
Pi Lambda Theta — Omni/July 26-29/30

Williamsburg

International Association of Baptist Colleges and Universities — Marriott Williamsburg/June 3-5
National Lieutenant Governors Association — Kingsmill Resort/July 25-27

WASHINGTON

Portland

Accrediting Council on Education in Journalism and Mass Communications — Westin/May 4-5/100

Seattle

Academy of Criminal Justice Sciences — Sheraton/March 13-17/1800
American Association of Clinical Endocrinologists — Sheraton/Apr. 11-15
American Association of Orthodontists — Washington State Convention Center/May 18-22
American College of Emergency Physicians — Convention Center/Oct. 8-11/4000
American Geriatrics Society — Seattle Convention Center/May 2-5/2500
American Radiological Nurses Association — Sheraton Seattle Hotel/March 1-6
American Society of Gene Therapy — Convention Center/May 30-June 3
American Society of Head and Neck Radiology — The Fairmont Olympic Hotel/Sept. 26-30
Association for Library and Information Science Education — Jan. 16-19
Association of Clinical Research Professionals — Washington State Convention Center/Apr. 20-24
Association of Vascular and Interventional Radiographers — March 1-6/450
Council of Multiple Listing Service — (Dates TBA)
EDUCAUSE — Oct. 23-26
Financial Planning Association — Sept. 8-11/3000
Institute for Operations Research and the Management Sciences — Nov. 4-7
International Society of Certified Employee Benefit Specialists — The Westin Seattle/Sept. 16-19
Miniature Book Society — Oct. 12-15
National Association of College and University Food Services — Sheraton/July 11-14
National Association of Educational Office Professionals — July 16-20
National Association of Schools of Public Affairs and Administration — The Westin(Dates TBA)
National Career Development Association — Sheraton/July 6-8/1000
National Property Management Association — June 3-7
Physician Insurers Association of America — Westin/May 23-26
Society for Public Health Education — Renaissance Hotel/June 6-9/600

Spokane

Conference of Radiation Control Program Directors — Red Lion/May 21-24/400

Tacoma

Western Literature Association — (Dates TBA)

WEST VIRGINIA

Pipestem

North American Mycological Association — TBD/Aug. 16-19/300

Wheeling

National Golf Foundation — Ogelbay Resort/Jan. 14-19

White Sulphur Springs

Apple Processors Association — Greenbrier/June 20-22/100

WISCONSIN

Milwaukee

Association of Collegiate Schools of Planning — Hilton Milwaukee City Center/Oct. 18-21
Federation of Environmental Technologists — Four Points Sheraton/March 12-14
Pickle Packers International — Hilton City Center/Apr. 17-19
Society of Pediatric Nurses — Hyatt Regency/Apr. 14-15/500

Oshkosh

National Association of Flight Instructors — July 24-30

WYOMING

Cody

Association of Official Seed Analysts — June 8-11/300

Laramie

American Ornithologists' Union — University of Wyoming/Aug. 8-11

ALBERTA

Banff

Industrial Truck Association — Sept. 8-10/300
Society for Obstetric Anesthesia and Perinatology — Fairmont Banff Springs/May 16-19/500

Calgary

American Orthopaedic Society for Sports Medicine — Telus Convention Centre/July 12-15/1000

Association for Arid Lands Studies — Hyatt Regency/Apr. 11-14
Association for Borderlands Studies — Hyatt Regency/Apr. 10-16

BRITISH COLUMBIA

Kelowna

National Tour Association — Apr. 26-28

Penticton

National Institute for Farm Safety — June 24-26

Vancouver

American Academy for Cerebral Palsy and Developmental Medicine — Oct. 10-13/800
American Judges Association — Sheraton Wall Centre(Dates TBA)
International Clarinet Association — University of British Columbia/July 4-8
Qualitative Research Consultants Association — Oct. 27-30/350
Structural Board Association — (Dates TBA)

Victoria

Association for Hose and Accessories Distribution — Fairmont Hotel/May 18-22
Society for Organic Petrology — University of Victoria/Aug. 19-25

ONTARIO

Toronto

American Orthopaedic Foot and Ankle Society — Westin Harbor Castle/July 12-15/450
American Pediatric Society — Convention Center/May 5-8/6000
American Society of Pediatric Nephrology — May 5-8
Association for Convention Operations Management — Westin Harbour Castle/Jan. 5-7
Council of American Jewish Museums — Jan. 21-24
GAMA International — March 18-21
Health & Sciences Communications Association — Sheraton Centre Toronto/June 14-17
International League of Electrical Associations — Novotel/July 18-21
International Reading Association — May 13-17
Music Teachers National Association — Sheraton Centre Toronto/March 23-27
North American Academy of Liturgy — Park Hyatt/Jan. 4-7
Professional Convention Management Association — Jan. 7-10/3000
Society for Pediatric Research — Metro Convention Center/May 5-8
Society of Critical Care Medicine — Fairmont/June 14-16/300
Society of General Internal Medicine — Sheraton/Apr. 25-28
Surgical Infection Society — Westin Harbour Castle/Apr. 18-20
U.S. Grains Council — Marriott/July 21-25
University and College Designers Association — Hilton/September

QUEBEC

Montreal

American Peptide Society — (Dates TBA)
ASME International Gas Turbine Institute — Palais de Congres/May 14-17/2500
Commission on Accreditation for Law Enforcement Agencies — (Dates TBA)
Flexographic Technical Association — Palais des Congres/May 6-9
International Society for Adolescent Psychiatry & Psychology — Fairmont Queen Elizabeth Hotel/July 4-7
Society for Biomolecular Sciences — Apr. 15-19
Society for Clinical Trials — Hyatt/May 20-23
Society for Pediatric Radiology — May 17-20
Society of Financial Service Professionals — Hilton Montreal Bonaventure/Sept. 27-29

Quebec City

American Folklore Society — Hilton/Oct. 17-21
American Oil Chemists' Society — Quebec City Convention Center/May 13-16
American Risk and Insurance Association — Loews Le Concordia Hotel/Aug. 5-8
LOMA — Quebec City Hilton Hotel/Sept. 16-18

SASKATCHEWAN

Saskatoon

Association of Cooperative Educators — Univ. of Saskatchewan/May 29-June 2

AUSTRALIA

Melbourne

Association for the Advancement of Automotive Medicine — Oct. 14-17/200

BAHAMAS

Bahamas

Metal Treating Institute — The Atlantis/Aug. 24-29/150

Grand Bahama Island

National Church Goods Association — Westin Sheraton Our Lucaya Resort/Jan. 4-10

Paradise Island

Community Financial Services Association of America — Feb. 28-March 4
Distribution Contractors Association — Atlantis/Jan. 20-25/300

BELGIUM

Brussels

International Society for the Performing Arts — June 7-10

BERMUDA

Bermuda

Society for the Preservation of Oral Health — Southhampton Fairmont/March 27-Feb. 30/65

CHINA

Hong Kong

International Society of Hospitality Consultants — Intercontinental/Oct. 5-11/150

Shangai

Perlite Institute — May 5-9/25

Shanghai

CIES, The Food Business Forum — June 20-22

ETHIOPA

Addis Ababa

American Incense Manufacturers Association — July 2-4/20

FRANCE

Lyon

Engineering in Medicine and Biology Society — Convention Center/Aug. 22-27

GERMANY

Berlin

International Society for Magnetic Resonance in Medicine — ICC Berlin/May 19-25/5500
Law and Society Association — July 25-28/1500
Marketing Agencies Association Worldwide — May

Frankfurt

International Listening Association — July 18-21

Jena

International Society of Chemical Ecology — (Dates TBA)

INDIA

New Delhi

International Institute of Synthetic Rubber Producers — Hyatt/Apr. 16-19/150

ITALY

Florence

International Society of Arthroscopy, Knee Surgery and Orthopaedic Sports Medicine — May 27-31

Lucca

WACRA - World Association for Case Method Research and Application — Jan. 3-6

JAPAN

Kyoto

International Society of Applied Intelligence — June 6-29/250

Osaka

International Psychogeriatric Association — Oct. 14-18/1500

MEXICO

Acapulco

American Geophysical Union — May 22-25/3000

Cancun

American Galvanizers Association — La Meridian/March 26-30/150

Association of Private Enterprise Education — Hilton(Dates TBA)

International Pediatric Transplant Association — (Dates TBA)

Society for Developmental Biology — Hotel Gran Melia/June 16-20

Cozumel

National Association of Reunion Managers — Splendor of the Seas/Jan. 10-15

Guadalajara

WACRA - World Association for Case Method Research and Application — July 1-4

Xalapa

American Bryological and Lichenological Society — Aug. 12-16

NETHERLANDS

Amsterdam

Institute of Internal Auditors — June

NEW ZEALAND

Auckland

Society for the Study of Evolution — (Dates TBA)

PORTUGAL

Lisbon

Society for the Exploration of Psychotherapy Integration — July 5-8

SOUTH AFRICA

Port Elizabeth

Society for Conservation Biology — July 1-5/1500

Somerset West

Association of Seventh-Day Adventist Librarians — Helderberg College(Dates TBA)

SPAIN

Barcelona

Geoscience and Remote Sensing Society — (Dates TBA)

Madrid

Society of Allied Weight Engineers — Malia Princesa/May 26-30/150

SWEDEN

Stockholm

Interferry — The Grand Hotel/Sept. 28-30

The Protein Society — May 12-16

SWITZERLAND

La-Chaux-de-Fonds

International Horn Society — Music Conservatory/July 8-14/450

TAIWAN

Taipei

International Association of School Librarianship — Gis Convention Center/July 16-20

THAILAND

Bangkok

World Allergy Organization - IACCI — Dec. 2-6/4000

UNITED KINGDOM

Edinburgh

Scoliosis Research Society — Sept. 4-8

London

Ultrasonic Industry Association — Nat Physical Lab/March 19-21/150

2007 National Trade and Professional Associations

Association Management Firms Index

Listed here are over 350 firms providing administrative and management services to associations on a contract basis. In addition to contact information and the names and titles of firm principals, a list of clients managed on a full-time basis by the firm is included, when available.

ABLE MANAGEMENT SOLUTIONS, INC.

5310 E. Main St., Suite 104
Columbus, OH 43213-2598
Tel: (614)868-1144 *Fax:* (614)868-1177
Email: info@ablemgt.com
website: www.ablemgt.com

Sammi Soutar CAE, *President*

American Association of Code Enforcement
American Soc. of Architectural Illustrators
Central Ohio Retail Grocers Ass'n
Ohio Bed and Breakfast Association
Ohio Planning Conference

ACCENT ON MANAGEMENT

17 S. High St., Suite 200
Columbus, OH 43215-3458
Tel: (614)221-1900 *Fax:* (614)221-1989
Email: accent@assnoffices.com
website: www.assnoffices.com

David W. Field, *President*

AIA Ohio
AIA Ohio Foundation
Association for Corporate Growth
Community Development Society
Gamma Iota Sigma
Great Lakes Association of Orthodontists
Mid-Atlantic Society of Orthodontists
National Association of Insurance and Financial Advisors - Ohio
Ohio Association of Civil Trial Attorneys
Ohio Association of Textile Services
Ohio Auctioneers Association
Ohio Cleaners Association
Ohio Economic Development Association
Ohio Educational Library/Media Association
Ohio Government Finance Officers Association
Ohio Propane Foundation and Research Council
Ohio Propane Gas Association
Ohio State Association of Nurse Anesthetists
School Nutrition Association of Ohio
Society of Financial Service Professionals - Columbus Chapter

ACCURATE IMAGE MARKETING INC.

212 S. Henry St.
Alexandria, VA 22314-3522
Tel: (703)549-9500 *Fax:* (703)549-9074
Toll Free: (888)899-4653
website: www.aimmeetings.com

Walter E. Galanty Jr., *President*

National Association of Golf Tournament Directors

ADMINISTRATIVE MANAGEMENT SERVICES, INC.

28790 Chagrin Blvd., Suite 350
Cleveland, OH 44122-4630
Tel: (216)464-2137 *Fax:* (216)464-0397
Email: dwilliams@admgt.com
website: www.admgt.com

David L. Williams, *President*

Conference of Business Economists
International Association for Energy Economics
U.S. Combined Heat and Power Ass'n
United States Association for Energy Economics

ADMINISTRATIVE OFFICE

2545 Ridgeway Dr., Suite B
National City, CA 91950-7733
Tel: (619)267-2236
Email: prattc@adminoff.com
website: www.adminoff.com

Charles A. Pratt CAE, *President*

San Diego Dry Cleaners Ass'n

ADMINISTRATIVE SYSTEMS, INC.

5204 Fairmont Ave.
Downers Grove, IL 60515
Tel: (630)655-0112 *Fax:* (630)493-0798
Email: info@asihq.com
website: www.asihq.com

Judith Keel, *President*

Association of Women Surgeons
Association of Women Surgeons Foundation
Independent Medical Distributors Association

ADVANCED MANAGEMENT CONCEPTS

136 S. Keowee St.
Dayton, OH 45402-2241
Tel: (937)222-1024 *Fax:* (937)222-5794
Email: amc@advmgtconcepts.com
website: www.advmgtconcepts.com

Daniel Lea, *Chief Executive Officer*

American Woman's Society of Certified Public Accountants
Association for Accounting Administration
Cellulose Insulation Manufacturers Association
Inflatable Advertising Dealers Association
Materials Marketing Associates
Miami Valley NARI
National Associated CPA Firms
National Guild of Professional Paperhangers
National Society of Accountants for Cooperatives
Ohio Pest Control Association
Ohio Valley NARI
SAVE International

ADVANCEMENT PLANNING GROUP

2041 Riverside Dr., Suite 102
Columbus, OH 43221-4024
Tel: (614)486-6634 *Fax:* (614)486-5845
Email: mvild@rrohio.com

Margaret H. Vild, *President*

Columbus Academy of Osteopathic Medicine
Columbus Osteopathic Foundation
Ohio State Society of the American College of Osteopathic Family Physicians

AGRI WASHINGTON

1100 17th St., N.W., 10th Floor
Washington, DC 20036
Tel: (202)785-6710 *Fax:* (202)331-4212
Email: agriwash@aol.com
website: www.agriwashington.org

Paul S. Weller Jr., *President*

Agriculture Biotechnology Forum
Apple Processors Association
Canadian-American Business Council
Financial Executives International
Maryland Dairy Industry Association
National Grange
Riley Memorial Foundation
Washington Agricultural Roundtable
Washington Caucus

ALAMPI & ASSOCIATES MANAGEMENT CORP.

66 Morris Ave., Suite 2-A
Springfield, NJ 07081-1450
Tel: (973)379-1100 *Fax:* (973)379-6507
Email: rickaaamc@earthlink.net
website: www.alampimgt.com

Richard Alampi, *President*

Atlantic Coast Veterinary Foundation
Converting Equipment Manufacturers Association

Golf Course Superintendents Association of New Jersey
Irrigation Association of New Jersey
Metropolitan New York Paint and Coatings Ass'n
New Jersey Health Underwriters Association
New Jersey Lumber Dealers Association
New Jersey Veterinary Foundation
New Jersey Veterinary Medical Association
New York Society for Coatings Technology
Sales Association of the Chemical Industry

THE ALEXANDRIA GROUP, INC.

P.O. Box 142089
Austin, TX 78714-2089
Tel: (512)973-0040 *Fax:* (512)973-0043
Email: alexgrp@alexandriagroup.com
website: www.alexandriagroup.com

M. Lynn Mitchel, *Managing Partner*

National Council on Qualifications for the Lighting Professions
National Magazine, Book, and Film Carriers
Stencil Artisans League Foundation
Stencil Artisans League, Inc.

ALLEN MARKETING & MANAGEMENT

P.O. Box 1897
Lawrence, KS 66044
Tel: (785)843-1234 Ext: 260 *Fax:* (785)843-1274
Toll Free: (800)627-0629 Ext: 260
Email: amm@allenpress.com
website: www.allenmm.com

Susan Metzger, *Manager*

PETER ALLEN, INC.

66 Morris Ave., Suite 1-A
Springfield, NJ 07081
Tel: (973)564-5859 *Fax:* (973)564-7480

Peter Allen CAE, *President*

National Council of Acoustical Consultants

ALTERNATIVE MANAGEMENT

6725 Via Austi Pkwy., #250
Las Vegas, NV 89119
Tel: (702)798-5156 *Fax:* (702)798-8653
Email: katrina@alternativemanagement.net

Katrina Ferry, *Owner*

Building Owners and Managers Association of Nevada
Commercial Real Estate Women of Southern Nevada
Institute of Real Estate Management - Las Vegas Chapter
Nat'l Ass'n of Industrial and Office Properties - Southern Nevada Chapter
Nevada Association of Land Surveyors
Nevada Professional Facility Managers Ass'n
Soc. for Marketing Professional Services-Las Vegas Chapter
Southern Nevada CCIM Chapter
Southern Nevada Multihousing Association
Technology Business Alliance of Nevada
Urban Land Institute - Las Vegas Chapter

ALTERNATIVE MANAGEMENT SOLUTIONS, INC.

100 Webster St., Suite 101
Oakland, CA 94607-3724
Tel: (510)832-7200 *Fax:* (510)832-7300
Email: bsanders@amsinc.org
website: www.amsinc.org

Bruce A. Sanders CAE, *President*

American College of Phlebology
Ass'n of Dermatology Administrators/Managers
San Francisco Chapter - American Marketing Ass'n

AMERICAN MEDICAL SYSTEMS PROFESSIONAL SERVICES

1250 Long Beach Ave., Suite 323
Los Angeles, CA 90021
Tel: (213)624-2225 *Fax:* (213)624-2229

Lorraine P. Auerbach, *President and Chief Executive Officer*

California Association of Health Plans
California Nursing Students Ass'n
Foundation of the California Nursing Students Ass'n

AMERICAN TRADE AND PROFESSIONAL ASSOCIATION MANAGEMENT

P.O. Box 59811
Potomac, MD 20859-9811
Tel: (301)365-2521 *Fax:* (301)365-7705

Russell E. Barker, *President*

Peanut and Tree Nut Processors Association

PAT AMICK AND ASSOCIATES

204 E. High St.
Jefferson City, MO 65101
Tel: (573)632-6662 *Fax:* (573)636-5783

Patricia S. Riner Amick, *President*

AIA Missouri
Missouri Economic Development Council
Missouri Travel Council

AMP MANAGEMENT SERVICES

8310 Nieman Road
Lenexa, KS 66214-1598
Tel: (913)541-0400 *Fax:* (913)541-0156
Email: info-amp@goamp.com
website: www.goamp.com

Cathy Berra MBA, *Manager, Operations*

American Board of Histocompatability and Immunogenetics
American Board of Transplant Coordinators
Association of Genetic Technologists
Nat'l Credentialing Agency for Laboratory Personnel
National Association of EMS Physicians
North American Transplant Coordinators Organization
Oak Park Homes Ass'n
Transportation Lawyers Association

AMR MANAGEMENT SERVICES

201 E. Main St., Suite 1405
Lexington, KY 40507
Tel: (859)514-9150 *Fax:* (859)514-9207
Email: info@amrms.com
website: www.amrms.com

Jack Gallt, *Association Director*

Bluegrass Hospitality Association
Nat'l Ass'n of State Chief Information Officers
National Association of Government Defined Contribution Administrators
National Association of State Chief Administrators
National Association of State Chief Information Officers
National Association of State Procurement Officials
Nursing Organizations Alliance

ANDERSON MANAGEMENT SERVICES, INC.

1335 H St., Suite 100
Lincoln, NE 68508-2882
Tel: (402)476-1528 *Fax:* (402)476-1259

Robert L. Anderson, *President*

American Society of Interior Designers - Nebraska/Iowa Chapter
Automotive Recycling Industry of Nebraska
Nebraska Agri-Business Association
Nebraska Auctioneers Association
Nebraska Hotel and Motel Association
Nebraska State Pest Control Association

APT, INC.

P.O. Box 2264
2900 E. Broadway
Bismarck, ND 58502-2264
Tel: (701)224-1815 *Fax:* (701)224-9824
Email: aptinc@aptnd.com
website: www.aptnd.com

Kendrick P. Tupa, *Chief Executive Officer*

Association of Former Public Employees
Bismarck/Mandan Apartment Ass'n
Independent North Dakota State Employees Association
National Association of Social Workers - North Dakota Chapter
National Association of Social Workers - Wyoming Chapter
North Dakota Ass'n of Nurse Anesthetists
North Dakota Association for Home Care
North Dakota Board of Clinical Lab Practice
North Dakota Board of Occupational Therapy Practice
North Dakota Board of Social Work Examiners
North Dakota Dietetic Ass'n
North Dakota Lumbermans Ass'n
North Dakota Occupational Therapists Ass'n
North Dakota Pawnbrokers Ass'n
North Dakota Retired Teachers Ass'n

ARDMORE MANAGEMENT GROUP, LLC

2500 E. Main St., Suite 100
Columbus, OH 43209-2483
Tel: (614)235-5001 *Fax:* (614)235-0880
Email: dan@ardmore-group.com
website: www.ardmore-group.com

Daniel H. Dozer CAE, *President*

Central Ohio Chapter - Community Ass'ns Institute
Ohio Lake Communities Ass'n
Ohio Land Title Association

ASSOCIATED MANAGEMENT SERVICES

444 E. Algonquin Ave.
Arlington Heights, IL 60005-4654
Tel: (847)228-8375

Laura M. Downes CAE, *Director, Management Services*

American Association for Hand Surgery
American Society for Reconstructive Microsurgery
American Society of Maxillofacial Surgeons
Association of Plastic Surgery Assistants
Microcirculatory Society of America
Plastic Surgery Admininstrative Association

ASSOCIATED SERVICES

20 Surrey Ct.
Columbia, SC 29212
Tel: (803)772-5354 *Fax:* (803)798-0670
Toll Free: (800)344-4518
Email: contact@as-irmo.com
website: http://associatedservices-irmo.com

Kelly Smith, *Executive Director*

Independent Banks of South Carolina
Mining Association of South Carolina
Motorcoach Ass'n of South Carolina
South Carolina Association of Special Purpose Districts
South Carolina Campground Owners Ass'n
South Carolina Dairy Association

ASSOCIATION ADMINISTRATIVE MANAGEMENT SERVICES, INC.

502 E. 11th St., Suite 400
Austin, TX 78701-2619
Tel: (512)708-0611 *Fax:* (512)708-0627
Email: aams@aams-texas.com
website: www.aams-texas.com

Cheryl Wiles, *Executive Vice President*

Austin Ass'n of Remodeling Contractors
Society of Infectious Diseases Pharmacists
Texas Association of Acupuncturists
Texas Association of Addiction Professionals
Texas Association of Pawnbrokers
Texas Concrete Pipe Association
Texas Rural Health Association
Texas Society of Health-System Pharmacists

ASSOCIATION ADMINISTRATORS

4035 E. Fanfol Dr.
Phoenix, AZ 85028
Tel: (602)912-5310

Pauline Wampler, *President*

American Soc. for Interior Designers - Arizona North Chapter
Arizona Physical Therapy Association
Arizona Water Well Association

THE ASSOCIATION ADVANTAGE LLC

Lakeside Office Park, Suite 3-2
591 North Ave.
Wakefield, MA 01880-1617
Tel: (781)245-6485 *Fax:* (781)245-6487
Email: association.advantage@verizon.net

Sherri L. Oken CAE, *Principal*

Connecticut Academy of Physician Assistants
International Special Events Society - New England
New England Carwash Association

ASSOCIATION AND GOVERNMENT RELATIONS MANAGEMENT

4900-B S. 31st St.
Arlington, VA 22206
Tel: (703)820-7400

Thomas Fise, *President*

American College of Gastroenterology
Association of Program Directors in Surgery
Society of Head and Neck Surgeons
Southeastern Society of Plastic and Reconstructive Surgeons

ASSOCIATION AND SOCIETY MANAGEMENT INTERNATIONAL, INC.

201 Park Washington Ct.
Falls Church, VA 22046-4527
Tel: (703)533-0251 *Fax:* (703)241-5603
Email: info@asmii.com
website: www.asmii.com

Harry W. Buzzerd Jr., CAE, *Chairman*

American Textile Machinery Association
Capital Equipment Export Council
Cyanide Poisoning Treatment Coalition
International Association of Emergency Managers
International Aviation Ground Support Association
National Association of Government Communicators
National Association of State Emergency Medical Services Officials
Process Equipment Manufacturers' Association
Product Liability Prevention and Defense Group

ASSOCIATION AND SOCIETY MANAGEMENT, INC.

1306-A W. Anderson Lane
Austin, TX 78757
Tel: (512)454-8626 *Fax:* (512)454-3036
Email: info@assnmgmt.com
website: www.assnmgmt.com

Don R. McCullough CAE, *President and Chief Executive Officer*

Automobile Insurance Agents of Texas
Lone Star Chapter Certified Residential Specialists
National Barbecue Association
Texas Ass'n of Alternative Education
Texas Association of Professional Geoscientists
Texas Golf Course Owners Ass'n
Texas Independent Insurance Adjusters Association
Texas Indoor Air Quality Ass'n
Texas Jewelers Association
Texas Professional Benefit Administrators Association

ASSOCIATION ASSOCIATES, INC.

One AAA Dr., Suite 102
Trenton, NJ 08691
Tel: (609)890-9207 *Fax:* (609)581-8244
Email: aai@hq4u.com
website: www.hq4u.com

Debbie Hart CAE, APR, *President*

New Jersey Dietetic Association

ASSOCIATION CONCEPTS

315 New Salem
Park Forest, IL 60466
Tel: (708)748-3330 *Fax:* (708)748-3335
Email: office325@aol.com

Sarah Robertson, *President*

Broadcast Advertising Club of Chicago
Chicago Interactive Marketing Association

ASSOCIATION EXCHANGE

P.O. Box 1519
Winter Haven, FL 33882-1519
Tel: (863)293-5710

David Boozer, *President*

Florida Aquaculture Association
Florida Ground Water Association
Florida Tropical Fish Farms Association

ASSOCIATION EXECUTIVES, LLC

6610 Hwy.100, Suite 203
Nashville, TN 37205
Tel: (615)353-9200

Elliott W McNiel, *Executive Officer*

ASSOCIATION EXPOSITIONS & SERVICES

383 Main Ave.
Norwalk, CT 06852-6059
Tel: (203)840-5404

Margaret Pederson, *Senior Vice President*

ASSOCIATION HEADQUARTERS OF CALIFORNIA

5355 Parkford Circle
Granite Bay, CA 95746
Tel: (916)791-6613 *Fax:* (916)772-3781

Skip Daum, *President*

American Subcontractors Association - California
California Recreation Vehicle Dealers Association
Community Ass'ns Institute/California Legislative Action Committee

ASSOCIATION HEADQUARTERS, INC.

1500 Commerce Pkwy.
Mount Laurel, NJ 08054
Tel: (856)439-0500
website: www.associationheadquarters.com

William L. MacMillan CAE, *Chief Executive Officer*

American Association for Aerosol Research
American Society for Histocompatability and Immunogenetics
American Society of Transplantation
American Transplant Congress
Attention Deficit Disorder Association
Church Benefits Ass'n
Flag Manufacturers Ass'n of America
International Liver Transplantation Society
International Pediatric Transplant Association
Juvenile Products Manufacturers Association
Kids in Distressed Situations (KIDS)
Legal Netlink Alliance
National Association of Professional Pet Sitters
Office Business Center Association International
Product Development and Management Association
Receptive Services Association of America
Society for Biomaterials
Unfinished Furniture Association
Wound, Ostomy and Continence Nurses Society
Writing Instrument Manufacturers Association

ASSOCIATION INNOVATION AND MANAGEMENT

1821 Michael Faraday Dr., #300
Reston, VA 20190-5332
Tel: (703)438-3103 *Fax:* (703)438-3113
Email: cwilson@aim-hq.com
website: www.aim-hq.com

Shawn D. Lamb, *Chief Executive Officer*

Academy of Toxicological Sciences
Environmental Mutagen Society
Internat'l Union of Toxicology
Soc. of Toxicologic Pathology
Society of Toxicology
Teratology Society

ASSOCIATION INSIGHT

4536 114th St.
Urbandale, IA 50322
Tel: (515)727-0648 *Fax:* (515)251-8657
Email: kleeds@associationinsight.com
website: www.associationinsight.com

Kirk A. Leeds, *President*

Agriculture's Clean Water Alliance
Iowa Independent Crop Consultants Ass'n
Iowa Public Airports Ass'n
Iowa Soybean Association

ASSOCIATION ISSUES AND MANAGEMENT

2111 Wilson Blvd., Suite 700
Arlington, VA 22201
Tel: (703)875-8650 *Fax:* (703)351-9750

Marshall Cohen, *President*

Aseptic Packaging Council

ASSOCIATION MANAGEMENT & COMMUNICATIONS

349 Granada Road
West Palm Beach, FL 33401
Tel: (561)802-9310 *Fax:* (561)802-4310
Email: assomgmt@association-management.net
website: www.association-management.net

Alison Pruitt, *President*

Appraisal Institute - East Florida Chapter
Ass'n of Eminent Domain Professionals
Billiard and Bowling Institute of America
Executives' Ass'n of The Palm Beaches
Florida Nursery, Growers and Landscape Association
Marine Industries Ass'n of Palm Beach County

Paralegal Ass'n of Florida
Rotary Club of West Palm Beach

ASSOCIATION MANAGEMENT ALLIANCE, INC.

950 S. Cherry St., Suite 508
Denver, CO 80246-2664
Tel: (303)758-3513 *Fax:* (303)758-0190
Email: dslothower@amainc.net

Douglas W. Slothower, *President and Chief Executive Officer*

American Society of Agricultural Consultants
American Society of Farm Managers and Rural Appraisers
Educational Foundation of the American Soc. of Farm Managers and Rural Appraisers
Nat'l Sheep Association

ASSOCIATION MANAGEMENT AND MARKETING RESOURCES

5807 Grosvenor Lane, Suite 100
Bethesda, MD 20814-1835
Tel: (301)530-9066 *Fax:* (301)530-9076
Email: scarey@ammr.com
website: www.ammr.com

Karen Clayton, *Executive Vice President*

Independent Living Strategists Ass'n

ASSOCIATION MANAGEMENT BUREAU

8405 Greensboro Dr., Suite 800
Vienna, VA 22102
Tel: (703)506-3260
website: www.ambnet.org

Maria Brennan, *Executive Vice President*

American Society of Women Accountants
American Women in Radio and Television
Audio Publishers Association
Emergency Department Practice Management Association
Foundation of American Women in Radio and Television
Internat'l Alliance for Women
National Association of Telecommunications Officers and Advisors
National Association of Women Business Owners
Society of National Association Publications

ASSOCIATION MANAGEMENT CENTER

4700 W. Lake Ave.
Glenview, IL 60025-1485
Tel: (847)375-4700 *Fax:* (888)240-7626
Email: info@connect2amc.com
website: www.connect2amc.com

Mark T. Engle CAE, *Vice President*

American Academy of Hospice and Palliative Medicine
American Academy of Pain Medicine
American Association of Neuroscience Nurses
American Board of Neuroscience Nurses
American Board of Pain Medicine
American Pain Society
American Society for Bioethics and Humanities
American Society of Pediatric Hematology/Oncology
Association of Pediatric Hematology/Oncology Nurses
Association of Rehabilitation Nurses
Awards and Recognition Association
Awards & Recognition Industry Educational Foundation
Chicago Advertising Federation
Christian Stewardship Association
Freestanding Insert Council of North America
Giving Institute
Giving USA Foundation
Healthcare Quality Foundation
Metal Construction Association
Midwest Pain Society
National Association for Healthcare Quality
National Association of Neonatal Nurses
National Association of Professional Organizers
Neuroscience Nursing Foundation
North American Neuromodulation Society
North American Retail Dealers Association
Rehabilitation Nursing Certification Board
Rehabilitation Nursing Foundation

ASSOCIATION MANAGEMENT GROUP, INC.

8201Greensboro Dr., Suite 300
McLean, VA 22102
Tel: (703)610-9000 *Fax:* (703)610-9005
website: www.amg-inc.com

J. Bruce Wardle CAE, *President and Chief Executive Officer*

American Ambulance Association
American Council of Engineering Companies of Metropolitan Washington
Ass'n of Fundraising Professionals - D.C. Chapter
Association of Fundraising Professionals - Washington, D.C. Metro Area Chapter
Association of Hispanic Advertising Agencies
Association of Legal Administrators - Capital Chapter
Association of Water Technologies
Chronic Disease Directors
Convention Industry Council
Hospitality Sales and Marketing Association International
International Society for the Study of Dissociation
Nat'l Certification Board for Therapeutic Massage and Bodywork
National Adult Day Services Association
National Association of Mortgage Brokers
Board of Registered Polysomnographic Technologists
World Airline Entertainment Association

ASSOCIATION MANAGEMENT PLUS

9959 Allisonville Road
Fishers, IN 46038
Tel: (317)578-7768 *Fax:* (317)578-7718

Kimberly Williams, *Executive Officer*

Indiana Academy of Ophthalmology

ASSOCIATION MANAGEMENT PLUS, INC.

P.O. Box 6322
Helena, MT 59604
Tel: (406)442-5490
Email: stuart@initco.net

Stuart H. Doggett, *Owner*

Montana Inn-Keepers Association
Montana Land Title Association
Montana Manufactured Housing and Recreational Vehicle Association
Montana Veterinary Medical Association

ASSOCIATION MANAGEMENT RESOURCES

3300 Washtenaw Ave., Suite 222
Ann Arbor, MI 48104
Tel: (734)971-0000 *Fax:* (734)677-2407
Email: info@amr-hq.com
website: www.amr-hq.com

Richard A. Correll, *President*

CHIME Foundation
College of Healthcare Information Management Executives
Health Level Seven
Meeting Professionals International - Michigan Chapter
Michigan Ass'n of Nurse Anesthetists
Michigan Ass'n of Public Employment Retirement Systems
Michigan Association of Professional Court Reporters
Michigan Council of Teachers of Mathematics
Michigan Mortgage Brokers Association
Michigan Occupational Therapy Association
Michigan Science Teachers Ass'n
Michigan Society of Respiratory Care
Microsoft Healthcare Users Group
National Association of Industrial Technology
School Nutrition Association of Michigan
Society of Automotive Analysts

ASSOCIATION MANAGEMENT RESOURCES INTERNATIONAL

121 Cayuga St.
Seneca Falls, NY 13148-1117
Tel: (315)568-0082

Edward D. Shanken CAE, *President*

ACCRA - West Rotary Club, Ghana, West Africa
American Insurance Attorneys
Ass'n of Ghana Industries
Federation of Ass'ns of Ghanaian Exporters
Ghana Soc. of Ass'n Executives
Internat'l Center for Professional Development
Internat'l Executive Service Corps
Philanthropic Development Group
Seneca County Chamber of Commerce
USAID

ASSOCIATION MANAGEMENT SERVICES/PAMCO

207 Shelby St.
P.O. Box 1183
Frankfort, KY 40602
Tel: (502)875-5858

D. Ray Gillespie, *President*

Kentucky Beverage Association
Kentucky Business Industry Recycling Program
Kentucky Hotel and Lodging Association
Kentucky Self-Insurers Association

ASSOCIATION MANAGEMENT SERVICES, INC.

33 S. Catalina Ave., Suite 202
Pasadena, CA 91106-2426
Tel: (626)449-4356 *Fax:* (626)564-8540
Email: pam@assnmgmt.net
website: www.assnmgmt.net

Pamela Hemann CAE, *President*

Building Industry Ass'n of Southern California - LA County East Chapter
Leadership California
Pasadena Child Health Foundation

ASSOCIATION MANAGEMENT SOLUTIONS

39355 California St., Suite 307
Fremont, CA 94538
Tel: (510)608-5900 *Fax:* (510)608-5917
Email: info@amsl.com
website: www.amsl.com

Karen Moreland, *Principal*

Coral Constortium
Digital Subscriber Line Forum
FLO Forum
Gaming Standards Association
International Packet Communications Consortium
IPsphere Forum
MPEG Industry Forum
Multiservice Switching Forum
Network Processing Forum
NIFA Forum
Optical Internetworking Forum
Service Creation Community

ASSOCIATION MANAGEMENT SYSTEMS

214 N. Hale St.
Wheaton, IL 60187
Tel: (630)510-4500 *Fax:* (630)510-4501
Email: info@association-mgmt.com
website: www.association-mgmt.com

Michael D. Hansen, *President*

American Academy of Oral and Maxillofacial Pathology
American Society of Business Publication Editors
Association of Industrial Real Estate Brokers
Association of Pool and Spa Professionals - Region Service Center 5
Calendar Marketing Association
Casual Furniture Retailers
Commanderie de Bordeaux a Chicago
Illinois CCIM Chapter
Lambda Alpha Internat'l
National Association of Ticket Brokers
National Independent Flag Dealers Association
National Retail Hobby Stores Association
Northern Illinois Commercial Ass'n of Realtors
Small Business Financial Exchange
Soc. of Industrial and Office Retailers - Chicago Chapter

ASSOCIATION MANAGEMENT SYSTEMS

P.O. Box 15215
Hattiesburg, MS 39404-5215
Tel: (601)582-3330 *Fax:* (601)582-3354
Email: ams@megagate.com

F. Lamar Evans, *Chief Executive Officer*

American Society of Landscape Architects - Mississippi Chapter
Bent Creek Homeowners Ass'n
Hattiesburg Home Builders Ass'n
Mississippi Contract Poultry Growers Association
Mississippi Recreation and Parks Association
National Government Publishing Association

ASSOCIATION MANAGEMENT, INC.

P.O. Box 35128
Albuquerque, NM 87176
Tel: (505)888-0752 *Fax:* (505)884-0668

David M. McCoy, *President*

Rio Grande Underground Contractors Ass'n

ASSOCIATION MANAGERS

P.O. Box 370
Bath, MI 48808-0370
Tel: (517)641-6554

Jon Hayes, *President*

Independent Accountants Association of Michigan

ASSOCIATION MANAGERS, INC.

3900 E. Timrod
Tucson, AZ 85711-4170
Tel: (520)881-1778
Email: ami@dakotacom.net

Phillip A. Gutt CAE, *President*

Executive Referral Club

ASSOCIATION MANAGERS, INC.

9001 Braddock Road, Suite 380
Springfield, VA 22151-1002
Tel: (703)426-8100 *Fax:* (703)426-8400
Toll Free: (800)403-3374
website: www.assnmgrs.com

Dennis W. Boyd, *President*

Federal Criminal Investigators Ass'n
National Ass'n of Assistant U.S. Attorneys

ASSOCIATION MAX

3702 Nathan Hale Court
P.O. Box 620830
Middleton, WI 53562-0830
Tel: (608)836-3851 *Fax:* (608)836-3890
Email: associationmax@aol.com

Maxine D. O'Brien, *Owner*

Illinois State Auctioneers Association
Missouri Professional Auctioneers Association
National Air/Vac Association
Wisconsin Amusement and Music Operators
Wisconsin Auctioneers Association

ASSOCIATION PARTNERS, INC.

P.O. Box 60128
Nashville, TN 37206
Tel: (615)254-1233 *Fax:* (615)254-1186
Email: connie@associationpartners.com
website: www.associationpartners.com

Connie C. Wallace CAE, *President*

AIA Tennessee
American Institute of Architects - Gulf States Region
Tennessee Association of Convention and Visitors Bureaus
Tennessee Association of Nurse Anesthetists
Tennessee Foundation for Architecture
Tennessee Lobbyists Association

ASSOCIATION PROFESSIONAL MANAGEMENT SERVICES

532 42nd St.
Des Moines, IA 50312
Tel: (515)440-6057 *Fax:* (515)440-6055
Email: apmsthomas@aol.com

Beverly V. Thomas, *President*

Ingersoll Area Ass'n
Iowa Hearing Aid Society
Iowa Public Transit Association
National Independent Fire Alarm Distributors
Opticians Association of Iowa
UNICON

ASSOCIATION RESOURCE CENTER, INC.

785 Orchard Dr., Suite 225
Folsom, CA 95630
Email: arc@4arc.com
website: www.assocresourcecenter.com

Stephen Hamilton, *President*

California Association of Mortgage Brokers
California Integrated Waste Management Board
California Resource Recovery Association
California Sign Association
El Dorado Winery Ass'n
Funeral Directors Service Corp.
Reno Market
Structural Engineers Association of California
Taxicab Paratransit Association of California
Unified Wine and Grape Symposium
West Coast Western Wear and Equipment Association
Western Association of Convention and Visitors Bureaus

ASSOCIATION RESOURCES, INC.

342 N. Main St.
West Hartford, CT 06117-2507
Tel: (860)586-7500 Ext: 510 *Fax:* (860)586-7550
website: www.associationresources.com

M. Suzanne C. Berry CAE, *Executive Vice President*

American Epilepsy Society
Association of College and University Auditors
Association of Connecticut Career Schools
Connecticut Podiatric Medical Association
Connecticut Police Chiefs Association
Connecticut Police Foundation
Connecticut Psychological Association
Internat'l League Against Epilepsy
International Association of Campus Law Enforcement Administrators
International Society for Clinical Densitometry

ASSOCIATION RESOURCES, INC.

P.O. Box 6082
Gainesville, GA 30504
Tel: (770)534-1155 *Fax:* (770)534-3550

Frank R. Rizzo, *President*

Southern Wholesalers Association

ASSOCIATION SERVICES

30575 Trabuco Canyon Road, Suite 104
Trabuco Canyon, CA 92678
Tel: (949)459-8735

Lyn Paymer, *Principal*

Chlorine Gas Disinfection Ass'n
National Plasterers Council
Professional Refinishing Conferences
Swimming Pool Water Treatment Professionals

ASSOCIATION SERVICES CORP.

2945 S.W. Wanamaker Dr., Suite A
Topeka, KS 66614-5321
Tel: (785)271-0208 *Fax:* (785)271-0166
Email: stan@glasswebsite.com

Stanley L. Smith, *President*

Glass Week
Glazing Industry Code Committee
National Sunroom Association
Protective Glazing Council

ASSOCIATION SERVICES GROUP

P.O. Box 2945
LaGrange, GA 30241-2945
Tel: (706)845-9085 *Fax:* (706)883-8215
Email: chall@asginfo.net
website: www.associationservicesgroup.net

Charles T. Hall Jr., *President*

Association of Fundraising Professionals - Atlanta Chapter
Garden Centers of America
Georgia Association of Training, Education and Support
Georgia Enterprises for Products and Services
Georgia Forestry Association
Georgia Fruit and Vegetable Growers Association
Georgia Interpretive Services Network
Georgia Sanitary Suppliers Association
Keep Troup Beautiful
Plant Growth Regulators Society of America
Society for the Preservation of Oral Health
Southeast Greenhouse Conference and Trade Show
Southeast Society of American Foresters

ASSOCIATION SERVICES GROUP INC.

P.O. Box 1515
Milwaukee, WI 53201
Tel: (414)475-7022

Alan J. Carlson, *President*

Wisconsin Association of Behavioral Health Services
Wisconsin Network Administrators Group

ASSOCIATION SERVICES GROUP, INC.

595 S. 14th St.
Boise, ID 83702
Tel: (208)344-0781
Email: association@iiabi.org

Wendy J. Tippetts, *President*

Idaho Insurance Council
Independent Insurance Agents and Brokers of Idaho
Surplus Line Association of Idaho

ASSOCIATION SERVICES INTERNATIONAL, INC.

2412 Cobblestone Way
Frederick, MD 21702
Tel: (301)663-4252 *Fax:* (301)694-4948

Gloria Parsley, *President*

Bioelectromagnetics Society
Society for Physical Regulation in Biology and Medicine

ASSOCIATION SERVICES OF MICHIGAN

412 W. Ottawa St.
Lansing, MI 48933-1518
Tel: (517)372-8270 *Fax:* (517)372-1731

Brian P. Lovellette CAE, *President*

Michigan Association of Ambulance Services
Michigan Association of Emergency Medical Technicians

ASSOCIATION SERVICES, INC.

P.O. Box 2524
Fargo, ND 58108
Tel: (701)293-6822

Robert L. Lamp, *Executive Vice President*

Automobile Dealers Association of North Dakota
North Dakota Implement Dealers Association

ASSOCIATIONS INTERNATIONAL, INC.

6516 Truman Lane, Suite 100
Falls Church, VA 22043
Tel: (703)237-1104
Email: aiboss@aol.com

Dr. Armand B. Weiss CAE, *President*

Daniel Heumann Fund for Spinal Cord Research
Washington Management and Business Association
Wharton School Club of Washington

ASSOCIATIONS OF GEORGIA, INC.

168 N. Johnston St., Suite 304
Dallas, GA 30132
Tel: (770)445-3180 Ext: 22 *Fax:* (770)445-3893
Email: AOG1998@AOL.COM
website: http://aoginc.org/

Melissa Pelfrey, *Management Executive*

Georgia Auctioneers Association
Georgia Speakers Association
Greythorne/Mt. Vernon Pointe Homeowners Ass'n
Home Builders Ass'n of Carroll County
Home Builders Ass'n of Rome
Independent Funeral Directors of Georgia
Paulding County Builders Ass'n
West Georgia Green Ass'n

ASSOCIATIONS PLUS INC.

P.O. Box 11035
Columbia, SC 29211-1035
Tel: (803)252-7128
Email: leigh@assnsplus.com

Leigh M. Burns Faircloth, *President and Owner*

American Fats and Oil Association
South Carolina Association of Heating and Air Conditioning Contractors
South Carolina Aviation Association
South Carolina Soybean Board
South Carolina Tire Dealers and Retreaders Association

ATTACHE INTERNATIONAL

1912 Clay St.
North Kansas City, MO 64116
Tel: (816)421-1991 *Fax:* (816)421-1991
website: www.attacheinternational.com

James A. Spawn, *Executive Officer*

American Federation of Aviculture
American Lowline Registry
American Tarentaise Association
Garand Collectors Association
Kansas City Paralegal Ass'n
North American Corriente Association

AVERY MANAGEMENT GROUP

5530 Wisconsin Ave., Suite 1210
Chevy Chase, MD 20815
Tel: (301)941-1063 *Fax:* (301)986-9313
website: www.averymanagement.com

Andrew Avery, *President*

ABF Educational Foundation
American Association of Oriental Medicine
Independent Inventors Discussion and Educatiuon Ass'n

BACHNER COMMUNICATIONS, INC.

8811 Colesville Road, Suite G-106
Silver Spring, MD 20910
Tel: (301)589-9121 *Fax:* (301)589-2017
Email: info@bachner.com

John P. Bachner, *President*

ASFE/The Best People on Earth
Engineers Leadership Foundation
National Lighting Bureau

BAI, INC.

10015 Old Columbia Road, Suite B-215
Columbia, MD 21046
Tel: (301)596-2584
Email: mlevin0986@aol.com
website: www.baileadership.com

Mark Levin CAE, *President*

Chain Link Fence Manufacturers Institute
Montgomery Blair Alumni Ass'n

BANNISTER & ASSOCIATES, INC.

34 N. High St.
New Albany, OH 43054-8507
Tel: (614)895-1355 *Fax:* (614)895-3466
Email: jim@bannister.com
website: www.bannister.com

James R. Bannister CEM, *Chairman and Chief Executive Officer*

Association for Financial Technology
National Industrial Fashion Show & Conference
Ohio Dietetic Association

BARRACK ASSOCIATION MANAGEMENT

21165 Whitfield Place, Suite 105
Potomac Falls, VA 20165
Tel: (703)433-2520 *Fax:* (703)433-0369
website: www.bam-inc.com

David Barrack, *President*

American Edged Products Manufacturers Association
National Association of Public Insurance Adjusters
Washington Technical Professional Forum

WILLIAM BELL ASSOCIATES

P.O. Box 152
Hallowell, ME 04347
Tel: (207)622-4443
Email: feedalliance@gwi.net

William A. Bell, *President*

Maine Association of Conservation Districts
Maine Veterinary Medical Association
New England Brown Egg Council
New England Veterinary Medical Association
Northeast Ag and Feed Alliance

WILLIAM S. BERGMAN ASSOCIATES

1726 M St., N.W., Suite 1101
Washington, DC 20036-4502
Tel: (202)452-1520
Email: dlb@wsba.com

William S. Bergman CAE, *President*

Consumers for World Trade
Friends of the National Institute of Nursing Research
North American Association of State and Provincial Lotteries
NOVA Foundation
Nurses Organization of Veterans Affairs
Outdoor Power Equipment Aftermarket Association

BIRENBAUM AND ASSOCIATES

906 Olive St., Suite 1200
St. Louis, MO 63101-1434
Tel: (314)241-1445 *Fax:* (314)241-1449
Email: birenbaum@birenbaum.org

Dr. Mark Birenbaum, *President*

American Association of Bioanalysts
American Board of Bioanalysis
Association of Corporate Counsel - St. Louis Chapter
Association of Defensive Spray Manufacturers
WaterJet Technology Association

SHIRLEY BISHOP, INC.

2150 107 St. Ave., Suite 205
Seattle, WA 98133-9009
Tel: (206)367-8704
Email: shirley@shirleybishopinc.com
website: www.shirleybishopinc.com

Shirley Bishop, *President*

Association of Academic Health Sciences Library Directors
Association of Fundraising Professionals
Burke Gilman PDA
Commercial Real Estate Women - Seattle Chapter
Council of International Investigators
Greater Seattle Business Ass'n
International Council on Systems Engineering
International Sprout Growers Association
Leave a Legacy of Western WA
Marine Insurance Ass'n of Seattle
National Association of Judiciary Interpreters and Translators
Northwest Development Officers Association
Puget Sound Grantwriters Ass'n
Seattle Soc. of Financial Analysts
United Ways of Washington
Washington Psychiatric Society
Washington Speech and Hearing Association
Washington State Planned Giving Council
Washington State Society of Anesthesiologists

S.J. BLAIR ASSOCIATION MANAGEMENT

P.O. Box 70027
Shawnee Mission, KS 66207
Tel: (913)661-0084

Sharon J. Blair, *Executive Director*

Iowa Jewelers Association
Kansas Jewelers Association
Missouri Jewelers and Watchmakers Association
Nebraska and South Dakota Jewelers Association
Oklahoma Jewelers Association

RALPH J. BLOCH & ASSOCIATES, INC.

1430 N. Astor St., Suite 7A
Chicago, IL 60610-5717
Tel: (312)640-0465 *Fax:* (312)896-5094
Toll Free: (877)551-1984

Ralph J. Bloch, *President*

Association of Pool and Spa Professionals Region 5
Association of Pool and Spa Professionals Region 6

BOSTROM CORP.

230 E. Ohio St., Suite 400
Chicago, IL 60611-3625
Tel: (312)644-0828 *Fax:* (202)216-9646
Email: solutions@bostrom.com
website: www.bostrom.com

1444 I St., N.W., Suite 700
Washington, DC 20005

Jeanne Sheehy, *C.M.O.*

Accreditation Council for Continuing Medical Education
American Society of Access Professionals
Association for Commuter Transportation
Association of Commuter Transportation
Electronic Financial Services Council
Employee Assistance Society of North America
Illinois Speech-Language-Hearing Association
Interlocking Concrete Pavement Institute
International Biometric Society
Microscopy Society of America
Monterey Wine Festival
National Association of Boards of Examiners of Long Term Care Administrators
Society of Women Engineers
Tile Roofing Institute

BRENDEN & ASSOCIATES, INC.

2799 Stratford Road
Richmond, VA 23225
Tel: (804)272-9004

Brenda Ferguson CMP, CAE, *President*

Architectural Woodwork Institute - Virginia Chapter
Recreational Vehicle Dealers Association of Virginia
Virginia Community Colleges Association
Virginia Floorcovering Association
Virginia Horse Council

BROCK AND ASSOCIATES

6114 LaSalle Ave., Box 296
Oakland, CA 94611
Tel: (510)531-7087 *Fax:* (510)531-6759
Email: brock.assoc@att.net
website: www.brockassoc.com

Holly Brock-Cohn, *Principal*

National Association of Temple Administrators

R. FRANKLIN BROWN, JR., INC.

994 Old Eagle School Road, Suite 1019
Wayne, PA 190871802
Tel: (610)971-4850 *Fax:* (610)971-4859
Email: fbrown@cbsa.copper-brass.org

R. Franklin Brown Jr., *President*

Copper and Brass Servicenter Association

BURK AND ASSOCIATES, INCORPORATED

1313 Dolley Madison Blvd., Suite 402
McLean, VA 22101-3926
Tel: (703)790-1745
Email: society@burkinc.com

Brett J. Burk, *President*

American Academy of Health Physics
American Institute of Biological Sciences
Health Physics Society
Semiconductor Environmental Safety and Health Association
Society for Integrative and Comparative Biology
Society for Risk Analysis
Society of Wetland Scientists

THE BURROUGHS MANAGEMENT GROUP, INC.

107 Kilmayne Dr., Suite C
Cary, NC 27511
Tel: (919)469-5858 *Fax:* (919)469-5870

Terence V. Burroughs, *President*

National Pharmaceutical Association

CAIN ASSOCIATES

P.O. Box 1290
New Market, VA 22844
Tel: (540)740-3329 *Fax:* (540)740-4556
Email: jcain@well-drillers.com

Jane Cain, *Executive Officer*

South Atlantic Well Drillers Association
Virginia Water Well Association

CALMETTO MANAGEMENT GROUP, INC.

883 NE Main St.
Simpsonville, SC 29681
Tel: (864)962-2201
Toll Free: (800)605-4633
website: www.calmetto.com

1250 H St. N.W., Suite 901
Washington, DC 20005
Tel: (202)463-8162 *Fax:* (202)463-8155

Ashley Neumann, *Director, Government Relations*

Captive Insurance Council of the District of Columbia, Inc.
Montana Captive Insurers Association
Self Insurance Educational Foundation
Self Insurance Institute of America, Inc.
Self Insurers Publishing Corporation
South Carolina Captive Insurance Association

CAPITAL PUBLIC AFFAIRS, INC.

Five Mapleton Road, Suite 200
Princeton, NJ 08540
Tel: (609)514-2600 *Fax:* (609)514-2660
Email: pzita@cpanj.com
website: www.cpanj.com

Patrizia Zita, *Principal*

Athletic Trainers Society of New Jersey
Building Contractors Association of New Jersey
Community Associations Institute - New Jersey
Driving School Association of New Jersey
Garden State Employment and Training Association
Independent Energy Producers of New Jersey
New Jersey Apartment Association
New Jersey Association of School Administrators
New Jersey Counselors Association
New Jersey Health Officers Association
New Jersey Hemophilia Ass'n
New Jersey Retail Merchants Association
Test Boring Association

CAPITOL CONNECTIONS

26 Exchange St., East, Suite 414
St. Paul, MN 55101-2264
Tel: (651)293-9295
website: www.capitolconnections.com

Ruby Knuton, *Office Manager*

Minnesota Association of County Officers
Minnesota Concrete and Masonry Contractors Association

CAPITOL HILL MANAGEMENT SERVICES, INC.

90 State St., Suite 1009
Albany, NY 12207
Tel: (518)463-8644 *Fax:* (518)463-8656
Email: chms@caphill.com
website: www.caphill.com/

John A. Graziano Jr., *President*

Academy of Certified Archivists
Albany Executives Ass'n
Capitol Region Human Resource Ass'n
National Association of Government Archives and Records Administrators
New York State Cosmetology Association
New York State Society of Opticians
Veterinary Hospital Managers Association

CAPITOL INSIGHTS

P.O. Box 615
45 Memorial Circle, 301
Augusta, ME 04332
website: www.capitolinsights.com/

Cheryl C. Timberlake, *President*

Biotechnology Association of Maine
Center for Innovation in Biotechnology
Maine Beer and Wine Wholesalers

CARUSO ASSOCIATES INC., ASSOCIATION MANGEMENT SERVICES

7853 Arapahoe Court, Suite 2100
Englewood, CO 80112-1361
Tel: (303)694-4728

Fred Caruso CAE, *Chief Executive Officer*

American Physical Therapy Association - Colorado Chapter
Colorado Funeral Directors Association
Colorado Funeral Service Board
Home Care Association of Colorado

CAVANAGH AND ASSOCIATES

600 Cameron St., Suite 309
Alexandria, VA 22314
Tel: (703)340-1654 *Fax:* (703)340-1658

Michael Cavanagh, *Principal*

Council for Electronic Revenue Communication Advancement

CENTER FOR ASSOCIATION GROWTH

1926 Waukegan Road, Suite 1
Glenview, IL 60025-1770
Tel: (847)657-6700 *Fax:* (847)657-6819
Toll Free: (800)492-6462
Email: info@tcag.com
website: www.tcag.com

Carl A. Wangman CAE, *Chairman and Chief Executive Officer*

Commission on Accreditation of Ambulance Services
Illinois Home Care Council
Legal Marketing Association
Society of Trauma Nurses

CENTER FOR ASSOCIATION MANAGEMENT, INC.

77 Rutherford Ave., Suite 3B
Waltham, MA 02453
Tel: (781)647-7004 *Fax:* (781)647-7222
Email: theoffice@camihq.com

Scott Goffstein, *President*

American Marketing Ass'n, Boston Chapter
CASE, District I
Community Running Ass'n
English-Speaking Union - Boston Chapter
Healthcare Financial Management Association
Human Resources Council
International Society for Pharmaceutical Engineering
Massachusetts Speech-Language-Hearing Association
New England Ass'n of Healthcare Philanthropy
Planned Giving Group of Connecticut
Planned Giving Group of New England
SPRI, Inc.

CENTER FOR ASSOCIATION RESOURCES, INC.

1901 N. Roselle Road, Suite 920
Schaumburg, IL 60195
Tel: (847)885-5680 *Fax:* (847)885-5681
Email: rob@associaton-resources.com
website: www.association-resources.com

Robert O. Patterson, *Principal*

Kite Trade Association International
National Association of Executive Recruiters
National Organization of Bar Counsel
Self-Insurance Guaranty Funds of America
Seventh Circuit Bar Association

CERTIFIED ASSOCIATION MANAGEMENT CO.

195 Wekiva Springs Road, Suite 200
Longwood, FL 32779-2552
Tel: (407)774-0207
website: www.associationoffice.net

Thomas A. Monahan CAE, *President*

American Association of Independent News Distributors
Association of Healthcare Internal Auditors
National Concrete Burial Vault Association

CHALLENGE MANAGEMENT, INC.

12300 Ford Road, Suite 135
Dallas, TX 75234
Tel: (972)755-2560 *Fax:* (972)755-2561
Email: info@challenge-management.com
website: www.challenge-management.com

Janine K. Bethscheider Ph.D., *Executive Vice President*

American Soc. for Training and Development - Dallas Chapter
Embroidery Trade Association
International Association for Exhibition Management - Dallas-Fort Worth Chapter
Mystery Shopping Providers Association
Texas Dietetic Association
Texas Society for Medical Staff Services

THE CHARLES GROUP

373 Route 46 W
Buildling E, Suite 215
Fairfield, NJ 07004
Tel: (973)575-1444 *Fax:* (973)575-1445

Carol Davis-Grossman, *Managing Partner*

Healthcare Businesswomen's Association
Public Relations Society of America - New York Chapter

THE CHRISTOPHER GROUP

2300 Bethards Dr., Suite K
Santa Rosa, CA 95045
Tel: (707)544-9639 *Fax:* (707)575-8620
Toll Free: (888)682-2997
website: www.chrisgroup.com

Linda E. Christopher CAE, MPA, *President and Chief Executive Officer*

California Association for Nurse Practitioners

CL ASSOCIATION SERVICES

7208 Forestburg Dr.
Arlington, TX 76001
Tel: (682)518-6008 *Fax:* (682)518-6476

Pamela Bess, *President*

BMC - A Foodservice Sales and Marketing Council
Financial Planning Ass'n - Dallas/Ft. Worth Chapter
Manufacturers Representatives of America
Network of Ingredient Marketing Specialists
Paper and Plastic Representatives Management Council
Power-Motion Technology Representatives Association

CLARION MANAGEMENT RESOURCES, INC.

515 King St., Suite 420
Alexandria, VA 22314-3103
Tel: (703)684-5570 *Fax:* (703)684-6048
website: www.clarionmanagement.com

Carole M. Rogin, *President*

Association of Women in the Metal Industries
Better Hearing Institute
Council of Glass and Ceramic Manufacturers
EPDM Roofing Association
Glass Packaging Institute
Hearing Industries Association
International Society of Hospitality Consultants
Virginia Wineries Association

CLEAN LISTS ASSOCIATES, INC.

122 E. 42nd St., 17th Fl.
New York, NY 10168
Tel: (212)551-1013 *Fax:* (212)551-1107
Email: cleanlists@mindspring.com
website: http://cleanlistsassociates.homestead.com

Burton P. Beck, *Principal*

Nat'l Investor Relations Institute - NYC Chapter
Nat'l Realty Club

CLEMONS & ASSOCIATES, INC.

5024-R Campbell Blvd.
Baltimore, MD 21236-5974
Tel: (410)931-8100
Email: clemonsc@clemonsmgmt.com
website: www.clemonsmgmt.com

Calvin K. Clemons CAE, *President*

Fire Suppression Systems Association
FSSA Educational Foundation
International Society of Restaurant Association Executives
National Association of Sign Supply Distributors
Office Products Manufacturers Association
Office Products Wholesalers Association
OPWA Educational Foundation
Ordinary Citizen
Register of Professional Archeologists

CM SERVICES

800 Roosevelt Road, Suite 312
Glen Ellyn, IL 60137-5839
Tel: (630)858-7337
Email: partner@cmservices.com
website: www.cmservices.com

Rick Church, *President*

American Fence Association
American Fence Association Education Foundation
Automotive Glass Repair Safety Standard Committee
Bearing Specialist Association
Ceramic Tile Distributors Association
Composite Fence and Deck Association
National Church Goods Association
Plastic Pipe and Fittings Association
Plastic Piping Education Foundation
Thermoset Resin Formulators Ass'n
Vinyl Fence, Deck and Railing Manufacturers Association

CMA ASSOCIATION SERVICES GROUP

191 Clarksville Road
Princeton Junction, NJ 08550
Tel: (609)799-6000 *Fax:* (609)799-7032
website: www.thinkcma.com

Jeffrey E. Barnhart, *President and Chief Executive Officer*

Alpha Omega International Dental Fraternity
Association for Convention Operations Management
Communications Advertising and Marketing Association of New Jersey
International Card Manufacturers Association
International Function Point Users Group
International Furnishings and Design Association
Northeast Window and Door Association
Professional Association of Investment Communications Resrouces
Professional Systems Network
Smart Card Alliance

MARSHALL R. COLLINS & ASSOCIATES

117 New London Tpk.
Glastonbury, CT 06033-2457
Tel: (860)657-8587 *Fax:* (860)659-3452
Email: info@marshallrcollins.com
website: www.marshallrcollins.com

Marshall R. Collins, *Executive Officer*

American Society of Travel Agents - Connecticut Chapter
Chamber of Commerce of Northwest Connecticut
Connecticut Association of Not-for-Profit Providers For the Aging
Connecticut Association of Schools/Connecticut Interscholastic Athletic Conference
Connecticut Irrigation Contractors Association
Eastern Connecticut Chamber of Commerce
Greater Danbury Chamber of Commerce
Greater Hartford Property Owners Ass'n
Greater Waterbury Chamber of Commerce
Milford Chamber of Commerce
Quinnipac Chamber of Commerce
YMCAs of Connecticut Public Policy Committee

COMMUNICATION MANAGEMENT, INC.

5443 N. Broadway, Suite 101
Chicago, IL 60640
Tel: (773)561-0802 *Fax:* (773)561-1343
Email: kgboyer@ix.netcom.com

Kevin G. Boyer, *President*

American Soc. for Training & Development - Chicagoland Chapter
Chicago Books Clinic
Organization Development Network of Chicago
Third Coast Marketing
Women's Treatment Center

COMPASS MANAGEMENT COMPANY

8833 Perimeter Park Blvd., Suite 301
Jacksonville, FL 32216
Tel: (904)998-0853 *Fax:* (904)998-0855
website: www.leadingstar.com

Christopher R. Seymour, *Executive Director*

Florida Lipid Associates
Florida Obstetric and Gynecologic Society
Florida Society of Ophthalmology
Florida Surgical Society
National Lipid Association
Southeast Lipid Society
Vitreous Soc. Foundation

COMPREHENSIVE ASSOCIATION CONSULTANTS

P.O. Box 545
Garrisonville, VA 22463
Tel: (540)752-7600 *Fax:* (540)752-9300
Email: cacinfo@cbc.org
website: www.cbc.org/cac

Mary Ann Emely CAE, *Chief Operating Officer*

American Council for Technology
Nat'l Economists Club
Nat'l Economists Club Education Foundation
Univ. of Connecticut Alumni Ass'n - Washington, DC Chapter
Washington Foundation for Psychiatry

CONFERENCE AND MANAGEMENT SPECIALISTS

6740 E. Hampden Ave., Suite 306
Denver, CO 80224
Tel: (303)756-5120
Toll Free: (800)745-3976
Email: karenh@mgmtoffice.com

Karen A. Hone, *Executive Director*

Community Associations Institute - Rocky Mountain Chapter
Health Industry Representatives Association
International Society of Arboriculture
ProGreen Expo
Rocky Mountain Chapter - Electronics Representatives Association
Rocky Mountain Manufacturing and Design Expo

CONVEXX

2260 Corporate Circle, Suite 400
Henderson, NV 89074-7701
Tel: (702)450-7662 *Fax:* (702)450-7732
Toll Free: (877)792-3722
website: www.convexx.com

Susan L. Schwartz CEM, *President*

Exhibition Services and Contractors Association

CONWAY DATA, INC.

35 Technology Pkwy., Suite 150
Norcross, GA 30092
Tel: (770)325-3470 *Fax:* (770)263-8825
Email: larry.edge@conway.com
website: www.conway.com

Lawrence L. Edge, *Vice President*

Industrial Asset Management Council
National Association of Professional Organizers
U.S.-Cuba Trade Association
World Development Federation

CORNERSTONE ASSOCIATION MANAGEMENT

76 S. State St.
Concord, NH 03301-3520
Tel: (603)228-1231 *Fax:* (603)228-2118

Walter Perry, *Owner*

American College of Cardiology - Northern New England Tri-State Chapter
American Society of Home Inspectors - New England Chapter
Association of Pool and Spa Professionals
Granite State Designers and Installers Association
New England Pest Management Association
New Hampshire Association of Residential Care Homes
New Hampshire Estate Planning Council
New Hampshire School Transportation Association

CORNERSTONE COMMUNICATIONS GROUP, INC.

1231 Collier Road, N.W., Suite J
Atlanta, GA 30318
Tel: (404)249-8833
Email: leann@cstone1.com
website: www.cstone1.com

James E. Toney, *President*

Council of Superior Court Clerks of Georgia
Georgia Association of Community Service Bonds
Georgia Society of Anesthesiologists

COURTESY ASSOCIATES

2025 M St. NW
Suite 800
Washington, DC 20036
Tel: (202)331-2000 Ext: 2426 *Fax:* (202)331-0111
Email: info@courtesyassoc.com
website: www.courtesyassociates.com

Leslie Thornton, *Director, Operations*

Association of Meeting Professionals
Commercial Real Estate Women - Washington DC Chapter
International Society for Antiviral Research
Training Officers Conference

THE CRAIG GROUP INC.

37 W. Broad St., Suite 480
Columbus, OH 43215
Tel: (614)241-2222

Philip A. Craig, *President*

American Association of Veterinary Clinicians
Franklin County Trial Lawyers Ass'n
Ohio Association of Convention and Visitor Bureaus
Ohio Licensed Beverage Association
Opticians Association of Ohio
Professional Photographers of Ohio

CRAVEN MANAGEMENT ASSOCIATES

800 Perry Hwy., Suite 3
Pittsburgh, PA 15229
Tel: (412)366-1177 *Fax:* (412)366-8804
Email: info@robertcraven.com
website: www.robertcraven.com

Robert Craven, *Principal*

Council of State Association Presidents

CROW-SEGAL MANAGEMENT COMPANY

1133 W. Morse Blvd., Suite 201
Winter Park, FL 32789-3743
Tel: (407)647-8839

Pat Crow-Segal CAE, *President*

Florida Apartment Association
Florida Auto Dismantlers and Recyclers Association
Florida Library Association
Florida Motorcoach Association
Florida Society of Facial Plastic and Reconstructive Surgery
Florida Society of Otolaryngology-Head and Neck Surgery
Florida Urological Society
MISER Users Group
Mortgage Bankers Association of Florida
National Association of Minority Engineering Program Administrators
Society of University Surgeons

DANCY, PUETZ & ASSOCIATES

7794 Grow Dr.
Pensacola, FL 32514
Tel: (850)484-9987 *Fax:* (850)484-8762
website: www.puetzamc.com/

Jon Dancy, *Chief Executive Officer*

American Radiological Nurses Association
National Gerontological Nursing Association
National Nursing Staff Development Organization
Pediatric Endocronology Nursing Society
Society for Vascular Nursing
Society of Pediatric Nurses

DAVIS/REPLOGLE & ASSOCIATES

4929 Wilshire Blvd., Suite 428
Los Angeles, CA 90010
Tel: (323)937-5514 *Fax:* (323)937-0959

C. James Dowden, *President*

Alliance of Area Business Publications
American Academy of Medical Acupuncture
American College of Surgeons - Southern California Chapter
American Property Tax Counsel
City and Regional Magazine Association
International Facility Management Association - Los Angeles Chapter
Los Angeles OB-GYN Soc.
Los Angeles Surgical Soc.
Medical Acupuncture Research Foundation
OB-GYN Assembly of Southern California
Parenting Publications of America
Shakey's Franchised Dealers Ass'n

DEGNON ASSOCIATES, INC.

6728 Old McLean Village Dr.
McLean, VA 22101-3906
Tel: (703)556-9222
Email: info@degnon.org
website: www.degnon.org

George K. Degnon CAE, *President*

Ambulatory Pediatric Association
American Psychosomatic Society
Association of Christian Therapists
Association of Pediatric Program Directors
International Society for Quality of Life Research
Lawson Wilkins Pediatric Endocrine Society
Rome Foundation
Society for Developmental and Behavioral Pediatrics
Society for Occupational and Environmental Health

DEMPSEY MANAGEMENT SERVICES, INC.

2336 Wisteria Dr., Suite 240
Snellville, GA 30078
Tel: (678)344-6283 *Fax:* (678)344-6299
Email: tdempsey@dempsey-mgt.com
website: www.dempsey-mgt.com

F.G. (Terry) Dempsey Jr., CAE, CEM, *President*

DeckExpo
Professional Deck Builder Magazine

DESANTIS MANAGEMENT GROUP

1950 Old Tustin Ave.
Santa Ana, CA 92705-7812
Tel: (714)550-9155 *Fax:* (714)550-9234
Email: info@desantisgroup.com
website: www.desantisgroup.com

Frank DeSantis CAE, *President*

American Urological Association - Western Section
Asociacion National de Sacerdotes Hispanos
California Urological Association
Inland Empire Urological Society
Orange County Renaissance Foundation

DG&A MANAGEMENT SERVICES, LLC

582 New Loudon Road
Latham, NY 12110
Tel: (518)785-0721
Email: dga@taconic.net

Daniel A. Goldstein CAE, CMP, *Principal*

DILLEHAY MANAGEMENT INC.

295 W. Crossville Road, Suite 130
Roswell, GA 30075
Tel: (770)640-1022 *Fax:* (770)640-1095
website: www.dillehaymgt.com

Charles B. Dillehay, *President*

DON DILLON ASSOCIATES

13140 Coit Road, Suite 320, LB 120
Dallas, TX 75240-5737
Tel: (972)233-9107 *Fax:* (972)490-4219
Email: don@dondillon.com
website: www.dondillon.com

Donald W. Dillon, *President*

Academic Language Therapy Association
American College of Cardiology - Texas Chapter
American Marketing Ass'n-Dallas/Fort Worth Chapter
American Viola Society
Internat'l Dyslexia Ass'n - Dallas Branch
International Society of Bassists
IT Service Management Forum USA
Music Industry Conference
Nat'l Gay Pilots Ass'n
Nat'l Piano Foundation
Nat'l Speakers Ass'n of North Texas
National Association of School Music Dealers
Piano Manufacturers Association International
Retail Print Music Dealers Association
Society of Atherosclerosis Imaging
Texas Art Education Association

DIVERSIFIED CONSULTANTS

P.O. Box 36972
Birmingham, AL 35236
Tel: (256)985-9488

Bob Mosca, *President*

Alabama Association of Temporary and Staffing Services
Alabama Pawnbrokers Association
Alabama Veterans Memorial Foundation
American Ass'n of Physicians
Southern Dental Association

DIVERSIFIED CONSULTANTS, INC.

6405 Metcalf, Suite 503
Shawnee Mission, KS 66202-3929
Tel: (913)384-2345 *Fax:* (913)384-5112
Toll Free: (888)337-6623
Email: tunderwood@dci-kansascity.com
website: www.dci-kansascity.com

Terry Kay Underwood, *President*

DIVERSIFIED MANAGEMENT SERVICES, INC.

525 S.W. Fifth St., Suite A
Des Moines, IA 50309-4501
Tel: (515)282-8192 *Fax:* (515)282-9117
Email: dms@assoc-mgmt.com
website: www.assoc-mgmt.com

Richard L. Goodson Jr., *Chief Executive Officer*

Alliance Bank Group
American Institute of Floral Designers Foundation
Association of Former Agents of the U.S. Secret Service
Florida Staffing Association
International Association of Professional Security Consultants
International Network of Merger and Acquisition Partners
Iowa Greenhouse Growers Association
Iowa Physician Assistants Society
Iowa Podiatric Medical Society
Iowa Rural Health Association
Iowa Speech-Language-Hearing Association
Iowa's Community Bankers
Midwest Conference of Community Bankers
Morris Scholarship Fund, Inc.
National Association for Poetry Therapy
Plumbing-Heating-Cooling Contractors of Iowa
Stadium Managers Association
Temp Net

DOLCI MANAGEMENT SERVICES, INC.

322 Eighth Ave., Suite 501
New York, NY 10001-8001
Tel: (212)206-8301 Ext: 108 *Fax:* (212)645-1147
Email: brandon@dolcimanagement.com
website: www.dolcimanagement.com

Joel A. Dolci CAE, *President*

7 x 24 Exchange
Association of Real Estate Women
Contact Group, The
New York Executive Women in Real Estate
New York Society of Association Executives
New York Society of Association Executives Education and Research Foundation

DRAKE AND COMPANY

16020 Swinging Ridge Road, Suite 300
Chesterfield, MO 63017
Tel: (636)449-5050 *Fax:* (636)449-5051
Email: info@drakeco.com
website: www.drakeco.com

Steven Drake, *President*

Alpha Zeta Foundation
Alpha Zeta Fraternity
American Academy on Communication in Healthcare
Employer Health Network
Middle States Hearth Patio and Barbeque Association
National Christmas Tree Association

DROHAN MANAGEMENT GROUP

12100 Sunset Hills Road, Suite 130
Reston, VA 20190-3221
Tel: (703)437-4377 *Fax:* (703)435-4390
Email: wmd@drohanmgmt.com
website: www.drohanmgmt.com

William M. Drohan CAE, *President*

American Brachytherapy Society
American College of Medical Physics
Association of Insurance Compliance Professionals
Association of University Research Parks
Association of Vascular and Interventional Radiographers
Council of Science Editors
Eastern North American Region of the Biometric Soc.
National Alliance for Accessible Golf
National Association of Corporate Treasurers
National Society of Certified Business Healthcare Consultants
North American Skull Base Society
Sports Lawyers Association

THE DROZ GROUP, LLC

770 Hillcrest Dr., Suite 2
Laguna Beach, CA 92651
Tel: (949)715-6932 *Fax:* (949)715-6931
website: www.thedrozgroup.com

Fred Droz, *President*

Council of Communication Management
Laguna Institute
City of Malibu
Vision Laguna 2030

DYNAMIC MANAGEMENT SERVICES, INC.

551 Fifth Ave., Suite 3025
New York, NY 10176-3099
Tel: (212)687-4010
Email: info@dynamicmanagement.com
website: www.dynamicmanagement.com

Arlene Stock CAE, *President*

Association of Real Estate Women
Capital Markets Credit Analysts Society
Contingency Planning Exchange
Mortgage Bankers Ass'n of New York
Real Estate Lenders Ass'n
Society of Quantitative Analysts

DYNAMIC RESOURCES, INC.

8345 University Blvd., Suite F-1
Des Moines, IA 50325-1168
Tel: (515)225-2323 *Fax:* (515)225-6363

Alda Helvey, *President*

American Society of Landscape Architects - Iowa Chapter
Cosmetologists and Barbers of Iowa
Greater Des Moines Heating & Cooling Association
Institute of Real Estate Management
International Facilities Management Association - Iowa Chapter
Iowa Court Reporters Ass'n
Iowa Heat Pump Association
Iowa Motion Picture Ass'n
Iowa Society of Association Executives
Iowa Talented and Gifted Ass'n
Iowa-Nebraska Drycleaning and Laundry Association
Leave a Legacy - Iowa
Mothers Against Drunk Driving (MADD) - Polk County
Parent Teacher Ass'n of Iowa
United States Ombudsman Association

EASTER ASSOCIATES

630 Country Green Lane
Charlottesville, VA 22902
Tel: (804)977-3716
Email: easter@easterassociates.com

Peter Easter CAE, *President*

Car and Truck Renting and Leasing Association of Virginia
Intelligent Transportation Society of Virginia
Old Dominion Highway Contractors Association
Virginia Aggregates Association
Virginia Association of Broadcasters
Virginia Association of Marine Industries
Virginia Automotive Recyclers Association
Virginia Ready-Mixed Concrete Association

EDUCATION MANAGEMENT AND ACCREDITATION CONSULTING

9739 Denton Dr.
Dallas, TX 75220
Tel: (214)351-0330 *Fax:* (214)351-0354

Philip A. Von Der Heydt, *Contact*

THE ENGINEERING CENTER

One Walnut St.
Boston, MA 02108-3616
Tel: (617)227-5551
Email: tec@engineers.org
website: www.engineers.org

Abbie R. Goodman, *Executive Director*

American Council of Engineering Companies of Massachusetts
Boston Soc. of Civil Engineers Section, ASCE
LSP Ass'n
Massachusetts Association of Land Surveyors and Civil Engineers

BARRY R. EPSTEIN ASSOCIATES, INC.

11922 Waterwood Dr.
Boca Raton, FL 33428-1026
Tel: (561)852-0000 *Fax:* (561)451-0000
Email: pr@publicrelations.nu
website: www.publicrelations.nu

Barry R. Epstein APR, CCE, *President*

Boca Raton Roundtable
Gold Coast Public Relations Council
Together Against Gangs
West Boca Leaders

J. EDGAR EUBANKS AND ASSOCIATES, INC.

3008 Millwood Ave.
Columbia, SC 29205-1807
Tel: (803)252-5646
Toll Free: (800)445-8629
website: www.jee.com

MaryAnn S. Crews, *President*

Audiology Awareness Campaign
Flying Scot Sailing Ass'n
National Association of Bankruptcy Trustees
National Association of Chapter 13 Trustees
National Association of Decorative Fabric Distributors
Reprographic Services Association
South Carolina Defense Trial Attorneys Association
Trustees' Education Network

EURICH MANAGEMENT SERVICES LLC

3225 W. St. Joseph
Lansing, MI 48917
Tel: (517)327-9207 *Fax:* (517)321-0495
Toll Free: (800)984-2884
Email: info@eurich.com
website: www.eurich.com

Donnelly K. Eurich CAE, CMP, *President*

Affiliated Building Services Contractors in Michigan
Air Conditioning Contractors of America - Michigan Chapter
Grand Rapids New Car Dealers Ass'n
Michigan Alliance of Recreational Property Owners
Michigan Institute of Laundering and Dry Cleaning
Michigan Motorcycle Dealers Association
Michigan Movers Association
Michigan Recycling Coalition
Mid American Health Organization
Midwest Carwash Ass'n
Professional Ski Instructors of America - Central

EWALD CONSULTING GROUP

26 E. Exchange St., Suite 500
St. Paul, MN 55101-2264
Tel: (651)290-6260
website: www.ewald.com

David C. Ewald CAE, *President*

American College of Cardiology - Minnesota Chapter
Economic Development Association of Minnesota
Mid-America Economic Development Council
Minnesota Council of Child Caring Agencies
Minnesota Fabricare Institute
Minnesota Forestry Association
Minnesota Glass Association
Minnesota Internet Services Trade Association
Minnesota Legislative Society
Minnesota Magazine and Publications Association
Minnesota Sign Association
Minnesota Water Well Association
United Concrete and Masonry Contractors Ass'n

KATHLEEN EWING & ASSOCIATES

1609 Connecticut Ave., N.W., Suite 200
Washington, DC 20009
Tel: (202)986-0105

Kathleen Ewing, *President*

Art Dealers Association of Greater Washington
Association of International Photography Art Dealers
Institutional and Service Textile Distributors Association

EXECUTIVE ADMINISTRATION, INC.

85 W. Algonquin Road, Suite 550
Arlington Heights, IL 60005-4425
Tel: (847)427-9600 *Fax:* (847)427-9656
Email: mail@execadmin.com

James R. Slawny, *President*

Academy of Osseointegration
American Association of Certified Allergists
American College of Allergy, Asthma and Immunology
American Society for Blood and Marrow Transplantation
American Society of Colon and Rectal Surgeons
Foundation of ACAAI
Illinois Society of Allergy, Asthma and Immunology
James Ewing Foundation
Research Foundation of the American Soc. of Colon and Rectal Surgeons
Society of Surgical Oncology

EXECUTIVE ASSOCIATION MANAGEMENT, INC.

823 Congress Ave., Suite 1300
Austin, TX 78701
Tel: (512)479-0425 *Fax:* (512)495-9031
Email: mmarks@eami.com
website: www.eami.com

Michael T. Marks, *President*

Austin Auto Show
Austin Automobile Dealers Ass'n
College Band Directors National Association
Metro Houston Ford Dealers Advertising Committee
National Association of Professional Employer Organizations - Texas Chapter
Recreational Vehicle Dealers Association of Texas
South Texas Ford Dealers Advertising Fund
South Texas Lincoln Mercury Dealers Advertising Fund
Southwestern Ice Association
Texas Assisted Living Association
Texas Automotive Recyclers Association
Texas Motorcycle Dealers Association

EXECUTIVE DIRECTOR, INC.

555 E. Wells St., Suite 1100
Milwaukee, WI 53202-3823
Tel: (414)276-6445
Email: info@execinc.com
website: www.execinc.com

David Baumann, *Chief Operating Officer*

American Academy of Allergy, Asthma, and Immunology
American Academy of Emergency Medicine
American Academy of Nursing
American Association of Medical Society Executives
American College of Mohs Micrographic Surgery and Cutaneous Oncology
American Society for Experimental NeuroTherapeutics
American Society of Gene Therapy
Cancer Vaccine Consortium
Central Society for Clinical Research
Clinical Immunology Society
Collegium Internationale Allergologicum
Council for Accreditation in Occupational Hearing Conservation
Federation of Clinical Immunology Societies
Internat'l Soc. for Biological Therapy of Cancer
International Society for Biological Therapy of Cancer
Movement Disorder Society
Nat'l Anemia Action Council
Scoliosis Research Society
Society for Clinical Data Management
Society for the Advancement of Blood Management
Society of Behavioral Medicine
World Allergy Organization - IACCI
Wound Ostomy Continence Nursing Certification Board

EXECUTIVE MANAGEMENT ASSOCIATES

1804 W. Burbank Blvd.
Burbank, CA 91506-1315
Tel: (818)843-5660
Email: exmgtassoc@aol.com
website: www.emaoffice.com/

Larry Newell, *Partner*

Association of Educational Therapists
California School Food Services Association
Financial Planning Ass'n - Los Angeles Chapter
Los Angeles Business Travel Ass'n
Risk and Insurance Management Soc. - Los Angeles Chapter
Soc. of Logistics Engineers - District 9
Southern California Ass'n for Financial Professionals
Western Pension and Benefits Conference - Los Angeles Chapter

EXECUTIVE MANAGEMENT SERVICES, INC.

P.O. Box 13089
Tallahassee, FL 32317
Tel: (850)878-3134 *Fax:* (850)878-1291
Toll Free: (800)530-3134
Email: ems-rac@hotmail.com
website: www.ems-mp.com

Robert S. Rhinehart, *President*

American Association of Business Valuation Specialists
American Association of Physicians and Health Care Professionals
American Association of Processors
Amusement and Music Owners Association of Florida
Elephant Marketing Services, Inc.

EXECUTIVE SUPPORT, INC.

202 Forest Ave.
Oak Park, IL 60302
Tel: (708)383-0620 *Fax:* (708)383-2095
website: www.executivesupportinc.com

Susan Roberts, *President*

Association of Specialized and Professional Accreditors
Canadian Club of Chicago
Chicago Jewelers Ass'n
International Association of Corporate and Professional Recruitment

EXECUTIVES CONSULTANTS, INC.

10210 Leatherleaf Court
Manassas, VA 20111-4245
Tel: (703)257-1512
website: www.assnctr.com

Robert C. LaGasse, *President*

Garden Writers Association
Hydroponic Merchants Association
Mulch and Soil Council

FANNING GROUP, INC.

P.O. Box 479
Hanson, MA 02341-0479
Tel: (781)293-4100 *Fax:* (781)294-0808
website: www.fanningnet.com

Deborah Fanning CAE, *President*

The Art and Creative Materials Institute
Council for Art Education

NORMAN FERACHI AND ASSOCIATES, INC.

603 Europe St.
Baton Rouge, LA 70802
Tel: (225)387-3261
Email: ferachi@aol.com

Norman C. Ferachi, *Principal*

Association of Louisiana Lobbyists
Louisiana Association of Chiefs of Police
Louisiana Association of Criminal Defense Lawyers
Louisiana Association of Plumbing-Heating-Cooling Contractors
Louisiana Soft Drink Association

FERNLEY & FERNLEY, INC.

100 N. 20th St., 4th Floor
Philadelphia, PA 19103-1443
Tel: (215)564-3484
Email: spine@fernley.com
website: www.fernley.com

Suzanne C. Pine, *Executive Vice President*

AMCinstitute
Association for High Technology Distribution
Aviation Distributors and Manufacturers Association International
CFA of Philadelphia
Commercial Development and Marketing Association
Craft Retailers Association for Tomorrow
Federation of Exchange Accomodators
Gases and Welding Distributors Association
Hatteras 1510 Club
Industrial Supply Association
International Association of Ice Cream Vendors
National Distributor Alliance
National Field Selling Association
North American Horticultural Supply Association
Security Hardware Distributors Association
Tin Stabilizers Association
Water and Sewer Distributors of America
Wharton Private Equity Partners
Wheeltime Network
Wood Machinery Manufacturers of America

FIRSTPOINT MANAGEMENT RESOURCES

1500 Sunday Dr., Suite 102
Raleigh, NC 27607
Tel: (919)787-5181 *Fax:* (919)787-4916
Email: dfeild@firstpointresources.com

David Feild, *Executive Vice President*

American College of Cardiology - North Carolina Chapter
American College of Epidemiology
American Society for Cytotechnology
American Society of Echocardiography
Cardiovascular Credentialing International
Controlled Environment Testing Association
Internat'l Soc. for Adult Congenital Cardiac Disease
International Lactation Consultant Association
Multi-Housing Laundry Association
National Board of Echocardiography
North Carolina Board of Dietetics and Nutrition
North Carolina Board of Podiatry Examiners
North Carolina Dietetic Association
North Carolina Land Title Association
North Carolina Soc. of Healthcare Attorneys
Society of American Travel Writers
Southern Innkeepers Association
Triangle Area Hotel-Motel Ass'n
U.S. Breast Feeding Committee

FITZGERALD MANAGEMENT CORP.

2850 S. Ocean Blvd., Suite 114
Palm Beach, FL 33480-6205
Tel: (561)533-0991 *Fax:* (561)533-7466
Email: fitzgeraldfscott@bellsouth.net
website: www.smacentral.org

Kathryn R. Fitzgerald, *Executive Vice President*

Screen Manufacturers Association
Window Council

FLYNN MANAGEMENT ASSOCIATES

100 Roscommon Dr., Suite 320
Middletown, CT 06457
Tel: (860)635-6300 *Fax:* (860)635-6400
Toll Free: (877)521-0103
Email: simon.flynn@worldnet.att.net
website: www.flynnmgt.com/about.html

Simon A. Flynn, *President*

American College of Cardiology - Connecticut Chapter
Connecticut Lodging Association
Connecticut Restaurant Association
Connecticut Tooling and Machining Association
Connecticut Veterinary Medical Association

FSA GROUP

304 W. Liberty St., Suite 201
Louisville, KY 40202-3011
Tel: (502)583-3783 *Fax:* (502)589-3602
Email: fsa@hqtrs.com
website: www.fsagroup.net

Lieann O'Brien, *Chairman*

American Cheese Society
American Institute of Wine and Food
American Society for Healthcare Food Service Administrators
Council of Independent Restaurants of America
Foodservice Consultants Society International
Internat'l Ass'n of Culinary Professionals Foundation
International Association of Culinary Professionals
International Food Service Executives' Association
Mobile Industrial Caterers' Association International
National Association of Equipment Leasing Brokers
Society for Foodservice Management
Women Chefs and Restaurateurs

G GROUP MANAGEMENT FOR ASSOCIATIONS

P.O. Box 330520
San Francisco, CA 94133
Tel: (415)399-9702

George LaBar, *President*

GACHES BRADEN BARBEE & ASSOCIATES

825 S. Kansas Ave., Suite 500
Topeka, KS 66612
Tel: (781)233-4512 *Fax:* (781)233-2206

Ron Gaches, *President*

ACEC of Kansas
Kansas Association of Defense Counsel
Kansas Association of Dental Hygienists' Associations
Kansas Association of Financial Services
Kansas Association of Insurance and Financial Advisors
Kansas Self-Insurers Association
Kansas Society of Professional Engineers

GATEKEEPER MANAGEMENT SERVICES

20335 Ventura Blvd., Suite 310
Woodland Hills, CA 91364-2144
Tel: (818)610-0320 *Fax:* (818)610-0323

Gary W. Larson, *President*

North American Society of Scaffold Professionals
Scaffold Industry Association
SIA Educational Foundation
SIA Training Program

DONALD H. GILBERT & ASSOCIATES

5360 Workman Mill Road
Whittier, CA 90601-2258
Tel: (562)908-6131
Email: dongilbertassoc@aol.com

Jane A. Gilbert, *Principal*

American Concrete Institute - Southern California Chapter
Southern California KFC Franchisee Association
Structural Engineers Ass'n of Southern California

GIUFFRIDA ASSOCIATES

204 E St., N.E.
Washington, DC 20002
Tel: (202)547-6340 *Fax:* (202)547-6348
Email: info@giuffrida.com
website: www.giuffrida.com

Annette Summers, *Chief Operating Officer*

Ass'n of Career Management Consulting Firms - North America Chapter
Association for Convention Marketing Executives
Association of Career Firms International
Association of Career Professionals International
Institute of Career Certification International

GREAT NORTH MOUNTAIN MANAGEMENT

P.O. Box 76
Bayse, VA 22810
Tel: (540)856-2111 *Fax:* (540)856-2441
Email: gnmm@lbjunlimited.com

Betty Wilson, *Principal*

GREAT WESTERN ASSOCIATION MANAGEMENT, INC.

7995 E. Prentice Ave., Suite 100
Greenwood Village, CO 80111
Tel: (303)770-2220 *Fax:* (303)770-1614
Email: info@gwami.com
website: www.gwami.com

Karen Wojdyla, *President*

Air and Surface Transport Nurses Ass'n
Colorado Payphone Association
Colorado Turfgrass Foundation
National Hearing Conservation Association
Real Estate Service Providers Council - Colorado Chapter
Rocky Mountain Regional Turfgrass Association

GROOME MARKETING ASSOCIATES

36 Taylor Road
Princeton, NJ 08540
Tel: (908)329-6706

James J. Groome CMP, CAE, *President*

GROUP CONCEPTS, INC.

1240 N. Jefferson, Suite G
Anaheim, CA 92807
Tel: (714)632-6800
Email: gci@speed.net

Kelly William Ramirez, *President*

California Associated Truckers
California Furniture Manufacturers Association
California Locksmiths Association
Industrial Caterers Association

GROUP MANAGEMENT SERVICES, LLC

P.O. Box 11594
Montgomery, AL 36111-0594
Tel: (334)260-7970 *Fax:* (334)272-7128
Email: larry@gmsal.com

Larry A. Vinson CAE, *Principal*

Alabama Civil Justice Reform Committee
Alabama Council of Association Executives
Alabama Dietetic Association
Alabama Food Service and Nutrition Expo
Alabama Self-Insurers Association
Solid Waste Association of North America - Alabama Chapter

GROUP MANAGEMENT, INC.

4633 E. Broadway Blvd., Suite 101
Tucson, AZ 85711-3511
Tel: (520)323-1115 *Fax:* (520)323-3399

Donna Rainville, *Director, Administration*

American Institute of Architects - Southern Arizona Chapter
Arizona Multihousing Ass'n - Souther Arizona Chapter
Arizona Travel Parks Association
Cornerstone Building Foundation

GROUP MANAGMENT RESOURCES

132 Great Road, Suite 200
Stow, MA 01775-1189
Tel: (978)897-9808 *Fax:* (978)897-5442
Email: laurenhunt@mindspring.com

Lauren Hunte, *President*

Nat'l Commission for Electrologist Certification

THE GUILD ASSOCIATES, INC.

389 Main St., Suite S-202
Malden, MA 02148-5017
Tel: (781)397-8870 *Fax:* (781)397-8887
Email: lguild@guildassoc.com

Richard S. Guild CAE, *President*

Association of Fundraising Professionals - Massachusetts Chapter
Boston Economic Club
Coin Machine Industries Association of Massachusetts
New England Marine Trade Association

HAB ASSOCIATES, INC.

142 E. Ontario, #1700
Chicago, IL 60611
Tel: (312)475-3719 *Fax:* (312)951-9475
Email: bburns@nccnet.org

Betty Burns CAE, *President*

Center for Certification Preparation and Review
Nat'l Certification Corp. for the Obstetric, Gynecologic, and Neonatal Nursing Specialties

HARRY HANSEN MANAGEMENT, INC.

151 Herricks Road, Suite 1
Garden City Park, NY 11040
Tel: (516)739-2510 *Fax:* (516)739-3803
Toll Free: (800)284-6228
Email: info@hansen-management.com
website: www.hansen-management.com

Harry A. Hansen, *President*

Fixed Income Analysts Society
Risk Management Ass'n - New York Chapter

the HARRINGTON co.

4248 Park Glen Road
Minneapolis, MN 55416-4758
Tel: (952)928-4666 *Fax:* (952)929-1318
Email: jharrington@harringtoncompany.com
website: www.harringtoncompany.com

Ed A. Harrington CAE, *Chairman*

Aircraft Builders Council
American Institute of Professional Association Group Insurance Administrators
Association Correctional Food Service Affiliates
Captive Insurance Companies Association
Coalition of Alternative Risk Funding Mechanisms
Dr. Anthony Downs Annual Real Estate Outlook
Harmonie Group
Harrington Foundation
Indoor Environmental Standards Organization
Institute of Real Estate Management - Minnesota Chapter #45
Midwest Direct Marketing Association
Minnesota Academy of Physician Assistants
Minnesota Heating and Cooling Association
Minnesota Public Health Association
Minnesota Real Estate Services Association
Nat'l Ass'n of Subrogation Professionals
National Association of Home Inspectors
National Association of Industrial and Office Properties - Minnesota Chapter
National Association of Minority Contractors
National Risk Retention Association
Northland Heat Pump Association
PLUS Foundation
Professional Liability Underwriting Society
Registered Professional Liability Underwriters
World Captive Forum

HARRINGTON MANAGEMENT, INC.

305 Second Ave.
Waltham, MA 02451
Tel: (781)895-9080 *Fax:* (781)895-9088
Email: wharrington@harringtoninc.com
website: www.harringtoninc.com

Wesley E. Harrington CAE, *President*

American Lithotripsy Society
Meeting Professionals International - New England Chapter
Urology Society of America

HARRIS MANAGEMENT GROUP, INC.

335 Beard St.
Tallahassee, FL 32303-6227
Tel: (850)222-6000 *Fax:* (850)222-6002

Robert Skrob CAE, *President*

Automatic Merchandising Association of Florida
Florida Dental Hygiene Association
Florida Motorcycle Dealers Association
Florida Movers and Warehousemen's Association
Florida Occupational Therapy Association
Florida Skin Cancer Foundation
Florida Society of Anesthesiologists
Florida Society of Dermatologists
Florida Society of OB-GYN
Professional Opticians of Florida

HAUCK & ASSOCIATES, INC.

1255 23rd St. NW, Suite 200
Washington, DC 20037-1174
Tel: (202)452-8100 *Fax:* (202)833-3636
Email: hauckinfo@hauck.com
website: www.hauck.com

Sheldon J. Hauck, *President and Chief Executive Officer*

American Academy of Wound Management
American Coke and Coal Chemicals Institute
Association for Governmental Leasing and Finance
Association of Cancer Executives
DFK Internat'l/USA
Intellectual Property Owners Association
International Intellectual Property Association
International Oxygen Manufacturers Association
Nat'l Ass'n of Healthcare Consultants Foundation
National Association of Healthcare Consultants
National Council of Intellectual Property Law Associations
Open Travel Alliance
Soy Protein Council

ROBERT HERZOG INC./ASSOCIATION MANAGEMENT SERVICES

N 27 W 23957 Paul Road, Suite 202
Pewaukee, WI 53072
Tel: (262)650-0583

Michael J. Herzog, *Vice President*

RICHARD HESS AND ASSOCIATES

6412 N. Santa Fe
Suite C
Oklahoma City, OK 73116
Tel: (405)424-1775 *Fax:* (405)424-1781
Email: rhess@rhess.com

Dan Fitzpatrick, *Account Executive*

Metro Area Development Corporation
Nat'l Ass'n of Sonic Drive-In Franchisees
Natural Resources Education Foundation
Oklahoma L-P Gas Research, Marketing and Safety Commission
Oklahoma Propane Gas Association
Oklahoma Psychological Association
Oklahoma Society of Association Executives
Oklahomans for Energy and Jobs

HILL MANAGEMENT COMPANY

175 W. 200 South, Suite 2012
Salt Lake City, UT 84101
Tel: (801)521-8340 *Fax:* (801)521-8360
Email: hillmgmt@aol.com

John P. Hill, *Executive Director*

Rocky Mountain Gas Association
Utah Petroleum Marketers and Retailers Association

HILLIARD ASSOCIATION MANAGEMENT, INC.

P.O. Box 6524
Raleigh, NC 27628
Tel: (919)787-5859

William N. Hilliard, *President*

American College of Physicians-North Carolina Chapter
North Carolina College of Emergency Physicians
North Carolina College of Internal Medicine
North Carolina Society of Anesthesiologists

HOLLAND-PARLETTE ASSOCIATES, INC

575 Market St., #2125
San Francisco, CA 94105-3411
Tel: (415)927-5725 *Fax:* (415)927-5726
Email: info@hp-assoc.com
website: www.hp-assoc.com

Kerry Parker CAE, *Principal*

American Soc. of Civil Engineers - San Francisco Section
American Society of Orthopaedic Physician's Assistants
California Society of Addiction Medicine
Marketing Association of Credit Unions
Medical Marketing Association
National Association of Orthopedic Technicans

Pacific Dermatologic Association
Society for Free Radical Biology and Medicine
Society for Pediatric Dermatology
Structural Engineers Ass'n of Northern California
Western Occupational and Environmental Medical Association
Western Occupational Health Conference
Women's Dematologic Society
Women's Dermatologic Society Foundation

HOST MANAGEMENT GROUP

2365 Harrodsburg Road, Suite A-325
Lexington, KY 40509
Tel: (859)226-4260 *Fax:* (859)226-4445
Email: hostpr@hostcommunications.com
website: www.hostcommunications.com

Lynne Walker McNees, *Vice President*

American Volleyball Coaches Association
International Coach Federation
International Spa Association
National Tour Association
Quest/J.D. Edwards User Group

BETSY HOUSTON

910 17th St., N.W., Suite 800
Washington, DC 20036
Tel: (202)466-8744
Email: betsyhou@ix.netcom.com

Betsy Houston, *Principal*

Federation of Materials Socs.

HUGHES & CRONIN PUBLIC AFFAIRS STRATEGIES

700 Plaza Middlesex
Middletown, CT 06457
Tel: (860)347-9955 *Fax:* (860)343-0014
Email: cjhughes@hughesandcronin.com
website: www.hughesandcronin.com

Carroll J. Hughes, *President*

Connecticut Bus Association
Connecticut Catholic Hospital Council
Connecticut Package Stores Association

HUNT MANAGEMENT SYSTEMS

Two Wisconsin Circle, Suite 670
Chevy Chase, MD 20815
Tel: (301)718-7722
Email: fred@spbatpa.com

Frederick D. Hunt Jr., *President*

Society of Professional Benefit Administrators

IDP ASSOCIATION MANAGEMENT

P.O. Box 1420
Cherry Hill, NJ 08034
Email: askus@idpcreative.com
website: www.idpcreative.com

3245 Freemansburg Ave.
Palmer, PA 18045-7118

Paul Prass, *President*

Fluid Power Distributors Association
Fluid Power Society
Philadelphia Suburban Gas Ass'n

IMI ASSOCIATION EXECUTIVES

P.O. Box 3159
Durham, NC 27715-3159
Tel: (919)383-0044
website: www.imiae.com

Stevie Hughes, *President and Chief Executive Officer*

Atlantic Coast Exposition
Carolina/Virginia Dairy Products Association
Council of Multiple Listing Service
National Association of County Recorders, Election Officials and Clerks
National Association of Professional Background Screeners
National Public Records Research Association
North Carolina Amusement Machine Association
North Carolina Pest Control Association
North Carolina School Counselor Association
North Carolina Vending Association
Property Records Industry Association
Real Estate Information Professionals Association
South Carolina Automatic Merchandising Association
Virginia Automatic Merchandising Association

INFORM, INC.

P.O. Box 1708
Hickory, NC 28603
Tel: (828)322-7766

Paul F. Fogleman, *Executive Director*

Carolina Hosiery Association

INNOVATIVE ASSOCIATION SERVICES, INC.

P.O. Box 130220
Birmingham, AL 35213
Tel: (205)802-7551 *Fax:* (205)802-7553

Byron W. McCain CAE, *President*

Alabama Information Technology Ass'n
Alabama Marine and Recreation Ass'n
Birmingham Hospitality Ass'n
Speech and Hearing Ass'n of Alabama

INNOVATIVE MANAGEMENT ASSOCIATES, INC.

P.O. Box 589
Olney, MD 20830-0589
Tel: (301)924-0633 *Fax:* (301)924-4124
Email: ima@imaservices.net

Jean R. Rankin CAE, *President*

Mortgage Bankers Association of Metropolitan Washington

INTEGRATED CAPITOL STRATEGIES

120 Perkins Road
Madbury, NH 03823
Tel: (603)742-2212 *Fax:* (603)742-2116
Email: intcapstrat@comcast.net

Clark T. Corson, *President*

Council of Independent Tobacco Manufacturers of America (CITMA)
New Hampshire Wholesale Beverage Association
Personal Watercraft Industry Association

INTEGRATED SOLUTIONS AND SERVICES, INC.

506 Green Hill Beach Road
Wakefield, RI 02879
Tel: (914)635-2388
Email: jhpowers@ibm.net

John H. Powers, *President*

International Association of Electronics Recyclers

INTERACTIVE MANAGEMENT, INC.

11166 Huron St., Suite 27
Aurora, CO 80234-3339
Tel: (303)433-4446 *Fax:* (303)458-0002

Roberta Bourn, *President*

American Planning Association - Colorado Chapter
Colorado Open Systems Consortium
Portfolio Management Institute
Professional Engineers of Colorado
Rocky Mountain Fabricare Association
Rocky Mountain Hearth Products Association

INTERNATIONAL ASSOCIATION MANAGERS

1224 N. Nokomis NE
Alexandria, MN 56308
Tel: (320)763-5190 *Fax:* (320)763-9290
Email: iami@iami.org

Robert G. Johnson, *Executive Director*

Association of Construction Inspectors
Environmental Assessment Association
Housing Inspection Foundation
Internat'l Trade Ass'n
International Real Estate Institute
International Society of Meeting Planners
International Travel Writers and Editors Association
National Association of Real Estate Appraisers
National Association of Review Appraisers and Mortgage Underwriters
Professional Women's Appraisal Association

INTERNATIONAL MEETINGS, INC.

7315 Wisconsin Ave.
Suite 215E
Washington, DC 20814-3202
Tel: (301)718-9757 *Fax:* (301)718-9756
Toll Free: (800)227-5210
Email: imi@imimtg.com
website: www.imimtg.com

Suzette Gomolisky, *Chief Executive Officer*

American Association for Women Radiologists
American Society of Emergency Radiology
Fleischner Society
International Pension and Employee Benefits Lawyers Association
Princeton Club of Washington
Society for Pediatric Radiology
Society for Uroradiology
Society of Gastrointestinal Radiologists

JAFIC ASSOCIATION MANAGEMENT, INC.

P.O. Box 180458
Casselberry, FL 32718-0458
Tel: (407)260-1313

Janice Ficarrotto, *President*

Air Conditioning Contractors Ass'n - Central Florida
Air Conditioning Contractors Ass'n Apprenticeship Program
Florida Air Conditioning Contractors Association
Florida Ass'n of Electrical Contractors - Central Florida
Florida Ass'n of Electrical Contractors Apprenticeship Program
Florida Association of Electrical Contractors

ANTHONY J. JANNETTI, INC.

E. Holly Ave.
P.O. Box 56
Pitman, NJ 08071-0056
Tel: (856)256-2300
Email: ajjinc@ajj.com
website: www.ajj.com

Anthony J. Jannetti, *President*

Academy of Medical-Surgical Nurses
American Academy of Ambulatory Care Nursing
American Nephrology Nurses Association
Certification Board for Urologic Nurses and Associates
Dermatology Nurses' Association
Dermatology Nursing Certification Board
International Association of Forensic Nurses
NAON Foundation
Nephrology Nursing Certification Commission
Plastic Surgical Nursing Certification Board
Society of Urologic Nurses and Associates

JONES McADEN AND ASSOCIATES

P.O. Box 11937
Columbia, SC 29211-1937
Tel: (803)771-4271
Email: joe@jma-associations.com
website: www.jma-associations.com

Joe S. Jones III, *Owner*

Consulting Engineers of South Carolina
South Carolina Civil Justice Coalition
South Carolina Society of Professional Engineers

JTL & ASSOCIATES, INC.

6057 Arlington Expwy.
P.O. Box 8826
Jacksonville, FL 32239
Tel: (904)724-3003

John T. Lowe, *President*

Jacksonville Marine Ass'n

KANE GLOBAL COMMUNICATIONS

6081 Central Park Dr.
Columbus, OH 43231
Tel: (614)797-2262 *Fax:* (614)797-2264
website: www.superabrasives.org

Kathryn A. Kane, *Manager, Business*

Industrial Diamond Association of America

KARE ASSOCIATION MANAGEMENT SERVICES

2170 S. Parker Road, Suite 255
Denver, CO 80231-5710
Tel: (303)750-9764

Karen M. Renshaw CAE, *President*

Colorado Association of Chiefs of Police
Colorado Association of Insurance and Financial Advisors
Colorado Human Resource Association
Nat'l Ass'n of Insurance and Financial Advisors - Denver Chapter
Rocky Mountain Region Professional Products Association
Soc. of Financial Service Professionals - Rocky Mountain Chapter

KAUTTER MANAGEMENT GROUP, INC.

222 S. Westmonte Dr., Suite 101
Altamonte Springs, FL 32714
Tel: (407)774-7880
Email: kmg-assn@worldnet.att.net

Willard S. Kautter CAE, *President*

American Society of Ophthalmic Plastic and Reconstructive Surgery
Florida Academy of Physicians Assistants
Florida Association of Nurse Anesthetists
Florida Association of Self Insurance
Florida Association of Special Districts
Florida Association of Speech-Language Pathologists and Audiologists
Florida CCIM Chapter
Florida Court Reporters Association
Florida Lipid Associates
Florida Magazine Association
Florida Vacation Rental Managers Association
Legal Image Network Communications
Michael J. Reid Memorial Scholarship Fund
NAPR Services, Inc.
Nat'l Ass'n of Indistrial and Office Properties - Central Florida
National Association of Physician Recruiters
Society for Technological Advancement of Reporting
Space Coast Apartment Ass'n
U.S. Optimist Dinghy Ass'n

KEENEY CORPORATION, INC.

118 N. Eighth St.
Richmond, VA 23219-2306
Tel: (804)643-0312
Email: keeneycorp@aol.com

Bruce B. Keeney Sr., *President*

Association of Independent Funeral Homes of Virginia
Virginia Automotive Repair Association
Virginia Gasoline Marketers Council
Virginia Optometric Association

THE KELLEN COMPANY

5775G Peachtree-Dunwoody Road, Suite 500
Atlanta, GA 30342-1507
Email: kco@kellencompany.com
website: www.kellencompany.com

1156 15th St., N.W., Suite 900
Washington, DC 20005

Peter S. Rush, *Chief Executive Officer*

American College of Tax Counsel
American Tax Policy Institute
Apple Products Research and Education Council
Asphalt Roofing Manufacturers Association
Association for Dressings and Sauces
Association of Fund-Raising Distributors and Suppliers
Builders Hardware Manufacturers Association
Calorie Control Council
Comics Magazine Association of America
Concord Grape Association
Distinguished Restaurants of North America
Educational Leaders, Inc.
Exhibit Designers and Producers Association
Exhibit Designers and Producers Foundation
Food Update
Food Update Foundation
GCM Guild
Greeting Card Association
Healthcare Convention and Exhibitors Association
Home Fashion Products Association
Home Fashion Products Foundation
Home Infusion Therapy Franchise Owners Ass'n
Horseradish Information Council
International Food Additives Council
International Formula Council
International Glutamate Technical Committee
International Inflight Food Service Association
International Interior Design Association - New York Chapter
International Jelly and Preserve Association
Juice Products Association
Lignin Institute
Messenger Courier Association of the Americas
Nat'l Elder Law Foundation
Nat'l Guardianship Foundation
National Academy of Elder Law Attorneys
National Association of Margarine Manufacturers
National Candle Association
National Guardianship Association
National Institute of Oilseed Products
National Pasta Association
National Pecan Shellers Association
National Society for Healthcare Foodservice Management
New York Women in Communications
New York Women in Communications Foundation
New York Women's Agenda
Pima Dental Study Club
Research Chefs Association
Research Chefs Foundation
Roof Coatings Manufacturers Association
Saguaro Business Club
Southern Arizona Veterinary Medical Ass'n
Southern Arizona Veterinary Medical Ass'n Foundation
Vinegar Institute
Weather Risk Management Ass'n
Window Covering Manufacturers Association
Window Covering Safety Council
Window Coverings Manufacturers Association
Worldwide Printing Thermographers Ass'n

KELLEN COMPANY

1604 N. Country Club Road
Tucson, AZ 85716
Tel: (520)325-1055

Deborah J. Barnett, *Vice President*

Nat'l Elder Law Foundation
National Academy of Elder Law Attorneys
National Association of Professional Geriatric Care Managers
Southern Arizona Veterinary Medical Ass'n

KELSEY MANAGEMENT SERVICES

1726 M St., N.W., Suite 403
Washington, DC 20036
Tel: (202)822-8600 *Fax:* (202)822-8686
website: www.kelseymgmt.com/

Eric G. Scharf CAE, *President*

College Savings Foundation

KIMBALL & ASSOCIATES INTERNATIONAL

8233 Old Courthouse Road, Suite 210
Vienna, VA 22182
Tel: (703)556-9300 *Fax:* (703)556-9301
Email: pkimball@kimbal.com
website: www.kimbal.com

Philip Kimball, *President*

Nat'l Honey Board Export Program
National Association of the Remodeling Industry - Metropolitan Washington Chapter
National Dry Bean Council
United States Apple Export Council

KING STRINGFELLOW GROUP

2105 Laurel Bush Road, Suite 200
Bel Air, MD 21015
Tel: (443)640-1030 *Fax:* (443)640-1031
Email: info@ksgroup.org
website: www.ksgroup.org/contact.htm

Jackwelyn King, *Account Executive*

American Veterinary Distributors Association
Flexographic Prepress Platemakers Association
Lawn and Garden Marketing and Distribution Association
Maryland Recyclers Coalition
National States Geographic Information Council
Pet Industry Distributors Association
Postcard and Souvenir Distributors Association
Safety Equipment Distributors Association
Spill Control Association of America
Web Sling and Tiedown Association

KLEIN & SAKS GROUP

1200 G St. NW
Suite 800
Washington, DC 20005
Tel: (202)835-0952 *Fax:* (202)835-0155

Michael DiRienzo, *Managing Director*

Internat'l Cyanide Management Institute
Silver Institute

KNIGHT ENTERPRISES LTD.

4840 Bob Billings Pkwy., Suite 1000
Lawrence, KS 660493876
Tel: (785)843-5511 *Fax:* (785)843-7555
Email: knight@knightltd.com
website: www.knightltd.com

Scott L. McKinney, *Executive Vice President*

Midwest Roofing Contractors Association
National Frame Builders Association

KRISSOFF & ASSOCIATES, INC.

Three Church Circle, PMB 250
Annapolis, MD 21401-1933
Tel: (410)267-0023 *Fax:* (410)267-7546
Email: krissoff@krissoff.org

Michael R. Krissoff, *President*

Asphalt Emulsion Manufacturers Association
Asphalt Recycling and Reclaiming Association
International Slurry Surfacing Association
Transportation Lawyers Association

L&L MANAGEMENT SERVICES, INC.

5841 Cedar Lake Road, Suite 204
Minneapolis, MN 55416
Tel: (952)545-6204 *Fax:* (952)545-6073
website: www.llmsi.com

Linda Scher, *President*

American Neurological Association
American Society of Neuroimaging
American Society of Neurorehabilitation
Ass'n of University Professors of Neurology
International Academy of Trial Lawyers
North American Neuro-Ophthalmology Society
Organization of Human Brain Mapping

LAGNIAPPE ASSOCIATES, INC.

1016 Rosser St.
Conyers, GA 30012
Tel: (770)388-7979
Email: laillw@mindspring.com

Lynn L. White, *President*

Atlanta Ass'n of Insurance and Financial Advisors
Child Care Consortium
Georgia Child Care Leadership Forum

LARIMER ASSOCIATION & SPECIAL EVENTS RESOURCES/EUREKA CONNECTION

37 W. Broad St., Suite 480
Columbus, OH 43215
Tel: (614)358-2828 *Fax:* (614)241-2215
Toll Free: (888)538-7352
Email: larimer@eurekaconnection.com
website: www.eurekaconnection.com

Ted Pierce, *President*

Antique and Amusement Photographers International

C.A. LARSEN AND ASSOCIATES

309 E. Rand Road, Suite 365
Arlington Heights, IL 60004
Tel: (847)577-7200 *Fax:* (847)577-7276
Toll Free: (800)424-8737
Email: clarsen3@earthlink.net

C. Andrew Larsen CAE, CCM, *President*

Lightning Protection Institute
Wiring Harness Manufacturers Association

LEGISLATIVE AND ASSOCIATION MANAGEMENT

P.O. Box 50025
Austin, TX 78763
Tel: (512)345-8299
Email: csb@capitolsuretybond.com
website: www.capitolsurety.com

Charles H. Huff CAE, *President*

LEGISLATIVE INFORMATION SERVICES OF HAWAII

677 Ala Moana Blvd., Suite 815
Honolulu, HI 96813-5416
Tel: (808)533-6750 *Fax:* (808)599-2606

Richard C. Botti CAE, *President*

Hawaii Automotive Repair and Retail Gasoline Dealers Association
Hawaii Food and Beverage Association
Hawaii Food Industry Association
Retail Liquor Dealers Association of Hawaii

LEIPPER MANAGEMENT GROUP

P.O. Box 21481
Reno, NV 89515
Tel: (775)972-5011 *Fax:* (775)972-5011
Email: headquarters@leipper.org
website: http://leipper.org

Bryan R. Leipper, *Partner*

Child Abuse and Neglect Prevention Task Force
Fallen Leaf Tract Ass'n
Nevada Chiropractic Ass'n
Washoe County Concert Ass'n

LESTER MANAGEMENT SERVICES

P.O. Box 15322
Long Beach, CA 90815-0322
Tel: (562)425-1721
Email: lestermgmt@aol.com

Vickie Lester CAE, *President*

California Decorating Products Association
Independent Pool and Spa Service Association
Los Angeles Fastener Ass'n
Western Association of Fastener Distributors

LIVENGOOD AND ASSOCIATES

200 S. Meridian St., Suite 350
Indianapolis, IN 46225
Tel: (317)673-4200 *Fax:* (317)673-4210
website: www.livengood-associates.com

John Livengood, *President*

Indiana Alliance of Boys and Girls Clubs
Indiana Association of Beverage Retailers
Indiana Hospitality and Tourism Foundation
Indiana Hotel and Lodging Association
Restaurant and Hospitality Association of Indiana

LOBUE & MAJDALANY MANAGEMENT GROUP

P.O. Box 29920
San Francisco, CA 94129-0920
Tel: (415)561-6110 *Fax:* (415)561-6120
Email: info@lm-mgmt.com
website: www.lm-mgmt.com

Michael LoBue, *President*

ATM Forum
Fibre Channel Industry Association
SCSI Trade Association
Transaction Processing Performance Council

LONG & ASSOCIATES, INC.

28 Lowry Dr.
West Milton, OH 45383
Tel: (937)698-4188 *Fax:* (937)698-6153
Email: roelong@wesnet.com
website: www.longmgt.com

Roe Long-Wagner, *Chief Executive Officer*

American Rolling Door Institute
Institute of Door Dealers Accreditation
International Door Association
Metal Building Contractors and Erectors Association

LOVELESS MANAGEMENT & LEGISLATIVE SERVICES, INC.

600 Wharfside Way
Jacksonville, FL 32207
Tel: (904)435-0599 *Fax:* (904)396-9928

Gary W. Loveless CAE, *President*

Community Resource Institute
Florida Enterprise Zone Coalition
Jacksonville Wrecker Ass'n
TECHNET Internat'l - Atlantic Coast Chapter

'M COMPANIES

3942 N. Upland St.
Arlington, VA 22207-4642
Tel: (703)533-9539 *Fax:* (703)533-1612
Email: themcos@aol.com

Milton M. Bush CAE, *Principal*

Independent Association of Accredited Registrars
International Federation of Inspection Agencies - Americas Committee

MACKIN AND COMPANY

139 Lancaster St.
Albany, NY 12210-1903
Tel: (518)449-4698 *Fax:* (518)432-5651
website: www.mackinco.com

Robert E. Mackin, *Principal*

Association of Financial Guaranty Insurors
Industry Education Council to the National Conference of Insurance Legislators

MAGELLAN MANAGEMENT COMPANY

1650 S. Dixie Hwy., Suite 500
Boca Raton, FL 33432
Tel: (561)750-8558 *Fax:* (561)395-8557
Email: d.ferreira@magellanmanagement.com

Don Ferreira, *Executive Director*

ACCA - Gold Coast Chapter
ARW Research and Educational Foundation
Electrical Generating Systems Association
Midwest Association of Colleges and Employers

MANAGEMENT CONCEPTS, INC.

605 Poole Dr.
Garner, NC 27529-4547
Tel: (919)779-7516 *Fax:* (919)779-5642
Email: cbarbour@mgmt4u.com
website: www.mgmt4u.com

Charlene B. Barbour, *President and Chief Executive Officer*

American Academy of Psychotherapists
Carolinas Association of RV Parks and Campgrounds
International Society for Pharmaceutical Engineering - Carolina/South Atlantic Chapter
National Federation of Licensed Practical Nurses
North Carolina Association of Nurse Anesthetists
North Carolina Board of Licensed Professional Counselors
North Carolina Interpreters & Transliterators Licensing Board
North Carolina Society of Oral and Maxillofacial Surgeons
North Carolina Society of Radiologic Technologists

MANAGEMENT EXCELLENCE, INC.

11 W. Monument Ave., Suite 510
P.O. Box 2307
Dayton, OH 45401-2307
Tel: (937)586-3700
Email: mei@meinet.com
website: www.meinet.com

Francine W. Rickenbach C.A.E., *President*

Association of Destination Management Executives
Construction Business Development Association
Employee Involvement Association
GMV Emergency Medical Services Council
National Association of Nephrology Technologists and Technicians
Sonitrol Nat'l Dealers Ass'n
Ultrasonics Industry Association

MANAGEMENT OPTIONS, INC.

107 S. West St., Suite 110
Alexandria, VA 22314-2891
Tel: (703)486-8722
Toll Free: (888)441-5454
Email: managementoption@aol.com
website: www.moinc.com/

Thomas C. Osina CAE, *President and Chief Executive Officer*

Mid-Atlantic Propane Gas Association
Virginia Propane Gas Association
West Virginia Propane Gas Association

MANAGEMENT PLUS, INC.

71 Pinon Hill Place, N.E.
Albuquerque, NM 87122-1914
Tel: (505)856-6810
Email: viviennemattox@mpinm.com

Vivienne Harwood Mattox, *Executive Officer*

Association of Vacuum Equipment Manufacturers International
Society of Vacuum Coaters

MANAGEMENT RESOURCE SPECIALISTS, INC.

P.O. Box 7389
Springfield, IL 62791-7389
Tel: (217)793-5143

Pamela Tolson CAE, *President*

American Association of Public Health Dentistry
American Soc. for Pharmacy Law
Association for Preservation Technology International
Georgian Ass'n in the U.S.A.
Hispanic Dental Association
Illinois Petroleum Equipment Contractors Association
Illinois Rural Health Association
Illinois Society of Association Executives
National Oral Health Conference

MANAGEMENT SERVICES

716 Randall Ave.
Cheyenne, WY 82001
Tel: (307)637-7575 *Fax:* (307)638-8472
Email: managementservic@qwest.net

Dan J. Lex CAE, *President*

Northern Rockies Optometric Conference
Quality Health Care Foundation of Wyoming
Wyoming Optometric Association

MANAGEMENT SERVICES TO ASSOCIATIONS

P.O. Box 220
Annandale, VA 22003
Tel: (703)850-8552 *Fax:* (703)532-1798
Email: kentonp1@aol.com

Kenton Pattie, *President*

Association Chief Executive Council
Nat'l Center for Fair Competition
National Association of Police Equipment Distributors
National Emergency Equipment Dealers Association
National Emergency Medical Services Distributors Association

MANAGEMENT SOLUTION FOR ASSOCIATIONS

152 Madison Ave., Suite 801
New York, NY 10016
Tel: (212)481-3038
Email: mgmtoffice@aol.com

Rosemarie Sharpe, *President*

MANAGEMENT SOLUTIONS PLUS, INC.

15245 Shady Grove Road, Suite 130
Rockville, MD 20850-3222
Tel: (301)258-9210
Email: bpalys@mgmtsol.com
website: www.mgmtsol.com

Beth W. Palys CAE, *President*

American Academy of Appellate Lawyers
American College of Mortgage Attorneys
American Society of Consulting Arborists
Association of Water Technologies
Council of Tree and Landscape Appraisers
Landscape Contractors Association of Maryland, District of Columbia and Virginia
National Conference on Weights and Measures
Society for Historical Archaeology

MAPLE STREET MANAGEMENT

224 W. Maple Ave.
Orange, CA 92866-1322
Tel: (714)771-3685 *Fax:* (714)744-8975
Email: sandraeven@aol.com
website: www.maplestreet.org

Sandra A. Even CAE, CMP, *President*

California Association of Nurse Anesthetists
Forum for Corporate Directors
Kaiser Permanente Nurse Anesthetists Ass'n
Meeting Professionals International - Orange County Chapter

MARION ASSOCIATES

131 N.W. First Ave.
Delray Beach, FL 33444-2611
Tel: (561)266-9016 *Fax:* (561)266-9017

P.O. Box 100
Ho-Ho-Kus, NJ 07423
Tel: (561)266-9016 *Fax:* (561)266-9017

Ruth Stramberg, *Manager, New Jersey Office*

Association of Service and Computer Dealers International
Florida Internet Service Providers Association
North-American Association of Telecommunications Dealers

MARKETSHARE, INC.

2 Wisconsin Circle, Suite 700
Chevy Chase, MD 20815
Tel: (240)235-6060 *Fax:* (240)235-6061
Email: assocmail@aol.com
website: www.marketshareinc.net

Jay McCrensky, *President*

Contemporary Kabbalah Institute
International Private Infrastructure Association
Moldovan-American Chamber of Commerce
Romanian-American Chamber of Commerce

THE MATTISON CORPORATION

430 N. Park Ave., Suite 210
Indianapolis, IN 46202-3677
Tel: (317)685-8433
Email: garya.price@aol.com

Gary A. Price, *President*

Indiana Academy of Family Physicians Foundation
Indiana Construction Roundtable
Indiana Subcontractors Association
Indiana Water Environment Association
Metro Indianapolis Coalition for Construction Safety

MAYBERRY & ASSOCIATES

252 N. Washington St., Suite A
Falls Church, VA 22046-4500
Tel: (703)538-8804 *Fax:* (703)538-6305

Peter G. Mayberry, *President*

Healthcare Compliance Packaging Council
Pharmaceutical Printed Literature Association

McBRIDE & ASSOCIATES, INC.

1633 Normandy Ct.
Suite A
Lincoln, NE 68512
Tel: (402)476-3852
Email: dmcbride@assocoffice.net
website: www.mcbridemanagement.com

David S. McBride, *President and Chief Executive Officer*

National Association of Insurance and Financial Advisors - Nebraska
Nebraska Arborists Association
Nebraska Foundation for Children's Vision
Nebraska Funeral Directors Association
Nebraska Optometric Association
North Central States Optometric Council

MCCULLOCH AND ASSOCIATES, INC.

1205 Stonewood Court
Annapolis, MD 21409-5440
Tel: (410)974-4472
Email: mcc@mdassn.com

Mary Jo McCulloch, *Executive*

Association of Pool and Spa Professionals - Chesapeake Chapter
Capitol Region USA
Maryland Hotel and Lodging Association
Maryland State Child Care Association
Maryland Tourism Council

MEDICAL EDUCATION COLLABORATIVE

1800 Jackson St., Suite 200
Golden, CO 80401
Tel: (303)278-1900 *Fax:* (303)278-1985

P.O. Box 6256
Freehold, NJ 07728-9998
Tel: (732)863-5581 *Fax:* (732)863-5589

Robert Orsetti, *Director, N.J. Office*

Prostate Cancer Education Council

MEETING EXPECTATIONS

415 E. Paces Ferry Road, N.E., Suite 200
Atlanta, GA 30305
Tel: (404)240-0999 Ext: 229 *Fax:* (404)240-0998
Toll Free: (866)240-0999
Email: bwolfert@meetingexpectations.com
website: www.meetingexpectations.com

Barry Wolfert CMP, *Director, Business Development*

MELBY CAMERON AND HULL, INC.

23607 Hwy. 99, Suite 2-C
P.O. Box 2016
Edmonds, WA 98020-9516
Tel: (425)774-7479 *Fax:* (425)771-9588
Email: info@melbycameronhull.com
website: www.melbycameronhull.com

Lynn L. Melby CAE, *Chief Executive Officer*

Alliance for Healthy Communities
American Academy of Oral Medicine
American Holistic Medical Association
Home Care Association of Washington
Independent Insurance Agents and Brokers of King County
National Association of Industrial and Office Properties - Washington State Chapter
National Association of Professional Mortgage Women

National Federation of Paralegal Associations
Northwest Hearth Patio and Barbecue Association
Washington Land Title Association
Washington Society of Association Executives

MEREDITH AND HOPKINS, INC.

10 Drs James Parker Blvd., Suite 103
Red Bank, NJ 07701-2315
Tel: (732)842-5070 *Fax:* (732)219-1938
Email: info@merhop.com
website: www.merhop.com

Gerri Hopkins, *President*

Industrial and Commercial Real Estate Women of New Jersey
Radio Club of America

THE MERIDIAN GROUP

P.O. Box 160
Del Mar, CA 92014
Tel: (858)792-3883 *Fax:* (858)792-3884

Katherine Clark, *Partner*

Information Technologies Credit Union Association
National Association of Credit Union Chairmen
National Association of Credit Union Supervisory and Auditing Committees
National Council of Postal Credit Unions
Western Association of Technology Credit Unions

MILDE, ROLLINS & ASSOCIATES

505 Beach St., Suite 130
San Francisco, CA 94133
Tel: (415)674-4500 *Fax:* (415)674-4539
Email: j.milde@mra-sf.com
website: www.mra-sf.com

Jeffrey L. Milde CAE, *President*

Bay Area OD Network
CAMUS International
NCB-IDA
PC/104 Consortium

MILLIRON AND ASSOCIATES

200 N. Third St., Suite 1500
Harrisburg, PA 17101
Tel: (717)232-5322

Ken Brandt, *Account Executive*

Bowling Proprietors Association of Pennsylvania
Pennsylvania Amusement and Music Machine Association
Pennsylvania State Council of Farm Organizations

MISSISSIPPI ASSOCIATION MANAGERS, INC.

419 E. Broadway
Yazoo City, MS 39194
Tel: (662)751-4626 *Fax:* (662)751-4628

Misty Moore, *President*

American Institute of Architects - Mississippi
Mississippi Architectural Foundation
Mississippi Board of Psychology
Mississippi Society of Association Executives
Mississippi State Board of Examiners for Licensed Professional Counselors
Mississippi Tourism Association
Mississippians Emergency Medical Services

MITCHELL MANAGEMENT COMPANY

2101 Libbie Ave.
Richmond, VA 23210
Tel: (804)288-7172 *Fax:* (804)288-7174

Ashton D. Mitchell III, *President*

Virginia Golf Club
Virginia Hospitality and Travel Association

MULTISERVICE MANAGEMENT COMPANY

994 Old Eagle School Road, Suite 1019
Wayne, PA 19087-1802
Tel: (610)971-4850
Email: info@multiservicemgmt.com
website: www.multiservicemgmt.com

Robert H. Ecker, *President and Chief Executive Officer*

Aircraft Locknut Manufacturers Association
American Society of Heating, Refrigerating and Air-Conditioning Engineers
Building Maintenance Contractors Association
Cordage Institute
Delaware Valley Chapter - Air Conditioning Contractors of America
Fluid Sealing Association
Gasket Fabricators Association
National Association of Diaper Services
National Classification Management Society
Professional Apparel Association
Textile Maintenance Council
Vibration Isolation and Seismic Control Mfrs Ass'n

MYERS/SMITH, INC.

799 N. Beverly Glen
Los Angeles, CA 90077
Tel: (310)446-8360 *Fax:* (310)446-8390

Robert Myers, *President*

Autotestcon Conference
IEEE Industry Applications Society
IEEE Instrumentation and Measurement Society
IEEE Instrumentation and Measurement Technology Conference
IEEE Power Electronics Society
Power Electronics Specialists Conference
Sensors for Industry Conference

NEFF & DOWNING MANAGEMENT SERVICES

P.O. Box 579
Moorestown, NJ 08057
Tel: (856)234-0330
Email: associationmgr@comcast.net
website: www.neffdowning.com

June P. Neff, *President*

Direct Store Distributors Association
International Hard Anondizing Association
Philadelphia Area Meeting Professionals Internat'l
Philadelphia Ass'n of Metal Finishers
Philadelphia Business Executives
Philadelphia Estate Planning Council
Philadelphia Public Relations Association
Planned Giving Council of Greater Philadelphia
Wise Foods Distributors Ass'n

NEXT WAVE GROUP, LLC

550M #217
Severna Park, MD 21146
Tel: (410)647-5002 *Fax:* (410)544-4640
Email: pat@nextwavegroup.com
website: www.nextwavegroup.com

Patricia H. Troy CAE, *President and Chief Executive Officer*

Entrepreneur's Exchange, Inc.
Facetswoman, Inc.
Mid-Atlantic Carwash Ass'n

NIKE ASSOCIATION MANAGEMENT, INC.

P.O. Box 647
Northbrook, IL 60065-0647
Tel: (847)559-9233 *Fax:* (847)559-9235

Pamela W. Franzen, *President*

Sump and Sewage Pump Manufacturers Association

NON-PROFIT SERVICES CORP.

P.O. Box 631206
Houston, TX 77263-1206
Tel: (713)776-1307 *Fax:* (713)776-1308
Email: npsc@npscmgmt.com
website: www.npscmgmt.com

Dean Newton, *President and Chief Executive Officer*

Affordable Housing Management Ass'n - East Texas Chapter
Financial Executives International - Houston Chapter
Healthcare Financial Management Ass'n - Region 9
Planned Giving Council of Houstion

NONPROFIT MANAGEMENT INC.

1555 Connecticut Ave., N.W., Suite 200
Washington, DC 20036-1111
Tel: (202)462-9600
Email: tbryantsr@nonprofitmgt.com
website: www.nonprofitmgt.com

Thomas E. Bryant Sr., *President*

Aspirin Foundation of America
Consortium for School Networking
Friends of the Nat'l Library of Medicine
National Foundation for Mental Health

NONPROFIT RESOURCES, INC.

410 20th St., Suite 102, Box 1456
Glenwood Springs, CO 81601
Tel: (970)945-1478 *Fax:* (970)384-0512
Email: info@nprweb.org
website: www.nprweb.org

Cindy Challis Orr CAE, *Senior Partner*

Ass'n of Equipment Management Professionals Foundation
Association of Equipment Management Professionals

NONPROFIT SOLUTIONS

1821 University Ave. West, Suite S-256
St. Paul, MN 55104-2804
Tel: (651)917-6240 *Fax:* (651)917-1835
Email: office@nonprofitsolutions.com
website: www.nonprofitsolutions.com

Jim Thalhuber, *President*

Advertising Federation of Minnesota
American Marketing Association - Minnesota Chapter
American Soc. for Training and Development - Twin Cities Chapter
Association of Fundraising Professionals - Minnesota Chapter
Human Resource Professionals of Minnesota
International Association of Business Communicators - Minnesota Chapter
League of Women Voters - St. Paul
Meeting Professionals International - Minnesota Chapter
Minnesota Association of Health Underwriters
Minnesota Global Trade Association
Minnesota Medical Group Management Association
Minnesota Planned Giving Council
Myasthenia Gravis Foundation
Public Relations Society of America - Minnesota Chapter
Soc. of Financial Service Professionals - Twin Cities

NORTHEAST ASSOCIATION MANAGEMENT, INC.

100 Conifer Hill Dr., Suite 307
Danvers, MA 01923
Email: bwilkes@neami.com
website: www.neami.com

P.O. Box 12250
Albany, NY 12212-2250
Tel: (518)458-1026 *Fax:* (518)458-7811

Kevin Hume, *Executive Vice President*

Public Employer Risk Management Association

O'BRIEN INTERNATIONAL., INC.

11001 Danka Way North, Suite 1
St. Petersburg, FL 33716
Tel: (727)577-5002 *Fax:* (727)577-5012

Patrick A. O'Brien, *President*

Concrete Sawing and Drilling Association
National Drilling Association

O'BRYON AND COMPANY

4424 Montgomery Ave., Suite 102
Bethesda, MD 20814
Tel: (301)652-5066 *Fax:* (301)913-9146
Email: obryonco@aol.com

David S. O'Bryon CAE, *President*

American Association of Limited Partners
Association of Chiropractic Colleges

OEI - AN ASSOCIATION MANAGEMENT COMPANY

1711 W. County Road B, Suite 300-North
Roseville, MN 55113-4036
Tel: (651)635-0206 *Fax:* (651)635-0307
Email: oei@assocmgmt.org

John Arlandson, *President*

OFFINGER MANAGEMENT COMPANY

1100-H Brandywine Blvd.
Zanesville, OH 43701-7303
Tel: (740)452-4541 *Fax:* (740)452-2552
Toll Free: (888)878-6334
Email: omc.info@offinger.com
website: www.offinger.com

746 Morrison Road
Columbus, OH 43230-6649
Tel: (740)452-4541 *Fax:* (740)452-2552

Kim Vierstra, *Executive Vice President*

American Coaster Enthusiasts
American Massage Therapy Association - Ohio Chapter
Crochet Guild of America
The Knitting Guild Association
The National NeedleArts Association
Ohio Lawn Care Association
Ohio Turfgrass Foundation
Ohio Turfgrass Research Trust
Opticians Association of Ohio
Professional Retail Store Maintenance Association
Restaurant Facility Management Association

ORGANIZATION MANAGEMENT

2971 Flowers Road South, Suite 266
Atlanta, GA 30341
Tel: (770)452-0660
Email: info@organizationmanagement.net
website: www.organizationmanagement.net

Judy Stokes, *President*

Refrigerated Foods Association

ORGANIZATION MANAGEMENT GROUP, INC.

184 Business Park Dr., Suite 200-A
Virginia Beach, VA 23462
Tel: (757)473-8701 *Fax:* (757)473-9897
website: www.managegroup.com

J. Michael Reitelbach, *President*

ORGANIZATION MANAGEMENT SERVICES OF WEST VIRGINIA

P.O. Box 1335
Charleston, WV 253251335
Tel: (304)342-4441

Ruth Sayre, *Contact*

Charleston Public Safety Council
West Virginia Public Accountants Association
West Virginia Tire Dealers Association

ORGANIZATION MANAGEMENT, INC.

P.O. Box 896
Olympia, WA 98507-0896
Tel: (360)943-8155 *Fax:* (360)586-5538
Email: jcrabill@comcast.net

Jerry Crabill, *President*

Corvette and High Performance Soc.
Washington Association of Building Officials

ORGANIZATIONAL SERVICES, INC.

P.O. Box 6
Kearney, NJ 07032
Tel: (201)998-5133

Marianne H. Carney, *President*

Art Directors Club of New Jersey
Building Owners and Managers Ass'n of Westchester County
Building Owners and Managers Association - New Jersey Chapter
Middle Atlantic Conference of Building Owners and Managers
New Jersey Advertising Club

OSBORN & BARR COMMUNICATIONS

One N. Brentwood, 8th Fl.
St. Louis, MO 63105
Tel: (314)726-5511 *Fax:* (314)726-6350
Toll Free: (888)235-4332
Email: whaleyh@osborn-barr.com
website: www.osborn-barr.com

Steve Barr, *Chief Executive Officer*

Cattlemens' Beef Board
Nat'l Pork Board
Ohio Soybean Council
Propane Education and Research Council
U.S. Potato Board
United Soybean Board
Wisconsin Soybean Council

OUTSOURCING MANAGEMENT GROUP

2400 22nd St., Suite 110
Sacramento, CA 95818
Tel: (916)443-1566 *Fax:* (916)451-9150
Email: omgs@omgs.com
website: www.omgs.com

Sandra K. Virago CAE, *President*

Ass'n of Commercial Real Estate - Sacramento
California Court Reporters Association
California Mortuary Alliance
CCIM - Northern California Chapter
Financial Planning Ass'n of Northern California
Interment Association of California
Internat'l Conference of Building Officials - Sacramento Valley Chapter
Nat'l Network Reporting Company
Promotional Marketing Ass'n of Northern California
Sacramento Area Human Resource Ass'n
Western Cemetery Alliance

PAI MANAGEMENT CORPORATION

5272 River Road, Suite 630
Bethesda, MD 20816
Tel: (301)656-4224 Ext: 6539 *Fax:* (301)656-0989
Email: pai@paimgmt.com
website: www.paimgmt.com

Norman E. Wallis Ph.D., *President*

Academy of Psychosomatic Medicine
American College of Foot and Ankle Orthopedics and Medicine
American College of Radiation Oncology
International Society for Pharmacoepidemiology
Society for Mucosal Immunology
Society for Radiation Oncology Administrators

PARTNERS IN ASSOCIATION MANAGEMENT

1530 Metropolitan Blvd.
Tallahassee, FL 32308
Tel: (850)224-0711
Email: piam@executiveoffice.org
website: www.executiveoffice.org

Bennett E. Napier CAE, *Partner*

Florida Aviation-Aerospace Alliance
Florida Dental Laboratory Association
Florida Fire Equipment Dealers Association
Florida Life Care Residents Association
Florida Rental Association
Florida Society of Ambulatory Surgical Centers
Georgia Association of Fire Safety Equipment Dealers
Georgia Society of Ambulatory Surgical Centers
National Association of Dental Laboratories
National Board for Certification in Dental Technology

PENCOR MAZUR LTD.

111 E. Wacker Dr., Suite 990
Chicago, IL 60601
Tel: (312)729-9900 *Fax:* (312)729-9800

Joel Shiffrin, *Chief Executive Officer*

Alliance for Merger and Acquisition Advisors
CPA Auto Dealer Consultants Association
CPA Construction Industry Association
CPA Manufacturing Services Association
Law Firm Services Association
National CPA Health Care Advisors Association
National Litigation Support Services Association
Not-for-Profit Services Association

PERIPHERAL SERVICES, INC.

P.O. Box 539
Webster, NY 14580
Tel: (585)545-6920
Email: mail@peripheralservices.com
website: www.peripheralservices.com

Nancy C. Carleton CAE, *President*

Diversified Marketing Group
Financial Planning Ass'n of Upstate New York
Society of Quantitative Analysts

PHYLLIS PERRON & ASSOCIATES, INC.

450 Laurel St., Suite 1400
Baton Rouge, LA 70801
Tel: (225)344-0620 *Fax:* (225)344-1132
website: www.pperron.com

Phyllis Perron, *President*

Louisiana Insurers' Conference
Louisiana Life and Health Insurance Guaranty Association

Louisiana Pharmacists Association
Louisiana United Businesses Association

PETRICK OUTSOURCING UNLIMITED, INC.

679 Hottel Road
Woodstock, VA 22664
Tel: (540)459-8390 *Fax:* (540)459-3440
Email: annette@petrickoutsourcing.com
website: www.petrickoutsourcing.com

Annette E. Petrick CAE, *President*

J.W. PRENDERGAST & ASSOCIATES

Grand Central Station
P.O. Box 3139
New York, NY 10163-3139
Tel: (212)217-6824
Email: jwpgroup@ren.com

James W. Prendergast, *Principal*

Direct Marketing Day Foundation
Graphic Arts Professionals Educational Foundation

PRICE MANAGEMENT CORP.

815 Quarrier St., Suite 345
Charleston, WV 25301-2641
Tel: (304)345-4710 *Fax:* (304)346-6416
Email: rprice0851@aol.com

Roger K. Price, *President*

West Virginia Funeral Directors Association
West Virginia Optometric Association

PROFESSIONAL ASSOCIATION MANAGEMENT SERVICES, INC.

225 E. Cook St.
Springfield, IL 62704
Tel: (217)528-5230 *Fax:* (217)241-4683
Email: mike@p-a-m-s.com
website: www.p-a-m-s.com

Michael R. Lane, *President*

Alliance of Automotive Service Providers of Illinois
Illinois Hearing Society
Illinois Land Title Association
Illinois Mini Storage Ass'n

PROFESSIONAL ASSOCIATION MANAGEMENT, INC.

3461 Lawrenceville-Suwanee Road, Suite F
Suwanee, GA 30024
Tel: (770)271-5320 *Fax:* (770)271-0634

J.W. Holderfield CAE, *President*

American College of Cardiology - Georgia Chapter
DeKalb Medical Soc.
Georgia Academy of General Dentistry
Georgia Society of Oral and Maxillofacial Surgeons
InSight
Northern District Dental Soc.
Southeastern Society of Oral and Maxillofacial Surgeons

PROFESSIONAL ASSOCIATION MANAGEMENT, LLC

1231 E. Grandview Road
Phoenix, AZ 85022
Tel: (602)588-0028 *Fax:* (602)993-2900
Toll Free: (888)265-7627
Email: pattiherington@cox.net

Patricia W. Herington CAE, *Owner*

Arizona Millwright Employers Association
Arizona Coalition for Tomorrow
Arizona Policy Forum
Multi-State Highway Transportation Agreement

PROFESSIONAL EXCHANGE SERVICE CORP.

P.O. Box 1071
Fresno, CA 93714
Tel: (559)228-6140
Toll Free: (800)835-3924

Cynthia Downing, *President and Chief Executive Officer*

California Ass'n of Health Underwriters
California Ass'n of Senior Estate Planners
California Professional Association of Specialty Contractors
Central California Nikkei Foundation
Central California Psychiatric Soc.
Fresno Ass'n of Insurance and Financial Advisors
Fresno Estate Planning Council
Fresno Society of Financial Service Professionals
Golden Gate Ass'n of Health Underwriters
North Coast Association of Health Underwriters
North County Personnel Association
Sacramento Ass'n of Insurance and Financial Advisors
Silicon Valley Ass'n of Health Underwriters
The Junior League of Fresno

PROFESSIONAL MANAGEMENT ASSOCIATES, L.L.C.

203 Towne Center Dr.
Hillsborough, NJ 08844
Tel: (908)359-1184
website: www.profmgmt.com

Joanne Cole CAE, CMP, *Managing Member*

Internal Securities Ass'n for Institutional Trade Communication
New Jersey Ass'n of Professional Mediators
New Jersey Association of School Psychologists
New Jersey Dietetic Association
New Jersey Speech-Language-Hearing Association
New York Metro Chapter, American Soc. of Interior Designers
Ombudsman Association, The
Oracle Clinical Users Group

PROFESSIONAL RELATIONS AND RESEARCH INSTITUTE

900 Cummings Ctr., Suite 221-U
Beverly, MA 01915-6183
Tel: (978)927-8330 *Fax:* (978)524-0461
website: www.prri.com

William T. Maloney CAE, *President*

American Association for Thoracic Surgery
American Association of Plastic Surgeons
American College of Surgeons - Massachusetts Chapter
American Federation for Medical Research
American Surgical Association
American Urological Association - Mid-Atlantic Section
American Urological Association - New England Section
Congenital Heart Surgeons Society
Innovation in Cancer Therapies
International Society for Minimally-Invasive Cardiac Surgery
New England Society for Vascular Surgery
New England Society of Association Executives
New England Surgical Society
Society for Clinical Vascular Surgery
Society for Pediatric Urology
Society for Surgery of the Alimentary Tract
Southern Association for Vascular Surgery
Thoracic Surgery Foundation for Research and Education
Western Thoracic Surgical Association

PROGRAM MANAGEMENT GROUP, INC.

P.O. Box 669
Annapolis, MD 21404-0669
Tel: (410)268-2011
Email: jreilly@pmgamc.com

James P. Reilly, *President*

European Ass'n of the Plasma Products Industry
Plasma Protein Therapeutics Association

PUBLIC STRATEGIES IMPACT LLC

414 River View Plaza
Trenton, NJ 08611
Tel: (609)393-7799 *Fax:* (609)393-9891
Email: info@njlobbyist.com
website: www.njlobbyist.com

Joseph A. Simonetta CAE, *Partner*

AIA New Jersey
American Society of Landscape Architects - New Jersey Chapter
New Jersey Hotel and Lodging Association
New Jersey Soc. of Professional Engineers Educational Foundation
New Jersey Society of Municipal Engineers
New Jersey Society of Professional Engineers
New Jersey Travel Industry Association
Opticians Association of New Jersey

ROBERT N. PYLE & ASSOCIATES

1223 Potomac St. NW
Washington, DC 20007-3212
Tel: (202)333-8190

Robert N. Pyle, *Chairman*

Independent Bakers Association
National Grape Cooperative Association

RAMCO/REESE ASSOCIATION MANAGEMENT COMPANY

P.O. Box 1144
Highland Park, IL 60035
Tel: (847)433-1335

Gerald H. Reese CAE, *President*

CASMI Educational Foundation
Chicago Ass'n of Spring Manufacturers

RAYBOURN GROUP INTERNATIONAL, INC.

7150 Winton Dr., Suite 300
Indianapolis, IN 46268
Tel: (312)923-8500 *Fax:* (317)280-8527
Toll Free: (800)362-2546
Email: sgorup@raybourn.com
website: www.raybourn.com

One E. Wacker Dr., Suite 2410
Chicago, IL 60601
Tel: (312)923-8500 *Fax:* (317)280-8527

1001 Connecticut Ave., Suite 528
Washington, DC 20036
Tel: (312)923-8500 *Fax:* (317)280-8527

James D. Montoya CAE, *Association Executive*

Corporate Housing Providers Association
Custom Electronic Design and Installation Association
Electronics Representatives Association - Indiana/Kentucky Chapter
Indiana Society of Association Executives
Interior Design Educators Council
International Association of Speakers Bureaus
International Furniture Rental Association
Mobile Electronic Retailers Ass'n
Northern Indiana Apartment Council
Society for Nutrition Education

THE REBEDEAU GROUP

7000 W. Southwest Hwy.
Chicago Ridge, IL 60415
Tel: (708)361-6000
Email: trg@tradeshownet.com

Mary Beth Rebedeau, *President*

American Society of Anesthesiologists

REES GROUP INC., THE

2810 Crossroads Dr., Suite 3000
Madison, WI 53718
Tel: (608)443-2468 *Fax:* (608)443-2474
Email: srees@reesgroupinc.com
website: www.reesgroupinc.com

Susan M. Rees, *Chief Executive Officer*

American College of Veterinary Pathologists
American Osteopathic Academy for Sports Medicine
Association for the Advancement of Applied Sport Psychology
International Neural Network Society
National Council on Measurement in Education
Society for Psychophysiological Research
Society for Research on Nicotine and Tobacco
Society of Clinical and Medical Hair Removal
Wisconsin Winery Association

REGNET ENVIRONMENTAL SERVICES

1250 Connecticut Ave., N.W., Suite 700
Washington, DC 20036
Tel: (202)419-1500 *Fax:* (202)659-8037
Email: info@regnet.com
website: www.regnet.com

Robert Fensterheim, *President*

Acrylonitrile Group
Alkylphenols and Ethoxylates Research Council
Chlorinated Paraffins Industry Association
Emulsion Polymers Council
North American Polyelectrolyte Producers Association
Phosphite Manufacturers Consortium
Propylene Carbonate/T-Butyl Alcohol HPV Committee
QUAT HPV Challenge Task Group
SB Latex Council
Vinyl Acetate Council

REINFRIED AND ASSOCIATES, INC.

6724 Lone Oak Blvd.
Naples, FL 34109
Tel: (239)514-3441 *Fax:* (239)514-3470
Email: reinfried@earthlink.net

Robert A. Reinfried, *President*

American Chain Association
Conveyor Equipment Manufacturers Association
Mechanical Power Transmission Association
Scale Manufacturers Association

RENAISSANCE ASSOCIATION MANAGEMENT

3459 Lawrenceville-Suwanee Road
Suwanee, GA 30024-6427
Tel: (770)932-3263 *Fax:* (770)932-3276

Greg Martin, *President*

Georgia Shorthand Reporters Association
Southern Association of Wholesale Distributors

RESOURCE CENTER FOR ASSOCIATIONS LIMITED

10200 W. 44th Ave., Suite 304
Wheat Ridge, CO 80033-2840
Tel: (303)422-2615
Email: rc@resourcenter.com
website: http://resourcenter.com

Francine Butler Ph.D., CAE, *President*

American Society of Indexers
Association for Applied Psychophysiology and Biofeedback
Association of Community Health Nursing Educators
Biofeedback Certification Institute of America
Midwest Nursing Research Society
North American Nature Photography Association
Society for Scholarly Publishing
Southern Nursing Research Society

RESOURCE MANAGEMENT PLUS

1211 Locust St.
Philadelphia, PA 19107-5409
Tel: (215)545-1985 *Fax:* (215)545-8107
Toll Free: (800)408-8951
website: www.rmpinc.com

Joseph Braden, *President*

Association of Oncology Social Work
Robert O. Gilbert Foundation
Health Care Compliance Association
Health Care Conference Administrators
International Society of Psychiatric-Mental Health Nurses
NANDA Foundation
NANDA International
Society for Medical Decision Making
Society for Social Work Leadership in Health Care

K.W. REYNOLDS & ASSOCIATES

P.O. Box 76533
Atlanta, GA 30358
Tel: (770)977-1476
Email: kwr@mindspring.com

Kenneth W. Reynolds, *President*

The Foodservice Group, Inc.

RIGHT DIRECTIONS CONSULTING

2001 Midwest Road, Suite 106
Oak Brook, IL 60521-1335
Tel: (630)495-8597

Ken Boyce, *President*

Spring Manufacturers Institute

ROBSTAN GROUP, INC.

14 W. Third St., Suite 200
Kansas City, MO 64105
Tel: (816)472-8870 *Fax:* (816)472-7765
website: www.robstan.com

Kenneth R. Bowman, *President*

Association for Accounting Marketing
Aviation Insurance Association
Internat'l Midas Dealers Ass'n
Internat'l Window Cleaners Association
Mass Marketing Insurance Institute
North American Specialty Printing Manufacturers Association
Polyurea Development Association
Sealant, Waterproofing and Restoration Institute

ROCKY MOUNTAIN MANAGEMENT SERVICES, INC.

P.O. Box 4553
Missoula, MT 59806-4553
Tel: (406)251-5232 *Fax:* (406)251-5270
Email: robin@rmms.net
website: www.rmms.net

Robin L. Childers CAE, *President*

Home Health Section of the American Physical Therapy Ass'n
Montana Nursery and Landscape Association
Rehabilitation Association of Montana
Section on Health Policy and Administration of the American Physical Therapy Ass'n

ROGERS ENTERPRISES

13577 Grain Lane
San Diego, CA 92129-2581
Tel: (858)484-1681
Email: spirits99@aol.com

Frederick J. Rogers, *President*

RUGGLES SERVICE CORP.

2209 Dickens Road
P.O. Box 11086
Richmond, VA 23230-1086
Tel: (804)282-0062
Email: stewart@societyhq.com

John A. Hinckley, *President*

American College of Osteopathic Pediatricians
Eastern Pain Ass'n
New England Pain Association
Society for Obstetric Anesthesia and Perinatology
Society for Pediatric Anesthesia
Society of Cardiovascular Anesthesiologists
Society of Neurosurgical Anesthesia and Critical Care
Virginia Orthopaedic Society
Virginia Society of Anesthesiologists

S & S MANAGEMENT SERVICES, INC.

One Regency Dr.
P.O. Box 30
Bloomfield, CT 06002-0030
Tel: (860)243-3977
Email: aschuman@ssmgt.com
website: www.ssmgt.com

C. Mitchell Sorensen, *Executive Vice President*

American Academy of Emergency Psychiatrists
American Academy of Psychiatry and the Law
American Academy of Psychoanalysis and Dynamic Psychiatry
American Clinical Neurophysiology Society
Associated Sheet Metal/Roofing Contractors - Connecticut Chapter
Building Owners and Managers Association of Southern Connecticut
Committee of Concerned Psychiatrists
Connecticut Academy of Family Physicians
Connecticut Association of Personnel Consultants
Connecticut Psychiatric Society
Connecticut Roofing Contractors Association
Connecticut Subcontractors Association
Core Content Review of Family Medicine (Internat'l)
Eastern Connecticut Physician Delivery Services
Family Medicine Political Action Committee
Greater Hartford Building and Owners Association
Mason Contractors Association of Connecticut
Middlesex County Medical Ass'n
New England Council, Painting and Decorating Contractors of America
New London County Medical Ass'n
Professional Show Managers Association
Real Estate Finance Ass'n of Connecticut
Tolland County Medical Ass'n
Waterbury Medical Ass'n
Windham County Medical Ass'n

THE SANFORD ORGANIZATION, INC.

1000 N. Rand Road, Suite 214
Wauconda, IL 60084-1188
Tel: (847)526-2010 *Fax:* (847)526-3993
Email: tso@tso.net
website: www.tso.net

Rand Baldwin CAE, *President*

Aluminum Anodizers Council
Aluminum Extruders Council
Extrusion Technology Foundation
Mid-America Horticulture Trade Show
Public Relations Soc. of America - Chicago

SCHLOSSER MANAGEMENT COMPANY

3271 Springcrest Dr.
Hamilton, OH 45011-8229
Tel: (513)895-0695 *Fax:* (513)895-1739
Email: dan310@eartlink.net

Dan L. Schlosser, *President*

North Central Wholesalers Association
Ohio Water Quality Association
Ohio Water Well Association

THE SCHNEIDER GROUP, INC.

5400 Bosque Blvd., Suite 680
Waco, TX 76710-4446
website: www.sgmeet.com

Helen Schneider Lemay, *President*

American Society of Limnology and Oceanography
Ass'n for Women in Science
Estuarine Research Federation

SDI MANAGEMENT CO.

5777 W. Century Blvd., Suite 503
Los Angeles, CA 90045-5675
Tel: (310)417-3929
Email: sdi1@ix.netcom.com

Raymond P. Delrich CAE, CEM, *Chief Executive Officer*

Harbor Ass'n of Industry and Commerce
Maritime Coalition for Clean Air

THE JOSEPH E. SHANER COMPANY

720 Light St.
Baltimore, MD 21230-3816
Tel: (410)752-3318
website: www.jeshaner.com

Thomas C. Shaner CAE, APR, *President*

American Institute of Floral Designers
Baltimore City Dental Soc.
Baltimore Life Underwriters Charitable Foundation
Building Owners and Managers of Greater Baltimore
Chesapeake Human Resources Ass'n
Criminal Defense Attorneys Ass'n of MD
Maryland Association of Mortgage Brokers
Maryland Chiropractic Association
Maryland Improvement Contractors Association
Maryland Optometric Association
MD Chapter of the Appraisal Institute
National Association of Industrial and Office Properties - Maryland/D.C. Chapter
Professional Grounds Management Society

SHAW/YODER INC.

1414 K St., Suite 320
Sacramento, CA 95814
Tel: (916)446-4656 *Fax:* (916)446-4318

Paul J. Yoder, *President*

California Coalition on Workers' Compensation
California Transit Association
California Transit Insurance Pool
California Travel Industry Association
Solid Waste Association of North America - California Chapters

THE SHERWOOD GROUP, INC.

60 Revere Dr., Suite 500
Northbrook, IL 60062-1577
Tel: (847)480-9080
website: www.sherwood-group.com

John R. Waxman, *President*

SHORE MANAGEMENT SERVICES

11271 Ventura Blvd., Suite 514
Studio City, CA 91604-3136
Tel: (818)761-5755 *Fax:* (818)761-5009
Email: info@shoremanagement.com
website: www.shoremanagement.com

Barbara Shore, *President*

American Soc. of Travel Agents - Southern California Chapter
Public Relations Soc. of America - Los Angeles Area Chapter

SIMONELLI & ASSOCIATES

1011 St. Andrews Dr., Suite I
El Dorado Hills, CA 95762
Tel: (916)933-3061
Email: fjs@foundryhistory.com

Frederick J. Simonelli Ph.D., *Chairman of the Board*

California Cast Metals Association
California Foundry History Institute
Metalcasting Stormwater Monitoring Group

SLACK INC.

6900 Grove Road
Thorofare, NJ 08086-9447
Tel: (856)848-1000 *Fax:* (856)848-6891
website: www.slackinc.com

Peter Slack, *President*

American Society of PeriAnesthesia Nurses
American Society of Transplant Surgeons
CenterSpan
Gynecologic Surgery Society
Impact Americas
International Association of Forensic Nurses
North American Society for Pediatric Gastroenterology, Hepatology and Nutrition
Pan-Pacific Surgical Ass'n

SmithBucklin Corporation

401 N. Michigan Ave.
Chicago, IL 60611-4267
Tel: (312)644-6610 *Fax:* (312)321-6869
Toll Free: (866)722-7655
Email: info@smithbucklin.com
website: www.smithbucklin.com

2025 M St., N.W., Suite 800
Washington, DC 20036-3309

540 Maryville Center Dr., LLF
St. Louis, MO 63141

Henry Givray, *Chairman and Chief Executive Officer*

Academy of Dispensing Audiologists
American Academy of Esthetic Dentistry
American Association of Cardiovascular and Pulmonary Rehabilitation
American Association of Legal Nurse Consultants
American Bearing Manufacturing Association
American Ladder Institute
American Society for Bone and Mineral Research
American Society of Hand Therapists
American Spice Trade Association
American Urogynecologic Society
American Zinc Association
Americas SAP Users Group
Assistive Technology Industry Association
Association of Information Technology Professionals
Association of Professional Researchers for Advancement
Association of Steel Distributors
Battery Council International
Business Higher Education Forum
CATIA Operators Exchange
Center for Exhibition Industry Research
Certifying Board of Gastroenterology Nurses and Associates
Check Payment Systems Association
Chemical Industry Data Exchange
Chicago Estate Planning Council
Cosmetologists Chicago
Cremation Association of North America
EDGE - Computer Associates Users Group
Encompass - a Hewlett-Packard Users Group
Financial and Insurance Conference Planners
Illinois Cosmetology Association
Indoor Tanning Association
Information Users Association
InSight Users Group
Institute of Management Consultants USA
International Association of Airport Duty Free Stores
International Bone and Mineral Society
International Business Brokers Association
International Carwash Association
International Customer Service Association
International DB2 Users Group
International Formalwear Association
International Forum
International Nortel Networks Users Group
International Oracle Users Group
International Reprographic Association
International Society for Experimental Hematology
International Special Events Society
ITUG - A Hewlett-Packard Users Group
Joint Users of Siemens Technology
Lamaze International
Managed Funds Association
Metal Framing Manufacturers Association
Monument Builders of North America
Museum Trustee Association
National Association for County Community and Economic Development
National Association Medical Staff Services
National Association of Floor Covering Distributors
National Association of Healthcare Access Management
National Association of Independent Fee Appraisers
National Association of Local Housing Finance Agencies
National Association of Orthopaedic Nurses
National Child Care Association
National Cosmetology Association
National Fastener Distributors Association
National Institute of Pension Administrators
National Organization for Competency Assurance
National Society of Genetic Counselors
North American Building Material Distribution Association
North American Building Materials Association Education Foundation
Orthopaedic Nurses Certification Board
Pet Food Institute
Popcorn Borad
Popcorn Institute
Professional Association for SQL Server
Regional Airline Association
SHARE - an IBM Users Group
Society for Information Management
Society of Gastroenterology Nurses and Associates
Society of Gynecologic Oncologists
Society of Incentive & Travel Executives
Southwestern Surgical Congress
Special Care Dentistry Association
SSA Global Users Forum North America
U.S. Breastfeeding Committee
Wallcoverings Association

SOCIAL ENGINEERING ASSOCIATES

28 E. Jackson Blvd., Room 910
Chicago, IL 60604
Tel: (312)939-4987
Email: socialeng@ameritech.net

Richard Lockhart, *President*

Ass'n of Condominium, Townhouse, and Homeowners' Ass'ns
Community Health Charities of Illinois
Illinois Soft Drink Association

SOLUTIONS FOR ASSOCIATIONS, INC.

140 N. Bloomingdale Road
Bloomingdale, IL 60108-1017
Tel: (630)351-8669 *Fax:* (630)351-8490
website: www.solutions-for-assoc.com

John E. Kasper Ph.D., CAE, *President*

SOUTHEASTERN MANAGEMENT SERVICES

P.O. Box 95564
Atlanta, GA 30347

Thomas G. Cook, *President*

SOUTHERN ASSOCIATION SERVICES

P.O. Box 801
Macon, GA 31202-0801
Tel: (478)743-8612 *Fax:* (478)743-8278
Email: terikremer@southernassociationservices.com

Patricia Tisdale, *Administrator*

Georgia Automotive Recyclers Association
Georgia Dairy Products Association
Georgia Equity Lenders Association
Georgia Industrial Loan Association
Mortgage Bankers Association of Georgia

SPECIALIZED ASSOCIATION SERVICES

130 E. John Carpenter Fwy.
Irving, TX 75062
Tel: (469)524-5000 *Fax:* (469)524-5121
website: www.1sas.com

Lisa Davis, *Director*

Alliance for Affordable Services
Americans for Financial Security
National Association for the Self-Employed
Soho America

SPECIALTY SOCIETY SERVICES

6300 N. River Road, Suite 727
Rosemont, IL 60018-4226
Tel: (847)384-4238

Karen Jared, *Executive Officer*

American Academy for Cerebral Palsy and Developmental Medicine
American Shoulder and Elbow Surgeons
Association of Bone and Joint Surgeons
Association of Children's Prosthetic-Orthotic Clinics
Bones Society
Cervical Spine Research Society
Clinical Orthopaedics and Related Research Journal
Council of Musculoskeletal Specialty Socs.
Federation of Spine Associations
Orthopaedic Research Society
Orthopaedic Trauma Association
Pediatric Orthopedic Society of North America
Ruth Jackson Orthopaedic Society

SPECTRUM MANAGEMENT, INC.

P.O. Box 7010
Silver Spring, MD 20907

Glenn L. Northup, *President*

ST. AUBIN AND ASSOCIATES, LLC

12835 Pembroke Circle
Leawood, KS 66209
Tel: (913)345-2811 *Fax:* (913)345-8008
Email: sainte@kc.rr.com

Barbara St. Aubin, *Managing Partner*

GAYLE STEWART ENTERPRISES

1450 Warner Ave.
Tustin, CA 92780
Tel: (714)258-8390 *Fax:* (714)258-8391
Email: info@associationplanet.com

Gayle Stewart CAE, *President*

American Marketing Association
American Society of Civil Engineers
Association for Corporate Growth
Executives Ass'n of Orange County
Institute of Real Estate Management - Orange County Chapter
International Facility Management Association
Painting and Decorating Contractors of America - Golden State Council
Painting and Decorating Contractors of America - Southern California Chapter
Southern California Ass'n of Civil Engineers and Land Surveyors

STYGAR ASSOCIATES, INC.

1202 Allanson Road
Mundelein, IL 60060-3808
Tel: (847)566-4566
Email: estygariii@aol.com
website: http://stygarassociates.com

Edward J. Stygar Jr., *President*

American Art Therapy Association
American Association for Accreditation of Ambulatory Surgery Facilities
American Biological Safety Association
American Pathology Foundation
Illinois Soc. of Pathologists
Rhinoplasty Soc.

SUFKA AND ASSOCIATES

1518 K St., N.W., Suite 503
Washington, DC 20005-1203
Tel: (202)628-5336
Email: sufka1@aol.com
website: www.sufka.com

Kenneth M. Sufka, *President*

AABC Commissioning Group
Associated Air Balance Council
National Air Duct Cleaners Association

SVINICKI ASSOCIATION SERVICES

1123 N. Water St.
Milwaukee, WI 53202
Tel: (414)276-8788 *Fax:* (414)276-7704
Email: info@svinicki.com
website: www.svinicki.com

Jane A. Svinicki CAE, *President*

American College of Cardiology - Wisconsin Chapter
American Marketing Ass'n - Milwaukee Chapter
Association of Manpower Franchise Owners
Association of Wisconsin Cleaning Contractors
Brick Distributors of Wisconsin
Civil Trial Counsel of Wisconsin
Milwaukee Press Club
Plumbing-Heating-Cooling Contractors of Wisconsin
Residential Services Association of Wisconsin
Soc. of Financial Service Professionals - Milwaukee Chapter
Wisconsin Association of Personnel Services
Wisconsin Concrete Masonry Association
Wisconsin Direct Marketing Association
Wisconsin School Food Service Ass'n
Wisconsin Society of Association Executives

SYNERGY RESOURCE GROUP, INC.

3131 Fernbrook Lane North, Suite 111
Plymouth, MN 55447
Tel: (763)566-5999 *Fax:* (763)566-5780
Toll Free: (888)990-9959
Email: carnold@synergy-resource.com
website: www.synergy-resource.com

Charles Arnold, *Chief Executive Officer*

Construction Specifications Institute
International Facilities Management Association - Minnesota Chapter
International Interior Design Association
Minnesota Outdoor Heritage Ass'n
Minnesota Precision Manufacturing Association
Nat'l "M" Club
Pennsylvania Builder Magazine
Precision Manufacturing Magazine
Producers Council Midwest
Society for Marketing Professional Services

TAC, INC.

2321 W. Olive Ave., Suite I
Burbank, CA 91506
Tel: (818)558-7182 *Fax:* (818)558-7906
Email: vero@apala.org

Veronica Thompson, *President*

Advertising Production Ass'n of Los Angeles
American Institute Graphic Arts

TAI/EXPOGROUP

867 Sussex Blvd.
Broomall, PA 19008-0800
Tel: (610)604-4500

Stephen E. Markowitz, *President and Chief Executive Officer*

Midlantic Business Alliance
Philadelphia Ass'n of Retail Druggists

STAN TAIT & ASSOCIATES

2952 Wellington Circle
Tallahassee, FL 32309
Tel: (850)906-9220

Teri Besse, *Meeting Planner*

Economic Club of Florida
Florida Shore and Beach Preservation Ass'n
Int'l Conference on Disaster Management
Nat'l Conference on Beach Preservation Technology
Nat'l Hurricane Conference

TALLEY AND ASSOCIATES, INC.

25241 Paseo de Alicia, Suite 120
Laguna Hills, CA 92653
Tel: (949)380-3300 *Fax:* (949)380-3310
Email: info@talleyassoc.com
website: www.talleyassoc.com

Robert L. Evans, *Associate*

California Mobilehome Parkowners Association
Cypress Economic Development Council
Manufactured Housing Educational Trust of Orange, Riverside, and San Bernardino Counties
National Association of Industrial and Office Properties, Inland Empire
Urban Land Institute, Inland Empire

TALLEY MANAGEMENT GROUP, INC.

19 Mantua Road
Mt. Royal, NJ 08061
Tel: (856)423-7222 *Fax:* (856)423-3420
Email: gtalley@talley.com
website: www.talley.com

Gregg Talley, *President and Chief Executive Officer*

American Academy of Orofacial Pain
American Association for Paralegal Education

American Association for Vascular Surgery
American Cancer Society
American Council for Headache Education
American Geriatrics Society
American Headache Society
American Society for Reproductive Medicine
Association for Research in Otolaryngology
Custom Tailors and Designers Association of America
Internat'l Jewelry Design Guild
National Society for Experiential Education
New York State Society of Physicians Assistants
Real Estate Educators Association
Snack Food Association
Society for Cardiovascular Magnetic Resonance
Society for Healthcare Epidemiology of America
Women's Jewelry Association

TASC, INC. ASSOCIATION MANAGEMENT

1800 K St., N.W., Suite 718
Washington, DC 20006
Tel: (202)466-4214 *Fax:* (202)466-7414

Randy Dyer CAE, *President*

Conservation Council
Early Childhood Education Institute
International Electronic Article Surveillance Manufacturers Association
National Structured Settlements Trade Association
NSSTA Political Action Committee

TECHNICAL ENTERPRISES FOR ASSOCIATION MANAGEMENT

850 Dogwood Road, Suite A-400636
Lawrenceville, GA 30044-7218
Tel: (770)972-3011 *Fax:* (770)972-3012

Mimi Harlan, *President*

Cast Stone Institute
WAM Marketplace

TECHNICAL ENTERPRISES, INC.

7044 S. 13th St.
Oak Creek, WI 53154-1429
Tel: (414)768-8000
Email: sherer@techenterprises.net
website: www.techenterprises.net

Scott P. Sherer, *President*

Ass'n of Contingency Planners
Eastern Association of Colleges and Employers
Information Systems Security Association
Login Internat'l
NaSPA Education Foundation
NASPA Internet
NaSPA: the Network and System Professionals Association
National Reading Conference
Wisconsin Society of Professional Engineers

TEI ANALYTICAL, INC.

7177 N. Austin Ave.
Niles, IL 60714
Tel: (847)647-1345 *Fax:* (847)647-0844
website: www.teianalytical.com

Gayle E. O'Neill Ph.D., *President*

American Concrete Institute - Illinois Section
American Institute of Chemical Engineers - Chicago Section
Chicago Chromatography Discussion Group
Commercial Development and Marketing Ass'n Educational Foundation
Soc. of Automotive Engineers - Chicago Section

TH MGMT, INC.

P.O. Box 34155
Charlotte, NC 28234-4155
Tel: (704)365-3622 *Fax:* (704)365-3678
website: www.associationoffices.com

Theresa Salmen CAE, *Principal*

America Institute of Architects - Charlotte Section
Association of Philanthropic Counsel
Charlotte Region Commercial Board of REALTORS
Construction Financial Management Ass'n - Charlotte Chapter
Metrolina Business Council
NAIOP - Charlotte Chapter
North Carolina Medical Group Managers
Urban Land Institute - Charlotte Chapter

the ARDEL group

13355 Tenth Ave. North, Suite 108
Minneapolis, MN 55441-5554
Tel: (763)765-2300 *Fax:* (763)765-2329
Email: info@ardel.com
website: www.ardel.com

Rosealee M. Lee CAE, *Chief Executive Officer*

Controlled Release Society
Surfaces in Biomaterials Foundation
Wound Healing Society

THOMAS ASSOCIATES, INC.

1300 Sumner Ave.
Cleveland, OH 44115-2851
Tel: (216)241-7333 *Fax:* (216)241-0105
website: www.taol.com

Charles M. Stockinger, *Chairman*

American Association of Automatic Door Manufacturers
American Measuring Tool Manufacturers Association
Ass'n of Ingersoll-Rand Distributors
Chemical Fabrics and Film Association
Compressed Air and Gas Institute
Door and Access Systems Manufacturers' Association, International
Fire Equipment Manufacturers' Association
Fluid Controls Institute
Heat Exchange Institute
Metal Building Manufacturers Association
National Association of Graphic and Product Identification Manufacturer's, Inc.
North American Sawing Association
Power Tool Institute
Scaffolding, Shoring and Forming Institute
Steel Window Institute
United States Cutting Tool Institute

THOMPSON MANAGEMENT ASSOCIATES

105 Eastern Ave., Suite 104
Annapolis, MD 21403-3300
Tel: (410)263-1014
Email: jthompson@thompsonmanagement.com
website: www.thompsonmanagement.com

Joseph M. Thompson Jr., *President*

Association for Hose and Accessories Distribution
Independent Sealing Distributors
University of Industrial Distribution
Yacht Brokers Association of America

TLC - THE LEGISLATIVE CENTER, INC.

677 Ala Moana Blvd., Suite 815
Honolulu, HI 96813-5416
Tel: (808)537-4308 *Fax:* (808)533-2739

Tim Lyons CAE, *President*

Hawaii Business League
Hawaii Flooring Association
Hawaii Pest Control Association
Pacific Insulation Contractors Association
Roofing Contractors Association of Hawaii
Subcontractors Association of Hawaii

TORII PHILLIPS ASSOCIATION MANAGEMENT, LLC

12342 W. Layton Ave.
Greenfield, WI 53228
Tel: (414)529-4702 *Fax:* (414)529-4722
Email: bswingle@toriiphillips.com

Brian Swingle, *Executive Director*

Illinois Sign Association
Wisconsin Association of Textile Services
Wisconsin Fabricare Institute
Wisconsin Green Industry Federation
Wisconsin Nursery Association

TOUCHSTONE PARTNERSHIP, LTD.

300 W. State St.
Media, PA 19063
Tel: (610)566-6516 *Fax:* (610)566-8313
website: www.touchstonepartners.com

Dual Membership Council

TRADE ASSOCIATION MANAGEMENT

P.O. Box 778
Douglasville, GA 30134
Tel: (770)489-1440 *Fax:* (770)489-1425

Ski Bashinski, *President*

Greater Atlanta Fabricare Ass'n
Southeast Sign Association
Southern States Sign Council
Surveying and Mapping Society of Georgia

TRADE ASSOCIATION MANAGEMENT, INC.

25 N. Broadway
Tarrytown, NY 10591-3201
Tel: (914)332-0040
Email: info@taminc.com
website: www.taminc.com

Richard C. Byrne, *President*

Alliance for Fire and Smoke Containment and Control
American Wire Cloth Institute
Capital Markets Credit Analysts Society
Cold Formed Parts and Machine Institute
Expansion Joint Manufacturers Association
Hand Tools Institute
Institute of Store Planners
New York Association of Mortgage Brokers
Risk Management Ass'n - New York Chapter
Tubular Exchanger Manufacturers Association

UPDATE MANAGEMENT, INC.

147 S.E. 102nd Ave.
Portland, OR 97216-2703
Tel: (503)253-9385
website: www.updatemanagement.com

Michael A. Fisher CAE, *President*

National Association of Consumer Shows
Northwest Supply Management Association
Oregon Association of Defense Counsel
Oregon Dental Executives Association
Oregon Landscape Contractors Association
Oregon Physical Therapy Association
Oregon Psychological Association
Oregon Soc. of Health-Systems Pharmacists
Oregon Society of Association Management
Pacific Association for Medical Equipment Services
Pacific Northwest Precast Concrete Association
Pacific Northwest Steel Fabricators Association
Structural Roof Erectors Association

VANNATTA PUBLIC RELATIONS & ASSOCIATION MANAGEMENT

P.O. Box 135
3340 Commercial St. SE, Suite 210
Salem, OR 97308-0135
Tel: (503)585-8254
website: www.vannattapr.com

Mary L. VanNatta-Gail, *Chief Executive Officer*

Appraisal Institute - Greater Oregon Chapter
Association of Engineering Employees of Oregon
Oregon Association of Health Underwriters
Oregon Hearth Patio and Barbecue Association
Oregon Highway Users Alliance

VIRTUAL, INC.

401 Edgewater Place, Suite 600
Wakefield, MA 01880
Tel: (781)246-0500 *Fax:* (781)224-1239
Email: brogers@virtualmgmt.com
website: www.virtualmgmt.com

Bruce Rogers, *President*

VK ASSOCIATION MANAGEMENT

908 Main St., Suite 608
Tiburon, CA 94920-2517
Tel: (415)459-2234 *Fax:* (415)366-3255

Cres Van Keulen CAE, *Principal*

American Camping Ass'n - Northern California Section
ESOP Association - California/Western States Chapter
Security Analysts of San Francisco
Western Pension and Benefits Conference - San Francisco Chapter

WALKER MANAGEMENT GROUP

618 Church St., Suite 220
Nashville, TN 37219
Tel: (615)254-3687 *Fax:* (615)254-7047
Email: dawalker@walkermgt.com
website: www.walkermgt.com

Dee Ann Walker CAE, *President*

American Board of Veterinary Practitioners
American Veterinary Dental Society
Community Housing Developers Association of Tennessee
Phi Delta Chi
Tennessee Consumer Finance Association
Tennessee Osteopathic Medical Association
Tennessee Veterinary Medical Association
Veterinary Emergency & Critical Care Society

DON WALLACE ASSOCIATES

1156 15th St., N.W., Suite 315
Washington, DC 20005
Tel: (202)331-1331 *Fax:* (202)331-2112

Donald L. Wallace Jr., *President*

Cotton Warehouse Association of America

WALTER AND ASSOCIATES

9001 Hickman Road, Suite 220
Des Moines, IA 50322
Tel: (515)278-8700
Email: walter1@netins.net

Craig D. Walter, *President*

Iowa Assisted Living Ass'n
Iowa Bed and Breakfast Guild
Iowa Lodging Association
Iowa Natural Gas Association
Iowa One Call
Iowa Utility Contractors Association

WANNER ASSOCIATES

908 N. Second St.
Harrisburg, PA 17102-3119
Tel: (717)236-2050 *Fax:* (717)236-2046
Email: jwanner@wannerassoc.com
website: www.wannerassoc.com

John D. Wanner CAE, *President*

American Society of Landscape Architects - Pennsylvania/Delaware Chapter
Chiropractic Fellowship of Pennsylvania
Eastern Building Material Dealers Association
General Contractors Association of Pennsylvania
Pennsylvania Dietetic Association
Pennsylvania Economic Development Association
Pennsylvania Federation of Fraternal and Social Organizations
Pennsylvania Propane Gas Association
Pennsylvania Self Storage Association
Pennsylvania Society of Professional Engineers
Pupil Transportation Association of Pennsylvania
Sheet Metal and Air Conditioning Contractors Association of Pennsylvania

THE WARD MANAGEMENT GROUP, INC.

10293 N. Meridian St., Suite 175
Indianapolis, IN 46290-1073
Tel: (317)816-1619
Email: mfw@wardmanage.com
website: www.wardmanage.com

Michael F. Ward CAE, *President and Chief Executive Officer*

AAFRC Trust for Philanthropy
Biomedical Marketing Association
D.A.R.E. Indiana
Giving Institute
Indiana Ass'n of Chiefs of Police Foundation
Indiana Association of Chiefs of Police

WASHINGTON POLICY ASSOCIATES, INC.

1600 Duke St., Suite 400
Alexandria, VA 22314
Tel: (703)519-1715 *Fax:* (410)263-3186
Toll Free: (866)847-3609
website: www.wpa.org

Jeffrey C. Smith, *President*

Air and Expedited Motor Carriers Association
Airforwarders Association
Committee for Private Offshore Rescue and Towing (C-PORT)
Drug and Alcohol Testing Industry Association
Maritime Consortium
National Marine Charter Association

WATSON AND ASSOCIATES

13102 Laurinda Way
Santa Ana, CA 92705-1821
Tel: (714)744-6789

Lita L. Watson, *President*

American College of Cardiology - California Chapter
American Society of General Surgeons - California Chapter

M. WEGENER AND ASSOCIATES

P.O. Box 4250
Sunland, CA 91041-4250
Tel: (818)951-2842 *Fax:* (818)353-5976

Monika Wegener, *Owner*

Foreign Trade Association of So. Calif.
Harbor Association of Industry and Commerce
Los Angeles Customs Brokers and Freight Forwarders Ass'n
Los Angeles-Vancouver Sister City Ass'n
Propeller Club - Los Angeles/Long Beach
Women in International Trade - Los Angeles

WESTENBERGER MANAGEMENT, INC.

201 Indian Hills Court
Marietta, GA 30068-3972
Tel: (770)977-3918

John Westenberger CAE, *President*

Alabama Association of RV Parks and Campgrounds
Georgia Association of RV Parks and Campgrounds
Georgia Recreation Coalition
Tennessee Association of RV Parks and Campgrounds
Tennessee Recreation Coalition

WHERRY ASSOCIATES

30200 Detroit Road
Cleveland, OH 44145-1967
Tel: (440)899-0010 *Fax:* (440)892-1404
website: www.wherryassoc.com

J. Jeffery Wherry, *President*

Cemented Carbide Producers Association
Machine Knife Association
Nat'l Tooling and Machining Ass'n - Cleveland Chapter
National Association of Industrial and Office Properties
Ohio Mortgage Bankers Association
Steel Door Institute
Unified Abrasives Manufacturers Association

WHITING MANAGEMENT RESOURCES

1720 S. Bellaire St., Suite 110
Denver, CO 80222
Tel: (303)820-3151 *Fax:* (303)820-3844
Email: kbarstnar@wmrdever.com

Kathie Barstnar, *President*

Common Cents Fund - NAIOP, Colorado
Denver Security Traders Ass'n
Environmental and Engineering Geophysical Society
Nat'l Ass'n of Industrial and Office Properties - Colorado Chapter

WIDENER & ASSOCIATES, INC.

P.O. Box 1928
Duluth, GA 30096-0034
Tel: (678)646-0369
Email: bruce@widener-associates.com

Bruce Widener, *President*

Conditioned Air Association of Georgia
Georgia Drillers Association
Georgia Equipment Distributors Association
Georgia On-Site Waste Association

WILKES MANAGEMENT ASSOCIATES

P.O. Box 536544
Orlando, FL 32853-6544
Tel: (407)898-1695 *Fax:* (407)894-2312
Email: wilkesmgmt@aol.com

Shelburn M. Wilkes, *President*

American Hernia Society
Florida Healthcare Engineering Association

WILLIAMS MANAGEMENT RESOURCES

1755 Park St., Suite 260
Naperville, IL 60563
Tel: (630)416-1166 *Fax:* (630)416-9798
Email: pwilliams@wmrhq.com
website: www.wmrhq.com

Pamela Williams CAE, *President*

Ass'n of Fundraising Professionals - Chicago Chapter
Cable and Telecommunications Human Resources Association
Chicago Dematological Society

International Association for Exhibition Management - Midwestern Chapter
Midwest Healthcare Marketing Association

STEVEN WINTER ASSOCIATES, INC.

50 Washington St.,
Norwalk, CT 06854
Tel: (203)857-0200 *Fax:* (203)852-0741
Email: henglish@swinter.com

1112 16th Street, NW, Suite 240
Washington, DC 20036
Tel: (202)628-6100 *Fax:* (202)393-5043

Steven Winter, *President*

Federal Network for Sustainability
Sustainable Buildings Industry Council

WV CROSS ENTERPRISES, INC.

114 Coolidge St.
Silverton, OR 97381-2008
Tel: (503)873-5384 *Fax:* (503)873-9389
Email: wvce@teleport.com
website: www.wvcross.com

William V. Cross, *President*

Oregon Association of Convention and Visitors Bureaus
Oregon Building Officials Association
Oregon Mechanical Officials Association
Oregon Self-Insurers Association

BEVERLY ZIEGLER & ASSOCIATES

3315 Griffith Park Blvd., Suite 108
Los Angeles, CA 90027-2231
Tel: (323)664-4408

Beverly Ziegler, *Executive Officer/Owner*

Apartment Ass'n of Greater Los Angeles
Apartment Ass'n of San Fernando Valley/Ventura
Beverly Hills Gun Club and Rifle Range
Botach Management
Calibre Collision Centers
Epicentre Restaurant
Jeskor Research
Kawada Company of America/Kawada Hotel
Los Angeles Water and Power Ass'n
Mar-Scott Properties
Sign Users Council of California

Washington Representatives Directory

MAIL LIST ORDER FORM

SELECTIONS:

☐ **INDIVIDUALS •** Includes both in-house and contract lobbyists and government relations personnel. (Approximate Count: 18,000)

☐ **ORGANIZATIONS REPRESENTED •** Includes the organizations with DC offices who retain federal government representation here in the nation's capital. (Approximate Count: 3,400)

☐ **FIRMS •** Includes the DC law and lobbying firms who have been hired to represent the interests of their clients before the federal government. (Approximate Count: 1,500)

☐ **FEDERAL GOVERNMENT LEGISLATIVE AFFAIRS PERSONNEL •** Includes the individuals doing legislative and congressional affairs work for each of the Executive Branch departments and regulatory agencies. (Approximate Count: 500)

☐ **CUSTOMIZED LIST •** Sort by issue area or industry -- Please call (301) 986-1455 or visit us on the web at www.bethesda-list.com/columbiabooks.html for more info.

___

___

___

___

PRICING:

$175 per thousand ($350 minimum) base rate plus applicable selection charges.
Multiple use license also available. Please inquire for pricing.

ADDITIONAL OPTIONS:

☐ **PHONE/FAX •** $300/thousand

☐ **EMAIL/WEB •** $300/thousand

Applicable selection charges and other fees may apply. For a complete list of selections and pricing, please visit us on the web at www.bethesda-list.com/columbiabooks.html or call 301-986-1455.

LIST FORMAT:

☐ **EMAIL •** (Add $35)

☐ **DISKETTE •** (Add $50)

NOTE: Check, money order or credit card information MUST accompany order, along with a clear copy of your mail piece.

SEND TO:

Bethesda List Center, Inc.
4833 Rugby Avenue, Suite 501
Bethesda, MD 20814-3910
PHONE: 301-986-1455 FAX 301-907-4870
EMAIL: info@bethesda-list.com
WEB: www.bethesda-list.com/columbiabooks.html

Order will not be processed without valid contact information

NAME: ___
TITLE: ___
COMPANY: ___
ADDRESS: ___
CITY/STATE/ZIP: ___
TELEPHONE: ___
FAX: ___
EMAIL: ___

☐ Check/Money Order enclosed

☐ Charge to credit card:

☐ VISA ☐ MASTERCARD

Complete Name on card: ___
Expiration Date: ___ CVN#: ___
Signature: ___
Date: ___